Toll-Free Phone Book USA

A Directory of Toll-Free Telephone Numbers for Businesses and Organizations Nationwide

2006

10th Edition

Containing Toll-Free Numbers, Telephone Numbers, and Mailing Addresses for Leading U.S. Businesses, Organizations, Agencies, and Institutions, Including Companies, Associations, Educational Institutions, Media, Political Organizations, Societies, Travel Providers, and U.S. Government Agencies. Arranged Alphabetically by Name of Organization and in a Classified Section by Type of Business.

615 Griswold Street • Detroit, Michigan 48226

Omnigraphics, Inc.

Darren L. Smith, *Managing Editor*

Penny J. Hoffman, *Editor*

Aaron Borowicz, Michael Davidson, Sharlene C. Glassman, Mark Mandell, Lori Perez, and Elisha M. Sullivan, *Assistant Editors*

Nancy V. Kniskern, *Contributing Editor*

Alicia Elkiss, *Editorial Associate*

Melissa Ann Becerra, Marilyn Berg, Tiffany Delano, Jacqueline Elkiss, Jennie Hummel, Dena Kelly, Sue Lynch, and Rhonda J. Oxman, *Verification Assistants*

* * *

Peter E. Ruffner, *Publisher*
Frederick G. Ruffner, Jr., *Chairman*
Matthew P. Barbour, *Senior Vice President*
Kay Gill, *Vice President—Directories*

* * *

Elizabeth Barbour, *Research and Permissions Coordinator*
David P. Bianco, *Marketing Director*
Leif A. Gruenberg, *Development Manager*
Kevin Hayes, *Operations Manager*
Barry Puckett, *Librarian*
Cherry Stockdale, *Permissions Assistant*

Shirley Amore, Kevin Glover, Martha Johns, Kirk Kauffman, and Angelesia Thorington, *Administrative Staff*

ISBN 0-7808-0807-X
ISSN 1092-0285

Printed in the United States of America

OMNIGRAPHICS, INC.
615 Griswold Street • Detroit, MI 48226
Phone Orders: 800-234-1340 • Fax Orders: 800-875-1340
Mail Orders: P.O. Box 625 • Holmes, PA 19043
www.omnigraphics.com

Table of Contents

How To Use This Directory

Toll-Free Phone Book USA provides toll-free numbers, along with other key contact information, for some of the largest and most important corporations, organizations, and institutions in the United States. This tenth edition contains **more than 46,200** individual listings, presented alphabetically by company or organization name as well as in a classified subject arrangement according to business or organization type. The directory is intended as a convenient resource for toll-free calling nationwide, with supplemental contact data provided as an aid to follow-up correspondence or additional research.

What's Included in Toll-Free Phone Book USA?

Toll-free phone numbers, addresses, and local telephone numbers are provided for major businesses and industries located throughout the United States, as well as for organizations that serve as important information resources for businesses. Included also are listings for top Canadian companies and organizations.

Types of businesses listed in *Toll-Free Phone Book USA* include:

- manufacturing, retail, and wholesale companies;
- construction, mining, transportation, and utilities industries;
- agricultural interests;
- media and communications;
- and a full range of service industries.

Examples of other types of organizations listed include:

- associations;
- colleges and universities;
- libraries;
- research centers; and
- US Government agencies and offices.

How Do I Find What I'm Looking For?

Toll-Free Phone Book USA is organized in two main sections: an **Alphabetical Section,** in which listings are presented alphabetically according to company or organization name; and a **Classified Section,** where listings are organized under subject headings and subheadings according to business or organization type. All of the 46,200 plus entries are listed in each section.

- **Alphabetizing in *Toll-Free Phone Book USA***

  Alphabetizing throughout *Toll-Free Phone Book USA* is on a word-by-word, rather than letter-by-letter, basis. No distinction is made between upper and lower case letters, and articles, conjunctions, and most prepositions are ignored for sorting purposes. Names that begin with symbols or numerals rather than letters file first. Symbols that may accompany numerals (e.g., a pound sign [#] or dollar sign [$]) are ignored for alphabetical sorting.

  The following example illustrates these alphabetizing rules:

  1 on 1 Computing
  $1 Sunglasses Ltd
  3M Co
  All Weather Vacuuming
  C & S Inc
  Calido Hotels
  Cambridge Fire Insurance
  Damon Corp
  DAS Co
  Data Generation Inc
  La Quinta Motor Inns
  Laacke Co

- **Index to Classified Headings**

  All of the subject headings under which listings are organized in the Classified Section of *Toll-Free Phone*

Book USA are identified in the Index to Classified Headings located at the back of the directory. Page numbers given for each index citation refer to the page on which a particular subject category begins, rather than to a specific company or organization name. "See" and "See also" references are included to help guide users to appropriate subject categories.

Content of Individual Listings

Each listing in *Toll-Free Phone Book USA* provides the official name of the company, organization, or institution; street or other mailing address; city, state, and zip code; toll-free telephone number; and local telephone number (with area code). For publicly traded companies, stock exchange information is provided as well.

Classification Codes

In addition to these items of contact information, each listing in *Toll-Free Phone Book USA* contains a **classification code.** Classification codes are numbers that appear to the left of subject headings in the Classified Section and in a "Class" column to the right of listings in the Alphabetical Section, thus providing a common element that links the two sections. Users can determine a company's business activity by matching a number in a "Class" column to the corresponding subject heading number in the Classified Section.

Some listings in the Classified Section may be organized under a second level of subheadings within the broader category named in a heading. In situations where there are two levels of headings, two levels of classification codes are given as well. For instance, if a heading numbered as 200 is followed by a series of subheadings, the first subheading would be numbered 200-1, the second would be 200-2, and so on. Headings that have been created only to provide a reference to another heading category—i.e., "See" and "See also" references—are ***not*** numbered.

- **Company Names**

  As a general rule, complete official names are given for companies and organizations listed in *Toll-Free Phone Book USA*. In the case of listings for companies that are clearly named after individuals, information usually is presented both by the person's first name and by the last name. For example, LL Bean Inc would also be listed as Bean LL Inc.

  Companies that are well-known by an acronym or initialism—for example, IBM—usually are listed both by acronym and by full name (i.e., "IBM" and "International Business Machines Corp").

- **Addresses**

  Most of the addresses provided in this directory are street addresses, unless mail cannot be accepted at a particular location, in which case a post office box or other mailing address is provided. All listings include the city, state, and five-digit zip code as well.

- **Toll-Free Numbers**

  All ten digits, including the area code (800, 866, 877, or 888), are given for each listing's toll-free number. If the toll-free number is intended for a specific use (e.g., customer service, human resources, or technical support) rather than for general calling, an asterisk is printed to the right of the toll-free number and an explanatory note (e.g., *Cust Svc) is printed on the line below the name/address data.

- **Telephone Numbers**

  Local telephone numbers given in *Toll-Free Phone Book USA* are usually for the main switchboard of a company or organization, and area codes are included with all phone numbers listed.

- **Stock Exchange Information**

  Trading symbols and corresponding stock exchanges for publicly traded companies are provided below the company's name and address.

Comments Welcome

Comments from readers concerning this publication, including suggestions for additions and improvements, are welcome.

1. Area Codes in Numerical Order

201 ... New Jersey
202 ... District of Columbia
203 ... Connecticut
204 ... Manitoba
205 ... Alabama
206 ... Washington
207 ... Maine
208 ... Idaho
209 ... California
210 ... Texas
212 ... New York
213 ... California
214 ... Texas
215 ... Pennsylvania
216 ... Ohio
217 ... Illinois
218 ... Minnesota
219 ... Indiana
224 ... Illinois
225 ... Louisiana
228 ... Mississippi
229 ... Georgia
231 ... Michigan
234 ... Ohio
239 ... Florida
240 ... Maryland
242 ... Bahamas
246 ... Barbados
248 ... Michigan
250 ... British Columbia
251 ... Alabama
252 ... North Carolina
253 ... Washington
254 ... Texas
256 ... Alabama
260 ... Indiana
262 ... Wisconsin
264 ... Anguilla
267 ... Pennsylvania
268 ... Antigua and Barbuda
269 ... Michigan
270 ... Kentucky
276 ... Virginia
281 ... Texas
284 ... British Virgin Islands
289 ... Ontario
301 ... Maryland
302 ... Delaware
303 ... Colorado
304 ... West Virginia
305 ... Florida
306 ... Saskatchewan
307 ... Wyoming
308 ... Nebraska
309 ... Illinois
310 ... California
312 ... Illinois
313 ... Michigan
314 ... Missouri
315 ... New York
316 ... Kansas
317 ... Indiana
318 ... Louisiana
319 ... Iowa
320 ... Minnesota
321 ... Florida
323 ... California
325 ... Texas
330 ... Ohio
334 ... Alabama
336 ... North Carolina
337 ... Louisiana
339 ... Massachusetts
340 ... US Virgin Islands
345 ... Cayman Islands
347 ... New York
351 ... Massachusetts
352 ... Florida
360 ... Washington
361 ... Texas
386 ... Florida
401 ... Rhode Island
402 ... Nebraska
403 ... Alberta
404 ... Georgia
405 ... Oklahoma
406 ... Montana
407 ... Florida
408 ... California
409 ... Texas
410 ... Maryland
412 ... Pennsylvania
413 ... Massachusetts
414 ... Wisconsin
415 ... California
416 ... Ontario
417 ... Missouri
418 ... Quebec
419 ... Ohio
423 ... Tennessee
425 ... Washington
430 ... Texas
432 ... Texas
434 ... Virginia
435 ... Utah
440 ... Ohio
441 ... Bermuda
443 ... Maryland
450 ... Quebec
469 ... Texas
470 ... Georgia
473 ... Grenada
475 ... Connecticut
478 ... Georgia
479 ... Arkansas
480 ... Arizona
484 ... Pennyslvania
501 ... Arkansas
502 ... Kentucky
503 ... Oregon
504 ... Louisiana
505 ... New Mexico
506 ... New Brunswick
507 ... Minnesota
508 ... Massachusetts
509 ... Washington
510 ... California
512 ... Texas
513 ... Ohio
514 ... Quebec
515 ... Iowa
516 ... New York
517 ... Michigan
518 ... New York
519 ... Ontario
520 ... Arizona
530 ... California
540 ... Virginia
541 ... Oregon
551 ... New Jersey
559 ... California
561 ... Florida
562 ... California
563 ... Iowa
567 ... Ohio
570 ... Pennsylvania
571 ... Virginia
573 ... Missouri
574 ... Indiana
580 ... Oklahoma
585 ... New York
586 ... Michigan
601 ... Mississippi
602 ... Arizona
603 ... New Hampshire
604 ... British Columbia
605 ... South Dakota
606 ... Kentucky
607 ... New York
608 ... Wisconsin
609 ... New Jersey
610 ... Pennsylvania
612 ... Minnesota
613 ... Ontario
614 ... Ohio
615 ... Tennessee
616 ... Michigan
617 ... Massachusetts
618 ... Illinois
619 ... California
620 ... Kansas
623 ... Arizona
626 ... California
630 ... Illinois
631 ... New York
636 ... Missouri
641 ... Iowa
646 ... New York
647 ... Ontario
649 ... Turks and Caicos
650 ... California
651 ... Minnesota
660 ... Missouri
661 ... California
662 ... Mississippi
664 ... Montserrat
671 ... Guam
678 ... Georgia
682 ... Texas
684 ... American Samoa
689 ... Florida
701 ... North Dakota
702 ... Nevada
703 ... Virginia
704 ... North Carolina
705 ... Ontario
706 ... Georgia
707 ... California
708 ... Illinois
709 ... Newfoundland
712 ... Iowa
713 ... Texas
714 ... California
715 ... Wisconsin
716 ... New York
717 ... Pennsylvania
718 ... New York
719 ... Colorado
720 ... Colorado
724 ... Pennsylvania
727 ... Florida
731 ... Tennessee
732 ... New Jersey
734 ... Michigan
740 ... Ohio
754 ... Florida
757 ... Virginia
758 ... Saint Lucia
760 ... California
763 ... Minnesota
765 ... Indiana
767 ... Dominica
769 ... Mississippi
770 ... Georgia
772 ... Florida
773 ... Illinois
774 ... Massachusetts
775 ... Nevada
778 ... British Columbia
780 ... Alberta
781 ... Massachusetts
784 ... Saint Vincent & the Grenadines
785 ... Kansas
786 ... Florida
787 ... Puerto Rico
800 ... Toll-free; all states
801 ... Utah
802 ... Vermont
803 ... South Carolina
804 ... Virginia
805 ... California
806 ... Texas
807 ... Ontario
808 ... Hawaii
809 ... Dominican Republic
810 ... Michigan
812 ... Indiana
813 ... Florida
814 ... Pennsylvania
815 ... Illinois
816 ... Missouri
817 ... Texas
818 ... California
819 ... Quebec
828 ... North Carolina
830 ... Texas
831 ... California
832 ... Texas
843 ... South Carolina
845 ... New York
847 ... Illinois
848 ... New Jersey
850 ... Florida
856 ... New Jersey
857 ... Massachusetts
858 ... California
859 ... Kentucky
860 ... Connecticut
862 ... New Jersey
863 ... Florida
864 ... South Carolina
865 ... Tennessee
866 ... Toll-free; all states
867 ... Northwest Territories
868 ... Trinidad and Tobago
869 ... Saint Kitts and Nevis
870 ... Arkansas
876 ... Jamaica
877 ... Toll-free; all states
878 ... Pennsylvania
888 ... Toll-free; all states
901 ... Tennessee
902 ... Nova Scotia
903 ... Texas
904 ... Florida
905 ... Ontario
906 ... Michigan
907 ... Alaska
908 ... New Jersey
909 ... California
910 ... North Carolina
912 ... Georgia
913 ... Kansas
914 ... New York
915 ... Texas
916 ... California
917 ... New York
918 ... Oklahoma
919 ... North Carolina
920 ... Wisconsin
925 ... California
928 ... Arizona
931 ... Tennessee
936 ... Texas
937 ... Ohio
939 ... Puerto Rico
940 ... Texas
941 ... Florida
947 ... Michigan
949 ... California
951 ... California
952 ... Minnesota
954 ... Florida
956 ... Texas
959 ... Connecticut
970 ... Colorado
971 ... Oregon
972 ... Texas
973 ... New Jersey
978 ... Massachusetts
979 ... Texas
980 ... North Carolina
985 ... Louisiana
989 ... Michigan

2. Area Codes in State Order

Alabama
205 Birmingham & Tuscaloosa
251 southwest
256 north & east central
334 south

Alaska
907 all locations

American Samoa
684 all locations

Arizona
480 east of Phoenix including Tempe & Scottsdale
520 southeast
602 Phoenix
623 west of Phoenix including Glendale
928 most of state except south central & southeast areas

Arkansas
479 west central & northwest
501 Little Rock & surrounding areas
870 east & south

California
209 central
213 Los Angeles
310 Long Beach/west
323 Los Angeles
408 west central
415 San Francisco
510 Oakland
530 north
559 central
562 Long Beach
619 San Diego & surrounding area (except north)
626 Pasadena/east
650 south of San Francisco
661 Bakersfield & northern LA county
707 northwest
714 northern Orange County
760 southeast except San Diego area
805 south
818 Burbank & Glendale area
831 west central
858 San Diego/north
909 San Bernardino & surrounding area
916 Sacramento & surrounding area
925 east of Oakland
949 southern Orange County
951 Riverside & surrounding area (except north)

Canada
204 all locations in Manitoba
250 outside Vancouver area including Vancouver Island
289 north of Toronto
306 all locations in Saskatchewan
403 southern Alberta
416 Toronto
418 eastern Quebec
450 outside Montreal metro area
506 all locations in New Brunswick
514 Montreal metro area
519 southern Ontario
604 Vancouver area
613 northeast of Toronto
647 Toronto
705 eastern Ontario
709 all locations in Newfoundland
778 Vancouver area
780 central & northern Alberta
807 western Ontario
819 western Quebec
867 all locations in Yukon & Northwest Territories
902 all locations in Nova Scotia & Prince Edward Island
905 north of Toronto

Caribbean, Bahamas & Bermuda
242 Bahamas
246 Barbados
264 Anguilla
268 Antigua & Barbuda
284 British Virgin Islands
340 US Virgin Islands
345 Cayman Islands
441 Bermuda
473 Grenada
649 Turks & Caicos
664 Montserrat
758 Saint Lucia
767 Dominica
784 Saint Vincent & Grenadines
787 Puerto Rico
809 Dominican Republic
868 Trinidad & Tobago
869 Saint Kitts & Nevis
876 Jamaica
939 Puerto Rico

Colorado
303 Denver
719 south & east
720 Denver
970 west & north

Connecticut
203 southwest
475 southwest
860 except southwest
959 except southwest

Delaware
302 all locations

District of Columbia
202 all locations

Florida
239 southwest (Lee, Collier & part of Monroe counties)
305 southeast
321 central & east central
352 Gainesville, Ocala & surrounding areas
386 northeast except Jacksonville, St. Augustine, & surrounding areas
407 central
561 Palm Beach County
689 central and east central
727 Saint Petersburg/ Clearwater
754 Fort Lauderdale & surrounding area
772 Martin, St Lucie, Indian River & part of Brevard counties
786 southeast
813 Tampa
850 northwest
863 south central
904 Jacksonville, St. Augustine, & surrouding areas
941 southwest (Sarasota, Charlotte & Manatee counties)
954 Fort Lauderdale & surrounding area

Georgia
229 southwest
404 Atlanta
470 Atlanta & surrounding area
478 central
678 Atlanta area
706 north except Atlanta area
770 Atlanta suburbs
912 southeast

Guam
671 all locations

Hawaii
808 all locations

Idaho
208 all locations

Illinois
217 central
224 suburban Chicago
309 west
312 Chicago
618 south
630 northeast
708 northeast
773 Chicago (outside central commercial area)
815 north
847 suburban Chicago

Indiana
219 northwest
260 northeast
317 Indianapolis metro area
574 north central
765 central except Indianapolis metro area
812 south

Iowa
319 east central
515 central including Des Moines & Ames
563 east
641 south central & east central
712 west

Kansas
316 Wichita & surrounding area
620 south except Wichita & surrounding area
785 north except Kansas City
913 Kansas City

Kentucky
270 west & central
502 north including Louisville
606 east
859 north central

Louisiana
225 east central
318 north & west
337 west central & southwest
504 New Orleans area
985 southeast except New Orleans area

Maine
207 all locations

Maryland
240 west
301 west
410 east
443 east

Massachusetts
339 outside metro Boston
351 north
413 west
508 southeast
617 Boston metro area
774 southeast
781 outside metro Boston
857 Boston metro area
978 north

Michigan
231 northwest
248 east (Oakland County)
269 southwest
313 Detroit & inner suburbs
517 south central
586 east (Macomb County)
616 west/southwest
734 west of Detroit
810 east (except Oakland & Macomb counties)
906 north
947 east (Oakland County)
989 central

Minnesota
218 north
320 central except Minneapolis/Saint Paul metro area
507 south
612 Minneapolis
651 Saint Paul & east central
763 suburbs north & northwest of Minneapolis
952 suburbs south & southwest of Minneapolis

Mississippi
228 Gulfport/Biloxi & surrounding area
601 south except Gulfport/ Biloxi & surrounding area
662 north
769 south except Gulfport/ Biloxi & surrounding area

Missouri
314 Saint Louis
417 southwest
573 east except Saint Louis metro area
636 east (outside Saint Louis)
660 north except Kansas City & Saint Joseph
816 Kansas City & Saint Joseph

Montana
406 all locations

Nebraska
308 west
402 east

Nevada
702 Las Vegas area
775 all locations except Las Vegas

New Hampshire
603 all locations

New Jersey
201 northeast
551 northeast
609 southeast
732 east central
848 east central
856 southwest
862 northwest
908 west central
973 northwest

New Mexico
505 all locations

New York
212 New York City
315 north central
347 New York City
516 Nassau County
518 northeast
585 west-central
607 south central
631 Suffolk County
646 New York City
716 west
718 New York City
845 north & west of Westchester County
914 Westchester County
917 New York City

North Carolina
252 east
336 Greensboro & Winston-Salem areas
704 southwest
828 west
910 south central
919 north central
980 southwest

North Dakota
701 all locations

Ohio
216 Cleveland metro area
234 northeast except Cleveland
330 northeast except Cleveland
419 northwest
440 north central except Cleveland metro area
513 southwest
567 northwest
614 Columbus area
740 east & central except Columbus area
937 southwest except Cincinnati area

Oklahoma
405 central
580 south and west
918 northeast

Oregon
503 Portland area
541 outside Portland area
971 Portland area

Pennsylvania
215 Philadelphia
267 Philadelphia
412 Pittsburgh metro area
484 southeast
570 northeast
610 southeast
717 southeast
724 outside Pittsburgh metro area
814 west
878 Pittsburgh & surrounding area

Rhode Island
401 all locations

South Carolina
803 central
843 east
864 northwest

South Dakota
605 all locations

Tennessee
423 northeast & southeast
615 north central
731 west except Shelby, Fayette, & Tipton counties
865 Knoxville & surrounding area
901 southwest (Shelby, Fayette, & Tipton counties)
931 Nashville & north central

Texas
210 San Antonio metro area
214 Dallas
254 north central
281 Houston

2. Area Codes in State Order (continued)

325 central
361 Corpus Christi & surrounding area
409 east of Houston area
430 northeast
432 west central
469 Dallas
512 Austin & surrounding area
682 Fort Worth metro area & Arlington
713 Houston
806 northwest
817 Fort Worth metro area & Arlington
830 south central
832 Houston
903 northeast
915 west (including El Paso)
936 north of Houston area
940 north
956 south
972 Dallas
979 west of Houston area

Toll calls: from Canada & the Caribbean

880
881

Toll-free; all states

800
866
877
888

Utah

435 all locations except Salt Lake City/Ogden/Provo metro areas
801 Salt Lake City, Ogden & Provo metro areas

Vermont

802 all locations

Virginia

276 southwest
434 south & central
540 north
571 northeast
703 northeast
757 Norfolk & surrounding area
804 east

Washington

206 Seattle area
253 Tacoma area
360 west except Seattle, Tacoma & Everett areas
425 east of Seattle between Everett & Kent
509 east

West Virginia

304 all locations

Wisconsin

262 southeast except Milwaukee
414 Milwaukee
608 southwest
715 north
920 southeast except Milwaukee & surrounding area (south)

Wyoming

307 all locations

Toll-Free Phone Book USA

Alphabetical Section

Listings here are presented in alphabetical order by company or organization name. Alphabetizing is on a word-by-word rather than letter-by-letter basis. For a detailed explanation of the scope and arrangement of listings in this directory, please refer to "How To Use This Directory" at the beginning of this book. An explanation of individual page elements is also provided under the "Sample Entry" on the back inside cover of the book.

SYMBOLS & NUMERALS

Company	City	State	Zip	Toll-Free	Phone	Class
@INR.net 379 Amherst St Suite 218	Nashua	NH	03063	**877-880-8120**	603-880-8120	795
@Road Inc 47200 Bayside Pkwy	Fremont	CA	94538	**877-428-7623**	510-668-1638	222
NASDAQ: ARDI						
1 2 3 HostMe! 3864 Courtney St Suite 130	Bethlehem	PA	18017	**888-321-3278**	610-266-6700	795
1-800-ATTORNEY Inc 186 Industrial Center Dr	Lake Helen	FL	32744	**800-644-3458**	386-228-1000	623-6
1-800 Contacts Inc 66 E Wadsworth Pk Dr 3rd Fl	Draper	UT	84020	**800-266-8228**	801-924-9800	451
NASDAQ: CTAC						
1-800-Flowers.com Inc 1600 Stewart Ave	Westbury	NY	11590	**800-356-9377**	516-237-6000	287
NASDAQ: FLWS						
1-800-Mattress 31-10 48th Ave	Long Island City	NY	11101	**800-999-1000**	718-472-1200	361
#1 Cochran of Monroeville 4520 William Penn Hwy	Monroeville	PA	15146	**877-262-4726**	412-373-3333	57
1-Day Paint & Body Centers Inc 21801 S Western Ave	Torrance	CA	90501	**800-448-1908**	310-328-0390	62-4
1 Hour Martinizing Dry Cleaning Stores 422 Wards Corner Rd	Loveland	OH	45140	**800-827-0207**	513-351-6211	305
1st AAA Factors Inc 321 N Mall Dr	Saint George	UT	84790	**888-216-1235**		268
1st Community Bank 2911 N Westwood Blvd	Poplar Bluff	MO	63901	**888-831-3620**	573-778-0101	71
1st Corporate Limousine DBA Carey Executive Limousine 245 University Ave SW	Atlanta	GA	30315	**800-743-5466**	770-933-9000	433
1st Rochdale Co-op Group Ltd 465 Grand St 2nd Fl	New York	NY	10002	**877-624-3253**	212-673-3900	244
1st Source Corp 100 N Michigan St	South Bend	IN	46601	**800-513-2360***	574-235-2000	355-2
NASDAQ: SRCE ■ *Cust Svc						
2 Places At 1 Time Inc 512 Means St Suite 350	Atlanta	GA	30318	**877-275-2237**	404-815-9980	455
2nd Ave Design 737 W 2nd Ave	Mesa	AZ	85210	**800-843-1602**	480-464-8366	482
3 Strikes Inc 1905 Elizabeth Ave	Rahway	NJ	07065	**888-725-8483**	732-382-3820	338
3CI Complete Compliance Corp 1517 W North Carrier Pkwy Suite 104	Grand Prairie	TX	75050	**800-863-0345**	972-375-0006	653
3Com Corp 5403 Betsy Ross Dr	Santa Clara	CA	95054	**800-638-3266***	408-326-5000	174
NASDAQ: COMS ■ *Cust Svc						
3D Exhibits Inc 2800 Lively Blvd	Elk Grove Village	IL	60007	**800-471-9617**	847-250-9000	230
3D Systems Inc 26081 Ave Hall	Valencia	CA	91355	**800-653-1993**	661-295-5600	176-8
NASDAQ: TDSC						
3Dlabs Inc 1901 McCarthy Blvd	Milpitas	CA	94035	**800-464-3348**	408-432-6700	613
3M Abrasive Systems Div 3M Center Bldg 223-6N-01	Saint Paul	MN	55144	**800-742-9546**	651-737-6501	1
3M Adhesives & Tapes Div 3M Ctr Bldg 220-8E-04	Saint Paul	MN	55144	**800-362-3550**		717
3M Automotive Aftermarket Div 3M Center Bldg 223-6N-01	Saint Paul	MN	55144	**800-364-3577**		149
3M Canada Co PO Box 5757	London	ON	N6A4T1	**800-265-1840**	519-451-2500	717
3M Co 3M Ctr	Saint Paul	MN	55144	**800-364-3577**	651-733-1110	184
NYSE: MMM						
3M Commercial Care Div 3M Center Bldg 223-4N-14	Saint Paul	MN	55144	**800-847-3021**	800-626-8578	149
3M Commercial Graphics Div 3M General Offices Bldg 220-6W-06	Saint Paul	MN	55144	**800-328-3908**		589
3M Consumer & Office Div 3M Ctr	Saint Paul	MN	55144	**800-364-3577**	651-733-1110	523
NYSE: MMM						
3M Display & Graphics Div 3M Ctr	Saint Paul	MN	55144	**800-364-3577**	651-733-1110	717
3M Electrical Products Div 6801 River Place Blvd 3M Austin Ctr	Austin	TX	78726	**800-245-3573**		252
3M Electro & Communications Div 3M Ctr	Saint Paul	MN	55144	**800-364-3577**	651-733-1110	252
3M Electronic Handling & Protection Div 6801 River Place Blvd	Austin	TX	78726	**800-328-1368**		252
3M ESPE Dental Products Div 3M Ctr Bldg 275-2SE-03	Saint Paul	MN	55144	**888-364-3577**		226
3M Health Care Solutions 3M Ctr Health Care Service Ctr	Saint Paul	MN	55144	**800-364-3577***	651-733-1110	469
*Prod Info						
3M Industrial Mineral Products Div 3M Ctr Bldg 225-2N-07	Saint Paul	MN	55144	**800-447-2914**		490
3M Interconnect Solutions Div 6801 River Place Blvd	Austin	TX	78726	**800-225-5373**	512-984-1800	252
3M Manufacturing & Industry Solutions 3M Ctr	Saint Paul	MN	55144	**888-364-3577**	651-733-1110	1
3M Medical-Surgical Markets Div 3M Health Care Ctr Bldg 275-4 W-02	Saint Paul	MN	55144	**800-228-3957**		469
3M Meeting & Presentation Solutions Div 6801 River Place Blvd 3M Austin Ctr	Austin	TX	78726	**800-328-1371**		580
3M Occupational Health & Environmental Safety Products Div 3M Ctr Bldg 235-2W-75	Saint Paul	MN	55144	**800-328-1667**	651-733-8029	566
3M Personal Care & Related Products Div 3M Ctr Bldg 220-3W-10	Saint Paul	MN	55144	**866-212-5083**		717
3M Precision Optics Inc 4000 McMann Rd	Cincinnati	OH	45245	**800-877-0787**	513-752-7000	534
3M Safety Security & Protection Services Div 3M Ctr	Saint Paul	MN	55144	**800-364-3577**	651-733-1110	566
3M Touch Systems 300 Griffin Brook Dr	Methuen	MA	01844	**866-407-6666**	978-659-9000	171-1
3M Traffic Control Materials Div 3M Ctr Bldg 225-5S-08	Saint Paul	MN	55144	**800-553-1380**		589
3M Transportation Div 3M Ctr	Saint Paul	MN	55144	**888-364-3577**	651-733-1110	149
3M Unitek 2724 South Peck Rd	Monrovia	CA	91016	**800-634-5300**	626-445-7960	226
4-Star Trailers Inc 10000 NW 10th St	Oklahoma City	OK	73127	**800-848-3095**	405-324-7827	768
4-Wheel & Off-Road Magazine 6420 Wilshire Blvd	Los Angeles	CA	90048	**800-800-4294**	323-782-2000	449-3
4D Inc 3031 Tisch Way Suite 902	San Jose	CA	95128	**800-785-3303**	408-557-4600	176-1
4Life Research 9850 S 300 West	Sandy	UT	84070	**800-776-9898***	801-562-3600	361
*Sales						
4WARD Intellect Inc 550 Alden Rd Suite 107	Markham	ON	L3R6A8	**866-892-6297**	905-513-7360	4
5-7-9 Shops 1000 Pennsylvania Ave	Brooklyn	NY	11207	**800-435-5556**	718-485-3000	155-6
5th Avenue Suites Hotel 506 SW Washington St	Portland	OR	97204	**800-711-2971**	503-222-0001	373
7 D Ranch PO Box 100	Cody	WY	82414	**888-587-9885**	307-587-9885	238
7-Eleven Inc PO Box 711	Dallas	TX	75221	**800-255-0711**	214-828-7011	203
NYSE: SE						
9to5 National Assn of Working Women 152 W Wisconsin Ave Suite 408	Milwaukee	WI	53203	**800-522-0925**	414-274-0925	48-24
11th Hour Vacations 15 Century Dr	Greenville	SC	29607	**888-740-1998**	864-331-1140	762
21st Century Casualty Co 6301 Owensmouth Ave	Woodland Hills	CA	91367	**800-443-3100**	818-704-3700	384-4
21st Century Holding Co 4161 NW 5th St	Plantation	FL	33317	**800-333-3477**	954-581-9993	355-4
NASDAQ: TCHC						
21st Century Insurance Co 6301 Owensmouth Ave	Woodland Hills	CA	91367	**800-443-3100**	818-704-3700	384-4
21st Century Insurance Group 6301 Owensmouth Ave	Woodland Hills	CA	91367	**800-443-3100**	818-704-3700	355-4
NYSE: TW						
21st Services Inc 200 S 6th St Suite 350	Minneapolis	MN	55402	**877-371-3008**	612-371-3008	783
24 Hour Fitness Worldwide Inc 12647 Alcosta Blvd 5th fl	San Ramon	CA	94583	**888-256-5485**	925-543-3100	349
63 Ranch Box 979	Livingston	MT	59047	**888-395-5151**	406-222-0570	238
70 Park Avenue Hotel 70 Park Ave at 38th St	New York	NY	10016	**877-707-2752**	212-973-2400	373
84 Lumber Co 1019 Rte 519	Eighty Four	PA	15330	**800-664-1984**	724-228-8820	190-3
100 Fountain Spa at the Pillar & Post Inn 48 John St PO Box 1011	Niagara-on-the-Lake	ON	L0S1J0	**888-669-5566**	905-468-0515	698
101 Publishing 1033 Oregon Ave Suite 101	Palo Alto	CA	94303	**800-852-4890***	650-493-2221	623-2
*Orders						
180s Inc 720 S Montford Ave	Baltimore	MD	21224	**877-725-4386**	410-534-6320	153-9
24/7 Real Media Inc 132 W 31st St 9th Fl	New York	NY	10001	**877-247-2477**	212-231-7100	7
NASDAQ: TFSM						
360Commerce 11400 Burnet Rd Suite 5200	Austin	TX	78758	**800-897-8663**	512-491-2600	176-11
500 West Hotel 500 W Broadway	San Diego	CA	92101	**866-500-7533**	619-234-5252	373
711.NET Inc 2063 N Lecanto Hwy	Lecanto	FL	34461	**866-558-6778**		390
724 Solutions Inc 4101 Yonge St Suite 702	Toronto	ON	M2P1N6	**877-241-7378**	416-226-2900	222
NASDAQ: SVNX						
800-JR Cigar Inc 301 Rt 10 E	Whippany	NJ	07981	**800-572-4427**	973-884-9555	744
1800CHEAPSEATS 11145 Tampa Ave Suite 17-B	Northridge	CA	91326	**800-243-2773**		762
1928 Jewelry Co 3000 W Empire Ave	Burbank	CA	91504	**800-227-1928**	818-841-1928	400

A

Company	City	State	Zip	Toll-Free	Phone	Class
A-1 Carbide Corp 1649 Miraloma Ave	Placentia	CA	92870	**800-222-9422**	714-630-9422	609
A-1 Components Corp 625 W 18th St	Hialeah	FL	33010	**800-759-2872**	305-885-1911	650
A & B Aerospace Inc 612 Ayon Ave	Azusa	CA	91702	**888-999-9397**	626-334-2976	22
A-B-C Packaging Machine Corp 811 Live Oak St	Tarpon Springs	FL	34689	**800-237-5975**	727-937-5144	537
A & B Smith Co 1383 Frey Industrial Pk	Pittsburgh	PA	15235	**800-288-1776**	412-242-5400	44
A & B Wiper Supply Inc 5601 Paschall Ave	Philadelphia	PA	19143	**800-333-7247**	215-482-6100	497

Name / Address	City	State	ZIP	Toll-Free	Phone	Class
A Better Chance 240 W 35th St 9th Fl	New York	NY	10001	**800-543-7181**	646-346-1310	48-11
A Camacho Inc 2502 Walden Woods Dr	Plant City	FL	33566	**800-881-4534**	813-305-4534	291-33
A Daigger Co Inc 620 Lakeview Pkwy	Vernon Hills	IL	60061	**800-621-7193**	847-816-5060	592
A-dec Inc 2601 Crestview Dr *Cust Svc	Newberg	OR	97132	**800-547-1883***	503-538-9471	226
A Duchini Inc 2550 McKinley Ave	Erie	PA	16503	**800-937-7317**	814-456-7027	181
A Duie Pyle Distribution & Warehousing Inc 650 Westtown Rd	West Chester	PA	19381	**800-523-5020**	610-696-5800	790-1
A Duie Pyle Inc PO Box 564	West Chester	PA	19381	**800-523-5020**	610-696-5800	440
A & E Products Group Inc 1 Harmon Meadow Blvd	Secaucus	NJ	07094	**800-762-1167**		344
A & E Transport Services Inc 101 W Utica St Suite 2	Oswego	NY	13126	**800-724-0614**	315-343-2804	110
A & E Travel 3307 Northland Dr Suite 220	Austin	TX	78731	**877-238-6877**	512-244-9883	762
A Family Limousine 6311 Stirling Rd	Davie	FL	33314	**877-599-5466**	954-522-7455	433
A Finkl & Sons Co 2011 N Southport Ave	Chicago	IL	60614	**800-343-2562**	773-975-2510	709
A & K Railroad Materials Inc PO Box 30076	Salt Lake City	UT	84130	**800-453-8812**	801-974-5484	759
A & L Distributing Co 7933 SW Cirrus Dr	Beaverton	OR	97008	**800-234-9556**	503-684-9384	270
A & M Tape & Packaging 5201 Nob Hill Rd	Sunrise	FL	33351	**800-231-8806**	954-572-2500	549
A & M Tool & Die Co Inc 64 Mill St	Southbridge	MA	01550	**800-848-4628**	508-764-3241	745
A Matter of Fax 105 Harrison Ave	Harrison	NJ	07029	**800-433-3329**	973-482-3700	177
A Meyers & Sons Corp 325 W 38th St	New York	NY	10018	**800-666-5577**	212-279-6632	583
A Nose For Clothes 13100 SW 128th St	Miami	FL	33186	**877-870-6673**	305-253-8631	155-6
A Pomerantz & Co 701 Market St Suite 7000	Philadelphia	PA	19106	**800-344-9135**	215-408-2100	315
A Rifkin Co 1400 Sans Souci Pkwy *Cust Svc	Wilkes-Barre	PA	18706	**800-458-7300***	570-825-9551	68
A Schulman Inc 3550 W Market St *NASDAQ: SHLM*	Akron	OH	44333	**800-662-3751**	330-666-3751	594-2
A Sheftel & Sons Inc 2121 31st St SW *Cust Svc	Allentown	PA	18103	**800-542-2426***	610-797-9420	730-8
A Stucki Co 2600 Neville Rd	Pittsburgh	PA	15225	**800-771-7302**	412-771-7300	636
A & W Products Co Inc 14 Gardner St	Port Jervis	NY	12771	**800-223-5156**	845-856-5156	523
A Yankee Line 370 W 1st St	Boston	MA	02127	**800-942-8890**	617-268-8890	108
A & Z Hayward Co 655 Waterman Ave	East Providence	RI	02914	**800-556-7462**	401-438-0550	400
A+Net Internet Services 10350 Barnes Canyon Rd	San Diego	CA	92121	**877-275-8763**	858-410-6929	390
A1 Worldwide Limousine Inc 69 Yorkville Ave Suite 205	Toronto	ON	M5R1B8	**877-537-5466**	416-922-5466	433
A1Books.com 35 Love Ln *Cust Svc	Netcong	NJ	07857	**877-212-6657***	973-426-9995	96
A1SuperCruises.com 3380 Fairline Farms Rd Suite 7	West Palm Beach	FL	33414	**866-878-8785**	561-204-2669	760
A2Z Science & Nature Store 57 King St	Northampton	MA	01060	**877-261-6171**	413-586-1611	518
AA Importing Co Inc 7700 Hall St *Cust Svc	Saint Louis	MO	63147	**800-325-0602***	314-383-8800	356
AAA (American Academy of Audiology) 11730 Plaza America Dr Suite 300	Reston	VA	22190	**800-222-2336**	703-790-8466	49-8
AAA (American Ambulance Assn) 8201 Greensboro Dr Suite 300	McLean	VA	22102	**800-523-4447**	703-610-9018	49-21
AAA (American Arbitration Assn Inc) 335 Madison Ave 10th Fl	New York	NY	10017	**800-778-7879**	212-716-5800	41
AAA Alabama 2400 Acton Rd	Birmingham	AL	35243	**800-521-8124**	205-978-7000	53
AAA Allied Group Inc 15 W Central Pkwy	Cincinnati	OH	45202	**800-543-2345**	513-762-3100	53
AAA Arizona 3144 N 7th Ave	Phoenix	AZ	85013	**800-352-5382**	602-274-1116	53
AAA Ashland County 502 Claremont Ave	Ashland	OH	44805	**800-222-4357**	419-289-8133	53
AAA Blue Grass/Kentucky 155 N MLK Blvd	Lexington	KY	40507	**800-568-5222**	859-233-1111	53
AAA Carolinas 6600 AAA Dr	Charlotte	NC	28212	**800-477-4222**	704-569-3600	53
AAA Central Penn 2023 Market St	Harrisburg	PA	17103	**877-848-9990**	717-236-4021	53
AAA Chicago Motor Club 975 Meridian Lake Dr	Aurora	IL	60504	**866-968-7222**	630-328-7000	53
AAA Co Inc 6232 Bragg Blvd	Fayetteville	NC	28303	**800-850-8776**	910-867-6111	35
AAA Colorado 4100 E Arkansas Ave	Denver	CO	80222	**877-244-9790**	303-753-8800	53
AAA Columbiana County 516 Broadway St	East Liverpool	OH	43920	**800-222-4357**	330-385-2020	53
AAA Cooper Transportation 1751 Kinsey Rd	Dothan	AL	36303	**800-633-7571**	334-793-2284	769
AAA East Penn 1020 Hamilton St	Allentown	PA	18105	**800-552-6679**	610-434-5141	53
AAA East Tennessee 100 W 5th Ave	Knoxville	TN	37917	**800-234-1222**	865-637-1910	53
AAA Financial Corp 9601 W Sample Rd	Coral Springs	FL	33065	**800-881-2530**	954-344-2530	498
AAA Hawaii 1130 N Nimitz Hwy Suite A-170	Honolulu	HI	96817	**800-736-2886**	808-593-2221	53
AAA Hoosier Motor Club 3750 Guion Rd	Indianapolis	IN	46222	**800-624-9820**	317-923-3311	53
AAA Kentucky 435 E Broadway	Louisville	KY	40202	**800-727-2552**	502-582-3311	53
AAA Massillon Auto Club 1972 Wales Rd NE	Massillon	OH	44646	**800-222-4357**	330-833-1084	53
AAA Miami Valley 825 S Ludlow St	Dayton	OH	45402	**800-624-2321**	937-224-2801	53
AAA Michigan 1 Auto Club Dr	Dearborn	MI	48126	**800-222-6424**	313-336-1234	53
AAA Mid-Atlantic 2040 Market St	Philadelphia	PA	19103	**888-859-5161**	215-864-5000	53
AAA Minnesota/Iowa 600 W Travelers Trail	Burnsville	MN	55337	**800-222-1333**	952-707-4500	53
AAA Missouri 12901 N Forty Dr	Saint Louis	MO	63141	**800-222-4357**	314-523-7350	53
AAA MountainWest 2100 11th Ave	Helena	MT	59601	**800-332-6119**	406-447-8100	53
AAA Nebraska 910 N 96th St	Omaha	NE	68114	**800-222-6327**	402-390-1000	53
AAA New Mexico Inc 10501 Montgomery Blvd NE	Albuquerque	NM	87111	**800-846-0377**	505-291-6611	53
AAA North Dakota 1801 38th St SW	Fargo	ND	58103	**800-342-4254**	701-282-6222	53
AAA North Jersey 418 Hamburg Tpke	Wayne	NJ	07470	**800-222-4357**	973-956-2200	53
AAA of Northern California Nevada & Utah 150 Van Ness Ave *Cust Svc	San Francisco	CA	94102	**800-922-8228***	415-565-2012	53
AAA Northern New England 68 Marginal Way	Portland	ME	04104	**800-222-4357**	207-780-6800	53
AAA Northwest Ohio 7150 W Central Ave	Toledo	OH	43617	**800-428-0060**	419-843-1200	53
AAA Ohio Auto Club 90 E Wilson Bridge Rd	Worthington	OH	43085	**800-282-0585**	614-431-7800	53
AAA Oklahoma 2121 E 15th St	Tulsa	OK	74104	**800-222-2582**	918-748-1000	53
AAA Oregon/Idaho 600 SW Market St *Cust Svc	Portland	OR	97201	**800-452-1643***	503-222-6734	53
AAA Reservation Services 1740 Jackson Ave	New Orleans	LA	70113	**888-840-2331**	504-522-1785	368
AAA South Dakota 1300 Industrial Ave	Sioux Falls	SD	57104	**800-222-4545**	605-336-3690	53
AAA Southern New England 110 Royal Little Dr	Providence	RI	02904	**800-222-7448**	401-868-2000	53
AAA Southern Pennsylvania 2840 Eastern Blvd	York	PA	17402	**800-222-1469**	717-600-8700	53
AAA Travel Topics Magazine 2023 Market St	Harrisburg	PA	17103	**877-848-9990**	717-236-4021	449-22
AAA Washington-Inland 1745 114th Ave SE	Bellevue	WA	98004	**800-562-2582**	425-462-2222	53
AAA Western & Central New York 100 International Dr	Buffalo	NY	14221	**800-836-2582**	716-633-9860	53
AAA Wisconsin 8401 Excelsior Dr	Madison	WI	53717	**800-236-1300**	608-836-6555	53
AAAAI (American Academy of Allergy Asthma & Immunology) 611 E Wells St 4th Fl	Milwaukee	WI	53202	**800-822-2762**	414-272-6071	49-8
AAACN (American Academy of Ambulatory Care Nursing) 200 E Holly Ave Box 56	Pitman	NJ	08080	**800-262-6877**	856-256-2350	49-8
AAAS (American Assn for the Advancement of Science) 1200 New York Ave NW	Washington	DC	20005	**800-731-4939**	202-326-6400	49-19
AABP (American Assn of Bovine Practitioners) PO Box 1755	Rome	GA	30162	**800-269-2227**	706-232-2220	48-2
AABT (Association for Advancement of Behavior Therapy) 305 7th Ave 16th Fl	New York	NY	10001	**800-685-2228**	212-647-1890	49-15
AACAP (American Academy of Child & Adolescent Psychiatry) 3615 Wisconsin Ave NW	Washington	DC	20016	**800-333-7636**	202-966-7300	49-15
AACC (American Assn for Clinical Chemistry Inc) 2101 L St NW Suite 202 *Cust Svc	Washington	DC	20037	**800-892-1400***	202-857-0717	49-19
AACD (American Academy of Cosmetic Dentistry) 5401 World Dairy Dr	Madison	WI	53718	**800-543-9220**	608-222-8583	49-8
AACE International - Assn for the Advancement of Cost Engineering (AACE) 209 Prairie Ave Suite 100	Morgantown	WV	26501	**800-858-2678**	304-296-8444	49-1
AACN (American Assn of Critical-Care Nurses) 101 Columbia	Aliso Viejo	CA	92656	**800-809-2273**	949-362-2000	49-8
AACPM (American Assn of Colleges of Podiatric Medicine) 1350 Piccard Dr Suite 322	Rockville	MD	20850	**800-922-9266**	301-990-7400	49-8
AACT (American Assn of Community Theatre) 8402 BriarWood Cir	Lago Vista	TX	78645	**866-687-2228**	512-267-0711	48-4
AADE (American Assn of Diabetes Educators) 100 W Monroe St Suite 400	Chicago	IL	60603	**800-338-3633**	312-424-2426	49-8
AADEP (American Academy of Disability Evaluating Physicians) 150 N Wacker Dr Suite 1420	Chicago	IL	60606	**800-456-6095**	312-658-1171	49-8
AADP (American Assn of Drugless Practitioners) 2705 61st St	Galveston	TX	77551	**888-764-2237**	409-741-9000	48-17
AAE (American Assn of Endodontists) 211 E Chicago Ave Suite 1100	Chicago	IL	60611	**800-872-3636**	312-266-7255	49-8
AAEP (American Assn of Equine Practitioners) 4075 Iron Works Pkwy	Lexington	KY	40511	**800-443-0177**	859-233-0147	48-3
AAES (American Assn of Engineering Societies) 1828 L St NW Suite 906 *Orders	Washington	DC	20036	**888-400-2237***	202-296-2237	49-19
AAF (American Advertising Federation) 1101 Vermont Ave NW Suite 500	Washington	DC	20005	**800-999-2231**	202-898-0089	49-18
AAF International Corp 10300 Ormsby Park Pl Suite 600	Louisville	KY	40223	**888-223-2003**	502-637-0011	19
AAFA (American Apparel & Footwear Assn) 1601 N Kent St Suite 1200	Arlington	VA	22209	**800-520-2262**	703-524-1864	49-4
AAFA (Asthma & Allergy Foundation of America) 1233 20th St NW Suite 402	Washington	DC	20036	**800-727-8462**	202-466-7643	48-17
AAFCS (American Assn of Family & Consumer Sciences) 400 N Columbus St Suite 202	Alexandria	VA	22314	**800-424-8080**	703-706-4600	49-5
AAFD (American Assn of Franchisees & Dealers) 3500 5th Ave Suite 103	San Diego	CA	92103	**800-733-9858**	619-209-3775	49-18
AAFES (Army & Air Force Exchange Service) 3911 S Walton Walker Blvd	Dallas	TX	75236	**800-527-6790**	214-312-2011	778
AAFP (American Academy of Family Physicians) 11400 Tomahawk Creek Pkwy	Leawood	KS	66211	**800-274-2237**	913-906-6000	49-8
AAFPRS (American Academy of Facial Plastic & Reconstructive Surgery) 310 S Henry St	Alexandria	VA	22314	**800-332-3223**	703-299-9291	49-8
AAGL (American Assn of Gynecological Laparoscopists) 13021 E Florence Ave	Santa Fe Springs	CA	90670	**800-554-2245**	562-946-8774	49-8
AAHA (American Animal Hospital Assn) PO Box 150899	Denver	CO	80215	**800-252-2242**	303-986-2800	48-3

Name / Address	City	State	ZIP	Toll-Free	Phone	Class
AAHC (American Assn of Healthcare Consultants) 5938 N Drake Ave	Chicago	IL	60659	**888-350-2242**		49-8
AAHPERD (American Alliance for Health Physical Education Recreation & Dance) 1900 Association Dr	Reston	VA	20191	**800-213-7193**	703-476-3400	48-22
AAHSA (American Assn of Homes & Services for the Aging) 2519 Connecticut Ave NW	Washington	DC	20008	**800-508-9442**	202-783-2242	48-6
AAI (Africa-America Institute) 420 Lexington Ave Suite 1706	New York	NY	10170	**800-745-3899**	212-949-5666	48-14
AAI ACL Technologies Inc 3200 Enterprise St	Brea	CA	92821	**800-521-4987**	714-223-5100	464
AAI Corp PO Box 126	Hunt Valley	MD	21030	**800-626-6283**	410-666-1400	519
AAI Foster Grant 500 George Washington Hwy	Smithfield	RI	02917	**800-388-0258**	401-231-3800	531
AAII (American Assn of Individual Investors) 625 N Michigan Ave	Chicago	IL	60611	**800-428-2244**	312-280-0170	49-2
aaiPharma Inc 2320 Scientific Pk Dr *NASDAQ: AAIIE*	Wilmington	NC	28405	**800-575-4224**	910-254-7000	572
AAIS (American Assn of Insurance Services) 1745 S Naperville Rd	Wheaton	IL	60187	**800-564-2247**	630-681-8347	49-9
Aakron Rule Corp 8 Indianola Ave	Akron	NY	14001	**800-828-1570**	716-542-5483	10
AALBC (African American Literature Book Club) 55 W 116th St Suite 195	Harlem	NY	10026	**866-603-8394**		94
Aalfs Mfg Co 1005 4th St	Sioux City	IA	51101	**888-412-2537**	712-252-1877	153-11
AALR (American Assn for Leisure & Recreation) 1900 Association Dr	Reston	VA	20191	**800-213-7193**	703-476-3400	48-23
AALU (Association for Advanced Life Underwriting) 2901 Telestar Ct	Falls Church	VA	22042	**888-275-0092**	703-641-9400	49-9
AAMA (American Assn of Medical Assistants) 20 N Wacker Dr Suite 1575	Chicago	IL	60606	**800-228-2262**	312-899-1500	49-8
AAMCO Transmissions Inc 1 Presidential Blvd *Cust Svc	Bala Cynwyd	PA	19004	**800-523-0401***	610-668-2900	62-6
Aames Financial Corp 350 S Grand Ave 43rd Fl	Los Angeles	CA	90071	**800-829-2929**	323-210-5000	498
AAMI (Association for the Advancement of Medical Instrumentation) 1110 N Glebe Rd Suite 220	Arlington	VA	22201	**800-332-2264**	703-525-4890	49-8
Aamp of America Inc 13160 56th Ct Suite 508	Clearwater	FL	33760	**800-477-2267**	727-572-9255	60
AAMR (American Assn on Mental Retardation) 444 N Capitol St NW Suite 846	Washington	DC	20001	**800-424-3688**	202-387-1968	48-17
AAMT (American Assn for Medical Transcription) 100 Sycamore Ave	Modesto	CA	95354	**800-982-2182**	209-527-9620	49-8
AAMVA (American Assn of Motor Vehicle Administrators) 4301 Wilson Blvd Suite 400	Arlington	VA	22203	**800-515-8881**	703-522-4200	49-7
AAN (American Academy of Neurology) 1080 Montreal Ave	Saint Paul	MN	55116	**800-879-1960**	651-695-2717	49-8
AANC (American Assn of Nutritional Consultants) 401 Kings Hwy	Winona Lake	IN	46590	**888-828-2262**	574-269-6165	49-8
AANN (American Assn of Neuroscience Nurses) 4700 W Lake Ave	Glenview	IL	60025	**888-557-2266**	847-375-4733	49-8
AANP (American Assn of Naturopathic Physicians) 3201 New Mexico Ave NW Suite 350	Washington	DC	20016	**866-538-2267**	202-895-1392	48-17
AANS (American Assn of Neurological Surgeons) 5550 Meadowbrook Dr	Rolling Meadows	IL	60068	**888-566-2267**	847-378-0500	49-8
AAO (American Assn of Orthodontists) 401 N Lindbergh Blvd	Saint Louis	MO	63141	**800-424-2841**	314-993-1700	49-8
AAOHN (American Assn of Occupational Health Nurses) 2920 Brandywine Rd Suite 100	Atlanta	GA	30341	**888-646-4631**	770-455-7757	49-8
AAOM (American Assn of Oriental Medicine) PO Box 162340	Sacramento	CA	95816	**866-455-7999**	916-443-4770	48-17
AAOMS (American Assn of Oral & Maxillofacial Surgeons) 9700 W Bryn Mawr Ave	Rosemont	IL	60018	**800-822-6637**	847-678-6200	49-8
AAP (American Academy of Pediatrics) 141 Northwest Point Blvd	Elk Grove Village	IL	60007	**800-433-9016**	847-434-4000	49-8
AAP (American Academy of Periodontology) 737 N Michigan Ave Suite 800	Chicago	IL	60611	**800-282-4867**	312-787-5518	49-8
AAPB (Association for Applied Psychophysiology & Biofeedback) 10200 W 44th Ave Suite 304	Wheat Ridge	CO	80033	**800-477-8892**	303-422-8436	49-8
AAPCC (American Assn of Poison Control Centers) 3201 New Mexico Ave Suite 330	Washington	DC	20016	**800-222-1222**	202-362-7217	49-8
AAPG (American Assn of Petroleum Geologists) 1444 S Boulder Ave	Tulsa	OK	74119	**800-364-2274**	918-584-2555	48-12
AAPG Explorer Magazine 1444 S Boulder Ave	Tulsa	OK	74119	**800-364-2274**	918-584-2555	449-21
AAPL (American Academy of Psychiatry & the Law) 1 Regency Dr PO Box 30	Bloomfield	CT	06002	**800-331-1389**	860-242-5450	49-15
AAPS (American Assn of Pharmaceutical Scientists) 2107 Wilson Blvd Suite 700	Arlington	VA	22201	**877-998-2277**	703-243-2800	49-19
AAPS (American Assn of Physician Specialists Inc) 2296 Henderson Mill Rd Suite 206	Atlanta	GA	30345	**800-447-9397**	770-939-8555	49-8
AAR (Association of American Railroads) 50 F St NW *Cust Svc	Washington	DC	20001	**800-544-7245***	202-639-2100	49-21
AAR Aircraft Turbine Center 1100 N Wood Dale Rd 1 AAR Pl	Wood Dale	IL	60191	**800-422-2213**	630-227-2000	759
AAR Cargo Systems 12633 Inkster Rd	Livonia	MI	48150	**800-247-1273**	734-522-2000	23
AAR Composites 14201 Myerlake Cir	Clearwater	FL	33760	**888-227-3597**	727-539-8585	23
AAR Corp 1100 N Wood Dale Rd 1 AAR Pl *NYSE: AIR*	Wood Dale	IL	60191	**800-422-2213**	630-227-2000	22
AAR Distribution 1100 N Wood Dale Rd 1 AAR Pl	Wood Dale	IL	60191	**800-422-2213**	630-227-2000	759
AARDA (American Autoimmune Related Disease Assn) 22100 Gratiot Ave	Eastpointe	MI	48021	**800-598-4668**	586-776-3900	48-17
Aaron Brothers Inc 1221 S Beltline Rd	Coppell	TX	75019	**888-372-6464**	972-409-1300	45
Aaron Rents Inc 309 E Paces Ferry Rd NE *NYSE: RNT*	Atlanta	GA	30305	**800-551-6015**	404-231-0011	261-3
AARP 601 'E' St NW	Washington	DC	20049	**888-687-2277**	202-434-2277	48-6
AARP Broadcast Dept 601 'E' St NW	Washington	DC	20049	**888-687-2277**	202-434-2600	632
AARP Health Care Options PO Box 1017	Montgomeryville	PA	18936	**800-523-5800**		384-3
AARP Investment Funds PO Box 219735	Kansas City	MO	64121	**800-253-2277**		517
AARP The Magazine 601 'E' St NW	Washington	DC	20049	**800-424-3410**	202-434-6880	449-10
AARP Motoring Plan 200 N Martingale Rd	Schaumburg	IL	60173	**800-555-1121**		53
AARP Public Policy Institute 601 'E' St NW	Washington	DC	20049	**888-687-2277**	202-434-2277	654
AASA (American Assn of School Administrators) 801 N Quincy St Suite 700	Arlington	VA	22203	**800-771-1162**	703-528-0700	49-5
AASL (American Assn of School Librarians) 50 E Huron St	Chicago	IL	60611	**800-545-2433**	312-280-4386	49-11
AASR Inc 2219 McKinney St *Cust Svc	Houston	TX	77003	**800-621-0685***	713-223-4474	590
AATBS (Association for Advanced Training in the Behavioral Sciences) 5126 Ralston St	Ventura	CA	93003	**800-472-1931**	805-676-3030	49-5
AAUP (American Assn of University Professors) 1012 14th St NW Suite 500	Washington	DC	20005	**800-424-2973**	202-737-5900	49-5
AAUW Outlook Magazine 1111 16th St NW	Washington	DC	20036	**800-326-2289**	202-785-7700	449-10
AAVSO (American Assn of Variable Star Observers) 25 Birch St	Cambridge	MA	02138	**800-223-0138**	617-354-0484	49-19
AB Dick Co 7400 Caldwell Ave	Niles	IL	60714	**800-422-3616**	847-779-1900	617
AB Watley Inc 90 Park Ave 26th Fl	New York	NY	10016	**888-229-2853**	212-500-6500	679
AB Young Cos Inc 15305 Stony Creek Way	Noblesville	IN	46060	**800-886-7001**	317-565-5000	601
ABA (American Bankers Assn) 1120 Connecticut Ave NW *Cust Svc	Washington	DC	20036	**800-226-5377***	202-663-5000	49-2
ABA (American Baptist Assn) 4605 N State Line Ave	Texarkana	TX	75503	**800-264-2482**	903-792-2783	48-20
ABA (American Bar Assn) 750 N Lake Shore Dr	Chicago	IL	60611	**800-285-2221**	312-988-5000	49-10
ABA (American Bicycle Assn) 1645 W Sunrise Blvd	Gilbert	AZ	85233	**800-886-1269**	480-961-1903	48-22
ABA (American Booksellers Assn) 828 S Broadway	Tarrytown	NY	10591	**800-637-0037**	914-591-2665	49-18
ABA (American Burn Assn) 625 N Michigan Ave Suite 1530	Chicago	IL	60611	**800-548-2876**	312-642-9260	49-8
ABA (American Businesspersons Assn) 350 Fairway Dr Suite 200	Deerfield Beach	FL	33441	**800-221-2168**	954-571-1877	49-12
ABA Commission on Domestic Violence 740 15th St NW 9th Fl	Washington	DC	20005	**800-799-7233**	202-662-1737	49-10
ABA Journal 750 N Lake Shore Dr	Chicago	IL	60611	**800-285-2221**	312-988-5000	449-15
ABA Marketing Network 1120 Connecticut Ave NW	Washington	DC	20036	**800-226-5377**	202-663-5268	49-2
ABA Museum of Law 321 N Clark St	Chicago	IL	60610	**800-285-2221**	312-988-5000	509
Abacus Communications LC 4456 Corporation Ln Suite 200	Virginia Beach	VA	23462	**800-866-2004**	757-497-2004	722
Abacus Software Inc 5130 Patterson St SE *Sales	Grand Rapids	MI	49512	**800-451-4319***	616-698-0330	176-6
Abacus Technology Corp 5454 Wisconsin Ave Suite 1100	Chevy Chase	MD	20815	**800-225-2135**	301-907-8500	178
Abalon Precision Mfg Corp 1040 Home St	Bronx	NY	10459	**800-888-2225**	718-589-5682	688
Abatement Technologies 2220 Northmont Pkwy Suite 100	Duluth	GA	30096	**800-634-9091**	770-689-2600	37
Abatix Corp 8201 Eastpoint Dr Suite 500 *NASDAQ: ABIX*	Dallas	TX	75227	**800-426-3983**	214-381-1146	378
Abaxis Inc 3240 Whipple Rd *NASDAQ: ABAX*	Union City	CA	94587	**800-822-2947**	510-675-6500	410
ABB Inc 501 Merritt 7 *Prod Info	Norwalk	CT	06851	**800-626-4999***	203-750-2200	379
ABB SSAC Inc 8220 Loop Rd *Tech Supp	Baldwinsville	NY	13027	**800-377-7722***	315-638-1300	202
ABB Vetco Gray Inc 3010 Briarpark Dr Suite 300	Houston	TX	77042	**800-231-6828**	713-821-5000	526
Abbco Inc 26 N Garden Ave	Bensenville	IL	60106	**866-986-6546**	630-595-7115	447
Abbey Delray 2000 Lowson Blvd	Delray Beach	FL	33445	**800-936-7397**	561-454-2000	659
Abbey Hotel 300 21st St	Miami Beach	FL	33139	**888-612-2239**	305-531-0031	373
Abbey Press Inc 1 Hill Dr *Sales	Saint Meinrad	IN	47577	**800-962-4760***	812-357-6611	623-4
Abbey Resort & Fontana Spa 269 Fontana Blvd	Fontana	WI	53125	**800-558-2405**	262-275-6811	655
Abbot & Abbot Box Corp 37-11 10th St	Long Island City	NY	11101	**800-377-0037**	718-392-2600	199
Abbott Industries Inc 95-25 149th St	Jamaica	NY	11435	**800-232-5676**	718-291-0800	75
Abbott Laboratories 100 Abbott Pk Rd *NYSE: ABT*	Abbott Park	IL	60064	**800-323-9100**	847-937-6100	572
Abbott Laboratories Abbott Diagnostics Div 100 Abbott Pk Rd	Abbott Park	IL	60064	**800-323-9100**	847-937-6100	229
Abbott Laboratories Animal Health Div 1401 Sheridan Rd	North Chicago	IL	60064	**888-299-7416**	847-937-6100	574

Name / Address	City	State	ZIP	Toll-Free	Phone	Class
Abbott Laboratories Pharmaceutical Products Div 100 Abbott Park Rd	Abbott Park	IL	60064	800-255-5162	847-937-6100	572
Abbott Laboratories Ross Products Div 625 Cleveland Ave *PR	Columbus	OH	43215	800-227-5767*	614-624-7677	291-10
Abbott Sysco Food Service 2400 Harrison Rd	Columbus	OH	43204	800-686-3663	614-272-0658	292-8
ABC (American Bowling Congress) 5301 S 76th St	Greendale	WI	53129	800-514-2695	414-421-6400	48-22
ABC (America's Blood Centers) 725 15th St NW Suite 700	Washington	DC	20005	888-872-5663	202-393-5725	49-8
ABC Bancorp PO Box 3668 *NASDAQ: ABCB*	Moultrie	GA	31776	888-556-2701	229-890-1111	355-2
ABC-CLIO Inc 130 Cremona Dr	Santa Barbara	CA	93117	800-368-6868	805-968-1911	623-2
ABC Compounding Co Inc 6970 Jonesboro Rd	Morrow	GA	30260	800-795-9222	770-968-9222	149
ABC Corporate Services 6400 Shafer Ct Suite 310	Rosemont	IL	60018	800-722-5179	847-384-6868	760
ABC Fine Wines & Spirits 8989 S Orange Ave	Orlando	FL	32824	800-854-7283	407-851-0000	435
ABC Metals Inc 500 W Clinton St	Logansport	IN	46947	800-238-8470	574-753-0471	483
ABC News VideoSource 125 West End Ave 5th Fl	New York	NY	10023	800-789-1250	212-456-5421	500
ABC Photo & Imaging Services Inc 9016 Prince William St	Manassas	VA	20110	800-368-4044	703-369-2566	577
ABC School Supply Inc 3312 N Berkeley Lake Rd	Duluth	GA	30096	800-669-4222	770-497-0001	673
ABC Seamless Siding 3001 Fiechtner Dr	Fargo	ND	58103	800-732-6577	701-293-5952	188-12
ABC Supply Co Inc 1 ABC Pkwy	Beloit	WI	53511	800-366-2227	608-362-7777	190-4
Abco Distribution Inc 6282 Proprietors Rd	Worthington	OH	43085	800-821-9435	614-848-4899	616
Abco Inc 1621 Wall St	Dallas	TX	75215	800-969-2226	214-565-1191	87
Abco Laboratories Inc 2450 S Watney Way	Fairfield	CA	94533	800-678-2226	707-432-2200	291-37
ABCO Products Corp 6800 NW 36th Ave	Miami	FL	33147	888-694-2226	305-694-2226	497
Abco Refrigeration Supply Corp 49-70 31st St	Long Island City	NY	11101	800-786-2075	718-937-9000	651
ABD Insurance & Financial Services 305 Walnut St	Redwood City	CA	94063	800-542-7676	650-839-6000	383
Abduction. Jimmy Ryce Center for Victims of Predatory 908 Coquina Ln	Vero Beach	FL	32963	800-546-7923	772-492-0200	48-6
Abel Cigar Co 165 Aviador St	Camarillo	CA	93010	800-848-7335	805-484-8789	741-2
Abel Quality Products 165 Aviador St	Camarillo	CA	93010	800-848-7335	805-484-8789	701
Abell-Howe Crane Inc 375 W South Frontage Rd Suite A	Bolingbrook	IL	60440	800-366-0068	630-626-5520	462
Abercrombie & Fitch Co 6301 Fitch Pass *NYSE: ANF*	New Albany	OH	43054	800-666-2595	614-283-6500	155-4
Abercrombie & Kent International Inc 1520 Kensington Rd Suite 212	Oak Brook	IL	60523	800-323-7308	630-954-2944	748
Aberdeen American News 124 S 2nd St	Aberdeen	SD	57402	800-925-4100	605-225-4100	522-2
Aberdeen Area Chamber of Commerce 516 S Main St	Aberdeen	SD	57401	800-874-9038	605-225-2860	137
Aberdeen Convention & Visitors Bureau PO Box 78	Aberdeen	SD	57402	800-645-3851	605-225-2414	205
Aberdeen & Rockfish Railroad Co 101 E Main St	Aberdeen	NC	28315	800-849-5713	910-944-2341	634
Aberdeen Woods Conference Center 201 Aberdeen Pkwy	Peachtree City	GA	30269	800-285-6338	770-487-2666	370
Abe's of Maine Cameras & Electronics 1957 Coney Island Ave	Brooklyn	NY	11223	800-227-0400	718-645-0900	119
ABF Inc (Advanced Business Fulfillment Inc) 3183 Rider Trail S	Earth City	MO	63045	800-804-7430	314-770-2986	114
Abigail Adams National Bancorp Inc 1130 Connecticut Ave NW Suite 200 *NASDAQ: AANB*	Washington	DC	20036	877-442-3267	202-772-3600	355-2
Abilene Christian University ACU Box 29000 *Admissions	Abilene	TX	79699	800-460-6228*	325-674-2000	163
Abilene Convention & Visitors Bureau 201 NW 2nd St PO Box 146	Abilene	KS	67410	800-569-5915	785-263-2231	205
Abilene Convention & Visitors Bureau 1101 N 1st St	Abilene	TX	79601	800-727-7704	325-676-2556	205
Abilene Philharmonic Orchestra 402 Cypress St Suite 130	Abilene	TX	79601	800-460-0610	325-677-6710	563-3
Abilene Reporter-News 101 Cypress St	Abilene	TX	79601	800-588-6397	325-673-4271	522-2
Abingdon Convention & Visitors Bureau 335 Cummings St	Abingdon	VA	24210	800-435-3440	276-676-2282	205
ABIOMED Inc 22 Cherry Hill Dr *NASDAQ: ABMD*	Danvers	MA	01923	800-422-8666	978-777-5410	249
Abita Brewing Co 21084 Hwy 36	Covington	LA	70433	800-737-2311	985-893-3143	103
Abitec Corp Inc PO Box 569 *Sales	Columbus	OH	43216	800-555-1255*	614-429-6464	291-29
Abitibi-Consolidated Sales Corp 4 Gannett Dr	White Plains	NY	10604	800-848-7213	914-640-8600	543
ABKA (American Boarding Kennels Assn) 1702 E Pikes Peak Ave	Colorado Springs	CO	80909	877-570-7788	719-667-1600	48-3
Abkit Inc 61 Broadway Suite 1310	New York	NY	10006	800-226-6227	212-292-1550	786
Able Builders Equipment Inc 7475 NW 63rd St	Miami	FL	33166	800-864-5387	305-592-5940	261-4
Able Energy Inc PO Box 630 *NASDAQ: ABLE*	Rockaway	NJ	07866	800-564-1012	973-625-1012	311
Ableauctions.com Inc 1963 Lougheed Hwy *AMEX: AAC*	Coquitlam	BC	V3K3T8	888-599-2253	604-521-2253	51
ABMP (Associated Bodywork & Massage Professionals) 1271 Sugarbush Dr	Evergreen	CO	80439	800-458-2267	303-674-8478	48-17
ABN AMRO Funds PO Box 9765	Providence	RI	02940	800-992-8151		517
ABN AMRO Inc 135 S La Salle St	Chicago	IL	60603	800-643-9600	312-904-2000	679
ABN AMRO Mortgage Group Inc 1643 N Harrison Pkwy Bldg H	Sunrise	FL	33323	877-406-2967	954-320-1000	498
Abortion Federation. National 1755 Massachusetts Ave NW Suite 600	Washington	DC	20036	800-772-9100	202-667-5881	49-8
About Web Services 1253 N Research Way Suite Q-2500	Orem	UT	84097	800-396-1999	801-437-6000	795
AboveNet Communications Inc 1735 Lundy Ave	San Jose	CA	95131	866-859-6971	408-521-5619	387
AboveNet Inc 360 Hamilton Ave 7th Fl	White Plains	NY	10601	866-859-6971	914-421-6700	721
ABPA (American Book Producers Assn) 160 5th Ave	New York	NY	10010	800-209-4575	212-645-2368	49-16
ABRA (American Bio-Recovery Assn) 2020 Pennsylvania Ave NW Suite 456	Washington	DC	20006	888-979-2217	888-979-2272	49-4
ABRA Therapeutics Inc 10365 Hwy 116	Forestville	CA	95436	800-745-0761	707-869-0761	211
Abracadabra! Cruises 1735 Roswell Rd Suite 100	Marietta	GA	30062	800-474-5678	770-509-8080	760
Abraham Baldwin Agricultural College 2802 Moore Hwy ABAC 3	Tifton	GA	31793	800-733-3653	229-386-3236	160
Abraham Lincoln Insurance Co 5250 S 6th St	Springfield	IL	62703	800-323-0050	217-241-6300	384-2
Abrams Aerial Survey Corp 9659 W Grand Ledge Hwy Suite 1	Sunfield	MI	48890	800-826-7518	517-372-8100	713
Abrams & Co Publishers Inc PO Box 10025 *Cust Svc	Waterbury	CT	06725	800-227-9120*	203-756-3580	623-2
Abrams Construction Inc 1945 The Exchange Suite 350	Atlanta	GA	30339	800-935-9350	770-952-3555	185
Abrams Harry N Inc 100 5th Ave 7th Fl	New York	NY	10011	800-345-1359	212-206-7715	623-2
Abravanel Maurice Hall 123 W South Temple	Salt Lake City	UT	84101	888-451-2787	801-533-5626	562
Abrisa USPG PO Box 3258	Ventura	CA	93006	800-350-5000	805-525-4902	328
ABRY Partners LLC 111 Huntington Ave 30th Fl	Boston	MA	02199	800-578-2279	617-859-2959	397
ABS-CBN Global Ltd DBA Filipino Channel 859 Cowan Rd	Burlingame	CA	94010	800-345-2465	650-697-3700	725
ABS Computer Technologies Inc 9997 E Rosehills Rd *Sales	Whittier	CA	90601	800-876-8088*	562-695-8823	171-3
ABS Global Inc 1525 River Rd *Cust Svc	DeForest	WI	53532	800-356-5331*	608-846-3721	12-2
Abso-Clean Industries Inc 199 Wales Ave	Tonawanda	NY	14150	800-837-5000	716-693-2111	149
Absolut Aire Inc 5496 N Riverview Dr	Kalamazoo	MI	49004	800-804-4000	269-382-1875	15
Absopure Water Co 8835 General Dr	Plymouth	MI	48170	800-422-7678		792
ABT Internet 525 Northern Blvd Suite 302	Great Neck	NY	11021	800-367-3414	516-829-5484	390
ABTA (American Brain Tumor Assn) 2720 River Rd	Des Plaines	IL	60018	800-886-2282	847-827-9910	48-17
Abuse America. Prevent Child 200 S Michigan Ave 17th Fl	Chicago	IL	60604	800-244-5373	312-663-3520	48-6
Abuse of Children. American Professional Society on the 107 Amberside Dr	Goose Creek	SC	29445	877-402-7722	843-764-2905	48-6
Abuse & Incest National Network. Rape 635-B Pennsylvania Ave SE	Washington	DC	20003	800-656-4673	202-544-1034	48-6
Abused by Priests. Survivors Network of Those PO Box 6416	Chicago	IL	60680	877-409-2720	312-409-2720	48-21
ABWA (American Business Women's Assn) 9100 Ward Pkwy	Kansas City	MO	64114	800-228-0007	816-361-6621	49-12
AC Dellovade Inc 108 Cavasina Dr	Canonsburg	PA	15317	800-245-1556	724-873-8190	188-12
AC Miller Concrete Products Inc PO Box 199	Spring City	PA	19475	800-229-2922	610-948-4600	181
AC & S Inc 120 N Lime St	Lancaster	PA	17602	800-487-7255	717-397-3631	188-9
AC & T Co Inc 11535 Hopewell Rd	Hagerstown	MD	21740	800-458-3835	301-582-2700	311
ACA (Agriculture Council of America) 11020 King St Suite 205	Overland Park	KS	66210	888-982-4329	913-491-1895	48-2
ACA (American Camp Assn) 5000 SR-67 N	Martinsville	IN	46151	800-428-2267	765-342-8456	48-23
ACA (American Canoe Assn) 7432 Alban Station Blvd Suite B-232	Springfield	VA	22150	800-929-5162	703-451-0141	48-22
ACA (American Chiropractic Assn) 1701 Clarendon Blvd 2nd Fl	Arlington	VA	22209	800-986-4636	703-276-8800	49-8
ACA (American Correctional Assn) 4380 Forbes Blvd	Lanham	MD	20706	800-222-5646	301-918-1800	49-7
ACA (American Counseling Assn) 5999 Stevenson Ave	Alexandria	VA	22304	800-347-6647	703-823-9800	49-15
ACA (Auto Club of America Corp) 9411 N Georgia St	Oklahoma City	OK	73120	800-411-2007	405-751-4430	53
ACA-PAC (American Chiropractic Assn PAC) 1701 Clarendon Blvd	Arlington	VA	22209	800-986-4636	703-276-8800	604
ACAAI (American College of Allergy Asthma & Immunology) 85 W Algonquin Rd Suite 550	Arlington Heights	IL	60005	800-842-7777	847-427-1200	49-8
Acacia Federal Savings Bank 7600 Leesburg Pike East Bldg Suite 200	Falls Church	VA	22043	800-950-0270	703-506-8100	71
Acacia Life Insurance Co 7315 Wisconsin Ave	Bethesda	MD	20814	800-444-1889	301-280-1000	384-2
Acacia National Life 7315 Wisconsin Ave	Bethesda	MD	20814	800-444-1889	301-280-1000	384-2
Academe Magazine 1012 14th St NW Suite 500	Washington	DC	20005	800-424-2973	202-737-5900	449-8
Academic Choir Apparel 20644 Superior St	Chatsworth	CA	91311	800-626-5000	818-886-8697	153-14
Academy of Art University 79 New Montgomery St	San Francisco	CA	94105	800-544-2787	415-274-2200	163
Academy Bus Tours Inc 111 Paterson Ave	Hoboken	NJ	07030	800-442-7272	201-339-6000	740

Listing	City	State	ZIP	Toll-Free	Phone	Class
Academy of General Dentistry (AGD) 211 E Chicago Ave Suite 900	Chicago	IL	60611	**888-243-3368**	312-440-4300	49-8
Academy for Guided Imagery Inc 30765 Pacific Coast Hwy Suite 369	Malibu	CA	90265	**800-726-2070**		754
Academy of Managed Care Pharmacy (AMCP) 100 N Pitt St Suite 400	Alexandria	VA	22314	**800-827-2627**	703-683-8416	49-8
Academy of Model Aeronautics (AMA) 5161 E Memorial Dr	Muncie	IN	47302	**800-435-9262**	765-287-1256	48-18
Academy of Music Broad & Locust Sts	Philadelphia	PA	19102	**800-457-8354**	215-893-1935	562
Academy of Osseointegration 85 W Algonquin Rd Suite 550	Arlington Heights	IL	60005	**800-656-7736**	847-439-1919	49-8
Academy Sports & Outdoors 1800 N Mason Rd	Katy	TX	77449	**877-999-9856**	281-646-5200	702
Academy of Students of Pharmacy American Pharmacists Assn 2215 Constitution Ave NW	Washington	DC	20037	**800-237-2742**	202-628-4410	49-8
Acadia Inn 98 Eden St	Bar Harbor	ME	04609	**800-638-3636**	207-288-3500	373
Acadia National Park Rt 233 Eagle Lake Rd *Campground Resv	Bar Harbor	ME	04609	**800-365-2267***	207-288-3338	554
Acadia Polymers Inc Park at Valley Pointe 5251 Concourse Dr Suite 3	Roanoke	VA	24019	**800-444-6165**	540-265-2700	60
Acadia Realty Trust 1311 Mamaroneck Ave Suite 260 *NYSE: AKR*	White Plains	NY	10605	**800-227-5570**	914-288-8100	641
Acadian Ambulance & Air Med Services Inc PO Box 98000	Lafayette	LA	70509	**800-259-3333**	337-291-3333	31
ACAM (American College for Advancement in Medicine) 23121 Verdugo Dr Suite 204	Laguna Hills	CA	92653	**800-532-3688**	949-583-7666	49-8
Acapulco Restaurants Inc 4001 Via Oro Ave Suite 200	Long Beach	CA	90810	**800-735-3501**	310-513-7500	657
ACAT (Accreditation Council for Accountancy & Taxation) 1010 N Fairfax St	Alexandria	VA	22314	**888-289-7763**	703-549-2228	48-1
ACB (American Council of the Blind) 1155 15th St NW Suite 1004	Washington	DC	20005	**800-424-8666**	202-467-5081	48-17
ACBL (American Contract Bridge League) 2990 Airways Blvd *Sales	Memphis	TN	38116	**800-264-2743***	901-332-5586	48-18
ACC (American College of Cardiology) 9111 Old Georgetown Rd *Cust Svc	Bethesda	MD	20814	**800-253-4636***	301-897-5400	49-8
ACCE (American Chamber of Commerce Executives) 4875 Eisenhower Ave Suite 250	Alexandria	VA	22304	**800-394-2223**	703-998-0072	49-12
Accel Graphic Systems Inc 11103 Indian Trail	Dallas	TX	75229	**800-666-8803**	972-484-6808	617
Accelerated Business Credit Corp 101 N Westlake Blvd Suite 204	Westlake Village	CA	91362	**866-446-2888**	805-370-0234	268
Accelerated Genetics E 10890 Penny Ln	Baraboo	WI	53913	**800-451-9275**	608-356-8357	12-2
Accelerated Technology Inc 734 N University Blvd	Mobile	AL	36608	**800-468-6853**	251-208-3400	176-2
Accellent 200 W 7th Ave	Collegeville	PA	19426	**800-321-6285**	610-489-0300	610
Accelr8 Technology Corp 7000 Broadway Bldg 3-307 *AMEX: AXK*	Denver	CO	80221	**800-582-8898**	303-863-8088	176-12
Accelrys Inc 9685 Scranton Rd *NASDAQ: ACCL*	San Diego	CA	92121	**800-756-4674**	858-799-5000	176-5
Accent Inns Vancouver Airport 10551 St Edwards Dr	Richmond	BC	V6X3L8	**800-663-0298**	604-273-3311	372
Accent Inns Vancouver-Burnaby 3777 Henning Dr	Burnaby	BC	V5C6N5	**800-663-0298**	604-473-5000	372
Acceptance Insurance Cos Inc 300 W Broadway Suite 3600	Council Bluffs	IA	51503	**800-228-7217**	712-329-3600	384-4
Acceris Communications Solutions 1001 Brinton Rd	Pittsburgh	PA	15221	**800-447-2111**	412-244-6600	721
Access America 673 Emery Valley Rd	Oak Ridge	TN	37830	**800-860-2140**	865-482-2140	721
Access America 2805 N Parham Rd	Richmond	VA	23294	**800-729-6021**	804-285-3300	384-7
Access Anytime Bancorp Inc 801 Pile St *NASDAQ: AABC*	Clovis	NM	88101	**888-299-4310**	505-762-4417	355-2
Access Board 1331 F St NW Suite 1000	Washington	DC	20004	**800-872-2253**	202-272-0080	336-16
Access Business Group LLC 7575 Fulton St E *Cust Svc	Ada	MI	49355	**800-253-6500***	616-787-5358	440
Access Communications 101 Howard St	San Francisco	CA	94105	**800-393-7737**	415-904-7070	622
Access Data Corp 2 Chatham Ctr 11th Fl	Pittsburgh	PA	15219	**888-799-1744**	412-201-6000	39
Access Energy Co-op 907 E Washington St	Mount Pleasant	IA	52641	**866-242-4232**	319-385-1577	244
Access Group PO Box 250367	Atlanta	GA	30325	**877-353-9837**	770-234-3600	384-4
Access Industries Inc 4001 E 138th St	Grandview	MO	64030	**800-669-9047**	816-763-3100	255
Access Innovations Inc 131 Adams St NE	Albuquerque	NM	87108	**800-926-8328**	505-265-3591	175
Access Intelligence LLC 1201 Seven Locks Rd Suite 300	Potomac	MD	20854	**800-777-5006**	301-354-2000	623-9
Access US 712 N 2nd St Suite 300	Saint Louis	MO	63102	**800-638-6373**	314-655-7700	390
Access Worldwide Communications Inc 4950 Communications Ave Suite 300	Boca Raton	FL	33431	**800-867-2340**	561-226-5000	722
Accessories Assoc Inc 500 George Washington Hwy	Smithfield	RI	02917	**800-388-0258**	401-231-3800	400
Accident Fund Co 232 S Capitol Ave	Lansing	MI	48901	**800-888-0616**	517-342-4200	384-4
Acclaim Energy Trust 255 5th Ave SW Suite 1900 *TSE: AE.DB*	Calgary	AB	T2P2Z1	**877-539-6300**	403-539-6300	662
ACCO Brands Inc 300 Tower Pkwy	Lincolnshire	IL	60069	**800-222-6462**	847-541-9500	87
ACCO Canada Inc 5 Precido Ct	Brampton	ON	L6S6B7	**800-268-3447**	905-595-3100	87
Acco Chain & Lifting PO Box 792	York	PA	17405	**800-967-7333**	717-741-4863	462
ACCO Engineered Systems 6265 San Fernando Rd *Cust Svc	Glendale	CA	91201	**800-998-2226***	818-244-6571	188-10
Acco Feeds Inc 1025 China St	Abilene	TX	79602	**800-592-4472**	325-672-3271	438
Acco Systems Inc 12755 E Nine-Mile Rd	Warren	MI	48089	**800-521-3423**	586-755-7500	206
Accommodations Plus 4230 Merrick Rd	Massapequa	NY	11758	**800-733-7666**	718-995-4444	368
Accor Economy Lodging						
Motel 6 LP 4001 International Pkwy	Carrollton	TX	75007	**800-466-8356**	972-360-9000	369
Red Roof Inns Inc 4001 International Pkwy	Carrollton	TX	75007	**800-733-7663**	972-360-9000	369
Studio 6 4001 International Pkwy	Carrollton	TX	75007	**800-466-8356**	972-360-9000	369
Accord Financial Corp 77 Bloor St W *TSE: ACD*	Toronto	ON	M5S1M2	**800-967-0015**	416-961-0007	268
Accord Financial Inc 25 Woods Lake Rd Suite 102	Greenville	SC	29607	**800-231-2757**	864-271-4384	268
Accord Human Resources Inc 210 Park Ave Suite 1200	Oklahoma City	OK	73102	**800-725-4004**	405-232-9888	619
Accord Industries 4001 Forsyth Rd	Winter Park	FL	32792	**800-477-7675**	407-671-5200	181
Account Funding Inc 16055 Ventura Blvd Suite 924	Encino	CA	91436	**800-666-3928**		268
Accountancy. National Assn of State Boards of 150 4th Ave N Suite 700	Nashville	TN	37219	**800-272-3926**	615-880-4200	49-1
Accountancy & Taxation. Accreditation Council for 1010 N Fairfax St	Alexandria	VA	22314	**888-289-7763**	703-549-2228	48-1
Accountants. American Institute of Certified Public 1211 Ave of the Americas	New York	NY	10036	**888-777-7077**	212-596-6200	49-1
Accountants. American Woman's Society of Certified Public 136 S Keowee St	Dayton	OH	45402	**800-297-2721**	937-222-1872	49-1
Accountants. Association of Government 2208 Mt Vernon Ave	Alexandria	VA	22301	**800-242-7211**	703-684-6931	49-1
Accountants Global Network 2851 S Parker Rd Suite 850	Aurora	CO	80014	**800-782-2272**	303-743-7880	49-1
Accountants Inc. Institute of Management 10 Paragon Dr	Montvale	NJ	07645	**800-638-4427**	201-573-9000	49-1
Accountants. National Society of 1010 N Fairfax St	Alexandria	VA	22314	**800-966-6679**	703-549-6400	49-1
Accounting Dept Management & Administration Report 3 Park Ave 30th Fl	New York	NY	10016	**800-401-5937**	212-244-0360	521-2
Accounting Education. Foundation for 3 Park Ave 18th Fl	New York	NY	10016	**800-537-3635**	212-719-8300	49-1
Accounting for Law Firms Newsletter 345 Park Ave S	New York	NY	10010	**800-888-8300**	212-779-9200	521-2
Accounting Office Management & Administration Report 3 Park Ave 30th Fl	New York	NY	10016	**800-401-5937**	212-244-0360	521-2
Accounting Today Magazine PO Box 4871	Chicago	IL	60694	**800-260-2793**		449-5
AccountingSolutions Div Career Blazers Inc 222 W Las Colinas Blvd Suite 1250E	Irving	TX	75039	**800-787-6750**	214-296-6700	707
Accounts Receivable Funding Corp 317 Peoples St Suite 600	Corpus Christi	TX	78401	**800-992-1717**	361-884-7196	268
Accoutrements PO Box 30811	Seattle	WA	98113	**800-886-2221**	425-349-3838	323
ACCP (American College of Chest Physicians) 3300 Dundee Rd	Northbrook	IL	60062	**800-343-2227**	847-498-1400	49-8
Accraply Div Barry-Wehmiller Cos Inc 3580 Holly Ln N	Plymouth	MN	55447	**800-328-3997**	763-557-1313	537
Accreditation Commission. Continuing Care 1730 Rhode Island Ave NW Suite 209	Washington	DC	20036	**866-888-1122**	202-587-5001	48-1
Accreditation. Commission on Office Laboratory 9881 Broken Land Pkwy Suite 200	Columbia	MD	21046	**800-981-9883**	410-381-6581	49-8
Accreditation. Council on 120 Wall St 11th Fl	New York	NY	10005	**866-262-8088**	212-797-3000	48-1
Accreditation Council for Accountancy & Taxation (ACAT) 1010 N Fairfax St	Alexandria	VA	22314	**888-289-7763**	703-549-2228	48-1
Accreditation for Law Enforcement Agencies. Commission on 10302 Eaton Pl Suite 100	Fairfax	VA	22030	**800-368-3757**	703-352-4225	49-7
Accreditation Program Inc. Community Health 39 Broadway Suite 710	New York	NY	10006	**800-656-9656**	212-480-8828	48-1
Accreditation of Rehabilitation Facilities. Commission on 4891 E Grant Rd	Tucson	AZ	85712	**888-281-6531**	520-325-1044	48-1
Accredited Home Lenders Inc 15030 Ave of Science Suite 100 *NASDAQ: LEND*	San Diego	CA	92128	**800-690-6000**	858-676-2100	498
Accrediting Commission Inc. National League for Nursing 61 Broadway 33rd Fl	New York	NY	10006	**800-669-1656**	212-363-5555	48-1
Accredo Health Inc 1640 Century Center Pkwy Suite 101 *NASDAQ: ACDO*	Memphis	TN	38134	**877-222-7336**	901-385-3688	576
ACCU-GLASS Div Becton Dickinson & Co 10765 Trenton Ave	Saint Louis	MO	63132	**800-325-4796**	314-423-0300	328
Accu-Sort Systems Inc 511 School House Rd	Telford	PA	18969	**800-227-2633**	215-723-0981	171-7
AccuBanc Mortgage Corp 12377 Merit Dr Suite 600	Dallas	TX	75251	**800-457-1600**	972-982-7000	498
Accucaps Industries Ltd 2125 Ambassador Dr	Windsor	ON	N9C3R5	**800-665-7210**	519-969-5404	572
Accufax PO Box 35563	Tulsa	OK	74153	**800-256-8898**	918-627-2226	621
Accuracy in Media Inc (AIM) 4455 Connecticut Ave NW Suite 330	Washington	DC	20008	**800-787-4567**	202-364-4401	49-14
Accuracy in Media Report 4455 Connecticut Ave NW Suite 330	Washington	DC	20008	**800-787-4567**	202-364-4401	521-11

Company / Address	City	State	ZIP	Toll-Free	Phone	Class
Accurate Air Engineering Inc 2712 N Alameda St	Compton	CA	90224	**800-438-5577**	310-537-1350	378
Accurate Arms Co Inc 5891 Hwy 230 W	McEwen	TN	37101	**800-416-3006**	931-729-4207	264
Accurate Bushing Co Inc 443 North Ave *Sales	Garwood	NJ	07027	**800-932-0076***	908-789-1121	77
Accurate Chemical & Scientific Corp 300 Shames Dr	Westbury	NY	11590	**800-645-6264**	516-333-2221	229
Accurate Flannel Bag Co 35-37 36th St 6th Fl	Long Island City	NY	11106	**800-234-9200**	718-784-7600	343
Accurate Mailings Inc 215 O'Neill Ave	Belmont	CA	94002	**800-732-3290**	650-591-5601	5
Accurate Perforating Co 3636 S Kedzie Ave	Chicago	IL	60632	**800-621-0273**	773-254-3232	479
Accurate Surgical & Scientific Instruments Corp 300 Shames Dr	Westbury	NY	11590	**800-645-3569**	516-333-2570	468
Accuride Corp 7140 Office Cir *NYSE: ACW* ■ *Cust Svc	Evansville	IN	47715	**800-626-7096***	812-962-5000	60
Accursio Sam S & Sons Farms PO Box 901767	Homestead	FL	33090	**800-233-6826**	305-246-3455	11-11
Accutec Inc 168 Main Ave	Wallington	NJ	07057	**800-222-8832**	973-471-3131	560
Accutest Laboratories 2235 Rt 130 Bldg B	Dayton	NJ	08810	**800-329-0204**	732-329-0200	728
Accutrade Inc PO Box 2227 *Cust Svc	Omaha	NE	68103	**800-228-3011***	402-970-7400	679
AccuWeather Inc 385 Science Park Rd *Sales	State College	PA	16803	**800-566-6606***	814-235-8650	520
ACD (American College of Dentists) 839 Quince Orchard Blvd Suite J	Gaithersburg	MD	20878	**888-223-1920**	301-977-3223	49-8
ACD Systems International Inc PO Box 36 *TSE: ASA*	Saanichton	BC	V8M2C3	**800-579-5309**	250-544-6700	176-8
ACDE (American Council for Drug Education) c/o Phoenix House 164 W 74th St	New York	NY	10023	**800-378-4435**	212-595-5810	48-17
ACDI/VOCA (ACDI/VOCA) 50 F St NW Suite 1075	Washington	DC	20001	**800-929-8622**	202-638-4661	48-5
ACE (Altamont Commuter Express) 5000 Airport Way Stockton Metropolitan Airport Suite 201	Stockton	CA	95206	**800-411-7245**	209-468-5600	460
ACE (American Council on Exercise) 4851 Paramount Dr	San Diego	CA	92123	**800-825-3636**	858-279-8227	48-17
ACE Cash Express Inc 1231 Greenway Dr Suite 800 *NASDAQ: AACE* ■ *Sales	Irving	TX	75038	**800-713-3338***	972-550-5000	139
ACE Conference Center & Country Club 800 Ridge Pike	Lafayette Hill	PA	19444	**800-523-3000**	610-825-8000	370
Ace Doran Hauling & Rigging Co Inc 1601 Blue Rock St	Cincinnati	OH	45223	**800-829-0929**	513-681-7900	769
Ace Forms of Kansas Inc 2900 N Rotary Terr	Pittsburg	KS	66762	**800-223-9287**	620-232-9290	111
Ace Glass Inc 1430 Northwest Blvd PO Box 688	Vineland	NJ	08360	**800-223-4524**	856-692-3333	329
Ace Mortgage Funding Inc 777 Beachway Dr	Indianapolis	IN	46224	**888-223-9975**	317-246-5740	498
Ace Parking Management Inc 645 Ash St	San Diego	CA	92101	**800-925-7275**	619-233-6624	552
Ace Rent-A-Car 5806 W Washington St	Indianapolis	IN	46241	**800-242-7368**	317-243-6336	126
Ace Sign Systems Inc 3621 W Royerton Rd	Muncie	IN	47304	**800-607-6010**	765-288-1000	692
Ace Tank & Equipment Co PO Box 9039	Seattle	WA	98109	**877-223-8265**	206-281-5000	92
Ace-Tex Enterprises 7601 Central St	Detroit	MI	48210	**800-444-3800**	313-834-4000	434
Ace Tool Co 7337 Bryan Dairy Rd	Largo	FL	33777	**800-777-5910**	727-544-4331	61
Ace World Wide Moving 1900 E College Ave	Cudahy	WI	53110	**800-223-6683**	414-764-1000	508
ACE*COMM Corp 704 Quince Orchard Rd Suite 100 *NASDAQ: ACEC*	Gaithersburg	MD	20878	**800-989-5566**	301-721-3000	720
Aceco Industrial Packaging 166 Frelinghuysen Ave	Newark	NJ	07114	**800-832-2247**	973-242-2200	68
ACEI (Association for Childhood Education International) 17904 Georgia Ave Suite 215	Olney	MD	20832	**800-423-3563**	301-570-2111	49-5
ACEP (American College of Emergency Physicians) PO Box 619911	Dallas	TX	75261	**800-798-1822**	972-550-0911	49-8
Acer America Corp 2641 Orchard Pkwy Bldg 1	San Jose	CA	95134	**800-733-2237**	408-432-6200	171-3
ACES (American College of Eye Surgeons) 334 E Lake Rd Suite 135	Palm Lake Harbor	FL	34685	**888-335-0077**	727-480-8542	49-8
ACES (Association for Children for Enforcement of Support) PO Box 7842	Fredericksburg	VA	22404	**800-738-2237**		48-6
ACF (American Culinary Federation Inc) 180 Sector Place Way	Saint Augustine	FL	32095	**800-624-9458**	904-824-4468	49-6
ACF (Association of Consulting Foresters of America) 312 Montgomery St Suite 208	Alexandria	VA	22314	**888-540-8733**	703-548-0990	48-2
ACF Components & Fasteners Inc 31012 Huntwood Ave *Cust Svc	Hayward	CA	94544	**800-227-2901***	510-487-2100	245
ACFAS (American College of Foot & Ankle Surgeons) 8725 W Higgins Rd Suite 555	Chicago	IL	60631	**800-421-2237**	773-693-9300	49-8
ACFC (American Coalition for Fathers & Children) 1420 Spring Hill Rd	McLean	VA	22102	**800-978-3237**		48-6
ACG (Association for Corporate Growth) 1926 Waukegan Rd Suite 1	Glenview	IL	60025	**800-699-1331**	847-657-6730	49-12
ACG Direct 14660 23-Mile Rd	Shelby Township	MI	48315	**800-968-7101**	586-247-7100	378
ACH Food Cos Inc 7171 Goodlet Farms Pkwy	Cordova	TN	38016	**800-691-1106**	901-381-3000	291-30
ACHCA (American College of Health Care Administrators) 300 N Lee St Suite 301	Alexandria	VA	22314	**888-882-2422**	703-739-7900	49-8
ACHE (American Council for Headache Education) 19 Mantua Rd	Mount Royal	NJ	08061	**800-255-2243**	856-423-0258	48-17
ACHE (Association for Continuing Higher Education) 2001 Mabelene Rd	Charleston	SC	29406	**800-807-2243**	843-574-6658	49-5
Acheson Colloids Co 1600 Washington Ave	Port Huron	MI	48060	**800-255-1908**	810-984-5581	530
AchieveGlobal Inc 8875 Hidden River Pkwy Suite 400	Tampa	FL	33637	**800-659-6090**	813-631-5500	753
ACI Distribution 965 Ridge Lake Blvd Suite 300	Memphis	TN	38120	**800-238-6057**	901-767-7111	325
ACI Electronics Inc 125 Michael Dr Suite 105	Syosset	NY	11791	**800-645-4955**	516-730-8182	245
ACI Telecentrics Inc 3100 W Lake St Suite 300	Minneapolis	MN	55416	**800-735-1224**	612-928-4700	722
Acic Fine Chemicals Inc 131 Clarence St Suite 200	Brantford	ON	N3T2V6	**800-265-6727**	519-751-3668	470
ACIPCO (American Cast Iron Pipe Co) 2916 16th St N	Birmingham	AL	35207	**800-442-2347**	205-325-7701	302
Ackerman Mfg Co/Spring Air 4140 Park Ave	Saint Louis	MO	63110	**800-264-3052**	314-771-3052	463
Ackermann Public Relations & Marketing 1111 Northshore Dr Suite N-400	Knoxville	TN	37919	**888-414-7787**	865-584-0550	622
ACLARA BioSciences Inc 1288 Pear Ave *NASDAQ: ACLA*	Mountain View	CA	94043	**800-257-7121**	650-210-1200	410
ACM (Association for Computing Machinery) 1515 Broadway 17th Fl	New York	NY	10036	**800-342-6626**	212-869-7440	48-9
ACM Aviation Inc 1475 Airport Blvd	San Jose	CA	95110	**800-359-7538**	408-286-3832	63
ACMA Computers Inc 1505 Reliance Way *Sales	Fremont	CA	94539	**800-786-6888***	510-623-1212	171-3
ACMA USA Inc 501 Southlake Blvd	Richmond	VA	23236	**800-525-2735**	804-794-9777	537
ACME (Association for Couples in Marriage Enrichment) PO Box 10596	Winston-Salem	NC	27108	**800-634-8325**	336-724-1526	48-6
Acme Brick Co 2821 W 7th St	Fort Worth	TX	76107	**800-433-5650**	817-332-4101	148
Acme Construction Co Inc 7695 Bond St	Cleveland	OH	44139	**800-938-2263**	440-232-7474	187-8
Acme Dynamics Inc 3608 Sydney Rd	Plant City	FL	33566	**800-622-9355**	813-752-3137	627
Acme Farms Inc PO Box 3065	Seattle	WA	98114	**800-542-8309**	206-323-4300	292-10
Acme Group 1750 Telegraph Rd	Bloomfield Hills	MI	48302	**800-521-8565**	248-203-2000	730-3
Acme Industrial Co 441 Maple Ave	Carpentersville	IL	60110	**800-323-5582**	847-428-3911	484
Acme Linen Co Inc 5136 E Triggs St	City of Commerce	CA	90022	**800-255-2263**	323-266-4000	356
Acme Markets Inc 75 Valley Stream Pkwy	Malvern	PA	19355	**800-767-2312**	610-889-4000	339
Acme Metal Cap Inc Co 33-53 62nd St	Woodside	NY	11377	**800-338-3581**	718-335-3000	479
Acme Mfg Co 4240 N Atlantic Blvd	Auburn Hills	MI	48326	**888-340-2263**	248-393-7300	447
Acme Mfg Co 7601 State Rd	Philadelphia	PA	19136	**800-899-2850**	215-338-2850	688
Acme Pizza & Bakery Equipment Inc 7039 E Slauson Ave	Commerce	CA	90040	**800-428-2263**	323-722-7900	293
Acme Printing Co Inc 30 Industrial Way	Wilmington	MA	01887	**800-829-0800**	978-658-0800	615
Acme Spirally Wound Paper Products Inc 4810 W 139th St PO Box 35320	Cleveland	OH	44135	**800-274-2797**	216-267-2950	125
Acme Truck Line Inc 121 Pailet Dr	Harvey	LA	70058	**800-825-6246**	504-368-2510	769
Acme United Corp 1931 Black Rock Tpke *AMEX: ACU*	Fairfield	CT	06825	**800-835-2263**	203-332-7330	468
ACMI Corp 136 Turnpike Rd	Southborough	MA	01772	**866-879-0640**	508-804-2600	375
ACOFP (American College of Osteopathic Family Physicians) 330 E Algonquin Rd Suite 1	Arlington Heights	IL	60005	**800-323-0794**	847-228-6090	49-8
ACOM Solutions Inc 2850 E 29th St	Long Beach	CA	90806	**800-347-3638**	562-424-7899	176-1
Acor Orthopaedic Inc 18530 S Miles Pkwy	Cleveland	OH	44128	**800-237-2267**	216-662-4500	296
ACORD PO Box 1529	Pearl River	NY	10965	**800-444-3341**	845-620-1700	49-9
Acordia Inc 150 N Michigan Ave Suite 4100	Chicago	IL	60601	**866-226-7342**	312-423-2500	383
Acordis Celluosic Fibers Ltd US Hwy 43 N PO Box 171	Axis	AL	36505	**800-633-6720**	251-679-2200	730-8
ACORN (Association of Community Organizations for Reform Now) 739 8th St SE	Washington	DC	20003	**877-552-2676**	202-547-2500	48-7
Acorn Engineering Co Inc PO Box 3527	City of Industry	CA	91744	**800-488-8999**	626-336-4561	598
Acorn Products Inc 390 W Nationwide Blvd	Columbus	OH	43215	**800-888-4196**	614-222-4400	746
Acorn Wire & Iron Works Inc 4940 S Kilbourn Ave	Chicago	IL	60632	**800-552-2676**	773-585-0600	275
Acosta Sales & Marketing Co 500 Waters Edge Oak Creek Ctr	Lombard	IL	60148	**800-843-2750**	630-620-7600	194
Acoustic Systems Inc 415 E St Elmo Rd	Austin	TX	78745	**800-749-1460**	512-444-1961	382
Acoustical Material Services Inc 1620 S Maple Ave	Montebello	CA	90640	**800-486-3517**	323-721-9011	190-2
ACP (American College of Physicians) 190 N Independence Mall W	Philadelphia	PA	19106	**800-523-1546**	215-351-2400	49-8
ACPA (American Chronic Pain Assn) PO Box 850	Rocklin	CA	95677	**800-533-3231**	916-632-0922	48-17
ACPE (American College of Physician Executives) 4890 W Kennedy Blvd Suite 200	Tampa	FL	33609	**800-562-8088**	813-287-2000	49-8

Name / Address	City	State	ZIP	Toll-Free	Phone	Class
Acqua Hotel 555 Redwood Hwy	Mill Valley	CA	94941	**800-738-7477**	415-380-0400	373
ACR (American College of Radiology)						
1891 Preston White Dr.	Reston	VA	20191	**800-227-5463**	703-648-8900	49-8
ACR Electronics Inc						
5757 Ravenswood Rd	Fort Lauderdale	FL	33312	**800-432-0227**	954-981-3333	666
ACRL (Association of College &						
Research Libraries) 50 E Huron St	Chicago	IL	60611	**800-545-2433**	312-280-2519	49-11
Acro Labels Inc						
2530 Wyandotte Rd	Willow Grove	PA	19090	**800-355-2235**	215-657-5366	404
Acrodyne Industries Inc						
200 Schell Ln	Phoenixville	PA	19460	**800-523-2596**	610-917-1300	633
ACRS (Associated Communications						
& Research Services Inc)						
817 NE 63rd St.	Oklahoma City	OK	73105	**800-442-3341**	405-843-9966	195
Acrylic Design Assoc						
6050 Nathan Ln N	Plymouth	MN	55442	**800-445-2167**	763-559-8395	231
ACS (American Cancer Society)						
1599 Clifton Rd NE.	Atlanta	GA	30329	**800-227-2345**	404-320-3333	48-17
ACS (American Chemical Society)						
1155 16th St NW	Washington	DC	20036	**800-227-5558**	202-872-4600	49-19
ACS (American College of Surgeons)						
633 N Saint Clair St	Chicago	IL	60611	**800-621-4111**	312-202-5000	49-8
ACS Industries Inc 191 Social St	Woonsocket	RI	02895	**800-237-1939**	401-769-4700	676
ACSI (Association of Christian						
Schools International)						
731 Chapel Hills Dr	Colorado Springs	CO	80920	**800-367-0798***	719-528-6906	49-5
*Cust Svc						
AcSys Biometrics Corp 399 Pearl St.	Burlington	ON	L7R2M8	**877-842-7687**	905-634-4111	85
ACT Teleconferencing Inc						
1526 Cole Blvd Bldg 3 Suite 300	Golden	CO	80401	**800-228-2554**	303-235-9000	721
NASDAQ: ACTT						
ACTE (Association for Career &						
Technical Education)						
1410 King St.	Alexandria	VA	22314	**800-826-9972**	703-683-3111	49-5
ACTE (Association of Corporate Travel						
Executives) 515 King St						
Suite 340	Alexandria	VA	22314	**800-228-3669**	703-683-5322	48-23
Actel Corp 2061 Stierlin Ct	Mountain View	CA	94043	**800-262-1060**	650-318-4200	686
NASDAQ: ACTL						
Acterna Corp						
1 Milestone Center Dr	Germantown	MD	20876	**800-543-1550**	301-353-1550	720
Acteva.com 1 Bush St 15th Fl.	San Francisco	CA	94104	**877-855-8646***	415-374-8222	735
*Cust Svc						
Action Against Hunger						
247 W 37th St Suite 1201	New York	NY	10018	**877-777-1420**	212-967-7800	48-5
Action Capital Corp						
230 Peachtree St Suite 910	Atlanta	GA	30303	**800-525-7767**	404-524-3181	268
Action Co 1425 N Tennessee St	McKinney	TX	75069	**800-937-3700***	972-542-8700	423
*Sales						
Action Products International Inc						
1101 N Keller Rd Suite E.	Orlando	FL	32810	**800-772-2846**	407-481-8007	750
NASDAQ: APII						
Action Sports Systems Inc						
617 Carbon City Rd	Morganton	NC	28655	**800-631-1091**	828-584-8000	153-19
Action Technologies Inc						
10970 International Blvd 2nd Fl	Oakland	CA	94603	**800-967-5356**	510-638-8300	176-1
ActionTec Electronics Inc						
760 N Mary Ave	Sunnyvale	CA	94085	**800-752-7820**	408-752-7700	496
Activant Solutions Inc						
804 Las Cimas Pkwy	Austin	TX	78746	**800-678-5266**	512-328-2300	176-10
ActivCard Inc 6623 Dumbarton Cir	Fremont	CA	94555	**800-529-9499**	510-574-0100	176-12
NASDAQ: ACTI						
Active Aero Group 2068 E St	Belleville	MI	48111	**800-872-5387***	734-547-7200	14
*Cust Svc						
Active Decisions Inc						
1400 Fashion Island Blvd						
Suite 500	San Mateo	CA	94404	**866-662-3847**	650-342-0500	7
Active Industries Inc 20 Solar Dr	Clifton Park	NY	12065	**800-403-2284**	518-371-2020	804
Active Network						
1020 Prospect St Suite 250	La Jolla	CA	92037	**888-543-7223***	858-551-9916	7
*Cust Svc						
Active Parenting Publishers						
810 Franklin Ct SE Suite B.	Marietta	GA	30067	**800-825-0060**	770-429-0565	502
Active Services Corp						
1500 Urban Center Dr						
Suite 200	Vestavia Hills	AL	35242	**800-805-7430**	205-970-3300	442
Active Transportation Co						
3050 W Broadway	Louisville	KY	46211	**800-685-5638**	502-775-6401	769
Active Voice LLC						
2033 6th Ave Suite 500	Seattle	WA	98121	**877-864-8948***	206-441-4700	176-7
*Sales						
Active Web Corp						
3-304 Stone Rd W Suite 155	Guelph	ON	N1G4W4	**866-837-2711**	519-837-2711	796
activePDF Inc						
27405 Puerta Real Suite 100	Mission Viejo	CA	92691	**866-468-6733**	949-582-9002	176-12
Actors Theatre of Louisville						
316 W Main St	Louisville	KY	40202	**800-428-5849**	502-584-1265	734
Actown-Electrocoil Inc						
2414 Highview St	Spring Grove	IL	60081	**800-531-6366**	815-675-6641	252
Actron Mfg Co						
15825 Industrial Pkwy	Cleveland	OH	44135	**800-228-7667**	216-898-9200	247
Actuate Corp						
701 Gateway Blvd						
6th Fl	South San Francisco	CA	94080	**800-914-2259***	650-837-2000	176-1
NASDAQ: ACTU ■ *Sales						
ACU (American Conservative Union)						
1007 Cameron St	Alexandria	VA	22314	**800-228-7345**	703-836-8602	48-7
Acuity Insurance PO Box 58	Sheboygan	WI	53082	**800-242-7666**	920-458-9131	384-4
Acura Div American Honda Motor Co Inc						
1919 Torrance Blvd	Torrance	CA	90501	**800-382-2238**	310-783-2000	59
Acushnet Co 333 Bridge St	Fairhaven	MA	02719	**800-225-8500**	508-979-2000	701
AcuSport Corp 1 Hunter Pl	Bellefontaine	OH	43311	**800-543-3150**	937-593-7010	701
AD Industries Inc						
12160 Sherman Way	North Hollywood	CA	91605	**800-233-4201**	818-765-4200	87
AD Schinner Co Inc						
4901 W State St	Milwaukee	WI	53208	**800-776-4709**	414-771-4300	549
ADA (American Diabetes Assn)						
1701 N Beauregard St	Alexandria	VA	22311	**800-232-3472**	703-549-1500	48-17
ADA (American Dietetic Assn)						
120 S Riverside Plaza Suite 2000	Chicago	IL	60606	**800-877-1600**	312-899-0040	49-8
ADA (Americans for Democratic						
Action) 1625 K St NW						
Suite 210	Washington	DC	20006	**800-787-2734**	202-785-5980	48-7
Ada Resources Inc 6603 Kirbyville St	Houston	TX	77033	**800-945-6113**	713-644-2111	569
Adair Printing Technologies						
7850 2nd St	Dexter	MI	48130	**800-637-5025**	734-426-2822	614
ADAM Inc						
1600 RiverEdge Pkwy Suite 100	Atlanta	GA	30328	**800-755-2326**	770-980-0888	351
NASDAQ: ADAM						
Adamatic Corp						
607 Industrial Way W.	Eatontown	NJ	07724	**800-526-2807**	732-544-8400	293
Adams Abigail National Bancorp Inc						
1130 Connecticut Ave NW						
Suite 200	Washington	DC	20036	**877-442-3267**	202-772-3600	355-2
NASDAQ: AANB						
Adams & Brooks Inc						
1915 S Hoover St PO Box 7303	Los Angeles	CA	90007	**800-999-9808***	213-749-3226	291-8
*Orders						
Adams-Burch Inc 1901 Stanford Ct.	Landover	MD	20785	**800-347-8093***	301-341-1600	295
*Cust Svc						
Adams Business Forms Inc						
200 Jackson St.	Topeka	KS	66603	**800-444-0038**	785-233-4101	111
Adams-Columbia Electric Co-op						
401 E Lake St.	Friendship	WI	53934	**800-831-8629**	608-339-3346	244
Adams Construction Co						
523 Rutherford Ave NE	Roanoke	VA	24016	**800-523-4417**	540-982-2366	187-4
Adams County Chamber of Commerce						
PO Box 398	West Union	OH	45693	**888-223-5454**	937-544-5454	137
Adams Electric Co-op						
700 Eastwood St	Camp Point	IL	62320	**800-232-4797**	217-593-7701	244
Adams Electric Co-op Inc						
1338 Biglerville Rd	Gettysburg	PA	17325	**888-232-6732**	717-334-9211	244
Adams Elevator Equipment Co						
6310 W Howard St.	Niles	IL	60714	**800-323-0796**	847-581-2900	255
Adams Express Co						
7 Saint Paul St Suite 1140	Baltimore	MD	21202	**800-638-2479**	410-752-5900	397
NYSE: ADX						
Adams Harkness Inc						
99 High St 12th Fl	Boston	MA	02110	**800-225-6201**	617-371-3900	679
Adams John J Die Corp						
10 Nebraska St.	Worcester	MA	01604	**800-356-0110**	508-757-3894	447
Adams Keegan Inc						
6055 Primacy Pkwy Suite 300	Memphis	TN	38119	**800-621-1308**	901-683-5353	619
Adams Laboratories Inc DBA Adams						
Respiratory Therapeutics						
14801 Sovereign Rd	Fort Worth	TX	76155	**800-770-5270**	817-354-3858	470
Adam's Mark Hotels Gold Mark						
Rewards 11330 Olive Blvd	Saint Louis	MO	63141	**800-444-2326**	314-567-9000	371
Adam's Mark Hotels & Resorts						
11330 Olive Blvd	Saint Louis	MO	63141	**800-444-2326**	314-567-9000	369
Adams Media Corp 57 Littlefield St.	Avon	MA	02322	**800-872-5627**		623-2
Adams Oceanfront Resort						
4 Read St	Dewey Beach	DE	19971	**800-448-8080**	302-227-3030	373
Adams Products Co PO Box 189	Morrisville	NC	27560	**800-672-3131**	919-467-2218	181
Adams & Reese LLP						
1 Shell Sq Suite 4500	New Orleans	LA	70139	**800-725-1990**	504-581-3234	419
Adams Respiratory Therapeutics						
14801 Sovereign Rd	Fort Worth	TX	76155	**800-770-5270**	817-354-3858	470
Adams Rite Mfg Co						
260 W Santa Fe St	Pomona	CA	91767	**800-872-3267**	909-632-2300	345
Adams RL Plastics Inc						
5955 Crossroads Commerce Pkwy	Wyoming	MI	49517	**800-968-2241**	616-261-4400	590
Adams Rural Electric Co-op Inc						
4800 SR 125	West Union	OH	45693	**800-283-1846**	937-544-2305	244
Adams State College						
208 Edgemont Blvd	Alamosa	CO	81102	**800-824-6494**	719-587-7712	163
Adams USA Inc 610 S Jefferson Ave	Cookeville	TN	38501	**800-251-6857**	931-526-2109	701
Adamson Global Technology Corp						
13200 Ramblewood Dr.	Chester	VA	23836	**800-525-7703**	804-748-6453	92
Adaptec Inc 691 S Milpitas Blvd	Milpitas	CA	95035	**800-959-7274***	408-945-8600	613
NASDAQ: ADPT ■ *Tech Supp						
Adaptive Micro Systems Inc						
7840 N 86th St.	Milwaukee	WI	53224	**800-558-7022**	414-357-2020	176-7
Adaptive Solutions Inc						
1301 Azalea Rd Suite 101	Mobile	AL	36693	**800-299-3045**	251-666-3045	176-12
Adapto Storage Products						
625 E 10th Ave.	Hialeah	FL	33010	**800-923-2786**	305-499-4800	281
ADB Systems International Inc						
302 East Mall Suite 300	Etobicoke	ON	M9B6C7	**888-287-7467**	416-640-0400	176-7
ADC Telecommunications Inc						
13625 Technology Dr.	Eden Prairie	MN	55344	**800-366-3891**	952-938-8080	720
NASDAQ: ADCT						
AdCare Hospital of Worcester						
107 Lincoln St	Worcester	MA	01605	**800-345-3552**	508-799-9000	712
Adco Inc 900 W Main St	Sedalia	MO	65301	**800-821-7556**	660-826-3300	149
Adco Inc 13911 Distribution Way	Dallas	TX	75234	**800-486-4583**	972-484-6177	43
Adco Litho Line Inc						
2700 W Roosevelt Rd	Broadview	IL	60155	**800-875-2326**	708-345-8200	10
Adcole Corp 669 Forest St	Marlborough	MA	01752	**800-858-5802**	508-485-9100	464
Adcom Worldwide Inc PO Box 390048	Edina	MN	55439	**800-747-7424**	952-829-7990	306
ADDCO Inc 240 Arlington Ave E.	Saint Paul	MN	55117	**888-616-4408**	651-488-8600	691
Adden Furniture Inc 26 Jackson St.	Lowell	MA	01852	**800-625-3876**	978-454-7848	314-3
Addiction Professionals. NAADAC -						
Assn for 901 N Washington St						
Suite 600	Alexandria	VA	22314	**800-548-0497**	703-741-7686	49-15
Addicts Anonymous. Sex						
PO Box 70949	Houston	TX	77270	**800-477-8191**	713-869-4902	48-21
Addison Avenue Federal Credit Union						
1501 Pagemill Rd.	Palo Alto	CA	94303	**877-233-4766**		216
Addison Biological Laboratory Inc						
507 N Cleveland Ave	Fayette	MO	65248	**800-331-2530**	660-248-2215	574
Addison County Chamber of						
Commerce 2 Court St	Middlebury	VT	05753	**800-733-8376**	802-388-7951	137
Addison Insurance Co						
118 2nd Ave SE	Cedar Rapids	IA	52401	**800-332-7977**	319-399-5700	384-4
Addison-Wesley Higher Education Group						
75 Arlington St.	Boston	MA	02116	**800-447-2226**	617-848-6000	623-2

Name / Address	City	State	Zip	Toll-Free	Phone	Class
ADE Corp 80 Wilson Way; *NASDAQ: ADEX*	Westwood	MA	02090	**800-343-2332**	781-467-3500	685
ADEA (American Dental Education Assn) 1400 K St NW Suite 1100	Washington	DC	20005	**800-353-2237**	202-289-7201	49-5
ADEAR Center PO Box 8250	Silver Spring	MD	20907	**800-438-4380**	301-495-3311	196
Adecco Inc 175 Broad Hollow Rd; *NYSE: ADO*	Melville	NY	11747	**877-632-9169**	631-844-7800	707
Adelman Travel Group 6980 N Port Washington Rd	Milwaukee	WI	53217	**800-231-3999**	414-352-7600	760
Adelphi University 1 South Ave	Garden City	NY	11530	**800-233-5744**	516-877-3000	163
Adelphia Communications Corp 5619 DTC Pkwy	Greenwood Village	CO	80111	**800-892-7300**	303-268-6300	117
Adelphia PowerLink 1 N Main St; *Cust Svc	Coudersport	PA	16915	**888-683-1000***	888-233-5638	390
Adelphia Steel Equipment Co 7372 State Rd	Philadelphia	PA	19136	**800-865-8211**	215-333-6300	314-1
Adelson Nathan Hospice 4141 S Swenson St	Las Vegas	NV	89119	**888-281-8646**	702-733-0320	365
ADESA Inc 13085 Hamilton Crossing Blvd; *NYSE: KAR*	Carmel	IN	46032	**800-862-7882**	317-815-1100	51
Adeza Biomedical Corp 1240 Elko Dr; *NASDAQ: ADZA* ■ *Cust Svc	Sunnyvale	CA	94089	**877-945-0208***	408-745-0975	229
ADHA (American Dental Hygienists' Assn) 444 N Michigan Ave Suite 3400	Chicago	IL	60611	**800-243-2342**	312-440-8900	49-8
Adhesives Research Inc 400 Seaks Run Rd	Glen Rock	PA	17327	**800-445-6240**	717-235-7979	3
ADI Meetings & Incentives Inc 1223 E Broadway Rd Suite 100	Tempe	AZ	85282	**800-944-2359**	480-350-9090	377
adidas America 5055 N Greeley Ave	Portland	OR	97217	**888-234-3270**	971-234-2300	296
Adimage Promotional Group 2300 Main St	Hugo	MN	55038	**800-344-8809**	651-426-0820	10
Adirondack Chair Co Inc 31-01 Vernon Blvd	Long Island City	NY	11106	**800-477-1330**	718-932-4003	315
Adirondack Council 103 Hand Ave Suite 3	Elizabethtown	NY	12932	**877-873-2240**	518-873-2240	48-13
Adirondack Direct 31-01 Vernon Blvd	Long Island City	NY	11106	**800-221-2444**	718-204-4500	315
Adirondack Mountain Club 814 Goggins Rd; *Orders	Lake George	NY	12845	**800-395-8080***	518-668-4447	48-23
Adirondack Regional Chambers of Commerce 5 Warren St	Glens Falls	NY	12801	**888-516-7247**	518-798-1761	137
Adirondack Trailways 499 Hurley Ave	Hurley	NY	12443	**800-858-8555**	845-339-4230	109
Adirondack Wire & Cable Co Inc 191 Social St	Woonsocket	RI	02895	**800-237-4542**	401-769-1600	800
Adjusta-Post Lighting Co 3960 Summit Rd	Norton	OH	44203	**800-321-2132**	330-745-1692	431
Adler Coleman E & Sons Inc 722 Canal St	New Orleans	LA	70130	**800-925-7912**	504-523-5292	402
Adleta Co 1645 Diplomat Dr Suite 200	Carrollton	TX	75006	**800-423-5382**	972-620-5600	356
Adlon Hotel 1275 N 4th St	San Jose	CA	95112	**888-452-3566**	408-282-1000	373
ADM (Archer Daniels Midland Co) 4666 E Faries Pkwy; *NYSE: ADM*	Decatur	IL	62526	**800-637-5824**	217-424-5200	184
ADM Alliance Nutrition Inc 1000 N 30th St	Quincy	IL	62301	**800-292-3333**	217-222-7100	438
ADM Animal Health & Nutrition Div 1877 NE 58th Ave	Des Moines	IA	50313	**800-247-5450**	515-262-9763	574
ADM Arkady Products 100 Paniplus Rd	Olathe	KS	66061	**800-255-6637**	913-782-8800	291-17
ADM Corp 100 Lincoln Blvd	Middlesex	NJ	08846	**800-327-0718**	732-469-0900	260
ADM Investor Services Inc 141 W Jackson Blvd 1610A Board of Trade Bldg	Chicago	IL	60604	**800-243-2649**	312-435-7000	167
ADM Milling Co 8000 W 110th St Suite 300	Overland Park	KS	66210	**800-637-5843**	913-491-9400	291-23
ADM Nutraceutical Div 4666 Faries Pkwy	Decatur	IL	62526	**800-637-5843**	217-424-5200	786
ADM Oil Refinery 1940 E Hull Ave	Des Moines	IA	50316	**800-637-5843**	515-263-2112	291-29
AdMasters 16901 Dallas Pkwy Suite 204	Addison	TX	75001	**877-236-2783**	972-866-9300	9
ADM/GROWMARK River System Inc 4666 E Faries Pkwy	Decatur	IL	62526	**800-637-5843**	217-424-5900	271
Administaff Inc 19001 Crescent Springs Dr; *NYSE: ASF*	Kingwood	TX	77339	**800-465-3800**	281-358-8986	619
Administrators. American Assn of School 801 N Quincy St Suite 700	Arlington	VA	22203	**800-771-1162**	703-528-0700	49-5
Administrators. American Federation of School 1729 21st St NW	Washington	DC	20009	**800-354-2372**	202-986-4209	49-5
Admiral Benbow Inns of America Inc 2160 Kingston Ct Suite N	Marietta	GA	30067	**800-451-1986**	770-952-9145	369
Admiral Craft Equipment Corp 940 S Oyster Bay Rd	Hicksville	NY	11801	**800-223-7750**	516-433-3535	479
Admiral Fell Inn 888 S Broadway	Baltimore	MD	21231	**800-292-4667**	410-522-7377	373
Admiral Hotel 2 Baltimore Ave	Rehoboth Beach	DE	19971	**888-882-4188**	302-227-2103	373
Admiral Lehigh Golf Resort & Spa 225 E Joel Blvd	Lehigh Acres	FL	33972	**888-465-3222**	239-369-2121	655
Admiral-Merchants Motor Freight Inc 215 S 11th St	Minneapolis	MN	55403	**800-972-8864**	612-332-4819	769
Ado Corp 851 Simuel Rd; *Cust Svc	Spartanburg	SC	29301	**800-845-0918***	864-574-2731	731
Adobe Systems Inc 345 Park Ave; *NASDAQ: ADBE*	San Jose	CA	95110	**800-833-6687**	408-536-6000	176-8
Adolescent Psychiatry. American Academy of Child & 3615 Wisconsin Ave NW	Washington	DC	20016	**800-333-7636**	202-966-7300	49-15
Adolphus The 1321 Commerce St	Dallas	TX	75202	**800-221-9083**	214-742-8200	373
Adopt America Network 1025 N Reynolds Rd	Toledo	OH	43615	**800-246-1731**	419-534-3350	48-6
Adoption ARC Inc 4701 Pine St Suite J-7	Philadelphia	PA	19143	**800-884-4004**	215-748-1441	48-6
Adoption Center. National 1500 Walnut St Suite 701	Philadelphia	PA	19102	**800-862-3678**	215-735-9988	48-6
Adoption. Dave Thomas Foundation for 4288 W Dublin Granville Rd	Dublin	OH	43017	**800-275-3832**	614-764-8454	300
Adoption Information Clearinghouse. National 330 C St SW	Washington	DC	20447	**888-251-0075**	703-352-3488	336-6
Adoption. National Council for 225 N Washington St	Alexandria	VA	22314	**866-212-3678**	703-299-6633	48-6
Adoptive Families Magazine 39 W 37th St	New York	NY	10018	**800-372-3300**	646-366-0830	449-10
Adorama Camera Inc 42 W 18th St	New York	NY	10011	**800-223-2500**	212-741-0052	119
ADP (Association of Directory Publishers) 116 Cass St	Traverse City	MI	49684	**800-267-9002**		49-16
ADP (Automatic Data Processing Inc) 1 ADP Blvd; *NYSE: ADP*	Roseland	NJ	07068	**800-225-5237**	973-994-5000	223
ADP TotalSource Co 10200 Sunset Dr	Miami	FL	33173	**800-447-3237**	305-630-1000	619
ADRA (Adventist Development & Relief Agency International) 12501 Old Columbia Pike	Silver Spring	MD	20904	**800-424-2372**	301-680-6380	48-5
Adray Appliance Photo & Sound Center 20219 Carlysle St	Dearborn	MI	48124	**800-652-3729**	313-274-9500	35
Adrian College 110 S Madison St	Adrian	MI	49221	**800-877-2246**	517-265-5161	163
Adrian Fabricators Inc Cargotainer Div PO Box 518	Adrian	MI	49221	**800-221-3794**	517-266-5700	462
Adrian Home Builders Inc PO Box 266	Adrian	GA	31002	**800-642-7380**	478-668-3231	107
ADS Corp 5030 Bradford Dr NW Bldg 1 Suite 210	Huntsville	AL	35805	**800-633-7246**	256-430-3366	200
AdStar Inc 4553 Glencoe Ave Suite 325; *NASDAQ: ADST*	Marina del Rey	CA	90292	**800-752-5187**	310-577-8255	176-1
ADT Security Systems Inc 14200 E Exposition Ave	Aurora	CO	80012	**800-662-5378**	303-338-8200	681
ADTRAN Inc 901 Explorer Blvd; *NASDAQ: ADTN*	Huntsville	AL	35806	**800-923-8726**	256-963-8000	720
ADTRAV Travel Management 4555 S Lake Pkwy	Birmingham	AL	35244	**800-476-2952**	205-444-4800	760
Adult Day Services Assn. National 8201 Greensboro Dr Suite 300	McLean	VA	22102	**800-424-9046**	703-610-9000	48-6
Advance America Cash Advance Centers Inc 135 N Church St; *NYSE: AEA*	Spartanburg	SC	29306	**866-640-4227**	864-342-5600	139
Advance Carbon Products Inc 2036 National Ave	Hayward	CA	94545	**800-283-1249**	510-293-5930	127
Advance Corp Braille-Tac Div 8200 97th St S	Cottage Grove	MN	55016	**800-328-9451**	651-771-9297	692
Advance Energy Technologies Inc 1 Solar Dr	Clifton Park	NY	12065	**800-724-0198**	518-371-2140	650
Advance Fiber Technologies Corp 344 Lodi St	Hackensack	NJ	07601	**800-631-1930**	201-488-2700	730-5
Advance Financial Bancorp 1015 Commerce St; *NASDAQ: AFBC*	Wellsburg	WV	26070	**800-569-7650**	304-737-3531	355-2
Advance Food Service Equipment Inc 200 Heartland Blvd	Edgewood	NY	11717	**800-645-3166**	631-242-4800	293
Advance Lifts Inc 701 S Kirk Rd	Saint Charles	IL	60174	**800-843-3625**	630-584-9881	462
Advance Reservations Inn Arizona PO Box 950	Tempe	AZ	85280	**800-456-0682**	480-990-0682	368
Advance Transformer Co 10275 W Higgins Rd	Rosemont	IL	60018	**800-322-2086**	847-390-5000	756
Advanced American Pharmaceuticals Inc DBA Peak Nutrition 1097 11th St	Syracuse	NE	68446	**800-600-2069**	402-269-2825	786
Advanced Biotechnologies Inc 9108 Guilford Rd Rivers Pk II	Columbia	MD	21046	**800-426-0764**	301-470-3220	229
Advanced Business Fulfillment Inc (ABF Inc) 3183 Rider Trail S	Earth City	MO	63045	**800-804-7430**	314-770-2986	114
Advanced Coatings & Surface Technology Newsletter 7550 W I-10 Suite 400	San Antonio	TX	77229	**877-463-7678**	210-348-1000	521-12
Advanced Data-Comm Inc 301 Data Ct	Dubuque	IA	52003	**800-582-9501**	563-582-9501	722
Advanced Design & Packaging Inc 5090 McDougall Dr SW	Atlanta	GA	30336	**800-333-2487**	404-699-1952	101
Advanced Digital Information Corp 11431 Willows Rd NE; *NASDAQ: ADIC*	Redmond	WA	98052	**800-336-1233**	425-881-8004	174
Advanced Drainage Systems Inc 4640 Trueman Blvd	Hilliard	OH	43026	**800-821-6710**	614-658-0050	585
Advanced Electronic Support Products Inc 1810 NE 144th St; *NASDAQ: AESP*	North Miami Beach	FL	33181	**800-446-2377**	305-944-7710	252
Advanced Energy Industries Inc 1625 Sharp Pt Dr; *NASDAQ: AEIS*	Fort Collins	CO	80525	**800-446-9167**	970-221-4670	685
Advanced Fibre Communications Inc 1465 N McDowell Blvd; *NASDAQ: AFCI*	Petaluma	CA	94954	**800-690-2324**	707-794-7700	720
Advanced Information Systems Group Inc 2180 W SR 434 Suite 6150	Longwood	FL	32779	**800-780-2598**	407-774-7181	178
Advanced Input Devices Inc 600 W Wilbur Ave	Coeur d'Alene	ID	83815	**800-444-5923**	208-765-8000	171-1
Advanced Lighting Technologies Inc 32000 Aurora Rd	Solon	OH	44139	**800-965-2677**	440-248-3510	429
Advanced Looseleaf Technologies Inc 1424 Somerset Ave	Dighton	MA	02715	**800-339-6354**	508-669-6354	87
Advanced Machine & Engineering Co 2500 Latham St	Rockford	IL	61103	**800-255-2331**	815-962-6076	484
Advanced Marketing Services Inc 5880 Oberlin Dr Suite 400; *NYSE: MKT*	San Diego	CA	92121	**800-695-3580**	858-457-2500	97
Advanced Materials Group Inc 20211 S Susana Rd; *Cust Svc	Rancho Dominguez	CA	90221	**800-395-3626***	310-537-5444	590
Advanced Measurement Technology 801 S Illinois Ave	Oak Ridge	TN	37831	**800-251-9750**	865-482-4411	410
Advanced Mfg Technology Newsletter 7550 W I-10 Suite 400	San Antonio	TX	77229	**877-463-7678**	210-348-1000	521-12
Advanced Micro Devices Inc PO Box 3453; *NYSE: AMD*	Sunnyvale	CA	94088	**800-538-8450**	408-732-2400	686

Name / Address	City	State	ZIP	Toll-Free	Phone	Class
Advanced Microelectronics Inc 6001 E Old Hwy 50	Vincennes	IN	47591	**800-264-8851**	812-726-4500	173
Advanced MP Technology 1010 Calle Sombra	San Clemente	CA	92673	**800-492-3113**	949-492-3113	245
Advanced Neuromodulation Systems Inc 6901 Preston Rd *NASDAQ: ANSI*	Plano	TX	75024	**800-727-7846**	972-309-8000	249
Advanced Ozone Engineering Inc 6038 Oakwood Ave.	Cincinnati	OH	45224	**800-588-3871**	513-681-3871	84
Advanced Photographic Solutions LLC 1525 Hardeman Ln NE	Cleveland	TN	37312	**800-241-9234**	423-479-5481	577
Advanced Power Technology Inc 405 SW Columbia St *NASDAQ: APTI*	Bend	OR	97702	**800-522-0809**	541-382-8028	686
Advanced Processing Laboratories Inc 16868 Via del Campo Ct	San Diego	CA	92127	**800-822-7522**	858-674-2850	171-3
Advanced Products Co 1021 Spring Garden St.	Philadelphia	PA	19123	**800-755-9852**	215-232-5926	104
Advanced Research Laboratories 1063 McGaw Ave Suite 100	Irvine	CA	92614	**800-966-6960**	949-221-8238	211
Advanced Reservation Systems Inc 1059 1st Ave	San Diego	CA	92101	**800-434-7894**	619-238-0900	368
Advanced Resource Technologies Inc 2800 Eisenhower Ave 4th Fl E	Alexandria	VA	22314	**800-796-9936**	703-836-8811	178
Advanced Security Link 1000 Scenic Ave.	Costa Mesa	CA	92626	**800-576-4275**	714-825-1818	681
Advanced Settlements Inc 2101 Park Center Dr Suite 220	Orlando	FL	32835	**800-561-4148**	407-296-7373	783
Advanced Sports Nutrition (ASN) 1813 Cascade St.	Hood River	OR	97031	**800-800-9119**	541-387-4500	786
Advanced Sterilization Products 33 Technology Dr.	Irvine	CA	92618	**800-595-0200**	949-581-5799	469
Advanced Technology Marketing 6053 W Century Blvd Suite 200	Los Angeles	CA	90045	**800-624-4303**	310-642-1881	5
Advanced TelCom Group Inc 463 Aviation Blvd Suite 120 *Cust Svc	Santa Rosa	CA	95403	**800-285-6100***	707-284-5000	721
Advanced Test Products Inc 3270 Executive Way	Miramar	FL	33025	**800-327-5060**	954-499-5400	247
Advanced Visual Systems Inc 300 5th Ave *Sales	Waltham	MA	02451	**800-728-1600***	781-890-4300	176-5
Advanstar Communications Inc 7500 Old Oak Blvd	Cleveland	OH	44130	**800-225-4569**	440-243-8100	623-9
Advanstar Medical Economics Healthcare Communications 5 Paragon Dr	Montvale	NJ	07645	**800-526-4870**	201-358-7200	623-9
Advanstar Veterinary Healthcare Communications 8033 Flint St.	Lenexa	KS	66214	**800-255-6864**	913-492-4300	623-9
Advanta Corp PO Box 844 *NASDAQ: ADVNA*	Spring House	PA	19477	**800-327-5998**	215-657-4000	214
Advanta Leasing Services 40 E Clementon Rd	Gibbsboro	NJ	08026	**800-255-0022**		214
Advanta National Bank PO Box 15555	Wilmington	DE	19850	**800-441-7306**		71
Advantage Cellular Systems Inc 3040 Nashville Hwy	Alexandria	TN	37012	**800-772-8645**	615-464-2355	721
Advantage Credit International 15 W Strong St Suite 20A	Pensacola	FL	32501	**800-600-2510**	850-470-9336	176-10
Advantage Funding Corp 1000 Parkwood Cir Suite 300	Atlanta	GA	30339	**800-241-2274**	770-955-2274	268
Advantage Limousine Services Inc DBA ALS Transportation Inc 4605 Post Oak Pl Suite 211	Houston	TX	77027	**866-355-5466**	713-355-5466	433
Advantage Payroll Services Inc 126 Merrow Rd PO Box 1330 *Cust Svc	Auburn	ME	04211	**800-876-0178***	207-784-0178	559
Advantage Rent-A-Car 1343 Hallmark Dr *Cust Svc	San Antonio	TX	78216	**800-777-5500***	210-344-4712	126
Advantec MFS Inc 6723 Sierra Ct Suite A	Dublin	CA	94568	**800-334-7132**	925-479-0625	19
AdvanTech Solutions 1410 N Westshore Blvd Suite 600	Tampa	FL	33607	**888-340-9442**	813-289-9442	619
Advantis Technologies 1400 Bluegrass Lakes Pkwy	Alpharetta	GA	30004	**888-452-7678**	770-521-5999	258
Advantor Systems Corp 1707 Orlando Central Pkwy Suite 350 *Sales	Orlando	FL	32809	**800-238-2686***	407-859-3350	681
Advent Capital Management LLC 1065 Ave of the Americas 31st Fl	New York	NY	10018	**888-523-8368**	212-482-1600	393
Advent Software Inc 301 Brannan St 6th Fl *NASDAQ: ADVS*	San Francisco	CA	94107	**800-727-0605**	415-543-7696	176-10
Adventa Hospice 684 Hwy 91 Suite 1	Elizabethton	TN	37643	**800-774-1404**	423-547-0852	365
Adventa Hospice 1423 W Morris Blvd	Morristown	TN	37814	**800-659-2633**	423-587-9484	365
Adventist Community Services 12501 Old Columbia Pike	Silver Spring	MD	20904	**877-227-2702**	301-680-6438	48-5
Adventist Development & Relief Agency International (ADRA) 12501 Old Columbia Pike	Silver Spring	MD	20904	**800-424-2372**	301-680-6380	48-5
Adventist Health System 111 N Orlando Ave	Winter Park	FL	32789	**800-327-9290**	407-647-4400	348
Adventure 16 Inc 4620 Alvarado Canyon Rd	San Diego	CA	92120	**800-854-2672**	619-283-2362	702
Adventure Alaska Tours Inc PO Box 64	Hope	AK	99605	**800-365-7057**	907-782-3730	748
Adventure Center 40 N Main St	Ashland	OR	97520	**800-444-2819**	541-488-2819	748
Adventure Center Inc 1311 63rd St Suite 200	Emeryville	CA	94608	**800-227-8747**	510-654-1879	748
Adventure Connection PO Box 475	Coloma	CA	95613	**800-556-6060**	530-626-7385	748
Adventure Cycling Assn 150 E Pine St PO Box 8308	Missoula	MT	59802	**800-755-2453**	406-721-1776	48-22
Adventure Library 141 Tompkins Ave *Cust Svc	Pleasantville	NY	10570	**800-823-7323***	914-747-0777	94

Name / Address	City	State	ZIP	Toll-Free	Phone	Class
Adventure Life South America 1655 S 3rd St W Suite 1	Missoula	MT	59801	**800-344-6118**	406-541-2677	748
Adventure Magazine 1145 17th St NW	Washington	DC	20036	**800-647-5463**	202-857-7000	449-11
Adventureland Inn I-80 & Hwy 65	Des Moines	IA	50316	**800-910-5382**	515-265-7321	373
Adventureland Park 5091 NE 56th St	Altoona	IA	50009	**800-532-1286**	515-266-2121	32
Adventures in Advertising 101 Commerce St.	Oshkosh	WI	54901	**800-460-7836**	920-236-7272	10
Adventures Out West 15001 N 74th St. *Resv	Scottsdale	AZ	85260	**800-755-0935***	602-996-6100	748
Advertising Age Magazine 360 N Michigan Ave	Chicago	IL	60601	**800-678-2724**	312-649-5200	449-5
Advertising Bureau. Radio 261 Madison Ave 23rd Fl	New York	NY	10016	**800-252-7234**	212-681-7200	49-18
Advertising Federation. American 1101 Vermont Ave NW Suite 500	Washington	DC	20005	**800-999-2231**	202-898-0089	49-18
Advertising International. Point-of-Purchase 1660 L St NW 10th Fl	Washington	DC	20036	**888-407-6724**	202-530-3000	49-18
Advertising & Marketing Assn. Retail 325 7th St NW Suite 1100	Washington	DC	20004	**800-673-4692**	202-661-3052	49-18
Advest Group Inc 90 State House Sq	Hartford	CT	06103	**800-243-8115**	860-509-1000	679
Advisor Media Inc 4849 Viewridge Ave Suite 200	San Diego	CA	92123	**800-336-6060**	858-278-5600	623-9
Advisor Today 2901 Telestar Ct.	Falls Church	VA	22042	**800-247-4074**	703-770-8477	449-5
Advisory Board Co 2445 M St NW *NASDAQ: ABCO*	Washington	DC	20037	**800-672-6620**	202-672-5600	193
Advitech Inc 1165 boul Lebourgneuf Suite 140	Quebec	QC	G2K2C9	**888-686-7498**	418-686-7498	470
ADVO Inc 1 Targeting Ctr. *NYSE: AD*	Windsor	CT	06095	**800-238-6462**	860-285-6100	5
Advocacy Coalition. National Youth 1638 R St NW Suite 300	Washington	DC	20009	**800-541-6922**	202-319-7596	48-6
Advocat Inc 277 Mallory Station Rd Suite 130	Franklin	TN	37067	**800-771-7576**	615-771-7575	442
Advocate The 22 N 1st St.	Newark	OH	43055	**800-555-8350**	740-345-4053	522-2
Advocate Assn. National Court Appointed Special 100 W Harrison St North Tower Suite 500	Seattle	WA	98119	**800-628-3233**	206-270-0072	48-6
Advocate Health Care 2025 Windsor Dr	Oak Brook	IL	60523	**800-323-8622**	630-572-9393	348
Advocate Hospice 1441 Branding Ave Suite 310	Downers Grove	IL	60515	**800-564-2025**	630-963-6800	365
Advocate Magazine 100 E Edwards St.	Springfield	IL	62704	**800-252-8076**	217-544-0706	449-8
Advocate Messenger 330 S 4th St	Danville	KY	40423	**800-428-0409**	859-236-2551	522-2
AdWare Systems Inc 5111 Commerce Crossings Dr Suite 200	Louisville	KY	40229	**800-626-2027**	502-810-5000	176-1
Adweek Directories 770 Broadway	New York	NY	10003	**800-468-2395**	646-654-5000	623-9
Adweek Magazine 770 Broadway	New York	NY	10003	**800-722-6658**	646-654-5500	449-5
AE Petsche Co Inc 2112 W Division St	Arlington	TX	76012	**800-777-9280**	817-461-9473	245
AEA (Aquatic Exercise Assn) PO Box 1609	Nokomis	FL	34274	**888-232-9283**	941-486-8600	48-22
AeA: Advancing the Business of Technology 5201 Great America Pkwy Suite 520	Santa Clara	CA	95054	**800-284-4232**	408-987-4200	49-4
AEA Advocate Magazine 4000 N Central Ave Suite 1600	Phoenix	AZ	85012	**800-352-5411**	602-264-1774	449-8
Aearo Co 5457 W 79th St *Cust Svc	Indianapolis	IN	46268	**800-327-3431***	317-692-6666	566
AEC Inc 801 AEC Dr.	Wood Dale	IL	60191	**800-966-1060**	630-595-1060	15
AEC Southern Ohio College 309 Buttermilk Pike	Fort Mitchell	KY	41017	**800-888-1445**	859-341-5627	158
AEC Southern Ohio College 1011 Glendale Milford Rd	Cincinnati	OH	45215	**800-888-1445**	513-771-2424	158
AECT (Association for Educational Communications & Technology) 1800 N Stonelake Dr Suite 2	Bloomington	IN	47404	**877-677-2328**	812-335-7675	49-5
AED (Associated Equipment Distributors) 615 W 22nd St	Oak Brook	IL	60523	**800-388-0650**	630-574-0650	49-18
AEDC Federal Credit Union 550 William Northern Blvd PO Box 1210	Tullahoma	TN	37388	**800-342-3086**	931-455-5441	216
Aegis The PO Box 189	Bel Air	MD	21014	**888-879-1710**	410-838-4400	522-4
Aegis Communications Group Inc 7880 Bent Branch Dr Suite 150	Irving	TX	75063	**800-332-0266**	972-830-1800	722
Aegon Special Markets Group Inc 20 Moores Rd.	Frazer	PA	19355	**800-523-7900**	610-648-5000	384-2
Aehr Test Systems 400 Kato Terr *NASDAQ: AEHR*	Fremont	CA	94539	**800-522-7200**	510-623-9400	685
AEI (American Enterprise Institute for Public Policy Research) 1150 17th St NW Suite 1100	Washington	DC	20036	**800-862-5801**	202-862-5800	654
AEI Speakers Bureau 214 Lincoln St Suite 113	Boston	MA	02134	**800-447-7325**	617-782-3111	699
AEL Inc PO Box 1348	Charleston	WV	25325	**800-624-9120**	304-347-0400	654
AELE (Americans for Effective Law Enforcement) 841 W Touhy Ave	Park Ridge	IL	60068	**800-763-2802**	847-685-0700	48-8
AEM Inc 11525 Sorrento Valley Rd	San Diego	CA	92121	**888-323-6462**	858-481-0210	252
Aeolian Enterprises Inc PO Box 888	Latrobe	PA	15650	**800-269-4672**	724-539-9460	647
AEP (Association of Emergency Physicians) 911 Whitewater Dr	Mars	PA	16046	**866-772-1818**	724-772-1818	49-8
AEP Colloids Div SARCOM Inc 393 Church St PO Box 3425	Saratoga Springs	NY	12866	**800-848-0658**	518-584-4105	144
AEP Industries Inc 125 Phillips Ave *NASDAQ: AEPI*	South Hackensack	NJ	07606	**800-999-2374**	201-641-6600	589
AEP Pro Serv 1 Riverside Plaza	Columbus	OH	43215	**800-777-1131**	614-716-1000	258
AEP Public Service Co of Oklahoma PO Box 201	Tulsa	OK	74102	**888-216-3523**		774
AEP-Span Corp 5100 E Grand Ave	Dallas	TX	75223	**800-527-2503**	214-827-1740	482

Alphabetical Section

Name / Address	City	State	Zip	Toll-Free	Phone	Class
AEP Texas 1 Riverside Dr	Columbus	OH	43215	**866-322-5563**		774
Aer Lingus 538 Broadhollow Rd Suite 3	Melville	NY	11747	**800-474-7424**	631-577-5700	26
Aer Lingus Airlines Gold Circle Club 538 Broadhollow Rd.	Melville	NY	11747	**800-474-7424**		27
AERA (Automotive Engine Rebuilders Assn) 330 Lexington Dr	Buffalo Grove	IL	60089	**888-326-2372**	847-541-6550	49-21
Aerco International Inc 159 Paris Ave	Northvale	NJ	07647	**800-526-0288**	201-768-2400	352
Aerial Co Inc 2300 Aerial Dr	Marinette	WI	54143	**800-950-9565**	715-735-9323	78
Aerie Resort PO Box 108	Malahat	BC	V0R2L0	**800-518-1933**	250-743-7115	655
Aermotor Pumps Inc 293 Wright St	Delavan	WI	53115	**800-265-7241**	800-230-1816	627
Aero Air LLC 2050 NE 25th Ave	Hillsboro	OR	97124	**800-448-2376**	503-640-3711	14
Aero-Fast Bicycle Co PO Box 3812	Jacksonville	FL	32206	**800-656-2376**	904-354-3339	83
Aero Industries Inc 3010 W Morris St. *Sales	Indianapolis	IN	46241	**800-535-9545***	317-244-2433	718
Aero Industries Inc 5690 Clarkson Rd Richmond International Airport	Richmond	VA	23250	**800-845-1308**	804-222-7211	63
Aero Pharmaceuticals Inc 3040 FAU Blvd Suite 100	Boca Raton	FL	33431	**800-223-6837**	561-208-2200	229
Aero Plastics Inc 163 Pioneer Dr	Leominster	MA	01453	**800-458-0116**	978-537-4303	590
Aero Products International Inc 1225 Karl Ct *Cust Svc	Wauconda	IL	60084	**800-237-6233***	847-487-7158	463
Aero-Smith Inc 214 Aviation Way	Martinsburg	WV	25401	**800-550-2507**	304-262-2507	63
Aero Systems Engineering Inc 358 E Fillmore Ave *NASDAQ: AERS*	Saint Paul	MN	55107	**800-321-0288**	651-227-7515	464
Aero Tec Labs Inc 45 Spear Rd Industrial Pk	Ramsey	NJ	07446	**800-526-5330**	201-825-1400	663
Aerobic Life Industries Inc 2800 E Chambers Suite 700 *Orders	Phoenix	AZ	85044	**800-798-0707***	602-283-0755	451
Aerobics & Fitness Assn of America (AFAA) 15250 Ventura Blvd Suite 200	Sherman Oaks	CA	91403	**877-968-7263**	818-905-0040	48-22
Aerodynamics Inc 6544 Highland Rd.	Waterford	MI	48327	**800-235-9234**	248-666-3500	63
Aerofin Corp 4621 Murray Pl PO Box 10819	Lynchburg	VA	24506	**800-237-6346**	434-845-7081	92
Aeroglide Corp PO Box 29505	Raleigh	NC	27626	**800-722-7483**	919-851-2000	293
Aerolineas Argentinas 51 E 42nd St Suite 1600	New York	NY	10017	**800-333-0276**	212-542-8880	26
AeroMexico 3663 N Sam Houston Pkwy E Suite 500	Houston	TX	77032	**800-237-6639**	281-372-3420	26
AeroMexico Club Premier 3663 N Sam Houston Pkwy E Suite 500	Houston	TX	77032	**800-247-3737**		27
Aeronautic Assn. National 1815 N Fort Myer Dr Suite 500	Arlington	VA	22209	**800-644-9777**	703-527-0226	48-22
Aeronautics. Academy of Model 5161 E Memorial Dr	Muncie	IN	47302	**800-435-9262**	765-287-1256	48-18
Aeronautics & Astronautics. American Institute of 1801 Alexander Bell Dr Suite 500	Reston	VA	20191	**800-639-2422**	703-264-7500	49-19
Aeronca Inc 2320 Wedekind Dr	Middletown	OH	45042	**800-991-1387**	513-422-2751	23
Aeronet Worldwide PO Box 17239	Irvine	CA	92623	**800-552-3869**	949-474-3000	13
Aeroshade Inc 433 Oakland Ave	Waukesha	WI	53186	**800-331-7179**	262-547-2101	88
Aerosoles 201 Meadow Rd	Edison	NJ	08817	**800-798-9478**	732-985-6900	296
Aerospace America Inc 900 Harry Truman Pkwy PO Box 189	Bay City	MI	48707	**800-237-6414**	989-684-2121	471
Aerospace America Magazine 1801 Alexander Bell Dr Suite 500	Reston	VA	20191	**800-639-2422**	703-264-7500	449-21
Aerospace & Electronics Systems Society. IEEE IEEE Operations Ctr 445 Hoes Ln	Piscataway	NJ	08854	**800-678-4333**	732-981-0060	49-19
Aerotech World Trade Corp 11 New King St	White Plains	NY	10604	**800-499-2982**	914-681-3000	759
Aerotek Inc 7301 Parkway Dr	Hanover	MD	21076	**800-435-2029**	410-540-7000	707
AeroThrust Corp PO Box 522236	Miami	FL	33152	**800-228-0665**	305-871-1790	25
Aerovox Inc 167 John Vertente Blvd	New Bedford	MA	02745	**800-343-3348**	508-994-9661	252
AESC (Association of Energy Service Companies) 10200 Richmond Ave Suite 275	Houston	TX	77042	**800-692-0771**	713-781-0758	48-12
AESC (Association of Executive Search Consultants) 12 E 41st St 17th Fl	New York	NY	10017	**877-843-2372**	212-398-9556	49-12
AESCULAP Inc 3773 Corporate Pkwy *Cust Svc	Center Valley	PA	18034	**800-282-9000***	800-258-1946	468
Aesthetic Plastic Surgery. American Society for 11081 Winners Cir	Los Alamitos	CA	90720	**800-364-2147**	562-799-2356	49-8
AESU Travel Inc 3922 Hickory Ave	Baltimore	MD	21211	**800-638-7640**	410-366-5494	760
AETEA Information Technology Inc 1445 Research Blvd Suite 300	Rockville	MD	20850	**888-772-3832**	301-721-4200	178
AETEK UV Systems 1200 Windham Pkwy *Sales	Romeoville	IL	60446	**800-333-2304***	630-226-4200	429
Aether Systems Inc 11460 Cronridge Dr *NASDAQ: AETH*	Owings Mills	MD	21117	**888-812-6767**	410-654-6400	222
AETN (Arkansas Educational Television Network) PO Box 1250	Conway	AR	72033	**800-662-2386**	501-682-2386	620
Aetna Felt Corp 2401 W Emaus Ave.	Allentown	PA	18103	**800-526-4451**	610-791-0900	730-6
Aetna Freight Lines Inc PO Box 350	Warren	OH	44482	**800-837-4995**	330-369-5201	769
Aetna Health & Life Insurance Co 151 Farmington Ave	Hartford	CT	06156	**800-872-3862**	860-273-0123	384-2
Aetna Inc 151 Farmington Ave *NYSE: AET*	Hartford	CT	06156	**800-872-3862**	860-273-0123	384-3
Aetna Life Insurance & Annuity Co 151 Farmington Ave	Hartford	CT	06156	**800-872-3862**	860-273-0123	384-2
Aetna Plastics Corp 1702 Saint Clair Ave	Cleveland	OH	44114	**800-634-3074**	216-781-4421	592
Aetna US Healthcare Inc 980 Jolly Rd	Blue Bell	PA	19422	**800-962-6842**		384-3
Aetna US Healthcare Pharmacy Management 11100 Wayzata Blvd Suite 400 MC F615	Minnetonka	MN	55035	**800-872-3862**	952-594-6250	575
Aetrium Inc 2350 Helen St *NASDAQ: ATRM*	North Saint Paul	MN	55109	**800-274-3500**	651-770-2000	247
AF Comm Supply 8238 Neiman Rd	Lenexa	KS	66214	**800-255-6222**	913-492-6212	245
AFA (Air Force Assn) 1501 Lee Hwy	Arlington	VA	22209	**800-727-3337**	703-247-5800	48-19
AFA (American Federation of Astrologers) 6535 S Rural Rd.	Tempe	AZ	85283	**888-301-7630**	480-838-1751	48-18
AFA (American Fence Assn) 800 Roosevelt Rd Bldg C-20	Glen Ellyn	IL	60137	**800-822-4342**	630-942-6598	49-3
AFAA (Aerobics & Fitness Assn of America) 15250 Ventura Blvd Suite 200	Sherman Oaks	CA	91403	**877-968-7263**	818-905-0040	48-22
AFAR (American Federation for Aging Research) 70 W 40th St 11th Fl	New York	NY	10018	**888-582-2327**	212-703-9977	49-8
AFB (American Foundation for the Blind) 11 Penn Plaza Suite 300	New York	NY	10001	**800-232-5463**	212-502-7600	48-17
AFC (Automotive Finance Corp) 13085 Hamilton Crossing Blvd.	Carmel	IN	46032	**888-335-6675**	317-815-9645	214
AFC Cable Systems Inc 272 Duchaine Blvd	New Bedford	MA	02745	**800-767-6006**	508-998-1131	800
AFC Enterprises Inc 6 Concourse Pkwy Suite 1700 *NASDAQ: AFCE*	Atlanta	GA	30328	**866-232-4401**	770-391-9500	656
AFCEA (Armed Forces Communications & Electronics Assn) 4400 Fair Lakes Ct	Fairfax	VA	22033	**800-336-4583**	703-631-6100	48-19
AFCO Credit Corp 110 William St 29th Fl	New York	NY	10038	**800-288-2313**	212-401-4400	214
Afco Industries Inc 3400 Roy Ave	Alexandria	LA	71302	**800-551-6576**	318-448-1651	473
Afco Mfg Corp 428 Cogshall St PO Box 230	Holly	MI	48442	**800-743-4415**	248-634-4415	471
Affholder Inc 17988 Edison Ave	Chesterfield	MO	63005	**800-325-1159**	636-532-2622	187-10
Affiliated Car Rental LC DBA Sensible Car Rental Inc 96 Freneau Ave Suite 2	Matawan	NJ	07747	**800-367-5159**	732-583-8500	126
Affiliated Foods Inc 1401 Farmers Ave	Amarillo	TX	79118	**800-234-3661**	806-372-3851	292-8
AFFINA 2001 Ruppman Plaza	Peoria	IL	61614	**800-787-7626**	309-685-5901	722
Affina Dumont Plaza 150 E 34th St	New York	NY	10016	**866-233-4642**	212-481-7600	373
Affinia Hospitality 500 W 37th St. *Resv	New York	NY	10018	**866-246-2203***	212-465-3700	369
Affinity Bioreagents Inc 4620 Technology Dr Suite 600	Golden	CO	80403	**800-527-4535**	303-278-4535	229
Affinity Federal Credit Union 73 Mountain View Blvd Bldg 200	Basking Ridge	NJ	07920	**800-325-0808**	908-860-7300	216
Affordable Car Rental System Inc 96 Freneau Ave Suite 2	Matawan	NJ	07747	**800-631-2290**	732-290-8300	126
Affordable Residential Communities Inc 600 Grant St Suite 900 *NYSE: ARC*	Denver	CO	80203	**800-245-5415**	303-291-0222	640
Affymetrix Inc 3380 Central Expy *NASDAQ: AFFX* ■ *Tech Supp	Santa Clara	CA	95051	**888-362-2447***	408-731-5503	249
AFG Industries Inc PO Box 929	Kingsport	TN	37662	**800-251-0441**	423-229-7200	325
AFGC (American Forage & Grassland Council) PO Box 94	Georgetown	TX	78627	**800-944-2342**		48-2
AFI (Armed Forces Insurance Exchange) PO Box G	Fort Leavenworth	KS	66027	**800-828-7732**	913-651-5000	384-4
AFI Fest American Film Institute 2021 N Western Ave	Los Angeles	CA	90027	**866-231-3378**	323-856-7600	278
AFLAC (American Family Life Assurance Co of Columbus) 1932 Wynnton Rd	Columbus	GA	31999	**800-992-3522**	706-323-3431	384-2
AFLAC Inc 1932 Wynnton Rd *NYSE: AFL*	Columbus	GA	31999	**800-992-3522**	706-323-3431	355-4
AFM (American Federation of Musicians of the US & Canada) 1501 Broadway Suite 600	New York	NY	10036	**800-762-3444**	212-869-1330	405
AFM Hospitality Corp Inc 135 Queens Plate Suite 410 *TSE: AFM*	Toronto	ON	M9W6V1	**800-249-3656**	416-361-1010	369
AFP (Association of Fundraising Professionals) 1101 King St Suite 700	Alexandria	VA	22314	**800-666-3863**	703-684-0410	49-12
AFP Imaging Corp 250 Clearbrook Rd.	Elmsford	NY	10523	**800-592-6666**	914-592-6100	580
AFP Transformers Inc 206 Talmedge Rd	Edison	NJ	08817	**800-843-1215**	732-248-0305	756
Africa Adventure Co 5353 N Federal Hwy Suite 300	Fort Lauderdale	FL	33308	**800-882-9453**	954-491-8877	748
Africa-America Institute (AAI) 420 Lexington Ave Suite 1706	New York	NY	10170	**800-745-3899**	212-949-5666	48-14
African American Historical Museum & Cultural Center of Iowa 55 12th Ave SE	Cedar Rapids	IA	52406	**877-526-1863**	319-862-2101	509
African American Literature Book Club (AALBC) 55 W 116th St Suite 195	Harlem	NY	10026	**866-603-8394**		94
African Lion Safari & Game Farm RR 1	Cambridge	ON	N1R5S2	**800-461-9453**	519-623-2620	811
African Safari Wildlife Park 267 Lightner Rd	Port Clinton	OH	43452	**800-521-2660**	419-732-3606	811
African Travel Inc 1100 E Broadway 2nd Fl	Glendale	CA	91205	**800-421-8907**	818-507-7893	748
African Wildlife Foundation (AWF) 1400 16th St NW Suite 120	Washington	DC	20036	**888-494-5354**	202-939-3333	48-3
Afro World Hair Goods Inc 7276 Natural Bridge Rd	Saint Louis	MO	63121	**800-228-9424**	314-389-5194	342
Afromart Gift Enterprises PO Box 7814	Long Beach	CA	90807	**877-215-0284**	562-426-0055	322
AFS (American Foundry Society) 1695 N Penny Ln	Schaumburg	IL	60173	**800-537-4237**	847-824-0181	49-13
AFSA (Air Force Sergeants Assn) 5211 Auth Rd	Suitland	MD	20746	**800-638-0594**	301-899-3500	48-19

Name / Address	City	State	ZIP	Toll-Free	Phone	Class
AFSA (American Federation of School Administrators) 1729 21st St NW	Washington	DC	20009	**800-354-2372**	202-986-4209	49-5
AFSP (American Foundation for Suicide Prevention) 120 Wall St 22nd Fl	New York	NY	10005	**888-333-2377**	212-363-3500	48-17
AFT (American Farmland Trust) 1200 18th St NW Suite 800	Washington	DC	20036	**800-431-1499**	202-331-7300	48-2
AFT (American Federation of Teachers) 555 New Jersey Ave NW	Washington	DC	20001	**800-238-1133**	202-879-4400	405
AFT Healthcare 555 New Jersey Ave NW	Washington	DC	20001	**800-238-1133**	202-879-4491	405
After Six Inc 240 Collins Industrial Dr *Cust Svc	Athens	GA	30601	**800-554-8212***	706-543-5286	153-12
Afton Pumps Inc 7335 Ave N	Houston	TX	77011	**800-829-9731**	713-923-9731	627
AFUD (American Foundation for Urologic Disease) 1000 Corporate Blvd Suite 410	Linthicum	MD	21090	**800-828-7866**	410-689-3990	48-17
A/G (Assemblies of God) 1445 N Boonville Ave	Springfield	MO	65802	**800-641-4310**	417-862-2781	48-20
AG Edwards Inc 1 N Jefferson Ave *NYSE: AGE*	Saint Louis	MO	63103	**877-835-7877**	314-955-3000	355-3
AG Partners Inc PO Box 467	Lake City	MN	55041	**800-772-2990**	651-345-3328	438
AG Processing Inc PO Box 2047	Omaha	NE	68103	**800-247-1345**	402-496-7809	291-29
Ag States Agency 5500 Cenex Dr	Inver Grove Heights	MN	55077	**800-548-1494**	651-355-3700	384-4
Ag Valley Co-op 103 S Commercial St	Maywood	NE	69038	**800-233-4551**	308-362-4244	272
Ag West Supply 9055 Rickreall Rd	Rickreall	OR	97371	**800-842-2224**	503-363-2332	270
AGA (American Galvanizers Assn) 6881 S Holly Cir Suite 108	Centennial	CO	80112	**800-468-7732**	720-554-0900	49-13
AGA (Association of Government Accountants) 2208 Mt Vernon Ave	Alexandria	VA	22301	**800-242-7211**	703-684-6931	49-1
Agape Tours Inc 1210 US Hwy 281	Wichita Falls	TX	76310	**800-460-2641**	940-767-4935	748
Agar Supply Co Inc 225 John Hancock Rd	Taunton	MA	02780	**800-669-6040**	508-821-2060	292-9
Agave the Arizona Spa at the Westin Kierland Resort & Spa 6902 E Greenway Pkwy	Scottsdale	AZ	85254	**888-625-5144**	480-624-1500	698
AGB (Association of Governing Boards of Universities & Colleges) 1 Dupont Cir NW Suite 400	Washington	DC	20036	**800-356-6317**	202-296-8400	49-5
AGC (Associated General Contractors of America) 333 John Carlyle St Suite 200	Alexandria	VA	22314	**800-242-1766**	703-548-3118	49-3
AGC Life Insurance Co 2000 American General Way	Brentwood	TN	37027	**800-888-2452**	615-749-1000	384-2
AGC PAC (Associated General Contractors PAC) 333 John Carlyle St Suite 200	Alexandria	VA	22314	**800-242-1766**	703-548-3118	604
Agency for Healthcare Research & Quality 540 Gaither Rd	Rockville	MD	20850	**800-358-9295**	301-427-1200	654
Agency for Toxic Substances & Disease Registry Centers for Disease Control & Prevention 1600 Clifton Rd NE Bldg 37 MS E-29	Atlanta	GA	30333	**888-422-8737**	404-498-0110	654
AGENCY.COM Ltd 20 Exchange Pl 9th Fl	New York	NY	10005	**800-736-4644**	212-358-2600	193
Agere Systems Inc 1110 American Pkwy NE *NYSE: AGR*	Allentown	PA	18109	**800-372-2447**	610-712-6011	686
Aget Mfg Co 1408 E Church St	Adrian	MI	49221	**800-832-2438**	517-263-5781	19
AGF Management Ltd 2920 Matheson Blvd E	Mississauga	ON	L4W5J4	**800-268-8583**	905-214-8203	393
Agfa Corp 100 Challenger Rd	Ridgefield Park	NJ	07660	**800-581-2432**	201-440-2500	580
Aggregate Industries Inc 888 Dunbarton Rd	Manchester	NH	03102	**800-322-7665**	603-627-7666	180
AGI Inc 1950 N Ruby St	Melrose Park	IL	60160	**800-677-9110**	708-344-9100	102
AGI Schutz Merchandising Co 376 Pine St	Forest City	NC	28043	**800-662-2150**	828-245-9871	281
Agie Ltd 9009-G Perimeter Woods Dr	Charlotte	NC	28016	**800-438-5021**	704-927-8900	447
Agile Mfg Inc 720 Industrial Park Rd	Anderson	MO	64831	**800-704-7356**	417-845-6065	269
Agile Software Corp 6373 San Ignacio Ave *NASDAQ: AGIL*	San Jose	CA	95119	**888-594-5736**	408-284-4000	176-1
Agilent Technologies Inc 395 Page Mill Rd *NYSE: A*	Palo Alto	CA	94306	**877-424-4536**	650-752-5000	247
Agiliti Inc 1125 Energy Pk Dr Suite 100 *Tech Supp	Saint Paul	MN	55108	**866-244-5484***	952-918-2000	39
AgilQuest Corp 9407 Hull St	Richmond	VA	23236	**888-745-7455**	804-745-0467	176-1
Agilysys Inc 6065 Parkland Blvd *NASDAQ: AGYS*	Cleveland	OH	44124	**800-362-9127**	440-720-8500	172
Aging. American Assn of Homes & Services for the 2519 Connecticut Ave NW	Washington	DC	20008	**800-508-9442**	202-783-2242	48-6
Aging. American Society on 833 Market St Suite 511	San Francisco	CA	94103	**800-537-9728**	415-974-9600	48-6
Aging. Christian Foundation for Children & 1 Elmwood Ave	Kansas City	KS	66103	**800-875-6564**	913-384-6500	48-6
Aging. National Center on Women & Brandeis University Heller Graduate School MS 035	Waltham	MA	02454	**800-929-1995**	781-736-3866	48-6
Aging. National Council on the 300 D St SW Suite 801	Washington	DC	20024	**800-424-9046**	202-479-1200	48-6
Aging. National Interfaith Coalition on 300 D St SW	Washington	DC	20024	**800-424-9046**	202-479-1200	48-6
Aging. National Resource Center on Native American 501 N Columbia Rd Rm 4531	Grand Forks	ND	58202	**800-896-7628**	701-777-3437	48-6
Aging News Alert Newsletter 8204 Fenton St	Silver Spring	MD	20910	**800-666-6380**	301-588-6380	521-8
Aging Parents. Children of 1609 Woodbourne Rd Suite 302A	Levittown	PA	19057	**800-227-7294**	215-945-6900	48-6

Name / Address	City	State	ZIP	Toll-Free	Phone	Class
Aging Research. Alliance for 2021 K St NW Suite 305	Washington	DC	20006	**800-639-2421**	202-293-2856	48-17
Aging Research. American Federation for 70 W 40th St 11th Fl	New York	NY	10018	**888-582-2327**	212-703-9977	49-8
Agissar Corp 526 Benton St	Stratford	CT	06615	**800-627-8256**	203-375-8662	112
AGL Corp 2202 Redmond Rd	Jacksonville	AR	72076	**800-643-9696**	501-982-4433	416
AGL Resources Inc 10 Peachtree Pl *NYSE: ATG* ■ *Cust Svc	Atlanta	GA	30309	**800-427-5463***	404-584-4000	774
AGM Industries Inc 16 Jonathan Dr	Brockton	MA	02301	**800-225-9990**	508-587-3900	798
AGMA (American Guild of Musical Artists) 1430 Broadway 14th Fl	New York	NY	10018	**800-543-2462**	212-265-3687	48-4
AGN International-North America (AGN) 2851 S Parker Rd Suite 850	Aurora	CO	80014	**800-782-2272**	303-743-7880	49-1
Agnes Scott College 141 E College Ave	Decatur	GA	30030	**800-868-8602**	404-471-6000	163
Agora Publishing Inc 14 W Monument St	Baltimore	MD	21201	**800-433-1528**	410-783-8499	623-9
AGPA (American Group Psychotherapy Assn) 25 E 21st St 6th Fl	New York	NY	10010	**877-668-2472**	212-477-2677	49-15
Agralite Electric Co-op 320 E Hwy 12	Benson	MN	56215	**800-950-8375**	320-843-4150	244
Agresso Americas 8150 Corporate Park Dr Suite 130	Cincinnati	OH	45242	**888-848-3776**	513-564-0400	176-1
Agri Beef Co 1555 Shoreline Dr 3rd Fl	Boise	ID	83702	**800-657-6305**	208-338-2500	11-1
Agri Co-op 310 Logan St	Holdrege	NE	68949	**800-658-4089**	308-995-8626	272
Agri-King Inc 18246 Waller Rd	Fulton	IL	61252	**800-435-9560**	815-589-2525	438
Agri-Mark Inc 100 Milk St	Methuen	MA	01844	**800-225-0532**	978-689-4442	291-27
Agri-Marketing Assn. National 11020 King St Suite 205	Overland Park	KS	66210	**800-530-5646**	913-491-6500	49-18
AGRIcareers Inc PO Box 140	Massena	IA	50853	**888-224-5621**	712-779-3300	257
Agricredit Acceptance LLC PO Box 2000	Johnston	IA	50131	**800-873-2474**	515-251-2800	214
Agricultural Commodities Inc 2224 Oxford Rd	New Oxford	PA	17350	**800-359-8899**	717-624-8249	276
Agricultural Engineers. American Society of 2950 Niles Rd. *Orders	Saint Joseph	MI	49085	**800-695-2723***	269-429-0300	48-2
Agricultural Speakers Network 10436 Oak Ridge Dr. *Sales	Zionsville	IN	46077	**800-222-1556***	317-873-9797	699
Agricultural Statistics Service. National 1400 Independence Ave SW Rm 4117	Washington	DC	20250	**800-727-9540**	202-720-2707	336-1
Agriculture Council of America (ACA) 11020 King St Suite 205	Overland Park	KS	66210	**888-982-4329**	913-491-1895	48-2
Agriflora Corp 9475 NW 13th St	Miami	FL	33172	**800-851-2098**	305-477-0291	288
AgriGold Hybrids RR 1 Box 203	Saint Francisville	IL	62460	**800-262-7333**	618-943-5776	684
AgriNorthwest 7404 W Hood Pl Suite B	Kennewick	WA	99336	**800-333-8175**	509-734-1195	11-5
Agripro Seeds Inc 2369 330th St	Slater	LA	50244	**877-247-4776**		11-5
AGRIS Corp 1600 N Lorraine St	Hutchinson	KS	67501	**800-795-7995**	620-669-9811	176-10
Agrium Inc 13131 Lake Fraser Dr SE *NYSE: AGU*	Calgary	AB	T2J7E8	**877-247-4861**	403-225-7000	276
AGRM (Association of Gospel Rescue Missions) 1045 Swift Ave	Kansas City	MO	64116	**800-624-5156**	816-471-8020	48-20
Agropur Co-op Agro-alimentaire 510 rue Principale	Granby	QC	J2G7G2	**800-363-6190**	450-375-1991	291-27
AGS Publishing 4201 Woodland Rd	Circle Pines	MN	55014	**800-471-8457**	651-287-7220	242
AGSI 3390 Peachtree Rd NE Suite 350	Atlanta	GA	30326	**800-768-2474**	404-816-7577	178
AGTA (American Gem Trade Assn) 3030 LBJ Fwy Suite 840	Dallas	TX	75234	**800-972-1162**	214-742-4367	49-4
AGU (American Geophysical Union) 2000 Florida Ave NW	Washington	DC	20009	**800-966-2481**	202-462-6900	49-19
Aguirre Engineers Inc 13276 E Fremont Pl	Centennial	CO	80112	**800-403-7066**	303-799-8378	728
AH Rice Corp 55 Spring St *Sales	Pittsfield	MA	01201	**800-765-7423***	413-443-6477	730-5
AH Schreiber Co 460 W 34th St 10th Fl	New York	NY	10001	**800-724-1612**	212-564-2700	153-17
AHA (American Heart Assn) 7272 Greenville Ave	Dallas	TX	75231	**800-242-8721**	214-373-6300	48-17
AHA (American Homeowners Assn) 1100 Summer St 1st Fl *Cust Svc	Stamford	CT	06905	**800-470-2242***	203-323-7715	48-10
AHA (American Hospital Assn) 1 N Franklin St	Chicago	IL	60606	**800-424-4301**	312-422-3000	49-8
AHA (American Humane Assn) 63 Inverness Dr E	Englewood	CO	80112	**800-227-4645**	303-792-9900	48-6
AHA News 1 N Franklin St Suite 2800	Chicago	IL	60606	**800-621-6902**	312-893-6800	449-5
Ahaus Tool & Engineering Inc PO Box 280	Richmond	IN	47375	**800-962-3571**	765-962-3571	745
AHCA (American Health Care Assn) 1201 L St NW	Washington	DC	20005	**800-321-0343**	202-842-4444	49-8
Ahead 270 Samuel Barnet Blvd	New Bedford	MA	02745	**800-282-2246**	508-999-4466	153-9
AheadTek Inc 6410 Via Del Oro	San Jose	CA	95119	**800-971-9191**	408-226-9991	633
Ahearn & Soper Inc 100 Woodbine Downs Blvd	Rexdale	ON	M9W5S6	**800-263-4258**	416-675-3999	172
AHI International 6400 Shafer Ct	Rosemont	IL	60018	**800-323-7373**	847-384-4500	748
AHIA (Association of Healthcare Internal Auditors) PO Box 449	Onsted	MI	49265	**888-275-2442**	517-467-7729	49-1
AHIMA (American Health Information Management Assn) 233 N Michigan Ave Suite 2150	Chicago	IL	60601	**800-335-5535**	312-233-1100	49-8
AHNA (American Holistic Nurses' Assn) 2733 E Lakin Dr Suite 2	Flagstaff	AZ	86004	**800-278-2462**	928-526-2196	48-17
AHPC Holdings Inc 500 Park Blvd Suite 1260 *NASDAQ: GLOV*	Itasca	IL	60143	**800-828-2964**	630-285-9191	566
AHRA (American Healthcare Radiology Administrators) 490-B Boston Post Rd Suite 101	Sudbury	MA	01776	**800-334-2472**	978-443-7591	49-8
AHS (American Hiking Society) 1422 Fenwick Ln	Silver Spring	MD	20910	**800-972-8608**	301-565-6704	48-23
AHS (American Horticultural Society) 7931 E Boulevard Dr	Alexandria	VA	22308	**800-777-7931**	703-768-5700	48-18
Al Friedman Co Inc 44 W 18th St	New York	NY	10011	**800-204-6352**	212-243-9000	45

Alphabetical Section

Name / Address	City	State	Zip	Toll-Free	Phone	Class
Ai Miami International University of Art & Design 1501 Biscayne Blvd	Miami	FL	33132	**800-225-9023**	305-428-5700	159
AIA (American Institute of Architects) 1735 New York Ave NW *Orders	Washington	DC	20006	**800-365-2724***	202-626-7300	48-4
AIAA (American Institute of Aeronautics & Astronautics) 1801 Alexander Bell Dr Suite 500	Reston	VA	20191	**800-639-2422**	703-264-7500	49-19
AIADA (American International Automobile Dealers Assn) 211 N Union St Suite 300	Alexandria	VA	22314	**800-462-4232**	703-519-7800	49-18
AIB College of Business 2500 Fleur Dr	Des Moines	IA	50321	**800-444-1921**	515-244-4221	158
AIBS (American Institute of Biological Sciences) 1444 'I' St NW Suite 200	Washington	DC	20005	**800-992-2427**	202-628-1500	49-19
AIC Investment Bulletin 30 Stockbridge Rd	Great Barrington	MA	01230	**800-532-4999**	413-528-9779	521-9
AIChE (American Institute of Chemical Engineers) 3 Park Ave *Cust Svc	New York	NY	10016	**800-242-4363***	212-591-7338	49-19
AICPA (American Institute of Certified Public Accountants) 1211 Ave of the Americas	New York	NY	10030	**800-777-7077**	212-596-6200	49-1
AICPCU/IIA (American Institute for CPCU & Insurance Institute of America) 720 Providence Rd PO Box 3016	Malvern	PA	19355	**800-644-2101**	610-644-2100	49-9
AICR Newsletter 1759 R St NW	Washington	DC	20009	**800-843-8114**	202-328-7744	521-8
Aid & Development Inc. Mercy-USA for 44450 Pinetree Dr Suite 201	Plymouth	MI	48170	**800-556-3729**	734-454-0011	48-5
Aid for Education Report 8204 Fenton St	Silver Spring	MD	20910	**800-666-6380**	301-588-6380	521-4
Aid Inc. International 17011 W Hickory St	Spring Lake	MI	49456	**800-968-7490**	616-846-7490	48-5
AIDS Care. Association of Nurses in 3538 Ridgewood Rd	Akron	OH	44333	**800-260-6780**	330-670-0101	49-8
AIDS Foundation. Elizabeth Glaser Pediatric 2950 31st St Suite 125	Santa Monica	CA	90405	**888-499-4673**	310-314-1459	48-17
AIDS Prevention Center. National Native American 436 14th St Suite 1020	Oakland	CA	94612	**800-283-6880**	510-444-2051	48-17
AIDS Research. American Foundation for 120 Wall St 13th Fl	New York	NY	10005	**800-392-6327**	212-806-1600	48-17
AIDSinfo PO Box 6303	Rockville	MD	20849	**800-448-0440**	301-519-0459	336-6
AIFS (American Institute for Foreign Study) 9 W Broad St	Stamford	CT	06902	**800-727-2437**	203-399-5000	48-11
AIG Life Insurance Co PO Box 2226	Wilmington	DE	19899	**800-441-7468**	302-594-2000	384-2
AIG SunAmerica Inc 1 SunAmerica Ctr 37th Fl	Los Angeles	CA	90067	**800-445-7862**	310-772-6000	355-4
AIGA (American Institute of Graphic Arts) 164 5th Ave	New York	NY	10010	**800-548-1634**	212-807-1990	48-4
Aigner Index Inc 218 MacArthur Ave	New Windsor	NY	12553	**800-242-3919**	845-562-4510	597
AIIM - Enterprise Content Management Assn 1100 Wayne Ave Suite 1100	Silver Spring	MD	20910	**800-477-2446**	301-587-8202	49-19
Aiken Electric Co-op Inc 2790 Wagener Rd	Aiken	SC	29802	**800-922-1262**	803-649-6245	244
Aiken (Greater) Chamber of Commerce PO Box 892	Aiken	SC	29802	**800-542-4536**	803-641-1111	137
Aiken Regional Medical Centers 302 University Pkwy	Aiken	SC	29802	**800-245-3679**	803-641-5000	366-2
AIM (Accuracy in Media Inc) 4455 Connecticut Ave NW Suite 330	Washington	DC	20008	**800-787-4567**	202-364-4401	49-14
AIM (Association for Interactive Marketing) 1430 Broadway 8th Fl	New York	NY	10018	**888-337-0008**	212-790-1406	48-9
Aim Electronics Corp 3103 N Andrews Ave	Pompano Beach	FL	33064	**800-327-8663**	954-984-3400	252
AIM Family of Funds 11 Greenway Plaza Suite 100	Houston	TX	77046	**800-347-1919**	713-626-1919	517
AIM Global - Assn for Automatic Identification & Mobility (AIM) 125 Warrendale-Bayne Rd	Warrendale	PA	15086	**800-338-0206**	724-934-4470	49-19
AIM Mail Centers 15550-D Rockfield Blvd	Irvine	CA	92618	**800-669-4246**	949-837-4151	114
AIM Supply Co 7337 Bryan Dairy Rd	Largo	FL	33777	**800-999-0125**		378
Aimco 10000 SE Pine St	Portland	OR	97216	**800-852-1368**	503-255-7364	378
AimNet Solutions Inc 125 Jeffrey Ave	Holliston	MA	01746	**888-332-5746**	508-429-0700	455
Aims Community College 5401 20th St	Greeley	CO	80634	**800-301-5388**	970-330-8008	160
AIMS Logistics 311 Moore Ln	Collierville	TN	38017	**877-406-9966**	901-854-5777	440
Aims Multimedia 20765 Superior St	Chatsworth	CA	91311	**800-367-2467**	818-773-4300	500
AIN Plastics Inc 23235 Telegraph Rd *Cust Svc	Southfield	MI	48034	**800-521-1757***	248-356-4000	592
Ainsworth Feed Yards Co PO Box 267	Ainsworth	NE	69210	**800-438-3148**	402-387-2455	11-1
Ainsworth Lumber Co Ltd 1055 Dunsmuir St Suite 3194 *TSE: ANS*	Vancouver	BC	V7X1L3	**877-661-3200**	604-661-3200	671
AIP Inc 1290 Maplelawn St	Troy	MI	48084	**800-247-5551**	248-649-7300	745
AIPB (American Institute of Professional Bookkeepers) 6001 Montrose Rd Suite 500	Rockville	MD	20852	**800-622-0121**	301-770-7300	49-1
AIR (Association of Independents in Radio) 328 Flatbush Ave Suite 322	Brooklyn	NY	11238	**888-937-2477**		620
Air America Jet Charter Inc 9000 Randolph St	Houston	TX	77061	**888-423-9110**	713-640-2900	14
Air Brook Limousine Inc 318 Overlook Ave	Rochelle Park	NJ	07662	**800-800-1990**	201-843-6100	433
Air Canada 7373 Cote Vertu W	Saint-Laurent	QC	H4Y1H4	**888-247-2262**	514-422-5000	26
Air Canada Aeroplan PO Box 15000 Station Airport	Dorval	QC	H4Y1H5	**866-689-8080**	800-361-5373	27
Air Canada Cargo LaGuardia International Airport Hangar 5B	Flushing	NY	11371	**800-688-2274**	718-899-9128	13
Air Canada Jazz 310 Goudey Dr *Cust Svc	Enfield	NS	B2T1E4	**866-222-6688***	902-873-5000	26
Air Cargo International & Domestic 180 Admiral Cochrane Dr Suite 305	Annapolis	MD	21401	**800-747-6505**	410-280-5578	306
Air Charter Team 10015 NW Ambassador Dr Suite 202	Kansas City	MO	64153	**800-205-6610**	816-283-3280	14
Air China 150 E 52 St	New York	NY	10022	**800-982-8802**	212-371-9898	26
Air China Companion Club 150 E 52nd St	New York	NY	10022	**800-982-8802**	212-371-9898	27
Air Comfort Corp 2550 Braga Dr	Broadview	IL	60155	**800-466-3779**	708-345-1900	188-10
Air-Conditioning Engineers Inc. American Society of Heating Refrigerating & 1791 Tullie Cir NE *Cust Svc	Atlanta	GA	30329	**800-527-4723***	404-636-8400	49-3
Air Conditioning Heating & Refrigeration News 2401 W Big Beaver Rd Suite 700	Troy	MI	48084	**800-837-8337**	248-362-3700	449-21
Air Courier Dispatch 1700 Enterprise Way Suite 110	Atlanta	GA	30348	**800-257-7162**	770-933-9496	536
Air Force Assn (AFA) 1501 Lee Hwy	Arlington	VA	22209	**800-727-3337**	703-247-5800	48-19
Air Force Magazine 1501 Lee Hwy	Arlington	VA	22209	**800-727-3337**	703-247-5800	449-12
Air Force Sergeants Assn (AFSA) 5211 Auth Rd	Suitland	MD	20746	**800-638-0594**	301-899-3500	48-19
Air Force Times Magazine 6883 Commercial Dr	Springfield	VA	22159	**800-424-9335**	703-750-9000	449-12
Air France 125 W 55th St *Resv	New York	NY	10019	**800-237-2747***	212-830-4000	26
Air France Frequence Plus 235 King St E	Kitchener	ON	N2G4N5	**800-375-8723**	519-772-3570	27
Air India 570 Lexington Ave 15th Fl	New York	NY	10022	**800-223-7776**	212-407-1300	26
Air Jamaica 7th Heaven 8300 NW 33rd St Suite 440	Miami	FL	33122	**800-523-5585**	305-670-3222	27
Air Jamaica 95-25 Queens Blvd 7th FL	Rego Park	NY	11374	**800-523-5585**	718-830-0622	26
Air Line Pilots Assn 535 Herndon Pkwy	Herndon	VA	20170	**800-359-2572**	703-689-2270	405
Air Liquide America LP 2700 Post Oak Blvd Suite 1800	Houston	TX	77056	**877-855-9533**	713-624-8000	141
Air Logistics Inc 4605 Industrial Dr	New Iberia	LA	70560	**800-365-6771**	337-365-6771	354
Air Midwest Inc DBA US Airways Express 2203 Air Cargo Rd	Wichita	KS	67209	**800-428-4322**	316-942-8137	26
Air Monitor Corp 1050 Hopper Ave	Santa Rosa	CA	95403	**800-247-3569**	707-544-2706	601
Air New Zealand Airpoints 1960 E Grand Ave Suite 300	El Segundo	CA	90245	**800-223-9494**	800-262-1234	27
Air New Zealand Cargo Sales JFK International Airport Cargo Plaza Bldg 87	Jamaica	NY	11430	**800-400-0153**	718-244-1333	13
Air New Zealand Ltd 1960 E Grand Ave Suite 900	El Segundo	CA	90245	**800-262-1234**	310-648-7000	26
Air by Pleasant 4025 Camino del Rio S Suite 210	San Diego	CA	92108	**800-877-8111**	619-282-3455	17
Air Products & Chemicals Inc 7201 Hamilton Blvd *NYSE: APD* ■ *Prod Info	Allentown	PA	18195	**800-345-3148***	610-481-4911	141
Air Quality Engineering Inc 7140 Northland Dr N	Brooklyn Park	MN	55428	**800-328-0787**	763-531-9823	19
Air Response Inc 7211 S Peoria St Suite 200	Englewood	CO	80112	**800-631-6565**	303-858-9967	31
Air Royale International Inc 9100 Wilshire Blvd Suite 420	Beverly Hills	CA	90212	**800-776-9253**	310-289-9800	14
AIR-serv Group LLC 1370 Mendota Heights Rd	Mendota Heights	MN	55120	**800-227-5336**	651-454-0518	55
Air Sunshine Inc PO Box 22237	Fort Lauderdale	FL	33335	**800-327-8900**	954-434-8900	26
Air-Supply Inc 350 5th Ave Empire State Bldg Suite 6724	New York	NY	10118	**800-671-9961**	212-695-1647	17
Air Systems Inc 7400 S 28th St	Fort Smith	AR	72908	**800-643-2980**	479-646-8386	688
Air Tahiti Nui 1990 E Grand Ave *Cust Svc	El Segundo	CA	90245	**877-824-4846***	310-662-1860	26
Air Technical Industries 7501 Clover Ave	Mentor	OH	44060	**800-321-9680**	440-951-5191	462
Air Tool Service Co (ATSCO) 7722 Metric Dr	Mentor	OH	44060	**800-321-3554**	440-942-4475	747
Air Traffic Controllers Assn. National 1325 Massachusetts Ave NW	Washington	DC	20005	**800-266-0895**	202-628-5451	405
Air Traffic Management Inc 16550 Air Ctr Blvd *Cust Svc	Houston	TX	77032	**800-231-0221***	281-821-2002	13
Air Transport Assn of America (ATA) 1301 Pennsylvania Ave NW Suite 1100	Washington	DC	20004	**800-319-2463**	202-626-4000	49-21
Air Transport World Magazine 1350 Connecticut Ave NW Suite 902	Washington	DC	20036	**800-366-1901**	202-659-8500	449-21
Air Transportation Assn. National 4226 King St	Alexandria	VA	22302	**800-808-6282**	703-845-9000	49-21
Air Van Moving Group 10510 NE Northup Way Suite 110	Kirkland	WA	98033	**800-877-1442**	425-629-4101	508
Air & Waste Management Assn (A&WMA) 420 Fort Duquesne Blvd 1 Gateway Ctr 3rd Fl	Pittsburgh	PA	15222	**800-270-3444**	412-232-3444	48-12
Air-Way Mfg Co 586 N Main St *Cust Svc	Olivet	MI	49076	**800-253-1036***	269-749-2161	777
Air2Web Inc 1230 Peachtree St NE 12th Fl	Atlanta	GA	30309	**877-238-3637**	404-815-7707	222
AirBoss Polymer Products Corp 200 Veterans Blvd	South Haven	MI	49090	**888-258-7252**	269-637-2181	664
Aircom Mfg Inc 6205 E 30th St	Indianapolis	IN	46219	**800-925-2426**	317-545-5383	688
Aircon Filter Mfg Co 441 Green St	Philadelphia	PA	19123	**800-833-3019**	215-922-5222	19
Airconditioning & Refrigeration Distributors International. Heating 1389 Dublin Rd	Columbus	OH	43215	**888-253-2128**	614-488-1835	49-18
Aircraft Assn. Experimental 3000 Poberezny Rd	Oshkosh	WI	54902	**800-236-4800**	920-426-4800	48-18
Aircraft Instrument & Radio Co Inc 1853 S Eisenhower Ct	Wichita	KS	67209	**800-835-2243**	316-945-0445	759

Toll-Free | Phone | Class

Aircraft Owners & Pilots Assn (AOPA)
421 Aviation Way ... Frederick MD 21701 **800-872-2672** 301-695-2000 49-21
Aircraft Parts Corp 100 Corporate Dr.. Holtsville NY 11742 **877-427-2634** 631-289-0077 22
Aircraft Service International Group
201 S Orange Ave Suite 205 ... Orlando FL 32801 **800-557-2744** 407-648-7373 294
Aircraft Specialists Inc
6005 Propeller Ln ... Sellersburg IN 47172 **800-356-3723** 812-246-4696 63
Aircraft Technical Publishers
101 S Hill Dr ... Brisbane CA 94005 **800-227-4610** 415-330-9500 623-11
AirEvac Services Inc
2630 Sky Harbor Blvd ... Phoenix AZ 85034 **800-421-6111** 602-244-9327 31
AirFlite Inc 3250 AirFlite Way ... Long Beach CA 90807 **800-241-3548** 562-490-6200 14
Airfloat Systems Inc
2230 Brush College Rd ... Decatur IL 62526 **800-888-0018** 217-423-6001 206
Airflow Systems Inc 11221 Pagemill Rd... Dallas TX 75243 **800-818-6185** 214-503-8008 19
Airgas Inc
259 N Radnor-Chester Rd Suite 100... Radnor PA 19087 **800-255-2165** 610-687-5253 144
NYSE: ARG
Airguard Industries Inc
3807 Bishop Ln ... Louisville KY 40218 **800-999-3458** 502-969-2304 19
AirLiance Materials LLC
PO Box 661008 ... Chicago IL 60666 **877-233-5800** 847-233-5800 759
Airlie Conference Center
6809 Airlie Rd ... Warrenton VA 20187 **800-288-9573** 540-347-1300 370
Airline History Museum
201 Lou Holland Dr Hangar 9 ... Kansas City MO 64116 **800-513-9484** 816-421-3401 509
Airline Passengers Assn. International
5204 Tennyson Pkwy ... Plano TX 75024 **800-821-4272** 972-404-9980 48-23
Airlines Travel Agent Network. International 300 Garden City
Plaza Suite 342 ... Garden City NY 11530 **800-294-2826** 516-663-6000 49-21
Airmate Co Inc 16280 County Rd D ... Bryan OH 43506 **800-544-3614** 419-636-3184 675
AirNet Communications Corp
3950 Dow Rd ... Melbourne FL 32934 **800-984-1990** 321-984-1990 720
NASDAQ: ANCC
AirNet Systems Inc
3939 International Gateway ... Columbus OH 43219 **888-888-8463** 614-237-2057 536
NYSE: ANS
Airolite Co 114 Westview Ave ... Marietta OH 45750 **800-247-6548** 740-373-7676 482
Airosol Co Inc
1101 Illinois PO Box 120 ... Neodesha KS 66757 **800-633-9576** 620-325-2666 143
Airparts Co Inc PO Box 9268 ... Fort Lauderdale FL 33310 **800-392-4999** 954-739-3575 759
Airport Hotel Halifax
60 Bell Blvd Halifax
International Airport ... Enfield NS B2T1K3 **800-667-3333** 902-873-3000 372
Airport Regency Hotel
1000 NW Lejeune Rd ... Miami FL 33126 **800-367-1039** 305-441-1600 373
Airports Newsletter
1200 G St NW Suite 900 ... Washington DC 20005 **800-752-4959** 202-383-2350 521-13
AirportsPickup.com PO Box 652 ... New York NY 10040 **877-800-6500** 212-927-7152 433
Airtech Corp 4260 W Artesia Ave ... Fullerton CA 92833 **800-634-4453** 714-562-9295 19
Airtechnics Inc 3851 N Webb Rd ... Wichita KS 67226 **800-544-4070** 316-315-1200 245
Airtek Inc 4087 Walden Ave ... Lancaster NY 14086 **800-451-6023** 716-685-4040 15
Airtek Inc PO Box 466 ... Irwin PA 15642 **800-424-7835** 724-863-1350 526
Airtel Plaza Hotel 7277 Valjean Ave ... Van Nuys CA 91406 **800-224-7835** 818-997-7676 373
Airtex Consumer Products a Division of Federal Foam Technologies
150 Industrial Pk Blvd ... Cokato MN 55321 **800-851-8887** 320-286-2696 730-6
Airtex Products 407 W Main St ... Fairfield IL 62837 **800-880-3056** 618-842-2111 60
AirTran Airways 9955 AirTran Blvd ... Orlando FL 32827 **800-247-8726** 407-251-5600 26
AirTran Airways A-Plus Rewards
1224 Bob Harman Rd ... Savannah GA 31408 **888-327-5878** 27
Airwalk International LLC
603 Park Point Dr Suite 100 ... Golden CO 80401 **800-677-1545** 303-526-2100 296
Airway Industries Inc/Atlantic Products Corp Airway Pk ... Ellwood City PA 16117 **800-245-1750*** 724-752-0012 444
*Cust Svc
Airways Freight Corp
3849 W Wedington Dr ... Fayetteville AR 72704 **800-643-3525** 479-442-6301 306
Aisin World Corp of America
24330 Garnier St ... Torrance CA 90505 **800-822-2726** 310-326-8681 60
AITDomains 421 Maiden Ln ... Fayetteville NC 28301 **877-549-2881** 910-321-1327 389
Aitken Products Inc PO Box 151 ... Geneva OH 44041 **800-569-9341** 440-466-5711 15
AIUM (American Institute of Ultrasound in Medicine) 14750 Sweitzer Ln
Suite 100 ... Laurel MD 20707 **800-638-5352** 301-498-4100 49-8
AIUSA (Amnesty International USA)
5 Penn Plaza 14th Fl ... New York NY 10001 **800-266-3789** 212-807-8400 48-5
AJ Daw Printing Ink Co
3559 Greenwood Ave ... Los Angeles CA 90040 **800-432-9465** 323-723-3253 381
AJ Desmond & Sons Funeral Directors
2600 Crooks Rd ... Troy MI 48084 **800-210-7135** 248-362-2500 499
AJ Funk & Co Inc 1471 Timber Dr ... Elgin IL 60123 **877-225-3865** 847-741-6760 149
AJ Plastic Products
19919 Shawnee Mission Pkwy ... Shawnee KS 66218 **800-999-5518** 913-422-2027 593
AJ Siris Corp Inc PO Box AV ... Paterson NJ 07509 **800-526-5300** 973-684-7700 597
Ajax Tocco Magnethermic Corp
1745 Overland Ave NE ... Warren OH 44483 **800-321-0153** 330-372-8511 313
AJC International
5188 Roswell Rd NW ... Atlanta GA 30342 **800-252-3663** 404-252-6750 292-8
Ajilon Communications
3039 Premiere Pkwy Suite 900 ... Duluth GA 30097 **800-843-6910** 678-584-2511 195
Ajilon Services Inc
210 W Pennsylvania Ave 5th Fl ... Towson MD 21204 **800-626-8082** 410-821-0435 455
AJLI (Association of Junior Leagues International Inc) 90 William St
Suite 200 ... New York NY 10038 **800-955-3248** 212-683-1515 48-15
AJS Assoc 1003 Jordan Ln ... Huntsville AL 35816 **800-227-0340** 256-830-2423 656
AJWS (American Jewish World Service)
45 W 36th St 10th Fl ... New York NY 10018 **800-889-7146** 212-736-2597 48-5
AK Bommer Custom Snowboards
PO Box 1444 ... Valdez AK 99686 **888-252-6637** 907-835-3846 701
AK Stamping Inc 1159 US Rt 22... Mountainside NJ 07092 **800-227-3258*** 908-232-7300 479
*Cust Svc
AK Steel Holding Corp
703 Curtis St ... Middletown OH 45043 **800-331-5050** 513-425-5000 709
NYSE: AKS
AK Tube LLC 30400 E Broadway ... Walbridge OH 43465 **800-955-8031** 419-661-4150 481

Akal Security Inc PO Box 1197 ... Santa Cruz NM 87567 **888-325-2527** 505-753-7832 683
Akamai Technologies Inc
8 Cambridge Ctr ... Cambridge MA 02142 **877-425-2624** 617-444-3000 176-7
NASDAQ: AKAM
Akcros Chemicals America
500 Jersey Ave ... New Brunswick NJ 08903 **800-500-7890*** 732-247-2202 594-2
*Cust Svc
Akers Packaging Service Inc
2820 Lefferson Rd ... Middletown OH 45044 **800-327-7308** 513-422-6312 101
AKF (American Kidney Fund)
6110 Executive Blvd Suite 1010 ... Rockville MD 20852 **800-638-8299** 301-881-3052 48-17
Akorn Inc 2500 Millbrook Dr ... Buffalo Grove IL 60089 **800-932-5676** 847-279-6100 229
AkPharma Inc PO Box 111 ... Pleasantville NJ 08232 **800-994-4711** 609-645-5100 572
Akrochem Corp 255 Fountain St ... Akron OH 44304 **800-321-2260** 330-535-2108 594-3
Akron Beacon Journal
44 E Exchange St ... Akron OH 44309 **800-777-2442** 330-996-3000 522-2
Akron-Canton Regional Airport (CAK) ... North Canton OH 44720 **888-434-2359** 330-896-2385 28
Akron Gasket & Packing Enterprises Inc
1244 Home Ave ... Akron OH 44310 **800-289-7318** 330-633-3742 321
Akron General Medical Center
400 Wabash Ave ... Akron OH 44307 **800-221-4601** 330-344-6000 366-2
Akron Paint & Varnish Inc
1390 Firestone Pkwy ... Akron OH 44301 **800-772-3452** 330 773-0911 540
Akron/Summit County Convention & Visitors Bureau 77 E Mill St ... Akron OH 44308 **800-245-4254** 330-374-7560 205
Aksys Ltd 2 Marriott Dr ... Lincolnshire IL 60069 **877-229-5700** 847-229-2020 468
NASDAQ: AKSY
Akzo Nobel Inc 525 W Van Buren St ... Chicago IL 60607 **800-227-7070*** 312-544-7000 141
*Cust Svc
Al-Anon Family Group Headquarters Inc
1600 Corporate
Landing Pkwy ... Virginia Beach VA 23454 **888-425-2666** 757-563-1600 48-21
AL Bazzini Co Inc 200 Food Center Dr ... Bronx NY 10474 **800-228-0172*** 718-842-8644 291-28
*Cust Svc
Al Copeland Investments
1405 Airline Hwy ... Metairie LA 70001 **800-401-0401** 504-830-1000 656
AL Gilbert Co 304 N Yosemite Ave ... Oakdale CA 95361 **800-847-1721** 209-847-1721 438
Al Neyer Inc
10151 Carver Rd Suite 100 ... Cincinnati OH 45242 **877-271-6400** 513-271-6400 639
ALA (American Library Assn)
50 E Huron St ... Chicago IL 60611 **800-545-2433** 312-944-6780 49-11
ALA (American Lighting Assn)
2050 Stemmons Fwy Suite 10046 ... Dallas TX 75342 **800-605-4448** 214-698-9898 49-4
ALA (American Lung Assn)
61 Broadway 6th Fl ... New York NY 10006 **800-586-4872** 212-315-8700 48-17
Ala Moana Hotel 410 Atkinson Dr ... Honolulu HI 96814 **800-367-6025** 808-955-4811 373
Alabama
Conservation & Natural Resources Dept 64 N Union St PO
Box 301450 ... Montgomery AL 36130 **800-262-3151** 334-242-3486 335
Homeland Security Dept
PO Box 304115 ... Montgomery AL 36130 **800-361-4454** 334-956-7250 335
Prepaid Affordable College Tuition (PACT) Program 100 N Union
St Suite 660 ... Montgomery AL 36130 **800-252-7228** 334-242-7514 711
Public Service Commission
PO Box 304260 ... Montgomery AL 36130 **800-392-8050** 334-242-5218 335
Rehabilitation Services Dept
2129 E South Blvd ... Montgomery AL 36116 **800-441-7607** 334-281-8780 335
Securities Commission
770 Washington Ave
Suite 570 ... Montgomery AL 36130 **800-222-1253** 334-242-2984 335
Senior Services Dept
770 Washington Ave
Suite 470 ... Montgomery AL 36130 **877-425-2243** 334-242-5743 335
State Parks Div 64 N Union St ... Montgomery AL 36130 **800-252-7275** 334-242-3334 335
Tourism & Travel Bureau
401 Adams Ave Suite 126 ... Montgomery AL 36104 **800-252-2262** 334-242-4169 335
Alabama Art Supply Inc
1006 23rd St S ... Birmingham AL 35205 **800-749-4741*** 205-322-4741 45
*Cust Svc
Alabama Business Council
PO Box 76 ... Montgomery AL 36101 **800-665-9647** 334-834-6000 138
Alabama Constitution Village
109 Gates Ave ... Huntsville AL 35801 **800-678-1819** 256-564-8100 509
Alabama Correctional Industries
1400 Lloyd St ... Montgomery AL 36107 **800-224-7007** 334-261-3600 618
Alabama Crown Distributing
421 Industrial Ln ... Birmingham AL 35211 **800-548-1869** 205-941-1155 82-3
Alabama Democratic Party
PO Box 950 ... Montgomery AL 36104 **800-995-3386** 334-262-2221 605-1
Alabama Educational Television Commission 2112 11th Ave S
Suite 400 ... Birmingham AL 35205 **800-239-5233** 205-328-8756 620
Alabama Eye Bank
500 Robert Jemison Rd ... Birmingham AL 35209 **800-423-7811** 205-942-2120 265
Alabama Farmers Co-op Inc
121 Somerville Rd NE ... Decatur AL 35601 **800-737-6843** 256-353-6843 276
Alabama Gas Corp (Alagasco)
605 Richard Arrington Jr
Blvd N ... Birmingham AL 35203 **800-292-4005** 205-326-8100 774
Alabama Gulf Coast Convention & Visitors Bureau PO Drawer 457 .. Gulf Shores AL 36547 **800-745-7263** 251-968-7511 205
Alabama Library Assn (ALLA)
400 S Union St Suite 395 ... Montgomery AL 36104 **877-563-5146** 334-263-1272 427
Alabama MD 19 S Jackson St ... Montgomery AL 36104 **800-239-6272** 334-263-6441 449-16
Alabama Medical Assn
19 S Jackson St ... Montgomery AL 36104 **800-239-6272** 334-263-6441 466
Alabama Metal Industries Corp
3245 Fayette Ave ... Birmingham AL 35208 **800-366-2642** 205-787-2611 482
Alabama National BanCorporation
1927 1st Ave N ... Birmingham AL 35203 **888-583-3200** 205-583-3600 355-2
NASDAQ: ALAB
Alabama Power Co PO Box 2641 ... Birmingham AL 35291 **800-245-2244** 205-257-1000 774
Alabama Public Television (APT)
2112 11th Ave S Suite 400 ... Birmingham AL 35205 **800-239-5233** 205-328-8756 620

Name / Address	City	State	Zip	Toll-Free	Phone	Class
Alabama Republican Party 2019 Holland Ave S	Birmingham	AL	35255	**877-919-2002**	205-212-5900	605-2
Alabama School Journal PO Box 4177	Montgomery	AL	36103	**800-392-5839**	334-834-9790	449-8
Alabama Shakespeare Festival 1 Festival Dr	Montgomery	AL	36117	**800-841-4273**	334-271-5300	734
Alabama State University 915 S Jackson St	Montgomery	AL	36104	**800-253-5037**	334-229-4100	163
Alabama Theatre 4750 Hwy 17 S	North Myrtle Beach	SC	29582	**800-342-2262**	843-272-1111	562
Alabama Tissue Center 1900 University Blvd 855 Tinsley Harrison Towers	Birmingham	AL	35294	**800-227-2907**	205-934-4314	535
Alacare Home Health Services Inc 4752 Hwy 280 E	Birmingham	AL	35242	**800-852-4724**	205-981-8000	358
ALACO Ladder Co 5167 G St	Chino	CA	91710	**888-310-7040**	909-591-7561	412
Aladdin Knowledge Systems Ltd 2920 N Arlington Heights Rd	Arlington Heights	IL	60004	**800-562-2543**	847-818-3800	176-12
NASDAQ: ALDN						
Aladdin Mills Inc 2001 Antioch Rd	Dalton	GA	30720	**800-241-4072**	706-277-1100	131
Aladdin Resort & Casino 3667 Las Vegas Blvd S	Las Vegas	NV	89109	**877-333-9474**	702-785-5555	655
Alagasco (Alabama Gas Corp) 605 Richard Arrington Jr Blvd N	Birmingham	AL	35203	**800-292-4005**	205-326-8100	774
Alaglass Pools 165 Sweet Bay Rd	Saint Matthews	SC	29135	**877-655-7179**	803-655-7179	367
Alaka'i Mechanical Corp 2655 Waiwai Loop	Honolulu	HI	96819	**800-600-1085**	808-834-1085	188-10
Alamar Resort Inn 311 16th St	Virginia Beach	VA	23451	**800-346-5681**	757-428-7582	373
Alameda Newspaper Group PO Box 28884	Oakland	CA	94604	**800-595-9595**	510-208-6300	623-8
Alamo Group Inc 1502 E Walnut St	Seguin	TX	78155	**800-356-6286***	830-379-1480	269
NYSE: ALG ■ *Cust Svc						
Alamo Inn 2203 E Commerce St	San Antonio	TX	78203	**888-222-7666**	210-227-2203	373
Alamo Iron Works Inc 943 SBC Center Pkwy	San Antonio	TX	78219	**800-292-7817***	210-223-6161	378
*Cust Svc						
Alamo Music Center 425 N Main Ave	San Antonio	TX	78205	**800-822-5010**	210-224-1010	515
Alamo Rent A Car Inc 6929 N Lakewood Ave Suite 100	Tulsa	OK	74117	**800-327-9633**	918-401-6000	126
Alamo Steel Co 2784 Old Dallas Rd	Waco	TX	76705	**800-810-3166**	254-799-2471	471
Alamo Tissue Service Ltd 4414 Centerview Suite 167	San Antonio	TX	78228	**800-226-9091**	210-738-2663	535
Alamo Title Insurance 10010 San Pedro Blvd Suite 700	San Antonio	TX	78216	**800-292-5320**	210-340-0456	384-6
Alamo Travel Group Inc 9000 Wurzbach Rd	San Antonio	TX	78240	**800-692-5266**	210-593-0084	760
Alamo Water Refiners Inc 13700 Hwy 90 W	San Antonio	TX	78245	**800-659-8400**	210-677-8400	793
Alamodome 100 Montana St	San Antonio	TX	78203	**800-884-3663**	210-207-3663	706
Alamogordo Chamber of Commerce 1301 N White Sands Blvd	Alamogordo	NM	88310	**800-826-0294**	505-437-6120	137
Alan Gordon Enterprises Inc 5625 Melrose Ave	Hollywood	CA	90038	**800-825-6684**	323-466-3561	580
Alan Preuss Florists 17680-E W Bluemound Rd	Brookfield	WI	53045	**800-839-8400**	262-786-7900	287
Alan Ritchey Inc 740 S I-35 E Frontage Rd	Valley View	TX	76272	**800-877-0273**	940-726-3276	769
Alanco Technologies Inc 15575 N 83rd Way Suite 3	Scottsdale	AZ	85260	**800-303-7566**	480-607-1010	19
NASDAQ: ALAN						
ALARIS Medical Systems Inc 10221 Wateridge Cir	San Diego	CA	92121	**800-854-7128**	858-458-7000	468
Alaska						
Postsecondary Education Commission 3030 Vintage Blvd	Juneau	AK	99801	**800-441-3293***	907-465-6740	335
*Cust Svc						
Student Aid Office 3030 Vintage Blvd	Juneau	AK	99801	**800-441-2962**	907-465-2962	711
Vocational Rehabilitation Div 801 W 10th St Suite 200	Juneau	AK	99801	**800-478-2815**	907-465-2814	335
Alaska Airlines Cargo Services 19300 International blvd	Seattle	WA	98188	**800-426-0333**	206-433-3200	13
Alaska Airlines Inc PO Box 68900	Seattle	WA	98168	**800-252-7522***	206-433-3200	26
*Resv						
Alaska Airlines Mileage Plan PO Box 24948 Customer Service Ctr	Seattle	WA	98124	**800-654-5669**		27
Alaska Bible College PO Box 289	Glennallen	AK	99588	**800-478-7884**	907-822-3201	163
Alaska Bingo Supply 3707 Woodland Dr Suite 3	Anchorage	AK	99517	**800-478-7003**	907-243-7003	317
Alaska Business Monthly 501 W Northern Lights Blvd Suite 100	Anchorage	AK	99503	**800-770-4373**	907-276-4373	449-5
Alaska Commercial Co 550 W 64th Ave Suite 200	Anchorage	AK	99518	**800-478-4484**	907-273-4600	339
Alaska Communications Systems Group Inc 600 Telephone Ave	Anchorage	AK	99503	**800-478-7121**	907-297-3000	721
NASDAQ: ALSK						
Alaska Diesel Electric Inc 4420 14th Ave NW	Seattle	WA	98107	**800-762-0165**	206-789-3880	259
Alaska Industrial Hardware Inc 2192 Viking Dr	Anchorage	AK	99501	**800-478-7201**	907-276-7201	359
Alaska Magazine 301 Arctic Slope Ave Suite 300	Anchorage	AK	99518	**800-458-4010**	907-272-6070	449-22
Alaska Marine Highway System	Juneau	AK	99801	**800-642-0066**	907-465-3941	460
Alaska Marine Lines Inc 5615 W Marginal Way SW	Seattle	WA	98106	**800-950-4265**	206-763-4244	307
Alaska Native Heritage Center 8800 Heritage Center Dr	Anchorage	AK	99506	**800-315-6608**	907-330-8000	509
Alaska One PO Box 755620	Fairbanks	AK	99775	**800-727-6543**	907-474-7491	620
Alaska Pacific University 4101 University Dr	Anchorage	AK	99508	**800-252-7528**	907-564-8248	163
Alaska Power & Telephone Co 193 Otto St	Port Townsend	WA	98368	**800-982-0136***	360-385-1733	774
*Cust Svc						
Alaska Stock Images 2505 Fairbanks St	Anchorage	AK	99503	**800-487-4285**	907-276-1343	582
Alaska Tour & Travel 9170 Jewel Lake Rd Suite 202	Anchorage	AK	99502	**800-208-0200**	907-245-0200	760
Alaska Travel Adventures Inc 18384 Redmond Way	Redmond	WA	98052	**800-323-5757**	425-497-1212	760
Alaska USA Federal Credit Union 4000 Credit Union Dr	Anchorage	AK	99503	**800-525-9094**	907-563-4567	216
Alaska Vacation Packages PO Box 622	Palmer	AK	99645	**888-745-8872**	907-745-8872	760
Alaska Wildlife Conservation Center Milepost 79 Seward Hwy	Portage Glacier	AK	99587	**866-773-2025**	907-783-2025	811
Alaskan Copper & Brass Co 3223 6th Ave S	Seattle	WA	98134	**800-552-7661**	206-623-5800	483
Alateen 1600 Corporate Landing Pkwy	Virginia Beach	VA	23454	**888-425-2666**	757-563-1600	48-21
Alban Tractor Co 8531 Pulaski Hwy	Baltimore	MD	21237	**800-492-6994**	410-686-7777	353
Albany Area Chamber of Commerce 225 W Broad Ave	Albany	GA	31701	**800-475-8700**	229-434-8700	137
Albany County Convention & Visitors Bureau 25 Quackenbush Sq	Albany	NY	12207	**800-258-3582**	518-434-1217	205
Albany Democrat-Herald 600 Lyons St SW	Albany	OR	97321	**800-677-3993**	541-926-2211	522-2
Albany Herald 126 N Washington St	Albany	GA	31701	**800-685-4639**	229-888-9300	522-2
Albany Herald Publishing Co Inc 126 N Washington St	Albany	GA	31702	**800-685-4639**	229-888-9300	623-8
Albany International Corp 1373 Broadway	Albany	NY	12204	**800-833-3836**	518-445-2200	730-3
NYSE: AIN						
Albany International Corp Appleton Wire Div 435 6th St	Menasha	WI	54952	**800-558-3526**	920-725-2600	730-3
Albany International Corp Engineered Fabrics Div 214 Kirby Dr	Portland	TN	37148	**800-833-3836**	615-325-6767	730-3
Albany International Corp Mount Vernon Dryer Fabrics Div 1373 Broadway	Albany	NY	12204	**800-833-3836**	518-445-2200	730-3
Albany State University 504 College Dr	Albany	GA	31705	**800-822-7267**	229-430-4600	163
Albany Steel Inc 566 Broadway	Albany	NY	12204	**800-342-9317**	518-436-4851	188-14
Albany Visitors Assn 250 Broadalbin St SW Suite 110	Albany	OR	97321	**800-526-2256**	541-928-0911	205
AlbanyDoor Systems 975A Old Norcross Rd	Lawrenceville	GA	30045	**800-252-2691**	770-962-7997	233
Albemarle Electric Membership Corp 159 Creek Dr	Hertford	NC	27944	**800-215-9915**	252-426-5735	244
Albert at Bay Suite Hotel 435 Albert St	Ottawa	ON	K1R7X4	**800-267-6644**	613-238-8858	372
Albert Einstein Healthcare Network 5501 Old York Rd	Philadelphia	PA	19141	**800-346-7834**	215-456-7010	348
Albert Guarnieri Co 1133 E Market St	Warren	OH	44483	**800-686-2639**	330-394-5636	744
Albert H Notini & Sons Inc 225 Aiken St	Lowell	MA	01854	**800-366-8464**	978-459-7151	744
Albert Lea Newspapers Inc PO Box 60	Albert Lea	MN	56007	**800-657-4996**	507-373-1411	623-8
Albert Lea Seed House 1414 W Main St	Albert Lea	MN	56007	**800-352-5247**	507-373-3161	684
Albert Lea Tribune 808 W Front St PO Box 60	Albert Lea	MN	56007	**800-657-4996**	507-373-1411	522-2
Albert Screen Print Inc 3704 Summit Rd	Norton	OH	44203	**800-759-2774**	330-753-1252	730-7
Albert Whitman & Co 6340 Oakton St	Morton Grove	IL	60053	**800-255-7675**	847-581-0033	623-2
Alberta Bair Theater for the Performing Arts 2722 3rd Ave N Suite 400	Billings	MT	59101	**877-321-2074**	406-256-8915	562
Alberta Blue Cross 10009 108th St NW	Edmonton	AB	T5J3C5	**800-661-6995**	780-498-8100	384-3
Alberta. Library Assn of 80 Baker Crescent NW	Calgary	AB	T2L1R4	**877-522-5550**	403-284-5818	427
Alberta-Pacific Forest Industries Inc Hwy 63 N	Boyle	AB	T0A0M0	**800-661-5210**	780-525-8000	624
Alberta Place Suite Hotel 10049 103rd St	Edmonton	AB	T5J2W7	**800-661-3982**	780-423-1565	372
Alberto-Culver Co 2525 W Armitage Ave	Melrose Park	IL	60160	**800-333-0005**	708-450-3000	184
NYSE: ACV						
Albertson College of Idaho 2112 Cleveland Blvd	Caldwell	ID	83605	**800-224-3246**	208-459-5011	163
Albertson's Inc 250 E Parkcenter Blvd	Boise	ID	83706	**888-746-7252**	208-395-6200	339
NYSE: ABS						
Albertus Magnus College 700 Prospect St	New Haven	CT	06511	**800-578-9160**	203-773-8550	163
Albinism & Hypopigmentation. National Organization for PO Box 959	East Hampstead	NH	03826	**800-473-2310**	603-887-2310	48-17
Albion College 611 E Porter St	Albion	MI	49224	**800-858-6770**	517-629-1000	163
Albion Hotel 1650 James Ave	Miami Beach	FL	33139	**888-665-0008**	305-913-1000	373
Albion Laboratories Inc 101 N Main St	Clearfield	UT	84015	**800-453-2406**	801-773-4631	438
Albis Plastics Corp 445 Hwy 36 N PO Box 711	Rosenberg	TX	77471	**888-252-4748**	281-342-3311	594-2
Albright College PO Box 15234	Reading	PA	19612	**800-252-1856**	610-921-2381	163
Albuquerque Convention Center 401 2nd St NW	Albuquerque	NM	87102	**800-733-9918***	505-768-4575	204
*Mktg						
Albuquerque Convention & Visitors Bureau 20 First Plaza Suite 601	Albuquerque	NM	87102	**800-733-9918**	505-842-9918	205
Albuquerque Journal 7777 Jefferson St NE	Albuquerque	NM	87109	**800-990-5765**	505-823-7777	522-2
Albuquerque Tribune 7777 Jefferson St NE	Albuquerque	NM	87109	**800-665-8742**	505-823-3653	522-2
Alcas Corp 1116 E State St	Olean	NY	14760	**800-828-0448**	716-373-6141	219
Alcatel Canada Inc 600 March Rd PO Box 13600	Kanata	ON	K2K2E6	**888-662-3425**	613-591-3600	720
Alcatel USA Inc 3400 W Plano Pkwy	Plano	TX	75075	**800-252-2835**	972-519-3000	720
Alchemy International Inc 14909 Community St	Panorama City	CA	91402	**800-798-4801***	818-830-3374	211
*Orders						
Alcoa Fastening Systems DBA Huck Fasteners 3724 E Columbia St	Tucson	AZ	85714	**800-326-1799**	520-519-7400	274

Listing	City	State	ZIP	Toll-Free	Phone	Class
Alcoa Fujikura Ltd 830 Crescent Ctr Dr Suite 600	Franklin	TN	37067	**800-627-7854**	615-778-6000	202
Alcoa Home Exteriors 1590 Omega Dr	Pittsburgh	PA	15205	**866-496-0370**	412-249-6000	190-4
Alcoa Mill Products 4879 State St	Riverdale	IA	52722	**800-237-3254**	563-459-3000	476
Alcoa Primary Metals 900 S Gay St Riverview Tower Suite 1100	Knoxville	TN	37902	**800-852-0238**	865-594-4700	476
Alcoa Wheel Products International 1600 Harvard Ave	Cleveland	OH	44105	**800-242-9898**	216-641-3600	474
Alcoa World Chemicals 501 W Park Rd	Leetsdale	PA	15056	**800-643-8771**	412-630-2800	141
Alcohol & Tobacco Tax & Trade Bureau (TTB) 650 Massachusetts Ave NW	Washington	DC	20226	**877-882-3277**	202-927-8100	336-14
National Revenue Center 550 Main St	Cincinnati	OH	45202	**800-937-8864**	513-684-3334	336-14
Alcoholic Beverage Control Newsletter PO Box 7376	Alexandria	VA	22307	**800-876-2545**	703-768-9600	521-7
Alcoholism & Drug Dependence. National Council on 20 Exchange Pl Suite 2902	New York	NY	10005	**800-622-2255**	212-269-7797	48-17
Alcon Laboratories Inc 6201 South Fwy *NYSE: ACL*	Fort Worth	TX	76134	**800-757-9195**	817-293-0450	572
Alcon Laboratories Inc Surgical Div 6201 South Fwy *Orders	Fort Worth	TX	76134	**800-862-5266***	817-293-0450	531
Alcon Research Ltd 6201 S Fwy	Fort Worth	TX	76134	**800-757-9195**	817-551-6929	265
Alcott Group 71 Executive Blvd PO Box 160	Farmingdale	NY	11735	**888-425-2688**		619
ALCTS (Association for Library Collections & Technical Services) 50 E Huron St	Chicago	IL	60611	**800-545-2433**	312-280-5038	49-11
Aldag Honold Mechanical Inc 3509 S Business Dr	Sheboygan	WI	53082	**800-967-1712**	920-458-8777	188-10
Aldelano Packaging Corp 3525 Walnut Ave Suite A	Chino	CA	91710	**800-509-9212**	909-861-3970	538
Alden Beach Resort 5900 Gulf Blvd	Saint Pete Beach	FL	33706	**800-237-2530**	727-360-7081	373
Alden Curtis & Michaels Ltd 1170 Broadway Suite 316	New York	NY	10001	**800-569-3877**	212-532-7996	157
Alderbrook Resort 7101 E SR-106	Union	WA	98592	**800-622-9370**	360-898-2200	655
Alderfer Bologna Co Inc PO Box 2 *Sales	Harleysville	PA	19438	**800-341-1121***	215-256-8818	291-26
Alderman Cave Feeds 158 N Main St PO Box 217	Winters	TX	79567	**800-588-3333**	325-754-4546	438
Aldershot of New Mexico Inc 3905 Meadow Lark Ln	Mesilla Park	NM	88047	**888-768-6867**	505-523-8621	363
Alderson-Broaddus College College Hill Rd *Admissions	Philippi	WV	26416	**800-263-1549***	304-457-1700	163
Alderson Reporting Co 1111 14th St NW Suite 400	Washington	DC	20004	**800-367-3376**	202-289-2260	436
Alderwoods Group Inc 259 Yorkland Rd *NASDAQ: AWGI*	Toronto	ON	M2J5R2	**800-206-6404**	416-498-2430	499
ALDF (American Lyme Disease Foundation Inc) 293 Rt 100	Somers	NY	10589	**800-876-5963**	914-277-6970	48-17
ALDI Inc 1200 N Kirk Rd	Batavia	IL	60510	**800-388-2534**	630-879-8100	339
Aldila Inc 13450 Stowe Dr *NASDAQ: ALDA*	Poway	CA	92064	**800-854-2786**	858-513-1801	701
Aldine Metal Products Corp PO Box 246	Brookfield	CT	06804	**877-775-2551**	203-775-2551	473
Aldo Shoes 2300 Emile Belanger	Saint-Laurent	QC	H4R3J4	**888-818-2536**	514-747-2536	296
Ale House Management Inc 612 N Orange Ave Suite C-6	Jupiter	FL	33458	**866-743-2299**	561-743-2299	657
Alef Judaica 8440 Warner Dr	Culver City	CA	90232	**800-262-2533**	310-202-0024	130
ALerCHEK Inc 203 Anderson St	Portland	ME	04101	**877-282-9542**	207-775-2574	229
Aleris International Inc 500 W Jefferson St 19th Fl *NYSE: ARS*	Louisville	KY	40202	**866-266-2586**	502-589-8100	709
Alert Mfg & Supply Co 520 S 18th St	West Des Moines	IA	50265	**800-247-4178**	515-223-5843	664
AlertOne Services Inc 24 W 4th St	Williamsport	PA	17701	**800-693-5433**	570-321-5433	565
Aleutians East Borough PO Box 349	Sand Point	AK	99661	**888-383-2699**	907-383-2699	334
Alex C Fergusson Inc 5000 Letterkenny Rd Suite 220	Chambersburg	PA	17201	**800-345-1329**	717-264-9147	143
Alex R Masson Inc 12819 198th St	Linwood	KS	66052	**800-444-6210**	913-301-3281	363
Alexa Internet PO Box 29141	San Francisco	CA	94129	**888-882-5392**	415-561-6900	176-7
Alexa On Royal 119 Royal St	New Orleans	LA	70130	**888-487-9643**	504-962-0600	373
Alexander Communications Group Inc 28 W 25th St 8th Fl	New York	NY	10010	**800-232-4317**	212-228-0246	623-9
Alexander Doll Co Inc DBA Madame Alexander 615 W 131st St	New York	NY	10027	**800-229-5192**	212-283-5900	750
Alexander Group Inc 14635 N Kierland Blvd Suite 200	Scottsdale	AZ	85254	**800-327-8525**	480-998-9644	194
Alexander & Hamilton Inc 2618 Edenborn Ave	Metairie	LA	70002	**800-627-2539**	504-887-9153	157
Alexander Hamilton Institute Inc 70 Hilltop Rd *Orders	Ramsey	NJ	07446	**800-879-2441***	201-825-3377	623-9
Alexander Hotel 5225 Collins Ave	Miami Beach	FL	33140	**800-327-6121**	305-865-6500	373
Alexander Mfg Co 12978 Tesson Ferry Rd	Saint Louis	MO	63128	**800-467-5343**	314-842-3344	10
Alexander Palms Court 715 South St	Key West	FL	33040	**800-858-1943**	305-296-6413	373
Alexander Plastics Inc 11937 Denton Dr	Dallas	TX	75234	**800-421-4171**	972-241-4171	597
Alexander/Ryan Marine & Safety Co of Louisiana 7759 Townsend Pl	New Orleans	LA	70126	**800-743-0501**	504-243-0501	759
Alexandria & Arlington Bed & Breakfast Network 512 S 25th St	Arlington	VA	22202	**888-549-3415**	703-549-3415	368
Alexandria Convention & Visitors Assn 221 King St	Alexandria	VA	22314	**800-388-9119**	703-838-4200	205
Alexandria Daily Town Talk PO Box 7558	Alexandria	LA	71306	**800-523-8391**	318-487-6397	522-2
Alexandria Lakes Area Chamber of Commerce 206 Broadway	Alexandria	MN	56308	**800-235-9441**	320-763-3161	137
Alexandria Moulding 95 Lochiel St E	Alexandria	ON	K0C1A0	**800-267-1773**	613-525-2784	304
Alexandria Technical College 1601 Jefferson St	Alexandria	MN	56308	**888-234-1222**	320-762-0221	160
Alexandria/Pineville Area Convention & Visitors Bureau 707 Main St	Alexandria	LA	71301	**800-551-9546**	318-442-9546	205
Alexis Hotel 1007 1st Ave	Seattle	WA	98104	**800-264-8482**	206-624-4844	373
Alexis Park Resort 375 E Harmon Ave	Las Vegas	NV	89109	**800-582-2228**	702-796-3300	373
Alexis Playsafe 999 Chestnut St SE	Gainesville	GA	30503	**800-253-9476**	770-535-3000	153-4
ALF (American Liver Foundation) 75 Maiden Ln Suite 603	New York	NY	10038	**800-465-4837**	212-668-1000	48-17
Alfa Aesar Co 26 Parkridge Rd 2nd Fl	Ward Hill	MA	01835	**800-343-0660**	978-521-6300	143
Alfa Corp PO Box 11000 *NASDAQ: ALFA*	Montgomery	AL	36191	**888-964-2532**	334-288-3900	355-4
Alfa Leisure Inc 13501 5th St	Chino	CA	91710	**800-373-3372**	909-628-5574	120
Alfalfa Electric Co-op Inc 121 E Main St	Cherokee	OK	73728	**888-736-3837**	580-596-3333	244
ALFCO Div Home Care Industries Inc 1 Lisbon Ct *Cust Svc	Clifton	NJ	07013	**800-240-7998***	973-365-1600	19
Alfery Sausage Co Inc RD 6 Box 2060	Mount Pleasant	PA	15666	**800-648-2547**	724-547-5270	291-26
Alfieri Charles Studio 4390 N Federal Hwy Suite 203	Fort Lauderdale	FL	33308	**800-321-2413**	954-928-1755	342
Alflex Inc 2630 El Presidio St	Long Beach	CA	90810	**800-755-4232**	310-886-8300	804
Alford Group Inc 1603 Orrington Ave 2nd Fl	Evanston	IL	60201	**800-291-8913**	847-425-9800	312
Alfred Angelo Inc 1301 Virginia Dr Suite 110	Fort Washington	PA	19034	**800-504-7263**	215-659-5300	153-21
Alfred Benesch & Co 205 N Michigan Ave Suite 2400	Chicago	IL	60601	**877-222-9995**	312-565-0450	258
Alfred Dunhill North America Ltd 645 5th Ave	New York	NY	10022	**800-776-4053**	212-888-4000	155-3
Alfred Heller Heat Treating Co 5 Wellington St	Clifton	NJ	07015	**800-946-8847**	973-772-4200	475
Alfred Hitchcock Mystery Magazine 475 Park Ave S 11th Fl	New York	NY	10016	**800-333-3311**	212-686-7188	449-11
Alfred Mainzer Inc 27-08 40th Ave	Long Island City	NY	11101	**800-222-2737**	718-392-4200	130
Alfred Nickles Bakery Inc 26 N Main St	Navarre	OH	44662	**800-635-1110**	330-879-5635	291-1
Alfred Publishing Co 16320 Roscoe Blvd Suite 100	Van Nuys	CA	91406	**800-292-6122**	818-891-5999	623-7
Alfred State College 10 Upper College Dr	Alfred	NY	14802	**800-425-3733**	607-587-4215	160
Alfred University Saxon Dr	Alfred	NY	14802	**800-541-9229**	607-871-2115	163
ALG Admiral Inc 1101 Ellis St	Bensenville	IL	60106	**800-323-0289**	630-766-3900	306
Alger Delta Co-op Electric Assn 426 N 9th St	Gladstone	MI	49837	**800-562-0950**	906-428-4141	244
Alger Fred Management Inc 30 Montgomery St 11th Fl	Jersey City	NJ	07302	**800-223-3810**	201-547-3600	393
Alger Fund 30 Montgomery St	Jersey City	NJ	07302	**800-992-3863**	201-547-3600	517
Alger Mfg Co Inc 724 S Bon View Ave	Ontario	CA	91761	**800-854-9833**	909-986-4591	610
Algoma Hardwoods Inc 1001 Perry St	Algoma	WI	54201	**800-678-8910**	920-487-5221	234
Algoma Steel Inc 105 West St *TSE: AGA*	Sault Sainte Marie	ON	P6A7B4	**800-387-9495**	705-945-2351	709
Algonquin. Fairmont 184 Adolphus St	Saint Andrews	NB	E5B1T7	**800-441-1414**	506-529-8823	655
Algonquin Travel Corp 130 Merton St *Cust Svc	Toronto	ON	M4S1A4	**888-599-0789***	416-485-1700	761
Algor Inc 150 Beta Dr	Pittsburgh	PA	15238	**800-482-5467**	412-967-2700	176-5
Algy Costume & Uniform Co 440 NE 1st Ave	Hallandale	FL	33009	**800-458-2549**	954-457-8100	153-19
ALI (American Law Institute) 4025 Chestnut St	Philadelphia	PA	19104	**800-253-6397**	215-243-1600	49-10
Aliant Inc PO Box 880 *TSE: AIT*	Halifax	NS	B3J2W3	**800-688-9811**	877-225-4268	721
Alias Systems Corp 210 King St E	Toronto	ON	M5A1J7	**800-447-2542**	416-362-9181	176-8
Alice Chamber of Commerce 612 E Main St	Alice	TX	78332	**877-992-5423**	361-664-3454	137
Alice Lloyd College 100 Purpose Rd *Admissions	Pippa Passes	KY	41844	**888-280-4252***	606-368-2101	163
Alienware Corp 12400 SW 134 Ct Bay 8	Miami	FL	33186	**866-287-6727**	305-251-9797	176-6
Align Technology Inc 881 Martin Ave *NASDAQ: ALGN*	Santa Clara	CA	95050	**888-822-5446**	408-470-1000	226
Alikar Gardens Resort 1123 Verde Dr	Colorado Springs	CO	80910	**800-456-1123**	719-475-2564	373
Alimentation Couche-Tard Inc 1600 boul St Martin E Suite 200 Tower B *TSE: ATD*	Laval	QC	H7G4S7	**800-361-2612**	450-662-3272	203
Alinabal Inc 28 Woodmont Rd	Milford	CT	06460	**800-254-6763**	203-877-3241	77
ALIR Co 814 Hwy A1A Suite 303	Ponte Vedra Beach	FL	32082	**888-599-1112**	904-280-1112	783
Alisal Guest Ranch & Resort 1054 Alisal Rd	Solvang	CA	93463	**800-425-4725**	805-688-6411	655
Alitalia Airlines 350 5th Ave 37th Fl	New York	NY	10118	**800-223-5730**	212-903-3300	26
Alitalia Airlines MilleMiglia Club 350 5th Ave 36th Fl *Cust Svc	New York	NY	10118	**800-223-5730***	888-525-4825	27
Alitalia Executive Cargo Div JFK International Airport N Boundry Rd Bldg 79	Jamaica	NY	11430	**800-221-4745**	718-244-8500	13
Alive Hospice Inc 1718 Patterson St	Nashville	TN	37203	**800-327-1085**	615-327-1085	365
Alkinco 264 W 40th St	New York	NY	10018	**800-424-7118**	212-719-3070	342
All Aboard Benefits 6162 E Mockingird Ln Suite 104	Dallas	TX	75214	**800-462-2322**	214-821-6677	384-7

Name / Address	City	State	ZIP	Toll-Free	Phone	Class
All Aboard Cruise Center PO Box 540685	Grand Prairie	TX	75054	**800-567-5379**	972-262-4638	760
All Aboard Cruises Inc 11114 SW 127th Ct	Miami	FL	33186	**800-883-8657**	305-385-8657	760
All American Homes of Kansas LLC DBA All American KanBuild PO Box 259	Osage City	KS	66523	**800-343-2783**	785-528-4163	107
All American Life Insurance Co PO Box 4373	Houston	TX	77210	**800-487-5433**		384-2
All American Semiconductor Inc 16115 NW 52nd Ave *NASDAQ: SEMI*	Miami	FL	33014	**800-762-2095**	305-621-8282	245
All American Ticket Service 2616 Philadelphia Pike Suite E	Claymont	DE	19703	**800-669-0571**	302-798-8556	735
All Around the Town 270 Lafayette St Suite 804	New York	NY	10012	**800-443-3800**	212-675-5600	368
All-Bilt Uniform Fashion 30-00 47th Ave	Long Island City	NY	11101	**800-221-2980**	718-706-1414	153-19
All Broward Hurricane Panel Co 450 W McNab Rd	Fort Lauderdale	FL	33309	**800-432-1803**	954-974-3300	690
All Children's Hospital 801 6th St S	Saint Petersburg	FL	33701	**800-456-4543**	727-898-7451	366-1
All-Clad Metalcrafters Inc 424 Morganza Rd *Cust Svc	Canonsburg	PA	15317	**800-255-2523***	724-745-8300	477
All Cruise Travel 1213 Lincoln Ave Suite 205	San Jose	CA	95125	**800-227-8473**	408-295-1200	760
All-Inclusive Vacations Inc 1595 Iris St	Lakewood	CO	80215	**866-980-6483**	303-980-6483	760
All Keys Reservation Service PO Box 269	Norfolk	CT	06058	**800-255-5397**		368
All Medical Personnel 4651 Sheridan St	Hollywood	FL	33021	**800-706-2378**	954-922-9696	707
All Nation Insurance Co Inc 29621 Northwestern Hwy	Southfield	MI	48034	**800-254-8144**		384-4
All New Stamping Co 10801 Lower Azusa Rd	El Monte	CA	91731	**800-877-7775**	626-443-8813	479
All Nippon Airways Co Ltd 1251 Ave of the Americas 8th Fl	New York	NY	10020	**800-235-9262**		26
All Nippon Airways Mileage Club (ANA) 2050 W 190th St Suite 100	Torrance	CA	90504	**800-262-4653**	310-782-3000	27
All Pro Exercise Products Inc 2110 Harbourside Dr Suite 528	Longboat Key	FL	34228	**800-735-9287**	941-387-9432	263
All-Pro Fasteners Inc 1916 Peyco Dr N	Arlington	TX	76001	**800-361-6627**	817-467-5700	346
All Saints' Episcopal School 2717 Confederate Ave	Vicksburg	MS	39180	**800-748-9957**	601-636-5266	611
All Saints Health Care 3801 Spring St	Racine	WI	53405	**800-526-9309**	262-687-4011	366-2
All-Search & Inspection Inc 1108 E South Union Ave	Midvale	UT	84047	**800-227-3152**	801-984-8160	621
All Seasons Services Inc 1265 Belmont St Suite 2	Brockton	MA	02301	**888-558-2557**	508-559-9000	294
All Service Computer Rental 600 Sylvan Ave	Englewood Cliffs	NJ	07632	**800-927-6555**	201-568-6555	261-1
All Staffing Inc 100 W Ridge St PO Box 219	Lansford	PA	18232	**800-442-4538**	570-645-5000	619
All-Star Agency Speakers Bureau 4829 Powell Rd	Fairfax	VA	22032	**800-736-0031**	703-503-9438	699
All Star Glass Co Inc 1845 Morena Blvd	San Diego	CA	92110	**800-225-4185**	619-275-3343	62-2
All States Inc 1801 W Foster Ave *Cust Svc	Chicago	IL	60640	**800-621-5837***	773-728-0525	597
All Tune & Lube Brakes & More Inc 8334 Veteran's Hwy	Millersville	MD	21108	**800-935-8863**	410-987-1011	62-5
All Tune Transmissions 8334 Veteran's Hwy	Millersville	MD	21108	**800-935-8863**	410-987-1011	62-6
All-Waves Cruise & Travel 20381 Lake Forest Dr Suite B-3	Lake Forest	CA	92630	**800-449-0767**	949-829-8031	760
All West Coachlines Inc 7701 Wilbur Way	Sacramento	CA	95828	**800-843-2121**	916-423-4000	108
All West Registry 329 E 2100 S	Salt Lake City	UT	84115	**877-734-6263**		389
ALLA (Alabama Library Assn) 400 S Union St Suite 395	Montgomery	AL	36104	**877-563-5146**	334-263-1272	427
Alladin Plastics Inc 140 Industrial Dr	Surgoinsville	TN	37873	**800-960-2351**	423-345-2351	596
Allan Hancock College 800 S College Dr	Santa Maria	CA	93454	**800-338-8731**	805-922-6966	160
Allan Vigil Ford 6790 Mt Zion Blvd	Marrow	GA	30260	**800-222-3597**	678-364-3673	57
Allegacy Federal Credit Union 700 Highland Oaks Dr	Winston-Salem	NC	27103	**800-782-4670**	336-774-3400	216
Allegan County Tourist & Recreational Council 3255 122nd Ave Suite 102	Allegan	MI	49010	**888-425-5342**	269-686-9088	205
Alleghany Pharmacal Corp 277 Northern Blvd	Great Neck	NY	11022	**800-645-6190**	516-466-0660	211
Allegheny College 520 N Main St	Meadville	PA	16335	**800-521-5293**	814-332-3100	163
Allegheny Energy Inc 800 Cabin Hill Dr *NYSE: AYE* ■ *Cust Svc	Greensburg	PA	15601	**800-255-3443***	724-837-3000	355-5
Allegheny Ludlum Corp 100 River Rd *Sales	Brackenridge	PA	15014	**800-258-3586***	412-394-2800	709
Allegheny Paper Shredders Corp PO Box 80	Delmont	PA	15626	**800-245-2497**	724-468-4300	112
Allegheny Plastics Inc 17 Ave A	Leetsdale	PA	15056	**800-966-5152**	412-749-0700	593
Allegheny Power 800 Cabin Hill Dr *Cust Svc	Greensburg	PA	15601	**800-255-3443***	724-837-3000	774
Allegheny Technologies Inc 6 PPG Pl Suite 1000 *NYSE: ATI* ■ *Sales	Pittsburgh	PA	15222	**800-258-3586***	412-394-2800	709
Allegheny Wesleyan College 2161 Woodsdale Rd	Salem	OH	44460	**800-292-3153**	330-337-6403	163
Allegiance Insurance Co 1 Horace Mann Plaza	Springfield	IL	62715	**800-999-1030**	217-789-2500	384-4
Allegiant Air 3301 N Buffalo Dr Suite B-9 *Resv	Las Vegas	NV	89129	**800-432-3810***	702-851-7300	26
Allegra Network LLC 21680 Haggerty Rd	Northville	MI	48167	**800-726-9050**	248-596-8600	114
Allegria Spa at the Park Hyatt Beaver Creek 100 E Thomas Pl	Beaver Creek	CO	81620	**800-233-1234**	970-748-7500	698
Allegria Spa at the Ventana Inn & Spa Hwy 1	Big Sur	CA	93920	**800-628-6500**	831-667-4222	698
Allegro Coffee Co 12799 Claude Ct *Cust Svc	Thornton	CO	80241	**800-530-3993***	303-444-4844	291-7
Allegro Corp 14134 NE Airport Way	Portland	OR	97230	**800-288-2007**	503-257-8480	512
Allegro Mfg Inc 7250 E Oxford Way	Commerce	CA	90040	**800-833-5562**	323-724-0101	343
Allen Alva Industries Inc 1001-15 N 3rd St PO Box 427 *Cust Svc	Clinton	MO	64735	**800-343-5657***	660-885-3331	448
Allen Brothers Inc 3737 S Halsted St	Chicago	IL	60609	**800-548-7777**	773-890-5100	465
Allen Canning Co 305 E Main St	Siloam Springs	AR	72761	**800-234-2553**	479-524-6431	291-20
Allen Co 712 E Main St	Blanchester	OH	45107	**800-783-2491**	937-783-2491	675
Allen Co Inc PO Box 537	Winchester	KY	40392	**888-744-3361**	859-744-3361	187-4
Allen Daniel Assoc Inc 411 Waverly Oaks Rd Suite 113	Waltham	MA	02454	**800-882-2100**	781-647-7722	157
Allen-Edmonds Shoe Corp 201 E Seven Hills Rd *Cust Svc	Port Washington	WI	53074	**800-235-2348***	262-235-6000	296
Allen Extruders Inc 1305 Lincoln Ave	Holland	MI	49423	**800-833-1305**	616-392-9004	589
Allen Foods Inc 8543 Page Ave	Saint Louis	MO	63114	**800-888-4855**	314-426-4100	292-8
Allen Fred Florist 310 E Broad St	Gadsden	AL	35903	**800-824-9181**	256-546-0437	287
Allen Group 2965 W State Rd 434 Suite 100	Longwood	FL	32779	**800-272-7252**	407-788-8822	454
Allen & Hoshall Inc 1661 International Dr Suite 100	Memphis	TN	38120	**888-819-5005**	901-820-0820	258
Allen Industries Corp 6434 Burnt Poplar Rd	Greensboro	NC	27409	**800-967-2553**	336-668-2791	692
Allen & John Inc 2505 N Shirk Rd	Visalia	CA	93278	**800-803-7527**		130
Allen Marketing & Management 810 E 10th St	Lawrence	KS	66044	**800-627-0932**	785-843-1235	47
Allen Millwork Inc PO Box 6480	Shreveport	LA	71136	**800-551-8737**	318-868-6541	489
Allen Robert Fabrics Inc 55 Cabot Blvd	Mansfield	MA	02048	**800-333-3777**	508-339-9151	583
Allen Samuels Auto Group 301 Owen Ln	Waco	TX	76710	**800-762-8850**	254-761-6800	57
Allen-Sherman-Hoff Co 185 Great Valley Pkwy	Malvern	PA	19355	**888-274-7278**	610-647-9900	379
Allen Systems Group Inc (ASG) 1333 3rd Ave S	Naples	FL	34102	**800-932-5536**	239-435-2200	176-12
Allen University 1530 Harden St	Columbia	SC	29204	**877-625-5368**	803-376-5700	163
Allen Ventures Inc 517 State Farm Rd	Deerfield	WI	53531	**877-423-9800**	608-423-9800	647
Allenberry Resort 1559 Boiling Springs Rd	Boiling Springs	PA	17007	**800-430-5468**	717-258-3211	655
Allen's Hatchery Inc 126 N Shipley St	Seaford	DE	19973	**800-777-8966**	302-629-9163	11-8
Allentown Beverage Co Inc 1249 N Quebec St *Cust Svc	Allentown	PA	18109	**800-852-2337***	610-432-4581	82-1
Allentown Business School 2809 E Saucon Valley Rd	Center Valley	PA	18034	**800-227-9109**	610-791-5100	158
Allentown Equipment 421 Schantz Rd	Allentown	PA	18104	**800-553-3414**	610-398-0451	379
Allentown State Hospital 1600 Hanover Ave	Allentown	PA	18109	**800-256-3571**	610-740-3200	366-3
Allerderm Laboratories Inc PO Box 9295	Phoenix	AZ	85010	**800-365-6868**	707-664-8777	573
Allergan Canada Inc 110 Cochrane Dr	Markham	ON	L3R9S1	**800-668-6424**	905-940-1660	572
Allergan Inc PO Box 19534 *NYSE: AGN*	Irvine	CA	92623	**800-347-4500**	714-246-4500	572
Allergan Inc North America Region PO Box 19534	Irvine	CA	92623	**800-347-4500**	714-246-4500	572
Allergan Inc Worldwide Operations PO Box 19534	Irvine	CA	92623	**800-347-4500**	714-246-4500	572
Allergy & Anaphylaxis Network. Food 11781 Lee Jackson Hwy Suite 160	Fairfax	VA	22033	**800-929-4040**	703-691-3179	48-17
Allergy Asthma & Immunology. American Academy of 611 E Wells St 4th Fl	Milwaukee	WI	53202	**800-822-2762**	414-272-6071	49-8
Allergy Asthma & Immunology. American College of 85 W Algonquin Rd Suite 550	Arlington Heights	IL	60005	**800-842-7777**	847-427-1200	49-8
Allergy Foundation of America. Asthma & 1233 20th St NW Suite 402	Washington	DC	20036	**800-727-8462**	202-466-7643	48-17
Allergy Research Foundation. Practical 1421 Colvin Blvd	Buffalo	NY	14223	**800-787-8780**	716-875-5578	48-17
Allermed Laboratories Inc 7203 Convoy Ct	San Diego	CA	92111	**800-221-2748**	858-292-1060	229
Alley Theatre 615 Texas Ave	Houston	TX	77002	**800-259-2553**	713-228-9341	562
Alliance The PO Box 1089	Corinth	MS	38835	**877-347-0545**	662-287-5269	137
Alliance for Aging Research 2021 K St NW Suite 305	Washington	DC	20006	**800-639-2421**	202-293-2856	48-17
Alliance Atlantis Communications Inc 121 Bloor St E Suite 1500 *NASDAQ: AACB*	Toronto	ON	M4W3M5	**877-345-9195**	416-967-1174	503
Alliance Bank 541 Lawrence Rd *NASDAQ: ALLB*	Broomall	PA	19008	**800-550-4387**	610-353-2900	71
Alliance for Better Campaigns 1990 M St NW Suite 200	Washington	DC	20036	**888-637-3389**	202-659-1300	48-7
Alliance Blue Cross Blue Shield 1831 Chestnut St	Saint Louis	MO	63103	**800-366-2583**	314-923-4444	384-3
Alliance Capital Management Holding LP 1345 Ave of the Americas *NYSE: AC*	New York	NY	10105	**800-221-5672**	212-969-1000	355-3
Alliance Capital Management LP 1345 Ave of the Americas *Cust Svc	New York	NY	10105	**800-221-5672***	212-969-1000	393
Alliance Carolina Tool & Mold Corp 125 Glenn Bridge Rd	Arden	NC	28704	**800-684-7831**	828-684-7831	745
Alliance Commerce Inc 11950 NW 39th St Suite A	Coral Springs	FL	33065	**877-638-2777**	954-575-2300	39
Alliance Consulting 2005 Market St 32nd Fl	Philadelphia	PA	19103	**800-706-3339**	215-569-8722	175

Company / Address	City	State	ZIP	Toll-Free	Phone	Class
Alliance Entertainment Corp 4250 Coral Ridge Dr	Coral Springs	FL	33065	**800-329-7664**	954-255-4000	512
Alliance Gaming Corp 6601 S Bermuda Rd *NYSE: AGI*	Las Vegas	NV	89119	**877-462-2559**	702-896-7700	317
Alliance Grain Co 1306 W 8th St	Gibson City	IL	60936	**800-222-2451**	217-784-4284	271
Alliance Imaging Inc 1900 S State College Blvd Suite 600 *NYSE: AIQ*	Anaheim	CA	92806	**800-544-3215**	714-688-7100	376
Alliance Insurance Co 5250 S 6th St	Springfield	IL	62705	**800-323-0050**	217-241-6300	384-2
Alliance Investigations LLC 240 S Montezuma St Suite 100	Prescott	AZ	86303	**800-717-1196**	928-717-1196	392
Alliance Library System 600 High Point Ln Suite 1	Eask Peoria	IL	61611	**800-700-4857**	309-694-9200	426
Alliance Limousine Inc 1800 N Highland Ave Suite 220	Los Angeles	CA	90028	**800-679-5466**	323-465-9406	433
Alliance Mid-West Co 640 Keystone St *Cust Svc	Alliance	OH	44601	**800-521-9694***	330-821-5700	481
Alliance Plastics Inc 3123 Station Rd	Erie	PA	16510	**877-728-9227**	814-899-7671	152
Alliance PPO LLC 4 Taft Ct	Rockville	MD	20850	**800-544-2853**	301-762-8205	384-3
Alliance Reservations Network 14435 N 7th St	Phoenix	AZ	85022	**800-802-2100**	602-952-2100	000
Alliance for Retired Americans 888 16th St NW Ste 520	Washington	DC	20006	**888-373-6497**	202-974-8222	48-6
Alliance Rubber Co 210 Carpenter Dam Rd	Hot Springs	AR	71901	**800-626-5940**	501-262-2700	663
Alliance Semiconductor Corp 2575 Augustine Dr *NASDAQ: ALSC*	Santa Clara	CA	95054	**888-383-4900**	408-855-4900	686
Alliant Energy Corp 4902 N Biltmore Ln *NYSE: LNT* ■ *Cust Svc	Madison	WI	53707	**800-521-1725***	608-458-3311	774
Alliant International University 10455 Pomerado Rd	San Diego	CA	92131	**866-825-5426**	858-271-4300	163
Alliant Powder PO Box 6	Radford	VA	24143	**800-276-9337**	540-639-7800	264
Allianz Global Investors of America LP 800 Newport Ctr Dr Suite 100	Newport Beach	CA	92660	**800-225-1970**	949-219-2200	393
Allianz Insurance Co 2350 Empire Ave	Burbank	CA	91504	**800-421-0504**	818-260-7500	384-4
Allianz Life Insurance Co of North America 5701 Golden Hills Dr	Minneapolis	MN	55416	**800-328-5600**	763-765-6500	384-2
Allied Body Works Inc 625 S 96th St	Seattle	WA	98108	**800-733-7450**	206-763-7811	505
Allied Building Products Corp 15 E Union Ave	East Rutherford	NJ	07073	**800-541-2198**	201-507-8400	190-3
Allied Business Documents 333 Bucklin St	Providence	RI	02907	**800-556-6310**	401-461-1700	111
Allied Capital Corp 1919 Pennsylvania Ave NW 3rd Fl *NYSE: ALD*	Washington	DC	20006	**888-818-5298**	202-331-1112	779
Allied Construction Products LLC 3900 Kelley Ave *Cust Svc	Cleveland	OH	44114	**800-321-1046***	216-431-2600	189
Allied Construction Services & Color Inc PO Box 937	Des Moines	IA	50304	**800-365-4855**	515-288-4855	188-9
Allied Controls Inc 150 E Aurora St	Waterbury	CT	06708	**800-648-8871**	203-757-4200	202
Allied Court Reporters Inc 115 Phenix Ave	Cranston	RI	02920	**888-443-3767**	401-946-5500	436
Allied Defense Group Inc 8000 Towers Crescent Dr Suite 260 *AMEX: ADG*	Vienna	VA	22182	**800-847-5322**	703-847-5268	794
Allied Diagnostic Imaging Resources Inc 5440-A Oakbrook Pkwy	Norcross	GA	30093	**800-262-9333**	770-448-0250	143
Allied Employer Group 4400 Buffalo Gap Rd Suite 4500	Abilene	TX	79606	**800-729-7823**	325-695-5822	619
Allied Equipment Rentals 4969 Santa Monica Blvd	Los Angeles	CA	90029	**800-975-7368**	323-663-3251	261-2
Allied Erecting & Dismantling Co Inc 2100 Poland Ave	Youngstown	OH	44502	**800-624-2867**	330-744-0808	188-17
Allied Fire & Security Inc 425 W 2nd Ave	Spokane	WA	99201	**800-448-8338**	509-624-3152	665
Allied Health Group 145 Technology Pkwy NW	Norcross	GA	30092	**800-741-4674**	770-246-9191	707
Allied Healthcare Products Inc 1720 Sublette Ave *NASDAQ: AHPI*	Saint Louis	MO	63110	**800-444-3940**	314-771-2400	469
Allied Insurance 3820 109th St	Des Moines	IA	50391	**800-532-1436**	515-508-4211	384-4
Allied International 13207 Bradley Ave	Sylmar	CA	91342	**800-533-8333**	818-364-2333	346
Allied International Credit Corp 16635 Young St Suite 26	Newmarket	ON	L3X1V6	**888-478-8181**	905-470-8181	157
Allied International NA Inc 700 Oakmont Ln	Westmont	IL	60559	**800-323-1909**	630-570-3500	508
Allied-Locke Industries 1088 Corregidor Rd	Dixon	IL	61021	**800-435-7752**	815-288-1471	609
Allied Machine & Engineering Corp 120 Deeds Dr	Dover	OH	44622	**800-321-5537**	330-343-4283	484
Allied Marketing Group Inc 1555 Regal Row *Cust Svc	Dallas	TX	75247	**800-762-3302***	214-915-7000	451
Allied Mechanical Services Inc 2211 Miller Rd	Kalamazoo	MI	49001	**888-237-3017**	269-344-0191	188-10
Allied North America 390 N Broadway	Jericho	NY	11753	**800-861-9452**	516-733-9200	383
Allied Office Products Inc 100 Delawanna Ave	Clifton	NJ	07014	**800-275-2554**	973-594-3000	524
Allied Oil & Supply Inc 2209 S 24th St	Omaha	NE	68103	**800-333-3717**	402-344-4343	569
Allied Plastics Co Inc 2001 Walnut St *Cust Svc	Jacksonville	FL	32206	**800-999-0386***	904-359-0386	314-1
Allied Plastics Inc 9445 E River Rd	Coon Rapids	MN	55433	**800-328-3113**	763-862-4500	597
Allied Steel Construction Co Inc PO Box 1111	Oklahoma City	OK	73101	**800-522-4658**	405-232-7531	261-2
Allied Supply Co Inc 1100 E Monument Ave	Dayton	OH	45402	**800-589-5690**	937-224-9833	651
Allied Systems Co 2300 Oregon St	Sherwood	OR	97140	**800-627-0429**	503-625-2560	269
Allied Telesyn International Corp 19800 North Creek Pkwy Suite 200	Bothell	WA	98011	**800-424-4284**	425-487-8880	174
Allied Tool Products 9334 N 107th St	Milwaukee	WI	53224	**800-558-5147**	414-355-8280	447
Allied Tower Co 4646 Mandale Rd	Alvin	TX	77511	**800-207-4623**	281-331-9627	187-1
Allied Towing Corp 500 E Indian River Rd	Norfolk	VA	23523	**800-446-8241**	757-545-7301	457
Allied Tube & Conduit Inc 16100 S Lathrop Ave	Harvey	IL	60426	**800-882-5543**	708-339-1610	481
Allied Van Lines Inc 700 Oakmont Ln *Cust Svc	Westmont	IL	60559	**800-762-4689***	630-570-3000	508
Allied Vaughn Inc 7951 Computer Ave	Bloomington	MN	55435	**800-323-0281**	952-832-3200	644
AlliedBarton Security Services 3606 Horizon Dr	King of Prussia	PA	19406	**888-239-1104**	610-239-1100	682
Allina Hospice & Palliative Care 2550 University Ave W Suite 180-S	Saint Paul	MN	55114	**800-261-0879**	651-635-9173	365
Allington International Inc 20160 Center Ridge Rd Suite 206	Cleveland	OH	44116	**800-747-5202**	440-333-0505	392
Allison-Erwin Co PO Box 32308 *Sales	Charlotte	NC	28232	**800-253-0370***	704-334-8621	38
Allison Payment Systems LLC 2200 Production Dr	Indianapolis	IN	46241	**800-755-2440**	317-808-2400	111
AllMeds Inc 151 Lafayette Dr Suite 401	Oak Ridge	TN	37830	**888-343-6337**	865-482-1999	39
Allmerica Financial Corp 440 Lincoln St *NYSE: AFC*	Worcester	MA	01653	**800-533-7881**	508-855-1000	355-4
Allmerica Life Insurance Co 440 Lincoln St	Worcester	MA	01653	**800-533-7881**	508-855-1000	384-2
Allmerica Property & Casualty Cos Inc 440 Lincoln St	Worcester	MA	01653	**800-407-5222**	508-855-1000	384-4
Allor Mfg Inc 12534 Emerson Dr	Brighton	MI	48116	**888-244-4028**	248-486-4500	206
Allos Therapeutics Inc 11080 Circle Point Rd Suite 200 *NASDAQ: ALTH*	Westminster	CO	80020	**888-255-6702**	303-426-6262	86
AlloSource 6278 S Troy Cir	Centennial	CO	80111	**888-873-8330**	720-873-0213	535
Alloy Inc 151 W 26th St 11th Fl *NASDAQ: ALOYE* ■ *Cust Svc	New York	NY	10001	**888-452-5569***	212-244-4307	169
Alloy Stainless Products Co 611 Union Blvd	Totowa	NJ	07512	**800-631-8372**	973-256-1616	584
Alloy Wire Belt Co 2318 Tenaya Dr	Modesto	CA	95354	**800-538-7933**	209-575-4900	206
Allpets Inc 1 Maplewood Dr *Orders	Hazleton	PA	18201	**800-346-0749***	570-384-5555	451
Allred Douglas Co 11512 El Camino Real Suite 100	San Diego	CA	92130	**800-555-6214**	858-793-0202	641
Allscripts Healthcare Solutions 2401 Commerce Ave *NASDAQ: MDRX*	Libertyville	IL	60048	**800-654-0889**	847-680-3515	176-10
Allstar Fire Equipment Inc 12328 Lower Azusa Rd	Arcadia	CA	91006	**800-425-5787**	626-652-0900	667
Allstate Corp 2775 Sanders Rd Allstate Plaza *NYSE: ALL*	Northbrook	IL	60062	**800-255-7828**	847-402-5000	355-4
Allstate Indemnity Co 2775 Sanders Rd	Northbrook	IL	60062	**800-366-2958**	847-402-5000	384-4
Allstate Insurance Co 2775 Sanders Rd Allstate Plaza	Northbrook	IL	60062	**800-366-2958**	847-402-5000	384-4
Allstate Life Insurance Co 3100 Sanders Rd Allstate West Plaza *Cust Svc	Northbrook	IL	60062	**800-366-1411***	847-402-5000	384-2
Allstate Life Insurance Co of New York PO Box 80469	Lincoln	NE	68501	**800-347-5433**		384-2
Allstate Motor Club 51 W Higgins Rd	South Barrington	IL	60010	**800-255-2582**	847-551-2300	53
Allstate Power Vac Inc 928 E Hazelwood Ave	Rahway	NJ	07065	**800-876-9699**	732-815-0220	653
Allstate Steel Co Inc 130 S Jackson Ave	Jacksonville	FL	32220	**888-781-6040**	904-781-6040	188-14
AllStates Technical Services 1777 Sentry Pkwy W Suite 304	Blue Bell	PA	19422	**800-432-8006**	215-591-3870	707
Allstates WorldCargo Inc 4 Lakeside Dr S	Forked River	NJ	08731	**800-575-5575**	609-693-5950	306
Allsteel Inc 2210 2nd Ave *Cust Svc	Muscatine	IA	52761	**888-255-7833***	563-262-4800	314-1
Allstream Corp 200 Wellington St W	Toronto	ON	M5V3G2	**888-288-2273**	416-345-2000	721
Alltech Assoc Inc 2051 Waukegan Rd *Cust Svc	Deerfield	IL	60015	**800-255-8324***	847-948-8600	410
Alltech Inc 3031 Catnip Hill Pike	Nicholasville	KY	40356	**800-289-8324**	859-885-9613	574
ALLTEL Communications Products Inc 13560 Morris Rd 1 ALLTEL Ctr	Alpharetta	GA	30004	**800-501-1754**	678-351-4000	245
ALLTEL Communications Services 1 Allied Dr *Cust Svc	Little Rock	AR	72202	**800-255-8351***	501-905-8500	721
ALLTEL Corp 1 Allied Dr *NYSE: AT*	Little Rock	AR	72202	**800-255-8351**	501-905-8000	721
ALLTEL Publishing Corp 100 Executive Pkwy	Hudson	OH	44236	**800-235-3386**	330-650-7100	623-6
Alltel Stadium 1 Alltel Stadium Pl	Jacksonville	FL	32202	**877-452-4784**	904-633-6000	706
Alltex Inc 324 Taylor St	Manchester	NH	03103	**800-255-8391**	603-625-9722	434
Alltype Fire Protection Co 9495 Page Ave PO Box 32432	Saint Louis	MO	63132	**800-369-7101**	314-426-7100	667
Allume Systems Inc 245 Westridge Dr	Watsonville	CA	95076	**800-732-8881**	831-761-6200	176-12
Allure Magazine 4 Times Sq	New York	NY	10036	**800-223-0780**	212-286-2860	449-11
Allvac Inc 2020 Ashcraft Ave	Monroe	NC	28110	**800-537-5551**	704-289-4511	476
Allway Tools Inc 1255 Seabury Ave	Bronx	NY	10462	**800-422-5592**	718-792-3636	746
Allwire Inc PO Box 12602	Fresno	CA	93778	**800-255-3828**	559-485-8120	800
Ally Industries Inc 30-A Progress Ave	Seymour	CT	06483	**800-772-3389**	203-888-7873	667
Allyn & Bacon/Longman Publishers Pearson Education Inc 75 Arlington St Suite 300 *Orders	Boston	MA	02116	**800-852-8024***	617-848-7090	623-2

Alphabetical Section

Name / Address	City	State	ZIP	Toll-Free	Phone	Class
ALM (American Leprosy Missions) 1 ALM Way	Greenville	SC	29601	**800-543-3135**	864-271-7040	48-5
Alma College 614 W Superior St	Alma	MI	48801	**800-321-2562**	989-463-7111	163
Alma Iron & Metal Co Inc PO Box 729	Alma	MI	48801	**800-572-6357**	989-463-2131	674
Alma Products Co 2000 Michigan Ave	Alma	MI	48801	**877-427-2625**	989-463-1151	60
Almay Inc 237 Park Ave	New York	NY	10017	**800-473-8566**	212-527-4700	211
Almo Corp 2709 Commerce Way	Philadelphia	PA	19154	**800-345-2566**	215-698-4000	38
Almost Family Inc 9510 Ormsby Station Rd Suite 300 *NASDAQ: AFAM*	Louisville	KY	40223	**800-845-6987**	502-899-5355	358
ALOA (Associated Locksmiths of America) 3003 Live Oak St	Dallas	TX	75204	**800-532-2562**	214-827-1701	49-3
Aloette Cosmetics Inc 4900 Highlands Pkwy	Smyrna	GA	30082	**800-256-3883**	678-444-2563	211
Alogent Corp 4005 Windward Plaza 2nd Fl	Alpharetta	GA	30005	**888-333-6030**	770-752-6400	176-10
Aloha Airlines AlohaPass PO Box 30028	Honolulu	HI	96820	**800-367-5250**		27
Aloha Airlines Inc PO Box 30028	Honolulu	HI	96820	**800-367-5250**	808-484-1111	26
ALP Industries Inc 1229 W Lincoln Hwy	Coatesville	PA	19320	**800-220-2515**	610-384-1300	802
ALP Lighting Components Inc 6333 Gross Point Rd	Niles	IL	60714	**877-257-5841**	773-774-9550	803
Alpena Area Chamber of Commerce 235 W Chisholm St PO Box 65	Alpena	MI	49707	**800-425-7362**	989-354-4181	137
Alpena Area Convention & Visitors Bureau 235 W Chisholm St	Alpena	MI	49707	**800-425-7362**	989-354-4181	205
Alpena Community College 666 Johnson St	Alpena	MI	49707	**888-468-6222**	989-356-9021	160
Alpenhof Lodge 3255 W Village Dr	Teton Village	WY	83025	**800-732-3244**	307-733-3242	373
Alpha 1 Induction Service Center Inc 1525 Old Alum Creek Dr	Columbus	OH	43209	**800-991-2599**	614-253-8900	313
Alpha Assoc Inc 2 Amboy Ave	Woodbridge	NJ	07095	**800-563-3136**	732-634-5700	730-2
Alpha Chi National College Honor Scholarship Society Harding University PO Box 12249	Searcy	AR	72149	**800-477-4225**	501-279-4443	48-16
Alpha Epsilon Pi Fraternity Inc 8815 Wesleyan Rd	Indianapolis	IN	46268	**800-223-2374**	317-876-1913	48-16
Alpha Omega International Dental Fraternity 500 Commonwealth Dr	Warrendale	PA	15086	**800-677-8468**	724-778-3419	48-16
Alpha Omega Tours & Charters PO Box 97	Medical Lake	WA	99022	**800-351-1060**	509-624-4116	748
Alpha Plastics Inc 1555 Page Industrial Blvd	Saint Louis	MO	63132	**800-421-4772**	314-427-4300	99
Alpha Sigma Phi National Fraternity 710 Adams St	Carmel	IN	46032	**800-800-1845**	317-843-1911	48-16
Alpha Technologies Inc 3767 Alpha Way	Bellingham	WA	98226	**800-322-5742**	360-647-2360	252
Alpha Technologies Services LLC 2689 Wingate Ave	Akron	OH	44314	**800-356-9886**	330-745-1641	200
Alpha Wire Co 711 Lidgerwood Ave	Elizabeth	NJ	07207	**800-522-5742**	908-925-8000	801
AlphaGary Corp 170 Pioneer Dr	Leominster	MA	01453	**800-232-9741**	978-537-8071	594-2
AlphaGraphics Inc 268 S State St Suite 300	Salt Lake City	UT	84111	**800-955-6246**	801-595-7270	615
Alpharma Inc 1 Executive Dr *NYSE: ALO*	Fort Lee	NJ	07024	**800-645-4216**	201-947-7774	572
Alpharma Inc Animal Health Div 1 Executive Dr 3rd Fl	Fort Lee	NJ	07024	**800-834-6470**	201-947-7774	574
Alpharma Inc Fine Chemicals Div 1 Executive Dr 4th Fl	Fort Lee	NJ	07024	**800-645-4216**	201-947-7774	470
Alpharma Inc US Pharmaceuticals Div 7205 Windsor Blvd *Cust Svc	Baltimore	MD	21244	**800-638-9096***	410-298-1000	470
AlphaStaff Inc 1801 Clint Moore Rd Suite 115	Boca Raton	FL	33487	**888-335-9545**	561-241-9545	619
Alphin Brothers Inc 2302 US 301 S	Dunn	NC	28334	**800-672-4502**	910-892-8751	291-36
Alpina Sports USA PO Box 23	Hanover	NH	03755	**800-425-7462**	603-448-3101	702
Alpine Adventure Trails Tours Inc 7495 Lower Thomaston Rd	Macon	GA	31220	**888-478-4004**	478-477-4004	748
Alpine Electronics of America 19145 Gramercy Pl	Torrance	CA	90501	**800-257-4631**	310-326-8000	52
Alpine Engineered Products Inc PO Box 2225	Pompano Beach	FL	33061	**800-735-8055**	954-781-3333	92
Alpine Helen/White County Convention & Visitors Bureau PO Box 730	Helen	GA	30545	**800-858-8027**	706-878-2181	205
Alpine Lumber Co 1120 W 122nd Ave Suite 301	Westminster	CO	80234	**800-275-2365**	303-451-8001	190-3
Alpine Meadows Ski Resort 2600 Alpine Meadows Rd PO Box 5279	Tahoe City	CA	96145	**800-441-4423**	530-583-4232	655
Alpine Packing Co 9900 Lower Sacramento Rd	Stockton	CA	95210	**800-399-6328**	209-477-2691	465
Alps Sportswear Mfg Co 15 Union St	Lawrence	MA	01840	**800-262-7010**	978-683-2438	153-3
Alro Steel Corp 3100 E High St	Jackson	MI	49203	**800-877-2576**	517-787-5500	483
ALS Assn 27001 Agoura Rd Suite 150	Calabasas Hills	CA	91301	**800-782-4747**	818-880-9007	48-17
ALS Transportation Inc 4605 Post Oak Pl Suite 211	Houston	TX	77027	**866-355-5466**	713-355-5466	433
ALSAC (American Lebanese Syrian Associated Charities) 501 St Jude Pl	Memphis	TN	38105	**800-822-6344**	901-578-2000	48-5
ALSC (Association for Library Service to Children) 50 E Huron St	Chicago	IL	60611	**800-545-2433**	312-280-2163	49-11
Alside Div Associated Materials Inc PO Box 2010	Akron	OH	44309	**800-922-6009**	330-929-1811	233
Alsons Corp PO Box 282	Hillsdale	MI	49242	**800-421-0001**	517-439-1411	598
ALSTOM Signaling Inc 1025 John St *Cust Svc	West Henrietta	NY	14586	**800-717-4477***	585-783-2000	691
ALTA (American Land Title Assn) 1828 L St NW Suite 705	Washington	DC	20036	**800-787-2582**	202-296-3671	49-10
ALTA (Association for Library Trustees & Advocates) 50 E Huron St	Chicago	IL	60611	**800-545-2433**	312-280-2161	49-11
Alta Dena Dairy 17637 E Valley Blvd *Orders	City of Industry	CA	91744	**800-533-2479***	626-964-6401	291-27
Alta Genetics Inc RR 2	Balzac	AB	T0M0E0	**800-932-2855**	403-226-0666	12-2
Alta Lodge 1 Main St PO Box 8040	Alta	UT	84092	**800-707-2582**	801-742-3500	655
Alta Peruvian Lodge PO Box 8017 Little Cottonwood Canyon	Alta	UT	84092	**800-453-8488**	801-742-3000	373
Alta Resources 1 Neenah Ctr Suite 500	Neenah	WI	54956	**800-756-7298**	920-727-9925	722
Altadis USA 5900 N Andrews Ave Suite 1100 *Orders	Fort Lauderdale	FL	33309	**800-446-5797***	954-772-9000	741-2
Altamaha Electric Membership Corp 611 W Liberty St	Lyons	GA	30436	**800-822-4563**	912-526-8181	244
Altamont Commuter Express (ACE) 5000 Airport Way Stockton Metropolitan Airport Suite 201	Stockton	CA	95206	**800-411-7245**	209-468-5600	460
Altamonte Billiard Factory Inc 700 N Hwy 17-92	Longwood	FL	32750	**800-780-7799**	407-339-8700	701
Altana Inc 60 Baylis Rd	Melville	NY	11747	**800-645-9833**	631-454-7677	573
Altana Inc Savage Laboratories Div 60 Baylis Rd	Melville	NY	11747	**800-231-0206**	631-454-7677	572
Altana Pharma Inc 435 N Service Rd W 1st Fl	Oakville	ON	L6M4X8	**888-367-3331**	905-469-9333	86
Altec Lansing Technologies Inc PO Box 277 Rt 6	Milford	PA	18337	**800-258-3288**	570-296-6444	171-5
Alten Engineering Div Westerman Cos 245 N Broad St	Bremen	OH	43107	**800-338-8265**	740-569-4143	700
Alter Group 5500 W Howard St	Skokie	IL	60077	**800-637-4842**	847-676-4300	639
Alter Trading Corp 689 Craig Rd	Saint Louis	MO	63141	**888-887-6005**	314-872-2400	674
Altera Corp 101 Innovation Dr *NASDAQ: ALTR* ■ *Cust Svc	San Jose	CA	95134	**800-767-3753***	408-544-7000	686
Alternative Distribution Alliance 72 Spring St 12th Fl	New York	NY	10012	**800-239-3232**	212-343-2485	512
Alternative Medicine. National Center for Complementary & National Institutes of Health 31 Center Dr Bldg 31	Bethesda	MD	20892	**888-644-6226**	301-435-5042	336-6
Alternative Medicine.com 2995 Wilderness Pl Suite 205	Boulder	CO	80301	**800-333-4325**	800-515-4325	351
Alternative Networking Inc DBA ANI Site Development 1300 Riverland Rd	Fort Lauderdale	FL	33312	**800-733-9929**	954-581-9929	168
Althoff Industries Inc 8001 S Rt 31	Crystal Lake	IL	60014	**800-225-2443**	815-455-7000	188-10
AltiGen Communications Inc 4555 Cushing Pkwy *NASDAQ: ATGN*	Fremont	CA	94538	**888-258-4436**	510-252-9712	720
Altiris Inc 588 W 400 South *NASDAQ: ATRS*	Lindon	UT	84042	**888-252-5551**		176-12
Altium Inc 17140 Bernardo Center Dr Suite 100	San Diego	CA	92128	**800-488-0680**	858-485-4600	176-5
Altius Health Plans 10421 S Jordan Gateway Suite 400	South Jordan	UT	84095	**800-365-1334**	801-355-1234	384-3
Altman Specialty Plants Inc 3742 Bluebird Canyon Rd	Vista	CA	92084	**800-348-4881**	760-744-8191	363
Altman Weil Inc PO Box 625	Newtown Square	PA	19073	**800-947-2875**	610-359-9900	193
Altmeyer Home Stores Inc Rt 22 461 William Penn Hwy	Delmont	PA	15626	**800-394-6628**	724-468-3434	357
Alto-Shaam Inc PO Box 450	Menomonee Falls	WI	53052	**800-329-8744**	262-251-3800	293
Altoona Center 1515 4th St	Altoona	PA	16601	**800-398-3202**	814-946-6900	228
Altoona Mirror 301 Cayuga Ave	Altoona	PA	16602	**800-222-1962**	814-946-7411	522-2
Altoona Regional Health System Altoona Hospital 620 Howard Ave	Altoona	PA	16601	**800-946-1902**	814-946-2011	366-2
Altour-Classic Cruise & Travel 19720 Ventura Blvd Suite A	Woodland Hills	CA	91364	**800-688-8500**	818-346-8747	760
Altran Corp 451 D St	Boston	MA	02210	**800-281-2506**	617-204-1000	728
Altrec.com Inc 135 Lake St S Suite 1000	Kirkland	WA	90833	**800-369-3949**	425-827-5159	702
ALTRES Inc 967 Kapiolani Blvd	Honolulu	HI	96814	**800-373-1955**	808-591-4900	707
Altru Hospice 1380 S Columbia Rd	Grand Forks	ND	58206	**800-545-5615**	701-780-5258	365
Altru Hospital 1200 S Columbia Rd	Grand Forks	ND	58201	**800-732-4277**	701-780-5000	366-2
Altus Times 218 W Commerce St PO Box 578	Altus	OK	73522	**800-303-1221**	580-482-1221	522-2
Aluma-Glass Industries Inc 16265 Star Rd	Nampa	ID	83687	**800-321-8273**	208-467-4491	232
Aluma Shield Industries Inc 725 Summer Hill Dr	Deland	FL	32724	**888-882-5862**	386-626-6789	106
Aluma Shield Industries Inc Butcher Boy Doors Div 725 Summerhill Dr	Deland	FL	32724	**888-882-5862**	386-626-6789	650
Aluminum Line Products Co 24460 Sperry Cir	Westlake	OH	44145	**800-321-3154**	440-835-8880	688
Aluminum Precision Products Inc 3333 W Warner St	Santa Ana	CA	92704	**800-411-8983**	714-546-8125	474
Alva Allen Industries Inc 1001-15 N 3rd St PO Box 427 *Cust Svc	Clinton	MO	64735	**800-343-5657***	660-885-3331	448
Alva-Amco Pharmacal Cos Inc 7711 N Merrimac Ave	Niles	IL	60714	**800-792-2582**	847-663-0700	572
Alvadora Spa at the Royal Palms Resort & Spa 5200 E Camelback Rd	Phoenix	AZ	85018	**800-672-6011**	602-977-6400	698
Alvah Bushnell Co 519 E Chelten Ave	Philadelphia	PA	19144	**800-255-7434**	215-842-9520	550
Alvan Motor Freight Inc 3600 Alvan Rd	Kalamazoo	MI	49001	**800-632-4172**	269-382-1500	769
Alvarado Mfg Co Inc 12660 Colony St	Chino	CA	91710	**800-423-4143**	909-591-8431	482
Alvernia College 400 Saint Bernadine St	Reading	PA	19607	**888-258-3764**	610-796-8200	163
Alverno College PO Box 343922	Milwaukee	WI	53234	**800-933-3401**	414-382-6100	163
Alvey Systems Inc 9301 Olive Blvd	Saint Louis	MO	63132	**800-325-1596**	314-993-4700	206
Alvin & Co Inc 1335 Blue Hills Ave	Bloomfield	CT	06002	**800-444-2584**	860-243-8991	43
Alvin Convention & Visitors Bureau 105 W Willis St	Alvin	TX	77511	**800-331-4063**	281-585-3359	205
Alvin Hollis & Co Inc 1 Hollis St	South Weymouth	MA	02190	**800-649-5090**	781-335-2100	311
Alvin-Manvel Area Chamber of Commerce 105 W Willis St	Alvin	TX	77511	**800-331-4063**	281-331-3944	137

				Toll-Free	Phone	Class
Alyeska Prince Hotel & Resort						
PO Box 249	Girdwood	AK	99587	**800-880-3880**	907-754-1111	655
Alyson Adventures Inc 923 White St	Key West	FL	33040	**800-825-9766**	305-296-9935	748
Alzheimer's Assn						
225 N Michigan Ave Suite 1700	Chicago	IL	60601	**800-272-3900**	312-335-8700	48-17
Alzheimer's Disease Education &						
Referral Center PO Box 8250	Silver Spring	MD	20907	**800-438-4380**	301-495-3311	196
AM Appliance Group						
789 N Grove Rd Suite 103	Richardson	TX	75081	**800-898-1879**	972-644-8595	36
AM Braswell Jr Food Co Inc						
226 N Zetterower Ave	Statesboro	GA	30458	**800-673-9388**	912-764-6191	291-20
AM Castle & Co 3400 N Wolf Rd	Franklin Park	IL	60131	**800-289-2785**	847-455-7111	483
AMEX: CAS						
AM Communications Inc						
1900 AM Dr	Quakertown	PA	18951	**800-248-9004**	215-538-8700	174
Am-Pac Tire Pros Inc						
917 6th Ave N	Birmingham	AL	35203	**800-875-4655**	205-322-4651	54
Am-Pack Tasco Distributing Ltd						
PO Box 20305	Waco	TX	76702	**800-548-1075**	254-772-9144	740
Am-Safe Inc 1043 N 47th Ave	Phoenix	AZ	85043	**800-228-1567**	602-850-2850	666
AM Todd Co 1717 Douglas Ave	Kalamazoo	MI	49005	**800-968-2603**	269-343-2603	470
AMA (Academy of Model Aeronautics)						
5161 E Memorial Dr	Muncie	IN	47302	**800-435-9262**	765-287-1256	48-18
AMA (American Management Assn)						
1601 Broadway	New York	NY	10019	**800-262-9699**	212-586-8100	753
AMA (American Marketing Assn)						
311 S Wacker Dr Suite 5800	Chicago	IL	60606	**800-262-1150**	312-542-9000	49-18
AMA (American Medical Assn)						
515 N State St	Chicago	IL	60610	**800-621-8335**	312-464-5000	49-8
AMA (American Motorcyclist Assn)						
13515 Yarmouth Dr	Pickerington	OH	43147	**800-262-5646**	614-856-1900	48-22
AMACO (American Art Clay Co Inc)						
66 Guion Rd	Indianapolis	IN	46254	**800-374-1600**	317-244-6871	43
Amada America						
7025 Firestone Blvd	Buena Park	CA	90621	**800-854-3567**	714-739-2111	447
Amada America Inc						
7025 Firestone Blvd	Buena Park	CA	90621	**800-626-6612**	714-739-2111	448
Amada Cutting Technologies						
14849 E Northam St	La Mirada	CA	90638	**800-877-4729**	714-670-1704	447
Amadeus North America LLC						
9250 NW 36 St	Miami	FL	33178	**800-888-7971**	305-499-6000	332
Amador County Chamber of Commerce						
PO Box 596	Jackson	CA	95642	**800-649-4988**	209-223-0350	137
AMAG Technology Inc						
20701 Manhattan Pl	Torrance	CA	90501	**800-889-9138**	310-518-2380	681
Amalgamated Transit Union (ATU)						
5025 Wisconsin Ave NW 3rd Fl	Washington	DC	20016	**888-240-1196**	202-537-1645	405
Amana Appliances Inc						
2800 220th Trail	Amana	IA	52204	**800-843-0304***	319-622-5511	16
*Cust Svc						
Amana Colonies Convention & Visitors						
Bureau 622 46th Ave	Amana	IA	52203	**800-245-5465**	319-622-7622	205
Amana Woolen Mill 800 48th Ave	Amana	IA	52203	**800-222-6430**	319-622-3432	731
Amanda Co						
4079 Govenor Dr Suite 320	San Diego	CA	92122	**800-410-2745**		721
Amangani Resort 1535 NE Butte Rd	Jackson	WY	83001	**877-734-7333**	307-734-7333	655
Amano Cincinnati Inc						
140 Harrison Ave	Roseland	NJ	07068	**800-526-2559**	973-403-1900	112
Amarillo Convention & Visitor Council						
PO Box 9480	Amarillo	TX	79105	**800-692-1338**	806-374-1497	205
Amarillo Hardware Co Inc						
PO Box 1891	Amarillo	TX	79172	**800-949-4722**	806-376-4722	346
Amarillo National Bank						
410 S Taylor St Plaza One	Amarillo	TX	79101	**800-262-3733**	806-378-8000	71
Amarillo Ritz Plaza Hotel 7909 I-40 E	Amarillo	TX	79118	**800-274-5315**	806-373-3303	373
Amarillo Wind Machine Co						
20513 Ave 256	Exeter	CA	93221	**800-311-4498**	559-592-4256	269
AmAsia International Ltd						
34 3rd Ave	Burlington	MA	01803	**888-877-3338**	781-229-6611	296
Amateur Softball Assn of America						
Inc (ASA) 2801 NE 50th St	Oklahoma City	OK	73111	**800-654-8337**	405-424-5266	48-22
Amatex Corp 1032 Stambridge St	Norristown	PA	19404	**800-441-9680**	610-277-6100	730-3
Amatom Electronic Hardware LLC						
5 Pasco Hill Rd	Cromwell	CT	06416	**800-243-6032**	860-828-0847	478
Amax Engineering Corp						
1565 Reliance Way	Fremont	CA	94539	**800-889-2629***	510-651-8886	171-3
*Cust Svc						
Amazon Herb Co						
1002 Jupiter Park Ln Suite 1	Jupiter	FL	33458	**800-535-0850**	561-575-7663	786
Amazon.com Inc PO Box 81226	Seattle	WA	98108	**800-201-7575***	206-622-2335	96
NASDAQ: AMZN ■ *Cust Svc						
AMBAC Assurance Corp						
1 State St Plaza 15th Fl	New York	NY	10004	**800-221-1854**	212-668-0340	384-5
AMBAC Financial Group Inc						
1 State Street Plaza 15th Fl	New York	NY	10004	**800-221-1854**	212-668-0340	355-4
NYSE: ABK						
AMBAC International Inc						
594 Spears Creek Church Rd	Pontiac	SC	29045	**800-628-6894**	803-735-1400	60
Ambassador Envelope Co						
6705 Keaton Corp Pkwy	Saint Charles	MO	63304	**800-325-4510**	636-477-1300	260
Ambassador Hotel						
535 Tchoupitoulas St	New Orleans	LA	70130	**888-527-5271**	504-527-5271	373
Ambassador Hotel 3100 I-40 W	Amarillo	TX	79102	**800-817-0521**	806-358-6161	373
Ambassador Limousine						
3215 S Cinder Ln	Las Vegas	NV	89103	**888-519-5466**	702-362-6200	433
Ambassador Theatre 215 W 49th St	New York	NY	10019	**800-432-7250**	212-239-6200	732
Ambassadors International Inc						
1071 Camelback St	Newport Beach	CA	92660	**800-325-7103**	949-759-5900	748
NASDAQ: AMIE						
AmBath Corp 1055 S Country Club Dr	Mesa	AZ	85210	**888-826-2284**	480-844-2596	599
Ambec Inc 1320 Wards Ferry Rd	Lynchburg	VA	24502	**800-899-4406**	434-582-1200	206
Amber Lotus Publishing						
1250 Addison St Studio 214	Berkeley	CA	94702	**800-326-2375**	510-225-0149	130
Amberley Greeting Card Co						
11510 Goldcoast Dr	Cincinnati	OH	45249	**800-262-3759**	513-489-2775	130
Amberley Suite Hotel						
7620 Pan American Fwy NE	Albuquerque	NM	87109	**800-333-9806**	505-823-1300	373
AMBEST Inc						
5250 Virginia Way Suite 250	Brentwood	TN	37027	**800-910-7220**	615-371-5187	319

				Toll-Free	Phone	Class
Ambion Inc						
2130 Woodward St Suite 200	Austin	TX	78744	**800-888-8804**	512-651-0200	229
Amboy National Bank						
3590 US Hwy 9 S	Old Bridge	NJ	08857	**800-942-6269**	732-591-8700	71
Ambriola Co Inc 2 Burma Rd	Jersey City	NJ	07305	**800-962-8224**	201-434-6289	292-4
Ambrosi & Assoc						
200 W Jackson Blvd 6th Fl	Chicago	IL	60606	**888-262-7674**	312-666-9200	338
Ambrosia House Tropical Lodging						
615 Fleming St	Key West	FL	33040	**800-535-9838**	305-296-9838	373
Ambulance Assn. American						
8201 Greensboro Dr Suite 300	McLean	VA	22102	**800-523-4447**	703-610-9018	49-21
Ambulatory Care Nursing. American						
Academy of 200 E Holly Ave Box 56	Pitman	NJ	08080	**800-262-6877**	856-256-2350	49-8
AMC (Appalachian Mountain Club)						
5 Joy St	Boston	MA	02108	**800-262-4455***	617-523-0636	48-13
*Orders						
AMC Cancer Research Center						
1600 Pierce St	Denver	CO	80214	**800-321-1557**	303-233-6501	654
AMC Entertainment Inc						
920 Main St	Kansas City	MO	64105	**800-326-2432**	816-221-4000	733
AMEX: AEN						
Amco Corp 901 N Kilpatrick Ave	Chicago	IL	60651	**800-621-4023**		281
AMCO Engineering Co						
3801 N Rose St	Schiller Park	IL	60176	**800-833-3156***	847-671-6670	253
*Mktg						
Amco McLean Corp						
548 S Fulton Ave	Mount Vernon	NY	10550	**800-431-2010**	914-237-4000	38
AMCOL International Corp						
1500 W Shure Dr	Arlington Heights	IL	60004	**800-323-0629**	847-392-4600	493-2
NYSE: ACO						
Amcom Software Inc						
5555 W 78th St	Minneapolis	MN	55439	**800-852-8935**	952-829-7445	176-7
AMCON Distributing Co						
7405 Irvington Rd	Omaha	NE	68122	**800-369-0047**	402-331-3727	744
AMEX: DIT						
Amcor Precast 801 W 12th St	Ogden	UT	84404	**800-776-8760**	801-399-1171	181
AMCORE Bank NA 501 7th St	Rockford	IL	61104	**888-426-2673**	815-968-1259	71
AMCORE Financial Inc 501 7th St	Rockford	IL	61104	**800-521-5150**	815-968-2241	355-2
NASDAQ: AMFI						
AMCP (Academy of Managed Care						
Pharmacy) 100 N Pitt St						
Suite 400	Alexandria	VA	22314	**800-827-2627**	703-683-8416	49-8
AMD (Association of Millwork						
Distributors) 10047 Robert						
Trent Jones Pkwy	New Port Richey	FL	34655	**800-786-7274**	727-372-3665	49-3
AMD Industries Inc 4620 W 19th St	Cicero	IL	60804	**800-367-9999**	708-863-8900	231
AMDA (American Medical Directors						
Assn) 10480 Little Patuxent Pkwy						
Suite 760	Columbia	MD	21044	**800-876-2632**	410-740-9743	49-8
AME Inc PO Box 909	Fort Mill	SC	29716	**800-849-7766**	803-548-7766	187-6
AME Ready Mix Div AVR Inc						
PO Box 307	Elk River	MN	55330	**800-374-8544***	763-441-2800	180
*Cust Svc						
Amedisys Inc						
11100 Mead Rd Suite 300	Baton Rouge	LA	70816	**800-467-2662**	225-292-2031	347
NASDAQ: AMED						
Amegy Bancorp Inc						
4400 Post Oak Pkwy	Houston	TX	77027	**800-324-6705**	713-235-8800	355-2
NASDAQ: ABNK						
Amegy Bank of Texas						
4400 Post Oak Pkwy	Houston	TX	77027	**800-287-0301**	713-235-8800	71
Amekor Industries						
500 Brook Rd Suite 100	Conshohocken	PA	19428	**800-345-6332**	610-825-6747	342
Amelco Corp 19208 S Vermont Ave	Gardena	CA	90248	**800-788-8838**	310-327-3070	188-4
Amelia Island Co 1501 Lewis St	Amelia Island	FL	32034	**888-261-6161**	904-261-6161	639
Amelia Island-Fernandina						
Beach-Yulee Chamber of						
Commerce 961687 Gateway						
Blvd Suite 101-G	Amelia Island	FL	32034	**800-226-3542**	904-261-3248	137
Amelia Island Plantation						
1501 Lewis St	Amelia Island	FL	32034	**800-874-6878**	904-261-6161	655
AmerCable Corp 350 Bailey Rd	El Dorado	AR	71730	**800-643-1516**	870-862-4919	800
Ameren Corp 1901 Chouteau Ave	Saint Louis	MO	63103	**800-552-7583**	314-621-3222	355-5
NYSE: AEE						
AmerenUE PO Box 66149	Saint Louis	MO	63166	**800-552-7583**	314-621-3222	774
Amerex Industries Inc						
665 Molly Ln Suite 110	Woodstock	GA	30189	**800-359-2586**	770-693-2100	19
Ameri-Fax Corp 7709 W 20th Ave	Hialeah	FL	33014	**800-969-1601**	305-828-1701	544
Ameriana Bancorp						
2118 Bundy Ave	New Castle	IN	47362	**800-487-2118**	765-529-2230	355-2
NASDAQ: ASBI						
Americ Disc Inc						
2525 rue Canadien	Drummondville	QC	J2C7W2	**800-263-0419**	819-474-2655	644
America the Beautiful Fund						
725 15th St NW Suite 605	Washington	DC	20005	**800-522-3557**	202-638-1649	48-13
America First Apartment Investors Inc						
1004 Farnam St Suite 100	Omaha	NE	68102	**800-283-2357**	402-444-1630	641
NASDAQ: APRO						
America First Assoc						
94 Covert Ave	Stewart Manor	NY	11530	**888-588-0400**	516-437-0866	679
America First Credit Union						
1344 W 4675 South	Riverdale	UT	84405	**800-999-3961**	801-627-0900	216
America II Corp Inc						
2600 118th Ave N	Saint Petersburg	FL	33716	**800-767-2637**	727-573-0900	245
America II Electronics Inc						
2600 118th Ave N	Saint Petersburg	FL	33716	**800-767-2637**	727-573-0900	245
America Online Inc (AOL)						
22000 AOL Way	Dulles	VA	20166	**888-265-8002***	703-265-1000	390
*Orders						
America Online Latin America Inc						
6600 N Andrews Ave						
Suite 400	Fort Lauderdale	FL	33309	**800-827-6364**	954-689-3000	390
America Outdoors						
5816 Kingston Pike	Knoxville	TN	37919	**800-524-4814**	865-558-3595	48-23
America Service Group Inc						
105 Westpark Dr Suite 200	Brentwood	TN	37027	**800-729-0069**	615-373-3100	384-3
NASDAQ: ASGR						
America West Airlines FlightFund						
PO Box 20050	Phoenix	AZ	85036	**800-247-5691**		27

Name / Address	City	State	ZIP	Toll-Free	Phone	Class
America West Airlines Inc 4000 E Sky Harbor Blvd	Phoenix	AZ	85034	**800-235-9292**	480-693-0800	26
America West Cargo 1329 S 27th St	Phoenix	AZ	85034	**800-292-2274**	480-693-2900	13
America West Holdings Corp 111 W Rio Salado Pkwy *NYSE: AWA*	Tempe	AZ	85281	**800-235-9292**	480-693-0800	355-1
Americal Corp 389 Americal Rd PO Box 1419	Henderson	NC	27536	**800-633-9707**	252-762-2000	153-10
AmeriCall Corp 550 E Diehl Rd	Naperville	IL	60563	**800-688-0078**	630-955-9100	722
American AAdvantage Funds 4151 Amon Carter Blvd MD 2450	Fort Worth	TX	76155	**800-388-3344**	817-967-3509	517
American Academy of Allergy Asthma & Immunology (AAAAI) 611 E Wells St 4th Fl	Milwaukee	WI	53202	**800-822-2762**	414-272-6071	49-8
American Academy of Ambulatory Care Nursing (AAACN) 200 E Holly Ave Box 56	Pitman	NJ	08080	**800-262-6877**	856-256-2350	49-8
American Academy of Art 332 S Michigan Ave Suite 300	Chicago	IL	60604	**888-461-0600**	312-461-0600	159
American Academy of Audiology (AAA) 11730 Plaza America Dr Suite 300	Reston	VA	22190	**800-222-2336**	703-790-8466	49-8
American Academy of Child & Adolescent Psychiatry (AACAP) 3615 Wisconsin Ave NW	Washington	DC	20016	**800-333-7636**	202-966-7300	49-15
American Academy of Cosmetic Dentistry (AACD) 5401 World Dairy Dr	Madison	WI	53718	**800-543-9220**	608-222-8583	49-8
American Academy of Disability Evaluating Physicians (AADEP) 150 N Wacker Dr Suite 1420	Chicago	IL	60606	**800-456-6095**	312-658-1171	49-8
American Academy of Dramatic Arts 1336 N La Brea Ave	Hollywood	CA	90028	**800-222-2867**	323-464-2777	159
American Academy of Dramatic Arts 120 Madison Ave	New York	NY	10016	**800-463-8990**	212-686-9244	159
American Academy of Facial Plastic & Reconstructive Surgery (AAFPRS) 310 S Henry St	Alexandria	VA	22314	**800-332-3223**	703-299-9291	49-8
American Academy of Family Physicians (AAFP) 11400 Tomahawk Creek Pkwy	Leawood	KS	66211	**800-274-2237**	913-906-6000	49-8
American Academy of Neurology (AAN) 1080 Montreal Ave	Saint Paul	MN	55116	**800-879-1960**	651-695-2717	49-8
American Academy of Ophthalmology 655 Beach St	San Francisco	CA	94109	**800-222-3937**	415-561-8500	49-8
American Academy of Pediatrics (AAP) 141 Northwest Point Blvd	Elk Grove Village	IL	60007	**800-433-9016**	847-434-4000	49-8
American Academy of Periodontology (AAP) 737 N Michigan Ave Suite 800	Chicago	IL	60611	**800-282-4867**	312-787-5518	49-8
American Academy of Psychiatry & the Law (AAPL) 1 Regency Dr PO Box 30	Bloomfield	CT	06002	**800-331-1389**	860-242-5450	49-15
American Ace Inc 2500 Heiman St	Nashville	TN	37208	**800-309-0079**	615-329-0079	291-7
American Advertising Federation (AAF) 1101 Vermont Ave NW Suite 500	Washington	DC	20005	**800-999-2231**	202-898-0089	49-18
American Agent & Broker Magazine 6000 Lombardo Center Dr Suite 420	Seven Hills	OH	44131	**888-772-8926**		449-5
American Air Charter Network PO Box 569	Melville	NY	11747	**800-393-2538**	516-768-3202	14
American Airlines AAdvantage Program PO Box 619620	DFW Airport	TX	75261	**800-882-8880**		27
American Airlines Duty Free 1166 Kane Concourse Suite 301	Bay Harbor Islands	FL	33154	**888-388-9373**	305-864-5788	240
American Airlines Employees Federal Credit Union PO Box 155489	Fort Worth	TX	76155	**800-533-0035**	817-963-6000	216
American Airlines Inc PO Box 619616	DFW Airport	TX	75261	**800-433-7300**	817-963-1234	26
American Airlines Inc Cargo Div PO Box 619616	DFW Airport	TX	75261	**800-227-4622**	817-967-2400	13
American Alliance for Health Physical Education Recreation & Dance (AAHPERD) 1900 Association Dr	Reston	VA	20191	**800-213-7193**	703-476-3400	48-22
American Alternative Insurance Corp 685 College Rd E	Princeton	NJ	08543	**800-305-4954**	609-951-8295	384-4
American Aluminum Co Inc 230 Sheffield St	Mountainside	NJ	07092	**800-315-3977**	908-233-3500	473
American Ambulance Assn (AAA) 8201 Greensboro Dr Suite 300	McLean	VA	22102	**800-523-4447**	703-610-9018	49-21
American Amicable Life Insurance Co PO Box 2549	Waco	TX	76702	**800-736-7311**	254-297-2777	384-2
American Angus Assn (AAA) 3201 Frederick Ave	Saint Joseph	MO	64506	**800-821-5478**	816-383-5100	48-2
American Animal Hospital Assn (AAHA) PO Box 150899	Denver	CO	80215	**800-252-2242**	303-986-2800	48-3
American Anti-Slavery Group Inc 198 Tremont St Suite 421	Boston	MA	02116	**800-884-0719**	617-426-8161	48-5
American Apparel & Footwear Assn (AAFA) 1601 N Kent St Suite 1200	Arlington	VA	22209	**800-520-2262**	703-524-1864	49-4
American Arbitration Assn Inc (AAA) 335 Madison Ave 10th Fl	New York	NY	10017	**800-778-7879**	212-716-5800	41
American Art Clay Co Inc (AMACO) 66 Guion Rd	Indianapolis	IN	46254	**800-374-1600**	317-244-6871	43
American Artist Magazine 770 Broadway	New York	NY	10003	**800-745-8922**	646-654-5500	449-2
American Asphalt Paving Co 500 Chase Rd	Shavertown	PA	18708	**800-326-9362**	570-696-1181	46
American Assn for the Advancement of Science (AAAS) 1200 New York Ave NW	Washington	DC	20005	**800-731-4939**	202-326-6400	49-19
American Assn of Bovine Practitioners (AABP) PO Box 1755	Rome	GA	30162	**800-269-2227**	706-232-2220	48-2
American Assn for Clinical Chemistry Inc (AACC) 2101 L St NW Suite 202 *Cust Svc	Washington	DC	20037	**800-892-1400***	202-857-0717	49-19
American Assn of Colleges of Podiatric Medicine (AACPM) 1350 Piccard Dr Suite 322	Rockville	MD	20850	**800-922-9266**	301-990-7400	49-8
American Assn of Community Theatre (AACT) 8402 BriarWood Cir	Lago Vista	TX	78645	**866-687-2228**	512-267-0711	48-4
American Assn of Critical-Care Nurses (AACN) 101 Columbia	Aliso Viejo	CA	92656	**800-809-2273**	949-362-2000	49-8
American Assn of Diabetes Educators (AADE) 100 W Monroe St Suite 400	Chicago	IL	60603	**800-338-3633**	312-424-2426	49-8
American Assn of Drugless Practitioners (AADP) 2705 61st St	Galveston	TX	77551	**888-764-2237**	409-741-9000	48-17
American Assn of Endodontists (AAE) 211 E Chicago Ave Suite 1100	Chicago	IL	60611	**800-872-3636**	312-266-7255	49-8
American Assn of Engineering Societies (AAES) 1828 L St NW Suite 906 *Orders	Washington	DC	20036	**888-400-2237***	202-296-2237	49-19
American Assn of Equine Practitioners (AAEP) 4075 Iron Works Pkwy	Lexington	KY	40511	**800-443-0177**	859-233-0147	48-3
American Assn of Family & Consumer Sciences (AAFCS) 400 N Columbus St Suite 202	Alexandria	VA	22314	**800-424-8080**	703-706-4600	49-5
American Assn of Franchisees & Dealers (AAFD) 3500 5th Ave Suite 103	San Diego	CA	92103	**800-733-9058**	610-209-3775	49-18
American Assn of Fund-Raising Counsel (AAFRC) 4700 W Lake Ave	Glenview	IL	60025	**800-462-2372**	847-375-4709	48-5
American Assn of Gynecological Laparoscopists (AAGL) 13021 E Florence Ave	Santa Fe Springs	CA	90670	**800-554-2245**	562-946-8774	49-8
American Assn of Healthcare Consultants (AAHC) 5938 N Drake Ave	Chicago	IL	60659	**888-350-2242**		49-8
American Assn of Homes & Services for the Aging (AAHSA) 2519 Connecticut Ave NW	Washington	DC	20008	**800-508-9442**	202-783-2242	48-6
American Assn of Individual Investors (AAII) 625 N Michigan Ave	Chicago	IL	60611	**800-428-2244**	312-280-0170	49-2
American Assn of Insurance Services (AAIS) 1745 S Naperville Rd	Wheaton	IL	60187	**800-564-2247**	630-681-8347	49-9
American Assn for Leisure & Recreation (AALR) 1900 Association Dr	Reston	VA	20191	**800-213-7193**	703-476-3400	48-23
American Assn of Medical Assistants (AAMA) 20 N Wacker Dr Suite 1575	Chicago	IL	60606	**800-228-2262**	312-899-1500	49-8
American Assn of Medical Review Officers (AAMRO) PO Box 12873	Research Triangle Park	NC	27709	**800-489-1839**	919-489-5407	49-8
American Assn for Medical Transcription (AAMT) 100 Sycamore Ave	Modesto	CA	95354	**800-982-2182**	209-527-9620	49-8
American Assn on Mental Retardation (AAMR) 444 N Capitol St NW Suite 846	Washington	DC	20001	**800-424-3688**	202-387-1968	48-17
American Assn of Motor Vehicle Administrators (AAMVA) 4301 Wilson Blvd Suite 400	Arlington	VA	22203	**800-515-8881**	703-522-4200	49-7
American Assn of Naturopathic Physicians (AANP) 3201 New Mexico Ave NW Suite 350	Washington	DC	20016	**866-538-2267**	202-895-1392	48-17
American Assn of Neurological Surgeons (AANS) 5550 Meadowbrook Dr	Rolling Meadows	IL	60068	**888-566-2267**	847-378-0500	49-8
American Assn of Neuroscience Nurses (AANN) 4700 W Lake Ave	Glenview	IL	60025	**888-557-2266**	847-375-4733	49-8
American Assn of Nutritional Consultants (AANC) 401 Kings Hwy	Winona Lake	IN	46590	**888-828-2262**	574-269-6165	49-8
American Assn of Occupational Health Nurses (AAOHN) 2920 Brandywine Rd Suite 100	Atlanta	GA	30341	**888-646-4631**	770-455-7757	49-8
American Assn of Oral & Maxillofacial Surgeons (AAOMS) 9700 W Bryn Mawr Ave	Rosemont	IL	60018	**800-822-6637**	847-678-6200	49-8
American Assn of Oriental Medicine (AAOM) PO Box 162340	Sacramento	CA	95816	**866-455-7999**	916-443-4770	48-17
American Assn of Orthodontists (AAO) 401 N Lindbergh Blvd	Saint Louis	MO	63141	**800-424-2841**	314-993-1700	49-8
American Assn of Orthodontists PAC 401 N Lindbergh Blvd	Saint Louis	MO	63141	**800-424-2841**	314-993-1700	604
American Assn of Petroleum Geologists (AAPG) 1444 S Boulder Ave	Tulsa	OK	74119	**800-364-2274**	918-584-2555	48-12
American Assn of Pharmaceutical Scientists (AAPS) 2107 Wilson Blvd Suite 700	Arlington	VA	22201	**877-998-2277**	703-243-2800	49-19
American Assn of Physician Specialists Inc (AAPS) 2296 Henderson Mill Rd Suite 206	Atlanta	GA	30345	**800-447-9397**	770-939-8555	49-8
American Assn of Poison Control Centers (AAPCC) 3201 New Mexico Ave Suite 330	Washington	DC	20016	**800-222-1222**	202-362-7217	49-8
American Assn of Professional Landmen (AAPL) 4100 Fossil Creek Blvd	Fort Worth	TX	76137	**888-566-2275**	817-847-7700	48-12
American Assn of Retired Persons 601 'E' St NW	Washington	DC	20049	**888-687-2277**	202-434-2277	48-6
American Assn of School Administrators (AASA) 801 N Quincy St Suite 700	Arlington	VA	22203	**800-771-1162**	703-528-0700	49-5
American Assn of School Librarians (AASL) 50 E Huron St	Chicago	IL	60611	**800-545-2433**	312-280-4386	49-11
American Assn of University Professors (AAUP) 1012 14th St NW Suite 500	Washington	DC	20005	**800-424-2973**	202-737-5900	49-5
American Assn of University Women (AAUW) 1111 16th St NW	Washington	DC	20036	**800-326-2289**	202-785-7700	49-5
American Assn of Variable Star Observers (AAVSO) 25 Birch St	Cambridge	MA	02138	**800-223-0138**	617-354-0484	49-19

Name / Address	City	State	Zip	Toll-Free	Phone	Class
American Athletic Inc 200 American Ave	Jefferson	IA	50129	**800-247-3978**	515-386-3125	340
American Autoimmune Related Disease Assn (AARDA) 22100 Gratiot Ave	Eastpointe	MI	48021	**800-598-4668**	586-776-3900	48-17
American Avionics Inc 7023 Perimeter Rd S *Sales	Seattle	WA	98108	**800-518-5858***	206-763-8530	25
American Axle & Mfg Holdings Inc 1840 Holbrook Ave *NYSE: AXL*	Detroit	MI	48212	**800-299-2953**	313-758-3600	60
American Baby Magazine 125 Park Ave	New York	NY	10017	**800-678-1208**	212-557-6600	449-11
American Background Information Services Inc 629 Cedar Creek Grade Suite C	Winchester	VA	22601	**800-669-2247**	540-665-8056	621
American Baler Co 800 E Centre St	Bellevue	OH	44811	**800-843-7512**	419-483-5790	379
American Bank 4029 W Tilghman St	Allentown	PA	18104	**888-366-6622**	610-366-1800	71
American Banker Newsletters 1 State St Plaza 27th Fl	New York	NY	10004	**800-221-1809**	212-803-8350	623-9
American Banker/Bond Buyer 1 State Street Plaza 26th Fl	New York	NY	10004	**800-362-3807**	212-803-8200	623-9
American Bankers Assn (ABA) 1120 Connecticut Ave NW *Cust Svc	Washington	DC	20036	**800-226-5377***	202-663-5000	49-2
American Baptist Assn (ABA) 4605 N State Line Ave	Texarkana	TX	75503	**800-264-2482**	903-792-2783	48-20
American Baptist Churches USA PO Box 851	Valley Forge	PA	19482	**800-222-3872**	610-768-2000	48-20
American Baptist News Service PO Box 851	Valley Forge	PA	19482	**800-222-3872**	610-768-2077	520
American Bar Assn (ABA) 750 N Lake Shore Dr	Chicago	IL	60611	**800-285-2221**	312-988-5000	49-10
American Bedding Industries 500 S Falkenburg Rd	Tampa	FL	33619	**800-780-1084**	813-651-2233	463
American Behavioral Benefits Managers 550 Montgomery Hwy	Birmingham	AL	35216	**800-677-4544**	205-871-7814	454
American Beverage Licensees (ABL) 5101 River Rd Suite 108	Bethesda	MD	20816	**800-311-8999**	301-656-1494	49-6
American Bible Society 1865 Broadway	New York	NY	10023	**800-322-4253**	212-408-1200	623-4
American Bicycle Assn (ABA) 1645 W Sunrise Blvd	Gilbert	AZ	85233	**800-886-1269**	480-961-1903	48-22
American Bio-Recovery Assn (ABRA) 2020 Pennsylvania Ave NW Suite 456	Washington	DC	20006	**888-979-2217**	888-979-2272	49-4
American Biologics 1180 Walnut Ave	Chula Vista	CA	91911	**800-227-4458**	619-429-8200	410
American Biophysics Corp 140 Frenchtown Rd	North Kingstown	RI	02852	**877-699-8727**	401-884-3500	420
American Blind & Wallpaper Factory 909 N Sheldon Rd *Cust Svc	Plymouth	MI	48170	**800-575-9019***	734-207-5800	451
American Boarding Kennels Assn (ABKA) 1702 E Pikes Peak Ave	Colorado Springs	CO	80909	**877-570-7788**	719-667-1600	48-3
American Body Armor & Equipment Inc 13386 International Pkwy	Jacksonville	FL	32218	**800-654-9943**	904-741-5400	566
American Bone Marrow Donor Registry 2733 North St	Mandeville	LA	70448	**800-745-2452**	985-626-1749	48-17
American Book Producers Assn (ABPA) 160 5th Ave	New York	NY	10010	**800-209-4575**	212-645-2368	49-16
American Booksellers Assn (ABA) 828 S Broadway	Tarrytown	NY	10591	**800-637-0037**	914-591-2665	49-18
American Borate Corp 5700 Cleveland St Suite 420	Virginia Beach	VA	23462	**800-486-1072**	757-490-2242	493-1
American Botanical Council 6200 Manor Rd	Austin	TX	78723	**800-373-7105**	512-926-4900	48-17
American Bowling Congress (ABC) 5301 S 76th St	Greendale	WI	53129	**800-514-2695**	414-421-6400	48-22
American Brain Tumor Assn (ABTA) 2720 River Rd	Des Plaines	IL	60018	**800-886-2282**	847-827-9910	48-17
American Brass Mfg Co 5000 Superior Ave	Cleveland	OH	44103	**800-431-6440**	216-431-6565	598
American Brush Co Inc 112 Industrial Blvd	Claremont	NH	03743	**800-225-0392**	603-542-9951	104
American Burn Assn (ABA) 625 N Michigan Ave Suite 1530	Chicago	IL	60611	**800-548-2876**	312-642-9260	49-8
American Business Financial Services Inc PO Box11716 Suite 215	Philadelphia	PA	19101	**800-776-4001**		498
American Business Systems Inc 315 Littleton Rd	Chelmsford	MA	01824	**800-356-4034**	978-250-9600	176-1
American Business Women's Assn (ABWA) 9100 Ward Pkwy	Kansas City	MO	64114	**800-228-0007**	816-361-6621	49-12
American Businesspersons Assn (ABA) 350 Fairway Dr Suite 200	Deerfield Beach	FL	33441	**800-221-2168**	954-571-1877	49-12
American Cabaret Theatre 401 E Michigan St	Indianapolis	IN	46204	**800-375-8887**	317-631-0334	562
American Cafe 150 W Church Ave	Maryville	TN	37801	**800-325-0755**	865-379-5700	657
American Camp Assn (ACA) 5000 SR-67 N	Martinsville	IN	46151	**800-428-2267**	765-342-8456	48-23
American Canadian Caribbean Line Inc 461 Water St	Warren	RI	02885	**800-556-7450**	401-247-0955	217
American Cancer Society (ACS) 1599 Clifton Rd NE	Atlanta	GA	30329	**800-227-2345**	404-320-3333	48-17
American Canoe Assn (ACA) 7432 Alban Station Blvd Suite B-232	Springfield	VA	22150	**800-929-5162**	703-451-0141	48-22
American Capital Group Inc 500 N State College Blvd Suite 950	Orange	CA	92868	**800-305-0224**	714-937-4126	779
American Capitol Insurance Co 10555 Richmond Ave 2nd Fl	Houston	TX	77042	**800-527-2567**	713-974-2242	384-2
American Car Services 10853 N Central Expy Suite 2125	Dallas	TX	75231	**800-410-1399**	214-637-6600	433
American Carrier Equipment Corp 2285 E Date Ave	Fresno	CA	93706	**800-344-2174**	559-442-1500	768

Name / Address	City	State	Zip	Toll-Free	Phone	Class
American Casein Co 109 Elbow Ln	Burlington	NJ	08016	**800-699-6455**	609-387-3130	291-10
American Cash Flow Assn (ACFA) 255 S Orange Ave Suite 600	Orlando	FL	32801	**800-253-1294**	407-206-6523	49-12
American Cast Iron Pipe Co (ACIPCO) 2916 16th St N	Birmingham	AL	35207	**800-442-2347**	205-325-7701	302
American Casting & Mfg Corp 51 Commercial St	Plainview	NY	11803	**800-342-0333**	516-349-7010	321
American Century Funds PO Box 419200	Kansas City	MO	64141	**800-345-2021**	816-531-5575	517
American Century Investments Inc 4500 Main St	Kansas City	MO	64111	**800-345-2021**	816-531-5575	393
American Chamber of Commerce Executives (ACCE) 4875 Eisenhower Ave Suite 250	Alexandria	VA	22304	**800-394-2223**	703-998-0072	49-12
American Chemical Society (ACS) 1155 16th St NW	Washington	DC	20036	**800-227-5558**	202-872-4600	49-19
American Chemical Society Publications 1155 16th St NW Publications Support Services	Washington	DC	20036	**800-227-5558**	202-872-4600	623-11
American Chiropractic Assn (ACA) 1701 Clarendon Blvd 2nd Fl	Arlington	VA	22209	**800-986-4636**	703-276-8800	49-8
American Chiropractic Assn PAC (ACA-PAC) 1701 Clarendon Blvd	Arlington	VA	22209	**800-986-4636**	703-276-8800	604
American Chronic Pain Assn (ACPA) PO Box 850	Rocklin	CA	95677	**800-533-3231**	916-632-0922	48-17
American Cinematographer Magazine 1782 N Orange Dr	Hollywood	CA	90028	**800-448-0145**	323-969-4333	449-9
American City Business Journals Inc 120 W Moorehead St Suite 400	Charlotte	NC	28202	**800-704-3757**	704-973-1000	623-9
American Civil War Museum 297 Steinwehr Ave	Gettysburg	PA	17325	**800-877-7775**	717-334-6245	509
American Classic Sales 1142 S 2475 West	Salt Lake City	UT	84104	**888-733-5763**	801-977-3935	701
American Classic Sanitation LLC 242 E Live Oak Ave	Irwindale	CA	91706	**877-340-0004**	626-462-9110	261-4
American Cleaning Co 39-30 Review Ave	Long Island City	NY	11101	**888-929-7587**	718-392-8080	149
American Cleanroom Supply LLC 1042-B El Camino Real Suite 414	Encinitas	CA	92024	**888-901-3220**		667
American Cleft Palate-Craniofacial Assn 104 S Estes Dr Suite 204	Chapel Hill	NC	27514	**800-242-5338**	919-933-9044	49-8
American Club The 444 Highland Dr	Kohler	WI	53044	**800-344-2838**	920-457-8000	655
American Coach Limousine 1433 W Jeffrey Dr	Addison	IL	60101	**888-709-5466**	630-629-0001	433
American Coach Lines Inc 2328 10th Ave N Suite 501	Lake Worth	FL	33460	**800-593-1818**	561-721-1170	748
American Coalition for Fathers & Children (ACFC) 1420 Spring Hill Rd	McLean	VA	22102	**800-978-3237**		48-6
American Coffee Co Inc 800 Magazine St	New Orleans	LA	70130	**800-554-7234**	504-581-7234	291-7
American College 270 S Bryn Mawr Ave	Bryn Mawr	PA	19010	**888-263-7265**	610-526-1000	787
American College for Advancement in Medicine (ACAM) 23121 Verdugo Dr Suite 204	Laguna Hills	CA	92653	**800-532-3688**	949-583-7666	49-8
American College of Allergy Asthma & Immunology (ACAAI) 85 W Algonquin Rd Suite 550	Arlington Heights	IL	60005	**800-842-7777**	847-427-1200	49-8
American College of Cardiology (ACC) 9111 Old Georgetown Rd *Cust Svc	Bethesda	MD	20814	**800-253-4636***	301-897-5400	49-8
American College of Chest Physicians (ACCP) 3300 Dundee Rd	Northbrook	IL	60062	**800-343-2227**	847-498-1400	49-8
American College of Dentists (ACD) 839 Quince Orchard Blvd Suite J	Gaithersburg	MD	20878	**888-223-1920**	301-977-3223	49-8
American College of Emergency Physicians (ACEP) PO Box 619911	Dallas	TX	75261	**800-798-1822**	972-550-0911	49-8
American College of Eye Surgeons (ACES) 334 E Lake Rd Suite 135	Palm Lake Harbor	FL	34685	**888-335-0077**	727-480-8542	49-8
American College of Foot & Ankle Surgeons (ACFAS) 8725 W Higgins Rd Suite 555	Chicago	IL	60631	**800-421-2237**	773-693-9300	49-8
American College of Health Care Administrators (ACHCA) 300 N Lee St Suite 301	Alexandria	VA	22314	**888-882-2422**	703-739-7900	49-8
American College of Osteopathic Family Physicians (ACOFP) 330 E Algonquin Rd Suite 1	Arlington Heights	IL	60005	**800-323-0794**	847-228-6090	49-8
American College of Physician Executives (ACPE) 4890 W Kennedy Blvd Suite 200	Tampa	FL	33609	**800-562-8088**	813-287-2000	49-8
American College of Physicians (ACP) 190 N Independence Mall W	Philadelphia	PA	19106	**800-523-1546**	215-351-2400	49-8
American College of Radiology (ACR) 1891 Preston White Dr	Reston	VA	20191	**800-227-5463**	703-648-8900	49-8
American College of Surgeons (ACS) 633 N Saint Clair St	Chicago	IL	60611	**800-621-4111**	312-202-5000	49-8
American Colloid Co 1500 W Shure Dr	Arlington Heights	IL	60004	**800-323-0629**	847-392-4600	493-2
American Color Graphics Inc 100 Winners Cir Suite 300	Brentwood	TN	37027	**800-621-7746**	615-377-0377	615
American Commerce Insurance Co 3590 Twin Creeks Dr	Columbus	OH	43204	**800-848-2945**	614-272-6951	384-4
American Commercial Barge Lines Co 1701 E Market St	Jeffersonville	IN	47130	**800-457-6377**	812-288-0100	309
American Commercial Lines Inc 1701 E Market St	Jeffersonville	IN	47130	**800-457-6377**	812-288-0100	309
American Community Mutual Insurance Co 39201 Seven-Mile Rd	Livonia	MI	48152	**800-991-2642**	734-591-9000	384-2
American Conservative Union (ACU) 1007 Cameron St	Alexandria	VA	22314	**800-228-7345**	703-836-8602	48-7

Name / Address	City	State	ZIP	Toll-Free	Phone	Class
American Contact Lens Inc 15970 Bernardo Ctr	San Diego	CA	92127	**800-959-4448**	858-487-8684	531
American Contract Bridge League (ACBL) 2990 Airways Blvd *Sales	Memphis	TN	38116	**800-264-2743***	901-332-5586	48-18
American Converters Inc 5360 Main St NE	Fridley	MN	55421	**888-360-8050**	763-574-1044	590
American Correctional Assn (ACA) 4380 Forbes Blvd	Lanham	MD	20706	**800-222-5646**	301-918-1800	49-7
American Council of the Blind (ACB) 1155 15th St NW Suite 1004	Washington	DC	20005	**800-424-8666**	202-467-5081	48-17
American Council for Drug Education (ACDE) c/o Phoenix House 164 W 74th St	New York	NY	10023	**800-378-4435**	212-595-5810	48-17
American Council on Exercise (ACE) 4851 Paramount Dr	San Diego	CA	92123	**800-825-3636**	858-279-8227	48-17
American Council for Headache Education (ACHE) 19 Mantua Rd	Mount Royal	NJ	08061	**800-255-2243**	856-423-0258	48-17
American Council of Hypnotist Examiners 700 S Central Ave	Glendale	CA	91204	**800-894-9766**	818-242-1159	49-15
American Counseling Assn (ACA) 5999 Stevenson Ave	Alexandria	VA	22304	**800-347-6647**	703-823-9800	49-15
American Country Collection of Bed & Breakfast Homes 1353 Union St	Schenectady	NY	12308	**800-810-4948**	518-370-4948	368
American Court Motel 85 Merrimon Ave	Asheville	NC	28801	**800-233-3582**	828-253-4427	373
American Craft Council 72 Spring St 6th Fl	New York	NY	10012	**800-836-3470**	212-274-0630	48-4
American Crane & Equipment Corp 531 Old Swede Rd	Douglassville	PA	19518	**877-877-6778**	610-385-6061	462
American Cruise Lines 741 Boston Post Rd Suite 200	Guilford	CT	06437	**800-814-6880**	203-453-6800	218
American Culinary Federation Chef & Child Foundation 180 Center Place Way	Saint Augustine	FL	32095	**800-624-9458**	904-824-4468	48-6
American Culinary Federation Inc (ACF) 180 Sector Place Way	Saint Augustine	FL	32095	**800-624-9458**	904-824-4468	49-6
American Cutting Edge Inc 4455 Infirmary Rd	West Carrollton	OH	45449	**800-543-6860**	937-866-5986	484
American Dental Education Assn (ADEA) 1400 K St NW Suite 1100	Washington	DC	20005	**800-353-2237**	202-289-7201	49-5
American Dental Hygienists' Assn (ADHA) 444 N Michigan Ave Suite 3400	Chicago	IL	60611	**800-243-2342**	312-440-8900	49-8
American Dental Partners Inc 201 Edgewater Dr Suite 285 *NASDAQ: ADPI*	Wakefield	MA	01880	**877-252-7414**	781-224-0880	455
American Desk Mfg Co Inc PO Box 608	Temple	TX	76503	**800-433-3142**	254-778-1811	314-3
American Diabetes Assn (ADA) 1701 N Beauregard St	Alexandria	VA	22311	**800-232-3472**	703-549-1500	48-17
American Diagnostica Inc 500 West Ave	Stamford	CT	06902	**888-234-4435**	203-602-7777	229
American Dietetic Assn (ADA) 120 S Riverside Plaza Suite 2000	Chicago	IL	60606	**800-877-1600**	312-899-0040	49-8
American Distilling & Mfg Inc 31 E High St	East Hampton	CT	06424	**800-203-4444**	860-267-4444	470
American Drill Bushing Co 2000 Camfield Ave	Los Angeles	CA	90040	**800-423-4425**	323-725-1515	484
American Driving Records Inc 2860 Gold Tailings Ct	Rancho Cordova	CA	95670	**800-766-6877**	916-456-3200	621
American Dynamics Corp 6795 Flanders Dr	San Diego	CA	92121	**800-854-2057**	858-642-2400	681
American Eagle Federal Credit Union 417 Main St	East Hartford	CT	06118	**800-842-0145**	860-568-2020	216
American Eagle Outfitters 150 Thorn Hill Dr *NASDAQ: AEOS* ■ *Cust Svc	Warrendale	PA	15086	**888-232-4535***	724-776-4857	155-4
American Education Corp 7506 N Broadway Ext Suite 505 *Sales	Oklahoma City	OK	73116	**800-222-2811***	405-840-6031	176-3
American Educational Products Inc 401 W Hickory St PO Box 2121	Fort Collins	CO	80522	**800-446-8767**	970-484-7445	242
American Educational Products LLC Hubbard Scientific Div 401 Hickory St *Cust Svc	Fort Collins	CO	80522	**800-289-9299***	970-484-7445	242
American Educational Products LLC National Teaching Aids Div 401 Hickory St *Cust Svc	Fort Collins	CO	80522	**800-289-9299***	970-484-7445	242
American Educational Products LLC Scott Resources Div 401 Hickory St *Cust Svc	Fort Collins	CO	80522	**800-289-9299***	970-484-7445	242
American Educator Magazine 555 New Jersey Ave NW	Washington	DC	20001	**800-238-1133**	202-879-4400	449-8
American & Efird Inc PO Box 507	Mount Holly	NC	28120	**800-438-6781**	704-827-4311	730-9
American Electric Power Co Inc 1 Riverside Plaza *NYSE: AEP* ■ *Cust Svc	Columbus	OH	43215	**800-277-2177***	614-716-1000	355-5
American Electric Supply Inc 1872 W Pomona Rd	Corona	CA	92880	**800-877-8346**	951-734-7910	245
American Enterprise Institute for Public Policy Research (AEI) 1150 17th St NW Suite 1100	Washington	DC	20036	**800-862-5801**	202-862-5800	654
American Equity Investment Life Insurance Co 5000 Westown Pkwy Suite 440	West Des Moines	IA	50266	**888-221-1234**	515-221-0002	384-2
American Eurocopter Corp 2701 Forum Dr	Grand Prairie	TX	75052	**800-873-0001**	972-641-0000	21
American Excelsior Co PO Box 5067	Arlington	TX	76005	**800-777-7645**	817-640-1555	590
American Express Asset Management Group AXP Financial Ctr	Minneapolis	MN	55440	**800-328-8300**	612-671-3131	393
American Express Brokerage 70400 AXP Financial Ctr	Minneapolis	MN	55474	**800-297-7378**	612-671-3131	679
American Express Business Finance 390 N Sepulveda Blvd Suite 1000	El Segundo	CA	90245	**800-234-8975**	800-774-5855	214
American Express Centurion Bank 4315 S 2700 W	Salt Lake City	UT	84130	**888-356-1006**	801-945-3000	71
American Express Co Inc World Financial Ctr 200 Vesey St *NYSE: AXP*	New York	NY	10285	**800-666-1775**	212-640-2000	213
American Express Credit Corp 301 N Walnut St 1 Christina Centre Suite 1002	Wilmington	DE	19801	**800-525-5450**	302-594-3350	214
American Express Financial Advisors Inc AXP Financial Ctr	Minneapolis	MN	55440	**800-328-8300**	612-671-3131	393
American Express Financial Corp AXP Financial Ctr	Minneapolis	MN	55440	**800-328-8300**	612-671-3131	393
American Express Mutual Funds 70100 AXP Financial Ctr	Minneapolis	MN	55474	**800-328-8300**	612-671-3131	517
American Family Insurance Group 6000 American Pkwy	Madison	WI	53783	**800-374-0008**	608-249-2111	355-4
American Family Life Assurance Co of Columbus (AFLAC) 1932 Wynnton Rd	Columbus	GA	31999	**800-992-3522**	706-323-3431	384-2
American Family Life Insurance Co 6000 American Pkwy	Madison	WI	53783	**800-374-0008**	608-249-2111	384-2
American Family Mutual Insurance Co 6000 American Pkwy *Cust Svc	Madison	WI	53783	**800-374-0008***	608-249-2111	384-2
American Family Physician Magazine 11400 Tomahawk Creek Pkwy	Leawood	KS	66211	**800-274-2237**	913-906-6000	449-16
American Family Radio PO Drawer 2440	Tupelo	MS	38803	**800-326-4543**	662-844-8888	630
American Farmland Trust (AFT) 1200 18th St NW Suite 800	Washington	DC	20036	**800-431-1499**	202-331-7300	48-2
American Federation for Aging Research (AFAR) 70 W 40th St 11th Fl	New York	NY	10018	**888-582-2327**	212-703-9977	49-8
American Federation of Arts (AFA) 41 E 65th St	New York	NY	10021	**800-232-0270**	212-988-7700	48-4
American Federation of Astrologers (AFA) 6535 S Rural Rd	Tempe	AZ	85283	**888-301-7630**	480-838-1751	48-18
American Federation Insurance Co 25400 US Hwy 19 N Suite 185	Clearwater	FL	33763	**800-527-3907**	727-712-2115	384-4
American Federation of Musicians of the US & Canada (AFM) 1501 Broadway Suite 600	New York	NY	10036	**800-762-3444**	212-869-1330	405
American Federation of School Administrators (AFSA) 1729 21st St NW	Washington	DC	20009	**800-354-2372**	202-986-4209	49-5
American Federation of Teachers (AFT) 555 New Jersey Ave NW	Washington	DC	20001	**800-238-1133**	202-879-4400	405
American Federation of Teachers Committee on Political Education 555 New Jersey Ave NW	Washington	DC	20001	**800-238-1133**	202-879-4400	604
American Fence Assn (AFA) 800 Roosevelt Rd Bldg C-20	Glen Ellyn	IL	60137	**800-822-4342**	630-942-6598	49-3
American Fence Co 2502 N 27th Ave	Phoenix	AZ	85009	**888-691-4565**	602-734-0500	190-2
American Fidelity Assurance Co 2000 N Classen Blvd	Oklahoma City	OK	73106	**800-654-8489**	405-523-2000	384-2
American Fidelity Group 2000 N Classen Blvd	Oklahoma City	OK	73106	**800-654-8489**	405-523-2000	355-4
American Fire & Casualty Co 9450 Seward Rd	Fairfield	OH	45014	**800-843-6446**	513-867-3000	384-4
American Fitness Magazine 15250 Ventura Blvd Suite 200	Sherman Oaks	CA	91403	**800-446-2322**	818-905-0040	449-13
American Flight Group 1974 Baltimore Annapolis Blvd	Annapolis	MD	21401	**877-234-5387**	410-757-6329	14
American Floor Products Co Inc 7977 Cessna Ave	Gaithersburg	MD	20879	**800-342-0424**	301-987-0490	286
American Fluorescent Corp 2345 N Ernie Krueger Cir	Waukegan	IL	60087	**800-873-2326**	847-249-5970	431
American Foods Group Inc PO Box 8547	Green Bay	WI	54308	**800-345-0293**	920-437-6330	465
American Forage & Grassland Council (AFGC) PO Box 94	Georgetown	TX	78627	**800-944-2342**		48-2
American Foreign Service Assn 2101 'E' St NW	Washington	DC	20037	**800-704-2372**	202-338-4045	49-7
American Forest Foundation (AFF) 1111 19th St NW Suite 780	Washington	DC	20036	**888-889-4466**	202-463-2462	48-2
American Forest & Paper Assn (AF&PA) 1111 19th St NW Suite 800	Washington	DC	20036	**800-878-8878**	202-463-2700	48-2
American Forests 734 15th St NW Suite 800 PO Box 2000	Washington	DC	20013	**800-368-5748**	202-955-4500	48-13
American Forests Magazine 734 15th St NW Suite 800	Washington	DC	20005	**800-368-5748**	202-955-4500	449-19
American Foundation for AIDS Research (amfAR) 120 Wall St 13th Fl	New York	NY	10005	**800-392-6327**	212-806-1600	48-17
American Foundation for the Blind (AFB) 11 Penn Plaza Suite 300	New York	NY	10001	**800-232-5463**	212-502-7600	48-17
American Foundation for Suicide Prevention (AFSP) 120 Wall St 22nd Fl	New York	NY	10005	**888-333-2377**	212-363-3500	48-17
American Foundation for Urologic Disease (AFUD) 1000 Corporate Blvd Suite 410	Linthicum	MD	21090	**800-828-7866**	410-689-3990	48-17
American Founders Life Insurance Co PO Box 52121	Phoenix	AZ	85072	**800-531-5067**	480-425-5100	384-2
American Foundry Society (AFS) 1695 N Penny Ln	Schaumburg	IL	60173	**800-537-4237**	847-824-0181	49-13
American Frozen Foods Inc 155 Hill St	Milford	CT	06460	**800-233-5554**	203-882-6200	292-6
American Funds Group 135 S State College Blvd	Brea	CA	92821	**800-421-0180**	714-671-7000	517

				Toll-Free	Phone	Class
American Furniture Warehouse Co 8501 Grant St	Thornton	CO	80229	**800-992-7997**	303-289-3311	316
American Galvanizers Assn (AGA) 6881 S Holly Cir Suite 108	Centennial	CO	80112	**800-468-7732**	720-554-0900	49-13
American Gaming & Electronics 9500 W 55th St	McCook	IL	60525	**800-336-6630**	708-290-2100	317
American Gem Trade Assn (AGTA) 3030 LBJ Fwy Suite 840	Dallas	TX	75234	**800-972-1162**	214-742-4367	49-4
American General Financial Services 601 NW 2nd St	Evansville	IN	47701	**800-457-3741**	812-424-8031	215
American General Life & Accident Insurance Co 2000 American General Way	Brentwood	TN	37027	**800-888-2452**	615-749-1000	384-2
American General Life Insurance Co 2929 Allen Pkwy	Houston	TX	77019	**800-231-3655**	713-522-1111	384-2
American Geophysical Union (AGU) 2000 Florida Ave NW	Washington	DC	20009	**800-966-2481**	202-462-6900	49-19
American Golf Corp 2951 28th St	Santa Monica	CA	90405	**800-345-4259**	310-664-4000	641
American Gramaphone LLC 9130 Mormon Bridge Rd	Omaha	NE	68152	**800-348-3434**	402-457-4341	643
American Granby Inc 7645 Henry Clay Blvd	Liverpool	NY	13088	**800-776-2266**	315-451-1100	601
American Grandprix Assn (AGA) 1301 6th Ave W Suite 406	Bradenton	FL	34205	**800-237-8924**	941-744-5466	48-22
American Grease Stick Co 2651 Hoyt St	Muskegon Heights	MI	49444	**800-253-0403**	231-733-2101	530
American Greetings Corp 1 American Rd *NYSE: AM* ■ *Sales	Cleveland	OH	44144	**800-321-3040***	216-252-7300	130
American Greetings Corp Carlton Cards Div 1 American Rd *Sales	Cleveland	OH	44144	**800-321-3040***	216-252-7300	129
American Greetings Corp Learning Horizons Div 1 American Rd	Cleveland	OH	44144	**800-321-3040**	216-252-7300	242
American Grinding & Machine Co 2000 N Mango Ave	Chicago	IL	60639	**877-988-4343**	773-889-4343	446
American Group Psychotherapy Assn (AGPA) 25 E 21st St 6th Fl	New York	NY	10010	**877-668-2472**	212-477-2677	49-15
American Guidance Service Inc DBA AGS Publishing 4201 Woodland Rd	Circle Pines	MN	55014	**800-471-8457**	651-287-7220	242
American Guild of Musical Artists (AGMA) 1430 Broadway 14th Fl	New York	NY	10018	**800-543-2462**	212-265-3687	48-4
American Guild of Organists (AGO) 475 Riverside Dr Suite 1260	New York	NY	10115	**800-246-5115**	212-870-2310	48-4
American Gypsum Co 3811 Turtlecreek Blvd Suite 1200	Dallas	TX	75219	**800-545-6302**	214-530-5500	341
American Hagstrom Langenscheidt DBA Hagstrom Map 46-35 54th Rd	Maspeth	NY	11378	**800-432-6277**	718-784-0055	623-1
American Hardware Mutual Insurance Co PO Box 435	Minneapolis	MN	55440	**800-227-4663**	952-935-1400	384-4
American Health Care Assn (AHCA) 1201 L St NW	Washington	DC	20005	**800-321-0343**	202-842-4444	49-8
American Health Information Management Assn (AHIMA) 233 N Michigan Ave Suite 2150	Chicago	IL	60601	**800-335-5535**	312-233-1100	49-8
American Health & Life Insurance Co PO Box 1876	Fort Worth	TX	76101	**800-711-3454**	817-348-7573	384-2
American Health Products Corp 500 Park Blvd Suite 1260	Itasca	IL	60143	**800-828-2964**	630-285-9191	566
American Healthcare Radiology Administrators (AHRA) 490-B Boston Post Rd Suite 101	Sudbury	MA	01776	**800-334-2472**	978-443-7591	49-8
American Healthcare Specialty Insurance Co 1888 Century Pk E Suite 800	Los Angeles	CA	90067	**800-962-5549**	310-551-5900	384-5
American HealthNet 2110 S 169th Plaza	Omaha	NE	68130	**800-745-4712**	402-733-2700	176-11
American Healthways Inc 3841 Greenhills Village Dr Suite 300 *NASDAQ: AMHC*	Nashville	TN	37215	**800-327-3822**	615-665-1122	347
American Heart Assn (AHA) 7272 Greenville Ave	Dallas	TX	75231	**800-242-8721**	214-373-6300	48-17
American Heller Corp 15825 Leone Dr	Macomb	MI	48042	**800-950-2487**	586-677-2300	447
American Herbal Products 1440 JFK Causeway Suite 400	North Bay Village	FL	33141	**888-446-6884**	305-865-2919	237
American Heritage Life Insurance Co 1776 American Heritage Life Dr	Jacksonville	FL	32224	**800-521-3535**	904-992-1776	384-2
American Heritage Magazine 90 5th Ave	New York	NY	10011	**800-777-1222**	212-206-5500	449-11
American Hiking Society (AHS) 1422 Fenwick Ln	Silver Spring	MD	20910	**800-972-8608**	301-565-6704	48-23
American History Illustrated Magazine 6405 Flank Dr	Harrisburg	PA	17112	**800-829-3340**	717-657-9555	449-14
American Holistic Nurses' Assn (AHNA) 2733 E Lakin Dr Suite 2	Flagstaff	AZ	86004	**800-278-2462**	928-526-2196	48-17
American Home Base 428 Childers St	Pensacola	FL	32534	**800-422-4663**	850-857-0860	723
American Home Furnishings 3535 Menaul Blvd NE	Albuquerque	NM	87107	**800-876-4454**	505-883-2211	316
American Home Mortgage Investment Corp 520 Broadhollow Rd *NYSE: AHM*	Melville	NY	11747	**800-755-3100**	516-949-3900	498
American Home Shield 889 Ridge Lake Blvd	Memphis	TN	38120	**800-247-1644**	901-537-8000	687
American Homeowners Assn (AHA) 1100 Summer St 1st Fl *Cust Svc	Stamford	CT	06905	**800-470-2242***	203-323-7715	48-10
American Homeowners Foundation (AHF) 6776 Little Falls Rd	Arlington	VA	22213	**800-489-7776**	703-536-7776	49-17
American HomePatient Inc 5200 Maryland Way Suite 400	Brentwood	TN	37027	**800-890-7271**	615-221-8884	358
American Honda Motor Co Inc Acura Div 1919 Torrance Blvd	Torrance	CA	90501	**800-382-2238**	310-783-2000	59
American Horticultural Society (AHS) 7931 E Boulevard Dr	Alexandria	VA	22308	**800-777-7931**	703-768-5700	48-18
American Hose & Industrial Rubber Inc 2545 N Broad St	Philadelphia	PA	19132	**800-533-1134**	215-223-7710	364
American Hospital Assn (AHA) 1 N Franklin St	Chicago	IL	60606	**800-424-4301**	312-422-3000	49-8
American Hotel Register Co 100 S Milwaukee Ave	Vernon Hills	IL	60061	**800-323-5686**	847-743-3000	549
American Household Products Inc 8220 Dunnavant Rd SE PO Box 310	Leeds	AL	35094	**800-325-3895**	205-699-5144	596
American Humane Assn (AHA) 63 Inverness Dr E	Englewood	CO	80112	**800-227-4645**	303-792-9900	48-6
American Hunter Magazine 11250 Waples Mill Rd	Fairfax	VA	22030	**800-672-3888**	703-267-1300	449-20
American Identity 7500 W 110th St	Overland Park	KS	66210	**800-848-8028**	913-319-3100	10
American Imaging Management 40 Skokie Blvd Suite 500	Northbrook	IL	60062	**800-340-0010**	847-564-8500	455
American Income Life Insurance Co 1200 Wooded Acres	Waco	TX	76710	**800-433-3405**	254-772-3050	384-2
American Indian College of the Assemblies of God 10020 N 15th Ave	Phoenix	AZ	85021	**800-933-3828**	602-944-3335	163
American Indian College Fund 8333 Greenwood Blvd	Denver	CO	80221	**800-776-3863**	303-426-8900	48-11
American Indian Housing Council. National 900 2nd St NE Suite 305	Washington	DC	20002	**800-284-9165**	202-789-1754	49-7
American Ingredients Co 3947 Broadway	Kansas City	MO	64111	**800-669-4092**	816-561-9050	291-17
American Institute of Aeronautics & Astronautics (AIAA) 1801 Alexander Bell Dr Suite 500	Reston	VA	20191	**800-639-2422**	703-264-7500	49-19
American Institute of Architects (AIA) 1735 New York Ave NW *Orders	Washington	DC	20006	**800-365-2724***	202-626-7300	48-4
American Institute of Baking 1213 Bakers Way PO Box 3999	Manhattan	KS	66505	**800-633-5137**	785-537-4750	654
American Institute of Biological Sciences (AIBS) 1444 'I' St NW Suite 200	Washington	DC	20005	**800-992-2427**	202-628-1500	49-19
American Institute for Cancer Research 1759 R St NW	Washington	DC	20009	**800-843-8114**	202-328-7744	654
American Institute of Certified Public Accountants (AICPA) 1211 Ave of the Americas	New York	NY	10036	**888-777-7077**	212-596-6200	49-1
American Institute of Chemical Engineers (AIChE) 3 Park Ave *Cust Svc	New York	NY	10016	**800-242-4363***	212-591-7338	49-19
American Institute for CPCU & Insurance Institute of America (AICPCU/IIA) 720 Providence Rd PO Box 3016	Malvern	PA	19355	**800-644-2101**	610-644-2100	49-9
American Institute for Foreign Study (AIFS) 9 W Broad St	Stamford	CT	06902	**800-727-2437**	203-399-5000	48-11
American Institute of Graphic Arts (AIGA) 164 5th Ave	New York	NY	10010	**800-548-1634**	212-807-1990	48-4
American Institute of Professional Bookkeepers (AIPB) 6001 Montrose Rd Suite 500	Rockville	MD	20852	**800-622-0121**	301-770-7300	49-1
American Institute of Ultrasound in Medicine (AIUM) 14750 Sweitzer Ln Suite 100	Laurel	MD	20707	**800-638-5352**	301-498-4100	49-8
American Insulated Wire Corp 95 Grand Ave	Pawtucket	RI	02861	**800-366-2492**	401-726-0700	801
American InterContinental University *Atlanta* 3330 Peachtree Rd NE	Atlanta	GA	30326	**800-255-6839**	404-965-5700	163
Los Angeles 12655 W Jefferson Blvd	Los Angeles	CA	90066	**800-333-2652**	310-302-2000	163
American International Automobile Dealers Assn (AIADA) 211 N Union St Suite 300	Alexandria	VA	22314	**800-462-4232**	703-519-7800	49-18
American International College 1000 State St *Admissions	Springfield	MA	01109	**800-242-3142***	413-737-7000	163
American International Forest Products LLC 5560 SW 107th St	Beaverton	OR	97005	**800-366-1611**	503-641-1611	190-3
American Investors Life Insurance Co 555 S Kansas Ave	Topeka	KS	66603	**800-435-4884**	785-232-6945	384-2
American Isuzu Motors Inc 13340 183rd St *Cust Svc	Cerritos	CA	90702	**800-255-6727***	562-229-5000	59
American Jet Charter 5901 Philip J Rhoads Hanger 14 Wiley Post Airport	Bethany	OK	73008	**800-495-5453**	405-495-5453	14
American Jewish World Service (AJWS) 45 W 36th St 10th Fl	New York	NY	10018	**800-889-7146**	212-736-2597	48-5
American Journal of Nursing 345 Hudson St 16th Fl	New York	NY	10014	**800-777-2295**	212-886-1200	449-16
American Journal of Psychiatry 1000 Wilson Blvd Suite 1825	Arlington	VA	22209	**800-368-5777**	703-907-7300	449-16
American Journalism Review University of Maryland 1117 Journalism Bldg Room 2116	College Park	MD	20742	**800-827-0771**	301-405-8803	449-5
American Kidney Fund (AKF) 6110 Executive Blvd Suite 1010	Rockville	MD	20852	**800-638-8299**	301-881-3052	48-17
American Laboratories Inc 4410 S 102nd St *Cust Svc	Omaha	NE	68127	**800-445-5989***	402-339-2494	470
American LaFrance Corp 8500 Palmetto Commerce Pkwy	Lodson	SC	29456	**888-253-8725**	843-486-7400	505
American Land Lease Inc 29399 US 19 N Suite 320 *NYSE: ANL*	Clearwater	FL	33761	**800-826-6069**	727-726-8868	641
American Land Title Assn (ALTA) 1828 L St NW Suite 705	Washington	DC	20036	**800-787-2582**	202-296-3671	49-10
American Law Institute (ALI) 4025 Chestnut St	Philadelphia	PA	19104	**800-253-6397**	215-243-1600	49-10

Name / Address	City	State	Zip	Toll-Free	Phone	Class
American Law Label Inc 4135 S Pulaski Rd	Chicago	IL	60632	**800-529-5223**	773-523-2222	404
American Lawyer Magazine 345 Park Ave S	New York	NY	10010	**800-888-8300**	212-779-9200	449-15
American Lawyer Media Inc 345 Park Ave S 8th Fl	New York	NY	10010	**800-888-8300**	212-545-6000	623-9
American Leak Detection Inc 888 Research Dr Suite 100	Palm Springs	CA	92262	**800-755-6697**	760-320-9991	188-10
American Lebanese Syrian Associated Charities (ALSAC) 501 St Jude Pl	Memphis	TN	38105	**800-822-6344**	901-578-2000	48-5
American Lecithin Co Inc 115 Hurley Rd Unit 2B	Oxford	CT	06478	**800-364-4416**	203-262-7100	291-29
American Legion 700 N Pennsylvania St *Cust Svc	Indianapolis	IN	46204	**800-433-3318***	317-630-1200	48-19
American Leprosy Missions (ALM) 1 ALM Way	Greenville	SC	29601	**800-543-3135**	864-271-7040	48-5
American Libraries Magazine 50 E Huron St	Chicago	IL	60611	**800-545-2433**	312-944-6780	449-8
American Library Assn (ALA) 50 E Huron St	Chicago	IL	60611	**800-545-2433**	312-944-6780	49-11
American Licorice Co 3701 W 128th Pl	Alsip	IL	60803	**800-220-2399**	708-371-1414	291-8
American Life & Casualty Insurance Co 11815 N Pennsylvania St	Carmel	IN	46032	**800-544-0467**	317-817-6300	384-2
American Life Insurance Co 600 King St 1 ALICO Plaza	Wilmington	DE	19801	**800-441-7468**	302-594-2000	384-2
American Lifts 601 W McKee St	Greensburg	IN	47240	**800-426-9772**	812-663-4085	462
American Light 4401 Westgate Blvd Suite 310	Austin	TX	78745	**800-854-6465**	512-440-7985	245
American Lighting Assn (ALA) 2050 Stemmons Fwy Suite 10046	Dallas	TX	75342	**800-605-4448**	214-698-9898	49-4
American Liver Foundation (ALF) 75 Maiden Ln Suite 603	New York	NY	10038	**800-465-4837**	212-668-1000	48-17
American Locker Group Inc 608 Allen St *NASDAQ: ALGI*	Jamestown	NY	14701	**800-828-9118**	716-664-9600	665
American Locker Security Systems Inc 608 Allen St *Sales	Jamestown	NY	14701	**800-828-9118***	716-664-9600	665
American Louver Co 7700 Austin Ave	Skokie	IL	60077	**800-323-4250**	847-470-3300	431
American Lung Assn (ALA) 61 Broadway 6th Fl	New York	NY	10006	**800-586-4872**	212-315-8700	48-17
American Lyme Disease Foundation Inc (ALDF) 293 Rt 100	Somers	NY	10589	**800-876-5963**	914-277-6970	48-17
American Machine & Tool Co Inc 400 Spring St	Royersford	PA	19468	**888-268-7867**	610-948-3800	627
American Machine Tool Distributors' Assn (AMTDA) 1445 Research Blvd Suite 450	Rockville	MD	20850	**800-878-2683**	301-738-1200	49-18
American Management Assn (AMA) 1601 Broadway	New York	NY	10019	**800-262-9699**	212-586-8100	753
American Management Assn International Keye Productivity Center Div 600 AMA Way *Cust Svc	Saranac Lake	NY	12983	**800-262-9699***	518-891-1500	753
American Manufacturers Mutual Insurance Co 1 Kemper Dr	Long Grove	IL	60049	**800-833-0355**	847-320-2000	384-4
American Marketing Assn (AMA) 311 S Wacker Dr Suite 5800	Chicago	IL	60606	**800-262-1150**	312-542-9000	49-18
American Marking Systems Inc PO Box 1677	Clifton	NJ	07015	**800-782-6766**	973-478-5600	459
American Mat & Frame Co PO Box 2064	Morgan Hill	CA	95038	**800-537-0984**	408-778-1150	43
American Materials LLC PO Box 1246	Eau Claire	WI	54702	**866-421-7625**	715-835-2251	180
American Mathematical Society (AMS) 201 Charles St PO Box 6248 *Cust Svc	Providence	RI	02940	**800-321-4267***	401-455-4000	49-19
American Media Inc 1000 American Media Way	Boca Raton	FL	33464	**800-749-7733**	561-997-7733	623-9
American Medical Alert Corp 3265 Lawson Blvd *NASDAQ: AMAC*	Oceanside	NY	11572	**800-645-3244**	516-536-5850	565
American Medical Assn (AMA) 515 N State St	Chicago	IL	60610	**800-621-8335**	312-464-5000	49-8
American Medical Directors Assn (AMDA) 10480 Little Patuxent Pkwy Suite 760	Columbia	MD	21044	**800-876-2632**	410-740-9743	49-8
American Medical Laboratories Inc 14225 Newbrook Dr	Chantilly	VA	20153	**800-336-3718**	703-802-6900	409
American Medical Rehabilitation Providers Assn (AMRPA) 1710 'N' St NW	Washington	DC	20036	**888-346-4624**	202-223-1920	49-8
American Medical Response 6200 S Syracuse Way Suite 200	Greenwood Village	CO	80111	**800-375-0564**	303-614-8500	31
American Medical Security Group Inc 3100 AMS Blvd *NYSE: AMZ*	Green Bay	WI	54313	**800-232-5432**	920-661-1111	355-4
American Medical Student Assn (AMSA) 1902 Association Dr	Reston	VA	20191	**800-767-2266**	703-620-6600	49-5
American Medical Systems Holdings Inc 10700 Bren Rd W *NASDAQ: AMMD*	Minnetonka	MN	55343	**800-328-3881**	952-933-4666	469
American Medical Technologies Inc 5555 Bear Ln *NASDAQ: ADLI*	Corpus Christi	TX	78405	**800-440-0310**	361-289-1145	226
American Medical Technologists (AMT) 710 Higgins Rd	Park Ridge	IL	60068	**800-275-1268**	847-823-5169	49-8
American Megatrends Inc 6145-F Northbelt Pkwy	Norcross	GA	30071	**800-828-9264**	770-263-8181	174
American Mensa Ltd 1229 Corporate Dr W	Arlington	TX	76006	**800-666-3672**	817-607-0060	48-15
American Mental Health Counselors Assn (AMHCA) 801 N Fairfax St Suite 304	Alexandria	VA	22314	**800-326-2642**	703-548-6002	49-15
American Metal Bearing Co 7191 Acacia Ave	Garden Grove	CA	92841	**800-888-3048**	714-892-5527	609
American Metalcraft Inc 2074 George St	Melrose Park	IL	60160	**800-333-9133**	708-345-1177	479
American Meter Co 132 Welsh Rd Suite 140	Horsham	PA	19044	**888-295-7928**	215-830-1800	486
American Mortgage Express 3570 Camino Del Rio N Suite 300	San Diego	CA	92108	**800-700-0263**	619-521-3000	498
American Motorcyclist Assn (AMA) 13515 Yarmouth Dr	Pickerington	OH	43147	**800-262-5646**	614-856-1900	48-22
American Motorcyclist Magazine 13515 Yarmouth Dr	Pickerington	OH	43147	**800-262-5646**	614-856-1900	449-3
American Motorists Insurance Co 1 Kemper Dr	Long Grove	IL	60049	**800-833-0355**	847-320-2000	384-4
American Moulding & Millwork Co 2801 West Ln	Stockton	CA	95204	**800-441-8231**	209-946-5800	314-2
American Multi-Cinema Inc 920 Main St	Kansas City	MO	64105	**800-326-2432**	816-221-4000	733
American Musical Supply PO Box 152	Spicer	MN	56288	**800-458-4076**	320-796-2088	515
American National Bankshares Inc 628 Main St *NASDAQ: AMNB*	Danville	VA	24541	**800-240-8190**	434-792-5111	355-2
American National Insurance Co 1 Moody Plaza *NASDAQ: ANAT* ■ *Cust Svc	Galveston	TX	77550	**800-899-6806***	409-763-4661	384-2
American National Rubber Co Main & High St *Cust Svc	Ceredo	WV	25507	**800-624-3410***	304-453-1311	664
American Needle Inc 1275 Bush Pkwy	Buffalo Grove	IL	60089	**800-356-7589**	847-215-0011	153-9
American Nephrology Nurses' Assn (ANNA) 200 E Holly Ave	Pitman	NJ	08080	**888-600-2662**	856-256-2320	49-8
American Nickeloid Co 2900 W Main St	Peru	IL	61354	**800-645-5643**	815-223-0373	472
American Nonwovens Corp 221 Fabritek Dr	Columbus	MS	39702	**800-628-7961**	662-327-0745	34
American Nuclear Insurers (ANI) 95 Glastonbury Blvd	Glastonbury	CT	06033	**888-561-3433**	860-682-1301	49-9
American Nuclear Society (ANS) 555 N Kensington Ave	La Grange Park	IL	60526	**800-323-3044**	708-352-6611	49-19
American Numismatic Assn (ANA) 818 N Cascade Ave	Colorado Springs	CO	80903	**800-367-9723**	719-632-2646	48-18
American Numismatic Assn Money Museum 818 N Cascade Ave	Colorado Springs	CO	80903	**800-367-9723**	719-632-2646	509
American Nurse Magazine 600 Maryland Ave SW Suite 100W	Washington	DC	20024	**800-274-4262**	202-651-7000	449-16
American Nurse Newsletter 8515 Georgia Ave Suite 400	Silver Spring	MD	20910	**800-274-4262**	301-628-5000	521-2
American Nurses Assn (ANA) 8515 Georgia Ave Suite 400	Silver Spring	MD	20910	**800-274-4262**	301-628-5000	49-8
American Nutrition Inc 2890 Reeves Ave	Ogden	UT	84402	**800-257-4530**	801-394-3477	568
American Obesity Assn (AOA) 1250 24th St NW Suite 300	Washington	DC	20037	**800-986-2373**	202-776-7711	48-17
American Oil Chemists Society (AOCS) 2211 W Bradley Ave	Champaign	IL	61821	**800-336-2627**	217-359-2344	48-12
American ORT 817 Broadway 10th Fl	New York	NY	10003	**800-364-9678**	212-353-5800	48-5
American Orthodontics Corp 1714 Cambridge Ave	Sheboygan	WI	53081	**800-558-7687**	920-457-5051	226
American Orthopaedic Society for Sports Medicine (AOSSM) 6300 N River Rd Suite 500	Rosemont	IL	60018	**877-321-3500**	847-292-4900	49-8
American Osteopathic Assn (AOA) 142 E Ontario St	Chicago	IL	60611	**800-621-1773**	312-202-8000	49-8
American Packing & Gasket Co 6039 Armour Dr	Houston	TX	77020	**800-888-5223**	713-675-5271	321
American Pad & Paper Co LLC 3101 E George Bush Hwy Suite 200	Plano	TX	75082	**800-426-1368**		542-3
American Pallet Inc 1001 Knox Rd	Oakdale	CA	95361	**800-840-6122**	209-847-6122	541
American Panel Corp 5800 SE 78th St	Ocala	FL	34472	**800-327-3015**	352-245-7055	650
American Paper Recycling Corp 301 W Lake St *Cust Svc	Northlake	IL	60164	**800-762-6790***	708-344-6789	646
American Paper & Twine Co 7400 Cockrill Bend Blvd	Nashville	TN	37209	**800-251-2437**	615-350-9000	549
American Park 'n Swap 40 Fountain Plaza	Buffalo	NY	14202	**800-828-7240**	716-858-5185	267
American Park & Recreation Society (APRS) c/o National Recreation & Park Assn 22377 Belmont Ridge Rd	Ashburn	VA	20148	**800-626-6772**	703-858-4741	48-23
American Parkinson Disease Assn (APDA) 1250 Hyland Blvd Suite 4B	Staten Island	NY	10305	**800-223-2732**	718-981-8001	48-17
American Parkinson's Disease Assn Newsletter 1250 Hylan Blvd Suite 4B	Staten Island	NY	10305	**800-223-2732**	718-981-8001	521-8
American Payment Systems Inc 15 Sterling Dr PO Box 5044	Wallingford	CT	06492	**800-309-7668**	203-679-4400	254
American Performance Industries 109 McNeil Rd PO Box 250	Sanford	NC	27330	**800-438-3348**	919-775-7321	729
American Permanent Ware Inc 729 3rd Ave	Dallas	TX	75226	**800-527-2100**	214-421-7366	293
American Pet Products Manufacturers Assn (APPMA) 255 Glenville Rd	Greenwich	CT	06831	**800-452-1225**	203-532-0000	49-4
American Pharmaceutical Partners Inc 2020 Ruby St *NASDAQ: APPX*	Melrose Park	IL	60160	**800-888-7704**	708-345-6170	573
American Pharmacists Assn (APhA) 2215 Constitution Ave NW	Washington	DC	20037	**800-237-2742**	202-628-4410	49-8
American Pharmacists Assn PAC 2215 Constitution Ave NW	Washington	DC	20037	**800-237-2742**	202-628-4410	604
American Photo Magazine 1633 Broadway	New York	NY	10019	**800-274-4514**	212-767-6006	449-14
American Physical Therapy Assn (APTA) 1111 N Fairfax St	Alexandria	VA	22314	**800-999-2782**	703-684-2782	49-8
American Physicians Assurance Corp 1301 N Hagadorn Rd	East Lansing	MI	48823	**800-748-0465**	517-351-1150	384-4

Name / Address	City	State	ZIP	Toll-Free	Phone	Class
American Physicians Capital Inc (APCapital) 1301 N Hagadorn Rd	East Lansing	MI	48823	**800-748-0465**	517-351-1150	355-4
NASDAQ: ACAP						
American Physicians Insurance Exchange (API) 1301 S Capitol of Texas Hwy Suite C-300	Austin	TX	78746	**800-252-3628**	512-328-0888	384-5
American Physicians Service Group Inc 1301 Capitol of Texas Hwy S Suite C-300	Austin	TX	78746	**800-252-3628**	512-328-0888	355-4
NASDAQ: AMPH						
American PIE 316 Oak St PO Box 676	Northfield	MN	55057	**800-320-2743**	507-645-5613	48-13
American Pilots Assn 499 S Capitol St SW Suite 409	Washington	DC	20003	**800-527-4568**	202-484-0700	49-21
American Plastic Molding Corp 965 S Elm St	Scottsburg	IN	47170	**877-527-8427**	812-752-7000	593
American Plastic Toys Inc 799 Ladd Rd	Walled Lake	MI	48390	**800-521-7080**	248-624-4881	750
American Playground Corp 6406 Production Dr	Anderson	IN	46013	**800-541-1602**	765-642-0288	340
American Pneumatic Tool Inc 14710 S Maple Ave	Gardena	CA	90248	**800-532-7402**	310-538-2600	747
American Podiatric Medical Assn (APMA) 9312 Old Georgetown Rd	Bethesda	MD	20814	**800-275-2762**	301-571-9200	49-8
American Polarity Therapy Assn (APTA) PO Box 19858	Boulder	CO	80308	**800-359-5620**	303-545-2080	48-17
American Polywater Corp 5630 Memorial Ave Suite 2	Stillwater	MN	55082	**800-328-9384**	651-430-2270	530
American Poolplayers Assn (APA) 1000 Lake St Louis Blvd Suite 325	Lake Saint Louis	MO	63367	**800-372-2536**	636-625-8611	48-22
American Power Conversion Corp (APC) 132 Fairgrounds Rd	West Kingston	RI	02892	**800-788-2208***	401-789-5735	252
NASDAQ: APCC ■ *Cust Svc						
American Power Products Inc 5525 Brooks St	Montclair	CA	91763	**800-533-2929**	909-988-0819	429
American Power Pull Corp PO Box 109	Wauseon	OH	43567	**800-808-5922**	419-335-7050	462
American President Lines Ltd 1111 Broadway	Oakland	CA	94607	**800-999-7733**	510-272-8000	308
American Presidential Museum 3107 W Hwy 76	Branson	MO	65616	**866-334-8683**	417-334-8683	509
American Press 4900 Hwy 90 E	Lake Charles	LA	70615	**800-531-4080***	337-494-4000	522-2
*News Rm						
American Press LLC 1 American Pl	Gordonsville	VA	22942	**800-289-4602**	540-832-2253	615
American Printing House for the Blind 1839 Frankfort Ave PO Box 6085	Louisville	KY	40206	**800-223-1839**	502-895-2405	623-10
American Professional Practice Assn (APPA) 350 Fairway Dr Suite 200	Deerfield Beach	FL	33441	**800-221-2168**	954-571-1877	49-8
American Professional Services Inc 5350 S Western Ave Suite 500	Oklahoma City	OK	73109	**800-219-9120**	405-636-4222	392
American Professional Society on the Abuse of Children (APSAC) 107 Amberside Dr	Goose Creek	SC	29445	**877-402-7722**	843-764-2905	48-6
American Profile Magazine 341 Cool Springs Blvd Suite 400	Franklin	TN	37067	**800-720-6323**	615-468-6000	449-11
American Program Bureau Inc 36 Crafts St	Newton	MA	02458	**800-225-4575**	617-965-6600	699
American Progressive Life & Health Insurance Co of New York 6 International Dr Suite 190	Rye Brook	NY	10573	**800-332-3377**	914-934-8300	384-2
American Prostate Society 7188 Ridge Rd PO Box 870	Hanover	MD	21076	**800-308-1106**	410-859-3735	48-17
American Prosthodontic Society (APS) 426 Hudson St	Hackensack	NJ	07601	**877-499-3500**	201-440-7699	49-8
American Protection Insurance Co 1 Kemper Dr	Long Grove	IL	60049	**800-833-0355**	847-320-2000	384-4
American Proteins Inc 4705 Leland Dr	Cumming	GA	30041	**800-346-7476**	770-886-2250	438
American Psych Systems 8403 Colesville Rd Suite 1600	Silver Spring	MD	20910	**800-305-3720**	301-571-0633	454
American Psychiatric Assn (APA) 1000 Wilson Blvd Suite 1825	Arlington	VA	22209	**888-357-7924**	703-907-7300	49-15
American Psychological Assn (APA) 750 1st St NE	Washington	DC	20002	**800-374-2721**	202-336-5500	49-15
American Psychologist Magazine 750 1st St NE	Washington	DC	20002	**800-374-2721**	202-336-5500	449-16
American Public Communications Council Inc (APCC) 625 Slaters Ln Suite 104	Alexandria	VA	22314	**800-868-2722**	703-739-1322	49-20
American Public Gas Assn (APGA) 201 Massachusetts Ave NE Suite C-4	Washington	DC	20002	**800-927-4204**	202-464-2742	48-12
American Public Information on the Environment 316 Oak St PO Box 676	Northfield	MN	55057	**800-320-2743**	507-645-5613	48-13
American Public Media 45 7th St E	Saint Paul	MN	55101	**877-276-8400**	651-290-1225	630
American Qualex International Inc 920-A Calle Negocio	San Clemente	CA	92673	**800-772-1776**	949-492-8298	229
American Quality Products 9115-1 Dice Rd	Santa Fe Springs	CA	90670	**800-245-3737**	562-946-1616	99
American Quarter Horse Assn (AQHA) PO Box 200	Amarillo	TX	79168	**800-414-7433**	806-376-4811	48-3
American Quarter Horse Heritage Center & Museum 2601 I-40 E	Amarillo	TX	79104	**888-209-8322**	806-376-5181	509
American Quarter Horse Journal PO Box 200	Amarillo	TX	79168	**800-291-7323**	806-376-4811	449-1
American Racing Equipment Inc 19067 S Reyes Ave	Rancho Dominguez	CA	90221	**800-421-5800**	310-635-7806	60
American Railcar Industries Inc 100 Clark St	Saint Charles	MO	63301	**800-933-7937**	636-940-6000	636
American Re Corp 555 College Rd E	Princeton	NJ	08543	**800-255-5676**	609-243-4200	355-4
American Recreation Products Inc 1224 Fern Ridge Pkwy	Saint Louis	MO	63141	**800-325-4121**	314-576-8000	718
American Recycled Plastic Inc 1500 Main St	Palm Bay	FL	32905	**866-674-1525**	321-674-1525	647
American Red Ball International Inc 9750 3rd Ave NE Suite 200	Seattle	WA	98115	**800-669-6424**	206-526-1730	508
American Red Ball Transit Co Inc 1335 Sadlier Circle E Dr	Indianapolis	IN	46239	**800-733-8077**	317-353-8331	508
American Reeling Devices Inc 15 Airpark Vista Blvd	Dayton	NV	89403	**800-354-7335***	775-246-1000	118
*Sales						
American Refugee Committee (ARC) 430 Oak Grove St Suite 204	Minneapolis	MN	55403	**800-875-7060**	612-872-7060	48-5
American Registry of Diagnostic Medical Sonographers (ARDMS) 51 Monroe St Plaza East 1	Rockville	MD	20850	**800-541-9754**	301-738-8401	49-8
American Reinsurance Co 555 College Rd E	Princeton	NJ	08543	**800-255-5676**	609-243-4200	384-4
American Religious Town Hall Inc 745 N Buckner Blvd	Dallas	TX	75218	**800-783-9828**	214-328-9828	442
American Rental Assn (ARA) 1900 19th St	Moline	IL	61265	**800-334-2177**	309-764-2475	49-4
American Republic Insurance Co 601 6th Ave	Des Moines	IA	50309	**800-247-2190**	515-245-2000	384-2
American Research Corp 602 Monterey Pass Rd	Monterey Park	CA	91754	**888-462-3899**	626-284-1904	174
American Retirement Corp 111 Westwood Pl Suite 200	Brentwood	TN	37027	**888-221-7317**	615-221-2250	659
NYSE: ACR						
American Ribbon & Toner Co 2895 W Prospect Rd	Fort Lauderdale	FL	33309	**800-327-1013**	954-733-4552	616
American Rifleman Magazine 11250 Waples Mill Rd	Fairfax	VA	22030	**800-672-3888**	703-267-1379	449-20
American River Transportation Co 4666 E Faries Pkwy	Decatur	IL	62526	**800-637-5824**	217-424-5200	309
American Rivers 1025 Vermont Ave NW Suite 720	Washington	DC	20005	**800-296-6900**	202-347-7550	48-13
American Rivers Cruise Lines 2101 4th Ave Suite 2200	Seattle	WA	98121	**800-901-9152**	206-388-0444	218
American Road Insurance Co 4 Park Ln Blvd Suite 460	Dearborn	MI	48126	**800-234-2722**	313-845-5850	384-4
American Roentgen Ray Society (ARRS) 44211 Slatestone Ct	Leesburg	VA	20176	**800-438-2777**	703-729-3353	49-8
American Rose Society (ARS) 8877 Jefferson Paige Rd	Shreveport	LA	71119	**800-637-6534**	318-938-5402	48-18
American Royal Assn 1701 American Royal Ct	Kansas City	MO	64102	**800-821-5857**	816-221-9800	48-2
American Royal Museum & Visitors Center 1701 American Royal Ct	Kansas City	MO	64102	**800-821-5857**	816-221-9800	509
American Rubber Products Corp 315 Brighton St	La Porte	IN	46350	**800-348-8842**	219-326-1315	60
American Running Assn 4405 East-West Hwy Suite 405	Bethesda	MD	20814	**800-776-2732**	301-913-9517	48-22
American Saddlebred Museum 4083 Iron Works Pkwy	Lexington	KY	40511	**800-829-4438**	859-259-2746	509
American Safari Cruises Inc 19221 36th Ave W Suite 208	Lynnwood	WA	98036	**888-862-8881**	425-776-4700	217
American Safety Razor Co 1 Razor Blade Ln	Verona	VA	24482	**800-445-9284**	540-248-8000	211
American Safety Technologies Inc 565 Eagle Rock Ave	Roseland	NJ	07068	**800-631-7841**	973-403-2600	540
American Salon Magazine 1 Park Ave 2nd Fl	New York	NY	10016	**800-342-8244**	212-951-6600	449-21
American Sanitary Inc (AmSan) 3 Parkway N Suite 120 N	Deerfield	IL	60015	**888-468-1555**	847-607-2300	398
American Savings Bank FSB 915 Fort St	Honolulu	HI	96804	**800-272-2566**	808-531-6262	71
American Scholar Magazine 1606 New Hampshire Ave NW	Washington	DC	20009	**800-821-4567**	202-265-3808	449-10
American School Counselor Assn (ASCA) 1101 King St Suite 625	Alexandria	VA	22314	**800-306-4722**	703-683-2722	49-5
American School Health Assn (ASHA) 7263 State Rt 43 PO Box 708	Kent	OH	44240	**800-445-2742**	330-678-1601	49-5
American Science & Engineering Inc 829 Middlesex Tpke	Billerica	MA	01821	**800-225-1608**	978-262-8700	681
NASDAQ: ASEI						
American Scientist Magazine PO Box 13975	Research Triangle Park	NC	27709	**800-282-0444**	919-549-0097	449-19
American Seafoods Holdings LLC 2025 1st Ave Suite 900	Seattle	WA	98121	**800-275-2019**	206-448-0300	280
AMEX: SEA						
American Seafoods International 40 Herman Melville Blvd	New Bedford	MA	02740	**800-343-8046**	508-997-0031	291-14
American Seating Co 401 American Seating Ctr	Grand Rapids	MI	49504	**800-748-0268***	616-732-6600	314-3
*Cust Svc						
American Security Products Inc 11925 Pacific Ave	Fontana	CA	92337	**800-421-6142**	951-685-9680	665
American Seed Trade Assn (ASTA) 225 Reinekers Ln Suite 650	Alexandria	VA	22314	**888-890-7333**	703-837-8140	48-2
American Seminar Leaders Assn (ASLA) 2405 E Washington Blvd	Pasadena	CA	91104	**800-735-0511**	626-791-1211	49-12
American Senior Fitness Assn (SFA) PO Box 2575	New Smyrna Beach	FL	32170	**800-243-1478**	386-423-6634	48-6
American Shared Hospital Services 4 Embarcadero Ctr Suite 3700	San Francisco	CA	94111	**800-735-0641**	415-788-5300	261-5
AMEX: AMS						
American SIDS Institute 509 Augusta Dr	Marietta	GA	30067	**800-232-7437**	770-426-8746	48-6
American Skandia PO Box 8012	Boston	MA	02266	**800-752-6342**		517
American Small Businesses Assn (ASBA) 206 E College St Suite 201B	Grapevine	TX	76051	**800-942-2722**	817-488-8770	49-12
American Social Health Assn (ASHA) PO Box 13827	Research Triangle Park	NC	27709	**800-277-8922**	919-361-8400	48-17
American Society for Aesthetic Plastic Surgery (ASAPS) 11081 Winners Cir	Los Alamitos	CA	90720	**800-364-2147**	562-799-2356	49-8

Name	Address	City	State	ZIP	Toll-Free	Phone	Class
American Society on Aging (ASA)	833 Market St Suite 511	San Francisco	CA	94103	**800-537-9728**	415-974-9600	48-6
American Society of Agricultural Engineers (ASAE)	2950 Niles Rd *Orders	Saint Joseph	MI	49085	**800-695-2723***	269-429-0300	48-2
American Society of Appraisers (ASA)	555 Herndon Pkwy Suite 125	Herndon	VA	20170	**800-272-8258**	703-478-2228	49-17
American Society of Association Executives (ASAE)	1575 'I' St NW	Washington	DC	20005	**888-950-2723**	202-626-2723	49-12
American Society of Cataract & Refractive Surgery (ASCRS)	4000 Legato Rd Suite 850	Fairfax	VA	22033	**800-451-1339**	703-591-2220	49-8
American Society of Cinematographers (ASC)	1782 N Orange Dr	Hollywood	CA	90028	**800-448-0145**	323-969-4333	48-4
American Society for Clinical Investigation (ASCI)	35 Research Dr Suite 300	Ann Arbor	MI	48103	**866-660-2724**	734-222-6050	49-8
American Society of Clinical Oncology (ASCO)	1900 Duke St Suite 200	Alexandria	VA	22314	**888-282-2552**	703-299-0150	49-8
American Society for Clinical Pathology (ASCP)	2100 W Harrison St *Cust Svc	Chicago	IL	60612	**800-621-4142***	312-738-1336	49-8
American Society for Colposcopy & Cervical Pathology (ASCCP)	20 W Washington St Suite 1	Hagerstown	MD	21740	**800-787-7227**	301-733-3640	49-8
American Society of Composers Authors & Publishers (ASCAP)	1 Lincoln Plaza	New York	NY	10023	**800-952-7227**	212-621-6000	48-4
American Society of Consultant Pharmacists (ASCP)	1321 Duke St	Alexandria	VA	22314	**800-355-2727**	703-739-1300	49-8
American Society of Contemporary Medicine Surgery & Ophthalmology	820 N Orleans St Suite 208	Chicago	IL	60610	**800-621-4002**	312-440-0699	49-8
American Society of Heating Refrigerating & Air-Conditioning Engineers Inc (ASHRAE)	1791 Tullie Cir NE *Cust Svc	Atlanta	GA	30329	**800-527-4723***	404-636-8400	49-3
American Society of Home Inspectors (ASHI)	932 Lee St Suite 101	Des Plaines	IL	60016	**800-743-2744**	847-759-2820	49-3
American Society of Human Genetics (ASHG)	9650 Rockville Pike	Bethesda	MD	20814	**866-486-4363**	301-571-1825	49-19
American Society of Landscape Architects (ASLA)	636 'I' St NW	Washington	DC	20001	**800-787-2752**	202-898-2444	48-2
American Society of Limnology & Oceanography (ASLO)	5400 Bosque Blvd Suite 680	Waco	TX	76710	**800-929-2756**	254-399-9635	49-19
American Society of Mechanical Engineers (ASME)	3 Park Ave *Cust Svc	New York	NY	10016	**800-843-2763***	212-591-7722	49-19
American Society of Military Comptrollers (ASMC)	415 N Alfred	Alexandria	VA	22314	**800-462-5637**	703-549-0360	48-19
American Society for Nondestructive Testing Inc (ASNT)	1711 Arlingate Ln *Orders	Columbus	OH	43228	**800-222-2768***	614-274-6003	49-19
American Society for Parenteral & Enteral Nutrition (ASPEN)	8630 Fenton St Suite 412	Silver Spring	MD	20910	**800-727-4567**	301-587-6315	49-8
American Society of PeriAnesthesia Nurses (ASPAN)	10 Melrose Ave Suite 110	Cherry Hill	NJ	08003	**877-737-9696**	856-616-9600	49-8
American Society for Photobiology (ASP)	810 E 10th St	Lawrence	KS	66044	**800-627-0629**	785-843-1235	49-19
American Society of Plastic Surgeons (ASPS)	444 E Algonquin Rd	Arlington Heights	IL	60005	**888-475-2784**	847-228-9900	49-8
American Society of Professional Estimators (ASPE)	2525 Perimeter Place Dr Suite 102	Nashville	TN	37214	**888-378-6283**	615-316-9200	49-3
American Society for Quality (ASQ)	600 N Plankinton Ave	Milwaukee	WI	53201	**800-248-1946**	414-272-8575	49-13
American Society of Radiologic Technologists (ASRT)	15000 Central Ave SE	Albuquerque	NM	87123	**800-444-2778**	505-298-4500	49-8
American Society for Surgery of the Hand (ASSH)	6300 N River Rd Suite 600	Rosemont	IL	60018	**888-576-2774**	847-384-8300	49-8
American Society for Therapeutic Radiology & Oncology (ASTRO)	12500 Fair Lakes Cir Suite 375	Fairfax	VA	22033	**800-962-7876**	703-502-1550	49-8
American Society for Training & Development (ASTD)	1640 King St Box 1443	Alexandria	VA	22313	**800-628-2783**	703-683-8100	49-5
American Society of Travel Agents (ASTA)	1101 King St Suite 200	Alexandria	VA	22314	**800-440-2782**	703-739-2782	48-23
American Society of Travel Agents PAC	1101 King St Suite 200	Alexandria	VA	22314	**800-275-2782**	703-739-2782	604
American Software Inc	470 E Paces Ferry Rd *NASDAQ: AMSWA*	Atlanta	GA	30305	**800-726-2946**	404-261-4381	176-1
American Solenoid Co Inc	760 New Brunswick Rd	Somerset	NJ	08873	**800-526-3966**	732-560-1240	715
American Solutions for Business	31 E Minnesota Ave	Glenwood	MN	56334	**800-862-3690**	320-634-5471	523
American Southern Insurance Co	3715 Northside Pkwy NW Bldg 400 8th Fl	Atlanta	GA	30327	**800-241-1172**	404-266-9599	384-4
American Soybean Assn (ASA)	12125 Woodcrest Executive Dr Suite 100	Saint Louis	MO	63141	**800-688-7692**	314-576-1770	48-2
American Spectator Magazine	1611 N Kent St Suite 901	Arlington	VA	22209	**800-524-3469**	703-807-2011	449-17
American Speech-Language-Hearing Assn (ASHA)	10801 Rockville Pike	Rockville	MD	20852	**800-498-2071**	301-897-5700	49-8
American Speech-Language-Hearing Assn PAC	10801 Rockville Pike	Rockville	MD	20852	**800-638-8255**	301-897-5700	604
American Spoon Foods Inc	1668 Clarion Ave	Petoskey	MI	49770	**800-222-5886**	231-347-9030	291-20
American Sporting Goods Corp	2323 Main St	Irvine	CA	92614	**800-848-8698**	949-752-6688	296
American Sports	74 Albe Dr Suite 1	Newark	DE	19702	**800-977-6786**	302-369-9480	701
American Sports Nutrition Inc	1501 E Main St	Meriden	CT	06450	**888-462-5671**	203-639-8189	786
American Square Dance Magazine	34 E Main St	Apopka	FL	32703	**888-588-2362**	407-886-7151	449-14
American Stair Corp Inc	642 Forestwood Dr	Romeoville	IL	60446	**800-872-7824**	815-886-9600	482
American Standard Building Systems Inc	PO Box 4908	Martinsville	VA	24115	**800-888-4908**	276-638-3991	107
American Standard Cos Inc	1 Centennial Ave *NYSE: ASD*	Piscataway	NJ	08854	**800-223-0068**	732-980-6000	355-3
American Standard Inc	1 Centennial Ave PO Box 6820	Piscataway	NJ	08855	**800-223-0068**	732-980-6000	598
American Standard Insurance Co of Wisconsin	6000 American Pkwy	Madison	WI	53783	**800-374-0008**	608-249-2111	384-2
American Standards Testing Bureau Inc	PO Box 583	New York	NY	10274	**800-221-5170**	212-943-3160	728
American Star Cork Co	33-53 62nd St	Woodside	NY	11377	**800-338-3581**	718-335-3000	208
American States Water Co	630 E Foothill Blvd *NYSE: AWR*	San Dimas	CA	91773	**800-999-4033**	909-394-3600	774
American Stationery Co Inc	100 N Park Ave *Sales	Peru	IN	46970	**800-822-2577***	765-473-4438	615
American Statistical Assn (ASA)	1429 Duke St	Alexandria	VA	22314	**888-231-3473**	703-684-1221	49-19
American Statistician	1429 Duke St	Alexandria	VA	22314	**888-231-3473**	703-684-1221	449-5
American Steel Building Co Inc	12218 Robin Blvd	Houston	TX	77045	**800-877-8335**	713-433-5661	106
American Steel LLC	4033 NW Yeon Ave	Portland	OR	97210	**800-547-9032**	503-226-1511	483
American Stock Exchange (AMEX)	86 Trinity Pl	New York	NY	10006	**800-843-2639**	212-306-1000	680
American Strip Steel Inc	55 Passaic Ave	Kearny	NJ	07032	**800-526-1216**	201-991-1500	483
American Student List LLC	330 Old Country Rd	Mineola	NY	11501	**888-462-5600**	516-248-6100	5
American Swedish Institute	2600 Park Ave *Sales	Minneapolis	MN	55407	**800-579-3336***	612-871-4907	509
American Synthetic Rubber Corp	PO Box 32960 *Cust Svc	Louisville	KY	40232	**800-262-9253***	502-449-8300	594-3
American Systems Corp	13990 Parkeast Cir	Chantilly	VA	20151	**800-733-2721**	703-968-6300	178
American Teacher Magazine	555 New Jersey Ave NW	Washington	DC	20001	**800-238-1133**	202-879-4400	449-8
American Technical Publishers Inc	1155 W 175th St	Homewood	IL	60430	**800-323-3471**	708-957-1100	623-11
American Technology Corp	13114 Evening Creek Dr S *NASDAQ: ATCO*	San Diego	CA	92128	**800-417-2346**	858-679-2114	245
American Textile Co	10 N Linden St *Cust Svc	Duquesne	PA	15110	**800-289-2826***	412-948-1020	731
American Theological Library Assn (ATLA)	250 S Wacker Dr Suite 1600	Chicago	IL	60606	**888-665-2852**	312-454-5100	48-20
American Thermoplastic Co	106 Gamma Dr	Pittsburgh	PA	15238	**800-245-6600**	412-967-0900	87
American Thermoplastic Extrusion Co	4851 NW 128th Street Rd	Opa Locka	FL	33054	**800-426-9605**	305-769-9566	588
American Tinnitus Assn (ATA)	65 SW Yamhill	Portland	OR	97205	**800-634-8978**	503-248-9985	48-17
American Tire Distributors Inc	12200 Herbert Wayne Ct Suite 150	Huntersville	NC	28078	**800-277-8473**	704-992-2000	740
American Tissue Corp	80 Orville Dr	Bohemia	NY	11716	**800-282-7922**	631-435-9000	548-2
American Tower Corp	116 Huntington Ave 11th Fl *NYSE: AMT*	Boston	MA	02116	**877-282-7483**	617-375-7500	168
American Tract Society (ATS)	1624 N 1st St	Garland	TX	75040	**800-548-7228**	972-276-9408	48-20
American Traffic Safety Services Assn (ATSSA)	15 Riverside Pkwy Suite 100	Fredericksburg	VA	22406	**800-272-8772**	540-368-1701	49-21
American Trails West	92 Middle Neck Rd	Great Neck	NY	11021	**800-645-6260**	516-487-2800	748
American Transparent Plastics Corp	180 National Rd *Orders	Edison	NJ	08817	**800-942-8725***	732-287-3000	538
American Trauma Society	8903 Presidential Pkwy Suite 512	Upper Marlboro	MD	20772	**800-556-7890**	301-420-4189	49-8
American Trucker Magazine	7355 N Woodland Dr	Indianapolis	IN	46278	**800-827-7468**	317-297-5500	449-21
American Trucking Assns (ATA)	2200 Mill Rd	Alexandria	VA	22314	**800-282-5463**	703-838-1700	49-21
American Type Culture Collection (ATCC)	10801 University Blvd PO Box 1549	Manassas	VA	20108	**800-638-6597**	703-365-2700	654
American United Life Insurance Co	PO Box 368	Indianapolis	IN	46206	**800-537-6442**	317-285-1877	384-2
American Urological Assn (AUA)	1000 Corporate Blvd	Linthicum	MD	21090	**866-746-4282**	410-689-3700	49-8
American Vending Sales Inc	750 Morse Ave	Elk Grove Village	IL	60007	**800-441-0009**	847-439-9400	55
American Viatical Services	280 Heritage Walk	Woodstock	GA	30188	**800-699-5326**	770-926-8880	783

Name / Address	City	State	ZIP	Toll-Free	Phone	Class
American Volkssport Assn (AVA) 1001 Pat Booker Rd Suite 101	Universal City	TX	78148	**800-830-9255**	210-659-2112	48-22
American Watchmakers-Clockmakers Institute (AWI) 701 Enterprise Dr	Harrison	OH	45030	**866-367-2924**	513-367-9800	49-4
American Water Ski Hall of Fame & Museum 1251 Holy Cow Rd	Polk City	FL	33868	**800-533-2972**	863-324-2472	511
American Water Works Assn (AWWA) 6666 W Quincy Ave	Denver	CO	80235	**800-926-7337**	303-794-7711	48-12
American Watercraft Assn PO Box 1993	Ashburn	VA	20147	**800-913-2921**		48-22
American Way. People for the 2000 M St NW Suite 400	Washington	DC	20036	**800-326-7329**	202-467-4999	48-7
American Welding Society (AWS) 550 NW Le Jeune Rd	Miami	FL	33126	**800-443-9353**	305-443-9353	49-3
American Welding & Tank Co PO Box 8870	Camp Hill	PA	17001	**800-445-6709**	717-763-5080	92
American West Steamboat Co 2101 4th Ave Suite 1150	Seattle	WA	98121	**800-434-1232**	206-292-9606	218
American West Trading Co 1751 Alpine Dr	Clarksville	TN	37040	**800-340-4466**	931-645-4466	296
American Whirlpool Products Corp 3050 N 29th Ct	Hollywood	FL	33020	**800-327-1394**	954-921-4400	367
American Whitewater (AW) 1424 Fenwick Ln	Silver Spring	MD	20910	**866-262-8429**	301-589-9453	48-23
American WholeHealth Networks Inc 45999 Ctr Oak Plaza Suite 100	Sterling	VA	20166	**800-274-7526**	703-547-5100	384-3
American Wholesale Marketers Assn (AWMA) 2750 Prosperity Ave Suite 550	Fairfax	VA	22031	**800-482-2962**	703-208-3358	49-18
American Woman's Society of Certified Public Accountants (AWSCPA) 136 S Keowee St	Dayton	OH	45402	**800-297-2721**	937-222-1872	49-1
American Woodmark Corp 3102 Shawnee Dr *NASDAQ: AMWD*	Winchester	VA	22601	**800-677-8182**	540-665-9100	116
American Youth Soccer Organization (AYSO) 12501 S Isis Ave *Cust Svc	Hawthorne	CA	90250	**800-872-2976***	310-643-6455	48-22
Americana Tickets NY 115 W 45th St 8th Fl	New York	NY	10036	**800-833-3121**	212-581-6660	735
AmericanChurch Div AmericanPaper Group Inc PO Box 3132	Youngstown	OH	44513	**800-250-7112**	330-758-4545	260
AmericanGreetings.com Inc 1 American Rd	Cleveland	OH	44144	**888-749-5884**	216-889-5000	129
Americanna Co 29 Aldrin Rd *Cust Svc	Plymouth	MA	02360	**888-747-5550***	508-747-5550	10
Americano Beach Resort 1260 N Atlantic Ave	Daytona Beach	FL	32118	**800-874-1824**	386-255-7431	373
AmericanPaper Group Inc PO Box 3120	Youngstown	OH	44513	**800-431-4134**	330-758-4545	260
AmericanPaper Group Inc AmericanChurch Div PO Box 3132	Youngstown	OH	44513	**800-250-7112**	330-758-4545	260
AmericanPaper Group Inc AmericanPaper Products Co Div 8401 Southern Blvd	Youngstown	OH	44512	**800-431-4134**	330-758-4545	260
AmericanPaper Products Co Div AmericanPaper Group Inc 8401 Southern Blvd	Youngstown	OH	44512	**800-431-4134**	330-758-4545	260
Americans for Democratic Action (ADA) 1625 K St NW Suite 210	Washington	DC	20006	**800-787-2734**	202-785-5980	48-7
Americans for Effective Law Enforcement (AELE) 841 W Touhy Ave	Park Ridge	IL	60068	**800-763-2802**	847-685-0700	48-8
Americans for Fair Taxation PO Box 27487	Houston	TX	77227	**800-324-7829**	713-963-9023	48-7
Americans United for Separation of Church & State 518 C St NE	Washington	DC	20002	**800-875-3707**	202-466-3234	48-7
Americans with Disabilities Act Information 950 Pennsylvania Ave NW	Washington	DC	20530	**800-514-0301**		336-10
AmericanTours International Inc (ATI) 6053 W Century Blvd	Los Angeles	CA	90045	**800-800-8942**	310-641-9953	748
AmeriCares Foundation 88 Hamilton Ave	Stamford	CT	06902	**800-486-4357**	203-658-9500	48-5
America's Best Contacts & Eyeglasses 7255 N Crescent Blvd	Pennsauken	NJ	08110	**800-896-7247**	856-486-4300	533
America's Blood Centers (ABC) 725 15th St NW Suite 700	Washington	DC	20005	**888-872-5663**	202-393-5725	49-8
America's Car-Mart Inc 1501 SE Walton Blvd Suite 213 *NASDAQ: CRMT*	Bentonville	AR	72712	**800-264-2535**	479-464-9944	57
America's Cash Express 1231 Greenway Dr Suite 800 *NASDAQ: AACE* ■ *Sales	Irving	TX	75038	**800-713-3338***	972-550-5000	139
America's Catch Inc PO Box 584	Itta Bena	MS	38941	**800-242-0041**	662-254-7207	291-14
Americas. Council of the 680 Park Ave	New York	NY	10021	**800-733-2342**	212-628-3200	48-7
America's Double Seal Ring Co 2065 Montgomery St	Fort Worth	TX	76107	**800-397-7777**	817-738-6581	128
America's Health Insurance Plans (AHIP) 601 Pennsylvania Ave NW Suite 500 *Cust Svc	Washington	DC	20004	**877-291-2247***	202-778-3200	49-9
America's Hobby Center Inc 8300 Tonnelle Ave	North Bergen	NJ	07047	**800-242-1931**	201-662-8500	451
Americas. Partners of the 1424 K St NW Suite 700	Washington	DC	20005	**800-322-7844**	202-628-3300	48-5
America's Promise - The Alliance for Youth 909 N Washington St Suite 400	Alexandria	VA	22314	**800-365-0153**	703-684-4500	48-6
America's Second Harvest 35 E Wacker Dr Suite 2000	Chicago	IL	60601	**800-771-2303**	312-263-2303	48-5
AmericasMart 240 Peachtree St NW Suite 2200	Atlanta	GA	30303	**800-285-6278**	404-220-2659	204
Americast Div Valley Blox Inc 11352 Virginia Precast Rd	Ashland	VA	23005	**800-999-2279**	804-798-6068	181

Name / Address	City	State	ZIP	Toll-Free	Phone	Class
Americh Corp 13212 Saticoy St	North Hollywood	CA	91605	**800-453-1463**	818-982-1711	367
Americhem Inc 225 Broadway St E	Cuyahoga Falls	OH	44221	**800-228-3476**	330-929-4213	141
AmericInn International LLC 250 Lake Dr E	Chanhassen	MN	55317	**800-634-3444**	952-294-5000	369
Americo Financial Life & Annuity Insurance Co PO Box 410288 *Cust Svc	Kansas City	MO	64141	**800-366-6565***	816-391-2000	384-2
Americo Life Inc 1055 Broadway	Kansas City	MO	64105	**800-982-8144**	816-391-2000	355-4
AmeriCom Inc 870 E 9400 S	Sandy	UT	84094	**800-820-6296**	801-571-2446	721
Americomm Direct Marketing 1065 Bristol Rd	Mountainside	NJ	07092	**888-737-5478**	908-232-3800	5
AmeriCorps USA 1201 New York Ave NW 8th Fl	Washington	DC	20525	**800-942-2677**	202-606-5000	336-16
AmeriCredit Corp 801 Cherry St Suite 3900 *NYSE: ACF*	Fort Worth	TX	76102	**800-937-3635**	817-302-7000	215
Americus Dental Lab Inc 150-15 Hillside Ave	Jamaica	NY	11432	**888-263-7428**	718-658-6655	406
Americus Times-Recorder 101 Hwy 27 E	Americus	GA	31709	**800-924-2751**	229-924-2751	522-2
AmeriFactors 215 Celebration Pl Suite 150	Celebration	FL	34747	**800-884-3863**	407-566-1150	268
Ameriflight Inc 4700 Empire Ave Hangar 1	Burbank	CA	91505	**800-800-4538**	818-980-5005	13
Amerifresh 4025 Delridge Way SW Suite 550	Seattle	WA	98106	**800-568-3235**	206-933-4900	292-7
AMERIGROUP Corp 4425 Corporation Ln *NYSE: AGP*	Virginia Beach	VA	23462	**800-600-4441**	757-490-6900	384-3
AmeriHost Franchise Systems Inc 1 Sylvan Way	Parsippany	NJ	07054	**800-889-8847**	973-428-9700	369
Amerijet International Inc 2800 S Andrews Ave	Fort Lauderdale	FL	33316	**800-786-6944**	954-359-0077	13
Amerilink LLC 2 Easton Oval Suite 500	Columbus	OH	43219	**800-669-8765**	614-479-2500	633
Amerimax Building Products Inc 5208 Tennyson Pkwy Suite 100	Plano	TX	75024	**800-258-6295**	469-366-3200	471
Amerimax Home Products Inc 450 Richardson Dr	Lancaster	PA	17603	**800-347-2586**	717-299-3711	471
Amerindo Investment Advisors Inc 1 Embarcadero Ctr Suite 2300	San Francisco	CA	94111	**888-832-4386**	415-362-0292	393
AmeriPath Inc 7111 Fairway Dr Suite 400	Palm Beach Gardens	FL	33418	**800-330-6565**	561-845-1850	455
AmeriPride Service Inc 10801 Wayzata Blvd *Cust Svc	Minnetonka	MN	55305	**800-595-3913***	952-738-4252	434
Ameriquest Field in Arlington 1000 Ballpark Way Suite 400	Arlington	TX	76011	**888-968-3927**	817-273-5222	706
AMERISAFE Inc 2301 Hwy 190 W	DeRidder	LA	70634	**800-256-9052**	337-463-9052	384-4
AmeriScript Inc 4301 Darrow Rd	Stow	OH	44224	**800-681-6912**	330-686-7000	575
AmeriSearch 1232 Q St	Sacramento	CA	95814	**800-877-2877**	916-443-0795	621
Ameriserv Financial 216 Franklin St	Johnstown	PA	15901	**800-837-2265**	814-533-5300	71
AmeriServe Financial Inc 216 Franklin St *NASDAQ: ASRV* ■ *Cust Svc	Johnstown	PA	15901	**800-837-2265***	814-533-5300	355-2
AmerisourceBergen Corp 1300 Morris Dr Suite 100 *NYSE: ABC*	Chesterbrook	PA	19087	**800-829-3132**	610-727-7000	237
AmeriSpan Unlimited PO Box 58129	Philadelphia	PA	19102	**800-879-6640**	215-751-1100	414
AmeriSpec Inc 889 Ridgelake Blvd	Memphis	TN	38120	**800-426-2270**	901-820-8500	360
Ameristar Casino Hotel Council Bluffs 2200 River Rd	Council Bluffs	IA	51501	**877-462-7827**	712-328-8888	133
Ameristar Casino Hotel Kansas City 3200 N Ameristar Dr	Kansas City	MO	64161	**800-499-4961**	816-414-7000	373
Ameristar Casino Hotel Vicksburg 4116 Washington St	Vicksburg	MS	39180	**800-700-7770**	601-638-1000	133
Ameristar Casino Saint Charles 1260 S Main St PO Box 720	Saint Charles	MO	63301	**800-325-7777**	636-940-4300	133
Ameristar Casinos Inc 3773 Howard Hughes Pkwy Suite 490-S *NASDAQ: ASCA*	Las Vegas	NV	89109	**866-921-9229**	702-567-7000	132
Ameristar Financial 1795 N Butterfield Rd	Libertyville	IL	60048	**800-784-1535**	847-855-2000	215
AmeriSuites 700 Rt 46 E	Fairfield	NJ	07004	**800-833-1516**	973-882-1010	369
AmeriSuites West 11777 W Silver Spring Dr	Milwaukee	WI	53225	**800-723-8280**	414-462-3500	373
Amerisure Insurance Co PO Box 2060	Farmington Hills	MI	48333	**800-257-1900**	248-615-9000	384-4
Ameritas Acacia Mutual Holding Co 5900 O St	Lincoln	NE	68510	**800-311-7871**	402-467-1122	355-4
Ameritas Direct 5900 'O' St	Lincoln	NE	68510	**800-283-9588**	402-467-1122	384-2
Ameritas Holding Co 5900 O St	Lincoln	NE	68510	**800-311-7871**	402-467-1122	355-4
Ameritas Investment Corp PO Box 81889	Lincoln	NE	68501	**800-228-8712**	402-466-4565	679
Ameritas Life Insurance Corp 5900 'O' St	Lincoln	NE	68510	**800-283-9588**	402-467-1122	384-2
Ameritas Managed Dental Plan Inc 5900 'O' St	Lincoln	NE	68510	**800-404-8019**	402-467-1122	384-3
Ameritas Variable Life Insurance Co 5900 'O' St	Lincoln	NE	68510	**800-634-8353**	402-467-1122	384-2
Ameritel Inn Boise Spectrum 7499 W Overland Rd	Boise	ID	83709	**877-800-5876**	208-323-2500	373
Ameritel Inn Boise Towne Square 7965 W Emerald St	Boise	ID	83704	**800-600-6001**	208-378-7000	373
Ameritel Inn Pocatello 1440 Bench Rd	Pocatello	ID	83201	**800-600-6001**	208-234-7500	373
Ameritours 5018 William Flynn Hwy	Gibsonia	PA	15044	**800-466-3868**	724-443-5600	748
Ameritrade Holding Corp PO Box 3288 *NASDAQ: AMTD*	Omaha	NE	68103	**800-237-8692**	402-331-2744	355-3
Ameritrade Inc 4211 S 102nd St *Cust Svc	Omaha	NE	68127	**800-237-8692***	402-331-2744	679

Company / Address	City	State	ZIP	Toll-Free	Phone	Class
Ameriwood Industries Inc 305 E South 1st St	Wright City	MO	63390	**800-454-0283**	636-745-3351	314-2
AmerLink Log Homes Ltd 7991 Beasley Rd	Whitakers	NC	27891	**800-872-4254**	252-977-2545	107
Amerock Corp PO Box 7018 *Cust Svc	Rockford	IL	61125	**800-435-6959***	815-963-9631	345
Ameron International Fiberglass Composite Pipe Group PO Box 801148	Houston	TX	77280	**800-542-4070**	713-690-7777	585
Ameron International Performance Coatings & Finishes Group 13010 Morris Road Suite 400	Alpharetta	GA	30004	**800-926-3766**	678-393-0653	143
Amersham Biosciences 800 Centennial Ave PO Box 1327	Piscataway	NJ	08854	**800-526-3593**	732-457-8000	410
AmerSuites Milwaukee Airport 200 W Grange Ave	Milwaukee	WI	53207	**800-833-1516**	414-744-3600	373
AmerUs Group Co 699 Walnut St *NYSE: AMH*	Des Moines	IA	50309	**800-367-3669**	515-362-3600	355-4
AmerUs Life Insurance Co 611 5th Ave	Des Moines	IA	50309	**800-800-9882**	515-283-2371	384-2
Ames Rubber Corp 19 Ames Blvd	Hamburg	NJ	07419	**800-697-9101**	973-827-9101	664
Ames Safety Envelope Co 12 Tyler St	Somerville	MA	02143	**800-225-1138**	617-776-1142	260
Ames Supply Co 1936 University Ln	Lisle	IL	60532	**800-323-3856**	630-964-2440	378
Ames Taping Tools Inc 3305 Breckenridge Blvd Suite 122 *Cust Svc	Duluth	GA	30096	**800-408-2801***	770-243-2637	746
Ames True Temper Inc 465 Railroad Ave	Camp Hill	PA	17011	**800-393-1846**	717-737-1500	746
AMETEK Inc 37 N Valley Rd Bldg 4 PO Box 1764 *NYSE: AME*	Paoli	PA	19301	**800-473-1286**	610-647-2121	355-3
AMETEK Inc Chemical Products Div 455 Corporate Blvd *Orders	Newark	DE	19702	**800-441-7777***	302-456-4400	730-3
AMETEK Inc Dixson Div 287 27 Rd	Grand Junction	CO	81503	**888-302-0639**	970-244-1241	486
AMETEK Inc Test & Calibration Instruments Div 8600 Somerset Dr	Largo	FL	33773	**800-527-9999**	727-536-7831	464
AMETEK National Controls Corp 1725 Western Dr	West Chicago	IL	60185	**800-323-2593**	630-231-5900	202
AMETEK Power Instruments Panalarm Div 1725 Western Dr	West Chicago	IL	60185	**800-213-9568**	630-231-5900	200
AMETEK Prestolite Power & Switch 2220 Corporate Dr	Troy	OH	45373	**800-367-2002**	937-440-0800	252
AMETEK Sensor Technology Automation & Process Technologies Div 1080 N Crooks Rd	Clawson	MI	48017	**800-635-0289**	248-435-0700	200
AMETEK Sensor Technology Drexelbrook Div 205 Keith Valley Rd *Cust Svc	Horsham	PA	19044	**800-527-6297***	215-674-1234	486
AMETEK Solidstate Controls 875 Dearborn Dr	Columbus	OH	43085	**800-635-7300**	614-846-7500	252
AMEX (American Stock Exchange) 86 Trinity Pl	New York	NY	10006	**800-843-2639**	212-306-1000	680
AMF Bakery Systems 2115 W Laburnum Ave	Richmond	VA	23227	**800-225-3771**	804-355-7961	206
AMF Bowling Worldwide Inc 8100 AMF Dr	Mechanicsville	VA	23111	**800-342-5263**	804-730-4000	100
AMF Funds 230 W Monroe St Suite 2810	Chicago	IL	60606	**800-527-3713**		517
amfAR (American Foundation for AIDS Research) 120 Wall St 13th Fl	New York	NY	10005	**800-392-6327**	212-806-1600	48-17
AMG Resources Corp 4100 Grand Ave	Pittsburgh	PA	15225	**800-633-3606**	412-331-0770	674
Amgen Canada Inc 6755 Mississauga Rd Suite 400	Mississauga	ON	L5N7Y2	**800-665-4273**	905-542-7277	86
Amgen Inc 1 Amgen Ctr Dr *NASDAQ: AMGN*	Thousand Oaks	CA	91320	**800-926-4369**	805-447-1000	86
AMG/Neuma Inc 7366 N Lincoln Ave Suite 202	Lincolnwood	IL	60712	**800-457-7828**	847-674-1150	783
AMHCA (American Mental Health Counselors Assn) 801 N Fairfax St Suite 304	Alexandria	VA	22314	**800-326-2642**	703-548-6002	49-15
Amherst-Merritt International 5565 Red Bird Ctr Dr Suite 150	Dallas	TX	75237	**800-627-7752**	214-339-0753	198
Amherst Systems Inc 1740 Wehrle Dr *Cust Svc	Buffalo	NY	14221	**800-477-0181***	716-631-0610	694
AMI Leasing PO Box 986	Worcester	MA	01613	**800-468-9993**	508-852-5311	284
AMI Metals Inc 1738 General George Patton Dr	Brentwood	TN	37027	**800-727-1903**	615-377-0400	483
Amica Life Insurance Co PO Box 6008	Providence	RI	02940	**800-242-6422**		384-2
Amica Mutual Insurance Co 100 Amica Way	Lincoln	RI	02865	**800-652-6422**		384-4
Amicalola Electric Membership Corp 544 Hwy 515 S	Jasper	GA	30143	**800-992-6471**	706-253-5200	244
AMICAS Inc 239 Ethan Allen Hwy *NASDAQ: AMCS*	Ridgefield	CT	06877	**800-278-0037**	203-438-3654	176-10
Amick Farms Inc PO Box 2309	Leesville	SC	29070	**800-926-4257**	803-532-1400	11-8
Amidon Graphics 1966 Benson Ave	Saint Paul	MN	55116	**800-328-6502**	651-690-2401	614
Amigos Canning Co Inc PO Box 37347	San Antonio	TX	78237	**800-580-3477**	210-434-0433	291-36
Amigos de las Americas 5618 Star Ln	Houston	TX	77057	**800-231-7796**	713-782-5290	48-5
Amigos Library Services 14400 Midway Rd	Dallas	TX	75244	**800-843-8482**	972-851-8000	380
Amital Spinning Corp 197 Bosch Blvd	New Bern	NC	28562	**800-548-1922**	252-636-3435	730-9
Amivest Capital Management 275 Broad Hollow Rd	Melville	NY	11747	**800-426-4837**	631-844-0572	393
AMK Drives & Controls Inc 5631 S Laburnum Ave	Richmond	VA	23231	**800-385-3929**	804-222-0323	507
Amlings Flowerland 540 W Ogden Ave	Hinsdale	IL	60521	**888-265-4647**	630-850-5070	287
Ammeraal Beltech USA 7501 N St Louis Ave *Cust Svc	Skokie	IL	60076	**800-323-4170***	847-673-6720	364
AMN Healthcare Services Inc 12400 High Bluff Dr Suite 100 *NYSE: AHS*	San Diego	CA	92130	**866-510-1904**		707
Amnesty Action Newsletter 322 8th Ave	New York	NY	10001	**800-266-3789**	212-807-8400	521-8
Amnesty International USA (AIUSA) 5 Penn Plaza 14th Fl	New York	NY	10001	**800-266-3789**	212-807-8400	48-5
AMOA (Amusement & Music Operators Assn) 33 W Higgins Rd Suite 830	South Barrington	IL	60010	**800-937-2662**	847-428-7699	48-23
Amodio Moving & Storage Inc 1 Hartford Sq	New Britain	CT	06052	**800-326-6346**	860-223-2725	508
Amon Carter Museum 3501 Camp Bowie Blvd	Fort Worth	TX	76107	**800-573-1933**	817-738-1933	509
Amorim Industrial Solutions 26112 110th St PO Box 25	Trevor	WI	53179	**800-558-3206**	262-862-2311	208
Amoroso's Baking Co 845 S 55th St	Lansdowne	PA	19143	**800-377-6557**	215-471-4740	291-1
Amos Press Inc PO Box 4129	Sidney	OH	45365	**800-327-1259**	937-498-2111	623-9
Ampac Packaging LLC 12025 Tricon Rd	Cincinnati	OH	45246	**800-543-7030**	513-671-1777	67
Ampac Seed Co 32727 Hwy 99 E	Tangent	OR	97389	**800-547-3230**	541-928-1651	684
Ampacet Corp 660 White Plains Rd *Cust Svc	Tarrytown	NY	10591	**800-888-4267***	914-631-6600	141
Ampco Metal Inc 1117 E Algonquin Rd	Arlington Heights	IL	60005	**800-437-6100**	847-437-6000	476
Ampersand Art Supply 1500 E 4th St	Austin	TX	78702	**800-822-1939**	512-322-0278	43
Ampex Corp 1228 Douglas Ave	Redwood City	CA	94063	**800-227-8333**	650-367-2011	644
Amphastar Pharmaceuticals Inc 11570 6th St	Rancho Cucamonga	CA	91730	**800-423-4136**	909-980-9484	572
Amphenol Aerospace 40-60 Delaware Ave	Sidney	NY	13838	**800-678-0141**	607-563-5011	252
Amphenol Corp 358 Hall Ave *NYSE: APH*	Wallingford	CT	06492	**877-267-4366**	203-265-8900	803
Amphenol RF 4 Old Newtown Rd *Sales	Danbury	CT	06810	**800-825-5577***	203-743-9272	252
Amphenol Sine Systems 25371 Joy Blvd	Mount Clemens	MI	48046	**800-394-7732**	586-465-3131	252
Amphenol Spectra-Strip 720 Sherman Ave	Hamden	CT	06514	**800-846-6400**	203-281-3200	252
AMPI 315 N Broadway	New Ulm	MN	56073	**800-533-3580**	507-354-8295	292-4
Amplivox Inc 3149 MacArthur Blvd	Northbrook	IL	60062	**800-267-5486**	847-498-9000	52
APMP Inc 1380 E Wackerly Rd	Midland	MI	48642	**800-530-9100**	989-837-8800	4
AMR Investment Services Inc PO Box 619003 MD 2450	DFW Airport	TX	75261	**800-967-9009**	817-967-3509	393
AmRad Engineering Inc 32 Hargrove Grade	Palm Coast	FL	32137	**800-445-6033**	386-445-6000	252
AmREIT 8 Greenway Plaza Suite 1000 *AMEX: AMY*	Houston	TX	77046	**800-888-4400**	713-850-1400	640
AmRent PO Box 771176	Houston	TX	77215	**800-324-3681**	713-266-1870	621
AMREP Inc 990 Industrial Park Dr *Cust Svc	Marietta	GA	30062	**800-241-7766***	770-422-2071	143
Amresco Inc 30175 Solon Industrial Pkwy	Solon	OH	44139	**800-366-1313**	440-349-1313	229
Amro Music Stores 2918 Poplar Ave	Memphis	TN	38111	**800-661-2676**	901-323-8888	515
AMRPA (American Medical Rehabilitation Providers Assn) 1710 'N' St NW	Washington	DC	20036	**888-346-4624**	202-223-1920	49-8
AMS (American Mathematical Society) 201 Charles St PO Box 6248 *Cust Svc	Providence	RI	02940	**800-321-4267***	401-455-4000	49-19
AMS (ASI) Inc 11300 W 89th St	Overland Park	KS	66214	**800-765-0861**	913-495-2600	519
AMS Entertainment 1213 State St Suite J	Santa Barbara	CA	93101	**800-267-3548**	805-899-4000	179
AMS Health Sciences Inc 2601 Northwest Expy Suite 1210W PO Box 12940 *AMEX: AMM*	Oklahoma City	OK	73157	**800-426-4267**	405-842-0131	291-11
AMS Services Inc 3 Waterside Crossing *Sales	Windsor	CT	06095	**800-444-4813***	860-602-6000	176-10
AMSA (American Medical Student Assn) 1902 Association Dr	Reston	VA	20191	**800-767-2266**	703-620-6600	49-5
AmSan (American Sanitary Inc) 3 Parkway N Suite 120 N	Deerfield	IL	60015	**888-468-1555**	847-607-2300	398
Amscan Inc 80 Grasslands Rd	Elmsford	NY	10523	**800-284-4333**	914-345-2020	548-1
Amsco Windows Inc 1880 S 1045 West	Salt Lake City	UT	84104	**800-748-4661**	801-978-5000	232
Amsco-Wire Products Co 610 Grand Ave	Ridgefield	NJ	07657	**800-255-7467**	201-945-5700	610
Amsoil Inc 925 Tower Ave *Sales	Superior	WI	54880	**800-777-7094***	715-392-7101	530
AmSouth Bancorporation PO Box 11007 *NYSE: ASO*	Birmingham	AL	35288	**800-267-6884**	205-320-7151	355-2
AmSouth Bank 1900 5th Ave N	Birmingham	AL	35203	**800-284-4100**	205-326-5164	71
AmSouth Funds 3435 Stelzer Rd	Columbus	OH	43219	**800-451-8382**	614-470-8000	517
AmStaff Human Resources Inc 6723 Plantation Rd	Pensacola	FL	32504	**800-888-0472**	850-477-7022	619
Amster-Kirtz Co 2830 Cleveland Ave NW	Canton	OH	44709	**800-257-9338**	330-493-1800	744
Amsterdam Printing & Litho Corp 166 Wallins Corners Rd	Amsterdam	NY	12010	**800-833-6231**	518-842-6000	10
Amsterdam Recorder 1 Venner Rd	Amsterdam	NY	12010	**800-453-6397**	518-843-1100	522-2
Amstore Corp 540 Danforth St	Coopersville	MI	49404	**800-933-6681**	616-837-3700	281
AmSurg Corp 20 Burton Hills Blvd 5th Fl *NASDAQ: AMSG*	Nashville	TN	37215	**800-945-2301**	615-665-1283	347
AMSUS (Association of Military Surgeons of the US) 9320 Old Georgetown Rd	Bethesda	MD	20814	**800-761-9320**	301-897-8800	49-8
AMT (American Medical Technologists) 710 Higgins Rd	Park Ridge	IL	60068	**800-275-1268**	847-823-5169	49-8
AMT (Association for Manufacturing Technology) 7901 Westpark Dr	McLean	VA	22102	**800-524-0475**	703-893-2900	49-12
AMT Datasouth Corp 4765 Calle Quetzal	Camarillo	CA	93012	**800-215-9192**	805-388-5799	171-6
AMTDA (American Machine Tool Distributors' Assn) 1445 Research Blvd Suite 450	Rockville	MD	20850	**800-878-2683**	301-738-1200	49-18

Name / Address	City	State	ZIP	Toll-Free	Phone	Class
Amtech Lighting Services 2390 E Orangewood Ave Suite 100	Anaheim	CA	92806	**800-423-4481**	714-940-4000	150
Amtelco 4800 Curtin Dr	McFarland	WI	53558	**800-356-9148**	608-838-4194	720
Amtico International Inc 6480 Roswell Rd	Atlanta	GA	30328	**800-268-4260**	404-267-1900	286
Amtote International Inc 11200 Pepper Rd	Hunt Valley	MD	21031	**800-345-1566**	410-771-8700	317
Amtrak 60 Massachusetts Ave NE	Washington	DC	20002	**800-872-7245**	202-906-3000	635
Amusement Business Magazine 5055 Wilshire Blvd	Los Angeles	CA	90036	**800-745-8922**	323-525-2350	449-9
Amusement & Music Operators Assn (AMOA) 33 W Higgins Rd Suite 830	South Barrington	IL	60010	**800-937-2662**	847-428-7699	48-23
Amvac Chemical Corp 4100 E Washington Blvd	Los Angeles	CA	90023	**888-468-2726**	323-264-3910	276
AmVestors Financial Corp 555 S Kansas Ave	Topeka	KS	66603	**800-255-2405**	785-232-6945	355-4
AMVETS 4647 Forbes Blvd	Lanham	MD	20706	**877-726-8387**	301-459-9600	48-19
Amway Corp 7575 Fulton St E	Ada	MI	49355	**800-253-6500**	616-787-6000	361
Amway Grand Plaza Hotel 187 Monroe Ave NW	Grand Rapids	MI	49503	**800-253-3590**	616-774-2000	373
AMX Corp 3000 Research Dr	Richardson	TX	75082	**800-222-0193**	469-624-8000	202
AN Deringer Inc PO Box 1309	Saint Albans	VT	05478	**800-448-8108**	802-524-8110	440
ANA (American Numismatic Assn) 818 N Cascade Ave	Colorado Springs	CO	80903	**800-367-9723**	719-632-2646	48-18
ANA (American Nurses Assn) 8515 Georgia Ave Suite 400	Silver Spring	MD	20910	**800-274-4262**	301-628-5000	49-8
ANAC (Association of Nurses in AIDS Care) 3538 Ridgewood Rd	Akron	OH	44333	**800-260-6780**	330-670-0101	49-8
Anachemia Chemicals Inc 3 Lincoln Blvd	Rouses Point	NY	12979	**800-323-1414**	518-297-4444	229
Anacom General Corp 1240 S Claudina St	Anaheim	CA	92805	**800-955-9540**	714-774-8080	385
Anacom Med-Tek 1240 S Claudina St	Anaheim	CA	92805	**800-955-9540**	714-774-8484	385
Anadarko Daily News 117-119 E Broadway	Anadarko	OK	73005	**800-256-2763**	405-247-3331	522-2
Anaheim Automation 910 E Orangefair Ln *Sales	Anaheim	CA	92801	**800-345-9401***	714-992-6990	202
Anaheim Custom Extruders 4640 E La Palma Ave *Cust Svc	Anaheim	CA	92807	**800-229-2760***	714-693-8508	589
Anaheim Extrusion Co Inc 1330 N Kraemer Blvd	Anaheim	CA	92806	**800-660-3318**	714-630-3111	476
Anaheim Mfg Co 4240 E La Palma Ave *Cust Svc	Anaheim	CA	92807	**800-854-3229***	714-524-7770	36
Anaheim Plaza Hotel 1700 S Harbor Blvd	Anaheim	CA	92802	**800-532-4517**	714-772-5900	373
Anaheim/Orange County Visitor & Convention Bureau 800 W Katella Ave	Anaheim	CA	92802	**888-598-3200**	714-765-8888	205
Analog Devices Inc 1 Technology Way PO Box 9106 *NYSE: ADI*	Norwood	MA	02062	**800-262-5643**	781-329-4700	686
Analysts Inc 20505 Earl St	Torrance	CA	90503	**800-336-3637**	310-370-2345	728
Analysts International Corp 3601 W 76th St *NASDAQ: ANLY*	Minneapolis	MN	55435	**800-800-5044**	952-835-5900	178
Analytic Investors Inc 500 S Grand Ave 23rd Fl	Los Angeles	CA	90017	**800-618-1872**	213-688-3015	393
Analytic Services Inc 2900 S Quincy St Suite 800	Arlington	VA	22206	**866-226-5697**	703-416-2000	682
Analytical Computer Services 11500 Northwest Fwy Suite 320	Houston	TX	77092	**888-744-9451**	713-681-0039	172
ANALYTICI 150 E 42nd St 25th Fl	New York	NY	10017	**877-568-8032**		194
Anaphylaxis Network. Food Allergy & 11781 Lee Jackson Hwy Suite 160	Fairfax	VA	22033	**800-929-4040**	703-691-3179	48-17
Anarad Inc 3405 Wiley Post Rd	Carrollton	TX	75006	**888-626-3763**	972-458-6100	200
Anaren Microwave Inc 6635 Kirkville Rd *NASDAQ: ANEN*	East Syracuse	NY	13057	**800-544-2414**	315-432-8909	252
AnaSpec Inc 2149 O'Toole Ave Suite L	San Jose	CA	95131	**800-452-5530**	408-452-5055	229
Anastasia Inn 218 Anastasia Blvd	Saint Augustine	FL	32080	**888-226-6181**	904-825-2879	373
Ancestry.com Inc 360 W 4800 North *Cust Svc	Provo	UT	84606	**800-262-3787***	801-705-7000	677
Anchor Bay Entertainment Inc 1699 Stutz Dr	Troy	MI	48084	**800-786-8777**	248-816-0909	500
Anchor Computer Inc 1900 New Hwy	Farmingdale	NY	11735	**800-728-6262**	631-293-6100	176-10
Anchor Crane & Hoist Service Co Inc 2020 E Grauwyler Rd	Irving	TX	75061	**800-275-2624**	972-438-5100	462
Anchor Gasoline 114 E 5th St	Tulsa	OK	74103	**800-321-4086**	918-584-5291	527
Anchor Glass Container Corp 4343 Anchor Plaza Pkwy *NASDAQ: AGCC*	Tampa	FL	33634	**800-326-2467**	813-882-0000	327
Anchor-Harvey Components Inc 600 W Lamm Rd	Freeport	IL	61032	**888-367-4464**	815-235-4400	474
Anchor Hospital 5454 Yorktowne Dr	Atlanta	GA	30349	**800-444-2273**	770-991-6044	712
Anchor Industries Inc 1100 Burch Dr	Evansville	IN	47725	**800-544-4445**	812-867-2421	718
Anchor Paper Co Inc 480 Broadway St	Saint Paul	MN	55101	**800-652-9755**	651-298-1311	543
Anchor Tobacco Co Inc 605 Capitol St	Charleston	WV	25301	**800-213-6134**	304-342-6134	744
Anchorage Alaska Bed & Breakfast Assn PO Box 242623	Anchorage	AK	99524	**888-584-5147**	907-272-5909	368
Anchorage Convention & Visitors Bureau 524 W 4th Ave	Anchorage	AK	99501	**800-478-1255**	907-276-4118	205
Anchorage Daily News 1001 Northway Dr	Anchorage	AK	99508	**800-555-1212**	907-257-4200	522-2
Anchorage Inn 26 Vendue Range	Charleston	SC	29401	**800-421-2952**	843-723-8300	373
AnchorBank PO Box 7933	Madison	WI	53707	**800-252-6246**	608-252-8700	71
Anchors Away Cruise Center 3702 Independence Pl	Rocklin	CA	95677	**888-516-6306**	916-625-0722	760
Anchors Away Cruise Outlet 3750 Caribou St PO Box 871723	Wasilla	AK	99687	**800-580-3494**	907-373-3494	760
Ancient Cedars Spa at the Wickaninnish Inn Osprey Ln at Chesterman Beach Box 250	Tofino	BC	V0R2Z0	**800-333-4604**	250-725-3113	698
Ancient Images Greeting Cards 44 N 100 West	Moab	UT	84532	**800-891-6635**	435-259-4087	130
Ancira Enterprises Inc 6111 Bandera Rd	San Antonio	TX	78238	**800-299-5286**	210-681-4900	57
Anco Insurance Managers Inc 1733 Briarcrest Dr	Bryan	TX	77802	**800-749-1733**	979-776-2626	383
Anco Products Inc 2500 S 17th St	Elkhart	IN	46517	**800-837-2626**	574-293-5574	382
Ancra International LLC 4880 W Rosecrans Ave	Hawthorne	CA	90250	**800-973-5091**	310-973-5000	462
Andalusia Star News 207 Dunson St PO Box 430	Andalusia	AL	36420	**866-735-5289**	334-222-2402	522-2
Andavo Travel Inc 5325 S Valentia Way	Greenwood Village	CO	80111	**800-685-0038**	303-694-3322	760
Anderol Inc 215 Merry Ln PO Box 518	East Hanover	NJ	07936	**888-263-3765**	973-887-7410	530
Andersen 2000 Inc 306 Dividend Dr	Peachtree City	GA	30269	**800-241-5424**	770-486-2000	19
Andersen Corp 100 4th Ave N	Bayport	MN	55003	**877-229-2677**	651-264-5150	234
Anderson Area Medical Center 800 N Fant St	Anderson	SC	29621	**800-825-6688**	864-261-1000	366-2
Anderson Automatics Inc 6401 Welcome Ave N	Minneapolis	MN	55429	**800-959-0316**	763-533-2206	610
Anderson Brass Co 1629 W Bobo Newsome Hwy	Hartsville	SC	29550	**800-476-9876**	843-332-4111	776
Anderson Chemical Co PO Box 1041	Litchfield	MN	55355	**800-366-2477**	320-693-2477	143
Anderson Coach & Tour Co 1 Anderson Plaza	Greenville	PA	16125	**800-345-3435**	724-588-8310	748
Anderson College 316 Blvd	Anderson	SC	29621	**800-542-3594**	864-231-2030	163
Anderson Copper & Brass Co 4325 Frontage Rd	Oak Forest	IL	60452	**800-323-5284**	708-535-9030	598
Anderson-DuBose Co 6575 Davis Industrial Pkwy	Solon	OH	44139	**800-248-1080**	440-248-8800	295
Anderson Electrical Products Inc PO Box 455	Leeds	AL	35094	**800-423-0730**	205-699-2411	345
Anderson Erickson Dairy Co 2420 E University Ave	Des Moines	IA	50317	**800-234-7257**	515-265-2521	291-27
Anderson Independent-Mail PO Box 2507	Anderson	SC	29622	**800-859-6397**	864-224-4321	522-2
Anderson Instrument Co 156 Auriesville Rd	Fultonville	NY	12072	**800-833-0081**	518-922-5315	200
Anderson International Corp 6200 Harvard Ave	Cleveland	OH	44105	**800-336-4730**	216-641-1112	293
Anderson Lithograph Co 3217 S Garfield Ave	Los Angeles	CA	90040	**800-727-5846**	323-727-7767	615
Anderson Machinery Co Inc 6535 Leopard St	Corpus Christi	TX	78409	**800-308-6043**	361-289-6043	353
Anderson Products Inc 1040 Southbridge St	Worcester	MA	01610	**800-755-6101**	508-755-6100	104
Anderson Roy Corp 11400 Reichold Rd	Gulfport	MS	39503	**800-688-4003**	228-896-4000	185
Anderson-Snow Corp 9225 Ivanhoe St	Schiller Park	IL	60176	**800-346-2645**	847-678-3823	15
Anderson Symphony Orchestra PO Box 741	Anderson	IN	46015	**888-644-9490**	765-644-2111	563-3
Anderson Trucking Service Inc 203 Cooper Ave N PO Box 1377	Saint Cloud	MN	56302	**800-328-2307**	320-255-7400	769
Anderson University 1100 E 5th St *Admissions	Anderson	IN	46012	**800-428-6414***	765-649-9071	163
Anderson Wholesale Co PO Box 69	Muskogee	OK	74402	**800-324-9656**	918-682-5568	237
Anderson/Madison County Visitors & Convention Bureau 6335 S Scatterfield Rd	Anderson	IN	46013	**800-533-6569**	765-643-5633	205
Andersons DBA Erny's PO Box 452	Walton	IN	46994	**800-552-3769**	574-626-2522	276
Andersons Inc 480 W Dussel Dr *NASDAQ: ANDE*	Maumee	OH	43537	**800-537-3370**	419-893-5050	184
Andersons Inc Agriculture Group 480 W Dussel Dr	Maumee	OH	43537	**800-537-3370**	419-893-5050	271
Andersons Inc Processing Group 480 W Dussel Dr	Maumee	OH	43537	**800-537-3370**	419-893-5050	276
Andersons Inc Rail Group 480 W Dussel Dr	Maumee	OH	43537	**866-234-0505**	419-893-5050	261-6
Andersons Inc Retail Group 480 W Dussel Dr	Maumee	OH	43537	**800-537-3370**	419-893-5050	778
Andex Industries Inc 1911 4th Ave N	Escanaba	MI	49829	**800-338-9882**	906-786-6070	89
Andis Co 1800 Renaissance Blvd *Cust Svc	Sturtevant	WI	53177	**800-558-9441***	262-884-2600	37
Andover College 901 Washington Ave	Portland	ME	04103	**800-639-3110**	207-774-6126	158
Andover Newton Theological School 210 Herrick Rd	Newton Centre	MA	02459	**800-964-2687**	617-964-1100	164-3
Andrea Electronics Corp 65 Orville Dr Suite 110 *AMEX: AND*	Bohemia	NY	11716	**800-442-7787**	631-719-1800	52
Andreini & Co 220 W 20th Ave	San Mateo	CA	94403	**800-969-2522**	650-573-1111	383
Andrew College 413 College St	Cuthbert	GA	39840	**800-664-9250**	229-732-2171	160
Andrew Corp 10500 W 153rd St *NASDAQ: ANDW* ■ *Cust Svc	Orland Park	IL	60462	**800-255-1479***	708-349-3300	633
Andrew Corp Decibel Products Div 2601 Telecom Pkwy	Richardson	TX	75082	**800-676-5342**	972-952-9700	633
Andrews Federal Credit Union PO Box 4000	Clinton	MD	20735	**800-487-5500**	301-702-5500	216
Andrews Hotel 624 Post St	San Francisco	CA	94109	**800-926-3739**	415-563-6877	373
Andrews Publications Inc 175 Strafford Ave Bldg 4 Suite 140	Wayne	PA	19087	**800-345-1101**	610-225-0510	623-9
Andrews School 38588 Mentor Ave	Willoughby	OH	44894	**800-753-4683**	440-942-3606	611
Andrews University 100 US 31	Berrien Springs	MI	49104	**800-253-2874**	269-471-7771	163
Andrews Van Lines Inc 310 S 7th St *Cust Svc	Norfolk	NE	68701	**800-228-8146***	402-371-5440	508
Andritz-Ruthner Inc 1010 Commercial Blvd S	Arlington	TX	76001	**800-433-5161**	817-465-5611	793
Andrology Laboratory & Sperm Bank 9500 Euclid Ave Cleveland Clinic Foundation Desk A19.1	Cleveland	OH	44195	**800-223-2273**	216-444-3019	535
Andrx Corp 4955 Orange Dr *NASDAQ: ADRX*	Davie	FL	33314	**800-331-2632**	954-585-1400	573

Name / Address	City	State	ZIP	Toll-Free	Phone	Class
Andy Williams Moon River Theatre 2500 W Hwy 76	Branson	MO	65616	**800-666-6094**	417-334-4500	562
Anemostat 1220 Watsoncenter Rd	Carson	CA	90745	**800-982-9000**	310-835-7500	232
Anetsberger Brothers Inc 180 N Anets Dr	Northbrook	IL	60062	**800-837-2638**	847-272-0770	293
Angel Fire Resort PO Drawer B	Angel Fire	NM	87710	**800-633-7463**	505-377-6401	655
ANGELCARE PO Box 600370	San Diego	CA	92160	**888-264-5227**	619-795-6234	48-5
Angelo State University 2601 West Ave N Box 11014	San Angelo	TX	76909	**800-946-8627**	325-942-2041	163
Angelus Shoe Polish Co 8640 National Blvd PO Box 883	Culver City	CA	90232	**800-722-4848**	310-836-3314	149
AngioDynamics Inc 603 Queensbury Ave *NASDAQ: ANGO*	Queensbury	NY	12804	**800-772-6446**	518-798-1215	468
Angler's Inn 265 N Millward St PO Box 1247	Jackson	WY	83001	**800-867-4667**	307-733-3682	373
Angler's Roslyn Group Ltd 45-25 162nd St	Flushing	NY	11358	**800-221-0675**	718-961-7744	523
Angola Wire Products Inc 803 Wohlert St	Angola	IN	46703	**800-800-7225**	260-665-9447	281
Angstrom Lighting 837 N Cahuenga Blvd	Hollywood	CA	90038	**866-275-9211**	323-462-4246	708
Angstrom Technologies Inc 1895 Airport Exchange Blvd Suite 110 *Cust Svc	Erlanger	KY	41018	**800-543-7358***	859-282-0020	143
Anguil Environmental Systems Inc 8855 N 55th St	Milwaukee	WI	53223	**800-488-0230**	414-365-6400	19
Angus Assn. American 3201 Frederick Ave	Saint Joseph	MO	64506	**800-821-5478**	816-383-5100	48-2
Angus Buffers & Biochemicals 2236 Liberty Dr	Niagara Falls	NY	14304	**800-648-6689**	716-283-1434	229
Anheuser-Busch Cos Inc 1 Busch Pl *NYSE: BUD*	Saint Louis	MO	63118	**800-342-5283**	314-577-2000	184
Anheuser-Busch Inc 1 Busch Pl *Cust Svc	Saint Louis	MO	63118	**800-342-5283***	314-577-2000	103
ANI (American Nuclear Insurers) 95 Glastonbury Blvd	Glastonbury	CT	06033	**888-561-3433**	860-682-1301	49-9
ANI Printing Inks 15500 28th Ave N	Plymouth	MN	55447	**800-328-7838**	763-559-5911	381
ANI Site Development 1300 Riverland Rd	Fort Lauderdale	FL	33312	**800-733-9929**	954-581-9929	168
Animal Hospital Assn. American PO Box 150899	Denver	CO	80215	**800-252-2242**	303-986-2800	48-3
Animal Poison Control Center. ASPCA 1717 S Philo Rd Suite 36	Urbana	IL	61802	**888-426-4435**	217-337-5030	48-3
Animal Protection Institute (API) 1122 'S' St	Sacramento	CA	95814	**800-348-7387**	916-447-3085	48-3
Animal Rights. International Society for 965 Griffin Pond Rd	Clarks Summit	PA	18411	**800-543-4727**	570-586-2200	48-3
Animal Welfare. International Fund for 411 Main St PO Box 193	Yarmouth Port	MA	02675	**800-932-4329**	508-744-2000	48-3
Animals Inc. Friends of 777 Post Rd Suite 205	Darien	CT	06820	**800-321-7387**	203-656-1522	48-3
Animals. People for the Ethical Treatment of 501 Front St *Orders	Norfolk	VA	23510	**800-483-4366***	757-622-7382	48-3
Animals. World Society for the Protection of 34 Deloss St	Framingham	MA	01702	**800-883-9772**	508-879-8350	48-3
Animas Corp 200 Lawrence Dr *NASDAQ: PUMP*	West Chester	PA	19380	**877-937-7867**	610-644-8990	469
Animation Factory Inc 2000 W 42nd St Suite C	Sioux Falls	SD	57105	**800-525-2475**	605-339-4722	176-8
Anixter Inc 2301 Patriot Blvd	Glenview	IL	60025	**800-323-8166**	847-677-2600	188-4
Anixter International Inc 2301 Patriot Blvd *NYSE: AXE*	Glenview	IL	60025	**800-264-9837**	224-521-8000	245
Ankle Surgeons. American College of Foot & 8725 W Higgins Rd Suite 555	Chicago	IL	60631	**800-421-2237**	773-693-9300	49-8
Ann Arbor Area Convention & Visitors Bureau 120 W Huron St	Ann Arbor	MI	48104	**800-888-9487**	734-995-7281	205
Ann Arbor News 340 E Huron St	Ann Arbor	MI	48104	**800-466-6989**	734-994-6989	522-2
Ann Sacks Tile & Stone Inc 8120 NE 33rd Dr	Portland	OR	97211	**800-278-8453**	503-281-7751	736
ANNA (American Nephrology Nurses' Assn) 200 E Holly Ave	Pitman	NJ	08080	**888-600-2662**	856-256-2320	49-8
Anna Griffin Inc 733 Lambert Dr	Atlanta	GA	30324	**888-817-8170**	404-817-8170	130
Anna Maria College 50 Sunset Ln	Paxton	MA	01612	**800-344-4586**	508-849-3300	163
Annaco Inc PO Box 1148	Akron	OH	44309	**800-394-1300**	330-376-1400	674
Annalee Mobilitee Dolls Inc 50 Reservoir Rd *Cust Svc	Meredith	NH	03253	**800-433-6557***	603-279-6544	750
Annals of Internal Medicine Magazine 190 North Independence Mall W	Philadelphia	PA	19106	**800-523-1546**	215-351-2400	449-16
Annaly Mortgage Management Inc 1211 Ave of the Americas Suite 2902 *NYSE: NLY*	New York	NY	10036	**800-487-9947**	212-696-0100	640
Annapolis Accommodations 41 Maryland Ave	Annapolis	MD	21401	**800-715-1000**	410-280-0900	368
Annapolis Bancorp Inc 1000 Bestgate Rd Suite 400 *NASDAQ: ANNB*	Annapolis	MD	21401	**800-582-2651**	410-224-4483	355-2
Annenberg/CPB Projects c/o Learner Online 1301 Pennsylvania Ave NW Suite 302	Washington	DC	20004	**800-532-7637**	202-783-0500	620
Annie E Casey Foundation 701 Saint Paul St	Baltimore	MD	21202	**800-222-1099**	410-547-6600	300
Annie Wright School 827 N Tacoma Ave	Tacoma	WA	98403	**800-847-1582**	253-272-2216	611
Annin & Co 105 Eisenhower Pkwy	Roseland	NJ	07068	**800-526-1390**	973-228-9400	282
Anniston Star 4305 McClellan Blvd PO Box 189	Anniston	AL	36202	**888-649-1551**	256-236-1551	522-2
Ann's Haven VNA 216 W Mulberry St	Denton	TX	76201	**800-383-5435**	940-566-6550	365
AnnTaylor Inc 142 W 57th St	New York	NY	10019	**800-677-6788**	212-541-3300	155-6
AnnTaylor Stores Corp 142 W 57th St *NYSE: ANN*	New York	NY	10019	**800-677-6788**	212-541-3300	155-6
Annual Reviews 4139 El Camino Way	Palo Alto	CA	94303	**800-523-8635**	650-493-4400	623-9
Ano-Coil Corp 60 E Main St	Rockville	CT	06066	**800-492-7286**	860-871-1200	770
Anonymizer Inc 5694 Mission Ctr Rd Box 426	San Diego	CA	92108	**888-270-0141**	619-725-3180	176-7
ANR Pipeline Co PO Box 2511	Houston	TX	77011	**800-827-5267**		320
ANR Storage Inc 27725 Stansbury Blvd Suite 200	Farmington Hills	MI	48334	**800-998-3847**	248-994-4100	320
Anron Heating & Air Conditioning Inc 440 Wyandanch Ave	North Babylon	NY	11704	**800-924-3336**	631-643-3433	188-10
ANS (American Nuclear Society) 555 N Kensington Ave	La Grange Park	IL	60526	**800-323-3044**	708-352-6611	49-19
Ansell Healthcare Inc 200 Schulz Dr	Red Bank	NJ	07701	**800-232-1309**	732-345-5400	566
Ansell Occupational Healthcare 1300 Walnut St *Cust Svc	Coshocton	OH	43812	**800-800-0444***	740-622-4311	153-8
Ansonborough Inn 21 Hassell St	Charleston	SC	29401	**800-522-2073**	843-723-1655	373
Ansonia Copper & Brass Inc 75 Liberty St *Cust Svc	Ansonia	CT	06401	**800-521-1703***	203-732-6600	476
Ansul Inc 1 Stanton St	Marinette	WI	54143	**800-862-6785**	715-735-7411	681
Answer Products Inc 28209 Ave Stanford *Cust Svc	Valencia	CA	91355	**800-423-0273***	661-257-4411	506
AnswerNet Network 345 Witherspoon St	Princeton	NJ	08542	**800-411-5777**	609-921-7450	723
Answerthink Inc 1001 Brickell Bay Dr Suite 3000 *NASDAQ: ANSR*	Miami	FL	33131	**888-844-6504**	305-375-8005	193
ANSYS Inc 275 Technology Dr *NASDAQ: ANSS*	Canonsburg	PA	15317	**800-937-3321**	724-746-3304	176-5
Antares Pharma Inc 13755 1st Ave N Suite 100 *NASDAQ: ANTR*	Minneapolis	MN	55441	**800-328-3077**	763-475-7700	468
Antec Inc 47900 Fremont Blvd *Cust Svc	Fremont	CA	94538	**888-542-6832***	510-770-1200	252
Antelope Valley Press 37404 Sierra Hwy PO Box 4050	Palmdale	CA	93590	**888-874-2527**	661-273-2700	522-2
Antennas & Propagation Society. IEEE IEEE Operations Ctr 445 Hoes Ln	Piscataway	NJ	08854	**800-678-4333**	732-981-0060	49-19
Anteon International Corp 3211 Jermantown Rd Suite 700 *NYSE: ANT*	Fairfax	VA	22030	**800-242-0230**	703-246-0200	178
Anter Brothers Co 12501 Elmwood Ave	Cleveland	OH	44111	**800-331-5000**	216-252-4555	744
Antex Electronics Corp 1125 W 190th St	Gardena	CA	90248	**800-338-4231**	310-532-3092	613
Anthem Blue Cross & Blue Shield 2015 Staples Mill Rd *Hum Res	Richmond	VA	23230	**888-744-6647***	804-354-7000	384-3
Anthem Blue Cross Blue Shield in Colorado 700 Broadway	Denver	CO	80273	**800-654-9338**	303-831-2131	384-3
Anthem Blue Cross & Blue Shield of Connecticut 370 Bassett Rd	North Haven	CT	06473	**800-545-0948**	203-239-4911	384-3
Anthem Blue Cross & Blue Shield of Maine 2 Gannett Dr *Cust Svc	South Portland	ME	04106	**800-482-0966***	207-822-7272	384-3
Anthem Blue Cross & Blue Shield of the Midwest 1351 William Howard Taft Rd	Cincinnati	OH	45204	**888-426-8436**	513-872-8100	384-3
Anthem Blue Cross & Blue Shield of Nevada 6900 Westcliffe Dr Suite 600 *Cust Svc	Las Vegas	NV	89145	**800-992-6907***	702-228-2583	384-3
Anthem Blue Cross & Blue Shield of New Hampshire 3000 Goffs Falls Rd	Manchester	NH	03111	**800-225-2666**	603-695-7000	384-3
Anthem Blue Cross & Blue Shield of Virginia 277 Bendix Rd Suite 100	Virginia Beach	VA	23452	**800-640-0007**	757-326-5130	384-3
Anthem Insurance Cos Inc 120 Monument Cir Suite 200	Indianapolis	IN	46204	**800-331-1476**	317-488-6000	384-2
Anthony Farms Inc 290 Depot St	Scandinavia	WI	54977	**800-826-0456**	715-467-2212	11-11
Anthony Forest Products Co 309 N Washington Ave	El Dorado	AR	71730	**800-221-2326**	870-862-3414	671
Anthony International 12812 Arroyo St	San Fernando	CA	91342	**800-772-0900**	818-365-9451	325
Anthony Michael Jewelers Inc 124 S Terrace Ave	Mount Vernon	NY	10550	**800-966-8800**	914-699-0000	401
Anthony-Thomas Candy Co 1777 Arlingate Ct	Columbus	OH	43228	**877-226-3921**	614-274-8405	291-8
Anthony's Florist & Gifts Inc 701 E Hallandale Beach Blvd	Hallandale	FL	33009	**800-989-8765**	954-457-8520	287
Anthony's Inc 5000 Georgia Ave	West Palm Beach	FL	33405	**800-324-1380**	561-588-7336	155-6
Anthro Corp 10450 SW Manhasset Dr	Tualatin	OR	97062	**800-325-3841**	503-691-2556	314-1
Anti-Vivisection Society. National 53 W Jackson Blvd Suite 1552	Chicago	IL	60604	**800-888-6287**	312-427-6065	48-3
Antibodies Inc PO Box 1560	Davis	CA	95617	**800-824-8540**	530-758-4400	86
AntiCancer Inc 7917 Ostrow St	San Diego	CA	92111	**800-511-2555**	858-654-2555	229
Antigua & Barbuda Dept of Tourism & Trade 610 5th Ave Suite 311	New York	NY	10020	**888-268-4227**	212-541-4117	764
Antigua Sportswear Inc 16651 N 84 Ave	Peoria	AZ	85382	**800-528-3133**	623-523-6000	153-12
Antillas Air JFK International Airport Cargo Bldg 68	Jamaica	NY	11430	**800-447-0417**	718-917-6855	13
Antimite Assoc Inc 7365 Hellman Ave	Rancho Cucamonga	CA	91730	**800-675-6483**	909-483-5300	567
Antioch College 795 Livermore St	Yellow Springs	OH	45387	**800-543-9436**	937-767-7331	163
Antioch Publishing Co 888 Dayton St	Yellow Springs	OH	45387	**800-543-2397**	937-767-7379	87

Name / Address	City	State	Zip	Toll-Free	Phone	Class
Antioch University 2326 6th Ave.	Seattle	WA	98121	**888-268-4477**	206-441-5352	163
Antique Car Museum/Grovewood Gallery 111 Grovewood Rd.	Asheville	NC	28804	**877-622-7238**	828-253-7651	509
Antique Collectors' Club 116 Pleasant St Eastworks Bldg	Easthampton	MA	01027	**800-252-5231**	413-529-0861	623-2
Antiques Magazine 575 Broadway 5th Fl *Cust Svc	New York	NY	10012	**800-925-9271***	212-941-2800	449-14
Antler Inn 43 W Pearl St PO Box 575	Jackson	WY	83001	**800-483-8667**	307-733-2535	373
Antonelli Institute 300 Montgomery Ave	Erdenheim	PA	19038	**800-722-7871**	215-836-2222	159
Antwerp Diamond Distributors 6 E 45th St Suite 302	New York	NY	10017	**800-223-0444**	212-319-3300	403
Anvil Cases 15730 Salt Lake Ave.	City of Industry	CA	91745	**800-359-2684**	626-968-4100	444
Any Mountain Ltd 71 Tamal Vista Blvd	Corte Madera	CA	94925	**800-992-4844**	415-927-2400	702
AnyDoc Software Inc 401 E Jackson St Suite 1200	Tampa	FL	33602	**800-775-3222**	813-222-0414	176-7
AnyWho Online Directory c/o AT & T Corp 1 AT & T Way	Bedminster	NJ	07921	**800-222-0300**	908-221-2000	677
AO Smith Corp 11270 W Park Pl Suite 170 *NYSE: AOS*	Milwaukee	WI	53224	**800-359-4065**	414-359-4000	507
AO Smith Water Products Co 500 Lindahl Pkwy	Ashland City	TN	37015	**800-365-8170**	615-792-4371	36
AOA (American Obesity Assn) 1250 24th St NW Suite 300	Washington	DC	20037	**800-986-2373**	202-776-7711	48-17
AOA (American Osteopathic Assn) 142 E Ontario St	Chicago	IL	60611	**800-621-1773**	312-202-8000	49-8
AOAC International 481 N Frederick Ave Suite 500	Gaithersburg	MD	20877	**800-379-2622**	301-924-7077	49-19
AOC (Association of Old Crows) 1000 N Payne St Suite 300	Alexandria	VA	22314	**888-653-2769**	703-549-1600	48-19
AOCA (Automotive Oil Change Assn) 12810 Hillcrest Rd Suite 221	Dallas	TX	75230	**800-331-0329**	972-458-9468	49-21
AOCS (American Oil Chemists Society) 2211 W Bradley Ave	Champaign	IL	61821	**800-336-2627**	217-359-2344	48-12
AOL (America Online Inc) 22000 AOL Way *Orders	Dulles	VA	20166	**888-265-8002***	703-265-1000	390
Aon Risk Services Inc 200 E Randolph St	Chicago	IL	60601	**800-432-3672**	312-381-4000	383
Aon Warranty Group Inc 1000 Milwaukee Ave 6th Fl	Glenview	IL	60025	**800-747-5152**	847-953-2025	687
Aonix North America Inc 5040 Shoreham Pl Suite 100	San Diego	CA	92122	**800-972-6649**	858-457-2700	176-12
AOPA (Aircraft Owners & Pilots Assn) 421 Aviation Way	Frederick	MD	21701	**800-872-2672**	301-695-2000	49-21
AOPA Pilot Magazine 421 Aviation Way	Frederick	MD	21701	**800-872-2672**	301-695-2000	449-14
AORN Inc 2170 S Parker Rd Suite 300	Denver	CO	80231	**800-755-2676**	303-755-6300	49-8
AOSSM (American Orthopaedic Society for Sports Medicine) 6300 N River Rd Suite 500	Rosemont	IL	60018	**877-321-3500**	847-292-4900	49-8
AP Broadcast Services 1825 K St NW Suite 800	Washington	DC	20006	**800-821-4747**	202-736-1100	632
APA (American Poolplayers Assn) 1000 Lake St Louis Blvd Suite 325	Lake Saint Louis	MO	63367	**800-372-2536**	636-625-8611	48-22
APA (American Psychiatric Assn) 1000 Wilson Blvd Suite 1825	Arlington	VA	22209	**888-357-7924**	703-907-7300	49-15
APA (American Psychological Assn) 750 1st St NE	Washington	DC	20002	**800-374-2721**	202-336-5500	49-15
APAC Atlantic Inc PO Box 399	Kinston	NC	28502	**800-849-1400**	252-527-8021	187-4
APAC Customer Services Inc 6 Parkway N *NASDAQ: APAC*	Deerfield	IL	60015	**800-776-2722**	847-374-4980	722
APAC Inc 900 Ashwood Pkwy Suite 700	Atlanta	GA	30338	**800-241-7074**	770-392-5300	187-4
Apache Corp 2000 Post Oak Blvd Suite 100 *NYSE: APA*	Houston	TX	77056	**800-272-2434**	713-296-6000	525
Apache Hose & Belting Co Inc 4805 Bowling St SW *Cust Svc	Cedar Rapids	IA	52406	**800-553-5455***	319-365-0471	364
Apache Junction Chamber of Commerce 567 W Apache Trail	Apache Junction	AZ	85220	**800-252-3141**	480-982-3141	137
Apartment Investment & Management Co 4582 S Ulster Street Pkwy Suite 1100 *NYSE: AIV*	Denver	CO	80237	**888-789-8600**	303-757-8101	641
APC (American Power Conversion Corp) 132 Fairgrounds Rd *NASDAQ: APCC* ■ *Cust Svc	West Kingston	RI	02892	**800-788-2208***	401-789-5735	252
APC Hegeman 50 Dietz St Suite K	Oneonta	NY	13820	**800-327-0085**	607-432-9039	454
APCapital (American Physicians Capital Inc) 1301 N Hagadorn Rd *NASDAQ: ACAP*	East Lansing	MI	48823	**800-748-0465**	517-351-1150	355-4
APCC (American Public Communications Council Inc) 625 Slaters Ln Suite 104	Alexandria	VA	22314	**800-868-2722**	703-739-1322	49-20
APCO Bulletin 351 N Williamson Blvd	Daytona Beach	FL	32114	**888-272-6911**	386-322-2500	521-8
APCO Employees Credit Union 1608 7th Ave N	Birmingham	AL	35203	**800-249-2726**	205-257-3601	216
Apco Products Inc PO Box 236	Essex	CT	06426	**800-640-2726**	860-767-2108	75
APCOM Inc 125 Southeast Pkwy	Franklin	TN	37064	**800-251-3535**	615-794-5574	201
APDA (American Parkinson Disease Assn) 1250 Hyland Blvd Suite 4B	Staten Island	NY	10305	**800-223-2732**	718-981-8001	48-17
APDIM (Association of Program Directors in Internal Medicine) 2501 M St NW Suite 550	Washington	DC	20037	**800-622-4558**	202-887-9450	49-8
Apex Color 200 N Lee St	Jacksonville	FL	32204	**800-367-6790**	904-358-2928	111

Name / Address	City	State	Zip	Toll-Free	Phone	Class
Apex CoVantage LLC 198 Van Buren St Suite 120	Herndon	VA	20170	**800-628-2739**	703-709-3000	176-12
Apex Fitness Group 100 Camino Ruiz	Camarillo	CA	93012	**800-656-2739**	805-449-1330	347
Apex Microtechnology Corp 5980 N Shannon Rd	Tucson	AZ	85741	**800-421-1865**	520-690-8600	252
Apex Mills Corp 168 Doughty Blvd	Inwood	NY	11096	**800-989-2739**	516-239-4400	730-4
Apex Office Products Inc 5209 N Howard Ave	Tampa	FL	33603	**800-227-1563**	813-871-2010	523
Apex Paper Box Co 5601 Walworth Ave *Cust Svc	Cleveland	OH	44102	**800-438-2269***	216-631-4000	102
APEX Systems Inc 2235 Staples Mill Rd Suite 200	Richmond	VA	23230	**800-452-7391**	804-254-2600	707
Apex Voice Communications Inc 15250 Ventura Blvd 3rd Fl	Sherman Oaks	CA	91403	**800-727-3970**	818-379-8400	176-7
APF Energy Trust 144 4th Ave SW Suite 2100	Calgary	AB	T2P3N4	**800-838-9206**	403-294-1000	662
APGA (American Public Gas Assn) 201 Massachusetts Ave NE Suite C-4	Washington	DC	20002	**800-927-4204**	202-464-2742	48-12
APhA (American Pharmacists Assn) 2215 Constitution Ave NW	Washington	DC	20037	**800-237-2742**	202-628-4410	49-8
Aphton Corp 80 SW 8th St *NASDAQ: APHT*	Miami	FL	33130	**877-274-8660**	305-374-7338	86
API (American Physicians Insurance Exchange) 1301 S Capitol of Texas Hwy Suite C-300	Austin	TX	78746	**800-252-3628**	512-328-0888	384-5
API (Animal Protection Institute) 1122 'S' St	Sacramento	CA	95814	**800-348-7387**	916-447-3085	48-3
API Construction Co 2366 Rose Pl	Saint Paul	MN	55113	**800-223-4922**	651-636-4320	188-9
API Electric 4631 Mike Colaillo Dr	Duluth	MN	55807	**866-624-0064**	218-624-0064	188-4
API Group Inc Fire Protection Group 2366 Rose Pl	Saint Paul	MN	55113	**800-223-4941**	651-636-4320	188-13
API Group Inc Materials Distribution Group 2366 Rose Pl	Saint Paul	MN	55113	**800-223-4922**	651-636-4320	190-2
API Heat Transfer 2777 Walden Ave	Buffalo	NY	14225	**877-274-4328**	716-684-9700	92
API Systems Group Inc 2366 Rose Pl	Saint Paul	MN	55113	**800-223-4922**	651-636-4320	681
APIC (Association for Professionals in Infection Control & Epidemiology Inc) 1275 K St NW Suite 1000	Washington	DC	20005	**888-278-2742**	202-789-1890	49-8
APICS - Assn for Operations Management 5301 Shawnee Rd	Alexandria	VA	22312	**800-444-2742**	703-354-8851	49-13
APL Ltd 1111 Broadway	Oakland	CA	94607	**800-999-7733**	510-272-8000	308
Aplix Inc PO Box 7505	Charlotte	NC	28241	**800-438-0424**	704-588-1920	583
APMA (American Podiatric Medical Assn) 9312 Old Georgetown Rd	Bethesda	MD	20814	**800-275-2762**	301-571-9200	49-8
Apogee Software Inc 1999 S Bascom Ave Suite 325	Campbell	CA	95008	**800-337-3256**	408-369-9001	176-6
Apollo Chemical Corp 1105 Southerland St	Graham NC	NC	27253	**800-374-3827**	336-226-1161	143
Apollo Design Technology Inc 4130 Fourier Dr	Fort Wayne	IN	46818	**800-288-4626**	260-497-9191	708
Apollo Metals Ltd 1001 14th Ave	Bethlehem	PA	18018	**800-338-0199**	610-867-5826	472
Apollo Park Executive Suites 805 S Circle Dr Suite 2B	Colorado Springs	CO	80910	**800-279-3620**	719-634-0286	373
Apollo Presentation Products 300 Tower Pkwy	Lincolnshire	IL	60069	**800-777-3750**		580
Apollo's Axes LLC 19228 Wind Dancer St	Lutz	FL	33558	**800-827-9196**	813-920-7363	515
Apotex Inc 150 Signet Dr	Weston	ON	M9L1T9	**800-268-4623**	416-749-9300	572
Apothecus Pharmaceutical Corp 220 Townsend Sq	Oyster Bay	NY	11771	**800-227-2393**	516-624-8200	572
Appairent Technologies Inc 150 Lucius Gordon Dr Suite 211	West Henrietta	NY	14586	**866-357-6210**	585-214-2460	720
Appalachian Bible College PO Box ABC	Bradley	WV	25818	**800-678-9222**	304-877-6428	163
Appalachian Life Insurance Co PO Box 5147	Springfield	IL	62705	**800-323-0050**	217-241-6300	384-2
Appalachian Mountain Club (AMC) 5 Joy St *Orders	Boston	MA	02108	**800-262-4455***	617-523-0636	48-13
Appalachian Project. Christian 322 Crab Orchard St	Lancaster	KY	40446	**866-270-4227**	859-792-3051	48-5
Appalachian School of Law PO Box 2825	Grundy	VA	24614	**800-895-7411**	276-935-4349	164-1
Apparel & Footwear Assn. American 1601 N Kent St Suite 1200	Arlington	VA	22209	**800-520-2262**	703-524-1864	49-4
Apparel Ventures Inc 13809 S Figueroa St	Los Angeles	CA	90061	**800-289-7946**	310-538-4980	153-17
Apparelmaster 123 Harrison Ave	Harrison	OH	45030	**877-543-1678**	513-202-1600	417
Appeal-Democrat 1530 Ellis Lake Dr	Marysville	CA	95901	**800-831-2345**	530-741-2345	522-2
Apperson Print Management Services 6855 E Gage Ave	Los Angeles	CA	90040	**800-877-2341**	562-927-4718	111
Appert's Foodservice 900 S Hwy 10	Saint Cloud	MN	56304	**800-225-3883**	320-251-3200	291-13
Appian Graphics Inc 18047 NE 68th St Suite B-100 *Tech Supp	Redmond	WA	98052	**800-422-7369***	425-882-2020	613
Apple Assn. US 8233 Old Courthouse Rd Suite 200	Vienna	VA	22182	**800-781-4443**	703-442-8850	48-2
Apple Bank for Savings 122 E 42nd St 9th Fl	New York	NY	10168	**800-722-6888**	212-224-6400	71
Apple Computer Inc 1 Infinite Loop *NASDAQ: AAPL* ■ *Cust Svc	Cupertino	CA	95014	**800-275-2273***	408-996-1010	171-3
Apple & Eve Inc 2 Seaview Blvd	Port Washington	NY	11050	**800-969-8018**	516-621-1122	291-20
Apple Rubber Products Inc 310 Erie St *Cust Svc	Lancaster	NY	14086	**800-828-7745***	716-684-6560	321
Apple Tree Inn 9508 N Division St	Spokane	WA	99218	**800-323-5796**	509-466-3020	373
Apple Vacations Inc 101 NW Point Blvd	Elk Grove Village	IL	60007	**800-365-2775**	847-640-1150	760
Apple Valley Chamber of Commerce 7300 W 147th St Suite 101	Apple Valley	MN	55124	**800-301-9435**	952-432-8422	137
Applegate Insulation Mfg Inc 1000 Highview Dr	Webberville	MI	48892	**800-627-7536**	517-521-3545	382

Name / Address	City	State	ZIP	Toll-Free	Phone	Class
AppleOne Employment Services Inc 327 W Broadway	Glendale	CA	91204	**800-872-2677**	818-240-8688	707
AppleOne Employment Services Inc 50 Paxman Rd Unit 8	Etobicoke	ON	M9C1B7	**800-564-5644**	416-622-0100	707
Applera Corp 301 Merritt 7	Norwalk	CT	06856	**800-761-5381**	203-840-2000	86
AppleSeeds Magazine 30 Grove St Suite C	Peterborough	NH	03458	**800-821-0115**	603-924-7209	449-6
Appleton Medical Center 1818 N Meade St	Appleton	WI	54911	**800-236-4101**	920-731-4101	366-2
Appleton Papers Inc PO Box 359	Appleton	WI	54912	**800-558-8390**	920-734-9841	542-1
Appletree Orchards Inc 12025 Four-Mile Rd NE	Lowell	MI	49331	**800-922-0635**	616-897-9216	310-3
Applewood Estates 1 Applewood Dr	Freehold	NJ	07728	**800-438-0888***	732-780-7370	659
*Mktg						
Applewood Manor Inn 62 Cumberland Cir	Asheville	NC	28801	**800-442-2197**	828-254-2244	373
Applewood Seed Co 5380 Vivian St	Arvada	CO	80002	**888-778-7333**	303-431-7333	684
Appliance Recycling Centers of America Inc 7400 Excelsior Blvd	Minneapolis	MN	55426	**800-452-8680**	952-930-9000	646
Applica Consumer Products Inc 3633 Flamingo Rd	Miramar	FL	33027	**800-231-9786***	954-883-1000	37
*Cust Svc						
Applica Inc 3633 Flamingo Rd	Miramar	FL	33027	**800-557-9463**	954-883-1000	37
NYSE: APN						
Applicant Insight Ltd PO Box 458	New Port Richey	FL	34656	**800-771-7703**		621
Applied Biosystems Group 850 Lincoln Ctr Dr	Foster City	CA	94404	**800-874-9868**	650-570-6667	410
NYSE: ABI						
Applied Computer Research Inc PO Box 82266	Phoenix	AZ	85071	**800-234-2227**	602-216-9100	623-11
Applied Concepts Inc 100 Rudolph Ln	Wexford	PA	15090	**800-466-5028**	724-776-5595	746
Applied Drilling Technology Inc 15375 Memorial Dr Suite A-200	Houston	TX	77079	**800-990-2384**	281-925-7100	529
Applied Energy Co Inc 11431 Chairman Dr	Dallas	TX	75243	**800-284-3166**	214-349-1171	626
Applied Extrusion Technologies Inc 15 Reads Way	New Castle	DE	19720	**800-688-2044**	302-326-5500	589
NASDAQ: AETC						
Applied Fiber Inc 1300 W Oakridge Dr	Albany	GA	31707	**800-226-5394**	229-888-3212	534
Applied Imaging Corp 2380 Walsh Ave Bldg B	Santa Clara	CA	95051	**800-634-3622**	408-562-0250	375
NASDAQ: AICX						
Applied Information Management Sciences Inc PO Box 2970	Monroe	LA	71207	**800-729-2467**	318-323-2467	176-10
Applied Innovation Inc 5800 Innovation Dr	Dublin	OH	43016	**800-247-9482**	614-798-2000	720
NASDAQ: AINN						
Applied Micro Circuits Corp 6290 Sequence Dr	San Diego	CA	92121	**800-935-2622**	858-450-9333	686
NASDAQ: AMCC						
Applied Plastics Co Inc 7320 S 6th St	Oak Creek	WI	53154	**800-959-0445**	414-764-2900	588
Applied Systems Inc 200 Applied Pkwy	University Park	IL	60466	**800-999-5368**	708-534-5575	176-11
Applix Inc 289 Turnpike Rd	Westborough	MA	01581	**800-827-7549**	508-870-0300	176-1
NASDAQ: APLX						
APPMA (American Pet Products Manufacturers Assn) 255 Glenville Rd	Greenwich	CT	06831	**800-452-1225**	203-532-0000	49-4
Appraisers. American Society of 555 Herndon Pkwy Suite 125	Herndon	VA	20170	**800-272-8258**	703-478-2228	49-17
Appraisers. Institute of Business 6950 Cypress Rd Suite 209	Plantation	FL	33317	**800-299-4130**	954-584-1144	49-17
Appraisers. National Assn of Master 303 W Cypress St	San Antonio	TX	78212	**800-229-6262**	210-271-0781	49-17
Appshop Inc 48089 Fremont Blvd	Fremont	CA	94538	**800-277-7467**	510-353-2900	39
AppTec Laboratory Services 2540 Executive Dr	Saint Paul	MN	55120	**888-794-0077**	651-675-2000	535
Apptis Inc 14155 Newbrook Dr	Chantilly	VA	20151	**800-338-8866**	703-279-3000	176-4
APPX Software Inc 11363 San Jose Blvd Suite 301	Jacksonville	FL	32223	**800-879-2779**	904-880-5560	176-1
APQC 123 Post Oak Ln 3rd Fl	Houston	TX	77024	**800-776-9676**	713-681-4020	49-12
Apria Healthcare Group Inc 26220 Enterprise Ct	Lake Forest	CA	92630	**800-647-5404**	949-639-2000	358
NYSE: AHG						
Apricorn Inc 12191 Kirkham Rd	Poway	CA	92064	**800-458-5448**	858-513-2000	171-8
APRO (Association of Progressive Rental Organizations) 1504 Robin Hood Trail	Austin	TX	78703	**800-204-2776**	512-794-0095	49-18
Apropos Technology Inc 1 Tower Ln 28th Fl	Oakbrook Terrace	IL	60181	**877-277-6767**	630-472-9600	176-7
NASDAQ: APRS						
APRS (American Park & Recreation Society) c/o National Recreation & Park Assn 22377 Belmont Ridge Rd	Ashburn	VA	20148	**800-626-6772**	703-858-4741	48-23
APS (American Prosthodontic Society) 426 Hudson St	Hackensack	NJ	07601	**877-499-3500**	201-440-7699	49-8
APS (Arizona Public Service Co) 400 N 5th St	Phoenix	AZ	85004	**800-253-9405***	602-250-1000	774
*Cust Svc						
APS Healthcare Inc 8403 Colesville Rd	Silver Spring	MD	20910	**800-305-3720**	301-563-5633	454
APSAC (American Professional Society on the Abuse of Children) 107 Amberside Dr	Goose Creek	SC	29445	**877-402-7722**	843-764-2905	48-6
Apscreen Inc 2043 Westcliff Dr Suite 300	Newport Beach	CA	92660	**800-277-2733**	949-646-4003	621
APSP (Association of Pool & Spa Professionals) 2111 Eisenhower Ave	Alexandria	VA	22314	**800-323-3996**	703-838-0083	49-4
APT (Alabama Public Television) 2112 11th Ave S Suite 400	Birmingham	AL	35205	**800-239-5233**	205-328-8756	620
APTA (American Physical Therapy Assn) 1111 N Fairfax St	Alexandria	VA	22314	**800-999-2782**	703-684-2782	49-8

Name / Address	City	State	ZIP	Toll-Free	Phone	Class
APTA (American Polarity Therapy Assn) PO Box 19858	Boulder	CO	80308	**800-359-5620**	303-545-2080	48-17
Aptech Computer Systems Inc 135 Delta Dr	Pittsburgh	PA	15238	**800-245-0720**	412-963-7440	176-11
APV Canada Inc 3280 Langstaff Rd	Concord	ON	L4K4Z8	**800-263-3958**	905-760-1852	293
APW Electronic Solutions 14100 Danielson St	Poway	CA	92064	**800-854-7086**	858-679-4550	253
APW Ltd N 22 W 23685 Ridgeview Pkwy W	Waukesha	WI	53188	**800-599-5556**	262-523-7600	253
AQHA (American Quarter Horse Assn) PO Box 200	Amarillo	TX	79168	**800-414-7433**	806-376-4811	48-3
Aqua-Aerobic Systems Inc 6306 N Alpine Rd	Rockford	IL	61111	**800-940-5008**	815-654-2501	793
Aqua Bamboo 2425 Kuhio Ave	Honolulu	HI	96815	**800-367-5004**	808-922-7777	373
Aqua Glass Corp 320 Industrial Park Dr	Adamsville	TN	38310	**800-632-0911**	731-632-0911	367
Aqua-Leisure Industries Inc 525 Bodwell St Ext PO Box 239	Avon	MA	02322	**888-807-2998**	508-587-5400	714
AquaCell Technologies Inc 10410 Trademark St	Rancho Cucamonga	CA	91730	**800-326-5222**	909-987-0456	793
AMEX: AQA						
Aquae Sulis Spa at the JW Marriott Resort Las Vegas 221 N Rampart Blvd	Las Vegas	NV	89145	**877-869-8777**	702-869-7807	698
Aquagenix Inc 1460 SW 3rd St Suite B2	Pompano Beach	FL	33069	**800-832-5253**	954-943-5118	653
Aqualung America Inc 2340 Cousteau Ct	Vista	CA	92083	**800-635-3483**	760-597-5000	701
Aquanaut Cruise Line Ltd 241 E Commercial Blvd	Fort Lauderdale	FL	33334	**800-327-8223**	954-491-0333	217
Aquapore Moisture Systems Inc 610 S 80th Ave	Tolleson	AZ	85353	**800-426-8419**	623-936-8083	364
Aquarion Co 835 Main St	Bridgeport	CT	06604	**800-732-9678**	203-336-7624	774
Aquarium of the Bay Pier 39	San Francisco	CA	94133	**888-732-3483**	415-623-5300	40
Aquarium Fish Magazine 3 Burroughs	Irvine	CA	92618	**800-365-4421***	949-855-8822	449-14
*Cust Svc						
Aquarium of the Pacific 100 Aquarium Way	Long Beach	CA	90802	**888-826-7257**	562-590-3100	40
Aquasport Marine Corp 1651 Whitfield Ave	Sarasota	FL	34243	**800-755-1099**	941-755-5800	91
Aquatherm Industries Inc 1940 Rutgers University Blvd	Lakewood	NJ	08701	**800-535-6307**	732-905-0440	352
Aquatic Exercise Assn (AEA) PO Box 1609	Nokomis	FL	34274	**888-232-9283**	941-486-8600	48-22
Aquatic Industries PO Box 889	Leander	TX	78646	**800-928-3707***	512-259-2255	367
*Cust Svc						
Aquatrol Inc 237-H N Euclid Way	Anaheim	CA	92801	**800-237-7735**	714-533-3381	568
Aquent LLC 711 Boylston St	Boston	MA	02116	**800-878-0900**	617-535-6000	707
Aquila Group of Funds 380 Madison Ave Suite 2300	New York	NY	10017	**800-762-5955**	212-697-6666	517
Aquila Inc 20 W 9th St	Kansas City	MO	64105	**800-303-0752**	816-421-6600	774
NYSE: ILA						
Aquinas College 1607 Robinson Rd SE	Grand Rapids	MI	49506	**800-678-9593**	616-459-8281	163
Aquinas Institute of Theology 3642 Lindell Blvd	St. Louis	MO	63108	**800-977-3869**	314-977-3882	164-3
AR Wilfley & Sons Inc 7350 E Progress Pl Suite 200	Englewood	CO	80111	**800-525-9930**	303-779-1777	627
ARA (American Rental Assn) 1900 19th St	Moline	IL	61265	**800-334-2177**	309-764-2475	49-4
ARA (Awards & Recognition Assn) 4700 W Lake Ave	Glenview	IL	60025	**800-344-2148**	847-375-4800	49-4
Araban Coffee Co Inc 2 Keith Way	Hingham	MA	02043	**800-225-2474**	781-740-4441	291-7
Arabia Steamboat Museum 400 Grand Blvd	Kansas City	MO	64106	**800-471-1856**	816-471-1856	509
Arabian Horse World Magazine 1316 Tamson Drive Suite 101	Cambria	CA	94328	**800-955-9423**	805-771-2300	449-14
Arachnid Inc 6212 Material Ave	Loves Park	IL	61111	**800-435-8319**	815-654-0212	317
ARAMARK Corp 1101 Market St Aramark Tower	Philadelphia	PA	19107	**800-999-8989**	215-238-3000	184
NYSE: RMK						
ARAMARK Food & Support Services 1101 Market St	Philadelphia	PA	19107	**800-999-8989**	215-238-3000	294
ARAMARK Harrison Lodging 580 White Plains Rd	Tarrytown	NY	10591	**800-422-6338**	914-631-8100	267
ARAMARK Uniform & Career Apparel 1101 Market St	Philadelphia	PA	19107	**800-999-8989**	215-238-3000	267
Aramco Services Co 9009 West Loop S	Houston	TX	77096	**800-343-4272**	713-432-4000	525
Arandell Corp PO Box 405	Menomonee Falls	WI	53052	**800-558-8724**	262-255-4400	615
ARB Inc 26000 Commercentre Dr	Lake Forest	CA	92630	**800-622-2699**	949-598-9242	187-9
Arbella Indemnity Insurance Co PO Box 699103	Quincy	MA	02269	**800-972-5348**	617-328-2800	384-4
Arbella Mutual Insurance Co PO Box 699103	Quincy	MA	02269	**800-972-5348**	617-328-2800	384-4
Arbella Protection Insurance Co PO Box 699103	Quincy	MA	02269	**800-972-5348**	617-328-2800	384-4
Arbeter Ring. Workmen's Circle/ 45 E 33rd St 4th Fl	New York	NY	10016	**800-922-2558**	212-889-6800	49-9
Arbinet-thexchange Inc 120 Albany St Tower II 4th Fl	New Brunswick	NJ	08901	**800-272-4638**	732-509-9100	680
NASDAQ: ARBX						
Arbitration Assn Inc. American 335 Madison Ave 10th Fl	New York	NY	10017	**800-778-7879**	212-716-5800	41
Arbitration Forums Inc 3350 Buschwood Park Dr Suite 295	Tampa	FL	33618	**800-967-8889***	813-931-4004	41
*Cust Svc						
Arbor Day Foundation. National 211 N 12th St	Lincoln	NE	68508	**888-448-7337**	402-474-5655	48-13
Arbor Hospice & Home Care 2366 Oak Valley Dr	Ann Arbor	MI	48103	**888-992-2273**	734-662-5999	365
Arbor Tree Surgery Inc 802 Paso Robles St	Paso Robles	CA	93446	**800-238-9494**	805-239-1239	765
Arboriculture. International Society of 1400 W Anthony Dr PO Box 3129	Champaign	IL	61826	**888-472-8733**	217-355-9411	48-2
Arbors The 403 W Center St	Manchester	CT	06040	**888-227-2677**	860-647-9343	659

Name / Address	City	State	ZIP	Toll-Free	Phone	Class
Arbour Hospital 49 Robinwood Ave	Jamaica Plain	MA	02130	**800-828-3934**	617-522-4400	366-3
Arby's Inc 1000 Corporate Dr	Fort Lauderdale	FL	33334	**800-487-2729**	954-351-5100	657
ARC (American Refugee Committee) 430 Oak Grove St Suite 204	Minneapolis	MN	55403	**800-875-7060**	612-872-7060	48-5
Arc Electric Inc PO Box 1667	Chesapeake	VA	23327	**800-989-1053**	757-424-5164	188-4
ARC Energy Trust 440 2nd Ave SW Suite 2100	Calgary	AB	T2P5E9	**888-272-4900**	403-503-8600	662
TSE: AET.UN						
ARC Inc. Adoption 4701 Pine St Suite J-7	Philadelphia	PA	19143	**800-884-4004**	215-748-1441	48-6
ARC Industries Inc 2879 Johnstown Rd	Columbus	OH	43219	**800-734-7007**	614-475-7007	707
ARC International 2025 Gateway Pl Suite 140	San Jose	CA	95110	**866-272-3344**	408-437-3400	176-2
ARC Traders Inc PO Box 3429	Scottsdale	AZ	85271	**800-528-2374**	480-945-0769	399
Arc of the US 1010 Wayne Ave Suite 650	Silver Spring	MD	20910	**800-433-5255**	301-565-3842	48-17
Arcadia Financial Ltd PO Box 1437	Eden Prairie	MN	55440	**800-486-1750**	952-944-4520	215
Arcadia Health Care 26777 Central Park Blvd Suite 200	Southfield	MI	48076	**800-733-8427**	248-352-7530	358
Arcadia University 450 S Easton Rd	Glenside	PA	19038	**888-232-8373**	215-572-2900	163
Arch Coal Inc 1 City Place Suite 300	Saint Louis	MO	63141	**800-238-7398**	314-994-2700	491
NYSE: ACI						
Arch Crown Tags Inc 177 Main St	West Orange	NJ	07052	**800-526-8353**	973-731-6300	404
Archadeck 2112 W Laburnum Ave Suite 100	Richmond	VA	23227	**800-722-4668**	804-353-6999	188-2
Archaeology Magazine 36-36 33rd St	Long Island City	NY	11106	**877-275-9782***	718-472-3050	449-19
*Cust Svc						
Archambault Group Inc 500 rue Sainte-Catherine E	Montreal	QC	H2L2C6	**877-849-8589**	514-849-6206	514
Archbold Container Corp 800 W Barre Rd PO Box 10	Archbold	OH	43502	**800-446-2520**	419-445-8865	231
Archer Daniels Midland Co (ADM) 4666 E Faries Pkwy	Decatur	IL	62526	**800-637-5824**	217-424-5200	184
NYSE: ADM						
Archipelago Holdings LLC 100 S Wacker Dr Suite 1800	Chicago	IL	60606	**888-514-7284**	312-960-1696	251
Architects. American Institute of 1735 New York Ave NW	Washington	DC	20006	**800-365-2724***	202-626-7300	48-4
*Orders						
Architects. American Society of Landscape 636 'I' St NW	Washington	DC	20001	**800-787-2752**	202-898-2444	48-2
Architects & Designers Book Service Doubleday Select Inc 101 Park Ave 23rd Fl	New York	NY	10178	**800-321-7323**		94
Architectural Bronze & Aluminum Corp 3638 W Oakton St	Skokie	IL	60076	**800-339-6581**	847-674-3638	766
Architectural Digest 6300 Wilshire Blvd 11th Fl	Los Angeles	CA	90048	**800-234-2347**	323-965-3400	449-2
Architectural Record Magazine 2 Penn Plaza 9th Fl	New York	NY	10121	**888-867-6395***	212-904-2594	449-2
*Cust Svc						
Architectural Shapes & Colors Custom Tile 1201 Millerton St SE	Canton	OH	44707	**877-497-4273**	330-484-0429	736
Architectural & Transportation Barriers Compliance Board 1331 F St NW Suite 1000	Washington	DC	20004	**800-872-2253**	202-272-0080	336-16
Architecture Magazine 770 Broadway	New York	NY	10003	**800-745-8922**	646-654-5500	449-2
Archstone-Smith Trust 9200 E Panorama Cir Suite 400	Englewood	CO	80112	**877-272-4786**	303-708-5959	641
NYSE: ASN						
Archway Cookies LLC 67 W Michigan Ave Suite 608	Battle Creek	MI	49017	**800-444-6205**	269-962-6205	291-9
Archway & Mother's Cookie Co 810 81st Ave	Oakland	CA	94621	**800-538-4842**	510-569-2323	291-9
Arco Electric Products Corp 2325 E Michigan Rd	Shelbyville	IN	46176	**800-428-4370**	317-398-9713	507
Arcom Control Systems 7500 W 161st St	Overland Park	KS	66085	**888-941-2224**	913-549-1000	174
Arcos Industries 1 Arcos Dr	Mount Carmel	PA	17851	**800-233-8460**	570-339-5200	798
ArcRon Div IEA W 141 N 9501 Fountain Blvd	Menomonee Falls	WI	53051	**800-886-4151**	262-255-4150	688
Arctic Office Products 100 W Fireweed Ln	Anchorage	AK	99503	**800-478-2322**	907-276-2322	524
Arctic Slope Regional Corp PO Box 129	Barrow	AK	99723	**800-770-2772**	907-852-8633	527
Arctic Star Refrigeration Mfg Co Inc 3540 W Pioneer Pkwy	Arlington	TX	76013	**800-229-6562**	817-274-1396	650
Arctic Storm Inc 400 N 34th St Suite 306	Seattle	WA	98103	**800-929-0908**	206-547-6557	280
Arcturus Engineering Inc 400 Logue Ave	Mountain View	CA	94043	**888-446-7911**	650-962-3020	410
Ardaman & Assoc Inc 8008 S Orange Ave	Orlando	FL	32809	**800-432-3143**	407-855-3860	258
Ardan Group Ltd 111 St Joseph's Terr	Woodbridge	NJ	07095	**800-699-3522**	732-855-0670	783
Ardco Corp 8250 E 40th Ave	Denver	CO	80207	**800-544-9013**	303-399-2934	472
Ardinger HT & Son Co 1990 Lake Point Dr	Lewisville	TX	75057	**800-683-0498**	214-631-9830	288
Ardmore Farms Inc 1915 N Woodland Blvd	DeLand	FL	32720	**800-365-8423**	386-734-4634	291-20
ARDMS (American Registry of Diagnostic Medical Sonographers) 51 Monroe St Plaza East 1	Rockville	MD	20850	**800-541-9754**	301-738-8401	49-8
ARE (Association for Research & Enlightenment) 215 67th St	Virginia Beach	VA	23451	**800-333-4499**	757-428-3588	48-17
Area Development Magazine 400 Post Ave Suite 304	Westbury	NY	11590	**800-735-2732**	516-338-0900	449-5
Area Development Partnership 1 Convention Center Plaza	Hattiesburg	MS	39401	**800-238-4288**	601-296-7500	137
Areba Casriel Institute 500 W 57th St	New York	NY	10019	**800-724-4444**	212-293-3000	712
Arena Hotel 817 The Alameda	San Jose	CA	95126	**800-954-6835**	408-294-6500	373
Arends & Sons Inc 715 S Sangamon Ave	Gibson City	IL	60936	**800-637-6052**	217-784-4241	270
Arescom Inc 47338 Fremont Blvd	Fremont	CA	94538	**800-575-4736**	510-445-3638	496
ARG Trucking Corp 369 Bostwick Rd	Phelps	NY	14532	**800-334-1314**	315-789-8871	769
Argent Hotel 50 3rd St	San Francisco	CA	94103	**877-222-6699**	415-974-6400	373
Argents Express Group 7025 Metroplex Dr	Romulus	MI	48174	**800-229-2231**	734-326-9499	306
Argo International Corp 140 Franklin St	New York	NY	10013	**877-274-6468**	212-431-1700	245
Argonaut Group Inc 10101 Reunion Pl Suite 500	San Antonio	TX	78216	**800-470-7958**	210-321-8400	355-4
NASDAQ: AGII						
Argonaut Hotel 495 Jefferson St.	San Francisco	CA	94109	**800-790-1415**	415-563-0800	373
Argonaut Insurance Co 250 Middlefield Rd	Menlo Park	CA	94025	**800-222-7811**	650-326-0900	384-4
Argonaut Technologies Inc 220 Saginaw Dr	Redwood City	CA	94063	**877-655-4200**	650-716-1600	229
NASDAQ: AGNT						
Argosy Casino Cincinnati 777 Argosy Pkwy	Lawrenceburg	IN	47025	**888-274-6797***	812-539-8000	133
*Resv						
Argosy Casino Kansas City 777 NW Argosy Pkwy	Riverside	MO	64150	**800-900-3423**	816-746-3100	133
Argosy Gaming Co 219 Piasa St	Alton	IL	62002	**800-336-7568**	618-474-7500	132
NYSE: AGY						
Argosy University/Twin Cities 1515 Central Pkwy	Eagan	MN	55121	**888-844-2004**	651-846-2882	787
Argosy's Alton Belle Casino 219 Piasa St	Alton	IL	62002	**800-336-7568**		133
Argus The 39737 Paseo Padre Pkwy	Fremont	CA	94538	**800-595-9595**	510-661-2600	522-2
Argus International Ltd 108 Whispering Pines Dr Suite 110	Scotts Valley	CA	95066	**800-862-7487**	831-461-4700	798
Argus Leader 200 S Minnesota Ave	Sioux Falls	SD	57104	**800-530-6397**	605-331-2200	522-2
Argus Observer 1160 SW 4th St	Ontario	OR	97914	**800-945-4223**	541-889-5387	522-2
Argus-Press 201 E Exchange St	Owosso	MI	48867	**800-444-4850**	989-725-5136	522-2
Argyle Hotel 8358 Sunset Blvd	West Hollywood	CA	90069	**800-225-2637**	323-654-7100	373
ARI Network Services Inc 11425 W Lake Pk Dr Suite 900	Milwaukee	WI	53224	**800-233-6997**	414-278-7676	176-10
Aria Spa & Club at the Vail Cascade Resort 1300 Westhaven Dr	Vail	CO	81657	**888-824-5772**	970-479-5942	698
Ariba Inc 807 11th Ave	Sunnyvale	CA	94089	**888-237-3131**	650-390-1000	39
NASDAQ: ARBA						
Ariel Capital Management LLC 200 E Randolph Dr Suite 2900	Chicago	IL	60601	**800-292-7435**	312-726-0140	393
Aries Research Inc 46791 Fremont Blvd	Fremont	CA	94538	**800-282-7437**	510-413-0288	171-3
Arima Marine International Inc 47 37th St NE	Auburn	WA	98002	**800-811-6440**	253-939-7980	91
ARINC Inc 2551 Riva Rd	Annapolis	MD	21401	**800-492-2182**	410-266-4000	669
Aristocrat Hotel. Holiday Inn 1933 Main St	Dallas	TX	75201	**800-231-4235**	214-741-7700	373
Aristocrat Technologies 7230 Amigo St	Las Vegas	NV	89119	**800-748-4156**	702-269-5000	317
Aristos International 319 S 11th St	McAllen	TX	78501	**800-527-4786**	956-631-2000	369
Aristotle Publishing Inc 205 Pennsylvania Ave SE	Washington	DC	20003	**800-243-4401**	202-543-8345	176-11
Arizant Inc 10393 W 70th St	Eden Prairie	MN	55344	**800-800-4346**	952-947-1200	469
Arizona						
Attorney General 1275 W Washington St	Phoenix	AZ	85007	**888-377-6108**	602-542-5025	335
Bill Status Capitol Complex 1700 W Washington St	Phoenix	AZ	85007	**800-352-8404**	602-542-4900	425
Children Youth & Families Div 1789 W Jefferson St	Phoenix	AZ	85007	**877-543-7633**	602-542-2277	335
Environmental Quality Dept 1110 W Washington St	Phoenix	AZ	85007	**800-234-5677**	602-207-2300	335
Legislature Capitol Complex 1700 W Washington St	Phoenix	AZ	85007	**800-352-8404**	602-542-4900	335
Rehabilitation Services Administration 1789 W Jefferson St 2nd Fl NW	Phoenix	AZ	85007	**800-563-1221**	602-542-3332	335
Tourism Office 1110 W Washington St Suite 155	Phoenix	AZ	85007	**888-520-3434**	602-364-3700	335
Arizona Assn of Realtors 255 E Osborne Rd Suite 200	Phoenix	AZ	85012	**800-426-7274**	602-248-7787	642
AriZona Beverage Co 5 Dakota Dr Suite 205	Lake Success	NY	11024	**800-832-3775**	516-812-0300	81-2
Arizona Biltmore Resort & Spa 2400 E Missouri Ave	Phoenix	AZ	85016	**800-950-0086**	602-955-6600	655
Arizona Cardinals 8701 S Hardy Dr	Tempe	AZ	85284	**800-999-1402**	602-379-0101	703
Arizona Chamber of Commerce 1221 E Osborne Rd Suite 100	Phoenix	AZ	85014	**800-498-6973**	602-248-9172	138
Arizona Charlie's Hotel & Casino 740 S Decatur Blvd	Las Vegas	NV	89107	**800-342-2695**	702-258-5111	133
Arizona Community Foundation 2122 E Highland Suite 400	Phoenix	AZ	85016	**800-222-8221**	602-381-1400	298
Arizona Correctional Industries 3701 W Cambridge Ave	Phoenix	AZ	85009	**800-992-1738**	602-272-7600	618
Arizona Daily Star 4850 S Park Ave	Tucson	AZ	85714	**800-695-4111**	520-573-4220	522-2
Arizona Dental Assn 4131 N 36th St	Phoenix	AZ	85018	**800-866-2732**	602-957-4777	225
Arizona Federal Credit Union PO Box 60070	Phoenix	AZ	85082	**800-523-4603**	602-683-1000	216
Arizona Golf Resort & Conference Center 425 S Power Rd	Mesa	AZ	85206	**800-528-8282**	480-832-3202	655
Arizona Highways Magazine 2039 W Lewis Ave	Phoenix	AZ	85009	**800-543-5432**	602-712-2000	449-22
Arizona Inn 2200 E Elm St	Tucson	AZ	85719	**800-933-1093**	520-325-1541	373
Arizona Insights Relocation Center Inc 10446 N 74th St Suite 100	Scottsdale	AZ	85258	**800-899-7356**	480-481-8401	652
Arizona Land Income Corp 2999 N 44th St Suite 100	Phoenix	AZ	85018	**800-999-1818**	602-952-6800	640
AMEX: AZL						

	City	State	ZIP	Toll-Free	Phone	Class
Arizona Limousines Inc 8900 N Central Ave Suite 101	Phoenix	AZ	85020	**800-678-0033**	602-267-7097	433
Arizona Medical Assn 810 W Bethany Home Rd	Phoenix	AZ	85013	**800-482-3480**	602-246-8901	466
Arizona Memorial Museum Assn 1 Arizona Memorial Pl	Honolulu	HI	96818	**888-485-1941**	808-422-5664	509
Arizona Opera Co 4600 N 12th St	Phoenix	AZ	85014	**877-473-1497**	602-266-7464	563-2
Arizona Portland Cement Co 2400 N Central Ave	Phoenix	AZ	85004	**800-462-2475**	602-271-0069	190-1
Arizona Precision Sheet Metal 2140 W Pinnacle Peak Rd	Phoenix	AZ	85027	**800-443-7039**	623-516-3700	688
Arizona Public Service Co (APS) 400 N 5th St *Cust Svc	Phoenix	AZ	85004	**800-253-9405***	602-250-1000	774
Arizona Republic 200 E Van Buren	Phoenix	AZ	85004	**800-331-9303**	602-444-8000	522-2
Arizona Republican State Committee 3501 N 24th St	Phoenix	AZ	85016	**800-844-4065**	602-957-7770	605-2
Arizona. State Bar of 4201 N 24th St Suite 200	Phoenix	AZ	85016	**866-482-9227**	602-252-4804	73
Arizona State Capitol Museum 1700 W Washington St	Phoenix	AZ	85007	**800-255-5841**	602-542-4675	509
Arizona State Hospital 2500 E Van Buren St	Phoenix	AZ	85008	**877-588-5163**	602-244-1331	366-3
Arizona Western College PO Box 929	Yuma	AZ	85366	**888-293-0392**	928-317-6000	160
Arizona Wholesale Supply Co 2020 E University Dr	Phoenix	AZ	85062	**800-877-4954**	602-258-7901	601
Ark Agency Animal Insurance Services PO Box 223	Paynesville	MN	56362	**800-328-8894**	320-243-7250	384-1
Ark-Les Corp 95 Mill St	Stoughton	MA	02072	**800-342-6472**	781-297-6000	803
Ark-La-Tex Antique & Classic Vehicle Museum 601 Spring St	Shreveport	LA	71101	**888-664-4854**	318-222-0227	509
Ark Valley Electric Co-op Assn 10 E 10th St	South Hutchinson	KS	67505	**888-297-9212**	620-662-6661	244
Arkansas						
Attorney General 323 Center St Suite 200 *Consumer Info	Little Rock	AR	72201	**800-482-8982***	501-682-2007	335
Consumer Protection Div 323 Center St Tower Bldg Suite 200	Little Rock	AR	72201	**800-482-8982**	501-682-6150	335
Crime Victims Reparations Board 323 Center St Suite 200	Little Rock	AR	72201	**800-448-3014**	501-682-1323	335
Economic Development Dept 1 Capitol Mall Suite 4C-300	Little Rock	AR	72201	**800-275-2672**	501-682-1121	335
Financial Aid Office 114 E Capitol St	Little Rock	AR	72201	**800-547-8839**	501-371-2013	711
Insurance Dept 1200 W 3rd St	Little Rock	AR	72201	**800-282-9134**	501-371-2600	335
Parks & Tourism Dept 1 Capitol Mall	Little Rock	AR	72201	**800-628-8725**	501-682-7777	335
Rehabilitation Services 1616 Brookwood Dr	Little Rock	AR	72202	**800-330-0632**	501-296-1600	335
Vital Records Div 4815 W Markham St Slot 44	Little Rock	AR	72205	**800-637-9314**	501-661-2174	335
Worker's Compensation Commission PO Box 950	Little Rock	AR	72203	**800-622-4472**	501-682-3930	335
Arkansas Alligator Farm & Petting Zoo 847 Whittington Ave	Hot Springs	AR	71901	**800-750-7891**	501-623-6172	811
Arkansas Aluminum Alloys Inc 4400 Malvern Rd *Cust Svc	Hot Springs	AR	71901	**800-643-1302***	501-262-3420	476
Arkansas Arts Center 501 E 9th St	Little Rock	AR	72202	**800-264-2787**	501-372-4000	509
Arkansas Blue Cross Blue Shield PO Box 2181	Little Rock	AR	72203	**800-238-8379**	501-378-2000	384-3
Arkansas Business Journal 122 E 2nd St	Little Rock	AR	72203	**888-322-6397**	501-372-1443	449-5
Arkansas Capital Corp Group 200 S Commerce St Suite 400	Little Rock	AR	72201	**800-216-7237**	501-374-9247	214
Arkansas Democrat-Gazette 121 E Capital St *Cust Svc	Little Rock	AR	72201	**800-482-1121***	501-378-3400	522-2
Arkansas Distributing Co LLC 800 E Barton	West Memphis	AR	72301	**877-735-3506**	870-735-3506	82-1
Arkansas Educational Television Network (AETN) PO Box 1250	Conway	AR	72033	**800-662-2386**	501-682-2386	620
Arkansas Lime Co 600 Limedale Rd *Cust Svc	Batesville	AR	72501	**800-252-5580***	870-793-2301	432
Arkansas Medical Society PO Box 55088	Little Rock	AR	72215	**800-542-1058**	501-224-8967	466
Arkansas Museum of Science & History Museum of Discovery 500 President Clinton Ave Suite 150	Little Rock	AR	72201	**800-880-6475**	501-396-7050	509
Arkansas Realtors Assn 204 Executive Ct Suite 300	Little Rock	AR	72205	**888-333-2206**	501-225-2020	642
Arkansas Repertory Theatre 601 Main St	Little Rock	AR	72203	**866-684-3737**	501-378-0445	562
Arkansas River Historical Society Museum 5350 Cimarron Rd	Catoosa	OK	74015	**888-512-7678**	918-266-2291	509
Arkansas State Dental Assn 2501 Crestwood Dr Suite 205	North Little Rock	AR	72116	**800-501-2732**	501-771-7650	225
Arkansas State University PO Box 1630	State University	AR	72467	**800-643-0080**	870-972-3024	163
Beebe 1000 Iowa St	Beebe	AR	72012	**800-632-9985**	501-882-6452	160
Newport 7648 Victory Blvd	Newport	AR	72112	**800-976-1676**	870-512-7800	160
Arkansas Tech University 1605 Coliseum Dr	Russellville	AR	72801	**800-582-6953**	479-968-0389	163
Arkansas Trailer Mfg Co 3200 S Elm St	Little Rock	AR	72204	**800-666-5417**	501-666-5417	768
Arkansas Valley Electric Co-op Corp 1811 W Commercial St	Ozark	AR	72949	**800-468-2176**	479-667-2176	244
Arkansas Valley Petroleum Inc 8336 E 73rd St Suite 100	Tulsa	OK	74133	**800-888-1389**	918-252-0508	569
Arkansas Western Gas Co 1001 Sain St	Fayetteville	AR	72703	**800-773-2113**	479-521-5400	774
Arkwright Inc 538 Main St *Cust Svc	Fiskeville	RI	02823	**800-942-5900***	401-821-1000	542-1
ARL (US Army Research Laboratory) ATTN: AMSRL-CS-PA 2800 Powder Mill Rd	Adelphi	MD	20783	**800-276-9522**	301-394-1178	654
Arley Corp 1115 W Chestnut St *Cust Svc	Brockton	MA	02301	**800-628-7872***	508-580-4245	731
Arlington Chamber of Commerce 505 E Border St	Arlington	TX	76010	**800-834-3928**	817-275-2613	137
Arlington Coal & Lumber Co Inc 41 Park Ave	Arlington	MA	02476	**800-649-8101**	781-643-8100	359
Arlington Computer Products Inc 851 Commerce Ct *Orders	Buffalo Grove	IL	60089	**800-548-5105***	847-541-6333	178
Arlington Convention & Visitors Bureau 1905 E Randol Mill Rd	Arlington	TX	76011	**800-433-5374**	817-265-7721	205
Arlington Convention & Visitors Service 1100 N Glebe Rd Suite 1500	Arlington	VA	22201	**800-296-7996**	703-228-0888	205
Arlington Industries Inc 1001 Technology Way	Libertyville	IL	60048	**800-323-4147**	847-362-1001	523
Arlington Industries Inc 1 Stauffer Industrial Pk	Scranton	PA	18517	**800-233-4717**	570-562-0270	803
Arlington Resort Hotel & Spa 239 Central Ave	Hot Springs	AR	71901	**800-643-1502**	501-623-7771	655
Arlins Aircraft Service Inc 36 Gallatin Field	Belgrade	MT	59714	**800-953-2471**	406-388-1351	63
Arlon Adhesives & Films 2811 S Harbor Blvd	Santa Ana	CA	92704	**800-854-0361**	714-540-2811	3
Arm Wrestling Assn. New York PO Box 670952	Flushing	NY	11367	**877-892-2707**	718-544-4592	48-22
ARMA International 13725 W 109th St Suite 101	Lenexa	KS	66215	**800-422-2762**	913-341-3808	49-12
Armaclad Inc 6806 Anthony Hwy	Waynesboro	PA	17268	**800-541-6666**	717-749-3141	232
Armada Funds PO Box 8421	Boston	MA	02266	**800-622-3863**		517
Armada Rubber Mfg Co 24586 Armada Ridge Rd PO Box 579	Armada	MI	48005	**800-842-8311**	586-784-9135	664
Armada/Hoffler Construction Co 222 Central Pk Ave Suite 2100	Virginia Beach	VA	23462	**800-766-0543**	757-366-4000	185
Armand Mfg Inc 2399 Silver Wolf Dr	Henderson	NV	89015	**800-343-7982**	702-565-7500	67
Armani Exchange 568 Broadway	New York	NY	10012	**800-717-2929**	212-431-6000	273
Armanino Foods of Distinction Inc 30588 San Antonio St *NASDAQ: ARMF*	Hayward	CA	94544	**800-255-5855**	510-441-9300	291-36
Armatron International Inc 15 Highland Ave	Malden	MA	02148	**800-343-3280**	781-321-2300	420
Armbrust International 735 Allens Ave	Providence	RI	02905	**800-255-2631**	401-781-3300	401
Armed Forces Communications & Electronics Assn (AFCEA) 4400 Fair Lakes Ct	Fairfax	VA	22033	**800-336-4583**	703-631-6100	48-19
Armed Forces Insurance Exchange (AFI) PO Box G	Fort Leavenworth	KS	66027	**800-828-7732**	913-651-5000	384-4
Armed Services Mutual Benefit Assn (ASMBA) PO Box 160384	Nashville	TN	37216	**800-251-8434**	615-851-0800	48-19
Armellini Express Lines Inc 3446 SW Armellini Ave	Palm City	FL	34990	**800-626-1815**	772-287-0575	769
Armin Industries 1500 N La Fox St	South Elgin	IL	60177	**800-427-3607**	847-742-1864	745
Armor All Products Corp PO Box 24305	Oakland	CA	94623	**800-222-7784**	510-271-7000	149
Armor Forensics 13386 International Pkwy	Jacksonville	FL	32218	**800-852-0300**	904-485-1836	229
Armor Safe Technologies LLC PO Box 560275	The Colony	TX	75056	**800-487-2766**	972-624-5734	665
Armour Tommy Golf Co 36 Dufflaw Rd *Cust Svc	Toronto	ON	M6A2W1	**800-723-4653***	416-630-4996	701
Arms Acres 75 Seminary Hill Rd	Carmel	NY	10512	**800-989-7581**	845-225-3400	712
Arms. Citizens Committee for the Right to Keep & Bear 12500 NE 10th Pl	Bellevue	WA	98005	**800-426-4302**	425-454-4911	48-7
Armstrong Air Conditioning Inc 421 Monroe St	Bellevue	OH	44811	**800-448-5872**	419-483-4840	16
Armstrong Atlantic State University 11935 Abercorn St	Savannah	GA	31419	**800-633-2349**	912-927-5275	163
Armstrong-Blum Mfg Co Inc 3501 Marvel Dr	Oshkosh	WI	54902	**800-472-9464**	920-236-7200	670
Armstrong County Chamber of Commerce 124 Market St	Kittanning	PA	16201	**800-979-3348**	724-543-1305	137
Armstrong County Tourist Bureau 125 Market St Suite 2	Kittanning	PA	16201	**888-265-9954**	724-548-3226	205
Armstrong Garden Centers Inc 2200 E Rt 66 Suite 200	Glendora	CA	91740	**800-229-1707**	626-914-1091	318
Armstrong Holdings Inc 2500 Columbia Ave	Lancaster	PA	17603	**800-446-8066**	717-397-0611	355-3
Armstrong Industrial Hose Products LLC 96 Stokes Ave	Trenton	NJ	08638	**800-275-6547**	609-883-3030	364
Armstrong Lumber Co Inc 2709 Auburn Way N	Auburn	WA	98002	**800-868-9066**	253-833-6666	805
Armstrong Medical Industries Inc 575 Knightsbridge Pkwy *Cust Svc	Lincolnshire	IL	60069	**800-323-4220***	847-913-0101	467
Armstrong Teasdale LLP 1 Metropolitan Sq Suite 2600	Saint Louis	MO	63102	**800-243-5070**	314-621-5070	419
Armstrong World Industries Inc 2500 Columbia Ave *Cust Svc	Lancaster	PA	17603	**800-233-3823***	717-397-0611	286
Army & Air Force Exchange Service (AAFES) 3911 S Walton Walker Blvd	Dallas	TX	75236	**800-527-6790**	214-312-2011	778
Army. Association of the US 2425 Wilson Blvd	Arlington	VA	22201	**800-336-4570**	703-841-4300	48-19
Army Distaff Foundation 6200 Oregon Ave NW	Washington	DC	20015	**800-541-4255**	202-541-0105	48-19
ARMY Magazine 2425 Wilson Blvd	Arlington	VA	22201	**800-336-4570**	703-841-4300	449-12
Army & Navy Academy 2605 Carlsbad Blvd PO Box 3000	Carlsbad	CA	92018	**888-762-2338**	760-729-2385	611
Army Times Magazine 6883 Commercial Dr	Springfield	VA	22159	**800-424-9335**	703-750-9000	449-12
Army Times Publishing Co 6883 Commercial Dr	Springfield	VA	22159	**800-424-9335**	703-750-9000	623-9
Arnie's Inc 722 Leonard St NW	Grand Rapids	MI	49504	**800-343-4361**	616-458-1107	291-1
Arnoff Moving & Storage Inc 1282 Dutchess Tpke	Poughkeepsie	NY	12603	**800-633-6683**	845-471-1504	508

Company / Address	City	State	ZIP	Toll-Free	Phone	Class
Arnold Ben Sunbelt Beverage Co PO Box 480	Ridgeway	SC	29130	888-262-9787	803-337-3500	82-3
Arnold Engineering Co 300 N West St	Marengo	IL	60152	800-545-4578	815-568-2000	450
Arnold Lumber Co 251 Fairgrounds Rd	West Kingston	RI	02892	800-339-0116	401-783-2266	190-3
Arnold Machinery Co 2955 W 2100 South *Cust Svc	Salt Lake City	UT	84119	800-821-0548*	801-972-4000	353
Arnold Pen Co 15 N Union St	Petersburg	VA	23803	800-296-6612	804-733-6612	10
Arnold SM Inc 7901 Michigan Ave *Cust Svc	Saint Louis	MO	63111	800-325-7865*	314-544-4103	104
Arnold Transportation Services Inc 9523 Florida Mining Blvd	Jacksonville	FL	32257	800-388-8320	904-262-4285	769
Arnold Truman Cos 701 S Robison Rd	Texarkana	TX	75504	800-243-5343	903-794-3835	569
Arnold Worldwide 101 Huntington Ave	Boston	MA	02199	800-782-4893	617-587-8000	4
ARO Fluid Products Div Ingersoll-Rand Co 1 Aro Ctr PO Box 151 *Cust Svc	Bryan	OH	43506	800-495-0276*	419-636-4242	220
Aromat Corp 629 Central Ave	New Providence	NJ	07974	800-276-6289	908-464-3550	202
Aromatherapy. National Assn for Holistic 3327 W Indian Trail Rd	Spokane	WA	99208	888-275-6242	509-325-3419	48-17
Aron M Corp 350 5th Ave Suite 3005	New York	NY	10118	800-899-2766	212-643-8883	153-2
Aronson Furniture Co 3401 W 47th St	Chicago	IL	60632	800-610-5678	773-376-3400	316
Aroostook Home Health Services 22 Birdseye Ave	Caribou	ME	04736	877-688-9977	207-492-8290	358
Arosa Suites Hotel 163 McLaren St	Ottawa	ON	K2P2G4	866-238-6783	613-238-6783	372
Arotech Corp 250 W 57th St Suite 310 *NASDAQ: ARTX*	New York	NY	10017	888-996-4440	212-258-3222	76
AroundCampus Inc 1000 Conshohocken Rd 4th Fl	Conshohocken	PA	19428	800-466-2221	610-940-1515	623-6
Arpin Paul Van Lines 99 James P Murphy Hwy	West Warwick	RI	02893	800-343-3500	401-828-8111	508
ArQule Inc 19 Presidential Way *NASDAQ: ARQL*	Woburn	MA	01801	800-644-5000	781-994-0300	86
Arranaga Robert & Co Inc 216 S Alameda St	Los Angeles	CA	90012	800-639-0059	213-622-1261	295
Array BioPharma Inc 1885 33rd St *NASDAQ: ARRY*	Boulder	CO	80301	877-633-2436	303-381-6600	86
Array Marketing 555 W 5th St 30th Fl	Los Angeles	CA	90013	866-452-1200	213-533-4189	231
Arribas Brothers Inc PO Box 809	Windermere	FL	34786	888-828-4840	407-828-4840	322
Arris Group Inc 3871 Lakefield Dr *NASDAQ: ARRS*	Suwanee	GA	30024	800-469-6569	770-622-8400	633
Arrow Air Inc 2000 NW 62nd Ave Bldg 711	Miami	FL	33122	800-871-3370	305-871-3116	13
Arrow Business Forms & Labels PO Box 297	Medfield	MA	02052	800-468-3676	508-359-2344	111
Arrow Electronics Inc 25 Hub Dr *NYSE: ARW* ■ *Sales	Melville	NY	11747	800-777-2776*	516-391-1300	245
Arrow Electronics Inc SBM Div 11455 Lakefield Dr	Duluth	GA	30097	888-228-2101	770-623-3430	172
Arrow Enterprise Computing Solutions MOCA Div 5230 Pacific Concourse Dr Bldg 2 4th Fl *Sales	Los Angeles	CA	90045	800-786-3425*	310-643-1400	172
Arrow Enterprise Storage Solutions 18750 Lake Dr E	Chanhassen	MN	55317	800-229-3475	952-949-0053	172
Arrow Exterminators Inc 8613 Roswell Rd	Atlanta	GA	30350	800-281-8978	770-993-8705	567
Arrow Florist & Park Avenue Greenhouses Inc 757 Park Ave	Cranston	RI	02910	800-556-7097	401-785-1900	287
Arrow Group Industries Inc 1680 Rt 23 N	Wayne	NJ	07474	800-851-1085	973-696-6900	106
Arrow International Inc 2400 Bernville Rd *NASDAQ: ARRO*	Reading	PA	19605	800-233-3187	610-378-0131	468
Arrow Line Inc 19 George St	East Hartford	CT	06108	800-243-9560	860-289-1531	108
Arrow Lock Co 325 Duffy Ave	Hicksville	NY	11801	800-221-6529	516-704-2700	345
Arrow-Magnolia International 2646 Rodney Ln *NASDAQ: ARWM*	Dallas	TX	75229	800-527-2101	972-247-7111	149
Arrow Publishing Co 50 Scotland Blvd	Bridgewater	MA	02324	800-343-7500	508-279-1177	623-1
Arrow Specialty Co 2301 E Independence St	Tulsa	OK	74110	800-331-3662	918-583-5711	259
Arrow Speed Warehouse 686 S Adams St	Kansas City	KS	66105	800-255-4606	913-321-1200	61
Arrow Stage Lines 720 E Norfolk Ave	Norfolk	NE	68701	800-672-8302	402-371-3850	108
Arrow Tank & Engineering Co 650 N Emerson St	Cambridge	MN	55008	888-892-7769	763-689-3360	92
Arrow Tru-Line Inc 2211 S Defiance St	Archbold	OH	43502	877-285-7253	419-446-2785	479
Arrow Uniform Rental Inc 6400 Monroe Blvd	Taylor	MI	48180	800-552-7769	313-299-5000	434
Arrowhead Electric Co-op Inc 5401 W Hwy 61	Lutsen	MN	55612	800-864-3744	218-663-7239	244
Arrowhead Mills Inc PO Box 2059	Hereford	TX	79045	800-749-0730	806-364-0730	291-23
Arrowhead Regional Medical Center 400 N Pepper Ave	Colton	CA	92324	877-873-2762	909-580-1000	366-2
Arrowsmith Eye Institute 210 25th Ave N Suite 900	Nashville	TN	37203	800-844-2019	615-327-2020	785
Arrowwood Conference Resort. Doral 975 Anderson Hill Rd	Rye Brook	NY	10573	800-223-6725	914-939-5500	370
Arrowwood Resort 2100 Arrowwood Ln NW	Alexandria	MN	56308	866-386-5263	320-762-1124	655
ARRS (American Roentgen Ray Society) 44211 Slatestone Ct	Leesburg	VA	20176	800-438-2777	703-729-3353	49-8
ARS (American Rose Society) 8877 Jefferson Paige Rd	Shreveport	LA	71119	800-637-6534	318-938-5402	48-18
Art Academy of Cincinnati 1125 Saint Gregory St	Cincinnati	OH	45202	800-323-5692	513-721-5205	163
Art in America Magazine 575 Broadway *Cust Svc	New York	NY	10012	800-925-8059*	212-941-2800	449-2

Company / Address	City	State	ZIP	Toll-Free	Phone	Class
Art & Antiques Magazine 9 E 40th St 7th Fl	New York	NY	10016	800-533-8484	212-686-5557	449-2
Art & Auction Magazine 11 E 36th St 9th Fl *Cust Svc	New York	NY	10016	800-777-8718*	212-447-9555	449-2
Art Concepts on Broadway 924 Broadway Plaza	Tacoma	WA	98402	800-758-7459	253-272-2202	50
Art-Craft Optical Co Inc 57 Goodway Dr S	Rochester	NY	14623	800-828-8288	585-546-6640	531
Art Essentials 32 E Victoria St	Santa Barbara	CA	93101	877-965-5456	805-965-5456	45
Art Hardware 402 S Nevada Ave	Colorado Springs	CO	80903	800-355-4229	719-635-2348	45
Art Institute of Atlanta 6600 Peachtree Dunwoody Rd 100 Embassy Row	Atlanta	GA	30328	800-275-4242	770-394-8300	159
Art Institute of California-San Diego 7650 Mission Valley Rd	San Diego	CA	92108	800-591-2422	858-598-1200	159
Art Institute of California-San Francisco 1170 Market St	San Francisco	CA	94102	888-493-3261	415-865-0198	163
Art Institute of Colorado 1200 Lincoln St	Denver	CO	80203	800-275-2420	303-837-0825	159
Art Institute of Dallas 8080 Park Ln Suite 100	Dallas	TX	75231	800-275-4243	214-692-8080	159
Art Institute of Fort Lauderdale 1799 SE 17th St	Fort Lauderdale	FL	33316	800-275-7603	954-463-3000	159
Art Institute of Houston 1900 Yorktown St	Houston	TX	77056	800-275-4244	713-623-2040	159
Art Institute of Minnesota 15 S 9th St	Minneapolis	MN	55402	800-777-3643	612-332-3361	159
Art Institute of Philadelphia 1622 Chestnut St	Philadelphia	PA	19103	800-275-2474	215-567-7080	159
Art Institute of Pittsburgh 420 Blvd of the Allies	Pittsburgh	PA	15219	800-275-2470	412-263-6600	159
Art Institute of Portland 1122 NW Davis St	Portland	OR	97209	888-228-6528	503-228-6528	163
Art Institute of Seattle 2323 Elliott Ave	Seattle	WA	98121	800-275-2471	206-448-0900	159
Art Institute of Tampa 4401 N Himes Ave Suite 150	Tampa	FL	33614	866-703-3277	813-873-2112	159
Art Iron Inc 860 Curtis St	Toledo	OH	43609	800-472-1113	419-241-1261	483
Art Leather Mfg Co Inc 45-10 94th St	Elmhurst	NY	11373	888-252-5286	718-699-6300	87
Art-O-Rama Inc 510 5th Ave	Pelham	NY	10803	800-421-2438	914-738-1138	304
Art-Phyl Creations 16250 NW 48th Ave	Hialeah	FL	33014	800-327-8318	305-624-2333	231
Art Publishing Group 165 Chubb Ave	Lyndhurst	NJ	07071	800-760-3058	201-842-8500	623-10
Art Stone Enterprises 1795 Express Dr N	Smithtown	NY	11787	800-522-8897	631-582-9500	153-6
ART Studio Clay Co 9320 Michigan Ave	Sturtevant	WI	53177	800-323-0212	262-884-4278	43
Art Style Printing Inc Dataware Div 7570 Renwick Dr	Houston	TX	77081	800-426-4844	713-432-1023	404
Art Supply Warehouse 6672 Westminster Blvd	Westminster	CA	92683	800-854-6467	714-891-3626	45
Art & Woodcrafters Supply 671 Hwy 165 *Orders	Branson	MO	65616	800-786-4818*	417-335-8382	45
ARTA (Association of Retail Travel Agents) 73 White Bridge Rd Box 238	Nashville	TN	37205	800-969-6069		49-21
Artco-Bell Corp PO Box 608	Temple	TX	76503	800-950-5850	254-778-1811	314-3
Artcraft Signs Co 1717 S Acoma St	Denver	CO	80223	800-278-7771	303-777-7771	692
Artcraft Wire Works Inc 7026 Camden Ave	Pennsauken	NJ	08110	800-356-2830	856-663-9334	75
Artesian Resources Corp 664 Churchmans Rd *NASDAQ: ARTNA*	Newark	DE	19702	800-332-5114	302-453-6900	355-5
Artex International Inc 1405 Walnut St	Highland	IL	62249	800-851-8671	618-654-2113	730-7
Artforum International Magazine 350 7th Ave 19th Fl	New York	NY	10001	800-783-4903	212-475-4000	449-2
Arthrex Inc 1370 Creekside Blvd	Naples	FL	34108	800-934-4404	239-643-5553	469
Arthritis Foundation 1330 W Peachtree St Suite 100	Atlanta	GA	30309	800-283-7800	404-872-7100	48-17
ArthroCare Corp 680 Vaqueros Ave *NASDAQ: ARTC*	Sunnyvale	CA	94085	800-348-8929	408-736-0224	249
Arthur Blank & Co Inc 225 Rivermoor St	Boston	MA	02132	800-776-7333	617-325-9600	10
Arthur Brown & Brother Inc 2 W 46th St	New York	NY	10036	800-772-7367	212-575-5555	523
Arthur G James Cancer Hospital & Richard J Solove Research Institute 300 W 10th Ave	Columbus	OH	43210	888-293-3118	614-293-5485	366-5
Arthur R. Outlaw Mobile Convention Center 1 S Water St	Mobile	AL	36602	800-566-2453	251-208-2100	204
Arthur Rutenberg Homes Inc 13922 58th St N	Clearwater	FL	33760	800-274-6637	727-536-5900	186
Artisan Funds PO Box 8412	Boston	MA	02266	800-344-1770		517
Artisan Press 726 Jefferson Ave	Ashland	OR	97520	800-424-9364	541-482-3373	404
Artisans Inc 716 River St	Calhoun	GA	30701	800-311-8756	706-629-9265	131
Artist Brand Canvas 2448 Loma Ave *Orders	South El Monte	CA	91733	888-579-2704*	626-579-2740	43
Artistic Carton Co 1975 Big Timber Rd	Elgin	IL	60123	877-784-7842	847-741-0247	101
Artistic Checks Inc PO Box 1000	Mabelvale	AR	72103	800-243-2577		140
Artistic Direct Inc 1316 College Ave *Cust Svc	Elmira	NY	14901	800-845-3720*	607-733-5541	404
Artistic Industries Inc 6395 SR 103 N Bldg 5	Lewistown	PA	17044	800-424-4433	717-242-2926	544
Artistic Products Inc 125 Commerce Dr	Hauppauge	NY	11788	800-223-8336	718-665-5510	542-3
Artists Alternative 10 Sims Rd	West Hartford	CT	06117	800-927-8258	860-236-3803	45
Artists. American Guild of Musical 1430 Broadway 14th Fl	New York	NY	10018	800-543-2462	212-265-3687	48-4
Artist's Magazine The 4700 E Galbraith Rd	Cincinnati	OH	45236	800-283-0963	513-531-2690	449-2
ARTnews Magazine 48 W 38th St 9th Fl *Cust Svc	New York	NY	10018	800-284-4625*	212-398-1690	449-2

Name / Address	City	State	ZIP	Toll-Free	Phone	Class
ARTnewsletter 48 W 38th St 9th Fl *Cust Svc	New York	NY	10018	**800-284-4625***	212-398-1690	521-6
Artpark 450 S 4th St	Lewiston	NY	14092	**800-659-7275**	716-754-9000	562
Arts. American Federation of 41 E 65th St	New York	NY	10021	**800-232-0270**	212-988-7700	48-4
Arts. American Institute of Graphic 164 5th Ave	New York	NY	10010	**800-548-1634**	212-807-1990	48-4
Arts & Letters Corp 4306 Sunbelt Dr	Addison	TX	75001	**888-853-9292**	972-661-8960	176-8
Aruba Tourism Authority 1200 Harbor Blvd	Weehawken	NJ	07086	**800-862-7822**	201-330-0800	764
Arvco Container Corp 845 Gibson St	Kalamazoo	MI	49001	**800-968-9128**	269-381-0900	101
Arvinyl Metal Laminates Corp 233 N Sherman Ave	Corona	CA	92882	**800-278-4695**	951-371-7800	476
AS Pratt & Sons 1901 Fort Myer Dr Suite 501 *Cust Svc	Arlington	VA	22209	**800-572-2797***	703-528-0145	623-9
ASA (Amateur Softball Assn of America Inc) 2801 NE 50th St	Oklahoma City	OK	73111	**800-654-8337**	405-424-5266	48-22
ASA (American Society on Aging) 833 Market St Suite 511	San Francisco	CA	94103	**800-537-9728**	415-974-9600	48-6
ASA (American Society of Appraisers) 555 Herndon Pkwy Suite 125	Herndon	VA	20170	**800-272-8258**	703-478-2228	48-17
ASA (American Soybean Assn) 12125 Woodcrest Executive Dr Suite 100	Saint Louis	MO	63141	**800-688-7692**	314-576-1770	48-2
ASA (American Statistical Assn) 1429 Duke St	Alexandria	VA	22314	**888-231-3473**	703-684-1221	49-19
ASA (Autism Society of America) 7910 Woodmont Ave Suite 300	Bethesda	MD	20814	**800-328-8476**	301-657-0881	48-17
ASA (Automotive Service Assn) 1901 Airport Fwy *Cust Svc	Bedford	TX	76021	**800-272-7467***	817-283-6205	49-21
ASA Computers Inc 2354 Calle del Mundo	Santa Clara	CA	95054	**800-732-5727**	408-654-2901	174
ASAE (American Society of Agricultural Engineers) 2950 Niles Rd *Orders	Saint Joseph	MI	49085	**800-695-2723***	269-429-0300	48-2
ASAE (American Society of Association Executives) 1575 'I' St NW	Washington	DC	20005	**888-950-2723**	202-626-2723	49-12
Asahi Thermofil Inc 1 Thermofil Way	Fowlerville	MI	48836	**800-444-4408**	517-223-2000	594-2
ASAHP (Association of Schools of Allied Health Professions) 1730 M St NW Suite 500	Washington	DC	20036	**800-497-8080**	202-293-4848	49-8
Asante Technologies Inc 2223 Oakland Rd	San Jose	CA	95131	**800-303-9121**	408-435-8388	174
ASAPS (American Society for Aesthetic Plastic Surgery) 11081 Winners Cir	Los Alamitos	CA	90720	**800-364-2147**	562-799-2356	49-8
ASB Financial Corp 503 Chillicothe St *NASDAQ: ASBP*	Portsmouth	OH	45662	**866-866-3177**	740-354-3177	355-2
ASBA (American Small Businesses Assn) 206 E College St Suite 201B	Grapevine	TX	76051	**800-942-2722**	817-488-8770	49-12
Asbestos & Lead Abatement Report 8737 Colesville Rd Suite 1100	Silver Spring	MD	20910	**800-274-6737**	301-589-5103	521-5
Asbury College 1 Macklem Dr	Wilmore	KY	40390	**800-888-1818**	859-858-3511	163
Asbury Methodist Village 201 Russell Ave	Gaithersburg	MD	20877	**800-327-2879**	301-330-3000	659
ASC (American Society of Cinematographers) 1782 N Orange Dr	Hollywood	CA	90028	**800-448-0145**	323-969-4333	48-4
ASC Inc 1 ASC Ctr	Southgate	MI	48195	**800-640-0191**	734-285-4911	60
ASC Profiles Inc 2110 Enterprise Blvd *Cust Svc	West Sacramento	CA	95691	**800-726-2727***	916-372-6851	688
ASCA (American School Counselor Assn) 1101 King St Suite 625	Alexandria	VA	22314	**800-306-4722**	703-683-2722	49-5
ASCAP (American Society of Composers Authors & Publishers) 1 Lincoln Plaza	New York	NY	10023	**800-952-7227**	212-621-6000	48-4
ASCCP (American Society for Colposcopy & Cervical Pathology) 20 W Washington St Suite 1	Hagerstown	MD	21740	**800-787-7227**	301-733-3640	49-8
ASCD (Association for Supervision & Curriculum Development) 1703 N Beauregard St	Alexandria	VA	22311	**800-933-2723**	703-578-9600	49-5
ASCE News 1801 Alexander Bell Dr Suite 100	Reston	VA	20191	**800-548-2723**	703-295-6215	449-21
Ascenia Bank PO Box 436029	Louisville	KY	40253	**877-369-2265**	502-499-4800	71
Aschinger Electric Co PO Box 26322	Fenton	MO	63026	**800-280-4061**	636-343-1211	188-4
ASCI (American Society for Clinical Investigation) 35 Research Dr Suite 300	Ann Arbor	MI	48103	**866-660-2724**	734-222-6050	49-8
ASCLA (Association of Specialized & Cooperative Library Agencies) 50 E Huron St	Chicago	IL	60611	**800-545-2433**	312-280-4395	49-11
ASCO (American Society of Clinical Oncology) 1900 Duke St Suite 200	Alexandria	VA	22314	**888-282-2552**	703-299-0150	49-8
Ascot Inn 1025 S Tryon St	Charlotte	NC	28203	**800-333-9417**	704-377-3611	373
ASCP (American Society for Clinical Pathology) 2100 W Harrison St *Cust Svc	Chicago	IL	60612	**800-621-4142***	312-738-1336	49-8
ASCP (American Society of Consultant Pharmacists) 1321 Duke St	Alexandria	VA	22314	**800-355-2727**	703-739-1300	49-8
ASCR (Association of Specialists in Cleaning & Restoration) 8229 Cloverleaf Dr Suite 460	Millersville	MD	21108	**800-272-7012**	410-729-9900	49-4
ASCRS (American Society of Cataract & Refractive Surgery) 4000 Legato Rd Suite 850	Fairfax	VA	22033	**800-451-1339**	703-591-2220	49-8

Name / Address	City	State	ZIP	Toll-Free	Phone	Class
Ascutney Mountain Resort 485 Hotel Rd	Brownsville	VT	05037	**800-243-0011**	802-484-7711	655
ASD Data Services LLC 180 Freedom Ave	Murfreesboro	TN	37129	**800-929-2612**	866-273-7297	623-6
ASD Specialty Healthcare 4006 Beltline Rd Suite 200	Addison	TX	75001	**800-746-6273**	972-490-5551	237
ASD/AMD Merchandise Group 2950 31st St Suite 100	Santa Monica	CA	90405	**800-421-4511**	310-396-6006	183
Asel Art Supply 2701 Cedar Springs Rd	Dallas	TX	75201	**888-273-5278**	214-871-2425	45
AseraCare Hospice 1212 Palm Valley Blvd	Round Rock	TX	78664	**800-332-3982**	512-467-7423	365
ASG (Allen Systems Group Inc) 1333 3rd Ave S	Naples	FL	34102	**800-932-5536**	239-435-2200	176-12
Ash Grove Cement Co PO Box 25900	Overland Park	KS	66225	**800-545-1886**	913-451-8900	135
Ash Jacob Co Inc 301 Munson Ave	McKees Rocks	PA	15136	**800-245-6111**	412-331-6660	154
Ash Sam Music Corp PO Box 9047	Hicksville	NY	11802	**888-615-5904**	516-932-6400	515
ASHA (American School Health Assn) 7263 State Rt 43 PO Box 708	Kent	OH	44240	**800-445-2742**	330-678-1601	49-5
ASHA (American Social Health Assn) PO Box 13827	Research Triangle Park	NC	27709	**800-277-8922**	919-361-8400	48-17
ASHA (American Speech-Language-Hearing Assn) 10801 Rockville Pike	Rockville	MD	20852	**800-498-2071**	301-897-5700	49-8
Ashaway Line & Twine Mfg Co PO Box 549	Ashaway	RI	02804	**800-556-7260**	401-377-2221	207
Ashbrook Center Ashland University	Ashland	OH	44805	**877-289-5411**	419-289-5411	654
Asher Winer Co 208 Lurgan Ave	Shippensburg	PA	17257	**800-556-8001**	717-532-4146	153-12
Asheville Area Chamber of Commerce 151 Haywood St	Asheville	NC	28801	**800-257-1300**	828-258-6101	137
Asheville Area Convention & Visitors Bureau PO Box 1010	Asheville	NC	28802	**800-257-5583**	828-258-6102	205
Asheville Citizen Times 14 O'Henry Ave	Asheville	NC	28801	**800-800-4204**	828-252-5622	522-2
Ashford.com 14001 NW 4th St	Sunrise	FL	33325	**888-922-9039**	954-453-2874	402
Ashford/Dromoland Castles PO Box 28966	Atlanta	GA	30358	**800-553-3719**	770-612-1701	369
ASHG (American Society of Human Genetics) 9650 Rockville Pike	Bethesda	MD	20814	**866-486-4363**	301-571-1825	49-19
ASHI (American Society of Home Inspectors) 932 Lee St Suite 101	Des Plaines	IL	60016	**800-743-2744**	847-759-2820	49-3
Ashland Alliance Chamber of Commerce PO Box 830	Ashland	KY	41105	**888-524-6860**	606-324-5111	137
Ashland Community College 1400 College Dr	Ashland	KY	41101	**800-370-7191**	606-329-2999	160
Ashland Office Supply Co Inc 2100 29th St	Ashland	KY	41101	**800-926-1267**	606-329-1400	524
Ashland Times-Gazette 40 E 2nd St	Ashland	OH	44805	**888-463-9711**	419-281-0581	522-2
Ashland University 401 College Ave	Ashland	OH	44805	**800-882-1548**	419-289-4142	163
Ashlar Inc 12731 Research Blvd Bldg A	Austin	TX	78759	**800-877-2745**	512-250-2186	176-5
Ashley-Chicot Electric Co-op Inc 307 E Jefferson St	Hamburg	AR	71646	**800-281-5212**	870-853-5212	244
Ashley Furniture Industries Inc 1 Ashley Way	Arcadia	WI	54612	**800-477-2222**	608-323-3377	314-2
Ashley Lighting Inc 405 Industrial Dr	Trumann	AR	72472	**800-343-5267**	870-483-6181	431
Ashman Court Marriott Conference Hotel 111 W Main St	Midland	MI	48642	**877-645-3643**	989-839-0500	370
Ashmore Brothers Inc PO Box 529	Greer	SC	29652	**800-601-5884**	864-879-7311	187-4
Ashmore Inn & Suites 4019 S Loop 289	Lubbock	TX	79423	**800-785-0061**	806-785-0060	373
ASHRAE (American Society of Heating Refrigerating & Air-Conditioning Engineers Inc) 1791 Tullie Cir NE *Cust Svc	Atlanta	GA	30329	**800-527-4723***	404-636-8400	49-3
Ashta Chemicals Inc 3509 Middle Rd *Cust Svc	Ashtabula	OH	44004	**800-492-5082***	440-997-5221	141
Ashworth Inc 2765 Loker Ave W *NASDAQ: ASHW*	Carlsbad	CA	92008	**800-800-8443**	760-438-6610	153-1
ASI Corp 48289 Fremont Blvd	Fremont	CA	94538	**800-210-0274**	510-226-8000	172
ASI DataMyte Inc 2800 Campus Dr Suite 60	Plymouth	MN	55441	**800-207-5631**	763-553-1040	176-10
Asian American Legal Defense & Education Fund (AALDEF) 99 Hudson St 12th Fl	New York	NY	10013	**800-966-5946**	212-966-5932	48-8
Asiana Airlines Asiana Club 3530 Wilshire Blvd Suite 1700 *Resv	Los Angeles	CA	90010	**800-227-4262***	213-365-4500	27
Asiana Airlines Inc 3530 Wilshire Blvd Suite 1700	Los Angeles	CA	90010	**800-227-4262**	213-365-4500	26
Asics Tiger Corp 16275 Laguna Canyon Rd	Irvine	CA	92618	**800-333-8404**	949-453-8888	296
ASID Professional Designer Magazine 608 Massachusetts Ave NE	Washington	DC	20002	**800-775-2743**	202-546-3480	449-5
Asimov's Science Fiction Magazine 475 Park Ave S 11th Fl	New York	NY	10016	**800-333-4108**	212-686-7188	449-11
Ask Magazine 30 Grove St Suite C	Peterborough	NH	03458	**800-821-0115**	603-924-7209	449-6
ASK Plastics Inc 9750 Ashton Rd	Philadelphia	PA	19114	**888-948-1862**	215-969-0800	593
Ask USGS 12201 Sunrise Valley Dr	Reston	VA	20192	**888-275-8747**		336-9
Askins Kitty Hospice Center 2402 Wayne Memorial Dr	Goldsboro	NC	27534	**800-260-4442**	919-735-1387	365
ASKO Inc 501 W 7th Ave	Homestead	PA	15120	**800-321-1310**	412-461-4110	484
AskSam Systems Inc 121 S Jefferson St	Perry	FL	32347	**800-800-1997**	850-584-6590	176-1
ASLA (American Seminar Leaders Assn) 2405 E Washington Blvd	Pasadena	CA	91104	**800-735-0511**	626-791-1211	49-12
ASLA (American Society of Landscape Architects) 636 'I' St NW	Washington	DC	20001	**800-787-2752**	202-898-2444	48-2
ASLO (American Society of Limnology & Oceanography) 5400 Bosque Blvd Suite 680	Waco	TX	76710	**800-929-2756**	254-399-9635	49-19
ASM Industries Inc Pacer Pumps Div 41 Industrial Cir *Cust Svc	Lancaster	PA	17601	**800-233-3861***	717-656-2161	627

Name / Address	City	State	ZIP	Toll-Free	Phone	Class
ASM International 9639 Kinsman Rd	Materials Park	OH	44073	**800-336-5152**	440-338-5151	49-13
ASMBA (Armed Services Mutual Benefit Assn) PO Box 160384	Nashville	TN	37216	**800-251-8434**	615-851-0800	48-19
ASMC (American Society of Military Comptrollers) 415 N Alfred	Alexandria	VA	22314	**800-462-5637**	703-549-0360	48-19
ASME (American Society of Mechanical Engineers) 3 Park Ave *Cust Svc	New York	NY	10016	**800-843-2763***	212-591-7722	49-19
ASML 8555 S River Pkwy *NASDAQ: ASML*	Tempe	AZ	85284	**800-227-6462**	480-383-4422	685
ASN (Advanced Sports Nutrition) 1813 Cascade St	Hood River	OR	97031	**800-800-9119**	541-387-4500	786
ASNT (American Society for Nondestructive Testing Inc) 1711 Arlingate Ln *Orders	Columbus	OH	43228	**800-222-2768***	614-274-6003	49-19
Asnuntuck Community College 170 Elm St	Enfield	CT	06082	**800-501-3967**	860-253-3000	160
Asolo Theatre Co 5555 N Tamiami Tr	Sarasota	FL	34243	**800-361-8388**	941-351-9010	734
ASP Westward LP 907B E Main St	Humble	TX	77338	**866-446-5979**	281-446-5979	623-8
ASPAN (American Society of PeriAnesthesia Nurses) 10 Melrose Ave Suite 110	Cherry Hill	NJ	08003	**877-737-9696**	856-616-9600	49-8
ASPCA Animal Poison Control Center 1717 S Philo Rd Suite 36	Urbana	IL	61802	**888-426-4435**	217-337-5030	48-3
ASPE (American Society of Professional Estimators) 2525 Perimeter Place Dr Suite 102	Nashville	TN	37214	**888-378-6283**	615-316-9200	49-3
Aspect Business Solutions 7550 IH-10 W 14th Fl	San Antonio	TX	78229	**800-609-8113**	210-256-8300	85
Aspect Communications Corp 1310 Ridder Park Dr *NASDAQ: ASPT*	San Jose	CA	95131	**800-391-2341**	408-325-2200	720
Aspect Medical Systems Inc 141 Needham St *NASDAQ: ASPM*	Newton	MA	02464	**888-247-4633**	617-559-7000	249
ASPEN (American Society for Parenteral & Enteral Nutrition) 8630 Fenton St Suite 412	Silver Spring	MD	20910	**800-727-4567**	301-587-6315	49-8
Aspen Canyon Ranch 13206 County Rd 3	Parshall	CO	80468	**800-321-1357**	970-725-3600	238
Aspen Daily News 517 E Hopkins Ave	Aspen	CO	81611	**800-889-9020**	970-925-2220	522-2
Aspen Group Inc 10325 N Rt 47	Hebron	IL	60034	**888-227-7361**	815-648-2001	786
Aspen Hotel & Suites 2900 S 68th St	Fort Smith	AR	72903	**800-627-9417**	479-452-9000	373
Aspen Meadows Resort 845 Meadows Rd	Aspen	CO	81611	**800-452-4240**	970-925-4240	655
Aspen Publishers Inc 111 8th Ave 7th Fl *Orders	New York	NY	10011	**800-638-8437***	212-771-0600	623-2
Aspen Skiing Co LLC PO Box 1248 *Sales	Aspen	CO	81612	**800-525-6200***	970-925-1220	369
Aspen Sports Ltd 408 E Cooper Ave	Aspen	CO	81611	**800-544-6648**	970-925-6331	702
Aspen Systems Corp 2277 Research Blvd	Rockville	MD	20850	**800-685-6867**	301-519-5000	455
Aspire Group 4510 Executive Dr Suite 206	San Diego	CA	92121	**800-487-2967**	858-526-1530	707
Aspirin Foundation of America 1555 Connecticut Ave NW Suite 200	Washington	DC	20036	**800-432-3247**		49-4
Asplundh Tree Expert Co 708 Blair Mill Rd	Willow Grove	PA	19090	**800-248-8733**	215-784-4200	765
ASPPB (Association of State & Provincial Psychology Boards) 7177 Halcyon Summit Dr	Montgomery	AL	36117	**800-448-4069**	334-832-4580	49-7
ASPR (Association of Staff Physician Recruiters) 1711 W County Rd B Suite 300N	Roseville	MN	55113	**800-830-2777**	651-635-0359	49-8
ASPS (American Society of Plastic Surgeons) 444 E Algonquin Rd	Arlington Heights	IL	60005	**888-475-2784**	847-228-9900	49-8
ASQ (American Society for Quality) 600 N Plankinton Ave	Milwaukee	WI	53201	**800-248-1946**	414-272-8575	49-13
ASRT (American Society of Radiologic Technologists) 15000 Central Ave SE	Albuquerque	NM	87123	**800-444-2778**	505-298-4500	49-8
ASSA ABLOY Door Security Solutions 110 Sargent Dr	New Haven	CT	06511	**800-377-3948**	203-624-5225	232
ASSA Inc 110 Sargent Dr	New Haven	CT	06511	**800-235-7482**	203-603-5959	345
Assault Prevention. National Center for 606 Delsea Dr	Sewell	NJ	08080	**800-258-3189**	856-582-7000	48-17
Assemblies of God (A/G) 1445 N Boonville Ave	Springfield	MO	65802	**800-641-4310**	417-862-2781	48-20
Assemblies of God Theological Seminary 1435 N Glenstone Ave	Springfield	MO	65802	**800-467-2487**	417-268-1000	164-3
Assembly Managers. International Assn of 635 Fritz Dr	Coppell	TX	75019	**800-935-4226**	972-906-7441	49-12
Assembly Technology & Test 12841 Stark Rd	Livonia	MI	48150	**800-373-8634**	734-522-9680	379
Asset Management Fund 230 W Monroe St Suite 2810	Chicago	IL	60606	**800-527-3713**		517
Asset Sales Report 1 State St Plaza	New York	NY	10004	**888-280-4820**	212-803-8200	521-1
Assignable Life Assets 601 N New York Ave Suite 202	Winter Park	FL	32789	**800-334-3211**		783
Assist-2-Sell Inc 1610 Meadow Wood Ln	Reno	NV	89502	**800-528-7816**	775-688-6060	638
Assn of Veterinarians. South Carolina 1226 Pickens St Suite 203	Columbia	SC	29201	**800-441-7228**		782
Associated Agencies Inc 1701 Golf Rd Tower 3 Suite 700	Rolling Meadows	IL	60008	**800-443-2827**	847-427-8400	383
Associated Bag Co 400 W Boden St	Milwaukee	WI	53207	**800-926-6100**	414-769-1000	67
Associated Banc-Corp 1200 Hansen Rd *NASDAQ: ASBC* ■ *PR	Green Bay	WI	54304	**800-236-2722***	920-491-7000	355-2
Associated Bank Green Bay NA 200 N Adams St	Green Bay	WI	54301	**800-236-3479**	920-433-3200	71
Associated Bank Illinois NA 612 N Main St *Cust Svc	Rockford	IL	61103	**800-358-6064***	815-987-3500	71
Associated Bank Milwaukee 401 E Kilbourn Ave	Milwaukee	WI	53202	**800-236-8866**	414-271-1786	71
Associated Bank North 303 S 1st Ave	Wausau	WI	54402	**800-236-7160**	715-845-4301	71
Associated Behavioral Health Care Inc 4701 41st Ave SW Suite 120	Seattle	WA	98116	**800-858-6702**	206-935-1282	454
Associated Bodywork & Massage Professionals (ABMP) 1271 Sugarbush Dr	Evergreen	CO	80439	**800-458-2267**	303-674-8478	48-17
Associated Communications & Research Services Inc (ACRS) 817 NE 63rd St	Oklahoma City	OK	73105	**800-442-3341**	405-843-9966	195
Associated Creditors Exchange Inc 3443 N Central Ave Suite 1100	Phoenix	AZ	85012	**800-280-3800**	602-954-6554	157
Associated Equipment Corp 5043 Farlan Ave	Saint Louis	MO	63115	**800-949-1472**	314-385-5178	247
Associated Equipment Distributors (AED) 615 W 22nd St	Oak Brook	IL	60523	**800-388-0650**	630-574-0650	49-18
Associated Estates Realty Corp 5025 Swetland Ct *NYSE: AEC*	Richmond Heights	OH	44143	**800-440-2372**	216-261-5000	641
Associated Food Stores Inc 1850 W 2100 South *Cust Svc	Salt Lake City	UT	84119	**888-574-7100***	801-973-4400	292-8
Associated General Contractors of America (AGC) 333 John Carlyle St Suite 200	Alexandria	VA	22314	**800-242-1766**	703-548-3118	49-3
Associated General Contractors PAC (AGC PAC) 333 John Carlyle St Suite 200	Alexandria	VA	22314	**800-242-1766**	703-548-3118	604
Associated Global Systems Inc 3333 New Hyde Park Rd *Cust Svc	New Hyde Park	NY	11042	**800-645-8300***	516-627-8910	440
Associated Grocers of Florida Inc 7000 NW 32nd Ave	Miami	FL	33147	**800-275-8181**	305-696-0080	292-8
Associated Grocers Inc 8600 Anselmo Ln	Baton Rouge	LA	70810	**800-637-2021**	225-769-2020	292-8
Associated Grocers Inc 3301 S Norfolk St	Seattle	WA	98118	**800-562-9729**	206-762-2100	292-8
Associated Grocers of New England Inc 725 Gold St	Manchester	NH	03108	**800-242-2248**	603-669-3250	292-8
Associated Grocers of the South 3600 Vanderbilt Rd	Birmingham	AL	35217	**800-695-6051**	205-841-6781	292-8
Associated Hygienic Products LLC 3400 River Green Ct Suite 600	Duluth	GA	30096	**888-639-5863**	770-497-9800	548-2
Associated Locksmiths of America (ALOA) 3003 Live Oak St	Dallas	TX	75204	**800-532-2562**	214-827-1701	49-3
Associated Materials Inc 3773 State Rd	Cuyahoga Falls	OH	44223	**800-257-4335**	330-929-1811	688
Associated Materials Inc Alside Div PO Box 2010	Akron	OH	44309	**800-922-6009**	330-929-1811	233
Associated Pathologists Laboratories 4230 Burnham Ave	Las Vegas	NV	89119	**800-433-2750**	702-733-7866	409
Associated Petroleum Carriers Inc PO Box 2808	Spartanburg	SC	29304	**800-573-9301**	864-573-9301	769
Associated Press Information Services 450 W 33rd St	New York	NY	10001	**800-272-2551**	212-621-1585	623-10
Associated Rollx Vans 6591 Hwy 13 W	Savage	MN	55378	**800-956-6668**	952-890-7851	62-7
Associated Rubber Co PO Box 245	Tallapoosa	GA	30176	**800-277-8231**	770-574-2321	594-3
Associated Steel Corp 18200 Miles Rd	Cleveland	OH	44128	**800-441-9303**	216-475-8000	346
Associated Wholesalers Inc PO Box 67	Robesonia	PA	19551	**800-927-7771**	610-693-3161	292-8
Association for Advanced Life Underwriting (AALU) 2901 Telestar Ct	Falls Church	VA	22042	**888-275-0092**	703-641-9400	49-9
Association for Advanced Training in the Behavioral Sciences (AATBS) 5126 Ralston St	Ventura	CA	93003	**800-472-1931**	805-676-3030	49-5
Association for Advancement of Behavior Therapy (AABT) 305 7th Ave 16th Fl	New York	NY	10001	**800-685-2228**	212-647-1890	49-15
Association for the Advancement of Medical Instrumentation (AAMI) 1110 N Glebe Rd Suite 220	Arlington	VA	22201	**800-332-2264**	703-525-4890	49-8
Association of American Railroads (AAR) 50 F St NW *Cust Svc	Washington	DC	20001	**800-544-7245***	202-639-2100	49-21
Association for Applied Psychophysiology & Biofeedback (AAPB) 10200 W 44th Ave Suite 304	Wheat Ridge	CO	80033	**800-477-8892**	303-422-8436	49-8
Association of Boarding Schools (TABS) 4455 Connecticut Ave NW Suite A-200	Washington	DC	20008	**800-541-5908**	202-966-8705	48-11
Association for Career & Technical Education (ACTE) 1410 King St	Alexandria	VA	22314	**800-826-9972**	703-683-3111	49-5
Association Casualty Insurance Co PO Box 9728	Austin	TX	78766	**800-252-9641**	512-345-7500	384-4
Association of Certified Fraud Examiners (ACFE) 716 West Ave	Austin	TX	78701	**800-245-3321**	512-478-9070	49-1
Association for Childhood Education International (ACEI) 17904 Georgia Ave Suite 215	Olney	MD	20832	**800-423-3563**	301-570-2111	49-5
Association for Children for Enforcement of Support (ACES) PO Box 7842	Fredericksburg	VA	22404	**800-738-2237**		48-6
Association of Christian Schools International (ACSI) 731 Chapel Hills Dr *Cust Svc	Colorado Springs	CO	80920	**800-367-0798***	719-528-6906	49-5
Association of College & Research Libraries (ACRL) 50 E Huron St	Chicago	IL	60611	**800-545-2433**	312-280-2519	49-11

Listing	City	State	ZIP	Toll-Free	Phone	Class
Association of Community Organizations for Reform Now (ACORN) 739 8th St SE	Washington	DC	20003	**877-552-2676**	202-547-2500	48-7
Association for Computing Machinery (ACM) 1515 Broadway 17th Fl	New York	NY	10036	**800-342-6626**	212-869-7440	48-9
Association of Consulting Foresters of America (ACF) 312 Montgomery St Suite 208	Alexandria	VA	22314	**888-540-8733**	703-548-0990	48-2
Association for Continuing Higher Education (ACHE) 2001 Mabelene Rd	Charleston	SC	29406	**800-807-2243**	843-574-6658	49-5
Association for Corporate Growth (ACG) 1926 Waukegan Rd Suite 1	Glenview	IL	60025	**800-699-1331**	847-657-6730	49-12
Association of Corporate Travel Executives (ACTE) 515 King St Suite 340	Alexandria	VA	22314	**800-228-3669**	703-683-5322	48-23
Association for Couples in Marriage Enrichment (ACME) PO Box 10596	Winston-Salem	NC	27108	**800-634-8325**	336-724-1526	48-6
Association of Directory Publishers (ADP) 116 Cass St	Traverse City	MI	49684	**800-267-9002**		49-16
Association for Educational Communications & Technology (AECT) 1800 N Stonelake Dr Suite 2	Bloomington	IN	47404	**877-677-2328**	812-335-7675	49-5
Association of Emergency Physicians (AEP) 911 Whitewater Dr	Mars	PA	16046	**866-772-1818**	724-772-1818	49-8
Association of Energy Service Companies (AESC) 10200 Richmond Ave Suite 275	Houston	TX	77042	**800-692-0771**	713-781-0758	48-12
Association of Executive Search Consultants (AESC) 12 E 41st St 17th Fl	New York	NY	10017	**877-843-2372**	212-398-9556	49-12
Association Executives. American Society of 1575 'I' St NW	Washington	DC	20005	**888-950-2723**	202-626-2723	49-12
Association of Fundraising Professionals (AFP) 1101 King St Suite 700	Alexandria	VA	22314	**800-666-3863**	703-684-0410	49-12
Association of Gospel Rescue Missions (AGRM) 1045 Swift Ave	Kansas City	MO	64116	**800-624-5156**	816-471-8020	48-20
Association of Governing Boards of Universities & Colleges (AGB) 1 Dupont Cir NW Suite 400	Washington	DC	20036	**800-356-6317**	202-296-8400	49-5
Association of Government Accountants (AGA) 2208 Mt Vernon Ave	Alexandria	VA	22301	**800-242-7211**	703-684-6931	49-1
Association of Healthcare Internal Auditors (AHIA) PO Box 449	Onsted	MI	49265	**888-275-2442**	517-467-7729	49-1
Association of Independents in Radio (AIR) 328 Flatbush Ave Suite 322	Brooklyn	NY	11238	**888-937-2477**		620
Association for Interactive Marketing (AIM) 1430 Broadway 8th Fl	New York	NY	10018	**888-337-0008**	212-790-1406	48-9
Association of Junior Leagues International Inc (AJLI) 90 William St Suite 200	New York	NY	10038	**800-955-3248**	212-683-1515	48-15
Association for Library Collections & Technical Services (ALCTS) 50 E Huron St	Chicago	IL	60611	**800-545-2433**	312-280-5038	49-11
Association for Library Service to Children (ALSC) 50 E Huron St	Chicago	IL	60611	**800-545-2433**	312-280-2163	49-11
Association for Library Trustees & Advocates (ALTA) 50 E Huron St	Chicago	IL	60611	**800-545-2433**	312-280-2161	49-11
Association Management Consultants Inc 409 Granville St Suite 218	Vancouver	BC	V6C1T2	**866-668-5344**	604-669-5344	47
Association Managers Inc 9001 Braddock Rd Suite 380	Springfield	VA	22151	**800-403-3374**	703-426-8100	47
Association for Manufacturing Technology (AMT) 7901 Westpark Dr	McLean	VA	22102	**800-524-0475**	703-893-2900	49-12
Association of Military Surgeons of the US (AMSUS) 9320 Old Georgetown Rd	Bethesda	MD	20814	**800-761-9320**	301-897-8800	49-8
Association of Millwork Distributors (AMD) 10047 Robert Trent Jones Pkwy	New Port Richey	FL	34655	**800-786-7274**	727-372-3665	49-3
Association of Nurses in AIDS Care (ANAC) 3538 Ridgewood Rd	Akron	OH	44333	**800-260-6780**	330-670-0101	49-8
Association of Old Crows (AOC) 1000 N Payne St Suite 300	Alexandria	VA	22314	**888-653-2769**	703-549-1600	48-19
Association of Pool & Spa Professionals (APSP) 2111 Eisenhower Ave	Alexandria	VA	22314	**800-323-3996**	703-838-0083	49-4
Association of Professional Flight Attendants 1004 W Euless Blvd	Euless	TX	76040	**800-395-2732**	817-540-0108	405
Association for Professionals in Infection Control & Epidemiology Inc (APIC) 1275 K St NW Suite 1000	Washington	DC	20005	**888-278-2742**	202-789-1890	49-8
Association of Program Directors in Internal Medicine (APDIM) 2501 M St NW Suite 550	Washington	DC	20037	**800-622-4558**	202-887-9450	49-8
Association of Progressive Rental Organizations (APRO) 1504 Robin Hood Trail	Austin	TX	78703	**800-204-2776**	512-794-0095	49-18
Association of Public-Safety Communications Officials International Inc 351 N Williamson Blvd	Daytona Beach	FL	32114	**888-272-6911**	386-322-2500	49-7
Association for Research & Enlightenment (ARE) 215 67th St	Virginia Beach	VA	23451	**800-333-4499**	757-428-3588	48-17
Association of Retail Marketing Services 10 Drs James Parker Blvd Suite 103	Red Bank	NJ	07701	**866-231-6310**	732-842-5070	49-18
Association of Retail Travel Agents (ARTA) 73 White Bridge Rd Box 238	Nashville	TN	37205	**800-969-6069**		49-21
Association Risk Management General Agency PO Box 9728 Suite 160	Austin	TX	78766	**800-252-9641**	512-345-7500	384-4
Association of Schools of Allied Health Professions (ASAHP) 1730 M St NW Suite 500	Washington	DC	20036	**800-497-8080**	202-293-4848	49-8
Association for Services Management International (AFSMI) 1342 Colonial Blvd Suite 25	Fort Myers	FL	33907	**800-333-9786**	239-275-7887	49-12
Association of Social Work Boards (ASWB) 400 Southridge Pkwy Suite B	Culpeper	VA	22701	**800-225-6880**	540-829-6880	49-7
Association of Specialists in Cleaning & Restoration (ASCR) 8229 Cloverleaf Dr Suite 460	Millersville	MD	21108	**800-272-7012**	410-729-9900	49-4
Association of Specialized & Cooperative Library Agencies (ASCLA) 50 E Huron St	Chicago	IL	60611	**800-545-2433**	312-280-4395	49-11
Association of Staff Physician Recruiters (ASPR) 1711 W County Rd B Suite 300N	Roseville	MN	55113	**800-830-2777**	651-635-0359	49-8
Association of State & Provincial Psychology Boards (ASPPB) 7177 Halcyon Summit Dr	Montgomery	AL	36117	**800-448-4069**	334-832-4580	49-7
Association for Supervision & Curriculum Development (ASCD) 1703 N Beauregard St	Alexandria	VA	22311	**800-933-2723**	703-578-9600	49-5
Association of Test Publishers 1201 Pennsylvania Ave Suite 300	Washington	DC	20004	**866-240-7909**		49-5
Association of Trial Lawyers of America (ATLA) 1050 31st St NW	Washington	DC	20007	**800-424-2725**	202-965-3500	49-10
Association of the US Army (AUSA) 2425 Wilson Blvd	Arlington	VA	22201	**800-336-4570**	703-841-4300	48-19
Association of Washington Business PO Box 658	Olympia	WA	98507	**800-521-9325**	360-943-1600	138
Association of Water Technologies (AWT) 8201 Greensboro Dr Suite 300	McLean	VA	22102	**800-858-6683**	703-610-9012	48-2
Association for Women in Science Inc (AWIS) 1200 New York Ave NW Suite 650	Washington	DC	20005	**800-886-2947**	202-326-8940	49-19
Association of Women's Health Obstetric & Neonatal Nurses (AWHONN) 2000 L St NW Suite 740	Washington	DC	20036	**800-673-8499**	202-261-2400	49-8
Assouline & Ting Inc 2050 Richmond St	Philadelphia	PA	19125	**800-521-4491**	215-627-3000	291-41
Assumption College 500 Salisbury St	Worcester	MA	01609	**888-882-7786**	508-767-7000	163
Assurant Employee Benefits 2323 Grand Blvd	Kansas City	MO	64108	**800-733-7879**	816-474-2345	384-2
Assurant Group 11222 Quail Roost Dr	Miami	FL	33157	**800-852-2244**	305-253-2244	355-4
Assurant Inc 1 Chase Manhattan Plaza 41st Fl *NYSE: AIZ*	New York	NY	10005	**800-859-5676**	212-859-7000	355-4
Assurant Life Insurance Co 308 Maltbie St Suite 200	Syracuse	NY	13204	**800-745-7100**	315-451-0066	384-2
AST Bearings 115 Main Rd	Montville	NJ	07045	**800-526-1250**	973-335-2230	77
AST Sports Science Inc 120 Capitol Dr	Golden	CO	80401	**800-627-2788**	303-278-1420	786
ASTA (American Seed Trade Assn) 225 Reinekers Ln Suite 650	Alexandria	VA	22314	**888-890-7333**	703-837-8140	48-2
ASTA (American Society of Travel Agents) 1101 King St Suite 200	Alexandria	VA	22314	**800-440-2782**	703-739-2782	48-23
Astaire Fred Dance Studios Inc 10 Bliss Rd	Longmeadow	MA	01106	**800-278-2473**	413-567-3200	754
ASTD (American Society for Training & Development) 1640 King St Box 1443	Alexandria	VA	22313	**800-628-2783**	703-683-8100	49-5
Astea International Inc 240 Gibraltar Rd *NASDAQ: ATEA*	Horsham	PA	19044	**800-878-4657**	215-682-2500	176-1
Astec America Inc 5810 Van Allen Way	Carlsbad	CA	92008	**888-412-7832**	760-930-4600	252
Astec Industries Inc 4101 Jerome Ave *NASDAQ: ASTE*	Chattanooga	TN	37407	**800-468-5938**	423-867-4210	189
Asthma & Allergy Foundation of America (AAFA) 1233 20th St NW Suite 402	Washington	DC	20036	**800-727-8462**	202-466-7643	48-17
Asthma & Immunology. American Academy of Allergy 611 E Wells St 4th Fl	Milwaukee	WI	53202	**800-822-2762**	414-272-6071	49-8
Asthma & Immunology. American College of Allergy 85 W Algonquin Rd Suite 550	Arlington Heights	IL	60005	**800-842-7777**	847-427-1200	49-8
Asticou Inn 15 Peabody Dr	Northeast Harbor	ME	04662	**800-258-3373**	207-276-3344	373
Aston Coconut Plaza Hotel 450 Lewers St	Honolulu	HI	96815	**877-997-6667**	808-923-8828	373
Aston Hotels & Resorts 2155 Kalakaua Ave Suite 500	Honolulu	HI	96815	**800-922-7866**	808-931-1400	369
Aston Waikiki Circle Hotel 2464 Kalakaua Ave	Honolulu	HI	96815	**877-997-6667**	808-923-1571	373
Astor Crowne Plaza-French Quarter 739 Canal St	New Orleans	LA	70130	**800-684-1127**	504-962-0500	373
Astor Hotel The 924 E Juneau Ave	Milwaukee	WI	53202	**800-558-0200**	414-271-4220	373
Astral Industries Inc 7375 US 27 S PO Box 638 *Sales	Lynn	IN	47355	**800-874-1070***	765-874-2525	134
AstraZeneca Canada Inc 1004 Middlegate Rd	Mississauga	ON	L4Y1M4	**800-565-5877**	905-277-7111	572
AstraZeneca LP PO Box 15437 *NYSE: AZN*	Wilmington	DE	19850	**800-456-3669**	302-886-3000	572
Astrex Inc 205 Express St	Plainview	NY	11803	**800-633-6360**	516-433-1700	245
ASTRO (American Society for Therapeutic Radiology & Oncology) 12500 Fair Lakes Cir Suite 375	Fairfax	VA	22033	**800-962-7876**	703-502-1550	49-8

Name / Address	City	State	Zip	Toll-Free	Phone	Class
Astro Chemicals Inc 64-94 Shaw's Ln	Springfield	MA	01104	**800-223-0776**	413-781-7240	144
Astro Homes PO Box 190	Shippenville	PA	16254	**800-222-7876**	814-226-6822	495
Astro Industries Inc 4403 Dayton-Xenia Rd	Dayton	OH	45432	**800-543-5810**	937-429-5900	800
Astro-Med Inc 600 E Greenwich Ave; *NASDAQ: ALOT*	West Warwick	RI	02893	**800-343-4039**	401-828-4000	171-6
Astro Pak Corp 12201 Pangborn Ave	Downey	CA	90241	**800-743-5444**	562-803-3400	728
Astrocom Corp 3500 Holly Ln N Suite 60	Minneapolis	MN	55447	**800-669-6242**	763-694-9949	720
AstroCosmos Metallurgical Div 4047 E Lincoln Way	Wooster	OH	44691	**800-231-6601**	330-264-8639	92
Astrofoam Molding Co Inc 4117 Calle Tesoro	Camarillo	CA	93012	**800-339-0967**	805-482-7276	590
Astrologers. American Federation of 6535 S Rural Rd	Tempe	AZ	85283	**888-301-7630**	480-838-1751	48-18
Astronautics. American Institute of Aeronautics & 1801 Alexander Bell Dr Suite 500	Reston	VA	20191	**800-639-2422**	703-264-7500	49-19
Astronics Corp 1801 Elmwood Ave; *NASDAQ: ATRO*	Buffalo	NY	14207	**800-666-3722**	716-447-9013	430
Astronomy Magazine 21027 Crossroads Cir	Waukesha	WI	53186	**888-350-2413**	262-796-8776	449-14
AstroTurf Industries Inc 809 Kenner St	Dalton	GA	30721	**800-723-8873**	706-272-4200	286
Astrup Drugs Inc 905 N Main St	Austin	MN	55912	**800-888-9069**	507-433-7447	236
ASV Inc 840 Lilly Ln; *NASDAQ: ASVI*	Grand Rapids	MN	55744	**800-346-5954**	218-327-3434	505
ASWB (Association of Social Work Boards) 400 Southridge Pkwy Suite B	Culpeper	VA	22701	**800-225-6880**	540-829-6880	49-7
Asyst Technologies Inc 48761 Kato Rd; *NASDAQ: ASYT*	Fremont	CA	94538	**800-345-7643**	510-661-5000	685
AT Clayton & Co Inc 2 Pickwick Plaza	Greenwich	CT	06830	**800-282-5298**	203-861-1190	543
AT Cross Co 1 Albion Rd; *AMEX: ATX*	Lincoln	RI	02865	**800-722-1719**	401-333-1200	560
At Health Inc 14241 NE Woodinville-Duvall Rd Suite 104	Woodinville	WA	98072	**888-284-3258**	360-668-3808	351
At Last Naturals Inc 401 Columbus Ave	Valhalla	NY	10595	**800-527-8123**	914-747-3599	211
AT & T Business Internet Services PO Box 30021	Tampa	FL	33630	**877-485-1500**		390
AT & T Corp 1 AT & T Way	Bedminster	NJ	07921	**800-222-0300**	908-221-2000	721
AT & T Foundation 32 Ave of the Americas Rm 2417	New York	NY	10013	**800-428-8652**	212-387-4801	299
AT & T Universal Card Services PO Box 44167	Jacksonville	FL	32231	**800-235-3549**	904-954-7500	213
AT & T WorldNet Service 32 Ave of the Americas; *Tech Supp	New York	NY	10013	**800-400-1447***	800-967-5363	390
AT Williams Oil Co 5446 University Pkwy	Winston-Salem	NC	27105	**800-642-0945**	336-767-6280	319
At Your Service 4400 Airport Fwy	Fort Worth	TX	76117	**888-777-7115**	817-831-3113	35
ATA (American Tinnitus Assn) 65 SW Yamhill	Portland	OR	97205	**800-634-8978**	503-248-9985	48-17
ATA (American Trucking Assns) 2200 Mill Rd	Alexandria	VA	22314	**800-282-5463**	703-838-1700	49-21
ATA Airlines Inc 7337 W Washington St; *Resv	Indianapolis	IN	46231	**800-435-9282***	317-247-4000	26
ATA Holdings Corp 7337 W Washington St	Indianapolis	IN	46231	**800-435-9282**	317-247-4000	355-1
ATA Travel Awards 7337 W Washington St	Indianapolis	IN	46231	**800-435-9282**	317-247-4000	27
Atari Inc 417 5th Ave 8th Fl; *NASDAQ: ATAR*	New York	NY	10016	**800-898-1438**	212-726-6500	176-3
ATAS International Inc 6612 Snowdrift Rd	Allentown	PA	18106	**800-468-1441**	610-395-8445	482
ATC Assoc Inc 104 E 25th St 10th Fl	New York	NY	10010	**800-725-3282**	212-353-8280	191
ATC Diversified Electronics Inc 1827 Freedom Rd; *Cust Svc	Lancaster	PA	17601	**800-874-0619***	717-295-0500	202
ATC Lighting & Plastics Inc 107 N Eagle St	Geneva	OH	44041	**800-543-1943**	440-466-7670	430
ATC Travelers 1983 Marcus Ave Suite E122	Lake Success	NY	11042	**800-797-8707**		707
ATCC (American Type Culture Collection) 10801 University Blvd PO Box 1549	Manassas	VA	20108	**800-638-6597**	703-365-2700	654
Atchison Daily Globe 1015 Main St PO Box 247	Atchison	KS	66002	**800-748-7615**	913-367-0583	522-2
Atchison-Holt Electric Co-op 18585 Industrial Rd	Rock Port	MO	64482	**888-744-5366**	660-744-5344	244
Atco Rubber Products Inc 7101 Atco Dr	Fort Worth	TX	76118	**800-877-3828**	817-595-2894	364
Atcom Business Telecom Solutions PO Box 13476	Research Triangle Park	NC	27709	**800-849-8266**	919-314-1001	195
ATD-American Co 111-149 Greenwood Ave	Wyncote	PA	19095	**800-283-9327**	215-576-1380	315
ATEC Inc 12600 Executive Dr	Stafford	TX	77477	**866-753-2384**	281-240-1919	610
Ateeco Inc DBA Mrs T's Pierogies 600 E Center St PO Box 606	Shenandoah	PA	17976	**800-233-3170**	570-462-2745	291-36
ATEK Medical Mfg 620 Watson St SW	Grand Rapids	MI	49504	**800-253-1540**	616-643-5200	468
Atex Media Command Inc 24 Crosby Dr	Bedford	MA	01730	**800-872-2839**	781-275-2323	176-10
ATG Group Inc 463 Aviation Blvd Suite 120; *Cust Svc	Santa Rosa	CA	95403	**800-285-6100***	707-284-5000	721
Athabasca University 1 University Dr	Athabasca	AB	T9S3A3	**800-788-9041**	780-675-6111	773
Athana Inc 24045 Frampton Ave	Harbor City	CA	90710	**800-421-1591**	310-539-7280	644
Athea Laboratories Inc 7855 N Faulkner Rd PO Box 240014	Milwaukee	WI	53224	**800-743-6417**	414-354-6417	143
Athena Controls Inc 5145 Campus Dr	Plymouth Meeting	PA	19462	**800-782-6776**	610-828-2490	200
Athena Diagnostics Inc 377 Plantation St 4 Biotech Pk	Worcester	MA	01605	**800-394-4493**	508-756-2886	229
Atheneum Suite Hotel & Conference Center 1000 Brush Ave	Detroit	MI	48226	**800-772-2323**	313-962-2323	373
Athens Banner-Herald 1 Press Pl	Athens	GA	30601	**800-533-4252**	706-549-0123	522-2
Athens Convention & Visitors Bureau 300 N Thomas St	Athens	GA	30601	**800-653-0603**	706-357-4430	205
Athens County Convention & Visitors Bureau 667 E State St	Athens	OH	45701	**800-878-9767**	740-592-1819	205
Athens Disposal Co Inc 14048 Valley Blvd; *Cust Svc	City of Industry	CA	91746	**888-336-6100***	626-336-3636	791
Athens Pastries & Frozen Foods Inc 13600 Snow Rd	Cleveland	OH	44142	**800-837-5683**	216-676-8500	291-2
Athens State University 300 N Beaty St	Athens	AL	35611	**800-522-0272**	256-233-8100	163
Athletes. Fellowship of Christian 8701 Leeds Rd	Kansas City	MO	64129	**800-289-0909**	816-921-0909	48-22
Athlete's Foot Group Inc 1950 Vaughn Rd	Kennesaw	GA	30144	**800-524-6444**	770-514-4500	296
Athletic Supporter Ltd 24601 Hallwood Ct	Farmington Hills	MI	48335	**800-521-6500**	248-474-0000	500
Athletic Trainers Assn. National 2952 Stemmons Fwy Suite 200	Dallas	TX	75247	**800-879-6282**	214-637-6282	48-22
Athletics. National Assn of Collegiate Directors of 24651 Detroit Rd	Westlake	OH	44145	**800-996-2232**	440-892-4000	48-22
ATI 30575 Trabuco Canyon Rd Suite 200	Trabuco Canyon	CA	92679	**877-757-0000**	949-265-2000	721
ATI (AmericanTours International Inc) 6053 W Century Blvd	Los Angeles	CA	90045	**800-800-8942**	310-641-9953	748
ATI Health Education Center 1395 NW 167th St Suite 200	Miami	FL	33169	**800-275-2725**	305-628-1000	787
ATI Inc 361 Sinclair-Frontage Rd	Milpitas	CA	95035	**800-536-2212**	408-942-1780	176-8
ATI Tools Div Snap-on Inc 2425 Vineyard Ave	Escondido	CA	92029	**800-284-4460**	760-746-8301	746
ATK Integrated Defense Co 4700 Nathan Ln N	Plymouth	MN	55442	**800-456-8933**	763-744-5000	494
Atkin Air 1420 Flightline Dr Suite B	Lincoln	CA	95648	**800-924-2471**	916-645-6242	14
Atkins & Pearce Inc 1 Braid Way	Covington	KY	41017	**800-837-7477**	859-356-2001	207
Atkinson-Baker Inc 330 N Brand Blvd Suite 250	Glendale	CA	91203	**800-288-3376**	818-551-7300	436
Atkinson Brooks Theatre 256 W 47th St	New York	NY	10036	**800-755-4000**	212-307-4100	732
Atkinson Candy Co 1608 W Frank Ave	Lufkin	TX	75904	**800-231-1203**	936-639-2333	291-8
Atkinson Freight Lines Co 2950 State Rd PO Box 984	Bensalem	PA	19020	**800-345-8052**	215-638-1130	769
ATL International Inc 8334 Veterans Hwy	Millersville	MD	21108	**800-935-8863**	410-987-1011	62-5
ATLA (American Theological Library Assn) 250 S Wacker Dr Suite 1600	Chicago	IL	60606	**888-665-2852**	312-454-5100	48-20
ATLA (Association of Trial Lawyers of America) 1050 31st St NW	Washington	DC	20007	**800-424-2725**	202-965-3500	49-10
ATLA Advocate Newsletter 1050 31st St NW	Washington	DC	20007	**800-424-2727**	202-965-3500	521-2
ATLA Law Reporter Newsletter 1050 31st St NW	Washington	DC	20007	**800-424-2727**	202-965-3500	521-7
Atlanta Architectural Textile 737 Miami Cir NE	Atlanta	GA	30324	**800-241-0178**	404-237-4246	386
Atlanta Bread Co International Inc 1955 Lake Park Dr Suite 400	Smyrna	GA	30080	**800-398-3728**	770-432-0933	69
Atlanta Christian College 2605 Ben Hill Rd	East Point	GA	30344	**800-776-1222**	404-761-8861	163
Atlanta College of Art 1280 Peachtree St NE	Atlanta	GA	30309	**800-832-2104**	404-733-5001	163
Atlanta Convention & Visitors Bureau 233 Peachtree St NE Suite 100	Atlanta	GA	30303	**800-285-2682**	404-521-6600	205
Atlanta Cutlery Corp 2147 Gees Mill Rd	Conyers	GA	30012	**800-883-0300**	770-922-3700	219
Atlanta Falcons 4400 Falcon Pkwy	Flowery Branch	GA	30542	**800-241-3489**	770-965-3115	703
Atlanta Fixture & Sales Co 3185 Northeast Expy	Atlanta	GA	30341	**800-282-1977**	770-455-8844	295
Atlanta Journal-Constitution 72 Marietta St	Atlanta	GA	30303	**800-846-6672**	404-526-5151	522-2
Atlanta Life Insurance Co PO Box 2222	Decatur	AL	35609	**800-235-5422**	404-659-2100	384-2
Atlanta Magazine 2600 Peachtree St Suite 300	Atlanta	GA	30303	**800-930-3019**	404-527-5500	449-22
Atlanta Opera 728 West Peachtree St NW	Atlanta	GA	30308	**800-356-7372**	404-881-8801	563-2
Atlanta Postal Credit Union 3900 Crown Rd	Atlanta	GA	30380	**800-849-8431**	404-768-4126	216
Atlanta Sharptech 1594 Evans Dr SW	Atlanta	GA	30310	**800-241-5296**	404-752-6000	670
Atlanta's DeKalb Convention & Visitors Bureau 1957 Lakeside Pkwy Suite 510	Tucker	GA	30084	**800-999-6055**	770-492-5000	205
Atlanta's Gwinnett Convention & Visitors Bureau 6500 Sugarloaf Pkwy Suite 200	Duluth	GA	30097	**888-494-6638**	770-623-3600	205
Atlantic American Corp PO Box 105480; *NASDAQ: AAME*	Atlanta	GA	30348	**800-241-1439**	404-266-5500	355-4
Atlantic Bank of New York 960 Ave of the Americas	New York	NY	10001	**800-535-2269**	212-967-7425	71
Atlantic Battery Co Inc 80 Elm St	Watertown	MA	02472	**800-924-2450**	617-924-2868	76
Atlantic Book Warehouse 979 Bethlehem Pike	Montgomeryville	PA	18936	**800-237-7323**	215-661-0450	96
Atlantic City Convention & Visitors Authority 2314 Pacific Ave	Atlantic City	NJ	08401	**888-228-4748**	609-449-7130	205
Atlantic City Hilton Boston & Pacific Ave	Atlantic City	NJ	08401	**877-432-7139**	609-347-7111	133
Atlantic City Toll-Free Reservations PO Box 665	Northfield	NJ	08225	**800-833-7070**	609-646-7070	368
Atlantic Coach 600 S Military Hwy	Virginia Beach	VA	23464	**800-258-9061**	757-420-3135	108

Name / Address	City	State	Zip	Toll-Free	Phone	Class
Atlantic Coast Schooner Co 391 Hatchet Mountain Rd	Hope	ME	04847	**800-500-6077**	207-763-4255	217
Atlantic Container Line 194 Wood Ave S Suite 500	Iselin	NJ	08830	**800-225-1235**	732-452-5400	308
Atlantic Corp 806 N 23rd St	Wilmington	NC	28405	**800-722-5841**	910-343-0624	543
Atlantic Corporate Interiors Inc 4600 Powder Mill Rd Suite 300	Beltsville	MD	20705	**800-564-3228**	301-931-3600	316
Atlantic Envelope Co 1420 Peachtree St NE Suite 200	Atlanta	GA	30309	**800-225-4636**	404-853-6700	260
Atlantic Exchange Inc 10405 NW 37th Terr	Miami	FL	33178	**800-327-2822**	305-593-1176	616
Atlantic Express Transportation Group Inc 7 North St	Staten Island	NY	10302	**800-336-3886**	718-442-7000	110
Atlantic Extrusions Corp 96 Swampscott Rd	Salem	MA	01970	**800-331-8441**	978-744-8000	589
Atlantic Eyrie Lodge 6 Norman Rd	Bar Harbor	ME	04609	**800-422-2883**	207-288-9786	373
Atlantic FEC Fertilizer & Chemical Co 18375 SW 260 St	Homestead	FL	33031	**800-432-3413**	305-247-8800	276
Atlantic Gasket Corp 3908 Frankford Ave	Philadelphia	PA	19124	**800-229-8881**	215-533-6400	321
Atlantic Group 5426 Robin Hood Rd	Norfolk	VA	23513	**800-446-8131**	757-857-6400	707
Atlantic India Rubber Co 1437 Kentucky Rt 1428	Hager Hills	KY	41222	**800-476-6638**	606-789-9115	664
Atlantic Information Services Inc 1100 17th St NW Suite 300	Washington	DC	20036	**800-521-4323**	202-775-9008	623-9
Atlantic Marine Inc 8500 Heckscher Dr	Jacksonville	FL	32226	**800-395-6446**	904-251-1545	689
Atlantic Meeco Inc 1501 E Gene Stipe Blvd	McAlester	OK	74501	**800-627-4621**	918-423-6833	107
Atlantic Mobile Home & RV Supplier Corp 4828 High Point Rd	Greensboro	NC	27407	**800-334-6976**	336-299-4691	61
Atlantic Monthly Magazine 711 3rd Ave 12th Fl	New York	NY	10017	**800-234-2411**	646-695-8500	449-11
Atlantic Oakes 119 Eden St	Bar Harbor	ME	04609	**800-336-2463**	207-288-5801	655
Atlantic Palace Suites Hotel 1507 Boardwalk	Atlantic City	NJ	08401	**800-527-8483**	609-344-1200	373
Atlantic Relocation Systems Inc 1314 Chattahoochee Ave NW *Cust Svc	Atlanta	GA	30318	**800-241-1140***	404-351-5311	508
Atlantic Salmon Federation (ASF) PO Box 5200	Saint Andrews	NB	E5B3S8	**800-565-5666**	506-529-1033	48-3
Atlantic Sands Hotel 101 N Boardwalk	Rehoboth Beach	DE	19971	**800-422-0600**	302-227-2511	373
Atlantic Service & Supply 130 Selig Dr	Atlanta	GA	30336	**800-859-1474**	404-699-8740	190-2
Atlantic Shutter Systems 3239 Hwy 301 N	Latta	SC	29565	**877-437-0608**		690
Atlantic Speakers Bureau 980 Rt 730	Scotch Ridge	NB	E3L5L2	**866-465-0990**	506-465-0990	699
Atlantic States Cast Iron Pipe Co 183 Sitgreaves St	Phillipsburg	NJ	08865	**800-859-1161**	908-454-1161	302
Atlantic Tower Corp 10197 Maple Leaf Ct	Ashland	VA	23005	**800-826-8616**	804-550-7490	168
Atlantic Track & Turnout Co PO Box 1589 *Cust Svc	Bloomfield	NJ	07003	**800-631-1274***	973-748-5885	759
Atlantic Trust 300 E Lombard St Suite 1100	Baltimore	MD	21202	**888-880-1621**	410-539-4660	393
Atlantic Union College 338 Main St	South Lancaster	MA	01561	**800-282-2030**	978-368-2239	163
Atlantic Veneer Corp 2457 Lennoxville Rd PO Box 660	Beaufort	NC	28516	**800-334-7723**	252-728-3169	602
Atlantic Whirlpools Inc 8721 Glenwood Ave	Raleigh	NC	27617	**800-849-8827**	919-783-7447	367
Atlantis Casino Resort 3800 S Virginia St	Reno	NV	89502	**800-723-6500**	775-825-4700	373
Atlantis Plastics Inc 1870 The Exchange Suite 200 *NASDAQ: ATPL*	Atlanta	GA	30339	**800-497-7659**	770-953-4567	589
Atlantis Plastics Inc Linear Films Div 6940 W 76th St S *Cust Svc	Tulsa	OK	74157	**800-332-4437***	918-446-1651	588
Atlantix Global Systems 1 Sun Ct	Norcross	GA	30092	**888-786-2727**	770-248-7700	172
Atlas Air Conditioning Co 4133 Southerland Rd	Houston	TX	77092	**800-460-9973**	713-460-7300	188-10
Atlas Bolt & Screw Co 1628 Troy Rd	Ashland	OH	44805	**800-321-6977**	419-289-6171	274
Atlas Carpet Mills Inc 2200 Saybrook Ave	City of Commerce	CA	90040	**800-272-8527**	323-724-9000	131
Atlas Container Corp 8140 Telegraph Rd	Severn	MD	21144	**800-394-4894**	410-551-6300	101
Atlas Copco Tools & Assembly Systems 2998 Dutton Rd	Auburn Hills	MI	48326	**800-859-3746**	248-373-3000	747
Atlas Distributing Corp 44 Southbridge St	Auburn	MA	01501	**800-649-6221**	508-791-6221	82-1
Atlas Food Systems & Services Inc 205 Woods Lake Rd	Greenville	SC	29607	**800-476-1123**	864-232-1885	294
Atlas Hotels Inc 500 Hotel Cir N	San Diego	CA	92108	**800-772-8527**	619-291-2232	369
Atlas Match LLC 1801 S Airport Cir	Euless	TX	76040	**800-628-2426**	817-267-1500	461
Atlas Metal Industries 1135 NW 159th Dr *Cust Svc	Miami	FL	33169	**800-762-7565***	305-625-2451	293
Atlas Minerals & Chemicals Inc 1227 Valley Rd *Cust Svc	Mertztown	PA	19539	**800-523-8269***	610-682-7171	3
Atlas Model Railroad Co Inc 378 Florence Ave *Orders	Hillside	NJ	07205	**800-872-2521***	908-687-0880	750
Atlas Pacific Engineering Co 1 Atlas Ave	Pueblo	CO	81001	**800-227-0682**	719-948-3040	293
Atlas Pen & Pencil Corp 3040 N 29th Ave	Hollywood	FL	33020	**800-327-3232**	954-920-4444	10
Atlas Railroad Construction Co 1253 SR 519 PO Box 8	Eighty Four	PA	15330	**800-245-4980**	724-228-4500	187-8
Atlas Roofing Falcon Foam Div 8240 Byron Center Rd SW	Byron Center	MI	49315	**800-917-9138**	616-878-1568	589
Atlas Sound 1601 Jack McKay Blvd	Ennis	TX	75119	**800-876-3333**	972-875-8413	52
Atlas Tag & Label Inc 2361 Industrial Dr	Neenah	WI	54956	**800-634-2705**	920-722-1557	404
Atlas Technologies Inc 201 S Alloy Dr	Fenton	MI	48430	**800-536-3162**	810-629-6663	448
Atlas Van Lines Inc 1212 St George Rd	Evansville	IN	47711	**800-638-9797**	812-424-2222	508
Atlas Welding & Boiler Repair 2960 Webster Ave	Bronx	NY	10458	**800-476-0556**	718-365-6600	188-10
Atlas World Group Inc 1212 St George Rd	Evansville	IN	47711	**800-252-8885**	812-424-2222	355-3
ATMI Inc 7 Commerce Dr *NASDAQ: ATMI*	Danbury	CT	06810	**800-766-2681**	203-794-1100	685
Atmos Energy Corp PO Box 650205 *NYSE: ATO*	Dallas	TX	75265	**888-954-4321**	972-934-9227	774
ATOFINA Chemicals Inc 2000 Market St	Philadelphia	PA	19103	**800-533-5552**	215-419-7000	276
Atomic Ski USA Inc 9 Columbia Dr	Amherst	NH	03031	**800-258-5020**	603-880-6143	701
Atos Origin 5599 San Felipe Suite 300	Houston	TX	77056	**866-875-8902**	713-513-3000	176-1
ATP Mfg LLC 761 Great Rd	North Smithfield	RI	02896	**800-315-5246**	401-765-8600	296
ATP Tour Inc 201 ATP Tour Blvd	Ponte Vedra Beach	FL	32082	**800-527-4811**	904-285-8000	48-22
Atria Retirement & Assisted Living 501 S 4th St Suite 140	Louisville	KY	40202	**877-719-1600**	502-719-1600	442
Atrion Corp 1 Allentown Pkwy *NASDAQ: ATRI*	Allen	TX	75002	**800-627-0226**	972-390-9800	468
Atrium Cos Inc 3890 W Northwest Hwy Suite 500	Dallas	TX	75220	**800-421-6292**	214-630-5757	232
Atrium Hotel 18700 MacArthur Blvd	Irvine	CA	92612	**800-854-3012**	949-833-2770	373
Atrium Inn 2889 E Hastings St	Vancouver	BC	V5K2A1	**888-428-7486**	604-254-1000	372
Atrium Suites Hotel Las Vegas 4255 S Paradise Rd	Las Vegas	NV	89109	**800-330-7728**	702-369-4400	373
Atrium Windows & Doors 9001 Ambassador Rd	Dallas	TX	75247	**800-938-2000**		233
ATS (American Tract Society) 1624 N 1st St	Garland	TX	75040	**800-548-7228**	972-276-9408	48-20
ATS Medical Inc 3905 Annapolis Ln Suite 105 *NASDAQ: ATSI*	Minneapolis	MN	55447	**866-287-6331**	763-553-7736	469
ATS Services Inc 9700 Phillips Hwy Suite 101	Jacksonville	FL	32256	**800-346-5574**	904-645-9505	707
ATS Tours 2381 Rosecrans Ave Suite 325	El Segundo	CA	90245	**800-423-2880**	310-643-0044	748
ATSCO (Air Tool Service Co) 7722 Metric Dr	Mentor	OH	44060	**800-321-3554**	440-942-4475	747
ATSSA (American Traffic Safety Services Assn) 15 Riverside Pkwy Suite 100	Fredericksburg	VA	22406	**800-272-8772**	540-368-1701	49-21
Attachmate Corp 3617 131st Ave SE	Bellevue	WA	98006	**800-426-6283**	425-644-4010	176-7
Attention-Deficit/Hyperactivity Disorder. Children & Adults with 8181 Professional Pl Suite 201	Landover	MD	20785	**800-233-4050**	301-306-7070	48-17
Attorneys General. National Assn of 750 1st St NE Suite 1100	Washington	DC	20002	**888-245-6224**	202-326-6000	49-7
Attorneys Inc. National Network of Estate Planning 1 Valmont Plaza 4th Fl	Omaha	NE	68154	**888-837-4090**	402-964-3700	49-10
Attorney's Title Insurance Fund Inc 6545 Corporate Ctr Blvd	Orlando	FL	32822	**800-336-3863**	407-240-3863	384-6
Attracta Sign Co 1468 James Rd	Rogers	MN	55374	**866-339-0603**	763-428-6377	8
Attraction Inc 672 rue du Parc	Lac-Drolet	QC	G0Y1C0	**800-567-6095**	819-549-2477	153-3
Atwood Lake Resort PO Box 96	Dellroy	OH	44620	**800-362-6406**	330-735-2211	655
Atwood Oceanics Inc 15835 Park Ten Place Dr Suite 200 *NYSE: ATW*	Houston	TX	77084	**800-231-5924**	281-749-7800	529
ATX Communications Inc 2100 Renaissance Blvd	King of Prussia	PA	19406	**800-220-2891**	610-755-4000	721
Au Bon Pain 19 Fid Kennedy Ave	Boston	MA	02210	**800-825-5227**	617-423-2100	69
Au Naturel Wellness & Medical Spa at the Brookstreet Hotel 525 Legget Dr	Ottawa	ON	K2K2W2	**888-826-2220**	613-271-3393	698
Au Sable Woodworking Co PO Box 108	Frederic	MI	49733	**800-248-9261**	989-348-7086	766
AUA (American Urological Assn) 1000 Corporate Blvd	Linthicum	MD	21090	**866-746-4282**	410-689-3700	49-8
Auberge Saint-Antoine 8 rue Saint-Antoine	Quebec	QC	G1K4C9	**888-692-2211**	418-692-2211	372
Auberge du Soleil 180 Rutherford Hill Rd	Rutherford	CA	94573	**800-348-5406**	707-963-1211	373
Auberge du Vieux-Port 97 de la Commune E	Montreal	QC	H2Y1J1	**888-660-7678**	514-876-0081	372
Aubrey Silvey Enterprises Inc 371 Hamp Jones Rd	Carrollton	GA	30117	**800-206-3815**	770-834-0738	187-10
Aubuchon WE Co Inc 95 Aubuchon Dr	Westminster	MA	01473	**800-282-4393**	978-874-0521	359
Auburn Leather Co PO Box 338	Auburn	KY	42206	**800-635-0617**	270-542-4116	423
Auburn Mfg Co 29 Stack St	Middletown	CT	06457	**800-427-5387**	860-346-6677	321
Auburn National Bancorporation Inc PO Box 3110 *NASDAQ: AUBN*	Auburn	AL	36831	**888-988-2162**	334-821-9200	355-2
Auburn Publishers Inc 25 Dill St	Auburn	NY	13021	**800-878-5311**	315-253-5311	623-8
Auburn University 202 Mary Martin Hall	Auburn University	AL	36849	**800-282-8769**	334-844-6425	163
Montgomery PO Box 244023	Montgomery	AL	36124	**800-227-2649**	334-244-3000	163
Auburn University Hotel & Dixon Conference Center 241 S College St	Auburn	AL	36830	**800-228-2876**	334-821-8200	370
Auburn/Opelika Convention & Visitors Bureau 714 E Glenn Ave	Auburn	AL	36830	**800-321-8880**	334-887-8747	205
Auction Block 1502 S I-35 Suite 200	Lancaster	TX	75146	**866-890-0400**	972-230-0400	51
Auction Systems Auctioneers & Appraisers Inc 3030 E Washington St	Phoenix	AZ	85034	**800-801-8880**	602-252-4842	51
Auctioneers Assn. National 8880 Ballentine St	Overland Park	KS	66214	**888-541-8084**	913-541-8084	49-18
Audi of America 3800 Hamlin Rd	Auburn Hills	MI	48326	**800-367-2834**	248-340-5000	59
Audible Inc 65 Willowbrook Blvd 3rd Fl *NASDAQ: ADBL*	Wayne	NJ	07470	**888-283-5051**	973-890-4070	388
Audio Book Club Inc 2 Ridgedale Ave	Cedar Knolls	NJ	07927	**800-688-4442**	973-539-9528	94
Audio Command Systems 694 Main St	Westbury	NY	11590	**800-382-2939**	516-997-5800	52
Audio-Digest Foundation DBA Cme Unlimited; Infomedix 1577 E Chevy Chase Dr	Glendale	CA	91206	**800-423-2308**	818-240-7500	754

Name / Address	City	State	ZIP	Toll-Free	Phone	Class
Audio Direct 460 W Roger Rd Suite 105	Tucson	AZ	85705	**888-628-3467**		35
Audio Engineering Society 60 E 42nd St Rm 2520	New York	NY	10165	**800-541-7299**	212-661-8528	49-19
Audio Graphic Systems Inc 2131 S Grove Ave Suite A	Ontario	CA	91761	**800-854-8547**	909-673-0070	35
Audio King Corp 321 W 84th Ave Suite A	Thornton	CO	80260	**800-260-2660**	303-412-2500	35
Audiology. American Academy of 11730 Plaza America Dr Suite 300	Reston	VA	22190	**800-222-2336**	703-790-8466	49-8
Audiosears Corp 2 South St	Stamford	NY	12167	**800-533-7863**	607-652-7305	52
Audiovox Corp 150 Marcus Blvd *NASDAQ: VOXX*	Hauppauge	NY	11788	**800-645-4994**	631-231-7750	52
Auditors. Association of Healthcare Internal PO Box 449	Onsted	MI	49265	**888-275-2442**	517-467-7729	49-1
Audrain Medical Center 620 E Monroe St	Mexico	MO	65265	**800-748-7098**	573-582-5000	366-2
Audubon Aquarium of the Americas 1 Canal St	New Orleans	LA	70130	**800-774-7394**	504-565-3033	40
Audubon Insurance Group PO Drawer 15989	Baton Rouge	LA	70895	**800-274-9830**	225-293-5900	384-4
Audubon Magazine 700 Broadway 5th Fl *Cust Svc	New York	NY	10003	**800-274-4201***	212-979-3000	449-19
Audubon Trails Coach Lines Inc 1807 Moll Ln	Evansville	IN	47725	**800-255-5234**	812-867-2098	108
Audubon Zoo 6500 Magazine St	New Orleans	LA	70118	**800-774-7394**	504-581-4629	811
Auerbach Publications 2000 NW Corporate Blvd *Cust Svc	Boca Raton	FL	33431	**800-272-7737***	561-994-0555	623-2
Auglaize Farmers Co-op Inc 601 S Logan St	Wapakoneta	OH	45895	**800-472-9286**	419-739-4600	272
Auglaize & Mercer Counties Convention & Visitors Bureau 900 Edgewater Dr	Saint Marys	OH	45885	**800-860-4726**	419-394-1294	205
Augsburg College 2211 Riverside Ave S CB 143	Minneapolis	MN	55454	**800-788-5678**	612-330-1000	163
Augsburg Fortress Publishers PO Box 1209	Minneapolis	MN	55440	**800-426-0115**	612-330-3300	623-4
August Max 100 Phoenix Ave	Enfield	CT	06082	**800-662-8042**	860-741-0771	155-6
August Winter & Sons Inc 2323 N Roemer Rd	Appleton	WI	54911	**800-236-8882**	920-739-8881	188-13
Augusta Chronicle 725 Broad St	Augusta	GA	30901	**800-822-4077**	706-724-0851	522-2
Augusta Medical Center 78 Medical Ctr Dr	Fishersville	VA	22939	**800-932-0262**	540-932-4000	366-2
Augusta Metropolitan Convention & Visitors Bureau 1450 Greene St Suite 110	Augusta	GA	30901	**800-726-0243**	706-823-6600	205
Augusta State University 2500 Walton Way	Augusta	GA	30904	**800-341-4373**	706-737-1632	163
Augustana College 639 38th St	Rock Island	IL	61201	**800-798-8100**	309-794-7000	163
Augustana College 2001 S Summit Ave	Sioux Falls	SD	57197	**800-727-5516**	605-274-0770	163
Augustana University College 4901 46th Ave	Camrose	AB	T4V2R3	**800-661-8714**	780-679-1100	773
Augustine Casino 84-001 Ave 54	Coachella	CA	92236	**888-752-9294**	760-391-9500	133
Aun Michael A 2901 E Irlo Bronson Memorial Hwy Suite D	Kissimmee	FL	34744	**800-356-0567**	407-870-0030	561
Aura Systems Inc 2335 Alaska Ave *Cust Svc	El Segundo	CA	90245	**800-909-2872***	310-643-5300	507
Aurafin OroAmerica 6701 N Nob Hill Rd	Tamarac	FL	33321	**800-327-1808**	954-718-3200	401
Auriton Solutions 1700 W Hwy 36 Suite 301	Roseville	MN	55113	**877-332-8700**	651-631-8000	48-10
Aurora Area Convention & Visitors Bureau 43 W Galena Blvd	Aurora	IL	60506	**800-477-4369**	630-897-5581	205
Aurora Cable Internet 350 Industrial Pkwy S	Aurora	ON	L4G3H3	**877-452-6743**	905-727-1981	390
Aurora Casket Co Inc 10944 Marsh Rd PO Box 29 *Cust Svc	Aurora	IN	47001	**800-457-1111***	812-926-1111	134
Aurora Co-op Elevator Co PO Box 209	Aurora	NE	68818	**800-642-6795**	402-694-2106	271
Aurora Inn 51 Holland Ave	Bar Harbor	ME	04609	**800-841-8925**	207-288-3771	373
Aurora Modular Industries 17300 Perris Blvd	Moreno Valley	CA	92551	**800-670-4515**	951-571-2200	107
Aurora National Life Assurance Co PO Box 4490	Hartford	CT	06147	**800-265-2652**		384-2
Aurora Textile Finishing Co PO Box 70	Aurora	IL	60507	**800-864-0303**	630-892-7651	730-7
Aurora University 347 S Gladstone Ave	Aurora	IL	60506	**800-742-5281**	630-844-5533	163
AUS Inc PO Box 1050	Moorestown	NJ	08057	**800-925-4287**	856-234-9200	623-8
AUSA (Association of the US Army) 2425 Wilson Blvd	Arlington	VA	22201	**800-336-4570**	703-841-4300	48-19
AUSA Life Insurance Co Inc 4333 Edgewood Rd NE *Cust Svc	Cedar Rapids	IA	52499	**800-625-4213***	319-398-8511	384-2
Austin College 900 N Grand Ave	Sherman	TX	75090	**800-442-5363**	903-813-3000	163
Austin Convention & Visitors Bureau 301 Congress Suite 200	Austin	TX	78701	**800-926-2282**	512-474-5171	205
Austin Film Festival 1604 Nueces	Austin	TX	78701	**800-310-3378**	512-478-4795	278
Austin Graduate School of Theology 1909 University Ave	Austin	TX	78705	**866-287-4723**	512-476-2772	163
Austin (Greater) Chamber of Commerce 210 Barton Springs Rd Suite 400	Austin	TX	78704	**800-856-5602**	512-478-9383	137
Austin Hotel & Spa 305 Malvern Ave	Hot Springs	AR	71901	**877-623-6697**	501-623-6600	373
Austin Industrial Inc 8031 Airport Blvd	Houston	TX	77061	**800-460-3402**	713-641-3400	187-9
Austin James Co 115 Downieville Rd PO Box 827	Mars	PA	16046	**800-245-1942**	724-625-1535	149
Austin News Agency Inc 4414 E Saint Elmo Rd	Austin	TX	78744	**800-542-0060**	512-447-6026	97
Austin Peay State University 601 College St	Clarksville	TN	37044	**800-844-2778**	931-221-7661	163
Austin Powder Co 25800 Science Park Dr Suite 300	Cleveland	OH	44122	**800-321-0752**	216-464-2400	264
Austin Symphony Orchestra 1101 Red River St	Austin	TX	78701	**888-462-3787**	512-476-6064	563-3
Austin Travel 265 Spagnoli Rd	Melville	NY	11747	**800-645-7466**	516-465-1000	760
Austin White Lime Co PO Box 9556 *Sales	Austin	TX	78766	**800-553-5463***	512-255-3646	432
Austin Zoo 10807 Rawhide Trail	Austin	TX	78736	**800-291-1490**	512-288-1490	811
Australian Pacific Tours (USA) Ltd 4605 Lankershim Blvd Suite 712	North Hollywood	CA	91602	**888-299-1428**	818-755-6392	748
Austrian Airlines 1720 Whitestone Expy Suite 500	Whitestone	NY	11357	**800-843-0002**	718-670-8600	26
Austrian Airlines Cargo JFK International Airport Cargo Bldg 67 Rm 3111	Jamaica	NY	11430	**800-637-2957**	718-995-2274	13
Autco Distributing Inc 10900 Midwest Industrial Blvd	Saint Louis	MO	63132	**800-443-0044**	314-426-6524	38
Auth Brothers Inc 1905 Clarkson Way	Landover	MD	20785	**800-424-2610**	301-322-8400	292-9
Auth-Florence Mfg 591 Mitchell Rd	Glendale Heights	IL	60139	**800-275-1747**	630-545-5500	385
Authentic Specialty Foods Inc 4340 Eucalyptus Ave	Chino	CA	91710	**888-236-2272**	909-631-2000	291-20
AuthentiDate Holding Corp 2165 Technology Dr *NASDAQ: ADAT*	Schenectady	NY	12308	**800-367-5906**	518-346-7799	355-3
Authentium Inc 7121 Fairway Dr Suite 102	Palm Beach Gardens	FL	33418	**800-423-9147**	561-575-3200	176-12
Author House 1663 Liberty Dr	Bloomington	IN	47403	**800-839-8640**	812-339-6000	623-2
Authoria Inc 300 5th Ave	Waltham	MA	02451	**877-628-8467**	781-530-2000	176-3
Authorize.Net Corp 915 S 500 East Suite 200 *Tech Supp	American Fork	UT	84003	**877-447-3938***	801-492-6450	176-7
Authors & Publishers. American Society of Composers 1 Lincoln Plaza	New York	NY	10023	**800-952-7227**	212-621-6000	48-4
Autism Society of America (ASA) 7910 Woodmont Ave Suite 300	Bethesda	MD	20814	**800-328-8476**	301-657-0881	48-17
Auto Accents 6550 Pearl Rd	Cleveland	OH	44130	**800-567-3120**	440-888-8886	35
Auto Club of America Corp (ACA) 9411 N Georgia St	Oklahoma City	OK	73120	**800-411-2007**	405-751-4430	53
Auto Club Ltd 106 E 6th St Suite 900	Austin	TX	78701	**866-247-3728**	512-343-4588	53
Auto Collision Repair. I-CAR Inter-Industry Conference on 3701 Algonquin Rd Suite 400	Rolling Meadows	IL	60008	**800-422-7872**	847-590-1191	49-21
Auto Dealer Consultants Assn. CPA 10831 Old Mill Rd Suite 400	Omaha	NE	68154	**888-475-4476**	402-778-7922	49-1
Auto Europe 39 Commercial St	Portland	ME	04101	**800-223-5555**	207-842-2000	126
Auto FX Software 141 Village St Suite 2	Birmingham	AL	35242	**800-839-2008**	205-980-0056	176-8
Auto Glass National 1537 W Alameda	Denver	CO	80223	**800-388-0104**	303-722-9600	62-2
Auto Glass Specialists Inc 1200 John Q Hammons Dr Suite 300	Madison	WI	53717	**800-558-1000**	608-271-5484	62-2
Auto-Graphics Inc 3201 Temple Ave	Pomona	CA	91768	**800-776-6939**	909-595-7204	770
Auto-Owners Insurance Co PO Box 30660	Lansing	MI	48909	**800-346-0346**	517-323-1200	384-4
Auto-Owners Life Insurance Co 6101 Anacapri Blvd	Lansing	MI	48917	**800-288-8740**	517-323-1200	384-2
Auto Repair Equality. Coalition for 119 Oronoco St Suite 300	Alexandria	VA	22314	**800-229-5380**	703-519-7555	49-21
Auto Shred Recycling LLC PO Box 17188	Pensacola	FL	32522	**800-277-6964**	850-432-0977	674
Auto-trol Technology Corp 12500 N Washington St	Denver	CO	80241	**800-233-2882**	303-452-4919	176-12
Auto Truck Inc 1200 N Ellis St	Bensenville	IL	60106	**877-284-4440**	630-860-5600	505
Autobell Car Wash Inc 1521 E 3rd St	Charlotte	NC	28204	**800-582-8096**		62-1
Autobytel Inc 18872 MacArthur Blvd *NASDAQ: ABTL*	Irvine	CA	92612	**888-422-8999**	949-225-4500	58
Autocam Corp 4070 E Paris Ave	Kentwood	MI	49512	**800-747-6978**	616-698-0707	60
Autoclave Engineers Div Snap-Tite 8325 Hessinger Dr	Erie	PA	16509	**800-458-0409**	814-838-5700	92
Autocrat Coffee Inc PO Box 285	Lincoln	RI	02865	**800-288-6272**	401-333-3300	291-7
Autodesk Inc 111 McInnis Pkwy *NASDAQ: ADSK* ■ *Prod Info	San Rafael	CA	94903	**800-964-6432***	415-507-5000	176-5
Autographic Business Forms Inc 31 Industrial Ave	Mahwah	NJ	07430	**800-526-5309**	201-327-6200	617
Autoimmune Related Disease Assn. American 22100 Gratiot Ave	Eastpointe	MI	48021	**800-598-4668**	586-776-3900	48-17
Autolog Corp 1701 E Linden Ave	Linden	NJ	07036	**800-526-6078**	908-587-9400	769
Automark Marking Systems 13475 Lakefront Dr	Earth City	MO	63045	**888-777-2303**	314-739-0430	459
Automated Office Products Inc 9730-EE ML King Jr Hwy	Lanham	MD	20706	**800-929-2528**	301-731-4000	616
Automated Packaging Systems Inc 10175 Phillip Pkwy *Sales	Streetsboro	OH	44241	**800-527-0733***	330-528-2000	537
Automated Training Systems Corp 4545 E Industrial St Suite 5B	Simi Valley	CA	93063	**800-426-8737**	805-520-1509	176-3
Automated Voice Systems Inc (AVSI) 17059 El Cajon Ave	Yorba Linda	CA	92886	**888-505-2026**	714-524-4488	52
Automatic Data Processing Inc (ADP) 1 ADP Blvd *NYSE: ADP*	Roseland	NJ	07068	**800-225-5237**	973-994-5000	223
Automatic Equipment Mfg Co 1 Mill Rd Industrial Pk	Pender	NE	68047	**800-228-9289**	402-385-3051	269
Automatic Firing Co Inc 2100 Fillmore Ave	Buffalo	NY	14214	**866-836-0300**	716-836-0300	601
Automatic Funds Transfer Services 151 S Landers St Suite C	Seattle	WA	98134	**800-275-2033**	206-254-0975	70
Automatic Ice & Beverage Inc PO Box 110159	Birmingham	AL	35211	**800-476-4242**	205-787-9640	651
Automatic Identification & Mobility. AIM Inc - Assn for 125 Warrendale-Bayne Rd	Warrendale	PA	15086	**800-338-0206**	724-934-4470	49-19
Automatic Products Corp 2735 Forest Ln	Garland	TX	75042	**800-788-2726**	972-272-6422	610
Automatic Products International Ltd 75 Plato Blvd W	Saint Paul	MN	55107	**800-523-8363**	651-224-4391	55

Name / Address	City	State	ZIP	Toll-Free	Phone	Class
Automatic Switch Co 50-60 Hanover Rd	Florham Park	NJ	07932	**800-524-1023**	973-966-2000	776
Automatic Systems Inc 9230 E 47th St	Kansas City	MO	64133	**800-366-3488**	816-356-0660	206
Automation Assoc Inc 416 Campus Dr	Arlington Heights	IL	60004	**800-927-7348**	847-255-4500	447
Automation Service Equipment Inc 23850 Pinewood St	Warren	MI	48091	**800-735-5940**	586-754-7480	206
Automation Society. IEEE Robotics & IEEE Operations Ctr 445 Hoes Ln	Piscataway	NJ	08854	**800-678-4333**	732-981-0060	49-19
Automation Technology Inc 2001 Gateway Pl Suite 100 *Sales	San Jose	CA	95110	**888-805-6322***	408-350-7020	176-7
Automobile Club of Southern California 2601 S Figueroa St	Los Angeles	CA	90007	**800-400-4222**	213-741-3686	53
Automobile Consumer Services Inc 6249 Stewart Rd	Cincinnati	OH	45227	**800-223-4882**	513-527-7700	58
Automobile Dealers Assn. American International 211 N Union St Suite 300	Alexandria	VA	22314	**800-462-4232**	703-519-7800	49-18
Automobile Dealers Assn. National 8400 Westpark Dr	McLean	VA	22102	**800-252-6232**	703-821-7000	49-18
Automobile Dealers Assn. National Independent 2521 Brown Blvd	Arlington	TX	76006	**800-682-3837**	817-640-3838	49-18
Automobile Protection Corp 6010 Atlantic Blvd	Norcross	GA	30071	**800-458-7071**	770-394-6610	383
Automotive Carrier Services Co LLC 402 S Main St 7th Fl	Joplin	MO	64801	**800-685-7904**	417-206-5900	769
Automotive Distribution Network DBA Parts Plus 5050 Poplar Ave Suite 2020	Memphis	TN	38157	**800-727-8112**	901-682-9090	49-18
Automotive Engine Rebuilders Assn (AERA) 330 Lexington Dr	Buffalo Grove	IL	60089	**888-326-2372**	847-541-6550	49-21
Automotive Engineers Inc. Society of 400 Commonwealth Dr	Warrendale	PA	15096	**877-606-7323**	724-776-4841	49-21
Automotive Executive Magazine 8400 Westpark Dr	McLean	VA	22102	**800-252-6232**	703-821-7150	449-21
Automotive Finance Corp (AFC) 13085 Hamilton Crossing Blvd	Carmel	IN	46032	**888-335-6675**	317-815-9645	214
Automotive Information Center 18872 MacArthur Blvd	Irvine	CA	92612	**888-422-8999**	949-862-1335	58
Automotive News Magazine 1155 Gratiot Ave	Detroit	MI	48207	**800-678-9595**	313-446-6000	449-21
Automotive Oil Change Assn (AOCA) 12810 Hillcrest Rd Suite 221	Dallas	TX	75230	**800-331-0329**	972-458-9468	49-21
Automotive Parts Headquarters 125 29th Ave S	Saint Cloud	MN	56301	**800-247-0339**	320-252-5411	61
Automotive Radiator Service Assn. National 15000 Commerce Pkwy Suite C	Mount Laurel	NJ	08054	**800-551-3232**	856-439-1575	49-21
Automotive Service Assn (ASA) 1901 Airport Fwy *Cust Svc	Bedford	TX	76021	**800-272-7467***	817-283-6205	49-21
Automotive Service Inc PO Box 2157	Reading	PA	19608	**800-383-3421**	610-678-3421	311
Automotive Services. Cross Country 4040 Mystic Valley Pkwy	Medford	MA	02155	**800-833-5500**		53
Automotive Services Training Network 4101 International Pkwy	Carrollton	TX	75007	**800-223-2786**	972-309-4000	502
AutoNation Financial Services 110 SE 6th St *Cust Svc	Fort Lauderdale	FL	33301	**888-825-8929***	954-769-7000	215
AutoNation Inc 110 SE 6th St *NYSE: AN*	Fort Lauderdale	FL	33301	**800-899-4911**	954-769-7000	57
Autoquip Corp PO Box 1058	Guthrie	OK	73044	**888-811-9876**	405-282-5200	462
AutoTrader.com LLC 5775 Peachtree Dunwoody Rd Suite A-200	Atlanta	GA	30342	**800-353-9350**	404-269-8000	58
Autotrol Corp PO Box 557	Crystal Lake	IL	60039	**800-228-6207**	815-459-3080	507
AutoVantage 100 Connecticut Ave	Norwalk	CT	06850	**800-876-7787**		53
AutoVIN Inc 50 Mansell Ct Suite 200	Roswell	GA	30076	**877-428-8684**	678-585-8000	58
Autoweb.com Inc 18872 MacArthur Blvd	Irvine	CA	92612	**888-422-8999**	949-225-4500	58
AutoWeek Magazine 1155 Gratiot Ave *Circ	Detroit	MI	48207	**800-678-9595***	313-446-6000	449-3
Autry Greer & Sons Inc 2850 W Main St	Prichard	AL	36612	**800-477-9490**	251-457-8655	339
Autumn Industries Inc 518 Perkins-Jones Rd	Warren	OH	44483	**800-447-2116**	330-372-5002	769
Av-Med Health Plan Inc PO Box 749	Gainesville	FL	32602	**800-535-9355**	352-372-8400	384-3
AV Video & Multi Media Producer Magazine 701 Westchester Ave Suite 101 W *Cust Svc	White Plains	NY	10604	**800-800-5474***	914-328-9157	449-21
AVA (American Volkssport Assn) 1001 Pat Booker Rd Suite 101	Universal City	TX	78148	**800-830-9255**	210-659-2112	48-22
AVA Electronics Corp 4000 Bridge St *Sales	Drexel Hill	PA	19026	**800-331-8838***	610-284-2500	803
Avado Brands Inc 150 Hancock St	Madison	GA	30650	**800-609-1255**	706-342-4552	656
Avalon Correctional Services Inc PO Box 57012 *NASDAQ: CITY*	Oklahoma City	OK	73157	**800-919-9113**	405-752-8802	210
Avalon Executive Transportation Inc 6611 Hillcrest Ave Suite 333	Dallas	TX	75205	**866-513-5466**	214-824-1455	433
Avalon Hotel 16 W 10th St	Erie	PA	16501	**800-822-5011**	814-459-2220	373
Avalon Hotel & Spa 0455 SW Hamilton Ct	Portland	OR	97239	**888-556-4402**	503-802-5800	373
Avalon Inn & Resort 9519 E Market St	Warren	OH	44484	**800-828-2566**	330-856-1900	655
Avalon Majestic 700 Ocean Dr	Miami Beach	FL	33139	**800-933-3306**	305-538-0133	373
Avalon Natural Cosmetics Inc 1105 Industrial Ave Suite 200	Petaluma	CA	94952	**800-227-5120**	707-769-5120	211
Avant Inc 238 Bemis Rd	Fitchburg	MA	01420	**800-433-6843**	978-345-8200	580
Avant Ministries 10000 N Oak Trafficway	Kansas City	MO	64155	**800-468-1892**	816-734-8500	48-20
Avanti Destinations Inc 851 SW 6th St	Portland	OR	97204	**800-422-5053**	503-295-1100	760

Name / Address	City	State	ZIP	Toll-Free	Phone	Class
Avanti Press Inc 155 W Congress St Suite 200	Detroit	MI	48226	**800-228-2684**	313-961-0022	130
Avanyu Spa at the Casa Madrona Hotel 801 Bridgeway	Sausalito	CA	94965	**866-709-7625**	415-354-8308	698
Avanyu Spa at the Cheeca Lodge Mile Marker 82 PO Box 527	Islamorada	FL	33036	**800-327-2888**	305-517-4485	698
Avanyu Spa at the Equinox Resort 3567 Main St	Manchester Village	VT	05254	**800-362-4747**	802-362-7881	698
Avanyu Spa at the Lodge at Rancho Mirage Resort 68-900 Frank Sinatra Dr	Rancho Mirage	CA	92270	**866-518-6870**	760-321-8989	698
Avanyu Spa at La Posada de Santa Fe Resort 330 E Palace Ave	Santa Fe	NM	87501	**866-331-7625**	505-954-9630	698
Avanyu Spa at the Rosario Resort 1400 Rosario Rd	Eastsound	WA	98245	**800-562-8820**	360-376-2222	698
Avanyu Spa at the Snake River Lodge 7710 Granite Loop Rd PO Box 348	Teton Village	WY	83025	**800-445-4655**	307-732-6070	698
Avatar Holdings Inc 201 Alhambra Cir 12th Fl *NASDAQ: AVTR*	Coral Gables	FL	33134	**800-736-6660**	305-442-7000	639
Avatar Studios Inc 2675 Scott Ave Suite G	Saint Louis	MO	63103	**800-737-6065**	314-533-2242	503
Avatech Solutions Inc 10715 Red Run Blvd Suite 101	Owings Mills	MD	21117	**800-520-8000**	410-581-8080	39
Avatex Corp 5910 N Central Expy Suite 1780	Dallas	TX	75206	**800-654-3808**	214-365-7450	237
Avatier Corp 12647 Alcosta Blvd Suite 400	San Ramon	CA	94583	**800-609-8610**	925-831-4746	176-12
AVCON Corp 4640 Ironwood Dr	Franklin	WI	53132	**877-423-8725**	414-817-6160	803
Ave Maria University 1025 Commons Cir	Naples	FL	34119	**877-283-8648**	239-280-2511	162
Aveda Corp 4000 Pheasant Ridge Dr	Blaine	MN	55449	**800-283-3224**	763-783-4000	211
Avedis Zildjian Co 22 Longwater Dr	Norwell	MA	02061	**800-229-8672**	781-871-2200	516
Avemco Insurance Co 411 Aviation Way	Frederick	MD	21701	**800-874-9125**	301-694-5700	384-4
Aventail Corp 808 Howell St 2nd Fl	Seattle	WA	98101	**877-283-6824**	206-215-1111	176-12
Aventis Pasteur Inc Discovery Dr *Orders	Swiftwater	PA	18370	**800-822-2463***	570-839-7187	86
Aventis Pharma Inc 2150 St Elzear Blvd W	Laval	QC	H7L4A8	**800-363-6364**	514-331-9220	572
Aventis Pharmaceuticals Inc 300 Somerset Corp Blvd *NYSE: AVE*	Bridgewater	NJ	08807	**800-981-2491**	908-231-4000	86
Avenue Inn & Spa 33 Wilmington Ave	Rehoboth Beach	DE	19971	**800-433-5870**	302-226-2900	373
Avenue Plaza Hotel & Spa 2111 St Charles Ave	New Orleans	LA	70130	**800-535-9575**	504-566-1212	373
Avenue Stores Inc 365 W Passaic St	Rochelle Park	NJ	07662	**877-708-8740**	201-845-0880	155-6
Avera Saint Luke's Hospital 305 S State St	Aberdeen	SD	57401	**800-225-8537**	605-622-5000	366-2
Averett University 420 W Main St	Danville	VA	24541	**800-283-7388**	434-791-4996	163
Averitt Express Inc PO Box 3166	Cookeville	TN	38502	**800-283-7488**	931-526-3306	769
Averitt Hardwoods International PO Box 2217	Clarksville	TN	37042	**800-647-8394**	931-647-8394	671
Avery Dennison Business Media Div 685 Howard St	Buffalo	NY	14206	**800-777-2879**	716-852-2155	404
Avery Dennison Corp 150 N Orange Grove Blvd *NYSE: AVY* ■ *Cust Svc	Pasadena	CA	91103	**800-252-8379***	626-304-2000	717
Avery Dennison Fastener Div 224 Industrial Rd	Fitchburg	MA	01420	**800-225-5913**	978-353-2100	597
Avery Dennison Microreplication Div 7590 Auburn Rd MS 16X	Painesville	OH	44077	**866-358-4862**	440-358-4862	239
Avery Dennison Printer Systems Div 7722 Dungan Rd	Philadelphia	PA	19111	**800-395-2282**	215-725-4700	171-6
Avery Dennison Worldwide Graphics Div 250 Chester St Bldg 6	Painesville	OH	44077	**800-443-9380**	440-358-3700	542-1
Avery Dennison Worldwide Office Products Div 50 Pointe Dr	Brea	CA	92821	**800-462-8379**	714-674-8500	523
Avery James Craftsman Inc PO Box 291367	Kerrville	TX	78029	**800-283-1770**	830-895-1122	401
Avexus 10182 Telesis Ct Suite 600 *Sales	San Diego	CA	92121	**800-413-2797***	858-352-3300	176-1
AVG Automation 343 Saint Paul Blvd	Carol Stream	IL	60188	**800-527-2841**	630-668-3900	252
Aviagen Group 5015 Bradford Dr	Huntsville	AL	35805	**800-826-9685**	256-890-3800	11-8
Aviall Inc 2750 Regent Blvd *NYSE: AVL*	Dallas	TX	75261	**800-284-2551**	972-586-1000	759
Avianca Airlines 8125 NW 53rd St Suite 111	Miami	FL	33166	**800-284-2622**		26
Aviation Charter Services 6551 Pierson Dr	Indianapolis	IN	46241	**800-522-2296**	317-244-7200	14
Aviation Daily Newsletter 1200 G St NW Suite 900	Washington	DC	20005	**800-752-4959**	202-383-2350	521-13
Aviation Fellowship. Mission 1849 N Wabash Ave	Redlands	CA	92374	**800-359-7623**	909-794-1151	48-20
Aviation Maintenance Assn. Professional 717 Princess St	Alexandria	VA	22314	**866-865-7262**	703-683-3171	49-21
Aviation Week & Space Technology Magazine 1200 G St NW Suite 922	Washington	DC	20005	**800-525-5003**	202-383-2314	449-19
Avici Systems Inc 101 Billerica Ave *NASDAQ: AVCI*	North Billerica	MA	01862	**877-292-8424**	978-964-2000	174
Avicis Inc 21670 Ridgetop Cir	Sterling	VA	20166	**888-591-9985**	703-480-3000	176-10
Avid Technology Inc 1 Park W Metropolitan Technology Pk *NASDAQ: AVID*	Tewksbury	MA	01876	**800-949-2843**	978-640-6789	176-8
Avila University 11901 Wornall Rd	Kansas City	MO	64145	**800-462-8452**	816-942-8400	163
Avion Flight Centre Inc 2506 N Pliska Dr	Midland	TX	79711	**800-759-3359**	432-563-2033	63
Aviron 297 N Bernardo Ave	Mountain View	CA	94043	**877-633-4411**	650-691-9214	86

Name / Address	City	State	ZIP	Toll-Free	Phone	Class
Avis Rent A Car System Inc 6 Sylvan Way	Parsippany	NJ	07054	**800-331-1212**	973-496-3500	126
Avista Advantage 1313 N Atlantic St 5th Fl	Spokane	WA	99201	**800-767-4197**		176-12
Avista Corp 1411 E Mission St *NYSE: AVA*	Spokane	WA	99202	**800-727-9170**	509-495-4817	774
Avista Utilities 1411 E Mission St	Spokane	WA	99202	**800-227-9187**	509-495-4817	774
Avitar Inc 65 Dan Rd *AMEX: AVR*	Canton	MA	02021	**800-255-0511**	781-821-2440	469
AvMed PO Box 749	Gainesville	FL	32602	**800-346-0231**	352-372-8400	384-3
Avnet Electronics Marketing 2211 S 47th St	Phoenix	AZ	85034	**888-822-8638**	480-643-2000	252
Avnet Inc 2211 S 47th St *NYSE: AVT*	Phoenix	AZ	85034	**888-822-8638**	480-643-2000	245
Avnet Technology Solutions 8700 S Price Rd	Tempe	AZ	85284	**800-409-1483**	480-794-6900	172
Avocent Corp 4991 Corporate Dr *NASDAQ: AVCT*	Huntsville	AL	35805	**800-932-9239**	256-430-4000	496
Avolent Inc 444 De Haro St Suite 100	San Francisco	CA	94107	**800-553-5505**	415-553-6400	176-1
Avomark Insurance Co 9450 Seward Rd	Fairfield	OH	45014	**800-843-6446**	513-603-7400	384-4
Avon Bearings 1500 Nagle Rd	Avon	OH	44011	**800-286-6274**	440-871-2500	609
Avon Books Div HarperCollins Pubishers 10 E 53rd St	New York	NY	10022	**800-242-7737**	212-207-7000	623-2
Avon Old Farms School 500 Old Farms Rd	Avon	CT	06001	**800-464-2866**	860-404-4100	611
Avon Products Inc 1251 Ave of the Americas *NYSE: AVP* ■ *Cust Svc	New York	NY	10020	**800-367-2866***	212-282-5000	211
AVR Inc AME Ready Mix PO Box 307 *Cust Svc	Elk River	MN	55330	**800-374-8544***	763-441-2800	180
AVS Inc 60 Fitchburg Rd	Ayer	MA	01432	**800-272-0710**	978-772-0710	313
AVSC International Inc 440 9th Ave 3rd Fl	New York	NY	10001	**800-564-2872**	212-561-8000	48-17
AVSI (Automated Voice Systems Inc) 17059 El Cajon Ave	Yorba Linda	CA	92886	**888-505-2026**	714-524-4488	52
Avstar Aviation 12 N Haven Ln	East Northport	NY	11731	**800-575-2359**	631-499-0048	14
Avtec Inc 6 Industrial Park	Cahokia	IL	62206	**800-552-8832**	618-337-7800	430
Avtron Mfg Inc 7900 E Pleasant Valley Rd	Independence	OH	44131	**800-922-9751**	216-641-8310	247
AVW - TELAV Audio Visual Solutions 4545 W Davis St	Dallas	TX	75211	**800-225-5289**	214-634-9060	35
AW Imported Auto Parts Inc 52 Hwy 35	Eatontown	NJ	07724	**800-631-5589**	732-542-5600	61
AW Marshall Co PO Box 16127	Salt Lake City	UT	84116	**800-273-4713**	801-328-4713	744
Award Products Inc 4830 N Front St	Philadelphia	PA	19120	**800-972-2562**	215-324-0414	766
Award Software International Div Phoenix Technologies Ltd 411 E Plumeria Dr	San Jose	CA	95134	**800-677-7305**	408-570-1000	176-12
Awards & Recognition Assn (ARA) 4700 W Lake Ave	Glenview	IL	60025	**800-344-2148**	847-375-4800	49-4
AWC Commercial Window Coverings Inc 825 W Williamson Way	Fullerton	CA	92832	**800-252-2280**	714-879-3880	188-1
AWF (African Wildlife Foundation) 1400 16th St NW Suite 120	Washington	DC	20036	**888-494-5354**	202-939-3333	48-3
AWHONN (Association of Women's Health Obstetric & Neonatal Nurses) 2000 L St NW Suite 740	Washington	DC	20036	**800-673-8499**	202-261-2400	49-8
AWI (American Watchmakers-Clockmakers Institute) 701 Enterprise Dr	Harrison	OH	45030	**866-367-2924**	513-367-9800	49-4
AWIS (Association for Women in Science Inc) 1200 New York Ave NW Suite 650	Washington	DC	20005	**800-886-2947**	202-326-8940	49-19
A&WMA (Air & Waste Management Assn) 420 Fort Duquesne Blvd 1 Gateway Ctr 3rd Fl	Pittsburgh	PA	15222	**800-270-3444**	412-232-3444	48-12
AWMA (American Wholesale Marketers Assn) 2750 Prosperity Ave Suite 550	Fairfax	VA	22031	**800-482-2962**	703-208-3358	49-18
Awrey Bakeries Inc 12301 Farmington Rd	Livonia	MI	48150	**800-950-2253**	734-522-1100	69
AWS (American Welding Society) 550 NW Le Jeune Rd	Miami	FL	33126	**800-443-9353**	305-443-9353	49-3
AWSCPA (American Woman's Society of Certified Public Accountants) 136 S Keowee St	Dayton	OH	45402	**800-297-2721**	937-222-1872	49-1
AWT (Association of Water Technologies) 8201 Greensboro Dr Suite 300	McLean	VA	22102	**800-858-6683**	703-610-9012	48-2
AWWA (American Water Works Assn) 6666 W Quincy Ave	Denver	CO	80235	**800-926-7337**	303-794-7711	48-12
AXA Canada Inc 2020 University St 6th Fl	Montreal	QC	H3A2A5	**800-361-1594**	514-282-1914	384-4
AXA Equitable Life Insurance Co 1290 Ave of the Americas	New York	NY	10104	**888-855-5100**	212-554-1234	384-2
Axcan Pharma Inc 597 Laurier Blvd *NASDAQ: AXCA*	Mont-Saint-Hilaire	QC	J3H6C4	**800-565-3255**	450-467-5138	572
Axcera Corp 103 Freedom Dr	Lawrence	PA	15055	**800-215-2614**	724-873-8100	633
Axeda Systems Inc 277 Great Valley Pkwy *NASDAQ: XEDA*	Malvern	PA	19355	**800-700-0362**	610-407-7300	176-7
Axiom HR Solutions 8345 Lenexa Dr Suite 100	Lenexa	KS	66214	**800-801-7557**	913-383-2999	619
Axis Communications Inc 100 Apollo Dr	Chelmsford	MA	01824	**800-444-2947**	978-614-2000	174
AXS-One Inc 301 Rt 17 N *AMEX: AXO* ■ *Sales	Rutherford	NJ	07070	**800-828-7660***	201-935-3400	176-1
Axsys Technologies Motion Control Products 7603 St Andrew Ave Suite H *Cust Svc	San Diego	CA	92154	**800-777-3393***	619-671-5400	507
Axton Candy & Tobacco Co PO Box 32219	Louisville	KY	40232	**800-633-7816**	502-634-8000	744

Name / Address	City	State	ZIP	Toll-Free	Phone	Class
AY McDonald Mfg Co 4800 Chavenelle Rd *Cust Svc	Dubuque	IA	52002	**800-292-2737***	563-583-7311	584
AYSO (American Youth Soccer Organization) 12501 S Isis Ave *Cust Svc	Hawthorne	CA	90250	**800-872-2976***	310-643-6455	48-22
Azalea Trace 10100 Hillview DR	Pensacola	FL	32514	**800-828-8274**	850-478-5200	659
Azar Nut Co 1800 Northwestern Dr	El Paso	TX	79912	**800-351-8178**	915-877-4079	291-28
Azerty Inc 13 Centre Dr	Orchard Park	NY	14127	**800-888-8080**	716-662-0200	172
Azon Corp 720 Azon Rd	Johnson City	NY	13790	**800-847-9374**		542-1
Azonix Corp 900 Middlesex Tpke Bldg 6	Billerica	MA	01821	**800-967-5558**	978-670-6300	200
Azteca Milling Co 501 W Chapin St	Edinburg	TX	78539	**800-262-7322**	956-383-4911	291-23
Aztech Labs Inc 43264 Christy St	Fremont	CA	94538	**800-886-8859**	510-683-9800	496
Aztex Wax Products 5225 Middlebrook Pike	Knoxville	TN	37921	**800-369-5357**	865-588-5357	149
AzTx Cattle Co PO Box 390	Hereford	TX	79045	**800-999-5065**	806-364-8871	11-1
Azumano Travel Service Inc 400 SW 4th Ave	Portland	OR	97204	**800-777-2018**	503-294-2000	760
Azusa Pacific University 1915 W Orangewood Ave	Orange	CA	92868	**800-272-0111**	714-935-0260	163

B

Name / Address	City	State	ZIP	Toll-Free	Phone	Class
B & B Adcrafters Inc 1712 Marshall St NE	Minneapolis	MN	55413	**888-788-9461**	612-788-9461	675
B & B Agency of Boston 47 Commercial Wharf #3	Boston	MA	02110	**800-248-9262**	617-720-3540	368
B & B Media Group 109 S Main St	Corsicana	TX	75110	**800-927-0517**	903-872-0517	622
B Berger Co 1380 Highland Rd *Cust Svc	Macedonia	OH	44056	**800-288-8400***	330-425-3838	583
B Braun of America Inc 824 12th Ave	Bethlehem	PA	18018	**800-523-9676**	610-691-5400	468
B & C Bus Lines 427 Continental Dr	Maryville	TN	37804	**877-812-2287**	865-983-4653	108
B & D Litho Inc 3820 N 38th Ave *Cust Svc	Phoenix	AZ	85019	**800-735-0375***	602-269-2526	111
B Designs Inc 23 Noel St Suite 2	Amesbury	MA	01913	**800-978-3575**	978-388-1052	130
B Frank Joy LLC 5335 Kilmer Pl	Hyattsville	MD	20781	**800-992-3569**	301-779-9400	187-10
B & G Equipment Inc 301 E 8th St	Greeley	CO	80631	**800-382-9024**	970-352-9141	270
B-G Mechanical Service Inc 32 North Rd	East Windsor	CT	06088	**800-992-7386**	860-623-7911	188-10
B & G Mfg Co Inc 3067 Unionville Pike	Hatfield	PA	19440	**800-366-3067**	215-822-1925	274
B & H Flowers Inc 3516 Foothill Rd	Carpinteria	CA	93014	**800-682-5666**	805-684-4550	363
B & H Mfg Co 3461 Roeding Rd	Ceres	CA	95307	**888-643-0444**	209-537-5785	537
B & H Mfg Inc 141 County Rd 34 E	Jackson	MN	56143	**800-240-3288**	507-847-2802	269
B & H Photo-Video-Pro Audio Corp 420 9th Ave	New York	NY	10001	**800-947-9954**	212-444-6600	119
B & K Corp 5675 Dixie Hwy	Saginaw	MI	48601	**800-977-3775**	989-777-2111	247
B Moss Clothing Co Ltd 550 Meadowland Pkwy	Secaucus	NJ	07094	**800-524-0639**	201-866-6677	658
B & S Distributing 1911 Rice St	Roseville	MN	55113	**800-328-9653**	651-488-7261	78
B Shackman Co Inc 9964 W Miller Dr	Galesburg	MI	49053	**800-221-7656**	269-484-1000	130
B Von Paris & Sons Inc 8691 Larkin Rd	Savage	MD	20763	**800-866-6355**	410-888-8500	508
BA Ballou & Co Inc 800 Waterman Ave	East Providence	RI	02914	**800-729-3347**	401-438-7000	399
BA Mason 1251 1st Ave	Chippewa Falls	WI	54774	**800-826-7030**	715-723-1871	296
BA Merchant Services LLC 1231 Durrett Ln	Louisville	KY	40213	**800-949-7379**	502-315-2000	254
Baader-Johnson 2955 Fairfax Trafficway	Kansas City	KS	66115	**800-288-3434**	913-621-3366	293
BAB Inc 500 Lake Cook Rd Suite 475	Deerfield	IL	60015	**800-251-6101**	847-948-7522	656
Babcock-Davis 9300 73rd Ave N	Brooklyn Park	MN	55428	**888-412-3726**	763-488-9200	232
Babcock & Wilcox Co 20 S Van Buren Ave	Barberton	OH	44203	**800-222-2625**	330-753-4511	92
Babe Winkelman Productions PO Box 407	Brainerd	MN	56401	**800-333-0471**	218-822-4424	727
Babies 'R' Us 545 Rt 17 S	Paramus	NJ	07652	**800-869-7787**	201-251-3191	155-1
Babin Machine Works Inc PO Box 2007	Beaumont	TX	77704	**800-269-1274**	409-892-1231	447
Babson College 231 Forest St	Babson Park	MA	02457	**800-488-3696**	781-235-1200	163
Babson David L & Co Inc 1 Memorial Dr Suite 1100	Cambridge	MA	02142	**877-766-0014**	617-225-3800	393
Babson-United Inc 400 Talcott Ave	Watertown	MA	02472	**888-223-7412**	781-235-0900	393
Baby Einstein Co LLC 1201 Grand Central Ave	Glendale	CA	91201	**800-793-1454**	818-265-6050	502
Babybug Magazine 30 Grove St Suite C	Peterborough	NH	03458	**800-821-0115**	603-924-7209	449-6
BabyCenter LLC 163 Freelon St	San Francisco	CA	94107	**866-241-2229**	415-537-0900	351
Baby's Dream Furniture Inc PO Box 579	Buena Vista	GA	31803	**800-835-2742**	229-649-4404	314-2
BabyTalk Magazine 530 5th Ave 4th Fl	New York	NY	10036	**800-234-0847**	212-522-8989	449-11
BAC (International Union of Bricklayers & Allied Craftworkers) 1776 'I' St NW Suite 500	Washington	DC	20006	**888-880-8222**	202-783-3788	405
Bacara Resort & Spa 8301 Hollister Ave	Santa Barbara	CA	93117	**877-422-4245**	805-968-0100	655
Bacardi USA Inc 2100 Biscayne Blvd	Miami	FL	33137	**800-222-2734**	305-573-8511	81-1
Bacharach Inc 621 Hunt Valley Cir	New Kensington	PA	15068	**800-736-4666**	724-334-5000	200
Bachem Bioscience Inc 3700 Horizon Dr	King of Prussia	PA	19406	**800-634-3183**	610-239-0300	470
Bachem-Peninsula Laboratories Inc 305 Old Country Rd	San Carlos	CA	94070	**800-650-4442**	650-592-5392	229

Name / Address	City	State	ZIP	Toll-Free	Phone	Class
Bachman Co 50 N 4th St	Reading	PA	19601	**800-523-8253**	610-320-7800	291-35
Bachmann Industries Inc 1400 E Erie Ave *Cust Svc	Philadelphia	PA	19124	**800-356-3910***	215-533-1600	750
Bachman's Inc 6010 Lyndale Ave S	Minneapolis	MN	55419	**888-222-4626**	612-861-7600	287
Bachrach Clothing Inc 1 Bachrach Ct	Decatur	IL	62526	**800-222-4722**	217-875-1020	155-3
Back Bay Restaurant Group Inc 284 Newberry St	Boston	MA	02115	**800-367-2424**	617-536-2800	656
Back Country Horsemen of America (BCHA) PO Box 1367	Graham	WA	98338	**888-893-5161**	360-832-2461	48-23
Back Porch Records 4650 N Port Washington Rd	Milwaukee	WI	53212	**800-966-3699**	414-961-8350	643
Back Stage Magazine 770 Broadway *Subscriptions	New York	NY	10003	**800-437-3183***	646-654-5500	449-9
Back Yard Burgers Inc 1657 Shelby Oaks Dr N Suite 105 *NASDAQ: BYBI*	Memphis	TN	38134	**800-292-6939**	901-367-0888	657
Backcountry.com 1136 S 3600 W Suite 600 *Orders	Salt Lake City	UT	84104	**800-409-4502***	801-973-4553	451
Background Bureau Inc 2019 Alexandria Pike	Highland Heights	KY	41076	**800-854-3990**	859-781-3400	621
Background Information Services Inc 1800 30th St Suite 204	Boulder	CO	80301	**800-433-6010**	303-442-3960	621
Backpacker Magazine 33 E Minor St *Subcriptions	Emmaus	PA	18098	**800-666-3434***	610-967-5171	449-14
Backroads 801 Cedar St	Berkeley	CA	94710	**800-462-2848**	510-527-1555	748
BackWeb Technologies Inc 2077 Gateway Pl Suite 500 *NASDAQ: BWEB*	San Jose	CA	95110	**800-863-0100**	408-933-1700	176-7
Backyard Oaks 401 E 8th St Suite 310	Sioux Falls	SD	57103	**800-456-8208**	605-338-1968	130
Bacon RS Veneer Co 6951 High Grove Blvd	Burr Ridge	IL	60527	**800-443-7995**	630-323-1414	602
Bacone College 2299 Old Bacone Rd	Muskogee	OK	74403	**888-682-5514**	918-683-4581	160
Bacon's Information Inc 332 S Michigan Ave Suite 900	Chicago	IL	60604	**800-621-0561**	312-922-2400	623-6
Bacou-Dalloz 910 Douglas Pike	Smithfield	RI	02917	**800-343-3411**	401-233-0333	566
Badcock's Economy Furniture Store Inc 512 Clematis St	West Palm Beach	FL	33401	**800-223-2625**	561-659-1370	316
Badge A Minit Ltd 345 N Lewis Ave	Oglesby	IL	61348	**800-223-4103**	815-883-8822	448
Badger Air Brush Co 9128 W Belmont Ave	Franklin Park	IL	60131	**800-222-7553**	847-678-3104	43
Badger Bus 200 W Beltline Hwy	Madison	WI	53713	**800-442-8259**	608-255-1511	460
Badger Daylighting Inc 6740 65th Ave	Red Deer	AB	T4P1A5	**800-465-4273**	403-343-0303	528
Badger Fire Protection Inc 4251 Seminole Tr	Charlottesville	VA	22911	**800-446-3857**		666
Badger Meter Inc 4545 W Brown Deer Rd *AMEX: BMI*	Milwaukee	WI	53223	**800-876-3837**	414-355-0400	486
Badger Paper Mills Inc 200 W Front St *NASDAQ: BPMI*	Peshtigo	WI	54157	**800-826-0494**	715-582-4551	547
Badger Sportswear Inc 850 Meacham Rd	Statesville	NC	28677	**800-868-0105**	704-876-4648	153-3
Badger West Wine & Spirits LLC PO Box 869	Eau Claire	WI	54701	**800-472-6674**	715-836-8600	82-3
BadgerTour & Travel 200 W Beltline Hwy	Madison	WI	53713	**800-442-8259**	608-255-4040	748
Badorf Shoe Co Inc PO Box 367	Lititz	PA	17543	**800-325-1545**	717-626-8521	296
BAE SYSTEMS Infrared Imaging Systems 2 Forbes Rd	Lexington	MA	02421	**800-250-9494**	781-863-3199	519
Baer Howard F Inc 1301 Foster Ave	Nashville	TN	37210	**800-447-7430**	615-255-7351	769
Baer Supply Co 909 Forest Edge Dr	Vernon Hills	IL	60061	**800-944-2237**	847-913-2237	346
Baer's Furniture 1589 NW 12th Ave	Pompano Beach	FL	33069	**800-543-2092**	954-946-3792	316
BAF Industries Inc 1910 S Yale St	Santa Ana	CA	92704	**800-437-9893**	714-540-3850	149
Bagcraft Packaging LLC 3900 W 43rd St	Chicago	IL	60632	**800-621-8468**	773-254-8000	66
Bagdad Roller Mills Inc 5740 Elmburg Rd PO Box 7	Bagdad	KY	40003	**800-928-3333**	502-747-8968	438
Baggett Transportation Co 2 S 32nd St	Birmingham	AL	35233	**800-633-8982**	205-322-6501	769
Baghouse & Industrial Sheet Metal Services Inc 1731 Pomona Rd	Corona	CA	92880	**866-997-3784**	951-272-6610	19
Bagshaw WH Co Inc PO Box 766	Nashua	NH	03061	**800-343-7467**	603-883-7758	478
Bahama Breeze 5900 Lake Ellenor Dr	Orlando	FL	32809	**866-475-5666**	407-245-4000	657
Bahama House 2001 S Atlantic Ave	Daytona Beach Shores	FL	32118	**800-571-2001**	386-248-2001	373
Bahamas Tourism Office 11400 W Olympic Blvd Suite 204	Los Angeles	CA	90064	**800-439-6993**	310-312-9544	764
Bahamas Tourism Office 1200 S Pine Island Rd Suite 750	Plantation	FL	33324	**800-224-3681**	954-236-9292	764
Bahamas Tourism Office 150 E 52nd St 28th Fl N	New York	NY	10022	**800-823-3136**	212-758-2777	764
Bahia Beach Resort 611 Destiny Dr	Ruskin	FL	33570	**800-327-2773**	813-645-3291	655
Bahia Mar Resort & Conference Center 6300 Padre Blvd	South Padre Island	TX	78597	**800-997-2373**	956-761-1343	655
Bahia Resort Hotel 998 W Mission Bay Dr	San Diego	CA	92109	**800-576-4229**	858-488-0551	655
BAI (Bank Administration Institute) 1 N Franklin St Suite 1000 *Cust Svc	Chicago	IL	60606	**800-224-9889***	312-553-4600	49-2
Bailard Biehl & Kaiser Group 950 Tower Ln Suite 1900	Foster City	CA	94404	**800-882-8383**	650-571-5800	393
Bailey Banks & Biddle Div Zale Corp 901 W Walnut Hill Ln *Cust Svc	Irving	TX	75038	**800-651-4222***	972-580-4000	402
Bailey County Electric Co-op Inc 305 East Ave B	Muleshoe	TX	79347	**800-869-7049**	806-272-4504	244
Bailey Matthews Shell Museum 3075 Sanibel-Captiva Rd PO Box 1580	Sanibel	FL	33957	**888-679-6450**	239-395-2233	509
Bailey's Sports Grill 1551 N Waterfront Pkwy Suite 310	Wichita	KS	67206	**800-229-2118**	316-634-0505	657
Bain & Co 2 Copley Pl	Boston	MA	02116	**800-800-8338**	617-572-2000	193
Bainbridge-Decatur County Chamber of Commerce PO Box 755	Bainbridge	GA	39818	**800-243-4774**	229-246-4774	137
Bair Alberta Theater for the Performing Arts 2722 3rd Ave N Suite 400	Billings	MT	59101	**877-321-2074**	406-256-8915	562
Baird Patrick & Co Inc 20 Exchange Pl 11th Fl	New York	NY	10005	**800-221-7747**	212-493-6600	679
Baird Robert W & Co Inc PO Box 672	Milwaukee	WI	53201	**800-792-2473**	414-765-3500	679
Baja Duty Free 4590 Border Village Rd	San Ysidro	CA	92173	**877-438-8937**	619-428-6671	240
Baja Expeditions Inc 2625 Garnet Ave	San Diego	CA	92109	**800-843-6967**	858-581-3311	217
Baja Fresh Mexican Grill 100 Moody Ct Suite 200	Thousand Oaks	CA	91360	**800-932-5309**	805-495-4704	657
Baja Products 4065 N Romero Rd	Tucson	AZ	85705	**800-845-2252**	520-887-1154	367
BakBone Software Inc 10145 Pacific Heights Blvd Suite 500	San Diego	CA	92121	**877-939-2663**	858-450-9009	176-12
Bake'n Joy Foods Inc 351 Willow St S	North Andover	MA	01845	**800-666-4937**	978-683-1414	291-16
Baker Book House Co Inc 6030 E Fulton St *Orders	Ada	MI	49301	**800-877-2665***	616-676-9185	623-4
Baker Book House Co Inc Revell Div 6030 E Fulton St *Orders	Ada	MI	49301	**800-877-2665***	616-676-9185	623-4
Baker City Herald 1915 1st St PO Box 807	Baker City	OR	97814	**888-318-7508**	541-523-3673	522-2
Baker Co Inc 161 Gatehouse Rd PO Drawer E	Sanford	ME	04073	**800-992-2537**	207-324-8773	411
Baker College						
Auburn Hills Campus 1500 University Dr	Auburn Hills	MI	48326	**888-429-0410**	248-340-0600	158
Cadillac Campus 9600 E 13th St	Cadillac	MI	49601	**888-313-3463**	231-876-3100	163
Clinton Township Campus 34950 Little Mack Ave	Clinton Township	MI	48035	**888-272-2842**	586-791-6610	163
Flint Campus 1050 W Bristol Rd	Flint	MI	48507	**800-964-4299**	810-767-7600	163
Jackson Campus 2800 Springport Rd	Jackson	MI	49202	**888-343-3683**	517-788-7800	163
Muskegon Campus 1903 Marquette Ave	Muskegon	MI	49442	**800-937-0337**	231-777-8800	163
Owosso Campus 1020 S Washington St	Owosso	MI	48867	**800-879-3797**	989-729-3300	163
Port Huron Campus 3403 Lapeer Rd	Port Huron	MI	48060	**888-262-2442**	810-985-7000	163
Baker Commodities Inc 4020 Bandini Blvd	Los Angeles	CA	90023	**800-427-0696**	323-268-2801	291-12
Baker County Visitors & Convention Bureau 490 Campbell St	Baker City	OR	97814	**800-523-1235**	541-523-3356	205
Baker & Daniels 300 N Meridian St Suite 2700	Indianapolis	IN	46204	**800-428-9506**	317-237-0300	419
Baker Distributing Co 7892 Baymeadows Way	Jacksonville	FL	32256	**877-733-9633**	904-733-9633	601
Baker Drywall Co Inc PO Box 38299	Dallas	TX	75238	**800-458-3480**	972-289-5534	188-9
Baker Electric Inc 111 SW Jackson Ave	Des Moines	IA	50315	**800-779-6774**	515-288-6774	188-4
Baker Furniture 1661 Monroe Ave NW	Grand Rapids	MI	49505	**800-592-2537**	616-361-7321	314-2
Baker Group 4224 Hubbell Ave	Des Moines	IA	50317	**800-789-8933**	515-262-4000	188-10
Baker Hughes Inc 3900 Essex Ln Suite 1200 *NYSE: BHI*	Houston	TX	77027	**800-229-7447**	713-439-8600	528
Baker Hughes Inc Baker Petrolite Div 12645 W Airport Blvd	Sugar Land	TX	77478	**800-231-3606**	281-276-5400	143
Baker HW Linen Co Inc 500 Corporate Dr	Mahwah	NJ	07430	**800-631-0122**	201-825-2000	356
Baker Hydro Filtrations Inc 1864 Tobacco Rd	Augusta	GA	30906	**800-247-7291**	706-793-7291	793
Baker Iron & Metal Co Inc 740 Rock Castle Ave	Lexington	KY	40505	**800-398-2537**	859-255-5676	674
Baker Mfg Corp 7460 Chancellor Dr	Orlando	FL	32809	**800-881-2284**	407-816-9559	367
Baker Michael Corp 100 Airsite Dr Airsite Business Pk *AMEX: BKR*	Moon Township	PA	15108	**800-553-1153**	412-269-6300	258
Baker Oil Tools Inc PO Box 40129	Houston	TX	77240	**800-229-7447**	713-466-1322	526
Baker Petrolite Div Baker Hughes Inc 12645 W Airport Blvd	Sugar Land	TX	77478	**800-231-3606**	281-276-5400	143
Baker Roofing Co 517 Mercury St	Raleigh	NC	27603	**800-849-4096**	919-828-2975	188-12
Baker & Taylor Books 2709 Water Ridge Pkwy Suite 500	Charlotte	NC	28217	**800-775-1800**	704-357-3500	97
Baker & Taylor Inc 2550 W Tyvola Rd Suite 300	Charlotte	NC	28217	**800-775-1800**	704-998-3100	97
Baker University 618 8th St	Baldwin City	KS	66006	**800-873-4282**	785-594-6451	163
Bakers Square Restaurants Inc 400 W 48th Ave	Denver	CO	80216	**800-800-3644**	303-296-2121	657
Bakersfield Californian 1707 Eye St	Bakersfield	CA	93302	**800-953- 533**	661-395-7500	522-2
Bakersfield (Greater) Convention & Visitors Bureau 515 Truxtun Ave	Bakersfield	CA	93301	**866-425-7353**	661-325-5051	205
Bakery Assn. RBA - Retailer's 14239 Park Center Dr	Laurel	MD	20707	**800-638-0924**	301-725-2149	49-6
Bakery Resources -Ms Desserts 2275 Rolling Run Dr *Cust Svc	Baltimore	MD	21244	**800-876-7117***	410-281-2000	291-9
Baking. American Institute of 1213 Bakers Way PO Box 3999	Manhattan	KS	66505	**800-633-5137**	785-537-4750	654
Bal Seal Engineering Co Inc 19650 Pauling	Foothill Ranch	CA	92610	**800-366-1006**	949-460-2100	321
Balance Bar Co 800 W Chester Ave *Cust Svc	Rye Brook	NY	10573	**800-678-4246***	914-335-8400	291-11
Balance Rock Inn 21 Albert Meadow	Bar Harbor	ME	04609	**800-753-0494**	207-288-2610	373
Balanced Care Corp 1215 Manor Dr	Mechanicsburg	PA	17055	**888-227-3145**	717-796-6100	442

Name / Address	City	State	ZIP	Toll-Free	Phone	Class
Balanced Line Casket Co 15 S Boundary St	Cambridge City	IN	47327	**800-382-6934**	765-478-3501	134
Balboa Bay Club & Resort 1221 W Coast Hwy	Newport Beach	CA	92663	**888-445-7153**	949-645-5000	655
Balboa Life & Casualty Insurance Co 3349 Michelson Dr Suite 200	Irvine	CA	92612	**800-854-6115**	949-222-8000	384-5
Balboa Travel Management Inc 5414 Oberlin Dr Suite 300	San Diego	CA	92121	**800-359-8773**	858-678-3700	760
Baldwin Contracting Co Inc 4509 Skyway Dr	Marysville	CA	95901	**800-682-5726**	530-742-5141	187-4
Baldwin County Electric Membership Corp 19600 Hwy 59	Summerdale	AL	36580	**800-837-3374**	251-989-6247	244
Baldwin Filters Inc 4400 E Hwy 30	Kearney	NE	68848	**800-822-5394**	308-234-1951	60
Baldwin Hardware Corp 841 E Wyomissing Blvd	Reading	PA	19611	**800-437-7448**	610-777-7811	345
Baldwin & Lyons Inc 1099 N Meridian St Suite 700 *NASDAQ: BWINB*	Indianapolis	IN	46204	**800-231-6024**	317-636-9800	384-4
Baldwin Piano Co 309 Plus Park Blvd	Nashville	TN	37219	**800-444-2766**	615-871-4500	516
Baldwin Richardson Foods Co Inc 20201 S La Grange Rd Suite 200 *Cust Svc	Frankfort	IL	60423	**800-762-6458***	815-464-9994	291-25
Baldwin-Wallace College 275 Eastland Rd	Berea	OH	44017	**877-292-7759**	440-826-2900	163
Balfour LG Co 7211 Circle S Rd	Austin	TX	78745	**888-225-3687**	512-444-2090	401
Bali Co 5660 University Pkwy *Cust Svc	Winston-Salem	NC	27105	**800-225-4872***	336-519-6053	153-18
Ball Homes LLC 3609 Walden Dr	Lexington	KY	40517	**888-268-1101**	859-268-1191	186
Ball Horticultural Co 622 Town Rd	West Chicago	IL	60185	**800-879-2255**	630-231-3600	288
Ball Park Brands 10151 Carver Rd *Cust Svc	Cincinnati	OH	45242	**888-317-5867***	513-936-2000	291-26
Ball Seed Co 622 Town Rd	West Chicago	IL	60185	**800-879-2255**	630-231-3500	684
Ball State University	Muncie	IN	47306	**800-482-4278**	765-285-8300	163
Ball Tire & Gas Inc 620 S Ripley Blvd	Alpena	MI	49707	**800-322-3016**	989-354-4186	740
Ballantines Hotels in Palm Springs 1420 N Indian Canyon Dr	Palm Springs	CA	92262	**800-485-2808**	760-320-1178	373
Ballantyne of Omaha Inc 4350 McKinley St	Omaha	NE	68112	**800-262-5016**	402-453-4444	580
Ballantyne Resort Hotel 10000 Ballantyne Commons Pkwy	Charlotte	NC	28277	**866-248-4824**	704-248-4000	655
Ballard Medical Products 12050 Lone Peak Pkwy	Draper	UT	84020	**800-528-5591**	801-572-6800	468
Ballard SB Construction Co 2828 Shipps Corner Rd	Virginia Beach	VA	23453	**800-296-0209**	757-440-5555	188-3
Ballard's Farm Sausage Inc PO Box 699	Wayne	WV	25570	**800-346-7675**	304-272-5147	291-26
Ballet Arizona 3645 E Indian School Rd	Phoenix	AZ	85018	**888-322-5538**	602-381-0184	563-1
Ballet Florida 500 Fern St	West Palm Beach	FL	33401	**800-540-0172**	561-659-1212	563-1
Ballet Makers Inc. Capezio/ 1 Campus Rd	Totowa	NJ	07512	**800-595-9002**	973-595-9000	296
Balliet's Inc 1900 NW Expy	Oklahoma City	OK	73118	**877-841-8078**	405-848-7811	155-6
Balloons Everywhere Inc 16474 Greeno Rd	Fairhope	AL	36532	**800-239-2000**	251-210-2100	555
BalloonZone 1 American Rd *Sales	Cleveland	OH	44144	**800-321-3040***	216-252-7300	323
Ballou BA & Co Inc 800 Waterman Ave	East Providence	RI	02914	**800-729-3347**	401-438-7000	399
Bally Gaming & Systems 6601 S Bermuda Rd	Las Vegas	NV	89119	**877-462-2559**	702-896-7700	317
Bally-Sierra Design Group 300 Sierra Manor Dr	Reno	NV	89511	**888-404-8838**	775-850-1500	317
Ballymore Co 220 Garfield Ave	West Chester	PA	19380	**800-762-8327**	610-696-3250	412
Bally's Atlantic City 1900 Boardwalk & Park Pl	Atlantic City	NJ	08401	**800-772-7777**	609-340-2000	655
Bally's Casino New Orleans 1 Stars & Stripes Blvd	New Orleans	LA	70126	**800-572-2559**	504-248-3200	133
Bally's Casino Tunica 1450 Bally's Blvd Casino Ctr	Robinsonville	MS	38664	**800-382-2559**	662-357-1500	133
Bally's Las Vegas 3645 Las Vegas Blvd S *Resv	Las Vegas	NV	89109	**800-225-5977***	702-739-4111	133
Balmoral Inn 120 Balmoral Ave	Biloxi	MS	39531	**800-393-9131**	228-388-6776	373
BALSAMS The Rt 26	Dixville Notch	NH	03576	**800-255-0600**	603-255-3400	655
Baltex Swimsuits 1350 Mazurette St	Montreal	QC	H4N1H2	**888-225-8391**	514-383-1850	153-17
Baltimore Area Convention & Visitors Assn 100 Light St 12th Fl	Baltimore	MD	21202	**800-343-3468**	410-659-7300	205
Baltimore City Community College 2901 Liberty Heights Ave	Baltimore	MD	21215	**888-203-1261**	410-462-8000	160
Baltimore County Conference & Visitors Bureau PO Box 5426	Lutherville	MD	21094	**877-782-9630**	410-296-4886	205
Baltimore Gas & Electric Co 39 W Lexington St	Baltimore	MD	21201	**800-685-0123**	410-234-5000	774
Baltimore Hebrew University 5800 Park Heights Ave	Baltimore	MD	21215	**888-248-7420**	410-578-6900	163
Baltimore International College 17 Commerce St	Baltimore	MD	21202	**800-624-9926**	410-752-4710	787
Baltimore Life Cos 10075 Red Run Blvd	Owings Mills	MD	21117	**800-628-5433**	410-581-6600	384-2
Baltimore Magazine 1000 Lancaster St Suite 400 *Cust Svc	Baltimore	MD	21202	**800-935-0838***	410-752-4200	449-22
Baltimore Orioles 333 W Camden St Oriole Pk at Camden Yards	Baltimore	MD	21201	**888-848-2473**	410-685-9800	703
Baltimore Rigging Co Inc 7475 Lake Dr	Baltimore	MD	21237	**800-626-2150**	410-574-7300	188-1
Baltimore Spice Inc 9740 Reisterstown Rd	Owings Mills	MD	21117	**800-365-3229**	410-363-1700	291-37
Baltimore Sun 501 N Calvert St	Baltimore	MD	21278	**800-829-8000**	410-332-6000	522-2
Baltimore Symphony Orchestra 1212 Cathedral St	Baltimore	MD	21201	**800-422-1198**	410-783-8100	563-3
Baltimore Tool Works PO Box 27149	Baltimore	MD	21230	**800-752-5533**	410-752-5297	746
Baltimore-Washington International Airport (BWI)	Baltimore	MD	21240	**800-435-9294**	410-859-7111	28
Balzer Pacific Equipment Co 2136 SE 8th Ave	Portland	OR	97214	**800-442-0966**	503-232-5141	353
Bama Pie Ltd 2745 E 11th St	Tulsa	OK	74104	**800-756-2262**	918-592-0778	291-1
Bamberger Polymers Inc 2 Jericho Plaza	Jericho	NY	11753	**800-888-8959**	516-622-3600	592
Banacol Marketing Corp 2655 Le Jeune Rd Suite 1015	Coral Gables	FL	33134	**800-824-6585**	305-441-9036	292-7
Banana Bay Resort 2319 N Roosevelt Blvd	Key West	FL	33040	**800-226-2621**	305-296-6925	655
Banana Republic 1 Harrison St	San Francisco	CA	94105	**800-333-7899**	650-952-4400	155-4
Banc Corp 17 N 20th St *NASDAQ: TBNC*	Birmingham	AL	35203	**877-326-2365**	205-326-2265	355-2
Banco Comercial Portugues 2 Wall St	New York	NY	10005	**800-746-7828**	212-306-7800	71
Banco Popular de Puerto Rico PO Box 36-2708	San Juan	PR	00936	**888-724-3650**	787-765-9800	71
Banco Santander Puerto Rico PO Box 362589 GPO	San Juan	PR	00936	**800-726-8263**	787-759-7070	71
Bancorp Bank 405 Silverside Rd *NASDAQ: TBBK* ■ *Cust Svc	Wilmington	DE	19809	**800-545-0289***	302-385-5000	71
BancorpSouth 2910 W Jackson St	Tupelo	MS	38801	**888-797-7711**	662-680-2000	71
BancorpSouth Inc 1 Mississippi Plaza *NYSE: BXS*	Tupelo	MS	38802	**888-797-7711**	662-680-2000	355-2
Bancroft Bag Inc 425 Bancroft Blvd	West Monroe	LA	71292	**800-551-4950**	318-387-2550	66
Bancroft Cap Co Inc 1122 S 2nd St	Cabot	AR	72023	**800-345-8784**	501-843-6561	153-9
BancTec Inc 4435 Spring Valley Rd	Dallas	TX	75244	**800-226-2832**	972-960-1666	176-10
BancWest Corp PO Box 3200	Honolulu	HI	96847	**888-844-4444**	808-525-7000	355-2
Band Fraternity. Kappa Kappa Psi National Honorary PO Box 849	Stillwater	OK	74076	**800-543-6505**	405-372-2333	48-16
Band-It-IDEX Inc 4799 Dahlia St	Denver	CO	80216	**800-525-0758**	303-320-4555	345
Band Sorority. Tau Beta Sigma National Honorary PO Box 849	Stillwater	OK	74076	**800-543-6505**	405-372-2333	48-16
Bandera County Convention & Visitors Bureau PO Box 171	Bandera	TX	78003	**800-364-3833**	830-796-3045	205
Bandera Electric Co-op Inc 3172 State Hwy 16 N	Bandera	TX	78003	**866-226-3372**	830-796-3741	244
Bandimere Speedway 3051 S Rooney Rd	Morrison	CO	80465	**800-664-8946**	303-697-6001	504
Bandit Industries Inc 6750 Millbrook Rd	Remus	MI	49340	**800-952-0178**	989-561-2270	189
Bands of America Inc (BOA) 39 W Jackson Pl	Indianapolis	IN	46225	**800-848-2263**	317-636-2263	48-11
Banff Adventures Unlimited 207 Caribou St	Banff	AB	T1L1A8	**800-644-8888**	403-762-4554	748
Banff Centre 107 Tunnel Mountain Dr	Banff	AB	T1L1H5	**800-884-7574**	403-762-6100	370
Banff National Park Box 900	Banff	AB	T1L1K2	**800-762-1599**	403-762-1550	553
Banfi Vintners USA 1111 Cedar Swamp Rd	Old Brookville	NY	11545	**800-645-6511**	516-626-9200	81-3
Banfield The Pet Hospital 11815 NE Glenn Widing Dr	Portland	OR	97220	**800-394-6117**	503-256-7299	781
Bang Printing Inc 3323 Oak St	Brainerd	MN	56401	**800-328-0450**	218-829-2877	614
Bangor Hydro Electric Co 33 State St	Bangor	ME	04402	**800-499-6600**	207-945-5621	774
Bangor Public Library 145 Harlow St	Bangor	ME	04401	**800-427-8336**	207-947-8336	426
Bangor Savings Bank PO Box 930	Bangor	ME	04402	**877-226-4671**	207-942-5211	71
Bangor Symphony Orchestra 51-A Main St PO Box 1441	Bangor	ME	04402	**800-639-3221**	207-942-5555	563-3
Bangor Theological Seminary 300 Union St	Bangor	ME	04401	**800-287-6781**	207-942-6781	164-3
Bank Administration Institute (BAI) 1 N Franklin St Suite 1000 *Cust Svc	Chicago	IL	60606	**800-224-9889***	312-553-4600	49-2
Bank of America Card Services 1 Commercial Plaza	Norfolk	VA	23510	**800-732-9194**	757-441-4770	213
Bank of America Corp 100 N Tryon St Suite 200 Corporate Ctr *NYSE: BAC*	Charlotte	NC	28202	**800-299-2265**		355-2
Bank of America Foundation 315 Montgomery St 8th Fl MS CA5-704-08-03	San Francisco	CA	94104	**888-488-9802**	415-953-3175	299
Bank of America Insurance Services Inc PO Box 21848	Greensboro	NC	27420	**800-288-7647**	336-805-8800	384-2
Bank of America Leasing Corp 2059 Northlake Pkwy 4th Fl	Tucker	GA	30084	**800-299-2265**	770-270-8400	214
Bank of America NA 699 S Mill Ave Suite 101	Tempe	AZ	85281	**800-299-2265**	480-804-9481	71
Bank of America NA 101 S Tryon St	Charlotte	NC	28255	**800-432-1000**	704-386-5478	71
Bank of America Securities LLC 600 Montgomery St	San Francisco	CA	94111	**800-227-4786**	415-627-2000	679
Bank Asset/Liability Management Newsletter 807 Las Cimas Pkwy Suite 300	Austin	TX	78746	**800-572-2797**		521-1
Bank Financial 21110 S Western Ave	Olympia Fields	IL	60461	**800-244-2265**	708-747-2000	71
Bank-Fund Staff Federal Credit Union PO Box 27755	Washington	DC	20038	**800-923-7328**	202-458-4300	216
Bank of Hawaii 111 S King St	Honolulu	HI	96813	**888-643-3888**	808-538-4171	71
Bank of Hawaii Corp PO Box 2900 *NYSE: BOH*	Honolulu	HI	96846	**888-643-3888**	808-537-8272	355-2
Bank of Ireland Asset Management (US) Ltd 75 Holly Hill Ln	Greenwich	CT	06830	**888-473-2275**	203-869-0111	393
Bank Leumi USA 420 Lexington Ave	New York	NY	10170	**800-892-5430**	917-542-2343	71
Bank of Marin 50 Madera Blvd *NASDAQ: BMRC*	Corte Madera	CA	94925	**800-654-5111**	415-927-2265	71
Bank of Montreal 3 Times Sq	New York	NY	10036	**800-363-9992**	212-758-6300	71
Bank of Montreal 119 Saint Jacques St *NYSE: BMO*	Montreal	QC	H2Y1L6	**800-363-9992**	514-877-7373	71
Bank Mutual Corp 4949 W Brown Deer Rd *NASDAQ: BKMU*	Milwaukee	WI	53223	**888-358-5070**	414-354-1500	355-2
Bank Network News 1 State Street Plaza 27th Fl	New York	NY	10004	**800-535-8403**	212-803-8200	521-1
Bank of New Hampshire NA PO Box 487 *Cust Svc	Farmington	NH	03835	**800-224-5563***	603-755-2255	71
Bank of New York 1 Wall St	New York	NY	10286	**800-225-5269**	212-635-6748	71

Name / Address	City	State	ZIP	Toll-Free	Phone	Class
Bank of Newport PO Box 450	Newport	RI	02840	**800-234-8586**	401-846-3400	71
Bank of North Dakota 700 E Main Ave	Bismarck	ND	58501	**800-472-2166**	701-328-5600	71
Bank of Oklahoma NA PO Box 2300 *Cust Svc	Tulsa	OK	74192	**800-234-6181***	918-588-6000	71
Bank One 1 Bank One Plaza	Chicago	IL	60670	**877-226-5663**	312-732-4000	71
Bank of the Ozarks Inc 12615 Chenal Pkwy Suite 3100 *NASDAQ: OZRK*	Little Rock	AR	72211	**800-628-3552**	501-978-2265	355-2
Bank Supervisors. Conference of State 1155 Connecticut Ave NW 5th Fl	Washington	DC	20036	**800-886-2727**	202-296-2840	49-7
Bank of the West 180 Montgomery St	San Francisco	CA	94104	**800-575-6677**	925-942-8300	71
BankAtlantic 1750 E Sunrise Blvd	Fort Lauderdale	FL	33304	**800-741-1700**	954-760-5000	71
BankAtlantic Bancorp Inc 1750 E Sunrise Blvd *NYSE: BBX*	Fort Lauderdale	FL	33304	**800-741-1700**	954-760-5000	355-2
Bankers Assn. American 1120 Connecticut Ave NW *Cust Svc	Washington	DC	20036	**800-226-5377***	202-663-5000	49-2
Bankers Assn. Mortgage 1919 Pennsylvania Ave NW	Washington	DC	20006	**800-793-6222**	202-557-2700	49-2
Bankers Fidelity Life Insurance Co PO Box 105652	Atlanta	GA	30348	**800-241-1439**		384-2
Bankers Insurance Co 360 Central Ave	Saint Petersburg	FL	33701	**800-627-0000**	727-823-4000	384-2
Bankers Life & Casualty Co 222 Merchandise Mart Plaza	Chicago	IL	60654	**800-621-3724**	312-396-6000	384-2
Bankers National Life Insurance Co 11815 N Pennsylvania St	Carmel	IN	46032	**800-888-4918**	317-817-6300	384-2
Bankers Systems Inc 6815 Saukview Dr	Saint Cloud	MN	56303	**800-397-2341**	320-251-3060	176-11
Bankers Training & Consulting Co 12250 Weber Hill Rd Suite 200	Saint Louis	MO	63127	**800-264-7600**	314-843-5656	502
Bankers United Life Assurance Co 4333 Edgewood Rd NE *Cust Svc	Cedar Rapids	IA	52499	**800-625-4213***	319-398-8511	384-2
Banking Advisory Network. Community 10831 Old Mill Rd Suite 400	Omaha	NE	68154	**888-475-4476**	402-778-7922	49-2
Banking Law Journal 1901 Fort Myer Dr Suite 702 *Cust Svc	Arlington	VA	22209	**800-572-2797***	703-528-0145	449-15
Banknorth Massachusetts 295 Park Ave *Cust Svc	Worcester	MA	01610	**800-390-6443***	508-752-2584	71
Banko Beverage Co 2124 Hanover Ave	Allentown	PA	18109	**800-322-9295**	610-434-0147	82-1
Bankrate Inc 11760 US Hwy 1 Suite 101 *NASDAQ: RATE*	North Palm Beach	FL	33408	**800-243-7720**	561-630-2400	677
Bankrate.com 11811 US Hwy 1 Suite 101	North Palm Beach	FL	33408	**800-243-7720**	561-630-2400	115
Bankruptcy Law Letter 610 Opperman Dr	Eagan	MN	55123	**800-937-8529**	651-687-7000	521-7
Bankruptcy Strategist Newsletter 345 Park Ave S	New York	NY	10010	**800-888-8300**	212-779-9200	521-7
Bankserv 222 Kearny St Suite 400	San Francisco	CA	94108	**888-354-3535**	415-217-4581	70
Bankshot Organization 785 F Rockville Pike Suite 504	Rockville	MD	20852	**800-933-0140**	301-309-0260	701
BankUnited Financial Corp 255 Alhambra Cir *NASDAQ: BKUNA*	Coral Gables	FL	33134	**800-440-9646**	305-569-2000	355-2
BankUnited FSB 255 Alhambra Cir Suite 100	Coral Gables	FL	33134	**800-440-9646**	305-569-2000	71
Banneker-Douglas Museum 84 Franklin St	Annapolis	MD	21401	**866-521-6173**	410-216-6180	509
Banner Bank PO Box 907	Walla Walla	WA	99362	**800-272-9933**	509-526-8734	71
Banner Candy Mfg Corp 700 Liberty Ave	Brooklyn	NY	11208	**800-221-0934**	718-647-4747	291-8
Banner Engineering Corp 9714 10th Ave N	Minneapolis	MN	55441	**888-373-6767**	763-544-3164	252
Banner-Graphic 100 N Jackson St PO Box 509	Greencastle	IN	46135	**888-778-8877**	765-653-5151	522-2
Banner Home Care & Hospice 1325 N Fiesta Blvd Suite 1	Gilbert	AZ	85233	**800-293-6989**	480-497-5535	365
Banner Life Insurance Co 1701 Research Blvd	Rockville	MD	20850	**800-638-8428**	301-279-4800	384-2
Banner Pharmacaps Inc 4125 Premier Dr	High Point	NC	27265	**800-447-1140**	336-812-4729	572
Banner Pharmacaps Ltd 5807 47th Ave	Olds	AB	T4H1S7	**866-507-3483**	403-556-2531	572
Banta Book Group PO Box 60	Menasha	WI	54952	**800-291-1171**	920-751-7771	614
Banta Catalog Group 7401 Kilmer Ln	Maple Grove	MN	55369	**888-882-2682**	763-424-7446	615
Banta Direct Marketing Group 12 Salt Creek Ln Suite 350 *Cust Svc	Hinsdale	IL	60521	**800-323-6112***	630-323-9490	615
Banta Foods Inc 1620 N Packer Rd	Springfield	MO	65803	**800-492-2682**	417-862-6644	292-8
Banyan Air Service Inc 1575 W Commercial Blvd	Fort Lauderdale	FL	33309	**800-200-2031**	954-491-3170	63
Banyan Resort 323 Whitehead St	Key West	FL	33040	**800-853-9937**	305-296-7786	373
Baptist Assn. American 4605 N State Line Ave	Texarkana	TX	75503	**800-264-2482**	903-792-2783	48-20
Baptist Bible College 628 E Kearney St	Springfield	MO	65803	**800-228-5754**	417-268-6060	163
Baptist Churches USA. American PO Box 851	Valley Forge	PA	19482	**800-222-3872**	610-768-2000	48-20
Baptist College of Florida 5400 College Dr	Graceville	FL	32440	**800-328-2660**	850-263-3261	163
Baptist Convention Inc. Progressive National 601 50th St NE	Washington	DC	20019	**800-876-7622**	202-396-0558	48-20
Baptist Convention USA Inc. National 1700 Baptist World Ctr Dr	Nashville	TN	37207	**866-531-3054**	615-228-6292	48-20
Baptist General Conference (BGC) 2002 S Arlington Heights Rd	Arlington Heights	IL	60005	**800-323-4215**	847-228-0200	48-20
Baptist Health of South Florida 8900 N Kendall Dr	Miami	FL	33176	**800-327-2491**	786-596-1960	366-2
Baptist Health Systems Inc 1225 N State St	Jackson	MS	39202	**800-948-6262**	601-968-1000	366-2
Baptist Health Systems of South Florida 6855 Red Rd Suite 600	Coral Gables	FL	33143	**800-327-2491**	786-662-7111	348
Baptist Hospice 11900 Colonel Glenn Rd Suite 2000	Little Rock	AR	72210	**800-900-7474**	501-202-7474	365
Baptist Medical Center 800 Prudential Dr	Jacksonville	FL	32207	**800-874-8567**	904-202-2000	366-2
Baptist Saint Anthony's Hospice PO Box 950	Amarillo	TX	79176	**800-315-6209**	806-212-8000	365
Baptists International. Conservative 1501 W Mineral Ave	Littleton	CO	80120	**800-487-4224**	720-283-2000	48-20
Baptists. National Assn of Free Will 5233 Mt View Rd	Antioch	TN	37013	**877-767-7659**	615-731-6812	48-20
Bar of Arizona. State 4201 N 24th St Suite 200	Phoenix	AZ	85016	**866-482-9227**	602-252-4804	73
Bar Assn. American 750 N Lake Shore Dr	Chicago	IL	60611	**800-285-2221**	312-988-5000	49-10
Bar Assn. Hispanic National 815 Connecticut Ave NW Suite 500	Washington	DC	20006	**877-221-6569**	202-223-4777	49-10
Bar Assn Inc. Maryland State 520 W Fayette St	Baltimore	MD	21201	**800-492-1964**	410-685-7878	73
Bar Assn. Indiana State 1 Indiana Sq Suite 530	Indianapolis	IN	46204	**800-266-2581**	317-639-5465	73
Bar Assn. Louisiana State 601 St Charles Ave	New Orleans	LA	70130	**800-421-5722**	504-566-1600	73
Bar Assn. Massachusetts 20 West St	Boston	MA	02111	**866-627-7577**	617-338-0500	73
Bar Assn. Minnesota State 600 Nicollet Mall Suite 380	Minneapolis	MN	55402	**800-882-6722**	612-333-1183	73
Bar Assn. National 1225 11th St NW	Washington	DC	20001	**800-621-2988**	202-842-3900	49-10
Bar Assn. Nebraska State 635 S 14th St	Lincoln	NE	68501	**800-927-0117**	402-475-7091	73
Bar Assn. New York State 1 Elk St	Albany	NY	12207	**800-342-3661**	518-463-3200	73
Bar Assn. Ohio State 1700 Lake Shore Dr	Columbus	OH	43204	**800-282-6556**	614-487-2050	73
Bar Assn. Oklahoma PO Box 53036	Oklahoma City	OK	73152	**800-522-8065**	405-416-7000	73
Bar Assn. Pennsylvania 100 South St	Harrisburg	PA	17101	**800-932-0311**	717-238-6715	73
Bar Assn. Tennessee 221 4th Ave N Suite 400	Nashville	TN	37219	**800-899-6993**	615-383-7421	73
Bar Assn. Washington State 2101 4th Ave Suite 400	Seattle	WA	98121	**800-945-9722**	206-727-8200	73
Bar. District of Columbia 1250 H St NW 6th Fl	Washington	DC	20005	**877-333-2227**	202-737-4700	73
Bar. Florida 651 E Jefferson St	Tallahassee	FL	32399	**800-342-8060**	850-561-5600	73
Bar of Georgia. State 104 Marietta St NW Suite 100	Atlanta	GA	30303	**800-334-6865**	404-527-8700	73
Bar Harbor Bankshares 82 Main St PO Box 400 *AMEX: BHB*	Bar Harbor	ME	04609	**800-237-9601**	207-288-3314	355-2
Bar Harbor Chamber of Commerce 93 Cottage St PO Box 158	Bar Harbor	ME	04609	**888-540-9990**	207-288-5103	137
Bar Harbor Hotel-Bluenose Inn 90 Eden St	Bar Harbor	ME	04609	**800-445-4077**	207-288-3348	373
Bar Harbor Inn Oceanfront Resort Newport Dr Box 7	Bar Harbor	ME	04609	**800-248-3351**	207-288-3351	373
Bar Harbor Regency Resort. Holiday Inn SunSpree 123 Eden St	Bar Harbor	ME	04609	**800-234-6835**	207-288-9723	655
Bar Lazy J Guest Ranch PO Box N	Parshall	CO	80468	**800-396-6279**	970-725-3437	238
Bar M Dude Ranch 58840 Bar M Ln	Adams	OR	97810	**888-824-3381**	541-566-3381	238
Bar of Michigan. State 306 Townsend St	Lansing	MI	48933	**800-968-1442**	517-372-9030	73
Bar of Nevada. State 600 E Charleston Blvd	Las Vegas	NV	89104	**800-254-2797**	702-382-2200	73
Bar of New Mexico. State 5121 Masthead St NE	Albuquerque	NM	87109	**800-876-6227**	505-797-6000	73
Bar. North Carolina State 208 Fayetteville St Mall	Raleigh	NC	27601	**800-662-7407**	919-828-4620	73
Bar of Texas. State 1414 Colorado St	Austin	TX	78701	**800-204-2222**	512-463-1463	73
Bar of Wisconsin. State 5302 Eastpark Blvd	Madison	WI	53718	**800-728-7788**	608-257-3838	73
Baraboo News Republic 219 1st St PO Box 9	Baraboo	WI	53913	**800-773-4808**	608-356-4808	522-2
Barbados Tourism Authority 3440 Wilshire Blvd Suite 1215	Los Angeles	CA	90010	**800-221-9831**	213-380-2198	764
Barbados Tourism Authority 150 Alhambra Cir Suite 1000	Coral Gables	FL	33134	**800-221-9831**	305-442-7471	764
Barbados Tourism Authority 800 2nd Ave 2nd Fl	New York	NY	10017	**800-221-9831**	212-986-6516	764
Barbara Ann Karmanos Cancer Institute 4110 John R St	Detroit	MI	48201	**800-527-6266**	313-833-0710	654
Barbara B Mann Performing Arts Hall 8099 College Pkwy SW	Fort Myers	FL	33919	**800-440-7469**	239-489-3033	562
Barbary Coast Hotel & Casino 3595 S Las Vegas Blvd	Las Vegas	NV	89109	**888-227-2279**	702-737-7111	373
Barbeques Galore 10 Orchard Rd Suite 200 *NASDAQ: BBQZ*	Lake Forest	CA	92630	**800-752-3085**	949-597-2400	322
Barber Pure Milk Co 19 Green Briar Rd	Anniston	AL	36201	**800-264-4157**	256-240-9141	291-27
Barber-Scotia College 145 Cabarrus Ave W *Admissions	Concord	NC	28025	**800-267-3910***	704-789-2902	163
Barber Shop Quartet Singing in America. Society for the Preservation & Encouragement of 7930 Sheridan Rd	Kenosha	WI	53143	**800-876-7464**	262-653-8440	48-18
Barber Supply Institute. Beauty & 15825 N 71st St Suite 100	Scottsdale	AZ	85254	**800-468-2274**	480-281-0424	49-18
Barberton Citizens Hospital 155 5th St NE	Barberton	OH	44203	**877-227-8745**	330-745-1611	366-2
Barbizon Suites 530 Ocean Dr	Miami Beach	FL	33139	**800-478-6082**	305-673-1173	373

Name / Address	City	State	ZIP	Toll-Free	Phone	Class
Barbour Welting Co Div Barbour Corp 1001 N Montello St	Brockton	MA	02301	800-955-9649	508-583-8200	296
BARC Electric Co-op 100 High St	Millboro	VA	24460	800-846-2272	540-997-9124	244
Barclay The 111 E 48th St	New York	NY	10017	800-327-0200	212-755-5900	373
Barclay College 607 N Kingman St	Haviland	KS	67059	800-862-0226	620-862-5252	163
Barclay International Group 6800 Jericho Tpke	Syosset	NY	11791	800-845-6636	516-364-0064	368
Barclay Steven Agency 12 Western Ave	Petaluma	CA	94952	888-965-7323	707-773-0654	699
Barclay Towers 809 Atlantic Ave	Virginia Beach	VA	23451	800-344-4473	757-491-2700	373
Barclays Capital Inc 200 Park Ave	New York	NY	10166	888-227-2275	212-412-4000	679
Barclays Global Investors Funds 45 Fremont St 5th Fl	San Francisco	CA	94105	888-204-3956	415-597-2000	517
Barco of California 350 W Rosecrans Ave	Gardena	CA	90248	800-421-1874	310-323-7315	153-19
Barco Folsom LLC 11101 Trade Center Dr	Rancho Cordova	CA	95670	888-414-7226	916-859-2500	171-4
BARCO Industries Inc 1020 MacArthur Rd *Cust Svc	Reading	PA	19605	800-234-8665*	610-374-3117	746
Barco Media LLC 1651 N 10 West	Logan	UT	84321	800-543-7904	435-753-2224	171-4
Barcus LG & Sons Inc 1430 State Ave	Kansas City	KS	66102	800-255-0180	913-621-1100	188-3
Bard Access Systems Inc 5425 W Amelia Earhart Dr	Salt Lake City	UT	84116	800-443-5505	801-595-0700	468
Bard CR Inc 730 Central Ave *NYSE: BCR* ■ *Cust Svc	Murray Hill	NJ	07974	800-526-4455*	908-277-8000	468
Bard CR Inc Endoscopic Technologies Div 129 Concord Rd Bldg 3 PO Box 7031	Billerica	MA	01821	800-225-1332	978-663-8989	468
Bard CR Inc Medical Div 8195 Industrial Blvd	Covington	GA	30014	800-526-4455	770-784-6100	468
Bard CR Inc Peripheral Vascular Div PO Box 1740	Tempe	AZ	85281	800-321-4254		468
Bard CR Inc Urological Div 8195 Industrial Blvd	Covington	GA	30014	800-526-4455	770-786-9051	468
Bard Optical 7722 N Crestline Dr	Peoria	IL	61615	800-752-3295	309-693-9540	533
Barden Corp 200 Park Ave	Danbury	CT	06813	800-243-1060	203-744-2211	609
Barden & Robeson Corp 103 Kelly Ave	Middleport	NY	14105	800-724-0141	716-735-3732	107
Bardes Plastics Inc 5225 W Clinton Ave *Cust Svc	Milwaukee	WI	53223	800-558-5161*	414-354-5300	591
Bardstown-Nelson County Chamber of Commerce 1 Court Sq	Bardstown	KY	40004	866-894-9545	502-348-9545	137
Bardstown-Nelson County Tourist & Convention Commission PO Box 867	Bardstown	KY	40004	800-638-4877	502-348-4877	205
Bare Sportswear Corp 1755 Grant Ave	Blaine	WA	98230	800-663-0111	360-332-2700	701
Barefoot Landing 4898 Hwy 17 S	North Myrtle Beach	SC	29582	800-272-2320	843-272-8349	50
Barenbrug USA Inc 33477 Hwy 99 E	Tangent	OR	97389	800-547-4101	541-926-5801	684
Baring Asset Management Co Inc 125 High St High St Tower Suite 2700	Boston	MA	02110	800-533-7432	617-951-0052	393
Barix Clinics 135 S Prospect St	Ypsilanti	MI	48198	800-282-0066	734-547-4700	797
Barker Steel Co Inc 55 Sumner St	Milford	MA	01757	800-370-0132	508-473-8484	471
Barkley Farling Corp 5370 Hwy 42	Hattiesburg	MS	39401	800-522-0297	601-545-2200	260
Barksdale Inc 3211 Fruitland Ave	Los Angeles	CA	90058	800-835-1060	323-589-6181	200
Barlovento LLC 165 Hostdale Dr Suite 1	Dothan	AL	36303	877-498-6039	334-983-9979	185
Barlow Promotional Products Inc 8700 Bellanca Ave	Los Angeles	CA	90045	800-227-5691	310-670-6363	766
Barn Furniture Mart Inc 6206 N Sepulveda Blvd	Van Nuys	CA	91411	888-302-2276	818-780-4070	316
Barnebey & Sutcliffe Corp 835 N Cassady Ave	Columbus	OH	43219	800-886-2272	614-258-9501	19
Barnes Engineering Co 2715 Delta Pl	Colorado Springs	CO	80910	800-995-6050	719-390-6500	77
Barnes Group Inc 123 Main St *NYSE: B*	Bristol	CT	06011	800-877-8803	860-583-7070	704
Barnes-Jewish Hospital Bone Marrow & Stem Cell Transplant Program 1 Barnes-Jewish Hospital Plaza Steinberg Bldg 5th Fl	Saint Louis	MO	63110	800-635-2371	314-454-8304	758
Barnes Jhane Inc 119 W 40th St 20th Fl	New York	NY	10018	888-465-4263	212-575-2448	273
Barnes & Thornburg 11 S Meridian St	Indianapolis	IN	46204	800-753-5139	317-236-1313	419
Barnes Wholesale Inc PO Box 17010	Inglewood	CA	90308	800-227-4845	310-641-1885	237
Barnet-Dulaney Eye Center 4800 N 22nd St	Phoenix	AZ	85016	800-966-7000	602-955-1000	785
Barnet William & Son Inc 1300 Hayne St	Arcadia	SC	29320	800-922-7638	864-576-7154	594-1
Barnett Implement Co Inc 4220 Old Hwy 99 S	Mount Vernon	WA	98273	800-453-9274	360-424-7995	270
Barnett Inc 3333 Lenox Ave	Jacksonville	FL	32254	800-288-2000	904-384-6530	601
Barnett International 1400 N Providence Rd Rose Tree Corporate Ctr Suite 2000	Media	PA	19063	800-856-2556	610-565-9400	193
Barnhart Crane & Rigging Inc 938 E 4th St	Richmond	VA	23224	800-787-4767	804-233-9221	261-2
Barnhill's Buffet Inc 226 Palafox Pl 5th Fl	Pensacola	FL	32502	888-738-3808	850-435-9914	657
Barnie's Coffee & Tea Co Inc 2126 Landstreet Rd Suite 300	Orlando	FL	32809	800-456-1416	407-854-6600	156
Barnsley Gardens 597 Barnsley Gardens Rd	Adairsville	GA	30103	877-773-2447	770-773-7480	655
Barnstead Inn PO Box 988 Bonnet St	Manchester Center	VT	05255	800-331-1619	802-362-1619	373
Barnstead/Thermolyne Corp 2555 Kerper Blvd	Dubuque	IA	52001	800-446-6060	563-556-2241	411
Baron Drawn Steel Corp 1420 Baron Steel Ave	Toledo	OH	43607	800-537-8850	419-531-5525	709
Baron Funds 767 5th Ave 49th Fl	New York	NY	10153	800-992-2766	212-583-2000	517
Baron Mfg Co 1200 Capitol Dr	Addison	IL	60101	800-368-8585	630-628-9110	345
Barona Valley Ranch Resort & Casino 1932 Wildcat Canyon Rd	Lakeside	CA	92040	888-722-7662	619-443-2300	133
Baronne Plaza Hotel 201 Baronne St	New Orleans	LA	70112	888-756-0083	504-522-0083	373
Barouh Eaton Allen Corp 67 Kent Ave	Brooklyn	NY	11211	800-366-6767	718-782-2601	616
Barr Engineering Co 4700 W 77th St	Minneapolis	MN	55435	800-632-2277	952-832-2600	258
Barr Enterprises Inc 7276 W Chickadee Rd	Greenwood	WI	54437	800-826-2341	715-267-6335	568
Barr Pharmaceuticals Inc 2 Quaker Rd PO Box 2900 *NYSE: BRL*	Pomona	NY	10970	800-222-4043	845-362-1100	573
Barr WM & Co Inc 205 Channel Ave	Memphis	TN	38113	800-782-9928	901-775-0100	540
Barratt American Inc 5950 Priestly Dr Suite 101	Carlsbad	CA	92008	800-675-0440	760-431-0800	639
Barrecrafters 700 Bernard	Granby	QC	J269H7	800-451-3240		701
Barrel O' Fun Snack Foods Co 800 4th St NW	Perham	MN	56573	800-346-4910	218-346-7000	291-35
Barren River Lake State Resort Park 1149 State Park Rd	Lucas	KY	42156	800-325-0057	270-646-2151	554
Barrett Business Services Inc 4724 SW Macadam Ave *NASDAQ: BBSI*	Portland	OR	97239	800-676-4710	503-220-0988	619
Barrett Carpet Mills Inc 2216 Abutment Rd	Dalton	GA	30721	800-241-4064	706-277-2114	131
Barrett Holdings Inc 15423 I-10 W	San Antonio	TX	78249	800-234-3466	210-341-2800	57
Barrett LW Co Inc 55 S Zuni St PO Box 19430	Denver	CO	80219	888-312-0888	303-934-5755	10
Barrett Moving & Storage Co 7100 Washington Ave S	Eden Prairie	MN	55344	800-879-1283	952-944-6550	508
Barrett Trailers Inc 1831 Hardcastle Blvd	Purcell	OK	73080	888-405-4050	405-527-5050	768
Barrick Gold Corp 161 Bay St BCE Place Suite 3700 *NYSE: ABX*	Toronto	ON	M5J2S1	800-720-7415	416-861-9911	492
Barrie Pace Catalog 101 N Wacker Dr	Chicago	IL	60606	800-441-6011	312-372-6300	451
Barringer RH Distributing Inc 1620 Fairfax Rd	Greensboro	NC	27407	800-273-0555	336-854-0555	82-1
Barrit BK Corp 1850 E Sedgley Ave	Philadelphia	PA	19124	888-256-2020	215-533-3900	314-1
Barron Electric Co-op 1456 E LaSalle Ave	Barron	WI	54812	800-322-1008	715-537-3171	244
Barron Industries Inc 105 19th St S	Irondale	AL	35210	800-226-3267	205-956-3441	19
Barron's The Dow Jones Business & Financial Weekly Magazine 200 Liberty St	New York	NY	10281	800-369-2834	212-416-2700	449-5
Barron's Educational Series Inc 250 Wireless Blvd	Hauppauge	NY	11788	800-645-3476	631-434-3311	623-2
Barron's Wholesale Tire Inc 1302 Eastport Rd	Jacksonville	FL	32218	800-245-1899	904-751-2449	740
Barrow Industries 3 Edgewater Dr	Norwood	MA	02062	800-332-2776	781-828-6750	583
Barrow Mfg Co Inc 83 Horton St	Winder	GA	30680	800-476-0047	770-867-2121	153-12
Barry Callebaut USA Inc 400 Industrial Pk Rd	Saint Albans	VT	05478	800-556-8845	802-524-9711	291-8
Barry Controls 40 Guest St	Brighton	MA	02135	800-227-7962	617-787-1555	663
Barry Electric Co-op 4015 Main St PO Box 307	Cassville	MO	65625	866-847-2333	417-847-2131	244
Barry Jon & Associates Inc PO Box 127	Concord	NC	28026	800-264-0384	704-723-4200	157
Barry RG Corp 13405 Yarmouth Dr NW	Pickerington	OH	43147	800-848-7560	614-864-6400	296
Barry Shuster Information Services 1157 Tucker Rd	North Dartmouth	MA	02747	877-852-2507	508-999-5436	621
Barry Trucking Inc 120 E National Ave	Milwaukee	WI	53204	800-279-8395	414-274-6150	769
Barry University 11300 NE 2nd Ave	Miami Shores	FL	33161	800-756-6000	305-899-3000	163
Barry-Wehmiller Cos Inc 8020 Forsyth Blvd	Clayton	MO	63105	800-862-8200	314-862-8000	537
Barry-Wehmiller Cos Inc Accraply Div 3580 Holly Ln N	Plymouth	MN	55447	800-328-3997	763-557-1313	537
Barrymore Theatre 243 W 47th St	New York	NY	10036	800-432-7250	212-239-6200	732
Bar's Products 720 W Rose St	Holly	MI	48442	800-521-7475	248-634-8278	321
Barstow College 2700 Barstow Rd	Barstow	CA	92311	877-336-6868	760-252-2411	160
Bartech Group 17199 N Laurel Pk Dr Suite 224	Livonia	MI	48152	800-828-4410	734-953-5050	707
Bartech Technical Services 3980 Chicago Dr	Grandville	MI	49418	800-968-5776	616-532-5555	707
Bartell Drug Co 4727 Denver Ave S	Seattle	WA	98134	877-227-8355	206-763-2626	236
Bartells EJ Co PO Box 4160	Renton	WA	98057	800-468-9528	425-228-4111	190-4
Bartender Magazine PO Box 158 *Sales	Liberty Corner	NJ	07938	800-463-7465*	908-766-6006	449-21
Bartholomew County Rural Electric Membership Corp 801 2nd St	Columbus	IN	47201	800-927-5672	812-372-2546	244
Bartizan Corp 217 Riverdale Ave	Yonkers	NY	10705	800-431-2682	914-965-7977	523
Bartlett & Co 4800 Main St Suite 600	Kansas City	MO	64112	800-888-6300	816-753-6300	291-23
Bartlett & Co 36 E 4th St	Cincinnati	OH	45202	800-800-4612	513-621-4612	393
Bartlett FA Tree Expert Co 476 Canal St	Stamford	CT	06902	877-227-8538	203-323-1131	765
Bartlett & West Engineers Inc 1200 SW Executive Dr	Topeka	KS	66615	888-200-6464	785-272-2252	258
Barton College PO Box 5000	Wilson	NC	27893	800-345-4973	252-399-6300	163
Barton Cotton Inc 1405 Parker Rd	Baltimore	MD	21227	800-638-4652	410-247-4800	130
Barton County Community College 245 NE 30th Rd	Great Bend	KS	67530	800-722-6842	620-792-2701	160
Barton County Electric Co-op 91 W Hwy 160	Lamar	MO	64759	800-286-5636	417-682-5636	244
Barton Creek Conference Resort 8212 Barton Club Dr	Austin	TX	78735	800-336-6158	512-329-4000	655
Barton Inc 55 E Monroe St 26th Fl	Chicago	IL	60603	800-949-7837	312-346-9200	82-3
Barton JF Contracting Co PO Box 73525	Houston	TX	77273	800-222-1472	281-443-3800	258
Barton Nelson Inc 13700 Wyandotte St	Kansas City	MO	64145	800-821-6697	816-942-3100	675

Company / Address	City	State	ZIP	Toll-Free	Phone	Class
Barton Solvents Inc 1920 NE Broadway Ave	Des Moines	IA	50313	**800-383-6488**	515-265-7998	144
Barudan America Inc 29500 Fountain Pkwy	Solon	OH	44139	**800-627-4776**	440-248-8770	729
Basco Co 7201 Snider Rd	Mason	OH	45040	**800-543-1938**	513-573-1900	325
Bascom Palmer Eye Institute 900 NW 17th St	Miami	FL	33136	**800-329-7000**	305-326-6000	366-5
Baseball Digest 990 Grove St	Evanston	IL	60201	**800-877-5893**	847-491-6440	449-20
Baseball Express Inc 1051 E Nakoma St *Cust Svc	San Antonio	TX	78216	**800-937-4824***	210-348-7000	702
Baseball Hall of Fame 910 S 3rd St	Minneapolis	MN	55415	**888-375-9707**	612-375-9707	511
Baseball Hall of Fame & Museum. Canadian 386 Church St PO Box 1838	Saint Marys	ON	N4X1C2	**877-250-2255**	519-284-1838	511
Baseball Hall of Fame & Museum. National 25 Main St	Cooperstown	NY	13326	**888-425-5633**	607-547-7200	511
Baseball Museum. Negro Leagues 1616 E 18th St	Kansas City	MO	64108	**888-221-6526**	816-221-1920	511
Basell North America Inc 912 Appleton Rd	Elkton	MD	21921	**800-458-1416**	410-996-1600	594-2
BASF Canada 345 Carlingview Dr *Cust Svc	Toronto	ON	M9W6N9	**800-267-2955***	416-675-3611	141
BASF Corp 3000 Continental Dr N *NYSE: BF*	Mount Olive	NJ	07828	**800-526-1072**	973-426-2600	141
BASF Corp Chemical Div 333 Mount Hope Ave *Cust Svc	Rockaway	NJ	07866	**800-669-2273***	973-895-8000	594-2
Bashas' Inc PO Box 488	Chandler	AZ	85244	**800-755-7292**	480-895-9350	339
Basic American Foods 2999 Oak Rd Suite 100	Walnut Creek	CA	94597	**800-227-4050**	925-472-4000	291-18
Basic Chemicals Solutions LLC (BCS) 525 Seaport Blvd	Redwood City	CA	94063	**888-810-4787**	650-363-1661	144
Basic Comfort Inc 5151 Franklin St	Denver	CO	80216	**800-456-8687**	303-778-7535	64
Basic Commodities Inc 863 S Orlando Ave	Winter Park	FL	32789	**800-338-7006**	407-629-2000	167
Basiclink Inc 761 D Ave Suite B	Coronado	CA	92118	**877-238-1770**	619-522-6771	795
Basin Harbor Club 4800 Basin Harbor Rd	Vergennes	VT	05491	**800-622-4000**	802-475-2311	655
Basis International Ltd 5901 Jefferson St NE *Orders	Albuquerque	NM	87109	**800-423-1394***	505-345-5232	176-12
Basketball Digest 990 Grove St *Cust Svc	Evanston	IL	60201	**800-877-5893***	847-491-6440	449-20
Basketball Hall of Fame. Naismith Memorial 1000 W Columbus Ave	Springfield	MA	01105	**877-446-6752**	413-231-5490	511
Basketville Inc PO Box 710	Putney	VT	05346	**800-258-4553**	802-387-5509	74
Baskin-Robbins 130 Royall St	Canton	MA	02021	**800-859-5339**	781-737-3000	221
Basler Turbo Conversions Inc PO Box 2305	Oshkosh	WI	54903	**800-558-0254**	920-236-7820	25
Basler Turbo Conversions Inc Basler Flight Service Div PO Box 2464	Oshkosh	WI	54903	**800-558-0254**	920-236-7827	63
Bass GH & Co Inc 600 Sable Oaks Dr *Cust Svc	South Portland	ME	04106	**800-950-2277***	207-791-4000	296
Bass Player Magazine 2800 Campus Dr *Cust Svc	San Mateo	CA	94403	**800-234-1831***	650-513-4300	449-9
Bassett Russ Co 8189 Byron Rd	Whittier	CA	90606	**800-350-2445**	562-945-2445	281
Bassett WE Co 100 Trap Falls Rd Ext	Shelton	CT	06484	**800-394-8746**	203-929-8483	211
Basta Sole 5 Marconi *Cust Svc	Irvine	CA	92618	**800-654-7000***	949-951-2010	314-4
Bastian Co 122 N Genesee St	Geneva	NY	14456	**800-609-0097**	315-789-8000	10
Bat Conservation International (BCI) PO Box 162603	Austin	TX	78716	**800-538-2287**	512-327-9721	48-3
Batavia Downs 8315 Park Rd	Batavia	NY	14020	**800-724-2000**	585-343-3750	628
Bates Container Inc 6433 Davis Blvd	North Richland Hills	TX	76180	**800-792-8736**	817-498-3200	101
Bates of Maine 2 Cedar St	Lewiston	ME	04240	**800-552-2837**		731
Batesville Guard 258 W Main St PO Box 2036	Batesville	AR	72503	**800-559-2383**	870-793-2383	522-2
Bath Assn. National Kitchen & 687 Willow Grove St	Hackettstown	NJ	07840	**800-843-6522**	908-852-0033	49-3
Bath & Body Works 7 Limited Pkwy E	Reynoldsburg	OH	43068	**888-856-1616**	614-856-6000	211
Bath-and-Body.com 1021 Bay Blvd Suite S	Chula Vista	CA	91911	**888-935-2639**	619-425-0829	211
Bath-Tec Inc PO Box 1118	Ennis	TX	75120	**800-526-3301**	972-646-5279	367
Bath Unlimited 1578 Sussex Tpk	Randolph	NJ	07869	**800-635-2731**	973-598-4300	598
Bathcrest Inc 5195 W 4700 S	Salt Lake City	UT	84118	**800-826-6790**	801-972-1110	188-11
Bathhouse at Calistoga Ranch 580 Lommel Rd	Calistoga	CA	94515	**800-942-4220**	707-254-2820	698
Bathroom World Mfg Co 3569 NW 10th Ave	Fort Lauderdale	FL	33309	**800-566-0541**	954-566-0451	367
Batliner Paper Stock Co Inc 2501 Front St	Kansas City	MO	64120	**800-821-8512**	816-483-3343	646
Baton Rouge Convention & Visitors Bureau 730 North Blvd	Baton Rouge	LA	70802	**800-527-6843**	225-383-1825	205
Battered Women's Justice Project 2104 4th Ave S Suite B	Minneapolis	MN	55404	**800-903-0111**	612-824-8768	49-10
Batteries Plus 925 Walnut Ridge Dr Suite 100	Hartland	WI	53029	**800-274-9155**	262-369-0690	35
Battery Manufacturers Assn. Independent 401 N Michigan Ave 24th Fl	Chicago	IL	60611	**800-237-6126**	312-245-1074	49-13
Battle Creek Enquirer 155 W Van Buren St	Battle Creek	MI	49017	**800-333-4139**	269-964-7161	522-2
Battle Creek Equipment Co 307 W Jackson St *Cust Svc	Battle Creek	MI	49017	**800-253-0854***	269-962-6181	263
Battle Creek Farmers Co-op 400 W Front St Box 10	Battle Creek	NE	68715	**800-233-6679**	402-675-2055	272
Battle Creek Inn 5050 Beckley Rd	Battle Creek	MI	49015	**800-232-3405**	269-979-1100	373
Battle Creek/Calhoun County Visitors & Convention Bureau 77 E Michigan Ave Suite 100	Battle Creek	MI	49017	**800-397-2240**	269-962-2240	205
Battle Green Inn 1720 Massachusetts Ave	Lexington	MA	02420	**800-343-0235**	781-862-6100	373
Battlefield Farms Inc 23190 Clarks Mountain Rd	Rapidan	VA	22733	**800-722-0744**	540-854-6485	363
Battles for Chattanooga Museum 1110 E Brow Rd	Lookout Mountain	TN	37350	**800-854-0675**	423-821-2812	509
Bauder College 384 N Yard Blvd Suite 190	Atlanta	GA	30313	**800-241-3797**	404-237-7573	787
Baudville Inc 5380 52nd St SE *Orders	Grand Rapids	MI	49512	**800-728-0888***	616-698-0888	176-1
Baue Funeral Homes 620 Jefferson St	Saint Charles	MO	63301	**888-724-0073**	636-724-0073	499
Bauer Built Inc PO Box 248	Durand	WI	54736	**800-999-0123**	715-672-4295	740
Bauer Nike Hockey Inc 150 Ocean Rd	Greenland	NH	03840	**800-362-3146**	603-430-2111	701
Bauer Premium Fly Reels 401 Corral de Tierra Rd	Salinas	CA	93908	**888-484-4165**	831-484-0536	701
Baum George K & Co 120 W 12th St 8th Fl	Kansas City	MO	64105	**800-821-7195**	816-474-1100	679
Baume & Mercier Inc 645 5th Ave	New York	NY	10022	**800-683-2286**	212-593-0444	151
Baumer Foods Inc 4301 Tulane Ave PO Box 19166 *Sales	New Orleans	LA	70179	**800-222-0694***	504-482-5761	291-20
Baumfolder Corp 1660 Campbell Rd	Sidney	OH	45365	**800-543-6107**	937-492-1281	546
Baumgarten's 144 Ottley Dr	Atlanta	GA	30324	**800-247-5547**	404-874-7675	523
Bausch & Lomb Inc 1 Bausch & Lomb Pl *NYSE: BOL*	Rochester	NY	14604	**800-344-8815**	585-338-6000	531
Bausch & Lomb Inc Vision Care Div 1400 N Goodman St	Rochester	NY	14609	**800-344-8815**	585-338-6000	531
Bausch & Lomb Pharmaceuticals Inc 8500 Hidden River Pkwy	Tampa	FL	33637	**800-323-0000**	813-975-7700	572
Bausch & Lomb Surgical Inc 180 Via Verde Dr *Cust Svc	San Dimas	CA	91773	**800-338-2020***	909-971-5100	468
Bavarian Inn PO Box 152	Custer	SD	57730	**800-657-4312**	605-673-2802	373
Bavarian Specialty Foods 22417 S Vermont Ave	Torrance	CA	90502	**800-421-0301**	310-212-6199	291-2
BAX Global Inc 440 Exchange	Irvine	CA	92602	**800-225-5229**	714-442-4500	440
Baxter JH & Co 1700 S El Camino Real Suite 200	San Mateo	CA	94402	**800-780-7073**	650-349-0201	806
Bay Area Anesthesia Inc PO Box 1547	Ukiah	CA	95482	**800-327-8427**	707-462-1557	707
Bay Area Chamber of Commerce 50 Central Ave	Coos Bay	OR	97420	**800-824-8486**	541-269-0215	137
Bay Area Chamber of Commerce/Visitor Bureau 145 Central Ave	Coos Bay	OR	97420	**800-824-8486**	541-266-0868	205
Bay Area Medical Center 3100 Shore Dr	Marinette	WI	54143	**888-788-2070**	715-735-6621	366-2
Bay City Flower Co Inc PO Box 186 *Sales	Half Moon Bay	CA	94019	**800-399-5858***	650-726-5535	363
Bay Club Hotel & Marina 2131 Shelter Island Dr	San Diego	CA	92106	**800-672-0800**	619-224-8888	373
Bay Concepts Inc PO Box 7229	Oakland	CA	94601	**888-534-4511**	510-534-4511	314-3
Bay Hill Golf Club & Lodge 9000 Bay Hill Blvd	Orlando	FL	32819	**888-422-9445**	407-876-2429	655
Bay Houston Towing Co 2243 Milford St	Houston	TX	77098	**800-324-3755**	713-529-3755	457
Bay Microfilm Inc DBA BMI Imaging Systems 1115 E Arques Ave *Cust Svc	Sunnyvale	CA	94085	**800-359-3456***	408-736-7444	487
Bay Mills Community College 12214 W Lakeshore Dr	Brimley	MI	49715	**800-844-2622**	906-248-3354	161
Bay News 1733 Sheepshead Bay Rd	Brooklyn	NY	11235	**800-564-5433**	718-615-2500	522-4
Bay de Noc Community College 2001 N Lincoln Rd	Escanaba	MI	49829	**800-221-2001**	906-786-5802	160
Bay Park Hotel 1425 Munras Ave	Monterey	CA	93940	**800-338-3564**	831-649-1020	373
Bay Path College 588 Longmeadow St	Longmeadow	MA	01106	**800-782-7284**	413-567-0621	163
Bay Point Resort Village Marriott Golf & Yacht Club 4200 Marriott Dr	Panama City Beach	FL	32408	**800-874-7105**	850-236-6000	655
Bay Regional Medical Center 1900 Columbus Ave	Bay City	MI	48708	**800-726-0666**	989-894-3000	366-2
Bay Ship & Yacht Co 310 W Cutting Blvd	Point Richmond	CA	94804	**800-900-6646**	510-237-0140	689
Bay State College 122 Commonwealth Ave	Boston	MA	02116	**800-815-3276**	617-236-8000	158
Bay State Computers Inc 4601 Presidents Dr Suite 130	Lanham	MD	20706	**800-266-3783**	301-306-0008	178
Bay State Gas Co 300 Friberg Pkwy	Westborough	MA	01581	**800-882-5454**	508-836-7000	774
Bay State Milling Co 100 Congress St	Quincy	MA	02169	**800-553-5687**	617-328-4400	291-23
Bay State Moving Systems Inc 60 Haynes Cir	Chicopee	MA	01020	**800-388-7411**	413-592-6381	508
Bay Swiss Mfg Co Inc 5 Airpark Vista Blvd	Dayton	NV	89403	**800-247-3207**	775-246-7100	610
Bay Valley Hotel & Resort 2470 Old Bridge Rd	Bay City	MI	48706	**800-292-5028**	989-686-3500	655
Bay View Capital Corp 1840 Gateway Dr Suite 300 *NYSE: BVC*	San Mateo	CA	94404	**800-229-8439**	650-312-7300	355-2
Bayada Nurses Home Care Specialists 290 Chester Ave	Moorestown	NJ	08057	**800-305-3000**	856-231-1000	358
Bayer Corp 100 Bayer Rd *NYSE: BAY*	Pittsburgh	PA	15205	**800-662-2927**	412-777-2000	572
Bayer Corp Agricultural Div 8400 Hawthorn Rd	Kansas City	MO	64120	**800-821-8556**	816-242-2000	276
Bayer Corp Chemicals Div 100 Bayer Rd	Pittsburgh	PA	15205	**800-662-2927**	412-777-2000	142
Bayer CropScience 2 Alexander Dr	Research Triangle Park	NC	27709	**800-523-0258**	919-549-2000	86
Bayer Healthcare Diagnostics Div 511 Benedict Ave	Tarrytown	NY	10591	**800-431-1970**	914-631-8000	468
Bayer Inc 77 Belfield Rd	Toronto	ON	M9W1G6	**800-622-2937**	416-248-0771	572
Bayer MaterialScience LLC 100 Bayer Rd	Pittsburgh	PA	15205	**800-662-2927**	412-777-2000	594-2
Bayfront Inn 138 Avenida Menendez	Saint Augustine	FL	32084	**800-558-3455**	904-824-1681	373

Name / Address	City	State	ZIP	Toll-Free	Phone	Class
Bayhead Products Corp 173 Crosby Rd	Dover	NH	03820	**800-603-0053**	603-742-3000	462
Bayley Construction Co PO Box 9004	Mercer Island	WA	98040	**800-598-8884**	206-621-8884	185
Bayley Seton Hospital 75 Vanderbilt Ave	Staten Island	NY	10304	**800-273-1114**	718-818-6000	366-2
Baylor Institute for Rehabilitation 3505 Gaston Ave	Dallas	TX	75246	**800-242-2334**	214-820-9300	366-4
Baylor School PO Box 1337	Chattanooga	TN	37401	**800-222-9567**	423-267-5902	611
Baylor University 1311 S 5th St	Waco	TX	76798	**800-229-5678**	254-710-1011	163
Bayly Inc 4151 N 29th Ave	Hollywood	FL	33020	**800-882-0255**	954-923-0255	153-9
Baymont Guest Ovations Program 100 E Wisconsin Ave	Milwaukee	WI	53202	**866-464-2321**	414-905-2000	371
Baymont Inns & Suites Inc 100 E Wisconsin Ave Suite 1800	Milwaukee	WI	53202	**877-229-6668**	414-905-2000	369
Bayonne Plumbing 250 Ave E	Bayonne	NJ	07002	**800-713-7473**	201-339-8000	601
Bayou Steel Corp PO Box 5000	LaPlace	LA	70069	**800-535-7692**	985-652-0370	709
Baystate VNA & Hospice 50 Maple St	Springfield	MA	01102	**800-249-8298**	413-781-2317	365
Bayview Hotel 111 Eden St	Bar Harbor	ME	04609	**800-356-3585**	207-288-5861	373
Bayview Limousine Service 15701 Nelson Pl S	Seattle	WA	98188	**800-606-7880**	206-824-6200	433
Bayview Press 30 Knox St PO Box 153	Thomaston	ME	04861	**800-903-2346**	207-354-9919	130
Bazaar Co 801 3rd Ave	Huntington	WV	25701	**877-764-0305**	304-522-0305	357
Bazz Houston Co 12700 Western Ave	Garden Grove	CA	92841	**800-385-9608**	714-898-2666	479
Bazzini AL Co Inc 200 Food Center Dr *Cust Svc	Bronx	NY	10474	**800-228-0172***	718-842-8644	291-28
BB & T Bank 3233 Thomasville Rd	Tallahassee	FL	32308	**888-385-3301**	850-385-3300	71
BB & T Capital Markets 2 S 9th St	Richmond	VA	23219	**800-476-3819**	804-649-3900	679
BB & T Insurance Services Inc 3605 Glenwood Ave	Raleigh	NC	27612	**800-821-1284**	919-716-9777	383
BB & T Sales Finance 6402 Arlington Blvd	Falls Church	VA	22042	**800-348-6189**	703-241-3500	215
BBI Source Scientific Inc 7390 Lincoln Way	Garden Grove	CA	92841	**800-888-9285**	714-898-9001	410
BBSI (Beauty & Barber Supply Institute) 15825 N 71st St Suite 100	Scottsdale	AZ	85254	**800-468-2274**	480-281-0424	49-18
BCAA (British Columbia Automobile Assn) 4567 Canada Way	Burnaby	BC	V5G4T1	**800-222-4357**	604-268-5000	53
BCBG Max Azria 2761 Fruitland Ave	Vernon	CA	90058	**888-636-2224**	323-589-2224	273
BCE Inc 1000 de la Gauchetiere St W Suite 3700 *NYSE: BCE*	Montreal	QC	H3B4Y7	**888-932-6666**	514-870-8777	355-3
BCHA (Back Country Horsemen of America) PO Box 1367	Graham	WA	98338	**888-893-5161**	360-832-2461	48-23
BCI (Bat Conservation International) PO Box 162603	Austin	TX	78716	**800-538-2287**	512-327-9721	48-3
BCI Burke Co Inc 660 Van Dyne Rd	Fond du Lac	WI	54937	**800-356-2070**	920-921-9220	340
BCM Engineers 920 Germantown Pike Suite 200	Plymouth Meeting	PA	19462	**800-221-1226**	610-313-3100	258
BCN Chemicals Inc 1320 Rt 9	Champlain	NY	12919	**800-661-1226**	514-630-1044	470
BCS Cuyahoga LLC 31000 Solon Rd	Solon	OH	44139	**800-362-9132**	440-248-0290	709
BD Biosciences 2350 Qume Dr	San Jose	CA	95131	**800-223-8226**	408-432-9475	410
BD Diagnostics 7 Loveton Cir	Sparks	MD	21152	**800-666-6433**	410-316-4000	229
BD Medical 9450 S State St	Sandy	UT	84070	**888-237-2762**	801-565-2300	468
BDP International Inc 510 Walnut St	Philadelphia	PA	19106	**888-999-2379**	215-629-8900	440
BDS Worldwide Inc 9362 Dielman Industrial Dr	Saint Louis	MO	63132	**800-325-4074**	314-817-0051	440
B/E Aerospace Inc 1400 Corporate Ctr Way *NASDAQ: BEAV*	Wellington	FL	33414	**888-223-2376**	561-791-5000	23
BE Implement Co PO Box 752	Brownfield	TX	79316	**800-725-5435**	806-637-3594	270
BEA (Broadcast Education Assn) 1771 'N' St NW	Washington	DC	20036	**888-380-7222**	202-429-5354	49-5
BEA Systems Inc 2315 N 1st St *NASDAQ: BEAS*	San Jose	CA	95131	**800-817-4232**	408-570-8000	176-12
Beach Colony Resort 5308 N Ocean Blvd	Myrtle Beach	SC	29577	**800-222-2141**	843-449-4010	655
Beach House Suites by the Don Cesar 3680 Gulf Blvd	Saint Pete Beach	FL	33706	**800-282-1116**	727-363-0001	373
Beach Patrol Inc 1165 E 230th St	Carson	CA	90745	**800-446-1101**	310-522-2700	153-17
Beach Plaza Hotel 625 N Atlantic Blvd	Fort Lauderdale	FL	33304	**800-451-4711**	954-566-7631	373
Beach-Russ Co 544 Union Ave	Brooklyn	NY	11211	**800-543-3903**	718-388-4090	170
Beachcomber Hotel 1340 Collins Ave	Miami Beach	FL	33139	**866-859-4177**	305-531-3755	373
Beachcomber Resort 2000 N Atlantic Ave	Daytona Beach	FL	32118	**800-245-3575**	386-252-8513	373
Beacher's Lodge 6970 US Hwy A1A S	Saint Augustine	FL	32080	**800-527-8849**	904-471-8849	373
Beaches of South Walton Tourist Development Council PO Box 1248	Santa Rosa Beach	FL	32459	**800-822-6877**	850-267-1216	205
Beacon Container Corp 700 W 1st St	Birdsboro	PA	19508	**888-211-5530**	610-582-2222	101
Beacon Education Management Inc 112 Turnpike Rd Suite 107	Westborough	MA	01581	**800-789-1258**	508-836-4461	241
Beacon Hotel 720 Ocean Dr	Miami Beach	FL	33139	**877-674-8200**	305-674-8200	373
Beacon News 101 S River St	Aurora	IL	60506	**800-244-5844**	630-844-5800	522-2
Beacon Power Corp 234 Ballardvale St *NASDAQ: BCON*	Wilmington	MA	01887	**888-938-9112**	978-694-9121	252
Beacon Roofing Supply Inc 1 Lakeland Park Dr	Peabody	MA	01960	**877-645-7663**	978-535-7668	190-4
Beacon Shoe Co Inc 213 Lions Estates Dr	Jonesburg	MO	63351	**800-325-7463**	636-488-5444	296
Bead Industries Inc 11 Cascade Blvd	Milford	CT	06460	**800-297-4851**	203-301-0270	478
Beadles Lumber Co Inc PO Box 3457	Moultrie	GA	31776	**800-763-2400**	229-985-6996	671
Beadwork Magazine 201 E 4th St *Cust Svc	Loveland	CO	80537	**800-849-8753***	970-669-7672	449-14
Beal Bank SSB 6000 Legacy Dr	Plano	TX	75024	**800-404-4494**	469-467-5000	71
Beal College 99 Farm Rd	Bangor	ME	04401	**800-660-7351**	207-947-4591	158
Beam Industries PO Box 788	Webster City	IA	50595	**800-369-2326**	515-832-4620	775
Bean DD & Sons Co 207 Peterborough St	Jaffrey	NH	03452	**800-326-8311**	603-532-8311	461
Bean John Co 309 Exchange Ave	Conway	AR	72032	**800-362-8326**	501-450-1500	60
Bean LL Inc 15 Casco St *Cust Svc	Freeport	ME	04033	**800-341-4341***	207-865-4761	451
Bear Creek Canoes Inc 72 Swamp Rd & Rt 107	Sebago	ME	04029	**800-241-2268**	207-647-5850	701
Bear Stearns & Co Inc 383 Madison Ave	New York	NY	10179	**800-999-2000**	212-272-2000	679
Bear Stearns Cos Inc 383 Madison Ave *NYSE: BSC*	New York	NY	10179	**800-999-2000**	212-272-2000	679
Bear Stearns Inc 383 Madison Ave	New York	NY	10179	**800-766-4111**	212-272-2000	517
BearCom Building Services 7022 South 400 W	Midvale	UT	84047	**888-569-9533**	801-569-9500	150
Bearcom Inc 4009 Distribution Dr Suite 200 *Sales	Garland	TX	75041	**800-527-1670***	214-340-8876	245
Beard Miller Co LLP 2609 Keiser Blvd PO Box 311	Reading	PA	19603	**800-267-9405**	610-376-2833	2
Bearing Inspection Inc 4422 Corporate Ctr Dr	Los Alamitos	CA	90720	**800-416-8881**	714-484-2400	77
Bearing Service Co of Pennsylvania 630 Alpha Dr CIDC Industrial Pk	Pittsburgh	PA	15238	**800-783-2327**	412-963-7710	77
BearingPoint Inc 1676 International Dr *NYSE: BE*	McLean	VA	22102	**866-276-4768**	703-747-3000	178
Bearskin Airlines PO Box 1447	Sioux Lookout	ON	P8T1C1	**800-465-2327**	807-737-3474	26
Beartooth Electric Co-op Inc 1306 N Broadway St	Red Lodge	MT	59068	**800-472-9821**	406-446-2310	244
Beatnik Inc 2600 S El Camino Real	San Mateo	CA	94403	**877-295-6593**	650-295-2300	514
Beatrice Daily Sun 200 N 7th St PO Box 847	Beatrice	NE	68310	**800-666-5233**	402-223-5233	522-2
Beatty Group International 9800 SW Beaverton Hillsdale Hwy Suite 105	Beaverton	OR	97005	**800-285-6215**	503-644-3340	377
Beau Rivage Resort & Casino 875 Beach Blvd	Biloxi	MS	39530	**888-750-7111**	228-386-7111	655
Beauchamp Distributing Co 1911 S Santa Fe Ave	Compton	CA	90221	**800-734-5102**	310-639-5320	82-1
Beaufort Memorial Hospital 955 Ribaut Rd	Beaufort	SC	29902	**877-532-6472**	843-522-5200	366-2
Beaulieu of America Inc 1414 Cleveland Hwy	Dalton	GA	30721	**800-633-2328**	706-370-4000	131
Beaulieu Vineyard 1960 St Helena Hwy	Rutherford	CA	94573	**800-264-6918**	707-967-5200	81-3
Beaumont Civic Center Complex 701 Main St	Beaumont	TX	77701	**800-782-3081**	409-838-3435	204
Beaumont Convention & Visitors Bureau 801 Main St Suite 100	Beaumont	TX	77701	**800-392-4401**	409-880-3749	205
Beaumont Vivian Theatre 150 W 65th St	New York	NY	10023	**800-432-7250**	212-239-6200	732
Beauregard Electric Co-op Inc 1010 E 1st St	DeRidder	LA	70634	**800-367-0275**	337-463-6221	244
Beaute Craft Supply Co 600 W Maple Rd	Troy	MI	48084	**800-331-8277**	248-362-0400	78
Beauti-Vue Products Inc 8555 194th Ave Bristol Industrial Pk	Bristol	WI	53104	**800-558-9431**	262-857-2306	88
BeautiControl Cosmetics Inc 2121 Midway Rd	Carrollton	TX	75006	**800-232-8841**	972-458-0601	211
Beauty & Barber Supply Institute (BBSI) 15825 N 71st St Suite 100	Scottsdale	AZ	85254	**800-468-2274**	480-281-0424	49-18
Beauvoir-Jefferson Davis Home 2244 Beach Blvd	Biloxi	MS	39531	**800-570-3818**	228-388-9074	50
Beaver Coaches Inc PO Box 5639 *Sales	Bend	OR	97708	**800-423-2837***	541-389-1144	120
Beaver County Chamber of Commerce 300 S Walnut Ln 202300	Beaver	PA	15009	**888-832-7591**	724-775-3944	137
Beaver Creek Lodge 26 Avon Dale Ln	Beaver Creek	CO	81620	**800-525-7280**	970-845-9800	373
Beaver Creek Resort & Spa. Park Hyatt 136 E Thomas Pl	Beaver Creek	CO	81620	**800-233-1234**	970-949-1234	655
Beaver Dam Community Hospital 707 S University Ave	Beaver Dam	WI	53916	**800-870-7181**	920-887-7181	366-2
Beaver Excavating Co Inc 4650 Southway St SW	Canton	OH	44706	**800-255-3767**	330-478-2151	188-5
Beaver Express Service LLC PO Box 1147	Woodward	OK	73802	**800-593-2328**	580-256-6460	769
Beaver Run Resort & Conference Center 620 Village Rd	Breckenridge	CO	80424	**800-525-2253**	970-453-6000	655
Beaver Street Fisheries Inc 1741 W Beaver St	Jacksonville	FL	32209	**800-874-6426**	904-354-8533	291-13
Beaverite Corp 128 Main St *Cust Svc	Beaver Falls	NY	13305	**800-424-6337***	315-346-6011	538
Beaverton Foods Inc PO Box 687	Beaverton	OR	97075	**800-223-8076**	503-646-8138	291-19
Beavertown Block Co Inc PO Box 337 *Cust Svc	Middleburg	PA	17842	**800-597-2565***	570-837-1744	181
bebe stores Inc 400 Valley Dr *NASDAQ: BEBE*	Brisbane	CA	94005	**877-232-3777**	415-715-3900	153-21
Becharas Brothers Coffee Co Inc 14501 Hamilton Ave	Highland Park	MI	48203	**800-944-9675**	313-869-4700	292-2
Bechik Products Inc 1140 Homer St	Saint Paul	MN	55116	**800-328-6569**	651-698-0364	463
Beck Mfg 330 E 9th St	Waynesboro	PA	17268	**800-742-6621**	717-762-9141	584
Beck RW Inc 1001 4th Ave Suite 2500	Seattle	WA	98154	**800-285-2325**	206-695-4700	191
Becker College 61 Sever St	Worcester	MA	01609	**877-523-2537**	508-791-9241	160
Becker DB Co Inc 54 Old Hwy 22	Clinton	NJ	08809	**800-394-3991**	908-730-6010	144
Becker Electric Supply Inc 1341 E 4th St	Dayton	OH	45402	**800-762-9515**	937-226-1341	245
Becket Fund for Religious Liberty 1350 Connecticut Ave NW Suite 605	Washington	DC	20036	**800-232-5385**	202-955-0095	48-8
Beckett Air Inc 37850 Taylor Industrial Pkwy	North Ridgeville	OH	44039	**800-831-7839**	440-327-9999	19
Beckett Corp 5931 Campus Circle Dr W	Irving	TX	75063	**888-232-5388**	972-871-8000	627
Beckett RW Corp PO Box 1289	Elyria	OH	44036	**800-645-2876**	440-327-1060	352

Name / Address	City	State	Zip	Toll-Free	Phone	Class
Beckley Newspapers Inc 801 N Kanawha St	Beckley	WV	25801	**800-950-0250**	304-255-4400	623-8
Beckley-Raleigh County Chamber of Commerce 245 N Kanawha St	Beckley	WV	25801	**800-718-1474**	304-252-7328	137
Beckman Coulter Inc 4300 N Harbor Blvd — *NYSE: BEC* ■ *Cust Svc	Fullerton	CA	92835	**800-742-2345***	714-871-4848	410
Beckwith Machinery Co 4565 William Penn Hwy	Murrysville	PA	15668	**888-232-5948**	724-327-1300	353
Becton Dickinson & Co 1 Becton Dr — *NYSE: BDX* ■ *Cust Svc	Franklin Lakes	NJ	07417	**888-237-2762***	201-847-6800	469
Becton Dickinson & Co ACCU-GLASS Div 10765 Trenton Ave	Saint Louis	MO	63132	**800-325-4796**	314-423-0300	328
Becton Dickinson Consumer Healthcare 1 Becton Dr	Franklin Lakes	NJ	07417	**888-237-2762**	201-847-6800	469
Becton Dickinson Pharmaceutical Systems 1 Becton Dr	Franklin Lakes	NJ	07417	**888-237-2762**	201-847-6800	468
BECU (Boeing Employees' Credit Union) PO Box 97050	Seattle	WA	98124	**800-233-2328**	206-439-5700	216
Bed Bath & Beyond Inc 650 Liberty Ave — *NASDAQ: BBBY*	Union	NJ	07083	**800-462-3966**	908-688-0888	357
Bed & Breakfast Accommodations Ltd PO Box 12011	Washington	DC	20005	**877-893-3233**	202-328-3510	368
Bed & Breakfast Assoc Bay Colony Ltd PO Box 57166 Babson Park Branch	Boston	MA	02457	**888-486-6018**	781-449-5302	368
Bed & Breakfast Atlanta Reservation Services 790 North Ave Suite 202	Atlanta	GA	30306	**800-967-3224**	404-875-0525	368
Bed & Breakfast & Beyond Reservation Service 3115 Napoleon Ave	New Orleans	LA	70125	**800-886-3709**	504-896-9977	368
Bed & Breakfast Cape Cod PO Box 1312	Orleans	MA	02653	**800-541-6226**	508-255-3824	368
Bed & Breakfast Directory for San Diego PO Box 3292	San Diego	CA	92163	**800-619-7666**		368
Bed & Breakfast of Hawaii PO Box 449	Kapaa	HI	96746	**800-733-1632**	808-822-7771	368
Bed & Breakfast Inc-A Reservation Service 1021 Moss St	New Orleans	LA	70152	**800-729-4640**	504-488-4640	368
Bed & Breakfast of Philadelphia PO Box 21	Devon	PA	19333	**800-448-3619**	610-687-3565	368
Bed & Breakfast Reservations 11A Beach Rd	Gloucester	MA	01930	**800-832-2632**	617-964-1606	368
Bed & Breakfast Reservations 11A Beach Rd	Gloucester	MA	01930	**800-832-2632**	978-281-9505	368
Bed & Breakfast San Francisco PO Box 420009	San Francisco	CA	94142	**800-452-8249**	415-899-0060	368
BedandBreakfast.com 700 Brazos St Suite B-700 — *Sales	Austin	TX	78701	**800-462-2632***	512-322-2710	762
Bedenbaugh Products Corp 105 Lisbon Rd	Laurens	SC	29360	**800-679-9419**	864-682-3136	198
Bedford Area Chamber of Commerce 305 E Main St	Bedford	VA	24523	**800-933-9535**	540-586-9401	137
Bedford County Visitors Bureau 131 S Juliana St	Bedford	PA	15522	**800-765-3331**	814-623-1771	205
Bedford Fair Lifestyles 421 Landmark Dr	Wilmington	NC	28410	**800-964-9030**		451
Bedford Gazette 424 W Penn St	Bedford	PA	15522	**800-242-4250**	814-623-1151	522-2
Bedford Industries Inc 1659 Rowe Ave — *Cust Svc	Worthington	MN	56187	**800-533-5314***	507-376-4136	538
Bedford Laboratories Inc 300 Northfield Rd	Bedford	OH	44146	**800-562-4797**	440-232-3320	470
Bedford Materials Co Inc 7676 Allegheny Rd	Manns Choice	PA	15550	**800-773-4276**	814-623-9014	804
Bedford Regional Medical Center 2900 W 16th St	Bedford	IN	47421	**800-755-3734**	812-275-1200	366-2
Bedford Rural Electric Co-op Inc 8846 Lincoln Hwy	Bedford	PA	15522	**800-808-2732**	814-623-5101	244
Beech-Nut Nutrition Corp 100 S 4th St Suite 1010	Saint Louis	MO	63102	**800-233-2468**	314-436-7667	291-36
Beecher Katharine Candies 1250 Slate Hill Rd	Camp Hill	PA	17011	**800-708-3641**	717-761-5440	291-8
Beechwood Hotel 363 Plantation St	Worcester	MA	01605	**800-344-2589**	508-754-5789	373
Beef Magazine 7900 International Dr Suite 300 — *Cust Svc	Minneapolis	MN	55425	**800-441-0294***	952-851-9329	449-1
Beef O'Bradys 5510 W LaSalle St Suite 200	Tampa	FL	33607	**800-728-8878**	813-226-2333	657
Beehive Botanicals Inc 16297 W Nursery Rd	Hayward	WI	54843	**800-233-4483**	715-634-4274	786
Beehive Machinery Inc PO Box 5002	Sandy	UT	84091	**800-621-8438**	801-561-4211	293
Beekman Hotel-Suites on the Ocean 9499 Collins Ave	Miami Beach	FL	33154	**800-237-9367**	305-861-4801	373
Beekman Tower Hotel 3 Mitchell Pl	New York	NY	10017	**866-233-4642**	212-355-7300	373
Beelman Truck Co 4 Caine Dr — *Sales	Madison	IL	62060	**800-541-5918***	618-452-8187	769
Beemak Plastics Inc 18554 S Susana Rd	Rancho Dominguez	CA	90221	**800-421-4393**	310-886-5880	597
Beeman Precision Airguns 5454 Argosy Dr	Huntington Beach	CA	92649	**800-227-2744**	714-890-4800	279
Beemer Precision Inc 230 New York Dr PO Box 3080	Fort Washington	PA	19034	**800-836-2340**	215-646-8440	609
Beer Institute 122 C St NW Suite 750	Washington	DC	20001	**800-379-2739**	202-737-2337	49-6
Beer Nuts Inc 103 N Robinson St	Bloomington	IL	61701	**800-233-7688**	309-827-8580	291-28
Beer Solutions 138313 W Laurel Dr	Lake Forest	IL	60045	**800-842-4050**	847-247-0121	82-1
Beer Wholesalers Assn. National 1101 King St Suite 600	Alexandria	VA	22314	**800-300-6417**	703-683-4300	49-6
Beere Precision Medical Instruments Inc 5307 95th Ave	Kenosha	WI	53144	**800-295-8505**	262-657-2800	468
BEGINNINGS for Parents of Children Who Are Deaf or Hard of Hearing Inc 3714 A Benson Dr	Raleigh	NC	27619	**800-541-4327**	919-850-2746	48-17
Behavior. Institute for the Advancement of Human 4370 Alpine Rd Suite 209	Portola Valley	CA	94028	**800-258-8411**	650-851-8411	49-8

Name / Address	City	State	Zip	Toll-Free	Phone	Class
Behavior Therapy. Association for Advancement of 305 7th Ave 16th Fl	New York	NY	10001	**800-685-2228**	212-647-1890	49-15
Behavioral Science Book Service Doubleday Select Inc 101 Park Ave 23rd Fl	New York	NY	10178	**800-321-7323**		94
Behavioral Science. NTL Institute for Applied 300 N Lee St Suite 300	Alexandria	VA	22314	**800-777-5227**	703-548-8840	753
Behavioral Sciences. Association for Advanced Training in the 5126 Ralston St	Ventura	CA	93003	**800-472-1931**	805-676-3030	49-5
Behlen Mfg Co 4025 E 23rd St	Columbus	NE	68601	**800-553-5520**	402-564-3111	106
Behr Climate Systems 5020 Augusta Dr	Fort Worth	TX	76106	**800-247-6558**	817-624-7273	16
Behr Joseph & Sons Inc PO Box 740	Rockford	IL	61105	**800-332-2347**	815-987-2600	674
Behr Lawrence Assoc Inc PO Box 8026	Greenville	NC	27835	**800-522-4464**	252-757-0279	195
Behr Process Corp 3400 W Segerstrom Ave	Santa Ana	CA	92704	**800-854-0133**	714-545-7101	540
BEI Technologies Inc Industrial Encoder Div 7230 Hollister Ave — *Sales	Goleta	CA	93117	**800-350-2727***	805-968-0782	252
BEI Technologies Inc Systron Donner Inertial Div 2700 Syctron Dr	Conoord	CA	04510	**000-227-1025**	925-071-0400	519
Beiderbecke Bix Memorial Society PO Box 3688	Davenport	IA	52808	**888-249-5487**	563-324-7170	48-4
Beiersdorf North America 187 Danbury Rd	Wilton	CT	06897	**800-233-2340**	203-563-5800	211
Bekins Van Lines LLC 330 S Mannheim Rd	Hillside	IL	60162	**800-723-5467**	708-547-2000	508
Bel Air Athletic Club 8400 E Crescent Pkwy Suite 200	Greenwood Village	CO	80111	**888-458-0489**	303-866-0800	349
Bel-Art Products Inc 6 Industrial Rd	Pequannock	NJ	07440	**800-423-5278**	973-694-0500	411
Bel Fuse Inc 206 Van Vorst St — *NASDAQ: BELFA*	Jersey City	NJ	07302	**800-235-3873**	201-432-0463	715
Bel-Rea Institute of Animal Technology 1681 S Dayton St	Denver	CO	80247	**800-950-8001**	303-751-8700	787
Belair Packing House 1626 90th Ave	Vero Beach	FL	32966	**800-567-1154**	772-567-1151	12-1
Belair Produce Co Inc 7226 Parkway Dr	Hanover	MD	21076	**888-782-8008**	410-782-8000	292-7
Belaire Products Inc 763 S Broadway St	Akron	OH	44311	**800-886-3224**	330-253-3116	10
Belarus Tractor International Inc 7842 N Faulkner Rd	Milwaukee	WI	53224	**800-356-2336**	414-355-2000	270
Belasco Theatre 111 W 44th St	New York	NY	10036	**800-432-7250**	212-239-6200	732
Belcam Inc Delagar Div 27 Montgomery St	Rouses Point	NY	12979	**800-848-9281**		211
Belcan Engineering Group Inc 10200 Anderson Way	Cincinnati	OH	45242	**800-423-5226**	513-891-0972	258
Belco Mfg Co 2303 Taylors Valley Rd	Belton	TX	76513	**800-251-8265**	254-933-9000	198
Belco Packaging Systems Inc 910 S Mountain Ave	Monrovia	CA	91016	**800-833-1833**	626-357-9566	537
Belden & Blake Corp 5200 Stoneham Rd	North Canton	OH	44720	**800-837-4344**	330-497-5471	525
Belden Wire & Cable Co PO Box 1980	Richmond	IN	47375	**800-235-3362**	765-983-5200	801
Belhaven College 1500 Peachtree St	Jackson	MS	39202	**800-960-5940**	601-968-5928	163
Believe In Tomorrow National Children's Foundation 6601 Frederick Rd	Baltimore	MD	21228	**800-933-5470**	410-744-1032	48-6
Bel/Kaukauna USA 1500 E North Ave	Little Chute	WI	54140	**800-558-3500**	920-788-3524	291-5
Belkin Corp 501 W Walnut St	Compton	CA	90220	**800-223-5546**	310-898-1100	252
Belknap Business Forms Inc 215 W Lake Rd — *Cust Svc	Mayville	NY	14757	**800-828-8350***	716-753-5300	111
Bell Canada 1000 rue de la Gauchetiere O Bureau 3700	Montreal	QC	H3B4Y7	**888-932-6666**	514-870-8777	721
Bell-Carter Foods Inc 3742 Mount Diablo Blvd	Lafayette	CA	94549	**800-252-3557**	925-284-5933	291-20
Bell Electrical Contractors Inc 128 Millwell Dr	Maryland Heights	MO	63043	**800-717-2355**	314-739-7744	188-4
Bell Equipment Inc PO Box 230	Grangeville	ID	83530	**800-753-3373**	208-983-1730	270
Bell Harbor International Conference Center 2211 Alaskan Way Pier 66	Seattle	WA	98121	**888-772-4422**	206-441-6666	204
Bell Helicopter Textron Inc PO Box 482	Fort Worth	TX	76101	**800-359-2355**	817-280-2011	21
Bell Industries Inc 1960 E Grand Ave Suite 560 — *AMEX: BI*	El Segundo	CA	90245	**800-782-2355**	310-563-2355	178
Bell Industries Inc Recreational Products Group 580 Yankee Doodle Rd Suite 1200	Eagan	MN	55121	**800-388-2355**	651-450-9020	61
Bell Industries Inc Tech.logix Group 3502 Woodview Trace Suite 100	Indianapolis	IN	46268	**800-722-1599**	317-227-6700	178
Bell Labs 600 Mountain Ave	Murray Hill	NJ	07974	**877-894-4647**	908-582-8500	654
Bell Microproducts Inc 1941 Ringwood Ave — *NASDAQ: BELM*	San Jose	CA	95131	**800-800-1513**	408-451-9400	245
Bell Optical Laboratory Inc 2510 Lance Dr	Kettering	OH	45409	**800-543-4864**	937-294-8022	532
Bell Pharmaceuticals PO Box 128	Belle Plaine	MN	56011	**800-328-5890**	952-873-2288	574
Bell Sports Corp 6225 N State Hwy 161 Suite 300	Irving	TX	75038	**866-525-2355**	469-417-6600	566
Bell Tower Hotel 300 S Thayer St	Ann Arbor	MI	48104	**800-562-3559**	734-769-3010	373
Bell Tower Inn 1235 2nd St SW	Rochester	MN	55902	**800-448-7583**	507-289-2233	373
Bella Automotive Group 5895 NW 167th St	Hialeah	FL	33015	**800-779-8696**	305-364-9800	57
Bellacino's Corp 10096 Shaver Rd	Portage	MI	49024	**877-379-0700**	269-329-0782	657
Bellagio Hotel & Casino 3600 Las Vegas Blvd S	Las Vegas	NV	89109	**888-987-7111**	702-693-7111	655
Bellarmine University 2001 Newburg Rd	Louisville	KY	40205	**800-274-4723**	502-452-8000	163

Listing	City	State	ZIP	Toll-Free	Phone	Class
Bellco First Federal Credit Union PO Box 6611	Greenwood Village	CO	80155	800-235-5261	303-689-7800	216
Bellco Glass Inc 340 Edrudo Rd	Vineland	NJ	08360	800-257-7043	856-691-1075	329
Belle Bonfils Memorial Blood Center 717 Yosemite St	Denver	CO	80230	800-365-0006	303-341-4000	90
Belle Meade Plantation 5025 Harding Rd *Info	Nashville	TN	37205	800-270-3991*	615-356-0501	509
Belle of Orleans LLC DBA Bally's Casino New Orleans 1 Stars & Stripes Blvd	New Orleans	LA	70126	800-572-2559	504-248-3200	133
Belle Tire Inc 3500 Enterprise Dr	Allen Park	MI	48101	800-352-3553	313-271-9400	62-5
Belleview Biltmore Resort & Spa 25 Belleview Blvd	Clearwater	FL	33756	800-237-8947	727-442-6171	655
Belleville & District Chamber of Commerce 5 Moira St E	Belleville	ON	K8N5B3	888-852-9992	613-962-4597	136
Belleville News-Democrat 120 S Illinois St	Belleville	IL	62220	877-338-7416	618-234-1000	522-2
Belleville Wire Cloth Inc 18 Rutgers Ave	Cedar Grove	NJ	07009	800-631-0490	973-239-0074	676
Bellevue Area Tourism & Visitors Bureau PO Box 63	Bellevue	OH	44811	800-562-6978	419-483-5359	205
Bellevue Club Hotel 11200 SE 6th St	Bellevue	WA	98004	800-579-1110	425-454-4424	373
Bellevue University 1000 Galvin Rd S	Bellevue	NE	68005	800-756-7920	402-291-8100	163
Bellingham Marine Industries Inc 1001 C St	Bellingham	WA	98225	800-733-5679	360-676-2800	187-5
Bellingrath Gardens & Home 12401 Bellingrath Garden Rd	Theodore	AL	36582	800-247-8420	251-973-2217	98
Bellmoor The 6 Christian St	Rehoboth Beach	DE	19971	800-425-2355	302-227-5800	373
BellSouth Advertising & Publishing Corp 2247 Northlake Pkwy	Tucker	GA	30084	877-573-2597		623-6
BellSouth Directory Sales Center 2200 Riverchase Ctr Suite 600	Birmingham	AL	35244	800-241-4558		97
BellSouth Long Distance Inc 28 Perimeter Ctr E	Atlanta	GA	30346	877-271-7795	770-352-3000	721
Belmont Abbey College 100 Belmont-Mt Holly Rd	Belmont	NC	28012	888-222-0110	704-825-6700	163
Belmont Crystal Springs Water Cos PO Box 3229	Lancaster	PA	17604	800-444-7873	717-560-6674	792
Belmont University 1900 Belmont Blvd	Nashville	TN	37212	800-563-6765	615-460-6000	163
Belo Corp 400 Record St *NYSE: BLC*	Dallas	TX	75202	800-431-0010	214-977-8222	623-8
Belo Corp Newspaper Group 400 S Record St	Dallas	TX	75205	800-431-0010	214-977-6606	623-8
Belo Corp Television Group 400 S Record St	Dallas	TX	75202	800-431-0010	214-977-6606	724
Beloit Beverage Co Inc 4059 W Bradley Rd	Milwaukee	WI	53209	800-345-0005	414-362-5000	82-1
Beloit College 700 College St	Beloit	WI	53511	800-356-0751	608-363-2500	163
Beloit Convention & Visitors Bureau 1003 Pleasant St	Beloit	WI	53511	800-423-5648	608-365-4838	205
Beloit Daily News 149 State St	Beloit	WI	53511	800-356-3411	608-365-8811	522-2
Beloit (Greater) Chamber of Commerce 520 E Grand Ave	Beloit	WI	53511	800-683-2774	608-365-8835	137
Beloit Memorial Hospital 1969 W Hart Rd	Beloit	WI	53511	800-637-2641	608-364-5011	366-2
Beloit Regional Hospice 655 3rd St Suite 200	Beloit	WI	53511	877-363-7421	608-363-7200	365
Belson Outdoors Inc 111 N River Rd	North Aurora	IL	60542	800-323-5664	630-897-8489	314-4
Belstra Milling Co Inc 424 15th St PO Box 460	Demotte	IN	46310	800-276-2789	219-987-4343	438
Belterra Casino Resort 777 Belterra Dr *Resv	Belterra	IN	47020	888-235-8377*	812-427-7777	655
Belting Industries Co Inc 20 Boright Ave	Kenilworth	NJ	07033	800-843-2358	908-272-8591	364
Belton Industries 1205 Hanby Rd PO Box 127	Belton	SC	29627	800-845-8753	864-338-5711	730-3
Beltone Electronics Corp 4201 W Victoria St	Chicago	IL	60646	800-235-8663	773-583-3600	469
Beltrami Electric Co-op Inc 4111 Technology Dr NW	Bemidji	MN	56601	800-955-6083	218-444-2540	244
Beltservice Corp 4143 Rider Trail N	Earth City	MO	63045	800-727-2358	314-344-8500	206
Belvac Production Machinery Inc 237 Graves Mill Rd	Lynchburg	VA	24502	800-423-5822	434-239-0358	485
Belvedere Hotel 319 W 48th St	New York	NY	10036	888-468-3558	212-245-7000	373
Belvedere USA Corp 1 Belvedere Blvd	Belvidere	IL	61008	800-435-5491	815-544-3131	78
Belwith International Ltd 3100 Broadway Ave	Grandville	MI	49418	800-235-9484		345
Bema Film Systems Inc 744 N Oaklawn Ave	Elmhurst	IL	60126	800-833-6657	630-279-7800	67
Bemidji Area Chamber of Commerce 300 Bemidji Ave	Bemidji	MN	56601	800-458-2223	218-444-3541	137
Bemidji State University 1500 Birchmont Dr NE	Bemidji	MN	56601	888-345-1721	218-755-2001	163
Bemis Co Inc Bemis Polyethylene Packaging Div 1350 N Fruitridge Ave	Terre Haute	IN	47804	800-457-0861	812-466-2213	589
Bemis Co Inc Industrial Products Div 2200 Badger Ave PO Box 2968	Oshkosh	WI	54903	800-328-4550	920-303-7830	717
Bemis Mfg Co PO Box 901	Sheboygan Falls	WI	53085	800-558-7651	920-467-4621	314-4
Bemis Pet Products PO Box 9066	Omaha	NE	68109	800-541-4303	402-734-6262	66
Ben Arnold Sunbelt Beverage Co PO Box 480	Ridgeway	SC	29130	888-262-9787	803-337-3500	82-3
Ben Bridge Jeweler Inc PO Box 1908 *Cust Svc	Seattle	WA	98111	888-448-1912*	206-448-8800	402
Ben E Keith Co 7650 Will Rogers Blvd	Fort Worth	TX	76140	877-317-6100	817-759-6000	292-8
Ben Elias Industries Corp 1400 Broadway 29th Fl	New York	NY	10018	800-354-2769	212-354-8300	154
Ben Franklin Stores 7601 Durand Ave	Racine	WI	53408	800-992-9307	262-681-7000	305
Ben Hogan Co 425 Meadow St	Chicopee	MA	01021	800-772-5346	413-536-1200	701
Ben Lippen School 7401 Monticello Rd	Columbia	SC	29203	888-236-5476	803-786-7200	611
Ben Moss Jewellers 300-201 Portage Ave	Winnipeg	MB	R3B3K6	888-236-6677	204-947-6682	402
Ben Myerson Candy Co Inc 928 Towne Ave	Los Angeles	CA	90021	800-421-8448	213-623-6266	291-8
Ben Tire Distributors Ltd Inc 203 E Madison St PO Box 158	Toledo	IL	62468	800-252-8961	217-849-3331	740
Benchmark Imaging & Display 640 Busse Hwy	Park Ridge	IL	60068	800-626-3069	847-292-5150	338
Benchmark Inc 4660 13th St	Wyandotte	MI	48192	800-521-9107	734-285-0900	143
Benchmark Industries Inc 630 Hay Ave	Brookville	OH	45309	800-833-4096	937-833-4091	107
BenchmarkQA Inc 3800 American Blvd W Suite 1580	Minneapolis	MN	55431	877-425-2581	952-392-2381	176-12
BENCO Electric Co-op 20946 549 Ave	Mankato	MN	56001	888-792-3626	507-387-7963	244
Bend Chamber of Commerce 777 NW Wall St Suite 200	Bend	OR	97701	800-905-2363	541-382-3221	137
Bend Industries Inc 2200 S Main St	West Bend	WI	53095	800-686-2363	262-338-5700	181
Bendel Executive Suites 213 Bendel Rd	Lafayette	LA	70503	800-990-5708	337-261-0604	373
Bender Group 345 Parr Cir	Reno	NV	89512	800-621-9402	775-788-8800	440
Bendix Commercial Vehicle Systems LLC 901 Cleveland St	Elyria	OH	44035	800-247-2725	440-329-9000	61
Benedict College 1600 Harden St	Columbia	SC	29204	800-868-6598	803-256-4220	163
Benedictine College 1020 N 2nd St	Atchison	KS	66002	800-467-5340	913-367-5340	163
Benedictine Health System 503 E 3rd St Suite 400	Duluth	MN	55805	800-833-7208	218-786-2370	348
Benedictine University 5700 College Rd	Lisle	IL	60532	888-829-6363	630-829-6000	163
Beneficial Life Insurance Co 36 S State St	Salt Lake City	UT	84136	800-233-7979	801-933-1100	384-2
Beneficial Mutual Savings Bank 530 Walnut St	Philadelphia	PA	19106	800-784-8490	215-864-6000	71
Beneficial Standard Life Insurance Co 11815 N Pennsylvania St	Carmel	IN	46032	800-288-4096	317-817-6200	384-2
Benefit Assn. Armed Services Mutual PO Box 160384	Nashville	TN	37216	800-251-8434	615-851-0800	48-19
Benefit Assn. Military PO Box 221110	Chantilly	VA	20153	800-336-0100	703-968-6200	48-19
BeneFit Cosmetics 685 Market St 7th Fl *Cust Svc	San Francisco	CA	94105	800-781-2336*	415-781-8153	211
Benefit Plans. International Foundation of Employee 18700 W Bluemond Rd PO Box 69	Brookfield	WI	53008	888-334-3327	262-786-6700	49-12
Benefit Specialists. International Society of Certified Employee 18700 W Bluemond Rd PO Box 209	Brookfield	WI	53008	888-334-3327	262-786-8771	49-12
Benefits America 415 East Paces Ferry Rd NE	Atlanta	GA	30305	800-777-8878	404-233-5411	783
Benesch Alfred & Co 205 N Michigan Ave Suite 2400	Chicago	IL	60601	877-222-9995	312-565-0450	258
BeneScript Services Inc 3720 DaVinci Ct Suite 200	Norcross	GA	30092	800-345-3189	770-448-4344	575
Benevolent Life Insurance Co Inc 1624 Milam St	Shreveport	LA	71103	800-435-1522	318-425-1522	384-2
Benfield Blanch Inc 500 N Akard St Suite 3700	Dallas	TX	75201	866-236-3435	214-756-7000	355-4
Bengard Tom Ranch Inc PO Box 80090	Salinas	CA	93912	800-546-3517	831-422-9021	11-11
Benihana Inc 8685 NW 53rd Terr Suite 201 *NASDAQ: BNHN*	Miami	FL	33166	800-327-3369	305-593-0770	656
Benjamin The 125 E 50th St	New York	NY	10022	800-637-8483	212-715-2500	373
Benjamin F Rich Co PO Box 6031	Newark	DE	19714	800-237-4241	302-894-0498	233
Benjamin & Marian Schuster Performing Arts Center 109 Main St	Dayton	OH	45402	888-228-3630	937-228-3630	562
Benjamin Moore & Co 51 Chestnut Ridge Rd	Montvale	NJ	07645	800-344-0400	201-573-9600	540
Benner-Nawman Inc 3450 Sabin Brown Rd	Wickenburg	AZ	85390	800-992-3833	928-684-2813	281
Bennett Auto Supply Inc 3141 SW 10th St	Pompano Beach	FL	33069	800-723-6638	954-335-8700	54
Bennett College 900 E Washington St *Admissions	Greensboro	NC	27401	800-413-5323*	336-273-4431	163
Bennett Mfg Co Inc 13315 Railroad St	Alden	NY	14004	800-345-2142	716-937-9161	281
Bennett Pump Co 1218 E Pontaluna Rd	Spring Lake	MI	49456	800-423-6638	231-798-1310	625
Bennigan's 6500 International Pkwy Suite 1000	Plano	TX	75093	800-727-8355	972-588-5000	657
Bennington Area Chamber of Commerce 100 Veterans Memorial Dr	Bennington	VT	05201	800-229-0252	802-447-3311	137
Bennington Banner 245 Main St PO Box 5027	Bennington	VT	05201	800-491-7567	802-447-7567	522-2
Bennington College 1 College Dr	Bennington	VT	05201	800-833-6845	802-442-5401	163
BenQ America Corp 53 Discovery	Irvine	CA	92618	866-600-2367	949-255-9500	171-7
Benrus Watch Co Inc 33-00 Northern Blvd	Long Island City	NY	11101	800-221-0131		151
BENS (Business Executives for National Security) 1717 Pennsylvania Ave NW Suite 350	Washington	DC	20006	800-296-2125	202-296-2125	49-12
Bensinger DuPont & Assoc 20 N Wacker Dr Suite 920	Chicago	IL	60606	800-227-8620	312-726-8620	454
Benson Industries Inc 1650 NW Naito Pkwy Suite 250	Portland	OR	97209	800-999-5113	503-226-7611	188-6
Benson International Inc Rt 14 S PO Box 970	Mineral Wells	WV	26150	877-489-9020	304-489-9020	505
Benson's Gourmet Seasonings PO Box 638	Azusa	CA	91702	800-325-5619	626 969 4443	291-37
Bent Tube Inc 9649 W Van Buren Rd	Fowlerville	MI	48836	888-797-1931	517-521-4330	584
Bentex Group Inc 100 W 33rd St Suite 1030	New York	NY	10001	800-451-0285	212-594-4250	153-4
Benthos Inc 49 Edgerton Dr *NASDAQ: BTHS* ■ *Sales	North Falmouth	MA	02556	800-446-1222*	508-563-1000	519
Bentley Beach Hotel 101 Ocean Dr	Miami Beach	FL	33139	866-236-8539	305-938-4600	373

Alphabetical Section

Name / Address	City	State	Zip	Toll-Free	Phone	Class
Bentley College 175 Forest St	Waltham	MA	02452	800-523-2354	781-891-2244	163
Bentley Hotel 510 Ocean Dr	Miami Beach	FL	33139	800-236-8510	305-538-1700	373
Bentley Mfg Co Inc 15123 Colorado Ave	Paramount	CA	90723	800-424-2425	562-634-4051	321
Bentley Mills Inc 14641 E Don Julian Rd	City of Industry	CA	91746	800-423-4709	626-333-4585	131
Bentley Systems Inc 685 Stockton Dr	Exton	PA	19341	800-236-8539	610-458-5000	176-5
Bently Nevada Corp 1631 Bently Pkwy S	Minden	NV	89423	800-227-5514	775-782-3611	464
Benton Convention Center 301 W 5th St	Winston-Salem	NC	27101	800-289-5670	336-727-2976	204
Benton Express Inc PO Box 16709	Atlanta	GA	30321	888-423-6866	404-267-2200	769
Benton Rural Electric Assn 402 7th	Prosser	WA	99350	800-221-6987	509-786-2913	244
Bentz Whaley Flessner 7251 Ohms Ln	Minneapolis	MN	55439	800-921-0111	952-921-0111	312
Benz Oil Inc 2724 W Hampton Ave	Milwaukee	WI	53209	800-991-2369	414-442-2900	530
Benzel's Pretzel Bakery Inc 5200 6th Ave	Altoona	PA	16602	800-344-4438	814-942-5062	291-9
Benziger Family Winery 1883 London Ranch Rd	Glen Ellen	CA	95442	888-490-2739	707-935-3000	81-3
BER Plastic Corp PO Box 2	Riverdale	NJ	07457	877-237-3456	973-839-2100	589
Berbee Information Networks Corp 5520 Research Pk Dr	Madison	WI	53711	888-888-8835	608-288-3000	178
Bercen Inc 1381 Cranston St	Cranston	RI	02920	800-525-0595	401-943-7400	143
Berea College 101 Chestnut St	Berea	KY	40403	800-326-5948	859-985-3000	163
Berendsen Fluid Power 401 S Boston Ave 1200 Mid Continent Tower	Tulsa	OK	74103	800-360-2327	918-592-3781	378
Beretta USA Corp 17601 Beretta Dr	Accokeek	MD	20607	800-636-3420	301-283-2191	279
Berg Equipment Co 2700 W Veterans Pkwy	Marshfield	WI	54449	800-494-1738	715-384-2151	269
Berg Steel Pipe Corp 5315 W 19th St	Panama City	FL	32401	800-874-0384	850-769-2273	481
Bergamot Inc 820 Wisconsin St *Cust Svc	Delavan	WI	53115	800-922-6733*	262-728-5572	10
Bergdorf Goodman Inc 754 5th Ave *Cust Svc	New York	NY	10019	800-218-4918*	212-753-7300	155-4
Berger Bros Co 805 Pennsylvania Blvd *Cust Svc	Feasterville	PA	19053	800-523-8852*	215-355-1200	688
Berger Holdings Ltd 805 Pennsylvania Blvd	Feasterville	PA	19053	800-523-8852	215-355-1200	688
Berger Louis Group Inc 100 Halsted St	East Orange	NJ	07018	800-323-4098	973-678-1960	258
Berger MZ & Co Inc 33-00 Northern Blvd	Long Island City	NY	11101	800-221-0131		151
Berger Transfer & Storage Inc 2950 Long Lake Rd	Saint Paul	MN	55113	800-328-2459	651-639-2260	508
Bergman Marilyn Pres & Chm ASCAP 1 Lincoln Plaza	New York	NY	10023	800-952-7227	212-621-6000	561
Bergmann Assoc Inc 200 First Federal Plaza	Rochester	NY	14614	800-724-1168	585-232-5135	258
Bergquist Co 18930 W 78th St	Chanhassen	MN	55317	800-347-4572	952-835-2322	252
Berk O Co 3 Milltown Ct	Union	NJ	07083	800-631-7392	908-851-9500	378
Berkeley College New York City Campus 3 E 43rd St	New York	NY	10017	800-446-5400	212-986-4343	158
Berkeley Convention & Visitors Bureau 2015 Center St 1st Fl	Berkeley	CA	94704	800-847-4823	510-549-7040	205
Berkeley County Chamber of Commerce PO Box 968	Moncks Corner	SC	29461	800-882-0337	843-761-8238	137
Berkeley Hotel 1200 E Cary St	Richmond	VA	23219	888-780-4422	804-780-1300	373
Berkeley Pumps 293 Wright St *Cust Svc	Delavan	WI	53115	888-237-5353*	262-728-5551	627
Berklee College of Music 1140 Boylston St	Boston	MA	02215	800-421-0084	617-747-2221	163
Berkley Publishing Group 375 Hudson St *Cust Svc	New York	NY	10014	800-631-8571*	212-366-2000	623-2
Berks Packing Co Inc PO Box 5919	Reading	PA	19610	800-882-3757	610-376-7291	291-26
Berks Products Corp 726 Spring St	Reading	PA	19604	800-282-2375	610-374-5131	493-5
Berks VNA Hospice Program 1170 Berkshire Blvd	Wyomissing	PA	19610	800-346-7848	610-378-0481	365
Berkshire Bank PO Box 1308	Pittsfield	MA	01202	800-773-5601	413-443-5601	71
Berkshire Eagle 75 S Church St PO Box 1171	Pittsfield	MA	01202	800-234-7404	413-447-7311	522-2
Berkshire Foods Inc 4600 S Packers Ave	Chicago	IL	60609	800-621-5042	773-254-2424	790-2
Berkshire Gas Co Inc 115 Cheshire Rd	Pittsfield	MA	01201	800-292-5012	413-442-1511	774
Berkshire Hathaway Life Insurance Co of Nebraska 3024 Harney St	Omaha	NE	68131	800-786-6426	402-536-3000	384-2
Berkshire Income Realty Inc 1 Beacon St *AMEX: BIR_pa*	Boston	MA	02108	888-867-0100	617-523-7722	641
Berkshire Life Insurance Co of America 700 South St	Pittsfield	MA	01201	800-819-2468	413-499-4321	384-2
Berkshire Property Advisors LLC 1 Beacon St Suite 1550	Boston	MA	02108	888-867-0100	617-646-2300	641
Berkshire Theatre Festival PO Box 797	Stockbridge	MA	01262	866-811-4111	413-298-5536	734
Berle Mfg Co 1411 Folly Rd	Charleston	SC	29412	800-845-4503	843-762-7150	153-12
Berlex Laboratories Inc 6 W Belt	Wayne	NJ	07470	888-237-2394	973-694-4100	229
Berlin Glove Co Inc 150 W Franklin St	Berlin	WI	54923	800-236-3367	920-361-5050	153-8
Berliner & Marx Inc 275 Morgan Ave	Brooklyn	NY	11211	800-222-8325	718-599-6400	465
Berlitz International Inc 400 Alexander Pk	Princeton	NJ	08540	800-257-9449	609-514-9650	305
Berman Leather Co 117 Beaver St	Waltham	MA	02453	800-992-3762	781-736-0870	422
Bermil Industries Corp DBA Wascomat of America PO Box 960338	Inwood	NY	11096	800-645-2205	516-371-4400	38
Bermuda Dept of Tourism 245 Peachtree Ctr Ave NE Suite 803	Atlanta	GA	30303	800-223-6106	404-524-1541	764
Bermuda Dept of Tourism 675 3rd Ave 20th Fl	New York	NY	10017	800-223-6106	212-818-9800	764
Bermuda Village 142 Bermuda Village Dr *Mktg	Advance	NC	27006	800-843-5433*	336-998-6535	659
Bernadette Business Forms Inc 8950 Pershall Rd	Saint Louis	MO	63042	800-862-7288	314-522-1700	111

Name / Address	City	State	Zip	Toll-Free	Phone	Class
Bernan Assoc 4611 F Assembly Dr	Lanham	MD	20706	800-865-3457	301-459-2255	623-10
Bernard C Harris Publishing Co Inc 2500 Westchester Ave Suite 400	Purchase	NY	10577	800-326-6600		623-2
Bernard Food Industries Inc 1125 Hartrey Ave	Evanston	IL	60204	800-323-3663	847-869-5222	291-18
Bernard Hodes Group 220 E 42 St	New York	NY	10017	888-438-9911	212-999-9000	4
Bernard L Madoff Investment Securities Co 885 3rd Ave 18th Fl	New York	NY	10022	800-334-1343	212-230-2424	679
Bernards Inn 27 Mine Brook Rd	Bernardsville	NJ	07924	888-766-0002	908-766-0002	373
Bernardus Lodge 415 Carmel Valley Rd	Carmel Valley	CA	93924	888-648-9463	831-658-3400	373
Berne Apparel Co 2100 Summit St	New Haven	IN	46774	800-843-7657	260-469-3136	153-19
Berner Foods Inc 2034 E Factory Rd	Dakota	IL	61018	800-819-8199	815-563-4222	291-5
Berney-Karp Inc 3350 E 26th St	Los Angeles	CA	90023	800-237-6395	323-260-7122	331
Bernhard Mechanical Contractors Inc 10321 Airline Hwy	Baton Rouge	LA	70816	888-773-2791	225-293-2791	188-10
Berns Co 1250 W 17th St	Long Beach	CA	90813	800-421-3773	562-437-0471	462
Bernstein-Rein 4600 Madison Ave Suite 1500	Kansas City	MO	64112	800-571-6246	816-756-0640	4
Berry Aviation Inc 1807 Airport Dr	San Marcos	TX	78666	800-229-2379	512-353-2379	14
Berry Co 3170 Kettering Blvd	Dayton	OH	45401	800-366-2379	937-296-2121	6
Berry College 2277 Martha Berry Hwy	Mount Berry	GA	30149	800-237-7942	706-232-5374	163
Berry Plastics Corp 101 Oakley St	Evansville	IN	47710	800-234-1930	812-429-9522	198
Berryman & Henigar 11590 W Bernardo Ct Suite 100	San Diego	CA	92127	800-964-4274	858-451-6100	258
Berryville Graphics PO Box 272	Berryville	VA	22611	800-606-6467	540-955-2750	614
Bertek Pharmaceuticals Inc 781 Chestnut Ridge Rd	Morgantown	WV	26505	888-823-7835	304-598-5420	572
Bertels Can Co 485 Stuart Rd *Cust Svc	Wilkes-Barre	PA	18706	800-829-0578*	570-829-0524	124
Bertolini's 350 W Hubbard St Suite 610	Chicago	IL	60610	800-486-4791	312-923-0030	657
Bertolli USA Inc 800 Sylvan Ave	Englewood Cliffs	NJ	07632	800-908-9789		291-41
Berwanger Overmyer Assoc 2245 Northbank Dr	Columbus	OH	43220	800-837-0503	614-457-7000	383
Berwick Electric Co 3450 N Nevada Ave Suite 100	Colorado Springs	CO	80907	800-442-0854	719-632-7683	188-4
Berwick Offray Inc Bombay Ln & 9th St	Berwick	PA	18603	800-327-0350	570-752-5934	730-5
Besco Electric Supply Co 711 S 14th St	Leesburg	FL	34748	800-541-6618	352-787-4542	357
Beseler Charles Co 1501 Oakland Ave	Millville	NJ	08332	800-237-3537		580
Besl Transfer Co 5700 Este Ave	Cincinnati	OH	45232	800-456-2375	513-242-3456	769
Besly Products Corp 100 Dearborn Ave	South Beloit	IL	61080	800-435-2965	815-389-2231	484
Bessemer Area Chamber of Commerce 321 N 18th St	Bessemer	AL	35020	888-423-7736	205-425-3253	137
Besser Appco 442 North WW White Rd	San Antonio	TX	78219	800-330-5590	210-333-1111	189
Besser Co 801 Johnson St	Alpena	MI	49707	800-530-9980	989-354-4111	379
Besser Lithibar Co 13521 Quality Dr	Holland	MI	49424	800-626-0415	616-399-5215	379
Best Block Co PO Box 13707	Milwaukee	WI	53213	800-782-7708	262-781-7200	181
Best Brands Corp 1765 Yankee Doodle Rd	Eagan	MN	55121	800-328-2068	651-454-5850	291-16
Best Buy Co Inc 7601 Penn Ave S *NYSE: BBY*	Richfield	MN	55423	800-369-5050	612-291-1000	35
Best Computer Supplies 895 E Patriot Blvd Suite 110	Reno	NV	89511	800-544-3472	775-850-2600	523
Best Fares USA Inc 1301 S Bowen Rd Suite 400	Arlington	TX	76013	800-880-1234	817-860-5573	762
Best Inns & Suites 13 Corporate Sq Suite 250	Atlanta	GA	30329	800-237-8466	404-321-4045	369
Best Kosher Foods Corp PO Box 25111	Cincinnati	OH	45225	888-800-0072	513-936-2000	291-26
Best Label Co 2943 Whipple Rd	Union City	CA	94587	800-637-5333	510-489-5400	404
Best Mfg Co 579 Edison St *Cust Svc	Menlo	GA	30731	800-241-0323*	706-862-2302	566
Best Mfg Inc 10 Exchange Pl 22nd Fl	Jersey City	NJ	07302	800-843-3233	201-356-3800	153-19
Best Packers Inc 1122 Bronson St *Sales	Palatka	FL	32177	800-771-9378*	386-328-5127	465
Best Price Cruises 8930 S Federal Hwy	Port Saint Lucie	FL	34952	800-672-7485	772-344-3330	760
Best Provision Co Inc 144 Avon Ave	Newark	NJ	07108	800-631-4466	973-242-5000	291-26
Best Registration Services Inc DBA BestRegistrar.com 1418 S 3rd St	Louisville	KY	40208	800-977-3475	502-637-4528	389
Best Rest Inn 1206 W 21st St	Ogden	UT	84401	800-343-8644	801-393-8644	373
Best-Rite Mfg PO Box D	Temple	TX	76503	866-886-6935		281
Best Sand Corp PO Box 87	Chardon	OH	44024	800-237-4986	440-285-3132	493-4
Best Software Inc 56 Technology Dr	Irvine	CA	92618	866-308-2378	949-753-1222	176-1
Best Software Inc CRM Div 8800 N Gainey Ctr Dr Suite 200	Scottsdale	AZ	85258	800-643-6400	480-368-3700	176-1
Best Software Inc Nonprofit & Government Div 12301 Research Blvd Bldg 4 Suite 350	Austin	TX	78759	800-647-3863	512-454-5004	176-1
Best Software Inc Small Business Div 1505 Pavilion Pl *Sales	Norcross	GA	30093	800-285-0999*	770-492-6414	176-1
Best Software Inc Specialty Products Div 2325 Dulles Corner Blvd Suite 800	Herndon	VA	20171	800-424-9392	703-793-2700	176-1
Best Sweet Inc 288 Mazeppa Rd	Mooresville	NC	28115	888-211-5530	704-664-4300	291-8
Best Travel Inc 8600 W Bryn Mawr Ave	Chicago	IL	60631	800-323-3015	773-380-0150	760
Best Traveler Program 13 Corporate Sq Suite 250	Atlanta	GA	30329	800-237-8466	404-321-4045	371
Best Western Blue Rock Golf Resort 39 Todd Rd	South Yarmouth	MA	02664	800-227-3263	508-398-6962	655
Best Western Dogwood Hills Resort Inn & Golf Club 1252 State Hwy KK	Osage Beach	MO	65065	800-528-1234	573-348-1735	655
Best Western Gold Crown Club International 20400 N 29th Ave	Phoenix	AZ	85027	800-237-8483		371
Best Western Inn of the Ozarks 297 W Van Buren	Eureka Springs	AR	72632	800-552-3785	479-253-9768	655

Name / Address	City	State	Zip	Toll-Free	Phone	Class
Best Western International Inc 6201 N 24th Pkwy	Phoenix	AZ	85016	**800-528-1234**	602-957-4200	369
Best Western Pelican Beach Resort 2000 N Atlantic Blvd.	Fort Lauderdale	FL	33305	**800-525-6298**	954-568-9431	373
Best Western Riverchase Inn 1800 Riverchase Dr	Birmingham	AL	35244	**800-937-8376**	205-985-7500	373
Bestar Inc 4220 Villeneuve St *TSE: BES*	Lac-Megantic	QC	G6B2C3	**888-823-7827**	819-583-1017	314-1
BestCalls.com 12 Clock Tower Pl	Maynard	MA	01754	**800-990-6397**		396
Besteman JA Co Inc 1060 Hall St SW	Grand Rapids	MI	49503	**800-253-4620**	616-452-2101	292-7
Bestforms Inc 1135 Avenida Acaso	Camarillo	CA	93012	**800-350-0618**	805-388-0503	111
BestRegistrar.com 1418 S 3rd St	Louisville	KY	40208	**800-977-3475**	502-637-4528	389
Bestt Liebco Corp 1201 Jackson St	Philadelphia	PA	19148	**800-523-9095**	215-336-3400	104
Bestway Inc 7800 N Stemmons Fwy Suite 320 *NASDAQ: BSTW*	Dallas	TX	75247	**800-520-1107**	214-630-6655	261-3
Bestway Tours & Safaris 8678 Greenall Ave Suite 206	Burnaby	BC	V5J3M6	**800-663-0844**	604-264-7378	748
BET Holdings II Inc 1235 'W' St NE	Washington	DC	20018	**800-626-9911**	202-608-2000	355-3
Beta LaserMike Inc 8001 Technology Blvd	Dayton	OH	45424	**800-886-9935**	937-233-9935	464
Beta Screen Corp 707 Commercial Ave	Carlstadt	NJ	07072	**800-272-7336**	201-939-2400	580
Beta Systems Software Inc 6411 Ivy Ln Suite 610	Greenbelt	MD	20770	**800-475-1168**	301-486-4600	176-12
Beta Theta Pi 5134 Bonham Rd	Oxford	OH	45056	**800-800-2382**	513-523-7591	48-16
Betar Inc 1524 Millstone River Rd	Hillsborough	NJ	08844	**800-841-8841**	908-359-4200	610
BETCO (Builders Equipment & Tool Co) 1617 Enid St	Houston	TX	77009	**800-908-8778**	713-869-3491	482
Betco Block & Products Inc 5400 Butler Rd	Bethesda	MD	20816	**800-486-2312**	301-654-2312	181
Bete Channing L Co Inc 1 Community Pl	South Deerfield	MA	01373	**800-628-7733**	413-665-7611	623-10
Bete Fog Nozzle Inc 50 Greenfield St	Greenfield	MA	01301	**800-235-0049**	413-772-0846	345
Beth-El College of Nursing & Health Sciences 1420 Austin Bluffs Pkwy	Colorado Springs	CO	80933	**800-990-8227**	719-262-4422	163
Bethany College 421 N 1st St	Lindsborg	KS	67456	**800-826-2281**	785-227-3311	163
Bethany College Main St	Bethany	WV	26032	**800-922-7611**	304-829-7000	163
Bethany College of the Assemblies of God 800 Bethany Dr	Scotts Valley	CA	95066	**800-843-9410**	831-438-3800	163
Bethany House Publishers 11400 Hampshire Ave S *Cust Svc	Bloomington	MN	55438	**800-328-6109***	952-829-2500	623-4
Bethany Limousine & Bus 2120 West Virginia Ave NE	Washington	DC	20037	**800-424-2971**	202-857-0440	433
Bethany Lutheran College 700 Luther Dr	Mankato	MN	56001	**800-944-3066**	507-344-7000	160
Bethany Theological Seminary 615 National Rd W	Richmond	IN	47374	**800-287-8822**	765-983-1800	164-3
Bethel College 1001 W McKinley Ave	Mishawaka	IN	46545	**800-422-4101**	574-257-3339	163
Bethel College 300 E 27th St	North Newton	KS	67117	**800-522-1887**	316-283-2500	163
Bethel Inn & Country Club PO Box 49	Bethel	ME	04217	**800-654-0125**	207-824-2175	655
Bethel University 3900 Bethel Dr	Saint Paul	MN	55112	**800-255-8706**	651-638-6400	163
Bethesda Hospital 2951 Maple Ave	Zanesville	OH	43701	**800-322-4762**	740-454-4000	366-2
Bethesda Iron Works Inc 650 Lofstrand Ln	Rockville	MD	20850	**800-762-1383**	301-762-9100	471
Bethpage Federal Credit Union 899 S Oyster Bay Rd	Bethpage	NY	11714	**800-628-7070**	516-349-6700	216
Bethune-Cookman College 640 Mary McLeod Bethune Blvd	Daytona Beach	FL	32114	**800-448-0228**	386-255-1401	163
Betlin Inc 4411 Marketing Pl	Groveport	OH	43125	**800-923-8546**	614-443-0248	153-1
Betson Enterprises Inc 303 Patterson Plank Rd	Carlstadt	NJ	07072	**800-524-2343**	201-438-1300	55
Better Brands of Atlanta Inc 755 Jefferson St NW	Atlanta	GA	30318	**800-273-4926**	404-872-4731	82-1
Better Business Bureau of Ark-La-Tex 401 Edwards St Suite 125	Shreveport	LA	71101	**800-372-4222**	318-222-7575	80
Better Business Bureau of Blountville PO Box 1178 Tri-City Airport	Blountville	TN	37617	**888-437-4222**	423-325-6616	80
Better Business Bureau of Central Alabama & the Wiregrass Area Montgomery Branch 1210 S 20th St	Birmingham	AL	35205	**800-824-5274**	205-558-2222	80
Better Business Bureau of Central East Texas 3600 Old Bullard Rd Bldg 1	Tyler	TX	75701	**800-443-0131**	903-581-5704	80
Better Business Bureau of Central & Eastern Kentucky 1460 Newton Pike	Lexington	KY	40511	**800-866-6668**	859-259-1008	80
Better Business Bureau of Central Louisiana 5220-C Rue Verdun	Alexandria	LA	71303	**800-256-2225**	318-473-4494	80
Better Business Bureau of Central Northeast Northwest & Southwest Arizona 4428 N 12th St	Phoenix	AZ	85014	**877-291-6222**	602-264-1721	80
Better Business Bureau of Central Ohio 1335 Dublin Rd Suite 30-A	Columbus	OH	43215	**800-759-2400**	614-486-6336	80
Better Business Bureau of Eastern Missouri & Southern Illinois 12 Sunnen Dr Suite 121	Saint Louis	MO	63143	**866-996-3887**	314-645-3300	80
Better Business Bureau of Eastern Oklahoma 1722 S Carson Ave Suite 3200	Tulsa	OK	74119	**800-928-4222**	918-492-1266	80
Better Business Bureau of Eastern Ontario & the Outaouais Inc 130 Albert St Suite 603	Ottawa	ON	K1P5G4	**877-889-8566**	613-237-4856	80
Better Business Bureau of Kansas (Except the Northeast) 328 Laura St	Wichita	KS	67211	**800-856-2417**	316-263-3146	80
Better Business Bureau of the Mountain States 1730 S College Ave Suite 303	Fort Collins	CO	80525	**800-564-0371**	970-484-1348	80
Better Business Bureau of Northeast Florida 4417 Beach Blvd Suite 202	Jacksonville	FL	32207	**800-940-1315**	904-721-2288	80
Better Business Bureau of Northeastern & Central Pennsylvania 4099 Birney Ave	Moosic	PA	18507	**888-229-3222**	570-342-9129	80
Better Business Bureau Serving Mid-Western Ontario 354 Charles St E	Kitchener	ON	N2G4L5	**800-459-8875**	519-579-3080	80
Better Business Bureau of the Sioux City Area 600 4th St Suite 904	Sioux City	IA	51101	**888-845-4222**	712-252-4501	80
Better Business Bureau of the Southeast Atlantic 6606 Abercorn St Suite 108C	Savannah	GA	31405	**800-353-1192**	912-354-7522	80
Better Business Bureau of Southern Alabama 3361 Cottage Hill Rd Suite E	Mobile	AL	36606	**800-544-4714**	251-433-5494	80
Better Business Bureau of Southern Colorado 25 N Wahsatch Ave	Colorado Springs	CO	80903	**866-206-1800**	719-636-1155	80
Better Business Bureau of Southern Piedmont Carolinas 5200 Park Rd Suite 202	Charlotte	NC	28209	**877-317-7236**	704-527-0012	80
Better Business Bureau of Southwest Georgia PO Box 808	Albany	GA	31702	**800-868-4222**	229-883-0744	80
Better Business Bureau of Southwest Louisiana 2309 E Crown Lake Rd	Lake Charles	LA	70606	**800-542-7085**	337-478-6253	80
Better Business Bureau of West Florida PO Box 7950	Clearwater	FL	33758	**800-525-1447**	727-535-5522	80
Better Hearing Institute (BHI) 515 King St Suite 420	Alexandria	VA	22314	**888-432-7435**	703-684-3391	48-17
Better Homes & Gardens Magazine 1716 Locust St	Des Moines	IA	50309	**800-374-4244**	515-284-3000	449-11
Better Homes & Gardens WOOD Magazine 1716 Locust St	Des Moines	IA	50309	**800-374-9663**		449-14
Better Investing Magazine PO Box 220	Royal Oak	MI	48068	**877-275-6242**	248-583-6242	449-11
Better Management Corp PO Box 9755	Youngstown	OH	44513	**877-293-4300**	330-758-5757	646
Better Packages Inc 255 Canal St	Shelton	CT	06484	**800-237-9151**	203-926-3700	112
Better Vision Institute (BVI) Vision Council of America 1700 Diagonal Rd Suite 500	Alexandria	VA	22314	**800-424-8422**	703-548-4560	48-17
Betteravia Farms PO Box 5845	Santa Maria	CA	93456	**800-328-8816**	805-925-2417	11-11
Bettis Laboratory 814 Pittsburgh-McKeeseport Blvd	West Mifflin	PA	15122	**800-296-5002**	412-476-5000	654
Betty Ford Center 39000 Bob Hope Dr	Rancho Mirage	CA	92270	**800-854-9211**	760-773-4100	712
Betty Machine Co 324 Freehill Rd	Hendersonville	TN	37075	**800-264-3480**	615-826-6004	610
Beulah Park Race Track 3664 Grant Ave	Grove City	OH	43123	**800-433-6905**	614-871-9600	628
Beutler Corp 4700 Lang Ave	McClellan	CA	95652	**800-238-8537**	916-646-2222	188-10
Bevan Mfg Co 4451 Rt 130	Burlington	NJ	08016	**800-222-8125**	609-386-6501	153-6
Bevco Precision Mfg Co 2246A Bluemound Rd	Waukesha	WI	53186	**800-864-2991**	262-798-9200	314-1
Beverage Corp International 3505 NW 107th St	Miami	FL	33167	**800-226-5061**	305-714-7000	81-2
Beverage Licensees. American 5101 River Rd Suite 108	Bethesda	MD	20816	**800-311-8999**	301-656-1494	49-6
Beverage Marketing Corp 850 3rd Ave	New York	NY	10022	**800-275-4630**	212-688-7640	194
Beverly Enterprises Inc 1000 Beverly Way *NYSE: BEV*	Fort Smith	AR	72919	**877-238-3759**	479-201-2000	442
Beverly Garland's Holiday Inn at Universal Studios Hollywood 4222 Vineland Ave	North Hollywood	CA	91602	**800-238-3759**	818-980-8000	373
Beverly Heritage Hotel 1820 Barber Ln	Milpitas	CA	95035	**800-443-4455**	408-943-9080	373
Beverly Hills Chamber of Commerce 239 S Beverly Dr	Beverly Hills	CA	90212	**800-345-2210**	310-248-1000	137
Beverly Hills Conference & Visitors Bureau 239 S Beverly Dr	Beverly Hills	CA	90212	**800-345-2210**	310-248-1000	205
Beverly Hills Hotel 9641 Sunset Blvd	Beverly Hills	CA	90210	**800-283-8885**	310-276-2251	373
Beverly Hills Transfer & Storage Co 15500 S Main St	Gardena	CA	90248	**800-999-7114**	310-276-1121	508
Beverly Hilton 9876 Wilshire Blvd.	Beverly Hills	CA	90210	**800-445-8667**	310-274-7777	373
Beverly Motel 703 N Ocean Blvd	Myrtle Beach	SC	29577	**800-843-0415**	843-448-9496	373
BeVocal Inc 685 Clyde Ave	Mountain View	CA	94043	**800-428-6225**	650-210-8600	606
BFI Innovations 420-C Airport Rd	Elgin	IL	60123	**800-323-7009**	847-214-4860	291-15
BG Products Inc 740 S Wichita St PO Box 1282	Wichita	KS	67201	**800-961-6228**	316-265-2686	530
BGC (Baptist General Conference) 2002 S Arlington Heights Rd	Arlington Heights	IL	60005	**800-323-4215**	847-228-0200	48-20
BGD Cos Inc 275 Market St Suite 192	Minneapolis	MN	55405	**800-699-3537**	612-338-6804	314-1
BGE Home Products & Services Inc 7161 Columbia Gateway	Columbia	MD	21046	**888-243-4663**	410-720-6619	359
BGF Industries Inc 3802 Robert Porcher Way	Greensboro	NC	27410	**800-476-4845**	336-545-0011	730-3
BGS & G Cos 44 Baltimore St *Cust Svc	Cumberland	MD	21502	**800-684-2474***	301-784-2410	383
BH Thermal Corp 1055 Gibbard Ave	Columbus	OH	43201	**800-848-7673**	614-294-3376	313
BHA Group Inc 8800 E 63rd St	Kansas City	MO	64133	**800-821-2222**	816-356-8400	19
BHI (Better Hearing Institute) 515 King St Suite 420	Alexandria	VA	22314	**888-432-7435**	703-684-3391	48-17
BHN Corp 435 Madison Ave	Memphis	TN	38103	**800-238-9046**	901-521-9500	188-9
Bi-County Community Hospital 13355 E Ten-Mile Rd	Warren	MI	48089	**800-423-1948**	586-759-7300	366-2
BI Inc 6400 Lookout Rd	Boulder	CO	80301	**800-241-2911**	303-218-1000	681
Biamp Systems Inc 10074 SW Arctic Dr	Beaverton	OR	97005	**800-826-1457**	503-641-7287	52
Biathlon Assn. US 29 Ethan Allen Ave	Colchester	VT	05446	**800-242-8456**	802-654-7833	48-22
Bible Broadcasting Network Inc 11530 Carmel Commons Blvd	Charlotte	NC	28226	**800-888-7077**	704-523-5555	629

Alphabetical Section

Name / Address	City	State	Zip	Toll-Free	Phone	Class
Bible League PO Box 28000	Chicago	IL	60628	**866-825-4636**	708-367-8500	48-20
Bible Society. American 1865 Broadway	New York	NY	10023	**800-322-4253**	212-408-1200	623-4
Bible Society. International 1820 Jet Stream Dr *Cust Svc	Colorado Springs	CO	80921	**800-524-1588***	719-488-9200	48-20
Bible Translators. Wycliffe PO Box 628200	Orlando	FL	32862	**800-992-5433**	407-852-3611	48-20
Biblical Archaeology Review 4710 41st St NW	Washington	DC	20016	**800-221-4644**	202-364-3300	449-18
Biblical Theological Seminary 200 N Main St	Hatfield	PA	19440	**800-235-4021**	215-368-5000	164-3
BIC Corp 500 BIC Dr	Milford	CT	06460	**800-546-1111**	203-783-2000	560
Bickel's Snack Foods 1120 Zinns Quarry Rd	York	PA	17404	**800-233-1933**	717-843-0738	291-35
Bickford's Family Restaurants Inc 1330 Soldiers Field Rd	Boston	MA	02135	**800-969-5653**	617-782-4010	657
Bick's Supermarkets 1540 Vision Dr	Platteville	WI	53818	**800-793-8089**	608-348-2343	339
Bicron 12345 Kinsman Rd	Newbury	OH	44065	**800-472-5656**	440-564-2251	464
Bicycle Assn. American 1645 W Sunrise Blvd	Gilbert	AZ	85233	**800-886-1269**	480-961-1903	48-22
Bicycle Casino 7301 Eastern Ave	Bell Gardens	CA	90201	**800-292-0015**	562-806-4646	133
Bicycling Assn. International Mountain 207 Canyon Blvd Suite 301 PO Box 7578	Boulder	CO	80306	**888-442-4622**	303-545-9011	48-23
Bicycling Magazine 33 E Minor St *Cust Svc	Emmaus	PA	18098	**800-666-2806***	610-967-5171	449-14
Bid-Well Corp PO Box 97	Canton	SD	57013	**800-843-9824**	605-987-2603	189
Biddeford-Saco-OOB Courier PO Box 1894	Biddeford	ME	04005	**800-617-3984**	207-282-4337	522-4
Biddle Precision Components Inc 701 S Main St	Sheridan	IN	46069	**800-428-4387**	317-758-4451	610
BidWay.com Inc 401 N Brand Blvd Suite 540	Glendale	CA	91203	**877-424-3229**	818-956-2040	51
Bidwell Industrial Group Inc 2055 S Main St	Middletown	CT	06457	**800-235-0999**	860-346-9283	112
Bieber Carl R Tourways Inc 320 Fair St	Kutztown	PA	19530	**800-243-2374**	610-683-7333	108
Bieber Lighting Corp 970 W Manchester Blvd	Inglewood	CA	90301	**800-243-2375**	310-645-6789	431
Bienville House Hotel 320 Decatur St	New Orleans	LA	70130	**800-535-7836**	504-529-2345	373
Bierlein Cos Inc 2000 Bay City Rd	Midland	MI	48642	**800-336-6626**	989-496-0066	188-17
Biesanz Stone Co Inc 4600 Goodview Rd	Winona	MN	55987	**800-247-8322**	507-454-4336	710
Biesemeyer Mfg Corp 216 S Alma School Rd Suite 1	Mesa	AZ	85210	**800-782-1831**	480-835-9300	809
Big 5 Sporting Goods Corp 2525 E El Segundo Blvd *NASDAQ: BGFV*	El Segundo	CA	90245	**800-367-2445**	310-536-0611	702
Big Apple Bagels 500 Lake Cook Rd Suite 475	Deerfield	IL	60015	**800-251-6101**	847-948-7520	69
Big Apple Circus 505 8th Ave 19th Fl	New York	NY	10018	**800-922-3772**	212-268-2500	147
Big Bad Inc 321 Summer St	Boston	MA	02210	**877-296-4287**	617-338-7770	7
Big Bowl 6820 LBJ Fwy	Dallas	TX	75240	**800-983-4637**	972-980-9917	657
Big Boy Restaurants International LLC 4199 Marcy St	Warren	MI	48091	**800-837-3003**	586-759-6000	656
Big Country Electric Co-op 1010 W South 1st St	Roby	TX	79543	**888-662-2232**	325-776-2244	244
Big-D Construction Corp 404 W 400 South Suite 550	Salt Lake City	UT	84101	**877-415-6009**	801-415-6000	187-7
Big Daddy's South Boston Speedway 1188 James D Hagood Hwy PO Box 1066	South Boston	VA	24592	**877-440-1540**	434-572-4947	504
Big Dog Holdings Inc 121 Gray Ave *NASDAQ: BDOG* ■ *Sales	Santa Barbara	CA	93101	**800-244-3647***	805-963-8727	153-3
Big Dog Sportswear 121 Gray Ave *Orders	Santa Barbara	CA	93101	**800-642-3647***	805-963-8727	153-3
Big Easy/Gulf Coast Reservation Service 233 Cottonwood Dr	Gretna	LA	70056	**800-368-4876**	504-433-2563	368
Big EZ Lodge PO Box 160070 7000 Beaver Creek Rd	Big Sky	MT	59716	**877-244-3299**	406-995-7000	370
Big Five Tours & Expeditions 1551 SE Palm Ct	Stuart	FL	34994	**800-244-3483**	772-287-7995	748
Big Flat Electric Co-op Inc 333 S 7th St E	Malta	MT	59538	**800-242-2040**	406-654-2040	244
Big G Cereals PO Box 9452	Minneapolis	MN	55440	**800-328-1144**	763-764-7600	291-4
Big Horn Rural Electric Co-op 208 S 5th St	Basin	WY	82410	**800-564-2419**	307-568-2419	244
Big House Products & Services PO Box 47	Camp Hill	PA	17001	**877-673-3724**	717-731-7132	618
Big Lots Inc 300 Phillipi Rd *NYSE: BLI*	Columbus	OH	43228	**800-877-1253**	614-278-6800	778
Big O Tires Inc 12650 E Briarwood Ave Suite 2D	Englewood	CO	80112	**800-321-2446**	303-728-5500	62-5
Big Red/Seven Up Bottling of South Texas 4518 Seguin Rd	San Antonio	TX	78219	**800-580-7333**	210-661-4271	81-2
Big River Industries Inc PO Box 66377	Baton Rouge	LA	70896	**800-969-5634**	225-627-4242	490
Big River Zinc Corp 2401 Mississippi Ave	Sauget	IL	62201	**800-274-4002**	618-274-5000	476
Big Sandy Community & Technical College 1 Bert T Combs Dr	Prestonsburg	KY	41653	**888-641-4132**	606-886-3863	160
Big Sky Airlines 1601 Aviation Pl	Billings	MT	59105	**800-237-7788**	406-247-3910	26
Big Sky Distributors Inc 14220 Wyandotte St	Kansas City	MO	64145	**800-926-4233**	816-941-3300	82-1
Big Sky Laser Technologies Inc 601 Haggerty Ln	Bozeman	MT	59715	**800-224-4759**	406-586-0131	416
Big Sky Resort 1 Lone Mountain Trail	Big Sky	MT	59716	**800-548-4486**	406-995-5000	655
Big Sky Technologies 9325 Sky Park Ct Suite 120	San Diego	CA	92123	**800-736-2751**	858-715-5000	176-7
Big Spring Convention & Visitor Bureau PO Box 1391	Big Spring	TX	79721	**800-734-7641**	432-263-7641	205
Big Stone Co-op PO Box 362	Clinton	MN	56225	**800-325-1132**	320-325-5466	311
Big Texan Motel 7701 I-40 E	Amarillo	TX	79118	**800-657-7177**	806-372-5000	373
Big Y Foods Inc 2145 Roosevelt Ave *Cust Svc	Springfield	MA	01102	**800-828-2688***	413-784-0600	339
Bigbend Hospice 1723 Mahan Ctr Blvd	Tallahassee	FL	32308	**800-772-5862**	850-878-5310	365
Bigelow Commercial Div Mohawk Industries Inc 160 S Industrial Blvd *Cust Svc	Calhoun	GA	30703	**800-233-4490***	706-629-7721	131
Bigfoot Adventure Tours Inc 360 Edworthy Way Suite 104	New Westminster	BC	V3L5T8	**888-244-6673**	604-278-8224	748
Bigge Crane & Rigging Co Inc 10700 Bigge St PO Box 1657	San Leandro	CA	94577	**888-337-2444**	510-638-8100	188-1
Bigstep 2601 Mission St Suite 500	San Francisco	CA	94110	**866-499-2799**		796
Bijan Boutique 420 N Rodeo Dr	Beverly Hills	CA	90210	**800-992-4526**	310-273-6544	564
Bike Athletic Co 3303 Cumberland Blvd	Atlanta	GA	30339	**800-251-9230**	678-742-8255	153-1
Bil-Jax Inc 125 Taylor Pkwy	Archbold	OH	43502	**800-537-0540**	419-445-8915	482
Bilkays Express Co 400 S 2nd St	Elizabeth	NJ	07206	**800-526-4006**	908-289-2400	769
Bill Doran Co Inc 619 W Jefferson St	Rockford	IL	61103	**800-822-8815**	815-965-6042	288
Bill Heard Enterprises 200 Brookstone Ctr Pkwy Suite 205	Columbus	GA	31904	**800-833-0479**	706-323-1111	57
Bill & Melinda Gates Foundation PO Box 23350	Seattle	WA	98102	**888-452-6352**	206-709-3100	300
Bill Miller Bar-B-Q 430 S Santa Rosa St	San Antonio	TX	78207	**800-339-3111**	210-225-4461	657
Billboard Magazine 770 Broadway *Cust Svc	New York	NY	10003	**800-437-3183***	646-654-5500	449-9
Billings Area Chamber of Commerce 815 S 27th St	Billings	MT	59101	**800-735-2635**	406-245-4111	137
Billings Convention & Visitors Bureau PO Box 31177	Billings	MT	59107	**800-735-2635**	406-245-4111	205
Billings Freight Systems Inc PO Box 2000	Lexington	NC	27293	**800-438-2151**	336-956-1111	769
Billings Gazette 401 N Broadway	Billings	MT	59107	**800-543-2505**	406-657-1200	522-2
Billings Hotel & Convention Center 1223 Mullowney Ln	Billings	MT	59101	**800-537-7286**	406-248-7151	373
Billings Inn 880 N 29th St	Billings	MT	59101	**800-231-7782**	406-252-6800	373
Billy Graham Evangelistic Assn 1 Billy Graham Pkwy PO Box 1270	Charlotte	NC	28201	**877-247-2426**	704-401-2432	48-20
Biloxi Beach Resort Inn 2736 Beach Blvd	Biloxi	MS	39531	**800-345-1570**	228-388-3310	373
Biltmore Estate 1 Approach Rd *Resv	Asheville	NC	28803	**800-858-4130***	828-225-1333	50
Biltmore Greensboro Hotel 111 W Washington St	Greensboro	NC	27401	**800-332-0303**	336-272-3474	373
Biltmore Hotel & Conference Center of the Americas 1200 Anastasia Ave	Coral Gables	FL	33134	**800-727-1926**	305-445-1926	655
Biltmore Hotel Los Angeles. Millennium 506 S Grand Ave	Los Angeles	CA	90071	**800-245-8673**	213-624-1011	373
Biltmore Hotel Oklahoma 401 S Meridian Ave	Oklahoma City	OK	73108	**800-522-6620**	405-947-7681	373
Biltmore Hotel & Suites 2151 Laurelwood Rd	Santa Clara	CA	95054	**800-255-9925**	408-988-8411	373
Biltmore House One N Pack Sq	Asheville	NC	28801	**800-543-1895**	828-225-6300	509
Biltmore Resort & Spa. Arizona 2400 E Missouri Ave	Phoenix	AZ	85016	**800-950-0086**	602-955-6600	655
Biltmore Resort & Spa. Belleview 25 Belleview Blvd	Clearwater	FL	33756	**800-237-8947**	727-442-6171	655
Biltmore Suites 205 W Madison St	Baltimore	MD	21201	**800-868-5064**	410-728-6550	373
Biltrite Corp 51 Sawyer Rd	Waltham	MA	02454	**800-245-8748**	781-647-1700	663
Bimba Mfg Co PO Box 68	Monee	IL	60449	**800-442-4622**	708-534-8544	220
Binax Inc 217 Read St	Portland	ME	04103	**800-323-3199**	207-772-3988	229
Bind-It Corp 150 Commerce Dr	Hauppauge	NY	11788	**800-645-5110**	631-234-2500	112
Bindagraphics Inc 2701 Wilmarco Ave	Baltimore	MD	21223	**800-326-0300**	410-362-7200	93
BindView Development Corp 5151 San Felipe 22nd Fl *NASDAQ: BVEW*	Houston	TX	77056	**800-813-5869**	713-561-4000	176-12
Bing Metals Group Steel Processing Div 1500 E Euclid	Detroit	MI	48211	**800-521-1564**	313-875-2022	483
Bingham Co 12827 E Imperial Hwy *Sales	Santa Fe Springs	CA	90670	**800-635-9490***	562-903-3006	617
Binion's Horseshoe Hotel & Casino 128 E Fremont St	Las Vegas	NV	89101	**800-237-6537**	702-382-1600	133
Binkley & Ober Inc PO Box 7	East Petersburg	PA	17520	**800-860-0441**	717-569-0441	181
Binney & Smith Inc 1100 Church Ln	Easton	PA	18044	**800-272-9652**	610-253-6271	43
Binswanger Glass 965 Ridge Lake Blvd Suite 300	Memphis	TN	38120	**800-238-6057**	901-767-7111	325
Binswanger Mirror PO Box 1400	Grenada	MS	38902	**800-221-8408**	662-226-5551	325
Bio-Botanica Inc 75 Commerce Dr	Hauppauge	NY	11788	**800-645-5720**	631-231-5522	470
Bio Cleaning Specialists Inc PO Box 18622	Minneapolis	MN	55418	**888-283-8898**	651-765-2429	84
Bio-Imaging Technologies Inc 826 Newtown-Yardley Rd Suite 101 *NASDAQ: BITI*	Newtown	PA	18940	**800-748-9032**	267-757-3000	375
Bio-Lab Inc 1735 N Brown Rd	Lawrenceville	GA	30043	**800-859-7946**	404-378-1753	141
Bio-logic Systems Corp 1 Bio-logic Plaza *NASDAQ: BLSC* ■ *Cust Svc	Mundelein	IL	60060	**800-323-8326***	847-949-5200	249
Bio Medic Data Systems Inc 1 Silas Rd	Seaford	DE	19973	**800-526-2637**	302-628-4100	85
Bio Online Inc 1900 Powell St Suite 230	Emeryville	CA	94608	**800-246-3010**	510-601-7194	677
Bio-Recovery Assn. American 2020 Pennsylvania Ave NW Suite 456	Washington	DC	20006	**888-979-2217**	888-979-2272	49-4
Bio-Recovery Corp 51-49 47th St	Woodside	NY	11377	**877-246-2532**	718-729-2600	84
Bio-Recovery Services of America LLC 552 Danberry St	Toledo	OH	43609	**800-699-6522**	419-381-8255	84
Bio-Reference Laboratories Inc 481 Edward H Ross Dr *NASDAQ: BRLI*	Elmwood Park	NJ	07407	**800-229-5227**	201-791-2600	407

Toll-Free | Phone | Class

Bio-Scene Recovery Inc 13191 Meadow St NE Suite A, Alliance OH 44601 **877-380-5500** 330-823-5500 84
Bio-Serv 1 8th St Suite 1, Frenchtown NJ 08825 **800-996-9908** 908-996-2155 574
Bio-Tissue 7000 SW 97th Ave Suite 211, Miami FL 33173 **888-296-8858** 305-412-4430 535
Bioanalytical Systems Inc 2701 Kent Ave, West Lafayette IN 47906 **800-845-4246** 765-463-4527 410
NASDAQ: BASI
Bioanalytical Systems Inc Clinical Research Unit 302 W Fayette St, Baltimore MD 21201 **800-787-7800** 410-385-4500 728
Biocare Inc PO Box 817, Easley SC 29641 **800-875-9396** 864-855-3400 84
Biocine Div Chiron Corp 4560 Horton St, Emeryville CA 94608 **800-524-4766** 510-655-8730 86
BioClean Inc PO Box 3062, Arlington WA 98223 **888-412-6300** 360-435-8170 84
BioCore Medical Technologies Inc 11800 Tech Rd Suite 240, Silver Spring MD 20904 **888-689-5655** 301-625-6818 469
Biodesign International 60 Industrial Pk Rd, Saco ME 04072 **888-530-0140** 207-283-6500 229
Bioethics Center. Midwest 1100 Walnut St Suite 2900, Kansas City MO 64106 **800-344-3829** 816-221-1100 48-17
Biofeedback. Association for Applied Psychophysiology & 10200 W 44th Ave Suite 304, Wheat Ridge CO 80033 **800-477-8892** 303-422-8436 49-8
Biofit Engineered Products 15500 Biofit Way, Bowling Greene OH 43402 **800-597-0246** 419-823-1089 314-1
Biogen Idec Inc 14 Cambridge Ctr, Cambridge MA 02142 **800-262-4363** 617-679-2000 86
NASDAQ: BIIB
BioGenex Laboratories Inc 4600 Norris Canyon Rd, San Ramon CA 94583 **800-421-4149** 925-275-0550 229
BioHorizons Implant Systems Inc One Perimeter Pk S Suite 230 S, Birmingham AL 35243 **888-246-8338** 205-967-7880 469
Bioject Medical Technologies Inc 20245 SW 95 Ave, Tualatin OR 97062 **800-683-7221** 503-692-8001 468
NASDAQ: BJCT
Biola University 13800 Biola Ave, La Mirada CA 90639 **800-652-4652*** 562-903-6000 163
*Admissions
BioLase Technology Inc 981 Calle Amanecer, San Clemente CA 92673 **800-699-9462** 949-361-1200 415
NASDAQ: BLTI
BioLink Technologies International Inc 599 Lexington Ave 38th Fl, New York NY 10022 **866-994-3843** 212-572-6344 85
Biological Sciences. American Institute of 1444 'I' St NW Suite 200, Washington DC 20005 **800-992-2427** 202-628-1500 49-19
Biology. Federation of American Societies for Experimental 9650 Rockville Pike, Bethesda MD 20814 **800-433-2732** 301-530-7000 49-19
Biology Teachers. National Assn of 12030 Sunrise Valley Dr Suite 110, Reston VA 20191 **800-406-0775** 703-264-9696 49-5
Biomarine Inc 456 Creamery Way, Exton PA 19341 **800-378-2287** 610-524-8800 566
Biomeda Corp 1851 Vanderbilt Rd, Texarkana AR 71854 **800-341-8787** 870-779-8787 229
Biomerica Inc 1533 Monrovia Ave, Newport Beach CA 92663 **800-854-3002*** 949-645-2111 229
*Cust Svc
BioMerieux Inc 595 Anglum Rd, Hazelwood MO 63042 **800-638-4835** 314-731-8500 468
Biomet Inc 56 E Bell Dr, Warsaw IN 46582 **800-348-9500** 574-267-6639 469
NASDAQ: BMET
Biometric Access Corp 2555 IH-35 Suite 200, Round Rock TX 78664 **800-873-4133** 512-246-3760 85
Biomira Inc 2011 94th St, Edmonton AB T6N1H1 **877-234-0444** 780-450-3761 86
NASDAQ: BIOM
Biomune Inc 8906 Rosehill Rd, Lenexa KS 66215 **800-846-0230** 913-894-0230 574
Bionetics Corp 11833 Cannon Blvd Suite 100, Newport News VA 23606 **800-868-0330** 757-873-0900 258
Bionetics Corp Ketron Div 44425 Pecan Ct Suite 200, California MD 20619 **800-922-3278** 301-862-3092 176-5
Bioniche Animal Health Canada Inc 231 Dundas St E, Belleville ON K8N1E2 **800-265-5464** 613-966-8058 574
Bioniche Life Sciences Inc PO Box 1570, Belleville ON N8N5J2 **800-265-5464** 613-966-8058 86
TSE: BNC
Bionutrics Inc 2415 E Cambelback Rd Suite 700, Phoenix AZ 85016 **800-508-7432** 602-508-0112 86
Bioproducts Inc 320 Springside Dr Suite 300, Fairlawn OH 44333 **800-722-7242** 330-665-1999 438
Biopure Corp 11 Hurley St, Cambridge MA 02141 **888-337-0929*** 617-234-6500 86
NASDAQ: BPUR ■ *Cust Svc
BioReliance Corp 14920 Broschart Rd, Rockville MD 20850 **800-553-5372** 301-738-1000 86
Bioscan Inc 4590 MacArthur Blvd NW, Washington DC 20007 **800-255-7226** 202-338-0974 375
BioScience 1444 'I' St NW Suite 200, Washington DC 20005 **800-992-2427** 202-628-1500 449-19
BioScrip Inc 100 Clearbrook Rd, Elmsford NY 10523 **888-818-3939** 914-460-1600 575
NASDAQ: BIOS
Bioscrypt Inc 5450 Explorer Dr Suite 500, Mississauga ON L4W5M1 **800-845-0096** 905-624-7700 85
TSE: BYT
Biosense Webster Inc 3333 Diamond Canyon Rd, Diamond Bar CA 91765 **800-729-9010** 909-839-8500 468
Biosite Inc 11030 Roselle St, San Diego CA 92121 **888-246-7483*** 858-455-4808 229
NASDAQ: BSTE ■ *Cust Svc
BioSource International Inc 542 Flynn Rd, Camarillo CA 93012 **800-242-0607** 805-987-0086 229
NASDAQ: BIOI
BioSpace Inc 564 Market St, San Francisco CA 94104 **888-246-7722** 239-659-0100 677
BiosPacific Inc 5980 Horton St Suite 225, Emeryville CA 94608 **800-344-6686** 510-652-6155 229
BioSphere Medical Inc 1050 Hingham St, Rockland MA 02370 **800-394-0295** 781-681-7900 86
NASDAQ: BSMD
Biotechnology Software Newsletter 140 Huguenot St 3rd Fl, New Rochelle NY 10801 **800-654-3237** 914-740-2100 521-3
Biotest Diagnostics Corp 66 Ford Rd Suite 220, Denville NJ 07834 **800-522-0090** 973-625-1300 229
Biovet Inc 2900 ave Beaudry, Saint-Hyacinthe QC J2S8W2 **888-824-6838** 450-771-7291 574
Biovet USA Inc 3055 Old Hwy 8 Suite 100, Saint Anthony MN 55418 **877-824-6838** 612-781-2952 574

BioZyme Inc 6010 Stockyards Expy, Saint Joseph MO 64504 **800-821-3070** 816-238-3326 438
Bipolar Support Alliance. Depression & 730 N Franklin St Suite 501, Chicago IL 60610 **800-826-3632** 312-642-0049 48-17
Birch Telecom Inc 2300 Main St Suite 600, Kansas City MO 64108 **888-422-4724** 816-300-3000 721
Birchcraft Studios Inc 10 Railroad St, Abington MA 02351 **800-333-0405** 781-878-5152 130
Birchcraft Studios Inc PO Box 328, Rockland MA 02370 **800-333-0405** 781-878-5151 130
Birchwood Laboratories Inc 7900 Fuller Rd, Eden Prairie MN 55344 **800-328-6156** 952-937-7900 143
Bird Breeder Magazine 3 Burroughs, Irvine CA 92618 **800-365-4421*** 949-855-8822 449-14
*Cust Svc
Bird Electronic Corp 30303 Aurora Rd, Solon OH 44139 **866-695-4569** 440-248-1200 247
Bird Precision PO Box 540569, Waltham MA 02454 **800-454-7369*** 781-894-0160 609
*Cust Svc
Bird Studies Canada PO Box 160, Port Rowan ON N0E1M0 **888-448-2473** 519-586-3531 48-3
Bird Talk Magazine 3 Burroughs, Irvine CA 92618 **800-365-4421*** 949-855-8822 449-14
*Cust Svc
Birdair Inc 65 Lawrence Bell Dr, Amherst NY 14221 **800-622-2246** 716-633-9500 188-12
Birds Eye Foods Inc 90 Linden Oaks, Rochester NY 14625 **800-999-5044** 585-383-1850 291-21
Birdwell Co 3708 Greenhouse Rd, Houston TX 77084 **800-237-2095** 281-492-1786 15
Birkenstock Footprint Sandals Inc 8171 Redwood Blvd, Novato CA 94945 **800-487-9255** 415-892-4200 296
Birmingham Civil Rights Institute 520 16th St N, Birmingham AL 35203 **866-328-9696** 205-328-9696 509
Birmingham Electric Battery Co 2230 2nd Ave S, Birmingham AL 35233 **800-446-0919** 205-458-0581 61
Birmingham (Greater) Convention & Visitors Bureau 2200 9th Ave N, Birmingham AL 35203 **800-458-8085** 205-458-8000 205
Birmingham International Forest Products LLC 1800 International Park Dr Suite 200, Birmingham AL 35243 **800-767-2437** 205-972-1500 190-3
Birmingham-Jefferson Convention Complex 2100 Richard Arrington Jr Blvd, Birmingham AL 35203 **877-843-2522** 205-458-8400 204
Birmingham News 2200 4th Ave N, Birmingham AL 35203 **800-283-4015** 205-325-2222 522-2
Birmingham Post-Herald 2200 4th Ave N, Birmingham AL 35203 **800-283-4255** 205-325-2343 522-2
Birmingham Rail & Locomotive Co Inc PO Box 530157, Birmingham AL 35253 **800-241-2260** 205-424-7245 759
Birmingham-Southern College 900 Arkadelphia Rd, Birmingham AL 35254 **800-523-5793** 205-226-4600 163
Birmingham Vending Co 540 2nd Ave N, Birmingham AL 35204 **800-288-7635** 205-324-7526 55
Birmingham Zoo 2630 Cahaba Rd, Birmingham AL 35223 **888-966-2426** 205-879-0409 811
Birthday Express 11220 120th Ave NE, Kirkland WA 98033 **800-424-7843** 425-250-1064 555
NASDAQ: BDAY
Birthparents Inc. Concerned United PO Box 230457, Encinitas CA 92023 **800-822-2777** 48-21
Biscayne Rod Manufacturing Inc 425 E 9th St, Hialeah FL 33010 **888-866-7637** 305-884-0808 701
Biscom Inc 321 Billerica Rd, Chelmsford MA 01824 **800-477-2472** 978-250-1800 496
Bishop Distributing Co 5200 36th St SE, Grand Rapids MI 49512 **800-748-0363*** 616-942-9734 356
*Cust Svc
Bishop-Wisecarver Corp 2104 Martin Way, Pittsburg CA 94565 **888-580-8272** 925-439-8272 609
Bishop's Buffet 1520 Midland Ct NE Suite 300, Cedar Rapids IA 52402 **866-393-4766** 319-393-4766 657
Bishop's Lodge Resort & Spa 1297 Bishop's Lodge Rd PO Box 2367, Santa Fe NM 87501 **800-732-2240** 505-983-6377 655
Bishops Services Inc 20283 SR 7 Suite 400, Boca Raton FL 33498 **800-373-5294** 561-237-4242 392
Bishop's University rue College, Lennoxville QC J1M1Z7 **800-567-2792** 819-822-9600 773
Bismarck-Mandan Convention & Visitors Bureau 1600 Burnt Boat Dr, Bismarck ND 58503 **800-767-3555** 701-222-4308 205
Bismarck Municipal Airport (BIS) Bismarck ND 58502 **800-453-4244** 701-222-6502 28
Bismarck State College 1500 Edwards Ave, Bismarck ND 58501 **800-445-5073** 701-224-5400 160
Bismarck Tribune 707 E Front Ave, Bismarck ND 58506 **866-476-5348** 701-223-2500 522-2
Bison Gear & Engineering Corp 3850 Ohio Ave, Saint Charles IL 60174 **800-282-4766** 630-377-4327 700
Bison Inc 603 L St, Lincoln NE 68508 **800-247-7668** 402-474-3353 701
Bison Products Co Inc PO Box 87, Buffalo NY 14240 **800-248-2705** 716-826-2700 291-26
Bissman Co Inc 30 W 5th St, Mansfield OH 44901 **800-321-2337*** 419-524-2337 82-1
*Cust Svc
Bisson Moving & Storage 76 New Meadows Rd, West Bath ME 04530 **800-370-4011** 207-442-7991 508
BISYS Education Services 1100 Circle 75 Pkwy Suite 1300, Atlanta GA 30339 **800-241-9095** 770-659-6000 243
BISYS Fund Services 3435 Stelzer Rd Suite 1000, Columbus OH 43219 **800-852-0045** 614-470-8000 679
Bite Communications 345 Spear St Suite 750, San Francisco CA 94105 **888-329-7059** 415-365-0222 622
Bitstream Inc 245 1st St, Cambridge MA 02142 **800-522-3668** 617-497-6222 176-8
NASDAQ: BITS
BIW Cable Systems Inc 22 Joseph E Warner Blvd, North Dighton MA 02764 **800-333-4248** 508-822-5444 800
BIW Ltd 230 Beaver St, Ansonia CT 06401 **800-481-0141** 203-735-1888 774
AMEX: BIW
Bix Beiderbecke Memorial Society PO Box 3688, Davenport IA 52808 **888-249-5487** 563-324-7170 48-4
Bix Produce Co 1415 L'Orient St, Saint Paul MN 55117 **800-642-9514** 651-487-8000 292-7
Bixby International Corp 1 Preble Rd, Newburyport MA 01950 **800-466-4102** 978-462-4100 589
Bizamo Music 12524 W Atlantic Blvd, Coral Springs FL 33071 **888-924-9266** 515
BizLand Inc 70 Blanchard Rd, Burlington MA 01803 **866-599-9964** 781-272-5585 39
Bizzack Inc 2265 Executive Dr, Lexington KY 40505 **800-599-0424** 859-299-8001 187-4
BJ Services Co 5500 NW Central Dr, Houston TX 77092 **800-234-6487** 713-462-4239 528
NYSE: BJS
BJJ Co Inc PO Box 30010, Stockton CA 95213 **800-776-2551** 209-941-8361 769
BJ's Restaurants Inc 16162 Beach Blvd Suite 100, Huntington Beach CA 92647 **800-223-1255** 714-848-3747 657
NASDAQ: BJRI

Name / Address	City	State	Zip	Toll-Free	Phone	Class
BJ's Wholesale Club 1 Mercer Rd *NYSE: BJ*	Natick	MA	01760	**800-257-2582**	508-651-7400	799
BK Barrit Corp 1850 E Sedgley Ave	Philadelphia	PA	19124	**888-256-2020**	215-533-3900	314-1
BK Miller Co Inc 4501 B Auth Place	Suitland	MD	20746	**800-801-7632**	301-423-6200	435
BKF Capital Group Inc 1 Rockefeller Plaza 19th Fl *NYSE: BKF*	New York	NY	10020	**800-253-1891**	212-332-8400	397
BKR International 19 Fulton St Suite 306	New York	NY	10038	**800-257-4685**	212-964-2115	49-1
Blach Distributing Co 131 Main St	Elko	NV	89801	**888-812-5224**	775-738-7111	82-1
Blachford Corp 401 Center Rd	Frankfort	IL	60423	**800-435-5942**	815-464-2100	530
Blachly-Lane Electric Co-op 90680 Hwy 99	Eugene	OR	97402	**800-446-8418**	541-688-8711	244
Black America's Political Action Committee 2029 P St NW Suite 202	Washington	DC	20036	**877-722-6722**	202-785-9619	604
Black Angus Inn 1430 Gambell St	Anchorage	AK	99501	**800-770-0707**	907-272-7503	373
Black Bear Casino 1785 Hwy 210 PO Box 777	Carlton	MN	55718	**888-771-0777**	218-878-2327	133
Black Box Corp 1000 Park Dr *NASDAQ: BBOX*	Lawrence	PA	15055	**877-877-2269**	724-746-5500	174
Black Butte Ranch 12930 Hawks Beard Rd	Black Butte Ranch	OR	97759	**800-452-7455**	541-595-6211	655
Black Classic Press PO Box 13414	Baltimore	MD	21203	**800-476-8870**	410-358-0980	623-2
Black Cultural Centre for Nova Scotia 1149 Main St	Dartmouth	NS	B2Z1A8	**800-465-0767**	902-434-6223	509
Black Data Processing Associates (BDPA) 6301 Ivy Ln Suite 700	Greenbelt	MD	20770	**800-727-2372**	301-220-2180	48-9
Black Enterprise Magazine 130 5th Ave	New York	NY	10011	**800-727-7777**	212-242-8000	449-5
Black Expressions Doubleday Direct Inc 1225 S Market St	Mechanicsburg	PA	17055	**800-688-4442**		94
Black Hawk College						
East Campus 1501 Illinois Hwy 78	Kewanee	IL	61443	**800-233-5671**	309-852-5671	160
Quad Cities Campus 6600 34th Ave	Moline	IL	61265	**800-334-1311**	309-796-5000	160
Black Hills Bentonite Co 55 Saltcreek Hwy *Orders	Casper	WY	82601	**800-788-9443***	307-265-3740	493-2
Black Hills Caverns 2600 Cavern Rd	Rapid City	SD	57702	**800-837-9358**	605-343-0542	50
Black Hills Corp 625 9th St *NYSE: BKH*	Rapid City	SD	57701	**800-843-8849**	605-721-1700	355-5
Black Hills Electric Co-op Inc 25197 Cooperative Way	Custer	SD	57730	**800-742-0085**	605-673-4461	244
Black Hills Health & Education Center Box 19	Hermosa	SD	57744	**800-658-5433**	605-255-4101	697
Black Hills Jewelry Mfg Co DBA Landstroms Blackhills Gold Creations 405 Canal St	Rapid City	SD	57701	**800-843-0009**	605-343-0157	401
Black Hills Pioneer 315 Seaton Cir	Spearfish	SD	57783	**800-676-2761**	605-642-2761	522-2
Black Hills State University 1200 University St	Spearfish	SD	57799	**800-255-2478**	605-642-6011	163
Black Hills Trucking Inc PO Drawer 2360	Casper	WY	82602	**800-253-8080**	307-237-9301	769
Black Knight USA 5355 Sierra Rd	San Jose	CA	95132	**800-535-3300**	408-923-7777	701
Black Millwork Co Inc 230 W Crescent Ave	Allendale	NJ	07401	**800-864-2356**	201-934-0100	489
Black Mountain Ranch PO Box 219	McCoy	CO	80463	**800-967-2401**	970-653-4226	238
Black Mountain-Swannanoa Chamber of Commerce 201 E State St	Black Mountain	NC	28711	**800-669-2301**	828-669-2300	137
Black Photo Corp 371 Gough Rd	Markham	ON	L3R4B6	**800-668-3826**	905-475-2777	119
Black Point Inn Resort 510 Black Point Rd	Scarborough	ME	04074	**800-258-0003**	207-883-2500	655
Black River Electric Co-op 2600 Hwy 67	Fredericktown	MO	63645	**800-392-4711**	573-783-3381	244
Black Romance Magazine 333 7th Ave 11th Fl	New York	NY	10001	**888-668-8783**	212-979-4800	449-11
Blackbaud Inc 2000 Daniel Island Dr *NASDAQ: BLKB* ■ *Cust Svc	Charleston	SC	29492	**800-468-8996***	843-216-6200	176-1
Blackbeard Cruises PO Box 661091	Miami	FL	33266	**800-327-9600**	305-888-1226	217
BlackBerry 295 Phillip St	Waterloo	ON	N2L3W8	**877-255-2377**	519-888-7465	222
Blackberry Farm 1471 W Millers Cove Rd	Walland	TN	37886	**800-273-6004**	865-380-2260	655
Blackboard Inc 1899 L St NW 5th Fl *NASDAQ: BBBB*	Washington	DC	20036	**800-424-9299**	202-463-4860	176-3
Blackbourn Media Packaging Div Fey Industries 200 4th Ave N	Edgerton	MN	56128	**800-842-7550**		87
Blackburn College 700 College Ave	Carlinville	IL	62626	**800-233-3550**	217-854-3231	163
Blackburn Don & Co Inc 13335 Farmington Rd	Livonia	MI	48150	**800-448-0528**	734-261-9100	245
Blackfeet Community College PO Box 819	Browning	MT	59417	**800-549-7457**	406-338-5421	161
Blackfoot Inn 5940 Blackfoot Trail SE	Calgary	AB	T2H2B5	**800-661-1151**	403-252-2253	372
Blackhawk Foundry & Machine Co 323 S Clark St	Davenport	IA	52802	**800-325-4766**	563-323-3621	302
Blackman Uhler LLC 2155 W Croft Cir	Spartanburg	SC	29302	**800-832-8985**	864-585-3661	142
BlackRock Funds 40 E 52nd St	New York	NY	10022	**888-825-2257**	212-754-5300	517
Blackstone Industries Inc 16 Stoney Hill Rd	Bethel	CT	06801	**800-441-0625**	203-792-8622	747
Blackstone Valley Chamber of Commerce 110 Church St	Whitinsville	MA	01588	**800-841-0919**	508-234-9090	137
Blackvoices.com Inc 435 N Michigan Ave Suite L2	Chicago	IL	60611	**877-765-1350**	312-222-4326	169
Blackwell North America Inc 6024 SW Jean Rd Bldg G	Lake Oswego	OR	97035	**800-547-6426**	503-684-1140	97
Blackwell Publishers Inc 350 Main St	Malden	MA	02148	**800-835-6770**	781-388-8250	623-2
Blackwell Publishing Professional 2121 S State Ave	Ames	IA	50014	**800-862-6657**	515-292-0140	623-2
Blackwell Sanders Peper Martin LLP 4801 Main St Suite 1000	Kansas City	MO	64112	**800-437-7309**	816-983-8000	419
Blackwell's Information Services 160 9th Ave	Runnemede	NJ	08078	**800-221-3306**	856-312-2690	97
Blade 541 N Superior St	Toledo	OH	43660	**888-252-3301**	419-724-6000	522-2
Blaine Construction Corp PO Box 10147	Knoxville	TN	37939	**800-424-0426**	865-693-8900	185
Blair Cedar & Novelty Works Inc 345 W Hwy 54	Camdenton	MO	65020	**800-325-3943**	573-346-2235	323
Blair College 1815 Jet Wing Dr	Colorado Springs	CO	80916	**888-741-4271**	719-574-1082	158
Blair Corp 220 Hickory St *AMEX: BL* ■ *Cust Svc	Warren	PA	16366	**800-458-6057***	814-723-3600	451
Blair Industries Inc 116 E Missouri St	Scott City	MO	63780	**800-624-3150**	573-264-2146	87
Blair Milling & Elevator Co 1000 Main St PO Box 437	Atchison	KS	66002	**800-633-2931**	913-367-2310	438
Blair Mills LP 115 Little St *Cust Svc	Belton	SC	29627	**800-458-8038***	864-338-6611	731
Blair William Capital Partners 222 W Adams St	Chicago	IL	60606	**800-621-0687**	312-236-1600	779
Blair William & Co LLC 222 W Adams St	Chicago	IL	60606	**800-621-0687**	312-236-1600	679
Blakely Hotel 136 W 55th St	New York	NY	10019	**800-735-0710**	212-245-1800	373
Blakeslee Construction 200 N Branford Rd	Branford	CT	06405	**800-922-6203**	203-488-2500	181
Blakeslee Inc 1844 S Laramie Ave	Cicero	IL	60804	**800-652-5889**	708-656-0660	293
Blanchard Compact Equipment 1410 Ashville Hwy	Spartanburg	SC	29303	**800-397-9075**	864-582-1245	270
Blanchard Ken Ken Blanchard Cos 125 State Pl	Escondido	CA	92029	**800-728-6000**	760-839-8070	561
Blanchard Machinery Inc 14301 NE 19th Ave	North Miami	FL	33181	**800-330-4242**	305-949-2581	261-2
Blank Arthur & Co Inc 225 Rivermoor St	Boston	MA	02132	**800-776-7333**	617-325-9600	10
Blank Joseph Inc 62 W 47th St Suite 808	New York	NY	10036	**800-223-7666**	212-575-9050	403
Blank Textiles Inc 2 Bridge St Suite 220	Irvington	NY	10533	**800-237-3717**	914-478-3100	583
Blanks Color Imaging 2343 N Beckley Ave	Dallas	TX	75208	**800-325-7651**	214-741-3905	770
Blanks/USA Inc 8625 Xylon Ct	Minneapolis	MN	55445	**800-328-7311**	763-391-8001	550
Blast Inc 220 Chatham Business Dr	Pittsboro	NC	27312	**800-242-5278**	919-542-3007	176-7
Blattner Brunner Inc 11 Stanwix St 5th Fl	Pittsburgh	PA	15222	**800-545-5372**	412-995-9500	7
Blattner DH & Sons Inc 400 CR 50	Avon	MN	56310	**800-877-2866**	320-356-7351	187-4
Blauer Mfg Co Inc 20 Aberdeen St	Boston	MA	02215	**800-225-6715**	617-536-6606	153-19
Blaupunkt Div Robert Bosch Corp 2800 S 25th Ave *Sales	Broadview	IL	60155	**800-323-1943***	708-865-5200	52
Blendex Co Inc 11208 Electron Dr	Louisville	KY	40299	**800-253-6339**	502-267-1003	291-23
Blenko Glass Co Inc Fairground Rd	Milton	WV	25541	**877-425-3656**	304-743-9081	330
Blessed Herbs Inc 109 Barre Plains Rd	Oakham	MA	01068	**800-489-4372**	508-882-3839	470
Blessing Hospice PO Box 7005	Quincy	IL	62305	**800-382-8833**	217-228-5521	365
Bleyhl Farm Service Inc 940 E Wine Country Rd	Grandview	WA	98930	**800-862-6806**	509-882-2248	272
Bleyle Inc 14 St John Cir *Cust Svc	Newnan	GA	30265	**800-241-3437***	770-253-2792	153-21
BLF Management Ltd 1152 Goodale Blvd	Columbus	OH	43216	**866-298-3576**	614-221-9580	47
Blick Dick Co PO Box 1267 *Orders	Galesburg	IL	61402	**800-447-8192***	309-343-6181	45
Blimpie International Inc 145 Huguenot St Suite 410	New Rochelle	NY	10801	**800-447-6258**	914-576-1006	657
Blind. American Council of the 1155 15th St NW Suite 1004	Washington	DC	20005	**800-424-8666**	202-467-5081	48-17
Blind. American Foundation for the 11 Penn Plaza Suite 300	New York	NY	10001	**800-232-5463**	212-502-7600	48-17
Blind. American Printing House for the 1839 Frankfort Ave PO Box 6085	Louisville	KY	40206	**800-223-1839**	502-895-2405	623-10
Blind & Dyslexic. Recording for the 20 Roszel Rd	Princeton	NJ	08540	**800-221-4792**	609-452-0606	48-17
Blind. Guide Dogs for the 350 Los Ranchitos Rd	San Rafael	CA	94903	**800-295-4050**	415-499-4000	48-17
Blind Inc. Guide Dog Foundation for the 371 E Jericho Tkpe	Smithtown	NY	11787	**800-548-4337**	631-265-2121	48-17
Blind Maker 2013 Centimeter Cir	Austin	TX	78758	**800-999-5444**	512-835-5333	88
Blind Mission International. Christian 450 E Park Ave	Greenville	SC	29601	**800-937-2264**	864-239-0065	48-5
Blind. National Industries for the 1901 N Beauregard St Suite 200 *Cust Svc	Alexandria	VA	22311	**800-433-2304***	703-998-0770	48-17
Blind Students Inc. National Alliance of 1155 15th St NW Suite 1004	Washington	DC	20005	**800-424-8666**	202-467-5081	48-11
Blindness America. Prevent 211 W Wacker Dr Suite 1700	Chicago	IL	60606	**800-331-2020**	312-363-6001	48-17
Blindness. Foundation Fighting 11435 Cron Hill Dr	Owings Mills	MD	21117	**800-683-5555**	410-568-0150	48-17
Blindness Inc. Research to Prevent 645 Madison Ave 21st Fl	New York	NY	10022	**800-621-0026**	212-752-4333	48-17
Blish-Mize Co 223 S 5th St	Atchison	KS	66002	**800-995-0525**	913-367-1250	346
Bliss Clearing Niagara 1004 E State St	Hastings	MI	49058	**800-642-5477**	269-948-3300	448
Blissfield Mfg Co 626 Depot St *Cust Svc	Blissfield	MI	49228	**800-626-1772***	517-486-2121	15
Blissworld LLC 50 Washington St 7th Fl	Brooklyn	NY	11201	**888-243-8825**	212-219-8970	211
Blistex Inc 1800 Swift Dr *Cust Svc	Oak Brook	IL	60523	**800-837-1800***	630-571-2870	572
Blitz USA Inc 404 26th Ave NW *Cust Svc	Miami	OK	74354	**800-331-3795***	918-540-1515	596
BloApCo (Blower Application Co Inc) N 114 W 19125 Clinton Dr	Germantown	WI	53022	**800-959-0880**	262-255-5580	462
Bloch Berman Brothers Inc 345 7th Ave 19th Fl *Cust Svc	New York	NY	10001	**800-382-3877***	212-255-0940	153-7
Bloch Industries 140 Commerce Dr	Rochester	NY	14623	**800-992-5624**	585-334-9600	116
Bloch RA Cancer Foundation 4400 Main St	Kansas City	MO	64111	**800-433-0464**	816-932-8453	48-17
Block Distributing Co Inc 6511 Tri County Pkwy	Schertz	TX	78154	**800-749-7532**	210-224-7531	82-3

Name / Address	City	State	Zip	Toll-Free	Phone	Class
Block H & R Inc 4400 Main St *NYSE: HRB*	Kansas City	MO	64111	800-829-7733	816-753-6900	184
Block M & Sons Inc 5020 W 73rd St	Bedford Park	IL	60638	800-621-8845	708-728-8400	356
Block USA 1572 Chelsea Ave	Memphis	TN	38108	888-942-5625	901-754-5115	181
Block WG Co 1414 Mississippi Blvd PO Box 280	Bettendorf	IA	52722	800-397-1651	563-823-2080	180
Blocklite Corp PO Box 540	Selma	CA	93662	800-896-0753	559-896-0753	181
Blocksom & Co 450 St John Rd Suite 710	Michigan City	IN	46360	800-745-1408	219-874-3231	19
Blodgett GS Corp 44 Lakeside Ave	Burlington	VT	05401	800-331-5842	802-658-6600	293
Blodgett Supply Co Inc PO Box 759	Williston	VT	05495	800-223-6911	802-864-9831	38
Blommer Chocolate Co 600 W Kinzie St	Chicago	IL	60610	800-621-1606	312-226-7700	291-8
Blondell's Crown Square 1406 2nd St SW	Rochester	MN	55902	800-441-5209	507-282-9444	373
Blonder Tongue Laboratories Inc 1 Jake Brown Rd *AMEX: BDR*	Old Bridge	NJ	08857	800-523-6049	732-679-4000	633
Blood Assurance Inc 700 E 3rd St	Chattanooga	TN	37403	800-962-0628	423-756-0966	90
Blood Center of Central Iowa 431 E Locust St	Des Moines	IA	50309	800-287-4903	515-288-0276	90
Blood Center of Southeastern Wisconsin PO Box 2178	Milwaukee	WI	53201	800-257-3840	414-933-5000	90
Blood Centers. America's 725 15th St NW Suite 700	Washington	DC	20005	888-872-5663	202-393-5725	49-8
Blood Centers of the Pacific 270 Masonic Ave	San Francisco	CA	94118	888-393-4483	415-567-6400	90
Blood-Horse Magazine PO Box 911088	Lexington	KY	40591	800-866-2361	859-278-2361	449-14
Blood Research Inc. Center for 800 Huntington Ave	Boston	MA	02115	800-850-2466	617-278-3000	654
Blood Systems Laboratories 2424 W Erie Dr	Tempe	AZ	85282	866-342-4275	602-343-7000	408
Blood's Hammock Groves 4600 Linton Blvd	Delray Beach	FL	33445	800-255-5188	561-498-3400	310-2
Bloomberg News 499 Park Ave 15th Fl	New York	NY	10022	800-448-5678	212-318-2000	520
Bloomberg Radio Network 499 Park Ave 15th Fl	New York	NY	10022	800-448-5678	212-318-2350	630
Bloomfield College 467 Franklin St	Bloomfield	NJ	07003	800-848-4555	973-748-9000	163
Bloomingdale's 1000 3rd Ave	New York	NY	10022	800-950-0047	212-705-2000	227
Bloomingdale's Credit Services 9111 Duke Blvd	Mason	OH	45040	800-456-9529	513-398-5221	213
Bloomington Convention & Visitors Bureau 7900 International Dr Suite 990	Bloomington	MN	55425	800-346-4289	952-858-8500	205
Bloomington-Normal Area Convention & Visitors Bureau 3201 CIRA Dr Suite 201	Bloomington	IL	61704	800-433-8226	309-665-0033	205
Bloomington/Monroe County Convention & Visitors Bureau 2855 N Walnut St	Bloomington	IN	47404	800-800-0037	812-334-8900	205
Blossman Gas Inc PO Box 1110	Ocean Springs	MS	39566	800-234-1110	228-875-2261	311
Blount Inc Oregon Cutting Systems Div 4909 SE International Way	Portland	OR	97222	800-223-5168	503-653-8881	747
Blount Mansion 200 W Hill Ave	Knoxville	TN	37901	888-654-0016	865-525-2375	50
Blount Outdoor Products Group 4909 SE International Way	Portland	OR	97222	800-223-5168	503-653-8881	420
Blount Seafood Corp PO Box 327	Warren	RI	02885	800-274-2526	401-245-8800	291-14
Blower Application Co Inc (BloApCo) N 114 W 19125 Clinton Dr	Germantown	WI	53022	800-959-0880	262-255-5580	462
Blue Bell Lodge & Resort Hwy 87 Custer State Pk	Custer	SD	57730	800-658-3530	605-255-4535	655
Blue Bird Corp 402 Blue Bird Blvd	Fort Valley	GA	31030	800-486-7122	478-825-2021	505
Blue Care Network of Michigan 25925 Telegraph Rd	Southfield	MI	48086	800-662-6667	248-354-7450	384-3
Blue Cat Design 4753 Mast Woods Rd	Port Hope	ON	L1A3V5	888-258-8228	905-753-1017	7
Blue Chip Casino Inc 2 Easy St	Michigan City	IN	46350	888-879-7711	219-879-7711	133
Blue Chip Economic Indicators Newsletter 1333 H St NW Suite 100E *Cust Svc	Washington	DC	20005	800-234-1660*	202-312-6112	521-9
Blue Chip Financial Forecasts Newsletter 1333 H St NW Suite 100E *Cust Svc	Washington	DC	20005	800-234-1660*	202-312-6112	521-9
Blue & Co LLC 12800 N Meridian St Suite 400	Carmel	IN	46032	800-717-2583	317-848-8920	2
Blue Coat Systems Inc 650 Almanor Ave *NASDAQ: BCSI*	Sunnyvale	CA	94085	888-462-3569	408-220-2200	174
Blue Cross & Blue Shield of Alabama 450 Riverchase Pkwy E	Birmingham	AL	35298	800-292-8868	205-988-2200	384-3
Blue Cross & Blue Shield of Alaska PO Box 91080	Seattle	WA	98111	800-345-6784	425-670-4000	384-3
Blue Cross Blue Shield of Arizona PO Box 2924	Phoenix	AZ	85062	800-232-2345	602-864-4400	384-3
Blue Cross & Blue Shield of Delaware PO Box 1991	Wilmington	DE	19899	800-633-2563	302-421-3000	384-3
Blue Cross & Blue Shield of Florida Health Options Div PO Box 1798	Jacksonville	FL	32231	800-734-6656		384-3
Blue Cross & Blue Shield of Florida Inc PO Box 1798	Jacksonville	FL	32231	800-477-3736	904-791-6111	384-3
Blue Cross & Blue Shield of Georgia 3350 Peachtree Rd NE *Cust Svc	Atlanta	GA	30326	800-441-2273*	404-842-8000	384-3
Blue Cross & Blue Shield of Kansas 1133 SW Topeka Blvd	Topeka	KS	66629	800-432-0216	785-291-7000	384-3
Blue Cross & Blue Shield of Kansas City 2301 Main St	Kansas City	MO	64108	800-892-6048	816-395-2222	384-3
Blue Cross & Blue Shield of Louisiana 5525 Reitz Ave	Baton Rouge	LA	70898	800-599-2583	225-295-3307	384-3
Blue Cross & Blue Shield of Massachusetts 401 Park Dr	Boston	MA	02215	800-262-2583		384-3

Name / Address	City	State	Zip	Toll-Free	Phone	Class
Blue Cross & Blue Shield of Minnesota PO Box 64560	Saint Paul	MN	55164	800-382-2000	651-662-8000	384-3
Blue Cross & Blue Shield of Mississippi PO Box 1043	Jackson	MS	39215	800-222-8046	601-932-3704	384-3
Blue Cross & Blue Shield of Montana 404 Fuller Ave	Helena	MT	59601	800-447-7828	406-444-8200	384-3
Blue Cross & Blue Shield of Nebraska 7261 Mercy Rd	Omaha	NE	68180	800-642-8980	402-390-1820	384-3
Blue Cross & Blue Shield of New Mexico PO Box 27630	Albuquerque	NM	87125	800-835-8699	505-291-3500	384-3
Blue Cross & Blue Shield of North Carolina PO Box 2291 *Cust Svc	Durham	NC	27702	800-311-2583*	919-489-7431	384-3
Blue Cross Blue Shield of North Dakota 4510 13th Ave SW	Fargo	ND	58121	800-342-4718	701-282-1100	384-3
Blue Cross & Blue Shield of Oklahoma 1215 S Boulder Ave *Cust Svc	Tulsa	OK	74119	800-942-5837*	918-560-3500	384-3
Blue Cross & Blue Shield of Rhode Island 444 Westminster St	Providence	RI	02903	800-527-7290	401-459-1000	384-3
Blue Cross & Blue Shield of South Carolina I-20 E at Alpine Rd	Columbia	SC	29219	800-288-2227	803-788-0222	384-3
Blue Cross Blue Shield of Tennessee 801 Pine St	Chattanooga	TN	37402	800-565-9140	423-755-5600	384-3
Blue Cross & Blue Shield of Texas Inc PO Box 655730 *Cust Svc	Dallas	TX	75265	800-521-2227*	972-766-6900	384-3
Blue Cross & Blue Shield United of Wisconsin 401 W Michigan St	Milwaukee	WI	53203	800-558-1584	414-226-5000	384-3
Blue Cross & Blue Shield of Vermont 445 Industrial Ln	Montpelier	VT	05602	800-457-6648	802-223-6131	384-3
Blue Cross & Blue Shield of Western New York PO Box 80	Buffalo	NY	14240	800-888-0757	716-887-6900	384-3
Blue Cross & Blue Shield of Wyoming PO Box 2266 *Cust Svc	Cheyenne	WY	82003	800-851-9145*	307-634-1393	384-3
Blue Cross of California 21555 Oxnard St	Woodland Hills	CA	91365	800-999-3643	818-703-2345	384-3
Blue Cross of Idaho 3000 E Pine Ave *Cust Svc	Meridian	ID	83642	800-365-2345*	208-345-4550	384-3
Blue Cross of Northeastern Pennsylvania 19 N Main St *Cust Svc	Wilkes-Barre	PA	18711	800-829-8599*	570-200-4300	384-3
Blue Diamond Growers 1802 C St	Sacramento	CA	95814	888-285-1351	916-442-0771	11-10
Blue Grass Chemical Specialties LP 895 Industrial Blvd	New Albany	IN	47150	800-638-7197	812-948-1115	580
Blue Grass Energy Co-op Corp PO Box 990	Nicholasville	KY	40340	888-546-4243	859-885-4191	244
Blue Grass Quality Meats PO Box 17658	Crescent Springs	KY	41017	888-236-4455	859-331-7100	291-26
Blue Grass Stockyard 375 Lisle Industrial Ave	Lexington	KY	40511	800-621-3972	859-255-7701	437
Blue Grass Tours Inc 817 Enterprise Dr	Lexington	KY	40510	800-755-6956	859-233-2152	748
Blue & Gray Transportation Co Inc 1111 Commerce Rd	Richmond	VA	23234	800-368-2583	804-232-2324	769
Blue Heron Paper 427 Main St	Oregon City	OR	97045	800-331-9991	503-650-4211	547
Blue Horizon Hotel 1225 Robson St	Vancouver	BC	V6E1C3	800-663-1333	604-688-1411	372
Blue Lakes Charters & Tours 12154 N Saginaw Rd	Clio	MI	48420	800-282-4287	810-686-4287	108
Blue Lance Inc 1700 W Loop S Suite 1100	Houston	TX	77027	800-856-2583	713-680-1187	176-12
Blue Line Foodservice Distribution 24120 Haggerty Rd	Farmington Hills	MI	48335	866-414-2583	248-478-6200	294
Blue Marlin Motel 1320 Simonton St	Key West	FL	33040	800-523-1698	305-294-2585	373
Blue Martini Software Inc 2600 Campus Dr	San Mateo	CA	94403	800-258-3627	650-356-4000	39
Blue Moon Hotel 944 Collins Ave	Miami Beach	FL	33139	800-724-1623	305-673-2262	373
Blue Mountain Arts Inc PO Box 4549 *Sales	Boulder	CO	80306	800-545-8573*	303-449-0536	130
Blue Mountain College PO Box 160	Blue Mountain	MS	38610	800-235-0136	662-685-4771	163
Blue Mountain Wallcoverings Inc 15 Akron Rd	Toronto	ON	M8W1T3	800-219-2424	416-251-1678	789
Blue Nile Inc 705 5th Ave S Suite 900 *NASDAQ: NILE*	Seattle	WA	98104	800-242-2728	206-336-6700	402
Blue North Fisheries 2930 Westlake Ave N Suite 300	Seattle	WA	98109	877-878-3263	206-352-9252	280
Blue Parrot Inn 916 Elizabeth St	Key West	FL	33040	800-231-2473	305-296-0033	373
Blue Pumpkin Software Inc 884 Hermosa Ct Suite 100	Sunnyvale	CA	94086	877-257-6756	408-830-5400	176-1
Blue Rhino Corp 104 Cambridge Plaza Dr	Winston-Salem	NC	27104	800-258-7466	336-659-6900	569
Blue Ribbon Home Warranty Inc 95 S Wadsworth Blvd	Lakewood	CO	80226	800-571-0475	303-986-3900	687
Blue Ribbon Label Corp 241 Hudson St	Hackensack	NJ	07601	800-223-2400	201-489-6003	404
Blue Ribbon Tag & Label Corp 4035 N 29th Ave	Hollywood	FL	33020	800-433-4974	954-922-9292	404
Blue Ridge Beverage Co Inc PO Box 700 *Cust Svc	Salem	VA	24153	800-868-0354*	540-380-2000	82-1
Blue Ridge Business Journal 347 W Campbell Ave	Roanoke	VA	24016	866-542-6198	540-777-6460	449-5
Blue Ridge Carpet Mills 1546 Progress Rd	Ellijay	GA	30540	800-241-5945	706-276-2001	131
Blue Ridge Electric Co-op Inc 734 W Main St	Pickens	SC	29671	800-240-3400	864-878-6326	244
Blue Ridge Electric Membership Corp 1216 Blowing Rock Blvd NE	Lenoir	NC	28645	800-451-5474	828-758-2383	244
Blue Ridge Growers Inc 21409 Germanna Hwy	Stevensburg	VA	22741	800-368-2030	540-399-1636	363
Blue Ridge Mountain Electric Membership Corp 1360 Main St	Young Harris	GA	30582	800-292-6456	706-379-3121	244
Blue Ridge Products Inc PO Box 2028	Hickory	NC	28603	800-345-1367	828-322-7990	590

Name / Address	City	State	ZIP	Toll-Free	Phone	Class
Blue Ridge Public Television 1215 McNeil Dr	Roanoke	VA	24015	**888-332-7788**	540-344-0991	620
Blue Rock Golf Resort. Best Western 39 Todd Rd	South Yarmouth	MA	02664	**800-227-3263**	508-398-6962	655
Blue Rock Industries 58 Main St	Westbrook	ME	04092	**800-439-2561**	207-854-2561	188-3
Blue Seal Feeds Inc 15 Buttrick Rd *Cust Svc	Londonderry	NH	03053	**800-367-2730***	603-437-3400	438
Blue Sky Swimwear 729 E International Speedway Blvd *Orders	Daytona Beach	FL	32118	**800-799-6445***	386-255-9009	153-17
Blue Water Area Convention & Visitors Bureau 520 Thomas Edison Pkwy	Port Huron	MI	48060	**800-852-4242**	810-987-8687	205
Blue Water Resort 2001 S Ocean Blvd	Myrtle Beach	SC	29577	**800-845-6994**	843-626-8345	655
Blue Wave Boats Hwy 69 S	Checotah	OK	74426	**800-432-6768**	918-473-6768	91
Blueberry Assn of North America. Wild 59 Cottage St po bOX 180	Bar Harbor	ME	04609	**800-233-9453**	207-288-2655	48-2
Bluebonnet Electric Co-op Inc 426 E Austin St	Giddings	TX	78942	**800-842-7708**	979-542-3151	244
Bluebonnet Savings Bank FSB 8150 N Central Expy Suite 1900	Dallas	TX	75206	**800-878-3111**	214-365-1300	71
BlueCross BlueShield of the Rochester Area 165 Court St	Rochester	NY	14647	**800-847-1200**	585-454-1700	384-3
Bluefield College 3000 College Dr	Bluefield	VA	24605	**800-872-0175**	276-326-3682	163
Bluefield Daily Telegraph 928 Bluefield Ave	Bluefield	WV	24701	**800-763-2459**	304-327-2800	522-2
Bluefield State College 219 Rock St	Bluefield	WV	24701	**800-654-7798**	304-327-4000	163
Bluefly Inc 42 W 39th St 9th Fl *NASDAQ: BFLY*	New York	NY	10018	**877-258-3359**	212-944-8000	155-6
Bluegrass Cellular Inc 2902 Ring Rd	Elizabethtown	KY	42701	**800-928-2355**	270-769-0339	721
Bluegrass Cooperage Co Inc PO Box 37210	Louisville	KY	40233	**800-364-6004**	502-368-1626	199
Bluegreen Corp 4960 Conference Way N Suite 100 *NYSE: BXG*	Boca Raton	FL	33431	**800-456-2582**	561-912-8000	738
BlueLinx Holdings Inc 4300 Wildwood Pkwy *NYSE: BXC*	Atlanta	GA	30339	**888-502-2583**	770-953-7000	190-3
Bluemkes Inc PO Box 149	Rosendale	WI	54974	**800-236-2133**	920-872-2131	420
Bluenose Inn 636 Bedford Hwy	Halifax	NS	B3M2L8	**800-565-2301**	902-443-3171	372
Bluenose Inn. Bar Harbor Hotel- 90 Eden St	Bar Harbor	ME	04609	**800-445-4077**	207-288-3348	373
BluePoint Data Storage Inc 6633 NW 25th Terr	Boca Raton	FL	33496	**866-786-7390**	561-417-0324	39
BlueRibbon.com 625 Walnut Ridge Dr Suite 108	Hartland	WI	53029	**800-788-1298**	262-369-0600	390
Bluestem Electric Co-op Inc 614 E Hwy 24	Wamego	KS	66547	**800-558-1580**	785-456-2212	244
Bluewater Adventures Ltd 252 E 1st St Suite 3	North Vancouver	BC	V7L1B3	**888-877-1770**	604-980-3800	217
Bluewater Bay Resort 1940 Bluewater Blvd	Niceville	FL	32578	**800-874-2128**	850-897-3613	655
Bluewater Inc 811 E Maple Ave	Mora	MN	55051	**800-733-7127**	320-679-3811	91
Bluffs Run Casino 2701 23rd Ave	Council Bluffs	IA	51501	**800-238-2946**	712-323-2500	133
Bluffton Flying Service Co 1080 Navajo Dr	Bluffton	OH	45817	**800-468-6359**	419-358-7045	14
Bluffton University 1 University Dr	Bluffton	OH	45817	**800-488-3257**	419-358-3257	163
Blume Tree Services 708 Blair Mill Rd	Willow Grove	PA	19090	**800-248-8733**	215-784-4200	765
Blumenthal-Kahn Electric LP 10233 S Dolfield Rd	Owings Mills	MD	21117	**800-238-8012**	410-363-1200	188-4
Blumenthal Lansing Co 1 Palmer Terr	Carlstadt	NJ	07072	**800-448-9749**	201-935-6220	583
Blumenthal Print Works Inc 905 S Broad St	New Orleans	LA	70125	**800-535-8590**	504-822-4620	730-7
BMA (Business Marketing Assn) 400 N Michigan Ave 15th Fl	Chicago	IL	60611	**800-664-4262**	312-822-0005	49-18
BMC Software Inc 2101 City West Blvd *NYSE: BMC*	Houston	TX	77042	**800-841-2031**	713-918-8800	176-1
BMDA (Building Material Dealers Assn) 12540 SW Main St Suite 200	Tigard	OR	97223	**800-666-2632**	503-624-0561	49-3
BMG Aviation Inc 984 S Kirby Rd	Bloomington	IN	47403	**888-457-3787**	812-825-7979	63
BMG Heritage 1540 Broadway	New York	NY	10036	**877-264-7744**		643
BMI Educational Services PO Box 800	Dayton	NJ	08810	**800-222-8100**	732-329-6991	97
BMI Imaging Systems 1115 E Arques Ave *Cust Svc	Sunnyvale	CA	94085	**800-359-3456***	408-736-7444	487
BMJ Mold & Engineering Co Inc 1104 N Touby Pike	Kokomo	IN	46901	**800-238-7785**	765-457-1166	593
BMW of North America Inc PO Box 1227	Westwood	NJ	07675	**800-526-0818**	201-307-4000	59
BNA Books Div Bureau of National Affairs Inc 1231 25th St *Sales	Washington	DC	20037	**800-960-1220***	202-452-4200	623-2
BNA Software Div Tax Management Inc 1250 23rd St NW	Washington	DC	20037	**800-424-2938**	202-728-7962	176-10
B'nai B'rith International 2020 K St NW 7th Fl	Washington	DC	20006	**888-388-4224**	202-857-6600	48-20
BNS Co 200 Frenchtown Rd Precision Pk	North Kingstown	RI	02852	**800-283-3600**	401-886-2000	176-10
BNSF (Burlington Northern & Santa Fe Railway) 2650 Lou Menk Dr	Fort Worth	TX	76131	**800-795-2673**		634
BNX Systems Corp 1953 Gallows Rd Suite 500	Vienna	VA	22182	**800-397-7561**	703-734-9200	85
BNY Hamilton Funds PO Box 182785	Columbus	OH	43218	**800-426-9363**		517
BNZ Materials Inc 6901 S Pierce St Suite 260	Littleton	CO	80128	**800-999-0890**	303-978-1199	648
Bo-Buck Mills Inc 921 East Blvd	Chesterfield	SC	29709	**800-690-7474**	843-623-2158	730-5
Bo-Jac Seed Co 245 1500th Ave	Mount Pulaski	IL	62548	**800-397-2069**	217-792-5001	11-11
Bo-Mer Mfg Co 13 Pulaski St	Auburn	NY	13021	**800-221-6563**	315-252-7216	591
BOA (Bands of America Inc) 39 W Jackson Pl	Indianapolis	IN	46225	**800-848-2263**	317-636-2263	48-11
Boarding Schools. Association of 4455 Connecticut Ave NW Suite A-200	Washington	DC	20008	**800-541-5908**	202-966-8705	48-11
Boardwalk Hotel & Casino 3750 Las Vegas Blvd S	Las Vegas	NV	89109	**800-635-4581**	702-735-2400	133
Boardwalk Inn 5757 Palm Blvd	Isle of Palms	SC	29451	**800-845-8880**	843-886-6000	373
Boardwalk Plaza Hotel 2 Olive Ave	Rehoboth Beach	DE	19971	**800-332-3224**	302-227-7169	373
Boar's Head Inn 200 Ednam Dr	Charlottesville	VA	22903	**800-476-1988**	434-296-2181	655
Boart Longyear Co 2640 W 1700 South *Cust Svc	Salt Lake City	UT	84104	**800-457-5778***	801-972-6430	189
Boat Owners Assn of the US 880 S Pickett St	Alexandria	VA	22304	**800-937-9307**	703-823-9550	48-23
Boat Owners Warehouse 311 SW 24th St	Fort Lauderdale	FL	33315	**888-262-8799**	954-522-7998	759
Boating Industry Magazine 6420 Sycamore Ln Suite 100	Maple Grove	MN	55369	**800-848-6247**	763-383-4400	449-21
Boating Magazine 1633 Broadway 41st Fl *Cust Svc	New York	NY	10019	**800-289-0399***	212-767-4823	449-4
BoatUS 880 S Pickett St	Alexandria	VA	22304	**800-937-9307**	703-823-9550	48-23
Bob Bullock Texas State History Museum 1800 N Congress Ave	Austin	TX	78701	**866-369-7108**	512-936-8746	509
Bob Evans Farms Inc 3776 S High St *NASDAQ: BOBE*	Columbus	OH	43207	**800-272-7675**	614-491-2225	657
Bob Feller Museum 310 Mill St PO Box 95	Van Meter	IA	50261	**866-996-2806**	515-996-2806	511
Bob Jones University 1700 Wade Hampton Blvd *Admissions	Greenville	SC	29614	**800-252-6363***	864-242-5100	163
Bob Pike Group 7620 W 78th St	Edina	MN	55439	**800-383-9210**	952-829-1954	753
Bob Rohrman Auto Group 701 Sagamore Pkwy S	Lafayette	IN	47905	**800-488-3534**	765-448-1000	57
Bob Sumerel Tires & Service Inc 3646 E Broad St	Columbus	OH	43213	**800-858-0421**	614-237-6325	740
Bob Ward & Sons Inc 3015 Paxson St	Missoula	MT	59801	**800-800-5083**	406-728-3220	702
Bobbi Brown Professional Cosmetics Inc 767 5th Ave	New York	NY	10153	**877-310-9222**		211
Bobby Cox Cos Inc 4055 International Plaza Suite 450	Fort Worth	TX	76109	**800-897-8723**	817-377-6200	656
Bobby Jones Retail Corp 1155 N Clinton Ave *Cust Svc	Rochester	NY	14621	**888-603-8968***	800-295-2000	153-3
Bobco Metals Co 2000 S Alameda St	Los Angeles	CA	90058	**800-262-2605**		483
Bobley Harmann Publishing Co 311 Crossways Park Dr *Cust Svc	Woodbury	NY	11797	**800-323-1692***	516-364-1800	87
Bobs Candies Inc 1315 W Oakridge Dr	Albany	GA	31707	**800-841-3602**	229-430-8300	291-8
Bob's Cruises 635 Fourth Line	Oakville	ON	L6L5W4	**800-361-6688**	905-338-2077	760
Bob's Merchandise Inc 1111 Hudson St	Longview	WA	98632	**800-292-5551**	360-425-3870	227
Bob's Red Mill Natural Foods Inc 5209 SE International Way	Milwaukie	OR	97222	**800-553-2258**	503-654-3215	291-4
Bob's Stores Inc 160 Corporate Ct	Meriden	CT	06450	**866-333-2627**	203-235-5775	155-2
Bobsled & Skeleton Federation. US 196 Old Military Rd	Lake Placid	NY	12946	**800-262-7533**	518-523-1842	48-22
BOC Edwards 301 Ballardvale St	Wilmington	MA	01887	**800-848-9800**	978-658-5410	685
BOC Gases America 575 Mountain Ave *Cust Svc	Murray Hill	NJ	07974	**800-262-4273***	908-464-8100	141
BOC Group 575 Mountain Ave	Murray Hill	NJ	07974	**800-932-0803**	908-665-2400	141
Boca Raton Resort & Club 501 E Camino Real	Boca Raton	FL	33431	**800-327-0101**	561-447-3000	655
Boca Times 1701 Green Rd Suite B	Deerfield Beach	FL	33064	**800-275-8820**	954-698-6397	522-4
Bodega Bay Lodge & Spa 103 Coast Hwy 1	Bodega Bay	CA	94923	**800-368-2468**	707-875-3525	373
Boden Store Fixtures Inc 5335 NE 109th Ave	Portland	OR	97220	**800-733-1923**	503-252-4728	281
Bodine Co 236 S Mount Pleasant Rd	Collierville	TN	38027	**800-223-5778**	901-853-7211	756
Bodine Electric Co 2500 W Bradley Pl	Chicago	IL	60618	**800-726-3463**	773-478-3515	507
Bodine Electric of Decatur Inc PO Box 976	Decatur	IL	62525	**800-252-3369**	217-423-2593	188-4
Bodine's Inc 6436 Penn Ave S	Richfield	MN	55423	**800-535-6424**	612-866-2025	515
Bodum Inc 1860 Renaissance Blvd Suite 201	Sturtevant	WI	53177	**800-232-6386**	262-884-4650	37
Body Masters Sports Industries Inc 700 E Texas Ave	Rayne	LA	70578	**800-325-8964**	337-334-9611	263
Body Shop The 5036 One World Way *Cust Svc	Wake Forest	NC	27587	**800-747-4827***	919-554-4900	211
Body-Solid Inc 1900 S Des Plaines Ave	Forest Park	IL	60130	**800-833-1227**	708-427-3500	263
Body & Soul 42 Pleasant St	Watertown	MA	02472	**800-755-1178**	617-926-0200	449-18
Bodycote North America Inc 5001 LBJ Fwy Suite 800	Dallas	TX	75244	**800-234-8422**	214-904-2420	475
Bodywork & Massage Professionals. Associated 1271 Sugarbush Dr	Evergreen	CO	80439	**800-458-2267**	303-674-8478	48-17
BOE Financial Services of Virginia Inc 323 Prince St *NASDAQ: BSXT*	Tappahannock	VA	22560	**800-443-5524**	804-443-4343	355-2
Boehm Edward Marshall Inc 25 Princess Diana Ln	Trenton	NJ	08638	**800-257-9410**	609-392-2207	330
Boehringer Ingelheim Chemicals Inc 2820 N Normandy Dr	Petersburg	VA	23805	**800-820-6015**	804-504-8700	470
Boehringer Ingelheim Ltd 5180 S Service Rd	Burlington	ON	L7L5H4	**800-263-9107**	905-639-0333	572
Boehringer Ingelheim Pharmaceuticals Inc 900 Ridgebury Rd	Ridgefield	CT	06877	**800-243-0127**	203-798-9988	572

Listing	City	State	ZIP	Toll-Free	Phone	Class
Boehringer Ingelheim Pharmaceuticals Inc Pharmaton Natural Health Products Div 900 Ridgebury Rd	Ridgefield	CT	06877	**800-451-6688**	203-798-9988	786
Boehringer Ingelheim Vetmedica Inc 2621 N Belt Hwy	Saint Joseph	MO	64506	**800-821-7467**	816-233-2571	574
Boeing Employees' Credit Union (BECU) PO Box 97050	Seattle	WA	98124	**800-233-2328**	206-439-5700	216
Boeing Sunnyvale 84 Hermosa Ct	Sunnyvale	CA	94086	**800-332-2201**	408-737-1000	519
Boeing Travel Management Co 325 JS McDonnell Blvd Bldg 303 M-S3069236	Hazelwood	MO	63042	**800-243-8292**	314-551-4025	760
Boekel Industries Inc 855 Pennsylvania Blvd	Feasterville	PA	19053	**800-336-6929**	215-396-8200	411
Boelter Cos Inc 11100 W Silver Spring Rd	Milwaukee	WI	53225	**800-392-3278**	414-461-3400	295
Boesen the Florist 3422 Beaver Ave	Des Moines	IA	50310	**800-274-4761**	515-274-4761	287
Boettcher Edgar Mason Contractors Inc 1616 S Airport Rd	Traverse City	MI	49686	**800-562-3827**	231-941-5802	188-7
Bogen Communications International Inc 50 Spring St	Ramsey	NJ	07446	**800-999-2809**	201-934-8500	52
Boggis-Johnson Electric Co 2900 N 112th St PO Box 26068	Milwaukee	WI	53226	**800-333-7650**	414-475-6900	245
Boh Brothers Construction Co LLC 730 S Tonti St	New Orleans	LA	70119	**800-284-3377**	504-821-2400	187-4
Bohannan Huston Inc 7500 Jefferson St NE Courtyard 1	Albuquerque	NM	87109	**800-877-5332**	505-823-1000	176-5
Bohler-Uddeholm North America 4902 Tollview Dr	Rolling Meadows	IL	60008	**800-638-2520**	847-577-2220	483
Bohrens United Van Lines 3 Applegate Dr	Robbinsville	NJ	08691	**800-326-4736**	609-208-1470	508
Boise Bible College 8695 W Marigold St	Boise	ID	83714	**800-893-7755**	208-376-7731	163
Boise Convention & Visitors Bureau 312 S 9th St Suite 100	Boise	ID	83702	**800-635-5240**	208-344-7777	205
Boise State Radio 1910 University Drive	Boise	ID	83725	**888-859-5278**	208-947-5660	620
Boise State University 1910 University Dr	Boise	ID	83725	**800-824-7017**	208-426-1156	163
Boise-Winnemucca Stage Lines Inc 1105 La Pointe St	Boise	ID	83706	**800-448-5692**	208-336-3300	108
Bojangles' Restaurants Inc 9432 Southern Pine Blvd	Charlotte	NC	28273	**800-366-9921**	704-527-2675	657
Boland Marine & Mfg Co Inc 1000 Tchoupitoulas St	New Orleans	LA	70130	**888-265-2631**	504-581-5800	689
Bolander Carl & Sons Co Inc 251 Starkey St	Saint Paul	MN	55107	**800-676-6504**	651-224-6299	188-5
Bolivar County Library 104 S Leflore Ave	Cleveland	MS	38732	**888-268-8076**	662-843-2774	426
Bolle Inc 9200 Cody St	Overland Park	KS	66214	**800-222-6553**	913-752-3400	531
Bolliger Inc 120 Viaduct Rd	Stamford	CT	06907	**800-243-9517**	203-324-5999	508
Bollinger Insurance 101 JFK Pkwy	Short Hills	NJ	07078	**800-526-1379**	973-467-0444	383
Bollman Hat Co 110 E Main St	Adamstown	PA	19501	**800-451-4287**	717-484-4361	153-9
Bolsa Chica Ecological Reserve 3842 Warner Ave	Huntington Beach	CA	92649	**888-265-7248**	714-846-1114	811
Bolton & Co 245 S Los Robles Ave Suite 105	Pasadena	CA	91101	**888-700-1444**	626-799-7000	383
Bolton Corp 919 W Morgan St	Raleigh	NC	27603	**800-438-1098**	919-828-9021	188-10
Bolton & Hay Inc 2701 Delaware Ave	Des Moines	IA	50317	**800-362-1861**	515-265-2554	295
BOMA (Building Owners & Managers Assn International) 1201 New York Ave NW Suite 300	Washington	DC	20005	**800-426-6292**	202-408-2662	49-17
Bomag Americas Inc 2000 Kentville Rd	Kewanee	IL	61443	**800-782-6624**	309-853-3571	189
Bomark Inks Inc 601 S 6th Ave	City of Industry	CA	91746	**800-323-5174**	626-968-1666	381
Bomb Magazine 594 Broadway Suite 905	New York	NY	10012	**888-475-5987**	212-431-3943	449-2
Bombard Society Inc 333 Pershing Way	West Palm Beach	FL	33401	**800-862-8537**	561-837-6610	748
Bombardier Aerospace Learjet 1 Learjet Way	Wichita	KS	67209	**800-289-5327**	316-946-2000	21
Bombardier Capital Group 261 Mountain View Dr	Colchester	VT	05446	**800-525-5871**	802-654-8100	214
Bombardier Skyjet 3040 Williams Dr Suite 404 *Cust Svc	Alexandria	VA	22031	**888-275-9538***	703-584-3330	762
Bombay Co Inc 550 Bailey Ave *NYSE: BBA*	Fort Worth	TX	76107	**800-829-7789**	817-347-8200	316
Bombet Cashio & Assoc 11220 N Harrells Ferry Rd	Baton Rouge	LA	70816	**800-256-5333**	225-275-0796	392
BOMI Institute 1521 Ritchie Hwy	Arnold	MD	21012	**800-235-2664**	410-974-1410	49-17
Bommer Industries Inc PO Box 187	Landrum	SC	29356	**800-334-1654**	864-457-3301	345
Bon Appetit Magazine 6300 Wilshire Blvd 10th Fl	Los Angeles	CA	90048	**800-765-9419**	323-965-3400	449-11
Bon Secour Fisheries Inc 17449 County Rd 49 S PO Box 60	Bon Secour	AL	36511	**800-633-6854**	251-949-7411	292-5
Bon Secours Cottage Hospital 468 Cadieux Rd	Grosse Pointe	MI	48230	**888-331-0954**	313-343-1000	366-2
Bon Secours Memorial Regional Medical Center 8260 Atlee Rd	Mechanicsville	VA	23116	**888-455-3766**	804-764-6000	366-2
Bon Secours Saint Mary's Hospital 5801 Bremo Rd	Richmond	VA	23226	**800-472-2011**	804-285-2011	366-2
Bon Voyage Travel 1640 E River Rd Suite 115	Tucson	AZ	85718	**800-439-7963**	520-797-1110	760
Bonair Daydreams PO Box 3741	Farmington	NM	87499	**888-226-6247**	505-326-1684	130
Bonaire Government Tourist Office 10 Rockefeller Plaza Suite 900	New York	NY	10020	**800-266-2473**	212-956-5911	764
Bonanza Beverage Co 6333 Ensworth St *Cust Svc	Las Vegas	NV	89119	**800-677-4166***	702-361-4166	82-1
Bonanza Bus Lines Inc 1 Bonanza Way	Providence	RI	02904	**888-331-7500**	401-331-7500	109
Bonanza Creek Country Guest Ranch 523 Bonanza Creek Rd	Martinsdale	MT	59053	**800-476-6045**	406-572-3366	238
Bonanza Restaurants 6500 International Pkwy Suite 1000	Plano	TX	75093	**800-727-8355**	972-588-5000	657
Bonanzaville USA 1351 W Main Ave	West Fargo	ND	58078	**800-700-5317**	701-282-2822	509
Bonaventure Resort & Spa 250 Racquet Club Rd	Weston	FL	33326	**800-996-3426**	954-389-3300	655
Bonaventure Tours 8 Boudreau Ln	Haute-Aboujagane	NB	E4P5N1	**800-561-1213**	506-532-3674	748
Boncosky Oil Co Inc 739 N State St	Elgin	IL	60123	**800-628-7231**	847-741-2577	569
Bond Charles Co 11 Green St PO Box 105 *Cust Svc	Christiana	PA	17509	**800-922-0125***	610-593-5171	700
Bond Place Hotel 65 Dundas St E	Toronto	ON	M5B2G8	**800-268-9390**	416-362-6061	372
Bondanza Michael Inc 10 W 46th St 12th Fl	New York	NY	10036	**800-835-0041**	212-869-0043	401
Bonded Concrete Inc 303 Rt 155	Watervliet	NY	12189	**800-252-8589**	518-273-5800	180
Bondhus Corp 1400 E Broadway St *Cust Svc	Monticello	MN	55362	**800-328-8310***	763-295-2162	746
Bondo Corp 3700 Atlanta Industrial Pkwy NW	Atlanta	GA	30331	**800-622-8754**	404-696-2730	3
Bondweek Newsletter 225 Park Ave S 7th Fl	New York	NY	10003	**800-543-4444**	212-224-3800	521-9
Bone Bank Allografts 4808 Research Dr	San Antonio	TX	78240	**800-397-0088**	210-696-7616	535
Bone Care International Inc 1600 Aspen Commons *NASDAQ: BCII*	Middleton	WI	53562	**888-389-3300**	608-662-7800	86
Bone Diseases - National Resource Center. NIH Osteoporosis & Related Osteoporosis & Related Bone Diseases - National Resource Center 1232 22nd St NW	Washington	DC	20037	**800-624-2663**	202-223-0344	336-6
Bone Marrow Donor Registry. American 2733 North St	Mandeville	LA	70448	**800-745-2452**	985-626-1749	48-17
Bone Marrow Foundation. Gift of Life 7700 Congress Ave Suite 2201	Boca Raton	FL	33487	**800-962-7769**	561-988-0100	48-17
Bone & Related Disorders. Paget Foundation for Paget's Disease of 120 Wall St Suite 1602	New York	NY	10005	**800-237-2438**	212-509-5335	48-17
Bonefish Grill 2202 N West Shore Blvd	Tampa	FL	33607	**866-880-2226**	813-282-1225	657
Bonell Mfg Co 13521 S Halsted St	Riverdale	IL	60827	**800-323-3110**	708-849-1770	745
Bonfit America Inc 8460 Higuera St	Culver City	CA	90232	**800-526-6348**	310-204-7880	557
Bongrain Cheese USA 400 S Custer Ave	New Holland	PA	17557	**800-253-6637**	717-355-8500	291-5
Bonita Pioneer Packaging Products Inc 7333 SW Bonita Rd	Portland	OR	97224	**800-677-7725**	503-684-6542	66
Bonita Springs Area Chamber of Commerce 25071 Chamber of Commerce Dr	Bonita Springs	FL	34135	**800-226-2943**	239-992-2943	137
Bonitz Contracting Co Inc 645 Rosewood Dr	Columbia	SC	29201	**800-452-7281**	803-799-0181	188-2
Bonland Industries Inc 50 Newark-Pompton Tpke	Wayne	NJ	07474	**800-289-7482**	973-694-3211	188-12
Bonn FH Co 4300 Gateway Blvd	Springfield	OH	45502	**800-323-0143**	937-323-7024	730-3
Bonne Bell Inc 18519 Detroit Ave	Lakewood	OH	44107	**800-321-1006**	216-221-0800	211
Bonnell William L Co 25 Bonnell St	Newnan	GA	30263	**800-846-8885**	770-253-2020	476
Bonneville Billing & Collection Inc PO Box 150621	Ogden	UT	84415	**800-660-6138**	801-621-7880	157
Bonneville Power Administration 905 NE 11th Ave	Portland	OR	97232	**800-282-3713**	503-230-3000	336-5
Bonney Forge Corp US Rt 522 S *Cust Svc	Mount Union	PA	17066	**800-345-7546***	814-542-2545	776
Bonnie Castle Resort 31 Holland St	Alexandria Bay	NY	13607	**800-955-4511**	315-482-4511	655
Bonsal American 8201 Arrowridge Blvd PO Box 241148	Charlotte	NC	28224	**800-738-1621**	704-525-1621	181
Bontecou Investigative Services Inc PO Box 2448	Jackson	WY	83001	**877-733-2639**	307-733-2637	392
Bontex Inc 1 Bontex Dr	Buena Vista	VA	24416	**800-733-4234**	540-261-2181	590
Bonus Building Care Inc PO Box 300	Indianola	OK	74442	**800-931-1102**	918-823-4990	150
Book Council. Children's 12 W 37th St 2nd Fl *Orders	New York	NY	10018	**800-999-2160***	212-966-1990	49-16
Book Marketing Update Newsletter 135 E Plumstead Ave	Lansdowne	PA	19050	**800-989-1400**	610-259-1070	521-10
Book Passage 51 Tamal Vista Blvd	Corte Madera	CA	94925	**800-999-7909**	415-835-1020	96
Book Producers Assn. American 160 5th Ave	New York	NY	10010	**800-209-4575**	212-645-2368	49-16
Book Publishing Report 11 River Bend Dr S	Stamford	CT	06907	**800-307-2529**	203-358-4100	521-11
Book Soup 8818 Sunset Blvd	West Hollywood	CA	90069	**800-764-2665**	310-659-3110	96
Book Wholesalers Inc DBA BWI 1847 Mercer Rd Suite D	Lexington	KY	40511	**800-888-4478**	859-231-9789	97
Bookazine Co Inc 75 Hook Rd	Bayonne	NJ	07002	**800-221-8112**	201-339-7777	97
Booker-Price Co 1318 McHenry St	Louisville	KY	40217	**800-928-1080**	502-637-2531	315
Booker T Washington Insurance Co PO Box 697	Birmingham	AL	35201	**800-228-4180**	205-328-5454	384-2
Bookkeepers. American Institute of Professional 6001 Montrose Rd Suite 500	Rockville	MD	20852	**800-622-0121**	301-770-7300	49-1
Booklist Magazine 50 E Huron St	Chicago	IL	60611	**800-545-2433**	312-944-6780	449-11
BookPeople 603 N Lamar	Austin	TX	78703	**800-853-9757**	512-472-5050	96
Books & Books 265 Aragon Ave	Coral Gables	FL	33134	**888-626-6576**	305-442-4408	96
Books on the Square 471 Angell St	Providence	RI	02906	**888-669-9660**	401-331-9097	96
Books On Tape Inc PO Box 25122	Santa Ana	CA	92799	**800-882-6657**	714-825-0021	623-2
Booksellers Assn. American 828 S Broadway	Tarrytown	NY	10591	**800-637-0037**	914-591-2665	49-18
BookSense.com 828 S Broadway	Tarrytown	NY	10591	**800-637-0037**	914-591-2665	96
Booksource Inc 1230 Macklind Ave	Saint Louis	MO	63110	**800-444-0435**	314-647-0600	97
Boomtown Casino Biloxi 676 Bayview Ave	Biloxi	MS	39530	**800-627-0777**	228-435-7000	133
Boomtown Casino & Hotel Reno 2100 Garson Rd	Verdi	NV	89439	**800-648-3790**	775-345-6000	133
Boomtown Casino New Orleans 4132 Peters Rd	Harvey	LA	70058	**800-366-7711**	504-366-7711	133

Name / Address	City	State	ZIP	Toll-Free	Phone	Class
Boomtown Hotel Casino 300 Riverside Dr	Bossier City	LA	71111	**877-862-4428**	318-746-0711	133
Boomtown Inc PO Box 399	Verdi	NV	89439	**800-648-3790**	775-345-6000	132
Boone Convention & Visitors Bureau 208 Howard St	Boone	NC	28607	**800-852-9506**	828-262-3516	205
Boone County Rural Electric Membership Corp 1207 Indianapolis Ave	Lebanon	IN	46052	**800-897-7362**	765-482-2390	244
Boone Daniel Regional Library 100 W Broadway	Columbia	MO	65203	**800-324-4806**	573-443-3161	426
Boone Electric Co-op 1413 Rangeline St	Columbia	MO	65205	**800-225-8143**	573-449-4181	244
Boone News-Republican 2136 E Mamie Eisenhower Ave	Boone	IA	50036	**888-270-0090**	515-432-1234	522-2
Boone Tavern Hotel of Berea College 100 Main St	Berea	KY	40404	**800-366-9358**	859-985-3700	373
Boos Dental Laboratories 801 12th Ave N	Minneapolis	MN	55411	**800-333-2667**	612-529-9655	406
Booth Theatre 222 W 45th St	New York	NY	10036	**800-432-7250**	212-239-6200	732
Boral Bricks Inc 1630 Arthern Rd	Augusta	GA	30903	**800-580-3842**	706-823-8802	148
Borbon Inc 7312 Walnut Ave	Buena Park	CA	90620	**800-929-1467**	714-994-0170	188-8
Border States Electric Supply 105 25th St N	Fargo	ND	58102	**800-676-5833**	701-293-5834	245
Borderland Tours 2550 W Calle Padilla	Tucson	AZ	85745	**800-525-7763**	520-882-7650	740
Borders Group Inc 100 Phoenix Dr *NYSE: BGP* ■ *Cust Svc	Ann Arbor	MI	48108	**800-566-6616***	734-477-1100	96
Borders Inc 100 Phoenix Dr *Cust Svc	Ann Arbor	MI	48108	**800-566-6616***	734-477-1100	96
Borg Produce Co 1601 E Olympic Blvd Bldg 100 Suite 101	Los Angeles	CA	90021	**800-808-2674**	213-688-9388	12-1
Boride Products Inc 2879 Aero Park Dr	Traverse City	MI	49686	**800-662-2131**	231-946-2100	1
Borland Software Corp 100 Enterprise Way *NASDAQ: BORL* ■ *Cust Svc	Scotts Valley	CA	95066	**800-331-0877***	831-431-1000	176-2
BORN Information Services Group 301 Carlson Pkwy Suite 500	Minnetonka	MN	55305	**800-469-2676**	952-258-6000	178
Bornhoft Concrete Products Inc 150 County Rd 8	Tyler	MN	56178	**800-257-5576**	507-247-5575	180
Bornstein Louis & Co 321 Washington St *Sales	Somerville	MA	02143	**800-842-1111***	617-776-3555	356
Borough of Manhattan Community College 199 Chambers St Rm S-300	New York	NY	10007	**877-669-2622**	212-220-1265	160
Borroughs Corp 3002 N Burdick St	Kalamazoo	MI	49004	**800-748-0227**	269-342-0161	281
Borsheim's Inc 120 Regency Pkwy	Omaha	NE	68114	**800-642-4438**	402-391-0400	402
Borzynski Brothers Distributing Inc PO Box 133	Franksville	WI	53126	**800-248-0420**	262-886-1623	11-11
Bosca Hugo Co Inc 1905 W Jefferson St	Springfield	OH	45506	**800-732-6722**	937-323-5523	422
Bosch Rexroth Corp 5150 Prairie Stone Pkwy	Hoffman Estates	IL	60192	**800-860-1055**	847-645-3600	507
Bosch Rexroth Corp Mobile Hydraulics Div PO Box 394	Wooster	OH	44691	**866-230-2790**	330-263-3300	777
Bosch Robert Corp Packaging Technology Div 9890 Red Arrow Hwy	Bridgman	MI	49106	**800-292-6724**	269-466-4000	537
Bosch Robert Tool Corp 4300 W Peterson Ave1800 W Central Rd	Mount Prospect	IL	60056	**800-301-8255**	224-223-2000	747
Bosch Security Systems 130 Perinton Pkwy	Fairport	NY	14450	**800-289-0096**	585-223-4060	681
Bose Corp The Mountain *Sales	Framingham	MA	01701	**800-444-2673***	508-879-7330	52
Boss Hugo Fashions Inc 601 W 26th St Suite 845	New York	NY	10001	**800-484-6207**	212-940-0600	153-12
Boss Mfg Co 221 W 1st St *Cust Svc	Kewanee	IL	61443	**800-447-4581***	309-852-2131	153-8
Bossier Civic Center 620 Benton Rd	Bossier City	LA	71111	**800-522-4842**	318-741-8900	204
Bossong Hosiery Mills Inc 840 W Salisbury St	Asheboro	NC	27203	**800-833-8895**	336-625-2175	153-10
Bost Neckwear Co Inc 503 Industrial Pk PO Box 1065	Asheboro	NC	27204	**800-334-8441**	336-625-6650	153-13
Bostik Inc 11320 Watertown Plank Rd	Wauwatosa	WI	53226	**800-558-4302**	414-774-2250	3
Boston Acoustics Inc 300 Jubilee Dr *NASDAQ: BOSA*	Peabody	MA	01960	**800-288-6148**	978-538-5000	52
Boston Advisors Inc 1 Federal St 26th Fl	Boston	MA	02110	**800-523-5903**	617-348-3100	393
Boston Beer Co 75 Arlington St *NYSE: SAM*	Boston	MA	02116	**800-372-1131**	617-368-5000	103
Boston College 140 Commonwealth Ave	Chestnut Hill	MA	02467	**800-360-2522**	617-552-8000	163
Boston Consulting Group Inc 53 State St 31st Fl	Boston	MA	02109	**800-367-1989**	617-973-1200	193
Boston Federal Savings Bank 17 New England Executive Park	Burlington	MA	01803	**800-688-2372**	781-272-0230	71
Boston Financial Data Services 2 Heritage Dr	North Quincy	MA	02171	**888-772-2337**	617-483-5000	393
Boston Gear 14 Hayward St *Cust Svc	Quincy	MA	02171	**888-999-9860***	617-328-3300	700
Boston (Greater) Convention & Visitors Bureau 2 Copley Pl Suite 105	Boston	MA	02116	**888-733-2678**	617-536-4100	205
Boston Harbor Hotel 70 Rowes Wharf	Boston	MA	02110	**800-752-7077**	617-439-7000	373
Boston Herald 1 Herald Sq	Boston	MA	02118	**800-225-2040**	617-426-3000	522-2
Boston Institutional Services Inc 100 Summer St 16th Fl	Boston	MA	02110	**800-325-5323**	617-223-5600	679
Boston Magazine 300 Massachusetts Ave	Boston	MA	02115	**800-333-2003**	617-262-9700	449-22
Boston Market Corp 14103 Denver West Pkwy	Golden	CO	80401	**800-877-2870**	303-278-9500	657
Boston Mutual Life Insurance Co 120 Royall St	Canton	MA	02021	**800-669-2668**	781-828-7000	384-2
Boston Park Plaza Hotel & Towers 64 Arlington St	Boston	MA	02116	**800-225-2008**	617-426-2000	373
Boston Pops 301 Massachusetts Ave Symphony Hall	Boston	MA	02115	**888-266-1200**	617-266-1492	563-3
Boston Proper 6500 Park of Commerce Blvd	Boca Raton	FL	33487	**800-327-3627**	561-241-1700	451
Boston Retail Products 400 Riverside Ave	Medford	MA	02155	**800-225-1633**	781-395-7417	281
Boston Sand & Gravel Co Inc 169 Portland St PO Box 9187	Boston	MA	02114	**800-624-2724**	617-227-9000	180
Boston Scientific Corp 1 Boston Scientific Pl *NYSE: BSX*	Natick	MA	01760	**800-272-3737**	508-650-8000	468
Boston Symphony Orchestra 301 Massachusetts Ave Symphony Hall	Boston	MA	02115	**888-266-1200**	617-266-1492	563-3
Boston Towing & Transportation Co LP 36 New St	East Boston	MA	02128	**800-836-8847**	617-567-9100	457
Boston Warehouse Trading Corp 59 Davis Ave	Norwood	MA	02062	**888-923-2982**	781-769-8550	356
BostonCoach 69 Norman St	Everett	MA	02149	**800-672-7676**	617-394-3900	433
Bostonian Hotel. Millennium 26 North St Faneuil Hall Marketplace	Boston	MA	02109	**800-343-0922**	617-523-3600	373
Boston's Best Chimney Sweep 80 Rear Bacon St	Waltham	MA	02451	**800-660-6708**	781-893-6611	150
BostonWorks.com c/o Boston Globe PO Box 2378	Boston	MA	02107	**888-566-4562**	617-929-2000	257
Bostrom Seating Inc 50 Nances Creek Industrial Blvd	Piedmont	AL	36272	**800-459-7328**	256-447-9051	678
Bostwick-Braun Co PO Box 912	Toledo	OH	43697	**800-777-9640**	419-259-3600	346
Botanical Council. American 6200 Manor Rd	Austin	TX	78723	**800-373-7105**	512-926-4900	48-17
Bott Radio Network 10550 Barkley St	Overland Park	KS	66212	**800-875-1903**	913-642-7770	629
Bottega Veneta Inc 635 Madison Ave	New York	NY	10022	**877-362-1715**	212-371-5511	422
Bottineau Convention & Visitor Bureau 519 Main St	Bottineau	ND	58318	**800-735-6932**	701-228-3849	205
Bottled Water Assn. International 1700 Diagonal Rd Suite 650	Alexandria	VA	22314	**800-928-3711**	703-683-5213	49-6
Bottom Line/Health Newsletter 281 Tresser Blvd *Cust Svc	Stamford	CT	06901	**800-289-0409***	203-973-5900	521-8
Bottom Line/Personal Newsletter 281 Tresser Blvd *Cust Svc	Stamford	CT	06901	**800-274-5611***	203-973-5900	521-6
Bottomline Technologies Inc 325 Corporate Dr *NASDAQ: EPAY*	Portsmouth	NH	03801	**800-243-2528**	603-436-0700	176-1
Bouchard John & Sons Co 1024 Harrison St	Nashville	TN	37203	**800-842-9156**	615-256-0112	188-10
Boucher Communications Inc 1300 Virginia Dr Suite 400	Fort Washington	PA	19034	**800-306-6332**	215-643-8000	623-9
Boulder Book Store 1107 Pearl St	Boulder	CO	80302	**800-244-4651**	303-447-2074	96
Boulder Convention & Visitors Bureau 2440 Pearl St	Boulder	CO	80302	**800-444-0447**	303-442-2911	205
Boulder Daily Camera 1048 Pearl St	Boulder	CO	80302	**800-783-1202**	303-442-1202	522-2
Boulder Mountain Lodge 91 Four-Mile Canyon Rd	Boulder	CO	80302	**800-458-0882**	303-444-0882	373
Boulder Station Hotel & Casino 4111 Boulder Hwy	Las Vegas	NV	89121	**800-683-7777**	702-432-7777	133
Boulders Resort & Golden Door Spa - A Wyndham Luxury Resort 34631 N Tom Darlington Dr PO Box 2090	Carefree	AZ	85377	**800-553-1717**	480-488-9009	655
Bouma Corp 4101 Roger B Chaffee Memorial Blvd	Grand Rapids	MI	49548	**800-813-9208**	616-538-3600	188-9
Bound to Stay Bound Books Inc 1880 W Morton Ave	Jacksonville	IL	62650	**800-637-6586**	217-245-5191	93
Boundless Corp 100 Marcus Blvd	Hauppauge	NY	11788	**800-342-7400**	631-342-7400	171-3
Bounty Trading Corp 1370 Broadway 14th Fl	New York	NY	10018	**800-526-8689**	212-279-5900	154
Bouras Industries Inc 25 DeForest Ave	Summit	NJ	07901	**800-631-1215**	908-277-1617	483
Boutique Spa at the Ritz-Carlton Georgetown 3100 South St NW	Washington	DC	20007	**800-241-3333**	202-912-4175	698
Bouton HL Co Inc 11 Kendrick Rd *Cust Svc	Wareham	MA	02571	**800-426-1881***	508-295-3300	531
Bovie Aaron Medical Industries 7100 30th Ave N	Saint Petersburg	FL	33710	**800-537-2790**	727-384-2323	249
Bovie Medical Corp 734 Walt Whitman Rd Suite 207 *AMEX: BVX*	Melville	NY	11747	**800-888-4999**	631-421-5452	249
Bovine Practitioners. American Assn of PO Box 1755	Rome	GA	30162	**800-269-2227**	706-232-2220	48-2
Bowater Inc Newsprint & Directory Div PO Box 1028	Greenville	SC	29602	**800-845-6002**	864-271-7733	547
Bowdon Mfg Co 127 N Carrol St	Bowdon	GA	30108	**800-937-7242**	770-258-7201	153-21
BOWE Bell + Howell Co 760 S Wolf Rd	Wheeling	IL	60090	**800-327-4608**	847-675-7600	171-7
BOWE Bell & Howell Mail & Messaging Technologies 3791 S Alston Ave	Durham	NC	27713	**800-220-3030**	919-767-7595	112
Bowe Machine Co 2527 State St	Bettendorf	IA	52722	**800-822-2693**	563-355-4777	446
Bowhunting World Magazine 14505 21st Ave N Suite 202	Plymouth	MN	55447	**800-766-0039**	763-473-5800	449-20
Bowie-Cass Electric Co-op Inc 117 North St	Douglassville	TX	75560	**800-794-2919**	903-846-2311	244
Bowie Industries Inc 1004 E Wise	Bowie	TX	76230	**800-433-0934**	940-872-1106	269
Bowie Mfg Inc 313 S Hancock	Lake City	IA	51449	**800-831-0960**	712-464-3191	595
Bowie State University 14000 Jericho Park Rd	Bowie	MD	20715	**877-772-6943**	301-860-4000	163
Bowl New England Inc 215 Lower Mountain View Dr	Colchester	VT	05446	**800-633-3535**	802-655-3468	100
Bowles Group of Cos DBA Workforce 2000 1903 Central Dr Suite 200	Bedford	TX	76021	**800-522-9778**	817-868-7277	619
Bowles Mattress Co Inc 1220 Watt St	Jeffersonville	IN	47130	**800-223-7509**	812-288-8614	463
Bowlin Travel Centers Inc 150 Louisiana Blvd NE	Albuquerque	NM	87108	**800-334-2236**	505-266-5985	8

Name / Address	City	State	ZIP	Toll-Free	Phone	Class
Bowling Congress. American 5301 S 76th St	Greendale	WI	53129	**800-514-2695**	414-421-6400	48-22
Bowling Congress. Women's International 5301 S 76th St	Greendale	WI	53129	**800-514-2695**	414-421-9000	48-22
Bowling Digest 990 Grove St	Evanston	IL	60201	**800-877-5893**	847-491-6440	449-20
Bowling Museum & Hall of Fame. International 111 Stadium Plaza Dr	Saint Louis	MO	63102	**800-966-2695**	314-231-6340	511
Bowling Proprietors Assn of America Inc (BPAA) 615 Six Flags Dr PO Box 5802	Arlington	TX	76005	**800-343-1329**	817-649-5105	48-23
Bowman Hollis Mfg Inc 2925 Old Steele Creek Rd	Charlotte	NC	28208	**888-269-2358**	704-374-1500	729
Bowne DecisionQuest 2050 W 190th St Suite 205	Torrance	CA	90504	**800-327-2449**	310-618-9600	436
Bowne Global Solutions 6500 Wilshire Blvd Suite 700	Los Angeles	CA	90048	**800-336-9898**	323-866-1000	193
Bowstreet Inc 200 Ames Pond Dr	Tewksbury	MA	01876	**877-663-2978**	978-863-1500	39
Boxley Co Inc PO Box 13527	Roanoke	VA	24035	**800-442-8878**	540-777-7600	493-5
Boxlight Corp 19472 Powder Hill Pl NE Suite 100	Poulsbo	WA	98370	**800-762-5757**	360-779-7901	580
Boyajian Inc 144 Will Dr	Canton	MA	02021	**800-419-4677**	781-828-9966	291-41
Boyar-Schultz Div WA Whitney Corp 650 Race St	Rockford	IL	61105	**800-435-2823**	815-964-6771	447
Boyd-Bluford Inc PO Box 12240	Norfolk	VA	23541	**800-985-2828**	757-855-6036	744
Boyd Bros Transportation Inc 3275 Hwy 30 *NASDAQ: BOYD*	Clayton	AL	36016	**800-338-2693**	334-775-1400	769
Boyd Coffee Co 19730 NE Sandy Blvd *Cust Svc	Portland	OR	97230	**800-545-4077***	503-666-4545	291-7
Boyd Corp 600 S McClure Rd	Modesto	CA	95357	**800-554-0200**	209-236-1111	664
Boyd Gaming Corp 2950 Industrial Rd *NYSE: BYD*	Las Vegas	NV	89109	**800-695-2455**	702-792-7200	132
Boyd Printing Co Inc 49 Sheridan Ave	Albany	NY	12210	**800-877-2693**	518-436-9686	614
Boyd Ty Ty Boyd Executive Learning Systems 1727 Garden Terr	Charlotte	NC	28203	**800-336-2693**	704-333-9999	561
Boyland Auto Group Inc 710 W Marine Dr	Astoria	OR	97103	**888-760-9303**	503-325-6411	57
Boyle Father Gregory J Homeboy Industries 1916 E 1st St	Los Angeles	CA	90033	**800-526-1254**		561
Boyle Investment Co 5900 Poplar Ave Suite 100	Memphis	TN	38119	**888-862-6953**	901-767-0100	641
Boyle John & Co Inc 1803 Salisbury Rd *Cust Svc	Statesville	NC	28677	**800-438-1061***	704-872-8151	730-2
Boyle's Famous Corned Beef Co 1638 St Louis Ave	Kansas City	MO	64101	**800-821-3626**	816-221-6283	291-26
Boyne Country Sports 1200 Bay View Rd	Petoskey	MI	49770	**800-462-6963**	231-439-4906	702
Boyne Highlands Resort 600 Highlands Dr	Harbor Springs	MI	49740	**800-462-6963**	231-526-3000	655
Boyne Mountain Resort PO Box 19	Boyne Falls	MI	49713	**800-462-6963**	231-549-6000	655
Boyne USA Inc PO Box 19	Boyne Falls	MI	49713	**800-462-6963**	231-549-6000	369
Boynton Beach Times 1701 Green Rd Suite B	Deerfield Beach	FL	33064	**800-275-8820**	954-698-6397	522-4
Boys & Girls Clubs of America 1230 W Peachtree St NW	Atlanta	GA	30309	**800-854-2582**	404-487-5700	48-15
Boys Ranch. Cal Farley's 600 W 11th St	Amarillo	TX	79174	**800-687-3722**	806-372-2341	48-6
Bozzuto Group 7850 Walker Dr Suite 400	Greenbelt	MD	20770	**800-718-0200**	301-220-0100	186
BP Amoco Credit Card 4300 Westown Pkwy	West Des Moines	IA	50266	**800-850-6266**	800-462-6626	213
BP Chemicals 150 W Warrenville Rd	Naperville	IL	60563	**877-701-2726**	630-420-5111	142
BP MotorClub 200 N Martingale Rd	Schaumburg	IL	60196	**800-334-3300**		53
BP Solvay Polyethylene North America 3333 Richmond Ave	Houston	TX	77098	**800-231-6313**	713-525-4000	594-2
BPAA (Bowling Proprietors Assn of America Inc) 615 Six Flags Dr PO Box 5802	Arlington	TX	76005	**800-343-1329**	817-649-5105	48-23
BPB 2424 Lakeshore Rd W	Mississauga	ON	L5J1K4	**866-272-8722**	905-823-9881	341
BPB Gypsum 27442 Portola Pkwy Suite 100	Foothill Ranch	CA	92610	**800-426-3669**	949-282-5300	341
BR Kreider & Son Inc 63 Kreider Ln	Manheim	PA	17545	**800-689-7651**	717-898-7651	188-5
Brabston Legal Investigations Inc 3746 Halls Mills Rd	Mobile	AL	36693	**800-239-4939**	251-666-5666	392
Brach's Confections Inc 19111 N Dallas Pkwy Suite 200	Dallas	TX	75287	**800-999-0204**	972-930-3600	291-8
Bracker's Department Store 68 N Morley Ave	Nogales	AZ	85621	**800-635-5431**	520-287-3631	227
Brackett Inc PO Box 19306	Topeka	KS	66619	**800-255-3506**	785-862-2205	617
Braco Window Cleaning Service Inc 1 Braco International Blvd	Wilder	KY	41076	**877-878-7091**	859-442-6000	150
Bradbury Co Inc PO Box 667	Moundridge	KS	67107	**800-397-6394**	620-345-6394	448
Braden Mfg LLC 5199 N Mingo Rd	Tulsa	OK	74117	**800-272-3360**	918-272-5371	471
Braden Sutphin Ink Co 3650 E 93rd St	Cleveland	OH	44105	**800-289-6872**	216-271-2300	381
Bradenton Area Convention & Visitors Bureau PO Box 1000	Bradenton	FL	34206	**800-822-2017**	941-729-9177	205
Bradford & Bigelow Inc 1 Electronic Ave Danvers Industrial Pk	Danvers	MA	01923	**800-882-9503**	978-777-1200	614
Bradford Health Services 2101 Magnolia Ave S Suite 518	Birmingham	AL	35205	**800-217-2849**	205-251-7753	712
Bradford School 2469 Stelzer Rd	Columbus	OH	43219	**800-678-7981**	614-416-6200	158
Bradford White Corp 725 Talamore Dr	Ambler	PA	19002	**800-523-2931**	215-641-9400	36
Bradley Academy for Visual Arts 1409 Williams Rd	York	PA	17402	**800-864-7725**	717-755-2300	159
Bradley Boulder 2040 16th St	Boulder	CO	80302	**800-858-5811**	303-545-5200	373
Bradley Caldwell Inc 200 Kiwanis Blvd	Hazleton	PA	18202	**800-257-9100**	570-455-7511	272
Bradley Corp PO Box 309	Menomonee Falls	WI	53051	**800-272-3539**	262-251-6000	598
Bradley Direct 7100 Jamesson Rd	Midland	GA	31820	**800-252-8248**		36
Bradley EB Co 5080 S Alameda St	Los Angeles	CA	90058	**800-533-3030**	323-585-9201	346
Bradley Inn 3063 Bristol Rd	New Harbor	ME	04554	**800-942-5560**	207-677-2105	373
Bradley Pharmaceuticals Inc 383 Rt 46 W *NYSE: BDY*	Fairfield	NJ	07004	**800-929-9300**	973-882-1505	572
Bradley University 1501 W Bradley Ave	Peoria	IL	61625	**800-447-6460**	309-676-7611	163
Bradmark Technologies Inc 4265 San Felipe Suite 800	Houston	TX	77027	**800-621-2808**	713-621-2808	176-1
Bradner Smith & Co 2300 Arthur Ave	Elk Grove Village	IL	60007	**800-678-1852**	847-290-8485	543
Brady Coated Products 6555 W Good Hope Rd	Milwaukee	WI	53223	**800-635-7557**	414-358-6600	717
Brady Corp 6555 W Good Hope Rd *NYSE: BRC* ■ *Cust Svc	Milwaukee	WI	53223	**800-537-8791***	414-358-6600	404
Brady Enterprises Inc 167 Moore Rd	East Weymouth	MA	02189	**800-225-5126**	781-337-5000	291-15
Brady Identification Solutions 6555 W Good Hope Rd *Cust Svc	Milwaukee	WI	53223	**800-537-8791***	414-358-6600	176-1
Brady Industries Inc 4175 S Arville St	Las Vegas	NV	89103	**800-293-4698**	702-876-3990	398
Brady Marketing Co 80 Berry Dr Suite A	Pacheco	CA	94553	**800-326-6080**	925-676-1300	38
Brady's Sportsman's Surplus Inc 2315 Brooks St	Missoula	MT	59801	**800-473-4867**	406-721-5501	702
Braemar Inc 11481 Rupp Dr	Burnsville	MN	55337	**800-328-2719**	952-890-5135	468
Bragg-Mitchell Mansion 1906 Springhill Ave	Mobile	AL	36607	**866-471-6364**	251-471-6364	509
Braid Electric Co Inc 299 Cowan St	Nashville	TN	37213	**800-342-1115**	615-242-6511	245
Braille-Tac Div Advance Corp 8200 97th St S	Cottage Grove	MN	55016	**800-328-9451**	651-771-9297	692
Brain Injury Assn of America 8201 Greensboro Dr Suite 611	McLean	VA	22102	**800-444-6443**	703-761-0750	48-17
Brain Tumor Assn. American 2720 River Rd	Des Plaines	IL	60018	**800-886-2282**	847-827-9910	48-17
Brainerd Dispatch 506 James St	Brainerd	MN	56401	**800-432-3703**	218-829-4705	522-2
Brainerd Lakes Area Chamber of Commerce PO Box 356	Brainerd	MN	56401	**800-450-2838**	218-829-2838	137
Brainerd Lakes Area Convention & Visitors Bureau 124 N 6th St	Brainerd	MN	56401	**800-450-2838**	218-829-2838	205
Brainerd Mfg Co Inc 140 Business Pk Dr	Winston-Salem	NC	27107	**800-652-7277**		345
BrainLAB Inc 3 Westbrook Corp Ctr Suite 400	Westchester	IL	60154	**800-784-7700**	708-409-1343	375
Braintree Landing Skilled Nursing & Rehabilitation Center 95 Commercial St	Braintree	MA	02184	**800-498-8322**	781-848-3678	441
Brake Roller Co 730 E Michigan Ave	Battle Creek	MI	49016	**800-537-9940**	269-968-9311	206
Brake Supply Co Inc 1300 W Lloyd Expy	Evansville	IN	47708	**800-457-5788**	812-467-1000	378
Brake & Wheel Parts Industries Inc 2415 W 21st St	Chicago	IL	60608	**800-621-8836**	773-847-7000	61
Brakeley Briscoe Inc 51 Locust Ave Suite 204	New Canaan	CT	06804	**800-486-5171**	203-972-0282	312
Brakewell Steel Fabricator Inc 55 Leone Ln	Chester	NY	10918	**888-914-9131**	845-469-9131	473
Bralco Metals Div Reliance Steel & Aluminum Co 15090 Northam St	La Mirada	CA	90638	**800-628-1864**	714-736-4800	483
Brame Specialty Co Inc 2021 S Briggs Ave	Durham	NC	27703	**800-672-0011**	919-598-1500	549
Bramwell Capital Management 745 5th Ave 16th Fl	New York	NY	10151	**800-272-6227**	212-308-0505	393
Branch Banking & Trust Co of South Carolina PO Box 408	Greenville	SC	29602	**800-226-5228**	864-242-8000	71
Branch Banking & Trust Co of Virginia 109 E Main St	Norfolk	VA	23510	**800-226-5228**	757-823-7800	71
Brand Flowers Inc 5300 Foothill Rd	Carpinteria	CA	93013	**800-549-0089**	805-684-5531	363
Branded Emblem Co Inc 7920 Foster St	Overland Park	KS	66204	**800-747-7920**	913-648-7920	256
Brandeis Machinery & Supply Co 1801 Watterson Trail	Louisville	KY	40299	**800-274-7253**	502-493-4380	353
Brandeis University 415 South St	Waltham	MA	02454	**800-622-0622**	781-736-2000	163
BrandEquity International 2330 Washington St	Newton	MA	02462	**800-969-3150**	617-969-3150	338
Brandermill Inn 13550 Harbour Pointe Pkwy	Midlothian	VA	23112	**800-554-0130**	804-739-8871	373
Brandes Investment Partners LP 11988 El Camino Real Suite 500	San Diego	CA	92191	**800-237-7119**	858-755-0239	393
Brandom Cabinets Co 211 Campus Dr *Cust Svc	Keene	TX	76059	**800-366-8001***	817-645-8841	116
BrandsMart USA Corp 3200 SW 42nd St	Hollywood	FL	33312	**800-432-8579**	954-797-4000	35
Brandtjen & Kluge Inc 539 Blanding Woods Rd	Saint Croix Falls	WI	54024	**800-826-7320**	715-483-3265	617
Brandywine Asset Management Inc 201 N Walnut St Suite 1200	Wilmington	DE	19801	**800-348-2499**	302-654-6162	393
Brandywine Conference & Visitors Bureau 1 Beaver Valley Rd	Chadford	PA	19317	**800-343-3983**	610-565-3679	205
Brandywine Funds PO Box 701	Milwaukee	WI	53201	**800-656-3017**		517
Brandywine Investment Group Homalite Div 11 Brookside Dr	Wilmington	DE	19804	**800-346-7802**	302-652-3686	589
Brandywine Suites Hotel 707 N King St	Wilmington	DE	19801	**800-756-0070**	302-656-9300	373
Branscome Inc 4551 John Tyler Hwy	Williamsburg	VA	23185	**888-229-2504**	757-229-2504	493-4
Branson Daily News 200 Industrial Pk Dr	Hollister	MO	65672	**800-490-8020**	417-334-3161	522-2
Branson Deals 152 Christie Ln	Walnut Shade	MO	65771	**800-221-5692**		760
Branson Nights Reservations 109 N Business 65	Branson	MO	65616	**800-329-9999**	417-335-6971	368
Branson/Lakes Area Chamber of Commerce PO Box 1897	Branson	MO	65615	**800-214-3661**	417-334-4136	137
Branson/Lakes Area Convention & Visitors Bureau PO Box 1897	Branson	MO	65615	**800-214-3661**	417-334-4136	205

Name / Address	City	State	ZIP	Toll-Free	Phone	Class
Branson/Lakes Area Lodging Assn PO Box 430	Branson	MO	65615	**888-238-6782**	417-332-1400	368
Branson's Best Reservations 3150 Green Mountain Dr	Branson	MO	65616	**800-800-2019**	417-339-2204	368
Branton Industries Inc 1101 Edwards Ave	Harahan	LA	70123	**800-548-5783**	504-733-7770	190-4
Brasfield & Gorrie LLC 729 S 30th St	Birmingham	AL	35233	**800-239-8017**	205-328-4000	185
Brass Eagle Inc 1201 SE 30th St	Bentonville	AR	72712	**877-877-4263**	479-464-8700	701
Brasseler USA 1 Brasseler Blvd	Savannah	GA	31419	**800-841-4522**	912-925-8525	226
BrassRing Inc 343 Winter St	Waltham	MA	02451	**888-265-6969**	781-530-5000	257
Brasstech Inc 2001 E Carnegie Ave	Santa Ana	CA	92705	**888-436-0805**	949-417-5207	598
Brasstown Valley Resort 6321 US Hwy 76	Young Harris	GA	30582	**800-201-3205**	706-379-9900	655
Braswell AM Jr Food Co 226 N Zetterower Ave	Statesboro	GA	30458	**800-673-9388**	912-764-6191	291-20
Brattleboro Area Chamber of Commerce 180 Main St	Brattleboro	VT	05301	**877-254-4565**	802-254-4565	137
Brattleboro Reformer 62 Black Mountain Rd Box 802	Brattleboro	VT	05302	**800-649-2311**	802-254-2311	522-2
Brauer Brothers Mfg Co 1520 Washington Ave 4th Fl	Saint Louis	MO	63103	**800-527-2837**	314-231-2864	423
Brauer Supply Co 4260 Forest Park Ave	Saint Louis	MO	63108	**800-392-8776**	314-534-7150	601
Braun Consulting Inc 20 W Kinzie St Suite 1600 *NASDAQ: BRNC*	Chicago	IL	60610	**800-682-7286**	312-984-7000	796
Braun GA Inc PO Box 70	Syracuse	NY	13205	**800-432-7286**	315-475-3123	418
Braun Intertec Corp 11001 Hampshire Ave S	Bloomington	MN	55438	**800-279-6100**	952-995-2000	258
Braun North America 1 Gillette Pk *Cust Svc	Boston	MA	02127	**800-272-8611***	617-463-3000	37
Bravo Cucina Italiana 4644 Kenny Rd	Columbus	OH	43220	**888-452-7286**	614-326-7944	657
Bravo Sports 6600 Katella Ave *Cust Svc	Cypress	CA	90630	**800-773-1111***	714-850-8800	588
Bravo! Development Inc 4644 Kenny Rd	Columbus	OH	43220	**888-452-7286**	614-326-7944	656
Brawn of California Inc 741 F St	San Diego	CA	92101	**800-293-9333**	619-544-9900	451
Brayton International Inc 250 Swathmoore St	High Point	NC	27263	**800-627-6770**	336-434-4151	314-1
Brazil Times 100 N Meridian St	Brazil	IN	47834	**800-489-5090**	812-446-2216	522-2
Brazilian Court Hotel 301 Australian Ave	Palm Beach	FL	33480	**800-552-0335**	561-655-7740	373
Brazos Mutual Funds 5949 Sherry Ln Suite 1600	Dallas	TX	75225	**800-426-9157**	214-365-5214	517
Brazosport Area Chamber of Commerce 420 W Hwy 332	Clute	TX	77531	**888-477-2505**	979-265-2505	137
Brazosport Facts 720 S Main St	Clute	TX	77531	**800-864-8340**	979-265-7411	522-2
BRB Publications Inc PO Box 27869	Tempe	AZ	85285	**800-929-3811**	480-829-7475	623-2
Bread for the World 50 F St NW Suite 500 *Cust Svc	Washington	DC	20001	**800-822-7323***	202-639-9400	48-5
Breadeaux Pisa Inc 3308 S Leonard Rd	Saint Joseph	MO	64503	**800-835-6534**	816-364-1088	657
Breadshop Inc 16100 Foothill Blvd	Irwindale	CA	91706	**800-334-3204**		291-4
Breakaway Tours 10 Kingsbridge Garden Cir Suite 400	Mississauga	ON	L5R3K6	**800-465-4257**	905-501-9774	748
Breakers The 1 S County Rd	Palm Beach	FL	33480	**800-833-3141**	561-655-6611	655
Breakers Hotel 3rd St & Boardwalk	Ocean City	MD	21843	**800-283-9165**	410-289-9165	373
Breakers Hotel & Suites 105 2nd St	Rehoboth Beach	DE	19971	**800-441-8009**	302-227-6688	373
Breakers Inn 2506 Beach Blvd	Biloxi	MS	39531	**800-624-5031**	228-388-6320	373
Breakers Resort Inn 1503 Atlantic Ave	Virginia Beach	VA	23451	**800-237-7532**	757-428-1821	373
Breakers Resort & Paradise Tower 2006 N Ocean Blvd	Myrtle Beach	SC	29577	**800-845-0688**	843-626-5000	373
Breakers at Waikiki 250 Beach Walk	Waikiki	HI	96815	**800-426-0494**	808-923-3181	373
Breakthrough Learning Inc 17800 Woodland Ave	Morgan Hill	CA	95037	**800-221-3637**	408-779-0701	753
Breakwater Inn 1711 Glacier Ave	Juneau	AK	99801	**800-544-2250**	907-586-6303	373
Breast Cancer Coalition. National 1101 17th St NW Suite 1300	Washington	DC	20036	**800-622-2838**	202-296-7477	48-17
Breast Cancer Foundation. Susan G Komen 5005 LBJ Fwy Suite 250	Dallas	TX	75244	**800-462-9273**	972-855-1600	48-17
Breast Cancer Organization. Y-ME National 212 W Van Buren St	Chicago	IL	60607	**800-221-2141**	312-986-8338	48-17
Brechet & Richter Co 6005 Golden Valley Rd *Sales	Minneapolis	MN	55422	**800-347-8700***	763-545-0201	292-11
Breckenridge Ski Resort 351 County Rd 708	Breckenridge	CO	80424	**800-789-7669**	970-453-5000	655
Brede Exposition Services Div Casey & Hayes Exhibits Inc 100 Industrial Pk Rd	Hingham	MA	02043	**800-835-0167**	781-741-5900	183
Breeden Homes Inc 366 E 40th Ave *Sales	Eugene	OR	97405	**800-322-3198***	541-686-9431	186
Breeders Assn. Thoroughbred Owners & PO Box 4367	Lexington	KY	40544	**888-606-8622**	859-276-2291	48-3
Breeders' & Exhibitors' Assn. Tennessee Walking Horse PO Box 286	Lewisburg	TN	37091	**800-359-1574**	931-359-1574	48-3
Breeders Journal 1525 River Rd	DeForest	WI	53532	**800-356-5331**	608-846-6211	449-1
Breeze-Eastern Div TransTechnology Corp 700 Liberty Ave *Sales	Union	NJ	07083	**800-929-1919***	908-686-4000	462
Breezy Point Resort 9252 Breezy Point Dr	Breezy Point	MN	56472	**800-432-3777**	218-562-7811	655
Bremen Castings Inc 500 N Baltimore St	Bremen	IN	46506	**800-837-2411**	574-546-2411	302
Bremner Biscuit Co 4600 Joliet St	Denver	CO	80239	**800-722-1871**	303-371-8180	291-9
Bremner Inc 800 Market St PO Box 618 *Cust Svc	Saint Louis	MO	63101	**800-725-7866***	314-877-7000	291-9
Brenau University 1 Centennial Cir	Gainesville	GA	30501	**800-252-5119**	770-534-6299	163
Brenco Inc PO Box 389	Petersburg	VA	23804	**800-238-4712**	804-732-0202	77
Brendan Worldwide Vacations 21625 Prairie St	Chatsworth	CA	91311	**800-421-8446**	818-428-6000	748
Brendle Sprinkler Co Inc PO Box 210609	Montgomery	AL	36121	**800-392-8021**	334-270-8571	188-13
Brenham Wholesale Grocery Co 602 W 1st St	Brenham	TX	77833	**800-324-3232**	979-836-7925	292-8
Brenham/Washington County Convention & Visitor Bureau 314 S Austin St	Brenham	TX	77833	**800-225-3695**	979-836-3695	205
Brennan International Transport Inc 2665 E Del Amo Blvd	Rancho Dominguez	CA	90221	**866-427-3662**	310-637-7000	308
Brennan Vacations 1402 3rd Ave Suite 717	Seattle	WA	98101	**800-237-7249**	206-622-9155	748
Brennco Travel Services Inc 6600 College Blvd Suite 130	Overland Park	KS	66211	**800-955-1909**	913-660-0121	760
Brenner Tank LLC 450 Arlington Ave	Fond du Lac	WI	54935	**800-558-9750**	920-922-5020	768
Brenner Tours 2535 132nd Ave	Hopkins	MI	49328	**800-338-5963**	269-793-7430	748
Brenntag Great Lakes LLC PO Box 444	Butler	WI	53007	**800-558-8501**	262-252-3550	144
Brenntag Mid-South Inc 1405 Hwy 136 W	Henderson	KY	42419	**800-950-7267**	270-830-1200	144
Brenntag Southwest Inc 610 Fisher Rd	Longview	TX	75604	**800-945-1858**	903-759-7151	144
Brent House Hotel 1512 Jefferson Hwy	New Orleans	LA	70121	**800-535-3986**	504-835-5411	373
Brentwood A Behavioral Health Co 1006 Highland Ave	Shreveport	LA	71101	**877-678-7500**	318-678-7500	366-3
Brescia University 717 Frederica St	Owensboro	KY	42301	**877-273-7242**	270-685-3131	163
Bresnan Communications Co 1 Manhattanville Rd	Purchase	NY	10577	**888-909-4357**	914-641-3300	117
Bresser's Cross Index Directory Co 684 W Baltimore St	Detroit	MI	48202	**800-878-3333**	313-874-0570	623-6
Bretford Mfg Inc 11000 Seymour Ave	Franklin Park	IL	60131	**800-521-9614**	847-678-2545	314-3
Brethren. Church of the 1451 Dundee Ave	Elgin	IL	60120	**800-323-8039**	847-742-5100	48-20
Brethren Missionary Herald 1104 Kings Hwy	Winona Lake	IN	46590	**800-348-2756**	574-267-7158	623-8
Brethren Press 1451 Dundee Ave	Elgin	IL	60120	**800-441-3712**	847-742-5100	623-4
Breuner's 3250 Buskirk Ave	Pleasant Hill	CA	94523	**800-865-6778**	925-472-4500	316
Brevard College 400 N Broad St	Brevard	NC	28712	**800-527-9090**	828-883-8292	160
Brevard Community College						
Cocoa 1519 Clearlake Rd	Cocoa	FL	32922	**888-747-2802**	321-632-1111	160
Melbourne 3865 N Wickham Rd	Melbourne	FL	32935	**888-747-2802**	321-632-1111	160
Palm Bay 250 Community College Pkwy	Palm Bay	FL	32909	**888-747-2802**	321-632-1111	160
Titusville 1311 N US 1	Titusville	FL	32796	**888-747-2802**	321-632-1111	160
Brevard-Transylvania Chamber of Commerce 35 W Main St	Brevard	NC	28712	**800-648-4523**	828-883-3700	137
Brewer Co 1354 US Hwy 50	Milford	OH	45150	**800-394-0017**	513-576-6300	46
Brewery Products Co Inc 1017 N Sherman St *Cust Svc	York	PA	17402	**800-233-9433***	717-757-3515	82-1
Brewmatic Co 20333 S Normandie Ave PO Box 2959	Torrance	CA	90509	**800-421-6860**	310-787-5444	293
Brewster Academy 80 Academy Dr	Wolfeboro	NH	03894	**800-842-9961**	603-569-7200	611
Brewster Dairy Inc PO Box 98	Brewster	OH	44613	**800-874-8874**	330-767-3492	291-5
Brewster Heights Packing Inc 908 Hwy 97	Brewster	WA	98812	**800-967-3634**	509-689-3424	310-3
Brewster Panel Inc PO Box 669	Vernon	AL	35592	**800-243-8198**		281
Brewster Rocky Mountain Adventures 208 Caribou St	Banff	AB	T1L1A9	**800-691-5085**	403-762-5454	748
Brewster Transport Co Ltd 100 Gopher St PO Box 1140	Banff	AB	T1L1J3	**800-661-1152**	403-762-6700	748
Brewster's Coffee Co Inc 500 Lake Cook Rd Suite 475	Deerfield	IL	60015	**800-251-6101**	847-948-7520	156
Brewton-Parker College Hwy 280	Mount Vernon	GA	30445	**800-342-1087**	912-583-2241	163
Bri-Mar Mfg LLC 1080 S Main St	Chambersburg	PA	17201	**800-732-5845**	717-263-6116	768
Briar Cliff University 3303 Rebecca St	Sioux City	IA	51104	**800-662-3303**	712-279-5321	163
Briarcliff Haven Healthcare & Rehabiliation Center 1000 Briarcliff Rd NE	Atlanta	GA	30306	**800-454-5909**	404-875-6456	441
Briarwood College 2279 Mount Vernon Rd	Southington	CT	06489	**800-952-2444**	860-628-4751	160
Brice's Crossroads National Battlefield Site 2680 Natchez Trace Pkwy	Tupelo	MS	38804	**800-305-7417**	662-680-4025	554
Brick Bodies Fitness Services Inc 201 Old Padonia Mill Rd	Cockeysville	MD	21030	**877-348-3861**	410-252-8058	349
Brick & Tile Corp of Lawrenceville 16024 Governor Harrison Pkwy	Lawrenceville	VA	23868	**877-274-2582**	434-848-3151	148
Brickell Financial Services Motor Club Inc DBA Road America Motor Club 7300 Corporate Ctr Dr Suite 601	Miami	FL	33126	**800-262-7262**	305-392-4300	53
BrickKicker Inc 849 N Ellsworth St	Naperville	IL	60563	**800-821-1820**	630-420-9900	360
Bricklayers & Allied Craftworkers. International Union of 1776 'I' St NW Suite 500	Washington	DC	20006	**888-880-8222**	202-783-3788	405
Brickman Group Ltd 375 S Flowers Mill Rd	Langhorne	PA	19047	**800-451-7272**	215-757-9400	413
Bridal Guide Magazine 3 E 54th St 15th Fl	New York	NY	10022	**800-472-7744**	212-838-2570	449-11
Bridal Originals 1700 Saint Louis Rd	Collinsville	IL	62234	**800-876-4696**	618-345-4499	153-21
Bride's Magazine 4 Times Sq	New York	NY	10036	**800-223-0780**	212-286-2860	449-11
Bridge Ben Jeweler Inc PO Box 1908 *Cust Svc	Seattle	WA	98111	**888-448-1912***	206-448-8800	402
Bridge Home Health & Hospice 15100 Birchaven Ln	Findlay	OH	45840	**800-982-3306**	419-423-5351	365
Bridge Kitchenware Inc 214 E 52nd St	New York	NY	10022	**800-274-3435**	212-688-4220	357
Bridge League. American Contract 2990 Airways Blvd *Sales	Memphis	TN	38116	**800-264-2743***	901-332-5586	48-18
Bridge Structural Ornamental & Reinforcing Iron Workers. International Assn of 1750 New York Ave NW Suite 400	Washington	DC	20006	**800-368-0105**	202-383-4800	405

				Toll-Free	Phone	Class
Bridge Travel Alliance 2200 Powell St Suite 130	Emeryville	CA	94608	**800-762-5885**	510-496-8266	760
Bridgeford Flying Services 2030 Airport Rd Napa County Airport	Napa	CA	94558	**800-229-6272**	707-224-0887	14
Bridgeman Foods Inc 1903 Stanley Gault Pkwy	Louisville	KY	40223	**800-254-7130**	502-254-7130	656
BridgePort Brewing Co 1318 NW Northrup St	Portland	OR	97209	**888-834-7546**	503-241-7179	103
Bridgeport News 1000 Bridgeport Ave	Shelton	CT	06484	**800-843-6791**	203-926-2080	522-4
Bridger Valley Electric Assn Inc 40014 Business Loop 1-80	Mountain View	WY	82939	**800-276-3481**	307-786-2800	244
Bridgestone Americas Holding Inc 535 Marriott Dr	Nashville	TN	37214	**800-543-7522***	615-937-5000	739
*Cust Svc						
Bridgestone Multimedia Group Inc 300 N McKemy Ave	Chandler	AZ	85226	**800-622-3070***	480-940-5777	500
*Cust Svc						
BridgeStreet Accommodations Inc 2242 Pinnacle Pkwy	Twinsburg	OH	44087	**800-278-7338**	330-405-6060	209
Bridgewater College 402 E College St	Bridgewater	VA	22812	**800-759-8328**	540-828-5375	163
Bridgewater Hotel 723 1st Ave	Fairbanks	AK	99701	**800-528-4916**	907-452-6661	373
Bridgford Foods Corp 1308 N Patt St	Anaheim	CA	92801	**800-854-3255**	714-526-5533	291-26
NASDAQ: BRID						
Bridon Cordage LLC 909 16th St	Albert Lea	MN	56007	**800-563-2170**	507-377-1601	207
Briefing.com Inc 555 S Airport Blvd Suite 150	Burlingame	CA	94010	**800-752-3013**	650-347-2220	396
Brielmaier House 710 Beach Blvd	Biloxi	MS	39530	**800-245-6943**	228-374-3105	50
Briercrest Seminary 510 College Dr	Caronport	SK	S0H0S0	**888-232-0531**	306-756-3200	164-3
Briggs Equipment 2777 Stemmons Fwy Suite 1525	Dallas	TX	75207	**800-606-1833**	214-630-0808	378
Briggs Plumbing Products 300 Eagle Rd	Goose Creek	SC	29445	**800-888-4458**	843-569-7887	600
Briggs & Stratton Corp PO Box 702	Milwaukee	WI	53201	**800-444-7774**	414-259-5333	259
NYSE: BGG						
Briggs & Stratton Power Products Group LLC PO Box 239	Jefferson	WI	53549	**800-270-1408**	920-674-3750	507
Brigham & Women's Hospital 75 Francis St	Boston	MA	02115	**800-722-5520**	617-732-5500	366-5
Brigham's Inc 30 Mill St	Arlington	MA	02476	**800-274-4426**	781-648-9000	291-25
Bright of America Inc 300 Greenbrier Rd	Summersville	WV	26651	**800-877-1925**	304-872-3000	548-2
Bright Chair Co 51 Railroad Ave PO Box 269	Middletown	NY	10940	**888-524-5997**	845-343-2196	314-1
Bright Coop Inc 803 W Seale St	Nacogdoches	TX	75964	**800-562-0730**	936-564-8378	75
Bright Horizons Family Solutions Inc 200 Talcott Ave S	Watertown	MA	02472	**800-324-4386**	617-673-8000	146
NASDAQ: BFAM						
Bright Image Corp 4900 Harrison St	Hillside	IL	60162	**800-733-5656**	708-449-5656	202
Brighton Hospital 12851 E Grand River Ave	Brighton	MI	48116	**800-523-8198**	810-227-1221	712
Brighton Ski Resort 12601 E Big Cottonwood Canyon	Brighton	UT	84121	**800-873-5512**	801-532-4731	655
Brightpoint Inc 501 Airtech Pkwy	Plainfield	IN	46168	**800-952-2355**	317-707-2355	245
NASDAQ: CELL						
Brightstar Corp 2010 NW 84th Ave	Miami	FL	33122	**800-381-8402**	305-477-8676	245
Brillion Iron Works Inc 200 Park Ave PO Box 127	Brillion	WI	54110	**800-409-9749**	920-756-2121	269
Brine Inc 47 Sumner St	Milford	MA	01757	**800-227-2722**	508-478-3250	701
Brinker International Inc 6820 LBJ Fwy	Dallas	TX	75240	**800-983-4637**	972-980-9917	656
NYSE: EAT						
Brinkmann Corp 4215 McEwen Rd	Dallas	TX	75244	**800-527-0717**	972-387-4939	431
Brinkmann Instruments Inc 1 Cantiague Rd PO Box 1019	Westbury	NY	11590	**800-645-3050**	516-334-7500	411
Brink's Co PO Box 18100	Richmond	VA	23226	**877-877-9119**	804-289-9600	184
NYSE: BCO						
Brink's Home Security Inc 8880 Esters Blvd	Irving	TX	75063	**800-874-1190**	972-871-3500	683
Brinly-Hardy Co Inc 3230 Industrial Pkwy	Jeffersonville	IN	47130	**800-626-5329**	812-218-6080	420
BRIO Corp N 120 W 18485 Freistadt Rd	Germantown	WI	53022	**888-274-6869***	262-250-3240	750
*Cust Svc						
Brio Tuscan Grille 4644 Kenny Rd	Columbus	OH	43220	**888-452-7286**	614-326-7944	657
Brioschi Inc 19-01 Pollitt Dr	Fair Lawn	NJ	07410	**800-274-6724**	201-796-4226	572
Briot 5360 NW 35th Ave	Fort Lauderdale	FL	33309	**800-852-8089**	954-733-2300	411
Brisco Inc 251 Buckeye Cove Rd	Swannanoa	NC	28778	**877-585-2737**	828-298-1510	446
Brisk Waterproofing Co Inc 720 Grand Ave	Ridgefield	NJ	07657	**800-942-9228**	201-945-0210	188-7
Bristol Babcock Inc 1100 Buckingham St	Watertown	CT	06795	**800-395-5497**	860-945-2200	200
Bristol Broadcasting Co Inc PO Box 1389	Bristol	VA	24203	**800-253-8112**	276-669-8112	629
Bristol Herald-Courier 320 Bob Morrison Blvd	Bristol	VA	24201	**888-228-2098**	276-669-2181	522-2
Bristol Hotel 1055 1st Ave	San Diego	CA	92101	**800-662-4477**	619-232-6141	373
Bristol Memorial Works Inc 508 Farmington Ave	Bristol	CT	06010	**877-225-7626**	860-583-1654	710
Bristol-Myers Squibb Canada Inc 2365 Cote de Liesse Rd	Montreal	QC	H4N2M7	**800-267-1088**	514-333-3200	572
Bristol Press 99 Main St	Bristol	CT	06010	**800-220-6229**	860-584-0501	522-2
Bristol Products Corp 700 Shelby St	Bristol	TN	37620	**800-336-8775***	423-968-4140	153-1
*Orders						
Britannica.com Inc 310 S Michigan Ave	Chicago	IL	60604	**800-747-8503***	312-347-7000	623-10
*Cust Svc						
Britax Child Safety Inc 13501 S Ridge Dr	Charlotte	NC	28273	**888-427-4829**	704-409-1700	64
BriteSmile Inc 490 N Wiget Ln	Walnut Creek	CA	94598	**800-274-8376**	925-941-6260	347
NASDAQ: BSML						
British Airways 75-20 Astoria Blvd	Jackson Heights	NY	11370	**800-247-9297**	347-418-4000	26
British Airways Executive Club PO Box 1757	Minneapolis	MN	55440	**800-955-2748**		27
British Columbia Automobile Assn (BCAA) 4567 Canada Way	Burnaby	BC	V5G4T1	**800-222-4357**	604-268-5000	53
British Heritage Magazine 6405 Flank Dr	Harrisburg	PA	17112	**800-829-3340**	717-657-9555	449-14
British Virgin Islands Tourist Board 3450 Wilshire Blvd Suite 1202	Los Angeles	CA	90010	**800-835-8530**	213-736-8931	764
British Virgin Islands Tourist Board 1270 Broadway Suite 705	New York	NY	10017	**800-835-8530**	212-696-0400	764
Britt Trucking Co Inc PO Drawer 707	Lamesa	TX	79331	**800-448-9098**	806-872-3353	769
BRK Brands Inc 3901 Liberty Street Rd	Aurora	IL	60504	**800-323-9005**	630-851-7330	681
Bro-Tex Inc 800 Hampden Ave	Saint Paul	MN	55114	**800-328-2282**	651-645-5721	497
Broad River Electric Co-op Inc 811 Hamrick St	Gaffney	SC	29342	**866-687-2667**	864-489-5737	244
Broadcast Education Assn (BEA) 1771 'N' St NW	Washington	DC	20036	**888-380-7222**	202-429-5354	49-5
Broadcast International Inc 7050 Union Pk Ctr Suite 650	Midvale	UT	84047	**800-722-0400**	801-562-2252	721
Broadcast Technology Society. IEEE IEEE Operations Ctr 445 Hoes Ln	Piscataway	NJ	08854	**800-678-4333**	732-981-0060	49-19
Broadcasters. National Federation of Community 970 Broadway Suite 1000	Oakland	CA	94612	**888-280-6322**	510-451-8200	49-14
Broadcasting & Cable Magazine 360 Park Ave S	New York	NY	10010	**800-554-5729**	646-746-6965	449-5
Broadcasting & Communications Assn. Satellite 1730 M St NW Suite 600	Washington	DC	20036	**800-541-5981**	202-349-3620	49-14
Broadcasting. Corporation for Public 401 9th St NW	Washington	DC	20004	**800-272-2190**	202-879-9600	300
Broadhurst Theatre 235 W 44th St	New York	NY	10036	**800-432-7250**	212-239-6200	732
Broadman & Holman Publishers 1 Lifeway Plaza	Nashville	TN	37234	**800-251-3225**	615-251-2000	623-4
Broadmoor The 1 Lake Ave	Colorado Springs	CO	80906	**800-634-7711**	719-634-7711	655
Broadspire Services 1200 W 7th St Suite 410	Los Angeles	CA	90017	**800-323-9585**	213-986-1050	795
Broadview International 520 Madison Ave	New York	NY	10022	**800-346-9616**	212-284-8100	679
Broadview Networks Holdings Inc 59 Maiden Ln 27th Fl	New York	NY	10038	**800-260-8766**	212-400-1000	721
BroadVision Inc 585 Broadway	Redwood City	CA	94063	**800-269-9375**	650-542-5100	39
NASDAQ: BVSN						
Broadwater Resort. President Casino 2110 Beach Blvd	Biloxi	MS	39531	**800-843-7737**	228-388-2211	655
Broadway Electrical Service Co Inc PO Box 3250	Knoxville	TN	37927	**800-516-6992**	865-524-1851	188-4
Broadway Inn 264 W 46th St	New York	NY	10036	**800-826-6300**	212-997-9200	373
Broadway Theatre 1681 Broadway	New York	NY	10019	**800-432-7250**	212-239-6200	732
Broadway.com 1650 Broadway Suite 910	New York	NY	10019	**800-276-2392**	212-541-8457	735
Broadwing Corp 7015 Albert Einstein Dr	Columbia	MD	21046	**877-926-7847**	443-259-4000	720
NASDAQ: BWNG						
Broan-NuTone LLC 926 W State St	Hartford	WI	53027	**800-558-1711***	262-673-4340	37
*Cust Svc						
Brocade Communications Systems Inc 1745 Technology Dr	San Jose	CA	95110	**877-501-2723**	408-333-8000	174
NASDAQ: BRCD						
Brock Grain Conditioning Group 1750 W SR-28	Frankfort	IN	46041	**800-541-7900**	765-654-8517	269
Brock-McVey Co Inc Refrigeration Supply Div PO Box 55487	Lexington	KY	40555	**800-955-1412**	859-255-1412	651
Brock Solutions Inc 86 Ardelt Ave	Kitchener	ON	N2C2C9	**877-702-7625**	519-571-1434	258
Brockman Forklift Inc 15800 Tireman Ave	Detroit	MI	48228	**800-228-1957**	313-584-4550	261-4
Brockway-Smith Co (BWAY) 146 Dascomb Rd	Andover	MA	01810	**800-225-7912**	978-475-7100	489
Broco Inc 8690 Red Oak St	Rancho Cucamonga	CA	91730	**800-845-7259**	909-483-3222	476
Brodart Co 500 Arch St	Williamsport	PA	17701	**800-233-8467**	570-326-2461	176-10
Brodart Co Automation Div 500 Arch St	Williamsport	PA	17701	**800-233-8467**	570-326-2461	623-10
Brodart Co Book Services Div 500 Arch St	Williamsport	PA	17701	**800-233-8467**	570-326-2461	97
Brodart Co Contract Library Furniture Div 500 Arch St	Williamsport	PA	17701	**800-233-8467**	570-326-2461	314-3
Brodart Co Library Supplies & Furnishings Div 500 Arch St	Williamsport	PA	17701	**800-233-8467**	570-326-2461	523
Brode WM Co 100 Elizabeth St PO Box 299	Newcomerstown	OH	43832	**800-848-9217**	740-498-5121	187-2
Broder Bros Co 45555 Port St	Plymouth	MI	48170	**800-521-0850**	734-454-4800	154
Broderbund LLC 500 Redwood Blvd	Novato	CA	94947	**800-395-0277**	415-382-4400	176-3
Brogan Byard F Inc 124 S Keswick Ave	Glenside	PA	19038	**800-232-7642**	215-885-3550	401
Brogdex Co 1441 W 2nd St	Pomona	CA	91766	**800-795-5225**	909-622-1021	293
Broken Arrow Electric Supply Inc 2350 W Vancouver	Broken Arrow	OK	74012	**877-999-2237**	918-258-3581	245
Broker Inn 555 30th St	Boulder	CO	80303	**800-338-5407**	303-444-3330	373
Brokerage Managers. Council of Real Estate 430 N Michigan Ave Suite 300	Chicago	IL	60611	**800-621-8738**	312-321-4400	49-17
Brolite Products Inc 1900 S Park Ave	Streamwood	IL	60107	**888-276-5483**	630-830-0340	291-42
Bromberg & Co Inc 123 N 20th St	Birmingham	AL	35203	**800-633-4616**	205-252-0221	357
Bronco Billy's Casino 233 E Bennett Ave	Cripple Creek	CO	80813	**877-989-2142**	719-689-2142	133
Bronco Wine Co 6342 Bystrum Rd	Ceres	CA	95307	**800-692-5780**	209-538-3131	81-3
Bronner Brothers Inc 2141 Powers Ferry Rd	Marietta	GA	30067	**800-241-6151**	770-988-0015	211
Bronx Zoo 2300 Southern Blvd	Bronx	NY	10460	**800-234-5128**	718-220-5100	811
Bronze Craft Corp 37 Will St	Nashua	NH	03060	**800-488-7747**	603-883-7747	345
Brook Environmental & Engineering Corp 11419 Cronridge Dr Suite 10	Owings Mills	MD	21117	**800-381-4434**	410-356-4875	728
Brook Furniture Rental Inc 100 Field Dr Suite 220	Lake Forest	IL	60045	**800-933-7368**	847-810-4000	261-3
Brook Mays Music Co 8605 John Carpenter Fwy	Dallas	TX	75247	**800-637-8966***	214-631-0928	515
*Cust Svc						
Brookdale on the Lake 1 Brookdale Rd	Scotrun	PA	18355	**800-233-4141**	570-839-8843	655

Name / Address	City	State	ZIP	Toll-Free	Phone	Class
Brooke Distributors Inc 16250 NW 52nd Ave	Miami	FL	33014	**800-275-8792**	305-624-9752	38
Brooke-Gould Memorial Library 450 S Barron St	Eaton	OH	45320	**800-241-7731**	937-456-4331	426
Brookfield Engineering Lab Inc 11 Commerce Blvd	Middleboro	MA	02346	**800-628-8139**	508-946-6200	200
Brookgreen Gardens 1931 Brookgreen Dr	Murrells Inlet	SC	29576	**800-849-1931**	843-235-6000	98
Brookhaven-Lincoln County Chamber of Commerce 230 S Whitworth Ave	Brookhaven	MS	39601	**800-613-4667**	601-833-1411	137
Brookings Area Chamber of Commerce 2308 6th St E	Brookings	SD	57006	**800-699-6125**	605-692-6125	137
Brookings Inn 2500 E 6th St PO Box 557	Brookings	SD	57006	**877-831-1562**	605-692-9471	373
Brookings Institution 1775 Massachusetts Ave NW	Washington	DC	20036	**800-275-1447**	202-797-6000	654
Brookline Bancorp Inc 160 Washington St *NASDAQ: BRKL*	Brookline	MA	02445	**877-668-2265**	617-730-3500	355-2
Brookline Savings Bank 160 Washington St	Brookline	MA	02445	**888-730-3554**	617-730-3500	71
Brooks Atkinson Theatre 256 W 47th St	New York	NY	10036	**800-755-4000**	212-307-4100	732
Brooks Brothers Inc 346 Madison Ave	New York	NY	10017	**800-444-1613**	212-682-8800	155-3
Brooks College 4825 E Pacific Coast Hwy	Long Beach	CA	90804	**800-421-3775**	562-498-2441	159
Brooks EJ Co 8 Microlab Rd	Livingston	NJ	07039	**800-458-7325**	973-597-2900	321
Brooks Equipment Co Inc 9700 Research Dr	Charlotte	NC	28262	**800-826-3473**	704-596-9438	667
Brooks Food Group Inc 940 Orange St	Bedford	VA	24523	**800-873-4934**	540-586-8284	291-2
Brooks Furniture Mfg Inc 110 Maples Ln	Tazewell	TN	37879	**800-427-6657**	423-626-1111	314-2
Brooks Institute of Photography 801 Alston Rd	Santa Barbara	CA	93108	**888-304-3456**	805-966-3888	163
Brooks Memorial Hospital 529 Central Ave	Dunkirk	NY	14048	**800-366-0717**	716-366-1111	366-2
Brooks Overton Veterans Affairs Medical Center 510 E Stoner Ave	Shreveport	LA	71101	**800-863-7441**	318-221-8411	366-6
Brooks Rehabilitation Hospital 3599 University Blvd S	Jacksonville	FL	32216	**800-487-7342**	904-858-7600	366-4
Brooks Resources Corp 296 SW Columbia St Suite A	Bend	OR	97702	**888-773-7553**	541-382-1662	639
Brooks Sports Inc 19820 North Creek Pkwy Suite 200	Bothell	WA	98011	**800-227-6657**	425-488-3131	296
Brooks Tropicals Inc PO Box 900160	Homestead	FL	33090	**800-327-4833**	305-247-3544	310-4
Brooks/Cole Publishing Co 60 Garden Ct Suite 205	Monterey	CA	93940	**800-354-0092**	831-373-0728	623-2
Brookshire Brothers Ltd 1201 Ellen Trout Dr	Lufkin	TX	75901	**800-364-6690**	936-634-8155	339
Brookshire Inner Harbor Suite Hotel 120 E Lombard St	Baltimore	MD	21202	**877-207-9046**	410-625-1300	373
Brookside Resort 463 East Pkwy	Gatlinburg	TN	37738	**800-251-9597**	865-436-5611	373
Brookstone Inc 1 Innovation Way *NASDAQ: BKST* ■ *Cust Svc	Merrimack	NH	03054	**800-846-3000***	603-880-9500	322
Brookstown Inn 200 Brookstown Ave	Winston-Salem	NC	27101	**800-845-4262**	336-725-1120	373
Brookstreet Hotel 525 Legget Dr	Ottawa	ON	K2K2W2	**888-826-2220**	613-271-1800	372
Brookville Glove Mfg Co Inc 5-15 Western Ave	Brookville	PA	15825	**800-322-7324**	814-849-7324	153-8
Brookwood Cos Inc 232 Madison Ave 10th Fl	New York	NY	10016	**800-426-5468**	212-551-0100	583
Brookwood Farms Dairy 1801 Hempstead Rd PO Box 7007	Lancaster	PA	17604	**800-233-2007**	717-233-6423	291-27
Broome Community College 901 Front St	Binghamton	NY	13902	**800-836-0689**	607-778-5000	160
Broome County Convention & Visitors Bureau PO Box 995	Binghamton	NY	13902	**800-836-6740**	607-772-8860	205
Brother International Corp 100 Somerset Corporate Blvd *Cust Svc	Bridgewater	NJ	08807	**800-276-7746***	908-704-1700	112
Brotherhood Mutual Insurance Co 6400 Brotherhood Way	Fort Wayne	IN	46825	**800-333-3735**	260-482-8668	384-4
Brother's Brother Foundation 1200 Galveston Ave	Pittsburgh	PA	15233	**888-323-1916**	412-321-3160	48-5
Broughton Foods Co 1701 Green St	Marietta	OH	45750	**800-283-2479**	740-373-4121	291-27
Broussard Brothers Inc 25817 Louisiana Hwy 333	Abbeville	LA	70510	**800-299-5303**	337-893-5303	261-4
Broward Center for the Performing Arts 201 SW 5th Ave	Fort Lauderdale	FL	33312	**800-564-9539**	954-462-0222	562
Broward Fire Equipment & Service Inc 101 SW 6th St	Fort Lauderdale	FL	33301	**800-866-3473**	954-467-6625	667
Broward General Medical Center 1600 S Andrews Ave	Fort Lauderdale	FL	33316	**866-293-7866**	954-355-4400	366-2
Broward Limousine & Airport Service Inc 7540 NW 5th St	Plantation	FL	33317	**800-276-9274**	954-791-3000	433
Brower CW Inc 413 S Riverside Dr	Modesto	CA	95354	**800-400-0477**	209-523-1828	203
Brown & Bigelow Inc 345 Plato Blvd E *Cust Svc	Saint Paul	MN	55107	**800-628-1755***	651-293-7000	10
Brown & Brown Inc 220 S Ridgewood Ave *NYSE: BRO*	Daytona Beach	FL	32114	**800-877-2769**	386-252-9601	383
Brown Capital Management Inc 1201 N Calvert St	Baltimore	MD	21202	**800-809-3863**	410-837-3234	393
Brown Citrus Systems Inc 333 M Ave NW	Winter Haven	FL	33881	**800-788-8225**	863-299-2111	293
Brown & Co Securities Corp 1 Beacon St 18th Fl	Boston	MA	02108	**800-822-2021**	617-357-4410	679
Brown & Cole PO Box 9797	Bellingham	WA	98227	**800-743-0437**	360-714-9797	339
Brown College 1440 Northland Dr	Mendota Heights	MN	55120	**800-627-6966**	651-905-3400	158
Brown Corp of America Inc 401 S Steele St	Ionia	MI	48846	**800-530-9570**	616-527-4050	480
Brown County Chamber of Commerce 110 E State St	Georgetown	OH	45121	**888-276-9664**	937-378-4784	137
Brown County Convention & Visitors Bureau PO Box 840	Nashville	IN	47448	**800-753-3255**	812-988-7303	205
Brown County Inn 51 E State Rd 46	Nashville	IN	47448	**800-772-5249**	812-988-2291	373
Brown County Rural Electric Assn PO Box 529	Sleepy Eye	MN	56085	**800-658-2368**	507-794-3331	244
Brown Dayton T Inc 1175 Church St	Bohemia	NY	11716	**800-232-6300**	631-589-6300	728
Brown DH Assoc Inc 222 Grace Church St	Port Chester	NY	10573	**800-253-1799**	914-937-4302	654
Brown DS Co 300 E Cherry St	North Baltimore	OH	45872	**800-848-1730**	419-257-3561	190-2
Brown Earle Heritage Center 6155 Earle Brown Dr	Minneapolis	MN	55430	**800-524-0239**	763-569-6300	204
Brown Guy Products 9003 Overlook Blvd	Brentwood	TN	37027	**877-794-5906**	615-777-1500	616
Brown & Haley 1940 E 11th St	Tacoma	WA	98421	**800-426-8400**	253-620-3000	291-8
Brown Hotel. Camberley 335 W Broadway St	Louisville	KY	40202	**800-555-8000**	502-583-1234	373
Brown International Corp 633 N Barranca Ave	Covina	CA	91723	**800-423-1843**	626-966-8361	293
Brown Joe Co Inc PO Box 1669	Ardmore	OK	73402	**800-444-4293**	580-223-4555	180
Brown Jordan Co Inc 9860 Gidley St	El Monte	CA	91731	**800-743-4252**	626-443-8971	314-4
Brown Les Les Brown Enterprises 20700 Civic Center Dr Suite 170	Southfield	MI	48076	**800-733-4226**	313-653-4110	561
Brown Mackie College 2106 S 9th St	Salina	KS	67401	**800-365-0433**	785-825-5422	158
Lenexa Campus 9705 Lenexa Dr	Lenexa	KS	66215	**800-635-9101**	913-768-1900	158
Brown Marine Service Inc 40 Audusson Ave	Pensacola	FL	32507	**800-234-3471**	850-453-3471	457
Brown Mfg Corp 6001 E Hwy 27	Ozark	AL	36360	**800-633-8909**	334-795-6603	269
Brown Packing Co Inc 1 Dutch Valley Dr	South Holland	IL	60473	**800-832-8325**	708-849-7990	465
Brown Palace Hotel 321 17th St	Denver	CO	80202	**800-321-2599**	303-297-3111	373
Brown Printing Co 2300 Brown Ave	Waseca	MN	56093	**800-533-0475**	507-835-2410	615
Brown & Saenger PO Box 84040 *Sales	Sioux Falls	SD	57118	**800-952-3509***	605-336-1960	315
Brown Shoe Co Inc 8300 Maryland Ave *NYSE: BWS* ■ *Cust Svc	Saint Louis	MO	63105	**800-766-6465***	314-854-4000	296
Brown Stove Works Inc 1422 Carolina Ave NE	Cleveland	TN	37311	**800-251-7485**	423-476-6544	36
Brown-Strauss Steel 2495 Uravan St *Sales	Aurora	CO	80011	**800-677-2778***	303-371-2200	483
Brown Tom Inc 555 17th St Suite 1850	Denver	CO	80202	**800-829-3408**	303-260-5000	525
Brown Tours 123 Saratoga Rd	Scotia	NY	12303	**800-424-4700**	518-853-4412	748
Brown WA & Son Inc 209 Long Meadow Dr	Salisbury	NC	28147	**800-438-2316**	704-636-5131	650
Brown Wood Preserving Co Inc 6201 Camp Ground Rd	Louisville	KY	40216	**800-537-1765**	502-448-2337	806
Brown Wood Products Co 7040 N Lawndale Ave	Lincolnwood	IL	60712	**800-328-5858**	847-673-4780	808
Browne-Halco Inc 2840 Morris Ave	Union	NJ	70783	**888-289-1005**	908-964-9200	295
Brownell & Co Inc 423 E Haddam-Moodus Rd	Moodus	CT	06469	**800-222-4007**	860-873-8625	207
Brownell World Travel 813 Shades Creek Pkwy	Birmingham	AL	35209	**800-999-3960**	205-802-6222	760
Brown's Bakery Inc 505 Downs St	Defiance	OH	43512	**800-468-2511**	419-784-3330	291-1
Brown's Chicken & Pasta Inc 489 W Fullerton Ave	Elmhurst	IL	60126	**888-582-7700**	630-617-8800	657
Brown's FM Sons Inc 127 S Furnace St PO Box 67	Birdsboro	PA	19508	**800-362-6455**	610-582-2741	438
Brown's Wharf Motel 121 Atlantic Ave	Boothbay Harbor	ME	04538	**800-334-8110**	207-633-5440	373
Brownstone Publishers Inc 149 5th Ave 16th Fl	New York	NY	10010	**800-643-8095**	212-473-8200	623-9
Brownsville Convention & Visitors Bureau PO Box 4697	Brownsville	TX	78523	**800-626-2639**	956-546-3721	205
Brownsville Herald The 1135 E Van Buren St	Brownsville	TX	78520	**800-488-4301**	956-542-4301	522-2
Brownsville Herald 11 E Van Buren St	Brownsville	TX	78520	**800-488-4301**	956-542-4301	522-2
Brownville Specialty Paper Products Inc 1 Bridge St	Brownville	NY	13615	**800-724-0299**	315-782-4500	551
Brownwood Bulletin 700 Carnegie PO Box 1189	Brownwood	TX	76804	**800-283-0998**	325-646-2541	522-2
Broyhill Co 1 N Market Sq	Dakota City	NE	68731	**800-228-1003**	402-987-3412	269
Broyhill Furniture Industries Inc 1 Broyhill Pk *Cust Svc	Lenoir	NC	28633	**800-327-6944***	828-758-3111	314-2
BRP Mfg Co 637 N Jackson St	Lima	OH	45801	**800-858-0482**	419-228-4441	663
BRT Laboratories Inc 400 W Franklin St	Baltimore	MD	21201	**800-765-5170**	410-225-9595	408
BRT Realty Trust 60 Cutter Mill Rd Suite 303 *NYSE: BRT*	Great Neck	NY	11021	**800-450-5816**	516-466-3100	498
Brubaker Tool Corp 200 Front St	Millersburg	PA	17061	**800-522-8665**	717-692-2113	484
Bruce Coleman Inc 117 E 24th St 5th Fl	New York	NY	10010	**800-942-7917**	212-979-6252	582
Bruce Donald & Co 3600 N Talman Ave	Chicago	IL	60618	**800-621-6017**	773-477-8100	400
Bruce Foods Corp PO Box 1030	New Iberia	LA	70562	**800-299-9082**	337-365-8101	291-20
Bruce Fox Inc 1909 McDonald Ln	New Albany	IN	47150	**800-289-3699**	812-945-3511	766
Bruce & Merrilees Electric Co 930 Cass St	New Castle	PA	16106	**800-652-5560**	724-652-5566	188-4
Bruchi's Cheesesteaks & Subs 11801 NE 65th St	Vancouver	WA	98682	**877-488-9045**	360-882-8823	657
Bruel & Kjaer Instruments Inc 2815-A Colonnades Ct	Norcross	GA	30071	**800-241-9188**	770-209-6907	247
Brueton Industries Inc 145-68 228th St *Cust Svc	Springfield Gardens	NY	11413	**800-221-6783***	718-527-3000	314-2
Brulin & Co Inc 2920 Dr AJ Brown Ave	Indianapolis	IN	46205	**800-776-7149**	317-923-3211	143
Bruner Ivory Handle Co PO Box 647	Hope	AR	71801	**800-233-1017**	870-777-2304	808
Brunner & Lay Inc 9300 King Ave	Franklin Park	IL	60131	**800-872-6899**	847-678-3232	746
Brunschwig & Fils 75 Virginia Rd	North White Plains	NY	10603	**800-538-8280**	914-684-5800	583

Name / Address	City	State	Zip	Toll-Free	Phone	Class
Brunswick Box Co Inc PO Box 7	Lawrenceville	VA	23868	**800-343-9913**	434-848-2222	541
Brunswick Community College PO Box 30	Supply	NC	28462	**800-754-1050**	910-754-6900	160
Brunswick County Chamber of Commerce PO Box 1185	Shallotte	NC	28459	**800-426-6644**	910-754-6644	137
Brunswick Electric Membership Corp 795 Ocean Hwy W	Supply	NC	28462	**800-842-5871**	910-754-4391	244
Brunswick New Technologies Marine Electronics 30 Sudbury Rd	Acton	MA	01720	**800-628-4487**	978-897-6600	519
Brush Creek Ranch HC 63 Box 10	Saratoga	WY	82331	**800-726-2499**	307-327-5241	238
Brush Engineered Materials Inc 17876 St Clair Ave *NYSE: BW* ■ *Cust Svc	Cleveland	OH	44110	**800-321-2076***	216-486-4200	492
Brushes Corp 5400 Smith Rd	Brook Park	OH	44142	**800-967-9697**	216-267-8084	104
Brushtech Inc PO Box 1130 *Cust Svc	Plattsburgh	NY	12901	**800-346-0818***	518-563-8420	104
Bruss Co 3548 N Kostner Ave	Chicago	IL	60641	**800-621-3882**	773-282-2900	292-9
Bry-Air Inc 10793 SR 37 W	Sunbury	OH	43074	**877-427-9247**	740-965-2974	15
Bryan Ashley International Inc 2601 Gateway Dr	Pompano Beach	FL	33069	**800-331-4225**	954-351-1199	314-2
Bryan College PO Box 7000	Dayton	TN	37321	**800-277-9522**	423-775-2041	163
Bryan-College Station Chamber of Commerce 4001 E 29th St Suite 175	Bryan	TX	77802	**800-777-8292**	979-260-5200	137
Bryan Foods Inc PO Box 1177 *Orders	West Point	MS	39773	**800-647-6342***	662-494-3741	291-26
Bryan LGH Medical Center West 2300 S 16th St	Lincoln	NE	68502	**800-742-7845**	402-475-1011	366-2
Bryan Times 127 S Walnut St	Bryan	OH	43506	**800-589-5520**	419-636-1111	522-2
Bryan/College Station Convention & Visitors Bureau 715 University Dr E	College Station	TX	77840	**800-777-8292**	979-260-9898	205
Bryant College 1150 Douglas Pike	Smithfield	RI	02917	**800-622-7001**	401-232-6000	163
Bryant Paul W Museum 300 Paul W Bryant Dr	Tuscaloosa	AL	35487	**866-772-2327**	205-348-4668	511
Bryant & Stratton College Richmond 8141 Hull St Rd	Richmond	VA	23235	**800-735-2420**	804-745-2444	158
Bryce Corp 4505 Old Lamar Ave PO Box 18338	Memphis	TN	38118	**800-238-7277**	901-369-4400	538
BryLin Hospitals 1263 Delaware Ave	Buffalo	NY	14209	**800-727-9546**	716-886-8200	366-3
Bryn-Alan Studios Inc 606 W Kennedy Blvd	Tampa	FL	33606	**800-749-2796**	813-253-2891	579
Bryn Mawr Bank Corp 801 Lancaster Ave *NASDAQ: BMTC*	Bryn Mawr	PA	19010	**888-732-2080**	610-525-1700	355-2
Bryn Mawr College 101 N Merion Ave	Bryn Mawr	PA	19010	**800-262-1885**	610-526-5000	163
Bryn Mawr Rehabilitation Hospital 414 Paoli Pike	Malvern	PA	19355	**888-734-2241**	610-251-5400	366-4
BSA (Business Software Alliance) 1150 18th St Suite 700	Washington	DC	20036	**888-667-4722**	202-872-5500	48-9
BSCAI (Building Service Contractors Assn International) 10201 Lee Hwy Suite 225	Fairfax	VA	22030	**800-368-3414**	703-359-7090	49-13
BSI Constructors Inc 6767 Southwest Ave	Saint Louis	MO	63143	**800-769-8090**	314-781-7820	185
BSN-Jobst Inc 5825 Carnegie Blvd	Charlotte	NC	28209	**800-221-7573**	704-554-9933	469
BSN Medical Inc 5825 Carnegie Blvd	Charlotte	NC	28209	**800-598-5370**	704-331-0600	469
BSQUARE Corp 110 110th Ave NE Suite 200 *NASDAQ: BSQR*	Bellevue	WA	98004	**888-820-4500**	425-519-5900	176-2
BSW International Inc 1 W 3rd St Suite 800	Tulsa	OK	74103	**800-749-8771**	918-582-8771	258
BT Mancini Co Inc 876 S Milpitas Blvd	Milpitas	CA	95036	**800-488-4286**	408-942-7900	188-12
BT Mancini Co Inc Brookman Div 876 S Milpitas Blvd Suite 81	Milpitas	CA	95035	**800-488-4286**	408-942-7900	185
BTA (Business Technology Assn) 12411 Wornall Rd	Kansas City	MO	64145	**800-316-9721**	816-941-3100	49-18
BTI Canada 370 King St W Suite 700	Toronto	ON	M5V1J9	**800-567-4337**	416-593-8866	761
BTS Travel & Tours 323 Silvergrove Dr NW	Calgary	AB	T3B4M4	**877-929-9019**	403-286-1205	760
BTU International Inc 23 Esquire Rd *NASDAQ: BTUI*	North Billerica	MA	01862	**800-998-0666**	978-667-4111	685
Bubba Gump Shrimp Co LLC 940 Calle Negocio Suite 250	San Clemente	CA	92673	**877-729-4867**	949-366-6260	657
Buca Inc 1300 Nicollet Mall Suite 5003 *NASDAQ: BUCA*	Minneapolis	MN	55403	**800-273-1388**	612-288-2382	656
Buccaneer Homes of Alabama Inc PO Box 1418	Hamilton	AL	35570	**800-326-2822**	205-921-3135	495
Buchan John F Homes 2821 Northup Way Suite 100	Bellevue	WA	98004	**866-528-2426**	425-827-2266	639
Buchanan Automotive Group 707 S Washington Blvd	Sarasota	FL	34236	**800-282-5633**	941-366-5230	57
Buchanan Ingersoll PC 301 Grant St 1 Oxford Ctr 20th Fl	Pittsburgh	PA	15219	**800-444-6738**	412-562-8800	419
Buchanan Metal Forming Inc 103 W Smith St	Buchanan	MI	49107	**800-253-0585**	269-695-3836	474
Buchart Horn Inc/Basco Assoc PO Box 15040	York	PA	17405	**800-274-2224**	717-852-1400	258
Bucher Willis & Ratliff Corp 609 W North St	Salina	KS	67401	**800-942-9807**	785-827-3603	258
Buchy Charles G Packing Co PO Box 899	Greenville	OH	45331	**800-762-1060**	937-548-2128	465
Buck Distributing Co Inc 15827 Commerce Ct *Cust Svc	Upper Marlboro	MD	20774	**800-750-2825***	301-952-0400	82-1
Buck Forkardt Inc 4169 Commercial Ave	Portage	MI	49002	**800-228-2825**	269-327-8200	484
Buck Knives Inc 660 S Lochsa St	Post Falls	ID	83854	**800-326-2825**	208-262-0500	219
Buckeye Business Products Inc 3830 Kelley Ave	Cleveland	OH	44114	**800-837-4323**	216-391-6300	616
Buckeye Container Inc 3350 Long Rd	Wooster	OH	44691	**800-686-8692**	330-264-6336	101
Buckeye Fire Equipment Co 110 Kings Rd	Kings Mountain	NC	28086	**800-438-1028**	704-739-7415	666
Buckeye International Inc 2700 Wagner Pl	Maryland Heights	MO	63043	**800-321-2583**	314-291-1900	149
Buckeye Nutrition 330 E Schultz Ave PO Box 505	Dalton	OH	44618	**800-417-6460**	330-828-2251	438
Buckeye Pacific LLC 4386 SW Macadam Ave Suite 200	Portland	OR	97207	**800-767-9191**	503-228-3330	190-3
Buckeye Rural Electric Co-op Inc 4848 SR 325 S	Patriot	OH	45658	**800-231-2732**	740-379-2025	244
Buckeye ShapeForm 555 Marion Rd	Columbus	OH	43207	**800-728-0776**	614-445-8433	253
Buckhead America Corp 50 Glen Lake Pkwy NE Suite 350	Atlanta	GA	30328	**800-432-7992**	770-393-2662	369
Buckhorn Inc 55 W TechneCenter Dr	Milford	OH	45150	**800-543-4454**	513-831-4402	198
Buckingham Hotel 1405 Baltimore Ave	Ocean City	MD	21842	**800-787-6246**	410-289-6246	373
Buckle Inc 2407 W 24th St *NYSE: BKE*	Kearney	NE	68845	**800-626-1255**	308-236-8491	155-4
Buckles-Smith 801 Savaker Ave	San Jose	CA	95126	**800-833-7362**	408-280-7777	245
Buckley Industries Inc 1850 E 53rd St N	Wichita	KS	67219	**800-835-2779**	316-744-7587	592
Buckley Powder Co 42 Inverness Dr E	Englewood	CO	80112	**800-333-2266**	303-790-7007	264
Buckman Laboratories Inc 1256 N McLean Blvd	Memphis	TN	38108	**800-282-5626**	901-278-0330	143
Bucks County Coffee Co 2250 W Cabot Blvd *Sales	Langhorne	PA	19047	**800-844-8790***	215-741-1855	156
Bucks County Conference & Visitors Bureau 3207 Street Rd	Bensalem	PA	19020	**800-836-2825**	215-639-0300	205
Buck's Pizza Franchising Corp Inc 53 Industrial Dr	Du Bois	PA	15801	**800-310-8848**	814-371-3076	657
Buckstaff Co PO Box 2506	Oshkosh	WI	54903	**800-755-5890**	920-235-5890	314-3
Bucyrus Blades Inc 260 E Beal Ave	Bucyrus	OH	44820	**800-532-5233**	419-562-6015	189
Buddig Carl & Co 950 W 175th St	Homewood	IL	60430	**800-621-0868**	708-798-0900	291-26
Buddy Rogers Music Inc 6891 Simpson Ave	Cincinnati	OH	45239	**888-276-8742**	513-729-1950	515
Buddy's Bar-B-Q 5806 Kingston Pike	Knoxville	TN	37919	**800-368-9208**	865-584-1924	657
Budget Blinds Inc 1927 N Glassell St	Orange	CA	92865	**800-420-5374**	714-637-2108	88
Budget Rent A Car System Inc 6 Sylvan Way	Parsippany	NJ	07054	**800-527-0700**	973-496-3500	126
Budgethotels.com Inc 1260 Hornby St Suite 104	Vancouver	BC	V6Z1W2	**800-548-4432**		368
Buehler Ltd 41 Waukegan Rd *Sales	Lake Bluff	IL	60044	**800-283-4537***	847-295-6500	410
Buehler Moving & Storage Co 3899 Jackson St	Denver	CO	80205	**800-234-6683**	303-388-4000	508
Buehner Block Co 2800 SW Temple	Salt Lake City	UT	84115	**800-999-2565**	801-467-5456	181
Buell Door Co Inc 5200 E Grand Ave	Dallas	TX	75223	**800-556-0155**	214-827-9260	234
Buena Park Convention & Visitors Office 6601 Beach Blvd Suite 200	Buena Park	CA	90621	**800-541-3953**	714-562-3560	205
Buena Vista Games 500 S Buena Vista St	Burbank	CA	91521	**800-228-0988**		176-6
Buena Vista Motel 1144 Mesaba Ave	Duluth	MN	55811	**800-569-8124**	218-722-7796	373
Buena Vista Suites 8203 World Center Dr	Orlando	FL	32821	**800-537-7737**	407-239-8588	373
Buena Vista University 610 W 4th St	Storm Lake	IA	50588	**800-383-2821**	712-749-2351	163
Buffalo Bill's Resort & Casino 31700 S Las Vegas Blvd	Primm	NV	89019	**800-386-7867**	702-382-1111	133
Buffalo China Inc 500 Bailey Ave *Cust Svc	Buffalo	NY	14210	**800-828-7033***	716-824-8515	716
Buffalo Convention Center 153 Franklin St Convention Center Plaza	Buffalo	NY	14202	**800-995-7570**	716-855-5555	204
Buffalo (Greater) Convention & Visitors Bureau 617 Main St Suite 200	Buffalo	NY	14203	**800-283-3256**	716-852-2356	205
Buffalo Horn Ranch 13825 County Rd 7	Meeker	CO	81641	**877-878-5450**	970-878-5450	238
Buffalo Hospital Supply Co Inc 4039 Genesee St	Buffalo	NY	14225	**800-724-0530**	716-626-9400	467
Buffalo Hotel Supply Co Inc 375 Commerce Dr PO Box 646	Amherst	NY	14226	**800-333-1678**	716-691-8080	295
Buffalo News 1 News Plaza PO Box 100	Buffalo	NY	14240	**800-777-8680**	716-849-3434	522-2
Buffalo Niagara Partnership 665 Main St Suite 200	Buffalo	NY	14203	**800-241-0474**	716-852-7100	137
Buffalo & Pittsburgh Railroad 1200-C Scottsville Rd Suite 200	Rochester	NY	14624	**800-603-3385**	585-463-3308	634
Buffalo Rock Co PO Box 10048 *Sales	Birmingham	AL	35202	**800-822-9799***	205-942-3435	82-2
Buffalo Sabres HSBC Arena 1 Seymour H Knox III Plaza	Buffalo	NY	14203	**888-467-2273**	716-855-4100	703
Buffalo Sheet Metals Inc PO Box 191	Buffalo	NY	14240	**800-724-0750**	716-895-2324	688
Buffalo Wild Wings Inc 1600 Utica Ave S Suite 700 *NASDAQ: BWLD*	Minneapolis	MN	55416	**800-499-9586**	952-593-9943	657
Buffalo Wire Works Co 1165 Clinton St	Buffalo	NY	14206	**800-828-7028**	716-826-4666	676
Buffalo's Franchise Concepts Inc 707 Whitlock Ave SW Bldg H Suite 13	Marietta	GA	30064	**800-459-4647**	770-420-1800	657
Buffet Partners LP 2701 E Plano Pkwy	Plano	TX	75074	**800-804-7151**	214-291-2900	656
Bugaboo Creek Steak House Inc 8215 Roswell Rd Bldg 600	Atlanta	GA	30350	**800-434-6245**	770-399-9595	657
Buick Motor Div General Motors Corp 300 Renaissance Ctr *Cust Svc	Detroit	MI	48265	**800-521-7300***	313-556-5000	59
Build-A-Bear Workshop Inc 1954 Innerbelt Business Center Dr	Saint Louis	MO	63114	**888-560-2327**	314-423-8000	749
Builders Assn. National Frame 4840 Bob Billings Pkwy Suite 1000	Lawrence	KS	66049	**800-557-6957**	785-843-2444	49-3
Builders Equipment & Tool Co (BETCO) 1617 Enid St	Houston	TX	77009	**800-908-8778**	713-869-3491	482
Builders General Supply Co 15 Sycamore Ave	Little Silver	NJ	07739	**800-570-7227**	732-747-0808	190-3

Name / Address	City	State	Zip	Toll-Free	Phone	Class
Builders Hardware & Supply Co Inc PO Box C-79005	Seattle	WA	98119	**800-999-5158**	206-281-3700	346
Builders. National Assn of Home 1201 15th St NW	Washington	DC	20005	**800-368-5242**	202-266-8200	49-3
Builders Research Center. National Assn of Home 400 Prince Georges Blvd	Upper Marlboro	MD	20774	**800-638-8556**	301-249-4000	654
Building Blocks Pediatric Home Health Services 18003 Sky Park Cir Suite B	Irvine	CA	92614	**800-346-9490**	949-752-9595	358
Building Codes & Standards. National Conference of States on 505 Huntmar Park Dr Suite 210	Herndon	VA	20170	**800-362-2633**	703-437-0100	49-7
Building Material Dealers Assn (BMDA) 12540 SW Main St Suite 200	Tigard	OR	97223	**800-666-2632**	503-624-0561	49-3
Building Material Dealers Assn. National Lumber & 40 Ivy St SE	Washington	DC	20003	**800-634-8645**	202-547-2230	49-18
Building Material Distribution Assn. North American 401 N Michigan Ave Suite 2400	Chicago	IL	60611	**888-747-7862**	312-644-6610	49-18
Building No 19 Inc 319 Lincoln St	Hingham	MA	02043	**800-225-5061**	781-749-6900	778
Building Owners & Managers Assn International (BOMA) 1201 New York Ave NW Suite 300	Washington	DC	20005	**800-426-6292**	202-408-2662	49-17
Building Owners & Managers Institute 1521 Ritchie Hwy	Arnold	MD	21012	**800-235-2664**	410-974-1410	49-17
Building Products Corp 950 Freeburg Ave	Belleville	IL	62220	**800-233-1996**	618-233-4427	180
Building Products Plus 12317 Almeda Rd	Houston	TX	77045	**800-460-8627**	713-434-8008	806
Building Service Contractors Assn International (BSCAI) 10201 Lee Hwy Suite 225	Fairfax	VA	22030	**800-368-3414**	703-359-7090	49-13
Bulk Lift International Inc 1013 Tamarac Dr	Carpentersville	IL	60110	**800-879-2247**	847-428-6059	68
Bulkmatic Transport Co 2001 N Cline Ave	Griffith	IN	46319	**800-535-8505**	219-972-7630	769
BulkRegister.com 10 E Baltimore St Suite 1500	Baltimore	MD	21202	**800-361-2682**	410-779-1400	389
Bull Moose Tube Co 1819 Clarkson Rd Suite 100	Chesterfield	MO	63017	**800-325-4467**	636-537-2600	481
Bullard Abrasives Inc 50 Hopkinton Rd	Westborough	MA	01581	**800-227-4469**	508-366-4465	1
Bullard Co 1898 Safety Way	Cynthiana	KY	41031	**800-827-0423**	859-234-6611	566
Bullen Chemical Co PO Box 37	Folcroft	PA	19032	**800-444-8900**	610-534-8900	149
Bulletin The 1777 SW Chandler Ave	Bend	OR	97702	**800-503-3933**	541-382-1811	522-2
Bulletin The 24417 75th St	Paddock Lake	WI	53168	**800-846-1101**	262-843-1535	522-4
BulletProof Corp 2400 E Las Olas Blvd Suite 332	Fort Lauderdale	FL	33301	**800-505-0105**	954-828-9400	176-2
Bullhead Area Chamber of Commerce 1251 Hwy 95	Bullhead City	AZ	86429	**800-987-7457**	928-754-4121	137
Bullock Hotel 633 Main St	Deadwood	SD	57732	**800-336-1876**	605-578-1745	373
Bullwhackers Casino 101 Gregory St	Black Hawk	CO	80422	**800-426-2855**		133
Bumble Bee Seafoods Inc PO Box 85362	San Diego	CA	92186	**800-800-8572**	858-715-4000	291-13
Bumble & Bumble LLC 146 E 56th St	New York	NY	10022	**800-728-6253**	212-521-6500	79
Bunn-O-Matic Corp 1400 Stevenson Dr	Springfield	IL	62703	**800-637-8606**	217-529-6601	37
Bunning John Transfer Co Inc PO Box 128	Rock Springs	WY	82902	**800-443-2753**	307-362-3791	769
Bunting Bearings Corp 1001 Holland Park Blvd	Holland	OH	43528	**888-228-9899**	419-866-7000	303
Bunting Magnetics Co 500 S Spencer Ave *Cust Svc	Newton	KS	67114	**800-835-2526***	316-284-2020	476
Bunzl Extrusion Inc 1625 Ashton Park Dr	Colonial Heights	VA	23834	**800-755-7528**	804-518-1124	589
Bunzl/Grossman Paper Co Inc 1305 Jersey Ave	North Brunswick	NJ	08902	**800-234-0169**	732-846-6500	549
Bur-Bee Co PO Box 797	Walla Walla	WA	99362	**800-747-9726**	509-525-5040	292-3
Burch Fabrics Group 4200 Brockton Dr SE	Grand Rapids	MI	49512	**800-841-8111**	616-698-2800	583
Burch Industries Inc 16780 Airbase Rd	Maxton	NC	28364	**800-322-3688**	910-844-3688	650
Burd & Fletcher Co Inc 5151 E Geospace Dr	Independence	MO	64056	**800-821-2776**	816-257-0291	102
Bureau of Consular Affairs *Office of Children's Issues* 2201 C St NW MS SA-29	Washington	DC	20520	**888-407-4747**	202-736-9130	336-12
Overseas Citizens Services 2201 C St NW Rm 4811	Washington	DC	20520	**888-407-4747**	202-647-5225	336-12
Bureau of Health Professions Practitioner Data Banks Div 5600 Fishers Ln Parklawn Bldg *Cust Svc	Rockville	MD	20857	**800-767-6732***	301-443-2300	336-6
Bureau of Indian Affairs Regional Offices **Alaska Region** PO Box 25520	Juneau	AK	99802	**800-645-8397**	907-586-7177	336-9
Bureau of National Affairs Inc 1231 25th St NW	Washington	DC	20037	**800-372-1033**	202-452-4200	623-2
Bureau of National Affairs Inc BNA Books Div 1231 25th St *Sales	Washington	DC	20037	**800-960-1220***	202-452-4200	623-2
Bureau of the Public Debt US Savings Bonds Call Center PO Box 1328	Parkersburg	WV	26101	**800-487-2663**	304-480-6112	336-14
Bureau of Transportation Statistics 400 7th St SW	Washington	DC	20590	**800-853-1351**	202-366-1270	336-13
Burger CF Creamery Co 8101 Greenfield Rd	Detroit	MI	48228	**800-229-2322**	313-584-4040	291-27
Burger King Restaurants of Canada Inc 401 The West Mall 7th Fl	Etobicoke	ON	M9C5J4	**888-252-8280**	416-626-6464	657
Burger's Ozark Country Cured Hams Inc 32819 Hwy 87 S	California	MO	65018	**800-203-4424**	573-796-3134	291-26
Burgess Industries Inc 2700 Campus Dr *Cust Svc	Plymouth	MN	55441	**800-233-2589***	763-553-7800	580
Burgess & Niple Inc 5085 Reed Rd	Columbus	OH	43220	**800-282-1761**	614-459-2050	258
Burgess Pigment Co Inc PO Box 4146	Macon	GA	31208	**800-841-8999**	478-746-5658	490
Burggraf Corp 322 Main St	Quapaw	OK	74363	**800-331-2617**	918-674-2281	740
Burgundy Global 336 W Passaic St 2nd Fl	Rochelle Park	NJ	07662	**800-546-6236**	201-291-4290	433
Burke Cyril J Inc 36000 Mound Rd	Sterling Heights	MI	48310	**800-482-4952**	586-939-4400	261-2
Burke Inc 805 Central Ave 5th Fl	Cincinnati	OH	45202	**800-688-2674**	513-241-5663	458
Burke International Tours Inc DBA Christian Tours Inc PO Box 890	Newton	NC	28658	**800-476-3900**	828-465-3900	748
Burke Mobility Products Inc 1800 Merriam Ln *Sales	Kansas City	KS	66106	**800-255-4147***	913-722-5658	469
Burke-Parsons-Bowlby Corp Rt 21 S	Ripley	WV	25271	**800-745-7095**	304-372-2211	275
Burke Rehabilitation Hospital 785 Mamaroneck Ave	White Plains	NY	10605	**888-992-8753**	914-597-2500	366-4
Burkhart Dental Supply Co 2502 S 78th St *Cust Svc	Tacoma	WA	98409	**800-828-2089***	253-474-7761	467
Burklund Distributors Inc 2500 N Main St Suite 3	East Peoria	IL	61611	**800-322-2876**	309-694-1900	292-3
Burkshire Marriott Conference Hotel 10 W Burke Ave	Towson	MD	21204	**800-435-5986**	410-324-8100	370
Burlee Networks 303 Peachtree Ctr Ave Suite 500	Atlanta	GA	30303	**877-467-8464**	404-260-2477	795
Burley Design Co-op Inc 4020 Steward Rd	Eugene	OR	97402	**800-423-8445**	541-687-1644	83
Burlington Basket Co PO Box 808	Burlington	IA	52601	**800-553-2300**	319-754-6508	74
Burlington College 95 North Ave	Burlington	VT	05401	**800-862-9616**	802-862-9616	163
Burlington Convention & Visitors Bureau 60 Main St Suite 100	Burlington	VT	05401	**877-264-3503**	802-863-3489	205
Burlington Free Press 191 College St	Burlington	VT	05401	**800-427-3124**	802-863-3441	522-2
Burlington Hawk Eye Co PO Box 10	Burlington	IA	52601	**800-397-1708**	319-754-8461	623-8
Burlington Homes of Maine Inc 620 Main St	Oxford	ME	04270	**800-255-5218**	207-539-4406	495
Burlington House Group 3330 W Friendly Ave	Greensboro	NC	27410	**800-523-7888**	336-379-2000	730-1
Burlington Industries LLC 804 Green Valley Rd Suite 300	Greensboro	NC	27408	**800-523-7888**	336-379-6220	730-1
Burlington Northern Santa Fe Corp 2650 Lou Menk Dr *NYSE: BNI*	Fort Worth	TX	76131	**800-795-2673**		355-3
Burlington Northern & Santa Fe Railway (BNSF) 2650 Lou Menk Dr	Fort Worth	TX	76131	**800-795-2673**		634
Burlington/Alamance County Convention & Visitors Bureau PO Box 519	Burlington	NC	27216	**800-637-3804**	336-570-1444	205
Burlington/West Burlington Area Chamber of Commerce 610 N 4th St Suite 200	Burlington	IA	52601	**800-827-4837**	319-752-6365	137
Burly Seal Products Co 1865 W 'D' Ave *Cust Svc	Tooele	UT	84074	**800-877-7325***	435-843-4477	321
Burma Bibas Inc 597 5th Ave 10th Fl	New York	NY	10017	**800-362-0037**	212-750-2500	153-13
Burmax Co 28 Barretts Ave	Holtsville	NY	11742	**800-645-5118**	631-447-8700	78
Burn Assn. American 625 N Michigan Ave Suite 1530	Chicago	IL	60611	**800-548-2876**	312-642-9260	49-8
Burn James International 211 Cottage St	Poughkeepsie	NY	12601	**800-431-4610**	845-454-8200	112
Burn Survivors. Phoenix Society for 2153 Wealthy St SE Suite 215	East Grand Rapids	MI	49506	**800-888-2876**	616-458-2773	48-17
Burner Systems International Inc 3600 Cummings Rd	Chattanooga	TN	37419	**800-251-6318**	423-822-3600	352
Burnett WT & Co Inc 1500 Bush St	Baltimore	MD	21230	**800-638-0606**	410-837-3000	590
Burnham Corp PO Box 3245	Lancaster	PA	17603	**877-567-4328**	717-397-4701	352
Burnham John Insurance Services PO Box 85802	San Diego	CA	92186	**800-421-6744**	619-231-1010	383
Burns Motor Freight Inc PO Box 149	Marlinton	WV	24954	**800-598-5674**	304-799-6106	769
Burns Veterinary Supply Inc 635 Prior Ave N	Saint Paul	MN	55104	**800-922-8767**	651-646-8788	467
Burnside Hotel 739 Windmill Rd	Dartmouth	NS	B3B1C1	**800-830-4656**	902-468-7117	372
Burnsley Hotel 1000 Grant St	Denver	CO	80203	**800-231-3915**	303-830-1000	373
Burpee W Atlee Co 300 Park Ave *Cust Svc	Warminster	PA	18974	**800-333-5808***	215-674-4900	684
Burr & Forman LLP 420 N 20th St Suite 3100	Birmingham	AL	35203	**800-438-2877**	205-251-3000	419
Burr Patterson & Auld Co PO Box 800	Elwood	IN	46036	**800-422-4348**	765-552-7366	401
Burrell Professional Labs 1311 Merrillville Rd	Crown Point	IN	46307	**800-348-8732**	219-663-3210	577
Burrelle's/Luce LLC 75 E Northfield Rd	Livingston	NJ	07039	**800-631-1160**	973-992-6600	380
Burris Co Inc 331 E 8th St	Greeley	CO	80631	**888-228-7747**	970-356-1670	534
Burris Logistics 501 SE 5th St	Milford	DE	19963	**800-805-8135**	302-839-4531	790-2
Burro Program. National Wild Horse & PO Box 3270	Sparks	NV	89432	**866-468-7826**	775-475-2222	336-9
Burrows Paper Corp 501 W Main St	Little Falls	NY	13365	**800-272-7122**	315-823-2300	547
Burrows Paper Corp Packaging Div 1722 53rd St	Fort Madison	IA	52627	**800-779-7779**	319-372-4241	544
Burson-Marsteller 230 Park Ave S	New York	NY	10003	**800-342-5692**	212-614-4000	622
Burt Automotive Network 5200 S Broadway	Englewood	CO	80113	**800-535-2878**	303-761-0333	57
Burt County Public Power District 613 N 13th St	Tekamah	NE	68061	**888-835-1620**	402-374-2631	244
Burtco Inc PO Box 40	Westminster Station	VT	05159	**800-451-4401**	802-722-3358	181
Burton Golf Inc 654 Anchors St	Fort Walton Beach	FL	32548	**800-633-4630**	850-244-8651	701
Burton Medical Products Inc 21100 Lassen St *Cust Svc	Chatsworth	CA	91311	**800-444-9909***	818-701-8700	431
Burton Snowboards Inc 80 Industrial Pkwy	Burlington	VT	05401	**800-881-3138**	802-862-4500	701
Busch Fred Foods Corp 6278 N Cicero	Chicago	IL	60646	**800-323-3981**	773-545-2650	291-26

Name / Address	City	State	ZIP	Toll-Free	Phone	Class
Busch Gardens Tampa Bay 3605 Bougainvillea Ave	Tampa	FL	33164	**888-800-5447**	813-987-5082	32
Busch Gardens Williamsburg 1 Busch Gardens Blvd	Williamsburg	VA	23187	**800-772-8886**	757-253-3350	32
Buse Timber & Sales Inc 3812 28th Pl NE	Everett	WA	98205	**800-305-2577**	425-258-2577	671
Busey Bank 201 W Main St	Urbana	IL	61801	**888-384-1010**	217-384-4500	71
Bush Hog LLC PO Box 1039 2501 Griffin Ave	Selma	AL	36701	**800-363-6096**	334-872-6261	269
Bush Industries Inc 1 Mason Dr	Jamestown	NY	14701	**800-228-2874**	716-665-2000	314-2
Bushline Inc 707 Industrial Park Dr	New Tazewell	TN	37825	**800-627-1682**	423-626-5246	314-2
Bushnell Alvah Co 519 E Chelten Ave	Philadelphia	PA	19144	**800-255-7434**	215-842-9520	550
Bushnell Corp DBA Bushnell Performance Optics 9200 Cody St	Overland Park	KS	66214	**800-423-3537**	913-752-3400	534
Bushnell Performance Optics 9200 Cody St	Overland Park	KS	66214	**800-423-3537**	913-752-3400	534
Business Appraisers. Institute of 6950 Cypress Rd Suite 209	Plantation	FL	33317	**800-299-4130**	954-584-1144	49-17
Business Assn. National 5151 Beltline Rd Suite 1150	Dallas	TX	75254	**800-456-0440**	972-458-0900	49-12
Business Assn. National Small 1156 15th St NW Suite 1100	Washington	DC	20005	**800-345-6728**	202-393-8830	49-12
Business Aviation Services 3501 Aviation Ave	Sioux Falls	SD	57104	**800-888-1646**	605-336-7791	63
Business & Commercial Aviation Magazine 6 International Dr Suite 310 *Cust Svc	Rye Brook	NY	10573	**800-525-5003***	914-939-0300	449-21
Business Communicators. International Assn of 1 Hallidie Plaza Suite 600	San Francisco	CA	94102	**800-766-4222**	415-544-4700	49-12
Business Council of New York State Inc 152 Washington Ave	Albany	NY	12210	**800-358-1202**	518-465-7511	138
Business Credit Magazine 8840 Columbia 100 Pkwy	Columbia	MD	21045	**800-955-8815**	410-740-5560	449-5
Business Crimes Bulletin 1617 JFK Blvd Suite 1750	Philadelphia	PA	19103	**800-888-8300**	800-999-1916	521-2
Business Examiner 1517 S Fawcett Ave Suite 350	Tacoma	WA	98402	**800-540-8322**	253-404-0891	449-5
Business Executives for National Security (BENS) 1717 Pennsylvania Ave NW Suite 350	Washington	DC	20006	**800-296-2125**	202-296-2125	49-12
Business Facilities Magazine 44 Apple St Suite 3	Tinton Falls	NJ	07724	**800-524-0337**	732-842-7433	449-5
Business First 501 S 4th St Suite 130	Louisville	KY	40202	**800-704-3757**	502-583-1731	449-5
Business Forms Inc 3498 Grand Ave	Pittsburgh	PA	15225	**800-451-8086**	412-331-3300	111
Business Furniture Corp 6102 Victory Way	Indianapolis	IN	46278	**800-774-5544**	317-216-1600	315
Business & Health Magazine 5 Paragon Dr	Montvale	NJ	07645	**800-232-7379**	201-358-7200	449-5
Business & Home Safety. Institute for 4775 E Fowler Ave	Tampa	FL	33617	**866-675-4247**	813-286-3400	49-9
Business Inn 180 MacLaren St	Ottawa	ON	K2P0L3	**800-363-1777**	613-232-1121	372
Business Insurance Magazine 360 N Michigan Ave	Chicago	IL	60601	**800-678-2724**	312-649-5200	449-5
Business Intelligence Advisor 37 Broadway Suite 1	Arlington	MA	02474	**800-964-8702**	781-648-8700	521-3
Business Interiors Inc 4141 Colorado Blvd	Denver	CO	80216	**800-373-6994**	303-321-6671	315
Business Journal The 25 E Boardman St	Youngstown	OH	44501	**800-837-6397**	330-744-5023	449-5
Business Leaders of America - Phi Beta Lambda Inc. Future 1912 Association Dr	Reston	VA	20191	**800-325-2946**	703-860-3334	48-11
Business & Legal Reports Inc 141 Mill Rock Rd E	Old Saybrook	CT	06475	**800-727-5257**	860-510-0100	623-9
Business Loan Express LLC 645 Madison Ave	New York	NY	10022	**888-722-5626**	212-751-5626	214
Business Magazine 1450 Don Mills Rd	Don Mills	ON	M3B3R5	**800-668-7678**	416-383-2300	449-5
Business Management Assn. Radiology 8001 Irvine Center Dr Suite 1060	Irvine	CA	92618	**888-224-7262**	949-340-5000	49-8
Business Marketing Assn (BMA) 400 N Michigan Ave 15th Fl	Chicago	IL	60611	**800-664-4262**	312-822-0005	49-18
Business. National Federation of Independent 1201 F St NW Suite 200	Washington	DC	20004	**800-552-6342**	202-554-9000	49-12
Business News Publishing Co 2401 W Big Beaver Rd Suite 700	Troy	MI	48084	**800-837-7370**	248-362-3700	623-9
Business Objects SA 3030 Orchard Pkwy *NASDAQ: BOBJ*	San Jose	CA	95134	**800-527-0580**	408-953-6000	176-1
Business Opportunities Journal PO Box 60762	San Diego	CA	92166	**800-809-1763**		449-5
Business Owners. National Assn of Women 8405 Greensboro Dr Suite 800	McLean	VA	22102	**800-556-2926**	703-506-3268	49-12
Business Professionals of America 5454 Cleveland Ave	Columbus	OH	43231	**800-334-2007**	614-895-7277	49-5
Business Publishers Inc 8737 Colesville Rd Suite 1100	Silver Spring	MD	20910	**800-274-6737**	301-587-6300	623-9
Business Software Alliance (BSA) 1150 18th St Suite 700	Washington	DC	20036	**888-667-4722**	202-872-5500	48-9
Business of Technology. AeA: Advancing the 5201 Great America Pkwy Suite 520	Santa Clara	CA	95054	**800-284-4232**	408-987-4200	49-4
Business Technology Assn (BTA) 12411 Wornall Rd	Kansas City	MO	64145	**800-316-9721**	816-941-3100	49-18
Business Travel News 770 Broadway *Cust Svc	New York	NY	10003	**800-950-1314***	646-654-4500	449-22
Business in Vancouver 1155 W Pender St Suite 500	Vancouver	BC	V6E2P4	**800-208-2011**	604-688-2398	449-5
Business Wire 44 Montgomery St 39th Fl	San Francisco	CA	94104	**800-227-0845**	415-986-4422	520
Business Women's Assn. American 9100 Ward Pkwy	Kansas City	MO	64114	**800-228-0007**	816-361-6621	49-12
Businesses Assn. American Small 206 E College St Suite 201B	Grapevine	TX	76051	**800-942-2722**	817-488-8770	49-12
Businessmen to Christ. Connecting 5746 Marlin Rd Suite 602 Osborne Center	Chattanooga	TN	37411	**800-575-2262**	423-698-4444	48-20
Businesspersons Assn. American 350 Fairway Dr Suite 200	Deerfield Beach	FL	33441	**800-221-2168**	954-571-1877	49-12
BusinessWeek Magazine 1221 Ave of the Americas 43rd Fl *Cust Svc	New York	NY	10020	**800-635-1200***	212-512-2511	449-5
Buskirk Lumber Co 319 Oak St	Freeport	MI	49325	**800-860-9663**	616-765-5103	671
Busler Enterprises Inc PO Box 23610 *Whse	Evansville	IN	47724	**800-457-3232***	812-424-7511	319
BUSPAC 700 13th St NW Suite 575	Washington	DC	20005	**800-283-2877**	202-842-1645	604
Butchart Gardens 800 Benvenuto Ave	Brentwood Bay	BC	V8M1J8	**866-652-4422**	250-652-4422	98
Butcher Boy Doors Div Aluma Shield Industries Inc 725 Summerhill Dr	Deland	FL	32724	**888-882-5862**	386-626-6789	650
Butcher Co 8310 16th St	Sturtevant	WI	53177	**800-795-9550**		149
Butcher Distributors Inc 101 Boyce Rd	Broussard	LA	70518	**800-960-0008**	337-837-2088	601
Butler Automatic Inc 41 Leona Dr	Middleboro	MA	02346	**800-544-0070**	508-923-0544	546
Butler & Co Inc PO Box 570	Vernon	AL	35592	**800-633-8988**	205-695-7132	769
Butler County Community College PO Box 1203	Butler	PA	16003	**888-826-2829**	724-287-8711	160
Butler County Rural Electric Co-op 521 N Main St	Allison	IA	50602	**888-267-2726**	319-267-2726	244
Butler County Rural Public Power District 1331 N 4th St	David City	NE	68632	**800-230-0569**	402-367-3081	244
Butler Home Products Inc 311 Hopping Brook Rd PO Box 8000	Holliston	MA	01746	**800-343-3368**	508-429-8100	497
Butler Mfg Co Lester Building Systems Div 1111 2nd Ave S	Lester Prairie	MN	55354	**800-826-4439**	320-395-2531	107
Butler Motor Transit Co Inc PO Box 1602	Butler	PA	16003	**800-222-8750**	724-282-1000	108
Butler Printing & Laminating Inc 250 Hamburg Tpke PO Box 836	Butler	NJ	07405	**800-524-0786**	973-838-8550	789
Butler Rural Electric Co-op Assn Inc 216 S Vine St	El Dorado	KS	67042	**800-464-0060**	316-321-9600	244
Butler Rural Electric Co-op Inc 3888 Still-Beckett Rd	Oxford	OH	45056	**800-255-2732**	513-867-4400	244
Butler TB Publishing Co 410 W Erwin St	Tyler	TX	75702	**800-333-9141**	903-597-8111	623-8
Butler Trucking Co PO Box 88	Woodland	PA	16881	**800-458-3777**	814-857-7644	769
Butler University 4600 Sunset Ave	Indianapolis	IN	46208	**800-368-6852**	317-940-8000	163
Butler Vent-A-Matic Corp 100 Washington Rd	Mineral Wells	TX	76067	**800-433-1626**	940-325-7887	16
Butler WA Co 5600 Blazer Pkwy	Dublin	OH	43017	**800-848-5983**	614-761-9095	574
Butler Wick & Co Inc 100 Federal Plaza E City Ctr 1	Youngstown	OH	44503	**800-229-1643**	330-744-4351	679
Butte College 3536 Butte Campus Dr *Hum Res	Oroville	CA	95965	**800-933-8322***	530-895-2511	160
Butte Electric Co-op Inc 109 S Dartmouth Ave	Newell	SD	57760	**800-928-8839**	605-456-2494	244
Butte-Silver Bow Chamber of Commerce 1000 George St	Butte	MT	59701	**800-735-6814**	406-723-3177	137
Butter Krust Baking Co Inc 249 N 11th St	Sunbury	PA	17801	**800-332-8521**	570-286-5845	291-1
Butterfield & Robinson 70 Bond St Suite 300	Toronto	ON	M5B1X3	**800-678-1147**	416-864-1354	748
Butterfield Trail Village 1923 E Joyce Blvd	Fayetteville	AR	72703	**800-441-9996**	479-442-7220	659
Butterfields 220 San Bruno Ave	San Francisco	CA	94103	**800-223-2854**	415-861-7500	51
Butterfly Life 2404 San Ramon Valley Blvd Suite 200	San Ramon	CA	94583	**800-288-8373**		349
Buurma Farms Inc 3909 Kok Rd	Willard	OH	44890	**888-428-8762**	419-935-6411	11-11
Buxton Co PO Box 1650	Springfield	MA	01102	**800-962-2813**	413-734-5900	422
Buy Owner 1192 E Newport Ctr Dr Suite 200	Deerfield Beach	FL	33442	**800-940-7777**	954-771-7777	638
Buy.com Inc 85 Enterprise St	Aliso Viejo	CA	92656	**877-880-1030**	949-389-2000	452
BUYandHOLD.com Securities Corp PO Box 6498	Edison	NJ	08837	**800-646-8212**		679
Buyer's Agent Council. Real Estate 430 N Michigan Ave	Chicago	IL	60611	**800-648-6224**	312-329-8656	49-17
BVI (Better Vision Institute) Vision Council of America 1700 Diagonal Rd Suite 500	Alexandria	VA	22314	**800-424-8422**	703-548-4560	48-17
BW Fabricators LP 4140 Reilly Rd	Wichita Falls	TX	76305	**800-508-2710**	940-855-2710	471
BWAY (Brockway-Smith Co) 146 Dascomb Rd	Andover	MA	01810	**800-225-7912**	978-475-7100	489
BWAY Corp 8607 Roberts Dr Suite 250	Atlanta	GA	30350	**800-527-2267**	770-587-0888	124
BWAY Corp 8607 Roberts Dr Suite 250	Atlanta	GA	30350	**800-527-2267**	770-645-4800	124
BWC Financial Corp 1400 Civic Dr *NASDAQ: BWCF*	Walnut Creek	CA	94596	**888-278-1079**	925-932-5353	355-2
BWI 1847 Mercer Rd Suite D	Lexington	KY	40511	**800-888-4478**	859-231-9789	97
BWIA International Airways 5805 Blue Lagoon Dr Suite 340	Miami	FL	33126	**800-327-0204**	305-261-0393	26
bx.com Inc 3 Davol Sq	Providence	RI	02903	**800-344-8487**	401-274-8991	796
Bybee Stone Co Inc 6293 N Matthews Dr	Ellettsville	IN	47429	**800-457-4530**	812-876-2215	710
Byer California 66 Potrero Ave	San Francisco	CA	94103	**800-998-2937**	415-626-7844	153-4
Byrd Foods Inc PO Box 318	Parksley	VA	23421	**800-777-2973**	757-665-5194	11-11
Byrne MRG 22 Isle of Pines Dr	Hilton Head Island	SC	29928	**888-816-8080**		193
Byrnes & Kiefer Co 131 Kline Ave	Callery	PA	16024	**877-444-2240**	724-538-5200	291-1
Byrnes WJ & Co Inc 880 Mitten Rd Suite C	Burlingame	CA	94010	**800-733-1142**	650-692-1142	306
BYTE.com 600 Community Dr	Manhasset	NY	11030	**800-645-6278**	516-562-5000	449-7

Name / Address	City	State	ZIP	Toll-Free	Phone	Class
Bytex Corp 113 Cedar St 495 Commerce Pk Suite S2	Milford	MA	01757	**800-227-1145**	508-422-9422	174

C

Name / Address	City	State	ZIP	Toll-Free	Phone	Class
C & A Industries Inc 11825 Q St	Omaha	NE	68137	**800-574-9829**	402-891-0009	707
C-COR Inc 60 Decibel Rd *NASDAQ: CCBL*	State College	PA	16801	**800-233-2267**	814-238-2461	633
C Cowles & Co Inc 83 Water St	New Haven	CT	06511	**800-624-4483**	203-865-3117	480
C Cretors & Co 3243 N California Ave	Chicago	IL	60618	**800-228-1885**	773-588-1690	293
C & D Technologies Inc 1400 Union Meeting Rd PO Box 3053 *NYSE: CHP*	Blue Bell	PA	19422	**800-543-8630**	215-619-2700	76
C & E Motorcoach Inc 1470 Bolton Rd	Atlanta	GA	30331	**800-229-0976**	404-799-9979	748
C & F Financial Corp PO Box 391 *NASDAQ: CFFI*	West Point	VA	23181	**800-296-6246**	804-843-2360	355-2
C & H Chemical Inc 222 Starkey St	Saint Paul	MN	55107	**800-900-2909**	651-227-4343	149
C & H Die Casting Inc PO Box 1170	Temple	TX	76503	**800-433-3148**	254-938-2541	303
C & H Distributors LLC 770 S 70th St *Sales	Milwaukee	WI	53214	**800-558-9966***	414-443-1700	378
C & H International 4751 Wilshire Blvd Suite 201	Los Angeles	CA	90010	**800-833-8888**	323-933-2288	17
C & J Jewelry Co Inc 100 Dupont Dr	Providence	RI	02907	**800-556-7494**	401-944-2200	400
C Lee Cook Co 916 S 8th St	Louisville	KY	40203	**877-266-5226**	502-587-6783	128
C-Line Products Inc 1100 Business Ctr Dr	Mount Prospect	IL	60056	**800-323-6084**	847-827-6661	523
C-MAP USA Inc 133 Falmouth Rd	Mashpee	MA	02649	**800-424-2627**	508-477-8010	713
C-ME.com 4349 Baldwin Ave Suite A	El Monte	CA	91731	**888-564-6263**	626-636-2530	176-7
C-Mor Co 7 Jewell St	Garfield	NJ	07026	**800-631-3830**	973-478-3900	88
C & R Clothiers Inc 5803 Glenmont Dr	Houston	TX	77081	**800-447-8487**	713-295-7200	155-3
C & R Mechanical 12825 Pennridge Dr	Bridgeton	MO	63044	**800-233-3828**	314-739-1800	188-10
C & R Research Services Inc 500 N Michigan Ave Suite 1200	Chicago	IL	60611	**800-621-5022**	312-828-9200	458
C & S Cos 499 Col Eileen Collins Blvd	Syracuse	NY	13212	**877-277-6583**	315-455-2000	258
C & S Marketing 10360 Old Placerville Rd Suite 100	Sacramento	CA	95827	**888-288-2009**	916-362-9609	176-10
C-Street Bakery 2930 W Maple St	Sioux Falls	SD	57107	**800-336-1320**	605-336-6961	69
C2M Newsletter 858 Longview Rd	Burlingame	CA	94010	**800-221-2557**	650-342-1954	521-2
CA (Cocaine Anonymous World Services Inc) 3740 Overland Ave Suite C	Los Angeles	CA	90034	**800-347-8998**	310-559-5833	48-21
CA-A Cancer Journal for Clinicians 345 Hudson St 16th Fl	New York	NY	10014	**800-777-2295**	212-886-1226	449-16
CA Lawton Co Inc 1860 Enterprise Dr	De Pere	WI	54115	**800-842-6888**	920-337-2470	448
CA One Services 40 Fountain Plaza	Buffalo	NY	14202	**800-828-7240**	716-858-5000	267
CA Rasmussen Inc 2360 Shasta Way	Simi Valley	CA	93065	**800-479-2888**	805-527-9330	187-4
CA Short Co Inc 7221 Pineville Matthews Rd Suite 600	Charlotte	NC	28277	**800-535-5690**	704-752-0119	192
CAA Alberta Motor Assn 10310 39A Ave NW	Edmonton	AB	T6J6R7	**800-642-3810**	780-430-5555	53
CAA Central Ontario 60 Commerce Valley Dr E	Thornhill	ON	L3T7P9	**800-268-3750**	905-771-3000	53
CAA Manitoba 870 Empress St	Winnipeg	MB	R3C2Z3	**800-222-4357**	204-262-6166	53
CAA Maritimes 378 Westmorland Rd	Saint John	NB	E2J2G4	**800-561-8807**	506-634-1400	53
CAA Mid-Western Ontario 148 Manitou Dr	Kitchener	ON	N2G4W8	**800-265-8975**	519-894-2582	53
CAA Niagara 3271 Schmon Pkwy	Thorold	ON	L2V4Y6	**800-263-7272**	905-984-8585	53
CAA North & East Ontario 2525 Carling Ave	Ottawa	ON	K2B7Z2	**800-267-8713**	613-820-1890	53
CAA Quebec 444 Bouvier St	Quebec	QC	G2J1E3	**800-686-9243**	418-624-2424	53
CAA Saskatchewan 200 Albert St N	Regina	SK	S4R5E2	**800-564-6222**	306-791-4321	53
Cabarrus County Convention & Visitors Bureau 3003 Dale Earnhardt Blvd	Kannapolis	NC	28083	**800-848-3740**	704-782-4340	205
Cabarrus Regional Chamber of Commerce 3003 Dale Earnhardt Blvd	Kannapolis	NC	28083	**800-848-3702**	704-782-4000	137
Cabela's Inc 1 Cabela Dr *NYSE: CAB*	Sidney	NE	69160	**800-237-8888**	308-254-5505	702
Cabell-Huntington Convention & Visitors Bureau PO Box 347	Huntington	WV	25708	**800-635-6329**	304-525-7333	205
CabelTel International Corp 14185 Dallas Pkwy Suite 650 *AMEX: GBR*	Dallas	TX	75254	**888-407-8400**	972-407-8400	442
Cabernet Corporate Housing PO Box 18281	Oklahoma City	OK	73154	**888-413-3463**	405-236-0066	209
Cable Markers Co Inc 22600-F Lambert St Suite 1204	Lake Forest	CA	92630	**800-746-7655**	949-699-1636	459
Cable Radio Networks Inc (CRN) 10487 Sunland Blvd	Sunland	CA	91040	**800-336-2225**	818-352-7152	725
Cable Regulation Monitor Newsletter 2115 Ward Ct NW	Washington	DC	20037	**800-771-9200**	202-872-9200	521-11
Cable Telecommunications Engineers. Society of 140 Philips Rd	Exton	PA	19341	**800-542-5040**	610-363-6888	49-19
Cable Television Cooperative Inc. National 11200 Corporate Ave	Lenexa	KS	66219	**800-825-0357**	913-599-5900	49-14
CableAmerica Corp 4120 E Valley Auto Dr	Mesa	AZ	85206	**800-327-4375**	480-558-7260	117
Cables to Go Inc 1501 Webster St	Dayton	OH	45404	**800-826-7904**	937-224-8646	801
Cabletel Communications Corp 55 Valleywood Dr	Markham	ON	L3R5L9	**800-268-3231**	905-475-1030	245
Cabot Corp 2 Seaport Ln Suite 1300 *NYSE: CBT*	Boston	MA	02210	**800-853-5407**	617-345-0100	143
Cabot Corp Inkjet Colorants Div 157 Concord Rd *Cust Svc	Billerica	MA	01821	**800-526-7591***	978-663-3455	143
Cabot Creamery Co-op Inc 1 Home Farm Way	Montpelier	VT	05602	**888-792-2268**	802-229-9361	291-5
Cabot Lodge Tallahassee North 2735 N Monroe St	Tallahassee	FL	32303	**800-223-1964**	850-386-8880	373
Cabot Market Letter 176 North St PO Box 2049 *Orders	Salem	MA	01970	**800-777-2658***	978-745-5532	521-9
Cabot Microelectronics Corp 870 N Commons Dr *NASDAQ: CCMP*	Aurora	IL	60504	**800-811-2756**	630-375-6631	143
Cabot Specialty Fluids 10001 Woodlock Forest Dr Suite 275	The Woodlands	TX	77380	**888-273-7455**	281-298-9955	143
Cabot Supermetals County Line Rd PO Box 1608	Boyertown	PA	19512	**800-531-3676**	610-367-1500	476
Cabrini College 610 King of Prussia Rd	Radnor	PA	19087	**800-848-1003**	610-902-8100	163
CABT (Coalition Against Bigger Trucks) 901 N Pitt St Suite 310	Alexandria	VA	22314	**888-222-8123**	703-535-3131	49-21
Cachat MF Co 14600 Detroit Ave Suite 600	Lakewood	OH	44107	**800-729-0900**	216-226-0900	144
Cache Inc 1440 Broadway 5th Fl *NASDAQ: CACH*	New York	NY	10018	**800-788-2224**	212-575-3200	155-6
Cacique Inc 14923 Procter Ave	La Puente	CA	91746	**800-521-6987**	626-961-3399	291-5
Cactus Flower Florists 7077 E Bell Rd	Scottsdale	AZ	85254	**800-922-2887**	480-483-9200	287
Cactus Pete's Resort Casino 1385 Hwy 93 PO Box 508	Jackpot	NV	89825	**800-821-1103**	775-755-2321	133
CACTUS Software 7301 Mission Rd Suite 300	Prairie Village	KS	66208	**800-776-2305**	913-677-0092	176-11
Cadbury Retirement Community 2150 Rt 38	Cherry Hill	NJ	08002	**800-422-3287**	856-667-4550	659
CADCA (CPA Auto Dealer Consultants Assn) 10831 Old Mill Rd Suite 400	Omaha	NE	68154	**888-475-4476**	402-778-7922	49-1
Cadence Capital Management 265 Franklin St 11th Fl	Boston	MA	02110	**800-298-2194**	617-367-7400	393
Cadence Design Systems Inc 2655 Seely Ave *NYSE: CDN* ■ *Cust Svc	San Jose	CA	95134	**800-746-6223***	408-943-1234	176-5
Cadet Mfg Co Inc 2500 W 4th Plain	Vancouver	WA	98660	**800-442-2338**	360-693-2505	37
Cadillac Area Visitors Bureau 222 Lake St	Cadillac	MI	49601	**800-225-2537**	231-775-0657	205
Cadillac Coffee Co 1801 Michael St	Madison Heights	MI	48071	**800-438-6900**	248-545-2266	291-7
Cadillac Motor Car Div General Motors Corp 300 Renaissance Ctr *Cust Svc	Detroit	MI	48265	**800-458-8006***	313-556-5000	59
Cadillac News 130 N Mitchell St	Cadillac	MI	49601	**888-584-6564**	231-775-6565	522-2
Cadillac Winter Garden Theatre 1634 Broadway	New York	NY	10019	**800-432-7250**	212-239-6200	732
Cadman Inc PO Box 97038	Redmond	WA	98073	**888-322-6847**	425-868-1234	493-6
Cadmus Communications Corp 1801 Bayberry Ct Suite 200 *NASDAQ: CDMS*	Richmond	VA	23226	**800-476-2973**	804-287-5680	355-3
Cadmus Communications Corp Whitehall Group Div 2750 Whitehall Park Dr	Charlotte	NC	28273	**800-733-4318**	704-583-6600	615
Cadmus Communications Port City Press Div 1323 Greenwood Rd	Baltimore	MD	21208	**800-858-7678**	410-486-3000	614
Cadmus Professional Communications 1801 Bayberry Ct Suite 200	Richmond	VA	23226	**877-422-3687**	804-287-5680	615
CadmusCom 1801 Bayberry Ct Suite 200	Richmond	VA	23226	**800-476-2973**	804-287-5680	5
CadmusMack 2901 Byrdhill Rd	Richmond	VA	23228	**800-888-2973**	804-264-2711	615
CAE Inc Royal Bank Plaza Suite 3060 *TSE: CAE*	Toronto	ON	M5J2J1	**800-760-0667**	416-865-0070	694
CAEP (Canadian Assn of Emergency Physicians) 1785 Alta Vista Dr Suite 104	Ottawa	ON	K1G3Y6	**800-463-1158**	613-523-3343	49-8
Caesars Atlantic City 2100 Pacific Ave	Atlantic City	NJ	08401	**800-443-0104**	609-348-4411	655
Caesars Cove Haven Resort 194 Lakeview Dr	Lakeville	PA	18438	**800-233-4141**	570-226-4506	655
Caesars Indiana Casino Hotel 11999 Ave of the Emperors	Elizabeth	IN	47117	**888-766-2648**	812-969-6000	373
Caesars Palace Las Vegas 3570 Las Vegas Blvd S	Las Vegas	NV	89109	**800-634-6661**	702-731-7110	373
Caesars Paradise Stream Rt 940 PO Box 99	Mount Pocono	PA	18344	**800-233-4141**	570-839-8881	655
Caesars Pocono Palace Resort Rt 209	Marshalls Creek	PA	18335	**800-233-4141**	570-588-6692	655
Caesars Tahoe 55 Hwy 50 PO Box 5800	Stateline	NV	89449	**800-648-3353**	775-588-3515	373
Cafe Express LLC 5858 Westheimer Rd Suite 110	Houston	TX	77057	**800-552-1999**	713-977-1922	656
Caffall Brothers Forest Products Inc 25260 SW Pkwy PO Box 725	Wilsonville	OR	97070	**800-547-2011**	503-682-1910	275
Cagle's Inc 2000 Hills Ave NW *AMEX: CGLa*	Atlanta	GA	30318	**800-476-2820**	404-355-2820	608
CAGW (Citizens Against Government Waste) 1301 Connecticut Ave NW Suite 400	Washington	DC	20036	**800-232-6479**	202-467-5300	48-7
CAH Industries Inc 1500 Midway Ct Suite W-2	Elk Grove Village	IL	60007	**800-323-0300**	847-593-0727	281
CAI (Chrysler Aviation Inc) 7120 Hayvenhurst Ave Suite 309	Van Nuys	CA	91406	**800-995-0825**	818-989-7900	14
Cain Electrical Supply Corp 204 Johnson St PO Box 2158	Big Spring	TX	79721	**800-749-8421**	432-263-8421	245
Cain's Foods Inc 114 E Main St PO Box 347	Ayer	MA	01432	**800-225-0601**	978-772-0300	291-19
Caitlin Raymond International Registry University of Massachusetts Medical Ctr 55 Lake Ave N	Worcester	MA	01655	**800-726-2824**	508-334-8969	535
Cajun & Grill of America 4104 Aurora St	Coral Gables	FL	33146	**800-662-1668**	305-476-1611	657

Name / Address	City	State	Zip	Toll-Free	Phone	Class
Cal-a-Vie Spa 29402 Spa Havens Way	Vista	CA	92084	**866-772-4283**	760-945-2055	697
Cal-Air Inc 12393 Slauson Ave	Whittier	CA	90606	**800-222-5247**	562-698-8301	188-10
Cal-Coast Dairy Systems Inc 424 S Tegner Rd *Cust Svc	Turlock	CA	95380	**800-732-6826***	209-634-9026	269
Cal Dive International Inc 400 N Sam Houston Pkwy E Suite 400 *NASDAQ: CDIS*	Houston	TX	77060	**888-345-2347**	281-618-0400	528
Cal Door 5755 Rossi Ln Suite A	Gilroy	CA	95020	**888-225-3667**	408-846-9805	116
Cal Farley's Boys Ranch 600 W 11th St	Amarillo	TX	79174	**800-687-3722**	806-372-2341	48-6
Cal Info 316 W 2nd St Suite 1102	Los Angeles	CA	90012	**877-687-8710**	213-687-8710	380
Cal-Neva Resort 2 Stateline Rd PO Box 368	Crystal Bay	NV	89402	**800-225-6382**	775-832-4000	655
Cal-North Wireless PO Box 627	Fort Jones	CA	96032	**800-499-1863**	530-468-5222	721
Cal-Surance Associates Inc 681 S Parker St Suite 200	Orange	CA	92868	**800-762-7800**	714-939-0800	383
Cal-Van Tools 4300 Waterleaf Ct	Greensboro	NC	27410	**800-537-2636**	336-294-3259	746
Calabro Cheese Corp 580 Coe Ave	East Haven	CT	06512	**800-969-1311**	203-469-1311	291-5
Calais Regional Chamber of Commerce 39 Union St	Calais	ME	04619	**888-422-3112**	207-454-2308	137
CalAmp Corp 1401 N Rice Ave *NASDAQ: CAMP*	Oxnard	CA	93030	**888-767-7988**	805-987-9000	633
CalAmp Corp 12670 High Bluff Dr	San Diego	CA	92130	**888-554-2024**	858-554-1400	174
Calavo Growers Inc PO Box 26081 *NASDAQ: CVGW*	Santa Ana	CA	92799	**800-422-5286**	949-223-1111	310-4
Calbag Metals Co PO Box 10067	Portland	OR	97296	**800-398-3441**	503-226-3441	674
Calcarb Inc 110 Indel Ave	Rancocas	NJ	08073	**800-732-5432**	609-261-4325	127
Calco Insurance Brokers & Agents Inc 2000 Alameda de las Pulgas	San Mateo	CA	94403	**800-800-8290**	650-295-4600	383
Calculated Industries Inc 4840 Hytech Dr	Carson City	NV	89706	**800-854-8075**	775-885-4900	171-2
Calder Race Course Inc 21001 NW 27th Ave	Miami	FL	33056	**800-333-3227**	305-625-1311	628
Caldwell College 9 Ryerson Ave	Caldwell	NJ	07006	**888-864-9516**	973-228-4424	163
Caldwell Freight Lines Inc PO Box 1950	Lenoir	NC	28645	**800-438-8244**	828-728-9231	769
Caldwell Tanks Alliance LLC 57 E Broad St	Newnan	GA	30263	**800-241-1650**	770-253-2600	188-14
CALEA (Commission on Accreditation for Law Enforcement Agencies) 10302 Eaton Pl Suite 100	Fairfax	VA	22030	**800-368-3757**	703-352-4225	49-7
Caledonian-Record The 195 Federal St	Saint Johnsbury	VT	05819	**800-523-6397**	802-748-8121	522-2
Calence Inc 1620 W Fountainhead Pkwy Suite 400	Tempe	AZ	85282	**877-225-3623**	480-889-9500	178
CALEX Mfg Co 2401 Stanwell Dr	Concord	CA	94520	**800-542-3355**	925-687-4411	507
Calfee Co of Dalton DBA Favorite Market 1503 N Tibbs Rd	Dalton	GA	30720	**800-634-2944**	706-226-4834	203
CalFirst Bancorp 18201 Von Karman Ave Suite 700 *NASDAQ: CFNB*	Irvine	CA	92612	**800-496-4640**	949-255-0500	355-2
Calgary Flames Pengrowth Saddledome 555 Saddledome Rise SE	Calgary	AB	T2G2W1	**888-535-2637**	403-777-2177	703
Calgon Carbon Corp 500 Calgon Carbon Rd *NYSE: CCC* ■ *Cust Svc	Pittsburgh	PA	15205	**800-422-7266***	412-787-6700	141
Calhoun Community College PO Box 2216	Decatur	AL	35609	**800-626-3628**	256-306-2500	160
Calhoun County Chamber of Commerce 1330 Quintard Ave	Anniston	AL	36201	**800-489-1087**	256-237-3536	137
Calian Technology Ltd 2 Beaverbrook Rd *TSE: CTY*	Kanata	ON	K2K1L1	**877-225-4264**	613-599-8600	707
Caliber Collision Centers 17771 Cowan Ave Suite 100	Irvine	CA	92614	**888-225-3237**	949-224-0300	62-4
Caliber Computer Corp 45531 Northport Loop W	Fremont	CA	94538	**800-748-9834**	510-353-1220	172
Calibrated Forms Co Inc 537 N East Ave	Columbus	KS	66725	**800-237-7576**		111
Calico Corners 203 Gale Ln *Cust Svc	Kennett Square	PA	19348	**800-213-6366***	610-444-9700	266
California						
Arts Council 1300 'I' St Suite 930	Sacramento	CA	95814	**800-201-6201**	916-322-6555	335
Child Support Services Dept PO Box 269112	Sacramento	CA	95826	**866-249-0773**	916-464-5000	335
Fair Political Practices Commission 428 J St Suite 620	Sacramento	CA	95814	**866-275-3772**	916-322-5660	335
Financial Institutions Dept 111 Pine St Suite 1100 *Consumer Info	San Francisco	CA	94111	**800-622-0620***	415-263-8500	335
Military Dept 9800 Goethe Rd PO Box 269101	Sacramento	CA	95826	**800-321-2752**	916-854-3000	335
Parks & Recreation Dept PO Box 942896	Sacramento	CA	94296	**800-777-0369**	916-653-6995	335
Public Utilities Commission 505 Van Ness Ave	San Francisco	CA	94102	**800-848-5580**	415-703-2782	335
Student Aid Commission PO Box 419027	Rancho Cordova	CA	95741	**888-224-7268**	916-526-8999	711
Teacher Credentialing Commission 1900 Capitol Ave	Sacramento	CA	95814	**888-921-2682**	916-445-7254	335
Veterans Affairs Dept 1227 'O' St	Sacramento	CA	95814	**800-221-8998**	916-653-2158	335
Victim Compensation Program PO Box 3036	Sacramento	CA	95812	**800-777-9229**	916-324-0400	335
California Acrylic Industries Cal Spas 1462 E Ninth St	Pomona	CA	91766	**800-225-7727**	909-623-8781	367
California Automobile Insurance Co 4484 Wilshire Blvd	Los Angeles	CA	90010	**800-431-6654**	323-857-7191	384-4
California Bank & Trust 11622 El Camino Real Suite 200	San Diego	CA	92130	**800-400-6080**	858-793-7400	71
California Baptist University 8432 Magnolia Ave	Riverside	CA	92504	**877-228-8866**	951-689-5771	163
California Cartage Co Inc 3545 Long Beach Blvd 5th Fl	Long Beach	CA	90807	**888-537-1432**	562-427-1143	769
California Casualty Insurance Group PO Box M	San Mateo	CA	94402	**800-288-7765**	650-574-4000	384-4
California Center for the Arts 340 N Escondido Blvd	Escondido	CA	92025	**800-988-4253**	760-839-4138	562
California Chamber of Commerce PO Box 1736	Sacramento	CA	95812	**800-772-2399**	916-444-6670	138
California Closet Co 1000 4th St Suite 800	San Rafael	CA	94901	**800-873-4264**	415-256-8500	188-11
California College of Arts & Crafts 1111 8th St	San Francisco	CA	94107	**800-447-1278**	415-703-9500	163
California Commerce Bank 2029 Century Pk E 42nd Fl	Los Angeles	CA	90067	**800-222-1234**		71
California Credit Union The 3330 Cahuenga Blvd W Suite 115	Los Angeles	CA	90068	**800-334-8788**	818-291-6700	216
California Cryobank Inc 1019 Gayley Ave	Los Angeles	CA	90024	**800-231-3373**	310-443-5244	535
California Cryobank Inc 950 Massachusetts Ave	Cambridge	MA	02139	**800-231-3373**	617-497-8646	535
California Culinary Academy Inc 625 Polk St	San Francisco	CA	94102	**800-229-2433**	415-771-3500	787
California Dairies Inc 11709 E Artesia Blvd	Artesia	CA	90701	**800-821-5588**	562-865-1291	291-27
California Dental Assn PO Box 13749	Sacramento	CA	95853	**800-736-7071**	916-443-0505	225
California Endowment 21650 Oxnard St Suite 1200	Woodland Hills	CA	91367	**800-449-4149**	818-703-3311	298
California First National Bancorp 18201 Von Karman Ave Suite 700 *NASDAQ: CFNB*	Irvine	CA	92612	**800-496-4640**	949-255-0500	355-2
California Flexrake Corp 9620 Gidley St	Temple City	CA	91780	**800-266-4200**	626-443-4026	420
California Gasket & Rubber Corp 1601 W 134th St	Gardena	CA	90249	**800-635-7084**	310-323-4250	321
California Hotel & Casino 12 Ogden Ave	Las Vegas	NV	89101	**800-634-6255**	702-385-1222	133
California Institute of the Arts 24700 McBean Pkwy	Valencia	CA	91355	**800-545-2787**	661-255-1050	163
California Institute of Technology 1200 E California Blvd	Pasadena	CA	91125	**800-568-8324**	626-395-6811	163
California Kitchen Cabinet Door Corp 5755 Rossi Ln Suite A	Gilroy	CA	95020	**888-225-3667**	408-846-9805	116
California Lutheran University 60 W Olsen Rd	Thousand Oaks	CA	91360	**877-258-3678**	805-493-3135	163
California Maritime Academy 200 Maritime Academy Dr	Vallejo	CA	94590	**800-561-1945**	707-654-1000	163
California Micro Devices Corp 430 N McCarthy Blvd Suite 100 *NASDAQ: CAMD*	Milpitas	CA	95035	**800-325-4966**	408-263-3214	686
California Mortgage Service 400 N Tustin Ave Suite 220	Santa Ana	CA	92705	**800-995-8267**	714-835-1500	498
California Neon Products Inc 4530 Mission Gorge Pl	San Diego	CA	92120	**800-822-6366**	619-283-2191	692
California Newspaper Service Bureau 915 E 1st St	Los Angeles	CA	90012	**800-788-7840**	213-229-5500	520
California Office Furniture Inc 1724 10th St	Sacramento	CA	95814	**877-442-6959**	916-442-6959	315
California Optical Leather Inc 2992 Alvarado St	San Leandro	CA	94577	**800-523-5567**	510-352-4774	422
California Pacific Homes 38 Executive Pk Suite 200	Irvine	CA	92614	**800-999-0629**	949-833-6000	639
California Pacific University 1017 E Grand Ave	Escondido	CA	92025	**800-458-9667**	760-739-7730	163
California Pajarosa PO Box 684	Watsonville	CA	95077	**800-565-6374**	831-722-6374	363
California Panel & Veneer Co PO Box 3250	Cerritos	CA	90703	**800-451-1745**	562-926-5834	602
California Parlor Car Tours 1255 Post St	San Francisco	CA	94109	**800-227-4250**	415-474-7500	748
California Physician Magazine PO Box 7690	San Francisco	CA	94120	**800-882-1262**	415-541-0900	449-16
California Pizza Kitchen Inc 6053 W Century Blvd Suite 1100 *NASDAQ: CPKI*	Los Angeles	CA	90045	**800-275-8255**	310-342-5000	657
California Portland Cement Co 2025 E Financial Way Suite 200	Glendora	CA	91741	**800-272-1891**	626-852-6200	135
California Products Corp 150 Dascomb Rd	Andover	MA	01810	**800-225-1141**	978-623-9980	540
California Redwood Assn (CRA) 405 Enfrente Dr Suite 200	Novato	CA	94949	**888-225-7339**	415-382-0662	48-2
California School Law Digest 747 Dresher Rd Suite 500	Horsham	PA	19044	**800-341-7874**	215-784-0860	521-4
California Software Corp 1241 Puerta del Sol	San Clemente	CA	92673	**800-841-1532**	949-498-9300	176-2
California Speedway 9300 Cherry Ave	Fontana	CA	92335	**800-944-7223**	909-429-5000	504
California State Automobile Assn 150 Van Ness Ave *Cust Svc	San Francisco	CA	94102	**800-922-8228***	415-565-2012	53
California State University Bakersfield 9001 Stockdale Hwy	Bakersfield	CA	93311	**800-788-2782**	661-664-2011	163
California State University Chico	Chico	CA	95929	**800-542-4426**	530-898-6321	163
California Steel & Tube 16049 Stephens St	City of Industry	CA	91745	**800-338-8823**	626-968-5511	481
California Theatre of Performing Arts 562 W 4th St	San Bernardino	CA	92402	**800-511-6449**	909-386-7361	562
California University of Pennsylvania 250 University Ave	California	PA	15419	**888-412-0479**	724-938-4000	163
California Water Service Group 1720 N 1st St *NYSE: CWT*	San Jose	CA	95112	**800-750-8200**	408-367-8200	774
California Western School of Law 225 Cedar St	San Diego	CA	92101	**800-255-4252**		164-1
Caligari Corp 1959 Landings Dr	Mountain View	CA	94043	**800-351-7620**	650-390-9600	176-8
Caligor Medical & Office Supplies Inc 846 Pelham Pkwy	Pelham Manor	NY	10803	**800-225-9906**	914-738-8400	467

Name / Address	City	State	ZIP	Toll-Free	Phone	Class
Calista Corp 301 Calista Ct Suite A	Anchorage	AK	99518	**800-277-5516**	907-279-5516	641
Calistoga Mineral Water Co 2767 E Imperial Hwy	Brea	CA	92821	**800-365-4446**		792
Calistoga Ranch 580 Lommel Rd	Calistoga	CA	94515	**800-942-4220**	707-254-2800	655
Calistoga Spa Hot Springs 1006 Washington St	Calistoga	CA	94515	**866-822-5772**	707-942-6269	697
Calix Society 2555 Hazelwood Ave	Saint Paul	MN	55109	**800-398-0524**	651-773-3117	48-21
Call for Action 5272 River Rd Suite 300	Bethesda	MD	20816	**800-647-1756**	301-657-8260	48-10
Call-Net Enterprises Inc 2235 Sheppard Ave E Suite 1800 *TSE: FON*	Toronto	ON	M2J5G1	**800-500-7741**	416-496-1644	721
Callan Assoc Inc 101 California St Suite 3500	San Francisco	CA	94111	**800-227-3288**	415-974-5060	393
Callaway Electric Co-op 503 Truman Rd	Fulton	MO	65251	**888-642-4840**	573-642-3326	244
Callaway Gardens Resort PO Box 2000	Pine Mountain	GA	31822	**800-225-5292**	706-663-2281	655
Callaway Golf Co 2180 Rutherford Rd *NYSE: ELY*	Carlsbad	CA	92008	**800-228-2767**	760-931-1771	701
Callender Marie Inc 27081 Aliso Creek Rd Suite 200	Aliso Viejo	CA	92656	**800-776-7437**	949-448-5300	657
Caller-Times 820 N Lower Broadway	Corpus Christi	TX	78401	**800-827-2011**	361-884-2011	522-2
Callery-Judge Grove 4001 Seminole-Pratt Whitney Rd	Loxahatchee	FL	33470	**800-967-2643**	561-793-1676	310-2
Calling Solutions By Phone Power Inc 2200 McCullough Ave	San Antonio	TX	78212	**800-321-8582**	210-822-7400	722
Calliope Magazine 30 Grove St Suite C	Peterborough	NH	03458	**800-821-0115**	603-924-7209	449-6
Callware Technologies Inc 2755 E Cottonwood Pkwy 4th Fl	Salt Lake City	UT	84121	**800-888-4226**	801-937-6800	176-7
Call_Solutions.com Inc 20825 Swenson Dr Suite 200	Waukesha	WI	53186	**800-669-7711**	262-827-6400	722
Calolympic Glove & Safety Co Inc 1720 Delilah St	Corona	CA	92879	**800-421-6630**	951-340-2229	667
Calphalon Corp 6100 Benore Rd	Toledo	OH	43612	**800-955-7687**	419-666-8700	477
Calpico Inc 1387 San Mateo Ave	South San Francisco	CA	94080	**800-998-9115**	650-588-2241	321
Calpine Corp 50 W San Fernando St 5th Fl *NYSE: CPN*	San Jose	CA	95113	**800-359-5115**	408-995-5115	774
Calpine Energy Inc 717 Texas Ave Suite 1000	Houston	TX	77002	**800-251-6165**	713-830-2000	525
Calsak Corp 200 W Artesia Blvd *Sales	Compton	CA	90220	**800-743-2595***	310-637-2000	592
Caltag Laboratories Inc 1849 Bayshore Hwy	Burlingame	CA	94010	**800-874-4007**	650-652-0468	229
Calumet Breweries Inc 6535 Osborn Ave *Cust Svc	Hammond	IN	46320	**800-882-2739***	219-845-2242	82-1
Calumet College of Saint Joseph 2400 New York Ave	Whiting	IN	46394	**877-700-9100**	219-473-4215	163
Calumet Lubricants Co 2780 Waterfront Pkwy Dr E Suite 200	Indianapolis	IN	46214	**800-437-3188**	317-328-5660	570
Calumet Photographic Inc 890 Supreme Dr *Cust Svc	Bensenville	IL	60106	**800-453-2550***	630-860-7447	119
Calvary Bible College & Seminary 15800 Calvary Rd	Kansas City	MO	64147	**800-326-3960**	816-322-0110	163
Calvert Engineering Inc 28606 W Livingston Ave	Valencia	CA	91355	**800-225-1339**	661-257-7330	627
Calvert Group Mutual Funds 4550 Montgomery Ave Suite 1000N	Bethesda	MD	20814	**800-727-5578**	301-951-4800	517
Calvert House. Governor 58 State Cir	Annapolis	MD	21401	**800-847-8882**	410-263-2641	373
Calvert Laboratories Inc 100 Discovery Dr Scott Technology Pk	Olyphant	PA	18447	**800-300-8114**	570-586-2411	409
Calvert Retail LP PO Box 302 W Rockland Rd Suite A	Montchanin	DE	19710	**800-747-7224**	302-622-8811	357
Calvin College 3201 Burton St SE	Grand Rapids	MI	49546	**800-688-0122**	616-957-6000	163
Calvin Klein Cosmetics 725 5th Ave Trump Tower	New York	NY	10022	**800-715-4023**	212-326-6800	564
Calvin Theological Seminary 3233 Burton St SE	Grand Rapids	MI	49546	**800-388-6034**	616-957-6036	164-3
Cal/West Seeds Inc 41970 E Main St	Woodland	CA	95776	**800-327-3337**	530-666-3331	272
Calypte Biomedical Corp 5000 Hopyard Rd Suite 480 *AMEX: HIV*	Pleasanton	CA	94588	**877-225-9783**	925-730-7200	229
Calyx & Corolla 185 Berry St Suite 2400	San Francisco	CA	94107	**888-882-2599**	415-626-5511	287
Calzone Case Co 225 Black Rock Ave *Cust Svc	Bridgeport	CT	06605	**800-243-5152***	203-367-5766	444
CAM Commerce Solutions Inc 17075 Newhope St Suite A *NASDAQ: CADA*	Fountain Valley	CA	92708	**800-726-3282**	714-241-9241	176-10
Camasco Group 5000 Armand-Frappier St	Saint-Hubert	QC	J3Z1G5	**877-361-4472**	514-856-7750	119
Camber Corp 635 Discovery Dr NW	Huntsville	AL	35806	**800-998-7988**	256-922-0200	178
Camberley Brown Hotel 335 W Broadway St	Louisville	KY	40202	**800-555-8000**	502-583-1234	373
Camberley Hotel Co 4405 Northside Pkwy Suite 2124	Atlanta	GA	30327	**800-555-8000**	404-261-9600	369
Cambex Corp 115 Flanders Rd	Westborough	MA	01581	**800-325-5565**	508-983-1200	174
Cambiar Investors Inc 2401 E 2nd Ave Suite 400	Denver	CO	80206	**888-673-9950**	303-302-9000	393
Cambrex Bioscience 97 South St	Hopkinton	MA	01748	**877-676-5888**	508-497-0700	86
Cambrex Charles City Inc 1205 11th St	Charles City	IA	50616	**800-247-1833**	641-257-1000	470
Cambrex North Brunswick Inc 661 Hwy 1 Bldg 661 *Sales	North Brunswick	NJ	08902	**866-286-9133***	732-447-1900	470
Cambridge Camera 34 Franklin Ave	Brooklyn	NY	11205	**800-221-2253**	718-858-5002	119
Cambridge Chamber of Commerce 750 Hespeler Rd	Cambridge	ON	N3H5L8	**800-749-7560**	519-622-2221	136
Cambridge Heart Inc 1 Oak Park Dr *NASDAQ: CAMH*	Bedford	MA	01730	**888-226-9283**	781-271-1200	468
Cambridge Inc 105 Goodwill Rd	Cambridge	MD	21613	**800-638-9560**	410-228-3000	206
Cambridge Information Group 7200 Wisconsin Ave Suite 601	Bethesda	MD	20814	**800-843-7751**	301-961-6700	623-11
Cambridge-Lee Industries Inc 1340 Soldiers Field Rd	Brighton	MA	02135	**800-225-4378**	617-783-3100	483
Cambridge Manor 8530 Township Line Rd	Indianapolis	IN	46260	**800-454-5909**	317-876-9955	441
Cambridge Products Corp 299 Johnson Ave Suite 100	Waseca	MN	56093	**800-243-8814**	507-833-8822	252
Cambridge Soundworks Inc 100 Brickstone Sq 5th Fl	Andover	MA	01810	**800-945-4434**	978-623-4400	52
Cambridge Suites Hotel Halifax 1583 Brunswick St	Halifax	NS	B3J3P5	**800-565-1263**	902-420-0555	372
Cambridge Suites Hotel Toronto 15 Richmond St E	Toronto	ON	M5C1N2	**800-463-1990**	416-368-1990	372
Cambridge Tool & Mfg Co Inc 67 Faulkner St	North Billerica	MA	01862	**888-333-9798**	978-667-8400	303
Cambridge University Press 40 W 20th St	New York	NY	10011	**800-221-4512**	212-924-3900	623-5
CambridgeSoft Corp 100 CambridgePark Dr	Cambridge	MA	02140	**800-315-7300**	617-588-9100	176-5
Cambro Mfg Co 5801 Skylab Rd	Huntington Beach	CA	92647	**800-833-3003**	714-848-1555	295
Camco Chemical Co 8150 Holton Dr *Cust Svc	Florence	KY	41042	**800-354-1001***	859-727-3200	149
Camco Inc DBA SuperPawn 3021 Business Ln	Las Vegas	NV	89103	**800-511-2568**	702-735-4444	558
Camden-Clark Memorial Hospital 800 Garfield Ave	Parkersburg	WV	26102	**800-422-6437**	304-424-2111	366-2
Camden County College PO Box 200 College Dr	Blackwood	NJ	08012	**888-228-2466**	856-227-7200	160
Camden National Corp 2 Elm St *AMEX: CAC*	Camden	ME	04843	**800-860-8821**	207-236-8821	355-2
Camden Property Trust 3 Greenway Plaza Suite 1300 *NYSE: CPT*	Houston	TX	77046	**800-922-6336**	713-354-2500	641
Camden Publications 331 E Bell St	Camden	MI	49232	**800-222-6336**	517-368-0365	522-4
Camel Grinding Wheels 7525 N Oak Park Ave	Niles	IL	60714	**800-760-6987**	847-647-5994	1
Camelback Inn JW Marriott Resort Golf Club & Spa 5402 E Lincoln Dr	Scottsdale	AZ	85253	**800-242-2635**	480-948-1700	655
Camelback Mountain. Sanctuary on 5700 E McDonald Dr	Paradise Valley	AZ	85253	**800-245-2051**	480-948-2100	655
Camelot Carpet Mills Inc 17111 Red Hill Ave	Irvine	CA	92614	**800-854-3258**	949-477-2299	131
Cameo Container Corp 1415 W 44th St	Chicago	IL	60609	**800-621-1030**	773-254-1030	101
Cameo Marble 540 Central Ct	New Albany	IN	47150	**800-447-8558**	812-944-5055	367
Camera Corner Inc PO Box 1899	Burlington	NC	27216	**800-868-2462**	336-228-0251	119
Camera Expert 5000 Armand-Frappier St	Saint-Hubert	QC	J3Z1G5	**877-361-4472**	514-856-7750	119
CameraWorld.com 2010 Main St Suite 400	Irvine	CA	92614	**800-226-3721**	949-442-0202	119
Cameron Glass Inc 3550 W Tacoma St	Broken Arrow	OK	74012	**800-331-3666**	918-254-6000	325
Cameron M Harris & Co 6400 Fairview Rd	Charlotte	NC	28210	**800-868-8834**	704-366-8834	383
Cameron University 2800 W Gore Blvd	Lawton	OK	73505	**888-454-7600**	580-581-2200	163
Camfil Farr Co 2121 E Paulhan St	Rancho Dominguez	CA	90220	**800-333-7320**	310-668-6300	19
Camillus Cutlery Co 54 Main St *Sales	Camillus	NY	13031	**800-344-0456***	315-672-8111	219
Camin Cargo Control Inc 230 Marion Ave	Linden	NJ	07036	**800-756-8798**	908-862-1899	728
Camino Real Foods Inc 5785 Corporate Ave Suite 170	Cypress	CA	90630	**800-421-6201**	714-816-7900	291-36
Camp Assn. American 5000 SR-67 N	Martinsville	IN	46151	**800-428-2267**	765-342-8456	48-23
Camp Fire USA 4601 Madison Ave	Kansas City	MO	64112	**800-669-6884**	816-756-1950	48-15
Campaign Fund. Women's 734 15th St NW Suite 500	Washington	DC	20005	**800-446-8170**	202-393-8164	48-7
Campaign Insider Newsletter 1414 22nd St NW *Cust Svc	Washington	DC	20037	**800-432-2250***	202-887-6279	521-7
Campaign for Tobacco-Free Kids 1400 'I' St NW Suite 1200	Washington	DC	20005	**800-284-5437**	202-296-5469	48-17
Campaigns. Alliance for Better 1990 M St NW Suite 200	Washington	DC	20036	**888-637-3389**	202-659-1300	48-7
CampAlaska Tours PO Box 872247	Wasilla	AK	99687	**800-376-9438**	907-376-9438	748
Campbell Blueprint & Supply Co Inc PO Box 820344	Memphis	TN	38182	**800-238-7564**	901-327-7385	239
Campbell Concrete & Materials PO Box 1147	Cleveland	TX	77328	**800-749-1843**	281-592-5201	180
Campbell Foundry Co 800 Bergen St	Harrison	NJ	07029	**800-843-4766**	973-483-5480	302
Campbell House Inn 1375 Harrodsburg Rd	Lexington	KY	40504	**800-354-9235**	859-255-4281	373
Campbell John J Co Inc 6012 Resources Dr	Memphis	TN	38134	**800-274-7663**	901-372-8400	188-12
Campbell Mfg Inc 129 E Spring St	Bechtelsville	PA	19505	**800-523-0224**	610-367-2107	584
Campbell Oil Co Inc 611 Erie St S	Massillon	OH	44646	**800-589-8555**	330-833-8555	569
Campbell Soup Co 1 Campbell Pl *NYSE: CPB*	Camden	NJ	08103	**800-772-8467**	856-342-4800	291-36
Campbell Towing Co PO Box 170	Wrangell	AK	99929	**800-399-4869**	907-874-3318	457
Campbell Travel 14800 Landmark Blvd Suite 155	Dallas	TX	75254	**800-357-7972**	972-716-2500	760
Campbell University PO Box 546	Buies Creek	NC	27506	**800-334-4111**	910-893-1290	163
Campbell Wrapper Corp 1415 Fortune Ave	De Pere	WI	54115	**800-727-4210**	920-983-7100	537

				Toll-Free	Phone	Class
Campbell's Resort PO Box 278	Chelan	WA	98816	**800-553-8225**	509-682-2561	655
Campbellsville University 1 University Dr	Campbellsville	KY	42718	**800-264-6014**	270-789-5000	163
Campers & RVers. Family 4804 Transit Rd Bldg 2	Depew	NY	14043	**800-245-9755**	716-668-6242	48-23
Camping World Inc 650 Three Springs Rd	Bowling Green	KY	42104	**800-626-3636*** *Cust Svc	270-781-2718	702
Campmor Inc 28 Parkway	Upper Saddle River	NJ	07458	**800-526-4784*** *Orders	201-825-8300	702
Campton Place Hotel 340 Stockton St	San Francisco	CA	94108	**800-235-4300**	415-781-5555	373
Campus Activities. National Assn for 13 Harbison Way	Columbia	SC	29212	**800-845-2338**	803-732-6222	49-5
Campus Crime Newsletter 8737 Colesville Rd Suite 1100	Silver Spring	MD	20910	**800-274-6737**	301-587-6300	521-4
Campus Crusade for Christ International 100 Lake Hart Dr	Orlando	FL	32832	**877-924-7478**	407-826-2000	48-20
Campus Inn. Dahlmann 615 E Huron St	Ann Arbor	MI	48104	**800-666-8693**	734-769-2200	373
Campus Inn & Suites 390 E Broadway	Eugene	OR	97401	**800-888-6313**	541-343-3376	373
Campus Life Magazine 465 Gundersen Dr	Carol Stream	IL	60188	**800-678-6083*** *Cust Svc	630-260-6200	449-11
Campus Tower Suite Hotel 11145 87th Ave	Edmonton	AB	T6G0Y1	**888-962-2522**	780-439-6060	372
Camstar Systems Inc 900 E Hamilton Ave Suite 400	Campbell	CA	95008	**800-237-2841**	408-559-5700	176-11
Camtronics Medical Systems 900 Walnut Ridge Dr	Hartland	WI	53029	**800-634-5151**	262-367-0700	375
Can Corp of America Inc PO Box 170	Blandon	PA	19510	**800-441-0876**	610-926-3044	124
Can Lines Inc PO Box 7039	Downey	CA	90241	**800-233-4597**	323-773-5676	462
Canaan Valley Resort & Conference Center HC 70 Box 330	Davis	WV	26260	**800-622-4121**	304-866-4121	655
Canac A Kohler Co 360 John St	Thornhill	ON	L3T3M9	**800-226-2248**	905-881-2153	116
Canad Inns - Club Regent Casino Hotel 1415 Regent Ave W	Winnipeg	MB	R2C3B2	**888-332-2623**	204-667-5560	372
Canad Inns Fort Garry 1824 Pembina Hwy	Winnipeg	MB	R3T2G2	**888-332-2623**	204-261-7450	372
Canad Inns Garden City 2100 McPhillips St	Winnipeg	MB	R2V3T9	**888-332-2623**	204-633-0024	372
Canad Inns Polo Park 1405 St Matthews Ave	Winnipeg	MB	R3G0K5	**888-332-2623**	204-775-8791	372
Canada Colors & Chemicals Ltd 80 Scarsdale Rd	Don Mills	ON	M3B2R7	**800-387-8006**	416-449-7750	144
Canada Life Financial Corp 330 University Ave	Toronto	ON	M5G1R8	**888-252-1847**	416-597-1456	384-4
Canada. Nature 1 Nicholas St Suite 606	Ottawa	ON	K1N7B7	**800-267-4088**	613-562-3447	48-13
Canada Stockwatch 609 Granville St Suite 1550	Vancouver	BC	V7Y1J6	**800-268-6397**	604-687-1500	396
Canadian Academy of Sport Medicine 1010 Polytek St Unit 14 Suite 100	Ottawa	ON	K1J9H9	**877-585-2394**	613-748-5851	49-8
Canadian Assn of Emergency Physicians (CAEP) 1785 Alta Vista Dr Suite 104	Ottawa	ON	K1G3Y6	**800-463-1158**	613-523-3343	49-8
Canadian Assn of Retired Persons (CARP) 1304-27 Queen St E	Toronto	ON	M5C2M6	**800-363-9736**	416-363-8748	48-6
Canadian Baseball Hall of Fame & Museum 386 Church St PO Box 1838	Saint Marys	ON	N4X1C2	**877-250-2255**	519-284-1838	511
Canadian Bearings Ltd 1401 Courtney Park Dr E	Mississauga	ON	L5T2E4	**800-229-2327**	905-670-6700	378
Canadian Biker 735 Market St	Victoria	BC	V8T2E2	**800-667-5667**	250-384-0333	449-3
Canadian Broadcasting Corp (CBC) 181 Queen St	Ottawa	ON	K1P1K9	**866-306-4636**	613-288-6000	629
Canadian Business Magazine 1 Mt Pleasant Rd 11th Fl	Toronto	ON	M4Y2Y5	**800-465-0700**	416-764-1200	449-5
Canadian Federation of Humane Societies (CFHS) 30 Concourse Gate Suite 102	Ottawa	ON	K2E7V7	**888-678-2347**	613-224-8072	48-3
Canadian Fishing Co Foot of Gore Ave	Vancouver	BC	V6A2Y7	**888-526-2929**	604-681-0211	280
Canadian Golf Hall of Fame & Museum Glen Abbey Golf Club 1333 Dorval Dr	Oakville	ON	L6J4Z3	**800-310-7242**	905-849-9700	511
Canadian Imperial Bank of Commerce 199 Bay St Commerce Court W *NYSE: BCM*	Toronto	ON	M5L1A2	**800-465-2422**	416-980-2211	71
Canadian Kennel Club (CKC) 89 Skyway Ave Suite 100	Etobicoke	ON	M9W6R4	**800-250-8040**	416-675-5511	48-3
Canadian Livestock Insurance 75 The Donway W Suite 708	Don Mills	ON	M3C2E9	**800-727-1502**	416-510-8191	384-1
Canadian Living Magazine 25 Sheppard Ave W Suite 100	Toronto	ON	M2N6S7	**800-387-6332**	416-733-7600	449-11
Canadian Medical Laboratories Ltd 6560 Kennedy Rd	Mississauga	ON	L5T2X4	**800-263-0801**	905-565-0043	409
Canadian Museum of Civilization PO Box 3100 Station B	Hull	QC	J8X4H2	**800-555-5621**	819-776-7000	509
Canadian Museum of Contemporary Photography 1 Rideau Canal	Ottawa	ON	K1N9N6	**877-541-8888**	613-990-8257	509
Canadian Museum of Nature 240 McLeod St	Ottawa	ON	K1P6P4	**800-263-4433**	613-566-4700	509
Canadian Pacific Railway Co Gulf Canada Sq 401 9th Ave SW *NYSE: CP*	Calgary	AB	T2P4Z4	**888-333-6370**	403-319-7000	634
Canadian Peregrine Foundation 250 Merton St Suite 104	Toronto	ON	M4S1B1	**888-709-3944**	416-481-1233	48-3
Canadian Securities Registration Systems 4126 Norland Ave Suite 200	Burnaby	BC	V5G3S8	**800-561-1404**	604-637-4000	621
Canadian Southern Baptist Seminary 200 Seminary View	Cochrane	AB	T4C2G1	**877-922-2727**	403-932-6622	164-3
Canadian Superior Energy Inc 400 3rd Ave SW Suite 3300 *TSE: SNG*	Calgary	AB	T2P4H2	**877-294-1411**	403-294-1411	525
Canadian Tire Corp Ltd PO Box 770 Stn K *TSE: CTR*	Toronto	ON	M4P2V8	**800-387-8803**	416-480-3000	184
Canadian Wild Bird Watching Adventures PO Box 82	Nestor Falls	ON	P0X1K0	**800-561-3166**		748
Canadian Wildlife Federation (CWF) 350 Michael Cowpland Dr	Kanata	ON	K2M2W1	**800-563-9453**	613-599-9594	48-13
Canadians. Council of 170 Laurier Ave W Suite 700	Ottawa	ON	K1P5V5	**800-387-7177**	613-233-2773	48-7
Canal Park Inn 250 Canal Park Dr	Duluth	MN	55802	**800-777-8560**	218-727-8821	373
Canal Park Stadium 300 S Main St	Akron	OH	44308	**800-972-3767**	330-253-5151	706
Canal Wood LLC PO Box 260010	Conway	SC	29528	**866-587-1460**	843-488-9663	439
Canam Steel Corp 4010 Clay St	Point of Rocks	MD	21777	**800-638-4293**	301-874-5141	471
Canandaigua Inn on the Lake 770 S Main St	Canandaigua	NY	14424	**800-228-2801**	585-394-7800	373
Canandaigua Wine Co Inc 116 Buffalo St	Canandaigua	NY	14424	**888-659-7900**	585-396-7600	81-3
Canberra Industries Inc 800 Research Pkwy	Meriden	CT	06450	**800-243-4422**	203-238-2351	464
Cancer Care Inc 275 7th Ave 22nd Fl	New York	NY	10001	**800-813-4673**	212-712-8080	48-17
Cancer Center & Research Institute. H Lee Moffitt 12902 Magnolia Dr	Tampa	FL	33612	**800-456-3434**	813-972-4673	366-5
Cancer Coalition. National Breast 1101 17th St NW Suite 1300	Washington	DC	20036	**800-622-2838**	202-296-7477	48-17
Cancer Coalition. National Ovarian 500 NE Spanish River Blvd Suite 8	Boca Raton	FL	33431	**888-682-7426**	561-393-0005	48-17
Cancer Foundation. Candlelighters Childhood PO Box 498	Kensington	MD	20895	**800-366-2223**	301-962-3520	48-17
Cancer Foundation. RA Bloch 4400 Main St	Kansas City	MO	64111	**800-433-0464**	816-932-8453	48-17
Cancer Foundation. Skin 245 5th Ave Suite 1403	New York	NY	10016	**800-754-6490**	212-725-5176	48-17
Cancer Foundation. Susan G Komen Breast 5005 LBJ Fwy Suite 250	Dallas	TX	75244	**800-462-9273**	972-855-1600	48-17
Cancer Information Service (CIS) National Cancer Institute 9000 Rockville Pike Bldg 31	Bethesda	MD	20892	**800-422-6237**	301-496-4000	336-6
Cancer Institute. Barbara Ann Karmanos 4110 John R St	Detroit	MI	48201	**800-527-6266**	313-833-0710	654
Cancer Institute. Dana-Farber 44 Binney St	Boston	MA	02115	**800-757-3324**	617-632-3000	366-5
Cancer Institute. National 6116 Executive Blvd MSC 8322	Bethesda	MD	20892	**800-422-6237**	301-435-3848	654
Cancer Letter PO Box 9905	Washington	DC	20016	**800-513-7042**	202-362-1809	521-8
Cancer Letter Business & Regulatory Report PO Box 9905	Washington	DC	20016	**800-513-7042**	202-362-1809	521-8
Cancer Organization. Y-ME National Breast 212 W Van Buren St	Chicago	IL	60607	**800-221-2141**	312-986-8338	48-17
Cancer Prevention Resource Center. National HPV & Cervical PO Box 13827	Research Triangle Park	NC	27709	**800-277-8922**	919-361-8400	48-17
Cancer Registry. Gilda Radner Familial Ovarian Roswell Park Cancer Institute Elm & Carlton Sts	Buffalo	NY	14263	**800-682-7426**	716-845-4503	48-17
Cancer Research. American Institute for 1759 R St NW	Washington	DC	20009	**800-843-8114**	202-328-7744	654
Cancer Research Center. AMC 1600 Pierce St	Denver	CO	80214	**800-321-1557**	303-233-6501	654
Cancer Research. National Foundation for 4600 East West Hwy Suite 525	Bethesda	MD	20814	**800-321-2873**	301-654-1250	654
Cancer Research & Prevention Foundation 1600 Duke St Suite 500	Alexandria	VA	22314	**800-227-2732**	703-836-4412	48-17
Cancer Society. American 1599 Clifton Rd NE	Atlanta	GA	30329	**800-227-2345**	404-320-3333	48-17
Cancer Society. National Children's 1015 Locust St Suite 600	Saint Louis	MO	63101	**800-532-6459**	314-241-1600	48-17
cancerfacts.com 1725 Westlake Ave N Suite 300	Seattle	WA	98109	**877-422-3228*** *Cust Svc	206-270-0225	351
Candalero Resort at Palmas Del Mar 270 Harborside Dr Suite 1	Humacao	PR	00791	**800-725-6273**	787-852-6000	655
Candela Corp 530 Boston Post Rd *NASDAQ: CLZR*	Wayland	MA	01778	**800-733-8550**	508-358-7637	415
Candid Color Systems Inc 1300 Metropolitan Ave	Oklahoma City	OK	73108	**800-336-4550**	405-947-8747	577
Candie's Inc 400 Columbus Ave *NASDAQ: CAND*	Valhalla	NY	10595	**800-352-2634**	914-769-8600	296
Candies Otto LLC 17271 Hwy 90	Des Allemands	LA	70030	**800-535-4563**	504-469-7700	457
Candle-Lite Div Lancaster Colony Corp PO Box 42364	Cincinnati	OH	45242	**800-718-7018**	513-563-1113	122
Candlelighters Childhood Cancer Foundation PO Box 498	Kensington	MD	20895	**800-366-2223**	301-962-3520	48-17
Candleman Corp 1120 Industrial Pk Rd PO Box 731	Brainerd	MN	56401	**800-328-3453**	218-829-0592	122
Candy Bouquet International Inc 423 E 3rd St	Little Rock	AR	72201	**877-226-3901**	501-375-9990	123
Candy Care Inc W 58th St	New York	NY	10019	**888-423-8823**	212-421-1234	130
Cane Creek Cycling Components 355 Cane Creek Rd	Fletcher	NC	28732	**800-234-2725**	828-684-3551	83
Caney Fork Electric Co-op Inc 920 Smithville Hwy	McMinnville	TN	37111	**888-505-3030**	931-473-3116	244
Caney Valley Electric Co-op Assn 401 Lawrence St	Cedar Vale	KS	67024	**800-310-8911**	620-758-2262	244
Canfield Jack Canfield Group & Chicken Soup for the Soul Enterprises PO Box 30880	Santa Barbara	CA	93130	**800-237-8336**		561
Canfisco Foot of Gore Ave	Vancouver	BC	V6A2Y7	**888-526-2929**	604-681-0211	280
Cangro Industries Long Island Transmission Co 495 Smith St	Farmingdale	NY	11735	**800-899-2264**	631-454-9000	609
Canine Companions for Independence (CCI) 2965 Dutton Ave	Santa Rosa	CA	95407	**800-572-2275**	707-577-1700	48-17
Canisius College 2001 Main St	Buffalo	NY	14208	**800-843-1517**	716-883-7000	163
CanJet Airlines PO Box 980	Enfield	NS	B2T1R6	**800-809-7777*** *Resv	902-973-7800	26
Cankdeska Cikana Community College PO Box 269	Fort Totten	ND	58335	**888-783-1463**	701-766-4415	161

				Toll-Free	Phone	Class
Canlyte 3015 Louis Amos	Lachine	QC	H8T1C4	**800-565-5486**	514-636-0670	431
Cannon Equipment Co						
15100 Business Pkwy	Rosemount	MN	55068	**800-825-8501**	651-322-6300	462
Cannon-Muskegon Corp						
2875 Lincoln St	Muskegon	MI	49441	**800-253-0371**	231-755-1681	476
Cannon Sline Industrial Inc						
10 Industrial Hwy MS 38	Lester	PA	19113	**800-729-4600**	610-521-2100	188-8
Cano Corp 225 Industrial Rd	Fitchburg	MA	01420	**800-237-1358**	978-342-0953	281
Canoe Assn. American						
7432 Alban Station Blvd						
Suite B-232	Springfield	VA	22150	**800-929-5162**	703-451-0141	48-22
Canoga Camera Corp						
22065 Sherman Way	Canoga Park	CA	91303	**800-201-4201**	818-346-5506	119
Canon Business Solutions-Northeast						
Inc 125 Park Ave 7th Fl	New York	NY	10017	**800-627-2679**	212-850-1000	113
Canon Business Solutions-Southeast						
Inc 300 Commerce Sq Blvd	Burlington	NJ	08016	**800-220-4000**	609-387-8700	113
Cañon City Chamber of Commerce						
403 Royal Gorge Blvd	Canon City	CO	81212	**800-876-7922**	719-275-2331	137
Canon Consumer Imaging & Information						
Systems Group 15955 Alton Pkwy	Irvine	CA	92618	**800-848-4123***	949-753-4000	580
*Sales						
Canon USA Inc 1 Canon Plaza	Lake Success	NY	11042	**800-828-4040**	516-488-6700	580
NYSE: CAJ						
Canoochee Electric Membership Corp						
342 E Brazell St	Reidsville	GA	30453	**800-342-0134**	912-557-4391	244
Canopy Systems Inc 5501 Dillard Ave	Cary	NC	27511	**800-757-1354**	919-851-6177	39
Canson Inc 21 Industrial Dr	South Hadley	MA	01075	**800-628-9283**	413-538-9250	43
Cantec Industries Inc						
455 Cote Vertu Rd	Montreal	QC	H4N1E8	**800-334-1567***	514-334-1510	717
*Orders						
Canteen Correctional Services						
38 Pond St Suite 308	Franklin	MA	02030	**800-357-0012**	508-520-4334	294
Canteen Vending Services						
2400 Yorkmont Rd	Charlotte	NC	28217	**800-357-0012**	704-329-4000	294
Canter & Assoc Inc						
12975 Coral Tree Pl	Los Angeles	CA	90066	**800-733-1711***	310-578-4700	754
*Cust Svc						
Canterbury Consulting Group Inc						
352 Stokes Rd Suite 200	Medford	NJ	08055	**800-873-2040**	609-953-0044	753
NASDAQ: CITI						
Canterbury Hotel 123 S Illinois St	Indianapolis	IN	46225	**800-538-8186**	317-634-3000	373
Canterbury Park Holding Corp						
1100 Canterbury Rd	Shakopee	MN	55379	**800-340-6361**	952-445-7223	628
AMEX: ECP						
Canterbury Shaker Village						
288 Shaker Rd	Canterbury	NH	03224	**866-783-9511**	603-783-9511	509
CANTEX Inc PO Box 365	Auburndale	FL	33823	**800-765-8704**	863-967-4161	585
Canton Regional Chamber of Commerce						
222 Market Ave N	Canton	OH	44702	**800-533-4302**	330-456-7253	137
Canton/Stark County Convention &						
Visitors Bureau 222 Market Ave N	Canton	OH	44702	**800-533-4302**	330-454-1439	205
Cantrall & Assoc						
2517 Eastlake Ave E Suite 200	Seattle	WA	98102	**800-837-6186**	206-322-6990	47
Canvas Products Co						
2340 Lafayette Blvd W	Detroit	MI	48216	**800-624-6671***	313-496-1000	718
*Cust Svc						
Canyon Chamber of Commerce						
1518 5th Ave	Canyon	TX	79015	**800-999-9481**	806-655-1183	137
Canyon Creek Cabinet Co						
16726 Tye St SE	Monroe	WA	98272	**800-228-1830**	425-481-6860	116
Canyon Ranch in the Berkshires						
165 Kemble St	Lenox	MA	01240	**800-742-9000***	413-637-4100	697
*Resv						
Canyon Ranch Health Resort						
8600 E Rockcliff Rd	Tucson	AZ	85750	**800-742-9000**	520-749-9000	697
Canyon Ranch SpaClub at the Gaylord						
Palms Resort 6000 W						
Osceola Pkwy	Kissimmee	FL	34746	**800-742-9000**	407-586-2051	698
Canyon Ranch SpaClub at the						
Venetian 3355 Las Vegas Blvd S						
Suite 1159	Las Vegas	NV	89109	**877-220-2688**	702-414-3600	698
Canyons Resort						
4000 The Canyons Resort Dr	Park City	UT	84098	**888-226-9667**	435-615-8040	655
Canyonville Christian Academy						
250 E 1st St PO Box 1100	Canyonville	OR	97417	**888-222-6379**	541-839-4401	611
CAP (Children Awaiting Parents Inc)						
595 Blossom Rd Suite 306	Rochester	NY	14610	**888-835-8802**	585-232-5110	48-6
CAP (College of American						
Pathologists) 325 Waukegan Rd	Northfield	IL	60093	**800-323-4040**	847-832-7000	49-8
Cap Rock Energy Corp						
500 W Wall St Suite 400	Midland	TX	79701	**800-442-8688**	432-683-5422	774
AMEX: RKE						
CAP Warehouse						
3108 Losee Rd	North Las Vegas	NV	89030	**800-879-7901**	702-642-7801	61
Capacity of Texas Inc						
401 Capacity Dr	Longview	TX	75604	**800-323-0135**	903-759-0610	505
Cape Air 660 Barnstable Rd	Hyannis	MA	02601	**800-352-0714**	508-771-6944	26
Cape Ann Chamber of Commerce						
33 Commercial St	Gloucester	MA	01930	**800-321-0133**	978-283-1601	137
Cape Cod Chamber of Commerce						
Rt 6 & 132	Hyannis	MA	02601	**888-332-2732**	508-362-3225	137
Cape Cod Community College						
2240 Iyanough Rd	West Barnstable	MA	02668	**877-846-3672**	508-362-2131	160
Cape Cod Five Cents Savings Bank						
19 West Rd	Orleans	MA	02653	**888-333-0555**	508-240-0555	71
Cape Cod Life Magazine						
270 Communications Way Bldg 6	Hyannis	MA	02601	**800-698-1717**	508-775-9800	449-22
Cape Cod Potato Chip Co						
100 Breed's Hill Rd	Hyannis	MA	02601	**888-881-2447**	508-775-3358	291-35
Cape Cod Regional Transit Authority						
(CCRTA) PO Box 1988	Hyannis	MA	02601	**800-352-7155**	508-775-8504	460
Cape Codder Resort & Spa						
1225 Iyanough Rd	Hyannis	MA	02601	**888-297-2200**	508-771-3000	655
Cape Coral Chamber of Commerce						
2051 Cape Coral Pkwy E	Cape Coral	FL	33904	**800-226-9609**	239-549-6900	137
Cape Fear Coast Convention &						
Visitors Bureau 24 N 3rd St	Wilmington	NC	28401	**800-222-4757**	910-341-4030	205

				Toll-Free	Phone	Class
Cape Fear Rod Co						
302-A Raleigh St	Wilmington	NC	28412	**888-886-2064**	910-350-0494	701
Cape Hatteras Electric Co-op						
47109 Light Plant Rd	Buxton	NC	27920	**800-454-5616**	252-995-5616	244
Cape May Foods Inc						
35 Indian Trail Rd	Burleigh	NJ	08210	**800-922-1141**	609-465-4551	291-13
Capel Inc 831 N Main St	Troy	NC	27371	**800-334-3711**	910-572-7000	131
Capella Education Co						
222 S 9th St 20th Fl	Minneapolis	MN	55402	**888-227-3552**	612-339-7665	241
Capezio/Ballet Makers Inc						
1 Campus Rd	Totowa	NJ	07512	**800-595-9002**	973-595-9000	296
Capital Agricultural Property Services Inc						
801 Warrenville Rd Suite 150	Lisle	IL	60532	**800-243-2060**	630-434-9150	310-3
Capital Asset Research Corp						
Ltd 3960 RCA Blvd						
Suite 6002	Palm Beach Gardens	FL	33410	**800-888-8293**	561-776-5000	157
Capital Automotive REIT						
8270 Greensboro Dr Suite 950	McLean	VA	22102	**877-422-7288**	703-288-3075	640
NASDAQ: CARS						
Capital Bank Corp 4901 Glenwood Ave	Raleigh	NC	27612	**800-308-3971**	919-645-6400	355-2
NASDAQ: CBKN						
Capital Beverage Co						
2424 Del Monte St	West Sacramento	CA	95691	**800-954-2667***	916-371-8164	82-1
*Cust Svc						
Capital Blue Cross						
2500 Elmerton Ave	Harrisburg	PA	17110	**800-958-5558***	610-820-2700	384-3
*Cust Svc						
Capital Cargo International Airlines						
6200 Hazeltine National Dr	Orlando	FL	32822	**800-593-9119**	407-855-2004	13
Capital City Bank Group Inc						
217 N Monroe St	Tallahassee	FL	32301	**888-671-0400**	850-671-0400	355-2
NASDAQ: CCBG						
Capital Community College						
950 Main St	Hartford	CT	06103	**800-894-6126**	860-906-5000	160
Capital Crossing Bank 101 Summer St	Boston	MA	02110	**888-880-3880**	617-880-1000	71
NASDAQ: CAPX						
Capital District Physicians' Health Plan						
Inc 1223 Washington Ave	Albany	NY	12206	**800-777-2273**	518-641-3000	384-3
Capital Ford Inc 4900 Capital Blvd	Raleigh	NC	27616	**800-849-3166**	919-790-4600	57
Capital Grille						
8215 Roswell Rd Bldg 600	Atlanta	GA	30350	**800-434-6245**	770-399-9595	657
Capital Group Cos Inc						
333 S Hope St	Los Angeles	CA	90071	**800-421-8511**	213-486-9200	393
Capital Growth Management LP						
1 International Pl 45th Fl	Boston	MA	02110	**800-334-6440**	617-737-3225	393
Capital Health Plan						
2140 Centerville Pl	Tallahassee	FL	32308	**800-390-1434**	850-383-3333	384-3
Capital Hill Hotel & Suites						
88 Albert St	Ottawa	ON	K1P5E9	**800-463-7705**	613-235-1413	372
Capital Hilton 1001 16th St NW	Washington	DC	20036	**800-445-8667**	202-393-1000	373
Capital Hospice Inc						
9300 Lee Hwy Suite 200	Faifax	VA	22031	**888-583-1900**	703-383-9222	365
Capital Hotel 111 W Markham St	Little Rock	AR	72201	**800-766-7666**	501-374-7474	373
Capital Imaging Co Inc						
2745 W 5th North St	Summerville	SC	29483	**800-868-6780**	843-871-6084	616
Capital Journal 333 N Dakota Ave	Pierre	SD	57501	**800-658-3063**	605-224-7301	522-2
Capital Manor 1955 Dallas Hwy NW	Salem	OR	97304	**800-637-0327**	503-362-4101	659
Capital Medical Center						
3900 Capital Mall Dr SW	Olympia	WA	98502	**888-677-9757**	360-754-5858	366-2
Capital One Financial Corp						
1680 Capital One Dr	McLean	VA	22102	**800-801-1164**	703-720-1000	213
NYSE: COF						
Capital Research Center						
1513 16th St NW	Washington	DC	20036	**800-459-3950**	202-483-6900	654
Capital Resource Advisors						
200 W Adams Suite 1800	Chicago	IL	60606	**888-677-4272**		393
Capital Times 1901 Fish Hatchery Rd	Madison	WI	53713	**800-362-8333**	608-252-6400	522-2
Capital Tire Inc 1001-17 Cherry St	Toledo	OH	43608	**800-537-0190**	419-241-5111	740
Capital University 1 E Main St	Columbus	OH	43209	**800-289-6289**	614-236-6011	163
CapitalSource Inc						
4445 Willard Ave 12th Fl	Chevy Chase	MD	20815	**866-876-8723**	301-841-2700	498
NYSE: CSE						
Capitol Adhesives USA Dixie Mfg Co Div						
300 Cross Plains Blvd	Dalton	GA	30720	**800-831-8381**	706-277-6241	131
Capitol Advantage LLC						
2751 Prosperity Ave 6th Fl	Fairfax	VA	22031	**800-659-8708**	703-289-4670	623-6
Capitol Aggregates Ltd						
11551 Nacogdoches Rd	San Antonio	TX	78217	**800-292-5315**	210-655-3010	46
Capitol City Speakers Bureau						
1620 S 5th St	Springfield	IL	62703	**800-397-3183**	217-544-8552	699
Capitol City Steel Co Inc 900 N IH-35	Buda	TX	78610	**800-333-8820**	512-282-8820	471
Capitol College 11301 Springfield Rd	Laurel	MD	20708	**800-950-1992**	301-369-2800	163
Capitol Detective Agency						
2922 N 18th Pl	Phoenix	AZ	85016	**800-346-0347**	602-277-0770	392
Capitol Federal Financial						
700 Kansas Ave	Topeka	KS	66603	**888-822-7333**	785-235-1341	355-2
NASDAQ: CFFN						
Capitol Federal Savings Bank						
700 S Kansas Ave	Topeka	KS	66603	**800-432-2926**	785-235-1341	71
Capitol Hill Suites 200 C St SE	Washington	DC	20003	**888-627-7811**	202-543-6000	373
Capitol Indemnity Corp						
4610 University Ave Suite 1400	Madison	WI	53705	**800-475-4450**	608-231-4450	384-4
Capitol Lien Records & Research Inc						
1010 N Dale St	Saint Paul	MN	55167	**800-845-4077**	651-488-0100	621
Capitol Music Hall 1015 Main St	Wheeling	WV	26003	**800-624-5456**	304-234-0050	562
Capitol Plaza Hotel & Conference						
Center 100 State St	Montpelier	VT	05602	**800-274-5252**	802-223-5252	373
Capitol Plaza Hotel Jefferson City						
415 W McCarty St	Jefferson City	MO	65101	**800-338-8088**	573-635-1234	373
Capitol Plaza Hotel Topeka						
1717 SW Topeka Blvd	Topeka	KS	66612	**800-579-7937**	785-431-7200	373
Capitol Plywood Inc						
160 Commerce Cir	Sacramento	CA	95815	**800-326-1505**	916-922-8861	602
Capitol Reservations						
1730 Rhode Island Ave NW						
Suite 1210	Washington	DC	20036	**800-847-4832**	202-452-1270	368
Capitol Services Inc						
800 Brazos St Suite 1100	Austin	TX	78701	**800-345-4647**	512-474-8377	621

Name / Address	City	State	ZIP	Toll-Free	Phone	Class
Capitol Specialty Insurance Corp 4610 University Ave Suite 1400	Madison	WI	53705	**800-475-4450**	608-231-4450	384-4
Capitol Technologies Inc 3615 W Voorde Dr	South Bend	IN	46628	**800-270-5222**	574-232-3311	745
Capitol Theatre 50 W 200 South	Salt Lake City	UT	84101	**888-451-2787**	801-323-6800	562
Capitol Trailways Inc PO Box 3353	Harrisburg	PA	17105	**800-333-8444**	717-233-7673	109
Capitol Uniform & Linen Service 195 Commerce Way	Dover	DE	19901	**800-323-1511**	302-674-1511	434
CapitolWatch PO Box 71	Great Falls	VA	22066	**888-468-9282**	202-544-2600	48-7
Capp Inc 201 Marple Ave	Clifton Heights	PA	19018	**800-356-8000**	610-394-1100	201
Capper's Magazine 1503 SW 42nd St	Topeka	KS	66609	**800-678-5779**	785-274-4300	449-11
Capri Miami Beach Condo-Hotel 3010 Collins Ave	Miami Beach	FL	33140	**800-528-0823**	305-531-7742	373
Capricorn Coffees Inc 353 10th St	San Francisco	CA	94103	**800-541-0758**	415-621-8500	292-2
Capsonic Automotive Inc 460 S 2nd St	Elgin	IL	60123	**888-981-1500**	847-888-7300	60
Capstead Mortgage Corp 8401 N Central Expy Suite 800 *NYSE: CMO*	Dallas	TX	75225	**800-358-2323**	214-874-2323	640
Captain Bartlett Inn 1411 Airport Way	Fairbanks	AK	99701	**800-544-7528**	907-452-1888	373
Captain Daniel Stone Inn 10 Water St	Brunswick	ME	04011	**877-573-5151**	207-725-9898	373
Captain D's LLC 1717 Elm Hill Pike Suite A-1	Nashville	TN	37210	**800-314-4819**	615-391-5461	657
Captain Tony's Inc 2607 S Woodland Blvd Suite 300	DeLand	FL	32720	**800-332-8669**	386-736-9855	657
Captaris Inc 10885 NE 4th St Suite 400 *NASDAQ: CAPA*	Bellevue	WA	98004	**800-443-0806**	425-455-6000	176-7
Car Brite Inc 1910 S State Ave	Indianapolis	IN	46203	**800-347-2439**	317-788-9925	149
Car Clinic Productions 5675 N Davis Hwy	Pensacola	FL	32503	**800-264-5454**	850-478-3139	632
Car Craft Magazine 6420 Wilshire Blvd	Los Angeles	CA	90048	**800-800-8326**	323-782-2000	449-3
Car Dealer Insider Newsletter 11300 Rockville Pike Suite 1100 *Cust Svc	Rockville	MD	20852	**800-929-4824***	301-816-8950	521-13
Car & Driver Magazine 2002 Hogback Rd	Ann Arbor	MI	48105	**800-666-9485**	734-971-3600	449-3
Car-Freshner Corp 21205 Little Tree Dr	Watertown	NY	13601	**800-545-5454**	315-788-6250	149
Car Rental Express 3337 W 4th Ave	Vancouver	BC	V6R1N6	**888-557-8188**	604-714-5911	126
Car Seat Specialty PO Box 3194	Rock Hill	SC	29732	**877-912-1313**		64
Car Stereo Review Magazine 1633 Broadway 45th Fl	New York	NY	10019	**800-498-1993**	212-767-6000	449-3
CAR Transportation Brokerage Co PO Box 712	Springdale	AR	72765	**800-648-6588**	479-751-8747	769
Car-X Assoc Corp 1375 E Woodfield Rd Suite 500	Schaumburg	IL	60173	**800-359-2359**	847-273-8920	305
Cara Operations Ltd 6303 Airport Rd	Mississauga	ON	L4V1R8	**800-860-4082**	905-405-6500	294
Cara Operations Ltd Airport Services Div 6303 Airport Rd	Mississauga	ON	L4V1R8	**800-860-4082**	905-405-6500	294
Carabella Corp 17662 Armstrong Ave *Cust Svc	Irvine	CA	92614	**800-227-2235***	949-263-2300	153-21
Carando Inc 20 Carando Dr	Springfield	MA	01104	**800-628-9524**	413-781-5620	291-26
Carat USA 2450 Colorado Ave Suite 300 E	Santa Monica	CA	90404	**800-847-6334**	310-255-1000	6
Caravali Coffees Inc 717 Del Paso Rd	Sacramento	CA	95834	**800-647-5282**	916-565-5500	291-7
Caravan International & EthnoGraphics PO Box 768	Colleyville	TX	76034	**800-442-0036**	817-577-2988	130
Caravan Products Co Inc 100 Adams Dr	Totowa	NJ	07512	**800-526-5261**	973-256-8886	291-16
Caravelle Resort Hotel & Villas 6900 N Ocean Blvd	Myrtle Beach	SC	29572	**800-845-0893**	843-918-8000	655
Caravelle Travel Management Inc 1900 E Golf Rd Suite 1100	Schaumburg	IL	60173	**800-323-0902**	847-619-8300	760
Carboline Co 350 Hanley Industrial Ct	Saint Louis	MO	63144	**800-848-4645**	314-644-1000	540
CarboMedics Inc 1300 E Anderson Ln	Austin	TX	78752	**800-648-1579**	512-435-3200	469
Carbon Power & Light Inc 110 E Spring St	Saratoga	WY	82331	**800-359-0249**	307-326-5206	244
Carbon Technology Inc 659 S County Trail	Exeter	RI	02822	**800-222-7266**	401-295-8877	321
Carbondale Convention & Tourism Bureau 1185 E Main St Suite 1046	Carbondale	IL	62901	**800-526-1500**	618-529-4451	205
Carbone of America 400 Myrtle Ave *Cust Svc	Boonton	NJ	07005	**800-526-0877***	973-334-0700	127
CARCO Group Inc 17 Flowerfield Industrial Pk	Saint James	NY	11780	**800-645-4556**	631-862-9300	621
Carco International Inc 2721 Midland Blvd	Fort Smith	AR	72904	**800-824-3215**	479-441-3270	270
Carco National Lease Inc 2905 N 32nd St	Fort Smith	AR	72904	**800-643-2596**	479-441-3200	767
Card & Gift Gallery Inc 4200 S East St	Indianapolis	IN	46227	**800-893-3115**	317-783-1555	129
Card Pak Inc 29601 Solon Rd	Solon	OH	44139	**800-824-3342**	440-542-3100	89
Cardello Electric Supply Co 701 N Point Dr	Pittsburgh	PA	15233	**800-333-0454**	412-322-8031	245
Carder Concrete Products Co 8311 W Carder Ct	Littleton	CO	80125	**800-285-2902**	303-791-1600	181
Cardima Inc 47266 Benicia St *NASDAQ: CRDM*	Fremont	CA	94538	**888-354-0300**	510-354-0300	468
Cardinal Aluminum Co 6910 Preston Hwy *Cust Svc	Louisville	KY	40219	**800-398-7833***	502-969-9302	476
Cardinal Brands 643 Massachusetts Suite 200	Lawrence	KS	66044	**800-444-3508**	785-344-1400	87
Cardinal Detecto Scale Mfg Co PO Box 151 *Cust Svc	Webb City	MO	64870	**800-641-2008***	417-673-4631	672
Cardinal Financial Corp 8270 Greensboro Dr Suite 500 *NASDAQ: CFNL*	McLean	VA	22102	**800-473-3247**	703-279-5050	355-2
Cardinal Glass Co 1087 Research Pkwy	Rockford	IL	61109	**800-728-3468**	815-394-1400	325
Cardinal Health Automation & Information Services 3750 Torrey View Ct	San Diego	CA	92130	**800-367-9947**	858-480-6000	468
Cardinal Health Distribution 7000 Cardinal Pl	Dublin	OH	43017	**800-234-8701**	614-757-5000	237
Cardinal Health Inc 7000 Cardinal Pl *NYSE: CAH*	Dublin	OH	43017	**800-234-8701**	614-757-5000	355-3
Cardinal Health Specialty Pharmaceutical Distribution 401 Mason Rd	La Vergne	TN	37086	**800-879-5569**		237
Cardinal Hill Rehabilitation Hospital 2050 Versailles Rd	Lexington	KY	40504	**800-843-1408**	859-254-5701	366-4
Cardinal Industries Inc 37 W 750 Rt 64	Saint Charles	IL	60175	**800-323-5018**	630-513-5400	542-1
Cardinal Office Systems Inc 576 E Main St	Frankfort	KY	40601	**800-930-2280**	502-875-3300	523
Cardinal Stritch University 6801 N Yates Rd	Milwaukee	WI	53217	**800-347-8822**	414-410-4000	163
CardInTheBox 350 S Rohlwing Rd Suite 200	Addison	IL	60101	**877-212-1121**	630-953-8882	130
CardioDynamics International Corp 6175 Nancy Ridge Dr Suite 300 *NASDAQ: CDIC*	San Diego	CA	92121	**800-778-4825**	858-535-0202	249
CardioGenesis Corp 26632 Towne Centre Dr Suite 320	Foothill Ranch	CA	92610	**800-238-2205**	714-649-5000	415
Cardiology. American College of 9111 Old Georgetown Rd *Cust Svc	Bethesda	MD	20814	**800-253-4636***	301-897-5400	49-8
Cardiome Pharma Corp 6196 Agronomy Rd 6th Fl *NASDAQ: CRME*	Vancouver	BC	V6T1Z3	**800-330-9928**	604-677-6905	86
Cardone Industries Inc 5501 Whitaker Ave *Cust Svc	Philadelphia	PA	19124	**800-777-4780***	215-912-3000	60
CardScan Inc 810 Memorial Dr 3rd Fl	Cambridge	MA	02139	**800-942-6739**	617-492-4200	171-7
CardStore.com 1195 Park Ave Suite 211	Emeryville	CA	94608	**877-822-2737**	510-595-6775	129
Cardtronics Inc 3110 Hayes Rd Suite 300	Houston	TX	77082	**800-786-9666**	281-596-9988	56
CardWeb.com Inc 10 N Jefferson St	Frederick	MD	21701	**800-260-7448**	301-631-9100	115
CARE (Coalition for Auto Repair Equality) 119 Oronoco St Suite 300	Alexandria	VA	22314	**800-229-5380**	703-519-7555	49-21
Care Choices 34605 12-Mile Rd *Sales	Farmington Hills	MI	48331	**800-261-3452***	248-489-6203	455
Care-Tech Laboratories Inc 3224 S Kingshighway Blvd	Saint Louis	MO	63139	**800-325-9681**	314-772-4610	572
CARE USA 151 Ellis St NE	Atlanta	GA	30303	**800-422-7385**	404-681-2552	48-5
CareCentric Inc 2625 Cumberland Pkwy Suite 310 *Sales	Atlanta	GA	30339	**800-254-9872***	678-264-4400	176-10
Career Blazers Inc 222 W Las Colinas Blvd Suite 1250E	Irving	TX	75039	**800-787-6750**	214-296-6700	707
Career Blazers Inc AccountingSolutions Div 222 W Las Colinas Blvd Suite 1250E	Irving	TX	75039	**800-787-6750**	214-296-6700	707
Career Blazers Inc Learning Centers Div 290 Madison Ave	New York	NY	10017	**800-284-3232**	212-725-7900	752
Career Blazers Inc Personnel One Div 222 W Las Colinas Blvd Suite 1250E	Irving	TX	75039	**800-787-6750**	214-296-6700	707
Career Blazers Inc ProDrivers Div 222 W Las Colinas Blvd Suite 1250E	Irving	TX	75039	**800-787-6750**	214-296-6700	707
Career Blazers Inc ResourceMFG Div 222 W Las Colinas Blvd Suite 1250E	Irving	TX	75039	**800-787-6750**	214-296-6700	707
Career Blazers Inc StaffingSolutions Div 222 W Las Colinas Blvd Suite 1250E	Irving	TX	75039	**800-787-6750**	214-296-6700	707
Career Blazers Inc Telesource Div 222 W Las Colinas Blvd Suite 1250E	Irving	TX	75039	**800-787-6750**	214-296-6700	707
Career Colleges of Chicago 11 E Adams St 2nd Fl	Chicago	IL	60603	**877-859-6300**	312-895-6300	158
Career & Community Leaders of America. Family 1910 Association Dr	Reston	VA	20191	**800-234-4425**	703-476-4900	48-11
Career Education Corp 2895 Greenspoint Pkwy Suite 600 *NASDAQ: CECO*	Hoffman Estates	IL	60195	**888-781-3608**	847-781-3600	241
Career & Technical Education. Association for 1410 King St	Alexandria	VA	22314	**800-826-9972**	703-683-3111	49-5
CareerBuilder Inc 8420 W Bryn Mawr Ave Suite 900	Chicago	IL	60631	**888-622-9022**	773-527-3600	707
CareerPark c/o Parker Advertising Service Inc Box 5600	Lancaster	PA	17606	**800-396-3306**	717-581-1966	257
CareerShop Inc 12200 W Colonial Dr	Winter Garden	FL	34787	**800-639-2060**	407-877-5992	257
CareerStaff Unlimited Inc 2600 S Gessner Suite 300	Houston	TX	77063	**800-443-1221**	713-297-9000	707
Carefree of Colorado 2145 W 6th Ave	Broomfield	CO	80020	**800-621-2617**	303-469-3324	718
Carefree Lifestyle Inc 1031 5th St	Miami Beach	FL	33139	**866-589-8796**	305-534-3531	433
Carefree Vacations Inc 9710 Scranton Rd Suite 300	San Diego	CA	92121	**800-800-8505**	858-450-4060	760
Caregiver Alliance. Family 180 Montgomery St Suite 1100	San Francisco	CA	94104	**800-445-8106**	415-434-3388	48-17
Caregivers Assn. National Family 10400 Connecticut Ave Suite 500	Kensington	MD	20895	**800-896-3650**	301-942-6430	48-6
Caregivers on Call 50 Broadway	Lynbrook	NY	11563	**800-225-1200**	516-887-1200	65
Caregiving Foundation. National 801 N Pitt St Suite 116	Alexandria	VA	22314	**800-930-1357**	703-299-9300	48-6

Company / Address	City	St	ZIP	Toll-Free	Phone	Class
Carelink Health Plans 141 Summers Square PO Box 1711	Charleston	WV	25326	**800-348-2922**		384-3
Caremark Rx Inc 211 Commerce St Suite 800 *NYSE: CMX*	Nashville	TN	37201	**800-633-9509**	615-743-6600	575
CareScience Inc 3600 Market St 7th Fl	Philadelphia	PA	19104	**888-223-8247**	215-387-9401	39
CareSouth Homecare Professionals 3626 Walton Way Ext Suite 2	Augusta	GA	30909	**800-241-3363**	706-855-5533	358
Carey Digital 1718 Central Pkwy	Cincinnati	OH	45214	**800-767-6071**	513-241-5210	770
Carey Executive Limousine 245 University Ave SW	Atlanta	GA	30315	**800-743-5466**	770-933-9000	433
Carey International Inc 4530 Wisconsin Ave NW 5th Fl	Washington	DC	20016	**800-336-4646**	202-895-1200	433
Carey Limo International PO Box 3823	Bellevue	WA	98009	**888-227-3903**	212-777-2111	433
Carey WP & Co LLC 50 Rockefeller Plaza 2nd Fl *NYSE: WPC*	New York	NY	10020	**800-972-2739**	212-492-1100	641
CARF (Commission on Accreditation of Rehabilitation Facilities) 4891 E Grant Rd	Tucson	AZ	85712	**888-281-6531**	520-325-1044	48-1
Carfax Inc 10304 Eaton Pl Suite 500	Fairfax	VA	22030	**800-274-2277**	703-934-2664	58
Cargill AgHorizons PO Box 9300 MS 19	Minneapolis	MN	55440	**800-227-4455**	952-742-7575	194
Cargill Asset Investment & Finance Group 12700 Whitewater Dr	Minnetonka	MN	55343	**800-227-4455**	952-984-3444	393
Cargill Assoc Inc 4701 Altamesa Blvd	Fort Worth	TX	76133	**800-433-2233**	817-292-9374	312
Cargill Energy PO Box 9300	Minneapolis	MN	55440	**800-227-4455**	952-742-7575	569
Cargill Foods 15407 McGinty Rd	Wayzata	MN	55391	**800-227-4455**	952-742-7575	291-29
Cargill Inc 15407 McGinty Rd	Wayzata	MN	55391	**800-227-4455**	952-742-7575	271
Cargill Inc Animal Nutrition Div 15407 McGinty Rd W	Wayzata	MN	55391	**800-227-4455**	952-984-1920	438
Cargill Inc North America 15407 McGinty Rd	Wayzata	MN	55391	**800-227-4455**	952-742-7575	291-23
Cargill Investor Services Inc 233 S Wacker Dr Suite 2300	Chicago	IL	60606	**800-621-4475**	312-460-4000	167
Cargill Malt - Specialty Products Group 704 S 15th St *Sales	Sheboygan	WI	53081	**800-669-6258***	920-459-4148	453
Cargill Salt Inc 400 S Hwy 169 Suite 600	Saint Louis Park	MN	55426	**888-385-7258**	952-984-8280	668
Cargill Turkey Products 1 Kratzer Rd *Cust Svc	Harrisonburg	VA	22802	**800-233-8457***	540-568-1400	608
Cargo Kids 2900 W Seminary Dr Suite 100 *Cust Svc	Fort Worth	TX	76133	**800-333-1402***	817-252-6861	316
Cargo Magazine 4 Times Sq	New York	NY	10036	**800-223-0780**	212-286-2860	449-11
Cargo Services Inc 1601 NW 70th Ave	Miami	FL	33126	**800-597-6010**	305-599-9333	13
Cargocaire Div Munters Corp PO Box 640 *Sales	Amesbury	MA	01913	**800-843-5360***	978-388-0600	15
Cargolux Airlines International 238 Lawrence Ave	South San Francisco	CA	94080	**800-722-2023**	650-225-0747	13
Cargotainer Div Adrian Fabricators PO Box 518	Adrian	MI	49221	**800-221-3794**	517-266-5700	462
Carhartt Inc 5750 Mercury Dr	Dearborn	MI	48126	**800-358-3825**	313-271-8460	153-19
Caribbean Gardens 1590 Goodlette-Frank Rd	Naples	FL	34102	**888-520-3756**	239-262-5409	811
Caribbean Resort & Villas 3000 N Ocean Blvd	Myrtle Beach	SC	29577	**800-552-8509**	843-448-7181	655
Caribbean Transportation Services 7304 W Market St	Greensboro	NC	27409	**800-767-2494**	336-668-7500	536
Caribbean Travel & Life Magazine 460 N Orlando Ave Suite 200 *Circ	Winter Park	FL	32789	**800-588-1689***	407-628-5662	449-22
Caribe Hilton Los Rosales St San Geronimo Grounds	San Juan	PR	00901	**800-445-8667**	787-721-0303	655
Caribe Royale Resort Suites 8101 World Center Dr	Orlando	FL	32821	**800-823-8300**	407-238-8000	373
Caribiana Sea Skiffs 8920 County Rd 65	Foley	AL	36535	**888-203-4883**	251-981-4442	91
Caribou Coffee Co Inc 3900 Lakebreeze Ave N *Cust Svc	Brooklyn Center	MN	55429	**888-227-4268***	763-533-2525	156
Caribou Highlands Lodge 371 Ski Hill Rd	Lutsen	MN	55612	**800-642-6036**	218-663-7241	655
Carisch Inc 641 E Lake St Suite 226	Wayzata	MN	55391	**800-952-7297**	952-473-4291	656
Caritas Peace Center 2020 Newburg Rd	Louisville	KY	40205	**800-451-3637**	502-451-3330	366-3
Carithers Wallace Courtenay Co 4343 Northeast Expy	Atlanta	GA	30340	**800-292-8220**	770-493-8200	315
Carl Bolander & Sons Co Inc 251 Starkey St	Saint Paul	MN	55107	**800-676-6504**	651-224-6299	188-5
Carl Buddig & Co 950 W 175th St	Homewood	IL	60430	**800-621-0868**	708-798-0900	291-26
Carl Fischer Inc 65 Bleecker St	New York	NY	10012	**800-762-2328**	212-777-0900	623-7
Carl Greve Jeweler Inc 731 SW Morrison St	Portland	OR	97205	**800-284-2044**	503-223-7121	402
Carl R Bieber Tourways Inc 320 Fair St	Kutztown	PA	19530	**800-243-2374**	610-683-7333	108
Carl Sandburg College 2400 Tom L Wilson Blvd	Galesburg	IL	61401	**877-236-1862**	309-344-2518	160
Carl T Hayden Veterans Affairs Medical Center 650 E Indian School Rd	Phoenix	AZ	85012	**800-359-8262**	602-277-5551	366-6
Carl Vinson Veterans Affairs Medical Center 1826 Veterans Blvd	Dublin	GA	31021	**800-595-5229**	478-272-1210	366-6
Carl Zeiss Inc Industrial Measuring Technology Div 6250 Sycamore Ln N	Maple Grove	MN	55369	**800-752-6181**	763-744-2400	484
Carl Zeiss Optical Inc 13017 N Kingston Ave *Cust Svc	Chester	VA	23836	**800-338-2984***	804-530-8300	531
Carle Hospice 206-A W Anthony Dr	Champaign	IL	61822	**800-610-5547**	217-383-3151	365
Carlee Corp 28 Piermont Rd	Rockleigh	NJ	07647	**800-822-7533**	201-768-6800	594-1
Carleton College 1 N College St	Northfield	MN	55057	**800-995-2275**	507-646-4000	163
Carleton Technologies Inc 10 Cobham Dr	Orchard Park	NY	14127	**800-395-4074**	716-662-0006	566
Carlile Transportation Services Inc 1800 E 1st Ave	Anchorage	AK	99501	**800-478-1853**	907-276-7797	769
Carlisle FoodService Products Inc 4711 E Hefner Rd	Oklahoma City	OK	73131	**800-654-8210**	405-475-5600	295
Carlisle Industrial Brake 1031 E Hillside Dr	Bloomington	IN	47401	**800-873-6361**	812-336-3811	60
Carlisle Power Transmission Products Inc 1 Prestige Pl	Miamisburg	OH	45342	**866-773-2926**	937-229-8000	364
Carlisle Sanitary Maintenance Products 402 S Black River St	Sparta	WI	54656	**800-356-8366**	608-269-2151	104
Carlisle SynTec Inc PO Box 7000	Carlisle	PA	17013	**800-479-6832**	717-245-7000	190-4
Carlisle Tire & Wheel Mfg 23 Windham Blvd *Sales	Aiken	SC	29805	**800-827-1001***	803-643-2900	739
Carlo John Inc 45000 River Ridge Dr	Clinton Township	MI	48038	**800-465-6234**	586-416-4500	187-4
Carlon Products Co PO Box 377 *Cust Svc	Derby	CT	06418	**800-243-6682***	203-735-7474	590
Carlow College 3333 5th Ave	Pittsburgh	PA	15213	**800-333-2275**	412-578-6000	163
Carl's Jr Restaurants 401 W Carl Karcher Way	Anaheim	CA	92803	**800-422-4141**	714-774-5796	657
Carlsbad Chamber of Commerce 302 S Canal St	Carlsbad	NM	88220	**800-221-1224**	505-887-6516	137
Carlsbad Convention & Visitors Bureau 400 Carlsbad Village Dr	Carlsbad	CA	92008	**800-227-5722**	760-434-6093	205
Carlsbad Convention & Visitors Bureau 302 S Canal St	Carlsbad	NM	88220	**800-221-1224**	505-887-6516	205
Carlsbad by the Sea 2855 Carlsbad Blvd	Carlsbad	CA	92008	**800-255-1556**	760-729-2377	659
Carlson GO Inc 350 Marshallton Thorndale Rd	Downingtown	PA	19335	**800-338-5622**	610-384-2800	709
Carlson Hospitality Worldwide PO Box 59159	Minneapolis	MN	55459	**800-333-3333**	763-212-5000	369
Carlson Hotels Worldwide						
Country Inns & Suites by Carlson PO Box 59159 *Resv	Minneapolis	MN	55459	**800-456-4000***	763-212-1000	369
Park Inn PO Box 59159 *Resv	Minneapolis	MN	55459	**800-670-7275***	763-212-1000	369
Radisson Hotels & Resorts PO Box 59159	Minneapolis	MN	55459	**800-333-3333**	763-212-5526	369
Carlson Leisure Group 12755 State Hwy 55	Plymouth	MN	55441	**800-335-8747**	763-212-5000	761
Carlson Marketing Group PO Box 59159	Minneapolis	MN	55459	**888-521-2200**	763-212-4520	722
Carlson Restaurants Worldwide Inc 4201 Marsh Ln	Carrollton	TX	75007	**800-374-3297**	972-662-5400	656
Carlson Systems LLC PO Box 3036	Omaha	NE	68103	**800-325-8343**	402-593-5300	346
Carlson Tool & Mfg Corp PO Box 85	Cedarburg	WI	53012	**800-532-2252**	262-377-2020	446
Carlson Wagonlit Travel Assoc 701 Carlson Pkwy	Minnetonka	MN	55305	**800-335-8747**	763-212-4000	761
Carlson Wagonlit Travel Inc 701 Carlson Pkwy	Minnetonka	MN	55305	**800-335-8747**	763-212-5000	761
Carlstedt Oscar G Co 577 College St	Jacksonville	FL	32204	**800-654-5739**	904-354-8474	288
Carlton Bates Co 3600 W 69th St	Little Rock	AR	72209	**800-482-9313**	501-562-9100	245
Carlton Cards Div American Greetings Corp 1 American Rd *Sales	Cleveland	OH	44144	**800-321-3040***	216-252-7300	129
Carlton & Co 101 Federal St Suite 1900	Boston	MA	02110	**800-622-0194**	617-342-7257	312
Carlton Fields PA 4221 W Boy Scout Blvd	Tampa	FL	33607	**888-223-9191**	813-223-7000	419
Carlton Food Products Inc PO Box 311385	New Braunfels	TX	78131	**800-628-9849**	830-625-7583	291-26
Carlton Hotel 1075 Sutter St	San Francisco	CA	94109	**800-922-7586**	415-673-0242	373
Carlton House Hotel. Helmsley 680 Madison Ave	New York	NY	10021	**800-221-4982**	212-838-3000	373
Carlton on Madison Ave 22 E 29th St	New York	NY	10016	**800-542-1502**	212-532-4100	373
Carlyle The 35 E 76th St	New York	NY	10021	**800-227-5737**	212-744-1600	373
Carlyle Johnson Machine Co 291 Boston Tpke	Bolton	CT	06043	**888-629-4867**	860-643-1531	609
Carlyle Suites Hotel 1731 New Hampshire Ave NW	Washington	DC	20009	**800-964-5377**	202-234-3200	373
Carman Industries Inc 1005 W Riverside Dr PO box 579	Jeffersonville	IN	47131	**800-456-7560**	812-288-4700	206
Carmel River Inn Hwy 1 at Carmel River Bridge PO Box 221609	Carmel	CA	93922	**800-882-8142**	831-624-1575	373
Carmel Valley Manor 8545 Carmel Valley Rd	Carmel	CA	93923	**800-544-5546**	831-624-1281	659
Carmel Valley Ranch Resort - A Wyndham Luxury Resort 1 Old Ranch Rd	Carmel	CA	93923	**800-422-7635**	831-625-9500	655
Carmeuse North America 11 Stanwix St 11th Fl	Pittsburgh	PA	15222	**800-445-3930**	412-995-5500	432
Carmichael Lynch Spong 800 Hennepin Ave	Minneapolis	MN	55403	**800-835-9624**	612-334-6000	622
Carmike Cinemas Inc 1301 1st Ave *NASDAQ: CKEC*	Columbus	GA	31901	**800-241-0431**	706-576-3400	733
Carmody & Bloom Inc 947 Linwood Ave	Ridgewood	NJ	07450	**800-242-9000**	201-670-1700	193
Carnegie Body Co 9500 Brookpark Rd	Cleveland	OH	44129	**800-362-1989**	216-749-5000	505
Carnegie Regional Library 49 W 7th St	Grafton	ND	58237	**800-568-5964**	701-352-2754	426
Carnegie Science Center 1 Allegheny Ave	Pittsburgh	PA	15212	**877-975-6787**	412-237-3400	509
Carnival Corp 3655 NW 87th Ave *NYSE: CCL*	Miami	FL	33178	**800-438-6744**	305-599-2600	355-3
Carnival Cruise Lines Inc 3655 NW 87th Ave	Miami	FL	33178	**888-227-6482**	305-599-2600	217

Company / Address	City	State	ZIP	Toll-Free	Phone	Class
Caro Foods Inc 2324 Bayou Blue Rd	Houma	LA	70364	**800-395-2276**	985-872-1483	292-7
Carol Woods Retirement Community 750 Weaver Dairy Rd	Chapel Hill	NC	27514	**800-518-9333**	919-968-4511	659
Carolane Propane Gas Inc 339 S Main St	Lexington	NC	27292	**800-838-1982**	336-249-8981	311
Carole Fabrics Inc 633 NW Frontage Rd	Augusta	GA	30907	**800-241-0920**	706-863-4742	731
Carole Joy Creations Inc 6 Production Dr Unit 1 *Sales	Brookfield	CT	06804	**800-223-6945***	203-740-4490	130
Carolee Designs Inc 19 E Elm St	Greenwich	CT	06830	**800-227-6533**	203-629-1139	400
Carolina Biological Supply Co 2700 York Rd	Burlington	NC	27215	**800-334-5551**	336-584-0381	673
Carolina Business Furniture LLC 535 Archdale Blvd	Archdale	NC	27263	**800-763-0212**	336-431-9400	314-1
Carolina Casualty Insurance Co 4600 Touchton Rd E Bldg 100	Jacksonville	FL	32246	**800-874-8053**	904-363-0900	384-4
Carolina Container Co 909 Prospect St	High Point	NC	27260	**800-627-0825**	336-883-7146	101
Carolina First Bank 102 S Main St	Greenville	SC	29601	**800-476-6400**	864-255-7900	71
Carolina Foods Inc 1807 S Tryon St	Charlotte	NC	28203	**800-234-0441**	704-333-9812	291-1
Carolina Glove Co Inc PO Drawer 820	Newton	NC	28658	**800-438-6888**	828-464-1132	153-8
Carolina Group 714 Green Valley Rd *NYSE: CG*	Greensboro	NC	27408	**888-278-1133**	336-335-7000	741-1
Carolina Holdings Inc 4403 Bland Rd	Raleigh	NC	27609	**877-734-6365**	919-431-1000	190-3
Carolina Inn 211 Pittsboro St	Chapel Hill	NC	27516	**800-962-8519**	919-933-2001	373
Carolina Meadows 100 Carolina Meadows	Chapel Hill	NC	27517	**800-458-6756**	919-942-4014	659
Carolina Mirror Co 600 Elkin Hwy	North Wilkesboro	NC	28659	**800-334-7245**	336-838-2151	330
Carolina Mountain Water Co 150 Central Ave	Hot Springs	AR	71901	**800-643-1501**	501-623-6671	792
Carolina Opry 8901 Hwy 17 N Suite A	Myrtle Beach	SC	29577	**800-843-6779**	843-238-8888	562
Carolina Packers Inc PO Box 1109	Smithfield	NC	27577	**800-682-7675**	919-934-2181	465
Carolina By-Products 1309 Industrial Dr	Fayetteville	NC	28301	**800-476-8675**	910-483-0473	291-12
Carolina Rim & Wheel Co 1308 Upper Asbury Dr	Charlotte	NC	28206	**800-532-6219**	704-334-7276	61
Carolina Shoe Co PO Box 1079	Morganton	NC	28680	**800-438-7026**	828-437-7755	296
Carolina Skiff Inc 3231 Fulford Rd	Waycross	GA	31503	**800-422-7543**	912-287-0547	91
Carolina Steel Corp 1451 S Elm Eugene St	Greensboro	NC	27406	**800-632-0286**	336-275-9711	471
Carolina Turkeys 1628 Garner Chapel Rd PO Box 589	Mount Olive	NC	28365	**800-523-4559**	919-658-6743	608
Carolinas Auto Supply House Inc 2135 Tipton Dr	Charlotte	NC	28206	**800-438-4070**	704-334-4646	61
Caroline Distribution 104 W 29th St 4th Fl	New York	NY	10001	**800-275-2250**	212-886-7500	512
Carollo Engineers 3033 N 44th St Suite 101	Phoenix	AZ	85018	**800-523-5822**	602-263-9500	258
Carolyn Fabrics Inc 1948 W Green Dr	High Point	NC	27261	**800-333-8400**	336-887-3101	583
Caron International 111 W 40th St 28th Fl	New York	NY	10018	**800-868-9194**	212-382-6400	750
Carondelet Hospice Services 1802 W Saint Mary's Rd	Tucson	AZ	85745	**800-979-9290**	520-205-7700	365
Carousel Beachfront Hotel & Suites 11700 Coastal Hwy	Ocean City	MD	21842	**800-641-0011**	410-524-1000	373
Carousel Carpet Mills Inc 1 Carousel Ln	Ukiah	CA	95482	**866-227-6873**	707-485-0333	131
Carousel Inn & Suites 1530 S Harbor Blvd	Anaheim	CA	92802	**800-854-6767**	714-758-0444	373
Carowinds 14523 Carowinds Blvd	Charlotte	NC	28273	**800-888-4386**	704-588-2606	32
CARP (Canadian Assn of Retired Persons) 1304-27 Queen St E	Toronto	ON	M5C2M6	**800-363-9736**	416-363-8748	48-6
Carpenter Co 5016 Monument Ave	Richmond	VA	23230	**800-288-3830**	804-359-0800	590
Carpenter Co Morning Glory Div 302 Highland Dr	Taylor	TX	76574	**800-234-9105**		731
Carpenter Contractors of America 941 SW 12th Ave	Pompano Beach	FL	33069	**800-959-8805**	954-781-2660	188-2
Carpenter & Paterson Inc 225 Merrimac St	Woburn	MA	01801	**800-342-6437**	781-935-2950	584
Carpenter Special Products Corp 1717 Cuyamaca St	El Cajon	CA	92020	**866-466-6584**	619-448-1000	584
Carpenter Specialty Alloys Operations 101 W Bern St	Reading	PA	19601	**800-654-6543**	610-208-2000	709
Carpenter Technology Corp 2 Meridian Blvd 3rd Fl *NYSE: CRS* ■ *Sales	Wyomissing	PA	19610	**800-654-6543***	610-208-2000	709
Carpet Network Inc 109 Gaither Dr Suite 302	Mount Laurel	NJ	08054	**800-428-1067**	856-273-9393	285
Carpet & Rug Institute (CRI) 310 S Holiday Ave	Dalton	GA	30720	**800-882-8846**	706-278-3176	49-4
Carpigiani Corp of America 3760 Industrial Dr	Winston-Salem	NC	27105	**800-648-4389**	336-661-9893	293
Carpin Mfg Inc 411 Austin Rd	Waterbury	CT	06705	**800-227-7461**	203-574-2556	152
Carplugs LLC 2150 Elmwood Ave	Buffalo	NY	14207	**888-227-5847**	716-876-9855	152
CarPrices.com c/o AutoFusion Corp 9605 Scranton Rd Suite 450	San Diego	CA	92121	**800-410-7354**		58
Carr Corp 1547 11th St	Santa Monica	CA	90401	**800-952-2398**	310-587-1113	580
CarrAmerica Realty Corp 1850 K St NW Suite 500 *NYSE: CRE*	Washington	DC	20006	**800-417-2277**	202-729-1700	641
Carreker Corp 4055 Valley View Ln Suite 1000 *NASDAQ: CANI*	Dallas	TX	75244	**800-486-1981**	972-458-1981	178
Carriage House Cos Inc 196 Newton St	Fredonia	NY	14063	**800-828-8915**	716-673-1000	291-20
Carriage House Foods DBA Grand Choice Foods 1131 Dayton Ave	Ames	IA	50010	**800-250-3860**	515-232-2273	291-26
Carriage Services Inc 1900 St James Pl 4th Fl *NYSE: CSV*	Houston	TX	77056	**800-692-3092**	713-332-8450	499
Carrie Sweet Ingredients 400 Prairie Village Dr	New Century	KS	66031	**800-255-6312**	913-780-1212	291-8
Carrier Access Corp 5395 Pearl Pkwy *NASDAQ: CACS*	Boulder	CO	80301	**800-495-5455**	303-442-5455	720
Carrier Clinic PO Box 147	Belle Mead	NJ	08502	**800-933-3579**	908-281-1000	366-3
Carrier Corp 1 Carrier Pl	Farmington	CT	06034	**800-227-7437**	860-674-3000	15
Carrier Corp Carrier Transicold Div 6304 Thompson Rd Bldg TR-20	East Syracuse	NY	13057	**800-255-7382**	315-432-6000	16
Carrier Refrigeration Operations 700 Bluffington Rd	Spartanburg	SC	29303	**800-845-9800**	864-582-8111	650
Carrington Convention & Visitors Bureau PO Box 439	Carrington	ND	58421	**800-641-9668**	701-652-2524	205
Carrington Laboratories Inc 2001 Walnut Hill Ln *NASDAQ: CARN* ■ *Cust Svc	Irving	TX	75038	**800-527-5216***	972-518-1300	572
Carroll & Co 425 N Canon Dr	Beverly Hills	CA	90210	**800-238-9400**	310-273-9060	155-3
Carroll Co 2900 W Kingsley Rd	Garland	TX	75041	**800-527-5722**	972-278-1304	149
Carroll College 1601 N Benton Ave	Helena	MT	59625	**800-992-3648**	406-447-4300	163
Carroll College 100 N East Ave	Waukesha	WI	53186	**800-227-7655**	262-547-1211	163
Carroll Companies Inc PO Box 1549	Boone	NC	28607	**800-884-2521**	828-264-2521	423
Carroll County Chamber of Commerce & Economic Development 61 N Lisbon St	Carrollton	OH	44615	**800-956-4684**	330-627-4811	137
Carroll County Equipment Co 25921 Hwy 65	Carrollton	MO	64633	**800-214-3337**	660-542-2485	270
Carroll County Rural Electric Membership Corp 119 W Franklin St	Delphi	IN	46923	**800-506-7362**	765-564-2057	244
Carroll Electric Co-op Corp 920 Hwy 62 Spur	Berryville	AR	72616	**800-432-9720**	870-423-2161	244
Carroll Electric Co-op Inc 350 Canton Rd NW	Carrollton	OH	44615	**800-232-7697**	330-627-2116	244
Carroll Fulmer Logistics Corp 8340 American Way	Groveland	FL	34736	**800-468-9400**	352-429-5000	769
Carroll Independent Fuel Co 2700 Loch Raven Rd	Baltimore	MD	21218	**800-834-8590**	410-235-1066	311
Carroll JP Co Inc 310 N Madison Ave	Los Angeles	CA	90004	**800-660-0162**	323-660-9230	188-8
Carroll Publishing Co 4701 Sangamore Rd Suite S-155	Bethesda	MD	20816	**800-336-4240**	301-263-9800	623-2
Carroll Valley Golf Resort 121 Sanders Rd	Fairfield	PA	17320	**800-548-8504**	717-642-8211	655
Carrollton Bancorp 1589 Sulphur Spring Rd *NASDAQ: CRRB*	Baltimore	MD	21227	**800-222-6566**	410-536-4600	355-2
Carron Net Co Inc PO Box 177	Two Rivers	WI	54241	**800-558-7768**	920-793-2217	207
CarsDirect.com Inc 909 N Sepulveda Blvd *Cust Svc	El Segundo	CA	90245	**800-431-2500***	310-280-4000	58
CarSmart 18872 MacArthur Blvd	Irvine	CA	92612	**888-422-8999**	949-862-1335	58
Carson City Convention & Visitors Bureau 1900 S Carson St Suite 100	Carson City	NV	89701	**800-638-2321**	775-687-7410	205
Carson-Dellosa Publishing Co Inc 7027 Albert Pick Rd	Greensboro	NC	27409	**800-321-0943**	336-632-0084	242
Carson & Gebel Ribbon Co 17 Green Pond Rd	Rockaway	NJ	07866	**800-223-8283**	973-627-4200	730-5
Carson Helicopters 952 Blooming Glen Rd	Perkasie	PA	18944	**800-523-2335**	215-249-3535	354
Carson Hot Mineral Springs Resort 372 St Martin Rd	Carson	WA	98610	**800-607-3678**	509-427-8292	373
Carson Hot Springs 1500 Hot Springs Rd	Carson City	NV	89706	**888-917-3711**	775-885-8844	50
Carson-Newman College 1646 Russell Ave	Jefferson City	TN	37760	**800-678-9061**	865-475-9061	163
Carson Nugget Casino 507 N Carson St	Carson City	NV	89702	**800-426-5239**	775-882-1626	133
Carson Oil Co Inc 3125 NW 35th Ave	Portland	OR	97210	**800-998-7767**	503-224-8500	569
Carson Valley Chamber of Commerce & Visitors Authority 1513 Hwy 395 N	Gardnerville	NV	89410	**800-727-7677**	775-782-8144	137
Carsonite International Corp 605 Bob Gifford Blvd	Early Branch	SC	29916	**800-648-7974**	803-943-9115	666
Carson's Inc 5970 N Ridge Ave	Chicago	IL	60660	**888-999-7427**	773-271-4000	657
CARSTAR Quality Collision Service 8400 W 110th St Suite 200	Overland Park	KS	66210	**800-227-7827**	913-451-1294	62-4
Carter Amon Museum 3501 Camp Bowie Blvd	Fort Worth	TX	76107	**800-573-1933**	817-738-1933	509
Carter BloodCare 2205 Hwy 121	Bedford	TX	76021	**800-366-2834**	817-412-5000	90
Carter & Burgess Inc PO Box 901058	Fort Worth	TX	76101	**800-624-7959**	817-735-6000	258
Carter Caves State Resort Park 344 Caveland Dr	Olive Hill	KY	41164	**800-325-0059**	606-286-4411	655
Carter Cos 601 Tallmadge Rd	Kent	OH	44240	**877-586-2374**	330-673-6100	359
Carter Healthcare 4301 Will Rogers Pkwy Suite 100	Oklahoma City	OK	73108	**888-951-1112**	405-947-7700	358
Carter & Holmes 3645 W Irving Park Rd	Chicago	IL	60618	**800-621-4646**	773-588-2626	153-13
Carter-Horner Inc 6600 Kitimat Rd	Mississauga	ON	L5N1L9	**800-387-2130**	905-826-6200	572
Carter-Jones Lumber Co 601 Tallmadge Rd	Kent	OH	44240	**877-586-2374**	330-673-6100	359
Carter Lumber Co Inc 601 Tallmadge Rd	Kent	OH	44240	**877-586-2374**	330-673-6100	359
Carter-Waters Corp 2440 W Pennway St	Kansas City	MO	64108	**800-444-2570**	816-471-2570	135
Carteret County Chamber of Commerce 801 Arendell St Suite 1	Morehead City	NC	28557	**800-622-6278**	252-726-6350	137
Carteret-Craven Electric Co-op 1300 Hwy 24 W	Newport	NC	28570	**800-682-2217**	252-247-3107	244
Carteret Mortgage Corp 6211 Centreville Rd Suite 800	Centreville	VA	20121	**877-227-8373**	703-802-8000	498
Cartersville Bartow County Convention & Visitors Bureau PO Box 200397	Cartersville	GA	30120	**800-733-2280**	770-387-1357	205
Carthage College 2001 Alford Pk Dr	Kenosha	WI	53140	**800-351-4058**	262-551-8500	163
Carthage Cup 505 E Cotton St	Carthage	TX	75633	**800-527-8440**	903-693-7151	596
Carthage Fabrics Corp PO Box 398	Carthage	NC	28327	**800-541-4877**	910-947-2211	730-1
Carthage Mills 4243 Hunt Rd *Sales	Cincinnati	OH	45242	**800-543-4430***	513-794-1600	730-3

Name / Address	City	State	ZIP	Toll-Free	Phone	Class
Cartier Inc 2 E 52nd St *Sales	New York	NY	10022	**800-227-8437***	212-753-0111	402
Cartier Place Suite Hotel 180 Cooper St	Ottawa	ON	K2P2L5	**800-236-8399**	613-236-5000	372
Cartner Glass Systems Inc PO Box 7744	Charlotte	NC	28241	**800-968-2818**	704-588-1976	188-6
Carton Service Inc First Quality Dr	Shelby	OH	44875	**800-533-7744**	419-342-5010	102
Cartoon Bank Div. New Yorker Magazine 145 Palisade St Suite 373	Dobbs Ferry	NY	10522	**800-897-8666**	914-478-5527	520
Cartwright Hotel 524 Sutter St	San Francisco	CA	94102	**800-794-7661**	415-421-2865	373
Cartwright Transportation Services 11901 Cartwright Ave	Grandview	MO	64030	**877-455-5991**	816-763-2700	508
Carus Corp 315 5th St	Peru	IL	61354	**800-435-6856**	815-223-1500	141
Carvel Corp 175 Capital Blvd Suite 400	Rocky Hill	CT	06067	**800-322-4848**	860-257-4448	221
Carvel Franchising 200 Glenridge Point Pkwy Suite 200	Atlanta	GA	30342	**800-227-8353**	404-255-3250	221
Carver Inc 1 Lummus Dr	Savannah	GA	31407	**800-458-6687**	912-748-5000	269
Carvin Guitars 12340 World Trade Dr	San Diego	CA	92128	**800-854-2235**	858-487-1600	516
Cary Chamber of Commerce 307 N Academy St	Cary	NC	27513	**800-919-2279**	919-467-1016	137
Carylon Corp 2500 W Arthington St	Chicago	IL	60612	**800-621-4342**	312-666-7700	653
CAS (Chemical Abstracts Service) PO Box 3012	Columbus	OH	43210	**800-848-6538**	614-447-3600	380
CAS Inc PO Box 11190	Huntsville	AL	35814	**800-729-8686**	256-895-8600	258
CAS Medical Systems Inc 44 E Industrial Rd	Branford	CT	06405	**800-227-4414**	203-488-6056	468
CASA (National Court Appointed Special Advocate Assn) 100 W Harrison St North Tower Suite 500	Seattle	WA	98119	**800-628-3233**	206-270-0072	48-6
Casa Colina Center for Rehabilitation 255 E Bonita Ave	Pomona	CA	91767	**800-926-5462**	909-596-7733	441
Casa Grande Suite Hotel 834 Ocean Dr	Miami Beach	FL	33139	**800-688-7678**	305-672-7003	373
Casa Grande Valley Newspaper Inc PO Box 15002	Casa Grande	AZ	85230	**800-821-1746**	520-836-7461	623-8
Casa Herrerra Inc 2655 N Pine St	Pomona	CA	91767	**800-624-3916**	909-392-3930	293
Casa Madrona Hotel 801 Bridgeway	Sausalito	CA	94965	**800-567-9524**	415-332-0502	373
Casa Marina Resort. Wyndham 1500 Reynolds St	Key West	FL	33040	**800-626-0777**	305-296-3535	655
Casa Monica Hotel 95 Cordova St	Saint Augustine	FL	32084	**888-472-6312**	904-827-1888	373
Casa Munras Garden Hotel 700 Munras Ave	Monterey	CA	93940	**800-222-2558**	831-375-2411	373
Casa Ole 1135 Edgebrook St	Houston	TX	77034	**800-741-7574**	713-943-7574	657
Casa Palmero 1518 Cypress Dr	Pebble Beach	CA	93953	**800-654-9300**	831-647-7500	655
Casa Sirena Hotel & Marina 3605 Peninsula Rd	Oxnard	CA	93035	**800-447-3529**	805-985-6311	373
Casa Via Mar Inn & Tennis Club 377 W Channel Islands Blvd	Port Hueneme	CA	93041	**800-992-5522**	805-984-6222	373
Casa Ybel Resort 2255 W Gulf Dr	Sanibel	FL	33957	**800-276-4753**	239-472-3145	655
Casablanca Fan Co 761 Corporate Center Dr	Pomona	CA	91768	**888-227-2178**	909-629-1477	37
Casablanca Hotel 147 W 43rd St	New York	NY	10036	**888-922-7225**	212-869-1212	373
Casablanca Resort 950 W Mesquite Blvd	Mesquite	NV	89027	**800-459-7529**	702-346-7529	655
Casabyte Inc 222 Williams Ave S *Cust Svc	Renton	WA	98055	**888-352-9527***	425-254-9925	720
Cascade Bancorp 1100 NW Wall St *NASDAQ: CACB*	Bend	OR	97701	**877-617-3400**	541-385-6205	355-2
Cascade College 9101 E Burnside St	Portland	OR	97216	**800-550-7678**	503-255-7060	163
Cascade Corp PO Box 20187 *NYSE: CAE*	Portland	OR	97294	**800-227-2233**	503-669-6300	462
Cascade Designs Inc 4000 1st Ave S *Cust Svc	Seattle	WA	98134	**800-877-9677***	206-624-8573	701
Cascade Diesel Engine Co LLP 9800 40th Ave S	Seattle	WA	98118	**800-238-3850**	206-764-3850	259
Cascade Financial Corp 2828 Colby Ave *NASDAQ: CASB*	Everett	WA	98201	**800-326-8787**	425-339-5500	355-2
Cascade General Inc 5555 N Channel Ave	Portland	OR	97217	**800-505-1930**	503-285-1111	689
Cascade International Seed Co 8483 W Stayton Rd	Aumsville	OR	97325	**800-826-6799**	503-749-1822	684
Cascade Machinery & Electric Inc PO Box 3575	Seattle	WA	98124	**800-289-0500**	206-762-0500	378
Cascade Microtech Inc 2430 NW 206th Ave	Beaverton	OR	97006	**800-550-3279**	503-601-1000	247
Cascade School Supplies Inc 1 Brown St PO Box 780	North Adams	MA	01247	**800-628-5078**	413-663-3716	673
Cascade Steel Rolling Mills Inc 3200 N Hwy 99 W	McMinnville	OR	97128	**800-283-2776**	503-472-4181	709
Cascade Wholesale Hardware Inc PO Box 1659	Hillsboro	OR	97123	**800-877-9987**	503-614-2600	346
Cascades Inn 3226 Shepherd of the Hills Expy	Branson	MO	65616	**800-588-8424**	417-335-8424	373
Cascades Re-Plast Inc 1350 ch Quatre-Saisons PO Box 514	Notre-Dame-du-Bon-Conseil	QC	J0C1A0	**888-313-2440**	819-336-2440	647
Cascadian Farm Inc 719 Metcalf St	Sedro Woolley	WA	98284	**800-624-4123**	360-855-0100	291-21
CasChem Inc 40 Ave A	Bayonne	NJ	07002	**800-227-2436**	201-858-7900	142
Casco International Inc DBA CA Short Co Inc 7221 Pineville Matthews Rd Suite 600	Charlotte	NC	28277	**800-535-5690**	704-752-0119	192
CASE (Council for Advancement & Support of Education) 1307 New York Ave NW Suite 1000 *Orders	Washington	DC	20005	**800-554-8536***	202-328-5900	49-5
Case Design Corp 333 School Ln	Telford	PA	18969	**800-847-4176**	215-703-0130	198
Case Logic Inc 6303 Dry Creek Pkwy	Longmont	CO	80503	**800-447-4848**	303-652-1000	523
Case Paper Co Inc 500 Mamaroneck Ave 2nd Fl	Harrison	NY	10528	**800-222-2922**	718-361-9000	544

Name / Address	City	State	ZIP	Toll-Free	Phone	Class
Case Stationery Co Inc 179 Saw Mill River Rd	Yonkers	NY	10701	**800-431-2422**	914-965-5100	542-3
Case Western Reserve University 10900 Euclid Ave	Cleveland	OH	44106	**800-967-8898**	216-368-4450	163
Case WR & Sons Cutlery Co Owens Way	Bradford	PA	16701	**800-523-6350**	814-368-4123	219
Casella Waste Systems Inc PO Box 866 *NASDAQ: CWST*	Rutland	VT	05702	**800-227-3552**	802-775-0325	791
CaseStack Inc 2850 Ocean Pk Blvd Suite 100	Santa Monica	CA	90405	**800-684-0522**	310-473-8885	440
Casey Annie E Foundation 701 Saint Paul St	Baltimore	MD	21202	**800-222-1099**	410-547-6600	300
Casey Electric Inc 245 Preston St	Jackson	TN	38301	**800-424-0428**	731-424-7741	188-4
Casey & Hayes Exhibits Inc Brede Exposition Services Div 100 Industrial Pk Rd	Hingham	MA	02043	**800-835-0167**	781-741-5900	183
Casey's Bar & Grill 10 Kingsbridge Garden Cir Suite 600	Mississauga	ON	L5R3K6	**800-361-3111**	905-568-0000	657
Cash America International Inc 1600 W 7th St *NYSE: PWN*	Fort Worth	TX	76102	**800-223-8738**	817-335-1100	558
Cash Flow Assn. American 255 S Orange Ave Suite 600	Orlando	FL	32801	**800-253-1294**	407-206-6523	49-12
Cash Hardware Co Inc 406 W Main St	Coulee City	WA	99115	**800-835-8311**	509-632-5547	270
Cash Plus Inc 3002 Dow Ave Suite 120	Tustin	CA	92780	**888-707-2274**	714-731-2274	139
Cash Register Sales Inc 2909 Anthony Ln NE	Minneapolis	MN	55418	**800-333-4949**	612-781-3474	113
Cash Systems Inc 3201 W County Rd 42 Suite 106 *AMEX: CKN* ■ *Sales	Burnsville	MN	55306	**877-600-8399***	952-895-8399	56
Cash-Wa Distributing Co 401 W 4th St	Kearney	NE	68847	**800-652-0010**	308-237-3151	292-8
CASI (Computer Analytical Systems Inc) 1418 S 3rd St	Louisville	KY	40208	**800-977-3475**	502-635-2019	178
Casino Arizona at Salt River 524 N 92nd St	Scottsdale	AZ	85256	**877-724-4687**	480-850-7777	133
Casino Aztar 421 NW Riverside Dr	Evansville	IN	47708	**800-342-5386**	812-433-4000	133
Casino Aztar Hotel 421 NW Riverside Dr	Evansville	IN	47708	**800-544-0120**	812-433-4444	373
Casino Magic Bay Saint Louis 711 Casino Magic Dr	Bay Saint Louis	MS	39520	**800-562-4425**	228-467-9257	133
Casino Magic Biloxi 195 Beach Blvd	Biloxi	MS	39530	**800-562-4425**	228-386-4600	133
Casino Magic Corp 711 Casino Magic Dr	Bay Saint Louis	MS	39520	**800-562-4425**	228-467-9257	132
Casino Niagara 5705 Falls Ave	Niagara Falls	ON	L2G7M9	**888-946-3255**	905-374-3598	133
Casino Player Magazine 8025 Black Horse Pike Suite 470	West Atlantic City	NJ	08232	**800-969-0711**	609-484-8866	449-9
Casino Queen 200 S Front St	East Saint Louis	IL	62201	**800-777-0777**	618-874-5000	133
Casino Windsor 377 Riverside Dr E	Windsor	ON	N9A7H7	**800-991-7777**	519-258-7878	133
Casio Inc 570 Mt Pleasant Ave *Cust Svc	Dover	NJ	07801	**800-634-1895***	973-361-5400	171-2
Casket Royale 137 Lafayette Rd	Hampton Falls	NH	03844	**800-791-4169**	603-929-1515	134
Caspari Inc 116 E 27th St 11th Fl *Sales	New York	NY	10016	**800-227-7274***	212-685-9798	130
Casper Area Chamber of Commerce 500 N Center St	Casper	WY	82602	**866-234-5311**	307-234-5311	137
Casper Area Convention & Visitors Bureau 330 S Center St Suite 420	Casper	WY	82601	**800-852-1889**	307-234-5362	205
Casper College 125 College Dr	Casper	WY	82601	**800-442-2963**	307-268-2110	160
Casper Events Center 1 Events Dr	Casper	WY	82601	**800-442-2256**	307-235-8441	204
Caspian Holdings of Delaware DBA Guyan Machinery Co PO Box 150	Chapmanville	WV	25508	**800-999-3888**	304-855-4501	353
Cass County Electric Co-op Inc 491 Elm St	Kindred	ND	58051	**800-248-3292**	701-356-4400	244
Cass Tours 109 N Maple St Suite B	Corona	CA	92880	**800-593-6510**	951-371-3511	760
Casso-Solar Corp PO Box 163	Pomona	NY	10970	**800-988-4455**	845-354-2500	352
Cassville Area Chamber of Commerce 504 Main St	Cassville	MO	65625	**866-847-2814**	417-847-2814	137
Castaic Brick Inc 32201 Castaic Lake Dr	Castaic	CA	91384	**800-227-8242**	661-259-3066	148
Castalloy Inc 1701 Industrial Ln	Waukesha	WI	53189	**800-211-0900**	262-547-0070	302
Castaways Beach Resort 2043 S Atlantic Ave	Daytona Beach Shores	FL	32118	**866-254-2722**	386-254-8480	373
Castek Software Factory Inc 438 University Ave Suite 700	Toronto	ON	M5G2K8	**866-922-7835**	416-777-2550	176-10
Castelle 855 Jarvis Dr Suite 100 *NASDAQ: CSTL*	Morgan Hill	CA	95037	**800-289-7555**	408-852-8000	496
Castellini Co PO Box 721610	Newport	KY	41072	**800-233-8560**	859-442-4600	292-7
Caster & Wheel Manufacturers. Institute of 8720 Red Oak Blvd Suite 201	Charlotte	NC	28217	**800-345-1815**	704-676-1190	49-13
Castillo del Mar Resort 5445 Collins Ave	Miami Beach	FL	33140	**888-352-3224**	305-865-1500	373
Castine Movers 1235 Chestnut St	Athol	MA	01331	**800-225-8068**	978-249-9105	508
Castle AM & Co 3400 N Wolf Rd *AMEX: CAS*	Franklin Park	IL	60131	**800-289-2785**	847-455-7111	483
Castle Dental Centers Inc 3701 Kriby Dr Suite 550	Houston	TX	77098	**800-867-6453**	713-490-8400	455
Castle Group Inc 500 Ala Moana Blvd Suite 555 *Sales	Honolulu	HI	96813	**800-733-7753***	808-524-0900	369
Castle Hill Inn & Resort 590 Ocean Dr	Newport	RI	02840	**888-466-1355**	401-849-3800	373
Castle on the Hudson 400 Benedict Ave	Tarrytown	NY	10591	**800-616-4487**	914-631-1980	373
Castle Inn & Suites 1734 S Harbor Blvd	Anaheim	CA	92802	**800-521-5653**	714-774-8111	373
Castle Metals Inc 3400 N Wolf Rd	Franklin Park	IL	60131	**800-289-2785**	847-455-7111	483
Castle Resorts & Hotels 500 Ala Moana Blvd Suite 555	Honolulu	HI	96813	**800-367-5004**	808-545-3510	369
Castle in the Sand Hotel 3701 Atlantic Ave	Ocean City	MD	21842	**800-552-7263**	410-289-6846	373

Name / Address	City	State	Zip	Toll-Free	Phone	Class
Castle Worldwide Inc 900 Perimeter Park Rd Suite G	Morrisville	NC	27560	**866-422-7853**	919-572-6880	243
Castleberry's Food Co PO Box 1010	Augusta	GA	30903	**800-241-3520**	706-733-7765	291-36
Castleton State College 86 Seminary St	Castleton	VT	05735	**800-639-8521**	802-468-5611	163
Castleton Suites 9600 Southland Cir SW	Calgary	AB	T2V5A1	**888-227-8534**	403-640-3900	372
Casto Travel Inc 900 Lafayette St Suite 105	Santa Clara	CA	95050	**800-832-3445**	408-984-7000	760
Castrol Heavy Duty Lubricants 9300 Pulaski Hwy	Baltimore	MD	21220	**800-777-1466**	410-574-5000	530
Castrol Industrial North America Inc 1100 W 31st St	Downers Grove	IL	60515	**800-621-2661**	630-241-4000	530
Castrol North America Inc 1500 Valley Rd	Wayne	NJ	07470	**800-633-6163**	973-633-2200	530
Casual Corner Group Inc 100 Phoenix Ave	Enfield	CT	06082	**800-789-5348**	860-741-0771	155-6
Casual Lamps of California Inc 15000 S Broadway	Gardena	CA	90248	**800-824-8228**	310-323-0105	431
Casual Male Inc 555 Turnpike St	Canton	MA	02021	**800-767-0319**	781-828-9300	155-3
Caswell-Massey Co Ltd 121 Fieldcrest Ave	Edison	NJ	08837	**800-326-0500**	732-225-2181	211
Cat Fancy Magazine 3 Burroughs *Cust Svc	Irvine	CA	92618	**800-365-4421***	949-855-8822	449-14
Catalano's Stop & Shop 5612 Wilson Mills Rd	Highland Heights	OH	44143	**800-991-5444**	440-442-8800	339
Catalina Express Berth 95 *Resv	San Pedro	CA	90731	**800-481-3470***	310-519-1212	460
Catalina Graphic Films Inc 27001 Agoura Rd Suite 100	Calabasas Hills	CA	91301	**800-333-3136**	818-880-8060	589
Catalina Lighting Inc 18191 NW 68th Ave	Miami	FL	33015	**800-966-7074**	305-558-4777	431
Catalina Marketing Research Solutions 2845 Chancellor Dr	Crestview Hills	KY	41017	**800-801-2425**	859-344-0077	458
Catalog.com Inc 6404 International Pkwy Suite 2200	Plano	TX	75093	**888-932-4376**	972-380-2202	795
Catalyst International Inc 8989 N Deerwood Dr	Milwaukee	WI	53223	**800-236-4600**	414-362-6800	176-10
Catalyst Semiconductor Inc 1250 Borregas Ave *NASDAQ: CATS*	Sunnyvale	CA	94089	**800-258-5991**	408-542-1000	686
Cataract & Refractive Surgery. American Society of 4000 Legato Rd Suite 850	Fairfax	VA	22033	**800-451-1339**	703-591-2220	49-8
Catawba College 2300 W Innes St	Salisbury	NC	28144	**800-228-2922**	704-637-4111	163
Caterpillar Logistics Services Inc 500 N Morton Ave	Morton	IL	61550	**800-447-6434**	800-240-2126	440
Cathay Bank 777 N Broadway	Los Angeles	CA	90012	**800-922-8429**	213-625-4700	71
Cathay Pacific Airways 300 Continental Blvd Suite 500	El Segundo	CA	90245	**800-233-2742**	310-615-1113	26
Cathay Pacific Asia Miles 300 Continental Blvd Suite 500	El Segundo	CA	90245	**866-892-2598**		27
Cathay Pacific Cargo 6040 Avion Dr Suite 338	Los Angeles	CA	90045	**800-628-6960**	310-417-0052	13
Cathedral Hill Hotel 1101 Van Ness Ave	San Francisco	CA	94109	**800-622-0855**	415-776-8200	373
Cathedral Press Inc 600 NE 6th St *Cust Svc	Long Prairie	MN	56347	**800-874-8332***	320-732-6143	623-10
Catherines Stores Corp 3742 Lamar Ave	Memphis	TN	38118	**800-289-6372**	901-363-3900	155-6
Catholic Church Extension Society of the USA 150 S Wacker Dr 20th Fl	Chicago	IL	60606	**800-842-7804**	312-236-7240	48-20
Catholic Family Life Insurance PO Box 11563	Milwaukee	WI	53211	**800-227-2354**	414-961-0500	384-2
Catholic Healthcare Partners 615 Elsinore Pl	Cincinnati	OH	45202	**800-367-9212**	513-639-2800	348
Catholic Medical Center 100 McGregor St	Manchester	NH	03102	**800-437-9666**	603-668-3545	366-2
Catholic Medical Mission Board (CMMB) 10 W 17th St	New York	NY	10011	**800-678-5659**	212-242-7757	48-5
Catholic Relief Services (CRS) 209 W Fayette St	Baltimore	MD	21201	**800-235-2772**	410-625-2220	48-5
Catholic School Teachers. National Assn of 1700 Sansom St Suite 903	Philadelphia	PA	19103	**800-996-2278**	215-665-0993	49-5
Catholic University of America 620 Michigan Ave NE	Washington	DC	20064	**800-673-2772**	202-319-5000	163
Cato Corp 8100 Denmark Rd *NYSE: CTR*	Charlotte	NC	28273	**800-488-0619**	704-554-8510	155-6
Catoosa County Area Chamber of Commerce 264 Catoosa Cir	Ringgold	GA	30736	**877-965-5201**	706-965-5201	137
Cats USA Pest Control PO Box 151	North Hollywood	CA	91603	**800-924-3626**	818-506-1000	567
Cattaneo Brothers Inc 769 Caudill St	San Luis Obispo	CA	93401	**800-243-8537**	805-543-7188	291-26
Cattle Raisers Museum 1301 W 7th St	Fort Worth	TX	76102	**800-242-7420**	817-332-8551	509
Cattleman's Meat Co 1825 Scott St	Detroit	MI	48207	**800-766-5699**	313-833-2700	465
Causeway Lumber Co 2601 S Andrews Ave	Fort Lauderdale	FL	33316	**800-375-5050**	954-763-1224	190-3
Cauthorne Paper Co 205 Hull St	Richmond	VA	23224	**800-552-3011**	804-232-6736	547
Cav-Air LLC 2011 S Perimeter Rd Suite L	Fort Lauderdale	FL	33309	**800-537-4454**	954-491-4454	63
Cavalier Hotel 4201 Atlantic Ave	Virginia Beach	VA	23451	**800-446-8199**	757-425-8555	655
Cavalier Telephone 2134 W Laburnum Ave	Richmond	VA	23227	**800-683-3944**	804-422-4100	721
Cavco Industries Inc 1001 N Central Ave 8th Fl *NASDAQ: CVCO*	Phoenix	AZ	85004	**800-790-9111**	602-256-6263	495
Caves Assn. National PO Box 280	Park City	KY	42160	**866-552-2837**	270-749-2228	48-23
Caviness Woodworking Co 200 N Aycock Ave PO Box 710	Calhoun City	MS	38916	**800-626-5195**	662-628-5195	701
Cavs/Gund Arena Co 1 Center Ct	Cleveland	OH	44115	**800-332-2287**	216-420-2000	355-3
Cayenta Inc 2955 Virtual Way Suite 250	Vancouver	BC	V5M4X6	**866-229-3682**		39
Caylor-Nickel Clinic PC 1 Caylor-Nickel Sq	Bluffton	IN	46714	**800-756-2663**	260-824-3500	366-2
Cayman Airways Ltd 8400 NW 52nd St Suite 210	Miami	FL	33166	**800-422-9626**	305-266-6760	26
Cayman Islands Dept of Tourism 8300 NW 53rd St Suite 103	Miami	FL	33166	**800-346-3313**	305-599-9033	764
Cayne James E 383 Madison Ave Chm/CEO Bear Stearns Cos Inc	New York	NY	10179	**800-999-2000**	212-272-2000	561
Cayuse Networks Inc 3019 117th Ave Ct E	Edgewood	WA	98372	**888-245-9691**		390
Cazenovia College 22 Sullivan St	Cazenovia	NY	13035	**800-654-3210**	315-655-7000	163
CB Fleet Inc 4615 Murray Pl PO Box 11349	Lynchburg	VA	24502	**800-999-9711**	434-528-4000	572
CB & I Trusco Tank 4388 Santa Fe Rd	San Luis Obispo	CA	93401	**800-487-8265**	805-544-9155	92
CB Mills Div Chicago Boiler Co 1300 Northwestern Ave	Gurnee	IL	60031	**800-969-7343**	847-662-4000	92
CB & Potts 10013 59th Ave SW PO Box 99010	Lakewood	WA	98499	**888-898-4050**	253-588-1788	657
CB Ragland Co 2720 Eugenia Ave	Nashville	TN	37211	**800-234-4455**	615-259-4622	292-8
CBA Information Services 4 Executive Campus	Cherry Hill	NJ	08002	**800-248-0470**	856-532-6500	212
CBA International 9240 Explorer Dr PO Box 62000	Colorado Springs	CO	80962	**800-252-1950**	719-265-9895	49-18
CBAN (Community Banking Advisory Network) 10831 Old Mill Rd Suite 400	Omaha	NE	68154	**888-475-4476**	402-778-7922	49-2
CBC (Canadian Broadcasting Corp) 181 Queen St	Ottawa	ON	K1P1K9	**866-306-4636**	613-288-6000	629
CBC (Children's Book Council) 12 W 37th St 2nd Fl *Orders	New York	NY	10018	**800-999-2160***	212-966-1990	49-16
CBC Marketing Group 3000 Cameron St	Monroe	LA	71201	**800-256-6000**	318-387-4621	721
CBCI Inc 4150 International Plaza Suite 800	Fort Worth	TX	76109	**800-759-0101**	817-737-1700	383
CBI Laboratories 4201 Diplomacy Rd	Fort Worth	TX	76155	**800-822-7546**	972-241-7546	211
CBI Services Inc 24 Read's Way	New Castle	DE	19720	**800-642-8675**	302-325-8400	188-14
CBInternational (CBI) 1501 W Mineral Ave	Littleton	CO	80120	**800-487-4224**	720-283-2000	48-20
CBLT-TV Ch 5 (CBC) 250 Front St W	Toronto	ON	M5W1E6	**866-306-4636**	416-205-3311	726
CBMC (Connecting Businessmen to Christ) 5746 Marlin Rd Suite 602 Osborne Center	Chattanooga	TN	37411	**800-575-2262**	423-698-4444	48-20
CBMI (Christian Blind Mission International) 450 E Park Ave	Greenville	SC	29601	**800-937-2264**	864-239-0065	48-5
CBN (Christian Broadcasting Network) 977 Centerville Tpke CBN Ctr	Virginia Beach	VA	23463	**800-759-0700**	757-226-7000	725
CBOT (Chicago Board of Trade) 141 W Jackson Blvd	Chicago	IL	60604	**800-572-3276**	312-435-3500	680
CBR (Center for Blood Research Inc) 800 Huntington Ave	Boston	MA	02115	**800-850-2466**	617-278-3000	654
CBRL Group Inc 305 Hartmann Dr *NASDAQ: CBRL*	Lebanon	TN	37087	**800-333-9566**	615-444-5533	355-3
CBWF-TV Ch 3 (SRC) 541 Portage Ave	Winnipeg	MB	R3C2H1	**866-306-4636**	204-788-3222	726
CBWT-TV Ch 6 (CBC) 541 Portage Ave	Winnipeg	MB	R3C2H1	**866-306-4636**	204-788-3222	726
CCA (Coastal Conservation Assn) 6919 Portwest Dr Suite 100	Houston	TX	77024	**800-201-3474**	713-626-4234	48-13
CCA Industries Inc 200 Murray Hill Pkwy *AMEX: CAW* ■ *Cust Svc	East Rutherford	NJ	07073	**800-524-2720***	201-330-1400	211
CCAC (Continuing Care Accreditation Commission) 1730 Rhode Island Ave NW Suite 209	Washington	DC	20036	**866-888-1122**	202-587-5001	48-1
CCAR (Central Conference of American Rabbis) 355 Lexington Ave 18th Fl	New York	NY	10017	**800-935-2227**	212-972-3636	48-20
CCC Group Inc 5797 Dietrich Rd	San Antonio	TX	78219	**888-661-4251**	210-661-4251	187-7
CCC Information Services Group Inc 444 Merchandise Mart Plaza *NASDAQ: CCCG*	Chicago	IL	60654	**800-621-8070**	312-222-4636	223
CCCC (Conference on College Composition & Communication) 1111 W Kenyon Rd	Urbana	IL	61801	**800-369-6283**	217-328-3870	49-5
CCF (Christian Children's Fund Inc) 2821 Emerywood Pkwy	Richmond	VA	23294	**800-776-6767**	804-756-2700	48-6
CCFA (Crohn's & Colitis Foundation of America) 386 Park Ave S 17th Fl	New York	NY	10016	**800-932-2423**	212-685-3440	48-17
CCH Corsearch 345 Hudson St 16th Fl	New York	NY	10014	**800-732-7241**	917-408-5000	621
CCH Inc 2700 Lake Cook Rd *Cust Svc	Riverwoods	IL	60015	**800-835-5224***	847-267-7000	623-9
CCH Legal Information Services 111 8th Ave	New York	NY	10011	**800-223-7567**	212-894-8940	621
CCH Washington Service Bureau Inc 1015 15th St NW 10th Fl	Washington	DC	20005	**800-955-5219**	202-312-6600	621
CCI (Canine Companions for Independence) 2965 Dutton Ave	Santa Rosa	CA	95407	**800-572-2275**	707-577-1700	48-17
CCI Mechanical Inc 758 S Redwood Rd	Salt Lake City	UT	84104	**800-521-7600**	801-973-9000	188-10
CCI Thermal Technologies Inc 5918 Roper Rd	Edmonton	AB	T6B3E1	**800-661-8529**	780-466-3178	313
CCMA LLC 300 Corporate Pkwy Suite 216-N	Amherst	NY	14226	**800-828-6621**	716-446-8800	476
CCRKBA (Citizens Committee for the Right to Keep & Bear Arms) 12500 NE 10th Pl	Bellevue	WA	98005	**800-426-4302**	425-454-4911	48-7
CCRTA (Cape Cod Regional Transit Authority) PO Box 1988	Hyannis	MA	02601	**800-352-7155**	508-775-8504	460
CCX Inc 500 E Middle St	Hanover	PA	17331	**800-323-5585**	717-637-3795	182
CD Publications 8204 Fenton St	Silver Spring	MD	20910	**800-666-6380**	301-588-6380	623-9
CD Universe 101 N Plains Industrial Rd	Wallingford	CT	06492	**800-231-7937**	203-294-1648	514

Name / Address	City	State	Zip	Toll-Free	Phone	Class
CD Warehouse Inc 900 N Broadway	Oklahoma City	OK	73102	**800-641-9394**	405-236-8742	514
CDA (Chemically Dependent Anonymous) PO Box 4425	Annapolis	MD	21403	**800-232-4673**	410-369-6556	48-21
CDC (Centers for Disease Control & Prevention)						
National Center for Environmental Health 4770 Buford Hwy Bldg 101	Chamblee	GA	30341	**888-232-6789**	770-488-7000	336-6
National Immunization Program 1600 Clifton Rd NE MS E05	Atlanta	GA	30333	**800-232-2522**	404-639-8200	336-6
CDC Distributors 7235 Progress St PO Box 1267	Holland	OH	43528	**800-537-0154**	419-866-3567	356
CDC Nvest Funds PO Box 219579	Kansas City	MO	64121	**800-225-5478**		517
CDF (Children's Defense Fund) 25 'E' St NW	Washington	DC	20001	**800-233-1200**	202-628-8787	48-6
CDI Credit Inc 6160 Peachtree Dunwoody Rd NE Suite B-210	Atlanta	GA	30328	**800-633-3961**	770-350-5070	621
CD&L Inc 80 Wesley St	South Hackensack	NJ	07606	**800-899-7296**	201-487-7740	306
AMEX: CDV						
CDMA (Chain Drug Marketing Assn) 43157 W Nine-Mile Rd PO Box 995	Novi	MI	48376	**800-935-2362**	248-449-9300	49-18
CDP Computer Supplier Inc 378 Page St	Stoughton	MA	02072	**800-366-6283**	781-341-3985	523
CDP Corp 1399 Executive Dr W	Richardson	TX	75081	**800-527-4356**	972-234-8565	330
CDR Pigments & Dispersions 305 Ring Rd	Elizabethtown	KY	42701	**800-898-3421**	270-737-1700	141
CDW Corp 200 N Milwaukee Ave	Vernon Hills	IL	60061	**800-828-4239**	847-465-6000	177
NASDAQ: CDWC						
CE Conover & Co Inc 4106 Blanche Rd	Bensalem	PA	19020	**800-266-6837**	215-639-6666	321
CE Niehoff & Co 2021 Lee St	Evanston	IL	60202	**800-643-4633***	847-866-6030	246
*Tech Supp						
CE Thurston & Sons Inc 3335 Croft St	Norfolk	VA	23513	**800-444-7713***	757-855-7700	188-9
*Cust Svc						
CE Toland & Son 5300 Industrial Way	Benicia	CA	94510	**800-675-1166**	707-747-1000	188-14
Cebridge Connections PO Box 139400	Tyler	TX	75713	**877-423-2743**	800-999-8876	117
Cebridge Connections PO Box 139400	Tyler	TX	75713	**800-999-8876**		117
CEC (Council for Exceptional Children) 1110 N Glebe Rd Suite 300	Arlington	VA	22201	**888-232-7733**	703-620-3660	49-5
Cecil Saydah Co 2935 E 12th St	Los Angeles	CA	90023	**800-221-4617**	323-263-9321	731
Cecil Whig Newspaper PO Box 429	Elkton	MD	21922	**800-220-3311**	410-398-3311	522-2
Cecilware Corp 43-05 20th Ave	Long Island City	NY	11105	**800-935-2211**	718-932-1414	295
Cecorp 8 Chrysler	Irvine	CA	92618	**800-854-6861**	949-583-0792	70
Cedar Crest College 100 College Dr	Allentown	PA	18104	**800-360-1222**	610-437-4471	163
Cedar Crest Specialties Inc 7269 Hwy 60	Cedarburg	WI	53012	**800-877-8341**	262-377-7252	291-25
Cedar Rapids Area Convention & Visitors Bureau PO Box 5339	Cedar Rapids	IA	52406	**800-735-5557**	319-398-5009	205
Cedar Rapids Marriott 1200 Collins Rd NE	Cedar Rapids	IA	52402	**800-541-1067**	319-393-6600	373
Cedar Rapids Symphony Orchestra 119 3rd Ave Se	Cedar Rapids	IA	52401	**800-369-8863**	319-366-8206	563-3
Cedar Shake & Shingle Bureau 7101 Horne St Suite 2	Mission	BC	V2V7A2	**800-843-3578**	604-820-7700	49-3
Cedar Shopping Centers Inc 44 S Bayles Ave Suite 304	Port Washington	NY	11050	**800-564-3128**	516-767-6492	641
NYSE: CDR						
Cedar Valley Hospice 2101 Kimball Ave Suite 401	Waterloo	IA	50702	**800-617-1972**	319-272-2002	365
Cedara Software Corp 6509 Airport Rd	Mississauga	ON	L4V1S7	**800-724-5970**	905-672-2100	176-10
Cedarapids Inc 909 17th St NE	Cedar Rapids	IA	52402	**800-821-5600***	319-363-3511	189
*Cust Svc						
CEDARLANE Laboratories Inc 5516 8th Line RR 2	Hornby	ON	L0P1E0	**800-268-5058**	905-878-8891	229
Cedars-Sinai Medical Center 8700 Beverly Blvd	Los Angeles	CA	90048	**800-233-2771**	310-423-3277	366-2
Cedarville University 251 N Main St	Cedarville	OH	45314	**800-233-2784**	937-766-2211	163
CEDIA (Custom Electronic Design & Installation Assn) 7150 Winton Dr Suite 300	Indianapolis	IN	46268	**800-669-5329**	317-328-4336	49-19
CEF Industries Inc 320 S Church St	Addison	IL	60101	**800-888-6419**	630-628-2299	23
CEI Engineering Assoc Inc 3317 SW 'I' St	Bentonville	AR	72712	**800-433-4173**	479-273-9472	258
Ceiva Logic Inc 214 E Magnolia Blvd	Burbank	CA	91502	**877-693-7263***	818-562-1495	580
*Tech Supp						
Cejka & Co 222 S Central Ave Suite 400	Saint Louis	MO	63105	**800-678-7858**	314-726-1603	707
Celadon Trucking Services Inc 9503 E 33rd St	Indianapolis	IN	46235	**800-235-2366**	317-972-7000	769
Celebrate Express Inc DBA Birthday Express 11220 120th Ave NE	Kirkland	WA	98033	**800-424-7843**	425-250-1064	555
NASDAQ: BDAY						
Celebration Hotel 700 Bloom St	Celebration	FL	34747	**888-472-6312**	407-566-6000	373
Celebrity Cruises 1050 Caribbean Way	Miami	FL	33132	**800-722-5941**	305-539-6000	217
Celebrity Inc 4520 Old Troup Hwy Suite C	Tyler	TX	75707	**800-527-8446**	903-561-3981	288
Celebrity Resorts Orlando 2800 N Poinciana Blvd	Kissimmee	FL	34746	**800-423-8604**	407-997-5000	373
Celera Genomics Group 45 W Gude Dr	Rockville	MD	20850	**877-235-3721**	240-453-3000	86
NYSE: CRA						
Celestial Seasonings Inc 4600 Sleepytime Dr	Boulder	CO	80301	**800-351-8175**	303-581-1202	291-40
Celestica Inc 844 Don Mills Rd	Toronto	ON	M3C1V7	**888-899-9998**	416-448-5800	252
NYSE: CLS						
Celgene Corp 7 Powder Horn Dr	Warren	NJ	07059	**888-423-5436**	732-271-1001	86
NASDAQ: CELG						
Celia Corp 140 E Averill St	Sparta	MI	49345	**800-253-3664**	616-887-7341	675
Cell Genesys Inc 500 Forbes Blvd	South San Francisco	CA	94080	**800-648-6747**	650-266-3000	86
NASDAQ: CEGE						
Cell-Loc Inc 3015 5th Ave NE Franklin Atrium Suite 220	Calgary	AB	T2A6T8	**877-569-5700**	403-569-5700	222
Cell-Tel Government Systems Inc 8226 Phillips Hwy Suite 290	Jacksonville	FL	32256	**800-737-7545**	904-363-1111	245
Cell Therapeutics Inc 201 Elliott Ave W Suite 400	Seattle	WA	98119	**800-215-2355**	206-282-7100	86
NASDAQ: CTIC						
Cello-Pack Corp 55 Innsbruck Dr	Cheektowaga	NY	14227	**800-778-3111**	716-668-3111	538
Cellofoam North America Inc PO Box 406	Conyers	GA	30012	**800-241-3634**	770-929-3688	590
Cellotape Inc 47623 Fremont Blvd	Fremont	CA	94538	**800-231-0608**	510-651-5551	404
Cellox Corp 1200 Industrial St	Reedsburg	WI	53959	**888-217-6631**	608-524-2316	590
CellStar Corp 1730 Briercroft Ct	Carrollton	TX	75006	**800-723-9070**	972-466-5000	245
NASDAQ: CLST						
Cellular One 3650 131st Ave SE Suite 600	Bellevue	WA	98006	**800-873-2349**	425-313-5200	721
NASDAQ: WWCA						
Cellular One Group (Licensing Management Office) 3650 131St Ave SE Suite 600	Bellevue	WA	98006	**800-545-5982**	425-586-8700	721
Cellular & Wireless Wholesale Corp 8240 NW 30th Terr	Miami	FL	33122	**888-918-4299**	305-436-8999	245
Celsion Corp 10220-L Old Columbia Rd	Columbia	MD	21046	**800-262-0394**	410-290-5390	468
AMEX: CLN						
CEM Corp PO Box 200	Matthews	NC	28106	**800-726-3331**	704-821-7015	410
CemcoLift Inc 2801 Township Line Rd	Hatfield	PA	19440	**800-962-3626***	215-799-2900	255
*Sales						
Cement Industries Inc 2709 Jeffcott St	Fort Myers	FL	33901	**800-332-1440**	239-332-1440	181
Cemetery & Funeral Assn. International 1895 Preston White Dr Suite 220	Reston	VA	20191	**800-645-7700**	703-391-8400	49-4
Cemstone Products Co 2025 Centre Pointe Blvd Suite 300	Mendota Heights	MN	55120	**800-642-3887**	651-688-9292	180
Cenac Towing Co Inc PO Box 2617	Houma	LA	70361	**800-942-5476**	985-872-2413	457
Cenacle Retreat House & Spirituality Center 29 W 012 Batavia Rd	Warrenville	IL	60555	**800-240-6702**	630-393-1231	660
Cendant Corp 9 W 57th St 37th Fl	New York	NY	10019	**877-446-3623**	212-413-1800	184
NYSE: CD						
Cendant Corp Hospitality Div						
AmeriHost Franchise Systems Inc 1 Sylvan Way	Parsippany	NJ	07054	**800-889-8847**	973-428-9700	369
Days Inns Worldwide Inc 1 Sylvan Way	Parsippany	NJ	07054	**800-329-7466**	973-428-9700	369
Howard Johnson International Inc 1 Sylvan Way	Parsippany	NJ	07054	**800-446-4656**	973-428-9700	369
Ramada Franchise Systems Inc 1 Sylvan Way	Parsippany	NJ	07054	**800-932-6726**	973-428-9700	369
Super 8 Motels Inc 1910 8th Ave NE	Aberdeen	SD	57401	**800-800-8000**	605-225-2272	369
Cendant Corp Hospitality Services Div						
Travelodge Hotels Inc 1 Sylvan Way	Parsippany	NJ	07054	**800-578-7878**	973-428-9700	369
Villager Lodge Franchise Systems Inc 1 Sylvan Way	Parsippany	NJ	07054	**888-821-5738**	973-428-9700	369
Wingate Inns International Inc 1 Sylvan Way	Parsippany	NJ	07054	**800-228-1000**	973-428-9700	369
Cendant Mortgage 6000 Atrium Way	Mount Laurel	NJ	08054	**866-684-7334**		498
Cenex 5500 Cenex Dr	Inver Grove Heights	MN	55077	**800-232-3639**	651-355-6000	530
Centenary College 2911 Centenary Blvd	Shreveport	LA	71104	**800-234-4448**	318-869-5011	163
Centenary College 400 Jefferson St	Hackettstown	NJ	07840	**800-236-8679**	908-852-1400	163
Centene Corp 7711 Carondelet Ave Suite 800	Saint Louis	MO	63105	**800-225-2573**	314-725-4477	384-3
NYSE: CNC						
Centennial HealthCare Corp 303 Perimeter Ctr N Suite 500	Atlanta	GA	30346	**800-334-1488**	770-698-9040	442
Centennial Inn 96 Pleasant St	Concord	NH	03301	**800-360-4839**	603-225-7102	373
Centennial Travelers 1532 E Mulberry St Suite G	Fort Collins	CO	80524	**800-223-0675**	970-484-4988	748
Center for Association Growth 1926 Waukegan Rd Suite 1	Glenview	IL	60025	**800-492-6462**	847-657-6700	47
Center for Association Resources Inc 1901 N Roselle Rd	Schaumburg	IL	60195	**888-705-1434**	847-885-5680	47
Center Bancorp Inc 2455 Morris Ave	Union	NJ	07083	**800-862-3683**	908-688-9500	355-2
NASDAQ: CNBC						
Center for Blood Research Inc (CBR) 800 Huntington Ave	Boston	MA	02115	**800-850-2466**	617-278-3000	654
Center for Communications Management Information 11300 Rockville Pike Suite 1100	Rockville	MD	20852	**888-275-2264**	301-287-2835	623-11
Center for Community Inclusion University of Maine 5717 Corbett Hall Rm 114	Orono	ME	04469	**800-203-6957**	207-581-1084	654
Center Court Historic Inn & Cottages 915 Center St	Key West	FL	33040	**800-797-8787**	305-296-9292	373
Center for Devices & Radiological Health 9200 Corporate Blvd Suite 100E	Rockville	MD	20850	**800-638-2041**		336-6
Center for Diagnostic Imaging 5775 Wayzata Blvd Suite 400	Saint Louis Park	MN	55416	**877-566-6500**	952-543-6500	376
Center for Education Reform 1001 Connecticut Ave NW Suite 204	Washington	DC	20036	**800-521-2118**	202-822-9000	48-11
Center on Education & Training for Employment Ohio State University 1900 Kenny Rd	Columbus	OH	43210	**800-848-4815**	614-292-4353	654
Center Enterprises Inc 30 Shield St	West Hartford	CT	06110	**800-542-2214***	860-953-4423	242
*Orders						
Center for Food Safety & Applied Nutrition 5100 Paint Branch Pkwy	College Park	MD	20740	**888-723-3366**	301-436-1600	336-6
Center for Genetic Testing at Saint Francis OU Shusterman Ctr 4502 E 41st St	Tulsa	OK	74135	**800-299-7919**	918-660-3838	408
Center on Human Policy 805 S Crouse Ave	Syracuse	NY	13244	**800-894-0826**	315-443-3851	48-17
Center for Individual Rights (CIR) 1233 20th St NW Suite 300	Washington	DC	20036	**877-426-2665**	202-833-8400	48-8

Name / Address	City	State	ZIP	Toll-Free	Phone	Class
Center Mfg Co 540 Goodrich Rd	Bellevue	OH	44811	800-377-7736	419-483-4852	665
Center for Organ Recovery & Education (CORE) 204 Sigma Dr RIDC Park	Pittsburgh	PA	15238	800-366-6777	412-366-6777	265
Center for Practical Bioethics 1100 Walnut St Suite 2900	Kansas City	MO	64106	800-344-3829	816-221-1100	48-17
Center for Reproductive Rights 120 Wall St 14th Fl	New York	NY	10005	800-786-9711	917-637-3600	48-8
Center for Technology Commercialization (CTC) 1400 Computer Dr	Westborough	MA	01581	800-472-6785	508-870-0042	654
Center for Western Studies 2101 S Summit Ave Augustana College	Sioux Falls	SD	57197	800-727-2844	605-274-4007	509
Center for Youth & Communities Brandeis University 60 Turner St 2nd Fl	Waltham	MA	02453	800-343-4205	781-736-3770	654
Centerplate 201 E Broad St *AMEX: CVP*	Spartanburg	SC	29306	800-698-6992	864-598-8600	294
CenterPoint Energy Arkla PO Box 751	Little Rock	AR	72203	800-992-7552	501-377-4556	774
CenterPoint Energy Inc 1111 Louisiana St *NYSE: CNP* ■ *Cust Svc	Houston	TX	77002	866-735-4268*	713-207-1111	355-5
Centerpointe Communications 2106 W Pioneer Pkwy Suite 131	Arlington	TX	76013	877-277-6811	817-277-6811	168
CenterPointe Hospital 5931 Hwy 94 S	Saint Charles	MO	63304	800-345-5407	636-441-7300	366-3
Centers for Disease Control & Prevention (CDC)						
National Center for Environmental Health 4770 Buford Hwy Bldg 101	Chamblee	GA	30341	888-232-6789	770-488-7000	336-6
National Immunization Program 1600 Clifton Rd NE MS E05	Atlanta	GA	30333	800-232-2522	404-639-8200	336-6
National Institute for Occupational Safety & Health 200 Independence Ave SW	Washington	DC	20201	800-356-4674	202-401-6997	336-6
Centers for Medicare & Medicaid Services (CMS) Medicare Hotline	Baltimore	MD	21207	800-633-4227		336-6
Centex Corp 2728 N Harwood St *NYSE: CTX*	Dallas	TX	75201	888-847-5130	214-981-5000	186
Centex Home Equity Corp PO Box 199400	Dallas	TX	75219	888-480-2432	214-981-5000	498
Centillium Communications Inc 215 Fourier Ave *NASDAQ: CTLM*	Fremont	CA	94539	877-879-7500	510-771-3700	686
Centimark Corp 12 Grandview Cir	Canonsburg	PA	15317	800-558-4100	724-743-7777	188-12
Centinela Freeman Regional Medical Center Memorial Campus 333 N Prairie Ave	Inglewood	CA	90301	800-455-1933	310-674-7050	366-2
Centocor Inc 200 Great Valley Pkwy	Malvern	PA	19355	888-874-3083	610-651-6000	86
CenTra 12225 Stephens Rd	Warren	MI	48089	800-334-4883	586-939-7000	769
Central Alabama Community College 1675 Cherokee Rd	Alexander City	AL	35010	800-643-2657	256-215-4255	160
Central Alabama Electric Co-op PO Box 681570	Prattville	AL	36068	800-545-5735	334-365-6762	244
Central Allied Enterprises Inc 1243 Raff Rd SW	Canton	OH	44710	800-862-6011	330-477-6751	187-4
Central Arizona College 8470 N Overfield Rd	Coolidge	AZ	85228	800-237-9814	520-426-4444	160
Central Baptist Theological Seminary 741 N 31st St	Kansas City	KS	66102	800-677-2287	913-371-5313	164-3
Central Benefits Mutual Insurance Co PO Box 850658	Richardson	TX	75085	800-777-3377	614-797-5200	384-2
Central Bible College 3000 N Grant Ave	Springfield	MO	65803	800-831-4222	417-833-2551	163
Central Brass Mfg Co Inc 2950 E 55th St	Cleveland	OH	44127	800-321-8630	216-883-0220	598
Central Builders Supply Co Inc PO Box 152	Sunbury	PA	17801	800-326-9361	570-286-6461	180
Central California Blood Center 3445 N 1st St	Fresno	CA	93726	800-404-2500	559-224-2900	90
Central Camera Co 230 S Wabash Ave	Chicago	IL	60606	800-421-1899	312-427-5580	119
Central Carolina Hospital 1135 Carthage St	Sanford	NC	27330	800-292-2262	919-774-2100	366-2
Central Carolina Technical College 506 N Guignard Dr	Sumter	SC	29150	800-221-8711	803-778-1961	158
Central Christian College PO Box 1403	McPherson	KS	67460	800-835-0078	620-241-0723	160
Central Christian College of the Bible 911 E Urbandale Dr	Moberly	MO	65270	888-263-3900	660-263-3900	163
Central City Opera 400 S Colorado Blvd Suite 530	Denver	CO	80246	800-851-8175	303-292-6500	563-2
Central Coast Bancorp 301 Main St *NASDAQ: CCBN*	Salinas	CA	93901	800-660-1585	831-422-6642	355-2
Central College 812 University St	Pella	IA	50219	877-462-3687	641-628-5285	163
Central Conference of American Rabbis (CCAR) 355 Lexington Ave 18th Fl	New York	NY	10017	800-935-2227	212-972-3636	48-20
Central Connecticut Co-op Farmers Assn PO Box 8500	Manchester	CT	06040	800-640-4523	860-649-4523	271
Central Dairy & Ice Cream Co 610 Madison St	Jefferson City	MO	65101	800-422-2148	573-635-6148	291-25
Central Delaware Economic Development Council 435 N Dupont Hwy	Dover	DE	19903	800-624-2522	302-678-3028	137
Central Delivery Service 5501 Virginia Manor Rd	Beltsville	MD	20705	800-938-4151	301-210-0100	536
Central Distributors Inc 15 Foss Rd *Cust Svc	Lewiston	ME	04241	800-427-5757*	207-784-4026	82-1
Central DuPage Hospital 25 N Winfield Rd	Winfield	IL	60190	877-933-1600	630-933-1600	366-2
Central Electric Co-op 1420 N Main St	Mitchell	SD	57301	800-477-2892	605-996-7516	244
Central Electric Membership Corp 128 Wilson Rd	Sanford	NC	27331	800-446-7752	919-774-4900	244
Central Federal Corp PO Box 345 *NASDAQ: GCFC*	Wellsville	OH	43968	888-273-8255	330-532-1517	355-2
Central Financial Acceptance Corp 1900 S Main St	Los Angeles	CA	90007	800-273-3486		215
Central Florida Electric Co-op Inc 1124 N Young Blvd	Chiefland	FL	32644	800-227-1302	352-493-2511	244
Central Florida Investments Inc 5601 Windhover Dr	Orlando	FL	32819	800-925-9999	407-351-3383	738
Central Florida Lions Eye & Tissue Bank Inc 5523 W Cypress St Suite 100	Tampa	FL	33607	800-277-2020	813-289-1200	265
Central Florida Tissue & Eye Bank Inc 8663 Commodity Cir	Orlando	FL	32819	800-753-9109	407-226-3888	535
Central Florida Visitors & Convention Bureau 1339 Helena Rd	Winter Haven	FL	33884	800-828-7655	863-298-7565	205
Central Flying Service Inc 1501 Bond St	Little Rock	AR	72202	800-888-5387	501-375-3245	63
Central Freight Lines Inc PO Box 2638 *NASDAQ: CENF*	Waco	TX	76702	800-233-9226	254-772-2120	769
Central Georgia Electric Membership Corp 923 S Mulberry St	Jackson	GA	30233	800-222-4877	770-775-7857	244
Central Global Express PO Box 698	Taylor	MI	48180	800-982-3924	734-955-2555	306
Central Hudson Gas & Electric Corp 284 South Ave	Poughkeepsie	NY	12601	800-527-2714	845-452-2000	774
Central Indiana Power Corp 2243 Main St	Greenfield	IN	46140	800-382-5544	317-477-2200	244
Central Industries Inc PO Box 1380	Scott	LA	70583	800-326-3171	337-233-3171	528
Central Ink Corp 1100 N Harvester Rd	West Chicago	IL	60185	800-345-2541	630-231-6500	381
Central Insurance Cos 800 S Washington St	Van Wert	OH	45891	800-736-7000	419-238-1010	384-4
Central Iowa Co-op PO Box 190	Jewell	IA	50130	800-728-0017	515-827-5431	271
Central Kentucky Blood Center 330 Waller Ave	Lexington	KY	40504	800-775-2522	859-276-2534	90
Central Lakes College						
Brainerd Campus 501 W College Dr	Brainerd	MN	56401	800-933-0346	218-855-8000	160
Staples Campus 1830 Airport Rd	Staples	MN	56479	800-247-6836	218-894-5100	160
Central Livestock Assn 310 Market Ln	South Saint Paul	MN	55075	800-733-1844	651-451-1844	437
Central Maine Community College 1250 Turner St *Admissions	Auburn	ME	04210	800-891-2002*	207-755-5100	787
Central Maine Power Co 83 Edison Dr	Augusta	ME	04336	800-565-0121	207-623-3521	774
Central Maintenance & Welding Inc 2620 Keysville Rd PO Drawer 777	Lithia	FL	33547	877-704-7411	813-737-1402	188-14
Central Massachusetts Regional Library System 8 Flagg Rd	Shrewsbury	MA	01545	800-922-8326	508-757-4110	426
Central Methodist College 411 Central Methodist Sq	Fayette	MO	65248	888-262-1854	660-248-3391	163
Central Michigan Community Hospital 1221 South Dr	Mount Pleasant	MI	48858	800-671-1453	989-772-6700	366-2
Central Michigan University 102 Warriner Hall	Mount Pleasant	MI	48859	888-292-5366	989-774-4000	163
Central Mine Equipment Co Inc 4215 Rider Trail N	Earth City	MO	63045	800-325-8827	314-291-7700	189
Central Mississippi Medical Center 1850 Chadwick Dr	Jackson	MS	39204	800-844-0919	601-376-1000	366-2
Central Missouri State University	Warrensburg	MO	64093	800-729-2678	660-543-4111	163
Central Nebraska Packing Inc PO Box 550 *Cust Svc	North Platte	NE	69103	800-445-2881*	308-532-1250	465
Central New Mexico Electric Co-op Inc Hwy 55 PO Box 157	Mountainair	NM	87036	800-339-2521	505-847-2521	244
Central Ohio Lions Eye Bank 456 W 10th Ave Suite B-0903	Columbus	OH	43210	800-301-4960	614-293-8114	265
Central Pacific Bank 220 S King St PO Box 3590	Honolulu	HI	96811	800-342-8422	808-544-0500	71
Central Park Media Corp 250 W 57th St Suite 317	New York	NY	10107	800-833-7456	212-977-7456	500
Central Parking Corp 2401 21st Ave S Suite 200 *NYSE: CPC*	Nashville	TN	37212	800-423-6613	615-297-4255	552
Central Pennsylvania College College Hill Rd	Summerdale	PA	17093	800-759-2727	717-732-0702	158
Central Pet 301 Island Rd	Mahwah	NJ	07430	800-631-7724	201-529-5050	568
Central Petroleum Transport Inc 4036 Southgate Dr *Sales	Sioux City	IA	51111	800-798-6357*	712-258-6357	769
Central Ready-Mix Concrete Inc 5013 W State St	Milwaukee	WI	53208	800-258-0010	414-258-7000	180
Central Reservation Service 159 Lookout Pl Suite 201	Maitland	FL	32751	800-548-3311	407-740-6442	368
Central Reservation Service of New England Inc 300 Terminal C Logan International Airport	East Boston	MA	02128	800-332-3026	617-569-3800	368
Central Reserve Life 17800 Royalton Rd	Strongsville	OH	44136	800-321-3997	440-572-2400	384-3
Central Rural Electric Co-op 3304 S Boomer Rd	Stillwater	OK	74074	800-375-2884	405-372-2884	244
Central Security Life Insurance Co PO Box 833879	Richardson	TX	75083	866-629-2677	972-699-2770	384-2
Central Signaling Inc 2033 Hamilton Rd	Columbus	GA	31904	800-554-1104	706-322-3756	683
Central Soya 38 Colfax St	Pawtucket	RI	02860	800-556-6777	401-724-3800	291-30
Central Specialties Ltd 220-D Exchange Dr	Crystal Lake	IL	60014	800-873-4370	815-459-6000	64
Central Sprinkler Corp 451 N Cannon Ave	Lansdale	PA	19446	800-523-6512	215-362-0700	379
Central State University 1400 Brush Row Rd PO Box 1004	Wilberforce	OH	45384	800-388-2781	937-376-6011	163
Central States Business Forms Inc 2500 Industrial Pkwy	Dewey	OK	74029	800-331-0920	918-534-1280	111
Central States Health & Life Co of Omaha PO Box 34350	Omaha	NE	68134	800-541-2363	402-397-1111	384-2
Central States Indemnity Co of Omaha PO Box 34350	Omaha	NE	68134	800-445-6500	402-397-1111	384-5
Central Steel & Wire Co 3000 W 51st St	Chicago	IL	60632	800-621-8510	773-471-3800	483

Listing	City	State	ZIP	Toll-Free	Phone	Class
Central Texas College 6200 W Central Texas Expy	Killeen	TX	76549	**800-792-3348**	254-526-1595	160
Central Texas Electric Co-op Inc 386 Friendship Ln	Fredericksburg	TX	78624	**800-900-2832**	830-997-2126	244
Central Texas Medical Center 1301 Wonder World Dr	San Marcos	TX	78666	**800-508-8515**	512-353-8979	366-2
Central Texas Veteran's Health Care 1901 Veterans Memorial Dr	Temple	TX	76504	**800-423-2111**	254-778-4811	366-6
Central Tower Inc 2855 Hwy 261	Newburgh	IN	47630	**800-664-8222**	812-853-0595	168
Central Transport International Inc 12225 Stephens Rd	Warren	MI	48089	**800-334-4883**	586-939-7000	769
Central Vermont Chamber of Commerce 33 Stewart Rd	Barre	VT	05641	**877-887-3678**	802-229-5711	137
Central Vermont Public Service Corp 77 Grove St *NYSE: CV* ■ *Cust Svc	Rutland	VT	05701	**800-649-2877***	802-773-2711	774
Central Virginia Electric Co-op 800 Cooperative Way	Lovingston	VA	22949	**800-367-2832**	434-263-8336	244
Central Virginia Training Center PO Box 1098	Lynchburg	VA	24505	**866-897-6095**	434-947-6000	228
Central Washington Hospital PO Box 1887	Wenatchee	WA	98807	**800-365-6428**	509-662-1511	366-3
Central Washington University 400 E University Way	Ellensburg	WA	98926	**866-298-4968**	509-963-1111	163
Central West of Texas Inc 3426 W Gilbert Rd	Grand Prairie	TX	75050	**800-533-1939**	972-399-1059	108
Central Wholesale Electrical Distributors Inc 1183-A Quarry Ln PO Box 1210	Pleasanton	CA	94566	**800-834-8122**	925-417-6930	245
Central Woodwork Inc 870 Keough Rd	Collierville	TN	38017	**800-788-3775**	901-363-4141	489
Central Wyoming College 2660 Peck Ave	Riverton	WY	82501	**800-735-8418**	307-855-2000	160
Centralia Sentinel 232 E Broadway	Centralia	IL	62801	**800-371-9892**	618-532-5604	522-2
CentralVac International Inc 1525 E 5th St	Kimball	NE	69145	**800-666-3133**	308-235-4139	775
Centre College of Kentucky 600 W Walnut St	Danville	KY	40422	**800-423-6236**	859-238-5350	163
Centre County Convention & Visitors Bureau 800 E Park Ave	State College	PA	16803	**800-358-5466**	814-231-1400	205
Centre Daily Times 3400 E College Ave	State College	PA	16804	**800-327-5500**	814-238-5000	522-2
Centre for Well-Being at the Phoenician 6000 E Camelback Rd	Scottsdale	AZ	85251	**800-843-2392**	480-423-2452	698
CENTRIA 1005 Beaver Grade Rd	Moon Township	PA	15108	**800-759-7474**	412-299-8000	471
Centric Software Inc 50 Las Colinas Ln	San Jose	CA	95119	**800-644-1002**	408-574-7802	39
Centrifuge Research Center ATTN: CEERD-PA-Z 3909 Halls Ferry Rd	Vicksburg	MS	39180	**800-522-6937**	601-634-2502	654
Centrilift Inc 200 W Stuart Roosa Dr	Claremore	OK	74017	**800-633-5088**	918-341-9600	627
Centron Data Services Co 1175 Devin Dr *Cust Svc	Norton Shores	MI	49441	**800-732-8787***	231-798-1221	5
Centrovision 2088 Anchor Ct	Newbury Park	CA	91320	**800-700-2088**	805-499-5902	686
Centura Bank DBA RBC Centura 1417 Centura Hwy	Rocky Mount	NC	27804	**800-236-8872**	252-454-4400	71
Centurion Wireless Technologies Inc 3425 N 44th St	Lincoln	NE	68504	**800-228-4563**	402-467-4491	633
Century 21 Commercial Investment Network 1 Campus Dr	Parsippany	NJ	07054	**800-221-5737**	973-428-9700	638
Century 21 Real Estate Corp 1 Campus Dr	Parsippany	NJ	07054	**800-221-5737**	973-428-9700	638
Century Aluminum Co 2511 Garden Rd Bldg A Suite 200 *NASDAQ: CENX*	Monterey	CA	93940	**888-642-9300**	831-642-9300	476
Century Aluminum Inc Willow Grove Rd PO Box 68	Ravenswood	WV	26164	**800-258-6686**	304-273-6241	476
Century Bancorp Inc 400 Mystic Ave *NASDAQ: CNBKA*	Medford	MA	02155	**800-442-1859**	781-391-4000	355-2
Century Casinos Inc 200-220 E Bennett Ave *NASDAQ: CNTY*	Cripple Creek	CO	80813	**888-966-2257**	719-689-0333	132
Century College 3300 Century Ave N	White Bear Lake	MN	55110	**800-228-1978**	651-779-3200	160
Century Fasteners Corp 50-20 Ireland St	Elmhurst	NY	11373	**800-221-0769**	718-446-5000	245
Century Fence Co PO Box 466	Waukesha	WI	53187	**800-558-0507**	262-547-3331	275
Century Fireplace Furnishings Inc 856 N Main St Ext	Wallingford	CT	06492	**800-448-0409**	203-265-1686	676
Century Glass Inc 4620 Andrews St	North Las Vegas	NV	89031	**800-654-7027**	702-385-9309	325
Century Graphics & Metals Inc 3497 All American Blvd	Orlando	FL	32810	**800-327-5664**	407-295-7818	692
Century Group Inc PO Box 228	Sulphur	LA	70664	**800-527-5232**	337-527-5266	181
Century House Inn 997 New Loudon Rd Rt 9	Latham	NY	12110	**888-674-6873**	518-785-0931	373
Century II Staffing Inc 278 Franklin Rd Suite 350	Brentwood	TN	37027	**800-972-9630**	615-665-9060	619
Century III at Universal Studios 2000 Universal Studios Plaza Suite 100	Orlando	FL	32819	**800-281-7501**	407-354-1000	501
Century Inc 1000 Century Blvd *Sales	Midwest City	OK	73110	**800-626-2787***	405-732-2226	701
Century Insurance Group 465 Cleveland Ave	Westerville	OH	43082	**800-878-7389**	614-895-2000	384-5
Century Interactive LLC 7502 Greenville Ave Suite 300	Dallas	TX	75231	**800-256-3159**	214-360-6280	721
Century-National Insurance Co 12200 Sylvan St	North Hollywood	CA	91606	**800-733-0880**	818-760-0880	384-4
Century Plaza Hotel & Spa 1015 Burrard St	Vancouver	BC	V6Z1Y5	**800-663-1818**	604-687-0575	372
Century Precision Optics 7701 Haskell Ave	Van Nuys	CA	91406	**800-228-1254**	818-766-3715	580
Century Ready-Mix Corp 3250 Armand St PO Box 4420	Monroe	LA	71211	**800-732-3969**	318-322-4444	180
Century Software 5284 S Commerce Dr Suite C-134	Salt Lake City	UT	84107	**800-877-3088**	801-268-3088	176-7
Century Sports Inc 1995 Rutgers University Blvd *Sales	Lakewood	NJ	08701	**800-526-7548***	732-905-4422	701
Century Spring Corp PO Box 15287	Los Angeles	CA	90015	**800-237-5225**	213-749-1466	705
Century Steel Erectors Co 210 Washington Ave PO Box 490	Dravosburg	PA	15034	**888-601-8801**	412-469-8800	188-14
Century Suites Hotel 300 SR-446	Bloomington	IN	47401	**800-766-5446**	812-336-7777	373
Century Tool & Mfg Co Inc PO Box 188	Cherry Valley	IL	61016	**800-435-4525**	815-332-4951	701
Century Wilshire Hotel 10776 Wilshire Blvd	Los Angeles	CA	90024	**800-421-7223**	310-474-4506	373
CEO Report 11300 Rockville Pike Suite 1100 *Cust Svc	Rockville	MD	20852	**800-929-4824***	301-816-8950	521-1
Cephalon Inc 145 Brandywine Pkwy *NASDAQ: CEPH*	West Chester	PA	19380	**800-675-8415**	610-344-0200	86
Cepheid 904 E Caribbean Dr *NASDAQ: CPHD*	Sunnyvale	CA	94089	**888-838-3222**	408-541-4191	410
Cequent Towing Products 47774 Anchor Ct W	Plymouth	MI	48170	**800-521-0510**	734-656-3000	751
Cequent Trailer Products 1050 Indianhead Dr	Mosinee	WI	54455	**800-604-9466**	715-693-1700	751
Cera Services 10960 E Crystal Falls Pkwy Suite 500	Leander	TX	78641	**800-966-3070**	512-259-5151	173
Ceragon Networks Inc 10 Forest Ave *Tech Supp	Paramus	NJ	07652	**877-342-3247***	201-845-6955	720
Ceramaseal Div CeramTec North America 1033 US Rt 20	New Lebanon	NY	12125	**800-752-7325**	518-794-7800	248
Ceramco Div Dentsply International Inc 6 Terri Ln Suite 100	Burlington	NJ	08016	**800-487-0100**	609-386-8900	226
CeraMed Dental LLC 12860 W Cedar Dr Suite 110	Lakewood	CO	80228	**800-426-7836**	303-985-0800	406
Ceramo Co Inc 681 Kasten Dr	Jackson	MO	63755	**800-325-8303**	573-243-3138	330
CeramTec North America PO Box 89 1 Technology Pl	Laurens	SC	29360	**800-845-9761**	864-682-3215	248
CeramTec North America Ceramaseal Div 1033 US Rt 20	New Lebanon	NY	12125	**800-752-7325**	518-794-7800	248
CeramTec North America Electronic Applications Inc 1 Technology Pl PO Box 89	Laurens	SC	29360	**800-845-9761**	864-682-3215	248
Cereal Food Processors Inc 2001 Shawnee Mission Pkwy	Mission Woods	KS	66205	**800-743-5687**	913-890-6300	291-23
Cereal Foods Inc 416 N Main St	McPherson	KS	67460	**800-835-2067**	620-241-2410	291-23
Cerebral Palsy. United 1660 L St NW Suite 700	Washington	DC	20036	**800-872-5827**	202-776-0406	48-17
Ceres Group Inc 17800 Royalton Rd *NASDAQ: CERG*	Strongsville	OH	44136	**800-321-3997**	440-572-2400	355-4
Ceridian Canada Ltd 125 Garry St	Winnipeg	MB	R3C3P2	**866-975-1808**	204-946-0770	455
Ceridian Corp 3311 E Old Shakopee Rd *NYSE: CEN*	Minneapolis	MN	55425	**800-767-4969**	952-853-8100	619
Cermetek Microelectronics Inc 406 Tasman Dr	Sunnyvale	CA	94089	**800-882-6271**	408-752-5000	496
Cerner Corp 2800 Rockcreek Pkwy *NASDAQ: CERN* ■ *Hum Res	Kansas City	MO	64117	**800-255-1024***	816-221-1024	176-11
Cerner DHT Inc 2800 Rockcreek Pkwy	Kansas City	MO	64119	**866-221-8877**	816-221-1024	176-10
Cerro Coso Community College Mammoth Campus PO Box 1865	Mammoth Lakes	CA	93546	**888-537-6932**	760-934-2875	160
Cerro Flow Products Inc 3000 Mississippi Ave	Sauget	IL	62206	**888-237-7611**	618-337-6000	481
Cerro Wire & Cable Co Inc 1099 Thompson Rd SE	Hartselle	AL	35640	**800-523-3869**	256-773-2522	800
Cersosimo Lumber Co Inc 1103 Vernon St	Brattleboro	VT	05301	**800-326-5647**	802-254-4508	671
Certa ProPainters Ltd 150 Green Tree Rd Suite 1003	Oaks	PA	19456	**800-462-3782**	610-983-9411	188-8
CertainTeed Corp 750 E Swedesford Rd *Prod Info	Valley Forge	PA	19482	**800-782-8777***	610-341-7000	382
Certicom Corp 5520 Explorer Dr 4th Fl	Mississauga	ON	L4W5L1	**800-561-6100**	905-507-4220	176-12
Certification of Computing Professionals. Institute for 2350 E Devon Ave Suite 115	Des Plaines	IL	60018	**800-843-8227**	847-299-4227	48-9
Certified Alloy Products Inc 3245 Cherry Ave	Long Beach	CA	90807	**800-421-3763**	562-595-6621	476
Certified Coatings of California 1045 Detroit Ave	Concord	CA	94518	**888-686-5551**	925-686-1550	188-8
Certified Dental Laboratory Inc 3206 N Kilpatrick Ave	Chicago	IL	60641	**800-458-3384**	773-205-6600	406
Certified Electronic Display Inc 3121 N Adart Rd	Stockton	CA	95215	**800-350-7773**	209-931-7850	692
Certified Financial Planner Board of Standards Inc 1670 Broadway Suite 600	Denver	CO	80202	**888-237-6275**	303-830-7500	49-2
Certified Horsemanship Assn (CHA) 5318 Old Bullard Rd	Tyler	TX	75703	**800-399-0138**	903-509-2473	48-3
Certified HR Services 5101 NW 21st Ave Suite 350	Fort Lauderdale	FL	33309	**800-793-2872**	954-677-0202	619
Certified Power Inc 970 Campus Dr	Mundelein	IL	60060	**800-877-8350**	847-573-3800	609
Certified Professional Managers. Institute of James Madison University MSC 5504	Harrisonburg	VA	22807	**800-568-4120**	540-568-3247	49-12

Entry	City	State	ZIP	Toll-Free	Phone	Class
Certified Public Accountants. American Institute of 1211 Ave of the Americas	New York	NY	10036	**888-777-7077**	212-596-6200	49-1
Certified Public Accountants. American Woman's Society of 136 S Keowee St	Dayton	OH	45402	**800-297-2721**	937-222-1872	49-1
Certified Transmission Rebuilders Inc 1801 S 54th St	Omaha	NE	68106	**800-554-7520**	402-558-2117	62-6
Certified Vacations Group Inc 110 E Broward Blvd	Fort Lauderdale	FL	33301	**800-233-7260**	954-522-1440	760
CertifiedMail.com Inc 35 Airport Rd Suite 120	Morristown	NJ	07960	**800-672-7233**	973-455-1245	176-7
Certis USA 9145 Guilford Rd Suite 175	Columbia	MD	21046	**800-847-5620**	301-604-7340	276
Cervical Cancer Prevention Resource Center. National HPV & PO Box 13827	Research Triangle Park	NC	27709	**800-277-8922**	919-361-8400	48-17
Cervical Pathology. American Society for Colposcopy & 20 W Washington St Suite 1	Hagerstown	MD	21740	**800-787-7227**	301-733-3640	49-8
Cervitor Kitchens Inc 10775 Lower Azusa Rd	El Monte	CA	91731	**800-523-2666**	626-443-0184	36
Cesarean Awareness Network Inc. International 1304 Kingsdale Ave	Redondo Beach	CA	90278	**800-686-4226**	310-542-6400	48-17
Cessford Construction Co 3808 Old Hwy 61	Burlington	IA	52601	**800-747-2297**	319-753-2297	493-5
Cetac Technologies Inc 14306 Industrial Rd	Omaha	NE	68144	**800-369-2822**	402-733-2829	410
CETCO (Colloid Environmental Technologies Co) 1500 W Shure Dr	Arlington Heights	IL	60004	**800-527-9948**	847-392-5800	3
CF Burger Creamery Co 8101 Greenfield Rd	Detroit	MI	48228	**800-229-2322**	313-584-4040	291-27
CF Martin & Co Inc DBA Martin Guitar Co 510 Sycamore St	Nazareth	PA	18064	**800-345-3103**	610-759-2837	516
CFA Institute 560 Ray C Hunt Dr PO Box 3668	Charlottesville	VA	22903	**800-247-8132**	434-951-5499	49-2
CFC International Inc 500 State St *NASDAQ: CFCI*	Chicago Heights	IL	60411	**800-323-3399**	708-891-3456	3
CFCA (Christian Foundation for Children & Aging) 1 Elmwood Ave	Kansas City	KS	66103	**800-875-6564**	913-384-6500	48-6
CFHS (Canadian Federation of Humane Societies) 30 Concourse Gate Suite 102	Ottawa	ON	K2E7V7	**888-678-2347**	613-224-8072	48-3
CFO Magazine 253 Summer St	Boston	MA	02210	**800-877-5416**	617-345-9700	449-5
CFTC (Commodity Futures Trading Commission) 1155 21 St NW 3 Lafayette Ctr	Washington	DC	20581	**866-366-2382**	202-418-5080	336-16
CFTO-TV Ch 9 (CTV) 9 Channel 9 Ct	Toronto	ON	M4A2M9	**800-668-0060**	416-332-5000	726
CG Schmidt Inc 11777 W Lake Pk Dr	Milwaukee	WI	53224	**800-248-1254**	414-577-1177	185
CGAS Exploration Inc 4770 Indianola Ave	Columbus	OH	43214	**800-686-2427**	614-888-9588	525
CGI Information Systems 600 Federal St	Andover	MA	01810	**800-637-3799**	978-946-3000	176-11
CGM Funds 222 Berkeley St Suite 1013	Boston	MA	02116	**800-345-4048**	617-859-7714	517
CGM Inc 1445 Ford Rd	Bensalem	PA	19020	**800-523-6570**	215-638-4400	135
CH & E Mfg Co 3849 N Palmer St *Cust Svc	Milwaukee	WI	53212	**800-236-0666***	414-964-3400	627
CH Ellis Co Inc 2432 Southeastern Ave *Sales	Indianapolis	IN	46201	**800-466-3351***	317-636-3351	444
CH Hanson Co 3630 N Wolf Rd	Franklin Park	IL	60131	**800-827-3398**	847-451-0500	459
CH Robinson Worldwide Inc 8100 Mitchell Rd Suite 200 *NASDAQ: CHRW*	Eden Prairie	MN	55344	**800-247-5644**	952-937-8500	440
CHA (Certified Horsemanship Assn) 5318 Old Bullard Rd	Tyler	TX	75703	**800-399-0138**	903-509-2473	48-3
CHA (Craft & Hobby Assn) 319 E 54th St	Elmwood Park	NJ	07407	**800-822-0494**	201-794-1133	48-18
Chace Leather Products 507 Alden St	Fall River	MA	02723	**800-272-4223**	508-678-7556	423
Chad Therapeutics Inc 21622 Plummer St *AMEX: CTU*	Chatsworth	CA	91311	**800-423-8870**	818-882-0883	468
CHADD (Children & Adults with Attention-Deficit/Hyperactivity Disorder) 8181 Professional Pl Suite 201	Landover	MD	20785	**800-233-4050**	301-306-7070	48-17
Chadderton Trucking Inc PO Box 687	Sharon	PA	16146	**800-942-8074**	724-981-5050	769
Chadron State College 1000 Main St	Chadron	NE	69337	**800-242-3766**	308-432-6263	163
Chadwick-BaRoss Inc 160 Warren Ave	Westbrook	ME	04092	**800-477-4963**	207-854-8411	353
Chadwick's of Boston 35 United Dr	West Bridgewater	MA	02379	**800-677-0340**	508-583-8110	451
Chain Drug Marketing Assn (CDMA) 43157 W Nine-Mile Rd PO Box 995	Novi	MI	48376	**800-935-2362**	248-449-9300	49-18
Chain Drug Stores. National Assn of 413 N Lee St	Alexandria	VA	22314	**800-678-6223**	703-549-3001	49-18
Chalk & Vermilion Fine Arts Inc 55 Old Post Rd #2	Greenwich	CT	06830	**800-877-2250**	203-869-9500	623-10
Challenge Dairy Products Inc 11875 Dublin Blvd Suite B230	Dublin	CA	94568	**800-733-2374**	925-828-6160	291-3
Challenge Publications Inc 9509 Vassar Ave Suite A	Chatsworth	CA	91311	**800-562-9182**	818-700-6868	623-9
Challenger Center for Space Science Education 1250 N Pitt St	Alexandria	VA	22314	**800-987-8277**	703-683-9740	48-11
Challenger Learning Center 316 Washington Ave Wheeling Jesuit University	Wheeling	WV	26003	**800-624-6992**	304-243-4325	509
Chalmers & Kubeck Inc 150 Commerce Dr	Aston	PA	19014	**800-242-5637**	610-494-4300	446
Chamber of Commerce Executives. American 4875 Eisenhower Ave Suite 250	Alexandria	VA	22304	**800-394-2223**	703-998-0072	49-12
Chamber of Commerce - Grand Haven-Spring Lake-Ferrysburg 1 S Harbor Dr	Grand Haven	MI	49417	**800-303-4096**	616-842-4910	137
Chamber of Commerce of Kitchener & Waterloo 80 Queen St N PO Box 2367	Kitchener	ON	N2H6L4	**888-672-4282**	519-576-5000	136
Chamber of Commerce. US Hispanic 2175 K St NW Suite 100	Washington	DC	20037	**800-874-2286**	202-842-1212	48-14
Chamber of Commerce. US Junior PO Box 7	Tulsa	OK	74102	**800-529-2337**	918-584-2481	48-7
Chamber - Gadsden & Etowah County PO Box 185	Gadsden	AL	35902	**800-238-6924**	256-543-3472	137
Chamber International. Junior 15645 Olive Blvd	Chesterfield	MO	63017	**800-905-5499**	636-449-3100	48-7
Chamber Ogden/Weber 2484 Washington Blvd Suite 400	Ogden	UT	84401	**888-621-8306**	801-621-8300	137
Chamber of Schenectady County 306 State St	Schenectady	NY	12305	**800-962-8007**	518-372-5656	137
Chamberlain Group 845 Larch Ave	Elmhurst	IL	60126	**800-282-6225**	630-279-3600	681
Chamberlain Mfg Corp 845 N Larch Ave	Elmhurst	IL	60126	**800-528-9131**	630-279-3600	794
Chambers Belt Co Inc 3230 E Broadway Rd Suite A-200	Phoenix	AZ	85040	**800-528-1388**	602-276-0016	153-2
Chambre de Commerce du Quebec 576 E Saint Catherine St Suite 200	Montreal	QC	H2L2E1	**888-595-8110**	514-522-1885	136
Chaminade 1 Chaminade Ln	Santa Cruz	CA	95065	**800-283-6569**	831-475-5600	370
Chaminade College Preparatory School 425 S Lindbergh Blvd	Saint Louis	MO	63131	**877-378-6847**	314-993-4400	611
Chaminade University 3140 Waialae Ave	Honolulu	HI	96816	**800-735-3733**	808-735-4711	163
Champagne Theatre 1984 Hwy 165 Welk Resort Ctr	Branson	MO	65616	**800-505-9355**		562
Champaign County Chamber of Commerce 113 Miami St	Urbana	OH	43078	**877-873-5764**	937-653-5764	137
Champaign County Convention & Visitors Bureau 1817 S Neil St Suite 201	Champaign	IL	61820	**800-369-6151**	217-351-4133	205
Champion Air 8009 34th Ave S Suite 500	Bloomington	MN	55425	**800-922-2606**	952-814-8700	14
Champion Auto Stores Inc 2565 Kasota Ave	Saint Paul	MN	55108	**800-899-6528**	651-644-6448	54
Champion Awards Inc 3649 Winplace Rd	Memphis	TN	38118	**800-242-6781**	901-365-4830	675
Champion Bus Inc 331 Graham Rd	Imlay City	MI	48444	**800-776-4943**	810-724-6474	505
Champion Chemical Co 8319 S Greenleaf Ave	Whittier	CA	90602	**800-621-7868**	562-945-1456	149
Champion Co 400 Harrison St *Sales	Springfield	OH	45505	**800-328-0115***	937-324-5681	197
Champion Industries Inc 2450-90 1st Ave *NASDAQ: CHMP*	Huntington	WV	25703	**800-624-3431**	304-528-2791	615
Champion Irrigation Products Inc 3141 N Maxson Rd	El Monte	CA	91732	**800-332-4267**	323-221-2108	598
Champion Manufacturing Industries Inc. 6021 N Galena Rd	Peoria	IL	61614	**800-452-7473**	309-685-1031	584
Champion Nutrition 2615 Stanwell Dr	Concord	CA	94520	**800-225-4831**	925-689-1790	786
Champion Photochemistry 1760 Meyerside Dr	Mississauga	ON	L5T1A3	**800-387-3430**	905-670-7900	580
Champion Products Inc 1000 E Hanes Mill Rd	Winston-Salem	NC	27105	**800-999-2249**	336-519-6500	153-3
Champion Shuffleboard Ltd 7216 Burns St	Richland Hills	TX	76118	**800-598-2881**	817-284-3499	701
Champion Solutions Group 791 Park of Commerce Blvd	Boca Raton	FL	33487	**800-771-7000**	561-997-2900	172
Champion Turf Equipment Inc 330 S Mission Rd	Los Angeles	CA	90033	**800-421-6171**	323-264-0746	423
Champlain Cable Corp 175 Hercules Dr	Colchester	VT	05446	**800-451-5162**	802-654-4200	801
Champlain College PO Box 670	Burlington	VT	05402	**800-570-5858**	802-658-0800	160
Champps Entertainment Inc 10375 Park Meadows Dr Suite 560 *NASDAQ: CMPP*	Littleton	CO	80124	**800-461-5965**	303-804-1333	656
Champps Restaurants & Bar 10375 Park Meadows Dr Suite 560	Littleton	CO	80124	**800-461-5965**	303-804-1333	657
Champs Software Inc 1255 N Vantage Pt Dr	Crystal River	FL	34429	**800-322-6647**	352-795-2362	176-1
Champs Sports 311 Manatee Ave W	Bradenton	FL	34205	**800-991-6813**	941-748-0577	702
Chance Rides Mfg Inc 4219 Irving St	Wichita	KS	67209	**800-242-6231**	316-942-7411	505
Chancellor Hotel on Union Square 433 Powell St	San Francisco	CA	94102	**800-428-4748**	415-362-2004	373
Chandler Chamber of Commerce 25 S Arizona Pl Suite 201	Chandler	AZ	85225	**800-963-4571**	480-963-4571	137
Chandler Inn 26 Chandler St	Boston	MA	02116	**800-842-3450**	617-482-3450	373
Chandler Regional Hospital 475 S Dobson Rd	Chandler	AZ	85224	**800-350-4677**	480-963-4561	366-2
Chandlers Plywood Products Inc PO Box 9009	Huntington	WV	25704	**800-624-3502**	304-429-1311	116
Chanel Inc 9 W 57th St 44th Fl	New York	NY	10019	**800-550-0005**	212-688-5055	564
Chaney Enterprises PO Box 548	Waldorf	MD	20604	**800-492-3495**	301-932-5000	181
Chang Richard Assoc 15265 Alton Pkwy Suite 300	Irvine	CA	92618	**800-756-8096**	949-727-7477	193
Channel Inn Hotel 650 Water St SW	Washington	DC	20024	**800-368-5668**	202-554-2400	373
Channel Islands Inn & Suites 1001 E Channel Islands Blvd	Oxnard	CA	93033	**800-344-5998**	805-487-7755	373
Channell Commercial Corp 250 Ynez Rd *NASDAQ: CHNL*	Temecula	CA	92591	**800-423-1863**	951-719-2600	633
Channellock Inc 1306 S Main St *Cust Svc	Meadville	PA	16335	**800-724-3018***	814-724-8700	746
Channing L Bete Co Inc 1 Community Pl	South Deerfield	MA	01373	**800-628-7733**	413-665-7611	623-10
Chantal Cookware Corp 2030 West Sam Houston Pkwy N	Houston	TX	77043	**800-365-4354**	713-467-9949	477
Chanticleer Inn 1458 E Dollar Lake Rd	Eagle River	WI	54521	**800-752-9193**	715-479-4486	655

Name / Address	City	State	ZIP	Toll-Free	Phone	Class
CHAP (Community Health Accreditation Program Inc) 39 Broadway Suite 710	New York	NY	10006	**800-656-9656**	212-480-8828	48-1
Chaparral Suites Resort & Conference Center 5001 N Scottsdale Rd	Scottsdale	AZ	85250	**800-528-1456**	480-949-1414	655
Chapel Hill News 505 W Franklin St	Chapel Hill	NC	27516	**800-365-6115**	919-932-2000	522-4
Chapel Hill/Orange County Visitors Bureau 501 W Franklin St	Chapel Hill	NC	27516	**888-968-2060**	919-968-2060	205
Chapel Services Inc 1212 W Main St	Richmond	KY	40475	**888-747-4949**	859-623-1500	795
Chapin Watermatics Inc 740 Water St	Watertown	NY	13601	**800-242-7467**	315-782-1170	364
Chapman RE Co 30 N Main St	West Boylston	MA	01583	**800-727-6231**	508-835-6231	188-16
Chapman/Leonard Studio Equipment Inc 12950 Raymer St	North Hollywood	CA	91605	**888-883-6559**	818-764-6726	708
Char-Broil 1442 Belfast Ave *Cust Svc	Columbus	GA	31904	**800-352-4111***	706-324-0421	36
Charbert Inc 299 Church St	Alton	RI	02894	**800-570-2184**	401-364-7751	730-4
Chardon Rubber Co 373 Washington St	Chardon	OH	44024	**800-322-0193**	440-285-2161	664
Chargeurs Inc 421 S Union St	Troy	OH	45373	**800-561-7981**	937-335-5611	544
Charisma Magazine 600 Rinehart Rd	Lake Mary	FL	32746	**800-829-3346**	407-333-0000	449-10
Charitable Gift Fund. Fidelity Investments PO Box 55158	Boston	MA	02205	**800-682-4438**		397
Charitable Trusts. Pew 2005 Market St 1 Commerce Sq Suite 1700	Philadelphia	PA	19103	**800-634-4850**	215-575-9050	300
Charities of America. Independent 21 Tamal Vista Blvd Suite 209	Corte Madera	CA	94925	**800-477-0733**		48-5
Charities. American Lebanese Syrian Associated 501 St Jude Pl	Memphis	TN	38105	**800-822-6344**	901-578-2000	48-5
Charities. Community Health 200 N Glebe Rd Suite 801	Arlington	VA	22203	**800-654-0845**	703-528-1007	48-5
Charities. International Orthodox Christian 110 West Rd Suite 360	Baltimore	MD	21204	**877-803-4622**	410-243-9820	48-5
Charles Alfieri Studio 4390 N Federal Hwy Suite 203	Fort Lauderdale	FL	33308	**800-321-2413**	954-928-1755	342
Charles Beseler Co 1501 Oakland Ave	Millville	NJ	08332	**800-237-3537**		580
Charles Bond Co 11 Green St PO Box 105 *Cust Svc	Christiana	PA	17509	**800-922-0125***	610-593-5171	700
Charles C Thomas Publisher 2600 S 1st St *Sales	Springfield	IL	62704	**800-258-8980***	217-789-8980	623-2
Charles Craft Inc 21381 Charles Craft Ln PO Box 1049	Laurinburg	NC	28352	**800-277-1009**	910-844-3521	730-9
Charles E Smith Corporate Living 400 15th St S	Arlington	VA	22202	**888-234-7829**	703-920-9550	209
Charles G Buchy Packing Co PO Box 899	Greenville	OH	45331	**800-762-1060**	937-548-2128	465
Charles GG Schmidt & Co Inc 301 W Grand Ave	Montvale	NJ	07645	**800-724-6438**	201-391-5300	746
Charles Hotel Harvard Square 1 Bennett St	Cambridge	MA	02138	**800-882-1818**	617-864-1200	373
Charles House & Sons Inc 235 Singleton St	Woonsocket	RI	02895	**800-243-7063**	401-769-0189	730-8
Charles Inc 518 N 10th St	Council Bluffs	IA	51503	**800-831-5878**	712-328-2603	314-2
Charles Industries Ltd 5600 Apollo Dr	Rolling Meadows	IL	60008	**800-458-4747**	847-806-6300	720
Charles Jones Inc PO Box 8488	Trenton	NJ	08650	**800-792-8888**	609-538-1000	621
Charles L Crane Agency Co 100 S 4th St Suite 800	Saint Louis	MO	63102	**800-363-9827**	314-241-8700	383
Charles Leonard Inc 79-11 Cooper Ave	Glendale	NY	11385	**800-999-7202**	718-894-4851	345
Charles M Sledd Co 100 E Cove Ext	Wheeling	WV	26003	**800-333-0374**	304-243-1820	744
Charles Machine Works Inc PO Box 66	Perry	OK	73077	**800-654-6481**	580-336-4402	189
Charles Mix Electric Assn Inc 440 Lake St	Lake Andes	SD	57356	**800-208-8587**	605-487-7321	244
Charles of the Ritz 237 Park Ave *Consumer Info	New York	NY	10017	**800-473-8566***	212-527-4000	564
Charles River Laboratories Inc 251 Ballardvale St *NYSE: CRL*	Wilmington	MA	01887	**800-522-7287**	978-658-6000	654
Charles Ross & Son Co 710 Old Willets Path	Hauppauge	NY	11788	**800-243-7677**	631-234-0500	379
Charles Ryan Assoc Inc 300 Summer St Suite 1100	Charleston	WV	25301	**877-342-0161**	304-342-0161	622
Charles Schneider Furniture 518 N 10th St	Council Bluffs	IA	51503	**800-831-5878**	712-328-1587	314-2
Charles Schwab & Co Inc 101 Montgomery St *Cust Svc	San Francisco	CA	94104	**800-435-4000***	415-627-7000	679
Charles Schwab Corp 101 Montgomery St *NYSE: SCH*	San Francisco	CA	94104	**800-648-5300**	415-627-7000	355-3
Charles Stark Draper Laboratory Inc 555 Technology Sq	Cambridge	MA	02139	**800-676-1977**	617-258-1000	654
Charles Town Races & Slots US Rt 340	Charles Town	WV	25414	**800-795-7001**		628
Charleston Area Convention & Visitors Bureau 423 King St	Charleston	SC	29403	**800-868-8118**	843-853-8000	205
Charleston Auto Parts Inc DBA CAP Warehouse 3108 Losee Rd	North Las Vegas	NV	89030	**800-879-7901**	702-642-7801	61
Charleston Convention & Visitors Bureau 200 Civic Center Dr	Charleston	WV	25301	**800-733-5469**	304-344-5075	205
Charleston Daily Mail 1001 Virginia St E	Charleston	WV	25301	**800-982-6397**	304-348-5140	522-2
Charleston Gazette 1001 Virginia St E	Charleston	WV	25301	**800-982-6397**	304-348-5140	522-2
Charleston Harbor Resort & Marina. Hilton 20 Patriots Point Rd	Mount Pleasant	SC	29464	**800-445-8667**	843-856-0028	655

Name / Address	City	State	ZIP	Toll-Free	Phone	Class
Charleston Place 205 Meeting St	Charleston	SC	29401	**800-611-5545**	843-722-4900	373
Charleston Southern University 9200 University Blvd	Charleston	SC	29406	**800-947-7474**	843-863-7000	163
Charleston Stage Co 135 Church St	Charleston	SC	29401	**800-454-7093**	843-577-5967	563-4
Charley's Eating & Drinking Saloon 284 Newbury St	Boston	MA	02115	**800-424-2753**	617-536-2800	657
Charley's Grilled Subs 2500 Farmers Dr Suite 140	Columbus	OH	43235	**800-437-8325**	614-923-4700	657
Charley's Steakery 2500 Farmers Dr	Columbus	OH	43235	**800-437-8325**	614-923-4700	657
Charlie Brown's Steakhouse Inc 1450 Rt 22 W	Mountainside	NJ	07092	**800-518-1855**	908-518-1800	657
Charlotte Business Journal 120 W Morehead St Suite 200	Charlotte	NC	28202	**800-948-5323**	704-973-1100	449-5
Charlotte Convention & Visitors Bureau 500 S College St Suite 300	Charlotte	NC	28202	**800-722-1994**	704-334-2282	205
Charlotte County Memorial Auditorium 75 Taylor St	Punta Gorda	FL	33950	**800-329-9988**	941-639-5833	562
Charlotte Institute of Rehabilitation 1100 Blythe Blvd	Charlotte	NC	28203	**800-634-2256**	704-355-4300	366-4
Charlotte Nature Museum 1658 Sterling Rd	Charlotte	NC	28209	**800-935-0553**	704-372-6261	509
Charlotte Observer 600 S Tryon St	Charlotte	NC	28202	**800-332-0686**	704-358-5000	522-2
Charlotte Pipe & Foundry Co 2109 Randolph Rd	Charlotte	NC	28207	**800-432-6172**	704-372-5030	481
Charlotte Pipe & Foundry Co Plastics Div PO Box 1339 *Sales	Monroe	NC	28111	**800-438-6091***	704-289-2531	585
Charlotte Russe 4645 Morena Blvd	San Diego	CA	92117	**877-266-9327**	858-587-9900	155-6
Charmant Group Inc 400 American Rd	Morris Plains	NJ	07950	**800-645-2121**	973-538-1511	531
Charmer Industries Inc 19-50 48th St	Astoria	NY	11105	**800-834-3546**	718-726-2500	82-3
Charmilles Technologies Corp 560 Bond St	Lincolnshire	IL	60069	**800-282-1336**	847-913-5300	447
Charms Co 7401 S Cicero Ave	Chicago	IL	60629	**800-877-7655**	773-838-3400	291-8
Charnstrom WA Co 5391 12th Ave E *Cust Svc	Shakopee	MN	55379	**800-328-2962***	952-403-0303	462
Charrette Corp 31 Olympia Ave	Woburn	MA	01801	**800-747-3776**	781-935-6000	45
Chart House Restaurants 1510 W Loop South	Houston	TX	77027	**800-552-6379**	713-850-1010	657
Charter at Beaver Creek 120 Offerson Rd PO Box 5310	Avon	CO	81620	**800-525-6660**	970-949-6660	373
Charter Club Resort on Naples Bay 1000 10th Ave S	Naples	FL	34102	**800-494-5559**	239-261-5559	655
Charter Financial Corp 600 3rd Ave *NASDAQ: CHFN*	West Point	GA	31833	**800-763-4444**	706-645-1391	355-2
Charter Flight Inc 5400 Airport Dr	Charlotte	NC	28208	**800-521-3148**	704-359-9124	14
Charter One Bank 1215 Superior Ave	Cleveland	OH	44114	**800-553-8981**	216-566-5300	71
Charter One Mortgage 10561 Telegraph Rd	Glen Allen	VA	23059	**800-876-2434**	804-627-4000	498
Charter Services Inc 8400 Airport Blvd Bldg 31	Mobile	AL	36608	**800-657-1555**	251-633-6090	14
Charter Wire 114 N Jackson St	Milwaukee	WI	53202	**800-436-9074**	414-390-3000	800
CharterBank 600 3rd Ave	West Point	GA	31833	**800-763-4444**	706-645-1391	71
CharterMac 625 Madison Ave *AMEX: CHC*	New York	NY	10022	**800-600-6422**	212-421-5333	498
Chartist Newsletter 6621 E Pacific Coast Hwy Suite 200	Long Beach	CA	90803	**800-942-4278**	562-596-2385	521-9
Chartpak Inc 1 River Rd	Leeds	MA	01053	**800-628-1910**	413-584-5446	43
Charts Inc 12977 Arroyo St	San Fernando	CA	91340	**800-882-9357**	818-898-3707	616
Chartway Federal Credit Union 160 Newtown Rd	Virginia Beach	VA	23462	**800-678-8765**	757-552-1000	216
Chas Levy Circulating Co 1930 George St Unit 1	Melrose Park	IL	60160	**800-549-5389**		97
Chase Bank 1 Chase Manhattan Plaza	New York	NY	10081	**800-935-9935**	212-270-6000	71
Chase Brass & Copper Co 14212 County Rd 50 PO Box 152	Montpelier	OH	43543	**800-537-4291**	419-485-3193	476
Chase Hotel at Palm Springs 200 W Arenas Rd	Palm Springs	CA	92262	**877-532-4273**	760-320-8866	373
Chase Insurance Co 2500 Westfield Drive	Elgin	IL	60123	**800-321-9313**	847-930-7000	384-2
Chase Manhattan Mortgage Corp 343 Thornall St	Edison	NJ	08837	**800-848-9136**	732-205-0600	498
Chase Packaging Inc 1300 Marshall Ave *Cust Svc	Newport News	VA	23607	**800-532-3345***	757-247-6676	66
Chase Suite Hotels by Woodfin 12730 High Bluff Dr Suite 250	San Diego	CA	92130	**800-237-8811**	858-794-2338	369
Chase-Walton Elastomers Inc 29 Apsley St	Hudson	MA	01749	**800-448-6289**	978-562-0085	364
Chateau Bonne Entente 3400 ch Sainte-Foy	Sainte-Foy	QC	G1X1S6	**800-463-4390**	418-653-5221	372
Chateau Dupre Hotel 131 Rue Decatur	New Orleans	LA	70130	**800-256-0135**	504-569-0600	373
Chateau Edmonton Hotel & Suites 7230 Argyll Rd	Edmonton	AB	T6C4A6	**800-465-3648**	780-465-7931	372
Chateau Elan Resort & Conference Center 100 rue Charlemagne	Braselton	GA	30517	**800-233-9463**	678-425-0900	370
Chateau Elan Spa at the Chateau Elan Atlanta 100 Rue Charlemagne	Braselton	GA	30542	**800-233-9463**	678-425-6064	698
Chateau Elan Winery 100 Tour de France	Braselton	GA	30517	**800-233-9463**	678-425-0900	50
Chateau Hotel & Conference Center 1601 Jumer Dr	Bloomington	IL	61704	**800-285-8637**	309-662-2020	373
Chateau Inn 5113 E McKinley Ave	Fresno	CA	93727	**800-445-2428**	559-456-1418	373
Chateau Julien Wine Estate 8940 Carmel Valley Rd	Carmel	CA	93923	**800-966-2601**	831-624-2600	50
Chateau Lacombe Edmonton. Crowne Plaza Hotel 10111 Bellamy Hill	Edmonton	AB	T5J1N7	**800-661-8801**	780-428-6611	372
Chateau on the Lake 415 N State Hwy 265	Branson	MO	65616	**888-333-5253**	417-334-1161	373
Chateau LeMoyne. Holiday Inn New Orleans 301 Rue Dauphine	New Orleans	LA	70112	**800-747-3279**	504-581-1303	373

Name / Address	City	State	Zip	Toll-Free	Phone	Class
Chateau Louis Hotel & Conference Centre 11727 Kingsway	Edmonton	AB	T5G3A1	**800-661-9843**	780-452-7770	372
Chateau Marmont Hotel 8221 Sunset Blvd	Hollywood	CA	90046	**800-242-8328**	323-656-1010	373
Chateau de La Mer Resort Inn 1410 Beach Blvd	Gulfport	MS	39507	**800-257-5551**	228-896-1703	373
Chateau Royal Hotel Suites 1420 Rue Crescent	Montreal	QC	H3G2B7	**800-363-0335**	514-848-0999	372
Chateau Sonesta Hotel New Orleans 800 Iberville St	New Orleans	LA	70112	**800-766-3782**	504-586-0800	373
Chateau Ste Michelle Winery 14111 NE 145th St	Woodinville	WA	98072	**800-267-6793**	425-415-3300	50
Chateau Versailles 1659 Sherbrooke St W	Montreal	QC	H3H1E3	**888-933-8111**	514-933-8111	372
Châtelaine Magazine 1 Mt Pleasant Rd 8th Fl	Toronto	ON	M4Y2Y5	**800-268-9119**	416-764-1888	449-11
Chatham Bars Inn 297 Shore Rd	Chatham	MA	02633	**800-527-4884**	508-945-0096	655
Chatham College Woodland Rd	Pittsburgh	PA	15232	**800-837-1290**	412-365-1100	163
Chatham Steel Corp 501 W Boundary St	Savannah	GA	31402	**800-546-2650**	912-233-4182	483
Chatham Village Foods Div T Marzetti Co 15 Kendrick Rd	Wareham	MA	02571	**800-771-3888**	508-291-2304	291-9
Chatsworth Data Corp 20710 Lassen St	Chatsworth	CA	91311	**800-423-5217**	818-341-9200	247
Chatsworth-Murray County Chamber of Commerce 126 N 3rd Ave	Chatsworth	GA	30705	**800-969-9490**	706-695-6060	137
Chatsworth Products Inc 31425 Agoura Rd	Westlake Village	CA	91361	**800-834-4969**	818-735-6100	174
Chattanooga Area Convention & Visitors Bureau 2 Broad St	Chattanooga	TN	37402	**800-322-3344**	423-756-8687	205
Chattanooga Bakery Inc 900 Manufacture Rd	Chattanooga	TN	37401	**800-251-3404**	423-267-3351	291-1
Chattanooga Convention Center 1 Carter Plaza	Chattanooga	TN	37402	**800-962-5213**	423-756-0001	204
Chattanooga Group 4717 Adams Rd	Hixson	TN	37343	**800-592-7329**	423-870-2281	469
Chattanooga Publishing Co 400 E 11th St	Chattanooga	TN	37403	**800-733-2637**	423-756-6900	623-8
Chattanoogan The 1201 S Broad St	Chattanooga	TN	37402	**877-756-1684**	423-756-3400	370
Chattem Inc 1715 W 38th St *NASDAQ: CHTT*	Chattanooga	TN	37409	**800-366-6077**	423-821-4571	211
Chautauqua County Visitors Bureau PO Box 1441	Chautauqua	NY	14722	**800-242-4569**	716-357-4569	205
CHC Industries 3055 Ruen Dr	Palm Harbor	FL	34685	**800-242-3665**	727-789-3000	344
Cheap Tickets Inc 7 Sylvan Way	Parsippany	NJ	07054	**888-922-8849**		762
Check Point Software Technologies Ltd 800 Bridge Pkwy *NASDAQ: CHKP*	Redwood City	CA	94065	**800-429-4391**	650-628-2000	176-12
Check Printers Inc 1530 Antioch Pike	Antioch	TN	37013	**800-766-1217**	615-277-7100	140
CheckCrafters Inc PO Box 100	Edgewood	MD	21040	**888-404-5245**		140
Checkers Drive-In Restaurants Inc 4300 W Cypress St Suite 600 *NASDAQ: CHKR*	Tampa	FL	33607	**800-800-8072**	813-283-7000	657
CheckFree Corp 4411 E Jones Bridge Rd *NASDAQ: CKFR* ■ *Cust Svc	Norcross	GA	30092	**800-305-3716***	678-375-3000	250
CheckPoint HR 2035 Lincoln Hwy Suite 1080	Edison	NJ	08817	**800-385-0331**	732-287-8270	559
Checkpoint Systems Inc 101 Wolf Dr *NYSE: CKP*	Thorofare	NJ	08086	**800-257-5540**	856-848-1800	681
Checks & Balances Inc 10328 Battleview Pkwy	Manassas	VA	20109	**800-624-3698**	703-361-2220	619
Checks In The Mail Inc 2435 Goodwin Ln	New Braunfels	TX	78135	**800-639-2432**	830-609-5500	140
Checks Unlimited PO Box 35630	Colorado Springs	CO	80935	**800-565-8332**		140
Cheeburger Cheeburger Restaurants Inc 15951 McGregor Blvd Suite 2A	Fort Myers	FL	33908	**800-487-6211**	239-437-1611	657
Cheeca Lodge & Spa MM 82 81801 Overseas Hwy	Islamorada	FL	33036	**800-327-2888**	305-664-4651	655
Chef & Child Foundation. American Culinary Federation 180 Center Place Way	Saint Augustine	FL	32095	**800-624-9458**	904-824-4468	48-6
Chef Solutions Inc 1000 Universal Dr	North Haven	CT	06473	**800-877-1157**	203-234-0115	291-2
Chef's Catalog 5950 Cowell Blvd *Cust Svc	Irving	TX	75039	**800-884-2433***	972-969-3100	357
Chell Group Corp 14 Meteor Dr	Toronto	ON	M9W1A4	**866-455-2435**	416-675-0874	779
Chelsea Inn 46 W 17th St	New York	NY	10011	**800-640-6469**	212-645-8989	373
Chelsea Inn Hotel 3836 Spenard Rd	Anchorage	AK	99517	**800-770-5002**	907-276-5002	373
Chelsea Moore Co 8940 Glendale Milford Rd	Loveland	OH	45140	**888-621-1161**	513-561-5454	638
Chelsea Savoy Hotel 204 W 23rd St	New York	NY	10011	**866-929-9353**	212-929-9353	373
Chem-Dry Carpet Drapery & Upholstery Cleaning 1530 N 1000 W	Logan	UT	84321	**800-841-6583**	435-755-0099	150
Chem Lab Products Inc 5160 E Airport Dr	Ontario	CA	91761	**800-745-4536**	909-390-9912	143
Chem-Nuclear Systems Inc 140 Stoneridge Dr	Columbia	SC	29210	**800-925-1592**	803-256-0450	653
Chem-Tainer Industries Inc 361 Neptune Ave	North Babylon	NY	11704	**800-275-2436**	631-661-8300	198
Chem-Trend Inc PO Box 860	Howell	MI	48844	**800-727-7730**	517-546-4520	530
Chem USA Corp 8445 Central Ave	Newark	CA	94560	**800-866-2436**	510-608-8818	171-3
Chematics Inc Hwy 13 S PO Box 293	North Webster	IN	46555	**800-348-5174**	574-834-2406	229
Chemcentral Corp 7050 W 71st St	Bedford Park	IL	60499	**800-331-6174**	708-594-7000	144
Chemed Corp 255 E 5th St Chemed Ctr Suite 2600 *NYSE: CHE*	Cincinnati	OH	45202	**800-224-3633**	513-762-6900	184
Chemetal 39 O'Neil St	Easthampton	MA	01027	**800-807-7341**	413-529-0718	290
Chemetall Oakite 50 Valley Rd	Berkeley Heights	NJ	07922	**800-526-4473**	908-464-6900	143
Chemetron Fire Systems 4801 Southwick Dr 3rd Fl *Cust Svc	Matteson	IL	60443	**800-878-5631***	708-748-1503	681
Chemical Abstracts Service (CAS) PO Box 3012	Columbus	OH	43210	**800-848-6538**	614-447-3600	380
Chemical & Associated Technologies Assn. Drug 1 Washington Blvd Suite 7	Robbinsville	NJ	08691	**800-640-3228**	609-448-1000	49-19
Chemical Coatings Inc 22 S Center St	Hickory	NC	28603	**800-522-8266**	828-728-8266	540
Chemical Engineering Magazine 110 William St 11th Fl	New York	NY	10038	**800-340-6539**	212-621-4900	449-21
Chemical & Engineering News 1155 16th St NW	Washington	DC	20036	**800-227-5558**	202-872-4600	449-21
Chemical Engineers. American Institute of 3 Park Ave *Cust Svc	New York	NY	10016	**800-242-4363***	212-591-7338	49-19
Chemical Equipment Magazine 301 Gibraltar Dr *Cust Svc	Morris Plains	NJ	07950	**800-446-6551***	973-292-5100	449-21
Chemical Financial Corp 333 E Main St *NASDAQ: CHFC*	Midland	MI	48640	**800-722-6050**	989-839-5350	355-2
Chemical Lime Co PO Box 985004	Fort Worth	TX	76185	**800-365-6724**	817-732-8164	432
Chemical Manufacturers Assn. Synthetic Organic 1850 M St NW Suite 700	Washington	DC	20036	**888-377-0778**	202-721-4100	49-19
Chemical Packaging Corp 2700 SW 14th St *Cust Svc	Pompano Beach	FL	33069	**800-327-1835***	954-974-5440	143
Chemical Processing Magazine 555 W Pierce Rd Suite 301	Itasca	IL	60143	**800-984-7644**	630-467-1300	449-21
Chemical Safety Corp 5901 Christie Ave Suite 502	Emeryville	CA	94608	**888-594-1100**	510-594-1000	39
Chemical Society. American 1155 16th St NW	Washington	DC	20036	**800-227-5558**	202-872-4600	49-19
Chemical Specialties Mfg Corp (Chemspec) 901 N Newkirk St *Sales	Baltimore	MD	21205	**800-638-7370***	410-675-4800	149
Chemical Week Assoc 110 William St	New York	NY	10038	**800-774-5733**	212-621-4900	623-9
Chemical Week Magazine 110 William St *Cust Svc	New York	NY	10038	**800-927-3430***	212-621-4900	449-21
Chemically Dependent Anonymous (CDA) PO Box 4425	Annapolis	MD	21403	**800-232-4673**	410-369-6556	48-21
Chemicon International Inc 28820 Single Oak Dr	Temecula	CA	92590	**800-437-7500**	951-676-8080	229
Chemineer Inc 5870 Poe Ave	Dayton	OH	45414	**800-643-0641**	937-454-3200	379
Chemistry Inc. American Assn for Clinical 2101 L St NW Suite 202 *Cust Svc	Washington	DC	20037	**800-892-1400***	202-857-0717	49-19
Chemistry. Society of Environmental Toxicology & 1010 N 12th Ave	Pensacola	FL	32501	**888-899-2088**	850-469-1500	49-19
Chemlawn Canada 70 Ronson Dr *Cust Svc	Etobicoke	ON	M9W1B9	**800-565-5296***	416-614-6677	421
Chempower Inc 1501 Raff Rd SW	Canton	OH	44710	**800-442-4299**	330-479-4202	188-9
Chemprene Inc 483 Fishkill Ave	Beacon	NY	12508	**800-431-9981**	845-831-2800	364
ChemPro Inc 141 Venture Blvd PO Box 2708	Spartanburg	SC	29304	**800-835-3712**	864-587-9308	149
Chemroy Canada Inc 106 Summerlea Rd	Brampton	ON	L6T4X3	**888-243-6769**	905-789-0701	144
Chemsolv Inc 1140 Industry Ave SE	Roanoke	VA	24103	**800-523-3099**	540-427-4000	144
Chemspec (Chemical Specialties Mfg Corp) 901 N Newkirk St *Sales	Baltimore	MD	21205	**800-638-7370***	410-675-4800	149
Chemstar Products Co 3915 Hiawatha Ave	Minneapolis	MN	55406	**800-328-5037**	612-722-0079	142
Chemtex International Inc 1979 Eastwood Rd	Wilmington	NC	28403	**877-243-6839**	910-509-4400	258
Chemtrol Div NIBCO Inc 1516 Middlebury St	Elkhart	IN	46516	**800-343-5455**	574-295-3316	585
Chemung County Chamber of Commerce 400 E Church St	Elmira	NY	14901	**800-627-5892**	607-734-5137	137
Chenango County Chamber of Commerce 19 Eaton Ave	Norwich	NY	13815	**800-556-8596**	607-334-1400	137
Chenango Valley Bus Lines Inc 105 Chenango St	Binghamton	NY	13901	**800-647-6471**	607-723-9408	108
Cheney Lime & Cement 478 Graystone Rd	Allgood	AL	35013	**800-752-8282**	205-625-3031	432
Chenille Kraft Co 65 Ambrogio Dr	Gurnee	IL	60031	**800-621-1261**	847-249-2900	242
CHEP USA 8517 S Park Cir	Orlando	FL	32819	**800-432-2437**	407-370-2437	634
Cher-Make Sausage Co 2915 Calumet Ave	Manitowoc	WI	54220	**800-242-7679**	920-683-5980	291-26
Cherokee Brick & Tile Co Inc 3250 Waterville Rd	Macon	GA	31206	**800-277-2745**	478-781-6800	148
Cherokee Electric Co-op 1550 Clarence Chestnut Bypass	Centre	AL	35960	**800-952-2667**	256-927-5524	244
Cherokee Heritage Center & National Museum 21992 S Keeler Rd	Park Hill	OK	74451	**888-999-6007**	918-456-6007	509
Cherokee Park Ranch 436 Cherokee Hills Dr	Livermore	CO	80536	**800-628-0949**	970-493-6522	238
Cherokee Tribal Travel & Promotions 498 Tsali Blvd	Cherokee	NC	28719	**800-438-1601**	828-497-9195	205
Cherry Bekaert & Holland LLP 1700 Bayberry Ct Suite 300	Richmond	VA	23226	**800-849-8281**	804-673-4224	2
Cherry Central Co-op Inc 1771 N US Hwy 31 S PO Box 988	Traverse City	MI	49685	**800-678-1860**	231-946-1860	310-3
Cherry Demolition 6131 Selinsky Rd	Houston	TX	77048	**800-444-1123**	713-987-0000	188-17
Cherry Hill Construction Inc 8211 Washington Blvd	Jessup	MD	20794	**800-262-2606**	410-799-3577	187-4
Cherry-Todd Electric Co-op Inc Hwy 18 PO Box 169	Mission	SD	57555	**800-856-4417**	605-856-4416	244
Cherrydale Farms Inc 1035 Mill Rd	Allentown	PA	18106	**800-333-4525**	610-366-1606	291-8
Cherryland Electric Co-op 5930 US Hwy 31 S	Grawn	MI	49637	**800-442-8616**	231-486-9200	244
Cheryl & Co Inc 646 McCorkle Blvd	Westerville	OH	43082	**800-443-8124**	614-891-8822	69

Name / Address	City	State	ZIP	Toll-Free	Phone	Class
Chesapeake Bay Magazine 1819 Bay Ridge Ave Suite 158	Annapolis	MD	21403	**800-584-5066**	410-263-2662	449-22
Chesapeake Biological Laboratories Inc 1111 S Paca St	Baltimore	MD	21230	**800-441-4225**	410-843-5000	86
Chesapeake Hardwood Products Inc 201 Dexter St W	Chesapeake	VA	23324	**800-446-8162**	757-543-1601	602
Chesapeake Industrial Leasing Co Inc 9512 Harford Rd	Baltimore	MD	21234	**800-782-1022**	410-661-5000	261-4
Chesapeake Life Insurance Co 1331 W Memorial Rd Suite 112	Oklahoma City	OK	73114	**800-725-7887**	405-848-0179	384-2
Chesbro Music Co Inc PO Box 2009 *Cust Svc	Idaho Falls	ID	83403	**800-243-7276***	208-522-8691	516
Cheshire Inn & Lodge 6300 Clayton Rd	Saint Louis	MO	63117	**800-325-7378**	314-647-7300	373
Cheskin Research 255 Shoreline Dr Suite 350	Redwood City	CA	94065	**888-802-8300**	650-802-2100	458
Chess Federation. US 3068 US Rt 9 W Suite 100 *Sales	New Windsor	NY	12553	**800-388-5464***	845-562-8350	48-18
Chess Life Magazine 3068 Rt 9W Suite 100 *Sales	New Windsor	NY	12553	**800-388-5464***	845-562-8350	449-14
Chest Physicians. American College of 3300 Dundee Rd	Northbrook	IL	60062	**800-343-2227**	847-498-1400	49-8
Chester College of New England 40 Chester St	Chester	NH	03036	**800-974-6372**	603-887-4401	160
Chester County Tourist Bureau 400 Exton Square Pkwy	Exton	PA	19341	**800-228-9933**	610-280-6145	205
Chester Fritz Auditorium Yale Dr & University Ave PO Box 9028 University of North Dakota	Grand Forks	ND	58202	**800-375-4068**	701-777-3076	562
Chester-Jensen Co Inc PO Box 908	Chester	PA	19016	**800-685-3750**	610-876-6276	293
Chester Valley Bancorp Inc 100 E Lancaster Ave *NASDAQ: CVAL*	Downingtown	PA	19335	**800-687-4529**	610-269-9700	355-2
Chesterfield Chamber of Commerce 101 Chesterfield Business Pkwy	Chesterfield	MO	63005	**888-242-4262**	636-532-3399	137
Chesterfield Hotel 855 Collins Ave	Miami Beach	FL	33139	**800-244-6088**	305-531-5831	373
Chesterfield Hotel 363 Cocoanut Row	Palm Beach	FL	33480	**800-243-7871**	561-659-5800	373
Chesterfield Mfg Corp 2359 Perimeter Pointe Pkwy	Charlotte	NC	28208	**800-322-1746**	704-283-0001	153-12
Chestnut Hill College 9601 Germantown Ave	Philadelphia	PA	19118	**800-248-0052**	215-248-7000	163
Chestnut Hill Hotel 8229 Germantown Ave	Philadelphia	PA	19118	**800-628-9744**	215-242-5905	373
Chestnut Ridge Foam Inc PO Box 781	Latrobe	PA	15650	**800-234-2734**	724-537-9000	590
Chetola Resort PO Box 17 N Main St	Blowing Rock	NC	28605	**800-243-8652**	828-295-5500	655
Chevrolet Motor Div General Motors Corp 300 Renaissance Ctr *Cust Svc	Detroit	MI	48265	**800-222-1020***	313-556-5000	59
Chevron Canada Ltd 1050 W Pender St Suite 1500	Vancouver	BC	V6E3T4	**800-663-1650**	604-668-5300	570
Chevron Corp 6001 Bollinger Canyon Rd *NYSE: CVX* ■ *Cust Svc	San Ramon	CA	94583	**800-243-8766***	925-842-1000	525
Chevron Energy Solutions 345 California St 32nd Fl	San Francisco	CA	94104	**800-982-6887**		258
Chevron Phillips Chemical Co LP 10001 Six Pines Dr	The Woodlands	TX	77380	**800-231-1212**	832-813-4100	142
Chevron Phillips Chemical Co Performance Pipe Div 5085 W Park Blvd Suite 500	Plano	TX	75093	**800-527-0662**	972-599-6600	585
Chevron Travel Club Inc PO Box P	Concord	CA	94524	**800-222-0585**		53
ChevronTexaco Credit Card Center 2001 Diamond Blvd	Concord	CA	94520	**800-243-8766**	925-842-1000	213
Chevy Chase Bank FSB 7501 Wisconsin Ave	Bethesda	MD	20814	**800-987-2265**	240-497-4102	71
Chevys Inc 2000 Powell St Suite 300	Emeryville	CA	94608	**800-424-3897**	510-768-1400	657
Cheyenne Area Convention & Visitors Bureau 121 W 15th St Suite 202	Cheyenne	WY	82001	**800-426-5009**	307-778-3133	205
Cheyenne Mountain Conference Resort 3225 Broadmoor Valley Rd	Colorado Springs	CO	80906	**800-428-8886**	719-538-4000	370
Cheyenne Newspaper Inc 702 W Lincolnway	Cheyenne	WY	82001	**800-561-6268**	307-634-3361	623-8
Cheyney University of Pennsylvania 1837 University Cir PO Box 200	Cheyney	PA	19319	**800-243-9639**	610-399-2275	163
CHF Industries Inc 1 Park Ave 9th Fl	New York	NY	10016	**800-243-7090**	212-951-7800	731
CHI (Children's Hospice International) 901 N Pitt St Suite 230	Alexandria	VA	22314	**800-242-4453**	703-684-0330	49-8
Chi Omega Fraternity 3395 Players Club Pkwy	Memphis	TN	38125	**800-488-4664**	901-748-8600	48-16
Chicago Board Options Exchange 400 S La Salle St	Chicago	IL	60605	**800-678-4667**	312-786-5600	680
Chicago Board of Trade (CBOT) 141 W Jackson Blvd	Chicago	IL	60604	**800-572-3276**	312-435-3500	680
Chicago Boiler Co 1300 Northwestern Ave	Gurnee	IL	60031	**800-969-7343**	847-662-4000	92
Chicago Boiler Co CB Mills Div 1300 Northwestern Ave	Gurnee	IL	60031	**800-969-7343**	847-662-4000	92
Chicago Convention & Tourism Bureau 2301 S Lake Shore Dr McCormick Complex Lakeside Ctr	Chicago	IL	60616	**800-244-2246**	312-567-8500	205
Chicago Cutting Die Co 3555 Woodhead Dr	Northbrook	IL	60062	**800-747-3437**	847-509-5800	745
Chicago Decal Co 101 Tower Dr	Burr Ridge	IL	60527	**888-332-2577**	630-850-2122	404
Chicago Display Marketing Corp 1999 N Ruby St	Melrose Park	IL	60160	**800-681-4340**	708-681-4340	231
Chicago Dowel Co Inc 4700 W Grand Ave	Chicago	IL	60639	**800-333-6935**	773-622-2000	808
Chicago Extruded Metals Co 1601 S 54th Ave *Cust Svc	Cicero	IL	60804	**800-323-8102***	708-656-7900	476
Chicago Faucet Co 2100 S Clearwater Dr	Des Plaines	IL	60018	**800-323-5060**	847-803-5000	598
Chicago Fire 980 N Michigan Ave Suite 1998	Chicago	IL	60611	**888-657-3473**	312-705-7200	703
Chicago Gasket Co 1285 W North Ave	Chicago	IL	60622	**800-833-5666**	773-486-3060	321
Chicago Heights Steel Acquisition Corp 211 E Main St	Chicago Heights	IL	60411	**800-424-4487**	708-754-0410	709
Chicago Lakeshore Hospital 4840 N Marine Dr	Chicago	IL	60640	**800-888-0560**	773-878-9700	366-3
Chicago Lumber Co of Omaha 1324 Pierce St	Omaha	NE	68103	**800-642-8210**	402-342-0840	190-3
Chicago Manifold Products Co 171 E Marquardt Dr *Sales	Wheeling	IL	60090	**800-323-7735***	847-459-6000	664
Chicago Meat Authority Inc 1120 W 47th Pl	Chicago	IL	60609	**800-383-3811**	773-254-3811	291-26
Chicago Mercantile Exchange Holdings Inc (CME) 20 S Wacker Dr *NYSE: CME*	Chicago	IL	60606	**800-331-3332**	312-930-1000	680
Chicago Metallic Corp 4849 S Austin Ave	Chicago	IL	60638	**800-323-7164**	708-563-4600	482
Chicago Metallic Products Inc 800 Ela Rd	Lake Zurich	IL	60047	**800-323-3966**	847-438-2171	477
Chicago Office of Tourism 78 E Washington St	Chicago	IL	60602	**877-244-2246**	312-744-2400	205
Chicago Pneumatic Tool Co 1800 Overview Dr	Rock Hill	SC	29730	**800-367-2442**	803-817-7000	747
Chicago Rawhide Industries 900 N State St *Cust Svc	Elgin	IL	60123	**800-882-0008***	847-742-7840	321
Chicago Rush 8735 W Higgins Rd Suite 160	Chicago	IL	60631	**888-682-3434**	773-243-3434	703
Chicago Southland Convention & Visitors Bureau 2304 173rd St	Lansing	IL	60438	**888-895-8233**	708-895-8200	205
Chicago Story 401 W Superior St	Chicago	IL	60610	**800-642-3173**	312-642-3173	503
Chicago Symphony Orchestra 220 S Michigan Ave	Chicago	IL	60604	**800-223-7114**	312-294-3000	563-3
Chicago Title Insurance Co 171 N Clark St	Chicago	IL	60601	**800-621-1919**	312-223-2000	384-6
Chicago Title & Trust Co 171 N Clark St	Chicago	IL	60601	**800-621-1919**	312-223-2000	384-6
Chicago Tribune 435 N Michigan Ave	Chicago	IL	60611	**800-874-2863**	312-222-3232	522-2
Chicago Tube & Iron Co 2531 W 48th St *Cust Svc	Chicago	IL	60632	**800-972-0217***	773-523-1441	483
Chicago-Wilcox Mfg Co 16928 State St	South Holland	IL	60473	**800-323-5282**	708-339-5000	321
Chick-fil-A Inc 5200 Buffington Rd	Atlanta	GA	30349	**800-232-2677**	404-765-8000	657
Chick Packaging Inc PO Box 80	Silver Lake	NH	03875	**800-258-4692**	603-367-8857	199
Chickasaw Electric Co-op 17970 Hwy 64 PO Box 459	Somerville	TN	38068	**866-465-3591**	901-465-3591	244
Chicken Out Rotisserie 15952 Shady Grove Rd	Gaithersburg	MD	20877	**800-328-4663**	301-921-0600	657
Chicken of the Sea International Inc 9330 Scranton Rd Suite 500	San Diego	CA	92121	**800-456-1511**	858-558-9662	291-13
Chico Chamber of Commerce 300 Salem St	Chico	CA	95928	**800-852-8570**	530-891-5556	137
Chico Enterprise Record 400 E Park Ave PO Box 9	Chico	CA	95927	**800-827-1421**	530-891-1234	522-2
Chicopee Provision Co Inc 19 Sitarz St	Chicopee	MA	01014	**800-924-6328**	413-594-4765	291-26
Chico's FAS Inc 11215 Metro Pkwy *NYSE: CHS*	Fort Myers	FL	33912	**888-855-4986**	239-277-6200	155-6
Chief Automotive Systems Inc 1924 E 4th St	Grand Island	NE	68801	**800-445-9262**	308-384-9747	379
Chief Executives Organization 7920 Norfolk Ave Suite 400	Bethesda	MD	20814	**800-634-2655**	301-656-9220	49-12
Chiefs of Police. International Assn of 515 N Washington St	Alexandria	VA	22314	**800-843-4227**	703-836-6767	49-7
Chilcote Co 2140-60 Superior Ave *Sales	Cleveland	OH	44114	**800-827-5679***	216-781-6000	550
Chilcote Co Taprell Loomis Div 2160 Superior Ave	Cleveland	OH	44114	**800-827-5679**	216-781-6000	550
Child Abuse America. Prevent 200 S Michigan Ave 17th Fl	Chicago	IL	60604	**800-244-5373**	312-663-3520	48-6
Child & Adolescent Psychiatry. American Academy of 3615 Wisconsin Ave NW	Washington	DC	20016	**800-333-7636**	202-966-7300	49-15
Child Care Assn. National 1016 Rosser St	Conyers	GA	30012	**800-543-7161**	770-922-8198	48-6
Child Care Information Center. National 243 Church St NW 2nd Fl	Vienna	VA	22180	**800-616-2242**		336-6
Child Care. National Assn for Family 5202 Pinemont Dr	Salt Lake City	UT	84123	**800-359-3817**	801-269-9338	48-6
Child Care Professionals. National Assn of 7610 Hwy 71 W Suite E	Austin	TX	78735	**800-537-1118**	512-301-5557	48-6
Child Care Resource & Referral Agencies. National Assn of 1319 F St NW Suite 500	Washington	DC	20004	**800-424-2246**	202-393-5501	48-6
Child Find of America Inc 7 Cummings Ln	Highland	NY	12528	**800-426-5678**	845-691-4666	48-6
Child Find Canada 212-2211 McPhillips St	Winnipeg	MB	R3G0N4	**800-387-7962**	204-339-5584	48-6
Child Foundation. American Culinary Federation Chef & 180 Center Place Way	Saint Augustine	FL	32095	**800-624-9458**	904-824-4468	48-6
Child Life Magazine Children's Better Health Institute 1100 Waterway Blvd	Indianapolis	IN	46202	**800-558-2376**	317-636-8881	449-6
Child Magazine 375 Lexington Ave 9th Fl	New York	NY	10017	**800-777-0222**	212-499-2000	449-11
Child Protection Law Report 8737 Colesville Rd Suite 1100	Silver Spring	MD	20910	**800-274-6737**	301-587-6300	521-8
Child Quest International 307 Orchard City Dr Suite 108	Campbell	CA	95008	**888-818-4673**	408-287-4673	48-6
Child Safety Council. National 4065 Page Ave	Jackson	MI	49204	**800-327-5107**	517-764-6070	48-6

Name / Address	City	State	Zip	Toll-Free	Phone	Class
Child Welfare League of America (CWLA) 440 1st St NW 3rd Fl	Washington	DC	20001	**800-407-6273**	202-638-2952	48-6
Childbirth Education Assn. International 8060 26th Ave SE *Sales	Minneapolis	MN	55425	**800-624-4934***	952-854-8660	48-17
Childcraft Education Corp 2920 Old Tree Dr	Lancaster	PA	17603	**800-631-5652**	717-397-1717	451
Childers Products Co 1370 E 40th St	Houston	TX	77022	**800-231-1024**	713-691-7002	688
Childhelp USA 15757 N 78th St	Scottsdale	AZ	85260	**800-422-4453**	480-922-8212	48-6
Childhood Cancer Foundation. Candlelighters PO Box 498	Kensington	MD	20895	**800-366-2223**	301-962-3520	48-17
Childhood Education International. Association for 17904 Georgia Ave Suite 215	Olney	MD	20832	**800-423-3563**	301-570-2111	49-5
Children & Adults with Attention-Deficit/Hyperactivity Disorder (CHADD) 8181 Professional Pl Suite 201	Landover	MD	20785	**800-233-4050**	301-306-7070	48-17
Children & Aging. Christian Foundation for 1 Elmwood Ave	Kansas City	KS	66103	**800-875-6564**	913-384-6500	48-6
Children of Aging Parents 1609 Woodbourne Rd Suite 302A	Levittown	PA	19057	**800-227-7294**	215-945-6900	48-6
Children. American Coalition for Fathers & 1420 Spring Hill Rd	McLean	VA	22102	**800-978-3237**		48-6
Children. American Professional Society on the Abuse of 107 Amberside Dr	Goose Creek	SC	29445	**877-402-7722**	843-764-2905	48-6
Children Assn Inc. North America Missing 136 Rt 420 Hwy	South Esk	NB	E1V4N8	**800-260-0753**	506-627-1209	48-6
Children. Association for Library Service to 50 E Huron St	Chicago	IL	60611	**800-545-2433**	312-280-2163	49-11
Children Awaiting Parents Inc (CAP) 595 Blossom Rd Suite 306	Rochester	NY	14610	**888-835-8802**	585-232-5110	48-6
Children. Council for Exceptional 1110 N Glebe Rd Suite 300	Arlington	VA	22201	**888-232-7733**	703-620-3660	49-5
Children for Enforcement of Support. Association for PO Box 7842	Fredericksburg	VA	22404	**800-738-2237**		48-6
Children Federation Inc. Save the 54 Wilton Rd	Westport	CT	06880	**800-728-3843**	203-221-4000	48-5
Children. Feed the PO Box 36	Oklahoma City	OK	73101	**800-627-4556**	405-942-0228	48-5
Children. Find the 2656 29th St Suite 203	Santa Monica	CA	90405	**888-477-6721**	310-314-3213	48-6
Children. Healing the PO Box 9065	Spokane	WA	99209	**877-432-5543**	509-327-4281	48-5
Children Inc PO Box 5381	Richmond	VA	23220	**800-538-5381**	804-359-4562	48-6
Children. INMED Partnerships for 45449 Severn Way Suite 161	Sterling	VA	20166	**800-521-1175**	703-444-4477	48-5
Children International 2000 E Red Bridge Rd	Kansas City	MO	64131	**800-888-3089**	816-942-2000	48-5
Children. National Assn for the Education of Young 1509 16th St NW	Washington	DC	20036	**800-424-2460**	202-232-8777	49-5
Children. National Center for Missing & Exploited 699 Prince St	Alexandria	VA	22314	**800-843-5678**	703-274-3900	48-6
Children of the Night 14530 Sylvan St	Van Nuys	CA	91411	**800-551-1300**	818-908-4474	48-6
Children. Parents of Murdered 100 E 8th St Suite B-41	Cincinnati	OH	45202	**888-818-7662**	513-721-5683	48-6
Children Services. Jewish Board of Family & 120 W 57th St	New York	NY	10019	**888-523-2769**	212-582-9100	48-6
Children. Spaulding for 16250 Northland Dr Suite 120	Southfield	MI	48075	**877-767-5437**	248-443-7080	48-6
Children. Stand For 516 SE Morrison St Suite 206	Portland	OR	97214	**800-663-4032**	503-235-2305	48-6
Children Who Are Deaf or Hard of Hearing Inc. BEGINNINGS for Parents of 3714 A Benson Dr	Raleigh	NC	27619	**800-541-4327**	919-850-2746	48-17
Children with Disabilities. National Dissemination Center for 1825 Connecticut Ave	Washington	DC	20009	**800-695-0285**	202-884-8200	48-17
Children. World Opportunities International/Help the 1875 Century Park E Suite 700	Los Angeles	CA	90067	**800-464-7187**	323-466-7187	48-5
Children & Youth Funding Report 8204 Fenton St	Silver Spring	MD	20910	**800-666-6380**	301-588-6380	521-8
Children's Alliance. Vanished 991 W Hedding St Suite 101	San Jose	CA	95126	**800-826-4743**	408-296-1113	48-6
Children's Better Health Institute 1100 Waterway Blvd	Indianapolis	IN	46202	**800-558-2376**	317-636-8881	623-9
Children's Book Council (CBC) 12 W 37th St 2nd Fl *Orders	New York	NY	10018	**800-999-2160***	212-966-1990	49-16
Children's Book Insider Newsletter 901 Columbia Rd	Fort Collins	CO	80525	**800-807-1916**	970-495-0056	521-11
Children's Cancer Society. National 1015 Locust St Suite 600	Saint Louis	MO	63101	**800-532-6459**	314-241-1600	48-17
Children's Care Hospital & School 2501 W 26th St	Sioux Falls	SD	57105	**800-584-9294**	605-782-2300	366-1
Children's Defense Fund (CDF) 25 'E' St NW	Washington	DC	20001	**800-233-1200**	202-628-8787	48-6
Children's Digest Children's Better Health Institute 1100 Waterway Blvd	Indianapolis	IN	46202	**800-558-2376**	317-636-8881	449-6
Children's Foundation. Believe In Tomorrow National 6601 Frederick Rd	Baltimore	MD	21228	**800-933-5470**	410-744-1032	48-6
Children's Foundation. Starlight 5900 Wilshire Blvd Suite 2530	Los Angeles	CA	90036	**800-274-7827**	323-634-0080	48-17
Children's Fund Inc. Christian 2821 Emerywood Pkwy	Richmond	VA	23294	**800-776-6767**	804-756-2700	48-6
Children's Hands-On Museum 2213 University Blvd	Tuscaloosa	AL	35401	**877-349-4235**	205-349-4235	510
Children's Healthcare of Atlanta at Egleston 1405 Clifton Rd NE	Atlanta	GA	30322	**800-250-5437**	404-325-6000	366-1
Children's Healthcare of Atlanta at Scottish Rite 1001 Johnson Ferry Rd NE	Atlanta	GA	30342	**800-250-5437**	404-256-5252	366-1
Children's Hospice International (CHI) 901 N Pitt St Suite 230	Alexandria	VA	22314	**800-242-4453**	703-684-0330	49-8
Children's Hospital 1056 E 19th Ave	Denver	CO	80218	**800-624-6553**	303-861-8888	366-1
Children's Hospital 700 Children's Dr	Columbus	OH	43205	**800-792-8401**	614-722-2000	366-1
Children's Museum of Indianapolis 3000 N Meridian St	Indianapolis	IN	46208	**800-826-5431**	317-924-5431	509
Children's Museum of Richmond 2626 W Broad St	Richmond	VA	23220	**877-295-2667**	804-474-7000	510
Children's Orchard Inc 900 Victors Way Suite 200	Ann Arbor	MI	48108	**800-999-5437**	734-994-9199	155-1
Children's Organ Transplant Assn (COTA) 2501 Cota Dr	Bloomington	IN	47403	**800-366-2682**	812-336-8872	48-17
Children's Place Retail Stores Inc 915 Secaucus Rd *NASDAQ: PLCE*	Secaucus	NJ	07094	**800-527-5355**	201-558-2400	155-1
Children's Playmate Magazine Children's Better Health Institute 1100 Waterway Blvd.	Indianapolis	IN	46202	**800-558-2376**	317-636-8881	449-6
Children's Press 90 Old Sherman Tpke	Danbury	CT	06816	**800-621-1115**	203-797-3500	623-2
Children's Rights Council (CRC) 6200 Editors Park Dr Suite 103	Hyattsville	MD	20782	**800-787-5437**	301-559-3120	48-6
Children's Survival Fund Inc 4211 Surfside Cir	Missouri City	TX	77459	**800-426-9885**	281-403-3808	48-5
Children's Villages-USA. SOS 1317 F St NW Suite 550	Washington	DC	20004	**800-886-5767**	202-347-7920	48-6
Children's Wish Foundation International 8615 Roswell Rd	Atlanta	GA	30350	**800-323-9474**	770-393-9474	48-17
Chili's Grill & Bar 6820 LBJ Fwy	Dallas	TX	75240	**800-983-4637**	972-980-9917	657
Chiltern Inn 3 Cromwell Harbor Rd	Bar Harbor	ME	04609	**800-404-0114**	207-288-0114	373
Chilton County Chamber of Commerce 500 5th Ave N	Clanton	AL	35045	**800-553-0493**	205-755-2400	137
Chilton Products Div Western Industries Inc 300 E Breed St	Chilton	WI	53014	**877-671-7063**	920-849-2381	593
Chime Master Systems PO Box 936	Lancaster	OH	43130	**800-344-7464**	740-746-8500	516
Chimney Rock Park Hwy 64/74A PO Box 39	Chimney Rock	NC	28720	**800-277-9611**	828-625-9611	98
Chimney Rock Public Power District 805 W 8th St	Bayard	NE	69334	**877-773-6300**	308-586-1824	244
Chimo Hotel 1199 Joseph Cyr St	Ottawa	ON	K1J7T4	**800-387-9779**	613-744-1060	372
CHIN-AM 1540 (Ethnic) 622 College St	Toronto	ON	M6G1B6	**888-944-2446**	416-531-9991	631
CHIN-FM 100.7 (Ethnic) 622 College St	Toronto	ON	M6G1B6	**888-944-2446**	416-531-9991	631
Chin Leeann Inc 3600 American Blvd W Suite 418	Bloomington	MN	55431	**800-784-0029**	952-896-3606	657
China Airlines Cargo Sales & Service 11201 Aviation Blvd	Los Angeles	CA	90045	**800-421-1289**	310-646-4293	13
China Airlines Dynasty Flyer 6053 W Century Blvd Suite 800	Los Angeles	CA	90045	**800-227-5118**		27
China Airlines Ltd 6053 W Century Blvd Suite 800	Los Angeles	CA	90045	**800-227-5118**	310-641-8888	26
Chinatrust Bank USA 22939 Hawthorne Blvd	Torrance	CA	90505	**888-839-9000**	310-791-2828	71
Chinese Cafes of America 4104 Aurora St	Coral Gables	FL	33146	**800-662-1668**	305-476-1611	657
CHIP Hospitality Traveller's Reward Program 1600-1030 W Georgia St	Vancouver	BC	V6E2Y3	**800-431-0070**	604-646-2447	371
Chip Steak & Provision Co 232 Dewey St	Mankato	MN	56001	**888-244-7783**	507-388-6277	465
Chippewa Herald 321 Frenette Dr PO Box 9	Chippewa Falls	WI	54729	**800-236-5515**	715-723-5515	522-2
Chippewa Trails 510 E South Ave	Chippewa Falls	WI	54729	**800-657-4469**	715-726-2440	108
Chippewa Valley Convention & Visitors Bureau 3625 Gateway Dr Suite F	Eau Claire	WI	54701	**888-523-3866**	715-831-2345	205
Chippewa Valley Electric Co-op 317 S 8th St	Cornell	WI	54732	**800-300-6800**	715-239-6800	244
Chippewa Valley Technical College 620 W Clairemont Ave	Eau Claire	WI	54701	**800-547-2882**	715-833-6200	787
Chiquita Brands International Inc 250 E 5th St *NYSE: CQB*	Cincinnati	OH	45202	**800-541-8998**	513-784-8000	310-4
Chiron Corp 4560 Horton St *NASDAQ: CHIR*	Emeryville	CA	94608	**800-524-4766**	510-655-8730	86
Chiron Corp Biocine Div 4560 Horton St	Emeryville	CA	94608	**800-524-4766**	510-655-8730	86
Chiron Therapeutics 4560 Horton St	Emeryville	CA	94608	**800-524-4766**	510-655-8729	86
Chiron Vaccines 4560 Horton St	Emeryville	CA	94608	**800-524-4766**	510-655-8729	86
Chiropractic Assn. American 1701 Clarendon Blvd 2nd Fl	Arlington	VA	22209	**800-986-4636**	703-276-8800	49-8
Chiropractic Health Plan of California PO Box 190	Clayton	CA	94517	**800-995-2442**	925-672-0106	384-3
Chiropractors Assn. International 1110 N Glebe Rd Suite 1000	Arlington	VA	22201	**800-423-4690**	703-528-5000	49-8
ChiroSource Inc 6200 Center St Suite 260	Clayton	CA	94517	**800-680-9997**	925-844-3100	384-3
Chisesi Brothers Meat Packing Co PO Box 19083	New Orleans	LA	70179	**800-966-3550**	504-822-3550	465
Chittenden Bank 2 Burlington Sq	Burlington	VT	05402	**800-752-0006**	802-658-4000	71
Chittenden Corp PO Box 820 *NYSE: CHZ*	Burlington	VT	05402	**800-642-3158**	802-658-4000	355-2
Chittenden & Eastman Co 100 New Rand Rd *Cust Svc	Sweet Springs	MO	65351	**800-553-5623***	319-753-2811	463
Chloride Systems 272 W Stage Park Service Rd	Burgaw	NC	28425	**800-403-6927**	910-259-1000	431
Choate Hall & Stewart 53 State St Exchange Pl	Boston	MA	02109	**800-520-2427**	617-248-5000	419
Chocolate Manufacturers Assn (CMA) 8320 Old Courthouse Rd Suite 300	Vienna	VA	22182	**800-433-1200**	703-790-5011	49-6
Chocolates a la Carte Inc 28455 Livingston Ave *Cust Svc	Valencia	CA	91355	**800-818-2462***	661-257-3700	291-8
Choctaw Electric Co-op Inc Hwy 93 N PO Box 758	Hugo	OK	74743	**800-780-6486**	580-326-6486	244
Choctawhatchee Electric Co-op Inc 1350 W Baldwin Ave	De Funiak Springs	FL	32435	**800-342-0990**	850-892-2111	244

Name / Address	City	State	ZIP	Toll-Free	Phone	Class
Choi Brothers Inc 3401 W Division St	Chicago	IL	60651	**800-524-2464**	773-489-2800	153-1
Choice Hotels Canada Inc 5090 Explorer Dr Suite 500	Mississauga	ON	L4W4T9	**800-424-6423**	905-602-2222	369
Choice Hotels International Inc 10750 Columbia Pike	Silver Spring	MD	20901	**800-424-6423**	301-592-5000	369
NYSE: CHH						
Clarion Hotels 10750 Columbia Pike	Silver Spring	MD	20901	**800-424-6423**	301-592-5000	369
Comfort Inns 10750 Columbia Pike	Silver Spring	MD	20901	**800-424-6423**	301-592-5000	369
Comfort Suites 10750 Columbia Pike	Silver Spring	MD	20901	**800-424-6423**	301-592-5000	369
Econo Lodge 10750 Columbia Pike	Silver Spring	MD	20901	**800-424-6423**	301-592-5000	369
MainStay Suites 10750 Columbia Pike	Silver Spring	MD	20901	**800-424-6423**	301-592-5000	369
Quality Inns Hotels & Suites 10750 Columbia Pike	Silver Spring	MD	20901	**800-424-6423**	301-592-5000	369
Rodeway Inns 10750 Columbia Pike	Silver Spring	MD	20901	**800-424-6423**	301-592-5000	369
Sleep Inn & Suites 10750 Columbia Pike	Silver Spring	MD	20901	**800-424-6423**	301-592-5000	369
Choice Office Products 5090 State St	Saginaw	MI	48603	**866-726-2678**	989-793-9860	524
Choice One Communications Inc 100 Chestnut St Suite 600	Rochester	NY	14004	**000-002-5000**		721
Choice Privileges Reward Program 2697 US Hwy 50	Grand Junction	CO	81503	**800-521-2121***	888-770-6800	371
*Cust Svc						
ChoicePoint Inc 1000 Alderman Dr	Alpharetta	GA	30005	**877-317-5000**	770-752-6000	223
NYSE: CPS						
ChoicePoint Precision Marketing 8600 N Industrial Rd	Peoria	IL	61615	**800-786-6880**	309-689-1000	5
Cholestech Corp 3347 Investment Blvd	Hayward	CA	94545	**800-733-0404**	510-732-7200	229
NASDAQ: CTEC						
ChopHouse & Brewery 248 Centennial Pkwy	Louisville	CO	80027	**800-273-9827**	303-664-4000	657
Chopra Center at La Costa Resort & Spa 2013 Costa del Mar Rd	Carlsbad	CA	92009	**888-424-6772**	760-931-7566	660
Chopra Deepak Chopra Center at La Costa Resort & Spa 2013 Costa del Mar Rd	Carlsbad	CA	92009	**888-424-6772**	760-931-7566	561
Choptank Electric Co-op Inc 24820 Meeting House Rd	Denton	MD	21629	**877-892-0001**	410-479-0380	244
Chowan College 200 Jones Dr	Murfreesboro	NC	27855	**800-488-4101**	252-398-6500	163
CHQR-AM 770 (N/T) 630 3rd Ave SW Suite 105	Calgary	AB	T2P4L4	**800-563-7770**	403-716-6500	631
CHRI-FM 99.1 (Rel) 1010 Thomas Spratt Pl Suite 3	Ottawa	ON	K1G5L5	**866-247-1440**	613-247-1440	631
Chris Kaye Plastics Corp 715 W Park Rd	Union	MO	63084	**800-325-9927**	636-583-2583	593
Chrislin Industries Inc 31312 Via Colinas Suite 108	Westlake Village	CA	91362	**800-468-0736**	818-991-2254	613
Christ. Community of 1001 W Walnut St	Independence	MO	64050	**800-825-2806**	816-833-1000	48-20
Christ. Connecting Businessmen to 5746 Marlin Rd Suite 602 Osborne Center	Chattanooga	TN	37411	**800-575-2262**	423-698-4444	48-20
Christ Hospital 2139 Auburn Ave	Cincinnati	OH	45219	**800-527-8919**	513-585-2000	366-2
Christ International. Campus Crusade for 100 Lake Hart Dr	Orlando	FL	32832	**877-924-7478**	407-826-2000	48-20
Christ School 500 Christ School Rd	Arden	NC	28704	**800-422-3212**	828-684-6232	611
Christ Scientist. First Church of 175 Huntington Ave	Boston	MA	02115	**800-288-7090**	617-450-2000	48-20
Christchurch School 49 Seahorse Ln	Christchurch	VA	23031	**800-296-2306**	804-758-2306	611
Christel DeHaan Fine Arts Center 1400 E Hanna Ave University of Indianapolis	Indianapolis	IN	46227	**800-232-8634**	317-788-3566	562
Christen Fred & Sons Co 714 George St	Toledo	OH	43608	**800-243-4161**	419-243-4161	688
Christendom College 134 Christendom Dr	Front Royal	VA	22630	**800-877-5456**	540-636-2900	163
Christensen Joe Inc 1540 Adams St	Lincoln	NE	68521	**800-228-5030**	402-476-7535	614
Christian Appalachian Project 322 Crab Orchard St	Lancaster	KY	40446	**866-270-4227**	859-792-3051	48-5
Christian Assn of the USA. Young Women's 1015 18th St NW Suite 1100	Washington	DC	20036	**800-992-2871**	202-467-0801	48-6
Christian Athletes. Fellowship of 8701 Leeds Rd	Kansas City	MO	64129	**800-289-0909**	816-921-0909	48-22
Christian Blind Mission International (CBMI) 450 E Park Ave	Greenville	SC	29601	**800-937-2264**	864-239-0065	48-5
Christian Board of Publication PO Box 179 Suite 1200	Saint Louis	MO	63166	**800-366-3383**	314-231-8500	623-9
Christian Booksellers Assn 9240 Explorer Dr PO Box 62000	Colorado Springs	CO	80962	**800-252-1950**	719-265-9895	49-18
Christian Broadcasting Network (CBN) 977 Centerville Tpke CBN Ctr	Virginia Beach	VA	23463	**800-759-0700**	757-226-7000	725
Christian Brothers University 650 East Pkwy S	Memphis	TN	38104	**800-288-7576**	901-321-3000	163
Christian Charities. International Orthodox 110 West Rd Suite 360	Baltimore	MD	21204	**877-803-4622**	410-243-9820	48-5
Christian Children's Fund Inc (CCF) 2821 Emerywood Pkwy	Richmond	VA	23294	**800-776-6767**	804-756-2700	48-6
Christian Churches. National Assn of Congregational 8473 S Howell Ave	Oak Creek	WI	53154	**800-262-1620**	414-764-1620	48-20
Christian Coalition of America PO Box 37030	Washington	DC	20013	**888-440-2262**	202-479-6900	48-7
Christian Dior 712 5th Ave 37th Fl	New York	NY	10019	**800-929-3467**	212-582-0500	273
Christian Disaster Response International 922 Magnolia Ave	Auburndale	FL	33823	**800-430-1235**	863-967-4357	48-5
Christian Endeavor International 309 S Main St	Mount Vernon	OH	43050	**800-260-3234**	740-397-2622	48-20
Christian Foundation for Children & Aging (CFCA) 1 Elmwood Ave	Kansas City	KS	66103	**800-875-6564**	913-384-6500	48-6
Christian Heritage College 2100 Greenfield Dr	El Cajon	CA	92019	**800-676-2242**	619-441-2200	163
Christian Management Assn 635 Camino De Los Mares Suite 205	San Clemente	CA	92673	**800-727-4262**	949-487-0900	49-12
Christian Publications Inc 3825 Hartzdale Dr	Camp Hill	PA	17011	**800-233-4443***	717-761-7044	623-4
*Orders						
Christian Reader Magazine 465 Gundersen Dr	Carol Stream	IL	60188	**800-223-3161**	630-260-6200	449-18
Christian Reformed Church in North America (CRC) 2850 Kalamazoo Ave SE	Grand Rapids	MI	49560	**800-272-5125**	616-241-1691	48-20
Christian Reformed World Relief Committee (CRWRC) 2850 Kalamazoo Ave SE	Grand Rapids	MI	49560	**800-552-7972**	616-224-0740	48-5
Christian Relief Services 2550 Huntington Ave Suite 200	Alexandria	VA	22303	**800-337-3543**	703-317-9086	48-5
Christian Schools International (CSI) 3350 E Paris Ave SE	Grand Rapids	MI	49512	**800-635-8288**	616-957-1070	49-5
Christian Schools International. Association of 731 Chapel Hills Dr	Colorado Springs	CO	80920	**800-367-0798***	719-528-6906	49-5
*Cust Svc						
Christian Science Monitor 1 Norway St	Boston	MA	02115	**800-288-7090**	617-450-2000	522-3
Christian Science Publishing Society 1 Norway St	Boston	MA	02115	**800-288-7090**	617-450-2000	623-8
Christian Theological Seminary 1000 W 42nd St	Indianapolis	IN	46208	**800-585-0108**	317-924-1331	164-3
Christian & Timbers 25825 Science Pk Dr Suite 400	Cleveland	OH	44122	**800-380-9444**	216-464-8710	262
Christian Tours Inc PO Box 890	Newton	NC	28658	**800-476-3900**	828-465-3900	748
Christianity Today Inc 465 Gundersen Dr	Carol Stream	IL	60188	**800-999-1704***	630-260-6200	623-9
*Cust Svc						
Christianity Today Magazine 465 Gundersen Dr	Carol Stream	IL	60188	**800-999-1704***	630-260-6200	449-18
*Sales						
ChristianLiving.net 1302 Clear Springs Trace	Louisville	KY	40223	**877-486-2660***	888-772-7355	390
*Tech Supp						
Christiansen Aviation Inc PO Box 702412	Tulsa	OK	74170	**800-331-5550**	918-299-2687	25
Christianson Systems Inc 20421 15th St SE	Blomkest	MN	56216	**800-328-8896**	320-995-6141	206
Christie Cookie Co 1205 3rd Ave N	Nashville	TN	37208	**800-458-2447**	615-242-3817	291-9
Christina America Inc 9880 Rue Clark	Montreal	QC	H3L2R3	**800-463-7946***	514-381-2365	153-17
*Cust Svc						
Christopher Enterprises 155 W 250 N	Spanish Fork	UT	84660	**800-453-1406**	801-794-6800	350
Christopher Newport University 1 University Pl	Newport News	VA	23606	**800-333-4268**	757-594-7000	163
Christopher Ranch 305 Bloomfield Ave	Gilroy	CA	95020	**800-321-9333**	408-847-1100	11-11
Christopher Reeve Paralysis Foundation 500 Morris Ave	Springfield	NJ	07081	**800-225-0292**	973-379-2690	48-17
Christophers The 12 E 48th St	New York	NY	10017	**888-298-4050**	212-759-4050	48-20
CHRISTUS Schumpert Health System 1 St Mary Pl	Shreveport	LA	71101	**888-336-8115**	318-681-4500	348
CHRISTUS Spohn Hospice 1660 S Staples St	Corpus Christi	TX	78404	**800-371-0115**	361-881-3159	365
Christ/USA. Youth for PO Box 4478	Englewood	CO	80155	**800-735-3252**	303-843-9000	48-20
Christy Concrete Products Inc 5236 Arboga Rd	Marysville	CA	95901	**800-486-7070**	530-742-8368	181
Christy Estates Suites 3942 Holly Rd	Corpus Christi	TX	78415	**800-678-4836**	361-854-1091	373
CHRO-TV Ch 5 (Ind) 87 George St	Ottawa	ON	K1N9H7	**800-461-2476**	613-789-0606	726
Chromaline Corp 4832 Grand Ave	Duluth	MN	55807	**800-328-4261**	218-628-2217	616
Chromalox Inc 103 Gamma Dr Ext	Pittsburgh	PA	15238	**800-368-2493***	412-967-3800	37
*Cust Svc						
Chromaprobe Inc 378 Fee Fee Rd	Maryland Heights	MO	63043	**888-964-1400**	314-738-0001	229
Chronic Pain Assn. American PO Box 850	Rocklin	CA	95677	**800-533-3231**	916-632-0922	48-17
Chronicle The 1 Chronicle Rd	Willimantic	CT	06226	**800-992-8466**	860-423-8466	522-2
Chronicle The 321 N Pearl St	Centralia	WA	98531	**800-562-6084**	360-736-3311	522-2
Chronicle Books 85 2nd St 6th Fl	San Francisco	CA	94105	**800-722-6657**	415-537-4200	623-2
Chronicle of Higher Education 1255 23rd St NW Suite 700	Washington	DC	20037	**800-728-2803***	202-466-1000	449-8
*Sales						
Chronicle-Telegram 225 East Ave	Elyria	OH	44035	**800-633-4623**	440-329-7000	522-2
Chronicle-Tribune 610 S Adams St	Marion	IN	46953	**800-955-7888**	765-664-5111	522-2
Chronimed Inc 10900 Red Cir Dr Suite 300	Minnetonka	MN	55343	**800-444-5951**	952-979-3600	468
Chrysalis Inn & Spa 804 10th St	Bellingham	WA	98225	**888-808-0005**	360-756-1005	373
Chrysler Aviation Inc (CAI) 7120 Hayvenhurst Ave Suite 309	Van Nuys	CA	91406	**800-995-0825**	818-989-7900	14
Chrysler Financial Co LLC 27777 Franklin Rd	Southfield	MI	48034	**800-556-8172***	248-427-6424	215
*Cust Svc						
Chrysler Walter P Museum 1 Chrysler Dr	Auburn Hills	MI	48326	**888-456-1924**	248-944-0001	509
CHT R Beitlich Corp 5046 Old Pineville Rd	Charlotte	NC	28217	**800-277-4941**	704-523-4242	143
Chubb Americas Sector 5201 Explorer Dr	Mississauga	ON	L4W4H1	**800-661-4149**	905-629-2600	681
Chubb & Son 15 Mountain View Rd	Warren	NJ	07059	**800-252-4670**	908-903-2000	384-4
Chubb Specialty Insurance 82 Hopmeadow St	Simsbury	CT	06070	**800-432-8168**	860-408-2000	384-5
Chugach Electric Assn Inc 5601 Minnesota Dr	Anchorage	AK	99519	**800-478-7494**	907-563-7494	244
Chula Vista Resort 4031 N River Rd	Wisconsin Dells	WI	53965	**800-388-4782**	608-254-8366	655
Chumash Casino 3400 E Hwy 246	Santa Ynez	CA	93460	**800-728-9997**	805-686-0855	133

	City	State	ZIP	Toll-Free	Phone	Class
Church in America. Reformed 475 Riverside Dr 18th Fl	New York	NY	10115	**800-722-9977**	212-870-3071	48-20
Church of the Brethren 1451 Dundee Ave	Elgin	IL	60120	**800-323-8039**	847-742-5100	48-20
Church of Christ Scientist. First 175 Huntington Ave	Boston	MA	02115	**800-288-7090**	617-450-2000	48-20
Church of Christ. United 700 Prospect Ave	Cleveland	OH	44115	**866-822-8224**	216-736-2100	48-20
Church Divinity School of the Pacific 2451 Ridge Rd	Berkeley	CA	94709	**800-353-2377**	510-204-0700	164-3
Church of the Foursquare Gospel. International 1910 W Sunset Blvd Suite 200	Los Angeles	CA	90026	**888-635-4234**	213-989-4200	48-20
Church of God Ministries 1201 E 5th St	Anderson	IN	46012	**800-848-2464**	765-642-0256	48-20
Church of God World Missions PO Box 8016	Cleveland	TN	37320	**800-345-7492**	423-478-7190	48-20
Church Loans & Investment Trust PO Box 8203	Amarillo	TX	79114	**800-692-1111**	806-358-3666	214
Church Ministries. Wider 700 Prospect Ave NE 7th Fl	Cleveland	OH	44115	**866-822-8224**	216-736-3200	48-20
Church Mutual Insurance Co 3000 Schuster Ln	Merrill	WI	54452	**800-542-3465**	715-536-5577	384-4
Church & Stagg Office Supply Co Inc 3421 6th Ave	Birmingham	AL	35222	**800-239-5336**	205-251-2951	524
Church & State. Americans United for Separation of 518 C St NE	Washington	DC	20002	**800-875-3707**	202-466-3234	48-7
Church Women United (CWU) 475 Riverside Dr Rm 1626	New York	NY	10115	**800-298-5551**	212-870-2347	48-20
Church World Service 475 Riverside Dr 7th Fl	New York	NY	10115	**800-456-1310**	212-870-2061	48-5
Church World Service Emergency Response Program 475 Riverside Dr 7th Fl	New York	NY	10115	**800-297-1516**	212-870-3151	48-5
Churchill Capital Inc 333 S 7th St Suite 2400	Minneapolis	MN	55402	**888-782-3328**	612-673-6633	779
Churchill Corporate Services 56 Utter Ave	Hawthorne	NJ	07506	**800-941-7458**	973-636-9400	209
Churchill Hotel 1914 Connecticut Ave NW	Washington	DC	20009	**800-424-2464**	202-797-2000	373
Church's Chicken Inc 980 Hammond Dr NE Suite 1100	Atlanta	GA	30328	**866-232-9402**	770-350-3800	657
Churchwell Co 3031 E Bay St	Jacksonville	FL	32202	**800-245-0075**	904-356-5721	10
Chuy's Comida Deluxe 1623 Toomey Rd	Austin	TX	78704	**800-439-2489**	512-473-2783	657
CI Fund Management Inc 151 Yonge St 11th Fl *TSE: CIX*	Toronto	ON	M5C2W7	**800-268-9374**	416-364-1145	393
CI Host 1851 Central Dr Suite 110 *Tech Supp	Bedford	TX	76021	**888-820-0688***	817-868-6999	795
CI Travel 101 W Main St Suite 800	Norfolk	VA	23510	**800-222-3577**	757-627-8000	760
Ciba Specialty Chemicals 540 White Plains Rd	Tarrytown	NY	10591	**800-431-1900**	914-785-2000	143
CIBA Vision Corp 11460 Johns Creek Pkwy	Duluth	GA	30097	**800-227-1524**	770-476-3937	531
CIBC Mortgage Inc 100 University Ave	Toronto	ON	M5J2X4	**800-465-2422**	416-785-3255	498
CIBC World Markets 300 Madison Ave	New York	NY	10017	**800-999-6726**	212-856-4000	679
CIBER Inc 5251 DTC Pkwy Suite 1400 *NYSE: CBR*	Greenwood Village	CO	80111	**800-242-3799**	303-220-0100	178
CICA-TV Ch 19 (Ind) 2180 Yonge St Box 200 Stn Q	Toronto	ON	M4T2T1	**800-613-0513**	416-484-2600	726
Cicada Magazine 30 Grove St Suite C	Peterborough	NH	03458	**800-821-0115**	603-924-7209	449-6
CiDRA Corp 50 Barnes Park N	Wallingford	CT	06492	**877-243-7277**	203-265-0035	720
CIEE (Council on International Educational Exchange) 7 Custom House St 3rd Fl *Cust Svc	Portland	ME	04101	**888-268-6245***	207-553-7600	49-5
CIENA Corp 1201 Winterson Rd *NASDAQ: CIEN*	Linthicum	MD	21090	**800-921-1144**	410-694-5700	720
Cigar Aficionado Magazine 387 Park Ave S 8th Fl *Sales	New York	NY	10016	**800-992-2442***	212-684-4224	449-14
Cigar.com Inc 747 N LaSalle Ave 2nd Fl	Chicago	IL	60610	**800-357-9800**	312-334-1010	743
Cigarette Racing Team Inc 4355 NW 128th St	Opa Locka	FL	33054	**800-347-4327**	305-931-4564	91
Cigarettes Cheaper! PO Box 2400	Benicia	CA	94510	**800-243-2737**	707-745-6691	743
CIGNA Behavioral Health Inc 11095 Viking Dr Suite 350	Eden Prairie	MN	55344	**800-433-5768**	952-996-2000	454
CIGNA Healthcare 900 Cottage Grove Rd	Hartford	CT	06152	**800-832-3211**	860-226-6000	384-3
CIGNA Healthcare of Arizona 11001 N Black Canyon Hwy	Phoenix	AZ	85029	**800-572-9990**	602-942-4462	384-3
CIGNA Healthcare of California 400 N Brand Blvd	Glendale	CA	91203	**800-344-7421**	818-500-6262	384-3
CIGNA Healthcare of Florida Inc Tampa 5404 Cypress Ctr Dr	Tampa	FL	33609	**800-832-3211**		384-3
CIGNA Healthcare of New Hampshire 2 College Pk Dr	Hooksett	NH	03106	**800-531-3121**		384-3
CIGNA Healthcare of San Diego 3636 Noble Dr Suite 150	San Diego	CA	92122	**800-368-2471**	858-625-5600	384-3
CIGNA Healthcare of South Carolina Inc 146 Fairchild Dr	Charleston	SC	29492	**800-962-8811**	843-884-4063	384-3
CIGNA Reinsurance 900 Cottage Grove Rd	Hartford	CT	06152	**888-244-6237**	860-226-6000	384-2
Cimarron Electric Co-op Hwy 81 N PO Box 299	Kingfisher	OK	73750	**800-375-4121**	405-375-4121	244
Cimarron Express Inc 21611 SR-51 PO Box 185	Genoa	OH	43430	**800-759-8979**	419-855-7713	769
Cimpl Meats Inc PO Box 80	Yankton	SD	57078	**800-829-3311**	605-665-1665	465
Cinch Connectors Inc 1700 Findley Rd	Lombard	IL	60148	**800-323-9612**	630-705-6000	803
Cincinnati Art Museum 953 Eden Park Dr	Cincinnati	OH	45202	**877-472-4226**	513-721-5204	509
Cincinnati Bell Inc 201 E 4th St *NYSE: CBB*	Cincinnati	OH	45202	**800-422-1199**	513-397-9900	721
Cincinnati Bengals 1 Paul Brown Stadium	Cincinnati	OH	45202	**866-621-8383**	513-621-3550	703
Cincinnati Bible College & Seminary 2700 Glenway Ave	Cincinnati	OH	45204	**800-949-4222**	513-244-8100	163
Cincinnati Children's Hospital Medical Center 3333 Burnet Ave	Cincinnati	OH	45229	**800-344-2462**	513-636-4200	366-1
Cincinnati Children's Hospital Research Foundation Children's Hospital Medical Center 3333 Burnet Ave	Cincinnati	OH	45229	**800-344-2462**	513-636-4588	654
Cincinnati Enquirer 312 Elm St	Cincinnati	OH	45202	**800-876-4500**	513-721-2700	522-2
Cincinnati Floor Co Inc 5162 Broerman Ave	Cincinnati	OH	45217	**800-886-4501**	513-641-4500	188-2
Cincinnati (Greater) Convention & Visitors Bureau 300 W 6th St	Cincinnati	OH	45202	**800-246-2987**	513-621-2142	205
Cincinnati History Museum 1301 Western Ave Cincinnati Museum Ctr	Cincinnati	OH	45203	**800-733-2077**	513-287-7000	509
Cincinnati Industrial Machinery An Armor Metal Group Co 3280 Hageman St	Cincinnati	OH	45241	**800-677-0076**	513-769-0700	313
Cincinnati Lamb 2200 Litton Ln	Hebron	KY	41048	**800-934-0735**	859-534-4600	447
Cincinnati Lamb 5523 E Nine-Mile Rd	Warren	MI	48091	**800-521-0166**	586-497-6000	447
Cincinnati Life Insurance Co PO Box 145496	Cincinnati	OH	45250	**800-783-4479**	513-870-2000	384-2
Cincinnati Magazine 705 Central Ave 1 Centennial Plaza Suite 175 *Cust Svc	Cincinnati	OH	45202	**800-846-4333***	513-421-4300	449-22
Cincinnati Preserving Co Inc 3015 E Kemper Rd	Sharonville	OH	45241	**800-222-9966**	513-771-2000	291-20
Cincinnati State Technical & Community College 3520 Central Pkwy	Cincinnati	OH	45223	**877-569-0115**	513-569-1500	160
Cincinnati Zoo & Botanical Garden 3400 Vine St	Cincinnati	OH	45220	**800-944-4776**	513-281-4701	811
Cincinnatian Hotel 601 Vine St	Cincinnati	OH	45202	**800-942-9000**	513-381-3000	373
Cincom Systems Inc 55 Merchant St	Cincinnati	OH	45246	**800-888-0115**	513-612-2300	176-1
Cindus Corp 515 Station Ave	Cincinnati	OH	45215	**800-543-4691**	513-948-9951	544
Cindy Rowe Auto Glass 4750 Lindle Rd	Harrisburg	PA	17111	**800-882-4639**	717-939-7551	62-2
Cine Magnetics Inc 100 Business Pk Dr Suite 1	Armonk	NY	10504	**800-431-1102**	914-273-7500	644
CinemaNow 4553 Glencoe Ave Suite 200	Marina del Rey	CA	90292	**800-432-5216**	310-255-3700	784
Cinemark Inc 3900 Dallas Pkwy Suite 500	Plano	TX	75093	**800-950-2872**	972-665-1000	733
Cinematographers. American Society of 1782 N Orange Dr	Hollywood	CA	90028	**800-448-0145**	323-969-4333	48-4
Cinergy Children's Museum 1301 Western Ave Cincinnati Museum Ctr	Cincinnati	OH	45203	**800-733-2077**	513-287-7000	510
Cinergy Corp 139 E 4th St *NYSE: CIN*	Cincinnati	OH	45202	**800-544-6900**	513-421-9500	355-5
Cinergy/CG & E 139 E 4th St *Cust Svc	Cincinnati	OH	45201	**800-544-6900***	513-421-9500	774
Cinergy/PSI 139 E 4th St *Cust Svc	Cincinnati	OH	45201	**800-544-6900***	513-421-9500	774
Cinergy/ULH & P 139 E 4th St *Cust Svc	Cincinnati	OH	45202	**800-544-6900***	513-421-9500	774
Cingular Wireless 5565 Glenridge Connector Suite 1401	Atlanta	GA	30342	**866-246-4852**	404-236-6000	721
Cinnabar Solution Inc 155 Sunnynoll Ct Suite 300	Winston-Salem	NC	27106	**800-782-2171**		688
Cinnabon World Famous Cinnamon Rolls 6 Concourse Pkwy Suite 1700	Atlanta	GA	30328	**866-232-4401**	770-391-9500	69
Cinram International Inc 2255 Markham Rd	Scarborough	ON	M1B2W3	**800-387-5146**	416-298-8190	644
Cintas Corp 6800 Cintas Blvd *NASDAQ: CTAS*	Mason	OH	45262	**800-786-4367**	513-459-1200	434
CIO Magazine 492 Old Connecticut Path	Framingham	MA	01701	**800-788-4605**	508-872-8200	449-5
Ciphergen Biosystems Inc 6611 Dumbarton Cir *NASDAQ: CIPH*	Fremont	CA	94555	**888-864-3770**	510-505-2100	86
Ciprico Inc 17400 Medina Rd Suite 800 *NASDAQ: CPCI*	Plymouth	MN	55447	**800-727-4669**	763-551-4000	174
CIR (Center for Individual Rights) 1233 20th St NW Suite 300	Washington	DC	20036	**877-426-2665**	202-833-8400	48-8
Circa 1801 Doblin Fabrics 1 Jacquard Dr *Cust Svc	Connelly Springs	NC	28612	**800-462-9295***	828-397-7003	730-1
Circa Information Technologies Inc 12001 Woodruff Ave Suite H	Downey	CA	90241	**877-992-4722**	562-803-1594	176-10
Circadian Technologies Inc 24 Hartwell Ave	Lexington	MA	02421	**800-284-5001**	781-676-6900	193
Circle B Co Inc 5636 S Meridian St	Indianapolis	IN	46217	**800-775-5640**	317-787-5746	188-9
Circle Bar Guest Ranch HCR 81 Box 61	Utica	MT	59452	**888-570-0227**	406-423-5454	238
Circle Group Holdings Inc 1011 Campus Dr *AMEX: CXN*	Mundelein	IL	60060	**800-730-4880**	847-549-6002	779
Circle in the Square Theatre 1633 Broadway	New York	NY	10019	**800-432-7250**	212-239-6200	732
Circle Y of Yoakum Inc 201 W Morris St	Yoakum	TX	77995	**800-531-3600**	361-293-5251	423
Circle Z Ranch PO Box 194	Patagonia	AZ	85624	**888-854-2525**	520-394-2525	238
Circleville Bible College PO Box 458	Circleville	OH	43113	**800-701-0222**	740-474-8896	163
Circuit City Group 9950 Mayland Dr	Richmond	VA	23233	**800-251-2665**	804-527-4000	35
Circuit City Stores Inc 9950 Mayland Dr *NYSE: CC*	Richmond	VA	23233	**800-251-2665**	804-527-4000	355-3
Circuit Research Labs Inc 1302 W Drivers Way	Tempe	AZ	85284	**800-535-7648**	480-403-8300	633

Name / Address	City	State	ZIP	Toll-Free	Phone	Class
Circuits & Systems Society. IEEE IEEE Operations Ctr 445 Hoes Ln	Piscataway	NJ	08854	**800-678-4333**	732-981-0060	49-19
Circus Circus Hotel & Casino Las Vegas 2880 Las Vegas Blvd S *Resv	Las Vegas	NV	89109	**800-634-3450***	702-734-0410	133
Circus Circus Hotel & Casino Reno 500 N Sierra St	Reno	NV	89503	**800-648-5010**	775-329-0711	133
Circus World Museum 550 Water St	Baraboo	WI	53913	**866-693-1500**	608-356-8341	509
Cirelli Foods Inc 30 Commerce Blvd	Middleboro	MA	02346	**800-242-0939**	508-947-8778	292-6
Cirque Corp 2463 S 3850 West Suite A	Salt Lake City	UT	84120	**800-454-3375**	801-467-1100	171-1
Cirque du Soleil Inc 8400 2nd Ave	Montreal	QC	H1Z4M6	**800-678-2119**	514-722-2324	147
Cirrus Healthcare Products LLC 60 Main St PO Box 220	Cold Spring Harbor	NY	11724	**800-327-6151**	631-692-7600	572
Cirrus Logic Inc 2901 Via Fortuna *NASDAQ: CRUS*	Austin	TX	78746	**800-888-5016**	512-851-4000	686
CIS (Cancer Information Service) National Cancer Institute 9000 Rockville Pike Bldg 31	Bethesda	MD	20892	**800-422-6237**	301-496-4000	336-6
CIS (Communities in Schools Inc) 277 S Washington St Suite 210	Alexandria	VA	22314	**800-247-4543**	703-519-8999	48-6
Cisco Systems Foundation 170 W Tasman Dr	San Jose	CA	95134	**800-553-6387**	408-527-3040	299
Cisco Systems Inc 170 W Tasman Dr *NASDAQ: CSCO*	San Jose	CA	95134	**800-553-6387**	408-526-4000	174
Cissell Mfg Co 831 S 1st St	Louisville	KY	40203	**800-882-6665**	502-587-1292	418
Citadel The 171 Moultrie St	Charleston	SC	29409	**800-868-1842**	843-953-5230	163
Citadel Halifax Hotel 1960 Brunswick St	Halifax	NS	B3J2G7	**800-565-7162**	902-422-1391	372
Citadel Security Software Inc 8750 N Central Expy	Dallas	TX	75231	**800-962-0701**	214-520-9292	176-12
Citadon Inc 201 Mission St Suite 2700 *Sales	San Francisco	CA	94105	**800-351-5231***	415-882-1888	39
Citation Homes Inc 1100 Lake St	Spirit Lake	IA	51360	**800-831-5090**	712-336-2156	805
CITCO Operations 357 Washington St	Chardon	OH	44024	**800-242-7366**	440-285-9181	1
Citect Inc 30000 Mill Creek Ave Suite 300	Alpharetta	GA	30022	**888-248-3281**	770-521-7511	176-5
CITGO Asphalt Refining Co 620 W Germantown Pike	Plymouth Meeting	PA	19462	**800-443-4232**	484-530-4020	570
Citi Financial Mortgage Co 5901 E Fowler Ave	Tampa	FL	33617	**800-217-1000**	813-984-8801	498
Citibank (Delaware) 1 Penns Way	New Castle	DE	19720	**800-341-4727**	302-323-3801	71
Citibank FSB 245 Market St	San Francisco	CA	94105	**866-248-4937**		71
Citibank NA 399 Park Ave	New York	NY	10022	**800-627-3999**		71
Citibank (Nevada) NA 8701 W Sahara Ave	Las Vegas	NV	89117	**866-248-4937**		71
Citibank (New York State) 3330 Monroe Ave	Pittsford	NY	14618	**800-934-1609**		71
Citibank (South Dakota) NA 701 E 60th St N	Sioux Falls	SD	57117	**800-843-0777**	605-331-2626	71
Citibank (West) FSB 950 Market St	San Francisco	CA	94104	**866-248-4937**		71
Citicapital 1255 Wrights Ln	West Chester	PA	19380	**800-736-9033**	610-719-4500	261-3
Citicorp Venture Capital Ltd 399 Park Ave 14th Fl Zone 4	New York	NY	10022	**800-285-3000**	212-559-1127	679
Cities of Gold Casino 10-B Cities of Gold Rd	Santa Fe	NM	87506	**800-455-3313**	505-455-3313	133
CitiFinancial 300 St Paul Pl *Cust Svc	Baltimore	MD	21202	**800-922-6235***	410-332-3000	215
Citifunds PO Box 9083	Boston	MA	02266	**800-331-1792**		517
Citigroup Global Markets Holdings Inc 300 First Stamford Pl 2nd Fl *Sales	Stamford	CT	06902	**888-777-0102***	203-961-6000	393
CitiMortgage Inc 15851 Clayton Rd	Ballwin	MO	63011	**800-283-7918**		498
Citiplate Inc 1600 Stewart Ave Suite 201	Westbury	NY	11590	**800-280-9778**	516-484-2000	770
CitiStreet PO Box 6723	Summerset	NJ	08875	**800-537-6517**	732-514-2000	679
Citizen The 171 Fair St	Laconia	NH	03246	**800-564-3806**	603-524-3800	522-2
Citizen Publishing Co Inc 805 Park Ave PO box 558	Beaver Dam	WI	53916	**800-777-9470**	920-887-0321	623-8
Citizen Systems America Corp 363 Van Ness Way Suite 404	Torrance	CA	90501	**800-421-6516**	310-781-1460	171-6
Citizen Tribune 1609 W 1st North St PO Box 625	Morristown	TN	37815	**800-624-0281**	423-581-5630	522-2
Citizen Watch Co of America Inc 1200 Wall St W	Lyndhurst	NJ	07071	**800-321-1023**	201-438-8150	151
Citizens Against Government Waste (CAGW) 1301 Connecticut Ave NW Suite 400	Washington	DC	20036	**800-232-6479**	202-467-5300	48-7
Citizens Bank 919 Market St	Wilmington	DE	19801	**888-910-4100**	302-421-2228	71
Citizens Bank 328 S Saginaw St 1 Citizens Banking Ctr	Flint	MI	48502	**800-825-7200**	810-766-7500	71
Citizens Bank of Massachusetts 28 State St	Boston	MA	02109	**800-922-9999**	617-725-5900	71
Citizens Bank New Hampshire 875 Elm St	Manchester	NH	03101	**800-922-9999**	603-634-6000	71
Citizens Bank of Rhode Island 1 Citizens Plaza *Cust Svc	Providence	RI	02903	**800-922-9999***	401-456-7000	71
Citizens Banking Corp 328 S Saginaw St *NASDAQ: CBCF* ■ *Cust Svc	Flint	MI	48502	**800-825-7200***	810-766-7500	355-2
Citizens Business Bank 701 N Haven Ave Suite 350	Ontario	CA	91764	**888-222-5432**	909-980-4030	71
Citizens Committee for the Right to Keep & Bear Arms (CCRKBA) 12500 NE 10th Pl	Bellevue	WA	98005	**800-426-4302**	425-454-4911	48-7
Citizens Communications Co 3 High Ridge Pk *NYSE: CZN*	Stamford	CT	06905	**800-877-4390**	203-614-5600	721
Citizens Electric Corp 150 Merchant St	Sainte Genevieve	MO	63670	**877-876-3511**	573-883-5339	244

Name / Address	City	State	ZIP	Toll-Free	Phone	Class
Citizens Equity First Credit Union 5401 W Dirksen Pkwy	Peoria	IL	61607	**800-633-7077**	309-633-7000	216
Citizens Financial Corp 12910 Shelbyville Rd Suite 300 *NASDAQ: CNFL*	Louisville	KY	40243	**800-843-7752**	502-244-2420	355-4
Citizens Financial Group Inc 1 Citizens Dr	Providence	RI	02915	**800-922-9999**	401-456-7000	355-2
Citizens Financial Services 707 Ridge Rd	Munster	IN	46321	**800-334-5869**	219-836-5500	71
Citizens First Bancorp Inc 525 Water St *NASDAQ: CTZN*	Port Huron	MI	48060	**800-922-5308**	810-987-8300	355-2
Citizens First Savings Bank 525 Water St	Port Huron	MI	48060	**800-922-5308**	810-987-8300	71
Citizens Funds 1 Harbor Pl Suite 400	Portsmouth	NH	03801	**800-223-7010**	603-436-5152	517
Citizens Gas & Coke Utility 2020 N Meridian St	Indianapolis	IN	46202	**800-427-4217**	317-924-3341	774
Citizens Inc 400 E Anderson Ln *NYSE: CIA*	Austin	TX	78752	**800-880-5044**	512-837-7100	355-4
Citizens Insurance Co of America 645 W Grand River Ave	Howell	MI	48843	**800-388-1300**	517-546-2160	384-4
Citizens Insurance Co of America PO Box 149151	Austin	TX	78714	**800-880-5044**	512-836-9730	384-2
Citizens Network for Foreign Affairs (CNFA) 1111 19th St NW Suite 900	Washington	DC	20036	**888-872-2632**	202-296-3920	48-5
Citizens Security Life Insurance Co PO Box 436149	Louisville	KY	40253	**800-843-7752**	502-244-2420	384-2
Citizens Trust Bank PO Box 4485	Atlanta	GA	30303	**800-547-1344**	404-659-5959	71
Citra Trading Corp 590 5th Ave 14th Fl *Orders	New York	NY	10036	**800-223-6515***	212-354-1000	403
Citrix Systems Inc 851 W Cypress Creek Rd *NASDAQ: CTXS*	Fort Lauderdale	FL	33309	**800-393-1888**	954-267-3000	176-12
Citrus County Chronicle 1624 N Meadowcrest Blvd	Crystal River	FL	34429	**888-852-2340**	352-563-6363	522-2
Citrus Valley Hospice 820 N Phillips Ave	West Covina	CA	91791	**877-422-7301**	626-859-2263	365
Citterio USA Corp 5115 35th St	Long Island City	NY	11101	**800-435-8888**	718-706-7390	291-26
City Bank PO Box 97007 *NASDAQ: CTBK*	Lynnwood	WA	98046	**800-569-0006**	425-745-5933	71
City Beverage LLC 1105 E Lafayette St	Bloomington	IL	61701	**800-272-2635**	309-662-1373	82-1
City Beverages of Orlando 10928 Florida Crown Dr	Orlando	FL	32824	**800-717-7267**	407-851-7100	82-1
City Bus 1500 W 3rd St	Williamsport	PA	17701	**800-248-9287**	570-326-2500	109
City Center Motel 800 N Carson St	Carson City	NV	89701	**800-338-7760**	775-882-5535	373
City College of New York 138th St & Convent Ave	New York	NY	10031	**800-286-9937**	212-650-7000	163
City Escape Holidays 13470 Washington Blvd Suite 101	Marina del Rey	CA	90292	**800-222-0022**	310-827-5031	760
City Holding Co 25 Gatewater Rd *NASDAQ: CHCO*	Cross Lanes	WV	25313	**800-922-9236**	304-769-1100	355-2
City of Hope National Medical Center 1500 E Duarte Rd	Duarte	CA	91010	**866-434-4673**	626-256-4673	366-2
Beckman Research Institute 1500 E Duarte Rd	Duarte	CA	91010	**800-826-4673**	626-359-8111	366-5
Hematology & Hematopoietic Cell Transplantation Div 1500 E Duarte Rd	Duarte	CA	91010	**800-535-7119**	626-256-4673	758
City Lighting Products Co 4307 W Papin St	Saint Louis	MO	63109	**800-888-2572**	314-534-1090	245
City National Bancshares Inc 25 W Flagler St	Miami	FL	33130	**800-435-8839**	305-577-7333	355-2
City National Bank 400 N Roxbury Dr *Cust Svc	Beverly Hills	CA	90210	**800-773-7100***	310-888-6000	71
City National Bank of Florida 450 E Las Olas Blvd	Fort Lauderdale	FL	33301	**800-762-2489**	954-467-6667	71
City National Bank of West Virginia 3601 McCorckle Ave	Charleston	WV	25304	**877-203-8700**	304-926-3300	71
City Public Service Board 145 Navarro St	San Antonio	TX	78296	**800-773-3077**	210-353-2222	774
City Securities Corp PO Box 44992	Indianapolis	IN	46244	**800-800-2489**	317-634-4400	679
City Suites Hotel 933 W Belmont Ave	Chicago	IL	60657	**800-248-9108**	773-404-3400	373
City of Thomasville Tourism Authority 401 S Broad St	Thomasville	GA	31792	**800-704-2350**	229-227-7099	205
City University of Bellevue 11900 NE 1st St	Bellevue	WA	98005	**800-426-5596**	425-637-1010	163
City University Los Angeles PO Box 4277	Inglewood	CA	90309	**800-262-8388**	310-671-0783	163
Citywide Reservation Services 839 Beacon St Suite A	Boston	MA	02215	**800-468-3593**	617-267-7424	368
Civacon 4304 N Mattox Rd *Sales	Riverside	MO	64150	**888-526-5657***	816-741-6600	777
CIVCO Medical Instruments 102 1st St S	Kalona	IA	52247	**800-445-6741**	319-656-4447	375
Civil Engineering Magazine 1801 Alexander Bell Dr Suite 100	Reston	VA	20191	**800-548-2723**	703-295-6000	449-21
Civil & Environmental Consultants Inc 333 Baldwin Rd	Pittsburgh	PA	15205	**800-365-2324**	412-429-2324	258
Civil Rights Newsletter PO Box 7376	Alexandria	VA	22307	**800-876-2545**	703-768-9600	521-7
Civil Rights. US Commission on 624 9th St NW	Washington	DC	20425	**800-552-6843**	202-376-7700	336-16
Civil Service Employees Insurance Co 50 California St Suite 2550	San Francisco	CA	94111	**800-282-6848**	925-817-6300	384-4
Civil War Preservation Trust (CWPT) 1331 H St NW Suite 1001	Washington	DC	20005	**888-606-1400**	202-367-1861	48-13
Civista Medical Center 701 E Charles St	La Plata	MD	20646	**800-422-8585**	301-609-4000	366-2

Name / Address	City	State	ZIP	Toll-Free	Phone	Class
Civitan International 1 Civitan Pl PO Box 130744	Birmingham	AL	35213	**800-248-4826**	205-591-8910	48-15
Civitan Magazine 1 Civitan Pl PO Box 130744	Birmingham	AL	35213	**800-248-4826**	205-591-8910	449-10
CJ Duffey Paper Co Inc 528 Washington Ave N	Minneapolis	MN	55401	**800-752-8190**	612-338-8701	543
CJ Krehbiel Co Inc 3962 Virginia Ave	Cincinnati	OH	45227	**800-598-7808**	513-271-6035	614
CJ Systems Aviation Group Inc 57 Allegheny County Airport	West Mifflin	PA	15122	**800-245-0230**	412-466-2500	31
CJ Vitner & Co 4202 W 45th St	Chicago	IL	60632	**800-397-7629**	773-523-7900	291-35
CJ Winter Machine Technologies Inc 167 Ames St	Rochester	NY	14611	**800-288-7655**	585-429-5000	448
CJRT-FM 91.1 (Jazz) 150 Mutual St	Toronto	ON	M5B2M1	**888-595-0404**	416-595-0404	631
CJT Koolcarb Inc 494 Mission St	Carol Stream	IL	60188	**800-323-2299**	630-690-5933	484
CK Worldwide Inc PO Box 1636	Auburn	WA	98071	**800-426-0877**	253-854-5820	798
CKC (Canadian Kennel Club) 89 Skyway Ave Suite 100	Etobicoke	ON	M9W6R4	**800-250-8040**	416-675-5511	48-3
CKE Restaurants Inc 401 W Carl Karcher Way *NYSE: CKR*	Anaheim	CA	92801	**800-758-2275**	714-774-5796	656
CKIK-FM 107.3 (CHR) 630 3rd Ave SW Suite 105	Calgary	AB	T2P4L4	**800-563-7770**	403-716-6500	631
CKRY-FM 105.1 (Ctry) 630 3rd Ave SW Suite 105	Calgary	AB	T2P4L4	**800-563-7770**	403-716-6500	631
CKVU-TV Ch 10 (Ind) 180 W 2nd Ave	Vancouver	BC	V5Y3T9	**888-336-9978**	604-876-1344	726
CLA (Coin Laundry Assn) 1315 Butterfield Rd Suite 212	Downers Grove	IL	60515	**800-570-5629**	630-963-5547	49-4
Claflin University 400 Magnolia St	Orangeburg	SC	29115	**800-922-1276**	803-535-5339	163
Claiborne County Chamber of Commerce 3222 Hwy 25 E Suite 1	Tazewell	TN	37879	**800-332-8164**	423-626-4149	137
Claiborne Electric Co-op Inc 12525 Hwy 9	Homer	LA	71040	**800-929-3504**	318-927-3504	244
Claim Jumper Restaurants 16721 Millikan Ave	Irvine	CA	92606	**800-949-4538**	949-756-9001	657
Claimsnet.com Inc 14860 Montfort Dr Suite 250	Dallas	TX	75254	**800-356-1511**	972-458-1701	223
Clair Odell Group 2 W Lafayette St Suite 400	Norristown	PA	19401	**800-220-3008**	610-825-5555	383
Claire Mfg Co 500 Vista Ave *Sales	Addison	IL	60101	**800-252-4731***	630-543-7600	143
Claire's Accessories 2400 W Central Rd	Hoffman Estates	IL	60195	**800-252-4737**	847-765-1100	155-6
Clairol Div Procter & Gamble Co 1 Blachley Rd	Stamford	CT	06922	**800-223-5800**	203-357-5000	211
Claitor's Law Books & Publishing Inc 3165 S Acadian Thwy	Baton Rouge	LA	70808	**800-274-1403**	225-344-0476	614
Clamp Swing Pricing Co Inc 8386 Capwell Dr	Oakland	CA	94621	**800-227-7615**	510-567-1600	404
Clampitt Paper Co of Dallas 9207 Ambassador Row	Dallas	TX	75247	**800-856-0138**	214-638-3300	543
Clamshell Buildings 1990 Knoll Dr	Ventura	CA	93003	**800-360-8853**	805-650-1700	718
Clamshell Structures Inc DBA Clamshell Buildings 1990 Knoll Dr	Ventura	CA	93003	**800-360-8853**	805-650-1700	718
ClappDiCO Corp 6325 Industrial Pkwy	Whitehouse	OH	43571	**800-537-6445**	419-877-5358	484
Clarcor Inc 840 Crescent Ctr Dr Suite 600 *NYSE: CLC*	Franklin	TN	37067	**800-252-7267**	615-771-3100	19
Clare Rose Inc 72 Clare Rose Blvd	Patchogue	NY	11772	**800-427-2833**	631-475-1840	82-1
Claremont Co Inc 35 Winsome Dr PO Box 430	Durham	CT	06422	**800-222-4448**	860-349-4499	382
Claremont Inn 555 W Foothill Blvd	Claremont	CA	91711	**800-854-5733**	909-626-2411	373
Claremont Resort & Spa 41 Tunnel Rd	Berkeley	CA	94705	**800-551-7266**	510-843-3000	655
Claremont Restaurant Group 129 Fast Ln	Mooresville	NC	28117	**877-704-5939**	704-660-5939	656
Clarence House Imports Ltd Inc 3010 Westchester Ave	Purchase	NY	10577	**800-803-2890**	914-701-0100	356
Clarendon College PO Box 968	Clarendon	TX	79226	**800-687-9737**	806-874-3571	160
Clarendon County Chamber of Commerce 19 N Brooks St	Manning	SC	29102	**800-731-5253**	803-435-4405	137
Clariant Corp 4000 Monroe Rd *Cust Svc	Charlotte	NC	28205	**800-631-8077***	704-331-7000	142
Claridge Hotel 1244 N Dearborn Pkwy	Chicago	IL	60610	**800-245-1258**	312-787-4980	373
Clarient Inc 33171 Paseo Cerveza *NASDAQ: CLRT*	San Juan Capistrano	CA	92675	**888-443-3310**	949-443-3355	375
ClariNet Communications Corp 4880 Stevens Creek Blvd Suite 206 *Sales	San Jose	CA	95129	**800-873-6387***	408-296-0366	380
Clarion Books 215 Park Ave S *Cust Svc	New York	NY	10003	**800-225-3362***	212-420-5800	623-2
Clarion Commercial Holdings Inc 230 Park Ave 12th Fl	New York	NY	10169	**800-776-4696**	212-883-2500	640
Clarion Corp of America 661 W Redondo Beach Blvd	Gardena	CA	90247	**800-462-5274**	310-327-9100	52
Clarion Hospital 1 Hospital Dr	Clarion	PA	16214	**800-522-0505**	814-226-9500	366-2
Clarion Hotel & Conference Center Antietam Creek 901 Dual Hwy	Hagerstown	MD	21740	**888-528-6738**	301-733-5100	370
Clarion Hotel San Jose Airport 1355 N 4th St	San Jose	CA	95112	**800-453-5340**	408-453-5340	373
Clarion Hotels 10750 Columbia Pike	Silver Spring	MD	20901	**800-424-6423**	301-592-5000	369
Clarion-Ledger 201 S Congress St	Jackson	MS	39201	**800-367-3384**	601-961-7000	522-2
Clarion University of Pennsylvania 840 Wood St	Clarion	PA	16214	**800-672-7171**	814-393-2000	163
Venango Campus 1801 W 1st St	Oil City	PA	16301	**800-672-7171**	814-676-6591	163
Claritas Inc 1525 Wilson Blvd Suite 1200	Arlington	VA	22209	**800-234-5973**	703-812-2700	176-1
Clarity Systems Ltd 2 Sheppard Ave E Suite 800	Toronto	ON	M2N5Y7	**877-410-5070**	416-250-5500	176-1
Clark Atlanta University 223 James P Brawley Dr SW *Admissions	Atlanta	GA	30314	**800-688-3228***	404-880-8000	163

Name / Address	City	State	ZIP	Toll-Free	Phone	Class
Clark Construction Group LLC 7500 Old Georgetown Rd	Bethesda	MD	20814	**800-827-4422**	301-272-8100	185
Clark Consulting 102 S Wynstone Park Dr Suite 200 *NYSE: CLK*	North Barrington	IL	60010	**800-597-7976**	847-304-5800	192
Clark Cos NA 156 Oak St *Cust Svc	Newton Upper Falls	MA	02464	**800-425-2757***	617-964-1222	658
Clark County Rural Electric Membership Corp 7810 SR 60 PO Box L	Sellersburg	IN	47172	**800-462-6988**	812-246-3316	244
Clark-Cutler-McDermott Co 5 Fisher St PO Box 269	Franklin	MA	02038	**800-922-3019**	508-528-1200	730-6
Clark David Co Inc 360 Franklin St *Cust Svc	Worcester	MA	01615	**800-298-6235***	508-751-5800	385
Clark-Dunbar Carpets 3232 Empire Dr	Alexandria	LA	71301	**800-256-1467**	318-445-0262	285
Clark Electric Co-op 124 N Main St PO Box 190	Greenwood	WI	54437	**800-272-6188**	715-267-6188	244
Clark Energy Co-op Inc 264 Iron Works Rd	Winchester	KY	40392	**800-992-3269**	859-744-4251	244
Clark Enterprises Inc 7500 Old Georgetown Rd	Bethesda	MD	20814	**800-800-2242**	301-657-7100	355-3
Clark Grave Vault Co 375 E 5th Ave	Columbus	OH	43201	**800-848-3570**	614-294-3761	134
Clark HC Implement Co 4411 E Hwy 12	Aberdeen	SD	57401	**800-532-6747**	605-225-8170	270
Clark JL Mfg Co 923 23rd Ave	Rockford	IL	61104	**800-252-7267**	815-962-8861	124
Clark-Lindsey Village 101 W Windsor Rd	Urbana	IL	61802	**800-998-2581**	217-344-2144	659
Clark Material Handling Co 2317 Alumni Park Plaza Suite 500	Lexington	KY	40517	**866-252-5275**	859-422-6400	462
Clark & Mitchell Inc 7820 Bluffton Rd	Fort Wayne	IN	46809	**800-319-2366**	260-747-7431	285
Clark Specialty Co Inc 8440 Rt 54	Hammondsport	NY	14840	**888-569-2128**	607-569-2191	688
Clark Steel Framing Systems 101 Clark Blvd	Middle Town	OH	45044	**800-882-7883**	513-539-2900	471
Clark Tire & Auto Supply Co Inc 220 S Center St	Hickory	NC	28602	**800-968-3092**	828-322-2303	62-5
Clark University 950 Main St	Worcester	MA	01610	**800-462-5275**	508-793-7711	163
Clarke American Checks Inc 10931 Laureate Dr	San Antonio	TX	78249	**800-382-0818**	210-697-8888	140
Clarke Electric Co-op Inc 1103 N Main St	Osceola	IA	50213	**800-362-2154**	641-342-2173	244
Clarke Products Inc 1170 109th St	Grand Prairie	TX	75050	**800-426-8964**	972-660-1992	367
Clarke-Washington Electric Membership Corp 1307 College Ave	Jackson	AL	36545	**800-323-9081**	251-246-9081	244
Clarksburg Exponent Telegram 324 Hewes Ave	Clarksburg	WV	26301	**800-982-6034**	304-626-1400	522-2
Clarksdale-Coahoma County Chamber of Commerce & Industrial Foundation 1540 DeSoto Ave	Clarksdale	MS	38614	**800-626-3760**	662-627-7337	137
Clarkson College 101 S 42nd St	Omaha	NE	68131	**800-647-5500**	402-552-3100	163
Clarkson University 10 Clarkson Ave	Potsdam	NY	13699	**800-527-6577**	315-268-6400	163
Clarkston Consulting 1007 Slater Rd Suite 400	Durham	NC	27703	**800-652-4274**	919-484-4400	178
Clarksville Area Chamber of Commerce 312 Madison St	Clarksville	TN	37041	**800-530-2487**	931-647-2331	137
Clarksville/Montgomery County Tourist Commission PO Box 883	Clarksville	TN	37041	**800-530-2487**	931-648-0001	205
Classic Checks Inc PO Box 2	Edgewood	MD	21040	**800-354-3588**		140
Classic City Beverages Inc 530 Calhoun Dr	Athens	GA	30601	**800-300-0218**	706-353-1650	82-1
Classic Custom Vacations 5893 Rue Ferrari	San Jose	CA	95138	**800-221-3949**	408-287-4550	760
Classic Letter Co 2850 S Jefferson Ave	Saint Louis	MO	63118	**877-551-5596**	314-664-0023	5
Classic Residence by Hyatt 655 Pomander Walk	Teaneck	NJ	07666	**800-292-7474**	201-836-7474	659
Classic Sanitation Co Inc 375 Rt 1 & 9 S	Jersey City	NJ	07306	**800-386-7783**	201-547-4100	791
Classic Spas Inc 1400 Melody Rd	Marysville	CA	95901	**800-796-7727**	530-742-7304	367
Classic Toy Trains Magazine 21027 Crossroads Cir	Waukesha	WI	53186	**888-350-2413**	262-796-8776	449-14
Classic Transportation Group 1600 Locust Ave	Bohemia	NY	11716	**800-666-4949**	631-567-5100	433
Classroom Connect Inc 8000 Marina Blvd Suite 400	Brisbane	CA	94005	**800-638-1639**	650-351-5100	242
ClassroomDirect.com PO Box 830677	Birmingham	AL	35283	**800-599-3040**	205-251-9171	673
Clatsop Community College 1653 Jerome Ave	Astoria	OR	97103	**866-252-8767**	503-325-0910	160
Claude Gable Co 322 Fraley Rd	High Point	NC	27263	**800-422-5331**	336-883-1351	314-2
ClaudiaM Publications PO Box 925	Huntington	NY	11743	**800-241-0776**	631-424-7074	130
Clausen Miller PC 10 S La Salle St Suite 1600	Chicago	IL	60603	**800-826-3505**	312-855-1010	419
Clauss Cutlery Co 223 N Prospect St *Cust Svc	Fremont	OH	43420	**800-225-2877***	419-332-7344	219
Claussen Pickle Co 1300 Claussen Dr	Woodstock	IL	60098	**800-435-2817**	815-338-7000	291-19
Claverack Rural Electric Co-op Inc RR 2 Box 17	Wysox	PA	18854	**800-326-9799**	570-265-2167	244
Clawson Tank Co Inc 4545 Clawson Tank Dr	Clarkston	MI	48346	**800-272-1367**	248-625-8700	92
Clay Electric Co-op Inc 225 W Walker Dr *Cust Svc	Keystone Heights	FL	32656	**800-224-4917***	352-473-8000	244
Clay Lacy Aviation 7435 Valjean Ave	Van Nuys	CA	91406	**800-423-2904**	818-989-2900	14
Clay Today 1560 Kingsley Ave Suite 1	Orange Park	FL	32073	**888-424-6220**	904-264-3200	522-4
Clay-Union Electric Corp 1410 E Cherry St	Vermillion	SD	57069	**800-696-2832**	605-624-2673	244
Clayco Construction Co 2199 Innerbelt Business Ctr Dr	Saint Louis	MO	63114	**888-429-3330**	314-429-5100	187-7
Claymore C Sieck Wholesale Florist 311 E Chase St	Baltimore	MD	21202	**800-624-7134**	410-685-4660	288

Name / Address	City	State	Zip	Toll-Free	Phone	Class
Clayton Block Co 515 Lakewood New Egypt Rd *Orders	Lakewood	NJ	08701	**800-662-3044***	732-905-3131	181
Clayton AT & Co Inc 2 Pickwick Plaza	Greenwich	CT	06830	**800-282-5298**	203-861-1190	543
Clayton Corp 866 Horan Dr *Cust Svc	Fenton	MO	63026	**800-325-6180***	636-349-5333	590
Clayton Industries 4213 N Temple City Blvd	El Monte	CA	91731	**800-423-4585**	626-443-9381	464
Clayton Marcus Co Inc 166 Teague Town Rd *Cust Svc	Hickory	NC	28601	**800-893-2931***	828-495-2200	314-2
Clayton Metals Inc 546 Clayton Ct	Wood Dale	IL	60191	**800-323-7628**		483
Clayton on the Park 8025 Bonhomme Ave	Clayton	MO	63105	**800-323-7500**	314-721-6543	373
Clean Harbors Inc 1501 Washington St PO Box 859048 *NASDAQ: CLHB*	Braintree	MA	02185	**800-282-0058**	781-849-1800	653
Clean-Tech Co 2815 Olive St	Saint Louis	MO	63103	**800-852-2388**	314-652-2388	150
Clean Venture/Cycle Chem Inc 201 S 1st St	Elizabeth	NJ	07206	**800-347-7672**	908-355-5800	653
Clean Water Action 4455 Connecticut Ave NW Suite A-300	Washington	DC	20008	**800-709-2837**	202-895-0420	48-13
Clean Water Fund (CWF) 4455 Connecticut Ave NW Suite A300-16	Washington	DC	20008	**800-709-2837**	202-895-0432	48-13
Clean Water Report 8737 Colesville Rd Suite 1100	Silver Spring	MD	20910	**800-274-6737**	301-587-6300	521-5
Cleaning & Restoration. Association of Specialists in 8229 Cloverleaf Dr Suite 460	Millersville	MD	21108	**800-272-7012**	410-729-9900	49-4
CleanNet USA Inc 9861 Brokenland Pkwy Suite 208	Columbia	MD	21046	**800-735-8838**	410-720-6444	150
Cleanol Services Inc 60 Norelco Dr	Toronto	ON	M9L2X6	**800-263-9430**	416-745-5221	150
Cleanroom Systems 7000 Performance Dr	North Syracuse	NY	13212	**800-825-3268**	315-452-7400	19
Clear Brook Lodge 890 Bethel Hill Rd	Shickshinny	PA	18655	**800-582-6241**	570-864-3116	712
Clear Brook Manor 1100 E Northampton St	Wilkes-Barre	PA	18702	**800-582-6241**	570-823-1171	712
Clear Channel Communications Inc 200 E Basse Rd *NYSE: CCU*	San Antonio	TX	78209	**888-937-6131**	210-822-2828	184
Clear Channel Radio 200 E Basse Rd	San Antonio	TX	78209	**888-937-6131**	210-822-2828	629
Clear Channel Television 200 E Basse Rd	San Antonio	TX	78209	**888-937-6131**	210-822-2828	724
Clear Lake Convention & Visitors Bureau PO Box 188	Clear Lake	IA	50428	**800-285-5338**	641-357-2159	205
Clear Lam Packaging Inc 1950 Pratt Blvd	Elk Grove Village	IL	60007	**800-305-4409**	847-439-8570	538
Clear View Bag Co 7137 Prospect Church Rd	Thomasville	NC	27361	**800-670-6483**	336-885-8131	67
ClearCommerce Corp 11921 N Mopac Expy Suite 400	Austin	TX	78759	**888-725-9345**	512-832-0132	176-7
ClearOne Communications Inc 1825 W Research Way	Salt Lake City	UT	84119	**800-945-7730**	801-975-7200	720
Clearr Corp 6325 Sandburg Rd	Minneapolis	MN	55427	**800-948-3269**	763-398-5400	692
ClearSail Communications LLC DBA Family.NET 5160 Timber Creek Rd	Houston	TX	77017	**888-905-0888**	713-230-2800	390
ClearStory Systems 2 Westborough Business Pk Suite 2000	Westborough	MA	01581	**800-546-6600**	508-870-4000	176-1
Clearvue & SVE 6465 N Avondale Ave	Chicago	IL	60631	**800-829-1900**	773-775-9433	500
Clearwater Christian College 3400 Gulf to Bay Blvd	Clearwater	FL	33759	**800-348-4463**	727-726-1153	163
Clearwater Marine Aquarium 249 Windward Passage	Clearwater	FL	33767	**888-239-9414**	727-441-1790	40
Clearwater Mattress Inc 1185 Gooden Crossing	Largo	FL	33778	**800-274-6288**	727-539-1600	463
Clearwater-Polk Electric Co-op 315 N Main Ave PO Box O	Bagley	MN	56621	**888-694-3833**	218-694-6241	244
Clearwater Power Co 4230 Hatwai Rd PO Box 997	Lewiston	ID	83501	**888-743-1501**	208-743-1501	244
Cleary University 3601 Plymouth Rd	Ann Arbor	MI	48105	**800-589-1979**	734-332-4477	163
Cleary WA Corp 1049 Rt 27	Somerset	NJ	08873	**800-238-7813**	732-247-8000	276
Cleco Corp 1030 Donahue Ferry Rd *NYSE: CNL* ■ *Cust Svc	Pineville	LA	71360	**800-622-6537***	318-484-7400	355-5
Cleco Power LLC 2030 Donahue Ferry Rd *Cust Svc	Pineville	LA	71361	**800-622-6537***	318-484-7400	774
Cleft Palate-Craniofacial Assn. American 104 S Estes Dr Suite 204	Chapel Hill	NC	27514	**800-242-5338**	919-933-9044	49-8
Cleft Palate Foundation (CPF) 1504 E Franklin St Suite 102	Chapel Hill	NC	27514	**800-242-5338**	919-933-9044	48-17
Cleftstone Manor 92 Eden St	Bar Harbor	ME	04609	**888-288-4951**	207-288-8086	373
Clement Communications Inc 10 LaCrue Ave	Concordville	PA	19331	**888-358-5858**	610-459-4200	623-10
Clement Industries Inc PO Box 914 *Cust Svc	Minden	LA	71058	**800-562-5948***	318-377-2776	768
Clement Pappas & Co Inc 1045 N Parsonage Rd	Seabrook	NJ	08302	**800-257-7019**	856-455-1000	291-20
Clements National Co 6650 S Narragansett Ave	Chicago	IL	60638	**800-966-0016**	708-594-5890	19
Cleo Inc 4025 Viscount Ave	Memphis	TN	38118	**800-289-2536**	901-369-6300	542-2
Cleo Wallace Centers Westminster Campus 8405 Church Ranch Blvd	Westminster	CO	80021	**800-456-2536**	303-466-7391	366-1
Clerks. International Institute of Municipal 8331 Utica Ave Suite 200	Rancho Cucamonga	CA	91730	**800-251-1639**	909-944-4162	49-7
Clermont College 4200 Clermont College Dr	Batavia	OH	45103	**866-446-2822**	513-732-5200	160
Clermont County Convention & Visitors Bureau 410 E Main St PO Box 100	Batavia	OH	45103	**800-796-4282**	513-732-3600	205

Name / Address	City	State	Zip	Toll-Free	Phone	Class
Cleveland-Bolivar County Chamber of Commerce 600 3rd St	Cleveland	MS	38732	**800-295-7473**	662-843-2712	137
Cleveland Brothers Equipment Co Inc 5300 Paxton St	Harrisburg	PA	17111	**800-482-2378**	717-564-2121	353
Cleveland Browns 76 Lou Groza Blvd *Sales	Berea	OH	44017	**888-891-1999***	440-891-5000	703
Cleveland Browns Stadium 100 Alfred Lerner Way *Sales	Cleveland	OH	44114	**888-891-1999***	440-891-5000	706
Cleveland Cavaliers 1 Center Ct Gund Arena	Cleveland	OH	44115	**800-332-2260**	216-420-2000	703
Cleveland City Blue Printing Co 1937 Prospect Ave	Cleveland	OH	44115	**800-993-2583**	216-241-7344	239
Cleveland-Cliffs Inc 1100 Superior Ave 18th Fl *NYSE: CLF*	Cleveland	OH	44114	**800-521-5701**	216-694-5700	492
Cleveland Clinic 9500 Euclid Ave	Cleveland	OH	44195	**800-223-2273**	216-444-2200	366-2
Cleveland Convention Center 500 Lakeside Ave	Cleveland	OH	44114	**800-543-2489**	216-348-2200	204
Cleveland Gear Co 3249 E 80th St	Cleveland	OH	44104	**800-423-3169**	216-641-9000	700
Cleveland Golf Co 5630 Cerritos Ave *Cust Svc	Cypress	CA	90630	**800-999-6263***	714-821-4200	701
Cleveland (Greater) Growth Assn 50 Public Sq Suite 200	Cleveland	OH	44113	**800-562-7121**	216-621-3300	137
Cleveland Indians Jacobs Field 2401 Ontario St	Cleveland	OH	44115	**866-488-7743**	216-420-4200	703
Cleveland Institute of Art 11141 East Blvd	Cleveland	OH	44106	**800-223-4700**	216-421-7400	163
Cleveland Institute of Electronics 1776 E 17th St	Cleveland	OH	44114	**800-243-6446**	216-781-9400	787
Cleveland Legal Support PO Box 5358	Central Point	OR	97502	**800-888-6629**	541-665-5162	392
Cleveland Magazine 1422 Euclid Ave Suite 730	Cleveland	OH	44115	**800-210-7293**	216-771-2833	449-22
Cleveland Motion Controls Inc 7550 Hub Pkwy	Cleveland	OH	44125	**800-321-8072**	216-524-8800	202
Cleveland Motion Controls Inc Torque Systems Div 6 Enterprise Rd	Billerica	MA	01821	**800-669-5112**	978-667-5100	507
Cleveland Museum of Art 11150 East Blvd *Sales	Cleveland	OH	44106	**888-262-7175***	216-421-7340	509
Cleveland Museum of Natural History 1 Wade Oval Dr University Cir	Cleveland	OH	44106	**800-317-9155**	216-231-4600	509
Cleveland Orchestra 11001 Euclid Ave Severance Hall	Cleveland	OH	44106	**800-686-1141**	216-231-7300	563-3
Cleveland Plant & Flower Co 12920 Corporate Dr	Parma	OH	44130	**800-688-8012**	216-898-3500	288
Cleveland Plywood Co Inc 5900 Harvard Ave	Cleveland	OH	44105	**800-727-2759**	216-641-6600	602
Cleveland Punch & Die Co 666 Pratt St PO Box 769	Ravenna	OH	44266	**888-451-4342**	330-296-4342	745
Cleveland Range Co 1333 E 179th St	Cleveland	OH	44110	**800-338-2204**	216-481-4900	293
Cleveland State University 2121 Euclid Ave	Cleveland	OH	44115	**888-278-6446**	216-687-2000	163
Cleveland Steel Tool Co 474 E 105th St *Cust Svc	Cleveland	OH	44108	**800-446-4402***	216-681-7400	448
Cleveland Wire Cloth & Mfg Co 3573 E 78th St	Cleveland	OH	44105	**800-321-3234**	216-341-1832	676
Cleveland Wood Products 3871 W 150th St	Cleveland	OH	44111	**800-969-9695**	216-252-1190	104
Cleveland/Bradley Chamber of Commerce 225 Keith St	Cleveland	TN	37320	**800-472-6588**	423-472-6587	137
Cleveland/Bradley Convention & Visitors Bureau PO Box 2275	Cleveland	TN	37320	**800-472-6588**	423-472-6587	205
Clever Devices Ltd 5 Aerial Way	Syosset	NY	11791	**800-872-6129**	516-433-6100	385
Clevite Engine Parts 1350 Eisenhower Pl	Ann Arbor	MI	48108	**800-338-8786**	734-975-4777	60
Click Magazine 30 Grove St Suite C	Peterborough	NH	03458	**800-821-0115**	603-924-7209	449-6
Click Pharmacy 8790 SW 8th St *Orders	Miami	FL	33174	**800-838-9525***	305-226-8373	236
ClickSoftware Inc 35 Corporate Dr Suite 140 *NASDAQ: CKSW*	Burlington	MA	01803	**888-438-3308**	781-272-5903	176-7
ClientLogic Corp 3102 W End Ave Suite 900	Nashville	TN	37203	**877-935-6442**	615-301-7100	5
ClientSoft Inc 8323 NW 12th St Suite 216	Miami	FL	33126	**800-622-2684**	305-716-1007	39
Cliff House at Pikes Peak 306 Canon Ave	Manitou Springs	CO	80829	**888-212-7000**	719-685-3000	373
Cliff Spa at Snowbird Hwy 210 PO Box 929000	Snowbird	UT	84092	**800-453-3000**	801-933-2225	698
Cliff Weil Inc 8043 Industrial Pk Rd	Mechanicsville	VA	23116	**800-446-9345**	804-746-1321	403
Clifford of Vermont 1453 VT Route 107	Royalton	VT	05068	**800-451-4381**	802-234-9921	245
Cliffstar Corp 1 Cliffstar Ave	Dunkirk	NY	14048	**800-777-2389**	716-366-6100	291-20
Clift The 495 Geary St	San Francisco	CA	94102	**800-652-5438**	415-775-4700	373
Clifton Gunderson LLC 301 SW Adams St Suite 900	Peoria	IL	61656	**800-450-4565**	309-671-4500	2
Clifty Farm Country Ham Co Inc PO Box 1146	Paris	TN	38242	**800-486-4267**	731-642-9740	291-26
ClimateMaster Inc 7300 SW 44th St	Oklahoma City	OK	73179	**800-299-9747**	405-745-6000	15
Climax Mfg Co 7840 SR 26	Lowville	NY	13367	**800-225-4629**	315-376-8000	547
Climax Portable Machine Tools Inc 2712 E 2nd St	Newberg	OR	97132	**800-333-8311**	503-538-2185	484
Climbing Magazine 0326 Hwy 133 Suite 190	Carbondale	CO	81623	**800-493-4569**	970-963-9449	449-20
Clinch-Tite Corp PO Box 456	Sandy Lake	PA	16145	**800-241-0900**	724-376-7315	541
Clinical Cancer Letter PO Box 9905	Washington	DC	20016	**800-513-7042**	202-362-1809	521-8
Clinical Chemistry Inc. American Assn for 2101 L St NW Suite 202 *Cust Svc	Washington	DC	20037	**800-892-1400***	202-857-0717	49-19

Name / Address	City	State	Zip	Toll-Free	Phone	Class
Clinical Investigation. American Society for 35 Research Dr Suite 300	Ann Arbor	MI	48103	**866-660-2724**	734-222-6050	49-8
CliniComp International 9655 Towne Ctr Dr	San Diego	CA	92121	**800-350-8202**	858-546-8202	176-10
Cliniqa Corp 1432 S Mission Rd	Fallbrook	CA	92028	**800-728-5205**	760-728-5205	229
Clinton Area Chamber of Commerce 333 4th Ave S	Clinton	IA	52733	**800-828-5702**	563-242-5702	137
Clinton Community College 136 Clinton Point Dr	Plattsburgh	NY	12901	**800-552-1160**	518-562-4200	160
Clinton Convention & Visitors Bureau 333 4th Ave S	Clinton	IA	52732	**800-828-5702**	563-242-5702	205
Clinton County Economic Partnership 212 N Jay St	Lock Haven	PA	17745	**888-388-6991**	570-748-5782	137
Clinton County Electric Co-op Inc 475 N Main St	Breese	IL	62230	**800-526-7282**	618-526-7282	244
Clinton Herald 221 6th Ave S	Clinton	IA	52733	**800-729-7101**	563-242-7101	522-2
Clinton Memorial Hospital 610 W Main St	Wilmington	OH	45177	**800-803-9648**	937-382-6611	366-2
Clinton Milk Co Inc 353 Morris Ave	Newark	NJ	07108	**800-223-6455**	973-642-3000	291-27
Clinton Nursery Products Inc 114 W Main St	Clinton	CT	06413	**800-289-7645**	860-669-8611	276
Clio Awards Inc 770 Broadway 6th Fl	New York	NY	10003	**800-946-2546**	212-683-4300	49-18
Clippard Instrument Lab 7390 Colerain Ave	Cincinnati	OH	45239	**877-245-6247**	513-521-4261	220
Clipper Cruise Line Inc 11969 Westline Industrial Dr	Saint Louis	MO	63146	**800-325-0010**	314-655-6700	217
Clipper Exxpress Inc 9014 Heritage Pkwy Suite 300	Woodridge	IL	60517	**800-678-2547**	630-739-0700	440
Clipper Fund 9601 Wilshire Blvd Suite 800	Beverly Hills	CA	90210	**800-776-5033**	310-247-3940	517
Clipping Bureau of Florida PO Box 2190	Palm Harbor	FL	34682	**800-442-0332**	727-442-0332	612
CLLA (Commercial Law League of America) 150 N Michigan Ave Suite 600	Chicago	IL	60601	**800-978-2552**	312-781-2000	49-10
CLM Corp PO Box 16807	Duluth	MN	55816	**800-232-1302**	218-722-3981	432
Clock Conversions 6700 Clay Ave	Grand Rapids	MI	49548	**800-732-5625**	616-698-9400	62-7
Clockmakers Institute. American Watchmakers- 701 Enterprise Dr	Harrison	OH	45030	**866-367-2924**	513-367-9800	49-4
Clocktower Inn Hotel 181 E Santa Clara St	Ventura	CA	93001	**800-727-1027**	805-652-0141	373
Clofine Dairy Products Inc 1407 New Rd	Linwood	NJ	08221	**800-441-1001**	609-653-1000	292-4
Cloister The 100 Hudson Pl	Sea Island	GA	31561	**800-732-4752**	912-638-3611	655
Clola Enterprises LP 2324 Ridgepoint Dr Suite A	Austin	TX	78754	**800-833-2923**	512-615-3400	150
Clontech Laboratories Inc 1290 Terra Bella Ave	Mountain View	CA	94043	**877-232-8995**	800-662-2566	229
Clopay Building Products Inc PO Box 440	Baldwin	WI	54002	**800-621-3667**	715-684-3223	232
Clopay Corp 8585 Duke Blvd	Mason	OH	45040	**800-262-2260**	513-770-4800	489
Clopay Plastic Products Co 8585 Duke Blvd	Mason	OH	45040	**800-282-2260**	513-770-4800	589
Cloquet Area Chamber of Commerce 225 Sunnyside Dr	Cloquet	MN	55720	**800-554-4350**	218-879-1551	137
Clorox Co 1221 Broadway *NYSE: CLX* ■ *Cust Svc	Oakland	CA	94612	**800-292-2808***	510-271-7000	184
Clos du Bois Wines 19410 Geyserville Ave *Sales	Geyserville	CA	95441	**800-222-3189***	707-857-1651	81-3
Close Up Foundation Inc 44 Canal Ctr Plaza	Alexandria	VA	22314	**800-256-7387**	703-706-3300	48-7
Closerie Publishing 1952 S La Cienega Blvd	Los Angeles	CA	90034	**800-295-9909**	310-559-9704	130
Closet Factory 12800 S Broadway	Los Angeles	CA	90061	**800-692-5673**	310-516-7000	188-11
ClosetMaid PO Box 4400 *Cust Svc	Ocala	FL	34478	**800-874-0008***	352-401-6000	281
Cloud County Community College 2221 Campus Dr	Concordia	KS	66901	**800-729-5101**	785-243-1435	160
Clough Harbour & Assoc 3 Winners Circle	Albany	NY	12205	**800-836-0817**	518-453-4500	258
Clougherty Packing Co DBA Farmer John Meats 3049 E Vernon Ave *Sales	Los Angeles	CA	90058	**800-432-7637***	323-583-4621	465
Cloverdale Equipment Co 13133 Cloverdale St	Oak Park	MI	48237	**800-822-7999**	248-399-6600	261-2
Cloverdale Foods Co Inc 3015 34th St NW PO Box 667	Mandan	ND	58554	**800-669-9511**	701-663-9511	291-26
Cloverhill Bakery Inc 2035 N Narragansett Ave	Chicago	IL	60639	**800-745-9822**	773-745-9800	291-1
Cloverland Electric Co-op 2916 W Hwy M-28	Dafter	MI	49724	**800-562-4953**	906-635-6800	244
Cloverland Green Spring Dairy Inc 2701 Loch Raven Rd *Orders	Baltimore	MD	21218	**800-876-6455***	410-235-4477	291-27
Clovis News Journal 521 Pile St	Clovis	NM	88101	**800-819-9925**	505-763-3431	522-2
Clovis/Curry County Chamber of Commerce 215 N Main St	Clovis	NM	88101	**800-261-7656**	505-763-3435	137
Clow Valve Co 902 S 2nd St	Oskaloosa	IA	52577	**800-829-2569**	641-673-8611	776
Clowns of America International (COAI) PO Box C	Richeyville	PA	15358	**888-522-5696**		48-4
CLS Group 1015 Waterwood Pkwy Suite D	Edmond	OK	73034	**800-580-5460**	405-348-5460	187-1
CLS Inc 270 Locust St	Hartford	CT	06114	**800-842-8078**	860-549-1230	245
CLT Meetings/Publicis Events 340 N Primrose Dr	Orlando	FL	32803	**800-944-9797**	407-628-9700	183
Club Assn. National 1201 15th St NW Suite 450	Washington	DC	20005	**800-625-6221**	202-822-9822	48-23
Club Cal Neva Hotel Casino 38 E 2nd St	Reno	NV	89501	**877-777-7303**	775-954-4540	655
Club Car Inc PO Box 204658	Augusta	GA	30917	**800-227-0739**	706-863-3000	505
Club Deportivo Chivas USA Home Depot Center 18400 Avalon Blvd Suite 500	Carson	CA	90746	**877-244-8271**	310-630-4550	703
Club Europa 802 W Oregon St	Urbana	IL	61801	**800-331-1882**	217-344-5863	748
Club Intrawest 375 Water St Suite 326	Vancouver	BC	V6B5C6	**800-767-2166**	604-689-8816	738
Club Med Inc 75 Valencia Ave	Coral Gables	FL	33134	**800-258-2633**	305-925-9000	369
Club Med Sandpiper 3500 SE Morningside Blvd	Port Saint Lucie	FL	34952	**800-258-2633**	772-335-4400	655
Club Tiare 1990 E Grand Ave	El Segundo	CA	90245	**877-824-4846**	310-662-1860	27
ClubCorp Inc 3030 LBJ Fwy	Dallas	TX	75234	**800-346-7621**	972-243-6191	641
Clubhouse Inn & Suites Knoxville 208 Market Place Blvd	Knoxville	TN	37922	**800-258-2466**	865-531-1900	373
Clubhouse Inn & Suites Wichita 515 S Webb Rd	Wichita	KS	67207	**800-258-2466**	316-684-1111	373
ClubLink Corp 15675 Dufferin St *TSE: LNK*	King City	ON	L7B1K5	**800-661-1818**	905-841-3730	641
ClubMac Inc 19 Morgan St	Irvine	CA	92618	**800-258-2622**	949-768-8130	177
Clyde Peeling's Reptiland 18628 US Rt 15	Allenwood	PA	17810	**800-737-8452**	570-538-1869	811
CM Almy Inc 1 Ruth Rd	Pittsfield	ME	04967	**800-225-2569**	207-487-3232	153-14
CM Paula Co 6049 Hi-Tek Ct	Mason	OH	45040	**800-543-4464**	513-336-3100	322
CM Ranch 167 Fish Hatchery Rd	Dubois	WY	82513	**800-455-0721**	307-455-2331	238
CM Services Inc 800 Roosevelt Rd Bldg C Suite 312	Glen Ellyn	IL	60137	**800-613-6672**	630-858-7337	47
CM Trailers Inc 200 County Rd PO Box 680	Madill	OK	73446	**888-268-7577**	580-795-5536	768
CMA (Chocolate Manufacturers Assn) 8320 Old Courthouse Rd Suite 300	Vienna	VA	22182	**800-433-1200**	703-790-5011	49-6
CMA (Country Music Assn) 1 Music Cir S	Nashville	TN	37203	**800-998-4636**	615-244-2840	48-4
CMAA (Crane Manufacturers Assn of America) 8720 Red Oak Blvd Suite 201	Charlotte	NC	28217	**800-345-1815**	704-676-1190	49-13
CMD Products 1410 Flightline Dr Suite D	Lincoln	CA	95648	**800-210-9949**	916-434-0228	420
CME (Chicago Mercantile Exchange Holdings Inc) 20 S Wacker Dr *NYSE: CME*	Chicago	IL	60606	**800-331-3332**	312-930-1000	680
CMG (Computer Measurement Group) 151 Fries Mill Rd Suite 104	Turnersville	NJ	08012	**800-436-7264**	856-401-1700	48-9
CMI Group Inc 4200 International Pkwy	Carrollton	TX	75007	**800-377-7713**	972-862-4200	157
CMI Inc 316 E 9th St	Owensboro	KY	42303	**866-835-0690**	270-685-6545	519
CMI Schneible Co 714 N Saginaw St	Holly	MI	48442	**800-627-6508**	248-634-8211	19
CMMB (Catholic Medical Mission Board) 10 W 17th St	New York	NY	10011	**800-678-5659**	212-242-7757	48-5
C'mon Inn Billings 2020 Overland Ave	Billings	MT	59102	**800-655-1170**	406-655-1100	373
C'mon Inn Fargo 4338 20th Ave SW	Fargo	ND	58103	**800-334-1570**	701-277-9944	373
C'mon Inn Grand Forks 3051 32nd Ave S	Grand Forks	ND	58201	**800-255-2323**	701-775-3320	373
CMP Inc 3641 Pebble Beach	Northbrook	IL	60062	**888-848-6700**	847-564-8160	183
CMP Media LLC 600 Community Dr	Manhasset	NY	11030	**800-645-6278**	516-562-5000	623-9
CMS Electric Co-op Inc PO Box 790	Meade	KS	67864	**800-794-2353**	620-873-2184	244
CMS Electric & Gas Co 1 Energy Plaza	Jackson	MI	49201	**888-477-5050**	517-788-0550	774
CMS Energy Corp 1 Energy Plaza *NYSE: CMS*	Jackson	MI	49201	**800-477-5050**	517-788-0550	355-5
CMS Industries Ltd 1320 Alberta Ave	Saskatoon	SK	S7K1R5	**800-668-8821**	306-955-8821	469
CMS Panhandle Eastern Pipe Line Co 5444 Westheimer Rd	Houston	TX	77056	**800-275-7375**	713-627-4272	320
CMS Peripherals Inc 3095 Redhill Ave *Sales	Costa Mesa	CA	92626	**800-327-5773***	714-424-5520	171-8
CMS Trunkline Gas Co 5444 Westheimer Rd	Houston	TX	77056	**800-275-7375**	713-627-4272	320
CMT Cos Inc 125 Plantation Centre Dr S Suite 100	Macon	GA	31210	**800-767-7253**	478-474-5633	656
CNA 40 Wall St	New York	NY	10005	**800-331-6053**	212-440-3000	384-4
CNA Insurance Co 333 S Wabash Ave	Chicago	IL	60685	**800-262-2000**	312-822-5000	384-4
CNA Surety Corp 333 S Wabash Ave CNA Plaza *NYSE: SUR*	Chicago	IL	60604	**877-672-6115**	312-822-5000	384-5
CNA Valley Forge Life Insurance Co 100 CNA Dr	Nashville	TN	37214	**800-437-8854**	615-871-1400	384-2
CNB Financial Corp 1 S 2nd St *NASDAQ: CCNE*	Clearfield	PA	16830	**800-492-3221**	814-765-9621	355-2
CNBC Inc 900 Sylvan Ave	Englewood Cliffs	NJ	07632	**800-788-2622**	201-585-2622	725
CNet Technology Inc 1455 McCandless Dr	Milpitas	CA	95035	**800-486-2638**	408-934-0800	174
CNFA (Citizens Network for Foreign Affairs) 1111 19th St NW Suite 900	Washington	DC	20036	**888-872-2632**	202-296-3920	48-5
CNH LLC 600 E Peoria St	Goodfield	IL	61742	**800-432-7680**	309-965-2233	269
CNS Inc PO Box 39802 *NASDAQ: CNXS*	Minneapolis	MN	55439	**800-441-0417**	952-229-1500	468
CNT (Computer Network Technology Corp) 6000 Nathan Ln N *NASDAQ: CMNT*	Minneapolis	MN	55442	**800-638-8324**	763-268-6000	174
CNW Inc 4710 Madison Rd	Cincinnati	OH	45227	**800-327-5900**	513-321-2775	610
Co-Advantage Resources 111 W Jefferson St Suite 100	Orlando	FL	32801	**888-278-6055**	407-422-8448	619
Co-Anon Family Groups PO Box 12722	Tucson	AZ	85732	**800-898-9985**	520-513-5028	48-21
Co-Mo Electric Co-op Inc 29868 Hwy 5	Tipton	MO	65081	**800-781-0157**	660-433-5521	244
Co-op America 1612 K St NW Suite 600	Washington	DC	20006	**800-584-7336**	202-872-5307	48-13
Co-op Feed Dealers Inc 380 Broome Corporate Pkwy PO Box 670 *Cust Svc	Conklin	NY	13748	**800-333-0895***	607-651-9078	272
Co-op Reserve Supply Inc 1100 Iron Horse Pk *Cust Svc	North Billerica	MA	01862	**800-769-2667***	978-528-5320	190-4
COA (Council on Accreditation) 120 Wall St 11th Fl	New York	NY	10005	**866-262-8088**	212-797-3000	48-1
Coach House Motorhomes Inc 3480 Technology Dr	Nokomis	FL	34275	**800-235-0984**	941-485-0984	120
Coach Inc 516 W 34th St *NYSE: COH*	New York	NY	10001	**800-444-3611**	212-594-1850	422
Coach Tours Ltd 475 Federal Rd	Brookfield	CT	06804	**800-822-6224**	203-798-8687	748
Coaches Assn of America. National Soccer 6700 Squibb Rd Suite 215	Mission	KS	66202	**800-458-0678**	913-362-1747	48-22

Name / Address	City	State	ZIP	Toll-Free	Phone	Class
Coaches Assn. National Youth Sports 2050 Vista Pkwy	West Palm Beach	FL	33411	**800-729-2057**	561-684-1141	48-22
Coachman Inn 32959 SR-Hwy 20	Oak Harbor	WA	98277	**800-635-0043**	360-675-0727	373
Coachmen Recreational Vehicles Corp 423 N Main St	Middlebury	IN	46540	**800-353-7383**	574-825-8500	120
CoActive Marketing Group Inc 415 Northern Blvd *NASDAQ: CMKG*	Great Neck	NY	11021	**800-680-9998**	516-465-4600	4
Coahoma Community College 3240 Friars Point Rd	Clarksdale	MS	38614	**800-844-1222**	662-621-4205	160
COAI (Clowns of America International) PO Box C	Richeyville	PA	15358	**888-522-5696**		48-4
Coal & Energy, National Research Center for PO Box 6064	Morgantown	WV	26506	**800-624-8301**	304-293-2867	654
Coalition Against Bigger Trucks (CABT) 901 N Pitt St Suite 310	Alexandria	VA	22314	**888-222-8123**	703-535-3131	49-21
Coalition for Auto Repair Equality (CARE) 119 Oronoco St Suite 300	Alexandria	VA	22314	**800-229-5380**	703-519-7555	49-21
Coast Anaheim Hotel 1855 S Harbor Blvd	Anaheim	CA	92802	**800-663-1144**	714-750-1811	373
Coast Bastion Inn 11 Bastion St	Nanaimo	BC	V9R6E4	**800-663-1144**	250-753-6601	372
Coast Bellevue Hotel 625 116th Ave NE	Bellevue	WA	98004	**800-325-4000**	425-455-9444	373
Coast Casinos Inc 4500 W Tropicana Ave	Las Vegas	NV	89103	**888-365-7111**	702-365-7111	132
Coast to Coast Corporate Housing PO Box 1597	Cypress	CA	90630	**800-451-9466**	714-229-1881	209
Coast to Coast Moving & Storage Co 470 Pulaski St	Brooklyn	NY	11221	**800-872-6683**	718-443-5800	508
Coast Dental Services Inc 2502 Rocky Point Rd Suite 1000 *NASDAQ: CDEN*	Tampa	FL	33607	**800-983-3848**	813-288-1999	455
Coast Distribution System 350 Woodview Ave *AMEX: CRV*	Morgan Hill	CA	95037	**800-495-5858**	408-782-6686	61
Coast Edmonton Plaza Hotel 10155 105th St	Edmonton	AB	T5J1E2	**800-663-1144**	780-423-4811	372
Coast Electric Power Assn 302 Hwy 90 *Cust Svc	Bay Saint Louis	MS	39521	**800-624-3348***	228-467-6535	244
Coast Gateway Hotel 18415 International Blvd	Seattle	WA	98188	**800-663-1144**	206-248-8200	373
Coast Harbourside Hotel & Marina 146 Kingston St	Victoria	BC	V8V1V4	**800-663-1144**	250-360-1211	372
Coast International Inn 3333 W International Airport Rd	Anchorage	AK	99502	**800-663-1144**	907-243-2233	373
Coast Long Beach Hotel 700 Queensway Dr	Long Beach	CA	90802	**800-663-1144**	562-435-7676	373
Coast Plaza Hotel & Conference Center 1316 33rd St NE	Calgary	AB	T2A6B6	**800-663-1144**	403-248-8888	372
Coast Plaza Hotel & Suites at Stanley Park 1763 Comox St	Vancouver	BC	V6G1P6	**800-663-1144**	604-688-7711	372
Coast Santa Cruz Hotel 175 W Cliff Dr	Santa Cruz	CA	95060	**800-663-1144**	831-426-4330	373
Coast Terrace Inn Edmonton South 4440 Gateway Blvd	Edmonton	AB	T6H5C2	**800-663-1144**	780-437-6010	372
Coast Vancouver Airport Hotel 1041 SW Marine Dr	Vancouver	BC	V6P6L6	**800-263-1555**	604-263-1555	372
Coast Whistler Hotel 4005 Whistler Way	Whistler	BC	V0N1B4	**888-252-4454**	604-932-2522	372
Coastal Bend Blood Center 5025 Deepwood Cir	Corpus Christi	TX	78415	**800-299-4943**	361-855-4943	90
Coastal Bend College 3800 Charco Rd	Beeville	TX	78102	**866-722-2838**	361-358-2838	160
Coastal Beverage Co Inc 301 Harley Rd PO Box 10159	Wilmington	NC	28404	**800-229-3884**	910-799-3011	82-1
Coastal Caisson Corp 12290 US Hwy 19 N	Clearwater	FL	33764	**800-723-0015**	727-536-4748	187-2
Coastal Carolina University PO Box 261954	Conway	SC	29528	**800-277-7000**	843-349-2026	163
Coastal Cement Corp 36 Drydock Ave	Boston	MA	02210	**800-828-8352**	617-350-0183	135
Coastal Chem Inc 8305 Otto Rd	Cheyenne	WY	82009	**800-949-6377**	307-637-2700	276
Coastal Chemical Co Inc 3520 Veterans Memorial *Cust Svc	Abbeville	LA	70510	**800-535-3862***	337-893-3862	144
Coastal Communications 100 Ryon Ave	Hinesville	GA	31313	**877-702-3030**	912-368-3300	721
Coastal Conservation Assn (CCA) 6919 Portwest Dr Suite 100	Houston	TX	77024	**800-201-3474**	713-626-4234	48-13
Coastal Electric Co-op 1265 S Coastal Hwy PO Box 109	Midway	GA	31320	**800-421-2343**	912-884-3311	244
Coastal Electric Co-op Inc 2269 Jefferies Hwy	Walterboro	SC	29488	**877-538-5700**	843-538-5700	244
Coastal Federal Bank 2619 Oak St	Myrtle Beach	SC	29577	**800-613-8179**	843-205-2000	71
Coastal Federal Credit Union 333 St Albans Dr	Raleigh	NC	27609	**800-868-4262**	919-420-8000	216
Coastal Georgia Community College 3700 Altama Ave	Brunswick	GA	31520	**800-675-7235**	912-264-7235	160
Coastal Helicopters Inc 8995 Yandukin Dr	Juneau	AK	99801	**800-789-5610**	907-789-5600	354
Coastal & Hydraulics Laboratory ATTN: CEERD-PA-Z 3909 Halls Ferry Rd	Vicksburg	MS	39180	**800-522-6937**	601-634-2502	654
Coastal Inns Inc 515 Kennedy St Unit 5	Dieppe	NB	E1A7R9	**800-665-7829**	506-859-2486	369
Coastal Journal PO Box 705	Bath	ME	04530	**800-649-6241**	207-443-6241	522-4
Coastal Living Magazine 2100 Lakeshore Dr *Cust Svc	Birmingham	AL	35209	**888-252-3529***	205-445-6000	449-22
Coastal Mechanical Services LLC 394 East Dr	Melbourne	FL	32904	**800-391-5757**	321-725-3061	188-10
Coastal Mechanical Services Ltd 191 N Travis St	San Benito	TX	78586	**800-568-2612**	956-399-5157	188-10
Coastal Transport Co Inc 5714 Star Ln	Houston	TX	77057	**800-256-8897**	713-784-1010	769
Coastal Transportation Inc 4025 13th Ave W	Seattle	WA	98119	**800-544-2580**	206-282-9979	307
Coastal Tug & Barge Inc 1020 Port Blvd Suite 2	Miami	FL	33132	**800-323-2495**	305-579-5013	457
Coastal Wood Products Inc 13285 Temple Ave	City of Industry	CA	91746	**800-852-9663**	626-333-1104	602
Coastline Distribution Inc 317 S Northlake Blvd Suite 1024	Altamonte Springs	FL	32701	**800-741-5531**	407-323-8500	601
Coastline Inn 80 John Roberts Rd	South Portland	ME	04106	**800-470-9494**	207-772-3838	373
Coates Screen Inc 631 Central Ave	East Rutherford	NJ	07073	**800-999-4657**	201-933-6100	381
Coats North America 3430 Toringdon Way Suite 301	Charlotte	NC	28227	**800-631-0965**	704-329-5800	730-9
Cobalt Boats 1715 N 8th St	Neodesha	KS	66757	**800-835-0256**	620-325-2653	91
Cobalt Group Inc 2200 1st Ave S Suite 400	Seattle	WA	98134	**800-909-8244**	206-269-6363	176-10
COBA/Select Sires Inc 1224 Alton Darby Creek Rd	Columbus	OH	43228	**800-837-2621**	614-878-5333	12-2
Cobb County Convention & Visitors Bureau 1 Galleria Pkwy	Atlanta	GA	30339	**800-451-3480**	678-303-2622	205
Cobb Mechanical Contractors Inc PO Box 6729	Colorado Springs	CO	80934	**800-808-2622**	719-471-8958	188-10
Cobb-Vantress Inc PO Box 1030	Siloam Springs	AR	72761	**800-749-9719**	479-524-3166	12-2
Cobblestone Magazine 30 Grove St Suite C	Peterborough	NH	03458	**800-821-0115**	603-924-7209	449-6
Cobblestone Publishing Co 30 Grove St Suite C	Peterborough	NH	03458	**800-821-0115**	603-924-7209	623-9
COBE Cardiovascular Inc 14401 W 65th Way	Arvada	CO	80004	**800-650-2623**	303-425-5508	468
Cobra Golf Inc 1812 Aston Ave *Cust Svc	Carlsbad	CA	92008	**800-223-3537***	760-929-0377	701
Cobra Mfg 7909 E 148th St S PO Box 667	Bixby	OK	74008	**800-352-6272**	918-366-7624	701
Cobra Pipe Supply Inc 100 Brook St	Elmwood	CT	06110	**877-474-7332**	860-233-1231	584
Coburn Supply Co Inc 550 Fannin St Suite 950	Beaumont	TX	77701	**800-832-8492**	409-838-6363	601
Coca-Cola Bottling Co Consolidated 4100 Coca-Cola Plaza *NASDAQ: COKE*	Charlotte	NC	28211	**800-777-2653**	704-551-4400	82-2
Coca-Cola Co 1 Coca-Cola Plaza *NYSE: KO*	Atlanta	GA	30313	**800-438-2653**	404-676-2121	81-2
Coca-Cola Scholars Foundation PO Box 442	Atlanta	GA	30301	**800-306-2653**	404-733-5420	711
Cocaine Anonymous World Services Inc (CA) 3740 Overland Ave Suite C	Los Angeles	CA	90034	**800-347-8998**	310-559-5833	48-21
Cocca's Inn & Suites 2 Wolf Rd	Albany	NY	12205	**888-426-2227**	518-459-2240	373
Cochise College 4190 W Hwy 80	Douglas	AZ	85607	**800-966-7943**	520-364-7943	160
Sierra Vista Campus 901 N Colombo Ave	Sierra Vista	AZ	85635	**800-966-7943**	520-515-0500	160
Cocoa Beach Area Chamber of Commerce 400 Fortenberry Rd	Merritt Island	FL	32952	**877-321-8474**	321-459-2200	137
Coconino Community College 2800 S Lone Tree Rd	Flagstaff	AZ	86001	**800-350-7122**	928-527-1222	160
Coconino County 219 E Cherry Ave	Flagstaff	AZ	86001	**800-559-9289**	928-774-5011	334
Coconut Malorie 200 59th St	Ocean City	MD	21842	**800-767-6060**	410-723-6100	373
Coconuts Music & Movies 38 Corporate Cir	Albany	NY	12203	**800-540-1242**	518-452-1242	514
Codale Electric Supply Inc 3150 S 900 West	Salt Lake City	UT	84119	**800-300-6634**	801-975-7300	245
CodeCorrect Inc 1200 Chesterly Dr Suite 260	Yakima	WA	98902	**877-937-3600**	509-453-0400	176-10
Codington-Clark Electric Co-op 3 8th Ave	Watertown	SD	57201	**800-463-8938**	605-886-5848	244
Codman & Shurtleff Inc 325 Paramount Dr	Raynham	MA	02767	**800-225-0460**	508-880-8100	469
Cody's Books Inc 2454 Telegraph Ave	Berkeley	CA	94704	**800-995-1180**	510-845-7852	96
Coe College 1220 1st Ave NE	Cedar Rapids	IA	52402	**877-225-5263**	319-399-8500	163
COECO Office Systems Co PO Box 2088	Rocky Mount	NC	27804	**800-682-6844**	252-977-1121	315
Coeur d'Alene Area Chamber of Commerce 1621 N 3rd St Suite 100	Coeur d'Alene	ID	83814	**877-782-9232**	208-664-3194	137
Coeur d'Alene Mines Corp PO Box 'I' *NYSE: CDE*	Coeur d'Alene	ID	83816	**800-624-2824**	208-667-3511	492
Coeur d'Alene Resort 115 S 2nd St PO Box 7200	Coeur d'Alene	ID	83814	**800-688-5253**	208-765-4000	655
Coex Coffee International Inc 2121 Ponce de Leon Blvd Suite 930	Coral Gables	FL	33134	**800-426-0343**	305-444-0568	292-2
Coface Services North America Inc 121 Whitney Ave	New Haven	CT	06510	**800-929-8374**	203-781-3800	212
Coffee Bean International 2181 NW Nicolai St	Portland	OR	97210	**800-877-0474**	503-227-4490	292-2
Coffee Bean & Tea Leaf 1945 S La Cienega Blvd	Los Angeles	CA	90034	**800-832-5323**	310-237-2326	156
Coffee Beanery Ltd 3429 Pierson Pl	Flushing	MI	48433	**800-728-2326**	810-733-1020	156
Coffee Creek Ranch 4940 Coffee Creek Rd	Trinity Center	CA	96091	**800-624-4480**	530-266-3343	238
Coffee Holding Co Inc 4401 1st Ave *AMEX: JVA*	Brooklyn	NY	11232	**800-458-2233**	718-832-0800	291-7
Coffee Masters Inc 7606 Industrial Ct	Spring Grove	IL	60081	**800-334-6485**	815-675-0088	292-2
Coffee People Inc 28 Executive Park Suite 200	Irvine	CA	92614	**800-354-5282**	949-260-1600	156
Coffeyville Community College 400 W 11th St	Coffeyville	KS	67337	**800-782-4732**	620-251-7700	160
Coffeyville Convention & Visitors Bureau PO Box 457	Coffeyville	KS	67337	**800-626-3357**	620-251-1194	205
Coffeyville Regional Medical Center 1400 W 4th St	Coffeyville	KS	67337	**800-540-2762**	620-251-1200	366-2
Cogeco Cable Inc 5 Pl Ville-Marie Suite 915	Montreal	QC	H3B2G2	**866-384-4837**	514-874-2600	117
Cogent Communications Group Inc 1015 31st St NW *AMEX: COI*	Washington	DC	20007	**877-875-4432**	202-295-4200	387
Coghlin Electric/Electronics PO Box 5100	Westborough	MA	01581	**800-343-1201**	508-870-5000	245

Company	City	State	ZIP	Toll-Free	Phone	Class
Cognetics Corp						
PO Box 386	Princeton Junction	NJ	08550	**800-229-8437**	609-799-5005	176-12
Cognex Corp 1 Vision Dr	Natick	MA	01760	**877-926-4639**	508-650-3000	171-3
NASDAQ: CGNX						
Cognis Corp 5051 Estecreek Dr	Cincinnati	OH	45232	**800-543-7370***	513-482-3000	142
*Cust Svc						
Cognizant Technology Solutions Corp						
500 Glenpointe Ctr W 7th Fl	Teaneck	NJ	07666	**888-937-3277**	201-801-0233	178
NASDAQ: CTSH						
Cognos Corp 15 Wayside Rd	Burlington	MA	01803	**800-426-4667***	781-229-6600	176-1
*Orders						
Cognos Inc						
3755 Riverside Dr PO Box 9707						
Stn T	Ottawa	ON	K1V1B7	**800-637-7447**	613-738-1440	176-1
NASDAQ: COGN						
Cogswell Polytechnical College						
1175 Bordeaux Dr	Sunnyvale	CA	94089	**800-264-7955**	408-541-0100	163
Cohasset Harbor Inn 124 Elm St	Cohasset	MA	02025	**800-252-5287**	781-383-6650	373
Cohber Communication						
PO Box 93100	Rochester	NY	14692	**800-724-3032**	585-272-1100	770
Cohen Brothers Inc PO Box 957	Middletown	OH	45044	**800-878-3697**	513-422-3696	674
Cohen & Co CPA						
1350 Euclid Ave Suite 800	Cleveland	OH	44115	**800-229-1099**	216-579-1040	2
Cohen & Steers Inc						
757 3rd Ave 20th Fl	New York	NY	10017	**800-330-7348**	212-832-3232	393
NYSE: CNS						
Coherent Auburn Group						
2303 Lindbergh St	Auburn	CA	95602	**800-343-4912***	530-823-9550	534
*Sales						
Coherent Inc						
5100 Patrick Henry Dr	Santa Clara	CA	95054	**800-527-3786***	408-764-4000	416
NASDAQ: COHR ■ *Sales						
Cohesion Technologies Inc						
2500 Faber Pl	Palo Alto	CA	94303	**877-264-3746**	650-320-5500	86
Cohn JH LLP						
75 Eisenhower Pkwy 2nd Fl	Roseland	NJ	07068	**800-879-2571**	973-228-3500	2
Cohoes Fashions Inc 43 Mohawk St	Cohoes	NY	12047	**800-736-8765**	518-237-0524	155-4
Cohu Inc Electronics Div						
3912 Calle Fortunada	San Diego	CA	92123	**800-735-2648**	858-277-6700	633
COI Foodservice 2629 Eugenia Ave	Nashville	TN	37211	**877-503-5212**	615-231-4300	294
Coilcraft Inc 1102 Silver Lake Rd	Cary	IL	60013	**800-325-5045**	847-639-2361	252
Coilhose Pneumatics Inc						
19 Kimberly Rd	East Brunswick	NJ	08816	**800-526-2100**	732-390-8480	364
Coilplus Pennsylvania Inc						
5135 Bleigh St	Philadelphia	PA	19136	**800-355-5200**	215-331-5200	483
Coin Acceptors Inc						
300 Hunter Ave	Saint Louis	MO	63124	**800-325-2646**	314-725-0100	55
Coin Laundry Assn (CLA)						
1315 Butterfield Rd						
Suite 212	Downers Grove	IL	60515	**800-570-5629**	630-963-5547	49-4
Coin Prices Magazine 700 E State St	Iola	WI	54990	**800-258-0929**	715-445-2214	449-14
Coinstar Inc 1800 114th Ave SE	Bellevue	WA	98004	**800-928-2274**	425-943-8000	55
NASDAQ: CSTR						
Coker College 300 E College Ave	Hartsville	SC	29550	**800-950-1908**	843-383-8000	163
COLA (Commission on Office Laboratory						
Accreditation) 9881 Broken Land						
Pkwy Suite 200	Columbia	MD	21046	**800-981-9883**	410-381-6581	49-8
Colad Group 801 Exchange St	Buffalo	NY	14210	**800-950-1755**	716-961-1776	545
Colbert County Tourism & Convention						
Bureau PO Box 740425	Tuscumbia	AL	35674	**800-344-0783**	256-383-0783	205
Colborne Corp 28495 N Ballard Dr	Lake Forest	IL	60045	**800-279-1879**	847-371-0101	293
Colby Attorneys Service Co Inc						
41 State St	Albany	NY	12207	**800-832-1220**	518-463-4426	621
Colby College 4000 Mayflower Hill	Waterville	ME	04901	**800-723-3032**	207-872-3000	163
Colby Community College						
1255 S Range Ave	Colby	KS	67701	**888-634-9350**	785-462-3984	160
Colby Convention & Visitors Bureau						
350 S Range Ave Suite 10	Colby	KS	67701	**800-611-8835**	785-460-7643	205
Colby Hill Inn The Oaks PO Box 779	Henniker	NH	03242	**800-531-0330**	603-428-3281	373
Colby-Sawyer College						
541 Main St	New London	NH	03257	**800-272-1015**	603-526-2010	163
Colchester Bakery 96 Lebanon Ave	Colchester	CT	06415	**800-554-2440**	860-537-2415	291-1
Cold Spring Granite Inc						
202 S 3rd Ave	Cold Spring	MN	56320	**800-328-5040**	320-685-3621	493-6
Cold Spring Granite Inc Texas						
Granite Div 2400 Hwy 1431 W	Marble Falls	TX	78654	**800-247-2637**	830-693-4316	710
Coldwater Creek Inc						
1 Coldwater Creek Dr	Sandpoint	ID	83864	**800-262-0040***	208-263-2266	451
NASDAQ: CWTR ■ *Cust Svc						
Coldwell Banker Commercial						
1 Campus Dr	Parsippany	NJ	07054	**800-222-2162**	973-496-7651	641
Coldwell Banker Gundaker						
2458 Old Dorsett Rd						
Suite 300	Maryland Heights	MO	63043	**800-325-1978**	314-298-5000	638
Coldwell Banker Relocation						
27271 Las Ramblas Suite 233	Mission Viejo	CA	92691	**800-733-1380**	800-292-2656	638
Coldwell Banker Residential						
Brokerage 8490 E						
Crescent Pkwy Suite 250	Greenwood Village	CO	80111	**877-233-8657**	303-409-1500	638
Coldwell Banker Residential Real Estate						
5971 Cattleridge Blvd Suite 202	Sarasota	FL	34232	**800-624-5292**	941-378-8211	638
Cole-Haan 1 Cole Haan Dr	Yarmouth	ME	04096	**800-488-2000**	207-846-2500	296
Cole Hersee Co 20 Old Colony Ave	Boston	MA	02127	**800-365-2653**	617-268-2100	803
Cole Information Services						
901 W Bond St	Lincoln	NE	68521	**877-414-3332**	402-323-3500	623-6
Cole Kenneth Productions Inc						
603 W 50th St	New York	NY	10019	**800-536-2653**	212-265-1500	296
NYSE: KCP						
Cole Managed Vision						
1925 Enterprise Pkwy	Twinsburg	OH	44087	**800-282-3931**	330-486-4000	384-3
Cole Papers Inc 1300 N 38th St	Fargo	ND	58102	**800-800-8090**	701-282-5311	543
Cole Taylor Bank						
1965 N Milwaukee Ave	Chicago	IL	60647	**800-727-2265**	773-927-7000	71
Cole Vision Corp						
1925 Enterprise Pkwy	Twinsburg	OH	44087	**800-282-3931**	330-486-3000	658
Cole Warren & Long Inc						
2 Penn Ctr Plaza Suite 312	Philadelphia	PA	19102	**800-394-8517**	215-563-0701	262
Cole & Weber/Red Cell						
308 Occidental Ave S	Seattle	WA	98104	**800-262-8515**	206-447-9595	4
Coleman Bruce Inc						
117 E 24th St 5th Fl	New York	NY	10010	**800-942-7917**	212-979-6252	582
Coleman Cable Systems Inc						
1530 Shields Dr	Waukegan	IL	60085	**800-323-9355**	847-672-2300	800
Coleman Co Inc 211 E 37th St N	Wichita	KS	67219	**800-835-3278***	316-832-2653	701
*Cust Svc						
Coleman College 7380 Parkway Dr	La Mesa	CA	91942	**800-430-2030**	619-465-3990	163
Coleman County Electric Co-op Inc						
3300 N Hwy 84	Coleman	TX	76834	**800-560-2128**	325-625-2128	244
Coleman Dairy Inc 6901 I-30	Little Rock	AR	72209	**800-365-1551**	501-565-1551	291-27
Coleman E Adler & Sons Inc						
722 Canal St	New Orleans	LA	70130	**800-925-7912**	504-523-5292	402
Coleman Factory Outlet Store & Museum						
235 N Saint Francis St	Wichita	KS	67202	**800-835-3278**	316-264-0836	509
Coleman Natural Products Inc						
5140 Race Ct Unit 4	Denver	CO	80216	**800-442-8666**	303-297-9393	291-26
Coles-Moultrie Electric Co-op						
104 DeWitt Ave E PO Box 709	Mattoon	IL	61938	**888-661-2632**	217-235-0341	244
Colgan Air Services						
2709 Fanta Reed Rd	La Crosse	WI	54603	**800-658-9498**	608-783-8359	14
Colgate Oral Pharmaceuticals						
One Colgate Way	Canton	MA	02021	**800-225-3756**	781-821-2880	226
Colibri Group 100 Niantic Ave	Providence	RI	02907	**800-556-7354***	401-943-2100	401
*Cust Svc						
Colibri/Park Lane Assoc Inc Linden						
Div 100 Niantic Ave	Providence	RI	02907	**800-556-7354***	401-943-2100	151
*Sales						
Colin Service Systems Inc						
170 Hamilton Ave	White Plains	NY	10601	**800-873-2654**	914-289-2000	105
Colitis Foundation of America. Crohn's						
& 386 Park Ave S 17th Fl	New York	NY	10016	**800-932-2423**	212-685-3440	48-17
CollaGenx Pharmaceuticals Inc						
41 University Dr Suite 200	Newtown	PA	18940	**800-613-7847**	215-579-7388	86
NASDAQ: CGPI						
Collectcorp Corp						
300 International Dr Amherst						
Ctr Suite 100	Williamsville	NY	14221	**888-935-1104**	416-961-9622	157
Collection Co of America						
700 Longwater Dr	Norwell	MA	02061	**800-886-9177**	781-681-4300	157
Collection of Fine Properties						
PO Box 1190	Breckenridge	CO	80424	**800-627-3766**	970-453-9692	369
Collecto Inc DBA Collection Co of						
America 700 Longwater Dr	Norwell	MA	02061	**800-886-9177**	781-681-4300	157
Collector's Mart Magazine 700 E State St	Iola	WI	54990	**800-258-0929**	715-445-2214	449-14
College Admission Counseling.						
National Assn for 1631 Prince St	Alexandria	VA	22314	**800-822-6285**	703-836-2222	49-5
College of American Pathologists						
(CAP) 325 Waukegan Rd	Northfield	IL	60093	**800-323-4040**	847-832-7000	49-8
College of American Pathologists						
PAC 1350 'I' St NW Suite 590	Washington	DC	20005	**800-392-9994**	202-354-7100	604
College of the Atlantic						
105 Eden St	Bar Harbor	ME	04609	**800-528-0025**	207-288-5015	163
College Board 45 Columbus Ave	New York	NY	10023	**800-927-4302**	212-713-8000	243
College Composition & Communication.						
Conference on 1111 W Kenyon Rd	Urbana	IL	61801	**800-369-6283**	217-328-3870	49-5
College for Creative Studies						
201 E Kirby St	Detroit	MI	48202	**800-952-2787**	313-872-3118	163
College Directory Publishing Inc						
1000 Conshohocken Rd	Conshohocken	PA	19428	**800-466-2221**	610-940-1515	623-6
College of Eastern Utah						
451 E 400 North	Price	UT	84501	**800-336-2381**	435-637-2120	160
San Juan Campus 639 W 100 S	Blanding	UT	84511	**800-395-2969**	435-678-2201	160
College for Financial Planning						
Inc 6161 S Syracuse Way	Greenwood Village	CO	80111	**800-237-9990**	303-220-1200	241
College Football Hall of Fame						
111 Saint Joseph St	South Bend	IN	44601	**800-440-3263**	574-235-9999	511
College Fund. American Indian						
8333 Greenwood Blvd	Denver	CO	80221	**800-776-3863**	303-426-8900	48-11
College Fund Inc. United Negro						
8260 Willow Oaks Corporate Dr						
Suite 400	Fairfax	VA	22031	**800-331-2244**	703-205-3400	48-11
College of the Holy Cross						
1 College St	Worcester	MA	01610	**800-442-2421**	508-793-2011	163
College Hospital 10802 College Pl	Cerritos	CA	90703	**800-352-3301**	562-924-9581	366-3
College House Inc						
1400 Chamberlayne Ave	Richmond	VA	23222	**800-888-7606**	804-643-4240	675
College of the Menominee Nation						
PO Box 1179	Keshena	WI	54135	**800-567-2344**	715-799-5600	161
College Misericordia 301 Lake St	Dallas	PA	18612	**866-262-6363**	570-674-6400	163
College of Mount Saint Joseph						
5701 Delhi Rd	Cincinnati	OH	45233	**800-654-9314**	513-244-4200	163
College of New Rochelle						
29 Castle Pl	New Rochelle	NY	10805	**800-933-5923**	914-654-5452	163
College of Notre Dame of Maryland						
4701 N Charles St	Baltimore	MD	21210	**800-435-0300**	410-435-0100	163
College Outlook & Career						
Opportunities Magazine 20 E						
Gregory Blvd	Kansas City	MO	64114	**800-274-8867**	816-361-0616	449-11
College of the Ozarks						
PO Box 17	Point Lookout	MO	65726	**800-222-0525**	417-334-6411	163
College Parents of America (CPA)						
8300 Boone Blvd Suite 500	Vienna	VA	22182	**888-256-4627**	703-761-6702	48-11
College Pro Painters Ltd						
200 Dexter Ave 2nd Fl	Watertown	MA	02472	**800-327-2468**	617-924-1300	188-8
College of the Redwoods						
7351 Tompkins Hill Rd	Eureka	CA	95501	**800-641-0400**	707-476-4100	160
Del Norte Campus						
883 W Washington Blvd	Crescent City	CA	95531	**800-641-0400**	707-465-2300	160
Mendocino Coast Campus						
1211 Del Mar Dr	Fort Bragg	CA	95437	**800-641-0400**	707-961-1001	160
College & Research Libraries.						
Association of 50 E Huron St	Chicago	IL	60611	**800-545-2433**	312-280-2519	49-11
College of Saint Benedict						
37 S College Ave	Saint Joseph	MN	56374	**800-249-9840**	320-363-5011	163
College of Saint Catherine						
2004 Randolph Ave	Saint Paul	MN	55105	**800-945-4599**	651-690-6000	163
Minneapolis 601 25th Ave S	Minneapolis	MN	55454	**800-945-4599**	651-690-7700	160
College of Saint Elizabeth						
2 Convent Rd	Morristown	NJ	07960	**800-210-7900**	973-290-4000	163

				Toll-Free	Phone	Class
College of Saint Joseph in Vermont 71 Clement Rd	Rutland	VT	05701	**877-270-9998**	802-773-5900	163
College of Saint Mary 1901 S 72nd St	Omaha	NE	68124	**800-926-5534**	402-399-2400	163
College of Saint Rose 432 Western Ave	Albany	NY	12203	**800-637-8556**	518-454-5150	163
College of Saint Scholastica 1200 Kenwood Ave	Duluth	MN	55811	**800-447-5444**	218-723-6000	163
College of Santa Fe 1600 St Michaels Dr	Santa Fe	NM	87505	**800-456-2673**	505-473-6011	163
Albuquerque Campus 4501 Indian School Rd	Albuquerque	NM	87110	**800-456-2673**	505-884-2732	163
College Savings Bank 5 Vaughn Dr	Princeton	NJ	08540	**800-888-2723**	609-987-3700	71
College Savings Plans Network PO Box 11910	Lexington	KY	40578	**877-277-6496**	859-244-8175	711
College of the Siskiyous 800 College Ave	Weed	CA	96094	**888-397-4339**	530-938-4461	160
College of Southern Maryland PO Box 910	La Plata	MD	20646	**800-933-9177**	301-934-2251	160
Prince Frederick Campus 3205 Brooms Island Rd	Port Republic	MD	20676	**800-933-9177**	410-586-3056	160
Saint Mary's Campus 22950 Hollywood Rd	Leonardtown	MD	20650	**800-933-9177**	240-725-5300	160
College of the Southwest 6610 N Lovington Hwy	Hobbs	NM	88240	**800-530-4400**	505-392-6561	163
College Stores. National Assn of 500 E Lorain St	Oberlin	OH	44074	**800-622-7498**	440-775-7777	49-18
College of Westchester 325 Central Ave	White Plains	NY	10606	**800-333-4924**	914-948-4442	158
College of Wooster 1189 Beall Ave	Wooster	OH	44691	**800-877-9905**	330-263-2000	163
Colleges. Association of Governing Boards of Universities & 1 Dupont Cir NW Suite 400	Washington	DC	20036	**800-356-6317**	202-296-8400	49-5
Colleges & Employers. National Assn of 62 Highland Ave	Bethlehem	PA	18017	**800-544-5272**	610-868-1421	49-5
Colleges of Podiatric Medicine. American Assn of 1350 Piccard Dr Suite 322	Rockville	MD	20850	**800-922-9266**	301-990-7400	49-8
Colleges & Schools. Middle States Assn of 3624 Market St	Philadelphia	PA	19104	**800-355-1258**	215-662-5600	49-5
Colleges & Schools. Southern Assn of 1866 Southern Ln	Decatur	GA	30033	**800-248-7701**	404-679-4500	49-5
Colleges & Universities. Hispanic Assn of 8415 Datapoint Dr Suite 400	San Antonio	TX	78229	**800-780-4228**	210-692-3805	49-5
Collegiate Directors of Athletics. National Assn of 24651 Detroit Rd	Westlake	OH	44145	**800-996-2232**	440-892-4000	48-22
Collegiate Funding Services Inc 100 Riverside Pkwy Suite 125	Fredericksburg	VA	22406	**800-762-6441**	540-374-1600	215
NASDAQ: CFSI						
Collegiate Licensing Assn. International 24651 Detroit Rd	Westlake	OH	44145	**800-996-2232**	440-892-4000	48-22
Collegiate Pacific Inc 532 Luck Ave	Roanoke	VA	24016	**800-336-5996**	540-981-0281	282
AMEX: BOO						
Collette Travel Service Inc 162 Middle St	Pawtucket	RI	02860	**800-832-4656**	401-728-3805	748
Collette Vacations 162 Middle St	Pawtucket	RI	02860	**800-340-5158**	401-727-9000	760
Collex Collision Experts 44700 Enterprise Dr	Clinton Township	MI	48038	**888-426-5539**	586-954-3850	62-4
Collin Street Bakery Inc 401 W 7th Ave	Corsicana	TX	75110	**800-504-1896***	903-872-8111	69
*Sales						
Collins & Aikman Corp Floorcoverings Div PO Box 1447	Dalton	GA	30722	**800-241-4902**	706-259-9711	131
Collins Appliance Parts Inc 1533 Metropolitan St	Pittsburgh	PA	15233	**800-366-9969**	412-321-3700	38
Collins Auto Group 4220 Bardstown Rd	Lousiville	KY	40218	**800-258-2455**	502-459-9550	57
Collins Cos 1618 SW 1st Ave Suite 500	Portland	OR	97201	**800-329-1219**	503-227-1219	671
Collins Electric Co Inc 53 2nd Ave	Chicopee	MA	01020	**800-321-4459**	413-592-9221	188-4
Collins Mfg Co 2000 Bowser Rd	Cookeville	TN	38506	**800-292-6450**	931-528-5151	78
Collinsville Journal 2 Executive Dr	Collinsville	IL	62234	**800-766-3278**	618-344-0264	522-4
Collision Repair. I-CAR Inter-Industry Conference on Auto 3701 Algonquin Rd Suite 400	Rolling Meadows	IL	60008	**800-422-7872**	847-590-1191	49-21
Colloid Environmental Technologies Co (CETCO) 1500 W Shure Dr	Arlington Heights	IL	60004	**800-527-9948**	847-392-5800	3
Colmac Coil Mfg Inc PO Box 571	Colville	WA	99114	**800-845-6778**	509-684-2595	15
Colmac Industries Inc PO Box 72	Colville	WA	99114	**800-926-5622**	509-684-4506	418
Coloma Frozen Foods Inc PO Box 520	Coloma	MI	49038	**800-462-7608**	269-849-0500	291-21
Colombian Emeralds International PO Box 5868	Fort Lauderdale	FL	33310	**800-666-3889**	954-917-2547	240
Colonial Bag Co PO Box 929	Lake Park	GA	31636	**800-392-4875**	229-559-8484	66
Colonial Bank 1 Commerce St	Montgomery	AL	36104	**888-285-5886**	334-240-5000	71
Colonial Carbon Co PO Box 498	Barrington	IL	60011	**800-345-9313**	847-299-0111	616
Colonial Craft 2270 Woodale Dr	Mounds View	MN	55112	**800-727-5187**	763-231-4000	489
Colonial Diversified Polymer Products LLC 2055 Forrest St Ext	Dyersburg	TN	38024	**800-303-3606**	731-287-3636	664
Colonial Engineering Inc 6400 Corporate Ave	Portage	MI	49002	**800-374-0234**	269-323-2495	584
Colonial Freight Systems Inc 10924 McBride Ln	Knoxville	TN	37932	**800-826-1402**	865-966-9711	769
Colonial Holdings Inc 10515 Colonial Downs Pkwy	New Kent	VA	23124	**888-482-8722**	804-966-7223	628
Colonial Life & Accident Insurance Co 1200 Colonial Life Blvd	Columbia	SC	29210	**800-325-4368**	803-798-7000	384-2
Colonial Mechanical Corp 2820 Ackley Ave	Richmond	VA	23228	**800-849-5504**	804-916-1400	188-10
Colonial Oil Industries Inc PO Box 576	Savannah	GA	31402	**800-944-3835**	912-236-1331	569
Colonial Penn Life Insurance Co 399 Market St	Philadelphia	PA	19181	**800-523-9100**	215-928-8000	384-2
Colonial Pipeline Co PO Box 1624	Alpharetta	GA	30009	**800-275-3004**	678-762-2200	586
Colonial Williamsburg Reservation Center PO Box 1776	Williamsburg	VA	23187	**800-447-8679**	757-253-2277	368

				Toll-Free	Phone	Class
Colonnade Hotel 120 Huntington Ave	Boston	MA	02116	**800-962-3030**	617-424-7000	373
Colonna's Shipyard Inc 400 E Indian River Rd	Norfolk	VA	23523	**800-265-6627**	757-545-2414	689
Colony Beach & Tennis Resort 1620 Gulf of Mexico Dr	Longboat Key	FL	34228	**800-426-5669**	941-383-6464	655
Colony Capital Management 3060 Peachtree Rd NW Suite 1550	Atlanta	GA	30305	**877-365-5050**	404-365-5050	393
Colony Hotel 155 Hammon Ave	Palm Beach	FL	33480	**800-521-5525**	561-655-5430	373
Colony Hotel 140 Ocean Ave	Kennebunkport	ME	04046	**800-552-2363**	207-967-3331	655
Colony Hotel & Cabana Club 525 E Atlantic Ave	Delray Beach	FL	33483	**800-552-2363**	561-276-4123	373
Colony Mortgage Corp 22983 Lorraine Rd	Fairview Park	OH	44026	**800-423-3085**	440-777-9999	498
Colony Reef Club 4670 A1A S	Saint Augustine	FL	32080	**800-624-5965**	904-471-2233	655
Colony South Hotel 7401 Surratts Rd	Clinton	MD	20735	**800-537-1147**	301-856-4500	373
Color-Art Inc 10300 Watson Rd	Saint Louis	MO	63127	**800-800-8845**	314-966-2000	615
Color Arts Inc PO Box 081158	Racine	WI	53408	**800-236-7751**	262-633-7751	675
Color Communication Inc 4000 W Fillmore St	Chicago	IL	60624	**800-458-5743**	773-638-1400	770
Color Converting Industries Co 3535 SW 56th St	Des Moines	IA	50321	**800-728-8200**	515-471-2100	381
Color Film Corp 770 Connecticut Ave	Norwalk	CT	06854	**800-882-1120**	203-866-2711	644
Color-Glo International 7111 Ohms Ln	Minneapolis	MN	55439	**800-333-8523**	952-835-1338	62-1
Color Kinetics Inc 10 Milk St Suite 1100	Boston	MA	02108	**888-385-5742**	617-423-9999	431
NASDAQ: CLRK						
Color Me Beautiful Inc 14900 Conference Ctr Dr Suite 450	Chantilly	VA	20151	**800-265-6763**	703-471-6400	361
Color Resolutions International 575 Quality Blvd	Fairfield	OH	45014	**800-346-8570**	513-552-7200	381
Color Spot Nurseries Inc 2575 Olive Hill Rd	Fallbrook	CA	92028	**800-554-4065**	760-695-1430	363
Colorado						
Arts Council 750 Pennsylvania St	Denver	CO	80203	**800-291-2787**	303-894-2617	335
CollegeInvest 1801 Broadway Suite 1300	Denver	CO	80202	**800-478-5651**	303-295-1981	711
Labor & Employment Dept 1515 Arapahoe St Tower 2 Suite 400	Denver	CO	80202	**800-390-7936**	303-318-8000	335
Lottery 201 W 8th St Suite 600	Pueblo	CO	81003	**800-999-2959**	719-546-2400	443
Parks & Outdoor Recreation Div 1313 Sherman St Rm 618	Denver	CO	80203	**800-678-2267***	303-866-3437	335
*Campground Resv						
Tourism Office 1625 Broadway Suite 1700	Denver	CO	80202	**800-265-6723**	303-892-3885	335
Victims Programs Office 700 Kipling St Suite 3000	Denver	CO	80215	**888-282-1080**	303-239-4442	335
Colorado Assn of Realtors 309 Inverness Way S	Englewood	CO	80112	**800-944-6550**	303-790-7099	642
Colorado Belle Hotel & Casino 2100 S Casino Dr	Laughlin	NV	89029	**800-477-4837***	702-298-4000	133
*Resv						
Colorado Boxed Beef Co PO Box 899	Winter Haven	FL	33882	**800-955-0636**	863-967-0636	292-9
Colorado Charter Lines & Tours 4960 Locust St	Commerce City	CO	80022	**800-821-7491**	303-287-0239	108
Colorado Christian University 3800 Automation Way Suite 101	Fort Collins	CO	80525	**800-443-2484**	970-223-8505	163
Colorado Christian University 8787 W Alameda Ave	Lakewood	CO	80226	**800-443-2484**	303-963-3200	163
Colorado Classic Co DBA Pappy's Golf Shop 4030 N Sinton Rd	Colorado Springs	CO	80907	**800-530-2345**	719-633-2064	701
Colorado College 14 E Cache La Poudre St	Colorado Springs	CO	80903	**800-542-7214**	719-389-6344	163
Colorado Correctional Industries DBA Juniper Valley Products 2862 S Circle Dr	Colorado Springs	CO	80906	**800-685-7891***	719-226-4206	618
*Cust Svc						
Colorado-Denver Delivery Inc 7170 Dahlia St	Commerce City	CO	80022	**800-488-3077**	303-289-5577	769
Colorado Medical Society 7351 Lowry Blvd	Denver	CO	80230	**800-654-5653**	720-859-1001	466
Colorado Mountain College						
Alpine Campus 1330 Bob Adams Dr	Steamboat Springs	CO	80487	**800-621-8559**	970-870-4444	160
Roaring Fork Campus 3000 County Rd 114	Glenwood Springs	CO	81601	**800-621-8559**	970-945-7481	160
Colorado Northwestern Community College 500 Kennedy Dr	Rangely	CO	81648	**800-562-1105**	970-675-2261	160
Craig Campus 50 College Dr	Craig	CO	81625	**800-562-1105**	970-824-7071	160
Colorado Petroleum Products Co 4080 Globeville Rd	Denver	CO	80216	**800-580-4080**	303-294-0302	530
Colorado Prime Foods 500 Bi-County Blvd Suite 400	Farmingdale	NY	11735	**800-365-2404**	631-694-1111	361
Colorado Railroad Museum 17155 W 44th Ave	Golden	CO	80402	**800-365-6263**	303-279-4591	509
Colorado Republican Party 1777 S Harrison St Suite 100	Denver	CO	80210	**800-236-3769**	303-758-3333	605-2
Colorado Resort Services 2955 Village Dr	Steamboat Springs	CO	80487	**800-525-7654**	970-879-7654	368
Colorado Rockies Coors Field 2001 Blake St	Denver	CO	80205	**800-388-7625**	303-292-0200	703
Colorado Saddlery Co PO Box 8538	Denver	CO	80201	**800-521-2465***	303-572-8350	423
*Cust Svc						
Colorado School Journal 1500 Grant St	Denver	CO	80203	**800-332-5939**	303-837-1500	449-8
Colorado School of Mines 1500 Illinois St	Golden	CO	80401	**800-446-9488**	303-273-3000	163
Colorado Serum Co 4950 York St	Denver	CO	80216	**800-525-2065***	303-295-7527	86
*Orders						
Colorado Springs Convention & Visitors Bureau 515 S Cascade Ave	Colorado Springs	CO	80903	**800-368-4748**	719-635-7506	205
Colorado Springs Municipal Airport (COS)	Colorado Springs	CO	80916	**800-462-6774**	719-550-1900	28

Name / Address	City	State	ZIP	Toll-Free	Phone	Class
Colorado Springs Utilities 111 S Cascade Ave	Colorado Springs	CO	80903	**800-238-5434**	719-448-4800	774
Colorado State Veterans Nursing Home-Homelake 3749 Sherman Ave	Monte Vista	CO	81144	**888-838-2687**	719-852-5118	780
Colorado State Veterans Nursing Home-Walsenburg 23500 US Hwy 160	Walsenburg	CO	81089	**800-645-8387**	719-738-5133	780
Colorado Time Systems LLC 1551 E 11th St	Loveland	CO	80537	**800-920-9332**	970-667-1000	692
Colorado Trails Ranch 12161 County Rd 240	Durango	CO	81301	**800-323-3833**	970-247-5055	238
Colorado Trust 1600 Sherman St	Denver	CO	80203	**888-847-9140**	303-837-1200	298
Colorado Valley Transit Inc 108 Cardinal Ln PO Box 940	Columbus	TX	78934	**800-548-1068**	979-732-6281	109
Colorado Veterinary Medical Assn 789 Sherman St Suite 550	Denver	CO	80203	**800-228-5429**	303-318-0447	782
ColorDynamics 200 E Bethany Dr	Allen	TX	75002	**800-445-0017**	972-390-6500	615
Colored People. National Assn for the Advancement of 4805 Mount Hope Dr	Baltimore	MD	21215	**877-622-2798**	410-358-8900	48-8
Colorhouse Inc 13010 County Rd 6	Plymouth	MN	55441	**800-328-8046**	763-553-0100	770
ColorImaging Inc 4350 Peachtree Industrial Blvd Suite 100	Norcross	GA	30071	**800-783-1090**	770-840-1090	616
Colorite Plastics Co 101 Railroad Ave	Ridgefield	NJ	07657	**800-631-1577**	201-941-2900	364
Colorite Specialty Resins PO Box 116	Burlington	NJ	08016	**800-215-1497**	609-386-9200	594-2
Colors By Design 7723 Densmore Ave	Van Nuys	CA	91406	**800-832-8436**	818-376-1226	130
Colors on Parade 642 Century Cir	Conway	SC	29526	**800-929-3363**	843-347-8818	62-4
ColorTyme Inc 5700 Tennyson Pkwy Suite 180	Plano	TX	75024	**800-411-8963**	972-608-5376	305
Colposcopy & Cervical Pathology. American Society for 20 W Washington St Suite 1	Hagerstown	MD	21740	**800-787-7227**	301-733-3640	49-8
Colquitt Electric Membership Corp 15 Rowland Dr	Moultrie	GA	31768	**800-342-8694**	229-985-3620	244
Colquitt Regional Medical Center 3131 S Main St	Moultrie	GA	31768	**888-262-2762**	229-985-3420	366-2
Coltene/Whaledent Inc 235 Ascot Pkwy	Cuyahoga Falls	OH	44223	**800-221-3046**	330-916-8800	226
Colt's Mfg Co Inc PO Box 1868	Hartford	CT	06144	**800-962-2658**	860-236-6311	279
Colt's Plastics Co PO Box 429	Dayville	CT	06241	**800-222-2658**	860-774-2277	99
Columbia 300 Inc 5005 West Ave *Cust Svc	San Antonio	TX	78213	**800-531-5920***	210-344-9211	701
Columbia Air Services LLC 112 Caruso Dr	Trenton	ME	04605	**888-756-8648**	207-667-5534	63
Columbia Bancorp 7168 Columbia Gateway Dr *NASDAQ: CBMD*	Columbia	MD	21044	**888-822-2265**	410-423-8000	355-2
Columbia Bank 7168 Columbia Gateway Dr	Columbia	MD	21046	**800-314-7714**	410-730-5000	71
Columbia Banking System Inc PO Box 2156 *NASDAQ: COLB*	Tacoma	WA	98401	**800-305-1905**	253-305-1900	355-2
Columbia Cascade Co 1975 SW 5th Ave	Portland	OR	97201	**800-547-1940**	503-223-1157	340
Columbia City Ballet PO Box 11898	Columbia	SC	29211	**800-899-7408**	803-799-7605	563-1
Columbia College 1001 Rogers St	Columbia	MO	65216	**800-231-2391**	573-875-8700	163
Columbia College-Jefferson City 3314 Emerald Ln	Jefferson City	MO	65109	**800-231-2391**	573-634-3250	163
Columbia Convention & Visitors Bureau 300 S Providence Rd	Columbia	MO	65203	**800-652-0987**	573-875-1231	205
Columbia Daily Tribune 101 N 4th St	Columbia	MO	65201	**800-333-6799**	573-449-3811	522-2
Columbia Data Products Inc 925 Sunshine Ln Suite 1080 *Sales	Altamonte Springs	FL	32714	**800-613-6288***	407-869-6700	176-12
Columbia Elevator Products Co Inc 175 N Main St	Port Chester	NY	10573	**877-265-3538**	914-937-7100	188-1
Columbia Forest Products Inc 222 SW Columbia St Suite 1575	Portland	OR	97201	**800-547-4261**	503-224-5300	602
Columbia Forest Products Inc Columbia Plywood Div PO Box 1780	Klamath Falls	OR	97601	**800-547-1791**	541-882-7281	602
Columbia Funds Distributor Inc 1 Fincial Ctr	Boston	MA	02111	**800-225-2365**		393
Columbia Funds Services Inc PO Box 8081	Boston	MA	02266	**800-345-6611**		517
Columbia Gas of Kentucky Inc 2001 Mercer Rd	Lexington	KY	40511	**800-432-9345**	859-288-0210	774
Columbia Gas of Maryland Inc 501 Technology Dr *Cust Svc	Canonsburg	PA	15317	**888-460-4332***	724-416-6300	774
Columbia Gas of Ohio Inc 200 Civic Center Dr	Columbus	OH	43215	**800-282-3044**	614-460-6000	774
Columbia Gas of Pennsylvania Inc 501 Technology Dr *Cust Svc	Canonsburg	PA	15317	**888-460-4332***	724-416-6300	774
Columbia Gas Transmission Corp 1700 MacCorkle Ave SE	Charleston	WV	25314	**800-832-3242**	304-357-2000	320
Columbia Gas of Virginia Inc 1809 Coyote Dr *Cust Svc	Chester	VA	23836	**800-543-8911***	804-323-5300	774
Columbia Gear Corp 530 County Rd 50	Avon	MN	56310	**800-323-9838**	320-356-7301	700
Columbia Industries Inc DBA Columbia 300 Inc 5005 West Ave *Cust Svc	San Antonio	TX	78213	**800-531-5920***	210-344-9211	701
Columbia International University 7435 Monticello Rd	Columbia	SC	29203	**800-777-2227**	803-754-4100	163
Columbia Lakes Resort & Conference Center 188 Freeman Blvd	West Columbia	TX	77486	**800-231-1030**	979-345-5151	655
Columbia Management Assoc Inc 1 Financial Ctr	Boston	MA	02111	**800-225-2365**	617-426-3750	393

Name / Address	City	State	ZIP	Toll-Free	Phone	Class
Columbia Metropolitan Convention & Visitors Bureau PO Box 15	Columbia	SC	29202	**800-264-4884**	803-545-0000	205
Columbia Mfg Corp 14400 S San Pedro St	Gardena	CA	90248	**800-729-3667**	310-327-9300	232
Columbia-Montour Visitors Bureau 121 Papermill Rd	Bloomsburg	PA	17815	**800-847-4810**	570-784-8279	205
Columbia National Inc 7142 Columbia Gateway Dr	Columbia	MD	21046	**800-444-7963**	410-872-2000	498
Columbia Natural Resources Inc 900 Pennsylvania Ave	Charleston	WV	25302	**800-962-6645**	304-353-5000	528
Columbia News Times 4272 Washington Rd Suite 3B	Evans	GA	30809	**888-464-9988**	706-863-6165	522-4
Columbia ParCar Corp 350 N Dewey Ave	Reedsburg	WI	53959	**800-222-4653**	608-524-8888	505
Columbia Pipe & Supply Co 1120 W Pershing Rd	Chicago	IL	60609	**888-361-7700**	773-927-6600	483
Columbia Rafting Adventures Ltd PO Box 942	Fairmont Hot Springs	BC	V0B1L0	**877-706-7238**	250-345-4550	748
Columbia Rural Electric Assn Inc 115 E Main St	Dayton	WA	99328	**800-642-1231**	509-382-2578	244
Columbia Savings Bank 19-01 Rt 208 *Cust Svc	Fair Lawn	NJ	07410	**800-522-4167***	201-796-3600	71
Columbia State Bank PO Box 2156	Tacoma	WA	98401	**800-305-1905**	253-305-1900	71
Columbia Steel Casting Co Inc PO Box 83095	Portland	OR	97283	**800-547-9471**	503-286-0685	302
Columbia Union College 7600 Flower Ave	Takoma Park	MD	20912	**800-835-4212**	301-891-4000	163
Columbia University Press 61 W 62nd St 3rd Fl	New York	NY	10023	**800-944-8648**	212-459-0600	623-5
Columbia Ventures Corp 16703 SE McGillivray Blvd Suite 210	Vancouver	WA	98683	**866-204-0747**	360-882-1052	397
Columbia Winery 14030 NE 145th St	Woodinville	WA	98072	**800-488-2347**	425-488-2776	50
Columbian 701 W 8th St	Vancouver	WA	98660	**800-743-3391**	360-694-3391	522-2
Columbian Chemicals Co 1800 W Oak Commons Ct	Marietta	GA	30062	**800-235-4003**	770-792-9400	143
Columbian Distribution Services Inc 900 Hall St SW	Grand Rapids	MI	49503	**888-609-8542**	616-514-6000	790-1
Columbian Rope Co 145 Towery St	Guntown	MS	38849	**800-692-0151**	662-348-2241	207
Columbian Tectank 2101 S 21st St PO Box 996	Parsons	KS	67357	**800-421-2788**	620-421-0200	92
Columbus Area Visitors Center 506 5th St	Columbus	IN	47201	**800-468-6564**	812-378-2622	205
Columbus Bank & Trust Co 1148 Broadway	Columbus	GA	31901	**800-334-9007**	706-649-2012	71
Columbus Blue Jackets Nationwide Arena 200 W Nationwide Blvd 3rd Fl	Columbus	OH	43215	**800-645-2657**	614-246-4625	703
Columbus Cello-Poly Corp 4041 Roberts Rd	Columbus	OH	43228	**800-837-1204**	614-876-1204	588
Columbus Circle Investors Inc 1 Station Pl Metro Ctr 8th Fl	Stamford	CT	06902	**888-826-5247**	203-353-6000	393
Columbus City Center 111 S 3rd St	Columbus	OH	43215	**800-882-4900**	614-221-4900	452
Columbus Civic Center 400 4th St	Columbus	GA	31901	**800-711-3986**	706-653-4482	706
Columbus Convention & Visitors Bureau 900 Front Ave	Columbus	GA	31901	**800-999-1613**	706-322-1613	205
Columbus Convention & Visitors Bureau PO Box 789	Columbus	MS	39703	**800-327-2686**	662-329-1191	205
Columbus Crew Crew Stadium 1 Black & Gold Blvd	Columbus	OH	43211	**800-273-9326**	614-447-2739	703
Columbus Dispatch 34 S 3rd St	Columbus	OH	43215	**800-848-1110**	614-461-5000	522-2
Columbus Electric Co-op Inc 900 N Gold St	Deming	NM	88031	**800-950-2667**	505-546-8838	244
Columbus Electric Mfg Co PO Box 4973	Johnson City	TN	37602	**800-251-7828**	423-477-4131	201
Columbus (Greater) Chamber of Commerce 37 N High St	Columbus	OH	43215	**800-950-1321**	614-221-1321	137
Columbus (Greater) Convention & Visitors Bureau 90 N High St	Columbus	OH	43215	**800-354-2657**	614-221-6623	205
Columbus & Greenville Railway Co 201 19th St N PO Box 6000	Columbus	MS	39703	**888-601-1222**	662-327-8664	634
Columbus. Knights of 1 Columbus Plaza	New Haven	CT	06510	**800-524-3611**	203-752-4000	48-15
Columbus Ledger-Enquirer 17 W 12th St	Columbus	GA	31902	**800-282-7859**	706-324-5526	522-2
Columbus Life Insurance Co 400 E 4th St PO Box 5737 *Cust Svc	Cincinnati	OH	45201	**800-677-9595***	513-361-6700	384-2
Columbus Marble Works Corp PO Box 791	Columbus	MS	39703	**800-647-1055**	662-328-1477	710
Columbus McKinnon Corp 140 John James Audubon Pkwy *NASDAQ: CMCO*	Amherst	NY	14228	**800-888-0985**	716-689-5400	462
Columbus Races 822 15th St	Columbus	NE	68601	**800-314-2983**	402-564-0133	628
Columbus State Community College 550 E Spring St	Columbus	OH	43215	**800-621-6407**	614-287-2400	160
Columbus State University 4225 University Ave	Columbus	GA	31907	**866-264-2035**	706-568-2001	163
Columbus Telegram 1254 27th St PO Box 648	Columbus	NE	68602	**800-279-1123**	402-564-2741	522-2
Columbus Zoo & Aquarium 9990 Riverside Dr PO Box 400	Powell	OH	43065	**800-666-5397**	614-645-3400	811
Columns The 3811 St Charles Ave	New Orleans	LA	70115	**800-445-9308**	504-899-9308	373
Colwell Systems Inc 201 Kenyon Rd *Cust Svc	Champaign	IL	61821	**800-637-1140***	217-351-5400	111
Com21 Inc 750 Tasman Dr	Milpitas	CA	95035	**888-266-2111**	408-953-9100	496
Comair Delta Connection 77 Comair Blvd	Erlanger	KY	41018	**800-727-2550**	859-767-2550	26
Comanche Electric Co-op Assn PO Box 729	Comanche	TX	76442	**800-915-2533**	325-356-2533	244
Comarco Wireless Technologies Inc 2 Cromwell *Cust Svc	Irvine	CA	92618	**800-697-1500***	949-599-7400	720

Name / Address	City	State	ZIP	Toll-Free	Phone	Class
Comark Corp 93 West St	Medfield	MA	02052	**800-280-8522**	508-359-8161	171-3
Combe Inc 1101 Westchester Ave	White Plains	NY	10604	**800-873-7400**	914-694-5454	211
CombiMatrix Corp 6500 Harbour Heights Pkwy Suite 301 *NASDAQ: CBMX*	Mukilteo	WA	98275	**800-985-2269**	425-493-2000	86
Combined Insurance Co of America 5050 N Broadway	Chicago	IL	60640	**800-428-5466**		384-2
Combined Transport Inc 5656 Crater Lake Ave	Central Point	OR	97502	**800-547-2870**	541-734-7418	769
Comcar Industries Inc 502 E Bridgers Ave *Cust Svc	Auburndale	FL	33823	**800-524-1101***	863-967-1101	769
Comcast Business Communications Inc 650 Centerton Rd	Moorestown	NJ	08057	**888-262-7300**	856-638-4000	721
Comcast Cable Communications Inc 200 Cresson Blvd *Cust Svc	Oaks	PA	19456	**800-266-2278***	610-650-3000	117
Comco Inc 2151 N Lincoln St	Burbank	CA	91504	**800-796-6626**	818-841-5500	1
Comco Plastics Inc 98-34 Jamaica Ave	Woodhaven	NY	11421	**800-849-0731**	718-849-9000	591
Comdata Corp 5301 Maryland Way	Brentwood	TN	37027	**800-266-3282**	615-370-7000	70
Comdel Inc 11 Kondelin Rd	Gloucester	MA	01930	**800-468-3144**	978-282-0620	252
Comdial Corp 106 Cattlemen Rd	Sarasota	FL	34232	**800-266-3425**	941-554-5000	720
Comdisco Ventures Group 6111 N River Rd	Rosemont	IL	60018	**800-321-1111**	847-698-3000	779
ComEd An Exelon Co PO Box 87522	Chicago	IL	60680	**800-334-7661**	312-394-4321	774
Comer Packing PO Box 33	Aberdeen	MS	39730	**800-748-8916**	662-369-9325	465
Comerica Bank 500 Woodward Ave	Detroit	MI	48226	**800-643-4418**	248-371-5000	71
Comerica Bank-California 333 W Santa Clara St	San Jose	CA	95113	**800-888-3595**	408-556-5000	71
Comerica Bank-Texas 753 W Illinois Ave	Dallas	TX	75224	**800-925-2160**	214-630-3030	71
Comerica Inc 500 Woodward Ave *NYSE: CMA*	Detroit	MI	48226	**800-521-1190**		355-2
Comerica Securities 201 W Fort St 3rd Fl	Detroit	MI	48226	**800-232-6983**	313-222-5580	679
COMFORCE Corp 415 Crossways Park Dr *AMEX: CFS*	Woodbury	NY	11797	**877-266-3672**		707
Comfort Financial Services PO Box 1140	Evansville	IN	47706	**866-866-1331**		215
Comfort Inn Tuscaloosa 4700 Doris Pate Dr	Tuscaloosa	AL	35405	**877-424-6423**	205-556-3232	373
Comfort Inn University 6541 Hwy 49	Hattiesburg	MS	39401	**800-424-6423**	601-264-1881	373
Comfort Inns 10750 Columbia Pike	Silver Spring	MD	20901	**800-424-6423**	301-592-5000	369
Comfort Suites 10750 Columbia Pike	Silver Spring	MD	20901	**800-424-6423**	301-592-5000	369
Comfort Suites Albuquerque 900 Louisiana Blvd NE	Albuquerque	NM	87110	**800-424-6423**	505-255-5566	373
Comfort Supply Inc 407 Garden Oaks Blvd	Houston	TX	77018	**800-281-7511**	713-845-4705	601
Comfort Systems USA Inc 777 Post Oak Blvd Suite 500 *NYSE: FIX*	Houston	TX	77056	**800-723-8431**	713-830-9600	188-10
Comfortex Inc PO Box 850	Winona	MN	55987	**800-445-4007**	507-454-6579	463
Comfortex Window Fashions Inc 21 Elm St *Cust Svc	Maplewood	NY	12189	**800-843-4151***	518-273-3333	88
Comics.com 200 Madison Ave 4th Fl	New York	NY	10016	**800-221-4816**	212-293-8500	520
Command Alkon Inc 1800 International Park Dr Suite 400	Birmingham	AL	35243	**800-624-1872**	205-879-3282	176-10
Command Communications Inc 7025 S Fulton St Suite 120	Centennial	CO	80112	**800-288-3491**	303-792-0890	720
Command Plastic Corp 124 West Ave	Tallmadge	OH	44278	**800-321-8001**	330-434-3497	538
Command Web Offset Inc 100 Castle Rd	Secaucus	NJ	07094	**800-466-2932**	201-863-8100	614
Commander Hotel 1401 Atlantic Ave	Ocean City	MD	21842	**888-289-6166**	410-289-6166	373
Commence Corp 200 Tornillo Way	Tinton Falls	NJ	07712	**877-266-6362**	732-380-9100	176-1
Commentary Magazine 165 E 56th St	New York	NY	10022	**800-829-6270**	212-891-1400	449-10
Commerce Bancorp Inc 1701 Rt 70 E Commerce Atrium *NYSE: CBH* ■ *Cust Svc	Cherry Hill	NJ	08034	**800-751-9000***	856-751-9000	355-2
Commerce Bancshares Inc 1000 Walnut St *NASDAQ: CBSH*	Kansas City	MO	64106	**800-892-7100**	816-234-2000	355-2
Commerce Bank NA 1000 Walnut St *Cust Svc	Kansas City	MO	64106	**800-453-2265***	816-234-2000	71
Commerce Corp 7603 Energy Pkwy	Baltimore	MD	21226	**800-289-0982**	410-255-3500	420
Commerce Group Inc 211 Main St *NYSE: CGI*	Webster	MA	01570	**800-221-1605**	508-943-9000	355-4
Commerce Insurance Co 211 Main St	Webster	MA	01570	**800-221-1605**	508-943-9000	384-4
Commerce National Insurance Services Inc 1701 Rt 70 E Commerce Atrium	Cherry Hill	NJ	08034	**888-751-9000**	856-489-7000	383
Commerce One Inc One Market St Steuart Tower Suite 1300	San Francisco	CA	94105	**800-628-2761**	415-644-8700	176-4
Commerce Title Co 1551 N Tustin Ave Suite 430	Santa Ana	CA	92705	**800-244-4322**	714-347-7000	384-6
Commercebank NA 220 Alhambra Cir	Coral Gables	FL	33134	**888-629-4810**	305-460-8701	71
CommerceNet 510 Logue Ave	Mountain View	CA	94043	**888-255-1900**	650-962-2600	48-9
Commercial Appeal 495 Union Ave	Memphis	TN	38103	**800-444-6397**	901-529-2345	522-2
Commercial Art Supply 935 Erie Blvd E	Syracuse	NY	13210	**800-669-2787**	315-474-1000	45
Commercial Bankshares Inc 1550 SW 57th Ave *NASDAQ: CLBK*	Miami	FL	33144	**800-752-7999**	305-267-1200	355-2
Commercial Capital Bancorp Inc 8105 Irvine Ctr Dr 15th Fl *NASDAQ: CCBI*	Irvine	CA	92618	**877-387-5574**	949-585-7500	71
Commercial Contracting Corp 4260 N Atlantic Blvd	Auburn Hills	MI	48326	**800-521-4386**	248-209-0500	188-1
Commercial Dispatch 516 Main St	Columbus	MS	39703	**888-477-1555**	662-328-2424	522-2
Commercial Distributing Co Inc 46 S Broad St *Cust Svc	Westfield	MA	01086	**800-332-8999***	413-562-9691	82-1
Commercial Federal Bank FSB 13220 California St	Omaha	NE	68154	**800-228-5023**	402-514-5306	71
Commercial Forged Products Div Wozniak Industries Inc 5757 W 65th St	Bedford Park	IL	60638	**800-637-2695**	708-458-1220	474
Commercial Law League of America (CLLA) 150 N Michigan Ave Suite 600	Chicago	IL	60601	**800-978-2552**	312-781-2000	49-10
Commercial Lease Law Insider Newsletter 149 5th Ave 16th Fl	New York	NY	10010	**800-643-8095**	212-473-8200	521-7
Commercial Leasing Law & Strategy Newsletter 345 Park Ave S	New York	NY	10010	**800-888-8300**	212-779-9200	521-7
Commercial Lighting Industries 72650 Dinah Shore Dr	Palm Desert	CA	92260	**800-755-0155**	760-328-9431	431
Commercial Music Co Inc 1550 Edison St	Dallas	TX	75207	**800-442-7281**	214-741-6381	516
Commercial National Financial Corp 900 Ligonier St *NASDAQ: CNAF*	Latrobe	PA	15650	**800-803-2266**	724-539-3601	355-2
Commercial Net Lease Realty Inc 450 S Orange Ave *NYSE: NNN*	Orlando	FL	32801	**800-522-3863**	407-650-1000	641
Commercial-News 17 W North St	Danville	IL	61832	**800-729-2992**	217-446-1000	522-2
Commercial Properties Realty Trust 5630 Bankers Ave	Baton Rouge	LA	70808	**800-648-9064**	225-924-7206	640
Commercial Workers International Union. United Food & 1775 K St NW	Washington	DC	20006	**800-551-4010**	202-223-3111	405
Commission on Accreditation for Law Enforcement Agencies (CALEA) 10302 Eaton Pl Suite 100	Fairfax	VA	22030	**800-368-3757**	703-352-4225	49-7
Commission on Accreditation of Rehabilitation Facilities (CARF) 4891 E Grant Rd	Tucson	AZ	85712	**888-281-6531**	520-325-1044	48-1
Commission Junction Inc 530 E Montecito St	Santa Barbara	CA	93103	**800-761-1072**	805-730-8000	7
Commission on Office Laboratory Accreditation (COLA) 9881 Broken Land Pkwy Suite 200	Columbia	MD	21046	**800-981-9883**	410-381-6581	49-8
Committee for a Strong Economy 9300 Livingston Rd	Fort Washington	MD	20744	**800-248-6862**	301-248-6200	604
Commodity Futures Trading Commission (CFTC) 1155 21 St NW 3 Lafayette Ctr	Washington	DC	20581	**866-366-2382**	202-418-5080	336-16
Commodity Information Systems Inc 3030 Northwest Expy Suite 725	Oklahoma City	OK	73112	**800-231-0477**	405-604-8726	623-9
Commodore Corp 1423 Lincolnway E	Goshen	IN	46526	**800-554-4285**	574-533-7100	495
Commodore Hotel 825 Sutter St	San Francisco	CA	94109	**800-338-6848**	415-923-6800	373
Commodore Motor Hotel 2013 2nd Ave	Seattle	WA	98121	**800-714-8868**	206-448-8868	373
Common Cause 1250 Connecticut Ave NW Suite 600	Washington	DC	20036	**800-926-1064**	202-833-1200	48-7
Common Sense About Kids & Guns 1225 'I' St NW Suite 1100	Washington	DC	20005	**877-955-5437**	202-546-0200	48-6
Commonweal Magazine 475 Riverside Dr Suite 405	New York	NY	10115	**888-495-6755**	212-662-4200	449-17
Commonwealth Bancshares Inc 403 Boush St *NASDAQ: CWBS*	Norfolk	VA	23510	**888-446-9862**	757-446-6900	355-2
Commonwealth Biotechnologies Inc 601 Biotech Dr *NASDAQ: CBTE*	Richmond	VA	23235	**800-735-9224**	804-648-3820	408
Commonwealth Business College *Merrillville* 1000 E 80th Pl Suite 101N	Merrillville	IN	46410	**800-258-3321**	219-769-3321	158
Michigan City 325 E US Hwy 20	Michigan City	IN	46360	**800-519-2416**	219-877-3100	158
Commonwealth Business Media Inc 50 Millstone Rd Bldg 400 Suite 200	East Windsor	NJ	08520	**888-215-6084**	609-371-7700	623-6
Commonwealth Canvas Corp 310 Andover St	Danvers	MA	01923	**877-922-6827**	978-646-9400	718
Commonwealth Club of California 595 Market St 2nd Fl	San Francisco	CA	94105	**800-933-7548**	415-597-6700	620
Commonwealth Communications Inc 105 Carnegie Ctr	Princeton	NJ	08540	**800-746-4726**	609-734-3700	187-1
Commonwealth Land Title Insurance Co 101 Gateway Center Pkwy Gateway 1	Richmond	VA	23235	**800-388-8822**	804-267-8000	384-6
Commonwealth Metal Corp 560 Sylvan Ave	Englewood Cliffs	NJ	07632	**800-772-2119**	201-569-2000	483
Commonwealth Park Suites Hotel 901 Bank St	Richmond	VA	23219	**888-343-7301**	804-343-7300	373
Commonwealth Telephone Co 100 CTE Dr	Dallas	PA	18612	**800-544-1530**	570-675-1121	721
Commonwealth Telephone Enterprises Inc 100 CTE Dr *NASDAQ: CTCO*	Dallas	PA	18612	**800-225-5282**	570-631-2700	721
Commonwealth Wine & Spirits Corp PO Box 37100	Louisville	KY	40233	**800-292-3597**	502-254-8600	82-3
CommScope Inc PO Box 1729 *NYSE: CTV*	Hickory	NC	28603	**800-982-1708**	828-324-2200	801
CommTouch Software Ltd 1300 Crittenden Ln Suite 103 *NASDAQ: CTCH*	Mountain View	CA	94043	**800-638-6824**	650-864-2000	176-7
Communication Briefings Newsletter 1101 King St Suite 110	Alexandria	VA	22314	**800-888-2084**	703-548-3800	521-11
Communication. Conference on College Composition & 1111 W Kenyon Rd	Urbana	IL	61801	**800-369-6283**	217-328-3870	49-5
Communication Data Services 1901 Bell Ave	Des Moines	IA	50315	**800-378-9982**	515-247-7500	223

Name / Address	City	State	ZIP	Toll-Free	Phone	Class
Communication Devices Inc 1 Forstmann Ct	Clifton	NJ	07011	**800-359-8561**	973-772-6997	174
Communication Intelligence Corp 275 Shoreline Dr Suite 500	Redwood Shores	CA	94065	**800-888-8242***	650-802-7888	176-12
*Sales						
Communication Technologies Inc DBA COMTek 14151 Newbrook Dr Suite 400	Chantilly	VA	20151	**888-266-8358**	703-961-9080	720
Communication at Work Newsletter 360 Hiatt Dr	Palm Beach Gardens	FL	33418	**800-621-5463**	561-622-9914	521-2
Communications Assn. Satellite Broadcasting & 1730 M St NW Suite 600	Washington	DC	20036	**800-541-5981**	202-349-3620	49-14
Communications Corp of America 700 Saint John St Suite 300	Lafayette	LA	70501	**800-237-1142**	337-237-1142	724
Communications Council Inc. American Public 625 Slaters Ln Suite 104	Alexandria	VA	22314	**800-868-2722**	703-739-1322	49-20
Communications Daily Newsletter 2115 Ward Ct NW	Washington	DC	20037	**800-771-9202**	202-872-9200	521-11
Communications & Electronics Assn. Armed Forces 4400 Fair Lakes Ct	Fairfax	VA	22033	**800-336-4583**	703-631-6100	48-19
Communications Industries Assn. International 11242 Waples Mill Rd Suite 200	Fairfax	VA	22030	**800-659-7469**	703-273-7200	49-20
Communications Mfg Co 2234 Colby Ave	Los Angeles	CA	90064	**800-462-5532**	310-828-3200	247
Communications Officials International Inc. Association of Public-Safety 351 N Williamson Blvd	Daytona Beach	FL	32114	**888-272-6911**	386-322-2500	49-7
Communications & Power Industries Inc EIMAC Div DBA CPI Inc EIMAC Div 301 Industrial Rd	San Carlos	CA	94070	**800-423-4622**	650-592-1221	252
Communications Society. IEEE IEEE Operations Ctr 445 Hoes Ln	Piscataway	NJ	08854	**800-678-4333**	732-981-0060	49-19
Communications Supply Corp 200 E Lies Rd	Carol Stream	IL	60188	**800-468-2121**	630-221-6400	245
Communications Supply Service Assn (CSSA) 5700 Murray St	Little Rock	AR	72209	**800-252-2772**	501-562-7666	49-20
Communications Systems Inc 213 S Main St	Hector	MN	55342	**800-852-8662**	320-848-6231	720
AMEX: JCS						
Communications & Technology. Association for Educational 1800 N Stonelake Dr Suite 2	Bloomington	IN	47404	**877-677-2328**	812-335-7675	49-5
Communications Test Design Inc 1373 Enterprise Dr	West Chester	PA	19380	**800-223-3910**	610-436-5203	720
Communicators. International Assn of Business 1 Hallidie Plaza Suite 600	San Francisco	CA	94102	**800-766-4222**	415-544-4700	49-12
CommuniTech.Net Inc 303 Peachtree Ctr Ave Suite 500	Atlanta	GA	30303	**877-467-8464**	404-260-2477	795
Communities in Schools Inc (CIS) 277 S Washington St Suite 210	Alexandria	VA	22314	**800-247-4543**	703-519-8999	48-6
Community America Credit Union 9777 Ridge Dr	Lenexa	KS	66219	**800-892-7957**	913-905-7000	216
Community Asphalt Corp 14005 NW 186th St	Hialeah	FL	33018	**800-741-0806**	305-829-0700	46
Community Bancorp Inc 900 Canterbury Pl Suite 300	Escondido	CA	92025	**800-362-2252**	760-432-1100	355-2
NASDAQ: CMBC						
Community Bank NA PO Box 509	Canton	NY	13617	**800-835-2993**	315-386-4553	71
Community Bank of Northern Virginia 107 Free Ct	Sterling	VA	20164	**800-430-5305**	703-430-5600	71
Community Bank Shares of Indiana Inc 101 W Spring St	New Albany	IN	47150	**866-944-2004**	812-944-2224	355-2
NASDAQ: CBIN						
Community Bank System Inc 5790 Widewaters Pkwy	DeWitt	NY	13214	**800-724-2262**	315-445-2282	355-2
NYSE: CBU						
Community Banking Advisory Network (CBAN) 10831 Old Mill Rd Suite 400	Omaha	NE	68154	**888-475-4476**	402-778-7922	49-2
Community Banks Inc 750 E Park Dr 2nd Fl	Harrisburg	PA	17111	**800-331-8362**	717-920-1698	355-2
NASDAQ: CMTY						
Community Blood Center of Greater Kansas City-Saint Joseph 3122 Frederick Ave	Saint Joseph	MO	64506	**800-725-6791**	816-232-6791	90
Community Blood Center of the Ozarks 2230 S Glenstone	Springfield	MO	65804	**800-280-5337**	417-227-5000	90
Community Blood Services of Illinois 1408 W University Ave	Urbana	IL	61801	**800-217-4483**	217-367-2202	90
Community Blue HMO of Blue Cross & Blue Shield of Western New York Inc PO Box 159	Buffalo	NY	14240	**800-544-2583**	716-884-2800	384-3
Community Broadcasters. National Federation of 970 Broadway Suite 1000	Oakland	CA	94612	**888-280-6322**	510-451-8200	49-14
Community Care 218 W 6th St	Tulsa	OK	74119	**800-278-7563**	918-594-5200	384-3
Community of Christ 1001 W Walnut St	Independence	MO	64050	**800-825-2806**	816-833-1000	48-20
Community Coffee Co PO Box 791	Baton Rouge	LA	70821	**800-688-0990**	225-291-3900	291-7
Community College of Beaver County 1 Campus Dr	Monaca	PA	15061	**800-335-0222**	724-775-8561	160
Community College of Southern Nevada Cheyenne Campus 3200 E Cheyenne Ave	North Las Vegas	NV	89030	**800-492-5728**	702-651-4000	160
Community Counselling Service Co Inc 461 5th Ave 3rd Fl	New York	NY	10017	**800-223-6733**	212-695-1175	312
Community Credit Union PO Box 830742	Richardson	TX	75083	**800-578-9009**	972-578-5000	216
Community Development Credit Unions. National Federation of 120 Wall St 10th Fl	New York	NY	10005	**800-437-8711**	212-809-1850	49-2
Community Development Digest 8204 Fenton St	Silver Spring	MD	20910	**800-666-6380**	301-588-6380	521-7
Community Directory Publishing Service 2025 E Beltline Ave SE Suite 101	Grand Rapids	MI	49546	**888-831-2800**	616-831-2800	623-6
Community First National Bank 520 Main Ave	Fargo	ND	58124	**800-232-2318**	701-293-2200	71
Community Health Accreditation Program Inc (CHAP) 39 Broadway Suite 710	New York	NY	10006	**800-656-9656**	212-480-8828	48-1
Community Health Center of Branch County 274 E Chicago St	Coldwater	MI	49036	**888-774-1471**	517-279-5400	366-2
Community Health Charities 200 N Glebe Rd Suite 801	Arlington	VA	22203	**800-654-0845**	703-528-1007	48-5
Community Health Funding Report 8204 Fenton St	Silver Spring	MD	20910	**800-666-6380**	301-588-6380	521-7
Community Health Systems Inc 155 Franklin Rd Suite 400	Brentwood	TN	37027	**888-373-9600**	615-373-9600	348
NYSE: CYH						
Community Hospice 1538 Central Ave	Ashland	KY	41101	**800-926-6184**	606-329-1890	365
Community Hospice & Home Care Services 32932 Warren Rd Suite 100	Westland	MI	48185	**800-444-0425**	734-522-4244	365
Community Hospice of Texas 6100 Western Pl Suite 500	Fort Worth	TX	76107	**800-226-0373**	817-870-2795	365
Community Hospital of Anderson & Madison Counties 1515 N Madison Ave	Anderson	IN	46011	**800-430-4774**	765-298-4242	366-2
Community Inclusion. Center for University of Maine 5717 Corbett Hall Rm 114	Orono	ME	04469	**800-203-6957**	207-581-1084	654
Community Investors Bancorp Inc 119 S Sandusky Ave	Bucyrus	OH	44820	**800-222-4955**	419-562-7055	355-2
NASDAQ: CIBI						
Community & Justice. National Conference for 475 Park Ave S 19th Fl	New York	NY	10016	**800-352-6225**	212-545-1300	48-8
Community Leaders of America. Family Career & 1910 Association Dr	Reston	VA	20191	**800-234-4425**	703-476-4900	48-11
Community Light & Sound Inc 333 E 5th St	Chester	PA	19013	**800-523-4934**	610-876-3400	52
Community Memorial Hospital 855 Mankato Ave	Winona	MN	55987	**800-944-3960**	507-454-3650	366-2
Community Methodist Hospital 1305 N Elm St	Henderson	KY	42420	**800-467-7766**	270-827-7700	366-2
Community Newspaper Holdings Inc 3500 Colonnade Pkwy Suite 600	Birmingham	AL	35243	**800-951-2644**	205-298-7100	623-8
Community Organizations for Reform Now. Association of 739 8th St SE	Washington	DC	20003	**877-552-2676**	202-547-2500	48-7
Community Oriented Policing Services Office (COPS) 1100 Vermont Ave NW 10th Fl	Washington	DC	20530	**800-421-6770**	202-616-2888	336-10
Community Pharmacists Assn. National 100 Daingerfield Rd	Alexandria	VA	22314	**800-544-7447**	703-683-8200	49-8
Community Products LLC DBA Community Playthings 359 Gibson Hill Rd	Chester	NY	10918	**800-777-4244**	845-572-3410	750
Community Service Inc. Women in 1900 N Beauregard St Suite 103	Alexandria	VA	22311	**800-442-9427**	703-671-0500	48-24
Community Services. Adventist 12501 Old Columbia Pike	Silver Spring	MD	20904	**877-227-2702**	301-680-6438	48-5
Community Suffolk Inc 304 2nd St	Everett	MA	02149	**800-225-4470**	617-389-5200	292-7
Community Theatre. American Assn of 8402 BriarWood Cir	Lago Vista	TX	78645	**866-687-2228**	512-267-0711	48-4
Community Tissue Services 3425 N 1st St Suite 103	Fresno	CA	93726	**800-201-8477**	559-224-1168	535
Community Tissue Services 7770 E 88th St	Indianapolis	IN	46256	**800-984-7783**	317-842-0009	535
Community Tissue Services 349 S Main St	Dayton	OH	45402	**800-684-7783**	937-222-0228	535
Community Tissue Services 2736 N Holland-Sylvania Rd	Toledo	OH	43615	**866-684-7783**	419-536-4924	535
Community Tissue Services 16361 NE Cameron Blvd	Portland	OR	97230	**800-545-8668**	503-408-9394	535
Community Tissue Services 7821 Bartram Ave Suite E	Philadelphia	PA	19153	**800-456-5445**	215-937-9662	535
Community Tissue Services 328 S Adams St	Fort Worth	TX	76104	**800-905-2556**	817-332-1898	535
Community Title & Escrow Ltd 2600 State St Bldg D	Alton	IL	62002	**800-854-4049**	618-466-7755	384-6
Community Transportation Assn of America (CTAA) 1341 G St NW Suite 1000	Washington	DC	20005	**800-527-8279**	202-628-1480	49-21
Community Trust Bancorp Inc 346 N Mayo Trail	Pikeville	KY	41501	**800-422-1090**	606-432-1414	355-2
NASDAQ: CTBI						
Community Trust Bank NA 346 N Mayo Trail	Pikeville	KY	41501	**800-422-1090**	606-432-1414	71
Comox Valley Chamber of Commerce 2040 Cliffe Ave	Courtenay	BC	V9N2L3	**888-357-4471**	250-334-3234	136
Compac Corp 103 Bilby Rd	Hackettstown	NJ	07840	**800-631-9350**	908-498-0660	717
Compac Industries Inc 103 Bilby Rd	Hackettstown	NJ	07840	**800-631-9350**	908-498-0660	717
Companion Life Insurance Co 3316 Farnam St	Omaha	NE	68175	**800-775-6000**		384-2
Companion Life Insurance Co 7909 Parklane Rd Suite 200	Columbia	SC	29223	**800-753-0404**	803-735-1251	384-2
Company Store 500 Company Store Rd	La Crosse	WI	54601	**800-285-3696**	608-785-1400	451
Compass Bancshares Inc 15 S 20th St	Birmingham	AL	35233	**800-239-2265**	205-933-3000	355-2
NASDAQ: CBSS						
Compass Bank 15 S 20th St	Birmingham	AL	35233	**800-239-4357***	205-933-3000	71
*Cust Svc						
Compass Cove Ocean Resort 2311 S Ocean Blvd	Myrtle Beach	SC	29577	**800-228-9894**	843-448-8373	655
Compass Group North American Div 2400 Yorkmont Rd	Charlotte	NC	28217	**800-357-0012**	704-329-4000	294

Name / Address	City	State	ZIP	Toll-Free	Phone	Class
Compass Minerals International Inc 8300 College Blvd *NYSE: CMP* ■ *Cust Svc	Overland Park	KS	66210	**800-253-7934***	913-344-9200	668
Compass Travel Service Inc 840 Ogden Ave	Westmont	IL	60559	**800-300-1606**	630-986-1606	760
Compassion International PO Box 65000	Colorado Springs	CO	80962	**800-336-7539**	719-487-7000	48-5
Compassionate Care Hospice 66 Mt Prospect Ave Bldg C	Clifton	NJ	07013	**800-916-1494**	973-916-1400	365
Compassionate Care Hospice 600 Highland Dr Suite 624	West Hampton	NJ	08060	**800-844-4774**	609-267-1178	365
Compassionate Care Hospice 3333 Street Rd Suite 235	Bensalem	PA	19020	**800-584-8165**	215-245-3525	365
Compassionate Care Hospice of Delaware 5610 Kirkwood Hwy	Wilmington	DE	19808	**800-219-0092**	302-683-1000	365
Compassionate Friends PO Box 3696	Oak Brook	IL	60522	**877-969-0010**	630-990-0010	48-21
CompassLearning Inc 9920 Pacific Heights Blvd Suite 500 *Cust Svc	San Diego	CA	92121	**800-247-1380***	858-587-0087	176-3
CompDent Corp 100 Mansell Ct E Suite 400	Roswell	GA	30076	**800-633-1262**	770-552-7101	384-3
Compel Corp 10410 Pioneer Blvd Suite 7	Santa Fe Springs	CA	90670	**800-553-1162**	562-946-8321	188-4
CompetitivEdge 196 S Main St	Colchester	CT	06415	**888-881-3343**	860-537-6731	612
Compex Inc 840 Columbia St Suite B	Brea	CA	92821	**800-279-8891**	714-482-0333	174
Compex Legal Services Inc 325 Maple Ave *Cust Svc	Torrance	CA	90503	**800-426-6739***	310-782-1801	436
Compex Technologies Inc 1811 Old Hwy 8 *NASDAQ: CMPX*	New Brighton	MN	55112	**800-551-7939**	651-631-0590	249
CompHealth Inc 4021 S 700 E Suite 300	Salt Lake City	UT	84107	**800-453-3030**	801-264-6400	707
Complemar Partners 175 Humboldt St	Rochester	NY	14610	**800-388-5126**	585-647-5800	545
Complete Music Inc 7877 L St	Omaha	NE	68127	**800-843-3866**	402-339-0001	179
Component Hardware Group Inc PO Box 2020	Lakewood	NJ	08701	**800-526-3694**	732-363-4700	345
ComponentOne LLC 4516 Henry St Suite 500	Pittsburgh	PA	15213	**800-858-2739**	412-681-4343	176-12
Components Packaging & Manufacturing Technology Society. IEEE 445 Hoes Ln PO Box 1331	Piscataway	NJ	08855	**800-678-4333**	732-562-5529	49-19
Composers Authors & Publishers. American Society of 1 Lincoln Plaza	New York	NY	10023	**800-952-7227**	212-621-6000	48-4
Composing Room of Michigan Inc 678 Front Ave NW Suite 135	Grand Rapids	MI	49504	**800-253-4632**	616-776-7940	770
Composite Technology Inc 1001 Ave R	Grand Prairie	TX	75050	**888-284-1972**	972-606-4400	25
Composition & Communication. Conference on College 1111 W Kenyon Rd	Urbana	IL	61801	**800-369-6283**	217-328-3870	49-5
Composition Materials Co Inc 125 Old Gate Ln	Milford	CT	06460	**800-262-7763**	203-874-6500	1
Compounding Pharmacists. International Academy of PO Box 1365	Sugar Land	TX	77487	**800-927-4227**	281-933-8400	49-8
Comprehensive EAP 5 Militia Dr	Lexington	MA	02421	**800-344-1011**	781-863-8283	454
Comprehensive Health Services Inc DBA Wellness Plan The 2888 W Grand Blvd *Cust Svc	Detroit	MI	48202	**800-680-9355***	313-875-4200	384-3
Comprehensive Mfg Services LLC DBA Courion 3044 Lambdin Ave	Saint Louis	MO	63115	**800-533-5760**	314-533-5700	232
Comprehensive Video Group 55 Ruta Ct	South Hackensack	NJ	07606	**800-526-0242**	201-229-4270	801
Compressor Engineering Corp (CECO) 5440 Alder Dr	Houston	TX	77081	**800-879-2326**	713-664-7333	170
Compscript Inc 1225 Broken Sound Pkwy NW Suite A	Boca Raton	FL	33487	**800-832-8585**	561-994-8585	576
Compsee Inc 400 N Main St	Mount Gilead	NC	27306	**800-768-5248**	910-439-6141	174
ComPsych Corp 455 N City Front Plaza Dr NBC Tower 13th Fl	Chicago	IL	60611	**800-272-7255**	312-595-4000	454
Comptroller of the Currency 250 'E' St SW 9th Fl	Washington	DC	20219	**800-613-6743**	202-874-4900	336-14
Comptrollers. American Society of Military 415 N Alfred	Alexandria	VA	22314	**800-462-5637**	703-549-0360	48-19
CompuCom Systems Inc 7171 Forest Ln *Cust Svc	Dallas	TX	75230	**800-597-0555***	972-856-3600	174
CompuCom Systems Inc Excell Data Div 1756 114th Ave SE Suite 220	Bellevue	WA	98004	**800-539-2355**	425-974-2000	178
CompuMed Inc 5777 W Century Blvd Suite 1285	Los Angeles	CA	90045	**800-421-3395**	310-258-5000	410
Compumedics USA Ltd 7850 Paseo del Norte Suite 101	El Paso	TX	79912	**877-717-3975**	915-845-5600	249
Compunetix Inc 2420 Mosside Blvd	Monroeville	PA	15146	**800-879-4266**	412-373-8110	720
Compunnel Software Group Inc 1000 Rt 9 N Suite 102	Woodbridge	NJ	07095	**800-692-4440**	732-636-1999	707
CompUSA Inc 14951 N Dallas Pkwy	Dallas	TX	75254	**800-278-4685**	972-982-4000	177
CompuServe Interactive Services Inc 5000 Arlington Ctr Blvd *Cust Svc	Columbus	OH	43220	**800-848-8990***	614-457-8600	390
Computech Resources Inc 1375 W Main Ave	De Pere	WI	54115	**877-500-3330**	920-336-1387	178
Computer Analytical Systems Inc (CASI) 1418 S 3rd St	Louisville	KY	40208	**800-977-3475**	502-635-2019	178
Computer Assoc International Inc 1 Computer Assoc Plaza *NYSE: CA*	Islandia	NY	11749	**800-225-5224**	631-342-6000	176-1

Name / Address	City	State	ZIP	Toll-Free	Phone	Class
Computer Books Direct Doubleday Select Inc 101 Park Ave 2nd Fl	New York	NY	10178	**800-321-7323**		94
Computer Capacity Management. Institute for 1020 8th Ave S Suite 6	Naples	FL	34102	**800-531-6143**	239-261-8945	48-9
Computer Components Corp DBA Universal Battery 1702 Hayden Dr	Carrollton	TX	75006	**800-749-0222**	972-387-0850	245
Computer Consultants Assn. Independent 11131 S Towne Sq Suite F	Saint Louis	MO	63123	**800-774-4222**	314-892-1675	48-9
Computer Conversions Inc 13230 Evening Creek Dr Suite 202	San Diego	CA	92128	**800-328-2911**	858-746-3007	176-12
Computer Credit Inc 640 W 4th St	Winston-Salem	NC	27101	**800-942-2995**	336-761-1524	157
Computer Economics Report 2082 Business Center Dr Suite 240	Irvine	CA	92612	**800-326-8100**	949-831-8700	521-3
COMPUTER EXPLORERS Inc 12715 Telge Rd	Cypress	TX	77429	**800-531-5053**	281-256-4100	146
Computer Gaming World Magazine 28 E 28th St 9th Fl	New York	NY	10016	**800-827-4450**	212-503-5371	449-14
Computer Graphics World Magazine 98 Spit Brook Rd	Nashua	NH	03062	**800-331-4463**	603-891-0123	449-7
Computer & Hi-tech Management Inc 596 Lynnhaven Pkwy	Virginia Beach	VA	23452	**800-768-4111**	757-486-8838	178
Computer Horizons Corp 49 Old Bloomfield Ave *NASDAQ: CHRZ*	Mountain Lakes	NJ	07046	**800-321-2421**	973-299-4000	178
Computer Law Strategist Newsletter 345 Park Ave S	New York	NY	10010	**800-888-8300**	212-779-9200	521-7
Computer Library Center Inc. Online 6565 Frantz Rd	Dublin	OH	43017	**800-848-5878**	614-764-6000	49-11
Computer Magazine 10662 Los Vaqueros Cir *Orders	Los Alamitos	CA	90720	**800-272-6657***	714-821-8380	449-7
Computer Measurement Group (CMG) 151 Fries Mill Rd Suite 104	Turnersville	NJ	08012	**800-436-7264**	856-401-1700	48-9
Computer Methods Corp 525 Rt 73 S Suite 300	Marlton	NJ	08053	**800-969-4360**	856-596-4360	178
Computer Network Technology Corp (CNT) 6000 Nathan Ln N *NASDAQ: CMNT*	Minneapolis	MN	55442	**800-638-8324**	763-268-6000	174
Computer Parts Unlimited Inc 3949 Heritage Oak Ct	Simi Valley	CA	93063	**800-644-4494**	805-306-2500	172
Computer Process Controls Inc 1640 Airport Rd NW Suite 104	Kennesaw	GA	30144	**800-829-2724**	770-425-2724	201
Computer Programs & Systems Inc (CPSI) 6600 Wall St *NASDAQ: CPSI*	Mobile	AL	36695	**800-711-2774**	251-639-8100	39
Computer Sales International Inc (CSI) 9990 Old Olive St Rd	Saint Louis	MO	63141	**800-955-0960**	314-997-7010	261-1
Computer Science Innovations Inc 1235 Evans Rd	Melbourne	FL	32904	**800-289-2923**	321-676-2923	176-1
Computer Sciences Corp 2100 E Grand Ave *NYSE: CSC*	El Segundo	CA	90245	**800-342-5272**	310-615-0311	178
Computer Services Inc 3901 Technology Dr	Paducah	KY	42001	**800-545-4274**	270-442-7361	223
Computer Shopper Magazine 28 E 28th St	New York	NY	10016	**800-274-6384**	646-472-4000	449-7
Computer Specialists Inc 904 Wind River Ln Suite 100	Gaithersburg	MD	20878	**800-505-4365**	301-921-8860	173
Computer Stock Forms Inc 324 S Washington St	Greenfield	OH	45123	**800-543-5565**	937-981-7751	111
Computer Task Group Inc (CTG) 800 Delaware Ave *NYSE: CTG*	Buffalo	NY	14209	**800-992-5350**	716-882-8000	178
Computer Technology Assoc (CTA) 12530 Parklawn Dr Suite 300	Rockville	MD	20852	**800-753-9201**	301-581-3200	178
Computer Technology Corp DBA CACTUS Software 7301 Mission Rd Suite 300	Prairie Village	KS	66208	**800-776-2305**	913-677-0092	176-11
Computerized Security Systems Inc 1950 Austin Dr *Sales	Troy	MI	48083	**877-272-3565***	248-680-8484	681
ComputerJobs.com Inc 280 Interstate North Pkwy SE Suite 300	Atlanta	GA	30339	**800-850-0045**	770-850-0045	257
Computers4SURE.com Inc 6 Cambridge Dr *Cust Svc	Trumbull	CT	06611	**800-585-4080***	203-615-7000	177
Computers in Libraries Magazine 143 Old Marlton Pike	Medford	NJ	08055	**800-300-9868**	609-654-6266	449-7
ComputerUser.com Inc 220 S 6th St Suite 500	Minneapolis	MN	55402	**800-788-0204**	612-339-7571	623-9
Computerwise Inc 302 N Winchester Ln	Olathe	KS	66062	**800-255-3739**	913-829-0600	171-7
Computerwork.com c/o Internet Assn Group 4500 Salisbury Rd	Jacksonville	FL	32216	**800-691-8413**	904-296-1993	257
Computerworld Magazine 1 Speen St	Framingham	MA	01701	**800-343-6474**	508-879-0700	449-7
Computing Center. National Energy Research Scientific Lawrence Berkeley National Laboratory 1 Cyclotron Rd MS 50C3396	Berkeley	CA	94720	**800-847-6070**	510-486-5849	654
Computing Machinery. Association for 1515 Broadway 17th Fl	New York	NY	10036	**800-342-6626**	212-869-7440	48-9
Computing Professionals. Institute for Certification of 2350 E Devon Ave Suite 115	Des Plaines	IL	60018	**800-843-8227**	847-299-4227	48-9
Compuware Corp 1 Campus Martius *NASDAQ: CPWR*	Detroit	MI	48226	**800-292-7432**	313-227-7300	176-1
Compuware Corp Professional Services Div 505 Hwy 169 N Suite 750 *Cust Svc	Plymouth	MN	55441	**800-292-7432***	763-541-9575	707
Comspec Digital Products Inc PO Box 178	Jacksonville	TX	75766	**800-490-6893**	832-443-4487	496

Name / Address	City	State	ZIP	Toll-Free	Phone	Class
Comsquared Systems Inc 5125 Peachtree Industrial Blvd.	Norcross	GA	30092	**800-592-3766**	770-734-5300	176-1
Comstock Images Inc 244 Sheffield St	Mountainside	NJ	07092	**800-225-2722**	908-518-6200	582
Comstock Resources Inc 5300 Town & Country Blvd Suite 500 *NYSE: CRK*	Frisco	TX	75034	**800-877-1322**	972-668-8800	525
Comstor Inc 14850 Conference Ctr Dr Suite 200	Chantilly	VA	20151	**800-955-9590**	703-345-5100	172
Comstor Productivity Center Inc 2219 N Dickey Rd	Spokane	WA	99212	**800-776-2451**	509-534-5080	487
Comsys IT Partners Inc 4400 Post Oak Pkwy Suite 1800 *NASDAQ: CITP*	Houston	TX	77027	**877-626-6797**	713-386-1400	707
ComTal Machine & Engineering Inc 5000 Township Pkwy	Saint Paul	MN	55110	**800-635-2507**	651-426-0177	537
Comtech Publishing Ltd 2835 Juliann Way *Orders	Reno	NV	89509	**800-456-7005***	775-825-9000	176-12
COMTek 14151 Newbrook Dr Suite 400	Chantilly	VA	20151	**888-266-8358**	703-961-9080	720
Comtek Computer Systems 2751 Mercantile Dr Suite 100	Rancho Cordova	CA	95742	**800-823-4450**	916-859-7000	173
Comtrol Corp 6655 Wedgewood Rd Suite 120	Maple Grove	MN	55311	**800-926-6876**	763-494-4100	174
Comunale SA Co Inc 2900 Newpark Dr	Barberton	OH	44203	**800-776-7181**	330-706-3040	188-13
Con Forms PO Box 308	Port Washington	WI	53074	**800-223-3676**	262-268-6800	181
Con-Tech Lighting 2783 Shermer Rd	Northbrook	IL	60062	**800-728-0312**	847-559-5500	431
Con-Way Central Express Inc 4880 Venture Dr	Ann Arbor	MI	48108	**800-421-4007**	734-994-6600	769
Con-Way Southern Express 14500 Trinity Blvd Suite 118	Fort Worth	TX	76155	**800-525-3117**	817-358-3600	769
Con-Way Western Express 6301 Beach Blvd Suite 300	Buena Park	CA	90621	**800-545-9683**	714-562-0110	769
ConAgra Food Ingredients Co SpiceTec-USF Group 195 Alexandra Way	Carol Stream	IL	60188	**800-872-9236**	630-682-5600	291-37
ConAgra Foods International 2 Jericho Plaza Suite 304	Jericho	NY	11753	**800-275-5454**	516-949-7500	291-26
ConAgra Foods Retail Products Co Dairy Foods Group 215 W Diehl Rd	Naperville	IL	60563	**800-444-7360**	630-857-5200	291-5
ConAgra Foods Retail Products Co Deli Foods Group 2001 Butterfield Rd	Downers Grove	IL	60515	**800-325-7424**	630-512-1000	465
ConAgra Hunt-Wesson Foodservice Co 3353 Michelson Dr	Irvine	CA	92612	**800-633-0112**	949-437-1000	291-20
ConAgra Seafood Cos PO Box 2819	Tampa	FL	33601	**800-732-3663**	813-241-1500	291-14
Conair Corp 1 Cummings Pt Rd	Stamford	CT	06902	**800-726-6247**	203-351-9000	37
Conaway-Winter Inc 718 E Park St	Willow Springs	MO	65793	**800-331-9476**	417-469-3125	296
Conax Buffalo Technologies LLC 2300 Walden Ave	Buffalo	NY	14225	**800-223-2389**	716-684-4500	200
Concentra Inc 5080 Spectrum Dr Suite 400 W	Addison	TX	75001	**800-232-3550**	972-364-8000	455
Concept Boats Corp 2410 NW 147th St	Opalocka	FL	33054	**888-635-8712**	305-635-8712	91
Concept Plastics Inc PO Box 847	High Point	NC	27260	**800-225-9553**	336-889-2001	597
Concepts Direct Inc 2950 Colorful Ave *NASDAQ: CDIR*	Longmont	CO	80504	**800-773-0208**	303-772-9171	451
Conceptus Inc 1021 Howard Ave *NASDAQ: CPTS*	San Carlos	CA	94070	**800-434-7240**	650-802-7240	468
Concern America PO Box 1790	Santa Ana	CA	92702	**800-266-2376**	714-953-8575	48-5
Concerned United Birthparents Inc (CUB) PO Box 230457	Encinitas	CA	92023	**800-822-2777**		48-21
Concerto Software 6 Technology Pk Dr	Westford	MA	01886	**800-999-4458**	978-952-0200	720
Conch House Heritage Inn 625 Truman Ave	Key West	FL	33040	**800-207-5806**	305-293-0020	373
Conch House Marina Resort 57 Comares Ave	Saint Augustine	FL	32080	**800-940-6256**	904-829-8646	373
Concord Camera Corp 4000 Hollywood Blvd Suite 650N *NASDAQ: LENS*	Hollywood	FL	33021	**800-339-4215**	954-331-4200	580
Concord Chemical Co 1700 Federal St	Camden	NJ	08105	**800-282-2436**	856-966-1526	149
Concord Coalition 1011 Arlington Blvd Suite 300	Arlington	VA	22209	**888-333-4248**	703-894-6222	48-7
Concord Communications Inc 400-600 Nickerson Rd *NASDAQ: CCRD*	Marlborough	MA	01752	**800-851-8725**	508-460-4646	176-12
Concord Fabrics Inc 462 7th Ave	New York	NY	10018	**800-223-5678**	212-760-0300	730-4
Concord Group Insurance Co 4 Bouton St	Concord	NH	03301	**800-852-3380**	603-224-4086	384-4
Concord Litho Group 92 Old Turnpike Rd	Concord	NH	03301	**800-258-3662**	603-225-3328	615
Concord Mills 8111 Concord Mills Blvd	Concord	NC	28027	**877-626-4557**	704-979-3000	452
Concord Records Inc 270 N Canon Dr Suite 1212	Beverly Hills	CA	90210	**800-551-5299**	310-385-4455	643
Concord Regional Visiting Nurse Assoc Hospice Program PO Box 1797	Concord	NH	03302	**800-924-8620**	603-224-4093	365
Concord Resort & Golf Club Concord Rd.	Kiamesha Lake	NY	12751	**888-448-9686**	845-794-4000	655
Concord University PO Box 1000	Athens	WV	24712	**800-344-6679**	304-384-3115	163
Concorde Career Colleges Inc 5800 Foxridge Dr Suite 500 *NASDAQ: CCDC*	Mission	KS	66202	**800-515-1007**	913-831-9977	787
Concorde Hotels International 1 Penn Plaza Suite 2127	New York	NY	10119	**800-888-4747**	212-935-1045	369
Concorde Hotels International Prestige Card 1 Penn Plaza Suite 2127	New York	NY	10119	**800-888-4747**	212-935-1045	371
Concordia College 171 White Plains Rd.	Bronxville	NY	10708	**800-937-2655**	914-337-9300	163
Concordia College Moorhead 901 S 8th St.	Moorhead	MN	56562	**800-699-9897**	218-299-4000	163
Concordia Electric Co-op Inc 1865 Hwy 84 W	Jonesville	LA	71343	**800-617-6282**	318-339-7969	244
Concordia Publishing House Inc 3558 S Jefferson Ave *Cust Svc	Saint Louis	MO	63118	**800-325-3040***	314-268-1000	623-4
Concordia University 1530 Concordia W	Irvine	CA	92612	**800-229-1200**	949-854-8002	163
Concordia University 7400 Augusta St.	River Forest	IL	60305	**800-285-2668**	708-771-8300	163
Concordia University 4090 Geddes Rd.	Ann Arbor	MI	48105	**800-253-0680**	734-995-7300	163
Concordia University 275 Syndicate St N.	Saint Paul	MN	55104	**800-333-4705**	651-641-8278	163
Concordia University 800 N Columbia Ave.	Seward	NE	68434	**800-535-5494**	402-643-3651	163
Concordia University 2811 NE Holman St	Portland	OR	97211	**800-321-9371**	503-288-9371	163
Concordia University at Austin 3400 IH-35 N	Austin	TX	78705	**800-865-4282**	512-486-2000	163
Concordia University Wisconsin 12800 N Lake Shore Dr	Mequon	WI	53097	**888-628-9472**	262-243-5700	163
Concourse Exhibition Center 8th & Brannan Sts	San Francisco	CA	94103	**800-877-8522**	415-864-1500	204
Concourse Hotel & Conference Center 4300 International Gateway	Columbus	OH	43219	**800-541-4574**	614-237-2515	373
Concrete Assn. National Precast 10333 N Meridian St Suite 272	Indianapolis	IN	46290	**800-366-7731**	317-571-9500	49-3
Concrete Materials Corp 106 Industry Rd	Richmond	KY	40475	**877-623-4238**	859-623-4238	180
Concrete Pavement Institute. Interlocking 1444 'I' St NW Suite 700	Washington	DC	20005	**800-241-3652**	202-712-9036	49-3
Concur Technologies Inc 6222 185th Ave NE *NASDAQ: CNQR*	Redmond	WA	98052	**800-358-0610**	425-702-8808	176-1
Concurrent Computer Corp 4375 River Green Pkwy Suite 100 *NASDAQ: CCUR*	Duluth	GA	30096	**877-978-7363**	678-258-4000	176-8
Condat Corp 250 S Industrial Dr	Saline	MI	48176	**800-883-7876**	734-944-4994	530
Conde Nast Publications Inc 4 Times Sq	New York	NY	10036	**800-223-0780**	212-286-2860	623-9
Conde Nast Traveler Magazine 4 Times Sq	New York	NY	10036	**800-223-0780**	212-286-2860	449-22
Conditioning Assn. National Strength & 1885 Bob Johnson Dr	Colorado Springs	CO	80906	**800-815-6826**	719-632-6722	48-22
Condon Oil Co Inc PO Box 184	Ripon	WI	54971	**800-452-1212**	920-748-3186	569
Conduit Pipe Products Co 1504 W Main St	West Jefferson	OH	43162	**800-848-6125**	614-879-9114	804
Cone Mills Corp 804 Green Valley Rd Suite 300	Greensboro	NC	27408	**800-763-0123**	336-379-6220	730-1
Cone Mills Corp Denim Group 804 Green Valley Rd Suite 300	Greensboro	NC	27408	**800-763-0123**	336-379-6220	730-1
Conectiv 800 King St PO Box 231	Wilmington	DE	19899	**800-266-3284**	302-429-3018	355-5
Conectiv Power Delivery 630 Martin Luther King Blvd *Cust Svc	Wilmington	DE	19899	**800-375-7117***	302-454-0300	774
Conestoga Wood Specialties Inc 245 Reading Rd	East Earl	PA	17519	**800-964-3667**	717-445-6701	116
Conexant Systems Inc 4000 MacArthur Blvd *NASDAQ: CNXT*	Newport Beach	CA	92660	**800-854-8099**	949-483-4600	686
Confectioners Assn. National 8320 Old Courthouse Rd Suite 300	Vienna	VA	22182	**800-433-1200**	703-790-5750	49-6
Confectioners International. Retail 1807 Glenview Rd Suite 204	Glenview	IL	60025	**800-545-5381**	847-724-6120	49-6
Confer Plastics Inc 97 Witmer Rd	North Tonawanda	NY	14120	**800-635-3213**	716-693-2056	593
Conference Center of the Americas. Biltmore Hotel & 1200 Anastasia Ave	Coral Gables	FL	33134	**800-727-1926**	305-445-1926	655
Conference on College Composition & Communication (CCCC) 1111 W Kenyon Rd	Urbana	IL	61801	**800-369-6283**	217-328-3870	49-5
Conference Management Services PO Box 2506	Monterey	CA	93942	**800-882-1891**	831-646-3377	183
Conference of State Bank Supervisors (CSBS) 1155 Connecticut Ave NW 5th Fl	Washington	DC	20036	**800-886-2727**	202-296-2840	49-7
Conference & Travel Services Inc 5701 Coventry Ln	Fort Wayne	IN	46804	**800-393-0060**	260-434-6600	183
Conference & Visitors Bureau of Montgomery County 11820 Parklawn Dr Suite 380	Rockville	MD	20852	**800-925-0880**	301-428-9702	205
Confidential Services PO Box 91034	Columbus	OH	43209	**800-752-4581**	614-252-4646	392
ConFish Inc PO Box 271	Isola	MS	38754	**800-228-3474**	662-962-3101	291-14
Confluence Watersports Co 3761 Old Glenola Rd	Trinity	NC	27370	**800-311-7245**	336-434-7470	701
Conforma Laboratories Inc 4705 Colley Ave	Norfolk	VA	23508	**800-426-1700**	757-423-5807	531
Congoleum Corp PO Box 3127 *AMEX: CGM*	Mercerville	NJ	08619	**800-274-3266**	609-584-3000	286
Congregational Christian Churches. National Assn of 8473 S Howell Ave	Oak Creek	WI	53154	**800-262-1620**	414-764-1620	48-20
Congress Daily Newsletter 1501 'M' St NW Suite 300	Washington	DC	20005	**800-207-8001**	202-739-8541	521-7
Congress Financial Corp 1133 Ave of the Americas	New York	NY	10036	**800-223-6352**	212-840-2000	214
Congress Plaza Hotel & Convention Center 520 S Michigan Ave	Chicago	IL	60605	**800-635-1666**	312-427-3800	373
Congress Watch 215 Pennsylvania Ave SE 3rd Fl	Washington	DC	20003	**800-289-3787**	202-546-4996	48-7
Congress.Org Capitol Advantage PO Box 2018	Merrifield	VA	22116	**800-659-8708**	703-289-4670	677

Name / Address	City	State	Zip	Toll-Free	Phone	Class
Congressional Quarterly Inc 1255 22nd St NW	Washington	DC	20037	**800-432-2250**	202-419-8500	623-2
Conifer Park 79 Glenridge Rd	Glenville	NY	12302	**800-989-6446**	518-399-6446	712
Conimar Corp 1724 NE 22nd Ave	Ocala	FL	34470	**800-874-9735**	352-732-7235	588
Conklin Co Inc 551 Valley Park Dr	Shakopee	MN	55379	**800-888-8838**	952-445-6010	361
Conklin Corp 199 West Rd	Pleasant Valley	NY	12569	**800-266-5546**	845-635-2136	720
Conley Frog Switch & Forge Co 387 E Bodley St	Memphis	TN	38109	**800-332-4457**	901-948-4591	474
Conley Paper & Packaging 1312 4th St SE	Canton	OH	44707	**800-362-6001**	330-456-8243	549
Conley's Mfg & Sales Inc 4344 E Mission Blvd	Montclair	CA	91763	**800-377-8441**	909-627-0981	106
Conlin Travel Inc 3270 Washtenaw Ave	Ann Arbor	MI	48104	**800-426-6546**	734-677-0900	760
Conmed Corp 525 French Rd	Utica	NY	13502	**800-448-6506**	315-797-8375	468
NASDAQ: CNMD						
Conn-Selmer Inc 600 Industrial Pkwy	Elkhart	IN	46515	**800-759-9124**	574-295-0079	516
Connect For Kids 1625 K St NW Suite 1100	Washington	DC	20006	**877-236-8666**	202-638-5770	48-6
Connected Corp 100 Pennsylvania Ave	Framingham	MA	01701	**800-934-0956**	508-808-7300	39
ConnectiCare Inc 30 Batterson Park Rd	Farmington	CT	06032	**800-251-7722**	860-674-5700	384-3
Connecticut						
Banking Dept 260 Constitution Plaza	Hartford	CT	06103	**800-831-7225**	860-240-8299	335
Consumer Protection Dept 165 Capitol Ave	Hartford	CT	06106	**800-842-2649**	860-713-6020	335
Higher Education Dept 61 Woodland St	Hartford	CT	06105	**800-842-0229**	860-947-1800	335
Rehabilitation Services Bureau 25 Sigourney St 11th Fl	Hartford	CT	06106	**800-537-2549**	860-424-4844	335
Victim Services Office 31 Cookes St	Plainville	CT	06062	**800-822-8428**	860-747-3994	335
Connecticut Assn of Realtors 111 Founders Plaza 11th Fl	East Hartford	CT	06108	**800-335-4862**	860-290-6601	642
Connecticut College 270 Mohegan Ave	New London	CT	06320	**888-553-8760**	860-439-2000	163
Connecticut Eye Bank & Visual Research Foundation Inc 100 Grand St	New Britain	CT	06052	**800-355-5520**	860-224-5550	265
Connecticut General Life Insurance Co 900 Cottage Grove Rd	Hartford	CT	06152	**800-444-2363**	860-226-6000	384-2
Connecticut Hospice 100 Double Beach Rd	Branford	CT	06405	**800-315-7654**	203-315-7500	365
Connecticut Laminating Co Inc 162 James St	New Haven	CT	06513	**800-753-9119**	203-787-2184	588
Connecticut Light & Power Co 107 Selden St	Berlin	CT	06037	**800-286-2000***	860-665-5000	774
*Cust Svc						
Connecticut Limousine LLC 230 Old Gate Ln	Milford	CT	06460	**800-472-5466**	203-878-6867	433
Connecticut Magazine 35 Nutmeg Dr	Trumbull	CT	06611	**800-974-2001**	203-380-6600	449-22
Connecticut Medicine Magazine 160 Saint Ronan St	New Haven	CT	06511	**800-635-7740**	203-865-0587	449-16
Connecticut microComputer Inc 150 Pocono Rd	Brookfield	CT	06804	**800-426-2872**	203-740-9890	496
Connecticut Post 410 State St	Bridgeport	CT	06604	**800-542-5620***	203-333-0161	522-2
*Edit						
Connecticut Public Broadcasting Inc (CPBI) 1049 Asylum Ave	Hartford	CT	06105	**800-683-2112**	860-278-5310	620
Connecticut Republican Party 97 Elm St Rear	Hartford	CT	06106	**888-982-8467**	860-547-0589	605-2
Connecticut Spring & Stamping Corp 48 Spring Ln	Farmington	CT	06034	**800-255-8590**	860-677-1341	705
Connecticut Stamping & Bending Co 206 Newington Ave	New Britain	CT	06051	**800-966-6964**	860-225-4637	584
Connecticut State Medical Society 160 Saint Ronan St	New Haven	CT	06511	**800-635-7740**	203-865-0587	466
Connecticut Sun 1 Mohegan Sun Blvd	Uncasville	CT	06382	**877-786-8499**	860-862-4000	703
Connecticut Water Service Inc 93 W Main St	Clinton	CT	06413	**800-286-5700**	860-669-8636	355-5
NASDAQ: CTWS						
Connecticut's Mystic & More! PO Box 89	New London	CT	06320	**800-863-6569**	860-444-2206	205
Connecting Businessmen to Christ (CBMC) 5746 Marlin Rd Suite 602 Osborne Center	Chattanooga	TN	37411	**800-575-2262**	423-698-4444	48-20
Connection The 11351 Rupp Dr	Burnsville	MN	55337	**800-883-5777***	952-948-5488	722
*Sales						
Connection Tours Inc 3596 Lorna Ridge Dr	Birmingham	AL	35216	**888-287-7328**	205-822-7323	748
Connectria Corp 10845 Olive Blvd Suite 300	Saint Louis	MO	63141	**800-781-7820**	314-587-7000	39
ConnectTo.Net 150 Professional Ctr Dr Suite H	Rohnert Park	CA	94928	**877-586-3538**	707-696-2365	390
Connell Co 1 Connell Dr	Berkeley Heights	NJ	07922	**800-233-3240**	908-673-3700	184
Connell Communications Inc 86 Elm St	Peterborough	NH	03458	**800-677-8847**	603-924-7271	623-9
Connell Finance Co Inc 1 Connell Dr	Berkeley Heights	NJ	07922	**800-233-3240**	908-673-3700	214
Connell Gatco Co 1 Connell Dr	Berkeley Heights	NJ	07922	**800-233-3240**	908-673-3700	378
Connell LP 1 International Pl 31st Fl	Boston	MA	02110	**800-276-4746**	617-737-2700	674
Connell Realty & Development Co 1 Connell Dr	Berkeley Heights	NJ	07922	**800-233-3240**	908-673-3700	639
Connell Technologies Co LLC 350 Lindbergh Ave	Livermore	CA	94550	**888-301-0300**	925-455-6790	214
Connell's Flowers 2385 E Main St	Bexley	OH	43209	**800-790-8980**	614-237-8653	287
Connelly Billiard Mfg 1440 S Euclid Ave	Tucson	AZ	85713	**800-861-8619**	520-624-6000	701
Connelly Skis Inc 20621 52nd Ave W	Lynnwood	WA	98036	**800-234-7547**	425-775-5416	701
Conner Prairie Living History Museum 13400 Allisonville Rd	Fishers	IN	46038	**800-966-1836**	317-776-6000	509
Connersville News-Examiner 406 N Central Ave	Connersville	IN	47331	**888-906-1700**	765-825-0581	522-2
Connetics Corp 3290 W Bayshore Rd	Palo Alto	CA	94303	**888-969-2628**	650-843-2800	86
NASDAQ: CNCT						
Connexus Energy Co-op 14601 Ramsey Blvd	Ramsey	MN	55303	**800-642-1672**	763-323-2600	244
Conning Corp City Place II 185 Asylum St	Hartford	CT	06103	**888-266-6464**	860-527-1131	355-3
Conn's Inc 3295 College St	Beaumont	TX	77701	**800-511-5750***	409-832-1696	35
NASDAQ: CONN ■ *Cust Svc						
Conolog Corp 5 Columbia Rd	Somerville	NJ	08876	**800-526-3984**	908-722-8081	633
NASDAQ: CNLG						
Conover CE & Co Inc 4106 Blanche Rd	Bensalem	PA	19020	**800-266-6837**	215-639-6666	321
Conquest Systems Inc 1023 15th St NW Suite 500	Washington	DC	20005	**800-719-8817**	202-289-4240	176-7
Conrad-American Inc 609 Main St	Houghton	IA	52631	**800-553-1791**	319-469-4111	269
Conrad Hotels 9336 Civic Ctr Dr	Beverly Hills	CA	90210	**800-445-8667**	310-278-4321	369
Conroe Regional Medical Center 504 Medical Ctr Blvd	Conroe	TX	77304	**888-633-2687**	936-539-1111	366-2
Conroy & Knowlton Inc 2000 S Hoefner Ave	Commerce	CA	90040	**888-295-9500**	323-665-5288	591
Conroy's Inc 2550 N Hollywood Way Suite 206	Burbank	CA	91505	**800-266-7697**	818-843-8280	287
Conseco Annuity Assurance Co 11815 N Pennsylvania St	Carmel	IN	46032	**800-541-2254**	317-817-6100	384-2
Conseco Health Insurance Co 11815 N Pennsylvania St	Carmel	IN	46932	**800-541-2254**	317-817-6100	384-2
Conseco Inc 11825 N Pennsylvania St	Carmel	IN	46032	**800-541-2254**	317-817-6100	355-4
NYSE: CNO						
Conservation Assn. Coastal 6919 Portwest Dr Suite 100	Houston	TX	77024	**800-201-3474**	713-626-4234	48-13
Conservation Assn. Student 689 River Rd PO Box 550	Charlestown	NH	03603	**888-722-9675**	603-543-1700	48-13
Conservation Corps. National Assn of Service & 666 11th St NW Suite 1000	Washington	DC	20001	**800-666-2722**	202-737-6272	48-6
Conservation International (CI) 1919 M St NW Suite 600	Washington	DC	20036	**800-406-2306**	202-912-1000	48-13
Conservation Society. Soil & Water 945 SW Ankeny Rd	Ankeny	IA	50021	**800-843-7645**	515-289-2331	48-13
Conservation Treaty Support Fund (CTSF) 3705 Cardiff Rd	Chevy Chase	MD	20815	**800-654-3150**	301-654-3150	48-13
Conservative Book Club PO Box 97197	Washington	DC	20090	**877-222-1964**	202-216-0600	94
Conservative Union. American 1007 Cameron St	Alexandria	VA	22314	**800-228-7345**	703-836-8602	48-7
Conso International Corp 513 N Duncan Bypass	Union	SC	29379	**800-842-6676**	864-427-9004	730-5
Consolidated Beverages Inc 12 Saint Mark St	Auburn	MA	01501	**800-922-8128**	508-832-5311	82-1
Consolidated Communications Inc 121 S 17th St	Mattoon	IL	61938	**800-553-9981**	217-235-3311	721
Consolidated Cruises 300 Market St	Kingston	PA	18704	**800-732-2628**	570-283-8480	760
Consolidated Devices Inc 19220 San Jose Ave	City of Industry	CA	91748	**800-525-6319**	626-965-0668	746
Consolidated Disposal Services Inc 12949 Telegraph Rd	Santa Fe Springs	CA	90670	**800-299-4898**	562-946-6441	791
Consolidated Distilled Products 2600 W 35th St	Chicago	IL	60632	**800-944-9450**	773-254-9000	81-1
Consolidated Edison Co of New York 4 Irving Pl	New York	NY	10003	**800-752-6633**	212-460-4600	774
Consolidated Edison Inc 4 Irving Pl	New York	NY	10003	**800-752-6633**	212-460-4600	355-5
NYSE: ED						
Consolidated Electric Co-op Inc 5255 SR 95	Mount Gilead	OH	43338	**800-421-5863**	419-947-3055	244
Consolidated Electronic Wire & Cable Co 11044 King St	Franklin Park	IL	60131	**800-621-4278**	847-455-8830	801
Consolidated Graphics Group Inc 1614 E 40th St	Cleveland	OH	44103	**888-884-9191**	216-881-9191	615
Consolidated Looseleaf Inc 649 Alden St	Fall River	MA	02722	**800-289-3523**	508-676-8580	87
Consolidated Market Response 700 W Lincoln Ave Suite 200	Charleston	IL	61920	**800-500-6006**	217-348-7050	722
Consolidated Metco Inc 13940 N Rivergate Blvd	Portland	OR	97203	**800-547-9473***	503-286-5741	60
*Sales						
Consolidated Pipe & Supply Inc 1205 Hilltop Pkwy	Birmingham	AL	35201	**800-467-7261***	205-323-7261	483
*Sales						
Consolidated Restaurant Operations Inc 12200 N Stemmons Fwy Suite 100	Dallas	TX	75234	**800-275-1337**	972-241-5500	656
Consolidated Shoe Co Inc 22290 Timberlake Rd	Lynchburg	VA	24502	**800-368-7463**	434-239-0391	296
Consolidated Supply Co 7337 SW Kable Ln	Tigard	OR	97224	**800-929-5810**	503-620-7050	601
Consolidated Systems Inc 650 Rosewood Dr	Columbia	SC	29201	**800-654-1912**	803-771-7920	688
Consolidated Vision Group Inc DBA America's Best Contacts & Eyeglasses 7255 N Crescent Blvd	Pennsauken	NJ	08110	**800-896-7247**	856-486-4300	533
Consortium for School Networking (CoSN) 1710 Rhode Island Ave NW Suite 900	Washington	DC	20036	**866-267-8747**	202-861-2676	48-9
Constantine's Wood Center 1040 E Oakland Pk Blvd	Fort Lauderdale	FL	33334	**800-443-9667**	954-561-1716	602
Constellation Brands Inc 370 Woodcliff Dr Suite 300	Fairport	NY	14450	**888-724-2169**	585-218-3600	82-3
NYSE: STZ						
Constellation Copper Corp 1776 Lincoln St	Denver	CO	80203	**877-370-5400**	303-861-5400	492
TSE: CCU						
Constitution-Tribune The 818 Washington St PO Box 707	Chillicothe	MO	64601	**800-373-0256**	660-646-2411	522-2
Constitutional Rights Foundation 601 S Kingsley Dr	Los Angeles	CA	90005	**800-488-4273**	213-487-5590	48-7
Construction Claims Monthly 8737 Colesville Rd Suite 1100	Silver Spring	MD	20910	**800-274-6737**	301-589-5103	521-13
Construction Engineering Research Laboratory PO Box 9005	Champaign	IL	61826	**800-872-2375**	217-352-6511	654

	Toll-Free	Phone	Class
Construction. National Assn of Women in 327 S Adams St . . . Fort Worth TX 76104	**800-552-3506**	817-877-5551	49-3
Construction Specialties Inc 3 Werner Way . . . Lebanon NJ 08833	**800-972-7214**	908-236-0800	482
Construction Specifications Institute (CSI) 99 Canal Ctr Plaza Suite 300 . . . Alexandria VA 22314	**800-689-2900**	703-684-0300	49-3
Construction Systems Software Inc 494 Covered Bridge . . . Schertz TX 78154	**800-979-6494**	210-979-6494	176-10
Construction Technology Laboratories Inc 5400 Old Orchard Rd . . . Skokie IL 60077	**800-522-2285**	847-965-7500	728
Construction Testing & Engineering Inc 242 W Larch Rd Suite F . . . Tracy CA 95304	**800-576-2271**	209-839-2890	728
Construx Software 11820 Northup Way Suite E-200 . . . Bellevue WA 98005	**866-296-6300**	425-636-0100	175
Consultant Pharmacists. American Society of 1321 Duke St . . . Alexandria VA 22314	**800-355-2727**	703-739-1300	49-8
Consultants. American Assn of Healthcare 5938 N Drake Ave . . . Chicago IL 60659	**888-350-2242**		49-8
Consultants. American Assn of Nutritional 401 Kings Hwy . . . Winona Lake IN 46590	**888-828-2262**	574-269-6165	49-8
Consultants Assn. CPA Auto Dealer 10831 Old Mill Rd Suite 400 . . . Omaha NE 68154	**888-475-4476**	402-778-7922	49-1
Consultants Assn Inc. Qualitative Research PO Box 967 . . . Camden TN 38320	**888-674-7722**	731-584-8080	49-18
Consultants Assn. Independent Computer 11131 S Towne Sq Suite F . . . Saint Louis MO 63123	**800-774-4222**	314-892-1675	48-9
Consultants Assn. Independent Educational 3251 Old Lee Hwy Suite 510 . . . Fairfax VA 22030	**800-808-4322**	703-591-4850	49-5
Consultants. Association of Executive Search 12 E 41st St 17th Fl . . . New York NY 10017	**877-843-2372**	212-398-9556	49-12
Consultants News Newsletter 1 Phoenix Mill Ln 3rd FL . . . Peterborough NH 03458	**800-531-0007**	603-924-0900	521-2
Consultants. Society of Telecommunications PO Box 416 . . . Fall River Mills CA 96028	**800-782-7670**	530-336-7070	49-20
Consultants USA Inc. Institute of Management 2025 M St NW Suite 800 . . . Washington DC 20036	**800-221-2557**	202-367-1134	49-12
Consulting Foresters of America. Association of 312 Montgomery St Suite 208 . . . Alexandria VA 22314	**888-540-8733**	703-548-0990	48-2
Consultis 4401 N Federal Hwy Suite 100 . . . Boca Raton FL 33431	**800-275-2667**	561-362-9104	707
Consumer Credit & Truth-In-Lending Compliance Report 807 Las Cimas Pkwy Suite 300 . . . Austin TX 78756	**800-572-2797**	800-753-7577	521-1
Consumer Electronics Society. IEEE IEEE Operations Ctr 445 Hoes Ln . . . Piscataway NJ 08854	**800-678-4333**	732-981-0060	49-19
Consumer Health Network 3525 Quakerbridge Rd . . . Hamilton NJ 08619	**800-225-4246**		384-3
Consumer Product Safety Commission . . . Washington DC 20207	**800-638-2772**	301-504-7908	336-16
Consumer Reports Magazine 101 Truman Ave . . . Yonkers NY 10703 *Orders	**800-288-7898***	914-378-2000	449-11
Consumer Sciences. American Assn of Family & 400 N Columbus St Suite 202 . . . Alexandria VA 22314	**800-424-8080**	703-706-4600	49-5
Consumer.gov 600 Pennsylvania Ave NW . . . Washington DC 20580	**877-382-4357**	202-326-2222	336-16
Consumers Energy 2075 Marshalltown Blvd PO Box 1058 . . . Marshalltown IA 50158	**800-696-6552**	641-752-1593	244
Consumers Energy Co 1 Energy Plaza . . . Jackson MI 49201 *Cust Svc	**800-477-5050***	517-788-0550	774
Consumers League. National 1701 K St NW Suite 1200 . . . Washington DC 20006	**800-876-7060**	202-835-3323	48-10
Consumers Power Inc 6990 W Hills Rd . . . Philomath OR 97370	**800-872-9036**	541-929-3124	244
Consumers Produce Co 1 21st St . . . Pittsburgh PA 15222	**800-245-0698**	412-281-0722	292-7
Consumers Union of US Inc 101 Truman Ave . . . Yonkers NY 10703	**800-234-1645**	914-378-2000	623-9
Contact Behavioral Health Services 1400 E Southern Ave Suite 800 . . . Tempe AZ 85282	**800-888-1477**	480-730-3023	454
Contact Industries Inc 641 Dowd Ave . . . Elizabeth NJ 07201	**800-536-3170**	908-351-5900	143
Contact Lens Manufacturers Assn PO Box 29398 . . . Lincoln NE 68529	**800-344-9060**	402-465-4122	49-4
Contact Lumber Co 9200 SE Sunnybrook Blvd Suite 200 . . . Clackamas OR 97015	**800-547-1038**	503-228-7361	489
Container Freight Corp 6150 Paramount Blvd . . . Long Beach CA 90805	**800-252-7208**	562-220-2433	769
Container Store 500 Freeport Pkwy . . . Coppell TX 75019	**800-733-3532**	972-538-6000	357
Contech Construction Products Inc 1001 Grove St . . . Middletown OH 45044	**800-338-1122**	513-425-5896	688
Contemporary OB/GYN Magazine 5 Paragon Dr . . . Montvale NJ 07645	**888-581-8052**	973-944-7777	449-16
Contemporary Pediatrics Magazine 5 Paragon Dr . . . Montvale NJ 07645	**888-581-8052**	973-944-7777	449-16
Contemporary Tours 125 Mineola Ave Suite 305 . . . Roslyn Heights NY 11577	**800-627-8873**	516-484-5032	748
Contemporary Urology Magazine 5 Paragon Dr . . . Montvale NJ 07645	**888-581-8052**	973-944-7777	449-16
Contex Inc 8100 South Blvd . . . Charlotte NC 28273	**800-243-8621**	704-554-8621	594-1
Contico International LLC 305 Rock Industrial Pk Dr . . . Saint Louis MO 63044	**800-831-7077**	314-656-4349	596
Contiki Holidays 801 E Katella Ave 3rd Fl . . . Anaheim CA 92805	**888-266-8454**		748
Continence. National Assn for 62 Columbus St . . . Charleston SC 29403	**800-252-3337**	843-377-0900	48-17
Continence Nurses Society. Wound Ostomy & 4700 W Lake Ave . . . Glenview IL 60025	**888-224-9626**		49-8
Continence. Simon Foundation for PO Box 815 . . . Wilmette IL 60091	**800-237-4666**	847-864-3913	48-17
Continental AFA Corp 135 Pine St . . . Forest City NC 28043	**800-325-0005**	828-245-1160	420
Continental Airlines Inc 1600 Smith St . . . Houston TX 77002 *NYSE: CAL*	**800-525-0280**	713-324-5000	26
Continental Airlines Inc Cargo Div DBA Continental Cargo 1600 Smith St . . . Houston TX 77002	**800-421-2456**		13
Continental Airlines OnePass 900 Grand Plaza Dr . . . Houston TX 77067	**800-621-7467**	713-952-1630	27
Continental Art Supplies 7041 Reseda Blvd . . . Reseda CA 91335	**800-499-5146**	818-345-1044	45
Continental Battery Corp 4919 Woodall St . . . Dallas TX 75247	**800-442-0081**	214-631-5701	76
Continental Binder & Specialty Corp 407 W Compton Blvd . . . Gardena CA 90248	**800-872-2897**	310-324-8227	87
Continental Cabinet Inc 2841 Pierce St . . . Dallas TX 75233	**800-786-6421**	214-467-4444	116
Continental Candle Co Inc 1420 W Walnut St . . . Compton CA 90220	**800-421-1035**	310-537-9300	122
Continental Cargo 1600 Smith St . . . Houston TX 77002	**800-421-2456**		13
Continental Cast Stone Inc 22001 W 83rd St . . . Shawnee KS 66227	**800-989-7866**	913-422-7575	710
Continental Casualty Co 333 S Wabash Ave . . . Chicago IL 60685	**800-262-2000**	312-822-5000	384-4
Continental Cement Co LLC 14755 N Outer 40 Suite 514 . . . Chesterfield MO 63017	**800-625-1144**	636-532-7440	135
Continental Coin Corp 5627 Sepulveda Blvd . . . Van Nuys CA 91411	**888-367-9456**	818-781-4232	403
Continental Computer Corp 2200 East Matthews Ave . . . Jonesboro AR 72401	**800-874-1413**	870-932-0081	176-10
Continental DataGraphics 222 N Sepulveda Blvd Suite 300 . . El Segundo CA 90245	**800-862-5691**	310-662-2300	223
Continental Electronics Corp 4212 S Buckner Blvd . . . Dallas TX 75227	**800-733-5011**	214-381-7161	633
Continental Express 1600 Smith St HQSCE . . . Houston TX 77002 *NYSE: XJT*	**877-324-2639**	713-324-5000	26
Continental Florida Materials 13450 W Sunrise Blvd Suite 430 . . . Sunrise FL 33323	**888-969-9100**	954-858-0780	181
Continental General Insurance Co PO Box 247007 . . . Omaha NE 68124	**800-545-8905**	402-397-3200	384-2
Continental Glass & Plastic Inc 841 W Cermak Rd . . . Chicago IL 60608	**888-676-5277**	312-666-2050	258
Continental Graphics Corp DBA Continental DataGraphics 222 N Sepulveda Blvd Suite 300 . . . El Segundo CA 90245	**800-862-5691**	310-662-2300	223
Continental Identification Products Inc PO Box 98 . . . Sparta MI 49345	**800-247-2499**	616-887-7341	404
Continental Industries Inc 4102 S 74th East Ave . . . Tulsa OK 74145	**800-558-1373**	918-627-5210	584
Continental Linen Services 4200 Manchester Rd . . . Kalamazoo MI 49001	**800-875-4636**	269-343-2551	434
Continental Mfg Co 305 Rock Industrial Pk Dr . . . Bridgeton MO 63044	**800-325-1051**	314-656-4301	497
Continental Mills Inc PO Box 88176 . . . Seattle WA 98138	**800-457-7744**	253-872-8400	291-16
Continental Resources Inc 175 Middlesex Tpke . . . Bedford MA 01730	**800-937-4688**	781-275-0850	174
Continental Safety Equipment Inc 899 Apollo Rd . . . Eagan MN 55121	**800-844-7003**	651-454-7233	667
Continental Silverline Products Inc 710 N Drennan St . . . Houston TX 77003	**800-392-9205**	713-222-7394	463
Continental Sportswear 135 W 27th St . . . New York NY 10001	**800-543-5007**	212-966-3404	154
Continental Western Group 11201 Douglas Ave . . . Urbandale IA 50322	**800-235-2942**	515-278-3000	384-4
Continental Wingate Co Inc 63 Kendrick St . . . Needham MA 02494	**800-332-0372**	781-707-9000	498
Continucare Corp 80 SW 8th St Suite 2350 . . . Miami FL 33130 *AMEX: CNU*	**888-350-7515**	305-350-7515	358
Continuing Care Accreditation Commission (CCAC) 1730 Rhode Island Ave NW Suite 209 . . . Washington DC 20036	**866-888-1122**	202-587-5001	48-1
Continuing Higher Education. Association for 2001 Mabelene Rd . . . Charleston SC 29406	**800-807-2243**	843-574-6658	49-5
Continuum 3150 Central Expy . . . Santa Clara CA 95051	**800-956-7757**	408-727-3240	416
Contour Saws Inc 1217 Thacker St . . Des Plaines IL 60016 *Sales	**800-458-9034***	847-824-1146	670
Contours Express Inc 156 Imperial Way . . . Nicholasville KY 40356	**877-227-2282**	859-885-6441	349
Contract Bridge League. American 2990 Airways Blvd . . . Memphis TN 38116 *Sales	**800-264-2743***	901-332-5586	48-18
Contract Counsel 1025 N Campbell Rd . . . Royal Oak MI 48067	**877-526-8673**	248-597-0400	707
Contract Design Magazine 770 Broadway . . . New York NY 10003	**800-950-1314**	646-654-5500	449-5
Contract Freighters Inc PO Box 2547 . . . Joplin MO 64803	**800-641-4747**	417-623-5229	769
Contract Management Assn. National 8260 Greensboro Dr Suite 200 . . . McLean VA 22102	**800-344-8096**	571-382-0082	49-12
Contractors of America. Associated General 333 John Carlyle St Suite 200 . . . Alexandria VA 22314	**800-242-1766**	703-548-3118	49-3
Contractors' Assn. Engineering 8310 Florence Ave . . . Downey CA 90240	**800-293-2240**	562-861-0929	49-19
Contractors Machinery Co Inc 13200 Northend Ave . . . Oak Park MI 48237	**800-572-7479**	248-543-4770	353
Contractors. National Assn of Minority 666 11th St NW Suite 520 . . . Washington DC 20001	**866-688-6262**	202-347-8259	49-3
Contractors Register Inc 800 E Main St . . . Jefferson Valley NY 10535	**800-431-2584**	914-245-0200	623-6
Contractors Steel Co PO Box 33881 . . . Detroit MI 48232	**800-521-3946**	734-464-4000	483
Contractor's Warehouse 3222 Winona Way Suite 201 . . . North Highlands CA 95660	**800-789-8060**	916-331-5934	359
Control Components Inc 22591 Avenida Empresa . . . Rancho Santa Margarita CA 92688	**800-788-8762**	949-858-1877	776

Company	City	State	ZIP	Toll-Free	Phone	Class
Control Concepts Corp 328 Water St	Binghamton	NY	13902	**800-288-6169**	607-724-2484	803
Control Engineering Magazine 2000 Clearwater Dr.	Oak Brook	IL	60523	**800-862-2670**	630-320-7000	449-21
Control Magazine 555 W Pierce Rd Suite 301	Itasca	IL	60143	**800-984-7644**	630-467-1300	449-21
Control Screening LLC 2 Gardner Rd	Fairfield	NJ	07004	**800-231-6414**	973-276-6161	464
Control Systems Society. IEEE IEEE Operations Ctr 445 Hoes Ln	Piscataway	NJ	08854	**800-678-4333**	732-981-0060	49-19
Controller Magazine PO Box 85310	Lincoln	NE	68510	**800-247-4890**	402-479-2143	449-21
Controller's Report 3 Park Ave 30th Fl	New York	NY	10016	**800-401-5937**	212-244-0360	521-1
Controlotron Corp 155 Plant Ave.	Hauppauge	NY	11788	**800-275-8479**	631-231-3600	486
Convenience Stores. National Assn of 1600 Duke St *Cust Svc	Alexandria	VA	22314	**800-966-6227***	703-684-3600	49-18
Convenient Food Mart Inc 467 N State St	Painesville	OH	44077	**800-860-4844**		203
Convention Consultants Historic Savannah Foundation Special Tours & Meeting Services 117 W Perry St	Savannah	GA	31401	**800-627-5030**	912-234-4088	183
Convention Management Assn. Professional 2301 S Lake Shore Dr Suite 1001	Chicago	IL	60616	**877-827-7262**	312-423-7262	49-12
Convention Planning Services Inc 2453 Orlando Central Pkwy	Orlando	FL	32809	**800-777-5333**	407-851-5122	183
Convention & Visitors Assn of Lane County Oregon PO Box 10286	Eugene	OR	97440	**800-547-5445**	541-484-5307	205
Convention & Visitors Bureau of Greater Cleveland 50 Public Sq Terminal Tower Suite 3100	Cleveland	OH	44113	**800-321-1001**	216-621-4110	205
Convention & Visitors Bureau of Greater Kansas City 1100 Main St Suite 2200	Kansas City	MO	64105	**800-767-7700**	816-221-5242	205
Convention & Visitors Bureau of Henry County 2020 S Memorial Dr Suite I	New Castle	IN	47362	**800-676-4302**	765-593-0764	205
Convention & Visitors Bureau of Marion County 110 Adams St	Fairmont	WV	26554	**800-834-7365**	304-368-1123	205
Convention & Visitors Bureau-Village of Pinehurst Southern Pines Aberdeen Area PO Box 2270	Southern Pines	NC	28388	**800-346-5362**	910-692-3330	205
Convera Corp 1921 Gallows Rd Suite 200 *NASDAQ: CNVR*	Vienna	VA	22182	**800-755-7005**	703-761-3700	176-11
Converged Access Inc 31 Dunham Rd	Billerica	MA	08121	**888-748-2720**	978-436-9111	174
Convergent Laser Technologies 900 Alice St	Oakland	CA	94607	**800-848-8200**	510-832-2130	415
Convergent Media Systems Corp 190 Bluegrass Valley Pkwy 1 Convergent Ctr	Alpharetta	GA	30005	**800-254-7463**	404-262-1555	721
Convergys Corp 201 E 4th St *NYSE: CVG*	Cincinnati	OH	45202	**888-284-9900**	513-723-7000	722
Converium 1 Chase Manhattan Plaza	New York	NY	10005	**866-900-2762**	212-898-5000	384-4
Converse College 580 E Main St.	Spartanburg	SC	29302	**800-766-1125**	864-596-9000	163
Converse Inc 1 High St *Cust Svc	North Andover	MA	01845	**800-428-2667***	978-983-3300	296
Conversent Communications Inc 313 Boston Post Rd W Suite 140 *Cust Svc	Marlborough	MA	01752	**800-275-2088***	508-486-6300	721
Conveyor Components Co 130 Seltzer Rd *Cust Svc	Croswell	MI	48422	**800-233-3233***	810-679-4211	206
Conveyor & Material Handling Systems 4598 SR 37	Mitchell	IN	47446	**800-551-3195**	812-849-5647	206
Conway Import Co Inc 11051 West Addison St	Franklin Park	IL	60131	**800-323-8801**	847-455-5600	291-19
Conwed Corp 2810 Weeks Ave SE	Minneapolis	MN	55414	**800-426-0149**	612-623-1700	589
Conwood Co LP PO Box 217	Memphis	TN	38101	**800-238-2409**	901-248-1700	741-3
Cook Aviation Inc 970 S Kirby Rd	Bloomington	IN	47403	**800-880-3499**	812-825-2392	63
Cook Biotech Inc 1425 Innovation Pl	West Lafayette	IN	47906	**888-299-4224**	765-497-3355	86
Cook C Lee Co 916 S 8th St	Louisville	KY	40203	**877-266-5226**	502-587-6783	128
Cook Communications Ministries 4050 Lee Vance View	Colorado Springs	CO	80918	**800-708-5550**	719-536-0100	623-9
Cook Composites & Polymers Co 820 E 14th Ave	North Kansas City	MO	64116	**800-821-3590**	816-391-6000	594-2
Cook Critical Care 750 Daniels Way	Bloomington	IN	47404	**800-457-4500**	812-339-2235	468
Cook Group Inc PO Box 1608	Bloomington	IN	47402	**800-457-4500**	812-331-1025	184
Cook Inc PO Box 489	Bloomington	IN	47402	**800-457-4500**	812-339-2235	468
Cook Moving Systems Inc 1845 Dale Rd	Buffalo	NY	14225	**800-828-7144**	716-897-0700	508
Cook OB/GYN 1100 W Morgan St	Spencer	IN	47460	**800-541-5591**	812-829-6500	468
Cook Surgical PO Box 489	Bloomington	IN	47402	**800-457-4500**	812-339-2235	468
Cook Technologies Inc N 2nd St	Green Lane	PA	18054	**800-755-2856**	215-234-4535	745
Cook Urological Inc 1100 W Morgan St.	Spencer	IN	47460	**800-457-4500**	812-339-2235	468
Cook Vascular Inc Rt 66 River Rd PO Box 529	Leechburg	PA	15656	**800-245-4715**	724-845-8621	468
Cookbook Publishers Inc 10800 Lakeview Ave.	Lenexa	KS	66219	**800-227-7282**	913-492-5900	614
Cooke County Electric Co-op Assn 11799 W US Hwy 82 PO Box 530	Muenster	TX	76252	**800-962-0296**	940-759-2211	244
Cookeville Area-Putnam County Chamber of Commerce 1 W 1st St	Cookeville	TN	38501	**800-264-5541**	931-526-2211	137
Cookie Bouquet 6757 Arapaho Rd Suite 707	Dallas	TX	75248	**800-752-8412**	972-386-7334	69
Cookies in Bloom Inc 12700 Hillcrest Rd Suite 251	Dallas	TX	75230	**800-222-3104**	972-490-8644	69
Cookietree Bakeries PO Box 57888	Salt Lake City	UT	84157	**800-998-0111**	801-268-2253	291-2
Cooking Light Magazine 2100 Lakeshore Dr.	Birmingham	AL	35209	**800-366-4712**	205-445-6000	449-13
Cooking.com 2850 Ocean Park Blvd Suite 310	Santa Monica	CA	90405	**800-663-8810**	310-450-3270	357
Cook's Illustrated Magazine 17 Station St. *Circ	Brookline	MA	02445	**800-526-8442***	617-232-1000	449-11
Cook's Inc PO Box 205	Grand Haven	MI	49417	**800-499-6001**	616-842-0180	35
Cookson Co Inc 2417 S 50th Ave	Phoenix	AZ	85043	**800-294-4358**	602-272-4244	232
Cookson Electronics Assembly Materials 600 Rte 440.	Jersey City	NJ	07304	**800-367-5460**	201-434-6778	476
Cookson Hills Electric Co-op Inc 1002 E Main St.	Stigler	OK	74462	**800-328-2368**	918-967-4614	244
CookTek Inc 810 W Washington St	Chicago	IL	60607	**888-266-5835**	312-563-9600	36
Cool Amphibious Manufacturers International LLC 31 Hawkes Rd.	Bluffton	SC	29910	**888-926-6553**	843-757-4133	120
Cooley Godward LLP 1 Maritime Plaza 20th Fl	San Francisco	CA	94111	**866-226-6539**	415-693-2000	419
Cooley Group 50 Esten Ave *Cust Svc	Pawtucket	RI	02860	**800-333-3048***	401-724-9000	730-2
Coolfont Resort 3621 Cold Run Valley Rd	Berkeley Springs	WV	25411	**800-888-8768**	304-258-4500	655
CoolSavings Inc 360 N Michigan Ave Suite 1900	Chicago	IL	60601	**888-428-8854**	312-224-5000	7
Cooper Atkins Corp 33 Reeds Gap Rd *Sales	Middlefield	CT	06455	**800-835-5011***	860-349-3473	200
Cooper Cameron Valves 3250 Briarpark Dr Suite 300	Houston	TX	77042	**800-432-8511**	281-499-8511	776
Cooper Communities Inc 903 N 47th St	Rogers	AR	72756	**800-648-6401**	479-246-6500	639
Cooper Cos Inc 21062 Bake Pkwy Suite 200 *NYSE: COO*	Lake Forest	CA	92630	**888-822-2660**	949-597-4700	531
Cooper Decoration Co 200 Maple St.	Syracuse	NY	13217	**800-632-4997**	315-475-1661	555
Cooper Energy Services 11800 Charles St	Houston	TX	77041	**888-423-7463**	713-856-1500	170
Cooper Farms 22348 County Rd 140	Oakwood	OH	45873	**888-594-8759**	419-594-3325	11-8
Cooper Frederick Lamp Co Inc 2545 W Diversey Ave.	Chicago	IL	60647	**800-693-5234**	773-384-0800	431
Cooper Harry Supply Co Inc 605 N Sherman Pkwy.	Springfield	MO	65802	**800-426-6737**	417-865-8392	601
Cooper Jack Transport Co Inc 2345 Grand Blvd Suite 400	Kansas City	MO	64108	**866-449-6301**	816-983-4000	769
Cooper Mfg Corp 1221 E Houston St.	Broken Arrow	OK	74012	**866-496-0369**	918-258-7300	526
Cooper Tire & Rubber Co 701 Lima Ave *NYSE: CTB* ■ *Cust Svc	Findlay	OH	45840	**800-854-6288***	419-423-1321	739
Cooper Turbocompressor 3101 Broadway.	Buffalo	NY	14225	**877-805-7911**	716-896-6600	170
Cooper Wellness Program 12230 Preston Rd	Dallas	TX	75230	**800-444-5192**	972-386-4777	697
Cooper Wiring Devices Inc 203 Cooper Cir *Cust Svc	Peachtree City	GA	30269	**800-441-3177***		803
Cooper Wood Products Inc 2785 Grassy Hill Rd	Rocky Mount	VA	24151	**800-262-3453**	540-483-9201	304
Cooperative Bankshares Inc 201 Market St. *NASDAQ: COOP*	Wilmington	NC	28402	**800-672-0443**	910-343-0181	355-2
Cooperative Communciations Inc 412-420 Washington Ave.	Belleville	NJ	07109	**800-833-2700**	973-759-8100	721
Cooperative Elevator Co PO Box 619	Pigeon	MI	48755	**800-968-0601**	989-453-4500	271
Cooperative Finance Assn Inc 10100 N Ambassador Dr Suite 315 PO Box 901532	Kansas City	MO	64190	**877-835-5232**	816-214-4200	214
Cooperative Optical 2424 E Eight-Mile Rd.	Detroit	MI	48234	**800-368-5160**	313-366-5100	533
Cooperative Partners Magazine PO Box 64089	Saint Paul	MN	55164	**800-867-6747**	651-355-5151	449-1
Cooperheat-MQS Inc 4740 E Park Dr	Houston	TX	77028	**800-526-4233**	713-673-3660	798
CooperSurgical Inc 95 Corporate Dr	Trumbull	CT	06611	**800-645-3760**	203-929-6321	468
Cooper/T Smith Stevedoring Co 118 N Royal St Commerce Bldg Suite 1100	Mobile	AL	36602	**800-239-8484**	251-431-6100	457
CooperVision Inc 21062 Bake Pkwy Suite 200	Lake Forest	CA	92630	**800-341-2030**	949-597-8130	531
Coors Field 2001 Blake St.	Denver	CO	80205	**800-388-7625**	303-762-5437	706
CoorsTek Inc 16000 Table Mountain Pkwy	Golden	CO	80403	**800-821-6110**	303-278-4000	248
Coosa Valley Electric Co-op 69220 Alabama Hwy 77	Talladega	AL	35160	**800-273-7210**	256-362-4180	244
COPE Inc 1120 G St NW Suite 550	Washington	DC	20005	**800-247-3054**	202-628-5100	454
Cope Plastics Inc 4441 Industrial Dr	Godfrey	IL	62035	**800-851-5510**	618-466-0221	592
Cope TJ Inc 11500 Norcom Rd.	Philadelphia	PA	19154	**800-426-4293**	215-961-2570	804
Copeland Al Investments 1405 Airline Hwy	Metairie	LA	70001	**800-401-0401**	504-830-1000	656
Copeland's Enterprises Inc PO Box 1348	San Luis Obispo	CA	93406	**800-619-2853**	805-543-0660	702
Copeland's of New Orleans 1405 Airline Dr.	Metairie	LA	70001	**800-401-0401**	504-830-1000	657
Copesan Services Inc 3490 N 127th St.	Brookfield	WI	53005	**800-267-3726**	262-783-6261	567
Copia International Ltd 1220 Iroquois Dr Suite 180 *Sales	Naperville	IL	60563	**800-689-8898***	630-778-8898	496
Copic Insurance Co 7351 Lowry Blvd.	Denver	CO	80230	**800-421-1834**		384-5
Copley News Service 123 Camino de la Reina Suite E-250	San Diego	CA	92108	**800-238-6196**	619-293-1818	520
Copley Square Hotel 47 Huntington Ave	Boston	MA	02116	**800-225-7062**	617-536-9000	373
Copper Development Assn Inc 260 Madison Ave 16th Fl	New York	NY	10016	**800-232-3282**	212-251-7200	49-13
Copper Hills Youth Center 5899 W Rivendell Dr	West Jordan	UT	84088	**800-776-7116**	801-561-3377	366-1

Listing	Toll-Free	Phone	Class
Copper Mountain Community College			
6162 Rotary Way PO Box 1398...Joshua Tree CA 92252	**866-366-3791**	760-366-3791	160
Copper Mountain Networks Inc			
1850 Embarcadero Rd .... Palo Alto CA 94303	**888-267-7374**	650-687-3300	720
Copper Mountain Resort			
509 Copper Rd PO			
Box 3001 ....Copper Mountain CO 80443	**888-219-2441**	970-968-2882	655
CopperCom Inc 3600 FAU Blvd..... Boca Raton FL 33431	**866-267-7371**	561-322-4000	720
Copperplate Publishing Inc			
1901 Lexington Ave N .... Roseville MN 55113	**888-772-6001**	651-487-8575	130
CopperWynd Resort & Club			
13225 N Eagle Ridge Dr........Fountain Hills AZ 85268	**877-707-7760**	480-333-1900	655
Coppin State University			
2500 W North Ave............... Baltimore MD 21216	**800-635-3674**	410-951-3600	163
COPS (Community Oriented Policing			
Services Office) 1100 Vermont			
Ave NW 10th Fl .... Washington DC 20530	**800-421-6770**	202-616-2888	336-10
Coral Beach Resort & Suites			
1105 S Ocean Blvd............ Myrtle Beach SC 29577	**800-843-2684**	843-448-8421	655
Coral Chemical Co 135 Le Baron St.. Waukegan IL 60085	**800-228-4646**	847-336-8100	143
Coral Reef Hotel 2299 Kuhio Ave..... Honolulu HI 96815	**800-922-7866**	808-922-1262	373
Coral Reef Resort			
5800 Gulf Blvd .... Saint Pete Beach FL 33706	**800-352-4874**	727-363-1604	373
Coral Sales Co 9838 SE 17th Ave.....Milwaukie OR 97222	**800-538-7245**	503-655-6351	483
Coral Springs Marriott Hotel			
11775 Heron Bay Blvd ....Coral Springs FL 33076	**800-333-3333***	954-753-5598	655
*Resv			
Coram Healthcare Corp			
1675 Broadway Suite 900 .... Denver CO 80202	**800-267-2642**	303-292-4973	358
Corbett Lighting Inc			
14625 E Clark Ave .... City of Industry CA 91745	**800-533-8769**	626-336-4511	431
Corbett Package Co PO Box 210 ... Wilmington NC 28402	**800-334-0684**	910-763-9991	199
Corbin 2360 Technology Pkwy......... Hollister CA 95023	**800-538-5035**	831-634-1100	506
Corbin Ltd 208 Lurgan Ave ....Shippensburg PA 17257	**800-950-3330**	717-532-4146	153-12
Corbis Corp 710 2nd Ave Suite 200 ..... Seattle WA 98104	**800-260-0444**	206-373-6000	582
Corby Industries Inc			
1501 E Pennsylvania St ....Allentown PA 18109	**800-652-6729**	610-433-1412	681
Corcoran College of Art & Design			
500 17th St NW............... Washington DC 20006	**888-267-2672**	202-639-1800	163
Corcoran Gallery of Art			
500 17th St NW............... Washington DC 20006	**800-267-2672**	202-639-1700	509
Corcoran RS Co 500 N Vine St ......New Lenox IL 60451	**800-637-1067**	815-485-2156	627
Cord Sets Inc 1015 5th St N....... Minneapolis MN 55411	**800-752-0580**	612-337-9700	803
Cordele Dispatch			
306 W 13th Ave PO Box 1058........Cordele GA 31010	**888-273-2278**	229-273-2277	522-2
Cordis Corp PO Box 025700 ....Miami FL 33102	**800-327-2490**	786-313-2000	468
Cordova Inc PO Box 521831..........Flushing NY 11352	**800-221-0744***	718-961-1020	401
*Cust Svc			
CORE (Center for Organ Recovery &			
Education) 204 Sigma Dr			
RIDC Park.................... Pittsburgh PA 15238	**800-366-6777**	412-366-6777	265
Core-Mark International Inc			
395 Oyster Point Blvd			
Suite 415 .... South San Francisco CA 94080	**800-622-1713**	650-589-9445	744
CoreData Group			
2108 W Laburnum Ave .... Richmond VA 23227	**800-775-8118**	804-278-6700	623-10
Coregis Insurance Co			
525 W Van Buren St Suite 500 ...... Chicago IL 60607	**800-879-4428**	312-821-4000	384-5
Corel Centre 1000 Palladium Dr........ Kanata ON K2V1A5	**800-444-7367**	613-599-0250	706
Corel Corp 1600 Carling Ave........... Ottawa ON K1Z8R7	**800-772-6735***	613-728-8200	176-8
*Orders			
CoreNet Global Inc			
260 Peachtree St NW Suite 1500...... Atlanta GA 30303	**800-726-8111**	404-589-3200	49-17
Corey Delta Inc 610 Industrial Way ..... Benicia CA 94510	**800-707-2260**	707-747-7500	187-5
Corey Steel Co 2800 S 61st Ct..........Cicero IL 60804	**800-323-2750**	708-735-8000	709
Corhart Refractories Corp			
1600 W Lee St................. Louisville KY 40210	**800-233-1421**	502-778-3311	649
Coriell Institute for Medical Research			
403 Haddon Ave.................. Camden NJ 08103	**800-752-3805**	856-757-9758	654
Corillian Corp			
3400 NW John Olsen Pl........... Hillsboro OR 97124	**800-863-6445**	503-629-3500	176-7
NASDAQ: CORI			
Corinth Area Tourism Promotion Council			
PO Box 2158 ....Corinth MS 38835	**800-748-9048**	662-287-8300	205
Corinthian Colleges Inc			
6 Hutton Ctr Dr Suite 400 .... Santa Ana CA 92707	**800-611-2101**	714-427-3000	241
NASDAQ: COCO			
Corinthian Schools Inc			
6 Hutton Ctr Dr Suite 400 .... Santa Ana CA 92707	**888-741-4271**	714-427-3000	241
Corio Inc			
959 Skyway Rd Suite 100 ....San Carlos CA 94070	**877-737-3700***	650-232-3000	39
*Cust Svc			
Corixa Corp 1900 9th Ave Suite 1100.... Seattle WA 98101	**888-426-7492**	206-366-3700	86
NASDAQ: CRXA			
Corken Inc 3805 NW 36th St .... Oklahoma City OK 73112	**800-631-4929**	405-946-5576	627
Corn Belt Energy Corp			
1 Energy Way................ Bloomington IL 61704	**800-879-0339**	309-662-5330	244
Corn Palace 604 N Main St........... Mitchell SD 57301	**800-257-2676**	605-996-5031	50
Corn Stock Theatre 1700 Park Rd ....Peoria IL 61604	**800-220-1185**	309-676-2196	563-4
Cornelia de Lange Syndrome Foundation			
Inc (CdLS) 302 W Main St Suite 100.....Avon CT 06001	**800-753-2357**	860-676-8166	48-17
Cornell College 600 1st St W.... Mount Vernon IA 52314	**800-747-1112**	319-895-4215	163
Cornell Cos Inc			
1700 West Loop S Suite 1500.......Houston TX 77027	**888-624-0816**	713-623-0790	210
NYSE: CRN			
Cornell Forge Co 6666 W 66th St...... Chicago IL 60638	**800-356-0204**	708-458-1582	474
Cornell Iron Works Inc			
100 Elmwood Ave Crestwood			
Industrial Pk................ Mountain Top PA 18707	**800-233-8366***	570-474-6773	232
*Cust Svc			
Cornell Maritime Press PO Box 456.. Centreville MD 21617	**800-638-7641**	410-758-1075	623-2
Cornell Paper & Box Inc			
162 Van Dyke St.................Brooklyn NY 11231	**888-251-1297**	718-875-3202	102
Cornell University Press			
750 Cascadilla St ....Ithaca NY 14850	**800-666-2211***	607-277-2338	623-5
*Sales			
Cornerstone Bancorp Inc			
550 Summer St .... Stamford CT 06901	**800-378-6367**	203-356-0111	355-2
AMEX: CBN			

Listing	Toll-Free	Phone	Class
Cornerstone Family Services			
155 Rittenhouse Cir .... Bristol PA 19007	**877-857-8890**	215-826-2800	499
NASDAQ: STON			
Cornerstone Medical Arts Center			
Hospital 57 W 57th St............New York NY 10019	**800-233-9999**	212-755-0200	712
Cornerstone Propane Partners LP			
432 Westridge Dr............. Watsonville CA 95076	**800-288-5206**	831-724-1921	311
Cornerstone University			
1001 E Beltline Ave NE.........Grand Rapids MI 49525	**800-787-9778***	616-222-1426	163
*Admissions			
Cornhusker Casualty Co			
9290 W Dodge Rd Suite 300.........Omaha NE 68114	**800-488-2930**	402-393-7255	384-4
Cornhusker Hotel The 333 S 13th St ....Lincoln NE 68508	**800-793-7474**	402-474-7474	373
Cornhusker State Industries			
800 Pioneers Blvd ....Lincoln NE 68502	**800-348-7537**	402-471-4597	618
Corning Area (Greater) Chamber of			
Commerce 1 W Market St Suite 302.. Corning NY 14830	**866-463-6264**	607-936-4686	137
Corning Cable Systems PO Box 489.....Hickory NC 28603	**800-743-2671**	828-901-5000	801
Corning Gilbert Inc			
5310 W Camelback Rd.............Glendale AZ 85301	**800-528-0199***	623-245-1050	252
*Cust Svc			
Corning Hospital 176 Denison Pkwy E .. Corning NY 14830	**800-295-1122**	607-937-7200	366-2
Corning Inc Life Sciences Div			
45 Nagog Park .... Acton MA 01720	**800-492-1110**	978-635-2200	410
Corning Museum of Glass			
1 Museum Way .... Corning NY 14830	**800-732-6845***	607-937-5371	509
*Cust Svc			
Corning Optical Fiber PO Box 7429.... Endicott NY 13760	**800-525-2524**	607-786-8125	326
Cornish College of the Arts			
1000 Lenora St.................... Seattle WA 98121	**800-726-2787**	206-323-1400	163
Cornwell Quality Tools Co			
667 Seville Rd ....Wadsworth OH 44281	**800-321-8356***	330-336-3506	746
*Cust Svc			
Corona Clipper Co 1540 E 6th St ....Corona CA 92879	**800-847-7863**	951-737-6515	420
Corona Curtain Mfg Co Inc			
401 Neponset St................... Canton MA 02021	**800-828-8906**	617-350-6970	731
Coronado Paint Co Inc			
308 S Old County Rd............ Edgewater FL 32132	**800-883-4193**	386-428-6461	540
Coronet Lighting			
16210 S Avalon Blvd .... Gardena CA 90248	**800-421-2748**	310-327-6700	431
CorpCare Assoc Inc			
7000 Peachtree Dunwoody Rd Bldg			
4 Suite 300....................... Atlanta GA 30328	**800-728-9444**	770-396-5253	454
Corpedia Corp DBA Corpedia Education			
2020 N Central Ave Suite 1050 ...... Phoenix AZ 85004	**877-629-8724**	602-712-9919	753
CorpHealth Inc			
1300 Summit Ave Suite 600 ......Fort Worth TX 76102	**800-240-8388**	817-332-2519	454
Corporate Accountability International			
46 Plympton St.................... Boston MA 02118	**800-688-8797**	617-695-2525	48-8
Corporate Branding 470 West Ave .... Stamford CT 06902	**888-969-2726**	203-327-6333	194
Corporate Care Works			
8665 Baypine Rd Suite 100 ...... Jacksonville FL 32256	**800-327-9757**	904-296-9436	454
Corporate Counsellor Newsletter			
1617 JFK Blvd Suite 1750 .... Philadelphia PA 19103	**800-999-1916**	215-557-2310	521-2
Corporate Disk Co			
1226 Michael Dr Suite F..........Wood Dale IL 60191	**800-634-3475**	630-616-0700	239
Corporate Dynamics Inc			
200 E 5th Ave Suite 118 ....Naperville IL 60563	**888-267-7396**	630-778-9991	193
Corporate Executive Board Co			
2000 Pennsylvania Ave NW ...... Washington DC 20006	**888-777-9561**	202-777-5000	193
NASDAQ: EXBD			
Corporate Express Business & Charter			
Airline 445 Palmer Rd NE Calgary			
Esso Avitat ....Calgary AB T2E7G4	**800-661-8151**	403-216-4050	14
Corporate Express Document & Print			
Management 4205 S 96th St .... Omaha NE 68127	**800-228-9277**	402-339-0900	111
Corporate Express Imaging &			
Computer Graphic Supplies			
Inc 1096 E Newport Center			
Dr Suite 300............... Deerfield Beach FL 33442	**800-828-9949**	954-379-5500	616
Corporate Express Inc			
1 Environmental Way............Broomfield CO 80021	**888-664-3945**	303-664-2000	524
Corporate Express Promotional			
Marketing 1400 N Price Rd.......Saint Louis MO 63132	**800-325-1965**	314-432-1800	5
Corporate Flight Inc			
6150 Highland Rd................Waterford MI 48327	**800-767-2473**	248-666-8800	14
Corporate Growth. Association for			
1926 Waukegan Rd Suite 1 .... Glenview IL 60025	**800-699-1331**	847-657-6730	49-12
Corporate Helicopters of San Diego			
3753 John J Montgomery Dr			
Suite 2 .... San Diego CA 92123	**800-345-6737**	858-505-5650	354
Corporate Housing Systems			
6517 Constitution Dr .... Fort Wayne IN 46804	**800-430-7171**	260-436-7171	373
Corporate Solutions			
303 Riding Trail Ct............... Leesburg VA 20176	**800-622-4686**		752
Corporate Telephone 56 Roland St...... Boston MA 02129	**800-274-1211**	617-625-1200	245
Corporate Travel Executives.			
Association of 515 King St			
Suite 340 .... Alexandria VA 22314	**800-228-3669**	703-683-5322	48-23
Corporate Travel Management Group			
450 E 22nd St Suite 100 .... Lombard IL 60148	**800-323-3800**	630-691-9100	760
Corporation for National & Community Service			
AmeriCorps USA			
1201 New York Ave NW			
8th Fl .... Washington DC 20525	**800-942-2677**	202-606-5000	336-16
Senior Corps			
1201 New York Ave NW....... Washington DC 20525	**800-424-8867**	202-606-5000	336-16
Corporation for Public Broadcasting			
(CPB) 401 9th St NW........... Washington DC 20004	**800-272-2190**	202-879-9600	300
Corporation Service Co			
2711 Centerville Rd Suite 400 .... Wilmington DE 19808	**800-927-9800**	302-636-5400	621
Corporation Service Co			
801 Adlai Stevenson Dr .... Springfield IL 62703	**800-634-9738**	217-529-5599	621
Corpus Christi Convention &			
Visitors Bureau 1201 N			
Shoreline Blvd.............. Corpus Christi TX 78401	**800-678-6232**	361-881-1888	205
Corpus Christi Symphony Orchestra			
555 N Carancahua St			
Suite 410 .... Corpus Christi TX 78478	**877-286-6683**	361-882-2717	563-3

Name / Address / City	State	ZIP	Toll-Free	Phone	Class
Correct Craft Inc 6100 S Orange Ave... Orlando	FL	32809	**800-346-2092**	407-855-4141	91
Correctional Assn. American 4380 Forbes Blvd................. Lanham	MD	20706	**800-222-5646**	301-918-1800	49-7
Correctional Enterprises of Connecticut 24 Wolcott Hill Rd...Wethersfield	CT	06109	**800-842-1146**	860-692-7480	618
Correctional Medical Services Inc 12647 Olive Blvd ....Saint Louis	MO	63141	**800-325-4809**	314-878-1810	455
Correctional Properties Trust 3300 PGA Blvd Suite 750 .... Palm Beach Gardens	FL	33410	**877-774-7661**	561-630-6336	641
NYSE: CPV					
Correctional Services Corp 1819 Main St Suite 1000...........Sarasota	FL	34236	**800-275-3766**	941-953-9199	210
NASDAQ: CSCQ					
Corrections Corp of America 10 Burton Hills Blvd.............. Nashville	TN	37215	**800-624-2931**	615-263-3000	210
NYSE: CXW					
Correlated Products Inc PO Box 42387 ....Indianapolis	IN	46242	**800-428-3266**	317-243-3248	149
Corrigan Moving Systems 23923 Research Dr......... Farmington Hills	MI	48335	**800-446-1996**	248-471-4000	508
Corrpro Cos Inc 1055 W Smith Rd......Medina	OH	44256	**800-726-5082**	330-723-5082	258
NYSE: CO					
Corrugated Supplies Corp 5101 W 65th St.............. Bedford Park	IL	60638	**888-826-2738**	708-458-5525	101
Corsicana Area Chamber of Commerce 120 N 12th St...................Corsicana	TX	75110	**877-376-7477**	903-874-4731	137
Corsicana Bedding Inc PO Box 1050 ....Corsicana	TX	75151	**800-323-4349**	903-872-2591	463
Corsicana Technologies Inc 2733 E Hwy 31....................Corsicana	TX	75110	**800-477-5353**	903-874-9500	142
CORT Business Services Corp 11250 Waples Mill Rd Suite 500...... Fairfax	VA	22030	**800-962-2678**	703-968-8500	261-3
CORT Furniture Rental 11250 Waples Mill Rd Suite 500...... Fairfax	VA	22030	**800-962-2678**	703-968-8500	261-3
Cort Theatre 138 W 48th St.........New York	NY	10036	**800-432-7250**	212-239-6200	732
Cortec Corp 4119 White Bear Pkwy .. Saint Paul	MN	55110	**800-426-7832**	651-429-1100	143
Cortex Biochem Inc 1933 Davis St Suite 321 .... San Leandro	CA	94577	**800-888-7713**	510-568-2228	229
Cortina Inn & Resort 103 US Rt 4 .... Killington	VT	05751	**800-451-6108**	802-773-3333	373
Cortland Line Co Inc 3736 Kellogg Rd..................Cortland	NY	13045	**800-847-6787**	607-756-2851	701
Corus America Inc 475 N Martingale Rd Suite 400 .. Schaumburg	IL	60173	**800-542-6244**	847-619-0400	483
Corus Bank NA 2401 N Halsted St ..... Chicago	IL	60614	**800-555-5710**	773-935-6000	71
Corus Bankshares Inc 3959 N Lincoln Ave .... Chicago	IL	60613	**800-555-5710**	773-832-3462	355-2
NASDAQ: CORS					
Corvallis Convention & Visitors Bureau 553 NW Harrison Blvd.............Corvallis	OR	97330	**800-334-8118**	541-757-1544	205
Corvallis Gazette-Times 600 SW Jefferson St PO Box 368....Corvallis	OR	97339	**800-653-3755**	541-753-2641	522-2
CorVu Corp 3400 W 66th St Suite 445.... Edina	MN	55435	**800-610-0769**	952-944-7777	176-1
Corwin Press Inc 2455 Teller Rd .... Thousand Oaks	CA	91320	**800-818-7243***	805-499-9734	623-2
*Orders					
Cosanti Historic Site 6433 Doubletree Ranch Rd ... Paradise Valley	AZ	85253	**800-752-3187**	480-948-6145	50
Cosco Fire Protection Inc 321 E Gardena Blvd...............Gardena	CA	90248	**800-827-5612**	323-321-5155	188-13
Cosco Graphics PO Box 836........... Toledo	OH	43697	**800-837-4221**	419-243-4221	770
Cosco Industries Inc 7220 W Wilson Ave........Harwood Heights	IL	60706	**800-323-0253**	708-457-2410	459
CoServ Electric 7701 S Stemmons Fwy....................Corinth	TX	76210	**800-274-4014**	940-321-4640	244
Cosgrove Enterprises 16000 NW 49th Ave.................Miami	FL	33014	**800-888-3396**	305-623-6700	104
Coshocton County Chamber of Commerce 101 N Whitewoman St .... Coshocton	OH	43812	**800-589-2430**	740-622-5411	137
Coshocton Tribune 550 Main St PO Box 10.......... Coshocton	OH	43812	**800-589-8689**	740-622-1122	522-2
COSI Columbus 333 W Broad St......Columbus	OH	43215	**888-819-2674**	614-228-2674	509
Cosmetic Dentistry. American Academy of 5401 World Dairy Dr............Madison	WI	53718	**800-543-9220**	608-222-8583	49-8
Cosmo. Hotel 761 Post St....... San Francisco	CA	94109	**800-252-7466**	415-673-6040	373
Cosmolab Inc 1100 Garrett Pkwy .... Lewisburg	TN	37091	**800-359-6254**	931-359-6253	211
Cosmopolitan Cosmetics 909 3rd Ave 20th Fl..............New York	NY	10022	**800-589-1412**	212-980-6400	237
Cosmopolitan Hotel 95 W Broadway...New York	NY	10007	**888-895-9400**	212-566-1900	373
Cosmopolitan International 7341 W 80th St .... Overland Park	KS	66204	**800-648-4331**	913-648-4330	48-15
Cosmopolitan Limousine 1601 S Preston St .... Louisville	KY	40217	**800-603-6594**	502-634-5466	433
Cosmopolitan Magazine 224 W 57th St..................New York	NY	10019	**800-888-2676**	212-649-2000	449-11
CoSN (Consortium for School Networking) 1710 Rhode Island Ave NW Suite 900 .... Washington	DC	20036	**866-267-8747**	202-861-2676	48-9
Cosrich Group Inc 51 LaFrance Ave .. Bloomfield	NJ	07003	**888-898-9176**	973-566-6240	211
Cost Cutters Family Hair Care Div Regis Corp 7201 Metro Blvd ..... Minneapolis	MN	55439	**888-888-7778**	952-947-7777	79
Cost Engineering. AACE International - Assn for the Advancement of 209 Prairie Ave Suite 100.................Morgantown	WV	26501	**800-858-2678**	304-296-8444	49-1
Cost Plus Inc 200 4th St............. Oakland	CA	94607	**800-777-4665**	510-893-7300	357
NASDAQ: CPWM					
Costa Cruise Lines 200 S Park Rd Suite 200......... Hollywood	FL	33021	**800-462-6782**	954-266-5600	217
Costa Del Mar 123 N Orchard St Bldg 6......Ormond Beach	FL	32174	**800-447-3700**	386-677-3700	531
Costa Fruit & Produce Inc 18 Bunker Hill Industrial Pk......Charlestown	MA	02129	**800-343-0836**	617-241-8007	292-7
Costa Nursery Farms Inc 22290 SW 162nd Ave ....Miami	FL	33170	**800-327-7074**	305-247-3248	363
Costamar Travel Inc 1421 E Oakland Park Blvd .... Fort Lauderdale	FL	33334	**800-444-7171**	954-630-0060	760
Costanoa Coastal Lodge & Camp 2001 Rossi Rd .... Pescadero	CA	94060	**877-262-7848**	650-879-1100	655
Costco Wholesale Corp 999 Lake Dr .. Issaquah	WA	98027	**800-774-2678***	425-313-8100	799
NASDAQ: COST ■ *Cust Svc					
Costume Specialists Inc 211 N 5th St....................Columbus	OH	43215	**800-596-9357**	614-464-2115	153-6
COTA (Children's Organ Transplant Assn) 2501 Cota Dr .... Bloomington	IN	47403	**800-366-2682**	812-336-8872	48-17
Cotelligent Inc 655 Montgomery St Suite 1000 .... San Francisco	CA	94111	**888-683-6400**	415-477-9900	178
Cothern Computer Systems Inc 1640 Lelia Dr Suite 200............ Jackson	MS	39216	**800-844-1155**	601-969-1155	176-7
Cott Corp 207 Queen's Quay W Suite 340...... Toronto	ON	M5J1A7	**800-994-2688**	416-203-3898	81-2
NYSE: COT					
Cotterman Co PO Box 168 ....Croswell	MI	48422	**800-552-3337**	810-679-4400	412
Cottey College 1000 W Austin Blvd .....Nevada	MO	64772	**888-526-8839**	417-667-8181	160
Cottman Transmission Systems Inc 240 New York Dr....... Fort Washington	PA	19034	**800-394-6116**	215-643-5885	62-6
Cotton Belt Inc 401 E Sater St........Pinetops	NC	27864	**800-849-4192**	252-827-4192	463
Cotton Council of America. National 1918 North Pkwy .... Memphis	TN	38112	**800-377-9030**	901-274-9030	49-18
Cotton Electric Co-op Inc 226 N Broadway...................Walters	OK	73572	**800-522-3520**	580-875-3351	244
Cotton Inc 6399 Weston Pkwy .... Cary	NC	27513	**800-334-5868**	919-678-2220	48-2
Cotton States Life Insurance Co 244 Perimeter Center Pkwy NE .... Atlanta	GA	30346	**800-282-6536**	770-391-8600	384-2
Cotton States Mutual Insurance Co 244 Perimeter Ctr Pkwy NE.......... Atlanta	GA	30346	**800-282-6536**	770-391-8600	384-4
Cotton's Week 1918 North Pkwy ..... Memphis	TN	38112	**800-377-9030**	901-274-9030	521-13
Cottrell Inc 2125 Candler Rd........ Gainesville	GA	30507	**800-827-0132***	770-532-7251	768
*Sales					
Cottrell Paper Co Inc PO Box 35 ....Rock City Falls	NY	12863	**800-948-3559**	518-885-1702	804
Couch Distributing Co Inc 104 Lee Rd.................... Watsonville	CA	95076	**800-542-5555**	831-724-0649	82-1
Couch & Philippi Inc PO Box A .... Stanton	CA	90680	**800-854-3360***	714-527-2261	692
*Orders					
Coulter Cos Inc DBA Peoria Disposal Co PO Box 9071 ....Peoria	IL	61612	**888-988-0760**	309-688-0760	791
Coulter Lake Guest Ranch 80 County Rd 273 .... Rifle	CO	81650	**800-858-3046**	970-625-1473	238
Coulter Steel & Forge Co PO Box 8008 .... Emeryville	CA	94662	**800-648-4884**	510-420-3500	474
Council on Accreditation (COA) 120 Wall St 11th Fl ....New York	NY	10005	**866-262-8088**	212-797-3000	48-1
Council for Advancement & Support of Education (CASE) 1307 New York Ave NW Suite 1000........ Washington	DC	20005	**800-554-8536***	202-328-5900	49-5
*Orders					
Council of the Americas 680 Park Ave ....New York	NY	10021	**800-733-2342**	212-628-3200	48-7
Council of Better Business Bureaus Inc Dispute Resolution Services & Mediation Training 4200 Wilson Blvd Suite 800 .... Arlington	VA	22203	**800-537-4600**	703-276-0100	41
Council Bluffs Area Chamber of Commerce 7 N 6th St .... Council Bluffs	IA	51503	**800-228-6878**	712-325-1000	137
Council of Canadians 170 Laurier Ave W Suite 700......... Ottawa	ON	K1P5V5	**800-387-7177**	613-233-2773	48-7
Council for Exceptional Children (CEC) 1110 N Glebe Rd Suite 300........ Arlington	VA	22201	**888-232-7733**	703-620-3660	49-5
Council on Foundations 1828 L St NW Suite 300 .... Washington	DC	20036	**800-673-9036**	202-466-6512	48-5
Council Grove/Morris County Convention & Visitors Bureau 212 W Main St .... Council Grove	KS	66846	**800-732-9211**	620-767-5882	205
Council on International Educational Exchange (CIEE) 7 Custom House St 3rd Fl........................Portland	ME	04101	**888-268-6245***	207-553-7600	49-5
*Cust Svc					
Council on Occupational Education 41 Perimeter Ctr East NE Suite 640.... Atlanta	GA	30346	**800-917-2081**	770-396-3898	48-1
Council for Professional Recognition 2460 16th St NW.............. Washington	DC	20009	**800-424-4310**	202-265-9090	49-5
Council of Real Estate Brokerage Managers (CRB) 430 N Michigan Ave Suite 300.................... Chicago	IL	60611	**800-621-8738**	312-321-4400	49-17
Council of Residential Specialists 430 N Michigan Ave Suite 300 ...... Chicago	IL	60611	**800-462-8841**	312-321-4400	49-17
Council of State Governments (CSG) 2760 Research Park Dr PO Box 11910 ....Lexington	KY	40578	**800-800-1910***	859-244-8000	49-7
*Sales					
Counsel. American Assn of Fund-Raising 4700 W Lake Ave..... Glenview	IL	60025	**800-462-2372**	847-375-4709	48-5
Counseling Assn. American 5999 Stevenson Ave............. Alexandria	VA	22304	**800-347-6647**	703-823-9800	49-15
Counseling. National Assn for College Admission 1631 Prince St........ Alexandria	VA	22314	**800-822-6285**	703-836-2222	49-5
Counseling. National Foundation for Credit 801 Roeder Rd Suite 900 .... Silver Spring	MD	20910	**800-388-2227**	301-589-5600	48-10
Counselor Assn. American School 1101 King St Suite 625 .... Alexandria	VA	22314	**800-306-4722**	703-683-2722	49-5
Counselors Assn. American Mental Health 801 N Fairfax St Suite 304.. Alexandria	VA	22314	**800-326-2642**	703-548-6002	49-15
Counselors. International Assn of Marriage & Family c/o American Counseling Assn 5999 Stevenson Ave .... Alexandria	VA	22304	**800-545-2223**	703-823-9800	49-15
Count Me In LLC 601 W Golf Rd Suite 108.....Mount Prospect	IL	60056	**800-958-8779**	847-981-8779	85
Counter Technology Inc 4733 Bethesda Ave Suite 800 ...... Bethesda	MD	20814	**800-783-4284**	301-907-0127	681
Country Bank for Savings 75 Main St..... Ware	MA	01082	**800-322-8233**	413-967-6221	71
Country Casualty Insurance Co 1701 Towanda Ave............ Bloomington	IL	61701	**888-211-2555**	309-557-3000	384-4

Name / Address	City	State	Zip	Toll-Free	Phone	Class
Country Classic Dairies Inc DBA Darigold Farms of Montana PO Box 968	Bozeman	MT	59771	**800-321-4563**	406-586-5426	292-4
Country Cos 1701 N Towanda Ave	Bloomington	IL	61701	**888-211-2555**	309-557-3000	384-2
Country Fresh Inc 355 Mart St SW	Grand Rapids	MI	49548	**800-748-0480**	616-243-0173	291-27
Country Hearth Breads 3355 W Memorial Blvd	Lakeland	FL	33815	**800-283-8093**	863-682-1155	291-1
Country Hearth Inn Country Club 4243 Don Woody Club Dr Suite 200	Atlanta	GA	30350	**888-635-2582**	770-393-2662	371
Country Hedging Inc PO Box 64089	Saint Paul	MN	55164	**800-328-6530**	651-355-5151	167
Country Home Bakers Inc 3 Enterprise Dr Suite 404 *Cust Svc	Shelton	CT	06484	**800-243-0008***	203-225-2333	291-2
Country Home Magazine 1716 Locust St *Cust Svc	Des Moines	IA	50309	**800-374-9431***	515-284-3000	449-11
Country Inns & Suites by Carlson PO Box 59159 *Resv	Minneapolis	MN	55459	**800-456-4000***	763-212-1000	369
Country Kitchen International 801 Deming Way	Madison	WI	53717	**888-359-3235**	608-833-9633	657
Country Lane Flower Shops Inc 729 S Michigan Ave	Howell	MI	48843	**800-764-7673**	517-546-1111	287
Country Living Magazine 224 W 57th St	New York	NY	10019	**800-888-0128**	212-649-2000	449-11
Country Magazine 5400 S 60th St	Greendale	WI	53129	**800-344-6913**	414-423-0100	449-11
Country Mark Co-op 1200 Refinery Rd	Mount Vernon	IN	47620	**800-832-5490**	812-838-4341	586
Country Music Assn (CMA) 1 Music Cir S	Nashville	TN	37203	**800-998-4636**	615-244-2840	48-4
Country Music Hall of Fame & Museum 222 5th Ave S	Nashville	TN	37203	**800-852-6437**	615-416-2001	509
Country Mutual Insurance Co 1701 Towanda Ave	Bloomington	IL	61701	**888-211-2555**	309-557-3000	384-4
Country Pride Restaurants 24601 Center Ridge Rd Suite 200	Westlake	OH	44145	**800-872-7024**	440-808-9100	657
Country Springs Hotel & Conference Center 2810 Golf Rd	Pewaukee	WI	53072	**800-247-6640**	262-547-0201	370
Country Today PO Box 570	Eau Claire	WI	54702	**800-236-4004**	715-833-9270	522-4
Country Tonite Theatre 3600 W Hwy 76	Branson	MO	65616	**800-468-6648**	417-334-2422	562
Country Woman Magazine 5400 S 60th St	Greendale	WI	53129	**800-344-6913**	414-423-0100	449-14
CountryTyme Inc 4218 Hoover Rd	Grove City	OH	43123	**800-388-1349**	614-875-1423	639
Countrywide Financial Corp 4500 Park Granada *NYSE: CFC*	Calabasas	CA	91302	**800-669-6607**	818-225-3000	498
Counts Sausage Co Inc PO Box 390	Prosperity	SC	29127	**800-868-0041**	803-364-2392	291-26
County College of Morris 214 Center Grove Rd	Randolph	NJ	07869	**888-226-8001**	973-328-5000	160
Coup de Pouce Magazine 2001 ave University Suite 900	Montreal	QC	H3A2A6	**800-528-3836**	514-499-0561	449-11
Couples in Marriage Enrichment. Association for PO Box 10596	Winston-Salem	NC	27108	**800-634-8325**	336-724-1526	48-6
Courier The 201 E 2nd St PO Box 887	Russellville	AR	72811	**800-369-5252**	479-968-5252	522-2
Courier The 601 Pulaski St PO Box 740	Lincoln	IL	62656	**800-747-5462**	217-732-2101	522-2
Courier The PO Box 609	Conroe	TX	77305	**800-659-8313**	936-756-6671	522-2
Courier-Express The 500 Jeffers St	Du Bois	PA	15801	**800-442-4217**	814-371-4200	522-2
Courier Herald 115 S Jefferson St	Dublin	GA	31021	**800-833-2504**	478-272-5522	522-2
Courier-Journal 525 W Broadway	Louisville	KY	40202	**800-765-4011**	502-582-4011	522-2
Courier Kendallville Inc 2500 Marion Dr	Kendallville	IN	46755	**800-228-9577**	260-347-3044	614
Courier-News 300 Lake St PO Box 531	Elgin	IL	60121	**800-445-3538**	847-888-7800	522-2
Courier-News 1201 Rt 22 W	Bridgewater	NJ	08807	**800-675-0298**	908-722-8800	522-2
Courier-Post PO Box 5300	Cherry Hill	NJ	08034	**800-677-6289**	856-663-6000	522-2
Courier Times The 201 S 14th St	New Castle	IN	47362	**800-489-2472**	765-529-1111	522-2
Courier-Tribune 500 Sunset Ave	Asheboro	NC	27203	**800-967-1838**	336-625-2101	522-2
Courier Westford Inc 22 Town Farm Rd	Westford	MA	01886	**800-666-8772**	978-692-6321	614
Courion 3044 Lambdin Ave	Saint Louis	MO	63115	**800-533-5760**	314-533-5700	232
Couristan Inc 2 Executive Dr	Fort Lee	NJ	07024	**800-223-6186**	201-585-8500	131
Course Technology 25 Thomson Pl	Boston	MA	02210	**800-648-7450**	617-757-7900	623-11
Court The 130 E 39th St	New York	NY	10016	**877-946-8357**	212-685-1100	373
Court Appointed Special Advocate Assn. National 100 W Harrison St North Tower Suite 500	Seattle	WA	98119	**800-628-3233**	206-270-0072	48-6
Court Management. National Assn for National Ctr for State Courts 300 Newport Ave	Williamsburg	VA	23185	**800-616-6165**	757-259-1841	49-10
Court Reporters Assn. National 8224 Old Courthouse Rd	Vienna	VA	22182	**800-272-6272**	703-556-6272	49-10
Courtesy Chevrolet 1233 E Camelback Rd	Phoenix	AZ	85014	**800-555-9322**	602-279-3232	57
CourtEXPRESS 701 Pennsylvania Ave NW Suite C-100	Washington	DC	20004	**800-542-3320**	202-737-7111	621
Courts. National Center for State 300 Newport Ave	Williamsburg	VA	23185	**800-616-6164**	757-253-2000	49-7
Courtyard by Marriott 1 Marriott Dr	Washington	DC	20058	**800-321-2211**	301-380-3000	369
Courtyard New Haven 30 Whalley Ave	New Haven	CT	06511	**800-321-2211**	203-777-6221	373
Coushatta Casino Resort 777 Coushatta Dr PO Box 1510	Kinder	LA	70648	**800-584-7263**	337-738-7300	133
Cousins Properties Inc 2500 Windy Ridge Pkwy Suite 1600 *NYSE: CUZ*	Atlanta	GA	30339	**800-926-8746**	770-955-2200	641
Cousins Subs Inc N 83 W 13400 Leon Rd	Menomonee Falls	WI	53051	**800-238-9736**	262-253-7700	657
Cousteau Society 710 Settlers Landing Rd	Hampton	VA	23669	**800-441-4395**	757-722-9300	48-13
Coustic-Glo International 7111 Ohms Ln	Minneapolis	MN	55439	**800-333-8523**	952-835-1338	188-11
Covad Communications Group Inc 110 Rio robles *Tech Supp	San Jose	CA	95134	**888-642-6823***	408-952-6400	390
Covance Inc 210 Carnegie Ctr *NYSE: CVD*	Princeton	NJ	08540	**888-268-2623**	609-452-8550	86
Covansys Corp 32605 W 12 Mile Rd Suite 250 *NASDAQ: CVNSE*	Farmington Hills	MI	48334	**877-642-2274**	248-488-2088	178
Covanta Energy Corp 40 Lane Rd	Fairfield	NJ	07004	**866-268-2682**	973-882-9000	774
Cove Forge Behavioral Health Rt 1 Box 79	Williamsburg	PA	16693	**800-873-2131**	814-832-2121	712
Cove Inn 900 Broad Ave S	Naples	FL	34102	**800-255-4365**	239-262-7161	373
Covenant House 346 W 17th St	New York	NY	10011	**800-999-9999**	212-727-4000	48-6
Covenant Theological Seminary 12330 Conway Rd	Saint Louis	MO	63141	**800-264-8064**	314-434-4044	164-3
Covenant Transport Inc 400 Birmingham Hwy *NASDAQ: CVTI*	Chattanooga	TN	37419	**800-334-9686**	423-821-1212	769
Covenant Village of Turlock 2125 N Olive Ave	Turlock	CA	95382	**800-485-7844**	209-632-9976	659
Coventry First LLC 7111 Valley Green Rd Suite 320	Fort Washington	PA	19034	**877-836-8300**	215-233-5100	783
Coventry Health Care of Delaware Inc 2751 Centerville Rd Suite 400	Wilmington	DE	19808	**800-727-9951**	302-995-6100	384-3
Coventry Health Care of Georgia Inc 1100 Circle 75 Pkwy Suite 1400	Atlanta	GA	30339	**800-470-2004**	678-202-2100	384-3
Coventry Health Care Inc 6705 Rockledge Dr Suite 900 *NYSE: CVH*	Bethesda	MD	20817	**800-843-7421**	301-581-0600	384-3
Coventry Health Care of Iowa Inc 4600 Westown Pkwy Regency 6 Suite 200	West Des Moines	IA	50266	**800-470-6352**	515-225-1234	384-3
Coventry Health Care of Kansas Inc 2300 Main St Suite 700	Kansas City	MO	64108	**800-468-1442**	816-221-8400	384-3
Coventry Health Care of Louisiana Inc 2424 Edenborn Ave Suite 350	Metairie	LA	70001	**800-245-8327**	504-834-0840	384-3
Coventry Health Care of Nebraska Inc 13305 Birch Dr Suite 100	Omaha	NE	68164	**800-471-0420**	402-498-9030	384-3
Coventry HealthCare Management Corp 9881 Mayland Dr	Richmond	VA	23233	**800-424-0077**	804-747-3700	384-3
Coverall North America Inc 500 W Cypress Creek Rd Suite 580	Fort Lauderdale	FL	33309	**800-537-3371**	954-351-1110	150
Covington Electric Co-op Inc 18836 US Hwy 84	Andalusia	AL	36420	**800-239-4121**	334-222-4121	244
Covington Flooring Co Inc 288-A Oxmore Ct	Birmingham	AL	35209	**800-824-1229**	205-328-2330	188-2
Covington International Travel 4401 Dominion Blvd	Glen Allen	VA	23060	**800-922-9238**	804-747-7077	760
Covisint One Campus Martius	Detroit	MI	48226	**888-222-1700**	248-827-6000	176-4
Covista Communications Inc 4803 Hwy 58 N *NASDAQ: CVST*	Chattanooga	TN	37416	**800-805-1000**	423-648-9700	721
Cowboy Village Resort 120 S Flat Creek Dr PO Box 8040	Jackson	WY	83001	**800-962-4988**	307-733-3121	373
Cowboy Village Resort at Togwotee PO Box 91	Moran	WY	83013	**800-543-2847**	307-543-2847	655
Cowee WJ Inc 28 Taylor Ave	Berlin	NY	12022	**800-862-6933**	518-658-2233	808
Coweta-Fayette Electric Membership Corp 390 N Hwy 29	Newnan	GA	30264	**877-746-4362**	770-253-5626	244
Cowles C & Co Inc 83 Water St	New Haven	CT	06511	**800-624-4483**	203-865-3117	480
Cowley County Community College PO Box 1147	Arkansas City	KS	67005	**800-593-2222**	620-442-0430	160
Cowlitz Bancorporation 927 Commerce Ave *NASDAQ: CWLZ*	Longview	WA	98632	**800-340-8865**	360-423-9800	355-2
Cowtown Boot Co 11401 Gateway Blvd W	El Paso	TX	79936	**800-580-2668**	915-593-2565	296
Cowtown Coliseum 121 E Exchange Ave	Fort Worth	TX	76106	**888-269-8696**	817-625-1025	706
Cox Engineering Co 35 Industrial Dr	Canton	MA	02021	**800-538-0027**	781-302-3300	188-10
Cox Industries Inc 860 Cannon Bridge Rd	Orangeburg	SC	29115	**800-476-4401**	803-534-7467	806
Cox Interior Inc 1751 Old Columbia Rd	Campbellsville	KY	42718	**800-733-1751**	270-789-3129	489
Cox & Kings 25 Davis Blvd	Tampa	FL	33606	**800-999-1758**	813-258-3323	748
Cox Mfg Co 5500 N Loop 1604 E	San Antonio	TX	78247	**800-900-7981**	210-657-7731	610
Cox Newspapers Inc 6205 Peachtree Dunwoody Dr	Atlanta	GA	30328	**800-950-3739**	678-645-0000	623-8
Coxreels 6720 S Clementine Ct *Cust Svc	Tempe	AZ	85283	**800-269-7335***	480-820-6396	118
Coyle Carpet One Inc 250 W Beltline Hwy	Madison	WI	53713	**800-842-6953**	608-257-0291	285
Coyne George S Chemical Co 3015 State Rd	Croydon	PA	19021	**800-523-1230**	215-785-3000	144
Coyne Textile Services Inc 140 Cortland Ave	Syracuse	NY	13202	**800-672-6963**	315-475-1626	434
Coyote Lake Feedyard Inc 1287 FM 1731	Muleshoe	TX	79347	**800-299-3321**	806-946-3321	11-1
Cozen O'Connor 1900 Market St	Philadelphia	PA	19103	**800-523-2900**	215-665-2000	419
Cozy Acres Resort 1100 Cozy Acres Rd	Mountain Pine	AR	71956	**877-691-2699**	501-767-5023	373
CP Hall Co 311 S Wacker Dr Suite 4700	Chicago	IL	60606	**800-762-6198**	312-554-7400	142
CPA (College Parents of America) 8300 Boone Blvd Suite 500	Vienna	VA	22182	**888-256-4627**	703-761-6702	48-11
CPA Auto Dealer Consultants Assn (CADCA) 10831 Old Mill Rd Suite 400	Omaha	NE	68154	**888-475-4476**	402-778-7922	49-1
CPA Health Care Advisors Assn. National 10831 Old Mill Rd Suite 400	Omaha	NE	68154	**888-475-4476**	402-778-7922	49-1
CPA Journal 3 Park Ave 18th Fl	New York	NY	10016	**800-633-6320**	212-719-8300	449-5
CPA Manufacturing Services Assn 10831 Old Mill Rd Suite 400	Omaha	NE	68154	**888-475-4476**	402-778-7922	49-1
CPA Marketing Report 2700 Lake Cook Rd	Riverwoods	IL	60015	**800-224-7977**	847-267-7000	521-10

Name / Address	City	State	ZIP	Toll-Free	Phone	Class
CPAC Inc 2364 Leicester Rd .... *NASDAQ: CPAK* ■ *Cust Svc	Leicester	NY	14481	**800-828-6011***	585-382-3223	143
CPASoftware 125 W Romana St Suite 500	Pensacola	FL	32501	**800-272-7123**	850-434-2685	176-10
CPB (Corporation for Public Broadcasting) 401 9th St NW	Washington	DC	20004	**800-272-2190**	202-879-9600	300
CPC Logistics Inc 14528 S Outer 40 Rd Suite 210 ..	Chesterfield	MO	63017	**800-274-3746**	314-542-2266	707
CPCU & Insurance Institute of America. American Institute for 720 Providence Rd PO Box 3016.....	Malvern	PA	19355	**800-644-2101**	610-644-2100	49-9
CPCU Society 720 Providence Rd Kahler Hall PO Box 3009	Malvern	PA	19355	**800-932-2728**		49-9
CPF (Cleft Palate Foundation) 1504 E Franklin St Suite 102......	Chapel Hill	NC	27514	**800-242-5338**	919-933-9044	48-17
CPI Corp 1706 Washington Ave...... *NYSE: CPY*	Saint Louis	MO	63103	**800-669-9699**	314-231-1575	579
CPI Inc EIMAC Div 301 Industrial Rd	San Carlos	CA	94070	**800-423-4622**	650-592-1221	252
CPI Plastics Group Ltd 979 Gana Ct	Mississauga	ON	L5S1N9	**800-251-9566**	416-798-9333	67
CPP Inc 1055 Joaquin Rd Suite 200	Mountain View	CA	94043	**800-624-1765**	650-969-8901	623-10
CPP International LLC PO Box 7525...	Charlotte	NC	28241	**800-888-3190**	704-588-3190	542-3
CPSI (Computer Programs & Systems Inc) 6600 Wall St...................... *NASDAQ: CPSI*	Mobile	AL	36695	**800-711-2774**	251-639-8100	39
CR Bard Inc 730 Central Ave........ *NYSE: BCR* ■ *Cust Svc	Murray Hill	NJ	07974	**800-526-4455***	908-277-8000	468
CR Bard Inc Endoscopic Technologies Div 129 Concord Rd Bldg 3 PO Box 7031	Billerica	MA	01821	**800-225-1332**	978-663-8989	468
CR Bard Inc Medical Div 8195 Industrial Blvd	Covington	GA	30014	**800-526-4455**	770-784-6100	468
CR Bard Inc Peripheral Vascular Div PO Box 1740	Tempe	AZ	85281	**800-321-4254**		468
CR Bard Inc Urological Div 8195 Industrial Blvd..............	Covington	GA	30014	**800-526-4455**	770-786-9051	468
CR Daniels Inc 3451 Ellicott Ctr Dr..	Ellicott City	MD	21043	**800-933-2638**	410-461-2100	718
CR England & Sons Inc 4701 W 2100 South...........	Salt Lake City	UT	84120	**800-453-8826**	801-972-2712	769
CR Gibson Inc 404 BNA Dr Bldg 200 Suite 600	Nashville	TN	37217	**800-243-6004**	615-724-2900	87
CR Laurence Co Inc PO Box 58923	Los Angeles	CA	90058	**800-421-6144**	323-588-1281	190-2
CRA (California Redwood Assn) 405 Enfrente Dr Suite 200...........	Novato	CA	94949	**888-225-7339**	415-382-0662	48-2
Crab House 1510 W Loop South.......	Houston	TX	77027	**800-552-6379**	713-850-1010	657
Crabtree & Evelyn Ltd 102 Peake Brook Rd............	Woodstock	CT	06281	**800-624-5211**	860-928-2761	211
Crabtree Summit Hotel 3908 Arrow Dr...	Raleigh	NC	27612	**800-521-7521**	919-782-6868	373
Cracker Barrel Old Country Store Inc 305 Hartmann Dr	Lebanon	TN	37087	**800-333-9566**	615-444-5533	657
Crackin Good Bakers Inc 701 N Forrest St..................	Valdosta	GA	31601	**800-323-7850**	229-242-7850	291-9
Crafco Inc 420 N Roosevelt Ave.......	Chandler	AZ	85226	**800-528-8242**	602-276-0406	46
Craft Assn. National 2012 Ridge Rd E Suite 120........	Rochester	NY	14622	**800-715-9594**	585-266-5472	48-18
Craft Council. American 72 Spring St 6th Fl...............	New York	NY	10012	**800-836-3470**	212-274-0630	48-4
Craft & Hobby Assn (CHA) 319 E 54th St..............	Elmwood Park	NJ	07407	**800-822-0494**	201-794-1133	48-18
Craft House International 5570 Enterprise Blvd	Toledo	OH	43612	**800-537-0295**	419-536-8351	750
Craft Inc PO Box 3049	South Attleboro	MA	02703	**800-827-2388**	508-761-7917	345
Craft Machine Works Inc 2102 48th St....................	Hampton	VA	23661	**888-350-6006**	757-380-8615	446
Craft Wholesalers Inc 77 Cypress St SW	Reynoldsburg	OH	43068	**800-666-5858**	740-964-6210	44
Craftmade International Inc 650 S Royal Ln.................... *NASDAQ: CRFT*	Coppell	TX	75019	**800-527-2578**	972-393-3800	37
Craftmatic Organization Inc 2500 Interplex Dr .... *Cust Svc	Trevose	PA	19053	**800-677-8200***	215-639-1310	463
Crafts Etc Ltd 7717 SW 44th St ..	Oklahoma City	OK	73179	**800-888-0321**	405-745-1200	44
Crafts 'n Things Magazine PO Box 420235	Palm Coast	FL	32142	**800-444-0441**	386-447-6309	449-14
Crafts Technologies 91 Joey Dr	Elk Grove Village	IL	60007	**800-323-6802**	847-758-3100	447
Craftsman Inn 7300 E Genesee St....	Fayetteville	NY	13066	**800-797-4464**	315-637-8000	373
Cragun's Conference & Golf Resort 11000 Cragun's Dr.................	Brainerd	MN	56401	**800-272-4867**	218-829-3591	655
Craig-Botetourt Electric Co-op PO Box 265	New Castle	VA	24127	**800-760-2232**	540-864-5121	244
Craig Jenny International Inc 5770 Fleet St	Carlsbad	CA	92008	**800-443-2331**	760-696-4000	797
Craighead Electric Co-op Corp 4714 Stadium Blvd.............	Jonesboro	AR	72403	**800-794-5012**	870-932-8301	244
Crain Brothers Inc PO Box 118...	Grand Chenier	LA	70643	**800-737-2767**	337-538-2411	528
Crain's Chicago Business Magazine 360 N Michigan Ave...............	Chicago	IL	60601	**800-678-2724**	312-649-5200	449-5
Crain's Cleveland Business Magazine 700 W St Clair Ave Suite 310	Cleveland	OH	44113	**888-909-9111**	216-522-1383	449-5
Crain's Detroit Business Magazine 1155 Gratiot Ave..................	Detroit	MI	48207	**888-909-9111**	313-446-6000	449-5
Crain's New York Business Magazine 711 3rd Ave	New York	NY	10017	**800-283-2724**	212-210-0100	449-5
Cram George F Co Inc 301 S LaSalle St...............	Indianapolis	IN	46201	**800-227-4199**	317-635-5564	623-1
Cramer Dee Inc 4221 E Baldwin Rd	Holly	MI	48442	**888-342-6995**	810-238-2664	188-12
Cramer Inc 1222 Quebec St ..	North Kansas City	MO	64116	**800-366-6700**	816-471-4433	314-1
Cramer Products Inc PO Box 1001.....	Gardner	KS	66030	**800-345-2231**	913-856-7511	469
CranBarry Inc 330 C Lynnway............	Lynn	MA	01901	**800-992-2021**	781-586-0111	153-1
Cranbrook Art Museum 39221 Woodward Ave	Bloomfield Hills	MI	48303	**800-462-7262**	248-645-3319	509
Crane Charles L Agency Co 100 S 4th St Suite 800	Saint Louis	MO	63102	**800-363-9827**	314-241-8700	383
Crane Co Dynalco Controls Div 3690 NW 53rd St...........	Fort Lauderdale	FL	33309	**800-368-6666**	954-739-4300	200
Crane & Co Inc 30 South St........... *Cust Svc	Dalton	MA	01226	**800-572-0024***	413-684-2600	542-3
Crane Co Stockham Div 2129 3rd Ave SE	Cullman	AL	35055	**800-786-2542**	256-775-3800	776
Crane Environmental 2600 Eisenhower Ave.............	Trooper	PA	19403	**800-633-7435**	610-631-7700	793
Crane FL & Sons Inc PO Box 428........	Fulton	MS	38843	**800-748-9523**	662-862-2172	188-9
Crane Institute of America Inc 3880 St Johns Pkwy	Sanford	FL	32771	**800-832-2726**	407-322-6800	787
Crane John Canada 423 Green Rd................	Stoney Creek	ON	L8E3A1	**800-263-6860**	905-662-6191	321
Crane John Inc 6400 W Oakton St	Morton Grove	IL	60053	**800-732-5464**	847-967-2400	321
Crane Manufacturers Assn of America (CMAA) 8720 Red Oak Blvd Suite 201	Charlotte	NC	28217	**800-345-1815**	704-676-1190	49-13
Crane Merchandising Systems 12955 Enterprise Way	Bridgeton	MO	63044	**800-325-8811**	314-298-3500	55
Crane Nuclear Inc 2825 Cobb International Blvd.......	Kennesaw	GA	30152	**800-795-8013**	770-424-6343	464
Crane Performance Siding 1441 Universal Rd	Columbus	OH	43207	**800-366-8472**	614-443-4841	190-4
Craneveyor Corp 1524 N Potrero Ave PO Box 3727	South El Monte	CA	91733	**800-423-4180**	626-442-1524	462
Cranford Johnson Robinson Woods 303 W Capitol Ave	Little Rock	AR	72201	**888-383-2579**	501-975-6251	4
Craniofacial Assn. American Cleft Palate- 104 S Estes Dr Suite 204	Chapel Hill	NC	27514	**800-242-5338**	919-933-9044	49-8
Cranmore Mountain Resort 1 Skimobile Rd PO Box 1640 ..	North Conway	NH	03860	**800-786-6754**	603-356-5544	655
Cranston Machinery Co Inc 2251 SE Oak Grove Blvd PO Box 68207	Oak Grove	OR	97267	**800-547-1012**	503-654-7751	546
Cranston Print Works Co 1381 Cranston St................	Cranston	RI	02920	**800-876-2756**	401-943-4800	730-7
Cranwell Resort Spa & Golf Club 55 Lee Rd.........................	Lenox	MA	01240	**800-272-6935**	413-637-1364	655
CRAssociates Inc 8580 Cinderbed Rd Suite 2400	Newington	VA	22122	**877-272-8960**	703-550-8145	455
Craven County Convention & Visitors Bureau 203 S Front St...........	New Bern	NC	28560	**800-437-5767**	252-637-9400	205
Craven Tire & Auto Inc 2728 Dorr Ave...	Fairfax	VA	22031	**800-284-6211**	703-698-8505	62-5
Cravey Green & Wahlen Inc 12 Piedmont Ctr Suite 210..........	Atlanta	GA	30305	**800-249-6669**	404-816-3255	779
Crawford & Co 5620 Glenridge Dr NE.... *NYSE: CRDa*	Atlanta	GA	30342	**800-241-2541**	404-256-0830	383
Crawford Communications Inc 3845 Pleasantdale Rd...............	Atlanta	GA	30340	**800-831-8027**	404-876-7149	501
Crawford Electric Co-op Inc 10301 N Service Rd...............	Bourbon	MO	65441	**800-677-2667**	573-732-4415	244
Crazy Shirts Inc 99-969 Iwaena St	Aiea	HI	96701	**800-771-2720**	808-487-9919	153-3
Crazy Woman Creek Bancorp Inc PO Box 1020 .... *NASDAQ: CRZY*	Buffalo	WY	82834	**800-348-8971**	307-684-5591	355-2
CRB (Council of Real Estate Brokerage Managers) 430 N Michigan Ave Suite 300	Chicago	IL	60611	**800-621-8738**	312-321-4400	49-17
CRC (Children's Rights Council) 6200 Editors Park Dr Suite 103....	Hyattsville	MD	20782	**800-787-5437**	301-559-3120	48-6
CRC (Christian Reformed Church in North America) 2850 Kalamazoo Ave SE........	Grand Rapids	MI	49560	**800-272-5125**	616-241-1691	48-20
CRC Evans Pipeline International Inc 10700 E Independence St	Tulsa	OK	74116	**800-395-5192**	918-438-2100	189
CRC Industries Inc 885 Louis Dr.... *Cust Svc	Warminster	PA	18974	**800-272-4620***	215-674-4300	530
CRC Press LLC 6000 Broken Sound Pkwy NW Suite 300 .... *Cust Svc	Boca Raton	FL	33487	**800-272-7737***	561-994-0555	623-9
CRC Publications Co 2850 Kalamazoo Ave SE........	Grand Rapids	MI	49560	**800-333-8300**	616-224-0727	623-4
Cream-O-Land Dairy Inc 529 Cedar Ln Box 146.............	Florence	NJ	08518	**800-220-6455**	609-499-3601	292-4
Creamer J Fletcher & Son Inc 101 E Broadway...............	Hackensack	NJ	07601	**800-835-9801**	201-488-9800	188-5
Creamland Dairies Inc 010 Indian School Rd NW	Albuquerque	NM	87102	**800-334-3865**	505-247-0721	291-25
Creation Group Inc 53032 County Rd 13 PO Box 1025	Elkhart	IN	46515	**800-862-3131**	574-264-3131	232
Creative Alliance Inc 437 W Jefferson St	Louisville	KY	40202	**800-525-0294**	502-584-8787	4
Creative Automation Co 220 Fencl Ln ...	Hillside	IL	60162	**800-773-1588**	708-449-2800	5
Creative Card Co Inc 7700 W 79th St .... *Cust Svc	Bridgeview	IL	60455	**800-621-3684***	708-563-9780	130
Creative Computer Applications Inc 26115-A Mureau Rd............. *AMEX: CAP*	Calabasas	CA	91302	**800-437-9000**	818-880-6700	176-10
Creative Concepts International 3 Waters Park Dr Suite 213.......	San Mateo	CA	94403	**800-222-8882**	650-357-7800	183
Creative Convention Services 1008 7th Ave Suite 209.........	Beaver Falls	PA	15010	**800-365-8501**	724-843-7501	183
Creative Foam Corp 300 N Alloy Dr.....	Fenton	MI	48430	**800-837-0630**	810-629-4149	590
Creative Foods LLC PO Box 368.......	Osceola	AR	72370	**800-643-0006**	870-563-2601	291-30
Creative Hobbies Inc 900 Creek Rd ...	Bellmawr	NJ	08031	**800-843-5456**	856-933-2540	44
Creative Impact Group 155 Revere Dr Suite 1...........	Northbrook	IL	60062	**800-445-2171**	847-945-7401	183
Creative Kid Stuff 4313 Upton Ave S .... *Orders	Minneapolis	MN	55410	**800-353-0710***	612-929-2431	749
Creative Kids Magazine PO Box 8813	Waco	TX	76714	**800-998-2208**	254-756-3337	449-6
Creative Labs Inc 1901 McCarthy Blvd.. *Cust Svc	Milpitas	CA	95035	**800-998-1000***	408-428-6600	613

	Toll-Free	Phone	Class
Creative Leisure International 951 Transport Way............... Petaluma CA 94954	**800-426-6367**	707-778-1800	760
Creative Loafing Atlanta 750 Willoughby Way .... Atlanta GA 30312	**800-950-5623**	404-688-5623	522-4
Creative Marketing Strategies Inc 15 E Center St .... Woodbury NJ 08096	**800-793-2345**	856-853-7718	722
Creative Teaching Press Inc 15342 Graham St......... Huntington Beach CA 92649	**800-444-4287**	714-895-5047	242
Creative Training Techniques International Inc 7620 W 78th St................. Edina MN 55439	**800-383-9210**	952-829-1954	753
Creative Urethanes Inc PO Box 919 .... Purcellville VA 20134 *Sales	**800-343-6591***	540-338-7139	663
Creativity for Kids 9450 Allen Dr ..... Cleveland OH 44125	**800-311-8684**	216-643-4660	750
Credence Systems Corp 1421 California Cir .... Milpitas CA 95035 *NASDAQ: CMOS*	**800-328-7045**	408-635-4300	247
Credit Acceptance Corp 25505 W 12 Mile Rd ....Southfield MI 48034 *NASDAQ: CACC*	**800-634-1506**	248-353-2700	215
Credit Card News 1 State Street Plaza 27th Fl ....New York NY 10004	**800-535-8403**	212-803-8200	521-1
Credit Card Sentinel Inc PO Box 4401 .... Carol Stream IL 60197 *Cust Svc	**800-423-5166***	847-605-7485	213
Credit Card Systems Inc 180 Shepard Ave .... Wheeling IL 60090	**800-747-1269**	847-459-8320	695
Credit Collections Inc 2915 N Classen Blvd Suite 100 .... Oklahoma City OK 73106	**866-723-2455**	405-290-2000	157
Credit Control Services Inc 2 Wells Ave Suite 1 ....Newton MA 02459	**800-998-5000**	617-965-2000	157
Credit Counseling. National Foundation for 801 Roeder Rd Suite 900 .... Silver Spring MD 20910	**800-388-2227**	301-589-5600	48-10
Credit Management. National Assn of 8840 Columbia 100 Pkwy .... Columbia MD 21045	**800-955-8815**	410-740-5560	49-2
Credit Suisse First Boston Corp 11 Madison Ave ....New York NY 10010	**877-775-2732**	212-325-2000	679
Credit Union 24 Inc 2473 Care Dr Suite 1 .... Tallahassee FL 32308	**877-570-2824**	850-701-2824	70
Credit Union Directors Newsletter 5710 Mineral Point Rd.............Madison WI 53705	**800-356-8010**	608-231-4000	521-1
Credit Union Executives Society (CUES) 5510 Research Park Dr ....Madison WI 53711	**800-252-2664**	608-271-2664	49-2
Credit Union Magazine 5710 Mineral Pt Rd ....Madison WI 53705 *Cust Svc	**800-356-9655***	608-231-4000	449-5
Credit Union National Assn (CUNA) 5710 Mineral Point Rd.............Madison WI 53705	**800-356-9655**	608-231-4000	49-2
Credit Union of Texas PO Box 517028....Dallas TX 75251	**800-314-3828**	972-263-9497	216
Credit Unions Inc. World Council of 5710 Minerial Point Rd ....Madison WI 53705	**800-356-2644**	608-231-7130	49-2
Credit Unions. National Assn of Federal 3138 10th St N.................. Arlington VA 22201	**800-336-4644**	703-522-4770	49-2
Credit Unions. National Federation of Community Development 120 Wall St 10th Fl.......................New York NY 10005	**800-437-8711**	212-809-1850	49-2
Credo Petroleum Corp 1801 Broadway Suite 900 .... Denver CO 80202 *NASDAQ: CRED*	**800-297-2366**	303-297-2200	525
Cree Inc 4600 Silicon Dr............. Durham NC 27703 *NASDAQ: CREE*	**800-533-2583**	919-313-5300	686
Creed Rosary Mfg Inc 15 Kenneth Miner Rd............ Wrentham MA 02093 *Orders	**800-255-7439***	508-384-7600	401
Creek Hill Welding 50 Mill St........Christiana PA 17509	**866-593-8188**	610-593-8188	751
Creftcon Industries DBA Regal Mfg Co 900 S Ajax Ave ...... City of Industry CA 91748	**800-582-3092**	626-964-6534	804
Creighton Brothers LP PO Box 220......Atwood IN 46502	**800-847-3447**	574-267-3101	11-8
Creighton University 2500 California Plaza ....Omaha NE 68178	**800-282-5835**	402-280-2700	163
Cres-Cor 5925 Heisley Rd ....Mentor OH 44060	**877-273-7267**	440-350-1100	281
Crescent Banking Co PO Box 668 ...... Jasper GA 30143 *NASDAQ: CSNT*	**800-872-7941**	678-454-2265	355-2
Crescent Cardboard Co LLC 100 W Willow Rd................ Wheeling IL 60090	**800-323-1055**	847-537-3400	550
Crescent City Consultants 210 Baronne St Suite 1108 ..... New Orleans LA 70112	**800-899-1191**	504-561-1191	183
Crescent City-Del Norte County Chamber of Commerce 1001 Front St................Crescent City CA 95531	**800-343-8300**	707-464-3174	205
Crescent Hotel 75 Prospect Ave............ Eureka Springs AR 72632	**877-342-9766**	479-253-9766	373
Crescent Hotel 403 N Crescent Dr....................Beverly Hills CA 90210	**800-451-1566**	310-247-0505	373
Crescent Inc 527 Willson St PO Box 669.. Niota TN 37826	**877-807-7625**	423-568-2101	153-10
Crescent Jewelry Co 315 11th St...... Oakland CA 94607	**800-588-4367**	510-874-7600	402
Crescent Mfg Co 1310 Majestic Dr..... Fremont OH 43420	**800-537-1330**	419-332-6484	219
Crescent-News 624 W 2nd St PO Box 249 ....Defiance OH 43512	**800-589-5441**	419-784-5441	522-2
Crescent Towing & Salvage Co Inc 1240 Patterson St............. New Orleans LA 70130	**800-843-3930**	504-366-1521	457
Crescent Truck Lines 2480 Whipple Rd ....Hayward CA 94544	**800-722-3171**	510-471-8900	769
Cresco Lines Inc 15220 S Halsted St.... Harvey IL 60426	**800-323-4476**	708-596-8310	769
Cress Photo PO Box 4262............. Wayne NJ 07474	**888-480-3456**	973-694-1280	119
Crest Electronics Inc 3706 Alliance Dr.............. Greensboro NC 27407	**800-873-2121**	336-855-6422	681
Crest Fruit Co 100 N Tower Rd..........Alamo TX 78516	**800-695-2253**	956-787-9971	451
Crest Healthcare Supply 195 S 3rd St... Dassel MN 55325 *Cust Svc	**800-328-8908***	320-275-3382	385
Crest Hotel & Suites 1670 James Ave.............. Miami Beach FL 33139	**800-531-3880**	305-531-0321	373
Crest Mfg Co 5 Hood Dr PO Box 368....Lincoln RI 02865	**800-652-7378**	401-333-1350	152
Crest Ultrasonics Corp PO Box 7266.... Trenton NJ 08628	**800-992-7378**	609-883-4000	771
Crested Butte Academy 505 Whiterock Ave PO Box 1180 ....Crested Butte CO 81224	**888-633-0222**	970-349-1805	611

	Toll-Free	Phone	Class
Crested Butte Mountain Resort 12 Snowmass Rd PO Box 5700........ Mount Crested Butte CO 81225	**800-810-7669**	970-349-2201	655
Crestmark Bank 850 E Long Lake Rd...... Troy MI 48085	**888-999-6088**	248-740-0700	268
Crestwood Manor 50 Lacey Rd........ Whiting NJ 08759	**800-526-1665**	732-849-4900	659
Crete Carrier Corp 400 NW 56th St .....Lincoln NE 68528	**800-998-4095**	402-475-9521	769
Cretors C & Co 3243 N California Ave .. Chicago IL 60618	**800-228-1885**	773-588-1690	293
Creutzfeldt-Jakob Disease Foundation Inc PO Box 5312 .... Akron OH 44334	**800-659-1991**	330-665-5590	48-17
Crew Outfitters 579 W High St......... Aurora MO 65605	**888-567-2739**		154
CRI (Carpet & Rug Institute) 310 S Holiday Ave .... Dalton GA 30720	**800-882-8846**	706-278-3176	49-4
Crichton College 255 N Highland Ave.............. Memphis TN 38111	**800-960-9777**	901-320-9700	163
Cricket Magazine 30 Grove St Suite C ....Peterborough NH 03458	**800-821-0115**	603-924-7209	449-6
CRIIMI MAE Inc 11200 Rockville Pike... Rockville MD 20852 *NYSE: CMM*	**800-266-0535**	301-816-2300	498
Crime Bureau. National Insurance 10330 S Roberts Rd............ Palos Hills IL 60465	**800-447-6282**	708-430-2430	49-9
Crime & Death Scene Cleaning PO Box 828 .... Ipswich MA 01938	**877-366-8348**	978-356-7007	84
Crime. National Center for Victims of 2000 M St NW Suite 480........ Washington DC 20036	**800-394-2255**	202-467-8700	48-8
Crime Stoppers International PO Box 614 .... Arlington TX 76004	**800-245-0009**	817-451-9229	48-8
Criminal Politics Magazine PO Box 37432 ....Cincinnati OH 45222	**800-543-0486**	513-475-0100	449-17
Crisis Magazine 1814 1/2 'N' St NW .... Washington DC 20036 *Cust Svc	**800-746-8073***	202-861-7790	449-18
Crissey Field State Recreation Site c/o Harris Beach State Park 1655 Hwy 101.......................Brookings OR 97415	**800-551-6949**	541-469-0224	554
CRISTA Ministries 19303 Fremont Ave N .... Seattle WA 98133	**800-442-4003**	206-546-7200	48-5
Criswell College 4010 Gaston Ave ....Dallas TX 75246	**800-899-0012**	214-821-5433	163
Criterion Catalysts & Technologies 16825 Northchase Dr Suite 1000..... Houston TX 77060	**800-777-2650**	281-874-2600	141
Critical-Care Nurses. American Assn of 101 Columbia................ Aliso Viejo CA 92656	**800-809-2273**	949-362-2000	49-8
Criticare Systems Inc 20925 Crossroads Cir Suite 100 ... Waukesha WI 53186 *AMEX: CMD*	**800-458-4615**	262-798-8282	468
CRM Learning 2215 Faraday Ave Suite F...........Carlsbad CA 92008	**800-421-0833**	760-431-9800	502
CRN (Cable Radio Networks Inc) 10487 Sunland Blvd............... Sunland CA 91040	**800-336-2225**	818-352-7152	725
Croatian National Tourist Office 350 5th Ave Suite 4003...........New York NY 10118	**800-829-4416**	212-279-8672	764
Crockett Hotel 320 Bonham St..... San Antonio TX 78205	**800-292-1050**	210-225-6500	373
Croda Inc 300-A Columbus Cir .... Edison NJ 08837	**888-252-7632**	732-417-0800	143
Croft Metals LLC 107 Oliver Emmerich Dr........... McComb MS 39648	**800-222-3195**	601-684-6121	476
Crohn's & Colitis Foundation of America (CCFA) 386 Park Ave S 17th Fl ....New York NY 10016	**800-932-2423**	212-685-3440	48-17
Crom Corp 250 SW 36th Terr .... Gainesville FL 32607	**800-289-2766**	352-372-3436	181
Crombie Properties Ltd 115 King St... Stellarton NS B0K1S0	**800-463-2406**	902-755-4440	641
Cromers Inc PO Box 163............ Columbia SC 29202	**800-322-7688**	803-779-1147	291-36
Cromwell Harbor Motel 359 Main St ....Bar Harbor ME 04609 *Resv	**800-544-3201***	207-288-3201	373
Cronos Containers Inc 1 Front St Suite 925.......... San Francisco CA 94111	**800-821-7035**		261-6
Cronos Containers Inc 517 Rt 1 S Suite 1000............... Iselin NJ 08830	**800-221-4126**	732-602-0808	261-6
Crop Insurance Services. National 7201 W 129th St Suite 200.... Overland Park KS 66213	**800-951-6247**	913-685-2767	48-2
CropKing.com Inc 5050 Greenwich Rd... Seville OH 44273	**800-321-5656**	330-769-2002	272
Croplan Genetics PO Box 64281 MS 5850 .... Saint Paul MN 55164	**800-328-9680**	651-765-5712	684
CROPP Cooperative 1 Organic Way..... LaFarge WI 54639	**888-444-6455**	608-625-2602	11-11
Crosby McKissick PO Box 3128 .... Tulsa OK 74101	**800-772-1500**	918-834-4611	462
Crosby & Overton Inc 1610 W 17th St .... Long Beach CA 90813	**800-827-6729**	562-432-5445	653
Crosby Philip Assoc II Inc PO Box 2687 .... Winter Park FL 32790	**800-223-3932**	407-679-7796	193
Crosley Corp 675 N Main St .... Winston-Salem NC 27101	**800-849-1112**	336-722-1112	36
Crosman Corp Rts 5 & 20...... East Bloomfield NY 14443	**800-724-7486**	585-657-6161	279
Cross Automation Inc 2001 Oak Pkwy .. Belmont NC 28012	**800-866-4568**	704-523-2222	245
Cross Border Monitor Newsletter 111 W 57th St 9th Fl............New York NY 10019	**800-938-4685**	212-554-0600	521-2
Cross AT Co 1 Albion Rd.............Lincoln RI 02865 *AMEX: ATX*	**800-722-1719**	401-333-1200	560
Cross Country Automotive Services 4040 Mystic Valley Pkwy ....Medford MA 02155	**800-833-5500**		53
Cross Country Bank 800 Delaware Ave.............. Wilmington DE 19801	**800-334-3180**	302-326-4200	71
Cross Country Healthcare Inc 6551 Park of Commerce Blvd Suite 200 .... Boca Raton FL 33487 *NASDAQ: CCRN*	**800-530-6125**	561-998-2232	707
Cross Country Home Services 1625 NW 136th Ave Suite 200 .... Fort Lauderdale FL 33323	**800-327-9787**	954-845-9100	687
Cross Country Ski Areas Assn 259 Bolton Rd ....Winchester NH 03470	**877-779-2754**	603-239-4341	48-22
Cross Creek Apparel LLC 3330 Cumberland Blvd Suite 1000..... Atlanta GA 30339	**800-321-1138**	678-742-8000	153-3
Cross Creek Resort 3815 SR 8........Titusville PA 16354	**800-461-3173**	814-827-9611	373
Cross Huller 13900 Lakeside Cir..........Sterling Heights MI 48313	**800-243-8620**	586-566-2400	447
Cross Mfg Inc 11011 King St Suite 210 ...... Overland Park KS 66210	**800-542-7677**	913-451-1233	626
Cross Oil Refining & Marketing Inc 484 E 6th St......................Smackover AR 71762	**800-725-3066**	870-881-8700	570
Cross Timbers Royalty Trust 901 Main St Bank of America Plaza 17th Fl ....Dallas TX 75202 *NYSE: CRT*	**877-228-5084**	214-209-2400	662

Company / Address	City	State	ZIP	Toll-Free	Phone	Class
CrossCountry Energy Co 1331 Lamar St Suite 650	Houston	TX	77010	**800-973-6766**	713-853-0300	774
Crossed Sabres Ranch 829 N Fork Hwy	Wapiti	WY	82450	**800-535-8944**	307-587-3750	238
Crosset Co Inc 10295 Toebben Dr	Independence	KY	41051	**800-347-4902**	859-283-5830	292-7
Crossgates Mall 1 Crossgates Mall Rd	Albany	NY	12203	**800-439-2011**	518-869-9565	452
Crossland Economy Studios 100 Dunbar St	Spartanburg	SC	29306	**877-276-7752**	864-573-1600	369
Crossman Post Production LLC DBA Crossman Digital Post 35 Lone Hollow	Sandy	UT	84092	**888-553-1958**	801-553-1958	501
Crossroad Farms Dairy 400 S Shortridge Rd	Indianapolis	IN	46219	**800-334-7502**	317-229-7600	291-27
Crossroads College 920 Mayowood Rd SW	Rochester	MN	55902	**800-456-7651**	507-288-4563	163
Crossroads Pipeline Co 12801 Fair Lakes Pkwy	Fairfax	VA	22033	**888-499-3450**		320
Crossroads Systems Inc 8300 N MoPac Expy. *NASDAQ: CRDS*	Austin	TX	78759	**800-643-7148**	512-349-0300	174
CrossSphere 546 E Main St	Lexington	KY	40508	**800-682-8886**	859-226-4444	48-23
Crossville Cumberland County Chamber of Commerce 34 S Main St	Crossville	TN	38555	**877-465-3861**	931-484-8444	137
Croswell Bus Lines Inc 975 W Main St	Williamsburg	OH	45176	**800-782-8747**	513-724-2206	108
Crouch & Fitzgerald 400 Madison Ave	New York	NY	10017	**800-627-6824**	212-755-5888	445
Croushorn Equipment Co Inc PO Box 796	Harlan	KY	40831	**800-861-5070**	606-573-2454	353
Crow Executive Air Inc 28331 Lemoyne Rd Toledo Metcalf Airport	Millbury	OH	43447	**800-972-2769**	419-838-6921	63
Crow Wing Co-op Power & Light Co PO Box 507	Brainerd	MN	56401	**800-648-9401**	218-829-2827	244
Crowder College 601 Laclede Ave	Neosho	MO	64850	**866-238-7788**	417-451-3223	160
Crowder Construction Co Inc PO Box 30007	Charlotte	NC	28230	**800-849-2966**	704-372-3541	187-4
Crowe Chizek & Co LLP 330 E Jefferson Blvd PO Box 7	South Bend	IN	46624	**800-276-9301**	574-232-3992	2
Crowell Corp PO Box 3227	Newport	DE	19804	**800-441-7525**	302-998-0557	717
Crowell Weedon & Co 624 S Grand Ave 1 Wilshire Bldg Suite 2600	Los Angeles	CA	90017	**800-227-0319**	213-620-1850	679
Crowley Foods Inc 95 Court St	Binghamton	NY	13901	**800-637-0019**	607-779-3289	291-5
Crowley Logistics Inc 9487 Regency Sq Blvd	Jacksonville	FL	32225	**800-874-6769**	904-727-2200	440
Crowley Marine Services Inc 1102 SW Massachusetts St	Seattle	WA	98134	**800-248-8632**	206-332-8000	457
Crowley Maritime Corp 155 Grand Ave Suite 700	Oakland	CA	94612	**800-276-9539**	510-251-7500	307
Crowley's Ridge College 100 College Dr	Paragould	AR	72450	**800-264-1096**	870-236-6901	160
Crown Andersen Inc 306 Dividend Dr *NASDAQ: CRAN*	Peachtree City	GA	30269	**800-241-5424**	770-486-2000	19
Crown Battery Mfg Co 1445 Majestic Dr	Fremont	OH	43420	**800-487-2879**	419-334-7181	76
Crown Clothing Corp 340 Vanderbilt Ave	Norwood	MA	02062	**800-225-8950**	781-769-0001	153-12
Crown College 8700 College View Dr	Saint Bonifacius	MN	55375	**800-682-7696**	952-446-4100	163
Crown Cork & Seal Co 1 Crown Way *NYSE: CCK*	Philadelphia	PA	19154	**800-523-3644**	215-698-5100	124
Crown Crafts Infant Products Inc 711 W Walnut St	Compton	CA	90220	**800-421-0526**	310-763-8100	64
Crown Financial Group Inc 525 Washington Blvd	Jersey City	NJ	07303	**800-333-3113**	201-459-9600	679
Crown Financial Ministries 601 Broad St SE	Gainesville	GA	30501	**800-722-1976**	770-534-1000	393
Crown Holdings Inc DBA Crown Cork & Seal Co 1 Crown Way *NYSE: CCK*	Philadelphia	PA	19154	**800-523-3644**	215-698-5100	124
Crown Liquors of Fort Lauderdale 910 NW 10th Pl	Fort Lauderdale	FL	33311	**888-563-9463**	954-763-6831	435
Crown Media Holdings Inc 6430 S Fiddlers Green Cir Suite 225 *NASDAQ: CRWN*	Greenwood Village	CO	80111	**800-820-7990**	303-220-7990	725
Crown Products Co Inc 6390 Phillips Hwy	Jacksonville	FL	32216	**800-683-7144**	904-737-7144	688
Crown Products Inc 3107 Halls Mill Rd	Mobile	AL	36606	**800-367-2769**	251-476-7777	10
Crown Roll Leaf Inc 91 Illinois Ave	Paterson	NJ	07503	**800-631-3831**	973-742-4000	290
Crown Travel & Cruises 240 Newton Rd Suite 106	Raleigh	NC	27615	**800-869-7447**	919-870-1986	760
Crowne Plaza-French Quarter. Astor 739 Canal St	New Orleans	LA	70130	**800-684-1127**	504-962-0500	373
Crowne Plaza Hotel Albany City Center State & Lodge Sts	Albany	NY	12207	**800-227-6963**	518-462-6611	373
Crowne Plaza Hotel Atlanta Airport 1325 Virginia Ave	Atlanta	GA	30344	**800-227-6963**	404-768-6660	373
Crowne Plaza Hotel Atlanta-Perimeter NW 6345 Powers Ferry Rd NW	Atlanta	GA	30339	**800-554-0055**	770-955-1700	373
Crowne Plaza Hotel Atlanta-Ravinia 4355 Ashford-Dunwoody Rd	Atlanta	GA	30346	**800-554-0055**	770-395-7700	373
Crowne Plaza Hotel Birmingham-The Redmont 2101 5th Ave N	Birmingham	AL	35203	**800-227-6963**	205-324-2101	373
Crowne Plaza Hotel Boston-Natick 1360 Worcester St	Natick	MA	01760	**800-227-6963**	508-653-8800	373
Crowne Plaza Hotel Boston-Woburn 2 Forbes Rd	Woburn	MA	01801	**800-227-6963**	781-932-0999	373
Crowne Plaza Hotel Cedar Rapids 350 1st Ave NE	Cedar Rapids	IA	52401	**800-227-6963**	319-363-8161	373
Crowne Plaza Hotel Chateau Lacombe Edmonton 10111 Bellamy Hill	Edmonton	AB	T5J1N7	**800-661-8801**	780-428-6611	372
Crowne Plaza Hotel Chicago-Allerton 701 N Michigan Ave	Chicago	IL	60611	**800-227-6963**	312-440-1500	373
Crowne Plaza Hotel Chicago Silversmith 10 S Wabash Ave	Chicago	IL	60603	**800-227-6963**	312-372-7696	373
Crowne Plaza Hotel Cincinnati Downtown 15 W 6th St	Cincinnati	OH	45202	**888-279-8260**	513-381-4000	373
Crowne Plaza Hotel Columbus Downtown 33 Nationwide Blvd	Columbus	OH	43215	**800-227-6963**	614-461-4100	373
Crowne Plaza Hotel Dallas Market Center 7050 Stemmons Fwy	Dallas	TX	75247	**800-227-6963**	214-630-8500	373
Crowne Plaza Hotel Dayton 33 E 5th St	Dayton	OH	45402	**800-227-6963**	937-224-0800	373
Crowne Plaza Hotel Detroit Metro Airport 8000 Merriman Rd	Romulus	MI	48174	**800-227-6963**	734-729-2600	373
Crowne Plaza Hotel Georgia 801 W Georgia St	Vancouver	BC	V6C1P7	**800-663-1111**	604-682-5566	372
Crowne Plaza Hotel Grand Rapids 5700 28th St SE	Grand Rapids	MI	49546	**888-957-9575**	616-957-1770	373
Crowne Plaza Hotel Greenville 851 Congaree Rd	Greenville	SC	29607	**800-227-6963**	864-297-6300	373
Crowne Plaza Hotel Harrisburg-Hershey 23 S 2nd St	Harrisburg	PA	17101	**800-227-6963**	717-234-5021	373
Crowne Plaza Hotel Hartford Downtown 50 Morgan St	Hartford	CT	06120	**800-227-6963**	860-549-2400	373
Crowne Plaza Hotel Houston Brookhollow 12801 Northwest Fwy	Houston	TX	77040	**800-227-6963**	713-462-9977	373
Crowne Plaza Hotel Houston-Medical Center 6701 S Main St	Houston	TX	77030	**800-227-6963**	713-797-1110	373
Crowne Plaza Hotel Indianapolis Downtown-Union Station 123 W Louisiana St	Indianapolis	IN	46225	**800-227-6963**	317-631-2221	373
Crowne Plaza Hotel Irvine-Orange County Airport 17941 Von Karman Ave	Irvine	CA	92614	**800-227-6963**	949-863-1999	373
Crowne Plaza Hotel Jackson Downtown 200 E Amite St	Jackson	MS	39201	**800-227-6963**	601-969-5100	373
Crowne Plaza Hotel Lake Oswego 14811 Kruse Oaks Dr	Lake Oswego	OR	97035	**800-465-4329**	503-624-8400	373
Crowne Plaza Hotel Los Angeles Airport 5985 W Century Blvd	Los Angeles	CA	90045	**888-315-3700**	310-642-7500	373
Crowne Plaza Hotel Los Angeles-Commerce Casino 6121 E Telegraph Rd	Commerce	CA	90040	**800-227-6963**	323-728-3600	373
Crowne Plaza Hotel Macon 108 1st St	Macon	GA	31201	**800-227-6963**	478-746-1461	373
Crowne Plaza Hotel Madison-East Towne 4402 E Washington Ave	Madison	WI	53704	**800-404-7630**	608-244-4703	373
Crowne Plaza Hotel Manhattan Times Square 1605 Broadway	New York	NY	10019	**800-243-6969**	212-977-4000	373
Crowne Plaza Hotel Meadowlands 2 Harmon Plaza	Secaucus	NJ	07094	**800-227-6963**	201-348-6900	373
Crowne Plaza Hotel Miami International Airport 950 NW Le Jeune Rd	Miami	FL	33126	**800-227-6963**	305-446-9000	373
Crowne Plaza Hotel Montreal Metro Centre 505 rue Sherbrooke O	Montreal	QC	H2L4N3	**800-561-4644**	514-842-8581	372
Crowne Plaza Hotel Nashua 2 Somerset Pkwy	Nashua	NH	03063	**800-227-6963**	603-886-1200	373
Crowne Plaza Hotel New York-La Guardia 104-04 Ditmars Blvd	East Elmhurst	NY	11369	**800-227-6963**	718-457-6300	373
Crowne Plaza Hotel New York at the United Nations 304 E 42nd St	New York	NY	10017	**800-879-8836**	212-986-8800	373
Crowne Plaza Hotel North Dallas-Addison 14315 Midway Rd	Addison	TX	75001	**800-227-6963**	972-980-8877	373
Crowne Plaza Hotel Omaha Old Mill 655 N 108th Ave	Omaha	NE	68154	**800-227-6963**	402-496-0850	373
Crowne Plaza Hotel Palo Alto 4290 El Camino Real	Palo Alto	CA	94306	**800-227-6963**	650-857-0787	373
Crowne Plaza Hotel Philadelphia-Center City 1800 Market St	Philadelphia	PA	19103	**800-227-6963**	215-561-7500	373
Crowne Plaza Hotel Phoenix Metro Center 2532 W Peoria Ave	Phoenix	AZ	85029	**800-465-4329**	602-943-2341	373
Crowne Plaza Hotel Pittsburgh International Airport 1160 Thorn Run Rd Ext	Coraopolis	PA	15108	**800-627-6373**	412-262-2400	373
Crowne Plaza Hotel Pittsfield 1 West St	Pittsfield	MA	01201	**800-227-6963**	413-499-2000	373
Crowne Plaza Hotel Pleasanton 11950 Dublin Canyon Rd	Pleasanton	CA	94588	**800-227-6963**	925-847-6000	373
Crowne Plaza Hotel Providence-Warwick 801 Greenwich Ave	Warwick	RI	02886	**800-227-6963**	401-732-6000	373
Crowne Plaza Hotel Redondo Beach & Marina 300 N Harbor Dr	Redondo Beach	CA	90277	**800-227-6963**	310-318-8888	373
Crowne Plaza Hotel Richmond-E Canal 555 E Canal St	Richmond	VA	23219	**800-227-6963**	804-788-0900	373
Crowne Plaza Hotel Rochester 70 State St	Rochester	NY	14614	**800-227-6963**	585-546-3450	373
Crowne Plaza Hotel Saint Louis 11228 Lone Eagle Dr	Bridgeton	MO	63044	**800-227-7963**	314-291-6700	373
Crowne Plaza Hotel San Francisco-Union Square 480 Sutter St	San Francisco	CA	94108	**800-243-1135**	415-398-8900	373
Crowne Plaza Hotel San Francisco/Peninsula Airport 1221 Chess Dr	Foster City	CA	94404	**800-227-6963**	650-570-5700	373
Crowne Plaza Hotel San Jose Downtown 282 Almaden Blvd	San Jose	CA	95113	**800-227-6963**	408-998-0400	373
Crowne Plaza Hotel San Jose/Silicon Valley 777 Bellew Dr	Milpitas	CA	95035	**800-227-6963**	408-321-9500	373
Crowne Plaza Hotel Seattle Downtown 1113 6th Ave	Seattle	WA	98101	**800-521-2762**	206-464-1980	373
Crowne Plaza Hotel Springfield 3000 S Dirksen Pkwy	Springfield	IL	62703	**800-227-6963**	217-529-7777	373
Crowne Plaza Hotel Sunrise-Sawgrass Mills 13400 W Sunrise Blvd	Sunrise	FL	33323	**888-633-1956**	954-851-1020	373
Crowne Plaza Hotel Washington DC. Hamilton 1001 14th St NW	Washington	DC	20005	**800-263-9802**	202-682-0111	373
Crowne Plaza Hotel Washington National Airport 1480 Crystal Dr	Arlington	VA	22202	**800-465-4329**	703-416-1600	373
Crowne Plaza Hotel West Palm Beach 1601 Belvedere Rd	West Palm Beach	FL	33406	**800-227-6963**	561-689-6400	373
Crowne Plaza Hotel White Plains Downtown 66 Hale Ave	White Plains	NY	10601	**800-752-4672**	914-682-0050	373

Name / Address	City	State	ZIP	Toll-Free	Phone	Class
Crowne Plaza Hotel Worcester Downtown 10 Lincoln Sq	Worcester	MA	01608	**800-628-4240**	508-791-1600	373
Crowne Plaza Key West La Concha Hotel 430 Duval St	Key West	FL	33040	**800-745-2191**	305-296-2991	373
Crowne Plaza Minneapolis Northstar Hotel 618 2nd Ave S	Minneapolis	MN	55402	**800-556-7827**	612-338-2288	373
Crowne Plaza Oceanfront Singer Island 3200 N Ocean Dr	Singer Island	FL	33404	**800-327-0522**	561-842-6171	373
Crowne Plaza O'Hare International Airport 5440 N River Rd	Rosemont	IL	60018	**800-227-6963**	847-671-6350	373
Crowne Plaza Quaker Square Hotel 135 S Broadway St	Akron	OH	44308	**866-668-6689**	330-253-5970	373
Crowne Plaza Resort Anaheim-Garden Grove 12021 Harbor Blvd	Garden Grove	CA	92840	**800-227-6963**	714-867-5555	655
Crowne Plaza Resort Hilton Head Island 130 Shipyard Dr	Hilton Head Island	SC	29928	**800-334-1881**	843-842-2400	655
Crowne Plaza Resort Orlando 12000 International Dr	Orlando	FL	32821	**800-227-6963**	407-239-1222	655
Crowne Plaza San Francisco International Airport 1177 Airport Blvd	Burlingame	CA	94010	**800-411-7275**	650-342-9200	373
Crowne Plaza Suites Dallas 7800 Alpha Rd	Dallas	TX	75240	**800-227-6963**	972-233-7600	373
CrownTonka Inc 10700 Hwy 55 Suite 300	Plymouth	MN	55441	**800-523-7337**	763-541-1410	650
CRS (Catholic Relief Services) 209 W Fayette St	Baltimore	MD	21201	**800-235-2772**	410-625-2220	48-5
CRST International Inc 3930 16th Ave SW PO Box 68	Cedar Rapids	IA	52406	**800-366-8460**	319-396-4400	769
Crucial Technology 3475 E Commercial Ct	Meridian	ID	83642	**800-336-8915**	208-363-5790	613
Crucible Compaction Metals 1001 Robb Hill Rd	Oakdale	PA	15071	**888-923-2670**	412-923-2670	709
Crucible Materials Corp PO Box 977	Syracuse	NY	13201	**800-365-1180**	315-487-4111	709
Crucible Materials Corp Specialty Metals Div PO Box 977	Syracuse	NY	13201	**800-365-1180**	315-487-4111	709
Crucible Materials Corp Trent Tube Div 2015 Energy Dr PO Box 77	East Troy	WI	53120	**800-558-2260**	262-642-7321	481
Crucible Service Centers 5639 W Genesee St	Camillus	NY	13031	**800-365-1185**	315-487-0800	483
Cruise Brokers 4802 Gunn Hwy Suite 141	Tampa	FL	33624	**800-409-1919**	813-288-9597	760
Cruise Center The 11713 101st Ave E	Puyallup	WA	98373	**800-454-7174**	253-845-5330	760
Cruise Concepts 34034 US Hwy 19 N	Palm Harbor	FL	34684	**800-752-7963**	727-784-7245	760
Cruise Connection LLC 7932 N Oak Suite 210	Kansas City	MO	64118	**800-572-0004**	816-420-8688	760
Cruise Connections Inc 1422 S Stratford Rd	Winston-Salem	NC	27103	**800-248-7447**	336-659-9772	760
Cruise Holidays International Inc 701 Carlson Pkwy	Minnetonka	MN	55305	**800-866-7245**		760
Cruise Lines. International Council of 2111 Wilson Blvd 8th Fl	Arlington	VA	22201	**800-595-9338**	703-522-8463	48-23
Cruise Marketing International 3401 Investment Blvd Suite 3	Hayward	CA	94545	**800-578-7742**	510-784-8500	760
Cruise People Inc 10191 W Sample Rd Suite 215	Coral Springs	FL	33065	**800-642-2469**	954-753-0069	760
Cruise People Ltd 1252 Lawrence Ave E Suite 210	Don Mills	ON	M3A1C3	**800-268-6523**	416-444-2410	760
Cruise Planners Inc 3300 University Dr Suite 602	Coral Springs	FL	33065	**800-683-0206**	954-344-8060	761
Cruise Shop The 700 Pasquinelli Dr Suite C	Westmont	IL	60559	**800-622-6456**	630-325-7447	760
Cruise by Sue 1792 Whitecap Cir	Fort Myers	FL	33903	**888-486-1135**	239-997-7874	760
Cruise & Travel Inc 26212 Carmel St	Laguna Hills	CA	92656	**888-484-3732**	949-360-8081	760
Cruise Travel Magazine 990 Grove St	Evanston	IL	60201	**800-877-5893**	847-491-6440	449-22
Cruise & Travel Shoppe 5809 NW 48th Ave	Coconut Creek	FL	33073	**800-957-4477**	954-427-3216	760
Cruise Vacation Center PO Box 12304	Huntsville	AL	35815	**800-239-9997**	256-880-6700	760
Cruise Vacation Center 2042 Central Pk Ave	Yonkers	NY	10710	**800-803-7245**	914-337-8500	760
Cruise Value Center 6 Edgeboro Rd	East Brunswick	NJ	08816	**800-231-7447**	732-257-4545	760
Cruise Ventures DBA CI Travel 101 W Main St Suite 800	Norfolk	VA	23510	**800-222-3577**	757-627-8000	760
Cruise Web Inc 8100 Corporate Dr Suite 300	Landover	MA	20785	**800-377-9383**	240-487-0155	760
Cruise West 2301 5th Ave Suite 401	Seattle	WA	98121	**888-851-8133**	206-441-8687	217
Cruise.com 1701 Eller Dr	Port Everglades	FL	33316	**888-333-3116**	954-763-6828	762
CruiseOne Inc 1415 NW 62nd St Suite 205	Fort Lauderdale	FL	33309	**800-832-3592**	954-958-3700	761
Cruises Cruises 6604 Antoine Dr	Houston	TX	77091	**800-245-9806**	713-681-9866	760
Cruises Inc 1415 SW 62nd St *Cust Svc	Fort Lauderdale	FL	33309	**800-854-0500***	954-958-3700	760
Cruises by Kay 6903 California Ave SW	Seattle	WA	98136	**800-938-2602**	206-938-2602	760
Cruises.com 100 Sylvan Rd	Woburn	MA	01801	**800-288-6006**	617-424-7990	762
CruisesOnly 100 Sylvan Rd Suite 600	Woburn	MA	01801	**800-278-4737**	617-424-7990	760
Crum Electric Supply Co 1165 English Ave	Casper	WY	82601	**800-726-2239**	307-266-1278	245
Crum & Forster Insurance Inc 305 Madison Ave	Morristown	NJ	07962	**800-227-3745**	973-490-6600	384-4
Crusade for Christ International. Campus 100 Lake Hart Dr	Orlando	FL	32832	**877-924-7478**	407-826-2000	48-20
Crutchfield Corp 1 Crutchfield Pk *Sales	Charlottesville	VA	22911	**800-955-3000***	434-817-1000	451
CRWRC (Christian Reformed World Relief Committee) 2850 Kalamazoo Ave SE	Grand Rapids	MI	49560	**800-552-7972**	616-224-0740	48-5
Cryobiology Inc 4830D Knightsbridge Blvd	Columbus	OH	43214	**800-359-4375**	614-451-4375	535
Cryogenic Laboratories Inc 1944 Lexington Ave N	Roseville	MN	55113	**800-466-2796**	651-489-8000	535
Cryolife Inc 1655 Roberts Blvd NW *NYSE: CRY*	Kennesaw	GA	30144	**800-438-8285**	770-419-3355	86
Cryovac Div Sealed Air Corp 100 Rogers Bridge Rd Bldg A	Duncan	SC	29334	**800-845-7551**	864-433-2000	538
Crystal Beach Suites & Health Club 6985 Collins Ave	Miami Beach	FL	33141	**800-435-0766**	305-865-9555	373
Crystal Cabinet Works Inc 1100 Crystal Dr	Princeton	MN	55371	**800-347-5045**	763-389-4187	116
Crystal Cathedral 12141 Lewis St	Garden Grove	CA	92840	**877-456-7900**	714-971-4000	50
Crystal Clear Industries 2 Bergen Tpke *Orders	Ridgefield Park	NJ	07660	**800-841-4014***	201-440-4200	330
Crystal Cream & Butter Co 1013 D St	Sacramento	CA	95814	**800-272-7326**	916-444-7200	291-3
Crystal Cruises Inc 2049 Century Pk E Suite 1400	Los Angeles	CA	90067	**866-446-6625**	310-785-9300	217
Crystal Farms Refrigerated Distribution Co 6465 Wayzata Blvd Suite 200	Minneapolis	MN	55426	**800-344-7382**	952-544-8101	292-10
Crystal Flash Petroleum Corp 5221 Ivy Tech Dr	Indianapolis	IN	46268	**800-886-3835**	317-879-2849	319
Crystal Frank & Co Inc 40 Broad St 15th Fl	New York	NY	10004	**800-221-5830**	212-344-2444	383
Crystal Geyser Water Co 501 Washington St *Cust Svc	Calistoga	CA	94515	**800-443-9737***	707-942-0500	792
Crystal Group Inc 850 Kacena Rd	Hiawatha	IA	52233	**800-378-1636**	319-378-1636	174
Crystal Inc 601 W 8th St	Lansdale	PA	19446	**800-525-3842**	215-368-1661	143
Crystal Inn Gulfport 9379 Canal Rd	Gulfport	MS	39503	**888-822-9600**	228-822-9600	373
Crystal Inn Salt Lake City Downtown 230 W 500 South	Salt Lake City	UT	84101	**800-366-4466**	801-328-4466	373
Crystal Lake Mfg Inc 2225 Hwy 14 W PO Box 159	Autaugaville	AL	36003	**800-633-8720**	334-365-3342	104
Crystal Mountain Resort 12500 Crystal Mountain Dr	Thompsonville	MI	49683	**800-968-7686**	231-378-2000	655
Crystal Shamrock Inc 6000 Douglas Dr N	Minneapolis	MN	55429	**800-533-2214**	763-533-2214	63
Crystal Springs Apparel 206 W Railroad Ave	Crystal Springs	MS	39059	**800-633-4635**	601-892-4551	153-21
Crystals International Inc 600 W ML King Jr Blvd	Plant City	FL	33563	**800-237-7620**	813-754-2691	291-18
Crysteel Mfg Inc PO Box 178 *Orders	Lake Crystal	MN	56055	**800-533-0494***	507-726-2728	462
Crystek Crystals Corp 12730 Commonwealth Dr Unit 6	Fort Myers	FL	33913	**800-237-3061**	239-561-3311	252
CS Henry Transfer Inc PO Box 2306	Rocky Mount	NC	27802	**800-849-6400**	252-446-5116	769
CS Mott Children's Hospital 1500 E Medical Center Dr	Ann Arbor	MI	48109	**800-211-8181**	734-936-4000	366-1
CSA Travel Protection 5454 Ruffin Rd	San Diego	CA	92123	**800-873-9855**		384-7
CSBS (Conference of State Bank Supervisors) 1155 Connecticut Ave NW 5th Fl	Washington	DC	20036	**800-886-2727**	202-296-2840	49-7
CSG (Council of State Governments) 2760 Research Park Dr PO Box 11910 *Sales	Lexington	KY	40578	**800-800-1910***	859-244-8000	49-7
CSG Information Services 3922 Coconut Palm Dr	Tampa	FL	33619	**800-927-9292**	813-627-6800	623-6
CSG Systems International Inc 7887 E Belleview Ave Suite 1000 *NASDAQ: CSGS*	Englewood	CO	80111	**800-366-2744**	303-804-4000	176-10
CSI (Christian Schools International) 3350 E Paris Ave SE	Grand Rapids	MI	49512	**800-635-8288**	616-957-1070	49-5
CSI (Computer Sales International Inc) 9990 Old Olive St Rd	Saint Louis	MO	63141	**800-955-0960**	314-997-7010	261-1
CSI (Construction Specifications Institute) 99 Canal Ctr Plaza Suite 300	Alexandria	VA	22314	**800-689-2900**	703-684-0300	49-3
CSI Bath Accessories Div Moen Inc 25300 Al Moen Dr	North Olmsted	OH	44070	**800-321-8809**	440-962-2000	598
CSI Compressor Systems Inc 3809 S FM 1788 PO Box 60760	Midland	TX	79711	**800-365-1170**	432-563-1170	170
CSI Fabricated Metal Bins Inc 6910 W Ridge Rd	Fairview	PA	16415	**800-937-9033**	814-474-9353	197
CSI International Inc 8120 State Rt 138	Williamsport	OH	43164	**800-795-4914**	740-420-5400	176-12
CSM Metal Fabricating & Engineering Inc 1800 S San Pedro St	Los Angeles	CA	90015	**800-272-4806**	213-748-7321	473
CSM Worldwide Inc 269 Sheffield St Suite 305	Mountainside	NJ	07092	**800-952-5227**	908-233-2882	19
CSN International PO Box 391	Twin Falls	ID	83303	**800-357-4226**	208-734-2049	630
CSP Inc 43 Manning Rd *NASDAQ: CSPI*	Billerica	MA	01821	**800-325-3110**	978-663-7598	171-3
CSR Inc PO Box 389	York	PA	17405	**800-839-0931**	717-843-0931	674
CSS Laboratories Inc 1641 McGaw Ave	Irvine	CA	92614	**800-852-2680**	949-852-8161	171-3
CSSA (Communications Supply Service Assn) 5700 Murray St	Little Rock	AR	72209	**800-252-2772**	501-562-7666	49-20
CST Technologies Inc 55 Northern Blvd Suite 200	Great Neck	NY	11021	**800-448-4407**	516-482-9001	229
CST/Berger Corp 255 W Fleming St	Watseka	IL	60970	**800-435-1859**	815-432-5237	534
CSX Intermodal Inc 301 W Bay St	Jacksonville	FL	32202	**800-542-2754**	904-633-1000	440
CT Communications Inc 1000 Progress Pl *NASDAQ: CTCI* ■ *Cust Svc	Concord	NC	28025	**800-617-8595***	704-722-2500	721
CT Corp 3 Winners Cir 3rd Fl	Albany	NY	12205	**800-624-0099**	518-451-8000	436
CT Corp 111 8th Ave	New York	NY	10011	**800-223-7567**	212-894-8940	621
CT Harris Inc 9411 Deepstep Rd	Sandersville	GA	31082	**800-547-6404**	478-552-5070	493-2
CT-Nassau Corp 4101 S NC 62	Alamance	NC	27201	**800-397-0090**	336-570-0091	730-5
CTA (Computer Technology Assoc) 12530 Parklawn Dr Suite 300	Rockville	MD	20852	**800-753-9201**	301-581-3200	178
CTAA (Community Transportation Assn of America) 1341 G St NW Suite 1000	Washington	DC	20005	**800-527-8279**	202-628-1480	49-21

Name / Address	City	State	ZIP	Toll-Free	Phone	Class
CTB/McGraw-Hill Div McGraw-Hill Cos Inc 20 Ryan Ranch Rd	Monterey	CA	93940	**800-538-9547**	831-393-0700	243
CTC (Center for Technology Commercialization) 1400 Computer Dr	Westborough	MA	01581	**800-472-6785**	508-870-0042	654
CTC Communications Corp 220 Bear Hill Rd	Waltham	MA	02451	**800-883-6000**	781-466-8080	721
CTC Parker Automation 50 W TechneCenter Dr *Cust Svc	Milford	OH	45150	**800-233-3329***	513-831-2340	171-3
CTD News 747 Dresher Rd Suite 500	Horsham	PA	19044	**800-341-7874**	215-784-0860	521-8
CTG (Computer Task Group Inc) 800 Delaware Ave *NYSE: CTG*	Buffalo	NY	14209	**800-992-5350**	716-882-8000	178
CTI PO Box 397	Rillito	AZ	85654	**800-362-4952**	520-624-2348	769
CTI Molecular Imaging Inc 810 Innovation Dr	Knoxville	TN	37932	**800-841-7226**	865-218-2000	375
CTL Distribution Inc PO Drawer 437	Mulberry	FL	33860	**800-237-9088**	863-428-2373	769
CTS Corporate Travel Solutions 340 Cedar St Suite 1200	Saint Paul	MN	55101	**800-635-5488**	651-287-4900	760
CTS Cruise & Travel 5435 Scotts Valley Dr	Scotts Valley	CA	95066	**800-777-1677**	831-438-6662	761
CTSF (Conservation Treaty Support Fund) 3705 Cardiff Rd	Chevy Chase	MD	20015	**800-664-3150**	301-654-3150	48-13
CTX Mortgage Co 3100 McKinnon St	Dallas	TX	75201	**800-666-5363**	214-981-5000	498
CTX Technology Corp 16728 E Gale Ave *Cust Svc	City of Industry	CA	91745	**877-688-3288***	626-363-9328	171-4
CU24 19 British American Blvd	Latham	NY	12110	**800-453-1466**	518-437-8100	70
CUB (Concerned United Birthparents Inc) PO Box 230457	Encinitas	CA	92023	**800-822-2777**		48-21
Cub Cadet Corp 1620 Welch St	Brownsville	TN	38012	**888-986-2288**	731-772-5600	420
Cubic Simulation Systems 2001 W Oakridge Rd	Orlando	FL	32809	**800-327-1020**	407-859-7410	694
Cubist Pharmaceuticals Inc 65 Hayden Ave *NASDAQ: CBST*	Lexington	MA	02421	**877-528-2478**	781-860-8660	86
Cubix Corp 2800 Lockheed Way *Sales	Carson City	NV	89706	**800-829-0554***	775-883-7611	174
Cucina Classica Italiana Inc 2400 Main St Suite 12	Sayreville	NJ	08872	**800-524-2713**	732-727-7800	291-5
Cudahy Patrick Inc 1 Sweet Apple-Wood Ln	Cudahy	WI	53110	**800-486-6900**	414-744-2000	465
CUE Inc 11 Leonberg Rd	Cranberry Township	PA	16066	**800-283-4621**	724-772-5225	589
CUES (Credit Union Executives Society) 5510 Research Park Dr	Madison	WI	53711	**800-252-2664**	608-271-2664	49-2
CUH2A Inc 1000 Lenox Dr	Lawrenceville	NJ	08648	**877-992-8422**	609-844-1212	258
Cuisinart Corp 1 Cummings Pt Rd	Stamford	CT	06902	**800-726-0190**	203-975-4600	37
Cuisine Solutions Inc 85 S Bragg St Suite 600 *AMEX: FZN*	Alexandria	VA	22312	**888-285-4679**	703-270-2900	291-36
Cuivre River Electric Co-op 1112 E Cherry St	Troy	MO	63379	**800-392-3709**	636-528-8261	244
Culinary Federation Chef & Child Foundation. American 180 Center Place Way	Saint Augustine	FL	32095	**800-624-9458**	904-824-4468	48-6
Culinary Federation Inc. American 180 Sector Place Way	Saint Augustine	FL	32095	**800-624-9458**	904-824-4468	49-6
Culinary Foods Inc 4201 S Ashland Ave	Chicago	IL	60609	**800-621-4049**	773-650-4000	291-36
Culinary Institute of America 1946 Campus Dr *Admissions	Hyde Park	NY	12538	**800-285-4627***	845-452-9600	787
Cullen/Frost Bankers Inc 100 W Houston St *NYSE: CFR*	San Antonio	TX	78205	**800-562-6732**	210-220-4011	355-2
Culligan International Co 1 Culligan Pkwy	Northbrook	IL	60062	**800-285-5442**	847-205-6000	793
Cullman Area Chamber of Commerce 301 2nd Ave SW	Cullman	AL	35055	**800-313-5114**	256-734-0454	137
Cullman Electric Co-op 1749 Eva Rd NE	Cullman	AL	35055	**800-242-1806**	256-737-3200	244
Cullman Times 300 4th Ave SE	Cullman	AL	35055	**800-844-5369**	256-734-2131	522-2
Culpeper Baptist Retirement Community 12425 Village Loop	Culpeper	VA	22701	**800-894-2411**	540-825-2411	659
Culpeper County Chamber of Commerce & Visitors Center 109 S Commerce St	Culpeper	VA	22701	**888-285-7373**	540-825-8628	137
Cultural Center for Language Studies Corp 3191 Coral Way Suite 114	Miami	FL	33145	**800-704-3131**	305-529-8563	414
Cultural Experiences Abroad Inc 1400 E Southern Ave Suite B-108	Tempe	AZ	85282	**800-266-4441**	480-557-7900	748
Culver Academies 1300 Academy Rd	Culver	IN	46511	**800-528-5837**	574-842-7000	611
Culver Industries Inc 1000 Industrial Blvd Hopewell Industrial Park	Aliquippa	PA	15001	**800-862-0070**	724-857-5770	330
Culver-Stockton College 1 College Hill	Canton	MO	63435	**800-537-1883**	573-288-6000	163
Cumberland Casualty & Surety Co 4311 W Waters Ave Suite 401	Tampa	FL	33614	**800-723-0171**	813-885-2112	384-5
Cumberland College 816 Walnut St	Williamsburg	KY	40769	**800-343-1609**	606-549-2200	163
Cumberland Farms Inc 777 Dedham St	Canton	MA	02021	**800-225-9702**	781-828-4900	203
Cumberland Farms Inc Gulf Div 777 Dedham St	Canton	MA	02021	**800-843-8028**	781-828-4900	319
Cumberland Hospital for Children & Adolescents 9407 Cumberland Rd	New Kent	VA	23124	**800-368-3472**	804-966-2242	366-1
Cumberland Insurance Group 633 Shiloh Pike	Bridgeton	NJ	08302	**800-232-6992**	856-451-4050	384-4
Cumberland Mutual Fire Insurance Co 633 Shiloh Pike	Bridgeton	NJ	08302	**800-232-6992**	856-451-4050	384-4
Cumberland Optical Laboratory 806 Olympic St	Nashville	TN	37203	**800-888-8316**	615-254-5868	531
Cumberland Packing Corp 2 Cumberland St	Brooklyn	NY	11205	**800-221-1763**	718-858-4200	291-38
Cumberland Technologies Inc 4311 W Waters Ave Suite 401	Tampa	FL	33614	**800-723-0171**	813-885-2112	355-4
Cumberland Times-News 19 Baltimore St	Cumberland	MD	21502	**800-742-8149**	301-722-4600	522-2
Cumberland University 1 Cumberland Sq	Lebanon	TN	37087	**800-467-0562**	615-444-2562	163
Cumberland Valley Co-op Assn 908 Mt Rock Rd	Shippensburg	PA	17257	**800-488-2197**	717-532-2191	438
Cumberland Valley Electric Inc Cumberland Gap Pkwy PO Box 440	Gray	KY	40734	**800-513-2677**	606-528-2677	244
Cumberland Wood Products Inc PO Box 68	Helenwood	TN	37755	**800-635-7335**	423-569-6363	118
Cuming County Public Power District 500 S Main St	West Point	NE	68788	**877-572-2463**	402-372-2463	244
Cummins-Allison Corp 891 Feehanville Dr	Mount Prospect	IL	60056	**800-786-5528**	847-299-9550	112
Cummins Inc PO Box 3005 *NYSE: CMI*	Columbus	IN	47201	**800-343-7357**	812-377-5000	259
CUNA (Credit Union National Assn) 5710 Mineral Point Rd	Madison	WI	53705	**800-356-9655**	608-231-4000	49-2
CUNA Mutual Group 5910 Mineral Point Rd	Madison	WI	53705	**800-937-2644**	608-238-5851	355-4
Cunard Line Ltd 24303 Town Ctr Dr Suite 200	Valencia	CA	91355	**800-528-6273**	800-223-0764	217
Cunningham Brick Co Inc 701 N Main St	Lexington	NC	27292	**800-672-6181**	336-248-8541	148
CUNO Inc 400 Research Pkwy *NASDAQ: CUNO*	Meriden	CT	06450	**800-243-6894**	203-237-5541	379
Cupertino National Bank & Trust 20230 Stevens Creek Blvd	Cupertino	CA	95014	**888-650-8008**	408-996-1144	71
Curacao Tourist Board 7951 SW 6th St Suite 216	Plantation	FL	33324	**800-328-7222**	954-370-5887	764
CuraGen Corp 555 Long Wharf Dr 11th Fl *NASDAQ: CRGN*	New Haven	CT	06511	**888-436-6643**	203-401-3330	86
CuraScript Pharmacy Inc 6272 Lee Vista Blvd	Orlando	FL	32822	**800-950-2840**	407-852-4903	575
Curative Health Services Inc 150 Motor Pkwy 4th Fl *NASDAQ: CURE*	Hauppauge	NY	11788	**800-966-5656**	631-232-7000	347
Curiosities Greeting Cards 64 Heather Rd	Buffalo	NY	14225	**877-424-4401**	716-837-7256	130
Curlee Mfg Co 13639 Aldine Westfield Rd	Houston	TX	77039	**800-631-6815**		804
Curling Assn. US PO Box 866	Stevens Point	WI	54481	**888-287-5377**	715-344-1199	48-22
Curon Medical Inc 46117 Landing Pkwy *NASDAQ: CURN*	Fremont	CA	94538	**877-734-2873**		249
Curran Assoc 737 Miami Cir NE	Atlanta	GA	30324	**800-241-0178**	404-237-4246	386
Current Designs PO Box 247	Winona	MN	55987	**877-655-1822**	507-454-5430	701
Current Inc 30 Tyler St PO Box 120183	East Haven	CT	06512	**877-436-6542**	203-469-1337	588
Current USA Inc 1005 E Woodmen Rd *Cust Svc	Colorado Springs	CO	80920	**800-525-7170***	719-594-4100	451
Curriculum Assoc Inc PO Box 2001	North Billerica	MA	01862	**800-225-0248**	978-667-8000	623-2
Curriculum Development. Association for Supervision & 1703 N Beauregard St	Alexandria	VA	22311	**800-933-2723**	703-578-9600	49-5
Curry College 1071 Blue Hill Ave	Milton	MA	02186	**800-669-0686**	617-333-2210	163
Curtain Call Costumes 333 E 7th Ave	York	PA	17404	**888-808-0801**	717-852-6910	153-6
Curtis 1000 Inc 1725 Breckinridge Pkwy Suite 500	Duluth	GA	30096	**800-683-8162**	678-380-9095	260
Curtis Dyna-Fog Ltd 17335 US Hwy 31 N	Westfield	IN	46074	**800-544-8990**	317-896-2561	170
Curtis Industries Inc 2400 S 43rd St	Milwaukee	WI	53219	**800-657-0853**	414-649-4200	803
Curtis Restaurant Supply Co 6577 E 40th St	Tulsa	OK	74145	**800-766-2878**	918-622-7390	295
Curtis-Toledo Inc 1905 Kienlen Ave	Saint Louis	MO	63133	**800-925-5431**	314-383-1300	170
Curtis Tractor Cab Inc 111 Higgins St	Worcester	MA	01606	**800-343-7676**	508-853-2200	505
Curtis Wilbur Co Inc 6913 Acco St	Montebello	CA	90640	**800-421-6150**	323-837-2300	293
Curtis-Young Corp 2704 Cindel Dr	Cinnaminson	NJ	08077	**800-282-6650**	856-665-6650	616
Curtiss Arlin Trucking Inc PO Box 26	Montevideo	MN	56265	**800-328-8940**	320-269-5581	769
Curtiss-Wright Controls Inc 15800 John J Delaney Dr Suite 200	Charlotte	NC	28277	**877-319-8468**	704-869-4600	25
Curves International Inc 100 Ritchie Rd	Waco	TX	76712	**800-848-1096**	254-399-9285	349
Cusack Wholesale Meat Inc PO Box 25111	Oklahoma City	OK	73125	**800-241-6328**	405-232-2114	292-9
Cushing Daily Citizen 115 S Cleveland St PO Box 1031	Cushing	OK	74023	**800-780-6397**	918-225-3333	522-2
Cushing-Malloy Inc 1350 N Main St	Ann Arbor	MI	48104	**888-295-7244**	734-663-8554	614
Cushion Cut Inc 2565 W 237th St	Torrance	CA	90505	**800-421-2222**		484
Custer Public Power District 625 E South 'E' St	Broken Bow	NE	68822	**888-749-2453**	308-872-2451	244
Custom Aluminum Products Inc 414 W Division St	South Elgin	IL	60177	**800-745-6333**	847-741-6333	476
Custom Building Products 13001 Seal Beach Blvd	Seal Beach	CA	90740	**800-272-8786**	562-598-8808	3
Custom Business Forms Inc 210 Edge Pl	Minneapolis	MN	55418	**800-234-1221**	612-789-0002	111
Custom Chrome Inc 16100 Jacqueline Ct	Morgan Hill	CA	95037	**800-729-3332**	408-778-0500	61
Custom Coolers LLC 5609 Azle Ave	Fort Worth	TX	76114	**800-627-0488**	817-626-3737	650
Custom Direct 1802 Fashion Ct	Joppa	MD	21085	**800-354-3540**	410-679-3300	140
Custom Drapery Blinds & Shutters 3900 Polk St	Houston	TX	77023	**800-929-9211**	713-225-9211	731
Custom Electronic Design & Installation Assn (CEDIA) 7150 Winton Dr Suite 300	Indianapolis	IN	46268	**800-669-5329**	317-328-4336	49-19
Custom Fiberglass Mfg Corp 1711 Harbor Ave	Long Beach	CA	90813	**800-768-4867**	562-432-5454	120

Company / Address	City	State	ZIP	Toll-Free	Phone	Class
Custom Fold Doors Inc 110 W Ash Ave	Burbank	CA	91502	**800-913-3573**	323-849-3225	281
Custom Food Group 2627 Midway Ave	Shreveport	LA	71108	**800-256-8828**	318-632-8000	294
Custom Food Products Inc 5145 W 123rd St *Cust Svc	Alsip	IL	60803	**800-621-8827***	708-239-2766	291-18
Custom Medical Stock Photo Inc 3660 W Irving Park Rd	Chicago	IL	60618	**800-373-2677**	773-267-3100	582
Custom Metal Crafters Inc 815 N Mountain Rd	Newington	CT	06111	**800-262-3140**	860-953-4210	583
Custom Mold Engineering Inc 9780 S Franklin Dr	Franklin	WI	53132	**800-448-2005**		745
Custom Pack Inc 443 Creamery Way	Exton	PA	19341	**800-722-7005**	610-524-4222	590
Custom Paper Tubes Inc PO Box 35140	Cleveland	OH	44135	**800-766-2527**	216-362-2964	125
Custom Products of Litchfield Inc 1715 S Sibley Ave	Litchfield	MN	55355	**800-222-5463**	320-693-3221	269
Custom Tapes Inc 7125 W Gunnison St	Harwood Heights	IL	60706	**800-621-7994**	708-867-6060	717
Customcraft Binder Corp 21 Addison Ln	Greenvale	NY	11548	**800-428-0934**	516-484-4020	87
Customer Communicator Newsletter 28 W 25th St 8th Fl	New York	NY	10010	**800-232-4317**	212-228-0246	521-2
Customer Service Assn. International 401 N Michigan Ave 22nd Fl	Chicago	IL	60611	**800-360-4272**	312-321-6800	49-12
Customers First Newsletter 360 Hiatt Dr	Palm Beach Gardens	FL	33418	**800-621-5463**	561-622-9914	521-2
CustomerSat Inc 1049 Terra Bella Ave	Mountain View	CA	94043	**800-372-7772**	650-234-8000	39
Cut Flower Wholesale Inc 2122 Faulkner Rd	Atlanta	GA	30324	**888-997-8367**	404-320-1619	288
Cut-Heal Animal Care Products Inc 923 S Cedar Hill Rd	Cedar Hill	TX	75104	**800-288-4325**	972-293-9700	574
Cutco Cutlery Corp 1116 E State St	Olean	NY	14760	**800-828-0448**		361
Cuthbert Greenhouses Inc 4900 Hendron Rd	Groveport	OH	43125	**800-321-1939**	614-836-3866	363
Cutler at Abbeville LLC 496 Industrial Park Rd	Abbeville	AL	36310	**800-633-7565**	334-585-2268	608
Cutler-Dickerson Co Inc 507 College Ave	Adrian	MI	49221	**800-968-5191**	517-265-5191	438
Cutler-Magner Co PO Box 16807	Duluth	MN	55816	**800-232-1302**	218-722-3981	432
Cutter Aviation 2802 E Old Tower Rd Sky Harbor International Airport	Phoenix	AZ	85034	**800-234-5382**	602-273-1237	25
Cutter Benchmark Review 37 Broadway Suite 1	Arlington	MA	02474	**800-964-8702**	781-648-8702	521-3
Cutter & Buck Inc 701 N 34th St Suite 400 *NASDAQ: CBUK*	Seattle	WA	98103	**800-929-9299**	206-622-4191	153-1
Cutter Information Corp 37 Broadway Suite 1	Arlington	MA	02474	**800-964-5118**	781-648-8700	623-9
Cutting Edge Cruises & Tours 32 Toms Way	Lagrangeville	NY	12540	**888-345-6100**	845-227-2660	760
Cuyahoga Community College						
Eastern Campus 4250 Richmond Rd	Highland Hills	OH	44122	**800-954-8742**	216-987-2024	160
Metropolitan Campus 2900 Community College Ave	Cleveland	OH	44115	**800-954-8742**	216-987-4200	160
Western Campus 11000 Pleasant Valley Rd	Parma	OH	44130	**800-954-8742**	216-987-5000	160
Cuyahoga County Public Library 2111 Snow Rd	Parma	OH	44134	**800-749-5560**	216-398-1800	426
Cuyahoga Falls News-Press PO Box 1549	Stow	OH	44224	**800-966-6565**	330-688-0088	522-4
Cuyahoga Molded Plastics Corp 1265 Babbitt Rd	Cleveland	OH	44132	**800-805-9549**	216-261-2744	593
CV Technologies Inc 9411 20th Ave	Edmonton	AB	T6N1E5	**888-843-7239**	780-432-0022	786
CV Therapeutics Inc 3172 Porter Dr *NASDAQ: CVTX*	Palo Alto	CA	94304	**877-475-2790**	650-384-8500	86
CVB Financial Corp PO Box 51000 *NASDAQ: CVBF*	Ontario	CA	91761	**888-222-5432**	909-980-4030	355-2
cVideo Inc 10967 Via Frontera *Tech Supp	San Diego	CA	92127	**800-724-8562***	858-385-2000	176-8
CVS Corp 1 CVS Dr *NYSE: CVS* ■ *Cust Svc	Woonsocket	RI	02895	**800-746-7287***	401-765-1500	236
CW Brower Inc 413 S Riverside Dr	Modesto	CA	95354	**800-400-0477**	209-523-1828	203
CW Ohio Inc 1209 Maple Ave	Conneaut	OH	44030	**800-677-5801**	440-593-5800	489
CWF (Canadian Wildlife Federation) 350 Michael Cowpland Dr	Kanata	ON	K2M2W1	**800-563-9453**	613-599-9594	48-13
CWF (Clean Water Fund) 4455 Connecticut Ave NW Suite A300-16	Washington	DC	20008	**800-709-2837**	202-895-0432	48-13
CWLA (Child Welfare League of America) 440 1st St NW 3rd Fl	Washington	DC	20001	**800-407-6273**	202-638-2952	48-6
CWPT (Civil War Preservation Trust) 1331 H St NW Suite 1001	Washington	DC	20005	**888-606-1400**	202-367-1861	48-13
CWR Mfg Corp 7000 Fly Rd *Sales	Syracuse	NY	13220	**800-724-0311***	315-437-1032	688
CWU (Church Women United) 475 Riverside Dr Rm 1626	New York	NY	10115	**800-298-5551**	212-870-2347	48-20
CXR Telcom Corp 894 Faulstich Ct	San Jose	CA	95112	**800-537-5762**	510-657-8810	247
CXtec 5404 S Bay Rd *Orders	Syracuse	NY	13212	**800-767-3282***	315-476-3000	801
Cyan Inc 14617 N Newport Hwy	Mead	WA	99021	**800-219-4119**	509-468-0807	176-6
Cyanotech Corp 73-4460 Queen Kaahumanu Hwy Suite 102 *NASDAQ: CYAN* ■ *Sales	Kailua-Kona	HI	96740	**800-453-1187***	808-326-1353	470
Cyber Merchants Exchange Inc 4349 Baldwin Ave Suite A	El Monte	CA	91731	**888-564-6263**	626-636-2530	176-7
Cyberdata Corp 2555 Garden Rd	Monterey	CA	93940	**800-292-3723**	831-373-2601	174
CyberData Inc 20 Max Ave	Hicksville	NY	11801	**877-942-8100**	516-942-8000	39
CyberEdit Inc 2000 Lenox Dr 3rd Fl	Lawrenceville	NJ	08648	**888-438-2633**	609-896-5401	257
Cyberex LLC 6095 Parkland Blvd Suite 310	Mayfield Heights	OH	44124	**800-292-3739**	440-995-3200	252
CyberGuard Corp 350 SW 12th Ave *NASDAQ: CGFW*	Deerfield Beach	FL	33442	**800-666-4273**	954-958-3900	174
Cyberian Outpost Inc 25 N Main St	Kent	CT	06757	**877-688-7678**	860-927-2050	177
Cyberonics Inc Cyberonics Bldg 100 Cyberonics Blvd *NASDAQ: CYBX*	Houston	TX	77058	**800-332-1375**	281-228-7200	469
CyberOptics Corp 5900 Golden Hills Dr *NASDAQ: CYBE* ■ *Cust Svc	Minneapolis	MN	55416	**800-746-6315***	763-542-5000	247
CyberSource Corp 1295 Charleston Rd *NASDAQ: CYBS*	Mountain View	CA	94043	**888-802-9237**	650-965-6000	176-7
CyberStaff America Ltd 253 W 35th St 16th Fl	New York	NY	10001	**888-244-2300**	212-244-2300	707
CyberTeams Inc 5714-B Industry Ln *Sales	Frederick	MD	21704	**888-832-5575***	301-682-8885	176-12
Cybertech Systems Inc 1250 E Diehl Rd Suite 403	Naperville	IL	60563	**800-874-1985**	630-472-3200	178
CyberTrader Inc 12401 Research Blvd Bldg 2 Suite 350	Austin	TX	78759	**888-762-9237**		679
Cybex International Inc 10 Trotter Dr *AMEX: CYB*	Medway	MA	02053	**888-462-9239**	508-533-4300	263
Cycle Country Accessories Corp 2188 Hwy 86 PO Box 239 *AMEX: ATC*	Milford	IA	51351	**800-841-2222**	712-338-2701	30
Cycle Systems Inc PO Box 611	Roanoke	VA	24004	**800-542-7000**	540-981-1211	674
Cycle World Magazine 1499 Monrovia Ave	Newport Beach	CA	92663	**800-876-8316**	949-720-5300	449-3
Cycling Assn. Adventure 150 E Pine St PO Box 8308	Missoula	MT	59802	**800-755-2453**	406-721-1776	48-22
Cyclone Drilling Inc PO Box 908	Gillette	WY	82717	**800-318-3724**	307-682-4161	529
Cyclone Mfg Co Inc PO Box 67	Urbana	IN	46990	**800-972-6130**	260-774-3311	269
CycoActive Inc 701 34th Ave	Seattle	WA	98122	**800-491-2926**	206-323-2349	506
Cygnus Inc 400 Penobscot Dr	Redwood City	CA	94063	**866-459-2824**	650-369-4300	468
Cyma Systems Inc 2330 W University Dr Suite 7	Tempe	AZ	85281	**800-292-2962**	480-303-2962	176-1
Cypress Bioscience Inc 4350 Executive Dr Suite 325 *NASDAQ: CYPB*	San Diego	CA	92121	**800-452-7646**	858-452-2323	86
Cypress Communications Inc 15 Piedmont Ctr Suite 100	Atlanta	GA	30305	**888-205-6912**	404-869-2500	721
Cypress Gardens Adventure Park 6000 Cypress Gardens Blvd *Tech Supp	Winter Haven	FL	33884	**800-282-2123***	863-324-2111	32
Cypress Hotel 10050 S DeAnza Blvd	Cupertino	CA	95014	**800-499-1408**	408-253-8900	373
Cypress Semiconductor Corp 3901 N 1st St *NYSE: CY*	San Jose	CA	95134	**800-541-4736**	408-943-2600	686
Cypress Swamp Tours Inc 501 Laroussini St	Westwego	LA	70094	**800-633-0503**	504-581-4501	748
Cyr Bus Lines 153 Gilman Falls Ave	Old Town	ME	04468	**800-244-2335**	207-827-2335	108
Cyr John T & Sons Inc 153 Gilman Falls Ave	Old Town	ME	04468	**800-244-2335**	207-827-2335	110
Cyr Northstar Tours 153 Gilman Falls Ave	Old Town	ME	04468	**800-244-2335**	207-827-2335	748
Cyrano Inc 26 Parker St	Newburyport	MA	01950	**800-714-4900**	978-462-0737	176-12
Cyril Bath Co 1610 Airport Rd	Monroe	NC	28110	**800-801-1418**	704-289-8531	448
Cyril J Burke Inc 36000 Mound Rd	Sterling Heights	MI	48310	**800-482-4952**	586-939-4400	261-2
Cystic Fibrosis Foundation 6931 Arlington Rd Suite 200	Bethesda	MD	20814	**800-344-4823**	301-951-4422	48-17
Cytec Corp 10385 Brockwood Rd	Dallas	TX	75238	**888-349-8881**	214-349-8881	171-3
Cytogen Corp 650 College Rd E *NASDAQ: CYTO*	Princeton	NJ	08540	**800-833-3533**	609-750-8200	86
Cytokinetics Inc 280 E Grand Ave *NASDAQ: CYTK*	South San Francisco	CA	94080	**877-394-2986**	650-624-3000	86
CytoSport Inc 4795 Industrial Way	Benicia	CA	94510	**888-298-6629**	925-685-6600	786
Cytyc Corp 250 Campus Dr *NASDAQ: CYTC*	Marlborough	MA	01752	**800-442-9892**	508-263-2900	229
Cyveillance Inc 1555 Wilson Blvd Suite 404	Arlington	VA	22209	**888-243-0097**	703-351-1000	39
Czech Airlines 1350 Ave of the Americas Suite 601	New York	NY	10019	**800-223-2365**	212-765-6545	26
Czech Airlines OK Plus 1350 Ave of the Americas Suite 601	New York	NY	10019	**800-223-2365**	212-765-6545	27

D

Company / Address	City	State	ZIP	Toll-Free	Phone	Class
D-A Lubricant Co 1340 W 29th St	Indianapolis	IN	46208	**800-873-2582**	317-923-5321	530
D & B Plastics Inc PO Box 26	Fairmont	MN	56031	**800-405-2247**	507-235-5950	589
D & B Sales & Marketing Solutions 460 Totten Pond Rd 7th Fl *Prod Info	Waltham	MA	02451	**800-590-0065***	781-672-9200	176-1
D & D Equipment Rental Inc PO Box 2369	Santa Fe Springs	CA	90670	**866-446-1100**	562-595-4555	261-2
D Davis Kenny Co Inc 4810 Greatland	San Antonio	TX	78218	**800-594-2045**	210-662-9882	87
D & E Communications Inc 124 E Main St *NASDAQ: DECC* ■ *Cust Svc	Ephrata	PA	17522	**800-321-6112***	717-733-4101	721
D & F Corp 42455 Merrill Rd	Sterling Heights	MI	48314	**800-959-3456**	586-254-5300	556
D & H Distributing Co Inc 2525 N 7th St	Harrisburg	PA	17110	**800-877-1200**	717-236-8001	172

Company / Address	City	State	ZIP	Toll-Free	Phone	Class
D & K Healthcare Resources Inc 8235 Forsythe Blvd. *NASDAQ: DKHR*	Saint Louis	MO	63105	**888-727-3485**	314-727-3485	237
D & L Stained Glass Supply Inc 4939 N Broadway	Boulder	CO	80304	**800-525-0940**	303-449-8737	44
D-Link Systems Inc 17595 Mt Herrmann St	Fountain Valley	CA	92708	**800-326-1688**	949-788-0805	174
D-M-E Co 29111 Stephenson Hwy	Madison Heights	MI	48071	**800-626-6653**	248-398-6000	593
D Myers & Sons Inc 4311 Erdman Ave	Baltimore	MD	21213	**800-367-7463**	410-522-7500	296
D-Q University PO Box 409	Davis	CA	95617	**866-468-6378**	530-758-0470	161
D & R Sports Center Inc 8178 W Main St	Kalamazoo	MI	49009	**800-992-1520**	269-372-2277	702
D & S Cattle Co 2167 SR 66 PO Box 172	Zolfo Springs	FL	33890	**800-522-0534**	863-735-1112	437
D & W Food Centers Inc 3001 Orchard Vista Dr SE	Grand Rapids	MI	49546	**800-642-3728**	616-940-3580	339
D & W Inc 941 Oak St	Elkhart	IN	46514	**800-255-0829**	574-264-9674	325
Da Camera of Houston 1427 Branard St	Houston	TX	77006	**800-233-2226**	713-524-7601	563-3
DA Davidson & Co Inc 8 3rd St N	Great Falls	MT	59401	**800-332-5915**	406-727-4200	679
Da Kine International 408 Columbia St Suite 300	Hood River	OR	97031	**800-827-7466**	541-386-3166	701
Da Lite Screen Co Inc 3100 N Detroit St	Warsaw	IN	46581	**800-622-3737**	574-267-8101	580
DA Matot Inc 2501 Van Buren St	Bellwood	IL	60104	**800-369-1070**	708-547-1888	255
DA Stuart Co 4580 Weaver Pkwy	Warrenville	IL	60555	**800-323-1438**	630-393-0833	530
DAC International Inc 6702 McNeil Dr	Austin	TX	78729	**800-527-2531**	512-331-5323	759
DAC Vision 3930 Miller Park Dr.	Garland	TX	75042	**800-800-1550**	972-494-4555	531
Dacco Inc PO Box 2789	Cookeville	TN	38502	**800-443-2226**	931-528-7581	60
Daco Corp 1761 E Brooks Rd	Memphis	TN	38116	**800-824-7992**	901-332-4000	767
Dacotah Paper Co 3940 15th Ave NW	Fargo	ND	58102	**800-726-1767**	701-277-3300	549
Dacra Glass Inc 1144 S State Rd 3 S	Hartford City	IN	47348	**800-359-3189**	765-348-2190	330
Dadant & Sons Inc 51 S 2nd St	Hamilton	IL	62341	**800-637-7468**	217-847-3324	122
Dade Behring Holdings Inc 1717 Deerfield Rd. *NASDAQ: DADE*	Deerfield	IL	60015	**800-948-3233**	847-267-5300	229
Dad's Pet Care Inc 18746 Mill St	Meadville	PA	16335	**800-458-1801**	814-724-7710	568
Daedal Div Parker Hannifin Corp 1140 Sandy Hill Rd	Irwin	PA	15642	**800-245-6903**	724-861-8200	534
Daemen College 4380 Main St	Amherst	NY	14226	**800-462-7652**	716-839-3600	163
Daewoo Electronics Corp of America 120 Chubb Ave	Lyndhurst	NJ	07071	**800-323-9668**	201-460-2000	52
Daffodil 163 Pearl St	Essex Junction	VT	05452	**800-795-1305**	802-879-0212	155-6
DAG Media Inc 125-10 Queens Blvd Suite 14 *NASDAQ: DAGM*	Kew Gardens	NY	11415	**800-261-2799**	718-263-8454	623-6
Daggett Truck Line Inc PO Box 158	Frazee	MN	56544	**800-262-9393**	218-334-3711	769
Dahle North America Inc 375 Jaffrey Rd	Peterborough	NH	03458	**800-243-8145**	603-924-0003	523
Dahlgren & Co Inc 1220 Sunflower St	Crookston	MN	56716	**800-346-6050**	218-281-2985	291-28
Dahlmann Campus Inn 615 E Huron St	Ann Arbor	MI	48104	**800-666-8693**	734-769-2200	373
Dahlsten Truck Line Inc 101 W Edgar PO Box 95	Clay Center	NE	68933	**800-228-4313**	402-762-3511	769
Daifuku America Corp 6700 Tussing Rd	Reynoldsburg	OH	43068	**800-531-1888**	614-863-1888	206
Daig Corp 14901 DeVeau Pl	Minnetonka	MN	55345	**800-328-3873**	952-933-4700	468
Daigger A Co Inc 620 Lakeview Pkwy	Vernon Hills	IL	60061	**800-621-7193**	847-816-5060	592
Daiichi Pharmaceutical Corp 11 Philips Pkwy	Montvale	NJ	07645	**800-374-5589**	201-573-7000	572
Daikin America Inc 20 Olympic Dr *Cust Svc	Orangeburg	NY	10962	**800-365-9570***	845-365-9500	594-2
Daily American 111 S Emma St PO Box 617	Somerset	PA	15501	**800-452-0823**	814-444-5900	522-2
Daily Ardmoreite 117 W Broadway St.	Ardmore	OK	73401	**800-873-0211**	580-223-2200	522-2
Daily Astorian 949 Exchange St	Astoria	OR	97103	**800-781-3211**	503-325-3211	522-2
Daily Banner 1000 Goodwill Rd.	Cambridge	MD	21613	**800-282-8586**	410-228-3131	522-2
Daily Business Review 1 SE 3rd Ave Suite 900	Miami	FL	33131	**800-777-7300**	305-347-6672	449-5
Daily Capital News 210 Monroe St	Jefferson City	MO	65101	**866-865-1690**	573-636-3131	522-2
Daily Chronicle 1586 Barber Greene Rd.	DeKalb	IL	60115	**877-688-4841**	815-756-4841	522-2
Daily Citizen 3000 E Race Ave	Searcy	AR	72143	**800-400-3142**	501-268-8621	522-2
Daily Citizen 308 S Thornton Ave	Dalton	GA	30722	**877-217-6397**	706-217-6397	522-2
Daily Citizen 805 Park Ave PO Box 558	Beaver Dam	WI	53916	**888-887-0111**	920-887-0321	522-2
Daily Clay County Advocate-Press 105 W North Ave	Flora	IL	62839	**800-804-9383**	618-662-2108	522-2
Daily Comet 705 W 5th St	Thibodaux	LA	70301	**800-256-1305**	985-447-4055	522-2
Daily Commerce 915 E 1st St	Los Angeles	CA	90012	**800-788-7840**	213-229-5300	522-2
Daily Commercial 212 E Main St	Leesburg	FL	34748	**877-702-0600**	352-365-8200	522-2
Daily Courier 1958 Commerce Ctr Cir	Prescott	AZ	86304	**888-349-3436**	928-445-3333	522-2
Daily Courier 601 Oak St	Forest City	NC	28043	**888-761-1898**	828-245-6431	522-2
Daily Courier 409 SE 7th St	Grants Pass	OR	97526	**800-228-0457**	541-474-3700	522-2
Daily Courier 127 W Apple St	Connellsville	PA	15425	**800-801-9000**	724-628-2000	522-2
Daily Democrat 1226 Ave H PO Box 160	Fort Madison	IA	52627	**800-798-8819**	319-372-6421	522-2
Daily Express Inc 1072 Harrisburg Pike	Carlisle	PA	17013	**800-735-3136**	717-243-5757	769
Daily Gate City 1016 Main St	Keokuk	IA	52632	**800-779-8819**	319-524-8300	522-2
Daily Gazette 2345 Maxon Rd Ext.	Schenectady	NY	12308	**800-262-2211**	518-374-4141	522-2
Daily Globe 300 11th St	Worthington	MN	56187	**800-642-3243**	507-376-9711	522-2
Daily Grill 11661 San Vincente Blvd Suite 404	Los Angeles	CA	90049	**888-999-9156**	310-820-5559	657
Daily Herald 1067 Pennsylvania Ave PO Box 246	Tyrone	PA	16686	**800-524-7108**	814-684-4000	522-2
Daily Herald 1555 N Freedom Blvd	Provo	UT	84604	**800-880-8075**	801-373-5050	522-2
Daily Iberian 926 E Main St	New Iberia	LA	70560	**800-365-6773**	337-365-6773	522-2
Daily Independent 224 17th St	Ashland	KY	41105	**800-955-5860**	606-326-2600	522-2
Daily Item 200 Market St PO Box 607	Sunbury	PA	17801	**800-792-2303**	570-286-5671	522-2
Daily Jefferson County Union 28 W Milwaukee Ave PO Box 801	Fort Atkinson	WI	53538	**800-236-1013**	920-563-5553	522-2
Daily Journal 8 Dearborn Sq	Kankakee	IL	60901	**800-892-1861**	815-937-3300	522-2
Daily Journal 2575 N Morton St	Franklin	IN	46131	**888-736-7101**	317-736-7101	522-2
Daily Journal 1513 St Joe Dr	Park Hills	MO	63601	**800-660-8166**	573-431-2010	522-2
Daily Journal 891 E Oak Rd	Vineland	NJ	08360	**800-222-0104**	856-691-5000	522-2
Daily Journal Corp 915 E 1st St *NASDAQ: DJCO*	Los Angeles	CA	90012	**800-788-7840**	213-229-5300	623-8
Daily Juice Products 1 Daily Way	Verona	PA	15147	**800-245-2929**	412-828-9020	291-20
Daily Leader 128 N Railroad Ave PO Box 551	Brookhaven	MS	39602	**800-833-6961**	601-833-6961	522-2
Daily Local News 250 N Bradford Ave	West Chester	PA	19382	**800-456-6397**	610-696-1775	522-2
Daily Messenger 73 Buffalo St	Canandaigua	NY	14424	**800-724-2099**	585-394-0770	522-2
Daily Mining Gazette 206 Sheldon Ave	Houghton	MI	49931	**800-682-7607**	906-482-1500	522-2
Daily Mountain Eagle 1301 Viking Dr	Jasper	AL	35502	**800-518-6397**	205-221-2840	522-2
Daily News 813 Center St PO Box 90012	Bowling Green	KY	42102	**800-599-6397**	270-781-1700	522-2
Daily News PO Box 340	Greenville	MI	48838	**800-968-9301**	616-754-9301	522-2
Daily News 215 E Ludington St PO Box 460	Iron Mountain	MI	49801	**800-743-2088**	906-774-2772	522-2
Daily News 2 Apollo Dr PO Box 870	Batavia	NY	14021	**888-217-6397**	585-343-8000	522-2
Daily News 724 Bell Fork Rd PO Box 196	Jacksonville	NC	28541	**800-659-2873**	910-353-1171	522-2
Daily News PO Box 760	Wahpeton	ND	58074	**800-666-4492**	701-642-8585	522-2
Daily News 325 Penn St	Huntingdon	PA	16652	**800-634-5692**	814-643-4040	522-2
Daily News 770 11th Ave	Longview	WA	98632	**800-341-4745**	360-577-2500	522-2
Daily News 34 Courtney St PO Box 778	Rhinelander	WI	54501	**888-886-8135**	715-365-6397	522-2
Daily News 100 S 6th Ave PO Box 478	West Bend	WI	53095	**800-924-3142**	262-306-5000	522-2
Daily News of Los Angeles 21221 Oxnard St	Woodland Hills	CA	91367	**800-346-6397**	818-713-3000	522-2
Daily News-Tribune 254 Beckon Ave	Needham	MA	02494	**800-982-4023**	781-647-7898	522-2
Daily Nonpareil 535 W Broadway Suite 300	Council Bluffs	IA	51503	**800-283-1882**	712-328-1811	522-2
Daily Press 13891 Park Ave PO Box 1389	Victorville	CA	92393	**800-553-2006**	760-241-7744	522-2
Daily Press 600 Ludington St	Escanaba	MI	49829	**800-743-0609**	906-786-2021	522-2
Daily Racing Form 100 Broadway 7th Fl *Cust Svc	New York	NY	10005	**800-306-3676***	212-366-7600	449-14
Daily Record 212 E Liberty St PO Box 918	Wooster	OH	44691	**800-686-2958**	330-264-1125	522-2
Daily Record Co 11 E Saratoga St	Baltimore	MD	21202	**800-296-8181**	410-752-3849	623-8
Daily Reflector PO Box 1967	Greenville	NC	27835	**800-849-6166**	252-752-6166	522-2
Daily Reflector Inc PO Box 1967	Greenville	NC	27835	**800-849-6166**	252-752-6166	623-8
Daily Register 35 S Vine St PO Box 248	Harrisburg	IL	62946	**800-283-8117**	618-253-7146	522-2
Daily Register PO Box 470	Portage	WI	53901	**800-236-2110**	608-742-2111	522-2
Daily Report for Executives Newsletter 1231 25th St NW	Washington	DC	20037	**800-372-1033**	202-452-4262	521-2
Daily Reporter 310 E Milwaukee St PO Box 197	Spencer	IA	51301	**800-383-0964**	712-262-6610	522-2
Daily Review 22533 Foothill Blvd	Hayward	CA	94541	**800-595-9595**	510-783-6111	522-2
Daily Review 116 Main St	Towanda	PA	18848	**800-253-3662**	570-265-2151	522-2
Daily Rocket-Miner 215 D St PO Box 98	Rock Springs	WY	82902	**888-443-3736**	307-362-3736	522-2
Daily Sparks Tribune 1002 C St	Sparks	NV	89431	**800-669-1338**	775-358-8061	522-2
Daily Standard 123 E Market St	Celina	OH	45822	**877-525-3680**	419-586-2371	522-2
Daily Star 102 Chestnut St PO Box 250	Oneonta	NY	13820	**800-721-1000**	607-432-1000	522-2
Daily Sun 1153 Main St	The Villages	FL	32159	**800-726-6592**	352-753-1119	522-4
Daily Telegram 133 N Winter St	Adrian	MI	49221	**800-968-5111**	517-265-5111	522-2
Daily Times 115 E Carroll St	Salisbury	MD	21801	**877-335-6278**	410-749-7171	522-2
Daily Times 201 N Allen Ave	Farmington	NM	87401	**800-395-6397**	505-325-4545	522-2
Daily Times-Call 350 Terry St	Longmont	CO	80501	**800-796-8201**	303-776-2244	522-2
Daily Times Herald 508 N Court St	Carroll	IA	51401	**800-262-5495**	712-792-3573	522-2
Daily Tribune 210 E 3rd St	Royal Oak	MI	48067	**877-373-2387**	248-541-3000	522-2
Daily Tribune 220 1st Ave S	Wisconsin Rapids	WI	54495	**800-362-8315**	715-423-7200	522-2
Daily Union 222 W 6th St PO Box 129	Junction City	KS	66441	**800-657-6096**	785-762-5000	522-2
Daily World 315 S Michigan St	Aberdeen	WA	98520	**800-829-7880**	360-532-4000	522-2
DaimlerChrysler Canada Inc PO Box 1621 Stn A	Windsor	ON	N9A4H6	**800-265-6904**	519-973-2000	59
DaimlerChrysler Corp 1000 Chrysler Dr *NYSE: DCX*	Auburn Hills	MI	48326	**800-992-1997**	248-576-5741	59
DaimlerChrysler Corp Dodge Div 1000 Chrysler Dr *Cust Svc	Auburn Hills	MI	48326	**800-992-1997***	248-576-5741	59
DaimlerChrysler Corp Eagle Div 800 Chrysler Dr E. *Cust Svc	Auburn Hills	MI	48326	**800-992-1997***	248-576-5741	59
DaimlerChrysler Corp Jeep Div 800 Chrysler Dr E. *Cust Svc	Auburn Hills	MI	48326	**800-992-1997***	248-576-5741	59
DaimlerChrysler Corp Plymouth Div 800 Chrysler Dr E. *Cust Svc	Auburn Hills	MI	48326	**800-992-1997***	248-576-5741	59
Dairy Assn Co Inc 91 Williams St	Lyndonville	VT	05851	**800-232-3610**	802-626-3610	574
Dairy Council Digest 10255 W Higgins Rd Suite 900 *Cust Svc	Rosemont	IL	60018	**800-426-8271***	847-803-2000	521-8
Dairy Farmers of America Inc 10220 N Ambassador Dr Northpointe Tower	Kansas City	MO	64153	**888-332-6455**	816-801-6455	291-5
Dairy Herd Management Magazine 10901 W 84th Terr.	Shawnee Mission	KS	66201	**800-255-5113**	913-438-8700	449-1
Dairy One 730 Warren Rd	Ithaca	NY	14850	**800-344-2697**	607-257-1272	12-2
Dairyland Greyhound Park 5522 104th Ave	Kenosha	WI	53144	**800-233-3357**	262-657-8200	628
Dairylea Co-op Inc 5001 Brittonfield Pkwy	East Syracuse	NY	13057	**800-654-8838**	315-433-0100	292-4

Name	Address	City	State	ZIP	Toll-Free	Phone	Class
Dairymen's Feed & Supply Co-op	323 E Washington St	Petaluma	CA	94952	**800-862-4699**	707-763-1585	438
Dairymen's Milk Co	3068 W 106th St	Cleveland	OH	44111	**800-944-2301**	216-671-2300	291-27
Daishowa America Co Ltd	PO Box 271 *Sales	Port Angeles	WA	98362	**800-331-6314***	360-457-4474	624
Daisy Mfg Co Inc	400 W Stribling Dr	Rogers	AR	72756	**800-643-3458**	479-636-1200	701
Daisy Wheel Ribbon Co Inc	10742 Edison Ct	Rancho Cucamonga	CA	91730	**800-266-5585**	909-989-5585	578
Daiwa Corp	12851 Midway Pl	Cerritos	CA	90703	**800-736-4653**	562-802-9589	701
Dake Div JSJ Corp	724 Robbins Rd	Grand Haven	MI	49417	**800-846-3253**	616-842-7110	346
Dakin LLC	32942 Lyons Ave Suite 215 *Cust Svc	Newhall	CA	91321	**800-777-6990***	661-222-9900	750
DakoCytomation	6392 Via Real *Cust Svc	Carpinteria	CA	93013	**800-400-3256***	805-566-6655	229
Dakota Brands International	2121 13th St NE	Jamestown	ND	58401	**800-844-5073**	701-252-5073	291-1
Dakota Central Telecommunications Co-op	630 5th St N	Carrington	ND	58421	**800-771-0974**	701-652-3184	721
Dakota Drug Inc	28 Main St N	Minot	ND	58703	**800-437-2018**	701-852-2141	237
Dakota Electric Assn	4300 220th St W	Farmington	MN	55024	**800-874-3409**	651-463-6212	244
Dakota Energy Co-op Inc	40294 US Hwy 14 PO Box 830	Huron	SD	57350	**800-353-8591**	605-352-8591	244
Dakota Granite Co	14964 484th Ave PO Box 1351	Milbank	SD	57252	**800-843-3333**	605-432-5580	710
Dakota Homestead Title Insurance Co	315 S Phillips Ave	Sioux Falls	SD	57104	**800-425-0388**	605-336-0388	384-6
Dakota Imaging Inc	7130 Minstrel Way	Columbia	MD	21045	**800-833-3137**	410-381-3113	39
Dakota Marble Inc	902 W 19th St	Yankton	SD	57078	**800-697-7241**	605-665-7241	710
Dakota Mfg Co Inc	1909 S Rowley St	Mitchell	SD	57301	**800-232-5682**	605-996-5571	768
Dakota Smith Signature Eyewear	498 N Oak St	Inglewood	CA	90302	**800-765-3937**	310-330-2700	531
Dakota State University	820 N Washington Ave	Madison	SD	57042	**888-378-9988**	605-256-5139	163
Dakota Supply Group	2601 3rd Ave N	Fargo	ND	58102	**800-437-4702**	701-237-9440	245
Dakota Valley Electric Co-op	7296 Hwy 281	Edgeley	ND	58433	**800-342-4671**	701-493-2281	244
Dakota Wesleyan University	1200 W University Ave	Mitchell	SD	57301	**800-333-8506**	605-995-2600	163
DAKOTACARE	1323 S Minnesota Ave	Sioux Falls	SD	57105	**800-325-5598**	605-334-4000	384-3
Dakotah Direct Inc	9317 E Sinto Ave	Spokane	WA	99206	**800-433-3633**	509-789-4500	722
Dakotah Inc	530 Park Ln *Cust Svc	Webster	SD	57274	**800-261-1315***	605-345-4646	731
Daktronics Inc	331 32nd Ave *NASDAQ: DAKT*	Brookings	SD	57006	**800-843-9878**	605-697-4300	171-4
Dal-Tile International Inc	7834 Hawn Fwy	Dallas	TX	75217	**800-933-8453**	214-398-1411	736
Dale Laboratories	2960 Simms St	Hollywood	FL	33020	**800-327-1776**	954-925-0103	577
Dalhart Consumers Fuel Assn Inc	PO Box 610	Dalhart	TX	79022	**800-249-5695**	806-249-5695	271
Dali Salvador Museum	1000 3rd St S	Saint Petersburg	FL	33701	**800-442-3254**	727-823-3767	509
Dalis HL Inc	35-35 24th St	Long Island City	NY	11106	**800-453-2547**	718-361-1100	245
Dallas Area Rapid Transit Authority (DART)	PO Box 660163	Dallas	TX	75266	**888-557-6669**	214-749-3278	460
Dallas Baptist University	3000 Mountain Creek Pkwy	Dallas	TX	75211	**800-460-1328**	214-333-7100	163
Dallas Christian College	2700 Christian Pkwy	Dallas	TX	75234	**800-688-1029**	972-241-3371	163
Dallas Convention Center	650 S Griffin St	Dallas	TX	75202	**877-850-2100**	214-939-2700	204
Dallas Convention & Visitors Bureau	325 N Saint Paul St Suite 700	Dallas	TX	75201	**800-232-5527**	214-571-1000	205
Dallas-Fort Worth International Airport (DFW)		Dallas	TX	75261	**800-762-0238**	972-574-8888	28
Dallas Johnson Greenhouse Inc	2802 Twin City Dr	Council Bluffs	IA	51501	**800-445-4794**	712-366-0407	363
Dallas Market Center	2100 Stemmons Fwy Suite MS 150	Dallas	TX	75207	**800-325-6587**		204
Dallas & Mavis Specialized Carrier Co	625 55th St	Kenosha	WI	53140	**888-878-2504**		769
Dallas Morning News	508 Young St	Dallas	TX	75202	**800-431-0010**	214-977-8222	522-2
Dallas World Trade Center	2100 Stemmons Fwy	Dallas	TX	75207	**800-325-6587**	214-655-6100	810
Dalles Chronicle	315 Federal St	The Dalles	OR	97058	**800-375-7832**	541-296-2141	522-2
Dalton Auction Co Inc	PO Box 1462	Dalton	GA	30722	**888-249-5831**	706-278-7441	51
Dalton Enterprises Inc	131 Willow St	Cheshire	CT	06410	**800-851-5606**	203-272-3221	46
Dalton Gear Co	212 Colfax Ave N	Minneapolis	MN	55405	**800-328-7485**	612-374-2150	700
Dalton State College	213 N College Dr	Dalton	GA	30720	**800-829-4436**	706-272-4436	160
Daltons Best Maid Products Inc	1400 S Riverside Dr	Fort Worth	TX	76104	**800-447-3581**	817-335-5494	291-19
Daly Computers Inc	22521 Gateway Center Dr	Clarksburg	MD	20871	**800-955-3259**	301-670-0381	174
Daly MJ & Sons Inc	110 Mattatuck Heights	Waterbury	CT	06705	**800-992-3603**	203-753-5131	188-13
Damascus Bakery Inc	56 Gold St	Brooklyn	NY	11201	**800-367-7482**	718-855-1457	69
Damon Industries Inc	PO Box 2120	Alliance	OH	44601	**800-362-9850**	330-821-5310	149
Damon's International Inc	4645 Executive Dr	Columbus	OH	43220	**800-226-7427**	614-442-7900	657
Damrow Co	PO Box 750	Fond du Lac	WI	54936	**800-236-1501**	920-922-1500	537
Dan Hill & Assoc Inc DBA Flow Boy Mfg	PO Box 720660	Norman	OK	73070	**800-580-3260**	405-329-3765	768
Dan Schantz Farm & Greenhouses LLC	8025 Spinnerstown Rd	Zionsville	PA	18092	**800-451-3064**	610-967-2181	363
Dana College	2848 College Dr	Blair	NE	68008	**800-444-3262**	402-426-9000	163
Dana Design	19215 Vashon Hwy SW	Vashon	WA	98070	**888-357-3262**	206-463-3631	701
Dana-Farber Cancer Institute	44 Binney St	Boston	MA	02115	**800-757-3324**	617-632-3000	366-5
Dana Kepner Co Inc	700 Alcott St	Denver	CO	80204	**800-332-3079**	303-623-6161	601
Dana Point Chamber of Commerce	24681 La Plaza Suite 115	Dana Point	CA	92629	**800-290-4262**	949-496-1555	137

Name	Address	City	State	ZIP	Toll-Free	Phone	Class
Dana Transport Inc	210 Essex Ave E	Avenel	NJ	07001	**800-733-3262**	732-750-9100	769
Danafilms Inc	5 Otis St PO Box 624	Westborough	MA	01581	**800-634-8289**	508-366-8884	589
Danaher Controls	1675 Delany Rd	Gurnee	IL	60031	**800-873-8731**	847-662-2666	486
Danaher Motion	1500 Mittel Blvd	Wood Dale	IL	60191	**866-993-2624**	630-860-7300	507
Danbury Hospital	24 Hospital Ave	Danbury	CT	06810	**800-284-3262**	203-797-7000	366-2
Dance. American Alliance for Health Physical Education Recreation &	1900 Association Dr	Reston	VA	20191	**800-213-7193**	703-476-3400	48-22
Dance Magazine	333 7th Ave 11th Fl	New York	NY	10001	**800-331-1750**	212-979-4814	449-9
Dance Teacher Magazine	250 W 57th St Suite 420	New York	NY	10107	**800-362-6765**		449-8
Dancker Sellew & Douglas	100 Broadway 5th Fl	New York	NY	10005	**800-326-2537**	212-267-2200	315
Danco Industries Inc	PO Box 948	Westfield	MA	01086	**800-225-7960**	413-568-0980	538
Danfords Inn Marina & Conference Center	25 E Broadway	Port Jefferson	NY	11777	**800-332-6367**	631-928-5200	655
Danforth John W Co	2100 Colvin Blvd	Tonawanda	NY	14150	**800-888-6119**	716-832-1940	188-10
D'Angelo Sandwich Shops	600 Providence Hwy	Dedham	MA	02026	**800-727-2446**	781-461-1200	657
Dangerous Goods Advisory Council (DGAC)	1100 H St NW Suite 740	Washington	DC	20005	**800-634-1598**	202-289-4550	49-21
Daniel Boone Regional Library	100 W Broadway	Columbia	MO	65203	**800-324-4806**	573-443-3161	426
Daniel Edward W Co Inc	11700 Harvard Ave *Cust Svc	Cleveland	OH	44105	**800-338-2658***	216-295-2750	345
Daniel Lumber Co Inc	309 Pierce St PO Box 340	LaGrange	GA	30241	**800-251-0398**	706-884-5686	541
Daniel Weaver Co	PO Box 525	Lebanon	PA	17042	**800-932-8377**	717-274-6100	291-26
Daniel Webster College	20 University Dr	Nashua	NH	03063	**800-325-6876**	603-577-6000	163
Daniel & Yeager	6767 Old Madison Pike Suite 690	Huntsville	AL	35806	**800-955-1919**	256-551-1070	262
Daniele Hotel	216 N Meramec Ave	Clayton	MO	63105	**800-325-8302**	314-721-0101	373
Danisco Cultor USA	411 E Gano PO Box 470489	Saint Louis	MO	63147	**800-851-8100**	314-436-3133	291-15
Danisco Ingredients USA Inc	201 New Century Pkwy	New Century	KS	66031	**800-255-6837**	913-764-8100	291-37
Danka Office Imaging Co Inc	7940 Marshall Dr	Lenexa	KS	66214	**800-336-4323**	913-495-5000	113
Dan'l Webster Inn	149 Main St	Sandwich	MA	02563	**800-444-3566**	508-888-3622	373
Danline Inc	1 Silver Ct	Springfield	NJ	07081	**800-552-7874**	973-376-1000	104
Danly IEM	6779 Engle Rd Suite F	Middleburg Heights	OH	44130	**800-243-2659**	440-239-7600	745
Danly IEM Punchrite Div	16065 Industrial Ln SW	Cleveland	OH	44135	**800-232-2659**	216-267-1444	745
Dann Dee Display Fixtures Inc	7555 N Caldwell Ave	Niles	IL	60714	**800-888-8515**	847-588-1600	281
Dann Insurance	1500 S Lakeside Dr	Bannockburn	IL	60015	**800-323-0371**	847-444-1060	383
Danner Shoe Mfg Co	18550 NE Riverside Pkwy	Portland	OR	97230	**800-345-0430**	503-251-1100	296
Dannon Co	120 White Plains Rd	Tarrytown	NY	10591	**800-321-2174**	914-366-9700	291-27
Danone Waters of North America Inc	3280 E Foothill Blvd	Pasadena	CA	91107	**800-492-8377**	626-585-1000	792
Danos & Curole Marine Contractors Inc	PO Box 1460	Larose	LA	70373	**800-487-5971**	985-693-3313	528
Dansk International Designs Ltd	100 Lenox Dr *Cust Svc	Lawrenceville	NJ	08648	**800-293-2675***	609-896-2800	716
Danville Area Chamber of Commerce	28 W North St	Danville	IL	61832	**800-373-6201**	217-442-1887	137
Danville Area Community College	2000 E Main St	Danville	IL	61832	**888-455-3222**	217-443-3222	160
Danville News	14 E Mahoning St	Danville	PA	17821	**800-792-2303**	570-275-3235	522-2
Danville State Hospital	200 State Hospital Dr	Danville	PA	17821	**888-796-3476**	570-271-4500	366-3
Daou Systems Inc	412 Creamery Way Suite 300	Exton	PA	19341	**800-578-3268**	610-594-2700	178
DAP Inc	2400 Boston St Suite 200 *Cust Svc	Baltimore	MD	21224	**800-584-3840***	410-675-2100	3
DAP Technologies Corp	5525 W Cypress St Suite 205	Tampa	FL	33607	**800-229-2822**	813-969-3271	171-2
Dapper Tire Co Inc	4025 Lockridge St	San Diego	CA	92102	**800-266-7172**	619-266-1397	740
Dar-Ran Furniture Industries	2402 Shore St	High Point	NC	27263	**800-334-7891**	336-861-2400	314-1
Dar-tech Inc	16485 Rockside Rd	Cleveland	OH	44137	**800-228-7347**	216-663-7600	144
Darby Edward J & Son Inc	PO Box 50049	Philadelphia	PA	19133	**800-875-6374**	215-236-2203	676
Darby Group Cos Inc	300 Jericho Quad	Jericho	NY	11753	**800-468-1001**	516-683-1800	572
Darby Printing Co	6215 Purdue Dr	Atlanta	GA	30336	**800-241-5292**	404-344-2665	614
Dard Products Inc	912 Custer Ave	Evanston	IL	60202	**800-323-2925**	847-328-5000	10
Dardanelle & Russellville Railroad Co	4416 S Arkansas Ave	Russellville	AR	72802	**800-530-7526**	479-968-6455	634
Dare Products Inc	PO Box 157	Battle Creek	MI	49016	**800-922-3273**	269-965-2307	275
Darex	62 Whittemore Ave	Cambridge	MA	02140	**800-232-6100**	617-498-4571	3
Darex Corp	PO Box 277	Ashland	OR	97520	**800-547-0222**	541-488-2224	447
Darice Inc	13000 Darice Pkwy	Strongsville	OH	44149	**800-321-1494**	440-238-9150	44
Darigold Farms of Montana	PO Box 968	Bozeman	MT	59771	**800-321-4563**	406-586-5426	292-4
Dark Horse Comics Inc	10956 SE Main St	Milwaukie	OR	97222	**800-862-0052**	503-652-8815	623-3
Darke Rural Electric Co-op Inc	1120 Fort Jefferson Rd	Greenville	OH	45331	**800-776-5612**	937-548-4114	244
Darling LA Co	1401 Hwy 49B	Paragould	AR	72450	**800-643-3499**	870-239-9564	281
Darling International Inc	251 O'Connor Ridge Blvd Suite 300 *AMEX: DAR*	Irving	TX	75038	**800-800-4841**	972-717-0300	291-12
Darlington School	1014 Cave Spring Rd	Rome	GA	30161	**800-368-4437**	706-235-6051	611
Darlington Veneer Co Inc	PO Box 1087	Darlington	SC	29540	**800-845-2388**	843-393-3861	602
D'Arrigo Brothers Co of Massachusetts Inc	105 New England Produce Ctr	Chelsea	MA	02150	**800-327-7446**	617-884-0316	292-7

Name / Address	City	State	ZIP	Toll-Free	Phone	Class
D'Arrigo Brothers Co of New York Inc 315 NYC Terminal Market	Bronx	NY	10474	**800-223-8080**	718-991-5900	292-7
Darrow Russ Group W133 N8569 Executive Pkwy	Menomonee Falls	WI	53051	**800-732-7769**	262-250-9600	57
DART (Dallas Area Rapid Transit Authority) PO Box 660163	Dallas	TX	75266	**888-557-6669**	214-749-3278	460
Dart Assn. National 5613 W 74th St	Indianapolis	IN	46278	**800-808-9884**	317-387-1299	48-22
Dart Container Corp 500 Hogsback Rd	Mason	MI	48854	**800-248-5960**	517-676-3800	590
Dart Mfg Co Inc 4012 Bronze Way	Dallas	TX	75237	**800-345-3278**	214-333-4221	523
Dart Transit Co Inc PO Box 64110	Saint Paul	MN	55164	**800-366-9000**	651-688-2000	769
Dart Warehouse Corp 1430 S Eastman Ave	Los Angeles	CA	90023	**800-963-3278**	323-264-1011	790-1
Dartek Computer Supply Corp 175 Ambassador Dr	Naperville	IL	60540	**800-553-8223**	630-355-3000	177
Dartmouth Medical School 1 Rope Ferry Rd	Dartmouth	NH	03755	**877-367-1797**	603-650-1200	164-2
Darton College 2400 Gillionville Rd	Albany	GA	31707	**866-775-1214**	229-430-6742	160
Darue of California Inc 14102 S Broadway	Los Angeles	CA	90059	**800-733-3375**	310-323-1350	153-21
Darvin Furniture 15400 La Grange Rd	Orland Park	IL	60462	**800-232-7846**	708-460-4100	316
Darwin D Martin House. Frank Lloyd Wright's 125 Jewett Pkwy	Buffalo	NY	14214	**877-377-3858**	716-856-3858	50
Darwin Magazine 492 Old Connecticut Path PO Box 9208	Framingham	MA	01701	**800-942-4672**	508-872-0080	449-7
Dasco Pro Inc 340 Blackhawk Park Ave	Rockford	IL	61104	**800-327-2690**	815-962-3727	746
Dash Tours 1024 Winnipeg St	Regina	SK	S4R8P8	**800-265-0000**	306-352-2222	748
Dashiell Corp PO Box 1300	Deer Park	TX	77536	**800-736-6400**	281-479-7407	188-4
Dassault Falcon 191 N DuPont Hwy New Castle County Airport	New Castle	DE	19720	**800-441-9390**	302-322-7000	63
Data Access Corp 14000 SW 119th Ave	Miami	FL	33186	**800-451-3539**	305-238-0012	176-2
Data Control Systems 213 Perry Pkwy	Gaithersburg	MD	20877	**800-296-3333**	301-590-3300	247
Data Description Inc 840 Hanshaw Rd 2nd Fl	Ithaca	NY	14850	**800-573-5121**	607-257-1000	176-5
Data Device Corp 105 Wilbur Pl *Cust Svc	Bohemia	NY	11716	**800-332-5757***	631-567-5600	252
Data Exchange Corp 3600 Via Pescador	Camarillo	CA	93012	**800-237-7911**	805-388-1711	173
Data Impressions Inc 13180 Paramount Blvd	South Gate	CA	90280	**800-677-3031**	562-630-8788	172
Data I/O Corp 10525 Willows Rd NE *NASDAQ: DAIO*	Redmond	WA	98052	**800-426-1045**	425-881-6444	685
Data Label Inc 1000 Spruce St	Terre Haute	IN	47807	**800-457-0676**	812-232-0408	404
Data Management Inc 537 New Britain Ave *Orders	Farmington	CT	06034	**800-243-1969***	860-677-8586	87
Data Papers Inc 95 Line Bluff Rd	Muncy	PA	17756	**800-233-3032**	570-546-2201	111
Data Pro Accounting Software Inc 150 2nd Ave N 16th Fl	Saint Petersburg	FL	33701	**800-237-6377**	727-803-1500	176-1
Data Processing Associates. Black 6301 Ivy Ln Suite 700	Greenbelt	MD	20770	**800-727-2372**	301-220-2180	48-9
Data Return LLC 222 W Las Colinas Blvd Suite 350E	Irving	TX	75039	**800-767-1514**	972-869-0770	178
Data Sales Co Inc 3450 W Burnsville Pkwy	Burnsville	MN	55337	**800-328-2730**	952-890-8838	172
Data Source Inc 1400 Universal Ave	Kansas City	MO	64120	**800-829-3369**	816-483-3282	111
Data Technology Inc 260-J Fordham Rd	Wilmington	MA	01887	**800-331-5797**	978-694-0055	537
Data Translation Inc 100 Locke Dr	Marlborough	MA	01752	**800-525-8528**	508-481-3700	613
Data Transmission Network Corp 9110 W Dodge Rd Suite 200	Omaha	NE	68114	**800-485-4000**	402-390-2328	380
DataCard Corp 11111 Bren Rd W	Minnetonka	MN	55343	**800-328-8623**	952-933-1223	695
DataCert Inc 3100 Timmons Suite 310	Houston	TX	77027	**800-770-5121**	713-572-3282	176-10
Datacolor 5 Princess Rd	Lawrenceville	NJ	08648	**800-433-1885**	609-924-2189	410
DataDirect Networks 9320 Lurline Ave	Chatsworth	CA	91311	**888-438-6768**	818-700-7600	171-8
DataDirect Technologies 3202 Tower Oaks Blvd Suite 300	Rockville	MD	20852	**800-876-3101**	301-468-8501	176-12
Dataforth Corp 3331 E Hemisphere Loop	Tucson	AZ	85706	**800-444-7644**	520-741-1404	496
Datalink Corp 8170 Upland Cir *NASDAQ: DTLK*	Chanhassen	MN	55317	**800-448-6314**	952-944-3462	171-8
Datalux Corp 155 Aviation Dr	Winchester	VA	22602	**800-328-2589**	540-662-1500	171-3
Datamann Inc 1994 Hartford Ave	Wilder	VT	05088	**800-451-4263**	802-295-6600	176-11
Datamatics Management Services Inc 330 New Brunswick Ave	Fords	NJ	08863	**800-673-0366**	732-738-9600	176-1
Datamax Corp 4501 Parkway Commerce Blvd	Orlando	FL	32808	**800-321-2233**	407-578-8007	171-6
Datamax Office Systems Inc 6717 Waldemar Ave	Saint Louis	MO	63139	**800-325-9299**	314-647-2500	113
DataMirror Corp 3100 Steeles Ave E Suite 1100 *NASDAQ: DMCX*	Markham	ON	L3R8T3	**800-362-5955**	905-415-0310	176-12
DataNational 3800 Concorde Pkwy Suite 500	Chantilly	VA	20151	**800-888-7823**	703-818-0120	623-6
Datanautics Inc 2953 Bunker Hill Ln Suite 100	Santa Clara	CA	95054	**888-422-2783**	408-350-1300	176-1
DataPipe 80 River St	Hoboken	NJ	07030	**877-773-3306**	201-792-4847	795
Dataram Corp 186 Rt 571 *NASDAQ: DRAM*	West Windsor	NJ	08550	**800-328-2726**	609-799-0071	613
DataRealm Internet Services LLC PO Box 726	Glassboro	NJ	08028	**877-227-3783**	602-850-4044	795
Datascope Corp 14 Philips Pkwy *NASDAQ: DSCP*	Montvale	NJ	07645	**800-288-2121**	201-391-8100	249
DataServ LLC 12825 Flushing Meadows Dr Suite 100	Saint Louis	MO	63131	**877-700-3282**	314-842-1155	39

Name / Address	City	State	ZIP	Toll-Free	Phone	Class
Datashare Corp 9485 Priority Way W Dr	Indianapolis	IN	46240	**800-228-5465**	317-569-7485	178
Datastream Systems Inc 50 Datastream Plaza *NASDAQ: DSTM*	Greenville	SC	29605	**800-955-6775**	864-422-5001	176-10
Datastrip Inc 211 Welsh Pool Rd Suite 100	Exton	PA	19341	**800-548-2517**	610-594-6130	85
Datatec Systems Inc 1275 Alderman Dr *NASDAQ: DATC*	Alpharetta	GA	30005	**800-631-2524**	770-667-8488	178
Datatech Depot 1371 N Miller St	Anaheim	CA	92806	**800-888-8181**	714-996-7500	173
Datatel Inc 4375 Fair Lakes Ct	Fairfax	VA	22033	**800-328-2835**	703-968-9000	176-10
Datatel Resources Corp 1729 Pennsylvania Ave	Monaca	PA	15061	**800-245-2688**	724-775-5300	111
DataTrace Investigations Inc PO Box 95322	South Jordan	UT	84095	**800-748-5335**	801-253-2400	392
Datavision & Devices PO Box 7445	Charlottesville	VA	22906	**800-237-5658**	434-977-0651	523
DataViz Inc 612 Wheelers Farms Rd	Milford	CT	06460	**800-733-0030**	203-874-0085	176-12
Dataware Div Art Style Printing Inc 7570 Renwick Dr	Houston	TX	77081	**800-426-4844**	713-432-1023	404
Datawatch Corp 175 Cabot St Suite 503 *NASDAQ: DWCH*	Lowell	MA	01854	**800-445-3311**	978-441-2200	176-12
DataWave Systems Inc 13575 Commerce Pkwy Suite 110	Richmond	BC	V6V2L1	**888-388-7031**	604-295-1800	721
DataWorld Inc 7700 Old Georgetown Rd Bldg 2 Box 1	Bethesda	MD	20814	**800-368-5754**	301-652-8822	380
Datel Inc 11 Cabot Blvd	Mansfield	MA	02048	**800-233-2765**	508-339-3000	252
Datron World Communications Inc 3030 Enterprise Ct *Sales	Vista	CA	92081	**800-405-0744***	760-734-5454	633
DATTCO Inc 583 South St	New Britain	CT	06051	**800-229-4879**	860-229-4878	108
DATTCO Inc School Bus Div 583 South St	New Britain	CT	06051	**800-229-4879**	860-229-4878	110
Datum Filing Systems Inc 89 Church Rd	Emigsville	PA	17318	**800-828-8018**	717-764-6350	281
Daum Commercial Real Estate Services 4675 McArthur Ct Suite 220	Newport Beach	CA	92660	**888-659-3286**	949-724-1900	638
Dauphin County 2 S 2nd St	Harrisburg	PA	17101	**800-328-0058**	717-780-6300	334
Dauphin Graphic Machines Inc PO Box 573	Elizabethville	PA	17023	**800-346-6119**	717-362-3243	617
Dauphin North America 300 Myrtle Ave *Cust Svc	Boonton	NJ	07005	**800-631-1186***	973-263-1100	314-1
Dauphine Orleans Hotel 415 Dauphine St	New Orleans	LA	70112	**800-521-7111**	504-586-1800	373
DAV (Disabled American Veterans) 3725 Alexandria Pike	Cold Spring	KY	41076	**877-426-2838**	859-441-7300	48-19
Dav El Chauffeured Transportation Network 200 2nd St	Chelsea	MA	02150	**800-922-0343**	617-887-0900	433
DavCo Restaurants Inc 1657 Crofton Blvd	Crofton	MD	21114	**800-523-1411**	410-721-3770	656
Dave & Buster's Inc 2481 Manana Dr *NYSE: DAB*	Dallas	TX	75220	**800-842-5369**	214-357-9588	645
Dave Thomas Foundation for Adoption 4288 W Dublin Granville Rd	Dublin	OH	43017	**800-275-3832**	614-764-8454	300
Davel Communications Inc 200 Public Sq Suite 700	Cleveland	OH	44114	**800-333-9920**	216-241-2555	721
Davenport & Co LLC 901 E Cary St	Richmond	VA	23219	**800-846-6666**	804-780-2000	679
Davenport Hotel 10 S Post St	Spokane	WA	99201	**800-899-1482**	509-455-8888	373
Davenport Industries LLC 167 Ames St	Rochester	NY	14611	**800-344-5748**	585-235-4545	447
Davenport Insulation Inc 7400 Gateway Ct	Manassas	VA	20109	**800-328-9485**	703-631-7744	188-9
Davenport JT & Sons Inc PO Box 1105 *Cust Svc	Sanford	NC	27331	**800-868-7550***	919-774-9444	292-8
Davenport University						
Grand Rapids Campus 415 E Fulton St	Grand Rapids	MI	49503	**800-632-9569**	616-451-3511	163
Lansing Campus 220 E Kalamazoo St	Lansing	MI	48933	**800-686-1600**	517-484-2600	163
Warren Campus 27650 Dequindre Rd	Warren	MI	48092	**800-724-7708**	586-558-8700	163
Davey Tree Expert Co 1500 N Mantua St	Kent	OH	44240	**800-445-8733**	330-673-9511	765
Davey Tree Surgery Co Inc PO Box 5015	Livermore	CA	94551	**800-972-5261**	925-443-1723	765
David Brown Union Pumps Co 4600 W Dickman Rd	Battle Creek	MI	49015	**800-877-7867**	269-966-4600	627
David Clark Co Inc 360 Franklin St *Cust Svc	Worcester	MA	01615	**800-298-6235***	508-751-5800	385
David Evans & Assoc Inc 2100 SW River Pkwy	Portland	OR	97201	**800-721-1916**	503-223-6663	258
David H Fell & Co Inc 6009 Bandini Blvd	Commerce	CA	90040	**800-822-1996**	323-722-9992	399
David Industries Inc Petrotherm Div 4122 E Chapman Ave Suite 10	Orange	CA	92869	**888-468-8645**	714-744-9234	526
David L Babson & Co Inc 1 Memorial Dr Suite 1100	Cambridge	MA	02142	**877-766-0014**	617-225-3800	393
David L Lawrence Convention Center 1000 Fort Duquesne Blvd	Pittsburgh	PA	15222	**800-222-5200**	412-565-6000	204
David Michael & Co Inc 10801 Decatur Rd	Philadelphia	PA	19154	**800-523-3806**	215-632-3100	291-15
David Peyser Sportswear Inc 8890 Spence St	Bay Shore	NY	11706	**800-367-7900**	631-231-7788	153-12
David William Hotel 700 Biltmore Way	Coral Gables	FL	33134	**800-757-8073**	305-445-7821	373
David Yurman Designs Inc 729 Madison Ave	New York	NY	10021	**800-226-1400**	212-896-1550	401
David's Bridal Inc 1001 Washington St	Conshohocken	PA	19428	**800-823-2403**	610-943-5000	155-6
Davidsmeyer Bus Service 2513 E Higgins Rd	Elk Grove Village	IL	60007	**800-323-0312**	847-437-3767	110
Davidson College Box 7156	Davidson	NC	28035	**800-768-0380**	704-894-2000	163

Name / Address	City	State	ZIP	Toll-Free	Phone	Class
Davidson DA & Co Inc 8 3rd St N	Great Falls	MT	59401	**800-332-5915**	406-727-4200	679
Davidson Industries Inc PO Box 7	Mapleton	OR	97453	**800-845-5516**	541-268-4422	671
Davidson Lumber Co 2801 N Morton St	Franklin	IN	46131	**800-787-3211**	317-738-3211	805
Davidson Transfer & Storage Co 6600 Frankford Ave	Baltimore	MD	21206	**800-285-4387**	410-488-9200	508
Davies Consulting Inc 6935 Wisconsin Ave Suite 600	Chevy Chase	MD	20815	**800-535-6470**	301-652-4535	193
Daviess-Martin County Rural Electric Membership Corp 12628 E 75 N PO Box 430	Loogootee	IN	47553	**800-762-7362**	812-295-4200	244
Davis Beverage Group 1530-A Bobali Dr	Harrisburg	PA	17104	**800-360-7056**	717-914-1295	81-2
Davis College 4747 Monroe St	Toledo	OH	43623	**800-477-7021**	419-473-2700	158
Davis Cos 33 Boston Post Rd W	Marlborough	MA	01752	**800-482-9494**	508-481-9500	707
Davis Dick Publishing Co 3333 W Commercial Blvd Suite 113	Fort Lauderdale	FL	33309	**800-654-1514**	954-733-3996	623-9
Davis Electrical Constructors Inc PO Box 1907	Greenville	SC	29602	**800-849-3284**	864-250-2500	188-4
Davis Elen Advertising 865 S Figueroa St 12th Fl	Los Angeles	CA	90017	**800-729-4322**	213-688-7000	4
Davis & Elkins College 100 Campus Dr	Elkins	WV	26241	**800-624-3157**	304-637-1900	163
Davis FA Co 1915 Arch St	Philadelphia	PA	19103	**800-523-4049**	215-568-2270	623-2
Davis Funds PO Box 8406	Boston	MA	02266	**800-279-0279**		517
Davis Furniture Industries Inc 2401 S College St	High Point	NC	27260	**877-463-2847**	336-889-2009	314-1
Davis Hamilton Jackson & Assoc 1401 McKinney St Suite 1600	Houston	TX	77010	**800-594-0438**	713-853-2322	393
Davis Harry & Co 1725 Blvd of Allies	Pittsburgh	PA	15219	**800-775-2289**	412-765-1170	51
Davis Homes Inc 3755 E 82nd St Suite 120	Indianapolis	IN	46240	**888-595-2800**	317-595-2800	639
Davis Inotek Instruments LLC 4701 Mt Hope Dr Suite J	Baltimore	MD	21215	**800-368-2516**	410-358-3900	200
Davis J Rolfe Insurance Agency Inc 850 Concourse Pkwy S Suite 200	Maitland	FL	32751	**800-896-0554**	407-691-9600	383
Davis Paint Co Inc 1311 Iron St	Kansas City	MO	64116	**800-821-2029**	816-471-4447	540
Davis Paul Restoration Inc 1 Independence Dr Suite 2300	Jacksonville	FL	32202	**800-722-1818**	904-737-2779	305
Davis Polk & Wardwell 450 Lexington Ave	New York	NY	10017	**888-765-5529**	212-450-4000	419
Davis Vision Inc 159 Express St	Plainview	NY	11803	**800-328-4728**	516-932-9500	384-3
Davis Wink Equipment Co Inc 4938 S Atlanta Rd Suite 800	Atlanta	GA	30080	**800-341-5459**	404-266-2290	378
DavisBaldwin Inc 4600 W Cypress St 2nd Fl	Tampa	FL	33607	**800-282-0467**	813-287-1936	383
Davisco International Inc PO Box 69	Le Sueur	MN	56058	**800-323-4503**	507-665-8811	291-10
DaVita Inc 601 Hawaii St *NYSE: DVA*	El Segundo	CA	90245	**800-310-4872**	310-536-2400	347
Davitt & Hanser Music Co 4940 Delhi Pike	Cincinnati	OH	45238	**800-999-5558**	513-451-5000	516
Davol Inc PO Box 8500	Cranston	RI	02920	**800-556-6756**	401-463-7000	468
Daw AJ Printing Ink Co 3559 Greenwood Ave	Los Angeles	CA	90040	**800-432-9465**	323-723-3253	381
Daw Inc 12552 S 125 West *Sales	Draper	UT	84020	**800-748-4778***	801-553-9111	185
Daw Technologies Inc 1600 W 2200 S Suite 201	Salt Lake City	UT	84119	**800-596-0901**	801-977-3100	188-9
Dawahares Inc 1845 Alexandria Dr	Lexington	KY	40504	**800-677-9108**	859-278-0422	155-2
Dawes Arboretum 7770 Jacksontown Rd SE	Newark	OH	43056	**800-443-2937**	740-323-2355	98
Dawe's Laboratories Inc 3355 N Arlington Heights Rd	Arlington Heights	IL	60004	**800-323-4317**	847-577-2020	574
Dawn Food Products Inc 2021 Micor Dr	Jackson	MI	49203	**800-248-1144**	517-789-4400	291-16
Dawson Community College PO Box 421	Glendive	MT	59330	**800-821-8320**	406-377-3396	160
Dawson Geophysical Co 508 W Wall St Suite 800 *NASDAQ: DWSN*	Midland	TX	79701	**800-332-9766**	432-684-3000	527
Dawson Public Power District PO Box 777	Lexington	NE	68850	**800-752-8305**	308-324-2386	244
Day The 47 Eugene O'Neil Dr PO Box 1231	New London	CT	06320	**800-542-3354**	860-442-2200	522-2
Day-Brite/Capri/Omega 776 S Green St	Tupelo	MS	38804	**800-955-5352**	662-842-7212	431
Day-Glo Color Corp 4515 St Clair Ave	Cleveland	OH	44103	**800-289-3294**	216-391-7070	540
Day John Co 6263 Abbott Dr	Omaha	NE	68110	**800-767-2273**	402-455-8000	270
Day Michael Enterprise Inc PO Box 179	Wadsworth	OH	44282	**800-758-0960**	330-336-7611	594-2
Day Publishing Co 47 Eugene O'Neill Dr	New London	CT	06320	**800-542-3354**	860-442-2200	623-8
Day Runner Inc 101 O'Neil Rd	Sydney	NY	13838	**800-323-0500**	607-563-9411	87
Day Services Assn. National Adult 8201 Greensboro Dr Suite 300	McLean	VA	22102	**800-424-9046**	703-610-9000	48-6
Day-Timers Inc 1 Willow Ln	East Texas	PA	18046	**800-457-5702**	610-398-1151	87
Day & Zimmermann Group Inc 1818 Market St	Philadelphia	PA	19103	**800-523-0786**	215-299-8000	713
Daylight Corp 11707 E 11th St	Tulsa	OK	74128	**800-331-2245**	918-438-0800	69
Daylight Transport 1501 Hughes Way	Long Beach	CA	90810	**800-468-9999**	310-507-8200	769
Daymar College 3361 Buckland Sq	Owensboro	KY	42301	**800-960-4090**	270-926-4040	158
Days Hotel New York City Midtown 790 8th Ave	New York	NY	10019	**800-572-6232**	212-581-7000	373
Days Inns Worldwide Inc 1 Sylvan Way	Parsippany	NJ	07054	**800-329-7466**	973-428-9700	369
DaySpa Magazine 7628 Densmore Ave	Van Nuys	CA	91406	**800-442-5667**	818-782-7328	449-21
DaySpring Cards Inc PO Box 1010	Siloam Springs	AR	72761	**800-944-8000**	479-524-9301	130
DayStarter North America 2286 Capp Rd	Saint Paul	MN	55114	**800-328-6537**	651-646-2707	76
Dayton Art Institute 456 Belmonte Pk N	Dayton	OH	45405	**800-296-4426**	937-223-5277	509
Dayton Convention Center 22 E 5th St	Dayton	OH	45402	**800-822-3498**	937-333-4700	204
Dayton Foundation 2300 Kettering Tower	Dayton	OH	45423	**877-222-0410**	937-222-0410	298
Dayton International Airport (DAY)	Vandalia	OH	45377	**877-359-3291**	937-454-8200	28
Dayton Legal Blank Inc 875 Congress Pk Dr	Dayton	OH	45459	**800-262-8480**	937-435-4405	87
Dayton Opera 138 N Main St	Dayton	OH	45402	**888-228-3630**	937-228-0662	563-2
Dayton Parts Inc 3500 Industrial Rd PO Box 5795	Harrisburg	PA	17110	**800-225-2159**	717-255-8500	60
Dayton Power & Light Co PO Box 1247	Dayton	OH	45401	**800-433-8500**	937-331-3900	774
Dayton Reliable Air Filter Inc 2294 N Moraine Dr *Orders	Dayton	OH	45439	**800-699-0747***	937-293-4611	18
Dayton Rogers Mfg Co 8401 W 35 'W' Service Dr	Blaine	MN	55449	**800-677-8881**	763-784-7714	479
Dayton Superior Corp 7777 Washington Village Dr Suite 130	Dayton	OH	45459	**877-632-9866**	937-428-6360	345
Dayton T Brown Inc 1175 Church St	Bohemia	NY	11716	**800-232-6300**	631-589-6300	728
Dayton Technologies 351 N Garver Rd	Monroe	OH	45050	**800-432-9560**	513-539-4444	233
Daytona Beach Area Convention & Visitors Bureau 126 E Orange Ave	Daytona Beach	FL	32114	**800-544-0415**	386-255-0415	205
Daytona Beach Resort & Conference Center 2700 N Atlantic Ave	Daytona Beach	FL	32118	**800-654-6216**	386-672-3770	373
Daytona Inn Beach Resort 219 S Atlantic Ave	Daytona Beach	FL	32118	**800-874-1822**	386-252-3626	373
Dayton/Montgomery County Convention & Visitors Bureau 1 Chamber Plaza Suite A	Dayton	OH	45402	**800-221-8235**	937-226-8211	205
Dayton/Richmond Concrete Accessories 721 Richard St	Miamisburg	OH	45342	**800-745-3700**	937-866-0711	190-1
Dazel An HP Software Co 14231 Tandem Blvd	Austin	TX	78728	**800-357-8357**	512-494-7300	176-1
Dazor Mfg Corp 4483 Duncan Ave	Saint Louis	MO	63110	**800-345-9103**	314-652-2400	431
DB Aviation Inc 3550 N McAree Rd	Waukegan	IL	60087	**800-638-4990**	847-263-5600	63
DB Becker Co Inc 54 Old Hwy 22	Clinton	NJ	08809	**800-394-3991**	908-730-6010	144
DBI Golf 408 6th St	Prinsburg	MN	56281	**800-328-8949**	320-978-6011	187-3
DBI/SALA & Protecta 3965 Pepin Ave	Red Wing	MN	55066	**800-328-6146**	651-388-8282	666
DBK Concepts Inc 12905 SW 129 Ave	Miami	FL	33186	**800-725-7226**	305-596-7226	173
DBSA (Depression & Bipolar Support Alliance) 730 N Franklin St Suite 501	Chicago	IL	60610	**800-826-3632**	312-642-0049	48-17
DC Humphrys Inc 5744 Woodland Ave *Sales	Philadelphia	PA	19143	**800-523-4503***	215-724-8181	718
DC Taylor Co 312 29th St NE	Cedar Rapids	IA	52402	**800-333-7763**	319-363-2073	188-12
DCA (Diamond Council of America) 3212 West End Ave Suite 202	Nashville	TN	37203	**877-283-5669**	615-385-5301	49-4
DCAT (Drug Chemical & Associated Technologies Assn) 1 Washington Blvd Suite 7	Robbinsville	NJ	08691	**800-640-3228**	609-448-1000	49-19
DCC Services LLC 1100 Poydras St Suite 1350	New Orleans	LA	70163	**800-309-1213**	504-585-7346	178
DCI (Drum Corps International) 470 S Irmen Dr *Orders	Addison	IL	60101	**800-495-7469***	630-628-7888	48-4
DCI Marketing Inc 2727 W Good Hope Rd	Milwaukee	WI	53209	**800-778-4805**	414-228-7000	194
DCOTA (Design Center of the Americas) 1855 Griffin Rd	Dania Beach	FL	33004	**800-573-2682**	954-920-7997	452
DCS Information Services Inc 500 N Central Expy Suite 280	Plano	TX	75074	**800-299-3647**	972-422-3600	621
DD Bean & Sons Co 207 Peterborough St	Jaffrey	NH	03452	**800-326-8311**	603-532-8311	461
DD Jones Transfer & Warehouse Co Inc 2115 Portlock Rd	Chesapeake	VA	23324	**800-335-4787**	757-494-0200	790-1
DDB Worldwide 437 Madison Ave	New York	NY	10022	**800-332-3336**	212-415-2000	4
DDC-I Inc 400 N 5th St Suite 1050	Phoenix	AZ	85004	**800-221-8643**	602-275-7172	176-2
De Bruce Grain PO Box 329	Creston	IA	50801	**877-274-2676**	641-782-6411	271
De Lage Landen Inc 1111 Old Eagle School Rd	Wayne	PA	19087	**800-735-3273**	610-386-5000	214
De La Rue Retail Payment Solutions 25 Rockwood Pl	Englewood	NJ	07631	**800-526-0494**	201-894-1700	176-10
DE Wolfgang Candy Co 50 E 4th Ave	York	PA	17404	**800-248-4273**	717-843-5536	291-8
Deaconess Billings Clinic 2800 10th Ave N	Billings	MT	59101	**800-332-7201**	406-657-4000	366-2
Deaconess College of Nursing 6150 Oakland Ave	Saint Louis	MO	63139	**800-942-4310**	314-768-3044	163
Deaf or Hard of Hearing Inc. BEGINNINGS for Parents of Children Who Are 3714 A Benson Dr	Raleigh	NC	27619	**800-541-4327**	919-850-2746	48-17
Deaf Smith Electric Co-op Inc PO Box 753	Hereford	TX	79045	**800-687-8189**	806-364-1166	244
Deal LLC 105 Madison Ave 4th Fl *Cust Svc	New York	NY	10016	**888-667-3325***	212-313-9200	623-9
DealerNet c/o Cobalt Group Inc 2200 1st Ave S Suite 400	Seattle	WA	98134	**800-909-8244**	206-269-6363	58
Dealers Election Action Committee 8400 Westpark Dr 3rd Fl MS 3	McLean	VA	22102	**877-501-3322**	703-821-7110	604
Dealers Supply Co Inc 112 S Duke St	Durham	NC	27715	**800-776-6655**	919-383-7451	356
Dealers Truck Equipment Co 2460 Midway St	Shreveport	LA	71108	**800-259-7569**	318-635-7567	505
Dean Co Inc PO Box 1239	Princeton	WV	24740	**800-624-6153**	304-425-8701	602
Dean College 99 Main St	Franklin	MA	02038	**877-879-3326**	508-541-1508	160
Dean & DeLuca Inc 560 Broadway	New York	NY	10012	**800-999-0306**	212-226-6800	333
Dean Distributors Inc 1350 Bayshore Hwy Suite 400	Burlingame	CA	94010	**800-792-0816**	650-340-1738	291-18
Dean Health Plan 1277 Deming Way	Madison	WI	53717	**800-279-1301**	608-836-1400	384-3
Dean Investment Assoc Kettering Tower Suite 2480	Dayton	OH	45423	**800-327-3656**	937-222-0282	393
Dean Medical Center 1313 Fish Hatchery Rd	Madison	WI	53715	**800-279-9966**	608-252-8000	366-2
Dean Pickle & Specialty Products Co 857 School Pl	Green Bay	WI	54303	**800-558-4700**	920-497-7131	291-19

Name / Address	City	State	ZIP	Toll-Free	Phone	Class
Dean Transportation Inc 4812 Aurelius Rd	Lansing	MI	48910	**800-282-3326**	517-319-8300	110
Dean Word Co Ltd 1245 River Rd PO Box 310330	New Braunfels	TX	78131	**800-683-3926**	830-625-2365	187-4
Dearborn A Kaplan Professional Co 30 S Wacker Dr	Chicago	IL	60606	**800-621-9621**	312-836-4400	623-2
Dearborn County Chamber of Commerce 555 Eads Pkwy E Suite 175	Greendale	IN	47025	**800-322-8198**	812-537-0814	137
Dearborn Federal Credit Union 400 Town Center Dr	Dearborn	MI	48126	**888-336-2700**	313-336-2700	216
Dearborn Financial Publishing Inc DBA Dearborn A Kaplan Professional Co 30 S Wacker Dr	Chicago	IL	60606	**800-621-9621**	312-836-4400	623-2
Dearborn Wholesale Grocers Inc 2801 S Western Ave	Chicago	IL	60608	**800-999-3663**	773-254-4300	292-8
Dearing Beverage Co Inc 331 Victory Rd	Winchester	VA	22602	**800-552-9550***	540-662-0561	82-1
*Cust Svc						
Death Penalty. National Coalition to Abolish the 920 Pennsylvania Ave SE	Washington	DC	20003	**888-286-2237**	202-543-9577	48-8
Deaton-Kennedy Co Inc 927 Gardner St	Joliet	IL	60434	**800-637-9665**	815-726-6234	614
Deauville Beach Resort 6701 Collins Ave	Miami Beach	FL	33141	**800-327-6656**	305-865-8511	655
Deb Shops Inc 9401 Blue Grass Rd	Philadelphia	PA	19114	**800-676-6700**	215-676-6000	155-6
NASDAQ: DEBS						
DeBartolo Edward J Corp 7620 Marcus St	Youngstown	OH	44512	**888-965-3532**	330-965-2000	355-3
DeBeer J & Son Inc 5 Burdick Dr	Albany	NY	12205	**800-833-3535**	518-438-7871	701
Debit Card News 1 State Street Plaza 27th Fl	New York	NY	10004	**800-535-8403**	212-803-8200	521-1
Debitek Inc 2115 Chapman Rd Suite 159	Chattanooga	TN	37421	**800-332-4835**	423-894-6177	603
DeBourgh Mfg Co 27505 Otero Ave PO Box 981	La Junta	CO	81050	**800-328-8829**	719-384-8161	281
DeBra-Kuempel 3976 Southern Ave	Cincinnati	OH	45227	**800-395-5741**	513-271-6500	188-10
DeBruce Grain Inc 4100 N Mulberry Dr Suite 300	Kansas City	MO	64116	**800-821-5210**	816-421-8182	271
DeCarolis Truck Rental Inc 333 Colfax St	Rochester	NY	14606	**800-666-1169**	585-254-1169	767
Decatur Area Convention & Visitors Bureau 202 E North St	Decatur	IL	62523	**800-331-4479**	217-423-7000	205
Decatur County Rural Electric Membership Corp 1430 W Main St	Greensburg	IN	47240	**800-844-7362**	812-663-3391	244
Decatur Daily 201 1st Ave SE	Decatur	AL	35601	**888-353-4612**	256-353-4612	522-2
Decatur-Morgan County Chamber of Commerce 515 6th Ave NE	Decatur	AL	35602	**800-353-0005**	256-353-5312	137
Decatur/Morgan County Convention & Visitors Bureau 719 6th Ave SE PO Box 2349	Decatur	AL	35601	**800-524-6181**	256-350-2028	205
Deccofelt Corp 555 S Vermont Ave	Glendora	CA	91740	**800-543-3226***	626-963-8511	730-2
*Cust Svc						
Dechert-Hampe & Co 27101 Puerta Real Suite 400	Mission Viejo	CA	92691	**888-790-6626**	949-282-0035	193
Decibel Products Div Andrew Corp 2601 Telecom Pkwy	Richardson	TX	75082	**800-676-5342**	972-952-9700	633
Decisioneering Inc 1515 Arapahoe St Suite 1311	Denver	CO	80202	**800-289-2550**	303-534-1515	176-1
DecisionOne Corp 50 E Swedesford Rd	Frazer	PA	19355	**800-767-2876**	610-296-6000	173
Deck House Inc 930 Main St	Acton	MA	01720	**800-727-3325**	978-263-7000	107
Deck The Walls Inc 101 S Hanley Rd Suite 1280	Saint Louis	MO	63105	**866-719-8200**	314-719-8200	45
Decker Steel & Supply Inc 4500 Train Ave	Cleveland	OH	44102	**800-321-6100**	216-281-7900	483
Decker Tape Products Inc 6 Stewart Pl	Fairfield	NJ	07004	**800-227-5252**	973-227-5350	717
Deckers Outdoor Corp 495-A S Fairview Ave	Goleta	CA	93117	**800-858-5342**	805-967-7611	296
NASDAQ: DECK						
Decko Products Inc 2105 Superior St	Sandusky	OH	44870	**800-537-6143**	419-626-5757	291-8
Deco Products Co 506 Sanford St	Decorah	IA	52101	**800-327-9751**		303
DecoArt Inc PO Box 297	Stanford	KY	40484	**800-367-3047**	606-365-3193	43
Decorated Products Co 1 Arch Rd	Westfield	MA	01086	**800-639-4909**	413-568-0944	472
Decorating Contractors of America. Painting & 11960 Westline Industrial Dr Suite 201	Saint Louis	MO	63146	**800-332-7322**	314-514-7322	49-3
Decorating Den Systems Inc 19100 Montgomery Village Ave Suite 200	Montgomery Village	MD	20886	**800-428-1366**	301-272-1500	386
Decorating Retailers Assn. Paint & 403 Axminister Dr	Fenton	MO	63026	**800-737-0107**	636-326-2636	49-18
Decorative Artist's Workbook 4700 E Galbraith Rd	Cincinnati	OH	45236	**800-289-0963**	513-531-2690	449-14
Decorative Crafts Inc 50 Chestnut St	Greenwich	CT	06830	**800-431-4455**	203-531-1500	356
Decorator & Craft Corp (DC & C) 428 S Zelta St	Wichita	KS	67207	**800-835-3013**	316-685-6265	44
Decore-ative Specialties Inc 2772 S Peck Rd	Monrovia	CA	91016	**800-729-7277**	626-254-9191	116
Decorize Inc 1938 E Phelps	Springfield	MO	65802	**877-669-3326**	417-879-3326	315
AMEX: DCZ						
Decosimo Joseph & Co CPA 2 Union Sq Tallan Bldg Suite 1100	Chattanooga	TN	37402	**800-782-8382**	423-756-7100	2
DeCoty Coffee Co Inc 1920 Austin St	San Angelo	TX	76903	**800-588-8001**	325-655-5607	291-7
Dedicated Computing N26 W23880 Commerce Cir	Waukesha	WI	53188	**877-523-3301**	262-951-7200	171-3
Dee Cramer Inc 4221 E Baldwin Rd	Holly	MI	48442	**888-342-6995**	810-238-2664	188-12
Dee Electronics Inc 2500 16th Ave SW	Cedar Rapids	IA	52404	**800-747-3331**	319-365-7551	245
Dee Paper Co Inc 100 Broomall St	Chester	PA	19013	**800-359-0041**	610-876-9285	102
Dee Zee Inc 1572 NE 58th Ave	Des Moines	IA	50313	**800-779-2102**	515-265-7331	479

Name / Address	City	State	ZIP	Toll-Free	Phone	Class
Deen Wholesale Meats 813 E Northside Dr	Fort Worth	TX	76102	**800-333-3953**	817-335-2257	292-9
Deep East Texas Electric Co-op Inc PO Box 736	San Augustine	TX	75972	**800-392-5986**	936-275-2314	244
Deer Horn Aviation Ltd Co DBA Avion Flight Centre Inc 2506 N Pliska Dr	Midland	TX	79711	**800-759-3359**	432-563-2033	63
Deer Path Inn 255 E Illinois Rd	Lake Forest	IL	60045	**800-788-9480**	847-234-2280	373
Deer Trail Implement Inc 1411 S 81 Hwy Bypass PO Box 1326	McPherson	KS	67460	**800-364-4020**	620-241-3553	270
Deer Valley 1375 Deer Valley Dr S	Park City	UT	84060	**800-453-3833**	435-649-4040	655
Deer Valley Ranch 16825 County Rd 162	Nathrop	CO	81236	**800-284-1708**	719-395-2353	238
Deere Credit Services Inc 6400 NW 86th St PO Box 6600	Johnston	IA	50131	**800-362-8580**	515-224-2800	214
Deere John Credit Co PO Box 6600	Johnston	IA	50131	**800-275-5322**	515-267-3000	214
Deere John Health Plan Inc 1300 River Dr Suite 200	Moline	IL	61265	**800-224-6599**	309-765-1200	384-3
Deerfield Spa 650 Resica Falls Rd	East Stroudsburg	PA	18301	**800-852-4494**	570-223-0160	697
Deerfield Times 1701 Green Rd Suite B	Deerfield Beach	FL	33064	**800-275-8820***	954-698-6397	522-4
*Sales						
Deerfield.com 4241 Old US 27 S	Gaylord	MI	49735	**800-599-8856**	989-732-8856	176-7
Deerhaven Inn & Suites 740 Crocker Ave	Pacific Grove	CA	93950	**800-525-3373**	831-373-1114	373
Deerhurst Resort 1235 Deerhurst Dr	Huntsville	ON	P1H2E8	**800-461-4390**	705-789-6411	655
Deering Banjo Co 3733 Kenora Dr	Spring Valley	CA	91977	**800-845-7791**	619-464-8252	516
DeeSign Co 1010 Raymond Way	Anaheim	CA	92801	**800-824-2565**	714-871-5115	692
Defender Industries Inc 42 Great Neck Rd	Waterford	CT	06385	**800-628-8225**	860-701-3400	759
Defenders of Wildlife 1130 17th St NW	Washington	DC	20036	**800-989-8981**	202-682-9400	48-3
Defense Energy Support Center 8725 John J Kingman Rd Suite 4950	Fort Belvoir	VA	22060	**800-286-7633**	703-767-9700	336-3
Defense Fund. Children's 25 'E' St NW	Washington	DC	20001	**800-233-1200**	202-628-8787	48-6
Defense Information Systems Agency Network Information Center 7990 Science Applications Ct MS CV-50	Vienna	VA	22183	**800-365-3642**	703-676-1051	336-3
Defense Nuclear Facilities Safety Board 625 Indiana Ave NW Suite 700	Washington	DC	20004	**800-788-4016**	202-694-7000	336-16
Defense Research Institute (DRI) 150 N Michigan Ave Suite 300	Chicago	IL	60601	**800-667-8108**	312-795-1101	49-10
Defense Technology / Federal Laboratories 13386 International Pkwy	Jacksonville	FL	32218	**800-773-3832**	904-741-5400	279
Defense Threat Reduction Agency 8725 John T Kingman Rd MS 6201	Fort Belvoir	VA	22060	**800-701-5096**	703-767-5870	336-3
Defense Today 1325 G St NW Suite 1003	Washington	DC	20005	**800-926-5464**	202-638-4260	521-7
Defiance College 701 N Clinton St	Defiance	OH	43512	**800-520-4632**	419-784-4010	163
Defined Contribution News 225 Park Ave S 7th Fl	New York	NY	10003	**800-543-4444**	212-224-3800	521-1
Deflect-O Corp PO Box 50057	Indianapolis	IN	46250	**800-428-4328**	317-849-9555	523
Degerstrom NA Inc 3303 N Sullivan Rd	Spokane	WA	99216	**800-637-3773**	509-928-3333	492
DeGrazia Gallery in the Sun 6300 N Swan Rd	Tucson	AZ	85718	**800-545-2185**	520-299-9191	509
Degussa Admixtures Inc 23700 Chagrin Blvd	Beachwood	OH	44122	**800-628-9990**	216-839-7500	143
Degussa Building Systems 889 Valley Park Dr	Shakopee	MN	55379	**800-433-9517***	952-496-6000	3
*Cust Svc						
Degussa Corp 379 Interpace Pkwy Bldg 3	Parsippany	NJ	07054	**800-334-8772**	973-541-8000	143
Degussa Wall Systems Inc 3550 St Johns Bluff Rd S	Jacksonville	FL	32224	**800-322-7825**	904-996-6000	143
DeHaan Christel Fine Arts Center 1400 E Hanna Ave University of Indianapolis	Indianapolis	IN	46227	**800-232-8634**	317-788-3566	562
DEI (Development Exchange Inc) 1645 Hennepin Ave Suite 312	Minneapolis	MN	55403	**888-454-2314**	612-677-1505	620
DEI Inc 230 N Market Pl	Escondido	CA	92029	**800-732-8344**	760-743-8344	496
DeKalb Steel Inc 3476 Lawrenceville Hwy	Tucker	GA	30084	**877-646-7623**	770-939-2300	471
Dekker Marcel Inc 270 Madison Ave	New York	NY	10016	**800-228-1160***	212-696-9000	623-2
*Sales						
DeKorne Furniture Co Inc 2740 29th St SE	Grand Rapids	MI	49512	**800-968-4848**	616-949-4966	316
Dekoron Unitherm Inc 1531 Commerce Creek Blvd	Cape Coral	FL	33909	**800-633-5015**	239-995-8111	481
Del Amo Hospital 23700 Camino Del Sol	Torrance	CA	90505	**800-533-5266**	310-530-1151	366-3
Del Coronado. Hotel 1500 Orange Ave	Coronado	CA	92118	**800-582-2595**	619-522-8000	655
Del Frisco's 224 E Douglas Ave	Wichita	KS	67202	**800-234-0888**	316-264-8899	657
Del Laboratories Inc 178 EAB Plaza West Tower	Uniondale	NY	11556	**800-952-5080**	516-844-2020	211
Del Lago Waterfront Conference Center & Resort 600 Del Lago Blvd	Montgomery	TX	77356	**800-863-9208**	936-582-7510	370
Del Mar Avionics 1601-C Alton Pkwy	Irvine	CA	92606	**800-854-0481**	949-250-3200	519
Del Mar College						
East Campus 101 Baldwin Blvd	Corpus Christi	TX	78404	**800-652-3357**	361-698-1200	160
West Campus 101 Baldwin Blvd	Corpus Christi	TX	78404	**800-652-3357**	361-698-1737	160
Del Mar Die Casting Co 12901 S Western Ave	Gardena	CA	90249	**800-624-7468**	323-321-0600	303
Del Mar Medical Systems LLC 13 Whatney	Irvine	CA	92618	**800-423-0480**		249

Name / Address	City	State	Zip	Toll-Free	Phone	Class
Del Monte Foods Co 1 Market St The Landmark	San Francisco	CA	94105	**800-543-3090***	415-247-3000	291-20
NYSE: DLM ■ *Cust Svc						
Del Monte Trucking Operations 2 Nestle Way	Lathrop	CA	95330	**800-634-6300**	209-547-7275	769
Del-Pooled Trust Funds Delaware Investments 2005 Market St 1 Commerce Sq	Philadelphia	PA	19103	**800-231-8002**		517
Del Rio Chamber of Commerce 1915 Veterans Blvd	Del Rio	TX	78840	**800-889-8149**	830-775-3551	137
Del Taco Inc 25521 Commercentre Dr Suite 200	Lake Forest	CA	92630	**800-852-7204***	949-462-9300	657
*Cust Svc						
Del Webb Corp 15111 N Pima Rd Suite 100	Scottsdale	AZ	85260	**800-808-8088**		639
Delacorte Press 1745 Broadway	New York	NY	10019	**800-200-3552**	212-782-9000	623-2
Delagar Div Belcam Inc 27 Montgomery St	Rouses Point	NY	12979	**800-848-9281**		211
Delair Group LLC 8600 River Rd	Delair	NJ	08110	**800-235-0185**	856-663-2900	714
DELAMAR Greenwich Harbor 500 Steamboat Rd	Greenwich	CT	06830	**866-335-2627**	203-661-9800	373
Delano The 1685 Collins Ave	Miami Beach	FL	33139	**800-555-5001**	305-538-7881	373
Delavan Industries 199 Lein Rd	West Seneca	NY	14224	**888-508-0700**	716-677-4080	768
Delavan Spray Technologies Div Goodrich Corp PO Box 969	Bamberg	SC	29003	**800-621-9357**	803-245-4347	170
Delaware						
Higher Education Commission 820 N French St 5th Fl	Wilmington	DE	19801	**800-292-7935**	302-577-3240	335
Parks & Recreation Div 89 Kings Hwy	Dover	DE	19901	**877-987-2757***	302-739-4702	335
*Campground Resv						
Tourism Office 99 Kings Hwy	Dover	DE	19901	**866-284-7483**	302-739-4271	335
Delaware Assn of Realtors 9 E Loockerman St Suite 315	Dover	DE	19901	**800-305-4445**	302-734-4444	642
Delaware County Chamber of Commerce 114 Main St	Delhi	NY	13753	**800-642-4443**	607-746-2281	137
Delaware County Community College 901 S Media Line Rd	Media	PA	19063	**800-543-0146**	610-359-5000	160
Delaware Electric Co-op Inc PO Box 600	Greenwood	DE	19950	**800-282-8595**	302-349-4571	244
Delaware Importers Inc 615 Lambson Ln	New Castle	DE	19720	**800-292-7890**	302-656-4487	82-3
Delaware Investments 2005 Market St	Philadelphia	PA	19103	**800-362-7500**	215-255-1200	393
Delaware Investments Funds 2005 Market St	Philadelphia	PA	19103	**800-523-1918**	215-255-1200	517
Delaware Medical Society 131 Continental Dr Suite 405	Newark	DE	19713	**800-348-6800**	302-658-7596	466
Delaware Mfg Industries Corp 3775 Commerce Ct	Wheatfield	NY	14120	**800-248-3642**	716-743-4360	259
Delaware North Cos Gaming & Entertainment 40 Fountain Plaza	Buffalo	NY	14202	**800-828-7240**	716-858-5000	628
Delaware North Cos Inc 40 Fountain Plaza	Buffalo	NY	14202	**800-828-7240**	716-858-5000	184
Delaware Park Racetrack & Slots Casino 777 Delaware Pk Blvd	Wilmington	DE	19804	**800-417-5687**	302-994-2521	628
Delaware Pooled Trust Funds Delaware Investments 2005 Market St 1 Commerce Sq	Philadelphia	PA	19103	**800-231-8002**		517
Delaware Racing Assn 777 Delaware Park Blvd	Wilmington	DE	19804	**800-441-6587***	302-994-2521	628
*Mktg						
Delaware State Chamber of Commerce PO Box 671	Wilmington	DE	19899	**800-292-9507**	302-655-7221	138
Delaware State News PO Box 737	Dover	DE	19903	**800-282-8586**	302-674-3600	522-2
Delaware Transit Corp 400 S Madison St	Wilmington	DE	19801	**800-652-3278**	302-577-3278	460
Delaware Valley College of Science & Agriculture 700 E Butler Ave	Doylestown	PA	18901	**800-233-5825**	215-489-2211	163
Delaware Valley Wholesale Florist 520 Mantua Blvd N	Sewell	NJ	08080	**800-676-1212**	856-468-7000	288
Delco Office Systems 55 Old Field Point Rd PO Box 423	Greenwich	CT	06830	**800-243-8528**	203-661-5101	462
Delco Remy International Inc 2902 Enterprise Dr	Anderson	IN	46013	**800-372-5131**	765-778-6499	60
DeLeon's Bromeliads Co 13745 SW 216th St	Goulds	FL	33170	**800-448-8649**	305-238-6028	363
Delfield Co 980 S Isabella Rd	Mount Pleasant	MI	48858	**800-733-8821**	989-773-7981	293
Deli Express 16101 W 78th St	Eden Prairie	MN	55344	**866-787-8862**	952-937-9440	291-36
dELiA*s Corp 435 Hudson St 3rd Fl	New York	NY	10014	**800-335-4269**	212-807-9060	451
Delicato Vineyards 12001 S Hwy 99	Manteca	CA	95336	**888-599-4637**	209-824-3600	81-3
Delicious Living Magazine 1401 Pearl St Suite 200	Boulder	CO	80302	**800-431-1255**	303-939-8440	449-11
deLima Paul Co Inc PO Box 4813	Syracuse	NY	13221	**800-962-8864**	315-699-5282	291-7
Delimex 7878 Airway Rd	San Diego	CA	92154	**800-382-6253**	619-661-5440	291-36
Dell Inc 1 Dell Way	Round Rock	TX	78682	**800-854-6214**	512-338-4400	171-3
NASDAQ: DELL						
Delmar Learning 5 Maxwell Dr	Clifton Park	NY	12065	**800-998-7498**	518-464-3500	623-2
Delmont Laboratories Inc 715 Harvard Ave PO Box 269	Swarthmore	PA	19081	**800-562-5541**	610-543-3365	574
DeLoache Flowers 2927 Millwood Ave	Columbia	SC	29205	**800-922-2707**	803-256-1681	287
DeLong Sportswear Inc 821 5th Ave	Grinnell	IA	50112	**800-733-5664**	641-236-3106	153-1
DeLorme 2 DeLorme Dr	Yarmouth	ME	04096	**800-452-5931***	207-846-7000	623-1
*Sales						
Delphos Daily Herald 405 N Main St	Delphos	OH	45833	**800-589-6950**	419-695-0015	522-2
Delphos Herald Inc 405 N Main St	Delphos	OH	45833	**800-589-6950**	419-695-0015	623-8
Delray Beach Times 1701 Green Rd Suite B	Deerfield Beach	FL	33064	**800-275-8820**	954-698-6397	522-4
Delray Plants Inc 5700 Sims Rd	Delray Beach	FL	33484	**800-854-5393**	561-498-3200	363
Delsey Luggage 6735 Business Pkwy Suite A	Elkridge	MD	21075	**800-558-3344**	410-796-5655	444
DelStar Technologies Inc 220 E St Elmo Rd	Austin	TX	78745	**800-531-5112**	512-447-7000	597
Delta Air Cargo 1600 Aviation Blvd Hartsfield-Atlanta International Airport	Atlanta	GA	30320	**800-352-2746**		13
Delta Air Lines Inc PO Box 20706 Hartsfiled-Atlanta Airport	Atlanta	GA	30320	**800-221-1212**	404-715-2600	26
NYSE: DAL						
Delta Air Lines SkyMiles SkyMiles Service Ctr Dept 654 PO Box 20532	Atlanta	GA	30320	**800-323-2323**		27
Delta Apparel Inc 2750 Premier Pkwy Suite 100	Duluth	GA	30097	**800-285-4456**	678-775-6900	153-3
AMEX: DLA						
Delta Area Hospice Care Ltd 522 Arnold Ave	Greenville	MS	38701	**800-742-2641**	662-335-7040	365
Delta Blood Bank 65 N Commerce St	Stockton	CA	95201	**800-244-6794**	209-943-3831	90
Delta Carbona Products Co 376 Hollywood Ave Suite 208	Fairfield	NJ	07004	**888-746-5599**	973-808-6260	149
Delta Casket Co 821 Lone Oak Dr	West Point	MS	39773	**800-647-6310**	662-494-4151	134
Delta Centrifugal Corp PO Box 1043	Temple	TX	76503	**800-433-3100***	254-773-9055	302
*Sales						
Delta Chemical Corp 2601 Cannery Ave	Baltimore	MD	21226	**800-282-5322**	410-354-0100	143
Delta CompuTec Inc 900 Huyler St	Teterboro	NJ	07608	**800-477-8586**	201-440-8585	178
Delta Connection 444 S River Rd	Saint George	UT	84790	**800-221-1212**	435-634-3000	26
Delta Consolidated Industries Inc 2728 Capital Blvd	Raleigh	NC	27604	**800-643-0084**	919-832-6351	479
Delta Corporate Services Inc 129 Littleton Rd	Parsippany	NJ	07054	**800-335-8220**	973-334-6260	178
Delta Corrugated Paper Products Corp W Ruby & Railroad Ave	Palisades Park	NJ	07650	**800-932-6937**	201-941-1910	101
Delta County Area Chamber of Commerce 230 Ludington St	Escanaba	MI	49829	**888-335-8264**	906-786-2192	137
Delta Craft Paper Co 99 Bud-Mill Dr	Buffalo	NY	14206	**800-735-5735**	716-856-5135	544
Delta Dental Insurance Co PO Box 1809	Alpharetta	GA	30023	**800-521-2651**	770-645-8700	384-3
Delta Dental Insurance Co - Alaska 257 E 200 South Suite 375	Salt Lake City	UT	84111	**800-521-2651**	801-575-5168	384-3
Delta Dental of Pennsylvania 1 Delta Dr	Mechanicsburg	PA	17055	**800-932-0783**	717-766-8500	384-3
Delta Dental Plan of Alabama 1000 Mansell Exchange W Bldg 100 Suite 100	Alpharetta	GA	30022	**800-521-2651**	770-645-8700	384-3
Delta Dental Plan of Arizona PO Box 43026	Phoenix	AZ	85080	**800-352-6132**		384-3
Delta Dental Plan of Arkansas 1513 Country Club Rd	Sherwood	AR	72120	**800-462-5410**	501-835-3400	384-3
Delta Dental Plan of California PO Box 7736	San Francisco	CA	94120	**888-335-8227**	415-972-8300	384-3
Delta Dental Plan of Colorado 4582 S Ulster St Suite 800	Denver	CO	80237	**800-233-0860**	303-741-9300	384-3
Delta Dental Plan of Connecticut PO Box 222	Parsippany	NJ	07054	**800-346-5377**	973-285-4000	384-3
Delta Dental Plan of Delaware 1 Delta Dr	Mechanicsburg	PA	17055	**800-932-0783**	717-766-8500	384-3
Delta Dental Plan of Florida PO Box 1809	Alpharetta	GA	30022	**800-521-2651**		384-3
Delta Dental Plan of Georgia PO Box 1809	Alpharetta	GA	30023	**800-521-2651**		384-3
Delta Dental Plan of Idaho PO Box 2870	Boise	ID	83701	**800-388-3490**	208-344-4546	384-3
Delta Dental Plan of Illinois PO Box 5402	Lisle	IL	60532	**800-323-1743**	630-964-2400	384-3
Delta Dental Plan of Indiana PO Box 30416	Lansing	MI	48909	**800-524-0149**		384-3
Delta Dental Plan of Iowa 2401 SE Tones Dr Suite 13	Ankeny	IA	50021	**800-532-1514**	515-963-4100	384-3
Delta Dental Plan of Kansas PO Box 49198	Wichita	KS	67201	**800-234-3375**	316-264-4511	384-3
Delta Dental Plan of Kentucky PO Box 242810	Louisville	KY	40224	**800-955-2023**	502-736-5000	384-3
Delta Dental Plan of Louisiana PO Box 1809	Alpharetta	GA	30023	**800-521-2651**		384-3
Delta Dental Plan of Maine PO Box 2002	Concord	NH	03302	**800-832-5700**		384-3
Delta Dental Plan of Maryland 1 Delta Dr	Mechanicsburg	PA	17055	**800-932-0783**	717-766-8500	384-3
Delta Dental Plan of Massachusetts 465 Medford St	Boston	MA	02129	**800-872-0500***	617-886-1000	384-3
*Cust Svc						
Delta Dental Plan of Michigan PO Box 30416	Lansing	MI	48909	**800-524-0149**		384-3
Delta Dental Plan of Minnesota PO Box 330	Minneapolis	MN	55440	**800-553-9536**	651-406-5918	384-3
Delta Dental Plan of Minnesota Corp PO Box 59238	Minneapolis	MN	55459	**800-448-3815**	651-406-5901	384-3
Delta Dental Plan of Mississippi PO Box 1809	Alpharetta	GA	30023	**800-521-2651**		384-3
Delta Dental Plan of Missouri PO Box 8690	Saint Louis	MO	63126	**800-392-1167**	314-656-3000	384-3
Delta Dental Plan of Montana PO Box 1809	Alpharetta	GA	30023	**800-521-2651**		384-3
Delta Dental Plan of Nebraska PO Box 245	Minneapolis	MN	55440	**800-553-9536**		384-3
Delta Dental Plan of Nevada PO Box 1809	Alpharetta	GA	30023	**800-521-2651**		384-3
Delta Dental Plan of New Hampshire 1 Delta Dr PO Box 2002	Concord	NH	03302	**800-537-1715**	603-223-1000	384-3
Delta Dental Plan of New Jersey Inc 1639 Rt 10 E	Parsippany	NJ	07054	**800-346-5377**	973-285-4000	384-3
Delta Dental Plan of New Mexico 2500 Louisiana Blvd NE Suite 600	Albuquerque	NM	87110	**800-999-0963**	505-883-4777	384-3
Delta Dental Plan of New York 1 Delta Dr	Mechanicsburg	PA	17055	**800-932-0783**	717-766-8500	384-3
Delta Dental Plan of North Carolina 333 Six Forks Rd Suite 100	Raleigh	NC	27609	**800-662-8856**	919-832-6015	384-3
Delta Dental Plan of North Dakota 3560 Delta Dental Dr	Eagan	MN	55122	**800-328-1188**	651-406-5900	384-3
Delta Dental Plan of Ohio PO Box 30416	Lansing	MI	48909	**800-524-0149**		384-3

Name / Address	City	State	ZIP	Toll-Free	Phone	Class
Delta Dental Plan of Oklahoma 16 NW 63rd St Suite 301	Oklahoma City	OK	73116	**800-522-0188**	405-607-2100	384-3
Delta Dental Plan of South Carolina PO Box 8690	Saint Louis	MO	63126	**800-392-1167**	314-656-3000	384-3
Delta Dental Plan of South Dakota 720 N Euclid Ave PO Box 1157	Pierre	SD	57501	**800-627-3961**	605-224-7345	384-3
Delta Dental Plan of Tennessee 240 Venture Cir	Nashville	TN	37228	**800-223-3104**	615-255-3175	384-3
Delta Dental Plan of Texas 1000 Mansell Exchange W Bldg 100 Suite 100	Alpharetta	GA	30022	**800-521-2651**	770-645-8700	384-3
Delta Dental Plan of Utah 1000 Mansell Exchange W Bldg 100 Suite 100	Alpharetta	GA	30022	**800-521-2651**	770-645-8700	384-3
Delta Dental Plan of Virginia 4818 Starkey Rd SW	Roanoke	VA	24014	**800-367-3531**	540-989-8000	384-3
Delta Dental Plan of Wisconsin 2801 Hoover Rd	Stevens Point	WI	54481	**800-236-3713**	715-344-6087	384-3
Delta Dental Plan of Wyoming 320 W 25th St Suite 100	Cheyenne	WY	82001	**800-735-3379**	307-632-3313	384-3
Delta Dental of Rhode Island PO Box 1517	Providence	RI	02901	**800-843-3582**	401-752-6100	384-3
Delta Dental of West Virginia 1 Delta Dr	Mechanicsburg	PA	17055	**800-932-0783**	717-766-8500	384-3
Delta Design Inc 12367 Crosthwaite Cir	Poway	CA	92064	**800-776-0697**	858-848-8000	247
Delta Downs Racing Assn Inc 2717 Delta Downs Dr	Vinton	LA	70668	**800-589-7441**	337-589-7441	628
Delta Education LLC 80 Northwest Blvd	Nashua	NH	03063	**800-258-1302**	603-889-8899	242
Delta Employees Credit Union PO Box 20541	Atlanta	GA	30320	**800-544-3328**	404-715-4725	216
Delta Environmental Consultants Inc 5910 Rice Creek Pkwy	Shoreview	MN	55126	**800-477-7411**	651-639-9449	653
Delta Galil USA 150 Meadowlawn Pkwy	Secaucus	NJ	07094	**800-645-4461**	201-902-0055	153-18
Delta Hotels Canadian Pacific Tower PO Box 227 TD Centre *Resv	Toronto	ON	M5K1J3	**800-268-1133***	416-874-2000	369
Delta Hotels Privilege Program 100 Wellington St Suite 1200	Toronto	ON	M5K1J3	**888-321-3358**	416-874-2000	371
Delta Lodge at Kananaskis 1 Centennial Dr	Kananaskis Village	AB	T0L2H0	**888-244-8666**	403-591-7711	655
Delta Meadowvale Resort & Conference Centre 6750 Mississauga Rd	Mississauga	ON	L5N2L3	**800-268-1133**	905-821-1981	655
Delta Natural Gas Co Inc 3617 Lexington Rd *NASDAQ: DGAS*	Winchester	KY	40391	**800-262-2012**	859-744-6171	774
Delta & Pine Land Co PO Box 157 *NYSE: DLP*	Scott	MS	38772	**800-321-8989**	662-742-3351	11-2
Delta Pride Catfish Inc 1301 Industrial Pkwy	Indianola	MS	38751	**800-421-1045**	662-887-5401	291-14
Delta Queen Steamboat Co Inc 1380 Port of New Orleans Pl Robin St Wharf	New Orleans	LA	70130	**800-543-1949**	504-586-0631	218
Delta Star Inc 270 Industrial Rd	San Carlos	CA	94070	**800-892-8673**	650-508-2850	756
Delta State University 1003 W Sunflower Rd	Cleveland	MS	38732	**800-468-6378**	662-846-3000	163
Delta Theta Phi 38640 Butternut Ridge Rd	Elyria	OH	44035	**800-783-2600**	440-458-4381	48-16
Delta Vacations 110 E Broward Blvd	Fort Lauderdale	FL	33301	**800-654-6559**	954-522-1440	760
Delta Victoria Ocean Pointe Resort Hotel & Spa 45 Songhees Rd	Victoria	BC	V9A6T3	**800-667-4677**	250-360-2999	655
Delta Waterfowl Foundation 1305 E Central Ave	Bismarck	ND	58501	**888-987-3695**	701-222-8857	48-3
Delta Whistler Resort 4050 Whistler Way	Whistler	BC	V0N1B4	**888-244-8666**	604-932-1982	655
Delta Whistler Village Suites 4308 Main St	Whistler	BC	V0N1B4	**888-244-8666**	604-905-3987	655
Delta/Beckwith Elevator Co 274 Southampton St	Boston	MA	02118	**800-648-8767**	617-427-5525	188-1
deltathree Inc 75 Broad St 31st Fl *NASDAQ: DDDC*	New York	NY	10004	**888-335-8230**	212-500-4850	721
DeltaTRAK Inc PO Box 398	Pleasanton	CA	94566	**800-962-6776**	925-467-5940	201
Deltec Inc 1265 Grey Fox Rd	Saint Paul	MN	55112	**800-426-2448**	651-633-2556	468
Deltek Systems Inc 13880 Dulles Corner Ln	Herndon	VA	20171	**800-456-2009**	703-734-8606	176-1
Deltona Corp 8014 SW 135th St Rd	Ocala	FL	34473	**800-935-6378**	352-347-2322	639
Deltronic Corp 3900 W Segerstrom Ave	Santa Ana	CA	92704	**800-451-6922**	714-545-0401	484
Deluxe Business Forms 3680 Victoria St N *Cust Svc	Shoreview	MN	55126	**800-328-7205***	651-483-7111	140
Deluxe Carpet Cleaning Co Inc 5907 High Grove Rd	Grandview	MO	64030	**800-733-0078**	816-763-3331	150
Deluxe Corp 3680 N Victoria St *NYSE: DLX*	Shoreview	MN	55126	**800-328-7205**	651-483-7111	355-3
DeLuxe Laboratories Inc 1377 N Serrano Ave	Hollywood	CA	90027	**800-233-5893**	323-462-6171	501
Deluxe Media Services Inc 568 Atrium Dr	Vernon Hills	IL	60061	**800-745-7265**	847-990-4100	500
DEMA (Diving Equipment & Marketing Assn) 3750 Convoy St Suite 310	San Diego	CA	92111	**800-862-3483**	858-616-6408	49-4
Demag Cranes & Components 29201 Aurora Rd	Cleveland	OH	44139	**800-321-6560**	440-248-2400	189
Demakes Enterprises Inc DBA Old Neighborhood Foods 37 Waterhill St	Lynn	MA	01905	**800-628-3529**	781-595-1557	465
Demantra Inc 230 3rd Ave	Waltham	MA	02451	**866-336-2687**	781-810-1700	176-1
DEMCO (Dixie Electric Membership Corp) PO Box 15659	Baton Rouge	LA	70895	**800-262-0221**	225-261-1221	244
Demco Inc 4810 Forest Run Rd *Orders	Madison	WI	53704	**800-356-1200***	608-241-1201	550
Democrat & Chronicle 55 Exchange Blvd	Rochester	NY	14614	**800-473-5274**	585-232-7100	522-2
Democratic Action. Americans for 1625 K St NW Suite 210	Washington	DC	20006	**800-787-2734**	202-785-5980	48-7

Name / Address	City	State	ZIP	Toll-Free	Phone	Class
Democratic National Committee 430 S Capitol St SE	Washington	DC	20003	**800-934-8683**	202-863-8000	605
Democrats of America. Young PO Box 77496	Washington	DC	20013	**877-639-8585**	202-639-8585	48-7
DeMolay International 10200 N Ambassador Dr *Orders	Kansas City	MO	64153	**800-336-6529***	816-891-8333	48-15
DemoLetter 177 Bovet Rd Suite 400	San Mateo	CA	94402	**800-633-4312**	650-577-2700	521-3
DeMoulin Brothers & Co Inc 1025 S 4th St	Greenville	IL	62246	**800-228-8134**	618-664-2000	153-19
Dempster Industries Inc 711 S 6th St	Beatrice	NE	68310	**800-777-0212**	402-223-4026	627
Demsey Mfg Co 78 New Wood Rd	Watertown	CT	06795	**800-533-6739**	860-274-6209	473
Den-Mat Corp 2727 Skyway Dr	Santa Maria	CA	93455	**800-433-6628**	805-922-8491	226
Denali Ventures Inc 5613 DTC Pkwy Suite 200	Greenwood Village	CO	80111	**877-290-5590**		105
Denbury Resources Inc 5100 Tennyson Pkwy Suite 3000 *NYSE: DNR*	Plano	TX	75024	**800-364-5482**	972-673-2000	525
Dendreon Corp 3005 1st Ave *NASDAQ: DNDN*	Seattle	WA	98121	**877-256-4545**	206-256-4545	86
Denison University 100 Main St	Granville	OH	43023	**800-336-4766**	740-587-0810	163
Denman Tire Corp 400 Diehl South Rd *Cust Svc	Leavittsburg	OH	44430	**800-334-5543***	330-675-4242	739
Dennert H Distributing Corp 351 Wilmer Ave *Cust Svc	Cincinnati	OH	45226	**800-837-5659***	513-871-7272	82-1
Dennis Supply Co PO Box 3376	Sioux City	IA	51102	**800-352-4618**	712-255-7637	651
Dennis Trucking Co Inc 6951 Norwitch Dr	Philadelphia	PA	19153	**800-333-4961**	215-492-8200	769
Dennis Uniform Mfg Co Inc 135 SE Hawthorne Blvd *Orders	Portland	OR	97214	**800-544-7123***	503-238-7123	153-19
Denny's Corp 203 E Main St *Cust Svc	Spartanburg	SC	29319	**800-733-6697***	864-597-8000	656
Dent Clinic Canada Inc 711 48th Ave SE Suite 6	Calgary	AB	T2G4X2	**888-722-3368**	403-255-3111	62-4
Dent & Co 5800 E Mabry Dr	Clovis	NM	88101	**800-748-3368**	505-763-5517	270
Dent Doctor Inc 11301 W Markham St	Little Rock	AR	72211	**800-946-3368**	501-224-0500	62-4
Dent Wizard International 4710 Earth City Expway	Bridgeton	MO	63044	**800-336-8949**	314-592-1800	62-4
Dent-X Corp 250 Clearbrook Rd	Elmsford	NY	10523	**800-592-6666**	914-592-6100	375
Dental Assn. Arizona 4131 N 36th St	Phoenix	AZ	85018	**800-866-2732**	602-957-4777	225
Dental Assn. Arkansas State 2501 Crestwood Dr Suite 205	North Little Rock	AR	72116	**800-501-2732**	501-771-7650	225
Dental Assn. California PO Box 13749	Sacramento	CA	95853	**800-736-7071**	916-443-0505	225
Dental Assn. Florida 1111 E Tennessee St	Tallahassee	FL	32308	**800-877-9922**	850-681-3629	225
Dental Assn. Georgia 7000 Peachtree Dunwoody Rd NE Bldg 17 Suite 200	Atlanta	GA	30328	**800-432-4357**	404-636-7553	225
Dental Assn. Hawaii 1345 S Beretania St Suite 301	Honolulu	HI	96814	**800-359-6725**	808-593-7956	225
Dental Assn. Indiana 401 W Michigan St	Indianapolis	IN	46202	**800-562-5646**	317-634-2610	225
Dental Assn. Iowa 505 5th Ave Suite 333	Des Moines	IA	50309	**800-828-2181**	515-282-7250	225
Dental Assn. Louisiana 7833 Office Pk Blvd	Baton Rouge	LA	70809	**800-388-6642**	225-926-1986	225
Dental Assn. Minnesota 2236 Marshall Ave	Saint Paul	MN	55104	**800-950-3368**	651-646-7454	225
Dental Assn. Montana 17 1/2 S Last Chance Gulch St	Helena	MT	59601	**800-257-4988**	406-443-2061	225
Dental Assn. Nevada 8863 W Flamingo Rd Suite 102	Las Vegas	NV	89147	**800-962-6710**	702-255-4211	225
Dental Assn. Oklahoma 629 NW Grand Blvd	Oklahoma City	OK	73118	**800-876-8890**	405-848-8873	225
Dental Assn. Wisconsin 111 E Wisconsin Ave Suite 1300	Milwaukee	WI	53202	**800-364-7646**	414-276-4520	225
Dental Economics Magazine 1421 S Sheridan Rd	Tulsa	OK	74112	**800-331-4463**	918-835-3161	449-16
Dental Education Assn. American 1400 K St NW Suite 1100	Washington	DC	20005	**800-353-2237**	202-289-7201	49-5
Dental Fraternity. Alpha Omega International 500 Commonwealth Dr	Warrendale	PA	15086	**800-677-8468**	724-778-3419	48-16
Dental Hygienists' Assn. American 444 N Michigan Ave Suite 3400	Chicago	IL	60611	**800-243-2342**	312-440-8900	49-8
Dental Laboratories. National Assn of 325 John Knox Rd Suite L-103	Tallahassee	FL	32303	**800-950-1150**	850-205-5626	49-8
Dental Practice Report 2 Northfield Plaza Suite 300	Northfield	IL	60093	**800-323-3337**	847-441-3700	449-16
Dental Products Report 2 Northfield Plaza Suite 300	Northfield	IL	60093	**800-323-3337**	847-441-3700	449-16
Dental Society. Massachusetts 2 Willow St Suite 200	Southborough	MA	01745	**800-943-9200**	508-480-9797	225
Dentistry. Academy of General 211 E Chicago Ave Suite 900	Chicago	IL	60611	**888-243-3368**	312-440-4300	49-8
Dentistry. American Academy of Cosmetic 5401 World Dairy Dr	Madison	WI	53718	**800-543-9220**	608-222-8583	49-8
Dentistry for the Handicapped. National Foundation of 1800 15th St Unit 100	Denver	CO	80202	**888-471-6334**	303-534-5360	48-17
Dentists. American College of 839 Quince Orchard Blvd Suite J	Gaithersburg	MD	20878	**888-223-1920**	301-977-3223	49-8
Dentists Insurance Co 1201 K St 17th Fl	Sacramento	CA	95814	**800-733-0635**	916-443-4501	384-5
Denton Chamber of Commerce 414 Parkway St	Denton	TX	76202	**888-381-1818**	940-382-9693	137
Denton Record-Chronicle 314 E Hickory St	Denton	TX	76201	**800-275-1722**	940-387-3811	522-2
Dentrix Dental Systems Inc 727 E Utah Valley Dr Suite 500	American Fork	UT	84003	**800-336-8749**	801-763-9300	176-10

Name / Address	City	State	Zip	Toll-Free	Phone	Class
Dentsply-Ceramco 6 Terri Ln	Burlington	NJ	08016	**800-487-0100**	609-386-8900	226
Dentsply International Inc 221 W Philadelphia St PO Box 872 *NASDAQ: XRAY*	York	PA	17405	**800-877-0020**	717-845-7511	226
Dentsply International Inc Ceramco Div 6 Terri Ln Suite 100	Burlington	NJ	08016	**800-487-0100**	609-386-8900	226
Dentsply International Inc Gendex Products Div 901 W Oakton St	Des Plaines	IL	60018	**800-800-2888**	847-640-4800	375
Dentsply International Inc LD Caulk Div 38 W Clarke Ave	Milford	DE	19963	**800-532-2855**	302-422-4511	226
Dentsply International Inc Professional Care Div 1301 Smile Way	York	PA	17404	**800-989-8825**	717-767-8500	226
Dentsply International Inc Rinn Div 1212 Abbott Dr	Elgin	IL	60123	**800-323-0970**	847-742-1115	226
Dentsply International Inc Trubyte Div 221 W Philadelphia St PO Box 872	York	PA	17405	**800-877-0020**	717-845-7511	226
Dentsply International Inc Tulsa Dental Div 5100 E Skelly Dr Suite 300	Tulsa	OK	74135	**800-662-1202**	918-493-6598	226
Denver Automotive & Diesel College 460 S Lipan St	Denver	CO	80223	**800-347-3232**	303-722-5724	787
Denver Brick Co 401 Prairie Hawk Dr	Castle Rock	CO	80109	**800-332-7724**	303-688-6952	148
Denver Center for the Performing Arts 1245 Champa St	Denver	CO	80204	**800-641-1222**	303-893-4100	562
Denver Center Theatre Co 1245 Champa St	Denver	CO	80204	**800-641-1222**	303-893-4000	734
Denver International Airport (DEN)	Denver	CO	80249	**800-247-2336**	303-342-2000	28
Denver Museum of Nature & Science 2001 Colorado Blvd	Denver	CO	80205	**800-925-2250**	303-370-6357	509
Denver Newspaper Agency 1560 Broadway	Denver	CO	80202	**800-933-1990**	303-892-2745	623-8
Denver Post 1560 Broadway	Denver	CO	80202	**800-336-7678**	303-820-1010	522-2
Department 56 Inc 6436 City W Pkwy 1 Village Pl *NYSE: DFS*	Eden Prairie	MN	55344	**800-348-3749**	952-944-5600	323
Department of the Air Force Agency for National Security & Emergency Preparedness	Fort McPherson	GA	30330	**800-366-0051**		336-3
Department of the Army						
Judge Advocate General 1777 N Kent St	Rosslyn	VA	22209	**800-208-7178**	703-697-5151	336-3
US Army Reserve Personnel Center 1 Reserve Way	Saint Louis	MO	63132	**800-318-5298**	314-592-0200	336-3
US Army War College 122 Forbes Ave	Carlisle	PA	17013	**800-453-0992**	717-245-4101	336-3
Department of Defense (DOD) Inspector General 400 Army-Navy Dr Suite 1000	Arlington	VA	22202	**800-424-9098**	703-604-8300	336-3
Department of Education 400 Maryland Ave SW	Washington	DC	20202	**800-872-5327**	202-401-2000	336-4
Inspector General's Fraud & Abuse Hotline	Washington	DC	20202	**800-647-8733**		336-4
Office of Federal Student Aid 830 1st St NE Union Center Plaza	Washington	DC	20202	**800-433-3243**		711
Department of Energy (DOE)						
Clean Cities Program 1000 Independence Ave SW EE-2K	Washington	DC	20585	**800-224-8437**	202-586-1573	336-5
Office of Civilian Radioactive Waste Management 1000 Independence Ave SW	Washington	DC	20585	**800-225-6972**	202-586-6842	336-5
Office of Energy Efficiency & Renewable Energy 1000 Independence Ave SW	Washington	DC	20585	**877-337-3463**	202-568-9220	336-5
Department of Health & Human Services (HHS) Office on Women's Health 200 Independence Ave SW Rm 730B	Washington	DC	20201	**800-994-9662**	202-690-7650	336-6
Department of Homeland Security (DHS)						
National Disaster Medical System 500 C Street SW Suite 713	Washington	DC	20472	**800-872-6967**		336-7
Ready.gov Naval Security Stn	Washington	DC	20528	**800-237-3239**		336-7
Department of Housing & Urban Development (HUD)						
Housing Discrimination Hotline	Washington	DC	20410	**800-669-9777**		336-8
Office of Fair Housing & Equal Opportunity 451 7th St SW MC E	Washington	DC	20410	**800-669-9777**	202-708-4252	336-8
Office of the Inspector General 451 7th St SW	Washington	DC	20410	**800-347-3735**	202-708-0430	336-8
Office of Multifamily Housing Programs 451 7th St SW	Washington	DC	20410	**800-685-8470**	202-708-2495	336-8
Department of Housing & Urban Development Regional Offices						
Pacific/Hawaii Region 450 Golden Gate Ave 8th Fl	San Francisco	CA	94102	**800-436-6446**	415-436-6550	336-8
Rocky Mountain Region 633 17th St 14th Fl	Denver	CO	80202	**800-543-9378**	303-672-5440	336-8
Department of Justice (DOJ)						
Office of Justice Programs 810 7th St NW Suite 6400	Washington	DC	20531	**800-421-6770**	202-307-5933	336-10
Office of Special Counsel for Immigration-Related Unfair Employment Practices 950 Pennsylvania Ave NW *Hotline	Washington	DC	20038	**800-255-7688***	202-616-5594	336-10
Department of Justice Antitrust Div 950 Pennsylvania Ave NW	Washington	DC	20530	**888-647-3258**	202-514-2421	336-10
Department of Labor (DOL) 200 Constitution Ave NW	Washington	DC	20210	**866-487-2365**	202-693-4650	336-11
GovBenefits.gov	Washington	DC	20407	**800-333-4636**		336-11
Department of Labor Women's Bureau 200 Constitution Ave NW Rm S3002	Washington	DC	20210	**800-827-5335**	202-693-6710	336-11
Department of Labor Women's Bureau Regional Offices						
Region 1 JFK Federal Bldg Rm E-270	Boston	MA	02203	**800-518-3585**	617-565-1988	336-11
Region 2 201 Varick St Rm 708	New York	NY	10014	**800-827-5335**	212-337-2389	336-11
Region 3 170 S Independence Mall W Suite 880W	Philadelphia	PA	19106	**800-379-9042**	215-861-4860	336-11
Region 4 Federal Center 61 Forsyth St SW Suite 7T95	Atlanta	GA	30303	**800-672-8356**	404-562-2336	336-11
Region 5 Federal Bldg 230 S Dearborn St Rm 1022	Chicago	IL	60604	**800-648-8183**	312-353-6985	336-11
Region 6 Federal Bldg 525 Griffin St Rm 735	Dallas	TX	75202	**888-887-6794**	214-767-6985	336-11
Region 7 1100 Main St Suite 845	Kansas City	MO	64105	**800-252-4706**	816-426-6108	336-11
Region 8 1990 Broadway Suite 1620	Denver	CO	80201	**800-299-0886**	303-844-1285	336-11
Region 9 71 Stevenson St Suite 927	San Francisco	CA	94105	**877-923-6509**	415-975-4750	336-11
Region 10 1111 3rd Ave Rm 925	Seattle	WA	98101	**888-296-7011**	206-553-1534	336-11
Department of the Navy Military Sealift Command 914 Charles Morris Ct SE Washington Navy Yard	Washington	DC	20398	**888-732-5438**	202-685-5055	336-3
Department of Transportation (DOT) Small & Disadvantaged Business Utilization Office 400 7th St SW Rm 9414	Washington	DC	20590	**800-532-1169**	202-366-1930	336-13
Department of the Treasury Office of Foreign Assets Control Pennsylvania Ave & Madison Pl NW	Washington	DC	20220	**800-306-2822**	202-622-2500	336-14
Department of Veterans Affairs (VA) 810 Vermont Ave NW	Washington	DC	20420	**800-827-1000**	202-273-6000	336-15
Small & Disadvantaged Business Utilization Office 801 'I' St NW	Washington	DC	20005	**800-949-8387**	202-565-8124	336-15
Departures Magazine 1120 Ave of the Americas 11th Fl	New York	NY	10036	**800-333-7483**	212-382-5600	449-22
DePaul University 1 E Jackson Blvd 9th Fl	Chicago	IL	60604	**800-433-7285**	312-362-8300	163
DePauw University 313 S Locust St	Greencastle	IN	46135	**800-447-2495**	765-658-4800	163
Dependable Component Supply Corp 1003 E Newport Ctr Dr	Deerfield Beach	FL	33442	**800-336-7100**	954-283-5800	245
Deploy Solutions Inc 100 Lowder Brook Dr Suite 1100	Westwood	MA	02090	**877-463-3756**	781-461-9024	176-1
Depobook Reporting Services 713 10th St	Modesto	CA	95354	**800-830-8885**	209-544-6466	436
DepoNet 25 A Vreeland Rd	Florham Park	NJ	07932	**800-337-6638**		436
Depot The Saint Louis County Heritage & Arts Center 506 W Michigan St	Duluth	MN	55802	**888-733-5833**	218-727-8025	509
Depression & Bipolar Support Alliance (DBSA) 730 N Franklin St Suite 501	Chicago	IL	60610	**800-826-3632**	312-642-0049	48-17
DEPTCOR PO Box 863	Trenton	NJ	08625	**800-321-6524**	609-292-4036	618
Depuy Acromed Inc 325 Paramount Dr	Raynham	MA	02767	**800-451-2006**	508-880-8100	469
DePuy Inc 700 Orthopedic Dr	Warsaw	IN	46581	**800-473-3789**	574-267-8143	469
Der-Tex Corp 1 Lehner Rd	Saco	ME	04072	**800-669-0364**	207-284-5931	730-2
DER Travel Services 9501 W Devon Ave Suite 301	Rosemont	IL	60018	**800-782-2424**	847-430-0000	748
Deringer AN Inc PO Box 1309	Saint Albans	VT	05478	**800-448-8108**	802-524-8110	440
Derma Sciences Inc 214 Carnegie Ctr Suite 100	Princeton	NJ	08540	**800-825-4325**	609-514-4744	467
Dermik Laboratories Inc 1050 Westlakes Dr	Berwyn	PA	19312	**800-666-6030**	484-595-2700	572
DeRoyal Industries Inc 200 DeBusk Ln	Powell	TN	37849	**800-251-9864**	865-938-7828	469
DeRoyal Textiles Inc 125 E York St *Sales	Camden	SC	29020	**800-845-1062***	803-432-2403	730-1
Derrick The 1510 W 1st St PO Box 928	Oil City	PA	16301	**800-352-1002**	814-676-7444	522-2
Derrick Publishing Co 1510 W 1st St	Oil City	PA	16301	**800-352-1002**	814-676-7444	623-8
Derse Exhibits Inc 1234 N 62nd St	Milwaukee	WI	53213	**800-562-2300**	414-257-2000	230
Des Moines Area Community College 2006 S Ankeny Blvd	Ankeny	IA	50021	**800-362-2127**	515-964-6200	160
Des Moines Area Community College 1125 Hancock Dr	Boone	IA	50036	**800-362-2127**	515-432-7203	160
Des Moines (Greater) Convention & Visitors Bureau 405 6th Ave Suite 201	Des Moines	IA	50309	**800-451-2625**	515-286-4960	205
Des Moines (Greater) Partnership 700 Locust St Suite 100	Des Moines	IA	50309	**800-376-9059**	515-286-4950	137
Des Moines Register 715 Locust St	Des Moines	IA	50304	**800-247-5346**	515-284-8000	522-2
DESA (Diabetes Exercise & Sports Assn) 8001 Montcastle Dr	Nashville	TN	37221	**800-898-4322**		48-17
DESA International 2701 Industrial Dr *Cust Svc	Bowling Green	KY	42101	**800-432-5212***	270-781-9600	352
Desai Capital Management Inc 410 Park Ave	New York	NY	10022	**800-337-2484**	212-838-9191	779
DeSales University 2755 Station Ave	Center Valley	PA	18034	**800-228-5114**	610-282-1100	163
Descartes Systems Group Inc 120 Randall Dr *NASDAQ: DSGX*	Waterloo	ON	N2V1C6	**800-419-8495**	519-746-8110	176-12
Desco Inc 1205 Lincolnton Rd	Salisbury	NC	28145	**800-222-2140**	704-633-6331	245
DeSears Appliances Inc 6430 14th St W	Bradenton	FL	34207	**800-337-3277**	941-751-7525	35
Deseret Book Co PO Box 30178 *Sales	Salt Lake City	UT	84130	**800-453-4532***	801-534-1515	623-4
Desert Canyon Golf Resort 1201 Desert Canyon Blvd	Orondo	WA	98843	**800-258-4173**	509-784-1111	655
Desert Dispatch 130 Coolwater Ln	Barstow	CA	92311	**800-676-7585**	760-256-2257	522-2
Desert Hills Motel 1010 S Carson St	Carson City	NV	89701	**800-652-7785**	775-882-1932	373
Desert Hot Springs Spa Hotel 10805 Palm Dr	Desert Hot Springs	CA	92240	**800-808-7727**	760-329-6000	655
Desert Inn Resort 900 N Atlantic Ave	Daytona Beach	FL	32118	**800-826-1711**	386-258-6555	373

Name / Address	City	State	ZIP	Toll-Free	Phone	Class
Desert Island Films 11 Coggeshall Cir	Middletown	RI	02842	**800-766-8550**	401-846-3453	500
Desert Moon Cafe 612 Corporate Way Suite 1M	Valley Cottage	NY	10989	**877-564-6362**	845-267-3300	657
Desert Publications Inc 303 N Indian Canyon Dr PO Box 2724	Palm Springs	CA	92262	**800-775-7256**	760-325-2333	623-9
Desert Regional Medical Center 1150 N Indian Canyon Dr	Palm Springs	CA	92262	**800-962-3765**	760-323-6511	366-2
Desert Schools Federal Credit Union PO Box 2945 *Mktg	Phoenix	AZ	85062	**800-456-9171***	602-433-7000	216
Desert Springs Marriott Resort & Spa 74855 Country Club Dr	Palm Desert	CA	92260	**800-331-3112**	760-341-2211	655
Desert Sun 750 N Gene Autry Trail	Palm Springs	CA	92263	**800-233-3741**	760-322-8889	522-2
Desert Sun Publishing Co PO Box 2734 *Advertising	Palm Springs	CA	92263	**800-233-3741***	760-322-8889	623-8
Design Assn. International Interior 13-500 Merchandise Mart	Chicago	IL	60654	**888-799-4432**	312-467-1950	48-4
Design Center of the Americas (DCOTA) 1855 Griffin Rd	Dania Beach	FL	33004	**800-573-2682**	954-920-7997	452
Design Design Inc 19 La Grave SE	Grand Rapids	MI	49503	[illegible]	616-774-2448	130
Design Group Staffing Services Inc 10155 102nd St Suite 2380	Edmonton	AB	T5J4G8	**800-770-1228**	780-428-1505	707
Design Homes Inc 600 N Marquette Rd	Prairie du Chien	WI	53821	**800-627-9443**	608-326-6041	107
Design Options 5202 Eagle Trail Dr *Cust Svc	Tampa	FL	33634	**877-800-3560***	813-885-4950	314-1
Design Strategy Corp 600 3rd Ave 25th Fl	New York	NY	10016	**800-331-8726**	212-370-0000	178
Design Travel Management Group Inc 2168 Lake Shore Cir	Arlington Heights	IL	60004	**800-773-7930**	847-577-7930	761
Design Within Reach Inc 225 Bush St 20th Fl *NASDAQ: DWRI*	San Francisco	CA	94104	**800-944-2233**	415-676-6500	357
Designatronics Inc 2101 Jericho Tpke *Orders	New Hyde Park	NY	11040	**800-345-1144***	516-328-3300	700
Designer Decal Inc 1120 E 1st Ave	Spokane	WA	99202	**800-622-6333**	509-535-0267	675
Designer Greetings Inc 250 Arlington Ave PO Box 140729	Staten Island	NY	10314	**800-654-6960**	718-981-7700	130
Designware Inc 1 American Rd	Cleveland	OH	44144	**800-321-3040**	216-252-7300	548-1
Desjardins Financial Security Life Assurance Co 200 Ave des Commandeurs	Levis	QC	G6V6R2	**866-838-7553**		384-2
Deskey Assoc Inc 120 E 8th St	Cincinnati	OH	45202	**877-433-7539**	513-721-6800	338
Desktop Imagery 2733 Concession Rd 7	Bowmanville	ON	L1C3K6	**800-579-9253**	905-263-2666	4
DeskTop Labels 7277 Boone Ave N	Minneapolis	MN	55428	**800-241-9730**	763-531-5800	404
Desmond AJ & Sons Funeral Directors 2600 Crooks Rd	Troy	MI	48084	**800-210-7135**	248-362-2500	499
Desmond Albany 660 Albany-Shaker Rd	Albany	NY	12211	**800-448-3500**	518-869-8100	373
Desmond Great Valley 1 Liberty Blvd	Malvern	PA	19355	**800-575-1776**	610-296-9800	373
DeSoto Mills Inc 3850 Sand Valley Rd PO Box 680228	Fort Payne	AL	35968	**800-551-7625**	256-845-6700	153-10
Despatch Industries Inc 8860 207th St W	Lakeville	MN	55044	**800-473-7373**	952-469-5424	313
DesPeres Hospital 2345 Dougherty Ferry Rd	Kirkwood	MO	63122	**888-457-5203**	314-821-5850	366-2
Destination Direct PO Box 65119	Port Ludlow	WA	98365	**888-227-5225**		176-10
Destination Hotels & Resorts Inc 10333 E Dry Creek Rd Suite 450	Englewood	CO	80112	**800-633-8347**	303-799-3830	369
Destination Services of Colorado Inc 0150 E Beaver Creek Blvd	Avon	CO	81620	**800-372-7686**	970-476-6565	183
Destination Success 15 W Central Pkwy	Cincinnati	OH	45202	**888-301-3866**	513-763-3070	377
Destination Winnipeg 259 Portage Ave	Winnipeg	MB	R3B2B4	**800-665-0204**	204-943-1970	205
Destrehan Plantation 13034 River Rd	Destrehan	LA	70047	**877-453-2095**	985-764-9315	50
Destructive Decisions. Students Against 255 Main St	Marlborough	MA	01752	**877-723-3462**	508-481-3568	48-6
Detecto Scale Co 203 E Daugherty St PO Box 151	Webb City	MO	64870	**800-641-2008**	417-673-4631	672
Detector Electronics Corp 6901 W 110th St	Minneapolis	MN	55438	**800-765-3473**	952-941-5665	681
Deter Security Inc 233 S Main St	Rutland	VT	05701	**800-696-3383**	802-773-7305	682
Detex Corp 302 Detex Dr	New Braunfels	TX	78130	**800-729-3839**	830-629-2900	681
Dethmers Mfg Co Inc 4010 320th St	Boyden	IA	51234	**800-543-3626**	712-725-2302	751
Detroit Broach Co 2750 Paldan Dr	Auburn Hills	MI	48326	**800-383-6978**	248-370-0600	447
Detroit Edison Co 2000 2nd Ave *Cust Svc	Detroit	MI	48226	**800-477-4747***	313-235-8000	774
Detroit Free Press 600 W Fort St	Detroit	MI	48226	**800-678-6400**	313-222-6400	522-2
Detroit Hoist Co 6650 Sterling Dr N	Sterling Heights	MI	48312	**800-521-9126**	586-268-2600	462
Detroit Lakes Regional Chamber of Commerce 700 Washington Ave	Detroit Lakes	MN	56501	**800-542-3992**	218-847-9202	137
Detroit Legal News Co 2001 W Lafayette Blvd	Detroit	MI	48216	**800-875-5275**	313-961-3949	623-8
Detroit Lions 222 Republic Dr	Allen Park	MI	48101	**800-616-7627**	313-216-4000	703
Detroit Metropolitan Convention & Visitors Bureau 211 W Fort St Suite 1000	Detroit	MI	48226	**800-225-5389**	313-202-1800	205
Detroit News 615 W Lafayette Blvd	Detroit	MI	48226	**800-678-6400**	313-222-6400	522-2
Detroit Pump & Mfg Co 18943 John R St	Detroit	MI	48203	**800-686-1662**	313-893-4242	378
Detroit Quality Brush Mfg 32165 Schoolcraft Rd	Livonia	MI	48150	**800-722-3037**	734-525-5660	104
Detroit Radiant Product Co 21400 Hoover Rd	Warren	MI	48089	**800-222-1100**	586-756-0950	313
Detroit Stoker Co 1510 E 1st St	Monroe	MI	48161	**800-786-5374**	734-241-9500	313
Detroit Testing Lab Inc 7111 E 11-Mile Rd	Warren	MI	48092	**800-820-7009**	586-754-9000	728
Detroit-Wayne County Port Authority 8109 E Jefferson Ave	Detroit	MI	48214	**800-249-7678**	313-331-3842	607
Detyens Shipyards Inc 1670 Drydock Ave Bldg 236 Suite 200	North Charleston	SC	29405	**800-745-2811**	843-308-8000	689
Deutsch Inc 111 8th Ave 14th Fl	New York	NY	10011	**800-287-3457**	212-981-7600	4
Deutsche Asset Management 345 Park Ave	New York	NY	10154	**800-232-9727**	212-326-6200	393
Deutsche Bank Securities Inc 60 Wall St	New York	NY	10005	**800-334-1898**		679
Deutsche Post Global Mail Ltd 196 Van Buren St 2nd Fl	Herndon	VA	20170	**800-426-7478**	703-450-5777	536
Deutsche Telekom Inc 600 Lexington Ave 17th Fl *NYSE: DT*	New York	NY	10022	**888-382-4872**	212-424-2900	721
Devcon Inc 30 Endicott St	Danvers	MA	01923	**800-626-7226**	978-777-1100	3
Developers Diversified Realty Corp 3300 Enterprise Pkwy *NYSE: DDR*	Beachwood	OH	44122	**800-258-7289**	216-755-5500	641
Developers of Nevada 7448 W Sahara Ave	Las Vegas	NV	89117	**888-250-7033**	702-222-1410	639
Development. American Society for Training & 1640 King St Box 1443	Alexandria	VA	22313	**800-628-2783**	703-683-8100	49-5
Development Dimensions International 1225 Washington Pike *Mktg	Bridgeville	PA	15017	**800-933-4463***	412-257-0600	192
Development Director's Letter 8204 Fenton St	Silver Spring	MD	20910	**800-666-6380**	301-588-6380	521-7
Development Exchange Inc (DEI) 1645 Hennepin Ave Suite 312	Minneapolis	MN	55403	**888-454-2314**	612-677-1505	620
Development Inc. Mercy-USA for Aid & 44450 Pinetree Dr Suite 201	Plymouth	MI	48170	**800-556-3729**	734-454-0011	48-5
Development Institute. First Nations 2300 Fallhill Ave Suite 412	Fredericksburg	VA	22401	**800-682-5384**	540-371-5615	48-14
Development. Institute for Integral PO Box 2172	Colorado Springs	CO	80901	**800-544-9562**	719-634-7943	754
Development & Relief Agency International. Adventist 12501 Old Columbia Pike	Silver Spring	MD	20904	**800-424-2372**	301-680-6380	48-5
Devereux Foundation 2012 Renaissance Blvd	King of Prussia	PA	19406	**800-345-1292**	610-520-3000	228
Devil's Head Resort & Convention Center S6330 Bluff Rd	Merrimac	WI	53561	**800-472-6670**	608-493-2251	655
Devine Intermodal 3870 Channel Dr	West Sacramento	CA	95691	**800-371-4430**	916-371-4430	769
DeVlieg Bullard II Inc 10100 Forest Hills Rd	Rockford	IL	61115	**800-248-8120**	815-282-4100	447
Devon Consulting 950 W Valley Rd Suite 2602	Wayne	PA	19087	**800-229-5709**	610-964-2700	707
Devon Group DBA Devon Self Storage 2000 Powell St Suite 1240	Emeryville	CA	94068	**800-995-4480**	510-450-1300	790-3
Devon Self Storage 2000 Powell St Suite 1240	Emeryville	CA	94068	**800-995-4480**	510-450-1300	790-3
De'Vons Optics Inc 10823 Bell Ct	Rancho Cucamonga	CA	91730	**888-333-8667**	909-466-4700	532
DeVore & Sons Inc DBA Heirloom Bible Publishers PO Box 780189	Wichita	KS	67278	**800-676-2448**	316-267-3211	623-4
DeVries Moving Packing & Storage 3808 N Sullivan Rd Spokane Industrial Pk Bldg 22	Spokane Valley	WA	99216	**800-333-6352**	509-924-6000	508
DeVRY Inc 1 Tower Ln Suite 1000 *NYSE: DV*	Oakbrook Terrace	IL	60181	**800-733-3879**	630-571-7700	241
DeVRY University 2700 3rd Ave SE	Calgary	AB	T2A7W4	**800-363-5558**	403-235-3450	787
DeVRY University 2149 W Dunlap Ave *Cust Svc	Phoenix	AZ	85021	**800-528-0250***	602-870-9222	787
DeVRY University 6600 Dumbarton Cir	Fremont	CA	94555	**888-201-9941**	510-574-1200	787
DeVRY University 3880 Kilroy Airport Way	Long Beach	CA	90806	**800-597-1333**	562-997-5422	787
DeVRY University 901 Corporate Ctr Dr University Ctr	Pomona	CA	91768	**800-243-3660**	909-622-9800	787
DeVRY University 925 S Niagara St	Denver	CO	80224	**888-212-1857**	303-329-3340	787
DeVRY University 250 N Arcadia Ave	Decatur	GA	30030	**800-221-4771**	404-292-7900	787
DeVRY University 1221 N Swift Rd	Addison	IL	60101	**800-346-5420**	630-953-1300	787
DeVRY University 3300 N Campbell Ave	Chicago	IL	60618	**800-338-7940**	773-929-8500	787
DeVRY University 11224 Holmes Rd	Kansas City	MO	64131	**800-821-3766**	816-941-0430	787
DeVRY University 630 US Hwy 1	North Brunswick	NJ	08902	**800-333-3879**	732-435-4880	787
DeVRY University 1350 Alum Creek Dr	Columbus	OH	43209	**800-426-2206**	614-253-7291	787
DeVRY University 4800 Regent Blvd	Irving	TX	75063	**800-633-3879**	972-929-6777	787
DevX Inc 150 Executive Pk Blvd Suite 4100	San Francisco	CA	94134	**800-887-2702**	415-467-0305	623-11
DeWAL Industries Inc 15 Ray Trainor Dr	Narragansett	RI	02882	**800-366-8356**	401-789-9736	717
Dewied International Inc 5010 E IH-10	San Antonio	TX	78219	**800-992-5600**	210-661-6161	291-26
Dewitt Products Co 5860 Plumer Ave *Cust Svc	Detroit	MI	48209	**800-962-8599***	313-554-0575	46
DeWitt Wallace Decorative Arts Museum 325 Francis St	Williamsburg	VA	23185	**800-447-8679**	757-220-7724	509
Dex Media Inc 198 Inverness Dr W *NYSE: DEX*	Englewood	CO	80112	**800-243-2960**	303-784-2900	623-6
Dexter Chemical LLC 845 Edgewater Rd	Bronx	NY	10474	**800-339-9111**	718-542-7700	143
Dexterity Surgical Inc 5444 W Heimer Suite 1970	Houston	TX	77056	**800-840-3339**	713-622-0516	468
Dey LP 2751 Napa Valley Corporate Dr	Napa	CA	94558	**800-869-9005**	707-224-3200	572
DeZurik Water Controls 250 Riverside Ave N	Sartell	MN	56377	**800-788-0288**	320-259-2000	776

Name / Address	City	State	ZIP	Toll-Free	Phone	Class
DF Stauffer Biscuit Co PO Box 1426 Belmont & 6th Ave	York	PA	17405	**800-673-2473**	717-843-9016	291-9
DFI (Diamond Flower Electric Instrument Co USA Inc) 732-C Striker Ave	Sacramento	CA	95834	**800-909-4334**	916-568-1234	171-3
DFS Group 12 South St	Townsend	MA	01469	**800-225-9528**		111
DG Systems 750 W John Carpenter Fwy Suite 700 *NASDAQ: DGIT*	Irving	TX	75039	**800-335-4347**	972-581-2000	9
DGAC (Dangerous Goods Advisory Council) 1100 H St NW Suite 740	Washington	DC	20005	**800-634-1598**	202-289-4550	49-21
DGSE Cos Inc 2817 Forest Ln *NASDAQ: DGSE*	Dallas	TX	75234	**800-527-5307**	972-484-3662	402
DH Blattner & Sons Inc 400 CR 50	Avon	MN	56310	**800-877-2866**	320-356-7351	187-4
DH Brown Associates Inc 222 Grace Church St	Port Chester	NY	10573	**800-253-1799**	914-937-4302	654
DHB Industries Inc 4031 NE 12th Terr *AMEX: DHB*	Oakland Park	FL	33334	**800-979-4343**	954-566-0040	566
DHL Airways DBA DHL Worldwide Express 1200 S Pine Island Rd	Plantation	FL	33324	**800-225-5345**		536
DHL Logistics 3435 Airborne Rd	Wilmington	OH	45177	**800-637-5502**		440
DHL Worldwide Express 1200 S Pine Island Rd	Plantation	FL	33324	**800-225-5345**		536
DHR International 10 S Riverside Plaza Suite 2220	Chicago	IL	60606	**800-782-2210**	312-782-1581	262
Diabetes Advisor Magazine 1701 N Beauregard St	Alexandria	VA	22311	**800-342-2383**	703-549-1500	449-16
Diabetes Assn. American 1701 N Beauregard St	Alexandria	VA	22311	**800-232-3472**	703-549-1500	48-17
Diabetes Center. International 3800 Park Nicollet Blvd	Minneapolis	MN	55416	**888-825-6315**	952-993-3393	654
Diabetes Educators. American Assn of 100 W Monroe St Suite 400	Chicago	IL	60603	**800-338-3633**	312-424-2426	49-8
Diabetes Exercise & Sports Assn (DESA) 8001 Montcastle Dr	Nashville	TN	37221	**800-898-4322**		48-17
Diabetes Research Foundation International. Juvenile 120 Wall St	New York	NY	10005	**800-533-2873**	212-785-9500	48-17
Diabetes Self-Management Magazine 150 W 22nd St *Circ	New York	NY	10011	**800-234-0923***	212-989-0200	449-13
Diablo Mfg Co Inc PO Box 1108 *Sales	Grass Valley	CA	95945	**800-551-2233***	530-272-2241	401
Diageo North America 801 Main Ave	Norwalk	CT	06851	**800-847-4109**	203-359-7100	81-1
Diagnostic Chemicals Ltd 16 McCarville St	Charlottetown	PE	C1E2A6	**800-565-0265**	902-566-1396	229
Diagnostic Medical Sonographers. American Registry of 51 Monroe St Plaza East 1	Rockville	MD	20850	**800-541-9754**	301-738-8401	49-8
Diagnostic Medical Sonography. Society of 2745 N Dallas Pkwy Suite 350	Plano	TX	75093	**800-229-9506**	214-473-8057	49-8
Diagnostic Products Corp 5700 W 96th St *NYSE: DP*	Los Angeles	CA	90045	**800-678-6699**	310-645-8200	229
Diagnostic Systems Laboratories Inc 445 Medical Ctr Blvd	Webster	TX	77598	**800-231-7970**	281-332-9678	229
Diagraph Corp 1 Missouri Research Pk Dr	Saint Charles	MO	63304	**800-526-2531**		112
Diagrind Inc 10491 W 164th Pl	Orland Park	IL	60467	**800-790-4333**	708-460-4333	1
DiagXotics Inc PO Box 160295	Nashville	TN	37216	**800-676-2927**	615-226-1832	574
Dial-A-Mattress Operating Corp DBA 1-800-Mattress 31-10 48th Ave	Long Island City	NY	11101	**800-999-1000**	718-472-1200	361
Dial Corp 15501 N Dial Blvd *Cust Svc	Scottsdale	AZ	85260	**800-258-3425***	480-754-3425	211
Dial Industries Inc 3616 Noakes St	Los Angeles	CA	90023	**800-624-8682**	323-263-6878	596
Dial-Thru International Corp 17383 Sunset Blvd Suite 350	Pacific Palisades	CA	90272	**800-378-9045**	310-566-1700	721
DialAmerica Marketing Inc 960 MacArthur Blvd *Cust Svc	Mahwah	NJ	07495	**800-526-4679***	201-327-0200	722
Dialog Corp 11000 Regency Pkwy Suite 10	Cary	NC	27511	**800-334-2564**	919-462-8600	380
Dialysis Corp of America 27 Miller St Suite 2 *NASDAQ: DCAI*	Lemoyne	PA	17043	**888-730-6164**	717-730-6164	347
Dialysis. International Society for Peritoneal 66 Martin St	Milton	ON	L9T2R2	**888-834-1001**	905-875-2456	49-8
Diametrics Medical Inc 2658 Patton Rd *NASDAQ: DMED*	Saint Paul	MN	55113	**800-949-4762**	651-639-8035	229
Diamond Animal Health Inc 2538 SE 43rd St *Cust Svc	Des Moines	IA	50327	**800-924-8601***	515-263-8600	574
Diamond Brand Canvas Products 145 Cane Creek Industrial Pk Rd Suite 1 *Sales	Fletcher	NC	28732	**800-258-9811***	828-684-9848	718
Diamond Chain Co 402 Kentucky Ave *Cust Svc	Indianapolis	IN	46225	**800-872-4246***	317-638-6431	609
Diamond Chemical Co Inc PO Box 7428	East Rutherford	NJ	07073	**800-654-7627**	201-935-4300	149
Diamond Coach Corp 2300 W 4th St	Oswego	KS	67356	**800-442-4645**	620-795-2191	505
Diamond Council of America (DCA) 3212 West End Ave Suite 202	Nashville	TN	37203	**877-283-5669**	615-385-5301	49-4
Diamond Flower Electric Instrument Co USA Inc (DFI) 732-C Striker Ave	Sacramento	CA	95834	**800-909-4334**	916-568-1234	171-3
Diamond Holding Corp 150 Marr Ave	Marietta	GA	30060	**800-556-6211**	770-590-0152	355-3
Diamond Innovations 6325 Huntley Rd *Cust Svc	Worthington	OH	43085	**800-443-1455***	614-438-2000	1
Diamond J Ranch PO Box 577	Ennis	MT	59729	**877-929-4867**	406-682-4867	238
Diamond Mfg Co 243 W 8th St	Wyoming	PA	18644	**800-233-9601**	570-693-0300	479
Diamond Offshore Drilling Inc 15415 Katy Fwy *NYSE: DO*	Houston	TX	77094	**800-848-1980**	281-492-5300	529
Diamond Packaging Co Inc PO Box 23620	Rochester	NY	14692	**800-333-4079**	585-334-8030	102
Diamond Parking Inc 3161 Elliott Ave Suite 200	Seattle	WA	98121	**800-340-7275**	206-284-3100	552
Diamond Perforated Metals Inc 7300 W Sunnyview Ave	Visalia	CA	93291	**800-642-4334**	559-651-1889	479
Diamond Power International Inc 2600 E Main St	Lancaster	OH	43130	**800-848-5086**	740-687-6500	379
Diamond Resorts International 3745 Las Vegas Blvd S	Las Vegas	NV	89109	**866-309-7318**	702-261-1000	738
Diamond Roller 150 Marr Ave	Marietta	GA	30060	**800-247-5290**	770-590-0152	617
Diamond Saw Works Inc 12290 Olean Rd	Chaffee	NY	14030	**800-828-1180**	716-496-7417	670
Diamond Services Inc 503 S DeGravelle Rd	Amelia	LA	70340	**800-879-1162**	985-631-2187	528
Diamond Tool & Die Inc 508 29th Ave	Oakland	CA	94601	**800-227-1084**	510-534-7050	745
Diamond Transportation System Inc 5021 21st St	Racine	WI	53406	**800-927-5702**	262-554-5400	769
Diamond US Elastomer 161 Marble Mill Rd	Marietta	GA	30060	**800-394-8735**	770-424-4850	594-3
Diamond Vogel Paint & Wax Co 1020 Albany Pl SE	Orange City	IA	51041	**800-728-6435**	712-737-4116	540
Diamondback Div Raleigh America Inc 6004 S 190th St Suite 101	Kent	WA	98032	**800-222-5527**	253-395-1100	83
DiamondCluster International Inc 875 N Michigan Ave Suite 3000 *NASDAQ: DTPI*	Chicago	IL	60611	**800-455-5875**	312-255-5000	193
Diamond/Delchester 841 Lincoln Ave	West Chester	PA	19381	**888-835-3535**	610-692-3366	311
Diamond/Triumph Auto Glass Inc 220 Division St	Kingston	PA	18704	**800-452-7143**	570-287-9915	62-2
Dian Fossey Gorilla Fund International 800 Cherokee Ave SE	Atlanta	GA	30315	**800-851-0203**	404-624-5881	48-3
DIANON Systems Inc 200 Watson Blvd	Stratford	CT	06615	**800-328-2666**	203-381-4000	409
DiaSorin Inc 1951 Northwestern Ave	Stillwater	MN	55082	**800-328-1482**	651-439-9710	229
DiaSys Corp 81 W Main St 5th Fl *AMEX: DYX*	Waterbury	CT	06702	**800-360-2003**	203-755-5083	410
Diaz Wholesale & Mfg Co Inc 5500 Bucknell Dr	Atlanta	GA	30336	**800-394-4639**	404-344-5421	292-11
DiAZiT Co Inc PO Box 276 *Cust Svc	Youngsville	NC	27596	**800-334-6641***	919-556-5188	692
DiCarlo Distributors Inc 1630 N Ocean Ave	Holtsville	NY	11742	**800-342-2756**	631-758-6000	292-8
diCarta Inc 1 Circle Star Way	San Carlos	CA	94070	**888-342-2782**	650-474-3800	176-1
Dick AB Co 7400 Caldwell Ave	Niles	IL	60714	**800-422-3616**	847-779-1900	617
Dick Blick Co PO Box 1267 *Orders	Galesburg	IL	61402	**800-447-8192***	309-343-6181	45
Dick Corp 1900 SR 51	Largo	PA	15025	**800-245-6577**	412-384-1000	185
Dick Davis Publishing Co 3333 W Commercial Blvd Suite 113	Fort Lauderdale	FL	33309	**800-654-1514**	954-733-3996	623-9
Dick Jones Trucking PO Box 136	Swanton	VT	05488	**800-451-3535**	802-868-3381	769
Dickerson Florida Inc PO Drawer 719	Stuart	FL	34995	**800-772-6246**	772-287-6820	187-4
DICKEY-john Corp 5200 Dickey-john Rd	Auburn	IL	62615	**800-637-2952**	217-438-3371	200
Dickey's Barbecue Restaurants Inc 4514 Cole Ave Suite 1000	Dallas	TX	75205	**866-340-6188**	972-248-9899	657
Dickie Walker Marine Inc 1405 S Coast Hwy *NASDAQ: DWMA*	Oceanside	CA	92054	**800-548-2234**	760-450-0360	153-3
Dickinson Area Partnership 600 S Stephenson Ave	Iron Mountain	MI	49801	**800-236-2447**	906-774-2002	137
Dickinson Brands Inc 31 E High St	East Hampton	CT	06424	**888-860-2279**	860-267-2279	572
Dickinson College PO Box 1773	Carlisle	PA	17013	**800-644-1773**	717-245-1231	163
Dickinson Convention & Visitors Bureau 72 E Museum Dr	Dickinson	ND	58601	**800-279-7391**	701-483-4988	205
Dickinson Homes Inc 404 S Stephenson Ave	Iron Mountain	MI	49801	**800-343-8179**	906-774-5800	107
Dickinson Press 1815 1st St PO Box 1367	Dickinson	ND	58602	**800-279-9150**	701-225-8111	522-2
Dickinson State University 291 Campus Dr	Dickinson	ND	58601	**800-279-4295**	701-483-2090	163
Dickman Directories Inc 6145 Columbus Pike	Lewis Center	OH	43035	**877-836-4154**	740-548-6130	623-6
Dick's Sporting Goods Inc 300 Industry Dr *NYSE: DKS*	Pittsburgh	PA	15275	**800-690-7655**	412-809-0100	702
Dickson Co 930 S Westwood Ave	Addison	IL	60101	**800-323-2448**	630-543-3747	200
Dickson County Chamber of Commerce 119 Hwy 70 E	Dickson	TN	37055	**877-718-4967**	615-446-2349	137
Dictaphone Corp 3191 Broadbridge Ave	Stratford	CT	06614	**800-942-6374**	203-381-7000	112
Didax Educational Resources Inc 395 Main St	Rowley	MA	01969	**800-458-0024**	978-948-2340	242
Didde Press Systems 6499 S Potomac St	Centennial	CO	80112	**800-225-5799**	303-708-9044	617
Die-Namic Inc 12700 Delta Dr	Taylor	MI	48180	**800-817-1270**	734-946-6150	745
Diebold Inc 5995 Mayfair Rd *NYSE: DBD*	North Canton	OH	44720	**800-999-3600**	330-490-4000	788
Diedrich Coffee Inc 28 Executive Pk Suite 200 *NASDAQ: DDRX*	Irvine	CA	92614	**800-354-5282**	949-260-1600	156
Dielectric Communications 22 Tower Rd *Sales	Raymond	ME	04071	**800-341-9678***	207-655-4555	633
Dielectric Polymers Inc 218 Race St	Holyoke	MA	01040	**800-628-9007**	413-532-3288	717
Dielectrics & Electrical Insulation Society. IEEE IEEE Operations Ctr 445 Hoes Ln	Piscataway	NJ	08854	**800-678-4333**	732-981-0060	49-19
Dielectrics Industries Inc 300 Burnett Rd	Chicopee	MA	01020	**800-472-7286**	413-594-8111	589
Diet Center Worldwide Inc 395 Springside Dr	Akron	OH	44333	**800-656-3294**	330-665-5861	797

Company / Address	City	State	ZIP	Toll-Free	Phone	Class
Dieterich-Post Co 616 Monterey Pass Rd	Monterey Park	CA	91754	**800-955-3729**	626-289-5021	113
Dietetic Assn. American 120 S Riverside Plaza Suite 2000	Chicago	IL	60606	**800-877-1600**	312-899-0040	49-8
Dietrichs Milk Products Inc 100 McKinley Ave	Reading	PA	19605	**800-526-6455**	610-929-5736	291-10
Dietz & Watson Inc 5701 Tacony St	Philadelphia	PA	19135	**800-333-1974**	215-831-9000	291-26
Dietzgen 250 S Northwest Hwy Suite 203 *Cust Svc	Park Ridge	IL	60068	**800-473-1270***	800-473-1200	578
Diffenbaugh Inc 6865 Airport Dr	Riverside	CA	92504	**800-394-5334**	951-351-6865	185
Different Drumbeats 400 Murrasy Hollow Rd	Shushan	NY	12873	**800-957-6548**	518-854-7446	130
Dig Magazine 30 Grove St Suite C	Peterborough	NH	03458	**800-821-0115**	603-924-7209	449-6
Digene Corp 1201 Clopper Rd *NASDAQ: DIGE*	Gaithersburg	MD	20878	**800-344-3631**	301-944-7000	229
Digi International Inc 11001 Bren Rd E *NASDAQ: DGII*	Minnetonka	MN	55343	**800-344-4273**	952-912-3444	174
Digi-Key Corp 701 Brooks Ave S	Thief River Falls	MN	56701	**800-344-4539**	218-681-6674	245
Digicomp Research Corp 930 Danby Rd *Cust Svc	Ithaca	NY	14850	**800-457-6000***	607-273-5900	176-12
Digidesign Inc 2001 Junipero Serra Blvd	Daly City	CA	94014	**800-333-2137**	650-731-6300	52
Digilog Inc 2360 Maryland Rd *Cust Svc	Willow Grove	PA	19090	**800-344-4564***	215-830-9400	174
Digimarc Corp 9405 SW Gemini Dr *NASDAQ: DMRC*	Everton	OR	97008	**800-344-4627**	503-469-4800	176-12
Digirad Corp 13950 Stowe Dr *NASDAQ: DRAD*	Poway	CA	92064	**800-947-6134**	858-726-1600	375
Digit Professional Inc 3926 Varsity Dr	Ann Arbor	MI	48108	**877-767-8862**	734-677-0840	52
Digital Angel Corp 490 Villaume Ave S *AMEX: DOC*	South Saint Paul	MN	55075	**800-328-0118**	651-455-1621	633
Digital Design Inc 67 Sand Park Rd	Cedar Grove	NJ	07009	**800-967-7746**	973-857-0900	171-6
Digital Employees' Federal Credit Union 220 Donald Lynch Blvd	Marlborough	MA	01752	**800-328-8797**	508-263-6700	216
Digital Excellence 300 York Ave	Saint Paul	MN	55101	**800-608-8008**	651-772-5100	644
Digital Generation Systems Inc 750 W John Carpenter Fwy Suite 700 *NASDAQ: DGIT*	Irving	TX	75039	**800-335-4347**	972-581-2000	9
Digital Innovations 3436 N Kennicott Suite 200	Arlington Heights	IL	60004	**888-762-7858**	847-463-9000	52
Digital Insight Corp 26025 Mureau Rd *NASDAQ: DGIN*	Calabasas	CA	91302	**888-344-4674**	818-871-0000	176-7
Digital Lightwave Inc 15550 Lightwave Dr *NASDAQ: DIGL*	Clearwater	FL	33760	**800-548-9283**	727-442-6677	720
Digital Media Impressions 3489 W 2100 South Suite 150	Salt Lake City	UT	84119	**800-637-5546**	801-303-6100	644
Digital Peripheral Solutions Inc 8015 E Crystal Dr	Anaheim	CA	92807	**800-559-4777**	714-692-5573	171-8
Digital Persona Inc 720 Bay Rd Suite 100	Redwood City	CA	94063	**877-378-2738**	650-474-4000	85
Digital Printing & Imaging Assn (DPI) 10015 Main St	Fairfax	VA	22031	**888-385-3588**	703-385-1339	49-16
Digital Products of Delaware Inc 625 SW 9th Terr	Pompano Beach	FL	33069	**800-671-0299**	954-941-0903	681
Digital River Inc 9625 W 76th St Suite 150 *NASDAQ: DRIV*	Eden Prairie	MN	55344	**800-207-2755**	952-253-8400	39
Digital Solutions Inc 4200 Industrial Park Dr *Cust Svc	Altoona	PA	16602	**888-222-3081***	814-944-0405	176-11
Digital Storage Inc 7611 Green Meadows Dr	Lewis Center	OH	43035	**800-232-3475**	740-548-7179	172
Digital Video Services 4592 40th St SE	Grand Rapids	MI	49512	**800-747-8273**	616-975-9911	239
Digital Voice Corp 13700 Hutton Dr *Cust Svc	Farmers Branch	TX	75234	**800-777-8329***	972-888-6300	720
DigitalNet Holdings Inc 2525 Network Pl *NASDAQ: DNET*	Herndon	VA	20171	**800-999-3732**	703-563-7500	178
DigitalWork.com Inc 661 W Lake St Suite 2-N	Chicago	IL	60661	**877-496-7571**	312-277-4350	39
Dignity Memorial 1929 Allen Pkwy	Houston	TX	77019	**800-894-2024**	713-522-5141	499
DignityUSA Inc 1500 Massachusetts Ave NW	Washington	DC	20005	**800-877-8797**	202-861-0017	48-21
Dillard University 2601 Gentilly Blvd	New Orleans	LA	70122	**800-216-6637**	504-816-4670	163
Dillard's Credit Services Inc PO Box 4599	Carol Stream	IL	60197	**800-643-8278**		213
Dilley Mfg Co 215 E 3rd St	Des Moines	IA	50309	**800-247-5087**	515-288-7289	87
Dillon County Chamber of Commerce 100 N MacArthur Ave	Dillon	SC	29536	**800-444-6838**	843-774-8551	137
Dillon E & Co PO Box 160	Swords Creek	VA	24649	**800-234-8970**	276-873-6816	181
Dillon Poe Supply Corp 215 Pelham Davis Cir	Greenville	SC	29615	**800-849-4300**	864-213-9000	346
DiMare Brothers/New England Farms Packing Co 84 New England Produce Ctr	Chelsea	MA	02150	**800-510-3700**	617-889-3800	292-7
DiMare Fresh Inc 1049 Ave H East	Arlington	TX	76011	**800-322-2184**	817-385-3000	292-7
Dime Community Bancshares Inc 209 Havemeyer St *NASDAQ: DCOM*	Brooklyn	NY	11211	**800-321-3463**	718-782-6200	355-2
Dimension One Spas 2611 Business Park Dr	Vista	CA	92081	**800-345-7727**	760-727-7727	367
Dimensions Inc 1801 N 12th St	Reading	PA	19604	**800-523-8452**	610-939-9900	750
Dimethaid Research Inc 1405 Denison St *TSE: DMX*	Markham	ON	L3R5V2	**888-398-3463**	905-415-1446	86
Dimock Gould & Co 190 22nd St	Moline	IL	61265	**800-274-4013**	309-797-0650	356
Dinah's Garden Hotel 4261 El Camino Real	Palo Alto	CA	94306	**800-227-8220**	650-493-4542	373
Diners Club Carte Blanche 7958 S Chester St Waterview IV	Englewood	CO	80112	**800-234-6377**	303-799-9000	213
Diners Club International 8430 W Bryn Mawr Ave	Chicago	IL	60631	**800-234-6377**	773-380-5100	213
Dingley Press 119 Lisbon St	Lisbon	ME	04250	**888-346-4539**	207-353-4151	615
Dinico Products Inc 220 Goffle Rd	Hawthorne	NJ	07506	**800-225-0497**	973-636-9050	431
Dinkel's Bakery 3329 N Lincoln Ave	Chicago	IL	60657	**800-822-8817**	773-281-7300	291-1
Dinklage Feed Yards Inc PO Box 274	Sidney	NE	69162	**888-343-5940**	308-254-5941	11-1
Dionex Corp 1228 Titan Way *NASDAQ: DNEX* ■ *Cust Svc	Sunnyvale	CA	94085	**800-346-6390***	408-737-0700	410
Dior Christian 712 5th Ave 37th Fl	New York	NY	10019	**800-929-3467**	212-582-0500	273
Dipert Travel & Transportation Ltd PO Box 580	Arlington	TX	76004	**800-433-5335**	817-543-3710	748
Diplomat Country Club & Spa 501 Diplomat Pkwy	Hallandale Beach	FL	33009	**800-327-1212**	954-883-4000	655
Diplomat Resort & Spa. Westin 3555 S Ocean Dr	Hollywood	FL	33019	**888-627-9057**	954-602-6000	655
DirecPC 11717 Exploration Ln	Germantown	MD	20876	**800-347-3272**	301-428-5500	390
Direct Container Line Inc 857 E 230th St	Carson	CA	90745	**888-325-4325**	310-518-1773	308
Direct General Corp 1281 Murfreesboro Rd *NASDAQ: DRCT* ■ *Cust Svc	Nashville	TN	37217	**800-627-8006***	615-399-4700	384-4
Direct Insite Corp 80 Orville Dr Suite 100 *NASDAQ: DIRI*	Bohemia	NY	11716	**800-619-0757**	631-244-1500	176-12
Direct Internet Access PO Box 7263	Monroe	LA	71211	**800-296-2249**		390
Direct Relief International 27 S La Patera Ln	Santa Barbara	CA	93117	**800-676-1638**	805-964-4767	48-5
Direct Satellite Services 315 Quail Ridge Dr	Westmont	IL	60559	**888-475-3474**	630-887-0277	117
Directed Electronics Inc 1 Viper Way	Vista	CA	92081	**800-876-0800**	760-598-6200	52
Directors Guild of America 7920 W Sunset Blvd	Los Angeles	CA	90046	**800-421-4173**	310-289-2000	405
Directory Distributing Assoc 172 Distribution Dr	Birmingham	AL	35209	**800-682-4000**		97
Directory Distributing Assoc 160 Corporate Woods Ct	Bridgeton	MO	63044	**800-325-1964**	314-592-8600	97
Directory Publishers. Association of 116 Cass St	Traverse City	MI	49684	**800-267-9002**		49-16
DirectoryNet LLC 4555 Mansell Rd Suite 230	Alpharetta	GA	30022	**800-733-1212**	770-521-0100	623-6
DIRECTV Inc PO Box 956 *Cust Svc	El Segundo	CA	90245	**800-347-3288***	310-535-5000	117
Dirigo Spice Corp Thyme Square 750 Dorchester Ave	Dorchester	MA	02125	**800-345-9540**	617-436-9540	291-37
Dirt Rider Magazine 6420 Wilshire Blvd *Orders	Los Angeles	CA	90048	**800-800-3478***	323-782-2000	449-3
Dirt Wheels Magazine 25233 Anza Dr	Valencia	CA	91355	**800-767-0345**	661-295-1910	449-3
DIS Corp 1315 Cornwall Ave *Cust Svc	Bellingham	WA	98225	**800-426-8870***	360-733-7610	176-10
Disa Systems Inc 102 Transit Ave	Thomasville	NC	27360	**800-532-0830**	336-889-5599	19
Disabilities Assn of America. Learning 4156 Library Rd	Pittsburgh	PA	15234	**888-300-6710**	412-341-1515	48-17
Disabilities. National Dissemination Center for Children with 1825 Connecticut Ave	Washington	DC	20009	**800-695-0285**	202-884-8200	48-17
Disability Discrimination in the Workplace PO Box 64833	Saint Paul	MN	55164	**800-328-4880**	847-948-7000	521-8
Disability Evaluating Physicians. American Academy of 150 N Wacker Dr Suite 1420	Chicago	IL	60606	**800-456-6095**	312-658-1171	49-8
Disability Funding Week 8204 Fenton St	Silver Spring	MD	20910	**800-666-6380**	301-588-6380	521-8
Disability Law Compliance Report 610 Opperman Dr *Cust Svc	Saint Paul	MN	55123	**800-328-4880***	651-687-7000	521-7
Disability Rights Center Inc 18 Low Ave	Concord	NH	03301	**800-834-1721**	603-228-0432	48-17
Disabled & Alone/Life Services for the Handicapped 352 Park Ave S 11th Fl	New York	NY	10010	**800-995-0066**	212-532-6740	48-17
Disabled American Veterans (DAV) 3725 Alexandria Pike	Cold Spring	KY	41076	**877-426-2838**	859-441-7300	48-19
Disabled American Veterans Magazine 3725 Alexandria Pike	Cold Spring	KY	41076	**877-426-2838**	859-441-7300	449-10
Disaster Assistance. Presbyterian 100 Witherspoon St	Louisville	KY	40202	**888-728-7228**	502-569-5839	48-5
Disaster News Network 9195-C Red Branch Rd	Columbia	MD	21045	**888-203-9119**	410-884-7350	520
Disaster Response International. Christian 922 Magnolia Ave	Auburndale	FL	33823	**800-430-1235**	863-967-4357	48-5
Disaster Response. Lutheran 8765 W Higgins Rd	Chicago	IL	60631	**800-638-3522**	773-380-2822	48-5
Disco Inc 1895 Brannan Rd	McDonough	GA	30253	**800-548-5150**	770-474-7575	497
Discount Car & Truck Rentals Ltd 720 Arrow Rd	North York	ON	M9M2M1	**866-742-5968**	416-744-0123	126
Discount Labels Inc 4115 Profit Ct	New Albany	IN	47150	**800-995-9500**	812-945-2617	404
Discount Tire Co 20225 N Scottsdale Rd	Scottsdale	AZ	85255	**800-347-4348**	480-606-6000	54
Discover Bank 12 Read's Way	New Castle	DE	19720	**800-347-7000**	302-323-7110	71
Discover Financial Services Inc 2500 Lake Cook Rd *Cust Svc	Riverwoods	IL	60015	**800-347-2683***	224-405-0900	213
Discover Magazine 114 5th Ave 15th Fl *Circ	New York	NY	10011	**800-829-9132***	212-633-4400	449-19
Discovery Canada Outdoor Adventure Inc 331 Front St	Kaslo	BC	V0G1M0	**888-300-4453**	250-353-7349	748
Discovery Channel Book Club Doubleday Select Inc 101 Park Ave 2nd Fl	New York	NY	10178	**800-321-7323**		94

Listing	City	State	ZIP	Toll-Free	Phone	Class
Discovery Charter & Tours 8668 Sunrise Dr	Chilliwack	BC	V2R3J1	**888-468-6877**	604-795-6016	748
Discovery Communications Inc 7700 Wisconsin Ave	Bethesda	MD	20814	**800-762-2189**		725
Discovery Cove 6000 Discovery Cove Way Suite B	Orlando	FL	32821	**877-434-7268**	407-370-1280	811
Discovery Cruises Inc 1775 NW 70th Ave	Miami	FL	33126	**800-866-8687**	305-597-0336	217
Discovery Place 301 N Tryon St	Charlotte	NC	28202	**800-935-0553**	704-372-6261	510
Discovery Toys Inc 6400 Brisa St	Livermore	CA	94550	**800-426-4777***	925-606-2600	361
*Cust Svc						
Discovery YMCA Magazine 101 N Wacker Dr	Chicago	IL	60606	**800-872-9622**	312-977-0031	449-20
DISCUS (Distilled Spirits Council of the US Inc) 1250 'I' St NW Suite 400	Washington	DC	20005	**888-862-7597**	202-628-3544	49-6
Disguise 11906 Tech Ctr Ct	Poway	CA	92064	**800-786-4864**	858-391-3600	153-6
DISH Network 9601 S Meridian Blvd	Englewood	CO	80112	**800-333-3474**	303-723-1000	117
Disk Software Inc 109 S Murphy Rd	Plano	TX	75094	**800-635-7760**	972-423-7288	176-5
Disney Adventures Magazine 114 5th Ave	New York	NY	10011	**800-829-5146***	212-633-4400	449-6
*Cust Svc						
Disney Consumer Products 500 S Buena Vista St	Burbank	CA	91521	**800-723-4763***	818-560-1000	623-9
*PR						
Disney Cruise Line 210 Celebration Pl	Celebration	FL	34747	**800-511-1333**	407-566-3500	217
Disney Educational Productions 105 Terry Dr Suite 120	Newtown	PA	18940	**800-295-5010**		502
Disney Magazine Publishing 114 5th Ave	New York	NY	10011	**800-333-8734***	212-633-4400	623-9
*Cust Svc						
Disney Vacation Club 200 Celebration Pl	Celebration	FL	34747	**800-500-3990**	407-566-3100	738
Disney's Hilton Head Island Resort 22 Harborside Ln	Hilton Head Island	SC	29928	**800-453-4911**	843-341-4100	655
Disney's Saratoga Springs Resort & Spa 1960 Broadway St	Lake Buena Vista	FL	32830	**800-282-9282**	407-827-1100	373
Disorders. National Organization for Rare 55 Kenosia Ave PO Box 1968	Danbury	CT	06813	**800-999-6673**	203-744-0100	48-17
Disorders. Paget Foundation for Paget's Disease of Bone & Related 120 Wall St Suite 1602	New York	NY	10005	**800-237-2438**	212-509-5335	48-17
Dispatch The 116 E Market St	Blairsville	PA	15717	**888-636-1116**	724-459-6100	522-2
Dispatch Printing Co 34 S 3rd St	Columbus	OH	43215	**800-282-0263**	614-461-5000	623-8
DispatchOne 2835 Belvidere Rd Suite 309 PO Box 8787	Waukegan	IL	60079	**800-942-9363**	847-662-8802	433
Dispensers Optical Service Corp 1815 Plantside Dr	Louisville	KY	40299	**800-626-4545***	502-491-3440	531
*Cust Svc						
Display Smart LLC 801 W 27th Terr	Lawrence	KS	66046	**888-843-1870**	785-843-1869	231
Display Technology Inc 111-01 14th Ave 3rd Fl	College Point	NY	11356	**800-424-4220**	718-321-3100	231
Disston Precision Inc 6795 State Rd	Philadelphia	PA	19135	**800-238-1007***	215-338-1200	670
*Cust Svc						
Distaff Foundation. Army 6200 Oregon Ave NW	Washington	DC	20015	**800-541-4255**	202-541-0105	48-19
Distillata Co 1608 E 24th St	Cleveland	OH	44114	**800-999-2906***	216-771-2900	792
*Cust Svc						
Distilled Spirits Council of the US Inc (DISCUS) 1250 'I' St NW Suite 400	Washington	DC	20005	**888-862-7597**	202-628-3544	49-6
Distillerie Stock USA Ltd 58-58 Laurel Hill Blvd	Woodside	NY	11377	**800-323-1884**	718-651-9800	81-3
Distinctive Designs International Inc 120 Sibley Dr	Russellville	AL	35653	**800-243-4787**	256-332-7390	288
Distribution Center Management Newsletter 28 W 25th St 8th Fl	New York	NY	10010	**800-232-4317**	212-228-0246	521-2
Distribution Network. Automotive 5050 Poplar Ave Suite 2020	Memphis	TN	38157	**800-727-8112**	901-682-9090	49-18
Distribution Technologies Inc DBA DistTech 14841 Sperry Rd	Newbury	OH	44065	**800-321-3143**	440-338-1010	769
Distribution Technology Inc 1701 Continental Blvd	Charlotte	NC	28273	**800-264-4771**	704-588-2867	790-1
Distributors Warehouse Inc 1900 N 10th St	Paducah	KY	42001	**800-892-9966**	270-442-8201	61
District of Columbia						
Convention & Tourism Corp 1212 New York Ave Suite 200	Washington	DC	20005	**800-422-8644**	202-724-5644	335
Employment Services Dept 609 H St NE	Washington	DC	20002	**877-319-7346**	202-698-6044	335
Tuition Assistance Grant Program 441 4th St NW Rm 350N	Washington	DC	20001	**877-485-6751**	202-727-2824	711
District of Columbia Bar 1250 H St NW 6th Fl	Washington	DC	20005	**877-333-2227**	202-737-4700	73
DistTech 14841 Sperry Rd	Newbury	OH	44065	**800-321-3143**	440-338-1010	769
DIT-MCO International Corp 5612 Brighton Terr	Kansas City	MO	64130	**800-821-2168**	816-444-9700	247
Ditech Communications Corp 825 E Middlefield Rd	Mountain View	CA	94043	**800-770-0117**	650-623-1300	720
NASDAQ: DITC						
ditech.com 3200 Park Center Dr Suite 150	Costa Mesa	CA	92626	**800-803-7656**	714-800-5800	498
Divaris Real Estate Inc 1 Columbus Ctr Suite 700	Virginia Beach	VA	23462	**888-373-0023**	757-497-2113	638
Diversa Corp 4955 Directors Pl	San Diego	CA	92121	**800-523-2990**	858-526-5000	86
NASDAQ: DVSA						
Diversco Inc 105 Diversco Dr	Spartanburg	SC	29307	**800-277-3420**	864-579-3420	682
Diverse Power Inc PO Box 160	LaGrange	GA	30241	**800-845-8362**	706-845-2000	244
Diversified Account Systems of Georgia Inc 1331 Citizens Pkwy Suite 110	Morrow	GA	30260	**800-226-1464**	770-961-5400	157
Diversified Adjustment Service Inc 600 Coon Rapids Blvd	Coon Rapids	MN	55433	**800-279-3733**	763-780-1042	157

Listing	City	State	ZIP	Toll-Free	Phone	Class
Diversified Chemical Technologies Inc 15477 Woodrow Wilson St	Detroit	MI	48238	**800-243-1424**	313-867-5444	143
Diversified Collection Services Inc 333 N Canyons Pkwy Suite 100	Livermore	CA	94551	**800-327-9467**	925-960-4800	157
Diversified Conference Management Inc 1878 Cypress Point Ct	Ann Arbor	MI	48108	**800-458-2535**	734-665-2535	183
Diversified Funding Services Inc PO Box 873	Jonesboro	GA	30237	**888-603-0055**	770-603-0055	268
Diversified Funds 4 Manhattanville Rd	Purchase	NY	10577	**800-926-0044**	914-697-8000	517
Diversified Human Resources Inc 2735 E Camelback Rd	Phoenix	AZ	85016	**888-870-5588**	480-941-5588	619
Diversified Medical Staffing LLC 3410 Belle Chase Way Suite 600	Lansing	MI	48911	**800-881-3205**	517-702-4030	707
Diversified Optical Products Inc 282 Main St	Salem	NH	03079	**800-230-1600**	603-898-1880	534
Diversified Optical Products Inc Cairns Advanced Technologies Div 282 Main St	Salem	NH	03079	**800-230-1600**	603-898-1880	566
Diversified Search Cos 2005 Market St Suite 3300	Philadelphia	PA	19103	**800-423-3932**	215-732-6666	262
Diversified Senior Services Inc 915 W 4th St	Winston-Salem	NC	27101	**800-721-8182**	336-724-1000	442
Diversified Software Systems Inc 18635 Sutter Blvd	Morgan Hill	CA	95037	**800-273-3774**	408-778-9914	176-12
Diversified Technology Inc 476 Highland Colony Pkwy	Ridgeland	MS	39157	**800-443-2667**	601-856-4121	613
Diversified Title & Escrow Services Co 222 S Harbor Blvd 8th Fl	Anaheim	CA	92805	**800-266-9485**	714-999-1800	384-6
Diversifoam Products 9091 County Rd 50	Rockford	MN	55373	**800-669-0100**	763-477-5854	590
Diversinet Corp 2225 Sheppard Ave E Suite 1801	Toronto	ON	M2J5C2	**800-357-7050**	416-756-2324	176-12
DiversiTech Inc 2530 Lantrac Ct	Decatur	GA	30035	**800-995-2222**	770-593-0900	15
Divi Resorts Inc 6340 Quadrangle Dr Suite 300	Chapel Hill	NC	27517	**800-367-3484**	919-419-3484	369
Dividend Capital Trust 518 17th St Suite 1700	Denver	CO	80202	**866-324-7348**	303-228-2200	640
Diving Equipment & Marketing Assn (DEMA) 3750 Convoy St Suite 310	San Diego	CA	92111	**800-862-3483**	858-616-6408	49-4
Diving Instructors International. Professional Assn of 30151 Tomas St	Rancho Santa Margarita	CA	92688	**800-729-7234***	949-858-7234	48-22
*Sales						
Dix Corp 4024 S Grove Rd	Spokane	WA	99224	**800-827-8548**	509-838-4455	188-14
Dixie Bocock Sporting Goods DBA Dixie Sporting Goods 501 Deacon Blvd	Winston-Salem	NC	27105	**888-262-6251**	336-724-2421	702
Dixie Electric Co-op PO Box 30	Union Springs	AL	36089	**888-349-4332**	334-738-2500	244
Dixie Electric Membership Corp (DEMCO) PO Box 15659	Baton Rouge	LA	70895	**800-262-0221**	225-261-1221	244
Dixie Group Inc 345-B Nowlin Ln	Chattanooga	TN	37421	**800-241-4211**	706-876-5800	131
NASDAQ: DXYN						
Dixie Gun Works Inc PO Box 130	Union City	TN	38281	**800-238-6785***	731-885-0700	702
*Orders						
Dixie Industries PO Box 180600	Chattanooga	TN	37406	**800-933-4943**	423-698-3323	345
Dixie Mfg Co Div Capitol Adhesives USA 300 Cross Plains Blvd	Dalton	GA	30720	**800-831-8381**	706-277-6241	131
Dixie-Narco Inc PO Drawer 719	Williston	SC	29853	**800-688-9090**	803-266-5000	55
Dixie Produce & Packaging Inc 5801 G St	Harahan	LA	70123	**800-952-5637**	504-733-7500	292-7
Dixie Restaurants Inc 1215 Rebsamen Pk Rd	Little Rock	AR	72202	**800-508-1242**	501-666-3494	657
Dixie State College 225 S 700 East	Saint George	UT	84770	**888-324-2998**	435-652-7500	160
Dixie Store Fixtures Inc 2425 1st Ave N	Birmingham	AL	35203	**800-323-4943**	205-322-2442	281
Dixieline Lumber Co Inc 3250 Sports Arena Blvd	San Diego	CA	92110	**800-443-7386**	619-224-4120	359
Dixon Builders & Developers Inc 7924 Jessie's Way	Hamilton	OH	45011	**877-442-5888**	513-887-6400	639
Dixon Industries Inc Hwy 169 PO Box 1569	Coffeyville	KS	67337	**877-288-6673**	620-251-2000	420
Dixon Ticonderoga Co 195 International Pkwy	Heathrow	FL	32746	**800-824-9430**	407-829-9000	560
AMEX: DXT						
Dixon Valve & Coupling Co 800 High St	Chestertown	MD	21620	**800-876-3822**	410-778-2000	777
Dixson Div AMETEK Inc 287 27 Rd	Grand Junction	CO	81503	**888-302-0639**	970-244-1241	486
dj Orthopedics Inc 2985 Scott St	Vista	CA	92081	**800-321-9549**	760-727-1280	469
NYSE: DJO						
DL Lee & Sons Inc PO Box 206	Alma	GA	31510	**800-673-9339***	912-632-4406	465
*Cust Svc						
DLZ Corp 6121 Huntley Rd	Columbus	OH	43229	**800-336-5352**	614-888-0040	258
DM Industries Ltd 2320 NW 147th St	Miami	FL	33054	**800-848-2772**	305-685-5739	367
DMG World Media 27 N Jefferson St	Knightstown	IN	46148	**800-876-5133**	765-345-5133	623-8
DMI Furniture Inc 101 Bullitt Ln Suite 205	Louisville	KY	40222	**888-372-1927**	502-426-4351	314-2
DMI Tile & Marble Inc 3012 5th Ave S	Birmingham	AL	35233	**800-322-8449**	205-322-8473	188-15
DMIA (Document Management Industries Assn) 433 E Monroe Ave	Alexandria	VA	22301	**800-336-4641**	703-836-6232	48-9
DMJM & Harris 605 3rd Ave 31st Fl	New York	NY	10158	**800-729-3656**	212-973-2900	258
DMS Direct Marketing Services Inc 2324 E Bell Rd	Phoenix	AZ	85022	**888-225-5367**	602-308-1000	722
DMS Laboratories Inc 2 Darts Mill Rd	Flemington	NJ	08822	**800-567-4367**	908-782-3353	574
DMV USA 1285 Rudy St	Onalaska	WI	54650	**877-300-7676***	608-779-7676	291-10
*Cust Svc						
DMW Worldwide 1325 Morris Dr	Wayne	PA	19087	**877-744-3699**	610-407-0407	5
DMX Music Inc 11400 W Olympic Blvd Suite 1100	Los Angeles	CA	90064	**800-700-4412**	310-444-1744	513

Name / Address	City	State	ZIP	Toll-Free	Phone	Class
DNA Diagnostics Center 205 Corporate Ct	Fairfield	OH	45014	**800-362-2368**	513-881-7800	408
DNE World Fruit Sales 1900 Old Dixie Hwy	Fort Pierce	FL	34946	**800-327-6676**	772-465-1110	310-2
Do it Best Corp PO Box 868	Fort Wayne	IN	46801	**800-348-1785**	260-748-5300	346
Do+Able Products Inc 5150 Edison Ave	Chino	CA	91710	**800-829-3648**	909-590-4444	489
Doak Dermatologics 383 Rt 46 W	Fairfield	NJ	07004	**800-929-9300**	973-882-1505	572
Doak House Museum 690 Erwin Hwy	Greeneville	TN	37743	**800-729-0256**	423-636-8554	509
DoALL Co 254 N Laurel Ave	Des Plaines	IL	60016	**800-955-8191**	847-824-8191	447
Doane Agricultural Services 11701 Borman Dr Suite 300	Saint Louis	MO	63146	**800-535-2342**	314-569-2700	623-9
Doane College 1014 Boswell Ave	Crete	NE	68333	**800-333-6263**	402-826-2161	163
Lincoln Campus 303 N 52nd St New Century Bldg	Lincoln	NE	68504	**800-333-6263**	402-466-4774	163
Doane LC Co PO Box 975	Essex	CT	06426	**800-447-5006**	860-767-8295	431
Doane Pet Care Co 210 Westwood Pl S Suite 400	Brentwood	TN	37027	**800-789-4639**	615-373-7774	568
Doane's Agricultural Report 11701 Borman Dr Suite 300	Saint Louis	MO	63146	**800-535-2342**	314-569-2700	521-13
Dober Chemical Group 14461 S Waverly Ave	Midlothian	IL	60445	**800-323-4983**	708-388-7700	143
Dobson Communications Corp 14201 Wireless Way	Oklahoma City	OK	73134	**888-575-9427***	405-529-8500	721
NASDAQ: DCEL ■ *Cust Svc						
DOC Optics Corp 19800 W Eight-Mile Rd	Southfield	MI	48075	**800-289-3937**	248-354-7100	533
Doc-U-Search Inc 63 Pleasant St	Concord	NH	03301	**877-524-3034**	603-224-2871	621
Dock Street Theatre 135 Church St	Charleston	SC	29401	**800-454-7093**	843-577-5967	562
DocMan Technologies 31300 Bainbridge Rd	Cleveland	OH	44139	**888-636-2626**	440-542-9660	39
Doctor's Assoc Inc 325 Bic Dr	Milford	CT	06460	**800-888-4848**	203-877-4281	656
Doctors' Co The 185 Greenwood Rd	Napa	CA	94558	**800-421-2368**	707-226-0100	384-5
Doctors Foster & Smith Inc 2253 Air Pk Rd	Rhinelander	WI	54501	**800-381-7179**	715-369-3305	568
Doctors Without Borders USA Inc 333 7th Ave 2nd Fl	New York	NY	10001	**888-392-0392**	212-679-6800	48-5
DocuCorp International Inc 5910 N Central Expy Suite 800	Dallas	TX	75206	**800-928-6000**	214-891-6500	176-8
NASDAQ: DOCC						
Document Management Industries Assn (DMIA) 433 E Monroe Ave	Alexandria	VA	22301	**800-336-4641**	703-836-6232	48-9
Document Sciences Corp 6339 Paseo del Lago	Carlsbad	CA	92009	**800-420-2620**	760-602-1400	176-1
NASDAQ: DOCX						
Dodd Camera & Video 2077 E 30th St	Cleveland	OH	44115	**800-507-1676**	216-361-6817	119
Dodd Co DBA Dodd Camera & Video 2077 E 30th St	Cleveland	OH	44115	**800-507-1676**	216-361-6817	119
Dodge City Community College 2501 N 14th Ave	Dodge City	KS	67801	**800-367-3222**	620-225-1321	160
Dodge City Daily Globe 705 2nd Ave PO Box 820	Dodge City	KS	67801	**800-279-8795**	620-225-4151	522-2
Dodge County Convention & Visitors Bureau 605 N Broad St	Fremont	NE	68025	**800-727-8323**	402-721-2641	205
Dodge & Cox 555 California St 40th Fl	San Francisco	CA	94104	**800-621-3979**	415-981-1710	393
Dodge & Cox Funds 555 California St 40th Fl	San Francisco	CA	94104	**800-621-3979**	415-981-1710	517
Dodge Div DaimlerChrysler Corp 1000 Chrysler Dr	Auburn Hills	MI	48326	**800-992-1997***	248-576-5741	59
*Cust Svc						
Dodge NP Real Estate 8701 W Dodge Rd Suite 300	Omaha	NE	68114	**800-642-5008**	402-397-4900	638
Dodge-Regupol Inc 715 Fountain Ave	Lancaster	PA	17601	**800-322-1923**	717-295-3400	286
Dodger Industries 1702 21st St	Eldora	IA	50627	**800-247-7879**	641-939-5464	153-1
Dodson Aviation Inc 2110 Montana Rd	Ottawa	KS	66067	**800-255-0034**	785-242-4000	759
Dodson Brothers Exterminating Co Inc PO Box 10249	Lynchburg	VA	24506	**800-446-0977**	434-847-9051	567
Doe Run Co 1801 Park 270 Dr Suite 300	Saint Louis	MO	63146	**800-356-3786**	314-453-7110	476
Dofasco Inc 1330 Burlington St E po Box 2460	Hamilton	ON	L8N3J5	**800-363-2726**	905-544-3761	709
TSE: DFS						
Dog Fancy Magazine 3 Burroughs	Irvine	CA	92618	**800-365-4421***	949-855-8822	449-14
*Cust Svc						
Dog Registry. National PO Box 116	Woodstock	NY	12498	**800-637-3647**	845-679-2355	48-3
Dog World Magazine 3 Burroughs	Irvine	CA	92618	**800-365-4421**	949-855-8822	449-14
Dogs of America. Guide 13445 Glenoaks Blvd	Sylmar	CA	91342	**800-459-4843**	818-362-5834	48-17
Dogwood Hills Resort Inn & Golf Club. Best Western 1252 State Hwy KK	Osage Beach	MO	65065	**800-528-1234**	573-348-1735	655
Doheny Eye Institute 1450 San Pablo St	Los Angeles	CA	90033	**800-872-2273**	323-442-6300	366-5
Doheny Eye & Tissue Transplant Bank 1127 Wilshire Blvd Suite 602	Los Angeles	CA	90017	**877-348-2020**	213-482-3937	535
Doherty Employment Group 7625 Parklawn Ave	Edina	MN	55435	**800-910-8822**	952-832-8383	619
Dohmen F Co W 194 North 11381 McCormick Dr	Germantown	WI	53022	**877-848-4166**	262-255-0022	237
DOJ (Department of Justice)						
Office of Justice Programs 810 7th St NW Suite 6400	Washington	DC	20531	**800-421-6770**	202-307-5933	336-10
Office of Special Counsel for Immigration-Related Unfair Employment Practices 950 Pennsylvania Ave NW	Washington	DC	20038	**800-255-7688***	202-616-5594	336-10
*Hotline						
DOL (Department of Labor) 200 Constitution Ave NW	Washington	DC	20210	**866-487-2365**	202-693-4650	336-11
GovBenefits.gov	Washington	DC	20407	**800-333-4636**		336-11
Dolby Laboratories Inc 100 Potrero Ave	San Francisco	CA	94103	**800-983-6529**	415-558-0200	52
NYSE: DLB						
Dolce Hamilton Park 175 Park Ave	Florham Park	NJ	07932	**800-321-6000**	973-377-2424	370
Dolce Hayes Mansion 200 Edenvale Ave	San Jose	CA	95136	**800-420-3200**	408-226-3200	370
Dolce Heritage 522 Heritage Rd	Southbury	CT	06488	**800-932-3466**	203-264-8200	370
Dolce International 28 W Grand Ave	Montvale	NJ	07645	**888-993-6523**	201-307-8700	369
Dolce Skamania Lodge 1131 SW Skamania Lodge Way	Stevenson	WA	98648	**800-221-7117**	509-427-7700	370
Dolce Tarrytown House 49 E Sunnyside Ln	Tarrytown	NY	10591	**800-553-8118**	914-591-8200	370
Dolch Computer Systems 3178 Laurelview Ct	Fremont	CA	94538	**877-347-4938**	510-661-2220	171-3
Dole Distribution Center 607 Ala Moana Blvd CFS-3	Honolulu	HI	96813	**800-697-9100**	808-531-5911	292-7
Dole Food Co Inc 1 Dole Dr	Westlake Village	CA	91362	**800-232-8888**	818-879-6600	310-4
Dole Fresh Vegetables Co PO Box 1759	Salinas	CA	93902	**800-333-5454***	831-754-5244	11-11
*Sales						
Dole Refrigerating Co 1420 Higgs Rd	Lewisburg	TN	37091	**800-251-8990**	931-359-6211	650
Dolese Brothers Co 20 NW 13th St	Oklahoma City	OK	73103	**800-375-2311**	405-235-2311	181
Dollar Bank FSB 3 Gateway Ctr	Pittsburgh	PA	15222	**800-828-5527**	412-261-4900	71
Dollar Discount Stores of America Inc 1362 Naamans Creek Rd	Boothwyn	PA	19061	**800-227-5314**	610-497-1991	778
Dollar Rent A Car Inc 5330 E 31st St	Tulsa	OK	74135	**800-800-4000**	918-669-3000	126
Dollars for Scholars Scholarship America 1 Scholarship Way	Saint Peter	MN	56082	**800-537-4180**	507-931-1682	711
Dollhouse Miniatures Magazine PO Box 595	Boston	MA	02117	**800-437-5828**	617-536-0100	449-14
Dolly's Pizza Franchising Inc 1097-B Union Lake Rd	White Lake	MI	48386	**866-336-5597**	248-360-6440	657
Dolomite USA Corp 5 Commerce Ave	West Lebanon	NH	03784	**800-257-2008**	603-298-5592	701
Dolphin Beach Resort 4900 Gulf Blvd	Saint Pete Beach	FL	33706	**800-237-8916**	727-360-7011	373
Dolphin Inn 1705 Atlantic Ave	Virginia Beach	VA	23451	**800-365-3467**	757-491-1420	373
Dolphin Medical Inc 12525 Chadron Ave	Hawthorne	CA	90250	**866-588-9539**	310-978-3073	468
Domain Assoc 1 Palmer Sq Suite 515	Princeton	NJ	08542	**800-241-1901**	609-683-5656	779
Domain Bank Inc 23 W 4th St	Bethlehem	PA	18015	**888-583-3382**	610-317-9606	389
Domain Direct Div TUCOWS Inc 96 Mowat Ave	Toronto	ON	M6K3M1	**800-371-6992**	416-531-2697	389
Domain Inc 51 Morgan Dr	Norwood	MA	02062	**877-436-6246**	781-769-9130	316
Domain Registration Services DBA dotEarth.com PO Box 447	Palmyra	NJ	08065	**888-339-9001**		389
Domaine Chandon Inc 1 California Dr	Yountville	CA	94599	**800-736-2892**	707-944-8844	81-3
DomainPeople Inc 555 W Hastings St Harbour Ctr Suite 1440	Vancouver	BC	V6B4N6	**877-734-3667**	604-639-1680	389
Domainsearch.com 9525 Kenwood Rd Suite 328	Cincinnati	OH	45242	**866-927-3624**	513-351-4222	677
Domco Tarkett Inc 1139 Lehigh Ave	Whitehall	PA	18052	**800-367-8275**	610-266-5500	286
Domestic Capital Corp 815 Reservoir Ave	Cranston	RI	02910	**800-556-6600**	401-946-3310	394
Domestic Linen Supply & Laundry Inc 3800 18th St	Detroit	MI	48208	**800-430-0871**	313-831-6700	434
Domestic Securities Inc 160 Summit Ave	Montvale	NJ	07645	**877-429-2111**	201-782-0888	679
Domestic Violence. ABA Commission on 740 15th St NW 9th Fl	Washington	DC	20005	**800-799-7233**	202-662-1737	49-10
Domestic Violence Hotline. National PO Box 161810	Austin	TX	78716	**800-799-7233**	512-794-1133	48-6
Domestic Violence. National Resource Center on 6400 Flank Dr Suite 1300	Harrisburg	PA	17112	**800-537-2238**	717-545-6400	48-6
Domine Builders Supply Corp 100 E Highland Dr	Rochester	NY	14610	**800-836-2565**	585-271-6330	181
Domini Social Investments PO Box 9785	Providence	RI	02940	**800-582-6757**		517
Dominica Tourist Office 110-64 Queens Blvd Box 427	Forest Hills	NY	11375	**888-645-5637**	212-949-1711	764
Dominican College 470 Western Hwy	Orangeburg	NY	10962	**866-432-4636**	845-359-7800	163
Dominican Republic Tourist Board 248 NW 42nd Ave	Miami	FL	33126	**888-358-9594**	305-444-4592	764
Dominican Republic Tourist Board 136 E 57th St Suite 803	New York	NY	10022	**888-374-6361**	212-588-1012	764
Dominick's Finer Foods Inc 711 Jorie Blvd	Oak Brook	IL	60523	**877-723-3929**	630-891-5000	339
Dominion East Ohio 701 E Cary St	Richmond	VA	23219	**888-667-3000**	804-771-3000	774
Dominion Electric Supply Co Inc 5053 Lee Hwy	Arlington	VA	22207	**800-525-5006**	703-536-4400	245
Dominion Hope 701 E Cary St	Richmond	VA	23219	**888-667-3000**	304-623-8600	774
Dominion Hospital 2960 Sleepy Hollow Rd	Falls Church	VA	22044	**800-950-6463**	703-536-2000	366-3
Dominion North Carolina Power 701 E Cary St	Richmond	VA	23219	**888-667-3000**	804-771-3000	774
Dominion Peoples 625 Liberty Ave	Pittsburgh	PA	15222	**800-764-0111**	412-244-2626	774
Dominion Post 1251 Earl L Core Rd	Morgantown	WV	26505	**800-654-4676**	304-292-6301	522-2
Dominion Resources Black Warrior Trust 901 Main St Bank of America Plaza 17th Fl	Dallas	TX	75202	**800-365-6548**	214-209-2400	662
NYSE: DOM						
Dominion Resources Inc PO Box 26532	Richmond	VA	23261	**800-552-4034**	804-775-2500	355-5
NYSE: D						
Dominion Transmission PO Box 2450	Clarksburg	WV	26302	**800-624-3101**	304-623-8000	320
Dominion Ventures Inc 1656 N California Blvd Suite 300	Walnut Creek	CA	94596	**800-875-4890**	925-280-6300	779
Dominion Veterinary Laboratories Inc 1199 Sanford St	Winnipeg	MB	R3E3A1	**800-465-7122**	204-589-7361	574

Name / Address	City	State	ZIP	Toll-Free	Phone	Class
Dominion Virginia Power 701 E Cary St	Richmond	VA	23219	**888-667-3000**	804-771-3000	774
Domino Amjet Inc 1290 Lakeside Dr	Gurnee	IL	60031	**800-444-4512**	847-244-2501	616
Domino's Pizza Inc 30 Frank Lloyd Wright Dr *NYSE: DPZ*	Ann Arbor	MI	48106	**888-366-4667**	734-930-3030	657
Domtar Inc 395 boul de Maisonneuve O *NYSE: DTC*	Montreal	QC	H3A1L6	**800-267-2040**	514-848-5400	671
Don Blackburn & Co Inc 13335 Farmington Rd	Livonia	MI	48150	**800-448-0528**	734-261-9100	245
Don CeSar Beach Resort & Spa 3400 Gulf Blvd	Saint Pete Beach	FL	33706	**800-282-1116**	727-360-1881	655
Don Dye Co Inc PO Box 107	Kingman	KS	67068	**800-901-3131**	620-532-3131	609
Don Edward & Co 2500 S Harlem Ave *Cust Svc	North Riverside	IL	60546	**800-777-4366***	708-883-8000	295
Don Garlits Museums 13700 SW 16th Ave	Ocala	FL	34473	**877-271-3278**	352-245-8661	511
Don Hall's Guesthouse 1313 W Washington Center Rd	Fort Wayne	IN	46825	**800-348-1999**	260-489-2524	373
Don Harrington Discovery Center 1200 Streit Dr	Amarillo	TX	79106	**800-784-9548**	806-355-9547	510
Don Hutson Organization 516 Tennessee St Suite 219	Memphis	TN	38103	**800-647-9166**	901-767-0000	753
Don Laughlin's Riverside Resort & Casino 1650 Casino Dr	Laughlin	NV	89029	**800-227-3849**	702-298-2535	133
Don Pablo's Mexican Kitchen 150 Hancock St	Madison	GA	30650	**800-765-7894**	706-342-4552	657
Don Roberto Jewelers Inc 1020 Calle Recodo Suite 100	San Clemente	CA	92673	**888-466-5300**	949-361-6700	402
Don Shula's Hotel & Golf Club 6842 Main St	Miami Lakes	FL	33014	**800-247-4852**	305-821-1150	655
Don Stevens Inc 980 Discovery Rd	Eagan	MN	55121	**800-444-2299**	651-452-0872	651
Don Wan Florist Ltd 5644 W 63rd St	Chicago	IL	60638	**800-336-6926**	773-585-2225	287
Doña Ana Branch Community College Box 30001 Dept 3DA	Las Cruces	NM	88003	**800-903-7503**	505-527-7500	160
Donald Bruce & Co 3600 N Talman Ave	Chicago	IL	60618	**800-621-6017**	773-477-8100	400
Donaldson Brown Hotel & Conference Center 201 Otey St Virginia Tech Campus	Blacksburg	VA	24061	**877-200-3360**	540-231-8000	370
Donatello The 501 Post St	San Francisco	CA	94102	**800-227-3184**	415-441-7100	373
Donatos Pizza 935 Taylor Stn Rd	Columbus	OH	43230	**800-366-2867**	614-864-2444	657
Donegal Group Inc 1195 River Rd *NASDAQ: DGICB*	Marietta	PA	17547	**800-877-0600**	717-426-1931	355-4
Donegal Mutual Insurance Co 1195 River Rd PO Box 302	Marietta	PA	17547	**800-877-0600**	717-426-1931	384-4
Donek Snowboards Inc 35907 E 88 Ave PO Box 580	Watkins	CO	80137	**877-533-6635**	303-261-0100	701
Donham Craft Inc 15 E Waterbury Rd	Naugatuck	CT	06770	**800-739-1919**	203-729-8244	472
Doniphan Electric Co-op Assn Inc PO Box 699	Troy	KS	66087	**800-699-0810**	785-985-3523	244
Donlen Corp 2315 Sanders Rd	Northbrook	IL	60062	**800-323-1483**	847-714-1400	284
Donlin Co Inc 539 E Saint Germain St	Saint Cloud	MN	56302	**800-892-7015**	320-251-3680	234
Donna Karan International Inc 550 7th Ave 15th Fl	New York	NY	10018	**800-231-0884**	212-789-1500	153-21
Donnelley Marketing 5711 S 86th Cir	Omaha	NE	68127	**888-508-0866**	402-593-4500	5
Donning Co Publishers 184 Business Pk Dr Suite 206	Virginia Beach	VA	23462	**800-296-8572**	757-497-1789	623-2
Donohoe Cos Inc 2101 Wisconsin Ave NW	Washington	DC	20007	**877-366-6463**	202-333-0880	639
Donor Alliance Inc 720 Colorado Blvd Suite 800-N	Denver	CO	80246	**888-868-4747**	303-329-4747	535
Donor Network of Arizona 201 W Coolidge	Phoenix	AZ	85013	**800-447-9477**	602-222-2200	265
Donor Program. National Marrow 3001 Broadway St NE Suite 500	Minneapolis	MN	55413	**800-526-7809**	612-627-5800	48-17
Donor Registry. American Bone Marrow 2733 North St	Mandeville	LA	70448	**800-745-2452**	985-626-1749	48-17
Donovan Marine Inc 6316 Humphreys St	Harahan	LA	70123	**800-347-4464**	504-488-5731	759
Donzi Marine PO Box 987	Tallevast	FL	34270	**800-624-3304**	941-727-0622	91
Dooney & Bourke Inc 1 Regent St *Cust Svc	East Norwalk	CT	06855	**800-347-5000***	203-853-7515	422
Door Manufacturers Assn. Window & 1400 E Touhy Ave Suite 470	Des Plaines	IL	60018	**800-223-2301**	847-299-5200	49-3
Dor-O-Matic Inc 7350 W Wilson Ave	Harwood Heights	IL	60706	**800-543-4635**	708-867-7400	345
Dorado Beach Resort & Country Club. Hyatt Hwy 693	Dorado	PR	00646	**800-233-1234**	787-796-1234	655
Doral Arrowwood Conference Resort 975 Anderson Hill Rd	Rye Brook	NY	10573	**800-223-6725**	914-939-5500	370
Doral Dental USA LLC 12121 N Corporate Pkwy	Mequon	WI	53092	**800-417-7140**	262-241-7140	384-3
Doral Desert Princess Palm Springs Resort 67-967 Vista Chino	Cathedral City	CA	92234	**888-386-4677**	760-322-7000	655
Doral Eaglewood Conference Resort & Spa Chicago 1401 Nordic Rd	Itasca	IL	60143	**877-285-6150**	630-773-2750	655
Doral Forrestal Conference Center Hotel 100 College Rd E	Princeton	NJ	08540	**800-222-1131**	609-452-7800	370
Doral Golf Resort & Spa 4400 NW 87th Ave	Miami	FL	33178	**800-713-6725**	305-592-2000	655
Doral Tesoro Hotel & Golf Club 3300 Championship Pkwy	Fort Worth	TX	76177	**866-983-7676**	817-961-0800	373
Doran Bill Co Inc 619 W Jefferson St	Rockford	IL	61103	**800-822-8815**	815-965-6042	288
Dorchester Farmers Co-op 208 W Depot	Dorchester	NE	68343	**800-642-6439**	402-946-2211	272
Dordt College 498 4th Ave NE	Sioux Center	IA	51250	**800-343-6738**	712-722-6000	163
Dorel Industries Inc 12345 Albert Hudson St Suite 100 *NASDAQ: DIIB* ■ *Cust Svc	Montreal	QC	H1G3L1	**800-544-1108***	514-323-5701	64
Dorel Juvenile Group 2525 State St	Columbus	IN	47201	**800-544-1108**	812-372-0141	314-2
Dorignac's Food Center Inc 710 Veterans Memorial Blvd	Metairie	LA	70005	**877-712-2204**	504-837-4650	339
Dorland Healthcare Information 1500 Walnut St Suite 1000	Philadelphia	PA	19102	**800-784-2332**	215-875-1212	623-10
Dorling Kindersley Publishing 375 Hudson St *Cust Svc	New York	NY	10014	**877-342-5357***	212-213-4800	623-2
DORMA Group North America Dorma Dr	Reamstown	PA	17567	**800-523-8483**	717-336-3881	345
Dornier MedTech America Inc 1155 Roberts Blvd	Kennesaw	GA	30144	**800-367-6437**	770-426-1315	375
Dorothy's Ruffled Originals Inc 6721 Market St	Wilmington	NC	28405	**800-367-6849**		731
Dorr-Oliver Eimco USA Inc 2850 S Becker Lake Dr	Salt Lake City	UT	84119	**800-257-0552**	801-526-2000	379
Dorsett Industries Inc 1304 May St	Dalton	GA	30721	**800-241-4035**	706-278-1961	131
Dorsey & Whitney LLP 50 S 6th St Suite 1500	Minneapolis	MN	55402	**800-759-4929**	612-340-2600	419
Doskocil Mfg Co Inc 4209 Barnett Blvd	Arlington	TX	76017	**800-433-5185**	817-467-5116	568
Dosmatic USA Inc 1230 Crowley Cir	Carrollton	TX	75006	**800-344-6767**	972-245-9765	627
Dossert Corp 500 Captain Neville Dr	Waterbury	CT	06705	**800-890-8878**	203-573-1616	803
Dot Foods Inc PO Box 192	Mount Sterling	IL	62353	**800-366-3687**	217-773-4411	292-6
Dot Hill Systems Corp 6305 El Camino Real *NASDAQ: HILL*	Carlsbad	CA	92009	**800-872-2783**	760-931-5500	174
Dot Packaging Group Inc 1500 Paramount Pkwy	Batavia	IL	60510	**800-323-6160**	630-879-0121	89
dotEarth.com PO Box 447	Palmyra	NJ	08065	**888-339-9001**		389
Dothan Area Chamber of Commerce 102 Jamestown Blvd	Dothan	AL	36301	**800-221-1027**	334-792-5138	137
Dothan Area Convention & Visitors Bureau 3311 Ross Clark Cir NW PO Box 8765	Dothan	AL	36305	**888-449-0212**	334-794-6622	205
Dothan Chrysler-Dodge Inc 4074 Ross Clark Cir NW	Dothan	AL	36303	**800-792-3007**	334-794-0606	57
Dothan Eagle PO Box 1968	Dothan	AL	36302	**800-811-1771**	334-792-3141	522-2
Dotronix Inc 160 1st St SE	New Brighton	MN	55112	**800-720-7218**	651-633-1742	171-4
Double Cola Co USA 537 Market St Suite 100	Chattanooga	TN	37402	**877-325-2659**	423-267-5691	81-2
Double H Plastics Inc 50 W Street Rd	Warminster	PA	18974	**800-523-3932**	215-674-4100	593
Double Stay Inn Oceanfront 905 S Atlantic Ave	Daytona Beach	FL	32118	**888-558-5577**	386-255-5432	373
Doubleday Book Club Doubleday Direct Inc 1225 S Market St	Mechanicsburg	PA	17055	**800-688-4442**		94
Doubleday Broadway Publishing Group 1745 Broadway	New York	NY	10019	**800-726-0600**	212-782-9000	623-2
Doubleday Direct Inc 1225 S Market St	Mechanicsburg	PA	17055	**800-688-4442**		94
Doubleday Large Print Home Library Doubleday Direct Inc 1225 S Market St	Mechanicsburg	PA	17055	**800-688-4442**		94
Doubletree Golf Resort San Diego 14455 Penasquitos Dr	San Diego	CA	92129	**800-222-8733**	858-672-9100	655
Doubletree Grand Key Resort 3990 S Roosevelt Blvd	Key West	FL	33040	**888-844-0454**	305-293-1818	655
Doubletree Hotel & Conference Center Saint Louis 16625 Swingley Ridge Rd	Chesterfield	MO	63017	**800-222-8733**	636-532-5000	370
Doubletree Hotel & Conference Center. University of Florida 1714 SW 34th St	Gainesville	FL	32607	**800-774-1500**	352-371-3600	370
Doubletree Hotel & Executive Meeting Center Somerset 200 Atrium Dr	Somerset	NJ	08873	**800-222-8733**	732-469-2600	370
Doubletree Hotel Johnson City 211 Mockingbird Ln	Johnson City	TN	37604	**800-342-7336**	423-929-2000	373
Doubletree Hotel Norwalk 789 Connecticut Ave	Norwalk	CT	06854	**888-444-2582**	203-853-3477	373
Doubletree Hotel Roanoke & Conference Center 110 Shenandoah Ave	Roanoke	VA	24016	**866-594-4722**	540-985-5900	370
Doubletree Hotels 9336 Civic Ctr Dr	Beverly Hills	CA	90210	**800-222-8733**	310-278-4321	369
Doubletree International Plaza Hotel Toronto Airport 655 Dixon Rd	Toronto	ON	M9W1J3	**800-668-3656**	416-244-1711	372
Doubletree Ocean Point Resort & Spa 17375 Collins Ave	Sunny Isles Beach	FL	33360	**866-623-2678**	305-940-5422	373
Doubletree Paradise Valley Resort 5401 N Scottsdale Rd	Scottsdale	AZ	85250	**800-222-8733**	480-947-5400	655
Doubletree La Posada Resort 4949 E Lincoln Dr	Scottsdale	AZ	85253	**800-222-8733**	602-952-0420	655
Dougherty & Co LLC 90 S 7th St Suite 4300	Minneapolis	MN	55402	**800-328-4085**	612-376-4000	679
Douglas Allred Co 11512 El Camino Real Suite 100	San Diego	CA	92130	**800-555-6214**	858-793-0202	641
Douglas Baldwin & Assoc PO Box 1249	La Canada	CA	91012	**800-392-3950**	818-952-4433	392
Douglas Battery Mfg Co 500 Battery Dr	Winston-Salem	NC	27107	**800-368-4527**	336-650-7000	76
Douglas Brothers 423 Riverside Industrial Pkwy	Portland	ME	04103	**800-341-0927**	207-797-6771	584
Douglas-Coffee County Chamber of Commerce 211 S Gaskin Ave	Douglas	GA	31533	**888-426-3334**	912-384-1873	137
Douglas Cuddle Toys Co Inc 69 Krif Rd PO Box D	Keene	NH	03431	**800-992-9002**	603-352-3414	750
Douglas Electric Co-op Inc PO Box 1327	Roseburg	OR	97470	**800-233-2733**	541-673-6616	244
Douglas-Guardian Services Corp 14800 St Mary's Ln	Houston	TX	77079	**800-255-0552**	281-531-0500	391
Douglas Industries Co 3441 S 11th Ave	Eldridge	IA	52748	**800-553-8907**	563-285-4162	701
Douglas Laboratories Inc 600 Boyce Rd	Pittsburgh	PA	15205	**800-245-4440**	412-494-0122	786
Douglas Press Inc 2810 Madison St	Bellwood	IL	60104	**800-323-0705**	708-547-8400	317
Douglas Publications Inc 2807 N Parham Rd Suite 200	Richmond	VA	23294	**800-223-1797**	804-762-9600	623-2
Douglas Stewart Co 2402 Advance Rd	Madison	WI	53718	**800-279-2795**	608-221-1155	673

Company	City	State	ZIP	Toll-Free	Phone	Class
Douglas & Sturgess Inc 730 Bryant St	San Francisco	CA	94107	**888-278-7883**	415-896-6283	45
Douglas/Quikut Co 118 E Douglas Rd	Walnut Ridge	AR	72476	**800-982-5233**	870-886-6774	219
Douglass Truck Bodies Inc 231 21st St	Bakersfield	CA	93301	**800-635-7641**	661-327-0258	505
Doumak Inc 2201 Touhy Ave	Elk Grove Village	IL	60007	**800-323-0318**	847-437-2100	291-8
Douron Inc 30 New Plant Ct	Owings Mills	MD	21117	**888-833-8350**	410-363-2600	315
DoveBid Inc 1241 E Hillsdale Blvd	Foster City	CA	94404	**800-665-1042**	650-571-7400	51
Dover Downs Gaming & Entertainment Inc 1131 N DuPont Hwy	Dover	DE	19901	**800-711-5882**	302-674-4600	628
NYSE: DDE						
Dover Downs Hotel & Conference Center 1131 N DuPont Hwy	Dover	DE	19901	**800-711-5882**	302-674-4600	370
Dover Motorsports Inc 1131 N Dupont Hwy	Dover	DE	19901	**800-441-7223**	302-674-4600	628
NYSE: DVD						
Dover Post PO Box 664	Dover	DE	19903	**800-942-1616**	302-678-3616	522-4
Dover Publications Inc 31 E 2nd St	Mineola	NY	11501	**800-223-3130**	516-294-7000	623-2
Dow AgroSciences LLC 9330 Zionsville Rd	Indianapolis	IN	46268	**800-258-1470**	317-337-3000	276
Dow Chemical Canada Inc 250 6th Ave SW Suite 2200	Calgary	AB	T2P3H7	**800-433-4398**	403-267-3500	142
Dow Chemical Co 2030 Dow Ctr	Midland	MI	48674	**800-331-6451***	989-636-1000	142
NYSE: DOW ■ *Cust Svc						
Dow Chemical Employees' Credit Union 600 E Lyon Rd	Midland	MI	48640	**800-835-7794**	989-835-7794	216
Dow Cover Co Inc 373 Lexington Ave	New Haven	CT	06513	**800-735-8877**	203-469-5394	343
Dow Electronics Inc 8603 Adamo Dr	Tampa	FL	33619	**800-627-2900**	813-626-5195	245
Dow Gardens 1018 W Main St	Midland	MI	48640	**800-362-4874**	989-631-2677	98
Dow Herbert H & Grace A Foundation 1018 W Main St	Midland	MI	48640	**800-362-4849**	989-631-3699	300
Dow Jones Reuters Business Interactive LLC DBA Factiva PO Box 300	Princeton	NJ	08543	**800-369-7466***	609-627-2000	623-10
*Cust Svc						
Dow Liquid Separations PO Box 1206	Midland	MI	48642	**800-447-4369**	989-832-2442	793
Dow Thermoset Systems 1881 W Oak Pkwy	Marietta	GA	30062	**800-735-3129**	770-428-2684	590
Dowagiac Daily News 217 N 4th St	Niles	MI	49020	**888-725-0108**	269-782-2101	522-2
Dowling College 150 Idle Hour Blvd	Oakdale	NY	11769	**800-369-5464**	631-244-3000	163
Down Beat Magazine 102 N Haven Rd	Elmhurst	IL	60126	**800-535-7496**	630-941-2030	449-9
Down East: The Magazine of Maine 680 Commercial St	Rockport	ME	04856	**800-727-7422**	207-594-9544	449-22
Down Syndrome Congress. National 1370 Center Dr Suite 102	Atlanta	GA	30338	**800-232-6372**	770-604-9500	48-17
Down Syndrome Society. National 666 Broadway 8th Fl	New York	NY	10012	**800-221-4602**	212-460-9330	48-17
Downers Grove Tourism & Events 801 Burlington Ave	Downers Grove	IL	60515	**800-934-0615**	630-434-5921	205
Downing Displays Inc 550 TechneCenter Dr	Milford	OH	45150	**800-883-1800**	513-248-9800	230
Downs Crane & Hoist Co Inc 8827 S Juniper St	Los Angeles	CA	90002	**800-748-5994**	323-589-6061	462
Downs Food Group 400 Armstrong Blvd N	Saint James	MN	56081	**800-533-0452**	507-375-3111	608
Downtown Airpark Inc 1701-A N Cimarron Rd	Yukon	OK	73099	**800-253-1456**	405-350-1161	25
Downtown Idea Exchange Newsletter 28 W 25th St 8th Fl	New York	NY	10003	**800-232-4317**	212-228-0246	521-2
Downtown Promotion Reporter Newsletter 28 W 25th St 8th Fl	New York	NY	10010	**800-232-4317**	212-228-0246	521-10
Downtown Vancouver B & B Accommodations Group 515 W Pender St Suite 247	Vancouver	BC	V6B6H5	**877-454-8179**	604-454-8179	368
Downtowner Inns 1726 Montreal Cir	Tucker	GA	30084	**800-251-1962**	770-270-1180	369
Doyle New York 175 E 87th St	New York	NY	10128	**800-808-0902**	212-427-2730	509
Doyle Protective Services Inc 792 Calkins Rd	Rochester	NY	14623	**800-836-9538**	585-244-3400	682
Doyle Signs Inc 232 Interstate Rd	Addison	IL	60101	**800-344-9490**	630-543-9490	692
DPAC Technologies Corp 7321 Lincoln Way	Garden Grove	CA	92841	**800-642-4477**	714-898-0007	686
NASDAQ: DPAC						
DPE Systems Inc 425 Pontius Ave N Suite 430	Seattle	WA	98109	**800-541-6566**	206-223-3737	178
DPF Data Services Group Inc 1990 Swarthmore Ave	Lakewood	NJ	08701	**800-431-4416**	732-370-8840	223
DPI (Digital Printing & Imaging Assn) 10015 Main St	Fairfax	VA	22031	**888-385-3588**	703-385-1339	49-16
DPL Inc 1065 Woodman Dr	Dayton	OH	45432	**800-322-9244**	937-224-6000	355-5
NYSE: DPL						
DPSI Inc 4905 Koger Blvd Suite 101	Greensboro	NC	27409	**800-897-7233**	336-854-7700	176-11
Dr Delphinium Designs Inc 5806 Lovers Lane & Tollway	Dallas	TX	75225	**800-783-8790**	214-522-9911	287
Dr Dobb's Journal 2800 Campus Dr	San Mateo	CA	94403	**800-289-9839**	650-513-4300	449-7
DR Horton Inc 1901 Ascension Blvd Suite 100	Arlington	TX	76006	**800-846-7866**	817-856-8200	639
NYSE: DHI						
Dr Kern USA Inc 221 S Franklin Rd	Indianapolis	IN	46221	**800-908-9885**	317-472-0867	78
Dr Pepper Bottling Co of Texas 2304 Century Ctr Blvd	Irving	TX	75062	**800-696-5891**	972-579-1024	82-2
Dr Pepper/Seven-Up Inc 5301 Legacy Dr PO Box 869077	Plano	TX	75024	**800-527-7096**	972-673-7000	81-2
DR Sperry & Co 112 N Grant St	North Aurora	IL	60542	**888-997-9297**	630-892-4361	448
Dr Toy 268 Bush St	San Francisco	CA	94104	**800-551-8697**		115
Dr Vinyl & Assoc Ltd 821 NW Commerce Dr	Lee's Summit	MO	64086	**800-531-6600**	816-525-6060	62-1
Draeger Medical Inc 3135 Quarry Rd	Telford	PA	18969	**800-437-2437**	215-723-9824	249
DraftWorldwide 633 N Saint Clair St	Chicago	IL	60611	**800-288-8755**	312-944-3500	4
Dragon Products Co 38 Preble St	Portland	ME	04104	**800-828-8352**	207-774-6355	135
Drake Center 151 W Galbraith Rd	Cincinnati	OH	45216	**800-948-0003**	513-948-2500	366-4
Drake Hotel 140 E Walton Pl	Chicago	IL	60611	**800-553-7253**	312-787-2200	373
Drake Petroleum Co Inc PO Box 72616	Providence	RI	02907	**800-456-9427**	401-781-9900	569
Drake University 2507 University Ave	Des Moines	IA	50311	**800-443-7253**	515-271-3181	163
Drake University School of Law 2507 University Ave	Des Moines	IA	50311	**800-443-7253**	515-271-2824	164-1
Dramm & Echter Inc 1150 Quail Gardens Dr	Encinitas	CA	92024	**800-854-7021**	760-436-0188	363
Dranetz-BMI 1000 New Durham Rd	Edison	NJ	08818	**800-372-6832**	732-287-3680	247
Draper & Kramer Inc 33 W Monroe St Suite 1900	Chicago	IL	60603	**800-621-0776**	312-346-8600	641
Draper Laboratory 555 Technology Sq	Cambridge	MA	02139	**800-676-1977**	617-258-1000	654
Draper Shade & Screen Co 411 S Pearl St	Spiceland	IN	47385	**800-238-7999**	765-987-7999	580
Drapers & Damons 9 Pasteur	Irvine	CA	92618	**800-843-1174**	949-784-3000	155-6
Drawbridge Inn 2477 Royal Dr	Fort Mitchell	KY	41017	**800-354-9793**	859-341-2800	373
Draxis Health Inc 6870 Goreway Dr 2nd Fl	Mississauga	ON	L4V1P1	**877-550-4515**	905-677-5500	86
NASDAQ: DRAX						
Dream 210 W 55th St	New York	NY	10019	**866-437-3266**	212-247-2000	373
Dream Factory Inc 1218 S 3rd St	Louisville	KY	40203	**800-456-7556**	502-637-8700	48-6
Dreamline Mfg Co PO Box 1250	Cabot	AR	72023	**800-888-3585**	501-843-3585	463
Dreammaker Bath & Kitchen by Worldwide PO Box 3146	Waco	TX	76707	**800-583-9099**	254-745-2477	188-11
Dreamworld Backdrops 9450 Lusk Blvd Suite E-100	San Diego	CA	92121	**800-737-0860**	858-452-1022	708
Drees Co 211 Grandview Dr	Fort Mitchell	KY	41017	**800-647-1711**	859-578-4200	186
Dremel Inc 4915 21st St	Racine	WI	53406	**800-437-3635**	262-554-1390	747
Dresco Reproduction Inc 12603 Allard St	Santa Fe Springs	CA	90670	**800-423-5834**	562-863-6677	113
Dresdner Kleinwort Wasserstein 1301 Ave of the Americas	New York	NY	10019	**800-457-0245**	212-429-2000	679
Dresser Flow Solutions 16240 Port St NW	Houston	TX	77041	**800-847-1099**	832-590-2300	776
Dresser Inc Wayne Div 3814 Jarrett Way	Austin	TX	78728	**800-289-2963**	512-388-8311	625
Dresser-Rand Co Steam Products Div 37 Coats St PO Box 592	Wellsville	NY	14895	**800-828-2818**	585-596-3100	259
Drew James H Corp 8701 Zionsville Rd	Indianapolis	IN	46268	**800-772-7342**	317-876-3739	187-4
Drew Pearson Marketing Inc 15006 Beltway Dr	Addison	TX	75001	**800-879-0880**	972-702-8055	153-9
Drew Shoe Corp 252 Quarry Rd	Lancaster	OH	43130	**800-837-3739**	740-653-4271	296
Drexel Heritage Furnishings Inc 1925 Eastchester Dr	High Point	NC	27265	**866-450-3434**	336-888-4800	314-2
Drexel University 3141 Chestnut St	Philadelphia	PA	19104	**800-237-3935**	215-895-2000	163
Drexelbrook Div AMETEK Sensor Technology 205 Keith Valley Rd	Horsham	PA	19044	**800-527-6297***	215-674-1234	486
*Cust Svc						
Dreyer's Grand Ice Cream Holdings Inc 5929 College Ave	Oakland	CA	94618	**800-888-3442**	510-652-8187	291-25
NASDAQ: DRYR						
Dreyfus-Cortney & Lowery Brothers Rigging 4500 N Galvez St	New Orleans	LA	70117	**800-228-7660**	504-944-3366	759
Dreyfus Family of Funds 200 Park Ave	New York	NY	10166	**800-645-6561**	212-922-6000	517
Dreyfuss Planetarium 49 Washington St	Newark	NJ	07102	**800-768-7386**	973-596-6529	587
DRI (Defense Research Institute) 150 N Michigan Ave Suite 300	Chicago	IL	60601	**800-667-8108**	312-795-1101	49-10
Dri Mark Products Inc 15 Harbor Pk Dr	Port Washington	NY	11050	**800-645-9118**	516-484-6200	560
Dri-Steem Humidifier Co 14949 Technology Dr	Eden Prairie	MN	55344	**800-328-4447**	952-949-2415	15
Driehaus Capital Management Inc 25 E Erie St	Chicago	IL	60611	**800-688-8819**	312-587-3800	393
Driftwood Lodge 435 Willoughby Ave	Juneau	AK	99801	**800-544-2239**	907-586-2280	373
Driftwood Lodge 7105 Maddox Blvd	Chincoteague Island	VA	23336	**800-553-6117**	757-336-6557	373
Driftwood on the Oceanfront 1600 N Ocean Blvd	Myrtle Beach	SC	29578	**800-942-3456**	843-448-1544	373
Driftwood Resort 6020 Driftwood Ln	Pine River	MN	56474	**800-950-3540**	218-568-4221	655
Driftwood Shores Resort 88416 1st Ave	Florence	OR	97439	**800-422-5091**	541-997-8263	373
Drillers Service Inc PO Box 1407	Hickory	NC	28603	**800-334-2308**	828-322-1100	526
Driscoll Strawberry Assoc Inc PO Box 50045	Watsonville	CA	95077	**800-871-3333**	831-761-5301	310-1
Driskill Hotel 604 Brazos St	Austin	TX	78701	**800-252-9367**	512-474-5911	373
Drive Train Industries Inc 3301 Brighton Blvd	Denver	CO	80216	**800-525-6177**	303-292-5176	61
Driven Technologies 2345 S Michigan Ave	Chicago	IL	60616	**877-437-4836**	312-842-1880	681
Drivers Assn. Owner-Operator Independent 1 NW OOIDA Dr	Grain Valley	MO	64029	**800-444-5791**	816-229-5791	49-21
Drivers License Guide Co 1492 Oddstad Dr	Redwood City	CA	94063	**800-227-8827**	650-369-4849	623-10
Drives Inc 1009 1st St	Fulton	IL	61252	**800-435-0782**	815-589-2211	609
DriveTime Corp 4020 E Indian School Rd	Phoenix	AZ	85018	**800-863-7483**	602-852-6600	57
Driving Records Facilities PO Box 1086	Glen Burnie	MD	21061	**800-772-5510**	410-761-5510	621
Drowsy Water Ranch PO Box 147	Granby	CO	80446	**800-845-2292**	970-725-3456	238
DRS Hadland Inc 4000 Moorpark Ave Suite 110	San Jose	CA	95117	**800-248-4686**	408-244-0901	580
DRS Infrared Technologies LP 13544 N Central Expy	Dallas	TX	75243	**877-377-4783**	972-560-6000	519
DRS Training & Control Systems 645 Anchors St NW	Fort Walton Beach	FL	32548	**800-326-6724**	850-302-3000	519
Drug Chemical & Associated Technologies Assn (DCAT) 1 Washington Blvd Suite 7	Robbinsville	NJ	08691	**800-640-3228**	609-448-1000	49-19
Drug Dependence. National Council on Alcoholism & 20 Exchange Pl Suite 2902	New York	NY	10005	**800-622-2255**	212-269-7797	48-17
Drug Detection Report 8737 Colesville Rd Suite 1100	Silver Spring	MD	20910	**800-274-6737**	301-587-6300	521-8

Company / Address	City	State	ZIP	Toll-Free	Phone	Class
Drug Education. American Council for						
c/o Phoenix House 164 W						
74th St	New York	NY	10023	**800-378-4435**	212-595-5810	48-17
Drug-Free America. Partnership for a						
405 Lexington Ave Suite 1601	New York	NY	10174	**888-575-3115**	212-922-1560	48-17
Drug Law Institute. Food &						
1000 Vermont Ave NW						
Suite 200	Washington	DC	20005	**800-956-6293**	202-371-1420	49-10
Drug Marketing Assn. Chain						
43157 W Nine-Mile Rd PO Box 995	Novi	MI	48376	**800-935-2362**	248-449-9300	49-18
Drug Stores. National Assn of Chain						
413 N Lee St	Alexandria	VA	22314	**800-678-6223**	703-549-3001	49-18
Drug Topics Magazine 5 Paragon Dr	Montvale	NJ	07645	**800-232-7379**	201-358-7200	449-5
Drugless Practitioners. American Assn						
of 2705 61st St	Galveston	TX	77551	**888-764-2237**	409-741-9000	48-17
DRUGPROOF						
1229 Madison St Suite 500	Seattle	WA	98104	**800-898-0182**	206-386-2661	407
drugstore.com Inc						
13920 SE Eastgate Way Suite 300	Bellevue	WA	98005	**800-378-4786**	425-372-3200	236
NASDAQ: DSCM						
Drum Corps International (DCI)						
470 S Irmen Dr	Addison	IL	60101	**800-495-7469***	630-628-7888	48-4
*Orders						
Drummond Island Tourism Assn						
PO Box 200	Drummond Island	MI	49726	**800-737-8666**	906-493-5245	205
Drunk Driving. Mothers Against						
511 E John Carpenter Fwy Suite 700	Irving	TX	75062	**800-438-6233**	214-744-6233	48-6
Drury Inns Gold Key Club						
PO Box 910	Cape Girardeau	MO	63702	**800-325-0581**		371
Drury Inns Inc						
721 Emerson Rd Suite 400	Saint Louis	MO	63141	**800-378-7946**	314-429-2255	369
Drury University 900 N Benton Ave	Springfield	MO	65802	**800-922-2274**	417-873-7879	163
Dryclean USA Inc 290 NE 68th St	Miami	FL	33138	**800-746-4583**	305-758-0066	417
AMEX: DCU						
Dryden District Chamber of Commerce						
284 Government St	Dryden	ON	P8N2P3	**800-667-0935**	807-223-2622	136
Dryvit Systems Inc						
1 Energy Way	West Warwick	RI	02893	**800-556-7752**	401-822-4100	382
DS Brown Co 300 E Cherry St	North Baltimore	OH	45872	**800-848-1730**	419-257-3561	190-2
DS & O Rural Electric Co-op Assn						
129 W Main St PO Box 286	Solomon	KS	67480	**800-376-3533**	785-655-2011	244
DS Technology Inc 7861 Palace Dr	Cincinnati	OH	45249	**800-531-0135**	513-247-2590	447
DSAT 30151 Tomas St	Rancho Santa Margarita	CA	92688	**800-729-7234**		502
DSC Logistics Inc 1750 S Wolf Rd	Des Plaines	IL	60018	**800-372-1960**	847-390-6800	440
DSFI 450 S Lombard Rd	Addison	IL	60101	**800-828-1411***	630-627-7777	111
*Cust Svc						
DSI Payroll Services 300 Atrium Dr	Somerset	NJ	08873	**800-254-0780**	732-748-1700	559
DSL.net Inc						
545 Long Wharf Dr 5th Fl	New Haven	CT	06511	**800-455-5546**	203-772-1000	390
AMEX: BIZ						
DSLextreme.com						
20847 Sherman Way	Winnetka	CA	91306	**800-774-3379**	818-902-4821	390
DSM Chemicals North America Inc						
1 Columbia Nitrogen Rd	Augusta	GA	30901	**800-825-4376**	706-849-6600	142
DSM Desotech Inc 1122 Saint Charles St	Elgin	IL	60120	**800-223-7191**	847-697-0400	143
DSM Engineering Plastics Inc						
2267 W Mill Rd	Evansville	IN	47720	**800-333-4237**	812-435-7500	594-2
DSM Food Specialties Inc						
2675 Eisenhower Ave Valley Forge						
Corporate Ctr	Eagleville	PA	19403	**800-662-4478**	610-650-8480	291-42
DST Controls 651 Stone Rd	Benicia	CA	94510	**800-251-0773**	707-745-5117	202
DST Industries Inc						
34364 Goddard Rd	Romulus	MI	48174	**800-327-6174**	734-941-0300	505
DST Systems Inc 333 W 11th St	Kansas City	MO	64105	**888-378-4636**	816-435-8600	176-1
NYSE: DST						
DSW Shoe Warehouse						
4150 E 5th Ave	Columbus	OH	43219	**800-477-8595***	614-237-7100	296
*Cust Svc						
DTE Energy Co 2000 2nd Ave	Detroit	MI	48226	**800-477-4747**	313-235-4000	355-5
NYSE: DTE						
Dublin Convention & Visitors Bureau						
9 S High St	Dublin	OH	43017	**800-245-8387**	614-792-7666	205
DuBois Business College 1 Beaver Dr	Du Bois	PA	15801	**800-692-6213**	814-371-6920	158
Dubois Chemicals Inc						
200 Crowne Point Place	Sharonville	OH	45241	**800-543-4906**	513-326-8800	149
Dubuque Area Chamber of Commerce						
300 Main St	Dubuque	IA	52004	**800-798-4748**	563-557-9200	137
Dubuque Convention & Visitors Bureau						
300 Main St Suite 200	Dubuque	IA	52001	**800-798-4748**	563-557-9200	205
Dubuque Greyhound Park & Casino						
1855 Greyhound Park Dr	Dubuque	IA	52001	**800-373-3647**	563-582-3647	628
Duchini A Inc 2550 McKinley Ave	Erie	PA	16503	**800-937-7317**	814-456-7027	181
Duchossois Industries Inc						
845 Larch Ave	Elmhurst	IL	60126	**800-282-6225**	630-279-3600	355-3
Duck Head Apparel Co Inc						
4902 W Waters Ave	Tampa	FL	33634	**888-385-8825**	813-249-4900	153-3
Duckback Products Inc 2644 Hegan Ln	Chico	CA	95928	**800-825-5382**	530-343-3261	540
Ducks Carpet & Flooring						
1133 Hwy 45 Bypass	Jackson	TN	38301	**800-372-1000**	731-664-2871	285
Ducks Unlimited Inc						
1 Waterfowl Way	Memphis	TN	38120	**800-453-8257**	901-758-3825	48-3
Ducks Unlimited Magazine						
1 Waterfowl Way	Memphis	TN	38120	**800-453-8257**	901-758-3825	449-20
Duckwall-ALCO Stores Inc						
401 Cottage Ave	Abilene	KS	67410	**800-334-2526**	785-263-3350	778
NASDAQ: DUCK						
Ducommun Technologies Inc						
23301 Wilmington Ave	Carson	CA	90745	**800-421-5032**	310-513-7200	202
Duct-O-Wire Co PO Box 519	Corona	CA	92878	**800-752-6001**	951-735-8220	202
Dude Rancher Lodge 415 N 29th St	Billings	MT	59101	**800-221-3302**	406-259-5561	373
Dudley Products Inc						
1080 Old Greensboro Rd	Kernersville	NC	27284	**800-334-4150**	336-993-8800	211
Duff Norton Co 9415 Pioneer Ave	Charlotte	NC	28273	**800-477-5009**	704-588-0510	462
Duffens Langley Optical Co						
8140 Marshall Dr	Lenexa	KS	66214	**800-888-5379**	913-492-5379	531
Duffey CJ Paper Co Inc						
528 Washington Ave N	Minneapolis	MN	55401	**800-752-8190**	612-338-8701	543
Duff's Business Institute						
100 Forbes Ave Suite 1200	Pittsburgh	PA	15222	**888-279-3314**	412-261-4520	158
Duffy Brothers Inc PO Box 250	Columbus	WI	53925	**800-242-1887**	920-623-4160	769
Dugan Production Corp						
709 E Murray Dr	Farmington	NM	87499	**800-618-1821**	505-325-1821	525
Duggan Industries Inc 3901 S Lamar St	Dallas	TX	75215	**877-428-8336**	214-428-8336	674
Duhig & Co Inc PO Box 226966	Los Angeles	CA	90022	**800-690-1776**	323-263-7161	483
Duininck Brothers Inc PO Box 208	Prinsburg	MN	56281	**800-328-8949**	320-978-6011	187-4
Duke Diet & Fitness Center						
804 W Trinity Ave	Durham	NC	27701	**800-235-3853**	919-688-3079	697
Duke Energy North America						
5400 Westheimer Ct	Houston	TX	77056	**800-873-3853**	713-627-5400	774
Duke Energy Services Group						
5400 Westheimer Ct	Houston	TX	77056	**800-873-3853**	713-627-5400	774
Duke Energy Trading & Marketing						
5400 Westheimer Ct	Houston	TX	77056	**800-873-3853**	713-260-1800	774
Duke Mfg Co 2305 N Broadway	Saint Louis	MO	63102	**800-735-3853**	314-231-1130	293
Duke Realty Corp						
600 E 96th St Suite 100	Indianapolis	IN	46240	**800-875-3366**	317-808-6000	641
NYSE: DRE						
Duke Towers Residential Suites						
807 W Trinity Ave	Durham	NC	27701	**866-385-3869**	919-687-4444	373
Duke University Press 905 W Main St	Durham	NC	27701	**888-651-0122***	919-687-3600	623-5
*Cust Svc						
Duke/Fluor Daniel						
2300 Yorkmont Rd	Charlotte	NC	28217	**800-486-4518**	704-426-2000	258
DukeNet Communications Inc						
400 S Tryon St	Charlotte	NC	28202	**800-873-3853**	704-382-7111	168
Duke's 8th Avenue Hotel						
630 W 8th Ave	Anchorage	AK	99501	**800-478-4837**	907-274-6213	373
Dulles Aviation Inc						
10501 Observation Rd Manassas						
Regional Airport	Manassas	VA	20110	**888-835-8934**	703-361-2171	63
Duluth Business University						
4724 Mike Colalilo Dr	Duluth	MN	55807	**800-777-8406**	218-722-4000	158
Duluth Convention & Visitors Bureau						
21 W Superior St Suite 100	Duluth	MN	55802	**800-438-5884**	218-722-4011	205
Duluth Entertainment Convention Center						
350 Harbor Dr	Duluth	MN	55802	**800-628-8385**	218-722-5573	204
Duluth News-Tribune 424 W 1st St	Duluth	MN	55802	**800-456-8080***	218-723-5281	522-2
*Circ						
DuMor Inc PO Box 142	Mifflintown	PA	17059	**800-494-0706**	717-436-2106	314-4
Dumore Corp 1030 Veterans St	Mauston	WI	53948	**888-467-8288**	608-847-6420	507
Dun & Bradstreet Receivable						
Management Services						
899 Eaton Ave	Bethlehem	PA	18025	**800-999-3867**	610-882-7000	157
Dunbar Mechanical Inc						
2806 N Reynolds Rd	Toledo	OH	43615	**800-719-2201**	419-537-1900	188-10
Dunbar Paul Laurence House						
219 N Paul Laurence Dunbar St	Dayton	OH	45407	**800-860-0148**	937-224-7061	50
Dunbarton Corp 868 Murray Rd	Dothan	AL	36303	**800-633-7553**	334-794-0661	232
Duncan Aviation Inc PO Box 81887	Lincoln	NE	68501	**800-228-4277**	402-475-2611	25
Duncan Banner						
1001 W Elm St PO Box 1268	Duncan	OK	73534	**800-893-8718**	580-255-5354	522-2
Duncan Enterprises 5673 E Shields Ave	Fresno	CA	93727	**800-458-7010**	559-291-4444	43
Duncan Equipment Co Inc						
3450 S MacArthur Blvd	Oklahoma City	OK	73179	**800-375-5216**	405-688-2300	378
Duncan Machinery Movers Inc						
2004 Duncan Machinery Dr	Lexington	KY	40504	**800-331-0116**	859-233-7333	769
Duncan Oil Inc						
1777 S Harrison St Suite P1	Denver	CO	80210	**800-359-3303**	303-759-3303	525
Duncan Parking Technologies Inc						
340 Industrial Park Rd	Harrison	AR	72601	**800-338-6226***	870-741-5481	486
*Cust Svc						
Duncan-Parnell Inc						
900 S McDowell St	Charlotte	NC	28204	**800-849-7708**	704-372-7766	114
Duncan Supply Co Inc						
910 N Illinois St	Indianapolis	IN	46204	**800-382-5528**	317-634-1335	601
Duncan Valley Electric Co-op Inc						
PO Box 440	Duncan	AZ	85534	**800-669-2503**	928-359-2503	244
Duncan-Williams Inc						
6750 Poplar Ave Suite 300	Memphis	TN	38138	**800-827-0827**	901-260-6800	679
Duncaster 40 Loeffler Rd	Bloomfield	CT	06002	**800-545-5065**	860-726-2000	659
Dundee Citrus Growers Assn						
111 1st St N	Dundee	FL	33838	**800-447-1574**	863-439-1574	12-1
Dundee Wealth Management Inc						
40 King St W Suite 5500	Toronto	ON	M5H4A9	**800-301-6745**	416-350-3489	397
TSE: DW						
Dundick Corp 4616 W 20th St	Cicero	IL	60804	**800-322-4243**	708-656-6363	484
Dunes Hotel						
333 Fort Pickens Rd	Pensacola Beach	FL	32561	**800-833-8637**	850-932-3536	373
Dunes Manor Hotel						
2800 Baltimore Ave	Ocean City	MD	21842	**800-523-2888**	410-289-1100	373
Dunhill Alfred North America Ltd						
645 5th Ave	New York	NY	10022	**800-776-4053**	212-888-4000	155-3
Dunhill Staffing Systems Inc						
9190 Priority Way W Suite 204	Indianapolis	IN	46240	**800-386-7823**	317-818-4910	707
Dunkin' Donuts Inc						
14 Pacella Park Dr	Randolph	MA	02368	**800-859-5339***	781-961-4000	69
*Cust Svc						
Dunkirk Specialty Steel Corp						
830 Brigham Rd PO Box 319	Dunkirk	NY	14048	**800-916-9133**	716-366-1000	709
Dunlap Co 200 Bailey Ave	Fort Worth	TX	76107	**866-274-0163**	817-336-4985	227
Dunlap Industries Inc PO Box 459	Dunlap	TN	37327	**800-251-7214**	423-949-4021	583
Dunlap & Kyle Co Inc PO Box 720	Batesville	MS	38606	**800-647-6133**	662-563-7601	740
Dunlap Towing Co PO Box 593	La Conner	WA	98257	**800-476-3114**	360-466-3114	457
Dunlop Tire Corp PO Box 1109	Buffalo	NY	14240	**800-828-7428**	716-639-5200	739
Dunmore Corp 145 Wharton Rd	Bristol	PA	19007	**888-386-6673***	215-781-8895	589
*Cust Svc						
Dunn-Edwards Corp						
4885 E 52nd Pl	Los Angeles	CA	90040	**800-537-4098**	323-771-3330	540
Dunn Energy Co-op PO Box 220	Menomonie	WI	54751	**800-924-0630**	715-232-6240	244
Dunn Mfg Inc 1400 Goldmine Rd	Monroe	NC	28110	**800-868-7111**	704-283-2147	10
Dunn Safety Products Inc						
37 S Sangamon St	Chicago	IL	60607	**800-451-3866**	312-666-5800	467
Dunn School						
2555 Hwy 154 PO Box 98	Los Olivos	CA	93441	**800-287-9197**	805-688-6471	611
Dunnellon Area Chamber of Commerce						
PO Box 868	Dunnellon	FL	34430	**800-830-2087**	352-489-2320	137
Dunwoody College of Technology						
818 Dunwoody Blvd	Minneapolis	MN	55403	**800-292-4625**	612-374-5800	787

Alphabetical Section

Company / Address	City	State	ZIP	Toll-Free	Phone	Class
Duo-Fast Corp 2400 Galvin Dr *Cust Svc	Elgin	IL	60123	**888-386-3278***	847-783-5500	746
DuPage Convention & Visitors Bureau 915 Harger Rd Suite 240	Oak Brook	IL	60523	**800-232-0502**	630-575-8070	205
Dupli-Systems Inc 8260 Dow Cir	Strongsville	OH	44136	**800-321-1610**	440-234-9415	111
Duplication Factory Inc 4275 Norex Dr	Chaska	MN	55318	**800-279-2009**	952-448-9912	644
DuPont Agriculture & Nutrition 1007 Market St DuPont Bldg	Wilmington	DE	19898	**800-441-7515**	302-774-1000	276
DuPont Air Products NanoMaterials LLC 1969 Palomar Oaks Way	Carlsbad	CA	92009	**866-265-0058**	760-931-9555	594-2
DuPont Automotive 950 Stephenson Hwy	Troy	MI	48083	**800-441-0575**	248-583-8000	540
DuPont Crop Protection 1007 Market St DuPont Bldg	Wilmington	DE	19898	**800-441-7515**	302-774-1000	276
DuPont El de Nemours & Co Inc 1007 Market St *NYSE: DD*	Wilmington	DE	19898	**800-441-7515**	302-774-1000	594-2
DuPont Engineering Polymers Lancaster Pike Rt 141 Barley Mill Plaza Bldg 22	Wilmington	DE	19805	**800-441-0575**	302-999-4592	594-2
DuPont Flooring Systems 3445 Millennium Ct	Columbus	OH	43219	**800-572-7823**	614-476-1043	188-2
DuPont Nonwovens Bldg 728 PO Box 80728 Chestnut Run Plaza	Wilmington	DE	19805	**800-448-9835**		730-6
DuPont Packaging & Industrial Polymers Barley Mill Plaza 26-2122 PO Box 80026	Wilmington	DE	19880	**800-438-7225**	302-774-1161	538
DuPont Performance Coatings 1007 Market St	Wilmington	DE	19898	**800-441-7515**	302-774-1000	540
DuPont Personal Protection 884 S 7th St	McBee	SC	29101	**800-931-3456**	843-335-8211	566
DuPont Qualicon Rt 141 Henry Clay Rd Bldg 400	Wilmington	DE	19880	**800-863-6842**	302-695-5300	229
DuPont Surfaces 4417 Lancaster Pike Chestnut Run Plaza Maple Run 721	Wilmington	DE	19805	**800-426-7426**	302-774-1000	588
DuPont Theatre 10th & Market Sts DuPont Bldg	Wilmington	DE	19801	**800-338-0881**	302-656-4401	562
DuPont Titanium Technologies 1007 Market St PO Box 80036	Wilmington	DE	19898	**800-441-7515**	302-774-1000	141
Duquesne Light Co 411 7th Ave *Cust Svc	Pittsburgh	PA	15230	**888-393-7100***	412-393-6000	774
Duquesne Light Holdings Inc 411 7th Ave *NYSE: DQE*	Pittsburgh	PA	15219	**877-393-7800**	412-393-6000	355-5
Duquesne University 600 Forbes Ave	Pittsburgh	PA	15282	**800-456-0590**	412-396-6000	163
DuQuoin Evening Call 9 N Division St PO Box 184	DuQuoin	IL	62832	**800-455-2133**	618-542-2133	522-2
DuQuoin Tourism Commission PO Box 1037	DuQuoin	IL	62832	**800-455-9570**	618-542-8338	205
Dura Automotive Systems Inc 2791 Research Dr *NASDAQ: DRRA*	Rochester Hills	MI	48309	**800-362-3872**	248-299-7500	60
Dura-Bilt Products Inc PO Box 188	Wellsburg	NY	14894	**800-233-4251**	570-596-2000	688
Dura-Line Corp 835 Innovation Dr	Knoxville	TN	37932	**800-847-7661**	865-218-3460	585
Dura Plastics Products Inc PO Box 2097	Beaumont	CA	92223	**800-854-2323**	951-845-3161	585
Dura-Stress Inc PO Box 490779	Leesburg	FL	34749	**800-342-9239**	352-787-1422	181
Dura Wax Co 4101 W Albany St	McHenry	IL	60050	**800-435-5705**	815-385-5000	149
Duracell 14 Research Dr Berkshire Corporate Pk	Bethel	CT	06801	**800-551-2355**	203-796-4000	76
Duraclean International Inc 220 Campus Dr *Cust Svc	Arlington Heights	IL	60004	**800-251-7070***	847-704-7100	150
Duraco Inc 7400 W Industrial Dr	Forest Park	IL	60130	**800-852-1025**	708-488-1025	590
Duraco Products Inc 1109 E Lake St	Streamwood	IL	60107	**800-888-7687**	630-837-6615	596
Duracote Corp 350 N Diamond St	Ravenna	OH	44266	**800-321-2252**	330-296-9600	730-2
Durakon Industries Inc 2101 N Lapeer Rd *Cust Svc	Lapeer	MI	48446	**800-955-3993***	810-664-0850	60
Duralee Fabrics Ltd Inc 1775 5th Ave *Cust Svc	Bay Shore	NY	11706	**800-275-3872***	631-273-8800	583
DuraLine Imaging Inc 110 Commercial Blvd	Flat Rock	NC	28731	**800-982-3872**	828-692-1301	616
Duraloy Technologies Inc 120 Bridge St	Scottdale	PA	15683	**800-823-5101**	724-887-5100	302
Duramet Corp 11350 Stephens Dr	Warren	MI	48089	**800-783-2280**	586-759-2280	484
Durango Area Chamber of Commerce 111 S Camino del Rio	Durango	CO	81303	**888-414-0835**	970-247-0312	137
Durango Herald 1275 Main Ave	Durango	CO	81301	**800-530-8318**	970-247-3504	522-2
Durango Mountain Resort 1 Skier Pl	Durango	CO	81301	**800-693-0175**	970-247-9000	655
Durango Steakhouse 2325 Ulmerton Rd Suite 20	Clearwater	FL	33762	**800-525-8643**	727-576-6424	657
Durant Daily Democrat 200 W Beech St PO Box 250	Durant	OK	74702	**800-729-4388**	580-924-4388	522-2
DuraSwitch Industries Inc 234 S Extension Rd Suite 103 *NASDAQ: DSWT*	Mesa	AZ	85210	**800-729-3132**	480-586-3300	715
DuraTech Industries International Inc 3780 Hwy 281 SE	Jamestown	ND	58402	**800-243-4601**	701-252-4601	269
Duratek Inc 10100 Old Columbia Rd *NASDAQ: DRTK*	Columbia	MD	21046	**800-638-3838**	410-312-5100	653
Durbin Marshall Food Corp 2830 Commerce Blvd	Irondale	AL	35210	**800-768-2456**	205-956-3505	11-8
Durham Convention & Visitors Bureau 101 E Morgan St	Durham	NC	27701	**800-446-8604**	919-687-0288	205
Durham Cos Inc 6300 Transit Rd	Depew	NY	14043	**800-633-7724**	716-684-3333	707
Durham Meat Co 2026 Martin Ave	Santa Clara	CA	95050	**800-233-8742**	800-444-5687	292-9
Durham Mfg Co Inc PO Box 230	Durham	CT	06422	**800-243-3774**	860-349-3427	281
Durham School Services Inc 9011 Mountain Ridge Dr Suite 200	Austin	TX	78759	**800-950-0485**	512-343-6292	110
Durkan Patterned Carpet Inc 405 Virgil Dr	Dalton	GA	30721	**800-241-4580**	706-278-7037	131
Duro Art Industries Inc 1832 Juneway Terr	Chicago	IL	60626	**800-621-5144**	773-743-3430	43
Duro Bag Mfg Co 7600 Empire Dr	Florence	KY	41042	**800-879-3876**	859-581-8200	67
Duro Dyne Corp 81 Spence St	Bay Shore	NY	11706	**800-899-3876**	631-249-9000	15
Duron Inc 10406 Tucker St	Beltsville	MD	20705	**800-723-8766**	301-937-4700	540
Durr Marketing Assoc Inc 1300 Lower Rodi Rd	Turtle Creek	PA	15145	**800-937-3877**	412-829-2300	144
Dury's 701 Ewing Ave	Nashville	TN	37203	**800-824-2379**	615-255-3456	119
Dutch Wonderland Family Amusement Park 2249 Lincoln Hwy E	Lancaster	PA	17602	**866-386-2839**	717-291-1888	32
Dutchess Beer Distributors Inc 5 Laurel St *Cust Svc	Poughkeepsie	NY	12603	**800-427-6308***	845-452-0940	82-1
Dutchess Community College 53 Pendell Rd	Poughkeepsie	NY	12601	**800-763-3933**	845-431-8010	160
Dutt & Wagner of Virginia Inc PO Box 518	Abingdon	VA	24212	**800-688-2116**	276-628-2116	292-10
Dutton Family Theatre 3454 W Hwy 76	Branson	MO	65616	**800-942-4626**	417-332-2772	509
DUTYFREE.COM PO Box 5868	Fort Lauderdale	FL	33310	**800-666-3889**	954-978-5482	240
Duvall HB Inc 901 E Patrick St	Frederick	MD	21701	**800-423-4032**	301-662-1125	270
Duvinage Corp 60 W Oak Ridge Dr	Hagerstown	MD	21740	**800-541-2645**	301-733-8255	482
DV: Digital Video Magazine 7300 N Linder Ave	Skokie	IL	60076	**888-776-7002**	847-763-9581	449-7
DVC 44 Whippany Rd	Morristown	NJ	07960	**800-526-8712**	973 776 6700	4
DVD Avenue PO Box 820	Clinton	MD	20735	**800-990-4159**	301-856-4159	94
DVD Empire 2140 Woodland Rd	Warrendale	PA	15086	**888-383-1880**	724-933-0399	784
DVD Overnight Inc PO Box 4681	Philadelphia	PA	19127	**877-383-1099**	215-483-0733	94
DVM Pharmaceuticals Inc 50 NW 176th St	Miami	FL	33169	**800-367-4902**	305-575-6950	574
DWI Journal PO Box 340	Fanwood	NJ	07023	**800-359-6049**	908-889-6336	521-7
Dwight D Eisenhower Presidential Library & Museum 200 SE 4th St	Abilene	KS	67410	**877-746-4453**	785-263-6700	426
Dwight D Eisenhower Veterans Affairs Medical Center 4101 S 4th St	Leavenworth	KS	66048	**800-952-8387**	913-682-2000	366-6
Dwyer Group Inc 1010 N University Parks Dr	Waco	TX	76707	**800-490-7501**	254-745-2400	355-3
Dwyer Products Corp 418 N Calumet Ave	Michigan City	IN	46360	**800-348-8508**	219-874-5236	36
Dycam Inc 22425 Ventura Blvd Suite 12	Woodland Hills	CA	91364	**800-883-9226**	818-998-8008	580
Dycom Industries Inc 4440 PGA Blvd Suite 500 *NYSE: DY*	Palm Beach Gardens	FL	33410	**877-210-0347**	561-627-7171	188-4
Dye Don Co Inc PO Box 107	Kingman	KS	67068	**800-901-3131**	620-532-3131	609
Dyer Riddle Mills & Precourt Inc 1505 E Colonial Dr	Orlando	FL	32803	**800-375-3767**	407-896-0594	258
DYK Inc 351 Cypress Ln	El Cajon	CA	92020	**800-227-8181**	619-440-8181	181
Dylan Hotel 52 E 41st St	New York	NY	10017	**866-553-9526**	212-338-0500	373
Dylon Industries 7700 Clinton Rd	Cleveland	OH	44144	**800-237-8246**	216-651-1300	530
Dynabrade Inc 8989 Sheridan Dr *Cust Svc	Clarence	NY	14031	**800-828-7333***	716-631-0100	747
Dynaco Inc 2246 E Date Ave	Fresno	CA	93706	**800-230-4985**	559-485-8520	656
Dynacraft Golf Products Inc 107 Pine St *Cust Svc	Newark	OH	43058	**800-423-2968***	740-344-1191	701
Dynalco Controls Div Crane Co 3690 NW 53rd St	Fort Lauderdale	FL	33309	**800-368-6666**	954-739-4300	200
Dynalectric Corp 4462 Corporate Ctr Dr	Los Alamitos	CA	90720	**800-729-0444**	714-828-7000	188-4
Dynalogic Inc 2921 Eastlake Ave E	Seattle	WA	98102	**800-735-0433**	206-323-9050	176-1
Dynamet Inc 195 Museum Rd	Washington	PA	15301	**800-237-9655**	724-228-1000	476
DynaMetric Inc 717 S Myrtle Ave	Monrovia	CA	91016	**800-525-6925**	626-358-2559	720
Dynamic Concepts Inc 1730 17th St NE	Washington	DC	20002	**800-634-4385**	202-944-8787	720
Dynamic Decisions Inc 31 Suttons Ln	Piscataway	NJ	08854	**800-689-9908**	732-819-3946	178
Dynamic Graphics Group 6000 N Forest Park Dr	Peoria	IL	61614	**800-255-8800**	309-688-8800	338
Dynamic Homes Inc 525 Roosevelt Ave	Detroit Lakes	MN	56501	**800-492-4833**	218-847-2611	107
Dynamic Instruments Inc 3860 Calle Fortunada	San Diego	CA	92123	**800-793-3358**	858-278-4900	52
Dynamic Management LLC 1210 Briarville Rd	Madison	TN	37115	**800-306-1748**	615-277-1234	656
Dynamic Materials Corp 5405 Spine Rd *NASDAQ: BOOM*	Boulder	CO	80301	**800-821-2666**	303-665-5700	473
Dynamic Mobile Data Systems Inc 285 Davidson Ave Suite 501 *Tech Supp	Somerset	NJ	08873	**866-662-4363***	732-302-1700	222
Dynamic Recovery Services Inc 2775 Villa Creek Dr Suite 290	Dallas	TX	75234	**800-886-8088**	972-241-5611	157
Dynamics Inc 1455 Estes	Elk Grove Village	IL	60007	**800-323-6850**	847-264-2580	536
Dynamics Research Corp 60 Frontage Rd *NASDAQ: DRCO*	Andover	MA	01810	**800-522-4321**	978-475-9090	178
Dynaquip Controls 10 Harris Industrial Pk	Saint Clair	MO	63077	**800-545-3636**	636-629-3700	777
Dynarand LLC 55 Francisco St Suite 780	San Francisco	CA	94133	**888-794-4877**	415-293-1340	176-7
Dynaric Inc 5740 Bayside Rd	Virginia Beach	VA	23455	**800-526-0827**	757-363-5850	537
Dynasty Suites 3735 Iowa Ave	Riverside	CA	92507	**800-842-7899**	951-369-8200	373
Dynatem Inc 23263 Madero Suite C	Mission Viejo	CA	92691	**800-543-3830**	949-855-3235	613
Dynatronics Corp 7030 Park Centre Dr *NASDAQ: DYNT*	Salt Lake City	UT	84121	**800-874-6251**	801-568-7000	249
Dynea USA Inc 1600 Valley River Dr Suite 390	Eugene	OR	97401	**800-862-1332**	541-687-8840	3
Dynegy Global Communications 1000 Louisiana St Suite 5800	Houston	TX	77002	**800-922-2104**	713-507-6400	721
Dynegy Inc 1000 Louisiana St Suite 5800 *NYSE: DYN*	Houston	TX	77002	**800-922-2104**	713-507-6400	355-5
Dyneon LLC 50 Milton Dr	Aston	PA	19014	**800-554-6782**	610-497-8899	594-2
Dynetics Engineering Corp 515 Bond St	Lincolnshire	IL	60069	**800-888-8110**	847-541-7300	112

Name / Address	City	State	ZIP	Toll-Free	Phone	Class
Dynix Corp 400 W Dynix Dr	Provo	UT	84604	**800-288-8020**	801-223-5200	176-10
Dyno Nobel Inc 50 S Main St Crossroad Towers 11th Fl	Salt Lake City	UT	84144	**800-473-2626**	801-364-4800	264
Dynoptic Inc 4399 35th St N	Saint Petersburg	FL	33714	**800-648-7463**	727-812-3000	531
D'Youville College 320 Porter Ave	Buffalo	NY	14201	**800-777-3921**	716-881-3200	163
Dyslexia Assn. International 8600 LaSalle Rd Chester Bldg Suite 382	Baltimore	MD	21286	**800-222-3123**	410-296-0232	48-17
Dyslexic. Recording for the Blind & 20 Roszel Rd	Princeton	NJ	08540	**800-221-4792**	609-452-0606	48-17
Dystonia Medical Research Foundation 1 E Wacker Dr Suite 2430	Chicago	IL	60601	**800-377-3978**	312-755-0198	48-17

E

Name / Address	City	State	ZIP	Toll-Free	Phone	Class
E-A-R Specialty Composites 5457 W 79th St	Indianapolis	IN	46268	**800-544-5180**	317-692-6666	590
E-Access Inc 840 6th Ave *Sales	Huntington	WV	25701	**800-471-5087***	304-697-4410	795
E-Builder Inc 100 W Cypress Creek Rd Suite 845	Fort Lauderdale	FL	33309	**800-580-9322**	954-938-8032	39
E-centives Inc 6901 Rockledge Dr 6th Fl	Bethesda	MD	20817	**877-323-6848**	240-333-6100	7
E Com Ventures Inc 251 International Pkwy *NASDAQ: ECMV*	Sunrise	FL	33325	**866-600-3600**	954-335-9100	658
E-Commerce Times 15821 Ventura Blvd Suite 635	Encino	CA	91436	**877-328-5500**	818-461-9700	449-5
E & D Web Inc 4633 W 16th St	Cicero	IL	60804	**800-323-5733**	708-656-6600	615
E Dillon & Co PO Box 160	Swords Creek	VA	24649	**800-234-8970**	276-873-6816	181
e-doc Magazine 1100 Wayne Ave Suite 1100	Silver Spring	MD	20910	**800-477-2446**	301-587-8202	449-7
E-Force 7920 Arjons Dr Suite A	San Diego	CA	92126	**800-433-6723**	858-547-3720	701
E Fougera & Co 60 Baylis Rd	Melville	NY	11747	**800-645-9833**	631-454-6996	573
E & J Gallo Winery 600 Yosemite Blvd	Modesto	CA	95354	**800-322-2389**	209-341-3111	81-3
E & L Transport Co LLC 35005 W Michigan Ave	Wayne	MI	48184	**800-833-8322**	734-729-9500	769
E-LOAN Inc 6230 Stone Ridge Mall Rd *NASDAQ: EELN*	Pleasanton	CA	94588	**888-356-2622**	925-847-6900	498
E-Markets Inc 1606 Golden Aspen Dr Suite 110	Ames	IA	50010	**877-674-7419**	515-233-8720	39
E & O Mari Inc 256 Broadway	Newburgh	NY	12550	**800-750-3034**	845-562-4400	516
E Ritter & Co Inc 106 Frisco St	Marked Tree	AR	72365	**800-323-0355**	870-358-2200	11-2
E Sam Jones Distributor Inc 4898 S Atlanta Rd	Smyrna	GA	30080	**800-624-9849**	404-351-3250	245
E Shoe Sale Inc 60 Enterprise Ave N	Secaucus	NJ	07094	**877-474-6372**	201-319-0853	296
e-SIM Ltd 225 S Lake Ave Suite 300	Pasadena	CA	91101	**800-368-5835**	626-584-7810	176-7
E Stewart Mitchell Inc PO Box 2799	Baltimore	MD	21225	**800-870-6365**	410-354-0600	190-1
e-talk Corp 4040 W Royal Ln Suite 100	Irving	TX	75063	**800-835-6357**	972-819-3100	176-1
E Tour & Travel 3626 Quadrangle Blvd Suite 400	Orlando	FL	32817	**800-339-5120**	407-658-8285	760
E-Z-EM Inc 717 Main St *AMEX: EZM*	Westbury	NY	11590	**800-544-4624**	516-333-8230	229
E-Z Mart Stores Inc 602 W Falvey St	Texarkana	TX	75501	**800-234-6502**	903-832-6502	203
E*Trade Bank 671 N Glebe Rd	Arlington	VA	22203	**800-382-2651**	703-247-3700	71
E*Trade Financial Corp 4500 Bohannon Dr *NYSE: ET* ■ *Orders	Menlo Park	CA	94025	**800-786-2575***	650-331-6000	679
E*Trade Financial Corp Corporate Services 4500 Bohannon Dr	Menlo Park	CA	94025	**800-786-2575**	650-331-6000	176-1
e.Digital Corp 13114 Evening Creek Dr S	San Diego	CA	92128	**877-278-1574**	858-679-1504	52
E.piphany Inc 475 Concar Dr *NASDAQ: EPNY*	San Mateo	CA	94402	**877-764-4163**	650-578-7200	176-1
EA Engineering Science & Technology Inc 11019 McCormick Rd	Hunt Valley	MD	21031	**800-777-9750**	410-584-7000	258
ea inc 1130 Iron Point Rd Suite 288	Folsom	CA	95630	**800-399-2828**	916-608-1868	178
EA Miller Inc 410 N 200 West	Hyrum	UT	84319	**800-873-0939**	435-245-6456	465
EAA (Experimental Aircraft Assn) 3000 Poberezny Rd	Oshkosh	WI	54902	**800-236-4800**	920-426-4800	48-18
EADS Sogerma Barfield Inc 4101 NW 29th St	Miami	FL	33142	**800-321-1039**	305-894-5400	25
Eagan Convention & Visitors Bureau 1501 Central Pkwy	Eagan	MN	55121	**800-324-2620**	651-675-5546	205
Eager Beaver 14893 Hwy 27	Lake Wales	FL	33853	**800-257-8163**	863-638-1421	768
Eagle Affiliates Inc 1000 S 2nd St	Plainfield	NJ	07063	**800-221-0434**	908-757-4464	596
Eagle Asset Management 880 Carillon Pkwy	Saint Petersburg	FL	33716	**800-237-3101**	727-573-2453	393
Eagle Aviation 2861 Aviation Way Columbia Metropolitan Airport	West Columbia	SC	29170	**800-848-6359**	803-822-5577	63
Eagle Burgmann Industries LP 10035 Brookriver Dr	Houston	TX	77040	**800-303-7735**	713-939-9515	321
Eagle Claw Fishing Tackle 4245 E 46th Ave	Denver	CO	80216	**800-628-0108**	303-321-1481	701
Eagle Comtronics Inc 7665 Henry Clay Blvd	Liverpool	NY	13088	**800-448-7474**	315-622-3402	633
Eagle Creek Inc 3055 Enterprise Ct *Cust Svc	Vista	CA	92081	**800-874-9925***	760-599-6500	444
Eagle Div DaimlerChrysler Corp 800 Chrysler Dr E *Cust Svc	Auburn Hills	MI	48326	**800-992-1997***	248-576-5741	59
Eagle Electric Supply Co Inc 135 Will Dr	Canton	MA	02021	**800-462-5010**	781-302-2000	245
Eagle Global Logistics 15350 Vickery Dr *NASDAQ: EAGL*	Houston	TX	77032	**800-821-9956**	281-618-3100	440
Eagle Group 100 Industrial Blvd	Clayton	DE	19938	**800-441-8440**	302-653-3000	478
Eagle Marketing Inc Perfume Originals Products Div 2412 Sequoia Pk	Yukon	OK	73099	**800-233-7424**	405-354-1027	564
Eagle Mountain Casino 681 S Tule Rd	Porterville	CA	93257	**800-903-3353**	559-788-6220	133
Eagle Mountain House Carter Notch Rd Box E	Jackson	NH	03846	**800-966-5779**	603-383-9111	373
Eagle Pack Pet Foods Inc 1025 W 11th St	Mishawaka	IN	46544	**800-255-5959**	574-259-7834	568
Eagle Pass Chamber of Commerce 1511 W Henderson St	Eagle Pass	TX	78853	**888-355-3224**	830-773-3224	137
Eagle-Picher Minerals Inc PO Box 12130 *Cust Svc	Reno	NV	89510	**800-228-3865***	775-824-7600	490
Eagle Point Software Corp 4131 Westmark Dr	Dubuque	IA	52002	**800-678-6565**	563-556-8392	176-10
Eagle Pointe Golf Resort 2250 E Pointe Rd	Bloomington	IN	47401	**877-324-7683**	812-824-4040	655
Eagle Professional Resources Inc 67 Yonge St Suite 200	Toronto	ON	M5E1J8	**800-281-2339**	416-861-0636	707
Eagle Publications Inc RR 2 River Rd Box 301	Claremont	NH	03743	**800-545-0347**	603-542-5121	623-8
Eagle Ridge Inn & Resort 444 Eagle Ridge Dr	Galena	IL	61036	**800-892-2269**	815-777-2444	655
Eagle Roller Mill Co 1101 Airport Rd	Shelby	NC	28150	**800-223-9108**	704-487-5061	438
Eagle Sports 6020 N Sam Houston Pkwy E	Humble	TX	77396	**800-862-4424**	281-441-4220	701
Eagle Times 401 River Rd	Claremont	NH	03743	**800-545-0347**	603-543-3100	522-2
Eagle Window & Door Inc 2045 Kerper Blvd	Dubuque	IA	52001	**800-324-5354**	563-556-2270	234
EagleHerald The 1809 Dunlap Ave PO Box 77	Marinette	WI	54143	**800-777-0345**	715-735-6611	522-2
Eagle's Nest Resort 6103 LaVaque Rd	Duluth	MN	55803	**800-348-4575**	218-721-4147	655
Eagles Talent Connection Inc 57 W South Orange Ave	South Orange	NJ	07079	**800-345-5607**	973-376-3737	699
Eagleville Hospital 100 Eagleville Rd	Eagleville	PA	19408	**800-255-2019**	610-539-6000	712
Eakes Office Plus 617 W 3rd St	Grand Island	NE	68802	**800-652-9396**	308-382-8026	524
EANGUS (Enlisted Assn of the National Guard of the US) 3133 Mt Vernon Ave	Alexandria	VA	22305	**800-234-3264**	703-519-3846	48-19
EAP Consultants Inc 3901 Roswell Rd Suite 340	Marietta	GA	30062	**800-869-0276**	770-951-8021	454
EAP Systems 500 W Cummings Pk Suite 6000	Woburn	MA	01801	**800-327-6721**	781-935-8850	454
Earl G Graves Ltd 130 5th Ave 10th Fl	New York	NY	10011	**800-727-7777**	212-242-8000	623-9
Earl May Seed & Nursery 208 N Elm St	Shenandoah	IA	51603	**800-831-4193**	712-246-1020	318
Earl Scheib Inc 15206 Ventura Blvd Suite 200	Sherman Oaks	CA	91403	**800-639-3275**	818-981-9992	62-4
Earle Brown Heritage Center 6155 Earle Brown Dr	Minneapolis	MN	55430	**800-524-0239**	763-569-6300	204
Earle Industries Inc Hwys 149 & 64 PO Box 28	Earle	AR	72331	**888-944-8667**	870-792-8694	731
Earle M Jorgensen Co 10650 S Alameda St *NYSE: JOR*	Lynwood	CA	90262	**800-336-5365**	323-567-1122	481
Earlham College 801 National Rd W	Richmond	IN	47374	**800-327-5426**	765-983-1200	163
Earlham School of Religion 228 College Ave	Richmond	IN	47374	**800-432-1377**	765-983-1423	164-3
Earl's Apparel Inc 908 S 4th St PO Box 939	Crockett	TX	75835	**800-527-3148**	936-544-5521	153-19
Early Bird The 5312 Sebring Warner Rd	Greenville	OH	45331	**800-548-5312**	937-548-3330	522-4
Early Childhood Teachers' Club Doubleday Select Inc 101 Park Ave 2nd Fl	New York	NY	10178	**800-321-7323**		94
Earmark LLC 1125 Dixwell Ave *Cust Svc	Hamden	CT	06514	**888-327-6275***	203-777-2130	633
Earnest Machine Products Co 12502 Plaza Dr	Parma	OH	44130	**800-327-6378**	216-362-1100	346
Earnest Partners LLC 75 14th St Suite 2300	Atlanta	GA	30309	**800-322-0068**	404-815-8772	393
Earnhardt Auto Centers 1301 N Arizona Ave	Gilbert	AZ	85233	**800-497-8740**	480-926-4000	57
Earp Distribution Co 6550 Kansas Ave	Kansas City	KS	66111	**800-866-3277**	913-287-3311	292-9
Earth. Friends of the 1717 Massachusetts Ave NW Suite 600	Washington	DC	20036	**877-843-8687**	202-783-7400	48-13
Earth Share 7735 Old Georgetown Rd Suite 900	Bethesda	MD	20814	**800-875-3863**	240-333-0300	48-13
Earthbound Farm 1721 San Juan Hwy	San Juan Bautista	CA	95045	**800-690-3200**	831-623-7880	11-11
EarthLink Inc 1375 Peachtree St NE *NASDAQ: ELNK*	Atlanta	GA	30309	**800-332-4892**	404-815-0770	390
Earthman Funeral Directors 2420 Fannin St	Houston	TX	77002	**800-654-2609**	713-659-3000	499
Earthwatch Institute 3 Clock Tower Pl Suite 100	Maynard	MA	01754	**800-776-0188**	978-461-0081	48-13
EarthWay Products Inc PO Box 547	Bristol	IN	46507	**800-678-0671**	574-848-7491	420
EAS Inc (Experimental & Applied Science Inc) 555 Corporate Cir	Golden	CO	80401	**800-297-9776**	303-271-1002	786
Easi File Mfg Corp 6 Wrigley St	Irvine	CA	92618	**800-800-5563**	949-855-4121	314-1
East Arkansas Community College 1700 Newcastle Rd	Forrest City	AR	72335	**877-797-3222**	870-633-4480	160
East Aurora (Greater) Chamber of Commerce 431 Main St	East Aurora	NY	14052	**800-441-2881**	716-652-8444	137
East Bay Chamber of Commerce 16 Cutler St Suite 102	Warren	RI	02885	**888-278-9948**	401-245-0750	137
East Bay Tire Co 2200 Huntington Dr Unit C	Fairfield	CA	94533	**800-831-8473**	707-437-4700	740
East Canyon Hotel & Spa 288 E Camino Monte Vista	Palm Springs	CA	92262	**877-324-6835**	760-320-1928	373
East Central Community College PO Box 129	Decatur	MS	39327	**877-462-3222**	601-635-2126	160

				Toll-Free	Phone	Class
East Central Energy PO Box 39	Braham	MN	55006	**800-254-7944**		244
East-Central Iowa Rural Electric Co-op PO Box 248	Urbana	IA	52345	**877-850-4343**	319-443-4343	244
East Central Oklahoma Electric Co-op Inc PO Box 1178	Okmulgee	OK	74447	**800-783-9317**	918-756-0833	244
East Coast Air Charter Inc PO Box 7137	Statesville	NC	28687	**888-277-7434**	704-838-1991	13
East Coast Flight Services Inc 29111 Newman Rd Easton Municipal Airport	Easton	MD	21601	**800-554-0550***	410-820-6633	14
*Sales						
East Coast Fruit Co Inc 3335 Edgewood Ave N..........	Jacksonville	FL	32205	**800-541-4602**	904-355-7591	292-7
East Coast Metal Distributors Inc 1313 S Briggs Ave	Durham	NC	27703	**800-334-9708**	919-598-5030	483
East Hill Woods 611 E Hill Rd.......	Southbury	CT	06488	**800-435-4249**	203-262-6161	659
East Jordan Iron Works Inc 301 Spring St.................	East Jordan	MI	49727	**800-874-4100**	231-536-2261	302
East Mfg Corp 1871 State Rt 44 PO Box 277	Randolph	OH	44265	**888-405-3278**	330-325-9921	768
East Moline Metal Products Co 1201 7th St	East Moline	IL	61244	**800-325-4151***	309-752-1350	479
*Sales						
East Oregonian 211 SE Byers St PO Box 1089......	Pendleton	OR	97801	**800-522-0255**	541-276-2211	522-2
East Ridge Retirement Village 19301 SW 87th Ave.................	Miami	FL	33157	**800-605-7778**	305-256-3564	659
East Side Moving & Storage PO Box 86216	Portland	OR	97286	**800-547-4600**	503-777-4181	508
East Stroudsburg University 200 Prospect St	East Stroudsburg	PA	18301	**877-230-5547**	570-422-3600	163
East Tennessee Public Communications Corp 1611 E Magnolia Ave.........	Knoxville	TN	37917	**800-595-0220**	865-595-0220	620
East Tennessee State University PO Box 70731	Johnson City	TN	37614	**800-462-3878**	423-439-4213	163
East Valley Tribune The 120 W 1st Ave...	Mesa	AZ	85210	**888-887-4286***	480-898-6500	522-2
*Cust Svc						
East-West Bank 415 Huntington Dr	San Marino	CA	91108	**800-888-3932**	626-799-8998	71
East-West Label Co Inc 1000 E Hector St	Conshohocken	PA	19428	**800-441-7333**	610-825-0410	404
East-West Mortgage 1568 Spring Hill Rd Suite 100.......	McLean	VA	22102	**800-844-1015**	703-442-0150	394
Eastbay Inc PO Box 8066	Wausau	WI	54402	**800-628-6301**		451
Easter Seals 230 W Monroe St Suite 1800	Chicago	IL	60606	**800-221-6827**	312-726-6200	48-17
Eastern Alloys Inc Henry Henning Dr PO Box Q	Maybrook	NY	12543	**800-456-1496**	845-427-2151	476
Eastern Arizona College 615 N Stadium Ave	Thatcher	AZ	85552	**800-678-3808**	928-428-8472	160
Eastern Bank 195 Market St.............	Lynn	MA	01903	**800-327-8376**	781-599-2100	71
Eastern Bank Corp Inc 112 Market St	Lynn	MA	01901	**800-327-8376**	781-599-2100	355-2
Eastern Baptist Theological Seminary 6 Lancaster Ave	Wynnewood	PA	19096	**800-220-3287**	610-896-5000	164-3
Eastern Cement Corp 13250 Eastern Ave	Palmetto	FL	34221	**800-282-7798**	941-729-7311	135
Eastern Concrete Materials Inc 475 Market St...............	Elmwood Park	NJ	07407	**800-822-7242**	201-797-7979	180
Eastern Connecticut State University 83 Windham St.................	Willimantic	CT	06226	**877-353-3278**	860-465-5000	163
Eastern Data Paper Inc PO Box 202	Little Falls	NJ	07424	**800-524-2528**	973-472-5252	543
Eastern Farmers Co-op 401 S Railroad Ave.................	Jasper	MN	56144	**800-865-2773**	507-348-3911	438
Eastern Federal Corp 901 East Blvd...	Charlotte	NC	28203	**800-394-7368**	704-377-3495	733
Eastern Financial Florida Credit Union 3700 Lakeside Dr.................	Miramar	FL	33027	**800-882-5007**	954-704-5000	216
Eastern Floral & Gift Shop 2836 Broadmoor Ave SE	Grand Rapids	MI	49512	**800-494-2202**	616-949-2200	287
Eastern Foods Inc 1000 Naturally Fresh Blvd	Atlanta	GA	30349	**800-765-1950**	404-765-9000	291-19
Eastern Garage Door 417 Canal St	Lawrence	MA	01842	**800-766-6012**	978-683-3158	232
Eastern Idaho Technical College 1600 S 25th E	Idaho Falls	ID	83404	**800-662-0261**	208-524-3000	787
Eastern Illini Electric Co-op PO Box 96	Paxton	IL	60957	**800-824-5102**	217-379-2131	244
Eastern Illinois University 600 Lincoln Ave	Charleston	IL	61920	**800-252-5711**	217-581-5000	163
Eastern Insurance Agency Inc 233 W Central St	Natick	MA	01760	**800-333-7234**	508-651-7700	383
Eastern Iowa Light & Power Co-op 600 E 5th St Po Box 3003...........	Wilton	IA	52778	**800-728-1242**	563-732-2211	244
Eastern Kentucky University 521 Lancaster Ave	Richmond	KY	40475	**800-465-9191**	859-622-1000	163
Eastern Lift Truck Co Inc PO Box 307	Maple Shade	NJ	08052	**888-779-8880**	856-779-8880	378
Eastern Maine Electric Co-op Inc PO Box 425	Calais	ME	04619	**800-696-7444**	207-454-7555	244
Eastern Mennonite University 1200 Park Rd................	Harrisonburg	VA	22802	**800-368-2665***	540-432-4118	163
*Admissions						
Eastern Metal/USA-SIGN 1430 Sullivan St....................	Elmira	NY	14901	**800-872-7446***	607-734-2295	692
*Sales						
Eastern Michigan University	Ypsilanti	MI	48197	**800-468-6368**	734-487-1849	163
Eastern Mountain Sports Inc 1 Vose Farm Rd	Peterborough	NH	03458	**888-463-6367**	603-924-9571	702
Eastern Nazarene College 23 E Elm Ave	Quincy	MA	02170	**800-883-6288**	617-745-3000	163
Eastern New Mexico Medical Center 405 W Country Club Rd............	Roswell	NM	88201	**800-437-9275**	505-622-8170	366-2
Eastern New Mexico University Station 7.........................	Portales	NM	88130	**800-367-3668**	505-562-2178	163
Roswell Campus PO Box 6000	Roswell	NM	88202	**800-243-6687**	505-624-7000	160
Eastern Oregon University 1 University Blvd	La Grande	OR	97850	**800-452-8639**	541-962-3393	163
Eastern Pennsylvania Business Journal 65 E Elizabeth Ave Suite 700......	Bethlehem	PA	18018	**800-328-1026**	610-807-9619	449-5
Eastern Pennsylvania Supply Co 700 Scott St PO Box 1126......	Wilkes-Barre	PA	18773	**800-432-8075**	570-823-1181	601
Eastern Reproduction Corp 1250 Main St	Waltham	MA	02154	**800-343-0217**	781-893-0555	399
Eastern Shore Seafood PO Box 38...	Mappsville	VA	23407	**800-446-8550***	757-824-5651	291-14
*Sales						
Eastern Star. General Grand Chapter Order of the 1618 New Hampshire Ave NW	Washington	DC	20009	**800-648-1182**	202-667-4737	48-15
Eastern Tea Corp 1 Engelhard Dr...........	Monroe Township	NJ	08831	**800-221-0865**	609-860-1100	291-40
Eastern Virginia Bankshares Inc 330 Hospital Rd	Tappahannock	VA	22560	**866-443-8429**	804-443-8400	355-2
NASDAQ: EVBS						
Eastern Washington University 101 Sutton Hall....................	Cheney	WA	99004	**888-740-1914**	509-359-6200	163
Eastern Wire Products Co 498 Kinsley Ave	Providence	RI	02909	**800-486-3181**	401-861-1350	75
Eastern Wood Products Inc PO Box 1056	Williamsport	PA	17703	**800-445-5428**	570-326-1946	541
Eastern Wyoming College 3200 W 'C' St..................	Torrington	WY	82240	**800-658-3195**	307-532-8200	160
Eastgate Tower 222 E 39th St	New York	NY	10016	**800-637-8483**	212-687-8000	373
EastGroup Properties Inc 100 E Capitol St Suite 300..........	Jackson	MS	39201	**800-337-6602**	601-354-3555	641
NYSE: EGP						
Eastland Park Hotel 157 High St	Portland	ME	04101	**888-671-8008**	207-775-5411	373
Eastman Chemical Co PO Box 431....	Kingsport	TN	37662	**800-327-8626***	423-229-2000	142
NYSE: EMN ■ *Cust Svc						
Eastman Credit Union PO Box 1989...	Kingsport	TN	37662	**800-999-2328**	423-229-8200	216
Eastman Kodak Co 343 State St......	Rochester	NY	14650	**800-242-2424**	585-724-4000	580
NYSE: EK						
Eastman Kodak Co Commercial & Government Systems Div 1447 Saint Paul St..............	Rochester	NY	14653	**800-698-3324**		580
Eastman Kodak Co Digital & Applied Imaging Div 343 State St..........	Rochester	NY	14650	**800-242-2424**	800-698-3324	580
Eastman Kodak Co Health Imaging Div 343 State St Bldg 20 4th Fl	Rochester	NY	14650	**800-677-9933***	585-588-9003	375
*Cust Svc						
Eastman Kodak Co Kodak Professional Div 343 State St.................	Rochester	NY	14650	**800-242-2424**	800-698-3324	580
Eastman Kodak Co Professional Motion Imaging Div 343 State St ...	Rochester	NY	14650	**800-621-3456**	800-698-3324	580
Eastman Machine Co 779 Washington St.................	Buffalo	NY	14203	**800-872-5571**	716-856-2200	729
Easton Sports Inc 7855 Haskell Ave ...	Van Nuys	CA	91406	**800-632-7866**	818-782-6445	701
Easton Tru-Flite LLC 2709 S Freeman Rd	Monticello	IN	47960	**800-348-2224**	574-583-5131	701
Eastown Distributors 14400 Oakland Ave...........	Highland Park	MI	48203	**800-417-0080**	313-867-6900	82-1
Eastpak Corp PO Box 1817...........	Appleton	WI	54912	**800-222-5725**		343
Eastside Hospital 2700 152nd Ave NE..............	Redmond	WA	98052	**800-995-5658**	425-883-5151	366-2
Eastsider 1701 Green Rd Suite B	Deerfield Beach	FL	33064	**800-275-8820**	954-698-6397	522-4
Easy Spirit Shoes 1129 Westchester Ave	White Plains	NY	10604	**800-284-9955**	914-640-6400	296
EasyHeat Div EGS Electrical Group LLC 2 Connecticut S Dr	East Granby	CT	06026	**800-523-7636**	860-653-1600	15
EasyLink Services Corp 33 Kinghtbridge Rd	Piscataway	NJ	08854	**800-624-5266**	732-652-3500	176-12
NASDAQ: EASY						
Easyriders Magazine 28210 Dorothy Dr.............	Agoura Hills	CA	91301	**800-247-6246**	818-889-8740	449-3
EATELCORP Inc 913 S Burnside Ave ...	Gonzales	LA	70737	**800-621-4211**	225-621-4300	721
Eating Disorders Assn. National 603 Stewart St Suite 803............	Seattle	WA	98101	**800-931-2237**	206-382-3587	48-17
Eat'n Park Hospitality Group Inc 285 E Waterfront Dr PO Box 3000	Pittsburgh	PA	15230	**800-947-4033**	412-461-2000	657
Eaton Cutler-Hammer Inc 1 Tuscarawas Rd	Beaver	PA	15009	**800-354-2070**	724-775-2000	715
Eaton Farm Confectioners Inc 30 Burbank Rd	Sutton	MA	01590	**800-343-9300**	508-865-5235	291-8
Eaton Office Supply Co Inc 180 John Glenn Dr................	Amherst	NY	14228	**800-365-3237**	716-691-6100	523
Eaton Steel Corp 10221 Capital Ave ...	Oak Park	MI	48237	**800-527-3851**	248-398-3434	483
Eaton Vance Corp 255 State St.........	Boston	MA	02109	**800-225-6265**	617-482-8260	393
NYSE: EV						
Eaton Vance Distributors Inc 255 State St	Boston	MA	02109	**800-225-6265**	617-482-8260	679
Eaton Vance Mutual Funds 255 State St	Boston	MA	02109	**800-225-6265**	617-482-8260	517
Eatons' Ranch 270 Eatons' Ranch Rd......	Wolf	WY	82844	**800-210-1049**	307-655-9285	238
Eatsleepmusic Network 301 Moodie Dr Suite 306............	Ottawa	ON	K2H9C4	**877-867-8668**		388
eAttorney Inc 245 Peachtree Ctr Ave Suite 2415.....	Atlanta	GA	30303	**800-378-6101**		39
Eau Claire Electric Co-op PO Box 368	Fall Creek	WI	54742	**800-927-5090**	715-832-1603	244
eB2B Commerce Inc 665 Broadway ...	New York	NY	10012	**877-853-3222**	212-477-1700	176-4
EB Bradley Co 5080 S Alameda St.............	Los Angeles	CA	90058	**800-533-3030**	323-585-9201	346
Ebara Technologies Inc 51 Main Ave...................	Sacramento	CA	95838	**800-535-5376**	916-920-5451	685
eBay Inc 2145 Hamilton Ave.........	San Jose	CA	95125	**800-322-9266**	408-558-7400	51
NASDAQ: EBAY						
EBDS (Employee Benefits Data Services Inc) 420 Fort Duquesne Blvd 1 Gateway Ctr Suite 1250	Pittsburgh	PA	15222	**800-472-2738**	412-394-6300	619
eBenX Inc 605 N Hwy 169 Suite LL	Minneapolis	MN	55441	**800-810-2352**	763-614-2000	176-10
Eber Brothers Wine & Liquor Corp 155 Paragon Dr	Rochester	NY	14624	**800-776-3237**	585-349-7700	82-3
EBI Medical Systems LP 100 Interpace Pkwy	Parsippany	NJ	07054	**800-526-2579**	973-299-9300	249
Eblens Casual Clothing 299 Industrial Ln	Torrington	CT	06790	**800-464-2898**	860-489-3073	155-2

Name / Address	City	State	Zip	Toll-Free	Phone	Class
Ebonite International Inc PO Box 746	Hopkinsville	KY	42241	800-626-8350	270-881-1200	701
EBS Building Supplies 261 State St	Ellsworth	ME	04605	800-244-7134	207-667-7134	359
EBSCO Book Services PO Box 1943 *Cust Svc	Birmingham	AL	35201	800-815-9627*	205-991-6600	96
EBSCO Development Co 5 Mt Laurel Ave	Birmingham	AL	35242	888-408-8696	205-408-8696	639
EBSCO Industries Inc 5724 Hwy 280 E	Birmingham	AL	35242	800-527-5901	205-991-6600	184
EBSCO Industries Inc Luxor Div 2245 Delany Rd	Waukegan	IL	60087	800-323-4656	847-244-1800	281
EBSCO Industries Inc Military Service Co Div PO Box 1943	Birmingham	AL	35201	800-255-3722	205-991-6600	322
EBSCO Industries Inc PRADCO Outdoor Brands Div 3601 Jenny Lind Rd	Fort Smith	AR	72901	800-531-1201	479-782-8971	701
EBSCO Industries Inc Publisher Promotion & Fulfillment Div 5724 Hwy 280 E	Birmingham	AL	35242	800-633-4931	205-991-1177	5
EBSCO Industries Inc Vulcan Information Packaging Div PO Box 29	Vincent	AL	35178	800-633-4526	205-672-2241	87
EBSCO Media 801 5th Ave S	Birmingham	AL	35233	800-765-0852	205-323-1508	615
EBSCO Professional Partnership Group PO Box 830705	Birmingham	AL	35283	800-528-3476	205-991-1188	9
EBSCO Promotional Products 825 5th Ave S	Birmingham	AL	35233	800-756-7023	205-323-4618	10
EBSCO Publishing Inc 10 Estes St	Ipswich	MA	01938	800-653-2726	978-356-6500	623-10
EBSCO Reception Room Subscription Services PO Box 830460	Birmingham	AL	35283	800-527-5901		97
EBSCO TeleServices 4150 Belden Village Ave NW Suite 401	Canton	OH	44718	800-456-5105	330-492-5105	722
EBW Inc 2814 McCracken St	Muskegon	MI	49441	800-475-5151	231-755-1671	446
Eby-Brown Co 280 W Shuman Blvd Suite 280	Naperville	IL	60563	800-553-8249	630-778-2800	744
Eby Co 4300 H St	Philadelphia	PA	19124	800-329-3430	215-537-4700	252
EC Co PO Box 10286	Portland	OR	97296	800-462-3370	503-224-3511	188-4
EC Ernst Inc 1420 Ritchie Marlboro Rd	Capitol Heights	MD	20743	800-683-7770	301-350-7770	188-4
EC & M Magazine 9800 Metcalf Ave *Acctg	Overland Park	KS	66212	800-814-9511*	913-341-1300	449-21
ECA (Engineering Contractors' Assn) 8310 Florence Ave	Downey	CA	90240	800-293-2240	562-861-0929	49-19
ECB Bancorp Inc 35080 US Hwy 264 *NASDAQ: ECBE*	Engelhard	NC	27824	800-849-2265	252-925-9411	355-2
ECC Capital Corp 1833 Alton Pkwy *NYSE: ECR*	Irvine	CA	92606	800-472-2971	949-856-8300	640
ECCO 833 W Diamond St	Boise	ID	83705	800-635-5900	208-395-8000	691
Ecco Business Systems Inc 60 W 38th St 4th Fl	New York	NY	10018	800-682-3226	212-921-4545	112
ECFA (Evangelical Council for Financial Accountability) 440 W Jubal Early Dr Suite 130	Winchester	VA	22601	800-323-9473	540-535-0103	48-5
ECG Management Consultants Inc 1111 3rd Ave Suite 2700	Seattle	WA	98101	800-729-7635	206-689-2200	193
eChapman Inc 5850 Waterloo Rd Suite 140	Columbia	MD	21045	800-752-1013	410-480-7095	679
Echelon Corp 550 Meridian Ave *NASDAQ: ELON*	San Jose	CA	95126	800-324-3566	408-938-5200	174
ECHO (Electronic Clearing House Inc) 730 Paseo Camarillo *NASDAQ: ECHO*	Camarillo	CA	93010	800-262-3246		254
Echo Canyon Guest Ranch 12507 Echo Canyon Creek Rd PO Box 328	La Veta	CO	81055	800-341-6603	719-742-5524	238
Echo Design Group 10 E 40th St 16th Fl	New York	NY	10016	800-331-3246	212-686-8771	153-13
Echo Inc 400 Oakwood Rd	Lake Zurich	IL	60047	800-673-1558	847-540-8400	420
Echo Lake Farm Produce Co PO Box 279	Burlington	WI	53105	800-888-3447	262-763-9551	11-8
Echo Valley Ranch & Spa Clinton PO Box 16	Jesmond	BC	V0K1K0	800-253-8831	250-459-2386	655
ECI Telecom Ltd 605 Crescent Executive Ct Suite 416	Lake Mary	FL	32746	800-321-2662	407-829-8600	720
Ecke Paul Ranch Inc 441 Saxony Rd	Encinitas	CA	92024	800-468-3253	760-753-1134	363
Eckel Mfg Co Inc PO Box 1375	Odessa	TX	79760	800-654-4779	432-362-4336	220
Eckerd College 4200 54th Ave S	Saint Petersburg	FL	33711	800-456-9009	727-867-1166	163
Eckerd Ruth Hall 1111 McMullen Booth Rd	Clearwater	FL	33759	800-875-8682	727-791-7060	562
Eckhart & Co Inc 4011 W 54th St	Indianapolis	IN	46254	800-443-3791	317-347-2665	87
Eckhart House 810 Main St Old Town	Wheeling	WV	26003	888-700-0118	304-232-5439	50
Eckstein Marine Services LLC 5135 Storey St	Harahan	LA	70123	800-735-5845	504-733-5845	457
Eclectic Products Inc 1075 Arrowsmith St 2nd Fl Suite B	Eugene	OR	97402	800-693-4667	541-284-4667	3
Eclipse Funds 169 Lackawanna Ave	Parsippany	NJ	07054	866-232-5477	973-394-3000	517
Eclipse Inc 1665 Elmwood Rd	Rockford	IL	61103	800-676-3254	815-877-3031	313
Eclipsys Corp 1750 Clint Moore Rd *NASDAQ: ECLP*	Boca Raton	FL	33487	888-325-4779	561-322-4321	176-10
Eco-Air Products Inc 9455 Cabot Dr	San Diego	CA	92126	800-284-8111	858-271-8111	19
Ecodyne MRM Inc 607 1st St SW	Massillon	OH	44646	888-891-1201	330-832-5091	92
Ecolab Inc 370 N Wabasha St *NYSE: ECL*	Saint Paul	MN	55102	800-392-3392	651-293-2233	149
Ecolab Pest Elimination Services 370 N Wabasha St	Saint Paul	MN	55102	800-352-5326	651-293-2233	567
Ecology Control Industries Inc 255 Parr Blvd	Richmond	CA	94801	800-788-1393	510-235-1393	653
Econo Lodge 10750 Columbia Pike	Silver Spring	MD	20901	800-424-6423	301-592-5000	369
Econo Lube N' Tune Inc PO Box 2470	Newport Beach	CA	92658	800-478-3795	949-851-2259	62-5
Econoco Corp 300 Karin Ln	Hicksville	NY	11801	800-645-7032	516-935-7700	281
Economic Development Newsletter PO Box 7376	Alexandria	VA	22307	800-876-2545	703-768-9600	521-7
Economic Education. Foundation for 30 S Broadway	Irvington-on-Hudson	NY	10533	800-960-4333	914-591-7230	654
Economic Education. National Council on 1140 6th Ave 2nd Fl	New York	NY	10036	800-338-1192	212-730-7007	49-5
Economic Opportunity Report 8737 Colesville Rd Suite 1100	Silver Spring	MD	20910	800-274-6737	301-587-6300	521-2
Economist Intelligence Unit 111 W 57th St 7th Fl	New York	NY	10019	800-938-4685	212-554-0600	623-9
Economist Magazine 111 W 57th St 8th Fl	New York	NY	10019	800-456-6086	212-541-5730	449-5
Economy Forms Corp 1800 NE Broadway	Des Moines	IA	50313	888-289-3326	515-266-1141	471
EconoTax Inc 5846 Ridgewood Rd Suite B-101	Jackson	MS	39211	800-748-9106	601-956-0500	719
eContent Magazine 88 Danbury Rd Suite 1-D	Wilton	CT	06897	800-248-8466	203-761-1466	449-7
eCOST.com Inc 2555 W 190th St Suite 106	Torrance	CA	90504	800-555-3613	310-225-4044	35
EcoWater Systems Inc PO Box 64420 *Cust Svc	Saint Paul	MN	55164	800-942-5415*	651-739-5330	793
eCredit.com Inc 20 CareMatrix Dr	Dedham	MA	02026	800-276-2321	781-752-1200	176-1
Ectaco Inc 31-21 31st St	Long Island City	NY	11106	800-710-7920	718-728-6110	171-2
ED Etnyre & Co 1333 S Daysville Rd	Oregon	IL	61061	800-995-2116	815-732-2116	189
Ed Morse Automotive Group Inc 6363 NW 6th Way Suite 400	Fort Lauderdale	FL	33309	800-336-6773	954-351-0055	57
Ed Necco & Assoc 804 Solida Rd	South Point	OH	45680	877-506-3226	740-894-1520	754
ED Smith & Sons Ltd 944 Hwy 8	Winona	ON	L8E5S3	800-263-9246	905-643-1211	291-20
Edco & Arrowhead Products Inc 8700 Excelsior Blvd	Hopkins	MN	55343	800-333-2580	952-938-6313	688
Edcon/Imperial/AV 30 Montauk Blvd	Oakdale	NY	11769	888-553-3266	631-567-7227	242
Eddie Bauer Inc 15010 NE 36th St *Orders	Redmond	WA	98052	800-426-8020*	425-755-6100	155-4
Eddington Thread Mfg Co 3222 Knights Rd	Bensalem	PA	19020	800-220-8901	215-639-8900	730-9
Eddy Packing Co Inc PO Box 392	Yoakum	TX	77995	800-292-2361	361-293-2361	465
Edelbrock Corp 2700 California St *NASDAQ: EDEL*	Torrance	CA	90503	800-739-3737	310-781-2222	60
Eden Foods Inc 701 Tecumseh Rd *Cust Svc	Clinton	MI	49236	800-248-0320*	517-456-7424	291-36
Eden House 1015 Fleming St	Key West	FL	33040	800-533-5397	305-296-6868	373
Eden Roc - A Renaissance Resort & Spa 4525 Collins Ave	Miami Beach	FL	33140	800-327-8337	305-531-0000	655
Eden Theological Seminary 475 E Lockwood Ave	Saint Louis	MO	63119	800-969-3627	314-961-3627	164-3
Eder Flag Mfg Co Inc 1000 W Rawson Ave	Oak Creek	WI	53154	800-558-6044	414-764-3522	282
Edey Mfg Co Inc 2159 E 92nd St	Los Angeles	CA	90002	800-333-9634	323-566-6151	650
Edgar Allan Poe Museum 1914-16 E Main St	Richmond	VA	23223	888-213-2763	804-648-5523	509
Edgar Boettcher Mason Contractors Inc 1616 S Airport Rd	Traverse City	MI	49686	800-562-3827	231-941-5802	188-7
Edgar H Wilson Convention Centre 200 Coliseum Dr	Macon	GA	31217	877-532-6144	478-751-9152	204
Edgar Lomax Co 6564 Loisdale Ct Suite 310	Springfield	VA	22150	866-205-0524	703-719-0026	393
EDGAR Online Inc 50 Washington St *NASDAQ: EDGR*	Norwalk	CT	06854	800-416-6651	203-852-5666	396
Edgcomb Metals Co 555 State Rd	Bensalem	PA	19020	800-562-6777	215-639-4000	483
Edge Information Management Inc 100 Rialto Pl Suite 800	Melbourne	FL	32901	800-725-3343	321-722-3343	621
Edge Products 1080 S Depot Dr	Ogden	UT	84404	888-360-3343	801-476-3343	246
Edge Systems LLC 1805 High Point Dr Suite 103 *Tech Supp	Naperville	IL	60563	800-352-3343*	630-810-9669	175
Edge Technologies Inc 3702 Pender Dr Suite 420	Fairfax	VA	22030	888-771-3343	703-691-7900	176-1
Edgecombe-Martin County Electric Membership Corp PO Box 188	Tarboro	NC	27886	800-445-6486	252-823-2171	244
Edgewater The 666 Wisconsin Ave	Madison	WI	53703	800-922-5512	608-256-9071	373
Edgewater Beach Hotel 1901 Gulf Shore Blvd N	Naples	FL	34102	800-821-0196	239-403-2000	373
Edgewater Hotel & Casino 2020 Casino Dr	Laughlin	NV	89029	800-677-4837	702-298-2453	133
Edgewater Motel & Cottages Box 566	Bar Harbor	ME	04609	888-310-9920	207-288-3491	373
Edgewater Resort 200 Edgewater Cir	Hot Springs	AR	71913	800-234-3687	501-767-3311	373
Edgewater Technology Inc 20 Harvard Mill Sq *NASDAQ: EDGW*	Wakefield	MA	01880	800-233-7924	781-246-3343	178
Edgewood College 1000 Edgewood College Dr	Madison	WI	53711	800-444-4861	608-663-4861	163
eDiets.com Inc 3801 W Hillsboro Blvd *NASDAQ: DIET*	Deerfield Beach	FL	33442	800-265-6170	954-360-9022	351
Edify Corp 2840 San Thomas Expy	Santa Clara	CA	95051	800-944-0056	408-982-2000	176-7
Edinboro University of Pennsylvania	Edinboro	PA	16444	800-626-2203	814-732-2761	163
Edinburg Chamber of Commerce 602 W University	Edinburg	TX	78540	800-800-7214	956-383-4974	137
Edinburg Regional Medical Center 1102 W Trenton Rd	Edinburg	TX	78539	800-465-5585	956-388-6000	366-2
Edison Capital 18101 Von Karman Ave Suite 1700	Irvine	CA	92612	800-241-8101	949-757-2400	214
Edison Chouest Offshore LLC 16201 E Main St	Galliano	LA	70354	800-417-7144	985-632-7144	457
Edison Community College						
Charlotte Campus 26300 Airport Rd	Punta Gorda	FL	33950	800-749-2322	941-637-5629	160
Collier County Campus 7007 Lely Cultural Pkwy	Naples	FL	34113	800-749-2322	239-732-3701	160
Lee County Campus 8099 College Pkwy SW	Fort Myers	FL	33919	800-749-2322	239-489-9054	160

Name / Address	City	State	Zip	Toll-Free	Phone	Class
Edison Electric Institute (EEI) 701 Pennsylvania Ave NW	Washington	DC	20004	**800-334-4688**	202-508-5000	48-12
Edison International 2244 Walnut Grove Ave *NYSE: EIX*	Rosemead	CA	91770	**800-655-4555**	626-302-1212	355-5
Edison Price Lighting Inc 41-50 22nd St	Long Island City	NY	11101	**800-275-8548**	718-685-0700	431
Edison Properties LLC 100 Washington St	Newark	NJ	07102	**800-248-7275**	973-643-7700	552
Edison Sault Electric Co 725 E Portage Ave	Sault Sainte Marie	MI	49783	**800-562-4960**	906-632-2221	774
Edison State Community College 1973 Edison Dr	Piqua	OH	45356	**800-922-3722**	937-778-8600	160
Edison Walthall Hotel 225 E Capitol St	Jackson	MS	39201	**800-932-6161**	601-948-6161	373
Edisto Electric Co-op Inc PO Box 547	Bamberg	SC	29003	**800-433-3292**	803-245-5141	244
Edith Macy Conference Center 550 Chappaqua Rd	Briarcliff Manor	NY	10510	**800-442-6229**	914-945-8000	370
Editor & Publisher Magazine 770 Broadway	New York	NY	10003	**800-783-4903**	646-654-5270	449-5
Editorial Eye Newsletter 66 Canal Center Plaza Suite 200	Alexandria	VA	22314	**800-683-8380**	703-683-0683	521-11
Editorial Freelancers Assn (EFA) 71 W 23rd St Suite 1910	New York	NY	10010	**866-929-5400**	212-929-5400	49-10
Edlon Inc 150 Pomeroy Ave *Sales	Avondale	PA	19311	**800-753-3566***	610-268-3101	588
Edlong Corp 225 Scott St	Elk Grove Village	IL	60007	**888-698-2783**	847-439-9230	291-15
Edlund Co Inc 159 Industrial Pkwy	Burlington	VT	05401	**800-772-2126**	802-862-9661	293
Edmo Distributors Inc 12830 E Mirabeau Pkwy	Spokane	WA	99216	**800-235-3300**	509-535-8280	759
Edmonton Eskimos 9023 111th Ave	Edmonton	AB	T5B0C3	**800-667-3757**	780-448-1525	703
Edmonton House Suite Hotel 10205 100th Ave	Edmonton	AB	T5J4B5	**888-962-2522**	780-420-4000	372
Edmonton International Airport (YEG)	Edmonton	AB	T5J2T2	**800-268-7134**	780-890-8900	28
Edmonton Journal PO Box 2421	Edmonton	AB	T5J2S6	**800-663-7810**	780-429-5100	522-1
Edmonton Symphony Orchestra 4 Sir Winston Churchill Sq Winspear Centre	Edmonton	AB	T5J4X8	**800-563-5081**	780-428-1414	563-3
Edmonton Tourism 9990 Jasper Ave NW 3rd Fl	Edmonton	AB	T5J1P7	**800-463-4667**	780-426-4715	205
Edmund Optics Inc 101 E Gloucester Pike	Barrington	NJ	08007	**800-363-1992**	856-547-3488	534
EDN Magazine 275 Washington St *Orders	Newton	MA	02458	**800-446-6551***	617-964-3030	449-21
EDO Corp 60 E 42nd St 42nd Fl *NYSE: EDO*	New York	NY	10165	**800-621-3677**	212-716-2000	519
edocs Inc 1 Apple Hill Dr Suite 301	Natick	MA	01760	**877-336-3362**	508-652-8600	176-1
Edom Laboratories Inc 100-M E Jeffryn Blvd	Deer Park	NY	11729	**800-723-3366**	631-586-2266	786
EDP Weekly Newsletter 1150 Connecticut Ave NW	Washington	DC	20036	**888-739-8500**	202-862-4375	521-3
Edro Corp 37 Commerce St *Sales	East Berlin	CT	06023	**800-628-6434***	860-828-0311	418
EDS Canada 33 Yonge St Suite 500	Toronto	ON	M5E1G4	**800-814-9038**	416-814-4500	178
Edstrom Industries Inc 819 Bakke Ave	Waterford	WI	53185	**800-558-5913**	262-534-5181	411
EduCap Inc 1676 International Dr Suite 501 *Cust Svc	McLean	VA	22102	**800-865-3276***	703-442-3000	215
Educate Inc 1001 Fleet St	Baltimore	MD	21202	**888-338-2283**	410-843-8000	146
Education Assn. Broadcast 1771 'N' St NW	Washington	DC	20036	**888-380-7222**	202-429-5354	49-5
Education. Association for Career & Technical 1410 King St	Alexandria	VA	22314	**800-826-9972**	703-683-3111	49-5
Education. Association for Continuing Higher 2001 Mabelene Rd	Charleston	SC	29406	**800-807-2243**	843-574-6658	49-5
Education Center Inc 3515 W Market St Suite 200	Greensboro	NC	27403	**800-714-7991**	336-854-0309	242
Education. Council for Advancement & Support of 1307 New York Ave NW Suite 1000 *Orders	Washington	DC	20005	**800-554-8536***	202-328-5900	49-5
Education. Council on Occupational 41 Perimeter Ctr East NE Suite 640	Atlanta	GA	30346	**800-917-2081**	770-396-3898	48-1
Education Digest PO Box 8623	Ann Arbor	MI	48107	**800-530-9673**	734-975-2800	449-8
Education Foundation. Nellie Mae 1250 Hancock St Suite 205N	Quincy	MA	02169	**877-635-5436**	781-348-4200	300
Education International. Association for Childhood 17904 Georgia Ave Suite 215	Olney	MD	20832	**800-423-3563**	301-570-2111	49-5
Education. Lumina Foundation for 30 S Meridian St Suite 700	Indianapolis	IN	46204	**800-834-5756**	317-951-5704	300
Education. MENC: National Assn for Music 1806 Robert Fulton Dr	Reston	VA	20191	**800-336-3768**	703-860-4000	49-5
Education. National Assn of State Boards of 277 S Washington St Suite 100	Alexandria	VA	22314	**800-368-5023**	703-684-4000	49-5
Education Reform. Center for 1001 Connecticut Ave NW Suite 204	Washington	DC	20036	**800-521-2118**	202-822-9000	48-11
Education Resource Information Center (ERIC) 4483-A Forbes Blvd	Lanham	MD	20706	**800-538-3742**		196
Education Society. IEEE IEEE Operations Ctr 445 Hoes Ln	Piscataway	NJ	08854	**800-678-4333**	732-981-0060	49-19
Education Technology News 8737 Colesville Rd Suite 1100	Silver Spring	MD	20910	**800-274-6737**	301-587-6300	521-4
Education & Training for Employment. Center on Ohio State University 1900 Kenny Rd	Columbus	OH	43210	**800-848-4815**	614-292-4353	654
Education US Dept of 400 Maryland Ave SW	Washington	DC	20202	**800-872-5327**	202-401-2000	336-4
Education USA Newsletter 747 Dresher Rd Suite 500 *Cust Svc	Horsham	PA	19044	**800-341-7874***	215-784-0860	521-4
Education Week Magazine 6935 Arlington Rd	Bethesda	MD	20814	**800-346-1834**	301-280-3100	449-8
Education of Young Children. National Assn for the 1509 16th St NW	Washington	DC	20036	**800-424-2460**	202-232-8777	49-5
Educational Communications & Technology. Association for 1800 N Stonelake Dr Suite 2	Bloomington	IN	47404	**877-677-2328**	812-335-7675	49-5
Educational Consultants Assn. Independent 3251 Old Lee Hwy Suite 510	Fairfax	VA	22030	**800-808-4322**	703-591-4850	49-5
Educational & Cooperative Union of America. Farmers 11900 E Cornell Ave	Aurora	CO	80014	**800-347-1961**	303-337-5500	48-2
Educational Development Corp 10302 E 55th Pl *NASDAQ: EDUC*	Tulsa	OK	74146	**800-475-4522**	918-622-4522	97
Educational Employees Credit Union PO Box 5242	Fresno	CA	93755	**800-538-3328**	559-437-7700	216
Educational Exchange. Council on International 7 Custom House St 3rd Fl *Cust Svc	Portland	ME	04101	**888-268-6245***	207-553-7600	49-5
Educational Insights Inc 18730 S Wilmington Ave	Rancho Dominguez	CA	90220	**800-933-3277**	310-884-2000	242
Educational Laboratory. North Central Regional 1120 E Diehl Rd Suite 200	Naperville	IL	60563	**800-356-2735**	630-649-6500	654
Educational Leadership Magazine 1703 N Beauregard St	Alexandria	VA	22311	**800-933-2723**	703-578-9600	449-8
Educational Lending Group Inc 12760 High Bluff Dr Suite 210 *NASDAQ: EDLG* ■ *Cust Svc	San Diego	CA	92130	**866-311-8060***	858-793-4151	215
Educational Media Foundation 5700 W Oaks Blvd	Rocklin	CA	95765	**800-434-8400**	916-251-1600	629
Educational Resources 1550 Executive Dr *Orders	Elgin	IL	60123	**800-624-2926***	847-888-8300	242
Educational Supplies Inc 1506 S Salisbury Blvd	Salisbury	MD	21801	**800-797-8775**	410-543-2519	673
Educational Technology Inc 2224 Hewlett Ave *Cust Svc	Merrick	NY	11566	**800-942-2136***	516-623-3200	52
Educational Tours 1123 Sterling Rd	Inverness	FL	34450	**800-343-9003**	352-344-3589	748
Educational Tours Inc PO Box 828	Northbrook	IL	60065	**800-962-0060**	847-509-0088	748
Educational Travel Consultants PO Box 1580	Hendersonville	NC	28793	**800-247-7969**	828-693-0412	748
Educational Travel Tours Inc PO Box 9028	Trenton	NJ	08650	**800-959-9833**	609-587-1550	748
Educators' Advocate Magazine 411 E Capitol Ave	Pierre	SD	57501	**800-529-0090**	605-224-9263	449-8
Educators Publishing Service Inc PO Box 9031	Cambridge	MA	02139	**800-225-5750**	617-547-6706	623-2
Educators Resource Inc 2575 Schillingers Rd	Semmes	AL	36575	**800-868-8181**	251-645-8800	673
Educators. Society of Park & Recreation c/o National Recreation & Park Assn 22377 Belmont Ridge Rd	Ashburn	VA	20148	**800-626-6772**	703-858-0784	48-23
Edupress Inc W 5527 SR 106	Fort Atlinson	WI	53538	**800-835-7978**	920-563-9751	242
Edward A Sherman Publishing Co 101 Malbone Rd	Newport	RI	02840	**800-320-2378**	401-849-3300	623-8
Edward Don & Co 2500 S Harlem Ave *Cust Svc	North Riverside	IL	60546	**800-777-4366***	708-883-8000	295
Edward Hines Lumber Co 1000 Corporate Grove Dr	Buffalo Grove	IL	60089	**888-334-4637**	847-353-7700	190-3
Edward Howard & Co 1360 E 9th St 7th Fl	Cleveland	OH	44114	**800-868-2045**	216-781-2400	622
Edward J Darby & Son Inc PO Box 50049	Philadelphia	PA	19133	**800-875-6374**	215-236-2203	676
Edward J DeBartolo Corp 7620 Marcus St	Youngstown	OH	44512	**888-965-3532**	330-965-2000	355-3
Edward Marshall Boehm Inc 25 Princess Diana Ln	Trenton	NJ	08638	**800-257-9410**	609-392-2207	330
Edward W Daniel Co Inc 11700 Harvard Ave *Cust Svc	Cleveland	OH	44105	**800-338-2658***	216-295-2750	345
Edward Waters College 1658 Kings Rd *Admissions	Jacksonville	FL	32209	**888-898-3191***	904-366-2715	163
Edwardo's Natural Pizza Restaurants 600 W Jackson Blvd Suite 200	Chicago	IL	60661	**800-344-5455**	312-463-1210	657
Edwards AG Inc 1 N Jefferson Ave *NYSE: AGE*	Saint Louis	MO	63103	**877-835-7877**	314-955-3000	355-3
Edwards Frank Co 3626 Parkway Blvd	West Valley City	UT	84120	**800-366-8851**	801-736-8000	61
Edwards-Freeman Inc 441 E Hector St	Conshohocken	PA	19428	**877-448-6887**	610-828-7441	291-32
Edwards Instrument Co 530 S Hwy H	Elkhorn	WI	53121	**800-366-5584**	262-723-4221	516
Edwards Jet Center 1691 Aviation Pl	Billings	MT	59105	**800-755-9624**	406-252-0508	63
Edwards Lifesciences Corp 1 Edwards Way *NYSE: EW*	Irvine	CA	92614	**800-424-3278**	949-250-2500	572
Edwards Mfg Co 1107 Sykes St PO Box 166	Albert Lea	MN	56007	**800-373-8206**	507-373-8206	448
Edwards Products Inc 11385 Sebring Dr	Cincinnati	OH	45240	**800-543-1835**	513-851-3000	281
Edwards Systems Technology 90 Fieldstone Ct	Cheshire	CT	06410	**800-655-4497**	203-699-3000	681
Edwin Gaynor Corp 200 Charles St	Stratford	CT	06615	**800-342-9667**	203-378-5545	803
Edwin L Heim Co 1918 Greenwood St	Harrisburg	PA	17104	**800-692-7317**	717-233-8711	188-4
Edwin Watts Golf Shops Inc 20 Hill Ave NW	Fort Walton Beach	FL	32548	**800-874-0146**	850-244-2066	702
Edy's Grand Ice Cream 5929 College Ave	Oakland	CA	94618	**800-888-3442**	510-652-8187	291-25
EE Product News 45 Eisenhower Dr 5th Fl	Paramus	NJ	07652	**800-829-9028**	201-393-6060	449-21

Name / Address	City	State	Zip	Toll-Free	Phone	Class
EE Schenck Co PO Box 5200	Portland	OR	97208	**800-433-0722**	503-284-4124	583
EE Times Magazine 600 Community Dr	Manhasset	NY	10030	**800-645-6278**	516-562-5000	449-21
EEI (Edison Electric Institute) 701 Pennsylvania Ave NW	Washington	DC	20004	**800-334-4688**	202-508-5000	48-12
EEOC (Equal Employment Opportunity Commission) 1801 L St NW	Washington	DC	20507	**800-669-4000**	202-663-4900	336-16
Eerdmans William B Publishing Co 255 Jefferson Ave SE	Grand Rapids	MI	49503	**800-253-7521**	616-459-4591	623-2
EF Lane Hotel 30 Main St	Keene	NH	03431	**888-300-5056**	603-357-7070	373
EFA (Editorial Freelancers Assn) 71 W 23rd St Suite 1910	New York	NY	10010	**866-929-5400**	212-929-5400	49-16
EFC Bancorp Inc 1695 Larkin Ave *AMEX: EFC*	Elgin	IL	60123	**888-354-4632**	847-741-3900	355-2
EFCO Corp 1000 County Rd	Monett	MO	65708	**800-221-4169**	417-235-3193	232
Effanbee Doll Co 459 Hurley Ave	Hurley	NY	12443	**888-362-3655**	845-339-8246	750
Effective Telephone Techniques Newsletter 360 Hiatt Dr	Palm Beach Gardens	FL	33418	**800-621-5463**	561-622-9914	521-2
Effingham Convention & Visitors Bureau 201 E Jefferson Ave	Effingham	IL	62401	**800-772-0750**	217-342-5305	205
Effingham County Chamber of Commerce 520 W 3rd St PO Box 1078	Springfield	GA	31329	**866-754-3301**	912-754-3301	137
Effingham Daily News 201 N Bankers St	Effingham	IL	62401	**800-526-7205**	217-347-7151	522-2
Effingham Equity Inc 201 W Roadway	Effingham	IL	62401	**800-223-1337**	217-342-4101	271
EFI Electronics Corp 1751 S 4800 West	Salt Lake City	UT	84104	**800-877-1174**	801-977-9009	803
EFM Sales Co 302 S 4th St	Emmaus	PA	18049	**800-935-0933**	610-965-9041	352
eFollett.com 1818 Swift Dr	Oak Brook	IL	60522	**800-381-5151**		96
EFP Corp 223 Middleton Run Rd	Elkhart	IN	46516	**800-205-8537**	574-295-4690	593
EFTEC North America LLC 31601 Research Park Dr	Madison Heights	MI	48071	**800-633-7789**	248-585-2200	3
eGain Communications Corp 345 E Middlefield Rd *NASDAQ: EGAN*	Mountain View	CA	94043	**888-603-4246**	650-230-7500	39
Egan Bernard & Co DBA DNE World Fruit Sales 1900 Old Dixie Hwy	Fort Pierce	FL	34946	**800-327-6676**	772-465-1110	310-2
Egan Mechanical Contractors Inc 7625 Boone Ave N	Brooklyn Park	MN	55428	**800-275-3426**	763-544-4131	188-10
EGC Corp 11718 McGallion Rd	Houston	TX	77076	**800-342-7677**	281-774-6100	591
Egenera Inc 165 Forest St	Marlborough	MA	01752	**800-316-3976**	508-858-2600	174
EGL Inc DBA Eagle Global Logistics 15350 Vickery Dr *NASDAQ: EAGL*	Houston	TX	77032	**800-821-9956**	281-618-3100	440
Eglin Federal Credit Union 838 NE Eglin Pkwy	Fort Walton Beach	FL	32547	**800-367-6159**	850-862-0111	216
Egreetings Network Inc 1 American Rd	Cleveland	OH	44144	**800-321-3040**	216-252-7300	130
eGroupManager 1819 Clarkson Rd Suite 301	Chesterfield	MO	63017	**800-992-8044**	636-530-7700	47
EGS Electrical Group LLC EasyHeat Div 2 Connecticut S Dr	East Granby	CT	06026	**800-523-7636**	860-653-1600	15
EGW Publishing Co Inc 1041 Shary Cir **Cust Svc*	Concord	CA	94518	**800-546-4754***	925-671-9852	623-9
EgyptAir 720 5th Ave 11th Fl	New York	NY	10019	**800-334-6787**	212-581-5600	26
EgyptAir Plus 720 5th Ave 11th FL	New York	NY	10019	**800-334-6787**	212-581-5600	27
Egyptian Electric Co-op Assn PO Box 38	Steeleville	IL	62288	**800-606-1505**	618-965-3434	244
Egyptian Stationers Inc 107 W Main St	Belleville	IL	62220	**800-642-3949**	618-234-2323	524
Egyptian Tourist Authority 630 5th Ave Suite 2305	New York	NY	10111	**877-773-4978**	212-332-2570	764
EH Wachs Co 100 Shepard St	Wheeling	IL	60090	**800-323-8185**	847-537-8800	447
Ehlert Publishing Group Inc 6420 Sycamore Ln Suite 100	Maple Grove	MN	55369	**800-848-6247**	763-383-4400	623-9
Ehmer Karl Inc 63-35 Fresh Pond Rd	Ridgewood	NY	11385	**800-487-5275**	718-456-8100	291-26
EHRI (Employer's Human Resources Inc) PO Box 1072	Wagoner	OK	74477	**800-878-0515**	918-485-9404	619
Ehrlich JC Co Inc PO Box 13848	Reading	PA	19612	**800-488-9495**	610-372-9700	567
EI DuPont de Nemours & Co Inc 1007 Market St *NYSE: DD*	Wilmington	DE	19898	**800-441-7515**	302-774-1000	594-2
EI Products 52 2nd St	Maxwell	TX	78656	**800-669-6766**	512-357-2776	431
EIA (Environmental Information Assn) 6935 Wisconsin Ave Suite 306	Chevy Chase	MD	20815	**888-343-4342**	301-961-4999	48-13
Eide Industries Inc 16215 Piuma Ave	Cerritos	CA	90703	**800-422-6827**	562-402-8335	718
Eileen West 525 Brannan St Suite 410	San Francisco	CA	94107	**800-421-0731**	415-957-9378	153-15
Einstein/Noah Bagel Corp 1687 Cole Blvd **Cust Svc*	Golden	CO	80401	**800-660-3200***	303-568-8000	69
eircom (US) Ltd 1 Landmark Sq Suite 1105	Stamford	CT	06901	**888-387-6731**	203-363-7171	721
EIS Inc 13200 10th Ave N Suite E	Plymouth	MN	55441	**800-328-4662**	763-513-7300	245
Eisai Inc 500 Frank W Burr Blvd Glenpointe Ctr W 5th Fl	Teaneck	NJ	07666	**888-793-4724**	201-692-1100	572
Eisenhart Wallcoverings Co 400 Pine St PO Box 464	Hanover	PA	17331	**800-555-2554**	717-632-8024	789
Eisenhower Dwight D Presidential Library & Museum 200 SE 4th St	Abilene	KS	67410	**877-746-4453**	785-263-6700	426
Eisenhower Dwight D Veterans Affairs Medical Center 4101 S 4th St	Leavenworth	KS	66048	**800-952-8387**	913-682-2000	366-6
Eisenhower Inn & Conference Center 2634 Emmitsburg Rd	Gettysburg	PA	17325	**800-776-8349**	717-334-8121	373
Eitel Presses Inc 97 Pinedale Industrial Rd	Orwigsburg	PA	17961	**800-458-2218**	570-366-0585	448
Eizo Nanao Technologies Inc 5710 Warland Dr	Cypress	CA	90630	**800-800-5202**	562-431-5011	171-4
EJ Bartells Co PO Box 4160	Renton	WA	98057	**800-468-9528**	425-228-4111	190-4
EJ Brooks Co 8 Microlab Rd	Livingston	NJ	07039	**800-458-7325**	973-597-2900	321
EJ Footwear Corp 120 Plaza Dr Suite A	Vestal	NY	13850	**800-223-5029**	607-584-5000	296
eJiva Inc 1000 Commerce Dr Suite 500	Pittsburgh	PA	15275	**877-354-8226**	412-787-2100	39
EKK Eagle America 33 Plan Way Bldg 5	Warwick	RI	02886	**800-314-9246**	401-732-0333	777
El Al Israel Airlines Ltd 15 E 26th St 6th Fl	New York	NY	10010	**800-223-6700**	212-852-0600	26
El Al Israel Airlines Matmid Frequent Flyer Club 15 E 26th St	New York	NY	10010	**800-223-6700**	212-852-0604	27
El Chico Restaurants Inc 12200 N Stemmons Fwy Suite 100	Dallas	TX	75234	**800-275-1334**	972-241-5500	657
El Conquistador Golf & Tennis Resort. Hilton Tucson 10000 N Oracle Rd	Tucson	AZ	85737	**800-325-7832**	520-544-5000	655
El Conquistador Resort & Country Club. Wyndham 1000 El Conquistador Ave	Fajardo	PR	00738	**800-996-3426**	787-863-1000	655
El Cortez Hotel & Casino 600 E Fremont St	Las Vegas	NV	89101	**800-634-6703**	702-385-5200	133
El Dorado County Chamber of Commerce 542 Main St	Placerville	CA	95667	**800-457-6279**	530-621-5885	137
El Dorado Furniture Corp 4200 NW 167th St	Miami	FL	33054	**800-236-6256**	305-624-9700	316
El Dorado Trading Group Inc 760 San Antonio Rd	Palo Alto	CA	94303	**800-227-8292**	650-494-6600	113
El Encanto Hotel & Garden Villas 1900 Lasuen Rd	Santa Barbara	CA	93103	**800-346-7039**	805-687-5000	373
El Encanto Inc PO Box 293	Albuquerque	NM	87103	**800-888-7336**	505-243-2722	291-36
EL Farmer & Co PO Box 3512	Odessa	TX	79760	**800-592-4753**	432-332-1496	769
El Fenix Corp 11075 Harry Hines Blvd	Dallas	TX	75229	**877-591-1918**	972-241-2171	657
El Guapo Spice Inc 6200 E Slauson Ave	Commerce	CA	90040	**800-995-8906**	323-890-8900	291-37
EL Harvey & Sons 68 Hopkinton Rd	Westborough	MA	01581	**800-321-3002**	508-836-3000	791
El Mar Plastics Inc 840 E Walnut St	Carson	CA	90746	**800-255-5210**	310-327-3180	592
El Modeno Gardens 11911 Jeffrey Rd	Irvine	CA	92602	**800-776-8111**	949-559-1234	363
El Nuevo Herald 1 Herald Plaza	Miami	FL	33132	**800-437-2535**	305-376-3535	522-2
El Paso Convention & Performing Arts Center 1 Civic Center Plaza	El Paso	TX	79901	**800-351-6024**	915-534-0600	204
El Paso Convention & Visitors Bureau 1 Civic Center Plaza	El Paso	TX	79901	**800-351-6024**	915-534-0600	205
El Paso Corp 1001 Louisiana St *NYSE: EP ■ *Cust Svc*	Houston	TX	77002	**800-594-2018***	713-420-2131	320
El Paso Electric Co 123 W Mills St *NYSE: EE*	El Paso	TX	79901	**800-351-1621**	915-543-5711	774
El Paso (Greater) Chamber of Commerce 10 Civic Ctr Plaza	El Paso	TX	79901	**800-651-8065**	915-534-0500	137
El Paso Times 300 N Campbell St Times Plaza	El Paso	TX	79901	**800-351-6007**	915-546-6100	522-2
El Pomar Foundation 10 Lake Cir	Colorado Springs	CO	80906	**800-554-7711**	719-633-7733	298
El Ran Furniture Ltd 2751 Transcanada Hwy	Pointe-Claire	QC	H9R1B4	**800-361-6546**	514-630-5656	314-2
El Rey Inn 1862 Cerillos Rd	Santa Fe	NM	87505	**800-521-1349**	505-982-1931	373
El San Juan Hotel & Casino. Wyndham 6063 Isla Verde Ave	Carolina	PR	00979	**800-996-3426**	787-791-1000	655
El Torito Restaurants Inc 4001 Via Oro Ave Suite 200	Long Beach	CA	90810	**800-735-3501**	310-513-7500	657
El Tovar Hotel PO Box 699	Grand Canyon	AZ	86023	**888-297-2757**	928-638-2631	373
Elan USA 5 Commerce Ave	West Lebanon	NH	03784	**800-950-8900**	603-298-9017	701
Elantic Networks Inc 2134 W Laburnum Ave	Richmond	VA	23227	**888-854-2138**	804-422-4100	721
Elastic Corp of America Inc 455 Hwy 70 W	Columbiana	AL	35051	**800-633-4538**	205-669-3101	730-5
Elat Chayyim 99 Mill Hook Rd	Accord	NY	12404	**800-398-2630**	845-626-0157	660
Elbeco Inc 4203 Pottsville Pike	Reading	PA	19605	**800-468-4654**	610-921-0651	153-19
Elbow River Inn & Casino 1919 Macleod Trail SE	Calgary	AB	T2G4S1	**800-661-1463**	403-269-6771	372
ELCA (Evangelical Lutheran Church in America) 8765 W Higgins Rd	Chicago	IL	60631	**800-638-3522**	773-380-2700	48-20
Elco Corp 1000 Belt Line Ave	Cleveland	OH	44109	**800-321-0467**	216-749-2605	530
Elcom International Inc 10 Oceana Way	Norwood	MA	02062	**800-713-3993**	781-440-3333	176-1
Elder Automotive Group 777 John R	Troy	MI	48083	**800-585-4005**	248-585-4000	57
Elder Mfg Co Inc 999 Executive Pkwy Suite 300	Saint Louis	MO	63141	**800-829-8880**	314-469-1120	153-19
Eldercare Locator 927 15th St NW 6th Fl	Washington	DC	20005	**800-677-1116**	202-296-8130	196
Elderhostel Inc 11 Ave de Lafayette	Boston	MA	02111	**877-426-8056**	617-426-7788	48-23
Elderly Instruments 1100 N Washington Ave	Lansing	MI	48906	**888-473-5810**	517-372-7890	515
ElderWood Senior Care 7 Limestone Dr	Williamsville	NY	14221	**888-826-9663**	716-633-3900	442
Eldon 1401 W Badger Rd	Madison	WI	53713	**800-356-8368**	608-216-3000	523
Eldon Howard Ltd 20333 Gilmore St	Winnetka	CA	91306	**800-685-1533**	818-340-9371	400
Eldorado Gold Corp 550 Burrard St Suite 1188 *AMEX: EGO*	Vanouver	BC	V6C2B5	**888-353-8166**	604-687-4018	492
Eldorado Hotel 309 W San Francisco St	Santa Fe	NM	87501	**800-955-4455**	505-988-4455	373
Eldorado Hotel Casino 345 N Virginia St **Resv*	Reno	NV	89501	**800-648-5966***	775-786-5700	373
Eldridge Hotel 701 Massachusetts St	Lawrence	KS	66044	**800-527-0909**	785-749-5011	373
Election Data Direct Inc PO Box 302021	Escondido	CA	92030	**800-233-9953**	760-751-9900	788
Election Systems & Software Inc 11208 John Galt Blvd	Omaha	NE	68137	**800-247-8683**	402-593-0101	788
Election Works Inc 42W349 Hunters Hill Dr	Saint Charles	IL	60175	**888-619-0500**	630-377-1973	788
Elections USA Inc 1927 E Saw Mill Rd	Quakertown	PA	18951	**800-789-8683**	215-538-0779	788
Electra-Gear Div Regal-Beloit Corp 1110 N Anaheim Blvd	Anaheim	CA	92801	**800-877-4327**	714-535-6061	700
Electracash 4404 E Pacific Coast Hwy **Cust Svc*	Long Beach	CA	90804	**800-444-6952***	888-310-7312	254
Electralloy Corp 175 Main St	Oil City	PA	16301	**800-458-7273**	814-678-4100	709
Electri-Flex Co 222 W Central Ave **Cust Svc*	Roselle	IL	60172	**800-323-6174***	630-529-2920	804
Electric Cooperative Assn. National Rural 4301 Wilson Blvd	Arlington	VA	22203	**866-673-2299**	703-907-5500	48-12

Company / Address	City	State	ZIP	Toll-Free	Phone	Class
Electric Fixture & Supply Co 1006 N 20th St	Omaha	NE	68102	**800-642-9312**	402-342-3050	245
Electric Fuels Corp 1 Progress Plaza	Saint Petersburg	FL	33733	**800-999-3835**	727-824-6600	491
Electric Golf Car Co 1022 Douglas Blvd	Roseville	CA	95678	**800-700-8857**	916-773-2244	505
Electric Heater Co 45 Seymour St	Stratford	CT	06615	**800-647-3165**	203-378-2659	36
Electric Heating Equipment Co 1240 Oronoque Rd	Milford	CT	06460	**800-958-9998**	203-882-0199	313
Electric Institute. Edison 701 Pennsylvania Ave NW	Washington	DC	20004	**800-334-4688**	202-508-5000	48-12
Electric Lightwave 4400 NE 77th Ave	Vancouver	WA	98662	**800-622-4354**	360-816-3000	721
Electric Machinery Enterprises Inc 2515 E Hanna Ave	Tampa	FL	33610	**800-824-2557**	813-238-5010	188-4
Electric Mail Co Inc 3999 Henning Dr Suite 300	Burnaby	BC	V5C6P9	**800-419-7463**	604-482-1111	39
Electric Materials Co 50 S Washington St	North East	PA	16428	**800-356-2211**	814-725-9621	303
Electric Mobility Corp 1 Mobility Plaza *Cust Svc	Sewell	NJ	08080	**800-257-7955***	856-468-0270	469
Electric Regulator Corp 6189 El Camino Real	Carlsbad	CA	92009	**800-458-6566**	760-438-7873	202
Electric Supply & Equipment Co 1812 E Wendover Ave	Greensboro	NC	27405	**800-632-0268**	336-272-4123	245
Electric Supply of Tampa Inc 4407 N Manhattan Ave	Tampa	FL	33614	**800-678-1894**	813-872-1894	245
Electric Utility Week Newsletter 2 Penn Plaza 25th Fl	New York	NY	10121	**800-752-8878**	212-904-6410	521-5
Electrical Corp of America 7320 Arlington Ave	Raytown	MO	64133	**800-426-9453**	816-737-3206	188-4
Electrical Distributing Inc 4600 NW St Helens Rd	Portland	OR	97210	**800-932-3774**	503-226-4044	38
Electrical Distributors Inc. National Assn of 1100 Corporate Sq Dr Suite 100	Saint Louis	MO	63132	**888-791-2512**	314-991-9000	49-18
Electrical & Electronics Engineers. Institute of 3 Park Ave 17th Fl	New York	NY	10016	**800-678-4333**	212-419-7900	49-19
Electrical Inspectors. International Assn of 901 Waterfall Way Suite 602	Richardson	TX	75080	**800-786-4234**	972-235-1455	49-3
Electrical Insulation Society. IEEE Dielectrics & IEEE Operations Ctr 445 Hoes Ln	Piscataway	NJ	08854	**800-678-4333**	732-981-0060	49-19
Electrical Products Co 531 N 4th St	Tipp City	OH	45371	**800-543-9450**	937-667-2431	507
Electro-Flex Heat Inc PO Box 88	Bloomfield	CT	06002	**800-585-4213**	860-242-6287	352
Electro-Magnetic Products Inc 355 Crider Ave	Moorestown	NJ	08057	**800-234-0071**	856-235-3011	745
Electro-Matic Products Inc 23409 Industrial Park Ct	Farmington Hills	MI	48335	**888-879-1088**	248-478-1182	245
Electro Products Inc 26601 79th Ave S	Kent	WA	98032	**800-423-0646**	253-859-0575	801
Electro Rent Corp 6060 Sepulveda Blvd *NASDAQ: ELRC* ■ *Sales	Van Nuys	CA	91411	**800-688-1111***	818-787-2100	261-1
Electro Sales Inc 100 Fellsway W	Somerville	MA	02145	**888-789-0500**	617-666-0500	507
Electro Scientific Industries Inc 13900 NW Science Pk Dr *NASDAQ: ESIO* ■ *Cust Svc	Portland	OR	97229	**800-547-5746***	503-641-4141	416
Electro-Sensors Inc 6111 Blue Circle Dr *NASDAQ: ELSE*	Minnetonka	MN	55343	**800-328-6170**	952-930-0100	486
Electro Steam Generator Corp 7217 Lockport Pl Suite 207	Lorton	VA	22079	**800-634-8177**	703-549-0664	259
Electro-Tec Corp 1501 N Main St	Blacksburg	VA	24060	**800-382-5366**	540-552-2111	507
Electro-Term/Hollingsworth 90 Memorial Dr	Springfield	MA	01104	**800-274-6748**	413-734-6469	804
Electrocorp 595 Portal St Suite A	Cotati	CA	94931	**800-525-0711**	707-665-9616	19
Electroglas Inc 6024 Silver Creek Valley Rd *NASDAQ: EGLS*	San Jose	CA	95138	**800-538-5124**	408-528-3000	685
Electroid Co 45 Fadem Rd	Springfield	NJ	07081	**800-242-7184**	973-467-8100	202
Electrolux LLC 5956 Sherry Ln Suite 1500 *Cust Svc	Dallas	TX	75225	**800-243-9078***	214-361-4300	775
Electromagnetic Compatibility Society. IEEE IEEE Operations Ctr 445 Hoes Ln	Piscataway	NJ	08854	**800-678-4333**	732-981-0060	49-19
Electron Devices Society. IEEE IEEE Operations Ctr 445 Hoes Ln	Piscataway	NJ	08854	**800-678-4333**	732-981-0060	49-19
Electron Energy Corp 924 Links Ave	Landisville	PA	17538	**800-824-2735**	717-898-2294	450
Electronic Arts Inc 209 Redwood Shores Pkwy *NASDAQ: ERTS* ■ *Sales	Redwood City	CA	94065	**877-324-2637***	650-628-1500	176-6
Electronic Business Magazine 275 Washington St *Cust Svc	Newton	MA	02458	**800-446-6551***	617-964-3030	449-5
Electronic Cash Systems Inc 22512 Avenida Empresa	Rancho Santa Margarita	CA	92688	**888-327-2864**	949-888-9955	56
Electronic Clearing House Inc (ECHO) 730 Paseo Camarillo *NASDAQ: ECHO*	Camarillo	CA	93010	**800-262-3246**		254
Electronic Courseware Systems Inc 1713 S State St *Orders	Champaign	IL	61820	**800-832-4965***	217-359-7099	176-3
Electronic Design & Installation Assn. Custom 7150 Winton Dr Suite 300	Indianapolis	IN	46268	**800-669-5329**	317-328-4336	49-19
Electronic Design Magazine 45 Eisenhower Dr 5th Fl	Paramus	NJ	07652	**800-829-9028**	201-393-6060	449-21
Electronic Distributors Assn. National 1111 Alderman Dr Suite 400	Alpharetta	GA	30005	**800-347-6332**	678-393-9990	49-18
Electronic News PO Box 15908	Hollywood	CA	91615	**800-353-9118**	818-487-4555	449-21
Electronic Payments Assn. NACHA - 13665 Dulles Technology Dr Suite 300	Herndon	VA	20171	**800-487-9180**	703-561-1100	49-2

Company / Address	City	State	ZIP	Toll-Free	Phone	Class
Electronic Publishers Assn. Newsletter & 1501 Wilson Blvd Suite 509	Arlington	VA	22209	**800-356-9302**	703-527-2333	49-14
Electronic Publishing Magazine 1421 S Sheridan Rd	Tulsa	OK	74112	**800-331-4463**	918-835-3161	449-5
Electronic Retailing Assn (ERA) 2000 N 14th St Suite 300	Arlington	VA	22201	**800-987-6462**	703-841-1751	49-18
Electronic Systems USA Inc 9410 Bunsen Pkwy Suite 100	Louisville	KY	40220	**800-765-7773**	502-495-6700	201
Electronic Tele-Communications Inc 1915 MacArthur Rd	Waukesha	WI	53188	**888-746-4382**	262-542-5600	720
Electronic Theatre Controls Inc 3031 Pleasantview Rd	Middleton	WI	53562	**800-688-4116**	608-831-4116	202
Electronic Trend Publications 1975 Hamilton Ave Suite 6	San Jose	CA	95125	**800-726-6858**	408-369-7000	623-11
Electronic Warfare Assoc Inc (EWA Inc) 13873 Park Center Rd Suite 500	Herndon	VA	20171	**888-392-0002**	703-904-5700	178
Electronics Assn. Armed Forces Communications & 4400 Fair Lakes Ct	Fairfax	VA	22033	**800-336-4583**	703-631-6100	48-19
Electronics Engineers. Institute of Electrical & 3 Park Ave 17th Fl	New York	NY	10016	**800-678-4333**	212-419-7900	49-19
Electronics for Imaging Inc 303 Velocity Way *NASDAQ: EFII*	Foster City	CA	94404	**800-568-1917**	650-357-3500	174
Electronics Representatives Assn (ERA) 444 N Michigan Ave Suite 1960	Chicago	IL	60611	**800-776-7377**	312-527-3050	49-18
Electronics Service Dealers Assn. National 3608 Pershing Ave	Fort Worth	TX	76107	**800-946-0201**	817-921-9061	49-18
Electronics Society. IEEE Industrial IEEE Operations Ctr 445 Hoes Ln	Piscataway	NJ	08854	**800-678-4333**	732-981-0060	49-19
Electronics Technicians Assn International (ETA) 5 Depot St	Greencastle	IN	46135	**800-288-3824**	765-653-8262	49-19
Electronics Technicians. International Society of Certified 3608 Pershing Ave	Fort Worth	TX	76107	**800-946-0201**	817-921-9101	49-19
Electrophoresis Society 1202 Ann St	Madison	WI	53713	**800-462-3417**	608-258-1565	49-19
Electrorack Inc 1443 S Sunkist St	Anaheim	CA	92806	**800-433-6745**	714-776-5420	281
Electroswitch Electronic Products 2010 Yonkers Rd	Raleigh	NC	27604	**888-768-2797**	919-833-0707	803
Elegant Bebe PO Box 670235	Dallas	TX	75536	**888-886-8307**	972-239-0028	314-2
Elegant Voyages 6348 Skywalker Dr	San Jose	CA	95135	**800-555-3534**	408-239-0300	760
Elektrisola Inc 126 High St	Boscawen	NH	03303	**800-325-2022**	603-796-2114	800
Element K LLC 500 Canal View Blvd	Rochester	NY	14623	**800-434-3466**	585-240-7500	752
Elementary School Principals. National Assn of 1615 Duke St	Alexandria	VA	22314	**800-386-2377**	703-684-3345	49-5
Elementis Chromium 3800 Buddy Lawrence Dr PO Box 9912 *Cust Svc	Corpus Christi	TX	78469	**800-531-3188***	361-883-6421	141
Elementis Pigments Inc 2051 Lynch Ave *Cust Svc	East Saint Louis	IL	62204	**800-323-7796***	618-646-2110	141
Elenbaas Co 411 W Front St	Sumas	WA	98295	**800-808-6954**	360-988-5811	438
Elevator Equipment Corp 4035 Goodwin Ave	Los Angeles	CA	90039	**888-577-3326**	323-245-0147	255
Elgar Electronics Corp 9250 Brown Deer Rd	San Diego	CA	92121	**800-733-5427**	858-450-0085	252
Elgin Area Convention & Visitors Bureau 77 Riverside Dr	Elgin	IL	60120	**800-217-5362**	847-695-7540	205
Elgin Dairy Foods Inc 3707 W Harrison St	Chicago	IL	60624	**800-786-9900**	773-722-7100	291-25
Elgin Molded Plastics 909 Grace St	Elgin	IL	60120	**800-548-5483**	847-931-2455	593
Elgin Watch Co 33-00 Northern Blvd	Long Island City	NY	11101	**800-221-0131**		151
ELI (Environmental Law Institute) 2000 L St NW Suite 620	Washington	DC	20036	**800-433-5120**	202-939-3800	49-10
Eli Journals 2272 Airport Rd	Naples	FL	34112	**800-508-2582**	239-280-2383	623-9
Eli Lilly Canada Inc 3650 Danforth Ave	Toronto	ON	M1N2E8	**800-268-4446**	416-694-3221	572
Eli Lilly & Co Lilly Corporate Ctr *NYSE: LLY* ■ *Prod Info	Indianapolis	IN	46285	**800-545-5979***	317-276-2000	572
Eli Lilly & Co Foundation Lilly Corporate Ctr	Indianapolis	IN	46285	**800-545-5979**	317-276-0464	299
Elias Ben Industries Corp 1400 Broadway 29th Fl	New York	NY	10018	**800-354-2769**	212-354-8300	154
Eliason Corp 9229 Shaver Rd *Cust Svc	Portage	MI	49024	**800-828-3655***	269-327-7003	650
Eliason & Knuth Cos Inc 13324 Chandler Rd	Omaha	NE	68138	**800-365-5760**	402-896-1614	188-9
Eliot Hotel 370 Commonwealth Ave	Boston	MA	02215	**800-443-5468**	617-267-1607	373
Eli's Cheesecake Co 6701 W Forest Preserve Dr	Chicago	IL	60634	**800-999-8300**	773-736-3417	291-2
Elite Aviation LLC 7501 Hayvenhurst Pl	Van Nuys	CA	91406	**888-334-7777**	818-988-5387	14
Elite Business Services PO Box 9630	Rancho Santa Fe	CA	92067	**800-204-3548**		753
Elite Coach 1685 W Main St	Ephrata	PA	17522	**800-722-6206**	717-733-7710	108
Elite Limousine Service Inc 1059 12th Ave Suite E	Honolulu	HI	96816	**800-776-2098**	808-735-2431	433
Elite Sportswear LP 2136 N 13th St *Cust Svc	Reading	PA	19604	**800-345-4087***	610-921-1469	153-1
EliteGroup Computer Systems Inc 45401 Research Ave	Fremont	CA	94539	**800-829-8890**	510-226-7333	171-3
Elixir Industries Inc 17925 S Broadway	Gardena	CA	90247	**800-421-1942**	310-767-3400	232
Elixir Industries Inc Custom Aluminum Div 5600 NE 121st Ave	Vancouver	WA	98682	**800-426-1782**	360-254-5077	591
Elizabeth Arden Inc 14100 NW 60th Ave *NASDAQ: RDEN*	Miami Lakes	FL	33014	**800-227-2445**	305-818-8000	564
Elizabeth Arden Red Door Spa at Mystic Marriott Hotel & Spa 625 North Rd	Groton	CT	06340	**866-449-7390**	860-446-2500	698
Elizabeth Arden Red Door Spa at the Seaview Marriot Resort & Spa 400 E Fairway Ln	Galloway	NJ	08205	**800-205-6518**	609-404-4100	698
Elizabeth Arden Red Door Spas 3822 E University Dr Suite 5	Phoenix	AZ	85034	**800-592-7336**	602-864-8191	79

Name / Address	City	State	Zip	Toll-Free	Phone	Class
Elizabeth City Area Chamber of Commerce 502 E Ehringhaus St	Elizabeth City	NC	27909	**888-258-4832**	252-335-4365	137
Elizabeth City State University 1704 Weeksville Rd CB 901	Elizabeth City	NC	27909	**800-347-3278***	252-335-3305	163
*Admissions						
Elizabeth Glaser Pediatric AIDS Foundation 2950 31st St Suite 125	Santa Monica	CA	90405	**888-499-4673**	310-314-1459	48-17
Elizabeth Hospice 150 W Crest St	Escondido	CA	92025	**800-797-2050**	760-737-2050	365
Elizabethtown Community College 600 College Street Rd	Elizabethtown	KY	42701	**877-246-2322**	270-769-2371	160
Elizabethtown Gas Co 1 Elizabethtown Plaza	Union	NJ	07083	**800-242-5830**	908-289-5000	774
Eljer Plumbingware Inc 14801 Quorum Dr	Dallas	TX	75254	**800-423-5537**	972-560-2000	600
Elk Assoc Funding Corp 747 3rd Ave 4th Fl	New York	NY	10017	**800-214-1047**	212-355-2449	394
Elk Automotive Inc 3012 Mobile Dr	Elkhart	IN	46514	**800-289-3551**	574-264-0768	62-7
Elk Mountain Ranch PO Box 910	Buena Vista	CO	81211	**800-432-8812**	719-539-4430	238
Elk Regional Health Center 763 Johnsonburg Rd	Saint Marys	PA	15857	**877-391-6800**	814-781-7500	366-2
Elk River Concrete Products Co 6550 Wedgwood Rd	Maple Grove	MN	55311	**800-557-7473**	763-545-7473	181
Elkader Wire & Display Co 1802 Preston St	Rockford	IL	61102	**800-435-5709**	815-963-3414	231
Elkem Metals Co 2700 Lake Rd E PO Box 40	Ashtabula	OH	44004	**800-848-9795**	440-993-2300	476
Elkhart County Convention & Visitors Bureau 219 Caravan Dr	Elkhart	IN	46514	**800-262-8161**	574-262-8161	205
Elkhart County the Paper PO Box 188	Milford	IN	46542	**800-733-4111**	574-658-4111	522-4
Elkhart Products Corp 1255 Oak St	Elkhart	IN	46514	**800-284-4851**	574-264-3181	584
Elkhorn Rural Public Power District PO Box 310	Battle Creek	NE	68715	**800-675-2185**	402-675-2185	244
Elkins Builders Supply Co 5 11th St	Elkins	WV	26241	**800-339-2640**	304-636-2640	180
Elkins-Randolph County Chamber of Commerce 315 Railroad Ave Suite 1	Elkins	WV	26241	**800-422-3304**	304-636-2717	137
Elko Area Chamber of Commerce 1405 Idaho St	Elko	NV	89801	**800-428-7143**	775-738-7135	137
Elko Civic Auditorium & Convention Center 700 Moren Way	Elko	NV	89801	**800-248-3556**	775-738-4091	204
Elko Speedway 26350 France Ave	Elko	MN	55020	**800-479-3630**	952-461-7223	504
Elle Decor Magazine 1633 Broadway 44th Fl	New York	NY	10019	**800-274-4687**	212-767-5800	449-11
Elle Magazine 1633 Broadway 44th Fl	New York	NY	10019	**800-876-8775**	212-767-5800	449-11
Ellery Queen Mystery Magazine 475 Park Ave S 11th Fl	New York	NY	10016	**800-333-3053**	212-686-7188	449-11
Ellett Brothers Inc 267 Columbia Ave	Chapin	SC	29036	**800-845-3711***	803-345-3751	701
*Sales						
Elliott & Assoc Ltd PO Box 13282	Albuquerque	NM	87192	**800-538-0111**	505-293-8896	392
Elliott Aviation Inc 6601 74th Ave	Milan	IL	61264	**800-447-6711**	309-799-3183	25
Elliott Bay Book Company 101 S Main St	Seattle	WA	98104	**800-962-5311**	206-624-6600	96
Elliott Co of Indianapolis Inc 9200 Zionsville Rd	Indianapolis	IN	46268	**800-545-1213***	317-291-1213	590
*Orders						
Elliott Davis & Co 200 E Broad St PO Box 6286	Greenville	SC	29606	**800-503-4721**	864-242-3370	2
Elliott Electric Supply Co 2526 N Stallings Dr	Nacogdoches	TX	75964	**877-777-0242**	936-569-1184	245
Elliott Machine Works Inc 146 Rensch Ave	Galion	OH	44833	**800-299-0412**	419-468-4709	505
Elliott Metal Works Inc PO Box 8675	Greenville	SC	29604	**800-726-1542**	864-269-8930	729
Elliott Sales Corp 2502 S 12th St	Tacoma	WA	98405	**800-576-3945**	253-383-3883	10
Elliott Turbomachinery Co 901 N 4th St	Jeannette	PA	15644	**800-635-2208**	724-527-2811	170
Elliott Wave International PO Box 1618	Gainesville	GA	30503	**800-336-1618***	770-536-0309	623-9
*Sales						
Elliott Wave Theorist Newsletter PO Box 1618	Gainesville	GA	30503	**800-336-1618**	770-536-0309	521-9
Elliott-Williams Co Inc 3500 E 20th St	Indianapolis	IN	46218	**800-428-9303**	317-453-2295	650
Elliott's Designs Inc 18201 Santa Fe Ave S	Rancho Dominguez	CA	90221	**800-435-5468**	310-631-4931	314-2
Ellis CH Co Inc 2432 Southeastern Ave	Indianapolis	IN	46201	**800-466-3351***	317-636-3351	444
*Sales						
Ellis Corp 1400 W Bryn Mawr Ave	Itasca	IL	60143	**800-611-6806**	630-250-9222	418
Ellison Bakery 4108 W Ferguson Rd	Fort Wayne	IN	46809	**800-711-8091**	260-747-6136	291-9
Ellison Bronze Co Inc 125 W Main St	Falconer	NY	14733	**800-665-6445**	716-665-6522	232
Ellison Machine Co Inc 9912 S Pioneer Blvd	Santa Fe Springs	CA	90670	**800-358-4828**	562-949-8311	378
Ellsworth Community College 1100 College Ave	Iowa Falls	IA	50126	**800-322-9235**	641-648-4611	160
Ellwood City Forge PO Box 31	Ellwood City	PA	16117	**800-843-0166**	724-752-0055	474
Elm Packaging Co 1261 Brukner Dr	Troy	OH	45373	**800-962-0635***	937-339-2655	590
*Cust Svc						
Elmar Worldwide Inc PO Box 245	Depew	NY	14043	**800-433-3562***	716-681-5650	537
*Cust Svc						
Elmer Candy Corp 401 N 5th St	Ponchatoula	LA	70454	**800-843-9537**	985-386-6166	291-8
Elmer's Restaurants Inc 11802 SE Stark St	Portland	OR	97216	**800-325-5188**	503-252-1485	657
NASDAQ: ELMS						
Elmet Technologies Inc 1560 Lisbon St	Lewiston	ME	04240	**800-343-8008**	207-784-3591	476
Elmhurst College 190 Prospect Ave	Elmhurst	IL	60126	**800-697-1871**	630-617-3400	163
Elmira College 1 Park Place	Elmira	NY	14901	**800-935-6472**	607-735-1724	163
Elmore-Pisgah Inc 204 Oak St	Spindale	NC	28160	**800-633-7829**	828-286-3665	730-9
Elms College 291 Springfield St	Chicopee	MA	01013	**800-255-3567**	413-592-3189	163
Elo TouchSystems Inc 301 Constitution Dr	Menlo Park	CA	94025	**800-557-1458**	510-739-4600	171-1
Elon University PO Box 398	Elon	NC	27244	**800-334-8448**	336-278-2000	163
ELS Language Centers 400 Alexander Pk	Princeton	NJ	08540	**800-468-8978**	609-750-3500	414

Name / Address	City	State	Zip	Toll-Free	Phone	Class
Elsevier Science Ltd 360 Park Ave S	New York	NY	10010	**888-437-4636**	212-989-5800	623-9
Eltech Systems Corp 100 7th Ave Suite 300	Chardon	OH	44024	**800-795-6832**	440-285-0300	143
Eltek Energy LLC 115 Erick St	Crystal Lake	IL	60014	**800-447-3484**	815-459-9090	174
Elvis Presley Enterprises Inc 3734 Elvis Presley Blvd	Memphis	TN	38186	**800-238-2000**	901-332-3322	355-3
Elvis Presley's Heartbreak Hotel 3677 Elvis Presley Blvd	Memphis	TN	38116	**877-777-0606**	901-332-1000	373
Elward Construction Co 680 Harlan St	Lakewood	CO	80214	**800-933-5339**	303-239-6303	188-6
Elwell-Parker Ltd 6499 W 65th St	Bedford Park	IL	60638	**800-848-4373***	708-563-6200	462
*Cust Svc						
Elwood Corp Gettys Group 2701 N Green Bay Rd	Racine	WI	53404	**800-566-5274**	262-637-6591	507
eMachines Inc 14350 Myford Rd Bldg 100	Irvine	CA	92606	**877-566-3463**	714-481-2828	171-3
Emageon Inc 1200 Corporate Dr Suite 200	Birmingham	AL	35242	**866-362-4366**	205-980-9222	375
NASDAQ: EMAG						
eMarketer 75 Broad St 32nd Fl	New York	NY	10004	**800-405-0844**	212-763-6010	521-10
Embalming Chemical Manufacturers Assn 1370 Honeyspot Rd Ext	Stratford	CT	06615	**800-243-6104**	203-375-2984	49-13
Embarcadero Resort Hotel & Marina 1000 SE Bay Blvd	Newport	OR	97365	**800-547-4779**	541-265-8521	373
Embassy Hotel & Suites 25 Cartier St	Ottawa	ON	K2P1J2	**800-661-5495**	613-237-2111	372
Embassy Suites Inc 755 Crossover Ln	Memphis	TN	38117	**800-362-2779**	901-374-5000	369
Embassy Suites Lubbock 5215 S Loop 289	Lubbock	TX	79424	**800-362-2779**	806-794-5353	373
Embassy West Hotel 1400 Carling Ave	Ottawa	ON	K1Z7L8	**800-267-8696**	613-729-4331	372
Emblem & Badge Inc 747 N Main St	Providence	RI	02940	**800-875-5444**	401-331-5444	10
Embraer Aircraft Corp 276 SW 34th St	Fort Lauderdale	FL	33315	**800-362-7237**	954-359-3700	21
Embroidery Store 5081 Arden Ct	Ramseur	NC	27316	**800-727-4244***	336-824-4975	729
*Cust Svc						
Embry-Riddle Aeronautical University						
Daytona Beach Campus 600 S Clyde Morris Blvd	Daytona Beach	FL	32114	**800-862-2416**	386-226-6000	163
Prescott Campus 3700 Willow Creek Rd	Prescott	AZ	86301	**800-888-3728**	928-777-3728	163
Embry's & Co 3363 Tates Creek Rd Suite 212	Lexington	KY	40502	**800-236-2797**	859-266-9785	155-6
Emby Hosiery Corp 3905 2nd Ave	Brooklyn	NY	11232	**800-287-6916**	718-499-6300	153-10
EMC Insurance Group Inc 717 Mulberry St	Des Moines	IA	50309	**800-362-2227**	515-280-2511	355-4
NASDAQ: EMCI						
EMC Legato 2350 W El Camino Real	Mountain View	CA	94040	**877-534-2867***	650-210-7000	176-12
*Tech Supp						
EMC National Life Co 4095 NW Urbandale Dr	Urbandale	IA	50322	**800-232-5818**	515-645-4000	384-2
EMC-Paradigm Publishing Co 875 Montreal Way	Saint Paul	MN	55102	**800-328-1452**	651-290-2800	623-2
EmCare Holdings Inc 1717 Main St Suite 5200	Dallas	TX	75201	**800-527-2145**	214-712-2000	455
EMCO (Engineering Measurements Co) 1401 Ken Pratt Blvd	Longmont	CO	80501	**800-356-9362**	303-651-0550	486
EMCO Chemical Distributors Inc 2100 Commonwealth Ave	North Chicago	IL	60064	**800-267-3626**	847-689-2200	144
Emco Specialties Inc 2121 E Walnut St	Des Moines	IA	50317	**800-933-3626***	515-265-6101	232
*Cust Svc						
EMD Biosciences Inc 10394 Pacific Ctr Ct	San Diego	CA	92121	**800-854-3417***	858-450-5500	229
*Cust Svc						
EMD Chemicals Inc 480 S Democrat Rd	Gibbstown	NJ	08027	**800-222-0342***	856-423-6300	141
*Cust Svc						
Emeco Industries Inc 805 W Elm Ave PO Box 179	Hanover	PA	17331	**800-366-5951**	717-637-5951	314-1
eMed Technologies Corp 76 Blanchard Rd	Burlington	MA	01803	**800-883-8989**	781-862-0000	176-10
eMedicine.com Inc 1004 Farnam St Suite 300	Omaha	NE	68102	**866-363-3362**	402-341-3222	351
eMedicineHealth.com 1004 Farnam St Suite 300	Omaha	NE	68102	**866-363-3362**	402-341-3222	351
Emera Inc 1894 Barrington St	Halifax	NS	B3J2W5	**800-358-1995**	902-450-0507	355-5
TSE: EMA						
Emerald Hills Golf Resort 42618 Hwy 171 S	Florien	LA	71429	**800-533-5031**	318-586-4661	655
Emerald Pointe Resort 7000 Holiday Rd	Lake Lanier Islands	GA	30518	**800-768-5253**	770-945-8787	655
Emerald Queen Casino 2102 Alexander Ave	Tacoma	WA	98421	**888-831-7655**	253-594-7777	133
eMerge Interactive Inc 10305 102nd Terr	Sebastian	FL	32958	**800-945-5310**	772-581-9700	176-10
NASDAQ: EMRG						
EMERgency 24 Inc 4179 W Irving Park Rd	Chicago	IL	60641	**800-877-3624**	773-777-0707	683
Emergency Consultants Inc 2240 S Airport Rd W	Traverse City	MI	49684	**800-253-1795**	231-946-8970	707
Emergency Management Agency. Federal 500 C St SW	Washington	DC	20472	**800-462-9029**	202-646-4600	336-7
Emergency Medicine Magazine 26 Main St	Chatham	NJ	07928	**800-976-4040**	973-701-8900	449-16
Emergency Nurses Assn 915 Lee St	Des Plaines	IL	60016	**800-900-9659**	847-460-4000	49-8
Emergency Physicians. American College of PO Box 619911	Dallas	TX	75261	**800-798-1822**	972-550-0911	49-8
Emergency Physicians. Association of 911 Whitewater Dr	Mars	PA	16046	**866-772-1818**	724-772-1818	49-8
Emergency Physicians. Canadian Assn of 1785 Alta Vista Dr Suite 104	Ottawa	ON	K1G3Y6	**800-463-1158**	613-523-3343	49-8
Emergency Preparedness News 8737 Colesville Rd Suite 1100	Silver Spring	MD	20910	**800-274-6737**	301-587-6300	521-7

Name / Address	City	State	Zip	Toll-Free	Phone	Class
Emergency Response Program. Church World Service 475 Riverside Dr 7th Fl	New York	NY	10115	**800-297-1516**	212-870-3151	48-5
Emerging Information Systems Inc 500 - 330 Saint Mary Ave	Winnipeg	MB	R3C3Z5	**888-692-3474**	204-943-3474	176-10
Emerging Technology Solutions Inc 10698 Deerfield Rd Suite 100 PO Box 1024	Franktown	CO	80116	**800-558-4269**	303-688-1987	176-1
Emerging Vision Inc 100 Quentin Roosevelt Blvd Suite 508	Garden City	NY	11530	**800-332-6302**	516-390-2100	658
Emeritus Corp 3131 Elliott Ave Suite 500 *AMEX: ESC*	Seattle	WA	98121	**800-429-4828**	206-298-2909	442
Emerson Flutes USA 600 Industrial Pkwy	Elkhart	IN	46515	**800-759-9124**	574-522-1675	516
Emerson Process Management CSI 835 Innovation Dr.	Knoxville	TN	37932	**800-675-4726**	865-675-2110	464
Emerson-Swan Inc 300 Pond St	Randolph	MA	02368	**800-346-9219**	781-986-2000	601
Emerson WS Co Inc 15 Acme Rd	Brewer	ME	04412	**800-789-6120**	207-989-3410	154
Emery Air Charter Inc 1 Airport Cir.	Rockford	IL	61125	**800-435-8090**	815-968-8287	25
Emess Design Group LLC 1 Early St	Ellwood City	PA	16117	**800-688-2579**	724-758-0707	429
eMeta Corp 81 Franklin St Suite 500	New York	NY	10013	**800-804-0103**		176-11
EMI Christian Music Group 101 Winners Cir	Brentwood	TN	37024	**800-669-8586**	615-371-6800	512
Emigrant Mortgage Co Inc 5 E 42nd St	New York	NY	10017	**888-364-4726**	212-850-4361	498
EMILY's List 1120 Connecticut Ave NW Suite 1100	Washington	DC	20036	**800-683-6459**	202-326-1400	48-7
EMJA Co Inc PO Box 767189	Roswell	GA	30076	**800-992-3652**	770-992-9464	548-2
Emkay Inc 805 W Thorndale Ave.	Itasca	IL	60143	**800-621-2001**	630-250-7400	284
EMM (Episcopal Migration Ministries) 815 2nd Ave.	New York	NY	10017	**800-334-7626**	212-716-6252	48-5
Emmanuel College PO Box 129	Franklin Springs	GA	30639	**800-860-8800**	706-245-7226	160
Emmaus Bible College 2570 Asbury Rd	Dubuque	IA	52001	**800-397-2425**	563-588-8000	163
Emmert FL Co Inc 2007 Dunlap St	Cincinnati	OH	45214	**800-441-3343**	513-721-5808	438
Emmpak Foods Inc 200 S Emmber Ln	Milwaukee	WI	53233	**800-558-4242**	414-645-6500	291-26
Emory Conference Center Hotel 1615 Clifton Rd	Atlanta	GA	30329	**800-933-6679**	404-712-6000	370
Emory & Henry College PO Box 10	Emory	VA	24327	**800-848-5493**	276-944-4121	163
Emory Inn 1641 Clifton Rd.	Atlanta	GA	30329	**800-933-6679**	404-712-6720	373
Emory University 200 Jones Ctr	Atlanta	GA	30322	**800-727-6036**	404-727-6036	163
Oxford College PO Box 1418	Oxford	GA	30054	**800-723-8328**	770-784-8328	160
Emoteq Corp 10002 E 43rd St. *Sales	Tulsa	OK	74146	**800-221-7572***	918-627-1845	507
Emperor Clock LLC 328 S Greeno Rd *Orders	Fairhope	AL	36532	**800-642-0011***	251-928-2316	151
Empi Inc 599 Cardigan Rd.	Saint Paul	MN	55126	**800-328-2536**	651-415-9000	468
Empire Airlines Inc 2115 Government Way	Coeur d'Alene	ID	83814	**800-392-9233**	208-667-5400	13
Empire Beef Co Inc 171 Weidner Rd	Rochester	NY	14624	**800-462-6804**	585-235-7350	292-9
Empire Blue Cross & Blue Shield 11 W 42 St. *NYSE: WC*	New York	NY	10036	**800-261-5962**	212-476-1000	384-3
Empire Comfort Systems Inc 918 Freeburg Ave	Belleville	IL	62222	**800-851-3153**	618-233-7420	352
Empire Deluxe PPO 11 W 42nd St	New York	NY	10036	**800-261-5962**	212-476-1000	384-3
Empire Diamond Corp 350 5th Ave Suite 7619	New York	NY	10118	**800-728-3425**	212-564-4777	403
Empire Die Casting Co Inc 635 Highland Rd E	Macedonia	OH	44056	**800-297-5724**	330-467-0750	303
Empire District Electric Co 602 Joplin St *NYSE: EDE*	Joplin	MO	64801	**800-639-0077**	417-625-5100	774
Empire Electric Assn Inc PO Drawer K	Cortez	CO	81321	**800-709-3726**	970-565-4444	244
Empire Financial Group Inc 2170 W SR 434 Suite 100 *AMEX: EFH*	Longwood	FL	32779	**800-569-3337**	407-774-1300	355-2
Empire Financial Holding Co 2170 W SR 434 Suite 100 *AMEX: EFH*	Longwood	FL	32779	**800-569-3337**	407-774-1300	355-2
Empire General Life Assurance Corp 7400 W 130th St Suite 400	Overland Park	KS	66213	**800-688-3518**	913-897-9733	384-2
Empire Industries Inc 180 Olcott St	Manchester	CT	06040	**800-243-4844**	860-647-1431	584
Empire International Ltd 55 Walnut St.	Norwood	NJ	07648	**800-451-5466**	201-784-1200	433
Empire Kosher Poultry Inc RD 5 Box 228	Mifflintown	PA	17059	**800-233-7177**	717-436-5921	608
Empire Landmark Hotel & Conference Centre 1400 Robson St	Vancouver	BC	V6G1B9	**800-830-6144**	604-687-0511	372
Empire Level Mfg Corp 929 Empire Dr	Mukwonago	WI	53149	**800-558-0722**	262-368-2000	746
Empire Livestock Marketing LLC 5001 Brittonfield Pkwy	East Syracuse	NY	13035	**800-462-8802**	315-433-9129	437
Empire Office Inc 125 Maiden Ln	New York	NY	10038	**877-533-6747**	212-607-5500	315
Empire Pacific Industries 10255 SW Spokane Ct PO Box 4210	Tualatin	OR	97062	**800-473-7013**	503-692-6167	232
Empire Safety & Supply Inc 4321 Anthony Ct Unit 5	Rocklin	CA	95677	**800-376-6337**		667
Empire Silver Co Inc 6520 New Utrecht Ave	Brooklyn	NY	11219	**800-255-9475**	718-232-3389	693
Empire Southwest Co 1725 S Country Club Dr.	Mesa	AZ	85210	**800-367-4731**	480-633-4400	353
Empire State College 1 Union Ave	Saratoga Springs	NY	12866	**800-847-3000**	518-587-2100	163
Empire State News Corp 2800 Walden Ave	Cheektowaga	NY	14225	**800-414-6247**	716-681-1100	97
Empire Vision Centers 2921 Erie Blvd E	Syracuse	NY	13224	**877-446-3145**	315-446-5120	533

Name / Address	City	State	Zip	Toll-Free	Phone	Class
Empire West Inc 9270 Graton Rd PO Box 511	Graton	CA	95444	**800-521-4261**	707-823-1190	591
Emplawyernet.com 1940 Westwood Blvd Suite 153	Los Angeles	CA	90025	**800-270-2688**		257
Employease Inc 3295 River Exchange Dr Suite 500	Norcross	GA	30092	**888-327-3638**	770-325-7700	39
Employee Benefit News 1325 G St NW Suite 970	Washington	DC	20005	**888-280-4820**	202-504-1122	449-5
Employee Benefit Plans. International Foundation of 18700 W Bluemond Rd PO Box 69	Brookfield	WI	53008	**888-334-3327**	262-786-6700	49-12
Employee Benefit Specialists. International Society of Certified 18700 W Bluemond Rd PO Box 209	Brookfield	WI	53008	**888-334-3327**	262-786-8771	49-12
Employee Benefits Data Services Inc (EBDS) 420 Fort Duquesne Blvd 1 Gateway Ctr Suite 1250	Pittsburgh	PA	15222	**800-472-2738**	412-394-6300	619
Employee Information Services Inc 12600 W Colfax Ave Suite A 501	Lakewood	CO	80215	**800-373-2145**	303-238-0189	407
Employee Policy Newsletter PO Box 7376	Alexandria	VA	22307	**800-876-2545**	703-768-9600	521-7
Employee Professionals 6320 Trail Blvd	Naples	FL	34108	**888-592-9700**	239-592-9700	619
Employee Relocation Council (ERC) 1717 Pennsylvania Ave NW Suite 800	Washington	DC	20006	**888-372-2255**	202-857-0857	49-12
Employer Central c/o College Central Network Inc 141 W 28th St 9th Fl	New York	NY	10001	**800-442-3614**	212-967-0230	257
Employer Support of the Guard & Reserve. National Committee for 1555 Wilson Blvd Suite 200	Arlington	VA	22209	**800-336-4590**	703-696-1386	48-19
Employer's Human Resources Inc (EHRI) PO Box 1072	Wagoner	OK	74477	**800-878-0515**	918-485-9404	619
Employers Insurance Co of Wausau A Mutual Co 2000 Westwood Dr	Wausau	WI	54401	**800-435-4401**	715-845-5211	384-4
Employers. National Assn of Colleges & 62 Highland Ave	Bethlehem	PA	18017	**800-544-5272**	610-868-1421	49-5
Employers Reinsurance Corp 5200 Metcalf Ave	Overland Park	KS	66202	**800-255-6931**	913-676-5200	384-4
Employment Law Strategist Newsletter 345 Park Ave S.	New York	NY	10010	**800-888-8300**	212-779-9200	521-7
Employment Screening Services Inc 627 E Sprague St Suite 100	Spokane	WA	99202	**800-473-7778**	509-624-3851	621
Employment Security. International Assn of Personnel in 1801 Louisville Rd	Frankfort	KY	40601	**888-898-9960**	502-223-4459	49-12
Employment. Women Work! National Network for Women's 1625 K St NW Suite 300	Washington	DC	20006	**800-235-2732**	202-467-6346	48-24
EmploymentGuide.com 295 Bendix Rd 4th Fl	Virginia Beach	VA	23452	**877-876-4039**	757-446-2900	257
Emporia State University 1200 Commercial PO Box 34	Emporia	KS	66801	**877-468-6378**	620-341-1200	163
Empress Casino 2300 Empress Dr	Joliet	IL	60436	**888-436-7737**	815-744-9400	133
Empress Hotel 7766 Fay Ave	La Jolla	CA	92037	**888-369-9900**	858-454-3001	373
Empress International Ltd 10 Harbor Park Dr *Sales	Port Washington	NY	11050	**800-645-6244***	516-621-5900	292-5
Emulex Corp 3333 Susan St *NYSE: ELX*	Costa Mesa	CA	92626	**800-854-7112**	714-662-5600	174
Emulso Corp 301 Ellicott St.	Buffalo	NY	14203	**800-724-7667**	716-854-2889	149
En Pointe Technologies Inc 100 N Sepulveda Blvd 19th Fl *NASDAQ: ENPT*	El Segundo	CA	90245	**800-800-4214**	310-725-5200	172
Enbee Plastics Inc 31-35 31st St	Long Island City	NY	11106	**800-255-9170**	718-721-3700	589
Enbridge Energy Partners LP 1100 Louisiana Suite 3300 *NYSE: EEP* ■ *PR	Houston	TX	77002	**800-525-3999***	888-650-8900	586
Enbridge Midcoast Energy Inc 1100 Louisiana St Suite 3300	Houston	TX	77002	**888-650-8900**	713-650-8900	320
Encad Inc A Kodak Co 6059 Cornerstone Ct W	San Diego	CA	92121	**877-362-2387**	858-452-0882	171-6
EnCana Oil & Gas USA Inc 555 17th St Suite 1850	Denver	CO	80202	**800-829-3408**	303-260-5000	525
Encarta 1 Microsoft Way	Redmond	WA	98052	**800-426-9400**	425-882-8080	677
Enchantment Resort 525 Boynton Canyon Rd	Sedona	AZ	86336	**800-826-4180**	928-282-2900	655
Encinitas Chamber of Commerce 138 Encinitas Blvd	Encinitas	CA	92024	**800-953-6041**	760-753-6041	137
Enclave Suites of Orlando 6165 Carrier Dr.	Orlando	FL	32819	**800-457-0077**	407-351-1155	373
Enclos Corp 2770 Blue Water Rd	Eagan	MN	55121	**800-831-1108**	651-796-6100	188-6
Enco Materials Inc 110 N 1st St	Nashville	TN	37213	**800-876-3626**	615-256-3199	471
Encoder Products Co 464276 Hwy 95 S PO box 249	Sagle	ID	83860	**800-366-5412**	208-263-8541	200
Encompass 401 N Michigan Ave 22nd Fl	Chicago	IL	60611	**877-354-9887**	312-321-5151	48-9
Encompass Group LLC 615 Macon Rd	McDonough	GA	30253	**800-284-4540**	770-957-3981	153-19
Encon Safety Products Co 6825 W Sam Houston Pkwy N	Houston	TX	77041	**800-283-6266**	713-466-1449	666
Encore Bank 1220 Augusta Dr	Houston	TX	77057	**800-727-3193**	713-787-3100	71
Encore Capital Group Inc 5775 Roscoe Ct	San Diego	CA	92123	**888-327-7774**		157
Encore Real Time Computing Inc 305 East Dr Suite A *Cust Svc	Melbourne	FL	33204	**800-936-2673***	321-473-1008	171-3
Encore Ribbon Inc 3721 Santa Rosa Ave Suite B-1	Santa Rosa	CA	95407	**800-431-4969**	707-206-9600	616
Encore Wire Corp PO Box 1149 *NASDAQ: WIRE*	McKinney	TX	75069	**800-962-9473**	972-562-9473	800
Encyclopaedia Britannica Inc 310 S Michigan Ave	Chicago	IL	60604	**800-323-1229**	312-347-7000	623-2
End-of-Life Choices PO Box 101810	Denver	CO	80250	**800-247-7421**	303-639-1202	48-8
Enderes Tool Co Inc 14925 Energy Way	Apple Valley	MN	55124	**800-874-7776**	952-891-1200	746

	Toll-Free	Phone	Class
Endevco Corp 30700 Rancho Viejo Rd. . . San Juan Capistrano CA 92675	**800-982-6732**	949-493-8181	464
Endicott Clay Products Co 57120 707 Rd. . . . . Endicott NE 68350	**800-927-9179**	402-729-3315	148
Endicott College 376 Hale St . . . . . Beverly MA 01915	**800-325-1114**	978-927-0585	163
Endicott Tile LLC 57120 707 Rd. . . . . Endicott NE 68350	**800-927-9179**	402-729-3315	736
Endo Pharmaceuticals Holdings Inc 100 Endo Blvd . . . . . Chadds Ford PA 19317 *NASDAQ: ENDP*	**800-462-3636**	610-558-9800	572
Endocare Inc 201 Technology Dr . . . . . Irvine CA 92618	**800-683-8938**	949-450-5400	468
Endodontists. American Assn of 211 E Chicago Ave Suite 1100. . . . . Chicago IL 60611	**800-872-3636**	312-266-7255	49-8
Endologix Inc 13900 Alton Pkwy Suite 122 . . . . . Irvine CA 92618 *NASDAQ: ELGX*	**800-983-2284**	949-457-9546	468
Endometriosis Assn 8585 N 76th Pl . . Milwaukee WI 53223	**800-992-3636**	414-355-2200	48-17
Endress+Hauser Inc 2350 Endress Pl. . . . . Greenwood IN 46143	**800-428-4344**	317-535-7138	200
Ener-G Foods Inc 5960 1st Ave S PO box 84487 . . . . . Seattle WA 98124	**800-331-5222**	206-767-6660	291-36
Enercon Engineering Inc 1 Altorfer Ln. . . . . East Peoria IL 61611	**800-218-8831**	309-694-1418	202
Enerfab Inc 4955 Spring Grove Ave . . . Cincinnati OH 45232	**800-966-7322**	513-641-0500	92
Energen Corp 605 Richard Arrington Blvd N . . . . Birmingham AL 35203 *NYSE: EGN*	**800-292-4005**	205-326-2700	355-5
Energizer Holdings Inc 533 Maryville University Dr . . . . . Saint Louis MO 63141 *NYSE: ENR*	**800-383-7323**	314-985-2000	76
Energy America Inc 2225 Sheppard Ave E Main Fl . . . . . Toronto ON M2J5C2	**888-305-3828**		774
Energy Concepts Inc 404 Washington Blvd. . . . . Mundelein IL 60060	**800-621-1247**	847-837-8191	694
Energy Daily Newsletter 1325 G St NW Suite 1003 . . . . . Washington DC 20005	**800-926-5464**	202-638-4260	521-5
Energy Efficiency & Renewable Energy Information Center PO Box 43165 . . . Olympia WA 98504	**877-337-3463**		196
Energy Intelligence Group 5 E 37th St 5th Fl. . . . . New York NY 10016	**888-427-7496**	212-532-1112	623-9
Energy & Process Corp 2146B Flintstone Dr . . . . . Tucker GA 30084	**800-241-9460**	770-934-3101	483
Energy Service Companies. Association of 10200 Richmond Ave Suite 275 . . . Houston TX 77042	**800-692-0771**	713-781-0758	48-12
Energy Technology Laboratory. National US Dept of Energy 3610 Collins Ferry Rd PO Box 880 . . . . . Morgantown WV 26507	**800-432-8330**	304-285-4764	654
Energy West Inc 1 First Ave S . . . . . Great Falls MT 59401 *NASDAQ: EWST*	**800-570-5688**	406-791-7500	774
EnergyExplorium 13339 Hagers Ferry Rd MG03E . . . Huntersville NC 28078	**800-777-0003**	704-875-5600	509
EnergyUnited Electric Membership Corp PO Box 1831 . . . . . Statesville NC 28687	**800-522-3793**	704-873-5241	244
EnergyUSA-TPC Corp 1500 165th St. . Hammond IN 46324	**800-531-1193**	219-853-5929	774
Enerpac 6101 N Baker Rd. . . . . Milwaukee WI 53209 *Cust Svc	**800-433-2766***	262-781-6600	747
Enerplus Resources Fund 333 7th Ave SW Suite 3000. . . . . Calgary AB T2P2Z1 *TSE: ERF.UN*	**800-319-6462**	403-298-2200	397
EnerStar Power Corp 11597 Illinois Hwy 1 . . . . . Paris IL 61944	**800-635-4145**	217-463-4145	244
EnerSys 2366 Bernville Rd. . . . . Reading PA 19605 *NYSE: ENS*	**800-538-3627**	610-208-1991	76
EnerVision Inc 2100 E Exchange Pl . . . . . Tucker GA 30084	**888-999-8840**	770-270-7764	193
Enesco Corp 225 Windsor Dr . . . . . Itasca IL 60143	**800-436-3726**	630-875-5300	330
Enesco Group Inc 225 Windsor Dr . . . . . Itasca IL 60143 *NYSE: ENC* ■ *Cust Svc	**800-632-7968***	630-875-5300	323
Enflo Corp 315 Lake Ave. . . . . Bristol CT 06010	**888-887-4093**	860-589-0014	589
Engage Technologies Inc 8419 Sunstate St . . . . . Tampa FL 33634	**800-388-2219**	813-885-6615	665
Engel Industries Inc 8122 Reilly Ave. . . . . Saint Louis MO 63111	**800-428-6046**	314-638-0100	661
Engelhard Corp 101 Wood Ave . . . . . Iselin NJ 08830 *NYSE: EC*	**800-631-9505**	732-205-5000	141
Engelmann Hermann Greenhouses Inc 2009 Marden Rd. . . . . Apopka FL 32703	**800-722-6435**	407-886-3434	363
Engemann Asset Management 600 N Rosemead Blvd . . . . . Pasadena CA 91107	**800-882-2855**	626-351-9686	393
EngenderHealth 440 9th Ave 3rd Fl . . . New York NY 10001	**800-564-2872**	212-561-8000	48-17
Engenio Information Technologies Inc 1621 Barber Ln. . . . . Milpitas CA 95035 *Tech Supp	**866-625-3993***	408-433-8000	171-8
Enger Kress Co 6510 Aurora Rd Suite C. . . . . West Bend WI 53090 *Cust Svc	**800-367-7547***	262-629-1553	422
Engine Components Inc 9503 Middlex Dr. . . . . San Antonio TX 78217	**800-324-2359**	210-820-8100	22
Engine Rebuilders Assn. Automotive 330 Lexington Dr . . . Buffalo Grove IL 60089	**888-326-2372**	847-541-6550	49-21
Engineer Research & Development Center. US Army 3909 Halls Ferry Rd ATTN: CEERD-PA-Z. . . . . Vicksburg MS 39180	**800-522-6937**	601-634-2502	654
Engineered Components Co PO Box 8121 . . . . . San Luis Obispo CA 93403	**800-235-4144**	805-544-3800	252
Engineered Data Products Inc 2550 W Midway Blvd. . . . . Broomfield CO 80020	**800-432-1337**	303-465-2800	314-1
Engineered Plastics Inc 211 Chase St PO Box 227 . . . . . Gibsonville NC 27249	**800-711-1740**	336-449-4121	591
Engineered Polymer Solutions Inc 1400 N State St . . . . . Marengo IL 60152	**800-654-4242**	815-568-3020	594-2
Engineered Products Co PO Box 108. . . . . Flint MI 48501	**888-414-3726**	810-767-2050	345
Engineered Products Inc 1844 Ardmore Blvd . . . . . Pittsburgh PA 15221	**800-245-4814**	412-242-6900	232
Engineered Products Inc 355 Woodruff Rd Suite 204. . . . . Greenville SC 29607	**800-868-0145**	864-234-4888	206
Engineered Valves Div ITT Industries Inc 33 Centerville Rd . . . . . Lancaster PA 17603	**800-366-1111**	717-291-1901	776
Engineering Contractors' Assn (ECA) 8310 Florence Ave . . . . . Downey CA 90240	**800-293-2240**	562-861-0929	49-19
Engineering & Equipment Co Inc 910 N Washington St. . . . . Albany GA 31701	**800-688-8816**	229-435-5601	601
Engineering Fraternity. Theta Tau Professional 815 Brazos St Suite 710. . . Austin TX 78701	**800-264-1904**	512-472-1904	48-16
Engineering Management Society. IEEE IEEE Operations Ctr 445 Hoes Ln . . . . . Piscataway NJ 08854	**800-678-4333**	732-981-0060	49-19
Engineering Measurements Co (EMCO) 1401 Ken Pratt Blvd. . . . . Longmont CO 80501	**800-356-9362**	303-651-0550	486
Engineering in Medicine & Biology Society. IEEE IEEE Operations Ctr 445 Hoes Ln. . . . . Piscataway NJ 08854	**800-678-4333**	732-981-0060	49-19
Engineering & Refrigeration Inc 56 Baldwin Ave. . . . . Jersey City NJ 07306	**800-631-3000**	201-333-4200	188-10
Engineering Societies. American Assn of 1828 L St NW Suite 906 . . . . . Washington DC 20036 *Orders	**888-400-2237***	202-296-2237	49-19
Engineering. Society for the Advancement of Material & Process 1161 Park View Dr. . . . . Covina CA 91724	**800-562-7360**	626-331-0616	49-19
Engineering Society. IEEE Product Safety IEEE Operations Ctr 445 Hoes Ln . . . . . Piscataway NJ 08854	**800-678-4333**	732-981-0060	49-19
Engineering & Surveying. National Council of Examiners for 280 Seneca Creek Rd. . . . . Clemson SC 29631	**800-250-3196**	864-654-6824	49-3
Engineers. American Society of Mechanical 3 Park Ave . . . . . New York NY 10016 *Cust Svc	**800-843-2763***	212-591-7722	49-19
Engineers. National Society of Professional 1420 King St. . . . . Alexandria VA 22314	**800-285-6773**	703-684-2800	49-19
Engineers. Society of American Military 607 Prince St . . . . . Alexandria VA 22314	**800-336-3097**	703-549-3800	48-19
Engis Corp 105 W Hintz Rd. . . . . Wheeling IL 60090	**800-993-6447**	847-808-9400	379
England CR & Sons Inc 4701 W 2100 South. . . . . Salt Lake City UT 84120	**800-453-8826**	801-972-2712	769
Englefield Oil Co 447 James Pkwy. . . . . Heath OH 43056	**800-282-1675**	740-928-8215	319
Englewood Electrical Supply 716 Belvedere Dr . . . . . Kokomo IN 46901	**800-589-8886**	765-452-4087	245
Englewood/Cape Haze Chamber of Commerce 601 S Indiana Ave . . . . . Englewood FL 34223	**800-603-7198**	941-474-5511	137
English. National Council of Teachers of 1111 W Kenyon Rd . . . . . Urbana IL 61801	**800-369-6283**	217-328-3870	49-5
ENGlobal Corp 600 Century Plaza Dr Suite 140. . . . . Houston TX 77073 *AMEX: ENG*	**800-411-6040**	281-821-3200	171-3
Engman-Taylor Co Inc W142 N9351 Fountain Blvd . . . . . Menomonee Falls WI 53051	**800-236-1975**		378
Engraved Graphics Assn. International 305 Plus Park Blvd. . . . . Nashville TN 37217 *x209	**800-821-3138***	615-366-1094	49-4
Enhance Interactive Inc 360 West 4800 N. . . . . Provo UT 84604	**800-840-1012**	801-705-7125	7
Enhanced Memory Systems Inc 1850 Ramtron Dr. . . . . Colorado Springs CO 80921	**800-545-3726**	719-481-7000	686
enherent Corp 80 Lamberton Rd 1st Fl. . . . . Windsor CT 06095	**877-778-4768**	860-687-2200	707
Enid (Greater) Chamber of Commerce PO Box 907 . . . . . Enid OK 73702	**888-229-2443**	580-237-2494	137
Enid News & Eagle 227 W Broadway . . . . . Enid OK 73702	**800-299-6397**	580-233-6600	522-2
Enidine Inc 7 Centre Dr. . . . . Orchard Park NY 14127	**800-852-8508**	716-662-1900	464
Enjoy Life Foods LLC 1601 N Natchez Ave. . . . . Chicago IL 60707	**888-503-6569**	773-889-5070	291-11
Enlightenment. Association for Research & 215 67th St . . . . . Virginia Beach VA 23451	**800-333-4499**	757-428-3588	48-17
Enlisted Assn of the National Guard of the US (EANGUS) 3133 Mt Vernon Ave. . . . . Alexandria VA 22305	**800-234-3264**	703-519-3846	48-19
Enlisted Reserve Assn. Naval 6703 Farragut Ave . . . . . Falls Church VA 22042	**800-776-9020**	703-534-1329	48-19
Enloe Medical Center 1531 Esplanade. . . . Chico CA 95926	**800-822-8102**	530-332-7300	366-2
Ennis Automotive Inc 2400 N Preston St. . Ennis TX 75120	**800-624-8813**	972-878-3896	246
Ennis Tag & Label 118 W Main St . . . Wolfe City TX 75496	**800-527-1008**	903-496-2244	404
Ennis Transportation Co Inc PO Drawer 798. . . . . Ennis TX 75120	**800-527-6772**	972-878-5801	769
Enoch Mfg Co PO Box 98 . . . . . Clackamas OR 97015	**888-659-6565**	503-659-2660	610
Enochs Medical Furniture Inc PO Box 50559 . . . . . Indianapolis IN 46250 *Cust Svc	**800-428-2305***	317-580-2940	314-3
Enogex Inc 515 Central Park Dr Suite 600 . . . . . Oklahoma City OK 73105	**800-829-9922**	405-525-7788	320
Enovation Graphic Systems Inc 200 Summit Lake Dr . . . . . Valhalla NY 10595	**800-755-3854**	914-749-4800	378
Enpath Medical Inc 15301 Hwy 55 W . . . . . Plymouth MN 55447 *NASDAQ: NPTH*	**800-559-2613**	763-559-2613	468
EnPro Industries Inc 5605 Carnegie Blvd Suite 500 . . . . . Charlotte NC 28209 *NYSE: NPO*	**866-663-6776**	704-731-1500	321
EnPro Industries Inc Fairbanks Morse Engine 701 White Ave . . . . . Beloit WI 53511	**800-356-6955**	608-364-4411	259
ENR/Engineering News-Record 2 Penn Plaza 9th Fl . . . . . New York NY 10121	**800-525-5003**	212-904-2000	449-21
Enrolled Agents. National Assn of 1120 Connecticut Ave NW Suite 460 . . . . . Washington DC 20036	**800-424-4339**	202-822-6232	49-10
Enron Corp 1221 Lamar St . . . . . Houston TX 77010	**800-973-6766**	713-853-6161	774
EnSafe 5724 Summer Trees Dr. . . . . Memphis TN 38134	**800-588-7962**	901-372-7962	191
ENSCO Inc 5400 Port Royal Rd . . . . . Springfield VA 22151	**800-367-2682**	703-321-9000	258
Ensco International Inc 500 N Akard St Suite 4300 . . . . . Dallas TX 75201 *NYSE: ESV*	**800-423-8006**	214-397-3000	529
ENSCO Marine Co 620 Moulin Rd . . . . Broussard LA 70518	**800-322-8217**	337-837-9583	307
Ensearch Management Consultants 905 E Cotati Ave. . . . . Cotati CA 94931	**800-473-6776**	707-795-3800	707

Name / Address	City	State	ZIP	Toll-Free	Phone	Class
Ensemble Travel 29 W 36th St 8th Fl	New York	NY	10018	**800-442-6871**	212-545-7460	761
Ensinger Hyde Co 1 Main St	Grenloch	NJ	08032	**800-234-4933**	856-227-0500	591
ENSR International 2 Technology Pk Dr	Westford	MA	01886	**800-722-2440**	978-589-3000	258
Ent Federal Credit Union 7250 Campus Dr	Colorado Springs	CO	80920	**800-525-9623**	719-574-1100	216
Enteral Nutrition. American Society for Parenteral & 8630 Fenton St Suite 412	Silver Spring	MD	20910	**800-727-4567**	301-587-6315	49-8
Entergy Arkansas Inc 425 W Capitol Ave	Little Rock	AR	72201	**800-368-3749**	501-377-4000	774
Entergy Corp 639 Loyola Ave *NYSE: ETR*	New Orleans	LA	70113	**800-368-3749**	504-529-5262	355-5
Entergy Louisiana Inc 639 Loyola Ave *Cust Svc	New Orleans	LA	70113	**800-368-3749***	504-529-5262	774
Entergy New Orleans Inc 639 Loyola Ave *Cust Svc	New Orleans	LA	70113	**800-368-3749***	504-529-5262	774
Entergy Texas Inc 350 Pine St	Beaumont	TX	77701	**800-368-3749**	409-838-6631	774
Enterprise Content Management Assn. AIIM International - 1100 Wayne Ave Suite 1100	Silver Spring	MD	20910	**800-477-2446**	301-587-8202	49-19
Enterprise Fleet Services 5105 Johnson Rd	Coconut Creek	FL	33073	**800-325-8007**	954-354-5400	284
Enterprise Foundation 10227 Wincopin Cir Suite 500	Columbia	MD	21044	**800-624-4298**	410-964-1230	48-5
Enterprise Fredericton 570 Queen St	Fredericton	NB	E3B6Z6	**800-200-1180**	506-444-4686	136
Enterprise Group of Funds 3343 Peachtree Rd NE East Tower Suite 450	Atlanta	GA	30326	**800-432-4320**	404-261-1116	517
Enterprise Messaging Services 10 Mystic Ln	Malvern	PA	19355	**877-367-5050**	610-701-7002	176-7
Enterprise Newspapers 4303 198th St SW	Lynnwood	WA	98036	**800-944-3630**	425-673-6500	623-8
Enterprise Rent-A-Car 600 Corporate Pk Dr	Saint Louis	MO	63105	**800-325-8007**	314-512-5000	126
Enterprise Truck Line Inc 1000 Colfax St	Gary	IN	46406	**800-825-0833**	219-977-5200	769
Entertainment Design Magazine 249 W 17th St *Sales	New York	NY	10011	**800-827-0315***	212-204-1813	449-9
Entertainment Law & Finance Newsletter 345 Park Ave S	New York	NY	10010	**800-888-8300**	212-779-9200	521-11
Entertainment Properties Trust 30 W Pershing Rd Suite 201 *NYSE: EPR*	Kansas City	MO	64108	**888-377-7348**	816-472-1700	641
Entertainment Publications Inc 1414 E Maple Rd	Troy	MI	48083	**800-926-0565**	248-404-1000	623-10
Enterworks Inc 19886 Ashburn Rd	Ashburn	VA	20147	**888-242-8356**	703-723-6740	176-1
Enthone-OMI Inc 350 Frontage Rd	West Haven	CT	06516	**800-496-8326**	203-934-8611	143
ENTRANCO Inc 10900 NE 8th St Suite 300	Bellevue	WA	98004	**800-454-5601**	425-454-5600	258
EntreMed Inc 9640 Medical Ctr Dr *NASDAQ: ENMD*	Rockville	MD	20850	**888-368-7363**	240-864-2600	86
Entrepreneur Magazine 2445 McCabe Way	Irvine	CA	92614	**800-274-6229**	949-261-2325	449-5
Entrepreneur Media Inc 2445 McCabe Way	Irvine	CA	92614	**800-357-7299**	949-261-2325	623-9
Entrust Inc 16633 Dallas Pkwy Suite 800 *NASDAQ: ENTU* ■ *Sales	Addison	TX	75001	**888-690-2424***	972-713-5800	176-12
Eventis Telecom Inc 30 W Superior St	Duluth	MN	55802	**888-436-8683**	218-720-2686	721
Environics Communications Inc 33 Bloor St E Suite 900	Toronto	ON	M4W3H1	**888-863-3377**	416-920-9000	622
Environment. American Public Information on the 316 Oak St PO Box 676	Northfield	MN	55057	**800-320-2743**	507-645-5613	48-13
Environment Balance Inc. Population- 2000 P St NW Suite 600	Washington	DC	20036	**800-866-6269**	202-955-5700	48-7
Environment of Care Leader Newsletter 11300 Rockville Pike Suite 1100	Rockville	MD	20852	**800-929-4824**	301-287-2700	521-8
Environment Federation. Water 601 Wythe St	Alexandria	VA	22314	**800-666-0206**	703-684-2400	48-13
Environmental Career Opportunities c/o Brubach Corp PO Box 678	Stanardsville	VA	22973	**800-315-9777**		257
Environmental Compliance Bulletin 1231 25th St NW	Washington	DC	20037	**800-372-1033**	202-452-4200	521-5
Environmental Compliance & Litigation Strategy Newsletter 1617 JFK Blvd Suite 1750	Philadelphia	PA	19103	**800-999-1916**	215-557-2310	521-5
Environmental Compliance Services Inc (ECS) 7 Island Dock Rd	Haddam	CT	06438	**800-524-9256**	860-345-4578	191
Environmental Data Resources Inc 3530 Post Rd	Southport	CT	06890	**800-352-0050**	203-255-6606	380
Environmental Defense 257 Park Ave S 17th Fl	New York	NY	10010	**800-505-0703**	212-505-2100	48-13
Environmental Earthscapes Inc 5075 S Swan Rd	Tucson	AZ	85706	**800-571-1575**	520-571-1575	413
Environmental Elements Corp 3700 Koppers St	Baltimore	MD	21227	**800-333-4331**	410-368-7000	19
Environmental Enterprises Inc 10163 Cincinnati Dayton Rd	Cincinnati	OH	45241	**800-722-2818**	513-772-2818	653
Environmental Industry Assns 4301 Connecticut Ave NW Suite 300	Washington	DC	20008	**800-927-5007**	202-244-4700	48-12
Environmental Information Assn (EIA) 6935 Wisconsin Ave Suite 306	Chevy Chase	MD	20815	**888-343-4342**	301-961-4999	48-13
Environmental Law Institute (ELI) 2000 L St NW Suite 620	Washington	DC	20036	**800-433-5120**	202-939-3800	49-10
Environmental Media Broadcasting Radio Network 7302 Pierce Ave	Whittier	CA	90607	**800-963-9927**	562-945-6469	632
Environmental Power Corp 1 Cate St 4th Fl	Portsmouth	NH	03801	**888-430-3082**	603-431-1780	774
Environmental Protection Agency (EPA) 1200 Pennsylvania Ave NW	Washington	DC	20460	**888-372-8255**	202-564-4700	336-16
National Lead Information Center 422 S Clinton Ave	Rochester	NY	14620	**800-424-5323**		336-16
Office of Ground Water & Drinking Water 1200 Pennsylvania Ave NW	Washington	DC	20460	**800-426-4791**	202-564-3750	336-16
US National Response Team 1200 Pennsylvania Ave NW MC 5104A	Washington	DC	20460	**800-424-8802**	202-267-2675	336-16
Environmental Protection Agency Regional Offices						
Region 1 1 Congress St Suite 1100	Boston	MA	02114	**888-372-7341**	617-918-1111	336-16
Region 3 1650 Arch St	Philadelphia	PA	19103	**800-438-2474**	215-814-5000	336-16
Region 4 Federal Ctr 61 Forsyth St SW	Atlanta	GA	30303	**800-241-1754**	404-562-9900	336-16
Region 5 77 W Jackson Blvd	Chicago	IL	60604	**800-621-8431**	312-353-2000	336-16
Region 6 1445 Ross Ave Suite 1200	Dallas	TX	75202	**800-887-6063**	214-665-2100	336-16
Region 7 901 N 5th St	Kansas City	KS	66101	**800-233-0425**	913-551-7003	336-16
Region 8 999 18th St Suite 300	Denver	CO	80202	**800-227-8917**	303-312-6308	336-16
Region 9 75 Hawthorne St	San Francisco	CA	94105	**866-372-9378**	415-947-8000	336-16
Region 10 1200 6th Ave MS RA-140	Seattle	WA	98101	**800-424-4372**	206-553-1200	336-16
Environmental Regulation Newsletter PO Box 7376	Alexandria	VA	22307	**800-876-2545**	703-768-9600	521-5
Environmental & Safety Designs Inc DBA EnSafe 5724 Summer Trees Dr	Memphis	TN	38134	**800-588-7962**	901-372-7962	191
Environmental Systems Products Inc 11 Kripes Rd	East Granby	CT	06026	**800-446-4708**	860-653-0081	200
Environmental Systems Research Institute Inc 380 New York St *Sales	Redlands	CA	92373	**800-447-9778***	909-793-2853	176-10
Environmental Toxicology & Chemistry. Society of 1010 N 12th Ave	Pensacola	FL	32501	**888-899-2088**	850-469-1500	49-19
Envirosource Inc 1155 Business Center Dr Suite 200	Horsham	PA	19044	**800-523-0781**	215-956-5500	646
Envision Peripherals Inc 47490 Seabridge Dr *Tech Supp	Fremont	CA	94538	**888-838-6388***	510-770-9988	171-4
ENVOY Corp 26 Century Blvd Suite 601	Nashville	TN	37214	**800-366-5716**	615-885-3700	223
Enwood Structures Inc 5724 McCrimmon Pkwy	Morrisville	NC	27560	**800-777-8648**	919-467-6155	805
Enzo Biochem Inc 60 Executive Blvd *NYSE: ENZ*	Farmingdale	NY	11735	**800-522-5052**	631-755-5500	229
Enzymatic Therapy 825 Challenger Dr	Green Bay	WI	54311	**800-783-2286**	920-469-1313	786
Eoff Electric Co Inc 1095 25th St SE Suite A	Salem	OR	97301	**877-371-3633**	503-371-3633	245
EOG Resources Inc 333 Clay St Suite 4200 *NYSE: EOG*	Houston	TX	77002	**877-363-3647**	713-651-7000	527
Eola Hills Wine Cellars 501 S Pacific Hwy 99 West	Rickreall	OR	97371	**800-291-6730**	503-623-2405	50
eOn Communications Corp 4105 Royal Dr Suite 100 *NASDAQ: EONC*	Kennesaw	GA	30144	**800-955-5321**	770-423-2200	720
Eon Labs Inc 227-15 N Conduit Ave *NASDAQ: ELAB*	Laurelton	NY	11413	**800-526-0225**	718-276-8600	573
EOS International 2382 Faraday Ave Suite 350 *Tech Supp	Carlsbad	CA	92008	**888-728-8746***	760-431-8400	176-11
EP Henry Corp 201 Park Ave	Woodbury	NJ	08096	**800-444-3679**	856-845-6200	181
EP MedSystems Inc 575 Rt 73 N *NASDAQ: EPMD*	West Berlin	NJ	08091	**800-537-6285**	856-753-8533	249
EP Technologies 2710 Orchard Pkwy *Cust Svc	San Jose	CA	95134	**800-552-6700***	408-895-3500	468
EPA (Environmental Protection Agency) 1200 Pennsylvania Ave NW	Washington	DC	20460	**888-372-8255**	202-564-4700	336-16
ePartners Inc 1304 W Walnut Hill Ln Suite 300	Irving	TX	75038	**888-883-9797**	972-751-0078	176-1
Epcon Industrial Systems Inc 17777 Interstate 45 S	Conroe	TX	77385	**800-447-7872**	936-273-1774	19
EPCOS Inc 186 Wood Ave S *NYSE: EPC*	Iselin	NJ	08830	**800-689-3717**	732-906-4300	252
Epes Carriers Inc 3400 Edgefield Ct	Greensboro	NC	27409	**800-869-3737**	336-668-3358	769
Ephraim McDowell Regional Medical Center 217 S 3rd St	Danville	KY	40422	**800-686-4121**	859-236-4121	366-2
Epic Life Insurance Co 1765 W Broadway *Sales	Madison	WI	53713	**800-236-8809***	608-223-2100	384-2
Epicor Software Corp 18200 Von Karman Suite 1000 *NASDAQ: EPIC*	Irvine	CA	92612	**800-999-1809**	949-585-4000	176-1
Epidemiology Inc. Association for Professionals in Infection Control & 1275 K St NW Suite 1000	Washington	DC	20005	**888-278-2742**	202-789-1890	49-8
Epilepsy Foundation 4351 Garden City Dr	Landover	MD	20785	**800-332-1000**	301-459-3700	48-17
Episcopal Church USA 815 2nd Ave	New York	NY	10017	**800-334-7626**	212-716-6000	48-20
Episcopal High School 1200 N Quaker Ln	Alexandria	VA	22302	**877-933-4347**	703-933-4062	611
Episcopal Life Magazine 815 2nd Ave Episcopal Church Ctr	New York	NY	10017	**800-334-7626**		449-18
Episcopal Migration Ministries (EMM) 815 2nd Ave	New York	NY	10017	**800-334-7626**	212-716-6252	48-5
Episcopal Relief & Development 815 2nd Ave	New York	NY	10017	**800-334-7626**		48-5
ePlus Inc 13595 Dulles Technology Dr *NASDAQ: PLUS*	Herndon	VA	20171	**800-827-5711**	703-984-8400	39
EPM Communications Inc 160 Mercer St 3rd Fl	New York	NY	10012	**888-852-9467**	212-941-0099	623-9

	City	State	Zip	Toll-Free	Phone	Class
Epoch Biosciences Inc 21720 23rd Dr SE Suite 150 *NASDAQ: EBIO*	Bothell	WA	98021	**800-562-5544**	425-482-5555	86
Epoch Internet Inc 555 Anton Blvd.	Costa Mesa	CA	92626	**888-443-7624**	714-327-2000	387
Eppinger Mfg Corp 6340 Schaefer Rd.	Dearborn	MI	48126	**888-771-8277**	313-582-3205	701
Epps Aviation Inc 1 Aviation Way DeKalb Peachtree Airport	Atlanta	GA	30341	**800-462-0104**	770-458-9851	63
EPRI Journal 3412 Hillview Ave.	Palo Alto	CA	94304	**800-313-3774**	650-855-2000	449-21
Epro Inc 10890 E CR 6	Bloomville	OH	44818	**866-818-3776**		736
Epsilon Inc 601 Edgewater Dr.	Wakefield	MA	01880	**800-225-3333**	781-685-6000	176-1
Epson America Inc 3840 Kilroy Airport Way *Cust Svc	Long Beach	CA	90806	**800-533-3731***	562-981-3840	171-6
Epson Electronics America Inc 150 River Oaks Pkwy	San Jose	CA	95134	**800-228-3964**	408-922-0200	686
Epworth Villa 14901 N Pennsylvania Ave.	Oklahoma City	OK	73134	**800-579-8776**	405-752-1200	659
Epylon Corp 1340 Treat Blvd Suite 210	Walnut Creek	CA	94597	**888-211-7438**	925-407-1020	176-4
EQ-The Environmental Quality Co 36255 Michigan Ave.	Wayne	MI	48184	**800-592-5489**	734-329-8000	791
Equal Employment Opportunity Commission (EEOC) 1801 L St NW	Washington	DC	20507	**800-669-4000**	202-663-4900	336-16
Equant 400 Galleria Pkwy Tower 400	Atlanta	GA	30339	**888-731-3100**	678-346-3000	174
Equifax Inc 1550 Peachtree St NW *NYSE: EFX* ■ *Sales	Atlanta	GA	30309	**888-202-4025***	404-885-8000	212
Equine Practitioners. American Assn of 4075 Iron Works Pkwy.	Lexington	KY	40511	**800-443-0177**	859-233-0147	48-3
Equinox The 3567 Main St	Manchester Village	VT	05254	**800-362-4747**	802-362-4700	655
Equinox Fitness Holdings Inc 895 Broadway	New York	NY	10003	**866-332-6549**	212-677-0180	349
Equipment Corp of America PO Box 306	Coraopolis	PA	15108	**800-745-3872**	412-331-2000	261-2
Equipment Distributors. Associated 615 W 22nd St.	Oak Brook	IL	60523	**800-388-0650**	630-574-0650	49-18
Equipment Leasing Newsletter 1617 JFK Blvd Suite 1750	Philadelphia	PA	19103	**800-999-1916**	215-557-2310	521-1
Equipment Today Magazine 1233 Janesville Ave	Fort Atkinson	WI	53538	**800-547-7377**	920-563-6388	449-21
Equipto Co Inc 4550 Beltway Dr *Cust Svc	Addison	TX	75001	**800-323-0801***	214-443-9800	281
Equipto Electronics Corp 351 Woodlawn Ave.	Aurora	IL	60506	**800-204-7225**	630-897-4691	253
Equis International 90 S 400 W Suite 620 *Sales	Salt Lake City	UT	84101	**800-882-3040***	801-265-9996	176-10
Equisport Agency Inc PO Box 269	Bloomfield Hills	MI	48303	**800-432-1215**	248-644-1215	384-1
Equitable Distributors Inc 1290 Ave of the Americas	New York	NY	10104	**888-855-5100**	212-554-1234	384-2
Equitable Gas Co 200 Allegheny Ctr Mall	Pittsburgh	PA	15212	**800-654-6335**	412-395-3000	774
Equitable Life & Casualty Insurance Co 3 Triad Ctr Suite 200 *Cust Svc	Salt Lake City	UT	84180	**800-352-5150***	801-521-2500	384-2
Equitable Utilities 200 Allegheny Center Mall	Pittsburgh	PA	15212	**800-654-6335**	412-395-3000	774
Equity Co-op Livestock Sales Assn E 10890 Penny Ln	Baraboo	WI	53913	**800-362-3989**	608-356-8311	437
Equity Corporate Housing 913 Trinity Rd.	Raleigh	NC	27607	**800-533-2370**	919-851-1511	368
Equity One Inc 1696 NE Miami Gardens Dr *NYSE: EQY*	North Miami Beach	FL	33179	**800-867-2777**	305-947-1664	641
Equity Utility Service Co Inc 1060-D Triad Ct	Marietta	GA	30062	**800-282-9695**	770-422-1005	245
Equus Capital Corp 2727 Allen Pkwy 13th Fl	Houston	TX	77019	**800-856-0901**	713-529-0900	779
ER Wagner Mfg Co Inc 4611 N 32nd St	Milwaukee	WI	53209	**800-558-5596**	414-871-5080	345
ERA (Electronic Retailing Assn) 2000 N 14th St Suite 300	Arlington	VA	22201	**800-987-6462**	703-841-1751	49-18
ERA (Electronics Representatives Assn) 444 N Michigan Ave Suite 1960	Chicago	IL	60611	**800-776-7377**	312-527-3050	49-18
Era Aviation Inc 6160 Carl Brady Dr.	Anchorage	AK	99502	**800-866-8394**	907-243-6633	26
Era Aviation Inc Louisiana Lake Charles Municipal Airport PO Box 6550	Lake Charles	LA	70606	**800-256-2372**	337-478-6131	14
ERA Franchise Systems Inc 1 Campus Dr	Parsippany	NJ	07054	**800-869-1260**	973-428-9700	638
Era Helicopters Inc 6160 Carl Brady Dr.	Anchorage	AK	99502	**800-843-1947**	907-248-4422	354
Erachem Comilog Inc 610 Pittman Rd	Baltimore	MD	21226	**800-789-2686**	410-789-8800	141
ERC (Employee Relocation Council) 1717 Pennsylvania Ave NW Suite 800	Washington	DC	20006	**888-372-2255**	202-857-0857	49-12
ERDC (US Army Engineer Research & Development Center) 3909 Halls Ferry Rd ATTN: CEERD-PA-Z	Vicksburg	MS	39180	**800-522-6937**	601-634-2502	654
Centrifuge Research Center ATTN: CEERD-PA-Z 3909 Halls Ferry Rd	Vicksburg	MS	39180	**800-522-6937**	601-634-2502	654
Coastal & Hydraulics Laboratory ATTN: CEERD-PA-Z 3909 Halls Ferry Rd	Vicksburg	MS	39180	**800-522-6937**	601-634-2502	654
Geotechnical & Structures Laboratory ATTN: CEERD-PA-Z 3909 Halls Ferry Rd	Vicksburg	MS	39180	**800-522-6937**	601-634-2502	654
Information Technology Laboratory 3909 Halls Ferry Rd ATTN: CEERD-IV-Z	Vicksburg	MS	39180	**800-522-6937**	601-634-2502	654

	City	State	Zip	Toll-Free	Phone	Class
Erdle Perforating Co 100 Pixley Industrial Pkwy	Rochester	NY	14624	**800-627-4700**	585-247-4700	92
Erdman Marshall & Assoc 5117 University Ave	Madison	WI	53705	**800-550-5117**	608-238-0211	258
Erect-A-Tube Inc 701 W Park St.	Harvard	IL	60033	**800-624-9219**	815-943-4091	106
eResearch Technology Inc 30 S 17th St 8th Fl. *NASDAQ: ERES*	Philadelphia	PA	19103	**800-704-9698**	215-972-0420	176-10
Ergodyne Corp 1410 Energy Pk Dr Suite 1	Saint Paul	MN	55108	**800-225-8238**	651-642-9889	469
Ergon Inc 2829 Lakeland Dr	Jackson	MS	39232	**800-824-2626**	601-933-3000	184
Ergon Inc Petroleum Specialties Marketing Div PO Box 1639	Jackson	MS	39215	**800-824-2626**	601-933-3000	530
Ergotron Inc 1181 Trapp Rd *Sales	Eagan	MN	55121	**800-888-8458***	651-681-7600	314-1
ERIC (Education Resource Information Center) 4483-A Forbes Blvd.	Lanham	MD	20706	**800-538-3742**		196
Eric Electronics 2220 Lundy Ave	San Jose	CA	95131	**800-406-3742**	408-432-1111	245
Erickson Air-Crane Co 3100 Willow Springs Rd PO Box 3247	Central Point	OR	97502	**800-424-2413**	541-664-5544	21
Erickson Oil Products Inc 1231 Industrial St.	Hudson	WI	54016	**800-521-0104**	715-386-8241	319
Erickson Petroleum Corp 4567 American Blvd W.	Bloomington	MN	55437	**800-745-7411**	952-830-8700	203
Erickson Transport Corp PO Box 10068	Springfield	MO	65808	**800-641-4595**	417-862-6741	769
ERICO International Corp 30575 Bainbridge Rd Suite 300	Solon	OH	44139	**800-800-9301**	440-349-2630	803
ERICO Products Inc 34600 Solon Rd	Solon	OH	44139	**800-813-3378**	440-248-0100	803
Erie Area Convention & Visitors Bureau 208 E Bayfront Pkwy Suite 103	Erie	PA	16507	**800-524-3743**	814-454-7191	205
Erie Business Center *Main* 246 W 9th St.	Erie	PA	16501	**800-352-3743**	814-456-7504	158
South 170 Cascade Galleria	New Castle	PA	16101	**800-722-6227**	724-658-9066	158
Erie Community College 121 Ellicott St	Buffalo	NY	14203	**800-836-0981**	716-842-2770	160
South Campus 4041 Southwestern Blvd	Orchard Park	NY	14127	**800-836-0983**	716-851-1003	160
Erie County Medical Center 462 Grider St	Buffalo	NY	14215	**888-894-9444**	716-898-3000	366-2
Erie Family Life Insurance Co 100 Erie Insurance Pl.	Erie	PA	16530	**800-458-0811**	814-870-2000	384-2
Erie Foods International Inc 401 7th Ave	Erie	IL	61250	**800-447-1887**	309-659-2233	291-10
Erie Indemnity Co 100 Erie Insurance Pl *NASDAQ: ERIE*	Erie	PA	16530	**800-458-0811**	814-870-2000	355-4
Erie Insurance Co 100 Erie Insurance Pl	Erie	PA	16530	**800-458-0811**	814-870-2000	384-4
Erie Insurance Co of New York 100 Erie Insurance Pl.	Erie	PA	16530	**800-458-0811**	814-870-2000	384-4
Erie Insurance Exchange 100 Erie Insurance Pl	Erie	PA	16530	**800-458-0811**	814-870-2000	384-4
Erie Insurance Property & Casualty Co 100 Erie Insurance Pl.	Erie	PA	16530	**800-458-0811**	814-870-2000	384-4
Erie Power Technologies Inc 5300 Knowledge Pkwy Suite 200	Erie	PA	16510	**800-323-3743**	814-897-7000	352
Erie Press Systems 1253 W 12th St PO Box 4061	Erie	PA	16512	**800-222-3608**	814-455-3941	448
Erie Regional Chamber & Growth Partnership 208 E Bayfront Pkwy	Erie	PA	16507	**800-524-3743**	814-454-7191	137
Erie Scientific Co 20 Post Rd.	Portsmouth	NH	03801	**800-258-0834**	603-431-8410	329
Erie Sport Store Inc 701 State St	Erie	PA	16501	**800-333-6812**	814-452-2289	702
Erie Times-News 205 W 12th St.	Erie	PA	16534	**800-352-0043**	814-870-1600	522-2
Erie Vehicle Co 60 E 51st St	Chicago	IL	60615	**888-550-3743**	773-536-6300	505
ERM Group Inc 350 Eagle View Blvd.	Exton	PA	19341	**800-662-1124**	610-524-3500	258
Ernest F Mariani Co Inc 614 W 600 South	Salt Lake City	UT	84104	**800-453-2927**	801-359-3744	651
Ernest Paper Products 5777 Smithway St	Commerce	CA	90040	**800-233-7788**	323-583-6561	549
Ernie Ball 151 Suburban Rd	San Luis Obispo	CA	93401	**800-543-2255**		516
Ernst EC Inc 1420 Ritchie Marlboro Rd	Capitol Heights	MD	20743	**800-683-7770**	301-350-7770	188-4
Ernst Publishing Co LLC 1937 Delaware Tpke Suite B	Clarksville	NY	12041	**800-345-3822**		623-9
Erny's PO Box 452	Walton	IN	46994	**800-552-3769**	574-626-2522	276
ERS Industries Inc 1005 Indian Church Rd	West Seneca	NY	14224	**800-993-6446**	716-675-2040	759
Ershigs Inc PO Box 1707	Bellingham	WA	98227	**888-377-4447**	360-733-2620	595
Erskine College PO Box 338	Due West	SC	29639	**800-241-8721**	864-379-2131	163
Ervin Industries Inc 3893 Research Pk Dr	Ann Arbor	MI	48108	**800-748-0055**	734-769-4600	1
Erving Paper Mills 97 E Main St.	Erving	MA	01344	**800-225-8014**	413-422-2700	548-2
Erwin Distributing Co 530 Monocacy Blvd	Frederick	MD	21701	**800-352-9165**	301-662-0372	82-1
ES Originals Inc 450 W 33rd St 9th Fl	New York	NY	10001	**800-677-6577**	212-736-8124	296
ESA (Evangelicals for Social Action) 10 E Lancaster Ave.	Wynnewood	PA	19096	**800-650-6600**	610-645-9390	48-7
Esab Welding & Cutting Products Inc PO Box 100545	Florence	SC	29501	**800-372-2123**	843-669-4411	798
ESB Bank 600 Lawrence Ave.	Ellwood City	PA	16117	**800-533-4193**	724-758-5584	71
ESB Financial Corp 600 Lawrence Ave *NASDAQ: ESBF*	Ellwood City	PA	16117	**800-533-4193**	724-758-5584	355-2
Escalade Inc DBA Escalade Sports PO Box 889 *NASDAQ: ESCA* ■ *Cust Svc	Evansville	IN	47706	**800-426-1421***	812-467-1200	701
Escalade Sports PO Box 889. *NASDAQ: ESCA* ■ *Cust Svc	Evansville	IN	47706	**800-426-1421***	812-467-1200	701
Escalera Inc 708 S Industrial Dr.	Yuba City	CA	95993	**800-622-1359**	530-673-6318	462
Escalon Premier Brands 1905 McHenry Ave.	Escalon	CA	95320	**800-343-9556**	209-838-7341	291-20
Escambia River Electric Co-op Inc PO Box 428	Jay	FL	32565	**800-235-3848**	850-675-4521	244
Escapees RV Club 100 Rainbow Dr	Livingston	TX	77351	**888-757-2582**	936-327-8873	48-23
Esco Corp 2141 NW 25th Ave.	Portland	OR	97210	**800-523-3795**	503-228-2141	189
ESCO LLC 2 S Point Dr.	Lake Forest	CA	92630	**800-622-3726**	949-330-3602	245
ESCO Technologies Inc 8888 Ladue Rd Suite 200 *NYSE: ESE*	Saint Louis	MO	63124	**888-622-3726**	314-213-7200	355-3

Name / Address	City	State	Zip	Toll-Free	Phone	Class
Eseeola Lodge 175 Linville Ave PO Box 99	Linville	NC	28646	**800-742-6717**	828-733-4311	655
ESGR (National Committee for Employer Support of the Guard & Reserve) 1555 Wilson Blvd Suite 200	Arlington	VA	22209	**800-336-4590**	703-696-1386	48-19
eSignal 3955 Point Eden Way *Sales	Hayward	CA	94545	**800-367-4670***	510-266-6000	176-1
Eskaton Village 3939 Walnut Ave	Carmichael	CA	95608	**800-300-3929**	916-974-2000	659
Eskco Inc 700 Liberty Ln	Dayton	OH	45449	**800-783-7526**	937-865-0498	87
Esker Inc 100 E 7th Ave	Stillwater	OK	74074	**800-343-7070**	405-533-5500	176-12
ESL Federal Credit Union 100 Kings Hwy S Suite 1200	Rochester	NY	14617	**800-848-2265**	585-336-1000	216
Esmeralda Resort. Renaissance 44-400 Indian Wells Ln	Indian Wells	CA	92210	**800-552-4386**	760-773-4444	655
eSoft Inc 295 Interlocken Blvd Suite 500	Broomfield	CO	80021	**888-903-7638**	303-444-1600	174
ESOP Assn 1726 M St NW Suite 501	Washington	DC	20036	**866-366-3832**	202-293-2971	49-12
ESPE Mfg Co Inc 9220 Ivanhoe St *Cust Svc	Schiller Park	IL	60176	**800-367-3773***	847-678-8950	345
Especially 4-U Tours & Travel 7303 E Main St Suite 107	Mesa	AZ	85207	**800-331-4968**	480-985-4200	748
Esplanade Hotel 95 S Broadway	White Plains	NY	10601	**800-247-5322**	914-761-8100	373
Esplanade Tours 160 Commonwealth Ave Suite L3	Boston	MA	02116	**800-426-5492**	617-266-7465	748
ESPN Magazine 19 E 34th St *Cust Svc	New York	NY	10016	**888-267-3684***	212-515-1000	449-20
Esprit Miami 3043 NW 107th Ave	Miami	FL	33172	**800-327-2320**	305-591-2244	288
Esquire Magazine 250 W 55th St	New York	NY	10019	**800-888-5400**	212-649-2000	449-11
Esselte Corp 48 S Service Rd Suite 400 *Cust Svc	Melville	NY	11747	**800-645-6051***	631-675-5700	550
Esselte Pendaflex Corp 1625 E Duane Blvd	Kankakee	IL	60901	**800-888-2115**	815-933-3351	87
Essem Packing Co 14 Loon Hill Rd	Dracut	MA	01826	**800-272-0030**	978-452-2195	291-26
Essence Communications Inc 1500 Broadway 6th Fl *Circ	New York	NY	10036	**800-274-9398***	212-642-0600	623-9
Essence Magazine 1500 Broadway 6th Fl	New York	NY	10036	**800-274-9398**	212-642-0600	449-11
Essential Links Essentix Inc 13807 SE McLoughlin Suite 626	Portland	OR	97222	**800-401-6970**	503-659-0707	677
Essex Brownell Inc 84 Executive Ave	Edison	NJ	08817	**800-228-8026**	732-287-3355	245
Essex Community College 7201 Rossville Blvd	Baltimore	MD	21237	**800-832-0262**	410-682-6000	160
Essex Corp 9150 Guilford Rd *NASDAQ: KEYW*	Columbia	MD	21046	**800-533-7739**	301-939-7000	258
Essex Grain Products 9 Lee Blvd	Frazer	PA	19355	**800-441-1017**	610-647-3800	292-11
Essex House - A Westin Hotel 160 Central Park S	New York	NY	10019	**800-937-8461**	212-247-0300	373
Essex Investment Management Co LLC 125 High St 29th Fl	Boston	MA	02110	**800-342-3202**	617-342-3200	393
Essex Mfg Inc 350 5th Ave Suite 501	New York	NY	10118	**800-648-6010**	212-239-0080	153-5
Essilor of America Inc 2400 118th Ave N	Saint Petersburg	FL	33716	**800-843-3937**	727-572-0844	531
Esskay Inc PO Box 587	Riderwood	MD	21139	**800-638-7350**	410-823-2100	465
Essmueller Co 334 Ave A PO Box 1966	Laurel	MS	39440	**800-325-7175**	601-649-2400	206
ESSROC Materials Inc 3251 Bath Pike	Nazareth	PA	18064	**800-523-9238**	610-837-6725	135
Estate Planners & Councils. National Assn of 1120 Chester Ave Suite 470	Cleveland	OH	44114	**866-226-2224**		49-10
Estate Planning Attorneys Inc. National Network of 1 Valmont Plaza 4th Fl	Omaha	NE	68154	**888-837-4090**	402-964-3700	49-10
Esterline Mason 13955 Balboa Blvd	Sylmar	CA	91342	**800-232-7700**	818-361-3366	494
Estes-Cox Corp 1295 H St	Penrose	CO	81240	**800-525-7561**	719-372-6565	750
Estex Mfg Co Inc 402 E Broad St PO Box 368	Fairburn	GA	30213	**800-749-1224**	770-964-3322	718
Esther Price Candies Inc 1709 Wayne Ave	Dayton	OH	45410	**800-782-0326**	937-253-2121	291-8
Estimators. American Society of Professional 2525 Perimeter Place Dr Suite 102	Nashville	TN	37214	**888-378-6283**	615-316-9200	49-3
eStoreManager.com c/o American Digital Network Inc 9725 Scranton Rd	San Diego	CA	92121	**877-928-9376**	858-427-2400	795
Estorge Surgical Supplies 112 S Pierce St	Lafayette	LA	70501	**800-256-8990**	337-232-8920	467
Estrella 415 S Belardo Rd	Palm Springs	CA	92262	**800-237-3687**	760-320-4117	373
Estridge Cos 1041 W Main St	Carmel	IN	46032	**800-473-7326**	317-846-7311	639
Esurance Inc 747 Front St 4th Fl	San Francisco	CA	94111	**800-926-6012**	415-875-4500	383
ET3 LLC DBA ExecuTrain Corp 2500 Northwinds Pkwy Suite 600	Alpharetta	GA	30004	**800-908-7246**	770-521-1964	752
ET Horn Co 16141 Heron Ave	La Mirada	CA	90638	**800-442-4676**	714-523-8050	144
ET Wright & Co Inc 1356 Williams St	Chippewa Falls	WI	54729	**800-934-1022**		451
ETA (Electronics Technicians Assn International) 5 Depot St	Greencastle	IN	46135	**800-288-3824**	765-653-8262	49-19
ETA (Evangelical Training Assn) 1620 Penny Ln	Schaumburg	IL	60173	**800-369-8291**	630-540-7840	48-20
Eta Sigma Gamma 2000 University Ave	Muncie	IN	47306	**800-715-2559**	765-285-2258	48-16
eTEK International Inc 5445 DTC Pkwy PH-4	Greenwood Village	CO	80111	**800-888-6894**	303-488-3499	176-1
Eternabond 16 Saint John Dr	Hawthorn Woods	IL	60047	**888-336-2663**	847-540-0600	717
ETF (Extra Touch Florist Assn) 137 N Larchmont Blvd Suite 529	Los Angeles	CA	90019	**888-419-1515**	323-735-7272	49-4
Ethex Corp 10888 Metro Ct	Saint Louis	MO	63043	**800-321-1705**	314-567-3307	573
Ethical Products Inc 27 Federal Plaza	Bloomfield	NJ	07003	**800-223-7768**	973-748-8282	568
Ethical Treatment of Animals. People for the 501 Front St *Orders	Norfolk	VA	23510	**800-483-4366***	757-622-7382	48-3
Ethicon Endo-Surgery Inc 4545 Creek Rd	Cincinnati	OH	45242	**800-556-8451**	513-786-7000	468
Ethics Inc. Leave No Trace Center for Outdoor PO Box 997	Boulder	CO	80306	**800-332-4100**	303-442-8222	48-23
Ethiopian Airlines 336 E 45th St 3rd Fl	New York	NY	10017	**800-445-2733**	212-867-0095	26
Ethyl IMAX Dome & Planetarium 2500 W Broad St	Richmond	VA	23220	**800-659-1727**	804-864-1400	587
Etienne Aigner Group Inc 47 Brunswick Ave	Edison	NJ	08818	**800-537-7463**	732-248-9200	343
Etnyre ED & Co 1333 S Daysville Rd	Oregon	IL	61061	**800-995-2116**	815-732-2116	189
E'Town Corp 600 South Ave	Westfield	NJ	07090	**800-272-1325**	908-654-1234	355-5
ETS Inc 1115 E Brigadoon Ct	Salt Lake City	UT	84117	**800-387-7003**	801-265-2497	176-1
Ettore Products Co 8469 Pardee Dr	Oakland	CA	94621	**800-438-8673**	510-638-4870	497
EU Services 649 N Horners Ln	Rockville	MD	20850	**800-230-3362**	301-424-3300	615
Euclid Chemical Co 19218 Redwood Rd	Cleveland	OH	44110	**800-321-7628**	216-531-9222	3
Euclid Universal Corp 30500 Bruce Industrial Pkwy Suite B	Solon	OH	44139	**800-280-2616**	440-349-4083	700
Eufaula/Barbour County Chamber of Commerce 333 E Broad St	Eufaula	AL	36027	**800-524-7529**	334-687-6664	137
Eugene Area Bed & Breakfast Assn 2013 Charnelton St	Eugene	OR	97405	**800-507-1354**	541-343-3553	368
Eugene Bible College 2155 Bailey Hill Rd	Eugene	OR	97405	**800-322-2638**	541-485-1780	163
Eugene O'Neill Theatre 230 W 49th St	New York	NY	10019	**800-432-7250**	212-239-6200	732
Eugene Welding Co 2420 Wills St	Marysville	MI	48040	**800-959-0857**	810-364-7421	281
Euler American Credit Indemnity Co 800 Red Brook Blvd 4th Fl	Owings Mills	MD	21117	**800-866-5551**	410-753-0753	384-5
Euphonix Inc 220 Portage Ave	Palo Alto	CA	94306	**800-579-7836**	650-855-0400	52
Eureka Chemical Co 234 Lawrence Ave	South San Francisco	CA	94080	**888-387-3522**	650-761-3536	143
Eureka Co 807 N Main St *Cust Svc	Bloomington	IL	61701	**800-843-4324***	309-828-2367	775
Eureka College 300 E College Ave	Eureka	IL	61530	**888-438-7352**	309-467-6350	163
Eureka-GGN 39 Broadway 19th Fl	New York	NY	10006	**800-562-4206**	212-404-5000	721
Eureka (Greater) Chamber of Commerce 2112 Broadway	Eureka	CA	95501	**800-356-6381**	707-442-3738	137
Eureka Mfg Co 47 Elm St	Norton	MA	02766	**800-376-8209**	508-285-9881	693
Eureka School Div Paper Magic Group Inc 401 Adams Ave *Cust Svc	Scranton	PA	18510	**800-258-1044***	570-961-3863	242
Eureka Welding Alloys Inc 2000 E Avis Dr	Madison Heights	MI	48071	**800-962-8560**	248-588-0001	798
Eureka/Humboldt County Convention & Visitors Bureau 1034 2nd St	Eureka	CA	95501	**800-346-3482**	707-443-5097	205
Euro Lloyd Travel Inc 1640 Hempstead Tpke	East Meadow	NY	11554	**800-334-2724**	516-228-4970	760
Euro RSCG Worldwide 350 Hudson St 6th Fl	New York	NY	10014	**800-263-7590**	212-886-2000	4
Euro-Suites Hotel 501 Chestnut Ridge Rd	Morgantown	WV	26505	**800-678-4837**	304-598-1000	373
Europe by Car Inc 62 William St 7th Fl	New York	NY	10005	**800-223-1516**	212-581-3040	126
European Touch Ltd II 8301 W Parkland Ct	Milwaukee	WI	53223	**800-626-6912**	414-357-7016	78
European Travel Inc 301 Howard St 4th Fl	San Francisco	CA	94105	**800-635-6463**	415-981-5518	760
Europtics Inc 2960 E 2nd Ave Suite C	Denver	CO	80206	**800-564-2179**	303-322-7507	533
EuroSoft Inc 1705 Capital of Texas Hwy Suite 200	Austin	TX	78746	**888-329-8100**	512-329-8100	707
Eurostar Inc 13425 S Figueroa St *Cust Svc	Los Angeles	CA	90061	**800-276-2002***	310-354-1387	296
Eutectic Corp N 94 W 14355 Garwin Mace Dr	Menomonee Falls	WI	53051	**800-558-8524**		798
Euthanasia & Assisted Suicide. International Task Force on PO Box 760	Steubenville	OH	43952	**800-958-5678**	740-282-3810	48-8
ev3 Inc 4600 Nathan Ln N *NASDAQ: EVVV*	Plymouth	MN	55442	**800-716-6700**	763-398-7000	468
EV Global Motors Co 4826 4th St	Irwindale	CA	91706	**800-871-4545**	626-813-9505	83
EVA Air Evergreen Club 12440 E Imperial Hwy Suite 250	Norwalk	CA	90650	**800-695-1188**	562-565-6000	27
EVA Airways 12440 E Imperial Hwy Suite 250	Norwalk	CA	90650	**800-695-1188**	562-565-6000	26
Eva Gabor International Ltd 5900 Equitable Rd	Kansas City	MO	64120	**800-236-0326**	816-231-3700	342
Eva-Tone Soundsheets Inc 4801 Ulmerton Rd *Sales	Clearwater	FL	33762	**800-382-8663***	727-572-7000	239
Evan-Moor Educational Publishers Inc 18 Lower Ragsdale Dr	Monterey	CA	93940	**800-777-4489**	831-649-5901	242
Evangel University 1111 N Glenstone Ave	Springfield	MO	65802	**800-382-6435**	417-865-2811	163
Evangelical Council for Financial Accountability (ECFA) 440 W Jubal Early Dr Suite 130	Winchester	VA	22601	**800-323-9473**	540-535-0103	48-5
Evangelical Lutheran Church in America (ELCA) 8765 W Higgins Rd	Chicago	IL	60631	**800-638-3522**	773-380-2700	48-20
Evangelical School of Theology 121 S College St	Myerstown	PA	17067	**800-532-5775**	717-866-5775	164-3
Evangelical Training Assn (ETA) 1620 Penny Ln	Schaumburg	IL	60173	**800-369-8291**	630-540-7840	48-20
Evangelicals for Social Action (ESA) 10 E Lancaster Ave	Wynnewood	PA	19096	**800-650-6600**	610-645-9390	48-7
Evangelistic Assn. Billy Graham 1 Billy Graham Pkwy PO Box 1270	Charlotte	NC	28201	**877-247-2426**	704-401-2432	48-20
Evanite Fiber Corp PO Box E *Cust Svc	Corvallis	OR	97339	**800-441-5567***	541-753-1211	326
Evans Analytical Group 810 Kifer Rd	Sunnyvale	CA	94086	**800-321-4775**	408-530-3500	728
Evans Bob Farms Inc 3776 S High St *NASDAQ: BOBE*	Columbus	OH	43207	**800-272-7675**	614-491-2225	657
Evans David & Assoc Inc 2100 SW River Pkwy	Portland	OR	97201	**800-721-1916**	503-223-6663	258
Evans Distribution Systems 18765 Seaway Dr	Melvindale	MI	48122	**888-361-9850**	313-388-3200	790-1

Name / Address	City	State	Zip	Toll-Free	Phone	Class
Evans Environmental Corp 14505 Commerce Way Suite 400	Miami Lakes	FL	33016	**800-486-7458**	305-374-8300	191
Evans Food Products Co 4118 S Halsted St	Chicago	IL	60609	**866-254-7400**	773-254-7400	291-35
Evans Frozen Baked Goods Inc PO Box 284 *Cust Svc	Cozad	NE	69130	**800-222-5641***	308-784-2409	291-2
Evans Fruit Farm 200 Cowiche City Rd	Cowiche	WA	98923	**800-255-7513**	509-678-4127	310-3
Evans-Hydro 18128 S Santa Fe Ave	Rancho Dominguez	CA	90221	**800-429-7867**	310-608-5801	627
Evans Industries Inc 1255 Peters Rd	Harvey	LA	70058	**800-749-6012**	504-374-6000	197
Evans-Sherratt Co 13050 Northend Ave	Oak Park	MI	48237	**800-248-3826**	248-584-5500	467
Evans & Sutherland Computer Corp 600 Komas Dr *NASDAQ: ESCC* ■ *Sales	Salt Lake City	UT	84108	**800-367-7460***	801-588-1000	694
Evans Systems Inc PO Box 2480	Bay City	TX	77404	**800-392-6402**	979-245-2981	569
Evans Tempcon Inc 701 Ann St NW	Grand Rapids	MI	49504	**800-354-7088**	616-361-2681	16
Evanson Paul J 800 Cabin Hill Dr Chm/Pres/CEO Allegheny Energy Inc	Greensburg	PA	15601	**800-255-3443**	724-837-3000	561
Evanston Publishing Inc 4824 Brownsboro Ctr	Louisville	KY	40207	**800-594-5190**	502-899-1919	95
Evansville Convention & Visitors Bureau 401 SE Riverside Dr	Evansville	IN	47713	**800-433-3025**	812-425-5402	205
Evansville Courier & Press 300 E Walnut St	Evansville	IN	47713	**800-288-3200**	812-424-7711	522-2
Evant Solutions Corp 235 Montgomery St Suite 1300	San Francisco	CA	94104	**800-316-2747**	415-283-1880	39
Evco Plastics Inc 100 W North St	DeForest	WI	53532	**800-507-6000**	608-846-6000	593
Eveden Ltd 65 Sprague St	Hyde Park	MA	02136	**800-733-8964**	617-361-7559	153-18
Evenflo Co Inc 1801 Commerce Dr	Piqua	OH	45356	**800-233-5921**	937-415-3300	64
Evening Observer 8-10 E 2nd St PO Box 391	Dunkirk	NY	14048	**800-836-0931**	716-366-3000	522-2
Evening Sun PO Box 151	Norwich	NY	13815	**800-836-6780**	607-334-3276	522-2
Evening Sun 135 Baltimore St	Hanover	PA	17331	**800-877-3786**	717-637-3736	522-2
Event Planning International Corp 7731 Little Ave Suite A	Charlotte	NC	28226	**800-940-2164**	704-943-1003	183
Ever-Bloom Inc 4701 Foothill Rd	Carpinteria	CA	93013	**800-388-8112**	805-684-5566	363
Ever-Lite Co Inc 1717 N Bayshore Dr Unit 1632	Miami	FL	33132	**800-891-4670**	305-577-0819	10
Ever-Ready Oil Co PO Box 25845	Albuquerque	NM	87125	**800-259-6120**	505-842-6120	569
Everbrite Inc PO Box 20020	Greenfield	WI	53220	**800-558-3888**	414-529-3500	692
Evercom Inc 8201 Tristar Dr	Irving	TX	75063	**800-947-0899**	972-988-3737	721
Everdream Corp 6591 Dumbarton Cir	Fremont	CA	94555	**877-437-3264**	510-818-5500	178
Everest & Jennings 2935 Northeast Pkwy	Atlanta	GA	30360	**800-235-4661**	770-447-1609	469
Everest Re Group Ltd 477 Martinsville Rd *NYSE: RE*	Liberty Corner	NJ	07938	**800-551-6501**	908-604-3000	355-4
Everest Reinsurance Co 477 Martinsville Rd	Liberty Corner	NJ	07938	**800-269-6660**	908-604-3000	384-5
Everett J Prescott Inc 32 Prescott St	Gardiner	ME	04345	**800-876-1357**	207-582-1851	601
Everfast Inc DBA Calico Corners 203 Gale Ln *Cust Svc	Kennett Square	PA	19348	**800-213-6366***	610-444-9700	266
Everfresh Food Corp 501 Huron Blvd SE	Minneapolis	MN	55414	**800-428-9999**	612-331-6393	291-31
Everfresh/Lacroix Beverages Inc 6600 E 9-Mile Rd	Warren	MI	48091	**800-323-3416**	586-755-9500	81-2
Everglades Direct 720 International Pkwy	Sunrise	FL	33345	**800-999-9111**	954-846-8899	451
Everglades Holiday Park 21940 Griffin Rd	Fort Lauderdale	FL	33332	**800-226-2244**	954-434-8111	50
Evergreen Air Center Inc Pinal Air Pk Rd	Marana	AZ	85653	**800-624-6838**	520-682-4181	25
Evergreen Art Works 2388 Cumberland Sq Dr	Bettendorf	IA	52722	**800-468-7280**	563-359-8324	45
Evergreen Bank NA 237 Glen St	Glens Falls	NY	12801	**888-792-1151**	518-792-1151	71
Evergreen Community Hospice 12822 124th Ln NE	Kirkland	WA	98034	**800-442-4546**	425-899-1040	365
Evergreen FS Inc 402 N Hershey Rd	Bloomington	IL	61704	**877-963-2392**	309-663-2392	272
Evergreen Helicopters of Alaska Inc 1936 Merrill Field Dr	Anchorage	AK	99501	**800-958-2454**	907-257-1500	354
Evergreen International Airlines Inc 3850 Three-Mile Ln	McMinnville	OR	97128	**800-383-5338**	503-472-0011	13
Evergreen International Aviation Inc 3850 Three Mile Ln	McMinnville	OR	97128	**800-472-9361**	503-472-9361	13
Evergreen Investments PO Box 8400	Boston	MA	02266	**800-343-2898**		517
Evergreen Lodge 250 South Frontage Rd W	Vail	CO	81657	**800-284-8245**	970-476-7810	373
Evergreen Marriott Conference Resort 4021 Lakeview Dr	Stone Mountain	GA	30083	**800-228-9290**	770-879-9900	370
Evergreen Scientific Co 2300 E 49th St	Los Angeles	CA	90058	**800-421-6261**	323-583-1331	597
Evergreen Solar Inc 259 Cedar Hill St *NASDAQ: ESLR*	Marlborough	MA	01752	**800-357-2221**	508-357-2221	686
Evergreens The 309 Bridgeboro Rd	Moorestown	NJ	08057	**800-371-4918**	856-439-2000	659
EverHome Mortgage Co 8100 Nations Way *Cust Svc	Jacksonville	FL	32256	**800-669-9721***	904-281-6000	498
Everlite Inc 607 Fisher Rd	Longview	TX	75604	**800-600-3867**	903-297-3444	768
Everprint International Inc 18021 Cortney Ct	City of Industry	CA	91748	**800-984-5777**	626-913-2888	173
Everpure Inc 1040 Muirfield Dr	Hanover Park	IL	60133	**800-323-7873**	630-307-3000	793
Everypath Inc 2211 N 1st St Suite 200 *Sales	San Jose	CA	95131	**800-355-1068***	408-562-8000	222
EVH Mfg LLC 4895 Red Bluff Rd	Loris	SC	29569	**888-990-2555**	843-756-4051	269
Evoke Software Inc 12357 Riata Trace Pkwy Suite C-200	Austin	TX	78727	**877-333-3427**	512-372-9370	176-1
Evolution Computing 7000 N 16th St Suite 120 #514	Phoenix	AZ	85020	**800-874-4028**	602-749-9476	176-5
Evolutionary Technologies International Inc 816 Congress Ave Suite 1450	Austin	TX	78701	**800-856-8800**	512-383-3000	176-1
EVSCO Pharmaceuticals Div IGI Inc 101 Lincoln Ave	Buena	NJ	08310	**800-387-2607**		574
EW Knauss & Sons Inc 625 E Broad St	Quakertown	PA	18951	**800-648-4220**	215-536-4220	465
EW Scripps Co 312 Walnut St Suite 2800 *NYSE: SSP*	Cincinnati	OH	45202	**800-888-3000**	513-977-3000	623-8
EW Wylie Corp 222 40th St SW *Cust Svc	Fargo	ND	58103	**800-437-4132***	701-282-5550	769
Ewa Hotel Waikiki 2555 Cartwright Rd	Honolulu	HI	96815	**800-359-8639**	808-922-1677	373
EWA Inc (Electronic Warfare Assoc Inc) 13873 Park Center Rd Suite 500	Herndon	VA	20171	**888-392-0002**	703-904-5700	178
Ewald Red Inc PO Box 519	Karnes City	TX	78118	**800-242-3524**	830-780-3304	595
eWatch Report 810 7th Ave 35th Fl	New York	NY	10019	**888-857-6842**	212-832-9400	521-3
eWEEK Magazine 28 E 28th St 8th Fl	New York	NY	10016	**888-663-8438**	212-503-3500	449-7
Ewell HR Inc 4635 Division Hwy	East Earl	PA	17519	**800-233-0161**	717-354-4556	769
Ewing Marion Kauffman Foundation 4801 Rockhill Rd	Kansas City	MO	64110	**800-489-4900**	816-932-1000	300
Ex-Cell Home Fashion Inc 295 5th Ave Rm 612	New York	NY	10016	**800-223-1999**	212-213-8000	731
Ex-Cell Metal Products Inc 11240 Melrose St	Franklin Park	IL	60131	**800-392-3557**	847-451-0451	281
Ex-Cell-O Machine Tools 6015 Center Dr	Sterling Heights	MI	48312	**800-837-6277**	586-939-1330	447
Exabyte Corp 2108 55th St *NASDAQ: EXBT* ■ *Cust Svc	Boulder	CO	80301	**800-445-7736***	303-442-4333	171-8
Exact Software North America 8800 Lyra Dr Suite 350	Columbus	OH	43240	**800-468-0834**	614-410-2600	176-1
Exactech Inc 2320 NW 66th Ct *NASDAQ: EXAC*	Gainesville	FL	32653	**800-392-2832**	352-377-1140	469
Exalpha Biologicals Inc 5 Clock Tower Pl Suite 255	Maynard	MA	01754	**800-395-1137**	978-461-0435	229
Examiners. Association of Certified Fraud 716 West Ave	Austin	TX	78701	**800-245-3321**	512-478-9070	49-1
Examiners for Engineering & Surveying. National Council of 280 Seneca Creek Rd	Clemson	SC	29631	**800-250-3196**	864-654-6824	49-3
Exber Inc 600 E Freemont St	Las Vegas	NV	89101	**800-634-6703**	702-385-5200	132
Excalibur Extrusions Inc 110 E Crowther Ave	Placentia	CA	92670	**800-648-6804**	714-528-8834	585
Excalibur Hotel & Casino 3850 Las Vegas Blvd S *Resv	Las Vegas	NV	89109	**800-937-7777***	702-597-7777	133
Excel Group 1 Merrick Ave	Westbury	NY	11590	**800-252-3390**	516-794-3355	219
Excel Partnership Inc 75 Glen Rd	Sandy Hook	CT	06482	**800-374-3818**	203-426-3281	193
Excel Process Pork 1915 W Canal St	Milwaukee	WI	53233	**800-558-4242**	414-410-8200	465
Excel Telecommunications 2440 Marsh Ln *Tech Supp	Carrollton	TX	75006	**800-589-5884***	972-478-3000	721
ExceLine 2345 Vauxhall Rd	Union	NJ	07083	**800-334-2212**	908-964-7000	431
Excell Data Div CompuCom Systems Inc 1756 114th Ave SE Suite 220	Bellevue	WA	98004	**800-539-2355**	425-974-2000	178
Excell Mfg Co 70 Royal Little Dr	Providence	RI	02904	**800-343-8410**	401-854-1700	401
Excell Store Fixtures 80 Jutland Rd	Toronto	ON	M8Z2H1	**800-392-3551**	416-503-1234	281
Excellent Adventures Inc 6215 Commodity Ct	Fort Wayne	IN	46818	**800-552-3893**	260-489-3556	108
Excelligence Learning Corp 2 Lower Ragsdale Dr Suite 200 *NASDAQ: LRNS*	Monterey	CA	93940	**800-627-2829**	831-333-2000	242
Excellon Automation Inc 24751 Crenshaw Blvd	Torrance	CA	90505	**800-392-3556**	310-534-6300	462
Excellus BlueCross BlueShield of Central New York 344 S Warren St	Syracuse	NY	13202	**800-633-6066**	315-671-6400	384-3
Excellus BlueCross BlueShield of Utica 12 Rhoads Dr	Utica	NY	13502	**800-544-1450**		384-3
Excelsior College 7 Columbia Cir	Albany	NY	12203	**888-647-2388**	518-464-8500	163
Excelsior Funds PO Box 8529	Boston	MA	02266	**800-446-1012**		517
Excelsior Inc 720 Chestnut St	Rockford	IL	61102	**800-435-4671**	815-987-2940	321
Excelsior Marking Products 4524 Hudson Dr	Stow	OH	44224	**800-433-3615**	330-929-2802	459
Excelsior Mfg & Supply Corp 1465 E Industrial Dr	Itasca	IL	60143	**800-548-8135**	630-773-5500	584
Exceptional Children. Council for 1110 N Glebe Rd Suite 300	Arlington	VA	22201	**888-232-7733**	703-620-3660	49-5
Exchange The PO Box 459	Laurinburg	NC	28353	**800-334-2311**	910-276-2311	522-2
Exchange Club. National 3050 W Central Ave	Toledo	OH	43606	**800-924-2643**	419-535-3232	48-15
Exchange National Bancshares Inc 132 E High St *NASDAQ: EXJF*	Jefferson City	MO	65101	**800-761-8362**	573-761-6100	355-2
Exchangors. National Council of 630 Quintana Rd Suite 150	Morro Bay	CA	93442	**800-324-1031**		49-17
Exclusive Findings 29 Delaine St	Providence	RI	02909	**800-342-9560**	401-421-3661	10
Excursia.com PO Box 936	Augusta	GA	30903	**800-622-6358**		762
Exec Air Montana Inc 2430 Airport Rd	Helena	MT	59601	**800-513-2190**	406-442-2190	14
ExecSuites 702 3rd Ave SW	Calgary	AB	T2P3B4	**800-667-4980**	403-294-5800	209
ExecUNet Inc 295 Westport Ave	Norwalk	CT	06851	**800-637-3126**	203-750-1030	257
Executive Airport Plaza 7311 Westminster Hwy	Richmond	BC	V6X1A3	**800-663-2878**	604-278-5555	372
Executive Car Leasing Inc 7807 Santa Monica Blvd	Los Angeles	CA	90046	**800-994-2277**	323-654-5000	284
Executive Enterprises Institute 2 Shaw's Cove	New London	CT	06320	**800-831-8333**	860-701-5900	753
Executive Excellence Newsletter 1366 East 1120 S	Provo	UT	84604	**800-304-9782**	801-375-4060	521-2
Executive Fliteways 1 Clark Rd	Ronkonkoma	NY	11779	**800-533-3363**	631-588-5454	14
Executive Greetings Inc 120 Greenwoods Industrial Pk *Cust Svc	New Hartford	CT	06057	**800-562-5468***	860-379-9911	130
Executive Health Group 10 Rockefeller Plaza 4th Fl	New York	NY	10020	**800-362-8671**	212-332-3030	347

Name / Address	City	State	ZIP	Toll-Free	Phone	Class
Executive Hotel & Conference Centre Burnaby 4201 Lougheed Hwy	Burnaby	BC	V5C3Y6	**800-590-3932**	604-298-2010	372
Executive Hotel Vancouver Downtown 1379 Howe St.	Vancouver	BC	V6Z2R5	**888-388-3932**	604-688-7678	372
Executive Hotel Vintage Court 650 Bush St	San Francisco	CA	94108	**800-654-1100**	415-392-4666	373
Executive Housekeepers Assn. International 1001 Eastwind Dr Suite 301	Westerville	OH	43081	**800-200-6342**	614-895-7166	49-4
Executive Inn 978 Phillips Ln	Louisville	KY	40209	**800-626-2706**	502-367-6161	373
Executive Inn Evansville 600 Walnut St.	Evansville	IN	47708	**877-424-0888**	812-424-8000	373
Executive Inn Rivermont 1 Executive Blvd	Owensboro	KY	42301	**800-626-1936**	270-926-8000	373
Executive Inn Suites San Jose 3930 Monterey Rd	San Jose	CA	95111	**800-453-7755**	408-281-8700	373
Executive Jet 4556 Airport Rd	Cincinnati	OH	45226	**800-451-2822**	513-979-6600	14
Executive Newsletter 5710 Mineral Point Rd *Circ	Madison	WI	53705	**800-356-8010***	608-231-4000	521-1
Executive Office Concepts Inc 1715 S Anderson Ave.	Compton	CA	90220	**800-421-5927**	310-537-1657	314-1
Executive Recruiter News 1 Phoenix Mill Ln 5th Fl.	Peterborough	NH	03458	**800-531-0007**	603-924-0900	521-2
Executive Royal Inn West Edmonton 10010 178th St.	Edmonton	AB	T5S1T3	**800-661-4879**	780-484-6000	372
Executive Search Consultants. Association of 12 E 41st St 17th Fl	New York	NY	10017	**877-843-2372**	212-398-9556	49-12
Executive Software International Inc 7590 N Glenoaks Blvd *Sales	Burbank	CA	91504	**800-829-6468***	818-771-1600	176-12
Executive Speakers Bureau 8470 Deerfield Ln.	Germantown	TN	38138	**800-754-9404**	901-754-9404	699
Executive Staffing Group The 4101 Lake Boone Trail Suite 112	Raleigh	NC	27607	**888-374-4364**	919-783-6695	619
Executive Strategies Newsletter PO Box 9070	McLean	VA	22102	**800-543-2053**	703-905-8000	521-2
Executive Suite Hotel 4360 Spenard Rd	Anchorage	AK	99517	**800-770-6366**	907-243-6366	373
Executive Tower Hotel 1405 Curtis St	Denver	CO	80202	**800-525-6651**	303-571-0300	373
Executive Transportation Brokers Inc DBA AirportsPickup.com PO Box 652	New York	NY	10040	**877-800-6500**	212-927-7152	433
Executive Transportation Service Inc 7108 DeSoto Ave Suite 204	Canoga Park	CA	91303	**800-348-4010**	818-716-7727	433
Executive West Hotel 830 Phillips Ln	Louisville	KY	40209	**800-626-2708**	502-367-2251	373
Executives. American Society of Association 1575 'I' St NW	Washington	DC	20005	**888-950-2723**	202-626-2723	49-12
Executives. National Assn for Female 60 E 42nd St 27th Fl	New York	NY	10165	**800-927-6233**	212-351-6400	49-12
Exel 570 Polaris Pkwy	Westerville	OH	43082	**800-272-1052**	614-865-8500	440
Exel Inns of America Inc 4706 E Washington Ave	Madison	WI	53704	**800-367-3935**	608-241-5271	369
Exel Inns Insider's Program 4706 E Washington Ave	Madison	WI	53704	**800-367-3935**	608-241-5271	371
Exelon Corp 10 S Dearborn St 37th Fl *NYSE: EXC*	Chicago	IL	60690	**800-334-7661**	312-394-7398	355-5
Exenet Technologies Inc 387 Park Ave S 3rd Fl	New York	NY	10016	**877-393-6388**	212-684-7300	39
Exercise. American Council on 4851 Paramount Dr	San Diego	CA	92123	**800-825-3636**	858-279-8227	48-17
Exercise Assn. Aquatic PO Box 1609	Nokomis	FL	34274	**888-232-9283**	941-486-8600	48-22
Exercise & Sports Assn. Diabetes 8001 Montcastle Dr	Nashville	TN	37221	**800-898-4322**		48-17
EXFO Burleigh Products Group Inc 7647 Main St Fishers	Victor	NY	14564	**800-663-3936**	585-924-9355	534
EXFO Electro-Optical Engineering Inc 400 Godin Ave *NASDAQ: EXFO*	Vanier	QC	G1M2K2	**800-663-3936**	418-683-0211	247
Exhibitgroup/Giltspur 200 N Gary Ave	Roselle	IL	60172	**800-843-3944**	630-307-2400	230
Exhibitors' Assn. Tennessee Walking Horse Breeders' & PO Box 286	Lewisburg	TN	37091	**800-359-1574**	931-359-1574	48-3
Exide Technologies 210 Carnegie Ctr Suite 500 *NASDAQ: XIDE*	Princeton	NJ	08540	**866-289-0645**	609-627-7200	76
Exiss Aluminum Trailers Inc 900 Exiss Blvd Box D	El Reno	OK	73036	**877-993-9477**	405-262-6471	751
Exopack LLC 3070 Southport Rd PO Box 5687	Spartanburg	SC	29304	**877-447-3539**	864-596-7140	538
Exotic Animal Paradise 124 Jungle Dr.	Strafford	MO	65757	**888-570-9898**	417-859-2016	811
EXP Computer Inc 920 S Oyster Bay Rd Unit B *Sales	Hicksville	NY	11801	**800-397-6922***	516-942-0507	171-8
Expanding Light 14618 Tyler Foote Rd	Nevada City	CA	95959	**800-346-5350**	530-478-7518	660
Expanko Cork Co Inc 3135 Lower Valley Rd *Cust Svc	Parkesburg	PA	19365	**800-345-6202***	610-593-3000	208
Expansion Management Magazine 1300 E 9th St	Cleveland	OH	44114	**800-539-7263**	216-931-9860	449-5
Expedia Inc 3150 139th Ave SE	Bellevue	WA	98005	**800-397-3342**	425-564-7200	762
Expedient 40 24th St Suite 300	Pittsburgh	PA	15222	**800-969-0099**	412-316-7800	390
Expeditors International of Washington Inc 1015 3rd Ave 12th Fl *NASDAQ: EXPD*	Seattle	WA	98104	**800-284-7474**	206-674-3400	440
Experian Inc 475 Anton Blvd	Costa Mesa	CA	92626	**888-397-3742**	714-830-7000	212
Experience Works Inc 2200 Clarendon Blvd Suite 1000	Arlington	VA	22201	**866-397-9757**	703-522-7272	48-6
Experiential Education. National Society for 515 King St Suite 240	Alexandria	VA	22314	**800-803-4170**	703-706-9552	48-11
Experimental Aircraft Assn (EAA) 3000 Poberezny Rd	Oshkosh	WI	54902	**800-236-4800**	920-426-4800	48-18
Experimental & Applied Science Inc (EAS Inc) 555 Corporate Cir	Golden	CO	80401	**800-297-9776**	303-271-1002	786
Experimental Biology. Federation of American Societies for 9650 Rockville Pike	Bethesda	MD	20814	**800-433-2732**	301-530-7000	49-19
Expert Choice Inc 1501 Lee Hwy Suite 302	Arlington	VA	22209	**888-259-6400**	703-243-5595	176-12
Expetic Technology Service 12 2nd Ave SW	Aberdeen	SD	57401	**888-297-2292**	605-225-4122	173
Exploited Children. National Center for Missing & 699 Prince St	Alexandria	VA	22314	**800-843-5678**	703-274-3900	48-6
Exploration Co The 500 North Loop 1604 E Suite 250 *NASDAQ: TXCO*	San Antonio	TX	78232	**877-912-8926**	210-496-5300	529
Exploration Inc. Society for Mining Metallurgy & 8307 Shaffer Pkwy	Littleton	CO	80127	**800-763-3132**	303-973-9550	49-13
Exploration Place 300 N McLean Blvd	Wichita	KS	67203	**877-904-1444**	316-263-3373	510
Explore Information Services Inc 2945 Lone Oak Dr Suite 150	Eagan	MN	55121	**800-531-9125**	651-681-4460	621
EXPO Design Center 2455 Paces Ferry Rd *Cust Svc	Atlanta	GA	30339	**800-553-3199***	770-433-8211	359
Expo Group 1740 Hurd Dr	Irving	TX	75038	**800-736-7775**	972-580-9000	183
Expon Exhibits 1902 Channel Dr.	West Sacramento	CA	95691	**800-783-9766**	916-371-1600	230
Export-Import Bank of the US 811 Vermont Ave NW	Washington	DC	20571	**800-565-3946**	202-565-3946	336-16
Express 2 Limited Pkwy *Cust Svc	Columbus	OH	43230	**800-477-8844***	614-415-4000	155-3
Express Digital Graphics Inc DBA PhotoReflect 9780 Mt Pyramid Ct Suite 120	Englewood	CO	80112	**888-584-0089**	303-790-1004	577
Express Hotel Reservations 3825 Iris Ave Suite 200	Boulder	CO	80301	**800-356-1123**	303-440-8481	368
Express-News Corp Ave 'E' & 3rd St	San Antonio	TX	78205	**800-555-1551**	210-250-3000	623-8
Express Oil Change 190 W Valley Ave	Birmingham	AL	35209	**888-945-1771**	205-945-1771	62-5
Express Scripts Inc 13900 Riverport Dr. *NASDAQ: ESRX*	Maryland Heights	MO	63043	**800-332-5455**	314-770-1666	575
Express Services Inc 8516 Northwest Expy	Oklahoma City	OK	73162	**800-652-6400**	405-840-5000	707
Express Technologies Inc DBA HalfPrice Hosting PO Box 22789	Louisville	KY	40252	**800-284-9391**	502-214-4100	795
Express-Times 30 N 4th St	Easton	PA	18042	**800-360-3601**	610-258-7171	522-2
ExpressJet Airlines Inc 1600 Smith St HQSCE *NYSE: XJT*	Houston	TX	77002	**877-324-2639**	713-324-5000	26
Expressway Inn 1340 S 21st Ave	Fargo	ND	58103	**800-437-0044**	701-235-3141	373
Expressway Suites 180 E Bismarck Expy	Bismarck	ND	58504	**888-774-5566**	701-222-3311	373
Exprezit! Convenience Stores LLC 6320 Quadrangle Dr Suite 200	Chapel Hill	NC	27517	**800-424-2067**	919-477-4200	658
Extended Stay America Inc *Crossland Economy Studios* 100 Dunbar St	Spartanburg	SC	29306	**877-276-7752**	864-573-1600	369
Extended StayAmerica Efficiency Studios 100 Dunbar St.	Spartanburg	SC	29306	**800-398-7829**	864-573-1600	369
StudioPLUS Deluxe Studios 100 Dunbar St	Spartanburg	SC	29306	**888-788-3467**	864-573-1600	369
Extended Stay Deluxe-Orlando Convention Center 8750 Universal Blvd	Orlando	FL	32819	**888-387-8420**	407-903-1500	373
Extended Systems Inc 5777 N Meeker Ave *NASDAQ: XTND*	Boise	ID	83713	**800-235-7576**	208-322-7575	176-7
EXTOL International Inc 474 N Centre St PO Box 1010	Pottsville	PA	17901	**888-334-3986**	570-628-5500	176-7
Extra Packaging Corp 631 Golden Harbour Dr	Boca Raton	FL	33432	**800-872-7548**	561-416-2060	544
Extra Touch Florist Assn (ETF) 137 N Larchmont Blvd Suite 529	Los Angeles	CA	90019	**888-419-1515**	323-735-7272	49-4
Extraco Mortgage 7503 Bosque Blvd	Waco	TX	76712	**800-227-4894**	254-772-0202	498
Extreme Networks Inc 3585 Monroe St *NASDAQ: EXTR*	Santa Clara	CA	95051	**888-257-3000**	408-579-2800	174
Extron Electronics USA 1230 S Lewis St *Tech Supp	Anaheim	CA	92805	**800-633-9876***	714-491-1500	52
Extrude Hone Corp 1 Industry Blvd PO Box 1000	Irwin	PA	15642	**800-367-1109**	724-863-5900	447
Extruded Metals Inc 302 Ashfield St	Belding	MI	48809	**800-428-7296**	616-794-1200	476
Exxon Travel Club PO Box 660460	Dallas	TX	75266	**800-833-9966**		53
ExxonMobil Corp 5959 Las Colinas Blvd. *NYSE: XOM* ■ *Hum Res	Irving	TX	75039	**800-252-1800***	972-444-1000	525
ExxonMobil Credit Card Services PO Box 4598	Carol Stream	IL	60197	**800-344-4355**		213
Eyde Construction Co PO Box 4218	East Lansing	MI	48826	**800-442-3933**	517-351-2480	186
Eye Bank of British Columbia Vancouver General Hospital 2550 Willow St Eye Care Centre 3rd Fl.	Vancouver	BC	V5Z3N9	**800-667-2060**	604-875-4567	265
Eye Care Centers of America Inc 11103 West Ave	San Antonio	TX	78213	**800-669-1183**	210-340-3531	658
Eye Care Inc 5858 Line Ave	Shreveport	LA	71106	**800-533-9638**	318-869-4443	532
Eye Centers of Florida 4101 Evans Ave	Fort Myers	FL	33901	**800-226-3377**	239-939-3456	785
Eye Communication Systems Inc 455 E Industrial Dr	Hartland	WI	53029	**800-558-2153**	262-367-1360	487
Eye Glass World Inc 3801 S Congress Ave.	Lake Worth	FL	33461	**800-529-4345**	561-965-9110	533
Eye-Kraft Optical Inc PO Box 400	Saint Cloud	MN	56302	**888-455-2022**	320-251-0141	531
Eye Lighting International NA 9150 Hendricks Rd	Mentor	OH	44060	**888-665-2677**	440-350-7000	429
Eye-Mart Express Inc 2110 Hutton Dr Suite 100	Carrollton	TX	75006	**800-755-3936**	972-488-2002	533

Name / Address	City	State	Zip	Toll-Free	Phone	Class
Eye-Mate Inc 77 N Centre Ave	Rockville Centre	NY	11570	**800-393-6283**	516-678-9613	533
Eye Surgeons. American College of 334 E Lake Rd Suite 135	Palm Lake Harbor	FL	34685	**888-335-0077**	727-480-8542	49-8
EyeMed Vision Care 4000 Luxottica Pl	Mason	OH	45040	**888-439-3633**		384-3
Eyetech 7016 6th St N	Oakdale	MN	55128	**800-328-9060**	651-501-8114	531
Eyre Bus Service Inc 13600 Triadelphia Rd	Glenelg	MD	21737	**800-321-3973**	410-442-1330	108
EZ Loader Boat Trailers Inc 717 N Hamilton St	Spokane	WA	99202	**800-398-5623**	509-489-0181	751
EZ Trail Inc Hwy 133 E Box 168	Arthur	IL	61911	**800-677-2802**	217-543-3471	269
EZCORP Inc 1901 Capital Pkwy *NASDAQ: EZPW*	Austin	TX	78746	**800-873-7296**	512-314-3400	558
Ezenia! Inc 154 Middlesex Tpke *NASDAQ: EZEN*	Burlington	MA	01803	**800-966-2301**	781-505-2100	174
EZPAWN 1901 Capital Pkwy	Austin	TX	78746	**800-873-7296**	512-314-3400	558

F

Name / Address	City	State	Zip	Toll-Free	Phone	Class
F-11 Photographic Supplies 16 E Main St *Sales	Bozeman	MT	59715	**800-548-0203***	406-587-1300	119
F & A Cheese Corp PO Box 19127	Irvine	CA	92623	**800-634-4109**	949-221-8255	291-5
F Byard Brogan Inc 124 S Keswick Ave	Glenside	PA	19038	**800-232-7642**	215-885-3550	401
F & D Head Co 3040 E Peden Rd	Fort Worth	TX	76179	**800-451-2684**	817-236-8773	709
F Dohmen Co W 194 North 11381 McCormick Dr	Germantown	WI	53022	**877-848-4166**	262-255-0022	237
F & F Foods Inc 3501 W 48th Pl	Chicago	IL	60632	**800-621-0225**	773-927-3737	291-35
F Gavina & Sons Inc 2700 Fruitland Ave	Vernon	CA	90058	**800-428-4627**	323-582-0671	291-7
F & H Ribbon Co Inc PO Box 1338	Hurst	TX	76053	**800-877-5775**	817-283-5891	766
F & M Bank Wisconsin 205 E 4th St	Kaukauna	WI	54130	**800-806-1692**	920-766-8160	71
F & M Hat Co Inc 103 Walnut St PO Box 40	Denver	PA	17517	**800-953-4287**	717-336-5505	153-9
F Schumacher & Co 79 Madison Ave	New York	NY	10016	**800-556-0040**	212-213-7900	731
F & W Publications Inc 4700 E Galbraith Rd *Sales	Cincinnati	OH	45236	**800-289-0963***	513-531-2690	623-9
F5 Networks Inc 401 Elliott Ave W *NASDAQ: FFIV*	Seattle	WA	98119	**888-882-4447**	206-272-5555	174
FA (Families Anonymous) PO Box 3475	Culver City	CA	90231	**800-736-9805**	310-815-8010	48-21
FA Bartlett Tree Expert Co 476 Canal St	Stamford	CT	06902	**877-227-8538**	203-323-1131	765
FA Davis Co 1915 Arch St	Philadelphia	PA	19103	**800-523-4049**	215-568-2270	623-2
FAA (Federal Aviation Administration) 800 Independence Ave SW	Washington	DC	20591	**800-322-7873**	202-267-3484	336-13
FAAN (Food Allergy & Anaphylaxis Network) 11781 Lee Jackson Hwy Suite 160	Fairfax	VA	22033	**800-929-4040**	703-691-3179	48-17
Fabcon Inc 6111 Hwy 13 W	Savage	MN	55378	**800-727-4444**	952-890-4444	181
Fabian's Investment Resources Newsletter 2100 Main St Suite 300	Huntington Beach	CA	92648	**800-950-8765**	714-536-1931	521-9
Fabral Inc 3449 Hempland Rd	Lancaster	PA	17601	**800-477-2741**	717-397-2741	471
Fabreeka International Inc 1023 Turnpike St *Cust Svc	Stoughton	MA	02072	**800-322-7352***	781-341-3655	664
Fabri-Form Co 200 S Friendship Dr	New Concord	OH	43762	**800-837-2574**	740-826-5000	591
Fabri-Kal Corp Plastics Pl	Kalamazoo	MI	49001	**800-888-5054**	269-385-5050	591
Fabri-Quilt Inc 901 E 14th Ave PO Box 12479	North Kansas City	MO	64116	**800-279-0622**	816-421-2000	256
Fabri-Tech Inc 8236 N 600 W *Cust Svc	McCordsville	IN	46055	**800-332-4797***	317-335-9412	730-8
Fabric Place Inc 136 Howard St	Framingham	MA	01702	**800-556-3700**	508-872-4888	266
Fabricare Institute. International 12251 Tech Rd	Silver Spring	MD	20904	**800-638-2627**	301-622-1900	49-4
Fabricated Components Inc PO Box 431	Stroudsburg	PA	18360	**800-233-8163**	570-421-4110	473
Fabricators & Manufacturers Assn International (FMA) 833 Featherstone Rd	Rockford	IL	61107	**800-432-2832**	815-399-8700	49-13
Fabricon Products 4101 N American St	Philadelphia	PA	19140	**800-676-9727**	215-455-3300	544
Fabrics Assn International. Industrial 1801 County Rd 'B' W	Roseville	MN	55113	**800-225-4324**	651-222-2508	49-13
Fabricut Inc 9303 E 46th St	Tulsa	OK	74145	**800-999-8200**	918-622-7700	356
Fabriko Inc 318 E Confederate Blvd	Appomattox	VA	24522	**800-558-0242**	434-352-7145	343
Faces Magazine About People 30 Grove St Suite C	Peterborough	NH	03458	**800-821-0115**	603-924-7209	449-6
FaceTime Communications Inc 1159 Triton Dr	Foster City	CA	94404	**888-349-3223**	650-574-1600	39
Facets Multimedia Inc 1517 W Fullerton Ave	Chicago	IL	60614	**800-331-6197**	773-281-9075	500
Facial Plastic & Reconstructive Surgery. American Academy of 310 S Henry St	Alexandria	VA	22314	**800-332-3223**	703-299-9291	49-8
Facilities Engineering Service Center. Naval 1100 23rd Ave	Port Hueneme	CA	93043	**888-484-3372**	805-982-1393	654
Facility Group Inc 2233 Lake Pk Dr Suite 100	Smyrna	GA	30080	**800-525-2463**	770-437-2700	185
Facility Solutions Group 4401 Westgate Blvd Suite 310	Austin	TX	78704	**800-854-6465**		245
Facing History & Ourselves National Foundation Inc 16 Hurd Rd	Brookline	MA	02445	**800-856-9039**	617-232-1595	48-11
Factiva PO Box 300 *Cust Svc	Princeton	NJ	08543	**800-369-7466***	609-627-2000	623-10
Factory 2-U Stores Inc 4000 Ruffin Rd	San Diego	CA	92123	**877-443-2286**	858-627-1800	155-2
Factory Air Conditioning Corp 330 Culebra Rd	San Antonio	TX	78201	**800-487-1037**	210-732-9984	15
Factory Mutual Insurance Co 1301 Atwood Ave	Johnston	RI	02919	**800-343-7722**	401-275-3000	384-4
Facts & Comparisons Inc 77 W Port Plaza Suite 450	Saint Louis	MO	63146	**800-223-0554**	314-216-2100	623-10
Facts on File Inc 132 W 31st St 17th Fl *Cust Svc	New York	NY	10001	**800-322-8755***	212-967-8800	623-2
FactSet Research Systems Inc 1 Greenwich Plaza 2nd Fl *NYSE: FDS*	Greenwich	CT	06830	**877-322-8738**	203-863-1500	396
Faegre & Benson LLP 90 S 7th St Suite 20 Wells Fargo Bldg	Minneapolis	MN	55402	**800-328-4393**	612-766-7000	419
FAFSA (Free Application for Federal Student Aid) US Dept of Education 400 Maryland Ave SW	Washington	DC	20202	**800-433-3243**	319-337-5665	711
FAG Bearings Corp 200 Park Ave	Danbury	CT	06810	**800-243-7512**	203-790-5474	77
Fagan Co 3125 Brinkerhoff Rd	Kansas City	KS	66115	**800-966-1178**	913-621-4444	188-10
Fahlgren Inc 414 Walnut St Suite 1006	Cincinnati	OH	45202	**800-543-2663**	513-241-9200	4
Failing George E Co 2215 S Van Buren St	Enid	OK	73701	**800-759-7441**	580-234-4141	526
FAIR (Federation for American Immigration Reform) 1666 Connecticut Ave NW Suite 400	Washington	DC	20009	**877-627-3247**	202-328-7004	48-7
Fair Grounds Corp 1751 Gentilly Blvd	New Orleans	LA	70119	**800-786-0010**	504-944-5515	628
Fair Hills Resort 24270 County Hwy 20	Detroit Lakes	MN	56501	**800-323-2849**	218-847-7638	655
Fair Isaac Corp 200 Smith Ranch Rd *NYSE: FIC*	San Rafael	CA	94903	**800-444-5850**	415-472-2211	223
Fair-Rite Products Corp 1 Commerical Row PO Box J	Wallkill	NY	12589	**888-324-7748**	845-895-2055	248
Fairbank Richard D 1680 Capital One Dr Fndr/Chm/CEO Capital One Financial	McLean	VA	22102	**800-801-1164**	703-720-1000	561
Fairbanks Convention & Visitors Bureau 550 1st Ave	Fairbanks	AK	99701	**800-327-5774**	907-456-5774	205
Fairbanks Hospital 8102 Clearvista Pkwy	Indianapolis	IN	46256	**800-225-4673**	317-849-8222	712
Fairbanks Hotel 517 3rd Ave	Fairbanks	AK	99701	**888-329-4685**	907-456-6411	373
Fairbanks Morse Engine EnPro Industries Inc 701 White Ave	Beloit	WI	53511	**800-356-6955**	608-364-4411	259
Fairbanks Princess Riverside Lodge 4477 Pikes Landing Rd	Fairbanks	AK	99709	**800-426-0500**	907-455-4477	373
Fairbanks Scales Inc 821 Locust St	Kansas City	MO	64106	**800-451-4107**	816-471-0231	672
Fairchild Auto-mated Parts Inc 10 White St	Winsted	CT	06098	**800-927-2545**	860-379-2725	610
Fairchild Dornier Inc 10823 NE Entrance Rd	San Antonio	TX	78216	**800-327-2313**	210-824-2313	63
Fairchild Industrial Products Co 3920 West Point Blvd	Winston-Salem	NC	27103	**800-423-1093**	336-659-3400	200
Fairchild Publications Inc 7 W 34th St 3rd Fl	New York	NY	10001	**800-289-0273**	212-630-4000	623-9
Fairchild Semiconductor Corp 333 Western Ave *NYSE: FCS*	South Portland	ME	04106	**800-341-0392**	207-775-8100	686
Fairfax Hospital 10200 NE 132nd St	Kirkland	WA	98034	**800-435-7221**	425-821-2000	366-3
Fairfax Sand & Crushed Stone Co 8490 Garrett Hwy	Oakland	MD	21550	**800-325-8663**	301-334-8101	493-4
Fairfield County Business Journal 3 Gannett Dr Suite G7	White Plains	NY	10604	**800-784-4564**	914-694-3600	449-5
Fairfield Engineering Co Inc PO Box 526	Marion	OH	43302	**800-827-3364**	740-387-3327	462
Fairfield Industries Inc 14100 Southwest Frwy Suite 600	Sugar Land	TX	77478	**800-231-9809**	281-275-7500	464
Fairfield Inn by Marriott 1 Marriott Dr	Washington	DC	20058	**800-228-9290**	301-380-3000	369
Fairfield Ledger 112 E Broadway	Fairfield	IA	52556	**800-369-0340**	641-472-4129	522-2
Fairfield Line Inc 605 W Stone PO Box 500	Fairfield	IA	52556	**800-247-3383**	641-472-3191	153-8
Fairfield Medical Center 401 N Ewing St	Lancaster	OH	43130	**800-548-2627**	740-687-8000	366-2
Fairfield Ocean Ridge Resort 1 King Cotton Rd	Edisto Beach	SC	29438	**877-296-6335**	843-869-2561	655
Fairfield Processing Corp PO Box 1157	Danbury	CT	06813	**800-980-8000**	203-744-2090	594-1
Fairfield Resorts Inc 8427 S Park Cir *Cust Svc	Orlando	FL	32819	**800-251-8736***	407-370-5200	738
Fairhaven 7200 3rd Ave	Sykesville	MD	21784	**800-241-9997**	410-795-8800	659
Fairlane Town Center 18900 Michigan Ave	Dearborn	MI	48126	**800-992-9500**	313-593-3330	452
Fairleigh Dickinson University 285 Madison Ave	Madison	NJ	07940	**800-338-8803**	973-593-8500	163
Metropolitan Campus 1000 River Rd	Teaneck	NJ	07666	**800-338-8803**	201-692-2000	160
Fairman Drilling Co PO Box 288	Du Bois	PA	15801	**800-225-6540**	814-371-8410	529
Fairmont Algonquin 184 Adolphus St	Saint Andrews	NB	E5B1T7	**800-441-1414**	506-529-8823	655
Fairmont Banff Springs PO Box 960	Banff	AB	T1L1J4	**800-441-1414**	403-762-2211	655
Fairmont Chateau Lake Louise 111 Lake Louise Dr	Lake Louise	AB	T0L1E0	**800-441-1414**	403-522-3511	655
Fairmont Le Chateau Montebello 392 rue Notre Dame	Montebello	QC	J0V1L0	**800-441-1414**	819-423-6341	655
Fairmont Chateau Whistler 4599 Chateau Blvd	Whistler	BC	V0N1B4	**800-441-1414**	604-938-8000	655
Fairmont Convention & Visitors Bureau PO Box 976	Fairmont	MN	56031	**800-657-3280**	507-235-8585	205
Fairmont Corp 2245 W Pershing Rd	Chicago	IL	60609	**800-621-6907**	773-376-1300	590

Listing	City	State	ZIP	Toll-Free	Phone	Class
Fairmont Foods of Minnesota 905 E 4th St	Fairmont	MN	56031	**800-432-4411**	507-238-9001	291-36
Fairmont Hot Springs Resort 1500 Fairmont Rd	Fairmont	MT	59711	**800-332-3272**	406-797-3241	655
Fairmont Hotels & Resorts Inc 100 Wellington St W TD Centre Suite 1600 *NYSE: FHR*	Toronto	ON	M5K1B7	**800-866-5577**	416-874-2600	369
Fairmont Jasper Park Lodge 1 Lodge Rd	Jasper	AB	T0E1E0	**800-441-1414**	780-852-3301	655
Fairmont Kea Lani Maui 4100 Wailea Alanui Dr	Maui	HI	96753	**800-659-4100**	808-875-4100	655
Fairmont Orchid Hawaii 1 N Kaniku Dr	Kohala	HI	96743	**800-845-9905**	808-885-2000	655
Fairmont President's Club 650 California St 12th Fl	San Francisco	CA	94108	**800-663-7575**	415-772-7800	371
Fairmont Products Inc 15 Kishacoquillas St	Belleville	PA	17004	**800-525-9338**	717-935-2121	291-27
Fairmont Scottsdale Princess 7575 E Princess Dr	Scottsdale	AZ	85255	**800-344-4758**	480-585-4848	655
Fairmont Sonoma Mission Inn & Spa 100 Boyes Blvd PO Box 1447	Boyes Hot Springs	CA	95416	**800-862-4945**	707-938-9000	655
Fairmont State College 1201 Locust Ave	Fairmont	WV	26554	**800-641-5678**	304-367-4000	163
Fairmont Supply Co 401 Technology Dr	Canonsburg	PA	15317	**800-245-9900**	724-514-3900	378
Fairmont Vacation Villas PO Box 127 *Resv	Fairmont Hot Springs	BC	V0B1L0	**800-663-6333***	250-345-6321	738
Fairmount The - A Wyndham Historic Hotel 401 S Alamo St	San Antonio	TX	78205	**800-996-3426**	210-224-8800	373
Fairmount Behavioral Health System 561 Fairthorne St	Philadelphia	PA	19128	**800-235-0200**	215-487-4000	366-3
Fairmount Turnberry Isle Resort & Club 19999 W Country Club Dr	Aventura	FL	33180	**800-327-7028**	305-932-6200	655
FairPoint Communications Inc 521 E Morehead St Suite 250 *NYSE: FRP*	Charlotte	NC	28202	**888-235-3242**	704-344-8150	721
Fairs & Expositions. International Assn of 3043 E Cairo	Springfield	MO	65802	**800-516-0313**	417-862-5771	48-23
Fairview General Hospital 18101 Lorain Ave	Cleveland	OH	44111	**800-323-8434**	216-476-7000	366-2
Fairview Hospice 2450 26th Ave S	Minneapolis	MN	55406	**800-285-5647**	612-728-2380	365
Fairview Hospital & Healthcare Services 2450 Riverside Ave S	Minneapolis	MN	55454	**800-328-4661**	612-672-6000	348
Fairview-University Medical Center University Campus 420 Delaware St SE	Minneapolis	MN	55455	**800-688-5252**	612-273-3000	366-2
Fairwind Air Charter 2555 SE Dixie Hwy	Stuart	FL	34996	**800-989-9665**	772-288-4130	14
Fairwinds Federal Credit Union 3075 N Alafaya Trail	Orlando	FL	32826	**800-443-6887**	407-277-5045	216
Fairwinds Schooner Cove Resort & Marina 3521 Dolphin Dr	Nanoose Bay	BC	V9P9J7	**800-663-7060**	250-468-7691	655
Faith Popcorn's BrainReserve 59 E 64th St	New York	NY	10021	**800-873-6337**	212-772-7778	194
FaithTrust Institute 2400 N 45th St Suite 10	Seattle	WA	98103	**877-860-2255**	206-634-1903	48-17
Falcon Business Forms Inc PO Box 326	Corsicana	TX	75151	**800-442-6262**	903-874-6583	111
Falcon Financial Investment Trust 15 Commerce Rd	Stamford	CT	06902	**800-771-5400**	203-967-0000	640
Falcon Foam Div Atlas Roofing 8240 Byron Center Rd SW	Byron Center	MI	49315	**800-917-9138**	616-878-1568	589
Falcon Foundry Co 96 6th St	Lowellville	OH	44436	**800-253-8624**	330-536-6221	303
Falcon Products Inc 9387 Dielman Industrial Dr	Saint Louis	MO	63132	**800-873-3252**	314-991-9200	314-1
Falk Corp 3001 W Canal St	Milwaukee	WI	53208	**800-852-3255**	414-342-3131	700
Falken Tire Corp 10404 6th St	Rancho Cucamonga	CA	91730	**800-723-2553**	909-466-1116	740
Fall River Rural Electric Co-op Inc 1150 N 3400 East	Ashton	ID	83420	**800-632-5726**	208-652-7431	244
Fallbrook Hospital District 624 E Elder St	Fallbrook	CA	92028	**800-647-6464**	760-728-1191	366-2
Fallon 50 S 6th St Suite 2500	Minneapolis	MN	55402	**888-321-2345**	612-321-2345	4
Falmouth Chamber of Commerce 20 Academy Ln	Falmouth	MA	02540	**800-526-8532**	508-548-8500	137
False Claims Act Legal Center 1220 19th St NW Suite 501	Washington	DC	20036	**800-873-2573**	202-296-4826	49-10
Famfare Media Works Inc 25300 Rye Canyon Rd	Valencia	CA	91355	**800-935-0090**	661-257-4000	623-9
Families Anonymous (FA) PO Box 3475	Culver City	CA	90231	**800-736-9805**	310-815-8010	48-21
Families of Spinal Muscular Atrophy PO Box 196	Libertyville	IL	60048	**800-886-1762**	847-367-7620	48-17
Families USA 1334 G St NW Suite 300	Washington	DC	20005	**800-593-5041**	202-628-3030	48-7
Family Advocate Magazine 750 N Lake Shore Dr	Chicago	IL	60611	**800-285-2221**	312-988-5000	449-15
Family of the Americas Foundation PO Box 1170	Dunkirk	MD	20754	**800-443-3395**	301-627-3346	48-17
Family Brands International LLC PO Box 429	Lenoir City	TN	37771	**800-356-4455**	865-986-8005	291-26
Family Campers & RVers (FCRV) 4804 Transit Rd Bldg 2	Depew	NY	14043	**800-245-9755**	716-668-6242	48-23
Family Cards USA 892 Riverside St	Portland	ME	04103	**877-765-3422**	207-797-9738	130
Family Career & Community Leaders of America (FCCLA) 1910 Association Dr	Reston	VA	20191	**800-234-4425**	703-476-4900	48-11
Family Caregiver Alliance (FCA) 180 Montgomery St Suite 1100	San Francisco	CA	94104	**800-445-8106**	415-434-3388	48-17
Family Caregivers Assn. National 10400 Connecticut Ave Suite 500	Kensington	MD	20895	**800-896-3650**	301-942-6430	48-6
Family Child Care. National Assn for 5202 Pinemont Dr	Salt Lake City	UT	84123	**800-359-3817**	801-269-9338	48-6
Family & Children Services. Jewish Board of 120 W 57th St	New York	NY	10019	**888-523-2769**	212-582-9100	48-6

Listing	City	State	ZIP	Toll-Free	Phone	Class
Family Circle Magazine 375 Lexington Ave 9th Fl	New York	NY	10017	**800-627-4444**	212-499-2000	449-11
Family & Consumer Sciences. American Assn of 400 N Columbus St Suite 202	Alexandria	VA	22314	**800-424-8080**	703-706-4600	49-5
Family & Consumer Sciences Research Institute Iowa State University MacKay Hall Rm 126	Ames	IA	50011	**877-891-5349**	515-294-5982	654
Family Counselors. International Assn of Marriage & c/o American Counseling Assn 5999 Stevenson Ave	Alexandria	VA	22304	**800-545-2223**	703-823-9800	49-15
Family Farm Coalition. National 110 Maryland Ave NE Suite 307	Washington	DC	20002	**800-639-3276**	202-543-5675	48-2
Family. Focus on the 8605 Explorer Dr *Sales	Colorado Springs	CO	80920	**800-232-6459***	719-531-3400	48-6
Family Handyman Magazine Commerce Dr Suite 700	Eagan	MN	55121	**800-285-4961**	651-454-9200	449-14
Family Home Hospice 1701 W Charleston Blvd Suite 201	Las Vegas	NV	89102	**800-999-2536**	702-383-0887	365
Family Inns of America Inc PO Box 10	Pigeon Forge	TN	37868	**800-251-9752**	865-453-4988	369
Family Life Broadcasting System DBA Family Life Radio 7355 N Oracle Rd	Tucson	AZ	85704	**800-776-1070**	520-742-6976	629
Family Life Communications Inc PO Box 35300	Tucson	AZ	85740	**800-776-1070**	520-742-6976	630
Family Life Insurance Co 6500 River Place Blvd	Austin	TX	78730	**800-925-6000**	512-404-5000	384-2
Family Literacy. National Center for 325 W Main St Suite 300	Louisville	KY	40202	**877-326-5481**	502-584-1133	48-11
Family Motor Coach Assn (FMCA) 8291 Clough Pike	Cincinnati	OH	45244	**800-543-3622**	513-474-3622	48-23
Family Motor Coaching Magazine 8291 Clough Pike	Cincinnati	OH	45244	**800-543-3622**	513-474-3622	449-22
Family Pharmacy 300 Chesterfield Pkwy	Malvern	PA	19355	**877-892-1254**		237
Family Physicians. American Academy of 11400 Tomahawk Creek Pkwy	Leawood	KS	66211	**800-274-2237**	913-906-6000	49-8
Family Physicians. American College of Osteopathic 330 E Algonquin Rd Suite 1	Arlington Heights	IL	60005	**800-323-0794**	847-228-6090	49-8
Family Radio 290 Hegenberger Rd	Oakland	CA	94621	**800-543-1495**	510-568-6200	629
Family Recovery Inc 555 SW 148th Ave	Sunrise	FL	33325	**800-417-6237**	954-370-0200	712
Family Relations. National Council on 3989 Central Ave NE Suite 550	Minneapolis	MN	55421	**888-781-9331**	763-781-9331	48-6
Family Relations Newsletter PO Box 7376	Alexandria	VA	22307	**800-876-2545**	703-768-9600	521-8
Family Research Council (FRC) 801 G St NW	Washington	DC	20001	**800-225-4008**	202-393-2100	48-6
Family Sports Concepts Inc 5510 W La Salle St Suite 200	Tampa	FL	33607	**800-728-8878**	813-226-2333	656
Family Stations Radio Network 290 Hegenberger Rd	Oakland	CA	94621	**800-543-1495**	510-568-6200	629
Family.NET 5160 Timber Creek Rd	Houston	TX	77017	**888-905-0888**	713-230-2800	390
FamilyFun Magazine 114 5th Ave	New York	NY	10011	**800-829-5146**	212-633-3620	449-6
Familymeds.com Inc 312 Farmington Ave	Farmington	CT	06032	**800-203-2776**	860-676-1222	236
FamilyNet 6350 West Fwy	Fort Worth	TX	76116	**800-292-2287**	817-737-4011	725
Famous Craft Inc 7921 15th St E	Sarasota	FL	34243	**888-244-3244**	941-358-3121	91
Famous Dave's of America Inc 8091 Wallace Rd *NASDAQ: DAVE*	Eden Prairie	MN	55344	**800-210-4040**	952-294-1300	657
Famous Footwear 7010 Mineral Point Rd *Cust Svc	Madison	WI	53717	**800-888-7198***	608-829-3668	296
Fan-Tastic Vent Corp 2083 S Almont Ave	Imlay City	MI	48444	**800-521-0298**	810-724-3818	37
Fancy Feet Inc 26650 Harding St	Oak Park	MI	48237	**800-858-8460**	248-398-8460	296
Faneuil Group 1 Bridge St Suite 101	Newton	MA	02458	**800-932-6384**	617-742-4888	722
Fannie Mae 3900 Wisconsin Ave NW *NYSE: FNM*	Washington	DC	20016	**800-732-6643**	202-752-7000	498
Fannin County Electric Co-op Inc PO Drawer 250	Bonham	TX	75418	**800-695-9020**	903-583-2117	244
Fanning/Howey Assoc Inc 1200 Irmscher Blvd	Celina	OH	45822	**888-499-2292**	419-586-2292	258
Fansteel Hydro Carbide PO Box 363	Latrobe	PA	15650	**800-245-2476**	724-539-9701	745
Fantagraph Div Standard Textile Co Inc One Knollcrest Dr	Cincinnati	OH	45237	**800-888-5000**	513-761-9255	731
Fantagraphics Books 7563 Lake City Way NE	Seattle	WA	98115	**800-657-1100**	206-524-1967	623-3
Fantastic Tours & Travel 6143 Jericho Tpke	Commack	NY	11725	**800-552-6262**	631-462-6262	748
Fantasy Holidays 400 Jericho Tpke Suite 301	Jericho	NY	11753	**800-645-2555**	516-935-8500	760
Fantasy Inc 2600 10th St	Berkeley	CA	94710	**800-227-0466**	510-549-2500	643
Fantasy Springs Resort Casino 84-245 Indio Springs Pkwy	Indio	CA	92203	**800-827-2946**	760-342-5000	133
Fantasyland Hotel 17700 87th Ave West Edmonton Mall	Edmonton	AB	T5T4V4	**800-737-3783**	780-444-3000	372
Fantini Baking Co Inc 375 Washington St	Haverhill	MA	01832	**800-223-9037**	978-373-1273	291-1
Fantus Paper Products DBA PS Greetings Inc 5730 N Tripp Ave *Sales	Chicago	IL	60646	**800-621-8823***	773-267-6069	130
FANUC Robotics North America Inc 3900 W Hamlin Rd	Rochester Hills	MI	48309	**800-477-6268**	248-377-7000	379
Fanzz 1832 W 2770 South Suite 10	Salt Lake City	UT	84119	**888-326-9946**	801-325-2700	702
FAO Schwarz 767 5th Ave Suite 401	New York	NY	10153	**800-426-8697**		749
Fapco Inc 216 Post Rd	Buchanan	MI	49107	**800-782-0167**	269-695-6889	539
Far East Broadcasting Co Inc PO Box 1	La Mirada	CA	90637	**800-523-3480**	562-947-4651	629

Name / Address	City	ST	ZIP	Toll-Free	Phone	Class
Far East Capital Corp 350 S Grand Ave	Los Angeles	CA	90071	**800-753-8449**	213-687-1260	395
FAR Voice Inc 16645 W Greenfield Ave	New Berlin	WI	53154	**888-661-8885**	262-797-4550	176-7
Far West Regional Technology Transfer Center South Hope St Research Annex 3716 Rm 200	Los Angeles	CA	90007	**800-642-2872**	213-743-2353	654
Faraday LLC 805 S Maumee St	Tecumseh	MI	49286	**800-465-7115**	517-423-2111	681
Farber Plastics Inc 162 Hanse Ave	Freeport	NY	11520	**800-338-6315**	516-378-4860	589
Farberware Div Lifetime Hoan Corp 1 Merrick Ave	Westbury	NY	11590	**800-252-3390**	516-683-6000	477
Fargo Electronics Inc 6533 Flying Cloud Dr *NASDAQ: FRGO*	Eden Prairie	MN	55344	**800-327-4622**	952-941-9470	171-6
Fargo Glass & Paint Co Inc 1801 7th Ave N	Fargo	ND	58102	**800-437-4612**	701-235-4441	190-2
Fargo-Moorhead Community Theatre 333 4th St S	Fargo	ND	58103	**877-687-7469**	701-235-6778	563-4
Fargo-Moorhead Convention & Visitors Bureau 2001 44th St SW	Fargo	ND	58103	**800-235-7654**	701-282-3653	205
Faria Thomas G Corp 385 Norwich-New London Tpke	Uncasville	CT	06382	**800-473-2742**	860-848-9271	486
Faribault Mills PO Box 369	Faribault	MN	55021	**800-533-0444**	507-334-6444	730-1
Faris Brothers of California Inc 12801 Arroyo St	Sylmar	CA	91342	**800-433-2747**	818-898-2377	153-15
Farm Aid 11 Ward St Suite 200	Somerville	MA	02143	**800-327-6243**	617-354-2922	48-5
Farm Boy Meats PO Box 996	Evansville	IN	47706	**800-852-3976**	812-425-5231	465
Farm Bureau Life Insurance Co 5400 University Ave	West Des Moines	IA	50266	**800-247-4170**	515-225-5400	384-2
Farm & City Insurance Co PO Box 712	Des Moines	IA	50303	**800-362-2296**	515-362-7600	384-4
Farm Coalition. National Family 110 Maryland Ave NE Suite 307	Washington	DC	20002	**800-639-3276**	202-543-5675	48-2
Farm Credit Leasing 5500 Wayzata Blvd Colonnade Bldg Suite 1600	Minneapolis	MN	55416	**800-328-8863**	763-797-7400	214
Farm Family Casualty Insurance Co PO Box 656	Albany	NY	12201	**800-843-3276**	518-431-5000	384-4
Farm Family Holdings Inc PO Box 656 *Cust Svc	Albany	NY	12201	**800-843-3276***	518-431-5000	355-4
Farm Family Life Insurance Co PO Box 656	Albany	NY	12201	**800-948-3276**	518-431-5000	384-2
Farm & Home Oil Co PO Box 389	Telford	PA	18969	**800-473-1562**	215-257-0131	311
Farm Implement & Supply Co Inc 520 W Mill St	Plainville	KS	67663	**888-589-6029**	785-434-4824	270
Farm Industry News 7900 International Dr Suite 300 *Cust Svc	Minneapolis	MN	55425	**800-441-0294***	952-851-9329	449-1
Farm Journal 1818 Market St 31st Fl	Philadelphia	PA	19103	**800-523-1538**	215-557-8900	449-1
Farm Progress Co Inc 191 S Gary Ave	Carol Stream	IL	60188	**800-441-1410**	630-690-5600	623-9
Farm & Ranch Living Magazine 5400 S 60th St	Greendale	WI	53129	**800-344-6913**	414-423-0100	449-1
Farm Service Co-op 2308 Pine St	Harlan	IA	51537	**800-452-4372**	712-755-3185	272
Farm Service Elevator Co 3735 County Rd 5 SW	Willmar	MN	56201	**800-328-8842**	320-235-8870	438
Farm Show Magazine PO Box 1029	Lakeville	MN	55044	**800-834-9665**	952-469-5572	449-1
Farm Stores 5800 NW 74th Ave	Miami	FL	33166	**800-726-3276**	305-471-5141	203
Farmer Boys Food Inc 3452 University Ave	Riverside	CA	92501	**800-930-3276**	951-275-9900	657
Farmer Brothers Co 20333 S Normandie Ave *NASDAQ: FARM*	Torrance	CA	90502	**800-735-3226**	310-787-5200	291-7
Farmer EL & Co PO Box 3512	Odessa	TX	79760	**800-592-4753**	432-332-1496	769
Farmer Jack 18718 Borman Ave	Detroit	MI	48228	**877-327-5225**	313-270-1000	339
Farmer John Meats 3049 E Vernon Ave *Sales	Los Angeles	CA	90058	**800-432-7637***	323-583-4621	465
Farmer Mac (Federal Agricultural Mortgage Corp) 1133 21st St NW Suite 600 *NYSE: AGM*	Washington	DC	20036	**800-879-3276**	202-872-7700	498
Farmers Alliance Mutual Insurance Co PO Box 1401	McPherson	KS	67460	**800-362-1075**	620-241-2200	384-4
Farmers Automobile Insurance Assn 2505 Court St	Pekin	IL	61558	**800-322-0160**	309-346-1161	384-4
Farmers Casualty Insurance Co PO Box 65150	West Des Moines	IA	50265	**800-666-3226**	515-223-9438	384-4
Farmer's Co-op 201 E Orin St	Gordon	NE	69343	**800-252-0898**	308-282-0898	438
Farmers Co-op Assn 105 Jackson St	Jackson	MN	56143	**800-864-3847**	507-847-4160	272
Farmers Co-op Co 105 Garfield Ave	Farnhamville	IA	50538	**800-642-6815**	515-544-3213	271
Farmers Co-op Dairy Inc 104 Rotary Dr *Cust Svc	West Hazleton	PA	18202	**800-548-8787***	570-453-0203	291-27
Farmers Co-op Oil Co 6th & Logan	Newman Grove	NE	68758	**800-898-6292**	402-447-6292	272
Farmers Co-op Shipping Assn PO Box 250	Clifton	KS	66937	**800-562-4203**	785-455-3315	307
Farmers Co-op Supply & Shipping Assn 570 Commerce St	West Salem	WI	54669	**800-657-5189**	608-786-1100	272
Farmers Cooperative Elevator Co 208 W Depot	Dorchester	NE	68343	**800-642-6439**	402-946-2211	271
Farmers Educational & Cooperative Union of America 11900 E Cornell Ave	Aurora	CO	80014	**800-347-1961**	303-337-5500	48-2
Farmers Electric Co-op Corp PO Box 708	Newport	AR	72112	**800-834-9055**	870-523-3691	244
Farmers Electric Co-op Inc 1959 Yoder Ave SW	Kalona	IA	52247	**877-426-6540**	319-683-2510	244
Farmers' Electric Co-op Inc PO Box 680	Chillicothe	MO	64601	**800-279-0496**	660-646-4281	244
Farmers Electric Co-op Inc PO Box 6037	Greenville	TX	75403	**800-541-2662**	903-455-1715	244
Farmers First Bank 24 N Cedar St	Lititz	PA	17543	**800-311-3182**	717-626-4735	71
Farmers Furniture 2005 Veterans Blvd Suite 1	Dublin	GA	31040	**800-456-0424**	478-272-4000	316
Farmers Insurance Exchange 4680 Wilshire Blvd	Los Angeles	CA	90010	**888-516-5656**	323-932-3200	384-4
Farmers Livestock Marketing Assn 840 IL Rt 127 PO Box 435	Greenville	IL	62246	**800-743-9110**	618-664-1432	437
Farmers & Mechanics Bank 110 Thomas Johnson Dr	Frederick	MD	21702	**800-445-3626**	301-694-4000	71
Farmers & Mechanics Bank 3 Sunset Rd	Burlington	NJ	08016	**800-523-4175**	609-386-2400	71
Farmers Mutual Hail Insurance Co of Iowa 2323 Grand Ave	Des Moines	IA	50312	**800-247-5248**	515-282-9104	384-4
Farmers Mutual Insurance Co of Nebraska 1220 Lincoln Mall	Lincoln	NE	68508	**800-742-7433**	402-434-8300	384-4
Farmers Organization. National 528 Billy Sunday Rd Suite 100	Ames	IA	50010	**800-247-2110**	515-292-2000	48-2
Farmers Rice Co-op PO Box 15223	Sacramento	CA	95851	**800-326-2799**	916-923-5100	291-23
Farmers Rural Electric Co-op Corp PO Box 1298	Glasgow	KY	42141	**800-253-2191**	270-651-2191	244
Farmers Rural Electric Co-op Inc 102 SE 6th St	Greenfield	IA	50849	**800-397-4821**	641-743-6146	244
Farmers Telephone Co-op Inc 1101 E Main St	Kingstree	SC	29556	**888-218-5050**	843-382-2333	721
Farmers & Traders Life Insurance Co 960 James St PO Box 1056	Syracuse	NY	13201	**800-347-0960**	315-471-5656	384-2
Farmers Union Mutual Insurance Co PO Box 2020	Jamestown	ND	58402	**800-366-6338**	701-252-2701	384-4
Farmers Union Oil Co of Kenmare Hwy 52 S PO Box 726 *Cust Svc	Kenmare	ND	58746	**800-342-4418***	701-385-4277	311
Farmhouse Spa at Blackberry Farm 1471 W Millers Cove Rd	Walland	TN	37886	**800-273-6004**	865-379-9819	698
Farming Technology Corp 6950 Neuhaus St	Houston	TX	77061	**800-395-2004**	713-923-5807	11-11
Farmingdale State University 2350 Broad Hollow Rd	Farmingdale	NY	11735	**877-432-7646**	631-420-2000	160
Farmington Chamber of Commerce 105 N Orchard Ave	Farmington	NM	87401	**888-325-0279**	505-325-0279	137
Farmington Convention & Visitors Bureau 3041 E Main St	Farmington	NM	87402	**800-448-1240**	505-326-7602	205
Farmland Dairies LLC 520 Main Ave	Wallington	NJ	07057	**800-275-4645**	973-777-2500	291-27
Farmland Foods Inc 7501 NW Tiffany Springs Pkey	Kansas City	MO	64153	**888-327-6526**	816-801-4300	291-26
Farmland Industries Inc 12200 N Ambassador Dr	Kansas City	MO	64163	**800-821-8000**	816-713-7000	438
Farmland Mutual Insurance Co 1100 Locust St Dept 3010	Des Moines	IA	50391	**800-228-6700**	515-280-4211	384-4
Farmland Trust. American 1200 18th St NW Suite 800	Washington	DC	20036	**800-431-1499**	202-331-7300	48-2
Farmstead Telephone Group Inc 22 Prestige Park Cir *AMEX: FTG*	East Hartford	CT	06108	**800-243-0234**	860-282-0010	245
Farmway Co-op Inc 204 E Court St	Beloit	KS	67420	**800-748-7038**	785-738-2241	272
Farnam Cos Inc PO Box 34820	Phoenix	AZ	85067	**800-234-2269**	602-285-1660	574
Farner-Bocken Co 1751 US Hwy 30 E	Carroll	IA	51401	**800-274-8692**	712-792-3503	744
FARO Technologies Inc 125 Technology Pk *NASDAQ: FARO*	Lake Mary	FL	32746	**800-736-0234**	407-333-9911	464
Farrell Louis E Co Inc 20 Karen Dr	South Burlington	VT	05403	**800-473-7741**	802-864-6000	82-2
Farrens Tree Service 708 Blair Mill Rd	Willow Grove	PA	19090	**800-248-8733**	215-784-4200	765
Farwest Homes PO Box 480	Chehalis	WA	98532	**800-752-0500**	360-748-3351	107
Farwest Steel Corp 2000 Henderson Ave	Eugene	OR	97403	**800-542-5091**	541-686-2000	483
FASEB (Federation of American Societies for Experimental Biology) 9650 Rockville Pike	Bethesda	MD	20814	**800-433-2732**	301-530-7000	49-19
Fashion Institute of Design & Merchandising 919 S Grand Ave *Admissions	Los Angeles	CA	90015	**800-421-0127***	213-624-1200	159
San Francisco 55 Stockton St	San Francisco	CA	94108	**800-422-3436**	415-675-5200	159
Fashion Institute of Technology 227 W 27th St	New York	NY	10001	**800-468-6348**	212-217-7650	163
Fashion Island Shopping Center 401 Newport Ctr Dr	Newport Beach	CA	92660	**800-495-4753**	949-721-2000	452
Fashion Newsletter 9700 Philadelphia Ct	Lanham	MD	20706	**800-345-2611**	301-731-5200	521-13
Fashion Tech Inc 2010 SE 8th Ave	Portland	OR	97214	**800-444-8822**	503-238-0666	88
Fashion Wallcoverings 2040 W 110th St *Orders	Cleveland	OH	44102	**800-362-9930***	216-631-6700	789
FAST (Food Automation-Service Techniques Inc) 905 Honeyspot Rd	Stratford	CT	06615	**800-327-8766**	203-377-4414	201
Fast Heat Inc 776 Oaklawn Ave	Elmhurst	IL	60126	**800-982-4328**	630-833-5400	313
Fast Search & Transfer Inc 93 Worcester St	Wellesley Hills	MA	02481	**888-871-3839**	781-304-2400	176-7
Fastcut Tool Corp 200 Front St	Millersburg	PA	17061	**800-682-8832**	717-692-2222	484
Fastec Industrial Corp 23348 County Rd 6	Elkhart	IN	46514	**800-837-2505**	574-262-2505	346
Fasteners Distributors Assn. Specialty Tools & 500 Elm Grove Rd	Elm Grove	WI	53122	**800-352-2981**	262-784-4774	49-18
Fastframe USA Inc 1200 Lawrence Dr Suite 300	Newbury Park	CA	91320	**888-863-7263**	805-498-4463	45
FASTNET Corp 3864 Courtney St Suite 130	Bethlehem	PA	18017	**888-321-3278**	610-954-5910	390
FASTSIGNS International Inc 2550 Midway Rd Suite 150	Carrollton	TX	75006	**800-827-7446**	972-447-0777	692
FastWeb Inc 444 N Michigan Ave Suite 3100	Chicago	IL	60611	**800-327-8932**	312-832-2126	711
Fata Hunter Co Inc 1040 Iowa Ave Suite 100	Riverside	CA	92507	**800-248-6837**	951-328-0200	258
Fathers & Children. American Coalition for 1420 Spring Hill Rd	McLean	VA	22102	**800-978-3237**		48-6
Faulkner Information Services 7905 Browning Rd Suite 116	Pennsauken	NJ	08109	**800-843-0460**	856-662-2070	623-11
Faulkner State Community College *Bay Minette* 1900 US Hwy 31 S	Bay Minette	AL	36507	**800-231-3752**	251-580-2100	160

Name / Address	City	State	ZIP	Toll-Free	Phone	Class
Fairhope 440 Fairhope Ave	Fairhope	AL	36532	**800-231-3752**	251-990-0420	160
Gulf Shores 3301 Gulf Shores Pkwy	Gulf Shores	AL	36542	**800-231-3752**	251-968-3101	160
Faulkner University 5345 Atlanta Hwy	Montgomery	AL	36109	**800-879-9816**	334-272-5820	163
Faultless Caster Div FKI Industries 1421 N Garvin St	Evansville	IN	47711	**800-322-9329***	812-425-1011	345
*Cust Svc						
Faultless Nutting Co Div FKI Industries 505 W Airport Dr	Watertown	SD	57201	**800-533-0337**	605-882-3000	462
Faultless Starch/Bon Ami Co 1025 W 8th St	Kansas City	MO	64101	**800-821-5565***	816-842-1230	149
*Cust Svc						
Favorite Market 1503 N Tibbs Rd	Dalton	GA	30720	**800-634-2944**	706-226-4834	203
Favorite Plastic Corp 1465 Utica Ave	Brooklyn	NY	11234	**800-221-8077***	718-253-7000	589
*Cust Svc						
Fawcette Technical Publications 2600 S El Camino Real Suite 300	San Mateo	CA	94403	**800-848-5523**	650-378-7100	623-11
Fawn Vendors Inc 8040 University Blvd	Des Moines	IA	50325	**800-247-2801**	515-274-3641	55
Fax Source 2 W Dry Creek Cir Suite 270	Littleton	CO	80210	**800-256-2753**	303-730-9396	721
Faxaway 417 2nd Ave W	Seattle	WA	98119	**800-906-4329**	206-301-7000	721
FaxBack Inc 7405 SW Tech Ctr Dr Suite 100	Tigard	OR	97223	**800-329-2225**	503-645-1114	721
FaxBond International 112 Basaltic Rd Unit 3	Concord	ON	L4K1G6	**800-263-3175**	905-669-0966	542-1
Fay Paper Products Inc PO Box 38	Norwood	MA	02062	**800-765-4620**	781-769-4620	542-3
Fay School 48 Main St	Southborough	MA	01772	**800-933-2925**	508-485-0100	611
Fay Spofford & Thorndike LLC 5 Burlington Woods	Burlington	MA	01803	**800-835-8666**	781-221-1000	258
Fayette Chamber of Commerce 65 W Main St	Uniontown	PA	15401	**800-916-9365**	724-437-4571	137
Fayette County Chamber of Commerce 310 Oyler Ave	Oak Hill	WV	25901	**800-927-0263**	304-465-5617	137
Fayette Electric Co-op Inc PO Box 490	La Grange	TX	78945	**800-874-8290**	979-968-3181	244
Fayetteville Area Convention & Visitors Bureau 245 Person St	Fayetteville	NC	28301	**800-255-8217**	910-483-5311	205
Fayetteville Electric System 408 W College St	Fayetteville	TN	37334	**800-379-2534**	931-433-1522	244
Fayetteville-Lincoln County Chamber of Commerce 208 S Elk Ave	Fayetteville	TN	37334	**888-433-1238**	931-433-1234	137
Fayetteville Observer 458 Whitfield St	Fayetteville	NC	28306	**800-345-9895**	910-323-4848	522-2
Fayetteville State University 1200 Murchison Rd	Fayetteville	NC	28301	**800-222-2594***	910-672-1111	163
*Admissions						
Fayez Sarofim & Co 2 Houston Ctr Suite 2907	Houston	TX	77010	**800-288-7125**	713-654-4484	393
Faygo Beverages Inc 3579 Gratiot Ave	Detroit	MI	48207	**800-347-6591**	313-925-1600	81-2
Fayhee John & Sons Inc 360 E Main St	Prairie City	IL	61470	**800-637-2614**	309-775-3317	270
FB Johnston Graphics 300 E Boundary St	Chapin	SC	29036	**800-800-8160**	803-345-5481	675
FBG Service Corp 407 S 27th Ave	Omaha	NE	68131	**800-777-8326**	402-346-4422	105
FBLA (Future Business Leaders of America - Phi Beta Lambda Inc) 1912 Association Dr	Reston	VA	20191	**800-325-2946**	703-860-3334	48-11
FBO Weekly Release Newsletter 11300 Rockville Pike Suite 1100	Rockville	MD	20852	**800-824-1195***	301-287-2700	521-7
*Cust Svc						
FC Haab Co Inc 2314 Market St	Philadelphia	PA	19103	**800-486-5663**	215-563-0800	311
FCA (Family Caregiver Alliance) 180 Montgomery St Suite 1100	San Francisco	CA	94104	**800-445-8106**	415-434-3388	48-17
FCA (Fellowship of Christian Athletes) 8701 Leeds Rd	Kansas City	MO	64129	**800-289-0909**	816-921-0909	48-22
FCC (Federal Communications Commission) 445 12th St SW	Washington	DC	20554	**888-225-5322**	202-418-0200	336-16
Consumer & Government Affairs Bureau 445 12th St SW	Washington	DC	20554	**888-225-5322**	202-418-1400	336-16
FCCI Insurance Group 6300 University Pkwy	Sarasota	FL	34240	**800-226-3224**	941-907-3224	384-4
FCCI Mutual Insurance Co 6300 University Pkwy	Sarasota	FL	34240	**800-226-3224**	941-907-3224	384-4
FCCLA (Family Career & Community Leaders of America) 1910 Association Dr	Reston	VA	20191	**800-234-4425**	703-476-4900	48-11
FCN Publishing 1725 K St NW Suite 506	Washington	DC	20006	**888-732-7070**	202-887-6320	623-9
FCRV (Family Campers & RVers) 4804 Transit Rd Bldg 2	Depew	NY	14043	**800-245-9755**	716-668-6242	48-23
FCx Performance Inc 3000 E 14th Ave	Columbus	OH	43219	**800-253-6223**	614-253-1996	378
FD Lawrence Electric Co Inc 3450 Beekman St	Cincinnati	OH	45223	**800-582-4490***	513-542-1100	245
*Cust Svc						
FD Stella Products Co 7000 Fenkell St	Detroit	MI	48238	**800-447-7356**	313-341-6400	378
FDC Corp 360 Bonnie Ln	Elk Grove Village	IL	60007	**800-848-5622**	847-437-3990	113
FDC Reports Inc 5550 Friendship Blvd Suite 1	Chevy Chase	MD	20815	**800-332-1370**	301-657-9830	623-9
FDIC (Federal Deposit Insurance Corp) 550 17th St NW	Washington	DC	20429	**877-375-3342**	202-898-6947	336-16
FDLI (Food & Drug Law Institute) 1000 Vermont Ave NW Suite 200	Washington	DC	20005	**800-956-6293**	202-371-1420	49-10
FDN Communications 2301 Lucien Way Suite 200	Maitland	FL	32751	**877-225-5336**	407-835-0300	721
Fear. Freedom From 308 Seaview Ave	Staten Island	NY	10305	**888-442-2022**	718-351-1717	48-17
Feather River College 570 Golden Eagle Ave	Quincy	CA	95971	**800-442-9799**	530-283-0202	160
Featherlite Inc PO Box 320	Cresco	IA	52136	**800-800-1230**	563-547-6000	768
NASDAQ: FTHR						
Featherlite Luxury Coaches Inc 4441 Orange Blvd	Sanford	FL	32771	**888-826-8273**	407-323-1120	505

Name / Address	City	State	ZIP	Toll-Free	Phone	Class
Fechheimer Brothers Co Inc 4545 Malsbary Rd	Cincinnati	OH	45242	**800-543-1939**	513-793-5400	153-19
Fedco Systems Co Super Grain Div PO Box 769	Sidney	OH	45365	**800-922-6641**	937-492-4158	293
Fedder RP Corp 1237 E Main St	Rochester	NY	14609	**800-288-1660**	585-288-1600	19
Federal Action Affecting the States Newsletter PO Box 7376	Alexandria	VA	22307	**800-876-2545**	703-768-9600	521-7
Federal Agricultural Mortgage Corp (Farmer Mac) 1133 21st St NW Suite 600	Washington	DC	20036	**800-879-3276**	202-872-7700	498
NYSE: AGM						
Federal APD Inc 42775 Nine-Mile Rd	Novi	MI	48375	**800-521-9330**	248-374-9600	681
Federal Assistance Monitor Newsletter 8204 Fenton St	Silver Spring	MD	20910	**800-666-6380**	301-588-6380	521-7
Federal Aviation Administration (FAA) 800 Independence Ave SW	Washington	DC	20591	**800-322-7873**	202-267-3484	336-13
Safety Hotline	Washington	DC	20591	**800-255-1111**		336-13
Federal Block Corp 247 Walsh Ave	New Windsor	NY	12553	**800-724-1999**	845-561-4108	181
Federal Bureau of Prisons National Institute of Corrections 1860 Industrial Cir Suite A	Longmont	CO	80501	**800-877-1461**	303-682-0213	336-10
Federal Cartridge Co 900 Ehlen Dr	Anoka	MN	55303	**800-322-2342**	763-323-2300	279
Federal Citizen Information Center 201 W 8th St	Pueblo	CO	81003	**888-878-3256**	719-948-3334	336-16
Federal Communications Commission (FCC) 445 12th St SW	Washington	DC	20554	**888-225-5322**	202-418-0200	336-16
Consumer & Government Affairs Bureau 445 12th St SW	Washington	DC	20554	**888-225-5322**	202-418-1400	336-16
Federal Computer Market Report 1150 Connecticut Ave NW Suite 900	Washington	DC	20036	**888-739-8500**	202-862-4375	521-7
Federal Credit Unions. National Assn of 3138 10th St N	Arlington	VA	22201	**800-336-4644**	703-522-4770	49-2
Federal Deposit Insurance Corp (FDIC) 550 17th St NW	Washington	DC	20429	**877-375-3342**	202-898-6947	336-16
Federal Deposit Insurance Corp Regional Offices						
Atlanta Regional Office 10 10th St NE Suite 800	Atlanta	GA	30309	**800-765-3342**		336-16
Chicago Regional Office 500 W Monroe St Suite 330	Chicago	IL	60661	**800-944-5343**	312-382-7500	336-16
Dallas Regional Office 1910 Pacific Ave 2nd Fl	Dallas	TX	75201	**800-568-9161**	972-761-2092	336-16
Kansas City Regional Office 2345 Grand Blvd	Kansas City	MO	64108	**800-334-9593**	816-234-8000	336-16
New York Regional Office 20 Exchange Pl Rm 6014	New York	NY	10005	**800-334-9593**	917-320-2500	336-16
San Francisco Regional Office 25 Ecker St Suite 2300	San Francisco	CA	94105	**800-756-3558**	415-546-0160	336-16
Federal Election Commission 999 'E' St NW	Washington	DC	20463	**800-424-9530**	202-694-1100	336-16
Federal Emergency Management Agency (FEMA) 500 C St SW	Washington	DC	20472	**800-462-9029**	202-646-4600	336-7
National Flood Insurance Program 500 C St SW	Washington	DC	20472	**800-427-4661**	202-646-2500	336-7
Federal Employees. National Assn of Retired 606 N Washington St	Alexandria	VA	22314	**800-627-3394**	703-838-7760	604
Federal Express Corp DBA FedEx Express PO Box 727	Memphis	TN	38194	**800-463-3339**	901-369-3600	536
Federal Flange 4014 Pinemont St	Houston	TX	77018	**800-231-0150**	713-681-0606	474
Federal Foam Technologies Inc 600 Wisconsin Dr	New Richmond	WI	54017	**800-898-9559**	715-246-9500	590
Federal Forge Inc 2807 S ML King Jr Blvd	Lansing	MI	48910	**800-968-2932**	517-393-5300	474
Federal Fruit & Produce Co 1890 E 58th Ave	Denver	CO	80216	**800-621-7166**	303-292-1303	292-7
Federal Highway Administration (FHWA) National Highway Institute 4600 N Fairfax Dr	Arlington	VA	22203	**877-558-6873**	703-235-0500	336-13
Federal Home Loan Bank						
Atlanta 1475 Peachtree St NE	Atlanta	GA	30309	**800-536-9650**	404-888-8000	336-16
Cincinnati 221 E 4th St Suite 1000 PO Box 598	Cincinnati	OH	45201	**888-852-6500**	513-852-7500	336-16
Des Moines 907 Walnut St	Des Moines	IA	50309	**800-544-0200**	515-281-1000	336-16
Pittsburgh 601 Grant St	Pittsburgh	PA	15219	**800-288-3400**	412-288-3400	336-16
San Francisco 600 California St Suite 300 PO Box 7948	San Francisco	CA	94120	**800-283-0700**	415-616-1000	336-16
Seattle 1501 4th Ave 19th Fl	Seattle	WA	98101	**800-283-0700**	206-340-2300	336-16
Federal Home Loan Mortgage Corp 8200 Jones Branch Dr	McLean	VA	22102	**800-373-3343**	703-903-3000	498
NYSE: FRE						
Federal Housing Administration (FHA) 451 7th St SW Suite 9100	Washington	DC	20410	**800-767-7460**	202-708-3600	336-8
Federal Industries Div Standex Corp 215 Federal Ave PO Box 290	Belleville	WI	53508	**800-356-4206**	608-424-3331	650
Federal Insurance Co 15 Mountain View Rd	Warren	NJ	07059	**800-252-4670**	908-903-2000	384-4
Federal International Inc 7935 Clayton Rd	Saint Louis	MO	63117	**800-972-7277**	314-721-3377	646
Federal Laboratories. Defense Technology / 13386 International Pkwy	Jacksonville	FL	32218	**800-773-3832**	904-741-5400	279
Federal Machine Corp 8040 University Blvd	Des Moines	IA	50325	**800-247-2446**	515-274-1555	55
Federal-Mogul Corp 26555 Northwestern Hwy	Southfield	MI	48034	**800-560-1400***	248-354-7700	60
*Cust Svc						
Federal Motor Carrier Safety Administration (FMCSA) 400 7th St SW	Washington	DC	20590	**888-832-5660**	202-366-2519	336-13
Federal News Services 1000 Vermont Ave NW 5th Fl	Washington	DC	20005	**800-221-4020**	202-347-1400	520
Federal Railroad Administration Regional Offices						
Region 3 61 Forsyth St SW Suite 16T20	Atlanta	GA	30303	**800-724-5993**	404-562-3800	336-13
Region 6 901 Locust St Suite 464	Kansas City	MO	64106	**800-724-5996**	816-329-3840	336-13

Name / Address	City	State	ZIP	Toll-Free	Phone	Class
Federal Realty Investment Trust 1626 E Jefferson St	Rockville	MD	20852	**800-658-8980**	301-998-8100	641
NYSE: FRT						
Federal Research Corp 1030 15th St NW Suite 920	Washington	DC	20005	**800-846-3190**	202-783-2700	621
Federal Research Report 8737 Colesville Rd Suite 1100	Silver Spring	MD	20910	**800-274-6737**	301-587-6300	521-4
Federal Reserve Bank of Atlanta New Orleans Branch 525 St Charles Ave PO Box 61630	New Orleans	LA	70161	**800-562-9023**	504-593-3200	72
Federal Reserve Bank of Cleveland 1455 E 6th St PO Box 6387	Cleveland	OH	44101	**888-333-2538**	216-579-2000	72
Cincinnati Branch 150 E 4th St PO Box 45201	Cincinnati	OH	43229	**800-432-1343**	513-721-4787	72
Columbus Branch 965 Kingsmill Pkwy PO Box 16541	Columbus	OH	43216	**800-333-2439**	614-846-7055	72
Pittsburgh Branch 717 Grant St PO Box 867	Pittsburgh	PA	15230	**888-333-7488**	412-261-7800	72
Federal Reserve Bank of Dallas 2200 N Pearl St PO Box 655906	Dallas	TX	75265	**800-333-4460**	214-922-6000	72
Federal Reserve Bank of Kansas City 925 Grand Blvd	Kansas City	MO	64198	**800-333-1010**	816-881-2000	72
Denver Branch 1020 16th St	Denver	CO	80202	**800-333-1020**	303-572-2300	72
Oklahoma City Branch 226 Dean A McGee Ave PO Box 25129	Oklahoma City	OK	73125	**800-333-1030**	405-270-8400	72
Omaha Branch 2201 Farnam St PO Box 3958	Omaha	NE	68103	**800-333-1040**	402-221-5500	72
Federal Reserve Bank of Minneapolis 90 Hennepin Ave PO Box 291	Minneapolis	MN	55480	**800-553-9656**	612-204-5000	72
Federal Reserve Bank of New York Buffalo Branch 160 Delaware Ave	Buffalo	NY	14202	**800-234-2931**	716-849-5000	72
Federal Reserve Bank of Richmond Charleston Branch 1200 Airport Rd PO Box 2309	Charleston	WV	25328	**800-642-8587**	304-353-6100	72
Federal Reserve Bank of Saint Louis 411 Locust St PO Box 442	Saint Louis	MO	63166	**800-333-0810**	314-444-8444	72
Federal Reserve Bank of San Francisco 101 Market St PO Box 7702	San Francisco	CA	94120	**800-227-4133**	415-974-2000	72
Los Angeles Branch 950 S Grand Ave PO Box 2077	Los Angeles	CA	90051	**800-843-8123**	213-683-2300	72
Seattle Branch 1015 2nd Ave PO Box 3567	Seattle	WA	98124	**800-552-7244**	206-343-3600	72
Federal Square Suites 8781 Madison Blvd	Madison	AL	35758	**800-458-1639**	256-772-8470	373
Federal Student Aid Information Center PO Box 84	Washington	DC	20044	**800-433-3243**		711
Federal Trade Commission (FTC) 600 Pennsylvania Ave NW	Washington	DC	20580	**877-382-4357**	202-326-2222	336-16
Consumer.gov 600 Pennsylvania Ave NW	Washington	DC	20580	**877-382-4357**	202-326-2222	336-16
National Do Not Call Registry	Washington	DC	20580	**888-382-1222**		336-16
Federal Warehouse Co 101 National Rd	East Peoria	IL	61611	**800-747-4100**	309-694-4500	790-1
Federal White Cement Ltd PO Box 548	Woodstock	ON	N4S7Y5	**800-265-1806***	519-485-5410	135
*Sales						
Federated Funds PO Box 8606	Boston	MA	02266	**800-245-4770**		517
Federated Insurance Cos PO Box 328	Owatonna	MN	55060	**800-533-0472**	507-455-5200	355-4
Federated Investors 1001 Liberty Ave Federated Investors Tower	Pittsburgh	PA	15222	**800-245-0242**	412-288-1900	393
NYSE: FII						
Federated Life Insurance Co PO Box 328	Owatonna	MN	55060	**800-533-0472**	507-455-5200	384-2
Federated Mutual Insurance Co PO Box 328	Owatonna	MN	55060	**800-533-0472**	507-455-5200	384-2
Federated Rural Electric Assn PO Box 69	Jackson	MN	56143	**800-321-3520**	507-847-3520	244
Federated Service Insurance Co PO Box 328	Owatonna	MN	55060	**800-533-0472**	507-455-5200	384-4
Federation for American Immigration Reform (FAIR) 1666 Connecticut Ave NW Suite 400	Washington	DC	20009	**877-627-3247**	202-328-7004	48-7
Federation of American Societies for Experimental Biology (FASEB) 9650 Rockville Pike	Bethesda	MD	20814	**800-433-2732**	301-530-7000	49-19
Federation Co-op 108 N Water St	Black River Falls	WI	54615	**800-944-1784**	715-284-5354	272
Federation of State Medical Boards of the US Inc (FSMB) 400 Fuller Wiser Rd Suite 300	Euless	TX	76039	**800-876-5396**	817-868-4000	49-8
FedEx Corp 942 S Shady Grove Road	Memphis	TN	38120	**800-463-3339**	901-369-3600	355-3
NYSE: FDX						
FedEx Custom Critical Inc 1475 Boettler Rd	Uniontown	OH	44685	**800-762-3787***	234-310-4090	536
*Cust Svc						
FedEx Express PO Box 727	Memphis	TN	38194	**800-463-3339**	901-369-3600	536
FedEx Freight East PO Box 840	Harrison	AR	72602	**800-874-4723**	870-741-9000	769
FedEx Freight West 6411 Guadalupe Mines Rd	San Jose	CA	95120	**800-845-4647**	408-268-9600	769
FedEx Kinko's Office & Print Services Inc 13155 Noel Rd Suite 1600	Dallas	TX	75240	**800-254-6567***	214-550-7000	114
*Cust Svc						
FedEx Supply Chain Services Inc 5455 Darrow Rd	Hudson	OH	44236	**800-588-3020**	330-342-3000	440
Fedmet Resources Corp PO Box 278 Westmount Stn	Montreal	QC	H3Z2T2	**800-609-5711**	514-931-5711	649
Fednav Ltd 1000 rue de la Gauchetière O Bureau 3500	Montreal	QC	H3B4W5	**800-678-4842**	514-878-6500	308
Fedway Assoc Inc 56 Hackensack Ave	South Kearny	NJ	07032	**800-433-3929**	973-624-6444	82-3
FedWorld.gov US Dept of Commerce 5285 Port Royal Rd	Springfield	VA	22161	**800-553-6847**	703-605-6000	336-2
FEE (Foundation for Economic Education) 30 S Broadway	Irvington-on-Hudson	NY	10533	**800-960-4333**	914-591-7230	654
Fee Brothers Inc 453 Portland Ave	Rochester	NY	14605	**800-961-3337**	585-544-9530	291-40
Feeco International Inc 3913 Algoma Rd	Green Bay	WI	54311	**800-373-9347***	920-469-5100	206
*Mktg						
Feed Assn. National Grain & 1250 I St NW Suite 1003	Washington	DC	20005	**800-680-9223**	202-289-0873	48-2
Feed the Children PO Box 36	Oklahoma City	OK	73101	**800-627-4556**	405-942-0228	48-5
Feed Products Inc 1000 W 47th Ave	Denver	CO	80211	**800-332-8285**	303-455-3646	438
Feelbest.com 778 Bank St	Ottawa	ON	K1S3V6	**888-689-9890**	613-234-4643	236
Feenaughty Machinery Co 4800 NE Columbia Blvd	Portland	OR	97218	**800-875-2566**	503-282-2566	353
Feesers Inc 5561 Grayson Rd	Harrisburg	PA	17111	**800-326-2828**	717-564-4636	292-8
FEI Behavioral Health 11700 W Lake Park Dr	Milwaukee	WI	53224	**800-221-3726**	414-359-1055	454
FEI Co 5350 NE Dawson Creek Dr	Hillsboro	OR	97124	**888-466-6455**	503-640-7500	410
NASDAQ: FEIC						
Feingold Assn of the US 540 E Main St Suite N	Riverhead	NY	11901	**800-321-3287**	631-369-9340	48-17
Feist Publications Inc 306 Main St	Spearville	KS	67876	**800-536-2612**	620-385-2612	623-6
Feistritzer Publications 4401A Connecticut Ave NW Suite 212	Washington	DC	20008	**866-778-2784**	202-362-3444	623-9
Felbro Inc 3666 E Olympic Blvd	Los Angeles	CA	90023	**800-733-5276**	323-263-8686	231
Feld Entertainment Inc 8607 Westwood Center Dr	Vienna	VA	22182	**800-298-3858**	703-448-4000	147
Feldman Lumber Co Inc 228 Buckeye Rd	Lancaster	KY	40444	**800-325-0459**	859-792-2141	671
Felicita Resort 2201 Fishing Creek Valley Rd	Harrisburg	PA	17112	**888-321-3713**	717-599-5301	655
Felker Brothers Corp 22 N Chestnut Ave	Marshfield	WI	54449	**800-826-2304**	715-384-3121	481
Fell David H & Co Inc 6009 Bandini Blvd	Commerce	CA	90040	**800-822-1996**	323-722-9992	399
Fellowes Inc 1789 Norwood Ave	Itasca	IL	60143	**800-945-4545**	630-893-1600	112
Fellowship of Christian Athletes (FCA) 8701 Leeds Rd	Kansas City	MO	64129	**800-289-0909**	816-921-0909	48-22
Fellowship Hall Inc 5140 Dunstan Rd	Greensboro	NC	27405	**800-659-3381**	336-621-3381	712
Felly's Flowers Inc PO Box 6620	Madison	WI	53716	**800-993-7673**	608-223-3285	287
Felpausch Food Centers Corp 127 S Michigan Ave	Hastings	MI	49058	**800-648-6433**	269-945-3485	339
Felton Brush Inc 7 Burton Dr	Londonderry	NH	03053	**800-258-9702**	603-425-0200	104
Felts Field Aviation Inc 5829 E Rutter Ave	Spokane	WA	99212	**800-676-5538**	509-535-9011	63
FEMA (Federal Emergency Management Agency) 500 C St SW	Washington	DC	20472	**800-462-9029**	202-646-4600	336-7
Female Executives. National Assn for 60 E 42nd St 27th Fl	New York	NY	10165	**800-927-6233**	212-351-6400	49-12
Female Health Co 515 N State St Suite 2225	Chicago	IL	60610	**800-635-0844**	312-595-9123	469
Female Patient Magazine 26 Main St	Chatham	NJ	07928	**800-976-4040**	973-701-8900	449-16
Femco Machine Co 754 S Main St Ext	Punxsutawney	PA	15767	**800-458-3445**	814-938-9763	446
Fence Assn. American 800 Roosevelt Rd Bldg C-20	Glen Ellyn	IL	60137	**800-822-4342**	630-942-6598	49-3
Fender Musical Instruments Corp 8860 E Chaparral Rd Suite 100	Scottsdale	AZ	85250	**800-488-1818**	480-596-9690	516
Fendi NA Inc 720 5th Ave 5th Fl	New York	NY	10019	**800-336-3469**	212-767-0100	155-6
Fendrich Industries Inc 7025 Augusta Rd	Greenville	SC	29605	**800-845-2744**	864-299-0600	153-13
Fendt Builders Supply Inc 22005 Gill Rd	Farmington Hills	MI	48335	**888-706-9974**	248-474-3211	181
Fennell Promotions Inc 951 Hornet Dr	Hazelwood	MO	63042	**800-495-9765**	314-592-3300	377
Fenner Drives 311 W Stiegel St	Manheim	PA	17545	**800-243-3374***	717-665-2421	364
*Sales						
Fenner Dunlop Conveyor Belting Americas 10125 S Tryon St	Charlotte	NC	28273	**800-922-1735***	704-943-5669	364
*Cust Svc						
Fenton Art Glass Co 700 Elizabeth St	Williamstown	WV	26187	**800-933-6766***	304-375-6122	330
*Cust Svc						
Fenwick Inn 13801 Coastal Hwy	Ocean City	MD	21842	**800-492-1873**	410-250-1100	373
Fenwick & West LLP 801 California St	Mountain View	CA	94041	**800-816-6136**	650-988-8500	419
Fergus Falls Regional Treatment Center 1400 N Union Ave	Fergus Falls	MN	56537	**800-657-3854**	218-739-7200	366-3
Fergusson Alex C Inc 5000 Letterkenny Rd Suite 220	Chambersburg	PA	17201	**800-345-1329**	717-264-9147	143
Fernandez Guitars International Inc 8163 Lankershim Blvd	North Hollywood	CA	91605	**800-318-8599**	818-252-6799	516
Fernando's Foods Corp PO Box 4188	Compton	CA	90221	**800-388-5505**	310-223-1499	291-36
Fernco PlumbQwik Inc 300 S Dayton St	Davison	MI	48423	**800-521-1283**	810-653-9626	585
Ferndale Laboratories Inc 780 W Eight-Mile Rd	Ferndale	MI	48220	**800-621-6003**	248-548-0900	572
Fernlea Nurseries Inc 294 Buck Blunt Rd	Quincy	FL	32351	**800-428-9729**	850-442-6188	363
Ferno-Washington Inc 70 Weil Way	Wilmington	OH	45177	**800-733-3766**	937-382-1451	469
Fernwood Resort & Country Club Rt 209 N	Bushkill	PA	18324	**888-337-6966**	570-588-9500	655
Ferolito Vultaggio & Sons 5 Dakota Dr Suite 205	Lake Success	NY	11024	**800-832-3775**	516-812-0300	81-2
Ferrara Bakery & Cafe Inc 195 Grand St 3rd Fl	New York	NY	10013	**800-871-6068**	212-226-6150	291-9
Ferrara Pan Candy Co 7301 W Harrison St	Forest Park	IL	60130	**800-323-1768**	708-366-0500	291-8
Ferrero USA Inc 600 Cottontail Ln	Somerset	NJ	08873	**800-337-7376**	732-764-9300	291-8
Ferriday Farm Equipment Co Inc 503 Lake Dr Hwy 568	Ferriday	LA	71334	**800-256-4576**	318-757-4576	270

Name / Address	City	State	ZIP	Toll-Free	Phone	Class
Ferris Baker Watts Inc 1700 Pennsylvania Ave NW Suite 700	Washington	DC	20006	**800-227-0308**	202-661-9500	679
Ferris State University 420 Oak St	Big Rapids	MI	49307	**800-433-7747**	231-591-2000	163
Ferro Corp Grant Chemical Div 111 W Irene Rd	Zachary	LA	70791	**800-325-3578**	225-654-6801	142
Ferro Corp Liquid Coatings & Dispersions Div 1301 N Flora St	Plymouth	IN	46563	**800-882-1456**	574-935-5131	540
Ferro Corp Plastic Colorants Div 103 Railroad Ave	Stryker	OH	43557	**800-521-9094**	419-682-3311	540
Ferro Corp Polymer Additives Div 7050 Krick Rd	Walton Hills	OH	44146	**800-321-9946**	216-641-8580	142
Ferro Pfanstiehl Laboratories Inc 1219 Glen Rock Ave	Waukegan	IL	60085	**800-383-0126**	847-623-0370	470
FerroTec (USA) Corp 40 Simon St	Nashua	NH	03060	**800-258-1788**	603-883-9800	686
Ferrum College PO Box 1000	Ferrum	VA	24088	**800-868-9797**	540-365-2121	163
FESCO Agencies NA Inc 821 2nd Ave Suite 1100	Seattle	WA	98104	**800-275-3372**	206-583-0860	306
Festiva Resorts 1 Vance Gap Rd *Resv	Asheville	NC	28805	**877-933-7848***	828-254-3378	738
Festival Bay Mall at International Drive 5250 International Dr	Orlando	FL	32819	**800-481-1944**	407-351-7718	452
Feterl Mfg Co 411 Center Ave W	Salem	SD	57058	**800-367-8660**	605-425-2206	269
Fetzer Vineyards 13601 Old River Rd	Hopland	CA	95449	**800-846-8637**	707-744-1250	81-3
Feutz Contractors Inc 1120 N Main St PO Box 130	Paris	IL	61944	**800-252-0273**	217-465-8402	188-5
Fey Industries Blackbourn Media Packaging Div 200 4th Ave N	Edgerton	MN	56128	**800-842-7550**		87
Fey Industries Inc 200 4th Ave N	Edgerton	MN	56128	**800-533-5340**	507-442-4311	87
FFA Organization. National 6060 FFA Dr	Indianapolis	IN	46268	**800-772-0939**	317-802-6060	48-2
FFE Transportation Services Inc 1145 Empire Central Pl	Dallas	TX	75247	**800-569-9200**	214-630-8090	769
FFF (Freedom From Fear) 308 Seaview Ave	Staten Island	NY	10305	**888-442-2022**	718-351-1717	48-17
FFLC Bancorp Inc PO Box 490420	Leesburg	FL	34749	**877-955-2265**	352-787-3311	355-2
FFP Marketing Co Inc DBA Kwik Pantry 2801 Glenda Ave	Fort Worth	TX	76117	**800-695-3282**	817-838-4700	658
FFW Corp 1205 N Cass St *NASDAQ: FFWC*	Wabash	IN	46992	**800-377-4984**	260-563-3185	355-2
FH Bonn Co 4300 Gateway Blvd	Springfield	OH	45502	**800-323-0143**	937-323-7024	730-3
FHA (Federal Housing Administration) 451 7th St SW Suite 9100	Washington	DC	20410	**800-767-7460**	202-708-3600	336-8
FHC Health Systems 240 Corporate Blvd	Norfolk	VA	23502	**800-451-3581**	757-459-5100	454
FHN Memorial Hospital 1045 W Stephenson St	Freeport	IL	61032	**800-747-4131**	815-599-6000	366-2
Fi-Shock Inc 5360 N National Dr	Knoxville	TN	37914	**800-251-9288**	865-524-7380	275
Fiber Glass Industries Inc 69 Edson St	Amsterdam	NY	12010	**800-842-4413**	518-842-4000	326
Fiber Instruments Sales Inc 161 Clear Rd *Sales	Oriskany	NY	13424	**800-500-0347***	315-736-2206	464
Fiber-Tech Industries Inc 2000 Kenskill Ave	Washington Court House	OH	43160	**800-879-4377**	740-335-9400	602
FiberCast Inc 25 S Main St	Sand Springs	OK	74063	**800-331-4406**	918-245-6651	3
Fibercel Corp 46 Brooklyn St PO Box 610	Portville	NY	14770	**800-545-8546**	716-933-8703	538
Fiberglass Engineering Inc DBA Cobalt Boats 1715 N 8th St	Neodesha	KS	66757	**800-835-0256**	620-325-2653	91
Fiberglass Specialties Inc PO Box 1340	Henderson	TX	75653	**800-527-1459**	903-657-6522	597
Fiberglass Systems Inc 4545 Enterprise St	Boise	ID	83705	**800-727-9907**	208-342-6823	367
Fibergrate Composite Structures Inc 5151 Beltline Rd Suite 700	Dallas	TX	75254	**800-527-4043**	972-250-1633	595
FiberMark Inc Technical Specialities Div 1 CR 519 *Cust Svc	Bloomsbury	NJ	08804	**800-784-8558***	908-995-2424	551
FiberNet Telecom Group Inc 570 Lexington Ave *NASDAQ: FTGX*	New York	NY	10022	**800-342-3768**	212-405-6200	720
Fiberoptics Technology Inc 1 Quassett Rd	Pomfret	CT	06258	**800-433-5248**	860-928-0443	326
Fiberstars Inc 44259 Noble Dr *NASDAQ: FBST*	Fremont	CA	94538	**800-327-7877**	510-490-0719	431
Fibre-Metal Products Co Rt 1 at S Brinton Wake Rd PO Box 248	Concordville	PA	19331	**800-523-7048**	610-459-5300	566
Fibrex Insulations Inc 561 Scott Rd PO Box 2079 *Cust Svc	Sarnia	ON	N7T7L4	**800-265-7514***	519-336-7770	382
Fibromyalgia Partnership Inc. National 140 Zinn Way PO Box 160	Linden	VA	22642	**866-725-4404**		48-17
Fibron Products Inc 170 Florida St	Buffalo	NY	14208	**800-516-0285**	716-886-2378	808
FIC Insurance Group 6500 River Place Blvd Bldg 1	Austin	TX	78730	**800-925-6000**	512-404-5000	384-2
Fidelifacts 42 Broadway 15th Fl	New York	NY	10004	**800-678-0007**	212-425-1520	621
Fidelitone Inc 1260 Karl Ct *Cust Svc	Wauconda	IL	60084	**800-342-2112***	847-487-3300	245
Fidelity Advisor Funds PO Box 770002	Cincinnati	OH	45277	**800-522-7297**		517
Fidelity Bank 100 E English St	Wichita	KS	67202	**800-658-1637**	316-265-2261	71
Fidelity Bankshares Inc 205 Datura St *NASDAQ: FFFL*	West Palm Beach	FL	33401	**800-422-3675**	561-514-9222	355-2
Fidelity Brokerage Services Inc 82 Devonshire St	Boston	MA	02109	**800-828-6680**	617-563-7000	679
Fidelity Exploration & Production Co 1700 Lincoln St Suite 4600	Denver	CO	80203	**800-986-3133**	303-893-3133	527
Fidelity Federal Bank & Trust 205 Datura St	West Palm Beach	FL	33401	**800-422-3675**	561-659-9900	71
Fidelity Freedom Funds PO Box 770001	Cincinnati	OH	45277	**800-343-3548**		517
Fidelity & Guaranty Life Insurance Co PO Box 1137 *Sales	Baltimore	MD	21203	**800-445-6758***	410-895-0100	384-2
Fidelity Information Services Inc 601 Riverside Avenue	Jacksonville	FL	32204	**800-874-7359**		176-10
Fidelity Investment Funds PO Box 770001	Cincinnati	OH	45277	**800-343-3548**		517
Fidelity Investments 82 Devonshire St	Boston	MA	02109	**800-522-7297**	617-563-7000	393
Fidelity Investments Charitable Gift Fund PO Box 55158	Boston	MA	02205	**800-682-4438**		397
Fidelity National Financial Inc 601 Riverside Avenue *NYSE: FNF*	Jacksonville	FL	32204	**800-815-3969**	888-934-3354	355-4
Fidelity National Home Warranty Inc 2950 Euskirk Ave	Walnut Creek	CA	94596	**800-862-6837**	925-934-4450	687
Fidelity National Title Insurance Co 4050 Calle Real Suite 100	Santa Barbara	CA	93110	**800-815-3969**	805-696-7000	384-6
Fidelity Personal Investments & Brokerage Group 82 Devonshire St	Boston	MA	02109	**800-828-6680**	617-563-7000	679
Fidelity Select Funds PO Box 770002	Cincinnati	OH	45277	**800-544-8888**		517
Fidelity Southern Corp 3490 Piedmont Rd Suite 1550 *NASDAQ: LION*	Atlanta	GA	30305	**888-248-5466**	404-639-6500	355-2
Fidelity Spartan Brokerage Services Inc 82 Devonshire St	Boston	MA	02109	**800-828-6680**	617-563-7000	679
Fidelity Spartan Funds PO Box 770002	Cincinnati	OH	45277	**800-544-8888**		517
Fidlar Doubleday Inc 6255 Technology Ave	Kalamazoo	MI	49009	**800-632-2259**	269-544-3600	614
Fidlar Software 4450 48th Ave Ct PO Box 6248	Rock Island	IL	61204	**800-747-4600**	309-794-3200	788
Fiducial Franchising 10480 Little Patuxent Pkwy 3rd Fl	Columbia	MD	21044	**800-323-9000**	410-910-5885	719
Fiducial Inc 450 Park Ave 15th Fl	New York	NY	10022	**800-283-1040**	212-207-4700	719
Fiduciary Management Assoc LLC 55 W Monroe St Suite 2550	Chicago	IL	60603	**800-793-0848**	312-930-6850	393
Field Container Co LP 1500 Nicholas Blvd	Elk Grove Village	IL	60007	**888-343-5334**	847-437-1700	102
Field Container Co LP Saint Clair Pakwell Div 120 25th Ave *Cust Svc	Bellwood	IL	60104	**800-323-1922***	708-547-7500	542-2
Field of Flowers Inc 5101 S University Dr	Davie	FL	33328	**800-963-7374**	954-680-2406	287
Field & Stream Magazine 2 Park Ave *Cust Svc	New York	NY	10016	**800-999-0869***	212-779-5000	449-20
Fieldcrest Cannon Textile Museum Cannon Village Visitor Center 200 West Ave	Kannapolis	NC	28081	**800-438-6111**	704-938-3200	509
Fields Corp 2240 Taylor Way	Tacoma	WA	98421	**800-627-4098**	253-627-4098	46
Fields Group Inc 9124 Technology Dr	Fishers	IN	46038	**800-600-2969**	317-578-4414	377
Fieldstone Communities Inc 14 Corporate Plaza	Newport Beach	CA	92660	**800-665-0661**	949-640-9090	639
Fiesta Casino Hotel 2400 N Rancho Dr	Las Vegas	NV	89130	**800-731-7333**	702-631-7000	133
Fiesta Inn Resort 2100 S Priest Dr	Tempe	AZ	85282	**800-528-6481**	480-967-1441	373
Fiesta Mart Inc 5235 Katy Fwy	Houston	TX	77007	**877-256-5060**	713-869-5060	339
Fiesta Salons Inc 6363 Fiesta Dr	Columbus	OH	43235	**800-825-6363**	614-766-6363	79
Fife Corp 222 W Memorial Rd	Oklahoma City	OK	73114	**800-333-3433**	405-755-1600	202
Fifteen Beacon Hotel 15 Beacon St	Boston	MA	02108	**877-982-3226**	617-670-1500	373
Fifth Season Inn 2219 S Waldron Rd	Fort Smith	AR	72903	**877-452-4880**	479-452-4880	373
Fifth Third Bancorp 38 Fountain Sq Plaza *NASDAQ: FITB*	Cincinnati	OH	45263	**800-972-3030**	513-579-5300	355-2
Fifth Third Bank 38 Fountain Sq Plaza	Cincinnati	OH	45263	**800-972-3030**	513-579-5300	71
Fifth Third Bank Central Ohio 21 E State St	Columbus	OH	43215	**800-972-3030**	614-341-2595	71
Fifth Third Bank Inc 100 Brighton Park Blvd	Frankfort	KY	40601	**800-972-3030**	502-695-0882	71
Fifth Third Bank Northeastern Ohio 1404 E 9th St *Cust Svc	Cleveland	OH	44114	**800-972-3030***	216-696-5300	71
Fifth Third Bank Northwestern Ohio 606 Madison Ave	Toledo	OH	43604	**800-972-3030**	419-259-7890	71
Fifth Third Bank Western Michigan 830 Pleasant St	Saint Joseph	MI	49085	**800-972-3030**	269-983-6311	71
Fifth Third Bank Western Ohio 110 N Main St	Dayton	OH	45402	**800-972-3030**	937-227-6500	71
Fifth Third Funds PO Box 182706	Columbus	OH	43218	**800-282-5706**		517
Figaro's Italian Pizza Inc 1500 Liberty St SE Suite 160	Salem	OR	97302	**888-344-2767**	503-371-9318	657
Figi's Inc 3200 S Maple Ave	Marshfield	WI	54449	**800-344-4353**	715-387-1771	451
Figueroa Hotel 939 S Figueroa St	Los Angeles	CA	90015	**800-421-9092**	213-627-8971	373
Fiji Visitors Bureau 5777 W Century Blvd Suite 220	Los Angeles	CA	90045	**800-932-3454**	310-568-1616	764
Fiksdal Motel 1215 2nd St SW	Rochester	MN	55902	**800-366-3451**	507-288-2671	373
Fila USA Inc 1 Fila Way	Sparks	MD	21152	**800-787-3452**	410-773-3000	153-1
Filanc JR Construction Co Inc 4616 North Ave	Oceanside	CA	92056	**877-225-5428**	760-941-7130	187-10
File Keepers LLC 6277 E Slauson Ave	Los Angeles	CA	90040	**800-332-3453**	323-728-3151	455
FileMaker Inc 5201 Patrick Henry Dr *Cust Svc	Santa Clara	CA	95054	**800-325-2747***	408-987-7000	176-1
FileNet Corp 3565 Harbor Blvd *NASDAQ: FILE*	Costa Mesa	CA	92626	**800-345-3638**	714-327-3400	176-7
FileStream Inc 333 Glen Head Rd	Old Brookville	NY	11545	**800-732-3002**	516-759-4100	176-12
Fillip Metal Cabinet Co 701 N Albany Ave	Chicago	IL	60612	**800-535-0733**	773-826-7373	314-1
Fillmore-Piru Citrus Assoc 355 N Main St PO Box 350	Piru	CA	93040	**800-524-8787**	805-524-3551	12-1
Film Comment Magazine 70 Lincoln Ctr Plaza *Cust Svc	New York	NY	10023	**800-783-4903***	212-875-5610	449-9
Film Technologies International Inc 2544 Terminal Dr S	Saint Petersburg	FL	33712	**800-777-1770**	727-327-2544	589
Film & Video Stock Shots 10442 Burbank Blvd	North Hollywood	CA	91601	**888-436-6824**	818-760-2098	582

Name / Address	City	State	Zip	Toll-Free	Phone	Class
Films for the Humanities & Sciences PO Box 2053	Princeton	NJ	08543	**800-257-5126**	609-275-1400	242
Filterfresh Coffee Service Inc 378 University Ave	Westwood	MA	02090	**800-461-8734**	781-461-8734	294
Filterspun 624 N Fairfield St	Amarillo	TX	79107	**800-432-0108**	806-383-3840	793
Filtertek Inc 11411 Price Rd	Hebron	IL	60034	**800-248-2461**	815-648-2416	593
Filtration Group Inc 912 E Washington St	Joliet	IL	60433	**800-739-4600**	815-726-4600	19
Fina Michael C Inc 545 5th Ave	New York	NY	10017	**800-289-3462**	212-557-2500	357
Final Draft Inc 26707 W Agoura Rd Suite 205	Calabasas	CA	91302	**800-231-4055**	818-995-8995	176-10
Finance America 16802 Aston St	Irvine	CA	92606	**800-690-8200**	949-440-1000	498
Finance Co The 16355 Laguna Canyon Rd	Irvine	CA	92618	**800-966-5100**		215
Financial Accountability. Evangelical Council for 440 W Jubal Early Dr Suite 130	Winchester	VA	22601	**800-323-9473**	540-535-0103	48-5
Financial Advisors. National Assn of Insurance & 2901 Telestar Ct *Sales	Falls Church	VA	22042	**877-866-2432***	703-770-8100	49-9
Financial Advisors. National Assn of Personal 3250 N Arlington Suite 109	Arlington Heights	IL	60004	**800-366-2732**	847-537-7722	49-2
Financial Benefit Life Insurance Co 555 S Kansas Ave	Topeka	KS	66603	**800-332-7732**	785-232-6945	384-2
Financial Crimes Enforcement Network (FinCEN) 2070 Chain Bridge Rd PO Box 39	Vienna	VA	22183	**800-767-2825**	703-905-3520	336-14
Financial Engines Inc 1804 Embarcadero Rd	Palo Alto	CA	94303	**888-443-8577**	650-565-4900	176-10
Financial Federal Corp 733 3rd Ave 24th Fl *AMEX: FIF*	New York	NY	10017	**800-480-1003**	212-599-8000	214
Financial Forum 90 N 100 East Suite 4	Logan	UT	84321	**800-500-5119**	435-750-0062	699
Financial Freedom Senior Funding Corp 7595 Irvine Ctr Dr Suite 250	Irvine	CA	92618	**800-500-5150**	949-341-9200	498
Financial Fusion Inc 561 Virginia Rd Bldg 5	Concord	MA	01742	**800-842-0885**	978-287-1975	176-10
Financial Guaranty Insurance Co 125 Park Ave 6th Fl	New York	NY	10017	**800-352-0001**	212-312-3000	384-5
Financial Indemnity Co 21650 Oxnard St Suite 1800	Woodland Hills	CA	91367	**800-777-4342**	818-313-8500	384-4
Financial Industries Corp 6500 River Place Blvd Bldg 1	Austin	TX	78730	**800-925-6000**	512-404-5000	355-4
Financial Management Assn. Healthcare 2 Westbrook Corporate Ctr Suite 700	Westchester	IL	60154	**800-252-4362**	708-531-9600	49-8
Financial Managers Society (FMS) 100 W Monroe St Suite 810 *Cust Svc	Chicago	IL	60603	**800-275-4367***	312-578-1300	49-2
Financial Planner Board of Standards Inc. Certified 1670 Broadway Suite 600	Denver	CO	80202	**888-237-6275**	303-830-7500	49-2
Financial Planning Assn (FPA) 5775 Glenridge Dr NE Suite B300	Atlanta	GA	30328	**800-945-4237**	404-845-0011	49-2
Financial Publishing Co PO Box 570 *Cust Svc	South Bend	IN	46624	**800-247-3214***	574-243-6040	623-2
Financial Security Assurance Holdings Ltd 350 Park Ave 13th Fl	New York	NY	10022	**800-846-4372**	212-826-0100	355-4
Financial Security Assurance Inc 350 Park Ave 13th Fl	New York	NY	10022	**800-846-4372**	212-826-0100	384-5
Financial Service Corp 2300 Windy Ridge Pkwy Suite 1100	Atlanta	GA	30339	**800-352-4372**	770-916-6500	679
Financial Service Professionals. Society of 270 S Bryn Mawr Ave	Bryn Mawr	PA	19010	**800-392-6900**	610-526-2500	49-9
Financial & Technology Professionals. Hospitality 11709 Boulder Ln Suite 110	Austin	TX	78726	**800-856-4242**	512-249-5333	49-1
Financial Times 1330 Ave of the Americas	New York	NY	10019	**800-628-8088**	212-641-6500	522-2
FinancialCAD Corp 13450 102nd Ave Suite 1753	Surrey	BC	V3T5X3	**800-304-0702**	604-957-1200	39
FinCEN (Financial Crimes Enforcement Network) 2070 Chain Bridge Rd PO Box 39	Vienna	VA	22183	**800-767-2825**	703-905-3520	336-14
Finch Pruyn & Co Inc 1 Glen St	Glens Falls	NY	12801	**800-833-9981**	518-793-2541	547
Finck Cigar Co 414 Vera Cruz St *Orders	San Antonio	TX	78207	**800-221-0638***	210-226-4191	741-2
Fincor Automation Inc 3750 E Market St *Sales	York	PA	17402	**800-334-3040***	717-751-4200	202
Find the Children 2656 29th St Suite 203	Santa Monica	CA	90405	**888-477-6721**	310-314-3213	48-6
Find People Fast 4600 Chippewa Suite 244	Saint Louis	MO	63116	**800-829-1807**	314-351-4000	621
Findings Inc PO Box 462	Keene	NH	03431	**800-343-0806**	603-352-3717	399
Findlay-Hancock County Chamber of Commerce 123 E Main Cross St	Findlay	OH	45840	**800-424-3326**	419-422-3313	137
Findlay Inn & Conference Center 200 E Main Cross St	Findlay	OH	45840	**800-825-1455**	419-422-5682	373
FIND/SVP Inc 625 Ave of the Americas 2nd Fl *Cust Svc	New York	NY	10011	**800-346-3688***	212-645-4500	380
FindWhat.com Inc 143 Varick St *NASDAQ: FWHT*	New York	NY	10013	**800-823-3477**	212-255-1500	677
Fine Cooking Magazine 63 S Main St	Newtown	CT	06470	**800-477-8727**	203-426-8171	449-14
Fine Homebuilding Magazine 63 S Main St	Newtown	CT	06470	**800-888-8286**	203-426-8171	449-21
Fine Organics Corp 420 Kuller Rd PO Box 2277	Clifton	NJ	07015	**800-526-7480**	973-478-1000	149
Fine Woodworking Magazine 63 S Main St PO Box 5507	Newtown	CT	06470	**800-888-8286**	203-426-8171	449-14
FineScale Modeler Magazine 21027 Crossroads Cir	Waukesha	WI	53186	**888-350-2413**	262-796-8776	449-14
Finger Lakes Library System 119 E Green St	Ithaca	NY	14850	**800-909-3557**	607-273-4074	426
Finger Lakes Printing Co PO Box 393	Geneva	NY	14456	**800-388-6652**	315-789-3333	623-8
Finger Lakes Times 218 Genesee St	Geneva	NY	14456	**800-388-6652**	315-789-3333	522-2

Name / Address	City	State	Zip	Toll-Free	Phone	Class
Finger Lakes Visitors Connection 25 Gorham St Box 179	Canandaigua	NY	14424	**877-386-4669**	585-394-3915	205
Fingerhut Cos Inc 4400 Baker Rd *Orders	Minnetonka	MN	55343	**800-233-3588***	952-932-3100	451
Finish Line Inc 3308 N Mitthoeffer Rd *NASDAQ: FINL*	Indianapolis	IN	46235	**800-370-6061**	317-899-1022	296
FinishMaster Inc 54 Monument Cir Suite 600 *NASDAQ: FMST*	Indianapolis	IN	46204	**888-311-3678**	317-237-3678	540
Finjan Software Inc 2025 Gateway Pl Suite 180	San Jose	CA	95110	**888-346-5268**	408-452-9700	176-12
Finkl A & Sons Co 2011 N Southport Ave	Chicago	IL	60614	**800-343-2562**	773-975-2510	709
Finks Jewelry Inc 3545 Electric Rd	Roanoke	VA	24018	**800-699-7464**	540-342-2991	402
Finlandia University 601 Quincy St	Hancock	MI	49930	**800-682-7604**	906-482-5300	160
Finley Hospital 350 N Grandview Ave	Dubuque	IA	52001	**800-582-1891**	563-582-1881	366-2
Finn Corp 9281 Le Saint Dr	Fairfield	OH	45014	**800-543-7166**	513-874-2818	269
Finnair 228 E 45th St	New York	NY	10017	**800-950-5000**	212-499-9000	26
Finnair Plus 228 E 45th St	New York	NY	10017	**800-950-3387**		27
Finnaren & Haley Inc 901 Washington St	Conshohocken	PA	19428	**800-843-9800**	610-825-1900	540
Finzer Roller Co 129 Rawls Rd	Des Plaines	IL	60018	**888-486-1900**	847-390-6200	664
Fire Council. National Volunteer 1050 17th St NW Suite 490	Washington	DC	20036	**888-275-6832**	202-887-5700	49-4
Fire Electrical Services 2500 Brookpark Rd	Cleveland	OH	44134	**877-741-6001**	216-741-6001	683
Fire & Emergency Training Network 4101 International Pkwy	Carrollton	TX	75007	**800-845-2443**	972-309-4000	502
Fire-End & Croker Corp 7 Westchester Plaza	Elmsford	NY	10523	**800-759-3473**	914-592-3640	566
Fire Fighters Equipment Co 3038 Lenox Ave	Jacksonville	FL	32254	**800-488-8542**	904-388-8542	667
Fire-Lite Alarms 1 Fire-Lite Pl	Northford	CT	06472	**800-289-3473**	203-484-7161	681
Fire Marshals. National Assn of State PO Box 4137	Clifton Park	NY	12065	**877-996-2736**	518-371-0018	49-7
Fire Professionals of America. International Union Security Police & 25510 Kelly Rd	Roseville	MI	48066	**800-228-7492**	586-772-7250	405
Fire Protection Assn. National 1 Batterymarch Pk	Quincy	MA	02169	**800-344-3555**	617-770-3000	48-17
Fire Service Instructors. International Society of 2425 Hwy 49 E	Pleasant View	TN	37146	**800-435-0005**		49-7
Firearms Training Systems Inc 7340 McGinnis Ferry Rd	Suwanee	GA	30024	**800-813-9046**	770-813-0180	694
Firecom Inc 39-27 59th St	Woodside	NY	11377	**800-347-3266**	718-899-6100	681
FireKing International Inc 101 Security Pkwy	New Albany	IN	47150	**800-528-9900**	812-948-8400	665
Firelands Electric Co-op Inc 1 Energy Pl PO Box 32	New London	OH	44851	**800-533-8658**	419-929-1571	244
Fireman's Fund Insurance Co 777 San Marin Dr	Novato	CA	94998	**800-227-1700**	415-899-2000	384-5
Fireman's Fund McGee Marine Underwriters 75 Wall St	New York	NY	10005	**800-235-6029**	212-524-8600	384-4
Firemen's Insurance Co of Washington DC 420 Lake Brook Dr	Glen Allen	VA	23060	**800-283-1153**	804-285-2700	384-4
FirePond Inc 8009 S 34th Ave Suite 1050	Minneapolis	MN	55425	**888-662-7722**	952-229-2300	176-1
Fireside Bank 5050 Hopyard Rd Suite 200	Pleasanton	CA	94588	**800-825-1862**	925-460-9020	71
Fireside Inn & Suites 25 Airport Rd	West Lebanon	NH	03784	**800-962-3198**	603-298-5906	373
Firestone Fibers & Textiles Co 100 Firestone Ln	Kings Mountain	NC	28086	**800-441-1336**	704-734-2100	730-3
Firestone Industrial Products Co 12650 Hamilton Crossing Blvd	Carmel	IN	46032	**800-888-0650**	317-818-8600	60
Firestone Polymers 381 W Wilbeth Rd *Cust Svc	Akron	OH	44319	**800-282-0222***	330-379-7000	594-3
Fireworks Fine Crafts Gallery 3307 Utah Ave S	Seattle	WA	98134	**800-505-8882**	206-682-8707	509
Firmenich Inc PO Box 5880	Princeton	NJ	08543	**800-257-9591**	609-452-1000	291-15
FIRST 200 Bedford St	Manchester	NH	03101	**800-871-8326**	603-666-3906	48-11
First Action Security 18702 Crestwood Dr	Hagerstown	MD	21742	**800-342-4243**	301-797-2124	683
First Albany Corp 677 Broadway	Albany	NY	12207	**800-462-6242**	518-447-8500	679
First Albany Cos Inc 30 S Pearl St *NASDAQ: FACT*	Albany	NY	12207	**800-833-4168**	518-447-8500	355-3
First Alert Inc 3901 Liberty Street Rd	Aurora	IL	60504	**800-323-9005**	630-851-7330	681
First Alexander Hamilton Life Insurance Co PO Box 21008	Greensboro	NC	27420	**800-950-2454**	336-691-3000	384-2
First American Bank SSB 2800 S Texas Ave Suite 200	Bryan	TX	77802	**800-299-0062**	979-361-6200	71
First American Corp 2 First American Way *NYSE: FAF*	Santa Ana	CA	92707	**800-854-3643**	714-558-3211	384-6
First American Funds PO Box 3011	Milwaukee	WI	53201	**800-677-3863**		517
First American Home Buyers Protection Corp 7833 Haskell Ave PO Box 10180	Van Nuys	CA	91410	**800-444-9030**	818-781-5050	687
First American Real Estate Solutions 5601 E La Palma Ave	Anaheim	CA	92807	**800-345-7334**	714-701-2100	621
First American Title Co of Los Angeles 520 N Central Ave	Glendale	CA	91203	**800-328-2652**	818-242-5800	384-6
First American Title Insurance Co 2 First American Way	Santa Ana	CA	92707	**800-854-3643**	714-558-3211	384-6
First American Title Insurance Co of Oregon 1700 SW 4th Ave Suite 102	Portland	OR	97201	**800-929-3651**	503-222-3651	384-6
First American Title Insurance Co of Texas 1500 S Dairy Ashford St Suite 300	Houston	TX	77077	**800-347-7826**	281-588-2200	384-6
First Assist Inc 4720 Montgomery Ln Suite 300	Bethesda	MD	20814	**800-426-1724**	301-718-2200	707
First Bancorp 341 N Main St *NASDAQ: FBNC*	Troy	NC	27371	**800-548-9377**	910-576-6171	355-2
First Bank 11901 Olive Blvd	Creve Coeur	MO	63141	**800-279-3600**	314-995-8700	71
First Banks Inc 135 N Meramec Ave	Clayton	MO	63105	**800-760-2265**	314-854-4600	355-2
First Busey Corp PO Box 17125 *NASDAQ: BUSE*	Urbana	IL	61803	**800-672-8739**	217-365-4516	355-2

Company / Address	City	State	ZIP	Toll-Free	Phone	Class
First Calgary Savings 510 16th Ave NE Suite 200	Calgary	AB	T2E1K4	**866-923-4778**	403-230-2783	71
First Candle/SIDS Alliance 1314 Bedford Ave Suite 210	Baltimore	MD	21208	**800-221-7437**	410-653-8226	48-17
First Capital Inc 220 Federal Dr NW *NASDAQ: FCAP*	Corydon	IN	47112	**800-390-1465**	812-738-2198	355-2
First Charter Bank 10200 David Taylor Dr	Charlotte	NC	28262	**800-601-8471**	704-786-3300	71
First Charter Corp PO Box 37937 *NASDAQ: FCTR*	Charlotte	NC	28237	**800-422-4650**	704-688-4300	355-2
First Choice Distribution 1770 NE 58th Ave	Des Moines	IA	50313	**800-369-8733**	515-262-9776	549
First Choice Haircutters 6465 Millcreek Dr Suite 210	Mississauga	ON	L5N5R6	**800-361-2887**	905-821-8555	79
First Choice Health Plan 600 University St 13th Fl	Seattle	WA	98101	**800-783-7312**	206-268-2406	384-3
First Church of Christ Scientist 175 Huntington Ave	Boston	MA	02115	**800-288-7090**	617-450-2000	48-20
First Citizens Bancorporation Inc PO box 29	Columbia	SC	29202	**888-612-4444**	803-771-8700	355-2
First Citizens Bank & Trust Co 3128 Smoketree Ct. *Cust Svc	Raleigh	NC	27604	**888-323-4732***	919-716-7000	71
First Class International 27156 Burbank	Foothill Ranch	CA	92010	**800-222-9968**	949-829-5300	760
First Coast Technical Institute 2980 Collins Ave.	Saint Augustine	FL	32084	**866-462-3284**	904-824-4401	787
First Colony Life Insurance Co 3100 Albert Lankford Dr.	Lynchburg	VA	24501	**888-325-5433**	434-845-0911	384-2
First Commonwealth Financial Corp 22 N 6th St Old Courthouse Sq *NYSE: FCF*	Indiana	PA	15701	**800-711-2265**	724-349-7220	355-2
First Commonwealth Inc 444 N Wells St Suite 600	Chicago	IL	60610	**800-788-3384**	312-644-1800	384-3
First Communications Inc 3340 W Market St	Akron	OH	44333	**800-860-1261**	330-835-2323	195
First Community Financial Corp 4000 N Central Ave Suite 100	Phoenix	AZ	85012	**800-242-3232**	602-265-7714	214
First Community Village 1800 Riverside Dr.	Columbus	OH	43212	**888-328-9511**	614-486-9511	659
First Connecticut Capital Corp 1000 Bridgeport Ave.	Shelton	CT	06484	**800-401-3222**	203-944-5400	498
First Consulting Group Inc PO Box 22676 *NASDAQ: FCGI*	Long Beach	CA	90801	**800-251-8005**	562-624-5200	193
First Cooperative Assn 113 S Lewis Ave.	Cleghorn	IA	51014	**800-594-9424**	712-436-2224	438
First Counsel Inc 428 E 4th St Suite 100	Charlotte	NC	28202	**800-313-1645**	704-342-1100	312
First Data Corp 6200 S Quebec St *NYSE: FDC*	Greenwood Village	CO	80111	**800-735-3362**	303-488-8000	254
First Data Integrated Payment Systems Financial Services Div 6200 S Quebec St	Greenwood Village	CO	80111	**800-208-3131**	303-488-8000	70
First DataBank Inc 1111 Bayhill Dr Suite 350	San Bruno	CA	94066	**800-633-3453**	650-588-5454	176-10
First Defiance Financial Corp 601 Clinton St. *NASDAQ: FDEF*	Defiance	OH	43512	**800-472-6292**	419-782-5015	355-2
First Draft Newsletter 316 N Michigan Ave Suite 300	Chicago	IL	60601	**800-878-5331**	312-960-4100	521-11
First Eagle Funds PO Box 219324	Kansas City	MO	64121	**800-334-2143**		517
First Eagle SoGen Funds PO Box 219324	Kansas City	MO	64121	**800-334-2143**		517
First Eastern Mortgage Corp 100 Brickstone Sq	Andover	MA	01810	**800-777-2240**	978-749-3100	498
First Electric Co-op Corp PO Box 5018	Jacksonville	AR	72078	**800-489-7405**	501-982-4545	244
First Energy 76 S Main St *NYSE: FE*	Akron	OH	44308	**800-646-0400**		355-5
First Environment Inc 91 Fulton St.	Boonton	NJ	07005	**800-486-5869**	973-334-0003	191
First Federal Bancorporation PO Box 458	Bemidji	MN	56619	**800-749-9606**	218-751-5120	355-2
First Federal Bancshares of Arkansas Inc 128 W Stephenson Ave *NASDAQ: FFBH*	Harrison	AR	72601	**800-345-2539**	870-741-7641	355-2
First Federal Bank 329 Pierce St	Sioux City	IA	51101	**800-352-4620**	712-277-0200	71
First Federal Bank of Arkansas FA 1401 Hwy 62 65 N.	Harrison	AR	72601	**800-345-2539**	870-741-7641	71
First Federal Bank of California FSB 401 Wilshire Blvd	Santa Monica	CA	90401	**800-637-5540**	310-319-6000	71
First Federal Bank of the Midwest 601 Clinton St PO Box 248	Defiance	OH	43512	**800-472-6292**	419-782-5015	71
First Federal Bankshares Inc 329 Pierce St *NASDAQ: FFSX*	Sioux City	IA	51102	**800-352-4620**	712-277-0200	355-2
First Federal Capital Bank 605 State St *Cust Svc	La Crosse	WI	54601	**800-657-4636***	608-784-8000	71
First Federal Capital Corp 605 State St	La Crosse	WI	54601	**800-657-4636**	608-784-8000	355-2
First Federal Savings & Loan Assn of Charleston 34 Broad St	Charleston	SC	29401	**800-768-3248**	843-724-0800	71
First Federal Savings & Loan Assn of Lakewood 14806 Detroit Ave.	Lakewood	OH	44107	**800-529-2780**	216-221-7300	71
First Financial Bank 300 High St *Cust Svc	Hamilton	OH	45011	**800-543-2265***	513-867-4700	71
First Financial Corp 1 First Financial Plaza *NASDAQ: THFF*	Terre Haute	IN	47807	**800-511-0045**	812-238-6000	355-2
First Financial Holdings Inc PO Box 118068 *NASDAQ: FFCH*	Charleston	SC	29423	**800-768-3248**	843-529-5933	355-2
First Financial Service Corp 2323 Ring Rd *NASDAQ: FFKY*	Elizabethtown	KY	42701	**800-314-2265**	270-765-2131	355-2
First Funds PO Box 8050	Boston	MA	02266	**800-442-1941**		517
First Gold Hotel 270 Main St	Deadwood	SD	57732	**800-274-1876**	605-578-9777	373
First Hartford Realty Corp 149 Colonial Rd PO Box 1270	Manchester	CT	06045	**888-646-6555**	860-646-6555	639
First Hawaiian Bank 999 Bishop St	Honolulu	HI	96813	**800-843-8411**	808-525-7153	71
First Health Group Corp 3200 Highland Ave	Downers Grove	IL	60515	**800-445-1425**	630-241-7900	455
First Health Services Corp 4300 Cox Rd.	Glen Allen	VA	23060	**800-884-2822**	804-965-7400	223
First Horizon Pharmaceutical Corp 6195 Shiloh Rd. *NASDAQ: FHRX*	Alpharetta	GA	30005	**800-849-9707**	770-442-9707	572
First Indiana Bank 135 N Pennsylvania St First Indiana Plaza	Indianapolis	IN	46204	**800-888-8586**	317-269-1200	71
First Indiana Corp 135 N Pennsylvania St First Indiana Plaza Suite 1900 *NASDAQ: FINB* ■ *Cust Svc	Indianapolis	IN	46204	**800-888-8586***	317-269-1200	355-2
First Industrial Realty Trust Inc 311 S Wacker Dr Suite 4000 *NYSE: FR*	Chicago	IL	60606	**800-894-8778**	312-344-4300	641
First Insurance Co of Hawaii Ltd 1100 Ward Ave.	Honolulu	HI	96814	**800-272-5202**	808-527-7777	384-4
First Internet Bank of Indiana 7020 Innovation Blvd Suite 210	Indianapolis	IN	46278	**888-873-3424**		71
First Interstate Bank 401 N 31st St	Billings	MT	59101	**888-752-3330**	406-255-5000	71
First Interstate Inn 20 SE Wyoming Blvd	Casper	WY	82609	**800-462-4667**	307-234-9125	373
First Investors Financial Services Group Inc 675 Bering Dr Suite 710 *NASDAQ: FIFS*	Houston	TX	77057	**800-722-9112**	713-977-2600	215
First Investors Funds 95 Wall St.	New York	NY	10005	**800-423-4026**	212-858-8000	517
First Investors Life Insurance Co 95 Wall St 22nd Fl	New York	NY	10005	**800-832-7783**	212-858-8200	384-2
First Investors Management Co Inc 95 Wall St. *Cust Svc	New York	NY	10005	**800-423-4026***	212-858-8000	393
First Keystone Financial Inc 22 W State St. *NASDAQ: FKFS*	Media	PA	19063	**800-590-1414**	610-565-6210	355-2
First Lease Inc 185 Commerce Dr Unit 2	Fort Washington	PA	19034	**800-544-7607**	215-283-9727	261-5
First Line Supervisor Newsletter 360 Hiatt Dr	Palm Beach Gardens	FL	33418	**800-621-5463**	561-622-9914	521-2
First Marblehead Corp 800 Boylston St 34th Fl *NYSE: FMD*	Boston	MA	02199	**800-895-4238**	781-639-2000	215
First Marketing 3300 Gateway Dr	Pompano Beach	FL	33069	**800-641-9251**	954-979-0700	623-9
First Midwest Bancorp Inc 300 Park Blvd Suite 405 *NASDAQ: FMBI*	Itasca	IL	60143	**800-322-3623**	630-875-7200	355-2
First Midwest Bank NA 300 Park Blvd Suite 405 PO Box 459	Itasca	IL	60143	**800-322-3623**	630-875-7200	71
First Missouri State Capitol State Historic Site 200-216 S Main St.	Saint Charles	MO	63301	**800-334-6946**	636-946-9282	554
First Mutual Bancshares Inc 400 108th Ave NE *NASDAQ: FMSB*	Bellevue	WA	98004	**800-735-7303**	425-455-7300	355-2
First National Bank Alaska 101 W 36 Ave.	Anchorage	AK	99503	**800-856-4362**	907-276-6300	71
First National Bank of Florida PO Box 413043	Naples	FL	34101	**800-262-7600**	239-262-7600	71
First National Bank of Nevada 2510 S Maryland Pkwy Suite A	Las Vegas	NV	89109	**888-216-6888**	702-792-2200	71
First National Bank of Omaha 1620 Dodge St	Omaha	NE	68197	**800-228-4411**	402-341-0500	71
First National Insurance Co of America 4333 Brooklyn Ave NE Safeco Plaza	Seattle	WA	98185	**800-332-3226**	206-545-5000	384-4
First National Lincoln Corp PO Box 940 *NASDAQ: FNLC*	Damariscotta	ME	04543	**800-564-3195**	207-563-3195	355-2
First National of Nebraska Inc 1 First National Ctr	Omaha	NE	68197	**800-688-7070**	402-341-0500	355-2
First Nations Development Institute 2300 Fallhill Ave Suite 412	Fredericksburg	VA	22401	**800-682-5384**	540-371-5615	48-14
First Niagara Bank 6950 S Transit Rd.	Lockport	NY	14094	**800-421-0004**	716-625-7500	71
First NLC Financial Services Inc 700 W Hillsboro Blvd Bldg 1 Suite 204	Deerfield Beach	FL	33441	**800-950-3314**	954-420-0060	498
First Oak Brook Bancshares Inc 1400 W 16th St *NASDAQ: FOBB*	Oak Brook	IL	60523	**800-536-3000**	630-571-1050	355-2
First Options of Chicago Inc 440 S La Salle St Suite 1600	Chicago	IL	60605	**800-621-3436**	312-362-3000	679
First Pacific Advisors Inc 11400 W Olympic Blvd Suite 1200	Los Angeles	CA	90064	**800-982-4372**	310-473-0225	393
First Penn-Pacific Life Insurance Co 10 N Martingale Rd	Schaumburg	IL	60173	**800-450-3067**	847-466-8000	384-2
First Place Bank 185 E Market St.	Warren	OH	44481	**800-995-2646**	330-373-1221	71
First Place Financial Corp 185 E Market St *NASDAQ: FPFC*	Warren	OH	44481	**800-995-2646**	330-373-1221	355-2
First Priority Health 19 N Main St.	Wilkes-Barre	PA	18711	**800-822-8753**		384-3
First Professionals Insurance Co 1000 Riverside Ave Suite 800	Jacksonville	FL	32204	**800-741-3742**	904-354-5910	384-5
First Quantum Minerals Ltd 543 Granville St Suite 800 *TSE: FM*	Vancouver	BC	V6C1X8	**888-688-6577**	604-688-6577	492
First Republic Bank 111 Pine St 3rd Fl *NYSE: FRC*	San Francisco	CA	94111	**800-392-1400**	415-392-1400	71

Name / Address	City	State	Zip	Toll-Free	Phone	Class
First Republic Corp of America 302 5th Ave	New York	NY	10001	**800-578-2254**	212-279-6100	641
First Residential Mortgage Network Inc 9500 Ormsby Station Rd	Louisville	KY	40223	**800-585-9005**	502-315-4700	498
First Service Realty Inc 13155 SW 42nd St Suite 200	Miami	FL	33175	**800-899-8477**	305-551-9400	638
First South Bancorp Inc 1311 Carolina Ave *NASDAQ: FSBK*	Washington	NC	27889	**888-317-0097**	252-946-4178	355-2
First South Production Credit Assn 713 S Pear Orchard Rd Suite 300	Ridgeland	MS	39157	**888-297-1722**	601-977-8394	214
First Southern Bancshares Inc 102 S Court St	Florence	AL	35630	**800-625-7131**	256-764-7131	355-2
First Southwest Co 325 N Saint Paul St Suite 800	Dallas	TX	75201	**800-678-3792**	214-953-4000	679
First State Bancorporation 7900 Jefferson NE *NASDAQ: FSNM*	Albuquerque	NM	87190	**888-699-7500**	505-241-7500	355-2
First Supply LLC 6800 Gisholt Dr	Madison	WI	53713	**800-236-9795**	608-222-7799	601
First Tennessee Bank 165 Madison Ave	Memphis	TN	38103	**800-999-0110**	901-523-4444	71
First United Corp 19 S 2nd St *NASDAQ: FUNC*	Oakland	MD	21550	**800-296-9471**	301-334-9471	355-2
First UNUM Life Insurance Co 2211 Congress St	Portland	ME	04122	**800-658-8686**		384-2
First Watch Inc 6910 Professional Pkwy E	Sarasota	FL	34240	**800-774-0724**	941-907-9800	657
First Wave Marine Inc 2616 South Loop W Suite 665	Houston	TX	77054	**800-399-9283**	713-847-4600	689
First West Virginia Bancorp Inc 1701 Warwood Ave *AMEX: FWV*	Wheeling	WV	26003	**866-235-1923**	304-277-1100	355-2
First Years Inc 1 Kiddie Dr	Avon	MA	02322	**800-533-6708**	508-588-1220	64
FirstCom Music 1325 Capital Pkwy Suite 109	Carrollton	TX	75006	**800-858-8880**	972-446-8742	514
FirstEnergy Corp 76 S Main St *NYSE: FE*	Akron	OH	44308	**800-646-0400**		355-5
FirstFed - A Division of Webster Bank 1 First FedPark	Swansea	MA	02777	**877-679-8181**	508-991-2601	71
FirstFed Bancorp Inc 1630 4th Ave N *NASDAQ: FFDB*	Bessemer	AL	35020	**800-436-5112**	205-428-8472	355-2
FirstFed Financial Corp 401 Wilshire Blvd *NYSE: FED*	Santa Monica	CA	90401	**800-637-5540**	310-319-6000	355-2
FirstGov 1800 F St NW	Washington	DC	20405	**800-333-4636**		336-16
FirstGov en Espanol 1800 F St NW	Washington	DC	20405	**800-333-4636**		196
Firsthand Funds PO Box 8356	Boston	MA	02266	**888-883-3863**		517
Firstline Corp 511 Highland Ave	Valdosta	GA	31603	**800-243-2451**	229-247-1717	730-3
FirstLogic Inc 100 Harborview Plaza	La Crosse	WI	54601	**888-215-6442**	608-782-5000	176-7
FirstMerit Corp 3 Cascade Plaza *NASDAQ: FMER*	Akron	OH	44308	**888-554-4362**	330-384-8000	355-2
Firstrust Savings Bank 1931 Cottman Ave	Philadelphia	PA	19111	**800-220-2265**	215-836-5200	71
Firstwave Technologies Inc 2859 Paces Ferry Rd Suite 1000 *NASDAQ: FSTW*	Atlanta	GA	30339	**800-540-6061**	770-431-1200	176-11
Firth Rixson Viking 1 Erik Cir	Verdi	NV	89439	**800-648-4870**	775-345-0345	474
Fischer Carl Inc 65 Bleecker St	New York	NY	10012	**800-762-2328**	212-777-0900	623-7
Fischer Environmental Service Inc PO Box 1319	Mandeville	LA	70471	**800-391-2565**	985-626-7378	567
Fischer Francis Trees & Watts Inc 200 Park Ave 46th Fl	New York	NY	10166	**888-367-3389**	212-681-3000	393
Fischer Imaging Corp 12300 N Grant St *NASDAQ: FIMG*	Denver	CO	80241	**800-825-8434**	303-452-6800	375
Fischer International Systems Corp 3584 Mercantile Ave	Naples	FL	34104	**800-776-7258**	239-643-1500	176-1
Fiserv Inc 255 Fiserv Dr *NASDAQ: FISV*	Brookfield	WI	53045	**800-558-8413**	262-879-5000	223
Fiserv Insurance Solutions 2110 Wiley Blvd SW	Cedar Rapids	IA	52404	**800-943-2851**	319-398-1800	176-11
Fish & Richardson PC 225 Franklin St 31st Fl	Boston	MA	02110	**800-818-5070**	617-542-5070	419
Fishel Co 1810 Arlingate Ln	Columbus	OH	43228	**800-347-4351**	614-274-8100	187-10
Fisher Canvas Products Inc 415 Saint Mary St	Burlington	NJ	08016	**800-892-6688**	609-239-2733	718
Fisher College 118 Beacon St	Boston	MA	02116	**800-446-1226**	617-236-8800	160
Fisher Communications Inc 100 4th Ave N Suite 510 *NASDAQ: FSCI*	Seattle	WA	98109	**800-443-0073**	206-404-7000	724
Fisher Development Inc 1485 Bayshore Blvd Suite 152	San Francisco	CA	94124	**800-227-4392**	415-468-1717	185
Fisher Diagnostics 8365 Valley Pike PO Box 307	Middletown	VA	22645	**800-528-0494**	540-869-3200	229
Fisher Electric Technology 2801 72nd St N	Saint Petersburg	FL	33710	**800-789-2347**	727-345-9122	246
Fisher Hamilton Inc 1316 18th St	Two Rivers	WI	54241	**800-762-7587**	920-793-1121	411
Fisher Investments 13100 Skyline Blvd	Woodside	CA	94062	**800-851-8845**	650-851-3334	393
Fisher Island Hotel & Resort 1 Fisher Island Dr	Fisher Island	FL	33109	**800-537-3708**	305-535-6080	655
Fisher Mfg Co PO Box 60	Tulare	CA	93275	**800-421-6162**	559-685-5200	598
Fisher Nut Co 2299 Busse Rd	Elk Grove Village	IL	60007	**800-323-1288**	847-593-2300	291-28
Fisher & Paykel Appliances Inc 27 Hubble	Irvine	CA	92618	**800-863-5394**	949-790-8900	36
Fisher & Paykel Healthcare Inc 22982 Alcalde Dr Suite 101	Laguna Hills	CA	92653	**800-446-3908**	949-470-3900	249
Fisher-Price Inc 636 Girard Ave	East Aurora	NY	14052	**800-432-5437**	716-687-3000	750
Fisher Research Laboratory Inc 200 W Willmott Rd	Los Banos	CA	93635	**800-672-6738**	209-826-3292	464
Fisher Robert S & Co Inc 19 Liberty St	Newark	NJ	07102	**800-526-8052**	973-622-2658	401
Fisher Sand & Gravel Co PO Box 1034	Dickinson	ND	58602	**800-932-8740**	701-456-9184	493-4

Name / Address	City	State	Zip	Toll-Free	Phone	Class
Fisher Scientific International Inc HealthCare Div 9999 Veterans Memorial Dr	Houston	TX	77038	**800-766-7000**	281-405-4000	229
Fisher Scientific International Inc Safety Div 2000 Park Ln *Cust Svc	Pittsburgh	PA	15275	**800-766-7000***	412-490-8300	566
Fisher Scientific International Inc Science Education Div 4500 Turnberry Dr	Hanover Park	IL	60133	**800-955-1177**	630-259-1200	673
Fisher Skylights Inc 5005 Veterans Memorial Hwy	Holbrook	NY	11741	**800-431-1586**	631-563-4001	688
Fisher Space Pen Co 711 Yucca St	Boulder City	NV	89005	**800-634-3494**	702-293-3011	560
Fisheries Supply Co 1900 N Northlake Way	Seattle	WA	98103	**800-426-6930**	206-632-4462	759
Fisherman's Wharf Inn 22 Commercial St	Boothbay Harbor	ME	04538	**800-628-6872**	207-633-5090	373
Fishermen's Village 1200 W Retta Esplanade	Punta Gorda	FL	33950	**800-639-0020**	941-639-8721	655
Fishers Bakery & Sandwich Co 1519 Brookside Dr	Raleigh	NC	27604	**800-849-8093**	919-832-6494	291-34
Fishery Products International 18 Electronics Ave	Danvers	MA	01923	**800-374-4770**	978-777-2660	292-5
Fishking Alabama Inc PO Box 1068	Bayou La Batre	AL	36509	**800-445-0729**	251-824-2118	291-13
Fishman & Tobin Inc 625 Ridge Pike Bldg E Suite 320	Conshohocken	PA	19428	**800-367-2772**	610-828-8400	153-12
Fisk University 1000 17th Ave N	Nashville	TN	37208	**800-443-3475**	615-329-8500	163
Fiskars Brands Inc 2537 Daniels St	Madison	WI	53718	**800-500-4849**	608-259-1649	746
Fiskars Brands Inc Garden Tools Div 780 Carolina St	Sauk City	WI	53583	**800-500-4849**	608-643-4389	420
Fiskars Brands Inc Newpoint Div 17300 Medina Rd Suite 800	Plymouth	MN	55447	**800-639-7646**	763-557-8889	803
Fiskars Brands Inc Power Sentry Div 17300 Medina Rd Suite 800	Plymouth	MN	55447	**800-852-4312**	763-557-8889	803
Fiskars Brands Inc Royal Floor Mats Div 3000 W Orange Ave	Apopka	FL	32703	**800-621-4253**	407-889-5533	663
Fiske Brothers Refining Co 129 Lockwood St	Newark	NJ	07105	**800-733-4755**	973-589-9150	530
Fit America MD 401 Fairway Dr	Deerfield Beach	FL	33441	**800-940-7546**	954-570-3211	797
Fitch Co 2201 Russell St	Baltimore	MD	21230	**800-933-4824**	410-539-1953	398
Fitger's Brewery Complex Museum 600 E Superior St	Duluth	MN	55802	**888-348-4377**	218-722-0410	509
Fitger's Inn 600 E Superior St	Duluth	MN	55802	**888-348-4377**	218-722-8826	373
Fitness Assn of America. Aerobics & 15250 Ventura Blvd Suite 200	Sherman Oaks	CA	91403	**877-968-7263**	818-905-0040	48-22
Fitness Assn. American Senior PO Box 2575	New Smyrna Beach	FL	32170	**800-243-1478**	386-423-6634	48-6
Fitness Co 1602 Hgwy 35 South	Oakhurst	NJ	07755	**888-353-6754**	732-775-0955	349
Fitness Magazine 15 E 26th St 5th Fl *Cust Svc	New York	NY	10010	**800-888-1181***	646-758-0600	449-13
Fitness Quest Inc 1400 Raff Rd SW	Canton	OH	44750	**800-321-9236**	330-478-0755	263
Fitness Zone 2630 6th Ave S *Cust Svc	Birmingham	AL	35233	**800-875-9145***	205-324-1955	702
Fitz & Floyd Corp Inc 501 Corporate Dr	Lewisville	TX	75057	**800-243-2058**	972-874-3480	716
FitzGerald Communications Inc 855 Boylston St 5th Fl	Boston	MA	02116	**888-494-9501**	617-488-9500	622
Fitzgerald Hotel 620 Post St	San Francisco	CA	94109	**800-334-6835**	415-775-8100	373
Fitzgerald's Casino & Hotel Las Vegas 301 E Fremont St	Las Vegas	NV	89101	**800-274-5825**	702-388-2400	373
Fitzgeralds Casino & Hotel Reno 255 N Virginia St PO Box 40130	Reno	NV	89504	**800-535-5825**	775-785-3300	133
Fitzgeralds Casino & Hotel Tunica 711 Lucky Ln	Robinsonville	MS	38664	**888-766-5825**	662-363-5825	133
Fitzpatrick Chicago Hotel 166 E Superior St	Chicago	IL	60611	**800-367-7701**	312-787-6000	373
Fitzpatrick Electric Supply Co 444 Irwin Ave	Muskegon	MI	49442	**800-968-6621**	231-722-6621	245
Fitzpatrick Manhattan Hotel 687 Lexington Ave	New York	NY	10022	**800-367-7701**	212-355-0100	373
Five Star Food Service Inc 1400 17th St	Columbus	GA	31901	**800-327-0043**	706-327-0303	294
Five Star Trucking Inc 4380 Glenbrook Rd	Willoughby	OH	44094	**800-321-3658**	440-953-9300	769
Fixtures Furniture 1642 Crystal Ave *Cust Svc	Kansas City	MO	64126	**800-821-3500***	816-241-4500	314-1
Fixtures International Inc 501 Yale St PO Box 7774	Houston	TX	77007	**800-444-1253**	713-869-3228	281
FJ Gray & Co 217-44 98th Ave	Queens Village	NY	11429	**800-523-3320**	718-217-2943	325
Fjord Seafoods DBA Windward Seafoods 8550 NW 17 St Suite 105	Miami	FL	33126	**800-780-3474**	305-591-8550	292-5
FKI Industries Faultless Caster Div 1421 N Garvin St *Cust Svc	Evansville	IN	47711	**800-322-9329***	812-425-1011	345
FKI Industries Faultless Nutting Co Div 505 W Airport Dr	Watertown	SD	57201	**800-533-0337**	605-882-3000	462
FKI Logistex 1500 Lebanon Rd	Danville	KY	40422	**877-935-4564**		206
FKI Security Group 101 Security Pkwy	New Albany	IN	47150	**800-457-2424**	812-948-8400	665
FL Crane & Sons Inc PO Box 428	Fulton	MS	38843	**800-748-9523**	662-862-2172	188-9
FL Emmert Co Inc 2007 Dunlap St	Cincinnati	OH	45214	**800-441-3343**	513-721-5808	438
FL Roberts & Co Inc 93 W Broad St PO Box 1964	Springfield	MA	01102	**800-628-4004**	413-781-7444	319
FL Smithe Inc 2040 Ave C	Bethlehem	PA	18017	**800-523-9482**	610-264-6011	462
FLA (Forest Landowners Assn) 3776 La Vista Rd Suite 250	Tucker	GA	30084	**800-325-2954**	404-325-2954	48-13
Flack Tours PO Box 725	Waddington	NY	13694	**800-842-9747**	315-393-7160	748
Flag Dealers Assn. National Independent 214 N Hale St	Wheaton	IL	60187	**877-544-3524**	630-510-4500	49-18
Flag Fire Equipment Ltd 1 Stanton St	Marinette	WI	54143	**800-265-0804**		666
Flagler College 74 King St	Saint Augustine	FL	32084	**800-304-4208**	904-829-6481	163

Listing	City	State	ZIP	Toll-Free	Phone	Class
Flagler County Chamber of Commerce 20 Airport Rd	Bunnell	FL	32110	**800-881-1022**	386-437-0106	137
Flagler Hospital 400 Health Park Blvd	Saint Augustine	FL	32086	**866-834-3278**	904-829-5155	366-2
Flagship All Suites Resort 60 N Maine Ave	Atlantic City	NJ	08401	**800-647-7890**	609-343-7447	373
Flagship Hotel Over the Water 2501 Seawall Blvd	Galveston	TX	77550	**800-392-6542**	409-762-9000	373
Flagstaff Convention & Visitors Bureau 323 W Aspen Ave	Flagstaff	AZ	86001	**800-217-2367**	928-779-7611	205
Flagstaff Symphony Orchestra PO Box 122	Flagstaff	AZ	86002	**888-520-7214**	928-774-5107	563-3
Flagstar Bancorp Inc 5151 Corporate Dr *NYSE: FBC*	Troy	MI	48098	**800-945-7700**	248-312-2000	355-2
Flagstar Bank FSB 5151 Corporate Dr	Troy	MI	48098	**800-945-7700**	248-312-2000	71
Flaherty MJ Co 1 Gateway Ctr Suite 450	Newton	MA	02458	**800-370-2280**	617-969-1492	188-10
Flair Communications Agency Inc 214 W Erie St	Chicago	IL	60610	**800-621-8317**	312-943-5959	10
Flambeau Inc 15981 Valplast Rd	Middlefield	OH	44062	**800-457-5252**	440-632-1631	593
Flamingo Hotel Tucson 1300 N Stone Ave	Tucson	AZ	85705	**800-300-3533**	520-770-1910	373
Flamingo Las Vegas 3555 Las Vegas Blvd S *Resv	Las Vegas	NV	89109	**800-732-2111***	702-733-3111	655
Flamingo Laughlin 1900 S Casino Dr *Resv	Laughlin	NV	89029	**800-352-6464***	702-298-5111	133
Flamingo Motel 3100 Baltimore Ave	Ocean City	MD	21842	**800-394-7465**	410-289-6464	373
Flamingo Resort Hotel & Conference Center 2777 4th St	Santa Rosa	CA	95405	**800-848-8300**	707-545-8530	655
Flashes Publishers Inc 595 Jenner Dr	Allegan	MI	49010	**800-968-4415**	269-673-2141	623-8
Flashfold Carton Inc 1140 Hayden St	Fort Wayne	IN	46803	**800-589-9060**	260-423-9431	102
Flathead Convention & Visitors Bureau 15 Depot Pk	Kalispell	MT	59901	**800-543-3105**	406-756-9091	205
Flathead Electric Co-op Inc 2510 Hwy 2 E	Kalispell	MT	59901	**800-735-8489**	406-752-4483	244
Flathead Valley Community College 777 Grandview Dr	Kalispell	MT	59901	**800-313-3822**	406-756-3822	160
Flatiron Structures Co Inc PO Box 2239	Longmont	CO	80502	**800-333-1760**	303-485-4050	187-4
Flatotel International 135 W 52nd St	New York	NY	10019	**800-352-8683**	212-887-9400	373
Flav-O-Rich 1105 N William St	Goldsboro	NC	27530	**877-321-1158**	919-734-0728	291-27
Flavia Beverage Systems 1301 Wilson Dr	West Chester	PA	19380	**800-882-6629**	610-430-2500	82-2
Flavia Publishing Inc 924 Anacapa St Suite B4	Santa Barbara	CA	93101	**800-352-8424**	805-564-6907	338
Flavor House Products PO Box 8084	Dothan	AL	36304	**800-233-5979**	334-983-5643	291-28
Flax Art & Design 240 Valley Dr	Brisbane	CA	94005	**800-343-3529**		45
Fleck Controls Inc 20580 Enterprise Ave *Cust Svc	Brookfield	WI	53045	**888-784-9065***	262-784-4490	776
Fleer/Skybox International LP 1120 Rt 73 S Suite 300	Mount Laurel	NJ	08054	**800-343-6816**	856-231-6200	750
Fleet Bank 100 Federal St	Boston	MA	02110	**866-826-8989**	617-434-2200	71
Fleet CB Inc 4615 Murray Pl PO Box 11349	Lynchburg	VA	24502	**800-999-9711**	434-528-4000	572
Fleet Engineers Inc 1800 E Keating Ave *Cust Svc	Muskegon	MI	49442	**800-333-7890***	231-777-2537	505
Fleet Landing Retirement Community 1 Fleet Landing Blvd	Atlantic Beach	FL	32233	**800-872-8761**	904-246-9900	659
Fleet Owner Magazine 11 Riverbend Dr S PO Box 4211	Stamford	CT	06907	**800-776-1246**	203-358-9900	449-5
Fleet Reserve Assn (FRA) 125 N West St	Alexandria	VA	22314	**800-372-1924**	703-683-1400	48-19
Fleetguard Inc 2931 Elm Hill Pike	Nashville	TN	37214	**800-777-7064**	615-367-0040	60
Fleetline Products 784 Bill Jones Industrial Dr	Springfield	TN	37172	**800-332-6653**	615-384-4338	60
Fleetwash Inc 273 Passaic Ave	Fairfield	NJ	07004	**800-847-3735**	973-882-8314	62-1
Fleetwood Group Inc 11832 James St	Holland	MI	49424	**800-257-6390**	616-396-1142	314-3
Fleetwood Homes of California Inc 7007 Jurupa Ave	Riverside	CA	92504	**800-999-9265**	951-688-5353	107
Fleetwood Homes of Idaho Inc PO Box 1550	Nampa	ID	83653	**800-334-8958**	208-466-2438	495
Fleetwood Homes of Washington Inc 211 5th St *Sales	Woodland	WA	98674	**800-275-6869***	360-225-9461	495
Fleetwood Inc 1305 Lakeview Dr	Romeoville	IL	60446	**800-824-6609**	630-759-6800	206
Fleetwood-Signode 2222 Windsor Ct	Addison	IL	60101	**800-862-7997**	630-268-9999	549
Fleming Door Products Ltd 20 Barr Rd	Ajax	ON	L1S3X9	**800-263-7515**	905-683-3667	232
Fleming Mason Energy Co-op PO Box 328	Flemingsburg	KY	41041	**800-464-3144**	606-845-2661	244
Flender Corp 950 Tollgate Rd	Elgin	IL	60123	**800-867-3766**	847-931-1990	700
Flents Products Co 5401 S Graham Rd	Saint Charles	MI	48655	**800-262-8221**	989-865-8221	211
Flesh Co 2118 59th St	Saint Louis	MO	63110	**800-869-3330**	314-781-4400	111
Fletcher Aviation Inc 9000 Randolph St	Houston	TX	77061	**800-329-4647**	713-649-8700	63
Fletcher Granite Co Inc 534 Groton Rd	Westford	MA	01886	**800-253-8168**	978-251-4031	493-6
Fletcher Group DBA Fletcher Aviation Inc 9000 Randolph St	Houston	TX	77061	**800-329-4647**	713-649-8700	63
Fletcher Music Centers Inc 3966 Airway Cir	Clearwater	FL	33762	**800-258-1088**	727-571-1088	515
Fletcher-Terry Co Inc 65 Spring Ln *Cust Svc	Farmington	CT	06032	**800-843-3826***	860-677-7331	746
Fleur de Lait BC USA 400 S Custer Ave	New Holland	PA	17557	**800-322-2743**	717-355-8500	291-5
Flex Bon Paints 2131 Andrea Ln	Fort Myers	FL	33912	**800-226-3539**	239-489-2332	540
Flex Cable & Furnace Products Inc 20 W Huron St	Pontiac	MI	48342	**800-245-3539**	248-332-6900	804
Flex-Kleen Div Met-Pro Corp 955 Hawthorn Dr	Itasca	IL	60143	**800-621-0734**	630-775-0707	19
Flex Magazine 21100 Erwin St	Woodland Hills	CA	91367	**800-423-5590**	818-884-6800	449-13
Flex-O-Lators Inc 1460 Jackson Dr	Carthage	MO	64836	**800-641-4363**	417-358-4095	705
Flex-O-Lite Inc 801 Corporate Ctr Dr Suite 300	Saint Charles	MO	63304	**800-325-9525**	636-300-2700	328
Flex-Y-Plan Distinctive Office Furnitue PO Box CC *Cust Svc	Fairview	PA	16415	**800-458-0552***	814-474-1565	314-1
Flexaust Co 1510 Armstrong Rd	Warsaw	IN	46580	**800-343-0428**	574-267-7909	364
Flexfab LLC 1699 W M-43 Hwy	Hastings	MI	49058	**800-331-0003**	269-945-2433	364
Flexi-Mat Corp 14420 N Van Dyke Rd	Plainfield	IL	60544	**800-338-7392**	815-609-4600	463
Flexible Flyer Inc 100 Tubb Ave *Cust Svc	West Point	MS	39773	**800-521-6233***	662-494-4732	750
Flexible Furniture 323 Acorn St *Cust Svc	Plainwell	MI	49080	**800-875-6836***	269-685-6831	314-1
Flexible Material Handling 9501 Granger Rd	Cleveland	OH	44125	**800-669-1501**	216-587-1575	462
Flexible Materials Inc 1202 Port Rd	Jeffersonville	IN	47130	**800-359-9663**	812-280-7000	602
FlexiInternational Software Inc 2 Enterprise Dr	Shelton	CT	06484	**800-353-9492**	203-925-3040	176-1
Flexmag Industries Inc 107 Industry Rd	Marietta	OH	45750	**800-543-4426**	740-374-8024	450
Floxon Industries Corp 1 Flexon Plaza	Newark	NJ	07114	**800-327-4673**	973-824-5527	364
FlexSol Packaging Corp 560 Ferry St	Newark	NJ	07105	**800-490-1990**	973-466-0266	67
Flextron Industries Inc 720 Mount Rd	Aston	PA	19014	**800-633-2181**	610-459-4600	538
Flight Attendants. Association of Professional 1004 W Euless Blvd	Euless	TX	76040	**800-395-2732**	817-540-0108	405
Flight Form Cases Inc 5950 192nd St NE *Cust Svc	Arlington	WA	98223	**800-657-1199***	360-435-6688	199
Flight Options 26180 Curtiss Wright Pkwy	Richmond Heights	OH	44143	**800-433-1285**	216-261-3500	14
Flight Suits Ltd 1675 Pioneer Way	El Cajon	CA	92020	**800-748-6693**	619-440-6976	153-19
Flightcraft Inc 90454 Boeing Dr	Eugene	OR	97402	**800-776-6312**	541-688-9291	63
Flightstar Corp 7 Airport Rd Willard Airport	Savoy	IL	61874	**800-747-4777**	217-351-7700	14
Flint Area Convention & Visitors Bureau 316 Water St *Sales	Flint	MI	48502	**800-253-5468***	810-232-8900	205
Flint Cliffs Mfg Co 1600 Bluff Rd	Burlington	IA	52601	**800-445-1867**	319-752-2781	269
Flint Cultural Center 1178 Robert T Longway Blvd	Flint	MI	48503	**888-823-6837**	810-237-7333	50
Flint Energies PO Box 308	Reynolds	GA	31076	**800-342-3616**	478-847-3415	244
Flint Journal 200 E 1st St *Circulation	Flint	MI	48502	**800-875-6200***	810-766-6100	522-2
Flint River Mills Inc PO Box 280 *Cust Svc	Bainbridge	GA	39818	**800-841-8502***	229-246-2232	438
Flint Sausage Works Inc PO Box 86	Flint	MI	48501	**800-654-7280**	810-239-3179	291-26
Flint & Walling Inc 95 N Oak St *Sales	Kendallville	IN	46755	**800-927-0360***	260-347-1600	627
Flintco Inc 1624 W 21st St	Tulsa	OK	74107	**800-947-2828**	918-587-8451	185
FlipDog.com 5 Clock Tower Pl Suite 500	Maynard	MA	01754	**877-887-3547**		257
FLIR Systems Inc 16505 SW 72nd Ave *NASDAQ: FLIR*	Portland	OR	97224	**800-322-3731**	503-684-3731	519
FLM Graphics 123 Lehigh Dr	Fairfield	NJ	07004	**800-257-9757**	973-575-9450	577
Floor Covering Assn. World 2211 Howell Ave	Anaheim	CA	92806	**800-624-6880**	714-978-6440	49-4
Floor Coverings International 5182 Old Dixie Hwy Suite B *Sales	Forest Park	GA	30297	**800-955-4324***	404-361-5047	361
FLOORgraphics Inc 5 Vaughn Dr Suite 200	Princeton	NJ	08540	**888-356-6723**	609-514-0404	692
Flooring Assn. National Wood 111 Chesterfield Industrial Blvd	Chesterfield	MO	63005	**800-422-4556**	636-519-9663	49-3
FloraCraft Corp PO Box 400	Ludington	MI	49431	**800-253-0409**	231-845-5127	590
Floral Plant Growers LLC 1133 Ebenezer Church Rd	Rising Sun	MD	21911	**800-637-2107**	410-658-6100	363
Florence Area Chamber of Commerce 290 Hwy 101	Florence	OR	97439	**800-524-4864**	541-997-3128	137
Florence Convention & Visitors Bureau 3290 W Radio Dr	Florence	SC	29501	**800-325-9005**	843-664-0330	205
Florence-Darlington Technical College 2715 W Lucas St	Florence	SC	29501	**800-228-5745**	843-661-8324	787
Florence Events Center 715 Quince St	Florence	OR	97439	**888-968-4086**	541-997-1994	204
Florentine Opera Co 700 N Water St Suite 950	Milwaukee	WI	53202	**800-326-7372**	414-291-5700	563-2
Florestone Products Co Inc 2851 Falcon Dr	Madera	CA	93637	**800-446-8827**	559-661-4171	599
Florida						
Bill Status 111 W Madison St Rm 704	Tallahassee	FL	32399	**800-342-1827**	850-488-4371	425
Child Support Enforcement Program PO Box 8030	Tallahassee	FL	32314	**800-622-5437**		335
Consumer Services Div 2005 Apalachee Pkwy	Tallahassee	FL	32399	**800-435-7352**	850-922-2966	335
Financial Services Dept 200 E Gaines St	Tallahassee	FL	32399	**800-342-2762**	850-413-3100	335
Insurance Regulation Office 200 E Gaines St	Tallahassee	FL	32399	**800-342-2762**	850-413-3132	335
Prepaid College Board PO Box 6567	Tallahassee	FL	32314	**800-552-4723**	850-488-8514	711
Recreation & Parks Div 3900 Commonwealth Blvd MS 500 *Campground Resv	Tallahassee	FL	32399	**800-326-3521***	850-245-2157	335
Student Financial Assistance Office 1940 N Monroe St Suite 70	Tallahassee	FL	32303	**888-827-2004**	850-410-5200	711
Tourism Commission 661 E Jefferson St Suite 300	Tallahassee	FL	32301	**888-735-2872**	850-488-5607	335
Vocational Rehabilitation Services Div 2002 Old St Augustine Rd Bldg A	Tallahassee	FL	32301	**800-451-4327**	850-245-3399	335

Name / Address	City	State	Zip	Toll-Free	Phone	Class
Florida Aquarium 701 Channelside Dr	Tampa	FL	33602	**800-353-4741**	813-273-4000	40
Florida Atlantic University 777 Glades Rd	Boca Raton	FL	33431	**800-299-4328**	561-297-3000	163
Davie Campus 2912 College Ave	Davie	FL	33314	**800-764-2222**	954-236-1000	163
Fort Lauderdale Campus 111 E Las Olas Blvd	Fort Lauderdale	FL	33301	**800-764-2222**	954-762-5200	163
Florida Bar 651 E Jefferson St	Tallahassee	FL	32399	**800-342-8060**	850-561-5600	73
Florida Bar Journal 650 Apalachee Pkwy	Tallahassee	FL	32399	**800-342-8060**	850-561-5600	449-15
Florida Chamber of Commerce 136 S Bruno St	Tallahassee	FL	32301	**877-521-1200**	850-521-1200	138
Florida Christian College 1011 Bill Beck Blvd	Kissimmee	FL	34744	**888-468-6322**	407-847-8966	163
Florida City Gas 955 E 25th St	Hialeah	FL	33013	**800-993-7546**	305-691-8710	774
Florida College 119 N Glen Arven Ave	Temple Terrace	FL	33617	**800-326-7655**	813-988-5131	160
Florida Community College at Jacksonville Downtown Campus 101 W State St	Jacksonville	FL	32202	**877-633-5950**	904-633-8100	160
Florida Crushed Stone Co PO Box 490300	Leesburg	FL	34749	**800-767-0608**	352-787-0608	493-5
Florida Culinary Institute 2410 Metro Centre Blvd	West Palm Beach	FL	33407	**800-867-2433**	561-688-2001	787
Florida Democratic Party PO Box 1758	Tallahassee	FL	32302	**800-925-3411**	850-222-3411	605-1
Florida Dental Assn 1111 E Tennessee St	Tallahassee	FL	32308	**800-877-9922**	850-681-3629	225
Florida East Coast Industries Inc 1 Malaga St *NYSE: FLA*	Saint Augustine	FL	32084	**800-342-1131**	904-829-3421	634
Florida East Coast Railway 1 Malaga St	Saint Augustine	FL	32084	**800-342-1131**	904-829-3421	634
Florida Education Assn 213 S Adams St	Tallahassee	FL	32301	**888-807-8007**	850-201-2800	405
Florida Favorite Fertilizer Inc 1607 Olive St	Lakeland	FL	33815	**800-822-4474**	863-688-2442	272
Florida Georgia Blood Alliance 536 W 10th St	Jacksonville	FL	32206	**800-447-1479**	904-353-8263	90
Florida Grand Opera 1200 Coral Way	Miami	FL	33145	**800-741-1010**	305-854-1643	563-2
Florida Gulf Coast University 10501 FGCU Blvd S	Fort Myers	FL	33965	**888-889-1095**	239-590-1000	163
Florida Holocaust Museum 55 5th St S	Saint Petersburg	FL	33701	**800-960-7448**	727-820-0100	509
Florida Hotels & Discount Guide World Choice Travel 11300 US 1 Suite 300	North Palm Beach	FL	33408	**800-670-5445**	561-845-8856	368
Florida Institute of Technology 150 W University Blvd	Melbourne	FL	32901	**800-888-4348**	321-674-8000	163
Florida International Museum 100 2nd St N	Saint Petersburg	FL	33701	**800-777-9882**	727-821-1448	509
Florida Keys Electric Co-op Assn 91605 Overseas Hwy PO Box 377	Tavernier	FL	33070	**800-858-8845**	305-852-2431	244
Florida Marlins Dolphins Stadium 2267 Dan Marino Blvd	Miami	FL	33056	**877-627-5467**	305-626-7400	703
Florida Medical Assn 123 S Adams St	Tallahassee	FL	32301	**800-762-0233**	850-224-6496	466
Florida Medical Center 5000 W Oakland Park Blvd	Fort Lauderdale	FL	33313	**800-222-9355**	954-735-6000	366-2
Florida Metropolitan University 3319 W Hillsborough Ave	Tampa	FL	33614	**877-225-0009**	813-879-6000	158
Orlando North 5421 Diplomat Cir	Orlando	FL	32810	**800-628-5870**	407-628-5870	163
Pinellas 2471 McMullen Booth Rd Suite 200	Clearwater	FL	33759	**800-353-3687**	727-725-2688	163
Pompano Beach 225 N Federal Hwy	Pompano Beach	FL	33062	**800-468-0168**	954-783-7339	163
Florida Orchestra 101 S Hoover Blvd Suite 100	Tampa	FL	33609	**800-662-7286**	813-286-1170	563-3
Florida Playground & Steel Co 4701 S 50th St	Tampa	FL	33619	**800-444-2655**	813-247-2812	340
Florida Pneumatic Mfg Corp 851 Jupiter Park Ln	Jupiter	FL	33458	**800-327-9403**	561-744-9500	747
Florida Public Utilities Co 401 S Dixie Hwy *AMEX: FPU*	West Palm Beach	FL	33401	**800-427-7712**	561-832-0872	774
Florida Republican Party PO Box 311	Tallahassee	FL	32302	**800-777-7920**	850-222-7920	605-2
Florida Rock Industries Inc 155 E 21st St *NYSE: FRK*	Jacksonville	FL	32206	**800-874-8382**	904-355-1781	180
Florida Sanitary Suppliers 3031 N Andrews Ave Ext	Pompano Beach	FL	33064	**800-940-0900**	954-972-1700	398
Florida Smoked Fish Div SeaSpecialties Inc 1111 NW 159th Dr	Miami	FL	33169	**800-654-6682**	305-625-5112	291-13
Florida Southern College 111 Lake Hollingsworth Dr	Lakeland	FL	33801	**800-274-4131**	863-680-4131	163
Florida Stage 262 S Ocean Blvd	Manalapan	FL	33462	**800-514-3837**	561-585-3404	734
Florida State University Panama City Campus 4750 Collegiate Dr	Panama City	FL	32405	**866-539-7588**	850-872-4750	163
Florida SunBreak 90 Alton Rd Suite 16	Miami Beach	FL	33139	**800-786-2732**	305-532-1516	368
Florida Technical College 1450 S Woodland Blvd	DeLand	FL	32720	**888-724-6441**	386-734-3303	787
Florida Tile Industries Inc 1 Sikes Blvd	Lakeland	FL	33815	**800-352-8453**	863-687-7171	736
Florida Times-Union 1 Riverside Ave	Jacksonville	FL	32202	**800-472-6397**	904-359-4111	522-2
Florida Today 1 Gannett Plaza	Melbourne	FL	32940	**800-633-8449**	321-242-3500	522-2
Florida Veterinary Medical Assn 7131 Lake Ellenor Dr	Orlando	FL	32809	**800-992-3862**	407-851-3862	782
Florida West Coast Symphony 709 N Tamiami Trail	Sarasota	FL	34236	**800-287-9634**	941-953-4252	563-3
Florida's Blood Centers 345 W Michigan St Suite 106	Orlando	FL	32806	**888-936-6283**	407-999-8400	90
Florida's Space Coast Office of Tourism 2725 Judge Fran Jamieson Way Suite B-105	Viera	FL	32940	**877-572-3224**	321-637-5483	205

Name / Address	City	State	Zip	Toll-Free	Phone	Class
Florig Equipment Inc 906 W Ridge Pike	Conshohocken	PA	19428	**800-345-6172**	610-825-0900	768
Florist 800 Network 2820 La Mirada Dr Suite J	Vista	CA	92083	**800-688-1299**	760-599-5599	287
Florist Assn. Extra Touch 137 N Larchmont Blvd Suite 529	Los Angeles	CA	90019	**888-419-1515**	323-735-7272	49-4
Florist Distributing 2403 Bell Ave	Des Moines	IA	50321	**800-373-3741**	515-243-5228	288
Florist & Florist Supplier Assn. Wholesale 147 Old Solomons Island Rd Suite 302	Annapolis	MD	21401	**888-289-3372**	410-573-0400	49-18
Florists. Society of American 1601 Duke St	Alexandria	VA	22314	**800-336-4743**	703-836-8700	49-4
Florstar Sales Inc 1325 N Mittel Blvd	Wood Dale	IL	60191	**800-942-6285**	630-595-7500	356
Flow Boy Mfg PO Box 720660	Norman	OK	73070	**800-580-3260**	405-329-3765	768
Flow Dry Technology Ltd 379 Albert Rd	Brookville	OH	45309	**800-533-0077**	937-833-2161	321
Flow International Corp 23500 64th Ave S *NASDAQ: FLOW*	Kent	WA	98032	**800-446-3569**	253-850-3500	447
Flower City Tissue Mills Inc PO Box 13497	Rochester	NY	14613	**800-595-2030**	585-458-9200	542-2
Flower Pot Florists 2314 N Broadway St	Knoxville	TN	37917	**800-824-7792**	865-523-5121	287
Flower World 5201 Rt 38	Pennsauken	NJ	08109	**800-257-7880**	856-429-5800	287
FlowerClub PO Box 60910	Los Angeles	CA	90060	**800-800-7363**	405-440-6001	287
Flowers Auto Parts Co 935 Hwy 70 Se	Hickory	NC	28601	**800-395-6272*** *Cust Svc	828-322-5414	61
Flowers Construction Co Inc PO Box 1207	Hillsboro	TX	76645	**800-792-3295**	254-582-2501	188-4
Flowers from Holland Ltd 835A Franklin Ct	Marietta	GA	30067	**800-647-8182**	770-380-3000	287
Flowerwood Garden Center 7625 US Hwy 14	Crystal Lake	IL	60012	**800-852-3114**	815-459-6200	318
Flowery Beauty Products Inc 107 Mill Plain Rd Suite 303	Danbury	CT	06811	**800-545-5247**	203-205-0686	211
Floyd & Beasley Transfer Co Inc PO Box 8	Sycamore	AL	35149	**800-952-7599**	256-245-4385	769
Floyd College PO Box 1864	Rome	GA	30162	**800-332-2406**	706-802-5000	160
Floyd Memorial Hospital 1850 State St	New Albany	IN	47150	**800-423-1513**	812-944-7701	366-2
Fluid Components International 1755 La Costa Meadows Dr	San Marcos	CA	92078	**800-863-8703**	760-744-6950	200
Fluid Management Inc 1023 S Wheeling Rd	Wheeling	IL	60090	**800-462-2466**	847-537-0880	379
Fluid Metering Inc 5 Aerial Way Suite 500	Syosset	NY	11791	**800-223-3388**	516-922-6050	626
Fluidmaster Inc 30800 Rancho Viejo Rd	San Juan Capistrano	CA	92675	**800-631-2011**	949-728-2000	598
Fluidyne Ansonia 1 Riverside Dr	Ansonia	CT	06401	**800-765-2676*** *Cust Svc	203-735-9311	610
Fluke Biomedical 2000 Arrowhead Dr	Carson City	NV	89706	**800-648-7952**	775-883-3400	247
Fluke Biomedical Radiation Management Services 6045 Cochran Rd	Solon	OH	44139	**800-850-4608**	440-248-9300	464
Fluke Corp 6920 Seaway Blvd	Everett	WA	98203	**800-753-5853**	425-446-6100	247
Fluor Global Services Inc 1 Enterprise Dr	Aliso Viejo	CA	92656	**800-405-6637**	949-349-2000	193
Fluoro Plastics Inc 3601 G St	Philadelphia	PA	19134	**800-262-1910*** *Cust Svc	215-425-5500	589
Fluoroscan Imaging Systems Inc 35 Crosby Dr	Bedford	MA	01730	**800-343-9729**	781-999-7300	375
Fly Logic Inc PO Box 270	Melba	ID	83641	**888-359-5644**	208-495-2090	701
Flying A Ranch 771 Flying A Ranch Rd	Pinedale	WY	82941	**888-833-3348**	307-367-2385	238
Flying E Ranch 2801 W Wickenburg Way	Wickenburg	AZ	85390	**888-684-2650**	928-684-2690	238
Flying J Inc 1104 Country Hill Dr	Ogden	UT	84403	**800-842-6428**	801-624-1000	319
Flying Magazine 1633 Broadway 43rd Fl	New York	NY	10019	**800-274-6793*** *Cust Svc	212-767-6000	449-14
Flynn Canada Ltd 1500 Valley Rd	Winnipeg	MB	R3H1B3	**800-304-8751**	204-786-6951	188-12
FM Brown's Sons Inc 127 S Furnace St PO Box 67	Birdsboro	PA	19508	**800-362-6455**	610-582-2741	438
FM Global 1301 Atwood Ave	Johnston	RI	02919	**800-343-7722**	401-275-3000	384-4
FMA (Fabricators & Manufacturers Assn International) 833 Featherstone Rd	Rockford	IL	61107	**800-432-2832**	815-399-8700	49-13
FMC Corp Agricultural Products Group 1735 Market St	Philadelphia	PA	19103	**800-621-4500**	215-299-6000	276
FMC Corp Industrial Chemicals Group 1735 Market St	Philadelphia	PA	19103	**800-621-4500**	215-299-6000	141
FMC Measurement Solutions 1602 Wagner Ave	Erie	PA	16510	**800-867-6484**	814-898-5000	486
FMC Technologies Inc 1803 Gears Rd *NYSE: FTI*	Houston	TX	77067	**800-869-6999**	281-591-4000	526
FMCA (Family Motor Coach Assn) 8291 Clough Pike	Cincinnati	OH	45244	**800-543-3622**	513-474-3622	48-23
FMCSA (Federal Motor Carrier Safety Administration) 400 7th St SW	Washington	DC	20590	**888-832-5660**	202-366-2519	336-13
FMI Corp 5151 Glenwood Ave Suite 100	Raleigh	NC	27612	**800-669-1364**	919-787-8400	193
FMJ/Pad.Lock Computer Security Systems Inc 741 E 223rd St	Carson	CA	90745	**800-322-3365**	310-549-3221	681
FMP International 1800 Industrial Pk Dr PO Box 732	Grand Haven	MI	49417	**800-560-7795**	616-847-9121	701
FMR Corp 82 Devonshire St	Boston	MA	02109	**800-522-7297**	617-563-7000	393
FMS (Financial Managers Society) 100 W Monroe St Suite 810	Chicago	IL	60603	**800-275-4367*** *Cust Svc	312-578-1300	49-2
FMS Inc 8100 Boone Blvd Suite 310	Vienna	VA	22182	**888-367-7801**	703-356-4700	176-2
FNB Corp 101 Sunset Ave *NASDAQ: FNBN*	Asheboro	NC	27203	**800-873-1172**	336-626-8300	355-2
FNB Corp 105 Arbor Dr *NASDAQ: FNBP*	Christiansburg	VA	24073	**800-642-7416**	540-382-4951	355-2

Name	Address	City	State	Zip	Toll-Free	Phone	Class
FNF Construction Inc	115 S 48th St	Tempe	AZ	85281	**800-542-9490**	480-784-2910	187-4
FNT Industries Inc	927 1st St (*Cust Svc)	Menominee	MI	49858	**800-338-9860***	906-863-5531	207
FNW Industrial Plastics Inc	740 S 28th St	Washougal	WA	98671	**800-634-5082**	360-835-2129	591
FoA (Friends of Animals Inc)	777 Post Rd Suite 205	Darien	CT	06820	**800-321-7387**	203-656-1522	48-3
Foam Rubber Products Inc	2000 Troy Ave	New Castle	IN	47362	**800-878-3774**	765-521-2000	590
Foamade Industries Inc	2550 Auburn Ct	Auburn Hills	MI	48326	**800-221-7388**	248-852-6010	590
Foamex International Inc	1000 Columbia Ave (*NASDAQ: FMXI*)	Linwood	PA	19061	**800-355-3626**	610-859-3000	590
Focal Communications Corp	200 N LaSalle St 10th Fl	Chicago	IL	60601	**800-895-8400**	312-895-8400	721
FOCUS	1529 18th St NW	Washington	DC	20036	**800-741-9415**	202-387-5200	449-8
Focus Camera Inc	905 McDonald Ave	Brooklyn	NY	11219	**800-221-0828**	718-436-6262	119
Focus Direct Inc	9707 Broadway	San Antonio	TX	78217	**800-299-9185**	210-805-9185	5
FOCUS Enhancements Inc	1370 Dell Ave (*NASDAQ: FCSE*)	Campbell	CA	95008	**800-338-3348**	408-866-8300	171-5
Focus on the Family	8605 Explorer Dr (*Sales)	Colorado Springs	CO	80920	**800-232-6459***	719-531-3400	48-6
Focus Healthcare of Georgia	2927 Demere Rd	Saint Simons Island	GA	31522	**800-234-0420**	912-638-1999	366-3
Focus Healthcare Management Inc	720 Cool Springs Blvd Suite 300	Franklin	TN	37067	**800-873-0055**	615-778-4000	455
Fodor's Travel Publications Inc	1745 Broadway	New York	NY	10019	**800-726-0600**	212-751-2600	623-2
Fodors.com	1745 Broadway	New York	NY	10019	**888-264-1745**	212-751-2600	762
Fogarty Van Lines	1103 E Cumberland Ave	Tampa	FL	33602	**800-237-7529**	813-228-7481	508
Fogel MH & Co Inc	2839 Liberty Ave	Pittsburgh	PA	15222	**800-245-2954**	412-261-3921	38
Foland Jewelry Brokers	630 E 11 Mile Rd	Royal Oak	MI	48067	**877-365-2637**	248-336-6666	402
Folbot Inc	4209 Pace St	Charleston	SC	29405	**800-533-5099**	843-744-3483	701
Foldcraft Co	615 Centennial Dr	Kenyon	MN	55946	**800-759-6653**	507-789-5111	314-1
Foley Inn	14 W Hull St Chippewa Sq	Savannah	GA	31401	**800-647-3708**	912-232-6622	373
Foley & Lardner	777 E Wisconsin Ave	Milwaukee	WI	53202	**800-558-1548**	414-271-2400	419
Foley Products Co	PO Box 7877	Columbus	GA	31908	**800-762-6773**	706-563-7882	180
Folger Adam Security Inc	16300 W 103rd St	Lemont	IL	60439	**800-966-6739**	630-739-3900	345
Follett Corp	2233 West St	River Grove	IL	60171	**800-621-4345**	708-583-2000	97
Follett Corp	801 Church Ln (*Cust Svc)	Easton	PA	18040	**800-523-9361***	610-252-7301	650
Follett Educational Services	1433 International Pkwy	Woodridge	IL	60517	**800-621-4272**	630-972-5600	97
Follett Higher Education Group	1818 Swift Dr	Oak Brook	IL	60523	**800-323-4506**	630-279-2330	96
Follett Library Resources	1340 Ridgeview Dr	McHenry	IL	60050	**888-511-5114**	815-759-1700	97
Follett Software Co	1391 Corporate Dr	McHenry	IL	60050	**800-323-3397**	815-344-8700	176-10
Folsom Lake Ford Inc	12755 Folsom Blvd	Folsom	CA	95630	**800-655-0555**	916-353-2000	57
FOLUSA (Friends of Libraries USA)	1420 Walnut St Suite 450	Philadelphia	PA	19102	**800-936-5872**	215-790-1674	49-11
Fomo Products Inc	2775 Barber Rd	Norton	OH	44203	**800-321-5585**	330-753-4585	590
Fond du Lac Band of Lake Superior Chippewa	1720 Big Lake Rd	Cloquet	MN	55720	**800-365-1613**	218-879-4593	132
Fond du Lac Convention & Visitors Bureau	171 S Pioneer Rd	Fond du Lac	WI	54935	**800-937-9123**	920-923-3010	205
Fond du Lac Tribal & Community College	2101 14th St	Cloquet	MN	55720	**800-657-3712**	218-879-0800	161
Fonda Group Inc	2920 N Main St (*Cust Svc)	Oshkosh	WI	54901	**888-898-3988***	920-235-9330	548-1
Fontaine Modification Co	9827 Mt Holly Rd	Charlotte	NC	28214	**800-989-2113**	704-391-1355	505
Fontaine Specialized Inc	5398 US Hwy 11	Springville	AL	35146	**800-633-6551**	205-467-6171	768
Fontaine Trailer Co	430 Letson Rd PO Box 619	Haleyville	AL	35565	**800-821-6535**	205-486-5251	768
Fontaine Truck Equipment Co	2490 Pinson Valley Pkwy	Birmingham	AL	35217	**800-824-3033**	205-841-8582	505
Fontainebleau Hilton Resort	4441 Collins Ave	Miami Beach	FL	33140	**800-548-8886**	305-538-2000	655
Fontana Spa. Abbey Resort &	269 Fontana Blvd	Fontana	WI	53125	**800-558-2405**	262-275-6811	655
Fontana Steel Inc	12451 Arron Rt	Rancho Cucamonga	CA	91739	**800-877-8758**	909-899-9993	188-14
Fontana Village Resort	Hwy 28 PO Box 68	Fontana Dam	NC	28733	**800-849-2258**	828-498-2211	655
Fontbonne University	6800 Wydown Blvd	Saint Louis	MO	63105	**800-205-5862**	314-862-3456	163
Food for All	201 Park Washington Ct	Falls Church	VA	22046	**800-896-5101**	703-237-3677	48-5
Food Allergy & Anaphylaxis Network (FAAN)	11781 Lee Jackson Hwy Suite 160	Fairfax	VA	22033	**800-929-4040**	703-691-3179	48-17
Food Automation-Service Techniques Inc (FAST)	905 Honeyspot Rd	Stratford	CT	06615	**800-327-8766**	203-377-4414	201
Food Chemical News	1725 K St NW Suite 506	Washington	DC	20006	**888-272-7737**	202-887-6320	521-13
Food City	PO Box 488	Chandler	AZ	85244	**800-755-7292**	480-895-9350	339
Food & Commercial Workers International Union. United	1775 K St NW	Washington	DC	20006	**800-551-4010**	202-223-3111	405
Food & Drug Administration (FDA)							
Center for Devices & Radiological Health	9200 Corporate Blvd Suite 100E	Rockville	MD	20850	**800-638-2041**		336-6
Center for Food Safety & Applied Nutrition	5100 Paint Branch Pkwy	College Park	MD	20740	**888-723-3366**	301-436-1600	336-6
FoodSafety.gov	5600 Fishers Ln	Rockville	MD	20857	**888-723-3366**		336-6
MedWatch	5600 Fishers Ln HFD-410	Rockville	MD	20857	**888-463-6332**	301-827-7240	336-6
National Center for Toxicological Research	3900 NCTR Rd	Jefferson	AR	72079	**800-638-3321**	870-543-7000	336-6
Office of Orphan Products Development	5600 Fishers Ln	Rockville	MD	20857	**800-300-7469**	301-827-3666	336-6
Food & Drug Law Institute (FDLI)	1000 Vermont Ave NW Suite 200	Washington	DC	20005	**800-956-6293**	202-371-1420	49-10
Food Giant Supermarkets	120 Industrial Dr	Sikeston	MO	63801	**800-445-3740**	573-471-3500	339
Food for the Hungry Inc	1224 E Washington St Phoenix	Scottsdale	AZ	85034	**800-248-6437**	480-998-3100	48-5
Food Industries Center. Gould	Ohio State University Howlett Hall Suite 140 2001 Fyffe Ct	Columbus	OH	43210	**800-752-2751**	614-292-7004	654
Food & Nutrition Service Food Stamps Program	3101 Park Center Dr	Alexandria	VA	22302	**800-221-5689**	703-305-2022	336-1
Food Processing Machinery Assn (FPMA)	200 Daingerfield Rd	Alexandria	VA	22314	**800-833-4337**	703-684-1080	49-13
Food Producers International	10505 Wayzata Blvd Suite 400	Minnetonka	MN	55305	**800-443-1336**	952-544-2763	291-15
Food Products Assn (FPA)	1350 'I' St NW Suite 300	Washington	DC	20005	**800-355-0983**	202-639-5900	49-6
Food Protection. International Assn for	6200 Aurora Ave Suite 200W	Des Moines	IA	50322	**800-369-6337**	515-276-3344	49-6
Food Service Executives Assn. International	836 San Bruno Ave	Henderson	NV	89015	**888-234-3732**	702-564-0997	49-6
Food Service Supplies Inc	1020 2nd Ave	Columbia	SC	29209	**800-366-3774**	803-776-2658	293
Food Services of America Inc	4025 Delridge Way SW Suite 400	Seattle	WA	98106	**800-372-3663**	206-933-5000	292-8
Food Technologists. Institute of	525 W Van Buren St Suite 1000	Chicago	IL	60607	**800-438-3663**	312-782-8424	49-6
Food Trade Inc. National Assn for the Specialty	120 Wall St 27th Fl	New York	NY	10005	**800-627-3869**	212-482-6440	49-6
Food Warming Equipment Co Inc	7900 SR 31 (*Sales)	Crystal Lake	IL	60014	**800-222-4393***	815-459-7500	293
Food & Wine Magazine	1120 Ave of the Americas	New York	NY	10036	**800-333-6569**	212-382-5600	449-11
Foods Assn. National Nutritional	3931 MacArthur Blvd Suite 101	Newport Beach	CA	92660	**800-966-6632**	949-622-6272	49-6
Foods Inc	4343 Merle Hay Rd	Des Moines	IA	50310	**800-421-4355**	515-278-1657	339
FoodSafety.gov	5600 Fishers Ln	Rockville	MD	20857	**888-723-3366**		336-6
Foodscience Corp	20 New England Dr	Essex Junction	VT	05453	**800-451-5190**	802-878-5508	786
Foot & Ankle Surgeons. American College of	8725 W Higgins Rd Suite 555	Chicago	IL	60631	**800-421-2237**	773-693-9300	49-8
Foot Locker Inc	112 W 34th St (*NYSE: FL*)	New York	NY	10120	**800-991-6682**	212-720-3700	296
Foot of the Mountain Motel	200 W Arapahoe Ave	Boulder	CO	80302	**866-773-5489**	303-442-5688	373
Foot-So-Port Shoe Corp	PO Box 247	Oconomowoc	WI	53066	**800-679-7463**	262-567-4416	296
Footaction USA	112 W 34th St	New York	NY	10120	**800-863-8932**	212-720-3700	296
Football Digest	990 Grove St	Evanston	IL	60201	**800-877-5893**	847-491-6440	449-20
Football Hall of Fame. College	111 Saint Joseph St	South Bend	IN	44601	**800-440-3263**	574-235-9999	511
Football League Players Assn. National	2021 L St NW Suite 600	Washington	DC	20036	**800-372-2000**	202-463-2200	48-22
Foothill Group Inc	2450 Colorado Ave Suite 3000W	Santa Monica	CA	90404	**800-535-1811**	310-453-7300	214
Foothills Inn	1625 N La Crosse St	Rapid City	SD	57701	**877-428-5666**	605-348-5640	373
Footstar Inc	933 MacArthur Blvd	Mahwah	NJ	07430	**866-208-7027**	201-934-2000	658
Footsteps Magazine	30 Grove St Suite C	Peterborough	NH	03458	**800-821-0115**	603-924-7209	449-6
Footwear Assn. American Apparel &	1601 N Kent St Suite 1200	Arlington	VA	22209	**800-520-2262**	703-524-1864	49-4
Footwear Assn. Pedorthic	7150 Columbia Gateway Dr Suite G	Columbia	MD	21046	**800-673-8447**	410-381-7278	48-17
FOP (Fraternal Order of Police)	1410 Donelson Pike Suite A-17	Nashville	TN	37217	**800-451-2711**	615-399-0900	48-15
For Eyes/Insight Optical	285 W 74th Pl	Hialeah	FL	33014	**800-367-3937**	305-557-9004	533
For Your Entertainment	38 Corporate Cir	Albany	NY	12203	**800-540-1242**	518-452-1242	514
Forage & Grassland Council. American	PO Box 94	Georgetown	TX	78627	**800-944-2342**		48-2
Forbes Hospice	115 S Neville St	Pittsburgh	PA	15213	**800-381-8080**	412-325-7200	365
Forbes Inc	60 5th Ave	New York	NY	10011	**800-888-9896**	212-620-2200	623-9
Forbes Magazine	60 5th Ave	New York	NY	10011	**800-888-9896**	212-620-2200	449-5
Forbes Products Corp	45 High Tech Dr	Rush	NY	14543	**800-836-7237**	585-334-4800	87
Forbo Industries Inc	PO Box 667 (*Cust Svc)	Hazleton	PA	18201	**800-842-7839***	570-459-0771	286
Force 3 Inc	2147 Priest Bridge Dr Suite 1	Crofton	MD	21114	**800-391-0204**	301-261-0204	178
Force Control Industries Inc	3660 Dixie Hwy	Fairfield	OH	45014	**800-829-3244**	513-868-0900	609
Force Inc	825 Park St	Christiansburg	VA	24073	**800-732-5252**	540-382-0462	681
Ford Auto Club Inc	PO Box 660460	Dallas	TX	75226	**800-348-5220**		53
Ford Center for the Performing Arts	213 W 42nd St	New York	NY	10036	**800-755-4000**	212-307-4100	732
Ford County Feed Yard Inc	12466 US Hwy 400	Ford	KS	67842	**800-783-2739**	620-369-2252	11-1
Ford Fasteners Inc	110 S Newman St	Hackensack	NJ	07601	**800-272-3673**	201-487-3151	274
Ford Gum & Machine Co Inc	18 Newton Ave	Akron	NY	14001	**800-225-5535**	716-542-4561	291-6
Ford Henry Museum	20900 Oakwood Blvd	Dearborn	MI	48124	**800-835-5237**	313-271-1620	509

Name / Address	City	State	ZIP	Toll-Free	Phone	Class
Ford Motor Co PO Box 6248 *NYSE: F*	Dearborn	MI	48126	**800-392-3673**	313-322-3000	59
Ford Motor Credit Co 1 American Rd PO Box 1732	Dearborn	MI	48121	**800-727-7000**	313-322-3000	215
Fordham Equipment Co 3308 Edson Ave	Bronx	NY	10469	**800-249-5922**	718-379-7300	314-3
Fordham University 441 E Fordham Rd	Bronx	NY	10458	**800-367-3426**	718-817-1000	163
College at Lincoln Center 113 W 60th St	New York	NY	10023	**800-367-3426**	212-636-6710	163
Forecast 1600 Fleetwood Dr	Elgin	IL	60123	**800-234-0416**	847-622-0416	431
Forecast Group DBA Forecast Homes 3536 Concours St Suite 100	Ontario	CA	91764	**800-229-4117**	909-483-7320	639
Forecast International/DMS Inc 22 Commerce Rd	Newtown	CT	06470	**800-451-4975**	203-426-0800	623-10
Forecaster of Boston 1 Ace St	Fall River	MA	02720	**800-760-7000**	508-676-6200	153-5
Foreign Affairs. Citizens Network for 1111 19th St NW Suite 900	Washington	DC	20036	**888-872-2632**	202-296-3920	48-5
Foreign Affairs Magazine 58 E 68th St	New York	NY	10021	**800-829-5539**	212-434-9525	449-17
Foreign Candy Co Inc 1 Foreign Candy Dr	Hull	IA	51239	**800-767-4575**	712-439-1496	292-3
Foreign Policy Assn (FPA) 470 Park Ave S 2nd Fl	New York	NY	10016	**800-628-5754**	212-481-8100	48-7
Foreign Service Assn. American 2101 'E' St NW	Washington	DC	20037	**800-704-2372**	202-338-4045	49-7
Foreign Study. American Institute for 9 W Broad St	Stamford	CT	06902	**800-727-2437**	203-399-5000	48-11
Foremost Corp of America PO Box 2450	Grand Rapids	MI	49501	**877-444-6678**	616-942-3000	355-4
Foremost Farms USA E10889A Penny Ln	Baraboo	WI	53913	**800-362-9196**	608-356-8316	291-10
Foremost Industries Inc 2375 Buchanan Trail W	Greencastle	PA	17225	**877-284-5334**	717-597-7166	107
Foremost Insurance Co PO Box 2450 *Cust Svc	Grand Rapids	MI	49501	**800-527-3905***	616-942-3000	384-4
Foremost Property & Casualty Insurance Co PO Box 2450	Grand Rapids	MI	49501	**800-527-3905**	616-942-3000	384-4
Foremost Signature Insurance Co PO Box 2450	Grand Rapids	MI	49501	**800-527-3905**	616-942-3000	384-4
Foreside Co 33 Hutcherson Dr *Cust Svc	Gorham	ME	04038	**800-359-8380***	207-854-4000	357
Forest City Residential Group Inc 50 Public Sq Terminal Tower Suite 1100	Cleveland	OH	44113	**800-726-1800**	216-621-6060	641
Forest City Trading Group Inc PO Box 4209	Portland	OR	97208	**800-767-3284**	503-246-8500	190-3
Forest Corp 1665 Enterprise Pkwy	Twinsburg	OH	44087	**800-637-6434**	330-425-3805	282
Forest Foundation. American 1111 19th St NW Suite 780	Washington	DC	20036	**888-889-4466**	202-463-2462	48-2
Forest Foundation. National Fort Missoula Rd Bldg 27 Suite 3	Missoula	MT	59804	**866-733-4633**	406-542-2805	48-13
Forest Grove Lumber Co 2700 Orchard Ave	McMinnville	OR	97128	**800-647-9663**	503-472-3195	671
Forest Laboratories Inc 909 3rd Ave 23rd Fl *AMEX: FRX*	New York	NY	10022	**800-947-5227**	212-421-7850	572
Forest Landowners Assn (FLA) 3776 La Vista Rd Suite 250	Tucker	GA	30084	**800-325-2954**	404-325-2954	48-13
Forest Lawn Memorial-Parks & Mortuaries 1712 S Glendale Ave	Glendale	CA	91205	**800-204-3131**	323-254-7251	499
Forest Lawn Museum 1712 S Glendale Ave	Glendale	CA	91205	**800-204-3131**		509
Forest Manor Inn 866 Hendersonville Rd	Asheville	NC	28803	**800-866-3531**	828-274-3531	373
Forest & Paper Assn. American 1111 19th St NW Suite 800	Washington	DC	20036	**800-878-8878**	202-463-2700	48-2
Forest Park Hospital 6150 Oakland Ave	Saint Louis	MO	63139	**877-249-8557**	314-768-3000	366-2
Forest Pharmaceutical Inc 13600 Shoreline Dr	Saint Louis	MO	63045	**800-678-1605**	314-493-7000	572
Forest Products Society 2801 Marshall Ct	Madison	WI	53705	**800-354-7164**	608-231-1361	48-2
Foresters of America. Association of Consulting 312 Montgomery St Suite 208	Alexandria	VA	22314	**888-540-8733**	703-548-0990	48-2
Foresters. Independent Order of 789 Don Mills Rd	Toronto	ON	M3C1T9	**800-828-1540**	416-429-3000	48-5
Forestry Suppliers Inc 205 W Rankin St PO Box 8397 *Cust Svc	Jackson	MS	39201	**800-752-8460***	601-354-3565	451
Forests. American 734 15th St NW Suite 800 PO Box 2000	Washington	DC	20013	**800-368-5748**	202-955-4500	48-13
Forethought Financial Services Inc Forethought Ctr *Cust Svc	Batesville	IN	47006	**800-881-2430***	812-934-7139	384-2
Foretich House 710 Beach Blvd	Biloxi	MS	39530	**800-245-6943**	228-374-3105	50
Foretravel Inc 1221 NW Stallings Dr	Nacogdoches	TX	75964	**800-955-6226**	936-564-8367	120
Forever Living Products International Inc 7501 E McCormick Pkwy	Scottsdale	AZ	85258	**888-440-2563**	480-998-8888	211
Forever/NPC Resorts LLC 7500 McCormick Blvd	Scottsdale	AZ	85258	**800-455-3509**	480-998-8888	294
Forge Recording Studios Inc 200 Lincoln Ave	Phoenixville	PA	19460	**800-331-0405**	610-935-1422	644
Forged Products Inc 6505 N Houston Rosslyn Rd	Houston	TX	77091	**800-876-3416**	713-462-3416	474
Forged Vessel Connections Inc 2525 DeSoto St *Cust Svc	Houston	TX	77091	**800-231-2701***	713-688-9705	474
Forgent Networks Inc 108 Wild Basin Rd *NASDAQ: FORG*	Austin	TX	78746	**888-323-8835**	512-437-2700	176-7
Forklifts of Minnesota Inc 501 W 78th St	Bloomington	MN	55420	**800-752-4300**	952-887-5400	378
Forks of Cheat Winery Stewart Town Rd	Morgantown	WV	26508	**877-989-4637**	304-598-2019	50
Form-A-Feed Inc 740 Bowman St	Stewart	MN	55385	**800-422-3649**	320-562-2413	438
Form-You 3 International Inc 395 Springside Dr	Akron	OH	44333	**800-525-6315**	330-668-1461	797
Formall Inc 3908 Fountain Valley Ln	Knoxville	TN	37918	**800-643-3676**	865-922-7514	591
Formax Feeds Co 980 Molly Pond Rd	Augusta	GA	30901	**800-241-2200**	706-722-6681	438
Formax Mfg Corp 168 Wealthy St SW	Grand Rapids	MI	49503	**800-242-2833**	616-456-5458	1
Formflex Inc PO Box 218	Bloomingdale	IN	47832	**800-255-7659**	765-498-8900	87
Formica Corp 10155 Reading Rd	Cincinnati	OH	45241	**800-367-6422**	513-786-3400	588
Formost Construction Co 41220 Guava St	Murrieta	CA	92562	**800-247-7532**	951-698-7270	187-3
Forms Manufacturers Inc 312 E Forest Ave	Girard	KS	66743	**800-835-0614**	620-724-8225	111
Forms & Surfaces 30 Pine St	Pittsburgh	PA	15223	**800-553-7722**	412-781-9003	482
Formtek Metal Forming Inc 26565 Miles Rd Suite 200	Cleveland	OH	44128	**800-631-0520**	216-292-4460	661
Formulabs Inc 529 W 4th Ave	Escondido	CA	92025	**800-642-2345**	760-741-2345	381
Forney Corp 3405 Wiley Post Rd *Cust Svc	Carrollton	TX	75006	**800-356-7740***	972-458-6100	200
Forney Industries Inc PO Box 563	Fort Collins	CO	80522	**800-521-6038**	970-482-7271	798
Forrest Hills Mountain Resort & Conference Center 135 Forrest Hills Dr	Dahlonega	GA	30533	**800-654-6313**	706-864-6456	655
Forrestal Conference Center Hotel. Doral 100 College Rd E	Princeton	NJ	08540	**800-222-1131**	609-452-7800	370
Forsbergs Inc 1210 Pennington Ave *Cust Svc	Thief River Falls	MN	56701	**800-654-1927***	218-681-1927	269
Forster Inc PO Box 657 *Cust Svc	Wilton	ME	04294	**800-777-7942***	207-645-2574	808
Forsythe MacArthur Assoc Inc 7770 Frontage Rd	Skokie	IL	60077	**800-843-4488**	847-675-8000	261-1
Forsythe Technology Inc 7770 Frontage Rd	Skokie	IL	60077	**800-843-4488**	847-675-8000	174
Fort Collins Convention & Visitors Bureau 3745 E Prospect Rd Suite 200	Fort Collins	CO	80525	**800-274-3678**	970-491-3388	205
Fort Collins Mulberry Inn 4333 E Mulberry St	Fort Collins	CO	80524	**800-234-5548**	970-493-9000	373
Fort Collins Plaza Inn 3709 E Mulberry St	Fort Collins	CO	80524	**800-434-5548**	970-493-7800	373
Fort Dearborn Co 6035 W Gross Point Rd	Niles	IL	60714	**888-332-7746**	773-774-4321	615
Fort Dearborn Life Insurance Co 1020 W 31st St	Downers Grove	IL	60515	**800-633-3696**		384-2
Fort Dodge Animal Health 9225 Indian Creek Pkwy Bldg 32 Suite 400	Overland Park	KS	66210	**800-477-1365**	913-664-7000	574
Fort Edward Express Co Inc PO Box 394	Fort Edward	NY	12828	**800-342-1233**	518-792-6571	769
Fort Garry The 222 Broadway	Winnipeg	MB	R3C0R3	**800-665-8088**	204-942-8251	372
Fort Hays State University 600 Park St	Hays	KS	67601	**800-628-3478**	785-628-4000	163
Fort Henry Historic Site PO Box 213 *Cust Svc	Kingston	ON	K7L4V8	**800-437-2233***	613-542-7388	509
Fort Lauderdale (Greater) Convention & Visitors Bureau 100 E Broward Blvd Suite 200	Fort Lauderdale	FL	33301	**800-356-1662**	954-765-4466	205
Fort Lauderdale Hospital 1601 E Las Olas Blvd	Fort Lauderdale	FL	33301	**800-585-7527**	954-463-4321	366-3
Fort Lauderdale Jet Center 1100 Lee Wagner Blvd	Fort Lauderdale	FL	33315	**800-394-5388**	954-359-3200	63
Fort Madison Convention & Visitors Bureau PO Box 425	Fort Madison	IA	52627	**800-210-8687**	319-372-5472	205
Fort Marcy Hotel Suites 320 Artist Rd	Santa Fe	NM	87501	**800-745-9910**	505-988-2800	373
Fort McDowell Casino Fort McDowell Rd Hwy 87	Scottsdale	AZ	85264	**800-843-3678**	480-837-1424	133
Fort Meigs State Memorial 29100 W River Rd	Perrysburg	OH	43551	**800-283-8916**	419-874-4121	50
Fort Morgan Area Chamber of Commerce 300 Main St	Fort Morgan	CO	80701	**800-354-8660**	970-867-6702	137
Fort Myers Beach Chamber of Commerce 17200 San Carlos Blvd	Fort Myers Beach	FL	33931	**800-782-9283**	239-454-7500	137
Fort Myers (Greater) Chamber of Commerce PO Box 9289	Fort Myers	FL	33902	**800-366-3622**	239-332-3624	137
Fort Ranch PO Box 73	Golconda	NV	89414	**800-651-4567**	480-488-2775	238
Fort Recovery Industries Inc 2440 SR-49 *Sales	Fort Recovery	OH	45846	**800-445-5695***	419-375-4121	198
Fort Roofing & Sheet Metal Works Inc 4230 Domino Ave	North Charleston	SC	29405	**800-356-6716**	843-554-9711	188-12
Fort Scott Community College 2108 S Horton St	Fort Scott	KS	66701	**800-874-3722**	620-223-2700	160
Fort Scott Tribune 6 E Wall St PO Box 150	Fort Scott	KS	66701	**800-658-1753**	620-223-1460	522-2
Fort Smith Convention & Visitors Bureau 2 N 'B' St	Fort Smith	AR	72901	**800-637-1477**	479-783-8888	205
Fort Vancouver National Historic Site 10001 E 5th St	Vancouver	WA	98661	**800-832-3599**	360-696-7655	554
Fort Wayne Newspapers Inc 600 W Main St	Fort Wayne	IN	46802	**800-444-3303**	260-461-8444	623-8
Fort Worth Convention & Visitors Bureau 415 Throckmorton St	Fort Worth	TX	76102	**800-433-5747**	817-336-8791	205
Fort Worth Museum of Science & History 1501 Montgomery St	Fort Worth	TX	76107	**888-255-9300**	817-255-9300	509
Fort Worth Star-Telegram 685 John B Sias Pkwy	Fort Worth	TX	76134	**800-776-7827**	817-390-7400	522-2
Forten Corp 7815 Silverton Ave Suite 2-A	San Diego	CA	92126	**800-722-5588**	858-693-9888	207
Forth Inc 5155 W Rosecrans Ave Suite 1018	Hawthorne	CA	90250	**800-553-6784**	310-491-3356	176-2
Fortifiber Corp 1001 Tahoe Blvd	Incline Village	NV	89451	**800-443-4079**	775-833-6161	542-1
Fortifications of Quebec National Historic Site 100 Saint-Louis St PO Box 2474	Quebec	QC	G1R3Z7	**800-463-6769**	418-648-7016	50
Fortune Brands Inc 300 Tower Pkwy *NYSE: FO*	Lincolnshire	IL	60069	**800-225-2719**	847-484-4400	184

Name / Address	City	State	ZIP	Toll-Free	Phone	Class
Fortune Dogs Inc DBA Big Dog Sportswear 121 Gray Ave *Orders	Santa Barbara	CA	93101	**800-642-3647***	805-963-8727	153-3
Fortune Fashions Industries LLC 4700 S Boyle Ave	Vernon	CA	90058	**800-788-6550**	323-277-7740	153-3
Fortune Magazine Rockefeller Ctr Time & Life Bldg	New York	NY	10020	**800-621-8000**	212-522-1212	449-5
Fortune Plastics Inc Williams Ln PO Box 637	Old Saybrook	CT	06475	**800-243-0306**	860-388-3426	67
Fortune Practice Management 9888 Carroll Centre Rd Suite 100	San Diego	CA	92126	**800-628-1052**	858-535-6287	455
Fortunoff 70 Charles Lindbergh Blvd. *Cust Svc	Uniondale	NY	11553	**800-777-2807***	516-832-9000	402
Forum The 101 N 5th St	Fargo	ND	58102	**800-747-7311**	701-235-7311	522-2
Forum Communications Co 101 5th St N	Fargo	ND	58102	**800-747-7311**	701-235-7311	623-8
Forum Corp 265 Franklin St 4th Fl.	Boston	MA	02110	**800-367-8611**	617-523-7300	753
Forum Gazette 4801 S University Dr Suite 101	Davie	FL	33328	**800-275-8820**	954-680-4460	522-4
Forum Publishing Group 1701 Green Rd Suite B	Deerfield Beach	FL	33064	**800-275-8820**	954-698-6397	623-8
Forvus Research Inc 742-200 McKnight Dr.	Knightdale	NC	27545	**888-323-4887**	919-954-0063	176-12
Forward Air Corp PO Box 1058 *NASDAQ: FWRD*	Greeneville	TN	37744	**800-726-6654**	423-636-7100	769
Forward Corp 219 N Front St	Standish	MI	48650	**800-664-4501**	989-846-4501	319
Forward Industries Inc 1801 Green Rd Suite E *NASDAQ: FORD*	Pompano Beach	FL	33064	**800-872-3935**	954-419-9544	444
Forward Publishing 45 E 33rd St	New York	NY	10016	**800-266-0773**	212-889-8200	623-8
Forward Technology Industries Inc 3050 Ranchview Ln N *Cust Svc	Minneapolis	MN	55447	**800-307-6040***	763-559-1785	379
Foseco Metallurgical Inc 20200 Sheldon Rd	Cleveland	OH	44142	**800-321-3132**	440-826-4548	143
Foss Maritime Co 660 W Ewing St.	Seattle	WA	98119	**800-426-2885**	206-281-3800	457
Foss Mfg Co Inc 380 Lafayette Rd	Hampton	NH	03842	**800-343-3277**	603-929-6000	730-6
Fossey Dian Gorilla Fund International 800 Cherokee Ave SE	Atlanta	GA	30315	**800-851-0203**	404-624-5881	48-3
Fossil Inc 2280 N Greenville Ave. *NASDAQ: FOSL*	Richardson	TX	75082	**800-969-0900**	972-234-2525	151
Foster City Flowers & Gifts 1185 Chess Dr Suite G	Foster City	CA	94404	**800-970-7673**	650-573-6607	287
Foster George J Co Inc 333 Central Ave.	Dover	NH	03820	**800-660-8310**	603-742-4455	623-8
Foster LB Co 415 Holiday Dr. *NASDAQ: FSTR*	Pittsburgh	PA	15220	**800-255-4500**	412-928-3400	636
Foster Parent Assn. National 7512 Stanich Ave Suite 6	Gig Harbor	WA	98335	**800-557-5238**	253-853-4000	48-6
Foster Products Corp 601 Campus Dr Suite C-7	Arlington Heights	IL	60004	**800-231-9541**	847-358-9500	3
Foster's Daily Democrat 333 Central Ave	Dover	NH	03820	**800-660-8310**	603-742-4455	522-2
Fostoria Industries Inc 1200 N Main St	Fostoria	OH	44830	**800-495-4025**	419-435-9201	313
Foth Ron Advertising 8100 N High St.	Columbus	OH	43235	**888-766-3684**	614-888-7771	4
Foth & Van Dyke & Assoc Inc PO Box 19012	Green Bay	WI	54307	**800-236-8690**	920-497-2500	258
Fotofolio Inc 561 Broadway *Sales	New York	NY	10012	**800-955-3686***	212-226-0923	130
FotoTime Inc 6711 Atlanta Dr.	Colleyville	TX	76034	**888-705-0389**	469-361-3441	577
Fougera E & Co 60 Baylis Rd	Melville	NY	11747	**800-645-9833**	631-454-6996	573
Foundation for Accounting Education 3 Park Ave 18th Fl	New York	NY	10016	**800-537-3635**	212-719-8300	49-1
Foundation for the Carolinas 217 S Tryon St.	Charlotte	NC	28202	**888-335-9541**	704-973-4500	298
Foundation Center 79 5th Ave 2nd Fl.	New York	NY	10003	**800-424-9836**	212-620-4230	48-11
Foundation Constructors Inc 81 Big Break Rd PO Box 97	Oakley	CA	94561	**800-841-8740**	925-625-4455	188-5
Foundation for Economic Education (FEE) 30 S Broadway	Irvington-on-Hudson	NY	10533	**800-960-4333**	914-591-7230	654
Foundation for European Language & Educational Centres USA 101 N Union St Suite 300	Alexandria	VA	22314	**888-387-6236**	703-684-1494	414
Foundation Fighting Blindness 11435 Cron Hill Dr.	Owings Mills	MD	21117	**800-683-5555**	410-568-0150	48-17
Foundation for Moral Law Inc PO Box 231264	Montgomery	AL	36123	**866-317-0800**	334-262-1245	48-7
Foundation News & Commentary Magazine 1828 L St NW Suite 300	Washington	DC	20036	**800-771-8187**	202-467-0445	449-5
Foundations. Council on 1828 L St NW Suite 300	Washington	DC	20036	**800-673-9036**	202-466-6512	48-5
Founders Asset Management LLC 210 University Blvd Suite 800	Denver	CO	80206	**800-525-2440**	303-394-4404	393
Founders Federal Credit Union 607 N Main St	Lancaster	SC	29720	**800-845-1614**	803-283-5900	216
Founders Inn 5641 Indian River Rd	Virginia Beach	VA	23464	**800-926-4466**	757-424-5511	370
Foundry Networks Inc 2100 Gold St. *NASDAQ: FDRY*	Alviso	CA	95002	**888-887-2652**	408-586-1700	174
Foundry Society. American 1695 N Penny Ln	Schaumburg	IL	60173	**800-537-4237**	847-824-0181	49-13
Fountainhead College of Technology 3203 Tazewell Pike	Knoxville	TN	37918	**888-218-7335**	865-688-9422	787
Fountainhead Group Inc 23 Garden St	New York Mills	NY	13417	**800-311-9903**	315-736-0037	170
Fountainhead Water Co PO Box 570	Salem	SC	29676	**800-874-8595**	864-944-1993	792
Fountains at Millbrook 79 Flint Rd.	Millbrook	NY	12545	**800-433-6092**	845-677-8550	659
Four Flags Area Chamber of Commerce 321 E Main St.	Niles	MI	49120	**888-683-8361**	269-683-3720	137
Four Points by Sheraton Hotels 1111 Westchester Ave *Cust Svc	White Plains	NY	10604	**877-443-4585***	914-640-8100	369
Four Queens Hotel & Casino 202 Fremont St.	Las Vegas	NV	89101	**800-634-6045**	702-385-4011	373
Four Sails Resort Hotel 3301 Atlantic Ave	Virginia Beach	VA	23451	**800-227-4213**	757-491-8100	373

Name / Address	City	State	ZIP	Toll-Free	Phone	Class
Four Seasons Hotels Inc 1165 Leslie St. *NYSE: FS*	Toronto	ON	M3C2K8	**800-332-3442**	416-449-1750	369
Four Seasons Inc 1801 Waters Ridge Dr	Lewisville	TX	75057	**800-433-7508**	972-316-8100	601
Four Seasons Limousine Co 2432 W Peoria Ave Bldg 5 Suite 1112	Phoenix	AZ	85029	**877-548-1612**	623-979-8473	433
Four Seasons Resort Aviara 7100 Four Seasons Pt	Carlsbad	CA	92009	**800-332-3442**	760-603-6800	655
Four Seasons Resort & Club Dallas at Las Colinas 4150 N MacArthur Blvd	Irving	TX	75038	**800-332-3442**	972-717-0700	655
Four Seasons Resort Hualalai 100 Ka'upulehu Dr	Ka'upulehu-Kona	HI	96740	**888-340-5662**	808-325-8000	655
Four Seasons Resort Maui at Wailea 3900 Wailea Alanui Dr	Wailea	HI	96753	**800-334-6284**	808-874-8000	655
Four Seasons Resort Palm Beach 2800 S Ocean Blvd.	Palm Beach	FL	33480	**800-432-2335**	561-582-2800	655
Four Seasons Resort Santa Barbara 1260 Channel Dr.	Santa Barbara	CA	93108	**888-424-5866**	805-969-2261	655
Four Seasons Resort Scottsdale at Troon North 10600 E Crescent Moon Dr	Scottsdale	AZ	85262	**800-332-3442**	480-515-5700	655
Four Seasons Spa at the Four Seasons Hotel Las Vegas 3960 Las Vegas Blvd S	Las Vegas	NV	89119	**800-819-5053**	702-632-5302	698
Four Seasons Spa at the Four Seasons Hotel Los Angeles at Beverly Hills 300 S Doheny Dr	Los Angeles	CA	90048	**800-819-5053**	310-786-2229	698
Four Seasons Spa at the Four Seasons Resort Aviara 7100 Four Seasons Pt	Carlsbad	CA	92009	**800-819-5053**	760-603-6902	698
Four Seasons Spa at the Four Seasons Resort Jackson Hole 7680 Granite Loop Rd PO Box 544	Teton Village	WY	83025	**800-819-5053**	307-732-5120	698
Four Seasons Spa at the Four Seasons Resort Maui 3900 Wailea Alanui Dr	Kihei	HI	96753	**800-819-5053**	808-874-2925	698
Four Seasons Spa at the Four Seasons Resort Santa Barbara 1260 Channel Dr	Santa Barbara	CA	93108	**800-819-5053**	805-565-8250	698
Four Seasons Spa at the Four Seasons Scottsdale at Troon North 10600 E Crescent Moon Dr	Scottsdale	AZ	85262	**800-819-5053**	480-513-5145	698
Four Seasons Sunrooms 5005 Veterans Memorial Hwy	Holbrook	NY	11741	**800-368-7732**	631-563-4000	106
Four Seasons Vacation Ownership 1165 Leslie St.	Toronto	ON	M3C2K8	**800-332-3442**	416-449-1750	738
Four Wheel Campers 1460 Churchill Downs Ave	Woodland	CA	95776	**800-242-1442**	530-666-1442	120
Four Wheeler Magazine 6420 Wilshire Blvd	Los Angeles	CA	90048	**800-777-0555**	323-782-2000	449-3
Four Winds Hospital 800 Cross River Rd	Katonah	NY	10536	**800-528-6624**	914-763-8151	366-3
Foursome Inc 841 Lake St E	Wayzata	MN	55391	**888-368-7766**	952-473-4667	155-2
Foursquare Gospel. International Church of the 1910 W Sunset Blvd Suite 200	Los Angeles	CA	90026	**888-635-4234**	213-989-4200	48-20
Fourth Avenue 4th Ave-betw University Blvd & 9th St	Tucson	AZ	85705	**800-933-2477**	520-624-5004	50
Fourth R Inc 11410 NE 124th St Suite 142	Kirkland	WA	98034	**800-821-8653**	425-814-1001	754
Fourwinds Resort & Marina 9301 Fairfax Rd	Bloomington	IN	47401	**800-538-1187**	812-824-9904	655
Fowler MM Inc 4220 Neal Rd	Durham	NC	27705	**800-313-6635**	919-309-2925	319
Fowler's Chocolate Co 100 River Rock Dr	Buffalo	NY	14207	**800-824-2263**	716-877-9983	291-8
Fownes Brothers & Co Inc 16 E 34th St.	New York	NY	10016	**800-345-6837**	212-683-0150	153-8
Fox Bruce Inc 1909 McDonald Ln.	New Albany	IN	47150	**800-289-3699**	812-945-3511	766
Fox Chase Cancer Center 333 Cottman Ave	Philadelphia	PA	19111	**888-369-2427**	215-728-6900	366-5
Fox Cities Convention & Visitors Bureau 3433 W College Ave.	Appleton	WI	54914	**800-236-6673**	920-734-3358	205
Fox Henry A Sales Co 4494 36th St SE	Kentwood	MI	49512	**800-762-8730**	616-949-1210	82-1
Fox Hills Resort & Convention Center 250 W Church St	Mishicot	WI	54228	**800-950-7615**	920-755-2376	655
Fox & Hound Restaurant Group 1551 N Waterfront Pkwy Suite 310 *NASDAQ: FOXX*	Wichita	KS	67206	**800-229-2118**	316-634-0505	656
Fox Industries Inc 3100 Falls Cliff Rd	Baltimore	MD	21211	**888-760-0369**	410-243-8856	3
Fox Michael J Foundation for Parkinson's Research PO Box 4777 Grand Central Stn	New York	NY	10163	**800-708-7644**		300
Fox Packaging Co 2200 Fox Dr.	McAllen	TX	78504	**800-336-6369**	956-682-6176	68
Fox Pool Corp 3490 Board Rd.	York	PA	17402	**800-723-1011**	717-764-8581	714
Fox River Mills Inc 227 Poplar Stq PO Box 298	Osage	IA	50461	**800-247-1815**	641-732-3798	153-10
Fox River Paper Co 100 W Lawrence St	Appleton	WI	54911	**800-993-7300**	920-733-7341	547
Fox Valley Corp PO Box 727	Appleton	WI	54912	**800-993-7300**	920-739-8982	547
Fox Valley Technical College 1825 N Bluemound Dr	Appleton	WI	54912	**800-735-3882**	920-735-5600	787
Fox World Travel Inc 7936 Sheridan Rd. *Resv	Kenosha	WI	53143	**800-236-8475***	262-654-9116	760
Foxcroft School PO Box 5555	Middleburg	VA	20118	**800-858-2364**	540-687-5555	611
Foxdale Village 500 E Marylyn Ave	State College	PA	16801	**800-253-4951**	814-238-3322	659
Foxes Music Co 416 S Washington St	Falls Church	VA	22046	**800-446-4414**	703-533-7393	515
Fox's Distribution Inc 3243 Old Frankstown Rd	Pittsburgh	PA	15239	**800-899-3697**	724-733-7888	657
Fox's Pizza Den Inc 3243 Old Frankstown Rd	Pittsburgh	PA	15239	**800-899-3697**	724-733-7888	657

Name / Address	City	State	ZIP	Toll-Free	Phone	Class
Foxtail Foods 6075 Poplar Ave Suite 800 *Cust Svc	Memphis	TN	38119	**800-487-2253***	901-766-6400	291-23
Foxwoods Resort Casino 39 Norwich Westerly Rd	Ledyard	CT	06339	**800-752-9244**	860-312-3000	133
Foxworth-Galbraith Lumber Co 17111 Waterview Pkwy	Dallas	TX	75252	**800-688-8082**	972-437-6100	190-3
FP International 1090 Mills Way	Redwood City	CA	94063	**800-866-9946**	650-261-5300	590
FP Mailing Solutions 140 N Mitchell Ct	Addison	IL	60101	**800-341-6052**		113
FPA (Financial Planning Assn) 5775 Glenridge Dr NE Suite B300	Atlanta	GA	30328	**800-945-4237**	404-845-0011	49-2
FPA (Food Products Assn) 1350 'I' St NW Suite 300	Washington	DC	20005	**800-355-0983**	202-639-5900	49-6
FPA (Foreign Policy Assn) 470 Park Ave S 2nd Fl	New York	NY	10016	**800-628-5754**	212-481-8100	48-7
FPC Inc 6677 Santa Monica Blvd	Hollywood	CA	90038	**800-814-1333**	323-468-5774	501
FPI Thermoplastic Technologies PO Box 1907	Morristown	NJ	07962	**800-932-0715**	973-539-4200	593
FPIC Insurance Group Inc 225 Water St Suite 1400 *NASDAQ: FPIC*	Jacksonville	FL	32202	**800-221-2101**	904-354-2482	355-4
FPL Energy Inc 700 Universe Blvd	Juno Beach	FL	33408	**888-867-3050**	561-691-7171	774
FPM LLC 1501 S Lively Blvd	Elk Grove Village	IL	60007	**800-875-3316**	847-228-2525	475
FPMA (Food Processing Machinery Assn) 200 Daingerfield Rd	Alexandria	VA	22314	**800-833-4337**	703-684-1080	49-13
FRA (Fleet Reserve Assn) 125 N West St	Alexandria	VA	22314	**800-372-1924**	703-683-1400	48-19
Fraen Corp 80 Newcrossing Rd	Reading	MA	01867	**800-370-0078**	781-942-2223	479
Fraenkel Co Inc PO Box 15385	Baton Rouge	LA	70895	**800-847-2580**	225-275-8111	314-2
FragranceNet.com Inc 909 Motor Pkwy	Hauppauge	NY	11788	**800-987-3738**	631-582-5204	564
Fralin & Waldron Inc 2917 Penn Forest Blvd	Roanoke	VA	24018	**888-238-7459**	540-774-4415	639
Frame Builders Assn. National 4840 Bob Billings Pkwy Suite 1000	Lawrence	KS	66049	**800-557-6957**	785-843-2444	49-3
Frames Data Inc 100 Ave of the Americas 14th Fl	New York	NY	10013	**800-821-6069**	949-788-0150	532
Framesi USA Inc 400 Chess St	Coraopolis	PA	15108	**800-321-9648**	412-269-2950	211
FRAN-PAC 1350 New York Ave NW Suite 900	Washington	DC	20005	**800-543-1038**	202-628-8000	604
France Compressor Products 4410 Greenbriar Dr	Stafford	TX	77477	**800-675-6646**	281-207-4600	128
Franchise Assn. International 1350 New York Ave NW Suite 900	Washington	DC	20005	**800-543-1038**	202-628-8000	49-18
Franchisees & Dealers. American Assn of 3500 5th Ave Suite 103	San Diego	CA	92103	**800-733-9858**	619-209-3775	49-18
Franchising World Magazine 1350 New York Ave NW Suite 900	Washington	DC	20005	**800-543-1038**	202-628-8000	449-5
Francis & Lusky LLC 1450 Elm Hill Pike	Nashville	TN	37210	**800-251-3711**	615-242-0501	10
Francis Marion University PO Box 100547	Florence	SC	29501	**800-368-7551**	843-661-1362	163
Francis Scott Key Motel 12806 Ocean Gateway PO Box 468	Ocean City	MD	21842	**800-213-0088**	410-213-0088	373
Franciscan Estates 1178 Galleron Rd	Saint Helena	CA	94574	**800-529-9463**	707-963-7111	81-3
Franciscan Hospice 2901 Bridgeport Way W	University Place	WA	98466	**800-338-8305**	253-671-7000	365
Franciscan Shared & Medical Science Laboratories Inc 11020 W Plank Ct Suite 100	Wauwatosa	WI	53226	**800-256-1522**	414-476-3400	409
Franciscan University 400 N Bluff Blvd	Clinton	IA	52732	**800-242-4153**	563-242-4023	163
Franco Mfg Co Inc 555 Prospect St	Metuchen	NJ	08840	**800-631-4663**	732-494-0500	731
FRANdata Corp 1725 'I' St NW Suite 600	Washington	DC	20006	**800-485-9570**	202-336-7632	380
Frank B Fuhrer Wholesale Co 3100 E Carson St	Pittsburgh	PA	15203	**800-837-2212**	412-488-8844	82-1
Frank Crystal & Co Inc 40 Broad St 15th Fl	New York	NY	10004	**800-221-5830**	212-344-2444	383
Frank Edwards Co 3626 Parkway Blvd	West Valley City	UT	84120	**800-366-8851**	801-736-8000	61
Frank Lill & Son Inc 656 Basket Rd	Webster	NY	14580	**800-756-0490**	585-265-0490	188-10
Frank Liquor Co Inc PO Box 620710	Middleton	WI	53562	**800-362-9550**	608-836-6000	82-3
Frank Lloyd Wright's Darwin D Martin House 125 Jewett Pkwy	Buffalo	NY	14214	**877-377-3858**	716-856-3858	50
Frank M Booth Inc 222 3rd St	Marysville	CA	95901	**800-540-9369**	530-742-7134	188-10
Frank Mayer & Assoc Inc 1975 Wisconsin Ave	Grafton	WI	53024	**800-225-3987**	262-377-4700	231
Frank Miller & Sons Inc 13831 S Emerald Ave	Riverdale	IL	60827	**800-423-6358**	708-201-7200	149
Frank Parsons Paper Co Inc 2270 Beaver Rd	Landover	MD	20785	**800-944-9940**	301-386-4700	543
Frank Paxton Lumber Co 23925 Commerce Park Rd	Beachwood	OH	44122	**800-325-9800**	513-984-8200	190-3
Frank Phillips College PO Box 5118	Borger	TX	79008	**800-687-2056**	806-457-4200	160
Frank Russell Co PO Box 1616	Tacoma	WA	98402	**800-426-7969**	253-572-9500	393
Frank Schaffer Publications PO Box 141487	Grand Rapids	MI	49514	**800-253-5469**	800-417-3261	242
Frank W Mayborn Civic & Convention Center 3303 N 3rd St	Temple	TX	76501	**800-478-0338**	254-298-5720	204
Frank W Whitcomb Construction Corp PO Box 1000	Walpole	NH	03608	**800-238-7283**	603-445-5555	187-4
Franke Foodservice Systems 305 Tech Park Dr	La Vergne	TN	37086	**888-437-2653**	615-287-8200	314-1
Frankenmuth Convention & Visitors Bureau 635 S Main St	Frankenmuth	MI	48734	**800-386-8696**	989-652-6106	205
Frankenmuth Mutual Insurance Co 1 Mutual Ave *Cust Svc	Frankenmuth	MI	48787	**800-234-1133***	989-652-6121	384-4
Frankford Candy & Chocolate Co Inc 2101 Washington Ave	Philadelphia	PA	19146	**800-523-9090**	215-735-5200	291-8
Frankfort Convention Center 405 Mero St	Frankfort	KY	40601	**800-960-7200**	502-564-5335	204
Frankfort First Bancorp Inc 216 W Main St *NASDAQ: FKKY*	Frankfort	KY	40602	**888-818-3372**	502-223-1638	355-2
Frankfort Lew 516 W 34th St Chm/CEO Coach Inc	New York	NY	10001	**800-444-3611**	212-594-1850	561
Frankfort/Franklin County Tourist & Convention Commission 100 Capital Ave	Frankfort	KY	40601	**800-960-7200**	502-875-8687	205
Franklin The 164 E 87th St	New York	NY	10128	**877-847-4444**	212-369-1000	373
Franklin Area Chamber of Commerce 1259 Liberty St	Franklin	PA	16323	**888-547-2377**	814-432-5823	137
Franklin Bank NA 24725 W 12-Mile Rd	Southfield	MI	48034	**800-527-4447**	248-358-5170	71
Franklin College 101 Branigin Blvd	Franklin	IN	46131	**800-852-0232**	317-738-8000	163
Franklin County Tourism Bureau PO Box 1641	Benton	IL	62812	**800-661-9998**	618-439-0608	205
Franklin Covey Co 2200 W Parkway Blvd *NYSE: FC*	Salt Lake City	UT	84119	**800-827-1776**	801-975-1776	753
Franklin D Roosevelt Library & Museum 4079 Albany Post Rd	Hyde Park	NY	12538	**800-337-8474**	845-229-8114	426
Franklin Electric Co Inc 400 E Spring St *NASDAQ: FELE*	Bluffton	IN	46714	**800-269-0063**	260-824-2900	507
Franklin Electric Co-op Inc PO Box 10	Russellville	AL	35653	**800-451-1505**	256-332-2730	244
Franklin Electronic Publishers Inc 1 Franklin Plaza *AMEX: FEP*	Burlington	NJ	08016	**800-266-5626**	609-386-2500	171-2
Franklin Equipment Co 33551 Carver Rd	Franklin	VA	23851	**800-835-7503**	757-562-6111	189
Franklin Feed & Supply Co 1977 Philadelphia Ave	Chambersburg	PA	17201	**800-722-2074**	717-264-6148	438
Franklin Fibre-Lamitex Corp 903 E 13th St	Wilmington	DE	19802	**800-233-9739**	302-652-3621	588
Franklin Homes Inc 10655 Hwy 43	Russellville	AL	35653	**800-332-4511**	256-332-4510	495
Franklin Industrial Minerals 612 10th Ave N	Nashville	TN	37203	**800-626-8147**	615-259-4222	493-5
Franklin Industries Inc 612 10th Ave N	Nashville	TN	37203	**800-626-8147**	615-259-4222	190-1
Franklin Interiors Inc 2740 Smallman St Suite 600	Pittsburgh	PA	15222	**800-371-5001**	412-261-2525	316
Franklin International 2020 Bruck St	Columbus	OH	43207	**800-877-4583**	614-443-0241	3
Franklin Iron & Metal Corp 1939 E 1st St	Dayton	OH	45403	**800-255-8184**	937-253-8184	674
Franklin Life Insurance Co The 1 Franklin Sq	Springfield	IL	62713	**800-528-2011**	217-528-2011	384-2
Franklin & Marshall College PO Box 3003	Lancaster	PA	17604	**877-678-9111**	717-291-3911	163
Franklin Mills 1455 Franklin Mills Cir	Philadelphia	PA	19114	**800-336-6255**	215-632-1500	452
Franklin Mint Corp 105 Commerce Dr	Aston	PA	19014	**800-523-7622**	610-459-6000	451
Franklin Mutual Insurance Co PO Box 400	Branchville	NJ	07826	**800-842-0551**	973-948-3120	384-4
Franklin Park Conservatory & Botanical Garden 1777 E Broad St	Columbus	OH	43203	**800-241-7275**	614-645-8733	98
Franklin Pierce College						
Concord Campus 5 Chenell Dr	Concord	NH	03301	**800-325-1090**	603-228-1155	163
Keene Campus 17 Bradco St	Keene	NH	03431	**800-325-1090**	603-357-0079	163
Lebanon Campus 24 Airport Rd Suite 19	West Lebanon	NH	03784	**800-325-1090**	603-298-5549	163
Nashua Campus 20 Cotton Rd	Nashua	NH	03063	**800-325-1090**	603-889-4143	163
Portsmouth Campus 73 Corporate Dr	Portsmouth	NH	03801	**800-325-1090**	603-433-2000	163
Rindge Campus 20 College Rd Box 60	Rindge	NH	03461	**800-437-0048**	603-899-4000	163
Salem Campus 12 Industrial Way	Salem	NH	03079	**800-325-1090**	603-898-1263	163
Franklin Power Products Inc 400 Forsythe St *Cust Svc	Franklin	IN	46131	**800-837-7697***	317-738-2117	259
Franklin Resources Inc DBA Franklin Templeton Investments 1 Franklin Pkwy *NYSE: BEN*	San Mateo	CA	94403	**800-342-5236**	650-312-2000	393
Franklin Rural Electric Co-op PO Box 437	Hampton	IA	50441	**800-750-3557**	641-456-2557	244
Franklin Sports Industry Inc 17 Campanelli Pkwy	Stoughton	MA	02072	**800-225-8647**	781-344-1111	701
Franklin Supply Inc 75 Lee St	Franklin	LA	70538	**800-259-3208**	337-828-3208	744
Franklin Templeton Investments 3344 Quality Dr	Rancho Cordova	CA	95670	**800-632-2350**	650-312-2000	679
Franklin Templeton Investments 1 Franklin Pkwy *NYSE: BEN*	San Mateo	CA	94403	**800-342-5236**	650-312-2000	393
Franklin Templeton Mutual Funds PO Box 33030	Saint Petersburg	FL	33733	**800-632-2301**		517
Franklin University 201 S Grant Ave	Columbus	OH	43215	**877-341-6300**	614-797-4700	163
Franklin Watts PO Box 1795 *Cust Svc	Danbury	CT	06816	**800-621-1115***	203-797-3500	623-2
Frankoma Pottery 9549 Frankoma Rd	Sapulpa	OK	74066	**800-331-3650**	918-224-5511	716
Franks Industries Inc 924 S Meridian PO Box 127	Sunman	IN	47041	**800-446-4844**	812-623-1140	102
Franz Bakery 340 NE 11th Ave	Portland	OR	97232	**800-935-5679**	503-232-2191	291-1
Franz Family Bakeries Gai's Div 2006 Weller St	Seattle	WA	98144	**800-272-7323**	206-322-0931	291-1
Fraser & Hoyt Group Incentive Div 1505 Barrington St Suite 107	Halifax	NS	B3J3K5	**800-565-8747**	902-421-1113	377
Fraser Papers Inc 70 Seaview Ave	Stamford	CT	06902	**877-237-2737**	203-705-2800	542-1
Fraternal Order of Police (FOP) 1410 Donelson Pike Suite A-17	Nashville	TN	37217	**800-451-2711**	615-399-0900	48-15
Fraud Education Fun. Taxpayers Against 1220 19th St NW Suite 501	Washington	DC	20036	**800-873-2573**	202-296-4826	49-10
Fraud Examiners. Association of Certified 716 West Ave	Austin	TX	78701	**800-245-3321**	512-478-9070	49-1

Name / Address	Toll-Free	Phone	Class
Fraud Information Center. National 1701 K St NW Suite 1200 .... Washington DC 20006	**800-876-7060**	202-835-3323	48-10
Fraud Watch. Internet c/o National Fraud Information Ctr 1701 K St NW Suite 1200 .... Washington DC 20006	**800-876-7060**	202-835-3323	48-10
Frazee Industries Inc 6625 Miramar Rd .... San Diego CA 92121	**800-477-9991**	619-276-9500	540
Frazier & Co 601 Union St Suite 3200 ... Seattle WA 98101	**800-411-4499**	206-621-7200	779
Frazier Historical Arms Museum 829 W Main St .... Louisville KY 40202	**866-886-7103**	502-412-2280	509
Fred A Moreton & Co 709 E South Temple .... Salt Lake City UT 84102	**800-594-8949**	801-531-1234	383
Fred Alger Management Inc 30 Montgomery St 11th Fl .... Jersey City NJ 07302	**800-223-3810**	201-547-3600	393
Fred Allen Florist 310 E Broad St ..... Gadsden AL 35903	**800-824-9181**	256-546-0437	287
Fred Astaire Dance Studios Inc 10 Bliss Rd .... Longmeadow MA 01106	**800-278-2473**	413-567-3200	754
Fred Busch Foods Corp 6278 N Cicero .... Chicago IL 60646	**800-323-3981**	773-545-2650	291-26
Fred Christen & Sons Co 714 George St .... Toledo OH 43608	**800-243-4161**	419-243-4161	688
Fred Gutwein & Sons Inc 15691 W 600 S .... Francesville IN 47946 *Cust Svc	**800-457-2700***	219-567-9141	11-5
Fred M Schildwachter & Sons Inc 1400 Ferris Pl .... Bronx NY 10461	**800-642-3646**	718-828-2500	311
Fred Meyer Inc 3800 SE 22nd Ave ..... Portland OR 97202	**800-858-9202**	503-232-8844	339
Fred Meyer Jewelers Inc 3800 SE 22nd Ave .... Portland OR 97202	**800-858-9202**	503-797-5550	402
Fred Pryor Seminars 9757 Metcalf Ave .... Overland Park KS 66212	**800-780-8476**	913-967-8599	753
Fred Usinger Inc 1030 N Old World 3rd St .... Milwaukee WI 53203	**800-558-9997**	414-276-9100	291-26
Fred Weber Inc 2320 Creve Coeur Mill Rd ... Maryland Heights MO 63043	**800-808-0980**	314-344-0070	187-4
Freddie Mac 8200 Jones Branch Dr .... McLean VA 22102 *NYSE: FRE*	**800-373-3343**	703-903-3000	498
North Central Region 333 W Wacker Dr Suite 2500 ..... Chicago IL 60606	**800-373-3343**	312-407-7400	498
Northeast Region 8200 Jones Branch Dr .... McLean VA 22102	**800-373-3343**	703-902-7700	498
Southeast/Southwest Region 2300 Windy Ridge Pkwy Suite 200N .... Atlanta GA 30339	**800-373-3343**	770-857-8800	498
Frederick Aviation 330 Aviation Way .. Frederick MD 21701	**800-545-9393**	301-662-8156	63
Frederick Cooper Lamp Co Inc 2545 W Diversey Ave .... Chicago IL 60647	**800-693-5234**	773-384-0800	431
Frederick Mfg Corp 4840 E 12th St .... Kansas City MO 64127	**800-743-3150**	816-231-5007	420
Frederick News Post 200 E Patrick St .... Frederick MD 21701	**800-486-1177**	301-662-1177	522-2
Frederick Paul Inc 223 W Poplar St ... Fleetwood PA 19522	**800-247-1417**	610-944-0909	155-3
Frederick Wildman & Sons Ltd 311 E 53rd St .... New York NY 10022	**800-733-9463**	212-355-0700	82-3
Frederick's of Hollywood Inc 6608 Hollywood Blvd .... Hollywood CA 90028	**800-323-9525**	323-466-5151	155-6
Fredericksburg Convention & Visitors Bureau 302 E Austin St .... Fredericksburg TX 78624	**888-997-3600**	830-997-6523	205
Fredericksen Tank Lines Inc PO Box 235 .... West Sacramento CA 95691	**800-441-2109**	916-371-4655	769
Frederik Meijer Gardens & Sculpture Park 1000 East Beltline Ave NE .... Grand Rapids MI 49525	**888-974-1580**	616-957-1580	98
Fredman Brothers Furniture Co Inc 908 SW Washington St .... Peoria IL 61602	**800-248-5228**	309-674-2011	314-2
Fred's Inc 4300 New Getwell Rd PO Box 18356 .... Memphis TN 38118 *NASDAQ: FRED*	**800-374-7417**	901-365-8880	227
Free Application for Federal Student Aid (FAFSA) US Dept of Education 400 Maryland Ave SW .... Washington DC 20202	**800-433-3243**	319-337-5665	711
Free Enterprise System Inc 1254 S West St .... Indianapolis IN 46225	**800-255-1337**	317-634-7433	108
Free-Flow Packaging Corp DBA FP International 1090 Mills Way .. Redwood City CA 94063	**800-866-9946**	650-261-5300	590
Free Lance Star 616 Amelia St ... Fredericksburg VA 22401	**800-877-0500**	540-374-5000	522-2
Free Press 418 S 2nd St .... Mankato MN 56002	**800-657-4662**	507-625-4451	522-2
Free Will Baptist Bible College 3606 West End Ave .... Nashville TN 37205	**800-763-9222**	615-383-1340	163
Free Will Baptists. National Assn of 5233 Mt View Rd .... Antioch TN 37013	**877-767-7659**	615-731-6812	48-20
Freed-Hardeman University 158 E Main St .... Henderson TN 38340	**800-630-3480**	731-989-6000	163
Freedman Seating Co 4545 W Augusta Blvd .... Chicago IL 60651	**800-443-4540**	773-524-2440	678
Freedom Arms Inc 314 Hwy 239 .... Freedom WY 83120 *Orders	**800-833-4432***	307-883-2468	279
Freedom Capital LLC 1 Beacon St 5th Fl .... Boston MA 02108	**800-861-8088**	617-722-4700	393
Freedom From Fear (FFF) 308 Seaview Ave .... Staten Island NY 10305	**888-442-2022**	718-351-1717	48-17
Freedom Graphic Services Inc 1101 S Janesville St .... Milton WI 53563	**800-334-3540**	608-868-7007	111
Freedom Greeting Card Co Inc 774 American Dr .... Bensalem PA 19020 *Sales	**800-359-3301***	215-604-0300	130
Freedom from Hunger 1644 DaVinci Ct .... Davis CA 95616	**800-708-2555**	530-758-6200	48-5
Freedom. Institute for Health 1825 'I' St NW Suite 400 .... Washington DC 20006	**888-616-1976**	202-429-6610	48-8
Freedom Investments Inc 375 Raritan Ctr Pkwy .... Edison NJ 08837	**800-944-4033**	732-934-3113	679
Freedom Medical Inc 219 Welsh Pool Rd .... Exton PA 19341	**800-784-8849**	610-903-0200	261-5
Freedom Oil Co 814 W Chestnut St .... Bloomington IL 61701	**800-397-6147**	309-828-7750	319
Freedom Plastics Inc 3206 Enterprise Rd .... Fort Pierce FL 34982	**800-432-6143**	772-465-1222	585
Freedom Village 23442 El Toro Rd .. Lake Forest CA 92630	**800-584-8084**	949-472-4700	659
Freedom Village 6501 17th Ave W ... Bradenton FL 34209	**800-841-4676**	941-798-8122	659
FreedomWorks 1775 Pennsylvania Ave NW 11th Fl .... Washington DC 20006	**888-564-6273**	202-783-3870	48-7
Freehold Chevrolet 3712 Rt 9 S PO Box 6697 .... Freehold NJ 07728	**800-648-8656**	732-462-1324	57
Freehold Royalty Trust 144 4th Ave SW Suite 400 .... Calgary AB T2P3N4	**888-257-1873**	403-221-0848	662
Freelancers Assn. Editorial 71 W 23rd St Suite 1910 .... New York NY 10010	**866-929-5400**	212-929-5400	49-16
Freeman The 30 S Broadway .... Irvington-on-Hudson NY 10533 *Sales	**800-452-3518***	914-591-7230	449-17
Freeman H & Son Inc 411 N Cranberry Rd .... Westminster MD 21157	**800-468-0689**	410-857-5774	153-12
Freeman Harold & Co 275 7th Ave .... New York NY 10001	**800-221-4092**	212-989-9001	401
Freeman Hospital & Health Systems 1102 W 32nd St .... Joplin MO 64804	**800-477-6610**	417-623-2801	366-2
Freeman Jewelers Inc 76 Merchants Row .... Rutland VT 05701	**800-949-2792**	802-773-2792	402
Freeman Mfg Co 900 W Chicago Rd ..... Sturgis MI 49091	**800-253-2091**	269-651-2371	469
Freeman Mfg & Supply Co 1101 Moore Rd .... Avon OH 44011	**800-321-8511**	440-934-1902	556
Freeman WH & Co 41 Madison Ave 35th Fl .... New York NY 10010	**800-903-3019**	212-576-9400	623-2
Freescale Semiconductor Inc 6501 William Cannon Dr W .... Austin TX 78735 *NYSE: FSL* ■ *Tech Supp	**800-521-6274***	512-895-2000	686
Freeservers.com 1253 N Research Way Suite Q-2500 .... Orem UT 84097	**800-396-1999**	801-437-6000	795
Freestone Inn at Wilson Ranch 31 Early Winters Dr .... Mazama WA 98833	**800-639-3809**	509-996-3906	655
FreightCar America Inc 17 Johns St .... Johnstown PA 15901 *NASDAQ: RAIL*	**800-458-2235**		636
Freighter World Cruises Inc 180 South Lake Ave Suite 335 ...... Pasadena CA 91101	**800-531-7774**	626-449-3106	760
Freightliner Corp 4747 N Channel Ave .... Portland OR 97217 *Cust Svc	**800-385-4357***	503-735-8000	505
Freirich Foods Inc PO Box 1529 ...... Salisbury NC 28145	**800-554-4788**	704-636-2621	465
Fremont Hotel & Casino 200 E Fremont St .... Las Vegas NV 89101	**800-634-6182**	702-385-3232	133
Fremont Industries Inc 4400 Valley Industrial Blvd N PO Box 67 .... Shakopee MN 55379	**800-436-1238**	952-445-4121	143
Fremont Investment & Loan 2727 E Imperial Hwy .... Brea CA 92821	**800-373-6668**	714-961-5000	71
Fremont Life Insurance Co PO Box 410288 .... Kansas City MO 64141	**800-231-0801**	816-391-2000	384-2
Fremont Tribune 135 N Main St .... Fremont NE 68025	**800-927-7598**	402-721-5000	522-2
Fremont/Sandusky County Convention & Visitors Bureau 712 North St Suite 102 .... Fremont OH 43420	**800-255-8070**	419-332-4470	205
French Country Waterways Ltd PO Box 2195 .... Duxbury MA 02331	**800-222-1236**	781-934-2454	218
French Craft Leather Goods Co Inc 234 W 24th St .... Los Angeles CA 90007	**800-541-0088**	213-746-6771	153-2
French Hospital Medical Center 1911 Johnson Ave .... San Luis Obispo CA 93401	**800-775-5335**	805-543-5353	366-2
French Implement Co Inc 497 S Hwy 105 .... Charleston MO 63834	**800-325-8622**	573-649-3021	270
French Lick Springs Resort & Spa 8670 W SR-56 .... French Lick IN 47432	**800-457-4042**	812-936-9300	655
French Market Inn. Historic 501 Rue Decatur .... New Orleans LA 70130	**888-538-5651**	504-561-5621	373
French Meadow Bakery Inc 2610 Lyndale Ave S .... Minneapolis MN 55408	**877-669-3278**	612-870-4740	291-11
French Paper Co 100 French St .... Niles MI 49120	**800-253-5952**	269-683-1100	542-1
French Quarter Suites Hotel 2144 Madison Ave .... Memphis TN 38104	**800-843-0353**	901-728-4000	373
French Toast 100 W 33rd St Suite 1012 .... New York NY 10001	**800-262-5437**	212-594-4740	153-19
Frenchman Valley Farmers Co-op Exchange 143 Broadway .... Imperial NE 69033	**800-538-2667**	308-882-3200	272
Frequent Flyer Magazine 3025 Highland Pkwy Suite 200 .... Downers Grove IL 60515	**800-525-1138**	630-515-5300	449-22
Frequent Flyer Services 1930 Frequent Flyer Pt ...... Colorado Springs CO 80915	**800-209-2870**	719-597-8889	623-9
Fresenius Medical Care North America 95 Hayden Ave 2 Ledgemont Ctr .... Lexington MA 02420 *NYSE: FMS*	**800-662-1237**	781-402-9000	347
Fresh Choice Inc 485 Cochrane Cir .... Morgan Hill CA 95037	**800-859-8693**	408-776-0799	657
Fresh Del Monte Produce Inc 241 Sevilla Ave .... Coral Gables FL 33134 *NYSE: FDP* ■ *Cust Svc	**800-950-3683***	305-520-8400	310-4
Fresh Enterprises Inc 100 Moody Ct Suite 200 ..... Thousand Oaks CA 91360	**877-225-2373**	805-495-4704	656
Fresh Express Inc 950 E Blanco Rd ..... Salinas CA 93901 *Cust Svc	**800-242-5472***	831-422-5917	12-1
Fresh Mark Inc 1888 Southway St SE .... Massillon OH 44646	**800-860-6777**	330-832-7491	465
Fresh Water Fishing Hall of Fame. National 10360 Hall of Fame Dr ..... Hayward WI 54843	**866-268-4333**	715-634-4440	511
Freshens Frozen Treats 1750 The Exchange .... Atlanta GA 30339	**800-633-4519**	678-627-5400	657
Freshens Quality Brands 1750 The Exchange .... Atlanta GA 30339	**800-633-4519**	678-627-5400	221
Freshwater & Marine Aquarium Magazine 144 W Sierra Madre Blvd .... Sierra Madre CA 91024	**800-523-1736**	626-355-1476	449-14
Freshwater Society 2500 Shadywood Rd .... Excelsior MN 55331	**888-471-9773**	952-471-9773	48-13

Name / Address	City	State	Zip	Toll-Free	Phone	Class
Fresno Bee 1626 'E' St	Fresno	CA	93786	**800-877-7300**	559-441-6111	522-2
Fresno Convention & Visitors Bureau 848 M St 3rd Fl	Fresno	CA	93721	**800-788-0836**	559-233-0836	205
Fresno Distributing Co Inc 2055 E McKinley Ave	Fresno	CA	93703	**800-655-2542**	559-442-8800	601
Fresno Pacific University 1717 S Chestnut Ave	Fresno	CA	93702	**800-660-6089**	559-453-2039	163
Fretz Corp 2001 Woodhaven Rd	Philadelphia	PA	19116	**866-987-2121**	215-671-8300	38
Freudenberg-NOK General Partnership 47690 E Anchor Ct	Plymouth	MI	48170	**800-533-5656**	734-451-0020	321
Freundlich Supply Co Inc 2200 Arthur Kill Rd	Staten Island	NY	10309	**800-221-0260**	718-356-1500	759
Frey John M Co Inc 2735 62nd St Ct	Bettendorf	IA	52722	**800-397-3739**	563-332-9200	601
Frey John S Enterprises Inc 1900 E 64th St	Los Angeles	CA	90001	**800-377-3322**	323-583-4061	471
Friar Tuck Resort & Convention Center 4858 SR-32	Catskill	NY	12414	**800-832-7600**	518-678-2271	655
Friary of Lakeview Center 4400 Hickory Shores Blvd	Gulf Breeze	FL	32563	**800-332-2271**	850-932-9375	712
Frick Services Inc 3154 Depot St	Wawaka	IN	46794	**800-552-1754**	260-761-3311	271
Friday Report 224 7th St	Garden City	NY	11530	**800-229-6700**	516-746-6700	521-10
Fridgedoor.com 21 Dixwell Ave	Quincy	MA	02169	**888-463-3184**	617-770-7913	323
Fried Brothers Inc 467 N 7th St	Philadelphia	PA	19123	**800-523-2924**	215-627-3205	345
Frieda John Professional Hair Care Inc 333 Ludlow St *Cust Svc	Stanford	CT	06902	**800-521-3189***	203-762-1233	211
Frieda's Inc 4465 Corporate Ctr Dr	Los Alamitos	CA	90720	**800-421-9477**	714-826-6100	292-7
Friede Halter Inc PO Box 1328	Pascagoula	MS	39568	**800-877-0029**	228-696-6888	689
Friedland Ralph & Brothers Inc 17 Industrial Dr	Cliffwood Beach	NJ	07735	**800-631-2162**	732-290-9800	88
Friedman Al Co Inc 44 W 18th St	New York	NY	10011	**800-204-6352**	212-243-9000	45
Friedman Billings Ramsey Group Inc 1001 19th St N 18th Fl *NYSE: FBR*	Arlington	VA	22209	**800-846-5050**	703-312-9500	679
Friedman Brothers Decorative Arts Inc 9015 NW 105th Way	Medley	FL	33178	**800-327-1065**	305-887-3170	330
Friedman Electric Supply 1321 Wyoming Ave	Exeter	PA	18643	**800-545-5517**	570-654-3371	245
Friedman Industries Inc PO Box 21147 *AMEX: FRD*	Houston	TX	77226	**800-899-7695**	713-672-9433	483
Friedman's Inc 171 Crossroads Pkwy	Savannah	GA	31407	**800-545-9033**	912-233-9333	402
Friedrich Air Conditioning Co 4200 N Pan Am Expy PO Box 1540	San Antonio	TX	78295	**800-541-6645**	210-225-2000	15
Friel's Inc 100 Friel Pl	Queenstown	MD	21658	**800-739-2676**	410-827-8811	291-20
Friend HA & Co Inc 1535 Lewis Ave	Zion	IL	60099	**800-323-4394**	847-746-1248	524
Friend Tire Co 11 N Industrial Dr	Monett	MO	65708	**800-950-8473**	417-235-7836	740
Friendfinder Network Inc 445 Sherman Ave Suite C	Palo Alto	CA	94306	**800-388-0760**	650-847-3100	224
Friendly Cruises Inc 3081 S Sycamore Village Dr	Superstition Mountain	AZ	85218	**800-842-1786**	888-842-1786	760
Friendly's Restaurants 1855 Boston Rd	Wilbraham	MA	01095	**800-966-9970**	413-543-2400	657
Friends of Animals Inc (FoA) 777 Post Rd Suite 205	Darien	CT	06820	**800-321-7387**	203-656-1522	48-3
Friends of the Earth 1717 Massachusetts Ave NW Suite 600	Washington	DC	20036	**877-843-8687**	202-783-7400	48-13
Friends of the Earth Canada 260 Saint Patrick St Suite 300	Ottawa	ON	K1N5K5	**888-385-4444**	613-241-0085	48-13
Friends of the Earth Magazine 1717 Massachusetts Ave Suite 600	Washington	DC	20005	**877-843-8687**	202-783-7400	449-19
Friends Hospital 4641 Roosevelt Blvd	Philadelphia	PA	19124	**800-889-0548**	215-831-4600	366-3
Friends of Libraries USA (FOLUSA) 1420 Walnut St Suite 450	Philadelphia	PA	19102	**800-936-5872**	215-790-1674	49-11
Friends Research Institute Inc 505 Baltimore Ave	Baltimore	MD	21204	**800-822-3677**	410-823-5116	654
Friends of the River 915 20th St	Sacramento	CA	95814	**888-464-2477**	916-442-3155	48-13
Friends University 2100 University St	Wichita	KS	67213	**800-794-6945**	316-295-5000	163
Friendship Village 1400 N Drake Rd	Kalamazoo	MI	49006	**800-613-3984**	269-381-0560	659
Friendship Village of Tempe 2645 E Southern Ave	Tempe	AZ	85282	**800-824-1112**	480-831-5000	659
Frigidaire Home Products Co 250 Bobby Jones Expy *Sales	Augusta	GA	30907	**800-288-4924***	706-651-1751	36
Fringe Benefits Management Co 3101 Sessions Rd	Tallahassee	FL	32303	**800-847-8286**	850-425-6200	383
Friona Feedyard PO Box 806	Friona	TX	79035	**800-658-6086**	806-265-3574	11-1
Friona Industries LP 500 S Taylor St Suite 601	Amarillo	TX	79101	**800-658-6014**	806-374-1811	11-1
Fripp Patricia 527 Hugo St	San Francisco	CA	94122	**800-634-3035**	415-753-6556	561
Frisch's Restaurants Inc 2800 Gilbert Ave *AMEX: FRS*	Cincinnati	OH	45206	**800-873-3633**	513-961-2660	657
Frisco Bay Industries Ltd 160 Graveline St	Saint-Laurent	QC	H4T1R7	**800-463-7472**	514-738-7300	681
Frit Industries Inc PO Box 1589	Ozark	AL	36361	**800-633-7685**	334-774-2515	276
Frito-Lay Co 7701 Legacy Dr	Plano	TX	75024	**800-776-2257**	972-334-7000	291-35
Fritz Chester Auditorium Yale Dr & University Ave PO Box 9028 University of North Dakota	Grand Forks	ND	58202	**800-375-4068**	701-777-3076	562
Fritz Co Inc 1912 Hastings Ave	Newport	MN	55055	**800-328-1652**	651-459-9751	292-3
Fritz Industries Inc PO Box 170040	Dallas	TX	75217	**800-955-1323**	972-285-5471	181
Fritze Keyspan LLC 1 Chapin Rd *Cust Svc	Pine Brook	NJ	07058	**800-626-7799***	973-808-0411	15
FRM Weekly Newsletter 224 7th St	Garden City	NY	11530	**800-229-6700**	516-746-6700	521-6
Froedtert Hospital Bone Marrow Transplant Program 9200 W Wisconsin Ave	Milwaukee	WI	53226	**800-272-3666**	414-805-3666	758
Froedtert Malting Co PO Box 712	Milwaukee	WI	53201	**800-646-6258**	414-671-1166	453
Frog Street Press Inc 308 E Trunk St	Crandall	TX	75114	**800-884-3764**	972-472-6896	242
From 9 to 5 Newsletter 360 Hiatt Dr	Palm Beach Gardens	FL	33418	**800-621-5463**	561-622-9914	521-2
Fromm Electric Supply Corp 2101 Centre Ave PO Box 15147	Reading	PA	19612	**800-360-4441**	610-374-4441	245
Front Range Community College Larimer Campus 4616 S Shields St	Fort Collins	CO	80526	**800-289-3722**	970-226-2500	160
Front Row USA Entertainment Inc 18170 W Dixie Hwy 2nd Fl	North Miami Beach	FL	33160	**800-446-8499**	305-940-8499	735
Frontenac Co 135 S La Salle St Suite 3800	Chicago	IL	60603	**800-368-3681**	312-368-0044	779
Frontier Adjusters of America Inc PO Box 7610	Phoenix	AZ	85011	**800-528-1187**	602-264-1061	383
Frontier Airlines 7001 Tower Rd	Denver	CO	80249	**800-265-5505**	720-374-4200	26
Frontier Airlines EarlyReturns PO Box 17304 *Cust Svc	Denver	CO	80217	**800-265-5505***	866-263-2759	27
Frontier Airlines Inc 7001 Tower Rd *NASDAQ: FRNT*	Denver	CO	80249	**800-265-5505**	720-374-4200	355-1
Frontier Co-op Co 211 S Lincoln St	Brainard	NE	68626	**800-869-0379**	402-545-2811	271
Frontier Community College 2 Frontier Dr	Fairfield	IL	62837	**877-464-3687**	618-842-3711	160
Frontier Corp 180 S Clinton Ave	Rochester	NY	14646	**800-836-0342**	585-777-1000	721
Frontier Electronic Systems Corp 4500 W 6th Ave	Stillwater	OK	74074	**800-677-1769**	405-624-1769	519
Frontier Natural Products Co-op 3021 78th St PO Box 299	Norway	IA	52318	**800-669-3275**	319-227-7996	291-37
Frontier Power Co PO Box 280	Coshocton	OH	43812	**800-624-8050**	740-622-6755	244
Frontier Tours Inc 1923 N Carson St Suite 105	Carson City	NV	89701	**800-648-0912**	775-882-2100	748
Frontiers International PO Box 959	Wexford	PA	15090	**800-245-1950**	724-935-1577	748
FrontRange Solutions Inc 1125 Kelly Johnson Blvd	Colorado Springs	CO	80920	**800-776-7889**	719-531-5007	176-1
Frost Inc 2020 Bristol Ave NW *Cust Svc	Grand Rapids	MI	49504	**800-783-6633***	616-453-7781	206
Frost National Bank 100 W Houston	San Antonio	TX	78205	**800-562-6732**	210-220-4011	71
Frost & Sullivan Inc 7550 W I-10 Suite 400	San Antonio	TX	78229	**877-463-7678**	210-348-1000	194
Fru-Con Construction Corp 15933 Clayton Rd	Ballwin	MO	63011	**800-937-8266**	636-391-6700	185
Frullati Cafe & Bakery 7730 E Greenway Rd Suite 104	Scottsdale	AZ	85260	**800-438-2590**	480-443-0200	657
Frutarom Corp 9500 Railroad Ave	North Bergen	NJ	07047	**800-526-7147**	201-861-9500	291-15
FRx Software Corp 4700 S Syracuse Pkwy Suite 150	Denver	CO	80237	**800-379-8733**	303-741-8000	176-1
Fry Inc 650 Avis Dr	Ann Arbor	MI	48108	**800-379-6858**	734-741-0640	796
Frye Tech Inc 110 Industrial Rd	New Windsor	NY	12553	**800-705-3793**		616
Fryeburg Academy 152 Main St	Fryeburg	ME	04037	**877-935-2013**	207-935-2013	611
FSA Group LLC 304 W Liberty St Suite 201	Louisville	KY	40202	**800-620-6422**	502-583-3783	47
FSB Magazine Rockefeller Ctr 1271 Ave of the Americas 4th Fl *Cust Svc	New York	NY	10020	**800-771-1444***	212-522-3263	449-5
FSG Crest LLC 354 W Armory Dr	South Holland	IL	60473	**877-747-1225**	708-210-0800	130
FSI International Inc 3455 Lyman Blvd *NASDAQ: FSII*	Chaska	MN	55318	**800-274-5440**	952-448-5440	685
FSI/Fork Standards Inc 668 E Western Ave	Lombard	IL	60148	**800-468-6009**	630-932-9380	202
FSMB (Federation of State Medical Boards of the US Inc) 400 Fuller Wiser Rd Suite 300	Euless	TX	76039	**800-876-5396**	817-868-4000	49-8
FTC (Federal Trade Commission) 600 Pennsylvania Ave NW	Washington	DC	20580	**877-382-4357**	202-326-2222	336-16
FTD Group Inc 3113 Woodcreek Dr *NYSE: FTD*	Downers Grove	IL	60515	**800-788-9000**	630-719-7800	289
FTD Inc 3113 Woodcreek Dr	Downers Grove	IL	60515	**800-736-3383**	630-724-6200	287
FTI Consulting Inc 900 Bestgate Rd Suite 100 *NYSE: FCN*	Annapolis	MD	21401	**800-334-5701**	410-224-8770	436
FTZ Industries Inc 515 Palmetto Dr	Simpsonville	SC	29681	**800-336-8989**	864-963-5000	803
Fuchs Lubricants Co 17050 Lathrop Ave	Harvey	IL	60426	**800-323-7755**	708-333-8900	530
Fuchs Lubricants Co Grand Kal Div 760 36th St SE	Grand Rapids	MI	49548	**800-247-0364**	616-247-0363	530
Fuchs Lubricants Co LUBRITECH Div 2140 S 88th St	Kansas City	KS	66111	**800-800-6457**	913-422-4022	530
Fuchs Lubricants Co Midlantic Div 1700 S Caton Ave	Baltimore	MD	21227	**800-776-0368**	410-368-5000	530
Fuchs Lubricants Co Montgomery Div 17191 Chrysler Fwy	Detroit	MI	48203	**800-368-5991**	313-891-3700	530
Fuchs Lubricants Co Southeast Div 2601 New Cut Rd	Spartanburg	SC	29303	**800-442-5666**	864-574-9300	530
Fugazy International Travel 6006 SW 18th St Suite B3	Boca Raton	FL	33433	**800-852-7613**	954-481-2888	760
Fuhrer Frank B Wholesale Co 3100 E Carson St	Pittsburgh	PA	15203	**800-837-2212**	412-488-8844	82-1
Fuji Photo Film USA Inc 200 Summit Lake Dr	Valhalla	NY	10595	**800-755-3854**	914-789-8100	580
Fujicolor Processing Inc 174 S Main St	Mansfield	OH	44902	**800-558-1678**	419-525-1678	577
Fujikura America Inc 280 Interstate North Cir SE Suite 530	Atlanta	GA	30339	**888-385-4587**	770-956-7200	801
Fujinon Inc 10 High Point Dr	Wayne	NJ	07470	**800-872-0196**	973-633-5600	534
Fujisawa Canada Inc 625 Cochrane Dr Suite 1000 *Cust Svc	Markham	ON	L3R9R9	**800-888-7704***	905-470-7990	572
Fujisawa Healthcare 3 Parkway N	Deerfield	IL	60015	**800-888-7704**	847-317-8800	572
Fujitsu Computer Products of America Inc 2904 Orchard Pkwy	San Jose	CA	95134	**800-626-4686**	408-432-6333	171-8

Company / Address	City	State	ZIP	Toll-Free	Phone	Class
Fujitsu Computer Systems Corp 1250 E Arques Ave	Sunnyvale	CA	94085	**877-213-6674**	408-746-6000	174
Fujitsu Microelectronics America Inc 1250 E Arques Ave	Sunnyvale	CA	94088	**800-637-0683**	408-737-5600	686
Fujitsu Ten Corp of America 19600 S Vermont Ave	Torrance	CA	90502	**800-233-2216**	310-327-2151	52
Fulcrum Analytics 304 Hudson St 5th Fl	New York	NY	10013	**888-421-6655**	212-651-7000	194
Fulfillment Service Assn. Mailing & 1421 Prince St Suite 410	Alexandria	VA	22314	**800-333-6272**	703-836-9200	49-18
Fulflex Inc 652 George Washington Hwy	Lincoln	RI	02865	**800-222-1263**	401-333-1212	730-5
Fulghum Industries Inc 317 S Main St PO Box 909	Wadley	GA	30477	**800-841-5980**	478-252-5223	671
Full Circle Bookstore 50 Penn Pl	Oklahoma City	OK	73118	**800-683-7323**	405-842-2900	96
Full Sail Brewing Co 506 Columbia St	Hood River	OR	97031	**888-244-2337**	541-386-2281	103
Full Sail Center for the Recording Arts 3300 University Blvd Suite 160	Winter Park	FL	32792	**800-226-7625**	407-679-6333	787
Fuller Brush Co 1 Fuller Way *Cust Svc	Great Bend	KS	67530	**800-438-5537***	620-792-1711	104
Fuller George H & Son Co 151 Exchange St	Pawtucket	RI	02860	**800-237-0043**	401-722-6530	401
Fuller HB Co 1200 Willow Lake Blvd PO Box 64683 *NYSE: FUL*	Saint Paul	MN	55164	**800-828-2981**	651-236-5900	3
Fullerton Building Systems Inc 34620 250th St	Worthington	MN	56187	**800-450-9782**	507-376-3128	805
Fullerton Tool Co Inc 121 Perry St	Saginaw	MI	48602	**800-248-8315**	989-799-4550	484
FullWeb Inc 201 Robert S Kerr Ave Suite 210	Oklahoma City	OK	73102	**888-826-4687**	405-236-8200	795
Fulmer Carroll Logistics Corp 8340 American Way	Groveland	FL	34736	**800-468-9400**	352-429-5000	769
Fulmer Co 122 Gayoso Ave	Memphis	TN	38103	**800-467-2400**	901-525-5711	506
Fulton Bank 1 Penn Sq	Lancaster	PA	17602	**800-752-9580**	717-291-2411	71
Fulton Corp 303 8th Ave	Fulton	IL	61252	**800-252-0002**	815-589-3211	345
Fulton County Regional Chamber of Commerce 2 N Main St	Gloversville	NY	12078	**800-676-3858**	518-725-0641	137
Fulton-Denver Co 3500 Wynkoop St	Denver	CO	80216	**800-776-6715**	303-294-9292	68
Fulton Financial Corp 1 Penn Sq *NASDAQ: FULT*	Lancaster	PA	17602	**800-752-9580**	717-291-2411	355-2
Fulton Industries Inc 135 E Linfoot St	Wauseon	OH	43567	**800-537-5012**	419-335-3015	431
Fulton Opera House 12 N Prince St	Lancaster	PA	17608	**888-480-1265**	717-397-7425	562
Fund-Raising Counsel. American Assn of 4700 W Lake Ave	Glenview	IL	60025	**800-462-2372**	847-375-4709	48-5
Fundraising Professionals. Association of 1101 King St Suite 700	Alexandria	VA	22314	**800-666-3863**	703-684-0410	49-12
Fundy National Park PO Box 1001 *Campground Resv	Alma	NB	E4H1B4	**800-414-6765***	506-887-6000	553
Funeral Assn. International Cemetery & 1895 Preston White Dr Suite 220	Reston	VA	20191	**800-645-7700**	703-391-8400	49-4
Funeral Consumers Alliance 33 Patchen Rd	South Burlington	VT	05403	**800-765-0107**	802-865-8300	48-10
Funeral Directors Assn. National 13625 Bishop's Dr	Brookfield	WI	53005	**800-228-6332**	262-789-1880	49-4
Funeral Directors & Morticians Assn. National 3951 Snapfinger Pkwy Suite 570	Decatur	GA	30035	**800-434-0958**	404-286-6680	49-4
Funeral Homes. Selected Independent 500 Lake Cook Rd Suite 205	Deerfield	IL	60015	**800-323-4219**	847-236-9401	49-4
Funeral Service Consumer Assistance Program PO Box 486	Elm Grove	WI	53122	**800-662-7666**		48-10
Funeral Service Insider Newsletter 11300 Rockville Pike Suite 1100	Rockville	MD	20852	**800-929-4824**	301-287-2700	521-13
Funjet Vacations 8907 N Port Washington Rd	Milwaukee	WI	53217	**800-558-6654**	414-351-3553	760
Funk AJ & Co Inc 1471 Timber Dr	Elgin	IL	60123	**877-225-3865**	847-741-6760	149
Funk Mfg Co PO Box 577	Coffeyville	KS	67337	**800-844-1337**	620-251-3400	609
Funk Software Inc 222 3rd St	Cambridge	MA	02142	**800-828-4146**	617-497-6339	176-7
Fuqua Homes Inc 7100 S Cooper St	Arlington	TX	76001	**800-336-0874**	817-465-3211	495
Furama Hotel Los Angeles 8601 Lincoln Blvd	Los Angeles	CA	90045	**800-225-8126**	310-670-8111	373
Furmanite America 101 Old Underwood Rd Suite F	La Porte	TX	77571	**800-444-5572**	281-842-5100	446
Furmano Foods Inc 700 Cannery Rd PO Box 500	Northumberland	PA	17857	**877-877-6032**	570-473-3516	291-20
Furnishings Assn. National Home 3010 Tinsley Dr Suite 101	High Point	NC	27265	**800-888-9590**	336-886-6100	49-4
Furniture Medic Inc 3839 Forrest Hill Irene Rd	Memphis	TN	38125	**800-877-9933**	901-597-8600	305
FurnitureFind.com Inc 311 W Jefferson Blvd	South Bend	IN	46601	**800-362-7632**	574-299-2700	357
Furst-McNess Co 120 E Clark St	Freeport	IL	61032	**800-435-5131**	815-235-6151	438
Fusion Inc 4658 E 355th St	Willoughby	OH	44094	**800-626-9501**	440-946-3300	379
Fusion Telecommunications International Inc 420 Lexington Ave Suite 518 *AMEX: FSN*	New York	NY	10170	**800-503-3325**	212-972-2000	721
Fusz Lou Automotive Network Inc 925 N Lindbergh Blvd	Saint Louis	MO	63141	**800-371-7819**	314-994-1500	57
Futura Industries Corp Freeport Ctr Bldg H-11 PO Box 160350 *Cust Svc	Clearfield	UT	84016	**800-824-2049***	801-773-6282	476
Future Business Leaders of America - Phi Beta Lambda Inc (FBLA-PBL) 1912 Association Dr	Reston	VA	20191	**800-325-2946**	703-860-3334	48-11
Future Electronics 237 Hymus Blvd	Pointe-Claire	QC	H9R5C7	**800-388-8731**	514-694-7710	245
Future Foam Inc 400 N 10th St	Council Bluffs	IA	51503	**800-733-8067**	712-323-6718	590
Future Market Service Newsletter 330 S Wells St Suite 1112	Chicago	IL	60606	**800-621-5271**	312-554-8456	521-9
Future Metals Inc 10401 State St	Tamarac	FL	33321	**800-733-0960**	954-724-1400	483
Future Products Tool Corp 885 N Rochester Rd	Clawson	MI	48017	**800-237-5754**	248-588-1060	745
Future Shop Ltd 6200 McKay Ave Unit 144	Burnaby	BC	V5H4L7	**800-663-2275**	604-434-3844	35
Future Society. World 7910 Woodmont Ave Suite 450	Bethesda	MD	20814	**800-989-8274**	301-656-8274	49-19
Future Vacations Inc 110 E Broward Blvd 11th Fl	Fort Lauderdale	FL	33301	**800-456-2323**	954-522-1440	760
Futurebiotics Inc 70 Commerce Dr	Hauppauge	NY	11788	**800-367-5433**	631-272-6300	786
Futurekids Inc 1000 N Studebaker Rd Suite 1	Long Beach	CA	90815	**800-765-8000**	562-296-1111	146
Futures Assn. National 200 W Madison St	Chicago	IL	60606	**800-366-6321**	312-781-1300	49-2
Futures Magazine 833 W Jackson Blvd 7th Fl	Chicago	IL	60607	**800-972-9316**	312-846-4600	449-5
FutureSoft Inc 12012 Wickchester Ln Suite 600	Houston	TX	77079	**800-989-8908**	281-496-9400	176-7
Futuretech: Emerging Technologies Newsletter 7550 W I-10 Suite 400	San Antonio	TX	77229	**877-463-7678**	210-348-1000	521-12
Futurex Inc 864 Old Boerne Rd	Bulverde	TX	78163	**800-251-5112**	830-980-9782	174
Futurist Magazine 7910 Woodmont Ave Suite 450	Bethesda	MD	20814	**800-989-8274**	301-656-8274	449-11
FW Webb 237 Albany St	Boston	MA	02118	**800-453-1100**	617-227-2240	378
Fybroc Div Met-Pro Corp 700 Emlen Way	Telford	PA	18969	**800-392-7621**	215-723-8155	627
Fyda Freightliner Youngstown Inc 5260 76th Dr	Youngstown	OH	44515	**800-837-3932**	330-797-0224	62-5
Fypon Ltd 3846 Green Valley Rd	Seven Valleys	PA	17360	**800-955-5748**	717-993-2593	590
Fytokem Products Inc 110 Research Dr Suite 101	Saskatoon	SK	S7N3R3	**877-457-3986**	306-668-2552	470

G

Company / Address	City	State	ZIP	Toll-Free	Phone	Class
G & H Decoys Inc PO Box 1208 *Orders	Henryetta	OK	74437	**800-443-3269***	918-652-3314	701
G-I Holdings Inc 1361 Alps Rd	Wayne	NJ	07470	**800-766-3411**	973-628-4032	355-3
G & K Services Inc 5995 Opus Pkwy Suite 500 *NASDAQ: GKSRA*	Minnetonka	MN	55343	**800-452-2737**	952-912-5500	434
G-L Veneer Co Inc 2224 E Slauson Ave	Huntington Park	CA	90255	**800-588-5003**	323-582-5203	602
G Loomis Inc 1359 Down River Dr	Woodland	WA	98674	**800-456-6647**	360-225-6516	701
G & M Electrical Contractors Co 1746 N Richmond St	Chicago	IL	60647	**800-546-8050**	773-278-8200	188-4
G-S Supplies 408 Saint Paul St	Rochester	NY	14605	**800-295-3050**	585-295-0250	534
G & T Industries Inc 3413 Eastern Ave SE	Grand Rapids	MI	49508	**800-686-2659**	616-452-8611	590
G & W Laboratories Inc 111 Coolidge St	South Plainfield	NJ	07080	**800-922-1038**	908-753-2000	572
GA Braun Inc PO Box 70	Syracuse	NY	13205	**800-432-7286**	315-475-3123	418
GA Wintzer & Son Co 5 N Blackhoof St PO Box 406	Wapakoneta	OH	45895	**800-331-1801**	419-738-3771	291-12
GA Wright Inc Direct Marketing Div 4105 Holly St	Denver	CO	80216	**800-824-5886**	303-333-4453	5
Gabelli Asset Management Inc 1 Corporate Ctr *NYSE: GBL*	Rye	NY	10580	**800-422-3554**	914-921-5681	393
Gabelli Funds 1 Corporate Ctr	Rye	NY	10580	**800-422-3554**	914-921-5100	517
Gable Claude Co 322 Fraley Rd	High Point	NC	27263	**800-422-5331**	336-883-1351	314-2
GableSigns Inc 7440 Fort Smallwood Rd	Baltimore	MD	21226	**800-854-0568**	410-255-6400	692
Gabriel Mfg Co Inc 125 S Liberty Dr	Stony Point	NY	10980	**800-454-3387**	845-942-0100	597
Gachman Metals & Recycling Co Inc 2600 Shamrock Ave	Fort Worth	TX	76107	**800-749-0423**	817-334-0211	674
Gaco Western Inc PO Box 88698 *Cust Svc	Seattle	WA	98138	**800-456-4226***	206-575-0450	590
Gadabout Tours Inc 700 E Tahquitz Canyon Way	Palm Springs	CA	92262	**800-952-5068**	760-325-5556	748
GADCO (General American Door Co) 5050 Baseline Rd	Montgomery	IL	60538	**800-323-0813**	630-859-3000	232
Gadsden County Chamber of Commerce 208 N Adams St	Quincy	FL	32351	**800-627-9231**	850-627-9231	137
Gadsden Scaffold Co Inc 137 Ewing Ave	Gadsden	AL	35901	**800-538-1780**	256-547-6918	482
Gadsden State Community College PO Box 227	Gadsden	AL	35902	**800-226-5563**	256-549-8200	160
Gadsden Times 401 Locust St	Gadsden	AL	35901	**800-762-2464**	256-549-2000	522-2
Gage Industries Inc PO Box 1318	Lake Oswego	OR	97035	**800-443-4243**	503-639-2177	591
GAI Consultants Inc 570 Beatty Rd	Monroeville	PA	15146	**800-437-2150**	412-856-6400	258
GAI-Tronics Corp PO Box 1060	Reading	PA	19607	**800-492-1212**	610-777-1374	720
Gaiam Inc 360 Interlocken Blvd Suite 300 *NASDAQ: GAIA*	Broomfield	CO	80021	**800-869-3446**	303-464-3600	451
Gail & Rice Productions Inc 21301 Civic Ctr Dr	Southfield	MI	48076	**800-860-1931**	248-799-5000	502
Gainesville Area Chamber of Commerce 101 S Culberson St	Gainesville	TX	76241	**888-585-4468**	940-665-2831	137
Gainesville Sun 2700 SW 13th St *Circ	Gainesville	FL	32614	**800-443-9493***	352-378-1411	522-2
Gainesville Times 345 Green St NW	Gainesville	GA	30501	**800-395-5005**	770-532-1234	522-2
Gainey Ceramics Inc 1200 Arrow Hwy *Cust Svc	La Verne	CA	91750	**800-451-8155***	909-593-3533	330
Gainey Transportation Services Inc 6000 Clay Ave SW	Grand Rapids	MI	49548	**800-859-4072**	616-530-8551	769
GAINSCO Inc 5400 Airport Fwy Suite A	Fort Worth	TX	76117	**800-438-4246**	817-336-2500	355-4
Gai's Div Franz Family Bakeries 2006 Weller St	Seattle	WA	98144	**800-272-7323**	206-322-0931	291-1

Company / Address	City	State	Zip	Toll-Free	Phone	Class
GAL Mfg Corp 50 E 153rd St	Bronx	NY	10451	**877-425-3538**	718-292-9000	255
Galaxy Cablevision PO Box 1007 *Cust Svc	Sikeston	MO	63801	**800-365-6988***	573-472-8200	117
Galaxy Carpet Mills Inc 235 Industrial Blvd	Chatsworth	GA	30705	**800-835-6070**	706-695-9611	131
Galaxy Nutritional Foods Inc 2441 Viscount Row *AMEX: GXY* ■ *Cust Svc	Orlando	FL	32809	**800-808-2325***	407-855-5500	291-5
Galaxy Tire & Wheel Inc 730 Eastern Ave *Sales	Malden	MA	02148	**800-343-3276***	781-321-3910	739
Galbreath Inc 461 E Rosser Dr	Winamac	IN	46996	**800-285-0666**	574-946-6631	379
Galderma Laboratories Inc 14501 N Fwy	Fort Worth	TX	76177	**800-582-8225**	817-961-5000	572
Gale Group 27500 Drake Rd *Cust Svc	Farmington Hills	MI	48331	**800-877-4253***	248-699-4253	623-2
Galen Assoc 610 5th Ave 5th Fl	New York	NY	10020	**800-868-4195**	212-218-4990	779
Galena/Jo Daviess County Convention & Visitors Bureau 720 Park Ave	Galena	IL	61036	**800-747-9377**	815-777-3557	205
Galesburg Area Convention & Visitors Bureau 2163 East Main St	Galesburg	IL	61402	**800-916-3330**	309-343-2485	205
Galey & Lord Inc 7736 McCloud Rd Suite 300 *Cust Svc	Greensboro	NC	27409	**800-527-9548***	336-665-3000	730-1
Gallade Chemical Inc 1230 E St Gertrude Pl	Santa Ana	CA	92707	**800-325-8431**	714-546-9901	144
Gallagher Asphalt Corp 18100 S Indiana Ave	Thornton	IL	60476	**800-536-7160**	708-877-7160	187-4
Gallagher Corp 3908 Morrison Dr	Gurnee	IL	60031	**800-249-3473**	847-249-3440	594-2
Gallagher Financial Systems 1500 San Remo Ave Suite 251	Coral Gables	FL	33146	**800-989-9998**	305-665-5099	176-11
Gallagher Healthcare Insurance Services Inc 2000 W Sam Houston Pkwy S Suite 2000	Houston	TX	77042	**800-733-4474**	713-461-4000	383
Gallant Greetings Corp 4300 United Pkwy	Schiller Park	IL	60176	**800-621-4279**	847-671-6500	130
Gallard-Schlesinger Industries Inc 245 Newtown Rd Suite 305	Plainview	NY	11803	**800-645-3044**	516-683-6900	144
Galleon Resort & Marina 617 Front St	Key West	FL	33040	**800-544-3030**	305-296-7711	655
Galleria Park Hotel 191 Sutter St	San Francisco	CA	94104	**866-756-3036**	415-781-3060	373
Gallery Furniture Inc 6006 I-45 N Fwy	Houston	TX	77076	**800-518-0008**	713-694-5570	316
Gallery of History Inc 3601 W Sahara Ave Suite 207 *NASDAQ: HIST*	Las Vegas	NV	89102	**800-425-5379**	702-364-1000	51
Galliard Capital Management Inc 800 La Salle Ave Suite 2060	Minneapolis	MN	55402	**800-717-1617**	612-667-3210	394
Galliker Dairy Co Inc 143 Donald Ln	Johnstown	PA	15904	**800-477-6455**	814-266-8702	291-27
Gallo E & J Winery 600 Yosemite Blvd	Modesto	CA	95354	**800-322-2389**	209-341-3111	81-3
Gallo Salami 2411 Baumann Ave	San Lorenzo	CA	94580	**800-321-1097**	510-276-1300	291-26
Gallo Wine Distributors Inc 345 Underhill Blvd	Syosset	NY	11791	**800-272-4255**	516-921-9005	82-3
Galls Inc 2680 Palumbo Dr	Lexington	KY	40509	**800-477-7766**	859-266-7227	566
Gallup Convention & Visitors Bureau PO Box 600	Gallup	NM	87305	**800-242-4282**	505-863-3841	205
Gallup Independent 500 N 9th St	Gallup	NM	87305	**800-545-3817**	505-863-6811	522-2
Gallup Organization 901 F St NW	Washington	DC	20004	**877-242-5587**	202-715-3030	458
Gallup Sand & Gravel Co PO Box 1119	Gallup	NM	87305	**800-257-3818**	505-863-3818	180
Galpin Motors Inc 15505 Roscoe Blvd	North Hills	CA	91343	**800-464-2574**	818-787-3800	57
Galt House Hotel 140 N 4th St	Louisville	KY	40202	**800-626-1814**	502-589-5200	373
Galvanizers Assn. American 6881 S Holly Cir Suite 108	Centennial	CO	80112	**800-468-7732**	720-554-0900	49-13
Galveston County Daily News PO Box 628	Galveston	TX	77553	**800-561-3611**	409-683-5200	522-2
Galvin Flying Service 7149 Perimeter Rd	Seattle	WA	98108	**800-341-4102**	206-763-0350	63
Galyan's Trading Co Inc 1 Galyan's Pkwy *NASDAQ: GLYN*	Plainfield	IN	46168	**888-425-9267**	317-532-0200	702
GAMA International 2901 Telestar Ct *Cust Svc	Falls Church	VA	22042	**800-345-2687***	703-770-8184	49-9
Gamajet Cleaning Systems Inc PO Box 626 *Sales	Devault	PA	19432	**800-289-5387***	610-408-9940	379
Gambling Inc. National Council on Problem 208 G St NE 1st Fl	Washington	DC	20002	**800-522-4700**	202-547-9204	49-8
Gambro BCT 10811 W Collins Ave	Lakewood	CO	80215	**877-339-4228**	303-232-6800	410
Gambro Healthcare Inc 5200 Virginia Way	Brentwood	TN	37027	**800-467-4736**	615-320-4200	347
Gambro Renal Products 10810 W Collins Ave	Lakewood	CO	80215	**800-525-2623**	303-232-6800	249
Gamco Industries Inc 325 N Kirkwood Dr Suite 200	Saint Louis	MO	63122	**888-726-8100**	314-909-1670	176-3
Game Financial Corp 1550 Utica Ave S Suite 100	Saint Louis Park	MN	55416	**800-363-3372**	952-591-3000	70
Game-Time Inc 150 Gametime Dr *Sales	Fort Payne	AL	35968	**800-235-2440***	256-845-5610	340
GameFly Inc PO Box 6019	Inglewood	CA	90312	**888-986-6400**		94
GamePlan Financial Marketing LLC 300 ParkBrooke Pl Suite 200	Woodstock	GA	30189	**866-766-3855**	770-517-2765	394
GameStop Corp 2250 William D Tate Ave *NYSE: GME*	Grapevine	TX	76051	**800-288-9020**	817-424-2000	177
GameTech International Inc 900 Sandhill Rd *NASDAQ: GMTC*	Reno	NV	89521	**800-487-8510**	775-850-6000	317
Gamewell Co 12 Clintonville Rd	Northford	CT	06472	**800-866-1456**	203-484-7161	681
Gameznflix Inc 6960 Eastgate Blvd	Lebanon	TN	37088	**800-613-1543**		94
Gaming Assn. National Indian 224 2nd St SE	Washington	DC	20003	**800-286-6442**	202-546-7711	48-23
Gaming Partners International Corp 1700 Industrial Rd *NASDAQ: GPIC*	Las Vegas	NV	89102	**800-728-5766**	702-384-2425	317

Company / Address	City	State	Zip	Toll-Free	Phone	Class
Gamma Beta Phi Society 78-A Mitchell Rd Suite 204	Oak Ridge	TN	37830	**800-628-9920**	865-483-6212	48-16
Gamma Racquet Sports 200 Waterfront Dr	Pittsburgh	PA	15222	**800-333-0337**	412-323-0335	701
Gander Mountain Co 4567 American Blvd W *NASDAQ: GMTN*	Bloomington	MN	55437	**800-745-7411**	952-830-8700	702
Gandy Co 528 Gandrud Rd	Owatonna	MN	55060	**800-443-2476**	507-451-5430	269
Gandy's Dairies Inc PO Box 992	San Angelo	TX	76902	**800-200-3326**	325-655-6965	291-25
Ganin Tire Co Inc 1421 38th St	Brooklyn	NY	11218	**800-344-2788**	718-633-6300	740
Gannett Co Inc Gannett Offset Div 6883 Commercial Dr	Springfield	VA	22159	**800-255-1457**	703-642-1800	615
Gannett Fleming Inc PO Box 67100	Harrisburg	PA	17106	**800-233-1055**	717-763-7211	258
Gannett Media Technologies International 151 W 4th St Suite 201 *Sales	Cincinnati	OH	45202	**800-801-3771***	513-665-3777	176-10
Gannett Offset Div Gannett Co Inc 6883 Commercial Dr	Springfield	VA	22159	**800-255-1457**	703-642-1800	615
Gannett Welsh & Kotler Inc 222 Berkeley St Suite 1500	Boston	MA	02116	**800-225-4236**	617-236-8900	393
Gannon University 109 University Sq	Erie	PA	16541	**800-426-6668**	814-871-7000	163
Gans Ink & Supply Co Inc 1441 Boyd St	Los Angeles	CA	90033	**800-372-7410**	323-264-2200	381
Gant Travel Management 304 W Kirkwood Ave Suite 1	Bloomington	IN	47404	**800-742-4198**		760
Gantrade Corp 210 Summit Ave Bldg B	Montvale	NJ	07645	**800-426-8723**	201-573-1955	142
GAP Adventures 355 Eglinton Ave E	Toronto	ON	M4P1M5	**800-465-5600**	416-260-0999	748
Gap Inc 2 Folsom St *NYSE: GPS*	San Francisco	CA	94105	**800-333-7899**	650-952-4400	658
GapKids 1 Harrison St	San Francisco	CA	94105	**800-333-7899**	650-952-4400	155-1
Garan Inc 350 5th Ave 19th Fl	New York	NY	10118	**800-326-0225**	212-563-2000	153-4
Garban Corp 1100 Plaza 5 12th Fl	Jersey City	NJ	07311	**800-427-6859**	201-369-5663	679
Garber Travel Service Inc 27 Boylston St	Chestnut Hill	MA	02467	**800-359-4272**	617-739-2200	760
Garco Building Systems 2714 S Garfield Rd	Airway Heights	WA	99001	**800-941-2291**	509-244-5611	106
Garda World Security Corp 705 Bourget St Suite 200 *TSE: GW*	Montreal	QC	H4C2M6	**800-334-2732**	514-937-7487	682
Gardco Lighting 2661 Alvarado St	San Leandro	CA	94577	**800-227-0758**	510-357-6900	431
Garden City Community College 801 Campus Dr	Garden City	KS	67846	**800-658-1696**	620-276-7611	160
Garden City Feed Yard 1805 W Annie Scheer Rd	Garden City	KS	67846	**800-272-4191**	620-275-4191	11-1
Garden City Hotel 45 7th St	Garden City	NY	11530	**800-547-0400**	516-747-3000	373
Garden City Telegram 310 N 7th St	Garden City	KS	67846	**800-475-8600**	620-275-8500	522-2
Garden Clubs Inc. National 4401 Magnolia Ave Suite 1600	Saint Louis	MO	63110	**800-550-6007**	314-776-7574	48-18
Garden Court Hotel 520 Cowper St	Palo Alto	CA	94301	**800-824-9028**	650-322-9000	373
Garden Fresh Restaurant Corp 15822 Bernardo Ctr Dr Suite A	San Diego	CA	92127	**800-874-1600**	858-675-1600	656
Garden of the Gods Motel 2922 W Colorado Ave	Colorado Springs	CO	80904	**800-637-0703**	719-636-5271	373
Garden Grove Chamber of Commerce 12866 Main St Suite 102	Garden Grove	CA	92840	**800-959-5560**	714-638-7950	137
Garden Grove Playhouse 12001 Saint Mark St	Garden Grove	CA	92845	**866-468-3399**	714-897-5122	563-4
Garden Herbs Inc 26021 Business Center Dr	Redlands	CA	92374	**800-388-9397**	909-796-2569	291-37
Garden Island Newspaper 3-3137 Kuhio Hwy	Lihue	HI	96766	**800-296-2880**	808-245-3681	522-2
Garden Jewelry Co Inc 579 5th Ave Suite 420	New York	NY	10017	**800-321-0259**	212-421-7700	401
Garden & Landscape Design Book Club Doubleday Select Inc 101 Park Ave 23rd Fl	New York	NY	10178	**800-321-7323**		94
Garden of Life Inc 770 Northpoint Pkwy Suite 100 *Orders	West Palm Beach	FL	33407	**888-622-8986***	561-748-2477	786
Garden Place Hotel 6615 Transit Rd	Williamsville	NY	14221	**800-427-3361**	716-635-9000	373
Garden Ridge Corp 19411 Atrium Pl Suite 170	Houston	TX	77084	**800-216-4887**	281-579-7901	357
Garden Spa at MacArthur Place 29 E MacArthur St	Sonoma	CA	95476	**800-722-1866**	707-933-3193	698
Garden State Growers 99 Locust Grove Rd	Pittstown	NJ	08867	**800-288-8484**	908-730-8888	363
Garden State Life Insurance Co 2450 S Shore Blvd Suite 401	League City	TX	77573	**800-638-8565**	281-538-1037	384-2
Garden State Nutritionals 8 Henderson Dr	West Caldwell	NJ	07006	**800-526-9095**	973-575-9200	786
Gardena Valley News 16417 S Western Ave	Gardena	CA	90247	**800-329-6351**	310-329-6351	522-4
Gardenburger Inc 1411 SW Morrison St Suite 400	Portland	OR	97205	**800-636-0109**	503-205-1500	291-36
Gardener's Supply Co 128 Intervale Rd	Burlington	VT	05401	**800-863-1700**	802-660-3500	318
Gardening Assn. National 1100 Dorset St	South Burlington	VT	05403	**800-538-7476**	802-863-5251	48-18
Gardens of the American Rose Center 8877 Jefferson-Paige Rd	West Shreveport	LA	71119	**800-637-6534**	318-938-5402	98
Gardens Hotel 526 Angela St	Key West	FL	33040	**800-526-2664**	305-294-2661	373
Gardiner's Resort 114 Carmel Valley Rd	Carmel Valley	CA	93924	**800-453-6225**	831-659-2207	655
Gardner Asphalt Corp 4161 E 7th Ave	Tampa	FL	33605	**800-237-1155**	813-248-2101	46
Gardner & Benoit Inc PO Box 7246	Charlotte	NC	28241	**800-467-6676**	704-504-1151	295
Gardner Denver Blower Div 100 Gardner Pk	Peachtree City	GA	30269	**800-543-7736**	770-632-5000	19
Gardner Denver Inc 1800 Gardner Expy *NYSE: GDI*	Quincy	IL	62305	**800-682-9868**	217-222-5400	170
Gardner Denver Pump Div 4747 S 83rd E Ave	Tulsa	OK	74145	**800-637-8099**	918-664-1151	627

Name / Address	City	State	ZIP	Toll-Free	Phone	Class
Gardner Denver Water Jetting Systems Inc 12300 N Houston Rosslyn Rd	Houston	TX	77086	**800-231-3628**	281-448-5800	170
Gardner Glass Products Inc 600 Elkin Hwy	North Wilkesboro	NC	28659	**800-334-7267**	336-651-9300	330
Gardner Inc 3641 Interchange Rd	Columbus	OH	43204	**800-848-8946**	614-456-4000	270
Gardner Publications Inc 6915 Valley Ave	Cincinnati	OH	45244	**800-950-8020**	513-527-8800	623-9
Gardner-Webb University PO Box 817	Boiling Springs	NC	28017	**800-253-6472**	704-406-4498	163
Gardner-Webb University M Christopher White School of Divinity 110 S Main St Noel Hall	Boiling Springs	NC	28017	**800-619-3761**	704-406-4400	164-3
Gardners Candies Inc 2600 Adams Ave	Tyrone	PA	16686	**800-242-2639**	814-684-3925	123
Gare Inc 165 Rosemont St	Haverhill	MA	01832	**888-511-4273**	978-373-9131	43
Gared Sports Inc 1107 Mullanphy St	Saint Louis	MO	63106	**800-325-2682**	314-421-0044	701
Garelick Farms Inc 124 Grove St Franklin Oaks Office Pk Suite 100	Franklin	MA	02038	**800-343-4982**	508-528-9000	291-27
Garff Ken Automotive Group 195 E University Pkwy	Orem	UT	84058	**888-323-5869**	801-374-1751	57
Garfield County 55 S Main St	Panguitch	UT	84759	**800-636-8826**	435-676-8826	334
Garfield Suites Hotel 2 Garfield Pl	Cincinnati	OH	45202	**800-367-2155**	513-421-3355	373
GarKane Energy Inc PO Box 465	Loa	UT	84747	**800-747-5403**	435-836-2795	244
Garland C Norris Co 1101 Terry Rd	Apex	NC	27502	**800-331-8920**	919-387-1059	549
Garland Co Inc 3800 E 91st St	Cleveland	OH	44105	**800-321-9336**	216-641-7500	46
Garland Commercial Industries 185 E South St	Freeland	PA	18224	**800-424-2411**	570-636-1000	293
Garland Landmark Museum 200 Museum Plaza Dr	Garland	TX	75040	**888-879-0264**	972-205-2749	509
Garland Publishing Inc 270 Madison Ave	New York	NY	10016	**800-797-3803**	917-351-7100	623-2
Garland Resort 4700 N Red Oak Rd	Lewiston	MI	49756	**800-968-0042**	989-786-2211	655
Garlits Don Museums 13700 SW 16th Ave	Ocala	FL	34473	**877-271-3278**	352-245-8661	511
Garlock Sealing Technologies 1666 Division St	Palmyra	NY	14522	**800-448-6688**	315-597-4811	321
GARMCO USA 55 Triangle St	Danbury	CT	06810	**800-722-3645**	203-743-2731	476
Garment Corp of America 801 W 41st St 3rd Fl *Cust Svc	Miami Beach	FL	33140	**800-944-4500***	305-531-4040	153-19
Garment Council. UFCW Textile & 4207 Lebanon Pike Suite 200	Hermitage	TN	37076	**888-462-4892**	615-889-9221	405
Garmin Ltd 1200 E 151st St *NASDAQ: GRMN*	Olathe	KS	66062	**888-442-7646**	913-397-8200	519
Garr Tool Co 7800 N Alger Rd	Alma	MI	48801	**800-248-9003**	989-463-6171	484
Garrett Aviation 6201 W Imperial Hwy	Los Angeles	CA	90045	**800-942-7738**	310-568-3700	25
Garrett County Chamber of Commerce 15 Visitors Ctr Dr	McHenry	MD	21541	**800-387-5237**	301-387-4386	137
Garrett-Evangelical Theological Seminary 2121 Sheridan Rd	Evanston	IL	60201	**800-736-4627**	847-866-3900	164-3
Garrett Metal Detectors 1881 W State St	Garland	TX	75042	**800-234-6151**	972-494-6151	464
Garrett Speakers International Inc PO Box 153448	Irving	TX	75015	**800-787-2840**	972-513-0054	699
Garrett's Desert Inn 311 Old Santa Fe Trail	Santa Fe	NM	87501	**800-888-2145**	505-982-1851	373
Garrity Industries Inc 14 New Rd	Madison	CT	06443	**800-872-5483**	203-245-8383	431
Garry Packing Inc PO Box 249	Del Rey	CA	93616	**800-248-2126**	559-888-2126	291-18
Garst Seed Co 2369 230th St PO Box 500	Slater	IA	50244	**888-464-2778**	515-685-5000	684
Gartland Foundry Co Inc PO Box 1564	Terre Haute	IN	47808	**800-237-0226**	812-232-0226	302
Gartmore Funds PO Box 182205	Columbus	OH	43218	**800-848-0920**		517
Gartmore Morley Financial Services Inc 5665 SW Meadows Rd Suite 400	Lake Oswego	OR	97035	**800-548-4806**	503-620-7899	393
Gartner Inc 56 Top Gallant Rd *NYSE: IT*	Stamford	CT	06904	**800-328-2776**	203-316-1111	458
Garuda Indonesian Airlines 3050 Post Oak Blvd Suite 1320	Houston	TX	77056	**800-342-7832**	713-877-1942	26
Garvan Woodland Gardens 550 Arkridge Rd PO Box 22240	Hot Springs	AR	71903	**800-366-4664**	501-262-9300	98
Garvey Corp 208 S Rt 73	Blue Anchor	NJ	08037	**800-257-8581**	609-561-2450	206
Gary Plastic Packaging Corp 1340 Viele Ave	Bronx	NY	10474	**800-221-8150**	718-893-2200	589
Gas Assn. American Public 201 Massachusetts Ave NE Suite C-4	Washington	DC	20002	**800-927-4204**	202-464-2742	48-12
Gas Compact Commission. Interstate Oil & 900 NE 23rd St PO Box 53127	Oklahoma City	OK	73152	**800-822-4015**	405-525-3556	48-12
Gas Equipment Supply Co Inc 1440 Lakes Pkwy Suite 300	Lawrenceville	GA	30043	**800-241-4155**	770-995-1131	378
Gas-Fired Products Inc PO Box 36485	Charlotte	NC	28236	**800-438-4936**	704-372-3485	313
Gasboy International Inc 7300 W Friendly Ave *Sales	Greensboro	NC	27420	**800-444-5579***	336-547-5000	625
Gaska-Tape Inc 1810 W Lusher Ave	Elkhart	IN	46517	**800-423-1571**	574-294-5431	717
Gasket Mfg Co Inc 18001 S Main St	Gardena	CA	90248	**800-442-7538**	310-217-5600	321
Gaskets Inc 301 W Hwy 16 PO Box 398	Rio	WI	53960	**800-558-1833**	920-992-3137	321
Gaspard Robert Co Inc 200 N Janacek Rd	Brookfield	WI	53045	**800-784-6868**	262-784-6800	153-14
Gast Mfg Inc PO Box 97	Benton Harbor	MI	49023	**800-952-4278**	269-926-6171	170
Gaston Chamber of Commerce 601 W Franklin Blvd	Gastonia	NC	28052	**800-348-8461**	704-864-2621	137
Gaston County Travel & Tourism 620 N Main St	Belmont	NC	28012	**800-849-9994**	704-825-4044	205
Gaston Gazette 1893 Remount Rd	Gastonia	NC	28054	**800-273-3315**	704-869-1700	522-2
Gastonian The 220 E Gaston St	Savannah	GA	31401	**800-322-6603**	912-232-2869	373
Gastroenterology Nurses & Associates Inc. Society of 401 N Michigan Ave	Chicago	IL	60611	**800-245-7462**	312-321-5165	49-8
Gate City Beverage Distributors 2505 Steele St	San Bernardino	CA	92408	**800-500-4283**	909-799-1600	82-1
Gates of the Arctic National Park & Preserve 201 1st Ave	Fairbanks	AK	99701	**866-869-6887**	907-457-5752	554
Gates Bar-B-Q 4621 Paseo Blvd	Kansas City	MO	64110	**800-662-7427**	816-923-0900	657
Gates Bill & Melinda Foundation PO Box 23350	Seattle	WA	98102	**888-452-6352**	206-709-3100	300
Gateway Center 1 Gateway Dr	Collinsville	IL	62234	**800-289-2388**	618-345-8998	204
Gateway Foundation Inc 55 E Jackson St Suite 1500	Chicago	IL	60604	**800-444-1331**	312-663-1130	712
Gateway Funds 3805 Edwards Rd Suite 600	Cincinnati	OH	45209	**800-354-6339**	513-719-1100	517
Gateway Helicopters Ltd PO Box 21028 Aviation Ln Hangar 4	North Bay	ON	P1B9N8	**888-474-4214**	705-474-4214	354
Gateway Inc 7565 Irvine Center Dr *NYSE: GTW*	Irvine	CA	92618	**800-846-2000**	949-471-7000	171-3
Gateway Limousines 1550 Gilbreth Rd	Burlingame	CA	94010	**800-486-7077**	650-345-7077	433
Gateway Newstands Inc 9555 Yonge St Suite 400	Richmond Hill	ON	L4C9M5	**800-942-5351**	905-737-7755	743
Gateway Press 1619 Commerce Dr	Stow	OH	44224	**800-966-6565**	330-688-0088	522-4
Gateway Regional Medical Center 2100 Madison Ave	Granite City	IL	62040	**800-559-9992**	618-798-3000	366-2
Gateway Riverboat Cruises 707 N 1st St	Saint Louis	MO	63102	**877-982-1410**	314-621-4040	218
Gateway Safety Inc 4722 Spring Rd	Cleveland	OH	44131	**800-822-5347**	216-749-1100	531
Gateway Supply Co Inc 1312 Hamrick St	Columbia	SC	29202	**800-922-5312**	803-771-7160	601
Gateway Technical College 3520 30th Ave	Kenosha	WI	53144	**800-247-7122**	262-564-2200	787
Gateway Tire Co Inc 4 W Crescentville Rd	Cincinnati	OH	45246	**800-837-1405**	513-874-2500	740
Gateway Title Co 1405 N San Fernando Blvd	Burbank	CA	91504	**800-660-6992**	818-953-2300	384-6
Gateway Tourism Council PO Box 2011	Bayonne	NJ	07002	**877-428-3930**	201-436-6009	205
Gateway Travel Management 1501 Ardmore Blvd Suite 400	Pittsburgh	PA	15221	**800-553-0093**	412-244-3740	760
Gateways Inn 51 Walker St	Lenox	MA	01240	**888-492-9466**	413-637-2532	373
Gatlinburg Convention Center 303 Reagan Dr	Gatlinburg	TN	37738	**800-343-1475**	865-436-2392	204
Gatlinburg Dept of Tourism & Convention Ctr 234 Historic Nature Trail	Gatlinburg	TN	37738	**800-343-1475**	865-436-2392	205
Gator Park 24050 SW 8th St	Miami	FL	33184	**800-559-2205**	305-559-2255	811
Gatorade Sports Science Institute 617 W Main St	Barrington	IL	60010	**800-616-4774**	847-381-1980	654
Gatorade Worldwide PO Box 049003	Chicago	IL	60604	**800-884-2867**	312-821-1000	81-2
Gatorland 14501 S Orange Blossom Trail	Orlando	FL	32837	**800-393-5297**	407-855-5496	811
Gatsby Spas Inc 1003 S Alexander St Suite 7	Plant City	FL	33563	**800-393-7727**	813-754-4122	367
GATX Capital Corp 4 Embarcadero Ctr Suite 2200	San Francisco	CA	94111	**800-227-4289**	415-955-3200	214
GATX Corp 500 W Monroe St *NYSE: GMT*	Chicago	IL	60661	**800-525-4289**	312-621-6200	214
GATX Rail Canada 1600 Rene Levesque Blvd W Suite 1500	Montreal	QC	H3H1P9	**800-806-2489**	514-931-7343	261-6
Gaucher Foundation. National 5410 Edson Ln Suite 260	Rockville	MD	20852	**800-428-2437**	301-816-1515	48-17
Gaudenzia Inc Common Ground 2835 N Front St	Harrisburg	PA	17110	**888-237-8984**	717-238-5553	712
Gavel International Corp 2275 Half Day Rd Suite 190	Bannockburn	IL	60015	**800-544-2835**	847-945-8150	183
Gavina F & Sons Inc 2700 Fruitland Ave	Vernon	CA	90058	**800-428-4627**	323-582-0671	291-7
Gay & Lesbian Travel Assn. International 4331 N Federal Hwy Suite 304	Fort Lauderdale	FL	33308	**800-448-8550**	954-776-2626	48-23
Gay Men's Health Crisis (GMHC) 119 W 24th St	New York	NY	10011	**800-243-7692**	212-367-1000	48-17
Gayla Industries Inc 6401 Antoine Dr	Houston	TX	77291	**800-231-7508**	713-681-2411	750
Gaylor Electric 11711 N College Ave Suite 150	Carmel	IN	46032	**800-878-0577**	317-843-0577	188-4
Gaylord Brothers PO Box 4901 *Cust Svc	Syracuse	NY	13221	**800-634-6304***	315-457-5070	314-3
Gaylord Hospital Gaylord Farms Rd PO Box 400	Wallingford	CT	06492	**888-429-5673**	203-284-2800	366-4
Gaylord Industries Inc 10900 SW Avery St	Tualatin	OR	97062	**800-547-9696**	503-691-2010	19
Gaylord Mfg Co PO Box 547	Ceres	CA	95307	**800-375-0091**	209-538-3313	804
Gaymar Industries Inc 10 Centre Dr	Orchard Park	NY	14127	**800-828-7341**	716-662-2551	468
Gaynor Edwin Corp 200 Charles St	Stratford	CT	06615	**800-342-9667**	203-378-5545	803
Gaz Metro LP 1717 rue du Havre *TSE: GZM.un*	Montreal	QC	H2K2X3	**800-567-1313**	514-598-3444	774
Gazette The 30 S Prospect St *News Rm	Colorado Springs	CO	80903	**800-800-4899***	719-632-5511	522-2
Gazette The PO Box 319	Galena	IL	61036	**800-373-6397**	815-777-0019	522-4
Gazette The 500 3rd Ave SE	Cedar Rapids	IA	52401	**800-397-8212**	319-398-8313	522-2
Gazette The 1010 St Catherine St W Suite 200	Montreal	QC	H3B5L1	**800-361-8478**	514-987-2222	522-1
Gazette Newspapers Inc 1200 Quince Orchard Blvd	Gaithersburg	MD	20878	**888-670-7100**	301-948-3120	623-8
GB Products International Corp 5650 Imhoff Dr Suite B	Concord	CA	94520	**800-650-0341**	925-825-3040	459
GBA Systems 1501 Highwoods Blvd Suite 201	Greensboro	NC	27410	**800-422-3267**	336-668-4555	176-1
GBF Graphics Inc 7300 Niles Ctr Rd	Skokie	IL	60077	**800-423-8326**	847-677-1700	111
GBS Filing Systems 224 Morges Rd	Malvern	OH	44644	**800-873-4427**	330-863-1828	550
GC America Inc 3737 W 127th St	Alsip	IL	60803	**800-323-3386**	708-597-0900	226
GC Quality Lubricants Inc 1403 6th St	Macon	GA	31206	**800-768-5823**	478-738-3900	530
GC Services LP 6330 Gulfton St	Houston	TX	77081	**800-756-6524**	713-777-4441	157
GC Supply Inc 3587 Clover Ln	New Castle	PA	16105	**800-248-4653**	724-658-1741	759
GCA Services Group 100 Four Falls Corporate Ctr	West Conshohocken	PA	19428	**800-422-8760**	610-834-7555	150
GCC Dacotah 501 N Saint Onge St	Rapid City	SD	57702	**800-843-8324**	605-721-7100	135

Name / Address	City	State	ZIP	Toll-Free	Phone	Class
GCC Printers USA 209 Burlington Rd *Sales	Bedford	MA	01730	**800-422-7777***	781-275-5800	171-6
GCF Food Services Inc 658 Danforth Ave Suite 201	Toronto	ON	M4J5B9	**800-465-3324**	416-778-8028	656
GCI Group Inc 825 3rd Ave 24th Fl	New York	NY	10022	**800-883-9525**	212-537-8000	622
GCSAA (Golf Course Superintendents Assn of America) 1421 Research Park Dr	Lawrence	KS	66049	**800-472-7878**	785-841-2240	48-2
GDI Infotech Inc 3775 Varsity Dr	Ann Arbor	MI	48108	**800-608-7682**	734-477-6900	175
GE (General Electric Co) 3135 Easton Tpke *NYSE: GE* ■ *Cust Svc	Fairfield	CT	06828	**800-626-2000***	203-373-2211	184
GE Access 11300 Westmoor Cir *Sales	Westminster	CO	80031	**800-733-9333***	303-545-1000	172
GE Capital Assurance Co Long Term Care Div 1650 Los Gamos Dr	San Rafael	CA	94903	**800-456-7766**	415-492-7500	384-2
GE Capital Auto Financial Services 540 W Northwest Hwy *Cust Svc	Barrington	IL	60010	**800-488-5208***	847-277-4000	214
GE Capital Card Services PO Box 276	Dayton	OH	45401	**800-844-6543**	800-333-1071	213
GE Capital Fleet Services 3 Capital Dr	Eden Prairie	MN	55344	**800-469-0044**	952-828-1000	284
GE Capital IT Management Services 2480 Meadowvale Blvd	Mississauga	ON	L5N7Y1	**800-268-2106**	905-816-3000	178
GE Capital Public Finance 8400 Normandale Lake Blvd Suite 470	Minneapolis	MN	55437	**800-346-3164**	952-897-5649	214
GE Capital Small Business Finance 635 Maryville Ctr Dr Suite 120	Saint Louis	MO	63141	**800-447-2025**	314-205-3500	214
GE Colonial Penn PO Box 8110	Fort Washington	PA	19034	**800-523-4040**	267-468-2000	384-4
GE Commercial Equipment Financing 44 Old Ridgebury Rd	Danbury	CT	06810	**800-937-4322**	203-796-1000	214
GE Consumer Products Appliance Pk	Louisville	KY	40225	**800-626-2000**	502-452-4311	36
GE Elfun Funds 101 Savings St	Pawtucket	RI	02860	**800-242-0134**		517
GE Energy 4200 Wildwood Pkwy	Atlanta	GA	30339	**800-368-1316**		259
GE Fanuc Automation Corp 2500 Austin Dr *Cust Svc	Charlottesville	VA	22911	**800-432-7521***	434-978-5000	200
GE Financial Assurance Holdings Inc 6604 W Broad St	Richmond	VA	23230	**800-844-6543**	804-281-6000	384-2
GE Healthcare PO Box 414	Milwaukee	WI	53201	**800-558-5102**	262-544-3011	375
GE Healthcare Information Technologies 8200 W Tower Ave	Milwaukee	WI	53223	**800-558-5102**	414-355-5000	249
GE Information Technology Solutions Inc 1101 Pacific Ave	Erlanger	KY	41018	**877-505-5557**	859-815-7000	172
GE Infrastructure Security 205 Lowell St	Wilmington	MA	01887	**800-433-5346**	978-658-3767	464
GE Ion Track 205 Lowell St	Wilmington	MA	01887	**800-433-5346**	978-658-3767	464
GE Lighting Systems Inc 3010 Spartanburg Hwy	East Flat Rock	NC	28726	**877-798-6702**	828-693-2000	431
GE Mortgage Insurance Corp 6601 Six Forks Rd	Raleigh	NC	27615	**800-334-9270**	919-846-4100	384-5
GE Motor Club Inc 200 N Martingale Rd *Cust Svc	Schaumburg	IL	60173	**800-616-9286***	800-417-6368	53
GE Multilin 215 Anderson Ave	Markham	ON	L6E1B3	**800-547-8629**	905-294-6222	202
GE Mutual Funds 101 Savings St	Pawtucket	RI	02860	**800-242-0134**		517
GE Nuclear Energy 175 Curtner Ave	San Jose	CA	95150	**800-626-2004**	408-925-1000	92
GE OEC Medical Systems Inc 384 Wright Brothers Dr	Salt Lake City	UT	84116	**800-365-1366**	801-328-9300	375
GE Perfect Getaways PO Box 5007	Carol Stream	IL	60197	**800-621-5505**	800-452-7118	760
GE Petrochemicals Inc SR 892 *Cust Svc	Washington	WV	26181	**800-643-4346***	304-863-7778	142
GE Plastics 1 Plastics Ave	Pittsfield	MA	01201	**800-451-3147**	413-448-7484	594-2
GE Polymerland 9930 Kincey Ave	Huntersville	NC	28078	**800-752-7842**		592
GE Quartz 4901 Campbell Rd	Willoughby	OH	44094	**800-438-2100**	800-258-3803	490
GE Rail Car Services 161 N Clark St 7th Fl	Chicago	IL	60601	**888-272-5793**	312-853-5000	261-6
GE Security 300 W 6th St Suite 1850	Austin	TX	78701	**877-526-0885**	512-381-2760	681
GE Silicones 260 Hudson River Rd *Cust Svc	Waterford	NY	12188	**800-332-3390***	518-237-3330	142
GE Structured Products 1 Plastics Ave	Pittsfield	MA	01201	**800-451-3147**	413-448-5400	588
GE Transportation Rail 2901 E Lake Rd *Prod Info	Erie	PA	16531	**800-626-2000***	814-875-2234	636
GE Transportation Rail Global Signaling PO Box 8900	Melbourne	FL	32904	**800-342-5434**	321-435-7000	691
GE Vendor Financial Services 10 Riverview Dr	Danbury	CT	06810	**800-876-2033**	203-749-6000	214
GEA Niro Inc 9165 Rumsey Rd	Columbia	MD	21045	**800-446-4231**	410-997-8700	379
Geac AEC Business Solutions 3707 W Cherry St *Tech Supp	Tampa	FL	33607	**888-284-4232***	813-874-3344	176-1
Geac Restaurant Systems 175 Ledge St	Nashua	NH	03060	**888-432-2773**	603-889-5152	176-11
Gear for Sports Inc 9700 Commerce Pkwy	Lenexa	KS	66219	**800-423-5044**	913-693-3200	153-1
Gearench Inc PO Box 192	Clifton	TX	76634	**800-221-1848**	254-675-8651	526
Gearhart By The Sea PO Box 2700	Gearhart	OR	97138	**800-547-0115**	503-738-8331	655
Geary's Stores Inc 351 N Beverly Dr	Beverly Hills	CA	90210	**800-243-2797**	310-273-4741	357
Geauga County Transit 12555 Merritt Rd	Chardon	OH	44024	**888-287-7190**	440-285-2222	109
Geek Squad Inc 1213 Washington Ave N	Minneapolis	MN	55401	**888-237-8289**	612-343-4335	173
Geerlings & Wade Inc 960 Turnpike St	Canton	MA	02021	**800-782-9463**	781-821-4152	451
Gehl's Guernsey Farms Inc N116 W15970 Main St	Germantown	WI	53022	**800-521-2873**	262-251-8570	291-10
Gehr Industries 7400 E Slauson Ave	Los Angeles	CA	90040	**800-688-6606**	323-728-5558	800
GEICO 1 GEICO Plaza	Washington	DC	20076	**800-824-5404**	301-986-2500	355-4
GEICO (Government Employees Insurance Co) 1 GEICO Plaza	Washington	DC	20076	**800-841-3000**	301-986-3000	384-4
GEICO Casualty Co 1 GEICO Plaza	Washington	DC	20076	**800-841-3000**	301-986-2300	384-4
GEICO General Insurance Co 1 GEICO Plaza	Washington	DC	20076	**800-841-3000**	301-986-2300	384-4
Geiger 70 Mt Hope Ave	Lewiston	ME	04240	**888-222-4276**	207-755-2000	10
Geiger Brothers Promotional Marketing 2010 Oakgrove Rd	Hattiesburg	MS	39402	**800-264-9291**	601-264-1991	10
Geiger International Inc 6095 Fulton Industrial Blvd SW	Atlanta	GA	30336	**800-444-8812**	404-344-1100	314-1
Geisinger Health Plan 100 N Academy Ave	Danville	PA	17822	**800-447-4000**	570-271-8760	384-3
Gelco Information Network Inc 10700 Prairie Lakes Dr	Eden Prairie	MN	55344	**800-444-6588**	952-947-1500	39
Gelmart Industries Inc 136 Madison Ave 4th Fl	New York	NY	10016	**800-746-0014**	212-743-6900	153-18
Gem Dandy Inc 200 W Academy St	Madison	NC	27025	**800-334-5101**	336-548-9624	153-2
Gem East Corp 2124 2nd Ave	Seattle	WA	98121	**800-426-0605**	206-441-1700	401
GEM Group 9 International Way	Lawrence	MA	01843	**800-800-3200**	978-691-2000	68
GEM Industrial Inc 6842 Commodore Dr	Walbridge	OH	43465	**800-837-5909**	419-666-6554	188-10
Gem Refrigerator Co 650 E Erie Ave	Philadelphia	PA	19134	**800-922-1422**	215-426-8700	650
Gem Trade Assn. American 3030 LBJ Fwy Suite 840	Dallas	TX	75234	**800-972-1162**	214-742-4367	49-4
Gemini Air Cargo 44965 Aviation Dr Suite 300	Dulles	VA	20166	**888-359-4221**	703-260-8100	13
Gemini Fund Services LLC 150 Motor Pkwy Suite 205	Hauppauge	NY	11788	**800-368-3322**	631-951-0500	393
Gemini Inc 103 Mensing Ave	Cannon Falls	MN	55009	**800-533-3631**	507-263-3957	692
Gemini Valve Inc 2 Otter Ct	Raymond	NH	03077	**800-370-0936**	603-895-4761	776
Gemological Institute of America (GIA) 5345 Armada Dr	Carlsbad	CA	92008	**800-421-7250**	760-603-4000	49-4
Gemplus Corp 1350 Old Bayshore Hwy Suite 445	Burlingame	CA	94010	**888-436-7627**	650-373-0200	695
Gems Sensors Inc 1 Cowles Rd	Plainville	CT	06062	**800-378-1600**	860-747-3000	200
Gemtex 60 Belfield Rd	Toronto	ON	M9W1G1	**800-387-5100**	416-245-5605	1
GEMTOP Mfg Inc 8811 SE Herbert Ct	Clackamas	OR	97015	**800-547-9706**	503-659-3733	505
Gemtor Inc 1 Johnson Ave	Matawan	NJ	07747	**800-405-9048**	732-583-6200	666
Gemveto Jewelry Co Inc 16 E 52nd St	New York	NY	10022	**800-221-4438**	212-755-2522	401
Gen-Probe Inc 10210 Genetic Ctr Dr *NASDAQ: GPRO*	San Diego	CA	92121	**800-523-5001**	858-410-8000	229
Genaera Corp 5110 Campus Dr *NASDAQ: GENR*	Plymouth Meeting	PA	19462	**800-522-8973**	610-941-4020	86
Genaissance Pharmaceuticals Inc 5 Science Pk *NASDAQ: GNSC*	New Haven	CT	06511	**877-476-4363**	203-773-1450	86
GenBio 15222 Ave of Science Suite A *Tech Supp	San Diego	CA	92128	**800-288-4368***	858-592-9300	229
Genca 9600 18th St N	Saint Petersburg	FL	33716	**800-237-5448**	727-524-3622	745
Gencor Industries Inc 5201 N Orange Blossom Trail	Orlando	FL	32810	**800-234-3626**	407-290-6000	189
Genealogical Society. National 3108 Columbia Pike Suite 300	Arlington	VA	22204	**800-473-0060**	703-525-0050	48-18
Genealogy.com 360 W 4800 North	Provo	UT	84606	**800-262-3787**	801-705-7000	677
Genecare Medical Genetics Center 201 Sage Rd Suite 300	Chapel Hill	NC	27514	**800-277-4363**	919-942-0021	408
Genelex Corp 3000 1st Ave Suite 1	Seattle	WA	98121	**800-523-6487**	206-382-9591	408
Genencor International Inc 925 Page Mill Rd	Palo Alto	CA	94304	**800-847-5311**	650-846-7500	86
Genender International Imports Inc 44 Century Dr	Wheeling	IL	60090	**800-547-3333**	847-541-3333	403
Genentech Inc 1 DNA Way *NYSE: DNA*	South San Francisco	CA	94080	**800-551-2231**	650-225-1000	86
General Aluminum Co of Texas 1001 W Crosby Rd	Carrollton	TX	75006	**800-727-0835**	972-242-5271	232
General American Door Co (GADCO) 5050 Baseline Rd	Montgomery	IL	60538	**800-323-0813**	630-859-3000	232
General American Investors Co Inc 450 Lexington Ave Suite 3300	New York	NY	10017	**800-436-8401**	212-916-8400	397
General Aviation News PO Box 39099	Lakewood	WA	98439	**800-426-8538**	253-471-9888	449-14
General Bearing Corp 44 High St *NASDAQ: GNRL* ■ *Sales	West Nyack	NY	10994	**800-431-1766***	845-358-6000	77
General Beverage & Beer PO Box 44326	Madison	WI	53744	**800-362-3636**	608-271-1234	82-3
General Binding Corp 1 GBC Plaza *NASDAQ: GBND* ■ *Orders	Northbrook	IL	60062	**800-723-4000***	847-272-3700	112
General Butler State Resort Park PO Box 325	Carrollton	KY	41008	**866-462-8853**	502-732-4384	655
General Carbide Corp PO Box C	Greensburg	PA	15601	**800-245-2465**	724-836-3000	745
General Casualty Co of Wisconsin 1 General Dr	Sun Prairie	WI	53596	**800-362-5448**	608-837-4440	384-4
General Chemical Group Inc 90 E Halsey Rd *Cust Svc	Parsippany	NJ	07054	**800-631-8050***	973-515-0900	141
General Cigar Co Inc 387 Park Ave S	New York	NY	10016	**800-273-8044**	212-448-3800	741-2
General Coatings Technology Inc 24 Woodward Ave	Flushing	NY	11385	**800-522-3664**	718-821-1232	540
General Communication Inc 2550 Denali St Suite 1000 *NASDAQ: GNCMA*	Anchorage	AK	99503	**800-770-7886**	907-265-5600	721
General Contractors of America. Associated 333 John Carlyle St Suite 200	Alexandria	VA	22314	**800-242-1766**	703-548-3118	49-3
General Data Co Inc 4354 Ferguson Dr	Cincinnati	OH	45245	**800-733-5252**	513-752-7978	172
General Die Casters Inc 2150 Highland Rd	Twinsburg	OH	44087	**800-332-2278**	330-657-2300	303
General Digital Corp 8 Nutmeg Rd S	South Windsor	CT	06074	**800-952-2535**	860-282-2900	171-4
General Dynamics C4 Systems 400 John Quincy Adams Rd Bldg 80	Taunton	MA	02780	**888-483-2472**	508-880-4000	176-10
General Dynamics Decision Systems 8201 E McDowell Rd	Scottsdale	AZ	85257	**877-466-9467**	480-441-8630	519

	City	State	Zip	Toll-Free	Phone	Class
General Econopak Inc 1725 N 6th St	Philadelphia	PA	19122	**888-871-8568**	215-763-8200	566
General Electric Co (GE) 3135 Easton Tpke	Fairfield	CT	06828	**800-626-2000***	203-373-2211	184
NYSE: GE ■ *Cust Svc						
General Equipment Co PO Box 334	Owatonna	MN	55060	**800-533-0524***	507-451-5510	379
*Cust Svc						
General Equipment & Supplies Inc PO Box 2145	Fargo	ND	58107	**800-437-2924**	701-282-2662	353
General Fasteners Co Inc 11820 Globe Rd	Livonia	MI	48150	**800-945-2658**	734-452-2400	346
General Fiber Communications Inc 100 W Elm St Suite 300	Conshohocken	PA	19428	**866-285-3048**	610-772-2100	187-1
General Formulations Inc 309 S Union St	Sparta	MI	49345	**800-253-3664**	616-887-7387	589
General Grand Chapter Order of the Eastern Star 1618 New Hampshire Ave NW	Washington	DC	20009	**800-648-1182**	202-667-4737	48-15
General Loose Leaf Bindery Co 3811 Hawthorn Ct	Waukegan	IL	60087	**800-621-0493**	847-244-9700	87
General Machine Products Co Inc 3111 Old Lincoln Hwy	Trevose	PA	19053	**800-345-6009***	215-357-5500	746
*Tech Supp						
General Medical Laboratories 36 S Brook St	Madison	WI	53715	**800-236-0465**	608-267-6529	407
General Mills Inc 1 General Mills Blvd	Minneapolis	MN	55426	**800-328-1144**	763-764-7600	291-4
NYSE: GIS						
General Mills Inc International Foods Div 1 General Mills Blvd	Minneapolis	MN	55426	**800-328-1144**	763-764-7600	291-4
General Monitors Inc 26776 Simpatica Cir	Lake Forest	CA	92630	**866-686-0741**	949-581-4464	200
General Morgan Inn 111 N Main St	Greeneville	TN	37743	**800-223-2679**	423-787-1000	373
General Motors Acceptance Corp (GMAC) 200 Renaissance Ctr	Detroit	MI	48265	**800-200-4622**	313-556-5000	215
General Motors Acceptance Corp Canada (GMAC Canada) 3300 Bloor St W Suite 2800	Toronto	ON	M8X2X5	**800-616-4622**	416-234-6600	215
General Motors of Canada Ltd 1908 Colonel Sam Dr	Oshawa	ON	L1H8P7	**800-263-3777**	905-644-5000	59
General Motors Corp Buick Motor Div 300 Renaissance Ctr	Detroit	MI	48265	**800-521-7300***	313-556-5000	59
*Cust Svc						
General Motors Corp Cadillac Motor Car Div 300 Renaissance Ctr	Detroit	MI	48265	**800-458-8006***	313-556-5000	59
*Cust Svc						
General Motors Corp Chevrolet Motor Div 300 Renaissance Ctr	Detroit	MI	48265	**800-222-1020***	313-556-5000	59
*Cust Svc						
General Motors Corp Electro-Motive Div 9301 W 55th St	La Grange	IL	60525	**800-255-5354***	708-387-6000	636
*Cust Svc						
General Motors Corp Pontiac Div 300 Renaissance Ctr	Detroit	MI	48265	**800-762-2737***	313-556-5000	59
*Cust Svc						
General Motors Corp Pontiac-GMC Div 300 Renaissance Ctr	Detroit	MI	48265	**800-762-2737***	313-556-5000	59
*Cust Svc						
General Motors Corp Saturn Corp Div 100 Saturn Pkwy MD 371-999-S24	Spring Hill	TN	37174	**800-553-6000***	931-486-5000	59
*Cust Svc						
General Music Corp 1164 Tower Ln	Bensenville	IL	60106	**800-323-0280**	630-766-8230	516
General Physics Corp 6095 Marshalee Dr Suite 300	Elkridge	MD	21075	**800-727-6677**	410-379-3600	753
General Plastic Extrusions Inc 1238 Kasson Dr	Prescott	WI	54021	**800-532-3888**	715-262-3806	538
General Plastics Mfg Co 4910 Burlington Way	Tacoma	WA	98409	**800-806-6051**	253-473-5000	590
General Plug & Mfg Co Inc 455 N Main St PO Box 26	Grafton	OH	44044	**800-289-7584**	440-926-2411	584
General Polymeric Corp PO Box 380	Reading	PA	19607	**800-654-4391**	610-374-5171	597
General Produce Co Ltd 1330 N 'B' St	Sacramento	CA	95814	**800-366-4985**	916-441-6431	292-7
General Products 4045 N Rockwell St	Chicago	IL	60618	**800-888-1934**	773-463-2424	87
General Re Corp 695 E Main St Financial Ctr	Stamford	CT	06901	**800-431-9994**	203-328-5000	355-4
General Reinsurance Corp 695 E Main St Financial Ctr	Stamford	CT	06901	**800-431-9994**	203-328-5000	384-4
General Revenue Corp 11501 Northlake Dr	Cincinnati	OH	45249	**800-234-1472**	513-469-1472	157
General Ribbon Corp 20650 Prairie St	Chatsworth	CA	91311	**800-423-5400**	818-709-1234	616
General Services Administration (GSA) 1800 F St NW	Washington	DC	20405	**800-424-5210***	202-501-1231	336-16
*Fraud Hotline						
FCIC National Contact Center	Pueblo	CO	81009	**800-333-4636**		336-16
Federal Citizen Information Center 201 W 8th St	Pueblo	CO	81003	**888-878-3256**	719-948-3334	336-16
FirstGov 1800 F St NW	Washington	DC	20405	**800-333-4636**		336-16
General Shale Products LLC 3211 N Roan St	Johnson City	TN	37601	**800-414-4661***	423-282-4661	148
*Cust Svc						
General Sign Co PO Box 999	Cape Girardeau	MO	63702	**800-325-0205***	573-334-5041	692
*Cust Svc						
General Star National Insurance Co 695 E Main St Financial Ctr	Stamford	CT	06901	**800-431-9994**	203-328-5000	384-4
General Steel Fabricators 927 Schifferdecker Rd	Joplin	MO	64801	**800-820-8644**	417-623-2224	471
General Tool Co 101 Landy Ln	Cincinnati	OH	45215	**800-472-4406**	513-733-5500	745
General Tool & Supply Co Inc 2705 NW Nicolai St	Portland	OR	97210	**800-783-3411**	503-226-3411	378
General Tours 53 Summer St	Keene	NH	03431	**800-221-2216**	603-357-5033	748
General Trailer Parts LLC 1420 S B St	Springfield	OR	97477	**800-452-9532**	541-746-8218	768
General Truck Parts & Equipment Co 3835 W 42nd St	Chicago	IL	60632	**800-621-3914**	773-247-6900	61
General Valve Co 800 Koomey Rd	Brookshire	TX	77423	**800-926-2288**	281-934-6013	776
General Vision Services LLC 520 8th Ave 9th Fl	New York	NY	10018	**800-847-4661**	212-594-2580	533
General Wax & Candle Co 6858 Beck Ave PO Box 9398	North Hollywood	CA	91609	**800-543-0642**	818-765-5808	122
General Wholesale Co 1271 Tacoma Dr NW	Atlanta	GA	30318	**800-801-0772**	404-351-3626	82-1
General Wire Spring Co 1101 Thompson Ave	McKees Rocks	PA	15136	**800-245-6200**	412-771-6300	704
Generation 2 Worldwide 113 Anderson Ct Suite 1	Dothan	AL	36301	**800-736-1140**	334-792-1144	314-2
Generex Biotechnology Corp 33 Harbour Sq Suite 202	Toronto	ON	M5J2G2	**800-391-6755**	416-364-2551	86
NASDAQ: GNBT						
Genesee County Chamber of Commerce 210 E Main St	Batavia	NY	14020	**800-622-2686**	585-343-7440	137
Genesee Grande Hotel 1060 E Genesee St	Syracuse	NY	13210	**800-365-4663**	315-476-4212	373
Genesee Grande Hotel. 1060 E Genesee St	Syracuse	NY	13210	**800-365-4663**	315-476-4212	373
Genesis Computer Repair & Sales 121 F Grafton Station Ln	Yorktown	VA	23692	**866-289-4277**	757-833-6262	173
Genesis Consolidated Services Inc 76 Blanchard Rd	Burlington	MA	01803	**800-367-8367**	781-272-4900	619
Genesis ElderCare 101 E State St	Kennett Square	PA	19348	**800-699-1520**	610-444-6350	442
Genesis Energy LP 500 Dallas St Suite 2500	Houston	TX	77002	**800-284-3365**	713-860-2500	586
AMEX: GEL						
Genesis HealthCare Corp 101 E State St	Kennett Square	PA	19348	**800-699-1520**	610-444-6350	442
NASDAQ: GHCI						
Genesys Conferencing Inc 9139 S Ridgeline Blvd	Highlands Ranch	CO	80129	**800-685-1995**	303-267-1272	721
Genesys Hospice 7280 S State Rd	Goodrich	MI	48438	**888-943-9690**	810-762-4370	365
Genesys Regional Medical Center Health Park 1 Genesys Pkwy	Grand Blanc	MI	48439	**888-606-6556**	810-762-8000	366-2
Genesys Telecommunications Laboratories Inc 2001 Junipero Serra Blvd	Daly City	CA	94014	**888-436-3797**	650-466-1100	720
Genetic Alliance Inc 4301 Connecticut Ave NW Suite 404	Washington	DC	20008	**800-336-4363**	202-966-5557	48-17
Genetic Engineering News 2 Madison Ave	Larchmont	NY	10538	**800-654-3237**	914-834-3100	521-12
Genetic Profiles Corp 10675 Treena St Suite 103	San Diego	CA	92131	**800-551-7763**	858-623-0840	408
Genetic Technology News 7550 W I-10 Suite 400	San Antonio	TX	77229	**877-463-7678**	210-348-1000	521-12
Genetica DNA Laboratories Inc 8740 Montgomery Rd	Cincinnati	OH	45236	**800-433-6848**	513-985-9777	408
Genetics. American Society of Human 9650 Rockville Pike	Bethesda	MD	20814	**866-486-4363**	301-571-1825	49-19
Genetics & IVF Institute 3020 Javier Rd	Fairfax	VA	22031	**800-552-4363**	703-698-7355	408
Genetics Society of America (GSA) 9650 Rockville Pike	Bethesda	MD	20814	**866-486-4363**	301-634-7300	49-19
Geneva College 3200 College Ave	Beaver Falls	PA	15010	**800-847-8255**	724-846-5100	163
Geneva Cos 5 Park Plaza 18th Fl	Irvine	CA	92614	**800-854-4643***	949-756-2200	183
*Cust Svc						
Geneva on the Lake 1001 Lochland Rd	Geneva	NY	14456	**800-343-6382**	315-789-7190	373
Geneva Rock Products Inc PO Box 538	Orem	UT	84059	**800-464-2003**	801-765-7800	180
Geneva Steel Holdings Corp PO Box 2500	Provo	UT	84603	**800-877-9990**	801-227-9000	709
Genex Co-op Inc/CRI 100 MBC Dr	Shawano	WI	54166	**888-333-1783**	715-526-2141	12-2
Genie Co 22790 Lake Park Blvd	Alliance	OH	44601	**800-995-1111***	330-821-5360	681
*Cust Svc						
Genie Industries Inc PO Box 97030	Redmond	WA	98073	**800-536-1800***	425-881-1800	462
*Sales						
Genieco Inc 200 N Laflin St	Chicago	IL	60607	**800-223-8217**	312-421-2383	143
Genitope Corp 525 Penobscot Dr	Redwood City	CA	94063	**866-436-4867**	650-482-2000	86
NASDAQ: GTOP						
Genlyte Thomas Group LLC 10350 Ormsby Park Pl Suite 601	Louisville	KY	40223	**800-626-2847**	502-420-9500	431
Genmar Industries Inc 80 S 8th St 2900 IDS Ctr	Minneapolis	MN	55402	**800-328-5557**	612-339-7600	91
Genoa Business Forms Inc 445 Park Ave	Sycamore	IL	60178	**800-383-2801**	815-895-2800	111
Genome Resources. National Center for 2935 Rodeo Pk Dr E	Santa Fe	NM	87505	**800-450-4854**	505-982-7840	654
Genomic Solutions Inc 4355 Varsity Dr Suite E	Ann Arbor	MI	48108	**877-436-6642**	734-975-4800	86
Genova Products Inc 7034 E Court St	Davison	MI	48423	**800-521-7488**	810-744-4500	585
Genpak Corp 68 Warren St	Glens Falls	NY	12801	**800-626-6695**	518-798-9511	590
Genpak Processor Div PO Box 727	Glens Falls	NY	12801	**800-626-6695**	518-798-9511	544
Genpharm Inc 85 Advance Rd	Etobicoke	ON	M8Z2S6	**800-668-3174**	416-236-2631	573
GenQuest DNA Analysis Laboratory Univ of Nevada - Reno 1664 N Virginia St	Reno	NV	89557	**877-362-5227**	775-784-4494	408
Gensco Inc 4402 20th St E	Tacoma	WA	98424	**800-729-3003**	253-922-3003	601
Genta Inc 2 Connell Dr	Berkeley Heights	NJ	07922	**888-322-2264**	908-286-9800	86
NASDAQ: GNTA						
Gentek Building Products Inc 3773 State Rd	Cuyahoga Falls	OH	44223	**800-548-4542**		688
Gentex Corp 600 N Centennial St	Zeeland	MI	49464	**800-444-4689**	616-772-1800	324
NASDAQ: GNTX						
Gentex Optics Inc 324 Main St	Simpson	PA	18407	**800-343-6062**	570-282-3550	531
Gentiva Health Services Inc 3 Huntington Quadrangle Suite 200S	Melville	NY	11747	**866-436-8487**	631-501-7000	358
NASDAQ: GTIV						
Genuardi's Family Markets Inc 301 E Germantown Pike	Norristown	PA	19401	**877-723-3929**	610-277-6000	339
Genus Inc 1139 Karlstad Dr	Sunnyvale	CA	94089	**800-366-0989**	408-747-7120	685
GenVec Inc 65 W Watkins Mill Rd	Gaithersburg	MD	20878	**877-943-6832**	240-632-0740	86
NASDAQ: GNVC						

Listing	Toll-Free	Phone	Class
Genworth Financial Inc 6610 W Broad St ... Richmond VA 23230	**888-436-9678**	804-484-3821	384-2
NYSE: GNW			
Genzyme Biosurgery 1 Kendall Sq ... Cambridge MA 02139	**800-326-7002**	617-252-7500	469
Genzyme Corp 500 Kendall St ... Cambridge MA 02142	**800-326-7002**	617-252-7500	229
NASDAQ: GENZ			
Genzyme Diagnostics 1 Kendall Sq Bldg 1400 ... Cambridge MA 02139	**800-326-7002**	617-252-7500	229
Genzyme Genetics 3400 Computer Dr ... Westborough MA 01581	**800-326-7002**	508-898-9001	408
Geo-Centers Inc 7 Wells Ave ... Newton MA 02459	**800-347-7592**	617-964-7070	654
GEO Group Inc 621 NW 53rd St Suite 700 ... Boca Raton FL 33487	**800-666-5640**	561-893-0101	210
NYSE: GGI			
Geo M Robinson & Co 852 85th Ave ... Oakland CA 94621	**800-894-8942**	510-632-7017	188-13
Geocel Corp PO Box 398 ... Elkhart IN 46515	**800-348-7615**	574-264-0645	3
Geocomp Corp 1145 Massachusetts Ave ... Boxborough MA 01719	**800-822-2669***	978-635-0012	176-5
*Cust Svc			
GeoDesic Corp 400 Commerce Rd ... Alice TX 78332	**800-824-4153**	361-668-3766	343
Geographic Expeditions 1008 Gen Kennedy Ave ... San Francisco CA 94129	**800-777-8183**	415-922-0448	748
Geographic Society. National 1145 17th St NW ... Washington DC 20036	**800-647-5463***	202-857-7000	49-19
*Orders			
Geographics LLC 93 North Ave ... Garwood NJ 07027	**800-526-4280**		542-3
GeoGraphix 1805 Shea Ctr Dr Suite 400 ... Highlands Ranch CO 80129	**800-296-0596**	303-779-8080	176-10
Geological Society of America (GSA) 3300 Penrose Pl PO Box 9140 ... Boulder CO 80301	**800-472-1988**	303-447-2020	49-19
GeoLogistics Corp 1251 E Dyer Rd Suite 200 ... Santa Ana CA 92705	**888-543-1239**	714-513-3000	440
Geologists. American Assn of Petroleum 1444 S Boulder Ave ... Tulsa OK 74119	**800-364-2274**	918-584-2555	48-12
Geology. Society for Sedimentary 6128 E 38th St Suite 308 ... Tulsa OK 74135	**800-865-9765**	918-610-3361	49-19
Geomatrix Consultants Inc 2101 Webster St 12th Fl ... Oakland CA 94612	**800-999-6879**	510-663-4100	258
GeoPharma Inc 6950 Bryan Dairy Rd ... Largo FL 33777	**800-654-2347**	727-544-8866	786
NASDAQ: GORX			
Geophysical Research Letter 2000 Florida Ave NW ... Washington DC 20009	**800-966-2481**	202-462-6900	521-12
Geophysical Union. American 2000 Florida Ave NW ... Washington DC 20009	**800-966-2481**	202-462-6900	49-19
GeoResources Inc 1407 W Dakota Pkwy Suite 1-B ... Williston ND 58802	**800-735-5984**	701-572-2020	525
NASDAQ: GEOI			
George E Failing Co 2215 S Van Buren St ... Enid OK 73701	**800-759-7441**	580-234-4141	526
George F Cram Co Inc 301 S LaSalle St ... Indianapolis IN 46201	**800-227-4199**	317-635-5564	623-1
George Fischer Sloane Mfg Co Inc 7777 Sloane Dr ... Little Rock AR 72206	**800-423-2686**	501-490-7777	585
George Fox University 414 N Meridian St ... Newberg OR 97132	**800-765-4369**	503-538-8383	163
George H Fuller & Son Co 151 Exchange St ... Pawtucket RI 02860	**800-237-0043**	401-722-6530	401
George J Foster Co Inc 333 Central Ave ... Dover NH 03820	**800-660-8310**	603-742-4455	623-8
George J Igel & Co Inc 2040 Alum Creek Dr ... Columbus OH 43207	**800-345-4435**	614-445-8421	188-5
George K Baum & Co 120 W 12th St 8th Fl ... Kansas City MO 64105	**800-821-7195**	816-474-1100	679
George Koch Sons LLC 10 S 11th Ave ... Evansville IN 47744	**888-873-5624**	812-465-9600	379
George Mason University 4400 University Dr MS N3A4 ... Fairfax VA 22030	**888-627-6612**	703-993-1000	163
George Meany Center for Labor Studies; Meany George Center for Labor Studies 10000 New Hampshire Ave ... Silver Spring MD 20903	**800-462-4237**	301-431-6400	158
George Melhado & Co 10 Merchant St ... Sharon MA 02067	**800-635-4236**	781-784-5550	744
George PD Co Inc 5200 N 2nd St ... Saint Louis MO 63147	**800-325-7492**	314-621-5700	540
George R Brown Convention Center 1001 Avenida de Las Americas ... Houston TX 77010	**800-427-4697**	713-853-8000	204
George Risk Industries Inc 802 S Elm St ... Kimball NE 69145	**800-523-1227***	308-235-4645	681
*Sales			
George S Coyne Chemical Co 3015 State Rd ... Croydon PA 19021	**800-523-1230**	215-785-3000	144
George S May International Co 303 S Northwest Hwy ... Park Ridge IL 60068	**800-999-3020**	847-825-8806	193
George Uhe Co Inc 12 Rt 17 N ... Paramus NJ 07653	**800-850-4075**	201-843-4000	470
George Washington University 2121 'I' St NW ... Washington DC 20052	**800-447-3765**	202-994-1000	163
Mount Vernon College 2100 Foxhall Rd NW ... Washington DC 20007	**800-447-3765**	202-242-6672	163
George Washington University Inn 824 New Hampshire Ave NW ... Washington DC 20037	**800-426-4455**	202-337-6620	373
George Weston Bakeries Inc 55 Paradise Ln ... Bay Shore NY 11706	**800-842-9595**	631-273-6000	291-1
Georgetown College 400 E College St ... Georgetown KY 40324	**800-788-9985**	502-863-8000	163
Georgetown Convention & Visitors Bureau PO Box 409 ... Georgetown TX 78627	**800-436-8696**	512-930-3545	205
Georgetown County Chamber of Commerce 1001 Front St ... Georgetown SC 29442	**800-777-7705**	843-546-8436	137
Georgetown Inn 1310 Wisconsin Ave NW ... Washington DC 20007	**800-424-2979**	202-333-8900	373
Georgetown Railroad Co 5300 S IH-35 PO Box 529 ... Georgetown TX 78627	**800-772-8272**	512-863-2538	634
Georgetown Steel Corp 420 S Harard St ... Georgetown SC 29440	**800-472-7637***	843-546-2525	709
*Sales			
Georgetown University Conference Center 3800 Reservoir Rd NW ... Washington DC 20057	**800-228-9290**	202-687-3200	370
Georgette Klinger Inc 501 Madison Ave ... New York NY 10022	**800-554-6437**	212-838-3200	79
Georgia			
Environmental Protection Div 2 ML King Jr Dr SE Suite 1152E ... Atlanta GA 30334	**888-373-5947**	404-657-5947	335
Parks Recreation & Historic Sites Div 2 ML King Jr Dr SE Suite 1352E ... Atlanta GA 30334	**800-862-7275**	404-656-2770	335
Ports Authority PO Box 2406 ... Savannah GA 31402	**800-342-8012**	912-964-3811	607
Student Finance Commission 2082 E Exchange Pl Suite 200 ... Tucker GA 30084	**800-505-4732**	770-724-9000	711
Tourism Div 285 Peachtree Center Ave NE Suite 1000 ... Atlanta GA 30303	**800-847-4842**	404-656-2000	335
Georgia Boot Inc PO Box 10 ... Franklin TN 37068	**800-251-3388**	615-794-1556	296
Georgia Casualty & Surety Co 4370 Peachtree Rd NE ... Atlanta GA 30319	**866-458-7506**	404-266-5500	384-4
Georgia Chamber of Commerce 235 Peachtree St NE Suite 900 ... Atlanta GA 30303	**800-241-2286**	404-223-2264	138
Georgia College & State University 231 W Hancock St CB 23 ... Milledgeville GA 31061	**800-342-0471**	478-445-5004	163
Georgia Correctional Industries 2984 Clifton Springs Rd ... Decatur GA 30034	**800-282-7130**	404-244-5100	618
Georgia Crate & Basket Co Inc 1200 Parnell St ... Thomasville GA 31792	**800-841-0001**	229-226-2541	199
Georgia Crown Distributing 7 Crown Cir ... Columbus GA 31907	**800-332-4830**	706-568-4580	82-3
Georgia Democratic Party 1100 Spring St Suite 710 ... Atlanta GA 30309	**800-894-1996**	404-870-8201	605-1
Georgia Dental Assn 7000 Peachtree Dunwoody Rd NE Bldg 17 Suite 200 ... Atlanta GA 30328	**800-432-4357**	404-636-7553	225
Georgia Eye Bank Inc 3060 Peachtree Rd NW Suite 130 ... Atlanta GA 30305	**800-342-9812**	404-264-1900	265
Georgia Golf Hall of Fame 1 11th St ... Augusta GA 30901	**888-874-4443**	706-724-4443	511
Georgia Golf Hall of Fame Botanical Gardens 1 Eleventh St ... Augusta GA 30901	**888-874-4443**	706-724-4443	98
Georgia Healthcare Partnership Inc 7135 Hodgson Memorial Dr Suite 12 ... Savannah GA 31406	**800-566-6710**	912-350-6710	384-3
Georgia Lighting Supply Co 530 14th St NW ... Atlanta GA 30318	**800-282-0220**	404-875-4759	357
Georgia Medical Assn 1330 W Peachtree St NW Suite 500 ... Atlanta GA 30309	**800-282-0224**	404-876-7535	466
Georgia Military College 201 E Green St ... Milledgeville GA 31061	**800-342-0413**	478-445-2700	160
Georgia Music Hall of Fame 200 ML King Jr Blvd ... Macon GA 31202	**888-427-6257**	478-750-8555	509
Georgia Power Co 241 Ralph McGill Blvd NE ... Atlanta GA 30308	**888-660-5890***	404-506-6526	774
*Cust Svc			
Georgia Public Broadcasting (GPB) 260 14th St NW ... Atlanta GA 30318	**800-222-6006**	404-685-2400	620
Georgia Republican Party 3110 Maple Dr Suite 200-E ... Atlanta GA 30305	**877-464-2467**	404-257-5559	605-2
Georgia Southwestern State University 800 Wheatley St ... Americus GA 31709	**800-338-0082**	229-928-1273	163
Georgia. State Bar of 104 Marietta St NW Suite 100 ... Atlanta GA 30303	**800-334-6865**	404-527-8700	73
Georgia Telco Credit Union 1155 Peachtree St NE Suite 400 ... Atlanta GA 30309	**800-533-2062**	404-874-1166	216
Georgia Tufters LLC 416 S River St ... Calhoun GA 30701	**800-232-2607**	706-629-4516	131
Georgia Veterinary Medical Assn 2814 Spring Rd Suite 217 ... Atlanta GA 30339	**800-853-1625**	678-309-9800	782
Georgia Walker & Assoc Inc PO Box 584 ... Raymore MO 64083	**800-385-2423**	816-331-3211	384-1
Georgian Court Hotel 773 Beatty St ... Vancouver BC V6B2M4	**800-663-1155**	604-682-5555	372
Georgian Court University 900 Lakewood Ave ... Lakewood NJ 08701	**800-458-8422**	732-364-2200	163
Georgian Hotel 1415 Ocean Ave ... Santa Monica CA 90401	**800-538-8147**	310-395-9945	373
Georgian Resort 384 Canada St ... Lake George NY 12845	**800-525-3436**	518-668-5401	373
Georgian Terrace Hotel 659 Peachtree St ... Atlanta GA 30308	**800-651-2316**	404-897-1991	373
Georgie Boy Mfg Inc 69950 Hwy M 62 ... Edwardsburg MI 49112	**877-876-9024**	269-663-3415	120
Georgie's Ceramic & Clay Co Inc 756 NE Lombard St ... Portland OR 97211	**800-999-2529**	503-283-1353	43
Geoscience & Remote Sensing Society. IEEE IEEE Operations Ctr 445 Hoes Ln ... Piscataway NJ 08854	**800-678-4333**	732-981-0060	49-19
GeoSyntec Consultants Inc 621 NW 53rd St Suite 650 ... Boca Raton FL 33487	**800-765-4436**	561-995-0900	258
Geotechnical & Structures Laboratory ATTN: CEERD-PA-Z 3909 Halls Ferry Rd ... Vicksburg MS 39180	**800-522-6937**	601-634-2502	654
GeoTrust Inc 40 Washington St Suite 20 ... Wellesley Hills MA 02481	**800-944-0492**	781-235-4677	176-7
Gerald R Ford Conservation Center 1326 S 32nd St ... Omaha NE 68105	**800-833-6747**	402-595-1180	50
Gerard Daniel Worldwide 34 Barnhart Dr ... Hanover PA 17331	**800-233-3017**	717-637-5901	676
Gerber Auto Collision & Glass Centers Inc 8250 Skokie Blvd ... Skokie IL 60077	**800-479-1230**	847-679-0510	62-4
Gerber Childrenswear Inc 7005 Pelham Rd Suite D ... Greenville SC 29602	**800-642-4452**	864-987-5200	153-4
Gerber Coburn Optical Inc 1701 S Cherokee St ... Muskogee OK 74402	**800-262-8761**	918-683-4521	745
Gerber Legendary Blades Inc 14200 SW 72nd Ave ... Portland OR 97224	**800-950-6161**	503-639-6161	219
Gerber Life Insurance Co 1311 Mamaroneck Ave ... White Plains NY 10605	**800-704-2180**	914-272-4000	384-2
Gerber Metal Supply Co 2 Boundary Rd ... Somerville NJ 08876	**800-836-4672**	908-823-9150	483
Gerber Products Co 445 State St ... Fremont MI 49413	**800-443-7237**	231-928-2000	291-36
Gerber Technology Inc 24 Industrial Pk Rd W ... Tolland CT 06084	**800-826-3243**	860-871-8082	729
Gerber Tours Inc 1400 Old Country Rd Suite 100 ... Westbury NY 11590	**800-645-9145**	516-826-5000	748
Gerdau AmeriSteel Corp 5100 W Lemon St Suite 312 ... Tampa FL 33609	**800-637-8144***	813-286-8383	709
NYSE: GNA ■ *Sales			

Name / Address	City	State	ZIP	Toll-Free	Phone	Class
Gerhardts Inc 819 Central Ave	Jefferson	LA	70121	**800-722-6566**	504-733-2500	202
Germain Motor Co 4130 Morse Crossing	Columbus	OH	43219	**866-771-2178**	614-478-2002	57
German American Bancorp 711 Main St *NASDAQ: GABC*	Jasper	IN	47546	**800-482-1314**	812-482-1314	355-2
German-Bliss Equipment Co Inc 624 W Spring St	Princeville	IL	61559	**800-728-4734**	309-385-4316	270
Germania Farm Mutual Insurance Assn PO Box 645	Brenham	TX	77834	**800-392-2202**	979-836-5224	384-4
Germiphene Corp PO Box 1748	Brantford	ON	N3T5V7	**800-265-9931**	519-759-7100	572
Gerriets International 29 Hutchinson Rd	Allentown	NJ	08501	**800-369-3695**	609-758-9121	708
Gerry Cosby & Co Inc 3 Pennsylvania Plaza	New York	NY	10001	**877-563-6464**	212-563-6464	702
Gershman Investment Corp 7 N Bemiston Ave	Clayton	MO	63105	**800-457-2357**	314-889-0600	498
Gershwin Theatre 222 W 51st St	New York	NY	10019	**800-755-4000**	212-307-4100	732
Gerson Co 1450 S Lone Elm Rd	Olathe	KS	66061	**800-999-7401**	913-262-7400	403
Gerson Louis M Co Inc 15 Sproat St	Middleboro	MA	02346	**800-225-8623**	508-947-4000	566
Gertrude Hawk Chocolates Inc 9 Keystone Pk	Dunmore	PA	18512	**800-822-2032**	570-342-7556	291-8
GES Exposition Services 950 Grier Dr	Las Vegas	NV	89119	**800-443-9767**	702-263-1500	183
Geschmay Corp 525 Old Piedmont Hwy	Greenville	SC	29605	**800-845-6774**	864-220-7500	546
Gesipa Fasteners USA Inc 375 Phillips Blvd	Ewing	NJ	08618	**800-257-9404**	609-883-8300	274
Gesswein Paul H & Co 255 Hancock Ave	Bridgeport	CT	06605	**800-544-2043**	203-366-5400	399
Get Smart Products 578 Nepperham Ave	Yonkers	NY	10701	**800-827-0673**	914-709-0600	119
GET Travel Group LLC DBA Invasion Tours 3355 Vincent Dr	Pleasant Hill	CA	94523	**800-339-4723**	925-944-5844	748
Getinge USA Inc 1777 E Henrietta Rd *Cust Svc	Rochester	NY	14623	**800-950-9912***	585-475-1400	468
Getronics 290 Concord Rd	Billerica	MA	01821	**800-225-0654**	978-625-5000	178
Gettel Automotive Group 3480 Bee Ridge Rd	Sarasota	FL	34239	**888-468-8696**	941-921-2655	57
GetThere LC 3150 Sabre Dr	Southlake	TX	76092	**800-850-3906**	682-605-1000	762
Getting Along Newsletter 360 Hiatt Dr	Palm Beach Gardens	FL	33418	**800-621-5463**	561-622-9914	521-2
Gettysburg College 300 N Washington St	Gettysburg	PA	17325	**800-431-0803**	717-337-6000	163
Gettysburg Convention & Visitors Bureau PO Box 4117	Gettysburg	PA	17325	**800-337-5015**	717-334-6274	205
Gettysburg Review 300 N Washington St	Gettysburg	PA	17325	**800-431-0803**	717-337-6000	449-10
Getzen Co Inc 530 S Hwy H PO Box 440	Elkhorn	WI	53121	**800-366-5584**	262-723-4221	516
Gevity HR Inc 600 301 Blvd W *NASDAQ: GVHR*	Bradenton	FL	34205	**800-243-8489**	941-748-4540	619
Gexco 7209 Arlington Ave Suite D	Riverside	CA	92503	**800-829-8222**	951-637-0546	701
GF Office Furniture Ltd 6655 Seville Dr *Cust Svc	Canfield	OH	44406	**800-321-4005***	330-533-7799	314-1
GFC Leasing Co 2101 W Beltline Hwy	Madison	WI	53713	**800-333-5905**	608-274-7877	261-3
GFI America Inc 2815 Blaisdell Ave S	Minneapolis	MN	55408	**800-669-8996**	612-872-6262	465
GFK Custom Research Inc 8401 Golden Valley Rd PO Box 27900	Minneapolis	MN	55427	**800-328-6784**	763-542-0800	458
G/GPUSA (Greens/Green Party USA) PO Box 1406	Chicago	IL	60690	**866-473-3672**	708-524-1741	605
GGS Information Services Inc 3265 Farmtrail Rd	York	PA	17402	**800-927-4474**	717-764-2222	770
GH Bass & Co Inc 600 Sable Oaks Dr *Cust Svc	South Portland	ME	04106	**800-950-2277***	207-791-4000	296
Ghent Mfg Inc 2999 Henkle Dr	Lebanon	OH	45036	**800-543-0550**	513-932-3445	242
Ghirardelli Chocolate Co 1111 139th Ave	San Leandro	CA	94578	**800-877-9338**	510-483-6970	291-8
GHS Corp 2813 Wilber Ave	Battle Creek	MI	49015	**800-388-4447**	269-968-3351	516
GI Trucking Co 14727 Alondra Blvd	La Mirada	CA	90638	**800-541-1670**	714-523-1122	769
GIA (Gemological Institute of America) 5345 Armada Dr	Carlsbad	CA	92008	**800-421-7250**	760-603-4000	49-4
Giant Bicycle Inc 3587 Old Conejo Rd	Newbury Park	CA	91320	**800-874-4268**	805-267-4600	83
Giant Cement Holding Inc 320-D Midland Pkwy	Summerville	SC	29485	**800-845-1174**	843-851-9898	135
Giant Eagle Inc 101 Kappa Dr *Cust Svc	Pittsburgh	PA	15238	**800-553-2324***	412-963-6200	339
Giant Food Inc 6300 Sheriff Rd	Landover	MD	20785	**888-469-4426**	301-341-4100	339
Giant Food Stores Inc 1149 Harrisburg Pike	Carlisle	PA	17013	**800-814-4268**	717-249-4000	339
Giant Industries Arizona Inc 23733 N Scottsdale Rd	Scottsdale	AZ	85255	**800-937-4937**	480-585-8888	586
Giant Industries Inc 23733 N Scottsdale Rd *NYSE: GI*	Scottsdale	AZ	85255	**800-937-4937**	480-585-8888	570
Giant Van Lines 8215 Patuxent Range Rd	Jessup	MD	20794	**866-442-6863**	301-490-5790	508
Giantbank.com 6300 NE 1st Ave Suite 300	Fort Lauderdale	FL	33308	**877-446-4200**	954-958-0001	71
Giardinelli PO Box 4370	Medford	OR	97501	**800-249-8361**	541-772-5173	515
Gibb Robert & Sons Inc 205 SW 40th St	Fargo	ND	58103	**800-842-7366**	701-282-5900	188-10
Gibbon Packing Inc PO Box 730	Gibbon	NE	68840	**800-652-1910**	308-468-5771	465
Gibbs & Assoc 323 Science Dr	Moorpark	CA	93021	**800-654-9399**	805-523-0004	176-5
Gibbs College of Boston 126 Newbury St	Boston	MA	02116	**800-675-4557**	617-578-7100	158
Gibbs College of Norwalk 10 Norden Pl	Norwalk	CT	06855	**800-845-5333**	203-838-4173	158
Gibbs Oil Co LP PO Box 9151	Chelsea	MA	02150	**800-352-3558**	617-889-9000	203
Gibbs Wire & Steel Co Inc PO Box 520	Southington	CT	06489	**800-800-4422**	860-621-0121	483
Gibco Motor Express Inc PO Box 18	Elberfeld	IN	47613	**800-333-4285**	812-867-0069	769
Gibraltar Industries Inc 3556 Lakeshore Rd *NASDAQ: ROCK*	Buffalo	NY	14219	**800-777-0675**	716-826-6500	709
Gibraltar Metals Corp 1050 Military Rd	Buffalo	NY	14217	**800-873-6322**	716-875-7920	483
Gibraltar Packaging Group Inc DBA Great Plains Packaging Co 2000 Summit Ave	Hastings	NE	68902	**800-456-1366**	402-463-1366	102
Gibson Arnold & Assoc 1776 Yorktown St Suite 350	Houston	TX	77056	**800-879-2007**	713-572-3000	707
Gibson CR Inc 404 BNA Dr Bldg 200 Suite 600	Nashville	TN	37217	**800-243-6004**	615-724-2900	87
Gibson Guitar Corp DBA Gibson Musical Instruments 309 Plus Park Blvd	Nashville	TN	37217	**800-444-2766**	615-871-4500	516
Gibson Laboratories Inc 1040 Manchester St	Lexington	KY	40508	**800-477-4763**	859-254-9500	229
Gibson Musical Instruments 309 Plus Park Blvd	Nashville	TN	37217	**800-444-2766**	615-871-4500	516
Gibson Piano Ventures Inc DBA Baldwin Piano Co 309 Plus Park Blvd	Nashville	TN	37219	**800-444-2766**	615-871-4500	516
Giddings & Lewis LLC 142 Doty St PO Box 590	Fond du Lac	WI	54936	**800-343-2847**	920-921-9400	447
Giddings & Lewis Machine Tools 142 Doty St PO Box 590	Fond du Lac	WI	54936	**800-343-2847**	920-921-9400	447
Gideon Putnam Hotel & Conference Center 24 Gideon Putnam Rd	Saratoga Springs	NY	12866	**800-732-1560**	518-584-3000	373
Gietzen & Assoc Inc 1302 N Marion St	Tampa	FL	33602	**888-779-2345**	813-223-3233	392
Gift Box Corp of America 225 5th Ave Rm 1223	New York	NY	10010	**800-443-8269**	212-684-5113	102
Gift of Hope Organ & Tissue Donor Network 660 N Industrial Dr	Elmhurst	IL	60126	**800-545-4438**	630-758-2600	535
Gift of Life Bone Marrow Foundation 7700 Congress Ave Suite 2201	Boca Raton	FL	33487	**800-962-7769**	561-988-0100	48-17
Gift of Life Donor Program Eye Bank 2000 Hamilton St Rodin Pl Suite 201	Philadelphia	PA	19130	**800-543-6391**	215-557-8090	265
Gift Wrap Co 338 Industrial Blvd	Midway	GA	31320	**800-443-4429**	912-884-9727	542-2
GiftCertificates.com 315 5th Ave S Suite 100	Seattle	WA	98104	**800-773-7368**	206-568-2500	322
Giftco Inc 700 Woodlands Pkwy	Vernon Hills	IL	60061	**800-443-8261**	847-478-8400	323
Gifts & Novelties Trade Assn. Souvenirs 10 E Athens Ave Suite 208	Ardmore	PA	19003	**800-284-5451**	610-645-6940	49-18
Giftware News 20 W Kinzie 12th Fl	Chicago	IL	60610	**800-229-1967**	312-849-2220	449-21
Giga-Tronics Inc 4650 Norris Canyon Rd *NASDAQ: GIGA*	San Ramon	CA	94583	**800-726-4442**	925-328-4650	247
Giglio Distributing Co Inc 155 MLK Pkwy	Beaumont	TX	77701	**800-725-2337**	409-838-1654	82-1
Gilbane Building Co Mid-Atlantic Regional Office 7901 Sandy Spring Rd Suite 500	Laurel	MD	20707	**800-445-2263**	301-317-6100	185
Gilbane Building Co Southwest Regional Office 1331 Lamar St Suite 1170	Houston	TX	77010	**800-445-2263**	713-209-1873	185
Gilbert AL Co 304 N Yosemite Ave	Oakdale	CA	95361	**800-847-1721**	209-847-1721	438
Gilbert Mechanical Contractors Inc 4451 W 76th St	Edina	MN	55435	**800-701-0986**	952-835-3810	688
Gilbert Paper Co 100 W Lawrence St	Appleton	WI	54911	**866-452-8777**	920-733-7807	547
Gilbert Tweed Assoc Inc 415 Madison Ave 20th Fl	New York	NY	10017	**800-456-3932**	212-758-3000	262
Gilbreth Packaging Systems 3001 State Rd	Croydon	PA	19021	**800-758-5888**	215-785-3350	404
Gilco Inc 16000 Common Rd	Roseville	MI	48066	**800-424-4526**	586-779-5850	479
Gilcrease Museum 1400 N Gilcrease Museum Rd	Tulsa	OK	74127	**888-655-2278**	918-596-2700	509
Gilda Radner Familial Ovarian Cancer Registry Roswell Park Cancer Institute Elm & Carlton Sts	Buffalo	NY	14263	**800-682-7426**	716-845-4503	48-17
Gildan Activewear Inc 725 Montee de Liesse *NYSE: GSE*	Montreal	QC	H4T1P5	**800-668-8337**	514-735-2023	153-3
Gilead Sciences Inc 333 Lakeside Dr *NASDAQ: GILD*	Foster City	CA	94404	**800-445-3235**	650-574-3000	86
Giles & Ransome Inc Ransome Engine Power Div 2975 Galloway Rd	Bensalem	PA	19020	**800-753-4228**	215-639-4300	270
Gilfillan Div ITT Industries Inc 7821 Orion Ave	Van Nuys	CA	91406	**800-264-9234**	818-988-2600	519
Gilford Securities Inc 777 3rd Ave 17th Fl	New York	NY	10017	**800-445-3673**	212-888-6400	679
Gill Athletics Inc 2808 Gemini Ct *Cust Svc	Champaign	IL	61822	**800-637-3090***	217-367-8438	701
Gillespie Oil Inc PO Box 370	Bellefontaine	OH	43311	**800-686-3835**	937-599-2085	319
Gillette Children's Specialty Healthcare 200 E University Ave	Saint Paul	MN	55101	**800-719-4040**	651-291-2848	366-1
Gillette Co Prudential Tower Bldg *NYSE: G* ■ *Cust Svc	Boston	MA	02199	**800-445-5388***	617-421-7000	211
Gillette Dairy of the Black Hills Inc PO Box 2553	Rapid City	SD	57709	**800-933-3247**	605-348-1500	291-27
Gillig Corp 25800 Clawiter Rd	Hayward	CA	94545	**800-735-1500**	510-785-1500	505
Gillman Cos 10595 W Sam Houston Pkwy S	Houston	TX	77099	**800-933-7809**	713-776-7000	57
Gilman Brothers Co PO Box 38	Gilman	CT	06336	**800-852-4220**	860-889-8444	590
Gilman Russell T Inc 1230 Cheyenne Ave	Grafton	WI	53024	**800-445-6267**	262-377-2434	484
Gilmore Entertainment Group PO Box 7576	Myrtle Beach	SC	29572	**800-843-6779**	843-449-4444	179
Gilmour Mfg Group PO Box 838 *Cust Svc	Somerset	PA	15501	**800-458-0107***	814-443-4802	420
Gilster-Mary Lee Corp 1037 State St	Chester	IL	62233	**800-851-5371**	618-826-2361	291-16
Gina B Designs Inc 12700 Industrial Pk Blvd Suite 40	Plymouth	MN	55441	**800-228-4856**	763-559-7595	130
Gingrich Candace Youth Outreach Mgr Human Rights Campaign 1640 Rhode Island Ave NW	Washington	DC	20036	**800-777-4723**	202-628-4160	561
Ginseng Co 2279 Agate Ct	Simi Valley	CA	93065	**800-284-2598**	805-520-2592	786
Giorgio Foods Inc 1161 Park Rd	Reading	PA	19605	**800-220-2139**	610-926-2139	291-20
Girard College 2101 S College Ave Suite 311	Philadelphia	PA	19121	**877-344-7273**	215-787-2600	611

Name / Address	City	State	Zip	Toll-Free	Phone	Class
Girardi Distributors LLC 5 Railroad Pl.	Athol	MA	01331	800-322-1229	978-249-3581	82-1
Girl Power! Substance Abuse & Mental Health Services Administration 5600 Fishersn Ln.	Rockville	MD	20857	800-729-6686		196
Girl Scout Leader Magazine 420 5th Ave	New York	NY	10018	800-223-0624	212-852-8000	449-10
Girl Scouts of the USA 420 5th Ave	New York	NY	10018	800-223-0624	212-852-8000	48-15
Girlfriends Magazine 3415 Cesar Chavez Suite 101	San Francisco	CA	94110	800-475-3763	415-648-9464	449-10
Girls & Boys Town 14100 Crawford St.	Boys Town	NE	68010	800-448-3000	402-498-1300	48-6
Girls Inc 120 Wall St 3rd Fl.	New York	NY	10005	800-374-4475	212-509-2000	48-24
Girl's Life Magazine 4517 Hartford Rd	Baltimore	MD	21214	888-999-3222	410-426-9600	449-6
Girls & Women in Sport. National Assn for 1900 Association Dr.	Reston	VA	20191	800-213-7193	703-476-3400	48-22
Girlshop Inc 154 W 14th St 9th Fl	New York	NY	10011	888-450-7467	212-645-6240	155-6
Giroux Glass Inc 850 W Washington Blvd.	Los Angeles	CA	90015	800-684-5277	213-747-7406	188-6
Giselle's Travel Inc 1300 Ethan Way Suite 100.	Sacramento	CA	95825	800-782-5545	916-922-5500	760
Gish Biomedical Inc 22942 Arroyo Vista	Rancho Santa Margarita	CA	92688	800-938-0531	949-635-6200	469
Gitman Brothers Shirt Co Inc 1350 Ave of the Americas Suite 1115 *Cust Svc	New York	NY	10019	800-526-3929*	212-581-6968	153-12
Gitman & Co 2309 Chestnut St	Ashland	PA	17921	800-526-3929	570-875-3100	153-12
Givaudan Flavors Corp 1199 Edison Dr.	Cincinnati	OH	45216	800-892-1199	513-948-8000	291-15
Given Imaging Ltd 5555 Oakbrook Pkwy Oakbrook Technology Ctr Suite 355 *NASDAQ: GIVN*	Norcross	GA	30093	800-448-3644	770-662-0870	375
GIW Industries Inc 5000 Wrightsboro Rd.	Grovetown	GA	30813	800-241-2702	706-863-1011	627
GKG (Global Knowledge Group Inc) 2700 Earl Rudder Fwy S Suite 1300	College Station	TX	77845	800-617-0412	979-693-5447	795
GLA Integrated Network Solutions LLC 5555 Winghaven Blvd.	O'Fallon	MO	63366	800-896-3355	636-625-5700	195
Glacier Bancorp Inc 49 Commons Loop *NASDAQ: GBCI*	Kalispell	MT	59901	800-735-4371	406-756-4200	355-2
Glacier Bay Country Inn Mile 1 Tong Rd.	Gustavus	AK	99826	800-628-0912	907-697-2288	373
Glacier Bay Cruiseline 2101 4th Ave Suite 2200 *Resv	Seattle	WA	98121	800-451-5952*	206-623-7110	217
Glacier Clear Enterprises Inc 3291 Thomas St. *Cust Svc	Innisfil	ON	L9S3W3	800-668-5118*	705-436-6363	792
Glacier Electric Co-op Inc PO Box 2090	Cut Bank	MT	59427	800-347-6795	406-873-5566	244
Glacier Garlock Bearings 700 Mid Atlantic Pkwy PO Box 189	Thorofare	NJ	08086	800-222-0147	856-848-3200	60
Glacier Northwest Inc PO Box 1730	Seattle	WA	98111	800-750-0123	206-764-3000	180
Glade Springs Resort 200 Lake Dr	Daniels	WV	25832	800-634-5233	304-763-2000	655
Glades Electric Co-op Inc PO Box 519	Moore Haven	FL	33471	800-226-4024	863-946-0061	244
Glades Pharmaceuticals Inc 6340 Sugarloaf Pkwy Suite 400	Duluth	GA	30097	888-445-2337	770-945-0708	573
Glamis Gold Ltd 5190 Neil Rd Suite 310 *NYSE: GLG*	Reno	NV	89502	800-452-6472	775-827-4600	492
Glamos Wire Products Co Inc 5561 N 152nd St	Hugo	MN	55038	800-428-6353	651-429-5386	75
Glamour Magazine 4 Times Sq	New York	NY	10036	800-274-7410	212-286-2860	449-11
Glamour Shots 1300 Metropolitan Ave	Oklahoma City	OK	73108	800-336-4550		579
Glasforms Inc 271 Barnard Ave	San Jose	CA	95125	888-297-3800	408-297-9300	589
Glasgow-Barren County Chamber of Commerce 118 E Public Sq	Glasgow	KY	42141	800-264-3161	270-651-3161	137
Glasgow Inc PO Box 1089	Glenside	PA	19038	888-222-7570	215-884-8800	187-4
Glass Assn. National 8200 Greensboro Dr Suite 302	McLean	VA	22102	866-342-5642	703-442-4890	49-13
Glass Doctor 1020 N University Parks Dr	Waco	TX	76707	800-280-9959	254-745-2480	62-2
Glass House Inn 3202 W 26th St	Erie	PA	16506	800-956-7222	814-833-7751	373
Glass Specialty System Inc PO Box 737	Bloomington	IL	61702	800-500-0500	309-664-1087	62-2
GlassHouse Technologies Inc 200 Crossing Blvd	Framingham	MA	01702	800-767-4535	508-879-5729	174
Glassmere Fuel Service Inc 1967 Saxonburg Blvd.	Tarentum	PA	15084	800-235-9054	724-224-0880	311
Glasstite Inc 600 Hwy 4 N *Cust Svc	Dunnell	MN	56127	800-533-0450*	507-695-2378	324
Glastic Corp 4321 Glenridge Rd	Cleveland	OH	44121	800-360-1319	216-486-0100	595
Glastonbury Southern Gage Co Inc 46 Industrial Park Rd.	Erin	TN	37061	800-251-4243	931-289-4243	484
Glaucoma Research Foundation 490 Post St Suite 1427	San Francisco	CA	94102	800-826-6693	415-986-3162	48-17
GlaxoSmithKline PO Box 13398 *NYSE: GSK*	Research Triangle Park	NC	27709	888-825-5249	919-248-2100	572
GlaxoSmithKline Foundation 5 Moore Dr.	Research Triangle Park	NC	27709	888-825-5249	919-483-2140	299
Glazier Foods Co 1520 Oliver St	Houston	TX	77007	800-989-6411	713-869-6411	292-8
Gleason Reel Corp PO Box 26	Mayville	WI	53050	800-571-0166	920-387-4120	118
Glen Grove Suites 2837 Yonge St.	Toronto	ON	M4N2J6	800-565-3024	416-489-8441	372
Glen Oaks Community College 62249 Shimmel Rd.	Centreville	MI	49032	888-994-7818	269-467-9945	160
Glenayre Electronics Inc 11360 Lakefield Dr	Duluth	GA	30097	800-688-4001	770-283-1000	720
Glenayre Technologies Inc 11360 Lakefield Dr *NASDAQ: GEMS*	Duluth	GA	30097	800-866-4002	770-283-1000	720
Glenbeigh Health Source 2863 SR 45	Rock Creek	OH	44084	800-234-1001	440-563-3400	712
Glencoe/McGraw-Hill 8787 Orion Pl	Columbus	OH	43240	800-848-1567	614-430-4000	623-2
Glencrest Farm PO Box 4468	Midway	KY	40347	800-903-0136	859-233-7032	362
Glendale Chamber of Commerce 7105 N 59th Ave	Glendale	AZ	85301	800-437-8669	623-937-4754	137
Glendinning Marine Products 740 Century Cir	Conway	SC	29526	800-500-2380	843-399-6146	202
Glendorn 1000 Glendorn Dr.	Bradford	PA	16701	800-843-8568	814-362-6511	373
Glenerin Inn 1695 The Collegeway	Mississauga	ON	L5L3S7	877-991-9971	905-828-6103	372
Glenmede Funds 1650 Market St One Liberty Pl Suite 1200	Philadelphia	PA	19103	800-966-3200	215-419-6000	517
Glenmede Trust Co 1650 Market St Suite 1200	Philadelphia	PA	19103	800-966-3200	215-419-6000	393
Glenmoor Country Club 4191 Glenmoor Rd NW	Canton	OH	44718	888-456-6667	330-966-3600	655
Glenmore Inn 2720 Glenmore Trail SE	Calgary	AB	T2C2E6	800-661-3163	403-279-8611	372
Glenn O Hawbaker Inc 1952 Waddle Rd.	State College	PA	16803	800-221-1355	814-237-1444	46
Glenoit LLC 3002 Anaconda Rd.	Tarboro	NC	27886	800-829-0984	252-823-2124	730-4
Glenro Inc 39 McBride Ave	Paterson	NJ	07501	800-922-0106	973-279-5900	313
Glenrock International Inc 985 E Linden Ave	Linden	NJ	07036	800-442-6374	908-862-3433	130
Glens Falls Lehigh Cement Co 313 Warren St	Glens Falls	NY	12801	800-833-4157	518-792-1137	135
Glenshaw Glass Co Inc 1101 William Flynn Hwy.	Glenshaw	PA	15116	800-326-2467	412-486-9100	327
Glensheen Mansion 3300 London Rd.	Duluth	MN	55804	888-454-4536	218-726-8980	50
Glentek Inc 208 Standard St.	El Segundo	CA	90245	800-232-4485	310-322-3026	507
Glenville State College 200 High St.	Glenville	WV	26351	800-924-2010	304-462-7361	163
Glenwood LLC 111 Cedar Ln	Englewood	NJ	07631	800-542-0772	201-569-0050	573
Glenwood Springs Post Independent 2014 Grand Ave	Glenwood Springs	CO	81601	866-850-9937	970-945-8515	522-2
Glick Textiles Inc 2327 SW Fwy.	Houston	TX	77098	800-231-7246	713-942-9191	583
Glickenhaus & Co 6 E 43rd St 10th Fl.	New York	NY	10017	800-559-8540	212-953-7800	679
Glidden House 1901 Ford Dr.	Cleveland	OH	44106	800-759-8358	216-231-8900	373
Glidden Rural Electric Co-op PO Box 486	Glidden	IA	51443	800-253-6211	712-659-3649	244
Glindmeyer Distributing Co Inc 4141 Bienville St.	New Orleans	LA	70119	800-466-1754	504-486-6646	38
Glines & Rhodes Inc 189 East St	Attleboro	MA	02703	800-343-1196	508-226-2000	476
Glissen Chemical Co Inc 1321 58th St.	Brooklyn	NY	11219	800-356-9922	718-436-4200	149
Glit/Microtron 809 Broad St	Wrens	GA	30833	800-431-2976	706-547-6555	1
Glo-Quartz Electric Heater Co Inc 7084 Maple St *Sales	Mentor	OH	44060	800-321-3574*	440-255-9701	313
Global Computer Supplies 11 Harbor Pk Dr. *Sales	Port Washington	NY	11050	800-845-6225*	516-625-6200	172
Global Consultants Inc 25 Airport Rd	Morristown	NJ	07960	877-264-6424	973-889-5200	178
Global Cos LLC 800 South St Suite 200	Waltham	MA	02454	800-685-7222	781-894-8800	569
Global Crossing Conferencing 1499 W 121 Ave.	Westminster	CO	80234	800-525-8244	303-633-3000	721
Global DocuGraphix 2329 Circadian Way	Santa Rosa	CA	95407	800-325-3120	707-527-6022	111
Global Electronic Music Marketplace PO Box 4062	Palm Springs	CA	92262	800-207-4366	760-318-6250	514
Global Exchange 2017 Mission St Suite 303	San Francisco	CA	94110	800-497-1994	415-255-7296	48-7
Global eXchange Services Inc 100 Edison Park Dr	Gaithersburg	MD	20878	800-560-4347	301-340-4000	176-4
Global Finishing Solutions LLC 1625 W Crosby Rd Suite 124	Carrollton	TX	75006	800-389-5296		313
Global Imaging Systems Inc 3820 Northdale Blvd Suite 200A *NASDAQ: GISX*	Tampa	FL	33624	888-628-7834	813-960-5508	113
Global Incentives Inc 2120 Main St Suite 130	Huntington Beach	CA	92648	800-292-7348	714-960-2300	377
Global Industries Inc 17 W Stow Rd	Marlton	NJ	08053	800-220-1900	856-596-3390	314-1
Global Industries Ltd PO Box 442 *NASDAQ: GLBL*	Sulphur	LA	70664	800-525-3483	337-583-5000	528
Global Knowledge Group Inc (GKG) 2700 Earl Rudder Fwy S Suite 1300	College Station	TX	77845	800-617-0412	979-693-5447	795
Global Knowledge Network Corp 9000 Regency Pkwy Suite 500	Cary	NC	27512	800-268-7737	919-461-8600	752
Global Market Perspective Newsletter PO Box 1618	Gainesville	GA	30503	800-336-1618	770-536-0309	521-9
Global MetalForm LP 733 Davis St.	Scranton	PA	18505	800-233-4818	570-346-3871	253
Global Money Management Newsletter 225 Park Ave S 7th Fl	New York	NY	10003	800-715-9195	212-224-3800	521-1
Global Motorsport Group 16100 Jacqueline Ct.	Morgan Hill	CA	95037	800-359-5700	408-778-0500	61
Global Network Tours Inc DBA Air-Supply Inc 350 5th Ave Empire State Bldg Suite 6724	New York	NY	10118	800-671-9961	212-695-1647	17
Global Payment Technologies Inc 425 B Oser Ave *NASDAQ: GPTX*	Hauppauge	NY	11788	800-472-2506	631-231-1177	112
Global Payments Inc 10 Glenlake Pkwy North Tower *NYSE: GPN*	Atlanta	GA	30328	800-560-2960	770-829-8000	254
Global Philosophy Travel LLC 61 Parish Farm Rd	Branford	CT	06405	888-378-9276	203-315-8200	760
Global Power Report 2 Penn Plaza 25th Fl	New York	NY	10121	800-223-6180	800-752-8878	521-5
Global Response Corp 777 S SR-7	Margate	FL	33068	800-537-8000	954-973-7300	722
Global Shop Solutions Inc 975 Evergreen Cir. *Sales	The Woodlands	TX	77380	800-364-5958*	281-681-1959	176-1
Global Signal Inc 301 N Cattleman Rd Suite 300 *NYSE: GSE*	Sarasota	FL	34232	888-748-3482	941-364-8886	168

Name / Address	City	State	Zip	Toll-Free	Phone	Class
Global Software Inc 3200 Atlantic Ave Suite 200 *Mktg	Raleigh	NC	27604	**800-326-3444***	919-872-7800	176-1
Global Stone Chemstone Corp 1696 Oranda Rd	Strasburg	VA	22657	**800-541-3172**	540-465-5161	432
Global Stone Saint Clair PO Box 160	Marble City	OK	74945	**800-366-5106**	918-775-4466	432
Global Stone Tenn Luttrell 486 Clinch Valley Rd *Sales	Luttrell	TN	37779	**800-467-5463***	865-992-3841	432
Global Technovations Inc 7108 Fairway Dr Suite 130	Palm Beach Gardens	FL	33418	**800-285-7708**	561-775-5756	60
Global Travel 900 W Jefferson St	Boise	ID	83702	**800-584-8888**	208-387-1000	760
Global Travel International 2600 Lake Lucien Dr Suite 201	Maitland	FL	32751	**800-951-5979**	407-660-7800	761
Global Turnkey Systems Inc 2001 Rt 46 Suite 203 *Help Line	Parsippany	NJ	07054	**800-221-1746***	973-331-1010	176-10
Global University 1211 S Glenstone Ave	Springfield	MO	65804	**800-443-1083**	417-862-9533	754
Global Vacation Travel Packages 61 Parish Farm Rd	Branford	CT	06405	**888-378-9276**	203-315-8200	760
GlobalDie 1130 Minot Ave PO Box 1120	Auburn	ME	04211	**800-910-3747**		745
GlobalPass 6355 NW 36th St Suite 600	Miami	FL	33166	**877-946-4537**	305-870-7500	27
GlobalQuest Journeys Ltd 185 Willis Ave 2nd Fl	Mineola	NY	11501	**800-221-3254**	516-739-3690	748
GlobalSantaFe Corp 15375 Memorial Dr *NYSE: GSF*	Houston	TX	77079	**800-231-5754**	281-925-6000	529
Globalstar LP 461 S Milpitas Blvd Bldg 5	Milpitas	CA	95035	**877-245-6225**	408-933-4000	669
Globalware Solutions Inc 1089 Mills Way	Redwood City	CA	94063	**800-224-6326**	650-363-2200	239
Globe Amerada Glass Co 2001 Greenleaf Ave	Elk Grove Village	IL	60007	**800-323-8776**	847-364-2900	324
Globe Electronic Hardware Inc 34-24 56th St	Woodside	NY	11377	**800-221-1505**	718-457-0303	202
Globe Food Equipment Co PO Box 3209	Dayton	OH	45401	**800-347-5423**	937-299-5493	293
Globe-Gazette 300 N Washington St PO Box 271	Mason City	IA	50402	**800-421-0546**	641-421-0500	522-2
Globe Indemnity Co 9300 Arrowpoint Blvd *Cust Svc	Charlotte	NC	28273	**800-523-5451***	704-522-2000	384-4
Globe Life & Accident Insurance Co 204 N Robinson Ave Globe Life Ctr	Oklahoma City	OK	73102	**800-654-5433**	405-270-1400	384-2
Globe Magazine 1000 American Media Way	Boca Raton	FL	33467	**800-749-7733**	561-997-7733	449-11
Globe Mfg Co Inc PO Box 128 37 Loudon Rd	Pittsfield	NH	03263	**800-232-8323**	603-435-8323	566
Globe Motorists Supply Co Inc 560 S 3rd Ave	Mount Vernon	NY	10550	**888-884-7278**	914-668-6430	61
Globe Transportation Graphics 7127 Rutherford Rd	Baltimore	MD	21244	**800-755-6750**	410-685-6750	692
Globecomm Systems Inc 45 Oser Ave *NASDAQ: GCOM*	Hauppauge	NY	11788	**888-231-9800**	631-231-9800	633
Globus Cosmos & Monograms 5301 S Federal Cir	Littleton	CO	80123	**800-221-0090**	303-797-2800	748
Gloria Jean's Gourmet Coffees 28 Executive Pk Suite 200	Irvine	CA	92614	**800-354-5282**	949-260-1600	156
Glorietta Bay Inn 1630 Glorietta Blvd	Coronado	CA	92118	**800-283-9383**	619-435-3101	373
Glorybee Foods Inc PO Box 2744	Eugene	OR	97402	**800-456-7923**	541-689-0913	291-24
Gloss.com Inc 767 5th Ave *Orders	New York	NY	10153	**888-550-4567***	212-572-4200	211
Glover Equipment Inc 221 Cockeysville Rd PO Box 405	Cockeysville	MD	21030	**800-966-9016**	410-771-8000	315
Gloves Inc 50 Suffolk Rd	Mansfield	MA	02048	**800-225-6076**	508-339-2590	153-8
Glovia International LLC 1940 E Mariposa Ave	El Segundo	CA	90245	**888-245-6842**	310-563-7000	176-1
Glowpoint Inc 225 Long Ave *NASDAQ: GLOW*	Hillside	NJ	07205	**866-456-9764**	973-282-2000	39
GLS Corp 833 Ridgeview Dr	McHenry	IL	60050	**800-457-8777**	815-385-8500	592
GLU (Great Lakes United) Buffalo State College Cassety Hall 1300 Elmwood Ave	Buffalo	NY	14222	**800-846-0142**	716-886-0142	48-13
GlycoGenesys Inc 31 St James Ave Suite 810 *NASDAQ: GLGS*	Boston	MA	02116	**800-260-6843**	617-422-0674	572
GM Motor Club PO Box 3580	Southfield	MI	48037	**800-705-0055**		53
GM Nameplate Inc 2040 15th Ave W	Seattle	WA	98119	**800-366-7668**	206-284-2200	472
GMA Industries 444 Innovation Way	Allentown	PA	18109	**800-667-5531**	610-694-9494	537
GMAC (General Motors Acceptance Corp) 200 Renaissance Ctr	Detroit	MI	48265	**800-200-4622**	313-556-5000	215
GMAC Canada (General Motors Acceptance Corp Canada) 3300 Bloor St W Suite 2800	Toronto	ON	M8X2X5	**800-616-4622**	416-234-6600	215
GMAC Global Relocation Services 150 Mount Bethel Rd	Warren	NJ	07059	**800-589-7858**	908-542-5400	652
GMAC Insurance 500 W 5th St	Winston Salem	NC	27102	**877-468-3466**	336-770-2000	384-4
GMAC Insurance Holdings Inc 1 GMAC Insurance Plaza	Saint Louis	MO	63166	**877-468-3466**	314-493-8000	355-4
GMAC Mortgage Corp 100 Witmer Rd	Horsham	PA	19044	**800-627-0128**	215-682-1000	498
GMG Distributors Inc 1995 Davis St	San Leandro	CA	94577	**800-468-4420**	510-430-2940	540
GMHC (Gay Men's Health Crisis) 119 W 24th St	New York	NY	10011	**800-243-7692**	212-367-1000	48-17
GMI (Graphics Microsystems Inc) 484 Oakmead Pkwy	Sunnyvale	CA	94085	**800-336-1464**	408-745-7745	617
GMI Composites Inc 1355 W Sherman Blvd	Muskegon	MI	49441	**800-330-4045**	231-755-1611	595
GML Inc 500 Oak Grove Pkwy	Saint Paul	MN	55127	**800-344-8899**	651-490-0000	591
GN Netcom Inc 77 Northeastern Blvd	Nashua	NH	03062	**800-345-8639**	603-598-1100	720
GNC Corp 300 6th Ave *Cust Svc	Pittsburgh	PA	15222	**888-462-2548***	412-288-4600	350
GNC Franchising Inc 300 6th Ave	Pittsburgh	PA	15222	**800-259-5008**	412-288-4600	305
Go Ahead Vacations 1 Education St	Cambridge	MA	02141	**800-242-4686**	617-619-1000	748
GO Carlson Inc 350 Marshallton Thorndale Rd	Downingtown	PA	19335	**800-338-5622**	610-384-2800	709
GO Magazine 6600 AAA Dr	Charlotte	NC	28212	**800-477-4222**	704-377-3600	449-22
Go RVing Coalition 1896 Preston White Dr	Reston	VA	20191	**888-467-8464**	703-620-6003	48-23
Go...With Jo! Tours & Travel Inc 910 Dixieland Rd	Harlingen	TX	78552	**800-999-1446**	956-423-1446	748
Goal Oriented Inc 7935 E 14th Ave	Denver	CO	80220	**888-393-0888**	303-393-6040	701
Goal Sporting Goods Inc 37 Industrial Pk Rd Box 236	Essex	CT	06426	**800-334-4625**	860-767-9112	701
Goalsetter Systems Inc PO Box 552	Pella	IA	50219	**800-362-4625**	641-628-2628	701
GoAmerica Inc 401 Hackensack Ave *NASDAQ: GOAM*	Hackensack	NJ	07601	**888-462-4600**	201-996-1717	222
Go/Dan Industries 100 Gando Dr	New Haven	CT	06513	**800-755-2160**	203-562-5121	60
Goddard College 123 Pitkin Rd	Plainfield	VT	05667	**800-468-4888**	802-454-8311	163
Godfather's Pizza Inc 9140 W Dodge Rd	Omaha	NE	68114	**800-456-8347**	402-391-1452	657
Godfrey & Kahn SC 780 N Water St	Milwaukee	WI	53202	**877-455-2900**	414-273-3500	419
Godiva Chocolatier Inc 355 Lexington Ave 16th Fl	New York	NY	10017	**800-732-7333**	212-984-5900	291-8
Goebel Fixture Co 528 Dale St	Hutchinson	MN	55350	**800-727-4646**	320-587-2112	281
Goettl Air Conditioning Inc 1845 W 1st St	Tempe	AZ	85281	**800-334-6494**	602-275-1515	15
Goettle Construction Inc 12071 Hamilton Ave	Cincinnati	OH	45231	**800-248-8661**	513-825-8100	188-3
Goetze's Candy Co Inc 3900 E Monument St *Orders	Baltimore	MD	21205	**800-295-8058***	410-342-2010	291-8
Goffa International Corp 5301 11th St	Long Island City	NY	11101	**800-969-7864**	718-361-8883	750
GOG (Gynecologic Oncology Group) 1600 JFK Blvd Suite 1020	Philadelphia	PA	19103	**800-225-3053**	215-854-0770	49-8
Gogebic Community College E 4946 Jackson Rd	Ironwood	MI	49938	**800-682-5910**	906-932-4231	160
GOGO WorldWide Vacations 69 Spring St	Ramsey	NJ	07446	**888-271-1584**	201-934-3500	760
GoHip.com Inc 8306 Wilshire Blvd Suite 54	Beverly Hills	CA	90211	**866-739-5517**	213-596-6248	677
GOJO Industries Inc PO Box 991	Akron	OH	44309	**800-321-9647**	330-255-6000	211
Gold Banc Corp Inc 11301 Nall Ave *NASDAQ: GLDB*	Leawood	KS	66211	**866-842-4686**	913-451-8050	355-2
Gold Bond Mattress Co 261 Weston St	Hartford	CT	06120	**800-873-8498**	860-549-2000	463
Gold Canyon Golf Resort 6100 S Kings Ranch Rd	Gold Canyon	AZ	85218	**800-624-6445**	480-982-9090	655
Gold Coast Beverage Distributors Inc 3325 NW 70th Ave	Miami	FL	33122	**800-432-0463**	305-591-9800	82-1
Gold Coast Hotel & Casino 4000 W Flamingo Rd	Las Vegas	NV	89103	**888-402-6278**	702-367-7111	133
Gold Coast Railroad Museum 12450 SW 152nd St	Miami	FL	33177	**888-608-7246**	305-253-0063	509
Gold Eagle Co 4400 S Kildare Ave	Chicago	IL	60632	**800-621-1251**	773-376-4400	143
Gold Lake Mountain Resort & Spa 3371 Gold Lake Rd	Ward	CO	80481	**800-450-3544**	303-459-3544	655
Gold Lance Inc 148 E Broadway	Owatonna	MN	55060	**800-252-5777**	507-455-6100	401
Gold Medal Bakery Inc 21 Penn St	Fall River	MA	02724	**800-642-7568**	508-674-5766	69
Gold Medal Products Co 10700 Medallion Dr *Cust Svc	Cincinnati	OH	45241	**800-543-0862***	513-769-7676	293
Gold Mitchell Co 135 One Comfortable Pl	Taylorsville	NC	28681	**800-789-5401**	828-632-9200	314-2
Gold Newsletter 2400 Jefferson Hwy Suite 600	Jefferson	LA	70121	**800-877-8847**	504-837-3033	521-9
Gold Points Reward Network PO Box 59159	Minneapolis	MN	55459	**800-508-9000**	763-212-6900	371
Gold Pure Food Products Inc 1 Brooklyn Rd	Hempstead	NY	11550	**800-422-4681**	516-483-5600	291-19
Gold Reserve Inc 926 W Sprague Ave Suite 200 *AMEX: GRZ*	Spokane	WA	99201	**800-625-9550**	509-623-1500	492
Gold Star Chili 650 Lunken Pk Dr	Cincinnati	OH	45226	**800-643-0465**	513-231-4541	657
Gold Star FS Inc 101 N East St	Cambridge	IL	61238	**800-443-8497**	309-937-3369	272
Gold Star Sausage Co Inc PO Box 4245	Denver	CO	80204	**800-258-7229**	303-295-6400	291-26
Gold Strike Casino Resort 1010 Casino Ctr Dr *Resv	Robinsonville	MS	38664	**888-245-7829***	662-357-1111	133
Gold Strike Hotel & Gambling Hall 1 Main St PO Box 19278	Jean	NV	89019	**800-634-1359**	702-477-5000	133
Gold Toe Brands Inc 661 Plaid St *Cust Svc	Burlington	NC	27215	**800-523-8265***	336-229-3700	153-10
Goldbelt Hotel Juneau 51 Egan Dr	Juneau	AK	99801	**888-478-6909**	907-586-6900	373
Goldberg Co Inc 2423-A Grenoble Rd	Richmond	VA	23294	**800-365-6533**	804-228-5700	38
Goldberger Doll Mfg Co Inc 538 Johnson Ave	Brooklyn	NY	11237	**800-452-3655**	718-366-5800	750
Goldcorp Inc 145 King St W Suite 2700 *NYSE: GG*	Toronto	ON	M5H1J8	**800-813-1412**	416-865-0326	492
Goldcrest Wallcoverings 1526 New Scotland Rd	Slingerlands	NY	12159	**800-535-9513**	518-478-7214	789
Golden Age Festival Travel 5501 New Jersey Ave	Wildwood Crest	NJ	08260	**800-257-8920**	609-522-6316	748
Golden Artists Colors Inc 188 Bell Rd	New Berlin	NY	13411	**800-959-6543**	607-847-6154	43
Golden Bear Travel Inc 16 Digital Dr	Novato	CA	94949	**800-551-1000**	415-382-8900	760
Golden Books 1745 Broadway *Cust Svc	New York	NY	10019	**800-558-9427***	212-782-9000	623-2
Golden Cheese Co of California 1138 W Rincon St *Cust Svc	Corona	CA	92880	**800-842-0264***	951-493-4700	291-5

Name / Address	City	State	ZIP	Toll-Free	Phone	Class
Golden Corral Corp 5151 Glenwood Ave	Raleigh	NC	27612	**800-284-5673**	919-781-9310	657
Golden Door Spa at the Wyndham Peaks Resort 136 Country Club Dr Box 2702	Telluride	CO	81435	**800-772-5482**	970-728-2590	698
Golden Door Spa. Wyndham Peaks Resort & 136 Country Club Dr	Telluride	CO	81435	**800-789-2220**	970-728-6800	655
Golden Eagle Distributors Inc 705 E Ajo Way	Tucson	AZ	85726	**800-274-4283**	520-884-5999	82-1
Golden Eagle Insurance Corp 525 B St	San Diego	CA	92101	**800-688-8661**	619-744-6000	384-4
Golden Eagle Resort 511 Mountain Rd PO Box 1090	Stowe	VT	05672	**800-626-1010**	802-253-4811	373
Golden Flake Snack Foods Inc 1 Golden Flake Dr	Birmingham	AL	35205	**800-239-2447**	205-323-6161	291-35
Golden Foods/Golden Brands Inc PO Box 398	Louisville	KY	40201	**800-622-3055**	502-636-3712	291-30
Golden Gate University 536 Mission St	San Francisco	CA	94105	**800-448-4968**	415-442-7000	158
Golden Light Equipment Co 1010 W 6th St	Amarillo	TX	79101	**800-692-4098**	806-373-4277	295
Golden Neo-Life Diamite International 3500 Gateway Blvd	Fremont	CA	94538	**800-432-5848**	510-651-0405	361
Golden North Motel 4888 Old Airport Rd	Fairbanks	AK	99709	**800-447-1910**	907-479-6201	373
Golden Nugget Hotel 129 E Fremont St	Las Vegas	NV	89101	**800-634-3454**	702-385-7111	655
Golden Nugget Laughlin 2300 S Casino Dr	Laughlin	NV	89029	**800-237-1739**	702-298-7111	133
Golden Oaks Village 5801 N Oakwood Rd	Enid	OK	73703	**800-259-0914**	580-234-2817	659
Golden One Credit Union 6507 4th Ave	Sacramento	CA	95817	**800-521-0137**	916-732-2900	216
Golden Rule. International Order of the 13523 Lakefront Dr	Bridgeton	MO	63045	**800-637-8030**	314-209-7142	49-4
Golden Spike Equipment Co 1352 W Main St PO Box 70	Tremonton	UT	84337	**800-821-4474**	435-257-5346	270
Golden Spike Event Center 1000 N 1200 West	Ogden	UT	84404	**800-442-7362**	801-399-8544	204
Golden Sports Tours 301 W Parker Rd Suite 206	Plano	TX	75023	**800-966-8258**	972-578-1166	760
Golden Star Inc 400 E 10th Ave	North Kansas City	MO	64116	**800-821-2792**	816-842-0233	497
Golden State Cellular 17400 High School Rd	Jamestown	CA	95327	**800-453-8255**	209-533-8844	721
Golden State Mutual Life Insurance Co 1999 W Adams Blvd	Los Angeles	CA	90018	**800-225-5476**	323-731-1131	384-2
Golden State Warriors 1011 Broadway	Oakland	CA	94607	**888-479-4667**	510-986-2200	703
Golden States Engineering Inc 15338 S Garfield Ave	Paramount	CA	90723	**800-292-2838**	562-634-3125	610
Golden Stream Quality Foods 11899 Exit 5 Pkwy	Fishers	IN	46038	**800-837-2855**	317-845-5534	291-8
Golden Sun Feeds Inc 1842 Hwy 4 S	Estherville	IA	51334	**800-831-5040**	712-362-3551	568
Golden Temple Inc 2545 Prairie Rd	Eugene	OR	97402	**800-285-6457**	541-461-2160	291-11
Golden Theatre 252 W 45th St	New York	NY	10036	**800-432-7250**	212-239-6200	732
Golden Valley Electrical Assn Inc PO Box 71249	Fairbanks	AK	99707	**800-770-4832**	907-452-1151	244
Golden Valley Memorial Hospital 1600 N 2nd St	Clinton	MO	64735	**800-748-7681**	660-885-5511	366-2
Golden West Dental & Vision Plan Inc 888 W Ventura Blvd	Camarillo	CA	93010	**800-995-4124**	805-987-8941	384-3
Golden West Telecommunications Co-op Inc 415 Crown St	Wall	SD	57790	**877-610-7040**	605-279-2161	721
Goldener Hirsch Inn 7570 Royal St E	Park City	UT	84060	**800-252-3373**	435-649-7770	373
GoldenRAM Computer Products 8 Whatney	Irvine	CA	92618	**800-222-8861**	949-460-9000	613
Goldens' Foundry & Machine Co 600 12th St	Columbus	GA	31901	**800-328-8379**	706-323-0471	302
Goldey Beacom College 4701 Limestone Rd	Wilmington	DE	19808	**800-833-4877**	302-998-8814	163
Goldman Sachs Asset Management 32 Old Slip 17th Fl	New York	NY	10005	**800-292-4726**	212-902-1000	393
Goldman Sachs & Co 85 Broad St	New York	NY	10004	**800-323-5678**	212-902-1000	679
Goldman Sachs Funds PO Box 219711	Kansas City	MO	64121	**800-526-7384**	312-655-4435	517
Goldman Sachs Group Inc 85 Broad St *NYSE: GS*	New York	NY	10004	**800-323-5678**	212-902-1000	679
Gold'n Plump Poultry 4150 2nd St S	Saint Cloud	MN	56301	**800-328-8236**	320-251-6568	608
Gold's Gym International 358 Hampton Dr	Venice	CA	90291	**800-457-5375**	310-392-3005	349
Goldsboro Milling Co 938 Millers Chapel Rd	Goldsboro	NC	27534	**800-768-7823**	919-778-3130	438
Goldshield Elite 1501 Northpoint Pkwy Suite 100	West Palm Beach	FL	33407	**866-218-8142**		361
Goldsmith & Eggleton Inc 300 1st St	Wadsworth	OH	44281	**800-321-0954**	330-336-6616	594-2
Goleta Valley Chamber of Commerce PO Box 781 5582 Calle Real Suite A	Goleta	CA	93116	**800-646-5382**	805-967-4618	137
Golf Assn Museum. US 77 Liberty Corner Rd	Far Hills	NJ	07931	**800-222-8742**	908-234-2300	511
Golf Assn. National Senior 3672 Nottingham Way	Hamilton Square	NJ	08690	**800-282-6772**	609-631-8145	48-22
Golf Assn. US PO Box 708 *Orders	Far Hills	NJ	07931	**800-336-4446***	908-234-2300	48-22
Golf Course Owners Assn. National 291 Seven Farms Dr 2nd Fl	Charleston	SC	29492	**800-933-4262**	843-881-9956	48-23
Golf Course Superintendents Assn of America (GCSAA) 1421 Research Park Dr	Lawrence	KS	66049	**800-472-7878**	785-841-2240	48-2
Golf Digest 20 Westport Rd PO Box 850	Wilton	CT	06897	**800-962-5513**	203-761-5100	449-20
Golf Foundation. National 1150 S US Hwy 1 Suite 401	Jupiter	FL	33477	**800-733-6006**	561-744-6006	48-22
Golf Hall of Fame. Georgia 1 11th St	Augusta	GA	30901	**888-874-4443**	706-724-4443	511
Golf Hall of Fame & Museum. Canadian Glen Abbey Golf Club 1333 Dorval Dr	Oakville	ON	L6J4Z3	**800-310-7242**	905-849-9700	511
Golf Hosts Inc 36750 US Hwy 19 N	Palm Harbor	FL	34684	**800-456-2000**	727-942-2000	369
Golf Magazine 2 Park Ave	New York	NY	10016	**800-227-2224**	212-779-5000	449-20
Golf Packages of the Carolinas 218 Main St	North Myrtle Beach	SC	29582	**877-833-2255**	877-732-6999	760
Golf Resort. Westin Innisbrook 36750 US Hwy 19 N	Palm Harbor	FL	34684	**800-456-2000**	727-942-2000	655
Golf Shack Inc 1631 N Bell School Rd	Rockford	IL	61107	**888-446-5390**	815-397-3709	702
Golf Tips Magazine 12121 Wilshire Blvd Suite 1200	Los Angeles	CA	90025	**800-283-4330**	310-820-1500	449-20
Golf USA 3705 W Memorial Rd Suite 801	Oklahoma City	OK	73134	**800-488-1107**	405-751-0015	702
Golf for Women Magazine 201 Westport Rd PO Box 850	Wilton	CT	06897	**800-962-5513**	203-761-5100	449-20
Golf World Magazine 210 Westport Rd PO Box 850	Wilton	CT	06897	**800-962-5513**	203-761-5100	449-20
GolfCoach Inc 5060 N Royal Atlanta Dr Suite 28	Tucker	GA	30084	**800-772-3813**	770-414-9508	701
Golfsmith International Inc 11000 N IH-35 *Sales	Austin	TX	78753	**800-396-0099***	512-837-4810	702
Goltens New York Corp 160 Van Brunt St	Brooklyn	NY	11231	**877-204-1088**	718-855-7200	689
gomembers Inc 11720 Sunrise Valley Dr Suite 300	Reston	VA	20191	**888-288-4634**	703-620-9600	176-10
Gonnella Baking Co 2002 W Erie St	Chicago	IL	60612	**800-262-3442**	312-733-2020	69
Gonser Gerber Tinker Stuhr LLP 400 E Diehl Rd Suite 380	Naperville	IL	60563	**800-446-4487**	630-505-1433	312
Gonzaga University 502 E Boone Ave	Spokane	WA	99258	**800-986-9585**	509-328-4220	163
Gonzaga University School of Law 721 N Cincinnati St *Admissions	Spokane	WA	99258	**800-793-1710***	509-328-4220	164-1
Gonzales Automotive Group 5800 Firestone Blvd	South Gate	CA	90280	**888-318-5337**	562-776-2330	57
Gonzalez Henry B Convention Center 200 E Market St	San Antonio	TX	78205	**877-504-8895**	210-207-8500	204
Gonzer LJ Assoc Inc 1225 Raymond Blvd	Newark	NJ	07102	**800-631-4218**	973-624-5600	707
Gooch Brake & Equipment Co 506 Grand Blvd	Kansas City	MO	64106	**800-444-3216**	816-421-3085	61
Good Cook Book-of-the-Month Club Inc 1271 Ave of the Americas 3rd Fl	New York	NY	10020	**800-233-1066**	212-522-4200	94
Good Cos Inc 1118 E 223rd St	Carson	CA	90745	**800-666-8225**	310-549-2160	314-2
Good Earth Travel Adventures Reservations PO Box 8510	Canmore	AB	T1W2V2	**888-979-9797**	403-678-9358	368
Good Eats Inc 12200 Stemmons Fwy Suite 100	Dallas	TX	75234	**800-275-1337**	972-241-5500	657
Good Guys Inc 1600 Harbor Bay Pkwy Suite 200	Alameda	CA	94502	**800-229-4897**	510-747-6000	35
Good Housekeeping Magazine 250 W 55th St	New York	NY	10019	**800-888-7788**	212-649-2000	449-11
Good-Nite Inn Fremont 4135 Cushing Pkwy	Fremont	CA	94538	**800-648-3466**	510-656-9307	373
Good Sam Recreational Vehicle Club PO Box 6888	Englewood	CO	80155	**800-234-3450**		48-23
Good Samaritan Hospice 310 Allston St	Brighton	MA	02135	**800-425-8282**	617-566-6242	365
Good Samaritan Hospice 3825 Electric Rd SW Suite A	Roanoke	VA	24018	**888-466-7809**	540-776-0198	365
Good Samaritan Hospice Care 166 E Goodale Ave	Battle Creek	MI	49017	**800-254-5939**	269-660-3600	365
Good Samaritan Hospital 10 E 31st St	Kearney	NE	68847	**800-658-4250**	308-865-7100	366-2
Good Samaritan Medical & Rehabilitation Center 800 Forest Ave	Zanesville	OH	43701	**800-322-4762**	740-454-5843	366-2
Good Samaritan Regional Medical Center 3600 NW Samaritan Dr	Corvallis	OR	97330	**888-872-0760**	541-757-5111	366-2
Good Shepherd Hospice of Mid-Florida Inc 105 Arneson Ave	Auburndale	FL	33823	**800-753-1880**	863-297-1880	365
Good Time Tickets Inc 38 Hadden Field Rd	Palmyra	NJ	08065	**800-774-8499**	856-829-3900	735
Good Time Tours 455 Corday St	Pensacola	FL	32503	**800-446-0886**	850-476-0046	748
Good Times Travel Club Inc 17132 Magnolia St	Fountain Valley	CA	92708	**888-488-2287**	714-848-1255	748
Good Zoo & Benedum Planetarium Rt 88 N Oglebay Pk	Wheeling	WV	26003	**800-624-6988**	304-243-4030	811
Goodall Jane Institute for Wildlife Research Education & Conservation 8700 Georgia Ave Suite 500	Silver Spring	MD	20910	**800-592-5263**	301-565-0086	48-3
Goodall Mfg Co 7558 Washington Ave S	Eden Prairie	MN	55344	**800-328-7730**	952-941-6666	246
Goodall Rubber Co 790 Birney Hwy Suite 100	Aston	PA	19014	**800-562-8002**	610-361-0800	378
Goodell Inc 9440 Science Ctr Dr *Cust Svc	Minneapolis	MN	55428	**800-542-3906***	763-531-0053	219
Goodheart-Willcox Publisher 18604 W Creek Dr	Tinley Park	IL	60477	**800-323-0440**	708-687-5000	623-2
Goodhue County Co-op Electric Assn PO Box 99	Zumbrota	MN	55992	**800-927-6864**	507-732-5117	244
Goodin Co 2700 N 2nd St	Minneapolis	MN	55411	**800-328-8433**	612-588-7811	601
GoodLife TV Network 650 Massachusetts Ave NW	Washington	DC	20001	**800-446-6388**	202-289-6633	725
Goodman & Co LLP 1 Commercial Pl Suite 800	Norfolk	VA	23510	**888-899-5100**	757-624-5100	2
Goodman Factors 3010 LBJ Freeway Suite 140	Dallas	TX	75234	**877-446-6362**	972-241-3297	268
Goodman Holding Co 2550 N Loop W Suite 400	Houston	TX	77092	**888-593-9988**	713-861-2500	355-3
Goodman IB Mfg Co 120 E 3rd St	Newport	KY	41071	**800-543-1945**	859-261-2086	401
Goodrich Corp 2730 W Tyvola Rd 4 Coliseum Ctr *NYSE: GR*	Charlotte	NC	28217	**800-784-7009**	704-423-7000	519
Goodrich Corp Aircraft Interior Products Div 3414 S 5th St	Phoenix	AZ	85040	**888-419-4344**	602-232-4000	23

Listing	Toll-Free	Phone	Class
Goodrich Corp Delavan Spray Technologies Div PO Box 969 Bamberg SC 29003	800-621-9357	803-245-4347	170
Goodrich Corp Engineered Polymer Products Div 6061 Goodrich Blvd Jacksonville FL 32226	800-366-8945	904-757-3660	597
Goodrich Corp Fuel & Utility Systems Div 100 Patton Rd Vergennes VT 05491	800-722-7251	802-877-2111	464
Goodrich Corp Sterling Die Div 5565 Venture Dr Suite D Parma OH 44130	800-533-1300	216-267-1300	745
Goodrich Petroleum Corp 808 Travis St Suite 1320 Houston TX 77002 *NYSE: GDP*	800-256-2380	713-780-9494	528
Goodrich Quality Theaters Inc 4417 Broadmoor Ave SE Kentwood MI 49512	800-473-3523	616-698-7733	733
Goodwill Industries International Inc 15810 Industrial Dr Rockville MD 20855	800-741-0197	301-530-6500	48-5
Goodwin Biotechnology Inc 1850 NW 69th Ave Plantation FL 33313	800-814-8600	954-321-5300	229
Goodwin Hotel 1 Haynes St Hartford CT 06103	800-922-5006	860-246-7500	373
Goody Products Inc 400 Galleria Pkwy Suite 1100 Atlanta GA 30339	800-241-4324	770-615-4700	211
Goodyear Tire & Rubber Co 1144 E Market St Akron OH 44316 *NYSE: GT* ■ *Cust Svc	800-321-2136*	330-796-2121	739
Goody's Family Clothing Inc PO Box 22000 Knoxville TN 37933 *NASDAQ: GDYS*	800-224-3114	865-966-2000	155-2
Gooseneck Trailer Mfg Co 4400 E Hwy 21 Bryan TX 77808	800-688-5490	979-778-0034	751
Gopher Motor Rebuilding Inc 6530 James Ave N Minneapolis MN 55430	800-328-3994	763-746-3440	259
Gopher Sign Co 1310 Randolph Ave Saint Paul MN 55105	800-383-3156	651-698-5095	692
Gorant Candies Inc 8301 Market St Youngstown OH 44512	800-572-4139	330-726-8821	123
Gordman Inc 12100 W Center Rd Omaha NE 68144	800-456-7463	402-691-4000	227
Gordon Alan Enterprises Inc 5625 Melrose Ave Hollywood CA 90038	800-825-6684	323-466-3561	580
Gordon Brothers Corp 40 Broad St Suite 800 Boston MA 02109	800-487-4882	617-422-6542	51
Gordon Brush Mfg Co Inc 6247 Randolph St Commerce CA 90040	800-950-7950	323-724-7777	104
Gordon College 255 Grapevine Rd Wenham MA 01984	800-343-1379	978-927-2300	163
Gordon County Chamber of Commerce 300 S Wall St Calhoun GA 30701	800-887-3811	706-625-3200	137
Gordon Food Service 333 50th St SW Grand Rapids MI 49548	800-968-7500	616-530-7000	295
Henry Lee Div 3301 NW 125th St Miami FL 33167	800-274-4533	305-685-5851	295
Gordon Kenneth IAG 1209 Distributors Row New Orleans LA 70123 *Cust Svc	800-234-1433*	504-734-1433	153-12
Gordon-Piatt Group Inc PO Box 21220 Tulsa OK 74141	800-638-6940		352
Gordon Rj & Co 8730 W Sunset Blvd Suite 290 West Hollywood CA 90069	800-746-7366	310-734-3500	193
Gordon Sign Co Inc 2930 W 9th Ave Denver CO 80204	800-323-6121	303-629-6121	692
Gordon Trucking Inc 151 Stewart Rd SW Pacific WA 98047	800-426-8486	253-863-7777	769
Gordon's Jewelers Div Zale Corp 901 W Walnut Hill Ln Irving TX 75038 *Cust Svc	888-467-3661*	972-580-4000	402
Goria Enterprises PO Box 14489 Greensboro NC 27415	800-828-5879	336-375-5821	181
Gorilla Fund International. Dian Fossey 800 Cherokee Ave SE Atlanta GA 30315	800-851-0203	404-624-5881	48-3
Gorilla Sports 12440 E Imperial Hwy Suite 300 Norwalk CA 90651	800-447-7457	562-484-2000	349
Gorin's Homemade Cafe & Grill 4 Executive Pk E Suite 315 Atlanta GA 30329	888-489-7277	404-248-9900	657
Gorton Slade Co Inc 4433 W 42nd Pl Chicago IL 60632	800-524-8237	773-927-2400	292-5
Gorton's Inc 128 Rogers St Gloucester MA 01930	800-225-0572	978-283-3000	291-14
Goshen Chamber of Commerce 232 S Main St Goshen IN 46526	800-307-4204	574-533-2102	137
Goshen College 1700 S Main St Goshen IN 46526	800-348-7422	574-535-7000	163
Goshen News 114 S Main St PO Box 569 Goshen IN 46527	800-487-2151	574-533-2151	522-2
Gosiger Inc 108 McDonough St Dayton OH 45402	800-888-4188	937-228-5174	378
GoSolo Technologies Inc 1901 Ulmerton Rd Suite 400 Clearwater FL 33762	888-551-7656	727-821-6565	606
Gospel. International Church of the Foursquare 1910 W Sunset Blvd Suite 200 Los Angeles CA 90026	888-635-4234	213-989-4200	48-20
Gospel Light Publications 1957 Eastman Ave Ventura CA 93003	800-235-3415	805-644-9721	623-4
Gospel Publishing House 1445 N Boonville Ave Springfield MO 65802 *Orders	800-641-4310*	417-862-2781	614
Gospel Rescue Missions. Association of 1045 Swift Ave Kansas City MO 64116	800-624-5156	816-471-8020	48-20
Goss Inc 1511 Rt 8 Glenshaw PA 15116	800-367-4677	412-486-6100	798
Gossner Foods Inc 1051 N 1000 West Logan UT 84321	800-944-0454	435-752-9365	291-5
Gotham Distributing Corp 60 Portland Rd Conshohocken PA 19428	800-446-8426	610-649-7650	512
Gotham Insurance Co 913 3rd Ave 10th Fl New York NY 10022	800-367-0224	212-551-0600	384-4
GoTickets.com 201 Shannon Oaks Cir Cary NC 27512	800-775-1617	919-481-4868	735
Gottry Corp 175 Ensminger Rd Tonawanda NY 14150	800-836-6720	716-876-3800	571
Goucher College 1021 Dulaney Valley Rd Baltimore MD 21204	800-468-2437	410-337-6000	163
Gougler Industries Inc 705 Lake St Kent OH 44240	800-527-2282	330-673-5821	379
Gould & Eberhardt Gear Machinery Corp 2 Sutton Rd PO Box 190 Webster MA 01570	888-241-4757	508-943-5001	447
Gould Food Industries Center Ohio State University Howlett Hall Suite 140 2001 Fyffe Ct Columbus OH 43210	800-752-2751	614-292-7004	654
Gould & Goodrich Leather Inc 709 E McNeil St Lillington NC 27546	800-277-0732	910-893-2071	423
Gould JD Co Inc 4707 Massachusetts Ave Indianapolis IN 46218	800-634-6853	317-547-5289	777
Gould Paper Corp 11 Madison Ave 14th Fl New York NY 10010	800-275-4685	212-301-0000	543
Goulds Pumps Inc Goulds Water Technologies Group E Bayard St Ext Seneca Falls NY 13148	800-327-7700	315-568-2811	776
Gourmet Award Foods 7225 W Marcia Rd Milwaukee WI 53223	800-726-7205	414-365-7000	292-11
Gourmet Magazine 4 Times Sq New York NY 10036	800-365-2454	212-286-2860	449-11
Gouverneur Hotel Montreal (Place-Dupuis) 1415 rue Saint-Hubert Montreal QC H2L3Y9	888-910-1111	514-842-4881	372
Gouverneur Hotel Sainte-Foy 3030 Laurier Blvd Sainte-Foy QC G1V2M5	888-910-1111	418-651-3030	372
Gouverneur Talc Co Inc 1837 State Hwy 812 Gouverneur NY 13642	800-243-6064	315-287-0100	493-3
GovBenefits.gov Washington DC 20407	800-333-4636		336-11
Governing Boards of Universities & Colleges. Association of 1 Dupont Cir NW Suite 400 Washington DC 20036	800-356-6317	202-296-8400	49-5
Governing Magazine 1100 Connecticut Ave NW Suite 1300 Washington DC 20036	800-944-0922	202-862-8802	449-12
Government Accountants. Association of 2208 Mt Vernon Ave Alexandria VA 22301	800-242-7211	703-684-6931	49-1
Government Accounting & Auditing Update Newsletter 395 Hudson St New York NY 10014	800-431-9025	212-367-6300	521-7
Government Contracts Update Newsletter 11300 Rockville Pike Suite 1100 Rockville MD 20852 *Cust Svc	888-287-2223*	301-287-2700	521-7
Government Employees Credit Union of El Paso 7227 Viscount Blvd El Paso TX 79925	800-772-4328	915-778-9221	216
Government Employees Insurance Co (GEICO) 1 GEICO Plaza Washington DC 20076	800-841-3000	301-986-3000	384-4
Government Executive Magazine 1501 M St NW Suite 300 Washington DC 20005	800-207-8001	202-739-8400	449-12
Government Information Services 1725 K St NW Suite 700 Washington DC 20006	800-677-3789	202-872-4000	623-9
Government Liaison Services Inc 200 N Glebe Rd Suite 321 Arlington VA 22203	800-642-6564	703-524-8200	621
Government Micro Resources Inc 7403 Gateway Ct Manassas VA 20109 *Cust Svc	800-220-4672*	703-330-1199	178
Government Research Service PO Box 2067 Topeka KS 66601	800-346-6898	785-232-7720	623-2
Government Waste. Citizens Against 1301 Connecticut Ave NW Suite 400 Washington DC 20036	800-232-6479	202-467-5300	48-7
Governmental Purchasing. National Institute of 151 Spring St Suite 300 Herndon VA 20170	800-367-6447	703-736-8900	49-7
Governments. Council of State 2760 Research Park Dr PO Box 11910 Lexington KY 40578 *Sales	800-800-1910*	859-244-8000	49-7
Governor Calvert House 58 State Cir Annapolis MD 21401	800-847-8882	410-263-2641	373
Governor Hotel 611 SW 10th Ave Portland OR 97205	800-554-3456	503-224-3400	373
Governor's House Hotel 1615 Rhode Island Ave NW Washington DC 20036	800-821-4367	202-296-2100	373
Governor's House Hotel & Conference Center 2705 E South Blvd Montgomery AL 36116	866-535-5392	334-288-2800	373
Governor's Inn 210 Richards Blvd Sacramento CA 95814	800-999-6689	916-448-7224	373
Governor's Inn 700 W Sioux Ave Pierre SD 57501	888-315-2378	605-224-4200	373
Governors State University 1 University Pkwy University Park IL 60466	800-478-8478	708-534-5000	163
GovLoans.gov Washington DC 20405	800-333-4636		196
Gowan Inc 5550 Airline Dr Houston TX 77076	888-724-6926	713-696-5400	188-10
GP Deltapoint 6095 Marshalee Dr Elkridge MD 21075	888-843-4784	410-379-3600	193
GP Solo 750 N Lake Shore Dr Chicago IL 60611	800-285-2221	312-988-5000	449-15
GPA 1151 W 40th St Chicago IL 60609	800-395-9000	312-243-6860	543
GPB (Georgia Public Broadcasting) 260 14th St NW Atlanta GA 30318	800-222-6006	404-685-2400	620
GPB Education 260 14th St NW Atlanta GA 30318	888-501-8960	404-685-2550	620
GPO (US Government Printing Office) 732 N Capitol St NW Washington DC 20401	866-512-1800	202-512-0000	623-2
GQ: Gentlemen's Quarterly Magazine 4 Times Sq New York NY 10036	800-289-9330	212-286-2860	449-11
GR Herberger's Inc 600 W Saint Germain St Saint Cloud MN 56301	800-398-7896	320-251-5351	227
GR Sponaugle & Sons Inc 4391 Chambers Hill Rd Harrisburg PA 17111	800-866-7036	717-564-1515	188-10
Gra-Bell Truck Line Inc PO Box 1019 Holland MI 49422	800-632-5300	616-396-1453	769
GRABBER Performance Group 4600 Danvers Dr SE Grand Rapids MI 49512	800-423-1233	616-940-1914	566
Graber Olive House Inc 315 E 4th St Ontario CA 91764	800-996-5483	909-983-1761	333
Grace Bible College 1011 Aldon St SW Wyoming MI 49509	800-968-1887	616-538-2330	163
Grace College 200 Seminary Dr Winona Lake IN 46590	800-544-7223	574-372-5100	163
Grace University 1311 S 9th St Omaha NE 68108	800-383-1422	402-449-2800	163
Grace & Wild Inc 23689 Industrial Park Dr Farmington Hills MI 48335	800-451-6010	248-471-6010	502
Grace WR & Co 7500 Grace Dr Columbia MD 21044 *NYSE: GRA*	888-398-4646	410-531-4000	143
Graceland (Elvis Presley Mansion) 3734 Elvis Presley Blvd Memphis TN 38186	800-238-2000	901-332-3322	509
Graceland Fruit Inc 1123 Main St Frankfort MI 49635	800-352-7181	231-352-7181	291-18
Graceland University 1 University Pl Lamoni IA 50140	800-346-9208	641-784-5000	163
Graceland University 1401 W Truman Rd Independence MO 64050	800-833-0524	816-833-0524	163
GRACO Children's Products Inc 150 Oaklands Blvd Exton PA 19341	800-345-4109	610-884-8000	64
Graco Inc 88 11th Ave Minneapolis MN 55413 *NYSE: GGG* ■ *Cust Svc	800-328-0211*	612-623-6000	625
Grady Management Inc 8630 Fenton St Suite 625 Silver Spring MD 20910	800-544-7239	301-587-3330	641
Grady W Jones Co 3965 Old Getwell Rd Memphis TN 38118	800-727-5118	901-365-8830	378
Grady's American Grill 4220 Edison Lakes Pkwy Mishawaka IN 46545	800-589-3820	574-271-4600	657

Name / Address	City	State	ZIP	Toll-Free	Phone	Class
Graebel Van Lines Inc 16346 E Airport Circle	Aurora	CO	80011	**800-723-6683**	303-214-6680	508
Graef Windows Inc 365 McClurg Rd	Youngstown	OH	44512	**800-877-2911**	330-652-9999	232
Graff Californiawear 1515 E 15th St	Los Angeles	CA	90021	**800-421-8692**	213-749-0171	153-21
Graham Billy Evangelistic Assn 1 Billy Graham Pkwy PO Box 1270	Charlotte	NC	28201	**877-247-2426**	704-401-2432	48-20
Graham Co 1 Penn Sq W Graham Bldg	Philadelphia	PA	19102	**888-472-4262**	215-567-6300	383
Graham Corp 20 Florence Ave *AMEX: GHM* ■ *Orders	Batavia	NY	14020	**800-828-8150***	585-343-2216	379
Graham County Chamber of Commerce 1111 Thatcher Blvd	Safford	AZ	85546	**888-837-1841**	928-428-2511	137
Graham County Electric Co-op Inc PO Drawer B	Pima	AZ	85543	**800-577-9266**	928-485-2451	244
Graham-Field Health Products Inc 2935 Northeast Pkwy	Atlanta	GA	30360	**800-235-4661**	770-447-1609	469
Graham Professional Div Little Rapids Corp 2273 Larsen Rd PO Box 19100 *Cust Svc	Green Bay	WI	54304	**800-558-6765***	920-494-8701	566
Grain & Feed Assn. National 1250 I St NW Suite 1003	Washington	DC	20005	**800-680-9223**	202-289-0873	48-2
Grain Inspection Packers & Stockyards Administration 1400 Independence Ave SW 10th Fl.	Washington	DC	20250	**800-998-3447**	202-720-0219	336-1
Grain Marketing & Production Research Center USDA/ARS 1515 College Ave	Manhattan	KS	66502	**800-627-0388**	785-776-2701	654
Grainger WW Inc 100 Grainger Pkwy *NYSE: GWW*	Lake Forest	IL	60045	**888-361-8649**	847-535-1000	245
Gramercy Park Hotel 2 Lexington Ave	New York	NY	10010	**800-221-4083**	212-475-4320	373
GramTel USA PO Box 720	South Bend	IN	46624	**866-481-7622**	574-472-4726	178
Granby Zoo & Amazoo Water Park 525 St-Hubert St	Granby	QC	J2G5P3	**877-472-6299**	450-372-9113	811
Grand 1894 Opera House 2020 Postoffice St	Galveston	TX	77550	**800-821-1894**	409-765-1894	562
Grand Aire Express Inc 11777 W Airport Service Rd	Swanton	OH	43558	**800-704-7263**	419-865-1780	63
Grand America Hotel 555 S Main St	Salt Lake City	UT	84111	**800-621-4505**	801-258-6000	373
Grand Banks Yachts Ltd 2 Marina Plaza	Newport	RI	02840	**800-809-0909**	401-848-7550	91
Grand Beach Inn 198 E Grand Ave	Old Orchard Beach	ME	04064	**800-834-9696**	207-934-4621	373
Grand Blanc Cement Products 10709 S Center Rd	Grand Blanc	MI	48439	**800-875-7500**	810-694-7500	181
Grand Canyon National Park Lodges PO Box 699	Grand Canyon	AZ	86023	**888-297-2757**	928-638-2631	368
Grand Canyon Trust 2601 N Fort Valley Rd	Flagstaff	AZ	86001	**888-428-5550**	928-774-7488	48-13
Grand Canyon University 3300 W Camelback Rd	Phoenix	AZ	85017	**800-800-9776**	602-249-3300	163
Grand Casino Biloxi 265 Beach Blvd	Biloxi	MS	39530	**800-946-2946**	228-436-2946	133
Grand Casino Gulfport 3215 W Beach Blvd	Gulfport	MS	39501	**800-946-7777**	228-870-7777	133
Grand Casino Hinckley 777 Lady Luck Dr	Hinckley	MN	55037	**800-472-6321**	320-384-7777	133
Grand Casino Mille Lacs 777 Grand Ave PO Box 343	Onamia	MN	56359	**800-626-5825**	320-532-7777	133
Grand Casino Tunica 13615 Old Hwy 61 N	Robinsonville	MS	38664	**800-946-4946**	662-363-2788	133
Grand Champions Resort. Hyatt 44-600 Indian Wells Ln	Indian Wells	CA	92210	**800-233-1234**	760-341-1000	655
Grand Choice Foods 1131 Dayton Ave	Ames	IA	50010	**800-250-3860**	515-232-2273	291-26
Grand Country Inn Grand Country Sq 1945 W Hwy 76	Branson	MO	65616	**800-828-9068**	417-335-3535	373
Grand Cypress Resort. Hyatt Regency 1 Grand Cypress Blvd	Orlando	FL	32836	**800-233-1234**	407-239-1234	655
Grand Electric Co-op Inc PO Box 39	Bison	SD	57620	**800-592-1803**	605-244-5211	244
Grand European Tours 4000 Kruse Way Pl Bldg 2 Suite 355	Lake Oswego	OR	97035	**800-552-5545**	503-635-9627	748
Grand Forks (Greater) Convention & Visitors Bureau 4251 Gateway Dr	Grand Forks	ND	58203	**800-866-4566**	701-746-0444	205
Grand Geneva Resort & Spa 7036 Grand Geneva Way	Lake Geneva	WI	53147	**800-558-3417**	262-248-8811	655
Grand Harbor Resort & Waterpark 350 Bell St	Dubuque	IA	52001	**866-690-4006**	563-609-4000	655
Grand Haven Tribune 101 N 3rd St	Grand Haven	MI	49417	**800-874-7180**	616-842-6400	522-2
Grand Hotel 286 Grand Dr	Mackinac Island	MI	49757	**800-334-7263**	906-847-3331	655
Grand Hotel Minneapolis 615 2nd Ave S	Minneapolis	MN	55402	**866-843-4726**	612-339-3655	373
Grand Hyatt Hotels 71 S Walker Dr	Chicago	IL	60606	**800-233-1234**	312-750-1234	369
Grand Island Independent 422 W 1st St PO Box 1208	Grand Island	NE	68802	**800-658-3160**	308-382-1000	522-2
Grand Junction Area Chamber of Commerce 360 Grand Ave	Grand Junction	CO	81501	**800-352-5286**	970-242-3214	137
Grand Junction Visitors & Convention Bureau 740 Horizon Dr	Grand Junction	CO	81506	**800-962-2547**	970-244-1480	205
Grand Lodge Crested Butte 6 Emmons Rd	Mount Crested Butte	CO	81225	**888-823-4446**	970-349-8000	655
Grand Montana. Holiday Inn 5500 Midland Rd	Billings	MT	59101	**800-465-4329**	406-248-7701	373
Grand Oaks Hotel 2315 Green Mountain Dr	Branson	MO	65616	**800-553-6423**	417-336-6423	373
Grand Opera House 818 N Market St	Wilmington	DE	19801	**800-374-7263**	302-652-5577	562
Grand Pacific Palisades Resort & Hotel 5805 Armada Dr	Carlsbad	CA	92008	**800-725-4723**	760-827-3200	655
Grand Pacific Resorts 5900 Pasteur Ct Suite 200	Carlsbad	CA	92008	**800-444-3515**	760-431-8500	738
Grand Palms Hotel & Golf Resort 110 Grand Palms Dr	Pembroke Pines	FL	33027	**800-327-9246**	954-431-8800	655
Grand Portage Lodge & Casino PO Box 233	Grand Portage	MN	55605	**800-543-1384**	218-475-2401	655
Grand Prairie Co-op Inc 1 S Calhoun St	Tolono	IL	61880	**800-252-4724**	217-485-6630	271
Grand Rapids Area Chamber of Commerce 1 NW 3rd St	Grand Rapids	MN	55744	**800-472-6366**	218-326-6619	137
Grand Rapids Area Convention & Visitors Bureau 1 NW 3rd St	Grand Rapids	MN	55744	**800-355-9740**	218-326-9607	205
Grand Rapids Civic Theatre 30 N Division Ave	Grand Rapids	MI	49503	**866-455-4728**	616-222-6650	562
Grand Rapids Label Co 2351 Oak Industrial Dr NE	Grand Rapids	MI	49505	**800-552-5215**	616-459-8134	404
Grand Rapids Press 155 Michigan St NW	Grand Rapids	MI	49503	**800-878-1400**	616-459-1400	522-2
Grand Rapids Rampage 130 Fulton St W	Grand Rapids	MI	49503	**888-595-4878**	616-559-1871	703
Grand Rapids/Kent County Convention & Visitors Bureau 171 Monroe Ave NW Suite 700	Grand Rapids	MI	49503	**800-678-9859**	616-459-8287	205
Grand Rental Station 203 Jandus Rd	Cary	IL	60013	**800-833-3004**	847-462-5440	261-3
Grand River Infrastructure Inc 2701 Chicago Dr SW	Grand Rapids	MI	49519	**800-968-2662**	616-534-9645	181
Grand Strand Aviation DBA Ramp 66 2800 Terminal St	North Myrtle Beach	SC	29582	**800-433-8918**	843-272-5337	63
Grand Strand Regional Medical Ctr 809 82nd Pkwy	Myrtle Beach	SC	29572	**800-222-1859**	843-692-1000	366-2
Grand Summit Hotel 570 Springfield Ave	Summit	NJ	07901	**800-346-0773**	908-273-3000	373
Grand Targhee Resort PO Box SKI	Alta	WY	83422	**800-827-4433**	307-353-2300	655
Grand Teton Lodge Co PO Box 240	Moran	WY	83013	**800-628-9988**	307-543-3100	369
Grand Traverse Resort & Spa 100 Grand Traverse Village Blvd PO Box 404	Acme	MI	49610	**800-748-0303**	231-938-2100	655
Grand Valley State University 1 Campus Dr	Allendale	MI	49401	**800-748-0246**	616-331-2025	163
Grand Victoria Casino & Resort by Hyatt 600 Grand Victoria Dr	Rising Sun	IN	47040	**800-472-6311**	812-438-1234	133
Grand View College 1200 Grandview Ave	Des Moines	IA	50316	**800-444-6083**	515-263-2800	163
Grand View Lodge 23521 Nokomis Ave	Nisswa	MN	56468	**800-432-3788**	218-963-2234	655
Grand View Media Group Inc 200 Croft St Suite 1	Birmingham	AL	35242	**888-431-2877**	205-262-4600	623-9
Grand Wailea Resort & Spa 3850 Wailea Alanui Dr	Wailea	HI	96753	**800-888-6100**	808-875-1234	655
Grandmother's Buttons Museum 9814 Royal St	Saint Francisville	LA	70775	**800-580-6941**	225-635-4107	509
Grandoe Corp PO Box 713	Gloversville	NY	12078	**800-472-6363**	518-725-8641	153-8
Grandprix Assn. American 1301 6th Ave W Suite 406	Bradenton	FL	34205	**800-237-8924**	941-744-5465	48-22
Grandwell Industries Inc 121 Quantum St	Holly Springs	NC	27540	**800-338-6554**	919-557-1221	692
Grange Co-op Supply Assn 89 Alder St	Central Point	OR	97502	**800-888-6317**	541-664-1261	438
Grange Guardian 650 S Front St	Columbus	OH	43206	**800-422-0550**	614-445-2900	384-4
Grange Life Insurance Co 650 S Front St	Columbus	OH	43206	**800-422-0550**	614-445-2900	384-2
Grange Mutual Casualty Co 650 S Front St	Columbus	OH	43206	**800-422-0550**	614-445-2900	384-4
Grange. National 1616 H St NW	Washington	DC	20006	**888-447-2643**	202-628-3507	48-2
Grangeville Environmental Services 585 McAllister St	Hanover	PA	17331	**866-437-5151**	717-637-6152	84
Granit Bronz Inc 202 S 3rd Ave	Cold Spring	MN	56320	**800-328-2312**	320-685-4628	710
Granite City Electric Supply Co 19 Quincy Ave	Quincy	MA	02169	**800-850-9400**	617-472-6500	357
Granite City Journal 2 Executive Dr	Collinsville	IL	62234	**800-766-3278**	618-877-7700	522-4
Granite Furniture Co 1050 E 2100 South	Salt Lake City	UT	84106	**800-470-9077**	801-486-3333	316
Granite Group Wholesalers LLC 6 Storrs St	Concord	NH	03301	**800-258-3690**	603-224-1901	601
Granite Knitwear Inc 805 S Salberry Ave Hwy 52S	Granite Quarry	NC	28072	**800-476-9944**	704-279-5526	153-12
Granite State Electric Co 55 Bearfoot Rd	Northborough	MA	01532	**800-322-3223**	508-357-4501	774
Graniterock Co PO Box 50001	Watsonville	CA	95077	**800-327-1711**	831-768-2000	190-1
Granitize Products Inc 11022 Vulcan St	South Gate	CA	90280	**800-553-6866**	562-923-5438	149
Grant Assembly Technologies 90 Silliman Ave	Bridgeport	CT	06605	**800-227-2150**	203-366-4557	448
Grant Chemical Div Ferro Corp 111 W Irene Rd	Zachary	LA	70791	**800-325-3578**	225-654-6801	142
Grant Geophysical Inc PO Box 219950	Houston	TX	77218	**800-390-5530**	281-398-9503	258
Grant Piston Rings 1360 N Jefferson St	Anaheim	CA	92807	**800-854-3540**	714-996-0050	128
Grant Plaza Hotel 465 Grant Ave	San Francisco	CA	94108	**800-472-6899**	415-434-3883	373
Grant Prideco Inc 400 N San Houston Pkwy E Suite 900 *NYSE: GRP*	Houston	TX	77060	**866-472-6861**	281-878-8000	584
Grantham Distributing Co Inc 2685 Hansrob Rd	Orlando	FL	32804	**800-226-4010**	407-299-6446	82-3
Grants Pass Chamber of Commerce 1995 NW Vine St PO Box 970	Grants Pass	OR	97528	**800-547-5927**	541-476-7717	137
Grants Pass Visitors & Convention Bureau 1995 NW Vine St	Grants Pass	OR	97526	**800-547-5927**	541-476-5510	205
Grants.gov Dept of Health & Human Services 200 Independence Ave SW	Washington	DC	20201	**800-518-4726**		196
Grants/Cibola County Chamber of Commerce 100 N Iron St	Grants	NM	87020	**800-748-2142**	505-287-4802	137
Granville Market Letter PO Box 413006	Kansas City	MO	64141	**800-876-5388**	816-474-5353	521-9
Grapevine Canyon Ranch Inc PO Box 302	Pearce	AZ	85625	**800-245-9202**	520-826-3185	238

Name / Address	City	State	Zip	Toll-Free	Phone	Class
Grapevine Convention & Visitors Bureau 1 Liberty Pk Plaza	Grapevine	TX	76051	**800-457-6338**	817-410-3185	205
Graphel Corp 6115 Centre Pk Dr	West Chester	OH	45071	**800-255-1104**	513-779-6166	490
Graphic Arts. American Institute of 164 5th Ave	New York	NY	10010	**800-548-1634**	212-807-1990	48-4
Graphic Arts Mutual Insurance Co PO Box 530	Utica	NY	13503	**800-274-1914**	315-734-2000	384-4
Graphic Arts Technical Foundation. Printing Industries of America/ 200 Deer Run Rd	Sewickley	PA	15143	**800-910-4283**	412-741-6860	49-16
Graphic Converting Inc 6701 W Oakton St	Niles	IL	60714	**800-447-1935**	847-967-3300	544
Graphic Imaging Assn. Specialty 10015 Main St	Fairfax	VA	22031	**888-385-3588**	703-385-1335	49-16
Graphic Packaging International 4455 Table Mountain Dr	Golden	CO	80403	**800-677-2886**	303-215-4600	102
NYSE: GPK						
Graphic Sciences Inc 7515 NE Ambassador Pl Suite L	Portland	OR	97220	**888-546-4465**	503-460-0203	381
Graphic Specialties Inc 3110 Washington Ave N	Minneapolis	MN	55411	**800-486-4605**	612-522-5287	692
Graphic Technology Inc 301 Gardner Dr	New Century	KS	66031	**800-767-9930**	913-829-8000	404
Graphics Assn. International Engraved 306 Plus Park Blvd	Nashville	TN	37217	**800-821-3138***	615-366-1094	49-4
*x209						
Graphics Microsystems Inc (GMI) 484 Oakmead Pkwy	Sunnyvale	CA	94085	**800-336-1464**	408-745-7745	617
Graphique De France 9 State St	Woburn	MA	01801	**800-444-1464***	781-935-3405	130
*Sales						
Graphite Sales Inc 16710 W Park Circle Dr	Chagrin Falls	OH	44023	**800-321-4147**	440-543-8221	490
Graphnet Inc 40 Foltron St 28th Fl	New York	NY	10038	**800-327-1800**	212-994-1100	721
Grasan Equipment 440 S Illinois Ave	Mansfield	OH	44907	**800-526-4602**	419-526-4440	206
Grason PO Box 669007	Charlotte	NC	28254	**800-487-0433**		96
Grason-Stadler Inc 5225 Verona Rd Bldg 2	Madison	WI	53711	**800-700-2282**	608-441-2323	468
Grass Roots Publishing Co Inc Hochman Assoc 908 Oaktree Rd Suite H	South Plainfield	NJ	07080	**877-207-9007**	908-222-1811	623-9
Grassland Council. American Forage & PO Box 94	Georgetown	TX	78627	**800-944-2342**		48-2
Grassland Dairy Products Co Inc PO Box 160	Greenwood	WI	54437	**800-428-8837**	715-267-6182	291-3
Gratz College 7605 Old York Rd	Melrose Park	PA	19027	**800-475-4635**	215-635-7300	163
Graulich International Inc 6411 NW 35th Ave	Miami	FL	33147	**800-836-2709**	305-836-1700	306
Gravel Assn. National Stone Sand & 1605 King St	Alexandria	VA	22314	**800-342-1415**	703-525-8788	49-3
Gravely International Inc 655 W Ryan St	Brillion	WI	54110	**888-927-4367***	920-756-2141	420
*Cust Svc						
Graver Technologies Inc 200 Lake Dr	Glasgow	DE	19702	**800-249-1990**	302-731-1700	793
Graver Water Systems Inc 750 Walnut Ave	Cranford	NJ	07016	**877-472-8379**	908-653-4200	793
Graves Brothers Co 8465 Old Dixie Hwy PO Box 700277	Wabasso	FL	32970	**877-999-8499***	772-589-4356	310-2
*Sales						
Graves Earl G Ltd 130 5th Ave 10th Fl	New York	NY	10011	**800-727-7777**	212-242-8000	623-9
Graves Fire Protection PO Box 451	Lunenburg	MA	01462	**800-214-1456**	978-345-0165	667
Graves Lumber Co 1315 S Cleveland-Massillon Rd	Copley	OH	44321	**877-500-5515**	330-666-1115	489
Graves Piano & Organ Co Inc 5798 Karl Rd	Columbus	OH	43229	**800-686-4322**	614-847-4322	515
Gravograph-New Hermes Inc 2200 Northmont Pkwy	Duluth	GA	30096	**800-843-7637**	770-623-0331	617
Gray Cary Ware & Freidenrich LLP 401 B St Suite 2000	San Diego	CA	92101	**888-429-4293**	619-699-2700	419
Gray FJ & Co 217-44 98th Ave	Queens Village	NY	11429	**800-523-3320**	718-217-2943	325
Gray James N Construction Co Inc 10 Quality St	Lexington	KY	40507	**800-950-4729**	859-281-5000	185
Gray Line of Portland 11655 SW Pacific Hwy	Portland	OR	97223	**888-684-3322**	503-684-3322	748
Gray Panthers 733 15th St NW Suite 437	Washington	DC	20005	**800-280-5362**	202-737-6637	48-6
Gray Rocks Resort & Convention Center 2322 rue Labelle	Mont-Tremblant	QC	J8E1T8	**800-567-6767**	819-425-2771	655
Gray & Sons Inc PO Box 8	Butler	MD	21023	**800-254-0752**	410-771-4311	187-4
Gray Truck Line Co PO Box 1406	Lake Alfred	FL	33850	**800-282-6884**	863-956-3431	769
Graybar Electric Co Inc 34 N Meramec Ave	Saint Louis	MO	63105	**800-472-9227**	314-573-9200	245
Grayhill Inc 561 Hillgrove Ave	La Grange	IL	60525	**800-244-0559**	708-354-1040	715
Graymark Security Group 7301 NW 4th St Suite 110	Plantation	FL	33317	**800-881-3242**	954-581-5575	392
Graymont Dolime (OH) Inc PO Box 158	Genoa	OH	43430	**800-537-4489**	419-855-8336	432
Graymont PA Inc PO Box 448	Bellefonte	PA	16823	**888-472-9086***	814-355-4744	432
*Orders						
Graymont Western US Inc 3950 S 700 E Suite 301	Salt Lake City	UT	84107	**800-814-7532**	801-262-3942	432
Grays Harbor Chamber of Commerce 506 Duffy St	Aberdeen	WA	98520	**800-321-1924**	360-532-1924	137
Grayson-Collin Electric Co-op Inc PO Box 548	Van Alstyne	TX	75495	**800-967-5235**	903-482-7100	244
GRE America Inc 425 Harbor Blvd	Belmont	CA	94002	**800-233-5973**	650-591-1400	496
Grease Monkey International Inc 633 17th St Suite 400	Denver	CO	80202	**800-822-7706**	303-308-1660	62-5
Great American Bagel 519 N Cass Ave	Westmont	IL	60559	**888-224-3563**	630-963-3393	69
Great American Coach Co 4220 Howard Ave	New Orleans	LA	70125	**866-596-2698**	504-212-5925	108
Great American Cookie Co Inc 4685 Frederick Dr SW	Atlanta	GA	30336	**800-332-4856**	404-696-1700	69
Great American Country 9697 E Mineral Ave	Englewood	CO	80112	**800-727-5663**	303-792-3111	725
Great American Financial Resources Inc 250 E 5th St	Cincinnati	OH	45202	**800-438-3398**	513-333-5300	355-4
NYSE: GFR						
Great American Health Foods 4075 40th Ave SW	Fargo	ND	58108	**800-437-2733**	701-356-2760	291-11
Great American Life Assurance Co of Puerto Rico Inc PO Box 363786	San Juan	PR	00936	**800-980-7651**	787-758-4888	384-2
Great American Life Insurance Co 525 Vine St 7th Fl	Cincinnati	OH	45202	**800-854-3649**	513-357-3300	384-2
Great American Office LLC 337 Rt 101	Bedford	NH	03110	**888-596-9996**	603-472-9996	524
Great American Products Inc 1661 S Seguin Ave	New Braunfels	TX	78130	**800-341-4436**	830-620-4400	693
Great American Stock 5200 Pasadena Ave Suite C	Albuquerque	NM	87113	**800-624-5834**	505-892-7747	582
Great Arrow Graphics 2495 Main St Suite 457	Buffalo	NY	14214	**800-835-0490**	716-836-0408	130
Great Basin Gold Ltd 800 W Pender St Suite 1020	Vancouver	BC	V6C2V6	**800-667-2114**	604-684-6365	492
AMEX: GBN						
Great Basin Visitor Assn 507 Main St	Klamath Falls	OR	97601	**800-445-6728**	541-884-0666	205
Great Bay Distributors 2310 Starkey Rd	Largo	FL	33771	**800-231-4283**	727-584-8626	82-1
Great Bend Feeding Inc 355 NW 30 Ave	Great Bend	KS	67530	**800-792-2508**	620-792-2508	11-1
Great Bend Mfg Co Inc 2501 Griffin Ave	Selma	AL	36701	**800-825-1701**	334-872-6261	260
Great Bend Tribune 2012 Forest St PO Box 228	Great Bend	KS	67530	**800-950-8742**	620-792-1211	522-2
Great Books Foundation 35 E Wacker Dr Suite 2300	Chicago	IL	60601	**800-222-5870**	312-332-5870	48-11
Great Central Insurance Co 3625 N Sheridan Rd	Peoria	IL	61633	**800-447-1972**	309-688-8571	384-4
Great Clips Inc 7700 France Ave S Suite 425	Minneapolis	MN	55435	**800-999-5959**	952-893-9088	79
Great Divide Lodge 550 Village Rd	Breckenridge	CO	80424	**800-321-8444**	970-453-4500	373
Great Earth Vitamin Stores 1101 S Millikin Ave Suite A	Ontario	CA	91761	**800-374-7328**		350
Great Falls Area Chamber of Commerce 710 1st Ave N	Great Falls	MT	59401	**800-735-8535**	406-761-4434	137
Great Falls Tribune 205 River Dr S	Great Falls	MT	59405	**800-438-6600**	406-791-1444	522-2
Great Frame Up Systems Inc 101 S Hanley Rd Suite 1280	Saint Louis	MO	63105	**866-719-8200**	314-719-8200	45
Great Harvest Bread Co 28 S Montana St	Dillon	MT	59725	**800-442-0424**	406-683-6842	69
Great Lakes Airlines 1022 Airport Pkwy	Cheyenne	WY	82001	**800-554-5111**	307-432-7000	26
Great Lakes Aquarium 353 Harbor Dr	Duluth	MN	55802	**877-866-3474**	218-740-3474	40
Great Lakes Aviation Ltd DBA Great Lakes Airlines 1022 Airport Pkwy	Cheyenne	WY	82001	**800-554-5111**	307-432-7000	26
Great Lakes Cartage Co PO Box 4704	Youngstown	OH	44515	**800-228-4274***	330-793-9331	769
*Cust Svc						
Great Lakes Cheese Co Inc 17825 Great Lakes Pkwy	Hiram	OH	44234	**800-677-7181**	440-834-2500	291-5
Great Lakes Christian College 6211 W Willow Hwy	Lansing	MI	48917	**800-937-4522***	517-321-0242	163
*Admissions						
Great Lakes Cruise Co 3270 Washtenaw Ave	Ann Arbor	MI	48104	**888-891-0203**	734-677-0900	217
Great Lakes Dredge & Dock Co 2122 York Rd	Oak Brook	IL	60523	**800-323-7100**	630-574-3000	187-5
Great Lakes Energy Co-op 1323 Boyne Ave	Boyne City	MI	49712	**888-485-2537**		244
Great Lakes Filter 301 Arch Ave	Hillsdale	MI	49242	**800-521-8565**		19
Great Lakes Industrial Technology Center 20445 Emerald Pkwy SW Suite 200	Cleveland	OH	44135	**800-472-6785**	216-898-6400	654
Great Lakes Packaging Corp W 190 N 11393 Carnegie Dr	Germantown	WI	53022	**800-261-4572**	262-255-2100	101
Great Lakes Packers Inc 400 Great Lakes Pkwy PO Box 366	Bellevue	OH	44811	**800-624-8464**	419-483-2956	12-1
Great Lakes Towing Co 50 Public Sq 1800 Terminal Tower	Cleveland	OH	44113	**800-321-3663**	216-621-4854	457
Great Lakes United (GLU) Buffalo State College Cassety Hall 1300 Elmwood Ave	Buffalo	NY	14222	**800-846-0142**	716-886-0142	48-13
Great Mall of the Bay Area 447 Great Mall Dr	Milpitas	CA	95035	**800-625-5229**	408-945-4022	452
Great Mall of the Great Plains 20700 W 151st St	Olathe	KS	66061	**888-386-6255**	913-829-6748	452
Great Neck Saw Mfg Inc 165 E 2nd St	Mineola	NY	11501	**800-457-0600***	516-746-5352	670
*Cust Svc						
Great North American Cos 2828 Forest Ln Suite 2000	Dallas	TX	75234	**800-527-2782**	972-481-6100	523
Great Northern Corp 395 Stroebe Rd	Appleton	WI	54914	**800-236-3671**	920-739-3671	101
Great Northern Insurance Co 15 Mountain View Rd	Warren	NJ	07059	**800-252-4670**	908-903-2000	384-4
Great Plains Health Alliance Inc 625 3rd St	Phillipsburg	KS	67661	**800-432-2779**	785-543-2111	348
Great Plains Industries Inc 5252 E 36th St N	Wichita	KS	67220	**800-835-0113***	316-686-7361	627
*Sales						
Great Plains Packaging Co 2000 Summit Ave	Hastings	NE	68902	**800-456-1366**	402-463-1366	102
Great Plains Regional Medical Center 601 W Leota St	North Platte	NE	69101	**800-662-0011**	308-696-8000	366-2
Great Plains-Rocky Mountain Hazardous Substance Research Center Kansas State University Ward Hall Rm 104	Manhattan	KS	66506	**800-798-7796**	785-532-6519	654
Great Planes Model Distributors Co 1608 Interstate Dr	Champaign	IL	61826	**800-637-7660**	217-398-6300	750
Great River Medical Center PO Box 108	Blytheville	AR	72316	**800-557-5591**	870-838-7300	366-2
Great Seats Inc 7338 Baltimore Ave Suite 108A	College Park	MD	20740	**800-664-5056**	301-985-6250	735
Great Smokies Diagnostic Laboratory 63 Zillicoa St	Asheville	NC	28801	**800-522-4762**	828-253-0621	409

Name / Address	City	State	Zip	Toll-Free	Phone	Class
Great Source Education Group 181 Ballardvale St.	Wilmington	MA	01887	**800-289-4490**	978-661-1300	242
Great Southern Bancorp Inc PO Box 9009GS *NASDAQ: GSBC* ■ *Cust Svc	Springfield	MO	65808	**800-749-7113***	417-887-4400	355-2
Great Southern Bank FSB 1451 E Battlefield Rd	Springfield	MO	65804	**800-749-7113**	417-887-4400	71
Great Southern Coaches Inc 900 Burke Ave	Jonesboro	AR	72401	**800-251-5569**	870-935-5569	108
Great Southern Life Insurance Co PO Box 410288	Kansas City	MO	64141	**800-231-0801**	816-391-2000	384-2
Great Southern Wood Preserving Inc PO Box 610	Abbeville	AL	36310	**800-633-7539**	334-585-2291	806
Great Web Sites for Kids American Library Assn 50 E Huron St.	Chicago	IL	60611	**800-545-2433**	312-944-6780	677
Great West Casualty Co 1100 W 29th St	South Sioux City	NE	68776	**800-228-8602**	402-494-2411	384-4
Great-West Healthcare 8525 E Orchard Rd.	Greenwood Village	CO	80111	**800-839-6631**		384-3
Great-West Life & Annuity Insurance Co PO Box 1700	Denver	CO	80201	**800-537-2033**	303-737-3000	384-2
Great Western Mfg Co Inc PO Box 149	Leavenworth	KS	66048	**800-682-3121**	913-682-2291	293
Great Western Pet Supply 2001 N Black Canyon Hwy.	Phoenix	AZ	85009	**800-646-3611**	602-255-0166	568
Great Wraps! 4 Executive Pk E Suite 315	Atlanta	GA	30329	**888-489-7277**	404-248-9900	657
Greater Akron Chamber 1 Cascade Plaza 17th Fl.	Akron	OH	44308	**800-621-8001**	330-376-5550	137
Greater Alton/Twin Rivers Convention & Visitors Bureau 200 Piasa St	Alton	IL	62002	**800-258-6645**	618-465-6676	205
Greater Atlantic Financial Corp 10700 Parkridge Blvd Suite P50 *NASDAQ: GAFC*	Reston	VA	20191	**800-296-5581**	703-391-1300	355-2
Greater Bangor Convention & Visitors Bureau 1 Cumberland Pl Suite 300	Bangor	ME	04401	**800-916-6673**	207-947-5205	205
Greater Bay Bancorp 2860 W Bayshore Rd *NASDAQ: GBBK*	Palo Alto	CA	94301	**800-226-5262**	650-813-8200	355-2
Greater Big Rapids Convention & Visitors Bureau 246 N State St	Big Rapids	MI	49307	**888-229-4386**	231-796-7640	205
Greater Binghamton Chamber of Commerce 49 Court St	Binghamton	NY	13902	**800-836-6740**	607-772-8860	137
Greater Bridgeport Conference & Vistors Center 164 W Main St	Bridgeport	WV	26330	**800-368-4324**	304-842-7272	205
Greater Cedar Creek Lake Area Chamber of Commerce 1907 W Main St.	Gun Barrel City	TX	75156	**877-222-5253**	903-887-3152	137
Greater Columbus Chamber of Commerce 1200 6th Ave	Columbus	GA	31902	**800-360-8552**	706-327-1566	137
Greater Columbus Convention Center 400 N High St.	Columbus	OH	43215	**800-626-0241**	614-827-2500	204
Greater Conroe-Lake Conroe Area Chamber of Commerce 505 W Davis St	Conroe	TX	77301	**800-283-6645**	936-756-6644	137
Greater Conroe/Lake Conroe Area Chamber of Commerce PO Box 2347	Conroe	TX	77305	**800-283-6645**	936-756-6644	137
Greater Hutchinson Convention & Visitors Bureau 117 N Walnut St	Hutchinson	KS	67501	**800-691-4282**	620-662-3391	205
Greater Jackson County Chamber of Commerce PO Box 973	Scottsboro	AL	35768	**800-259-5508**	256-259-5500	137
Greater Johnstown/Cambria County Convention & Visitors Bureau 416 Main St Suite 100	Johnstown	PA	15901	**800-237-8590**	814-536-7993	205
Greater Laconia Transit Agency 50 Airport Rd	Gilford	NH	03249	**800-294-2496**	603-528-2496	109
Greater Lafayette Convention & Visitors Bureau 301 Frontage Rd	Lafayette	IN	47905	**800-872-6648**	765-447-9999	205
Greater Louisville Inc 614 W Main St.	Louisville	KY	40202	**800-500-1066**	502-625-0000	137
Greater Mankato Chamber & Convention Bureau 112 S Riverfront Dr.	Mankato	MN	56002	**800-657-4733**	507-345-4519	205
Greater Merrimack Valley Convention & Visitors Bureau 9 Central St Suite 201	Lowell	MA	01852	**800-443-3332**	978-459-6150	205
Greater Miami & the Beaches Hotel Assn 407 Lincoln Rd Suite 10G	Miami Beach	FL	33139	**800-531-3553**	305-531-3553	368
Greater Naples Marco Island Everglades Convention & Visitors Bureau 3050 N Horseshoe Dr Suite 218	Naples	FL	34104	**800-688-3600**	239-403-2425	205
Greater New Braunfels Chamber of Commerce PO Box 311417	New Braunfels	TX	78131	**800-572-2626**	830-625-2385	205
Greater North Dakota Assn PO Box 2639	Bismarck	ND	58502	**800-382-1405**	701-222-0929	138
Greater Oklahoma City Chamber of Commerce 123 Park Ave	Oklahoma City	OK	73102	**800-616-1114**	405-297-8900	137
Greater Omaha Packing Co PO Box 7566	Omaha	NE	68107	**800-747-5400**	402-731-3480	465
Greater Phoenix Convention & Visitors Bureau 400 E Van Buren St 1 Arizona Ctr Suite 600	Phoenix	AZ	85004	**877-225-5749**	602-254-6500	205
Greater Pueblo Chamber of Commerce 302 N Santa Fe Ave	Pueblo	CO	81003	**800-233-3446**	719-542-1704	137
Greater Pueblo Chamber of Commerce & Visitors Council 210 N Santa Fe	Pueblo	CO	81003	**800-233-3446**	719-542-1704	205
Greater Richmond Convention Center 403 N 3rd St	Richmond	VA	23219	**800-370-9004**	804-783-7300	204
Greater Rome Convention & Visitors Bureau PO Box 5823	Rome	GA	30162	**800-444-1834**	706-295-5576	205
Greater Saint Charles Convention & Visitors Bureau 230 S Main St	Saint Charles	MO	63301	**800-366-2427**	636-946-7776	205
Greater Shreveport Chamber of Commerce 400 Edwards St	Shreveport	LA	71101	**800-448-5432**	318-677-2500	137
Greater Susquehanna Valley Chamber of Commerce 104 S Susquehanna Trail PO Box 10	Shamokin Dam	PA	17876	**800-410-2880**	570-743-4100	137
Greater Tacoma Bed & Breakfast Reservation Service 619 N 'K' St	Tacoma	WA	98403	**800-406-4088**	253-752-8175	368
Greater Tacoma Convention & Trade Center 1500 Broadway Plaza	Tacoma	WA	98402	**888-227-3705**	253-830-6601	204
Greater Talent Network Inc 437 5th Ave 7th Fl	New York	NY	10016	**800-326-4211**	212-645-4200	699
Greater Winter Haven Area Chamber of Commerce 401 Ave 'B' NW	Winter Haven	FL	33881	**800-871-7027**	863-293-2138	137
Greater Woodfield Convention & Visitors Bureau 1430 N Meacham Rd Suite 1400	Schaumburg	IL	60173	**800-847-4849**	847-490-1010	205
Greater Yellowstone Coalition (GYC) 13 S Willson Ave Suite 2	Bozeman	MT	59775	**800-775-1834**	406-586-1593	48-13
Greek Hotel & Cruise Reservation Center 17280 Newhope St Suite 18	Fountain Valley	CA	92708	**800-736-5717**	714-641-3118	368
Greeley Convention & Visitors Bureau 902 7th Ave	Greeley	CO	80631	**800-449-3866**	970-352-3567	205
Greeley & Hansen 100 S Wacker Dr Suite 1400	Chicago	IL	60606	**800-837-9779**	312-558-9000	258
Greeley Tribune 501 8th Ave.	Greeley	CO	80631	**800-275-0321**	970-352-0211	522-2
Green Bay Botanical Garden PO Box 12644	Green Bay	WI	54307	**877-355-4224**	920-490-9457	98
Green Bay Dressed Beef Inc PO Box 8547	Green Bay	WI	54308	**800-345-0293**	920-437-4311	291-26
Green Bay Packaging Inc 1700 N Webster Ct.	Green Bay	WI	54302	**800-558-4008**	920-433-5111	538
Green Bay Packaging Inc Mill Div 1700 N Webster Ct.	Green Bay	WI	54302	**800-558-4008**	920-433-5111	551
Green Bay Press-Gazette PO Box 23430	Green Bay	WI	54305	**800-289-8221**	920-431-8400	522-2
Green Bearing Co 9801 Harvard Ave.	Cleveland	OH	44105	**800-367-9014**	216-883-7800	77
Green Bull Inc 11225 Bluegrass Pkwy	Louisville	KY	40299	**800-558-2855**	502-267-5577	412
Green Burrito 401 Carl Karcher Way	Anaheim	CA	92801	**800-422-4141**	714-774-5796	657
Green Circle Growers Inc 15650 SR-511	Oberlin	OH	44074	**800-533-4266**	440-775-1411	363
Green Hills Software Inc 30 W Sola St	Santa Barbara	CA	93101	**800-765-4733**	805-965-6044	176-2
Green Lawn Care 476 Evans Ave.	Etobicoke	ON	M8W2T9	**800-387-3426**	416-253-6540	421
Green Mountain Coffee Roasters Inc 33 Coffee Ln *NASDAQ: GMCR* ■ *Cust Svc	Waterbury	VT	05676	**800-432-4627***	802-244-5621	291-7
Green Mountain College 1 College Cir.	Poultney	VT	05764	**800-776-6675**	802-287-8000	163
Green Mountain Energy Co 3815 Capital of Texas Hwy Suite 100 *Cust Svc	Austin	TX	78704	**800-286-5856***	512-691-6100	774
Green Mountain at Fox Run PO Box 164	Ludlow	VT	05149	**800-448-8106**	802-228-8885	697
Green Mountain Inn 18 Main St PO Box 60	Stowe	VT	05672	**800-253-7302**	802-253-7301	373
Green Mountain Power Corp 163 Acorn Ln *NYSE: GMP*	Colchester	VT	05446	**888-835-4672**	802-864-5731	774
Green Oaks Hospital 7808 Clodus Fields Dr	Dallas	TX	75251	**800-866-6554**	972-991-9504	366-3
Green Oaks Hotel 6901 West Fwy.	Fort Worth	TX	76116	**800-433-2174**	817-738-7311	373
Green Park Inn 9239 Valley Blvd.	Blowing Rock	NC	28605	**800-852-2462**	828-295-3141	373
Green Theodore Francis State Airport (PVD)	Warwick	RI	02886	**888-268-7222**	401-737-4000	28
Green Tortoise Adventure Travel 494 Broadway	San Francisco	CA	94133	**800-867-8647**	415-956-7500	748
Green Tree Packing Co 65 Central Ave.	Passaic	NJ	07055	**800-221-5754**	973-473-1305	291-26
Green Tree Servicing LLC 345 Saint Peter St Suite 600	Saint Paul	MN	55102	**800-423-9527**	651-293-3400	215
Green Valley Floral Co 24999 Potter Rd	Salinas	CA	93908	**800-228-1255**	831-424-7691	363
Green Valley Pecan Co 1625 E Sahuarita Rd	Sahuarita	AZ	85629	**800-533-5269**	520-791-2852	11-10
Green Valley Resort 1871 W Canyon View Dr	Saint George	UT	84770	**800-237-1068**	435-628-8060	655
Green Valley Spa 1871 W Canyon View Dr	Saint George	UT	84770	**800-237-1068**	435-628-8060	697
Greenbelt Electric Co-op Inc PO Box 948	Wellington	TX	79095	**800-527-3082**	806-447-2536	244
Greenbrier The 300 W Main St	White Sulphur Springs	WV	24986	**800-453-4858**	304-536-1110	655
Greenbrier Co 1 Centerpointe Dr Suite 200 *NYSE: GBX*	Lake Oswego	OR	97035	**800-343-7188**	503-684-7000	636
Greenbrier County Convention & Visitors Bureau 540 N Jefferson St Suite N	Lewisburg	WV	24901	**800-833-2068**	304-645-1000	205
Greenbrier Farms Ltd 225 Sign Pine Rd	Chesapeake	VA	23322	**800-821-2141**	757-421-2141	318
Greenbrier (Greater) Chamber of Commerce 540 N Jefferson St Box 17 Suite N	Lewisburg	WV	24901	**800-833-2068**	304-645-1000	137
Greenbrier Resort Management Co 300 W Main St	White Sulphur Springs	WV	24986	**800-624-6070**	304-536-1110	369
Greene Coach Charters & Tours Inc 126 Bohannon Ave	Greeneville	TN	37745	**800-338-5469**	423-638-8271	748
Greene County Convention & Visitors Bureau 1221 Meadowbridge Dr	Beavercreek	OH	45434	**800-733-9109**	937-429-9100	205
Greene Henry M & Assoc Inc 28457 N Ballard Dr Suite A-1	Lake Forest	IL	60045	**800-356-1300**	847-816-9330	722
Greenerd Press & Machine Co Inc 41 Crown St	Nashua	NH	03061	**800-877-9110**	603-889-4101	448
Greenetrack Greyhound Park I-59 at Exit 45 - Union Rd PO Drawer 471	Eutaw	AL	35462	**800-633-5942**	205-372-9318	628

Name / Address	City	State	ZIP	Toll-Free	Phone	Class
Greenfield Industries Inc						
470 Old Evans Rd	Evans	GA	30809	**888-434-4311**	706-863-7708	484
Greenfield Online Inc						
21 River Rd Suite 2000	Wilton	CT	06897	**888-291-9997**	203-834-8585	458
NASDAQ: SRVY						
Greenfield Village						
20900 Oakwood Blvd	Dearborn	MI	48124	**800-835-5237**	313-271-1620	509
Greenheart Farms Inc						
PO Box 1510	Arroyo Grande	CA	93421	**800-549-5531**	805-481-2234	11-11
Greenhorn Creek Guest Ranch						
2116 Greenhorn Ranch Rd	Quincy	CA	95971	**800-334-6939**	530-283-0930	238
Greenhorn Creek Resort						
711 McCauley Ranch Rd	Angels Camp	CA	95222	**888-736-5900**	209-736-6201	655
Greenhorne & O'Mara Inc						
9001 Edmonston Rd	Greenbelt	MD	20770	**866-322-8905**	301-982-2800	258
Greenleaf Nursery Co 28406 Hwy 82	Park Hill	OK	74451	**800-331-2982**	918-457-5172	363
Greenleaf Wholesale Florists Inc						
13239 Weld County Rd 4	Brighton	CO	80601	**800-659-8000**	303-659-8000	288
Greenlee Textron Inc						
4455 Boeing Dr	Rockford	IL	61109	**800-435-0786**	815-397-7070	747
Greenline Equipment						
6068 S Redwood Rd	Salt Lake City	UT	84123	**888-201-5500**	801-966-4231	270
GreenLine Paper Co 631 S Pine St	York	PA	17403	**800-641-1117**	717-845-8697	543
Greenman-Pedersen Inc						
325 W Main St	Babylon	NY	11702	**800-347-9221**	631-587-5060	258
Greenpeace Canada						
250 Dundas St W Suite 605	Toronto	ON	M5T2Z5	**800-320-7183**	416-597-8408	48-13
Greenpeace USA						
702 H St NW Suite 300	Washington	DC	20001	**800-326-0959**	202-462-1177	48-13
Greensboro Area Convention & Visitors Bureau 317 S						
Greene St	Greensboro	NC	27401	**800-344-2282**	336-274-2282	205
Greensboro College						
815 W Market St	Greensboro	NC	27401	**800-346-8226**	336-272-7102	163
Greens/Green Party USA (G/GPUSA)						
PO Box 1406	Chicago	IL	60690	**866-473-3672**	708-524-1741	605
Greenspace Services Ltd						
70 Ronson Dr	Etobicoke	ON	M9W1B9	**800-565-5296**	416-614-6677	421
Greenville Advocate PO Box 507	Greenville	AL	36037	**888-246-8237**	334-382-3111	522-4
Greenville Area Central Reservations						
PO Box 10527	Greenville	SC	29603	**800-351-7180**	864-233-0461	368
Greenville Area Chamber of Commerce						
1 Depot Sq	Greenville	AL	36037	**800-959-0717**	334-382-3251	137
Greenville College						
315 E College Ave	Greenville	IL	62246	**800-345-4440**	618-664-7100	163
Greenville (Greater) Convention & Visitors Bureau 631 S Main St						
Suite 301	Greenville	SC	29601	**800-351-7180**	864-421-0000	205
Greenville News 305 S Main St	Greenville	SC	29601	**800-800-5116**	864-298-4100	522-2
Greenville-Pitt County Convention & Visitors Bureau 303 SW						
Greenville Blvd	Greenville	NC	27834	**800-537-5564**	252-329-4200	205
Greenville Technical College						
506 S Pleasantburg Dr	Greenville	SC	29606	**800-723-0673**	864-250-8000	160
Brashier Campus PO Box 5616	Greenville	SC	29606	**800-723-0673**	864-228-5000	160
Greer Campus PO Box 5616	Greenville	SC	29606	**800-723-0673**	864-848-2000	160
Greenwald Industries						
212 Middlesex Ave	Chester	CT	06412	**800-221-0982**	860-526-0800	486
Greenwillow Books						
1350 Ave of the Americas	New York	NY	10019	**800-242-7737**	212-261-6500	623-2
Greenwood Convention & Visitors Bureau 1902 Leflore Ave	Greenwood	MS	38930	**800-748-9064**	662-453-9197	205
Greenwood-Heinemann						
361 Hanover St	Portsmouth	NH	03801	**800-541-2086**	603-431-7894	623-2
Greenwood Inn						
10700 SW Allen Blvd	Beaverton	OR	97005	**800-289-1300**	503-643-7444	373
Greenwood Inn Calgary						
3515 26th St NE	Calgary	AB	T1Y7E3	**888-233-6730**	403-250-8855	372
Greenwood Inn Edmonton						
4485 Gateway Blvd	Edmonton	AB	T6H5C3	**888-233-6730**	780-431-1100	372
Greenwood Inn Winnipeg						
1715 Wellington Ave	Winnipeg	MB	R3H0G1	**888-233-6730**	204-775-9889	372
Greenwood Mills Inc						
300 Morgan Ave	Greenwood	SC	29646	**800-847-5929**	864-229-2571	730-1
Greenwood Mop & Broom Inc						
PO Drawer 1426	Greenwood	SC	29648	**800-635-6849**	864-227-8411	104
Greenwood Plantation						
6838 Highland Rd	Saint Francisville	LA	70775	**800-259-4475**	225-655-4475	50
Greenwood Publishing Group Inc						
88 Post Rd W	Westport	CT	06881	**800-225-5800***	203-226-3571	623-2
*Orders						
Greer Industries Inc						
PO Box 1900	Morgantown	WV	26507	**800-773-0412**	304-296-1751	493-5
Greer Laboratories Inc 639 Nuway Cir	Lenoir	NC	28645	**800-378-3906***	828-754-5327	470
*Cust Svc						
Greer Lime Co PO Box 1900	Morgantown	WV	26507	**800-773-0412**	304-296-1751	432
Greer Margolis Mitchell Burns & Assoc 1010 Wisconsin Ave NW						
Suite 800	Washington	DC	20007	**800-283-7606**	202-338-8700	4
Greer Steel Co 624 Boulevard	Dover	OH	44622	**800-388-2868***	330-343-8811	709
*Sales						
Greg Manning Auctions Inc						
775 Passaic Ave	West Caldwell	NJ	07006	**800-221-0243**	973-882-0004	51
NASDAQ: GMAI						
Gregg Investigations Inc						
6320 Monona Dr	Madison	WI	53716	**800-866-1976**	608-256-1074	392
Gregory Mfg Co Inc 506 Oak Dr	Lewiston	NC	27849	**800-233-4734**	252-348-2531	269
Greif Inc 425 Winter Rd	Delaware	OH	43015	**800-354-7343**	740-549-6000	197
NYSE: GEF						
Grenada Board of Tourism						
PO Box 1668	Lake Worth	FL	33460	**800-927-9554**	561-588-8176	764
Grenada Board of Tourism						
305 Madison Ave Suite 2145	New York	NY	10165	**800-927-9554**	212-687-9554	764
Grenelefe Golf & Tennis Resort						
3200 SR-546	Haines City	FL	33844	**888-808-7410**	863-422-7511	655
Grenoble House 329 Dauphine St	New Orleans	LA	70112	**800-722-1834**	504-522-1331	373
Gresham Smith & Partners						
511 Union St 1400 Nashville						
City Ctr	Nashville	TN	37219	**800-867-3384**	615-770-8100	258
Greshes Warren 202 Telluride Tr	Chapel Hill	NC	27514	**800-858-1516**	919-933-5900	561
Gretag Macbeth LLC						
617 Little Britain Rd	New Windsor	NY	12553	**800-622-2384**	845-565-7660	410
Gretz Beer Co 710 E Main St	Norristown	PA	19401	**866-473-8926**	610-275-0285	82-1
Greve Carl Jeweler Inc						
731 SW Morrison St	Portland	OR	97205	**800-284-2044**	503-223-7121	402
Grey Bonnet Inn 831 Rt 100 N	Killington	VT	05751	**800-342-2086**	802-775-2537	373
Grey House Publishing						
185 Millerton Rd PO Box 860	Millerton	NY	12546	**800-562-2139**	518-789-8700	623-6
Grey Wolf Inc						
10370 Richmond Ave Suite 600	Houston	TX	77042	**800-553-7563**	713-435-6100	525
AMEX: GW						
Greyhound Canada Transportation Corp						
180 Dundas St W Suite 300	Toronto	ON	M5G1Z8	**800-661-8747**	416-594-0343	108
Greyhound Hall of Fame						
407 S Buckeye Ave	Abilene	KS	67410	**800-932-7881**	785-263-3000	511
Greyling Area Visitor's Council						
213 N James St	Grayling	MI	49738	**800-937-8837**	989-348-2921	205
Greystone Inn Greystone Ln	Lake Toxaway	NC	28747	**800-824-5766**	828-966-4700	655
Gribetz International Inc						
13800 NW 4th St	Sunrise	FL	33325	**800-326-4742**	954-846-0300	729
Gries Seed Farms Inc 2348 N 5th St	Fremont	OH	43420	**800-472-4797**	419-332-5571	684
Griffin Anna Inc 733 Lambert Dr	Atlanta	GA	30324	**888-817-8170**	404-817-8170	130
Griffin Environmental Co Inc						
7066 Interstate Island Rd	Syracuse	NY	13209	**877-293-8789**	315-451-5300	19
Griffin Gate Resort. Marriott's						
1800 Newtown Pike	Lexington	KY	40511	**800-228-9290**	859-231-5100	655
Griffin Industries						
4221 Alexandria Pike	Cold Spring	KY	41076	**800-743-7413**	859-781-2010	438
Griffin Industries Inc						
4413 Tanner Church Rd	Ellenwood	GA	30294	**800-536-3935**	404-363-1320	291-12
Griffin Publishing Group 18022 Cowan	Irvine	CA	92614	**800-472-9741**	949-263-3733	614
Griffin Rip Truck Travel Center Inc						
PO Box 10128	Lubbock	TX	79408	**800-333-9330**	806-763-9349	319
Griffin Wayne J Electric Inc						
116 Hopping Brook Rd	Holliston	MA	01746	**800-421-0151**	508-429-8830	188-4
Griffith Energy Services Inc						
2510 Schuster Dr	Cheverly	MD	20781	**800-633-4328**	301-322-5100	311
Griffith Laboratories USA 1 Griffith Ctr	Alsip	IL	60803	**800-346-9494***	708-371-0900	291-37
*Cust Svc						
Griffith Rubber Mills						
2625 NW Industrial St	Portland	OR	97210	**800-321-9677**	503-226-6971	664
Grifols USA Inc 2410 Lillyvale Ave	Los Angeles	CA	90032	**800-421-0008**	323-225-2221	86
Grill Concepts Inc						
11661 San Vicente Blvd						
Suite 404	Los Angeles	CA	90049	**888-999-9156**	310-820-5559	656
NASDAQ: GRIL						
Grimmer Industries Inc DBA GrimmerSchmidt Compressors						
1015 N Hurricane Rd	Franklin	IN	46131	**800-428-9703**	317-736-8416	170
GrimmerSchmidt Compressors						
1015 N Hurricane Rd	Franklin	IN	46131	**800-428-9703**	317-736-8416	170
Grindmaster Crathco Systems Inc						
PO Box 35020	Louisville	KY	40232	**800-695-4500**	502-425-4776	293
Grinnell College 1103 Park St	Grinnell	IA	50112	**800-247-0113**	641-269-3600	163
Grinnell Mutual Reinsurance Co						
4215 Highway 146	Grinnell	IA	50112	**800-362-2041**	641-269-8000	384-4
Grisanti's Inc						
9300 Shelbyville Rd Suite 508	Louisville	KY	40222	**800-436-6323**	502-429-0341	657
Griswold Rubber Co Inc PO Box 638	Moosup	CT	06354	**800-472-8788***	860-564-3321	663
*Cust Svc						
Griswold ST & Co Inc PO Box 849	Williston	VT	05495	**800-339-4565**	802-658-0201	181
Grit Magazine 1503 SW 42nd St	Topeka	KS	66609	**800-678-7741**	785-274-4300	449-11
Grizzly & Wolf Discovery Center						
201 S Canyon	West Yellowstone	MT	59758	**800-257-2570**	406-646-7001	811
Grob Inc 1731 10th Ave	Grafton	WI	53024	**800-225-6481**	262-377-1400	447
Grobet File Co of America Inc						
750 Washington Ave	Carlstadt	NJ	07072	**800-847-4188**	201-939-6700	746
Grocers Supply Co Inc						
3131 E Holcombe Blvd	Houston	TX	77021	**800-352-8003**	713-747-5000	292-8
Grocery Supply Co						
130 Hillcrest Dr	Sulphur Springs	TX	75482	**800-231-1938**	903-885-7621	292-8
Groen 1055 Mendell Davis Dr	Jackson	MS	39272	**800-676-9040**	601-372-3903	295
Groendyk Mfg Co Inc						
19318 Main St	Buchanan	VA	24066	**800-879-4395**	540-254-1010	664
Groendyke Transport Inc						
2510 Rock Island Blvd	Enid	OK	73701	**800-843-2103**	580-234-4663	769
Grogans Health Care Supply Inc						
1016 S Broadway St	Lexington	KY	40504	**800-365-1020**	859-254-6661	467
Grolier Electronic Publishing Inc						
90 Old Sherman Tpke	Danbury	CT	06816	**800-955-9877**	203-797-3500	176-3
Grolier Inc 90 Old Sherman Tpke	Danbury	CT	06816	**800-955-9877***	203-797-3500	623-2
*Cust Svc						
Groovfold Inc						
1050 W State St	Newcomerstown	OH	43832	**800-367-1133**	740-498-8363	304
Gros-Ite Industries						
1790 New Britain Ave	Farmington	CT	06032	**800-242-1790**	860-677-2603	22
Gros Morne National Park						
PO Box 130	Rocky Harbour	NL	A0K4N0	**800-563-6353***	709-458-2417	553
*Campground Resv						
Grosch Irrigation Co Inc						
3110 33rd Rd	Silver Creek	NE	68663	**800-509-2261**	308-773-2261	188-16
Grosh Scenic Rentals						
4114 Sunset Blvd	Hollywood	CA	90029	**877-363-7998**	323-662-1134	708
Gross Mechanical Contractors Inc						
3622 Greenwood Blvd	Saint Louis	MO	63143	**800-641-0071**	314-645-0077	188-10
Grossenburg Implement Inc						
31341 US Hwy 18	Winner	SD	57580	**800-658-3440**	605-842-2040	270
Grosslein Beverages Inc						
13554 Tungsten St NW	Anoka	MN	55303	**800-421-5804***	763-421-5804	82-1
*Cust Svc						
Grossman Iron & Steel Co Inc						
5 N Market St	Saint Louis	MO	63102	**800-969-9423**	314-231-9423	674
Grossmont College						
8800 Grossmont College Dr	El Cajon	CA	92020	**866-476-7766**	619-644-7000	160
Grossmont-Cuyamaca Community College District 8800 Grossmont						
College Dr	El Cajon	CA	92020	**866-476-7766**	619-644-7010	160

	City	State	ZIP	Toll-Free	Phone	Class
Grosvenor Resort at Walt Disney World Village 1850 Hotel Plaza Blvd	Lake Buena Vista	FL	32830	**800-624-4109**	407-828-4444	373
Grote Industries Inc 2600 Lanier Dr	Madison	IN	47250	**800-457-9540**	812-273-2121	60
Groth Corp 13650 N Promenade Blvd	Stafford	TX	77477	**800-531-3140**	281-295-6800	776
Ground Source Heat Pump Assn. International Oklahoma State University 374 Cordell S	Stillwater	OK	74078	**800-626-4747**	405-744-5175	49-13
Ground Water Assn. National 601 Dempsey Rd	Westerville	OH	43081	**800-551-7379**	614-898-7791	48-12
Grounds For Play Inc 1401 E Dallas St	Mansfield	TX	76063	**800-552-7529**	817-477-5482	340
Groundskeeper PO Box 43820	Tucson	AZ	85706	**800-571-1575**	520-571-1575	421
Groundskeeper Tree Div PO Box 43820	Tucson	AZ	85733	**800-571-1575**	520-571-1575	765
Group 1 Software Inc 4200 Parliament Pl Suite 600	Lanham	MD	20706	**800-368-5806**	301-731-2300	176-1
Group Canam Inc 11505 1st Ave Bureau 500 *TSE: CAM*	Saint-Georges	QC	G5Y7X3	**877-499-6049**	418-228-8031	709
Group Dekko Services LLC 6928 N 400 E	Kendallville	IN	46755	**800-829-0700**	260-347-0700	803
Group Health Co-op 521 Wall St	Seattle	WA	98121	**888-901-4636**	206-448-5600	384-3
Group Health Plan Inc 111 Corporate Office Dr Suite 400	Earth City	MO	63045	**800-743-3901**	314-506-1700	384-3
Group Leaders of America Inc 460 E State St	Salem	OH	44460	**800-628-0993**	330-337-1027	748
Group Management Services Inc 3296 Columbia Rd Suite 101	Richfield	OH	44286	**800-456-2885**	330-659-0100	455
Group O Inc 4905 77th Ave	Milan	IL	61264	**800-752-0730**	309-736-8300	114
Group Tour Co Inc 1110 Vermont Ave NW Suite 407	Washington	DC	20005	**800-424-8895**	202-955-5667	748
Groupe Lacasse LLC 99 St-Pierre St	Sainte-Pie	QC	J0H1W0	**888-522-2773**	450-772-2495	314-1
Groupe TVA Inc 1600 Maisonneuve Blvd E	Montreal	QC	H2L4P2	**877-304-8828**	514-790-0461	724
GroupSystems.com 520 Zang St Suite 211	Broomfield	CO	80021	**800-368-6338**	303-468-8680	176-12
Grove Isle Club & Resort 4 Grove Isle Dr	Coconut Grove	FL	33133	**800-884-7683**	305-858-8300	373
Grove Park Inn Resort & Spa 290 Macon Ave	Asheville	NC	28804	**800-438-5800**	828-252-2711	655
Grover Corp PO Box 340080	Milwaukee	WI	53234	**800-776-3602**	414-384-9472	128
Growers Co-op Inc 2500 S 13th St	Terre Haute	IN	47802	**800-283-8123**	812-235-8123	271
Growers Equipment Co 8674 NW 58th St	Miami	FL	33166	**800-592-7890**	305-592-7891	270
Growers Fertilizer Corp PO Box 1407	Lake Alfred	FL	33850	**800-343-1101**	863-956-1101	276
Growers Marketing Service Inc PO Box 2595	Lakeland	FL	33806	**800-476-2037**	863-644-2414	11-11
Growing Edge Magazine PO Box 1027	Corvallis	OR	97339	**800-888-6785**	541-757-8477	449-14
Growth Foundation. Human 997 Glen Cove Ave Suite 5	Glen Head	NY	11545	**800-451-6434**	516-671-4041	48-17
Growth Fund Guide Newsletter PO Box 6600	Rapid City	SD	57709	**800-621-8322**	605-341-1971	521-9
Growth Stock Outlook Newsletter 4405 East-West Hwy Suite 305	Bethesda	MD	20814	**800-742-5476**	301-654-5205	521-9
Gruber Systems Inc 25636 Ave Stanford	Valencia	CA	91355	**800-257-4070**	661-257-4060	593
Gruet Winery 8400 Pan American Fwy NE	Albuquerque	NM	87113	**888-857-9463**	505-821-0055	50
Grunau Co Inc 1100 W Anderson Ct	Oak Creek	WI	53154	**800-365-1920**	414-216-6900	188-10
Grundfos Pumps Corp 5900 E Shields Ave *Cust Svc	Fresno	CA	93727	**800-333-1366***	559-292-8000	627
Grundy County Rural Electric Co-op 102 E 'G' Ave	Grundy Center	IA	50638	**800-390-7605**	319-824-5251	244
Grundy Electric Co-op Inc 4100 Oklahoma Ave	Trenton	MO	64683	**800-279-2249**	660-359-3941	244
Grupo Taca PO Box 590628	Miami	FL	33159	**800-251-1351**	305-871-1587	26
GS Blodgett Corp 44 Lakeside Ave	Burlington	VT	05401	**800-331-5842**	802-658-6600	293
GS Metals Corp 3764 Longspur Rd	Pinckneyville	IL	62274	**800-582-3643**	618-357-5353	482
GS Robins & Co 126 Chouteau Ave	Saint Louis	MO	63102	**800-777-5155**	314-621-5165	144
GSA (General Services Administration) 1800 F St NW *Fraud Hotline	Washington	DC	20405	**800-424-5210***	202-501-1231	336-16
GSA (Genetics Society of America) 9650 Rockville Pike	Bethesda	MD	20814	**866-486-4363**	301-634-7300	49-19
GSE Lining Technology Inc 19103 Gundle Rd	Houston	TX	77073	**800-435-2008**	281-443-8564	589
GSE Systems Inc 9189 Red Branch Rd *AMEX: GVP* ■ *Cust Svc	Columbia	MD	21045	**800-638-7912***	410-772-3500	176-1
GSE Tech-motive Tool 42860 Nine-Mile Rd	Novi	MI	48375	**800-795-7875**	248-596-0600	464
GSI Commerce Inc 935 1st Ave *NASDAQ: GSIC*	King of Prussia	PA	19406	**877-708-4305**	610-265-3229	7
GSL Electric Inc 8540 S Sandy Pkwy	Sandy	UT	84070	**800-221-4135**	801-565-0088	188-4
GST/E-Systems 2929 E Imperial Hwy Suite 170	Brea	CA	92821	**800-833-0128**	714-572-8020	172
GT Com 502 5th St Caller Box 9001	Port Saint Joe	FL	32456	**800-772-7288**	850-229-7231	721
GT Consultants 3050 Eagle Watch Dr	Woodstock	GA	30189	**800-659-0345**	770-591-1343	183
GT Water Products Inc 5239 N Commerce Ave	Moorpark	CA	93021	**800-862-5647**	805-529-2900	596
GTC Biotherapeutics Inc 175 Crossing Blvd Suite 410 *NASDAQ: GTCB*	Framingham	MA	01702	**800-326-7002**	508-620-9700	86
GTCO CalComp Inc 7125 Riverwood Dr	Columbia	MD	21046	**800-344-4723**	410-381-6688	171-1
GTE Federal Credit Union PO Box 172599	Tampa	FL	33672	**800-241-4120**	813-871-2690	216
GTN Inc 13320 Northend Ave	Oak Park	MI	48237	**888-225-5486**	248-548-2500	501
GTSI Corp 3901 Stonecroft Blvd *NASDAQ: GTSI*	Chantilly	VA	20151	**800-999-4874**	703-502-2000	172

	City	State	ZIP	Toll-Free	Phone	Class
Guadalupe Valley Electric Co-op Inc PO Box 118	Gonzales	TX	78629	**800-223-4832**	830-857-1200	244
Guadalupe Valley Telephone Co-op 36101 FM 3159	New Braunfels	TX	78132	**800-367-4882**	830-885-4411	721
Guam Visitors Bureau c/o Aviso Inc 1336-C Park St	Alameda	CA	94501	**800-873-4826**	510-865-0366	764
Guarantee Electrical Co 3405 Bent Ave	Saint Louis	MO	63116	**800-854-4326**	314-772-5400	188-4
Guarantee Trust Life Insurance Co 1275 Milwaukee Ave	Glenview	IL	60025	**800-338-7452**	847-699-0600	384-2
Guaranteed Air Freight & Forwarding Inc 4555 McDonnell Blvd	Saint Louis	MO	63134	**800-445-0738**	314-427-7709	306
Guaranty Bancshares Inc 100 W Arkansas St PO Box 1158 *NASDAQ: GNTY*	Mount Pleasant	TX	75455	**888-572-9881**	903-572-9881	355-2
Guaranty Bank 8333 Douglas Ave	Dallas	TX	75225	**800-999-1726**	214-360-3360	71
Guaranty Bank SSB 4000 W Brown Deer Rd	Brown Deer	WI	53209	**800-585-5264**	414-362-4000	71
Guaranty Insurance Services Inc 1300 S Mopac Expy	Austin	TX	78746	**800-331-8959**	512-434-8464	383
Guaranty Residential Lending Inc 1300 S Mopac Expy	Austin	TX	78746	**800-964-9420**	512-434-8000	498
Guard-Line Inc 215 S Louise St PO Box 1030	Atlanta	TX	75551	**800-527-8822**	903-796-4111	153-8
Guard & Reserve. National Committee for Employer Support of the 1555 Wilson Blvd Suite 200	Arlington	VA	22209	**800-336-4590**	703-696-1386	48-19
Guard Security Hardware 1 S Middlesex Ave *Sales	Monroe Township	NJ	08831	**800-523-1268***	609-860-9990	345
Guard Systems Inc 12124 Ramona Blvd	El Monte	CA	91732	**800-307-0031**	626-433-4999	682
Guardian Alarm Co 20800 Southfield Rd	Southfield	MI	48075	**800-782-9688**	248-423-1000	683
Guardian Chemical Co PO Box 93667	Atlanta	GA	30377	**800-241-6742**	404-873-1692	149
Guardian Electric Mfg Co Inc 1425 Lake Ave	Woodstock	IL	60098	**800-762-0369**	815-337-0050	202
Guardian Glass Co 24150 Haggerty Rd	Farmington Hills	MI	48335	**800-621-8682**	248-471-0180	62-2
Guardian Group of Funds PO Box 219611	Kansas City	MO	64121	**800-343-0817**		517
Guardian Industries Corp 2300 Harmon Rd	Auburn Hills	MI	48326	**800-327-5888**	248-340-1800	325
Guardian Insurance & Annuity Co 7 Hanover Sq	New York	NY	10004	**888-482-7342**	212-598-8000	384-2
Guardian Life Insurance Co of America 7 Hanover Sq	New York	NY	10004	**888-482-7342**	212-598-8000	384-2
Guardian Packaging Inc 3615 Security St	Garland	TX	75042	**800-259-1502**	214-349-1500	590
Guardian Voting Systems 1675 Delany Rd	Gurnee	IL	60031	**800-888-9527**	847-662-2666	788
Guardsman FurniturePro 4999 36th St SE	Grand Rapids	MI	49512	**800-253-3957**	616-285-7877	305
Guardsmark Inc 22 S 2nd St	Memphis	TN	38103	**800-238-5878**	901-522-6000	682
Guarnieri Albert Co 1133 E Market St	Warren	OH	44483	**800-686-2639**	330-394-5636	744
Guckenheimer Enterprises Inc 3 Lagoon Dr Suite 325	Redwood Shores	CA	94065	**800-466-5303**	650-592-3800	294
Guden HA Co Inc 99 Raynor Ave	Ronkonkoma	NY	11779	**800-344-6437**	631-737-2900	345
Guenther House 205 E Guenther St	San Antonio	TX	78204	**800-235-8186**	210-227-1061	50
Guernsey Bel Inc 4300 S Morgan St	Chicago	IL	60609	**800-621-0271**	773-927-4000	291-15
Guess? Inc 1444 S Alameda St *NYSE: GES*	Los Angeles	CA	90021	**800-394-8377**	213-765-3100	153-11
Guest Informant Inc 21200 Erwin St	Woodland Hills	CA	91367	**800-275-5885**	818-716-7484	623-9
Guest Informant Magazine 21200 Erwin St	Woodland Hills	CA	91367	**800-275-5885**	818-716-7484	449-22
Guest Lodge at Cooper Aerobic Center Clinic 12230 Preston Rd	Dallas	TX	75230	**800-444-5187**	972-386-0306	373
Guest Services Inc 3055 Prosperity Ave	Fairfax	VA	22031	**800-345-7534**	703-849-9300	294
Guest Supply Inc PO Box 902 *Cust Svc	Monmouth Junction	NJ	08852	**800-448-3787***	609-514-9696	211
Guhring Inc 1445 Commerce Ave	Brookfield	WI	53045	**800-776-6170**	262-784-6730	484
Guida-Seibert Dairy Co 433 Park St	New Britain	CT	06051	**800-832-8929**	860-224-2404	291-27
Guidant Corp PO Box 44906 *NYSE: GDT*	Indianapolis	IN	46244	**800-405-9611**	317-971-2000	468
Guide Dog Foundation for the Blind Inc 371 E Jericho Tkpe	Smithtown	NY	11787	**800-548-4337**	631-265-2121	48-17
Guide Dogs of America 13445 Glenoaks Blvd	Sylmar	CA	91342	**800-459-4843**	818-362-5834	48-17
Guide Dogs for the Blind 350 Los Ranchitos Rd	San Rafael	CA	94903	**800-295-4050**	415-499-4000	48-17
Guidecraft USA 66 Grand Ave Suite 207	Englewood	NJ	07631	**800-544-6526**	201-894-5401	750
Guided Imagery Inc. Academy for 30765 Pacific Coast Hwy Suite 369	Malibu	CA	90265	**800-726-2070**		754
GuideOne Insurance Co 1111 Ashworth Rd	West Des Moines	IA	50265	**877-448-4331**	515-267-5000	384-4
GuideOne Mutual Insurance Co 1111 Ashworth Rd	West Des Moines	IA	50265	**877-448-4331**	515-267-5000	384-4
GuideOne Specialty Mutual Insurance Co 1111 Ashworth Rd	West Des Moines	IA	50265	**800-247-4181**	515-267-5000	384-4
Guideposts Inc 39 Seminary Hill Rd *Cust Svc	Carmel	NY	10512	**800-431-2344***	845-225-3681	623-9
Guideposts Magazine 39 Seminary Hill Rd	Carmel	NY	10512	**800-431-2344**	845-225-3681	449-18
GuildCraft of California 18626 S Reyes Ave	Rancho Dominguez	CA	90221	**800-283-6716**	310-223-4200	314-2
Guilford College 5800 W Friendly Ave	Greensboro	NC	27410	**800-992-7759**	336-316-2100	163
Guilford Mills Inc 6001 W Market St *Cust Svc	Greensboro	NC	27409	**800-277-0987***	336-316-4000	730-4
Guilford Pharmaceuticals Inc 6611 Tributary St *NASDAQ: GLFD*	Baltimore	MD	21224	**800-453-3746**	410-631-6300	86

Name / Address	City	State	ZIP	Toll-Free	Phone	Class
Guillemot North America 5500 rue Saint-Laurent Suite 5000	Montreal	QC	H2T1S6	**877-484-5536**	514-279-9960	171-1
Guitar Center Inc 5795 Lindero Canyon Rd *NASDAQ: GTRC*	Westlake Village	CA	91362	**800-905-0585**	818-735-8800	515
Guitar Imports 887 N McCormick Way 3	Layton	UT	84041	**877-544-4060**	801-544-4060	515
Guitar Player Magazine 2800 Campus Dr *Cust Svc	San Mateo	CA	94403	**800-289-9839***	650-513-4300	449-9
Guittard Chocolate Co 10 Guittard Rd	Burlingame	CA	94010	**800-468-2462**	650-697-4427	291-8
Gulf Asphalt Corp 4116 US Hwy 231	Panama City	FL	32404	**800-300-0177**	850-785-4675	187-4
Gulf Business Forms Inc 2460 S IH-35	San Marcos	TX	78667	**800-433-4853**	512-353-8313	111
Gulf City Seafood Inc PO Box 1346	Pascagoula	MS	39568	**800-666-3300**	228-762-3271	291-14
Gulf Coast Collection Bureau Inc 3621 Webber St	Sarasota	FL	34232	**888-839-6999**	941-927-6999	157
Gulf Coast Community College 5230 W Hwy 98	Panama City	FL	32401	**800-311-3685**	850-769-1551	160
Gulf Coast Electric Co-op Inc PO Box 220	Wewahitchka	FL	32465	**800-333-9392**	850-639-2216	244
Gulf Coast Exploreum Science Center 65 Government St	Mobile	AL	36602	**877-625-4386**	251-208-6883	510
Gulf Coast Hospital 13681 Doctors Way	Fort Myers	FL	33912	**800-440-4481**	239-768-5000	366-2
Gulf Coast Hotel Reservations PO Box 116	Biloxi	MS	39533	**888-388-1006**	228-388-6117	368
Gulf Coast Machine & Supply Co Inc 6817 Industrial Rd	Beaumont	TX	77705	**800-231-3032**	409-842-1311	709
Gulf Coast Regional Blood Center 1400 La Concha Ln	Houston	TX	77054	**888-482-5663**	713-790-1200	90
Gulf Div Cumberland Farms Inc 777 Dedham St	Canton	MA	02021	**800-843-8028**	781-828-4900	319
Gulf Hills Hotel 13701 Paso Rd	Ocean Springs	MS	39564	**877-875-4211**	228-875-4211	655
Gulf Island Fabrication Inc 583 Thompson Rd *NASDAQ: GIFI*	Houma	LA	70363	**888-465-2100**	985-872-2100	526
Gulf Lumber Co Inc PO Box 1663	Mobile	AL	36633	**800-496-3307**	251-457-6872	671
Gulf Motor Club 929 N Plum Grove Rd	Schaumburg	IL	60173	**800-633-3224**		53
Gulf Oil LP 90 Everett Ave	Chelsea	MA	02150	**800-256-4853**	617-889-9000	569
Gulf Power Co 1 Energy Pl	Pensacola	FL	32520	**800-487-6937**	850-444-6111	774
Gulf Publishing Co Inc 2 Greenway Plaza Suite 1020	Houston	TX	77046	**800-231-6275**	713-529-4301	623-9
Gulf Reduction Corp 6020 Navigation Blvd	Houston	TX	77011	**800-899-1705**	713-926-1705	476
Gulf Refrigeration Supply Inc of Tampa 8920 Sabal Industrial Blvd	Tampa	FL	33619	**888-683-2111**	813-626-5111	651
Gulf South Medical Supply Inc 173 E Marketridge Dr	Ridgeland	MS	39157	**800-347-2456**	601-856-5900	467
Gulf South Pipeline Co LP 20 E Greenway Plaza Suite 900	Houston	TX	77046	**866-820-6000**	713-544-6000	320
Gulf States Asphalt Co Inc PO Box 508	South Houston	TX	77587	**800-662-0987**	713-941-4410	46
Gulf States Inc 6711 E Hwy 332	Freeport	TX	77541	**800-231-9849**	979-233-5555	188-10
Gulf States Manufacturers 101 Airport Rd PO Box 1128	Starkville	MS	39760	**800-844-4853**	662-323-8021	106
Gulf Stream Coach Inc 503 S Oakland Ave PO Box 1005	Nappanee	IN	46550	**800-289-8787**	574-773-7761	120
Gulf-Wandes Corp 8325 S Choctaw Dr	Baton Rouge	LA	70815	**800-211-7613**	225-927-1920	592
Gulf War Illness Information Helpline	Washington	DC	20420	**800-749-8387**		336-15
Gulfeagle Supply 1451 Channelside Dr *NASDAQ: EEGL*	Tampa	FL	33605	**800-986-3001**	813-636-9808	190-4
Gulfside Regional Hospice Inc 6117 Trouble Creek Rd	New Port Richey	FL	34653	**800-561-4883**	727-845-5707	365
GulfStream Hotel 1 Lake Ave	Lake Worth	FL	33460	**888-540-0669**	561-540-6000	373
Gulfstream International Airlines 1815 Griffin Rd Suite 400	Dania Beach	FL	33004	**800-457-4853**	954-266-3000	26
GulfTerra Energy Partners LP 1001 Louisiana St	Houston	TX	77002	**800-594-2018**	713-420-2131	320
Gulistan Carpet Inc 3140 Hwy 5	Aberdeen	NC	28315	**800-869-2727**	910-944-2371	131
Gull Industries 3404 4th Ave S	Seattle	WA	98134	**800-866-4855**	206-624-5900	569
Gump's 135 Post St	San Francisco	CA	94108	**800-766-7628**	415-982-1616	322
Gunbarrel Guest House 6901 Lookout Rd	Boulder	CO	80301	**800-530-1513**	303-530-1513	373
Gund Arena 1 Center Ct	Cleveland	OH	44115	**800-332-2287**	216-420-2000	706
Gund Inc 1 Runyons Ln *Cust Svc	Edison	NJ	08817	**800-448-4863***	732-248-1500	750
Gundaker Property Management 2458 Old Dorsett Rd Suite 300	Maryland Heights	MO	63043	**800-325-1978**	314-298-5000	641
Gundersen Lutheran at Home HomeCare & Hospice 811 Monitor St Suite 101	La Crosse	WI	54603	**800-848-5442**	608-775-8400	365
Gundersen Lutheran Medical Center 1900 South Ave	La Crosse	WI	54601	**800-362-9567**	608-785-0530	366-2
Gunderson Inc 4350 NW Front Ave	Portland	OR	97210	**800-253-4350**	503-972-5700	636
Gunite Corp 302 Peoples Ave	Rockford	IL	61104	**800-677-3786**	815-490-6364	60
Gunite Supply & Equipment Co 1726 S Magnolia Ave	Monrovia	CA	91016	**888-393-8635**	626-359-9361	321
Gunlocke Co LLC 1 Gunlocke Dr *Cust Svc	Wayland	NY	14572	**800-828-6300***	585-728-5111	314-1
Gunnebo-Johnson Corp 1240 N Harvard Ave *Sales	Tulsa	OK	74115	**800-331-5460***	918-832-8933	462
Gunnison County Electric Assn PO Box 180	Gunnison	CO	81230	**800-726-3523**	970-641-3520	244
Guns & Ammo Magazine 6420 Wilshire Blvd 14th Fl	Los Angeles	CA	90048	**800-800-2666**	323-782-2000	449-20
Guns. Common Sense About Kids & 1225 'I' St NW Suite 1100	Washington	DC	20005	**877-955-5437**	202-546-0200	48-6
Gunther-Nash Mining Construction Co 2 City Place Dr Suite 380	Saint Louis	MO	63141	**800-261-2611**	314-692-2611	187-6
Gupton-Jones College of Funeral Service 5141 Snapfinger Woods Dr	Decatur	GA	30035	**800-848-5352**	770-593-2257	787
Gurnee Mills 6170 W Grand Ave	Gurnee	IL	60031	**800-937-7467**	847-263-7500	452
Gurney's Inn Resort & Spa 290 Old Montauk Hwy	Montauk	NY	11954	**800-848-7639**	631-668-2345	655
Gusdorf Canada Ltd 2105 Dagenais Blvd W	Laval	QC	H7L5W9	**800-361-2304**	450-963-0808	314-2
Gusmer Corp 1 Gusmer Dr	Lakewood	NJ	08701	**800-367-4767**	732-370-9000	170
Gussco Mfg Inc 5112 2nd Ave	Brooklyn	NY	11232	**800-248-7726**	718-492-7900	550
Gustafson Inc PO Box 660065	Dallas	TX	75266	**800-248-6907**	972-985-8877	276
Gustafson's Dairy Inc 4169 County Rd 15-A	Green Cove Springs	FL	32043	**800-342-1092**	904-284-3750	291-27
Gustave A Larson Co PO Box 910	Pewaukee	WI	53072	**800-829-9609**	262-542-0200	651
Gustavus Adolphus College 800 W College Ave	Saint Peter	MN	56082	**800-487-8288**	507-933-8000	163
Gusto Brands Inc 707 Douglas St	LaGrange	GA	30240	**800-241-3232**	706-882-2573	82-1
Guthrie County Rural Electric Co-op Assn PO Box 7	Guthrie Center	IA	50115	**888-747-2206**	641-747-2206	244
Guthrie News Leader 107 W Harrison St PO Box 879	Guthrie	OK	73044	**888-851-8717**	405-282-2222	522-2
Guthrie Theater 725 Vineland Pl	Minneapolis	MN	55403	**877-447-8243**	612-347-1100	562
Guthy-Renker Corp 41550 Eclectic St Suite 200	Palm Desert	CA	92260	**800-321-4730**	760-773-9022	503
Guttenplans Frozen Dough 100 Hwy 36	Middletown	NJ	07748	**888-422-4357**	732-495-9480	291-2
Gutwein Fred & Sons Inc 15691 W 600 S *Cust Svc	Francesville	IN	47946	**800-457-2700***	219-567-9141	11-5
Guy Brown Products 9003 Overlook Blvd	Brentwood	TN	37027	**877-794-5906**	615-777-1500	616
Guyan Machinery Co PO Box 150	Chapmanville	WV	25508	**800-999-3888**	304-855-4501	353
Guymon Daily Herald 515 N Ellison St	Guymon	OK	73942	**866-430-6397**	580-338-3355	522-2
Gwaii Haanas National Park Reserve/Haida Heritage Site PO Box 37 *Resv	Queen Charlotte	BC	V0T1S0	**800-435-5622***	250-559-8818	553
Gwaltney of Smithfield Ltd 601 N Church St	Smithfield	VA	23430	**800-888-7521**	757-357-3131	465
Gwinnett Center 6400 Sugarloaf Pkwy Bldg 100	Duluth	GA	30097	**800-224-6422**	770-813-7500	204
Gwin's Travel Planners Inc 212 N Kirkwood Rd	Kirkwood	MO	63122	**800-325-1904**	314-822-1957	760
GWV International 300 1st Ave	Needham	MA	02494	**800-225-5498**	781-449-6500	760
Gwynedd-Mercy College PO Box 901	Gwynedd Valley	PA	19437	**800-342-5462**	215-646-7300	163
Gym Source 40 E 52nd St	New York	NY	10022	**800-496-7687**	212-688-4222	702
Gymboree Corp 500 Howard St *NASDAQ: GYMB*	San Francisco	CA	94105	**800-222-7758**	415-278-7000	155-1
Gymboree Corp Play & Music Program 700 Airport Blvd Suite 200	Burlingame	CA	94010	**800-222-7758**	650-579-0600	146
Gynecologic Oncology Group (GOG) 1600 JFK Blvd Suite 1020	Philadelphia	PA	19103	**800-225-3053**	215-854-0770	49-8
Gynecological Laparoscopists. American Assn of 13021 E Florence Ave	Santa Fe Springs	CA	90670	**800-554-2245**	562-946-8774	49-8
Gyrus Medical Inc 6655 Wedgwood Rd Suite 160	Maple Grove	MN	55311	**800-852-9361**	763-416-3000	468
Gyrus Medical Inc ENT Div 2925 Appling Rd	Bartlett	TN	38133	**800-262-3540**	901-373-0200	469

H

Name / Address	City	State	ZIP	Toll-Free	Phone	Class
H Dennert Distributing Corp 351 Wilmer Ave *Cust Svc	Cincinnati	OH	45226	**800-837-5659***	513-871-7272	82-1
H Freeman & Son Inc 411 N Cranberry Rd	Westminster	MD	21157	**800-468-0689**	410-857-5774	153-12
H & H Color Lab Inc 8906 E 67th St	Raytown	MO	64133	**800-821-1305**	816-358-6677	577
H & H Foods PO Box 358	Mercedes	TX	78570	**800-365-4632**	956-565-6363	291-26
H & H Industrial Corp 7612 N Rt 130	Pennsauken	NJ	08110	**800-982-0341**	856-663-4444	688
H & H Meat Products Inc DBA H & H Foods PO Box 358	Mercedes	TX	78570	**800-365-4632**	956-565-6363	291-26
H & H Music Co 10303 Katy Fwy	Houston	TX	77024	**800-446-8742**	281-531-9222	515
H & H Publishing Co Inc 1231 Kapp Drive	Clearwater	FL	33765	**800-366-4079**	727-442-7760	243
H & H Swiss Screw Machine Products Co Inc 1478 Chestnut Ave	Hillside	NJ	07205	**800-826-9985**	908-688-6390	610
H & H Tooling Inc 30505 Clemens Rd	Westlake	OH	44145	**800-808-6840**	440-250-3204	448
H Koch & Sons Co 5410 E La Palma Ave	Anaheim	CA	92807	**800-433-5787**	714-779-7000	666
H Kramer & Co 1345 W 21st St	Chicago	IL	60608	**800-621-2305**	312-226-6600	476
H Krevit & Co Inc 73 Welton St	New Haven	CT	06511	**800-922-6626**	203-772-3350	143
H & L Bloom Inc School Bus Div 28 Grovenor St	Taunton	MA	02780	**800-323-3009**	508-822-1442	110
H & L Tooth Co Inc 10055 E 56 St N	Tulsa	OK	74117	**800-458-6684**		474
H Lee Moffitt Cancer Center & Research Institute 12902 Magnolia Dr	Tampa	FL	33612	**800-456-3434**	813-972-4673	366-5
H & M Systems Software Inc 600 E Crescent Ave Suite 203 *Cust Svc	Upper Saddle River	NJ	07458	**800-367-3366***	201-934-3414	176-11
H Meyer Dairy Co 415 John St	Cincinnati	OH	45215	**800-347-6455**	513-948-8811	291-27
H Muehlstein & Co Inc 800 Connecticut Ave	Norwalk	CT	06854	**800-257-3746**	203-855-6000	592
H O Sports Inc 17622 NE 67th Ct	Redmond	WA	98052	**800-938-4040**	425-885-3505	701
H-P Products Inc 512 W Gorgas St	Louisville	OH	44641	**800-860-8823**	330-875-5556	584
H Poll Electric Co 8 N Saint Clair St	Toledo	OH	43697	**800-548-0196**	419-255-1660	245
H & R Block Financial Advisors Inc 719 Griswold St	Detroit	MI	48226	**800-521-1111**	313-628-1300	393

Company	City	State	ZIP	Toll-Free	Phone	Class
H & R Block Inc 4400 Main St NYSE: HRB	Kansas City	MO	64111	**800-829-7733**	816-753-6900	184
H & R Block Mortgage Corp 3 Burlington Woods 2nd Fl	Burlington	MA	01803	**800-974-1899**	781-852-5600	498
H & R Block Tax Services Inc 4400 Main St	Kansas City	MO	64111	**800-869-9220**	816-753-6900	719
H Reisman Corp 377 Crane St	Orange	NJ	07051	**800-631-3424**	973-677-9200	470
H & S Bakery Inc 601 S Caroline St	Baltimore	MD	21231	**800-959-7655**	410-558-3096	291-1
H Stern Jewelers Inc 645 5th Ave	New York	NY	10022	**800-747-8376**	212-688-0300	402
H & W Trucking Co Inc 1772 N Andy Griffith Pkwy PO Box 1545	Mount Airy	NC	27030	**800-334-9181**	336-789-2188	769
H Wilson Co 555 W Taft Dr	South Holland	IL	60473	**800-245-7224**	708-339-5111	314-1
H2O Plus Inc 845 W Madison St *Cust Svc	Chicago	IL	60607	**800-690-2284***	312-850-9283	211
HA Friend & Co Inc 1535 Lewis Ave	Zion	IL	60099	**800-323-4394**	847-746-1248	524
HA Guden Co Inc 99 Raynor Ave	Ronkonkoma	NY	11779	**800-344-6437**	631-737-2900	345
Haab FC Co Inc 2314 Market St	Philadelphia	PA	19103	**800-486-5663**	215-563-0800	311
Haas Baking Co 9769 Reavis Park Dr	Saint Louis	MO	63123	**800-325-3171**	314-631-6100	69
Haas Cabinet Co Inc 625 W Utica St	Sellersburg	IN	47172	**800-457-6458**	812-246-4431	116
Haas Walter & Sons Inc 123 W 23rd St	Hialeah	FL	33010	**800-552-3845**	305-883-2257	692
Haas & Wilkerson Inc PO Box 2946	Shawnee Mission	KS	66201	**800-821-7703**	913-432-4400	383
Habana Inn 2200 NW 39th Expy	Oklahoma City	OK	73112	**800-988-2221**	405-528-2221	373
Habasit ABT Inc 150 Industrial Park Rd	Middletown	CT	06457	**800-522-2358**	860-632-2211	364
Habasit Belting Inc 1400 Clinton St	Buffalo	NY	14206	**800-325-1585**	716-824-8484	364
Haber Fabrics Corp 1745 Hayden Dr	Carrollton	TX	75006	**800-527-1980**	972-416-8479	583
Habersham Bancorp 282 Historic Hwy 441 N NASDAQ: HABC	Cornelia	GA	30531	**800-822-0316**	706-778-1000	355-2
Habersham County Chamber of Commerce PO Box 366	Cornelia	GA	30531	**800-835-2559**	706-778-4654	137
Habersham Electric Membership Corp PO Box 25	Clarkesville	GA	30523	**800-640-6812**	706-754-2114	244
Habitat 3801 Old Seward Hwy Suite 5 University Ctr	Anchorage	AK	99503	**800-770-1856**	907-561-1856	357
Habitat for Humanity International Inc 121 Habitat St	Americus	GA	31709	**800-422-4828**	229-924-6935	48-5
Habitat Suites 500 E Highland Mall Blvd	Austin	TX	78752	**800-535-4663**	512-467-6000	373
HAC (Housing Assistance Council) 1025 Vermont Ave NW Suite 606	Washington	DC	20005	**800-989-4422**	202-842-8600	48-5
Hach Co PO Box 389	Loveland	CO	80539	**800-227-4224**	970-669-3050	410
Hacienda Hotel 525 N Sepulveda Blvd	El Segundo	CA	90245	**800-421-5900**	310-615-0015	373
Hacienda Mexican Restaurants 1501 N Ironwood Dr	South Bend	IN	46635	**800-541-3227**	574-272-5922	657
Hackett J Lee Co 23550 Haggerty Rd	Farmington Hills	MI	48335	**800-422-5388**	248-478-0200	378
Hackley Hospital 1700 Clinton St	Muskegon	MI	49442	**800-825-4677**	231-726-3511	366-2
Hackney HT Co 502 S Gay St	Knoxville	TN	37902	**800-406-1291**	865-546-1291	184
Hackney & Sons Inc 400 Hackney Ave	Washington	NC	27889	**800-763-0700**	252-946-6521	505
HACU (Hispanic Assn of Colleges & Universities) 8415 Datapoint Dr Suite 400	San Antonio	TX	78229	**800-780-4228**	210-692-3805	49-5
Hadassah Women's Zionist Organization of America Inc 50 W 58th St	New York	NY	10019	**888-303-3640**	212-355-7900	48-20
Hader/Seitz Inc PO Box 510260	New Berlin	WI	53151	**877-388-2101**	262-641-6000	220
Hadley Cos 11300 Hampshire Ave S *Sales	Bloomington	MN	55438	**800-927-0880***	952-943-8474	623-10
Hadley-Roma Watchband Corp 106 Corporate Pk Dr	White Plains	NY	10604	**800-800-7662**	914-694-2000	422
Haeger Industries Inc 7 Maiden Ln	Dundee	IL	60118	**800-288-2529**	847-426-3441	330
Haemonetics Corp 400 Wood Rd NYSE: HAE	Braintree	MA	02184	**800-225-5242**	781-848-7100	468
Hagemeyer North America 12117 Insurance Way	Hagerstown	MD	21740	**800-638-3552**	301-733-1212	245
Hager Hinge Co 139 Victor St	Saint Louis	MO	63104	**800-325-9995**	314-772-4400	345
Hagerstown Aviation Services Inc 18627 Jarkey Dr	Hagerstown	MD	21742	**800-889-6094**	301-733-5200	63
Hagerstown Business College 18618 Crestwood Dr	Hagerstown	MD	21742	**800-422-2670**	301-739-2670	158
Hagerstown Community College 11400 Robinwood Dr	Hagerstown	MD	21742	**866-422-2468**	301-790-2800	160
Hagerstown/Washington County Convention & Visitors Bureau 16 Public Sq Ellizabeth Hager Ctr	Hagerstown	MD	21740	**800-228-7829**	301-791-3246	205
Haggar Clothing Co 11511 Luna Rd Two Colinas Crossing NASDAQ: HGGR	Dallas	TX	75234	**800-942-4427**	214-352-8481	153-12
Haggard & Stocking Industrial Supplies 5318 Victory Dr	Indianapolis	IN	46203	**800-622-4824**	317-788-4661	378
Haggerty Enterprises Inc 321 W Lake St Suite G	Elmhurst	IL	60126	**800-352-5282**	630-315-3300	330
Hagie Mfg Co 721 Central Ave W	Clarion	IA	50525	**800-247-4885**	515-532-2861	269
Hagstrom Map 46-35 54th Rd	Maspeth	NY	11378	**800-432-6277**	718-784-0055	623-1
Hahn Automotive Warehouse Inc 415 W Main St	Rochester	NY	14608	**800-456-0365**	585-235-1595	61
Hahn & Bowersock Inc 151 Kalmus Dr Suite L-1	Costa Mesa	CA	92626	**800-660-3187**	714-549-3700	436
Hahn Systems Co Inc 2401 Production Dr	Indianapolis	IN	46241	**800-589-3796**	317-243-3796	378
HAI (Helicopter Assn International) 1635 Prince St	Alexandria	VA	22314	**800-435-4976**	703-683-4646	49-21
Haines City Citrus Growers Assn 8 Willard Ave *Sales	Haines City	FL	33845	**800-422-4245***	863-422-1174	12-1
Haines & Co Inc 8050 Freedom Ave NW	North Canton	OH	44720	**800-843-8452**	330-494-9111	623-6
Haines JJ & Co Inc 6950 Aviation Blvd	Glen Burnie	MD	21061	**800-922-9248**	410-760-4040	356
Haines Visitors Bureau PO Box 530	Haines	AK	99827	**800-458-3579**	907-766-2234	205
Hair Cuttery 2815 Hartland Rd	Falls Church	VA	22043	**800-874-6288**	703-698-7090	79
Haircrafters/Great Expectations 7201 Metro Blvd	Minneapolis	MN	55439	**888-888-7778**	952-947-7777	79
Hajoca Corp 127 Coulter Ave	Ardmore	PA	19003	**800-284-3164**	610-649-1430	601
Hajoca Corp Keenan Supply Div 1341 Philadelphia St	Pomona	CA	91766	**800-437-6593**	909-613-1363	601
Hal Leonard Corp PO Box 227	Winona	MN	55987	**800-321-3408**	507-454-2920	623-7
Hal Lewis Group 1700 Market St 6th Fl	Philadelphia	PA	19103	**888-778-6115**	215-563-4461	4
Haldeman-Homme Inc 430 Industrial Blvd NE	Minneapolis	MN	55413	**800-795-0696**	612-331-4880	315
Haldex Hydraulic Systems 2222 15th St	Rockford	IL	61104	**800-572-7867**	815-398-4400	626
Hale Farm & Village 2686 Oakhill Rd	Bath	OH	44210	**800-589-9703**	330-666-3711	509
Hale Products Inc 700 Spring Mill Ave	Conshohocken	PA	19428	**800-220-4253**	610-825-6300	627
Hale TJ Co W 139 N 9499 Hwy 145 PO Box 250	Menomonee Falls	WI	53051	**800-236-4253**	262-255-5555	281
Hale Trailer Brake & Wheel Service Inc 5361 Oakview Dr	Allentown	PA	18104	**800-383-8894**	610-395-0371	767
Halekulani Hotel 2199 Kalia Rd	Honolulu	HI	96815	**800-367-2343**	808-923-2311	373
Halex Co 23901 Aurora Rd	Bedford Heights	OH	44146	**800-749-3261**	440-439-1616	303
Haley Brothers Inc 6291 Orangethorpe Ave	Buena Park	CA	90620	**800-848-3240**	714-670-2112	234
Half Moon Bay Lodge & Conference Center 2400 S Cabrillo Hwy	Half Moon Bay	CA	94019	**800-710-0778**	650-726-9000	373
Half.com Inc 500 S Gravers Rd *Cust Svc	Plymouth Meeting	PA	19462	**800-545-9857***	610-567-1090	96
Halff Assoc Inc 8616 NW Plaza Dr	Dallas	TX	75225	**800-425-3387**	214-346-6200	258
HalfPrice Hosting PO Box 22789	Louisville	KY	40252	**800-284-9391**	502-214-4100	795
Halifax Corp 5250 Cherokee Ave AMEX: HX ■ *Cust Svc	Alexandria	VA	22312	**800-944-2543***	703-750-2202	261-1
Halkey-Roberts Corp 11600 Dr ML King Jr St N *Sales	Saint Petersburg	FL	33716	**800-303-4384***	727-577-1300	776
Hall Automotive 441 Viking Dr	Virginia Beach	VA	23452	**800-242-4255**	757-431-9944	57
Hall China Co 1 Anna St PO Box 989 *Cust Svc	East Liverpool	OH	43920	**800-445-4255***	330-385-2900	716
Hall Contracting Corp 6415 Lakeview Rd	Charlotte	NC	28269	**800-741-2117**	704-598-0818	187-10
Hall CP Co 311 S Wacker Dr Suite 4700	Chicago	IL	60606	**800-762-6198**	312-554-7400	142
Hall Industries Inc 514 Mecklem Ln	Ellwood City	PA	16117	**800-828-5519**	724-752-2000	610
Hall Signs Inc PO Box 2267 Dept 15 *Cust Svc	Bloomington	IN	47402	**800-284-7446***	812-332-9355	692
Hallamore Motor Transportation Inc 795 Plymouth St	Holbrook	MA	02343	**800-242-1300**	781-767-2000	769
Hallcrest Inc 1820 Pickwick Ln	Glenview	IL	60025	**800-527-1419**	847-998-8580	201
Halliburton Co Engineering & Construction Group DBA Kellogg Brown & Root 4100 Clinton Dr	Houston	TX	77020	**800-231-8166**	713-753-2000	258
Halliburton Screen Co 1815 Shearn St	Houston	TX	77007	**800-527-4772**	713-869-5771	676
Hallmark Cards Inc 2501 McGee St	Kansas City	MO	64108	**800-425-5627**	816-274-5111	130
Hallmark Channel 12700 Ventura Blvd Suite 200	Studio City	CA	91604	**888-390-7474**	818-755-2400	725
Hallmark Hall of Fame Productions Inc 12001 Ventura Pl Suite 300	Studio City	CA	91604	**800-425-5627**	818-505-9191	503
Hallmark International 2501 McGee St	Kansas City	MO	64108	**800-425-5627**	816-274-5111	130
Hallmark Resort PO Box 547	Cannon Beach	OR	97110	**800-345-5676**	503-436-1566	373
Hallmark Sweet 49 Pearl St	Attleboro	MA	02703	**800-225-2706**	508-222-9234	401
Halls Merchandising Inc 200 E 25th St	Kansas City	MO	64108	**888-545-2121**	816-274-8111	227
Hallwood Commercial Real Estate LLC 3710 Rawlins St Suite 1500	Dallas	TX	75219	**800-225-0135**	214-528-5588	641
Hallwood Group Inc 3710 Rawlins St Suite 1500 AMEX: HWG	Dallas	TX	75219	**800-225-0135**	214-528-5588	184
Halmode Apparel Inc 1400 Broadway 11th Fl	New York	NY	10018	**800-388-0938**	212-564-7800	153-21
HALO Branded Solutions 1980 Industrial Dr	Sterling	IL	61081	**800-683-4256**	815-625-0980	10
Halo Distributing Co 200 Lombrano St	San Antonio	TX	78207	**800-749-4256**	210-735-1111	82-1
Halogen Software Inc 17 Auriga Dr	Ottawa	ON	K2E7Y9	**866-566-7778**	613-744-2254	176-1
Halsey & Griffith Inc 313 Datura St	West Palm Beach	FL	33401	**800-466-1921**	561-820-8000	524
Halsted Corp 78 Halladay St	Jersey City	NJ	07304	**800-843-5184**	201-433-3323	68
HALT - An Organization of Americans for Legal Reform 1612 K St NW Suite 510	Washington	DC	20006	**888-367-4258**	202-887-8255	48-7
Haltoms Jewelers 317 Main St	Fort Worth	TX	76102	**800-850-2303**	817-336-4051	402
Halton Co PO Box 3377	Portland	OR	97208	**800-452-7676**	503-288-6411	353
Hambrecht WR & Co 539 Bryant St Suite 100 *Cust Svc	San Francisco	CA	94107	**877-673-6476***	415-551-8600	679
Hambro Forest Products Inc PO Box 129	Crescent City	CA	95531	**800-442-6276**	707-464-6131	286
Hamburg Brothers Inc 40 24th St	Pittsburgh	PA	15222	**800-568-4624**	412-227-6200	38
Hamburg Chamber of Commerce 8 S Buffalo St	Hamburg	NY	14075	**877-322-6890**	716-649-7917	137
Hamburg Sud North America Inc 465 South St	Morristown	NJ	07960	**800-901-7447**	973-775-5300	308
Hamilton Beach/Proctor-Silex Inc 4421 Waterfront Dr *Cust Svc	Glen Allen	VA	23060	**800-851-8900***	804-273-9777	37
Hamilton Caster & Mfg Co 1637 Dixie Hwy	Hamilton	OH	45011	**800-733-7665**	513-863-3300	345

Alphabetical Section

Name / Address	City	State	ZIP	Toll-Free	Phone	Class
Hamilton College 198 College Hill Rd	Clinton	NY	13323	**800-843-2655**	315-859-4421	163
Hamilton College - Lincoln 1821 K St	Lincoln	NE	68508	**800-742-7738**	402-474-5315	158
Hamilton College - Omaha 3350 N 90th St	Omaha	NE	68134	**800-642-1456**	402-572-8500	158
Hamilton County Convention & Visitors Bureau 11601 Municipal Dr	Fishers	IN	46038	**800-776-8687**	317-598-4444	205
Hamilton County Electric Co-op Assn PO Box 753	Hamilton	TX	76531	**800-595-3401**	254-386-3123	244
Hamilton Crowne Plaza Hotel Washington DC 1001 14th St NW	Washington	DC	20005	**800-263-9802**	202-682-0111	373
Hamilton Dorsey Alston Co 4401 Northside Pkwy Suite 400	Atlanta	GA	30327	**888-717-4393**	770-850-0050	383
Hamilton Fixture Co 3550 Symmes Rd	Hamilton	OH	45015	**800-889-2165**	513-874-2016	281
Hamilton Group 100 Elwood Davis Rd	North Syracuse	NY	13212	**800-351-3066**	315-413-0086	268
Hamilton Materials Inc 345 W Meats Ave	Orange	CA	92865	**800-331-5569**	714-637-2770	341
Hamilton Precision Metals Inc 1780 Rohrerstown Rd	Lancaster	PA	17601	**800-476-7065**	717-569-7061	478
Hamilton Printing Co Inc PO Box 232	Rensselaer	NY	12144	**800-242-4222**	518-732-4491	614
Hamilton Sorter Co Inc 3158 Production Dr	Fairfield	OH	45014	**800-503-9900**	513-870-4400	201
Hamilton Tiger-Cats 75 Balsam Ave N Ivor Wynne Stadium	Hamilton	ON	L8L8C1	**800-714-7627**	905-547-2418	703
Hamilton Watch Co Inc 1200 Harbor Blvd *Cust Svc	Weehawken	NJ	07086	**800-456-5354***	201-271-1400	151
Hamline University 1536 Hewitt Ave	Saint Paul	MN	55104	**800-753-9753**	651-523-2207	163
Hamline University School of Law 1536 Hewitt Ave	Saint Paul	MN	55104	**800-388-3688**	651-523-2461	164-1
Hamm NR Quarry Inc PO Box 17	Perry	KS	66073	**888-597-5464**	785-597-5111	493-5
Hammacher Schlemmer & Co 303 W Erie St	Chicago	IL	60610	**800-233-4800**	312-664-8170	357
Hammel Green & Abrahamson Inc 701 Washington Ave N	Minneapolis	MN	55401	**888-442-8255**	612-758-4000	258
Hammer Co Inc 9450 Rosemont Dr	Streetsboro	OH	44241	**800-258-9463**	330-422-9463	82-3
Hammer Nutrition Ltd 4952 Whitefish Stage Rd *Cust Svc	Whitefish	MT	59937	**800-336-1977***	406-862-1877	786
Hammerman Brothers Inc 40 W 57th St	New York	NY	10019	**800-223-6436**	212-956-2800	401
Hammett JL Co 1 Hammett Pl *Cust Svc	Braintree	MA	02184	**800-955-2200***	781-848-1000	673
Hammett's Learning World 1 Hammett Pl	Braintree	MA	02184	**800-955-2200**	781-848-1000	673
Hammond Communications Group Inc 173 Trade St	Lexington	KY	40511	**888-424-1878**	859-254-1878	502
Hammond Electronics Inc 1230 W Central Blvd *Sales	Orlando	FL	32805	**800-929-3672***	407-849-6060	245
Hammond Suzuki USA 733 Annoreno Dr	Addison	IL	60101	**800-466-2286**	630-543-0277	516
Hammond World Atlas Corp 95 Progress St	Union	NJ	07083	**800-526-4953**	908-206-1300	623-1
Hammons Juanita K Hall for the Performing Arts 901 S National Ave	Springfield	MO	65804	**888-476-7849**	417-836-6776	562
Hammons Products Co 105 Hammons Dr PO Box 140	Stockton	MO	65785	**888-429-6887**	417-276-5181	11-10
Hamon Research-Cottrell Inc 58 E Main St	Somerville	NJ	08876	**800-722-3048**	908-685-4000	379
Hampden Papers Inc PO Box 149	Holyoke	MA	01041	**800-456-0200**	413-536-1000	544
Hampden-Sydney College PO Box 667	Hampden-Sydney	VA	23943	**800-755-0733**	434-223-6120	163
Hampshire College 89 West St	Amherst	MA	01002	**877-937-4267**	413-549-4600	163
Hampshire Group Ltd PO Box 2667 *NASDAQ: HAMP*	Anderson	SC	29622	**800-275-3520**	864-225-6232	153-10
Hampshire House Hotel & Conference Center 30 Tri-County Pkwy	Cincinnati	OH	45246	**800-543-4211**	513-772-5440	373
Hampshire John H Inc 320 W 24th St	Baltimore	MD	21211	**800-638-0076**	410-366-8900	188-2
Hampstead Hospital 218 East Rd	Hampstead	NH	03841	**800-600-5311**	603-329-5311	366-3
Hampton Affiliates 9600 SW Barnes Rd Sunset Business Pk Suite 200	Portland	OR	97225	**888-310-1464**	503-297-7691	671
Hampton Conventions & Visitors Bureau 1919 Commerce Dr Suite 290	Hampton	VA	23666	**800-487-8778**	757-722-1222	205
Hampton Inn 755 Crossover Ln	Memphis	TN	38117	**800-426-7866**	901-374-5000	369
Hampton Inn & Suites 755 Crossover Ln	Memphis	TN	38117	**800-426-7866**	901-374-5000	369
Hampton Inn & Suites Santa Ana/Orange County Airport 2720 Hotel Terrace Dr	Santa Ana	CA	92705	**800-333-3333**	714-556-3838	373
Hampton Technologies LLC 19 Industrial Blvd	Medford	NY	11763	**800-229-1019**	631-924-1335	459
Hampton University 100 E Queen St *Admissions	Hampton	VA	23668	**800-624-3328***	757-727-5000	163
Hamrick Industries 742 Peachoid Rd	Gaffney	SC	29341	**800-487-5411**	864-489-6095	153-3
Hamworthy Peabody Combustion Inc 70 Shelton Technology Ctr	Shelton	CT	06484	**877-732-2639**	203-922-1199	352
Hana Hou Magazine (Hawaiian Airlines) 3465 Waialae Ave Suite 340	Honolulu	HI	96816	**888-733-3336**	808-733-3333	449-22
Hanafin Robert J Inc PO Box 509	Endicott	NY	13761	**800-448-4826**	607-754-3500	383
Hanalei Bay Resort & Suites 5380 Honoiki Rd	Princeville	HI	96722	**800-827-4427**	808-826-6522	655
Hanauer JB & Co 4 Gatehall Dr	Parsippany	NJ	07054	**800-631-1094**	973-829-1000	679
Hanchett Mfg Inc 900 N State St	Big Rapids	MI	49307	**800-454-7403**	231-796-7070	447
Hanco Corp 3650 Dodd Rd *Cust Svc	Eagan	MN	55123	**800-328-7400***	651-456-5600	740
Hancock Bank 2510 14th St	Gulfport	MS	39501	**800-522-6542**	228-868-4000	71
Hancock Concrete Products Inc 17 Atlantic Ave	Hancock	MN	56244	**800-992-8982**	320-392-5207	181
Hancock Holding Co 2510 14th St *NASDAQ: HBHC*	Gulfport	MS	39501	**800-522-6542**	228-868-4000	355-2
Hancock Memorial Hospital 801 N State St	Greenfield	IN	46140	**888-900-4677**	317-462-5544	366-2
Hancock-Wood Electric Co-op Inc PO Box 190	North Baltimore	OH	45872	**800-445-4840**	419-257-3241	244
Hand. American Society for Surgery of the 6300 N River Rd Suite 600	Rosemont	IL	60018	**888-576-2774**	847-384-8300	49-8
Hand Held Products Inc 700 Vision Dr	Skaneateles Falls	NY	13153	**800-782-4263**	315-685-4100	171-2
Handex Group Inc 30941 Suneagle Dr	Mount Dora	FL	32757	**800-989-3753**	352-735-1800	653
Handgards Inc 901 Hawkins Blvd	El Paso	TX	79915	**800-351-8161**	915-779-6606	566
Handicapped. Disabled & Alone/Life Services for the 352 Park Ave S 11th Fl	New York	NY	10010	**800-995-0066**	212-532-6740	48-17
Handicapped. National Foundation of Dentistry for the 1800 15th St Unit 100	Denver	CO	80202	**888-471-6334**	303-534-5360	48-17
Handle With Care Packaging Store 5675 DTC Blvd Suite 280	Greenwood Village	CO	80111	**800-525-6309**	303-741-6626	114
Handlery Hotel & Resort 950 Hotel Cir N	San Diego	CA	92108	**800-676-6567**	619-298-0511	655
Handlery Union Square Hotel 351 Geary St	San Francisco	CA	94102	**800-843-4343**	415-781-7800	373
Handley Industries Inc 2101 Brooklyn Rd	Jackson	MI	49203	**800-870-5088**	517-787-8821	198
Hands of Hope Hospice 105 N Far West Dr Suite 100	Saint Joseph	MO	64506	**800-443-1143**	816-271-7190	365
Handy Dandy Food Stores Inc 1800 Magnavox Way	Fort Wayne	IN	46804	**800-686-2836**	260-436-1415	203
Handy Hardware Wholesale Inc 8300 Tewantin Dr	Houston	TX	77061	**800-364-3835**	713-644-1495	346
Handy & Harman Tube Co Inc 701 W Township Line Rd	Norristown	PA	19403	**800-766-8823**	610-539-3900	481
Handy John T Co Inc PO Box 309	Crisfield	MD	21817	**800-426-3977**	410-968-1772	292-5
Handy NB Co 65 10th St	Lynchburg	VA	24504	**800-284-6242**	434-847-4495	601
Handyman Connection Inc 9403 Kenwood Rd Suite D-207	Cincinnati	OH	45242	**800-466-5530**	513-771-1122	188-11
Hanes Industries 500 N McLin Creek Rd	Conover	NC	28613	**800-438-9124**	828-464-4673	583
Hanes Mall 3320 Silas Creek Pkwy Suite 264	Winston-Salem	NC	27103	**800-443-6255**	336-765-8323	452
Hanger Orthopedic Group Inc 2 Bethesda Metro Ctr Suite 1200 *NYSE: HGR*	Bethesda	MD	20814	**800-765-3822**	301-986-0701	347
Hangsterfer's Laboratories Inc 175 Ogden Rd	Mantua	NJ	08051	**800-433-5823**	856-468-0216	530
Hanin Travel 2681 W Olympic Blvd Suite 101	Los Angeles	CA	90006	**800-839-5929**	213-388-4949	760
Hankook Tire America Corp 1450 Valley Rd	Wayne	NJ	07470	**800-426-5665**	973-633-9000	739
Hanley Co Inc 641 W Main St	Sun Prairie	WI	53590	**800-279-1422**	608-837-5111	270
Hanley-Hazelden 5200 East Ave	West Palm Beach	FL	33407	**800-444-7008**	561-841-1000	712
Hanna Andersson Corp 1010 NW Flanders St *Cust Svc	Portland	OR	97209	**800-222-0544***	503-242-0920	451
Hannaford Bros Co Inc 145 Pleasant Hill Rd	Scarborough	ME	04074	**800-341-6393**	207-883-2911	339
Hannay Reels Inc 553 SR 143	Westerlo	NY	12193	**877-467-3357**	518-797-3791	118
Hannibal Convention & Visitors Bureau 505 N 3rd St	Hannibal	MO	63401	**866-263-4825**	573-221-2477	205
Hannibal Courier-Post 200 N 3rd St PO Box A	Hannibal	MO	63401	**800-748-7025**	573-221-2800	522-2
Hannibal Industries Inc 3851 S Santa Fe Ave	Los Angeles	CA	90058	**800-433-3166**	323-588-4261	481
Hannibal-LaGrange College 2800 Palmyra Rd	Hannibal	MO	63401	**800-454-1119**	573-221-3675	163
Hannon Hydraulics Inc 625 N Loop 12	Irving	TX	75061	**800-333-4266**	972-438-2870	220
Hannover Life Reassurance Co of America 800 N Magnolia Ave Suite 1400	Orlando	FL	32803	**800-327-1910**	407-649-8411	384-2
Hanover Accessories Inc 3555 Holly Ln N Suite 60	Plymouth	MN	55447	**888-509-6100**	763-509-6100	750
Hanover College PO Box 108	Hanover	IN	47243	**800-213-2178**	812-866-7000	163
Hanover Compressor Co 8150 N Central Expy Suite 1550 *NYSE: HC* ■ *Sales	Dallas	TX	75206	**800-522-9270***	214-528-9270	378
Hanover Foods Corp 1550 York St PO Box 334	Hanover	PA	17331	**800-888-4646**	717-632-6000	291-36
Hanover Hospital 300 Highland Ave	Hanover	PA	17331	**800-673-2426**	717-637-3711	366-2
Hanover Inc 11000 Corporate Ctr Dr Suite 200	Houston	TX	77041	**800-366-0980**	281-854-3000	528
Hanover Inn PO Box 151	Hanover	NH	03755	**800-443-7024**	603-643-4300	373
Hanover Insurance Co 100 North Pkwy	Worcester	MA	01605	**800-922-8427**	508-853-7200	384-4
Hanover Lantern Inc 350 Kindig Ln	Hanover	PA	17331	**800-233-7196**	717-632-6464	431
Hanover Wire Cloth 500 E Middle St PO Box 473	Hanover	PA	17331	**800-323-5585**	717-637-3795	676
Hanovia Corp 825 Lehigh Ave	Union	NJ	07083	**800-229-3666**	908-688-0050	429
Hans Johnsen Co Inc 8901 Chancellor Row *Sales	Dallas	TX	75247	**800-879-1515***	214-879-1550	346
Hansel 'n Gretel Brand Inc 79-36 Cooper Ave	Glendale	NY	11385	**800-635-3354**	718-326-0041	465
Hansen Harry Management Inc 151 Herricks Rd Suite 1	Garden City Park	NY	11040	**800-284-6228**	516-739-2510	183
Hansen Natural Corp 1010 Railroad St *NASDAQ: HANS*	Corona	CA	92882	**800-426-7367**	951-739-6200	81-2
Hansen's Disease Programs. National 1770 Physicians Park Dr	Baton Rouge	LA	70816	**800-642-2477**	225-756-3773	654
Hansen's Furniture Inc 411 Fraine Barracks Rd	Bismarck	ND	58504	**888-221-2565**	701-223-2565	316
Hansgrohe Inc 1490 Bluegrass Lakes Pkwy Suite 200	Alpharetta	GA	30004	**800-334-0455**	770-360-9880	598

Name / Address	City	State	Zip	Toll-Free	Phone	Class
Hanson Brick & Tile 15720 John J Delany Dr	Charlotte	NC	28277	**877-426-7668**	704-341-8750	148
Hanson Building Products North America 3500 Maple Ave	Dallas	TX	75219	**800-527-2362**	214-525-5500	181
Hanson CH Co 3630 N Wolf Rd	Franklin Park	IL	60131	**800-827-3398**	847-451-0500	459
Hanson Engineers Inc 1525 S 6th St	Springfield	IL	62703	**800-788-2450**	217-788-2450	258
Hanson Pipe & Products PO Box 368	Green Cove Springs	FL	32043	**800-432-0030**	904-284-3213	181
Hanson Silo Co 11587 County Rd 8 SE	Lake Lillian	MN	56253	**800-450-4171**	320-664-4171	269
Hapco Inc 26252 Hillman Hwy	Abingdon	VA	24210	**800-368-7171**	276-628-7171	482
Hapman Conveyors 6002 E Kilgore Rd	Kalamazoo	MI	49048	**800-427-6260**	269-382-8200	206
Happy Harry's Inc 326 Ruthar Dr	Newark	DE	19711	**866-994-2779**	302-366-0335	236
Happy & Healthy Products Inc 1600 S Dixie Hwy Suite 200	Boca Raton	FL	33432	**800-378-4854**	561-367-0739	292-6
Happy Valley School PO Box 850	Ojai	CA	93024	**800-900-0437**	805-646-4343	611
Hapuna Beach Prince Hotel 62-100 Kauna'oa Dr	Kamuela	HI	96743	**800-882-6060**	808-880-1111	655
Har-Con Corp 551 N Shepherd Dr Suite 270	Houston	TX	77007	**800-438-0536**	713-869-8451	188-10
Harben Inc 2010 Ronald Regan Blvd.	Cumming	GA	30041	**800-327-5387**	770-889-9535	627
Harbison-Fischer Mfg PO Box 2477	Fort Worth	TX	76113	**800-364-7867**	817-297-2211	526
Harbor Beach Resort & Spa. Marriott 3030 Holiday Dr.	Fort Lauderdale	FL	33316	**800-228-9290**	954-525-4000	655
Harbor Court Hotel 165 Steuart St	San Francisco	CA	94105	**800-346-0555**	415-882-1300	373
Harbor Court Hotel 550 Light St	Baltimore	MD	21202	**800-824-0076**	410-234-0550	373
Harbor Federal Savings Bank 100 S 2nd St	Fort Pierce	FL	34950	**888-613-2262**	772-461-2414	71
Harbor Florida Bancshares Inc 100 S 2nd St *NASDAQ: HARB*	Fort Pierce	FL	34950	**800-234-1959**	772-461-2414	355-2
Harbor House 28 Pier 21	Galveston	TX	77550	**800-874-3721**	409-763-3321	373
Harbor House Village South Beach St.	Nantucket	MA	02554	**800-475-2637**	508-228-1500	655
Harbor Industries Inc 14130 172nd Ave	Grand Haven	MI	49417	**800-968-6993**	616-842-5330	231
Harbor Light Hospice 800 Roosevelt Rd Bldg C Suite 206	Glen Ellyn	IL	60137	**800-419-0542**	630-942-0100	365
Harbor Sales Co Inc 1000 Harbor Ct.	Sudlersville	MD	21668	**800-345-1712**		602
Harbor View Hotel 131 N Water St PO Box 7 Martha's Vineyard	Edgartown	MA	02539	**800-225-6005**	508-627-7000	373
Harborlite Corp PO Box 100	Vicksburg	MI	49097	**800-403-4869**	269-649-1352	490
HarborOne Credit Union 68 Legion Pkwy	Brockton	MA	02301	**800-244-7592**	508-895-1000	216
Harborplace & The Gallery 200 E Pratt St	Baltimore	MD	21202	**800-427-2671**	410-332-4191	50
Harborside Event Center 1375 Monroe St	Fort Myers	FL	33901	**800-294-9516**	239-332-7600	204
Harborside Hotel & Marina 55 West St	Bar Harbor	ME	04609	**800-328-5033**	207-288-5033	373
Harborside Inn Christie's Landing	Newport	RI	02840	**800-427-9444**	401-846-6600	373
Harborside Inn of Boston 185 State St.	Boston	MA	02109	**800-437-7668**	617-723-7500	373
Harbour Town Resort & Yacht Club 149 Lighthouse Rd	Hilton Head Island	SC	29928	**800-541-7375**	843-671-1400	655
Harbour's Edge 401 E Linton Blvd.	Delray Beach	FL	33483	**800-232-1358**	561-272-7979	659
Harbourtowne Golf Resort & Conference Center 9784 Martingham Dr	Saint Michaels	MD	21663	**800-446-9066**	410-745-9066	655
Harco National Insurance Co PO Box 68309	Schumburg	IL	60168	**800-448-4642**	847-321-4800	384-4
Harcourt Achieve 6277 Sea Harbor Dr	Orlando	FL	32887	**800-531-5015**		623-2
Harcourt Assessment Inc 19500 Bulverde Rd.	San Antonio	TX	78259	**800-228-0752**	210-339-5000	243
Harcourt Equipment 313 Hwy 169 & 175 E	Harcourt	IA	50544	**800-445-5646**	515-354-5331	270
Harcourt Inc 6277 Sea Harbor Dr	Orlando	FL	32887	**800-782-4479**	407-345-2000	623-2
Harcourt Outlines Inc 7765 S 175 West PO Box 128	Milroy	IN	46156	**800-428-6584**	765-629-2625	55
Harcourt Pencil Co 7765 S 175 W	Milroy	IN	46156	**800-215-4024**	765-629-2244	560
Harcros Chemicals Inc 5200 Speaker Rd	Kansas City	KS	66106	**800-765-4748**	913-321-3131	144
Harcum College 750 Montgomery Ave.	Bryn Mawr	PA	19010	**800-345-2600**	610-525-4100	160
Hard Mfg Co Inc 230 Grider St	Buffalo	NY	14215	**800-873-4273**	716-893-1800	314-3
Hard Rock Cafe International Inc 6100 Old Park Ln	Orlando	FL	32835	**800-235-7625**	407-445-7625	657
Hard Rock Hotel & Casino 4455 Paradise Rd.	Las Vegas	NV	89109	**800-473-7625**	702-693-5000	655
Hardee's Food Systems Inc 505 N 7th St.	Saint Louis	MO	63101	**800-711-4274**	314-259-6200	657
Hardel Mutual Plywood Corp PO Box 566	Chehalis	WA	98532	**800-562-6344**	360-740-0232	602
Harder Mechanical Contractors Inc PO Box 5118	Portland	OR	97208	**800-392-3729**	503-281-1112	188-10
Harder Paper & Packaging 5301 Verona Rd	Madison	WI	53711	**800-261-3400**	608-271-5127	549
HARDI (Heating Airconditioning & Refrigeration Distributors International) 1389 Dublin Rd.	Columbus	OH	43215	**888-253-2128**	614-488-1835	49-18
Hardie James Building Products 26300 La Alameda Ave Suite 250	Mission Viejo	CA	92691	**888-542-7343**	949-348-1800	190-4
Hardigg Industries Inc 147 N Main St	South Deerfield	MA	01373	**800-542-7344**	413-665-2163	198
Hardin County Convention & Visitors Bureau 495 Main St.	Savannah	TN	38372	**800-552-3866**	731-925-2364	205
Hardin-Simmons University 2200 Hickory St	Abilene	TX	79698	**800-568-2692**	325-670-1000	163
Harding University 900 E Center Ave	Searcy	AR	72149	**800-477-4407**	501-279-4000	163
Hardinge Inc 1 Hardinge Dr. *NASDAQ: HDNG*	Elmira	NY	14902	**800-843-8801**	607-734-2281	447

Name / Address	City	State	Zip	Toll-Free	Phone	Class
Hardware Assn. National Retail 5822 W 74th St *Cust Svc	Indianapolis	IN	46278	**800-772-4424***	317-290-0338	49-18
Hardware Distribution Warehouses Inc (HDW) 6900 Woolworth Rd *Cust Svc	Shreveport	LA	71129	**800-256-8527***	318-686-8527	346
Hardware Specialty Co Inc 4875 36th St.	Long Island City	NY	11101	**800-800-9269**	718-361-9393	245
Hardwick Clothes Inc 3800 Old Tasso Rd NE	Cleveland	TN	37312	**800-251-6392**	423-476-6534	153-12
Hardwood Lumber Assn. National 6830 Raleigh-LaGrange Rd	Memphis	TN	38134	**800-933-0318**	901-377-1818	49-3
Hardy Corp 430 12th St S	Birmingham	AL	35233	**800-289-4822**	205-252-7191	188-10
Hardy James G & Co 352 7th Ave Suite 1223	New York	NY	10001	**800-847-4076**	212-689-6680	356
Harford County Chamber of Commerce 108 S Bond St	Bel Air	MD	21014	**800-682-8536**	410-838-2020	137
Harford Systems Inc 2225 Pulaski Hwy PO Box 700	Aberdeen	MD	21001	**800-664-7620**	410-272-3400	473
Hargrave Military Academy 200 Military Dr	Chatham	VA	24531	**800-432-2480**	434-432-2481	611
Hargray Communications PO Box 5986	Hilton Head Island	SC	29938	**800-726-1266**	843-686-5000	721
Harker's Distribution Inc 801 6th St SW	Le Mars	IA	51031	**800-798-9800**	712-546-8171	292-10
Harkins Builders Inc 2201 Warwick Way	Marriottsville	MD	21104	**888-224-5697**	410-750-2600	185
Harlan Bioproducts for Science Inc PO Box 29176	Indianapolis	IN	46229	**800-972-4362**	317-353-8810	229
Harlan Materials Handling Corp PO Box 15159	Kansas City	KS	66115	**800-255-4262**	913-342-5650	462
Harlan Sprague Dawley Inc 298 S Carroll Rd.	Indianapolis	IN	46229	**800-793-7287**	317-894-7521	411
Harlem Globetrotters International Inc 400 E Van Buren St Suite 300	Phoenix	AZ	85004	**800-641-4667**	602-258-0000	179
Harlequin Enterprises Ltd 225 Duncan Mill Rd	Don Mills	ON	M3B3K9	**800-387-0112**	416-445-5860	623-2
Harlequin Enterprises Ltd Distribution Center 3010 Walden Ave	Depew	NY	14043	**800-873-8635**	716-684-1800	97
Harley-Davidson Inc 3700 W Juneau Ave *NYSE: HDI*	Milwaukee	WI	53208	**800-443-2153**	414-342-4680	506
Harley-Davison Financial Services 150 S Wacker Dr Suite 3100	Chicago	IL	60606	**800-538-3150**	312-368-9501	215
Harleysville Atlantic Insurance Co 107 Southern Blvd	Savannah	GA	31405	**800-543-6355**	912-234-1281	384-4
Harleysville Group Inc 355 Maple Ave *NASDAQ: HGIC*	Harleysville	PA	19438	**800-222-1981**	215-256-5000	355-4
Harleysville Insurance Co of New Jersey 308 Harper Dr Suite 200	Morristown	NJ	08057	**888-595-9876**	856-642-1646	384-4
Harleysville Insurance Co of New York 120 Washington St.	Watertown	NY	13601	**800-962-1006**	315-782-1160	384-4
Harleysville Mutual Insurance Co 355 Maple Ave	Harleysville	PA	19438	**800-523-6344**	215-256-5000	384-2
Harleysville National Bank & Trust Co 483 Main St	Harleysville	PA	19438	**800-423-3955**	215-256-8851	71
Harleysville National Corp 483 Main St *NASDAQ: HNBC*	Harleysville	PA	19438	**800-423-3955**	215-256-8851	355-2
Harleysville Savings Financial Corp 271 Main St *NASDAQ: HARL*	Harleysville	PA	19438	**888-256-8828**	215-256-8828	355-2
Harlingen Area Chamber of Commerce 311 E Tyler St.	Harlingen	TX	78550	**800-531-7346**	956-423-5440	137
Harlo Corp PO Box 129	Grandville	MI	49468	**800-391-4151**	616-538-0550	462
Harman International Industries Inc 1101 Pennsylvania Ave NW Suite 1010 *NYSE: HAR* ■ *Cust Svc	Washington	DC	20004	**800-336-4525***	202-393-1101	52
Harman Kardon Inc 250 Crossways Pk Dr.	Woodbury	NY	11797	**800-336-4525**	516-496-3400	52
Harmon Autoglass 4000 Olson Memorial Hwy Suite 600	Minneapolis	MN	55422	**800-352-0777**	763-521-5100	62-2
Harmon Electric Assn Inc PO Box 393	Hollis	OK	73550	**800-643-7769**	580-688-3342	244
Harmonic Inc 549 Baltic Way *NASDAQ: HLIT*	Sunnyvale	CA	94089	**800-788-1330**	408-542-2500	633
Harmony Blue Granite Co Inc PO Box 958	Elberton	GA	30635	**800-241-7000**	706-283-3111	710
Harmony Safari Park 431 Clouds Cove Rd.	Huntsville	AL	35803	**877-726-4625**		811
Harmony Sports 22 Village Dr	Riverside	RI	02915	**800-882-3448**	401-490-9334	701
Harnack Co 6016 Nordic Dr *Cust Svc	Cedar Falls	IA	50613	**800-772-2022***	319-277-0660	420
Harodite Finishing Co 66 South St.	Taunton	MA	02780	**800-328-5656**	508-824-6961	730-7
Harold Freeman & Co 275 7th Ave	New York	NY	10001	**800-221-4092**	212-989-9001	401
Harold LeMay Enterprises Inc 13502 Pacific Ave.	Tacoma	WA	98444	**800-345-3629**	253-537-8687	791
Harold Levinson Assoc Inc 21 Banfi Plaza	Farmingdale	NY	11735	**800-325-2512**	631-962-2400	744
Harold's Stores Inc 5919 Maple Ave. *AMEX: HLD*	Dallas	TX	75235	**800-949-3533**	214-366-0600	155-4
Harper Brush Works Inc 400 N 2nd	Fairfield	IA	52556	**800-223-7894**	641-472-5186	104
HarperCollins Canada Ltd 1995 Markham Rd	Scarborough	ON	M1B5M8	**800-387-0117**	416-321-2241	623-2
HarperCollins Children's Books Group 1350 Ave of the Americas *Cust Svc	New York	NY	10019	**800-242-7737***	212-261-6500	623-2
HarperCollins Publishers Avon Books Div 10 E 53rd St.	New York	NY	10022	**800-242-7737**	212-207-7000	623-2
HarperCollins Publishers Inc 10 E 53rd St. *Cust Svc	New York	NY	10022	**800-242-7737***	212-207-7000	623-2
Harper's Bazaar Magazine 1700 Broadway	New York	NY	10019	**800-888-3045**	212-903-5000	449-11
Harper's Magazine 666 Broadway	New York	NY	10012	**800-444-4653**	212-420-5720	449-11
Harpoon Brewery 306 Northern Ave	Boston	MA	02210	**888-427-7666**	617-574-9551	103

Company / Address	City	State	ZIP	Toll-Free	Phone	Class
Harrah's Ak-Chin Casino Resort 15406 Maricopa Rd	Maricopa	AZ	85239	**888-302-3293**	480-802-3091	655
Harrah's Atlantic City 777 Harrah's Blvd	Atlantic City	NJ	08401	**800-427-7247**	609-441-5000	133
Harrah's Cherokee Casino & Hotel 777 Casino Dr	Cherokee	NC	28719	**800-427-7247**	828-497-7777	133
Harrah's Council Bluffs 1 Harrah's Blvd	Council Bluffs	IA	51501	**888-598-8451**	712-329-6000	133
Harrah's Entertainment Inc 1 Harrah's Ct *NYSE: HET*	Las Vegas	NV	89119	**800-442-6443**	702-407-6000	132
Harrah's Joliet 151 N Joliet St	Joliet	IL	60432	**800-427-7247**	815-740-7800	133
Harrah's Lake Charles Casino & Hotel 505 N Lakeshore Dr	Lake Charles	LA	70601	**800-427-7247**	337-437-1500	133
Harrah's Lake Tahoe PO Box 8	Stateline	NV	89449	**800-427-7247**	775-588-6611	133
Harrah's Las Vegas 3475 Las Vegas Blvd S	Las Vegas	NV	89109	**800-427-7247**	702-369-5000	655
Harrah's Laughlin 2900 S Casino Dr PO Box 33000	Laughlin	NV	89029	**800-427-7247**	702-298-4600	133
Harrah's Metropolis Casino 100 E Front St	Metropolis	IL	62960	**800-929-5905**	618-524-2628	133
Harrah's New Orleans 512 S Peter St	New Orleans	LA	70130	**800-847-5299**	504-533-6000	133
Harrah's North Kansas City 1 Riverboat Dr	North Kansas City	MO	64116	**800-427-7247**	816-472-7777	373
Harrah's Phoenix Ak-Chin Casino Resort 15406 Maricopa Rd	Maricopa	AZ	85239	**800-427-7247**	480-802-5000	133
Harrah's Prairie Band Casino & Hotel 12305 150th Rd	Mayetta	KS	66509	**800-427-7247**	785-966-7777	133
Harrah's Reno 219 N Center St	Reno	NV	89501	**800-427-7247**	775-786-3232	373
Harrah's Rincon Casino & Resort 777 Harrah's Rincon Way	Valley Center	CA	92082	**877-777-2457**	760-751-3100	655
Harrah's Saint Louis Casino & Hotel 777 Casino Center Dr	Maryland Heights	MO	63043	**800-427-7247**	314-770-8100	133
Harrah's Vicksburg 1310 Mulberry St	Vicksburg	MS	39180	**800-843-2343**	601-636-3423	133
Harraseeket Inn 162 Main St	Freeport	ME	04032	**800-342-6423**	207-865-9377	373
Harrington College of Design 200 W Madison St Suite 200	Chicago	IL	60606	**877-939-4975**	312-939-4975	163
Harrington Don Discovery Center 1200 Streit Dr	Amarillo	TX	79106	**800-784-9548**	806-355-9547	510
Harrington Industrial Plastics LLC 14480 Yorba Ave	Chino	CA	91710	**800-669-8641**	909-597-8641	378
Harrington & King Perforating Co Inc 5655 W Fillmore St	Chicago	IL	60644	**800-621-3869**	773-626-1800	92
Harrington Signal Co 2519 4th Ave	Moline	IL	61265	**800-577-5758**	309-762-0731	681
Harrington Tools Inc PO Box 39879	Los Angeles	CA	90039	**800-331-6291**	323-245-2142	746
Harrington West Financial Group Inc 610 Alamo Pintado Rd *NASDAQ: HWFG*	Solvang	CA	93463	**800-525-4959**	805-688-6644	355-2
Harris Assoc LP 2 N La Salle St Suite 500	Chicago	IL	60602	**800-731-0700**	312-621-0600	393
Harris Bankcorp Inc 111 W Monroe St 18th Fl	Chicago	IL	60603	**888-340-2265**	312-461-2121	355-2
Harris Beach LLP 805 3rd Ave	New York	NY	10022	**888-999-0529**	212-687-0100	419
Harris Bernard C Publishing Co Inc 2500 Westchester Ave Suite 400	Purchase	NY	10577	**800-326-6600**		623-2
Harris Calorific Inc 2345 Murphy Blvd	Gainesville	GA	30504	**800-241-0804**	770-536-8801	798
Harris Cameron M & Co 6400 Fairview Rd	Charlotte	NC	28210	**800-868-8834**	704-366-8834	383
Harris Corp 1025 W NASA Blvd *NYSE: HRS*	Melbourne	FL	32919	**800-442-7747**	321-727-9100	633
Harris Corp Broadcast Communications Div 3200 Wismann Ln	Quincy	IL	62301	**800-622-0022**	217-222-8200	633
Harris Corp RF Communications Div 1680 University Ave	Rochester	NY	14610	**800-288-4277**	585-244-5830	633
Harris CT Inc 9411 Deepstep Rd	Sandersville	GA	31082	**800-547-6404**	478-552-5070	493-2
Harris Electric Supply Co Inc 656 Wedgewood Ave	Nashville	TN	37203	**800-342-1479**	615-255-4161	245
Harris Environmental Systems Inc 11 Connector Rd	Andover	MA	01810	**888-771-4200**	978-475-0104	650
Harris Farms Inc 23300 W Oakland Ave	Coalinga	CA	93210	**800-691-1199**	559-884-2477	11-11
Harris Group Inc 1000 Denny Way Suite 800	Seattle	WA	98109	**800-488-7410**	206-494-9400	258
Harris InfoSource 2057 E Aurora Rd	Twinsburg	OH	44087	**800-888-5900**	330-425-9000	623-6
Harris Interactive Inc 135 Corporate Woods *NASDAQ: HPOL*	Rochester	NY	14623	**800-866-7655**	585-272-8400	458
Harris Miniature Golf 141 W Burk Ave	Wildwood	NJ	08260	**888-294-6530**	609-522-4200	187-3
Harris Moran Seed Co 555 Codoni Ave	Modesto	CA	95352	**800-808-7333**	209-579-7333	684
Harris Ranch Beef Co PO Box 220	Selma	CA	93662	**800-742-1955**	559-896-3081	465
Harris Regional Hospital 68 Hospital Rd	Sylva	NC	28779	**800-496-2362**	828-586-7000	366-2
Harris-Tarkett Inc 2225 Eddie Williams Rd *Cust Svc	Johnson City	TN	37601	**800-842-7816***	423-928-3122	304
Harris Teeter Inc 701 Crestdale Dr *Cust Svc	Matthews	NC	28105	**800-432-6111***	704-844-3100	339
Harris Trust & Savings Bank 111 W Monroe St	Chicago	IL	60603	**888-340-2265**	312-461-2121	71
Harris Waste Management Group Inc 200 Clover Reach Dr	Peachtree City	GA	30269	**800-468-5657**	770-631-7290	791
Harrisburg Dairies Inc 2001 Herr St	Harrisburg	PA	17105	**800-692-7429**	717-233-8701	291-27
HarrisData 611 N Barker Rd Suite 200	Brookfield	WI	53045	**800-225-0585**	262-784-9099	178-1
Harrisdirect 501 Plaza II Harborside Financial Ctr	Jersey City	NJ	07311	**800-825-5873**		679
Harrison Conference Centers 755 Crossover Ln	Memphis	TN	38117	**800-422-6338**	901-374-5000	369
Harrison Hoge Industries 19 N Columbia St	Port Jefferson	NY	11777	**800-852-0925**	631-473-7308	701
Harrison Hot Springs Resort & Spa 100 Esplanade Ave	Harrison Hot Springs	BC	V0M1K0	**800-663-2266**	604-796-2244	655
Harrison Industries Inc PO Box 4009	Ventura	CA	93007	**800-418-7274**	805-647-1414	791
Harrison Paint Co 1329 Harrison Ave SW	Canton	OH	44706	**800-321-0680**	330-455-5125	540
Harrison Piping Supply Co Inc 38777 Schoolcraft Rd	Livonia	MI	48150	**800-482-3929**	734-464-4400	601
Harrison Rural Electrification Assn Inc Rt 6 Box 502	Clarksburg	WV	26301	**800-540-4732**	304-624-6365	244
Harrisonville Telephone Co 213 S Main St PO Box 149	Waterloo	IL	62298	**888-482-8353**	618-939-6112	721
Harry Cooper Supply Co Inc 605 N Sherman Pkwy	Springfield	MO	65802	**800-426-6737**	417-865-8392	601
Harry & David Co 2500 S Pacific Hwy *Cust Svc	Medford	OR	97501	**800-345-5655***	541-776-2121	333
Harry Davis & Co 1725 Blvd of Allies	Pittsburgh	PA	15219	**800-775-2289**	412-765-1170	51
Harry G Barr Co 6500 S Zero St	Fort Smith	AR	72903	**800-829-2277**	479-646-7891	233
Harry Hansen Management Inc 151 Herricks Rd Suite 1	Garden City Park	NY	11040	**800-284-6228**	516-739-2510	183
Harry Hynes Memorial Hospice 313 S Market St	Wichita	KS	67202	**800-767-4965**	316-265-9441	365
Harry L Murphy Inc 42 Bonaventura Dr	San Jose	CA	95134	**800-439-6777**	408-955-1100	285
Harry London Candies Inc 5353 Lauby Road *Cust Svc	North Canton	OH	44720	**800-321-0444***	330-494-0833	291-8
Harry Miller Co Inc 850 Albany St	Boston	MA	02119	**800-225-5598**	617-427-2300	718
Harry N Abrams Inc 100 5th Ave 7th Fl	New York	NY	10011	**800-345-1359**	212-206-7715	623-2
Harry Ritchie's Jewelers Inc 956 Willamette St *Cust Svc	Eugene	OR	97401	**800-935-2850***	541-686-1787	402
Harry S Truman Presidential Library & Museum 500 W Hwy 24	Independence	MO	64050	**800-833-1225**	816-833-1400	426
Harry Winston Inc 718 5th Ave	New York	NY	10019	**800-988-4110**	212-245-2000	401
Harsco Corp Gas Technologies Group PO Box 8316 *Cust Svc	Camp Hill	PA	17001	**800-821-2975***	717-763-5060	92
Harsco Track Technologies (HTT) 2401 Edmund Rd Box 20	West Columbia	SC	29171	**800-345-9160**	803-822-9160	636
Hart & Cooley Inc 500 E 8th St	Holland	MI	49423	**800-748-0392**	616-392-7855	482
Hart Crowser Inc 1910 Fairview Ave E	Seattle	WA	98102	**800-925-9530**	206-324-9530	258
Hart Electric Membership Corp PO Box 250	Hartwell	GA	30643	**800-241-4109**	706-376-4714	244
Hart Engineering Corp 29 Lark Industrial Pkwy	Greenville	RI	02828	**800-492-4278**	401-949-5300	258
Hart InterCivic 15500 Wells Port Dr PO Box 80649	Austin	TX	78708	**800-223-4278**	512-252-6400	788
Hart & Price Corp PO Box 36368	Dallas	TX	75235	**800-777-9129**	214-521-9129	651
Hart Publications Inc 4545 Post Oak Pl Suite 210	Houston	TX	77027	**800-874-2544**	713-993-9320	623-9
Hart Scientific Inc 799 E Utah Valley Dr	American Fork	UT	84003	**800-438-4278**	801-763-1600	200
Harte-Hanks Direct Marketing 55 5th Ave 14th Fl	New York	NY	10003	**800-543-2212**	212-889-5000	722
Harte-Hanks Inc PO Box 269 *NYSE: HHS*	San Antonio	TX	78291	**800-456-9748**	210-829-9000	5
Harte-Hanks Market Intelligence 9980 Huennekens St	San Diego	CA	92121	**800-854-8409**	858-450-1667	194
Harte-Hanks Response Management 2800 Wells Branch Pkwy	Austin	TX	78728	**800-333-3383**	512-434-1100	722
Harter Group Inc 11451 Harter Dr	Middlebury	IN	46540	**800-543-5449**	574-825-5871	314-1
Hartford Advocate 100 Constitution Plaza	Hartford	CT	06103	**800-442-4266**	860-548-9300	522-4
Hartford College for Women 1265 Asylum Ave *Admissions	Hartford	CT	06105	**866-468-6429***	860-768-5600	160
Hartford Computer Group Inc 1610 Colonial Pkwy	Inverness	IL	60067	**800-680-4424**	224-836-3000	178
Hartford Courant 285 Broad St	Hartford	CT	06115	**800-524-4242**	860-241-6200	522-2
Hartford Distributors Inc PO Box 8400	Manchester	CT	06040	**800-832-7211**	860-643-2337	82-1
Hartford Electric Supply Co (HESCO) 571 New Park Ave PO Box 331010	West Hartford	CT	06133	**800-969-5444**	860-236-6363	245
Hartford Life & Accident Insurance Co 200 Hopmeadow St	Simsbury	CT	06089	**800-833-5575**	860-525-8555	384-2
Hartford Mutual Funds PO Box 64387	Saint Paul	MN	55164	**888-843-7824**		517
Hartford Steam Boiler Inspection & Insurance Co 1 State St PO Box 5024	Hartford	CT	06102	**800-472-1866**	860-722-1866	384-4
Hartford Technologies 1022 Elm St	Rocky Hill	CT	06067	**888-840-9565**	860-571-3601	77
Hartford's Omni Auto Plan PO Box 105440	Atlanta	GA	30348	**800-777-6664**	770-952-4500	384-4
Hartgrove Hospital 520 N Ridgeway Ave	Chicago	IL	60624	**800-478-4783**	773-722-3113	366-3
Hartley Data Service Inc 1807 Glenview Rd	Glenview	IL	60025	**800-433-2796**	847-724-9280	223
Hartman-Walsh Painting Co 7144 N Market St	Saint Louis	MO	63133	**800-899-3535**	314-863-1800	188-8
Hartmarx Inc 101 N Wacker Dr	Chicago	IL	60606	**800-327-4466**	312-372-6300	153-12
Hartness House Inn 30 Orchard St	Springfield	VT	05156	**800-732-4789**	802-885-2115	373
Hartness International Inc PO Box 26509	Greenville	SC	29616	**800-845-8791**	864-297-1200	537
Harts Nursery of Jefferson Inc 4049 Jefferson-Scio Rd	Jefferson	OR	97352	**800-356-9335**	541-327-3366	363
Hartstone Inc PO Box 2310	Zanesville	OH	43701	**800-339-4278**	740-452-9000	716
Hartsville (Greater) Chamber of Commerce 214 N 5th St PO Box 578	Hartsville	SC	29550	**888-427-8720**	843-332-6401	137
Hartung Brothers Inc 918 Deming Way Suite 200	Madison	WI	53717	**800-362-2522**	608-829-6000	11-11
Hartz & Co 1341 Hughes Ford Rd	Frederick	MD	21701	**800-638-8170**	301-662-7500	153-12
Hartz Mountain Corp 400 Plaza Dr	Secaucus	NJ	07094	**800-929-6700**	201-271-4800	568
Hartzell Fan Inc 910 S Downing St	Piqua	OH	45356	**800-336-3267**	937-773-7411	19

Name / Address	City	State	ZIP	Toll-Free	Phone	Class
Harvard Bioscience Inc 84 October Hill Rd *NASDAQ: HBIO*	Holliston	MA	01746	**800-272-2775**	508-893-8999	410
Harvard Business Review 60 Harvard Way	Boston	MA	02163	**800-274-3214**	617-783-7500	449-5
Harvard Business School Publishing 60 Harvard Way	Boston	MA	02163	**800-545-7685**	617-783-7400	623-5
Harvard Coop Society 1400 Massachusetts Ave	Cambridge	MA	02138	**800-242-1882**	617-499-2000	96
Harvard Educational Review 8 Story St 1st Fl	Cambridge	MA	02138	**800-513-0763**	617-495-3432	449-8
Harvard Folding Box Co Inc 71 Linden St	Lynn	MA	01905	**800-876-1246**	781-598-1600	102
Harvard Management Co Inc 600 Atlantic Ave 16th Fl	Boston	MA	02210	**800-723-0044**	617-523-4400	779
Harvard Pilgrim Health Care Inc 93 Worcester St	Wellesley	MA	02481	**888-888-4742**	617-509-1000	384-3
Harvard Square Hotel 110 Mt Auburn St	Cambridge	MA	02138	**800-458-5886**	617-864-5200	373
Harvard University Press 79 Garden St *Cust Svc	Cambridge	MA	02138	**800-448-2242***	617-495-2600	623-5
Harvest Inn 1 Main St	Saint Helena	CA	94574	**800-950-8466**	707-963-9463	373
Harvest Land Co-op 711 Front St	Morgan	MN	56266	**800-245-5819**	507-249-3196	438
Harvest States Foods 1565 1st Ave NW	New Brighton	MN	55112	**800-700-0809**	651-697-5500	291-36
Harvey EL & Sons 68 Hopkinton Rd	Westborough	MA	01581	**800-321-3002**	508-836-3000	791
Harvey Electronics Inc 205 Chubb Ave *NASDAQ: HRVE*	Lyndhurst	NJ	07071	**800-254-7836**	201-842-0078	35
Harvey Industries Inc 1400 Main St	Waltham	MA	02451	**800-225-5724**	781-899-3500	190-4
Harvey Suites DFW Airport 4550 W John Carpenter Fwy	Irving	TX	75063	**800-922-9222**	972-929-4499	373
Harvey Watt & Co Atlanta Airport PO Box 20787	Atlanta	GA	30320	**800-241-6103**	404-767-7501	384-2
Harveys Resort Hotel & Casino Hwy 50 PO Box 128	Stateline	NV	89449	**800-427-8397**	775-588-2411	133
Hasbro Inc 1027 Newport Ave *NYSE: HAS*	Pawtucket	RI	02861	**800-242-7276**	401-431-8697	750
Hasbro Inc Parker Brothers Div 200 Narragansett Park Dr	Pawtucket	RI	02862	**888-836-7025**		750
Hasbro Inc Playskool Div 1027 Newport Ave	Pawtucket	RI	02861	**800-242-7276**	401-431-8697	750
Hasbro Inc Tiger Electronics Div 1027 Newport Ave	Pawtucket	RI	02861	**800-844-3733**	401-431-8697	750
Haskel International Inc 100 E Graham Pl	Burbank	CA	91502	**800-743-2720**	818-843-4000	627
Haskell Co 111 Riverside Ave	Jacksonville	FL	32202	**800-733-4275**	904-791-4500	187-7
Hassayampa Inn 122 E Gurley St	Prescott	AZ	86301	**800-322-1927**	928-778-9434	373
Hassenfritz Tom Equipment Co 1300 W Washington St	Mount Pleasant	IA	52641	**800-634-4885**	319-385-3114	270
Hassett Air Express 877 S Rt 83	Elmhurst	IL	60126	**800-323-9422**	630-530-6515	306
Hastings Area Chamber of Commerce & Tourism Bureau 111 E 3rd St	Hastings	MN	55033	**888-612-6122**	651-437-6775	137
Hastings Bus Co 425 31st St E	Hastings	MN	55033	**888-290-2429**	651-437-1888	110
Hastings College 710 N Turner Ave	Hastings	NE	68901	**800-532-7642**	402-463-2402	163
Hastings Entertainment Inc 3601 Plains Blvd *NASDAQ: HAST* ■ *Cust Svc	Amarillo	TX	79102	**877-427-8464***	806-351-2300	96
Hastings House 160 Upper Ganges Rd	Salt Spring Island	BC	V8K2S2	**800-661-9255**	250-537-2362	372
Hastings HVAC Inc PO Box 669 *Cust Svc	Hastings	NE	68902	**800-228-4243***	402-463-9821	15
Hastings Mfg Co 325 N Hanover St	Hastings	MI	49058	**800-776-1012**	269-945-2491	128
Hastings Pavement Co LLC PO Box 178	Islip	NY	11751	**800-669-9294**	631-669-4900	181
Hastings Tribune 908 W 2nd St	Hastings	NE	68901	**800-742-6397**	402-462-2131	522-2
Hastings Veterans Home 1200 E 18th St	Hastings	MN	55033	**877-838-3803**	651-438-8504	780
Hatch & Kirk Inc 5111 Leary Ave NW	Seattle	WA	98107	**800-426-2818**	206-783-2766	259
Hatco Inc 601 Marion Dr	Garland	TX	75042	**800-288-6579**	972-494-0511	153-9
Hatteras Hammocks Inc PO Box 1602	Greenville	NC	27835	**800-643-3522**	252-758-0641	314-4
Hattiesburg American 825 N Main St	Hattiesburg	MS	39401	**800-844-2637**	601-582-4321	522-2
Hatton Brown Publishing Co 225 Hanrick St	Montgomery	AL	36104	**800-669-5613**	334-834-1170	623-9
Hauppauge Computer Works Inc 91 Cabot Ct	Hauppauge	NY	11788	**800-443-6284**	631-434-1600	613
Hauppauge Digital Inc 91 Cabot Ct *NASDAQ: HAUP*	Hauppauge	NY	11788	**800-443-6284**	631-434-1600	613
Hause Machines Inc 809 S Pleasant St	Montpelier	OH	43543	**800-932-8665**	419-485-3158	447
Hausman Sam Meat Packer Inc PO Box 2422	Corpus Christi	TX	78403	**800-364-5521**	361-883-5521	465
Hausmann Industries Inc 130 Union St	Northvale	NJ	07647	**888-428-7626**	201-767-0255	314-1
Hautly Cheese Co Inc 5130 Northrup Ave	Saint Louis	MO	63110	**800-729-9339**	314-772-9339	292-4
Havana Riverwalk Inn 1015 Navarro St	San Antonio	TX	78205	**888-224-2008**	210-222-2008	373
Haven Business Forms Inc 6 Greek Ln	Edison	NJ	08817	**800-341-2245**	732-287-1750	111
Havens Steel Co 7219 E 17th St	Kansas City	MO	64126	**800-279-4283**	816-231-5724	471
Havenwyck Hospital 1525 University Dr	Auburn Hills	MI	48326	**800-401-2727**	248-373-9200	366-3
Haverhill Gazette PO Box 991	Haverhill	MA	01831	**800-370-0321**	978-374-0321	522-2
Haverty Furniture Cos Inc 780 Johnson Ferry Rd NE Suite 800 *NYSE: HVT*	Atlanta	GA	30342	**800-241-4599**	404-443-2900	316
Haviland Enterprises Inc 421 Ann St NW	Grand Rapids	MI	49504	**800-456-1134**	616-361-6691	144
Havre Daily News 119 2nd St PO Box 431	Havre	MT	59501	**800-993-2459**	406-265-6795	522-2
Hawaii Child Support Enforcement Agency 601 Kamokila Blvd Suite 251	Kapolei	HI	96707	**888-317-9081**	808-692-7000	335
Hawaii Chamber of Commerce 1132 Bishop St Suite 402	Honolulu	HI	96813	**800-464-2924**	808-545-4300	138
Hawaii Community Foundation 1164 Bishop St Suite 800	Honolulu	HI	96813	**888-731-3863**	808-537-6333	298
Hawaii Convention Center 1801 Kalakaua Ave	Honolulu	HI	96815	**800-295-6603**	808-943-3500	204
Hawaii Dental Assn 1345 S Beretania St Suite 301	Honolulu	HI	96814	**800-359-6725**	808-593-7956	225
Hawaii Medical Assn 1360 S Beretania St Suite 200	Honolulu	HI	96814	**866-536-8666**	808-536-7702	466
Hawaii Medical Service Assn 818 Keeaumoku St	Honolulu	HI	96814	**800-648-3190**	808-948-6111	384-3
Hawaii Pacific University 1164 Bishop St Suite 200	Honolulu	HI	96813	**866-225-5478**	808-544-0237	163
Windward Hawaii Loa Campus 45-045 Kamehameha Hwy	Kaneohe	HI	96744	**866-225-5478**	808-236-3500	163
Hawaii Prince Hotel Waikiki 100 Holomoana St	Honolulu	HI	96815	**800-321-6248**	808-956-1111	655
Hawaii Visitors & Convention Bureau 2270 Kalakaua Ave Suite 801	Honolulu	HI	96815	**800-464-2924**	808-923-1811	205
Hawaiian Airlines HawaiianMiles PO Box 30008	Honolulu	HI	96820	**877-426-4537**		27
Hawaiian Airlines Inc 3375 Koapaka St Suite G350 *AMEX: HA*	Honolulu	HI	96819	**800-367-5320**	808-835-3700	26
Hawaiian Inn 2301 S Atlantic Ave	Daytona Beach Shores	FL	32118	**800-457-0077**	386-255-5411	373
Hawaiian Isles Kona Coffee Co 2839 Mokumoa St *Orders	Honolulu	HI	96819	**800-749-9103***	808-833-2244	291-7
Hawaiian Tropic 1190 US Hwy 1 N	Ormond Beach	FL	32174	**800-874-4844**	386-677-9559	211
Hawaiian Tug & Barge PO Box 3288	Honolulu	HI	96801	**800-572-2743**	808-543-9311	457
Hawaiian Village. Hilton 2005 Kalia Rd	Honolulu	HI	96815	**800-445-8667**	808-949-4321	655
Hawaii's Best Bed & Breakfasts PO Box 485	Laupahoehoe	HI	96764	**800-262-9912**	808-962-0100	368
Hawbaker Glenn O Inc 1952 Waddle Rd	State College	PA	16803	**800-221-1355**	814-237-1444	46
Hawk Eye 800 S Main St	Burlington	IA	52601	**800-397-1708**	319-754-8461	522-2
Hawk Gertrude Chocolates Inc 9 Keystone Pk	Dunmore	PA	18512	**800-822-2032**	570-342-7556	291-8
Hawk Inn & Mountain Resort HCR 70 Box 64	Plymouth	VT	05056	**800-685-4295**	802-672-3811	655
Hawk Precision Components Group 31005 Solon Rd	Solon	OH	44139	**866-429-5724**	440-248-5456	476
Hawkeye Community College 1501 E Orange Rd	Waterloo	IA	50704	**800-670-4769**	319-296-2320	160
Hawkeye Leisure Trailers Ltd 1419 11th St N	Humboldt	IA	50548	**888-874-9943**	515-332-1802	751
Hawkeye REC PO Box 90	Cresco	IA	52136	**800-658-2243**	563-547-3801	244
Hawkeye Stages Inc 703 Dudley St	Decorah	IA	52101	**800-323-3368**	563-382-3639	108
Hawkins Inc 3100 E Hennepin Ave *NASDAQ: HWKN*	Minneapolis	MN	55413	**800-328-5460**	612-331-6910	141
Hawkins Traffic Safety Supply 1255 E Shore Hwy	Berkeley	CA	94710	**800-772-3995**	510-525-4040	666
Hawk's Cay Resort & Marina 61 Hawk's Cay Blvd	Duck Key	FL	33050	**800-432-2242**	305-743-7000	655
Haworth Inc 1 Haworth Ctr	Holland	MI	49423	**800-344-2600**	616-393-3000	314-1
Haws Corp 1455 Kleppe Ln	Sparks	NV	89431	**888-640-4297**	775-359-4712	650
Hawthorn Suites 13 Corporate Sq Suite 250	Atlanta	GA	30329	**800-527-1133**	404-321-4045	369
Hawthorne Hotel 18 Washington Sq W	Salem	MA	01970	**800-729-7829**	978-744-4080	373
Hawthorne Inn & Conference Center 420 High St	Winston-Salem	NC	27101	**800-972-3774**	336-777-3000	373
Hawthorne Race Course 3501 S Laramie Ave	Cicero	IL	60804	**800-780-0701**	708-780-3700	628
Hay-Adams Hotel 800 16th St NW	Washington	DC	20006	**800-424-5054**	202-638-6600	373
Hay Group Inc 100 Penn Sq E Wanamaker Bldg	Philadelphia	PA	19107	**800-776-1774**	215-861-2000	193
Hay House Inc PO Box 5100	Carlsbad	CA	92018	**800-654-5126**	760-431-7695	623-4
Hayden Automotive PO Box 77550	Corona	CA	92877	**800-621-3233**	951-736-2665	60
Hayden Carl T Veterans Affairs Medical Center 650 E Indian School Rd	Phoenix	AZ	85012	**800-359-8262**	602-277-5551	366-6
Hayden Twist Drill & Tool Co Inc 22822 Globe St	Warren	MI	48089	**800-521-1780**	586-754-7700	484
Hayes Helen Theatre 240 W 44th St	New York	NY	10036	**800-432-7250**	212-239-6200	732
Hayes Lemmerz International Inc 15300 Centennial Dr *NASDAQ: HAYZ*	Northville	MI	48167	**800-521-0515**	734-737-5000	60
Hayes Mfg Group Inc Core Div PO Box 595	Neenah	WI	54957	**800-236-8001**	920-725-7056	125
Hayes Rutherford B Presidential Center Spiegel Grove	Fremont	OH	43420	**800-998-7737**	419-332-2081	426
Hayes School Publishing Co Inc 321 Pennwood Ave	Pittsburgh	PA	15221	**800-245-6234**	412-731-4693	242
Hayes Seay Mattern & Mattern Inc PO Box 13446	Roanoke	VA	24034	**800-366-4766**	540-857-3100	258
Hayes Specialties Corp 1761 E Genesee	Saginaw	MI	48601	**800-248-3603**	989-755-6541	323
Hayes & Stolz Industrial Mfg Co Inc PO Box 11217	Fort Worth	TX	76110	**800-725-7272**	817-926-3391	293
Haynes Furniture Co Inc 5324 Virginia Beach Blvd	Virginia Beach	VA	23462	**800-768-0348**	757-497-9681	316
Haynes Herbert C Inc Box 96	Winn	ME	04495	**800-432-7867**	207-736-3412	439
Haynes International Inc 1020 W Park Dr PO Box 9013	Kokomo	IN	46901	**800-354-0806**	765-456-6000	476
Hays Convention & Visitors Bureau 1301 Pine St Suite B	Hays	KS	67601	**800-569-4505**	785-628-8202	205
Hays Daily News 507 Main St PO Box 857	Hays	KS	67601	**800-657-6017**	785-628-1081	522-2
Hays Fluid Controls PO Box 580	Dallas	NC	28034	**800-354-4297**	704-922-9565	777
Hays Medical Center 2220 Canterbury Dr	Hays	KS	67601	**800-248-0073**	785-623-5000	366-2
Hayward Baker Inc 1130 Annapolis Rd Suite 202	Odenton	MD	21113	**800-456-6548**	410-551-8200	188-5
Hayward Distributing Co 4061 Perimeter Dr	Columbus	OH	43228	**800-282-1585**	614-272-5953	270
Haywood County Chamber of Commerce PO Box 600	Waynesville	NC	28786	**877-456-3073**	828-456-3021	137
Haywood Electric Membership Corp 1560 Asheville Rd	Waynesville	NC	28786	**800-951-6088**	828-452-2281	244

Name / Address	City	State	Zip	Toll-Free	Phone	Class
Haywood Park Hotel 1 Battery Park Ave	Asheville	NC	28801	**800-228-2522**	828-252-2522	373
Hazard Community & Technical College 1 Community College Dr	Hazard	KY	41701	**800-246-7521**	606-436-5721	160
Hazard Campus 101 Vo Tech Dr	Hazard	KY	41701	**800-246-7521**	606-435-6101	787
Lees Campus 601 Jefferson Ave	Jackson	KY	41339	**800-246-7521**	606-666-7521	787
Hazardous Substance Research Center. Great Plains-Rocky Mountain Kansas State University Ward Hall Rm 104	Manhattan	KS	66506	**800-798-7796**	785-532-6519	654
Hazardous Waste News 8737 Colesville Rd Suite 1100	Silver Spring	MD	20910	**800-274-6737**	301-587-6300	521-5
Hazelden Foundation 15245 Pleasant Valley Rd	Center City	MN	55012	**800-257-7800**	651-257-4010	712
Hazelden Springbrook 1901 Esther St *Admissions	Newberg	OR	97132	**800-333-3712***	503-537-7000	712
Hazelnut Growers of Oregon 401 N 26th Ave	Cornelius	OR	97113	**800-273-4676**	503-648-4176	12-1
Hazelwood Enterprises Inc 402 N 32nd St	Phoenix	AZ	85008	**800-680-4667**	602-275-7709	322
Hazen & Sawyer PC 498 7th Ave 11th Fl	New York	NY	10018	**800-858-9876**	212-777-8400	258
Hazleton Standard Speaker 21 N Wyoming St	Hazleton	PA	18201	**800-843-6680**	570-455-3636	522-2
HazMat Transportation News 8737 Colesville Rd Suite 1100	Silver Spring	MD	20910	**800-274-6737**	301-587-6300	521-5
HB Duvall Inc 901 E Patrick St	Frederick	MD	21701	**800-423-4032**	301-662-1125	270
HB Fuller Co 1200 Willow Lake Blvd PO Box 64683 *NYSE: FUL*	Saint Paul	MN	55164	**800-828-2981**	651-236-5900	3
HB Hunter Co PO Box 1599	Norfolk	VA	23501	**800-446-8314**	757-664-5200	295
HB Maynard & Co Inc 8 Parkway Ctr	Pittsburgh	PA	15220	**888-629-6273**	412-921-2400	193
HB Reese Candy Co 925 Reese Ave *Cust Svc	Hershey	PA	17033	**800-468-1714***	717-534-4106	291-8
HB Rentals LC 5813 Hwy 90 E	Broussard	LA	70518	**800-262-6790**	337-839-1641	261-4
HB Stubbs Co 27027 Mound Rd	Warren	MI	48092	**800-968-2132**	586-574-9700	230
HB Williamson Co PO Box 1687 *Orders	Mount Vernon	IL	62864	**800-851-2467***	618-244-9000	304
HBD Inc 3901 Riverdale Rd	Greensboro	NC	27406	**800-403-2247**	336-275-4800	68
HBD Industries Inc 1301 W Sandusky Ave	Bellefontaine	OH	43311	**800-543-8070**	937-593-5010	364
HC Clark Implement Co 4411 E Hwy 12	Aberdeen	SD	57401	**800-532-6747**	605-225-8170	270
HC Miller Co 3030 Lowell Dr	Green Bay	WI	54311	**800-829-6555**		87
HC Osvold Co 2828 University Ave SE	Minneapolis	MN	55414	**800-328-4827**	612-331-1581	281
HC Schmeiding Produce Co PO Box 369	Springdale	AR	72765	**800-643-3607**	479-751-4517	292-7
HC Smith Ltd 20600 Chagrin Blvd Tower East Suite 200	Shaker Heights	OH	44122	**800-442-7583**	216-752-9966	262
HC Wainwright & Co Inc 245 Park Ave 44th Fl	New York	NY	10167	**800-727-7176**	212-856-5700	679
HCA Inc 1 Park Plaza *NYSE: HCA*	Nashville	TN	37203	**800-828-2561**	615-344-9551	348
HCAA (National CPA Health Care Advisors Assn) 10831 Old Mill Rd Suite 400	Omaha	NE	68154	**888-475-4476**	402-778-7922	49-1
HCF Inc 1100 Shawnee Rd	Lima	OH	45805	**800-999-2110**	419-999-2010	442
HCI (Health Communications Inc) 3201 SW 15th St *Cust Svc	Deerfield Beach	FL	33442	**800-851-9100***	954-360-0909	623-2
HCI Direct Inc 3050 Tillman Dr	Bensalem	PA	19020	**800-989-3695**	215-244-9600	153-10
HD Hudson Mfg Co 500 N Michigan Ave Suite 2300	Chicago	IL	60611	**800-523-9284**	312-644-2830	269
HD Smith Wholesale Drug Co 4650 Industrial Dr	Springfield	IL	62703	**800-252-8090**	217-529-0211	237
HD Vest Financial Services 6333 N State Hwy 161 4th Fl	Irving	TX	75038	**800-821-8254**	972-870-6000	393
HDR Engineering Inc 8404 Indian Hills Dr	Omaha	NE	68114	**800-366-4411**	402-399-1000	258
HDR Power Systems Inc 3563 Interchange Rd	Columbus	OH	43204	**888-797-2685**	614-308-5500	252
HDSA (Huntington's Disease Society of America) 158 W 29th St 7th Fl	New York	NY	10001	**800-345-4372**	212-242-1968	48-17
HDW (Hardware Distribution Warehouses Inc) 6900 Woolworth Rd *Cust Svc	Shreveport	LA	71129	**800-256-8527***	318-686-8527	346
HEAD USA 1 Selleck St	Norwalk	CT	06855	**800-874-3235**	203-855-0631	701
Headache Education. American Council for 19 Mantua Rd	Mount Royal	NJ	08061	**800-255-2243**	856-423-0258	48-17
Headache Foundation. National 820 N Orleans St Suite 217	Chicago	IL	60610	**888-643-5552**		48-17
Headington Oil Co 7557 Rambler Rd Suite 1100	Dallas	TX	75231	**800-245-5773**	214-696-0606	525
Headley-Whitney Museum 4435 Old Frankfort Pike	Lexington	KY	40510	**800-310-5085**	859-255-6653	509
HEAD/Penn Racquet Sports 306 S 45th Ave	Phoenix	AZ	85043	**800-289-7366**	602-269-1492	701
Headquarters.Com Inc 625 Walnut Ridge Dr Suite 108	Hartland	WI	53029	**800-788-1298**	262-369-0600	796
Heads & Threads International LLC 200 Kennedy Dr	Sayreville	NJ	08872	**800-929-1950**	732-727-5800	346
Headstart Hair For Men Inc 3395 Cypress Gardens Rd	Winter Haven	FL	33884	**800-645-6525**	863-324-5559	342
Heald College *Concord* 5130 Commercial Cir	Concord	CA	94520	**800-755-3550**	925-288-5800	158
Fresno 255 W Bullard Ave	Fresno	CA	93704	**800-284-0844**	559-438-4222	158
Hayward 25500 Industrial Blvd	Hayward	CA	94545	**800-755-3550**	510-783-2100	158
Honolulu 1500 Kapiolani Blvd	Honolulu	HI	96814	**800-755-3550**	808-955-1500	158
Portland 625 SW Broadway 2nd Fl	Portland	OR	97205	**800-432-5344**	503-229-0492	158
Salinas 1450 N Main St	Salinas	CA	93906	**800-755-3550**	831-443-1700	158
San Francisco 350 Mission St	San Francisco	CA	94105	**800-432-5398**	415-808-3000	158
Healing Center of Arizona 25 Wilson Canyon Rd	Sedona	AZ	86336	**877-723-2811**	928-282-7710	697
Healing the Children (HTC) PO Box 9065	Spokane	WA	99209	**877-432-5543**	509-327-4281	48-5

Name / Address	City	State	Zip	Toll-Free	Phone	Class
Health Accreditation Program Inc. Community 39 Broadway Suite 710	New York	NY	10006	**800-656-9656**	212-480-8828	48-1
Health Alliance Medical Plans 102 E Main St	Urbana	IL	61801	**800-851-3379**	217-337-8000	384-3
Health Alliance Plan 2850 W Grand Blvd	Detroit	MI	48202	**800-422-4641**	313-872-8100	384-3
Health Assn. American School 7263 State Rt 43 PO Box 708	Kent	OH	44240	**800-445-2742**	330-678-1601	49-5
Health Assn. American Social PO Box 13827	Research Triangle Park	NC	27709	**800-277-8922**	919-361-8400	48-17
Health Care Administrators. American College of 300 N Lee St Suite 301	Alexandria	VA	22314	**888-882-2422**	703-739-7900	49-8
Health Care Advisors Assn. National CPA 10831 Old Mill Rd Suite 400	Omaha	NE	68154	**888-475-4476**	402-778-7922	49-1
Health Care Assn. American 1201 L St NW	Washington	DC	20005	**800-321-0343**	202-842-4444	49-8
Health Care Property Investors Inc 3760 Kilroy Airport Way Suite 300 *NYSE: HCP*	Long Beach	CA	90806	**888-604-1990**	562-733-5100	641
Health Care Savings Inc 4530 Park Rd Suite 110	Charlotte	NC	28209	**800-833-8464**	704-527-6261	384-3
Health Care. Society for Social Work Leadership in 1211 Locust St	Philadelphia	PA	19107	**866-237-9542**	215-599-6134	49-15
Health Charities. Community 200 N Glebe Rd Suite 801	Arlington	VA	22203	**800-654-0845**	703-528-1007	48-5
Health Club Assn. National 640 Plaza Dr Suite 300	Highlands Ranch	CO	80129	**800-765-6422**	303-753-6422	48-22
Health Clubs of America 500 E Broward Blvd Suite 1650	Fort Lauderdale	FL	33394	**800-833-5239**	954-527-5373	349
Health Communications Inc (HCI) 3201 SW 15th St *Cust Svc	Deerfield Beach	FL	33442	**800-851-9100***	954-360-0909	623-2
Health Council. National 1730 M St NW Suite 500	Washington	DC	20036	**800-684-6814**	202-785-3910	48-17
Health Crisis. Gay Men's 119 W 24th St	New York	NY	10011	**800-243-7692**	212-367-1000	48-17
Health Employees. International Union of Industrial Service Transport 254 W 31st St	New York	NY	10001	**800-331-1070**	212-696-5545	405
Health Facilities Management Magazine 1 N Franklin Suite 2800	Chicago	IL	60606	**800-621-6902**	312-893-6800	449-5
Health Fitness Corp 3600 American Blvd West Suite 560	Bloomington	MN	55431	**800-639-7913**	952-831-6830	349
Health Foundation. People-to-People 255 Carter Hall Ln	Millwood	VA	22646	**800-544-4673**	540-837-2100	48-5
Health Freedom. Institute for 1825 'I' St NW Suite 400	Washington	DC	20006	**888-616-1976**	202-429-6610	48-8
Health & Healing Newsletter 7811 Montrose Rd	Potomac	MD	20854	**800-861-5967**	301-340-2100	521-8
Health Industry Distributors Assn (HIDA) 310 Montgomery St Suite 520	Alexandria	VA	22314	**800-549-4432**	703-549-4432	49-18
Health Information Center. National PO Box 1133	Washington	DC	20013	**800-336-4797**	301-565-4167	336-6
Health Information Management Assn. American 233 N Michigan Ave Suite 2150	Chicago	IL	60601	**800-335-5535**	312-233-1100	49-8
Health Insurance Plans. America's 601 Pennsylvania Ave NW Suite 500 *Cust Svc	Washington	DC	20004	**877-291-2247***	202-778-3200	49-9
Health Law Week Newsletter 590 Dutch Valley Rd NE	Atlanta	GA	30324	**800-926-7926**	404-881-1141	521-8
Health Net Inc 21650 Oxnard St *NYSE: HNT*	Woodland Hills	CA	91367	**800-291-6911**	818-676-6000	384-3
Health Nurses. American Assn of Occupational 2920 Brandywine Rd Suite 100	Atlanta	GA	30341	**888-646-4631**	770-455-7757	49-8
Health Occupations Students of America (HOSA) 6021 Morriss Rd Suite 111	Flower Mound	TX	75028	**800-321-4672**	972-874-0062	48-11
Health. Office on Women's Office on Women's Health 200 Independence Ave SW Rm 730B	Washington	DC	20201	**800-994-9662**	202-690-7650	336-6
Health Options Div Blue Cross & Blue Shield of Florida PO Box 1798	Jacksonville	FL	32231	**800-734-6656**		384-3
Health Physical Education Recreation & Dance. American Alliance for 1900 Association Dr	Reston	VA	20191	**800-213-7193**	703-476-3400	48-22
Health Plan of Upper Ohio Valley Inc 52160 National Rd E	Saint Clairsville	OH	43950	**800-624-6961**	740-695-3585	384-3
Health Professionals. National Assn of Certified Natural 714 E Winona Ave	Warsaw	IN	46580	**800-321-1005**		48-17
Health Professions. Association of Schools of Allied 1730 M St NW Suite 500	Washington	DC	20036	**800-497-8080**	202-293-4848	49-8
Health Racquet & Sportsclub Assn. International 263 Summer St 8th Fl	Boston	MA	02210	**800-228-4772**	617-951-0055	48-22
Health Resources Inc 10 E Baltimore St Suite 1404	Baltimore	MD	21202	**800-932-4648**	410-347-1540	575
Health Resources & Services Administration (HRSA) 5600 Fishers Ln	Rockville	MD	20857	**888-275-4772**	301-443-2216	336-6
Health Spa at Meadowood Napa Valley 900 Meadowood Ln	Saint Helena	CA	94574	**800-458-8080**	707-967-1275	698
Health Spa at the Regent Beverly Wilshire 9500 Wilshire Blvd	Beverly Hills	CA	90212	**800-545-4000**	310-385-7023	698
Health Watch Inc 6400 Park of Commerce Blvd Suite 1-A	Boca Raton	FL	33487	**888-994-1835**	561-994-6699	565

Name / Address	City	State	Zip	Toll-Free	Phone	Class
HealthAmerica Pennsylvania Inc 3721 Tecport Dr	Harrisburg	PA	17111	800-788-6445	717-540-4260	384-3
Healthcare. AFT 555 New Jersey Ave NW	Washington	DC	20001	800-238-1133	202-879-4491	405
Healthcare Consultants. American Assn of 5938 N Drake Ave	Chicago	IL	60659	888-350-2242		49-8
Healthcare Financial Management Assn (HFMA) 2 Westbrook Corporate Ctr Suite 700	Westchester	IL	60154	800-252-4362	708-531-9600	49-8
Healthcare Foodservice Magazine PO Box 470067	Celebration	FL	34747	800-525-2015	407-343-9333	449-21
Healthcare Informatics Magazine 4530 W 77th St Suite 350 *Cust Svc	Minneapolis	MN	55435	800-525-5003*	952-835-3222	449-5
Healthcare Internal Auditors. Association of PO Box 449	Onsted	MI	49265	888-275-2442	517-467-7729	49-1
Healthcare Quality. National Assn for 4700 W Lake Ave	Glenview	IL	60025	800-966-9392	847-375-4720	49-8
Healthcare Research & Quality. Agency for 540 Gaither Rd	Rockville	MD	20850	800-358-9295	301-427-1200	654
Healthcare Services Group Inc 3220 Tillman Dr Suite 300 *NASDAQ: HCSG*	Bensalem	PA	19020	800-523-2248	215-639-4274	434
Healthcare Strategy & Market Development. Society for American Hospital Assn 1 N Franklin St 28th Fl	Chicago	IL	60606	800-242-2626	312-422-3888	49-8
HealthCare USA Inc 10 S Broadway Suite 1200	Saint Louis	MO	63102	800-213-7792	314-241-5300	384-3
HealthCareSource Inc 8 Winchester Pl Suite 304	Winchester	MA	01890	888-289-9979		257
HealthDrive Corp 25 Needham St	Newton	MA	02461	888-964-6681	617-964-6681	347
HealthEssentials Solutions Inc 9510 Ormsby Station Rd Suite 101	Louisville	KY	40223	877-453-5307	502-429-7778	358
HealthExtras Inc 800 King Farm Blvd 4th Fl *NASDAQ: HLEX*	Rockville	MD	20850	800-323-6640	301-548-2900	384-2
HealthLink Inc 12443 Olive Blvd	Saint Louis	MO	63141	800-624-2356	314-989-6000	384-3
Healthlink Inc 13620 Reese Blvd E Suite 100	Huntersville	NC	28078	800-382-7094	704-947-8848	178
HealthMEDX 5100 N Towne Ctr Dr	Ozark	MO	65721	877-875-1200	417-582-1816	39
HealthPartners Inc PO Box 1309	Minneapolis	MN	55440	800-883-2177	952-883-5000	384-3
Healthplex Inc 60 Charles Lindbergh Blvd	Uniondale	NY	11553	800-468-0608	516-794-3000	384-3
HealthPlus of Michigan 2050 S Linden Rd	Flint	MI	48532	800-332-9161	810-230-2000	384-3
Healthpoint Ltd 3909 Hulen St	Fort Worth	TX	76107	800-441-8227	817-900-4000	573
HealthReach Homecare & Hospice PO Box 1568	Waterville	ME	04903	800-427-1127	207-873-1127	365
Healthrisk Group Inc 1551 N Tustin Ave Suite 300	Santa Ana	CA	92705	800-955-9600	714-953-9600	455
Healthsource North Carolina Inc 701 Corporate Center Dr	Raleigh	NC	27607	800-849-9300	919-854-7000	384-3
HealthSource Saginaw 3340 Hospital Rd	Saginaw	MI	48603	800-662-6848	989-790-7700	712
HealthSouth Braintree Rehabilitation Hospital 250 Pond St	Braintree	MA	02184	800-997-3422	781-848-5353	366-4
HealthSouth Chattanooga Rehabilitation Hospital 2412 McCallie Ave	Chattanooga	TN	37404	800-763-5189	423-698-0221	366-4
HealthSouth Corp 1 HealthSouth Pkwy	Birmingham	AL	35243	800-765-4772	205-967-7116	347
HealthSouth Mountainview Regional Rehabilitation Hospital 1160 Van Voorhis Rd	Morgantown	WV	26505	800-388-2451	304-598-1100	366-4
HealthSouth Nittany Valley Rehabilitation Hospital 550 W College Ave	Pleasant Gap	PA	16823	800-842-6026	814-359-3421	366-4
HealthSouth North Louisiana Rehabilitation Hospital 1401 Ezell St	Ruston	LA	71270	800-765-4772	318-251-3126	366-4
HealthSouth Reading Rehabilitation Hospital 1623 Morgantown Rd	Reading	PA	19607	800-755-8027	610-796-6000	366-4
HealthSouth Rehabilitation Hospital of Altoona 2005 Valley View Blvd	Altoona	PA	16602	800-873-4220	814-944-3535	366-4
HealthSouth Rehabilitation Hospital of Austin 1215 Red River	Austin	TX	78701	800-765-4772	512-474-5700	366-4
HealthSouth Rehabilitation Hospital of Erie 143 E 2nd St	Erie	PA	16507	800-234-4574	814-878-1200	366-4
HealthSouth Rehabilitation Hospital of Greater Pittsburgh 2380 McGinley Rd	Monroeville	PA	15146	800-695-4774	412-856-2400	366-4
HealthSouth Rehabilitation Hospital of Memphis 1282 Union Ave	Memphis	TN	38104	800-363-7342	901-722-2000	366-4
HealthSouth Rehabilitation Hospital of North Alabama 107 Governors Dr	Huntsville	AL	35801	800-467-3422	256-535-2300	366-4
HealthSouth Tri-State Rehabilitation Hospital 4100 Covert Ave	Evansville	IN	47714	800-677-3422	812-476-9983	366-4
HealthStream Inc 209 10th Ave S Suite 450 *NASDAQ: HSTM*	Nashville	TN	37203	800-933-9293	615-301-3100	753
HealthTronics Inc 1301 S Capital of Texas Hwy Suite B-200 *NASDAQ: HTRN*	Austin	TX	78746	888-252-6575	512-328-2892	249
HealthWeb Greater Midwest Region of the National Network Libraries of Medicine 1750 W Polk St MC 763	Chicago	IL	60612	800-338-7657	312-996-2464	351
Healthy Directions LLC 7811 Montrose Rd	Rockville	MD	20854	800-340-7788	301-340-2100	623-9
Healthy Planet Products Inc 43 Moraga Way Suite 205	Orinda	CA	94563	800-424-4422	925-253-9595	323
Healy SA Co 1910 S Highland Ave Suite 300	Lombard	IL	60148	888-724-3259	630-678-3110	258
Heard Bill Enterprises 200 Brookstone Ctr Pkwy Suite 205	Columbus	GA	31904	800-833-0479	706-323-1111	57
Hearing Assn. American Speech-Language- 10801 Rockville Pike	Rockville	MD	20852	800-498-2071	301-897-5700	49-8
Hearing Institute. Better 515 King St Suite 420	Alexandria	VA	22314	888-432-7435	703-684-3391	48-17
Hearing Society. International 16880 Middlebelt Rd Suite 4	Livonia	MI	48154	800-521-5247	734-522-7200	48-17
Hearn Kirkwood 7251 Standard Dr	Hanover	MD	21076	888-866-2905	410-712-6000	292-7
Hearn Paper Co 556 N Meridian Rd	Youngstown	OH	44509	800-225-2989	330-792-6533	543
Hearst Magazines Div 959 8th Ave	Manhattan	NY	10019	800-678-7767	212-649-2000	623-9
Heart Assn. American 7272 Greenville Ave	Dallas	TX	75231	800-242-8721	214-373-6300	48-17
Heart-Felt Greetings II Inc 1367 Fairview Blvd	Fairview	TN	37062	800-818-9099	615-799-8562	130
Heart Health & Nutrition Newsletter 7811 Montrose Rd	Potomac	MD	20854	800-861-5970	301-340-2100	521-8
Heart to Heart International 401 S Clairborne Rd Suite 302	Olathe	KS	66062	800-764-5220	913-764-5200	48-5
Heart of Iowa Co-op 229 E Ash St	Roland	IA	50236	800-662-4642	515-388-4341	271
Heart-Rate Inc 3190 Airport Loop Dr Bldg E	Costa Mesa	CA	92626	800-237-2271	714-850-9716	263
Heart Six Ranch 16985 Buffalo Valley Rd PO Box 70	Moran	WY	83013	888-543-2477	307-543-2477	238
Heart & Soul Magazine 315 Park Ave S 11th Fl	New York	NY	10010	800-666-1716	646-654-4200	449-13
Heartbreak Hotel. Elvis Presley's 3677 Elvis Presley Blvd	Memphis	TN	38116	877-777-0606	901-332-1000	373
Hearth & Home Technologies Inc 20802 Kensington Blvd	Lakeville	MN	55044	800-669-4328	952-985-6000	352
Hearthside by Villager 1 Sylvan Way	Parsippany	NJ	07054	888-821-5738	973-428-9700	369
HearthSong 3700 Wyse Rd *Orders	Dayton	OH	45414	800-533-4397*	540-948-7100	451
Heartlab Inc 1 Crosswind Rd	Westerly	RI	02891	800-959-3205	401-596-0592	176-10
Heartland Automotive Services Inc 11308 Davenport St	Omaha	NE	68154	800-417-7308	402-333-0990	62-5
Heartland Baptist Bible College 4700 NW 10th St Bldg D	Oklahoma City	OK	73127	877-943-9330	405-943-9330	163
Heartland Blood Centers 1200 N Highland Ave	Aurora	IL	60506	800-786-4483	630-892-7055	90
Heartland Business Intelligence 821 Marquette Ave 404 Foshay Tower	Minneapolis	MN	55402	800-967-1882	612-371-9255	392
Heartland China Inc PO Box 8156	Topeka	KS	66608	888-383-3163	785-354-8080	716
Heartland Co-op 2829 Westown Pkwy Suite 350	West Des Moines	IA	50266	800-513-3938	515-225-1334	271
Heartland Express Inc 2777 Heartland Dr *NASDAQ: HTLD*	Coralville	IA	52241	800-553-1201	319-545-2728	769
Heartland Express Inc 1515 Wherebottom Springs Rd	Chester	VA	23836	800-444-4929	804-768-0016	769
Heartland Funds 789 N Water St Suite 500	Milwaukee	WI	53202	800-432-7856	414-347-7777	517
Heartland Health Care Center Miami Lakes 5725 NW 186th St	Hialeah	FL	33015	800-427-4397	305-625-9857	441
Heartland Home Health Care & Hospice 901 Sun Valley Blvd Suite 220	Concord	CA	94520	800-675-2273	925-674-8610	365
Heartland Hospice 4070 Butler Pike Suite 100	Plymouth Meeting	PA	19462	800-807-3738	610-941-6700	365
Heartland Hospital East 5325 Faraon St	Saint Joseph	MO	64506	800-443-1143	816-271-6000	366-2
Heartland Information Services 3103 Executive Pkwy Suite 500	Toledo	OH	43606	800-626-3830	419-578-6300	755
Heartland Information Services Inc DBA Heartland Business Intelligence 821 Marquette Ave 404 Foshay Tower	Minneapolis	MN	55402	800-967-1882	612-371-9255	392
Heartland Inn Cedar Rapids 3315 Southgate Ct SW	Cedar Rapids	IA	52404	800-334-3277	319-362-9012	373
Heartland Inn Dubuque South 2090 Southpark Ct	Dubuque	IA	52003	800-334-3277	563-556-6555	373
Heartland Inn Dubuque West 4025 McDonald Dr	Dubuque	IA	52003	800-334-3277	563-582-3752	373
Heartland Paper Co 808 W Cherokee St *Cust Svc	Sioux Falls	SD	57104	800-843-7922*	605-336-1190	549
Heartland Park Topeka 1805 SW 71st St	Topeka	KS	66619	800-437-2237	785-862-4781	504
Heartland Payment Systems Inc 247 Hulfish St Suite 400	Princeton	NJ	08542	888-798-3131	609-683-3831	250
Heartland Power Co-op 216 Jackson St PO Box 65	Thompson	IA	50478	888-584-9732	641-584-2251	244
Heartland Rural Electric Co-op PO Box 40	Girard	KS	66743	888-835-9585	620-724-8251	244
Heartland Spa 1237 E 1600 North Rd	Gilman	IL	60938	800-545-4853		697
Heartline Fitness Products Inc 19209 Orbit Dr	Gaithersburg	MD	20879	800-262-3348	301-921-0661	263
HearUSA Inc 1250 Northpoint Pkwy *AMEX: EAR* ■ *Cust Svc	West Palm Beach	FL	33407	800-731-3277*	561-478-8770	469
Heat & Control Inc 21121 Cabot Blvd	Hayward	CA	94545	800-227-5980	510-259-0500	293
Heat Pump Assn. International Ground Source Oklahoma State University 374 Cordell S	Stillwater	OK	74078	800-626-4747	405-744-5175	49-13
Heatcraft Refrigeration Products 2175 W Park Place Blvd	Stone Mountain	GA	30087	800-321-1881	770-465-5600	650
Heath Consultants Inc 9030 Monroe Rd	Houston	TX	77061	800-432-8487	713-844-1300	191
Heath Marian Greeting Cards Inc 9 Kendrick Rd *Sales	Wareham	MA	02571	800-338-3740*	508-291-0766	130
Heath Mfg Co 140 Mill St	Coopersville	MI	49404	800-678-8183	616-997-8181	568
HEATH Resource Center George Washington Univ 2121 K St NW Suite 220	Washington	DC	20037	800-544-3284	202-973-0904	48-17

Listing	City	State	ZIP	Toll-Free	Phone	Class
Heatherbank Rehabilitation & Skilled Nursing Center 745 Chiques Hill Rd	Columbia	PA	17512	**800-840-9075**	717-684-7555	441
Heathman Hotel 1001 SW Broadway	Portland	OR	97205	**800-551-0011**	503-241-4100	373
Heathman Lodge 7801 NE Greenwood Dr	Vancouver	WA	98662	**888-475-3100**	360-254-3100	373
Heath's Inc 600 W Bridge St	Monticello	IL	61856	**800-443-2847**	217-762-2534	270
Heatilator Inc 1915 W Saunders St	Mount Pleasant	IA	52641	**800-843-2848**	319-385-9211	352
Heating Airconditioning & Refrigeration Distributors International (HARDI) 1389 Dublin Rd	Columbus	OH	43215	**888-253-2128**	614-488-1835	49-18
Heating & Plumbing Engineers Inc 407 W Fillmore Pl	Colorado Springs	CO	80907	**800-530-8592**	719-633-5414	188-10
Heating Refrigerating & Air-Conditioning Engineers Inc. American Society of 1791 Tullie Cir NE *Cust Svc	Atlanta	GA	30329	**800-527-4723***	404-636-8400	49-3
HeatMax Inc 505 Hill Rd	Dalton	GA	30721	**800-432-8629**	706-226-1800	566
Heatrex Inc PO Box 515	Meadville	PA	16335	**800-394-6589**	814-724-1800	313
Heavenly Ham 5445 Triangle Pkwy Suite 400	Norcross	GA	30092	**800-989-0509**	770-752-1999	333
Heaven's Best Carpet & Upholstery Cleaning PO Box 607	Roxburg	ID	83440	**800-359-2095**	208-359-1100	150
Heavy Duty Trucking Magazine 38 Executive Pk Suite 300	Irvine	CA	92614	**800-233-1911**	949-261-1636	449-21
Heavy Machines Inc 3926 E Rains Rd	Memphis	TN	38118	**800-238-5591**	901-260-2200	353
HEB Mfg Co Inc PO Box 188	Chelsea	VT	05038	**800-639-4187**	802-685-4821	75
Hebert Candy Mansion 575 Hartford Tpke	Shrewsbury	MA	01545	**800-642-7702**	508-845-8051	123
Hebrew College 160 Herrick Rd	Newton Center	MA	02459	**800-866-4814**	617-559-8600	163
Hebrew Immigrant Aid Society (HIAS) 333 7th Ave 17th Fl	New York	NY	10001	**800-442-7714**	212-967-4100	48-5
Hebrew Union College Los Angeles 3077 University Ave	Los Angeles	CA	90007	**800-899-0925**	213-749-3424	163
Hebron Academy Rt 119 PO Box 309	Hebron	ME	04238	**888-432-7664**	207-966-2100	611
Heckett Multiserv North America 612 N Main St	Butler	PA	16001	**800-999-7524**	724-283-5741	709
Heckman Bindery Inc 1010 N Sycamore St	North Manchester	IN	46962	**800-334-3628**	260-982-2107	93
Hecks Direct Mail & Printing Service Inc 202 W Florence Ave	Toledo	OH	43605	**800-997-4325**	419-661-6000	5
Hector Communications Corp 211 S Main St *AMEX: HCT*	Hector	MN	55342	**800-992-8857**	320-848-6611	721
Hector Turf & Garden Inc 1301 NW 3rd St	Deerfield Beach	FL	33442	**877-343-2867**	954-429-3200	270
Hedahls Inc 100 E Broadway	Bismarck	ND	58502	**800-433-2457**	701-223-8393	61
Hedwin Corp 1600 Roland Heights Ave	Baltimore	MD	21211	**800-638-1012**	410-467-8209	198
Heffel Gallery Ltd 2247 Granville St	Vancouver	BC	V6H3G1	**800-528-9608**	604-732-6505	42
Hegg & Hegg Elwha Fish Co 801 Marine Dr	Port Angeles	WA	98363	**800-435-3474**	360-457-3344	291-13
HEI Inc 1495 Steiger Lake Ln *NASDAQ: HEII*	Victoria	MN	55386	**800-778-7773**	952-443-2500	686
Heico Chemicals Inc PO Box 730	Delaware Water Gap	PA	18327	**800-344-3426**	570-420-3900	470
Heidel House Resort 643 Illinois Ave	Green Lake	WI	54941	**800-444-2812**	920-294-3344	655
Heidelberg College 310 E Market St	Tiffin	OH	44883	**800-434-3352**	419-448-2000	163
Heidelberg Distributing Co 1518 Dalton St *Cust Svc	Cincinnati	OH	45214	**800-486-1518***	513-421-5000	82-1
Heidelberg USA Inc 1000 Gutenberg Dr	Kennesaw	GA	30144	**800-437-7388**	770-419-6500	617
Heifer Project International (HPI) PO Box 1692	Merrifield	VA	22116	**800-422-0474**	501-907-2900	48-5
Heil Environmental Industries Ltd 5751 Cornelison Rd Bldg B	Chattanooga	TN	37411	**800-824-4345**	423-899-9100	505
Heil Trailer International 5741 Cornelison Rd Bldg A	Chattanooga	TN	37411	**800-400-6913**	423-499-1300	768
Heilind Electronics Inc 58 Jonspin Rd	Wilmington	MA	01887	**800-400-7041**	978-657-4870	245
Heim Edwin L Co 1918 Greenwood St	Harrisburg	PA	17104	**800-692-7317**	717-233-8711	188-4
Hein William S & Co Inc 1285 Main St	Buffalo	NY	14209	**800-828-7571**	716-882-2600	623-2
Heineken USA 360 Hamilton Ave Suite 1103	White Plains	NY	10601	**800-811-4951**	914-681-4100	103
Heineman Beverages Inc 407 Short St	Port Clinton	OH	43452	**800-734-9115**	419-734-9100	81-3
Heiners Bakery Inc 1300 Adams Ave	Huntington	WV	25704	**800-776-8411**	304-523-8411	291-1
Heinrich Envelope Corp 925 Zane Ave N	Minneapolis	MN	55422	**800-346-7957**	763-544-3571	260
Heinz Frozen Food Co 357 6th Ave *Cust Svc	Pittsburgh	PA	15222	**800-892-2401***	412-237-3600	291-21
Heinz HJ Co PO Box 57 *NYSE: HNZ*	Pittsburgh	PA	15230	**800-255-5750**	412-456-5700	291-20
Heirloom Bible Publishers PO Box 780189	Wichita	KS	67278	**800-676-2448**	316-267-3211	623-4
Heitman LLC 191 N Wacker Dr Suite 2500	Chicago	IL	60606	**800-225-5435**	312-855-5700	641
Heitman LLC 191 N Wacker Dr Suite 2500	Chicago	IL	60606	**800-225-5435**	312-855-5700	393
Hekman Furniture Co 1400 Buchanan Ave SW	Grand Rapids	MI	49507	**800-253-9249**	616-452-1411	314-2
Helen Hayes Hospital Rt 9W	West Haverstraw	NY	10993	**888-707-3422**	845-947-3000	366-4
Helen Hayes Theatre 240 W 44th St	New York	NY	10036	**800-432-7250**	212-239-6200	732
Helen Keller International 352 Park Ave S 12th Fl	New York	NY	10010	**877-535-5374**	212-532-0544	48-5
Helen of Troy Ltd 1 Helen of Troy Plaza *NASDAQ: HELE*	El Paso	TX	79912	**800-487-8432**	915-225-8000	38
Helena Area Chamber of Commerce 225 Cruse Ave	Helena	MT	59601	**800-743-5362**	406-442-4120	137
Helena Independent Record 317 Cruse Ave	Helena	MT	59604	**800-523-2272**	406-447-4000	522-2
Helena Laboratories Inc 1530 Lindbergh Dr	Beaumont	TX	77704	**800-231-5663**	409-842-3714	229
Helene Curtis Industries Inc 205 N Michigan Ave Suite 3200	Chicago	IL	60601	**800-621-2013**	312-661-0222	211
Heli-Mart Inc 3184 Airway Ave Suite E	Costa Mesa	CA	92626	**800-826-6899**	714-755-2999	759
Helicopter Assn International (HAI) 1635 Prince St	Alexandria	VA	22314	**800-435-4976**	703-683-4646	49-21
Helicopter Support Inc (HSI) 124 Quarry Rd PO Box 111068	Trumbull	CT	06611	**800-795-6051**	203-416-4000	759
Helikon Furniture Co Inc 607 Norwich Ave	Taftville	CT	06380	**800-824-6729**	860-886-2301	314-1
Helinet Aviation Services LLC 16425 Hart St Hangar 2	Van Nuys	CA	91406	**800-221-8389**	818-902-0229	354
Helix Electric Inc 8260 Camino Santa Fe Suite A	San Diego	CA	92121	**800-554-3549**	858-535-0505	188-4
Helix Ltd 310 S Racine Ave	Chicago	IL	60607	**800-334-3549**	312-421-6000	119
Heller Alfred Heat Treating Co 5 Wellington St	Clifton	NJ	07015	**800-946-8847**	973-772-4200	475
Heller Brothers Packing Corp 288 9th St	Winter Garden	FL	34787	**800-823-2124**	407-656-2124	310-2
Heller Seasonings & Ingredients Inc 150 S Wacker Dr Suite 3200	Chicago	IL	60606	**800-323-2726**	312-456-6800	291-37
Hello Direct Inc 74 Northeastern Blvd	Nashua	NH	03062	**800-444-3556**		451
Helly Hansen US Inc 3326 160th Ave SE Kenyon Ctr Suite 200	Bellevue	WA	98008	**800-435-5901**	425-378-8700	153-5
Helm Inc 14310 Hamilton Ave	Highland Park	MI	48203	**800-782-4356**	313-865-5000	451
Helmerich & Payne Inc 1437 S Boulder Ave *NYSE: HP*	Tulsa	OK	74119	**800-331-7250**	918-742-5531	529
Helmet House Inc 26855 Malibu Hill Rd	Calabasas Hills	CA	91301	**800-421-7247**	818-880-0000	566
Helmick Corp PO Box 71	Fairmont	WV	26555	**800-624-3808**	304-366-3520	478
Helmold JF & Brothers Inc 901 Morse Ave	Elk Grove Village	IL	60007	**800-323-8898**	847-437-7085	448
Helmsley Carlton House Hotel 680 Madison Ave	New York	NY	10021	**800-221-4982**	212-838-3000	373
Helmsley Hotel. New York 212 E 42nd St	New York	NY	10017	**800-221-4982**	212-490-8900	373
Helmsley Middletowne Hotel 148 E 48th St	New York	NY	10017	**800-221-4982**	212-755-3000	373
Helmsley Park Lane Hotel 36 Central Park S	New York	NY	10019	**800-221-4982**	212-371-4000	373
Helmsley Sandcastle Hotel 1540 Ben Franklin Dr	Sarasota	FL	34236	**800-225-2181**	941-388-2181	373
Help the Children. World Opportunities International/ 1875 Century Park E Suite 700	Los Angeles	CA	90067	**800-464-7187**	323-466-7187	48-5
Help At Home Inc 17 N State St 14th Fl	Chicago	IL	60602	**800-422-1755**	312-762-9680	358
Help-U-Sell Real Estate 6800 Jericho Tpke Suite 208 E	Syosset	NY	11791	**800-366-1177**	516-364-9650	638
Heluva Good Cheese Inc PO Box 410	Sodus	NY	14551	**800-323-2188**	315-483-6971	291-5
Helvoet Pharma Inc 9012 Pennsauken Hwy	Pennsauken	NJ	08110	**800-874-3586**	856-663-2202	469
Helwig Carbon Products Inc 8900 W Tower Ave	Milwaukee	WI	53224	**800-365-3113**	414-354-2411	127
Helzberg Diamonds 1825 Swift Ave	North Kansas City	MO	64116	**800-669-7780**	816-842-7780	402
Hemacare Corp 4954 Van Nuys Blvd	Sherman Oaks	CA	91403	**888-481-1538**	818-986-3883	90
Hemagen Diagnostics Inc 9033 Red Branch Rd	Columbia	MD	21045	**800-495-2180**	443-367-5500	229
Hemet Jacinto Valley Chamber of Commerce 615 N San Jacinto St	Hemet	CA	92543	**800-334-9344**	951-658-3211	137
Hemmings Motor News 222 Main St	Bennington	VT	05201	**800-227-4373**	802-442-3101	449-3
Hemophilia Foundation. National 116 W 32nd St 11th Fl	New York	NY	10001	**800-424-2634**	212-328-3700	48-17
Henderson Auctions Co 13340 Florida Blvd PO Box 336	Livingston	LA	70754	**800-850-2252**	225-686-2252	51
Henderson County Tourist Commission 101 N Water St Suite B	Henderson	KY	42420	**800-648-3128**	270-826-3128	205
Henderson County Travel & Tourism 201 S Main St	Hendersonville	NC	28792	**800-828-4244**	828-693-9708	205
Henderson Mfg Inc 1085 S 3rd St	Manchester	IA	52057	**800-359-4970**	563-927-2828	269
Henderson State University 1100 Henderson St	Arkadelphia	AR	71999	**800-228-7333**	870-230-5000	163
Henderson Wheel & Warehouse Supply 1825 S 300 West	Salt Lake City	UT	84115	**800-748-5111**	801-486-2073	61
Hendrick Hospice Care PO Box 1922	Abilene	TX	79601	**800-622-8516**	325-677-8516	365
Hendrick Mfg Co 1 7th Ave *Cust Svc	Carbondale	PA	18407	**800-225-7373***	570-282-1010	479
Hendrick Motorsports Museum 4411 Papa Joe Hendrick Blvd	Charlotte	NC	28262	**877-467-4890**	704-455-3400	511
Hendricks County Flyer 8109 Kingston St Suite 500	Avon	IN	46123	**800-359-3747**	317-272-5800	522-4
Hendricks Power Co-op PO Box 309	Danville	IN	46122	**800-876-5473**	317-745-5473	244
Hendrix College 1600 Washington Ave	Conway	AR	72032	**800-277-9017**	501-329-6811	163
Henig Inc 4135 Carmichael Rd	Montgomery	AL	36106	**800-521-2037**	334-277-7610	155-6
Henkel Consumer Adhesives Inc 32150 Just Imagine Dr	Avon	OH	44011	**800-321-1733**	440-937-7000	717
Henkel Corp 2200 Renaissance Blvd Suite 200	Gulph Mills	PA	19406	**800-521-5317**	610-270-8100	141
Henkel Corp Schwartzkopf & Henkel Div 1063 McGraw Ave Suite 100	Irvine	CA	92614	**800-326-2855**	949-794-5500	211
Henkel Surface Technologies 32100 Stephenson Hwy	Madison Heights	MI	48071	**800-521-6895**	248-583-9300	143
Henkels & McCoy Inc 985 Jolly Rd	Blue Bell	PA	19422	**800-523-2568**	215-283-7600	187-10
Henley Park Hotel 926 Massachusetts Ave NW	Washington	DC	20001	**800-222-8474**	202-638-5200	373
Henlopen Hotel 511 N Boardwalk	Rehoboth Beach	DE	19971	**800-441-8450**	302-227-2551	373
Hennessy Industries Inc 1601 JP Hennesey Dr	La Vergne	TN	37086	**800-688-6359**	615-641-5122	60
Henny Penny Corp 1219 US 35 W	Eaton	OH	45320	**800-417-8417**	937-456-4171	293

Name / Address	City	State	ZIP	Toll-Free	Phone	Class
Henri Bendel Inc 712 5th Ave	New York	NY	10019	**800-423-6335**	212-247-1100	155-6
Henri's Food Products Co Inc 8622 N 87th St. *Cust Svc	Milwaukee	WI	53224	**800-338-8831***	414-365-5720	291-19
Henry B Gonzalez Convention Center 200 E Market St	San Antonio	TX	78205	**877-504-8895**	210-207-8500	204
Henry Brick Co Inc 3409 Water Ave	Selma	AL	36703	**800-548-7576**	334-875-2600	148
Henry C Hitch Feedyards PO Box 1559	Guymon	OK	73942	**800-951-2533**	580-338-2533	11-1
Henry Co 2911 E Slauson Ave	Huntington Park	CA	90255	**800-486-1278**	323-583-5000	46
Henry Cogswell College 3002 Colby Ave	Everett	WA	98201	**866-411-4221**	425-258-3351	163
Henry County Chamber of Commerce 1709 Hwy 20 W West Ridge Business Ctr	McDonough	GA	30253	**800-436-7926**	770-957-5786	137
Henry CS Transfer Inc PO Box 2306	Rocky Mount	NC	27802	**800-849-6400**	252-446-5116	769
Henry EP Corp 201 Park Ave	Woodbury	NJ	08096	**800-444-3679**	856-845-6200	181
Henry Equestrian Insurance Brokers 28 Victoria St	Aurora	ON	L4G3L6	**800-565-4321**	905-727-1144	384-1
Henry Ford Community College 5101 Evergreen Rd	Dearborn	MI	48128	**800-585-4322**	313-845-9600	160
Henry Ford Museum 20900 Oakwood Blvd	Dearborn	MI	48124	**800-835-5237**	313-271-1620	509
Henry Ford OptimEyes 655 W 13-Mile Rd	Madison Heights	MI	48071	**800-792-3262**	248-588-9300	533
Henry H Stambaugh Auditorium 1000 5th Ave	Youngstown	OH	44504	**866-582-8963**	330-747-5175	562
Henry & Henry Inc 3765 Walden Ave	Lancaster	NY	14086	**800-828-7130**	716-685-4000	291-23
Henry John Co 5800 W Grand River Ave	Lansing	MI	48906	**800-748-0517**	517-323-9000	614
Henry M Greene & Assoc Inc 28457 N Ballard Dr Suite A-1	Lake Forest	IL	60045	**800-356-1300**	847-816-9330	722
Henry Mancini Institute 10811 Washington Blvd Suite 250	Culver City	CA	90232	**888-464-1903**	310-845-1900	563-3
Henry Margu Inc 540 Commerce Dr	Yeadon	PA	19050	**800-345-8284**	610-622-0515	342
Henry Pratt Co 401 S Highland Ave	Aurora	IL	60506	**877-436-7728**	630-844-4000	777
Henry Schein Inc 135 Duryea Rd *NASDAQ: HSIC*	Melville	NY	11747	**800-582-2702**	631-843-5500	467
Henry Technologies 701 S Main St	Chatham	IL	62629	**800-327-2272**	217-483-2406	15
Henry Wurst Inc 1331 Saline St	North Kansas City	MO	64116	**800-775-5851**	816-842-3113	615
Hensel Phelps Construction Co 420 6th Ave PO Box 0	Greeley	CO	80631	**800-826-6309**	970-352-6565	185
Henshaw's Electronics Co 7622 Wornall Rd	Kansas City	MO	64114	**888-445-3434**	816-444-3434	35
Hensley Industries Inc 2108 Joe Field Rd PO Box 29779	Dallas	TX	75229	**888-406-6262**	972-241-2321	189
Hepatitis Foundation International (HFI) 504 Blick Dr	Silver Spring	MD	20904	**800-891-0707**	301-622-4200	48-17
Her Interactive Inc 1150 114th Ave SE Suite 200 *Orders	Bellevue	WA	98004	**800-561-0908***	425-889-2900	176-6
Heraeus Electro-Nite Co 1 Summit Sq Suite 100	Langhorne	PA	19047	**800-220-1646**	215-464-4200	200
Heraeus Kulzer Inc Dental Products Div 99 Business Pk Dr	Armonk	NY	10504	**800-343-5336**	914-273-8600	226
Heraeus Tenevo 100 Heraeus Blvd	Buford	GA	30518	**800-848-4527**	770-945-2275	252
Herald The 216 E 4th St	Jasper	IN	47546	**877-482-2424**	812-482-2426	522-2
Herald The 52 S Dock St	Sharon	PA	16146	**800-981-1692**	724-981-6100	522-2
Herald Bulletin 1133 Jackson St	Anderson	IN	46015	**800-750-5049**	765-622-1212	522-2
Herald Democrat 603 S Sam Rayburn Fwy	Sherman	TX	75090	**800-827-7183**	903-893-8181	522-2
Herald-Dispatch 946 5th Ave	Huntington	WV	25720	**800-444-2446**	304-526-4000	522-2
Herald Journal 114 S Main St	Monticello	IN	47960	**800-541-7906**	574-583-5121	522-2
Herald Journal 75 W 300 North PO Box 487	Logan	UT	84323	**800-275-0423**	435-752-2121	522-2
Herald-Mail 100 Summit Ave	Hagerstown	MD	21740	**888-851-2553**	301-733-5131	522-2
Herald Mail Co Inc 100 Summit Ave	Hagerstown	MD	21740	**888-851-2553**	301-733-5131	623-8
Herald-News 300 Caterpillar Dr	Joliet	IL	60436	**800-397-9397**	815-729-6161	522-2
Herald & News PO Box 788	Klamath Falls	OR	97601	**800-275-0982**	541-885-4410	522-2
Herald-Palladium 7450 Hollywood Rd PO Box 128	Saint Joseph	MI	49085	**800-356-4262**	269-429-2400	522-2
Herald-Standard 8-18 E Church St PO Box 848	Uniontown	PA	15401	**800-342-8254**	724-439-7500	522-2
Herald-Star 401 Herald Sq	Steubenville	OH	43952	**800-526-7987**	740-283-4711	623-8
Herald-Sun 2828 Pickett Rd	Durham	NC	27705	**800-672-0061**	919-419-6500	522-2
Herald-Sun Newspapers PO Box 2092	Durham	NC	27702	**800-672-0061**	919-419-6900	623-8
Herald Times Reporter 902 Franklin St	Manitowoc	WI	54221	**800-783-7323**	920-684-4433	522-2
Herb Research Foundation (HRF) 4140 15th St	Boulder	CO	80304	**800-748-2617**	303-449-2265	48-17
Herbalist The 2106 NE 65th St	Seattle	WA	98115	**800-694-3727**	206-523-2600	786
Herberger's GR Inc 600 W Saint Germain St	Saint Cloud	MN	56301	**800-398-7896**	320-251-5351	227
Herbert C Haynes Inc Box 96	Winn	ME	04495	**800-432-7867**	207-736-3412	439
Herbert H & Grace A Dow Foundation 1018 W Main St	Midland	MI	48640	**800-362-4849**	989-631-3699	300
Herc-U-Lift Inc 5655 Hwy 12 W	Maple Plain	MN	55359	**800-362-3500**	763-479-2501	378
Hercules Chemical Co Inc 111 South St	Passaic	NJ	07055	**800-221-9330**	973-778-5000	3
Hercules Engine Components Co 2770 S Erie St	Massillon	OH	44646	**800-345-0662**	330-830-2498	259
Hercules Inc 1313 N Market St Hercules Plaza *NYSE: HPC*	Wilmington	DE	19894	**800-441-7600**	302-594-5000	142
Hercules Industries Inc 1310 W Evans Ave	Denver	CO	80223	**800-356-5350**	303-937-1000	601
Hercules Mfg Co 800 Bob Posey St	Henderson	KY	42420	**800-633-3031**	270-826-9501	505
Hercules Tire & Rubber Co 1300 Morrical Blvd	Findlay	OH	45840	**800-677-9535**	419-425-6400	739
Herculite Products Inc 105 E Sinking Springs Ln	Emigsville	PA	17318	**800-772-0036**	717-764-1192	730-2
Herff Jones Inc Cap & Gown Div 1000 N Market St	Champaign	IL	61820	**800-637-1124**	217-351-9500	153-14
Heritage Bags 1648 Diplomat Dr	Carrollton	TX	75006	**800-527-2247**	972-241-5525	67
Heritage Bible College PO Box 1628	Dunn	NC	28335	**800-297-6351**	910-892-4268	163
Heritage Center 1201 W Buena Vista Rd	Evansville	IN	47710	**800-704-0700**	812-429-0700	441
Heritage Christian University 3625 Helton Dr PO Box HCU	Florence	AL	35630	**800-367-3565**	256-766-6610	163
Heritage Club 2020 S Monroe St	Denver	CO	80210	**877-756-0025**	303-757-1404	659
Heritage College 3240 Fort Rd	Toppenish	WA	98948	**888-272-6190**	509-865-8500	163
Heritage Corridor Convention & Visitors Bureau 81 N Chicago St	Joliet	IL	60432	**800-926-2262**	815-727-2323	205
Heritage Environmental Services Inc 7901 W Morris St	Indianapolis	IN	46231	**877-436-8778**	317-243-0811	791
Heritage Exhibits 798 Albion Ave	Schaumburg	IL	60193	**800-966-9722**	847-301-4646	230
Heritage Financial Corp 201 5th Ave SW *NASDAQ: HFWA*	Olympia	WA	98501	**800-455-6126**	360-943-1500	355-2
Heritage Foods LLC 4002 Westminster Ave *Orders	Santa Ana	CA	92703	**800-321-5960***	714-775-5000	291-27
Heritage Foundation 214 Massachusetts Ave NE	Washington	DC	20002	**800-546-2843**	202-546-4400	654
Heritage Hill Living History Museum 2640 S Webster Ave	Green Bay	WI	54301	**800-721-5150**	920-448-5150	509
Heritage Hills Golf Resort & Conference Center 2700 Mount Rose Ave	York	PA	17402	**877-782-9752**	717-755-0123	655
Heritage Hotel 1780 Tribute Rd	Sacramento	CA	95815	**800-357-9913**	916-929-7900	373
Heritage House Inn 5200 N Hwy 1	Little River	CA	95456	**800-235-5885**	707-937-5885	373
Heritage Inn 1324 Richmond Rd	Williamsburg	VA	23185	**800-782-3800**	757-229-6220	373
Heritage Inn & Golf Club 2 Postal Ln	Lewes	DE	19958	**800-669-9399**	302-644-0600	373
Heritage Insurance Managers Inc PO Box 659570	San Antonio	TX	78265	**800-456-7480**	210-829-7467	384-5
Heritage Log Homes Inc PO Box 8080	Sevierville	TN	37864	**800-456-4663**	865-453-0140	107
Heritage Plastics Inc 1002 Hunt St	Picayune	MS	39466	**800-245-4623**	601-798-8663	594-2
Heritage Publishing Co 2402 Wildwood Ave	Sherwood	AR	72120	**800-643-8822**	501-835-5000	5
Heritage Summit HealthCare of Florida Inc PO Box 3623	Lakeland	FL	33802	**800-282-7644**	863-665-6629	384-3
Herkimer County Chamber of Commerce 28 W Main St	Mohawk	NY	13407	**877-984-4636**	315-866-7820	137
Herman H Sticht Co Inc 45 Main St Suite 701	Brooklyn	NY	11201	**800-221-3203**	718-852-7602	464
Herman Miller for Health Care 855 E Main Ave PO Box 302	Zeeland	MI	49464	**888-443-4357**		314-3
Herman Miller Inc 855 E Main Ave *NASDAQ: MLHR*	Zeeland	MI	49464	**888-443-4357**	616-654-3000	314-1
Hermann Engelmann Greenhouses Inc 2009 Marden Rd	Apopka	FL	32703	**800-722-6435**	407-886-3434	363
Hermann Oak Leather Co 4050 N 1st St	Saint Louis	MO	63147	**800-325-7950**	314-421-1173	424
Herman's Inc 2820 Blackhawk Rd *Cust Svc	Rock Island	IL	61201	**800-447-1295***	309-788-9568	154
Hermitage Hotel 231 6th Ave N	Nashville	TN	37219	**888-888-9414**	615-244-3121	373
Hermosa Inn 5532 N Palo Cristi Rd	Paradise Valley	AZ	85253	**800-241-1210**	602-955-8614	373
Hernando Pasco Hospice 12107 Majestic Blvd	Hudson	FL	34667	**800-486-8784**	727-863-7971	365
Herndon JE Co Inc 1020 J E Herndon Access Rd	Kings Mountain	NC	28086	**800-277-0500**	704-739-4711	730-8
Heroix Corp 57 Wells Ave	Newton	MA	02459	**800-229-6500**	617-527-1550	176-12
Heron Point of Chestertown 501 E Campus Ave	Chestertown	MD	21620	**800-327-9138**	410-778-7300	659
Herpes Resource Center. National PO Box 13827	Research Triangle Park	NC	27709	**800-227-8922**	919-361-8488	48-17
Herr Foods Inc PO Box 300	Nottingham	PA	19362	**800-344-3777**	610-932-9330	291-35
Herr Mfg Div Serta Inc 18 Prestige Ln	Lancaster	PA	17603	**800-626-6249**	717-392-4168	463
Herring Gas Co Inc 33 Main St	Meadville	MS	39653	**800-543-9049**	601-384-5833	311
HERS (Hysterectomy Educational Resources & Services Foundation) 422 Bryn Mawr Ave	Bala Cynwyd	PA	19004	**888-750-4377**	610-667-7757	48-17
Hersam Acorn Newspapers PO Box 1019	Ridgefield	CT	06877	**800-372-2790**	203-438-6545	623-8
Herschel-Adams Inc 1301 N 14th St *Cust Svc	Indianola	IA	50125	**800-247-2167***	515-961-7481	269
Hershey-Capital Region Visitors Bureau 4th & Chestnut Sts Suite 208 Harrisburg Transportation Ctr	Harrisburg	PA	17101	**800-995-0969**	717-231-7788	205
Hershey Co 100 Crystal A Dr *NYSE: HSY*	Hershey	PA	17033	**800-468-1714**		291-8
Hershey Creamery Co 301 S Cameron St	Harrisburg	PA	17101	**888-240-1905**	717-238-8134	291-25
Hershey Entertainment & Resorts Co PO Box 860	Hershey	PA	17033	**800-437-7439**	717-534-3131	369
Hershey. Hotel 100 Hotel Rd	Hershey	PA	17033	**800-533-3131**	717-533-2171	655
Hershey Lodge & Convention Center W Chocolate Ave & University Dr	Hershey	PA	17033	**800-533-3131**	717-533-3311	373
Hershey Mark Farms Inc 479 Horseshoe Pike	Lebanon	PA	17042	**888-801-3301**	717-867-4624	438
Hersheypark 100 W Hersheypark Dr	Hershey	PA	17033	**800-437-7439**	717-534-3900	32
Hertz Big 4 Rents Inc 5500 Commerce Blvd	Rohnert Park	CA	94928	**888-777-2700**	707-586-4444	261-2
Hertz Corp 225 Brae Blvd	Park Ridge	NJ	07656	**800-654-3131**	201-307-2000	126
Hertz Equipment Rental Corp 225 Brae Blvd	Park Ridge	NJ	07656	**800-654-3131**	201-307-2000	261-4
Herweck's Art & Drafting Supplies 300 Broadway St	San Antonio	TX	78205	**800-725-1349**	210-227-1349	45
Herzing College 280 W Valley Ave	Birmingham	AL	35209	**800-425-9432**	205-916-2800	787
Herzing College 3355 Lenox Rd Suite 100	Atlanta	GA	30326	**800-473-4533**	404-816-4533	158
Herzing College 5218 E Terrace Dr	Madison	WI	53718	**800-582-1227**	608-249-6611	787
Herzog Contracting Corp PO Box 1089	Saint Joseph	MO	64502	**800-950-1969**	816-233-9001	187-4
HESCO (Hartford Electric Supply Co) 571 New Park Ave PO Box 331010	West Hartford	CT	06133	**800-969-5444**	860-236-6363	245

Name / Address	City	State	ZIP	Toll-Free	Phone	Class
Heska Corp 2601 Midpoint Dr Suite D ... *NASDAQ: HSKA*	Fort Collins	CO	80525	**800-464-3752**	970-493-7272	574
Hess John R & Co Inc 400 Station St PO Box 3615 ...	Cranston	RI	02910	**800-828-4377**	401-785-9300	144
Hess Sweitzer Inc 2805 160th St ...	New Berlin	WI	53151	**800-491-4377**	262-641-9100	188-8
Hesse Inc 6700 St John Ave ...	Kansas City	MO	64123	**800-821-5562**	816-483-7808	768
Hesselbein Tire Co Inc 4299 Industrial Dr ...	Jackson	MS	39209	**800-685-6462**	601-974-5959	740
Hesselgrave International PO Box 30768 ...	Bellingham	WA	98228	**800-457-5522**	360-734-3570	748
Hesser College 3 Sundial Ave ...	Manchester	NH	03103	**800-526-9231**	603-668-6660	160
Hesston College PO Box 3000 ...	Hesston	KS	67062	**800-995-2757**	620-327-4221	160
Heuck ME Co Inc 3274 Beekman St ... *Cust Svc	Cincinnati	OH	45223	**800-359-3200***	513-681-1774	477
Heucotech Ltd 99 Newbold Rd ...	Fairless Hills	PA	19030	**800-438-2224**	215-736-0712	142
Hewitt Relocation Services Inc 7901 Stoneridge Dr Suite 390 ...	Pleasanton	CA	94588	**800-831-3444**	925-734-3434	652
Hewitt Soap Co Inc 333 Linden Ave ...	Dayton	OH	45403	**800-543-2245**	937-253-1151	211
Hewlett-Packard Co 3000 Hanover St ... *NYSE: HPQ* ■ *Sales	Palo Alto	CA	94304	**800-322-4772***	650-857-1501	171-3
Hexacon Electric Co 161 W Clay Ave ...	Roselle Park	NJ	07204	**888-439-2266**	908-245-6200	746
Hexcel Corp 281 Tresser Blvd 2 Stamford Plaza 16th Fl ... *NYSE: HXL*	Stamford	CT	06901	**800-444-3923**	203-969-0666	594-1
Heyco Products 1800 Industrial Way North ...	Toms River	NJ	08755	**800-526-4182**	732-286-1800	479
Heyman HospiceCare PO Box 163 ...	Rome	GA	30162	**800-324-1078**	706-232-0807	365
HF Financial Corp 225 S Main Ave ... *NASDAQ: HFFC*	Sioux Falls	SD	57104	**800-244-2149**	605-333-7556	355-2
HFB Financial Corp 1602 Cumberland Ave ... *NASDAQ: HFBA*	Middlesboro	KY	40965	**800-354-0182**	606-248-1095	355-2
HFG (Hospitality Furniture Group Mfg) 8180 NW 36th St Suite 418 ...	Miami	FL	33166	**800-772-8826**	305-477-2882	314-1
HFIA (Home Furnishings International Assn) 2050 Stemmons World Trade Center Suite 170 PO Box 420807 ...	Dallas	TX	75342	**800-942-4663**	214-741-7632	49-4
HFMA (Healthcare Financial Management Assn) 2 Westbrook Corporate Ctr Suite 700 ...	Westchester	IL	60154	**800-252-4362**	708-531-9600	49-8
HFN Magazine 7 W 34th St ...	New York	NY	10001	**800-424-8698**	212-630-4000	449-21
HFTP (Hospitality Financial & Technology Professionals) 11709 Boulder Ln Suite 110 ...	Austin	TX	78726	**800-856-4242**	512-249-5333	49-1
HGI Skydyne 100 River Rd ...	Port Jervis	NY	12771	**800-428-2273**	845-856-6655	198
HGTV (Home & Garden Television) 9721 Sherrill Blvd ...	Knoxville	TN	37932	**800-448-8275**	865-694-2700	725
Hi Pro International Inc 5049 S National Dr ...	Knowxville	TN	37914	**800-947-0997**	865-637-1711	688
Hi-Tec Sports USA Inc 4801 Stoddard Rd ...	Modesto	CA	95356	**800-521-1698**	209-545-1111	296
Hi-Tech Hose Inc 400 E Main St ...	Georgetown	MA	01833	**800-451-5985**	978-352-2077	364
Hi-Tech Pharmacal Co Inc 369 Bayview Ave ... *NASDAQ: HITK*	Amityville	NY	11701	**800-262-9010**	631-789-8228	572
HI TecMetal Group Inc 1101 E 55th St ...	Cleveland	OH	44103	**877-484-2867**	216-881-8100	475
Hi*Tech Electronic Displays 13900 US Hwy 19N ...	Clearwater	FL	33764	**800-723-9402**	727-531-4800	692
HIAS (Hebrew Immigrant Aid Society) 333 7th Ave 17th Fl ...	New York	NY	10001	**800-442-7714**	212-967-4100	48-5
Hiawatha Rubber Co 1700 67th Ave N ...	Minneapolis	MN	55430	**800-728-3845**	763-566-0900	664
Hiawatha World 607 Utah St ...	Hiawatha	KS	66434	**800-803-3321**	785-742-2111	522-2
Hibachi-San Japanese Grill 1683 Walnut Grove Ave ...	Rosemead	CA	91770	**800-487-2632**	626-799-9898	657
Hibbert Group 21 Muirhead Ave ...	Trenton	NJ	08638	**888-442-2378**	609-394-7500	5
Hibbing Community College 1515 E 25th St ...	Hibbing	MN	55746	**800-224-4422**	218-262-6700	160
Hibbs Hallmark & Co PO Box 8357 ...	Tyler	TX	75711	**800-765-6767**	903-561-8484	383
Hibco Plastics Inc PO Box 157 ...	Yadkinville	NC	27055	**800-849-8683**	336-463-2391	590
Hibernia Corp 313 Carondelet St ... *NYSE: HIB*	New Orleans	LA	70130	**800-245-4388**	504-533-2858	355-2
Hibernia National Bank 313 Carondelet St ...	New Orleans	LA	70130	**800-562-9007**	504-533-3333	71
HICAM (Hitachi Computer Products (America) Inc) 1800 E Imhoff Rd ...	Norman	OK	73071	**800-448-2244**	405-360-5500	613
Hickey-Freeman Co Inc 1155 N Clinton Ave ... *Cust Svc	Rochester	NY	14621	**800-295-2000***	585-467-7240	153-12
Hickman Williams & Co 550 Forest Ave Suite 16 ...	Plymouth	MI	48170	**800-862-1890**	734-414-9575	143
Hickman's Egg Ranch Inc 7403 N 91st Ave ...	Glendale	AZ	85305	**800-224-2123**	623-872-1120	11-8
Hickok Inc 10514 Dupont Ave ... *NASDAQ: HICKA*	Cleveland	OH	44108	**800-342-5080**	216-541-8060	247
Hickory Brands Inc 429 27th St NW ...	Hickory	NC	28601	**800-438-5777**	828-322-2600	730-5
Hickory Daily Record 1100 Park Pl ...	Hickory	NC	28603	**800-849-8586**	828-322-4510	522-2
Hickory Farms Inc 1505 Holland Rd ...	Maumee	OH	43537	**800-288-7327**	419-893-7611	333
Hickory Hill Furniture Corp 501 Hoyle St ...	Valdese	NC	28690	**800-737-4432**	828-874-2124	314-2
Hickory Metro Convention & Visitors Bureau 1960A 13th Ave Dr SE ...	Hickory	NC	28602	**800-509-2444**	828-322-1335	205
Hickory Point Bank & Trust FSB PO Box 2548 ... *Cust Svc	Decatur	IL	62525	**888-424-1976***	217-875-3131	71
Hickory Printing Group Inc PO Box 69 ...	Hickory	NC	28603	**800-442-5679**	828-465-3431	615
Hickory Publishing Co Inc PO Box 968 ...	Hickory	NC	28603	**800-849-8586**	828-322-4510	623-8
Hickory Ridge Marriott Conference Hotel 1195 Summerhill Dr ...	Lisle	IL	60532	**800-334-0344**	630-971-5000	370
Hickory Springs Mfg Co 235 2nd Ave NW ...	Hickory	NC	28601	**800-438-5341**	828-328-2201	705
Hickory Tech Corp 221 E Hickory St ... *NASDAQ: HTCO*	Mankato	MN	56002	**800-326-5789**	507-387-1151	355-3
Hickory Travel Systems Inc Park 80 Plaza East ...	Saddle Brook	NJ	07663	**800-448-0350**		761
Hicks Oil & Hicks Gas Inc 204 N Rt 54 ...	Roberts	IL	60962	**800-252-6871**	217-395-2281	569
HIDA (Health Industry Distributors Assn) 310 Montgomery St Suite 520 ...	Alexandria	VA	22314	**800-549-4432**	703-549-4432	49-18
Hidden Creek Ranch 11077 E Blue Lake Rd ...	Harrison	ID	83833	**800-446-3833**	208-689-3209	238
Hidden Valley Resort & Conference Center 1 Craighead Dr ...	Hidden Valley	PA	15502	**800-458-0175**	814-443-8000	370
Hideout at Flitner Ranch Resort PO Box 206 ...	Shell	WY	82441	**800-354-8637**	307-765-2080	238
Higbee Inc 6741 Thompson Rd N ...	Syracuse	NY	13221	**800-255-4800**	315-432-8021	321
Higdon Florist 201 E 32nd St ...	Joplin	MO	64804	**800-641-4726**	417-624-7171	287
Higgins JE Lumber Co 6999 S Front Rd ...	Livermore	CA	94550	**800-241-1883**	925-245-4300	190-3
High Concrete Structures Inc 125 Denver Rd ...	Denver	PA	17517	**800-773-2278**	717-336-9300	181
High Country Bancorp Inc 7360 W Hwy 50 ... *NASDAQ: HCBC*	Salida	CO	81201	**800-201-0557**	719-539-2516	355-2
High Country Inn 1785 Hwy 105 ...	Boone	NC	28607	**800-334-5605**	828-264-1000	373
High End Systems Inc 2105 Gracy Farms Ln ...	Austin	TX	78758	**800-890-8989**	512-836-2242	431
High Grade Beverage Inc 891 Old Georges Rd ...	South Brunswick	NJ	08852	**800-221-1194**	732-821-7600	82-1
High Hampton Inn & Country Club 1525 Hwy 107 S ...	Cashiers	NC	28717	**800-334-2551**	828-743-2450	655
High Plains Livestock Exchange LLC 28601 Hwy 34 PO Box 218 ...	Brush	CO	80723	**866-842-5115**	970-842-5115	437
High Plains Power Inc PO Box 713 ...	Riverton	WY	82501	**800-445-0613**	307-856-9426	244
High Plains Publishers Inc PO Box 760 ...	Dodge City	KS	67801	**800-452-7171**	620-227-7171	623-8
High Point 5960 SW 106th Ave ...	Cooper City	FL	33328	**800-523-7773**	954-680-2700	712
High Point Convention & Visitors Bureau 300 S Main St ...	High Point	NC	27260	**800-720-5255**	336-884-5255	205
High Point Enterprise 210 Church Ave ...	High Point	NC	27262	**800-933-5760**	336-888-3500	522-2
High Point Furniture Industries Inc 1104 Bedford St PO Box 2063 ...	High Point	NC	27261	**800-447-3462**	336-431-7101	314-1
High Point University 833 Montlieu Ave ...	High Point	NC	27262	**800-345-6993**	336-841-9216	163
High School Assns. National Federation of State PO Box 690 ... *Cust Svc	Indianapolis	IN	46206	**800-776-3462***	317-972-6900	48-22
High Sierra Sport Co 880 Corporate Woods Pkwy ...	Vernon Hills	IL	60061	**800-323-9590**	847-913-1100	444
High-Tech Materials Alert Newsletter 7550 W I-10 Suite 400 ...	San Antonio	TX	77229	**877-463-7678**	210-348-1000	521-12
High Technology Solutions Inc 9771 Clairmont Mesa Blvd Suite A ...	San Diego	CA	92124	**800-411-8483**	858-495-0508	258
High Vacuum Apparatus LLC 12880 Moya Blvd ...	Reno	NV	89506	**800-551-4422**	775-359-4442	776
High West Energy Inc PO Box 519 ...	Pine Bluffs	WY	82082	**888-834-1657**	307-245-3261	244
HighBridge Audio 33 S 6th St CC-2205 ...	Minneapolis	MN	55402	**800-755-8532**	612-304-7163	643
Higher Education. Association for Continuing 2001 Mabelene Rd ...	Charleston	SC	29406	**800-807-2243**	843-574-6658	49-5
Higher Learning Commission. North Central Assn 30 N La Salle St Suite 2400 ...	Chicago	IL	60602	**800-621-7440**	312-263-0456	49-5
Higher Octave Music 4650 N Port Washington Rd ...	Milwaukee	WI	53212	**800-966-3699**	414-961-8350	643
HighJump Software 6455 City West Pkwy ...	Eden Prairie	MN	55344	**800-328-3271**	952-947-4088	176-1
Highland Computer Forms Inc 1025 W Main St ...	Hillsboro	OH	45133	**800-669-5213**	937-393-4215	111
Highland Exchange Service Co-op 5916 SR 540 E PO Box K ...	Waverly	FL	33877	**800-237-3989**	863-439-3661	310-2
Highland Rim Regional Library Center 2118 E Main St ...	Murfreesboro	TN	37130	**800-257-7323**	615-893-3380	426
Highland Supply Corp 1111 6th St ...	Highland	IL	62249	**800-472-3645**	618-654-2161	538
Highlander Inn 2 Highlander Way ...	Manchester	NH	03103	**800-548-9248**	603-625-6426	373
Highlands Regional Medical Center 5000 KY Rt 321 ...	Prestonsburg	KY	41653	**800-533-4762**	606-886-8511	366-2
Highlights for Children Inc 1800 Watermark Dr ... *Cust Svc	Columbus	OH	43215	**800-255-9517***	614-486-0631	623-9
Highlights for Children Magazine 1800 Watermark Dr ... *Cust Svc	Columbus	OH	43215	**800-255-9517***	614-486-0631	449-6
Highlines Construction Co Inc 701 Bridge City Ave PO Box 408 ...	Westwego	LA	70096	**800-762-8860**	504-436-3961	188-4
HighMark Funds PO Box 8416 ...	Boston	MA	02266	**800-433-6884**		517
Highmark Life & Casualty 5th Ave Pl 120 5th Ave ...	Pittsburgh	PA	15222	**800-833-1115**	412-544-2000	384-2
Highsmith Inc W 5527 SR 106 PO Box 800 ...	Fort Atkinson	WI	53538	**800-558-3899**	920-563-9571	451
Highway To Health Inc 1 Radnor Corporate Ctr Suite 100 ...	Radnor	PA	19087	**888-243-2358**	610-254-8700	384-7
Highway Machine Co Inc (HMC) RR 1 Box 208A ...	Princeton	IN	47670	**800-803-0112**	812-385-3639	446
Highway Materials Inc 1750 Walton Rd ...	Blue Bell	PA	19422	**800-822-3779**	610-832-8000	46
Highwoods Properties Inc 3100 Smoketree Ct Suite 600 ... *NYSE: HIW*	Raleigh	NC	27604	**866-449-6637**	919-872-4924	641
Hiking Society. American 1422 Fenwick Ln ...	Silver Spring	MD	20910	**800-972-8608**	301-565-6704	48-23
Hiland Dairy 302 S Porter St ...	Norman	OK	73071	**800-366-6455**	405-321-3191	291-25
Hiland Dairy Co PO Box 2270 ...	Springfield	MO	65801	**800-641-4022**	417-862-9311	291-27
Hiland Dairy Foods Co 700 E Central St ...	Wichita	KS	67202	**800-336-0765**	316-267-4221	291-27

Name / Address	City	State	ZIP	Toll-Free	Phone	Class
Hilbert College 5200 S Park Ave.	Hamburg	NY	14075	**800-649-8003**	716-649-7900	163
Hilco Electric Co-op Inc PO Box 127	Itasca	TX	76055	**800-338-6425**	254-687-2331	244
Hildebrandt International 200 Cottontail Ln	Somerset	NJ	08873	**800-223-0937**	732-560-8888	193
Hilfiger Tommy Sportswear Inc 25 W 39th St	New York	NY	10018	**800-888-8802**	212-840-8888	153-3
Hilford Moving & Storage 1595 S Arundell Ave.	Ventura	CA	93003	**800-739-6683**	805-642-0221	508
Hilgard House Hotel & Suites 927 Hilgard Ave	Los Angeles	CA	90024	**800-826-3934**	310-208-3945	373
Hilgraeve Inc 111 Conant Avenue Suite A *Sales	Monroe	MI	48161	**800-826-2760***	734-243-0576	176-7
Hill Brothers Chemical Co 1675 N Main St	Orange	CA	92867	**800-994-8801**	714-998-8800	144
Hill Country Resort. Hyatt Regency 9800 Hyatt Resort Dr	San Antonio	TX	78251	**800-233-1234**	210-647-1234	655
Hill County Electric Co-op Inc PO Box 2330	Havre	MT	59501	**877-394-7804**	406-394-7802	244
Hill Crest Behavioral Health Services 6869 5th Ave S.	Birmingham	AL	35212	**800-292-8553**	205-833-9000	366-3
Hill Dan & Assoc Inc DBA Flow Boy Mfg PO Box 720660	Norman	OK	73070	**800-580-3260**	405-329-3765	768
Hill-Donnelly Information Services 10126 Windhorst Rd	Tampa	FL	33619	**800-925-4654**	813-832-1600	623-6
Hill Floral Products Inc 2117 Peacock Rd	Richmond	IN	47374	**800-526-4733**	765-973-6660	288
Hill & Griffith Co 1085 Summer St	Cincinnati	OH	45204	**800-543-0425**	513-921-1075	490
Hill James J House 240 Summit Ave	Saint Paul	MN	55102	**888-727-8386**	651-297-2555	50
Hill Mfg Co Inc 1500 Jonesboro Rd SE	Atlanta	GA	30315	**800-445-5123**	404-522-8364	149
Hill PHOENIX Inc 709 Sigman Rd	Conyers	GA	30013	**800-518-6630**	770-388-0706	650
Hill Physicians Medical Group Inc PO Box 5080	San Ramon	CA	94583	**800-445-5747**	925-820-8300	455
Hill School 717 E High St	Pottstown	PA	19464	**888-445-5150**	610-326-1000	611
Hill Top Research Inc PO Box 138	Miamiville	OH	45147	**800-785-2693**	513-831-3114	654
Hill York Corp 2125 S Andrews Ave	Fort Lauderdale	FL	33316	**800-777-2971**	954-525-2971	188-10
Hillbilly Inn Motel 1166 W Hwy 76	Branson	MO	65616	**800-535-0739**	417-334-3946	373
Hillcrest Homes 2705 Mountain View Dr *Mktg	La Verne	CA	91750	**800-566-4636***	909-593-4917	659
Hillcrest Terrace 200 Alliance Way	Manchester	NH	03102	**800-862-9490**	603-645-6500	659
Hillerich & Bradsby Co Inc 800 W Main St	Louisville	KY	40232	**800-282-2287**	502-585-5226	701
Hilliard JJB WL Lyons Inc 501 S 4th St Hilliard Lyons Ctr	Louisville	KY	40202	**800-444-1854**	502-588-8400	679
Hillman Co 330 Grant Bldg Suite 1900	Pittsburgh	PA	15219	**800-445-5626**	412-281-2620	397
Hillman Group Inc 10590 Hamilton Ave	Cincinnati	OH	45231	**800-800-4900**	513-851-4900	346
Hills Health Ranch PO Box 26	108 Mile Ranch	BC	V0K2Z0	**800-668-2233**	250-791-5225	697
Hill's Pet Nutrition Inc PO Box 148	Topeka	KS	66601	**800-255-0449**	785-354-8523	568
Hillsboro Equipment Inc E18898 State Hwy 33 E PO Box 583	Hillsboro	WI	54634	**800-521-5133**	608-489-2275	270
Hillshire Farm & Kahn's 3241 Spring Grove Ave	Cincinnati	OH	45225	**800-543-4465**	513-541-4000	291-26
Hillside Candy Co 35 Hillside Ave	Hillside	NJ	07205	**800-524-1304**	973-926-2300	291-8
Hilltop Basic Resources Inc 1 W 4th St Suite 1100	Cincinnati	OH	45202	**800-701-7973**	513-651-5000	180
Hillwood Museum & Gardens 4155 Linnean Ave NW	Washington	DC	20008	**877-445-5966**	202-686-8500	509
Hillyard Chemical Co Inc 302 N 4th St	Saint Joseph	MO	64501	**800-365-1555**	816-233-1321	149
Hilman Inc 12 Timber Ln *Cust Svc	Marlboro	NJ	07746	**888-276-5548***	732-462-6277	462
Hilo Hattie 700 N Nimitz Hwy	Honolulu	HI	96817	**800-233-8912**	808-524-3966	155-5
Hilsinger Co 33 W Bacon St	Plainville	MA	02762	**800-955-6544**	508-699-4406	531
Hilti Inc 5400 S 122nd East Ave *Cust Svc	Tulsa	OK	74146	**800-879-8000***	918-252-6000	747
Hilton Apparel Group 1859 Bowles Ave	Fenton	MO	63026	**800-323-5590**		153-1
Hilton. Atlantic City Boston & Pacific Ave	Atlantic City	NJ	08401	**877-432-7139**	609-347-7111	133
Hilton. Beverly 9876 Wilshire Blvd	Beverly Hills	CA	90210	**800-445-8667**	310-274-7777	373
Hilton. Capital 1001 16th St NW	Washington	DC	20036	**800-445-8667**	202-393-1000	373
Hilton. Caribe Los Rosales St San Geronimo Grounds	San Juan	PR	00901	**800-445-8667**	787-721-0303	655
Hilton Charleston Harbor Resort & Marina 20 Patriots Point Rd	Mount Pleasant	SC	29464	**800-445-8667**	843-856-0028	655
Hilton DFW Lakes Executive Conference Center 1800 Hwy 26 E	Grapevine	TX	76051	**800-445-8667**	817-481-8444	370
Hilton Galveston Island Resort 5400 Seawall Blvd	Galveston	TX	77551	**800-475-3386**	409-744-5000	655
Hilton Garden Inn 9336 Civic Ctr Dr	Beverly Hills	CA	90210	**800-445-8667**	310-278-4321	369
Hilton Garden Inn Albany Airport 800 Albany Shaker Rd	Albany	NY	12211	**877-782-9444**	518-464-6666	373
Hilton Garden Inn Albuquerque Airport 2601 Yale Blvd SE	Albuquerque	NM	87106	**877-782-9444**	505-765-1000	373
Hilton Garden Inn Albuquerque North/Rio Rancho 1771 Rio Rancho Blvd	Rio Rancho	NM	87124	**877-782-9444**	505-896-1111	373
Hilton Garden Inn Albuquerque/Journal Center 5320 San Antonio Blvd.	Albuquerque	NM	87109	**877-782-9444**	505-314-0800	373
Hilton Garden Inn Allentown Airport 1787-B Airport Rd	Allentown	PA	18109	**877-782-9444**	610-443-1400	373
Hilton Garden Inn Allentown West 230 Sycamore Rd	Breinigsville	PA	18031	**877-782-9444**	610-398-6686	373
Hilton Garden Inn Anaheim/Garden Grove 11777 Harbor Blvd	Garden Grove	CA	92840	**877-782-9444**	714-703-9100	373
Hilton Garden Inn Anchorage 100 W Tudor Rd	Anchorage	AK	99503	**877-782-9444**	907-729-7000	373
Hilton Garden Inn Arcadia/Pasadena 199 N 2nd Ave	Arcadia	CA	91006	**877-782-9444**	626-574-6900	373
Hilton Garden Inn Arlington Courthouse Plaza 1333 N Courthouse Rd	Arlington	VA	22201	**877-782-9444**	703-528-4444	373
Hilton Garden Inn Atlanta Airport/Millenium Center 2301 Sullivan Rd	College Park	GA	30337	**877-782-9444**	404-766-0303	373
Hilton Garden Inn Atlanta NE/Gwinnett Sugarloaf 2040 Sugarloaf Cir.	Duluth	GA	30097	**877-782-9444**	770-495-7600	373
Hilton Garden Inn Atlanta North/Alpharetta 4025 Winward Plaza	Alpharetta	GA	30005	**877-782-9444**	770-360-7766	373
Hilton Garden Inn Atlanta North/Johns Creek 11695 Medlock Bridge Rd	Duluth	GA	30097	**877-782-9444**	770-476-1966	373
Hilton Garden Inn Atlanta Northpoint 10975 Georgia Ln	Alpharetta	GA	30022	**877-782-9444**	678-566-3900	373
Hilton Garden Inn Atlanta Perimeter Center 1501 Lake Hearn Dr	Atlanta	GA	30319	**877-782-9444**	404-459-0500	373
Hilton Garden Inn Auburn/Opelika 2555 Hilton Garden Dr	Auburn	AL	36830	**877-782-9444**	334-502-3500	373
Hilton Garden Inn Austin NW/Arboretum 11617 Research Blvd	Austin	TX	78759	**877-782-9444**	512-241-1600	373
Hilton Garden Inn Austin/Round Rock 2310 N IH-35	Round Rock	TX	78681	**877-782-9444**	512-341-8200	373
Hilton Garden Inn Bakersfield 3625 Marriott Dr.	Bakersfield	CA	93308	**800-664-4321**	661-716-1000	373
Hilton Garden Inn Baton Rouge Airport 3330 Harding Blvd	Baton Rouge	LA	70807	**877-782-9444**	225-357-6177	373
Hilton Garden Inn Bentonville 2204 SE Walton Blvd	Bentonville	AR	72712	**877-782-9444**	479-464-7300	373
Hilton Garden Inn Birmingham/Lakeshore Drive 520 Wildwood Cir Dr N	Homewood	AL	35209	**877-782-9444**	205-314-0274	373
Hilton Garden Inn Boise Spectrum 7699 W Spectrum Rd.	Boise	ID	83709	**877-782-9444**	208-376-1000	373
Hilton Garden Inn Boise/Eagle 145 E Riverside Dr	Eagle	ID	83616	**877-782-9444**	208-938-9600	373
Hilton Garden Inn BWI Airport 1516 Aero Dr	Linthicum	MD	21090	**877-782-9444**	410-691-0500	373
Hilton Garden Inn Calabasas 24150 Park Sorrento	Calabasas	CA	91302	**877-782-9444**	818-591-2300	373
Hilton Garden Inn Calgary Airport 2335 Pegasus Rd NE	Calgary	AB	T2E8C3	**877-782-9444**	403-717-1999	372
Hilton Garden Inn Carlsbad Beach 6450 Carlsbad Blvd	Carlsbad	CA	92009	**877-782-9444**	760-476-0800	373
Hilton Garden Inn Charleston Airport 5265 International Blvd	North Charleston	SC	29418	**877-782-9444**	843-308-9330	373
Hilton Garden Inn Charlotte North 9315 Statesville Rd.	Charlotte	NC	28269	**877-782-9444**	704-597-7655	373
Hilton Garden Inn Charlotte Pineville 425 Towne Ctr Blvd	Pineville	NC	28134	**877-782-9444**	704-889-3279	373
Hilton Garden Inn Charlotte Uptown 508 E 2nd St	Charlotte	NC	28202	**877-782-9444**	704-347-5972	373
Hilton Garden Inn Chattanooga Downtown 311 Chestnut St	Chattanooga	TN	37402	**877-782-9444**	423-308-9000	373
Hilton Garden Inn Chattanooga/Hamilton Place 2343 Shallowford Village Dr.	Chattanooga	TN	37421	**877-782-9444**	423-308-4400	373
Hilton Garden Inn Chesapeake/Greenbrier 1565 Crossways Blvd	Chesapeake	VA	23320	**877-782-9444**	757-420-1212	373
Hilton Garden Inn Cincinnati Northeast 6288 Tri Ridge Blvd	Loveland	OH	45140	**877-782-9444**	513-576-6999	373
Hilton Garden Inn Cincinnati/Sharonville 11149 Dowlin Dr	Cincinnati	OH	45241	**877-782-9444**	513-772-2837	373
Hilton Garden Inn Cleveland Airport 4900 Emerald Ct SW	Cleveland	OH	44135	**877-782-9444**	216-898-1898	373
Hilton Garden Inn Cleveland Downtown 1100 Carnegie Ave	Cleveland	OH	44115	**877-782-9444**	216-658-6400	373
Hilton Garden Inn Cleveland/Twinsburg 8971 Wilcox Dr.	Twinsburg	OH	44087	**877-782-9444**	330-405-8448	373
Hilton Garden Inn Columbus 1500 Bradley Lakes Pkwy	Columbus	GA	31904	**877-782-9444**	706-660-1000	373
Hilton Garden Inn Columbus Airport 4265 Sawyer Rd	Columbus	OH	43219	**877-782-9444**	614-231-2869	373
Hilton Garden Inn Columbus/Dublin 500 Metro Pl N.	Dublin	OH	43017	**877-782-9444**	614-766-9900	373
Hilton Garden Inn Columbus/Grove City 3928 Jackpot Rd	Grove City	OH	43123	**877-782-9444**	614-539-8944	373
Hilton Garden Inn Cupertino 10741 N Wolfe Rd	Cupertino	CA	95014	**877-782-9444**	408-777-8787	373
Hilton Garden Inn Dallas/Allen 705 Central Expy S	Allen	TX	75013	**877-782-9444**	214-547-1700	373
Hilton Garden Inn Dallas/Market Center 2325 N Stemmons Fwy	Dallas	TX	75207	**877-782-9444**	214-634-8200	373
Hilton Garden Inn Daytona Beach Airport 189 Midway Ave	Daytona Beach	FL	32114	**877-782-9444**	386-944-4000	373
Hilton Garden Inn Denver Airport 16475 E 40th Cir	Aurora	CO	80011	**877-782-9444**	303-371-9393	373
Hilton Garden Inn Denver South/Meridian 9290 Meridian Blvd	Englewood	CO	80112	**877-782-9444**	303-824-1550	373
Hilton Garden Inn Detroit Downtown 351 Gratiot Ave.	Detroit	MI	48226	**877-782-9444**	313-967-0900	373
Hilton Garden Inn Detroit Metro Airport 31800 Smith Rd	Romulus	MI	48174	**877-782-9444**	734-727-6000	373
Hilton Garden Inn Fairfax 3950 Fair Ridge Dr.	Fairfax	VA	22033	**877-782-9444**	703-385-7774	373
Hilton Garden Inn Fairfield 2200 Gateway Ct	Fairfield	CA	94533	**877-782-9444**	707-426-6900	373
Hilton Garden Inn Flagstaff 350 W Forest Meadows St.	Flagstaff	AZ	86001	**877-782-9444**	928-226-8888	373
Hilton Garden Inn Folsom 221 Iron Point Rd.	Folsom	CA	95630	**877-782-9444**	916-353-1717	373
Hilton Garden Inn Fort Lauderdale/Hollywood Airport 180 SW 18th Ave	Dania Beach	FL	33004	**877-782-9444**	954-924-9204	373

Alphabetical Section

Listing	City	State	ZIP	Toll-Free	Phone	Class
Hilton Garden Inn Fort Lauderdale/Miramar 14501 Hotel Rd	Miramar	FL	33027	**877-782-9444**	954-438-7700	373
Hilton Garden Inn Fort Wayne 8615 US 24 W	Fort Wayne	IN	46804	**877-782-9444**	260-435-1777	373
Hilton Garden Inn Fort Worth North 4400 North Fwy	Fort Worth	TX	76137	**877-782-9444**	817-222-0222	373
Hilton Garden Inn Gettysburg 1061 York St	Gettysburg	PA	17325	**877-782-9444**	717-334-2040	373
Hilton Garden Inn Gilroy 6070 Monterey St.	Gilroy	CA	95020	**877-782-9444**	408-840-7000	373
Hilton Garden Inn Grand Forks/UND 4301 Dartmouth Dr	Grand Forks	ND	58203	**877-782-9444**	701-775-6000	373
Hilton Garden Inn Green Bay 1015 Lombardi Ave	Green Bay	WI	54304	**877-782-9444**	920-405-0400	373
Hilton Garden Inn Hartford North/Bradley International 555 Corporate Dr	Windsor	CT	06095	**877-782-9444**	860-688-6400	373
Hilton Garden Inn Hartford South/Glastonbury 85 Glastonbury Blvd	Glastonbury	CT	06033	**877-782-9444**	860-659-1025	373
Hilton Garden Inn Hilton Head 1575 Fording Island Rd	Hilton Head Island	SC	29926	**877-782-9444**	843-837-8111	373
Hilton Garden Inn Houston Northwest 7979 Willow Chase Blvd	Houston	TX	77070	**877-782-9444**	832-912-1000	373
Hilton Garden Inn Houston/Bush Intercontinental Airport 15400 John F Kennedy Blvd	Houston	TX	77032	**877-782-9444**	281-449-4148	373
Hilton Garden Inn Houston/Woodlands 9301 Six Pines Dr	Houston	TX	77380	**877-782-9444**	281-364-9300	373
Hilton Garden Inn Independence 19677 E Jackson Dr	Independence	MO	64057	**877-782-9444**	816-350-3000	373
Hilton Garden Inn Indianapolis Downtown 10 E Market St	Indianapolis	IN	46204	**877-782-9444**	317-955-9700	373
Hilton Garden Inn Indianapolis/Carmel 13090 Pennsylvania St.	Carmel	IN	46032	**877-782-9444**	317-581-9400	373
Hilton Garden Inn Irvine East/Lake Forest 27082 Towne Ctr Dr	Foothill Ranch	CA	92610	**877-782-9444**	949-859-4000	373
Hilton Garden Inn Jacksonville Airport 13503 Ranch Rd	Jacksonville	FL	32218	**877-782-9444**	904-421-2700	373
Hilton Garden Inn Jacksonville JTB/Deerwood Park 9745 Gate Pkwy N	Jacksonville	FL	32246	**877-782-9444**	904-997-6600	373
Hilton Garden Inn Jacksonville/Pointe Vedra 45 PGA Blvd	Ponte Vedra Beach	FL	32082	**877-782-9444**	904-280-1661	373
Hilton Garden Inn Kansas City/Kansas 520 Minnesota Ave.	Kansas City	KS	66101	**877-782-9444**	913-342-7900	373
Hilton Garden Inn Las Colinas 7516 Las Colinas Blvd	Irving	TX	75063	**877-782-9444**	972-444-8434	373
Hilton Garden Inn Las Vegas Strip South 7830 S Las Vegas Blvd	Las Vegas	NV	89123	**877-782-9444**	702-453-7830	373
Hilton Garden Inn LAX/El Segundo 2100 E Mariposa Ave	El Segundo	CA	90245	**877-782-9444**	310-726-0100	373
Hilton Garden Inn Lexington 1973 Plaudit Pl	Lexington	KY	40509	**877-782-9444**	859-543-8300	373
Hilton Garden Inn Livermore 2801 Constitution Dr	Livermore	CA	94551	**877-782-9444**	925-292-2000	373
Hilton Garden Inn Louisville Airport 2735 Crittenden Dr	Louisville	KY	40209	**877-782-9444**	502-637-2424	373
Hilton Garden Inn Louisville East 1530 Alliant Ave	Louisville	KY	40299	**877-782-9444**	502-297-8066	373
Hilton Garden Inn Madison West/Middleton 1801 Deming Way	Middleton	WI	53562	**877-782-9444**	608-831-2220	373
Hilton Garden Inn Milwaukee Park Place 11600 W Park Pl	Milwaukee	WI	53224	**877-782-9444**	414-359-9823	373
Hilton Garden Inn Minneapolis Eagan 1975 Rahncliff Ct	Eagan	MN	55122	**877-782-9444**	651-686-4605	373
Hilton Garden Inn Minneapolis Saint Paul/Shoreview 1050 Gramsie Rd	Shoreview	MN	55126	**877-782-9444**	651-415-1956	373
Hilton Garden Inn Minneapolis/Eden Prairie 6330 Point Chase	Eden Prairie	MN	55344	**877-782-9444**	952-995-9000	373
Hilton Garden Inn Minneapolis/Maple Grove 6350 Vinewood Ln N	Maple Grove	MN	55311	**877-782-9444**	763-509-9500	373
Hilton Garden Inn Mobile East Bay/Daphne 29546 N Main St	Daphne	AL	36526	**877-782-9444**	251-625-0020	373
Hilton Garden Inn Des Moines/Urbandale 8600 Northpark Dr	Urbandale	IA	50322	**877-782-9444**	515-270-8890	373
Hilton Garden Inn Montebello 801 N Via San Clemente	Montebello	CA	90640	**877-782-9444**	323-724-5900	373
Hilton Garden Inn Montgomery East 1600 Interstate Pk Dr	Montgomery	AL	36109	**877-782-9444**	334-272-2225	373
Hilton Garden Inn Montreal/Dorval Airport 7880 Cote De Liesse	Montreal	QC	H4T1E7	**877-782-9444**	514-788-5120	372
Hilton Garden Inn Mountain Inn 840 E El Camino Real	Mountain View	CA	94040	**877-782-9444**	650-964-1700	373
Hilton Garden Inn Napa 3585 Solano Ave.	Napa	CA	94558	**877-782-9444**	707-252-0444	373
Hilton Garden Inn Nashville Airport 412 Royal Pkwy	Nashville	TN	37214	**877-782-9444**	615-884-0088	373
Hilton Garden Inn New Orleans Airport 4535 Williams Blvd.	Kenner	LA	70065	**877-782-9444**	504-712-0504	373
Hilton Garden Inn New Orleans Convention Center 1001 S Peters St.	New Orleans	LA	70130	**877-782-9444**	504-525-0044	373
Hilton Garden Inn New Orleans French Quarter/CBD 821 Gravier St	New Orleans	LA	70130	**877-782-9444**	504-324-6000	373
Hilton Garden Inn Newport News 180 Regal Way	Newport News	VA	23602	**877-782-9444**	757-947-1080	373
Hilton Garden Inn Oakland/San Leandro 510 Lewelling Blvd	San Leandro	CA	94579	**877-782-9444**	510-346-5533	373
Hilton Garden Inn Oklahoma City Airport 801 S Meridian	Oklahoma City	OK	73108	**877-782-9444**	405-942-1400	373
Hilton Garden Inn Omaha Downtown/Old Market Area 1005 Dodge St	Omaha	NE	68102	**877-782-9444**	402-341-4400	373
Hilton Garden Inn Orange Beach Beachfront 23092 Perdido Beach Blvd	Orange Beach	AL	36561	**877-782-9444**	251-974-1600	373
Hilton Garden Inn Orlando Airport 7300 Augusta National Dr	Orlando	FL	32822	**877-782-9444**	407-240-3725	373
Hilton Garden Inn Orlando East/UCF 1959 N Alafaya Tr.	Orlando	FL	32826	**877-782-9444**	407-992-5000	373
Hilton Garden Inn Orlando International Drive North 5877 American Way	Orlando	FL	32819	**877-782-9444**	407-363-9332	373
Hilton Garden Inn Palm Springs/Rancho Mirage 71-700 Hwy 111	Rancho Mirage	CA	92270	**877-782-9444**	760-776-9700	373
Hilton Garden Inn Pensacola Beach 12 Via de Luna Dr.	Pensacola Beach	FL	32561	**866-916-2999**	850-916-2999	373
Hilton Garden Inn Philadelphia Center City 1100 Arch St	Philadelphia	PA	19107	**877-782-9444**	215-923-0100	373
Hilton Garden Inn Phoenix Airport 3422 E Elwood St.	Phoenix	AZ	85040	**877-782-9444**	602-470-0500	373
Hilton Garden Inn Phoenix Midtown 4000 N Central Ave	Phoenix	AZ	85012	**877-782-9444**	602-279-9811	373
Hilton Garden Inn Pittsburgh/Southpointe 1000 Corporate Dr	Canonsburg	PA	15317	**877-782-9444**	724-743-5000	373
Hilton Garden Inn Portland Airport 145 Jetport Blvd	Portland	ME	04102	**877-782-9444**	207-828-1117	373
Hilton Garden Inn Portland Airport 12048 NE Airport Way	Portland	OR	97220	**877-782-9444**	503-255-8600	373
Hilton Garden Inn Portland Downtown Waterfront 65 Commercial St	Portland	ME	04101	**877-782-9444**	207-780-0780	373
Hilton Garden Inn Portland/Beaverton 15520 NW Gateway Ct	Beaverton	OR	97006	**877-782-9444**	503-439-1717	373
Hilton Garden Inn Portland/Lake Oswego 14850 Kruse Oaks Dr	Lake Oswego	OR	97035	**877-782-9444**	503-684-8900	373
Hilton Garden Inn Redding 5050 Bechelli Ln.	Redding	CA	96002	**877-782-9444**	530-226-5111	373
Hilton Garden Inn Richmond Innsbrook 4050 Cox Rd.	Glen Allen	VA	23060	**877-782-9444**	804-521-2900	373
Hilton Garden Inn Richmond South/Southpark 800 Southpark Blvd	Colonial Heights	VA	23834	**877-782-9444**	804-520-0600	373
Hilton Garden Inn Rochester Downtown 225 S Broadway	Rochester	MN	55904	**877-782-9444**	507-285-1234	373
Hilton Garden Inn Roseville 1951 Taylor Rd.	Roseville	CA	95661	**877-782-9444**	916-773-7171	373
Hilton Garden Inn Sacramento/South Natomas 2540 Venture Oaks Way	Sacramento	CA	95833	**877-782-9444**	916-568-5400	373
Hilton Garden Inn Saint Augustine Beach 401 A1A Beach Blvd	Saint Augustine	FL	32080	**877-782-9444**	904-471-5559	373
Hilton Garden Inn Saint Louis/Chesterfield 16631 Chesterfield Grove Rd	Chesterfield	MO	63005	**877-782-9444**	636-532-9400	373
Hilton Garden Inn Saint Louis/O'Fallon 2310 Technology Dr	O'Fallon	MO	63366	**877-782-9444**	636-625-2700	373
Hilton Garden Inn San Francisco Airport North 670 Gateway Blvd	South San Francisco	CA	94080	**877-782-9444**	650-872-1515	373
Hilton Garden Inn San Francisco Airport/Burlingame 765 Airport Blvd	Burlingame	CA	94010	**877-782-9444**	650-347-7800	373
Hilton Garden Inn San Jose/Milpitas 30 Ranch Dr.	Milpitas	CA	95035	**877-782-9444**	408-719-1313	373
Hilton Garden Inn San Mateo 2000 Bridgepointe Cir.	San Mateo	CA	94404	**877-782-9444**	650-522-9000	373
Hilton Garden Inn Scottsdale Old Town 7324 E Indian School Rd	Scottsdale	AZ	85251	**877-782-9444**	480-481-0400	373
Hilton Garden Inn Seattle/Renton 1801 E Valley Rd	Renton	WA	98055	**877-782-9444**	425-430-1414	373
Hilton Garden Inn Spokane Airport 9015 W Hwy 2	Spokane	WA	99224	**877-782-9444**	509-244-5866	373
Hilton Garden Inn Springfield 800 W Columbus Ave.	Springfield	MA	01115	**877-782-9444**	413-886-8000	373
Hilton Garden Inn Syracuse 6004 Fair Lakes Rd	East Syracuse	NY	13057	**877-782-9444**	315-431-4800	373
Hilton Garden Inn Tallahassee 3333 Thomasville Rd	Tallahassee	FL	32308	**877-782-9444**	850-385-3553	373
Hilton Garden Inn Tampa East/Brandon 10309 Highland Manor Dr	Tampa	FL	33610	**877-782-9444**	813-626-6700	373
Hilton Garden Inn Toronto/Markham 300 Commerce Valley Dr E	Markham	ON	L3T7X3	**877-782-9444**	905-709-8008	372
Hilton Garden Inn Toronto/Mississauga 100 Traders Blvd	Mississauga	ON	L4Z2H7	**877-782-9444**	905-890-9110	372
Hilton Garden Inn Toronto/Oakville 2774 S Sheridan Way	Oakville	ON	L6J7T4	**877-782-9444**	905-829-1145	372
Hilton Garden Inn Tulsa Airport 7728 E Virgin Ct	Tulsa	OK	74115	**877-782-9444**	918-838-1444	373
Hilton Garden Inn Valencia Six Flags 2771o The Old Rd	Valencia	CA	91355	**877-782-9444**	661-254-8800	373
Hilton Garden Inn Virginia Beach Town Center 252 Town Center Dr	Virginia Beach	VA	23462	**877-782-9444**	757-326-6200	373
Hilton Garden Inn West Edmonton 17610 Stony Plain Rd	Edmonton	AB	T5S1A2	**877-782-9444**	780-443-2233	372
Hilton Garden Inn West Knoxville/Cedar Bluff 216 Peregrine Way	Knoxville	TN	37922	**877-782-9444**	865-690-6511	373
Hilton Garden Inn White Marsh 5015 Campbell Blvd	Baltimore	MD	21236	**877-782-9444**	410-427-0600	373
Hilton Garden Inn Wichita 2041 N Bradley Fair Pkwy	Wichita	KS	67206	**877-782-9444**	316-219-4444	373
Hilton Garden Inn Williamsburg 1624 Richmond Rd	Williamsburg	VA	23185	**877-782-9444**	757-253-9400	373
Hilton Grand Vacations Co LLC 6355 Metro West Blvd Suite 180	Orlando	FL	32835	**800-521-3144**	407-521-3100	738
Hilton Hartford 315 Trumbull St	Hartford	CT	06103	**800-445-8667**	860-728-5151	373
Hilton Hawaiian Village 2005 Kalia Rd	Honolulu	HI	96815	**800-445-8667**	808-949-4321	655
Hilton Head Health Institute 14 Valencia Rd	Hilton Head Island	SC	29928	**800-292-2440**	843-785-7292	697

Name / Address	City	State	Zip	Toll-Free	Phone	Class
Hilton Head Island Beach & Tennis Resort 40 Folly Field Rd	Hilton Head Island	SC	29928	**800-475-2631**	843-842-4402	655
Hilton Head Island - Bluffton Chamber of Commerce 1 Chamber Dr	Hilton Head Island	SC	29928	**800-523-3373**	843-785-3673	137
Hilton Head Island. Hilton Oceanfront Resort 23 Ocean Ln	Hilton Head Island	SC	29928	**800-845-8001**	843-842-8000	655
Hilton Head Island Visitors & Convention Bureau PO Box 5647	Hilton Head Island	SC	29938	**800-523-3373**	843-785-3673	205
Hilton Head Vacation Rentals 430 William Hilton Pkwy Suite 504	Hilton Head Island	SC	29926	**800-732-7671**	843-689-3010	368
Hilton HHonors Frequent Stay Program 2050 Chenault Dr	Carrollton	TX	75006	**800-548-8690**	972-788-0878	371
Hilton Hotels 9336 Civic Ctr Dr	Beverly Hills	CA	90210	**800-445-8667**	310-278-4321	369
Hilton Hotels Corp 9336 Civic Ctr Dr	Beverly Hills	CA	90210	**800-445-8667**	310-278-4321	369
NYSE: HLT						
Conrad Hotels 9336 Civic Ctr Dr	Beverly Hills	CA	90210	**800-445-8667**	310-278-4321	369
Doubletree Hotels 9336 Civic Ctr Dr	Beverly Hills	CA	90210	**800-222-8733**	310-278-4321	369
Embassy Suites Inc 755 Crossover Ln	Memphis	TN	38117	**800-362-2779**	901-374-5000	369
Hampton Inn 755 Crossover Ln	Memphis	TN	38117	**800-426-7866**	901-374-5000	369
Hampton Inn & Suites 755 Crossover Ln	Memphis	TN	38117	**800-426-7866**	901-374-5000	369
Harrison Conference Centers 755 Crossover Ln	Memphis	TN	38117	**800-422-6338**	901-374-5000	369
Hilton Garden Inn 9336 Civic Ctr Dr	Beverly Hills	CA	90210	**800-445-8667**	310-278-4321	369
Hilton Hotels 9336 Civic Ctr Dr	Beverly Hills	CA	90210	**800-445-8667**	310-278-4321	369
Homewood Suites by Hilton 755 Crossover Ln	Memphis	TN	38117	**800-225-5466**	901-374-5000	369
Hilton International Co 40 Wall St 41st Fl	New York	NY	10005	**800-445-8667**	212-820-1700	369
Hilton Key West Resort. Sunset Key Guest Cottages at 245 Front St	Key West	FL	33040	**888-477-7786**	305-292-5300	655
Hilton Lake Placid Resort 1 Mirror Lake Dr	Lake Placid	NY	12946	**800-755-5598**	518-523-4411	655
Hilton Longboat Key Beach Resort 4711 Gulf of Mexico Dr	Longboat Key	FL	34228	**800-445-8667**	941-383-2451	655
Hilton Marco Island Beach Resort 560 S Collier Blvd	Marco Island	FL	34145	**800-443-4550**	239-394-5000	655
Hilton Myrtle Beach Resort 10000 Beach Club Dr	Myrtle Beach	SC	29572	**877-887-9549**	843-449-5000	655
Hilton Oceanfront Resort Hilton Head Island 23 Ocean Ln	Hilton Head Island	SC	29928	**800-845-8001**	843-842-8000	655
Hilton Palm Springs Resort 400 E Tahquitz Canyon Way	Palm Springs	CA	92262	**800-522-6900**	760-320-6868	655
Hilton. Palmer House 17 E Monroe St	Chicago	IL	60603	**800-445-8667**	312-726-7500	373
Hilton Reno Resort & Casino 2500 E 2nd St	Reno	NV	89595	**800-501-2651**	775-789-2000	655
Hilton San Diego Airport/Harbor Island 1960 Harbor Island Dr	San Diego	CA	92101	**800-445-8667**	619-291-6700	373
Hilton San Diego Resort 1775 E Mission Bay Dr	San Diego	CA	92109	**877-414-8019**	619-276-4010	655
Hilton San Diego/Del Mar 15575 Jimmy Durante Blvd	Del Mar	CA	92014	**800-833-7904**	858-792-5200	373
Hilton Sandestin Beach Golf Resort & Spa 4000 Sandestin Blvd S	Destin	FL	32550	**800-367-1271**	850-267-9500	655
Hilton Seattle Airport & Conference Center 17620 Pacific Hwy S	Seattle	WA	98188	**800-445-8667**	206-244-4800	370
Hilton Sedona Resort & Spa 90 Ridge Trail Dr	Sedona	AZ	86351	**800-222-8733**	928-284-4040	655
Hilton Singer Island Oceanfront 3700 N Ocean Dr	Singer Island	FL	33404	**800-941-3592**	561-848-3888	373
Hilton Tucson El Conquistador Golf & Tennis Resort 10000 N Oracle Rd	Tucson	AZ	85737	**800-325-7832**	520-544-5000	655
Hilton University of Florida Conference Center 1714 SW 34th St	Gainesville	FL	32607	**800-774-1500**	352-371-3600	370
Hilton Waikoloa Village 425 Waikoloa Beach Dr	Waikoloa	HI	96738	**866-223-6574**	808-886-1234	655
Hilton Waterfront Beach Resort 21100 Pacific Coast Hwy	Huntington Beach	CA	92648	**800-822-7873**	714-845-8000	655
HiMEC Inc 1400 7th St NW	Rochester	MN	55901	**888-454-4632**	507-281-4000	188-10
Hinckley Springs 6055 S Harlem Ave	Chicago	IL	60638	**800-347-9283**	773-586-8600	792
Hinda Incentives Inc 2440 W 34th St	Chicago	IL	60608	**800-621-4412**	773-890-5900	753
Hindley Mfg Co Inc PO Box 38	Cumberland	RI	02864	**800-323-9031**	401-722-2550	345
Hinds Community College Utica Campus Hwy 18 W	Utica	MS	39175	**800-446-3722**	601-354-2327	160
Hinds Hospice 1616 W Shaw Ave Suite B-6	Fresno	CA	93711	**800-400-4677**	559-226-5683	365
Hines Edward Lumber Co 1000 Corporate Grove Dr	Buffalo Grove	IL	60089	**888-334-4637**	847-353-7700	190-3
Hines Horticulture Inc 12621 Jeffrey Rd	Irvine	CA	92620	**800-444-4499**	949-559-4444	363
NASDAQ: HORT						
Hines Nut Co Inc 990 S Saint Paul St	Dallas	TX	75201	**800-580-0580**	214-939-0253	291-28
Hingham Mutual Fire Insurance Co 230 Beal St	Hingham	MA	02043	**800-341-8200**	781-749-0841	384-4
Hiniker Co 58766 240th St	Mankato	MN	56002	**800-433-5620**	507-625-6621	269
Hinkley Lighting 12600 Berea Rd	Cleveland	OH	44111	**800-446-5539**	216-671-3300	431
Hintzsche Fertilizer Inc 2 S 181 County Line Rd PO Box 367	Maple Park	IL	60151	**800-446-3378**	630-557-2406	276
HIP Health Plans 7 W 34th St	New York	NY	10001	**800-447-8255**	212-630-5000	384-3
Hipotronics Inc 1650 Rt 22	Brewster	NY	10509	**800-727-4476**	845-279-8091	247
Hippocrates Health Institute Life-Change Center 1443 Palmdale Ct	West Palm Beach	FL	33411	**800-842-2125**	561-471-8876	697
Hipwell Mfg Co 831 W North Ave	Pittsburgh	PA	15233	**800-447-9355**	412-231-7310	431
Hiram College PO Box 67	Hiram	OH	44234	**800-362-5280**	330-569-5169	163
Hire.com Inc 200 Academy Dr	Austin	TX	78704	**800-953-4473**	512-583-4400	39
HireCheck Inc 805 Executive Center Dr W Suite 300	Saint Petersburg	FL	33702	**800-881-3924**	727-535-4473	621
HireKnowledge 1 Harry St	Providence	RI	02907	**800-937-3622**	401-942-0570	707
Hirschbach Motor Lines Inc 920 W 21st St PO Box 9	South Sioux City	NE	68776	**800-554-2969**	402-494-5000	769
Hirschfeld Steel Co Inc 112 W 29th St	San Angelo	TX	76902	**800-375-3216**	325-486-4201	471
Hirsh Industies Inc 1500 Delaware Ave	Des Moines	IA	50317	**800-872-3279**	515-265-7111	314-1
Hirsh Industries MEG Div 502 S Green St	Cambridge City	IN	47327	**800-645-3315***	765-478-3141	281
*Cust Svc						
Hirshleifer J & Son Inc 2080 Northern Blvd	Manhasset	NY	11030	**800-401-9313**	516-627-3566	155-4
Hirzel Canning Co Inc 411 Lemoyne Rd	Northwood	OH	43619	**800-837-1631**	419-693-0531	291-20
Hispanic Assn of Colleges & Universities (HACU) 8415 Datapoint Dr Suite 400	San Antonio	TX	78229	**800-780-4228**	210-692-3805	49-5
Hispanic Business Magazine 425 Pine Ave	Santa Barbara	CA	93117	**888-447-7287***	805-964-4554	449-5
*Sales						
Hispanic Chamber of Commerce. US 2175 K St NW Suite 100	Washington	DC	20037	**800-874-2286**	202-842-1212	48-14
Hispanic Journalists. National Assn of 529 14th St NW National Press Bldg Suite 1000	Washington	DC	20045	**888-346-6245**	202-662-7145	49-14
Hispanic Magazine 999 Ponce de Leon Blvd Suite 600	Coral Gables	FL	33134	**800-251-2688***	305-442-2462	449-10
*Cust Svc						
Hispanic National Bar Assn (HNBA) 815 Connecticut Ave NW Suite 500	Washington	DC	20006	**877-221-6569**	202-223-4777	49-10
Hispanic Scholarship Fund 55 2nd St Suite 1500	San Francisco	CA	94105	**877-473-4636**	415-808-2300	711
Historic Annapolis Foundation Museum 77 Main St	Annapolis	MD	21401	**800-603-4020**	410-268-5576	509
Historic Charleston Bed & Breakfast Reservations Service 57 Broad St	Charleston	SC	29401	**800-743-3583**	843-722-6606	368
Historic French Market Inn 501 Rue Decatur	New Orleans	LA	70130	**888-538-5651**	504-561-5621	373
Historic Huntsville Depot 404 Madison St	Huntsville	AL	35801	**800-678-1819**	256-564-8100	509
Historic Inns of Annapolis 58 State Cir	Annapolis	MD	21401	**800-847-8882**	410-263-2641	373
Historic Pines Ranch PO Box 311	Westcliffe	CO	81252	**800-446-9462**	719-783-9261	238
Historic Preservation. National Trust for 1785 Massachusetts Ave NW	Washington	DC	20036	**800-944-6847**	202-588-6000	48-13
Historic Roswell District 617 Atlanta St	Roswell	GA	30075	**800-776-7935**	770-640-3253	50
Historic Tours of America Inc 201 Front St Suite 224	Key West	FL	33040	**800-868-7482**	305-296-3609	748
Historical Lawmen Museum 750 N Motel Blvd	Las Cruces	NM	88007	**800-332-2121**	505-525-1911	509
Historical Research Center International Inc 2019 Corporate Dr	Boynton Beach	FL	33426	**800-940-7991**	561-732-5263	322
History & Ourselves National Foundation Inc. Facing 16 Hurd Rd	Brookline	MA	02445	**800-856-9039**	617-232-1595	48-11
Hit Promotional Products Inc 7150 Bryan Dairy Rd	Largo	FL	33777	**800-237-6305**	727-541-5561	10
Hitachi America Ltd 50 Prospect Ave	Tarrytown	NY	10591	**800-448-2244**	914-332-5800	184
Hitachi America Ltd Computer Div 2000 Sierra Pt Pkwy	Brisbane	CA	94005	**800-225-1741**	650-589-8300	171-8
Hitachi America Ltd Monitor Div 2000 Sierra Point Pkwy	Brisbane	CA	94005	**800-562-2552**	650-589-8300	171-4
Hitachi Canada Ltd 2495 Meadowpine Blvd	Mississauga	ON	L5N6C3	**800-906-4482**	905-821-4545	252
Hitachi Chemical Diagnostics 630 Clyde Ct	Mountain View	CA	94043	**800-233-6278**	650-961-5501	229
Hitachi Computer Products (America) Inc (HICAM) 1800 E Imhoff Rd	Norman	OK	73071	**800-448-2244**	405-360-5500	613
Hitachi Credit America Ltd 800 Connecticut Ave	Norwalk	CT	06854	**800-810-0952**	203-956-3000	261-1
Hitachi Data Systems Corp 750 Central Expy	Santa Clara	CA	95050	**800-227-1930**	408-970-1000	171-8
Hitachi Home Electronics Inc 900 Hitachi Way	Chula Vista	CA	91914	**800-981-2588**	619-591-5200	52
Hitachi Internetworking 2000 Sierra Point Pkwy	Brisbane	CA	94005	**800-927-9070**	650-244-7759	174
Hitachi Magnetics Corp 7800 Neff Rd	Edmore	MI	48829	**800-955-9321**	989-427-5151	450
Hitachi Medical Systems America Inc 1959 Summit Commerce Pk	Twinsburg	OH	44087	**800-800-3106**	330-425-1313	375
Hitch Enterprises Inc PO Box 1308	Guymon	OK	73942	**800-634-8678**	580-338-8575	355-3
Hitch Feeders II Inc 521 50th Rd	Satanta	KS	67870	**800-951-6181**	620-275-6181	11-1
Hitch Henry C Feedyards PO Box 1559	Guymon	OK	73942	**800-951-2533**	580-338-2533	11-1
Hitt Marking Devices Inc 3231 MacArthur Blvd Bldg 709	Santa Ana	CA	92704	**800-969-6699**	714-979-1405	459
Hiwassee College 225 Hiwassee College Dr	Madisonville	TN	37354	**800-356-2187**	423-442-2001	160
Hix Corp 1201 E 27th Terr	Pittsburg	KS	66762	**800-835-0606**	620-231-8568	729
HJ Heinz Co PO Box 57	Pittsburgh	PA	15230	**800-255-5750**	412-456-5700	291-20
NYSE: HNZ						
HK Systems Inc 2855 S James Dr	New Berlin	WI	53151	**800-424-7365**	262-860-7000	176-1
HL Bouton Co Inc 11 Kendrick Rd	Wareham	MA	02571	**800-426-1881***	508-295-3300	531
*Cust Svc						
HL Dalis Inc 35-35 24th St	Long Island City	NY	11106	**800-453-2547**	718-361-1100	245
HLC Hotels Inc PO Box 13069	Savannah	GA	31416	**800-358-6122**	912-352-4493	369
HLI (Human Life International) 4 Family Life Ln	Front Royal	VA	22630	**800-549-5433***	540-635-7884	48-6
*Orders						

Name / Address	City	State	Zip	Toll-Free	Phone	Class
HLW International 115 5th Ave 5th Fl	New York	NY	10003	**888-353-4601**	212-353-4600	258
HM Royal Inc 689 Pennington Ave	Trenton	NJ	08618	**800-257-9452**	609-396-9176	144
HMC (Highway Machine Co Inc) RR 1 Box 208A	Princeton	IN	47670	**800-803-0112**	812-385-3639	446
HMC Archtiect 3270 Inland Empire Blvd	Ontario	CA	91764	**800-350-9979**	909-989-9979	258
HMC Holdings LLC 720 Dartmouth Ln	Buffalo Grove	IL	60089	**800-874-6625**	847-541-5070	479
HME Inc 1950 Byron Ctr Ave	Wyoming	MI	49519	**800-669-9192**	616-534-1463	505
HMI Industries Inc 6000 Lombardo Ctr Genesis Bldg Suite 500 *Cust Svc	Seven Hills	OH	44131	**800-344-1840***	216-986-8008	775
HMN Financial Inc 1016 Civic Center Dr NW *NASDAQ: HMNF*	Rochester	MN	55901	**888-644-4142**	507-535-1200	355-2
HMO Illinois Inc 300 E Randolph St	Chicago	IL	60601	**800-892-2803**	312-938-6600	384-3
HMR Enterprises Inc DBA VIP Tickets 14515 Ventura Blvd Suite 210	Sherman Oaks	CA	91403	**800-328-4253**	818-907-1548	735
HMS National Inc 1625 NW 136th Ave Suite 200	Fort Lauderdale	FL	33323	**800-432-1033**	954-845-9100	687
HMS Partners 250 Civic Ctr Dr Suite 440	Columbus	OH	43215	**866-415-1010**	614-222-2548	4
HMXTailored Co 2020 Elmwood Ave	Buffalo	NY	14207	**800-874-5000**	716-874-5000	153-12
HNBA (Hispanic National Bar Assn) 815 Connecticut Ave NW Suite 500	Washington	DC	20006	**877-221-6569**	202-223-4777	49-10
HNI Corp PO Box 1109 *NYSE: HNI*	Muscatine	IA	52761	**800-336-8398**	563-264-7400	184
HNS International Inc 17662 Irvine Blvd Suite 20	Tustin	CA	92780	**877-474-6539**	714-508-6408	468
HO Bostrom Co Inc 818 Progress Ave	Waukesha	WI	53186	**800-332-5415**	262-542-0222	678
Ho-Chunk Casino S 3214 Hwy 12	Baraboo	WI	53913	**800-746-2486**	608-356-6210	133
Ho-Chunk Nation PO Box 667	Black River Falls	WI	54615	**800-294-9343**	715-284-9343	132
Ho-Lee-Chow 658 Danforth Ave Suite 201	Toronto	ON	M4J5B9	**800-465-3324**	416-778-8028	657
HO Trerice Co 12950 W Eight-Mile Rd	Oak Park	MI	48237	**888-873-7423**	248-399-8000	200
Hoak Capital Corp 13355 Noel Rd Suite 1050	Dallas	TX	75240	**800-755-0769**	972-960-4848	779
Hobart Corp 701 S Ridge Ave *Cust Svc	Troy	OH	45374	**800-333-7447***	937-332-3000	293
Hobart & William Smith Colleges 300 Pulteney St	Geneva	NY	14456	**800-852-2256**	315-781-3000	163
Hobbs Bonded Fibers Inc 200 S Commerce St	Waco	TX	76710	**800-433-3357**	254-741-0040	730-6
Hobbs Chamber of Commerce 400 N Marland Blvd	Hobbs	NM	88240	**800-658-6291**	505-397-3202	137
Hobbs Implement Co Inc PO Box 807	Edenton	NC	27932	**800-682-6457**	252-482-7411	270
Hobbs News-Sun PO Box 850	Hobbs	NM	88241	**800-993-2123**	505-393-2123	522-2
Hobbytown USA 6301 S 58th St	Lincoln	NE	68516	**800-869-0424**	402-434-5385	749
HobbyTron.com 1053 S 1675 W	Orem	UT	84058	**800-494-1778**	801-434-7664	749
Hobe Sound Bible College PO Box 1065	Hobe Sound	FL	33475	**800-881-5534**	772-546-5534	163
Hobie Cat Co 4925 Oceanside Blvd	Oceanside	CA	92056	**800-462-4349**	760-758-9100	91
Hoboken Floors PO Box 43205	Atlanta	GA	30336	**877-356-2687**	404-629-1425	356
Hobson & Motzer Inc 30 Air Line Dr PO Box 427	Durham	CT	06422	**800-476-5111**	860-349-1756	479
Hobsons CollegeView 10200 Alliance Rd Suite 301	Cincinnati	OH	45242	**800-927-8439**	513-891-5444	623-9
Hockey Co 3500 Maison Neuve W Suite 800 *Cust Svc	Westmount	QC	H3Z3C1	**800-451-4600***	514-932-1118	701
Hockey Digest 990 Grove St	Evanston	IL	60201	**800-877-5893**	847-491-6440	449-20
Hockey Hall of Fame. US PO Box 657	Eveleth	MN	55734	**800-443-7825**	218-744-5167	511
Hockey League Players Assn. National 777 Bay St Suite 2400	Toronto	ON	M5G2C8	**800-363-4625**	416-408-4040	48-22
Hockey News Magazine 100-25 Sheppard Ave W	Toronto	ON	M2N6F7	**888-361-9768**	416-733-7600	449-20
Hockey North America (HNA) PO Box 78	Sterling	VA	20167	**800-446-2539**	703-430-8100	48-22
Hocking College 3301 Hocking Pkwy	Nelsonville	OH	45764	**800-282-4163**	740-753-3591	787
Hodge Cramer & Assoc Inc 5400 Frantz Rd Suite 120	Dublin	OH	43016	**800-978-9212**	614-761-3005	312
Hodges Trucking Co Inc 4050 W I-40	Oklahoma City	OK	73108	**800-733-7765**	405-947-7764	769
Hodgson Russ LLP 1 M&T Plaza Suite 2000	Buffalo	NY	14203	**800-724-5184**	716-856-4000	419
Hoegemeyer Hybrids Inc 1755 Hoegemeyer Rd	Hooper	NE	68031	**800-245-4631**	402-654-3399	11-5
Hoenig Group Inc 4 International Dr 2nd Fl	Rye Brook	NY	10573	**800-999-9558**	914-312-2300	679
Hoerbiger Corp of America Inc 3350 Gateway Dr	Pompano Beach	FL	33069	**800-327-8961**	954-974-5700	776
Hoffco Inc 358 NW 'F' St	Richmond	IN	47374	**800-999-8161**	765-966-8161	420
Hoffman California Fabrics Inc 25792 Obrero Dr	Mission Viejo	CA	92691	**800-547-0100**	949-770-2922	583
Hoffman International Inc 300 S Randolphville Rd	Piscataway	NJ	08855	**800-446-3362**	732-752-3600	353
Hoffman Mills Inc 470 Park Ave S 7th Fl	New York	NY	10016	**800-582-1922**	212-684-3700	730-1
Hoffman Products 20700 Hubbell Ave	Oak Park	MI	48237	**800-445-6949**	248-395-8462	803
Hoffmann-LaRoche Inc 340 Kingsland St	Nutley	NJ	07110	**800-526-6367**	973-235-5000	572
Hoffmann-La Roche Ltd 2455 Meadowpine Blvd	Mississauga	ON	L5N6L7	**800-561-1759**	905-542-5555	572
Hoffmaster PO Box 2038	Oshkosh	WI	54903	**800-558-9300**	920-235-9330	548-2
Hoffritz Div Lifetime Hoan Corp 1 Merrick Ave	Westbury	NY	11590	**800-252-3390**	516-683-6000	477
Hofstra University 100 Hofstra University	Hempstead	NY	11549	**800-463-7872**	516-463-6700	163
Hog Slat 206 Fayetteville St	Newton Grove	NC	28366	**800-949-4647**	910-594-0219	11-6
Hogan Ben Co 425 Meadow St	Chicopee	MA	01021	**800-772-5346**	413-536-1200	701
Hoge-Warren-Zimmermann Co 40 W Cresentville Rd	Cincinnati	OH	45246	**800-322-3521**	513-671-3300	188-9
Hoggan Health Industries Inc 8020 S 1300 West	West Jordan	UT	84088	**800-678-7888**	801-572-6500	263
Hogi Yogi Corp 4833 N Edgewood Dr	Provo	UT	84604	**800-653-4581**	801-222-9004	657
Hogslat Midwest Inc 200 N Meridian Line Rd	Camden	IN	46917	**800-735-4135**	574-686-2573	438
Hogue Cellars 2800 Lee Rd	Prosser	WA	99350	**800-565-9779**	509-786-4557	81-3
Hohmann & Barnard Inc 30 Rasons Ct	Hauppauge	NY	11788	**800-323-7170**	631-234-0600	182
Hohner Inc 1000 Technology Pk Dr	Glen Allen	VA	23059	**800-446-6010**	804-515-1900	516
Hoist Fitness Systems Inc 9990 Empire St Suite 130	San Diego	CA	92126	**800-548-5438**	858-578-7676	263
Hoke Communications Inc 224 7th St	Garden City	NY	11530	**800-229-6700**	516-746-6700	623-9
Hoke County PO Box 210	Raeford	NC	28376	**800-597-8751**	910-875-8751	334
Hol-Mac Corp PO Box 349	Bay Springs	MS	39422	**800-844-3019**	601-764-4121	220
Holcim (US) Inc 1100 Victors Way Suite 50	Ann Arbor	MI	48108	**800-831-9507**	734-821-7000	135
Holcomb JR & Co Inc PO Box 94636	Cleveland	OH	44101	**800-362-9907**	216-341-3000	673
Holcomb's Education Resource 3205 Harvard Ave	Cleveland	OH	44105	**800-362-9907**	216-341-3000	673
Holden Graphic Services 607 Washington Ave N	Minneapolis	MN	55401	**800-423-1099**	612-339-0241	615
Holden MSS 5000 Lima St	Denver	CO	80239	**800-343-4717**	720-374-3700	722
Holga Inc 7901 Woodley Ave	Van Nuys	CA	91406	**800-544-4623**	818-782-0600	314-1
Holiday Acres Resort & Conference Center 4060 S Shore Dr	Rhinelander	WI	54501	**800-261-1500**	715-369-1500	655
Holiday Cos 4567 American Blvd W	Bloomington	MN	55437	**800-745-7411**	952-830-8700	184
Holiday Expeditions 544 East 3900 S	Salt Lake City	UT	84107	**800-624-6323**	801-266-2087	748
Holiday Inn Albany-Turf on Wolf Road 205 Wolf Rd	Albany	NY	12205	**800-465-4329**	518-458-7250	373
Holiday Inn Ann Arbor North Campus 3600 Plymouth Rd	Ann Arbor	MI	48105	**800-800-5560**	734-769-9800	373
Holiday Inn Aristocrat Hotel 1933 Main St	Dallas	TX	75201	**800-231-4235**	214-741-7700	373
Holiday Inn Arlington (Near Six Flags) 1507 N Watson Rd	Arlington	TX	76006	**877-622-5395**	817-640-7712	373
Holiday Inn Atlanta Downtown 101 Andrew Young International Blvd NW	Atlanta	GA	30303	**800-535-0707**	404-524-5555	373
Holiday Inn Atlantic City Boardwalk 115 S Chelsea Ave	Atlantic City	NJ	08401	**800-548-3030**	609-348-2200	373
Holiday Inn Augusta Civic Center 110 Community Dr	Augusta	ME	04330	**800-694-6404**	207-622-4751	373
Holiday Inn Augusta-Gordon Hwy 2155 Gordon Hwy	Augusta	GA	30909	**800-465-4329**	706-737-2300	373
Holiday Inn Austin-Town Lake 20 N IH-35	Austin	TX	78701	**800-465-4329**	512-472-8211	373
Holiday Inn Baltimore Inner Harbor 301 W Lombard St	Baltimore	MD	21201	**800-465-4329**	410-685-3500	373
Holiday Inn Bangor-Civic Center 500 Main St	Bangor	ME	04401	**800-799-8651**	207-947-8651	373
Holiday Inn Bangor-Odlin Rd 404 Odlin Rd	Bangor	ME	04401	**800-914-0101**	207-947-0101	373
Holiday Inn Baton Rouge South 9940 Airline Hwy	Baton Rouge	LA	70816	**800-465-4329**	225-924-7021	373
Holiday Inn Birmingham Airport 5000 Richard Arrington Blvd	Birmingham	AL	35212	**800-368-5533**	205-591-6900	373
Holiday Inn Birmingham-Homewood 260 Oxmoor Rd	Birmingham	AL	35209	**800-465-4329**	205-942-2041	373
Holiday Inn Boise Airport 3300 Vista Ave	Boise	ID	83705	**800-465-4329**	208-344-8365	373
Holiday Inn Boston-Brookline 1200 Beacon St	Brookline	MA	02446	**800-465-4329**	617-277-1200	373
Holiday Inn Boston-Logan Airport 225 McClellan Hwy	Boston	MA	02128	**800-465-4329**	617-569-5250	373
Holiday Inn Brentwood 760 Old Hickory Blvd	Brentwood	TN	37027	**800-465-4329**	615-373-2600	373
Holiday Inn Bridgeport 1070 Main St	Bridgeport	CT	06604	**800-465-4329**	203-334-1234	373
Holiday Inn BWI 890 Elkridge Landing Rd	Linthicum	MD	21090	**800-465-4329**	410-859-8400	373
Holiday Inn Calgary Downtown 119 12th Ave SW	Calgary	AB	T2R0G8	**800-661-9378**	403-266-4611	372
Holiday Inn Casper-Convention Center 300 W 'F' St	Casper	WY	82601	**800-465-4329**	307-235-2531	373
Holiday Inn Champaign/Urbana 1001 W Killarney St	Urbana	IL	61801	**800-465-4329**	217-328-7900	373
Holiday Inn Charleston Historic District 125 Calhoun St	Charleston	SC	29401	**877-805-7900**	843-805-7900	373
Holiday Inn Charleston House 600 Kanawha Blvd E	Charleston	WV	25301	**800-465-4329**	304-344-4092	373
Holiday Inn Charleston-Riverview 301 Savannah Hwy	Charleston	SC	29407	**800-465-4329**	843-556-7100	373
Holiday Inn Chesapeake 725 Woodlake Dr	Chesapeake	VA	23320	**800-465-4329**	757-523-1500	373
Holiday Inn Chevy Chase 5520 Wisconsin Ave	Chevy Chase	MD	20815	**800-465-4329**	301-656-1500	373
Holiday Inn Cheyenne 204 W Fox Farm Rd	Cheyenne	WY	82007	**800-465-4329**	307-638-4466	373
Holiday Inn Chicago City Center 300 E Ohio St	Chicago	IL	60611	**800-465-4329**	312-787-6100	373
Holiday Inn Chicago Mart Plaza 350 N Orleans St	Chicago	IL	60654	**800-465-4329**	312-836-5000	373
Holiday Inn Columbia Airport 500 Chris Dr	West Columbia	SC	29169	**800-465-4329**	803-794-9440	373
Holiday Inn Columbus-North I-85 2800 Manchester Expy	Columbus	GA	31904	**800-465-4329**	706-324-0231	373
Holiday Inn Crockett Hotel 320 Bonham St	San Antonio	TX	78205	**800-292-1050**	210-225-6500	373
Holiday Inn Daytona Beach Shores 3209 S Atlantic Ave	Daytona Beach Shores	FL	32118	**800-465-4329**	386-761-2050	373

Name / Address	City	State	ZIP	Toll-Free	Phone	Class
Holiday Inn Denver Downtown 1450 Glenarm Pl.	Denver	CO	80202	**800-423-5128**	303-573-1450	373
Holiday Inn Dubuque Five Flags 450 Main St	Dubuque	IA	52001	**800-465-4329**	563-556-2000	373
Holiday Inn Edmonton The Palace 4235 Gateway Blvd.	Edmonton	AB	T6J5H2	**800-565-1222**	780-438-1222	372
Holiday Inn Emerald Beach 1102 S Shoreline Blvd	Corpus Christi	TX	78401	**800-465-4329**	361-883-5731	373
Holiday Inn Fairborn Hotel & Conference Center 2800 Presidential Dr.	Fairborn	OH	45324	**800-465-4329**	937-426-7800	373
Holiday Inn Fargo 3803 13th Ave S	Fargo	ND	58106	**877-282-2700**	701-282-2700	373
Holiday Inn Flint 5353 Gateway Centre	Flint	MI	48507	**888-570-1770**	810-232-5300	373
Holiday Inn Fort Collins-University Park 425 W Prospect Rd.	Fort Collins	CO	80526	**800-465-4329**	970-482-2626	373
Holiday Inn Fort Lauderdale Beach 999 Fort Lauderdale Beach Blvd	Fort Lauderdale	FL	33304	**800-465-4329**	954-563-5961	373
Holiday Inn Fort Smith City Center 700 Rogers Ave	Fort Smith	AR	72901	**800-465-4329**	479-783-1000	373
Holiday Inn Fort Worth North Hotel & Conference Center 2540 Meacham Blvd.	Fort Worth	TX	76106	**800-465-4329**	817-625-9911	373
Holiday Inn Frankfort Capital Plaza 405 Wilkinson Blvd.	Frankfort	KY	40601	**800-465-4329**	502-227-5100	373
Holiday Inn Grand Forks 1210 N 43rd St.	Grand Forks	ND	58203	**800-465-4329**	701-772-7131	373
Holiday Inn Grand Island 100 Whitehaven Rd	Grand Island	NY	14072	**800-465-4329**	716-773-1111	373
Holiday Inn Grand Montana 5500 Midland Rd	Billings	MT	59101	**800-465-4329**	406-248-7701	373
Holiday Inn Great Falls 400 10th Ave S.	Great Falls	MT	59405	**800-257-1998**	406-727-7200	373
Holiday Inn Green Bay City Centre 200 E Main St.	Green Bay	WI	54301	**800-465-4329**	920-437-5900	373
Holiday Inn Gulfport Beachfront 1600 E Beach Blvd	Gulfport	MS	39501	**800-441-0887**	228-864-4310	373
Holiday Inn Harbourview 101 Wyse Rd	Dartmouth	NS	B3A1L9	**800-465-4329**	902-463-1100	372
Holiday Inn Helena Downtown 22 N Last Chance Gulch	Helena	MT	59601	**800-465-4329**	406-443-2200	373
Holiday Inn Hollywood Beach 2711 S Ocean Dr	Hollywood Beach	FL	33019	**800-237-4667**	954-923-8700	373
Holiday Inn Hotel & Suites Alexandria (Historic District) 625 1st St.	Alexandria	VA	22314	**877-732-3318**	703-548-6300	373
Holiday Inn Hotel & Suites Anaheim 1240 S Walnut St.	Anaheim	CA	92802	**800-465-4329**	714-535-0300	373
Holiday Inn Hotel & Suites Duluth Downtown Waterfront 200 W 1st St.	Duluth	MN	55802	**800-477-7089**	218-722-1202	373
Holiday Inn Hotel & Suites Elgin 495 Airport Rd	Elgin	IL	60123	**800-227-6963**	847-488-9000	373
Holiday Inn Hotel & Suites Fort Wayne Downtown 300 E Washington Blvd.	Fort Wayne	IN	46802	**800-465-4329**	260-422-5511	373
Holiday Inn Hotel & Suites Jackson North 5075 I-55 N	Jackson	MS	39206	**800-465-4329**	601-366-9411	373
Holiday Inn Hotel & Suites Madison West 1109 Fourier Dr.	Madison	WI	53717	**888-522-9472**	608-826-0500	373
Holiday Inn Hotel & Suites Overland Park 10920 Nall Ave.	Overland Park	KS	66211	**800-465-4329**	913-312-0900	373
Holiday Inn Hotel & Suites Overland Park West 8787 Reeder Rd	Overland Park	KS	66214	**888-825-7538**	913-888-8440	373
Holiday Inn Hotel & Suites Phoenix-Mesa 1600 S Country Club Dr.	Mesa	AZ	85210	**800-465-4329**	480-964-7000	373
Holiday Inn Hotel & Suites Saint Petersburg Beach 5250 Gulf Blvd	Saint Pete Beach	FL	33706	**800-448-0901**	727-360-1811	373
Holiday Inn Hotel & Suites Vancouver Downtown 1110 Howe St.	Vancouver	BC	V6Z1R2	**800-465-4329**	604-684-2151	372
Holiday Inn Huntsville-Madison 9035 Madison Blvd.	Madison	AL	35758	**800-826-9563**	256-772-7170	373
Holiday Inn Huntsville Research Park 5903 University Dr NW	Huntsville	AL	35806	**800-845-7275**	256-830-0600	373
Holiday Inn I-40 1911 I-40 E.	Amarillo	TX	79102	**800-465-4329**	806-372-8741	373
Holiday Inn at Indigo Lakes 2620 W International Speedway Blvd	Daytona Beach	FL	32114	**800-465-4329**	386-258-6333	373
Holiday Inn Jacksonville Airport 14670 Duval Rd	Jacksonville	FL	32218	**800-465-4329**	904-741-4404	373
Holiday Inn JFK Airport 144-02 135th Ave.	Jamaica	NY	11436	**800-465-4329**	718-659-0200	373
Holiday Inn Johnson City 101 W Springbrook Dr.	Johnson City	TN	37604	**800-465-4329**	423-282-4611	373
Holiday Inn Key West Beachside 3841 N Roosevelt Blvd.	Key West	FL	33040	**800-292-7706**	305-294-2571	373
Holiday Inn on King 370 King St W	Toronto	ON	M5V1J9	**800-263-6364**	416-599-4000	372
Holiday Inn on the Lane 328 W Lane Ave.	Columbus	OH	43201	**800-465-4329**	614-294-4848	373
Holiday Inn Lansing South/Convention Center 6820 S Cedar St.	Lansing	MI	48911	**800-465-4329**	517-694-8123	373
Holiday Inn de Las Cruces 201 E University Ave	Las Cruces	NM	88005	**800-465-4329**	505-526-4411	373
Holiday Inn Leesburg 1500 E Market St	Leesburg	VA	20176	**888-850-8545**	703-771-9200	373
Holiday Inn Lexington North 1950 Newtown Pike	Lexington	KY	40511	**800-465-4329**	859-233-0512	373
Holiday Inn Lincoln Downtown 141 N 9th St.	Lincoln	NE	68508	**800-465-4329**	402-475-4011	373
Holiday Inn Long Beach Airport 2640 Lakewood Blvd	Long Beach	CA	90815	**800-465-4329**	562-597-4401	373
Holiday Inn Louisville Airport East 4004 Gardiner Pt Dr.	Louisville	KY	40213	**800-465-4329**	502-452-6361	373
Holiday Inn Lubbock Hotel & Towers 801 Ave Q.	Lubbock	TX	79401	**800-465-4329**	806-763-1200	373
Holiday Inn Lubbock Park Plaza 3201 S Loop 289	Lubbock	TX	79423	**800-465-4329**	806-797-3241	373
Holiday Inn Macon Conference Center 3590 Riverside Dr.	Macon	GA	31298	**888-781-7666**	478-474-2610	373
Holiday Inn Macon West 4755 Chambers Rd.	Macon	GA	31206	**877-622-6693**	478-788-0120	373
Holiday Inn Madison East 3841 E Washington Ave.	Madison	WI	53704	**800-465-4329**	608-244-2481	373
Holiday Inn Manhattan-Downtown/SoHo 138 Lafayette St.	New York	NY	10013	**800-465-4329**	212-966-8898	373
Holiday Inn Matteson 500 Holiday Plaza Dr	Matteson	IL	60443	**800-465-4329**	708-747-3500	373
Holiday Inn Minneapolis Metrodome 1500 Washington Ave S.	Minneapolis	MN	55454	**800-448-3663**	612-333-4646	373
Holiday Inn Des Moines Airport 6111 Fleur Dr	Des Moines	IA	50321	**800-248-4013**	515-287-2400	373
Holiday Inn Montgomery East 1185 Eastern Bypass Blvd	Montgomery	AL	36117	**800-465-4329**	334-272-0370	373
Holiday Inn Montreal Midtown 420 Sherbrooke St W.	Montreal	QC	H3A1B4	**800-387-3042**	514-842-6111	372
Holiday Inn Morgantown 1400 Saratoga Ave	Morgantown	WV	26505	**800-465-4329**	304-599-1680	373
Holiday Inn Myrtle Beach Oceanfront/Downtown 415 S Ocean Blvd	Myrtle Beach	SC	29577	**800-845-0313**	843-448-4481	373
Holiday Inn New Orleans Chateau LeMoyne 301 Rue Dauphine	New Orleans	LA	70112	**800-747-3279**	504-581-1303	373
Holiday Inn New Orleans Downtown-Superdome 330 Loyola Ave.	New Orleans	LA	70112	**800-535-7830**	504-581-1600	373
Holiday Inn New Orleans French Quarter 124 Royal St.	New Orleans	LA	70130	**800-447-2830**	504-529-7211	373
Holiday Inn New Orleans-Metairie 3400 S I-10 Service Rd	Metairie	LA	70001	**800-465-4329**	504-833-8201	373
Holiday Inn North Canton 4520 Everhard Rd NW	North Canton	OH	44718	**800-465-4329**	330-494-2770	373
Holiday Inn North Vancouver 700 Old Lillooet Rd	North Vancouver	BC	V7J2H5	**877-985-3111**	604-985-3111	372
Holiday Inn Ocean City Oceanfront 6600 Coastal Hwy.	Ocean City	MD	21842	**800-837-3588**	410-524-1600	373
Holiday Inn Omaha 3321 S 72nd St	Omaha	NE	68124	**800-465-4329**	402-393-3950	373
Holiday Inn Peoria City Centre 500 Hamilton Blvd	Peoria	IL	61602	**800-465-4329**	309-674-2500	373
Holiday Inn Perrysburg-French Quarter 10630 Fremont Pike	Perrysburg	OH	43551	**888-874-2592**	419-874-3111	373
Holiday Inn Philadelphia City Line 4100 Presidential Blvd	Philadelphia	PA	19131	**800-465-4329**	215-477-0200	373
Holiday Inn Philadelphia Stadium 900 Packer Ave.	Philadelphia	PA	19148	**800-424-0291**	215-755-9500	373
Holiday Inn Phoenix-Midtown 4321 N Central Ave	Phoenix	AZ	85012	**800-465-4329**	602-200-8888	373
Holiday Inn Phoenix-Tempe/ASU 915 E Apache Blvd.	Tempe	AZ	85281	**800-553-1826**	480-968-3451	373
Holiday Inn Pittsburgh Airport 8256 University Blvd	Coraopolis	PA	15108	**800-333-4835**	412-262-3600	373
Holiday Inn Plantation/Sawgrass 1711 N University Dr	Plantation	FL	33322	**800-465-4329**	954-472-5600	373
Holiday Inn Plaza La Chaudiere 2 rue Montcalm	Hull	QC	J8X4B4	**800-567-1962**	819-778-3880	372
Holiday Inn Pocatello 1399 Bench Rd.	Pocatello	ID	83201	**800-200-8944**	208-237-1400	373
Holiday Inn Portland by the Bay 88 Spring St.	Portland	ME	04101	**800-345-5050**	207-775-2311	373
Holiday Inn Portsmouth Olde Towne Waterfront 8 Crawford Pkwy	Portsmouth	VA	23704	**800-465-4269**	757-393-2573	373
Holiday Inn Providence Downtown 21 Atwells Ave	Providence	RI	02903	**800-465-4329**	401-831-3900	373
Holiday Inn Provo 1460 S University Ave.	Provo	UT	84601	**800-465-4329**	801-374-9750	373
Holiday Inn Raleigh-Brownstone 1707 Hillsborough St	Raleigh	NC	27605	**800-331-7919**	919-828-0811	373
Holiday Inn Raleigh-Durham Airport 4810 Old Page Rd	Research Triangle Park	NC	27709	**800-465-4329**	919-941-6000	373
Holiday Inn Richmond 6531 W Broad St	Richmond	VA	23230	**800-465-4329**	804-285-9951	373
Holiday Inn Rochester Airport 911 Brooks Ave	Rochester	NY	14624	**800-465-4329**	585-328-6000	373
Holiday Inn Rochester City Centre 220 S Broadway	Rochester	MN	55904	**800-241-1597**	507-252-8200	373
Holiday Inn Rocky Mountain Park 101 S St Vrain Ave.	Estes Park	CO	80517	**800-803-7837**	970-586-2332	373
Holiday Inn Rushmore Plaza 505 N 5th St.	Rapid City	SD	57701	**800-465-4329**	605-348-4000	373
Holiday Inn Sacramento Capitol Plaza 300 J St	Sacramento	CA	95814	**800-465-4329**	916-446-0100	373
Holiday Inn Sacramento I-80 Northeast 5321 Date Ave.	Sacramento	CA	95841	**800-465-4329**	916-338-5800	373
Holiday Inn Saint Louis-Westport 1973 Craigshire Rd.	Saint Louis	MO	63146	**800-465-4329**	314-434-0100	373
Holiday Inn Saint Paul North 1201 W County Rd 'E'	Saint Paul	MN	55112	**800-777-2232**	651-636-4123	373
Holiday Inn Salt Lake City Downtown 999 S Main St	Salt Lake City	UT	84111	**800-465-4329**	801-359-8600	373
Holiday Inn San Antonio Riverwalk 217 N Saint Mary's St	San Antonio	TX	78205	**800-465-4329**	210-224-2500	373
Holiday Inn San Diego on the Bay 1355 N Harbor Dr.	San Diego	CA	92101	**800-877-8920**	619-232-3861	373
Holiday Inn San Diego Bayside 4875 N Harbor Dr. *Resv	San Diego	CA	92106	**800-345-9995***	619-224-3621	373
Holiday Inn San Francisco Civic Center 50 8th St	San Francisco	CA	94103	**800-243-1135**	415-626-6103	373
Holiday Inn San Francisco Financial District 750 Kearny St.	San Francisco	CA	94108	**800-424-8292**	415-433-6600	373
Holiday Inn San Francisco-Fisherman's Wharf 1300 Columbus Ave	San Francisco	CA	94133	**800-465-4329**	415-771-9000	373
Holiday Inn San Francisco-Oakland Bay Bridge 1800 Powell St	Emeryville	CA	94608	**800-465-4329**	510-658-9300	373

Name / Address	City	State	Zip	Toll-Free	Phone	Class
Holiday Inn San Pedro-Los Angeles Harbor 111 S Gaffey St	San Pedro	CA	90731	**800-248-3188**	310-514-1414	373
Holiday Inn Santa Ana-Orange County Airport 2726 S Grand Ave	Santa Ana	CA	92705	**800-465-4329**	714-966-1955	373
Holiday Inn Santa Monica 120 Colorado Ave	Santa Monica	CA	90401	**800-947-9175**	310-451-0676	373
Holiday Inn Seattle-Tacoma Airport 17338 International Blvd	Seattle	WA	98188	**800-465-4329**	206-248-1000	373
Holiday Inn Select Alexandria Old Town 480 King St	Alexandria	VA	22314	**800-465-4329**	703-549-6080	373
Holiday Inn Select Atlanta 450 Capitol Ave SW	Atlanta	GA	30312	**800-442-6011**	404-591-2000	373
Holiday Inn Select Bakersfield-Convention Center 801 Truxtun Ave	Bakersfield	CA	93301	**800-465-4329**	661-323-1900	373
Holiday Inn Select Baltimore North 2004 Greenspring Dr	Timonium	MD	21093	**800-465-4329**	410-252-7373	373
Holiday Inn Select Bethesda 8120 Wisconsin Ave	Bethesda	MD	20814	**877-888-3001**	301-652-2000	373
Holiday Inn Select Boston-Government Center 5 Blossom St	Boston	MA	02114	**800-465-4329**	617-742-7630	373
Holiday Inn Select Brampton 30 Peel Centre Dr	Brampton	ON	L6T4G3	**800-465-4329**	905-792-9900	372
Holiday Inn Select Cleveland City Center-Lakeshore 1111 Lakeside Ave	Cleveland	OH	44114	**800-465-4329**	216-241-5100	373
Holiday Inn Select Cleveland (Strongsville) 15471 Royalton Rd	Strongsville	OH	44136	**800-465-4329**	440-238-8800	373
Holiday Inn Select Clinton 111 Rt 173	Clinton	NJ	08809	**800-465-4329**	908-735-5111	373
Holiday Inn Select Dallas LBJ NE 11350 LBJ Fwy	Dallas	TX	75238	**800-346-0660**	214-341-5400	373
Holiday Inn Select Dallas Love Field 3300 W Mockingbird Ln	Dallas	TX	75235	**800-465-4329**	214-357-8500	373
Holiday Inn Select Dallas North Park 10650 N Central Expy	Dallas	TX	75231	**800-465-4329**	214-373-6000	373
Holiday Inn Select Dallas/Fort Worth Airport South 4440 W Airport Fwy	Irving	TX	75062	**800-465-4329**	972-399-1010	373
Holiday Inn Select Decatur Conference Center 4191 W US Hwy 36	Decatur	IL	62522	**800-465-4329**	217-422-8800	373
Holiday Inn Select Denver-Cherry Creek 455 S Colorado Blvd	Denver	CO	80246	**800-465-4329**	303-388-5561	373
Holiday Inn Select Diamond Bar 21725 E Gateway Ctr Dr	Diamond Bar	CA	91765	**800-988-3587**	909-860-5440	373
Holiday Inn Select Executive Center Columbia Mall 2200 I-70 Dr SW	Columbia	MO	65203	**800-465-4329**	573-445-8531	373
Holiday Inn Select Fort Myers Airport 13051 Bell Tower Dr	Fort Myers	FL	33907	**800-465-4329**	239-482-2900	373
Holiday Inn Select Fredericksburg 2801 Plank Rd	Fredericksburg	VA	22401	**800-682-1049**	540-786-8321	373
Holiday Inn Select Halifax Centre 1980 Robie St	Halifax	NS	B3H3G5	**800-465-4329**	902-423-1161	372
Holiday Inn Select Houston-Greenway Plaza Area 2712 Southwest Fwy	Houston	TX	77098	**800-465-4329**	713-523-8448	373
Holiday Inn Select Houston I-10 W 14703 Park Row	Houston	TX	77079	**800-465-4329**	281-558-5580	373
Holiday Inn Select Indianapolis Airport 2501 S High School Rd	Indianapolis	IN	46241	**800-465-4329**	317-244-6861	373
Holiday Inn Select Indianapolis-North 3850 DePauw Blvd	Indianapolis	IN	46268	**800-465-4329**	317-872-9790	373
Holiday Inn Select Knoxville-Cedar Bluff 304 Cedar Bluff Rd	Knoxville	TN	37923	**800-465-4329**	865-693-1011	373
Holiday Inn Select Knoxville Downtown 525 Henley St	Knoxville	TN	37902	**800-465-4329**	865-522-2800	373
Holiday Inn Select Memphis Airport 2240 Democrat Rd	Memphis	TN	38132	**800-465-4329**	901-332-1130	373
Holiday Inn Select Memphis Downtown 160 Union Ave	Memphis	TN	38103	**888-300-5491**	901-525-5491	373
Holiday Inn Select Minneapolis/Saint Paul International Airport 3 Appletree Sq	Bloomington	MN	55425	**800-465-4329**	952-854-9000	373
Holiday Inn Select La Mirada 14299 Firestone Blvd	La Mirada	CA	90638	**800-356-6873**	714-739-8500	373
Holiday Inn Select Mississauga 2565 Argentia Rd	Mississauga	ON	L5N5V4	**800-465-4329**	905-542-2121	372
Holiday Inn Select Montreal Centre-Ville 99 ave Viger O	Montreal	QC	H2Z1E9	**888-878-9888**	514-878-9888	372
Holiday Inn Select Naperville 1801 N Naper Blvd	Naperville	IL	60563	**800-465-4329**	630-505-4900	373
Holiday Inn Select Nashville-Vanderbilt (Downtown) 2613 West End Ave	Nashville	TN	37203	**800-465-4329**	615-327-4707	373
Holiday Inn Select New Orleans Airport 2929 Williams Blvd	Kenner	LA	70062	**800-465-4329**	504-467-5611	373
Holiday Inn Select New Orleans Convention Center 881 Convention Center Blvd	New Orleans	LA	70130	**888-524-1881**	504-524-1881	373
Holiday Inn Select Niagara Falls 300 3rd St	Niagara Falls	NY	14303	**800-953-2557**	716-285-3361	373
Holiday Inn Select North Dallas 2645 LBJ Fwy	Dallas	TX	75234	**800-465-4329**	972-243-3363	373
Holiday Inn Select Opryland/Airport 2200 Elm Hill Pike	Nashville	TN	37214	**800-633-4427**	615-883-9770	373
Holiday Inn Select Orlando International Airport 5750 TG Lee Blvd	Orlando	FL	32822	**800-465-4329**	407-851-6400	373
Holiday Inn Select Orlando-University Central 12125 High Tech Ave *Resv	Orlando	FL	32817	**800-465-4329***	407-275-9000	373
Holiday Inn Select Ottawa West (Kanata) 101 Kanata Ave	Kanata	ON	K2T1E6	**800-465-4329**	613-271-3057	372
Holiday Inn Select Philadelphia-Bucks County 4700 Street Rd	Trevose	PA	19053	**800-873-7263**	215-364-2000	373
Holiday Inn Select Pittsburgh-University Center 100 Lytton Ave	Pittsburgh	PA	15213	**800-465-4329**	412-682-6200	373
Holiday Inn Select Quebec City Downtown 395 rue de la Couronne	Quebec	QC	G1K7X4	**800-267-2002**	418-647-2611	372
Holiday Inn Select Richardson 1655 N Central Expy	Richardson	TX	75080	**800-465-4329**	972-238-1900	373
Holiday Inn Select Richmond/Koger South Conference Center 1021 Koger Center Blvd	Richmond	VA	23235	**800-465-4329**	804-379-3800	373
Holiday Inn Select Saint Louis Convention Center 811 N 9th St	Saint Louis	MO	63101	**800-289-8338**	314-421-4000	373
Holiday Inn Select Saint Peters/Saint Charles Area 4341 Veteran's Memorial Pkwy	Saint Peters	MO	63376	**800-767-3837**	636-928-1500	373
Holiday Inn Select San Antonio International Airport 77 NE Loop 410	San Antonio	TX	78216	**800-445-8475**	210-349-9900	373
Holiday Inn Select San Diego North-Miramar 9335 Kearny Mesa Rd	San Diego	CA	92126	**800-262-2301**	858-695-2300	373
Holiday Inn Select Seattle-Renton 1 S Grady Way	Renton	WA	98055	**800-521-1412**	425-226-7700	373
Holiday Inn Select Stamford Downtown 700 Main St	Stamford	CT	06901	**800-408-7640**	203-358-8400	373
Holiday Inn Select Tallahassee Downtown Capitol 316 W Tennessee St	Tallahassee	FL	32301	**800-648-6135**	850-222-9555	373
Holiday Inn Select Toronto Airport 970 Dixon Rd	Toronto	ON	M9W1J9	**800-465-4329**	416-675-7611	372
Holiday Inn Select Tulsa 5000 E Skelly Dr	Tulsa	OK	74135	**800-836-9635**	918-622-7000	373
Holiday Inn Select Wichita 549 S Rock Rd	Wichita	KS	67207	**800-465-4329**	316-686-7131	373
Holiday Inn Select Wilmington (Claymont) 630 Naamans Rd	Claymont	DE	19703	**800-465-4329**	302-792-2700	373
Holiday Inn Select Windsor (Ambassador Bridge) 1855 Huron Church Rd	Windsor	ON	N9C2L6	**800-465-4329**	519-966-1200	372
Holiday Inn Select Winston-Salem 5790 University Pkwy	Winston-Salem	NC	27105	**800-553-9595**	336-767-9595	373
Holiday Inn Shreveport Financial Plaza 5555 Financial Plaza	Shreveport	LA	71129	**800-465-4329**	318-688-3000	373
Holiday Inn Siegen 10455 Reiger Rd	Baton Rouge	LA	70809	**800-465-4329**	225-293-6880	373
Holiday Inn Sioux Falls City Centre 100 W 8th St	Sioux Falls	SD	57104	**800-465-4329**	605-339-2000	373
Holiday Inn South Beach 2201 Collins Ave	Miami Beach	FL	33139	**800-356-6902**	305-779-3200	373
Holiday Inn Spearfish-Northern Black Hills Hotel & Convention Center PO Box 399	Spearfish	SD	57783	**800-999-3541**	605-642-4683	373
Holiday Inn Springfield-Holyoke Holidome & Conference Center 245 Whiting Farms Rd	Holyoke	MA	01040	**800-465-4329**	413-534-3311	373
Holiday Inn Springfield-North I-44 2720 N Glenstone Ave	Springfield	MO	65803	**800-465-4329**	417-865-8600	373
Holiday Inn SunSpree Bar Harbor Regency Resort 123 Eden St	Bar Harbor	ME	04609	**800-234-6835**	207-288-9723	655
Holiday Inn SunSpree Resort Corpus Christi 15202 Windward Dr	Corpus Christi	TX	78418	**888-949-8041**	361-949-8041	373
Holiday Inn SunSpree Resort Fort Walton Beach 573 Santa Rosa Blvd	Fort Walton Beach	FL	32548	**800-238-8686**	850-244-8686	373
Holiday Inn SunSpree Resort Gatlinburg 520 Historic Nature Trail	Gatlinburg	TN	37738	**800-435-9201**	865-436-9201	373
Holiday Inn SunSpree Resort Great Smokies 1 Holiday Inn Dr	Asheville	NC	28806	**800-733-3211**	828-254-3211	655
Holiday Inn SunSpree Resort Jacksonville Beach 1617 N 1st St	Jacksonville Beach	FL	32250	**800-590-4767**	904-249-9071	655
Holiday Inn SunSpree Resort Lake Buena Vista 13351 SR 535	Orlando	FL	32821	**800-366-6299**	407-239-4500	655
Holiday Inn SunSpree Resort Lake Ozark 120 Holiday Ln PO Box 1930	Lake Ozark	MO	65049	**800-532-3575**	573-365-2334	655
Holiday Inn SunSpree Resort Marina Cove 6800 Sunshine Skyway Ln	Saint Petersburg	FL	33711	**800-227-8045**	727-867-1151	655
Holiday Inn SunSpree Resort Myrtle Beach 1601 N Ocean Blvd	Surfside Beach	SC	29575	**877-245-1360**	843-238-5601	655
Holiday Inn SunSpree Resort South Padre Island 100 Padre Blvd	South Padre Island	TX	78597	**800-531-7405**	956-761-5401	655
Holiday Inn SunSpree Resort Virginia Beach 3900 Atlantic Ave	Virginia Beach	VA	23451	**800-942-3224**	757-428-1711	655
Holiday Inn SunSpree Resort Whistler Village 4295 Blackcomb Way	Whistler	BC	V0N1B4	**800-229-3188**	604-938-0878	655
Holiday Inn SunSpree Resort Wrightsville Beach 1706 N Lumina Ave	Wrightsville Beach	NC	28480	**877-330-5050**	910-256-2231	655
Holiday Inn Swan Court 2950 Pea Soup Andersen Blvd	Selma	CA	93662	**800-462-5363**	559-891-8000	373
Holiday Inn Tallahassee NW 2714 Graves Rd	Tallahassee	FL	32303	**800-465-4329**	850-562-2000	373
Holiday Inn Toledo West 2340 S Reynolds Rd	Toledo	OH	43614	**800-465-4329**	419-865-1361	373
Holiday Inn Topeka West 605 SW Fairlawn Rd	Topeka	KS	66606	**800-822-0216**	785-272-8040	373
Holiday Inn Toronto Yorkdale 3450 Dufferin St	Toronto	ON	M6A2V1	**800-465-4329**	416-789-5161	372
Holiday Inn at Universal Studios Hollywood. Beverly Garland's 4222 Vineland Ave	North Hollywood	CA	91602	**800-238-3759**	818-980-8000	373
Holiday Inn Vancouver Airport 10720 Cambie Rd	Richmond	BC	V6X1K8	**800-465-4329**	604-821-1818	372
Holiday Inn Virginia Beach Executive Center Hotel 5655 Greenwich Rd	Virginia Beach	VA	23462	**800-465-4329**	757-499-4400	373
Holiday Inn Virginia Beach Oceanside 2101 Atlantic Ave	Virginia Beach	VA	23451	**800-882-3224**	757-491-1500	373

Name / Address	City	State	Zip	Toll-Free	Phone	Class
Holiday Inn Washington-Capitol 550 C St SW	Washington	DC	20024	**800-465-4329**	202-479-4000	373
Holiday Inn Washington-Downtown 1155 14th St NW	Washington	DC	20005	**800-465-4329**	202-737-1200	373
Holiday Inn Washington-Georgetown 2101 Wisconsin Ave NW	Washington	DC	20007	**800-465-4329**	202-338-4600	373
Holiday Inn Washington on the Hill 415 New Jersey Ave NW	Washington	DC	20001	**800-465-4329**	202-638-1616	373
Holiday Inn Westlake 1100 Crocker Rd	Westlake	OH	44145	**800-465-4329**	440-871-6000	373
Holiday Inn Winnipeg Airport West 2520 Portage Ave	Winnipeg	MB	R3J3T6	**800-665-0352**	204-885-4478	372
Holiday Inn Woodlawn-Airport South 212 W Woodlawn Rd	Charlotte	NC	28217	**800-465-4329**	704-525-8350	373
Holiday Inn Worthington Hotel & Conference Center 175 Hutchinson Ave	Columbus	OH	43235	**800-465-4329**	614-885-3334	373
Holiday Inn Youngstown-Boardman 7410 South Ave	Boardman	OH	44512	**800-465-4329**	330-726-1611	373
Holiday Isle Beach Resort & Marina 84001 Overseas Hwy	Islamorada	FL	33036	**800-327-7070**	305-664-2321	655
Holiday Rambler Div Monaco Coach Corp 606 Nelson's Pkwy	Wakarusa	IN	46573	**800-650-7337**	574-862-7211	120
Holiday Retirement Corp 2250 McGilchrist St SE	Salem	OR	97302	**800-860-2249**	503-370-7070	641
Holiday Tours Inc 10367 Randleman Rd	Randleman	NC	27317	**800-733-9011**	336-498-9000	748
Holiday Travel Inc DBA Holiday Vacations 2727 Henry Ave	Eau Claire	WI	54701	**800-826-2266**	715-834-5555	748
Holiday Tree Farms Inc 800 NW Cornell Ave	Corvallis	OR	97330	**800-289-3684**	541-753-3236	737
Holiday Vacations 2727 Henry Ave	Eau Claire	WI	54701	**800-826-2266**	715-834-5555	748
Holiday Valley Resort PO Box 370 Rt 219	Ellicottville	NY	14731	**800-323-0020**	716-699-2345	655
Holiday World & Splashin' Safari 452 E Christmas Blvd	Santa Claus	IN	47579	**800-467-2682**	812-937-4401	32
Holistic Aromatherapy. National Assn for 3327 W Indian Trail Rd	Spokane	WA	99208	**888-275-6242**	509-325-3419	48-17
Holistic Nurses' Assn. American 2733 E Lakin Dr Suite 2	Flagstaff	AZ	86004	**800-278-2462**	928-526-2196	48-17
Holland America Line 300 Elliott Ave W	Seattle	WA	98119	**800-426-0327**	206-281-3535	217
Holland American Wafer Co 3300 Roger B Chaffee Blvd SE	Grand Rapids	MI	49548	**800-253-8350**	616-243-0191	291-9
Holland Area Convention & Visitors Bureau 76 E 8th St	Holland	MI	49423	**800-506-1299**	616-394-0000	205
Holland Capital Management LP 1 N Wacker Dr Suite 700	Chicago	IL	60606	**800-522-2711**	312-553-4830	393
Holland Co 1000 Holland Dr	Crete	IL	60417	**800-899-7754**	708-672-2300	636
Holland House Furniture 9420 E 33rd St	Indianapolis	IN	46235	**800-634-4666**	317-895-4300	315
Holland M Co 400 Skokie Blvd Suite 600	Northbrook	IL	60062	**800-872-7370**	847-272-7370	592
Holland Mfg Co Inc 15 Main St PO Box 404	Succasunna	NJ	07876	**800-454-2606**	973-584-8141	717
Holland Sentinel 54 W 8th St	Holland	MI	49423	**800-968-3495**	616-392-2311	522-2
Holland USA 1950 Industrial Blvd	Muskegon	MI	49442	**800-237-8932**	231-773-3271	60
Hollander Home Fashions Corp 6560 W Rogers Cir Suite 19	Boca Raton	FL	33487	**800-233-7666**	561-997-6900	731
Hollandia Dairy Inc 622 E Mission Rd	San Marcos	CA	92069	**800-794-0978**	760-744-3222	11-3
Holley Performance Products Inc 1801 Russellville Rd *Sales	Bowling Green	KY	42101	**800-638-0032***	270-782-2900	128
Hollingsworth Inc 1775 SW 30th St	Ontario	OR	97914	**800-541-1612**	541-889-7254	270
Hollins University 7916 Williamson Rd	Roanoke	VA	24020	**800-456-9595**	540-362-6401	163
Hollis Alvin & Co Inc 1 Hollis St	South Weymouth	MA	02190	**800-649-5090**	781-335-2100	311
Hollister Inc 2000 Hollister Dr	Libertyville	IL	60048	**800-323-4060**	847-680-1000	469
Hollister Moving & Storage 1650 Lana Way	Hollister	CA	95023	**800-696-6250**	831-637-6250	508
Holliswood Hospital 87-37 Palermo St	Holliswood	NY	11423	**800-486-3005**	718-776-8181	366-3
Hollow Inn 278 S Main St	Barre	VT	05641	**800-998-9444**	802-479-9313	373
Holloway Sportswear Inc 2633 Campbell Rd	Sidney	OH	45365	**800-331-5156**	937-596-6193	153-5
Holly Hill Hospital 3019 Falstaff Rd	Raleigh	NC	27610	**800-422-1840**	919-250-7000	366-3
Hollyhock Box 127	Mansons Landing	BC	V0P1K0	**800-933-6339**	250-935-6576	660
Hollywood Casino & Hotel 1150 Casino Strip Blvd PO Box 218	Robinsonville	MS	38664	**800-871-0711**	662-357-7700	133
Hollywood Entertainment Corp DBA Hollywood Video 9275 SW Peyton Ln	Wilsonville	OR	97070	**877-325-8687**	503-570-1600	784
Hollywood (Greater) Chamber of Commerce 330 N Federal Hwy	Hollywood	FL	33020	**800-231-5562**	954-923-4000	137
Hollywood Media Corp 2255 Glades Rd Suite 221A *NASDAQ: HOLL*	Boca Raton	FL	33431	**888-861-8898**	561-998-8000	677
Hollywood Metropolitan Hotel 5825 Sunset Blvd	Hollywood	CA	90028	**800-962-5800**	323-962-5800	373
Hollywood Rentals Production Services 19731 Nordhoff St	Northridge	CA	91324	**800-233-7830**	818-407-7800	708
Hollywood Roosevelt Hotel 7000 Hollywood Blvd	Hollywood	CA	90028	**800-950-7667**	323-466-7000	373
Hollywood Video 9275 SW Peyton Ln	Wilsonville	OR	97070	**877-325-8687**	503-570-1600	784
Hollywood Wax Museum 3030 W Hwy 76	Branson	MO	65616	**800-720-4110**	417-337-8277	509
Holm Industries Inc Saint Charles Div 315 N 9th St	Saint Charles	IL	60174	**800-221-2209**	630-584-1880	589
Holman Aviation Co 1940 Airport Ct	Great Falls	MT	59404	**800-843-7613**	406-453-7613	63
Holman Boiler Works Inc 1956 Singleton Blvd *Sales	Dallas	TX	75212	**800-331-1956***	214-637-0020	92
Holman Group 21050 Vanowen St	Canoga Park	CA	91303	**800-321-2843**	818-704-1444	454

Name / Address	City	State	Zip	Toll-Free	Phone	Class
Holme Roberts & Owen LLP 1700 Lincoln St Suite 4100	Denver	CO	80203	**800-334-4124**	303-861-7000	419
Holmes Community College PO Box 369	Goodman	MS	39079	**800-465-6374**	662-472-2312	160
Holmes Group Inc 1 Holmes Way	Milford	MA	01757	**800-546-5637**	508-634-8050	37
Holmes Murphy & Assoc Inc 3001 Westown Pkwy	West Des Moines	IA	50266	**800-247-7756**	515-223-6800	383
Holmes Regional Medical Center 1350 S Hickory St	Melbourne	FL	32901	**888-434-3730**	321-434-7000	366-2
Holmes-Wayne Electric Co-op Inc PO Box 112	Millersburg	OH	44654	**877-520-1055**	330-674-1055	244
Hologic Inc 35 Crosby Dr *NASDAQ: HOLX*	Bedford	MA	01730	**800-343-9729**	781-999-7300	375
Holoubek Inc W 238 N 1800 Rockwood Dr	Waukesha	WI	53188	**800-558-0566**	262-547-0500	675
Holox Ltd 1500C Indian Trail Rd	Norcross	GA	30093	**800-554-8306**	770-925-4640	378
Holstein Assn USA Inc 1 Holstein Pl *Orders	Brattleboro	VT	05302	**800-952-5200***	802-254-4551	48-2
Holt Co of Texas 3302 South WW White Rd	San Antonio	TX	78220	**800-275-4658**	210-648-1111	270
Holt Rinehart & Winston Inc 10801 N MoPac Expy Bldg 3	Austin	TX	78759	**800-992-1627**	512-721-7000	623-2
Holten Meat Inc 1682 Sauget Business Blvd	Sauget	IL	62206	**800-851-4684**	618-337-8400	292-9
Holts Cigar Co 1522 Walnut St	Philadelphia	PA	19102	**800-523-1641**	215-732-8500	743
Holum & Sons Co Inc 740 N Burr Oak Dr	Westmont	IL	60559	**800-447-4479**	630-654-8222	87
Holy Cross Energy PO Box 2150	Glenwood Springs	CO	81602	**888-347-4425**	970-945-5491	244
Holy Land Experience 4655 Vineland Rd	Orlando	FL	32811	**866-872-4659**	407-872-2272	32
Holy Redeemer Hospital & Medical Center 1648 Huntingdon Pike	Meadowbrook	PA	19046	**800-818-4747**	215-947-3000	366-2
Holy Rosary Medical Center 351 SW 9th St	Ontario	OR	97914	**877-225-4762**	541-881-7000	366-2
Holyoke Card & Paper Co 95 Fisk Ave	Springfield	MA	01107	**877-217-2737**	413-732-2107	544
Holyoke Rehabilitation Center 260 Easthampton Rd	Holyoke	MA	01040	**800-394-9733**	413-538-9733	441
Holz Rubber Co Inc 1129 S Sacramento St	Lodi	CA	95240	**800-285-1600**	209-368-7171	664
Homaco Inc 1875 W Fullerton Ave	Chicago	IL	60614	**888-446-6226**	773-384-5575	804
Homalite Div Brandywine Investment Group 11 Brookside Dr	Wilmington	DE	19804	**800-346-7802**	302-652-3686	589
Homasote Co PO Box 7240	West Trenton	NJ	08628	**800-257-9491**	609-883-3300	807
Home & Away Magazine 10703 J St	Omaha	NE	68127	**800-842-7294**	402-592-5000	449-22
Home Builders. National Assn of 1201 15th St NW	Washington	DC	20005	**800-368-5242**	202-266-8200	49-3
Home Capital Group Inc 145 King St W Suite 1910 *TSE: HCG*	Toronto	ON	M5H1J8	**800-990-7881**	416-360-4663	355-3
Home Care Accreditation Alert Newsletter 11300 Rockville Pike Suite 1100	Rockville	MD	20852	**800-929-4824**	301-287-2700	521-8
Home Care Industries Inc 1 Lisbon St	Clifton	NJ	07013	**888-772-2100**	973-365-1600	67
Home Care Industries Inc ALFCO Div 1 Lisbon St *Cust Svc	Clifton	NJ	07013	**800-240-7998***	973-365-1600	19
Home Care Supply 2155 IH-10 E	Beaumont	TX	77701	**800-871-1386**	409-835-3939	358
Home Depot Inc 2455 Paces Ferry Rd *NYSE: HD* ■ *Cust Svc	Atlanta	GA	30339	**800-553-3199***	770-433-8211	359
Home Depot Supply 10641 Scripps Summit Ct	San Diego	CA	92131	**800-233-6166**	858-831-2000	346
Home Diagnostics Inc 2400 NW 55th Ct	Fort Lauderdale	FL	33309	**800-342-7226**	954-677-9201	229
Home Equity Mortgage Assn. National 1301 Pennsylvania Ave NW Suite 500	Washington	DC	20004	**800-342-1121**	202-347-1210	49-2
Home Federal Bancorp 501 Washington St *NASDAQ: HOMF*	Columbus	IN	47201	**800-876-4372**	812-376-3323	355-2
Home Federal Bank 225 S Main Ave PO Box 5000	Sioux Falls	SD	57117	**800-244-2149**	605-333-7500	71
Home Financial Bancorp 279 E Morgan St *NASDAQ: HWEN*	Spencer	IN	47460	**800-690-2095**	812-829-2095	355-2
Home Fragrance Holdings 8323 Fairbanks White Oak Rd *Cust Svc	Houston	TX	77040	**800-256-5689***	713-466-4600	122
Home Furnishings Assn. National 3010 Tinsley Dr Suite 101	High Point	NC	27265	**800-888-9590**	336-886-6100	49-4
Home Furnishings Corp DBA Breuner's 3250 Buskirk Ave	Pleasant Hill	CA	94523	**800-865-6778**	925-472-4500	316
Home Furnishings International Assn (HFIA) 2050 Stemmons World Trade Center Suite 170 PO Box 420807	Dallas	TX	75342	**800-942-4663**	214-741-7632	49-4
Home Furnishings Representatives Assn. International 209 S Main St	High Point	NC	27260	**800-889-3920**	336-889-3920	49-18
Home & Garden Showplace 8600 W Bryn Mawr	Chicago	IL	60631	**888-474-9752**		318
Home & Garden Television (HGTV) 9721 Sherrill Blvd	Knoxville	TN	37932	**800-448-8275**	865-694-2700	725
Home Health Corp of America Inc 620 Freedom Business Center Suite 105	King of Prussia	PA	19406	**800-872-5230**	610-205-2440	358
Home Health & Hospice Care 22 Prospect St	Nashua	NH	03060	**800-887-5973**	603-882-2941	365
Home Health Line Newsletter 11300 Rockville Pike Suite 1100	Rockville	MD	20852	**800-929-4824**	301-287-2700	521-8
Home Health/Van Dyke Hospice 99 Rt 37 W	Toms River	NJ	08755	**800-338-3131**	732-818-6800	365
Home Helpers Inc 10700 Montgomery Rd	Cincinnati	OH	45242	**800-216-4196**	513-563-8339	358
Home Infusion Assn. National 205 Daingerfield Rd	Alexandria	VA	22314	**800-544-7447**	703-549-3740	49-8
Home Inspectors. American Society of 932 Lee St Suite 101	Des Plaines	IL	60016	**800-743-2744**	847-759-2820	49-3

Name / Address	City	State	ZIP	Toll-Free	Phone	Class
Home Inspectors Inc. National Assn of 4248 Park Glen Rd	Minneapolis	MN	55416	**800-448-3942**	952-928-4641	49-3
Home Instead Inc 604 N 109th Ct.	Omaha	NE	68154	**888-484-5759**	402-498-4466	358
Home IV Care & Nutritional Service PO Box 700	Stuarts Draft	VA	24477	**800-552-6576**	540-932-3000	358
Home Magazine 1633 Broadway 44th Fl	New York	NY	10019	**800-950-7370**	212-767-6000	449-11
Home News Enterprises 333 2nd St	Columbus	IN	47201	**800-876-7811**	812-372-7811	623-8
Home News Tribune 35 Kennedy Blvd.	East Brunswick	NJ	08816	**800-627-4663**	732-246-5500	522-2
Home & Office Products Assn. School 3131 Elbee Rd	Dayton	OH	45439	**800-854-7467**	937-297-2250	49-4
Home Paramount Pest Control Companies Inc 2011 Rock Spring Rd PO Box 850	Forest Hill	MD	21050	**800-492-5544**	410-510-0700	567
Home Products International Inc 4501 W 47th St *NASDAQ: HOMZ*	Chicago	IL	60632	**800-327-3534**	773-890-1010	596
Home Run Inn Inc 1300 Internationale Pkwy	Woodridge	IL	60517	**800-636-9696**	630-783-9696	657
Home Safety. Institute for Business & 4775 E Fowler Ave	Tampa	FL	33617	**866-675-4247**	813-286-3400	49-9
Home Savings & Loan Co of Youngstown 275 Federal Plaza W.	Youngstown	OH	44503	**888-999-4707**	330-742-0500	71
Home Security of America Inc 310 N Midvale Blvd	Madison	WI	53705	**800-367-1448**	608-231-0010	687
Home & Store News PO Box 329	Ramsey	NJ	07446	**877-237-7855**	201-327-1212	522-4
Home Street Bank Inc 601 Union St Suite 2000	Seattle	WA	98101	**800-654-1075**	206-623-3050	355-2
Home-Style Inn 6461 Edsall Rd	Alexandria	VA	22312	**888-223-9454**	703-354-4400	373
Home Town Newspapers PO Box 230	Howell	MI	48844	**888-999-1288**	517-548-2000	623-8
Home Vision Entertainment 4423 N Ravenswood Ave	Chicago	IL	60640	**800-826-3456**	773-878-2600	500
HomeAdvisor 1 Microsoft Way	Redmond	WA	98052	**800-642-7676**	425-882-8080	498
HomeBanc Mortgage Corp 2002 Summit Blvd Suite 100	Atlanta	GA	30319	**866-926-8466**	404-459-7400	498
HOMECALL Inc 92 Thomas Johnson Dr Suite 150	Frederick	MD	21702	**800-444-0097**	301-663-8818	358
HomeCare & Hospice 1225 W State St	Olean	NY	14760	**800-339-7011**	716-372-5735	365
Homecrest Industries Inc PO Box 350	Wadena	MN	56482	**888-346-4852**	218-631-1000	314-4
HomeFederal 218 W 2nd St	Seymour	IN	47274	**877-626-7000**	812-522-1592	71
HomeGain.com Inc 1250 45th St Suite 200	Emeryville	CA	94608	**888-542-0800**	510-655-0800	638
Homeland Stores Inc 28 E 33 St	Edmond	OK	73013	**800-522-5658**	405-216-2200	339
Homelessness & Mental Illness. National Resource Center on 345 Delaware Ave	Delmar	NY	12054	**800-444-7415**	518-439-7415	49-15
Homelessness. National Student Campaign Against Hunger & 233 N Pleasant St Suite 32	Amherst	MA	01002	**800-664-8647**	413-253-6417	48-5
HomeLife Realty Services Inc 5752 176th St Unit 203	Surrey	BC	V3S4C8	**800-667-6329**	604-575-3130	638
Homeopathy. National Center for 801 N Fairfax St Suite 306	Alexandria	VA	22314	**877-624-0613**	703-548-7790	48-17
Homeowners Assn. American 1100 Summer St 1st Fl *Cust Svc	Stamford	CT	06905	**800-470-2242***	203-323-7715	48-10
Homeowners Foundation. American 6776 Little Falls Rd	Arlington	VA	22213	**800-489-7776**	703-536-7776	49-17
HomePath c/o FannieMae 3900 Wisconsin Ave NW	Washington	DC	20016	**800-732-6643**	202-752-7016	498
Homeplace Ranch RR 1 Site 2 Box 6	Priddis	AB	T0L1W0	**877-931-3245**	403-931-3245	238
Homer Laughlin China Co 672 Fiesta Dr	Newell	WV	26050	**800-452-4462**	304-387-1300	716
Homer Optical Co Inc 2401 Linden Ln	Silver Spring	MD	20910	**800-627-2710**	301-585-9060	532
Homereach Hospice 3595 Olentangy River Rd	Columbus	OH	43214	**800-300-7075**	614-566-5377	365
Homes by Keystone Inc 13338 Midvale Rd PO Box 69	Waynesboro	PA	17268	**800-890-7926**	717-762-1104	107
Homes & Land Magazine/Rental Guide 1600 Capital Cir SW *Cust Svc	Tallahassee	FL	32310	**800-277-4357***	850-574-2111	449-21
Homes & Land Publishing Ltd 1830 E Park Ave.	Tallahassee	FL	32301	**800-466-3546**	850-574-2111	623-9
Homes of Merit Inc PO Box 1606	Bartow	FL	33831	**800-589-8942**	863-533-0593	495
Homes & Services for the Aging. American Assn of 2519 Connecticut Ave NW	Washington	DC	20008	**800-508-9442**	202-783-2242	48-6
Homeshield PO Box 907	Chatsworth	IL	60921	**800-323-2512**	815-635-3171	232
Homestead The 700 N Homestead Dr	Midway	UT	84049	**800-327-7220**	435-654-1102	655
Homestead The Rt 220 Main St PO Box 2000	Hot Springs	VA	24445	**800-838-1766**	540-839-1766	655
Homestead House Inc PO Box 6010	Broomfield	CO	80021	**800-275-0345**	303-425-6544	316
Homestead Mills PO Box 1115	Cook	MN	55723	**800-652-5233**	218-666-5233	291-4
Homestead Ravioli Co Inc 315 S Maple Ave	South San Francisco	CA	94080	**800-334-3397**	650-615-0750	291-36
Homestead Village Inc 100 Dunbar St	Spartanburg	SC	29306	**888-782-9473**	864-573-1600	369
Homestead/Florida City (Greater) Chamber of Commerce 43 N Krome Ave	Homestead	FL	33030	**888-352-4891**	305-247-2332	137
HomeSteps 500 Plano Pkwy	Carrollton	TX	75010	**800-972-7555**		498
HomeStore Inc 30700 Russell Ranch Rd *NASDAQ: HOMS* ■ *Cust Svc	Westlake Village	CA	91362	**800-878-4166***	805-557-2300	795
HomeStreet Bank 601 Union St 2 Union Sq Suite 2000	Seattle	WA	98101	**800-654-1075**	206-623-3050	71
HomeStyle Books Book-of-the-Month Club Inc 1271 Ave of the Americas 3rd Fl.	New York	NY	10020	**800-233-1066**	212-522-4200	94
HomeTeam Inspection Service 575 Chamber Dr	Milford	OH	45150	**800-598-5297**	513-831-1300	360
Hometown Inc 1518 E North Ave	Milwaukee	WI	53202	**800-242-9238**	414-276-9311	311
Homewood Suites by Hilton 755 Crossover Ln	Memphis	TN	38117	**800-225-5466**	901-374-5000	369
HomeWorks Tri-County Electric Co-op 7973 E Grand River Ave PO Box 350	Portland	MI	48875	**800-848-9333**	517-647-7554	244
HON Co 200 Oak St	Muscatine	IA	52761	**800-553-8230**	563-264-7400	314-1
Honduras Tourism Institute 299 Alhambra Cir Suite 226	Coral Gables	FL	33134	**800-410-9608**	305-461-0601	764
Honey Acres 1557 Hwy 67 N	Ashippun	WI	53003	**800-558-7745**	920-474-4411	291-24
Honey Dew Assoc Inc 35 Braintree Hill Office Park Suite 205	Braintree	MA	02184	**800-946-6393**	781-849-3000	69
Honeybaked Ham Co 5445 Triangle Pkwy Suite 400	Norcross	GA	30092	**800-367-2426**	678-966-3100	333
Honeymead Products Co PO Box 3247	Mankato	MN	56002	**800-328-3445**	507-625-7911	291-29
Honeytree Inc PO Box 310	Onsted	MI	49265	**800-968-1889**	517-467-2482	291-24
Honeyville Grain Inc 11600 Dayton Dr	Rancho Cucamonga	CA	91730	**888-810-3212**	909-980-9500	291-4
Honeywell ACS 11 W Spring St	Freeport	IL	61032	**800-328-5111**		200
Honeywell Aerospace 1944 E Sky Harbor Cir	Phoenix	AZ	85034	**800-601-3099**		23
Honeywell Aerospace Electronic Systems 1944 E Sky Harbor Cir	Phoenix	AZ	85034	**800-601-3099**		519
Honeywell Airport Systems 2162 Union Pl	Simi Valley	CA	93065	**800-581-5591**	805-581-5591	431
Honeywell Automation & Control Solutions 11 W Spring St	Freeport	IL	61032	**800-328-5111**		200
Honeywell Defense Avionics Systems 9201 San Mateo Blvd NE	Albuquerque	NM	87113	**800-376-5311**	505-828-5000	519
Honeywell Fire Solutions DBA Fire-Lite Alarms 1 Fire-Lite Pl	Northford	CT	06472	**800-289-3473**	203-484-7161	681
Honeywell Inc Aircraft Landing Systems 3520 Westmoor St	South Bend	IN	46628	**800-707-4555**	574-231-2000	23
Honeywell International Inc 101 Columbia Rd *NYSE: HON* ■ *Cust Svc	Morristown	NJ	07962	**800-707-4555***	973-455-2000	184
Honeywell Nylon Inc 4824 Pkwy Plaza Blvd Suite 300	Charlotte	NC	28217	**800-247-0557**	704-423-2000	594-1
Honeywell Security Inc 165 Eileen Way *Cust Svc	Syosset	NY	11791	**800-573-0154***	516-921-6704	681
Honeywell Sensing & Control 11 W Spring St *Cust Svc	Freeport	IL	61032	**800-537-6945***	815-235-5500	202
Honeywell Sensotec 2080 Arlingate Ln	Columbus	OH	43228	**800-298-9228**	614-850-5000	464
Honeywell Space Systems 13350 US Hwy 19 N	Clearwater	FL	33764	**888-561-5665**	727-539-4000	494
Honeywell Specialty Chemicals 101 Columbia Rd	Morristown	NJ	07962	**800-222-0094**	973-455-2145	143
Honeywell Specialty Films 98 Westwood Rd *Cust Svc	Pottsville	PA	17901	**800-934-5679***	570-621-6000	538
Honeywell Specialty Materials 101 Columbia Rd	Morristown	NJ	07962	**800-222-0094**	973-455-2145	594-1
Honeywood Winery 1350 Hines St SE	Salem	OR	97302	**800-726-4101**	503-362-4111	50
Hong Kong Tourism Board 10940 Wilshire Blvd Suite 2050	Los Angeles	CA	90024	**800-282-4582**	310-208-4582	764
Honkamp Krueger Financial Services 2355 JFK Rd	Dubuque	IA	52002	**800-791-8994**	563-582-2855	2
Honolulu Advertiser PO Box 3110	Honolulu	HI	96801	**877-233-1133**	808-525-8000	522-2
Honolulu Airport Hotel 3401 N Nimitz Hwy	Honolulu	HI	96819	**800-800-3477**	808-836-0661	373
Honolulu Magazine 1000 Bishop St Suite 405	Honolulu	HI	96813	**800-788-4230**	808-537-9500	449-22
Honolulu Publishing Co Ltd 707 Richards St Suite 525	Honolulu	HI	96813	**800-272-5245**	808-524-7400	623-9
Honolulu Star-Bulletin 500 Ala Moana Blvd 7 Waterfront Plaza Suite 210	Honolulu	HI	96813	**800-417-3484**	808-529-4700	522-2
Honor Society. National 1904 Association Dr	Reston	VA	20191	**800-253-7746**	703-860-0200	48-11
Hoo-Hoo International PO Box 118	Gurdon	AR	71743	**800-979-9950**	870-353-4997	48-2
Hoober Inc 3452 Old Philadelphia Pike	Intercourse	PA	17534	**800-732-0017**	717-768-8231	270
Hood College 401 Rosemont Ave	Frederick	MD	21701	**800-922-1599**	301-696-3400	163
Hood HP Inc 90 Everett Ave. *Cust Svc	Chelsea	MA	02150	**800-662-4468***	617-887-3000	291-27
Hood Packaging Corp 25 Woodgreen Pl	Madison	MS	39110	**800-321-8115**	601-853-7260	66
Hooker Furniture Corp 440 E Commonwealth Blvd *NASDAQ: HOFT* ■ *Cust Svc	Martinsville	VA	24112	**888-462-6877***	276-632-0459	314-2
Hook's Discovery & Learning Center 1305 W 29th St	Indianapolis	IN	46208	**877-924-5886**	317-951-2222	509
Hooper Corp 2030 Pennsylvania Ave	Madison	WI	53704	**800-999-0451**	608-249-0451	188-10
Hooper Holmes Inc 170 Mt Airy Rd. *AMEX: HH*	Basking Ridge	NJ	07920	**800-782-7373**	908-766-5000	347
Hoops Sporting Equipment Inc 22047 Lutheran Church Rd	Tomball	TX	77375	**800-294-4667**	281-351-9822	701
Hoosier Co 5421 W 86th St PO Box 681064	Indianapolis	IN	46268	**800-521-4184**	317-872-8125	281
Hoosier Gasket Corp 3333 Massachusetts Ave	Indianapolis	IN	46218	**800-442-7705**	317-545-2000	321
Hoosier Park 4500 Dan Patch Cir	Anderson	IN	46013	**800-526-7223**	765-642-7223	628
Hooters Air 1704 Oak St	Myrtle Beach	SC	29577	**888-359-4668**	843-916-4600	26
Hooven Allison Co 677 Cincinnati Ave	Xenia	OH	45385	**800-543-0736**	937-372-4421	207
Hooven-Dayton Corp 8060 Technology Blvd	Dayton	OH	45424	**800-621-9291**	937-233-4473	404
Hoover Dam Hwy 93	Boulder City	NV	89006	**866-291-8687**	702-294-3517	50
Hoover Institution on War Revolution & Peace Stanford University 434 Galvez Mall	Stanford	CA	94305	**877-466-8374**	650-723-1754	654
Hoover Materials Handling Group Inc 2001 Westside Pkwy Suite 155	Alpharetta	GA	30004	**800-391-3561**	770-664-4047	197
Hoover & Strong Inc 10700 Trade Rd *Cust Svc	Richmond	VA	23236	**800-759-9997***	804-794-3700	476

Name / Address	City	State	Zip	Toll-Free	Phone	Class
Hoover's Inc 5800 Airport Blvd	Austin	TX	78752	**800-486-8666**	512-374-4500	396
Hop-A-Jet Inc 5525 NW 15th Ave Suite 150	Fort Lauderdale	FL	33309	**800-556-6633**	954-771-5779	14
Hope Center. Kristin Brooks 2001 N Beauregard St 12th Fl	Alexandria	VA	22311	**800-784-2433**	703-684-7722	48-17
Hope College 141 E 12th St DeWitt Ctr	Holland	MI	49423	**800-968-7850**	616-395-7850	163
Hope Hospice 9470 HealthPark Cir	Fort Myers	FL	33908	**800-835-1673**	239-482-4673	365
Hope International University 2500 E Nutwood Ave	Fullerton	CA	92831	**800-762-1294**	714-879-3901	163
Hope Magazine PO Box 160	Brooklin	ME	04616	**800-513-0869***	207-359-4651	449-18
*Cust Svc						
Hope Pharmaceuticals Inc 8260 E Gelding Dr Suite 104	Scottsdale	AZ	85260	**800-755-9595**	480-607-1970	572
Hopkins County Chamber of Commerce 1200 Houston St	Sulphur Springs	TX	75482	**888-300-6623**	903-885-6515	137
Hopkins Mfg Corp 428 Peyton St	Emporia	KS	66801	**800-524-1458**	620-342-7320	60
Hopkins Tom Tom Hopkins International 7531 E 2nd St	Scottsdale	AZ	85251	**800-528-0446**	480-949-0786	561
Hopkinsville-Christian County Chamber of Commerce 2800 Port Campbell Blvd	Hopkinsville	KY	42240	**800-842-9959**	270-885-9096	137
Hoppe Tool Inc 107 1st Ave	Chicopee	MA	01020	**800-742-6571***	413-592-9213	484
*Sales						
Hoppmann Corp 13129 Airpark Dr Suite 120	Elkwood	VA	22718	**800-368-3582***	540-829-2654	537
*Cust Svc						
Horace Mann Educators Corp 1 Horace Mann Plaza	Springfield	IL	62715	**800-999-1030**	217-789-2500	355-4
NYSE: HMN						
Horace Mann Growth Fund 1 Horace Mann Plaza	Springfield	IL	62715	**800-999-1030**	217-789-2500	517
Horace Mann Insurance Co 1 Horace Mann Plaza	Springfield	IL	62715	**800-999-1030**	217-789-2500	384-2
Horace Mann Life Insurance Co 1 Horace Mann Plaza	Springfield	IL	62715	**800-999-1030**	217-789-2500	384-2
Horiba Instruments Inc 17671 Armstrong Ave	Irvine	CA	92614	**800-446-7422**	949-250-4811	410
Horizon Air Freight 152-15 Rockaway Blvd	Jamaica	NY	11434	**800-221-6028**	718-528-3800	440
Horizon Air Industries Inc 19521 International Blvd S PO Box 68977	Seattle	WA	98168	**800-523-1223**	206-241-6757	26
Horizon Bank 1500 Cornwall Ave	Bellingham	WA	98225	**800-955-9194**	360-733-3050	71
Horizon Behavioral Services 1500 Waters Ridge Dr	Lewisville	TX	75057	**800-931-4646**	972-420-8200	454
Horizon Blue Cross Blue Shield of New Jersey 3 Penn Plaza E	Newark	NJ	07105	**800-466-2583**	973-466-4000	384-3
Horizon Convention Center 401 S High St	Muncie	IN	47305	**888-288-8860**	765-288-8860	204
Horizon Financial Corp 1500 Cornwall Ave	Bellingham	WA	98225	**800-955-9194**	360-733-3050	355-2
NASDAQ: HRZB						
Horizon Fleet Services Inc 341 NW 122nd St	Oklahoma City	OK	73114	**800-357-2444**	405-755-9703	261-4
Horizon Health Corp 1500 Waters Ridge Dr	Lewisville	TX	75057	**800-931-4646**	972-420-8200	454
NASDAQ: HORC						
Horizon House Publications Inc 685 Canton St	Norwood	MA	02062	**800-225-9977**	781-769-9750	623-9
Horizon Lines LLC 4064 Colony Rd Suite 200	Charlotte	NC	28211	**877-678-7447***	704-973-7000	307
*Cust Svc						
Horizon Media Inc 630 3rd Ave 3rd Fl	New York	NY	10017	**800-633-4201**	212-916-8600	6
Horizon Offshore Inc 2500 Citywest Blvd Suite 2200	Houston	TX	77042	**877-361-2600**	713-361-2600	187-5
Horizon Snack Foods 443 W 400 North	Salt Lake City	UT	84103	**800-453-4575**	801-533-9550	291-1
Horizon Solutions Corp 4 Access Rd	Albany	NY	12205	**800-345-4621**	518-452-6904	245
Horizon Termite & Pest Control Corp 45 Cross Ave	Midland Park	NJ	07432	**888-612-2847**	201-447-2530	567
Horizons Inc 2618 Mid America Dr	Junction City	KS	66441	**800-235-3140**	785-238-7575	120
Horlander Enterprises Inc DBA Nu-Yale Cleaners 6300 Hwy 62	Jeffersonville	IN	47130	**888-644-7400**	812-285-7400	417
Hormel Foods Corp 1 Hormel Pl	Austin	MN	55912	**800-523-4635**	507-437-5611	291-26
NYSE: HRL						
Hormel Foods International Corp 1 Hormel Pl	Austin	MN	55912	**800-523-4635**	507-437-5478	291-26
Horn ET Co 16141 Heron Ave	La Mirada	CA	90638	**800-442-4676**	714-523-8050	144
Hornady Mfg Co 3625 Old Potash Hwy	Grand Island	NE	68803	**800-338-3220***	308-382-1390	279
*Cust Svc						
Horner Millwork Corp 1255 Grand Army Hwy	Somerset	MA	02726	**800-543-5403**	508-679-6479	489
Hornung's Golf Products Inc 815 Morris St	Fond du Lac	WI	54935	**800-323-3569**	920-922-2640	323
Horry Telephone Co-op Inc 3480 Hwy 701 N	Conway	SC	29526	**800-824-6779**	843-365-2151	721
Horse Assn. American Quarter PO Box 200	Amarillo	TX	79168	**800-414-7433**	806-376-4811	48-3
Horse Breeders' & Exhibitors' Assn. Tennessee Walking PO Box 286	Lewisburg	TN	37091	**800-359-1574**	931-359-1574	48-3
Horse & Burro Program. National Wild PO Box 3270	Sparks	NV	89432	**866-468-7826**	775-475-2222	336-9
Horse Illustrated Magazine 3 Burroughs	Irvine	CA	92618	**800-365-4421**	949-855-8822	449-14
Horse. International Museum of the 4089 Iron Works Pkwy	Lexington	KY	40511	**800-678-8813**	859-259-4231	509
Horse Prairie Ranch 3300 Bachelor Mountain Rd	Dillon	MT	59725	**888-726-2454**	406-681-3155	238
Horse & Rider Magazine 4101 International Pkwy	Carrollton	TX	75007	**877-717-8928**	972-309-5700	449-14
Horsehead Resource Development Co Inc 900 Delaware Ave	Palmerton	PA	18071	**800-962-7500***	610-826-2111	674
*Sales						

Name / Address	City	State	Zip	Toll-Free	Phone	Class
Horsemanship Assn. Certified 5318 Old Bullard Rd	Tyler	TX	75703	**800-399-0138**	903-509-2473	48-3
Horsemen of America. Back Country PO Box 1367	Graham	WA	98338	**888-893-5161**	360-832-2461	48-23
Horseshoe Bay Resort & Conference Center PO Box 7766	Horseshoe Bay	TX	78657	**800-531-5105**	830-598-2511	655
Horseshoe Canyon Ranch 3900 Lochridge Rd	North Little Rock	AR	72116	**800-480-9635**	501-791-2679	238
Horseshoe Casino & Hotel 1021 Casino Ctr Dr	Robinsonville	MS	38664	**800-303-7463**	662-357-5500	133
Horspool & Romine Mfg Inc 5850 Marshall St	Oakland	CA	94608	**800-446-2263**	510-652-1844	610
Hortica Insurance PO Box 428	Edwardsville	IL	62025	**800-851-7740**	618-656-4240	384-4
Horticultural Society. American 7931 E Boulevard Dr	Alexandria	VA	22308	**800-777-7931**	703-768-5700	48-18
Horton DR Inc 1901 Ascension Blvd Suite 100	Arlington	TX	76006	**800-846-7866**	817-856-8200	639
NYSE: DHI						
Horton DR Inc 1901 Ascension Blvd Suite 100	Arlington	TX	76006	**800-846-7866**	817-856-8200	639
NYSE: DHI						
Horton Grand Hotel 311 Island Ave	San Diego	CA	92101	**800-542-1886**	619-544-1886	373
Horton Homes Inc 101 Industrial Blvd	Eatonton	GA	31024	**800-282-2680**	706-485-8506	495
Horton Inc 2565 Walnut St	Roseville	MN	55113	**800-843-7445**	651-361-6400	609
HOSA (Health Occupations Students of America) 6021 Morriss Rd Suite 111	Flower Mound	TX	75028	**800-321-4672**	972-874-0062	48-11
Hosokawa Micron Group 10 Chatham Rd	Summit	NJ	07901	**800-526-4491**	908-273-6360	293
Hosokawa Polymer Systems 63 Fuller Way	Berlin	CT	06037	**800-233-6112**	860-828-0541	379
Hospice of Acadiana 2600 Johnston St Suite 200	Lafayette	LA	70503	**800-738-2226**	337-232-1234	365
Hospice of Alamance Caswell 914 Chapel Hill Rd	Burlington	NC	27215	**800-588-8879**	336-532-0100	365
Hospice Alliance 10220 Prairie Ridge Blvd	Pleasant Prairie	WI	53158	**800-830-8344**	262-652-4400	365
Hospice of Arizona 2222 W Northern Ave Suite A100	Phoenix	AZ	85021	**800-890-9046**	602-678-1313	365
Hospice Atlanta-Visiting Nurse Health System 1244 Park Vista Dr	Atlanta	GA	30319	**800-287-7849**	404-869-3000	365
Hospice Austin 4107 Spicewood Springs Rd Suite 100	Austin	TX	78759	**800-445-3261**	512-342-4700	365
Hospice of Baton Rouge 9063 Siegen Ln	Baton Rouge	LA	70810	**800-349-8833**	225-767-4673	365
Hospice of the Bluegrass 2312 Alexandria Dr	Lexington	KY	40504	**800-876-6005**	859-276-5344	365
Hospice Care 41 Montvale Ave	Stoneham	MA	02180	**866-279-7103**	781-279-4100	365
Hospice Care of the District of Columbia 4401 Connecticut Ave Suite 700	Washington	DC	20008	**800-869-2136**	202-347-1700	365
Hospice Care Inc 4277 Middle Settlement Rd	New Hartford	NY	13413	**800-317-5661**	315-735-6484	365
Hospice Care of Nebraska 1600 S 70th St Suite 201	Lincoln	NE	68506	**800-826-3841**	402-488-1363	365
Hospice Care of Rhode Island 169 George St	Pawtucket	RI	02860	**800-338-6555**	401-444-9070	365
Hospice Care in Westchester & Putnam Inc 100 S Bedford Rd	Mount Kisco	NY	10549	**800-298-6341**	914-666-4228	365
Hospice of the Central Coast 2 Upper Ragsdale Bldg D Suite 210	Monterey	CA	93941	**800-492-3037**	831-649-7750	365
Hospice of Central Georgia 3780 Eisenhower Pkwy	Macon	GA	31206	**800-211-1084**	478-633-5660	365
Hospice of Central Iowa 401 Railroad Pl	West Des Moines	IA	50265	**800-806-9934**	515-274-3400	365
Hospice of Central Ohio 2269 Cherry Valley Rd	Newark	OH	43055	**800-804-2505**	740-344-0311	365
Hospice of the Chesapeake 445 Defense Hwy	Annapolis	MD	21401	**800-745-6132**	410-987-2003	365
Hospice of Cincinnati 4310 Cooper Rd	Cincinnati	OH	45242	**800-691-7255**	513-891-7700	365
Hospice Community Care PO Box 993	Rock Hill	SC	29731	**800-895-2273**	803-329-4663	365
Hospice of Community Visiting Nurse Agency 141 Park St	Attleboro	MA	02703	**800-220-0110**	508-222-0118	365
Hospice of Dayton 324 Wilmington Ave	Dayton	OH	45420	**800-653-4490**	937-256-4490	365
Hospice Education Institute 3 Unity Sq PO Box 98	Machiasport	ME	04655	**800-331-1620**	207-255-8800	48-17
Hospice Family Care 310 S Williams Blvd Suite 210	Tucson	AZ	85711	**800-839-3288**	520-790-9299	365
Hospice Foundation of America (HFA) 1621 Connecticut Ave NW Suite 300	Washington	DC	20009	**800-854-3402**	202-638-5419	49-8
Hospice of Greater New Orleans 3616 S I-10 Service Rd W Suite 109	Metairie	LA	70001	**800-960-3016**	504-838-8944	365
Hospice & Health Services Inc 1111 E Main St	Lancaster	OH	43130	**800-994-7077**	740-654-7077	365
Hospice of Holland Inc 270 Hoover Blvd	Holland	MI	49423	**800-255-3522**	616-396-2972	365
Hospice at Home PO Box 297	Stevensville	MI	49127	**800-717-3811**	269-429-7100	365
Hospice Home Care 1501 N University Ave Suite 340	Little Rock	AR	72207	**800-479-2503**	501-666-9697	365
Hospice Home Health of Olathe Medical Center 20333 W 151st St TDB 2 Suite 301	Olathe	KS	66061	**800-467-4451**	913-324-8515	365
Hospice of Huntington 1101 6th Ave	Huntington	WV	25701	**800-788-5480**	304-529-4217	365
Hospice International. Children's 901 N Pitt St Suite 230	Alexandria	VA	22314	**800-242-4453**	703-684-0330	49-8
Hospice of Lake Cumberland 100 Pkwy Dr	Somerset	KY	42503	**800-937-9556**	606-679-4389	365
Hospice of Lake & Sumter Inc 12300 Lane Park Rd	Tavares	FL	32778	**888-728-6234**	352-343-1341	365
Hospice of Lancaster County 685 Good Dr PO Box 4125	Lancaster	PA	17604	**800-924-7610**	717-295-3900	365

Name / Address	City	State	Zip	Toll-Free	Phone	Class
Hospice Longview 1306 Pine Tree Rd	Longview	TX	75604	**800-371-1016**	903-295-1680	365
Hospice of Medina County 797 N Court St	Medina	OH	44256	**800-700-4771**	330-722-4771	365
Hospice of Miami County PO Box 502	Troy	OH	45373	**800-372-0009**	937-335-5191	365
Hospice of Michigan 400 Mack Ave	Detroit	MI	48201	**888-466-5656**	313-578-5000	365
Hospice Ministries PO Box 1228	Ridgeland	MS	39158	**800-273-7724**	601-898-1053	365
Hospice of North Central Florida Inc 4200 NW 90th Blvd	Gainesville	FL	32606	**800-727-1889**	352-378-2121	365
Hospice of North Central Ohio 1605 County Rd 1095	Ashland	OH	44805	**800-952-2207**	419-281-7107	365
Hospice of Northeastern Illinois 410 S Hager Ave	Barrington	IL	60010	**800-425-4444**	847-381-5599	365
Hospice of Northern Colorado 2726 W 11th Street Rd	Greeley	CO	80634	**800-564-5563**	970-352-8487	365
Hospice & Palliative Care Organization. National 1700 Diagonal Rd Suite 625	Alexandria	VA	22314	**800-658-8898***	703-837-1500	49-8
*Help Line						
Hospice & Palliative Care of Southern Indiana 624 E Market St	New Albany	IN	47150	**800-895-5633**	812-945-4596	365
Hospice & Palliative Care of Western Colorado 2754 Compass Dr Suite 377	Grand Junction	CO	81506	**866-310-8900**	970-241-2212	365
Hospice of Palm Beach County 5300 East Ave	West Palm Beach	FL	33407	**800-287-4722**	561-848-5200	365
Hospice of the Panhandle 122 Waverly Ct	Martinsburg	WV	25401	**800-345-6538**	304-264-0406	365
Hospice of the Piedmont 2200 Old Ivy Rd Suite 2	Charlottesville	VA	22903	**800-975-5501**	434-817-6900	365
Hospice Preferred Choice 1235 N Loop W Suite 215	Houston	TX	77008	**888-646-8696**	713-864-2626	365
Hospice of the Rapidan PO Box 1715	Culpeper	VA	22701	**800-676-2012**	540-825-4840	365
Hospice of the Red River Valley 1701 38th St SW Suite 201	Fargo	ND	58102	**800-237-4629**	701-356-1500	365
Hospice Saint John 123 N Vine St	Hazleton	PA	18201	**877-438-3511**	570-459-6778	365
Hospice Savannah Inc PO Box 13190	Savannah	GA	31416	**888-355-4911**	912-355-2289	365
Hospice by the Sea 1531 W Palmetto Park Rd	Boca Raton	FL	33486	**800-633-2577**	561-395-5031	365
Hospice of Siouxland 224 4th St	Sioux City	IA	51101	**800-383-4545**	712-233-4100	365
Hospice of South Central Indiana 2626 E 17th St	Columbus	IN	47201	**800-841-4938**	812-376-5813	365
Hospice of South Louisiana 7932 Park Ave	Houma	LA	70364	**800-256-1611**	985-851-4273	365
Hospice of Southeastern Connecticut Inc PO Box 902	Uncasville	CT	06382	**877-654-4035**	860-848-5699	365
Hospice of Southern Illinois 305 S Illinois St	Belleville	IL	62220	**800-233-1708**	618-235-1703	365
Hospice of Southern Kentucky 1027 Broadway Ave	Bowling Green	KY	42104	**800-344-9479**	270-782-3402	365
Hospice of Southwest Florida 5955 Rand Blvd	Sarasota	FL	34238	**800-959-4291**	941-923-5822	365
Hospice of Southwest Georgia 818 Gordon Ave	Thomasville	GA	31792	**800-290-6567**	229-227-5520	365
Hospice of Spokane 121 S Arthur	Spokane	WA	99202	**888-459-0438**	509-456-0438	365
Hospice of Stanly County 960 N 1st St	Albemarle	NC	28001	**800-230-4236**	704-983-4216	365
Hospice at the Texas Medical Center 1905 Holcombe Blvd	Houston	TX	77030	**800-630-7894**	713-467-7423	365
Hospice of the Treasure Coast 2500 Virginia Ave Suite 202	Fort Pierce	FL	34981	**800-375-4682**	772-465-0660	365
Hospice of Tuscarawas County 201 W 3rd St	Dover	OH	44622	**800-947-7247**	330-343-7605	365
Hospice of the Upstate 1835 Rogers Rd	Anderson	SC	29621	**800-261-8638**	864-224-3358	365
Hospice of the Valley PO Box 2745	Decatur	AL	35602	**877-260-3657**	256-350-5585	365
Hospice of the Valley 5190 Market St	Youngstown	OH	44512	**800-640-5180**	330-788-1992	365
Hospice of Visiting Nurse Service 3358 Ridgewood Rd	Akron	OH	44333	**800-335-1455**	330-665-1455	365
Hospice VNA 46 S Main St	White River Junction	VT	05001	**800-858-1696**	802-295-2604	365
Hospice of Volusia/Flagler 3800 Woodbriar Trail	Port Orange	FL	32129	**800-272-2717**	386-322-4701	365
Hospice of Wake County Inc 1300 Saint Mary's St 4th Fl	Raleigh	NC	27605	**888-900-3959**	919-828-0890	365
Hospice of Wayne County 2525 Back Orrville Rd	Wooster	OH	44691	**800-884-6547**	330-264-4899	365
Hospice of Wichita Falls 4909 Johnson Rd	Wichita Falls	TX	76308	**800-378-2822**	940-691-0982	365
HospiceCare 5395 E Cheryl Pkwy	Madison	WI	53711	**800-553-4289**	608-276-4660	365
HospiceCare of the Piedmont 408 W Alexander Ave	Greenwood	SC	29646	**800-450-6646**	864-227-9393	365
HospiceCare of South Jersey 2848 S Delsea Dr	Vineland	NJ	08360	**800-584-1515**	856-794-1515	365
Hospira Inc 275 N Field Dr	Lake Forest	IL	60045	**877-946-7747**	224-212-2000	469
NYSE: HSP						
Hospital Assn. American 1 N Franklin St	Chicago	IL	60606	**800-424-4301**	312-422-3000	49-8
Hospital Billing & Collection Service Ltd 118 Lukens Dr	New Castle	DE	19720	**877-254-9580**	302-552-8000	157
Hospital Forms & Systems Corp 8900 Ambassador Row	Dallas	TX	75247	**800-527-5081**	214-634-8900	111
Hospital Housekeeping Systems 322 Congress Ave 2nd Fl	Austin	TX	78701	**800-229-2028**	512-478-1888	150
Hospital for Joint Diseases Orthopedic Institute 301 E 17th St	New York	NY	10003	**800-372-2887**	212-598-6000	366-5
Hospital Litigation Reporter 590 Dutch Valley Rd NE	Atlanta	GA	30324	**800-926-7926**	404-881-1141	521-7
Hospital of Saint Raphael 1450 Chapel St	New Haven	CT	06511	**800-662-2366**	203-789-3000	366-2
Hospital for Sick Children 1731 Bunker Hill Rd NE	Washington	DC	20017	**800-226-4444**	202-832-4400	366-1
Hospital Specialty Co 7501 Carnegie Ave	Cleveland	OH	44103	**800-321-9832**	216-361-1230	548-2
Hospitalite Canada 651 Notre Dame W Suite 260	Montreal	QC	H3C1H9	**800-665-1528**	514-287-9049	368
Hospitality Financial & Technology Professionals (HFTP) 11709 Boulder Ln Suite 110	Austin	TX	78726	**800-856-4242**	512-249-5333	49-1
Hospitality Furniture Group Mfg (HFG) 8180 NW 36th St Suite 418	Miami	FL	33166	**800-772-8826**	305-477-2882	314-1
Hospitality Inn 4400 S 27th St	Milwaukee	WI	53221	**800-825-8466**	414-282-8800	373
Hospitality International Inc 1726 Montreal Cir	Tucker	GA	30084	**800-251-1962**	770-270-1180	369
Downtowner Inns 1726 Montreal Cir	Tucker	GA	30084	**800-251-1962**	770-270-1180	369
Master Hosts Inns & Resorts 1726 Montreal Cir	Tucker	GA	30084	**800-247-4677**	770-270-1180	369
Passport Inn 1726 Montreal Cir	Tucker	GA	30084	**800-251-1962**	770-270-1180	369
Red Carpet Inn 1726 Montreal Cir	Tucker	GA	30084	**800-251-1962**	770-270-1180	369
Scottish Inns 1726 Montreal Cir	Tucker	GA	30084	**800-251-1962**	770-270-1180	369
Hospitality International INNcentive Card Program 1726 Montreal Cir	Tucker	GA	30084	**800-247-4677**		371
Hospitality Marketing Concepts Inc 15751 Rockfield Blvd Suite 200	Irvine	CA	92618	**866-212-4462**	949-454-1800	9
Hospitality Suites Resort 409 N Scottsdale Rd	Scottsdale	AZ	85257	**800-445-5115**	480-949-5115	373
Hospitality Tours 2 Academy Pl	Orleans	MA	02653	**800-966-1331**	508-240-3333	748
Hospitals & Health Networks Magazine 1 N Franklin Suite 2700	Chicago	IL	60606	**800-621-6902**	312-893-6800	449-5
Hoss's Steak & Sea House 170 Patch Way Rd	Duncansville	PA	16635	**800-992-4677**	814-695-7600	657
Host Airport Hotel 6945 Airport Blvd	Sacramento	CA	95837	**800-903-4678**	916-922-8071	373
Host Communications Inc 546 E Main St	Lexington	KY	40508	**888-484-4678**	859-226-4678	183
Host Depot Inc 9732 W Sample Rd	Coral Springs	FL	33065	**888-340-3527**	954-340-3527	795
Hostcentric Inc 6757 Edgewater Commerce Pkwy	Orlando	FL	32810	**800-467-8669**	407-445-3033	795
Hostedware Corp 16 Technology Dr Suite 116	Irvine	CA	92618	**800-211-6967**	949-585-1500	795
Hostway Corp 1 N State St 12th Fl	Chicago	IL	60602	**800-397-2449**	312-236-2132	795
Hot Dog on a Stick 5601 Palmer Way	Carlsbad	CA	92008	**800-321-8400**	760-930-0456	657
Hot Rod Magazine 6420 Wilshire Blvd	Los Angeles	CA	90048	**800-800-4681***	323-782-2000	449-3
*Orders						
Hot Rooms 1 E Erie St Suite 225	Chicago	IL	60611	**800-468-3500**	773-468-7666	368
Hot Springs Convention Center 134 Convention Blvd	Hot Springs	AR	71901	**800-543-2284**	501-321-1705	204
Hot Springs Convention & Visitors Bureau 134 Convention Blvd	Hot Springs	AR	71901	**800-543-2284**	501-321-2277	205
Hot Springs (Greater) Chamber of Commerce 659 Ouachita Ave	Hot Springs	AR	71901	**800-467-4636**	501-321-1700	137
Hot Springs Lodge & Pool 415 E 6th St PO Box 308	Glenwood Springs	CO	81602	**800-537-7946**	970-945-6571	655
Hot Stuff Pizza 2930 W Maple St	Sioux Falls	SD	57107	**800-648-6227**	605-336-6961	657
Hotel 71 Chicago 71 E Wacker Dr	Chicago	IL	60601	**800-621-4005**	312-346-7100	373
Hotel Acadia 43 rue Sainte-Ursule	Quebec	QC	G1R4E4	**800-463-0280**	418-694-0280	372
Hotel Adagio 550 Geary St	San Francisco	CA	94102	**800-228-8830**	415-775-5000	373
Hotel Alex Johnson 523 6th St	Rapid City	SD	57701	**800-888-2539**	605-342-1210	373
Hotel Allegro Chicago 171 W Randolph St	Chicago	IL	60601	**800-643-1500**	312-236-0123	373
Hotel Ambassador 1324 S Main St	Tulsa	OK	74119	**888-408-8282**	918-587-8200	373
Hotel Andra 2000 4th Ave	Seattle	WA	98121	**877-448-8600**	206-448-8600	373
Hotel Andrew Jackson 919 Royal St	New Orleans	LA	70116	**800-654-0224**	504-561-5881	373
Hotel de Anza 233 W Santa Clara St	San Jose	CA	95113	**800-843-3700**	408-286-1000	373
Hotel Astor 956 Washington Ave	Miami Beach	FL	33139	**800-270-4981**	305-531-8081	373
Hotel Avante 860 E El Camino Real	Mountain View	CA	94040	**800-538-1600**	650-940-1000	373
Hotel Beacon 2130 Broadway	New York	NY	10023	**800-572-4969**	212-787-1100	373
Hotel Bel-Air 701 Stone Canyon Rd	Los Angeles	CA	90077	**800-648-4097**	310-472-1211	373
Hotel Bijou 111 Mason St	San Francisco	CA	94102	**800-771-1022**	415-771-1200	373
Hotel Boulderado 2115 13th St	Boulder	CO	80302	**800-433-4344**	303-442-4344	373
Hotel Britton 112 7th St	San Francisco	CA	94103	**800-444-5819**	415-621-7001	373
Hotel Burnham 1 W Washington St	Chicago	IL	60602	**877-294-9712**	312-782-1111	373
Hotel Cantlie Suites 1110 rue Sherbrooke O	Montreal	QC	H3A1G9	**800-567-1110**	514-842-2000	372
Hotel Le Capitole 972 rue Saint-Jean	Quebec	QC	G1R1R5	**800-363-4040**	418-694-4040	372
Hotel Captain Cook 939 W 5th Ave	Anchorage	AK	99501	**800-843-1950**	907-276-6000	373
Hotel Casa del Mar 1910 Ocean Way	Santa Monica	CA	90405	**800-898-6999**	310-581-5533	373
Hotel Chateau Bellevue 16 rue de la Porte	Quebec	QC	G1R4M9	**800-463-2617**	418-692-2573	372
Hotel Chateau Laurier 1220 Pl George V O	Quebec	QC	G1R5B8	**800-463-4453**	418-522-8108	372
Hotel Cheribourg 2603 ch du Parc	Orford	QC	J1X8C8	**800-567-6132**	819-843-3308	655
Hotel Le Cirque 2 Lee Circle	New Orleans	LA	70130	**888-487-8782**	504-962-0900	373
Hotel Clarendon 57 rue Sainte-Anne	Quebec	QC	G1R3X4	**888-554-6001**	418-692-2480	372
Hotel Classique 2815 boul Laurier	Sainte-Foy	QC	G1V4H3	**800-463-1885**	418-658-2793	372
Hotel Le Clos Saint-Louis 69 rue Saint-Louis	Quebec	QC	G1R3Z2	**800-461-1311**	418-694-1311	372
Hotel Club Tremblant 121 rue Cuttle	Mont-Tremblant	QC	J8E1B9	**800-567-8341**	819-425-2731	655
Hotel Colorado 526 Pine St	Glenwood Springs	CO	81601	**800-544-3998**	970-945-6511	373
Hotel Congress 311 E Congress St	Tucson	AZ	85701	**800-722-8848**	520-622-8848	373
Hotel Cosmo 761 Post St	San Francisco	CA	94109	**800-252-7466**	415-673-6040	373
Hotel Crescent Court 400 Crescent Ct	Dallas	TX	75201	**800-654-6541**	214-871-3200	373
Hotel Del Coronado 1500 Orange Ave	Coronado	CA	92118	**800-582-2595**	619-522-8000	655
Hotel Del Sol 3100 Webster St	San Francisco	CA	94123	**877-433-5765**	415-921-5520	373
Hotel Derek 2525 West Loop S	Houston	TX	77027	**866-292-4100**	713-961-3000	373
Hotel DeVille 319 W Miller St	Jefferson City	MO	65101	**800-392-3366**	573-636-5231	373
Hotel Drisco 2901 Pacific Ave	San Francisco	CA	94115	**800-634-7277**	415-346-2880	373
Hotel Durant 2600 Durant Ave	Berkeley	CA	94704	**800-238-7268**	510-845-8981	373
Hotel Edgewater 2411 Alaskan Way Pier 67	Seattle	WA	98121	**800-624-0670**	206-728-7000	373
Hotel Edison 960 Ocean Dr	Miami Beach	FL	33139	**800-961-9076**	305-531-2744	373
Hotel Edison 228 W 47th St	New York	NY	10036	**800-637-7070**	212-840-5000	373
Hotel Elysee 60 E 54th St	New York	NY	10022	**800-535-9733**	212-753-1066	373
Hotel du Fort 1390 Rue du Fort	Montreal	QC	H3H2R7	**800-565-6333**	514-938-8333	372

Name / Address	City	State	ZIP	Toll-Free	Phone	Class
Hotel Fort Des Moines 1000 Walnut St................	Des Moines	IA	50309	**800-532-1466**	515-243-1161	373
Hotel Galvez - A Wyndham Historic Hotel 2024 Seawall Blvd	Galveston	TX	77550	**800-996-3426**	409-765-7721	373
Hotel George 15 'E' St NW	Washington	DC	20001	**800-576-8831**	202-347-4200	373
Hotel Georgia. Crowne Plaza 801 W Georgia St...............	Vancouver	BC	V6C1P7	**800-663-1111**	604-682-5566	372
Hotel Germain des Pres 1200 ave Germain-des-Pres.......	Sainte-Foy	QC	G1V3M7	**800-463-5253**	418-658-1224	372
Hotel Giraffe 365 Park Ave S at 26th St.........	New York	NY	10016	**877-296-0009**	212-685-7700	373
Hotel Grand Pacific 463 Belleville St	Victoria	BC	V8V1X3	**800-663-7550**	250-386-0450	372
Hotel Grand Victorian 2325 W Hwy 76..................	Branson	MO	65616	**800-324-8751**	417-336-2935	373
Hotel Griffon 155 Steuart St	San Francisco	CA	94105	**800-321-2201**	415-495-2100	373
Hotel Hana-Maui PO Box 9..............	Hana	HI	96713	**800-321-4262**	808-248-8211	655
Hotel Helix 1430 Rhode Island Ave NW......	Washington	DC	20005	**866-508-0658**	202-462-9001	373
Hotel Hershey 100 Hotel Rd	Hershey	PA	17033	**800-533-3131**	717-533-2171	655
Hotel Huntington Beach 7667 Center Ave..........	Huntington Beach	CA	92647	**877-891-0123**	714-891-0123	373
Hotel Jerome 330 E Main St............	Aspen	CO	81611	**800-331-7213**	970-920-1000	373
Hotel La Jolla 7955 La Jolla Shores Dr	La Jolla	CA	92037	**800-666-0261**	858-459-0261	373
Hotel l'Appartement Montreal 455 rue Sherbrooke O	Montreal	QC	H3A1B7	**800-363-3010**	514-284-3634	372
Hotel Lawrence 302 S Houston St	Dallas	TX	75202	**877-396-0334**	214-761-9090	373
Hotel Locators.com 919 Garnet Ave Suite 216	San Diego	CA	92109	**800-576-0003**		368
Hotel Lombardy 2019 Pennsylvania Ave NW	Washington	DC	20006	**800-424-5486**	202-828-2600	373
Hotel Lord-Berri 1199 rue Berri........	Montreal	QC	H2L4C6	**888-363-0363**	514-845-9236	372
Hotel Loretto 211 Old Santa Fe Trail....	Santa Fe	NM	87501	**800-727-5531**	505-988-5531	373
Hotel Los Gatos 210 E Main St......	Los Gatos	CA	95030	**866-335-1700**	408-335-1700	373
Hotel Lucia 400 SW Broadway	Portland	OR	97205	**877-225-1717**	503-225-1717	373
Hotel Lusso 1 N Post St	Spokane	WA	99201	**800-525-4800**	509-747-9750	373
Hotel Maison de Ville 727 Toulouse St..............	New Orleans	LA	70130	**800-634-1600**	504-561-5858	373
Hotel Majestic 1500 Sutter St....	San Francisco	CA	94109	**800-869-8966**	415-441-1100	373
Hotel Manoir Lafayette 661 Grande Allee E.................	Quebec	QC	G1R2K4	**800-363-8203**	418-522-2652	372
Hotel Manoir Victoria 44 Cote du Palais..................	Quebec	QC	G1R4H8	**800-463-6283**	418-692-1030	372
Hotel Maritime Plaza 1155 rue Guy....	Montreal	QC	H3H2P5	**800-363-6255**	514-932-1411	372
Hotel Marlowe Cambridge 25 Edwind H Land Blvd	Cambridge	MA	02141	**800-825-7040**	617-868-8000	373
Hotel Mead 451 E Grand Ave	Wisconsin Rapids	WI	54494	**800-843-6323**	715-423-1500	373
Hotel Metro 411 E Mason St........	Milwaukee	WI	53202	**877-638-7620**	414-272-1937	373
Hotel Milano 55 5th St	San Francisco	CA	94103	**800-398-7555**	415-543-8555	373
Hotel Monaco Chicago 225 N Wabash Ave................	Chicago	IL	60601	**866-610-0081**	312-960-8500	373
Hotel Monaco Denver 1717 Champa St ..	Denver	CO	80202	**800-397-5380**	303-296-1717	373
Hotel Monaco New Orleans 333 Saint Charles Ave	New Orleans	LA	70130	**866-685-8359**	504-561-0010	373
Hotel Monaco Salt Lake City 15 W 200 South..............	Salt Lake City	UT	84101	**877-294-9710**	801-595-0000	373
Hotel Monaco San Francisco 501 Geary St................	San Francisco	CA	94102	**866-622-5284**	415-292-0100	373
Hotel Monaco Seattle 1101 4th Ave.....	Seattle	WA	98101	**800-715-6513**	206-621-1770	373
Hotel de la Montagne 1430 rue de la Montagne...........	Montreal	QC	H3G1Z5	**800-361-6262**	514-288-5656	372
Hotel Monte Vista 100 N San Francisco St............	Flagstaff	AZ	86001	**800-545-3068**	928-779-6971	373
Hotel Monteleone 214 Royal St ...	New Orleans	LA	70130	**800-535-9595**	504-523-3341	373
Hotel Monticello 1075 Thomas Jefferson St NW ...	Washington	DC	20007	**800-388-2410**	202-337-0900	373
Hotel Nikko San Francisco 222 Mason St...............	San Francisco	CA	94102	**800-645-5687**	415-394-1111	373
Hotel Normandin 4700 boul Pierre-Bertrand	Quebec	QC	G2J1A4	**800-463-6721**	418-622-1611	372
Hotel Northampton 36 King St	Northampton	MA	01060	**800-547-3529**	413-584-3100	373
Hotel Ocean 1230 Ocean Dr	Miami Beach	FL	33139	**800-783-1725**	305-672-2579	373
Hotel Oceana 202 W Cabrillo Blvd	Santa Barbara	CA	93101	**800-965-9776**	805-965-4577	373
Hotel Oceana 849 Ocean Ave	Santa Monica	CA	90403	**800-777-0758**	310-393-0486	373
Hotel at Old Town 830 E 1st St	Wichita	KS	67202	**877-265-3869**	316-267-4800	373
Hotel Pacific 300 Pacific St	Monterey	CA	93940	**800-554-5542**	831-373-5700	373
Hotel Palomar 12 4th St	San Francisco	CA	94103	**877-294-9711**	415-348-1111	373
Hotel Parisi 1111 Prospect	La Jolla	CA	92037	**877-472-7474**	858-454-1511	373
Hotel Pattee 1112 Willis Ave............	Perry	IA	50220	**888-424-4268**	515-465-3511	373
Hotel Pere Marquette 501 Main St.......	Peoria	IL	61602	**800-447-1676**	309-637-6500	373
Hotel Phillips 106 W 12th St	Kansas City	MO	64105	**800-433-1426**	816-221-7000	373
Hotel Plaza Athenee 37 E 64th St	New York	NY	10021	**800-447-8800**	212-734-9100	373
Hotel Plaza Quebec 3031 boul Laurier...............	Sainte-Foy	QC	G1V2M2	**800-567-5276**	418-658-2727	372
Hotel du Pont 11th & Market Sts ...	Wilmington	DE	19801	**800-441-9019**	302-594-3100	373
Hotel Pontchartrain 2 Washington Blvd...	Detroit	MI	48226	**800-227-6963**	313-965-0200	373
Hotel le Priori 15 rue du Sault-au-Matelot	Quebec	QC	G1K3Y7	**800-351-3992**	418-692-3992	372
Hotel Provincial 1024 Rue Chartres	New Orleans	LA	70116	**800-535-7922**	504-581-4995	373
Hotel Quartier 2955 boul Laurier.....	Sainte-Foy	QC	G1V2M2	**888-818-5863**	418-650-1616	372
Hotel Queen Mary 1126 Queens Hwy	Long Beach	CA	90802	**800-437-2934**	562-435-3511	373
Hotel Rex 562 Sutter St.........	San Francisco	CA	94102	**800-433-4434**	415-433-4434	373
Hotel Roanoke & Conference Center. Doubletree 110 Shenandoah Ave.....	Roanoke	VA	24016	**866-594-4722**	540-985-5900	370
Hotel La Rose 308 Wilson St	Santa Rosa	CA	95401	**800-527-6738**	707-579-3200	373
Hotel Royal Palace 775 Honore Mercier Ave	Quebec	QC	G1R6A5	**800-567-5276**	418-694-2000	372
Hotel Royal Plaza PO Box 22203	Lake Buena Vista	FL	32830	**800-248-7890**	407-828-2828	373
Hotel Ruby Foo's 7655 Decarie Blvd....	Montreal	QC	H4P2H2	**800-361-5419**	514-731-7701	372
Hotel Saint Francis 210 Don Gaspar Ave	Santa Fe	NM	87501	**800-529-5700**	505-983-5700	373
Hotel Saint Germain 2516 Maple Ave.....	Dallas	TX	75201	**800-683-2516**	214-871-2516	373
Hotel Saint Marie 827 Toulouse St..............	New Orleans	LA	70112	**800-366-2743**	504-561-8951	373

Name / Address	City	State	ZIP	Toll-Free	Phone	Class
Hotel Saint Pierre 911 Burgundy St	New Orleans	LA	70116	**800-225-4040**	504-524-4401	373
Hotel Saint Regis Detroit 3071 W Grand Blvd	Detroit	MI	48202	**800-848-4810**	313-873-3000	373
Hotel San Carlos 202 N Central Ave	Phoenix	AZ	85004	**866-253-4121**	602-253-4121	373
Hotel Santa Barbara 533 State St	Santa Barbara	CA	93101	**888-259-7700**	805-957-9300	373
Hotel Santa Fe 1501 Paseo de Peralta	Santa Fe	NM	87501	**800-825-9876**	505-982-1200	373
Hotel Saranac 100 Main St.......	Saranac Lake	NY	12983	**800-937-0211**	518-891-2200	373
Hotel Shelley 844 Collins Ave.....	Miami Beach	FL	33139	**800-414-0612**	305-531-3341	373
Hotel Sofitel Chicago O'Hare 5550 N River Rd...............	Rosemont	IL	60018	**800-763-4835**	847-678-4488	373
Hotel Sofitel Chicago Water Tower 20 E Chestnut St	Chicago	IL	60611	**800-763-4835**	312-324-4000	373
Hotel Sofitel Houston 425 N Sam Houston Pkwy E	Houston	TX	77060	**800-763-4835**	281-445-9000	373
Hotel Sofitel Lafayette Square 806 15th St NW..............	Washington	DC	20005	**800-763-4835**	202-730-8800	373
Hotel Sofitel Los Angeles 8555 Beverly Blvd..............	Los Angeles	CA	90048	**800-521-7772**	310-278-5444	373
Hotel Sofitel Miami 5800 Blue Lagoon Dr................	Miami	FL	33126	**800-763-4835**	305-264-4888	373
Hotel Sofitel Minneapolis 5601 W 78th St..............	Bloomington	MN	55439	**800-876-6303**	952-835-1900	373
Hotel Sofitel New York 45 W 44th St	New York	NY	10036	**877-565-9240**	212-354-8844	373
Hotel Sofitel Philadelphia 120 S 17th St.................	Philadelphia	PA	19103	**800-763-4835**	215-569-8300	373
Hotel Sofitel San Francisco Bay 223 Twin Dolphin Dr	Redwood City	CA	94065	**800-763-4835**	650-598-9000	373
Hotel Solamar 435 6th Ave	San Diego	CA	92101	**877-230-0300**	619-531-8740	373
Hotel Strasburg 213 S Holliday St.....	Strasburg	VA	22657	**800-348-8327**	540-465-9191	373
Hotel Teatro 1100 14th St.............	Denver	CO	80202	**888-727-1200**	303-228-1100	373
Hotel Triton 342 Grant Ave	San Francisco	CA	94108	**800-800-1299**	415-394-0500	373
Hotel Universel 2300 ch Sainte-Foy ...	Sainte-Foy	QC	G1V1S5	**800-463-4495**	418-653-5250	372
Hotel Utica 102 Lafayette St.............	Utica	NY	13502	**877-906-1912**	315-724-7829	373
Hotel Versailles 1808 rue Sherbrooke O	Montreal	QC	H3H1E5	**800-933-8111**	514-933-8111	372
Hotel Victoria 56 Yonge St...........	Toronto	ON	M5E1G5	**800-363-8228**	416-363-1666	372
Hotel Viking 1 Bellevue Ave	Newport	RI	02840	**800-556-7126**	401-847-3300	373
Hotel Vintage Park 1100 5th Ave.......	Seattle	WA	98101	**800-853-3914**	206-624-8000	373
Hotel Vintage Plaza 422 SW Broadway	Portland	OR	97205	**800-263-2305**	503-228-1212	373
Hotel Washington 515 15th St NW..............	Washington	DC	20004	**800-424-9540**	202-638-5900	373
Hotel@MIT - University Park 20 Sidney St........................	Cambridge	MA	02139	**800-222-2733**	617-577-0200	373
HotelNetDiscount.com 3070 Windward Plaza Suite F-302...	Alpharetta	GA	30005	**800-364-1528**	770-664-1316	368
Hotelrooms.com Inc 108-18 Queens Blvd.............	Forest Hills	NY	11375	**800-486-7000**	718-730-6000	677
Hotels & Resorts Worldwide Inc. Preferred 311 S Wacker Dr Suite 1900	Chicago	IL	60606	**800-323-7500**	312-913-0400	368
Hotels.com 10440 N Central Expy........ *Sales	Dallas	TX	75231	**800-964-6835***	214-361-7311	368
HotJobs.com Ltd 406 W 31st St 9th Fl.............	New York	NY	10001	**877-468-5627**	212-302-0060	257
Hotwire.com 333 Market St Suite 100	San Francisco	CA	94105	**877-468-9473**	415-343-8400	762
Houchens Industries Inc 700 Church St	Bowling Green	KY	42101	**800-846-3252**	270-843-3252	339
Houff Roy Co 6200 S Oak Park Ave	Chicago	IL	60638	**800-366-1769**	773-586-8118	288
Houff Transfer Inc PO Box 220....	Weyers Cave	VA	24486	**800-476-4683**	540-234-9233	769
Hougen Mfg Inc 3001 Hougen Dr... *Orders	Swartz Creek	MI	48473	**800-462-7818***	810-635-7111	484
Houghton Chemical Corp 52 Cambridge St...................	Boston	MA	02134	**800-777-2466**	617-254-1010	143
Houghton College 1 Willard Ave	Houghton	NY	14744	**800-777-2556**	585-567-9200	163
W Seneca Campus 810 Union Rd..............	West Seneca	NY	14224	**800-247-6448**	716-674-6363	163
Houghton International Inc 950 Madison St PO Box 930	Valley Forge	PA	19482	**888-459-9844**	610-666-4000	3
Houghton Lake Area Tourism & Convention Bureau 4482 W Houghton Lake Dr	Houghton Lake	MI	48629	**800-676-5330**	989-366-8474	205
Houma Industries PO Box 685	Harvey	LA	70059	**800-348-5340**	504-347-4585	528
Houma-Terrebonne Tourist Commission 114 Tourist Dr	Gray	LA	70359	**800-688-2732**	985-868-2732	205
Hound Dog Products Inc 6811 Shady Oak Rd	Eden Prairie	MN	55344	**800-694-6863**	952-828-9008	420
House-Autry Mills Inc 7000 US Hwy 301 S.............	Four Oaks	NC	27524	**800-849-0802**	919-963-6200	291-23
House Beautiful Magazine 1700 Broadway 29th Fl	New York	NY	10019	**800-444-6873**	212-903-5000	449-11
House of Blues Entertainment Inc 6255 Sunset Blvd 16th Fl.........	Hollywood	CA	90028	**800-843-2583**	323-769-4600	179
House of Blues Hotel - A Loews Hotel 333 N Dearborn St.............	Chicago	IL	60610	**800-235-6397**	312-245-0333	373
House of Broel's Historic Mansion & Dollhouse Museum 2220 St Charles Ave..................	New Orleans	LA	70130	**800-827-4325**	504-525-1000	509
House Charles & Sons Inc 235 Singleton St..............	Woonsocket	RI	02895	**800-243-7063**	401-769-0189	730-8
House Doctors 575 Chamber Dr	Milford	OH	45150	**800-319-3359**	513-831-0100	186
House-Hasson Hardware Inc 3125 Water Plant Rd SE	Knoxville	TN	37914	**800-333-0520**	865-525-0471	346
House of Raeford Farms Inc PO Box 100	Raeford	NC	28376	**800-888-7539**	910-875-5161	608
House of La Rose 4223 E 49th St...........	Cuyahoga Heights	OH	44125	**800-642-4379**	216-271-5500	82-1
House of Specialties 5451 Able Ct......	Mobile	AL	36693	**800-348-2422**	251-438-2422	10
House of White Birches Inc 306 E Parr Rd...................... *Orders	Berne	IN	46711	**800-347-9887***	260-589-8741	623-9
House of Windsor Inc PO Box 68.... *Cust Svc	Dallastown	PA	17313	**800-237-4715***	717-244-4501	741-2

Company / Address	City	State	ZIP	Toll-Free	Phone	Class
Household Retail Services USA Churman's Corporate Ctr 90 Christiana Rd	New Castle	DE	19720	**800-695-6950**	302-327-2400	213
Housekeepers Assn. International Executive 1001 Eastwind Dr Suite 301	Westerville	OH	43081	**800-200-6342**	614-895-7166	49-4
HouseMaster 421 W Union Ave.	Bound Brook	NJ	08805	**800-526-3939**	732-469-6565	360
HouseValues Inc 15 Lake Bellevue Dr Suite 100 *NASDAQ: SOLD*	Bellevue	WA	98005	**877-450-0088**	425-454-0088	7
Housing Assistance Council (HAC) 1025 Vermont Ave NW Suite 606	Washington	DC	20005	**800-989-4422**	202-842-8600	48-5
Housing Council. National American Indian 900 2nd St NE Suite 305	Washington	DC	20002	**800-284-9165**	202-789-1754	49-7
Housing & Development Reporter Newsletter 610 Opperman Dr	Eagan	MN	55123	**800-937-8529**	651-687-7000	521-7
Housing Institute. Manufactured 2101 Wilson Blvd Suite 610	Arlington	VA	22201	**800-505-5500**	703-558-0400	49-3
Housing & Redevelopment Officials. National Assn of 630 'I' St NW	Washington	DC	20001	**877-866-2476**	202-289-3500	49-7
Houston Art 10770 Moss Ridge Rd *Cust Svc	Houston	TX	77043	**800-272-3804***	713-462-1086	43
Houston Astros Minute Maid Park 501 Crawford St	Houston	TX	77002	**877-927-8768**	713-259-8000	703
Houston Baptist University 7502 Fondren Rd	Houston	TX	77074	**800-969-3210**	281-649-3000	163
Houston Chronicle 801 Texas Ave.	Houston	TX	77002	**800-735-3800**	713-362-7171	522-2
Houston County Electric Co-op Inc PO Box 52	Crockett	TX	75835	**800-657-2445**	936-544-5641	244
Houston Exploration Co 1100 Louisiana St Suite 2000 *NYSE: THX*	Houston	TX	77002	**800-261-3283**	713-830-6800	525
Houston Grand Opera 510 Preston St Suite 500	Houston	TX	77002	**800-626-7372**	713-546-0200	563-2
Houston (Greater) Convention & Visitors Bureau 901 Bagby St Suite 100	Houston	TX	77002	**800-446-8786**	713-437-5200	205
Houston Numismatic Exchange Inc 2486 Times Blvd.	Houston	TX	77005	**800-231-3650**	713-528-2135	451
Houston Paper & Janitorial Supply Inc 600 Monument St.	Dothan	AL	36303	**800-239-7561**	334-794-7561	549
Houston Wiper & Mill Supply Co 9800 Market St.	Houston	TX	77029	**800-633-5968**	713-672-0571	497
Houston Wire & Cable Co 10201 N Loop E	Houston	TX	77029	**800-468-9473**	713-609-2100	245
Houstonian Hotel Club & Spa 111 N Post Oak Ln.	Houston	TX	77024	**800-231-2759**	713-680-2626	655
Houston's Restaurants 2425 E Camelback Rd Suite 200	Phoenix	AZ	85016	**866-418-8583**	602-553-2111	657
Hoveround Corp 2151 Whitfield Industrial Way	Sarasota	FL	34243	**800-755-4331**	941-739-6200	469
HOW Design Magazine 4700 E Galbraith Rd *Cust Svc	Cincinnati	OH	45036	**800-333-1115***	513-531-2690	449-2
Howard Brothers Florists 7101 Southwestern Ave	Oklahoma City	OK	73139	**800-648-0524**	405-632-4747	287
Howard Community College 10901 Little Patuxent Pkwy	Columbia	MD	21044	**800-234-9981**	410-772-4800	160
Howard County Tourism Council 8267 Main St	Ellicott City	MD	21043	**800-288-8747**	410-313-1900	205
Howard Edward & Co 1360 E 9th St 7th Fl.	Cleveland	OH	44114	**800-868-2045**	216-781-2400	622
Howard Eldon Ltd 20333 Gilmore St	Winnetka	CA	91306	**800-685-1533**	818-340-9371	400
Howard F Baer Inc 1301 Foster Ave	Nashville	TN	37210	**800-447-7430**	615-255-7351	769
Howard Greeley Rural Public Power District PO Box 105	Saint Paul	NE	68873	**800-280-4962**	308-754-4457	244
Howard Johnson Franchise Canada Inc 135 Queens Plate Suite 410	Toronto	ON	M9W6V1	**800-249-4656**	416-361-1010	369
Howard Johnson International Inc 1 Sylvan Way	Parsippany	NJ	07054	**800-446-4656**	973-428-9700	369
Howard Johnson Plaza Hotel 7707 NW 103rd St	Hialeah	FL	33016	**800-446-4656**	305-825-1000	373
Howard Johnson Plaza Hotel Dezerland Beach & Spa 8701 Collins Ave	Miami Beach	FL	33154	**800-331-9346**	305-865-6661	373
Howard Payne University 1000 Fisk Ave	Brownwood	TX	76801	**800-950-8465**	325-646-2502	163
Howard Press Inc 450 W 1st Ave	Roselle	NJ	07203	**800-223-0648**	908-245-4400	111
Howard R Green Co 8710 Earhart Ln SW PO Box 9009	Cedar Rapids	IA	52409	**800-728-7805**	319-841-4000	258
Howard-Sloan Search Inc 1140 Ave of the Americas	New York	NY	10036	**800-221-1326**	212-704-0444	262
Howard Systems International 281 Tresser Blvd	Stamford	CT	06901	**800-326-4860**	203-324-4600	178
Howard Uniform Co Inc 313 W Baltimore St	Baltimore	MD	21201	**800-628-8299**	410-727-3086	153-19
Howard University 2400 6th St NW	Washington	DC	20059	**800-822-6363**	202-806-6100	163
Howard W Sams 9850 E 30th St *Cust Svc	Indianapolis	IN	46229	**800-428-7267***	317-396-9850	623-2
Howard Weil 1100 Poydras St Suite 3500	New Orleans	LA	70163	**800-322-3005**	504-582-2500	679
Howard's Express Inc 369 Bostwick Rd	Phelps	NY	14532	**800-274-1100**	315-789-1900	769
Howden Buffalo Inc 2029 W Dekalb St *Sales	Camden	SC	29020	**800-321-8885***	803-713-2200	19
Howe Barnes Investments Inc 222 S Riverside Plaza 7th Fl	Chicago	IL	60606	**800-275-4693**	312-655-3000	679
Howe Military Academy PO Box 240	Howe	IN	46746	**888-462-4693**	260-562-2131	611
Howell Electric Motors 900 North Ave	Plainfield	NJ	07061	**800-346-9350**	908-756-8800	507
Howell-Oregon Electric Co-op Inc PO Box 649	West Plains	MO	65775	**888-463-7693**	417-256-2131	244
Howell Playground Equipment Inc 1714 E Fairchild *Orders	Danville	IL	61832	**800-637-5075***	217-442-0482	340
Howells-Craftland 6030 NE 112th Ave	Portland	OR	97220	**800-547-0368**	503-255-2002	44
Howes S Co Inc 25 Howard St	Silver Creek	NY	14136	**888-255-2611**	716-934-2611	293
Hoxworth Blood Center University of Cincinnati Medical Center 3130 Highland Ave ML0055	Cincinnati	OH	45267	**800-265-1515**	513-558-1200	90
Hoyt Corp 251 Forge Rd	Westport	MA	02790	**800-343-9411**	508-636-8811	418
Hoyt Corp 520 S Dean St.	Englewood	NJ	07631	**800-255-4698**	201-894-0707	803
HP Hood Inc 90 Everett Ave. *Cust Svc	Chelsea	MA	02150	**800-662-4468***	617-887-3000	291-27
HP Neun Co Inc 75 N Main St.	Fairport	NY	14450	**800-724-2641**	585-388-1360	102
HP Pavilion at San Jose 525 W Santa Clara St.	San Jose	CA	95113	**800-366-4423**	408-287-7070	706
HP Products Corp 4220 Saguaro Trail	Indianapolis	IN	46268	**800-382-5326**	317-298-9950	398
HPC Global 14 Inudstrial Dr.	Hanover	PA	17331	**800-233-4463**	717-637-6681	560
HPD Systems 23562 W Main St.	Plainfield	IL	60544	**800-927-0319**	815-609-2000	258
HPH Corp 1529 SE 47th Terr	Cape Coral	FL	33904	**800-654-9884**	239-540-0085	342
HPI (Heifer Project International) PO Box 1692	Merrifield	VA	22116	**800-422-0474**	501-907-2900	48-5
HPR Bakers 290 Madsen Dr Suite 101	Bloomingdale	IL	60108	**800-366-6776**	630-671-4100	291-1
HPSC Inc 1 Beacon St 2nd Fl	Boston	MA	02109	**800-225-2488**	617-720-7200	214
HPV & Cervical Cancer Prevention Resource Center National PO Box 13827	Research Triangle Park	NC	27709	**800-277-8922**	919-361-8400	48-17
HQ Global Workplaces Inc 15305 N Dallas Pkwy Suite 1400	Addison	TX	75001	**800-633-4237**	972-361-8100	305
HR America 1833 Magnavox Way	Fort Wayne	IN	46804	**800-837-4787**	260-436-3878	619
HR Ewell Inc 4635 Division Hwy	East Earl	PA	17519	**800-233-0161**	717-354-4556	769
HR Meininger Co 499 Broadway	Denver	CO	80203	**800-950-2787**	303-698-3838	45
HR Nicholson Co 6320 Oakleaf Ave *Cust Svc	Baltimore	MD	21215	**800-638-3514***	410-764-2323	291-20
HRC (National Herpes Resource Center) PO Box 13827	Research Triangle Park	NC	27709	**800-227-8922**	919-361-8488	48-17
HRF (Herb Research Foundation) 4140 15th St.	Boulder	CO	80304	**800-748-2617**	303-449-2265	48-17
HRMagazine 1800 Duke St	Alexandria	VA	22314	**800-283-7476**	703-548-3440	449-5
HRPlus 2902 Evergreen Pkwy Suite 100	Evergreen	CO	80439	**800-827-2479**	303-670-8177	621
HRSA (Health Resources & Services Administration) 5600 Fishers Ln	Rockville	MD	20857	**888-275-4772**	301-443-2216	336-6
HSB Group Inc 1 State St PO Box 5024	Hartford	CT	06102	**800-472-1866**	860-722-1866	384-4
HSB Reliability Technologies 1701 N Beauregard St Suite 400	Alexandria	VA	22311	**800-368-3371**	703-671-3800	193
HSBC Asset Management Inc 452 5th Ave	New York	NY	10018	**800-759-0315**	212-525-5000	393
HSBC Bank Canada 885 W Georgia St Suite 200	Vancouver	BC	V6C3E9	**800-291-3888**	604-685-1000	71
HSBC Bank USA 1 HSBC Ctr	Buffalo	NY	14203	**800-975-4722**	716-841-2424	71
HSBC Mortgage Corp (USA) 2929 Walden Ave	Depew	NY	14043	**800-338-4626**		498
HSBC USA Inc 1 HSBC Ctr	Buffalo	NY	14203	**800-975-4722**	716-841-2424	355-2
HSI (Helicopter Support Inc) 124 Quarry Rd PO Box 111068	Trumbull	CT	06611	**800-795-6051**	203-416-4000	759
HSN Improvements 23297 Commerce Pk	Beachwood	OH	44122	**800-944-8870**	216-831-6191	451
HSN LP 1 HSN Dr	Saint Petersburg	FL	33729	**800-284-3900**	727-872-1000	725
HSQ Technology 26227 Research Rd	Hayward	CA	94545	**800-486-6684**	510-259-1334	200
HSR Business to Business 300 E-Business Way Suite 500	Cincinnati	OH	45241	**800-243-2648**	513-671-3811	4
HSS RentX 1001 E Sunrise Blvd	Fort Lauderdale	FL	33304	**877-711-7368**	954-766-2588	261-3
HT Ardinger & Son Co 1990 Lake Point Dr	Lewisville	TX	75057	**800-683-0498**	214-631-9830	288
HT Hackney Co 502 S Gay St	Knoxville	TN	37902	**800-406-1291**	865-546-1291	184
HTC (Healing the Children) PO Box 9065	Spokane	WA	99209	**877-432-5543**	509-327-4281	48-5
HTH Corp 2490 Kalakaua Ave	Honolulu	HI	96815	**800-367-6060**	808-922-1233	369
HTI Voice & Internet Solutions Inc 2 Mt Royal Ave	Marlborough	MA	01752	**800-255-4241**	508-485-8400	176-7
HTL Inc PO Box 988DTS	Omaha	NE	68101	**800-877-4136**	712-328-2393	769
HTT (Harsco Track Technologies) 2401 Edmund Rd Box 20	West Columbia	SC	29171	**800-345-9160**	803-822-9160	636
Hualalai Sports Club & Spa at the Four Seasons Resort Hualalai 100 Kaupulehu Dr	Kaupulehu-Kona	HI	96740	**888-340-5662**	808-325-8440	698
Hub City Distributing Co 6 Princess Rd	Lawrenceville	NJ	08648	**800-551-0668**	609-844-9600	82-1
Hub City Inc PO Box 1089	Aberdeen	SD	57402	**800-482-2489**	605-225-0360	700
Hub Folding Box Co Inc 774 Norfolk St	Mansfield	MA	02048	**800-334-1113**	508-339-0005	102
Hub Group Inc 3050 Highland Pkwy Suite 100 *NASDAQ: HUBG*	Downers Grove	IL	60515	**800-964-2515**	630-271-3600	440
HUB International Ltd 55 E Jackson Blvd Suite 14A	Chicago	IL	60604	**800-432-2558**	877-402-6601	383
Hub Pattern Corp 2113 Salem Ave	Roanoke	VA	24016	**800-482-3505**	540-342-3505	556
Hub Pen Co Inc 230 Quincy Ave	Quincy	MA	02169	**800-388-2323**	617-471-9900	560
Hub Supply Inc 2546 S Leonine St	Wichita	KS	67217	**800-482-8665**	316-265-9608	378
Hubbard Co Inc 208 Lurgan Ave	Shippensburg	PA	17257	**800-241-1226**	717-532-4146	153-12
Hubbard Construction Co 1936 Lee Rd 3rd Fl	Winter Park	FL	32789	**800-476-1228**	407-645-5500	187-4
Hubbard Feeds Inc 424 N Riverfront Dr	Mankato	MN	56001	**800-869-7219**	507-388-9400	438
Hubbard ISA PO Box 415	Walpole	NH	03608	**800-482-2442**	603-756-3311	11-8
Hubbard Scientific Div American Educational Products LLC 401 Hickory St *Cust Svc	Fort Collins	CO	80522	**800-289-9299***	970-484-7445	242
Hubbell Industrial Controls 4301 Cheyenne Dr	Archdale	NC	27263	**800-828-4032**	336-434-2800	202
Hubbell Killark 3940 ML King Dr	Saint Louis	MO	63113	**800-545-5275**	314-531-0460	804
Hubbell Premise Wiring Inc 14 Lord's Hill Rd	Stonington	CT	06378	**800-626-0005**		803
Hubbell RACO 3902 W Sample St	South Bend	IN	46619	**800-722-6437**	574-234-7151	804

Name / Address	City	State	Zip	Toll-Free	Phone	Class
Huber's Orchard & Winery 19816 Huber Rd	Starlight	IN	47106	**800-345-9463**	812-923-3463	50
Huck Fasteners 3724 E Columbia St	Tucson	AZ	85714	**800-326-1799**	520-519-7400	274
Huddle House Inc 2969 E Ponce de Leon Ave	Decatur	GA	30030	**800-418-9555**	404-377-5700	657
Hudson City Bancorp Inc W 80 Century Rd *NASDAQ: HCBK*	Paramus	NJ	07652	**800-967-2200**	201-967-1900	355-2
Hudson HD Mfg Co 500 N Michigan Ave Suite 2300	Chicago	IL	60611	**800-523-9284**	312-644-2830	269
Hudson Hotel 356 W 58th St	New York	NY	10019	**800-444-4786**	212-554-6000	373
Hudson Institute 1015 18th St NW Suite 300	Washington	DC	20036	**800-483-7660**	202-225-7770	654
Hudson Liquid Asphalts Inc 89 Ship St	Providence	RI	02903	**800-556-3406**	401-274-2200	190-1
Hudson Machinery Worldwide PO Box 831	Haverhill	MA	01831	**800-346-5113**	978-374-0303	448
Hudson RCI 27711 Diaz Rd *Cust Svc	Temecula	CA	92589	**800-848-3766***	951-676-5611	468
Hudson River Bank & Trust 1 Hudson City Ctr PO Box 76	Hudson	NY	12534	**800-352-7776**	518-828-4600	71
Hudson River Bank & Trust 1 Hudson City Ctr PO Box 76	Hudson	NY	12534	**800-352-7776**	518-828-4331	71
Hudson River Inlay 34 State Street	Ossining	NY	10562	**800-745-0744**	914-762-1134	808
Hudson River Psychiatric Center 10 Ross Cir	Poughkeepsie	NY	12601	**800-871-7910**	845-452-8000	366-3
Hudson United Bancorp 1000 MacArthur Blvd *NYSE: HU*	Mahwah	NJ	07430	**800-482-5465**	201-236-2600	355-2
Hudson United Bank 1000 MacArthur Blvd	Mahwah	NJ	07430	**800-482-5465**	201-236-2600	71
Hudson Valley Community College 80 Vandenburgh Ave	Troy	NY	12180	**877-325-4822**	518-629-4822	160
Hudson Valley Farms Inc 381 Vineyard Ave	Highland	NY	12528	**800-336-2252**	845-691-2181	310-3
Hudson Valley Federal Credit Union 159 Barnegat Rd	Poughkeepsie	NY	12601	**800-468-3011**	845-463-3011	216
Hudson Valley Magazine 22 IBM Rd Suite 108	Poughkeepsie	NY	12601	**800-274-7844**	845-463-0542	449-22
Hudson Valley Paper Co 981 Broadway	Albany	NY	12207	**800-473-5525**	518-471-5111	543
Hudson Valve Co Inc 5301 Office Pk Dr Suite 330	Bakersfield	CA	93390	**800-748-6218**	661-869-1126	776
Hueston Woods Resort & Conference Center 5201 Lodge Rd	College Corner	OH	45003	**800-282-7275**	513-664-3500	655
Hufcor Inc 2101 Kennedy Rd	Janesville	WI	53545	**800-356-6968**	608-756-1241	281
Huffines Auto Group 4500 W Plano Pkwy	Plano	TX	75093	**866-522-5138**	972-867-6000	57
Huffman Corp 1050 Huffman Way	Clover	SC	29710	**800-523-4833**	803-222-4561	447
Huffman Koos Inc Rt 4 & Main St *Cust Svc	River Edge	NJ	07661	**800-648-3362***	201-343-4300	316
Huffy Bicycle Co 901 Pleasant Valley Dr	Springboro	OH	45066	**800-872-2453**	937-743-5011	83
Huffy Corp 225 Byers Rd	Miamisburg	OH	45342	**800-872-2453**	937-866-6251	355-3
Huffy Sports Co N 53 W 24700 South Corporate Cir *Cust Svc	Sussex	WI	53089	**800-558-5234***	262-820-3440	701
Hugestore.com 427 S Illinois St	Indianapolis	IN	46225	**800-259-7283**	317-321-9999	155-3
Hughes Corp Weschler Instruments Div 16900 Foltz Pkwy	Cleveland	OH	44149	**800-557-0064**	440-238-2550	247
Hughes RS Co Inc 10639 Glenoaks Blvd	Pacoima	CA	91331	**877-774-8443**	818-686-9111	378
Hughes RS Co Inc Saunders Div 905 Allen Ave *Sales	Glendale	CA	91201	**800-845-6500***	818-953-3000	446
Hugo Boss Fashions Inc 601 W 26th St Suite 845	New York	NY	10001	**800-484-6207**	212-940-0600	153-12
Hugo Daily News 128 E Jackson St	Hugo	OK	74743	**800-900-3311**	580-326-3311	522-2
Hugoton Royalty Trust 901 Main St Bank of America Plaza 17th Fl *NYSE: HGT*	Dallas	TX	75202	**877-228-5083**	214-209-2400	662
Huhtamaki Americas 9201 Packaging Dr	DeSoto	KS	66018	**800-255-4243**	913-583-3025	548-1
Hull Lift Truck Inc 28747 Old US 33 W	Elkhart	IN	46516	**800-860-4855**	574-293-8651	378
Hultgren Implements Inc 5698 State Hwy 175	Ida Grove	IA	51445	**800-827-1650**	712-364-3105	270
HUM Div of Medical Liability Mutual Insurance Co 8 British-American Blvd	Latham	NY	12110	**800-635-0666**	518-786-2700	384-5
Human Capital 28777 Northwestern Hwy Suite 125	Southfield	MI	48034	**888-736-9071**	248-353-3444	619
Human Events Magazine 1 Massachusetts Ave NW Suite 600 *Cust Svc	Washington	DC	20001	**800-787-7557***	202-216-0600	449-17
Human Genetics. American Society of 9650 Rockville Pike	Bethesda	MD	20814	**866-486-4363**	301-571-1825	49-19
Human Growth Foundation 997 Glen Cove Ave Suite 5	Glen Head	NY	11545	**800-451-6434**	516-671-4041	48-17
Human Kinetics 1607 N Market St	Champaign	IL	61820	**800-747-4457**	217-351-5076	623-2
Human Life International (HLI) 4 Family Life Ln *Orders	Front Royal	VA	22630	**800-549-5433***	540-635-7884	48-6
Human Management Services Inc 1463 Dunwoody Dr	Westchester	PA	19380	**800-343-2186**	610-644-6000	454
Human Policy. Center on 805 S Crouse Ave	Syracuse	NY	13244	**800-894-0826**	315-443-3851	48-17
Human Resource Executive Magazine 747 Dresher Rd Suite 500	Horsham	PA	19044	**800-341-7874**	215-784-0860	449-5
Human Resource Information Management. International Assn for PO Box 1086	Burlington	MA	01803	**800-946-6363**	781-273-3697	49-12
Human Resource Management. Society for 1800 Duke St	Alexandria	VA	22314	**800-283-7476**	703-548-3440	49-12
Human Resource Profile Inc 8506 Beechmont Ave	Cincinnati	OH	45255	**800-969-4300**	513-388-4300	621
Human Resources Dept Management Report 3 Park Ave 30th Fl	New York	NY	10016	**800-401-5937**	212-244-0360	521-2
Human Resources. International Public Management Assn for 1617 Duke St	Alexandria	VA	22314	**800-220-4762**	703-549-7100	49-12
Human Rights Campaign 1640 Rhode Island Ave NW	Washington	DC	20036	**800-777-4723**	202-628-4160	48-8
Human Rights Campaign PAC 1640 Rhode Island Ave NW	Washington	DC	20036	**800-777-4723**	202-628-4160	604
Humana HMO 500 W Main St	Louisville	KY	40202	**800-448-6262**	502-580-1000	384-3
Humana Inc 500 W Main St *NYSE: HUM*	Louisville	KY	40202	**800-486-2620**	502-580-1000	384-3
Humana Military Healthcare Services 500 W Main St	Louisville	KY	40201	**800-964-5482**	502-580-3200	384-3
Humane Assn. American 63 Inverness Dr E	Englewood	CO	80112	**800-227-4645**	303-792-9900	48-6
Humane Societies. Canadian Federation of 30 Concourse Gate Suite 102	Ottawa	ON	K2E7V7	**888-678-2347**	613-224-8072	48-3
Humane Studies. Institute for 3301 N Fairfax Dr Suite 440	Arlington	VA	22201	**800-697-8799**	703-993-4880	654
Humboldt County Rural Electric Co-op 1210 13th St N	Humboldt	IA	50548	**800-994-3532**	515-332-1616	244
Humboldt State University 1 Harpst St	Arcata	CA	95521	**866-850-9556**	707-826-3011	163
Humco Holding Group Inc 7400 Alumax Dr	Texarkana	TX	75501	**800-662-3435**	903-831-7808	572
Hume Music Inc 3660 SW Topeka Blvd	Topeka	KS	66611	**800-657-5748**	785-266-6366	515
Hummel Gift Shop 1656 E Garfield Rd	New Springfield	OH	44443	**800-354-5438**	330-549-3728	322
Hummer Wayne Investments LLC 300 S Wacker Dr Suite 1500	Chicago	IL	60606	**800-621-4477**	312-431-1700	679
Hummingbird Ltd 1 Sparks Ave *NASDAQ: HUMC*	Toronto	ON	M2H2W1	**877-359-4866**	416-496-2200	176-12
Humor Project Inc 480 Broadway Suite 210 *Orders	Saratoga Springs	NY	12866	**800-225-0330***	518-587-8770	48-17
Humperdinks 10013 59th Ave SW	Lakewood	WA	98499	**888-898-4050**	253-588-1788	657
Humphrey Products Co 5070 East N Ave	Kalamazoo	MI	49048	**800-477-8707**	269-381-5500	776
Humphrey's Half Moon Inn & Suites 2303 Shelter Island Dr	San Diego	CA	92106	**800-542-7400**	619-224-3411	373
Humphreys Inc 2009 W Hastings St *Cust Svc	Chicago	IL	60608	**800-621-8541***	312-997-2358	153-2
Humpty Dumpty Snack Foods USA 88 Pleasant Hill Rd	Scarborough	ME	04074	**800-274-2447**	207-883-8422	291-35
Humpty Dumpty's Magazine 1100 Waterway Blvd	Indianapolis	IN	46202	**800-558-2376**	317-636-8881	449-6
Humpty's Restaurants International Inc 2505 Macleod Tr S	Calgary	AB	T2G5J4	**800-661-7589**	403-269-4675	657
Hunger. Action Against 247 W 37th St Suite 1201	New York	NY	10018	**877-777-1420**	212-967-7800	48-5
Hunger Clearinghouse. National 505 8th Ave Suite 2100	New York	NY	10018	**800-453-2648**	212-629-8850	48-5
Hunger. Freedom from 1644 DaVinci Ct	Davis	CA	95616	**800-708-2555**	530-758-6200	48-5
Hunger & Homelessness. National Student Campaign Against 233 N Pleasant St Suite 32	Amherst	MA	01002	**800-664-8647**	413-253-6417	48-5
Hunger Project The 15 E 26th St Suite 1401	New York	NY	10010	**800-228-6691**	212-251-9100	48-5
Hunger Year Inc. World 505 8th Ave Suite 2100	New York	NY	10018	**800-548-6479**	212-629-8850	48-5
Hungry Howie's Pizza & Subs Inc 30300 Stephenson Hwy Suite 200	Madison Heights	MI	48071	**800-624-8122**	248-414-3300	657
Hungry Inc. Food for the 1224 E Washington St Phoenix	Scottsdale	AZ	85034	**800-248-6437**	480-998-3100	48-5
Hunt Construction Group 2450 S Tibbs Ave	Indianapolis	IN	46241	**800-223-6301**	317-227-7800	185
Hunt Forest Products PO Box 1263	Ruston	LA	71273	**800-390-8589**	318-255-2245	671
Hunt JB Transport Services Inc 615 JB Hunt Corporate Dr *NASDAQ: JBHT*	Lowell	AR	72745	**800-643-3622**	479-820-0000	440
Hunt Midwest Residential Development 8300 NE Underground Dr	Kansas City	MO	64161	**800-551-6877**	816-455-2500	639
Hunt Oil Co 1445 Ross Ave Fountain Pl Suite 1500	Dallas	TX	75202	**800-435-7794**	214-978-8000	570
Hunt Pan Am Aviation Inc 505 S Minnesota Ave Brownsville/South Padre International Airport	Brownsville	TX	78521	**800-888-7524**	956-542-9111	63
Hunt Rodney Co Inc 46 Mill St	Orange	MA	01364	**800-448-8860**	978-544-2511	471
Hunt Valve Co Inc DBA Hunt Engineering 1913 E State St	Salem	OH	44460	**800-321-2757**	330-337-9535	777
Hunter Co Inc 3300 W 71st Ave	Westminster	CO	80030	**800-676-4868**	303-427-4626	701
Hunter & Co of North Carolina Inc 1945 W Green Dr	High Point	NC	27261	**800-523-8387**	336-883-4161	789
Hunter Display 14 Hewlett Ave	East Patchogue	NY	11772	**800-767-2110**	631-475-5900	231
Hunter Douglas 2 Parkway & Rt 17 S	Upper Saddle River	NJ	07458	**800-436-7366**	201-327-8200	88
Hunter Douglas Architectural Products Inc 5015 Oakbrook Pkwy Suite 100	Norcross	GA	30093	**800-366-4327**	770-806-9557	482
Hunter Fan Co 2500 Frisco Ave	Memphis	TN	38114	**800-448-6837**	901-743-1360	37
Hunter HB Co PO Box 1599	Norfolk	VA	23501	**800-446-8314**	757-664-5200	295
Hunter Holmes McGuire Veterans Affairs Medical Center 1201 Broad Rock Blvd	Richmond	VA	23249	**800-784-8381**	804-675-5000	366-6
Hunter Marine Corp PO Box 1030	Alachua	FL	32616	**800-771-5556**	386-462-3077	91
Hunter Woodworks Inc PO Box 4937	Carson	CA	90749	**800-966-4751**	323-775-2544	541
Huntingdon College 1500 E Fairview Ave	Montgomery	AL	36106	**800-763-0313**	334-833-4497	163
Huntingdon County Visitors Bureau 7 Points Rd RD 1 Box 222A	Hesston	PA	16647	**888-729-7869**	814-658-0060	205
Huntington Bancshares Inc 41 S High St *NASDAQ: HBAN*	Columbus	OH	43287	**800-480-2265**	614-480-8300	355-2
Huntington College 2303 College Ave	Huntington	IN	46750	**800-642-6493**	260-356-6000	163

Name / Address	City	State	ZIP	Toll-Free	Phone	Class
Huntington County Visitors & Convention Bureau 407 N Jefferson St	Huntington	IN	46750	**800-848-4282**	260-359-8687	205
Huntington Hotel 1075 California St	San Francisco	CA	94108	**800-227-4683**	415-474-5400	373
Huntington Junior College 900 5th Ave	Huntington	WV	25701	**800-344-4522**	304-697-7550	158
Huntington Learning Centers Inc 954 Kinderkamack Rd	River Edge	NJ	07661	**800-226-5327**	201-261-8600	146
Huntington Mortgage Co 7575 Huntington Park Dr	Columbus	OH	43235	**800-323-4695**	614-480-6505	498
Huntington National Bank 41 S High St	Columbus	OH	43287	**800-480-2265**	614-480-8300	71
Huntington Park Rubber Stamp 2761 E Slauson Ave	Huntington Park	CA	90255	**800-882-0129**	323-582-6461	459
Huntington Township Chamber of Commerce 164 Main St	Huntington	NY	11743	**888-361-5710**	631-423-6100	137
Huntington Wholesale Furniture Co Inc PO Box 1300 *Orders	Huntington	WV	25715	**800-788-3858***	304-523-9415	315
Huntington's Disease Society of America (HDSA) 158 W 29th St 7th Fl	New York	NY	10001	**800-345-4372**	212-242-1968	48-17
Huntsman Corp 500 Huntsman Way *NYSE: HUN*	Salt Lake City	UT	84108	**800-421-2411**	801-584-5700	594-2
Huntsville Botanical Garden 4747 Bob Wallace Ave	Huntsville	AL	35805	**877-930-4447**	256-830-4447	98
Huntsville Museum of Art 300 Church St S	Huntsville	AL	35801	**800-786-9095**	256-535-4350	509
Huntsville Times 2317 S Memorial Pkwy	Huntsville	AL	35801	**800-239-5271**	256-532-4000	522-2
Huntsville-Walker County Chamber of Commerce 1327 11th St	Huntsville	TX	77340	**800-289-0389**	936-295-8113	137
Huntsville/Madison County Convention & Visitor's Bureau 500 Church St	Huntsville	AL	35801	**800-772-2348**	256-551-2230	205
Huntwood Industries 3808 N Sullivan Rd Bldg 26	Spokane	WA	99216	**800-873-7350**	509-924-5858	116
Huot Mfg Co 550 Wheeler St N	Saint Paul	MN	55104	**800-832-3838**	651-646-1869	314-1
Hurco Cos Inc 1 Technology Way *NASDAQ: HURC* ■ *Sales	Indianapolis	IN	46268	**800-634-2416***	317-293-5309	447
Hurco Design & Mfg 200 W 33rd St	Ogden	UT	84401	**877-859-6840**	801-394-9471	281
Hurd Corp PO Box 1450	Greeneville	TN	37744	**800-877-2581**	423-787-8800	345
Hurd Millwork Co Inc 575 S Whelan Ave	Medford	WI	54451	**800-433-4873**	715-748-2011	234
Huron Chamber & Visitors Bureau 15 4th St SW	Huron	SD	57350	**800-487-6673**	605-352-0000	205
Huron Insurance Co 355 Maple Ave	Harleysville	PA	19438	**800-523-6344**	215-256-5000	384-4
Huron Machine Products Inc 228 SW 21st Terr	Fort Lauderdale	FL	33312	**800-327-8186**	954-587-4541	484
Huron Valley Steel Corp 41000 E Huron River Dr	Belleville	MI	48111	**800-783-3404**	734-697-3400	709
Hurst Awning Co Inc 6865 NW 36th Ave	Miami	FL	33147	**800-327-0905**		690
Hurst Chemical Co 2500 N San Fernando Rd	Los Angeles	CA	90065	**800-723-2004**	323-223-4121	616
Hurst Farm Supply Inc 105 Ave D	Abernathy	TX	79311	**800-535-8903**	806-298-2541	270
Hurst Office Suppliers Inc 257 E Short St	Lexington	KY	40507	**800-926-4423**	859-255-4422	524
Hurst Place 555 Sanatorium Rd	Hamilton	ON	L8N3Z5	**888-521-8300**	905-521-8300	454
Hurtt Fabricating Corp PO Box 128	Marceline	MO	64658	**800-844-3010**	660-376-3501	473
Hurwitz-Mintz Furniture Co 227 Chartres St	New Orleans	LA	70130	**800-597-9555**	504-568-9555	316
Huse Publishing Co PO Box 977	Norfolk	NE	68702	**800-672-8351**	402-371-1020	623-8
Hush Puppies Co 9341 Courtland Dr NE	Rockford	MI	49351	**800-626-8696**	616-866-5500	296
Husman Snack Foods Co 1621 Moore St	Cincinnati	OH	45202	**800-487-6267**	513-621-5614	291-35
Husqvarna Turf Care Co 700 Park St	Beatrice	NE	68310	**877-368-8873**	402-223-2391	420
Hussey Copper Ltd 100 Washington St	Leetsdale	PA	15056	**800-733-8866**	724-251-4200	476
Hussey Seating Co 38 Dyer St Ext	North Berwick	ME	03906	**800-341-0401**	207-676-2271	314-3
Hussmann Corp 12999 St Charles Rock Rd	Bridgeton	MO	63044	**800-879-1152**	314-291-2000	650
Husson College 1 College Cir	Bangor	ME	04401	**800-448-7766**	207-941-7000	163
Hutchens Industries Inc 215 N Patterson Ave	Springfield	MO	65802	**800-654-8824**	417-862-5012	60
Hutchens Industries Inc Steel Process Div 215 N Patterson Ave	Springfield	MO	65802	**800-654-8824**	417-935-2276	709
Hutchings Court Reporters LLC 5701 S Eastern Ave Suite 530	Los Angeles	CA	90040	**800-697-3210**	323-888-6300	436
Hutchinson Community College 1300 N Plum St	Hutchinson	KS	67501	**800-289-3501**	620-665-3500	160
Hutchinson Island Beach Resort & Marina. Marriott 555 NE Ocean Blvd	Stuart	FL	34996	**800-775-5936**	772-225-3700	655
Hutchinson News 300 W 2nd St	Hutchinson	KS	67504	**800-766-3311**	620-694-5700	522-2
Hutchinson Seal Corp National O-Ring Div 11634 Patton Rd	Downey	CA	90241	**800-421-3837**	562-862-8163	321
Hutchinson/Mayrath Industries 514 W Crawford St	Clay Center	KS	67432	**800-523-6993**	785-632-3133	269
Hutchinson/Reno County Chamber of Commerce 117 N Walnut St	Hutchinson	KS	67501	**800-691-4262**	620-662-3391	137
Huther Brothers Inc 1290 University Ave	Rochester	NY	14607	**888-448-8437**	585-473-9462	746
Hutson Don Don Hutson Organization 516 Tennessee St Suite 219	Memphis	TN	38103	**800-647-9166**	901-767-0000	561
Hutson Don Organization 516 Tennessee St Suite 219	Memphis	TN	38103	**800-647-9166**	901-767-0000	753
Huttig Building Products Inc 555 Maryville University Dr *NYSE: HBP*	Saint Louis	MO	63141	**800-325-4466**	314-216-2600	489
Hutton Communications Inc 2520 Marsh Ln	Carrollton	TX	75006	**800-435-9313**	972-417-0250	245
HW Baker Linen Co Inc 500 Corporate Dr	Mahwah	NJ	07430	**800-631-0122**	201-825-2000	356

Name / Address	City	State	ZIP	Toll-Free	Phone	Class
HW Lochner Inc 20 N Wacker Dr Suite 1200	Chicago	IL	60606	**800-327-7346**	312-372-7346	258
HW Wilson Co 950 University Ave	Bronx	NY	10452	**800-367-6770**	718-588-8400	623-2
Hy-Ko Products Co 60 Meadow Ln	Northfield	OH	44067	**800-292-0550**	330-467-7446	692
Hy-Tape International Inc PO Box 540	Patterson	NY	12563	**800-248-0101**	845-878-4848	469
Hyannis Area Chamber of Commerce 1481 Rt 132 PO Box 100	Hyannis	MA	02601	**800-449-6647**	508-362-5230	137
Hyatt Arlington 1325 Wilson Blvd	Arlington	VA	22209	**800-233-1234**	703-525-1234	373
Hyatt on Capitol Square 75 E State St	Columbus	OH	43215	**800-233-1234**	614-228-1234	373
Hyatt Charlotte 5501 Carnegie Blvd	Charlotte	NC	28209	**800-233-1234**	704-554-1234	373
Hyatt Deerfield 1750 Lake Cook Rd	Deerfield	IL	60015	**800-233-1234**	847-945-3400	373
Hyatt Dorado Beach Resort & Country Club Hwy 693	Dorado	PR	00646	**800-233-1234**	787-796-1234	655
Hyatt Dulles 2300 Dulles Corner Blvd	Herndon	VA	20171	**800-233-1234**	703-713-1234	373
Hyatt Fair Lakes 12777 Fair Lakes Cir	Fairfax	VA	22033	**800-233-1234**	703-818-1234	373
Hyatt at Fisherman's Wharf 555 N Point St	San Francisco	CA	94133	**800-233-1234**	415-563-1234	373
Hyatt Gold Passport Program PO Box 27089	Omaha	NE	68127	**800-544-9288**		371
Hyatt Grand Champions Resort 44-600 Indian Wells Ln	Indian Wells	CA	92210	**800-233-1234**	760-341-1000	655
Hyatt. Grand Victoria Casino & Resort by 600 Grand Victoria Dr	Rising Sun	IN	47040	**800-472-6311**	812-438-1234	133
Hyatt Harborside 101 Harborside Dr	Boston	MA	02128	**800-233-1234**	617-568-1234	373
Hyatt Hotel. Rickeys - A 4219 El Camino Real	Palo Alto	CA	94306	**800-233-1234**	650-493-8000	373
Hyatt Hotels Corp 71 S Walker Dr	Chicago	IL	60606	**800-233-1234**	312-750-1234	369
Grand Hyatt Hotels 71 S Walker Dr	Chicago	IL	60606	**800-233-1234**	312-750-1234	369
Hyatt Regency Hotels 71 S Walker Dr	Chicago	IL	60606	**800-233-1234**	312-750-1234	369
Park Hyatt Hotels 71 S Walker Dr	Chicago	IL	60606	**800-233-1234**	312-750-1234	369
Hyatt Key West Resort & Marina 601 Front St	Key West	FL	33040	**800-554-9288**	305-296-9900	655
Hyatt Lisle 1400 Corporetum Dr	Lisle	IL	60532	**800-233-1234**	630-852-1234	373
Hyatt Orlando 6375 W Irlo Bronson Memorial Hwy	Kissimmee	FL	34747	**800-233-1234**	407-396-1234	373
Hyatt on Printer's Row 500 S Dearborn St	Chicago	IL	60605	**800-233-1234**	312-986-1234	373
Hyatt Regency Boston 1 Ave de Lafayette	Boston	MA	02111	**800-233-1234**	617-912-1234	373
Hyatt Regency Coconut Point Resort & Spa 5001 Coconut Rd	Bonita Springs	FL	34134	**800-233-1234**	239-444-1234	655
Hyatt Regency Grand Cypress Resort 1 Grand Cypress Blvd	Orlando	FL	32836	**800-233-1234**	407-239-1234	655
Hyatt Regency Hill Country Resort 9800 Hyatt Resort Dr	San Antonio	TX	78251	**800-233-1234**	210-647-1234	655
Hyatt Regency Hotels 71 S Walker Dr	Chicago	IL	60606	**800-233-1234**	312-750-1234	369
Hyatt Regency Huntington Beach 21100 Pacific Coast Hwy	Huntington Beach	CA	92648	**800-233-1234**	714-698-1234	373
Hyatt Regency Jacksonville Riverfront 225 Coast Line Dr	Jacksonville	FL	32202	**800-233-1234**	904-588-1234	373
Hyatt Regency Kauai Resort & Spa 1571 Poipu Rd	Koloa	HI	96756	**800-233-1234**	808-742-1234	655
Hyatt Regency Lake Las Vegas Resort 101 MonteLago Blvd	Henderson	NV	89011	**800-233-1234**	702-567-1234	655
Hyatt Regency Lake Tahoe Resort & Casino 111 Country Club Dr	Incline Village	NV	89451	**800-233-1234**	775-832-1234	655
Hyatt Regency Maui Resort & Spa 200 Nohea Kai Dr	Lahaina	HI	96761	**800-233-1234**	808-661-1234	655
Hyatt Regency Newport Beach 1107 Jamboree Rd	Newport Beach	CA	92660	**800-233-1234**	949-729-1234	373
Hyatt Regency Pier 66 2301 SE 17th St Cswy Pier 66	Fort Lauderdale	FL	33316	**800-233-1234**	954-525-6666	655
Hyatt Regency Scottsdale Resort at Gainey Ranch 7500 E Doubletree Ranch Rd	Scottsdale	AZ	85258	**800-233-1234**	480-991-3388	655
Hyatt Regency Tamaya Resort & Spa 1300 Tuyuna Trail	Santa Ana Pueblo	NM	87004	**800-233-1234**	505-867-1234	655
Hyatt Regency Waikiki Resort & Spa 2424 Kalakaua Ave	Honolulu	HI	96815	**800-233-1234**	808-923-1234	655
Hyatt Rosemont 6350 N River Rd	Rosemont	IL	60018	**800-233-1234**	847-518-1234	373
Hyatt Sainte Claire 302 S Market St	San Jose	CA	95113	**800-233-1234**	408-298-1230	373
Hyatt San Jose 1740 N 1st St	San Jose	CA	95112	**800-975-1234**	408-993-1234	373
Hyatt Sarasota 1000 Blvd of the Arts	Sarasota	FL	34236	**800-233-1234**	941-953-1234	373
Hyatt Vacation Ownership Inc 450 Carillon Pkwy Suite 210 *Resv	Saint Petersburg	FL	33716	**800-926-4447***	727-803-9400	738
Hyatt Valencia & Santa Clarita Conference Center 24500 Town Center Dr	Valencia	CA	91355	**800-233-1234**	661-799-1234	373
Hyatt Vineyard Creek Hotel & Spa 170 Railroad St	Santa Rosa	CA	95401	**800-233-1234**	707-636-7100	373
Hyatt West Hollywood 8401 Sunset Blvd	West Hollywood	CA	90069	**800-233-1234**	323-656-1234	373
Hyatt Westlake Plaza in Thousand Oaks 880 S Westlake Blvd	Westlake Village	CA	91361	**800-233-1234**	805-557-1234	373
Hybridon Inc 345 Vassar St *AMEX: HBY*	Cambridge	MA	02139	**800-223-3771**	617-679-5500	654
Hycor Biomedical Inc 7272 Chapman Ave *Cust Svc	Garden Grove	CA	92841	**800-382-2527***	714-933-3000	229
Hyde Mfg Co 54 Eastford Rd	Southbridge	MA	01550	**800-872-4933**	508-764-4344	746
Hydratight Sweeney Products Inc 12508 E Briarwood Ave Unit 1-A *Cust Svc	Englewood	CO	80112	**800-448-2524***	303-749-6000	747
Hydrel 12881 Bradley Ave	Sylmar	CA	91342	**800-750-9773**	818-362-9465	431
Hydril Co 3300 N Sam Houston Pkwy E *NASDAQ: HYDL*	Houston	TX	77032	**800-231-0023**	281-449-2000	526

Name / Address	City	State	Zip	Toll-Free	Phone	Class
Hydrite Chemical Co 300 N Patrick Blvd	Brookfield	WI	53045	**800-558-9566**	262-792-1450	144
Hydro Agri North America Inc 100 N Tampa St Suite 3200	Tampa	FL	33602	**800-944-9376**	813-222-5700	272
Hydro Aluminum North America 801 International Dr	Linthicum	MD	21090	**888-935-5752**	410-487-4500	481
HYDRO-FIT Inc 160 Madison St	Eugene	OR	97402	**800-346-7295***	541-484-4361	263
*Cust Svc						
Hydro One Inc 483 Bay St	Toronto	ON	M5G2P5	**888-664-9376**	416-345-5000	774
HydroCAD Software Solutions LLC 216 Chocorua Mountain Hwy	Chocorua	NH	03817	**800-927-7246**	603-323-8666	176-8
HydroChem Industrial Services Inc 900 Georgia Ave	Deer Park	TX	77536	**800-934-9376**	713-393-5600	150
Hydro/Kirby Agri Service Inc PO Box 6277	Lancaster	PA	17607	**800-745-7524**	717-299-2541	276
Hydromat Inc 11600 Adie Rd	Saint Louis	MO	63043	**888-432-0070**	314-432-4644	447
Hydron Technologies Inc 2201 W Sample Rd Bldg 9 Suite 7B	Pompano Beach	FL	33073	**800-449-3766**	954-861-6400	211
Hydroseal Valve Co Inc 1610 US Hwy 259 N	Kilgore	TX	75662	**800-256-8574**	903-984-8574	776
Hydrotex Inc 1825 Monetary Ln Suite 100	Carrollton	TX	75006	**800-527-9439**	972-389-8500	530
Hygenic Corp 1245 Home Ave	Akron	OH	44310	**800-321-2135**	330-633-8460	226
Hygolet Inc 349 SE 2nd Ave	Deerfield Beach	FL	33441	**800-494-6538**	954-481-8601	597
Hygrade Business Group Inc 232 Entin Rd	Clifton	NJ	07014	**800-836-7714**	973-249-6700	111
Hygrade Metal Moulding Mfg Corp 1990 Highland Ave	Bethlehem	PA	18020	**800-645-9475**	610-866-2441	232
Hygrade Precision Technologies Inc 329 Cooke St	Plainville	CT	06062	**800-457-1666**	860-747-5773	745
Hylant Group 811 Madison Ave	Toledo	OH	43624	**800-449-5268**	419-255-1020	383
Hynes Harry Memorial Hospice 313 S Market St	Wichita	KS	67202	**800-767-4965**	316-265-9441	365
Hynes John B Veterans Memorial Convention Center 900 Boylston St	Boston	MA	02115	**800-845-8800**	617-954-2000	204
Hynix Semiconductor America Inc 3101 N 1st St	San Jose	CA	95134	**800-627-7978**	408-232-8000	686
Hyperactivity Disorder. Children & Adults with Attention-Deficit/ 8181 Professional Pl Suite 201	Landover	MD	20785	**800-233-4050**	301-306-7070	48-17
Hypercom Corp 2851 W Kathleen Rd	Phoenix	AZ	85053	**800-577-5501**	602-504-5000	603
NYSE: HYC						
HyperData Technology USA Corp 817 S Lemon Ave	Walnut	CA	91789	**800-786-3343**	909-468-2955	171-3
HyperFeed Technologies Inc 300 S Wacker Dr Suite 300	Chicago	IL	60606	**800-225-5657**	312-913-2800	520
NASDAQ: HYPR						
Hyperion Capital Management Inc 165 Broadway 36th Fl	New York	NY	10006	**800-497-3746**	212-549-8400	393
Hyperion Solutions Corp 1344 Crossman Ave	Sunnyvale	CA	94089	**800-858-1666**	408-744-9500	176-1
NASDAQ: HYSL						
Hypertension Diagnostics Inc 2915 Waters Rd Suite 108	Eagan	MN	55121	**888-785-7392**	651-687-9999	468
NASDAQ: HDII						
Hypertherm Inc PO Box 5010	Hanover	NH	03755	**800-643-0030**	603-643-3441	447
Hyphen Solutions Inc 5055 Keller Springs Rd Suite 200	Addison	TX	75001	**877-508-2547***	972-728-8100	176-10
*Cust Svc						
Hypnotist Examiners. American Council of 700 S Central Ave	Glendale	CA	91204	**800-894-9766**	818-242-1159	49-15
Hypopigmentation. National Organization for Albinism & PO Box 959	East Hampstead	NH	03826	**800-473-2310**	603-887-2310	48-17
Hypro 375 5th Ave NW	New Brighton	MN	55112	**800-424-9776***	651-766-6300	627
*Cust Svc						
Hyson Products 10367 Brecksville Rd	Brecksville	OH	44141	**800-876-4976**	440-526-5900	777
Hyster New England 159 Rangeway Rd	North Billerica	MA	01862	**800-234-5438**	978-670-3000	462
Hysterectomy Educational Resources & Services Foundation (HERS) 422 Bryn Mawr Ave	Bala Cynwyd	PA	19004	**888-750-4377**	610-667-7757	48-17
Hyundai Motor America 10550 Talbert Ave	Fountain Valley	CA	92728	**800-633-5151***	714-965-3000	59
*Cust Svc						
Hywet Stan Hall & Gardens 714 N Portage Path	Akron	OH	44403	**888-836-5533**	330-836-5533	509

I

Name / Address	City	State	Zip	Toll-Free	Phone	Class
I-Bus Corp 2391 Zanker Rd Suite 370	San Jose	CA	95131	**800-382-4229**	408-428-6100	613
I-Business Network LLC 2256 Northwest Pkwy Suite E	Marietta	GA	30067	**877-336-4426**	678-627-0646	39
I Can't Believe It's Yogurt 8300 Woodbine Ave 5th Fl	Markham	ON	L3R9Y7	**800-528-0727**	905-479-8762	657
I-CAR Inter-Industry Conference on Auto Collision Repair (I-CAR) 3701 Algonquin Rd Suite 400	Rolling Meadows	IL	60008	**800-422-7872**	847-590-1191	49-21
I-Flow Corp 20202 Windrow Dr	Lake Forest	CA	92630	**800-448-3569**	949-206-2700	469
NASDAQ: IFLO						
I-Go Van & Storage 9820 S 142nd St	Omaha	NE	68138	**800-228-9276**	402-891-1222	508
I & K Distributors Inc 1600 Gressel Dr	Delphos	OH	45833	**800-472-9920**	419-695-5015	292-11
I Levy & Assoc Inc 1630 Des Peres Rd Suite 300	Saint Louis	MO	63131	**800-297-6717**	314-822-0810	176-11
I Rice & Co Inc 11500 Roosevelt Blvd Bldg D	Philadelphia	PA	19116	**800-232-6022**	215-673-7423	291-15
I Spiewak & Sons Inc 469 7th Ave 10th Fl	New York	NY	10018	**800-223-6850***	212-695-1620	153-19
*Cust Svc						
i-STAT Corp 104 Windsor Center Dr	East Windsor	NJ	08520	**800-827-7828**	609-443-9300	410
i2 Technologies Inc One i2 Pl 11701 Luna Rd	Dallas	TX	75234	**800-800-3288**	469-357-1000	176-1
IAAM (International Assn of Assembly Managers) 635 Fritz Dr	Coppell	TX	75019	**800-935-4226**	972-906-7441	49-12
IABC (International Assn of Business Communicators) 1 Hallidie Plaza Suite 600	San Francisco	CA	94102	**800-766-4222**	415-544-4700	49-12
IAC Industries 895 Beacon St	Brea	CA	92821	**800-229-1422**	714-990-8997	314-1
IACP (International Academy of Compounding Pharmacists) PO Box 1365	Sugar Land	TX	77487	**800-927-4227**	281-933-8400	49-8
IACP (International Assn of Chiefs of Police) 515 N Washington St	Alexandria	VA	22314	**800-843-4227**	703-836-6767	49-7
IAEI (International Assn of Electrical Inspectors) 901 Waterfall Way Suite 602	Richardson	TX	75080	**800-786-4234**	972-235-1455	49-3
IAFE (International Assn of Fairs & Expositions) 3043 E Cairo	Springfield	MO	65802	**800-516-0313**	417-862-5771	48-23
IAHB (Institute for the Advancement of Human Behavior) 4370 Alpine Rd Suite 209	Portola Valley	CA	94028	**800-258-8411**	650-851-8411	49-8
IAMFC (International Assn of Marriage & Family Counselors) c/o American Counseling Assn 5999 Stevenson Ave	Alexandria	VA	22304	**800-545-2223**	703-823-9800	49-15
IAMGOLD Corp 220 Bay St 5th Fl	Toronto	ON	M5J2W4	**888-464-9999**	416-360-4710	492
AMEX: IAG						
Iams Co 7250 Poe Ave	Dayton	OH	45414	**800-525-4267***	937-898-7387	568
*Cust Svc						
IAPA (Inter American Press Assn) 1801 SW 3rd Ave 7th Fl	Miami	FL	33129	**877-747-4272**	305-634-2465	49-14
IAPA (International Airline Passengers Assn) 5204 Tennyson Pkwy	Plano	TX	75024	**800-821-4272**	972-404-9980	48-23
IAPES (International Assn of Workforce Professionals) 1801 Louisville Rd	Frankfort	KY	40601	**888-898-9960**	502-223-4459	49-12
IAPHC (International Assn of Printing House Craftsmen) 7042 Brooklyn Blvd	Minneapolis	MN	55429	**800-466-4274**	763-560-1620	49-16
IAPMO (International Assn of Plumbing & Mechanical Officials) 5001 E Philadelphia St	Ontario	CA	91761	**800-854-2766**	909-472-4100	49-7
IATAN (International Airlines Travel Agent Network) 300 Garden City Plaza Suite 342	Garden City	NY	11530	**800-294-2826**	516-663-6000	49-21
IATSE (International Alliance of Theatrical Stage Employees Moving Picture Technicians) 1430 Broadway 20th Fl	New York	NY	10018	**800-223-6872**	212-730-1770	405
IATSE PAC 1430 Broadway 20th Fl	New York	NY	10018	**800-223-6972**	212-730-1770	604
IB Goodman Mfg Co 120 E 3rd St	Newport	KY	41071	**800-543-1945**	859-261-2086	401
IBA (Institute of Business Appraisers) 6950 Cypress Rd Suite 209	Plantation	FL	33317	**800-299-4130**	954-584-1144	49-17
IBC Group Inc 730 W McNab Rd	Fort Lauderdale	FL	33309	**800-776-1166**	954-968-2333	463
Iberia Air Cargo 6065 NW 18th St Bldg 716D	Miami	FL	33122	**800-221-6002**	305-526-6771	13
Iberia Airlines Plus Program 5835 Blue Lagoon Dr Suite 350	Miami	FL	33126	**800-721-4122**	305-267-7747	27
Iberia Airlines of Spain 5835 Blue Lagoon Dr Suite 350	Miami	FL	33126	**800-772-4642**	305-267-7747	26
IBERIABANK 1101 E Admiral Doyle Dr	New Iberia	LA	70560	**888-447-0770**	337-365-2361	71
IBERIABANK Corp 1101 E Admiral Doyle Dr	New Iberia	LA	70560	**800-968-0801**	337-365-2361	355-2
NASDAQ: IBKC						
Iberville Parish Chamber of Commerce 23675 Church St	Plaquemine	LA	70764	**888-687-3560**	225-687-3560	137
IBHS (Institute for Business & Home Safety) 4775 E Fowler Ave	Tampa	FL	33617	**866-675-4247**	813-286-3400	49-9
iBill (Internet Billing Co Ltd) 2200 SW 10th St	Deerfield Beach	FL	33442	**888-237-1764**	954-363-4400	250
IBM (International Business Machines Corp) New Orchard Rd	Armonk	NY	10504	**800-426-4968**	914-766-1900	171-3
NYSE: IBM						
IBM Palisades Conference Center Rt 9 W	Palisades	NY	10964	**800-426-0889**	845-732-6000	370
IBMA (Independent Battery Manufacturers Assn) 401 N Michigan Ave 24th Fl	Chicago	IL	60611	**800-237-6126**	312-245-1074	49-13
IBS (International Bible Society) 1820 Jet Stream Dr	Colorado Springs	CO	80921	**800-524-1588***	719-488-9200	48-20
*Cust Svc						
IBS Electronics Inc 3506 Lake Center Dr Unit D	Santa Ana	CA	92704	**800-527-2888**	714-751-6633	245
IBT Inc 9400 W 55th St	Merriam	KS	66203	**800-332-2114**	913-677-3151	378
IbuyDigital.com Inc 252 Conover St	Brooklyn	NY	11231	**866-243-4289**	646-218-2200	35
IBWA (International Bottled Water Assn) 1700 Diagonal Rd Suite 650	Alexandria	VA	22314	**800-928-3711**	703-683-5213	49-6
IC Corp 751 S Harkrider St	Conway	AR	72032	**800-993-7686***	501-327-7761	505
*Cust Svc						
IC Isaacs & Co Inc 3840 Bank St	Baltimore	MD	21224	**800-537-5995**	410-342-8200	153-3
ICA (International Chiropractors Assn) 1110 N Glebe Rd Suite 1000	Arlington	VA	22201	**800-423-4690**	703-528-5000	49-8
iCAD inc 4 Townsend W Suite 17	Nashua	NH	03063	**800-444-6983**	603-882-5200	375
NASDAQ: ICAD						
ICAN (International Cesarean Awareness Network Inc) 1304 Kingsdale Ave	Redondo Beach	CA	90278	**800-686-4226**	310-542-6400	48-17
ICAP Family of Funds PO Box 2160	Milwaukee	WI	53201	**888-221-4227**		517
Icare Industries Inc 4399 35th St N	Saint Petersburg	FL	33714	**800-648-7463**	727-812-3000	531
ICC Chemical Corp 460 Park Ave	New York	NY	10022	**800-422-1720**	212-521-1700	144
ICC Industries Inc 460 Park Ave	New York	NY	10022	**800-422-1720**	212-521-1700	142
ICCA (Independent Computer Consultants Assn) 11131 S Towne Sq Suite F	Saint Louis	MO	63123	**800-774-4222**	314-892-1675	48-9

Name / Address	City	State	ZIP	Toll-Free	Phone	Class
ICCL (International Council of Cruise Lines) 2111 Wilson Blvd 8th Fl	Arlington	VA	22201	**800-595-9338**	703-522-8463	48-23
ICCP (Institute for Certification of Computing Professionals) 2350 E Devon Ave Suite 115	Des Plaines	IL	60018	**800-843-8227**	847-299-4227	48-9
ICE (US Immigration & Customs Enforcement) 425 'I' St NW	Washington	DC	20536	**866-347-2423**	202-514-1900	336-7
Ice Age Park & Trail Foundation 207 E Buffalo St Suite 515	Milwaukee	WI	53202	**800-227-0046**	414-278-8518	48-23
ICE-CAP Inc 275 Grand Blvd	Westbury	NY	11590	**800-782-2765**	516-704-0200	15
Ice Cream Specialties 8419 Hanley Industrial Dr	Saint Louis	MO	63144	**800-662-7550**	314-962-2550	291-25
ICE Gallery 10030 N 25th Ave	Phoenix	AZ	85021	**888-320-4234**	602-395-1995	760
Ice-O-Matic 11100 E 45th Ave	Denver	CO	80239	**800-423-3367**	303-371-3737	650
ICEA (International Childbirth Education Assn) 8060 26th Ave SE	Minneapolis	MN	55425	**800-624-4934***	952-854-8660	48-17
*Sales						
Icelandair 5950 Symphony Woods Rd Suite 410	Columbia	MD	21044	**800-223-5500**	410-715-1600	26
Icelandair Customer Club 5950 Symphony Woods Rd Suite 410	Columbia	MD	21044	**800-223-5500**	800-757-7242	27
Icemakers Inc PO Box 321755	Birmingham	AL	35232	**800-467-2181**	205-591-2791	374
ICFA (International Cemetery & Funeral Assn) 1895 Preston White Dr Suite 220	Reston	VA	20191	**800-645-7700**	703-391-8400	49-4
ICFG (International Church of the Foursquare Gospel) 1910 W Sunset Blvd Suite 200	Los Angeles	CA	90026	**888-635-4234**	213-989-4200	48-20
ICG Communications Inc 161 Inverness Dr W	Englewood	CO	80112	**888-424-1144**	303-414-5000	387
ICG/Holliston PO Box 478	Kingsport	TN	37662	**800-251-0251**	423-357-6141	730-2
ICI American Holdings Inc 10 Finderne Ave	Bridgewater	NJ	08807	**800-998-9986**	908-203-2800	143
ICI Paints North America 925 Euclid Ave	Cleveland	OH	44115	**800-221-4100***	216-344-8000	540
*Cust Svc						
ICIA (International Communications Industries Assn) 11242 Waples Mill Rd Suite 200	Fairfax	VA	22030	**800-659-7469**	703-273-7200	49-20
iCIMS Inc 1301 Concord Ctr Suite 2 Hwy 36	Hazlet	NJ	07730	**800-889-4422**	732-847-1941	176-1
ICLA (International Collegiate Licensing Assn) 24651 Detroit Rd	Westlake	OH	44145	**800-996-2232**	440-892-4000	48-22
ICM Asset Management Inc 601 W Main Ave Suite 600	Spokane	WA	99201	**800-488-4075**	509-455-3588	393
ICM Corp 4025 Steve Reynolds Blvd Suite 120	Norcross	GA	30093	**800-654-8013***	770-381-2947	173
*Cust Svc						
ICM School of Business 10 Wood St	Pittsburgh	PA	15222	**800-441-5222**	412-261-2647	158
ICO Inc 5333 Westheimer Rd Suite 600	Houston	TX	77056	**877-777-0877**	713-351-4100	528
NASDAQ: ICOC						
ICOI (International Congress of Oral Implantologists) 248 Lorraine Ave 3rd Fl	Upper Montclair	NJ	07043	**800-442-0525**	973-783-6300	49-8
icollector.com 1963 Lougheed Hwy	Coquitlam	BC	V3K3T8	**866-313-0123**	604-521-3369	51
ICOM (Internet Communications) 303 Peachtree Ctr Ave Suite 500	Atlanta	GA	30303	**877-504-0091**	404-260-2477	795
ICOM America Inc 2380 116th Ave NE	Bellevue	WA	98004	**800-306-1356**	425-454-8155	633
ICON Exhibits 8333 Clinton Pk Dr	Fort Wayne	IN	46825	**800-320-4266**	260-483-6441	230
ICON Health & Fitness Inc 1500 S 1000 West	Logan	UT	84321	**800-999-3756**	435-750-5000	263
Icon Identity Solutions 1418 Elmhurst Rd	Elk Grove Village	IL	60007	**800-633-8181**	847-364-2250	692
Iconixx Corp 5301 Hollister Suite 400	Houston	TX	77040	**877-426-6499**	713-934-0200	178
IconMedialab Inc 22 4th St 9th Fl	San Francisco	CA	94103	**866-426-6871**	415-278-0471	7
ICPI (Interlocking Concrete Pavement Institute) 1444 'I' St NW Suite 700	Washington	DC	20005	**800-241-3652**	202-712-9036	49-3
ICPM (Institute of Certified Professional Managers) James Madison University MSC 5504	Harrisonburg	VA	22807	**800-568-4120**	540-568-3247	49-12
ICS Blount Inc 4909 SE International Way	Portland	OR	97222	**800-321-1240**	503-653-8881	670
ICS Telecom Inc 125 Highpower Rd	Rochester	NY	14623	**800-836-8677**	585-427-7000	245
ICSA (International Customer Service Assn) 401 N Michigan Ave 22nd Fl	Chicago	IL	60611	**800-360-4272**	312-321-6800	49-12
ICT Group Inc 100 Brandywine Blvd	Newtown	PA	18940	**800-799-6880**	215-757-0200	722
NASDAQ: ICTG						
ICTA (International Center for Technology Assessment) 660 Pennsylvania Ave SE Suite 302	Washington	DC	20003	**800-600-6664**	202-547-9359	49-19
ICTV Inc 14600 Winchester Blvd	Los Gatos	CA	95032	**800-926-8398**	408-364-9200	633
ICU Medical Inc 951 Calle Amanecer	San Clemente	CA	92673	**800-824-7890**	949-366-2183	469
NASDAQ: ICUI						
ICW Group 11455 El Camino Real	San Diego	CA	92130	**800-877-1111**	858-350-2400	384-4
ICWM (Institute of Caster & Wheel Manufacturers) 8720 Red Oak Blvd Suite 201	Charlotte	NC	28217	**800-345-1815**	704-676-1190	49-13
IDA (International Dyslexia Assn) 8600 LaSalle Rd Chester Bldg Suite 382	Baltimore	MD	21286	**800-222-3123**	410-296-0232	48-17
Idaho						
Arts Commission 2410 Old Penitentiary Rd	Boise	ID	83712	**800-278-3863**	208-334-2119	335
Crime Victims Compensation Program PO Box 83720	Boise	ID	83720	**800-950-2110**	208-334-6000	335
Economic Development Div PO Box 83720	Boise	ID	83720	**800-842-5858**	208-334-2470	335
State Government Information		ID		**877-443-3468**	208-334-2411	335
Tourism Div PO Box 83720	Boise	ID	83720	**800-842-5858**	208-334-2470	335
Idaho Assn of Realtors 1450 W Bannock St	Boise	ID	83702	**800-621-7553**	208-342-3585	642
Idaho Botanical Garden 2355 N Penitentiary Rd	Boise	ID	83712	**877-527-8233**	208-343-8649	98
Idaho County Light & Power Co-op PO Box 300	Grangeville	ID	83530	**877-212-0424**	208-983-1610	244
Idaho Democratic Party PO Box 445	Boise	ID	83701	**800-542-4737**	208-336-1815	605-1
Idaho Falls (Greater) Chamber of Commerce 630 W Broadway	Idaho Falls	ID	83402	**866-365-6943**	208-523-1010	137
Idaho Fresh-Pak Inc DBA Idahoan Foods 529 N 3500 East PO Box 130	Lewisville	ID	83431	**800-635-6100**	208-754-4686	291-18
Idaho Historical Museum 610 N Julia Davis Dr	Boise	ID	83702	**877-653-4367**	208-334-2120	509
Idaho Lions Eye Bank 1055 N Curtis Rd	Boise	ID	83706	**800-546-6889**	208-367-2400	265
Idaho National Engineering & Environmental Laboratory (INEEL) Communications & Public Affairs 2525 Fremont Avenue PO Box 1625	Idaho Falls	ID	83415	**800-708-2680**	208-526-0111	654
Idaho-Pacific Corp 4723 E 100 North PO Box 478	Ririe	ID	83443	**800-238-5503***	208-538-6971	291-18
*Sales						
Idaho Pacific Lumber Co (IdaPac) 370 N Benjamin Ln Suite 120	Boise	ID	83704	**800-231-2310**	208-375-8052	190-3
Idaho Power Co 1221 W Idaho St	Boise	ID	83702	**800-488-6151**	208-388-2200	774
Idaho Public Television (IPTV) 1455 N Orchard St	Boise	ID	83706	**800-543-6868**	208-373-7220	620
Idaho Republican State Committee PO Box 2267	Boise	ID	83701	**800-658-3898**	208-343-6405	605-2
Idaho State Journal 305 S Arthur	Pocatello	ID	83204	**800-275-0774**	208-232-4161	522-2
Idaho Statesman 1200 N Curtis Rd	Boise	ID	83706	**800-635-8934**	208-377-6400	522-2
Idaho Steel Products Co 255 E Anderson St	Idaho Falls	ID	83401	**800-633-0022**	208-522-1275	293
IdaPac (Idaho Pacific Lumber Co) 370 N Benjamin Ln Suite 120	Boise	ID	83704	**800-231-2310**	208-375-8052	190-3
IDC (International Data Corp) 5 Speen St	Framingham	MA	01701	**800-343-4935**	508-872-8200	458
Idea Channel 1502 Powell Ave	Erie	PA	16505	**800-388-0662**	814-464-9068	725
IDEA Inc 10455 Pacific Ctr Ct	San Diego	CA	92121	**800-999-4332**	858-535-8979	48-22
Idea Integration Corp 1 Independent Dr 2nd Fl	Jacksonville	FL	32202	**800-433-2206**	904-360-2700	796
Ideal Bias Binding Corp 1637 N Main St	Fall River	MA	02720	**800-532-6600**	508-673-3212	730-5
Ideal Chemical & Supply Co 4025 Air Park St	Memphis	TN	38118	**800-232-6776**	901-363-7720	144
Ideal Clamp 3200 Parker Dr	Saint Augustine	FL	32084	**800-221-0100**	904-829-1000	345
Ideal Fastener Corp PO Box 548	Oxford	NC	27565	**800-334-6653**	919-693-3115	583
Ideal Industries Inc Becker Pl	Sycamore	IL	60178	**800-435-0705***	815-895-5181	804
*Cust Svc						
Ideal Tape Co 1400 Middlesex St	Lowell	MA	01851	**800-284-3325**	978-458-6833	469
Idealab 130 W Union St	Pasadena	CA	91103	**888-433-3522**	626-585-6900	779
IDEAS Simulation Inc 125 Clairemont Ave Suite 570	Decatur	GA	30030	**800-567-4332**	404-370-1350	694
Ideas Unlimited for Editors Newsletter 9700 Philadelphia Ct	Lanham	MD	20706	**800-774-6809**	301-731-5200	521-11
IDEC Corp 1175 Elko Dr	Sunnyvale	CA	94089	**800-262-4332**	408-747-0550	202
Identatronics Inc 165 Lively Blvd	Elk Grove Village	IL	60007	**800-323-5403***	847-437-2654	580
*Cust Svc						
IDenticard Systems Inc 40 Citation Ln	Lancaster	PA	17601	**800-233-0298**	717-569-5797	681
Identification & Mobility. AIM Inc - Assn for Automatic 125 Warrendale-Bayne Rd	Warrendale	PA	15086	**800-338-0206**	724-934-4470	49-19
Identigene Inc 5615 Kirby Dr Suite 800	Houston	TX	77005	**800-362-8973**	713-798-9510	408
Identity Genetics Inc 801 32nd Ave	Brookings	SD	57006	**800-861-1054**	605-697-5300	408
Idesign Greetings Inc 12020 W Ripley Ave	Milwaukee	WI	53226	**800-432-3301**	414-475-7176	130
IDEXX Laboratories Inc 1 IDEXX Dr	Westbrook	ME	04092	**800-932-4399**	207-856-0300	229
NASDAQ: IDXX						
IDEXX Pharmaceuticals Inc 1 Idexx Dr	Westbrook	ME	04092	**800-548-6733**	207-856-0300	574
IDF (Immune Deficiency Foundation) 40 W Chesapeake Ave Suite 308	Towson	MD	21204	**800-296-4433**	410-321-6647	48-17
iDirect Technologies Inc 10803 Parkridge Blvd	Reston	VA	20191	**888-362-5475**	703-648-8080	720
IE Discovery Inc 9101 Burnet Rd Suite 202	Austin	TX	78758	**800-656-8444**	512-833-5588	39
IEA ArcRon Div W 141 N 9501 Fountain Blvd	Menomonee Falls	WI	53051	**800-886-4151**	262-255-4150	688
IECA (Independent Educational Consultants Assn) 3251 Old Lee Hwy Suite 510	Fairfax	VA	22030	**800-808-4322**	703-591-4850	49-5
IEEE (Institute of Electrical & Electronics Engineers) 3 Park Ave 17th Fl	New York	NY	10016	**800-678-4333**	212-419-7900	49-19
IEEE Aerospace & Electronics Systems Society IEEE Operations Ctr 445 Hoes Ln	Piscataway	NJ	08854	**800-678-4333**	732-981-0060	49-19
IEEE Antennas & Propagation Society (APS) IEEE Operations Ctr 445 Hoes Ln	Piscataway	NJ	08854	**800-678-4333**	732-981-0060	49-19
IEEE Broadcast Technology Society (BTS) IEEE Operations Ctr 445 Hoes Ln	Piscataway	NJ	08854	**800-678-4333**	732-981-0060	49-19
IEEE Circuits & Systems Society (CAS) IEEE Operations Ctr 445 Hoes Ln	Piscataway	NJ	08854	**800-678-4333**	732-981-0060	49-19
IEEE Communications Society (COMSOC) IEEE Operations Ctr 445 Hoes Ln	Piscataway	NJ	08854	**800-678-4333**	732-981-0060	49-19
IEEE Components Packaging & Manufacturing Technology Society 445 Hoes Ln PO Box 1331	Piscataway	NJ	08855	**800-678-4333**	732-562-5529	49-19

Name / Address	City	State	ZIP	Toll-Free	Phone	Class
IEEE Computer Graphics & Applications Magazine 10662 Los Vaqueros Cir	Los Alamitos	CA	90720	**800-272-6657**	714-821-8380	449-7
IEEE Computer Society Publications Office 10662 Los Vaqueros Cir	Los Alamitos	CA	90720	**800-272-6657**	714-821-8380	623-9
IEEE Consumer Electronics Society (CES) IEEE Operations Ctr 445 Hoes Ln	Piscataway	NJ	08854	**800-678-4333**	732-981-0060	49-19
IEEE Control Systems Society (CSS) IEEE Operations Ctr 445 Hoes Ln	Piscataway	NJ	08854	**800-678-4333**	732-981-0060	49-19
IEEE Dielectrics & Electrical Insulation Society IEEE Operations Ctr 445 Hoes Ln	Piscataway	NJ	08854	**800-678-4333**	732-981-0060	49-19
IEEE Education Society (ES) IEEE Operations Ctr 445 Hoes Ln	Piscataway	NJ	08854	**800-678-4333**	732-981-0060	49-19
IEEE Electromagnetic Compatibility Society (EMC) IEEE Operations Ctr 445 Hoes Ln	Piscataway	NJ	08854	**800-678-4333**	732-981-0060	49-19
IEEE Electron Devices Society (EDS) IEEE Operations Ctr 445 Hoes Ln	Piscataway	NJ	08854	**800-678-4333**	732-981-0060	49-19
IEEE Engineering Management Society (EMS) IEEE Operations Ctr 445 Hoes Ln	Piscataway	NJ	08854	**800-678-4333**	732-981-0060	49-19
IEEE Engineering in Medicine & Biology Society (EMB) IEEE Operations Ctr 445 Hoes Ln	Piscataway	NJ	08854	**800-678-4333**	732-981-0060	49-19
IEEE Geoscience & Remote Sensing Society (GRSS) IEEE Operations Ctr 445 Hoes Ln	Piscataway	NJ	08854	**800-678-4333**	732-981-0060	49-19
IEEE Industrial Electronics Society (IES) IEEE Operations Ctr 445 Hoes Ln	Piscataway	NJ	08854	**800-678-4333**	732-981-0060	49-19
IEEE Industry Applications Society IEEE Operations Ctr 445 Hoes Ln	Piscataway	NJ	08854	**800-678-4333**	732-981-0060	49-19
IEEE Information Theory Society (IT) IEEE Operations Ctr 445 Hoes Ln	Piscataway	NJ	08854	**800-678-4333**	732-981-0060	49-19
IEEE Instrumentation & Measurement Society (IM) IEEE Operations Ctr 445 Hoes Ln	Piscataway	NJ	08854	**800-678-4333**	732-981-0060	49-19
IEEE Lasers & Electro-Optics Society (LEOS) IEEE Operations Ctr 445 Hoes Ln	Piscataway	NJ	08854	**800-678-4333**	732-981-0060	49-19
IEEE Magnetics Society IEEE Operations Ctr 445 Hoes Ln	Piscataway	NJ	08854	**800-678-4333**	732-981-0060	49-19
IEEE Micro Magazine 10662 Los Vaqueros Cir	Los Alamitos	CA	90720	**800-272-6657**	714-821-8380	449-7
IEEE Microwave Theory & Techniques Society (MTT-S) IEEE Operations Ctr 445 Hoes Ln	Piscataway	NJ	08854	**800-678-4333**	732-981-0060	49-19
IEEE Neural Networks Society (NNS) IEEE Operations Ctr 445 Hoes Ln	Piscataway	NJ	08854	**800-678-4333**	732-981-0060	49-19
IEEE Nuclear & Plasma Sciences Society (NPSS) IEEE Operations Ctr 445 Hoes Ln	Piscataway	NJ	08854	**800-678-4333**	732-981-0060	49-19
IEEE Oceanic Engineering Society (OES) IEEE Operations Ctr 445 Hoes Ln	Piscataway	NJ	08854	**800-678-4333**	732-981-0060	49-19
IEEE Power Electronics Society (PELS) IEEE Operations Ctr 445 Hoes Ln	Piscataway	NJ	08854	**800-678-4333**	732-981-0060	49-19
IEEE Power Engineering Society (PES) IEEE Operations Ctr 445 Hoes Ln	Piscataway	NJ	08854	**800-678-4333**	732-981-0060	49-19
IEEE Product Safety Engineering Society IEEE Operations Ctr 445 Hoes Ln	Piscataway	NJ	08854	**800-678-4333**	732-981-0060	49-19
IEEE Professional Communication Society (PCS) IEEE Operations Ctr 445 Hoes Ln	Piscataway	NJ	08854	**800-678-4333**	732-981-0060	49-19
IEEE Reliability Society (RS) IEEE Operations Ctr 445 Hoes Ln	Piscataway	NJ	08854	**800-678-4333**	732-981-0060	49-19
IEEE Robotics & Automation Society (RAS) IEEE Operations Ctr 445 Hoes Ln	Piscataway	NJ	08854	**800-678-4333**	732-981-0060	49-19
IEEE Signal Processing Society IEEE Operations Ctr 445 Hoes Ln	Piscataway	NJ	08854	**800-678-4333**	732-981-0060	49-19
IEEE Society on Social Implications of Technology (SSIT) IEEE Operations Ctr 445 Hoes Ln	Piscataway	NJ	08854	**800-678-4333**	732-981-0060	49-19
IEEE Solid State Circuits Society (SSCS) IEEE Operations Ctr 445 Hoes Ln	Piscataway	NJ	08854	**800-678-4333**	732-981-0060	49-19
IEEE Systems Man & Cybernetics Society (SMC) IEEE Operations Ctr 445 Hoes Ln	Piscataway	NJ	08854	**800-678-4333**	732-981-0060	49-19
IEEE Ultrasonics Ferroelectrics & Frequency Control Society IEEE Operations Ctr 445 Hoes Ln	Piscataway	NJ	08854	**800-678-4333**	732-981-0060	49-19
IEEE Vehicular Technology Society (VTS) IEEE Operations Ctr 445 Hoes Ln	Piscataway	NJ	08854	**800-678-4333**	732-981-0060	49-19
IEHA (International Executive Housekeepers Assn) 1001 Eastwind Dr Suite 301	Westerville	OH	43081	**800-200-6342**	614-895-7166	49-4
iEmployee 699 Fall River Ave	Seekonk	MA	02771	**800-884-6504**	508-336-4441	176-1
iEntertainment Network Inc 124 Quade Dr	Cary	NC	27513	**800-438-4263**	919-678-8301	176-6
iExplore Inc 954 W Washington Blvd Suite 3W	Chicago	IL	60607	**800-439-7567**	312-492-9443	762
IFA (International Franchise Assn) 1350 New York Ave NW Suite 900	Washington	DC	20005	**800-543-1038**	202-628-8000	49-18
IFAI (Industrial Fabrics Assn International) 1801 County Rd 'B' W	Roseville	MN	55113	**800-225-4324**	651-222-2508	49-13
IFAW (International Fund for Animal Welfare) 411 Main St PO Box 193	Yarmouth Port	MA	02675	**800-932-4329**	508-744-2000	48-3
IFCA International PO Box 810	Grandville	MI	49468	**800-347-1840**	616-531-1840	48-20
Ifco Systems 6829 Flintlock Rd	Houston	TX	77040	**800-771-1148**	713-332-6145	541
IFEBP (International Foundation of Employee Benefit Plans) 18700 W Bluemond Rd PO Box 69	Brookfield	WI	53008	**888-334-3327**	262-786-6700	49-12
IFG Corp 34 W 33rd St	New York	NY	10001	**800-930-9601**	212-629-9600	153-4
IFI (International Fabricare Institute) 12251 Tech Rd	Silver Spring	MD	20904	**800-638-2627**	301-622-1900	49-4
IFSEA (International Food Service Executives Assn) 836 San Bruno Ave	Henderson	NV	89015	**888-234-3732**	702-564-0997	49-6
IFT (Institute of Food Technologists) 525 W Van Buren St Suite 1000	Chicago	IL	60607	**800-438-3663**	312-782-8424	49-6
IGAF Worldwide 2250 Satellite Blvd Suite 115	Duluth	GA	30097	**800-272-4423**	678-417-7730	49-1
iGATE Corp 1000 Commerce Dr Parkridge 1 *NASDAQ: IGTE*	Pittsburgh	PA	15275	**800-627-8323**	412-506-1131	355-3
IGC-Medical Advances Inc 10437 Innovation Dr	Milwaukee	WI	53226	**800-657-0891**	414-258-3808	375
IGC Polycold Systems Inc 3800 Lakeville Hwy	Petaluma	CA	94954	**888-476-5926**	707-769-7000	15
Igel George J & Co Inc 2040 Alum Creek Dr	Columbus	OH	43207	**800-345-4435**	614-445-8421	188-5
IGI Earth Color Group 527 W 34th St	New York	NY	10001	**800-407-6449**	212-967-9720	615
Igloo Products Corp 777 Igloo Rd *Cust Svc	Katy	TX	77494	**800-324-2653***	713-465-2571	596
IGLTA (International Gay & Lesbian Travel Assn) 4331 N Federal Hwy Suite 304	Fort Lauderdale	FL	33308	**800-448-8550**	954-776-2626	48-23
IGN Entertainment Inc 8000 Marina Blvd 4th Fl	Brisbane	CA	94005	**800-994-2275**	415-508-2000	623-10
IGS (Industrial Gasket & Shim Co Inc) 200 Country Club Rd	Meadow Lands	PA	15347	**800-229-1447**	724-222-5800	321
IGSHPA (International Ground Source Heat Pump Assn) Oklahoma State University 374 Cordell S	Stillwater	OK	74078	**800-626-4747**	405-744-5175	49-13
IGT Inc 7115 Amigo St Suite 150	Las Vegas	NV	89119	**888-254-7568**	702-263-7588	317
IHC (Intermountain Health Care Inc) 36 S State St 22nd Fl *Hum Res	Salt Lake City	UT	84111	**800-843-7820***	801-442-2000	348
IHC Health Plans Inc PO Box 30192	Salt Lake City	UT	84130	**800-538-5038**	801-442-5000	384-3
IHC Home Care 2250 S 1300 W Suite A	Salt Lake City	UT	84119	**800-527-1118**	801-977-9900	365
IHETS (Indiana Higher Education Telecommunication System) 714 N Senate Ave	Indianapolis	IN	46202	**800-776-4438**	317-263-8900	620
IHFRA (International Home Furnishings Representatives Assn) 209 S Main St	High Point	NC	27260	**800-889-3920**	336-889-3920	49-18
ihispano.com 17 N State St Suite 1700	Chicago	IL	60602	**888-252-1220**		257
IHOP (International House of Pancakes) 450 N Brand Blvd 7th Fl	Glendale	CA	91203	**800-241-4467**	818-240-6055	657
IHOP Corp 450 N Brand Blvd 7th Fl *NYSE: IHP*	Glendale	CA	91203	**800-241-4467**	818-240-6055	656
IHRIM (International Assn for Human Resource Information Management) PO Box 1086	Burlington	MA	01803	**800-946-6363**	781-273-3697	49-12
IHRSA (International Health Racquet & Sportsclub Assn) 263 Summer St 8th Fl	Boston	MA	02210	**800-228-4772**	617-951-0055	48-22
IHS (International Hearing Society) 16880 Middlebelt Rd Suite 4	Livonia	MI	48154	**800-521-5247**	734-522-7200	48-17
IHS Energy Group 15 Inverness Way E	Englewood	CO	80112	**800-645-3282**	303-736-3000	176-10
IHS Group 15 Inverness Way E	Englewood	CO	80112	**800-320-4555**	303-790-0600	176-11
IHS Inc 5009 Rondo Dr	Fort Worth	TX	76106	**800-485-5577**	817-625-5577	798
IIABA (Independent Insurance Agents & Brokers of America Inc) 127 S Peyton St	Alexandria	VA	22314	**800-221-7917**	703-683-4422	49-9
IIDA (International Interior Design Assn) 13-500 Merchandise Mart	Chicago	IL	60654	**888-799-4432**	312-467-1950	48-4
IIE (Institute of Industrial Engineers) 3577 Parkway Ln Suite 200 *Cust Svc	Norcross	GA	30092	**800-494-0460***	770-449-0460	49-13
III (Insurance Information Institute) 110 William St 24th Fl	New York	NY	10038	**800-331-9146**	212-346-5500	49-9
IIMAK 310 Commerce Dr	Amherst	NY	14228	**888-464-4625**	716-691-6333	523
IIMC (International Institute of Municipal Clerks) 8331 Utica Ave Suite 200	Rancho Cucamonga	CA	91730	**800-251-1639**	909-944-4162	49-7
Iiyama North America Inc 65 West St Rd Suite 101-B	Warminster	PA	18974	**800-394-4335**	215-682-9050	171-4
IJ Co PO Box 51890	Knoxville	TN	37950	**800-251-9516**	865-970-7800	292-8
IKEA 496 W Germantown Pike	Plymouth Meeting	PA	19462	**800-434-4532**	610-834-0180	316
Ikegami Electronics USA Inc 37 Brook Ave	Maywood	NJ	07607	**800-368-9171**	201-368-9171	633
IKG Industries 1 Mack Ctr Dr *Cust Svc	Paramus	NJ	07652	**800-969-5600***	201-261-5600	482
IKON Office Solutions Inc 70 Valley Stream Pkwy *NYSE: IKN*	Malvern	PA	19355	**800-983-2898**	610-296-8600	113
Il Fornaio America Corp 770 Tamalpais Dr Suite 400	Corte Madera	CA	94925	**800-291-1505**	415-945-0500	657
ILA (Iowa Library Assn) 3636 Westown Pkwy Suite 202	West Des Moines	IA	50266	**800-452-5507**	515-273-5322	427
ILC Dover Inc 1 Moonwalker Rd	Frederica	DE	19946	**800-631-9567**	302-335-3911	566
ILD Telecommunications Inc 16200 Addison Rd Suite 180	Addison	TX	75001	**800-749-1229**	972-267-0100	721
Ilene Industries Inc 301 Stanley Blvd	Shelbyville	TN	37160	**800-251-1602**	931-684-8731	321

Name / Address	City	State	Zip	Toll-Free	Phone	Class
iLinc Communications Inc 2999 N 44th St Suite 650 *AMEX: ILC*	Phoenix	AZ	85018	**877-736-8347**	602-952-1200	174
Ilitch Holdings Inc 2211 Woodward Ave	Detroit	MI	48201	**800-722-3727**	313-983-6000	184
Illinois						
Arts Council 100 W Randolph St Suite 10-500	Chicago	IL	60601	**800-237-6994**	312-814-4831	335
Child Support Enforcement Div 509 S 6th St	Springfield	IL	62701	**800-447-4278**	217-524-4602	335
Crime Victims Services Div 100 W Randolf Rd 13th Fl	Chicago	IL	60601	**800-228-3368**	312-814-2581	335
Human Services Dept 100 S Grand Ave E 3rd Fl	Springfield	IL	62762	**800-843-6154**	217-557-1601	335
Lottery 101 W Jefferson St	Springfield	IL	62702	**800-252-1775**	217-524-5155	443
Mental Health Div 100 W Randolf St Suite 3-400	Chicago	IL	60601	**800-252-2923**	312-814-2811	335
Rehabilitation Services Office 100 S Grand Ave E 3rd Fl	Springfield	IL	62762	**800-641-3929**	217-557-2507	335
Revenue Dept 101 W Jefferson St	Springfield	IL	62702	**800-732-8866**	217-782-3336	335
Student Assistance Commission 1755 Lake Cook Rd	Deerfield	IL	60015	**800-899-4722**	847-948-8500	711
Tourism Bureau 100 W Randolph St Suite 3-400	Chicago	IL	60601	**800-226-6632**	312-814-4732	335
Veterans Affairs Dept 833 S Spring St	Springfield	IL	62794	**800-437-9824**	217-782-6641	335
Workers' Compensation Commission 100 W Randolph St 8th Fl	Chicago	IL	60601	**866-352-3033**	312-814-6611	335
Illinois American Historical Water Museum 100 Lorentz St	Peoria	IL	61614	**800-422-2782**	309-671-3701	509
Illinois Auto Electric Co 700 Enterprise St	Aurora	IL	60504	**800-683-9312**	630-862-3300	378
Illinois Capacitor Inc 3757 W Touhy Ave	Lincolnwood	IL	60712	**800-323-5420**	847-675-1760	252
Illinois Cereal Mills Inc 616 S Jefferson St *Sales	Paris	IL	61944	**800-331-1716***	217-465-5331	291-23
Illinois College 1101 W College Ave	Jacksonville	IL	62650	**866-464-5265**	217-245-3000	163
Illinois Glove Co 3701 Commercial Ave	Northbrook	IL	60062	**800-342-5458**	847-291-1700	153-8
Illinois Institute of Art 350 N Orleans St Suite 136-L	Chicago	IL	60654	**800-351-3450**	312-280-3500	163
Illinois Institute of Technology 10 W 33rd St	Chicago	IL	60616	**800-448-2329**	312-567-3025	163
Illinois International Port District 3600 E 95th St	Chicago	IL	60617	**800-843-7678**	773-646-4400	607
Illinois State Chamber of Commerce 311 S Wacker Dr Suite 1500	Chicago	IL	60606	**800-322-4722**	312-983-7100	138
Illinois State Medical Inter-Insurance Exchange (ISMIE) 20 N Michigan Ave Suite 700	Chicago	IL	60602	**800-782-4767**	312-782-2749	384-5
Illinois State University	Normal	IL	61790	**800-366-2478**	309-438-2111	163
Illinois Symphony Orchestra 524 1/2 Capitol Ave	Springfield	IL	62705	**800-401-7222**	217-522-2838	563-3
Illinois Tool Works Inc (ITW) 3600 W Lake Ave *NYSE: ITW*	Glenview	IL	60025	**800-724-6166**	847-724-7500	379
Illinois Tool Works Inc TACC Div 56 Air Station Industrial Pk	Rockland	MA	02370	**800-503-6991**	781-878-7015	3
Illinois Waste Management & Research Center 1 E Hazelwood Dr	Champaign	IL	61820	**800-407-0261**	217-333-8940	654
Illinois Wesleyan University PO Box 2900	Bloomington	IL	61702	**800-332-2498**	309-556-3031	163
Illumina Inc 9885 Towne Centre Dr *NASDAQ: ILMN*	San Diego	CA	92121	**800-809-4566**	858-202-4500	410
Illuminating Co 76 S Main St	Akron	OH	44308	**800-646-0400**	216-622-9800	774
Illuminations 775 Point Blvd	Petaluma	CA	94954	**800-226-3537**	707-769-2700	322
ILOG Inc 1080 Linda Vista Ave	Mountain View	CA	94043	**800-367-4564**	650-567-8000	176-2
ILSCO 4730 Madison Rd *Sales	Cincinnati	OH	45227	**800-776-9775***	513-533-6200	803
ILX Lightwave Corp 31950 E Frontage Rd	Bozeman	MT	59715	**800-459-9459**	406-586-1244	247
ILX Resorts Inc 2111 E Highland Ave Suite 210 *AMEX: ILX*	Phoenix	AZ	85016	**800-822-2589**	602-957-2777	738
IMA (Institute of Management Accountants Inc) 10 Paragon Dr	Montvale	NJ	07645	**800-638-4427**	201-573-9000	49-1
Image Checks Inc PO Box 548	Little Rock	AR	72203	**800-562-8768**		140
Image Entertainment Inc 20525 Nordhoff St Suite 200 *NASDAQ: DISK*	Chatsworth	CA	91311	**800-473-3475**	818-407-9100	500
Image Labs International 151 Evergreen Dr	Bozeman	MT	59715	**800-785-5995**	406-585-7225	176-8
Image National Inc 444 E Amity Rd	Boise	ID	83716	**800-592-8058**	208-345-4020	692
Image One Corp 13201 Capital Ave	Oak Park	MI	48237	**800-799-5377**	248-414-9955	616
Image Works 1679 Rt 212	Woodstock	NY	12498	**800-475-8801**	845-679-8500	582
ImageMax Inc 455 Pennsylvania Ave Suite 200	Fort Washington	PA	19034	**800-873-9426**	215-628-3600	223
ImagePoint Inc 445 S Gay St	Knoxville	TN	37902	**800-444-7446**	865-938-1511	692
ImageState New York 29 E 19th St 4th Fl	New York	NY	10003	**800-821-9600**	212-505-2500	582
ImageTek Corp 420 E Easy St Suite 2	Simi Valley	CA	93065	**800-584-2503**	805-584-2100	616
ImageWare Systems Inc 10883 Thornmint Rd *AMEX: IW*	San Diego	CA	92127	**800-842-4199**	858-673-8600	176-10
Imaging Assn. Digital Printing & 10015 Main St	Fairfax	VA	22031	**888-385-3588**	703-385-1339	49-16
Imaging Assn. Specialty Graphic 10015 Main St	Fairfax	VA	22031	**888-385-3588**	703-385-1335	49-16
Imaging Diagnostic Systems Inc 6531 NW 18th Ct	Plantation	FL	33313	**800-992-9008**	954-581-9800	375
Imagistics International Inc 100 Oakview Dr *NYSE: IGI*	Trumbull	CT	06611	**800-945-9708**	203-365-7000	112
Imaje Co 1650 Airport Rd Suite 101	Kennesaw	GA	30144	**800-462-5302**	770-421-7700	171-6
iMatchup.com Inc 1 Blue Hill Plaza 5th Fl	Pearl River	NY	10965	**800-222-4963**	845-620-1212	224
Imation Corp 1 Imation Pl *NYSE: IMN*	Oakdale	MN	55128	**888-466-3456**	651-704-4000	644
IMBA (International Mountain Bicycling Assn) 207 Canyon Blvd Suite 301 PO Box 7578	Boulder	CO	80306	**888-442-4622**	303-545-9011	48-23
IMC (International Medical Corps) 1919 Santa Monica Blvd Suite 300	Santa Monica	CA	90404	**800-481-4462**	310-826-7800	48-5
IMC Group 165 Township Line Rd 1 Pitcairn Pl Suite 1200	Jenkintown	PA	19046	**800-220-6800**	215-517-6000	476
IMC Networks Corp 19772 Pauling	Foothill Ranch	CA	92610	**800-624-1070**	949-465-3000	174
IMC USA (Institute of Management Consultants USA Inc) 2025 M St NW Suite 800	Washington	DC	20036	**800-221-2557**	202-367-1134	49-12
IMCOR-Interstate Mechanical Corp 1841 E Washington St	Phoenix	AZ	85034	**800-628-0211**	602-257-1319	188-10
Imecom Group 8 Governor Wentworth Hwy	Wolfeboro	NH	03894	**800-329-9099**	603-569-0600	176-7
IMERYS 100 Mansell Ct E Suite 300	Roswell	GA	30076	**800-374-3224**	770-594-0660	493-2
IMG (International Motor Coach Group Inc) 8645 College Blvd Suite 220	Overland Park	KS	66210	**888-447-3466**	913-906-0111	49-21
IMI (International Masonry Institute) James Brice House 42 East St	Annapolis	MD	21401	**800-803-0295**	410-280-1305	49-3
IMI Cornelius Inc 101 Broadway St W	Osseo	MN	55369	**800-238-3600**	763-488-8200	650
IMI Data Search Inc 275 E Hillcrest Dr Suite 102	Thousand Oaks	CA	91360	**800-860-7779**	805-495-1149	621
Immaculata University 1145 King Rd	Immaculata	PA	19345	**888-428-6329**	610-647-4400	163
Immanuel-Saint Joseph's Hospital 1025 Marsh St	Mankato	MN	56001	**800-327-3721**	507-625-4031	366-2
Immedient 4582 S Ulster St Pkwy Suite 200	Denver	CO	80237	**800-324-3469**	303-770-7200	178
Immersion Corp 801 Fox Ln *NASDAQ: IMMR*	San Jose	CA	95131	**888-467-1900**	408-467-1900	171-1
Immersion Medical 55 W Watkins Mills Rd	Gaithersburg	MD	20878	**800-929-4709**	301-984-3706	694
Immigrant Aid Society. Hebrew 333 7th Ave 17th Fl	New York	NY	10001	**800-442-7714**	212-967-4100	48-5
Immigration & Naturalization Service (now US Citizenship & Immigration Services) 20 Massachusetts Ave NW	Washington	DC	20536	**800-870-3676**	202-514-4600	336-7
Immigration Reform. Federation for American 1666 Connecticut Ave NW Suite 400	Washington	DC	20009	**877-627-3247**	202-328-7004	48-7
Immtech International Inc 150 Fairway Dr Suite 150 *AMEX: IMM*	Vernon Hills	IL	60061	**877-898-8038**	847-573-0033	572
ImmucorGamma Inc 3130 Gateway Dr PO Box 5625 *NASDAQ: BLUD* ■ *Cust Svc	Norcross	GA	30091	**800-829-2553***	770-441-2051	229
Immune Deficiency Foundation (IDF) 40 W Chesapeake Ave Suite 308	Towson	MD	21204	**800-296-4433**	410-321-6647	48-17
Immuno-Mycologics Inc 1236 E Redbud Rd	Goldsby	OK	73093	**800-654-3639**	405-288-2383	229
ImmunoDiagnostics Inc 21 F Olympia Ave	Woburn	MA	01801	**800-573-1700**	781-938-6300	229
Immunology. American Academy of Allergy Asthma & 611 E Wells St 4th Fl	Milwaukee	WI	53202	**800-822-2762**	414-272-6071	49-8
Immunology. American College of Allergy Asthma & 85 W Algonquin Rd Suite 550	Arlington Heights	IL	60005	**800-842-7777**	847-427-1200	49-8
Immunovision Inc 1820 Ford Ave	Springdale	AR	72764	**800-541-0960**	479-751-7005	229
IMMVAC Inc 6080 Bass Ln	Columbia	MO	65201	**800-944-7563**	573-443-5363	574
IMPAC Medical Systems Inc 100 W Evelyn Ave	Mountain View	CA	94041	**888-464-6722**	650-623-8800	176-10
Impac Mortgage Holdings Inc 1401 Dove St Suite 100 *NYSE: IMH*	Newport Beach	CA	92660	**800-597-4101**	949-475-3600	640
Impact Drug & Alcohol Treatment Center 1680 N Fair Oaks Ave	Pasadena	CA	91103	**888-400-4222**	626-798-0884	712
Impact Innovations Group 8850 Stanford Blvd Suite 4000	Columbia	MD	21045	**877-239-2333**	410-872-5400	178
Impact Label Corp 3434 S Burdick St	Kalamazoo	MI	49001	**800-820-0362**	269-381-4280	404
Impact Plastics Inc 154 West St Bldg 3 Unit C	Cromwell	CT	06416	**800-625-7224**	860-632-3550	589
Impact Seven Inc 147 Lake Almena Dr	Almena	WI	54805	**800-685-9353**	715-357-3334	394
Impath Inc 521 W 57th St 6th Fl	New York	NY	10019	**800-447-8881**	212-698-0300	409
Impax Laboratories Inc 3735 Castor Ave *NASDAQ: IPXL*	Philadelphia	PA	19124	**800-296-5227**	215-289-2220	573
Imperial-Deltah Inc 795 Waterman Ave	East Providence	RI	02914	**800-556-7738**	401-434-2250	400
Imperial Graphics Inc 3100 Walkent Dr NW	Grand Rapids	MI	49544	**800-777-2591**	616-784-0100	111
Imperial Headwear Inc 5200 E Evans Ave *Cust Svc	Denver	CO	80222	**800-933-9444***	303-757-1166	153-9
Imperial Industries Inc 505 Industrial Park Ave	Mosinee	WI	54455	**800-558-2945**	715-359-0200	106
Imperial Majesty Cruise Line 2950 Gateway Dr	Pompano Beach	FL	33069	**800-394-3865**	954-956-9505	217
Imperial Nurseries Inc 90 Salmon Brook St	Granby	CT	06035	**800-343-3132**	860-653-4541	363
Imperial Oil Ltd 111 St Clair Ave W *AMEX: IMO*	Toronto	ON	M5W1K3	**800-567-3776**		570
Imperial Palace Hotel & Casino 3535 Las Vegas Blvd S	Las Vegas	NV	89109	**800-634-6441**	702-731-3311	133
Imperial Palace Inc 3535 Las Vegas Blvd S	Las Vegas	NV	89109	**800-634-6441**	702-731-3311	132

Name / Address	City	State	Zip	Toll-Free	Phone	Class
Imperial Palace Mississippi 850 Bayview Ave	Biloxi	MS	39530	**800-436-3000**	228-436-3000	133
Imperial Pools Inc 615 Loudonville Rd	Latham	NY	12110	**800-444-9977**	518-786-1200	714
Imperial Sugar Co PO Box 9 *NASDAQ: IPSU*	Sugar Land	TX	77487	**800-727-8427**	281-491-9181	291-38
Imperial Theatre 249 W 45th St	New York	NY	10036	**800-432-7250**	212-239-6200	732
Imperial Trading Co Inc 701 Edwards Ave PO Box 23508 *Cust Svc	Elmwood	LA	70183	**800-743-1761***	504-733-1400	292-8
Imperial of Waikiki 205 Lewers St	Honolulu	HI	96815	**800-347-2582**	808-923-1827	373
Implantologists. International Congress of Oral 248 Lorraine Ave 3rd Fl	Upper Montclair	NJ	07043	**800-442-0525**	973-783-6300	49-8
Implement Sales Co LLC 1574 Stone Ridge Dr	Stone Mountain	GA	30083	**800-955-9592**	770-908-9439	270
Impo International Inc PO Box 639	Santa Maria	CA	93456	**800-367-4676**	805-922-7753	296
Impreso Inc 652 Southwestern Blvd *NASDAQ: ZCOM*	Coppell	TX	75019	**800-521-8781**	972-462-0100	355-3
ImproveNet Inc 10799 N 90th St Suite 200	Scottsdale	AZ	85260	**877-517-2928**	480-346-0000	677
IMS Inc 340 Progress Dr	Manchester	CT	06040	**800-666-1626**	860-649-4415	245
IMSA (International Municipal Signal Assn) 165 E Union St PO Box 539	Newark	NY	14513	**800-723-4672**	315-331-2182	49-7
IMT Insurance Co PO Box 1336	Des Moines	IA	50305	**800-274-3531**	515-327-2777	384-4
IMX Inc 2305 Camino Ramon Suite 200	San Ramon	CA	94583	**800-401-4639**		498
In-Fisherman Magazine 7819 Highland Scenic Rd	Baxter	MN	56425	**800-441-1740**	218-829-1648	449-20
In-N-Out Burger Inc 4199 Campus Dr Suite 900 *Cust Svc	Irvine	CA	92612	**800-786-1000***	949-509-6200	657
In-Sink-Erator 4700 21st St	Racine	WI	53406	**800-558-5712**	262-554-5432	36
In Step Promotions Inc 10821 Lakeview Ave	Lenexa	KS	66219	**800-321-1098**	913-599-5995	296
In The Swim Inc 320 Industrial Dr	West Chicago	IL	60185	**800-288-7946**		702
INAMED Aesthetics 700 Ward Dr	Santa Barbara	CA	93111	**800-624-4261**	805-683-6761	469
INAMED Corp 5540 Ekwill St Suite D *NASDAQ: IMDC*	Santa Barbara	CA	93111	**800-624-6261**	805-692-5400	469
InBev USA 101 Merritt 7 PO Box 5075 *Cust Svc	Norwalk	CT	06856	**800-268-2337***	203-750-6600	103
Inc Magazine 375 Lexington Ave	New York	NY	10017	**800-234-0999**	212-499-2000	449-5
Incara Pharmaceuticals Corp 79 TW Alexander Dr Bldg 4401 Suite 200	Research Triangle Park	NC	27709	**888-290-0528**	919-558-8688	86
Incentive Publications Inc 2400 Crestmoor Dr Suite 211 *Mktg	Nashville	TN	37215	**800-421-2830***	615-385-2934	242
Incentive Solutions 2337 Perimeter Park Dr Suite 220	Atlanta	GA	30341	**800-463-5836**	770-457-4597	377
Incentivecity 7370 Bramalea Rd Suite 3	Mississauga	ON	L5S1N6	**877-387-2529**	905-362-0951	39
Incest National Network. Rape Abuse & 635-B Pennsylvania Ave SE	Washington	DC	20003	**800-656-4673**	202-544-1034	48-6
Inches-A-Weigh North America Inc 4320 Alpine Ct	Rockford	IL	61107	**800-241-8663**	815-227-4623	797
Inclinator Co of America 2200 Paxton St	Harrisburg	PA	17105	**800-343-9007**	717-234-8065	255
Incline Village/Crystal Bay Convention & Visitors Bureau 969 Tahoe Blvd	Incline Village	NV	89451	**800-468-2463**	775-832-1606	205
Inco Inc PO Box 2705	Rocky Mount	NC	27802	**800-672-4626**	252-446-1174	187-10
Incyte Corp Rt 141 & Henry Clay Rd Bldg E-336 *NASDAQ: INCY* ■ *Sales	Wilmington	DE	19880	**877-746-2983***	302-498-6700	86
Indala 6850-B Santa Teresa Blvd. *Sales	San Jose	CA	95119	**800-779-8663***	408-361-4700	171-7
Indalex Aluminum Solutions Group 3000 Lakeside Dr Suite 309S	Bannockburn	IL	60015	**877-276-1802**	847-295-0895	476
Indel-Davis Inc 4401 S Jackson Ave	Tulsa	OK	74107	**800-331-6300**	918-587-2151	528
Indemnity Co of California 17780 Fitch Suite 200	Irvine	CA	92614	**800-782-1546**	949-263-3300	384-5
Independence Air iCLUB 45200 Business Ct	Dulles	VA	20166	**800-359-3594**	703-650-6000	27
Independence Blue Cross 1901 Market St	Philadelphia	PA	19103	**800-227-3114**	215-241-2400	384-3
Independence Community Bank 195 Montague St	Brooklyn	NY	11201	**800-732-3434**	718-722-5700	71
Independence Community Bank Corp 195 Montague St *NASDAQ: ICBC*	Brooklyn	NY	11201	**800-732-3434**	718-722-5300	355-2
Independence Community College PO Box 708	Independence	KS	67301	**800-842-6063**	620-331-4100	160
Independence Excavating Inc 5720 Schaaf Rd	Independence	OH	44131	**800-524-3478**	216-524-1700	188-5
Independence Federal Savings Bank 1229 Connecticut Ave NW *NASDAQ: IFSB*	Washington	DC	20036	**888-922-6537**	202-628-5500	71
Independence Investment LLC 53 State St 28th Fl	Boston	MA	02109	**800-858-6635**	617-228-8700	393
Independence Technology LLC 45 Technology Dr	Warren	NJ	07059	**888-463-3000**		469
Independent Agent Magazine 127 S Peyton St	Alexandria	VA	22314	**800-221-7917**	703-683-4422	449-5
Independent Bank Corp 288 Union St *NASDAQ: INDB*	Rockland	MA	02370	**800-826-6100**	781-878-6100	355-2
Independent Bank Corp 230 W Main St *NASDAQ: IBCP*	Ionia	MI	48846	**800-662-0102**	616-527-9450	355-2
Independent Battery Manufacturers Assn (IBMA) 401 N Michigan Ave 24th Fl	Chicago	IL	60611	**800-237-6126**	312-245-1074	49-13
Independent Business. National Federation of 1201 F St NW Suite 200	Washington	DC	20004	**800-552-6342**	202-554-9000	49-12
Independent Charities of America 21 Tamal Vista Blvd Suite 209	Corte Madera	CA	94925	**800-477-0733**		48-5
Independent Chemical Corp 79-51 Cooper Ave	Glendale	NY	11385	**800-892-2578**	718-894-0700	144
Independent Community Bankers of America (ICBA) 1 Thomas Cir NW Suite 400	Washington	DC	20005	**800-422-8439**	202-659-8111	49-2
Independent Community Bankers of America PAC 1 Thomas Cir NW Suite 400	Washington	DC	20005	**800-422-8439**	202-659-8111	604
Independent Computer Consultants Assn (ICCA) 11131 S Towne Sq Suite F	Saint Louis	MO	63123	**800-774-4222**	314-892-1675	48-9
Independent Educational Consultants Assn (IECA) 3251 Old Lee Hwy Suite 510	Fairfax	VA	22030	**800-808-4322**	703-591-4850	49-5
Independent Health Assn 511 Farber Lakes Dr	Buffalo	NY	14221	**800-247-1466**	716-631-3001	384-3
Independent Ink Inc 13700 S Gramercy Pl	Gardena	CA	90249	**800-446-5538**	310-523-4657	381
Independent Institute 100 Swan Way	Oakland	CA	94621	**800-927-8733**	510-632-1366	654
Independent Insurance Agents & Brokers of America Inc (IIABA) 127 S Peyton St	Alexandria	VA	22314	**800-221-7917**	703-683-4422	49-9
Independent Jewelers Organization (IJO) 25 Seir Hill Rd	Norwalk	CT	06850	**800-624-9252**	203-846-4215	49-4
Independent Order of Foresters (IOF) 789 Don Mills Rd	Toronto	ON	M3C1T9	**800-828-1540**	416-429-3000	48-5
Independent Order of Odd Fellows 422 Trade St	Winston-Salem	NC	27101	**800-235-8358**	336-725-5955	48-15
Independent Petroleum Assn of America (IPAA) 1201 15th St NW Suite 300	Washington	DC	20005	**800-433-2851**	202-857-4722	48-12
Independent Press Assn (IPA) 2729 Mission St Suite 201	San Francisco	CA	94110	**877-463-9624**	415-643-4401	49-16
Independent Protection Co Inc 1607 S Main St	Goshen	IN	46526	**800-860-8388**	574-533-4116	803
Independent Publishers Group 814 N Franklin St *Orders	Chicago	IL	60610	**800-888-4741***	312-337-0747	97
Independent Sector 1200 18th St NW Suite 200 *Orders	Washington	DC	20036	**888-860-8118***	202-467-6100	48-5
Independent Weekly PO Box 2690	Durham	NC	27715	**800-948-8699**	919-286-1972	522-4
Indera Mills Co 350 W Maple St PO Box 309	Yadkinville	NC	27055	**800-334-8605**	336-679-4440	153-18
Index Fresh Inc 18184 Slover Ave	Bloomington	CA	92316	**800-352-6931**	909-877-1577	12-1
Index Stock Imagery Inc 23 W 18th St 3rd Fl	New York	NY	10011	**800-729-7466**	212-929-4644	582
India Tourist Office 3550 Wilshire Blvd Suite 204	Los Angeles	CA	90010	**800-422-4634**	213-380-8855	764
India Tourist Office 1270 Ave of the Americas Suite 1808	New York	NY	10020	**800-953-9399**	212-586-4901	764
Indian College Fund. American 8333 Greenwood Blvd	Denver	CO	80221	**800-776-3863**	303-426-8900	48-11
Indian Country Inc 791 Airport Rd	Deposit	NY	13754	**800-414-3801**	607-467-3801	671
Indian Creek Hotel 2727 Indian Creek Dr	Miami Beach	FL	33140	**800-491-2772**	305-531-2727	373
Indian Electric Co-op Inc PO Box 49	Cleveland	OK	74020	**800-482-2750**	918-358-2514	244
Indian Gaming Assn. National 224 2nd St SE	Washington	DC	20003	**800-286-6442**	202-546-7711	48-23
Indian Harvest Specialtifoods Inc 1012 Paul Bunyan Dr Se *Orders	Bemidji	MN	56601	**800-346-7032***	218-751-8500	291-23
Indian Head Industries Inc 8530 Cliff Cameron Dr	Charlotte	NC	28269	**800-527-1534**	704-547-7411	60
Indian Head Industries Inc MGM Brakes Div 8530 Cliff Cameron Dr	Charlotte	NC	28269	**800-527-1534**	704-547-7411	60
Indian Hills Community College 525 Grandview Ave	Ottumwa	IA	52501	**800-726-2585**	641-683-5111	160
Indian Housing Council. National American 900 2nd St NE Suite 305	Washington	DC	20002	**800-284-9165**	202-789-1754	49-7
Indian Lakes Resort 250 W Schick Rd	Bloomingdale	IL	60108	**800-334-3417**	630-529-0200	655
Indian Point Lodge 71 Dogwood Pk Trail	Branson	MO	65616	**800-888-1891**	417-338-2250	655
Indian Pueblo Cultural Center 2401 12th St NW	Albuquerque	NM	87104	**800-766-4405**	505-843-7270	509
Indian River Community College 3209 Virginia Ave	Fort Pierce	FL	34981	**866-866-4722**	772-462-4700	160
Indian River Estates 2250 Indian Creek Blvd W *Mktg	Vero Beach	FL	32966	**800-544-0277***	772-562-7400	659
Indian River Memorial Hospital 1000 36th St	Vero Beach	FL	32960	**800-226-4764**	772-567-4311	366-2
Indian Springs School 190 Woodward Dr	Indian Springs	AL	35124	**888-843-3477**	205-988-3350	611
Indian Trails Inc 109 E Comstock St	Owosso	MI	48867	**800-292-3831**	989-725-5105	108
Indian Valley Industries Inc 60-100 Corliss Ave	Johnson City	NY	13790	**800-659-5111**	607-729-5111	68
Indian Wells Resort Hotel 76-661 Hwy 111	Indian Wells	CA	92210	**800-248-3220**	760-345-6466	655
Indiana						
Community Development Div 1 N Capitol Ave Suite 700	Indianapolis	IN	46204	**800-824-2476**	317-232-8911	335
Consumer Protection Div 402 W Washington St 5th Fl	Indianapolis	IN	46204	**800-382-5516**	317-232-6330	335
Disability Aging & Rehabilitative Services Div 402 W Washington St Rm W451	Indianapolis	IN	46207	**800-545-7763**	317-232-1147	335
Family & Social Services Administration 402 W Washington St Rm W461	Indianapolis	IN	46207	**800-545-7763**	317-233-4454	335
Health Professions Bureau 402 W Washington St Rm W041	Indianapolis	IN	46204	**888-333-7515**	317-232-2960	335

Name / Address	City	State	ZIP	Toll-Free	Phone	Class
Insurance Dept 311 W Washington St Suite 300 *Cust Svc	Indianapolis	IN	46204	**800-622-4461***	317-232-2385	335
Port Commission 150 W Market St Suite 100	Indianapolis	IN	46204	**800-232-7678**	317-232-9200	607
State Parks & Reservoirs Div 402 W Washington Rm W-298	Indianapolis	IN	46204	**800-622-4931**	317-232-4124	335
Students Assistance Commission 150 W Market St Suite 500	Indianapolis	IN	46204	**888-528-4719**	317-232-2350	711
Tourism Div 1 N Capitol Ave Suite 700	Indianapolis	IN	46204	**888-365-6946**	317-232-8860	335
Victims Services Div 302 W Washington St Rm E209	Indianapolis	IN	46204	**800-353-1484**	317-232-1233	335
Indiana Beach 5224 E Indiana Beach Rd	Monticello	IN	47960	**800-583-4306**	574-583-4141	32
Indiana Blood & Marrow Transplantation Saint Francis Hospital 1600 Albany St 6th Tower	Beech Grove	IN	46107	**800-361-0016**	317-782-7355	758
Indiana Business College 550 E Washington St	Indianapolis	IN	46204	**800-999-9229**	317-264-5656	158
Indiana Business Magazine 55 Monument Cir Suite 300	Indianapolis	IN	46204	**800-473-2526**	317-692-1200	449-5
Indiana County Tourist Bureau 2334 Oakland Ave Suite 7	Indiana	PA	15701	**877-746-3426**	724-463-7505	205
Indiana Democratic Party 1 N Capital St Suite 200	Indianapolis	IN	46204	**800-223-3387**	317-231-7100	605-1
Indiana Dental Assn 401 W Michigan St	Indianapolis	IN	46202	**800-562-5646**	317-634-2610	225
Indiana Dunes - The Casual Coast 1120 S Calumet Suite 1	Chesterton	IN	46304	**800-283-8687**	219-926-2255	205
Indiana Farm Bureau Insurance Co 225 S East St	Indianapolis	IN	46202	**800-866-1160**	317-692-7200	384-2
Indiana Farmers Mutual Insurance Group 10 W 106th St	Indianapolis	IN	46290	**800-666-6460**	317-846-4211	384-4
Indiana Furniture Industries Inc 1224 Mill St	Jasper	IN	47546	**800-422-5727**	812-482-5727	314-1
Indiana Higher Education Telecommunication System (IHETS) 714 N Senate Ave	Indianapolis	IN	46202	**800-776-4438**	317-263-8900	620
Indiana Institute of Technology 1600 E Washington Blvd	Fort Wayne	IN	46803	**888-666-8324**	260-422-5561	163
Indiana Lions Eye & Tissue Transplant Bank Indiana University Medical Center 702 Rotary Cir Rm 115	Indianapolis	IN	46202	**800-232-4384**	317-274-8527	265
Indiana Memorial Union Hotel & Conference Center 900 E 7th St	Bloomington	IN	47405	**800-209-8145**	812-855-2536	373
Indiana Organ Procurement Organization 429 N Pennsylvania St Suite 201	Indianapolis	IN	46204	**888-275-4676**	317-685-0389	535
Indiana Republican Party 47 S Meridian St Suite 200	Indianapolis	IN	46204	**800-466-1087**	317-635-7561	605-2
Indiana Ribbon Inc 106 N 2nd St	Wolcott	IN	47995	**800-531-3100**	219-279-2112	542-2
Indiana State Bar Assn 1 Indiana Sq Suite 530	Indianapolis	IN	46204	**800-266-2581**	317-639-5465	73
Indiana State Chamber of Commerce 115 W Washington St Suite 850-S PO Box 44926	Indianapolis	IN	46204	**800-824-6885**	317-264-3110	138
Indiana State Medical Assn 322 Canal Walk	Indianapolis	IN	46202	**800-257-4762**	317-261-2060	466
Indiana State University 210 N 7th St	Terre Haute	IN	47809	**800-742-0891**	812-237-2121	163
Indiana Sugars Inc 911 Virginia St	Gary	IN	46402	**800-333-9666**	219-886-9151	292-11
Indiana Supply Corp 3835 E 21st St	Indianapolis	IN	46218	**800-686-0195**	317-359-5451	601
Indiana University						
East Campus 2325 Chester Blvd	Richmond	IN	47374	**800-959-3278**	765-973-8200	163
Kokomo Campus PO Box 9003	Kokomo	IN	46904	**888-875-4485**	765-455-9217	163
Northwest Campus 3400 Broadway	Gary	IN	46408	**888-968-7486**	219-980-6500	163
South Bend Campus 1700 Mishawaka Ave Box 7111	South Bend	IN	46634	**877-462-4872**	574-237-4111	163
Indiana University Cancer Center Bone Marrow & Stem Cell Transplant Team 550 N University Blvd Suite 6611	Indianapolis	IN	46202	**877-814-7594**	317-274-1114	758
Indiana University of Pennsylvania Sutton Hall 1011 South Dr Suite 117	Indiana	PA	15705	**800-442-6830**	724-357-2230	163
Indiana University Press 601 N Morton St	Bloomington	IN	47404	**800-842-6796**	812-855-8817	623-5
Indiana University-Purdue University Fort Wayne 2101 E Coliseum Blvd	Fort Wayne	IN	46805	**800-324-4739**	260-481-6100	163
Indiana Wesleyan University 4201 S Washington St	Marion	IN	46953	**800-332-6901**	765-677-2138	163
Indianapolis Artsgarden Above the intersection of Washington & Illinois St	Indianapolis	IN	46204	**800-965-2787**	317-631-3301	562
Indianapolis Business Journal 41 E Washington St Suite 200	Indianapolis	IN	46204	**800-968-1225**	317-634-6200	449-5
Indianapolis Colts 7001 W 56th St	Indianapolis	IN	46254	**800-805-2658**	317-297-2658	703
Indianapolis Convention & Visitors Assn 200 S Capitol Ave 1 RCA Dome Suite 100	Indianapolis	IN	46225	**800-323-4639**	317-639-4282	205
Indianapolis Fruit Co Inc 4501 Massachusetts Ave	Indianapolis	IN	46218	**800-377-2425**	317-546-2425	292-7
Indianapolis Life Insurance Co 9200 Keystone Crossing Suite 800	Indianapolis	IN	46204	**800-428-7031**	317-927-6500	384-2
Indianapolis Monthly Magazine 40 Monument Cir Suite 100 *Circ	Indianapolis	IN	46204	**888-403-9005***	317-237-9288	449-22
Indianapolis Newspapers Inc 307 N Pennsylvania St	Indianapolis	IN	46204	**800-669-7827**	317-633-1240	623-8
Indianapolis Power & Light Co PO Box 1595 *Cust Svc	Indianapolis	IN	46206	**888-261-8222***	317-261-8261	774
Indianapolis Star 307 N Pennsylvania St	Indianapolis	IN	46204	**800-669-7827**	317-444-4000	522-2
Indianapolis Symphony Orchestra 32 E Washington St Suite 600	Indianapolis	IN	46204	**800-366-8457**	317-262-1100	563-3
Indianhead Mountain Resort 500 Indianhead Rd	Wakefield	MI	49968	**800-346-3426**	906-229-2229	655
Indies Spa at the Hawks Cay Resort & Marina 61 Hawk's Cay Blvd	Duck Key	FL	33050	**800-432-2242**	305-289-4810	698
Indigo Inn 1 Maiden Ln	Charleston	SC	29401	**800-845-7639**	843-577-5900	373
Indio Chamber of Commerce 82921 Indio Blvd	Indio	CA	92201	**800-444-6346**	760-347-0676	137
IndiSonic Inc 126 N 3rd St Suite 512	Minneapolis	MN	55401	**877-492-7916**	612-349-9013	514
Individual Rights. Center for 1233 20th St NW Suite 300	Washington	DC	20036	**877-426-2665**	202-833-8400	48-8
Individual Software Inc 4255 Hopyard Rd Suite 2	Pleasanton	CA	94588	**800-822-3522**	925-734-6767	176-3
Individualized Shirts Co 581 Cortland St	Perth Amboy	NJ	08861	**888-474-4787**	732-826-8400	153-12
Indoor Purification Systems Inc 887 N McCormick Way Suite 3	Layton	UT	84041	**888-812-1516**	801-444-0606	18
Indotronix International Corp 331 Main St	Poughkeepsie	NY	12601	**800-800-8442**	845-473-1137	178
Inductoheat Inc 32251 N Avis Dr	Madison Heights	MI	48071	**800-642-8903**	248-585-9393	313
Inductotherm Corp 10 Indel Ave	Rancocas	NJ	08073	**800-257-9527**	609-267-9000	313
Inductotherm Industries Inc 10 Indel Ave	Rancocas	NJ	08073	**800-257-9527**	609-267-9000	313
Indulgence Spa at Taboo 1209 Muskoka Beach Rd RR 1	Gravenhurst	ON	P1P1R1	**800-461-0236**	705-687-2233	698
Indus International Inc 3301 Windy Ridge Pkwy *NASDAQ: IINT*	Atlanta	GA	30339	**800-554-6387**	770-952-8444	176-1
Indus International Inc 340 S Oak St PO Box 890	West Salem	WI	54669	**800-843-9377**	608-786-0300	487
Indusco Group 1200 W Hamburg St	Baltimore	MD	21230	**800-727-0665**	410-727-0665	462
Industrial Adhesives Inc 4244 W 6th Ave	Eugene	OR	97402	**800-451-2580**	541-683-6677	717
Industrial Alliance Insurance & Financial Services Inc 1080 Chemin Saint-Louis *TSE: IAG*	Sillery	QC	G1K7M3	**800-463-6236**	418-684-5182	355-4
Industrial-Alliance Life Insurance Co 1080 Chemin Saint-Louis	Sillery	QC	G1K7M3	**800-463-6236**	418-684-5000	384-2
Industrial Alloys Inc 3880 W Valley Blvd	Walnut	CA	91789	**800-255-6974**	909-594-7511	476
Industrial Bioprocessing Newsletter 7550 W I-10 Suite 400	San Antonio	TX	77229	**877-463-7678**	210-348-1000	521-12
Industrial Brush Co Inc PO Box 869	Fairfield	NJ	07007	**800-241-9860**	973-575-0455	104
Industrial Brush Corp PO Box 2608	Pomona	CA	91769	**800-228-6146**	909-591-9341	104
Industrial Chemicals Inc 2042 Montreat Dr	Birmingham	AL	35216	**800-476-2042**	205-823-7330	144
Industrial Container Services 7152 1st Ave S	Seattle	WA	98108	**800-451-3471**	206-763-2345	197
Industrial Custom Products Inc 2801 37th Ave NE	Minneapolis	MN	55421	**800-654-0886**	612-781-2255	321
Industrial Data Systems Inc 590 W Freedom Ave	Orange	CA	92865	**800-854-3311**	714-921-9212	672
Industrial Dynamics Co Ltd 3100 Fujita St	Torrance	CA	90505	**888-434-5832**	310-325-5633	464
Industrial Electric Wire & Cable Inc 5001 S Towne Dr	New Berlin	WI	53151	**800-344-2323**	262-782-2323	245
Industrial Electronics Society. IEEE IEEE Operations Ctr 445 Hoes Ln	Piscataway	NJ	08854	**800-678-4333**	732-981-0060	49-19
Industrial Engineers. Institute of 3577 Parkway Ln Suite 200 *Cust Svc	Norcross	GA	30092	**800-494-0460***	770-449-0460	49-13
Industrial Fabrics Assn International (IFAI) 1801 County Rd 'B' W	Roseville	MN	55113	**800-225-4324**	651-222-2508	49-13
Industrial Fabrics Corp 7160 Northland Cir N	Minneapolis	MN	55428	**800-328-3036**	763-535-3220	730-3
Industrial Gasket Inc 720 S Sara Rd	Mustang	OK	73064	**800-654-8433**	405-376-9393	321
Industrial Gasket & Shim Co Inc (IGS) 200 Country Club Rd	Meadow Lands	PA	15347	**800-229-1447**	724-222-5800	321
Industrial Heater Corp 30 Knotter Dr	Cheshire	CT	06410	**800-822-4426**	203-250-0500	313
Industrial Louvers Inc 511 7th St S	Delano	MN	55328	**800-328-3421**	763-972-2981	688
Industrial & Office Properties. National Assn of 2201 Cooperative Way 3rd Fl	Herndon	VA	20171	**800-666-6780**	703-904-7100	49-17
Industrial Packaging Assn. Reusable 8401 Corporate Dr Suite 450	Landover	MD	20785	**800-533-3786**	301-577-3786	49-13
Industrial Paper Shredders Inc 707 Ellsworth Ave PO Box 180	Salem	OH	44460	**888-637-4733**	330-332-0024	112
Industrial Paper Tube Inc 1335 E Bay Ave	Bronx	NY	10474	**800-345-0960**	718-893-5000	125
Industrial Piping Inc 800 Culp Rd	Pineville	NC	28134	**800-951-0988**	704-588-1100	188-10
Industrial Power & Lighting Corp 701 Seneca St	Buffalo	NY	14210	**800-639-3702**	716-854-1811	188-4
Industrial Resources. National Assn for the Exchange of 560 McClure St	Galesburg	IL	61401	**800-562-0955**	309-343-0704	48-5
Industrial Safety & Supply Co Inc 176 Newington Rd	West Hartford	CT	06110	**800-243-2316**	860-233-9881	667
Industrial Scientific Corp 1001 Oakdale Rd	Oakdale	PA	15071	**800-338-3287**	412-788-4353	200
Industrial Service Transport Health Employees. International Union of 254 W 31st St	New York	NY	10001	**800-331-1070**	212-696-5545	405
Industrial Services of America Inc 7100 Grade Ln *NASDAQ: IDSA*	Louisville	KY	40213	**800-824-2144**	502-368-1661	791
Industrial Supply Solutions Inc 520 Elizabeth St	Charleston	WV	25311	**800-346-5341**	304-346-5341	378
Industrial Technology Center. Great Lakes 20445 Emerald Pkwy SW Suite 200	Cleveland	OH	44135	**800-472-6785**	216-898-6400	654

Name / Address	City	State	ZIP	Toll-Free	Phone	Class
Industrial Tectonics Bearings Corp 18301 S Santa Fe Ave	Rancho Dominguez	CA	90221	**800-654-2597**	310-537-3750	77
Industrial Tectonics Inc 7222 W Huron River Dr	Dexter	MI	48130	**800-482-2255**	734-426-4681	476
Industrial Telecommunications Assn Inc (ITA) 1110 N Glebe Rd Suite 500	Arlington	VA	22201	**800-482-8282**	703-528-5115	49-20
Industrial Timber & Land Co 23925 Commerce Pk	Beachwood	OH	44122	**800-829-9663**	216-831-3140	541
Industrial Tool Inc 9210 52nd Ave N *Sales	Minneapolis	MN	55428	**800-776-4455***	763-533-7244	446
Industrial Tools Inc 1111 S Rose Ave	Oxnard	CA	93033	**800-266-5561**	805-483-1111	484
Industrial Towel & Uniform Inc 2700 S 160th St	New Berlin	WI	53151	**800-767-2487**	262-782-1950	434
Industrial Training Systems Corp 4101 International Pkwy	Carrollton	TX	75007	**800-727-2487**	972-309-4000	502
Industrial Truck Sales & Service Inc 4100 Randleman Rd	Greensboro	NC	27401	**800-632-0333**	336-275-9121	378
Industrial Welders & Machinists Inc PO Box 16720	Duluth	MN	55806	**800-689-9520**	218-628-1011	798
Industrial Wire Products Corp 3880 W Valley Blvd	Walnut	CA	91787	**800-843-9561**	909-594-7511	800
Industrial Workers. International Union of Petroleum & 8131 E Rosecrans Ave	Paramount	CA	90723	**800-624-5842**	562-630-6232	405
Industries for the Blind 3220 W Vliet St	Milwaukee	WI	53208	**800-642-8778**	414-933-4319	104
Industries for the Blind. National 1901 N Beauregard St Suite 200 *Cust Svc	Alexandria	VA	22311	**800-433-2304***	703-998-0770	48-17
Industronics Service Co 489 Sullivan Ave PO Box 649	South Windsor	CT	06074	**800-878-1551**	860-289-1551	313
Industry Applications Society. IEEE IEEE Operations Ctr 445 Hoes Ln	Piscataway	NJ	08854	**800-678-4333**	732-981-0060	49-19
Industry-Railway Suppliers Inc 811 Golf Ln	Bensenville	IL	60106	**800-728-0029**	630-766-5708	759
Industry Report 301 N Fairfax St	Alexandria	VA	22314	**800-542-6672**	703-549-9040	521-13
Indy Lighting Inc 12001 Exit 5 Pkwy	Fishers	IN	46038	**800-428-5212**	317-849-1233	431
IndyMac Bancorp Inc 155 N Lake Ave *NYSE: NDE*	Pasadena	CA	91101	**800-669-2300**	626-535-5901	355-2
IndyMac Bank 1 Banting	Irvine	CA	92618	**800-731-0383**	949-585-3301	498
INEEL (Idaho National Engineering & Environmental Laboratory) Communications & Public Affairs 2525 Fremont Avenue PO Box 1625	Idaho Falls	ID	83415	**800-708-2680**	208-526-0111	654
INEOS Silicas Americas 111 Ingalls Ave	Joliet	IL	60435	**800-775-3651**	815-727-3651	141
Inergy LP 2 Brush Creek Blvd Suite 200 *NASDAQ: NRGY*	Kansas City	MO	64112	**877-446-3749**	816-842-8181	569
INetU Inc 744 Roble Rd Suite 70	Allentown	PA	18019	**888-664-6388**	610-266-7441	795
Infant Loss Support Inc. SHARE Pregnancy & St Joseph's Health Ctr 300 1st Capitol Dr	Saint Charles	MO	63301	**800-821-6819**	636-947-6164	48-21
Infection Control & Epidemiology Inc. Association for Professionals in 1275 K St NW Suite 1000	Washington	DC	20005	**888-278-2742**	202-789-1890	49-8
InfiMed Inc 121 Metropolitan Dr	Liverpool	NY	13088	**800-825-8845**	315-453-4545	376
Infineon Raceway Hwys 37 & 121	Sonoma	CA	95476	**800-870-7223**	707-938-8448	504
Infiniti Div Nissan Motor Corp USA PO Box 191	Gardena	CA	90248	**800-647-7263**	310-532-3111	59
Infinity Insurance Co PO Box 830189	Birmingham	AL	35283	**800-334-1661**	205-870-4000	384-4
Infinity Property & Casualty Corp 11700 Great Oaks Way *NASDAQ: IPCC*	Alpharetta	GA	30022	**800-225-8930**	678-627-6000	384-4
Inflazyme Pharamceuticals Ltd 5600 Parkwood Way Suite 425	Richmond	BC	V6V2M2	**800-315-3660**	604-279-8511	86
Info-Center Inc 940 North St Ext	Feeding Hills	MA	01030	**800-462-3033**	413-786-7987	621
Info Directions Inc 833 Phillips Rd	Victor	NY	14564	**888-924-4110**	585-924-4110	176-1
Infocrossing Inc 2 Christie Heights St *NASDAQ: IFOX*	Leonia	NJ	07605	**800-431-1912**	201-840-4700	455
InFocus Corp 27700-B SW Parkway Ave *NASDAQ: INFS*	Wilsonville	OR	97070	**800-294-6400**	503-685-8888	580
Infodata Systems Inc 12150 Monument Dr Suite 400 *Sales	Fairfax	VA	22033	**800-336-4939***	703-934-5205	176-1
Infoglide Software Corp 6300 Bridge Point Pkwy Bldg 3 Suite 200	Austin	TX	78730	**800-338-2441**	512-532-3500	176-1
Infolab Inc PO Box 1309	Clarksdale	MS	38614	**800-647-8222**	662-627-2283	411
Infonet Services Corp 2160 E Grand Ave *NYSE: IN*	El Segundo	CA	90245	**877-325-2876**	310-335-2600	387
Infor Global Solutions 11720 Amber Park Dr Suite 400	Alpharetta	GA	30004	**866-244-5479**	678-393-5000	176-11
Informatica Corp 2100 Seaport Blvd *NASDAQ: INFA*	Redwood City	CA	94063	**800-653-3871**	650-385-5000	176-1
Information Analysis Inc 11240 Waples Mill Rd Suite 400	Fairfax	VA	22030	**800-829-7614**	703-383-3000	178
Information Builders Inc 2 Penn Plaza	New York	NY	10121	**800-969-4636**	212-736-4433	176-7
Information on the Environment. American Public 316 Oak St PO Box 676	Northfield	MN	55057	**800-320-2743**	507-645-5613	48-13
Information Gatekeepers Inc 320 Washington St Suite 302	Brighton	MA	02135	**800-323-1088**	617-782-5033	623-11
Information Handling Services Group Inc 15 Inverness Way E	Englewood	CO	80112	**800-320-4555**	303-790-0600	176-11
Information Imaging Corp 20 S Linden Ave Bldg 2-B	South San Francisco	CA	94080	**800-373-1834**	650-244-9911	487
Information Management Systems Inc 114 W Main St Suite 202	New Britain	CT	06050	**888-403-8347**	860-229-1119	621
Information Security Corp 1141 Lake Cook Rd Suite D	Deerfield	IL	60015	**800-203-5563**	847-405-0500	176-12
Information Service. National Technical 5285 Port Royal Rd *Orders	Springfield	VA	22161	**800-553-6847***	703-605-6000	336-2
Information Services Management International. Professional Records & 605 Benson Rd Suite B	Garner	NC	27529	**800-336-9793**	919-771-0657	49-12
Information Source LLC 627 E Sprague Ave Suite 111	Spokane	WA	99202	**800-548-8847**	509-624-2229	621
Information Systems Support Inc 13 Firstfield Rd Suite 100	Gaithersburg	MD	20878	**800-288-2095**	301-896-0500	178
Information Technology Assn. Library & 50 E Huron St	Chicago	IL	60611	**800-545-2433**	312-280-4270	49-11
Information Technology Laboratory 3909 Halls Ferry Rd ATTN: CEERD-IV-Z	Vicksburg	MS	39180	**800-522-6937**	601-634-2502	654
Information Television Network 621 NW 53rd St Suite 350	Boca Raton	FL	33487	**800-463-6488**	561-997-5433	727
Information Theory Society. IEEE IEEE Operations Ctr 445 Hoes Ln	Piscataway	NJ	08854	**800-678-4333**	732-981-0060	49-19
Information Today Inc 143 Old Marlton Pike	Medford	NJ	08055	**800-300-9868**	609-654-6266	623-9
Information Today Magazine 143 Old Marlton Pike	Medford	NJ	08055	**800-300-9868**	609-654-6266	449-7
InformationWeek Magazine 600 Community Dr	Manhasset	NY	11030	**800-645-6278**	516-562-7911	449-7
Informative Inc 2000 Sierra Point Pkwy Suite 301 *Sales	Brisbane	CA	94005	**800-829-1979***	650-534-1010	39
Informer Computer Systems Inc 12711 Western Ave	Garden Grove	CA	92841	**800-650-4636**	714-891-1112	174
INFORMS (Institute for Operations Research & the Management Sciences) 7240 Parkway Dr Suite 310	Hanover	MD	21076	**800-446-3676**	443-757-3500	49-19
Inforum Inc 801 Crescent Ctr Dr Suite 400	Franklin	TN	37067	**800-829-0600**	615-778-6300	176-11
InfoSonics Corp 5880 Pacific Center Blvd *AMEX: IFO*	San Diego	CA	92121	**800-519-1599**	858-373-1600	245
Infosys Technologies Ltd 1 Spectrum Pointe Suite 350	Lake Forest	CA	92630	**800-485-4636**	949-455-9161	176-1
InfoTech USA Inc 7 Kingsbridge Rd	Fairfield	NJ	07004	**800-305-8201**	973-227-8772	178
Infotel Distributing 6990 SR 36	Fletcher	OH	45326	**800-682-0422**	937-368-2650	172
InfoTrack Information Services Inc 111 Deerlake Rd	Deerfield	IL	60015	**800-275-5594**	847-444-1177	621
Infotrieve Inc 10850 Wilshire Blvd 8th Fl	Los Angeles	CA	90024	**800-422-4633**	310-234-2000	380
infoUSA Inc 5711 S 86th Cir *NASDAQ: IUSA*	Omaha	NE	68127	**800-321-0869**	402-593-4500	380
Infowave Software Inc 4664 Lougheed Hwy Suite 200	Burnaby	BC	V5C5T5	**800-463-6928**	604-473-3600	176-7
InfoWorld Magazine 501 2nd St Suite 120	San Francisco	CA	94107	**800-227-8365**	415-243-4344	449-7
InfoWorld Media Group Inc 501 2nd St Suite 120	San Francisco	CA	94107	**800-227-8365**	415-243-4344	623-9
Infusion Assn. National Home 205 Daingerfield Rd	Alexandria	VA	22314	**800-544-7447**	703-549-3740	49-8
ING Altus Group 230 Park Ave 14th Fl	New York	NY	10169	**800-621-6626**	212-309-8200	679
ING Americas 5780 Powers Ferry Rd NW	Atlanta	GA	30327	**800-465-3330**	770-980-3300	355-4
ING Barings 1325 Ave of the Americas	New York	NY	10019	**800-221-5855**	646-424-6000	679
ING Canada Inc 181 University Ave 9th Fl	Toronto	ON	M5H3M7	**866-817-2138**	416-941-5151	384-4
ING Funds 7337 E Doubletree Ranch Rd	Scottsdale	AZ	85258	**800-334-3444**	480-477-3000	517
ING Life of Georgia PO Box 105006	Atlanta	GA	30348	**888-968-5433**	770-980-5100	384-2
ING Northern Annuity 2000 21st Ave NW	Minot	ND	58703	**877-884-5050**		384-2
ING Southland Life Insurance Co 2000 21st Ave NW	Minot	ND	58703	**877-241-5050**	701-858-2000	384-2
Ingalls Feed Yard 10505 US Hwy 50	Ingalls	KS	67853	**800-477-6907**	620-335-5174	11-1
Ingalls & Snyder 61 Broadway 31st Fl	New York	NY	10006	**800-221-2598**	212-269-7800	679
Ingenico Corp 1003 Mansell Rd	Roswell	GA	30076	**800-435-3014**	770-594-6000	603
Ingenix Inc 12125 Technology Dr	Eden Prairie	MN	55344	**888-445-8745**	952-833-7100	455
Ingersoll-Rand Co ARO Fluid Products Div 1 Aro Ctr PO Box 151 *Cust Svc	Bryan	OH	43506	**800-495-0276***	419-636-4242	220
Ingersoll-Rand Co Von Duprin Exit Device Div 2720 Tobey Dr *Cust Svc	Indianapolis	IN	46219	**800-999-0408***	317-897-9944	345
Ingle International 5255 Yonge St Suite 218	Toronto	ON	M2N6P4	**800-360-3234**	416-730-8488	384-7
Ingles Markets Inc 2913 US Hwy 70 W *NASDAQ: IMKTA*	Black Mountain	NC	28711	**800-635-5066**	828-669-2941	339
Ingleside Inn 200 W Ramon Rd	Palm Springs	CA	92264	**800-772-6655**	760-325-0046	373
Ingram Barge Co 4400 Harding Rd 1 Belle Meade Pl	Nashville	TN	37205	**800-876-2047**	615-298-8200	309
Ingram Book Group 1 Ingram Blvd	La Vergne	TN	37086	**800-937-8000**	615-793-5000	97
Ingram Entertainment Inc 2 Ingram Blvd	La Vergne	TN	37089	**800-759-5000**	615-287-4000	500
Ingram Industries Inc PO Box 23049	Nashville	TN	37202	**800-876-2047**	615-298-8200	184
Ingram Materials Co 1030 Visco Dr	Nashville	TN	37210	**800-421-6998**	615-256-5111	190-1
Ingram Micro Inc 1600 E St Andrew Pl *NYSE: IM* ■ *Sales	Santa Ana	CA	92705	**800-456-8000***	714-566-1000	172
Inhalant Prevention Coalition. National 2904 Kerbey Ln	Austin	TX	78703	**800-269-4237**	512-480-8953	48-17
Inhibitex Inc 1165 Sanctuary Pkwy Suite 400 *NASDAQ: INHX*	Alpharetta	GA	30004	**866-784-3510**	678-746-1100	86
Initial Security 3355 Cherry Ridge St Suite 200	San Antonio	TX	78230	**800-683-7771**	210-349-6321	682

Name / Address	City	State	ZIP	Toll-Free	Phone	Class
Initial Tropical Plant Services 3750 W Deerfield Rd	Riverwoods	IL	60015	**800-345-0551**	847-634-4250	261-3
Ink Jet Art Solutions Inc 346 S 500 East Suite 200	Salt Lake City	UT	84102	**800-777-2076**	801-363-9700	582
InKine Pharmaceutical Co 1787 Sentry Pkwy W Bldg 18 Suite 440 *NASDAQ: INKP*	Blue Bell	PA	19422	**800-759-9350**	215-283-6850	86
Inktomi 4100 E 3rd Ave	Foster City	CA	94404	**888-465-8664**	650-653-2800	176-7
Inland Cement Ltd PO Box 3961	Edmonton	AB	T5L4P8	**800-252-9304**	780-420-2500	135
Inland Empire Magazine 3769 Tibbetts St Suite A	Riverside	CA	92506	**877-357-2005**	951-682-3026	449-22
Inland Group Inc 2901 Butterfield Rd	Oak Brook	IL	60523	**800-828-8999**	630-218-8000	641
Inland Mortgage Corp 2901 Butterfield Rd	Oak Brook	IL	60523	**800-828-8999**	630-218-8000	498
Inland Northwest Blood Center 210 W Cataldo Ave	Spokane	WA	99201	**800-423-0151**	509-624-0151	90
Inland Plywood Co 375 N Cass Ave	Pontiac	MI	48342	**800-521-4355**	248-334-4706	602
Inland Power & Light Co Inc PO Box 4429	Spokane	WA	99220	**800-747-7151**	509-747-7151	244
Inland Real Estate Corp 2901 Butterfield Rd *NYSE: IRC*	Oak Brook	IL	60523	**888-331-4732**	630-218-8000	640
Inland Real Estate Development Corp 2901 Butterfield Rd	Oak Brook	IL	60523	**800-828-8999**	630-218-8000	639
Inland Real Estate Sales Inc 2901 Butterfield Rd	Oak Brook	IL	60523	**800-828-8999**	630-218-8000	638
Inland Refractories Co 38600 Chester Rd	Avon	OH	44011	**800-321-0767**	440-934-6600	649
Inland Seafood Corp 1222 Menlo Dr	Atlanta	GA	30318	**800-883-3474**	404-350-5850	292-5
Inland Valley Arbitration & Mediation Service (IVAMS) 300 S Park Ave Suite 780	Pomona	CA	91766	**800-944-8267**	909-629-6301	41
Inland Waters Pollution Control Inc 2021 S Schaefer Hwy	Detroit	MI	48217	**800-992-9118**	313-841-5800	258
Inlet Tower Suites 1200 L St	Anchorage	AK	99501	**800-544-0786**	907-276-0110	373
Inline Plastics Corp 42 Canal St	Shelton	CT	06484	**800-826-5567**	203-924-5933	591
Inmagic Inc 200 Unicorn Pk Dr 4th Fl *Sales	Woburn	MA	01801	**800-229-8398***	781-938-4442	176-10
INMED Partnerships for Children 45449 Severn Way Suite 161	Sterling	VA	20166	**800-521-1175**	703-444-4477	48-5
Inn on 7th 10001 107th St	Edmonton	AB	T5J1J1	**800-661-7327**	780-429-2861	372
Inn on the Alameda 303 E Alameda St	Santa Fe	NM	87501	**800-289-2122**	505-984-2121	373
Inn of the Anasazi 113 Washington Ave	Santa Fe	NM	87501	**800-688-8100**	505-988-3030	373
Inn at Aspen 38750 Hwy 82	Aspen	CO	81611	**800-952-1515**	970-925-1500	370
Inn at Bay Harbor 3600 Village Harbor Dr	Bay Harbor	MI	49770	**800-462-6963**	231-439-4000	655
Inn on the Beach 1615 S Atlantic Ave	Daytona Beach	FL	32118	**800-874-0975**	386-255-0921	373
Inn at Beaver Creek 10 Elk Track Ln	Beaver Creek	CO	81620	**800-859-8242**	970-845-7800	655
Inn at Camachee Harbor 201 Yacht Club Dr	Saint Augustine	FL	32084	**800-688-5379**	904-825-0003	373
Inn at the Colonnade 4 W University Pkwy	Baltimore	MD	21218	**800-222-8733**	410-235-5400	373
Inn & Conference Center of Exeter 90 Front St	Exeter	NH	03833	**800-782-8444**	603-772-5901	373
Inn on the Creek 375 Rainbow Lane PO Box 1000	Midway	UT	84049	**800-654-0892**	435-654-0892	655
Inn on the Creek 295 N Millward St PO Box 445	Jackson	WY	83001	**800-669-9534**	307-739-1565	373
Inn at Essex 70 Essex Way	Essex Junction	VT	05452	**800-727-4295**	802-878-1100	373
Inn at Ethan Allen 21 Lake Ave Ext	Danbury	CT	06811	**800-742-1776**	203-744-1776	373
Inn on Fifth 699 5th Ave S	Naples	FL	34102	**888-403-8778**	239-403-8777	373
Inn on Gitche Gumee 8517 Congdon Blvd	Duluth	MN	55804	**800-317-4979**	218-525-4979	373
Inn of the Governors 101 W Alameda St	Santa Fe	NM	87501	**800-234-4534**	505-982-4333	373
Inn on the Harbor 359 Thames St	Newport	RI	02840	**800-225-3522**	401-849-6789	655
Inn at Harbour Town 11 Lighthouse Ln	Hilton Head Island	SC	29928	**888-807-6873**	843-363-8100	373
Inn at Harvard 1201 Massachusetts Ave	Cambridge	MA	02138	**800-458-5886**	617-491-2222	373
Inn at Henderson's Wharf 1000 Fell St	Baltimore	MD	21231	**800-522-2088**	410-522-7777	373
Inn of the Hills River Resort 1001 Junction Hwy	Kerrville	TX	78028	**800-292-5690**	830-895-5000	655
Inn at Jarrett Farm 38009 US Hwy 75 N	Ramona	OK	74061	**877-371-1200**	918-371-1200	373
Inn by the Lake 3300 Lake Tahoe Blvd	South Lake Tahoe	CA	96150	**800-877-1466**	530-542-0330	373
Inn on Lake Superior 350 Canal Park Dr	Duluth	MN	55802	**888-668-4352**	218-726-1111	373
Inn at Lambertville Station 11 Bridge St	Lambertville	NJ	08530	**800-524-1091**	609-397-4400	373
Inn of Long Beach 185 Atlantic Ave	Long Beach	CA	90802	**800-230-7500**	562-435-3791	373
Inn on Long Wharf 142 Long Wharf	Newport	RI	02840	**800-225-3522**	401-847-7800	655
Inn at the Market 86 Pine St	Seattle	WA	98101	**800-446-4484**	206-443-3600	373
Inn at Mayo Clinic 4400 San Pablo Rd	Jacksonville	FL	32224	**888-255-4458**	904-992-9992	373
Inn at Montchanin Village Rte 100 & Kirk Rd	Montchanin	DE	19710	**800-269-2473**	302-888-2133	373
Inn at Morro Bay 60 State Park Rd	Morro Bay	CA	93442	**800-321-9566**	805-772-5651	373
Inn on Mount Ada 398 Wrigley Rd PO Box 2560	Avalon	CA	90704	**800-608-7669**	310-510-2030	373
Inn of the Mountain Gods 287 Carrizo Canyon Rd	Mescalero	NM	88340	**800-545-9011**	505-464-5141	655
Inn at Mystic 3 Williams Ave PO Box 216	Mystic	CT	06355	**800-237-2415**	860-536-9604	373
Inn at National Hall 2 Post Rd W	Westport	CT	06880	**800-628-4255**	203-221-1351	373
Inn at Newport Beach 30 Wave Ave	Middletown	RI	02842	**800-786-0310**	401-846-0310	373
Inn at Nichols Village 1101 Northern Blvd	Clarks Summit	PA	18411	**800-642-2215**	570-587-1135	373
Inn at the Opera 333 Fulton St	San Francisco	CA	94102	**800-325-2708**	415-863-8400	373
Inn at Otter Crest 301 Otter Crest Loop	Otter Rock	OR	97369	**800-452-2101**	541-765-2111	373
Inn at Oyster Point 425 Marina Blvd	South San Francisco	CA	94080	**800-642-2720**	650-737-7633	373
Inn of the Ozarks. Best Western 297 W Van Buren	Eureka Springs	AR	72632	**800-552-3785**	479-253-9768	655
Inn at the Park 3751 E Douglas Ave	Wichita	KS	67218	**800-258-1951**	316-652-0500	373
Inn at Pelican Bay 800 Vanderbilt Beach Rd	Naples	FL	34108	**800-597-8770**	239-597-8777	373
Inn at Perry Cabin 308 Watkins Ln	Saint Michaels	MD	21663	**800-722-2949**	410-745-2200	373
Inn at Queen Anne 505 1st Ave N	Seattle	WA	98109	**800-952-5043**	206-282-7357	373
Inn at Rancho Santa Fe 5951 Linea Del Cielo PO Box 869	Rancho Santa Fe	CA	92067	**800-843-4661**	858-756-1131	655
Inn at Reading 1040 Park Rd	Wyomissing	PA	19610	**800-383-9713**	610-372-7811	373
Inn at Saint John 939 Congress St	Portland	ME	04102	**800-636-9127**	207-773-6481	373
Inn at Saint Mary's 53993 US 31-33 N	South Bend	IN	46637	**800-947-8627**	574-232-4000	373
Inn at Sawmill Farm Crosstown Rd & Rt 100 PO Box 367	West Dover	VT	05356	**800-493-1133**	802-464-8131	373
Inn by the Sea 40 Bowery Beach Rd	Cape Elizabeth	ME	04107	**800-888-4287**	207-799-3134	655
Inn of the Seventh Mountain 18575 SW Century Dr	Bend	OR	97702	**800-452-6810**	541-382-8711	655
Inn of the Six Mountains 2617 Killington Rd	Killington	VT	05751	**800-228-4676**	802-422-4302	373
Inn at Spanish Bay 2700 17-Mile Dr	Pebble Beach	CA	93953	**800-654-9300**	831-647-7500	655
Inn at Spanish Head 4009 SW Hwy 101	Lincoln City	OR	97367	**800-452-8127**	541-996-2161	373
Inn at Stratton Mountain 61 Middle Ridge Rd	Stratton Mountain	VT	05155	**800-777-1700**	802-297-2500	655
Inn at Tallgrass 2280 N Tara Cir	Wichita	KS	67226	**800-684-3466**	316-684-3466	373
Inn at Temple Square 71 W South Temple	Salt Lake City	UT	84101	**800-843-4668**	801-531-1000	373
Inn at the Tides PO Box 640 800 Hwy 1	Bodega Bay	CA	94923	**800-541-7788**	707-875-2751	373
Inn at Union Square 440 Post St	San Francisco	CA	94102	**800-288-4346**	415-397-3510	373
Inn on Woodlake 705 Woodlake Rd	Kohler	WI	53044	**800-919-3600**	920-452-7800	655
Inner Harbour Hospitals 4685 Dorsett Shoals Rd	Douglasville	GA	30135	**800-255-8657**	770-942-2391	366-1
Inner Traditions International 1 Park St	Rochester	VT	05767	**800-246-8648**	802-767-3174	623-2
Innisbrook Golf Resort. Westin 36750 US Hwy 19 N	Palm Harbor	FL	34684	**800-456-2000**	727-942-2000	655
Innkeeper Motels/Hotels 4829 Riverside Dr	Danville	VA	24541	**800-466-5337**	434-822-2161	369
Innodata Isogen Inc 3 University Plaza Dr Suite 506 *NASDAQ: INOD*	Hackensack	NJ	07601	**800-567-4784**	201-488-1200	176-12
INNOLOG (Innovative Logistics Techniques Inc) 2010 Corporate Ridge 9th Fl	McLean	VA	22102	**800-466-6564**	703-506-1555	178
Innotrac Corp 6655 Sugarloaf Pkwy *NASDAQ: INOC*	Duluth	GA	30097	**800-827-4666**	678-584-4000	194
InnovAsian Travel Inc 10 North Ln	Armonk	NY	10504	**800-553-4665**	914-273-6716	760
Innovative Fluid Handling Systems Inc 200 E 3rd St	Rock Falls	IL	61071	**800-435-7003**	815-626-1018	197
Innovative Health Products Inc 6950 Bryan Dairy Rd	Largo	FL	33777	**800-654-2347**	727-544-8866	572
Innovative Logistics Techniques Inc (INNOLOG) 2010 Corporate Ridge 9th Fl	McLean	VA	22102	**800-466-6564**	703-506-1555	178
Innovative Resources Consultant Group Inc 1 Park Plaza Suite 600	Irvine	CA	92614	**800-945-4724**	949-252-0590	193
Innovative Stamping Corp 2068 Gladwick St	Compton	CA	90220	**800-400-0047**	310-537-6996	479
Innovative Systems Inc 790 Holiday Dr Bldg 11	Pittsburgh	PA	15220	**800-622-6390**	412-937-9300	176-1
Innovative Technologies Corp 1020 Woodman Dr Suite 100	Dayton	OH	45432	**800-745-8050**	937-252-2145	176-10
Innovo Group Inc 2633 Kingston Pike Suite 100 *NASDAQ: INNO*	Knoxville	TN	37919	**800-627-2621**	865-546-1110	343
Inns of America 755 Raintree Dr Suite 200	Carlsbad	CA	92009	**800-826-0778**	760-438-6661	369
Inns at Mill Falls 312 Daniel Webster Hwy	Meredith	NH	03253	**800-622-6455**	603-279-7006	373
InnSuites Hospitality Trust 1615 E Northern Ave Suite 102 *AMEX: IHT*	Phoenix	AZ	85020	**800-842-4242**	602-944-1500	640
InnSuites Hotels Inc 1615 E Northern Ave Suite 102	Phoenix	AZ	85020	**800-842-4242**	602-944-1500	369
InnSuites Hotels Inc 1615 E Northern Ave Suite 102	Phoenix	AZ	85020	**800-842-4242**	602-944-1500	369
Inolex Chemical Co Jackson & Swanson Sts *Cust Svc	Philadelphia	PA	19148	**800-521-9891***	215-271-0800	142
INOVA Corp 110 Avon St	Charlottesville	VA	22902	**800-637-1077**	434-817-8000	385
INOVA Fairfax Hospital Transplant Center 8503 Arlington Blvd Suite 200	Fairfax	VA	22031	**800-358-8831**	703-970-3178	758
InPath Devices 3610 Dodge St Suite 200	Omaha	NE	68131	**800-988-1914**	402-345-9200	171-7
InPhonic Inc 1010 Wisconsin Ave NW Suite 600 *NASDAQ: INPC* ■ *Sales	Washington	DC	20007	**800-300-7066***	202-333-0001	721
Insaco Inc 1365 Canary Rd	Quakertown	PA	18951	**800-497-4531**	215-536-3500	710
Insco Dico Group 17780 Fitch Suite 200	Irvine	CA	92614	**800-782-1546**	949-263-3300	384-5
Insco Distributing Inc 12501 Network Blvd	San Antonio	TX	78249	**800-203-8400**	210-690-8400	651
Insevo Inc 2600 Campus Dr *Sales	San Mateo	CA	94403	**888-243-8762***	650-571-9798	176-1
Inside Energy Newsletter 2 Penn Plaza 25th Fl	New York	NY	10121	**800-223-6180**	800-752-8872	521-5

Name / Address	City	State	ZIP	Toll-Free	Phone	Class
Inside FERC Newsletter 2 Penn Plaza 25th Fl	New York	NY	10121	**800-223-6180**	800-752-8872	521-5
Inside FERC's Gas Market Report 2 Penn Plaza 25th Fl	New York	NY	10121	**800-223-6180**	212-904-6410	521-5
Inside NRC Newsletter 2 Penn Plaza 25th Fl	New York	NY	10121	**800-223-6180**	800-752-8872	521-5
Inside Washington Publishers Inc 1225 South Clark St Suite 1400	Arlington	VA	22202	**800-424-9068**	703-416-8500	623-9
InsideFlyer Magazine 1930 Frequent Flyer Point	Colorado Springs	CO	80915	**800-767-8896**	719-597-8889	449-22
Insider Weekly for AS/400 Managers 990 Washington St Suite 308	Dedham	MA	02026	**888-400-4768**	781-320-9460	521-3
Insight Enterprises Inc 6820 S Harl Ave *NASDAQ: NSIT*	Tempe	AZ	85283	**800-467-4448**	480-333-3000	177
InSight Health Services Corp 26250 Enterprise Ct Suite 100	Lake Forest	CA	92630	**800-874-8634**	949-282-6000	376
Insight Information Co 214 King St W Suite 300	Toronto	ON	M5H3S6	**888-777-1707**	416-777-2020	753
Insight Media 2162 Broadway	New York	NY	10024	**800-233-9910**	212-721-6316	500
Insight Vacations Inc 801 Katella Ave	Anaheim	CA	92805	**800-582-8380**		748
Insightful Corp 1700 Westlake Ave N Suite 500 *NASDAQ: IFUL*	Seattle	WA	98109	**800-569-0123**	206-283-8802	176-3
Insignia Systems Inc 6470 Sycamore Ct N *NASDAQ: ISIG*	Maple Grove	MN	55369	**800-874-4648**	763-392-6200	692
Insinger Machine Co 6245 State Rd	Philadelphia	PA	19135	**800-344-4802**	215-624-4800	293
InSite Vision Inc 965 Atlantic Ave *AMEX: ISV*	Alameda	CA	94501	**800-726-7483**	510-865-8800	229
Insituform Technologies Inc 702 Spirit 40 Park Dr *NASDAQ: INSU* ■ *Cust Svc	Chesterfield	MO	63005	**800-234-2992***	636-530-8000	187-10
Insl-X Products Corp 50 Holt Dr	Stony Point	NY	10980	**800-225-5554**	845-786-5000	540
INSP (Inspirational Network The) 7910 Crescent Executive Dr Suite 500	Charlotte	NC	28217	**800-725-4677**	704-525-9800	725
InspecTech Inc 925 N Point Pkwy Suite 400	Alpharetta	GA	30005	**800-285-3001**		360
Inspectors. American Society of Home 932 Lee St Suite 101	Des Plaines	IL	60016	**800-743-2744**	847-759-2820	49-3
Inspectors Inc. National Assn of Home 4248 Park Glen Rd	Minneapolis	MN	55416	**800-448-3942**	952-928-4641	49-3
Inspiration Software Inc 7412 SW Beaverton Hillsdale Hwy Suite 102	Portland	OR	97225	**800-877-4292**	503-297-3004	176-1
Inspirational Network The (INSP) 7910 Crescent Executive Dr Suite 500	Charlotte	NC	28217	**800-725-4677**	704-525-9800	725
Inspire Pharmaceuticals Inc 4222 Emperor Blvd Suite 200 *NASDAQ: ISPH*	Durham	NC	27703	**877-800-4536**	919-941-9777	86
Inspired Corp 103 Eisenhower Pkwy	Roseland	NJ	07068	**800-738-3747**	973-226-1234	512
Inspired Distribution LLC 103 Eisenhower Pkwy	Roseland	NJ	07068	**800-272-4214**	973-226-1234	514
Instantwhip Foods Inc 2200 Cardigan Ave *Cust Svc	Columbus	OH	43215	**800-544-9447***	614-488-2536	291-10
Insteel Industries Inc 1373 Boggs Dr	Mount Airy	NC	27030	**800-334-9504**	336-786-2141	182
Instinet Group Inc 3 Times Sq *NASDAQ: INGP*	New York	NY	10036	**800-225-5008**	212-310-9500	251
Institute for the Advancement of Human Behavior (IAHB) 4370 Alpine Rd Suite 209	Portola Valley	CA	94028	**800-258-8411**	650-851-8411	49-8
Institute of American Indian Arts 83 Avan Nu Po *Admissions	Santa Fe	NM	87508	**800-804-6422***	505-424-2300	161
Institute of American Indian Arts Museum 108 Cathedral Pl	Santa Fe	NM	87501	**800-804-6423**	505-983-8900	509
Institute of Business Appraisers (IBA) 6950 Cypress Rd Suite 209	Plantation	FL	33317	**800-299-4130**	954-584-1144	49-17
Institute for Business & Home Safety (IBHS) 4775 E Fowler Ave	Tampa	FL	33617	**866-675-4247**	813-286-3400	49-9
Institute of Caster & Wheel Manufacturers (ICWM) 8720 Red Oak Blvd Suite 201	Charlotte	NC	28217	**800-345-1815**	704-676-1190	49-13
Institute for Certification of Computing Professionals (ICCP) 2350 E Devon Ave Suite 115	Des Plaines	IL	60018	**800-843-8227**	847-299-4227	48-9
Institute of Certified Professional Managers (ICPM) James Madison University MSC 5504	Harrisonburg	VA	22807	**800-568-4120**	540-568-3247	49-12
Institute for Computer Capacity Management 1020 8th Ave S Suite 6	Naples	FL	34102	**800-531-6143**	239-261-8945	48-9
Institute of Electrical & Electronics Engineers (IEEE) 3 Park Ave 17th Fl	New York	NY	10016	**800-678-4333**	212-419-7900	49-19
Institute of Food Technologists (IFT) 525 W Van Buren St Suite 1000	Chicago	IL	60607	**800-438-3663**	312-782-8424	49-6
Institute for Health Freedom 1825 'I' St NW Suite 400	Washington	DC	20006	**888-616-1976**	202-429-6610	48-8
Institute for Humane Studies 3301 N Fairfax Dr Suite 440	Arlington	VA	22201	**800-697-8799**	703-993-4880	654
Institute of Industrial Engineers (IIE) 3577 Parkway Ln Suite 200 *Cust Svc	Norcross	GA	30092	**800-494-0460***	770-449-0460	49-13
Institute for Integral Development PO Box 2172	Colorado Springs	CO	80901	**800-544-9562**	719-634-7943	754
Institute of Management Accountants Inc (IMA) 10 Paragon Dr	Montvale	NJ	07645	**800-638-4427**	201-573-9000	49-1
Institute of Management & Administration Inc (IOMA Inc) 3 Park Ave 30th Fl	New York	NY	10016	**800-401-5937**	212-244-0360	623-9

Name / Address	City	State	ZIP	Toll-Free	Phone	Class
Institute of Management Consultants USA Inc (IMC USA) 2025 M St NW Suite 800	Washington	DC	20036	**800-221-2557**	202-367-1134	49-12
Institute for Operations Research & the Management Sciences (INFORMS) 7240 Parkway Dr Suite 310	Hanover	MD	21076	**800-446-3676**	443-757-3500	49-19
Institute of Packaging Professionals (IoPP) 1601 N Bond St Suite 101	Naperville	IL	60563	**800-432-4085**	630-544-5050	49-13
Institute of Paper Science & Technology (IPST) 500 10th St NW	Atlanta	GA	30332	**800-558-6611**	404-894-5700	49-13
Institute of Real Estate Management (IREM) 430 N Michigan Ave	Chicago	IL	60611	**800-837-0706**	312-329-6000	49-17
Institute for Rehabilitation & Research 1333 Moursund St	Houston	TX	77030	**800-447-3422**	713-799-5000	366-4
Institute for Supply Management (ISM) 2055 Centennial Cir *Cust Svc	Tempe	AZ	85284	**800-888-6276***	480-752-6275	49-12
Institute of Texan Cultures 801 S Bowie St HemisFair Pk	San Antonio	TX	78205	**800-776-7651**	210-458-2300	509
Institute of World Politics 1521 16th St NW	Washington	DC	20036	**888-566-9497**	202-462-2101	654
Institution Food House Inc 543 12th Street Dr NW	Hickory	NC	28603	**800-487-2527**	828-323-4500	294
Institutional Distributors Inc PO Box 520	East Bernstadt	KY	40729	**800-442-7885**	606-843-2100	294
Institutional Investor Newsletters 225 Park Ave S 8th Fl	New York	NY	10003	**800-715-9197**	212-224-3800	623-9
Institutional Linen Management. National Assn of 2130 Lexington Rd Suite H	Richmond	KY	40475	**800-669-0863**	859-624-0177	49-4
Institutional & Office Services Inc 4 Cara Ct	Randolph	NJ	07869	**800-223-1210**	973-895-9002	314-1
Institutional Wholesale Co 535 Dry Valley Rd	Cookeville	TN	38503	**800-239-9588**	931-537-4000	294
Instron Corp Wilson Instruments Div 100 Royall St	Canton	MA	02021	**800-695-4273**	781-575-6000	464
Instron Industrial Products Group 900 Liberty St	Grove City	PA	16127	**800-726-8378**	724-458-9610	464
Instructor Magazine 557 Broadway	New York	NY	10012	**800-544-2917**	212-343-6100	449-8
Instructors. National Assn of Underwater 1232 Tech Blvd	Tampa	FL	33619	**800-553-6284**	813-628-6284	48-22
Instrumentation. Association for the Advancement of Medical 1110 N Glebe Rd Suite 220	Arlington	VA	22201	**800-332-2264**	703-525-4890	49-8
Instrumentation Laboratory Inc 101 Hartwell Ave *Sales	Lexington	MA	02421	**800-955-9525***	781-861-0710	410
Instrumentation & Measurement Society. IEEE IEEE Operations Ctr 445 Hoes Ln	Piscataway	NJ	08854	**800-678-4333**	732-981-0060	49-19
Insul-8 Corp 10102 F St	Omaha	NE	68127	**800-521-4888**	402-339-9300	118
Insulair Inc 35275 Welty Rd	Vernalis	CA	95385	**800-343-3402**	209-839-0911	548-1
Insulation Assn. National 99 Canal Center Plaza Suite 222	Alexandria	VA	22314	**877-968-7642**	703-683-6422	49-3
Insulfab Plastics Inc 834 Hayne St	Spartanburg	SC	29301	**800-845-7599**	864-582-7506	588
Insultab Inc 45 Industrial Pkwy *Cust Svc	Woburn	MA	01801	**800-468-4822***	781-935-0800	588
Insurance Agents & Brokers of America Inc. Independent 127 S Peyton St	Alexandria	VA	22314	**800-221-7917**	703-683-4422	49-9
Insurance Agents. National Assn of Professional 400 N Washington St	Alexandria	VA	22314	**800-742-6900**	703-836-9340	49-9
Insurance Auto Auctions Inc 850 E Algonquin Rd Suite 100	Schaumburg	IL	60173	**800-872-1501**	847-839-3939	51
Insurance Chronicle Newsletter 1 State St Plaza	New York	NY	10004	**800-221-1809**	212-803-8200	521-1
Insurance Co of the West 11455 El Camino Real	San Diego	CA	92130	**800-877-1111**	858-350-2400	384-4
Insurance Companies at American General Financial PO Box 39	Evansville	IN	47701	**800-325-2147**		384-2
Insurance Companies. National Assn of Mutual 3601 Vincennes Rd PO Box 875525	Indianapolis	IN	46268	**800-336-2642**	317-875-5250	49-9
Insurance Consultants International 7405 Campstool Dr Suite 101	Colorado Springs	CO	80922	**800-576-2674**	281-587-9884	384-7
Insurance Counselors. Society of Certified PO Box 27027	Austin	TX	78755	**800-633-2165**	512-345-7932	49-9
Insurance Crime Bureau. National 10330 S Roberts Rd	Palos Hills	IL	60465	**800-447-6282**	708-430-2430	49-9
Insurance Data Processing Inc 1 Washington Sq	Wyncote	PA	19095	**800-523-6745**	215-885-2150	176-11
Insurance Exchange. Armed Forces PO Box G	Fort Leavenworth	KS	66027	**800-828-7732**	913-651-5000	384-4
Insurance & Financial Advisors. National Assn of 2901 Telestar Ct *Sales	Falls Church	VA	22042	**877-866-2432***	703-770-8100	49-9
Insurance Information Institute (III) 110 William St 24th Fl	New York	NY	10038	**800-331-9146**	212-346-5500	49-9
Insurance Institute of America. American Institute for CPCU & 720 Providence Rd PO Box 3016	Malvern	PA	19355	**800-644-2101**	610-644-2100	49-9
Insurance Institute of America Inc. Self- PO Box 1237	Simpsonville	SC	29681	**800-851-7789**	864-962-2208	49-9
Insurance Management Assoc Inc 250 N Water St	Wichita	KS	67202	**800-333-8913**	316-267-9221	383
Insurance Management Society Inc. Risk & 655 3rd Ave 2nd Fl	New York	NY	10017	**800-711-0317**	212-286-9292	49-9
Insurance Plans. America's Health 601 Pennsylvania Ave NW Suite 500 *Cust Svc	Washington	DC	20004	**877-291-2247***	202-778-3200	49-9
Insurance Reference Systems Inc DBA SilverPlume 4775 Walnut St Suite 2-B	Boulder	CO	80301	**800-677-4442**	303-444-0695	380

Name / Address	City	State	ZIP	Toll-Free	Phone	Class
Insurance Regulation Newsletter PO Box 7376	Alexandria	VA	22307	**800-876-2545**	703-768-9600	521-7
Insurance Research Council (IRC) 718 Providence Rd PO Box 3025	Malvern	PA	19355	**800-644-2101**	610-644-2212	49-9
Insurance Services. American Assn of 1745 S Naperville Rd	Wheaton	IL	60187	**800-564-2247**	630-681-8347	49-9
Insurance Services. National Crop 7201 W 129th St Suite 200	Overland Park	KS	66213	**800-951-6247**	913-685-2767	48-2
Insurance Services Office Inc (ISO) 545 Washington Blvd	Jersey City	NJ	07310	**800-888-4476**	201-469-2000	383
Insurance Women (International). National Assn of 1847 E 15th St	Tulsa	OK	74104	**800-766-6249**	918-744-5195	49-9
Insurance.com Insurance Agency LLC 29001 Solon Rd	Solon	OH	44139	**866-533-0227**		383
InsurBanc 10 Executive Dr	Farmington	CT	06032	**866-467-2262**	860-677-9701	71
Insure Kids Now! Health Resources & Services Administration 5600 Fishers Ln	Rockville	MD	20857	**877-543-7669**		196
Insured Aircraft Title Service Inc 4848 SW 36th St	Oklahoma City	OK	73179	**800-654-4882**	405-681-6663	621
InsynQ Inc 1127 Broadway Plaza Suite 202	Tacoma	WA	98402	**866-796-9925**	253-284-2000	39
Intacct Corp 170 Knowles Dr Suite 120	Los Gatos	CA	95032	**877-704-3700**	408-884-3390	39
Intaglio Visual Arts & Technology 3855 Eastern Ave SE	Grand Rapids	MI	49508	**800-632-9153**	616-243-3300	502
Intalco Aluminum Corp 4050 Mountain View Rd	Ferndale	WA	98248	**800-752-0852**	360-384-7061	476
Integic Corp 14585 Avion Pkwy	Chantilly	VA	20151	**800-874-2344**	703-222-2840	176-12
Integra Bank Corp PO Box 868 *NASDAQ: IBNK*	Evansville	IN	47705	**800-467-1928**	812-464-9800	355-2
Integra Bank NA 21 SE 3rd St	Evansville	IN	47708	**800-467-1928**	812-464-9800	71
Integra LifeSciences Holdings Corp 311 Enterprise Dr *NASDAQ: IART*	Plainsboro	NJ	08536	**800-654-2873**	609-275-0500	86
Integra Telecom 1201 NE Lloyd Blvd Suite 500	Portland	OR	97232	**800-727-8484**	503-453-8000	721
IntegraColor PO Box 180218	Dallas	TX	75218	**800-433-8247**	972-289-0705	615
Integral Development. Institute for PO Box 2172	Colorado Springs	CO	80901	**800-544-9562**	719-634-7943	754
Integralis US 111 Founders Plaza 13th Fl	East Hartford	CT	06108	**877-557-1475**	860-291-0851	176-12
Integrated Alarm Services Group Inc 99 Pine St 5th Fl *NASDAQ: IASG*	Albany	NY	12207	**888-305-4090**	518-426-1515	683
Integrated Brands 4175 Veterans Memorial Hwy	Ronkonkoma	NY	11779	**800-423-2763**	631-737-9700	291-25
Integrated Computer Solutions Inc 201 Broadway	Cambridge	MA	02139	**800-800-4271**	617-621-0060	176-2
Integrated Device Technology Inc 2975 Stender Way *NASDAQ: IDTI*	Santa Clara	CA	95054	**800-345-7015**	408-727-6116	686
Integrated Electronics Corp 420 E 58th Ave	Denver	CO	80216	**800-876-8686**	303-292-5537	245
Integrated Fund Services Inc 221 E 4th St Suite 300	Cincinnati	OH	45202	**800-543-8721**		679
Integrated Information Systems Inc 2250 W 14th St	Tempe	AZ	85281	**877-447-7755**	480-752-5000	178
Integrated Insights 9370 Sky Park Ct Suite 140	San Diego	CA	92123	**800-372-4472**	858-571-1698	454
Integrated Silicon Solution Inc (ISSI) 2231 Lawson Ln *NASDAQ: ISSI*	Santa Clara	CA	95054	**800-379-4774**	408-969-6600	686
Integrated Systems Analysts Inc 2800 Shirlington Rd Suite 1100	Arlington	VA	22206	**800-929-3436**	703-824-0700	178
Integretel Inc 5883 Rue Ferrari	San Jose	CA	95138	**888-302-2750**	408-362-4000	722
Integris Metals Inc 455 85th Ave NW	Minneapolis	MN	55433	**800-328-7800**	763-717-9000	483
Integrity eLearning Inc 5500 Santa Ana Canyon Rd Suite 245	Anaheim Hills	CA	92807	**888-624-6464**	714-637-9480	39
Integrity Life Insurance Co 515 W Market St 8th Fl	Louisville	KY	40202	**800-325-8583**	502-582-7900	384-2
Integrity Media Inc 1000 Cody Rd S *Orders	Mobile	AL	36695	**800-533-6912***	251-633-9000	643
Integrix Inc 2001 Corporate Ctr Dr	Newbury Park	CA	91230	**800-300-8288**	805-376-1000	174
Integro Inc 1350 17th St Suite 300	Denver	CO	80202	**888-575-9300**	303-575-9300	178
Intek Plastic Inc 800 E 10th St *Cust Svc	Hastings	MN	55033	**800-451-4544***	651-437-7700	321
Intel Corp 2200 Mission College Blvd *NASDAQ: INTC* ■ *Cust Svc	Santa Clara	CA	95052	**800-628-8686***	408-765-8080	686
Intel Museum 2200 Mission College Blvd	Santa Clara	CA	95052	**800-628-8686**	408-765-0503	509
Intelect Technologies Inc 1225 Commerce Dr	Richardson	TX	75081	**888-477-7272**	972-367-2100	633
IntelliCoat Technologies 28 Gaylord St	South Hadley	MA	01075	**800-628-9285**	413-536-7800	542-1
InteliData Technologies Corp 11600 Sunrise Valley Dr Suite 100 *NASDAQ: INTD*	Reston	VA	20191	**800-878-1053**	703-259-3000	70
Intellectual Property Strategist Newsletter 345 Park Ave S	New York	NY	10010	**800-883-8300**	212-779-9200	521-7
Intelli-Check Inc 246 Crossways Park W *AMEX: IDN*	Woodbury	NY	11797	**800-444-9542**	516-992-1900	171-7
Intelligencer Journal 8 W King St	Lancaster	PA	17603	**800-809-4666**	717-291-8811	522-2
Intelligencer Printing Co 330 Eden Rd	Lancaster	PA	17601	**800-233-0107**	717-291-3100	615
Intelligent Enterprise Magazine 2800 Campus Dr *Cust Svc	San Mateo	CA	94403	**800-289-9839***	650-513-4300	449-7
Intelligent Health Systems 4275 Executive Sq Suite 550	La Jolla	CA	92037	**800-487-5772**	858-453-3600	176-11
Intelligent Transportation Society of America 1100 17th St NW Suite 1200	Washington	DC	20036	**800-374-8472**	202-484-4847	49-21
IntelliNet Technologies Inc 1990 W New Haven Ave Suite 307	Melbourne	FL	32904	**888-726-0686**	321-726-0686	176-7
Intellinex LLC 925 Euclid Ave Suite 1800	Cleveland	OH	44115	**866-835-3276**	216-685-6000	752
IntelliReach Corp 20 CareMatrix Dr	Dedham	MA	02026	**800-219-9838**	781-410-3000	176-7
Intellisync Corp 2550 N 1st St Suite 500 *NASDAQ: SYNC*	San Jose	CA	95131	**800-248-2795**	408-321-7650	176-7
Intelnet Inc 320 Westcott St Suite 108	Houston	TX	77007	**888-636-3693**	713-880-3693	621
Intelogistics Corp 8411 W Oakland Pk Blvd Suite 300	Fort Lauderdale	FL	33351	**877-453-5700**	954-343-5588	176-1
Inter American Press Assn (IAPA) 1801 SW 3rd Ave 7th Fl	Miami	FL	33129	**877-747-4272**	305-634-2465	49-14
Inter City Oil Co Inc PO Box 3048	Duluth	MN	55803	**800-642-5542**	218-728-3641	569
Inter-County Energy Co-op PO Box 87	Danville	KY	40423	**888-266-7322**	859-236-4561	244
Inter Parfums Inc 551 5th Ave Suite 1500 *NASDAQ: IPAR*	New York	NY	10176	**800-533-6010**	212-983-2640	564
Inter-Tel Inc 1615 S 52nd St *NASDAQ: INTL*	Tempe	AZ	85281	**800-669-5858**	480-449-8900	720
Interact Inc 1225 L St Suite 600	Lincoln	NE	68508	**800-242-8649**	402-476-8786	176-7
InterAct Public Safety Systems Inc 45 Patton Ave	Asheville	NC	28801	**800-768-3911**	828-254-9876	176-10
Interactive Intelligence Inc 7601 Interactive Way *NASDAQ: ININ*	Indianapolis	IN	46278	**800-267-1364**	317-872-3000	176-7
Interactive Management Inc 11166 Huron St Suite 27	Denver	CO	80234	**800-243-1233**	303-433-4446	47
Interactive Market Systems Inc 770 Broadway	New York	NY	10003	**800-223-7942**	646-654-5900	176-10
Interactive Marketing. Association for 1430 Broadway 8th Fl	New York	NY	10018	**888-337-0008**	212-790-1406	48-9
Interactive Media Corp DBA Kanguru Solutions 1360 Main St *Sales	Millis	MA	02054	**888-526-4878***	508-376-4245	171-8
Interactive Public Relations Newsletter 316 N Michigan Ave Suite 300	Chicago	IL	60601	**800-878-5331**	312-960-4100	521-11
Interactive Services Group Inc 600 Delran Pkwy Suite C	Delran	NJ	08075	**800-566-3310**		173
InterAmerica Technologies Inc 8150 Leesburg Pike Suite 1400	Vienna	VA	22182	**800-945-8329**	703-893-3514	176-1
InterAmerican Motor Corp 8901 Canoga Ave	Canoga Park	CA	91304	**800-874-8925**	818-678-1200	61
Interamerican Trading & Products Corp PO Box 402427	Miami Beach	FL	33140	**800-999-7123**	305-885-9666	292-5
InterArt Distribution DBA Sunrise Greetings 1145 Sunrise Greetings Ct *Sales	Bloomington	IN	47404	**800-457-4045***	812-336-9900	130
Interbond Corp of America 3200 SW 42nd St	Hollywood	FL	33312	**800-432-8579**	954-797-4000	35
Intercall Inc 8420 W Bryn Mawr Suite 400 *Resv	Chicago	IL	60631	**800-374-2441***	773-399-1600	721
Interchange Financial Services Corp Park 80 W Plaza 2 *NASDAQ: IFCJ*	Saddle Brook	NJ	07663	**800-701-7718**	201-703-2265	355-2
Intercim Corp 501 E Hwy 13	Burnsville	MN	55337	**800-343-3734**	952-894-9010	176-10
Intercoastal Mfg Co 10975 SW 11 St Bldg A Suite 150	Beaverton	OR	97005	**800-547-6644**	503-574-2200	128
Intercollegiate Studies Institute (ISI) 3901 Centerville Rd	Wilmington	DE	19807	**800-526-7022**	302-652-4600	48-11
Intercomp Co 14465 23rd Ave N	Minneapolis	MN	55447	**800-328-3336**	763-476-2531	672
InterContinental The Barclay New York 111 E 48th St	New York	NY	10017	**800-327-0200**	212-755-5900	373
Intercontinental Chemical Corp 4660 Spring Grove Ave	Cincinnati	OH	45232	**800-543-2075**	513-541-7100	143
InterContinental Chicago 505 N Michigan Ave	Chicago	IL	60611	**800-628-2112**	312-944-4100	373
InterContinental Dallas 15201 Dallas Pkwy	Addison	TX	75248	**800-327-0200**	972-386-6000	373
InterContinental Hotel & Conference Center Cleveland 9801 Carnegie Ave	Cleveland	OH	44106	**877-707-8999**	216-707-4100	373
InterContinental Hotels Group Staybridge Suites by Holiday Inn 3 Ravinia Dr Suite 100	Atlanta	GA	30346	**800-465-4329**	770-604-2000	369
InterContinental Houston 2222 West Loop S	Houston	TX	77027	**800-316-8645**	713-627-7600	373
InterContinental Life Corp PO Box 149138	Austin	TX	78714	**800-925-6000**	512-404-5000	355-4
InterContinental Mark Hopkins San Francisco 1 Nob Hill	San Francisco	CA	94108	**800-662-4455**	415-392-3434	373
InterContinental Miami 100 Chopin Plaza	Miami	FL	33131	**888-567-8725**	305-577-1000	373
InterContinental Montreal 360 rue Saint-Antoine O	Montreal	QC	H2Y3X4	**800-361-3600**	514-987-9900	372
InterContinental New Orleans 444 St Charles Ave	New Orleans	LA	70130	**800-327-0200**	504-525-5566	373
InterContinental San Juan Resort & Casino 5961 Isla Verde Ave	Carolina	PR	00979	**800-443-2009**	787-791-6100	373
InterContinental Stephen F Austin 701 Congress Ave	Austin	TX	78701	**800-327-0200**	512-457-8800	373
InterContinental Suites Cleveland 8800 Euclid Ave	Cleveland	OH	44106	**888-707-8999**	216-707-4300	373
InterContinental Toronto 220 Bloor St W	Toronto	ON	M5S1T8	**800-267-0010**	416-960-5200	372
Intercontinental Toronto Centre 225 Front St W	Toronto	ON	M5V2X3	**800-227-6963**	416-597-1400	372
Interdean.Interconex 55 Hunter Ln	Elmsford	NY	10523	**800-952-7230**	914-347-6600	508
InterDigital Communications Corp 781 3rd Ave *NASDAQ: IDCC*	King of Prussia	PA	19406	**800-669-4737**	610-878-7800	686
Interex PO Box 3439	Sunnyvale	CA	94088	**800-468-3739**	408-747-0227	48-9

Name / Address	City	State	ZIP	Toll-Free	Phone	Class
Interface EAP Inc 10370 Richmond Ave Suite 1100	Houston	TX	77042	**800-324-4327**	713-781-3364	454
Interface Flooring Systems Inc 1503 Orchard Hill Rd	LaGrange	GA	30240	**800-336-0225**	706-882-1891	131
Interface Inc 7401 E Butherus Dr	Scottsdale	AZ	85260	**800-947-5598**	480-948-5555	464
Interface Solutions Inc 216 Wohlsen Way	Lancaster	PA	17603	**800-942-7538**	717-207-6000	321
Interfaith Coalition on Aging. National 300 D St SW	Washington	DC	20024	**800-424-9046**	202-479-1200	48-6
Interfoods of America Inc 9400 S Dadeland Blvd Suite 720	Miami	FL	33156	**866-476-7393**	305-670-0746	656
Interform Solutions 1901 Mayview Rd	Bridgeville	PA	15017	**800-945-7746**	412-221-3300	111
Intergraph Corp 288 Dunlop Blvd	Huntsville	AL	35824	**800-345-4856**	256-730-2000	176-5
NASDAQ: INGR						
Interim HealthCare Inc 1601 Sawgrass Corporate Pkwy	Sunrise	FL	33323	**800-338-7786**	954-858-6000	707
Interior Design Assn. International 13-500 Merchandise Mart	Chicago	IL	60654	**888-799-4432**	312-467-1950	48-4
Interior Design Magazine PO Box 16898	North Hollywood	CA	91615	**800-900-0804**		449-2
Interlake Material Handling Inc 1230 E Diehl Rd Suite 400	Naperville	IL	60563	**800-282-8032***	630-245-8800	462
*Sales						
Interlaken Inn 74 Interlaken Rd	Lakeville	CT	06039	**800-222-2909**	860-435-9878	655
Interlaken Resort & Country Spa W 4240 SR-50	Lake Geneva	WI	53147	**800-225-5558**	262-248-9121	655
Interland Inc 303 Peachtree Ctr Ave Suite 500	Atlanta	GA	30303	**800-214-1460**	404-260-2477	795
NASDAQ: INLD						
Interlectric Corp 1401 Lexington Ave	Warren	PA	16365	**800-722-2184**	814-723-6061	429
Interline Brands Inc 801 W Bay St	Jacksonville	FL	32204	**800-288-2000**	904-421-1400	346
NYSE: IBI						
Interlink Electronics Inc 546 Flynn Rd	Camarillo	CA	93012	**800-340-1331**	805-484-8855	171-1
NASDAQ: LINK						
Interlink Group LLC 98 Inverness Dr E Suite 150	Englewood	CO	80112	**888-533-1307**	303-542-7100	178
InterLock Industries Inc 7800 State Rd 60	Sellersburg	IN	47172	**800-406-7387**	812-246-1935	471
Interlocking Concrete Pavement Institute (ICPI) 1444 'I' St NW Suite 700	Washington	DC	20005	**800-241-3652**	202-712-9036	49-3
Intermec Technologies Corp 6001 36th Ave W	Everett	WA	98203	**800-934-3163***	425-348-2600	222
*Sales						
InterMedi@ Marketing Solutions 204 Carter Dr	West Chester	PA	19382	**800-835-3466**	610-696-4646	722
InterMetro Industries Corp 651 N Washington St	Wilkes-Barre	PA	18705	**800-992-1776***	570-825-2741	281
*Cust Svc						
Intermex Inc 9330 LBJ Fwy Suite 260	Dallas	TX	75243	**800-527-2303**	214-575-0572	589
Intermountain Color Inc 1840 Range St	Boulder	CO	80301	**800-678-9785**	303-443-3800	615
Intermountain Farmers Assn 1147 W 2100 South	Salt Lake City	UT	84119	**800-748-4432**	801-972-2122	272
Intermountain Gas Co Inc 555 S Cole Rd	Boise	ID	83709	**800-548-3679***	208-377-6000	774
*Cust Svc						
Intermountain Health Care Inc (IHC) 36 S State St 22nd Fl	Salt Lake City	UT	84111	**800-843-7820***	801-442-2000	348
*Hum Res						
Intermountain Rural Electric Assn PO Box A	Sedalia	CO	80135	**800-332-9540**	303-688-3100	244
Internal Auditing Alert Newsletter 395 Hudson St 4th Fl	New York	NY	10014	**800-950-1205**	212-367-6300	521-1
Internal Medicine. Association of Program Directors in 2501 M St NW Suite 550	Washington	DC	20037	**800-622-4558**	202-887-9450	49-8
Internal Medicine News 12230 Wilkins Ave	Rockville	MD	20852	**800-445-6975**	301-816-8700	449-16
Internal Revenue Service (IRS) 1111 Constitution Ave NW	Washington	DC	20224	**800-829-1040**	202-622-9511	336-14
National Taxpayer Advocate 1111 Constitution Ave NW	Washington	DC	20224	**877-777-4778**	202-622-6100	336-14
Tax Forms & Publications Div 1111 Constitution Ave NW	Washington	DC	20224	**800-829-3676**	202-622-5200	336-14
Internap Network Services Corp 250 Williams St Suite E-100	Atlanta	GA	30303	**877-843-7627**	404-302-9700	387
AMEX: IIP						
International Academy of Compounding Pharmacists (IACP) PO Box 1365	Sugar Land	TX	77487	**800-927-4227**	281-933-8400	49-8
International Academy of Design 5225 Memorial Hwy	Tampa	FL	33634	**800-222-3369**	813-881-0007	163
International Academy of Design & Technology 1 N State St Suite 400	Chicago	IL	60602	**877-222-3369**	312-980-9200	163
International Aid Inc 17011 W Hickory St	Spring Lake	MI	49456	**800-968-7490**	616-846-7490	48-5
International Airline Passengers Assn (IAPA) 5204 Tennyson Pkwy	Plano	TX	75024	**800-821-4272**	972-404-9980	48-23
International Airlines Travel Agent Network (IATAN) 300 Garden City Plaza Suite 342	Garden City	NY	11530	**800-294-2826**	516-663-6000	49-21
International Alliance of Theatrical Stage Employees Moving Picture Technicians (IATSE) 1430 Broadway 20th Fl	New York	NY	10018	**800-223-6872**	212-730-1770	405
International Assn of Assembly Managers (IAAM) 635 Fritz Dr	Coppell	TX	75019	**800-935-4226**	972-906-7441	49-12
International Assn of Bridge Structural Ornamental & Reinforcing Iron Workers 1750 New York Ave NW Suite 400	Washington	DC	20006	**800-368-0105**	202-383-4800	405
International Assn of Business Communicators (IABC) 1 Hallidie Plaza Suite 600	San Francisco	CA	94102	**800-766-4222**	415-544-4700	49-12
International Assn of Chiefs of Police (IACP) 515 N Washington St	Alexandria	VA	22314	**800-843-4227**	703-836-6767	49-7
International Assn of Electrical Inspectors (IAEI) 901 Waterfall Way Suite 602	Richardson	TX	75080	**800-786-4234**	972-235-1455	49-3
International Assn of Fairs & Expositions (IAFE) 3043 E Cairo	Springfield	MO	65802	**800-516-0313**	417-862-5771	48-23
International Assn for Food Protection (IAFP) 6200 Aurora Ave Suite 200W	Des Moines	IA	50322	**800-369-6337**	515-276-3344	49-6
International Assn for Human Resource Information Management (IHRIM) PO Box 1086	Burlington	MA	01803	**800-946-6363**	781-273-3697	49-12
International Assn of Marriage & Family Counselors (IAMFC) c/o American Counseling Assn 5999 Stevenson Ave	Alexandria	VA	22304	**800-545-2223**	703-823-9800	49-15
International Assn of Ocular Surgeons 820 N Orleans St Suite 208	Chicago	IL	60610	**800-621-4002**	312-440-0699	49-8
International Assn of Plumbing & Mechanical Officials (IAPMO) 5001 E Philadelphia St	Ontario	CA	91761	**800-854-2766**	909-472-4100	49-7
International Assn of Printing House Craftsmen (IAPHC) 7042 Brooklyn Blvd	Minneapolis	MN	55429	**800-466-4274**	763-560-1620	49-16
International Assn of Workforce Professionals (IAPES) 1801 Louisville Rd	Frankfort	KY	40601	**888-898-9960**	502-223-4459	49-12
International Baptist College 2150 E Southern Ave	Tempe	AZ	85282	**800-422-4858**	480-838-7070	163
International Bible Society (IBS) 1820 Jet Stream Dr	Colorado Springs	CO	80921	**800-524-1588***	719-488-9200	48-20
*Cust Svc						
International Billiards Inc 2311 Washington Ave	Houston	TX	77007	**800-255-6386**	713-869-3237	701
International Biometric Group LLC 1 Battery Park Plaza	New York	NY	10004	**888-424-8424**	212-809-9491	85
International Bonded Couriers Inc 3333 New Hyde Park Rd Suite 300	New Hyde Park	NY	11042	**800-422-4124**	516-627-8200	536
International Bottled Water Assn (IBWA) 1700 Diagonal Rd Suite 650	Alexandria	VA	22314	**800-928-3711**	703-683-5213	49-6
International Bowling Museum & Hall of Fame 111 Stadium Plaza Dr	Saint Louis	MO	63102	**800-966-2695**	314-231-6340	511
International Brake Industries Inc 1840 McCullough St	Lima	OH	45801	**800-537-2838**	419-227-4421	61
International Business College 5699 Coventry Ln	Fort Wayne	IN	46804	**800-589-6363**	260-432-8702	158
International Business Machines Corp (IBM) New Orchard Rd	Armonk	NY	10504	**800-426-4968**	914-766-1900	171-3
NYSE: IBM						
International Business Systems Inc 431 Yerkes Rd	King of Prussia	PA	19406	**800-220-1255**	610-265-7997	111
International Cemetery & Funeral Assn (ICFA) 1895 Preston White Dr Suite 220	Reston	VA	20191	**800-645-7700**	703-391-8400	49-4
International Center for Technology Assessment (ICTA) 660 Pennsylvania Ave SE Suite 302	Washington	DC	20003	**800-600-6664**	202-547-9359	49-19
International Ceramic Engineering 235 Brooks St	Worcester	MA	01606	**800-779-3321**	508-853-4700	248
International Cesarean Awareness Network Inc (ICAN) 1304 Kingsdale Ave	Redondo Beach	CA	90278	**800-686-4226**	310-542-6400	48-17
International Chauffeured Service Worldwide 53 E 34th St	New York	NY	10016	**800-266-5254**	212-213-0302	433
International Chemical Co 2628 N Mascher St	Philadelphia	PA	19133	**800-541-2504**	215-739-2313	143
International Childbirth Education Assn (ICEA) 8060 26th Ave SE	Minneapolis	MN	55425	**800-624-4934***	952-854-8660	48-17
*Sales						
International Chimney Corp 55 S Long St	Williamsville	NY	14221	**800-828-1446**	716-634-3967	188-7
International Chiropractors Assn (ICA) 1110 N Glebe Rd Suite 1000	Arlington	VA	22201	**800-423-4690**	703-528-5000	49-8
International Church of the Foursquare Gospel (ICFG) 1910 W Sunset Blvd Suite 200	Los Angeles	CA	90026	**888-635-4234**	213-989-4200	48-20
International Civil Rights Center & Museum 134 S Elm St	Greensboro	NC	27401	**800-748-7116**	336-274-9199	509
International Claim Specialists 530 W Lockport St	Plainfield	IL	60544	**800-822-8220**	815-254-0600	682
International Coatings Co 13929 E 166th St	Cerritos	CA	90702	**800-423-4103**	562-926-1010	381
International Coffee & Tea Inc 1945 S La Cienega Blvd	Los Angeles	CA	90034	**800-854-6252**	310-237-2326	156
International Cold Storage Co Inc 215 E 13th St	Andover	KS	67002	**800-835-0001**	316-733-1385	650
International College Fort Myers Campus 8695 College Pkwy Suite 217	Fort Myers	FL	33919	**800-466-0019**	239-482-0019	163
International College of Hospitality Management Cesar Ritz 1760 Mapleton Ave	Suffield	CT	06078	**800-955-0809**	860-668-3515	787
International Collegiate Licensing Assn (ICLA) 24651 Detroit Rd	Westlake	OH	44145	**800-996-2232**	440-892-4000	48-22
International Comfort Products Corp 650 Heil Quaker Ave	Lewisburg	TN	37091	**800-458-6650**	931-359-3511	16
International Communication Materials Inc Rt 119 S	Connellsville	PA	15425	**800-438-2530**	724-628-1014	616
International Communications Industries Assn (ICIA) 11242 Waples Mill Rd Suite 200	Fairfax	VA	22030	**800-659-7469**	703-273-7200	49-20
International Communications Research 53 W Baltimore Pike	Media	PA	19063	**800-633-1986***	484-840-4300	458
*Cust Svc						

				Toll-Free	Phone	Class
International Congress of Oral Implantologists (ICOI) 248 Lorraine Ave 3rd Fl	Upper Montclair	NJ	07043	**800-442-0525**	973-783-6300	49-8
International Converter Inc 721 Farson St	Belpre	OH	45714	**800-962-8572**	740-423-7525	544
International Cornea Project 9444 Balboa Ave Suite 100	San Diego	CA	92123	**888-393-2265**	858-694-0444	265
International Council of Cruise Lines (ICCL) 2111 Wilson Blvd 8th Fl	Arlington	VA	22201	**800-595-9338**	703-522-8463	48-23
International Council of Employers of Bricklayers & Allied Craftworkers 1730 Rhode Island Ave NW Suite 419	Washington	DC	20036	**888-880-8222**	202-457-9040	49-3
International Cruise & Excursion Gallery DBA ICE Gallery 10030 N 25th Ave	Phoenix	AZ	85021	**888-320-4234**	602-395-1995	760
International Customer Service Assn (ICSA) 401 N Michigan Ave 22nd Fl	Chicago	IL	60611	**800-360-4272**	312-321-6800	49-12
International Cutlery Ltd 367 Madison Ave	New York	NY	10017	**866-487-6164**	212-924-7300	357
International Dairy Queen Inc 7505 Metro Blvd	Minneapolis	MN	55439	**866-793-7582**	952-830-0200	656
International Data Corp (IDC) 5 Speen St	Framingham	MA	01701	**800-343-4935**	508-872-8200	458
International Destinations Inc 2025 M St NW Suite 500	Washington	DC	20036	**800-833-5254**	202-797-1222	183
International Diabetes Center 3800 Park Nicollet Blvd	Minneapolis	MN	55416	**888-825-6315**	952-993-3393	654
International Display Systems Inc 5008 Veterans Memorial Hwy	Holbrook	NY	11741	**800-542-9779**	631-218-1802	692
International Dyslexia Assn (IDA) 8600 LaSalle Rd Chester Bldg Suite 382	Baltimore	MD	21286	**800-222-3123**	410-296-0232	48-17
International Educational Exchange. Council on 7 Custom House St 3rd Fl *Cust Svc	Portland	ME	04101	**888-268-6245***	207-553-7600	49-5
International Electronics Inc 427 Turnpike St *NASDAQ: IEIB*	Canton	MA	02021	**800-343-9502**	781-821-5566	681
International Engraved Graphics Assn 305 Plus Park Blvd *x209	Nashville	TN	37217	**800-821-3138***	615-366-1094	49-4
International Envelope Co 2 Tabas Lane *Cust Svc	Exton	PA	19341	**800-468-9835***	610-363-0900	260
International Exchange. Youth for Understanding 6400 Goldsboro Rd Suite 100	Bethesda	MD	20817	**800-424-3691**	240-235-2100	48-11
International Executive Housekeepers Assn (IEHA) 1001 Eastwind Dr Suite 301	Westerville	OH	43081	**800-200-6342**	614-895-7166	49-4
International Expeditions Inc 1 Environs Pk	Helena	AL	35080	**800-633-4734**	205-428-1700	748
International Fabricare Institute (IFI) 12251 Tech Rd	Silver Spring	MD	20904	**800-638-2627**	301-622-1900	49-4
International Fiber Corp 50 Bridge St	North Tonawanda	NY	14120	**888-698-1936**	716-693-4040	594-1
International Fidelity Insurance Co 1 Newark Center 20th Fl	Newark	NJ	07102	**800-333-4167**	973-624-7200	384-5
International Fine Arts College 1501 Biscayne Blvd	Miami	FL	33132	**800-225-9023**	305-373-4684	159
International Food Service Executives Assn (IFSEA) 836 San Bruno Ave	Henderson	NV	89015	**888-234-3732**	702-564-0997	49-6
International Foundation of Employee Benefit Plans (IFEBP) 18700 W Bluemond Rd PO Box 69	Brookfield	WI	53008	**888-334-3327**	262-786-6700	49-12
International Franchise Assn (IFA) 1350 New York Ave NW Suite 900	Washington	DC	20005	**800-543-1038**	202-628-8000	49-18
International Fund for Animal Welfare (IFAW) 411 Main St PO Box 193	Yarmouth Port	MA	02675	**800-932-4329**	508-744-2000	48-3
International Gay & Lesbian Travel Assn (IGLTA) 4331 N Federal Hwy Suite 304	Fort Lauderdale	FL	33308	**800-448-8550**	954-776-2626	48-23
International Ground Source Heat Pump Assn (IGSHPA) Oklahoma State University 374 Cordell S	Stillwater	OK	74078	**800-626-4747**	405-744-5175	49-13
International Group Inc 85 Old Eagle School Rd	Wayne	PA	19087	**800-852-6537**	610-687-9030	570
International Health Racquet & Sportsclub Assn (IHRSA) 263 Summer St 8th Fl	Boston	MA	02210	**800-228-4772**	617-951-0055	48-22
International Hearing Society (IHS) 16880 Middlebelt Rd Suite 4	Livonia	MI	48154	**800-521-5247**	734-522-7200	48-17
International Home Furnishings Representatives Assn (IHFRA) 209 S Main St	High Point	NC	27260	**800-889-3920**	336-889-3920	49-18
International Homes of Cedar Inc PO Box 886	Woodinville	WA	98072	**800-767-7674**	360-668-8511	107
International Hotel of Calgary 220 4th Ave SW	Calgary	AB	T2P0H5	**800-637-7200**	403-265-9600	372
International House Hotel 221 Camp St	New Orleans	LA	70130	**800-633-5770**	504-553-9550	373
International House of Pancakes (IHOP) 450 N Brand Blvd 7th Fl	Glendale	CA	91203	**800-241-4467**	818-240-6055	657
International Imaging Materials Inc 310 Commerce Dr	Amherst	NY	14228	**888-464-4625**	716-691-6333	523
International Immunology Corp 25549 Adams Ave	Murrieta	CA	92562	**800-843-2853**	951-677-5629	229
International Inn. Coast 3333 W International Airport Rd	Anchorage	AK	99502	**800-663-1144**	907-243-2233	373
International Innovations Inc 4107 Spicewood Springs Rd Suite 216	Austin	TX	78759	**800-708-2111**	512-502-0636	344
International Institute of Municipal Clerks (IIMC) 8331 Utica Ave Suite 200	Rancho Cucamonga	CA	91730	**800-251-1639**	909-944-4162	49-7

				Toll-Free	Phone	Class
International Interior Design Assn (IIDA) 13-500 Merchandise Mart	Chicago	IL	60654	**888-799-4432**	312-467-1950	48-4
International Investigators Inc 3216 N Pennsylvania St	Indianapolis	IN	46205	**800-403-8111**	317-925-1496	392
International Isotopes Inc 4137 Commerce Circle	Idaho Falls	ID	83401	**800-699-3108**	208-524-5300	229
International Jet Aviation Services 12401 Aviator Way	Englewood	CO	80112	**800-858-5891**	303-790-0414	14
International Knife & Saw Inc 3940 Olympic Blvd Suite 350	Erlanger	KY	41018	**800-354-9872**	859-371-0333	670
International Label & Printing Co Inc 2550 United Ln	Elk Grove Village	IL	60007	**800-244-1442**	630-595-1442	404
International Lighting 1825 N 19th St	Saint Louis	MO	63106	**800-235-7050**	314-621-0600	431
International Lutheran Laymen's League 660 Mason Ridge Ctr Dr	Saint Louis	MO	63141	**800-944-3450**	314-317-4100	48-20
International Male 741 F St	San Diego	CA	92101	**800-293-9333**	619-544-9900	155-3
International Masonry Institute (IMI) James Brice House 42 East St	Annapolis	MD	21401	**800-803-0295**	410-280-1305	49-3
International Master Care Janitorial Franchising Inc 555 6th St Suite 327	New Westminster	BC	V3L5H1	**800-889-2799**	604-525-8221	150
International Medical Corps (IMC) 1919 Santa Monica Blvd Suite 300	Santa Monica	CA	90404	**800-481-4462**	310-826-7800	48-5
International Medical Device Regulatory Monitor Newsletter 9700 Philadelphia Ct	Lanham	MD	20706	**800-774-6809**	301-731-5200	521-8
International Meeting Managers Inc 4550 Post Oak Pl Suite 342	Houston	TX	77027	**800-423-7175**	713-965-0566	183
International Metal Hose Co 520 Goodrich Rd	Bellevue	OH	44811	**800-458-6855**	419-483-7690	481
International Microcomputer Software Inc 100 Rowland Way Suite 300	Novato	CA	94945	**800-833-8082**	415-878-4000	176-8
International Mill Service Inc 1155 Business Ctr Dr Suite 200	Horsham	PA	19044	**800-523-0781**	215-956-5500	674
International Monetary Market 20 S Wacker Dr	Chicago	IL	60606	**800-331-3332**	312-930-3170	680
International Motor Coach Group Inc (IMG) 8645 College Blvd Suite 220	Overland Park	KS	66210	**888-447-3466**	913-906-0111	49-21
International Mountain Bicycling Assn (IMBA) 207 Canyon Blvd Suite 301 PO Box 7578	Boulder	CO	80306	**888-442-4622**	303-545-9011	48-23
International Multifoods Corp 110 Cheshire Ln Suite 300	Minnetonka	MN	55305	**800-866-3300**	952-594-3300	292-8
International Municipal Signal Assn (IMSA) 165 E Union St PO Box 539	Newark	NY	14513	**800-723-4672**	315-331-2182	49-7
International Museum of the Horse 4089 Iron Works Pkwy	Lexington	KY	40511	**800-678-8813**	859-259-4231	509
International Musician 1501 Broadway Suite 600	New York	NY	10036	**800-762-3444**	212-869-1330	449-9
International Order of the Golden Rule (OGR) 13523 Lakefront Dr	Bridgeton	MO	63045	**800-637-8030**	314-209-7142	49-4
International Orthodox Christian Charities (IOCC) 110 West Rd Suite 360	Baltimore	MD	21204	**877-803-4622**	410-243-9820	48-5
International Paper Co 400 Atlantic St *NYSE: IP* ■ *Prod Info	Stamford	CT	06921	**800-223-1268***	203-541-8000	547
International Paper Food Service Business 3 Paragon Dr	Montvale	NJ	07645	**800-852-2425**	201-391-1776	548-1
International Patterns Inc 50 Inez Dr	Bay Shore	NY	11706	**800-471-6368**	631-952-2000	692
International Peace Garden PO Box 419	Boissevain	MB	R0K0E0	**800-432-6733**	204-534-2510	98
International Peace Garden Rt 1 Box 116	Dunseith	ND	58329	**888-432-6733**	701-263-4390	98
International Pharmaceutical Regulatory Monitor Newsletter 9700 Philadelphia Ct	Lanham	MD	20706	**800-345-2611**	301-731-5200	521-12
International Playthings Inc 75D Lackawanna Ave	Parsippany	NJ	07054	**800-631-1272**	973-316-2500	750
International Poly Bag Inc 990 Park Ctr Dr Suite G	Vista	CA	92083	**800-976-5922**	760-598-2468	67
International Precious Metals Institute (IPMI) 4400 Bayou Blvd Suite 18	Pensacola	FL	32503	**866-289-8484**	850-476-1156	49-4
International Profit Assoc Inc 1250 Barclay Blvd	Buffalo Grove	IL	60089	**800-531-7100**	847-808-5590	193
International Public Management Assn for Human Resources (IPMA-HR) 1617 Duke St	Alexandria	VA	22314	**800-220-4762**	703-549-7100	49-12
International Renaissance Festivals Ltd PO Box 315	Crownsville	MD	21032	**800-296-7304**	410-266-7304	147
International Reprographic Assn (IRgA) 401 N Michigan Ave	Chicago	IL	60611	**800-833-4742**	312-245-1026	49-16
International Resistive Co Inc (IRC) 736 Greenway Rd	Boone	NC	28607	**800-472-6467**	828-264-8861	252
International Restaurant Management Group Inc 4104 Aurora St	Coral Gables	FL	33146	**800-662-1668**	305-476-1611	656
International Revolving Door Co 2100 N 6th Ave *Cust Svc	Evansville	IN	47710	**800-745-4726***	812-425-3311	232
International Safe Transit Assn (ISTA) 1400 Abbott Rd Suite 160	East Lansing	MI	48823	**888-367-4782**	517-333-3437	49-21
International Sanitary Supply Assn (ISSA) 7373 N Lincoln Ave	Lincolnwood	IL	60712	**800-225-4772**	847-982-0800	49-18
International Satellite Services Inc 1004 Collier Ctr Way Suite 205	Naples	FL	34110	**888-511-3403**	239-598-2241	669
International Sign Assn (ISA) 707 N Saint Asaph St	Alexandria	VA	22314	**888-472-7446**	703-836-4012	49-4
International Society for Animal Rights (ISAR) 965 Griffin Pond Rd	Clarks Summit	PA	18411	**800-543-4727**	570-586-2200	48-3
International Society of Arboriculture (ISA) 1400 W Anthony Dr PO Box 3129	Champaign	IL	61826	**888-472-8733**	217-355-9411	48-2

Name / Address	City	State	Zip	Toll-Free	Phone	Class
International Society of Certified Electronics Technicians (ISCET) 3608 Pershing Ave	Fort Worth	TX	76107	**800-946-0201**	817-921-9101	49-19
International Society of Certified Employee Benefit Specialists (ISCEBS) 18700 W Bluemond Rd PO Box 209	Brookfield	WI	53008	**888-334-3327**	262-786-8771	49-12
International Society of Fire Service Instructors (ISFSI) 2425 Hwy 49 E	Pleasant View	TN	37146	**800-435-0005**		49-7
International Society for Peritoneal Dialysis (ISPD) 66 Martin St	Milton	ON	L9T2R2	**888-834-1001**	905-875-2456	49-8
International Society for Technology in Education (ISTE) 480 Charnelton St	Eugene	OR	97401	**800-336-5191**	541-302-3777	49-5
International SOS Assistance Inc 3600 Horizon Blvd Suite 300	Trevose	PA	19053	**800-523-8930**	215-244-1500	384-7
International Speakers Bureau Inc 2528 Elm St Suite 200	Dallas	TX	75226	**800-842-4483**	214-744-3885	699
International Specialty Products Inc 1361 Alps Rd	Wayne	NJ	07470	**800-365-7353**	973-628-4000	142
International Sports Sciences Assn (ISSA) 400 E Gutierrez St	Santa Barbara	CA	93101	**800-892-4772**	805-884-8111	48-22
International Spy Museum 800 F St NW	Washington	DC	20004	**866-779-6873**	202-393-7798	509
International Staple & Machine Co 629 E Butler Rd	Butler	PA	16002	**800-378-3430**	724-287-7711	747
International Steel Group Inc 4020 Kinross Lakes Pkwy *NYSE: ISG*	Richfield	OH	44286	**866-474-8808**	330-659-9100	709
International Student Tours 999 W Broadway Ave Suite 720	Vancouver	BC	V5Z1K5	**888-472-3933**	604-714-1244	748
International Tandem Users' Group (ITUG) 401 N Michigan	Chicago	IL	60611	**800-845-4884**	312-321-6851	48-9
International Task Force on Euthanasia & Assisted Suicide PO Box 760	Steubenville	OH	43952	**800-958-5678**	740-282-3810	48-8
International Technidyne Corp 8 Olsen Ave	Edison	NJ	08820	**800-631-5945**	732-548-6677	469
International Tennis Hall of Fame & Museum 194 Bellevue Ave	Newport	RI	02840	**800-457-1144**	401-849-3990	511
International Thermal Systems LLC 4697 W Greenfield Ave	Milwaukee	WI	53214	**877-683-6797**	414-672-7700	313
International Trade Administration 1401 Constitution Ave NW Hoover Bldg	Washington	DC	20230	**800-872-2723**	202-482-3809	336-2
International Union of Bricklayers & Allied Craftworkers (BAC) 1776 'I' St NW Suite 500	Washington	DC	20006	**888-880-8222**	202-783-3788	405
International Union of Industrial Service Transport Health Employees 254 W 31st St	New York	NY	10001	**800-331-1070**	212-696-5545	405
International Union of Petroleum & Industrial Workers 8131 E Rosecrans Ave	Paramount	CA	90723	**800-624-5842**	562-630-6232	405
International Union of Police Associations 1421 Prince St Suite 400	Alexandria	VA	22314	**800-247-4872**	703-549-7473	405
International Union of Security Officers 2201 Broadway Suite 101	San Leandro	CA	94612	**800-772-3326**	510-625-9913	405
International Union Security Police & Fire Professionals of America 25510 Kelly Rd	Roseville	MI	48066	**800-228-7492**	586-772-7250	405
International Video-Conferencing Inc 180 Adams Ave	Hauppauge	NY	11788	**800-224-7083**	631-273-5800	52
International Violin Co Ltd 1421 Clarkview Rd	Baltimore	MD	21209	**800-542-3538**	410-832-2525	515
International Warehouse Logistics Assn (IWLA) 2800 River Rd Suite 260	Des Plaines	IL	60018	**800-525-0165**	847-813-4699	49-21
International Wildlife Coalition (IWC) 70 E Falmouth Hwy	East Falmouth	MA	02536	**800-548-8704**	508-548-8328	48-3
International Window Corp 5625 E Firestone Blvd	South Gate	CA	90280	**800-477-4032**	562-928-6411	232
International Women's Apparel 610 Uhler Rd *Cust Svc	Easton	PA	18040	**800-735-7848***	610-258-9143	154
International Women's Sports Hall of Fame Eisenhower Pk Parking Field 6	East Meadow	NY	11554	**800-227-3988**	516-542-4700	511
International Wood Industries Inc 250 D St	Turlock	CA	95380	**800-458-5545**	209-632-3300	602
Internet America Inc 350 N Saint Paul St 1 Dallas Ctr Suite 3000	Dallas	TX	75201	**800-232-4335**	214-861-2662	390
Internet Billing Co Ltd (iBill) 2200 SW 10th St	Deerfield Beach	FL	33442	**888-237-1764**	954-363-4400	250
Internet Commerce Corp 805 3rd Ave 9th Fl *NASDAQ: ICCA*	New York	NY	10022	**888-422-4401**	212-271-7640	496
Internet Communications (ICOM) 303 Peachtree Ctr Ave Suite 500	Atlanta	GA	30303	**877-504-0091**	404-260-2477	795
Internet Fraud Watch c/o National Fraud Information Ctr 1701 K St NW Suite 1200	Washington	DC	20006	**800-876-7060**	202-835-3323	48-10
Internet Newsletter 1617 JFK Blvd Suite 1750	Philadelphia	PA	19103	**800-999-1916**	215-557-2300	521-3
Internet Operations Center Inc 200 Galleria Officentre Suite 109	Southfield	MI	48034	**800-485-4462**	248-204-8800	39
Internet Security Systems Inc 6303 Barfield Rd *NASDAQ: ISSX*	Atlanta	GA	30328	**888-901-7477**	404-236-2600	176-12
Internet Shopping Outlet Inc 55 John St 11th Fl	New York	NY	10038	**800-757-3015**	212-619-3353	452
Interpersonal Dynamics Inc 2265 Teton Plaza	Idaho Falls	ID	83404	**800-658-3837**	208-529-1737	454
Interphase Corp 2901 N Dallas Pkwy Suite 200 *NASDAQ: INPH*	Plano	TX	75093	**800-327-8638**	214-654-5000	174

Name / Address	City	State	Zip	Toll-Free	Phone	Class
Interplastic Corp 1225 Willow Lake Blvd	Saint Paul	MN	55110	**800-736-5497**	651-481-6860	594-2
Interpoint Corp PO Box 97005	Redmond	WA	98073	**800-822-8782**	425-882-3100	252
Interpool Inc 211 College Rd E *NYSE: IPX*	Princeton	NJ	08540	**800-388-7485**	609-452-8900	261-6
Interpore Cross International 181 Technology Dr	Irvine	CA	92618	**800-722-4489**	949-453-3200	535
Interpore Spine Ltd 181 Technology Dr	Irvine	CA	92618	**800-722-4489**	949-453-3200	469
InterraTech Corp 11 Federal St	Camden	NJ	08103	**888-589-4889**	856-614-5400	176-1
Interroll Corp 3000 Corporate Dr *Sales	Wilmington	NC	28405	**800-830-9680***	910-799-1100	206
Interscope Records 2220 Colorado Ave	Santa Monica	CA	90404	**800-982-1812**	310-865-1000	643
Intersections Inc 14901 Bogle Dr *NASDAQ: INTX*	Chantilly	VA	20151	**800-695-7536**	703-488-6100	213
Intershop Communications Inc 410 Townsend St Suite 125	San Francisco	CA	94107	**800-736-5197**	415-844-1500	176-7
Interstate Battery System of America Inc 12770 Merit Dr Suite 400	Dallas	TX	75251	**800-541-8419**	972-991-1444	61
Interstate Brick Co 9780 S 5200 West	West Jordan	UT	84088	**800-233-8654**	801-280-5200	148
Interstate Chemical Co Inc 2797 Freedland Rd	Hermitage	PA	16148	**800-422-2436**	724-981-3771	141
Interstate Commodities Inc 7 Madison St	Troy	NY	12181	**800-833-3636**	518-272-7212	271
Interstate Distributor Co 11707 21st Ave S	Tacoma	WA	98444	**800-426-8560**	253-537-9455	769
Interstate Electrical Supply Inc 2300 2nd Ave	Columbus	GA	31901	**800-903-4409**	706-324-1000	245
Interstate Electronics Corp 602 E Vermont Ave	Anaheim	CA	92805	**800-854-6979**	714-758-0500	519
Interstate Fire & Casualty Co 33 W Monroe St 12th Fl	Chicago	IL	60603	**800-628-8574**	312-346-6400	384-4
Interstate Insurance Group 33 W Monroe St 12th Fl	Chicago	IL	60603	**800-255-2096**	312-346-6400	355-4
Interstate Mechanical Contractors Inc 3200 Henson Rd	Knoxville	TN	37921	**800-556-7072**	865-588-0180	188-10
Interstate National Corp 33 W Monroe St 12th Fl	Chicago	IL	60603	**800-255-2096**	312-346-6400	355-4
Interstate National Dealer Services Inc 333 Earle Ovington Blvd Suite 700	Uniondale	NY	11553	**800-942-0400**	516-228-8600	383
Interstate Oil & Gas Compact Commission (IOGCC) 900 NE 23rd St PO Box 53127	Oklahoma City	OK	73152	**800-822-4015**	405-525-3556	48-12
Interstate Restaurant Equipment Corp 37 Amoskeag St	Manchester	NH	03102	**800-258-3040**	603-669-3400	295
Interstate Steel Co 401 E Touhy Ave	Des Plaines	IL	60017	**800-323-9800**	847-827-5151	709
Interstate Supply Co 4445 Gustine Ave	Saint Louis	MO	63116	**800-324-3535**	314-481-2222	356
Interstates Electric & Engineering Co Inc PO Box 260	Sioux Center	IA	51250	**800-827-1662**	712-722-1662	188-4
InterStudy Publications 210 12th Ave S Suite 100	Nashville	TN	37203	**800-844-3351**	888-293-9675	623-6
Interstyle Ceramics & Glass Ltd 3625 Brighton Ave	Burnaby	BC	V5A3H5	**800-667-1566**	604-421-7229	736
Intertek Testing Services North America Inc 3933 US Rt 11	Cortland	NY	13045	**800-345-3851**	607-753-6711	728
Interval International Inc 6262 Sunset Dr PH 1	Miami	FL	33143	**800-828-8200**	305-666-1861	738
Interventional Radiology. Society of 10201 Lee Hwy Suite 500	Fairfax	VA	22030	**800-488-7284**	703-691-1805	49-8
Intervest Bancshares Corp 1 Rockefeller Plaza Suite 400 *NASDAQ: IBCA*	New York	NY	10020	**877-226-5462**	212-218-2800	355-2
Interview Magazine 575 Broadway 5th Fl	New York	NY	10012	**800-925-9574**	212-941-2900	449-11
Intervoice Inc 17811 Waterview Pkwy *NASDAQ: INTV*	Dallas	TX	75252	**800-955-3675**	972-454-8000	720
InterWest Insurance Services Inc 3636 American River Dr	Sacramento	CA	95864	**800-444-4134**	916-488-3100	383
InterWorks Systems Inc 1233 Old Walt Whitman Rd	Melville	NY	11747	**800-814-9757**	631-424-9757	720
Intevac Inc 3560 Bassett St *NASDAQ: IVAC*	Santa Clara	CA	95054	**800-468-3822**	408-986-9888	534
Intex Corp 4130 Santa Fe Ave	Long Beach	CA	90801	**800-234-6839**	310-549-5400	701
Intex Supply Co 670 Alpha Dr *Cust Svc	Highland Heights	OH	44143	**800-753-5822***	440-449-6550	497
Intracel Resources LLC 93 Monocacy Blvd Unit A 8	Frederick	MD	21701	**877-289-5476**	301-668-8400	229
Intraco Corp 530 Stephenson Hwy	Troy	MI	48083	**800-595-6900**	248-585-6900	61
IntraLase Corp 3 Morgan *NASDAQ: ILSE*	Irvine	CA	92618	**877-393-2020**	949-859-5230	415
IntraLinks Inc 1372 Broadway 11th Fl *Tech Supp	New York	NY	10018	**888-546-5383***	212-543-7700	39
Intranet Report 316 N Michigan Ave Suite 300	Chicago	IL	60601	**800-878-5331**	312-960-4100	521-3
Intranets.com Inc 1 Van de Graaff Dr 6th Fl	Burlington	MA	01803	**888-932-2600**	781-565-6000	39
Intrav Inc 11969 Westline Industrial Dr	Saint Louis	MO	63146	**800-825-2900**	314-655-6700	748
Intraware Inc 25 Orinda Way Suite 101 *NASDAQ: ITRA*	Orinda	CA	94563	**888-446-8729**	925-253-4500	176-1
Intrex LLC 40 Park St	Brooklyn	NY	11206	**877-946-8739**	718-455-5042	314-1
IntriCon Corp 2034 S Limekiln Pike *AMEX: IIN*	Dresher	PA	19025	**800-523-6500**	215-646-6600	313
Intrinsix Corp 33 Lyman St	Westborough	MA	01581	**800-783-0330**	508-836-4100	258
Introgen Therapeutics Inc 301 Congress Ave Suite 1850 *NASDAQ: INGN*	Austin	TX	78701	**800-320-5010**	512-708-9310	86
Intrusion Inc 1101 E Arapaho Rd *NASDAQ: INTZ*	Richardson	TX	75081	**800-862-6637**	972-234-6400	176-12
INTRUST Bank NA 105 N Main St	Wichita	KS	67202	**800-895-2265**	316-383-1111	71
INTRUST Financial Corp 105 N Main St	Wichita	KS	67202	**800-242-7111**	316-383-1111	355-2
Intuit Inc PO Box 7850 *NASDAQ: INTU* ■ *Cust Svc	Mountain View	CA	94039	**800-446-8848***	650-944-6000	176-9

Name / Address	City	State	ZIP	Toll-Free	Phone	Class
Intuit Lender Services Inc						
PO Box 7850	Mountain View	CA	94039	**888-565-2488**	650-944-6000	498
Intuitive Mfg Systems Inc						
12131 113th Ave NE Suite 200	Kirkland	WA	98034	**877-549-2149**	425-821-0740	176-1
Intuitive Surgical Inc 950 Kifer Rd	Sunnyvale	CA	94086	**888-868-4647**	408-523-2100	468
NASDAQ: ISRG						
Inuit Gallery of Vancouver Ltd						
206 Cambie St Gastown	Vancouver	BC	V6B2M9	**888-615-8399**	604-688-7323	42
Invacare Corp 1 Invacare Way	Elyria	OH	44036	**800-333-6900**	440-329-6000	469
NYSE: IVC						
Invacare ICCG 1644 Lotsie Blvd	Saint Louis	MO	63132	**800-347-5440**	314-253-5440	468
Invasion Tours 3355 Vincent Dr	Pleasant Hill	CA	94523	**800-339-4723**	925-944-5844	748
Invensys 33 Commercial St	Foxboro	MA	02035	**866-746-6477**	508-543-8750	201
Invensys APV 395 Fillmore Ave	Tonawanda	NY	14150	**800-828-7667**	716-692-3000	293
Inventure Place 221 S Broadway	Akron	OH	44308	**800-968-4332**	330-762-4463	509
Inverary Resort PO Box 190	Baddeck	NS	B0E1B0	**800-565-5660**	902-295-3500	655
Inveresk Research Group Inc						
11000 Weston Pkwy	Cary	NC	27709	**800-421-1952**	919-460-9005	86
Inverness Corp 17-10 Willow St	Fair Lawn	NJ	07410	**800-631-0860**	201-794-3400	468
Inverness Hotel & Golf Club						
200 Inverness Dr W	Englewood	CO	80112	**800-346-4891**	303-799-5800	655
Inverness Medical Innovations Inc						
51 Sawyer Rd Suite 200	Waltham	MA	02453	**877-696-2525**	781-647-3900	229
AMEX: IMA						
Inverrary Plaza Resort						
3501 Inverrary Blvd	Fort Lauderdale	FL	33319	**800-241-0363**	954-485-0500	655
INVESCO Capital Management Inc						
1360 Peachtree St NE 1 Midtown Plaza Suite 100	Atlanta	GA	30309	**800-241-5477**	404-892-0896	393
INVESCO Funds Group Inc						
4350 S Monaco St	Denver	CO	80237	**800-525-8085**	303-930-6300	517
INVESCO-NAM						
400 W Market St Suite 2500	Louisville	KY	40202	**877-581-6262**	502-581-7668	393
Investment Counselors of Maryland LLC						
803 Cathedral St	Baltimore	MD	21201	**800-638-7983**	410-539-3838	393
Investment Technology Group						
380 Madison Ave 4th Fl	New York	NY	10017	**800-215-4484**	212-588-4000	679
NYSE: ITG						
Investment Trusts. National Assn of Real Estate 1875 'I' St NW Suite 600	Washington	DC	20006	**800-362-7348**	202-739-9400	49-17
Investments Charitable Gift Fund. Fidelity						
PO Box 55158	Boston	MA	02205	**800-682-4438**		397
Investor Relations Newsletter						
1 Phoenix Mill Ln	Peterborough	NH	03458	**800-531-0007**	603-924-0900	521-9
Investors. American Assn of Individual						
625 N Michigan Ave	Chicago	IL	60611	**800-428-2244**	312-280-0170	49-2
Investor's Business Daily						
12655 Beatrice St	Los Angeles	CA	90066	**800-831-2525**	310-448-6000	522-2
Investors Capital Corp						
230 Broadway Suite 205	Lynnfield	MA	01940	**800-949-1422**	781-593-8565	679
Investors Capital Holdings Ltd						
230 Broadway Suite 205	Lynnfield	MA	01940	**800-949-1422**	781-593-8565	355-3
AMEX: ICH						
Investors Corp. National Assn of						
PO Box 220	Royal Oak	MI	48068	**877-275-6242**	248-583-6242	49-2
Investors Heritage Life Insurance Co						
200 Capital Ave	Frankfort	KY	40602	**800-422-2011**	502-223-2361	384-2
Investors Life Insurance Co of Indiana						
6500 River Pl Blvd Bldg 1	Austin	TX	78730	**800-925-6000**	512-404-5000	384-2
Investors Life Insurance Co of North America 6500 River Pl Blvd Bldg 1	Austin	TX	78730	**800-925-6000**	512-404-5000	384-2
Investors Management Corp						
5151 Glenwood Ave	Raleigh	NC	27612	**800-284-5673**	919-781-9310	656
Investors Savings Bank						
101 JFK Pkwy	Shorthills	NJ	07078	**800-252-8119**	973-376-5100	71
Investors Title Co						
121 N Columbia St	Chapel Hill	NC	27514	**800-326-4842**	919-968-2200	355-4
NASDAQ: ITIC						
Investors Title Insurance Co						
121 N Columbia St	Chapel Hill	NC	27514	**800-326-4842**	919-968-2200	384-6
Investors Underwriting Managers Inc						
310 Hwy 35S	Red Bank	NJ	07701	**800-243-6869**	732-224-0500	384-4
InvestPrivate.com						
500 5th Ave 56th Fl	New York	NY	10110	**877-669-4732**	212-739-7700	397
Investrade Discount Securities						
950 N Milwaukee Ave Suite 102	Glenview	IL	60025	**800-498-7120**	847-375-6080	679
Invincible Office Furniture Co						
842 S 26th St	Manitowoc	WI	54220	**800-558-4417**	920-682-4601	314-1
Invirex Demolition Co PO Box 481	Huntington	NY	11743	**800-783-2336**	631-368-4485	188-17
INVISTA 4123 E 37th St North	Wichita	KS	67220	**877-446-8478**	316-828-1000	594-1
InVitro International						
17751 Sky Park E Suite G	Irvine	CA	92614	**800-246-8487**	949-851-8356	229
Invitrogen Corp 1600 Faraday Ave	Carlsbad	CA	92008	**800-955-6288***	760-603-7200	86
NASDAQ: IVGN ■ *Sales						
Invo Spline Inc 2357 E Nine-Mile Rd	Warren	MI	48090	**800-959-0884***	586-757-8840	484
*Cust Svc						
Inwesco Inc 746 N Coney Ave	Azusa	CA	91702	**800-266-9304**	626-334-9304	345
Inwood Office Environments						
1108 E 15th St	Jasper	IN	47546	**800-786-6121**	812-482-6121	314-1
INX International Ink Co						
651 Bonnie Ln	Elk Grove Village	IL	60007	**800-631-7956**	847-981-9399	381
IOCC (International Orthodox Christian Charities) 110 West Rd Suite 360	Baltimore	MD	21204	**877-803-4622**	410-243-9820	48-5
IOF (Independent Order of Foresters)						
789 Don Mills Rd	Toronto	ON	M3C1T9	**800-828-1540**	416-429-3000	48-5
IOGCC (Interstate Oil & Gas Compact Commission)						
900 NE 23rd St PO Box 53127	Oklahoma City	OK	73152	**800-822-4015**	405-525-3556	48-12
Iola Register						
302 S Washington St PO Box 767	Iola	KS	66749	**800-365-1901**	620-365-2111	522-2
Ioline Corp 14140 NE 200th St	Woodinville	WA	98072	**800-598-0029**	425-398-8282	729
IOMA Inc (Institute of Management & Administration Inc) 3 Park Ave 30th Fl	New York	NY	10016	**800-401-5937**	212-244-0360	623-9
IOMED Inc						
2441 S 3850 West Suite A	Salt Lake City	UT	84120	**800-621-3347**	801-975-1191	86
AMEX: IOX						
Ion Networks Inc						
120 Corporate Blvd	Sout Plainfield	NJ	07080	**800-722-8986**	908-546-3900	176-7
Iona College 715 North Ave	New Rochelle	NY	10801	**800-231-4662**	914-633-2502	163
IONA Technologies Inc						
200 West St 4th Fl	Waltham	MA	02451	**800-672-4948**	781-902-8000	176-7
NASDAQ: IONA						
Ionics Inc 65 Grove St	Watertown	MA	02472	**800-446-6427**	617-926-2500	793
Ionix Internet 266 Sutter St	San Francisco	CA	94108	**888-884-6649**	415-288-9940	390
IoPP (Institute of Packaging Professionals) 1601 N Bond St Suite 101	Naperville	IL	60563	**800-432-4085**	630-544-5050	49-13
IOS Brands Corp						
3113 Woodcreek Dr	Downers Grove	IL	60515	**800-736-3383**	630-719-7800	287
Iowa						
Child Support Recovery Unit						
400 SW 8th St Suite M	Des Moines	IA	50309	**888-229-9223**	515-281-5580	335
College Student Aid Commission						
200 10th St 4th Fl	Des Moines	IA	50309	**800-383-4222**	515-281-3501	711
Crime Victim Assistance Div						
321 E 12th St Rm 018	Des Moines	IA	50319	**800-373-5044**	515-281-5044	335
Educational Examiners Board						
400 E 14th St	Des Moines	IA	50319	**800-778-7856**	515-281-5849	335
Motor Vehicle Div						
100 Euclid Ave	Des Moines	IA	50313	**800-532-1121**	515-237-3202	335
Tourism Office 200 E Grand Ave	Des Moines	IA	50309	**888-472-6035**	515-242-4705	335
Veterans Affairs Commission						
Camp Dodge 7700 NW Beaver Dr Bldg A6A	Johnston	IA	50131	**800-838-4692**	515-242-5331	335
Iowa 80 Group Inc PO Box 639	Walcott	IA	52773	**800-336-9889**	563-284-6965	319
Iowa Assn of Business & Industry						
904 Walnut St Suite 100	Des Moines	IA	50309	**800-383-4224**	515-280-8000	138
Iowa Assn of Realtors						
1370 NW 114th St Suite 100	Clive	IA	50325	**800-532-1515**	515-453-1064	642
Iowa Central Community College						
330 Ave M	Fort Dodge	IA	50501	**800-362-2793**	515-576-7201	160
Iowa City/Coralville Convention & Visitors Bureau 900 1st Ave	Coralville	IA	52241	**800-283-6592**	319-337-6592	205
Iowa Dental Assn						
505 5th Ave Suite 333	Des Moines	IA	50309	**800-828-2181**	515-282-7250	225
Iowa Farm Bureau Spokesman Magazine						
5400 University Ave	West Des Moines	IA	50266	**800-442-3276**	515-225-5413	449-1
Iowa Lakes Community College						
300 S 18th St	Estherville	IA	51334	**800-242-5106**	712-362-2604	160
Iowa Lakes Electric Co-op						
702 S 1st St	Estherville	IA	51334	**800-225-4532**	712-362-7870	244
Iowa Library Assn (ILA)						
3636 Westown Pkwy Suite 202	West Des Moines	IA	50266	**800-452-5507**	515-273-5322	427
Iowa Limestone Co						
500 New York Ave	Des Moines	IA	50313	**800-247-2133**	515-243-8106	493-5
Iowa Medical Society						
1001 Grand Ave	West Des Moines	IA	50265	**800-747-3070**	515-223-1401	466
Iowa Medicine Magazine						
1001 Grand Ave	West Des Moines	IA	50265	**800-747-3070**	515-223-1401	449-16
Iowa Mold Tooling Co Inc						
500 Hwy 18 W	Garner	IA	50438	**800-247-5958**	641-923-3711	462
Iowa Office Supply Inc						
731 Lake Ave	Storm Lake	IA	50588	**800-373-9182**	712-732-4801	524
Iowa Paint Mfg Co Inc						
1625 Grand Ave	Des Moines	IA	50309	**800-659-4455**	515-283-1501	540
Iowa Prestressed Concrete Inc						
601 SW 9th St Suite B	Des Moines	IA	50309	**800-826-0464**	515-243-5118	181
Iowa Prison Industries						
420 Watson Powell Jr Way	Des Moines	IA	50309	**800-670-4537***	515-242-5702	618
*Sales						
Iowa Public Television (IPTV)						
6450 Corporate Dr PO Box 6450	Johnston	IA	50131	**800-532-1290**	515-242-3100	620
Iowa Realty Co Inc						
3501 Westown Pkwy	West Des Moines	IA	50266	**800-247-2430**	515-453-6222	638
Iowa State University 100 Alumni Hall	Ames	IA	50011	**800-262-3810**	515-294-4111	163
Iowa Veterinary Supply Co						
124 Country Club Rd	Iowa Falls	IA	50126	**800-392-5636**	641-648-2529	467
Iowa Wesleyan College						
601 N Main St	Mount Pleasant	IA	52641	**800-582-2383**	319-385-8021	163
Iowa Western Community College						
Clarinda Campus						
923 E Washington St	Clarinda	IA	51632	**800-521-2073**	712-542-5117	160
Council Bluffs Campus						
2700 College Rd Box 4-C	Council Bluffs	IA	51502	**800-432-5852**	712-325-3200	160
IPA (Independent Press Assn)						
2729 Mission St Suite 201	San Francisco	CA	94110	**877-463-9624**	415-643-4401	49-16
IPAA (Independent Petroleum Assn of America) 1201 15th St NW Suite 300	Washington	DC	20005	**800-433-2851**	202-857-4722	48-12
IPAC 2000 PO Box 290	Niagara Falls	NY	14304	**800-388-3211**	716-283-6464	15
IPALCO Enterprises Inc						
PO Box 1595	Indianapolis	IN	46206	**888-261-8222**	317-261-8261	355-5
IParty Corp 270 Bridge St Suite 301	Dedham	MA	02026	**888-727-8970**	781-329-3952	555
AMEX: IPT						
IPayment Inc						
40 Burton Hills Blvd Suite 415	Nashville	TN	37215	**800-324-9825***	615-665-1858	213
NASDAQ: IPMT ■ *Cust Svc						
IPC Communications Services						
501 Colonial Dr	Saint Joseph	MI	49085	**888-563-3220**	269-983-7105	770
IPC International Corp						
2111 Waukegan Rd	Bannockburn	IL	60015	**800-323-1228**	847-444-2000	682
IPIX Corp						
1009 Commerce Park Dr Suite 400	Oak Ridge	TN	37830	**888-909-4749**	865-220-6500	176-8
NASDAQ: IPIX						
IPMA-HR (International Public Management Assn for Human Resources) 1617 Duke St	Alexandria	VA	22314	**800-220-4762**	703-549-7100	49-12
IPMI (International Precious Metals Institute) 4400 Bayou Blvd Suite 18	Pensacola	FL	32503	**866-289-8484**	850-476-1156	49-4
IPNet Solutions Inc						
4100 Newport Pl Suite 800	Newport Beach	CA	92660	**888-882-6600**	949-476-4451	176-1

Alphabetical Section

Name / Address	City	State	ZIP	Toll-Free	Phone	Class
IPO Monitor 5200 W Century Blvd Suite 470	Los Angeles	CA	90045	**800-266-0126**		396
iProspect.com Inc 311 Arsenal St	Watertown	MA	02472	**800-522-1152**	617-923-7000	7
IPS Corp 455 W Victoria St	Compton	CA	90220	**800-421-2677**	310-898-3300	3
IPSCO Inc PO Box 1670 *NYSE: IPS*	Regina	SK	S4P3C7	**800-667-1616**	306-924-7700	709
Ipsen International Inc PO Box 6266	Rockford	IL	61125	**800-727-7625**	815-332-4941	313
IPST (Institute of Paper Science & Technology) 500 10th St NW	Atlanta	GA	30332	**800-558-6611**	404-894-5700	49-13
Ipswich Shellfish Co Inc 8 Hayward St	Ipswich	MA	01938	**800-477-9424**	978-356-4371	292-5
Ipswitch Inc 10 Maguire Rd Suite 220	Lexington	MA	02421	**800-793-4825**	781-676-5700	176-12
IPTV (Idaho Public Television) 1455 N Orchard St	Boise	ID	83706	**800-543-6868**	208-373-7220	620
IPTV (Iowa Public Television) 6450 Corporate Dr PO Box 6450	Johnston	IA	50131	**800-532-1290**	515-242-3100	620
Ira Green Inc 177 Georgia Ave	Providence	RI	02905	**800-959-0180**	401-467-4770	401
Irby Construction Co Inc 815 S State St	Jackson	MS	39215	**866-687-4729**	601-960-7304	187-10
Irby Stuart C Co 815 S State St PO Box 1819	Jackson	MS	39215	**800-844-1811**	601-969-1811	245
IRC (Insurance Research Council) 718 Providence Rd PO Box 3025	Malvern	PA	19355	**800-644-2101**	610-644-2212	49-9
IRC (International Resistive Co Inc) 736 Greenway Rd	Boone	NC	28607	**800-472-6467**	828-264-8861	252
Ircon Inc 7300 N Natchez Ave	Niles	IL	60714	**800-323-7660**	847-967-5151	201
Ireland's Inn Resort Hotel 2220 N Atlantic Blvd	Fort Lauderdale	FL	33305	**800-347-7776**	954-565-6661	373
IREM (Institute of Real Estate Management) 430 N Michigan Ave	Chicago	IL	60611	**800-837-0706**	312-329-6000	49-17
Irex Contracting Group 120 N Lime St	Lancaster	PA	17602	**800-487-7255**	717-397-3633	188-9
IRgA (International Reprographic Assn) 401 N Michigan Ave	Chicago	IL	60611	**800-833-4742**	312-245-1026	49-16
Iridex Corp 1212 Terra Bella Ave *NASDAQ: IRIX* ■ *Cust Svc	Mountain View	CA	94043	**800-388-4747***	650-940-4700	415
Iridian Technologies Inc 1245 N Church St Suite 3	Moorestown	NJ	08057	**866-474-3426**	856-222-9090	85
IRIS Graphics Inc 3 Federal St	Billerica	MA	01821	**800-666-8990**	978-313-4747	616
IRIS International Inc 9172 Eton Ave *NASDAQ: IRIS*	Chatsworth	CA	91311	**800-776-4747**	818-709-1244	375
Irish America Magazine 875 Ave of the Americas Suite 2100	New York	NY	10001	**800-582-6642**	212-725-2993	449-10
Irish Tourist Board 345 Park Ave 17th Fl	New York	NY	10154	**800-669-9967**	212-418-0800	764
Iron Age Corp Robinson Plaza III Suite 400 *Cust Svc	Pittsburgh	PA	15205	**800-223-8912***	412-787-4100	296
Iron City Distributing Co 2670 Commercial Ave *Cust Svc	Mingo Junction	OH	43938	**800-759-2671***	740-598-4171	82-1
Iron City Uniform Rental 6640 Frankstown Ave	Pittsburgh	PA	15206	**800-532-2010**	412-661-2001	434
Iron County Tourism & Convention Bureau 581 N Main	Cedar City	UT	84720	**800-354-4849**	435-586-5124	205
Iron Horse Resort 101 Iron Horse Way	Winter Park	CO	80482	**800-621-8190**	970-726-8851	373
Iron & Metals Inc 5555 Franklin St	Denver	CO	80216	**800-776-7910**	303-292-5555	674
Iron Mountain Inc 745 Atlantic Ave *NYSE: IRM*	Boston	MA	02111	**800-899-4766**		790-1
Iron Skillet 6080 Surety Dr	El Paso	TX	79905	**800-331-8809**	915-779-4711	657
Iron Trail Convention & Visitors Bureau 403 1st St N	Virginia	MN	55792	**800-777-8497**	218-749-8161	205
Iron Workers. International Assn of Bridge Structural Ornamental & Reinforcing 1750 New York Ave NW Suite 400	Washington	DC	20006	**800-368-0105**	202-383-4800	405
Ironman Magazine 1701 Ives Ave	Oxnard	CA	93033	**800-570-4766**	805-385-3500	449-13
IronMaster LLC 21828 87th Ave SE Suite E	Woodinville	WA	98072	**800-533-3339**	425-408-9040	263
Ironrock Capital Inc 1201 Millerton St SE	Canton	OH	44707	**877-497-4273**	330-484-4887	736
Ironton Tribune 2903 S 5th St	Ironton	OH	45638	**866-532-1441**	740-532-1441	522-2
Ironworkers Political Action League 1750 New York Ave NW Suite 400	Washington	DC	20006	**800-368-0105**	202-383-4800	604
Ironworld Discovery Center 801 SW Hwy 169 Suite 1	Chisholm	MN	55719	**800-372-6437**	218-254-7959	509
Iroquois New York 49 W 44th St	New York	NY	10036	**800-332-7220**	212-840-3080	373
Iroquois Products of Chicago 2220 W 56th St	Chicago	IL	60636	**800-453-3355**	773-436-3900	198
Irresistibles 7 Hawkes St	Marblehead	MA	01945	**800-555-9865**	781-631-1248	155-6
IRS (Internal Revenue Service) 1111 Constitution Ave NW	Washington	DC	20224	**800-829-1040**	202-622-9511	336-14
IRS Practice & Policy Bulletin 1231 25th St NW *Cust Svc	Washington	DC	20037	**800-372-1033***	202-452-4200	521-7
Irvin Dick Inc 475 Wilson Ave	Shelby	MT	59474	**800-332-5131**	406-434-5583	769
Irvin H Whitehouse & Sons Co 4600 Jennings Ln	Louisville	KY	40218	**800-626-5859**	502-966-4176	188-8
Irvine Access Floors Inc 9425 Washington Blvd Suite Y-WW	Laurel	MD	20723	**800-969-8870**	410-781-7190	482
Irvine Chamber of Commerce 2485 McCabe Way Suite 150	Irvine	CA	92614	**800-558-4262**	949-660-9112	137
Irvine Sensors Corp 3001 Redhill Ave Bldg 3 Suite 108 *NASDAQ: IRSN*	Costa Mesa	CA	92626	**800-468-4612**	714-549-8211	686
Irving Convention & Visitors Bureau 222 W Las Colinas Blvd Suite 1550	Irving	TX	75039	**800-247-8464**	972-252-7476	205
Irvington-Moore Div USNR Corp PO Box 40666	Jacksonville	FL	32203	**800-289-8767**	904-354-2301	462
Irvins Interstate Brick & Block Co Inc 2301 N Hawthorne Ln	Indianapolis	IN	46218	**800-837-3384**	317-547-9511	148

Name / Address	City	State	ZIP	Toll-Free	Phone	Class
Irwin Electric Membership Corp 915 W 4th St	Ocilla	GA	31774	**800-237-3745**	229-468-7415	244
Irwin Financial Corp 500 Washington St PO Box 929 *NYSE: IFC*	Columbus	IN	47202	**888-879-5900**	812-376-1020	355-2
Irwin Mortgage Corp 10300 Kincaid Dr	Fishers	IN	46038	**800-984-5363**	317-594-8900	498
Irwin Naturals 5310 Beethoven St	Los Angeles	CA	90066	**866-544-7946**	310-306-3636	786
Irwin Seating Co Inc PO Box 2429	Grand Rapids	MI	49501	**800-759-7328**	616-784-2621	314-3
Irwin Union Bank & Trust Co 500 Washington St	Columbus	IN	47201	**888-879-5900**	812-372-0111	71
ISA (International Sign Assn) 707 N Saint Asaph St	Alexandria	VA	22314	**888-472-7446**	703-836-4012	49-4
ISA (International Society of Arboriculture) 1400 W Anthony Dr PO Box 3129	Champaign	IL	61826	**888-472-8733**	217-355-9411	48-2
Isaac Carter Cabin 1701 Old Richton Rd	Petal	MS	39465	**800-638-6877**	601-268-3220	50
ISAR (International Society for Animal Rights) 965 Griffin Pond Rd	Clarks Summit	PA	18411	**800-543-4727**	570-586-2200	48-3
ISCEBS (International Society of Certified Employee Benefit Specialists) 18700 W Bluemound Rd PO Box 209	Brookfield	WI	53008	**888-334-3327**	262-786-8771	49-12
ISCET (International Society of Certified Electronics Technicians) 3608 Pershing Ave	Fort Worth	TX	76107	**800-946-0201**	817-921-9101	49-19
Isco Inc 4700 Superior St PO Box 82531	Lincoln	NE	68501	**800-228-4250**	402-464-0231	410
Isco Industries 926 Baxter Ave	Louisville	KY	40204	**800-345-4726**	502-583-6591	585
ISCO International Inc 1001 Cambridge Dr *AMEX: ISO*	Elk Grove Village	IL	60007	**888-472-3458**	847-391-9400	720
iScribe 101 Redwood Shores Pkwy Suite 101	Redwood City	CA	94065	**877-483-1324**	650-620-0061	171-1
ISE America Inc 33335 Galena Sassafras	Galena	MD	21635	**800-343-7926**	410-755-6300	608
iSelect Internet Inc 420 W Pine St	Lodi	CA	95240	**888-677-8679**	209-334-0496	390
Isfel Co Inc 900 Hart St	Rahway	NJ	07065	**800-927-8760**	732-382-3100	153-4
ISFSI (International Society of Fire Service Instructors) 2425 Hwy 49 E	Pleasant View	TN	37146	**800-435-0005**		49-7
ISI (Intercollegiate Studies Institute) 3901 Centerville Rd	Wilmington	DE	19807	**800-526-7022**	302-652-4600	48-11
ISI Commercial Refrigeration LP 9136 Viscount Row	Dallas	TX	75247	**800-777-5070**	214-631-7980	651
ISITE Design Inc 615 SW Broadway Suite 200	Portland	OR	97205	**888-269-9103**	503-221-9860	796
iSky Inc 6100 Frost Pl	Laurel	MD	20707	**800-351-5055**	240-456-4300	722
Islamorada Chamber of Commerce PO Box 915	Islamorada	FL	33036	**800-322-5397**	305-664-4503	137
Island Express Helicopter Service 1175 Queens Hwy S	Long Beach	CA	90802	**800-228-2566**	310-510-2525	354
Island Grand Beach Resort. TradeWinds 5500 Gulf Blvd	Saint Pete Beach	FL	33705	**800-360-4016**	727-367-6461	655
Island One Resorts 2345 Sand Lake Rd Suite 100	Orlando	FL	32809	**800-892-7523**	407-859-8900	738
Island Pacific Inc 19800 MacArthur Blvd Suite 1200 *AMEX: IPI*	Irvine	CA	92612	**800-944-3847**	949-476-2212	176-10
Island Packet 10 Buck Island Rd	Bluffton	SC	29910	**877-706-8100**	843-706-8100	522-2
Island Press 1718 Connecticut Ave NW Suite 300	Washington	DC	20009	**800-828-1302**	202-232-7933	623-2
Island Water Sports Inc 1985 NE 2nd St	Deerfield Beach	FL	33441	**800-873-0375**	954-427-4929	702
Islands of Adventure 1000 Universal Studios Plaza	Orlando	FL	32819	**888-837-2273**	407-363-8000	32
Islands Magazine PO Box 4728	Santa Barbara	CA	93140	**800-284-7958**	805-745-7100	449-22
Islands in the Sun Cruises & Tours 348 Thompson Creek Mall Suite 107	Stevensville	MD	21666	**800-278-7786**	301-251-4457	760
Isle of Capri Casino 401 Main St	Black Hawk	CO	80422	**800-843-4753**		133
Isle of Capri Casino 777 Isle of Capri Pkwy	Lula	MS	38644	**800-789-5825**	662-363-4600	133
Isle of Capri Casino 1800 E Front St	Kansas City	MO	64120	**800-843-4753**	816-855-7777	133
Isle of Capri Casino & Hotel 711 Isle of Capri Blvd	Bossier City	LA	71111	**800-843-4753**	318-678-7777	133
Isle of Capri Casino Resort 151 Beach Blvd	Biloxi	MS	39530	**800-843-4753**	228-435-5400	133
Isle of Capri Casinos Inc 1641 Popps Ferry Rd Suite B-1 *NASDAQ: ISLE*	Biloxi	MS	39532	**800-843-4753**	228-396-7000	132
Isle of Capri Inn 3033 Hilton Dr	Bossier City	LA	71111	**800-525-5143**	318-747-2400	373
Isle of Capri Lake Charles 100 W Lake Ave	West Lake	LA	70669	**800-843-4753**	337-430-0711	133
ISM (Institute for Supply Management) 2055 Centennial Cir *Cust Svc	Tempe	AZ	85284	**800-888-6276***	480-752-6275	49-12
ISMIE (Illinois State Medical Inter-Insurance Exchange) 20 N Michigan Ave Suite 700	Chicago	IL	60602	**800-782-4767**	312-782-2749	384-5
ISO (Insurance Services Office Inc) 545 Washington Blvd	Jersey City	NJ	07310	**800-888-4476**	201-469-2000	383
Iso-Tex Diagnostics Inc PO Box 909	Friendswood	TX	77549	**800-477-4839**	281-482-1231	229
Isolatek International Inc 41 Furnace St	Stanhope	NJ	07874	**800-631-9600**	973-347-1200	382
IsoTis OrthoBiologics US 2 Goodyear	Irvine	CA	92618	**800-550-7155**	949-595-8710	535
Isotoner Corp. Totes 9655 International Blvd	Cincinnati	OH	45246	**800-762-8712**	513-682-8200	772
ISP Elastomers 1615 Main St	Port Neches	TX	77651	**800-847-1625**	409-722-8321	594-3
Ispat Inland Inc 3210 Watling St	East Chicago	IN	46312	**800-422-9422**	219-399-1200	709
ISPD (International Society for Peritoneal Dialysis) 66 Martin St	Milton	ON	L9T2R2	**888-834-1001**	905-875-2456	49-8

Listing	City	State	ZIP	Toll-Free	Phone	Class
Israel Government Tourist Office 6380 Wilshire Blvd Suite 1700	Los Angeles	CA	90048	**888-774-7723**	323-658-7463	764
Israel Government Tourist Office 800 2nd Ave 16th Fl	New York	NY	10017	**888-774-7723**	212-499-5650	764
Isram World of Travel 630 3rd Ave 4th Fl	New York	NY	10017	**800-223-7460**	212-661-1193	748
ISSA (International Sanitary Supply Assn) 7373 N Lincoln Ave	Lincolnwood	IL	60712	**800-225-4772**	847-982-0800	49-18
ISSA (International Sports Sciences Assn) 400 E Gutierrez St	Santa Barbara	CA	93101	**800-892-4772**	805-884-8111	48-22
ISSI (Integrated Silicon Solution Inc) 2231 Lawson Ln *NASDAQ: ISSI*	Santa Clara	CA	95054	**800-379-4774**	408-969-6600	686
Isspro Inc 2515 NE Riverside Way PO Box 11177	Portland	OR	97211	**888-447-7776**	503-288-4488	486
ISTA (International Safe Transit Assn) 1400 Abbott Rd Suite 160	East Lansing	MI	48823	**888-367-4782**	517-333-3437	49-21
ISTA Advocate Magazine 150 W Market St Suite 900	Indianapolis	IN	46204	**800-382-4037**	317-263-3400	449-8
ISTA Pharmaceuticals Inc 15279 Alton Pkwy Suite 100 *NASDAQ: ISTA*	Irvine	CA	92618	**866-264-8568**	949-788-6000	86
ISTE (International Society for Technology in Education) 480 Charnelton St	Eugene	OR	97401	**800-336-5191**	541-302-3777	49-5
ISTours 999 W Broadway Ave Suite 720	Vancouver	BC	V5Z1K5	**888-472-3933**	604-714-1244	748
(i)Structure Inc 11707 Miracle Hills Dr	Omaha	NE	68154	**888-757-7501**	402-496-8500	455
IT Group Inc 100 Executive Way Suite 202	Ponte Vedra Beach	FL	32082	**888-482-4636**	904-285-9796	761
ITA (Industrial Telecommunications Assn Inc) 1110 N Glebe Rd Suite 500	Arlington	VA	22201	**800-482-8282**	703-528-5115	49-20
ITAGroup 4800 Westown Pkwy Suite 300	West Des Moines	IA	50266	**800-257-1985**	515-224-3400	377
Italy in America. Order of the Sons of 219 'E' St NE	Washington	DC	20002	**800-547-6742**	202-547-2900	48-14
Itasca Community College 1851 E Hwy 169	Grand Rapids	MN	55744	**800-996-6422**	218-327-4460	160
ITB Solutions DBA CardInTheBox 350 S Rohlwing Rd Suite 200	Addison	IL	60101	**877-212-1121**	630-953-8882	130
ITC Learning Corp 1616 Anderson Rd Suite 109	McLean	VA	22102	**800-638-3757**	703-286-0756	753
ITC^DeltaCom Inc 1791 OG Skinner Dr	West Point	GA	31833	**800-239-3000**	706-385-8000	721
Iten Industries 4602 Benefit Ave *Orders	Ashtabula	OH	44004	**800-227-4836***	440-997-6134	588
ITG Inc 380 Madison Ave 4th Fl	New York	NY	10017	**800-215-4484**	212-588-4000	679
Ithaca College 953 Danby Rd	Ithaca	NY	14850	**800-429-4274**	607-274-3011	163
Ithaca/Tompkins County Convention & Visitors Bureau 904 E Shore Dr	Ithaca	NY	14850	**800-284-8422**	607-272-1313	205
ITLA Capital Corp 888 Prospect St Suite 110 *NASDAQ: ITLA*	La Jolla	CA	92037	**888-551-4852**	858-551-0511	355-2
Itron Inc 2818 N Sullivan Rd *NASDAQ: ITRI*	Spokane	WA	99216	**800-635-5461**	509-924-9900	247
Itronix Corp 801 S Stevens St	Spokane	WA	99204	**800-441-1309**	509-624-6600	171-3
ITS America 1100 17th St NW Suite 1200	Washington	DC	20036	**800-374-8472**	202-484-4847	49-21
ITT Industries Inc Engineered Valves Div 33 Centerville Rd	Lancaster	PA	17603	**800-366-1111**	717-291-1901	776
ITT Industries Inc Gilfillan Div 7821 Orion Ave	Van Nuys	CA	91406	**800-264-9234**	818-988-2600	519
ITT Industries Jabsco 20 Icon	Foothill Ranch	CA	92610	**800-235-6538**	949-609-5106	627
ITT Night Vision 7635 Plantation Rd	Roanoke	VA	24019	**800-533-5502**	540-563-0371	534
ITT Standard 175 Standard Pkwy	Cheektowaga	NY	14227	**800-447-7700**	716-897-2800	92
ITT Technical Institute 5005 S Wendler Dr	Tempe	AZ	85282	**800-879-4881**	602-437-7500	787
ITT Technical Institute 1455 W River Rd	Tucson	AZ	85704	**800-870-9730**	520-408-7488	787
ITT Technical Institute 10863 Gold Center Dr	Rancho Cordova	CA	95670	**800-488-8466**	916-851-3900	787
ITT Technical Institute 630 E Brier Dr Suite 150	San Bernardino	CA	92408	**800-888-3801**	909-889-3800	787
ITT Technical Institute 9680 Granite Ridge Dr	San Diego	CA	92123	**800-883-0380**	858-571-8500	787
ITT Technical Institute 12669 Encinitas Ave	Sylmar	CA	91342	**800-363-2086**	818-364-5151	787
ITT Technical Institute 3401 S University Dr	Fort Lauderdale	FL	33328	**800-488-7797**	954-476-9300	787
ITT Technical Institute 6600 Youngerman Cir Suite 10	Jacksonville	FL	32244	**800-318-1264**	904-573-9100	787
ITT Technical Institute 4809 Memorial Hwy	Tampa	FL	33634	**800-825-2831**	813-885-2244	787
ITT Technical Institute 12302 W Explorer Dr	Boise	ID	83713	**800-666-4888**	208-322-8844	787
ITT Technical Institute 4919 Coldwater Rd	Fort Wayne	IN	46825	**800-866-4488**	260-484-4107	787
ITT Technical Institute 9511 Angola Ct	Indianapolis	IN	46268	**800-937-4488**	317-875-8640	787
ITT Technical Institute 10999 Stahl Rd	Newburgh	IN	47630	**800-832-4488**	812-858-1600	787
ITT Technical Institute 13505 Lake Front Dr	Earth City	MO	63045	**800-235-5488**	314-298-7800	787
ITT Technical Institute 9814 M St	Omaha	NE	68127	**800-677-9260**	402-331-2900	787
ITT Technical Institute 3325 Stop Eight Rd	Dayton	OH	45414	**800-568-3241**	937-454-2267	787
ITT Technical Institute 1030 N Meridian Rd	Youngstown	OH	44509	**800-832-5001**	330-270-1600	787
ITT Technical Institute 6035 NE 78th Ct	Portland	OR	97218	**800-234-5488**	503-255-6500	787
ITT Technical Institute 10208 Technology Dr	Knoxville	TN	37932	**800-671-2801**	865-671-2800	787
ITT Technical Institute 2845 Elm Hill Pike	Nashville	TN	37214	**800-331-8386**	615-889-8700	787
ITT Technical Institute 551 Ryan Plaza Dr	Arlington	TX	76011	**888-288-4950**	817-794-5100	787
ITT Technical Institute 6330 Hwy 290 E Suite 150	Austin	TX	78723	**800-431-0677**	512-467-6800	787
ITT Technical Institute 15621 Blue Ash Dr Suite 160	Houston	TX	77090	**800-879-6486**	281-873-0512	787
ITT Technical Institute 2101 Water View Pkwy	Richardson	TX	75080	**888-488-5761**	972-690-9100	787
ITT Technical Institute 5700 Northwest Pkwy	San Antonio	TX	78249	**800-880-0570**	210-694-4612	787
ITT Technical Institute 920 W Levoy Dr	Murray	UT	84123	**800-365-2136**	801-263-3313	787
ITT Technical Institute 863 Glenrock Rd Suite 100	Norfolk	VA	23502	**888-253-8324**	757-466-1260	787
ITT Technical Institute 12720 Gateway Dr Suite 100	Seattle	WA	98168	**800-422-2029**	206-244-3300	787
ITT Technical Institute N 1050 Argonne Rd	Spokane	WA	99212	**800-777-8324**	509-926-2900	787
ITT Technical Institute 6300 W Layton Ave	Greenfield	WI	53220	**800-388-3368**	414-282-9494	787
ITT Technical Institute of West Covina 1530 W Cameron Ave	West Covina	CA	91790	**800-414-6522**	626-960-8681	787
ITUG (International Tandem Users' Group) 401 N Michigan	Chicago	IL	60611	**800-845-4884**	312-321-6851	48-9
ITW (Illinois Tool Works Inc) 3600 W Lake Ave *NYSE: ITW*	Glenview	IL	60025	**800-724-6166**	847-724-7500	379
ITW Amp 100 Fairway Dr Suite 114	Vernon Hills	IL	60061	**800-322-4204**	847-918-1970	809
ITW Angleboard 595 Telser Rd Suite 100	Lake Zurich	IL	60047	**800-252-4777**	800-457-5777	537
ITW Auto-Sleeve 2003 Case Pkwy S Unit 3	Twinsburg	OH	44087	**800-852-4571**	330-487-2200	404
ITW Automotive Refinishing 1724 Indian Wood Cir	Maumee	OH	43537	**800-445-3988**	419-891-8100	170
ITW Brands 955 National Pkwy Suite 95500	Schaumburg	IL	60173	**800-982-7178**	847-944-2260	274
ITW Buildex 1349 W Bryn Mawr	Itasca	IL	60143	**800-284-5339**	630-595-3500	274
ITW Chemtronics Inc 8125 Cobb Centre Dr	Kennesaw	GA	30152	**800-645-5244**	770-424-4888	143
ITW Dymon 805 E Old 56 Hwy	Olathe	KS	66061	**800-289-3966**	913-397-9889	149
ITW Fibre Glass-Evercoat 6600 Cornell Rd	Cincinnati	OH	45242	**800-729-7600**	513-489-7600	60
ITW Food Equipment Group 701 S Ridge Ave *Cust Svc	Troy	OH	45374	**800-333-7447***	937-332-3000	293
ITW Heartland 3600 W Lake Ave	Glenview	IL	60025	**800-724-6166**	847-724-7500	447
ITW Industrial Finishing 195 International Blvd	Glendale Heights	IL	60139	**800-992-4657**	630-237-5000	170
ITW Insulation Systems 919 N Trenton St	Ruston	LA	71270	**800-551-4866**	318-251-2920	382
ITW Insulcast Inc 565 Eagle Rock Ave	Roseland	NJ	07068	**800-631-7841**	973-403-0261	3
ITW Paktron PO Box 4539	Lynchburg	VA	24502	**888-227-7845**	434-239-6941	252
ITW Ransburg 320 Phillips Ave *Cust Svc	Toledo	OH	43612	**800-726-8097***	419-470-2000	170
ITW Shippers Products 1203 N Main St	Mount Pleasant	TN	38474	**800-933-7731**	931-379-7731	666
ITW Southland 5700 Ward Ave	Virginia Beach	VA	23455	**800-804-4744**	757-543-5701	321
ITW Switches 7301 W Ainslie Ave	Harwood Heights	IL	60706	**800-544-3354**	708-667-3370	715
ITW Texwipe 3000 E Rt 17 S	Mahwah	NJ	07430	**800-839-9473**	201-327-9100	143
ITW Vortec 10125 Carver Rd	Cincinnati	OH	45242	**800-441-7475**	513-891-7474	15
ITW Workholding Group 2155 Traverse Field Dr	Traverse City	MI	49686	**800-828-5755**	231-947-5755	484
iUniverse 2021 Pine Lake Rd Suite 100	Lincoln	NE	68512	**800-288-4677**	402-323-7800	623-2
IVAMS (Inland Valley Arbitration & Mediation Service) 300 S Park Ave Suite 780	Pomona	CA	91766	**800-944-8267**	909-629-6301	41
Ivanhoe Energy Inc 999 Canada Pl Suite 654 *TSE: IE*	Vancouver	BC	V6C3E1	**888-273-9999**	604-688-8323	525
IVAX Diagnostics Inc 2140 N Miami Ave *AMEX: IVD*	Miami	FL	33127	**800-327-4565**	305-324-2300	229
IVAX Pharmaceuticals Inc 4400 Biscayne Blvd	Miami	FL	33137	**800-327-4114**	305-575-4100	573
IVC Fixture Mfg 245 5th Ave	New York	NY	10016	**800-777-5286**	212-213-6007	281
iVillage Inc 500 7th Ave 14th Fl *NASDAQ: IVIL*	New York	NY	10018	**800-977-1436**	212-600-6000	169
Ivinson Memorial Hospital 255 N 30th St	Laramie	WY	82072	**800-854-1115**	307-742-2141	366-2
IVOW Inc 2101 Faraday Ave *NASDAQ: IVOW*	Carlsbad	CA	92008	**800-510-8090**	760-603-9120	375
Ivy Animal Health Inc 8857 Bond St	Overland Park	KS	66214	**800-828-2192**	913-888-2192	574
IVY Biomedical Systems Inc 11 Business Park Dr	Branford	CT	06405	**800-247-4614**	203-481-4183	249
Ivy Funds 6300 Lamar Ave	Overland Park	KS	66202	**888-923-3355**	913-236-2000	517
Ivy Tech State College Columbus 4475 Central Ave	Columbus	IN	47203	**800-922-4838**	812-372-9925	787
Ivy Tech State College Gary 1440 E 35th Ave	Gary	IN	46409	**800-843-4882**	219-981-1111	787
Ivy Tech State College Kokomo 1815 E Morgan St	Kokomo	IN	46901	**800-459-0561**	765-459-0561	787
Ivy Tech State College Muncie 4301 S Cowan Rd	Muncie	IN	47302	**800-589-8324**	765-289-2291	787
Ivy Tech State College Richmond 2325 Chester Blvd	Richmond	IN	47374	**800-659-4562**	765-966-2656	787
Ivy Tech State College South Bend 220 Dean Johnson Blvd	South Bend	IN	46601	**888-489-3478**	574-289-7001	787
Ivy Tech State College Terre Haute 7999 S US 41	Terre Haute	IN	47802	**800-377-4882**	812-299-1121	787
IW Industries Inc 35 Melville Park Rd	Melville	NY	11747	**800-252-8202**	631-293-9494	610
IWC (International Wildlife Coalition) 70 E Falmouth Hwy	East Falmouth	MA	02536	**800-548-8704**	508-548-8328	48-3
Iwerks Entertainment Inc 4520 W Valerio St	Burbank	CA	91505	**800-388-8628**	818-841-7766	733

Name / Address	City	State	ZIP	Toll-Free	Phone	Class
IWLA (International Warehouse Logistics Assn) 2800 River Rd Suite 260	Des Plaines	IL	60018	**800-525-0165**	847-813-4699	49-21
Ixia 26601 W Agoura Rd *NASDAQ: XXIA*	Calabasas	CA	91302	**877-367-4942**	818-871-1800	247
Izaak Walton League of America (IWLA) 707 Conservation Ln.	Gaithersburg	MD	20878	**800-453-5463**	301-548-0150	48-13
Izatys Golf & Yacht Club 40005 85th Ave	Onamia	MN	56359	**800-533-1728**	320-532-3101	655
izzydesign 1 Industrial Pk *Cust Svc	Belton	TX	76513	**800-551-3227***	254-939-3517	314-1

J

Name / Address	City	State	ZIP	Toll-Free	Phone	Class
J Alexander's Corp 3401 West End Ave Suite 260 *AMEX: JAX*	Nashville	TN	37203	**888-285-2539**	615-269-1900	657
J & B Supply Inc 4915 S Zero St	Fort Smith	AR	72903	**800-345-5752**	479-649-4915	601
J Crew Group Inc 770 Broadway	New York	NY	10003	**800-932-0043**	212-209-2500	451
J & D Mfg Inc 6200 Hwy 12 *Cust Svc	Eau Claire	WI	54701	**800-848-7998***	715-834-1439	15
J D'Addario & Co Inc 595 Smith St	Farmingdale	NY	11735	**800-323-2746**	631-439-3300	516
J DeBeer & Son Inc 5 Burdick Dr	Albany	NY	12205	**800-833-3535**	518-438-7871	701
J Edgar Eubanks & Assoc 1 Windsor Cove Suite 305	Columbia	SC	29223	**800-445-8629**	803-252-5646	47
J Fletcher Creamer & Son Inc 101 E Broadway	Hackensack	NJ	07601	**800-835-9801**	201-488-9800	188-5
J & H Oil Co PO Box 9464	Wyoming	MI	49509	**800-442-9110**	616-534-2181	319
J Hirshleifer & Son Inc 2080 Northern Blvd	Manhasset	NY	11030	**800-401-9313**	516-627-3566	155-4
J & J Industries Inc 818 J & J Dr	Dalton	GA	30721	**800-241-4585**	706-278-4454	131
J & J Restaurant Group LLC 505 W Roseville Rd	Lancaster	PA	17601	**800-233-0128**	717-299-0968	69
J & J Snack Foods Corp 6000 Central Hwy *NASDAQ: JJSF*	Pennsauken	NJ	08109	**800-486-9533**	856-665-9533	291-25
J Jenkins Sons Co Inc 1801 Whitehead Rd	Baltimore	MD	21207	**800-296-3468**	410-265-5200	401
J Jill Group 4 Batterymarch Park *NASDAQ: JILL*	Quincy	MA	02169	**800-642-9989**	617-376-4300	451
J Lee Hackett Co 23550 Haggerty Rd	Farmington Hills	MI	48335	**800-422-5388**	248-478-0200	378
J & M Industries 300 Ponchatoula Pkwy	Ponchatoula	LA	70454	**800-989-1002**	985-386-6000	68
J-M Mfg Co Inc 9 Peach Tree Hill Rd	Livingston	NJ	07039	**800-621-4404**	973-535-1633	585
J Polep Distribution Services Inc 705 Meadow St	Chicopee	MA	01013	**800-447-6537**	413-592-4141	744
J & R Music World 23 Park Row	New York	NY	10038	**800-221-8180**	212-732-8600	514
J Rolfe Davis Insurance Agency Inc 850 Concourse Pkwy S Suite 200	Maitland	FL	32751	**800-896-0554**	407-691-9600	383
J Smith Lanier & Co 300 W 10th St	West Point	GA	31833	**800-226-4522**	706-645-2211	383
J Sosnick & Sons Inc 258 Littlefield Ave	South San Francisco	CA	94080	**800-443-6737**	650-952-2226	292-11
J & W Seligman & Co Inc 100 Park Ave	New York	NY	10017	**800-221-7844**	212-850-1864	393
J Weston Walch Publisher PO Box 658	Portland	ME	04104	**800-558-2846**	207-772-2846	623-2
j2 Global Communications Inc 6922 Hollywood Blvd 8th Fl *NASDAQ: JCOM* ■ *Sales	Hollywood	CA	90028	**888-718-2000***	323-817-3217	721
JA (Jewelers of America) 52 Vanderbilt Ave 19th Fl	New York	NY	10017	**800-223-0673**	646-658-0246	49-4
JA Besteman Co Inc 1060 Hall St SW	Grand Rapids	MI	49503	**800-253-4620**	616-452-2101	292-7
JA Majors Co 1401 Lakeway Dr	Lewisville	TX	75057	**800-633-1851**	972-353-1100	97
JA Nearing Co Inc 9390 Davis Ave	Laurel	MD	20723	**800-323-6933**	301-498-5700	232
JA Richards Co 903 N Pitcher St	Kalamazoo	MI	49007	**800-253-3288**	269-343-4684	448
Jabel Inc 365 Coit St	Irvington	NJ	07111	**800-526-4597**	973-374-6000	401
Jabo Supply Corp 5164 Braley St	Huntington	WV	25705	**800-334-5226**	304-736-8333	378
JACAN (Junior Achievement of Canada) 2275 Lakeshore Blvd W Suite 306	Toronto	ON	M8V3Y3	**800-265-0699**	416-622-4602	48-11
Jack B Kelley Inc 8101 W 34th Ave	Amarillo	TX	79121	**800-225-5525**	806-353-3553	769
Jack B Parson Cos 2350 S 1900 West	Ogden	UT	84401	**888-672-7766**	801-731-1111	187-4
Jack in the Box Inc 9330 Balboa Ave *NYSE: JBX*	San Diego	CA	92123	**800-500-5225**	858-571-2121	656
Jack in the Box Restaurants 9330 Balboa Ave	San Diego	CA	92123	**800-500-5225**	858-571-2121	657
Jack Cooper Transport Co Inc 2345 Grand Blvd Suite 400	Kansas City	MO	64108	**866-449-6301**	816-983-4000	769
Jack & Jill Ice Cream Co 3100 Marwin Ave	Bensalem	PA	19020	**800-220-2300**	215-639-2300	292-4
Jack & Jill Magazine 1100 Waterway Blvd	Indianapolis	IN	46202	**800-558-2376**	317-636-8881	449-6
Jack London Inn 444 Embarcadero W	Oakland	CA	94607	**800-549-8780**	510-444-2032	373
Jack-Post Corp 810 E 3rd St *Cust Svc	Buchanan	MI	49107	**800-800-4950***	269-695-7000	314-2
Jack Rabbit Lines Inc 301 N Dakota Ave	Sioux Falls	SD	57104	**800-678-6543**	605-336-3339	108
Jack Richeson & Co Inc 557 Marcella Dr	Kimberly	WI	54136	**800-233-2404**	920-738-0744	43
Jack Williams Tire Co Inc PO Box 3655	Scranton	PA	18505	**800-833-5051**	570-457-5000	62-5
Jackalope Pottery 2820 Cerrillos Rd	Santa Fe	NM	87507	**800-753-7757**	505-471-8539	357
Jackie Gaughan's Plaza Hotel & Casino 1 Main St	Las Vegas	NV	89125	**800-634-6575**	702-386-2110	373
Jacknob Corp 290 Oser Ave	Hauppauge	NY	11788	**888-231-9333**	631-231-9400	345
Jackpot Convenience Stores Inc 2737 W Commodore Way	Seattle	WA	98199	**800-552-0748**	206-286-6436	203
Jackpot Junction Casino Hotel 39375 County Hwy 24 PO Box 420	Morton	MN	56270	**800-946-2274**	507-644-3000	133
Jack's Family Restaurants Inc 124 W Oxmoor Rd	Birmingham	AL	35209	**800-422-3893**	205-945-8167	657
Jackson Area Chamber of Commerce 197 Auditorium St	Jackson	TN	38301	**800-858-5596**	731-423-2200	137
Jackson & Blanc Inc 7929 Arjons Dr	San Diego	CA	92126	**800-236-1121**	858-831-7900	188-10
Jackson CB & Co Inc DBA Spec's Liquor Warehouse 2410 Smith St	Houston	TX	77006	**888-526-8787**	713-526-8787	435
Jackson Citizen Patriot 214 S Jackson St	Jackson	MI	49201	**800-878-6397**	517-787-2300	522-2
Jackson Community College 2111 Emmons Rd	Jackson	MI	49201	**888-522-7344**	517-787-0800	160
Jackson County Chamber of Commerce 773 W Main St	Sylva	NC	28779	**800-962-1911**	828-586-2155	137
Jackson County Convention & Visitors Bureau 6007 Ann Arbor Rd	Jackson	MI	49201	**800-245-5282**	517-764-4440	205
Jackson County Memorial Hospital 1200 E Pecan St	Altus	OK	73521	**800-250-9965**	580-482-4781	366-2
Jackson County Rural Electric Membership Corp PO Box K	Brownstown	IN	47220	**800-288-4458**	812-358-4458	244
Jackson Electric Co-op PO Box 546	Black River Falls	WI	54615	**800-370-4607**	715-284-5385	244
Jackson Electric Membership Corp PO Box 38	Jefferson	GA	30549	**800-462-3691**	706-367-5281	244
Jackson Energy Co-op PO Box 307	McKee	KY	40447	**800-262-7480**	606-364-1000	244
Jackson Harness Raceway 200 W Ganson St	Jackson	MI	49201	**877-316-0283**	517-788-4500	628
Jackson Hewitt Inc 7 Sylvan Way *NYSE: JTX*	Parsippany	NJ	07054	**800-234-1040**	973-496-1040	719
Jackson Hole Central Reservations 140 E Broadway Suite 24	Jackson	WY	83001	**800-443-6931**	307-733-4005	368
Jackson Hole Lodge 420 W Broadway PO Box 1805	Jackson	WY	83001	**800-604-9404**	307-733-2992	373
Jackson Hole Mountain Resort PO Box 290	Teton Village	WY	83025	**888-333-7766**	307-733-2292	655
Jackson Hole Racquet Club Resort 3535 Moose-Wilson Rd	Wilson	WY	83014	**800-443-8613**	307-733-3990	655
Jackson Hole Resort Reservations LLC PO Box 12739	Jackson	WY	83002	**800-329-9205**	307-733-6331	368
Jackson ImmunoResearch Laboratories Inc 872 W Baltimore Pike	West Grove	PA	19390	**800-367-5296**	610-869-4024	229
Jackson Lake Lodge PO Box 250	Moran	WY	83013	**800-628-9988**	307-543-2811	655
Jackson Marking Products Co 9105 N Rainbow Ln	Mount Vernon	IL	62864	**800-782-6722**	618-242-1334	459
Jackson Mattress Co Inc PO Box 64609	Fayetteville	NC	28306	**800-763-7378**	910-425-0131	463
Jackson-Mitchell Inc PO Box 934	Turlock	CA	95381	**800-343-1185**	209-667-2019	291-10
Jackson National Life Insurance Co 1 Corporate Way	Lansing	MI	48951	**800-644-4565**	517-381-5500	384-2
Jackson & Perkins 2500 S Pacific Hwy PO Box 1028 *Cust Svc	Medford	OR	97501	**800-872-7673***	541-776-2000	451
Jackson Products Inc 801 Corporate Ctr Dr Suite 300	Saint Charles	MO	63304	**800-253-7281**	636-300-2700	566
Jackson Purchase Energy Corp 2900 Irvin Cobb Dr	Paducah	KY	42002	**800-633-4044**	270-442-7321	244
Jackson Securities 100 Peachtree St NW Suite 2250	Atlanta	GA	30303	**866-888-4574**	404-522-5766	679
Jackson State University 1400 John R Lynch St	Jackson	MS	39217	**800-848-6817**	601-979-2121	163
Jackson Sun 245 W LaFayette St	Jackson	TN	38301	**800-372-3922**	731-427-3333	522-2
Jackson Tour & Travel Inc 4500 55 Highland Village Suite 258	Jackson	MS	39216	**800-873-8572**	601-981-8415	748
Jackson/Hinds Library System 300 N State St	Jackson	MS	39201	**800-968-5803**	601-968-5811	426
JacksonLea PO Box 699	Conover	NC	28613	**800-438-6880**	828-464-1376	1
Jacksonville Bancorp Inc 100 N Laura St *NASDAQ: JAXB*	Jacksonville	FL	32202	**888-699-5292**	904-421-3040	355-2
Jacksonville College 105 BJ Albritton Dr	Jacksonville	TX	75766	**800-256-8522**	903-586-2518	160
Jacksonville Convention & Visitors Bureau 550 Water St Suite 1000	Jacksonville	FL	32202	**800-733-2668**	904-798-9111	205
Jacksonville Convention & Visitors Bureau 155 W Morton Ave	Jacksonville	IL	62650	**800-593-5678**	217-243-5678	205
Jacksonville Jaguars 1 Alltel Stadium Pl	Jacksonville	FL	32202	**877-452-4784**	904-633-6000	703
Jacksonville Journal-Courier 235 W State St	Jacksonville	IL	62650	**800-682-9132**	217-245-6121	522-2
Jacksonville Magazine 534 Lancaster St *Circ	Jacksonville	FL	32204	**800-962-0214***	904-358-8330	449-22
Jacksonville State University 700 Pelham Rd N	Jacksonville	AL	36265	**800-231-5291**	256-782-5781	163
Jacksonville University 2800 University Blvd N	Jacksonville	FL	32211	**800-225-2027**	904-256-8000	163
Jaco Electronics Inc 145 Oser Ave *NASDAQ: JACO*	Hauppauge	NY	11788	**800-966-5226**	631-273-5500	245
Jacob Ash Co Inc 301 Munson Ave	McKees Rocks	PA	15136	**800-245-6111**	412-331-6660	154
Jacob Leinenkugel Brewing Co Hwy 124 N PO Box 368	Chippewa Falls	WI	54729	**888-534-6437**	715-723-5557	103
Jacob Stern & Sons Inc 1464 E Valley Rd	Santa Barbara	CA	93108	**800-223-7054**	805-565-1411	291-12
Jacobi Sales Inc 425 Main St NE	Palmyra	IN	47164	**800-489-3617**	812-364-6141	270
Jacobs Richard E Group Inc 25425 Center Ridge Rd	Cleveland	OH	44145	**800-852-9558**	440-871-4800	641
Jacobsen Homes PO Box 368 *Sales	Safety Harbor	FL	34695	**800-843-1559***	727-726-1138	495
Jacobson & Co Inc PO Box 511	Elizabeth	NJ	07207	**800-352-2627**	908-355-5200	188-9
Jacobson SI Mfg Co 1414 Jacobson Dr	Waukegan	IL	60085	**800-621-5492**	847-623-1414	538
Jacquelyn Wigs 15 W 37th St 4th Fl	New York	NY	10018	**800-272-2424**	212-302-2266	342
Jacquin Charles et Cie 2633 Trenton Ave	Philadelphia	PA	19125	**800-523-3811**	215-425-9300	81-1

Company / Address	City	State	Zip	Toll-Free	Phone	Class
Jade Corp 3063 Philmont Ave	Huntingdon Valley	PA	19006	**800-628-4370**	215-947-3333	745
Jaeckle Wholesale Inc 4101 Owl Creek Dr	Madison	WI	53718	**800-236-7225**	608-838-5400	190-1
Jafra Cosmetics International 2451 Townsgate Rd	Westlake Village	CA	91361	**800-551-2345**	805-449-3000	211
Jaguar Cars North America 555 MacArthur Blvd *Cust Svc	Mahwah	NJ	07430	**800-452-4827***	201-818-8500	59
Jaguar Computer Systems Inc 4135 Indus Way	Riverside	CA	92503	**800-540-0548**	951-273-7950	173
JAI Pulnix Inc 1330 Orleans Dr	Sunnyvale	CA	94089	**800-445-5444**	408-747-0300	681
Jailhouse Inn 13 Marlborough St	Newport	RI	02840	**800-427-9444**	401-847-4638	373
Jaindl Farms 3150 Coffeetown Rd	Orefield	PA	18069	**800-475-6654**	610-395-3333	11-8
Jake's Over the Top 4605 Harrison Blvd	Ogden	UT	84403	**800-207-5804**	801-476-9780	657
Jake's Pizza Enterprises Inc 1931 Rohlwing Rd Suite B	Rolling Meadows	IL	60008	**800-425-2537**	847-368-1990	657
JAKKS Pacific Inc 22619 Pacific Coast Hwy Suite 250 *NASDAQ: JAKK*	Malibu	CA	90265	**877-875-2557**	310-456-7799	750
JAMA (Journal of the American Medical Assn) 515 N State St	Chicago	IL	60610	**800-262-2350**	312-464-5000	449-16
Jamaica Tourist Board 1320 S Dixie Hwy Suite 1101	Coral Gables	FL	33146	**800-233-4582**	305-665-0557	764
Jamba Juice Co 1700 17th St	San Francisco	CA	94103	**800-545-9972**		350
Jamcracker Inc 4677 Old Ironsides Dr Suite 450	Santa Clara	CA	95054	**866-559-0035**	408-496-5500	39
James A Murphy & Son Inc PO Box 3006	South Attleboro	MA	02703	**800-422-3237**	508-761-5060	399
James Austin Co 115 Downieville Rd PO Box 827	Mars	PA	16046	**800-245-1942**	724-625-1535	149
James Avery Craftsman Inc PO Box 291367	Kerrville	TX	78029	**800-283-1770**	830-895-1122	401
James B Oswald Co 1360 E 9th St Suite 600	Cleveland	OH	44114	**800-466-0468**	216-241-0468	383
James Burn International 211 Cottage St	Poughkeepsie	NY	12601	**800-431-4610**	845-454-8200	112
James Cable Partners 38710 N Woodward Ave Suite 180	Bloomfield Hills	MI	48304	**877-834-9487**	248-647-1080	117
James Candy Co 1519 Boardwalk	Atlantic City	NJ	08401	**800-441-1404**	609-344-1519	291-8
James E Van Zandt Veterans Affairs Medical Center 2907 Pleasant Valley Blvd	Altoona	PA	16602	**877-626-2500**	814-943-8164	366-6
James G Hardy & Co 352 7th Ave Suite 1223	New York	NY	10001	**800-847-4076**	212-689-6680	356
James Gettys Hotel 27 Chambersburg St	Gettysburg	PA	17325	**888-900-5275**	717-337-1334	373
James H Drew Corp 8701 Zionsville Rd	Indianapolis	IN	46268	**800-772-7342**	317-876-3739	187-4
James Hardie Building Products 26300 La Alameda Ave Suite 250	Mission Viejo	CA	92691	**888-542-7343**	949-348-1800	190-4
James J Hill House 240 Summit Ave	Saint Paul	MN	55102	**888-727-8386**	651-297-2555	50
James Machine Works Inc 1521 Adams St	Monroe	LA	71201	**800-259-6104**	318-322-6104	92
James N Gray Co 10 Quality St	Lexington	KY	40507	**800-950-4729**	859-281-5000	185
James River Bus Lines 915 N Allen Ave	Richmond	VA	23220	**877-342-7300**	804-342-7300	108
James River Equipment 11047 Leadbetter Rd	Ashland	VA	23005	**800-969-6001**	804-798-6001	270
James River Technical Inc 4439 Cox Rd	Glen Allen	VA	23060	**800-296-0027**	804-935-0150	178
James Skinner Baking Co 4657 G St	Omaha	NE	68117	**800-358-7428**	402-734-1672	291-2
James Tom Co 424 S Lynn Riggs Blvd	Claremore	OK	74017	**800-237-2140**	918-341-3773	153-12
Jameson Inn 8 Perimeter Ctr E Suite 8050	Atlanta	GA	30346	**800-526-3766**	770-901-9020	369
Jameson Inns Inc 8 Perimeter Ctr E Suite 8050 *NASDAQ: JAMS*	Atlanta	GA	30346	**800-526-3766**	770-901-9020	369
Jameson Inn 8 Perimeter Ctr E Suite 8050	Atlanta	GA	30346	**800-526-3766**	770-901-9020	369
Signature Inn 8 Perimeter Ctr E Suite 8050	Atlanta	GA	30346	**800-822-5252**	770-901-9020	369
Jamestown College 6081 College Ln	Jamestown	ND	58405	**800-336-2554**	701-252-3467	163
Jamestown Community College 525 Faulkner St	Jamestown	NY	14702	**800-388-8557**	716-665-5220	160
Jamestown Promotions & Tourism Center PO Box 917	Jamestown	ND	58401	**800-222-4766**	701-251-9145	205
Jamestown Sun 121 3rd St NW	Jamestown	ND	58401	**800-657-8067**	701-252-3120	522-2
Jamieson Laboratories Ltd 2 St Clair Ave W Suite 1600	Toronto	ON	M4V1L5	**888-235-8213**	416-960-0052	786
Jamison Bedding Inc PO Box 681948	Franklin	TN	37068	**800-255-1883**	615-794-1883	463
Jamison Door Co 55 JV Jamison Dr	Hagerstown	MD	21740	**800-532-3667**	301-733-3100	232
JAMS/Endispute 500 N State College Blvd Suite 600	Orange	CA	92868	**800-352-5267**	714-939-1300	41
Jan Cos 35 Sockanosset Cross Rd	Cranston	RI	02920	**800-937-1800**	401-946-4000	656
Jan-Pro Franchising Systems International Inc 383 Strand Industrial Dr	Little River	SC	29566	**800-668-1001**	843-399-9895	150
Janazzo Services Corp 140 Norton St	Milldale	CT	06467	**800-297-3931**	860-621-7381	188-10
Jane Goodall Institute for Wildlife Research Education & Conservation (JGI) 8700 Georgia Ave Suite 500	Silver Spring	MD	20910	**800-592-5263**	301-565-0086	48-3
Jane Magazine 7 W 34th St 6th Fl *Cust Svc	New York	NY	10001	**800-219-5294***	212-630-4000	449-11
Jane Rose Reporting 74 5th Ave	New York	NY	10011	**800-825-3341**	715-472-4631	436
Jane's Information Group 110 N Royal St Suite 200	Alexandria	VA	22314	**800-824-0768**	703-683-3700	623-2
Janesville Gazette 1 S Parker Dr PO Box 5001	Janesville	WI	53547	**800-362-6712**	608-754-3311	522-2
Janesville Sand & Lycon Co 1110 Harding St	Janesville	WI	53547	**800-955-7702**	608-754-7701	493-4
Jani-King International Inc 16885 Dallas Pkwy	Addison	TX	75001	**800-552-5264**	972-991-0900	150
Janlynn Corp 2070 Westover Rd	Chicopee	MA	01022	**800-445-5565**	413-206-0002	583
Janney Montgomery Scott LLC 1801 Market St	Philadelphia	PA	19103	**800-526-6397**	215-665-6000	679
Jan's Mountain Outfitters 1600 Park Ave PO Box 280	Park City	UT	84060	**800-745-1020**	435-649-4949	702
Janson Industries 1200 Garfield Ave SW	Canton	OH	44706	**800-548-8982**	330-455-7029	708
JanSport Inc N 850 County Hwy CB *Cust Svc	Appleton	WI	54914	**800-558-8404***	920-734-5708	153-3
Janssen-Ortho Inc 19 Green Belt Dr	North York	ON	M3C1L9	**800-387-8781**	416-382-5000	572
Janssen Pharmaceutica Inc 1125 Trenton-Harbourton Rd	Titusville	NJ	08560	**800-526-7736**	609-730-2000	572
Janssen's Charters & Tours 1623 Woods Rd E	Port Orchard	WA	98366	**800-922-5044**	360-871-2446	748
Jantize America Inc 15449 Middlebelt Rd	Livonia	MI	48154	**800-968-9182**	734-421-4733	150
Jantzen Inc 424 NE 18th Ave	Portland	OR	97232	**800-626-0215**	503-238-5000	153-17
Janus Funds 100 Fillmore St	Denver	CO	80206	**800-525-3713**	303-333-3863	517
Japan Airlines 461 5th Ave 6th Fl	New York	NY	10017	**800-525-3663**	212-838-4400	26
Japan Airlines Mileage Bank 300 Continental Blvd Suite 401	El Segundo	CA	90245	**800-525-6453**		27
Japan Fund PO Box 446	Portland	ME	04112	**800-535-2726**		517
Japan Travel Bureau USA Inc 810 7th Ave 34th Fl	New York	NY	10019	**800-235-3523**	212-698-4900	760
Japanese American National Museum 369 E 1st St	Los Angeles	CA	90012	**800-461-5266**	213-625-0414	509
Japs-Olson Co 7500 Excelsior Blvd	Saint Louis Park	MN	55426	**800-548-2897**	952-932-9393	615
Jarden Plastic Solutions PO Box 2750	Greenville	SC	29602	**888-291-5755**	864-879-7600	593
Jardine Petroleum Co 1117 N 400 East	North Salt Lake	UT	84054	**800-777-9251**	801-298-3252	569
Jared Coffin House 29 Broad St	Nantucket	MA	02554	**800-248-2405**	508-228-2400	373
Jarke Corp 750 Pinecrest Dr	Prospect Heights	IL	60070	**800-722-5255**	847-541-6500	281
Jarob Design Inc 2601 Elmridge Dr NW	Grand Rapids	MI	49544	**800-843-2508**	616-453-5419	692
Jarvis Caster Group 60 Record Dr	Henderson	TN	38340	**800-995-9876**		345
Jarvis Supply Co Inc 114 W 8th St	Winfield	KS	67156	**800-522-8058**	620-221-3113	61
Jasc Software Inc 7905 Fuller Rd *Orders	Eden Prairie	MN	55344	**800-622-2793***	952-930-9800	176-8
Jasco Cutting Tools 195 Saint Paul St	Rochester	NY	14604	**800-868-1074**	585-546-1254	447
Jasco Products Inc 311 NW 122nd St	Oklahoma City	OK	73114	**800-654-8483**	405-752-0710	245
Jasco Tools Inc 1390 Mt Read Blvd PO Box 60497	Rochester	NY	14606	**800-724-5497**	585-254-7000	484
Jason Natural Cosmetics Inc 5500 W 83rd St	Los Angeles	CA	90045	**800-527-6605**	310-838-7543	211
Jasper County Farm Bureau Co-op Assn 2530 N McKinley	Rensselaer	IN	47978	**800-828-7516**	219-866-7131	272
Jasper County Rural Electric Membership Corp PO Box 129	Rensselaer	IN	47978	**888-866-7362**	219-866-4601	244
Jasper Desk Co 415 E 6th St *Cust Svc	Jasper	IN	47547	**800-365-7994***	812-482-4132	314-1
Jasper Engine & Transmission Exchange Inc 815 Wernsing Rd PO Box 650	Jasper	IN	47547	**800-827-7455**	812-482-1041	60
Jasper-Newton Electric Co-op Inc 812 S Margaret Ave	Kirbyville	TX	75956	**800-231-9340**	409-423-2241	244
Jasper Rubber Products Inc 1010 1st Ave W	Jasper	IN	47546	**800-457-7457**	812-482-3242	664
Jasper Seating Co Inc 225 Clay St	Jasper	IN	47546	**800-622-5661**	812-482-3204	314-1
Jasper Wyman & Son PO Box 100	Milbridge	ME	04658	**800-341-1758**	207-546-2311	310-1
Jax Car Wash Inc 28845 Telegraph Rd	Southfield	MI	48034	**866-529-5273**	248-353-4700	62-1
Jay County Rural Electric Membership Corp PO Box 904	Portland	IN	47371	**800-835-7362**	260-726-7121	244
Jay Peak Ski & Summer Resort 4850 Rt 242	Jay	VT	05859	**800-451-4449**	802-988-2611	655
Jayco Inc 903 S Main St *Cust Svc	Middlebury	IN	46540	**877-825-4782***	574-825-5861	120
Jayhawk Bowling Supply Inc 355 N Iowa St	Lawrence	KS	66044	**800-255-6436**	785-842-3237	701
Jaynes Corp 2906 Broadway NE	Albuquerque	NM	87107	**800-432-5204**	505-345-8591	185
Jaypro Sports Inc 976 Hartford Tpke *Cust Svc	Waterford	CT	06385	**800-243-0533***	860-447-3001	340
Jays Foods Inc 825 E 99th St	Chicago	IL	60628	**800-621-6152**	773-731-8400	291-35
Jazz Basketball Investors Inc 301 W South Temple St Delta Ctr	Salt Lake City	UT	84101	**800-358-7328**	801-325-2500	703
Jazzercise Inc 2460 Impala Dr *Cust Svc	Carlsbad	CA	92008	**800-348-4748***	760-476-1750	797
Jazziz Magazine 2650 N Military Trail Suite 140 Fountain Square II Bldg	Boca Raton	FL	33431	**800-742-3252**	561-893-6868	449-9
JazzTimes Magazine 8737 Colesville Rd 9th Fl	Silver Spring	MD	20910	**800-866-7664**	301-588-4114	449-9
JB Hanauer & Co 4 Gatehall Dr	Parsippany	NJ	07054	**800-631-1094**	973-829-1000	679
JB Hunt Transport Services Inc 615 JB Hunt Corporate Dr *NASDAQ: JBHT*	Lowell	AR	72745	**800-643-3622**	479-820-0000	440
JB Martin Co 10 E 53rd St	New York	NY	10022	**800-223-0525**	212-421-2020	730-1
JB Oxford Holdings Inc 9665 Wilshire Blvd 3rd Fl *NASDAQ: JBOH*	Beverly Hills	CA	90212	**800-799-8870**	310-777-8888	355-3
JB Sandlin Cos 5137 Davis Blvd	Fort Worth	TX	76180	**800-821-4663**	817-281-3509	186
JBFCS (Jewish Board of Family & Children Services) 120 W 57th St	New York	NY	10019	**888-523-2769**	212-582-9100	48-6
JBL Professional 8400 Balboa Blvd	Northridge	CA	91329	**800-852-5776**	818-894-8850	52
JC Ehrlich Co Inc PO Box 13848	Reading	PA	19612	**800-488-9495**	610-372-9700	567
JC Newman Cigar Co 2701 16th St *Orders	Tampa	FL	33605	**800-477-1884***	813-248-2124	741-2
JC Penney Co Inc PO Box 10001 *NYSE: JCP* ■ *Orders	Dallas	TX	75301	**800-222-6161***	972-431-1000	227
JC Penney Optical Co 1 Harmon Dr Glen Oaks Industrial Park	Glendora	NJ	08012	**800-524-0789**	856-228-1000	533

Listing	City	State	ZIP	Toll-Free	Phone	Class
JC Potter Sausage Co 1914 Hwy 70 E	Durant	OK	74702	**800-321-8549**	580-924-2414	291-26
JC Whitney & Co 225 N Michigan Ave	Chicago	IL	60601	**800-529-4486**	312-431-6000	451
JCI (Junior Chamber International) 15645 Olive Blvd	Chesterfield	MO	63017	**800-905-5499**	636-449-3100	48-7
JCI Jones Chemicals Inc 100 Sunny Sol Blvd	Caledonia	NY	14423	**800-255-3789**	585-538-2314	141
JD Calato Mfg Co Inc 4501 Hyde Park Blvd *Cust Svc	Niagara Falls	NY	14305	**800-358-4590***	716-285-3546	516
JD Equipment Inc 1660 US 42 NE	London	OH	43140	**800-659-5646**	614-879-6620	270
JD Factors 1611 S Pacific Coast Hwy Suite 203	Redondo Beach	CA	90277	**866-585-2274**	310-316-7170	268
JD Gould Co Inc 4707 Massachusetts Ave	Indianapolis	IN	46218	**800-634-6853**	317-547-5289	777
JD Heiskell & Co 116 W Cedar St	Tulare	CA	93274	**800-366-1886**	559-757-3135	438
JD Streett & Co Inc 144 Weldon Pkwy	Maryland Heights	MO	63043	**800-678-6600**	314-432-6600	530
JDR Microdevices Inc 1850 S 10th St *Sales	San Jose	CA	95112	**800-538-5000***	408-494-1450	451
JDRF (Juvenile Diabetes Research Foundation International) 120 Wall St	New York	NY	10005	**800-533-2873**	212-785-9500	48-17
JDS Uniphase Corp 1768 Automation Pkwy *NASDAQ: JDSU*	San Jose	CA	95131	**800-644-8674**	408-546-5000	252
JE Herndon Co Inc 1020 J E Herndon Access Rd	Kings Mountain	NC	28086	**800-277-0500**	704-739-4711	730-8
JE Higgins Lumber Co 6999 S Front Rd	Livermore	CA	94550	**800-241-1883**	925-245-4300	190-3
JE Morgan Knitting Mills Inc 143 Mahanoy Ave PO Box 390	Tamaqua	PA	18252	**800-448-8240**	570-668-3330	153-18
Jean Paree Weegs Inc 4041 S 700 East Suite 2 *Orders	Salt Lake City	UT	84107	**800-422-9447***	801-328-9756	342
Jeep Div DaimlerChrysler Corp 800 Chrysler Dr E *Cust Svc	Auburn Hills	MI	48326	**800-992-1997***	248-576-5741	59
Jeepers! Inc 800 South St Suite 355	Waltham	MA	02453	**800-533-7377**	781-890-1800	645
Jefferds Corp US Rt 35 W PO Box 757	Saint Albans	WV	25177	**800-735-8111**	304-755-8111	378
Jefferies & Co Inc 11100 Santa Monica Blvd	Los Angeles	CA	90025	**800-421-0160**	310-445-1199	679
Jefferies Group Inc 11100 Santa Monica Blvd *NYSE: JEF*	Los Angeles	CA	90025	**800-421-0160**	310-445-1199	679
Jefferies Socks LLC 1176 N Church St *Cust Svc	Burlington	NC	27217	**800-334-6831***	336-226-7315	153-10
Jefferson Barracks National Cemetery 2900 Sheridan Rd	Saint Louis	MO	63125	**800-535-1117**	314-260-8691	50
Jefferson City Convention & Visitors Bureau 213 Adams St	Jefferson City	MO	65101	**800-769-4183**	573-632-2820	205
Jefferson City Post-Tribune 210 Monroe St	Jefferson City	MO	65101	**866-896-8088**	573-636-3131	522-2
Jefferson College of Health Sciences 920 S Jefferson St PO Box 13186	Roanoke	VA	24031	**888-985-8483**	540-985-8483	787
Jefferson Community College 1220 Coffeen St	Watertown	NY	13601	**888-435-6522**	315-786-2200	160
Jefferson Community College 4000 Sunset Blvd	Steubenville	OH	43952	**800-682-6553**	740-264-5591	158
Jefferson County Chamber of Commerce PO Box 890	Dandridge	TN	37725	**877-237-3847**	865-397-9642	137
Jefferson County Chamber of Commerce PO Box 426	Charles Town	WV	25414	**800-624-0577**	304-725-2055	137
Jefferson County Convention & Visitors Bureau PO Box A	Harpers Ferry	WV	25425	**800-848-8687**	304-535-2627	205
Jefferson Davis Electric Co-op 906 N Lake Arthur Ave	Jennings	LA	70546	**800-256-5332**	337-824-4330	244
Jefferson Energy Co-op 3077 Hwy 17 PO Box 457	North Wrens	GA	30833	**800-342-0322**	706-547-2167	244
Jefferson Hotel 101 West Franklin St	Richmond	VA	23220	**800-424-8014**	804-788-8000	373
Jefferson Lines 2100 E 26th St *Cust Svc	Minneapolis	MN	55404	**800-767-5333***	612-332-8745	109
Jefferson Lodge 616 S Jefferson St	Roanoke	VA	24011	**800-950-2580**	540-342-2951	373
Jefferson Mills Inc 27 Valley St *Sales	Pulaski	VA	24301	**800-574-0069***	540-980-1530	730-9
Jefferson Partners LP 2100 E 26th St *Cust Svc	Minneapolis	MN	55404	**800-767-5333***	612-332-8745	109
Jefferson-Pilot Corp 100 N Greene St *NYSE: JP*	Greensboro	NC	27401	**800-487-1485**	336-691-3000	184
Jefferson-Pilot Financial Insurance Co 100 N Greene St	Greensboro	NC	27401	**800-487-1485**	336-691-3000	384-2
Jefferson-Pilot Life Insurance Co 100 N Greene St	Greensboro	NC	27401	**800-487-1485**	336-691-3000	384-2
Jefferson-Pilot Securities Corp PO Box 515	Concord	NH	03302	**800-258-3648**	603-226-5000	679
Jefferson State Community College 2601 Carson Rd	Birmingham	AL	35215	**800-239-5900**	205-853-1200	160
Jefferson Wells International 200 S Executive Dr Suite 440	Brookfield	WI	53005	**800-826-5099**	262-957-3400	2
Jeffrey Chain Corp 2307 Maden Dr	Morristown	TN	37813	**800-251-9012**	423-586-1951	206
Jeffries Michael S CEO Abercrombie & Fitch Co 6301 Fitch Pass	New Albany	OH	43054	**800-666-2595**	614-283-6500	561
Jekyll Island Club Hotel 371 Riverview Dr	Jekyll Island	GA	31527	**800-535-9547**	912-635-2600	655
Jekyll Island Convention Center 1 Beachview Dr	Jekyll Island	GA	31527	**877-453-5955**	912-635-3400	204
Jel Sert Co PO Box 261	West Chicago	IL	60186	**800-323-2592**	630-231-7590	291-15
Jeld-Wen Inc 401 Harbor Isles Blvd	Klamath Falls	OR	97601	**800-535-3462**	541-882-3451	489
Jelenko International 99 Business Pk Dr	Armonk	NY	10504	**800-431-1785**	914-273-8600	226
Jelliff Corp 354 Pequot Ave	Southport	CT	06890	**800-364-9502**	203-259-1615	676
Jelly Belly Candy Co 1 Jelly Belly Ln	Fairfield	CA	94533	**800-323-9380**	707-428-2800	291-8
Jemez Mountains Electric Co-op PO Box 128	Espanola	NM	87532	**888-755-2105**	505-753-2105	244
JEMS Communications Inc 525 B St Suite 1900 *Cust Svc	San Diego	CA	92101	**800-266-5367***	619-687-3272	449-21
Jencast 1004 W 14th	Coffeyville	KS	67337	**800-796-6630**	620-251-7802	302
Jenckes Machine Co PO Box 364	Warren	RI	02885	**866-941-1455**	401-247-1999	468
Jenkins Brick Co Inc 201 N 6th St PO Box 91	Montgomery	AL	36104	**888-215-5700**	334-834-2210	148
Jenkins J Sons Co Inc 1801 Whitehead Rd	Baltimore	MD	21207	**800-296-3468**	410-265-5200	401
Jenkins Mfg Co Inc PO Box 249	Anniston	AL	36202	**800-633-2323**	256-831-7000	234
Jenkins WL Co 1445 Whipple Ave SW	Canton	OH	44710	**800-426-7021**	330-477-3407	691
Jenn-Air Co 403 W 4th St N	Newton	IA	50208	**800-688-9900**	641-792-7000	36
Jennie-O Turkey Store 2505 Willmar Ave SW	Willmar	MN	56201	**800-328-1756**	320-235-2622	608
Jennie Stuart Medical Center 320 W 18th St PO Box 2400	Hopkinsville	KY	42241	**800-887-5762**	270-887-0100	366-2
Jennifer Convertibles Inc 419 Crossways Park Dr *AMEX: JEN*	Woodbury	NY	11797	**800-595-1422**	516-496-1900	316
Jenny Craig International Inc 5770 Fleet St	Carlsbad	CA	92008	**800-443-2331**	760-696-4000	797
Jenny Lake Lodge PO Box 250	Moran	WY	83013	**800-628-9988**	307-733-4647	655
Jenny Lee Bakery Inc 620 Island Ave	McKees Rocks	PA	15136	**888-536-6933**	412-331-8900	291-1
Jensen Distribution Services 314 W Riverside Ave	Spokane	WA	99201	**800-234-1321**	509-624-1321	346
Jensen Industries Inc 1946 E 46th St	Los Angeles	CA	90058	**800-325-8351**	323-235-6800	314-2
Jensen Luhr & Sons Inc 400 Portway Ave PO Box 297	Hood River	OR	97031	**800-366-3811**	541-386-3811	701
Jensen Precast 625 Bergin Way	Sparks	NV	89431	**800-648-1134**	775-359-6200	181
Jensen Tools Inc 7815 S 46th St *Orders	Phoenix	AZ	85044	**800-426-1194***	480-968-6241	746
Jenzabar Inc 5 Cambridge Ctr 11th Fl	Cambridge	MA	02142	**877-536-0222**	617-492-9099	176-10
Jeppesen Sanderson Inc 55 Inverness Dr E	Englewood	CO	80112	**800-621-5377**	303-799-9090	623-2
Jergens Inc 15700 S Waterloo Rd	Cleveland	OH	44110	**800-537-4367**	216-486-2100	484
Jerky Hut International PO Box 308	Hubbard	OR	97032	**800-223-5759**	503-981-7191	333
Jerome's Furniture Warehouse 1401 East St	San Diego	CA	92101	**800-698-3444**	619-231-1757	316
Jerr-Dan Corp 1080 Hykes Rd *Sales	Greencastle	PA	17225	**800-926-9666***	717-597-7111	505
Jerry L Pettis Memorial Veterans Affairs Medical Center 11201 Benton St *Mail Rm	Loma Linda	CA	92357	**800-741-8387***	909-825-7084	366-6
Jerry Lipps Trucking Inc 3888 Nash Rd PO Drawer F *Cust Svc	Cape Girardeau	MO	63702	**800-325-3331***	573-335-8204	769
Jerry's Artarama 248-12 Union Tpke	Bellerose	NY	11426	**800-221-2323**	718-343-0777	45
Jerry's Marine Service 100 SW 16th St	Fort Lauderdale	FL	33315	**800-432-2231**	954-525-0311	759
Jerry's Sport Center Inc PO Box 121 *Sales	Forest City	PA	18421	**800-234-2612***	570-785-9400	701
Jerry's Subs & Pizza 15942 Shady Grove Rd	Gaithersburg	MD	20877	**800-990-9176**	301-921-8777	657
Jersey Mike's Franchise Systems Inc 2251 Landmark Pl	Manasquan	NJ	08736	**800-321-7676**	732-282-2323	657
Jervis B Webb Co 34375 W 12-Mile Rd	Farmington Hills	MI	48331	**800-526-9322**	248-553-1220	206
Jesco Resources Inc PO Box 12337	North Kansas City	MO	64116	**800-421-4590**	816-471-4590	530
Jesco-Wipco Industries Inc PO Box 388	Litchfield	MI	49252	**800-455-0019**	517-542-2903	281
Jessamine County Hospice PO Box 873	Nicholasville	KY	40356	**800-279-0750**	859-887-2696	365
Jessica McClintock Inc 1400 16th St	San Francisco	CA	94103	**800-333-5301**	415-553-8200	153-21
Jesuit School of Theology at Berkeley 1735 LeRoy Ave	Berkeley	CA	94709	**800-824-0122**	510-549-5000	164-3
Jet Air Jet Charter 547 Perimeter Rd Hanger 2 PO Box 178207	Nashville	TN	37217	**888-812-6604**	615-361-1007	14
Jet Aviation 112 Charles A Lindbergh Dr	Teterboro	NJ	07608	**800-538-0832**	201-288-8400	25
Jet Aviation Business Jets Inc 112 Charles A Lindbergh Dr	Teterboro	NJ	07608	**800-736-8538**	201-462-4100	14
Jet Aviation International Inc 1515 Perimeter Rd	West Palm Beach	FL	33406	**800-758-5387**	561-233-7233	63
Jet Food Stores of Georgia 1106 S Harris St	Sandersville	GA	31082	**800-277-1168**	478-552-2588	203
Jet-Lube Inc PO Box 21258	Houston	TX	77226	**800-538-5823**	713-674-7617	530
Jet Plastica Inc 1100 Schwab Rd	Hatfield	PA	19440	**800-220-5381**	215-362-1501	596
Jet Resource Inc 455 Wilmer Ave Lunken Airport Hangar 27	Cincinnati	OH	45226	**800-404-5387**	513-762-6909	14
JetBlue Airways 118-29 Queens Blvd	Forest Hills	NY	11375	**800-538-2583**	718-286-7900	26
JetBlue Airways Corp 118-29 Queens Blvd *NASDAQ: JBLU*	Forest Hills	NY	11375	**800-538-2583**	718-286-7900	355-1
JetBlue TrueBlue 6322 S 3000 East Fl G-1 Suite G-10	Salt Lake City	UT	84121	**800-538-2583**	801-365-2528	27
JetCorp 18152 Edison Ave	Chesterfield	MO	63005	**800-325-4811**	636-530-7000	14
Jet's America Inc 37177 Mound Rd	Sterling Heights	MI	48130	**888-446-5870**	586-268-5870	657
Jetscape Inc 408 S Andrews Ave Suite 200	Fort Lauderdale	FL	33301	**800-355-5387**	954-763-4737	24

Listing	Toll-Free	Phone	Class
Jetstream of Houston LLP 4930 Cranswick ... Houston TX 77041	**800-231-8192**	713-462-7000	777
Jevic Transportation Inc 700 Creek Rd ... Delanco NJ 08075	**800-257-0427**	856-461-7111	769
Jewel Case Corp 300 Niantic Ave ... Providence RI 02907	**800-441-4447**	401-943-1400	198
Jewelers of America (JA) 52 Vanderbilt Ave 19th Fl ... New York NY 10017	**800-223-0673**	646-658-0246	49-4
Jewelers Organization. Independent 25 Seir Hill Rd ... Norwalk CT 06850	**800-624-9252**	203-846-4215	49-4
Jewelers Shipping Assn (JSA) 125 Carlsbad St ... Cranston RI 02920	**800-688-4572**	401-943-6490	49-21
Jewelers & Suppliers of America. Manufacturing 45 Royal Little Dr ... Providence RI 02904	**800-444-6572**	401-274-3840	49-4
Jewell Instruments LLC 850 Perimeter Rd ... Manchester NH 03103	**800-227-5955**	603-669-6400	519
Jewelmont Corp 119 W 40th St ... New York NY 10018	**800-328-7173**	212-220-4222	401
JewelryWeb.com Inc 305 Northern Blvd Suite 101 ... Great Neck NY 11021	**800-955-9245**		402
Jewett-Cameron Trading Co Ltd 32275 NW Hillcrest PO Box 1010 ... North Plains OR 97133 *NASDAQ: JCTCF*	**800-547-5877**	503-647-0110	190-3
Jewish Board of Family & Children Services (JBFCS) 120 W 57th St ... New York NY 10019	**888-523-2769**	212-582-9100	48-6
Jewish Family & Life Magazine 90 Oak St PO Box 9129 ... Newton Upper Falls MA 02464	**888-458-8535**	617-965-7700	449-18
Jewish Medical & Research Center. National 1400 Jackson St ... Denver CO 80206	**800-222-5864**	303-388-4461	654
Jewish Museum of Maryland 15 Lloyd St ... Baltimore MD 21202	**877-376-7190**	410-732-6400	509
Jewish National Fund (JNF) 42 E 69th St ... New York NY 10021	**888-563-0099**	212-879-9300	48-20
Jewish Publication Society 2100 Arch St 2nd Fl ... Philadelphia PA 19103	**800-234-3151**	215-832-0600	623-4
Jewish Women. National Council of 53 W 23rd St 6th Fl ... New York NY 10010	**800-829-6259**	212-645-4048	48-24
Jewish World Service. American 45 W 36th St 10th Fl ... New York NY 10018	**800-889-7146**	212-736-2597	48-5
JF Barton Contracting Co PO Box 73525 ... Houston TX 77273	**800-222-1472**	281-443-3800	258
JF Braun & Sons Inc 265 Post Ave ... Westbury NY 11590	**800-997-7177**	516-997-2200	292-11
JF Drake State Technical College 3421 Meridian St N ... Huntsville AL 35811	**888-413-7253**	256-539-8161	158
JF Helmold & Brothers Inc 901 Morse Ave ... Elk Grove Village IL 60007	**800-323-8898**	847-437-7085	448
JF Shea Co Inc 655 Brea Canyon Rd ... Walnut CA 91789	**800-755-7432**	909-594-9500	187-4
JFC Inc PO Box 1106 ... Saint Cloud MN 56302	**800-328-8236**	320-251-3570	11-8
JFC International Inc 540 Forbes Blvd ... South San Francisco CA 94080	**800-633-1004**	650-873-8400	292-11
JFG Coffee Co 3434 Mynatt Ave ... Knoxville TN 37919	**800-627-1988**	865-546-2120	291-7
JGI (Jane Goodall Institute for Wildlife Research Education & Conservation) 8700 Georgia Ave Suite 500 ... Silver Spring MD 20910	**800-592-5263**	301-565-0086	48-3
JH Baxter & Co 1700 S El Camino Real Suite 200 ... San Mateo CA 94402	**800-780-7073**	650-349-0201	806
JH Cohn LLP 75 Eisenhower Pkwy 2nd Fl ... Roseland NJ 07068	**800-879-2571**	973-228-3500	2
JH Industries Inc 1981 E Aurora Rd ... Twinsburg OH 44087	**800-321-4968**	330-963-4105	471
JH Larson Co 10200 51st Ave N ... Plymouth MN 55442	**800-292-7970**	763-545-1717	245
JH Routh Packing Co Inc 4413 W Bogart Rd ... Sandusky OH 44870	**800-446-6759**	419-626-2251	465
JH Walker Trucking Co Inc 152 N Hollywood Rd ... Houma LA 70364	**800-535-5992**	985-868-8330	769
JH Whitney & Co LLC 177 Broad St 15th Fl ... Stamford CT 06901	**800-881-6085**	203-973-1400	779
JH Williams Oil Co Inc 1237 E Twiggs St ... Tampa FL 33602	**800-683-0536**	813-228-7776	569
Jhane Barnes Inc 119 W 40th St 20th Fl ... New York NY 10018	**888-465-4263**	212-575-2448	273
JHB International Inc 1955 S Quince St ... Denver CO 80247	**800-525-9007**	303-751-8100	583
JHL Industries 10012 Nevada Ave ... Chatsworth CA 91311	**800-255-6636**	818-882-2233	717
JHM Enterprises Inc 880 S Pleasantburg Dr Suite 3G ... Greenville SC 29607	**800-763-1100**	864-232-9944	369
JI Kislak Inc 7900 Miami Lakes Dr W ... Miami Lakes FL 33016	**800-233-7164**	305-364-4100	498
Jiffy Lube International Inc 700 Milam St ... Houston TX 77002	**800-327-9532**	713-546-4000	62-5
Jill J Group Inc The 4 Batterymarch Park ... Quincy MA 02169 *NASDAQ: JILL*	**800-642-9989**	617-376-4300	451
Jillian's Restaurants 4500 Bowling Blvd Suite 200 ... Louisville KY 40207	**888-594-8231**	502-638-9008	657
Jim Stafford Theatre 3440 W Hwy 76 ... Branson MO 65616	**800-677-8533**	417-335-8080	562
Jim Walter Homes Inc PO Box 31601 ... Tampa FL 33631	**800-492-5837**	813-871-4811	186
Jimbo's Jumbos Inc PO Box 465 ... Edenton NC 27932	**800-334-4771**	252-482-2193	291-32
Jimco Lamp & Mfg Co PO Box 490 ... Bono AR 72416	**888-565-1388**	870-935-6820	431
Jimlar Corp 160 Great Neck Rd ... Great Neck NY 11021	**800-883-3453**	516-829-1717	296
Jimmy Dean Foods Inc PO Box 2511 ... Cincinnati OH 45225	**800-925-3326**		291-26
Jimmy John's Franchise Inc 600 Tollgate Rd ... Elgin IL 60123	**800-546-6904**	847-888-7206	657
Jimmy Ryce Center for Victims of Predatory Abduction (JRC) 908 Coquina Ln ... Vero Beach FL 32963	**800-546-7923**	772-492-0200	48-6
Jimmy Swaggart Ministries (JSM) 8919 World Ministry Blvd ... Baton Rouge LA 70810 *Orders	**800-288-8350***	225-768-8300	48-20
JJ Haines & Co Inc 6950 Aviation Blvd ... Glen Burnie MD 21061	**800-922-9248**	410-760-4040	356
JJ Keller & Assoc Inc PO Box 368 ... Neenah WI 54957	**800-558-5011**	920-722-2848	623-11
JJ MacIntyre Co 1801 California Ave ... Corona CA 92881	**800-621-9859**	951-898-4300	157
JJ Michael Inc 74 Industrial Ave ... Little Ferry NJ 07643	**800-879-0470**	201-641-3600	770
JJB Hilliard WL Lyons Inc 501 S 4th St Hilliard Lyons Ctr ... Louisville KY 40202	**800-444-1854**	502-588-8400	679
JKP Sports Inc 19333 SW 18th Ave ... Tualatin OR 97062	**800-547-6843**	503-692-1635	701

Listing	Toll-Free	Phone	Class
JL Clark Mfg Co 923 23rd Ave ... Rockford IL 61104	**800-252-7267**	815-962-8861	124
JL Hammett Co 1 Hammett Pl ... Braintree MA 02184 *Cust Svc	**800-955-2200***	781-848-1000	673
JL Industries Inc 4450 W 78th Street Cir ... Bloomington MN 55435	**800-554-6077**	952-835-6850	281
JLK Direct Distribution Inc 31800 Industrial Rd ... Livonia MI 48150	**800-645-6878**	734-458-7000	378
JLM Couture Inc 225 W 37th St 5th Fl ... New York NY 10018 *NASDAQ: JLMC*	**800-924-6475**	212-921-7058	153-21
JLM Industries Inc 8675 Hidden River Pkwy ... Tampa FL 33637	**800-457-3743**	813-632-3300	144
JLM Marketing Inc 8675 Hidden River Pkwy ... Tampa FL 33637	**800-457-3743**	813-632-3300	144
JM Clipper Corp 403 Industrial Dr PO Drawer 632340 ... Nacogdoches TX 75964	**800-233-3900**	936-560-8900	321
JM Smucker Co 1 Strawberry Ln ... Orrville OH 44667 *NYSE: SJM*	**888-550-9555**	330-682-3000	291-20
JM Stewart Corp 2201 Cantu Ct Suite 217-218 ... Sarasota FL 34232	**800-237-3928**	941-378-4242	692
JM Swank Co 520 W Penn St ... North Liberty IA 52317	**800-593-6375**	319-626-3683	292-8
JM Tull Metals Co Inc PO Box 4725 ... Norcross GA 30091	**800-243-8855**	770-368-4311	483
JMA Railroad Supply Co 381 S Main Pl ... Carol Stream IL 60188	**800-874-0643**	630-653-9224	759
JMC Communities 2201 4th St N Suite 200 ... Saint Petersburg FL 33704	**800-741-4106**	727-823-0022	639
JML Optical Industries Inc 690 Portland Ave ... Rochester NY 14621 *Sales	**800-456-5462***	585-342-8900	534
JNF (Jewish National Fund) 42 E 69th St ... New York NY 10021	**888-563-0099**	212-879-9300	48-20
Jo-Ann Fabrics & Crafts 5555 Darrow Rd ... Hudson OH 44236	**888-739-4120**	330-656-2600	266
Jo-Carroll Energy PO Box 390 ... Elizabeth IL 61028	**800-858-5522**	815-858-2207	244
Jo Mar Laboratories 583-B Division St ... Campbell CA 95008	**800-538-4545**	408-374-5920	786
Job Shop Technology Magazine 16 Waterbury Rd ... Prospect CT 06712	**800-317-0474**	203-758-4474	449-21
Jobmaster Corp 1505 Serpentine Rd ... Baltimore MD 21209 *Cust Svc	**800-642-1400***	410-655-1400	450
Jobs for Progress National Inc. SER - 5215 N O'Connor Blvd Suite 2550 ... Irving TX 75039	**800-427-2306**	972-506-7815	48-6
Jobscope Corp PO Box 6767 ... Greenville SC 29606	**800-443-5794**	864-458-3100	176-11
JobWeb c/o National Assn of Colleges & Employers 62 Highland Ave ... Bethlehem PA 18017	**800-544-5272**	610-868-1421	257
Jockey International Inc 2300 60th St PO Box 1417 ... Kenosha WI 53140	**800-562-5391**	262-658-8111	153-18
Jockeys' Guild Inc PO Box 150 ... Monrovia CA 91017	**866-465-6257**	626-305-5605	48-22
Jodon Inc 62 Enterprise Dr ... Ann Arbor MI 48103	**800-989-5636**	734-761-4044	416
Joe Brown Co Inc PO Box 1669 ... Ardmore OK 73402	**800-444-4293**	580-223-4555	180
Joe Christensen Inc 1540 Adams St ... Lincoln NE 68521	**800-228-5030**	402-476-7535	614
Joe G Maloof & Co Inc 701 Comanche Rd NE ... Albuquerque NM 87107	**800-760-2293**	505-243-2293	82-1
Joe Krentzman & Son Inc PO Box 508 ... Lewistown PA 17044	**800-543-2000**	717-543-5635	674
Joe Wheeler Resort Lodge & Convention Center Joe Wheeler State Park 201 McLean Dr ... Rogersville AL 35652	**800-544-5639**	256-247-5461	655
Joe's Crab Shack 1510 W Loop South ... Houston TX 77027	**800-552-6379**	713-850-1010	657
Joe's Ready Mix Inc PO Box 168 ... Sioux Center IA 51250	**800-888-2649**	712-722-1646	180
Joey's Only Seafood Franchising Corp 514-42nd Ave SE ... Calgary AB T2G1Y6	**800-661-2123**	403-243-4584	657
Jofco International 402 E 13th St ... Jasper IN 47546	**800-235-6326**	812-482-5154	314-1
Johanna Foods Inc Johanna Farm Rd ... Flemington NJ 08822	**800-727-6700**	908-788-2200	291-20
Johannes Flowers Inc 4998 Foothill Rd ... Carpinteria CA 93013	**800-365-9476**	805-684-5686	363
John A Van Den Bosch Co 4511 Holland Ave ... Holland MI 49422 *Cust Svc	**800-968-6477***	616-848-2000	438
John Ascuaga's Nugget Hotel Casino 1100 Nugget Ave ... Sparks NV 89431	**800-648-1177**	775-356-3300	655
John B Hynes Veterans Memorial Convention Center 900 Boylston St ... Boston MA 02115	**800-845-8800**	617-954-2000	204
John B Sanfilippo & Son Inc 2299 Busse Rd ... Elk Grove Village IL 60007 *NASDAQ: JBSS*	**800-323-6887**	847-593-2300	291-28
John Bean Co 309 Exchange Ave ... Conway AR 72032	**800-362-8326**	501-450-1500	60
John Bouchard & Sons Co 1024 Harrison St ... Nashville TN 37203	**800-842-9156**	615-256-0112	188-10
John Boyle & Co Inc 1803 Salisbury Rd ... Statesville NC 28677 *Cust Svc	**800-438-1061***	704-872-8151	730-2
John Burnham Insurance Services PO Box 85802 ... San Diego CA 92186	**800-421-6744**	619-231-1010	383
John Carlo Inc 45000 River Ridge Dr ... Clinton Township MI 48038	**800-465-6234**	586-416-4500	187-4
John Crane Canada Inc 423 Green Rd ... Stoney Creek ON L8E3A1	**800-263-6860**	905-662-6191	321
John Crane Inc 6400 W Oakton St ... Morton Grove IL 60053	**800-732-5464**	847-967-2400	321
John D Archbold Memorial Hospital PO Box 1018 ... Thomasville GA 31799	**800-341-1009**	229-228-2000	366-2
John D & Catherine T MacArthur Foundation 140 S Dearborn St Suite 1100 ... Chicago IL 60603	**800-662-8004**	312-726-8000	300
John Day Co 6263 Abbott Dr ... Omaha NE 68110	**800-767-2273**	402-455-8000	270
John Deere Credit Co PO Box 6600 ... Johnston IA 50131	**800-275-5322**	515-267-3000	214
John Deere Health Care Inc 1300 River Dr Suite 200 ... Moline IL 61265	**800-224-6599**	309-765-1200	384-3
John Dessauer's Investor's World Newsletter 7811 Montrose Rd ... Potomac MD 20854	**800-804-0942**	301-340-2100	521-9
John E Koerner & Co Inc PO Box 10218 ... New Orleans LA 70181	**800-333-1913**	504-734-1100	292-11
John F Buchan Homes 2821 Northup Way Suite 100 ... Bellevue WA 98004	**866-528-2426**	425-827-2266	639

Name / Address	City	State	ZIP	Toll-Free	Phone	Class
John F Kennedy Center for the Performing Arts 2700 F St NW	Washington	DC	20566	**800-444-1324**	202-416-8000	562
John F Kennedy Library & Museum Columbia Point	Boston	MA	02125	**866-535-1960**	617-514-1600	426
John F Kennedy University 100 Ellinwood Way	Pleasant Hill	CA	94523	**800-696-5358**	925-969-3300	163
John Fayhee & Sons Inc 360 E Main St	Prairie City	IL	61470	**800-637-2614**	309-775-3317	270
John Frieda Professional Hair Care Inc 333 Ludlow St *Cust Svc	Stanford	CT	06902	**800-521-3189***	203-762-1233	211
John H Hampshire Inc 320 W 24th St	Baltimore	MD	21211	**800-638-0076**	410-366-8900	188-2
John Hancock Funds 101 Huntington Ave 10th Fl	Boston	MA	02199	**800-338-8080**	617-375-1500	517
John Hancock Funds 101 Huntington Ave 10th Fl *Cust Svc	Boston	MA	02199	**800-225-5291***	617-375-1500	393
John Hancock Life Insurance Co PO Box 111	Boston	MA	02117	**800-732-5543**	617-572-6000	384-2
John Hancock Variable Life Insurance Co PO Box 111	Boston	MA	02117	**800-732-5543**	617-572-6000	384-2
John Heinz Institute of Rehabilitation Medicine 150 Mundy St	Wilkes-Barre	PA	18702	**877-727-3422**	570-826-3800	366-4
John Henry Co 5800 W Grand River Ave	Lansing	MI	48906	**800-748-0517**	517-323-9000	614
John J Adams Die Corp 10 Nebraska St	Worcester	MA	01604	**800-356-0110**	508-757-3894	447
John J Campbell Co Inc 6012 Resources Dr	Memphis	TN	38134	**800-274-7663**	901-372-8400	188-12
John Johnson Co 1481 14th St	Detroit	MI	48216	**800-991-1394**	313-496-0600	718
John K Burch Co 4200 Brockton Dr SE	Grand Rapids	MI	49512	**800-841-8111**	616-698-2800	583
John Kavanagh Homes 1810 Pembroke Rd	Greensboro	NC	27408	**800-940-9904**	336-272-9904	639
John Keeler & Co Inc 3000 NW 109th Ave	Miami	FL	33172	**888-663-2722**	305-836-6858	292-5
John-Kenyon Eye Center 1305 Wall St Suite 200	Jeffersonville	IN	47130	**800-342-5393**	812-288-9011	785
John Knox Village 400 NW Murray Rd	Lee's Summit	MO	64081	**800-892-5669**	816-524-8400	659
John Knox Village of the Rio Grande Valley 1300 S Border Ave *Mktg	Weslaco	TX	78596	**800-245-6526***	956-968-4575	659
John L Wortham & Son LLP 2727 Allen Pkwy	Houston	TX	77019	**888-896-5623**	713-526-3366	383
John M Frey Co Inc 2735 62nd St Ct	Bettendorf	IA	52722	**800-397-3739**	563-332-9200	601
John Maneely Co 900 Haddon Ave	Collingswood	NJ	08108	**800-257-8182**	856-854-5400	481
John Middleton Inc 418 W Church Rd	King of Prussia	PA	19406	**800-523-1126**	610-265-1400	741-3
John O Butler Co 4635 W Foster Ave	Chicago	IL	60630	**800-528-8537**	773-777-4000	226
John Paul Mitchell Systems 9701 Wilshire Blvd Suite 1205 *Cust Svc	Beverly Hills	CA	90212	**800-793-8790***	310-248-3888	211
John R Hess & Co Inc 400 Station St PO Box 3615	Cranston	RI	02910	**800-828-4377**	401-785-9300	144
John R Jurgensen Co 11641 Mosteller Rd	Cincinnati	OH	45241	**800-686-9725**	513-771-0820	187-4
John Reyer Shoe Store Reyers City Ctr 40 S Water Ave *Cust Svc	Sharon	PA	16146	**800-245-1550***	724-981-2200	296
John Roberts Co 9687 E River Rd	Coon Rapids	MN	55433	**800-551-1534**	763-755-5500	615
John Rohrer Contracting Co Inc 2820 Roe Lane Bldg S	Kansas City	KS	66103	**800-255-6119**	913-236-5005	188-3
John S Frey Enterprises Inc 1900 E 64th St	Los Angeles	CA	90001	**800-377-3322**	323-583-4061	471
John S & James L Knight Foundation 200 S Biscayne Blvd Suite 3300	Miami	FL	33131	**800-711-2004**	305-908-2600	300
John S Knight Convention Center 77 E Mill St	Akron	OH	44308	**800-245-4254**	330-374-8900	204
John Sterling Corp PO Box 469	Richmond	IL	60071	**800-367-5726**	815-678-2031	345
John T Cyr & Sons Inc 153 Gilman Falls Ave	Old Town	ME	04468	**800-244-2335**	207-827-2335	110
John T Handy Co Inc PO Box 309	Crisfield	MD	21817	**800-426-3977**	410-968-1772	292-5
John W Danforth Co 2100 Colvin Blvd	Tonawanda	NY	14150	**800-888-6119**	716-832-1940	188-10
John W McDougall Co Inc 3731 Amy Lynn Dr	Nashville	TN	37218	**800-264-1122**	615-321-3900	688
John Wayne Cancer Institute Saint John's Health Center 2200 Santa Monica Blvd	Santa Monica	CA	90404	**800-262-6259**		654
John Wieland Homes & Neighborhoods Inc 1950 Sullivan Rd	Atlanta	GA	30337	**800-376-4663**	770-996-2400	639
John Wiley & Sons Inc 111 River St *NYSE: JWa* ■ *Sales	Hoboken	NJ	07030	**800-225-5945***	201-748-6000	623-2
John Wolf Florist 6228 Waters Ave	Savannah	GA	31406	**800-944-6435**	912-352-9843	287
John Zink Co LLC PO Box 21220	Tulsa	OK	74121	**800-421-9242**	918-234-1800	352
Johnny Appleseed's Inc 30 Tozer Rd *Cust Svc	Beverly	MA	01915	**800-767-6666***	978-922-2040	451
Johnny Rockets Group Inc 26970 Aliso Viejo Pkwy Suite 100	Aliso Viejo	CA	92656	**888-236-9100**	949-643-6100	656
Johnny Rockets the Original Hamburger 26970 Aliso Viejo Pkwy Suite 100	Aliso Viejo	CA	92656	**888-236-9100**	949-643-6100	657
Johnny's Fine Foods Inc 319 E 25th St *Orders	Tacoma	WA	98421	**800-962-1462***	253-383-4597	291-37
Johnny's Pizza House Inc 2920 N 7th St	West Monroe	LA	71291	**800-256-5453**	318-323-0518	657
Johns Hopkins University Press 2715 N Charles St *Orders	Baltimore	MD	21218	**800-537-5487***	410-516-6900	623-5
Johns Manville Corp PO Box 5108 *Prod Info	Denver	CO	80217	**800-654-3103***	303-978-2000	382
John's Pass Village & Boardwalk 150 John's Pass Boardwalk Pl	Madeira Beach	FL	33708	**800-755-0677**	727-398-6577	50
Johns R Ltd PO Box 149107	Austin	TX	78714	**800-521-9493**		401
Johnsen Hans Co Inc 8901 Chancellor Row *Sales	Dallas	TX	75247	**800-879-1515***	214-879-1550	346
Johnsen Nurseries Inc 2897 Freedom Blvd	Watsonville	CA	95076	**800-322-6529**	831-728-4205	363
Johnson Asset Management 555 Main St Suite 440	Racine	WI	53403	**800-407-5500**	262-681-4770	393
Johnson Bank 4001 N Main St	Racine	WI	53402	**800-236-8586**	262-639-6010	71
Johnson Bible College 7900 Johnson Dr	Knoxville	TN	37998	**800-827-2122**	865-573-4517	163
Johnson C Smith University 100 Beatties Ford Rd *Admissions	Charlotte	NC	28216	**800-782-7303***	704-378-1000	163
Johnson City Convention & Visitors Bureau 603 E Market St	Johnson City	TN	37601	**800-852-3392**	423-461-8000	205
Johnson City/Jonesborough/ Washington County Chamber of Commerce 603 E Market St	Johnson City	TN	37601	**800-852-3392**	423-461-8000	137
Johnson College 3427 N Main Ave	Scranton	PA	18508	**800-293-9675**	570-342-6404	787
Johnson Controls Fire & Security Solutions 1757 Tapo Canyon Rd	Simi Valley	CA	93063	**800-229-4076**	805-522-5555	681
Johnson Controls Inc 5757 N Green Bay Ave *NYSE: JCI*	Milwaukee	WI	53209	**800-972-8040**	414-524-1200	201
Johnson Controls Inc Controls Group 507 E Michigan St	Milwaukee	WI	53202	**800-275-5676**	414-274-4000	201
Johnson Corp 805 Wood St	Three Rivers	MI	49093	**800-657-5940**	269-278-1715	379
Johnson County Community College 12345 College Blvd	Overland Park	KS	66210	**866-896-5893**	913-469-8500	160
Johnson Dallas Greenhouse Inc 2802 Twin City Dr	Council Bluffs	IA	51501	**800-445-4794**	712-366-0407	363
Johnson Electric Coil Co 821 Watson St	Antigo	WI	54409	**800-826-9741**	715-627-4367	756
Johnson Gas Appliance Co 520 E Ave NW	Cedar Rapids	IA	52405	**800-553-5422**	319-365-5267	313
Johnson Hosiery Mills Inc 2808 Main Ave NW	Hickory	NC	28601	**800-438-1511**	828-322-6185	153-10
Johnson Implement Co Inc 1904 Hwy 82 W	Greenwood	MS	38930	**800-898-0160**	662-453-6525	270
Johnson Industries 5944 Peachtree Corners E *Orders	Norcross	GA	33071	**800-922-8111***	770-441-1128	61
Johnson John Co 1481 14th St	Detroit	MI	48216	**800-991-1394**	313-496-0600	718
Johnson & Johnson 1 Johnson & Johnson Plaza *NYSE: JNJ*	New Brunswick	NJ	08933	**800-635-6789**	732-524-0400	184
Johnson & Johnson Consumer Products Co 199 Grandview Rd	Skillman	NJ	08558	**800-526-3967**	908-874-1000	211
Johnson & Johnson Health Care Systems Inc 425 Hoes Ln	Piscataway	NJ	08854	**800-255-2500**	732-562-3000	455
Johnson & Johnson Vision Care Inc 7500 Centurion Pkwy	Jacksonville	FL	32256	**800-874-5278**	904-443-1000	531
Johnson Ladders Inc 700 S Ewing St *Cust Svc	Dallas	TX	75203	**800-523-1881***	214-943-7494	412
Johnson Magic Foundation Inc 9100 Wilshire Blvd East Tower Suite 700	Beverly Hills	CA	90212	**888-624-4205**	310-246-4400	300
Johnson Matthey Inc Catalysts & Chemicals Div 2001 Nolte Dr	West Deptford	NJ	08066	**800-444-1411**	856-853-8000	141
Johnson Matthey Medical Products 1401 King Rd	West Chester	PA	19380	**800-442-1405**	610-648-8000	468
Johnson Matthey Noble Metals 1401 King Rd	West Chester	PA	19380	**800-441-8159**	610-648-8000	473
Johnson Outdoors Inc 555 Main St *NASDAQ: JOUT*	Racine	WI	53403	**800-299-2592**	262-631-6600	701
Johnson Outdoors Watercraft Sport & Leisure Group 4855 Broadmoor Ave SE	Grand Rapids	MI	49512	**800-552-6287**	616-698-3000	91
Johnson LE Products Inc 2100 Sterling Ave	Elkhart	IN	46516	**800-837-4697**	574-293-5664	345
Johnson & Quin Inc 7460 N Lehigh Ave	Niles	IL	60714	**800-272-3770**	847-588-4800	5
Johnson Rick & Assoc of Colorado 1649 Downing St	Denver	CO	80218	**800-530-2300**	303-296-2200	392
Johnson Robert House 58 State Cir	Annapolis	MD	21401	**800-847-8882**	410-263-2641	373
Johnson Rubber Co 16025 Johnson St PO Box 67	Middlefield	OH	44062	**800-362-1951**	440-632-1611	664
Johnson SC & Son Inc 1525 Howe St	Racine	WI	53403	**800-494-4855**	262-260-2000	149
Johnson Scale Co 235 Fairfield Ave	West Caldwell	NJ	07006	**800-572-2531**	973-226-2100	672
Johnson Spencer Who Moved My Cheese LLC 1775 West 2300 S Suite B	Salt Lake City	UT	84119	**800-851-9311**	801-924-0260	561
Johnson State College 337 College Hill	Johnson	VT	05656	**800-635-2356**	802-635-2356	163
Johnson Storage & Moving Co 221 Broadway	Denver	CO	80203	**800-289-6683**	303-785-4310	508
Johnson Supply & Equipment Inc 10151 Stella Link Rd	Houston	TX	77025	**800-833-5455**	713-661-6666	601
Johnson Truck Bodies LLC 215 E Allen St *Sales	Rice Lake	WI	54868	**800-922-8360***	715-234-7071	505
Johnson & Wales University 8 Abbott Park Pl	Providence	RI	02903	**800-342-5598**	401-598-1000	163
Charleston 701 E Bay St	Charleston	SC	29403	**800-868-1522**	843-727-3000	163
Johnson's Garden Centers 2707 W 13th St	Wichita	KS	67203	**888-542-8463**	316-942-1443	318
Johnston County Visitors Bureau 1115 Industrial Pk Dr	Smithfield	NC	27577	**800-441-7829**	919-989-8687	205
Johnston FB Group 300 E Boundary St	Chapin	SC	29036	**800-800-8160**	803-345-5481	675
Johnston the Florist Inc 14179 Lincoln Way	North Huntingdon	PA	15642	**800-232-4795**	412-751-2821	287
Johnston Industries Inc Finished Fabrics Div PO Box 1108	Phenix City	AL	36868	**800-566-0889**	334-298-9351	730-7
Johnston Lemon & Co Inc 1101 Vermont Ave NW Suite 800	Washington	DC	20005	**800-424-5158**	202-842-5500	679

Name / Address	City	State	ZIP	Toll-Free	Phone	Class
Johnston Mfg 753 Arrow Grand Cir	Covina	CA	91722	**877-891-8899**	626-967-1511	444
Johnston & Murphy Inc 1415 Murfreesboro Rd	Nashville	TN	37217	**800-424-2854**	615-367-8101	296
Johnston Paper Co 1 Eagle Dr	Auburn	NY	13021	**800-800-7123**	315-253-8435	549
Johnston Seed Co 415 W Chestnut St	Enid	OK	73701	**800-375-4613**	580-233-5800	684
Johnston Tombigbee Furniture Mfg Co 1402 Waterworks Rd	Columbus	MS	39701	**800-654-3876**	662-328-1685	314-2
Johnstown/Cambria County (Greater) Chamber of Commerce 111 Market St	Johnstown	PA	15901	**800-790-4522**	814-536-5107	137
Joie de Vivre Hospitality Inc 567 Sutter St	San Francisco	CA	94102	**800-738-7477**	415-835-0300	369
Joint Township District Memorial Hospital 200 Saint Clair St	Saint Marys	OH	45885	**877-564-6897**	419-394-3335	366-2
Joliet Area Community Hospice 250 Water Stone Cir	Joliet	IL	60431	**800-360-1817**	815-740-4104	365
Joliet Equipment Corp PO Box 114	Joliet	IL	60434	**800-435-9350**	815-727-6606	507
Joliet Junior College 1215 Houbolt Rd	Joliet	IL	60431	**800-636-9886**	815-729-9020	160
Jolly Roger Inn 640 W Katella Ave	Anaheim	CA	92802	**800-854-8700**	714-772-7621	373
Jon Barry & Associates Inc PO Box 127	Concord	NC	28026	**800-264-0384**	704-723-4200	157
Jon Renau Collection 2510 Island View Way	Vista	CA	92081	**800-462-9447**	760-598-0067	342
Jones Aviation Service Inc 1234 Clyde Jones Rd	Sarasota	FL	34243	**800-945-6637**	941-355-8100	24
Jones-Blair Co 2728 Empire Central	Dallas	TX	75235	**800-492-9400**	214-353-1600	540
Jones Charles Inc PO Box 8488	Trenton	NJ	08650	**800-792-8888**	609-538-1000	621
Jones LE Co 1200 34th Ave	Menominee	MI	49858	**800-535-6637**	906-863-4411	128
Jones Co 16640 Chesterfield Grove Rd Suite 200	Chesterfield	MO	63005	**866-675-6637**	636-537-7000	186
Jones College 5353 Arlington Expy	Jacksonville	FL	32211	**800-331-0176**	904-743-1122	163
Jones County Chamber of Commerce PO Box 527	Laurel	MS	39441	**800-392-9629**	601-428-0574	137
Jones Cyber Solutions Ltd 9697 E Mineral Ave	Englewood	CO	80112	**800-944-2923**	303-784-3600	176-7
Jones DD Transfer & Warehouse Co Inc 2115 Portlock Rd	Chesapeake	VA	23324	**800-335-4787**	757-494-0200	790-1
Jones Dick Trucking PO Box 136	Swanton	VT	05488	**800-451-3535**	802-868-3381	769
Jones Eye Clinic 4405 Hamilton Blvd PO Box 3246	Sioux City	IA	51104	**800-334-2015**	712-239-3937	785
Jones Grady W Co 3965 Old Getwell Rd	Memphis	TN	38118	**800-727-5118**	901-365-8830	378
Jones Hamilton Co 8400 Enterprise Dr	Newark	CA	94560	**877-797-5426**	510-797-2471	141
Jones International Ltd 9697 E Mineral Ave	Englewood	CO	80112	**800-525-7002**	303-792-3111	630
Jones International University Ltd 9697 E Mineral Ave	Englewood	CO	80112	**800-811-5663**	303-784-8045	158
Jones Ken Tire Inc PO Box 782	Worcester	MA	01613	**800-225-9513**	508-755-5255	740
Jones Knowledge Inc 9697 E Mineral Ave	Englewood	CO	80112	**800-453-5663**	303-792-3111	753
Jones Media Networks Ltd 9697 E Mineral Ave	Englewood	CO	80112	**800-525-7000**	303-792-3111	630
Jones Metal Products Co 200 N Center St	West Lafayette	OH	43845	**800-552-3468**	740-545-6381	745
Jones Metal Products Inc 3201 3rd Ave	Mankato	MN	56001	**800-967-1750**	507-625-4436	688
Jones Motor Co Inc 900 W Bridge St	Spring City	PA	19475	**800-825-6637**	610-948-7900	769
Jones-Onslow Electric Membership Corp 259 Western Blvd	Jacksonville	NC	28546	**800-682-1515**	910-353-1940	244
Jones Radio Network Inc 8200 S Akron St Suite 103	Englewood	CO	80112	**800-609-5663**	303-784-8700	513
Jones Wilson N Medical Center 500 N Highland Ave	Sherman	TX	75092	**877-870-6696**	903-870-4611	366-2
Jonesboro Sun 518 Carson St	Jonesboro	AR	72401	**800-237-5341**	870-935-5525	522-2
Joplin Convention & Visitors Bureau 602 S Main St	Joplin	MO	64801	**800-657-2534**	417-625-4789	205
Joplin Globe 117 E 4th St	Joplin	MO	64801	**800-444-8514**	417-623-3480	522-2
Jordache Ltd 1400 Broadway 15th Fl	New York	NY	10018	**888-295-3267**	212-643-8400	153-11
Jordan Co PO Box 18377	Memphis	TN	38181	**800-888-8848**	901-363-2121	232
Jordan Controls Inc 5607 W Douglas Ave *Prod Info	Milwaukee	WI	53218	**800-637-5547***	414-461-9200	220
Jordan Jones & Goulding Inc 6801 Governors Lake Pkwy	Norcross	GA	30071	**800-545-2373**	770-455-8555	258
Jordan Millwork Co 1820 E 54th St N *Cust Svc	Sioux Falls	SD	57104	**800-843-0076***	605-336-1910	234
Jordan Tourism Board 6867 Elm St Suite 102	McLean	VA	22101	**877-733-5673**	703-243-7404	764
Jordano's Inc 550 S Patterson Ave	Santa Barbara	CA	93111	**800-325-2278**	805-964-0611	292-8
Jordan's Furniture Co 100 Stockwell Dr	Avon	MA	02322	**800-846-3737**	508-580-4600	316
Jorgensen Conveyors Inc 10303 N Baehr Rd	Mequon	WI	53092	**800-325-7705**	262-242-3089	206
Jorgenson's Inn & Suites 1714 11th Ave	Helena	MT	59601	**800-272-1770**	406-442-1770	373
Jos A Bank Clothiers 500 Hanover Pike *NASDAQ: JOSB* ■ *Cust Svc	Hampstead	MD	21074	**800-999-7472***	410-239-2700	153-12
Josam Co PO Box T	Michigan City	IN	46361	**800-365-6726**	219-872-5531	598
Joseph Behr & Sons Inc PO Box 740	Rockford	IL	61105	**800-332-2347**	815-987-2600	674
Joseph Blank Inc 62 W 47th St Suite 808	New York	NY	10036	**800-223-7666**	212-575-9050	403
Joseph Decosimo & Co CPA 2 Union Sq Tallan Bldg Suite 1100	Chattanooga	TN	37402	**800-782-8382**	423-756-7100	2
Joseph McSweeney & Sons Inc PO Box 26409	Richmond	VA	23260	**800-552-6927**	804-359-6024	291-26
Joseph Merritt & Co 650 Franklin Ave	Hartford	CT	06114	**800-344-4477**	860-296-2500	580
Joseph Meyerhoff Symphony Hall 1212 Cathedral St	Baltimore	MD	21201	**800-442-1198**	410-783-8100	562
Joseph Simon & Sons 2202 E River St	Tacoma	WA	98421	**800-562-8464**	253-272-9364	674
Joseph Weil & Sons Inc 825 E 26th St	La Grange Park	IL	60526	**800-621-5955**	708-579-9595	549
Joslyn Clark Controls Inc 2013 W Meeting St	Lancaster	SC	29720	**800-476-6952**	803-286-8491	202
Joslyn Electronics 5900 Eastport Blvd	Richmond	VA	23231	**800-752-8068**	804-236-3300	803
Joslyn High Voltage Corp 4000 E 116th St	Cleveland	OH	44105	**800-621-5875**	216-271-6600	803
Joslyn Mfg Co 3700 S Morgan St	Chicago	IL	60609	**800-456-7596**	773-927-1420	804
Jostens Inc 5501 American Blvd W	Minneapolis	MN	55437	**800-235-4774**	952-830-3300	401
Joule Inc 1235 US Rt 1 S *AMEX: JOL*	Edison	NJ	08837	**800-341-0341**	732-548-5444	707
Journal The 207 W King St	Martinsburg	WV	25401	**800-448-1895**	304-263-8931	522-2
Journal of Accountancy 201 Plaza III Harborside Financial Ctr	Jersey City	NJ	07311	**888-777-7077**	201-938-3000	449-5
Journal of the American Dental Assn 211 E Chicago Ave	Chicago	IL	60611	**800-621-8099**	312-440-2740	449-16
Journal of the American Dietetic Assn 120 S Riverside Plaza Suite 2000	Chicago	IL	60606	**800-877-1600**	312-899-0040	449-16
Journal of the American Medical Assn (JAMA) 515 N State St	Chicago	IL	60610	**800-262-2350**	312-464-5000	449-16
Journal of the American Veterinary Medical Assn 1931 N Meacham Rd Suite 100	Schaumburg	IL	60173	**800-248-2862**	847-925-8070	449-16
Journal of the Arkansas Medical Society PO Box 55088	Little Rock	AR	72215	**800-524-1058**	501-224-8967	449-16
Journal of Commerce Group 33 Washington St 13th Fl *Cust Svc	Newark	NJ	07103	**800-223-0243***	973-848-7000	623-9
Journal Communications Inc 333 W State St *NYSE: JRN*	Milwaukee	WI	53203	**800-456-5943**	414-224-2000	623-8
Journal & Courier 217 N 6th St *News Rm	Lafayette	IN	47901	**800-407-5813***	765-423-5511	522-2
Journal of Financial Planning 4100 E Mississippi Ave Suite 400	Denver	CO	80246	**800-322-4237**	303-759-4900	449-5
Journal of the Florida Medical Assn 123 S Adams St	Tallahassee	FL	32301	**800-762-0233**	850-224-6496	449-16
Journal Francais 944 Market St Suite 210 *Cust Svc	San Francisco	CA	94102	**800-232-1549***	415-981-9088	449-10
Journal Gazette 600 W Main St	Fort Wayne	IN	46802	**800-444-3303**	260-461-8222	522-2
Journal of Housing & Community Development 630 'I' St NW	Washington	DC	20001	**877-866-2476**	202-289-3500	449-5
Journal Inquirer 306 Progress Dr PO Box 510	Manchester	CT	06045	**800-237-3606**	860-646-0500	522-2
Journal of the Louisiana State Medical Society 6767 Perkins Rd	Baton Rouge	LA	70808	**800-375-9508**	225-763-8500	449-16
Journal of the Medical Assn of Georgia 1330 W Peachtree St NW Suite 500	Atlanta	GA	30309	**800-282-0224**	404-876-7535	449-16
Journal of the Mississippi State Medical Assn PO Box 2548	Ridgeland	MS	39158	**800-898-0251**	601-853-6733	449-16
Journal News 1 Gannett Dr	White Plains	NY	10604	**800-942-1010**	914-694-9300	522-2
Journal of Oklahoma State Medical Assn 601 NW Grand Blvd	Oklahoma City	OK	73118	**800-522-9452**	405-843-9571	449-16
Journal of Petroleum Technology 222 Palisades Creek Dr	Richardson	TX	75080	**800-456-6863**	972-952-9393	449-21
Journal of the Philosophy of Sport 1607 N Market St	Champaign	IL	61820	**800-747-4457**	217-351-5076	449-20
Journal of Physical Education Recreation & Dance 1900 Association Dr	Reston	VA	20191	**800-213-7193**	703-476-3477	449-8
Journal of Property Management 430 N Michigan Ave 7th Fl	Chicago	IL	60611	**800-837-0706**	312-329-6000	449-5
Journal of Protective Coatings & Linings 2100 Wharton St Suite 310	Pittsburgh	PA	15203	**800-837-8303**	412-431-8300	449-21
Journal Publishing Co PO Box 909	Tupelo	MS	38802	**800-264-6397**	662-842-2611	623-8
Journal Review 119 N Green St	Crawfordsville	IN	47933	**800-488-4414**	765-362-1200	522-2
Journal of the South Carolina Medical Assn 3210 Fernandina Rd	Columbia	SC	29210	**800-327-1021**	803-798-6207	449-16
Journal-Standard 27 S State St	Freeport	IL	61032	**800-325-6397**	815-232-1171	522-2
Journal Tribune 457 Alfred St	Biddeford	ME	04005	**888-429-1535**	207-282-1535	522-2
Journalists. National Assn of Hispanic 529 14th St NW National Press Bldg Suite 1000	Washington	DC	20045	**888-346-6245**	202-662-7145	49-14
JourneyCorp 488 Madison Ave 3rd Fl	New York	NY	10022	**800-305-4911**	212-753-5511	760
Journyx Inc 9800 N Lamar Blvd Suite 340	Austin	TX	78753	**800-755-9878**	512-834-8888	39
Joy B Frank LLC 5335 Kilmer Pl	Hyattsville	MD	20781	**800-992-3569**	301-779-9400	187-10
Joy Cone Co 3435 Lamor Rd	Hermitage	PA	16148	**800-242-2663**	724-962-5747	291-9
Joyce Florist 2729 S Hampton Rd	Dallas	TX	75224	**800-527-1520**	214-942-1776	287
Joyce Leslie Inc 135 W Commercial Ave	Moonachie	NJ	07074	**800-526-6216**	201-804-7800	155-6
Joyner & Co Realtors 2727 Enterprise Pkwy PO Box 31355	Richmond	VA	23294	**800-446-3858**	804-270-9440	638
JP Carroll Co Inc 310 N Madison Ave	Los Angeles	CA	90004	**800-660-0162**	323-660-9230	188-8
JP Mascaro Inc 600 W Neversink Rd	Reading	PA	19606	**800-334-3403**	610-779-8807	791
JPMorgan Chase Vastera 45025 Aviation Dr Suite 200	Dulles	VA	20166	**800-275-1374**	703-661-9006	176-10
JPMorgan Fleming Asset Management PO Box 219392	Kansas City	MO	64121	**800-348-4782**	816-435-1000	393
JPMorgan H & Q 560 Mission St	San Francisco	CA	94105	**800-227-3958**	415-315-5000	779
JPS Elastomerics Corp 9 Sullivan Rd	Holyoke	MA	01040	**800-621-7663**	413-533-8100	589
JR Filanc Construction Co Inc 4616 North Ave	Oceanside	CA	92056	**877-225-5428**	760-941-7130	187-10
JR Holcomb & Co Inc PO Box 94636	Cleveland	OH	44101	**800-362-9907**	216-341-3000	673
JR Roberts Corp 7745 Greenback Ln Suite 300	Citrus Heights	CA	95610	**800-551-1534**	916-729-5600	185
JR Short Milling Co 150 S Wacker Dr	Chicago	IL	60606	**800-544-8734**	312-559-5450	291-23
JR Simplot Co 999 Main St	Boise	ID	83702	**800-635-5008**	208-336-2110	291-21
JR Simplot Co AgriBusiness Group PO Box 70013	Boise	ID	83707	**800-635-9444**	208-672-2700	276

Name / Address	City	State	ZIP	Toll-Free	Phone	Class
JR Simplot Co Food Group 6360 S Federal Way	Boise	ID	83716	**800-635-0408**	208-384-8000	291-21
JRH Biosciences Inc 13804 W 107th St	Lenexa	KS	66215	**800-255-6032**	913-469-5580	86
JRM Industries Inc 1 Mattimore St	Passaic	NJ	07055	**800-533-2697**	973-779-9340	730-5
JRN Inc 201 W 7th St	Columbia	TN	38401	**800-251-8035**	931-381-3000	656
JR's Executive Inn Riverfront 1 Executive Blvd	Paducah	KY	42001	**800-866-3636**	270-443-8000	373
JS & A Group Inc 3350 Palms Centre Dr	Las Vegas	NV	89103	**800-323-6400**	702-798-9000	5
JS West Milling Co Inc 501 9th St *Cust Svc	Modesto	CA	95353	**800-675-9378***	209-577-3221	438
JSA (Jewelers Shipping Assn) 125 Carlsbad St	Cranston	RI	02920	**800-688-4572**	401-943-6490	49-21
JSA (Junior State of America) 400 S El Camino Real Suite 300	San Mateo	CA	94402	**800-334-5353**	650-347-1600	48-11
JSJ Corp 700 Robbins Rd	Grand Haven	MI	49417	**800-867-3208**	616-842-6350	314-1
JSJ Corp Dake Div 724 Robbins Rd	Grand Haven	MI	49417	**800-846-3253**	616-842-7110	346
JT Davenport & Sons Inc PO Box 1105 *Cust Svc	Sanford	NC	27331	**800-868-7550***	919-774-9444	292-8
JT Thorpe & Son Inc 1060 Hensley St	Richmond	CA	94801	**800-577-1755**	510-233-2500	313
JTech Communications Inc 6413 Congress Ave Suite 150	Boca Raton	FL	33487	**800-321-6221**	561-997-0772	720
Juanita K Hammons Hall for the Performing Arts 901 S National Ave	Springfield	MO	65804	**888-476-7849**	417-836-6776	562
Jubitz Corp 33 NE Middlefield Rd	Portland	OR	97211	**800-399-5480**	503-283-1111	319
Judd Wire Inc 124 Turnpike Rd *Cust Svc	Turners Falls	MA	01376	**800-545-5833***	413-863-4357	801
Judge Group Inc 300 Conshohocken State Rd Suite 300	West Conshohocken	PA	19428	**888-228-7162**	610-667-7700	707
Judicate West 1851 E 1st St Suite 1450	Santa Ana	CA	92705	**800-488-8805**	714-834-1340	41
Judicial Watch Inc PO Box 44444	Washington	DC	20026	**888-593-8442**	202-646-5172	48-7
Judson College 302 Bibb St	Marion	AL	36756	**800-447-9472**	334-683-6161	163
Judson Park 23600 Marine View Dr S	Des Moines	WA	98198	**877-263-8484**	206-824-4000	659
Jules Jurgensen Helbros International 101 W City Ave	Bala Cynwyd	PA	19004	**800-220-1233**	610-667-3500	151
Julian Tours 1500 N Beauregard St Suite 110	Alexandria	VA	22311	**800-541-7936**	703-379-2300	748
Julie Hat Co Inc 5948 Industrial Blvd PO Box 518	Patterson	GA	31557	**800-841-2592**	912-647-2031	153-9
Julie Morgenstern's Professional Organizers 350 5th Ave Suite 828	New York	NY	10118	**866-742-6473**	212-544-8722	193
Julie Rogers Theatre 765 Pearl St	Beaumont	TX	77701	**800-782-3081**	409-838-3435	562
Julius Koch USA Inc 387 Church St *Sales	New Bedford	MA	02745	**800-522-3652***	508-995-9565	730-5
Juneau Convention & Visitors Bureau 101 Egan Dr	Juneau	AK	99801	**888-581-2201**	907-586-2201	205
Jung JW Seed Co 335 S High St	Randolph	WI	53956	**800-297-3123**	920-326-3121	684
Jungle Adventures 26205 E Hwy 50	Christmas	FL	32709	**877-424-2867**	407-568-1354	811
Juniata College 1700 Moore St	Huntingdon	PA	16652	**877-586-4282**	814-643-4310	163
Juniata River Valley Visitors Bureau Historic Court House 1 W Market St Suite 103	Lewistown	PA	17044	**877-568-9739**	717-248-6713	205
Juniata Valley Area Chamber of Commerce 1 W Market St Suite 119	Lewistown	PA	17044	**877-568-9739**	717-248-6713	137
Junior Achievement of Canada (JACAN) 2275 Lakeshore Blvd W Suite 306	Toronto	ON	M8V3Y3	**800-265-0699**	416-622-4602	48-11
Junior Chamber of Commerce. US PO Box 7	Tulsa	OK	74102	**800-529-2337**	918-584-2481	48-7
Junior Chamber International (JCI) 15645 Olive Blvd	Chesterfield	MO	63017	**800-905-5499**	636-449-3100	48-7
Junior Food Stores of West Florida Inc DBA Tom Thumb 619 8th Ave	Crestview	FL	32536	**800-682-8486**	850-682-5171	203
Junior Leagues International Inc. Association of 90 William St Suite 200	New York	NY	10038	**800-955-3248**	212-683-1515	48-15
Junior State of America (JSA) 400 S El Camino Real Suite 300	San Mateo	CA	94402	**800-334-5353**	650-347-1600	48-11
Juniper Industries Inc 72-15 Metropolitan Ave	Middle Village	NY	11379	**800-221-4664**	718-326-2546	688
Juniper Inn 1315 N 27th St	Billings	MT	59101	**800-826-7530**	406-245-4128	373
Juniper Networks Inc 1194 N Mathilda Ave *NASDAQ: JNPR*	Sunnyvale	CA	94089	**888-586-4737**	408-745-2000	174
Juniper Valley Products 2862 S Circle Dr *Cust Svc	Colorado Springs	CO	80906	**800-685-7891***	719-226-4206	618
Juno Lighting Inc 1300 S Wolf Rd *NASDAQ: JUNO*	Des Plaines	IL	60017	**800-323-5068**	847-827-9880	431
Jupiter Beach Resort 5 N Hwy A1A	Jupiter	FL	33477	**800-228-8810**	561-746-2511	655
Jupiter Realty Corp 919 N Michigan Ave Suite 1500	Chicago	IL	60611	**800-910-2276**	312-642-6000	639
Jupiter Tequesta Juno Beach Chamber of Commerce 800 N US Hwy 1	Jupiter	FL	33477	**800-616-7402**	561-746-7111	137
Jurgensen John R Co 11641 Mosteller Rd	Cincinnati	OH	45241	**800-686-9725**	513-771-0820	187-4
Jury Research Institute 2617 Danville Blvd PO Box 100	Alamo	CA	94507	**800-233-5879**	925-932-5663	436
Jurys Washington Hotel 1500 New Hampshire Ave NW	Washington	DC	20036	**800-423-6953**	202-483-6000	373
Just Born Inc 1300 Stefko Blvd	Bethlehem	PA	18017	**800-445-5787**	610-867-7568	291-8
Just Desserts Inc 550 85th Ave	Oakland	CA	94621	**800-253-4438**	510-567-2910	69
Justice Design Group Inc 261 S Figueroa St Suite 450 *Cust Svc	Los Angeles	CA	90012	**800-533-4799***	213-437-0102	431
Justice. National Conference for Community & 475 Park Ave S 19th Fl	New York	NY	10016	**800-352-6225**	212-545-1300	48-8
Justice Project. Battered Women's 2104 4th Ave S Suite B	Minneapolis	MN	55404	**800-903-0111**	612-824-8768	49-10
Justin Boot Co Inc 610 W Daggett St *Cust Svc	Fort Worth	TX	76104	**866-240-8853***	817-332-4385	296
Justiss Oil Co Inc PO Box 2990	Jena	LA	71342	**800-256-2501**	318-992-4111	529
Justrite Mfg Co 2454 Dempster St Suite 300	Des Plaines	IL	60016	**800-469-5382**	847-298-9250	197
Juvenile Diabetes Research Foundation International (JDRF) 120 Wall St	New York	NY	10005	**800-533-2873**	212-785-9500	48-17
Juvenile Justice. National Center for 3700 S Water St Suite 200	Pittsburgh	PA	15203	**800-577-6903**	412-227-6950	48-8
JV Wells Inc PO Box 520	Sharptown	MD	21861	**800-638-7697**	410-883-3196	671
JVC Co of America 1700 Valley Rd	Wayne	NJ	07470	**800-526-5308**	973-317-5000	52
JVC Disc America Co 2 JVC Rd	Tuscaloosa	AL	35405	**800-223-5081**	205-556-7111	644
JW Aluminum Co 435 Old Mount Holly Rd	Mount Holly	SC	29445	**800-568-1100**	843-572-1100	476
JW Harris Co Inc 4501 Quality Pl	Mason	OH	45040	**800-733-4043**	513-754-2000	798
JW Jung Seed Co 335 S High St	Randolph	WI	53956	**800-297-3123**	920-326-3121	684
JW Marriott Desert Ridge Resort & Spa Phoenix 5350 E Marriott Dr	Phoenix	AZ	85054	**800-898-4527**	480-293-5000	373
JW Marriott New Orleans 614 Canal St	New Orleans	LA	70130	**888-236-2427**	504-525-6500	373
JW Marriott Orlando Grande Lakes Resort 4040 Central Florida Pkwy	Orlando	FL	32837	**800-576-5750**	407-206-2300	655
JW Marriott Resort Golf Club & Spa. Camelback Inn 5402 E Lincoln Dr	Scottsdale	AZ	85253	**800-242-2635**	480-948-1700	655
JW Marriott Resort Ihilani 92-1001 Olani St	Kapolei	HI	96707	**800-626-4446**	808-679-0079	655
JW Marriott Resort Las Vegas 221 N Rampart Blvd	Las Vegas	NV	89145	**877-869-8777**	702-869-7777	655
JW Pepper & Son Inc 2480 Industrial Blvd	Paoli	PA	19301	**800-345-6296**	610-648-0500	515
JW Peters 500 W Market St	Burlington	WI	53105	**800-877-9040**	262-763-2401	181
JW Speaker Corp PO Box 489	Germantown	WI	53022	**800-558-7288**	262-251-6660	430
JWP/Hyre Electric Co of Indiana Inc 2655 Garfield Ave	Highland	IN	46322	**800-272-9659**	219-923-6100	188-4
JWT Specialized Communications 5200 W Century Blvd Suite 310	Los Angeles	CA	90045	**800-676-7080**	310-665-8700	4

K

Name / Address	City	State	ZIP	Toll-Free	Phone	Class
K-2 Skis 19215 Vashon Hwy SW	Vashon	WA	98070	**800-972-4937**	206-463-3631	701
K-Dee Supply Inc 621 E Lake St	Lake Mills	WI	53551	**800-221-6417**	920-648-8202	768
K & F Industries Inc PO Box 1206	Indianapolis	IN	46206	**800-359-2385**	317-783-4154	674
K & G Men's Center Inc 1225 Chattahoochee Ave NW	Atlanta	GA	30318	**800-351-7987**	404-351-7987	155-3
K Line America Inc 8730 Stony Point Pkwy Suite 400	Richmond	VA	23235	**800-609-3221**	804-560-3600	308
K & M Corporate Housing Inc 16060 Caputo Dr Suite 120	Morgan Hill	CA	95037	**800-646-0907**	408-782-1212	209
K & M Electronics Inc 11 Interstate Dr W	Springfield	MA	01089	**800-442-4334**	413-781-1350	252
K & M Mfg Co 308 NW 2nd St	Renville	MN	56284	**800-328-1752**	320-329-3301	269
K-Mac Enterprises Inc 1820 S Zero St	Fort Smith	AR	72906	**800-345-5622**	479-646-2053	656
K-Swiss Inc 31248 Oak Crest Dr *NASDAQ: KSWS*	Westlake Village	CA	91361	**800-938-8000**	818-706-5100	296
K-Systems Inc 5060 Ritter Rd Suite 2-A	Mechanicsburg	PA	17055	**800-221-0204**	717-795-7711	176-1
K-Tel International Inc 2655 Cheshire Ln N Suite 100	Plymouth	MN	55447	**800-328-6640**	763-559-5566	643
K-Tron International Inc Rts 55 & 553 *NASDAQ: KTII*	Pitman	NJ	08071	**800-355-8766**	856-589-0500	200
K-Tube Corp 13400 Kirkham Way	Poway	CA	92064	**800-394-0058**	858-513-9229	469
K-VA-T Food Stores Inc PO Box 1158	Grundy	VA	24614	**800-253-6684**	276-623-5100	339
K-Y Farms DBA Valley Fruit Inc PO Box 770	Pharr	TX	78577	**800-255-1486**	956-787-3241	310-2
K2 Bike 19215 Vashon Hwy SW	Vashon	WA	98070	**800-426-1617**	206-463-3631	83
K2 Inc 2051 Palomar Airport Rd Suite 100 *NYSE: KTO*	Carlsbad	CA	92009	**800-972-4063**	760-494-1000	701
KA-BAR Knives Inc 200 Homer St	Olean	NY	14760	**800-282-0130**	716-372-5952	219
KA Steel Chemicals Inc 15185 Main St PO Box 729	Lemont	IL	60439	**800-677-8335**	630-257-3900	144
KAAL-TV Ch 6 (ABC) 1701 10th Pl NE	Austin	MN	55912	**800-234-0776**	507-437-6666	726
Kaba Ilco Corp 400 Jeffreys Rd	Rocky Mount	NC	27804	**800-334-1381**	252-446-3321	345
Kacey Fine Furniture 900 S Santa Fe Dr Dock 4 Unit 25	Denver	CO	80223	**800-574-1979**	303-778-6400	316
KACV-FM 89.9 (Alt) 2408 S Jackson St	Amarillo	TX	79109	**800-766-0176**	806-371-5222	631
KACV-TV Ch 2 (PBS) PO Box 447	Amarillo	TX	79178	**800-999-9243**	806-371-5222	726
Kadlec Medical Center 888 Swift Blvd	Richland	WA	99352	**800-780-6067**	509-946-4611	366-2
KADN-TV Ch 15 (Fox) 1500 Eraste Landry Rd	Lafayette	LA	70506	**800-738-6736**	337-237-1500	726
Kaemark 1338 County Rd 28	Giddings	TX	78942	**800-766-3651**	979-542-3651	78
Kaepa USA Inc 9050 Autobahn Dr Suite 500	Dallas	TX	75237	**800-880-9200**	972-296-7300	296
KAFF-AM 930 (Ctry) 1117 W Rt 66	Flagstaff	AZ	86001	**888-893-5646**	928-774-5231	631
KAFF-FM 92.9 (Ctry) 1117 W Rt 66	Flagstaff	AZ	86001	**888-412-5233**	928-774-5231	631
KAFT-TV Ch 13 (PBS) 350 S Donaghey Ave	Conway	AR	72034	**800-662-2386**	501-682-2386	726
Kagan World Media 1 Lower Ragsdale Dr Bldg 1 Suite 130	Monterey	CA	93940	**800-307-2529**	831-624-1536	623-9
Kahala Mandarin Oriental Hotel Hawaii Resort 5000 Kahala Ave	Honolulu	HI	96816	**800-367-2525**	808-739-8888	373
Kahler Grand Hotel 20 SW 2nd Ave	Rochester	MN	55902	**800-533-1655**	507-282-2581	373
Kahunaville Management Inc 500 S Madison St	Wilmington	DE	19801	**888-453-3990**	302-571-6200	657
KAID-TV Ch 4 (PBS) 1455 N Orchard St	Boise	ID	83706	**800-543-6868**	208-373-7220	726

Listing	City	State	ZIP	Toll-Free	Phone	Class
Kaiser Electroprecision Corp 17000 S Red Hill Ave	Irvine	CA	92614	800-866-5775	949-250-1015	202
Kaiser Foundation Health Plan Inc 1 Kaiser Plaza 27th Fl.	Oakland	CA	94612	800-464-4000	510-271-5910	384-3
Kaiser Permanente 1 Kaiser Plaza 27th Fl.	Oakland	CA	94612	800-464-4000	510-271-5910	384-3
Kaiser Permanente California 1950 Franklin St	Oakland	CA	94612	800-464-4000	510-987-1000	384-3
Kaiser Permanente Colorado Denver/Boulder 10350 E Dakota Ave	Denver	CO	80231	800-632-9700	303-344-7200	384-3
Kaiser Permanente Hawaii 711 Kapiolani Blvd	Honolulu	HI	96813	800-966-5955	808-432-5955	384-3
Kaiser Permanente Hospital 441 N Lakeview Ave	Anaheim	CA	92807	800-464-4000	714-279-4000	366-2
Kaiser Permanente Hospital 99 Montecillo Rd	San Rafael	CA	94903	800-464-4000	415-444-2000	366-2
Kaiser Permanente Medical Center 25825 S Vermont Ave	Harbor City	CA	90710	800-464-4000	310-325-5111	366-2
Kaiser Permanente Medical Center 1150 Veterans Blvd	Redwood City	CA	94063	800-464-4000	650-299-2000	366-2
Kaiser Permanente Medical Center 1200 El Camino Real	South San Francisco	CA	94080	800-660-1231	650-742-2000	366-2
Kaiser Permanente Medical Center-South Sacramento 6600 Bruceville Rd	Sacramento	CA	95823	800-464-4000	916-688-2000	366-2
Kaiser Permanente Mid-Atlantic States Inc 2101 E Jefferson St	Rockville	MD	20849	800-368-5784	301-468-6000	384-3
Kaiser Permanente Northwest 500 NE Multnomah St Suite 100	Portland	OR	97232	800-813-2000	503-813-2800	384-3
Kaiser Permanente Ohio 1001 Lakeside Ave N Pt Tower Suite 1200	Cleveland	OH	44114	888-571-4141	216-621-5600	384-3
Kaiser Permanente Parma Medical Center 12301 Snow Rd	Parma	OH	44130	800-524-7372	216-362-2000	366-2
Kaiser Permanente Riverside Medical Center 10800 Magnolia Ave *Cust Svc	Riverside	CA	92505	800-464-4000*	951-353-2000	366-2
Kaiser Precision Tooling Inc 641 Fargo Ave	Elk Grove Village	IL	60007	800-553-5113	847-228-7660	484
Kaiser Ventures LLC 3633 E Inland Empire Blvd Suite 480	Ontario	CA	91764	800-889-3652	909-483-8500	791
Kaiser Walnut Creek Hospice 200 Muir Rd	Martinez	CA	94553	800-418-8300	925-229-7800	365
KaiserAir Inc 8735 Earhart Rd	Oakland	CA	94621	800-538-2625	510-569-9622	14
KAJA-FM 97.3 (Ctry) 6222 NW IH-10	San Antonio	TX	78201	800-707-5597	210-736-9700	631
Kalamazoo College 1200 Academy St	Kalamazoo	MI	49006	800-253-3602	269-337-7166	163
Kalamazoo County Convention & Visitors Bureau 346 W Michigan Ave	Kalamazoo	MI	49007	800-530-9192	269-381-4003	205
Kalamazoo Gazette 401 S Burdick St	Kalamazoo	MI	49007	800-466-6397	269-345-3511	522-2
Kalamazoo Technical Furniture 6450 Valley Industrial Dr	Kalamazoo	MI	49009	800-832-5227	269-372-6000	411
Kalani Oceanside Retreat RR 2 Box 4500	Pahoa	HI	96778	800-800-6886	808-965-7828	660
Kalispel Case Line PO Box 267	Cusick	WA	99119	800-398-0338	509-445-1121	701
Kalispell Regional Medical Ctr 310 Sunnyview Ln	Kalispell	MT	59901	800-228-1574	406-752-5111	366-2
Kalitta Flying Service 818 Willow Run Airport	Ypsilanti	MI	48198	800-845-3390	734-484-0088	13
Kallista Inc 444 Highland Dr	Kohler	WI	53044	888-452-5547	920-457-4441	367
Kalmbach Publishing Co 21027 Crossroads Cir *Cust Svc	Waukesha	WI	53187	800-446-5489*	262-796-8776	623-9
Kalsec Inc PO Box 50511	Kalamazoo	MI	49005	800-323-9320	269-349-9711	291-15
Kalva Corp 3940 Porett Dr	Gurnee	IL	60031	800-525-8220	847-336-1200	291-8
Kalwall Corp 1111 Candia Rd	Manchester	NH	03109	800-258-9777	603-627-3861	597
Kalyn/Siebert LP 1505 W Main St	Gatesville	TX	76528	800-525-9689	254-865-7235	768
KAMA-AM 750 (Span) 2211 E Missouri Ave Suite S-300	El Paso	TX	79903	800-880-9797	915-544-9797	631
Kama Corp 600 Dietrich Ave	Hazleton	PA	18201	800-628-7598	570-455-2022	589
Kaman Industrial Technologies Inc 1 Waterside Crossing	Windsor	CT	06095	800-526-2626	860-687-5000	378
Kaman Instrumentation Corp 3450 N Nevada Ave	Colorado Springs	CO	80907	800-552-6267	719-635-6867	252
Kaman Music Corp 20 Old Windsor Rd	Bloomfield	CT	06002	800-647-2244	860-509-8888	516
Kamatics Corp 1330 Blue Hills Ave	Bloomfield	CT	06002	800-468-4735	860-243-9704	609
KaMMCO (Kansas Medical Mutual Insurance Co) 623 SW 10th Ave Suite 200	Topeka	KS	66612	800-232-2259	785-232-2224	384-5
Kamminga & Roodvoets Inc 3435 Broadmoor Ave SE	Grand Rapids	MI	49512	800-632-9755	616-949-0800	188-5
Kanawha Hospice Care 1143 Dunbar Ave	Dunbar	WV	25064	800-560-8523	304-768-8523	365
Kanawha Insurance Co PO Box 610	Lancaster	SC	29721	800-635-4252	803-283-5300	384-2
Kandiyohi Power Co-op 1311 Hwy 71 NE	Willmar	MN	56201	800-551-4951	320-235-4155	244
Kane Graphical Corp 2255 W Logan Blvd	Chicago	IL	60647	800-992-2921	773-384-1200	338
Kane Mfg Corp 515 N Fraley St	Kane	PA	16735	800-952-6399	814-837-6464	232
Kane Steel Co PO Box 829	Millville	NJ	08332	800-223-5263	856-825-2200	483
Kaneb Pipe Line Partners LP 2435 N Central Expy Suite 700 *NYSE: KPP*	Richardson	TX	75080	866-769-2987	972-699-4000	586
Kane's Beverage Week Newsletter 313 South Ave Suite 202	Fanwood	NJ	07023	800-359-6049	908-889-6336	521-13
Kangaroo Products Co 111 Kangaroo Dr PO Box 607	Columbus	NC	28722	800-438-3011	828-894-8241	701
Kankakee Valley Rural Electric Membership Corp 114 S Main St	Wanatah	IN	46390	800-552-2622	219-733-2511	244
Kanox Inc 1200 N Grand St PO Box 3007	Hutchinson	KS	67501	800-333-6156	620-665-5551	798
Kansas						
Insurance Dept 420 SW 9th St	Topeka	KS	66612	800-432-2484	785-296-3071	335
Travel & Tourism Development Div 1000 SW Jackson St Suite 100	Topeka	KS	66612	800-252-6727	785-296-5403	335
Kansas Assn of Realtors 3644 SW Burlingame Rd	Topeka	KS	66611	800-366-0069	785-267-3610	642
Kansas Brick & Tile Inc PO Box 450 *Cust Svc	Hoisington	KS	67544	800-999-0480*	620-653-2157	148
Kansas City Art Institute 4415 Warwick Blvd	Kansas City	MO	64111	800-522-5224	816-474-5224	163
Kansas City Aviation Center Inc 15325 Pflumm Rd Johnson County Executive Airport *Sales	Olathe	KS	66062	800-720-5222*	913-782-0530	63
Kansas City Board of Trade 4800 Main St Suite 303	Kansas City	MO	64112	800-821-5228	816-753-7500	680
Kansas City Convention & Entertainment Centers 301 W 13th St	Kansas City	MO	64105	800-821-7060	816-513-5000	204
Kansas City Kansas/Wyandotte County Convention & Visitors Bureau 727 Minnesota Ave PO Box 171517	Kansas City	KS	66117	800-264-1563	913-321-5800	205
Kansas City Life Insurance Co PO Box 219139 *NASDAQ: KCLI*	Kansas City	MO	64121	800-821-6164	816-753-7000	355-4
Kansas City Music Hall 201 W 13th St	Kansas City	MO	64105	800-821-7060	816-513-5000	562
Kansas City Royals Kauffman Stadium 1 Royal Way *Sales	Kansas City	MO	64129	800-676-9257*	816-921-8000	703
Kansas City Southern 427 W 12th St *NYSE: KSU*	Kansas City	MO	64105	800-243-8624	816-983-1303	355-3
Kansas City Southern Railway Co 427 W 12th St	Kansas City	MO	69405	800-468-6527	816-983-1303	634
Kansas City Star 1729 Grand Ave	Kansas City	MO	64108	800-726-2340	816-234-4141	522-2
Kansas Cosmosphere & Space Center 1100 N Plum	Hutchinson	KS	67501	800-397-0330	620-662-2305	510
Kansas Gas Service 7421 W 129th St	Overland Park	KS	66213	800-794-4780	913-319-8600	774
Kansas Living Magazine 2627 KFB Plaza	Manhattan	KS	66503	800-406-3053	785-587-6000	449-1
Kansas Medical Mutual Insurance Co (KaMMCO) 623 SW 10th Ave Suite 200	Topeka	KS	66612	800-232-2259	785-232-2224	384-5
Kansas Medical Society 623 SW 10th Ave	Topeka	KS	66612	800-332-0156	785-235-2383	466
Kansas Republican Party 2025 SW Gage Blvd	Topeka	KS	66604	888-482-9051	785-234-3456	605-2
Kansas State University Anderson Hall	Manhattan	KS	66506	800-232-0133	785-532-6250	163
Kansas Wesleyan University 100 E Claflin Ave	Salina	KS	67401	800-874-1154	785-827-5541	163
KANU-FM 91.5 (NPR) 1120 W 11th St University of Kansas	Lawrence	KS	66044	888-577-5268	785-864-4530	631
Kao Brands Co 2535 Spring Grove Ave	Cincinnati	OH	45214	800-742-8798	513-421-1400	211
Kao Specialties Americas LLC 243 Woodline St PO Box 2316	High Point	NC	27261	800-727-2214	336-884-2214	143
Kapalua Bay Hotel 1 Bay Dr	Kapalua	HI	96761	800-367-8000	808-669-5656	373
Kapalua Land Co Ltd 700 Village Rd *Sales	Kapalua	HI	96761	800-545-8439*	808-669-5622	639
Kapalua Resort 300 Kapalua Dr	Kapalua	HI	96761	877-527-2582	808-669-8044	655
Kapalua Villas The 500 Office Rd	Maui	HI	96761	800-545-0018	808-669-8088	655
Kaplan Inc 888 7th Ave 21st Fl *Cust Svc	New York	NY	10106	800-527-8378*	212-492-5800	243
Kaplan Inc Test Preparation & Admissions Div 888 7th Ave 21st Fl	New York	NY	10106	888-527-5268	212-492-5800	243
Kaplan International 888 7th Ave 21st Fl	New York	NY	10106	800-527-8378	212-492-5800	414
Kaplan McLaughlin Diaz 222 Vallejo St 4th Fl	San Francisco	CA	94111	800-822-5191	415-398-5191	258
Kaplan School Supply Corp 1310 Lewisville-Clemmons Rd	Lewisville	NC	27023	800-334-2014	336-766-7374	673
Kappa Alpha Theta Fraternity 8740 Founders Rd	Indianapolis	IN	46268	800-526-1870	317-876-1870	48-16
Kappa Delta Pi 3707 Woodview Trace	Indianapolis	IN	46268	800-284-3167	317-871-4900	48-16
Kappa Delta Rho. National Fraternity of 331 S Main St	Greensburg	PA	15601	800-536-5371	724-838-7100	48-16
Kappa Delta Sorority 3205 Players Ln	Memphis	TN	38125	800-536-1897	901-748-1897	48-16
Kappa Kappa Gamma 530 E Town St PO Box 38	Columbus	OH	43216	866-554-1870	614-228-6515	48-16
Kappa Kappa Iota 1875 E 15th St	Tulsa	OK	74104	800-678-0389	918-744-0389	48-16
Kappa Kappa Psi National Honorary Band Fraternity PO Box 849	Stillwater	OK	74076	800-543-6505	405-372-2333	48-16
Kappler Protective Apparel & Fabrics 115 Grimes Dr	Guntersville	AL	35976	800-600-4019	256-505-4000	566
Kar Nut Products Co Inc 1525 Wanda Ave	Ferndale	MI	48220	800-527-6887	248-541-7870	291-28
Karan Donna International Inc 550 7th Ave 15th Fl	New York	NY	10018	800-231-0884	212-789-1500	153-21
Karas & Karas Glass Co Inc 455 Dorchester Ave	Boston	MA	02127	800-888-1235	617-268-8800	188-6
Karastan Div Mohawk Industries Inc 335 Summit Rd *Cust Svc	Eden	NC	27288	800-845-8877*	336-627-7200	131
Karatz Bruce 10990 Wilshire Blvd Chm/CEO KB Home	Los Angeles	CA	90024	800-344-6637	310-231-4000	561
Karbra Co 131 W 35th St 8th Fl	New York	NY	10001	800-527-2721	212-736-9300	399
Kardex Systems Inc PO Box 171	Marietta	OH	45750	800-234-3654	740-374-9300	281
Karem Inc 549 Karem Dr	Marshall	WI	53559	800-655-1705	608-655-3439	568
Karen Ann Quinlan Hospice 99 Sparta Ave	Newton	NJ	07860	800-882-1117	973-383-0115	365

Name / Address	City	State	ZIP	Toll-Free	Phone	Class
Karges Furniture Co Inc 1501 W Maryland St	Evansville	IN	47710	**800-252-7437**	812-425-2291	281
Karl Ehmer Inc 63-35 Fresh Pond Rd	Ridgewood	NY	11385	**800-487-5275**	718-456-8100	291-26
Karman Inc 14707 E 2nd Ave 3rd Fl	Aurora	CO	80011	**800-825-6555**	303-893-2320	153-20
Karmanos Barbara Ann Cancer Institute 4110 John R St	Detroit	MI	48201	**800-527-6266**	313-833-0710	654
Karmanos Cancer Institute Hospice 24601 Northwestern Hwy	Southfield	MI	48075	**800-527-6266**	248-827-1592	365
Karnak Chemical Corp 330 Central Ave	Clark	NJ	07066	**800-526-4236**	732-388-0300	46
Karnes Electric Co-op Inc PO Box 7	Karnes City	TX	78118	**888-807-3952**	830-780-3952	244
Karolina Polymers Inc 1508 S Center St	Hickory	NC	28602	**800-280-2247**	828-328-2247	589
Karsten Mfg Corp 2201 W Desert Cove Ave	Phoenix	AZ	85029	**800-474-6434**	602-870-5000	701
Karten's Jewelers 901 W Walnut Hill Ln	Irving	TX	75038	**800-333-6739**	972-580-4000	402
Karthauser & Sons Inc W 147 N 11100 Fond du Lac Ave	Germantown	WI	53022	**800-338-8620**	262-255-7815	288
Kasco Corp 1569 Tower Grove Ave	Saint Louis	MO	63110	**800-325-8940**	314-771-1550	293
Kasle Steel Corp 4343 Wyoming Ave	Dearborn	MI	48126	**800-225-2753**	313-943-2500	483
Kaslen Textiles 5899 Downey Rd	Vernon	CA	90058	**800-423-4448**	323-589-5337	731
Kason Industries Inc 57 Amlajack Blvd	Shenandoah	GA	30265	**800-935-2766**	770-251-1422	345
Kaspar & Esh Inc 11-25 45th Ave	Long Island City	NY	11101	**800-223-2614**	718-786-0771	401
Kaspar Wire Works Inc PO Box 667	Shiner	TX	77984	**800-337-0610**	361-594-3327	75
Kastar Inc PO Box 1616 *Cust Svc	Racine	WI	53401	**800-645-1142***	262-554-2300	746
Katharine Beecher Candies 1250 Slate Hill Rd	Camp Hill	PA	17011	**800-708-3641**	717-761-5440	291-8
Katharine Gibbs School New York 50 W 40th St 1st Fl	New York	NY	10018	**800-843-0738**	212-867-9300	158
Katmai Coastal Bear Tours PO Box 1501	Homer	AK	99603	**800-532-8338**		748
Kato Design 3650 Austin Bluffs Suite 190	Colorado Springs	CO	80918	**800-448-3383**	719-634-8300	287
Katolight Corp 100 Power Dr	Mankato	MN	56001	**800-325-5450**	507-625-7973	507
Katten Muchin Zavis Rosenman 525 W Monroe St Suite 1300	Chicago	IL	60661	**800-346-7400**	312-902-5200	419
KATU-TV Ch 2 (ABC) 2153 NE Sandy Blvd	Portland	OR	97232	**800-447-6397**	503-231-4222	726
KATZ-FM 100.3 (Urban) 1001 Highlands Plaza Dr W Suite 100	Saint Louis	MO	63110	**800-541-0036**	314-333-8300	631
Katz Group 10104 103rd Ave Suite 1702	Edmonton	AB	T5J0H8	**800-267-8877**	780-990-0505	658
Kaua'i Chamber of Commerce PO Box 1969	Lihue	HI	96766	**800-262-1400**	808-245-7363	137
Kauai Coffee Co Inc PO Box 8	Eleele	HI	96705	**800-545-8605**	808-335-5497	291-7
Kaua'i Marriott Resort & Beach Club 3610 Rice St	Lihue	HI	96766	**800-220-2925**	808-245-5050	655
Kauai Resort & Spa. Hyatt Regency 1571 Poipu Rd	Koloa	HI	96756	**800-233-1234**	808-742-1234	655
Kauffman Ewing Marion Foundation 4801 Rockhill Rd	Kansas City	MO	64110	**800-489-4900**	816-932-1000	300
Kaufman & Broad Mortgage Co 10990 Wilshire Blvd 9th Fl	Los Angeles	CA	90024	**800-446-2624**	310-893-7300	498
Kaufmann Fund 140 E 45th St 43rd Fl	New York	NY	10017	**800-261-0551**	212-922-0123	517
Kavanagh John Homes 1810 Pembroke Rd	Greensboro	NC	27408	**800-940-9904**	336-272-9904	639
Kaw Valley Electric Co-op Inc 1100 SW Auburn Rd	Topeka	KS	66615	**800-794-2011**	785-478-3444	244
Kawada Hotel 200 S Hill St	Los Angeles	CA	90012	**800-752-9232**	213-621-4455	373
Kawal America Corp 2055 E University Dr	Compton	CA	90220	**800-421-2177**	310-631-1771	516
Kaweah Delta Hospital 400 W Mineral King Ave	Visalia	CA	93291	**800-529-3244**	559-624-2000	366-2
Kay Chemical Co 8300 Capital Dr	Greensboro	NC	27409	**800-333-4300**	336-668-7290	149
Kay Dee Designs Inc 177 Skunk Hill Rd	Hope Valley	RI	02832	**800-537-3433**	401-539-2405	731
Kay Dee Feed Co Inc 1919 Grand Ave	Sioux City	IA	51106	**800-831-4815**	712-277-2011	438
Kay El Bar Guest Ranch PO Box 2480	Wickenburg	AZ	85358	**800-684-7583**	928-684-7593	238
Kay Electric Co-op PO Box 607	Blackwell	OK	74631	**800-535-1079**	580-363-1260	244
Kay Elemetrics Corp 2 Bridgewater Ln	Lincoln Park	NJ	07035	**800-289-5297**	973-628-6200	252
Kay Home Products 26210 Emery Rd Suite 101	Cleveland	OH	44128	**800-600-7009**	216-896-6900	106
Kay Jewelers 375 Ghent Rd	Akron	OH	44333	**800-681-8796**	330-668-5000	402
Kay Park Recreation Corp 1301 Pine St *Cust Svc	Janesville	IA	50647	**800-553-2476***	319-987-2313	314-4
Kaye Chris Plastics Corp 715 W Park Rd	Union	MO	63084	**800-325-9927**	636-583-2583	593
Kaye Group Inc 1065 Ave of the Americas	New York	NY	10018	**800-456-5293**	212-338-2000	383
Kaye-Smith 720 Lind Ave SW	Renton	WA	98055	**800-822-9987**	425-228-8600	111
Kayem Foods Inc 75 Arlington St	Chelsea	MA	02150	**800-426-6100**	617-889-1600	291-26
Kayline Processing Inc 31 Coates St *Sales	Trenton	NJ	08611	**800-367-5546***	609-695-1449	589
Kayo of California Inc 161 W 39th St	Los Angeles	CA	90037	**800-233-6140**	323-233-6107	153-11
Kaytee Products Inc 521 Clay St	Chilton	WI	53014	**800-669-9580**	920-849-2321	568
Kaz Inc 1775 Broadway Suite 2405 *Cust Svc	New York	NY	10019	**800-241-1131***	212-586-1630	37
KAZU-FM 90.3 (NPR) 167 Central Ave PO Box 210	Pacific Grove	CA	93950	**800-903-6624**	831-375-7275	631
KB Electronics Inc 12095 NW 39th St	Coral Springs	FL	33065	**800-221-6570**	954-346-4900	202
KB Home 10990 Wilshire Blvd 7th Fl *NYSE: KBH*	Los Angeles	CA	90024	**800-344-6637**	310-231-4000	639
KB Home Orlando 8403 S Park Cir Suite 670	Orlando	FL	32819	**800-615-2312**	321-354-2500	639
KBAK-TV Ch 29 (CBS) 1901 Westwind Dr	Bakersfield	CA	93301	**800-229-6397**	661-327-7955	726
KBDI-TV Ch 12 (PBS) 2900 Welton St 1st Fl	Denver	CO	80205	**800-727-8812**	303-296-1212	726
KBHC (Kristin Brooks Hope Center) 2001 N Beauregard St 12th Fl	Alexandria	VA	22311	**800-784-2433**	703-684-7722	48-17
KBHE-FM 89.3 (NPR) 555 N Dakota St	Vermillion	SD	57069	**800-456-0766**	605-677-5861	631
KBHE-TV Ch 9 (PBS) PO Box 5000	Vermillion	SD	57069	**800-456-0766**	605-677-5861	726
KBIA-FM 91.3 (NPR) 409 Jesse Hall	Columbia	MO	65211	**800-292-9136**	573-882-3431	631
KBIG-FM 104.3 (AC) 3400 W Olive Ave Suite 550	Burbank	CA	91505	**800-524-4104**	818-559-2252	631
KBLG-AM 910 (N/T) 2075 Central Ave	Billings	MT	59102	**866-627-5483**	406-652-8400	631
KBLX-FM 102.9 (Urban AC) 55 Hawthorne St Suite 900	San Francisco	CA	94105	**800-683-5259**	415-284-1029	631
KBM Office Furniture Co 320 S 1st St	San Jose	CA	95113	**800-578-4526**	408-351-7100	315
KBME-TV Ch 3 (PBS) 207 N 5th St	Fargo	ND	58102	**800-359-6900**	701-241-6900	726
KBMX-FM 107.7 (AC) 14 E Central Entrance	Duluth	MN	55811	**866-266-2649**	218-727-4500	631
KBMY-TV Ch 17 (ABC) 3128 E Broadway Ave	Bismarck	ND	58501	**877-563-9369**	701-223-1700	726
KBNA-FM 97.5 (Span AC) 2211 E Missouri Ave Suite S-300	El Paso	TX	79903	**800-880-9797**	915-544-9797	631
KBR Rural Public Power District PO Box 187	Ainsworth	NE	69210	**800-672-0009**	402-387-1120	244
KBSG-FM 97.3 (Oldies) 1820 Eastlake Ave E	Seattle	WA	98102	**877-668-9797**	206-726-7000	631
KBSX-FM 91.5 (NPR) 1910 University Dr	Boise	ID	83725	**888-859-5278**	208-947-5660	631
KBTC-TV Ch 28 (PBS) 2320 S 19th St	Tacoma	WA	98405	**888-596-5282**	253-680-7700	726
KBYU-TV Ch 11 (PBS) 2000 Ironton Blvd Brigham Young University	Provo	UT	84606	**800-298-5298**	801-422-8450	726
KC Electric Assn PO Box 8	Hugo	CO	80821	**800-700-3123**	719-743-2431	244
KC Masterpiece Restaurants 9537 Alden St	Lenexa	KS	66215	**800-467-9206**	913-888-5210	657
KC Photo Engraving Co 2666 E Nina St	Pasadena	CA	91107	**800-660-4127**	323-681-0203	770
KCBA-TV Ch 35 (Fox) 1550 Moffett St	Salinas	CA	93905	**800-321-5222**	831-422-3500	726
KCBS-AM 740 (N/T) 865 Battery St 3rd Fl	San Francisco	CA	94111	**800-400-3697**	415-765-4000	631
KCFR-AM 1340 (NPR) 7409 S Alton Ct	Centennial	CO	80112	**800-722-4449**	303-871-9191	631
KCHF-TV Ch 11 (Ind) 27556 I-25 E Frontage Rd	Santa Fe	NM	87508	**800-831-9673**	505-473-1111	726
KCI Communications 1750 Old Meadow Rd Suite 300 *Cust Svc	McLean	VA	22102	**800-832-2330***	703-905-8000	623-9
KCI Inc (Kinetic Concepts Inc) 8023 Vantage Dr *NYSE: KCI*	San Antonio	TX	78230	**800-531-5346**	210-524-9000	469
KCI Technologies Inc 10 N Park Dr	Hunt Valley	MD	21030	**800-572-7496**	410-316-7800	258
KCLR-FM 99.3 (Ctry) 3215 Lemone Industrial Blvd Suite 200	Columbia	MO	65201	**800-455-5257**	573-875-1099	631
KCMP-FM 89.3 (NPR) 45 E 7th St	Saint Paul	MN	55101	**888-798-9225**	651-290-1212	631
KCMQ-FM 96.7 (CR) 3215 Lemone Industrial Blvd Suite 200	Columbia	MO	65201	**800-455-1967**	573-875-1099	631
KCMS-FM 105.3 (Rel) 19303 Fremont Ave N	Shoreline	WA	98133	**877-275-1053**	206-546-7350	631
KCND-FM 90.5 (NPR) 1814 N 15th St	Bismarck	ND	58501	**800-359-5566**	701-224-1700	631
KCOL-AM 600 (N/T) 1612 LaPorte Ave	Fort Collins	CO	80521	**866-888-5449**	970-482-5991	631
KCPW-FM 88.3 (NPR) PO Box 510730	Salt Lake Cityu	UT	84151	**888-359-5279**	801-359-5279	631
KCRG-TV Ch 9 (ABC) 501 2nd Ave SE	Cedar Rapids	IA	52401	**800-332-5443**	319-398-8422	726
KCRW-FM 89.9 (NPR) 1900 Pico Blvd	Santa Monica	CA	90405	**888-600-5279**	310-450-5183	631
KCS Energy Inc 5555 San Felipe St Suite 1200 *NYSE: KCS*	Houston	TX	77056	**800-848-9844**	713-877-8006	525
KCS Industries Inc 340 Maple Ave	Hartland	WI	53029	**800-777-5111**	262-369-9995	692
KCSD-FM 90.9 (NPR) PO Box 5000	Vermillion	SD	57069	**800-456-0766**	605-677-5861	631
KCTS-TV Ch 9 (PBS) 401 Mercer St	Seattle	WA	98109	**800-443-9991**	206-728-6463	726
KDAF-TV Ch 33 (WB) 8001 John Carpenter Fwy	Dallas	TX	75247	**877-252-8233**	214-252-9233	726
KDAL-AM 610 (N/T) 715 E Central Entrance	Duluth	MN	55811	**888-532-5610**	218-722-4321	631
KDAL-FM 95.7 (AC) 715 E Central Entrance	Duluth	MN	55811	**800-532-5610**	218-722-4321	631
KDAQ-FM 89.9 (NPR) 1 University Pl	Shreveport	LA	71115	**800-552-8502**	318-797-5150	631
KDDI America 375 Park Ave 7th Fl	New York	NY	10152	**888-696-9533**	212-702-3720	721
KDF Inc 10 Volvo Dr	Rockleigh	NJ	07647	**877-533-3343**	201-784-5005	685
KDI Precision Products Inc 3975 McMann Rd	Cincinnati	OH	45245	**800-377-3334**	513-943-2000	803
KDIN-TV Ch 11 (PBS) 6450 Corporate Dr	Johnston	IA	50131	**800-532-1290**	515-242-3100	726
KDIndustries 1525 E Lake Rd	Erie	PA	16511	**800-840-9577**	814-453-6761	650
KDLT-TV Ch 46 (NBC) 3600 S Westport Ave	Sioux Falls	SD	57106	**800-727-5358**	605-361-5555	726
KDNW-FM 97.3 (Rel) 1101 E Central Entrance	Duluth	MN	55811	**888-322-5369**	218-722-6700	631
KDON-FM 102.5 (CHR) 903 N Main St	Salinas	CA	93906	**888-558-5366**	831-755-8181	631
KDS USA 7373 Hunt Ave	Garden Grove	CA	92841	**800-237-9988**	714-379-5599	171-4
KDSU-FM 91.9 (NPR) 1301 12th Ave N NDSU Memorial Union Bldg	Fargo	ND	58102	**800-359-6900**	701-241-6900	631
KDVR-TV Ch 31 (Fox) 100 E Speer Blvd	Denver	CO	80203	**888-369-4762**	303-595-3131	726
KDVV-FM 100.3 (Rock) 825 S Kansas Ave Suite 100	Topeka	KS	66612	**866-297-1003**	785-272-2122	631
KE Adventure Travel 1131 Grand Ave	Glenwood Springs	CO	81601	**800-497-9675**	970-384-0001	748
Kea Lani Spa at the Fairmont Kea Lani Maui 4100 Wailea Alanui Dr	Maui	HI	96753	**800-659-4100**	808-875-2229	698

Name / Address	City	State	Zip	Toll-Free	Phone	Class
KEA News 401 Capital Ave	Frankfort	KY	40601	800-231-4532	502-875-2889	449-8
KEAN-FM 105.1 (Ctry) 3911 S 1st St	Abilene	TX	79605	800-588-5326	325-676-7711	631
Keane Inc 100 City Sq. *NYSE: KEA*	Boston	MA	02129	800-365-3263	617-241-9200	178
Kearfott Guidance & Navigation Corp 150 Totowa Rd	Wayne	NJ	07470	800-785-6000	973-785-6000	519
Kearney Area Chamber of Commerce 1007 2nd Ave	Kearney	NE	68847	800-652-9435	308-237-3101	137
Kearny Federal Savings Bank 614 Kearny Ave	Kearny	NJ	07032	800-273-3406	201-991-4100	71
Keating PJ Co Inc 998 Reservoir Rd	Lunenburg	MA	01462	800-441-4119	978-582-9931	187-4
Kedem Food Products/Royal Wine Corp 63 Le Fante Ln	Bayonne	NJ	07002	800-382-8299	718-384-2400	81-3
Kedesh Guest Ranch 1940 Hwy 14	Shell	WY	82441	800-845-3320	307-765-2791	238
Keds Corp 191 Spring St	Lexington	MA	02421	800-428-6575	617-824-6000	296
KEDT-FM 90.3 (NPR) 4455 S Padre Island Dr Suite 38	Corpus Christi	TX	78411	800-307-5338	361-855-2213	631
KEDT-TV Ch 16 (PBS) 4455 S Padre Island Dr Suite 38	Corpus Christi	TX	78411	800-307-5338	361-855-2213	726
Keefe Bruyette & Woods Inc 1 Constitution Plaza 17th Fl	Hartford	CT	06103	800-726-0006	860-722-5900	679
Keeler Brass Co 955 Godfrey Ave SW	Grand Rapids	MI	49503	800-874-6522	616-247-4000	345
Keeler John & Co Inc 3000 NW 109th Ave	Miami	FL	33172	888-663-2722	305-836-6858	292-5
Keeley Investment Corp 401 S La Salle St Suite 1201	Chicago	IL	60605	800-533-5344	312-786-5000	167
Keenan Supply Div Hajoca Corp 1341 Philadelphia St	Pomona	CA	91766	800-437-6593	909-613-1363	601
Keene Publishing Corp PO Box 546	Keene	NH	03431	800-765-9994	603-352-1234	623-8
Keene Sentinel 60 West St PO Box 546	Keene	NH	03431	800-765-9994	603-352-1234	522-2
Keene State College 229 Main St	Keene	NH	03435	800-572-1909	603-352-1909	163
Keeney Mfg Co 1170 Main St *Cust Svc	Newington	CT	06111	800-243-0526*	860-666-3342	598
Keepers International Inc 20720 Marilla St	Chatsworth	CA	91311	800-797-6257	818-882-5000	153-10
Kehe Food Distributors Inc 900 N Schmidt Rd	Romeoville	IL	60446	800-995-5343	815-886-0700	292-8
Keilson-Dayton Co 107 Commerce Park Dr	Dayton	OH	45404	800-759-3174	937-236-1070	744
Keiser College 1500 NW 49th St	Fort Lauderdale	FL	33309	800-749-4456	954-776-4456	787
Keith Ben E Co 7650 Will Rogers Blvd	Fort Worth	TX	76140	877-317-6100	817-759-6000	292-8
Keith Cos Inc 19 Technology Dr *NASDAQ: TKCI*	Irvine	CA	92618	800-735-3484	949-923-6000	258
Keithley Instruments Inc 28775 Aurora Rd *AMEX: KEI*	Cleveland	OH	44139	800-552-1115	440-248-0400	247
Kell-Strom Tool Co Inc 214 Church St	Wethersfield	CT	06109	800-851-6851	860-529-6851	745
Keller Crescent Co Inc 1100 E Louisiana St	Evansville	IN	47711	800-457-3837	812-464-2461	4
Keller-Hall Inc 1247 Eastwood Ave	Tallmadge	OH	44278	800-831-6147	330-633-6160	188-14
Keller JJ & Assoc Inc PO Box 368	Neenah	WI	54957	800-558-5011	920-722-2848	623-11
Keller Laboratories Inc 10966 Gravois Industrial Ct	Saint Louis	MO	63128	800-325-3056	314-919-4000	406
Keller Mfg Co Inc 1010 Keller Dr NE	New Salisbury	IN	47161	800-738-2240	812-366-4001	314-2
Keller Supply Co Inc 3209 17th Ave W	Seattle	WA	98119	800-285-3302	206-285-3300	601
Keller Transfer Line Inc 5635 Clay Ave SW	Grand Rapids	MI	49548	800-666-0701	616-531-1850	769
Keller Transfer/Commerce Distribution Center 31750 Enterprise Dr	Livonia	MI	48151	800-666-0701	734-458-5116	790-1
Kellermeyer Co 1025 Brown Ave	Toledo	OH	43607	800-462-9552	419-255-3022	398
Kelley Automotive Group 633 Ave of Autos	Fort Wayne	IN	46804	800-434-4750	260-434-4700	57
Kelley Blue Book Co Inc 5 Oldfield	Irvine	CA	92618	800-258-3266	949-770-7704	58
Kelley Jack B Inc 8101 W 34th Ave	Amarillo	TX	79121	800-225-5525	806-353-3553	769
Kellogg Brown & Root 4100 Clinton Dr	Houston	TX	77020	800-231-8166	713-753-2000	258
Kellogg Co 1 Kellogg Sq *NYSE: K* ■ *Cust Svc	Battle Creek	MI	49016	800-962-1413*	269-961-2000	291-4
Kellogg Hotel & Conference Center S Harrison Rd Michigan State University Campus	East Lansing	MI	48824	800-875-5090	517-432-4000	373
Kellogg Marine Supply Inc 5 Enterprise Dr	Old Lyme	CT	06371	800-243-9303	860-434-6002	759
Kellogg Supply Inc 350 W Sepulveda Blvd *Cust Svc	Carson	CA	90745	800-232-2322*	310-830-2200	276
Kellwood New England 300 Manley St *Cust Svc	Brockton	MA	02303	800-225-6987*	508-588-7200	153-3
Kelly Home Care Services Inc 999 W Big Beaver Rd	Troy	MI	48084	800-937-5355	248-362-4444	358
Kelly Inns Ltd 3211 W Sencore Dr	Sioux Falls	SD	57107	800-635-3559	605-334-2371	369
Kelly-Moore Paint Co Inc 987 Commercial St	San Carlos	CA	94070	800-874-4436	650-592-8337	540
Kelly Paper Co 288 Brea Canyon Rd	City of Industry	CA	91789	800-675-3559	909-859-8200	543
Kelly Pipe Co LLC 11680 Bloomfield Ave	Santa Fe Springs	CA	90670	800-305-3559	562-868-0456	584
Kelly Ryan Equipment Co 900 Kelly Ryan Dr	Blair	NE	68008	800-640-6967	402-426-2151	269
Kelly Staff Leasing 110 W 'A' St Suite 1700	San Diego	CA	92101	800-877-8233	619-615-7500	619
Kelly Systems Inc 422 N Western Ave	Chicago	IL	60612	800-258-8237	312-733-3224	462
Kelly's Pipe & Supply Co Inc 2124 Industrial Rd	Las Vegas	NV	89102	888-382-4957	702-382-4957	601
KELO-AM 1320 (N/T) 500 S Phillips Ave	Sioux Falls	SD	57104	800-888-5356	605-331-5350	631
Kelowna Chamber of Commerce 544 Harvey Ave	Kelowna	BC	V1Y6C9	800-663-4345	250-861-1515	136
Kelsey's Operations Ltd 6303 Airport Rd	Mississauga	ON	L4V1R8	800-860-4082	905-405-6500	656
Kelso WR Co Inc 10201 N Hague Rd	Indianapolis	IN	46256	800-352-5859	317-845-5858	188-12
Kelter-Alliant Insurance Services Inc 210 S Old Woodward Ave Suite 200	Birmingham	MI	48009	800-888-9088	248-540-3131	383
KEM Electric Co-op Inc 107 S Broadway	Linton	ND	58552	800-472-2673	701-254-4666	244
KEM Mfg Co 18-35 River Rd	Fair Lawn	NJ	07410	800-289-5362	201-796-8000	246
KEMA Consulting 3 Burlington Woods	Burlington	MA	01803	800-892-2006	781-273-5700	193
KEMC-FM 91.7 (NPR) 1500 University Dr	Billings	MT	59101	800-441-2941	406-657-2941	631
Kemin Industries Inc 2100 Maury St	Des Moines	IA	50317	800-247-7496	515-266-2111	438
Kemira Chemicals Inc 245 TownPark Dr Suite 200	Kennesaw	GA	30144	800-347-1542	770-436-1542	141
Kemlite Co 23525 W Eames St	Channahon	IL	60410	800-435-0080	815-467-8600	595
Kemper Arena 1800 Genessee St	Kansas City	MO	64102	800-634-3942	816-513-4000	706
Kemper Insurance Cos 1 Kemper Dr	Long Grove	IL	60049	800-833-0355	847-320-2000	384-4
Kemps Food Inc PO Box 7007	Lancaster	PA	17604	800-233-2007	717-394-5601	291-25
Kemps LLC 2929 University Ave SE	Minneapolis	MN	55414	800-322-9566	612-331-3775	291-27
Kemron Environmental Services Inc 8150 Leesburg Pike Suite 1410	Vienna	VA	22182	800-777-1042	703-893-4106	191
Kemwel Inc 39 Commercial St	Portland	ME	04112	800-678-0678	207-842-2285	126
Ken Garff Automotive Group 195 E University Pkwy	Orem	UT	84058	888-323-5869	801-374-1751	57
Ken Jones Tire Inc PO Box 782	Worcester	MA	01613	800-225-9513	508-755-5255	740
Ken-Mac Metals Inc 17901 Englewood Dr	Cleveland	OH	44130	800-831-9503	440-234-7500	483
Ken Stanton Music Inc 119 Cobb Pkwy N	Marietta	GA	30062	800-282-9011	770-427-2491	515
Kenall Mfg 1020 Lakeside Dr	Gurnee	IL	60031	800-453-6255	847-360-8200	431
Kenan Advantage Group Inc 4895 Dressler Rd NW	Canton	OH	44718	800-969-5149	330-491-0474	769
Kenan Transport Co 100 Europa Ctr Suite 320	Chapel Hill	NC	27517	800-768-8765	919-967-8221	769
Kenco Group Inc 2001 Riverside Dr	Chattanooga	TN	37401	800-365-7189	423-756-5552	440
Kenda USA 7095 Americana Pkwy	Reynoldsburg	OH	43068	866-536-3287	614-866-9803	740
Kendal at Ithaca 2230 N Triphammer Rd	Ithaca	NY	14850	800-253-6325	607-266-5300	659
Kendal at Oberlin 600 Kendal Dr *Mktg	Oberlin	OH	44074	800-548-9469*	440-775-0094	659
Kendale Industries Inc 7600 Hub Pkwy	Cleveland	OH	44125	800-321-9308	216-524-5400	479
Kendall Co 15 Hampshire St *Cust Svc	Mansfield	MA	02048	800-962-9888*	508-261-8000	468
Kendall College 2408 Orrington Ave	Evanston	IL	60201	877-588-8860	847-866-1300	163
Kendall College of Art & Design of Ferris State University 17 Fountain St NW	Grand Rapids	MI	49503	800-676-2787	616-451-2787	163
Kendall Electric Inc 131 Grand Trunk Ave	Battle Creek	MI	49015	800-632-5422	269-963-5585	245
Kendall-Hartcraft PO Box 11670	Huntsville	AL	35814	800-421-7435	256-859-5533	304
Kendall-Hartcraft 1480 Independence Ave PO Box 270465	Hartford	WI	53027	800-558-7834	262-673-3440	304
Kendall Industrial Supplies Inc 4560 W Dickman Rd	Battle Creek	MI	49015	800-632-9606	269-965-2211	245
Kendall-Jackson Wine Estates Ltd 425 Aviation Blvd	Santa Rosa	CA	95403	800-544-4413	707-544-4000	81-3
Kendall Packaging Corp 10200 N Port Washington Rd	Mequon	WI	53092	800-237-0951	262-404-1200	589
Kendall/Hunt Publishing Co 4050 Westmark Dr *Cust Svc	Dubuque	IA	52002	800-228-0810*	563-589-1000	623-2
Kendallville Iron & Metal Inc PO Box 69	Kendallville	IN	46755	800-530-5564	260-347-1958	674
Kendle International Inc 441 Vine St 1200 Carew Tower *NASDAQ: KNDL*	Cincinnati	OH	45202	800-733-1572	513-381-5550	654
Kendro Laboratory Products 275 Aiken Rd	Asheville	NC	28804	800-252-7100	828-658-2711	411
Kenmore Air Harbor Inc 6321 NE 175th St	Kenmore	WA	98028	800-543-9595	425-486-1257	26
Kenmore Camera Inc 18031 67th Ave NE	Kenmore	WA	98028	888-485-7447	425-485-7447	119
Kenmore-Town of Tonawanda Chamber of Commerce 3411 Delaware Ave	Kenmore	NY	14217	888-281-1680	716-874-1202	137
Kennametal Inc 1600 Technology Way *NYSE: KMT* ■ *Cust Svc	Latrobe	PA	15650	800-446-7738*	724-539-5000	484
Kennametal Inc Metalworking Systems Development 1600 Technology Way	Latrobe	PA	15650	800-446-7738	724-539-5000	447
Kennametal Inc Mining & Construction Div 1600 Technology Way	Latrobe	PA	15650	800-446-7738	724-539-5000	189
Kennebec Journal 274 Western Ave	Augusta	ME	04330	800-537-5508	207-623-3811	522-2
Kennebec Valley Community College 92 Western Ave	Fairfield	ME	04937	800-528-5882	207-453-5000	160
Kennebunk Home Inc 25 Canal St	Suncook	NH	03275	800-242-1537	603-485-7511	731
Kennecott Energy Co PO Box 3009	Gillette	WY	82717	800-305-1142	307-687-6000	491
Kennedy Center for the Performing Arts 2700 F St NW	Washington	DC	20566	800-444-1324	202-416-8000	562
Kennedy Group PO Box 420136	Dallas	TX	75342	800-527-5724	214-748-0821	315
Kennedy Information 1 Phoenix Mill Ln 5th Fl	Peterborough	NH	03458	800-531-1026	603-924-1006	623-9
Kennedy John F Library & Museum Columbia Point	Boston	MA	02125	866-535-1960	617-514-1600	426
Kennedy Mfg Co 520 E Sycamore St	Van Wert	OH	45891	800-413-8665	419-238-2442	479
Kennedy Office Supply Co 4211-A Atlantic Ave	Raleigh	NC	27604	800-733-9401	919-878-5400	524
Kennedy Space Center Public Inquiries	Kennedy Space Center	FL	32899	800-561-8618	321-867-5000	654
Kennedy Valve 1021 E Water St	Elmira	NY	14902	800-782-5831	607-734-2211	776
Kennedy-Western University 30301 Agoura Rd	Agoura Hills	CA	91301	800-635-2900	818-707-4300	163

Name / Address	City	State	ZIP	Toll-Free	Phone	Class
Kennedy Wholesale Inc 205 W Harvard St	Glendale	CA	91204	**877-292-2639**	818-241-9977	292-3
Kennedy-Wilson Inc 9601 Wilshire Blvd Suite 220 *NASDAQ: KWIC*	Beverly Hills	CA	90210	**800-522-6664**	310-887-6400	51
Kennel-Aire Inc 801 E North St	Ottawa	KS	66067	**800-346-0134**	785-242-8484	568
Kennels Assn. American Boarding 1702 E Pikes Peak Ave	Colorado Springs	CO	80909	**877-570-7788**	719-667-1600	48-3
Kenneth Cole Productions Inc 603 W 50th St *NYSE: KCP*	New York	NY	10019	**800-536-2653**	212-265-1500	296
Kenneth Gordon IAG Inc 1209 Distributors Row *Cust Svc	New Orleans	LA	70123	**800-234-1433***	504-734-1433	153-12
Kenney Corp 8420 Zionsville Rd	Indianapolis	IN	46268	**800-878-8676**	317-872-4793	420
Kenney Mfg Co 1000 Jefferson Blvd *Cust Svc	Warwick	RI	02886	**800-753-6639***	401-739-2200	88
Kenny D Davis Co Inc 4810 Greatland	San Antonio	TX	78218	**800-594-2045**	210-662-9882	87
Kenny Rogers Roasters 1400 Old Country Rd Suite 400	Westbury	NY	11590	**800-628-4267**	516-338-8500	657
Kenosha Area Convention & Visitors Bureau 812 56th St	Kenosha	WI	53140	**800-654-7309**	262-654-7307	205
Kenosha News 5800 7th Ave	Kenosha	WI	53140	**800-292-2700**	262-657-1000	522-2
Ken's Flower Shop 140 W South Boundary St	Perrysburg	OH	43551	**800-253-0100**	419-874-4103	287
Ken's Foods Inc 1 D'Angelo Dr	Marlborough	MA	01752	**800-633-5800**	508-485-7540	291-19
Kensey Nash Corp 55 E Uwchlan Ave *NASDAQ: KNSY*	Exton	PA	19341	**800-524-1984**	610-524-0188	468
Kensington Home Furnishings Center 200 Tilton Rd	Northfield	NJ	08225	**800-641-4844**	609-641-4800	285
Kensington Park Hotel 450 Post St	San Francisco	CA	94102	**800-553-1900**	415-788-6400	373
Kensington Publishing Corp 850 3rd Ave	New York	NY	10022	**877-422-3665**	212-407-1500	623-2
Kensington Riverside Inn 1126 Memorial Dr NW	Calgary	AB	T2N3E3	**877-313-3733**	403-228-4442	372
Kensington Technology Group 333 Twin Dolphin Dr 6th Fl	Redwood Shores	CA	94065	**800-243-2972**	650-572-2700	171-1
Kensington Windows Inc 1136 Industrial Pk Rd	Vandergrift	PA	15690	**800-444-4972**	724-845-8133	233
Kent The 1131 Collins Ave	Miami Beach	FL	33139	**800-688-7678**	305-604-5068	373
Kent Corp 4446 Pinson Valley Pkwy	Birmingham	AL	35217	**800-252-5368**	205-853-3420	281
Kent Cos Inc 130 60th St SW	Grand Rapids	MI	49548	**800-968-2345**	616-534-4909	188-3
Kent County Tourism Corp 435 N DuPont Hwy	Dover	DE	19901	**800-233-5368**	302-734-1736	205
Kent Elastomer Products Inc 1500 St Claire Ave *Cust Svc	Kent	OH	44240	**800-331-4762***	330-673-1011	663
Kent Oil Inc PO Box 908001	Midland	TX	79708	**800-375-5368**	432-699-5822	319
Kent School PO Box 2006	Kent	CT	06757	**800-538-5368**	860-927-6111	611
Kent Sporting Goods Co Inc 433 Park Ave S	New London	OH	44851	**800-537-2970**	419-929-7021	701
Kent State University 500 E Main St	Kent	OH	44242	**800-988-5368**	330-672-2121	163
Kentec Inc 3250 Centerville Hwy	Snellville	GA	30039	**800-241-0148**	770-985-1907	346
Kentec Medical Inc 17871 Fitch	Irvine	CA	92614	**800-825-5996**	949-863-0810	467
Kenton Times 201 E Columbus St PO Box 230	Kenton	OH	43326	**800-886-2412**	419-674-4066	522-2
Kentucky						
Consumer Protection Div 1024 Capital Center Dr Suite 200	Frankfort	KY	40601	**888-432-9257**	502-696-5389	335
Education Professional Standards Board 1024 Capitol Center Dr Suite 225	Frankfort	KY	40601	**888-598-7667**	502-573-4606	335
Fish & Wildlife Resources Dept 1 Game Farm Rd	Frankfort	KY	40601	**800-858-1549**	502-564-3400	335
Higher Education Assistance Authority PO Box 798	Frankfort	KY	40602	**800-928-8926**	502-696-7200	711
Historical Society 100 W Broadway	Frankfort	KY	40601	**877-444-7867**	502-564-1792	335
Housing Corp 1231 Louisville Rd	Frankfort	KY	40601	**800-633-8896**	502-564-7630	335
Parks Dept 500 Mero St Suite 1100	Frankfort	KY	40601	**800-255-7275**	502-564-2172	335
Real Estate Commission 10200 Linn Station Rd Suite 201	Louisville	KY	40223	**888-373-3300**	502-425-4273	335
Travel Dept 500 Mero St Suite 2200	Frankfort	KY	40601	**800-225-8747**	502-564-4930	335
Vocational Rehabilitation Dept 209 Saint Clair St Rm 200	Frankfort	KY	40601	**800-372-7172**	502-564-4440	335
Kentucky Assn of Realtors 161 Prosperous Pl	Lexington	KY	40509	**800-264-2185**	859-263-7377	642
Kentucky Christian University 100 Academic Pkwy *Admissions	Grayson	KY	41143	**800-522-3181***	606-474-3000	163
Kentucky Dam Village State Resort Park PO Box 69	Gilbertsville	KY	42044	**800-325-0146**	270-362-4271	554
Kentucky Educational Television (KET) 600 Cooper Dr	Lexington	KY	40502	**800-432-0951**	859-258-7000	620
Kentucky Electric Steel LLC PO Box 2119	Ashland	KY	41105	**800-333-3012**	606-929-1200	709
Kentucky Horse Park 4089 Iron Works Pkwy	Lexington	KY	40511	**800-678-8813**	859-233-4303	811
Kentucky International Convention Center 221 4th St	Louisville	KY	40202	**800-701-5831**	502-595-4381	204
Kentucky Kingdom. Six Flags 937 Phillips Ln	Louisville	KY	40209	**800-727-3267**	502-366-2231	32
Kentucky Medical Assn 4965 US Hwy 42 KMA Bldg Suite 2000	Louisville	KY	40222	**800-686-9923**	502-426-6200	466
Kentucky Military History Museum 125 E Main St	Frankfort	KY	40601	**877-444-7867**	502-564-3265	509
Kentucky Opera Assn 101 S 8th St	Louisville	KY	40202	**800-690-9236**	502-584-4500	563-2
Kentucky Organ Donor Affiliates 106 E Broadway	Louisville	KY	40202	**800-525-3456**	502-581-9511	535

Name / Address	City	State	ZIP	Toll-Free	Phone	Class
Kentucky Post 125 E Court St	Cincinnati	OH	45202	**800-937-4954**	859-292-2600	522-2
Kentucky-Tennessee Clay Co 1441 Donelson Pike	Nashville	TN	37217	**800-814-4538**	615-365-0852	493-2
Kentucky Trailer 2601 S 3rd St	Louisville	KY	40217	**888-598-7245**	502-637-2551	768
Kentucky Trailer Technologies 1240 Pontiac Trail	Walled Lake	MI	48390	**800-521-9700**	248-960-9700	768
Kentucky Utilities Co 1 Quality St	Lexington	KY	40507	**800-981-0600**	859-255-2100	774
Kentucky Wesleyan College PO Box 1039	Owensboro	KY	42302	**800-999-0592**	270-852-3120	163
Kentucky West Virginia Gas Co LLC 748 N Lake Dr	Prestonsburg	KY	41653	**800-654-9754**	606-886-2311	320
Kentwood Spring Water Co PO Box 52043	New Orleans	LA	70152	**800-235-7873**	504-821-3333	792
Kenwal Steel Corp 8223 W Warren Ave	Dearborn	MI	48126	**800-521-7522**	313-935-7942	483
Kenwood Therapeutics 383 Rt 46 W	Fairfield	NJ	07004	**800-929-9300**	973-882-1505	572
Kenwood USA Corp PO Box 22745	Long Beach	CA	90801	**800-536-9663**	310-639-9000	633
Kenya Tourism Board c/o Carlson Destinationa Marketing Services PO Box 59159	Minneapolis	MN	55459	**866-445-3692**		764
Kenyon College 8854 Ranson Hall	Gambier	OH	43022	**800-848-2468**	740-427-5000	163
KEO Cutters Inc 25040 Easy St	Warren	MI	48089	**888-771-2062**	586-771-2050	484
Ker & Downey Inc 6703 Highway Blvd	Katy	TX	77494	**800-423-4236**	281-371-2500	748
KERA-FM 90.1 (NPR) 3000 Harry Hines Blvd	Dallas	TX	75201	**800-456-5372**	214-871-1390	631
Kerite Co 49 Day St	Seymour	CT	06483	**800-777-7483**	203-888-2591	800
Kerkau Mfg Co 910 Harry S Truman Pkwy	Bay City	MI	48706	**800-248-5060**	989-686-0350	474
KERN-AM 1410 (N/T) 1400 Easton Dr Suite 144	Bakersfield	CA	93309	**800-840-5376**	661-328-1410	631
Kern County Board of Trade PO Bin 1312	Bakersfield	CA	93302	**800-500-5376**	661-861-2367	137
Kern Schools Federal Credit Union PO Box 9506	Bakersfield	CA	93389	**800-221-3311**	661-833-7900	216
Kerotest Mfg Corp 5500 2nd Ave	Pittsburgh	PA	15207	**800-825-8371**	412-521-4200	776
Kerr Concrete Pipe Co Inc PO Box 312	Hammonton	NJ	08037	**800-642-3755**	609-561-3400	181
Kerr Drug Stores Inc 3220 Spring Forest Rd	Raleigh	NC	27616	**800-494-3053**	919-544-3896	236
Kerr Group Inc 1706 Hempstead Rd	Lancaster	PA	17601	**800-367-1876**	717-299-6511	590
Kerr Lakeside Inc 26841 Tungsten Rd	Euclid	OH	44132	**800-487-5377**	216-261-2100	610
Kerr-McGee Rocky Mountain Corp 1999 Broadway Suite 3600	Denver	CO	80202	**800-275-8966**	303-296-3600	525
Kerr Pump & Supply 12880 Cloverdale St	Oak Park	MI	48237	**800-482-8259**	248-543-3880	627
Kerr Walter Theatre 219 W 48th St	New York	NY	10036	**800-432-7250**	212-239-6200	732
Kerrville Convention & Visitors Bureau 2108 Sidney Baker St	Kerrville	TX	78028	**800-221-7958**	830-792-3535	205
Kerry's Bromeliad Nursery Inc 21840 SW 258th St	Homestead	FL	33031	**800-331-9127**	305-247-7096	363
Kershaw County Chamber of Commerce 607 S Broad St	Camden	SC	29020	**800-968-4037**	803-432-2525	137
Kerzner International Ltd 1000 S Pine Island Rd *NYSE: KZL*	Plantation	FL	33324	**800-321-3000**	954-809-2000	132
KESQ-TV Ch 3 (ABC) 42650 Melanie Pl	Palm Desert	CA	92211	**877-564-9729**	760-568-6830	726
Kessel Lumber Supply Inc HC 84 Box 4	Keyser	WV	26726	**800-543-9479**	304-788-3371	671
Kessler Institute for Rehabilitation 1199 Pleasant Valley Way	West Orange	NJ	07052	**888-537-7537**	973-731-3600	366-4
Kessler International 45 Rockefeller Plaza Suite 2000	New York	NY	10111	**800-932-2221**	212-286-9100	392
Kessler's Inc 1201 Hummel Ave	Lemoyne	PA	17043	**800-382-1328**	717-763-7162	291-26
Kester Solder Co 515 E Touhy Ave	Des Plaines	IL	60018	**800-253-7837**	847-297-1600	143
Keswick Hall at Monticello 701 Club Dr	Keswick	VA	22947	**800-274-5391**	434-979-3440	373
KET (Kentucky Educational Television) 600 Cooper Dr	Lexington	KY	40502	**800-432-0951**	859-258-7000	620
Ketchikan Visitors Bureau 131 Front St	Ketchikan	AK	99901	**800-770-2200**	907-225-6166	205
Ketchum Inc 5151 Belt Line Rd Suite 900	Dallas	TX	75254	**800-242-2161**	214-866-7600	312
KETG-TV Ch 9 (PBS) 350 S Donaghey Ave	Conway	AR	72034	**800-662-2386**	501-682-2386	726
KETS-TV Ch 2 (PBS) 350 S Donaghey Ave	Conway	AR	72032	**800-662-2386**	501-682-2386	726
Kettering College of Medical Arts 3737 Southern Blvd	Kettering	OH	45429	**800-433-5262**	937-395-8601	160
Kettering University 1700 W 3rd Ave	Flint	MI	48504	**800-955-4464**	810-762-9500	163
Kettle Country Kitchen Inc 350 Oaks Trail Suite 142	Garland	TX	75043	**800-929-2391**	972-203-6222	657
KETV-TV Ch 7 (ABC) 2665 Douglas St	Omaha	NE	68131	**800-279-5388**	402-345-7777	726
Keuka College 141Central Ave	Keuka Park	NY	14478	**800-355-3852**	315-279-5000	163
Kewadin Casinos 3039 Mackinac Tr	Saint Ignace	MI	49781	**800-539-2346**	906-643-7071	133
Kewanee Corp 1642 Burlington Ave	Kewanee	IL	61443	**800-666-4481**	309-853-4481	232
Keweenaw Peninsula Chamber of Commerce 902 College Ave	Houghton	MI	49931	**866-304-5722**	906-482-5240	137
Kewill Systems PLC 100 Nickerson Rd	Marlborough	MA	01752	**877-872-2379**	508-229-4400	176-10
KEX-AM 1190 (Var) 4949 SW Macadam Ave	Portland	OR	97239	**800-990-0750**	503-225-1190	631
Key Air Inc 3 Juliano Dr Waterbury-Oxford Airport	Oxford	CT	06478	**800-258-6975**	203-264-0605	14
Key Bank USA NA 22 Corporate Woods	Albany	NY	12211	**800-872-5553**		71
Key Container Corp 21 Campbell St	Pawtucket	RI	02861	**800-343-8811**	401-723-2000	101
Key Corporate Banking & Finance 601 Oakmont Ln Suite 110	Westmont	IL	60559	**800-877-2860**	630-655-7100	215
Key Curriculum Press 1150 65th St	Emeryville	CA	94608	**800-338-7638**	510-595-7000	623-2
Key Energy 2210 W Broadway	Sweetwater	TX	79556	**800-749-6613**	325-236-6611	769
Key Industries Inc 400 Marble Rd	Fort Scott	KS	66701	**800-835-0365**	620-223-2000	153-19
Key Largo Bay Marriott Beach Resort 103800 Overseas Hwy	Key Largo	FL	33037	**866-849-3753**	305-453-0000	655
Key Largo Casino & Hotel 377 E Flamingo Rd	Las Vegas	NV	89109	**800-634-6617**	702-733-7777	373

Name / Address	City	State	ZIP	Toll-Free	Phone	Class
Key Largo Casino & Quality Inn Hotel 377 E Flamingo Rd	Las Vegas	NV	89109	**800-634-6617**	702-733-7777	373
Key Lime Inn 725 Truman Ave	Key West	FL	33040	**800-594-4430**	305-294-5229	373
Key Polymer Corp 17 Shepherd St	Lawrence	MA	01843	**888-539-7659**	978-683-9411	3
Key West Aquarium 1 Whitehead St	Key West	FL	33040	**800-868-7482**	305-296-2051	40
Key West Chamber of Commerce 402 Wall St	Key West	FL	33040	**800-527-8539**	305-294-2587	137
Key West Fragrance & Cosmetics Factory Inc 540 Greene St *Orders	Key West	FL	33040	**800-445-2563***	305-293-1885	211
Key West Key 726 Passover Ln	Key West	FL	33040	**800-881-7321**	305-294-4357	368
Key West Resort & Marina. Hyatt 601 Front St	Key West	FL	33040	**800-554-9288**	305-296-9900	655
Key West Visitors Center 402 Wall St	Key West	FL	33040	**800-648-6269**	305-294-2587	205
KeyBank NA 127 Public Sq	Cleveland	OH	44114	**800-539-2968**	216-689-3000	71
Keyboard Magazine 2800 Campus Dr *Cust Svc	San Mateo	CA	94403	**800-289-9919***	650-513-4300	449-9
Keyboard World Inc 23-25 E Main St	Frostburg	MD	21532	**800-947-4266**	301-729-1817	515
KeyCorp 127 Public Sq *NYSE: KEY* ■ *Hum Res	Cleveland	OH	44114	**888-539-2562***	216-689-3000	355-2
Keydata International Inc 201 Circle Dr N Suite 101	Piscataway	NJ	08854	**800-486-4800**	732-868-0588	171-3
Keye Productivity Center Div American Management Assn International 600 AMA Way *Cust Svc	Saranac Lake	NY	12983	**800-262-9699***	518-891-1500	753
KEYE-TV Ch 42 (CBS) 10700 Metric Blvd	Austin	TX	78758	**800-563-9742**	512-835-0042	726
Keyes Automotive Group 5855 Van Nuys Blvd	Van Nuys	CA	91401	**800-974-7709**	818-782-0122	57
KeyLink Systems Group 6675 Parkland Blvd	Solon	OH	44139	**800-539-5465**	440-498-6900	172
Keymark Corp 1188 Cayadutta Rd	Fonda	NY	12068	**800-833-1609**	518-853-3421	476
Keynote Systems Inc 777 Mariners Island Blvd *NASDAQ: KEYN*	San Mateo	CA	94404	**888-539-7978**	650-522-1000	176-7
KeyPoint Credit Union 505 N Mathilda Ave	Sunnyvale	CA	94085	**888-844-3279**	408-731-4100	216
Keyport Life Insurance Co 1 Sun Life Executive Pk	Wellesley Hills	MA	02481	**800-225-3950**	781-237-6030	384-2
Keystone Automotive Industries Inc 700 E Bonita Ave *NASDAQ: KEYS*	Pomona	CA	91767	**800-772-5557**	909-624-8041	61
Keystone Cable Corp 8200 Lynch Rd	Detroit	MI	48234	**800-223-2996**	313-924-9720	803
Keystone Cement Co PO Box A	Bath	PA	18014	**800-523-5442**	610-837-1881	135
Keystone Center 2001 Providence Ave	Chester	PA	19013	**800-558-9600**	610-876-9000	712
Keystone College 1 College Green	La Plume	PA	18440	**877-426-5534**	570-945-6953	160
Keystone Consolidated Industries Inc 7000 SW Adams St *Sales	Peoria	IL	61641	**800-447-6444***	309-697-7020	800
Keystone Electronics Corp 31-07 20th Rd	Astoria	NY	11105	**800-221-5510**	718-956-8900	345
Keystone Filter Div Met-Pro Corp 2485 N Penn Rd	Hatfield	PA	19440	**800-811-4424**	215-822-1963	793
Keystone Food Products Co 3767 Hecktown Rd	Easton	PA	18045	**800-523-9426**	610-258-0888	291-35
Keystone Health Plan Central 3815 Tecport Dr	Harrisburg	PA	17111	**800-622-2843**		384-3
Keystone Health Plan East Inc 1901 Market St	Philadelphia	PA	19101	**800-227-3114**	215-241-2400	384-3
Keystone Honing Co PO Box 187	Titusville	PA	16354	**800-458-3847**	814-827-9641	446
Keystone Learning Systems Corp 5300 Westview Dr Suite 405	Frederick	MD	21703	**800-658-3358**	301-624-5590	502
Keystone Maax PO Box 544	Southampton	PA	18966	**800-355-5397**	215-825-5250	598
Keystone Plastics Inc 3451 S Clinton Ave	South Plainfield	NJ	07080	**800-635-5238**	908-561-1300	104
Keystone Pretzels 124 W Airport Rd Flyway Business Pk	Lititz	PA	17543	**888-572-4500**	717-560-1882	291-9
Keystone Printing Ink Co 2700 Roberts Ave	Philadelphia	PA	19129	**800-523-0111**	215-228-8100	381
Keystone Resort 21996 Hwy 6	Keystone	CO	80435	**800-239-1639**	970-496-2316	655
Keystone Steel & Wire Div Keystone Consolidated Industries Inc 7000 SW Adams St *Sales	Peoria	IL	61641	**800-447-6444***	309-697-7020	800
Keystone Tube Co 13527 S Halsted St *Cust Svc	Riverdale	IL	60827	**800-323-9493***	708-841-2450	481
Keystops LLC PO Box 2809	Franklin	KY	42135	**800-346-6456**	270-586-8283	569
KF Industries Inc 1500 SE 89th St	Oklahoma City	OK	73149	**800-654-4842**	405-631-1533	776
KFAL-AM 900 (Ctry) 1805 Westminster Ave	Fulton	MO	65251	**800-769-5274**	573-642-3341	631
KFBB-TV Ch 5 (ABC) PO Box 1139	Great Falls	MT	59403	**800-854-7720**	406-453-4377	726
KFC 1441 Gardiner Ln	Louisville	KY	40213	**800-544-5774**	502-874-8300	657
KFFG-FM 97.7 (AAA) 55 Hawthorne St Suite 1100	San Francisco	CA	94105	**800-300-5364**	415-543-1045	631
KFIS-FM 104.1 (Rel) 6400 SE Lake Rd Suite 350	Portland	OR	97222	**866-320-1041**	503-786-0600	631
KFLX-FM 105.1 (AAA) 112 E Rt 66 Suite 105	Flagstaff	AZ	86001	**877-600-5359**	928-779-1177	631
KFMB-AM 760 (N/T) 7677 Engineer Rd	San Diego	CA	92111	**800-760-5362**	858-292-7600	631
KFME-TV Ch 13 (PBS) PO Box 3240	Fargo	ND	58108	**800-359-6900**	701-241-6900	726
KFNK-FM 104.9 (Alt) 351 Elliott Ave W Suite 300	Seattle	WA	98119	**800-482-1049**	206-494-2000	631
KFNW-FM 97.9 (Rel) 5702 52nd Ave S	Fargo	ND	58104	**800-979-1200**	701-282-5910	631
KFOG-FM 104.5 (AAA) 55 Hawthorne St Suite 1100	San Francisco	CA	94105	**800-300-5304**	415-543-1045	631
Kforce Inc 75 Rowland Way Suite 200	Novato	CA	94945	**800-880-4611**	415-895-2200	707
Kforce Inc 1001 E Palm Ave *NASDAQ: KFRC*	Tampa	FL	33605	**888-663-3626**	813-552-5000	707
KFPW-AM 1230 (AC) 321 N Greenwood Ave	Fort Smith	AR	72901	**800-352-1047**	479-783-5379	631
KFRC-AM 610 (Oldies) 865 Battery St	San Francisco	CA	94111	**888-456-5372**	415-391-9970	631
KFRC-FM 99.7 (Oldies) 875 Battery St 4th Fl	San Francisco	CA	94111	**888-456-5372**	415-391-9970	631
KFSH-FM 95.9 (Rel) 701 N Brand Blvd Suite 550	Glendale	CA	91203	**866-347-4959**	818-956-5552	631
KFTV-TV Ch 21 (Uni) 3239 W Ashlan Ave	Fresno	CA	93722	**800-733-5388**	559-222-2121	726
KFUO-FM 99.1 (Clas) 85 Founders Ln	Clayton	MO	63105	**800-844-0524**	314-505-7899	631
KFXA-TV Ch 28 (Fox) 600 Old Marion Rd NE	Cedar Rapids	IA	52402	**800-642-6140**	319-393-2800	726
KGAN-TV Ch 2 (CBS) 600 Old Marion Rd NE	Cedar Rapids	IA	52402	**800-642-6140**	319-395-9060	726
KGFE-TV Ch 2 (PBS) PO Box 3240	Fargo	ND	58108	**800-359-6900**	701-241-6900	726
KGGN-AM 890 (Rel) 1734 E 63rd St Suite 600	Kansas City	MO	64110	**800-924-3177**	816-333-0092	631
KGMS-AM 940 (Rel) 3222 S Richey Ave	Tucson	AZ	85713	**866-725-5467**	520-790-2440	631
KGNC-AM 710 (N/T) PO Box 710	Amarillo	TX	79189	**800-285-0710**	806-355-9801	631
KGNC-FM 97.9 (Ctry) PO Box 710	Amarillo	TX	79189	**877-765-9790**	806-355-9801	631
KGNZ-FM 88.1 (Rel) 542 Butternut St	Abilene	TX	79602	**800-588-8801**	325-673-3045	631
KGON-FM 92.3 (CR) 0700 SW Bancroft St	Portland	OR	97239	**800-222-9236**	503-223-1441	631
KGW-TV Ch 8 (NBC) 1501 SW Jefferson St	Portland	OR	97201	**800-288-5498**	503-226-5000	726
KGWN-TV Ch 5 (CBS) 2923 E Lincolnway	Cheyenne	WY	82001	**877-672-8019**	307-634-7755	726
KGY-AM 1240 (AC) 1700 Marine Dr NW	Olympia	WA	98501	**800-310-7625**	360-943-1240	631
KGY-FM 96.9 (Ctry) 1700 Marine Dr NW	Olympia	WA	98501	**800-310-7625**	360-943-1240	631
KHAK-FM 98.1 (Ctry) 425 2nd St SE 4th Fl	Cedar Rapids	IA	52401	**800-747-5425**	319-365-9431	631
KHAR-AM 590 (Nost) 301 Arctic Slope Ave Suite 300	Anchorage	AK	99518	**800-896-1669**	907-344-9622	631
KHBS-TV Ch 40 (ABC) 2415 N Albert Pike	Fort Smith	AR	72904	**800-821-9170**	479-783-4040	726
KHCC-FM 90.1 (NPR) 815 N Walnut St Suite 300	Hutchinson	KS	67501	**800-723-4657**	620-662-6646	631
KHHO-AM 850 (Sports) 351 Elliott Ave W Suite 300	Seattle	WA	98119	**877-829-0850**	206-285-2295	631
Khoury Inc 1011 N Stephenson Ave *Cust Svc	Iron Mountain	MI	49801	**800-553-5446***	906-774-6333	314-2
KHOZ-FM 102.9 (Ctry) 1111 Radio Ave	Harrison	AR	72601	**800-553-6103**	870-741-3103	631
KHVN-AM 970 (Rel) 5787 S Hampton Rd Suite 285	Dallas	TX	75232	**866-856-5447**	972-572-5447	631
KI 1330 Bellevue St	Green Bay	WI	54302	**877-231-8555**	920-468-8100	314-1
Kiamichi Electric Co-op Inc PO Box 340	Wilburton	OK	74578	**800-888-2731**	918-465-2338	244
Kiawah Island Resort 12 Kiawah Beach Dr	Kiawah Island	SC	29455	**800-654-2924**	843-768-2121	655
Kichler Lighting 7711 E Pleasant Valley Rd PO Box 318010	Cleveland	OH	44131	**888-659-8809**	216-573-1000	431
KICU-TV Ch 36 (Ind) 2102 Commerce Dr	San Jose	CA	95131	**800-464-5428**	408-953-3636	726
Kidde-Fenwal Inc 400 Main St	Ashland	MA	01721	**800-872-6527**	508-881-2000	201
Kidde plc 700 Nickerson Rd	Marlborough	MA	01752	**800-309-6336**	508-481-0700	355-3
Kiddie Academy International Inc 108 Wheel Rd Suite 200	Bel Air	MD	21015	**800-554-3343**	410-515-0788	146
Kidney Foundation. National 30 E 33rd St Suite 1100	New York	NY	10016	**800-622-9010**	212-889-2210	48-17
Kidney Fund. American 6110 Executive Blvd Suite 1010	Rockville	MD	20852	**800-638-8299**	301-881-3052	48-17
Kidron Auction Inc 4885 Kidron Rd	Kidron	OH	44636	**800-589-9749**	330-857-2641	437
Kidron Inc PO Box 17	Kidron	OH	44636	**800-321-5421**	330-857-3011	505
Kids. Connect For 1625 K St NW Suite 1100	Washington	DC	20006	**877-236-8666**	202-638-5770	48-6
Kids & Guns. Common Sense About 1225 'I' St NW Suite 1100	Washington	DC	20005	**877-955-5437**	202-546-0200	48-6
Kids-World.net c/o SecurityBase.com PO Box 52282	Irvine	CA	92619	**877-801-0354**		145
KidsChairs 2201 Long Prairie Suite 107-195	Flower Mound	TX	75022	**800-993-5578**		314-2
Kiefer Built Inc 305 E 1st St	Kanawha	IA	50447	**888-254-3337**	641-762-3201	768
Kieffer & Co Inc 3322 Washington Ave	Sheboygan	WI	53081	**800-458-4354**	920-458-4394	692
Kienstra Inc 201 W Ferguson Ave	Wood River	IL	62095	**888-543-6787**	618-254-4366	180
KIII-TV Ch 3 (ABC) 5002 S Padre Island Dr	Corpus Christi	TX	78411	**800-874-5705**	361-986-8300	726
KIIN-TV Ch 12 (PBS) 6450 Corporate Dr	Johnston	IA	50131	**800-532-1290**	515-242-3100	726
Kilian Community College 300 E 6th St	Sioux Falls	SD	57103	**800-888-1147**	605-221-3100	160
Killeen (Greater) Chamber of Commerce 1 Santa Fe Plaza	Killeen	TX	76540	**800-869-8265**	254-526-9551	137
Killington Resort & Pico Mountain 4763 Killington Rd	Killington	VT	05751	**800-621-6867**	802-422-6200	655
Killion Industries Inc 1380 Poinsettia Ave	Vista	CA	92083	**800-421-5352**	760-727-5102	281
Kilmartin Industries DBA Roger Williams Mint 79 Walton St	Attleboro	MA	02703	**800-225-2734**	508-226-3310	479
Kimball Electronics Group 1038 E 15th St	Jasper	IN	47549	**800-634-4005**	812-634-4200	613
Kimball Home Furniture 2602 Newton St	Jasper	IN	47549	**800-482-1616**	812-482-1600	314-2
Kimball Hospitality 1205 Kimball Blvd	Jasper	IN	47549	**800-634-9510**		314-3
Kimball International Inc 1600 Royal St *NASDAQ: KBALB*	Jasper	IN	47549	**800-482-1616**	812-482-1600	184
Kimball International Inc Transwall Div 1220 Wilson Dr	West Chester	PA	19380	**800-441-9255**	610-429-1400	281
Kimball Midwest 582 W Goodale St	Columbus	OH	43215	**800-233-1294**	614-228-6701	378
Kimball Miles Co 41 W 8th Ave	Oshkosh	WI	54901	**800-546-2255**	920-231-3800	451
Kimball Office Furniture Co 1600 Royal St	Jasper	IN	47549	**800-482-1818**	812-482-1600	314-1
Kimball Terrace Inn 10 Huntington Rd	Northeast Harbor	ME	04662	**800-454-6225**	207-276-3383	373

Name / Address	City	State	ZIP	Toll-Free	Phone	Class
Kimberly-Clark 6625 Industrial Park Blvd	Fort Worth	TX	76180	**800-742-1996**	817-581-6424	469
Kimberly-Clark Corp 351 Phelps Dr *NYSE: KMB*	Irving	TX	75038	**800-544-1847**	972-281-1200	548-2
Kimberly-Clark Corp Professional Health Care Business 1400 Holcomb Bridge Rd	Roswell	GA	30076	**800-558-6452**	770-587-8000	469
Kimberly-Clark Corp Technical Paper Div 1400 Holcomb Bridge Rd	Roswell	GA	30076	**800-544-1847**	770-587-8000	542-1
Kimberly Hotel 145 E 50th St	New York	NY	10022	**800-683-0400**	212-755-0400	373
Kimble Glass Inc 537 Crystal Ave *Cust Svc	Vineland	NJ	08360	**888-546-2531***	856-692-3600	329
Kimbo Educational 10 N 3rd Ave	Long Branch	NJ	07740	**800-631-2187**	732-229-4949	242
Kimco Realty Corp 3333 New Hyde Pk Rd Suite 100 *NYSE: KIM*	New Hyde Park	NY	11042	**800-285-4626**	516-869-9000	641
KIMO-TV Ch 13 (ABC) 2700 E Tudor Rd	Anchorage	AK	99507	**877-304-1313**	907-561-1313	726
Kimpton Hotel & Restaurant Group LLC 222 Kearny St Suite 200	San Francisco	CA	94108	**800-546-2686**	415-397-5572	369
KimStaff HR 17872 Cowan Ave	Irvine	CA	92614	**800-601-4800**	949-752-2995	619
Kimwood Corp 77684 Hwy 99 S	Cottage Grove	OR	97424	**800-942-4401**	541-942-4401	809
Kincaid Coach Lines Inc 9207 Woodend Rd	Edwardsville	KS	66111	**800-998-1901**	913-441-6200	748
Kincaid Furniture Co Inc 240 Pleasant Hill Rd	Hudson	NC	28638	**800-438-8207**	828-728-3261	314-2
Kinco International 4286 NE 185th Ave	Portland	OR	97230	**800-547-8410**	503-674-9002	153-8
Kinco Ltd 5245 Old Kings Rd	Jacksonville	FL	32254	**800-342-0244**	904-355-1476	232
Kind & Knox Gelatine Inc PO Box 927	Sioux City	IA	51102	**888-443-5482**	712-943-5516	291-22
Kinder-Harris Inc 203 E 22nd St	Stuttgart	AR	72160	**800-688-8839**	870-673-1518	356
Kinder Morgan Bulk Terminals Inc 7116 Hwy 22	Sorrento	LA	70778	**800-535-8170**	225-675-5387	457
Kinder Morgan Energy Partners LP 500 Dallas St Suite 1000 *NYSE: KMP*	Houston	TX	77002	**888-844-5657**	713-369-9000	320
Kinder Morgan Inc 500 Dallas St Suite 1000 *NYSE: KMI*	Houston	TX	77002	**800-525-3752**	713-369-9000	774
Kinder Morgan Inc KN Energy Retail Div 370 Van Gordon St	Lakewood	CO	80228	**800-232-1627**	303-989-1740	774
Kinder Morgan Management LLC 500 Dallas St 1 Allen Ctr Suite 1000 *NYSE: KMR*	Houston	TX	77002	**800-324-2900**	713-369-9000	320
Kinder Morgan Texas Pipeline LP 500 Dallas St Suite 1000	Houston	TX	77002	**800-324-2900**	713-369-9000	320
KinderCam Inc 5500 Peachtree Pkwy	Norcross	GA	30092	**888-522-6123**	678-966-3000	145
KinderCare Learning Centers Inc 650 NE Holladay St Suite 1400	Portland	OR	97232	**800-633-1488**	503-872-1300	146
Kindred Healthcare Inc 680 S 4th Ave *NASDAQ: KIND*	Louisville	KY	40202	**800-545-0749**	502-596-7300	348
Kindred Hospital Greensboro 2401 Southside Blvd	Greensboro	NC	27406	**877-836-2671**	336-271-2800	441
Kindt-Collins Co 12651 Elmwood Ave	Cleveland	OH	44111	**800-321-3170**	216-252-4122	3
Kinecor 451 Lebeau Blvd	Saint-Laurent	QC	H4N1S2	**866-546-3267**	514-333-7010	378
Kinecta Federal Credit Union 1440 Rosecrans Ave	Manhattan Beach	CA	90266	**800-854-9846**	310-643-5400	216
Kinedyne Inc 151 Industrial Pkwy	North Branch	NJ	08876	**800-848-6057**	908-231-1800	666
Kinefac Corp 156 Goddard Memorial Dr	Worcester	MA	01603	**800-458-5941**	508-754-6891	448
Kinesiology Assn. Touch for Health PO Box 392	New Carlisle	OH	45344	**800-466-8342**	937-845-3404	48-17
Kinesis Corp 22121 17th Ave SE Suite 112	Bothell	WA	98021	**800-454-6374**	425-402-8100	171-1
Kinetic Concepts Inc (KCI Inc) 8023 Vantage Dr *NYSE: KCI*	San Antonio	TX	78230	**800-531-5346**	210-524-9000	469
Kinetics Systems Inc 26055 SW Canyon Creek Rd	Wilsonville	OR	97070	**800-888-7597**	503-224-5200	188-10
King Art & Craft Supply Co Inc 142 N Main St PO Box 671	Herkimer	NY	13350	**800-777-1975**	315-866-5500	44
King Bio Pharmaceuticals Inc 3 Westside Dr	Asheville	NC	28806	**888-827-6414**	828-255-9818	572
King & Co Inc PO Box 10 *Cust Svc	Clarksville	AR	72830	**800-643-9530***	479-754-6090	590
King College 1350 King College Rd *Admissions	Bristol	TN	37620	**800-362-0014***	423-968-1187	163
King County 701 5th Ave Suite 3210	Seattle	WA	98104	**800-325-6165**	206-296-4040	334
King County Journal 600 Washington Ave S	Kent	WA	98032	**888-399-3999**	253-872-6600	522-2
King Edward Inn 5780-88 West St	Halifax	NS	B3K1H9	**800-565-5464**	902-422-3266	372
King Electrical Mfg Co 9131 10th Ave S	Seattle	WA	98108	**800-603-5464**	206-762-0400	37
King Engineering Corp 3201 S State St *Cust Svc	Ann Arbor	MI	48106	**800-959-0128***	734-662-5691	19
King Estate Winery 80854 Territorial Rd	Eugene	OR	97405	**800-884-4441**	541-942-9874	50
King Features Syndicate Inc 888 7th Ave 2nd Fl	New York	NY	10019	**800-526-5464**	212-455-4000	520
King Fisher Marine Services Inc 159 Hwy 316	Port Lavaca	TX	77979	**888-553-6751**	361-552-6751	187-5
King Industries Inc Science Rd	Norwalk	CT	06852	**800-431-7900**	203-866-5551	143
King Kamehameha's Kona Beach Hotel 75-5660 Palani Rd	Kailua-Kona	HI	96740	**800-367-2111**	808-329-2911	373
King Koil Licensing Co Inc 15 Salt Creek Ln Suite 210	Hinsdale	IL	60521	**800-525-8331**	630-230-9744	463
King LC Mfg Co Inc 24 7th St PO Box 367	Bristol	TN	37620	**800-826-2510**	423-764-5188	153-19
King Louie International Inc 13500 15th St	Grandview	MO	64030	**800-521-5212**	816-765-5212	153-1
King Mountain Ranch PO Box 497	Granby	CO	80446	**800-476-5464**	970-887-2511	238
King Nut Co 31900 Solon Rd	Solon	OH	44139	**800-498-5690**	440-248-8484	291-28
King Pacific Lodge 255 W 1st St Suite 214	North Vancouver	BC	V7M3G8	**888-592-5464**	604-987-5452	372
King Pharmaceuticals Inc 501 5th St *NYSE: KG*	Bristol	TN	37620	**800-776-3637**	423-989-8000	572
King Plastics Inc 840 N Elm St	Orange	CA	92867	**800-997-7540**	714-997-7540	596
King & Prince Beach & Golf Resort 201 Arnold Rd	Saint Simons Island	GA	31522	**800-342-0212**	912-638-3631	655
King & Prince Seafood Corp 1 King & Prince Blvd	Brunswick	GA	31520	**800-841-0205**	912-265-5155	291-14
King Provision Corp 9009 Regency Square Blvd	Jacksonville	FL	32211	**888-781-5464**	904-781-9888	295
King Publishing Group 1325 G St NW Suite 1003	Washington	DC	20005	**800-926-5464**	202-638-4260	623-9
King Ranch Inc PO Box 1090	Kingsville	TX	78364	**800-375-6411**	361-592-6411	11-1
King Relocation Services 13535 Larwin Cir	Santa Fe Springs	CA	90670	**800-854-3679**	562-921-0555	508
King Sash & Door Inc PO Box 1029	Mocksville	NC	27028	**800-642-0886**	336-768-4650	234
King Ward Coach Lines 110 N Bridge St	Holyoke	MA	01040	**800-639-4805**	413-539-5858	108
King Wire Inc 2500 Commonwealth Ave	North Chicago	IL	60064	**800-453-5464**	847-688-1100	245
Kingbridge Centre 12750 Jane St	King City	ON	L7B1A3	**800-827-7221**	905-833-3086	370
Kingdom of Callaway Chamber of Commerce 409 Court St	Fulton	MO	65251	**800-257-3554**	573-642-3055	137
King's College 133 N River St	Wilkes-Barre	PA	18711	**800-955-5777**	570-208-5900	163
Kings County Truck Lines PO Box 1016	Tulare	CA	93275	**800-842-5285**	559-686-2857	769
Kings Courier 1733 Sheepshead Bay Rd	Brooklyn	NY	11235	**800-564-5433**	718-615-2500	522-4
King's Daughters' Hospital 1 King's Daughters' Dr	Madison	IN	47250	**800-272-5341**	812-265-5211	366-2
Kings Island 6300 Kings Island Dr	Kings Island	OH	45034	**800-288-0808**	513-754-5700	32
Kings Island Resort & Conference Center 5691 Kings Island Dr	Mason	OH	45040	**800-704-2439**	513-398-0115	373
Kings Landing Historical Settlement 20 Kings Landing Service Entrance Rd Unit 2	Kings Lndg Hist Settlemnt	NB	E6K3W3	**888-666-5547**	506-363-4999	509
King's Material Inc PO Box 368	Cedar Rapids	IA	52406	**800-332-5298**	319-363-0233	181
Kingsbury Inc 10385 Drummond Rd	Philadelphia	PA	19154	**800-898-8912**	215-824-4000	609
Kingsdown Inc PO Box 388 *Cust Svc	Mebane	NC	27302	**800-354-5464***	919-563-3531	463
Kingsley Hotel & Suites 39475 N Woodward Ave	Bloomfield Hills	MI	48304	**800-544-6835**	248-644-1400	373
Kingsmill Resort & Spa 1010 Kingsmill Rd	Williamsburg	VA	23185	**800-832-5665**	757-253-1703	655
Kingsport Convention & Visitors Bureau PO Box 1403	Kingsport	TN	37662	**800-743-5282**	423-392-8820	205
Kingsport Publishing Co 701 Lynn Garden Dr	Kingsport	TN	37660	**800-251-0328**	423-246-8121	623-8
Kingsport Times-News 701 Lynn Garden Dr	Kingsport	TN	37660	**800-251-0328**	423-246-8121	522-2
Kingston Oil Supply Corp PO Box 760	Port Ewen	NY	12466	**800-755-6726**	845-331-0770	311
Kingston Technology Co 17600 Newhope St	Fountain Valley	CA	92708	**800-835-6575**	714-435-2600	283
Kingsway Financial Services Inc 5310 Explorer Dr Suite 200 *NYSE: KFS*	Mississauga	ON	L4W5H8	**800-265-5458**	905-629-7888	384-4
Kingway Material Handling 240 Northpoint Pkwy	Acworth	GA	30102	**800-554-6632**	770-917-9700	462
Kingwood College 20000 Kingwood Dr	Kingwood	TX	77339	**800-883-7939**	281-312-1600	160
KINK-FM 101.9 (AAA) 1501 SW Jefferson St	Portland	OR	97201	**877-567-5465**	503-517-6000	631
Kinka Cards 1 Orchard Park Rd	Madison	CT	06443	**800-635-4652**		130
Kinko's (now FedEx Kinko's Office & Print Services Inc) 13155 Noel Rd Suite 1600 *Cust Svc	Dallas	TX	75240	**800-254-6567***	214-550-7000	114
Kinney AM Inc 150 E 4th St	Cincinnati	OH	45202	**800-265-3682**	513-421-2265	258
Kinney Brick Co 100 Prosperity Rd	Albuquerque	NM	87105	**800-464-4605**	505-877-4550	148
Kinney Drugs Inc 29 E Main St	Gouverneur	NY	13642	**800-552-8044**	315-287-1500	236
Kinnie Annex Cartage Co 32097 Hollingsworth Ave	Warren	MI	48092	**888-546-6432**	586-939-2880	769
Kinray Inc 152-35 10th Ave	Whitestone	NY	11357	**800-854-6729**	718-767-1234	237
Kinross Gold USA Inc 670 Sierra Rose Dr	Reno	NV	89511	**800-644-3547**	775-829-1000	492
Kinsley Construction Inc 2700 Water St	York	PA	17403	**800-546-7539**	717-741-3841	185
Kinsley & Sons Inc PO Box 8539	Saint Louis	MO	63126	**800-468-4428**	314-843-0400	401
Kinston Convention & Visitors Bureau PO Box 157	Kinston	NC	28502	**800-869-0032**	252-523-2500	205
Kintetsu World Express USA Inc 100 Jericho Quadrangle Suite 326	Jericho	NY	11753	**800-275-4045**	516-933-7100	440
Kinyo Co Inc 14235 Lomitas Ave	La Puente	CA	91746	**800-735-4696**	626-333-3711	171-5
Kinzan Inc 5857 Owens Ave Suite 112	Carlsbad	CA	92008	**800-963-8424**	760-602-2900	39
KIOI-FM 101.3 (AC) 340 Townsend St 4th Fl	San Francisco	CA	94107	**800-800-1013**	415-975-5555	631
KION-TV Ch 46 (CBS) 1550 Moffett St	Salinas	CA	93905	**800-321-5222**	831-422-3500	726
Kiplinger Agriculture Letter 1729 H St NW *Circ	Washington	DC	20006	**800-544-0155***	202-887-6400	521-13
Kiplinger California Letter 1729 H St NW	Washington	DC	20006	**800-544-0155**	202-887-6400	521-6
Kiplinger Retirement Report 1729 H St NW	Washington	DC	20006	**800-544-0155**	202-887-6400	521-6
Kiplinger Tax Letter 1729 H St NW	Washington	DC	20006	**800-544-0155**	202-887-6400	521-7
Kiplinger Washington Editors Inc 1729 H St NW	Washington	DC	20006	**800-544-0155**	202-887-6400	623-9
Kiplinger Washington Letter 1729 H St NW	Washington	DC	20006	**800-544-0155**	202-887-6400	521-7

Name / Address	City	State	ZIP	Toll-Free	Phone	Class
Kiplinger's Personal Finance Magazine 1729 H St NW	Washington	DC	20006	**800-544-0155**	202-887-6400	449-11
KIQK-FM 104.1 (Ctry) 306 1/2 E Saint Joseph St	Rapid City	SD	57701	**800-456-2613**	605-343-0888	631
Kirby Co 1920 W 114th St	Cleveland	OH	44102	**800-437-7170**	216-228-2400	775
Kirby Lithographic Co Inc 2900 S Eads St	Arlington	VA	22202	**800-932-3594**	703-684-7600	614
Kirchman Corp PO Box 2269 *Cust Svc	Orlando	FL	32802	**800-327-1892***	407-831-3001	176-11
Kirk & Blum Mfg Co Inc 3120 Forrer St	Cincinnati	OH	45209	**800-333-5475**	513-458-2600	188-12
Kirkegaard & Perry Laboratories Inc 2 Cessna Ct	Gaithersburg	MD	20879	**800-638-3167**	301-948-7755	229
Kirkpatrick Concrete Co 2909 3rd Ave N	Birmingham	AL	35203	**800-489-0205**	205-323-8327	180
Kirkpatrick Pettis Inc 10250 Regency Cir Suite 500	Omaha	NE	68114	**800-776-5777**	402-397-5777	679
Kirkpatrick Science & Air Space Museum at Omniplex 2100 NE 52nd St	Oklahoma City	OK	73111	**800-532-7652**	405-602-6664	509
Kirkwood Community College 6301 Kirkwood Blvd SW	Cedar Rapids	IA	52404	**800-332-2055**	319-398-5411	160
Kirkwood Industries Inc 4855 W 130th St *Cust Svc	Cleveland	OH	44135	**800-262-2266***	216-267-6200	507
Kirsch Div Newell Rubbermaid Inc 916 S Arcade Ave	Freeport	IL	61032	**800-328-7290**	815-235-4171	88
Kirschman Morris Co Inc 5050 Almonaster St	New Orleans	LA	70126	**800-289-9430**	504-947-6673	316
Kirtac Inc 111 Carey Dr	Noblesville	IN	46060	**800-776-1646**	317-773-7855	656
Kishwaukee Community Hospital 626 Bethany Rd	DeKalb	IL	60115	**800-397-1521**	815-756-1521	366-2
Kiski School 1888 Brett Ln	Saltsburg	PA	15681	**877-547-5448**	724-639-3586	611
Kislak JI Inc 7900 Miami Lakes Dr W	Miami Lakes	FL	33016	**800-233-7164**	305-364-4100	498
KISQ-FM 98.1 (Urban AC) 340 Townsend St 4th Fl	San Francisco	CA	94107	**888-354-7736**	415-975-5555	631
Kissimmee-Saint Cloud Convention & Visitors Bureau 1925 E Irlo Bronson Memorial Hwy	Kissimmee	FL	34744	**800-327-9159**	407-847-5000	205
Kistler Instrument Corp 75 John Glenn Dr	Amherst	NY	14228	**888-547-8537**	716-691-5100	464
Kistler-Morse Corp 150 Venture Blvd	Spartanburg	SC	29306	**800-426-9010**	864-574-2763	200
Kistner Concrete Products Inc 8713 Read Rd	East Pembroke	NY	14056	**800-809-2801**	585-762-8216	181
KISU-TV Ch 10 (PBS) Idaho State University CB 8111 921 S 8th Ave	Pocatello	ID	83209	**800-543-6868**	208-282-2857	726
Kit Carson Electric Co-op Inc PO Box 587	Taos	NM	87571	**800-688-6780**	505-758-2258	244
Kitano New York 66 Park Ave	New York	NY	10016	**800-548-2666**	212-885-7000	373
Kitayama Brothers Inc 13239 Weld County Rd 4	Brighton	CO	80601	**800-829-5323**	303-659-8005	363
Kitchen & Bath Assn. National 687 Willow Grove St	Hackettstown	NJ	07840	**800-843-6522**	908-852-0033	49-3
Kitchen Collection Inc 71 E Water St	Chillicothe	OH	45601	**800-292-9150**	740-773-9150	357
Kitchen Craft of Canada Ltd 1180 Springfield Rd	Winnipeg	MB	R2C2Z2	**800-463-9707**	204-224-3211	116
Kitchen Resource LLC 3767 S 150 East	Salt Lake City	UT	84115	**800-692-6724**	801-261-3222	35
Kitchen Solvers Inc 401 Jay St	La Crosse	WI	54601	**800-845-6779**	608-791-5516	188-11
Kitchen Tune-Up Inc 813 Circle Dr	Aberdeen	SD	57401	**800-333-6385**	605-225-4049	188-11
KitchenAid Div Whirlpool Corp 2000 M-63 N	Benton Harbor	MI	49022	**800-253-1301**	269-923-5000	37
Kitsap Regional Library 1301 Sylvan Way	Bremerton	WA	98310	**877-883-9900**	360-405-9110	426
Kittery Trading Post 301 US Rt 1	Kittery	ME	03904	**888-587-6246**	207-439-2700	155-2
Kittredge Equipment Co Inc 2155 Columbus Ave	Springfield	MA	01104	**800-423-7082**	413-788-6101	295
Kitty Askins Hospice Center 2402 Wayne Memorial Dr	Goldsboro	NC	27534	**800-260-4442**	919-735-1387	365
Kitty Hawk Inc 1515 W 20th St PO Box 612787 *AMEX: KHK*	DFW Airport	TX	75261	**800-486-3780**	972-456-2200	13
Kiwanis Magazine 3636 Woodview Trace	Indianapolis	IN	46268	**800-549-2647**	317-875-8755	449-10
Kiwash Electric Co-op Inc PO Box 100	Cordell	OK	73632	**888-832-3362**	580-832-3361	244
KIXI-AM 880 (Nost) 3650 131st Ave SE Suite 550	Bellevue	WA	98006	**866-880-5494**	425-373-5536	631
KIYX-FM 106.1 (AC) PO Box 1	Platteville	WI	53818	**800-362-2224**	608-348-2775	631
KJ Brewco Collision Repair Systems Inc 309 Exchange Ave	Conway	AR	72032	**800-582-5215**	501-505-2794	379
KJLA-TV Ch 57 (Ind) 2323 Corinth Ave	Los Angeles	CA	90064	**800-588-5788**	310-943-5288	726
KJMN-FM 92.1 (Span AC) 777 Grant St 5th Fl	Denver	CO	80203	**888-874-2656**	303-832-0050	631
KJR-AM 950 (Sports) 351 Elliott Ave W Suite 300	Seattle	WA	98119	**800-829-0950**	206-285-2295	631
KJTY-FM 88.1 (Rel) 1005 SW 10th St	Topeka	KS	66604	**888-569-5589**	785-357-8888	631
KJZZ-FM 91.5 (NPR) 2323 W 14th St	Tempe	AZ	85281	**800-266-1111**	480-834-5627	631
KKAD-AM 1550 (Nost) 888 SW 5th Ave Suite 790	Portland	OR	97204	**866-517-1550**	503-228-5523	631
KKCB-FM 105.1 (Ctry) 14 E Central Entrance	Duluth	MN	55811	**800-928-2105**	218-727-4500	631
KKDV-FM 95.7 (Ctry) 201 3rd St Suite 1200	San Francisco	CA	94103	**800-905-9570**	415-957-0957	631
KKE Architects Inc 300 1st Ave N	Minneapolis	MN	55401	**866-224-6499**	612-339-4200	258
KKHT-AM 1070 (Rel) 6161 Savoy St Suite 1200	Houston	TX	77036	**800-625-1070**	713-260-3600	631
KKJZ-FM 88.1 (Jazz) 1288 N Bellflower Blvd	Long Beach	CA	90815	**800-767-3688**	562-985-5566	631
KKPX-TV Ch 65 (PAX) 848 Battery St	San Francisco	CA	94111	**888-467-2988**	415-276-1400	726
KKRZ-FM 100.3 (CHR) 4949 SW Macadam Ave	Portland	OR	97239	**888-843-0100**	503-225-1190	631
KKSF-FM 103.7 (NAC) 340 Townsend St 4th Fl	San Francisco	CA	94107	**866-900-1037**	415-975-5555	631

Name / Address	City	State	ZIP	Toll-Free	Phone	Class
KL Industries 1790 Sun Dolphin Dr	Muskegon	MI	49444	**800-733-2727**	231-733-2725	701
Klamath Blue Green Inc 301 S Old Stage Rd	Mount Shasta	CA	96067	**800-327-1956**	530-926-6684	786
Klamath County Chamber of Commerce 706 Main St	Klamath Falls	OR	97601	**877-552-6284**	541-884-5193	137
Klarbrunn Inc 860 West St	Watertown	WI	53094	**800-910-2837**	920-262-6300	792
Klaus Radio Inc 8400 N Allen Rd	Peoria	IL	61615	**800-545-5287**	309-691-4840	38
Klaussner Furniture Industries Inc 405 Lewallen Rd *Cust Svc	Asheboro	NC	27205	**800-828-9534***	336-625-6174	314-2
KLC Inc DBA Unicapital Leasing 433 New Park Ave	West Hartford	CT	06110	**800-444-8333**	860-233-3663	214
KLDJ-FM 101.7 (Oldies) 14 E Central Entrance	Duluth	MN	55811	**888-564-1017**	218-727-4500	631
Klear-Vu Corp 135 Alden St	Fall River	MA	02723	**800-732-8723**	508-674-5723	731
Kleen Test Products Inc 8225 W Parkland Ct	Milwaukee	WI	53223	**800-558-6842**	414-357-7444	548-2
Kleen-Tex Industries Inc 1516 Orchard Hill Rd	LaGrange	GA	30240	**800-241-2323**	706-882-8134	497
Klein Calvin Cosmetics 725 5th Ave Trump Tower	New York	NY	10022	**800-715-4023**	212-326-6800	564
Klein & Co Corporate Housing Services Inc 6312 S Fiddlers Green Cir Suite 230E	Englewood	CO	80111	**800-208-9826**	303-796-2100	209
Klein Landau & Romm 1725 K St NW	Washington	DC	20006	**866-807-1931**	202-728-0100	262
Klein Steel Service 105 Vanguarden Pkwy	Rochester	NY	14606	**800-477-6789**	585-328-4000	483
Klein Tools Inc PO Box 599033 *Cust Svc	Skokie	IL	60659	**800-553-4676***	847-677-9500	746
Klein Tools Inc Fort Smith Div 5721-A S Zero St	Fort Smith	AR	72903	**800-325-5723**	479-646-7347	423
Klement Sausage Co Inc 207 E Lincoln Ave	Milwaukee	WI	53207	**800-553-6368**	414-744-2330	291-26
KLH Audio Systems 11131 Dora St	Sun Valley	CA	91352	**800-854-4441**	818-767-2843	52
Kline William J & Son Inc 1 Venner Rd	Amsterdam	NY	12010	**800-453-6397**	518-843-1100	623-8
Kling 2301 Chestnut St	Philadelphia	PA	19103	**800-888-2054**	215-569-2900	258
Klinger Georgette Inc 501 Madison Ave	New York	NY	10022	**800-554-6437**	212-838-3200	79
Klingspor Abrasives Inc 2555 Tate Blvd SE	Hickory	NC	28602	**800-645-5555**	828-322-3030	1
Klipsch LLC 137 County Rd 278	Hope	AR	71801	**800-554-7724**	870-777-6751	52
Klitzner Industries Inc 44 Warren St	Providence	RI	02907	**800-556-6860**	401-751-7500	401
KLJC-FM 88.5 (Rel) 15800 Calvary Rd	Kansas City	MO	64147	**800-466-5552**	816-331-8700	631
KLLC-FM 97.3 (AC) 865 Battery St 3rd Fl	San Francisco	CA	94111	**800-400-3697**	415-765-4000	631
KLLM Transport Services Inc 135 Riverview Dr	Richland	MS	39218	**800-925-1000**	601-939-2545	769
KLN Steel Products Co PO Box 34690	San Antonio	TX	78265	**800-624-9101**	210-227-4747	314-3
KLNV-FM 106.5 (Span) 600 W Broadway Suite 2150	San Diego	CA	92101	**877-570-1065**	619-235-0600	631
KLNZ-FM 103.5 (Span) 501 N 44th St Suite 425	Phoenix	AZ	85008	**888-874-2656**	602-266-2005	631
KLO-AM 1430 (N/T) 4155 Harrison Blvd Suite 206	Ogden	UT	84403	**866-627-1430**	801-627-1430	631
KLOB-FM 94.7 (Span) 41601 Corporate Way	Palm Desert	CA	92260	**888-331-2667**	760-341-5837	631
Klochko Equipment Rental Co 2782 Corbin Ave	Melvindale	MI	48122	**800-783-7368**	313-386-7220	261-2
KLOK-FM 99.5 (Span) 67 Garden Ct	Monterey	CA	93940	**888-874-2656**	831-333-9735	631
Kloppenberg & Co 2627 W Oxford Ave	Englewood	CO	80110	**800-346-3246**	303-761-1615	650
KLOS-FM 95.5 (CR) 3321 S La Cienega Blvd	Los Angeles	CA	90016	**800-955-5567**	310-840-4900	631
Klosterman Baking Co Inc 4760 Paddock Rd	Cincinnati	OH	45229	**877-301-1004**	513-242-1004	291-1
KLPB-TV Ch 24 (PBS) 7733 Perkins Rd	Baton Rouge	LA	70810	**800-272-8161**	225-767-5660	726
KLQV-FM 102.9 (Span AC) 600 W Broadway Suite 2150	San Diego	CA	92101	**877-570-1065**	619-235-0600	631
KLRN-TV Ch 9 (PBS) 501 Broadway St	San Antonio	TX	78215	**800-627-8193**	210-270-9000	726
KLSE-FM 91.7 (Clas) 206 S Broadway Suite 735	Rochester	MN	55904	**800-652-9700**	507-282-0910	631
KLSY-FM 92.5 (AC) 3650 131st Ave SE Suite 550	Bellevue	WA	98006	**866-649-9250**	425-653-9462	631
KLTY-FM 94.9 (Rel) 6400 N Beltline Rd Suite 120	Irving	TX	75063	**866-562-1949**	972-870-9949	631
Kluber Lubrication North America LP 32 Industrial Dr	Londonderry	NH	03053	**888-455-8237**	603-434-7704	530
Klukwan Inc PO Box 209	Haines	AK	99827	**800-558-5926**	907-766-2211	439
Klutz 455 Portage Ave	Palo Alto	CA	94306	**800-737-4123**	650-857-0888	623-2
KM Systems Inc 4910 Starcrest Dr *Sales	Monroe	NC	28111	**800-438-1937***	704-289-9212	681
KMA The Agency 7160 Dallas Pkwy Suite 400	Plano	TX	75024	**800-562-4161**	972-244-1900	312
KMAJ-AM 1440 (N/T) 825 S Kansas Ave Suite 100	Topeka	KS	66612	**877-297-1077**	785-272-2122	631
KMAJ-FM 107.7 (AC) 825 S Kansas Ave Suite 100	Topeka	KS	66612	**877-297-1077**	785-272-2122	631
Kmart Corp 3100 W Big Beaver Rd *NASDAQ: KMRT* ■ *Cust Svc	Troy	MI	48084	**866-562-7848***	248-643-1000	227
KMBX-AM 700 (Span Oldies) 67 Garden Ct	Monterey	CA	93940	**866-434-4084**	831-333-9735	631
KMC Telecom Holdings Inc 1545 Rt 206 Suite 300	Bedminster	NJ	07921	**877-470-2100**	908-470-2100	721
KME Fire Apparatus 68 Sicker Rd	Latham	NY	12110	**800-394-5593**	518-861-8535	505
KMEL-FM 106.1 (Urban) 340 Townsend St 4th Fl	San Francisco	CA	94107	**800-955-5635**	415-975-5555	631
KMFC-FM 92.1 (Rel) 1249 E Hwy 22	Centralia	MO	65240	**800-769-5632**	573-682-5525	631
KMGN-FM 93.9 (CR) 1117 W Rt 66	Flagstaff	AZ	86001	**888-893-5646**	928-774-5231	631
KMI Diagnostics Inc 8201 Central Ave NE Suite P	Minneapolis	MN	55432	**888-523-1246**	763-780-2955	229
KMIZ-TV Ch 17 (ABC) 501 Business Loop 70 E	Columbia	MO	65201	**800-441-4485**	573-449-0917	726

Name / Address	City	State	Zip	Toll-Free	Phone	Class
KMOS-TV Ch 6 (PBS) Central Missouri State University	Warrensburg	MO	64093	**800-753-3436**	660-543-4134	726
KMOV-TV Ch 4 (CBS) 1 Memorial Dr	Saint Louis	MO	63102	**800-477-5668**	314-621-4444	726
KMPS-FM 94.1 (Ctry) 1000 Dexter Ave N Suite 100	Seattle	WA	98109	**800-464-9436**	206-805-1100	631
KMTT-FM 103.7 (AAA) 1100 Olive Way Suite 1650	Seattle	WA	98101	**800-676-5688**	206-233-1037	631
KMVP-AM 860 (Sports) 5300 N Central Ave	Phoenix	AZ	85012	**800-729-3776**	602-274-6200	631
KMXA-AM 1090 (Span) 777 Grant St 5th Fl	Denver	CO	80203	**888-874-2656**	303-832-0050	631
KMZ Rosenman 525 W Monroe St Suite 1300	Chicago	IL	60661	**800-346-7400**	312-902-5200	419
KN Energy Retail Div Kinder Morgan Inc 370 Van Gordon St	Lakewood	CO	80228	**800-232-1627**	303-989-1740	774
Knaack Mfg Co 420 E Terra Cotta Ave	Crystal Lake	IL	60014	**800-456-7865**	815-459-6020	479
Knappen Milling Co 110 S Water St	Augusta	MI	49012	**800-562-7736**	269-731-4141	291-23
Knauf Insulation 1 Knauf Dr	Shelbyville	IN	46176	**800-825-4434**	317-398-4434	382
Knauss EW & Sons Inc 625 E Broad St	Quakertown	PA	18951	**800-648-4220**	215-536-4220	465
KNBT Bancorp Inc 90 Highland Ave *NASDAQ: KNBT*	Bethlehem	PA	18017	**800-996-2062**	610-861-5000	355-2
KNDD-FM 107.7 (Alt) 1100 Olive Way Suite 1650	Seattle	WA	98101	**800-423-1077**	206-622-3251	631
KNDR-FM 104.7 (Rel) 1400 NE 3rd St	Mandan	ND	58554	**800-767-5095**	701-663-2345	631
KNDX-TV Ch 26 (Fox) 3130 E Broadway Ave	Bismarck	ND	58501	**877-563-9369**	701-355-0026	726
K'NEX Industries 2990 Bergey Rd PO box 700	Hatfield	PA	19440	**800-543-5639**	215-997-7722	750
KNI Inc 1261 S State College Pkwy	Anaheim	CA	92806	**800-886-7301**	714-956-7300	614
Knickerbocker Hotel Chicago. Millennium 163 E Walton Pl	Chicago	IL	60611	**800-621-8140**	312-751-8100	373
Knife River Corp 1915 N Kavaney Dr	Bismarck	ND	58501	**800-982-5339**	701-223-1771	135
Knight Capital Group Inc 525 Washington Blvd Newport Tower 23rd Fl *NASDAQ: NITE*	Jersey City	NJ	07310	**800-544-7508**	201-222-9400	679
Knight & Hale Game Calls PO Box 1587	Fort Smith	AR	72901	**800-500-9357**	479-782-8971	701
Knight John S Convention Center 77 E Mill St	Akron	OH	44308	**800-245-4254**	330-374-8900	204
Knight John S & James L Foundation 200 S Biscayne Blvd Suite 3300	Miami	FL	33131	**800-711-2004**	305-908-2600	300
Knight Peggy Solutions Inc 180 Harbor Dr Suite 221	Sausalito	CA	94965	**800-997-7753**	415-289-1777	342
Knight Publishing Co 600 S Tryon St	Charlotte	NC	28202	**800-332-0686**	704-358-5000	623-8
Knight Ridder Digital 35 S Market St	San Jose	CA	95113	**877-732-5248**	408-938-6000	795
Knight Ridder/Tribune Information Services 700 12th St NW Suite 1000	Washington	DC	20005	**800-346-8798**	202-383-6080	520
Knight Transportation Inc 5601 W Buckeye Rd *NASDAQ: KNGT*	Phoenix	AZ	85043	**800-489-2000**	602-269-2000	769
Knights of Columbus 1 Columbus Plaza	New Haven	CT	06510	**800-524-3611**	203-752-4000	48-15
Knights of Columbus Museum 1 State St	New Haven	CT	06510	**800-524-3611**	203-772-2130	509
Knights Franchise Systems Inc Knights Inns 1 Sylvan Way	Parsippany	NJ	07054	**800-418-8977**	973-428-9700	369
Knights Inns 1 Sylvan Way	Parsippany	NJ	07054	**800-418-8977**	973-428-9700	369
KNIS-FM 91.3 (Rel) 6363 Hwy 50 E	Carson City	NV	89701	**800-541-5647**	775-883-5647	631
Knitting Guild of America (TKGA) 1100-H Brandywine Blvd PO Box 3388	Zanesville	OH	43702	**800-969-6069**	740-452-4541	48-18
Knitting Machine & Supply Co Inc 1257 Westfield Ave	Clark	NJ	07066	**877-898-2900**	732-382-9898	729
KNLE-FM 88.1 (Rel) 12703 Research Blvd Suite 222	Austin	TX	78759	**800-322-5653**	512-257-8881	631
KNLJ-TV Ch 25 (Ind) 9810 SR-AE	New Bloomfield	MO	65063	**800-228-5284**	573-896-5105	726
KNME-TV Ch 5 (PBS) 1130 University Blvd NE University of New Mexico	Albuquerque	NM	87131	**800-328-5663**	505-277-2121	726
KNML-AM 610 (Sports) 500 4th St NW Suite 500	Albuquerque	NM	87102	**888-922-0610**	505-767-6700	631
Knob Hill Inn 960 N Main St PO Box 800 *Resv	Ketchum	ID	83340	**800-526-8010***	208-726-8010	373
Knockout Pest Control Inc 1009 Front St	Uniondale	NY	11553	**800-244-7378**	516-489-7817	567
Knoebels Amusement Resort PO Box 317	Elysburg	PA	17824	**800-487-4386**	570-672-2572	32
Knoll Inc 1235 Water St *NYSE: KNL* ■ *Cust Svc	East Greenville	PA	18041	**800-343-5665***	215-679-7991	314-1
Knopp Inc 1307 66th St	Emeryville	CA	94608	**800-227-1848**	510-653-1661	247
Knorr Beeswax Products Inc 1965 Kellogg Ave	Carlsbad	CA	92008	**800-807-2337**	760-431-2007	122
Knott's Berry Farm Resort 7675 Crescent Ave	Buena Park	CA	90620	**866-752-2444**	714-995-1111	655
Knouse Foods Co-op Inc 800 Peach Glen-Idaville Rd	Peach Glen	PA	17375	**800-827-7537**	717-677-8181	291-20
knovel.com 13 Eaton Ave	Norwich	NY	13815	**888-238-1626**	607-337-5600	623-11
KNOW-FM 91.1 (NPR) 45 E 7th St	Saint Paul	MN	55101	**800-228-7123**	651-290-1500	631
Know Before You Go Reservations 4720 W Irlo Bronson Memorial Hwy	Kissimmee	FL	34746	**800-749-1993**	407-352-9813	368
KnowledgePlanet.com 5095 Ritter Rd Suite 400	Mechanicsburg	PA	17055	**800-869-5763**	717-790-0400	193
KnowX LLC 730 Peachtree St Suite 700	Atlanta	GA	30308	**877-317-5000**	404-541-0221	621
Knox College 2 E South St	Galesburg	IL	61401	**800-678-5669**	309-341-7100	163
Knox County Convention & Visitors Bureau 107 S Main St	Mount Vernon	OH	43050	**800-837-5282**	740-392-6102	205
Knox Nursery Inc 4349 N Hiawassee Rd	Orlando	FL	32818	**800-441-5669**	407-293-3721	363
Knox RC & Co Inc 1 Goodwin Sq 24th Fl	Hartford	CT	06103	**800-742-2765**	860-524-7600	383
Knox RF Co Inc PO Box 1337	Smyrna	GA	30081	**800-989-7401**	770-434-7401	688
Knoxville News-Sentinel 2332 News Sentinel Dr	Knoxville	TN	37921	**800-237-5821**	865-523-3131	522-2
Knoxville Tourism & Sports Corp 301 S Gay St	Knoxville	TN	37902	**866-790-5373**	865-523-7263	205
KNRK-FM 94.7 (Alt) 0700 SW Bancroft St	Portland	OR	97239	**800-777-0947**	503-223-1441	631
KNXV-TV Ch 15 (ABC) 515 N 44th St	Phoenix	AZ	85008	**800-803-3277**	602-273-1500	726
Ko-Rec-Type Div Barouh Eaton Allen Corp 67 Kent Ave	Brooklyn	NY	11211	**800-366-6767**	718-782-2601	616
Koala Corp 7881 S Wheeling Ct	Englewood	CO	80112	**888-733-3456**	303-539-8300	340
KOAT-TV Ch 7 (ABC) 3801 Carlisle Blvd NE	Albuquerque	NM	87107	**800-421-6159**	505-884-7777	726
Kobe Steel USA Inc 535 Madison Ave	New York	NY	10022	**888-562-3872**	212-751-9400	709
Kobuk Valley National Park PO Box 1029	Kotzebue	AK	99752	**800-478-7252**	907-442-3890	554
Kobussen Buses Ltd W914 County Rd CE	Kaukauna	WI	54130	**800-447-0116**	920-766-0606	110
Koch Air LLC PO Box 1167	Evansville	IN	47706	**877-456-2422**	812-962-5200	601
Koch Brothers 325 Grand Ave	Des Moines	IA	50309	**800-944-5624**	515-283-2451	524
Koch Entertainment Distribution 22 Harbor Pk Dr	Port Washington	NY	11050	**800-332-7553**	516-484-1000	512
Koch Financial Corp 17767 N Perimeter Dr Suite 101	Scottsdale	AZ	85255	**866-545-2327**	480-419-3600	214
Koch Foods LLC 1300 Higgins Rd Suite 100	Park Ridge	IL	60068	**800-837-2778**	847-384-5940	608
Koch George Sons LLC 10 S 11th Ave	Evansville	IN	47744	**888-873-5624**	812-465-9600	379
Koch H & Sons Co 5410 E La Palma Ave	Anaheim	CA	92807	**800-433-5787**	714-779-7000	666
Koch Julius USA Inc 387 Church St *Sales	New Bedford	MA	02745	**800-522-3652***	508-995-9565	730-5
Koch Membrane Systems Inc 850 Main St	Wilmington	MA	01887	**800-343-0499**	978-694-7000	379
Koch Specialty Plant Services 12221 E Sam Houston Pkwy N	Houston	TX	77044	**800-497-1789**	713-427-7700	528
Koch Supply & Trading LP 4111 E 37th St N	Wichita	KS	67220	**800-245-2243**	316-828-5500	384-4
Kocher Flower Growers 6211 Yarrow Dr Suite B	Carlsbad	CA	92009	**800-821-4421**	760-607-9100	363
KOCN-FM 105.1 (Urban) 903 N Main St	Salinas	CA	93906	**888-896-5626**	831-755-8181	631
Kocolene Marketing LLC 1725 E Tipton St	Seymour	IN	47274	**800-457-9886**	812-522-2224	311
Kocour Co 4800 S St Louis Ave	Chicago	IL	60632	**888-562-6871**	773-847-1111	490
Kodak Co 343 State St *NYSE: EK*	Rochester	NY	14650	**800-242-2424**	585-724-4000	580
Kodak Polychrome Graphics 770 Canning Pkwy	Victor	NY	14564	**800-677-9943**	585-742-5700	616
Kodiak College 117 Benny Benson Dr	Kodiak	AK	99615	**800-486-7660**	907-486-4161	160
Koehler-Bright Star Inc 380 Stewart Rd *Cust Svc	Hanover Township	PA	18706	**800-631-3814***	570-825-1900	431
Koerner Distributors Inc 1305 W Wabash St	Effingham	IL	62401	**800-475-5162**	217-347-7113	82-1
Koerner John E & Co Inc PO Box 10218	New Orleans	LA	70181	**800-333-1913**	504-734-1100	292-11
Koeze Co 2555 Burlingame Ave SW	Grand Rapids	MI	49509	**888-253-6887**	616-724-2601	291-8
Kohl & Madden Printing Ink Corp 651 Garden St	Carlstadt	NJ	07072	**800-793-0022**	201-886-1203	381
Kohler Canada Co 180 Creditview Rd	Vaughan	ON	L4L9N4	**800-964-5590**	905-762-6599	598
Kohler Co Inc 444 Highland Dr	Kohler	WI	53044	**800-456-4537**	920-457-4441	184
Kohler Engines 444 Highland Dr	Kohler	WI	53044	**800-544-2444**	920-457-4441	259
Kohler Plumbing North America 444 Highland Dr	Kohler	WI	53044	**800-456-4537**	920-457-4441	598
Kohler Rental Power Div of Kohler Co 4509 S Taylor Dr	Sheboygan	WI	53081	**888-769-3794**	920-459-1634	261-4
Kohler Waters Spa 501 Highlands Dr	Kohler	WI	53044	**866-928-3777**	920-457-7777	698
Kohl's Corp N 56 West 17000 Ridgewood Dr *NYSE: KSS*	Menomonee Falls	WI	53051	**800-837-6644**	262-703-7000	227
Kohnstamm V & E Inc 882 3rd Ave	Brooklyn	NY	11232	**800-847-4500**	718-788-6320	291-15
Koike Aronson Inc PO Box 307	Arcade	NY	14009	**800-252-5232**	585-492-2400	447
Koinonia Partners Inc 1324 Georgia Hwy 49 S	Americus	GA	31719	**800-569-4128**	229-924-0391	291-28
KOIT-AM 1260 (AC) 201 3rd St Suite 1200	San Francisco	CA	94103	**800-564-8965**	415-777-0965	631
KOIT-FM 96.5 (AC) 201 3rd St Suite 1200	San Francisco	CA	94103	**800-564-8965**	415-777-0965	631
Koko Inn 5201 Ave Q	Lubbock	TX	79412	**800-782-3254**	806-747-2591	373
Koko Interactive PO Box 55	Caldwell	NJ	07006	**877-468-5656**	212-333-5387	176-7
Kokomo Tribune 300 N Union St	Kokomo	IN	46901	**800-382-0696**	765-459-3121	522-2
Kokosing Construction Co Inc 17531 Waterford Rd	Fredericktown	OH	43019	**800-800-6315**	740-694-6315	187-4
Kokusai Semiconductor Equipment Group 2450 N 1st St Suite 290	San Jose	CA	95131	**800-800-5321**	408-456-2750	685
Kolcraft Enterprises Inc 10832 NC Hwy 211 E *Cust Svc	Aberdeen	NC	28315	**800-453-7673***	910-944-9345	463
Kolene Corp 12890 Westwood Ave	Detroit	MI	48223	**800-521-4182**	313-273-9220	143
Kollmann Monumental Works Inc 1915 W Division St	Saint Cloud	MN	56301	**800-659-8010**	320-251-8010	710
Kollsman Inc 220 Daniel Webster Hwy	Merrimack	NH	03054	**800-258-1350**	603-889-2500	519
KOLN-TV Ch 10 (CBS) PO Box 30350	Lincoln	NE	68503	**800-475-1011**	402-467-4321	726
Kolpak Inc 2915 Tennessee Ave N	Parsons	TN	38363	**800-826-7036**	731-847-6361	650
Kolpin Outdoors Inc 205 N Depot St	Fox Lake	WI	53933	**877-956-5746**	920-928-3118	701
Komag Inc 1710 Automation Pkwy *NASDAQ: KOMG*	San Jose	CA	95131	**800-576-2000**	408-576-2000	644
Komar Apparel Supply Co LLC 6900 Washington Blvd	Montebello	CA	90640	**800-872-7397**	323-890-3000	583
Komatsu America Corp Cutting Technologies Div 265 Ballardvale St	Wilmington	MA	01887	**800-707-2767**	978-658-1640	447

Name / Address	City	State	Zip	Toll-Free	Phone	Class
Komen Susan G Breast Cancer Foundation 5005 LBJ Fwy Suite 250	Dallas	TX	75244	**800-462-9273**	972-855-1600	48-17
Komline-Sanderson Engineering Corp 12 Holland Ave	Peapack	NJ	07977	**800-225-5457**	908-234-1000	379
KOMO-AM 1000 (N/T) 140 4th Ave N Suite 340	Seattle	WA	98109	**877-869-6469**	206-404-4000	631
KomTeK 40 Rockdale St	Worcester	MA	01606	**800-756-6835**	508-853-4500	474
KOMU-TV Ch 8 (NBC) 5550 Hwy 63 S	Columbia	MO	65201	**800-409-0292**	573-884-6397	726
Kona Village Resort Queen Kaahumanu Hwy	Kaupulehu-Kona	HI	96740	**800-367-5290**	808-325-5555	655
Konami of America Inc 1400 Bridge Pkwy Suite 101	Redwood City	CA	94065	**888-212-0573**		176-6
Konami Gaming Inc 7140 S Industrial Rd Suite 700	Las Vegas	NV	89118	**866-544-7568**	702-367-0573	317
KONE Inc 1 Kone Ct	Moline	IL	61265	**800-334-9556**	309-764-6771	255
Konecranes America 7300 Chippewa Blvd	Houston	TX	77086	**800-231-0241**	281-445-2225	462
Koneta Inc 1400 Lunar Dr	Wapakoneta	OH	45895	**800-331-0775**	419-739-4200	663
Konexx 5550 Oberlin Dr	San Diego	CA	92121	**800-275-6354**	858-622-1400	496
Konica Minolta Business Solutions 500 Day Hill Rd	Windsor	CT	06095	**800-456-6422**	860-683-2222	578
Konica Minolta Graphic Imaging USA Inc 71 Charles St	Glen Cove	NY	11542	**800-645-6252**	516-674-2500	580
Konica Minolta Photo Imaging USA Inc 725 Darlington Ave	Mahwah	NJ	07430	**800-285-6422**	201-574-4000	580
Konica Minolta Printing Solutions USA Inc 1 Magnum Pass	Mobile	AL	36618	**800-523-2696**	251-633-4300	171-6
Konop Cos 1725 Industrial Dr	Green Bay	WI	54302	**800-770-0477**	920-468-8517	291-34
Konsyl Pharmaceuticals Inc 8050 Industrial Park Rd	Easton	MD	21601	**800-356-6795**	410-822-5192	572
Kontron Communications Inc 616 Cure-Boivin	Boisbriand	QC	J7G2A7	**800-354-4223**	450-437-5682	613
Kontron Mobile Computing Inc 7631 Anagram Dr	Eden Prairie	MN	55344	**888-343-5396**	952-974-7000	171-2
Kool Seal Inc 1499 Enterprise Pkwy	Twinsburg	OH	44087	**888-321-5665**	330-425-4717	46
Kooltronic Inc 30 Pennington-Hopewell Rd	Pennington	NJ	08534	**800-321-5665**	609-466-3400	15
Koontz-Wagner Electric Co Inc 3801 Voorde Dr	South Bend	IN	46628	**800-345-2051**	574-232-2051	188-4
Kootenay National Park PO Box 220	Radium Hot Springs	BC	V0A1M0	**800-748-7275**	250-347-9615	553
Kootenay River Runners PO Box 81	Edgewater	BC	V0A1E0	**800-599-4399**	250-347-9210	748
Kopf Builders Inc 420 Avon Belden Rd	Avon Lake	OH	44012	**800-242-8913**	440-933-6908	186
Kopp Funds 7701 France Ave S Suite 500	Edina	MN	55435	**888-533-5677**	952-841-0400	517
Kopp Investment Advisors Inc 7701 France Ave S Suite 500	Edina	MN	55435	**800-333-9128**	952-841-0400	393
Kopper's Chocolate Specialty Co Inc 39 Clarkson St	New York	NY	10014	**800-325-0026**	212-243-0220	291-8
Koral Industries Inc PO Box 1270	Ennis	TX	75120	**800-627-2441**	972-875-6555	367
Korber Hats Inc 394 Kilburn St *Cust Svc	Fall River	MA	02724	**800-428-9911***	508-672-7033	153-9
Kordes Enrichment Center 841 E 14th St	Ferdinand	IN	47532	**800-880-2777**	812-367-2777	660
Korea National Tourism Organization 4801 Wilshire Blvd Suite 103	Los Angeles	CA	90010	**800-868-7567**	323-634-0280	764
Korea National Tourism Organization 737 N Michigan Ave Suite 910	Chicago	IL	60611	**800-868-7567**	312-981-1717	764
Korea National Tourism Organization 2 Executive Dr Suite 750	Fort Lee	NJ	07024	**800-868-7567**	201-585-0909	764
Korean Air 6101 W Imperial Hwy	Los Angeles	CA	90045	**800-438-5000**	310-417-5200	26
Korean Air Skypass 1813 Wilshire Blvd Suite 400	Los Angeles	CA	90057	**800-525-4480**		27
Korex Corp 50000 W Pontiac Trail PO Box 930339	Wixom	MI	48393	**800-678-7627**	248-624-0000	211
Kornylak Corp 400 Heaton St	Hamilton	OH	45011	**800-837-5676**	513-863-1277	462
Korry Electronics Co 901 Dexter Ave N	Seattle	WA	98109	**800-257-8921**	206-281-1300	715
Korshak Stanley 500 Crescent Ct Suite 100	Dallas	TX	75201	**800-972-5959**	214-871-3600	155-4
Kosciusko County Convention & Visitors Bureau 111 Capital Dr	Warsaw	IN	46582	**800-800-6090**	574-269-6090	205
Kosciusko County Rural Electric Membership Corp PO Box 588	Warsaw	IN	46581	**800-790-7362**	574-267-6331	244
Koss Corp 4129 N Port Washington Ave *NASDAQ: KOSS*	Milwaukee	WI	53212	**800-872-5677**	414-964-5000	52
Kost Tire Distributors Inc 335 Court St	Binghamton	NY	13904	**800-622-6672**	607-723-1230	740
Kotecki-Rock of Ages Inc 3636 Pearl Rd	Cleveland	OH	44109	**800-753-2880**	216-749-2880	710
Kott Koatings Inc 27161 Burbank St	Foothill Ranch	CA	92610	**800-452-6161**	949-770-5055	188-11
Kova Fertilizer Inc 1330 N Anderson St	Greensburg	IN	47240	**800-346-1569**	812-663-5081	276
Kovacevich Richard M Chm/Pres/CEO Wells Fargo & Co 420 Montgomery St	San Francisco	CA	94104	**800-869-3557**		561
Koval Marketing Inc 11208 47th Ave W	Mukilteo	WA	98275	**800-972-4782**	425-347-4249	356
Kowalski Sausage Co Inc 2270 Holbrook Ave	Hamtramck	MI	48212	**800-482-2400**	313-873-8200	291-26
Koyo Corp of USA 29570 Clemens Rd	Westlake	OH	44145	**800-321-3102**	440-835-1000	77
KozaK Auto DryWash Inc PO Box 910	Batavia	NY	14021	**800-237-9927**	585-343-8111	149
KOZK-TV Ch 21 (PBS) 901 S National Ave	Springfield	MO	65804	**866-684-5695**	417-836-3500	726
K/P Corp 12647 Alcosta Blvd Suite 425	San Ramon	CA	94583	**877-957-2677**	925-543-5200	615
KP Iron Foundry Inc 4731 E Vine Ave	Fresno	CA	93725	**800-655-2590**	559-233-2591	302
KPBS-TV Ch 15 (PBS) 5200 Campanile Dr	San Diego	CA	92182	**888-399-5727**	619-594-1515	726
KPBX-FM 91.1 (NPR) 2319 N Monroe St	Spokane	WA	99205	**800-328-5729**	509-328-5729	631
KPDQ-FM 93.7 (Rel) 6400 SE Lake Rd Suite 350	Portland	OR	97222	**800-845-2162**	503-786-0600	631
KPDX-TV Ch 49 (UPN) 14975 NW Greenbrier Pkwy	Beaverton	OR	97006	**866-906-1249**	503-906-1249	726
KPLO-TV Ch 6 (CBS) 501 S Phillips Ave	Sioux Falls	SD	57104	**800-888-5356**	605-336-1100	726
KPLU-FM 88.5 (NPR) Pacific Lutheran University	Tacoma	WA	98447	**800-677-5758**	253-535-7758	631
KPLZ-FM 101.5 (AC) 140 4th Ave N Suite 340	Seattle	WA	98109	**888-821-1015**	206-404-4000	631
KPOJ-AM 620 (N/T) 4949 SW Macadam Ave	Portland	OR	97239	**866-452-0620**	503-225-1190	631
KPRF-FM 98.7 (CHR) 6214 W 34th St	Amarillo	TX	79109	**888-368-1212**	806-355-9777	631
KPSI-FM 100.5 (AC) 2100 Tahquitz Canyon Way	Palm Springs	CA	92262	**877-282-2648**	760-325-2582	631
KPT/Kaiser Precision Tooling Inc 641 Fargo Ave	Elk Grove Village	IL	60007	**800-553-5113**	847-228-7660	484
KPTS-TV Ch 8 (PBS) 320 W 21 St	Wichita	KS	67203	**800-794-8498**	316-838-3090	726
KPTV-TV Ch 12 (Fox) 14975 NW Greenbrier Pkwy	Beaverton	OR	97006	**866-906-1249**	503-906-1249	726
KPVI-TV Ch 6 (NBC) 902 E Sherman St	Pocatello	ID	83201	**800-366-5784**	208-232-6666	726
KPXE-TV Ch 50 (PAX) 4720 Oak St	Kansas City	MO	64112	**800-646-7296**	816-924-5050	726
KPXN-TV Ch 30 (PAX) 1100 Air Way	Glendale	CA	91201	**800-646-7296**	818-840-2687	726
KQBZ-FM 100.7 (N/T) 1100 Olive Way suite 1650	Seattle	WA	98101	**888-647-1007**	206-285-7625	631
KQCV-AM 800 (Rel) 1919 N Broadway	Oklahoma City	OK	73103	**888-909-5728**	405-521-0800	631
KQV-AM 1410 (N/T) 650 Smithfield St Centre City Towers	Pittsburgh	PA	15222	**800-424-1410**	412-562-5900	631
KR Strikeforce Inc 1200 S 54th Ave	Cicero	IL	60804	**800-297-8555**	708-863-1200	701
Kraco Enterprises Inc 505 E Euclid Ave	Compton	CA	90224	**800-678-1910**	310-639-0666	663
Kraft Chemical Co 1975 N Hawthorne Ave	Melrose Park	IL	60160	**800-345-5200**	708-345-5200	144
Kraft Food Ingredients Corp 8000 Horizon Ctr Blvd	Memphis	TN	38133	**800-458-8324**	901-381-6500	291-29
Kraft Foods International Inc 800 Westchester Ave	Rye Brook	NY	10573	**800-323-0768**	914-335-2500	292-8
Kraft WA Corp 199 Wildwood Ave	Woburn	MA	01801	**800-969-6121**	781-938-9100	507
Kraftware Corp 270 Cox St	Roselle	NJ	07203	**800-221-1728**	908-259-8883	596
Kramer Beverage Co Inc 161 S 2nd Rd *Cust Svc	Hammonton	NJ	08037	**800-321-4522***	609-704-7000	82-1
Kramer H & Co 1345 W 21st St	Chicago	IL	60608	**800-621-2305**	312-226-6600	476
Kramer Ink Co Inc 9900 Jordan Cir	Santa Fe Springs	CA	90670	**800-543-8792**	562-946-8847	381
Kramer Laboratories Inc 8778 SW 8th St	Miami	FL	33174	**800-824-4894**	305-223-1287	572
Kramer Levin Naftalis & Frankel LLP 919 3rd Ave	New York	NY	10022	**800-766-4707**	212-715-9100	419
Krames Communication/Staywell 780 Township Line Rd *Sales	Yardley	PA	19067	**800-333-3032***	267-685-2500	623-10
Krannert Center for the Performing Arts 500 S Goodwin Ave	Urbana	IL	61801	**800-527-2849**	217-333-6700	562
Krasny-Kaplan Corp 4899 Commerce Pkwy	Cleveland	OH	44128	**800-631-0520**	216-292-6300	206
Kraus-Anderson Capital Inc 523 S 8th St Suite 523	Minneapolis	MN	55404	**888-547-3983**	612-305-2934	214
Kraus-Anderson Insurance 420 Gateway Blvd	Burnsville	MN	55337	**800-207-9261**	952-707-8200	383
Kraus-Anderson Realty Co 4210 W Old Shakopee Rd	Bloomington	MN	55437	**800-399-4220**	952-881-8166	641
Krause Corp 305 S Monroe St	Hutchinson	KS	67501	**800-957-2873**	620-663-6161	269
Krause Design Inc PO Box 240-319	Dorchester	MA	02124	**877-572-8730**	617-436-2661	130
Krause Publications Inc 700 E State St *Cust Svc	Iola	WI	54990	**800-942-0673***	715-445-2214	623-9
Kravet Fabrics Inc 225 Central Ave S *Cust Svc	Bethpage	NY	11714	**800-648-5728***	516-293-2000	583
Kravis Raymond F Center for the Performing Arts 701 Okeechobee Blvd	West Palm Beach	FL	33401	**800-572-8471**	561-832-7469	562
KRCC-FM 91.5 (NPR) 912 N Weber St	Colorado Springs	CO	80903	**800-748-2727**	719-473-4801	631
Kreber Enterprises 221 Swathmore Ave	High Point	NC	27263	**800-775-3801**	336-861-2700	581
Kreber Graphics Inc 2580 Westbelt Dr	Columbus	OH	43228	**800-777-3501**	614-529-5701	770
Krehbiel CJ Co Inc 3962 Virginia Ave	Cincinnati	OH	45227	**800-598-7808**	513-271-6035	614
Kreher Steel Co LLC 1550 N 25th Ave	Melrose Park	IL	60160	**800-323-0745**	708-345-8180	483
Krehling Industries Inc 1425 E Wiggins Pass Rd	Naples	FL	34108	**800-226-3162**	239-597-3162	180
Kreider BR & Son Inc 63 Kreider Ln	Manheim	PA	17545	**800-689-7651**	717-898-7651	188-5
Kreider Farms 1461 Lancaster Rd	Manheim	PA	17545	**888-665-4415**	717-665-4415	11-3
Krentzman Joe & Son Inc PO Box 508	Lewistown	PA	17044	**800-543-2000**	717-543-5635	674
Krevit H & Co Inc 73 Welton St	New Haven	CT	06511	**800-922-6626**	203-772-3350	143
Krieger Specialty Products Co 4880 Gregg Rd	Pico Rivera	CA	90660	**866-203-5060**	562-695-0645	232
Kripalu Center for Yoga & Health 57 Interlaken Rd	Stockbridge	MA	01262	**800-741-7353**	413-448-3400	697
Krise Bus Service Inc 119 Bus Ln	Punxsutawney	PA	15767	**800-782-9769**	814-938-5250	110
Krispy Kreme Doughnuts Inc 370 Knollwood St Suite 500 *NYSE: KKD*	Winston-Salem	NC	27103	**800-334-1243**	336-725-2981	69
Kristin Brooks Hope Center (KBHC) 2001 N Beauregard St 12th Fl	Alexandria	VA	22311	**800-784-2433**	703-684-7722	48-17
KRKX-FM 94.1 (Rock) 2075 Central Ave	Billings	MT	59102	**866-627-5483**	406-652-8400	631
KRLD-AM 1080 (N/T) 1080 Ballpark Way	Arlington	TX	76011	**800-289-1080**	817-543-5400	631
KRMA-TV Ch 6 (PBS) 1089 Bannock St	Denver	CO	80204	**800-274-6666**	303-892-6666	726
KRNV-TV Ch 4 (NBC) 1790 Vassar St	Reno	NV	89502	**877-377-0122**	775-322-4444	726
Krogh Pump Co 251 W Channel Rd	Benicia	CA	94510	**800-225-7644**	707-747-7585	627
Krohn Industries Inc 303 Veterans Blvd	Carlstadt	NJ	07072	**800-526-6299**	201-933-9696	399

Name / Address	City	State	ZIP	Toll-Free	Phone	Class
KROL-FM 99.5 (Rel) 6900 Commerce St.	El Paso	TX	79915	**800-840-5765**	915-779-0016	631
Kroll Background America Inc 1900 Church St Suite 400	Nashville	TN	37203	**800-697-7189**	615-320-9800	621
Kroll Factual Data Inc 5200 Hahns Peak Dr	Loveland	CO	80538	**800-929-3400**	970-663-5700	212
Kroll Laboratory Specialists Inc 1111 Newton St	Gretna	LA	70053	**800-433-3823**	504-361-8989	407
Kroll Ontrack Inc 9023 Columbine Rd *Sales	Eden Prairie	MN	55347	**800-872-2599***	952-937-1107	176-12
Krones Inc 9600 S 58th St PO Box 321801	Franklin	WI	53132	**800-752-3787**	414-409-4000	537
Kroy Industries 701 S 17th St.	Henderson	NE	68371	**800-228-2883**	402-723-5374	269
Kroy LLC 3830 Kelley Ave	Cleveland	OH	44114	**888-888-5769**	216-426-5600	171-6
KRQE-TV Ch 13 (CBS) 13 Broadcast Plaza SW	Albuquerque	NM	87104	**800-283-4227**	505-243-2285	726
KRSK-FM 105.1 (AC) 0700 SW Bancroft St	Portland	OR	97239	**888-733-5105**	503-223-1441	631
KRT Direct 700 12th St NW Suite 1000	Washington	DC	20005	**800-346-8798**	202-383-6080	520
KRTH-FM 101.1 (Oldies) 5670 Wilshire Blvd Suite 200	Los Angeles	CA	90036	**800-232-5834**	323-936-5784	631
Kruepke Trucking Inc 2881 Hwy P	Jackson	WI	53037	**800-798-5000**	262-677-3155	769
Kruger Street Toy & Train Museum 144 Kruger St	Wheeling	WV	26003	**877-242-8133**	304-242-8133	509
Krups North America 196 Boston Ave	Medford	MA	02155	**800-526-5377**		37
Kruse Adhesive Tape Inc 16582 Burke Ln	Huntington Beach	CA	92647	**800-992-7702**	714-596-0707	717
Kruse International 5540 County Rd 11A	Auburn	IN	46706	**800-968-4444**	219-925-5600	51
Kruysman Inc 32-00 Skillman Ave	Long Island City	NY	11101	**800-221-3218**	718-433-3800	550
KRVS-FM 88.7 (NPR) PO Box 42171	Lafayette	LA	70504	**800-892-6827**	337-482-5787	631
KRWG-FM 90.7 (NPR) PO Box 3000	Las Cruces	NM	88003	**800-245-5794**	505-646-4525	631
KRWG-TV Ch 22 (PBS) Jordan St PO Box 30001 MSC TV 22	Las Cruces	NM	88003	**866-457-9488**	505-646-2222	726
Krystal Co 1 Union Sq	Chattanooga	TN	37402	**800-458-5841**	423-757-1550	657
KRZN-FM 96.3 (Rock) 2075 Central Ave	Billings	MT	59102	**866-627-5483**	406-652-8400	631
KSAN-FM 107.7 (CR) 55 Hawthorne St Suite 1100	San Francisco	CA	94105	**888-303-2663**	415-981-5726	631
KSAZ-TV Ch 10 (Fox) 511 W Adams St	Phoenix	AZ	85003	**888-369-4762**	602-257-1234	726
KSB Inc 4415 Sarellen Rd	Richmond	VA	23231	**800-945-7867**	804-222-1818	627
KSCI-TV Ch 18 (Ind) 1990 S Bundy Dr Suite 850	Los Angeles	CA	90025	**800-841-1818**	310-478-1818	726
KSED-FM 107.5 (Ctry) 112 E Rt 66 Suite 105	Flagstaff	AZ	86001	**800-799-5658**	928-779-1177	631
KSEE-TV Ch 24 (NBC) 5035 E McKinley Ave	Fresno	CA	93727	**800-234-5733**	559-454-2424	726
KSES-FM 107.1 (Span) 67 Garden Ct	Monterey	CA	93942	**866-434-4084**	831-333-9735	631
KSGN-FM 89.7 (Rel) 11498 Pierce St	Riverside	CA	92505	**800-321-5746**	951-687-5746	631
KSHE-FM 94.7 (Rock) 800 St Louis Union Stn	Saint Louis	MO	63103	**800-842-5743**	314-621-0095	631
KSKY-AM 660 (N/T) 6400 N Beltline Rd Suite 110	Irving	TX	75063	**800-949-5973**	214-561-9660	631
KSLZ-FM 107.7 (CHR) 1001 Highlands Plaza Dr W Suite 1100	Saint Louis	MO	63110	**888-570-1077**	314-333-8000	631
KSMB-FM 94.5 (CHR) 202 Galbert Rd	Lafayette	LA	70506	**800-299-2100**	337-232-1311	631
KSMS-FM 90.5 (NPR) Southwest Missouri State University 901 S National Ave	Springfield	MO	65804	**800-767-5768**	417-836-5878	631
KSMU-FM 91.1 (NPR) Southwest Missouri State University 901 S National Ave	Springfield	MO	65804	**800-767-5768**	417-836-5878	631
KSNW-TV Ch 3 (NBC) 833 N Main St	Wichita	KS	67203	**800-949-5769**	316-265-3333	726
KSOL-FM 98.9 (Span) 750 Battery St Suite 200	San Francisco	CA	94111	**888-880-5765**	415-733-5765	631
KSON-FM 97.3 (Ctry) 1615 Murray Canyon Rd Suite 710	San Diego	CA	92108	**800-243-1973**	619-291-9797	631
KSPR-TV Ch 33 (ABC) 1359 Saint Louis St	Springfield	MO	65802	**800-220-8222**	417-831-1333	726
KSPS-TV Ch 7 (PBS) 3911 S Regal St	Spokane	WA	99223	**800-735-2377**	509-354-7800	726
KSTX-FM 89.1 (NPR) 8401 Datapoint Dr Suite 800	San Antonio	TX	78229	**800-622-8977**	210-614-8977	631
KSWV-AM 810 (Span) 102 Taos St	Santa Fe	NM	87505	**800-794-5798**	505-989-7441	631
KTBN-TV Ch 40 (TBN) 2442 Michelle Dr	Tustin	CA	92780	**888-731-1000**	714-832-2950	726
KTCY-FM 101.7 (Span CHR) 5307 E Mockingbird Ln Suite 500	Dallas	TX	75206	**800-420-2757**	214-887-9107	631
Ktech Corp 1300 Eubank Blvd SE	Albuquerque	NM	87123	**877-998-5830**	505-998-5830	654
KTGF-TV Ch 16 (NBC) 118 6th St S	Great Falls	MT	59405	**800-926-5401**	406-761-8816	726
KTLI-FM 99.1 (Rel) 125 N Market St Suite 1900	Wichita	KS	67202	**800-525-5683**	316-303-9999	631
KTNO-AM 1440 (Span Rel) 5787 S Hampton Rd Suite 340	Dallas	TX	75232	**877-292-2431**	214-330-5866	631
KTNV-TV Ch 13 (ABC) 3355 S Valley View Blvd	Las Vegas	NV	89102	**800-463-9713**	702-876-1313	726
KTOM-FM 92.7 (Ctry) 903 N Main St	Salinas	CA	93906	**888-660-5866**	831-755-8181	631
KTOO-FM 104.3 (NPR) 360 Egan Dr	Juneau	AK	99801	**800-870-5866**	907-586-1670	631
KTOO-TV Ch 3 (PBS) 360 Egan Dr	Juneau	AK	99801	**800-870-5866**	907-586-1670	726
KTOQ-AM 1340 (N/T) 306 1/2 E Saint Joseph St	Rapid City	SD	57701	**800-456-2613**	605-343-0888	631
KTPK-FM 106.9 (Ctry) 2121 SW Chelsea Dr	Topeka	KS	66614	**888-291-1069**	785-273-1069	631
KTRR-FM 102.5 (AC) 600 Main St	Windsor	CO	80550	**800-964-1025**	970-686-2791	631
KTRS-AM 550 (N/T) 638 W Port Plaza	Saint Louis	MO	63146	**888-550-5877**	314-453-5500	631
KTSA-AM 550 (N/T) 4050 Eisenhauer Rd	San Antonio	TX	78218	**800-299-5872**	210-599-5500	631
KTSD-FM 91.1 (NPR) PO Box 5000	Vermillion	SD	57069	**800-456-0766**	605-677-5861	631
KTSD-TV Ch 10 (PBS) PO Box 5000	Vermillion	SD	57069	**800-456-0766**	605-677-5861	726
KTSF-TV Ch 26 (Ind) 100 Valley Dr	Brisbane	CA	94005	**800-488-6226**	415-468-2626	726
KTTC-TV Ch 10 (NBC) 6301 Bandel Rd NW	Rochester	MN	55901	**800-288-1656**	507-288-4444	726
KTTS-FM 94.7 (Ctry) 2330 W Grand St	Springfield	MO	65802	**800-765-5887**	417-865-6614	631
KTVB-TV Ch 7 (NBC) PO Box 7	Boise	ID	83707	**800-559-7277**	208-375-7277	726
KTVI-TV Ch 2 (Fox) 5915 Berthold Ave	Saint Louis	MO	63110	**800-920-0222**	314-647-2222	726
KTXR-FM 101.3 (AC) 3000 E Chestnut Expy	Springfield	MO	65802	**800-749-8001**	417-862-3751	631
KTXS-TV Ch 12 (ABC) 4420 N Clack St	Abilene	TX	79601	**800-588-5897**	325-677-2281	726
KTXY-FM 106.9 (AC) 3215 Lemone Industrial Blvd Suite 200	Columbia	MO	65201	**800-500-9107**	573-875-1099	631
KUAD-FM 99.1 (Ctry) 600 Main St	Windsor	CO	80550	**800-500-2599**	970-686-2791	631
KUAF-FM 91.3 (NPR) 747 W Dickson St Suite 2	Fayetteville	AR	72701	**800-522-5823**	479-575-2556	631
KUAR-FM 89.1 (NPR) 2801 S University Ave	Little Rock	AR	72204	**800-952-2528**	501-569-8485	631
KUAT-FM 90.5 (Clas) PO Box 210067	Tucson	AZ	85721	**800-521-5828**	520-621-5828	631
KUAZ-FM 89.1 (NPR) PO Box 210067	Tucson	AZ	85721	**800-521-5828**	520-621-5828	631
KUBE-FM 93.3 (CHR) 351 Elliott Ave W	Seattle	WA	98119	**877-933-9393**	206-285-2295	631
Kubin-Nicholson Corp 5880 N 60th St	Milwaukee	WI	53218	**800-858-9557**	414-461-8100	8
Kubotek USA 100 Locke Rd	Marlborough	MA	01752	**800-372-3872**	508-229-2020	176-5
KUCV-FM 91.1 (Var) 1800 N 33rd St	Lincoln	NE	68583	**800-290-6850**	402-472-2200	631
KUED-TV Ch 7 (PBS) 101 Wasatch Dr Rm 215	Salt Lake City	UT	84112	**800-477-5833**	801-581-7777	726
KUER-FM 90.1 (NPR) 101 S Wasatch Dr Rm 270	Salt Lake City	UT	84112	**800-313-5937**	801-581-6625	631
Kuert Concrete Inc 3402 Lincoln Way W	South Bend	IN	46628	**866-465-8378**	574-232-9911	180
KUFO-FM 101.1 (Rock) 2040 SW 1st Ave	Portland	OR	97201	**800-344-5836**	503-222-1011	631
Kugler Co 209 W 3rd	McCook	NE	69001	**800-445-9116**	308-345-2280	272
Kuhlman Corp 650 Beaver Creek Cir	Maumee	OH	43537	**800-669-3309**	419-897-6000	180
Kuhlman Inc N 56 W 16865 Ridgewood Dr Suite 100	Menomonee Falls	WI	53051	**800-781-9229**	262-252-9400	188-10
KUHM-FM 91.7 (NPR) 32 Campus Dr University of Montana	Missoula	MT	59812	**800-325-1565**	406-243-4931	631
Kuhn Flowers Inc 3802 Beach Blvd	Jacksonville	FL	32207	**800-458-5846**	904-398-8601	287
KUHT-TV Ch 8 (PBS) 4343 Elgin St	Houston	TX	77204	**800-364-5848**	713-748-8888	726
Kulicke & Soffa Industries Inc 2101 Blair Mill Rd *NASDAQ: KLIC*	Willow Grove	PA	19090	**800-445-5671**	215-784-6000	685
KULL-FM 92.5 (Oldies) 3911 S 1st St	Abilene	TX	79605	**800-659-1965**	325-676-7711	631
Kultur International Films Ltd 195 Hwy 36	West Long Branch	NJ	07764	**800-458-5887**	732-229-2343	502
KUMD-FM 103.3 (Var) 1201 Ordean Ct Rm 130	Duluth	MN	55812	**800-566-5863**	218-726-7181	631
Kumho Tire USA Inc 14605 Miller Ave	Fontana	CA	92336	**800-445-8646**	909-428-3999	740
Kumon North America Inc 300 Frank W Burr Blvd Glenpointe Ctr E 5th Fl	Teaneck	NJ	07666	**800-222-6284**	201-928-0444	146
KUND-FM 89.3 (NPR) PO Box 8117	Grand Forks	ND	58202	**800-359-6900**	701-777-4595	631
Kunda Beverage 349 S Henderson Rd	King of Prussia	PA	19406	**800-262-2323**	610-265-3113	82-1
Kuner-Empson Co PO Box 309	Brighton	CO	80601	**888-201-6440**	303-659-1710	291-20
Kunz Business Products Co 1600 Penn St	Huntingdon	PA	16652	**800-458-3442**	814-643-4320	87
Kunzler & Co Inc 652 Manor St	Lancaster	PA	17604	**800-233-0203**	717-299-6301	291-26
KUON-TV Ch 12 (PBS) 1800 N 33rd St	Lincoln	NE	68583	**800-698-3426**	402-472-3611	726
KUOP-FM 91.3 (NPR) 7055 Folsom Blvd	Sacramento	CA	95826	**800-800-5867**	916-278-8900	631
KUOW-FM 94.9 (NPR) 4518 University Way NE Suite 310	Seattle	WA	98105	**800-289-5869**	206-543-2710	631
Kuraray America Inc 101 E 52nd St 26th Fl	New York	NY	10022	**800-879-1676**	212-986-2230	730-1
Kurt Mfg Co 5280 Main St NE	Minneapolis	MN	55421	**800-458-7811**	763-572-1500	446
Kurt Weiss Greenhouses Inc 95 Main St	Center Moriches	NY	11934	**800-858-2555**	631-878-2500	363
Kurtz Brothers Co Inc PO Box 392	Clearfield	PA	16830	**800-252-3811**	814-765-6561	87
Kurtzon Lighting 1420 S Talman Ave	Chicago	IL	60608	**800-837-8937**	773-277-2121	431
Kurz Electric Solutions Inc 736 Ford St	Kimberly	WI	54136	**800-776-3629**	920-734-5644	700
Kurzweil Technologies Inc 15 Walnut St	Wellesley Hills	MA	02481	**877-365-9633**	781-263-0000	654
KUSD-TV Ch 2 (PBS) PO Box 5000	Vermillion	SD	57069	**800-456-0766**	605-677-5861	726
KUSM-TV Ch 9 (PBS) Visual Communications Bldg Rm 183	Bozeman	MT	59717	**800-426-8243**	406-994-3437	726
KUSP-FM 88.9 (NPR) 203 8th Ave	Santa Cruz	CA	95026	**800-655-5877**	831-476-2800	631
Kuss Corp 2150 Industrial Dr *Sales	Findlay	OH	45840	**800-252-5877***	419-423-9040	60
KUT-FM 90.5 (NPR) University of Texas 1 University Station Box A-0704	Austin	TX	78712	**800-435-8836**	512-471-1631	631
Kutsher's Country Club Resort Kutchers Rd PO Box 432	Monticello	NY	12701	**800-431-1273**	845-794-6000	655
Kutztown University PO Box 730	Kutztown	PA	19530	**877-628-1915**	610-683-4000	163
KUVO-FM 89.3 (Jazz) PO Box 2040	Denver	CO	80201	**800-574-5886**	303-480-9272	631
KUWJ-FM 90.3 (NPR) PO Box 3984	Laramie	WY	82071	**800-729-5897**	307-766-4240	631
KUWR-FM 91.9 (NPR) 1000 E University Ave Dept 3984	Laramie	WY	82071	**800-729-5897**	307-766-4240	631
KUWS-FM 91.3 (NPR) 1800 Grand Ave PO Box 2000	Superior	WI	54880	**800-300-8530**	715-394-8530	631
Kux Graphic Systems Inc 12675 Burt Rd	Detroit	MI	48223	**800-521-9534**	313-255-6460	692
KVAL Inc 825 Petaluma Blvd S	Petaluma	CA	94952	**800-553-5825**	707-762-7367	809
KVH Industries Inc 50 Enterprise Ctr *NASDAQ: KVHI*	Middletown	RI	02842	**888-584-4773**	401-847-3327	519
KVI-AM 570 (N/T) 140 4th Ave N Suite 340	Seattle	WA	98109	**888-421-5757**	206-404-4000	631
KVIE-TV Ch 6 (PBS) 2595 Capitol Oaks Dr	Sacramento	CA	95833	**800-347-5843**	916-929-5843	726
KVII-TV Ch 7 (ABC) 1 Broadcast Ctr	Amarillo	TX	79101	**800-777-5844**	806-373-1787	726

Name	Address	City	State	Zip	Toll-Free	Phone	Class
KVLC-FM 101.1 (Oldies)	105 E Idaho Ave Suite B	Las Cruces	NM	88005	**800-527-1170**	505-527-1111	631
KVLY-TV Ch 11 (NBC)	1350 21st Ave S	Fargo	ND	58103	**800-450-5844**	701-237-5211	726
KVMX-FM 107.5 (Oldies)	2040 SW 1st Ave	Portland	OR	97201	**800-567-1075**	503-222-1011	631
KVOS-TV Ch 12 (Ind)	1151 Ellis St	Bellingham	WA	98225	**800-488-5867**	360-671-1212	726
KVPR-FM 89.3 (NPR)	3437 W Shaw Ave Suite 101	Fresno	CA	93711	**800-275-0764**	559-275-0764	631
KVRP-FM 97.1 (Ctry)	PO Box 1118	Haskell	TX	79521	**800-460-5877**	940-864-8505	631
KVTT-FM 91.7 (Rel)	11061 Shady Trail	Dallas	TX	75229	**866-787-1917**	214-351-6655	631
KVVA-FM 107.1 (Span AC)	501 N 44th St Suite 425	Phoenix	AZ	85008	**800-420-2757**	602-266-2005	631
KW Tunnell Co Inc	900 E 8th Ave Suite 106	King of Prussia	PA	19406	**800-532-2483**	610-337-0820	193
Kwal-Howells Paint	3900 Joliet St *Cust Svc	Denver	CO	80239	**800-383-8406***	303-371-5600	540
KWCH-TV Ch 12 (CBS)	2815 E 37th St North	Wichita	KS	67219	**888-512-6397**	316-838-1212	726
KWGS-FM 89.5 (NPR)	600 S College Ave	Tulsa	OK	74104	**888-594-5947**	918-631-2577	631
Kwik Goal Ltd	140 Pacific Dr	Quakertown	PA	18951	**800-531-4252**	215-536-2200	701
Kwik Lok Corp	PO Box 9548	Yakima	WA	98909	**800-688-5945**	509-248-4770	293
Kwik Pantry	2801 Glenda Ave	Fort Worth	TX	76117	**800-695-3282**	817-838-4700	658
Kwik-Sew Pattern Co Inc	3000 Washington Ave N	Minneapolis	MN	55411	**888-594-5739**	612-521-7651	557
Kwik-Wall Co	1010 E Edwards St	Springfield	IL	62703	**800-280-5945**	217-522-5553	281
Kwikee Kwiver Co	7292 Peaceful Valley Rd PO Box 130	Acme	MI	49610	**800-346-7001**	231-938-1690	701
KWJJ-FM 99.5 (Ctry)	0700 SW Bancroft St	Portland	OR	97239	**866-239-9653**	503-223-1441	631
KWRT-AM 1370 (Ctry)	1600 Radio Hill Rd	Boonville	MO	65233	**800-887-6686**	660-882-6686	631
KWS Mfg Co	3041 Conveyor Dr	Burleson	TX	76028	**800-543-6558**	817-295-2247	206
KWTO-AM 560 (N/T)	3000 E Chestnut Expy	Springfield	MO	65802	**800-749-8001**	417-862-3751	631
KWWK-FM 96.5 (Ctry)	122 SW 4th St	Rochester	MN	55902	**888-599-5965**	507-286-1010	631
KWWR-FM 95.7 (Ctry)	1705 E Liberty St	Mexico	MO	65265	**800-264-5997**	573-581-5500	631
KWYR-FM 93.7 (AC)	PO Box 491	Winner	SD	57580	**800-388-5997**	605-842-3333	631
KX Industries	269 S Lambert Rd	Orange	CT	06477	**800-462-8745**	203-799-9000	793
KXAS-TV Ch 5 (NBC)	3900 Barnett St	Fort Worth	TX	76103	**800-232-5927**	817-429-5555	726
KXEG-AM 1280 (Rel)	2800 N 44th St Suite 100	Phoenix	AZ	85008	**888-294-4321**	602-254-5001	631
KXJM-FM 95.5 (Urban)	0234 SW Bancroft St	Portland	OR	97239	**800-990-0750**	503-243-7595	631
KXJZ-FM 88.9 (NPR)	7055 Folsom Blvd	Sacramento	CA	95826	**877-480-5900**	916-278-8900	631
KXL-AM 750 (N/T)	0234 SW Bancroft St	Portland	OR	97239	**800-990-0750**	503-243-7595	631
KXLT-TV Ch 47 (Fox)	6301 Bandel Rd NW	Rochester	MN	55901	**877-369-4788**	507-252-4747	726
KXMB-TV Ch 12 (CBS)	1811 N 15th St	Bismarck	ND	58501	**800-223-9197**	701-223-9197	726
KXPK-FM 96.5 (Span)	777 Grant St 5th Fl	Denver	CO	80203	**888-874-2656**	303-832-0050	631
KXPR-FM 90.9 (Clas)	7055 Folsom Blvd	Sacramento	CA	95826	**877-480-5900**	916-278-8900	631
KXTA-AM 1150 (Sports)	3400 W Olive Ave Suite 550	Burbank	CA	91505	**866-987-8570**	818-559-2252	631
KYCC-FM 90.1 (Rel)	9019 West Ln	Stockton	CA	95210	**800-654-5254**	209-477-3690	631
KYLD-FM 94.9 (Urban)	340 Townsend St 4th Fl	San Francisco	CA	94107	**888-333-9490**	415-975-5555	631
Kyle RH Furniture Co	1352 Hansford St	Charleston	WV	25301	**800-624-9170**	304-346-0671	315
Kyocera Industrial Ceramics Corp	5713 E Fourth Plain Rd	Vancouver	WA	98661	**800-826-0527**	360-696-8950	248
Kyocera Optics Inc	2301-200 Cottontail Ln *Cust Svc	Somerset	NJ	08873	**800-526-0266***	732-560-0060	580
Kyocera Solar Inc	7812 E Acoma Dr Suite 2	Scottsdale	AZ	85260	**800-223-9580**	480-948-8003	686
Kyocera Tycom Corp	17862 Fitch Ave	Irvine	CA	92614	**888-848-9266**		447
Kyphon Inc	1221 Crossman Ave *NASDAQ: KYPH*	Sunnyvale	CA	94089	**877-459-7466**	408-548-6500	469
Kysor Panel Systems	3201 NE Loop 820 Suite 150	Fort Worth	TX	76137	**800-633-3426**	817-281-5121	650
KYTV-TV Ch 3 (NBC)	PO Box 3500	Springfield	MO	65807	**800-492-4335**	417-268-3000	726
KYXY-FM 96.5 (AC)	8033 Linda Vista Rd	San Diego	CA	92111	**888-560-9650**	858-571-7600	631
KYYA-FM 93.3 (AC)	2075 Central Ave	Billings	MT	59102	**866-627-5483**	406-652-8400	631
KZBD-FM 105.7 (CR)	1601 E 57th Ave	Spokane	WA	99223	**800-718-7874**	509-448-1000	631
KZKZ-FM 106.3 (Rel)	6420 S Zero St	Fort Smith	AR	72903	**800-583-7960**	479-646-6700	631
KZOK-FM 102.5 (CR)	1000 Dexter Ave N Suite 100	Seattle	WA	98109	**800-252-1025**	206-805-1100	631
KZSE-FM 90.7 (NPR)	206 S Broadway Suite 735	Rochester	MN	55904	**800-652-9700**	507-282-0910	631

L

Name	Address	City	State	Zip	Toll-Free	Phone	Class
L-3 Avionics Systems	5353 52nd St SE	Grand Rapids	MI	49512	**800-253-9525**	616-949-6600	519
L-3 Communications Corp Telemetry & Instrumentation Div	9020 Balboa Ave	San Diego	CA	92123	**800-351-8483**	858-694-7500	519
L-3 Communications Flight International Aviation LLC	1 Lear Dr	Newport News	VA	23602	**800-358-4685**	757-886-5500	25
L-3 Communications Narda Microwave (East)	435 Moreland Rd	Hauppauge	NY	11788	**800-666-7060**	631-272-5600	633
L & F Industries Corp Div of Erie Press Systems	1253 W 12th St PO Box 4061	Erie	PA	16512	**800-222-3608**	814-455-3941	448
L & H Packing Co	PO Box 813368	San Antonio	TX	78283	**800-999-3241**	210-532-3241	465
L & H Technologies Inc	11616 Wilmar Blvd	Charlotte	NC	28273	**800-753-4576**	704-588-3670	378
L & L Enterprises Inc	1307 E Maple Rd	Troy	MI	48083	**800-433-9486**	248-689-3850	292-3
L & L Nursery Supply Co Inc	5350 G St	Chino	CA	91710	**800-624-2517**	909-591-0461	288
L & L/Jiroch Distributing Co	1180 58th St	Wyoming	MI	49509	**800-874-5550**	616-530-6600	744
L & M Bo-Truc Rental Inc	18692 W Main St	Galliano	LA	70354	**800-256-1186**	985-475-5733	309
L Suzio Concrete Co Inc	PO Box 748	Meriden	CT	06450	**888-789-4626**	203-237-8421	180
L Thorn Co Inc	PO Box 198	New Albany	IN	47151	**800-662-4594**	812-246-4461	190-1
L & W Supply Corp	125 S Franklin St	Chicago	IL	60606	**800-621-9622**	312-606-4000	190-2
La Bella Strings	256 Broadway	Newburgh	NY	12550	**800-750-3034**	845-562-4400	516
La Calhene Inc	1325 Field Ave S	Rush City	MN	55069	**800-322-7604**	320-358-4713	19
La Casa del Zorro	3845 Yaqui Pass Rd	Borrego Springs	CA	92004	**800-824-1884**	760-767-5323	655
La Choy Foodservice	3353 Michelson Dr	Irvine	CA	92612	**800-663-0112**	949-437-1000	291-36
La-Co/Markal Co	1201 Pratt Blvd	Elk Grove Village	IL	60007	**800-621-4025**	847-956-7600	459
LA Computer Center	450 N Oak St	Inglewood	CA	90302	**800-689-3933**	310-671-4444	172
La Concha Hotel. Crowne Plaza Key West	430 Duval St	Key West	FL	33040	**800-745-2191**	305-296-2991	373
La Costa Resort & Spa	2100 Costa del Mar Rd	Carlsbad	CA	92009	**800-854-5000**	760-438-9111	655
La Crosse Area Convention & Visitors Bureau	410 Veterans Memorial Dr	La Crosse	WI	54601	**800-658-9424**	608-782-2366	205
La Crosse Area (Greater) Chamber of Commerce	712 Main St	La Crosse	WI	54601	**800-889-0539**	608-784-4880	137
La Crosse Tribune	401 N 3rd St	La Crosse	WI	54601	**800-262-0420**	608-782-9710	522-2
La Cross/Rainfair Inc	18550 NE Riverside Pkwy	Portland	OR	97230	**800-558-5990**	503-766-1005	153-5
LA Darling Co	1401 Hwy 49B	Paragould	AR	72450	**800-643-3499**	870-239-9564	281
LA Fitness International	8105 Irvine Ctr Dr Suite 200	Irvine	CA	92618	**800-600-2540**	949-255-7400	349
La Flora Hotel	1238 Collins Ave	Miami Beach	FL	33139	**877-523-5672**	305-531-3406	373
La Follette Utilities Board	PO Box 1411	La Follette	TN	37766	**800-352-1340**	423-562-3316	244
La Fonda	100 E San Francisco St	Santa Fe	NM	87501	**800-523-5002**	505-982-5511	373
La France Industries Div Mount Vernon Mills Inc	290 Old Anderson Hwy	La France	SC	29656	**800-845-9728**	864-646-3213	730-1
La Gard Inc	3330 Kashiwa St	Torrance	CA	90505	**800-523-9605**	310-325-5670	345
LA Gear Inc	844 Moraga Dr	Los Angeles	CA	90049	**800-252-4327**	310-253-7744	296
La Habra Products Inc	4125 E La Palma Ave Suite 250	Anaheim	CA	92807	**800-649-8933**	714-778-2266	490
La Hacienda Treatment Center	PO Box 1	Hunt	TX	78024	**800-749-6160**	830-238-4222	712
La Jolla Beach & Tennis Club	2000 Spindrift Dr	La Jolla	CA	92037	**800-237-5211**	858-454-7126	655
La Leche League International Inc (LLL)	1400 N Meacham Rd	Schaumburg	IL	60173	**800-525-3243**	847-519-7730	48-17
La Madeleine Inc	6688 N Central Expy Suite 700	Dallas	TX	75206	**800-400-5840**	214-696-6962	69
La Mancha Resort Village	444 Avenida Caballeros	Palm Springs	CA	92262	**800-255-1773**	760-323-1773	655
La Mansion del Rio	112 College St	San Antonio	TX	78205	**800-292-7300**	210-518-1000	373
La Paloma Resort & Spa. Westin	3800 E Sunrise Dr	Tucson	AZ	85718	**888-627-7201**	520-742-6000	655
La Pensione Hotel	606 W Date St	San Diego	CA	92101	**800-232-4683**	619-236-8000	373
La Petite Academy Inc	130 S Jefferson	Chicago	IL	60661	**800-527-3848**	312-789-1200	146
La Plata Electric Assn Inc	PO Box 2750	Durango	CO	81302	**888-839-5732**	970-247-5786	244
La Playa Beach & Golf Resort	9891 Gulf Shore Dr	Naples	FL	34108	**800-237-6883**	239-597-3123	655
La Playa Hotel & Cottages-by-the-Sea	PO Box 900	Carmel	CA	93921	**800-582-8900**	831-624-6476	373
La Porte Herald-Argus	701 State St	La Porte	IN	46350	**866-362-2167**	219-362-2161	522-2
La Posada de Albuquerque	125 2nd St NW	Albuquerque	NM	87102	**800-777-5732**	505-242-9090	373
La Posada Hotel & Suites	1000 Zaragoza St	Laredo	TX	78040	**800-444-2099**	956-722-1701	373
La Posada Resort. Doubletree	4949 E Lincoln Dr	Scottsdale	AZ	85253	**800-222-8733**	602-952-0420	655
La Posada de Santa Fe Resort & Spa	330 E Palace Ave	Santa Fe	NM	87501	**800-727-5276**	505-986-0000	655
La Prairie at the Ritz-Carlton Spa New York (Central Park)	50 Central Pk S 2nd Fl	New York	NY	10019	**800-241-3333**	212-521-6135	698
La Quinta Inns Inc	909 Hidden Ridge Suite 600	Irving	TX	75038	**877-204-9204**	214-492-6600	369
La Quinta Resort & Club	49-499 Eisenhower Dr	La Quinta	CA	92253	**800-598-3828**	760-564-4111	655
La Quinta Returns Club	PO Box 2636	San Antonio	TX	78299	**800-642-4258**		371
La Raza. National Council of	1111 19th St NW Suite 1000	Washington	DC	20036	**800-311-6257**	202-785-1670	48-14
La Rosa Del Monte Express Inc	1133-35 Tiffany St	Bronx	NY	10459	**800-452-7672**	718-991-3300	769
La Rue's Flower Shop	2600 N MacArthur Blvd	Oklahoma City	OK	73127	**800-847-1462**	405-943-3314	287
La Salle Farmers Grain Co	317 4th St NE	Madelia	MN	56062	**800-245-5857**	507-642-3276	272
La Salsa Inc	6307 Carpinteria Ave Suite A	Carpinteria	CA	93013	**800-527-2572**	805-745-7500	657
La Senorita	1135 Edgebrook St	Houston	TX	77034	**800-741-7574**	713-943-7574	657
La Sierra University	4500 Riverwalk Pkwy	Riverside	CA	92515	**800-874-5587**	951-785-2000	163
La Valencia Hotel	1132 Prospect St	La Jolla	CA	92037	**800-451-0772**	858-454-0771	373
La Veta/Cuchara Chamber of Commerce	PO Box 32	La Veta	CO	81055	**866-615-3676**	719-742-3676	137
La Vida Llena	10501 Lagrima de Oro NE	Albuquerque	NM	87111	**800-922-1344**	505-293-4001	659
LA Weekly	6715 Sunset Blvd	Los Angeles	CA	90028	**800-304-4414**	323-465-4414	522-4
LA Weight Loss Centers	747 Dresher Rd Suite 100	Horsham	PA	19044	**877-524-3571**	215-346-4300	797
LAA (Library Assn of Alberta)	80 Baker Crescent NW	Calgary	AB	T2L1R4	**877-522-5550**	403-284-5818	427

Name / Address	City	State	ZIP	Toll-Free	Phone	Class
LAB Airlines 225 SE 1st St	Miami	FL	33131	**800-337-0918**	305-374-4600	26
Lab Products Inc 742 Sussex Ave	Seaford	DE	19973	**800-526-0469**	302-628-4300	75
Lab Safety Supply Inc PO Box 1368	Janesville	WI	53547	**800-356-0783**	608-754-2345	667
Lab-Volt Systems 1710 Hwy 34 PO Box 686	Farmingdale	NJ	07727	**800-522-9658**	732-938-2000	694
LaBarge Pipe & Steel Co 500 N Broadway Suite 1600	Saint Louis	MO	63102	**800-325-3363**	314-231-3400	483
Labatt Breweries of Canada 207 Queen's Quay W Suite 299	Toronto	ON	M5J1A7	**800-268-2337**	416-361-5050	103
Labatt Food Service 4500 Industry Park Dr	San Antonio	TX	78218	**800-324-8732**	210-661-4216	292-8
Labconco Corp 8811 Prospect Ave *Cust Svc	Kansas City	MO	64132	**800-821-5525***	816-333-8811	411
LabCorp (Laboratory Corp of America Holdings) 1447 York Ct *NYSE: LH* ■ *Cust Svc	Burlington	NC	27215	**800-334-5161***	336-584-5171	409
Label Art 1 Riverside Way	Wilton	NH	03086	**800-258-1050**	603-654-6131	404
Label Art Southeast Div 100 Clover Green	Peachtree City	GA	30269	**800-232-7833**	770-631-7324	544
Labelmaster Co 5724 N Pulaski Rd	Chicago	IL	60646	**800-621-5808**	773-478-0900	404
Labeltape Inc 4489 E Paris Ave SE	Grand Rapids	MI	49512	**800-928-4537**	616-698-1830	404
Labette Community College 200 S 14th St	Parsons	KS	67357	**888-522-3883**	620-421-6700	160
Labette County Medical Center 1902 S US Hwy 59	Parsons	KS	67357	**800-843-5262**	620-421-4880	366-2
Labor Finders International Inc 3910 RCA Blvd Suite 1001	Palm Beach Gardens	FL	33410	**800-864-7749**	561-627-6507	707
Labor Ready Inc PO Box 2910 *NYSE: LRW*	Tacoma	WA	98401	**800-991-4991**	253-383-9101	707
Labor Studies. George Meany Center for 10000 New Hampshire Ave	Silver Spring	MD	20903	**800-462-4237**	301-431-6400	158
Labor US Dept of 200 Constitution Ave NW	Washington	DC	20210	**866-487-2365**	202-693-4650	336-11
Laboratories Assn. Optical 11096-A Lee Hwy Suite 101	Fairfax	VA	22030	**800-477-5652**	703-359-2830	49-8
Laboratories at Bonfils 717 Yosemite St 2nd Fl	Denver	CO	80230	**800-321-6088**	303-365-9000	408
Laboratory Accreditation. Commission on Office 9881 Broken Land Pkwy Suite 200	Columbia	MD	21046	**800-981-9883**	410-381-6581	49-8
Laboratory Corp of America Holdings (LabCorp) 1447 York Ct *NYSE: LH* ■ *Cust Svc	Burlington	NC	27215	**800-334-5161***	336-584-5171	409
Laboratory Corp of America Paternity Testing Services 1440 York Ct	Burlington	NC	27215	**800-742-3944**	336-222-7566	408
Laboratory Equipment Magazine 301 Gibraltar Dr	Morris Plains	NJ	07950	**800-547-7377**	973-292-5100	449-21
Laboratory Institute of Merchandising 12 E 53rd St	New York	NY	10022	**800-677-1323**	212-752-1530	163
Laboratory Medicine Magazine 2100 W Harrison St	Chicago	IL	60612	**800-621-4142**	312-738-1336	449-16
Laboratory for Student Success (LSS) Temple University/Center for Research in Human Development & Education 933 Ritter Annex 1301 Cecil B. Moore Ave	Philadelphia	PA	19122	**800-892-5550**	215-204-3030	654
Laboratory Supply Co 250 Ottawa Ave *Cust Svc	Louisville	KY	40209	**800-888-5227***	502-363-1891	467
Laborchex Co 2506 Lakeland Dr Suite 200	Jackson	MS	39232	**800-880-0366**	601-664-6760	621
Labrada Bodybuilding Nutrition 403 Century Plaza Dr Suite 440	Houston	TX	77073	**800-832-9948**	281-209-2137	786
Lac Courte Oreilles Ojibwa Community College 13466 W Trepania Rd	Hayward	WI	54843	**888-526-6221**	715-634-4790	161
Lacerte Software Corp 5601 Headquarters Dr	Plano	TX	75024	**800-765-4065**		176-10
Lackawanna College 501 Vine St	Scranton	PA	18509	**877-346-3552**	570-961-7810	160
Lack's Stores Inc PO Box 2088	Victoria	TX	77902	**800-242-1123**	361-578-3571	316
Laclede Electric Co-op PO Box M	Lebanon	MO	65536	**800-299-3164**	417-532-3164	244
Laclede Gas Co 720 Olive St	Saint Louis	MO	63101	**800-887-4173**	314-342-0500	774
Laclede Group Inc 720 Olive St *NYSE: LG*	Saint Louis	MO	63101	**800-887-4173**	314-342-0500	355-5
Laclede Groves Retirement Community 723 S Laclede Station Rd	Saint Louis	MO	63119	**877-363-1211**	314-968-5570	659
Lacreek Electric Assn Inc PO Box 220	Martin	SD	57551	**800-655-9324**	605-685-6581	244
LaCrosse Footwear Inc 18550 NE Riverside Pkwy *NASDAQ: BOOT* ■ *Cust Svc	Portland	OR	97230	**800-323-2668***	503-766-1010	296
LACSA 3600 Wilshire Blvd Suite 100P *Sales	Los Angeles	CA	90010	**800-225-2272***	213-385-9424	26
Lacto Milk Products Corp Johanna Farm Rd	Flemington	NJ	08822	**800-727-6700**	908-788-2200	291-27
Lactoprot USA Inc PO Box 7 *Cust Svc	Blue Mounds	WI	53517	**800-236-3300***	608-437-5598	291-5
Lacy Clay Aviation 7435 Valjean Ave	Van Nuys	CA	91406	**800-423-2904**	818-989-2900	14
Ladenburg Thalmann Financial Services Inc 590 Madison Ave *AMEX: LTS*	New York	NY	10022	**800-523-8425**	212-409-2000	679
Ladies' Home Journal 125 Park Ave	New York	NY	10017	**800-374-4545**	212-557-6600	449-11
Ladies Workout Express 500 E Broward Blvd Suite 1650	Fort Lauderdale	FL	33394	**800-833-5239**	954-527-5373	349
LaDuke Winona White Earth Land Recovery Project 32033 E Round Lake Rd	Ponsford	MN	56575	**888-779-3577**	218-573-3448	561
Lady of America Franchise Corp 500 E Broward Blvd Suite 1650	Fort Lauderdale	FL	33394	**800-833-5239**	954-527-5373	349
Lady Bird Johnson Wildflower Center 4801 LaCrosse Ave	Austin	TX	78739	**877-945-3357**	512-292-4200	98
Lady Ester Lingerie Corp 33 E 33rd St	New York	NY	10016	**800-937-2413**	212-684-4446	153-18
Lady Foot Locker 112 W 34th St	New York	NY	10120	**800-877-5239**	212-720-3700	296
Lady Grace Stores Inc 61 Exchange St	Malden	MA	02148	**800-922-0504**	781-322-1721	155-6
Ladybug Magazine 30 Grove St Suite C	Peterborough	NH	03458	**800-821-0115**	603-924-7209	449-6
Lafayette Convention & Visitors Commission 1400 NW Evageline Thwy	Lafayette	LA	70501	**800-346-1958**	337-232-3737	205
Lafayette Glass Co Inc 2841 Teal Rd *Cust Svc	Lafayette	IN	47905	**800-382-7862***	765-474-1402	188-6
Lafayette Hotel 101 Front St	Marietta	OH	45750	**800-331-9336**	740-373-5522	373
Lafayette. Hotel Manoir 661 Grande Allee E	Quebec	QC	G1R2K4	**800-363-8203**	418-522-2652	372
Lafayette Life Insurance Co PO Box 7007 *Cust Svc	Lafayette	IN	47903	**800-243-6631***	765-477-7411	384-2
Lafayette Park Hotel 3287 Mt Diablo Blvd	Lafayette	CA	94549	**800-368-2468**	925-283-3700	373
Lafayette Plaza Hotel 301 Government St	Mobile	AL	36602	**800-692-6662**	251-694-0100	373
Lafayette Wood-Works Inc 3004 Cameron St	Lafayette	LA	70506	**800-960-3311**	337-233-5250	489
Lafayette Yard Marriott Conference Hotel 1 W Lafayette St	Trenton	NJ	08608	**800-228-9290**	609-421-4000	370
LaForce Inc 1060 W Mason St	Green Bay	WI	54303	**800-236-8858**	920-497-7100	232
LaFrance Equipment Corp 516 Erie St	Elmira	NY	14904	**800-873-8808**	607-733-5511	667
Lagasse Inc 1122 Longford Rd	Oaks	PA	19456	**800-345-6020**	610-933-9015	549
Lago Mar Resort & Club 1700 S Ocean Ln	Fort Lauderdale	FL	33316	**800-524-6627**	954-523-6511	655
Lagoon & Pioneer Village 375 N Hwy 91	Farmington	UT	84025	**800-748-5246**	801-451-8000	32
LaGrange College 601 Broad St	LaGrange	GA	30240	**800-593-2885**	706-880-8000	163
LaGrange County Convention & Visitor Bureau 440 1/2 S Van Buren St	Shipshewana	IN	46565	**800-254-8090**	260-768-4008	205
LaGrange County Rural Electric Membership Corp PO Box 147	LaGrange	IN	46761	**877-463-7165**	260-463-7165	244
Laguna Beach Visitors & Conference Bureau 252 Broadway	Laguna Beach	CA	92651	**800-877-1115**	949-497-9229	205
Laguna Brisas Spa Hotel 1600 S Coast Hwy	Laguna Beach	CA	92651	**877-503-1461**	949-497-7272	373
Laguna Cliffs Marriott Resort 25135 Park Lantern	Dana Point	CA	92629	**800-228-9290**	949-661-5000	655
Laguna College of Art & Design 2222 Laguna Canyon Rd	Laguna Beach	CA	92651	**800-255-0762**	949-376-6000	163
Lahey Clinic 41 Mall Rd	Burlington	MA	01805	**800-524-3955**	781-744-5100	366-2
Laich Industries Corp 1000 Laich Pkwy	Cleveland	OH	44135	**800-551-0053**	216-898-9900	591
Laidlaw Corp 6625 N Scottsdale Rd	Scottsdale	AZ	85250	**800-528-8295**	480-951-0003	344
Laidlaw International Inc 55 Shuman Blvd Suite 400 *NYSE: LI*	Naperville	IL	60563	**800-524-3529**	630-848-3000	355-3
Laidlaw International Inc School Bus Div 3221 N Service Rd	Burlington	ON	L7R3Y8	**800-563-6072**	905-336-1800	110
Laidlaw Transit Services Inc 5360 College Blvd Suite 200	Overland Park	KS	66211	**800-821-3451**	913-345-1986	109
Laird Plastics Inc 1400 Centrepark Blvd Suite 500	West Palm Beach	FL	33401	**800-610-1016**	561-684-7000	592
Laird Technologies PO Box 650	Delaware Water Gap	PA	18327	**800-843-4556**	570-424-8510	321
Laitner Brush Co 1561 Laitner Dr *Cust Svc	Traverse City	MI	49686	**800-423-6805***	231-929-3300	104
Laitram Corp 220 Laitram Ln	Harahan	LA	70123	**800-533-8253**	504-733-6000	519
Lake Austin Spa Resort 1705 S Quinlan Pk Rd	Austin	TX	78732	**800-847-5637**	512-266-2444	697
Lake Barkley State Resort Park 3500 State Park Rd Box 790	Cadiz	KY	42211	**800-325-1708**	270-924-1131	655
Lake Beverage Corp 900 John St	West Henrietta	NY	14586	**800-476-4049**	585-427-0090	82-1
Lake Breeze Motel Resort 9000 Congdon Blvd	Duluth	MN	55804	**800-738-5884**	218-525-6808	655
Lake Catherine Footwear PO Box 6048	Hot Springs	AR	71902	**800-826-8676**	501-262-6000	296
Lake Champlain Regional Chamber of Commerce 60 Main St Suite 100	Burlington	VT	05401	**877-686-5253**	802-863-3489	137
Lake Country Power 2810 Elida Dr	Grand Rapids	MN	55744	**800-421-9959**		244
Lake County Convention & Visitors Bureau 7770 Corinne Dr	Hammond	IN	46323	**800-255-5253**	219-989-7770	205
Lake County Press Inc 98 Noll St	Waukegan	IL	60085	**800-369-4333**	847-336-4333	615
Lake Cumberland State Resort Park 5465 State Park Rd	Jamestown	KY	42629	**800-325-1709**	270-343-3111	655
Lake Erie College 391 W Washington St	Painesville	OH	44077	**800-533-4996**	440-375-7000	163
Lake Estes Inn & Suites 1650 Big Thompson Ave	Estes Park	CO	80517	**800-332-6867**	970-586-3386	373
Lake Forest College 555 N Sheridan Rd	Lake Forest	IL	60045	**800-828-4751**	847-234-3100	163
Lake Immunogenics Inc 348 Berg Rd	Ontario	NY	14519	**800-648-9990**	585-265-1973	574
Lake Las Vegas Resort. Hyatt Regency 101 MonteLago Blvd	Henderson	NV	89011	**800-233-1234**	702-567-1234	655
Lake Lawn Resort 2400 E Geneva St	Delavan	WI	53115	**800-338-5253**	262-728-7950	655
Lake Louise Inn 210 Village Rd	Lake Louise	AB	T0L1E0	**800-661-9237**	403-522-3791	372
Lake Lure Inn & Conference Center PO Box 10	Lake Lure	NC	28746	**888-434-4970**	828-625-2525	373
Lake Mancos Ranch 42688 County Rd 'N'	Mancos	CO	81328	**800-325-9462**	970-533-1190	238
Lake Morey Resort Club House Rd PO Box 48	Fairlee	VT	05045	**800-423-1211**	802-333-4311	655
Lake Murray Resort Park 3323 Lodge Rd	Ardmore	OK	73401	**800-257-0322**	580-223-6600	655
Lake Norman Chamber of Commerce 20916 Torrence Chapel Rd PO Box 760	Cornelius	NC	28031	**800-305-2508**	704-892-1922	137
Lake of the Ozarks Convention & Visitors Bureau 5815 Hwy 54	Osage Beach	MO	65065	**800-386-5253**	573-348-1599	205
Lake Placid Convention & Visitors Bureau 216 Main St Olympic Ctr	Lake Placid	NY	12946	**800-447-5224**	518-523-2445	205

Alphabetical Section

Name / Address	City	State	ZIP	Toll-Free	Phone	Class
Lake Placid Lodge Whiteface Inn Rd PO Box 550	Lake Placid	NY	12946	**877-523-2700**	518-523-2700	373
Lake Placid Resort. Hilton 1 Mirror Lake Dr.	Lake Placid	NY	12946	**800-755-5598**	518-523-4411	655
Lake Placid/Essex County Visitors Bureau 2610 Main St Suite 2 Olympic Ctr.	Lake Placid	NY	12946	**800-447-5224**	518-523-2445	137
Lake Powell Resorts & Marinas 100 Lakeshore Dr.	Page	AZ	86040	**800-528-6154**	928-645-2433	655
Lake Quinault Lodge 345 S Shore Rd PO Box 7	Quinault	WA	98575	**800-562-6672**	360-288-2900	655
Lake Region Co-op Electrical Assn 1401 S Broadway	Pelican Rapids	MN	56572	**800-552-7658**	218-863-1171	244
Lake Region Electric Assn Inc PO Box 341	Webster	SD	57274	**800-657-5869**	605-345-3379	244
Lake Region Packing Assn Inc 124 S Joanna Ave PO Box 1477	Tavares	FL	32778	**800-780-3400**	352-343-3111	12-1
Lake Region State College 1801 College Dr N	Devils Lake	ND	58301	**800-443-1313**	701-662-1514	160
Lake Shores Industries Inc PO Box 59	Erie	PA	16512	**800-458-0463**	814-456-4277	692
Lake States Insurance Co 12935 S West Bay Shore Dr	Traverse City	MI	49684	**800-968-2090**	231-946-6390	384-4
Lake Sun Leader 918 N State Hwy 5	Camdenton	MO	65020	**866-346-2132**	573-346-2132	522-2
Lake Superior College 2101 Trinity Rd	Duluth	MN	55811	**800-432-2004**	218-733-7600	160
Lake Superior State University 650 W Easterday Ave	Sault Sainte Marie	MI	49783	**888-800-5778**	906-632-6841	163
Lake Tahoe Resort & Casino. Hyatt Regency 111 Country Club Dr.	Incline Village	NV	89451	**800-233-1234**	775-832-1234	655
Lake Tahoe Visitors Authority 1156 Ski Run Blvd	South Lake Tahoe	CA	96150	**800-288-2463**	530-544-5050	205
Lake Texoma Resort Park PO Box 248	Kingston	OK	73439	**800-528-0593**	580-564-2311	655
Lake of the Torches Resort Casino 510 Old Abe Rd	Lac du Flambeau	WI	54538	**800-258-6724**	715-588-7070	133
Lake Winnepesaukah Amusement Park 1730 Lakeview Dr.	Rossville	GA	30741	**877-525-3946**	706-866-5681	32
Lake Worth Herald/Coastal Observer PO Box 191	Lake Worth	FL	33460	**888-544-0047**	561-585-9387	522-4
Lakeland Animal Nutrition 2725 S Combee Rd	Lakeland	FL	33803	**800-682-6144**	863-682-4995	438
Lakeland Center 701 W Lime St.	Lakeland	FL	33815	**800-200-4870**	863-834-8100	204
Lakeland College W 3718 South Dr	Plymouth	WI	53073	**800-569-2166**	920-565-2111	163
Lakeland Community College 7700 Clocktower Dr	Kirtland	OH	44094	**800-589-8520**	440-953-7000	160
Lakeland Financial Corp 202 E Center St *NASDAQ: LKFN*	Warsaw	IN	46580	**800-827-4522**	574-267-6144	355-2
Lakeland Industries Inc 711-2 Koehler Ave *NASDAQ: LAKE*	Ronkonkoma	NY	11779	**800-645-9291**	631-981-9700	566
Lakeland Plastics Inc 1550 McCormick Blvd	Mundelein	IL	60060	**800-225-2508**	847-680-1550	588
Lakeland Village Beach & Mountain Resort 3535 Lake Tahoe Blvd	South Lake Tahoe	CA	96150	**800-822-5969**	530-544-1685	655
Lakeport (Greater) Chamber of Commerce 875 Lakeport Blvd PO Box 295	Lakeport	CA	95453	**866-525-3767**	707-263-5092	137
Lakes Entertainment Inc 130 Cheshire Ln Suite 101 *NASDAQ: LACO*	Minnetonka	MN	55305	**800-946-9464**	952-449-9092	132
Lakeshore Automatic Products Inc 1865 Industrial Park Dr	Grand Haven	MI	49417	**800-851-6411**	616-846-5090	610
Lakeshore Technical College 1290 North Ave	Cleveland	WI	53015	**800-443-2129**	920-693-8213	787
Lakeside Inn 100 N Alexander St	Mount Dora	FL	32757	**800-556-5016**	352-383-4101	373
Lakeside Mall 14000 Lakeside Cir.	Sterling Heights	MI	48313	**800-334-5573**	586-247-4131	452
Lakeside Mfg Inc 4900 W Electric Ave	West Milwaukee	WI	53219	**800-558-8565**	414-902-6400	314-1
Lakeside Oil Co Inc 555 W Brown Deer Rd	Milwaukee	WI	53217	**800-289-3835**	414-540-4000	569
Lakeview-on-the-Lake Motel 8696 E Lake Rd	Erie	PA	16511	**888-558-8439**	814-899-6948	373
Lakeview Scanticon Resort & Conference Center 1 Lakeview Dr.	Morgantown	WV	26508	**800-624-8300**	304-594-1111	655
Lakeville Area Chamber of Commerce & Convention & Visitors Bureau PO Box 12	Lakeville	MN	55044	**888-525-3845**	952-469-2020	137
Lakeway Inn & Resort 101 Lakeway Dr	Austin	TX	78734	**800-525-3929**	512-261-6600	370
Lakewold Gardens 12317 Gravelly Lake Dr SW	Lakewood	WA	98499	**888-858-4106**	253-584-4106	98
Lakewood Engineering & Mfg Co 501 N Sacramento Blvd	Chicago	IL	60612	**800-621-4277**	773-722-4300	15
Lakewood Hospital 14519 Detroit Ave.	Lakewood	OH	44107	**800-521-3955**	216-521-4200	366-2
Lakewood Shores Resort 7751 Cedar Lake Rd.	Oscoda	MI	48750	**800-882-2493**	989-739-2073	655
Lakin Tire West Inc 15305 Spring Ave.	Santa Fe Springs	CA	90670	**800-488-2752**	562-802-2752	740
LallyPak Inc 1209 Central Ave.	Hillside	NJ	07205	**800-523-8484**	908-351-4141	538
Lam Research Corp 4650 Cushing Pkwy *NASDAQ: LRCX*	Fremont	CA	94538	**800-526-7678**	510-659-0200	685
LAMA (Library Administration & Management Assn) 50 E Huron St	Chicago	IL	60611	**800-545-2433**	312-280-5036	49-11
Lama Tony Boot Co Inc 1137 Tony Lama St	El Paso	TX	79915	**800-866-9526**	915-778-8311	296
Lamar Advertising Co 5551 Corporate Blvd. *NASDAQ: LAMR*	Baton Rouge	LA	70808	**800-235-2627**	225-926-1000	8
Lamar Community College 2401 S Main St	Lamar	CO	81052	**800-968-6920**	719-336-2248	160
Lamar County Chamber of Commerce 1125 Bonham St.	Paris	TX	75460	**800-727-4789**	903-784-2501	137
Lamar County Electric Co-op Assn 1485 N Main St	Paris	TX	75460	**800-782-9010**	903-784-4303	244
Lamar Electric Membership Corp 1367 Hwy 341 S PO Box 40	Barnesville	GA	30204	**877-358-1383**	770-358-1383	244
Lamar Outdoor Advertising 5953 Susquehanna Plaza Dr	York	PA	17406	**800-632-9014**	717-252-1528	8
Lamar State College *Orange* 410 Front St.	Orange	TX	77630	**800-884-7750**	409-883-7750	160
Port Arthur PO Box 310	Port Arthur	TX	77641	**800-477-5872**	409-983-4921	160
Lamart Corp 16 Richmond St	Clifton	NJ	07015	**800-526-2789**	973-772-6262	588
Lamartek Inc DBA Dive Right 175 NW Washington St *Orders	Lake City	FL	32055	**800-495-1046***	386-752-1087	701
Lamaze International 2025 M St NW Suite 800	Washington	DC	20036	**800-368-4404**	202-367-1128	49-8
Lambda Chi Alpha International Fraternity 8741 Founders Rd.	Indianapolis	IN	46268	**800-209-6837**	317-872-8000	48-16
Lambda Electronics An Invensys Co 45 Fairchild Ave Suite A	Plainview	NY	11803	**800-526-2325**	516-629-3000	252
Lambda Novatronics Inc 2855 W McNab Rd	Pompano Beach	FL	33069	**800-952-6909**	954-984-7000	252
Lambda Physik Inc 3201 W Commercial Blvd Suite 110	Fort Lauderdale	FL	33309	**800-392-4637**	954-486-1500	416
Lambuth University 705 Lambuth Blvd.	Jackson	TN	38301	**800-526-2884**	731-425-2500	163
Lamers Bus Lines Inc 2407 S Point Rd	Green Bay	WI	54313	**800-236-1240**	920-496-3600	108
Lamers Tour & Travel 1126 W Boden Ct	Milwaukee	WI	53221	**800-236-8687**	414-281-2002	748
Laminations 3010 E Venture Dr.	Appleton	WI	54911	**800-925-2626**	920-831-0596	538
Laminators Inc 3255 Souderton Pike	Hatfield	PA	19440	**800-523-2347**	215-723-8107	805
Lammes Candies Since 1885 Inc 200 B Parker Dr Suite 500	Austin	TX	78728	**800-252-1885**	512-310-1885	291-8
Lamons Gasket Co 7300 Airport Blvd	Houston	TX	77061	**800-231-6906**	713-222-0284	321
Lamothe House Hotel 621 Esplanade Ave	New Orleans	LA	70116	**800-367-5858**	504-947-1161	373
LaMotte Co 802 Washington Ave	Chestertown	MD	21620	**800-344-3100**	410-778-3100	410
Lampert Tours Inc 1359 N Wells St	Chicago	IL	60610	**800-331-9640**	312-951-2866	748
Lamplight Farms Inc 4900 N Lilly Rd	Menomonee Falls	WI	53051	**800-645-5267**	262-781-9590	431
Lamplighter Inn & Suites South 1772 S Glenstone Ave	Springfield	MO	65804	**800-749-7275**	417-882-1113	373
Lampus RI Co 816 RI Lampus Ave	Springdale	PA	15144	**800-872-7310**	724-274-5035	181
Lamson College 1126 N Scottsdale Rd Suite 17	Tempe	AZ	85281	**800-898-7017**	480-898-7000	158
Lamson & Goodnow Mfg Co 45 Conway St.	Shelburne Falls	MA	01370	**800-872-6564**	413-625-6331	219
Lamson & Sessions Co 25701 Science Park Dr. *NYSE: LMS*	Cleveland	OH	44122	**800-321-1970**	216-464-3400	804
Lan Supervision Inc (LSVi) 3000 Executive Pkwy Suite 200 *Tech Supp	San Ramon	CA	94583	**800-820-8188***	925-355-0234	176-7
Lancaster Bible College 901 Eden Rd PO Box 83403	Lancaster	PA	17608	**800-544-7335**	717-569-7071	163
Lancaster Colony Corp Candle-Lite Div PO Box 42364	Cincinnati	OH	45242	**800-718-7018**	513-563-1113	122
Lancaster Distributing Co 1310 Union St	Spartanburg	SC	29302	**800-845-8287**	864-583-3011	540
Lancaster Eagle-Gazette 138 W Chestnut St.	Lancaster	OH	43130	**888-420-3883**	740-681-4500	522-2
Lancaster Glass Corp 240 W Main St.	Lancaster	OH	43130	**800-264-6826**	740-653-0311	328
Lancaster Host Resort 2300 Lincoln Hwy E *Resv	Lancaster	PA	17602	**800-233-0121***	717-299-5500	655
Lancaster Hotel 701 Texas St.	Houston	TX	77002	**800-231-0336**	713-228-9500	373
Lancaster Knives Inc 165 Court St PO Box 268	Lancaster	NY	14086	**800-869-9666**	716-683-5050	484
Lancaster Leaf Tobacco Co PO Box 897	Lancaster	PA	17608	**800-767-6889**	717-394-2676	742
Lancaster New Era 8 W King St	Lancaster	PA	17608	**800-809-4666**	717-291-8733	522-2
Lancaster Newspapers Inc 8 W King St	Lancaster	PA	17603	**800-809-4666**	717-291-8811	623-8
Lancaster Theological Seminary 555 W James St.	Lancaster	PA	17603	**800-393-0654**	717-393-0654	164-3
Lance Camper Corp 43120 Venture St	Lancaster	CA	93535	**800-423-7996**	661-949-3322	120
Lance Inc 8600 South Blvd *NASDAQ: LNCE*	Charlotte	NC	28273	**800-438-1880**	704-554-1421	291-9
Lancer Corp 6655 Lancer Blvd *AMEX: LAN*	San Antonio	TX	78219	**800-729-1500**	210-310-7000	650
Lancer Label 301 S 74th St *Cust Svc	Omaha	NE	68114	**800-228-7074***	402-390-9119	404
Lancer Orthodontics Inc 253 Pawnee St *Cust Svc	San Marcos	CA	92069	**800-854-2896***	760-744-5585	226
LanChile Airlines 9700 S Dixie Hwy 11th Fl	Miami	FL	33156	**800-735-5526**	305-670-1961	26
LanChile Cargo Group PO Box 520846	Miami	FL	33152	**800-735-5526**	305-871-4980	13
Lancia Construction 9430 Lima Rd Suite A	Fort Wayne	IN	46818	**800-752-6242**	260-489-4433	639
Land Coast Insulation Inc 4017 2nd St	New Iberia	LA	70560	**800-333-9424**	337-367-7741	188-9
Land Institute. Realtors 430 N Michigan Ave	Chicago	IL	60611	**800-441-5263**	312-329-8440	49-17
Land Institute. Urban 1025 Thomas Jefferson St NW Suite 500W *Orders	Washington	DC	20007	**800-321-5011***	202-624-7000	48-8
Land & Legal Solutions Inc 300 S Hamilton Ave	Greensburg	PA	15601	**800-245-7900**	724-853-8992	176-10
Land Line Magazine 1 NW OOIDA Dr	Grain Valley	MO	64029	**800-444-5791**	816-229-5791	449-21
Land 'N' Sea Distributing Inc 3131 N Andrews Ave Ext	Pompano Beach	FL	33064	**800-432-7652**	954-792-5436	759
Land O'Frost Inc 16850 Chicago Ave	Lansing	IL	60438	**800-323-3308**	708-474-7100	465
Land O'Lakes Farmland Feed LLC 4001 Lexington Ave N	Arden Hills	MN	55112	**800-328-9680**	651-481-2222	438
Land O'Lakes Inc 4001 Lexington Ave N	Arden Hills	MN	55126	**800-328-9680**	651-481-2222	291-3

Company / Address	City	State	ZIP	Toll-Free	Phone	Class
Land O'Lakes Inc Western Feed Div PO Box 818	Caldwell	ID	83606	**800-452-4052**	208-459-3689	438
Land O'Sun Dairies LLC 2900 Bristol Hwy	Johnson City	TN	37601	**800-683-0765**	423-283-5700	291-25
Land Rover North America Inc 555 MacArthur Rd	Mahwah	NJ	07430	**800-637-6837**	201-818-8500	59
Land Span Inc 1120 W Griffin Rd	Lakeland	FL	33805	**800-248-4847**	863-688-1102	769
Land Title Assn. American 1828 L St NW Suite 705	Washington	DC	20036	**800-787-2582**	202-296-3671	49-10
Land Transportation 1901 Phoenix Blvd Suite 210	Atlanta	GA	30349	**888-831-4448**	678-251-2500	769
Land. Trust for Public 116 New Montgomery St 4th Fl	San Francisco	CA	94105	**800-729-6428**	415-495-4014	48-13
Land Use Law Report 8737 Colesville Rd Suite 1100	Silver Spring	MD	20910	**800-274-6767**	301-587-6300	521-5
Landair Corp 430 Airport Rd	Greeneville	TN	37745	**888-526-3247**	423-783-1300	769
LandAmerica Financial Group Inc 101 Gateway Center Pkwy Gateway 1 *NYSE: LFG*	Richmond	VA	23235	**800-388-8822**	804-267-8000	355-4
LandAmerica OneStop Inc 600 Clubhouse Dr	Moon Township	PA	15108	**866-226-8616**		384-6
Landata Inc of Illinois 2055 W Army Trail Rd	Addison	IL	60101	**888-534-4461**	630-889-4088	384-6
Landau Uniforms Inc 8410 W Sandidge Rd	Olive Branch	MS	38654	**800-238-7513**	662-895-7200	153-19
Landauer Inc 2 Science Rd *NYSE: LDR*	Glenwood	IL	60425	**800-323-8830**	708-755-7000	566
Landcare Network. Professional 950 Herndon Pkwy Suite 450	Herndon	VA	20170	**800-395-2522**	703-736-9666	48-2
Landell-Thelen Inc 323 E Hwy 30	Shelton	NE	68876	**800-694-5674**	308-647-6811	270
Lander Co Inc 200 Lenox Dr Suite 202 *Orders	Lawrenceville	NJ	08648	**800-452-6337***	609-219-0930	211
Lander University 320 Stanley Ave	Greenwood	SC	29649	**888-452-6337**	864-388-8307	163
Landers Segal Color Co 305 W Grand Ave	Montvale	NJ	07645	**888-452-6726**	201-307-5995	540
Landlord Law Report 8204 Fenton St	Silver Spring	MD	20910	**800-666-6380**	301-588-6380	521-7
Landmark Bancorp Inc 800 Poyntz Ave *NASDAQ: LARK*	Manhattan	KS	66502	**800-322-6344**	785-565-2000	355-2
Landmark Communications Inc 150 W Brambleton Ave	Norfolk	VA	23510	**800-446-2004**	757-446-2010	355-3
Landmark Community Newspapers Inc 601 Taylorsville Rd	Shelbyville	KY	40065	**800-939-9322**	502-633-4334	623-8
Landmark Graphics Corp 2101 CityWest Blvd	Houston	TX	77242	**800-207-3098**	713-839-2000	176-10
Landmark Inn 230 N Front St	Marquette	MI	49855	**800-752-6362**	906-228-2580	373
Landmark Medical Center 115 Cass Ave	Woonsocket	RI	02895	**800-722-0175**	401-767-3211	366-2
Landmark Resort 1501 S Ocean Blvd	Myrtle Beach	SC	29577	**800-845-0658**	843-448-9441	655
Landmark Resort 7643 Hillside Rd	Egg Harbor	WI	54209	**800-273-7877**	920-868-3205	655
Landmark Theater 6 N Laurel St	Richmond	VA	23220	**877-297-5729**	804-646-4213	562
Landmen. American Assn of Professional 4100 Fossil Creek Blvd	Fort Worth	TX	76137	**888-566-2275**	817-847-7700	48-12
Landoll Corp 1900 North St *Cust Svc	Marysville	KS	66508	**800-446-5175***	785-562-5381	462
Landowners Assn. Forest 3776 La Vista Rd Suite 250	Tucker	GA	30084	**800-325-2954**	404-325-2954	48-13
Landry's Restaurants Inc 1510 W Loop South *NYSE: LNY*	Houston	TX	77027	**800-552-6379**	713-850-1010	657
Lands' End Inc 1 Lands' End Ln *Orders	Dodgeville	WI	53595	**800-356-4444***	608-935-9341	451
Landscape Architects. American Society of 636 'I' St NW	Washington	DC	20001	**800-787-2752**	202-898-2444	48-2
Landscape Concepts Inc 31745 N Alleghany Rd	Grayslake	IL	60030	**866-655-3800**	847-223-3800	413
Landscape Structures Inc 601 7th St S	Delano	MN	55328	**800-328-0035**	763-972-3391	340
Landshire Inc 9200 W Main St	Belleville	IL	62223	**800-468-3354**	618-398-8122	291-34
Landstar Development Corp 120 Fairway Woods Blvd	Orlando	FL	32824	**800-327-9105**	407-240-0044	639
Landstar Express America Inc 13410 Sutton Park Dr S	Jacksonville	FL	32224	**800-872-3278**		769
Landstar Gemini Inc 13410 Sutton Park Dr S	Jacksonville	FL	32224	**800-862-9232**		769
Landstar Inway Inc 1000 Simpson Rd	Rockford	IL	61102	**800-435-4373**	815-972-5000	769
Landstar Ligon Inc 13410 Sutton Park Dr S	Jacksonville	FL	32224	**800-235-4466**	904-306-2440	769
Landstar Logistics Inc 13410 Sutton Park Dr S	Jacksonville	FL	32224	**800-872-9400**	904-399-8909	440
Landstar Ranger Inc 13410 Sutton Pk Dr S	Jacksonville	FL	32224	**800-872-9400**	904-398-9400	769
Landstar System Inc 13410 Sutton Park Dr S *NASDAQ: LSTR*	Jacksonville	FL	32224	**800-872-9400**	904-398-9400	769
Landstroms Blackhills Gold Creations 405 Canal St	Rapid City	SD	57701	**800-843-0009**	605-343-0157	401
Lane Aviation Corp 4389 International Gateway	Columbus	OH	43219	**800-848-6263**	614-237-3747	63
Lane Bryant Inc 8655 E Broad St	Reynoldsburg	OH	43068	**800-876-8728**	614-577-4000	155-6
Lane College 545 Lane Ave *Admissions	Jackson	TN	38301	**800-960-7533***	731-426-7500	163
Lane EF Hotel 30 Main St	Keene	NH	03431	**888-300-5056**	603-357-7070	373
Lane Ltd 2280 Mountain Industrial Blvd	Tucker	GA	30084	**800-221-4134**	770-934-8540	741-3
Lane Packing Inc Hwy 96 & 50 Ln Rd PO Box 1087	Fort Valley	GA	31030	**800-277-3224**	478-825-3592	310-3
Lane Press Inc PO Box 130	Burlington	VT	05402	**800-733-3740**	802-863-5555	615
Langan Engineering & Environmental Services Inc River Drive Ctr 1	Elmwood Park	NJ	07407	**800-352-6426**	201-794-6900	258
Langdale Forest Products Co PO Box 1088	Valdosta	GA	31603	**800-864-6909**	229-242-7450	671
Langdon Hall Country House Hotel & Spa 1 Langdon Dr	Cambridge	ON	N3H4R8	**800-268-1898**	519-740-2100	372
Langenwalter Carpet Dyeing 1111 S Richfield Rd	Placentia	CA	92870	**800-422-4370**	714-528-7610	150
Langer Inc 450 Commack Rd *NASDAQ: GAIT*	Deer Park	NY	11729	**800-233-2687**	631-667-1200	469
Langeveld Bulb Co Inc 725 Vassar Ave	Lakewood	NJ	08701	**800-526-0467**	732-367-2000	318
Langham Hotel Boston 250 Franklin St	Boston	MA	02110	**800-791-7781**	617-451-1900	373
Langhorne Ski Shop 543 Lincoln Hwy	Fairless Hills	PA	19030	**800-523-8850**	215-295-4240	702
Langley Federal Credit Union 1055 W Mercury Blvd	Hampton	VA	23666	**800-826-7490**	757-827-7200	216
Langlois Co 10810 San Sevaine Way	Mira Loma	CA	91752	**800-962-5993**	951-360-3900	291-16
Langston Cos Inc 1760 S 3rd St *Cust Svc	Memphis	TN	38101	**800-627-5224***	901-774-4440	68
Langstons Co 2224 Exchange Ave	Oklahoma City	OK	73108	**800-658-2831**	405-235-9536	227
Language Automation Inc 1670 S Amphlett Blvd Suite 214	San Mateo	CA	94402	**800-571-4685**	650-571-7877	176-7
Language Exchange International 500 NE Spanish River Blvd Suite 19	Boca Raton	FL	33431	**800-223-5836**	561-368-3913	414
Language-Hearing Assn. American Speech- 10801 Rockville Pike	Rockville	MD	20852	**800-498-2071**	301-897-5700	49-8
Language Line Services 1 Lower Ragsdale Dr Bldg 2	Monterey	CA	93940	**877-886-3885**	831-648-7541	757
Lanier J Smith & Co 300 W 10th St	West Point	GA	31833	**800-226-4522**	706-645-2211	383
Lanier Park Hospital 675 White Sulphur Rd	Gainesville	GA	30501	**800-388-1920**	678-343-4000	366-2
Lannett Co Inc 9000 State Rd *AMEX: LCI*	Philadelphia	PA	19136	**800-325-9994**	215-333-9000	470
LanPass 9700 S Dixie Hwy 11th FL	Miami	FL	33156	**866-435-9526**	305-670-9999	27
LanPeru Airlines 9700 S Dixie Hwy 11th Fl	Miami	FL	33156	**800-735-5526**	305-670-9999	26
LANSA Inc 3010 Highland Pkwy Suite 950	Downers Grove	IL	60515	**800-457-4083**	630-874-7000	176-2
Lansco Colors 305 W Grand Ave	Montvale	NJ	07645	**888-452-6726**	201-307-5995	540
Lansdowne Resort 44050 Woodridge Pkwy	Leesburg	VA	20176	**800-541-4801**	703-729-8400	370
Lansing Community College 520 N Washington Sq	Lansing	MI	48901	**800-644-4522**	517-483-1957	160
Lansing (Greater) Convention & Visitors Bureau 1223 Turner St Suite 200	Lansing	MI	48906	**800-648-6630**	517-487-0077	205
Lansing State Journal 120 E Lenawee St	Lansing	MI	48919	**800-234-1719**	517-377-1000	522-2
Lantal Textiles Inc 1300 Langenthal Dr PO Box 965	Rural Hall	NC	27045	**800-334-3309**	336-969-9551	730-1
Lantech Inc 11000 Bluegrass Pkwy	Louisville	KY	40299	**800-866-0322**	502-267-4200	537
Lanter Co PO Box 68	Madison	IL	62060	**800-966-6137**	618-452-9500	769
Lantern Lodge Motor Inn 411 N College St	Myerstown	PA	17067	**800-262-5564**	717-866-6536	373
Lantronix Corp 15353 Barranca Pkwy *NASDAQ: LTRX* ■ *Orders	Irvine	CA	92618	**800-422-7055***	949-453-3990	720
LanVision Systems Inc 10200 Alliance Rd Suite 200 *NASDAQ: LANV*	Cincinnati	OH	45242	**800-878-5262**	513-794-7100	39
Laparoendoscopic Surgeons. Society of 7330 SW 62nd Pl Suite 410	South Miami	FL	33143	**800-446-2659**	305-665-9959	49-8
Laparoscopists. American Assn of Gynecological 13021 E Florence Ave	Santa Fe Springs	CA	90670	**800-554-2245**	562-946-8774	49-8
Lapham-Hickey Steel Corp 5500 W 73rd St *Cust Svc	Chicago	IL	60638	**800-323-8443***	708-496-6111	483
LapLink Software Inc 10210 NE Points Dr Suite 400	Kirkland	WA	98033	**800-343-8080**	425-952-6000	176-12
LaPorte County Convention & Visitors Bureau 1503 S Meer Rd	Michigan City	IN	46360	**800-634-2650**	219-872-5055	205
Laramie Area Chamber of Commerce 800 S 3rd St	Laramie	WY	82070	**866-876-1012**	307-745-7339	137
Laramie County Community College 1400 E College Dr	Cheyenne	WY	82007	**800-522-2993**	307-778-5222	160
Laramie River Dude Ranch 25777 County Rd 103	Jelm	WY	82063	**800-551-5731**	970-435-5716	238
Laramie Tire Distributors Inc 2000 Campus Ln	East Norristown	PA	19403	**800-523-0430**	610-615-8000	740
Larchmont Engineering & Irrigation Co 11 Larchmont Ln	Lexington	MA	02420	**877-862-2550**	781-862-2550	270
Larco 1902 13th St SE *Cust Svc	Brainerd	MN	56401	**800-523-6996***	218-829-9797	681
Laredo Morning Times 111 Esperanza Dr	Laredo	TX	78041	**800-728-3118**	956-728-2500	522-2
Laredo National Bancshares Inc 700 San Bernardo Ave *Mktg	Laredo	TX	78040	**888-723-1151***	956-723-1151	355-2
Laredo National Bank 700 San Bernardo Ave	Laredo	TX	78040	**888-723-1151**	956-723-1151	71
Lario Oil & Gas Co 301 S Market St	Wichita	KS	67202	**800-865-5611**	316-265-5611	525
Lark Books 67 Broadway St *Orders	Asheville	NC	28801	**800-284-3388***	828-253-0467	623-2
Lark Technologies Inc 9441 W Sam Houston Pkwy S Suite 103	Houston	TX	77099	**800-288-3720**	713-779-3663	654
Larksfield Place 7373 E 29th St N	Wichita	KS	67226	**877-636-1234**	316-636-1000	659
LaRoche Industries Inc 1100 Johnson Ferry Rd	Atlanta	GA	30342	**800-226-4572**	404-851-0300	276
Larry's Inc 2020 Schoonover St	Gillette	WY	82718	**800-967-1473**	307-682-5394	188-5
Larscom Inc 39745 Eureka Dr *NASDAQ: LARS*	Newark	CA	94560	**888-527-7266**	510-492-0800	720
Larsen's Mfg Co 7421 Commerce Ln NE	Minneapolis	MN	55432	**800-527-7367**	763-571-1181	666

Name / Address	City	State	ZIP	Toll-Free	Phone	Class
Larson Allen Weishair & Co LLP 220 S 6th St Suite 300	Minneapolis	MN	55402	**888-335-6080**	612-376-4500	2
Larson Boats 700 Paul Larson Memorial Dr	Little Falls	MN	56345	**800-255-3622**	320-632-5481	91
Larson Distributing Co Inc 5925 N Broadway	Denver	CO	80216	**800-736-3750**	303-296-7253	356
Larson Gustave A Co PO Box 910	Pewaukee	WI	53072	**800-829-9609**	262-542-0200	651
Larson JH Co 10200 51st Ave N	Plymouth	MN	55442	**800-292-7970**	763-545-1717	245
Larson-Juhl 3900 Steve Reynolds Blvd	Norcross	GA	30093	**800-438-5031**	770-279-5200	304
Larson Mfg Co 2333 Eastbrook Dr *Cust Svc	Brookings	SD	57006	**800-352-3360***	605-692-6115	233
Las Casitas Village & Golden Door Spa 1000 El Conquistador Ave	Fajardo	PR	00738	**800-996-3426**	787-863-1000	655
Las Cruces Convention & Visitors Bureau 211 N Water St	Las Cruces	NM	88001	**800-343-7827**	505-541-2444	205
Las Cruces Sun-News 256 W Las Cruces Ave	Las Cruces	NM	88005	**800-745-5851**	505-541-5400	522-2
Las Encinas Hospital 2900 E Del Mar Blvd	Pasadena	CA	91107	**800-792-2345**	626-795-9901	366-3
LAS Enterprises Inc 2413 L & A Rd	Metairie	LA	70001	**800-264-1527**	504-887-1515	186
Las Vegas Club 18 E Fremont St	Las Vegas	NV	89101	**800-634-6532**	702-385-1664	133
Las Vegas Convention Center 3150 Paradise Rd	Las Vegas	NV	89109	**800-332-5333**	702-892-0711	204
Las Vegas Convention & Visitors Authority 3150 S Paradise Rd	Las Vegas	NV	89109	**800-332-5333**	702-892-0711	205
Las Vegas Hilton 3000 Paradise Rd	Las Vegas	NV	89109	**800-732-7117**	702-732-5111	373
Las Vegas Medical Center 3695 Hot Springs Blvd PO Box 1388	Las Vegas	NM	87701	**800-446-5970**	505-454-2100	366-3
Las Vegas Motor Speedway 7000 Las Vegas Blvd N	Las Vegas	NV	89115	**800-644-4444**	702-644-4444	504
Las Vegas Optic 614 Lincoln St	Las Vegas	NM	87701	**800-767-6796**	505-425-6796	522-2
Las Vegas-San Miguel Chamber of Commerce PO Box 128	Las Vegas	NM	87701	**800-832-5947**	505-425-8631	137
LaSalle Bank NA 135 S LaSalle St	Chicago	IL	60603	**800-643-9600**	312-443-2000	71
LaSalle Hotel 120 S Main St	Bryan	TX	77803	**866-822-2000**	979-822-2000	373
Lasco Bathware 8101 E Kaiser Blvd Suite 130	Anaheim	CA	92808	**800-877-2005**	714-993-1220	595
Lasco Fittings Inc PO Box 116	Brownsville	TN	38012	**800-776-2756**	731-772-3180	585
Lasell College 1844 Commonwealth Ave	Newton	MA	02466	**888-527-3554**	617-243-2000	163
Laser Institute of America (LIA) 13501 Ingenuity Dr Suite 128	Orlando	FL	32826	**800-345-2737**	407-380-1553	49-19
Laser Technology Inc 7070 S Tucson Way	Englewood	CO	80112	**800-280-6113**	303-649-1000	486
Laser Tek Industries 4909 US Hwy 12	Richmond	IL	60071	**800-322-8137**	815-675-1199	524
Laser Vision Centers Inc 540 Maryville Centre Dr Suite 200	Saint Louis	MO	63141	**800-852-1033**	314-434-6900	785
Lasers & Electro-Optics Society. IEEE IEEE Operations Ctr 445 Hoes Ln	Piscataway	NJ	08854	**800-678-4333**	732-981-0060	49-19
Laserscope 3070 Orchard Dr. *NASDAQ: LSCP*	San Jose	CA	95134	**800-356-7600**	408-943-0636	415
LaserSight Inc 6848 Stapoint Ct	Winter Park	FL	32792	**888-527-3235**	407-678-9900	415
LaserSight Technologies Inc 6848 Stapoint Ct	Winter Park	FL	32792	**888-527-3235**	407-678-9900	415
LaserSight of Wisconsin 240 1st St	Neenah	WI	54956	**888-774-3937**	920-729-6600	785
LaserVue Eye Center 3554 Round Barn Blvd Suite 200	Santa Rosa	CA	95430	**888-527-3745**	707-522-6200	785
Lasko Metal Products Inc 820 Lincoln Ave	West Chester	PA	19380	**800-394-3267**	610-692-7400	37
Lassen Community College PO Box 3000	Susanville	CA	96130	**800-461-9389**	530-257-6181	160
Lassus Brothers Oil Inc 1800 Magnavox Way	Fort Wayne	IN	46804	**800-686-2836**	260-436-1415	319
LastMinuteTravel.com Inc 220 E Central Pkwy Suite 4010	Altamonte Springs	FL	32701	**800-442-0568**	407-667-8700	762
Lastra America Inc 83 Wooster Heights Rd	Danbury	CT	06810	**800-325-3310**	203-744-6720	770
Latah County 522 S Adams PO Box 8068	Moscow	ID	83843	**800-691-2012**	208-882-8580	334
Latah Creek Winery 13030 E Indiana Ave	Spokane	WA	99216	**800-528-2427**	509-926-0164	50
Latham Hotel The 3000 M St NW	Washington	DC	20007	**800-368-5922**	202-726-5000	373
Latham Hotel Center City 135 S 17th St	Philadelphia	PA	19103	**877-528-4261**	215-563-7474	373
Latham Seed Co 131 180th St	Alexander	IA	50420	**800-798-3258**	641-692-3258	684
Lathem Time Corp 200 Selig Dr SW	Atlanta	GA	30336	**800-241-4990**	404-691-0400	112
Laticrete International Inc 91 Amity Rd	Bethany	CT	06524	**800-243-4788**	203-393-0010	3
Latigo Ranch PO Box 237	Kremmling	CO	80459	**800-227-9655**		238
Latrobe Brewing Co 119 Jefferson St	Latrobe	PA	15650	**800-245-7892**	724-537-5545	103
Latta Inc 1502 4th Ave	Huntington	WV	25701	**800-624-3501**	304-523-8400	524
Latter Day Saints Business College 411 E South Temple St	Salt Lake City	UT	84111	**800-999-5767**	801-524-8100	158
Lattice Inc 1751 S Naperville Rd Suite 100 *Sales	Wheaton	IL	60187	**800-444-4309***	630-949-3250	176-12
Lattice Semiconductor Corp 5555 NE Moore Ct *NASDAQ: LSCC*	Hillsboro	OR	97124	**800-327-8636**	503-681-0118	686
Lattner Boiler Mfg Co PO Box 1527	Cedar Rapids	IA	52406	**800-345-1527**	319-366-0778	352
L'Auberge Del Mar Resort & Spa 1540 Camino del Mar	Del Mar	CA	92014	**800-553-1336**	858-259-1515	655
L'Auberge de Sedona 301 L'Auberge Ln *Resv	Sedona	AZ	86336	**800-272-6777***	928-282-1661	373
Lauda Air 1155 Connecticut Ave NW Suite 602	Washington	DC	20036	**800-843-0002**	202-955-0023	26
Laufen USA 4244 Mt Pleasant St NW Suite 100	North Canton	OH	44720	**800-321-0684**	330-649-5000	736
Laughing Elephant 3645 Interlake Ave N	Seattle	WA	98103	**800-354-0400**	206-447-9229	130
Laughing Water Guest Ranch PO Box 157	Fortine	MT	59918	**800-847-5095**	406-882-4680	238
Laughlin Homer China Co 672 Fiesta Dr	Newell	WV	26050	**800-452-4462**	304-387-1300	716
Laundry Assn. Coin 1315 Butterfield Rd Suite 212	Downers Grove	IL	60515	**800-570-5629**	630-963-5547	49-4
Laura & Co Inc PO Box 1238	Yelm	WA	98597	**866-439-1715**	360-894-1418	130
Laura Ingalls Wilder Museum & Home 3068 Hwy A	Mansfield	MO	65704	**877-924-7126**	417-924-3626	509
Laurel Grocery Co Inc PO Box 4100	London	KY	40743	**800-467-6601**	606-878-6601	292-8
Laurel Highlands Chamber of Commerce 537 W Main St	Mount Pleasant	PA	15666	**888-547-7521**	724-547-7521	137
Laurel Highlands Visitors Bureau 120 E Main St	Ligonier	PA	15658	**800-333-5661**	724-238-5661	205
Laurel Ink 911 N 145th St	Seattle	WA	98133	**800-850-0081**	206-767-4300	130
Laurel Inn 444 Presidio Ave	San Francisco	CA	94115	**800-552-8735**	415-567-8467	373
Laurel Lake Retirement Community 200 Laurel Lake Dr	Hudson	OH	44236	**866-650-0681**	866-650-2100	659
Laurel Racing Assn Inc Rt 198 & Racetrack Rd	Laurel	MD	20724	**800-638-1859**	301-725-0400	628
Laurel Steel Products Co 1 Mount Pleasant Rd	Scottdale	PA	15683	**800-426-1983**	724-887-8090	482
Laurelville Mennonite Church Center Rt 5 Box 145	Mount Pleasant	PA	15666	**800-839-1021**	724-423-2050	660
Lauren Mfg 2228 Reiser Ave SE	New Philadelphia	OH	44663	**800-683-0676**	330-339-3373	664
Lauren Ralph 650 Madison Ave	New York	NY	10022	**888-475-7674**	212-318-7000	273
Lauren Ralph Chm/CEO/Dir Polo Ralph Lauren Corp 650 Madison Ave	New York	NY	10022	**800-377-7656**		561
Laurence CR Co Inc PO Box 58923	Los Angeles	CA	90058	**800-421-6144**	323-588-1281	190-2
Laurens Electric Co-op Inc PO Box 700	Laurens	SC	29360	**800-942-3141**	864-682-3141	244
Laurentian Bank of Canada 1981 ave McGill College *TSE: LB*	Montreal	QC	H3A3K3	**800-522-1846**	514-284-4500	71
Laurentian University 935 Ramsey Lake Rd	Sudbury	ON	P3E2C6	**800-461-4030**	705-675-4843	773
Lauri 51 Magnetic Ave	Smethport	PA	16749	**800-451-0520**	814-887-6921	242
Lausell Inc PO Box 938	Bayamon	PR	00960	**800-981-7724**	787-798-7610	232
Lava Hot Springs 430 E Main St PO Box 669	Lava Hot Springs	ID	83246	**800-423-8597**	208-776-5221	50
Lavanture Products Co PO Box 2058	Elkhart	IN	46515	**800-348-7625**	574-264-0658	589
Lavelle Industries Inc 665 McHenry St	Burlington	WI	53105	**800-528-3553**	262-763-2434	664
LaVelle Vineyards 89697 Sheffler Rd	Elmira	OR	97437	**800-645-8463**	541-935-9406	50
LaVezzi Precision Inc 999 Regency Dr	Glendale Heights	IL	60139	**800-323-1772**	630-582-1230	446
Lavitt Paul Mills Inc 1517 'F' Ave SE	Hickory	NC	28602	**800-825-7285**	828-328-2463	153-10
Law. American Academy of Psychiatry & the 1 Regency Dr PO Box 30	Bloomfield	CT	06002	**800-331-1389**	860-242-5450	49-15
Law Enforcement Agencies. Commission on Accreditation for 10302 Eaton Pl Suite 100	Fairfax	VA	22030	**800-368-3757**	703-352-4225	49-7
Law Enforcement. Americans for Effective 841 W Touhy Ave	Park Ridge	IL	60068	**800-763-2802**	847-685-0700	48-8
Law Enforcement Associates Corp 100 Hunter Pl	Youngsville	NC	27596	**800-354-9669**	919-554-4700	52
Law Enforcement Technology Magazine 1233 Janesville Ave	Fort Atkinson	WI	53538	**800-547-7377**	920-563-6388	449-5
Law Enforcement Television Network 4101 International Pkwy	Carrollton	TX	75007	**800-535-5386**	972-309-4000	502
Law Firm Partnership & Benefits Report 1617 JFK Blvd Suite 1750	Philadelphia	PA	19103	**800-999-1916**	215-557-2310	521-2
Law Firm Services Assn (LFSA) 10831 Old Mill Rd Suite 400	Omaha	NE	68154	**800-475-4476**	402-778-7922	49-10
Law Institute. American 4025 Chestnut St	Philadelphia	PA	19104	**800-253-6397**	215-243-1600	49-10
Law Institute. Environmental 2000 L St NW Suite 620	Washington	DC	20036	**800-433-5120**	202-939-3800	49-10
Law Institute. Food & Drug 1000 Vermont Ave NW Suite 200	Washington	DC	20005	**800-956-6293**	202-371-1420	49-10
Law Institute. Practising 810 7th Ave 26th Fl	New York	NY	10019	**800-260-4754**	212-824-5700	49-10
Law League of America. Commercial 150 N Michigan Ave Suite 600	Chicago	IL	60601	**800-978-2552**	312-781-2000	49-10
Law Office Management & Administration Report 3 Park Ave 30th Fl	New York	NY	10016	**800-401-5937**	212-244-0360	521-2
Law Officer's Bulletin 610 Opperman Dr	Eagan	MN	55123	**800-344-5008**	651-687-7000	521-2
Law Technology News 345 Park Ave S *Cust Svc	New York	NY	10010	**800-274-2893***	212-779-9200	449-7
Law.com Inc 10 United Nations Plaza 3rd Fl	San Francisco	CA	94102	**800-903-9872**		677
Law.com Lawjobs 10 Union Plaza 3rd Fl	San Francisco	CA	94102	**800-628-1160**		257
Lawjobs 10 Union Plaza 3rd Fl	San Francisco	CA	94102	**800-628-1160**		257
Lawn-Boy Inc 8111 S Lyndale Ave	Bloomington	MN	55420	**800-526-6937**	952-888-8801	420
Lawn Doctor Inc 142 SR 34	Holmdel	NJ	07733	**800-631-5660**	732-946-0029	421
Lawn & Golf Supply Co Inc 647 Nutt Rd	Phoenixville	PA	19460	**800-362-5650**	610-933-5801	420
Lawrence Behr Assoc Inc PO Box 8026	Greenville	NC	27835	**800-522-4464**	252-757-0279	195
Lawrence County Area (Greater) Chamber of Commerce PO Box 488	South Point	OH	45680	**800-408-1334**	740-377-4550	137
Lawrence County Chamber of Commerce 1609 N Locust Ave PO Box 86	Lawrenceburg	TN	38464	**877-388-4911**	931-762-4911	137

Alphabetical Section

Name / Address	City	State	Zip	Toll-Free	Phone	Class
Lawrence County Tourist Promotion Agency 229 S Jefferson St	New Castle	PA	16101	**888-284-7599**	724-654-8408	205
Lawrence Daily Journal-World Co 609 New Hampshire St	Lawrence	KS	66044	**800-578-8748**	785-843-1000	623-8
Lawrence David L Convention Center 1000 Fort Duquesne Blvd	Pittsburgh	PA	15222	**800-222-5200**	412-565-6000	204
Lawrence FD Electric Co Inc 3450 Beekman St *Cust Svc	Cincinnati	OH	45223	**800-582-4490***	513-542-1100	245
Lawrence Foods Inc 2200 Lunt Ave	Elk Grove Village	IL	60007	**800-323-7848**	847-437-2400	291-20
Lawrence Hardware 2 1st Ave	Sterling	IL	61081	**800-435-9568**	815-625-0360	345
Lawrence Journal-World 609 New Hampshire St	Lawrence	KS	66044	**800-578-8748**	785-843-1000	522-2
Lawrence & Memorial Hospital 365 Montauk Ave	New London	CT	06320	**888-777-9539**	860-442-0711	366-2
Lawrence Metal Products Inc 260 Spur Dr S PO Box 400-M *Sales	Bay Shore	NY	11706	**800-441-0019***	631-666-0300	482
Lawrence Paper Co 2801 Lakeview Rd	Lawrence	KS	66049	**800-535-4553**	785-843-8111	101
Lawrence Ragan Communications Inc 316 N Michigan Ave Suite 300	Chicago	IL	60601	**800-878-5331**	312-960-4140	623-9
Lawrence Sign Inc 945 Pierce Butler Rt	Saint Paul	MN	55104	**800-998-8901**	651-488-6711	692
Lawrence Technological University 21000 W 10-Mile Rd	Southfield	MI	48075	**800-225-5588**	248-204-3160	163
Lawrence Transportation Systems PO Box 7667	Roanoke	VA	24019	**800-336-9626**	540-966-4000	769
Lawrence University PO Box 599	Appleton	WI	54912	**888-201-6017**	920-832-7000	163
Lawrence Visitor Information Ctr 402 N 2nd St	Lawrence	KS	66044	**888-529-5267**	785-865-4499	205
Lawrence Welks Desert Oasis 34567 Cathedral Canyon Dr	Cathedral City	CA	92234	**800-824-8224**	760-321-9000	655
Lawrenceville Property & Casualty Co 2 Princess Rd	Lawrenceville	NJ	08648	**800-234-6449**	609-896-2404	384-4
Lawrenceville Re 2 Princess Rd	Lawrenceville	NJ	08648	**800-234-6449**	609-896-2404	384-4
Lawrenceville School 2500 Main St PO Box 6008	Lawrenceville	NJ	08648	**800-735-2030**	609-896-0400	611
Lawry's Foods Inc 222 E Huntington Dr	Monrovia	CA	91016	**800-952-9797**	626-930-8870	291-19
Lawson Mechanical Contractors 6090 S Watt Ave	Sacramento	CA	95829	**800-491-8808**	916-381-5000	188-10
Lawson Products Inc 1666 E Touhy Ave *NASDAQ: LAWS*	Des Plaines	IL	60018	**800-718-1221**	847-827-9666	378
Lawson Software Inc 380 Saint Peter St *NASDAQ: LWSN*	Saint Paul	MN	55102	**800-477-1357**	651-767-7000	176-1
Lawter International Inc 8601 95th St	Pleasant Prairie	WI	53158	**800-775-2983**	262-947-7300	143
Lawton CA Co Inc 1860 Enterprise Dr	De Pere	WI	54115	**800-842-6888**	920-337-2470	448
Lawton Chamber of Commerce & Industry 629 SW 'C' Ave Suite A	Lawton	OK	73501	**800-872-4540**	580-355-3541	137
Lawton Constitution 102 SW 3rd St Po Box 2069	Lawton	OK	73502	**800-364-3636**	580-353-0620	522-2
Lawton Industries Inc 4353 Pacific St	Rocklin	CA	95677	**800-692-2600**	916-624-7894	478
Lawyer Concierge Ltd 2155 Fairway Cir	Duluth	GA	30096	**888-852-5651**	770-638-1888	436
Lawyers of America. Association of Trial 1050 31st St NW	Washington	DC	20007	**800-424-2725**	202-965-3500	49-10
Lawyers Diary & Manual 240 Mulberry St	Newark	NJ	07102	**800-444-4041**	973-642-1440	623-2
Lawyers Title Co 251 S Lake Ave Suite 400	Pasadena	CA	91101	**800-347-7800**	626-304-2700	384-6
Lawyers Title Insurance Corp 101 Gateway Center Pkwy	Richmond	VA	23235	**800-446-7086**	804-267-8000	384-6
Lawyers' Travel Service 71 5th Ave 10th Fl	New York	NY	10003	**800-431-1112**	212-679-1166	760
lawyers.com Martindale-Hubbell 121 Chanlon Rd	New Providence	NJ	07974	**800-526-4902**	908-464-6800	169
Layton Mfg Corp 825 Remsen Ave	Brooklyn	NY	11236	**800-545-8002**	718-498-6000	15
Lazard Funds 30 Rockefeller Plaza 57th Fl	New York	NY	10112	**800-823-6300**		517
Lazare Kaplan International Inc 529 5th Ave 19th Fl *AMEX: LKI* ■ *Cust Svc	New York	NY	10017	**800-554-3325***	212-972-9700	399
Lazy K Bar Guest Ranch 8401 N Scenic Dr	Tucson	AZ	85743	**800-321-7018**	520-744-3050	238
Lazy L & B Ranch 1072 E Fork Rd	Dubois	WY	82513	**800-453-9488**	307-455-2839	238
LB Foster Co 415 Holiday Dr *NASDAQ: FSTR*	Pittsburgh	PA	15220	**800-255-4500**	412-928-3400	636
LB Furniture Industries LLC 99 S 3rd St	Hudson	NY	12534	**800-403-0833**	518-828-1501	314-3
LB White Co Inc W 6636 LB White Rd	Onalaska	WI	54650	**800-345-7200**	608-783-5691	352
LBA Group Inc 3400 Tupper Dr	Greenville	NC	27834	**800-522-4464**	252-757-0279	258
LBC Houston LP 11666 Port Rd	Seabrook	TX	77586	**888-922-4433**	281-474-4433	571
LBI Eyewear 20801 Nordhoff St	Chatsworth	CA	91311	**800-423-5175**	818-407-1890	531
LBU Inc 217 Brook Ave	Passaic	NJ	07055	**800-678-4528**	973-773-4800	68
LC Doane Co PO Box 975	Essex	CT	06426	**800-447-5006**	860-767-8295	431
LC Financial Inc 16119 Vanowen St	Van Nuys	CA	91406	**800-800-4523**	818-780-9300	157
LC Industries 401 N Western Ave	Chicago	IL	60612	**800-539-6255**	312-455-0500	444
LC King Mfg Co Inc 24 7th St PO Box 367	Bristol	TN	37620	**800-826-2510**	423-764-5188	153-19
LCA-Vision Inc 7840 Montgomery Rd *NASDAQ: LCAV*	Cincinnati	OH	45236	**888-529-2020**	513-792-9292	785
LCI Ltd 415 Pablo Ave N	Jacksonville Beach	FL	32240	**800-578-7891**	904-241-1200	144
LCMS (Lutheran Church Missouri Synod) 1333 S Kirkwood Rd	Saint Louis	MO	63122	**888-843-5267**	314-965-9000	48-20
LCT Transportation Services 26444 County Rd 33	Okahumpka	FL	34762	**800-874-3344**	352-326-8900	769
LDA (Learning Disabilities Assn of America) 4156 Library Rd	Pittsburgh	PA	15234	**888-300-6710**	412-341-1515	48-17
LDF (Lyme Disease Foundation Inc) Box 332	Tolland	CT	06084	**800-886-5963**	860-525-2000	48-17
LDS Test & Measurement LLC 8333 Rockside Rd *Sales	Valley View	OH	44125	**800-468-5365***	216-328-7000	247
Le Chateau Montebello. Fairmont 392 rue Notre Dame	Montebello	QC	J0V1L0	**800-441-1414**	819-423-6341	655
Le Creuset of America Inc 114 Bob Gifford Blvd	Early Branch	SC	29916	**800-827-1798**	803-943-4308	477
LE Johnson Products Inc 2100 Sterling Ave	Elkhart	IN	46516	**800-837-4697**	574-293-5664	345
LE Jones Co 1200 34th Ave	Menominee	MI	49858	**800-535-6637**	906-863-4411	128
Le Journal de Montreal 4545 rue Frontenac	Montreal	QC	H2H2R7	**800-521-4545**	514-521-4545	522-1
Le Mars Daily Sentinel 41 1st Ave NE	Le Mars	IA	51031	**800-728-0066**	712-546-7031	522-2
Le Meridien at Beverly Hills 465 S La Cienega Blvd	Los Angeles	CA	90048	**800-645-5624**	310-247-0400	373
Le Meridien Chicago 521 N Rush St	Chicago	IL	60611	**800-543-4300**	312-645-1500	373
Le Moyne College 1419 Salt Springs Rd	Syracuse	NY	13214	**800-333-4733**	315-445-4100	163
Le Nouvel Montreal Hotel & Spa 1740 boul Rene-Levesque W	Montreal	QC	H3H1R3	**800-363-6063**	514-931-8841	372
Le Parc Suite Hotel 733 N West Knoll Dr	West Hollywood	CA	90069	**800-578-4837**	310-855-8888	373
Le Parker Meridien 118 W 57th St	New York	NY	10019	**800-543-4300**	212-245-5000	373
Le Pavillon Hotel 833 Poydras St	New Orleans	LA	70112	**800-535-9095**	504-581-3111	373
LE Rabjohn Inc 1833 N Daly St	Los Angeles	CA	90031	**800-559-3737**	323-221-9163	15
Le Richelieu Hotel 1234 Chartres St	New Orleans	LA	70116	**800-535-9653**	504-529-2492	373
Le Royal Meridien King Edward 37 King St E	Toronto	ON	M5C1E9	**800-543-4300**	416-863-3131	372
Le Saint Sulpice 414 St Sulpice	Montreal	QC	H2Y2V5	**877-785-7423**	514-282-9942	372
LE Sauer Machine Co 3535 Tree Ct Industrial Blvd	Saint Louis	MO	63122	**800-745-4107**	636-225-5358	546
LE Smith Glass Co 1900 Liberty St	Mount Pleasant	PA	15666	**800-537-6484**	724-547-3544	330
Le Sueur Cheese Co Inc 719 N Main St	Le Sueur	MN	56058	**800-247-0871**	507-665-3353	291-5
Lea County Electric Co-op Inc PO Drawer 1447	Lovington	NM	88260	**800-510-5232**	505-396-3631	244
Lea & Perrins Inc 1501 Pollitt Dr	Fair Lawn	NJ	07410	**800-289-5797**	201-791-1600	291-19
Lea Regional Medical Center 5419 N Lovington Hwy	Hobbs	NM	88240	**877-492-8001**	505-392-6581	366-2
Leach & Garner General Findings 57 John L Dietsch Sq PO Box 200	North Attleboro	MA	02761	**800-345-1105**	508-695-7800	401
Lead Information Center. National **National Lead Information Center** 422 S Clinton Ave	Rochester	NY	14620	**800-424-5323**		336-16
Leader Insurance Co 5205 N O'Connor Blvd Suite 700	Irving	TX	75039	**877-953-2337**	214-526-3876	384-4
Leader-Telegram 701 S Farwell St	Eau Claire	WI	54701	**800-236-8808**	715-833-9200	522-2
Leaders Club Services Leading Hotels of the World 99 Park Ave *Resv	New York	NY	10016	**800-223-6800***	212-515-5600	371
Leadership For The Front Lines Newsletter 7201 McKinney Cir	Frederick	MD	21704	**800-243-0876**	301-698-7100	521-2
Leadership Journal 465 Gundersen Dr	Carol Stream	IL	60188	**800-777-3136**	630-260-6200	449-5
Leadership for Results Newsletter 316 N Michigan Ave Suite 300	Chicago	IL	60601	**800-878-5331**	312-960-4140	521-2
Leading Authorities Inc 1220 L St NW Suite 850	Washington	DC	20005	**800-773-2537**	202-783-0300	699
Leading Brands Inc 1500 W Georgia St Suite 1800 *NASDAQ: LBIX*	Vancouver	BC	V6G2Z6	**866-685-5200**	604-685-5200	82-2
Leading Hotels of the World 99 Park Ave	New York	NY	10016	**800-223-6800**	212-515-5600	368
Leading Lady Cos 24050 Commerce Pk *Cust Svc	Beachwood	OH	44122	**800-321-4804***	216-464-5490	153-18
League of Women Voters (LWV) 1730 M St NW Suite 1000	Washington	DC	20036	**800-249-8683**	202-429-1965	48-7
Leamington District Chamber of Commerce PO Box 321	Leamington	ON	N8H3W3	**800-250-3336**	519-326-2721	136
Leanin' Tree Inc 6055 Longbow Dr	Boulder	CO	80301	**800-777-8716**	303-530-1442	130
Leanin' Tree Museum of Western Art 6055 Longbow Dr	Boulder	CO	80301	**800-777-8716**	303-530-1442	509
Leap Wireless International Inc 10307 Pacific Center Ct	San Diego	CA	92121	**877-977-5327**	858-882-6000	721
LeapFrog Enterprises Inc 6401 Hollis St Suite 150 *NYSE: LF*	Emeryville	CA	94608	**800-701-5327**	510-420-5000	750
Learn.com Inc 14000 NW 4th St	Sunrise	FL	33325	**800-544-1023**	954-233-4000	754
LearnCom Inc 714 Industrial Dr	Bensenville	IL	60106	**800-824-8889**	630-227-1080	502
Learning Care Group Inc 38345 W Ten-Mile Rd Suite 100 *NASDAQ: LCGI*	Farmington Hills	MI	48335	**800-425-1212**	248-476-3200	146
Learning Channel The (TLC) 8516 Georgia Ave	Silver Spring	MD	20910	**888-404-5969**	240-662-2000	725
Learning Disabilities Assn of America (LDA) 4156 Library Rd	Pittsburgh	PA	15234	**888-300-6710**	412-341-1515	48-17
Learning Horizons Div American Greetings Corp 1 American Rd	Cleveland	OH	44144	**800-321-3040**	216-252-7300	242
Learning How 8895 McGaw Rd	Columbia	MD	21045	**800-675-7627**	410-381-0828	673
Learning Resources 380 N Fairway Dr	Vernon Hills	IL	60061	**800-222-3909**	847-573-8400	242
Learning Tree International Inc 6053 W Century Blvd Suite 200 *NASDAQ: LTRE* ■ *Cust Svc	Los Angeles	CA	90045	**800-843-8733***	310-417-9700	752
Learning Works 15342 Graham St	Huntington Beach	CA	92649	**800-235-5767**	714-895-5047	242
Learning Wrap-Ups Inc 1660 W Gordon Ave Suite 4	Layton	UT	84041	**800-992-4966**	801-497-0050	242
Learningstation.com Inc 8008 Corporate Ctr Dr Suite 210	Charlotte	NC	28217	**888-679-7058**	704-926-5400	39
Lease One Systems 7305 Manchester Rd Suite C-1	Saint Louis	MO	63143	**888-645-1300**	314-645-1300	261-3
Lease Plan USA 1165 Sanctuary Pkwy	Alpharetta	GA	30004	**800-457-8721**	770-933-9090	284
Leasing Assoc Inc PO Box 243	Houston	TX	77001	**800-449-4807**	713-522-9771	284

Name / Address	City	State	Zip	Toll-Free	Phone	Class
Leather Specialty Co 2690 W Airport Blvd	Sanford	FL	32771	**888-771-0200**	407-323-1830	444
Leathercraft Inc 102 Section House Rd	Conover	NC	28613	**800-951-3507**	828-322-3305	314-2
Leatherman Tool Group Inc 12106 NE Ainsworth Cir	Portland	OR	97220	**800-847-8665**	503-253-7826	746
Leave No Trace Center for Outdoor Ethics Inc PO Box 997	Boulder	CO	80306	**800-332-4100**	303-442-8222	48-23
Leavenworth Convention & Visitors Bureau 518 Shawnee St PO Box 44	Leavenworth	KS	66048	**800-844-4114**	913-682-4113	205
Leavenworth-Jefferson Electric Co-op Inc PO Box 70	McLouth	KS	66054	**888-796-6111**	913-796-6111	244
Leavenworth Times 422 Seneca St	Leavenworth	KS	66048	**800-466-0305**	913-682-0305	522-2
Lebanese Syrian Associated Charities. American 501 St Jude Pl	Memphis	TN	38105	**800-822-6344**	901-578-2000	48-5
Lebanon Area Chamber of Commerce 186 N Adams St	Lebanon	MO	65536	**888-588-5710**	417-588-3256	137
Lebanon Daily Record 100 E Commercial St	Lebanon	MO	65536	**800-665-8875**	417-532-9131	522-2
Lebanon Reporter 117 E Washington St	Lebanon	IN	46052	**888-482-4650**	765-482-4650	522-4
Lebanon Seaboard Corp 1000 E Cumberland St	Lebanon	PA	17042	**800-233-0628**	717-273-1685	276
Lebanon Valley College 101 N College Ave	Annville	PA	17003	**800-445-6181**	717-867-6100	163
Lebenthal & Co Inc 120 Broadway 12th Fl	New York	NY	10271	**800-425-6116**	212-425-6116	679
Leblanc Inc 7001 Leblanc Blvd	Kenosha	WI	53141	**800-558-9421**	262-658-1644	516
Leboeuf Brothers Towing Co Inc PO Box 9036	Houma	LA	70361	**800-256-5088**	985-594-6692	457
Lechler Inc 445 Kautz Rd *Cust Svc	Saint Charles	IL	60174	**800-777-2926***	630-377-6611	478
Leco Corp 3000 Lakeview Ave	Saint Joseph	MI	49085	**800-292-6141**	269-985-5496	410
LeCroy Corp 700 Chestnut Ridge Rd *NASDAQ: LCRY*	Chestnut Ridge	NY	10977	**800-553-2769**	845-425-2000	247
LecTec Corp 10701 Red Circle Dr	Minnetonka	MN	55343	**800-777-2291**	952-933-2291	469
Ledgelawn Inn 66 Mt Desert St	Bar Harbor	ME	04609	**800-274-5334**	207-288-4596	373
Ledger The 300 W Lime St	Lakeland	FL	33815	**888-431-7323**	863-802-7000	522-2
Ledger-Independent PO Box 518	Maysville	KY	41056	**800-264-9091**	606-564-9091	522-2
LedgerPlus Inc 401 Saint Francis St	Tallahassee	FL	32301	**888-643-1348**	850-681-1941	719
Ledtronics Inc 23105 Kashiwa Ct	Torrance	CA	90505	**800-579-4875**	310-534-1505	429
Lee Academy 26 Winn Rd	Mee	ME	04455	**888-433-2852**	207-738-2255	611
Lee Brass Co PO Box 1229	Anniston	AL	36202	**800-876-1811**	256-831-2501	303
Lee Brick & Tile Co 3704 Hawkins Ave	Sanford	NC	27330	**800-672-7559**	919-774-4800	148
Lee & Cates Glass Inc 142 Madison St	Jacksonville	FL	32203	**800-433-4188**	904-354-4643	188-6
Lee Co PO Box 424	Westbrook	CT	06498	**800-533-7584**	860-399-6281	776
Lee Co Inc 331 Mallory Station Rd	Franklin	TN	37067	**888-567-7747**	615-567-1000	188-10
Lee Construction Co PO Box 7667	Charlotte	NC	28241	**800-849-5272**	704-588-5272	187-4
Lee County Electric Co-op Inc PO Box 3455	North Fort Myers	FL	33918	**800-282-1643**	239-995-2121	244
Lee County Visitors & Convention Bureau 12800 University Dr Suite 550	Fort Myers	FL	33907	**800-237-6444**	239-338-3500	205
Lee Dan Communications Inc 155 Adams Ave	Hauppauge	NY	11788	**800-231-1414**	631-231-1414	385
Lee & Eastes Tank Lines Inc 2418 Airport Way S	Seattle	WA	98134	**800-552-7496**	206-623-5403	769
Lee Hecht Harrison LLC 50 Tice Blvd	Woodcliff Lake	NJ	07677	**800-611-4544**	201-782-3704	192
Lee Jeans 1 Lee Dr	Merriam	KS	66202	**800-453-3348**	913-384-4000	153-11
Lee Kum Kee Inc 14841 don Julian Rd *Orders	City of Industry	CA	91746	**800-654-5082***	626-709-1888	291-19
Lee Middleton Original Dolls Inc 480 Olde Worthington Rd Suite 110	Westerville	OH	43082	**800-242-3285**	614-901-0604	750
Lee Myles Transmissions 140 Rt 17 N	Paramus	NJ	07652	**800-426-5114**	201-262-0555	62-6
Lee Pharmaceuticals Inc 1434 Santa Anita Ave	South El Monte	CA	91733	**800-950-5337**	626-442-3141	211
Lee Products Co 800 E 80th St	Minneapolis	MN	55420	**800-989-3544**	952-854-3544	523
Lee Publications Inc 6113 State Hwy 5	Palatine Bridge	NY	13428	**800-218-5586**	518-673-3237	623-8
Lee Ray-Tarantino Co Inc PO Box 2408	South San Francisco	CA	94083	**800-321-1035**	650-761-2854	292-7
Lee Spring Co Inc 1462 62nd St	Brooklyn	NY	11219	**800-426-0272**	718-236-2222	705
Lee Supply Corp 6610 Guion Rd	Indianapolis	IN	46268	**800-873-1103**	317-290-2500	601
Lee Thomas H Co 100 Federal St Suite 3500	Boston	MA	02110	**800-227-1050**	617-227-1050	397
Lee University 1120 N Ocoee St	Cleveland	TN	37311	**800-533-9930**	423-614-8000	163
Lee Wholesale Floral Inc 917 N 8th St	Abilene	TX	79601	**800-677-2626**	325-673-7381	288
Leeann Chin Inc 3600 American Blvd W Suite 418	Bloomington	MN	55431	**800-784-0029**	952-896-3606	657
Leebaw Mfg Co Inc PO Box 553	Canfield	OH	44406	**800-841-8083**	330-533-3368	462
Leech Lake Area Chamber of Commerce PO Box 1089	Walker	MN	56484	**800-833-1118**	218-547-1313	137
Leech Lake Tribal College PO Box 180	Cass Lake	MN	56633	**888-829-4240**	218-335-4200	161
Leeches USA Ltd 300 Shames Dr	Westbury	NY	11590	**800-645-3569**	516-333-2570	467
Leed Plastics Corp 1425 Palomares Ave	La Verne	CA	91750	**800-421-9880**	909-596-1927	592
Leegin Creative Leather Co 14022 Nelson Ave	City of Industry	CA	91746	**800-235-8748**	626-961-9381	153-2
Leelanau Fruit Co 2900 SW Bayshore Dr	Suttons Bay	MI	49682	**800-431-0718**	231-271-3514	291-21
Leelanau Sands Casino 2521 NW Bayshore Dr	Suttons Bay	MI	49682	**800-922-2946**	231-271-4104	133
Leelanau School 1 Old Homestead Rd	Glen Arbor	MI	49636	**800-533-5262**	231-334-5800	611
Leer LP 206 Leer St *Cust Svc	New Lisbon	WI	53950	**800-766-5337***	608-562-3161	650
Leerink Swann & Co 1 Federal St 37th Fl	Boston	MA	02110	**800-808-7525**	617-248-1601	393
Lees Carpets Div Mohawk Industries Inc 706 Green Valley Rd	Greensboro	NC	27408	**800-523-5647**	336-378-9162	131
Lees Elite Club 130 N State St	North Vernon	IN	47265	**800-733-5337**	812-346-5072	371
Lees Inns of America Inc 130 N State St	North Vernon	IN	47265	**800-733-5337**	812-346-5072	369
Lees-McRae College PO Box 128	Banner Elk	NC	28604	**800-280-4562**	828-898-5241	163
Lee's Mfg Co 1700 Smith St	North Providence	RI	02911	**800-821-1700**	401-353-1740	399
Lee's Summit Chamber of Commerce 220 SE Main St	Lee's Summit	MO	64063	**888-816-5757**	816-524-2424	137
Leesport Financial Corp 1240 Broadcasting Rd *NASDAQ: FLPB*	Wyomissing	PA	19610	**888-238-3330**	610-208-0966	355-2
Leff H Electric Co Inc 1163 E 40th St	Cleveland	OH	44114	**800-686-5333**	216-432-3000	245
Leffelman WG & Sons Inc 340 N Metcalf Ave	Amboy	IL	61310	**800-957-2513**	815-857-2513	270
Leffler Energy Inc PO Box 278	Richland	PA	17087	**800-222-2531**	717-866-2105	569
LeFiell Mfg Co 13700 Firestone Blvd	Santa Fe Springs	CA	90670	**800-451-5971**	562-921-3411	481
Legacy Benefits Corp 350 5th Ave Suite 4320	New York	NY	10118	**800-875-1000**	212-643-1190	783
Legacy Cabinets LLC PO Box 730	Eastaboga	AL	36260	**800-813-1112**	256-831-4888	116
Legacy Golf Resort 6808 S 32nd St	Phoenix	AZ	85042	**888-828-3673**	602-305-5500	655
Legacy of Life Tissue Foundation 4804 Research Dr	San Antonio	TX	78240	**800-397-3077**	210-696-7677	535
Legacy Visiting Nurses Assn Hospice PO Box 3426	Portland	OR	97208	**800-896-6287**	503-225-6370	365
Legal Data Resources Inc 2816 W Summerdale Ave	Chicago	IL	60625	**800-735-9207**	773-561-2468	621
Legal Defense & Education Fund. Asian American 99 Hudson St 12th Fl	New York	NY	10013	**800-966-5946**	212-966-5932	48-8
Legal Defense Fund. Sierra 131 Water St Suite 214	Vancouver	BC	V6B4M3	**800-926-7744**	604-685-5618	48-13
Legal Fraternity. Phi Delta Phi International 1426 21st St NW	Washington	DC	20036	**800-368-5606**	202-223-6801	48-16
Legal & General America Inc 1701 Research Blvd	Rockville	MD	20850	**800-638-8428**	301-279-4800	355-4
Legal Network Ltd 425 6th Ave Suite 1830	Pittsburgh	PA	15219	**800-737-3436**	412-201-7470	707
Legal Reform. HALT - An Organization of Americans for 1612 K St NW Suite 510	Washington	DC	20006	**888-367-4258**	202-887-8255	48-7
Legal Sea Foods Inc 1 Seafood Way	Boston	MA	02210	**800-477-5342**	617-783-8088	657
Legal Tech Newsletter 1617 JFK Blvd Suite 1750	Philadelphia	PA	19103	**800-999-1916**	215-557-2310	521-3
LegalEase Inc 139 Fulton St Suite 1013	New York	NY	10038	**800-393-1277**	212-393-9070	621
LegaLink 160 Commonwealth Ave Suite U-3	Boston	MA	02116	**800-662-1466**	617-262-7717	436
Legends at Capitol Hill 2500 Legends Cir	Prattville	AL	36066	**888-250-3767**	334-290-1235	655
Legends of Harley Drag Racing Museum 1126 S Saunders St	Raleigh	NC	27603	**800-394-2758**	919-832-2261	509
Legends Resort 1500 Legends Dr PO Box 2038	Myrtle Beach	SC	29578	**888-246-9809**	843-236-9318	655
Legends Resort & Country Club 430 Rt 517 PO Box 637	McAfee	NJ	07428	**800-835-2555**	973-827-6000	655
Legends Theater 3216 W Hwy 76	Branson	MO	65616	**800-374-7469**	417-339-3003	562
Legerity Inc 4509 Frederick Ln Suite 200	Austin	TX	78744	**800-432-4009**	512-228-5400	686
Legg Co Inc 325 E 10th St *Sales	Halstead	KS	67056	**800-835-1003***	316-835-2256	364
Legg Mason Family of Funds 100 Light St	Baltimore	MD	21202	**800-368-2558**	410-539-0000	517
Legg Mason Inc 100 Light St *NYSE: LM*	Baltimore	MD	21202	**800-368-2558**	410-539-0000	679
Leggett & Platt Inc PO Box 757 *NYSE: LEG*	Carthage	MO	64836	**800-888-4569**	417-358-8131	705
Leggett & Platt Inc Textile & Fiber Products Div 400 Davidson St	Nashville	TN	37213	**800-888-4136**	615-734-1600	730-1
Leggett Wire Co 1 Leggett Rd	Carthage	MO	64836	**800-888-4569**	417-358-8131	800
Legion Insurance 1 Logan Sq Suite 1400	Philadelphia	PA	19103	**800-255-6738**	215-963-1200	384-4
Legion Lighting Co Inc 221 Glenmore Ave	Brooklyn	NY	11207	**800-453-4466**	718-498-1770	431
Legislative Network for Nurses Newsletter 8737 Colesville Rd Suite 1100	Silver Spring	MD	20910	**800-274-6737**	301-587-6300	521-2
LEGO Systems Inc 555 Taylor Rd	Enfield	CT	06082	**800-243-4870**	860-749-2291	750
LEGOLAND California 1 Legoland Dr	Carlsbad	CA	92008	**877-534-6526**	760-438-5346	32
LeGrand Johnson Construction Co Inc PO Box 248	Logan	UT	84323	**800-286-6820**	435-752-2000	187-4
Legum Home Health Care PO Box 700	Stuarts Draft	VA	24477	**800-552-6576**	540-932-3000	358
Lehigh Carbon Community College 4525 Education Pk Dr	Schnecksville	PA	18078	**800-414-3975**	610-799-2121	160
Lehigh Cement Co North America 7660 Imperial Way	Allentown	PA	18195	**800-523-5488**	610-366-4600	135
Lehigh Group 2834 Shoeneck Rd	Macungie	PA	18062	**800-523-9382**	610-966-9702	207
Lehigh Safety Shoe Co 120 Plaza Dr Suite A	Vestal	NY	13850	**800-444-4086**	607-584-5000	296
Lehigh Southwest Cement Co 2300 Clayton Rd Suite 300	Concord	CA	94520	**888-554-5010**	925-609-6920	135
Lehigh Valley Convention & Visitors Bureau 2200 Ave A	Bethlehem	PA	18017	**800-747-0561**	610-882-9200	205
Lehigh Valley Dairies Inc 880 Allentown Rd	Lansdale	PA	19446	**800-937-3233**	215-855-8205	291-27
Lehigh Valley Hospice 2166 S 12th St	Allentown	PA	18103	**800-944-4354**	610-402-7400	365
Lehigh Valley International Airport (ABE)	Allentown	PA	18103	**888-359-5842**	610-266-6000	28
Lehigh Valley Plastics Inc 1075 N Gilmore St	Allentown	PA	18109	**800-354-5344**	610-439-8573	593
Lehman Brothers Asset Management LLC 200 S Wacker Dr Suite 2100	Chicago	IL	60606	**800-764-9336**	312-559-2880	393

	City	State	ZIP	Toll-Free	Phone	Class
Lehman Brothers Bank FSB 1000 West St Suite 200	Wilmington	DE	19801	**800-372-8464**	302-654-6179	71
Lehman Brothers Holdings Inc 745 7th Ave *NYSE: LEH*	New York	NY	10019	**800-666-2388**	212-526-7000	355-3
Lehman Brothers Inc 70 Hudson St	Jersey City	NJ	07302	**800-666-2388**	201-524-2000	679
Lehman Communications Corp 350 Terry St	Longmont	CO	80501	**800-796-8201**	303-776-2244	623-8
Lehman Sugarfree Confections Inc 4512 Farragut Rd	Brooklyn	NY	11203	**800-438-3327**	718-469-3057	291-11
Lehr Precision Inc 11230 Deerfield Rd	Cincinnati	OH	45242	**800-966-5060**	513-489-9800	610
Lehrer's Flowers Inc 3191 W 38th Ave	Denver	CO	80211	**800-537-1308**	303-455-1234	287
Leica Geosystems LLC 6330 28th St SE *Sales	Grand Rapids	MI	49546	**800-367-9453***	616-949-7430	416
Leica Inc 2345 Waukegan Rd 3rd Fl	Bannockburn	IL	60015	**800-248-0123**	847-405-0123	410
Leicht Transfer & Storage Co 1401 State St PO Box 2447	Green Bay	WI	54306	**800-338-5665**	920-432-8632	440
Leidenheimer Baking Co 1501 Simon Bolivar Ave	New Orleans	LA	70113	**800-259-9099**	504-525-1575	291-1
Leidy's Inc 266 W Cherry Ln	Souderton	PA	18964	**800-222-2319**	215-723-4606	292-9
Leifer Group 9393 W 110th St Suite 500	Overland Park	KS	66210	**877-676-9200**	913-385-9200	5
Leigh Fibers Inc 1101 Syphrit Rd	Wellford	SC	29385	**800-274-7707**	864-439-4111	730-8
Leinenkugel Jacob Brewing Co Hwy 124 N PO Box 368	Chippewa Falls	WI	54729	**888-534-6437**	715-723-5557	103
Leiner Health Products Inc 901 E 233rd St	Carson	CA	90745	**800-421-1168**	310-835-8400	572
Leisure Hotel Group of Companies 1600 N Lorraine St Suite 211	Hutchinson	KS	67501	**888-250-1618**	620-663-9800	369
Leisure Hotels LLC 1600 N Lorraine St Suite 211	Hutchinson	KS	67501	**888-250-1618**	620-663-9800	369
Leisure Lift 1800 Merriam Ln	Kansas City	KS	66106	**800-255-0285**	913-722-5658	469
Leisure & Recreation. American Assn for 1900 Association Dr	Reston	VA	20191	**800-213-7193**	703-476-3400	48-23
Leisure Systems Inc DBA Yogi Bear's Jellystone Park Camp Resorts 50 W Techne Center Dr Suite G *Sales	Milford	OH	45150	**800-626-3720***	513-831-2100	121
Leisure Travel News 770 Broadway *Cust Svc	New York	NY	10003	**800-950-1314***	646-654-4500	449-22
Leitch Technology Corp 150 Ferrand Dr Suite 700 *TSE: LTV*	Toronto	ON	M3C3E5	**800-387-0233**	416-445-9640	633
LEK Consulting 28 State St 16th Fl	Boston	MA	02109	**800-929-4535**	617-951-9500	193
Leland Engineering Inc 501 S Miller Dr	White Pigeon	MI	49099	**800-669-7681**	269-483-7681	120
Leland Scott & Assoc Inc 4275 Little Rd Suite 101	Arlington	TX	76016	**800-808-5061**	817-478-1888	157
Lely USA Inc 1410 Vermeer Rd E PO Box 437	Pella	IA	50219	**888-245-4684**	641-621-7905	269
LeMay Harold Enterprises Inc 13502 Pacific Ave	Tacoma	WA	98444	**800-345-3629**	253-537-8687	791
Lemco Tool Corp 1850 Metzger Ave	Cogan Station	PA	17728	**800-233-8713**	570-494-0620	446
Lemon Tree Inc 1 Division Ave	Levittown	NY	11756	**800-345-9156**	516-735-2828	79
LeMoyne-Owen College 807 Walker Ave *Admissions	Memphis	TN	38126	**800-737-7778***	901-774-9090	163
Lemoyne Sleeper Co Inc PO Box 227	Lemoyne	PA	17043	**800-382-1217**	717-763-1630	463
Lempco Industries Inc 5490 Dunham Rd	Cleveland	OH	44137	**800-321-8632**	216-475-2400	745
Len-Dal Carpets Inc PO Box 39	Chatsworth	GA	30705	**800-241-4030**	706-695-4533	131
Lender Liability Law Report 1901 Fort Myer Dr Suite 501 *Cust Svc	Arlington	VA	22209	**800-572-2797***	703-528-0145	521-1
LendingTree Inc 11115 Rushmore Dr	Charlotte	NC	28277	**877-510-2659**	704-541-5351	498
Lenexa Convention & Visitors Bureau 11180 Lackman Rd	Lenexa	KS	66219	**800-950-7867**	913-888-1414	205
Lennar Financial Services Inc 700 NW 107th Ave 3rd Fl	Miami	FL	33172	**800-741-8262**	305-223-9966	498
Lennar Homes Inc 700 NW 107th Ave Suite 400	Miami	FL	33172	**800-741-4663**	305-559-4000	639
Lennox Hearth Products 1110 W Taft Ave	Orange	CA	92865	**800-854-0257**	714-921-6100	352
Lenoir Community College PO Box 188	Kinston	NC	28502	**800-848-5497**	252-527-6223	160
Lenoir Mirror Co Inc PO Box 1650	Lenoir	NC	28645	**800-438-8204**	828-728-3271	328
Lenoir-Rhyne College 510 7th Ave NE PO Box 7227	Hickory	NC	28603	**800-277-5721**	828-328-1741	163
Lenox Hotel 61 Exeter St	Boston	MA	02116	**800-225-7676**	617-536-5300	373
Lenox Inc 100 Lenox Dr *Cust Svc	Lawrenceville	NJ	08648	**800-635-3669***	609-896-2800	716
Lenox Suites Hotel 616 N Rush St	Chicago	IL	60611	**800-445-3669**	312-337-1000	373
Lenoxx Electronics Corp 2 Germak Dr	Carteret	NJ	07008	**800-315-5885**	718-633-4480	52
LensCrafters Inc 4000 Luxottica Pl	Mason	OH	45040	**800-283-5367**	513-765-6000	533
Leo Pharma Inc 123 Commerce Valley Dr E Suite 400	Thornhill	ON	L3T7W8	**800-668-7234**	905-886-9822	86
Leola Village Inn & Suites 38 Deborah Dr	Leola	PA	17540	**877-669-5094**	717-656-7002	373
Leon Farmer & Co PO Box 1352	Athens	GA	30603	**800-282-7009**	706-353-1166	82-1
Leon Levin Inc 250 W 39th St 5th Fl	New York	NY	10018	**800-822-3363**	212-575-1900	153-21
Leon Max Inc 3100 New York Dr	Pasadena	CA	91107	**800-345-3813**	626-797-6886	153-21
Leonard Charles Inc 79-11 Cooper Ave	Glendale	NY	11385	**800-999-7202**	718-894-4851	345
Leonard Hal Corp PO Box 227	Winona	MN	55987	**800-321-3408**	507-454-2920	623-7
Leonard Hudson Drilling Co 601 N Price Rd	Pampa	TX	79065	**800-826-9587**	806-665-1816	529
Leonard Paper Co 725 N Haven St *Cust Svc	Baltimore	MD	21205	**800-327-5547***	410-563-0800	549
Leonard Valve Co 1360 Elmwood Ave	Cranston	RI	02910	**888-797-4456**	401-461-1200	776
Leon's Texas Cuisine Co 2100 Redbud Blvd	McKinney	TX	75069	**800-527-1243**	972-529-5050	291-36
Leotek Electronics USA Corp 1330 Memorex Dr	Santa Clara	CA	95050	**888-806-1188**	408-988-4668	692
Leoti Greentech Inc PO Drawer L	Leoti	KS	67861	**800-783-2621**	620-375-2621	270
Lepercq de Neuflize & Co 40 W 57th St 19th Fl	New York	NY	10019	**800-697-3863**	212-698-0700	679
Leppla Moving & Storage Co 303 W Southern Ave	Mesa	AZ	85210	**800-922-6344**	480-964-1444	508
Leprechaun Lines PO Box 2628	Newburgh	NY	12550	**800-624-4217**	845-565-7900	108
Leprino Foods Co 1830 W 38th Ave	Denver	CO	80211	**800-537-7466**	303-480-2600	291-5
Leprosy Missions. American 1 ALM Way	Greenville	SC	29601	**800-543-3135**	864-271-7040	48-5
Lerman Container Co 10 Great Hill Rd	Naugatuck	CT	06770	**800-453-7626**	203-723-6681	99
L'Ermitage Beverly Hills. Raffles 9291 Burton Way	Beverly Hills	CA	90210	**800-800-2113**	310-278-3344	373
Lerner Research Institute Cleveland Clinic Foundation 9500 Euclid Ave NB 21	Cleveland	OH	44195	**800-223-2273**	216-444-3900	654
Leros First Class 6 Skyline Dr	Hawthorne	NY	10532	**800-825-3767**	914-747-2300	433
Les Entreprises Michel Corbeil Inc 830 12th Ave	Saint-Lin-Laurentides	QC	J5M2V9	**888-439-3577**	450-439-3577	505
Les Etoiles Barges 3355 Lenox Rd Suite 750	Atlanta	GA	30326	**800-280-1492**		218
Les Suites Hotel Ottawa 130 Besserer St	Ottawa	ON	K1N9M9	**800-267-1989**	613-232-2000	372
Lesaffre Yeast Corp 433 E Michigan St	Milwaukee	WI	53202	**877-677-7000**	414-615-4055	291-42
Lesbian Travel Assn. International Gay & 4331 N Federal Hwy Suite 304	Fort Lauderdale	FL	33308	**800-448-8550**	954-776-2626	48-23
Lescarden Inc 420 Lexington Ave Suite 212	New York	NY	10170	**888-581-2076**	212-687-1050	86
LESCO Inc 15885 Sprague Rd *NASDAQ: LSCO*	Strongsville	OH	44136	**800-321-5325**	440-783-9250	420
LeSea Broadcasting 61300 S Ironwood Rd	South Bend	IN	46614	**800-365-3732**	574-291-8200	724
Lesley University 29 Everett St	Cambridge	MA	02138	**800-999-1959**	617-868-9600	163
Leslie Controls Inc 12501 Telecom Dr	Tampa	FL	33637	**800-253-7543**	813-978-1000	776
Leslie's Swimming Pool Supplies 3925 E Broadway Rd Suite 100	Phoenix	AZ	85040	**800-233-8063**	602-366-3999	702
LeSportsac Inc 358 5th Ave 8th Fl	New York	NY	10001	**800-486-2247**	212-736-6262	444
Lester Building Systems Div Butler Mfg Co 1111 2nd Ave S	Lester Prairie	MN	55354	**800-826-4439**	320-395-2531	107
Lester Telemarketing Inc 19 Business Park Dr	Branford	CT	06405	**800-999-5265**	203-488-5265	722
Lester's Florist Inc 2100 Bull St	Savannah	GA	31401	**800-841-1103**	912-233-6066	287
LeSueur-Richmond Slate Corp PO Box 8 Rt 675	Arvonia	VA	23004	**800-235-8921**	434-581-3214	710
Letica Corp PO Box 5005	Rochester	MI	48308	**866-538-4221**	248-652-0557	548-1
LeTourneau University 2100 S Mobberly	Longview	TX	75602	**800-759-8811**	903-753-0231	163
Let's Live Magazine 11050 Santa Monica Blvd 3rd Fl	Los Angeles	CA	90025	**800-676-4333**	310-445-7500	449-13
Let's Talk Inc 410 Townsend St Suite 100 *Orders	San Francisco	CA	94107	**866-825-5460***	415-344-0227	35
Leukemia & Lymphoma Society 475 Park Ave S 8th Fl	New York	NY	10016	**800-955-4572**	212-448-9206	48-17
Levanta Inc 650 Townsend St Suite 225	San Francisco	CA	94103	**888-546-4878**	415-354-4878	178
Level 3 Communications Inc 1025 Eldorado Blvd *NASDAQ: LVLT*	Broomfield	CO	80021	**877-453-8353**	720-888-1000	387
Level 8 Systems Inc 8000 Regency Pkwy	Cary	NC	27511	**866-538-3588**	919-380-5000	176-1
Level Valley Creamery 807 Pleasant Valley Rd	West Bend	WI	53095	**800-558-1707**	262-675-6533	291-3
Levenger 420 S Congress Ave *Cust Svc	Delray Beach	FL	33445	**800-544-0880***	561-276-2436	451
Leventhal Ltd 1295 Northern Blvd	Manhasset	NY	11030	**800-847-4095**	516-365-9540	153-19
Leverock Seafood House PO Box 20466	Tampa	FL	33622	**888-538-3762**	813-637-8663	657
Levi Strauss & Co 1155 Battery St	San Francisco	CA	94111	**800-872-5384**	415-501-6000	153-11
Levin Management Corp 893 Rt 22 W	North Plainfield	NJ	07060	**800-488-0768**	908-755-2401	641
Levinson Harold Assoc Inc 21 Banfi Plaza	Farmingdale	NY	11735	**800-325-2512**	631-962-2400	744
Levinson Institute Inc 28 Main St Suite 100	Jaffrey	NH	03452	**800-290-5735**	603-532-4700	753
Leviton Mfg Co Inc 59-25 Little Neck Pkwy *Tech Supp	Little Neck	NY	11362	**800-824-3005***	718-229-4040	803
Levitt & Sons Corp 7777 Glades Rd Suite 410	Boca Raton	FL	33434	**800-741-5110**	561-482-5100	186
Levolor Div Newell Rubbermaid Inc 4110 Premier Dr	High Point	NC	27265	**800-232-2028**	336-812-8181	88
Levonian Brothers Inc PO Box 629 *Cust Svc	Troy	NY	12180	**800-538-6642***	518-274-3610	291-26
Levy Chas Circulating Co 1930 George St Unit 1	Melrose Park	IL	60160	**800-549-5389**		97
Levy Group Inc 512 7th Ave 3rd Fl	New York	NY	10018	**800-223-2073**	212-398-0707	153-5
Levy I & Assoc Inc 1630 Des Peres Rd Suite 300	Saint Louis	MO	63131	**800-297-6717**	314-822-0810	176-11
Levy Jewelers Inc 101 E Broughton St	Savannah	GA	31401	**800-237-5389**	912-233-1163	402
Levy Security Corp 8750 W Bryn Mawr Ave Suite 1200	Chicago	IL	60631	**800-649-5389**	773-867-9204	682
Lewan & Assoc Inc 1400 S Colorado Blvd	Denver	CO	80222	**800-553-9265**	303-759-5440	113
Lewcott Corp 86 Providence Rd *Sales	Millbury	MA	01527	**800-225-7725***	508-865-1791	594-2
Lewer Agency Inc 4534 Wornall Rd	Kansas City	MO	64111	**800-821-7715**	816-753-4390	383
Lewis & Clark College 0615 SW Palatine Hill Rd	Portland	OR	97219	**800-444-4111**	503-768-7040	163
Lewis & Clark Monument Frontier Park	Saint Charles	MO	63303	**800-366-2427**		50
Lewis & Clark National Historic Trail c/o National Park Service 601 Riverfront Dr	Omaha	NE	68102	**888-237-3252**	402-661-1804	50

Name / Address	City	State	Zip	Toll-Free	Phone	Class
Lewis-Clark State College 500 8th Ave	Lewiston	ID	83501	**800-933-5272**	208-792-2210	163
Lewis & Clark Trail Heritage Foundation PO Box 3434	Great Falls	MT	59404	**888-701-3434**	406-454-1234	48-23
Lewis Cos 28777 Northwestern Hwy Suite 100	Southfield	MI	48034	**800-968-6808**	248-354-9005	185
Lewis County Chamber of Commerce 7383-C Utica Blvd.	Lowville	NY	13367	**800-724-0242**	315-376-2213	137
Lewis County Rural Electric Co-op Assn PO Box 68	Lewistown	MO	63452	**888-454-4485**	573-215-4000	244
Lewis Dreyfus Citrus Inc PO Box 770399	Winter Garden	FL	34777	**800-549-4272**	407-656-1000	291-21
Lewis-Goetz & Co Inc 650 Washington Rd Suite 210	Pittsburgh	PA	15228	**800-289-1236**	412-787-4154	378
Lewis Industrial Supply Co 3307 N 6th St.	Harrisburg	PA	17110	**800-929-2400**	717-234-2409	730-8
Lewis Kenneth D Pres/CEO Bank of America Corp 100 N Tyron St.	Charlotte	NC	28255	**800-299-2265**		561
Lewis Marine Supply Co Inc 220 SW 32nd St.	Fort Lauderdale	FL	33315	**800-327-3792***	954-523-4371	759
*Sales						
Lewis RE Refrigeration Inc 803 S Lincoln St PO Box 92	Creston	IA	50801	**800-264-0767**	641-782-8183	651
Lewis Systems Inc 325 E Oliver St	Baltimore	MD	21202	**800-533-5394**	410-539-5100	5
Lewis Tree Service Inc 225 Ballantyne Rd	Rochester	NY	14623	**800-333-1593**	585-436-3208	765
Lewis Ultrasonics 102 Willenbroch Rd	Oxford	CT	06478	**800-243-5092**	203-264-3100	771
Lewis University 1 University Pkwy Box 295	Romeoville	IL	60446	**800-897-9000**	815-838-0500	163
Lewisohn Sales Co Inc PO Box 192	North Bergen	NJ	07047	**800-631-3196***	201-864-0300	671
*Orders						
Lewiston Chamber of Commerce 111 Main St Suite 120	Lewiston	ID	83501	**800-473-3543**	208-743-3531	137
Lewiston Daily Sun Corp 104 Park St	Lewiston	ME	04240	**800-482-0753**	207-784-5411	623-8
Lewiston Sales Inc 21241 Dutchmans Crossing Rd	Lewiston	MN	55952	**800-732-6334**	507-523-2112	437
Lewistown Hospital 400 Highland Ave	Lewistown	PA	17044	**800-248-0505**	717-248-5411	366-2
Lewisville Chamber of Commerce 551 N Valley Pkwy	Lewisville	TX	75067	**800-657-9571**	972-436-9571	137
Lewtan Industries Corp 30 High St	Hartford	CT	06103	**800-539-8268**	860-278-9800	10
Lexcom Communications 200 N State St PO Box 808	Lexington	NC	27293	**888-234-1663**	336-249-9901	721
Lexcom Inc DBA Lexcom Communications 200 N State St PO Box 808	Lexington	NC	27293	**888-234-1663**	336-249-9901	721
Lexicon Branding Inc 30 Liberty Ship Way Suite 3360	Sausalito	CA	94965	**800-783-9713**	415-332-1811	194
Lexicon Genetics Inc 8800 Technology Forest Pl.	The Woodlands	TX	77381	**800-578-1972**	281-863-3000	86
NASDAQ: LEXG						
Lexington Community College Cooper Dr 203 Oswald Bldg.	Lexington	KY	40506	**866-774-4872**	859-257-4872	160
Lexington Convention & Visitors Bureau 301 E Vine St.	Lexington	KY	40507	**800-845-3959**	859-233-7299	205
Lexington Group 185 Main St Suite 401	New Britain	CT	06051	**800-571-0197**	860-225-3993	454
Lexington Herald-Leader 100 Midland Ave.	Lexington	KY	40508	**800-274-7355**	859-231-3100	522-2
Lexington Home Brands PO Box 1008	Lexington	NC	27293	**800-539-4636**	336-249-5300	314-2
Lexington Insurance Co Inc 100 Summer St	Boston	MA	02110	**800-355-4891**	617-330-1100	384-4
Lexington Memorial Hospital 250 Hospital Dr	Lexington	NC	27292	**800-442-7381**	336-248-5161	366-2
Lexington Philharmonic 161 N Mill St	Lexington	KY	40507	**888-494-4226**	859-233-4226	563-3
Lexington Services 2120 Walnut Hill Ln Suite 100	Irving	TX	75038	**800-537-8483**	972-714-0585	368
LexisNexis Group 9443 Springboro Pike	Miamisburg	OH	45342	**800-227-9597**	937-865-6800	380
LexisNexis Martindale-Hubbell 121 Chanlon Rd	New Providence	NJ	07974	**800-526-4902**	908-464-6800	380
LexisNexis Matthew Bender 744 Broad St	Newark	NJ	07102	**800-252-9257**	973-820-2000	623-2
LexJet Corp 1680 Fruitville Rd Suite 202	Sarasota	FL	34236	**800-453-9538**	941-330-1210	616
Lexmark International Inc 740 W New Circle Rd.	Lexington	KY	40550	**800-539-6275***	859-232-2000	171-6
NYSE: LXK ■ *Cust Svc						
Lexus Div Toyota Motor Sales USA Inc 19001 S Western Ave.	Torrance	CA	90509	**800-331-4331***	310-468-4000	59
*Cust Svc						
LFA (Lupus Foundation of America Inc) 2000 L St Suite 710	Washington	DC	20036	**800-558-0121**	202-349-1155	48-17
LFSA (Law Firm Services Assn) 10831 Old Mill Rd Suite 400	Omaha	NE	68154	**800-475-4476**	402-778-7922	49-10
LG Balfour Co 7211 Circle S Rd	Austin	TX	78745	**888-225-3687**	512-444-2090	401
LG Barcus & Sons Inc 1430 State Ave	Kansas City	KS	66102	**800-255-0180**	913-621-1100	188-3
LG & E Energy Corp 220 W Main St	Louisville	KY	40202	**800-331-7370**	502-627-2000	355-5
LG Electronics USA Inc 1000 Sylvan Ave	Englewood Cliffs	NJ	07632	**800-243-0000***	201-816-2000	171-4
*Tech Supp						
LGC Wireless Inc 2540 Junction Ave	San Jose	CA	95134	**800-530-9960**	408-952-2400	174
LGInternational 6700 SW Bradbury Ct	Portland	OR	97224	**800-345-0534**	503-620-0520	404
LH Lincoln & Son Inc 87 West St	Galeton	PA	16922	**800-845-4626**	814-274-9200	423
LH Selman Ltd 123 Locust St	Santa Cruz	CA	95060	**800-538-0766**	831-427-1177	330
LHC Group LLC 420 W Pinhook Rd Suite A	Lafayette	LA	70503	**800-489-1307**	337-233-1307	358
NASDAQ: LHCG						
L'Hotel Quebec 3115 ave des Hotels	Sainte-Foy	QC	G1W3Z6	**800-567-5276**	418-658-5120	372
L'Hotel du Vieux-Quebec 1190 rue Saint-Jean	Quebec	QC	G1R1S6	**800-361-7787**	418-692-1850	372
LIA (Laser Institute of America) 13501 Ingenuity Dr Suite 128	Orlando	FL	32826	**800-345-2737**	407-380-1553	49-19
Liability Underwriting Society. Professional 5353 Wayzata Blvd Suite 600	Minneapolis	MN	55416	**800-845-0778**	952-746-2580	49-9
Libbey Inc 300 Madison Ave	Toledo	OH	43604	**888-794-8469**	419-325-2100	331
NYSE: LBY						
Libby Hill Seafood Restaurants Inc 4517-B W Market St.	Greensboro	NC	27407	**800-452-2071**	336-294-0505	657
Libertarian Party 2600 Virginia Ave NW Suite 100	Washington	DC	20037	**800-682-1776**	202-333-0008	605
Liberty Bank 315 Main St	Middletown	CT	06457	**800-622-6732**	860-344-7200	71
Liberty. Becket Fund for Religious 1350 Connecticut Ave NW Suite 605	Washington	DC	20036	**800-232-5385**	202-955-0095	48-8
Liberty Brass Turning Co Inc 38-01 Queens Blvd	Long Island City	NY	11101	**800-345-5939**	718-784-2911	610
Liberty Carton Co 870 Louisiana Ave S.	Minneapolis	MN	55426	**800-328-1784**	763-540-9600	101
Liberty Corporate Services Inc 11285 Elkins Rd Suite G1B	Roswell	GA	30076	**800-334-2735**	770-794-6600	621
Liberty Distributors Inc PO Box 48168	Wichita	KS	67201	**800-633-9211**	316-264-7393	38
Liberty Diversified Industries Inc 5600 Hwy 169 N	New Hope	MN	55428	**800-421-1270**	763-536-6600	355-3
Liberty FiTECH Systems 3098 Piedmont Rd NE Suite 200	Atlanta	GA	30305	**800-275-4374**	404-262-2298	176-11
Liberty Forge Inc PO Drawer 1210	Liberty	TX	77575	**800-231-2377**	936-336-5785	474
Liberty Funds Group 1 Financial Ctr	Boston	MA	02111	**800-225-2365**	617-426-3750	393
Liberty Hardware Mfg Corp 140 Business Park Dr.	Winston-Salem	NC	27107	**800-542-3789**	336-769-4077	345
Liberty Homes Inc 1101 Eisenhower Dr N	Goshen	IN	46526	**800-733-0431**	574-533-0431	495
NASDAQ: LIBHA						
Liberty Industries Inc 840 McClurg Rd	Youngstown	OH	44512	**800-860-4744**	330-729-2100	537
Liberty Iron & Metal Co PO Box 1391	Erie	PA	16512	**800-836-0259**	814-453-6758	674
Liberty Medical Supply Inc 10045 SE Federal Hwy	Port Saint Lucie	FL	34952	**800-633-2001**	772-398-5800	467
Liberty National Life Insurance Co PO Box 2612	Birmingham	AL	35202	**800-333-0637**	205-325-2722	384-2
Liberty Richter Inc 400 Lyster Ave	Saddle Brook	NJ	07663	**800-631-3650**	201-843-8900	292-11
Liberty Tax Service Inc 4575 Bonney Rd Suite 1040	Virginia Beach	VA	23462	**800-790-3863**	757-493-8855	719
Liberty Travel Inc 69 Spring St	Ramsey	NJ	07446	**800-899-9800**	201-934-3500	760
Liberty University 1971 University Blvd	Lynchburg	VA	24502	**800-543-5317**	434-582-2000	163
Liberty Wood & Construction Inc 3300 Benzing Rd	Orchard Park	NY	14127	**800-448-2200**	716-824-6067	489
LibertyTree 100 Swan Way	Oakland	CA	94621	**800-927-8733**	510-568-6047	96
Libman Co 220 N Sheldon St	Arcola	IL	61910	**800-646-6262**	217-268-4200	104
Librarians. American Assn of School 50 E Huron St.	Chicago	IL	60611	**800-545-2433**	312-280-4386	49-11
Libraries. Association of College & Research 50 E Huron St	Chicago	IL	60611	**800-545-2433**	312-280-2519	49-11
Libraries Div. Universal Service Administrative Co Schools & 2000 L St NW	Washington	DC	20036	**888-203-8100**		721
Libraries Group Inc. Research 2029 Stierlin Ct Suite 100	Mountain View	CA	94043	**800-537-7546**	650-962-9951	49-5
Libraries USA. Friends of 1420 Walnut St Suite 450	Philadelphia	PA	19102	**800-936-5872**	215-790-1674	49-11
Library Administration & Management Assn (LAMA) 50 E Huron St	Chicago	IL	60611	**800-545-2433**	312-280-5036	49-11
Library Agencies. Association of Specialized & Cooperative 50 E Huron St	Chicago	IL	60611	**800-545-2433**	312-280-4395	49-11
Library Assn. Alabama 400 S Union St Suite 395	Montgomery	AL	36104	**877-563-5146**	334-263-1272	427
Library Assn of Alberta (LAA) 80 Baker Crescent NW	Calgary	AB	T2L1R4	**877-522-5550**	403-284-5818	427
Library Assn. American 50 E Huron St	Chicago	IL	60611	**800-545-2433**	312-944-6780	49-11
Library Assn. American Theological 250 S Wacker Dr Suite 1600	Chicago	IL	60606	**888-665-2852**	312-454-5100	48-20
Library Assn. Iowa 3636 Westown Pkwy Suite 202	West Des Moines	IA	50266	**800-452-5507**	515-273-5322	427
Library Assn. Minnesota 1619 Dayton Ave Suite 314	Saint Paul	MN	55104	**877-867-0982**	651-641-0982	427
Library Assn. New York 252 Hudson Ave	Albany	NY	12210	**800-252-6952**	518-432-6952	427
Library Assn. Ontario 100 Lombard St Suite 303	Toronto	ON	M5CIM3	**866-873-9867**	416-363-3388	427
Library Assn. Public 50 E Huron St	Chicago	IL	60611	**800-545-2433**	312-280-5752	49-11
Library Assn. Texas 3355 Bee Cave Rd Suite 401	Austin	TX	78746	**800-580-2852**	512-328-1518	427
Library Binding Service 1801 Thompson Ave	Des Moines	IA	50316	**800-247-5323**	515-262-3191	93
Library Center Inc. Online Computer 6565 Frantz Rd	Dublin	OH	43017	**800-848-5878**	614-764-6000	49-11
Library Collections & Technical Services. Association for 50 E Huron St	Chicago	IL	60611	**800-545-2433**	312-280-5038	49-11
Library Corp The 3801 E Florida Ave Suite 300	Denver	CO	80210	**888-439-2275**	303-758-3030	176-10
Library Council. Ohio 2 Easton Oval Suite 525	Columbus	OH	43215	**800-436-5423**	614-416-2258	427
Library Hotel 299 Madison Ave	New York	NY	10017	**877-793-7323**	212-983-4500	373
Library & Information Technology Assn (LITA) 50 E Huron St	Chicago	IL	60611	**800-545-2433**	312-280-4270	49-11
Library Reproduction Service 14214 S Figueroa St	Los Angeles	CA	90061	**800-255-5002**	310-354-2610	614
Library of Science Book Club Doubleday Select Inc 101 Park Ave 2nd Fl	New York	NY	10178	**800-321-7323**		94
Library Service to Children. Association for 50 E Huron St	Chicago	IL	60611	**800-545-2433**	312-280-2163	49-11

Name / Address	City	State	ZIP	Toll-Free	Phone	Class
Library Services Assn. Young Adult 50 E Huron St	Chicago	IL	60611	**800-545-2433**	312-280-4390	49-11
Library of Speech-Language Pathology Doubleday Select Inc 101 Park Ave 2nd Fl	New York	NY	10178	**800-321-7323**		94
Library Trustees & Advocates. Association for 50 E Huron St	Chicago	IL	60611	**800-545-2433**	312-280-2161	49-11
Licensing Assn. International Collegiate 24651 Detroit Rd	Westlake	OH	44145	**800-996-2232**	440-892-4000	48-22
Lichtenberg S & Co Inc 295 5th Ave Rm 918 *Cust Svc	New York	NY	10016	**800-682-1959***	212-689-4510	731
Licking Rural Electrification Inc PO Box 4970	Newark	OH	43058	**800-255-6815**	740-892-2791	244
Liddell Trailers 100 Industrial Dr	Springville	AL	35146	**800-662-9216**	205-467-3990	768
LiDestri Foods Inc 815 Whitney Rd W	Fairport	NY	14450	**800-397-5222**	585-377-7700	291-20
Liebert Corp 1050 Dearborn Dr *Tech Supp	Columbus	OH	43085	**800-543-2778***	614-888-0246	803
Liebert Mary Ann Publishers Inc 140 Huguenot St 3rd Fl	New Rochelle	NY	10801	**800-654-3237**	914-740-2100	623-9
Liechty Farm Equipment Inc PO Box 67	Archbold	OH	43502	**800-272-5898**	419-445-1565	270
Life Alert 16027 Ventura Blvd Suite 400	Encino	CA	91436	**800-700-7000**	818-700-7000	565
Life Asset Group LLC 1111 Lincoln Rd Suite 801	Miami Beach	FL	33139	**800-481-3481**	305-534-9044	783
Life Fitness 5100 N River Rd	Schiller Park	IL	60176	**800-735-3867**	847-288-3300	263
Life Insurance Co of the Southwest PO Box 569080	Dallas	TX	75356	**800-543-3794**	214-638-7100	384-2
Life Investors Insurance Co of America 4333 Edgewood Rd NE	Cedar Rapids	IA	52499	**800-625-4213**	319-398-8511	384-2
Life Like Dental Laboratory 1640 Cobb International Blvd Suite 4	Kennesaw	GA	30152	**800-241-0632**	770-499-1024	406
Life-Like Products Inc 1600 Union Ave *Cust Svc	Baltimore	MD	21211	**800-638-1470***	410-889-1023	590
Life-Link International Inc PO Box 2913	Jackson	WY	83001	**800-443-8620**	307-733-2266	701
Life Magazine Rockefeller Ctr Time & Life Bldg	New York	NY	10020	**800-541-1000**	212-522-1212	449-11
Life Partners Holdings Inc 204 Woodhew Dr *NASDAQ: LPHI*	Waco	TX	76712	**800-368-5569**	254-751-7797	783
Life Sciences Inc 2900 72nd St N	Saint Petersburg	FL	33710	**800-237-4323**	727-345-9371	229
Life Settlement Assn of America. Viatical & 800 Mayfair Cir	Orlando	FL	32803	**800-842-9811**	407-894-3797	49-9
Life of the South Insurance Co 100 W Bay St	Jacksonville	FL	32202	**800-888-2738**	904-350-9660	384-5
Life Time Fitness Inc 6442 City West Pkwy *NYSE: LTM*	Eden Prairie	MN	55344	**800-368-7543**	952-947-0000	349
Life Underwriting. Association for Advanced 2901 Telestar Ct	Falls Church	VA	22042	**888-275-0092**	703-641-9400	49-9
Life Uniform Co 2132 Kratky Rd	Saint Louis	MO	63114	**800-325-8033**	314-824-2900	155-5
LifeBanc 20600 Chagrin Blvd Suite 350	Cleveland	OH	44122	**888-558-5433**	216-752-5433	535
Lifeblood/Mid-South Regional Blood Center 1040 Madison Ave	Memphis	TN	38104	**888-543-3256**	901-522-8585	90
Lifecare Inc 400 Nyala Farms Rd	Westport	CT	06880	**800-873-4636**	203-226-2680	65
LifeCell Corp 1 Millennium Way *NASDAQ: LIFC*	Branchburg	NJ	08876	**800-367-5737**	908-947-1100	535
LifeCore Biomedical Inc 3515 Lyman Blvd *NASDAQ: LCBM* ■ *Cust Svc	Chaska	MN	55318	**800-752-2663***	952-368-4300	86
LifeFone 16 Yellowstone Ave	White Plains	NY	10607	**800-882-2280**	914-948-0282	565
LifeGard of America Inc 141 W Main St	Westminster	MD	21157	**800-448-5697**	410-875-2126	565
LIFELINE Blood Services 828 North Pkwy	Jackson	TN	38305	**800-924-6572**	731-427-4431	90
Lifeline of Ohio 770 Kinnear Rd Suite 200	Columbus	OH	43212	**800-525-5667**	614-291-5667	535
Lifeline Program 1979 Lakeside Pkwy Suite 925	Tucker	GA	30084	**800-572-4346**	800-252-5282	783
Lifeline Systems Inc 111 Lawrence St *NASDAQ: LIFE*	Framingham	MA	01702	**800-451-0525**	508-988-1000	565
LifeLink Tissue Bank 8510 Sunstate St	Tampa	FL	33634	**800-683-2400**	813-886-8111	535
LifeNet 5809 Ward Ct	Virginia Beach	VA	23455	**800-847-7831**	757-464-4761	535
Lifepath Hospice 3010 W Azeele St	Tampa	FL	33609	**800-209-2200**	813-877-2200	365
LifeScan Inc 1000 Gibraltar Dr	Milpitas	CA	95035	**800-227-8862**	408-263-9789	229
LifeShare of the Carolinas 86 Victoria Rd Bldg B	Asheville	NC	28801	**800-932-4483**	828-258-9703	265
LifeShare of the Carolinas 5000 D Airport Ctr Pkwy	Charlotte	NC	28208	**800-932-4483**	704-697-3303	535
LifeShare Transplant Donor Services of Oklahoma 5801 N Broadway Suite 300	Oklahoma City	OK	73118	**888-580-5680**	405-840-5551	535
LifeSource Blood Services 1205 N Milwaukee Ave	Glenview	IL	60025	**800-486-0680**	847-298-9660	90
Lifestyle Center of America Rt 1 Box 4001	Sulphur	OK	73086	**800-213-8955**	580-993-2327	697
Lifetime Doors Inc 30700 Northwestern Hwy	Farmington	MI	48334	**800-521-0500**	248-851-7700	234
Lifetime Healthcare Cos 165 Court St	Rochester	NY	14647	**800-847-1200**	585-454-1700	355-4
Lifetime Hoan Corp 1 Merrick Ave *NASDAQ: LCUT*	Westbury	NY	11590	**800-252-3390**	516-683-6000	477
Lifetime Hoan Corp Farberware Div 1 Merrick Ave	Westbury	NY	11590	**800-252-3390**	516-683-6000	477
Lifetime Hoan Corp Hoffritz Div 1 Merrick Ave	Westbury	NY	11590	**800-252-3390**	516-683-6000	477
Lifetime Products Inc PO Box 160010 Freeport Ctr Bldg D-11	Clearfield	UT	84016	**800-225-3865**	801-776-1532	701
Lifetouch Church Directories 1371 State Rt 598	Galion	OH	44833	**800-521-4611**	419-468-4739	623-10
LifeWay Glorieta Conference Center PO Box 8 *Resv	Glorieta	NM	87535	**800-797-4222***	505-757-6161	204
Lift-All Co Inc 1909 McFarland Dr	Landisville	PA	17538	**800-433-0396**	717-898-6615	462
Lift-Tech International 414 W Broadway Ave *Cust Svc	Muskegon	MI	49443	**800-955-5541***	231-733-0821	462
Liftex Inc 443 Ivyland Rd	Warminster	PA	18974	**800-448-3079**	215-957-0810	462
Lifts West Condominium Resort Hotel PO Box 330	Red River	NM	87558	**800-221-1859**	505-754-2778	655
Ligand Pharmaceuticals Inc 10275 Science Ctr Dr *NASDAQ: LGND*	San Diego	CA	92121	**800-964-5793**	858-550-7500	572
Ligature 4909 Alcoa Ave	Los Angeles	CA	90058	**800-944-5440**	323-585-6000	770
Liggett Group Inc 100 Maple Ln	Mebane	NC	27302	**800-334-1686**	919-304-7700	741-1
Liggett-Stashower Inc 1228 Euclid Ave 2nd Fl	Cleveland	OH	44115	**800-877-4573**	216-348-8500	4
Light Impressions Inc PO Box 787	Brea	CA	92822	**800-828-6216**	714-441-4539	119
Light & Life Communications PO Box 535002	Indianapolis	IN	46253	**800-348-2513**	317-244-3660	623-4
Light Sources Inc 37 Robinson Blvd	Orange	CT	06477	**800-245-4458**	203-799-7877	429
Lighthouse Club Hotel 201 60th St	Ocean City	MD	21842	**888-371-5400**	410-524-5400	373
Lighthouse Computer Services Inc 6 Blackstone Valley Pl Suite 205	Lincoln	RI	02865	**888-542-8030**	401-334-0799	178
Lighthouse Electric Co-op Inc PO Box 600	Floydada	TX	79235	**800-657-7192**	806-983-2814	244
Lighthouse Hospice 1040 N Kings Hwy Suite 100	Cherry Hill	NJ	08034	**888-345-7742**	856-661-5600	365
Lighthouse Inn 6 Guthrie Pl	New London	CT	06320	**888-600-5681**	860-443-8411	373
Lighthouse International 111 E 59th St	New York	NY	10022	**800-829-0500**	212-821-9200	48-17
Lighthouse Lodge & Suites 1150 Lighthouse Ave	Pacific Grove	CA	93950	**800-858-1249**	831-655-2111	373
Lighting Assn. American 2050 Stemmons Fwy Suite 10046	Dallas	TX	75342	**800-605-4448**	214-698-9898	49-4
Lightolier 631 Airport Rd	Fall River	MA	02720	**800-217-7722**	508-679-8131	431
Lights of America 611 Reyes Dr *Cust Svc	Walnut	CA	91789	**800-321-8100***	909-594-7883	431
Lightspan Inc 10140 Campus Pt Dr	San Diego	CA	92121	**888-425-5543**	858-824-8000	176-3
Lightwave Electronics Corp 2400 Charleston Rd	Mountain View	CA	94043	**888-544-4892**	650-962-0755	416
Li'l Dino Corp 5601 Roanne Way Suite 100	Greensboro	NC	27409	**800-525-6782**	336-297-4440	657
Lilleys' Landing Resort 367 River Ln	Branson	MO	65616	**800-284-2916**	417-334-6380	655
Lillian Vernon Corp 1 Theall Rd	Rye	NY	10580	**800-545-5426**	914-925-1200	451
Lilly Conference Center. Marten House Hotel & 1801 W 86th St	Indianapolis	IN	46260	**800-736-5634**	317-872-4111	370
Lilly Eli Canada Inc 3650 Danforth Ave	Toronto	ON	M1N2E8	**800-268-4446**	416-694-3221	572
Lilly Eli & Co Lilly Corporate Ctr *NYSE: LLY* ■ *Prod Info	Indianapolis	IN	46285	**800-545-5979***	317-276-2000	572
Lily Guesthouse 835 Collins Ave	Miami Beach	FL	33139	**888-742-6600**	305-535-9900	373
Lima News 3515 Elida Rd	Lima	OH	45807	**800-686-9924**	419-223-1010	522-2
Lima/Allen County Convention & Visitors Bureau 147 N Main St	Lima	OH	45801	**888-222-6075**	419-222-6075	205
Lime Rock Park 497 Lime Rock Rd	Lakeville	CT	06039	**800-722-3577**	860-435-5000	504
Limestone College 1115 College Dr	Gaffney	SC	29340	**800-795-7151**	864-489-7151	163
Limited The 3 Limited Pkwy	Columbus	OH	43230	**800-945-9000**	614-415-2000	155-6
Limited Brands Inc 3 Limited Pkwy *NYSE: LTD*	Columbus	OH	43230	**800-945-9000**	614-415-7000	658
Limited Edition 2170 Sunrise Hwy *Orders	Merrick	NY	11566	**800-645-2864***	516-623-4400	322
Limited Too 8323 Walton Pkwy	New Albany	OH	43054	**800-934-4496**	614-775-3500	155-1
Limnology & Oceanography. American Society of 5400 Bosque Blvd Suite 680	Waco	TX	76710	**800-929-2756**	254-399-9635	49-19
Limo One 1342 Shoulder Creek Ln	San Bruno	CA	94066	**877-490-5466**	415-531-6180	433
Limoneira Co 1141 Cummings Rd	Santa Paula	CA	93060	**800-350-5541**	805-525-5541	310-2
Limpert Brothers Inc PO Box 1480	Vineland	NJ	08362	**800-691-1353**	856-691-1353	291-15
LIMRA International Inc 300 Day Hill Rd *Cust Svc	Windsor	CT	06095	**800-285-7792***	860-688-3358	49-9
Lincare Holdings Inc 19387 US 19 N *NASDAQ: LNCR*	Clearwater	FL	33764	**800-284-2006**	727-530-7700	358
Lincoln Bancorp 1121 E Main St PO Box 510 *NASDAQ: LNCB*	Plainfield	IN	46168	**888-895-6539**	317-839-6539	355-2
Lincoln Christian Seminary 100 Campus View Dr	Lincoln	IL	62656	**888-522-5228**	217-732-3168	164-3
Lincoln City Visitor & Convention Bureau 801 SW Hwy 101 Suite 1	Lincoln City	OR	97367	**800-452-2151**	541-994-8378	205
Lincoln Convention & Visitors Bureau 1135 M St 3rd Fl	Lincoln	NE	68508	**800-423-8212**	402-434-5335	205
Lincoln County 300 Central Ave PO Box 338	Carrizozo	NM	88301	**800-687-2705**	505-648-2394	334
Lincoln County Historical Society Museum of Pioneer History 717 Manvel Ave	Chandler	OK	74834	**888-258-2809**	405-258-2425	509
Lincoln Educational Services 200 Executive Dr	West Orange	NJ	07052	**877-693-8887**	973-736-9340	241
Lincoln Electric Co-op Inc PO Box 628	Eureka	MT	59917	**800-442-2994**	406-889-3301	244
Lincoln Financial Group 1500 Market St Centre Sq West Tower Suite 3900 *NYSE: LNC*	Philadelphia	PA	19102	**800-454-6265**	215-448-1400	355-4
Lincoln Insurance Group 1526 K St	Lincoln	NE	68508	**800-747-7191**	402-423-7191	384-2
Lincoln Journal-Star 926 P St	Lincoln	NE	68508	**800-742-7315**	402-475-4200	522-2
Lincoln Lakes Region (Greater) Chamber of Commerce 256 W Broadway	Lincoln	ME	04457	**888-794-8065**	207-794-8065	137
Lincoln Land Community College 5250 Shepherd Rd PO Box 19256	Springfield	IL	62794	**800-727-4161**	217-786-2200	160
Lincoln Land Oil Co 2026 Republic St	Springfield	IL	62702	**800-238-4912**	217-523-5050	311

Company	City	State	ZIP	Toll-Free	Phone	Class
Lincoln LH & Son Inc 87 West St	Galeton	PA	16922	**800-845-4626**	814-274-9200	423
Lincoln Logs Ltd 5 Riverside Dr	Chestertown	NY	12817	**800-833-2461**	518-494-5500	107
Lincoln Memorial University 6965 Cumberland Gap Pkwy	Harrogate	TN	37752	**800-325-0900**	423-869-3611	163
Lincoln-Mercury Co 16800 Executive Plaza Dr PO Box 6248	Dearborn	MI	48121	**800-521-4140**		59
Lincoln Motors 28300 Euclid Ave	Cleveland	OH	44092	**800-668-6748**	216-731-4790	507
Lincoln National Corp DBA Lincoln Financial Group 1500 Market St Centre Sq West Tower Suite 3900 *NYSE: LNC*	Philadelphia	PA	19102	**800-454-6265**	215-448-1400	355-4
Lincoln National Life Insurance Co 1300 S Clinton St	Fort Wayne	IN	46802	**800-454-6265**	260-455-2000	384-2
Lincoln Office Supply Co Inc 77 Commerce Dr	Morton	IL	61550	**800-468-6868**	309-263-7777	524
Lincoln Poultry & Egg Co 2005 'M' St	Lincoln	NE	68510	**800-477-4433**	402-477-3757	292-10
Lincoln Suites Downtown 1823 L St NW	Washington	DC	20036	**800-424-2970**	202-223-4320	373
Lincoln Technical Institute 7225 Winton Dr Bldg 128	Indianapolis	IN	46268	**800-554-4465**	317-632-5553	787
Lincoln Technical Institute 5151 Tilghman St	Allentown	PA	18104	**877-533-2592**	610-398-5301	787
Lincoln Technical Institute 9191 Torresdale Ave	Philadelphia	PA	19136	**800-806-1917**	215-335-0800	787
Lincoln Theater 200 Bloomfield Ave University of Hartford Campus	West Hartford	CT	06117	**800-274-8587**	860-768-4228	562
Lincoln Trail College 11220 State Hwy 1	Robinson	IL	62454	**866-582-4322**	618-544-8657	160
Lincoln University 820 Chestnut St *Admissions	Jefferson City	MO	65102	**800-521-5052***	573-681-5000	163
Lincoln University 1570 Old Baltimore Pike PO Box 179 *Admissions	Lincoln University	PA	19352	**800-790-0191***	610-932-8300	163
Lincoln Wood Products Inc PO Box 375	Merrill	WI	54452	**800-967-2461**	715-536-2461	234
Lincolnshire Resort. Marriott's 10 Marriott Dr	Lincolnshire	IL	60069	**800-228-9290**	847-634-0100	655
Linda Evans Fitness Centers 2491 San Ramon Valley Blvd Suite 1 PMB 203	San Ramon	CA	94583	**800-455-4632**	925-743-3399	349
Linda Hall Library 5109 Cherry St	Kansas City	MO	64110	**800-662-1545**	816-363-4600	426
Lindal Cedar Homes Inc PO Box 24426 *Prod Info	Seattle	WA	98124	**800-426-0536***	206-725-0900	107
Lindblad Expeditions 96 Morton St 9th Fl	New York	NY	10014	**800-397-3348**	212-765-7740	748
Linden Bulk Transportation Co Inc 4200 Tremley Point Rd	Linden	NJ	07036	**800-333-2855**	908-862-3883	769
Linden Div Colibri/Park Lane Assoc Inc 100 Niantic Ave *Sales	Providence	RI	02907	**800-556-7354***	401-943-2100	151
Linden Hall School for Girls 212 E Main St	Lititz	PA	17543	**800-258-5778**	717-626-8512	611
Linden Hill School 154 S Mountain Rd	Northfield	MA	01360	**888-254-6336**	413-498-2906	611
Linden Publishing 2006 S Mary St *Sales	Fresno	CA	93721	**800-345-4447***	559-233-6633	623-2
Linden Row Inn 100 E Franklin St	Richmond	VA	23219	**800-348-7424**	804-783-7000	373
Lindenmeyr Munroe Paper Corp 115 Moonachie Ave	Moonachie	NJ	07074	**800-631-0193**	201-440-6491	543
LINDO Systems Inc 1415 N Dayton St *Sales	Chicago	IL	60622	**800-441-2378***	312-988-7422	176-5
Lindquist Machine Corp PO Box 2327	Green Bay	WI	54306	**888-499-0831**	920-713-4100	446
Lindquist Steels Inc 1050 Woodend Rd	Stratford	CT	06615	**800-243-9637**	203-377-2828	483
Lindsay Mfg Co 214 E 2nd St *NYSE: LNN*	Lindsay	NE	68644	**800-829-5300**	402-428-2131	269
Lindsay Mfg Inc PO Box 1708	Ponca City	OK	74602	**800-546-3729**	580-762-2457	775
Lindsey Wilson College 210 Lindsey Wilson St	Columbia	KY	42728	**800-264-0138**	270-384-2126	163
Lindt & Sprungli USA 1 Fine Chocolate Pl	Stratham	NH	03885	**877-695-4638**	603-778-8100	291-8
Linear Films Div Atlantis Plastics Inc 6940 W 76th St S *Cust Svc	Tulsa	OK	74157	**800-332-4437***	918-446-1651	588
Linear LLC 2055 Corte del Nogal *Cust Svc	Carlsbad	CA	92009	**800-421-1587***	760-438-7000	681
Linen Management. National Assn of Institutional 2130 Lexington Rd Suite H	Richmond	KY	40475	**800-669-0863**	859-624-0177	49-4
Linens 'n Things Inc 6 Brighton Rd *NYSE: LIN*	Clifton	NJ	07015	**866-568-7378**	973-778-1300	357
Linens of the Week 713 Lamont St NW	Washington	DC	20010	**800-355-8874**	202-291-9200	434
Linfield College 900 SE Baker St	McMinnville	OR	97128	**800-640-2287**	503-883-2200	163
Lingo Mfg Co 7400 Industrial Rd *Cust Svc	Florence	KY	41042	**800-354-9771***	859-371-2662	231
Linguistics Systems Inc 201 Broadway	Cambridge	MA	02139	**800-654-5006**	617-864-3900	757
LINK2GOV Corp 1 Burton Hills Blvd Suite 300	Nashville	TN	37215	**800-483-7072**	615-297-2770	176-7
LinkShare Corp 215 Park Ave S 8th Fl	New York	NY	10003	**800-875-5645**	646-654-6000	7
Linksys 18582 Teller Ave	Irvine	CA	92612	**800-326-7114**	949-823-3000	174
Linn Gear Co 100 N 8th St PO Box 397	Lebanon	OR	97355	**800-547-2471**	541-259-1211	609
LINQ Industrial Fabrics Inc 2550 W 5th North St	Summerville	SC	29483	**800-822-8968**	843-873-5800	730-3
Lintern Corp 8685 Station St	Mentor	OH	44061	**800-321-3638**	440-255-9333	15
Linton Daily Citizen PO Box 129	Linton	IN	47441	**800-947-4487**	812-847-4487	522-2
Linvar LLC 245 Hamilton St	Hartford	CT	06106	**800-282-5288**	860-951-3818	462
Linvatec Corp 11311 Concept Blvd	Largo	FL	33773	**800-325-5900**	727-392-6464	468
Linville Caverns US 221 N	Marion	NC	28752	**800-419-0540**	828-756-4171	50

Company	City	State	ZIP	Toll-Free	Phone	Class
Linx Communications Inc 175 Crossing Blvd Suite 300	Framingham	MA	01702	**888-367-5469**	617-747-4200	222
Linzer Products Corp 248 Wyandanch Ave	Wyandanch	NY	11798	**800-221-0787**	631-253-3333	104
Lion Apparel Inc 6450 Poe Ave	Dayton	OH	45414	**800-548-6614**	937-898-1949	153-19
Lion Brand Yarn Co 34 W 15th St	New York	NY	10011	**800-795-5466**	212-243-8995	730-9
Lion Brewery Inc 700 N Pennsylvania Ave	Wilkes-Barre	PA	18705	**800-233-8327**	570-823-8801	103
Lion Brothers Co Inc 10246 Reisterstown Rd *Cust Svc	Owings Mills	MD	21117	**800-365-6543***	410-363-1000	256
Lion Inc 2000 S Colorado Blvd Suite 350	Denver	CO	80222	**800-786-8083**	303-455-1800	498
Lion Magazine 300 W 22nd St *Circ	Oak Brook	IL	60523	**800-710-7822***	630-571-5466	449-10
Lion Oil Co PO Box 1639	Jackson	MS	39215	**800-824-2626**	601-933-3000	570
Lion Square Lodge & Conference Center 660 W Lionshead Pl	Vail	CO	81657	**800-525-5788**	970-476-2281	655
Lionel LLC 26750 23 Mile Rd	Chesterfield	MI	48051	**800-454-6635**	586-949-4100	750
Lionmark Construction Cos 1620 Woodson Rd	Saint Louis	MO	63114	**800-392-4295**	314-991-2180	187-4
Lions Eye Bank of Central Texas Inc 103 E Wheeler PO Box 347	Manor	TX	78653	**800-977-3937**	512-457-0638	265
Lions Eye Bank of Delaware Valley 2000 Hamilton Ct Rodin Pl Suite 301	Philadelphia	PA	19130	**800-743-6667**	215-563-1679	265
Lions Eye Bank of Oregon 1010 NW 22nd Ave Suite N144	Portland	OR	97210	**800-843-7793**	503-413-7523	265
Lions Gate Entertainment Corp 595 Burrard St *NYSE: LGF*	Vancouver	BC	V7J3S5	**888-609-6120**	604-609-6100	503
Lions Gate Entertainment Corp Lions Gate Television Div 4553 Glencoe Ave Suite 200	Marina del Rey	CA	90292	**800-424-7070**	310-449-9200	503
Lions Gate Films Inc 4553 Glencoe Ave Suite 200	Marina del Rey	CA	90292	**800-424-7070**	310-449-9200	503
Lions Gate Television Div Lions Gate Entertainment Corp 4553 Glencoe Ave Suite 200	Marina del Rey	CA	90292	**800-424-7070**	310-449-9200	503
Lions Medical Eye Bank & Research Foundation of Eastern Virginia Inc 600 Gresham Dr	Norfolk	VA	23507	**800-453-6059**	757-668-2020	265
Lipe Automation Equipment 7650 Edgecomb Dr	Liverpool	NY	13088	**800-448-7822**	315-457-1052	206
LiphaTech Inc 3600 W Elm St	Milwaukee	WI	53209	**888-331-7900**		86
LipoScience Inc 2500 Sumner Blvd	Raleigh	NC	27616	**877-547-6837**	919-212-1999	229
Lipper International Inc 235 Washington St	Wallingford	CT	06492	**800-243-3129**	203-269-8588	716
Lippincott Williams & Wilkins 530 Walnut St	Philadelphia	PA	19106	**800-638-3030**	215-521-8300	623-2
Lipps Jerry Trucking Inc 3888 Nash Rd PO Drawer F *Cust Svc	Cape Girardeau	MO	63702	**800-325-3331***	573-335-8204	769
Lipscomb University 3901 Granny White Pike	Nashville	TN	37204	**800-333-4358**	615-269-1000	163
Liquent Inc 1300 Virginia Dr Suite 125	Fort Washington	PA	19034	**800-515-3777**	215-619-6000	176-11
Liquid Digital Media Inc 999 Main St	Redwood City	CA	94063	**866-443-6386**	650-549-2000	176-8
Liquid Drive Corp 418 Hadley St	Holly	MI	48442	**800-523-4443**	248-634-5382	626
Liquid Transport Corp 8470 Allison Pointe Blvd Suite 400	Indianapolis	IN	46250	**800-942-3175**	317-841-4200	769
Lisa Motor Lines Inc PO Box 4529	Fort Worth	TX	76164	**800-569-9234**	817-336-2900	769
Lisle Convention & Visitors Bureau 4746 Main St	Lisle	IL	60532	**800-733-9811**	630-769-1000	205
List Industries Inc 401 NW 12th Ave	Deerfield Beach	FL	33442	**800-776-1342**	954-429-9155	314-3
Lista International Corp 106 Lowland St *Cust Svc	Holliston	MA	01746	**800-722-3020***	508-429-1350	281
Listel Vancouver Hotel 1300 Robson St	Vancouver	BC	V6E1C5	**800-663-5491**	604-684-8461	372
Lister-Petter Inc 815 E 56 Hwy	Olathe	KS	66061	**800-888-3512**	913-764-3512	378
Listo Pencil Corp 1925 Union St	Alameda	CA	94501	**800-547-8648**	510-522-2910	560
LITA (Library & Information Technology Assn) 50 E Huron St	Chicago	IL	60611	**800-545-2433**	312-280-4270	49-11
Litchfield Beach & Golf Resort 14276 Ocean Highway	Pawleys Island	SC	29585	**800-845-1897**	843-237-3000	655
Litehouse Inc 1109 N Ella Ave	Sandpoint	ID	83864	**800-669-3169**	208-263-7569	291-19
Literacy. National Center for Family 325 W Main St Suite 300	Louisville	KY	40202	**877-326-5481**	502-584-1133	48-11
Literacy Worldwide. Pro 1320 Jamesville Ave	Syracuse	NY	13210	**800-448-8878**	315-422-9121	48-5
Literary Guild Doubleday Direct Inc 1225 S Market St	Mechanicsburg	PA	17055	**800-688-4442**		94
Litetronics International Inc 4101 W 123rd St	Alsip	IL	60803	**800-860-3392**	708-389-8000	429
Lith-O-Roll Corp 9521 Telstar Ave	El Monte	CA	91731	**800-423-4176**	626-579-0340	446
Litho-Krome Co 5700 Old Brim Dr	Midland	GA	31820	**800-572-8028**	706-225-6600	615
Lithographix Inc 13500 S Figueroa St	Los Angeles	CA	90061	**800-848-2449**	323-770-1000	615
Lithonia Lighting Co 1400 Lester Rd *Cust Svc	Conyers	GA	30012	**800-858-7763***	770-922-9000	431
Lititz Mutual Insurance Co 2 N Broad St	Lititz	PA	17543	**800-626-4751**	717-626-4751	384-4
Littell International Inc 145 N Swift Rd	Addison	IL	60101	**800-548-8355**	630-916-6662	661
Little America Hotels & Resorts 500 S Main St	Salt Lake City	UT	84101	**800-453-9450**	801-363-6781	369
Little Britches Rodeo Assn. National 1045 W Rio Grande St	Colorado Springs	CO	80906	**800-763-3694**	719-389-0333	48-22
Little Brown & Co 1271 Ave of the Americas *Cust Svc	New York	NY	10020	**800-759-0190***	212-522-1212	623-2
Little Caesars Inc 2211 Woodward Ave	Detroit	MI	48201	**800-722-3727**	313-983-6000	657
Little Crow Foods PO Box 1038	Warsaw	IN	46581	**800-288-2769**	574-267-7141	291-4

Name / Address	City	State	ZIP	Toll-Free	Phone	Class
Little Dutch Boy Bakery Inc 12349 S 970 East	Draper	UT	84020	**800-382-2594**	801-571-3800	291-9
Little Giant Pump Co 3810 N Tulsa Ave	Oklahoma City	OK	73112	**800-621-7264**	405-947-2511	627
Little Gym International Inc 8970 E Raintree Dr Suite 200	Scottsdale	AZ	85260	**888-228-2878**	480-948-2878	349
Little Inn by the Sea 4546 El Mar Dr	Lauderdale-by-the-Sea	FL	33308	**800-492-0311**	954-772-2450	373
Little King Inc 11811 'I' St	Omaha	NE	68137	**800-788-9478**	402-330-8019	657
Little Lady Foods Inc 2323 Pratt Blvd	Elk Grove Village	IL	60007	**800-439-1440**	847-806-1440	291-36
Little Nell The 675 E Durant Ave	Aspen	CO	81611	**888-843-6355**	970-920-4600	373
Little Palm Island 28500 Overseas Hwy MM 28.5	Little Torch Key	FL	33042	**800-343-8567**	305-872-2524	655
Little People of America (LPA) 5289 NE Elam Young Pkwy Suite F-700	Hillsboro	OR	97124	**888-572-2001**	503-846-1562	48-17
Little Professor Book Centers Inc PO Box 3160	Ann Arbor	MI	48106	**800-899-6232**	734-663-8733	96
Little Rapids Corp 2273 Larsen Rd	Green Bay	WI	54303	**800-496-3040**	920-496-3040	566
Little Rapids Corp Graham Professional Div 2273 Larsen Rd PO Box 19100	Green Bay	WI	54304	**800-558-6765***	920-494-8701	566
*Cust Svc						
Little River Electric Co-op Inc PO Box 220	Abbeville	SC	29620	**800-459-2141**	864-366-2141	244
Little Rock Convention & Visitors Bureau PO Box 3232	Little Rock	AR	72203	**800-844-4781**	501-376-4781	205
Little Switzerland Inc 6800 NW Broken Sound Pkwy	Boca Raton	FL	33487	**888-257-5488**	561-206-0080	240
Little Tikes Co 2180 Barlow Rd	Hudson	OH	44236	**800-321-0183***	330-650-3000	750
*Cust Svc						
Littlefield Feedyard RR 1 Box 26	Amherst	TX	79312	**800-687-5141**	806-385-5141	11-1
Littleford Day Inc 7451 Empire Dr	Florence	KY	41042	**800-365-8555**	859-525-7600	379
Littlestown Foundry Inc 150 Charles St PO Box 69	Littlestown	PA	17340	**800-471-0844**	717-359-4141	303
Littonian Shoe Co PO Box 95	Littlestown	PA	17340	**888-790-3930**	717-359-5194	296
Liturgical Publications Inc 2875 S James Dr	New Berlin	WI	53151	**800-876-4574**	262-785-1188	623-9
Liturgical Publications of Saint Louis Inc 160 Old State Rd	Ballwin	MO	63021	**800-876-7000**	636-394-7000	623-10
LiveBridge Inc 7303 SE Lake Rd	Portland	OR	97267	**800-783-6000**	503-652-6000	722
Livengrin Foundation 4833 Hulmeville Rd	Bensalem	PA	19020	**800-245-4746**	215-638-5200	712
Liver Foundation. American 75 Maiden Ln Suite 603	New York	NY	10038	**800-465-4837**	212-668-1000	48-17
Livermore Software Laboratories Inc 1830 S Kirkwood Rd Suite 205	Houston	TX	77077	**800-240-5754**	281-759-3274	176-12
Livestock Marketing Assn (LMA) 10510 NW Ambassador Dr	Kansas City	MO	64153	**800-821-2048**	816-891-0502	48-2
LiveVault Corp 201 Boston Post Rd W	Marlborough	MA	01752	**800-638-5518**	508-460-6670	39
Living Bank PO Box 6725	Houston	TX	77625	**800-528-2971**	713-961-9431	48-17
Living Earth Crafts 3210 Executive Ridge Dr	Vista	CA	92081	**800-358-8292**	760-597-2155	78
Living Earth Technology Co 5625 Crawford Rd	Houston	TX	77041	**800-665-3826**	713-466-7360	276
Living Water Worship & Teaching Center 595 N Aspaas Rd	Cornville	AZ	86325	**888-627-5631***	928-634-4421	660
*Mktg						
Livingston Boats PO Box 819	Elma	WA	98541	**866-482-5580**	360-482-5580	91
Livingston County Chamber of Commerce 4635 Millennium Dr	Geneseo	NY	14454	**800-538-7365**	585-243-2222	137
Livingston Enterprise 401 S Main St	Livingston	MT	59047	**800-345-8412**	406-222-2000	522-2
Livingston Memorial Visiting Nurse Assn Hospice 1996 Eastman Ave Suite 101	Ventura	CA	93003	**800-540-0543**	805-642-1608	365
Livingstone College 701 W Monroe St	Salisbury	NC	28144	**800-835-3435**	704-216-6000	163
LJ Gonzer Assoc Inc 1225 Raymond Blvd	Newark	NJ	07102	**800-631-4218**	973-624-5600	707
LJ Technical Systems Inc 85 Corporate Dr	Holtsville	NY	11742	**800-237-3482**	631-758-1616	176-3
LKG Industries Inc 3660 Publisher's Dr	Rockford	IL	61109	**800-645-2262**	815-874-2301	52
LKQ Corp 120 N LaSalle St Suite 3300	Chicago	IL	60602	**877-557-2677**	312-621-1950	61
NASDAQ: LKQX						
LL Bean Inc 15 Casco St	Freeport	ME	04033	**800-341-4341***	207-865-4761	451
*Cust Svc						
LL Building Products Inc 4501 Circle 75 Pkwy Suite E5300	Atlanta	GA	30339	**800-755-9397**	770-953-6366	688
LL Sams Inc 1203 Industrial Blvd	Cameron	TX	76520	**800-537-4723**	254-697-6754	314-3
Llano Estacado Winery FM 1585 3.2 miles E of US 87 S	Lubbock	TX	79404	**800-634-3854**	806-745-2258	50
Llewellyn Worldwide Inc PO Box 64383	Saint Paul	MN	55164	**800-843-6666**	651-291-1970	623-2
LLL (La Leche League International Inc) 1400 N Meacham Rd	Schaumburg	IL	60173	**800-525-3243**	847-519-7730	48-17
Lloyd Aereo Boliviano Airlines Cargo 1651 NW 68 Ave Bldg 706	Miami	FL	33131	**800-489-4118***	305-526-5565	13
*Cust Svc						
Lloyd Aereo Boliviano DBA LAB Airlines 225 SE 1st St	Miami	FL	33131	**800-337-0918**	305-374-4600	26
Lloyd Inc 604 W Thomas Ave	Shenandoah	IA	51601	**800-831-0004**	712-246-4000	574
Lloyd/Flanders Industries Inc 3010 10th St	Menominee	MI	49858	**800-526-9894**	906-863-4491	314-4
LM Becker & Co Inc PO Box 1459	Appleton	WI	54912	**888-869-6569**	920-739-5269	55
LMA (Livestock Marketing Assn) 10510 NW Ambassador Dr	Kansas City	MO	64153	**800-821-2048**	816-891-0502	48-2
LNB Bancorp Inc 457 Broadway	Lorain	OH	44052	**800-860-1007**	440-244-6000	355-2
NASDAQ: LNBB						
LNR Property Corp 1601 Washington Ave Suite 800	Miami Beach	FL	33139	**800-784-6380**	305-695-5600	641
Load King Div Terex Corp 701 E Rose St PO Box 427	Elk Point	SD	57025	**800-264-5522**	605-356-3301	768
Load King Mfg Co PO Box 40606	Jacksonville	FL	32203	**800-531-4975**	904-354-8882	293
Load Rite Trailers Inc 265 Lincoln Hwy	Fairless Hills	PA	19030	**800-562-3783**	215-949-0500	751
Loan Market Week 225 Park Ave S 7th Fl	New York	NY	10003	**800-543-4444**	212-224-3300	521-1
LoanSurfer.com 12140 Woodcrest Executive Dr	Saint Louis	MO	63141	**877-434-4555**	314-628-2000	498
Lobster Direct 97 Bedford Hills Rd	Bedford	NS	B4A1J8	**800-672-5297**	902-832-1680	292-5
Local Motion Inc 424 Sumner St	Honolulu	HI	96817	**800-841-7613**	808-523-7873	701
Loch Gallery 16 Hazelton Ave	Toronto	ON	M5R2E2	**877-227-9828**	416-964-9050	42
Lock Haven University	Lock Haven	PA	17745	**800-233-8978**	570-893-2011	163
Lock Joint Tube Inc 515 W Ireland Rd	South Bend	IN	46614	**800-257-6859**	574-299-5326	481
Lockheed Federal Credit Union 2340 Hollywood Way	Burbank	CA	91505	**800-328-5328**	818-565-2020	216
Lockheed Martin Management & Data Systems Western Region 3200 Zanker Rd	San Jose	CA	95134	**800-537-2188**	408-473-3000	519
Lockheed Martin Naval Electronics & Surveillance Systems Manassas 9500 Godwin Dr	Manassas	VA	20110	**800-325-4019**	703-367-2121	519
Lockheed Window Corp Rt 100 PO Box 166	Pascoag	RI	02859	**800-537-3061**	401-568-3061	232
Locksmiths of America. Associated 3003 Live Oak St	Dallas	TX	75204	**800-532-2562**	214-827-1701	49-3
Lockwood Bros Inc 220 Salters Creek Rd	Hampton	VA	23661	**800-367-5295**	757-722-1946	769
Lockwood Products Inc 5615 SW Willow Ln	Lake Oswego	OR	97035	**800-423-1625**	503-635-8113	364
Loctite Corp 1001 Trout Brook Crossing	Rocky Hill	CT	06067	**800-842-0041**	860-571-5100	3
Loctite Corp North American Group 1001 Trout Brook Crossing	Rocky Hill	CT	06067	**800-243-4874***	860-571-5100	3
*Cust Svc						
Locus Telecommunications Inc 111 Sylvan Ave	Englewood Cliffs	NJ	07632	**888-823-7587**	201-585-3600	721
Lodal Inc 620 N Hooper St	Kingsford	MI	49802	**800-435-3500**	906-779-1700	505
Lodge Alley Inn 195 E Bay St	Charleston	SC	29401	**800-456-0009**	843-722-1611	373
Lodge at Cloudcroft 1 Corona Pl	Cloudcroft	NM	88317	**800-395-6343**	505-682-2566	655
Lodge & Club at Ponte Vedra Beach 607 Ponte Vedra Blvd	Ponte Vedra Beach	FL	32082	**800-243-4304**	904-273-9500	655
Lodge on the Desert 306 N Alvernon Way	Tucson	AZ	85711	**800-456-5634**	520-325-3366	373
Lodge of Four Seasons Horseshoe Bend Pkwy PO Box 215	Lake Ozark	MO	65049	**800-843-5253**	573-365-3000	655
Lodge Hotel & Conference Center 900 Spruce Hills Dr	Bettendorf	IA	52722	**800-285-8637**	563-359-7141	373
Lodge at Koele PO Box 630310	Lanai City	HI	96763	**800-321-4666**	808-565-7300	655
Lodge at the Mountain Village 1415 Lowell Ave	Park City	UT	84060	**800-754-2002**	435-649-0800	373
Lodge of the Ozarks 3431 W Hwy 76	Branson	MO	65616	**800-213-2584**	417-334-7535	373
Lodge at Pebble Beach 1500 Cypress Dr	Pebble Beach	CA	93953	**800-654-9300**	831-624-3811	655
Lodge at Sonoma Renaissance Resort & Spa 1325 Broadway	Sonoma	CA	95476	**888-710-8008**	707-935-6600	373
Lodge & Spa at Breckenridge 112 Overlook Dr	Breckenridge	CO	80424	**800-736-1607**	970-453-9300	373
Lodge & Spa at Cordillera 2205 Cordillera Way	Edwards	CO	81632	**800-877-3529**	970-926-2200	373
Lodge at Tamarron 40292 Hwy 550 N	Durango	CO	81301	**800-678-1000**	970-259-2000	655
Lodge at Vail 174 E Gore Creek Dr	Vail	CO	81657	**800-331-5634**	970-476-5011	655
Lodge at Ventana Canyon - A Wyndham Luxury Resort 6200 N Clubhouse Ln	Tucson	AZ	85750	**800-828-5701**	520-577-1400	655
Lodge at Woodcliff 199 Woodcliff Dr	Fairport	NY	14450	**800-365-3065**	585-381-4000	655
LodgeNet Entertainment Corp 3900 W Innovation St	Sioux Falls	SD	57107	**888-563-4363**	605-988-1330	117
NASDAQ: LNET						
Lodging.com 4805 N 30th St Suite 103	Colorado Springs	CO	80919	**888-563-4434**		368
Lodi Conference & Visitors Bureau 2545 W Turner Rd	Lodi	CA	95242	**800-798-1810**	209-365-1195	205
Lodi Memorial Hospital 975 S Fairmont Ave	Lodi	CA	95241	**800-876-6750**	209-334-3411	366-2
Loeb Electric Co 915 Williams Ave	Columbus	OH	43212	**800-837-2852**	614-294-6351	245
Loewenstein Inc 206 E Frazier Ave	Liberty	NC	27298	**877-396-5356**	336-622-2201	314-1
Loews Coronado Bay Resort 4000 Coronado Bay Rd	Coronado	CA	92118	**800-815-6397**	619-424-4000	655
Loews Corp 667 Madison Ave	New York	NY	10021	**800-235-6397**	212-521-2000	184
NYSE: LTR						
Loews First Guest Recognition Program 2 2nd St Station Plaza	Rye	NY	10580	**800-563-9712**		371
Loews Hotel. House of Blues Hotel - A 333 N Dearborn St	Chicago	IL	60610	**800-235-6397**	312-245-0333	373
Loews Hotels 667 Madison Ave	New York	NY	10021	**800-235-6397**	212-521-2000	369
Loews Ventana Canyon Resort 7000 N Resort Dr	Tucson	AZ	85750	**800-234-5117**	520-299-2020	655
Lofland Co 2920 N Stemmons Fwy	Dallas	TX	75247	**800-288-5250**	214-631-5250	483
Loft Seed Inc 9327 US Rt 1 Suite J	Laurel	MD	20723	**800-732-3332**		684
Loftness Specialized Farm Equipment Inc 650 S Main St	Hector	MN	55342	**800-828-7624**	320-848-6266	269
Lofts Hotel & Suites 55 E Nationwide Blvd	Columbus	OH	43215	**800-735-6387**	614-461-2663	373
Logan Clay Products Co 201 S Walnut St	Logan	OH	43138	**800-848-2141**	740-385-2184	148
Logan Corp 555 7th Ave	Huntington	WV	25706	**888-853-4751**	304-526-4700	378
Logan Farms Honey Glazed Hams 10560 Westheimer Rd	Houston	TX	77042	**800-833-4267**	713-781-3773	333
Logan-Hocking Chamber of Commerce PO Box 838	Logan	OH	43138	**800-414-6731**	740-385-6836	137
Logan International Airport (BOS)	Boston	MA	02128	**800-235-6426**	617-561-1818	28
Logan's Roadhouse Inc 3011 Armory Dr Suite 300	Nashville	TN	37204	**800-815-9056**	615-885-9056	657
Logansport Financial Corp 723 E Broadway	Logansport	IN	46947	**800-436-5151**	574-722-3855	355-2
NASDAQ: LOGN						
Logansport/Cass County Chamber of Commerce 300 E Broadway Suite 103	Logansport	IN	46947	**800-425-2071**	574-753-6388	137

Name / Address	City	State	ZIP	Toll-Free	Phone	Class
Logantex Inc 70 W 36th St Suite 1001	New York	NY	10018	**800-223-2004**	212-221-3900	583
Logic Devices Inc 395 W Java Dr *NASDAQ: LOGC*	Sunnyvale	CA	94089	**800-851-0767**	408-542-5400	686
Logical Design Solutions Inc 131 Madison Ave	Morristown	NJ	07960	**800-275-5374**	973-971-0100	796
LogicVision Inc 101 Metro Dr 3rd Fl *NASDAQ: LGVN*	San Jose	CA	95110	**888-584-2478**	408-453-0146	685
Logiplex Corp 4855 N Lagoon	Portland	OR	97217	**800-735-0555**	503-978-6726	681
Logistics Assn. International Warehouse 2800 River Rd Suite 260	Des Plaines	IL	60018	**800-525-0165**	847-813-4699	49-21
Logitech Inc 6505 Kaiser Dr *Sales	Fremont	CA	94555	**800-231-7717***	510-795-8500	171-1
Logos Christian College 8159 Arlington Expy Suite 29	Jacksonville	FL	32211	**800-252-4253**	904-745-3311	163
Lois Paul & Partners 150 Presidential Way	Woburn	MA	01801	**800-989-1550**	781-782-5000	622
LoJack Corp 200 Lowder Brook Dr Suite 1000 *NASDAQ: LOJN*	Westwood	MA	02090	**800-456-5225**	781-326-4700	681
Lollytogs Ltd 100 W 33rd St Suite 1012	New York	NY	10001	**800-262-5437**	212-594-4740	153-4
LOMA 2300 Windy Ridge Pkwy Suite 600	Atlanta	GA	30339	**800-275-5662**	770-951-1770	400
Loma Linda University School of Medicine	Loma Linda	CA	92350	**800-422-4558**	909-558-4467	164-2
Lomanco Inc 2101 W Main St	Jacksonville	AR	72078	**800-643-5596**	501-982-6511	15
Lomar Distributing 2500 Dixon St	Des Moines	IA	50316	**800-369-3663**	515-244-3105	292-11
Lomax Michael Pres/CEO United Negro College Fund Inc 8260 Willow Oaks Corporate Dr	Fairfax	VA	22031	**800-331-2244**	703-205-3400	561
Lompoc Valley Chamber of Commerce & Visitors Bureau PO Box 626	Lompoc	CA	93438	**800-240-0999**	805-736-4567	137
Lon Morris College 800 College Ave Administrative Bldg	Jacksonville	TX	75766	**800-259-5753**	903-589-4000	160
London Fog Industries 1700 Westlake Ave N Suite 200	Seattle	WA	98109	**800-877-8878**	206-270-5300	153-5
London Harry Candies Inc 5353 Lauby Road *Cust Svc	North Canton	OH	44720	**800-321-0444***	330-494-0833	291-8
London Insurance Group Corp PO Box 29045	Phoenix	AZ	85038	**800-433-8181**		384-2
London Life Insurance Co 255 Dufferin Ave	London	ON	N6A4K1	**800-667-3733**	519-432-5281	384-2
London/Laurel County Tourist Commission 140 W Daniel Boone Pkwy	London	KY	40741	**800-348-0095**	606-878-6900	205
Lone Mountain Ranch PO Box 160069	Big Sky	MT	59716	**800-514-4644**	406-995-4644	238
Lone Oak Lodge 2221 N Fremont St	Monterey	CA	93940	**800-283-5663**	831-372-4924	373
Lone Star Corrugated Container Corp 700 N Wildwood	Irving	TX	75061	**800-552-6937**	972-579-1551	101
Lone Star Park at Grand Prairie 1000 Lone Star Pkwy	Grand Prairie	TX	75050	**800-795-7223**	972-263-7223	628
Lone Star Steakhouse & Saloon Inc 224 E Douglas Ave *NASDAQ: STAR*	Wichita	KS	67202	**800-234-0888**	316-264-8899	657
Lone Star Steel Co 15660 N Dallas Pkwy Suite 500	Dallas	TX	75248	**800-527-4615**	972-386-3981	709
Lone Star Technologies Inc 15660 N Dallas Pkwy Suite 500 *NYSE: LSS*	Dallas	TX	75248	**800-527-4615**	972-386-3981	355-3
Lonely Planet Online 150 Linden St	Oakland	CA	94607	**800-275-8555**	510-893-8555	762
Lonely Planet Publications 150 Linden St	Oakland	CA	94607	**800-275-8555**	510-893-8555	623-2
Loners on Wheels (LoW) PO Box 1060-WB	Cape Girardeau	MO	63702	**888-569-4478**		48-23
Long Beach Chamber of Commerce 350 National Blvd	Long Beach	NY	11561	**866-563-3275**	516-432-6000	137
Long Beach Convention & Visitors Bureau 1 World Trade Ctr Suite 300	Long Beach	CA	90831	**800-452-7829**	562-436-3645	205
Long Beach Genetics 2384 E Pacifica Pl	Rancho Dominguez	CA	90220	**800-824-2699**	310-632-8900	408
Long Distance Roses 8673 N Peacock Way	Hilmar	CA	95324	**800-537-6737**		287
Long Electric Co Inc 1310 S Franklin Rd	Indianapolis	IN	46239	**800-356-2450**	317-356-2455	188-4
Long & Foster Realtors 11351 Random Hills Rd	Fairfax	VA	22030	**800-237-8800**	703-359-1500	638
Long Hollow Ranch 71105 Holmes Rd	Sisters	OR	97759	**877-923-1901**	541-923-1901	238
Long House Alaskan Hotel 4335 Wisconsin St	Anchorage	AK	99517	**888-243-2133**	907-243-2133	373
Long Island Convention & Visitors Bureau 330 Motor Pkwy Suite 203	Hauppauge	NY	11788	**800-441-4601**	631-951-3440	205
Long Island Financial Corp 1601 Veterans Memorial Hwy Suite 120 *NASDAQ: LICB*	Islandia	NY	11749	**888-542-2888**	631-348-0888	355-2
Long Island Power Authority 333 Earle Ovington Blvd Suite 403 *Cust Svc	Uniondale	NY	11553	**877-275-5472***	516-222-7700	774
Long Island University *Brooklyn Campus* 1 University Plaza	Brooklyn	NY	11201	**800-548-7526**	718-488-1011	163
CW Post Campus 720 Northern Blvd	Greenvale	NY	11548	**800-548-7526**	516-299-2000	163
Southampton College 239 Montauk Hwy	Southampton	NY	11968	**800-548-7526**	631-287-8010	163
Long-Lewis Hardware Co 430 9th St N	Birmingham	AL	35203	**800-322-0492**	205-322-2561	346
Long Painting Co 21414 68th Ave S	Kent	WA	98032	**800-678-5664**	253-234-8050	188-8
Long Phil Dealerships 1212 Motor City Dr	Colorado Springs	CO	80906	**800-685-5664**	719-575-7100	57
Long Term Care. National Assn of Directors of Nursing Administration in 10101 Alliance Rd Suite 140	Cincinnati	OH	45242	**800-222-0539**	513-791-3679	49-8
Long Term Preferred Care Inc 801 Crescent Ctr Dr Suite 200	Franklin	TN	37067	**800-251-2148**		384-3
Long Wharf Theatre 222 Sargent Dr	New Haven	CT	06511	**800-782-8497**	203-787-4284	562
Long Wholesale Distribution Center PO Box 70	Meridian	MS	39301	**800-748-3847**	601-482-3144	744
Longacre Theatre 220 W 48th St	New York	NY	10036	**800-432-7250**	212-239-6200	732
LongAgribusiness LLC 111 Fairview St	Tarboro	NC	27886	**877-639-5194**	252-823-4151	269
Longboat Key Beach Resort. Hilton 4711 Gulf of Mexico Dr	Longboat Key	FL	34228	**800-445-8667**	941-383-2451	655
Longboat Key Club 301 Gulf of Mexico Dr	Longboat Key	FL	34228	**800-237-8821**	941-383-8821	655
Longhorn Mfg Co Inc PO Box 6060	Roswell	NM	88202	**800-248-3957**	505-347-5411	264
LongHorn Steakhouse 8215 Roswell Rd Bldg 600	Atlanta	GA	30350	**800-434-6245**	770-399-9595	657
Longust Distributing Inc 2432 W Birchwood Ave	Mesa	AZ	85202	**800-352-0521**	480-820-6244	356
Longview Fibre Co Central & Eastern Container Div 3832 N 3rd St	Milwaukee	WI	53212	**800-929-8111**	414-264-8100	101
Longview Inspection 5250 Mayfair Rd	North Canton	OH	44720	**800-321-0878**	330-494-9436	728
Longview News-Journal 320 E Methvin St	Longview	TX	75601	**800-825-9799**	903-757-3311	522-2
Longview Newspapers Inc 320 E Methvin St	Longview	TX	75601	**800-627-4716**	903-757-3311	623-8
Longwood Elastomers Inc 706 Green Valley Rd Suite 212	Greensboro	NC	27408	**800-374-2837**	336-272-3710	664
Longwood Gardens 1001 Conservatory Rd	Kennett Square	PA	19348	**800-737-5500**	610-388-1000	98
Longwood University 201 High St	Farmville	VA	23909	**800-281-4677**	434-395-2060	163
Lonsdale Quay Hotel 123 Carrie Cates Ct	North Vancouver	BC	V7M3K7	**800-836-6111**	604-986-6111	372
Look of Love International 555-A N Michigan Ave	Kenilworth	NJ	07033	**800-526-7627**	908-687-9502	342
LookSmart Ltd 625 2nd St *NASDAQ: LOOK*	San Francisco	CA	94107	**877-512-5665**	415-348-7000	677
Loomis Co 850 Park Rd	Wyomissing	PA	19610	**800-782-0392**	610-374-4040	383
Loomis Communities 246 N Main St	South Hadley	MA	01075	**800-865-7655**	413-532-5325	659
Loomis Fargo & Co 1655 Vilbig Rd	Dallas	TX	75208	**800-725-7475**	214-742-2554	682
Loomis G Inc 1359 Down River Dr	Woodland	WA	98674	**800-456-6647**	360-225-6516	701
Loomis Sayles & Co Inc LP 1 Financial Ctr	Boston	MA	02111	**800-225-2365**	617-482-2450	393
Loomis Sayles Funds 1 Financial Ctr	Boston	MA	02111	**800-633-3330**	617-482-2450	517
Loop Capital Markets LLC 200 W Jackson Blvd 16th Fl	Chicago	IL	60606	**888-294-8898**	312-913-4900	679
Loop-Loc Ltd 390 Motor Pkwy	Hauppauge	NY	11788	**800-562-5667**	631-582-2626	718
Lorain County Community College 1005 N Abbe Rd	Elyria	OH	44035	**800-995-5222**	440-365-5222	160
Lorain County Visitors Bureau 8025 Leavitt Rd	Amherst	OH	44001	**800-334-1673**	440-984-5282	205
Lorain-Medina Rural Electric Co-op Inc PO Box 158	Wellington	OH	44090	**800-222-5673**	440-647-2133	244
Lorain Public Library System 351 6th St	Lorain	OH	44052	**800-322-7323**	440-244-1192	426
Loral Skynet Ltd 500 Hills Dr	Bedminster	NJ	07921	**800-242-2422**	908-470-2300	669
Loras College 1450 Alta Vista St	Dubuque	IA	52001	**800-245-6727**	563-588-7100	163
Lord Abbett & Co 90 Hudson St	Jersey City	NJ	07302	**800-874-3733**		393
Lord Abbett Family of Funds 90 Hudson St	Jersey City	NJ	07302	**800-201-6984**	201-395-2000	517
Lord Corp 111 Lord Dr	Cary	NC	27511	**800-524-2885**	919-468-5979	3
Lord Elgin Hotel 100 Elgin St	Ottawa	ON	K1P5K8	**800-267-4298**	613-235-3333	372
Lord Fairfax Community College Middletown Campus 173 Skirmisher Ln	Middletown	VA	22645	**800-906-5322**	540-868-7000	160
Lord Nelson Hotel & Suites 1515 South Park St	Halifax	NS	B3J2L2	**800-565-0000**	902-423-6331	372
Lord Stanley Suites on the Park 1889 Alberni St	Vancouver	BC	V6G3G7	**888-767-7829**	604-688-9299	372
Lord & Taylor 424 5th Ave	New York	NY	10018	**800-223-7440**	212-391-3344	227
L'Oreal USA Inc Soft Sheen/Carson Products Div 8522 S LaFayette	Chicago	IL	60620	**800-342-7661**	800-621-6143	211
Loren Industries Inc 2801 Greene St	Hollywood	FL	33020	**800-772-8085**	954-920-6622	401
Loren Products 250 Canal St	Lawrence	MA	01840	**800-274-6068**	978-685-0911	149
Lorenz Corp PO Box 802	Dayton	OH	45401	**800-444-1144**	937-228-6118	623-7
Loretto Casket Co 110 W Commerce St	Loretto	TN	38469	**800-225-9105**	931-853-6921	134
Lorillard Tobacco Co 714 Green Valley Rd	Greensboro	NC	27408	**877-703-0386**	336-335-7000	741-1
Lorin Industries 125 E Keating Ave	Muskegon	MI	49443	**800-678-1215**	231-722-1631	472
Lorraine Travel 377 Alhambra Cir	Coral Gables	FL	33134	**800-666-8911**	305-446-4433	760
Lortz Direct Marketing Inc 13936 Gold Cir	Omaha	NE	68144	**800-366-7686**	402-334-9446	5
Los Abrigados Resort 160 Portal Ln	Sedona	AZ	86336	**800-521-3131**	928-282-1777	655
Los Angeles Athletic Club 431 W 7th St	Los Angeles	CA	90014	**800-421-8777**	213-625-2211	373
Los Angeles Avengers 12100 W Olympic Blvd Suite 400	Los Angeles	CA	90064	**888-283-6437**	310-788-7744	703
Los Angeles Convention Center 1201 S Figueroa St	Los Angeles	CA	90015	**800-448-7775**	213-741-1151	204
Los Angeles Convention & Visitors Bureau 333 S Hope St 18th Fl	Los Angeles	CA	90071	**800-228-2452**	213-624-7300	205
Los Angeles Galaxy 18400 Avalon Blvd Suite 200	Carson	CA	90746	**877-342-5299**	310-630-2200	703
Los Angeles International Film Festival American Film Institute 2021 N Western Ave	Los Angeles	CA	90027	**866-231-3378**	323-856-7600	278
Los Angeles Kings Staples Ctr 1111 S Figueroa St	Los Angeles	CA	90015	**888-546-4752**	213-742-7100	703
Los Angeles Magazine 5900 Wilshire Blvd 10th Fl *Cust Svc	Los Angeles	CA	90036	**800-876-5222***	323-801-0100	449-22
Los Angeles Times 202 W 1st St	Los Angeles	CA	90012	**800-528-4637**	213-237-5000	522-2
Los Angeles Times Festival of Books Los Angeles Times 202 W 1st St	Los Angeles	CA	90012	**800-528-4637**	213-237-5000	277

Name / Address	City	State	ZIP	Toll-Free	Phone	Class
Los Angeles Times Orange County 1375 Sunflower Ave	Costa Mesa	CA	92626	**800-528-4637**	714-966-5600	522-2
Los Willows Inn & Spa 530 Stewart Canyon Rd	Fallbrook	CA	92028	**888-731-9400**	760-728-8121	698
Loss Recovery Systems Inc 10 Dwight Pk Dr	Syracuse	NY	13209	**800-724-3473**	315-451-9111	84
Lost Mountain Tissue Bank 3175 Cherokee St NW	Kennesaw	GA	30144	**800-243-1070**	770-428-1070	535
LOT Polish Airlines 500 5th Ave Suite 408	New York	NY	10110	**800-223-0593**	212-869-1074	26
Lottery Channel Inc 425 Walnut St Suite 2300	Cincinnati	OH	45202	**800-733-2074**	513-381-0777	725
Lotus Cars USA Inc 2236 Northmont Pkwy	Duluth	GA	30096	**800-245-6887**	770-476-6540	59
Lotus Development Corp 55 Cambridge Pkwy	Cambridge	MA	02142	**800-343-5414***	617-577-8500	176-1
*Sales						
Lou Ana Foods Inc 715 N Railroad Ave	Opelousas	LA	70570	**800-551-9080**	337-948-6561	291-30
Lou Fusz Automotive Network Inc 925 N Lindbergh Blvd	Saint Louis	MO	63141	**800-371-7819**	314-994-1500	57
LOUD Technologies Inc 16220 Wood Red Rd NE	Woodinville	WA	98072	**800-258-6883**	425-487-4333	52
Loudoun County Chamber of Commerce 101 Blue Seal Dr Suite 100	Leesburg	VA	20177	**800-578-5222**	703-777-2176	137
Loudoun Hospital Center 44045 Riverside Pkwy	Leesburg	VA	20176	**888-542-8477**	703-858-6000	366-2
Loudoun House 209 Castlewood Dr	Lexington	KY	40505	**800-914-7990**	859-254-7024	50
Louis Allis Large Motor Corp PO Box 610	Hayden	AL	35079	**866-568-4700**	205-590-2986	507
Louis Berger Group Inc 100 Halsted St	East Orange	NJ	07018	**800-323-4098**	973-678-1960	258
Louis Bornstein & Co 321 Washington St	Somerville	MA	02143	**800-842-1111***	617-776-3555	356
*Sales						
Louis Boston 234 Berkeley St	Boston	MA	02116	**800-225-5135**	617-262-6100	155-3
Louis & Co 895 Columbia St	Brea	CA	92821	**800-422-4389**	714-529-1771	190-3
Louis E Farrell Co Inc 20 Karen Dr	South Burlington	VT	05403	**800-473-7741**	802-864-6000	82-2
Louis Ferre Inc 302 5th Ave 10th Fl	New York	NY	10001	**800-695-1061**	212-239-1600	342
Louis M Gerson Co Inc 15 Sproat St	Middleboro	MA	02346	**800-225-8623**	508-947-4000	566
Louis M Martini Winery 254 S St Helena Hwy PO Box 112	Saint Helena	CA	94574	**800-321-9463**	707-963-2736	81-3
Louis Padnos Iron & Metal Co PO Box 1979	Holland	MI	49422	**800-442-3509**	616-396-6521	674
Louis Rukeyser's Mutual Funds 1750 Old Meadow Rd Suite 300	McLean	VA	22102	**800-892-9702**	703-905-8000	521-9
Louis Trauth Dairy Inc 16 E 11th St	Newport	KY	41071	**800-544-6455**	859-431-7553	291-25
Louis Vuitton NA Inc 19 E 57th St	New York	NY	10022	**866-884-8866***	212-931-2000	155-6
*Cust Svc						
Louisburg College 501 N Main St	Louisburg	NC	27549	**800-775-0208**	919-496-2521	160
Louise Obici Memorial Hospital 2800 Godwin Blvd	Suffolk	VA	23434	**800-237-5788**	757-934-4000	366-2
Louisiana						
Bill Status State Capitol 13th Fl	Baton Rouge	LA	70804	**800-256-3793**	225-342-2456	425
Ethics Board 2415 Quail Dr 3rd Fl	Baton Rouge	LA	70808	**800-842-6630**	225-763-8777	335
Insurance Dept PO Box 94214	Baton Rouge	LA	70804	**800-259-5300**	225-342-5900	335
Rehabilitation Services 8225 Florida Blvd	Baton Rouge	LA	70806	**800-737-2958**	225-925-4131	335
State Parks Office PO Box 44426	Baton Rouge	LA	70804	**888-677-1400**	225-342-8111	335
Student Financial Assistance Office PO Box 91202	Baton Rouge	LA	70821	**800-259-5626**	225-922-1011	711
Louisiana Assn of Business & Industry 3113 Valley Creek Dr	Baton Rouge	LA	70808	**888-816-5224**	225-928-5388	138
Louisiana Dental Assn 7833 Office Pk Blvd	Baton Rouge	LA	70809	**800-388-6642**	225-926-1986	225
Louisiana Educational Television Authority 7733 Perkins Rd	Baton Rouge	LA	70810	**800-272-8161**	225-767-5660	620
Louisiana Industries PO Box 5396	Bossier City	LA	71171	**800-894-5422**	318-742-3111	181
Louisiana Life Magazine 111 Veterans Memorial Blvd Suite 1800	Metairie	LA	70005	**877-221-3512***	504-834-9292	449-22
*Edit						
Louisiana Medical Mutual Insurance Co 1 Galleria Blvd Suite 700	Metairie	LA	70001	**800-452-2120**	504-831-3756	384-5
Louisiana Office Supply Co 5550 Florida Blvd	Baton Rouge	LA	70806	**800-738-2218**	225-927-1110	524
Louisiana Organ Procurement Agency 3501 N Causeway Blvd Suite 940	Metairie	LA	70002	**800-521-4483**	504-837-3355	535
Louisiana-Pacific Corp 414 Union St Suite 2000	Nashville	TN	37219	**877-744-5600**	615-986-5600	671
NYSE: LPX						
Louisiana Public Broadcasting (LPB) 7733 Perkins Rd	Baton Rouge	LA	70810	**800-272-8161**	225-767-5660	620
Louisiana Realtors Assn 4639 Bennington Ave	Baton Rouge	LA	70808	**800-266-8538**	225-923-2210	642
Louisiana Republican Party 11440 N Lake Sherwood Ave Suite A	Baton Rouge	LA	70816	**800-376-7245**	225-928-2998	605-2
Louisiana State Bar Assn 601 St Charles Ave	New Orleans	LA	70130	**800-421-5722**	504-566-1600	73
Louisiana State Medical Society 6767 Perkins Rd Suite 100	Baton Rouge	LA	70808	**800-375-9508**	225-763-8500	466
Louisiana State Museum 751 Chartres St	New Orleans	LA	70116	**800-568-6968**	504-568-6968	509
Louisiana State University Alexandria Campus 8100 US Hwy 71 S	Alexandria	LA	71302	**888-473-6417***	318-445-3672	160
*Admissions						
Louisiana Superdome 1500 Poydras PO Box 52439	New Orleans	LA	70152	**800-756-7074**	504-587-3663	706
Louisiana Tech University 305 Wisteria St	Ruston	LA	71272	**800-528-3241**	318-257-0211	163
Louisiana Utilities Supply PO Box 3531	Baton Rouge	LA	70821	**800-743-8916**	225-383-8916	592
Louisiana Veterinary Medical Assn 8550 United Plaza Blvd Suite 1001	Baton Rouge	LA	70809	**800-524-2996**	225-928-5862	782
Louisville Bedding Co 10400 Bunsen Way	Louisville	KY	40299	**800-626-2594**	502-491-3370	731
Louisville Gas & Electric Co 220 W Main St	Louisville	KY	40202	**800-331-7370**	502-627-2000	774
Louisville Golf Co 2500 Grassland Dr	Louisville	KY	40299	**800-456-1631**	502-491-5490	701
Louisville & Jefferson County Convention & Visitors Bureau 401 W Main St Suite 2300	Louisville	KY	40202	**800-792-5595**	502-584-2121	205
Louisville Orchestra 300 W Main St Suite 100	Louisville	KY	40202	**800-775-7777**	502-587-8681	563-3
Louisville Presbyterian Theological Seminary 1044 Alta Vista Rd	Louisville	KY	40205	**800-264-1839**	502-895-3411	164-3
Louisville Science Center 727 W Main St	Louisville	KY	40202	**800-591-2203**	502-561-6100	509
Louisville Technical Institute 3901 Atkinson Square Dr	Louisville	KY	40218	**800-844-6528**	502-456-6509	787
Loup River Public Power District PO Box 988	Columbus	NE	68602	**888-564-3172**	402-564-3171	244
Loup Valleys Rural Public Power District 606 'S' St	Ord	NE	68862	**888-880-3633**	308-728-3633	244
Lourdes College 6832 Convent Blvd	Sylvania	OH	43560	**800-878-3210**	419-885-3211	163
Lourdes Homecare & Hospice 2855 Jackson St	Paducah	KY	42003	**800-870-7460**	270-444-2262	365
Lourdes Industries Inc 65 Hoffman Ave	Hauppauge	NY	11788	**800-368-3728**	631-234-6600	494
Love Box Co Inc PO Box 546	Wichita	KS	67201	**800-937-5229**	316-838-0851	101
Love Chrysler Plymouth Inc 4331 S Staples St	Corpus Christi	TX	78411	**866-460-5683**	361-991-5683	57
Love Envelopes Inc 10733 E Ute St	Tulsa	OK	74116	**800-532-9747**	918-836-3535	260
Lovejoy Hospice 939 NE 8th St	Grants Pass	OR	97526	**888-758-8569**	541-474-1193	365
Lovejoy Inc 2655 Wisconsin Ave	Downers Grove	IL	60515	**800-334-9659**	630-852-0500	609
Lovejoy Tool Co Inc 133 Main St	Springfield	VT	05156	**800-843-8376**	802-885-2194	484
Lovelace Health Plan 4101 Indian School Rd NE	Albuquerque	NM	87110	**800-877-7526***	505-262-7363	384-3
*Hum Res						
Loveland Daily Reporter-Herald 201 E 5th St	Loveland	CO	80537	**800-216-0680**	970-669-5050	522-2
Loveland Industries Inc 14520 WCR #64	Greeley	CO	80631	**800-356-8920**	970-356-8920	272
Love's Travel Stops & Country Stores Inc 10601 N Pennsylvania	Oklahoma City	OK	73120	**800-388-0983**	405-751-9000	203
Loveshaw Corp PO Box 83	South Canaan	PA	18459	**800-747-1586***	570-937-4921	537
*Cust Svc						
Lovitt & Touche Inc 7202 E Rosewood St	Tucson	AZ	85710	**800-426-2756**	520-722-3000	383
Lovotti Bros Distributing Co PO Box 15840	Sacramento	CA	95852	**800-473-3911**	916-441-3911	82-3
LoW (Loners on Wheels) PO Box 1060-WB	Cape Girardeau	MO	63702	**888-569-4478**		48-23
Lowell The 28 E 63rd St	New York	NY	10021	**800-221-4444**	212-838-1400	373
Lowell Health Care Center 19 Varnum St	Lowell	MA	01850	**800-966-5644**	978-454-5644	441
Lowell Mfg Co 100 Integram Dr	Pacific	MO	63069	**800-325-9660**	636-257-3400	52
Lowell Sun 15 Kearny Sq	Lowell	MA	01852	**800-694-7100**	978-458-7100	522-2
Lowell Sun Publishing Co 15 Kearney Sq	Lowell	MA	01852	**800-694-7100**	978-458-7100	623-8
Lower Cape Fear Hospice and Life Care 725-A Wellington Ave	Wilmington	NC	28401	**800-733-1476**	910-772-5444	365
Lower Keys Chamber of Commerce 31020 Overseas Hwy	Big Pine Key	FL	33043	**800-872-3722**	305-872-2411	137
Lower Valley Energy PO Box 188	Afton	WY	83110	**800-882-5875**	307-885-3175	244
Lowe's Cos Inc 1605 Curtis Bridge Rd	North Wilkesboro	NC	28697	**800-890-5932**	336-658-4000	359
NYSE: LOW						
Lowes Food Stores Inc 1381 Old Mill Cir Suite 200	Winston-Salem	NC	27103	**800-669-5693**	336-659-0180	339
Lowrance Electronics Inc 12000 E Skelly Dr	Tulsa	OK	74128	**800-234-4738**	918-437-6881	519
NASDAQ: LEIX						
Lowrey Organ Co 825 E 26th St	La Grange Park	IL	60526	**800-451-5939**	708-352-3388	516
Loxcreen Co Inc 1630 Old Dunbar Rd	West Columbia	SC	29172	**800-394-8667**	803-822-8200	476
Loyal American Life Insurance Co PO Box 559004	Austin	TX	78755	**800-633-6752**		384-2
Loyd's Aviation Services Inc 2813 Hangar Way	Bakersfield	CA	93308	**800-284-1334**	661-393-1334	63
Loyd's Electric Supply Inc 117 E College St	Branson	MO	65616	**800-492-4030**	417-334-2171	245
Loyola College 4501 N Charles St	Baltimore	MD	21210	**800-221-9107**	410-617-2000	163
Loyola Marymount University 1 LMU Dr	Los Angeles	CA	90045	**800-568-4636**	310-338-2700	163
Loyola University 6363 St Charles Ave	New Orleans	LA	70118	**800-456-9652**	504-865-2011	163
Loyola University Chicago 820 N Michigan Ave	Chicago	IL	60611	**800-262-2373**	312-915-6000	163
Lake Shore Campus 6525 N Sheridan Rd	Chicago	IL	60626	**800-262-2373**	773-274-3000	163
School of Professional Studies 6525 N Sheridan Rd	Chicago	IL	60626	**800-756-9652**	773-262-8100	163
Lozier Corp 6336 Pershing Dr	Omaha	NE	68110	**800-228-9882**	402-457-8000	281
Lozier's Box R Ranch PO Box 100	Cora	WY	82925	**800-822-8466**	307-367-4868	238
LP Thebault Co 249 Pomeroy Rd PO Box 169	Parsippany	NJ	07054	**800-843-2285**	973-884-1300	615
LPA (Little People of America) 5289 NE Elam Young Pkwy Suite F-700	Hillsboro	OR	97124	**888-572-2001**	503-846-1562	48-17
LPB (Louisiana Public Broadcasting) 7733 Perkins Rd	Baton Rouge	LA	70810	**800-272-8161**	225-767-5660	620
LPL Financial Services 1 Beacon St 22nd Fl	Boston	MA	02108	**800-775-4575**	617-423-3644	679
LPS Industries Inc 10 Caesar Pl	Moonachie	NJ	07074	**800-275-4577***	201-438-3515	538
*Sales						

Name / Address	City	State	Zip	Toll-Free	Phone	Class
LPS Laboratories 4647 Hugh Howell Rd	Tucker	GA	30084	**800-241-8334**	770-934-7800	530
LR Nelson Corp 1 Sprinkler Ln	Peoria	IL	61615	**800-635-7668*** *Sales	309-690-2200	420
LR Services 600 Hayden Cir	Allentown	PA	18109	**888-675-9650**	610-266-2500	14
LRP Publications 360 Hiatt Dr	Palm Beach Gardens	FL	33418	**800-621-5463**	561-622-6520	623-2
LSB Corp 30 Massachusetts Ave *NASDAQ: LSBX*	North Andover	MA	01845	**800-730-9660**	978-725-7500	355-2
LSB Financial Corp 101 Main St *NASDAQ: LSBI*	Lafayette	IN	47901	**800-704-3084**	765-742-1064	355-2
LSC LLC DBA Eileen West 525 Brannan St Suite 410	San Francisco	CA	94107	**800-421-0731**	415-957-9378	153-15
LSF Network Inc 395 Oyster Pt Blvd Suite 110	South San Francisco	CA	94080	**877-616-8226**		7
LSI Industries Inc 10000 Alliance Rd *NASDAQ: LYTS*	Cincinnati	OH	45242	**800-274-2840**	513-793-3200	431
LSI Logic Corp 1621 Barber Ln *NYSE: LSI*	Milpitas	CA	95035	**866-574-5741**	408-433-8000	686
LSI Metal Fabrication Inc 3871 Turkeyfoot Rd	Erlanger	KY	41018	**800-546-1513**	859-342-9944	471
LSI Midwest Lighting Co PO Box 15097	Kansas City	KS	66115	**800-743-5483**	913-281-1100	431
LSQ Funding Group LC 1403 W Colonial Dr Suite B	Orlando	FL	32804	**800-474-7606**	407-206-0022	268
LSS (Laboratory for Student Success) Temple University/Center for Research in Human Development & Education 933 Ritter Annex 1301 Cecil B. Moore Ave	Philadelphia	PA	19122	**800-892-5550**	215-204-3030	654
LTD Financial Services LP 7322 Southwest Fwy Suite 1600	Houston	TX	77074	**800-414-2101**	713-414-2100	157
LTS Wireless Inc 311 S LHS Dr	Lumberton	TX	77657	**800-255-5471**	409-755-4038	168
LTU International Airways 20803 Biscayne Blvd Suite 401	North Miami Beach	FL	33180	**866-266-5588**	305-932-1595	26
LTX Corp 50 Rosemont Rd *NASDAQ: LTXX*	Westwood	MA	02090	**800-451-2500**	781-461-1000	247
Lubbock Avalanche-Journal 710 Ave J	Lubbock	TX	79401	**800-692-4021**	806-762-8844	522-2
Lubbock Chamber of Commerce 1301 Broadway Suite 101	Lubbock	TX	79401	**800-321-5822**	806-761-7000	137
Lubbock Christian University 5601 19th St	Lubbock	TX	79407	**800-933-7601**	806-796-8800	163
Lubbock Convention & Visitors Bureau 1301 Broadway St Suite 200	Lubbock	TX	79401	**800-692-4035**	806-747-5232	205
Lubbock Inn 3901 19th St	Lubbock	TX	79410	**800-545-8226**	806-792-5181	373
Lubrication Engineers Inc 3851 Airport Fwy	Fort Worth	TX	76111	**800-537-7683**	817-834-6321	530
Lubrication Technologies Inc 900 Mendelssohn Ave N	Golden Valley	MN	55427	**800-328-5573**	763-545-0707	530
Lubriquip Inc 18901 Cranwood Pkwy	Cleveland	OH	44128	**800-872-5823**	216-581-2000	379
Lubrizol Corp 29400 Lakeland Blvd *NYSE: LZ*	Wickliffe	OH	44092	**800-522-4125**	440-943-4200	143
Luby's Inc PO Box 33069 *NYSE: LUB*	San Antonio	TX	78265	**800-886-4600**	210-654-9000	657
Lucas-Milhaupt Inc 5656 S Pennsylvania Ave	Cudahy	WI	53110	**800-558-3856**	414-769-6000	476
Lucasey Mfg Corp PO Box 14023	Oakland	CA	94614	**800-582-2739**	510-534-1435	473
Lucchese Boot Co Inc 40 Walter Jones Blvd	El Paso	TX	79906	**800-637-6888**	915-778-8585	296
Luce Press Clippings Inc 42 S Center St	Mesa	AZ	85210	**800-528-8226**	480-834-4884	612
Luce & Son Inc 2399 Valley Rd	Reno	NV	89512	**888-296-7570**	775-785-7810	82-1
Lucent Technologies Inc Bell Labs 600 Mountain Ave	Murray Hill	NJ	07974	**877-894-4647**	908-582-8500	654
Lucille Farms Inc 150 River Rd *NASDAQ: LUCY*	Montville	NJ	07045	**800-654-6844**	973-334-6030	291-5
Luckenbach & Johnson Inc 1828 Tilghman St	Allentown	PA	18104	**800-451-7451**	610-434-6235	38
Lucks Co 3003 S Pine St	Tacoma	WA	98409	**800-826-7409**	206-674-7200	291-8
Lucky Lady Oil Co 107 NW 28th St	Fort Worth	TX	76106	**800-303-1412**	817-740-7400	569
Lucky Magazine 4 Times Sq	New York	NY	10036	**800-223-0780**	212-286-2860	449-11
Lucor Inc 790 Pershing Rd	Raleigh	NC	27608	**800-216-2553**	919-828-9511	62-5
Lucta USA Inc 1829 Stanley St	Northbrook	IL	60062	**800-323-5341**	847-272-6650	438
Ludington Daily News 202 N Rath St	Ludington	MI	49431	**800-748-0407**	231-845-5181	522-2
Ludlow Composites Corp 2100 Commerce Dr	Fremont	OH	43420	**800-628-5463**	419-332-5531	663
Ludlow Tape 2 Ludlow Pk Dr	Chicopee	MA	01022	**800-445-5025**	413-593-6400	469
Ludlow Textiles Co Inc PO Box 559	Ludlow	MA	01056	**800-628-9048**	413-583-5051	730-9
Ludlum Measurements Inc 501 Oak St	Sweetwater	TX	79556	**800-622-0828**	325-235-5494	464
Ludowici Roof Tile Inc 4757 Tile Plant Rd PO Box 69	New Lexington	OH	43764	**800-945-8453*** *Cust Svc	740-342-1995	148
Ludwig Music House Inc 3600 Rider Trail S	Earth City	MO	63045	**800-783-7007**	314-298-9696	515
Lufkin Visitor & Convention Bureau 1615 S Chestnut	Lufkin	TX	75901	**800-409-5659**	936-634-6305	205
Lufkin/Angelina County Chamber of Commerce 1615 S Chestnut st	Lufkin	TX	75901	**800-409-5659**	936-634-6644	137
Lufthansa Cargo USA 3400 Peachtree Rd Lenox Towers Suite 1225	Atlanta	GA	30326	**877-542-2746**	404-814-5311	13
Lufthansa USA 1640 Hempstead Tpke	East Meadow	NY	11554	**800-581-6400*** *Resv	516-296-9200	26
Luggage Dealers Assn. National 1817 Elmdale Ave	Glenview	IL	60026	**866-998-6869**	847-998-6869	49-18
Lugz 155 6th Ave 9th Fl	New York	NY	10013	**800-648-8602**	212-691-4700	296
Luhr Jensen & Sons Inc 400 Portway Ave PO Box 297	Hood River	OR	97031	**800-366-3811**	541-386-3811	701
Luhrs Corp 255 Diesel Rd	Saint Augustine	FL	32084	**800-829-5847**	904-829-0500	91
Luigino's Inc 525 S Lake Ave	Duluth	MN	55802	**800-521-1281**	218-723-5555	291-36
Luitpold Pharmaceuticals Inc 1 Luitpold Dr PO Box 9001	Shirley	NY	11967	**800-645-1706**	631-924-4000	574
Lujan Manuel Insurance Inc PO Box 3727	Albuquerque	NM	87190	**888-652-7771**	505-758-2206	384-4
Luke Soules Acosta 1920 Westridge Dr	Irving	TX	75038	**800-486-0928**	972-518-1442	292-8
Luker Inc 514 National Ave	Augusta	GA	30901	**800-982-9534**	706-724-0244	293
Lumbee River Electric Membership Corp PO Box 830	Red Springs	NC	28377	**800-683-5571**	910-843-4131	244
Lumber Assn. National Hardwood 6830 Raleigh-LaGrange Rd	Memphis	TN	38134	**800-933-0318**	901-377-1818	49-3
Lumber Assn. North American Wholesale 3601 Algonquin Rd Suite 400	Rolling Meadows	IL	60008	**800-527-8258**	847-870-7470	49-18
Lumber & Building Material Dealers Assn. National 40 Ivy St SE	Washington	DC	20003	**800-634-8645**	202-547-2230	49-18
Lumber Liquidators Inc 1455 VFW Pkwy	West Roxbury	MA	02132	**877-645-5347**	617-327-1222	285
Lumbermens 3773 Martin Way E Bldg A	Olympia	WA	98506	**800-842-8256**	360-456-1880	359
Lumbermen's Underwriting Alliance 2501 N Military Trail	Boca Raton	FL	33431	**800-327-0630**	561-994-1900	384-4
Lumberton Area Visitors Bureau 3431 Lackey St	Lumberton	NC	28360	**800-359-6971**	910-739-9999	205
Lumenis Ltd 2400 Condensa St	Santa Clara	CA	95051	**800-227-1914**	408-764-3000	415
Lumi-Lite Candle Co Inc 102 Sundale Rd PO Box 97	Norwich	OH	43767	**800-288-2340**	740-872-3248	122
Lumina Foundation for Education 30 S Meridian St Suite 700	Indianapolis	IN	46204	**800-834-5756**	317-951-5704	300
Luminex Corp 12212 Technology Blvd *NASDAQ: LMNX*	Austin	TX	78727	**888-219-8020**	512-219-8020	410
Luminex Software Inc 6840 Indiana Ave Suite 130	Riverside	CA	92506	**888-586-4639**	951-781-4100	176-12
Lummus Corp 1 Lummus Dr PO Box 4259	Savannah	GA	31407	**800-458-6687**	912-447-9000	729
Luna Garcia 201 San Juan Ave	Venice	CA	90291	**800-905-9975**	310-396-8026	716
Lund International Holdings Inc 911 Lund Blvd Suite 100	Anoka	MN	55303	**800-377-5863**	763-576-4200	60
Lundbeck Canada Inc 413 St-Jacques St W Suite FB-230	Montreal	QC	H2Y1N9	**800-586-2325**	514-844-8515	86
Lundia Div MII Inc 600 Capitol Way	Jacksonville	IL	62650	**800-726-9663**	217-243-8585	281
Lung Assn. American 61 Broadway 6th Fl	New York	NY	10006	**800-586-4872**	212-315-8700	48-17
Lunt-Fontanne Theatre 205 W 46th St	New York	NY	10036	**800-755-4000**	212-307-4100	732
Lunt Silversmiths 298 Federal St	Greenfield	MA	01301	**800-242-2774**	413-774-2774	693
Lupient Automotive Group 750 Pennsylvania Ave S	Minneapolis	MN	55426	**800-328-0608**	763-544-6666	57
Lupus Foundation of America Inc (LFA) 2000 L St Suite 710	Washington	DC	20036	**800-558-0121**	202-349-1155	48-17
Luskey's/Ryon's Western Stores Inc 2601 N Main St	Fort Worth	TX	76106	**800-725-7966**	817-625-2391	155-5
Luster Products Inc 1104 W 43rd St	Chicago	IL	60609	**800-621-4255**	773-579-1800	211
Lutco Inc 677 Cambridge St	Worcester	MA	01610	**888-588-0099**	508-756-6296	77
Luther College 700 College Dr	Decorah	IA	52101	**800-458-8437**	563-387-2000	163
Lutheran Brotherhood Foundation 625 4th Ave S Suite 1415	Minneapolis	MN	55415	**800-365-4172**		299
Lutheran Church in America. Evangelical 8765 W Higgins Rd	Chicago	IL	60631	**800-638-3522**	773-380-2700	48-20
Lutheran Church Missouri Synod (LCMS) 1333 S Kirkwood Rd	Saint Louis	MO	63122	**888-843-5267**	314-965-9000	48-20
Lutheran Disaster Response 8765 W Higgins Rd	Chicago	IL	60631	**800-638-3522**	773-380-2822	48-5
Lutheran Laymen's League. International 660 Mason Ridge Ctr Dr	Saint Louis	MO	63141	**800-944-3450**	314-317-4100	48-20
Lutheran Magazine 8765 W Higgins Rd	Chicago	IL	60631	**800-638-3522**	773-380-2540	449-18
Lutheran School of Theology at Chicago 1100 E 55th St	Chicago	IL	60615	**800-635-1116**	773-256-0700	164-3
Lutheran Theological Seminary at Gettysburg 61 Seminary Ridge	Gettysburg	PA	17325	**800-658-8437**	717-334-6286	164-3
Lutheran Theological Seminary at Philadelphia 7301 Germantown Ave	Philadelphia	PA	19119	**800-286-4616**	215-248-4616	164-3
Lutheran World Relief (LWR) 700 Light St	Baltimore	MD	21230	**800-597-5972**	410-230-2700	48-5
Lutron Electronics Co Inc 7200 Suter Rd	Coopersburg	PA	18036	**800-523-9466*** *Tech Supp	610-282-3800	202
Lutsen Resort 5700 W Hwy 61 PO Box 9	Lutsen	MN	55612	**800-258-8736**	218-663-7212	655
Luv n' care Ltd PO Box 6050	Monroe	LA	71211	**800-588-6227**	318-388-4916	256
Lux Bond & Green Inc 46 Lasalle Rd	West Hartford	CT	06107	**800-524-7336**	860-521-3015	402
Luxe Hotel Sunset Boulevard 11461 Sunset Blvd	Los Angeles	CA	90049	**800-468-3541**	310-476-6571	373
Luxe Worldwide Hotels 11461 Sunset Blvd	Los Angeles	CA	90049	**866-589-3411**	310-440-3090	369
Luxo Corp 200 Clearbrook Rd	Elmsford	NY	10523	**800-222-5896**	914-345-0067	431
Luxor Div EBSCO Industries Inc 2245 Delany Rd	Waukegan	IL	60087	**800-323-4656**	847-244-1800	281
Luxor Hotel & Casino 3900 Las Vegas Blvd S	Las Vegas	NV	89119	**800-288-1000*** *Resv	702-262-4000	133
Luxottica Group 44 Harbor Park Dr	Port Washington	NY	11050	**800-422-2020**	516-484-3800	531
Luxury Collection 1111 Westchester Ave	White Plains	NY	10604	**877-443-4585*** *Cust Svc	914-640-8100	369
Luzenac America Inc 345 Inverness Dr S Suite 310	Centennial	CO	80112	**800-525-8252**	303-643-0400	493-3
Luzerne County Community College 1333 S Prospect St	Nanticoke	PA	18634	**800-377-5222**	570-740-0200	160
Luzier Personalized Cosmetics Inc 7910-12 Troost Ave	Kansas City	MO	64131	**800-821-6632**	816-531-8338	211
LW Barrett Co Inc 55 S Zuni St PO Box 19430	Denver	CO	80219	**888-312-0888**	303-934-5755	10
LW Robbins Assoc 201 Summer St	Holliston	MA	01746	**800-229-5972**	508-893-0210	312
LWB Refractories Co PO Box 1189	York	PA	17405	**800-233-1991**	717-848-1501	649

Name / Address	City	State	ZIP	Toll-Free	Phone	Class
LWR (Lutheran World Relief) 700 Light St	Baltimore	MD	21230	**800-597-5972**	410-230-2700	48-5
LWV (League of Women Voters) 1730 M St NW Suite 1000	Washington	DC	20036	**800-249-8683**	202-429-1965	48-7
LXE Inc 125 Technology Pkwy	Norcross	GA	30092	**800-664-4593**	770-447-4224	171-2
Lyceum Theatre 149 W 45th St	New York	NY	10036	**800-432-7250**	212-239-6200	732
Lycoming College 700 College Pl	Williamsport	PA	17701	**800-345-3920**	570-321-4000	163
Lycoming Engines 652 Oliver St	Williamsport	PA	17701	**800-258-3279**	570-323-6181	22
Lycon Inc PO Box 427	Janesville	WI	53547	**800-955-8758**	608-754-7701	180
Lyda Builders Inc 12400 Hwy 281 N Suite 200	San Antonio	TX	78216	**800-846-7026**	210-684-1770	185
Lydall Inc 1 Colonial Rd *NYSE: LDL*	Manchester	CT	06045	**800-365-9325**	860-646-1233	551
Lyden Gardens 215 E 64th St	New York	NY	10021	**800-637-8483**	212-355-1230	373
Lyden House 320 E 53rd St	New York	NY	10022	**800-637-8483**	212-888-6070	373
Lyden Oil Co Inc 3711 Lee Harps Rd	Youngstown	OH	44515	**800-362-9410**	330-792-1100	569
Lydian Trust Co 3801 PGA Blvd	Palm Beach Gardens	FL	33410	**866-659-5055**	561-776-8860	70
Lykes Bros Inc PO Box 2879	Tampa	FL	33601	**800-243-0494**	813-223-3981	355-4
Lykes Insurance Inc PO Box 2879	Tampa	FL	33601	**800-243-0491**	813-223-3911	384-4
Lykes Lines Ltd LLC PO Box 31244	Tampa	FL	33631	**800-242-7447**	813-276-4600	308
Lyle Signs Inc 6294 Bury Dr	Eden Prairie	MN	55346	**800-367-8560**	952-934-7653	692
Lyman Products Corp 475 Smith St	Middletown	CT	06457	**800-225-9626**	860-632-2020	279
Lyman-Richey Corp 4315 Cuming St	Omaha	NE	68131	**800-727-8432**	402-558-2727	190-1
Lyme Disease Foundation Inc (LDF) Box 332	Tolland	CT	06084	**800-886-5963**	860-525-2000	48-17
Lyme Disease Foundation Inc. American 293 Rt 100	Somers	NY	10589	**800-876-5963**	914-277-6970	48-17
Lymphoma Research Foundation 8800 Venice Blvd Suite 207	Los Angeles	CA	90034	**800-500-9976**	310-204-7040	48-17
Lymphoma Society. Leukemia & 475 Park Ave S 8th Fl	New York	NY	10016	**800-955-4572**	212-448-9206	48-17
Lynch Exhibits 7 Campus Dr Burlington Business Campus	Burlington	NJ	08016	**800-343-1666**	609-387-1600	230
Lynch Jones & Ryan Inc 3 Times Sq 8th Fl *Sales	New York	NY	10036	**800-992-7526***	212-310-9500	679
Lynch Systems Inc 601 Independent St	Bainbridge	GA	39817	**800-428-6333**	229-248-2345	379
Lynchburg College 1501 Lakeside Dr	Lynchburg	VA	24501	**800-426-8101**	434-544-8100	163
Lynches River Electric Co-op Inc PO Box 308	Pageland	SC	29728	**800-922-3486**	843-672-6111	244
Lynde-Ordway Co Inc 3308 W Warner Ave	Santa Ana	CA	92704	**800-762-7057**	714-957-1311	112
Lynden Air Cargo LLC 6441 S Airpark Pl	Anchorage	AK	99502	**888-243-7248**	907-243-6150	13
Lynden Inc 18000 International Blvd Suite 800	Seattle	WA	98188	**800-426-3201**	206-241-8778	306
Lynden Transport Inc 3027 Rampart Dr	Anchorage	AK	99501	**800-327-9390**	907-276-4800	769
Lyndon State College 1001 College Rd PO Box 919	Lyndonville	VT	05851	**800-225-1998**	802-626-6413	163
Lynk Systems Inc 600 Morgan Falls Rd Suite 260	Atlanta	GA	30350	**800-200-5965**	770-396-1616	254
Lynn Insurance Group 2501 N Military Trail	Boca Raton	FL	33431	**800-327-0630**	561-994-1900	384-4
Lynn Ladder & Scaffolding Co Inc PO Box 346	Lynn	MA	01905	**800-596-6717**	781-598-6010	412
Lynn Sign Co 3 Liberty St	Merrimac	MA	01860	**800-225-5764**	978-346-8182	692
Lynn University 3601 N Military Trail	Boca Raton	FL	33431	**800-544-8035**	561-237-7900	163
Lynx Air International 3402 SW 9th Ave	Fort Lauderdale	FL	33315	**888-596-9247**	954-772-9808	26
Lyon-Coffey Electric Co-op Inc PO Box 229	Burlington	KS	66839	**800-748-7395**	620-364-2116	244
Lyon College PO Box 2317	Batesville	AR	72503	**800-423-2542**	870-793-9813	163
Lyon Conklin & Co 7030 Troy Hill Dr Suite 700A	Elkridge	MD	21075	**800-759-5966**	410-540-2800	483
Lyon County Co-op Oil Co 1100 E Main St	Marshall	MN	56258	**888-532-9686**	507-532-9686	311
Lyon County Joint Tourism Commission 82 Days Inn Dr	Kuttawa	KY	42055	**800-355-3885**	270-388-5300	205
Lyon & Healy Harps Inc 168 N Ogden Ave	Chicago	IL	60607	**800-621-3881**	312-786-1881	516
Lyon-Lincoln Electric Co-op Inc PO Box 639	Tyler	MN	56178	**800-927-6276**	507-247-5505	244
Lyon Rural Electric Co-op PO Box 629	Rock Rapids	IA	51246	**800-658-3976**	712-472-2506	244
Lyon Work Space Products 420 N Main St	Montgomery	IL	60538	**800-433-8488**	630-892-8941	281
Lyons Lavey Nickel & Swift Inc 220 E 42nd St 3rd Fl	New York	NY	10017	**800-599-0188**	212-771-3000	4
Lyons Magnus Inc 1636 S 2nd St	Fresno	CA	93702	**800-344-7130**	559-268-5966	291-20
Lyric Street Records 1100 Demonbreun St Suite 100	Nashville	TN	37203	**888-814-4934**	615-963-4848	643
LZ Truck Equipment Co Inc 1881 Rice St	Roseville	MN	55113	**800-247-1082**	651-488-2571	505

M

Name / Address	City	State	ZIP	Toll-Free	Phone	Class
M Aron Corp 350 5th Ave Suite 3005	New York	NY	10118	**800-899-2766**	212-643-8883	153-2
M & B Hangers Co 1313 Parkway Dr SE	Leeds	AL	35094	**800-227-0436**	205-699-2171	344
M Block & Sons Inc 5020 W 73rd St	Bedford Park	IL	60638	**800-621-8845**	708-728-8400	356
M & C Leasing Co Inc 1050 Union Rd Suite 102	West Seneca	NY	14224	**800-416-9080**	716-873-6800	261-3
M & C Specialties Co 90 James Way *Cust Svc	Southampton	PA	18966	**800-441-6996***	215-322-1600	717
M-Care 2301 Commonwealth Blvd	Ann Arbor	MI	48105	**800-527-5549**	734-747-8700	384-3
M-Chem Industries Corp 1607 Derwent Way	Delta	BC	V3M6K8	**800-663-9925**		149
M Conley Co 1312 4th St SE	Canton	OH	44707	**800-362-6001**	330-456-8243	549
M-D Building Products Inc 4041 N Santa Fe Ave *Cust Svc	Oklahoma City	OK	73118	**800-654-8454***	405-528-4411	232
M & D Industries International Inc 7700 Anagram Dr	Eden Prairie	MN	55344	**888-469-5277**		597
M-D Pneumatics Div Tuthill Corp 4840 W Kearney St	Springfield	MO	65803	**800-825-6937**	417-865-8715	19
M & F Case International Inc 717 School St *Cust Svc	Pawtucket	RI	02860	**800-343-8820***	401-722-4830	87
M Holland Co 400 Skokie Blvd Suite 600	Northbrook	IL	60062	**800-872-7370**	847-272-7370	592
M & I Bank Northeast 310 W Walnut St	Green Bay	WI	54303	**888-464-5463**	920-436-1800	71
M & I First National Leasing Corp 250 E Wisconsin Ave Suite 1400	Milwaukee	WI	53202	**800-558-9840**	414-272-2374	214
M & I Home Lending Solutions 4121 NW Urbandale Dr	Urbandale	IA	50322	**800-827-2654**	515-281-2807	498
M & I Marshall & Ilsley Bank 770 N Water St	Milwaukee	WI	53202	**800-342-2265**	414-765-7700	71
M & I Mortgage Corp W 57 N 14280 Doerr Way	Cedarburg	WI	53012	**800-236-1221**	262-376-8484	498
M & I Wealth Management 1000 N Water St	Milwaukee	WI	53202	**800-342-2265**	414-287-8700	393
M & M Aerospace Hardware Inc 10000 NW 15th Terr	Miami	FL	33172	**800-533-5155**	305-592-5155	759
M & M Designs Inc 1981 Quality Blvd	Huntsville	TX	77320	**800-627-0656**	936-295-2682	675
M & M Livestock Products Co 310 E Broadway St	Eagle Grove	IA	50533	**800-247-4820**	515-448-5371	438
M & M Supply Co PO Box 548	Duncan	OK	73534	**800-404-7879**	580-252-7879	526
M Putterman & Co Inc 4834 S Oakley St	Chicago	IL	60609	**800-621-0146**	773-927-4120	718
M & Q Plastic Products 1120 Welsh Rd Suite 170	North Wales	PA	19454	**800-600-3068**	267-498-4000	593
M-R Sign Co Inc 1706 1st Ave N	Fergus Falls	MN	56537	**800-231-5564**	218-736-5681	692
M & S Systems Inc 2861 Congressman Ln	Dallas	TX	75220	**800-877-6631**	214-358-3196	385
M Shanken Communications Inc 387 Park Ave S 8th Fl	New York	NY	10016	**800-866-0775**	212-684-4224	623-9
M Swift & Sons Inc 10 Love Ln	Hartford	CT	06112	**800-628-0380**	860-522-1181	290
M & T Bank Corp 1 M & T Plaza 5th Fl *NYSE: MTB*	Buffalo	NY	14203	**800-724-2440**	716-842-4200	355-2
M & T Bank Corp 67 Jackson St	Fishkill	NY	12524	**800-433-2265**	845-896-7644	71
M & T Mortgage Corp 1 Fountain Plaza	Buffalo	NY	14203	**800-724-7575**	716-848-7600	498
M-Tron Industries Inc PO Box 630	Yankton	SD	57078	**800-762-8800**	605-665-9321	252
M-USA (Mercy-USA for Aid & Development Inc) 44450 Pinetree Dr Suite 201	Plymouth	MI	48170	**800-556-3729**	734-454-0011	48-5
M & W Gear Co 1020 S Sangamon Ave	Gibson City	IL	60936	**800-221-2855**	217-784-4261	269
M2 Collision Centers Inc 1100 Colorado Ave 2nd Fl	Santa Monica	CA	90401	**877-623-6796**	310-399-3887	62-4
MA (Marijuana Anonymous World Services) PO Box 2912	Van Nuys	CA	91404	**800-766-6779**		48-21
MAA (Mathematical Assn of America) 1529 18th St NW	Washington	DC	20036	**800-741-9415**	202-387-5200	49-19
Maaco Auto Painting & Body Works 381 Brooks Rd	King of Prussia	PA	19406	**800-523-1180**	610-265-6606	62-4
Maas-Hansen Steel Corp 2435 E 37th St	Vernon	CA	90058	**800-647-8335**	323-583-6321	483
Maas-Rowe Carillons Inc 2255 Meyers Ave	Escondido	CA	92029	**800-854-2023**	760-743-1311	516
Maass Midwest Inc 11283 Dundee Rd	Huntley	IL	60142	**800-323-6259**	847-669-5135	627
Maax Inc 1010 Sherbrooke St W Suite 1610 *TSE: MXA*	Montreal	QC	H3A2R7	**800-463-6229**		599
MAAX Pearl 9224 73rd Ave N	Brooklyn Park	MN	55428	**800-328-2531**	763-424-3335	367
MAB Paints 600 Reed Rd	Broomall	PA	19008	**800-622-1899**	610-353-5100	540
Mabis Healthcare Inc 1931 Norman Dr	Waukegan	IL	60085	**800-728-6811**	847-680-6811	467
Mabuhay Miles 116 McDonnell Rd	San Francisco	CA	94128	**800-747-1959**		27
Mac Equipment Inc 7901 NW 107 Terr	Kansas City	MO	64153	**800-821-2476**	816-891-9300	206
Mac-Gray Corp 22 Water St *NYSE: TUC*	Cambridge	MA	02141	**800-622-4729**	617-492-4040	378
Mac Paper Converters PO Box 5369	Jacksonville	FL	32247	**800-334-7026**	904-733-9660	544
Mac Papers Inc 3300 Phillips Hwy	Jacksonville	FL	32207	**800-622-2968**	904-348-3300	543
Mac Tools Inc 4635 Hilton Corporate Dr	Columbus	OH	43232	**800-622-8665**	614-755-7000	746
Mac Trailer Mfg Inc 14599 Commerce St NE	Alliance	OH	44601	**800-795-8454**	330-823-9900	768
Mac Valves Inc 30569 Beck Rd	Wixom	MI	48393	**800-622-8587**	248-624-7700	776
MacAddict Network c/o Imagine Media Inc 150 N Hill Dr Suite 40 *Cust Svc	Brisbane	CA	94005	**888-771-6222***	415-468-4684	623-9
Macalester College 1600 Grand Ave	Saint Paul	MN	55105	**800-231-7974**	651-696-6357	163
MacAllister Machinery Co Inc 7515 E 30th St PO Box 1941	Indianapolis	IN	46219	**800-227-3228**	317-545-2151	353
MacArthur Co 2400 Wycliff St	Saint Paul	MN	55114	**800-777-7507**	651-646-2773	190-4
MacArthur John D & Catherine T Foundation 140 S Dearborn St Suite 1100	Chicago	IL	60603	**800-662-8004**	312-726-8000	300
MacArthur Place 29 E MacArthur St	Sonoma	CA	95476	**800-722-1866**	707-938-2929	373
Macatawa Bank Corp 10753 Macatawa Dr *NASDAQ: MCBC*	Holland	MI	49422	**877-820-2265**	616-820-1444	355-2
Macau Government Tourist Office 3601 Aviation Blvd Suite 2100	Manhattan Beach	CA	90266	**866-656-2228**	310-643-2630	764

Name / Address	City	State	ZIP	Toll-Free	Phone	Class
MacBeath Hardwood Co 2150 Oakdale Ave	San Francisco	CA	94124	**800-233-0782**	415-401-7046	671
MACCO Adhesives 925 Euclid Ave Suite 900	Cleveland	OH	44115	**800-634-0015**	216-344-7304	3
MacConnect Inc 81 Larkfield Rd *Sales	East Northport	NY	11731	**866-622-2666***	888-660-3010	390
MacConnection 730 Milford Rd Rt 101A	Merrimack	NH	03054	**800-800-0014**	603-683-2000	177
MacCurrach Golf Construction Inc 3501 Faye Rd	Jacksonville	FL	32226	**800-646-1581**	904-646-1581	187-3
MacDermid Inc 245 Freight St *NYSE: MRD*	Waterbury	CT	06702	**800-325-4158**	203-575-5700	143
MacDill Federal Credit Union 6701 S Dale Mabry Hwy	Tampa	FL	33611	**800-839-6328**	813-837-2451	216
MacDonald-Miller Co Inc 7717 Detroit Ave SE	Seattle	WA	98106	**800-962-5979**	206-763-9400	188-10
Mace Group Inc 15861 Tapia St	Irwindale	CA	91706	**800-644-1132**	626-338-8787	171-1
Mace Security International Inc 160 Benmont Ave Suite 1 *NASDAQ: MACE*	Bennington	VT	05201	**800-255-2634**	802-447-1503	681
Macerich Co 401 Wilshire Blvd Suite 700 *NYSE: MAC*	Santa Monica	CA	90401	**800-421-7237**	310-394-6911	641
MacGill William V & Co 1000 N Lombard Rd	Lombard	IL	60148	**800-323-2841**	630-889-0500	467
MacGregor Golf Co Inc 1000 Pecan Grove Dr	Albany	GA	31707	**800-841-4358**	229-420-7000	701
MacGregor's Market 2930 W Maple St	Sioux Falls	SD	57107	**800-648-6227**	605-336-6961	657
Machine Specialty & Mfg Inc 215 Rousseau Rd	Youngsville	LA	70592	**800-256-1292**	337-837-0020	474
Machine Tool Distributors' Assn. American 1445 Research Blvd Suite 450	Rockville	MD	20850	**800-878-2683**	301-738-1200	49-18
Machine Works at Essex Inc 75 Crystal Ave	New London	CT	06320	**800-724-0528**	860-447-3935	446
Machinery Dealers National Assn (MDNA) 315 S Patrick St	Alexandria	VA	22314	**800-872-7807**	703-836-9300	49-18
Machining Assn. National Tooling & 9300 Livingston Rd	Fort Washington	MD	20744	**800-248-6862**	301-248-6200	49-13
MacHome 200 Folsom St Suite 150	San Francisco	CA	94105	**800-800-6542**	415-957-1911	449-7
MacIntire & Assoc Inc 531 W Plata St Suite 200	Tucson	AZ	85705	**800-641-2737**	520-622-2737	392
MacIntyre Assoc Inc 106 W State St	Kennett Square	PA	19348	**888-575-0903**	610-925-5925	312
MacIntyre JJ Co 1801 California Ave	Corona	CA	92881	**800-621-9859**	951-898-4300	157
Mack Energy Co 1202 N 10th St	Duncan	OK	73533	**800-299-5580**	580-252-5580	525
Mack-Miller Candle Co Inc 202 SHeridan Rd	Liverpool	NY	13090	**800-522-6353**	315-453-9665	122
Mackay Envelope Corp 2100 Elm St SE	Minneapolis	MN	55414	**800-622-5299**	612-331-9311	260
Mackenzie Financial Corp 150 Bloor St W Suite M111	Toronto	ON	M5S3B5	**888-653-7070**	416-922-5322	393
Mackinaw Area Visitors Bureau 10300 US 23 PO Box 160	Mackinaw City	MI	49701	**800-666-0160**	231-436-5664	205
MacLean-Fogg Co 1000 Allanson Rd	Mundelein	IL	60060	**800-323-4536**	847-566-0010	60
Maclean's Magazine 1 Mt Pleasant Rd 11th Fl	Toronto	ON	M4Y2Y5	**800-268-9119**	416-764-1300	449-17
Macmillan/McGraw-Hill Div McGraw-Hill Cos Inc 2 Pennsylvania Plaza	New York	NY	10121	**800-442-9685**	212-512-2000	242
MacMurray College 447 E College Ave	Jacksonville	IL	62650	**800-252-7485**	217-479-7000	163
MacNeal Hospital 3249 S Oak Pk Ave	Berwyn	IL	60402	**888-622-6325**	708-795-9100	366-2
Macomb Community College South Campus 14500 E 12-Mile Rd	Warren	MI	48088	**866-622-6624**	586-445-7000	160
Macomb Journal 203 N Randolph St	Macomb	IL	61455	**800-237-6858**	309-833-2114	522-2
Macon-Bibb County Convention/Visitors Bureau 200 Cherry St	Macon	GA	31201	**800-768-3401**	478-743-3401	205
Macon Cigar & Tobacco Co Inc DBA MCT Wholesale 575 12th St	Macon	GA	31201	**800-637-0190**	478-743-2236	744
Macon City Auditorium 415 1st St	Macon	GA	31201	**877-532-6144**	478-751-9152	562
Macon Electric Co-op PO Box 157	Macon	MO	63552	**800-553-6901**	660-385-3157	244
Macon Iron & Paper Stock Co Inc 950 Lower Poplar Rd	Macon	GA	31202	**800-342-1933**	478-743-6773	646
Macon State College 100 College Station Dr	Macon	GA	31206	**800-272-7619**	478-471-2700	160
Macon Telegraph 120 Broadway	Macon	GA	31201	**800-679-6397**	478-744-4200	522-2
Macpherson Meistergram Inc DBA Embroidery Store 5081 Arden Ct *Cust Svc	Ramseur	NC	27316	**800-727-4244***	336-824-4975	729
MacPherson's-Artcraft 1351 Ocean Ave	Emeryville	CA	94608	**800-289-9800**	510-428-9011	44
Macristy Industries Inc 206 Newington Ave	New Britain	CT	06051	**800-966-6964**	860-225-4637	598
Macro 4 Inc 35 Waterview Blvd *Cust Svc	Parsippany	NJ	07054	**800-866-6224***	973-402-8000	176-1
Macromedia Inc 600 Townsend St Suite 500-W *NASDAQ: MACR* ■ *Cust Svc	San Francisco	CA	94103	**800-470-7211***	415-252-2000	176-7
Macrovision Corp 2830 De La Cruz Blvd *NASDAQ: MVSN*	Santa Clara	CA	95050	**800-622-7686**	408-743-8600	176-12
Mac's Convenience Stores Inc 10 Commander Blvd	Scarborough	ON	M1S3T2	**800-268-5574**	416-291-4441	203
MACSTEEL 1 Jackson Sq Suite 500 *Sales	Jackson	MI	49204	**800-888-7833***	517-782-0415	709
Macsteel Service Centers USA 888 San Clemente Dr Suite 250	Newport Beach	CA	92660	**866-622-7833**	949-219-9000	483
MACtac 4560 Darrow Rd	Stow	OH	44224	**800-762-2822**	330-688-1111	3
Macworld Magazine 501 2nd St Suite 120 *Cust Svc	San Francisco	CA	94107	**800-873-4941***	415-243-4141	449-7

Name / Address	City	State	ZIP	Toll-Free	Phone	Class
Macy Edith Conference Center 550 Chappaqua Rd	Briarcliff Manor	NY	10510	**800-442-6229**	914-945-8000	370
Macy RH & Co Inc DBA Macy's 151 W 34th St *Cust Svc	New York	NY	10001	**800-526-1202***	212-695-4400	227
Macy's 151 W 34th St *Cust Svc	New York	NY	10001	**800-526-1202***	212-695-4400	227
Macy's Credit Services 5300 Kings Island Dr *Cust Svc	Mason	OH	45040	**800-743-6229***	513-459-1500	213
Mad Catz Interactive Inc 7480 Mission Valley Rd Suite 101 *AMEX: MCZ*	San Diego	CA	92108	**800-831-1442**	619-683-9830	171-1
Mad Magazine 1700 Broadway	New York	NY	10019	**800-462-3624**	212-506-4850	449-11
Mad Science Group 8360 Bougainville St Suite 201	Montreal	QC	H4P2G1	**800-586-5231**	514-344-4181	146
MADD (Mothers Against Drunk Driving) 511 E John Carpenter Fwy Suite 700	Irving	TX	75062	**800-438-6233**	214-744-6233	48-6
Madden Mfg Co 1317 Princeton Blvd	Elkhart	IN	46516	**800-369-6233**	574-295-4292	627
Madden Steven Ltd 52-16 Barnett Ave *NASDAQ: SHOO*	Long Island City	NY	11104	**800-747-6233**	718-446-1800	296
Madden's on Gull Lake 11266 Pine Beach Peninsula	Brainerd	MN	56401	**800-247-1040**	218-829-2811	655
Maddux Metal Works Inc 4116 Bronze Way	Dallas	TX	75237	**800-952-1984**	214-333-2311	688
Made2Manage Systems Inc 450 E 96th St Suite 300	Indianapolis	IN	46240	**800-626-0220**	317-249-1200	176-1
Madelaine Chocolate Novelties Inc 9603 Beach Channel Dr	Rockaway Beach	NY	11693	**800-322-1505**	718-945-1500	291-8
Maden Technologies 2110 Washington Blvd Suite 200	Arlington	VA	22204	**800-601-5112**	703-769-4440	178
Madico Inc 45 Industrial Pkwy *Cust Svc	Woburn	MA	01801	**800-456-4331***	781-935-7850	588
Madison The 1177 15th St NW	Washington	DC	20005	**800-424-8577**	202-862-1600	373
Madison Area Technical College 3550 Anderson St	Madison	WI	53704	**800-322-6282**	608-246-6100	787
Madison Bancshares Group Ltd 1767 Sentry Pkwy W	Blue Bell	PA	19422	**800-848-9867**	215-641-1111	355-2
Madison Cable Corp 125 Goddard Memorial Dr	Worcester	MA	01603	**877-623-4766**	508-752-2884	801
Madison Chemical Co Inc 3141 Clifty Dr	Madison	IN	47250	**800-345-1915**	812-273-6000	149
Madison Concourse Hotel & Governors Club 1 W Dayton St	Madison	WI	53703	**800-356-8293**	608-257-6000	373
Madison Convention & Visitors Bureau 115 E Jefferson St	Madison	GA	30650	**800-709-7406**	706-342-4454	205
Madison County Convention & Visitors Bureau 405 Madison Ave	Norfolk	NE	68701	**888-371-2932**	402-371-2932	205
Madison Courier 310 Courier Sq	Madison	IN	47250	**800-333-2885**	812-265-3641	522-2
Madison Cutting Die Inc 2547 Progress Rd	Madison	WI	53716	**800-395-9405**	608-221-3422	545
Madison Daily Leader PO Box 348	Madison	SD	57042	**877-635-7323**	605-256-4555	522-2
Madison Gas & Electric Co 133 S Blair St	Madison	WI	53703	**800-245-1125**	608-252-7000	774
Madison (Greater) Convention & Visitors Bureau 615 E Washington Ave	Madison	WI	53703	**800-373-6376**	608-255-2537	205
Madison Hotel 1 Convent Rd	Morristown	NJ	07960	**800-526-0729**	973-285-1800	373
Madison Hotel 79 Madison Ave	Memphis	TN	38103	**888-636-7447**	901-333-1200	373
Madison Newspapers Inc 1901 Fish Hatchery Rd *Classified	Madison	WI	53713	**800-252-7723***	608-252-6200	623-8
Madison Paper Industries PO Box 129	Madison	ME	04950	**800-323-3443**	207-696-3307	547
Madison Press PO Box 390	London	OH	43140	**800-282-3838**	740-852-1616	522-2
Madisonville Community College 2000 College Dr	Madisonville	KY	42431	**866-227-4812**	270-821-2250	160
Madix Store Fixtures 500 Airport Rd *Cust Svc	Terrell	TX	75160	**800-776-2349***	972-563-5744	281
Madoff Bernard L Investment Securities 885 3rd Ave 18th Fl	New York	NY	10022	**800-334-1343**	212-230-2424	679
Madonna Rehabilitation Hospital 5401 South St	Lincoln	NE	68506	**800-676-5448**	402-489-7102	366-4
Madonna University 36600 Schoolcraft Rd	Livonia	MI	48150	**800-852-4951**	734-432-5339	163
MAF (Mission Aviation Fellowship) 1849 N Wabash Ave	Redlands	CA	92374	**800-359-7623**	909-794-1151	48-20
Mafcote Industries Inc 108 Main St *Cust Svc	Norwalk	CT	06851	**800-526-4280***	203-847-8500	542-2
Mag Instrument Inc 1950 S Sterling Ave	Ontario	CA	91761	**800-289-6241**	909-947-1006	431
Mag-Nif Inc 8820 East Ave	Mentor	OH	44060	**800-869-5463**	440-946-4308	750
Magazine Publishers of America (MPA) 810 7th Ave 24th Fl	New York	NY	10019	**888-567-3228**	212-872-3700	49-16
Magdalen College 511 Kearsarge Mountain Rd	Warner	NH	03278	**877-498-1723**	603-456-2656	163
Magee Rehabilitation Hospital 6 Franklin Plaza	Philadelphia	PA	19102	**800-966-2433**	215-587-3000	366-4
Magellan Health Services Inc 6950 Columbia Gateway Dr *NASDAQ: MGLN*	Columbia	MD	21046	**800-458-2740**	410-953-1000	454
Magellan Midstream Partners LP 1 Williams Ctr *NYSE: MMP*	Tulsa	OK	74172	**800-574-6671**		586
Magenta Corp 3800 N Milwaukee Ave	Chicago	IL	60641	**800-387-4378**	773-777-5050	152
Maggie Valley Area Convention & Visitors Bureau 2487 Soco Rd PO Box 87	Maggie Valley	NC	28751	**800-785-8259**	828-926-1686	205
Maggie Valley Resort & Country Club 1819 Country Club Dr	Maggie Valley	NC	28751	**800-438-3861**	828-926-1616	655
Maggio Data Forms Printing Ltd 1735 Expy Dr N	Hauppauge	NY	11788	**800-783-6313**	631-348-0343	111
Magic American Corp 23700 Mercantile Rd *Cust Svc	Cleveland	OH	44122	**800-321-6330***	216-464-2353	149
Magic Bus Co 16 Roncesvalles Ave	Toronto	ON	M6R2K3	**877-371-8747**	416-516-7433	748
Magic Johnson Foundation Inc 9100 Wilshire Blvd East Tower Suite 700	Beverly Hills	CA	90212	**888-624-4205**	310-246-4400	300

	City	State	ZIP	Toll-Free	Phone	Class
Magic Software Enterprises Inc						
17310 Red Hill Ave Suite 270	Irvine	CA	92614	**800-345-6244**	949-250-1718	176-12
NASDAQ: MGIC						
Magic Valley Electric Co-op Inc						
PO Box 267	Mercedes	TX	78570	**800-880-6832**	866-225-5683	244
Magic Valley Newspapers						
132 Fairfield St W	Twin Falls	ID	83301	**800-658-3883**	208-733-0931	623-8
Magic Valley Regional Medical Center						
650 Addison Ave W	Twin Falls	ID	83301	**800-947-4852**	208-737-2000	366-2
Magid Glove & Safety Mfg Co						
2060 N Kolmar Ave	Chicago	IL	60639	**800-444-8010**	773-384-2070	153-8
Magie Brothers Oil Co						
9101 Fullerton Ave	Franklin Park	IL	60131	**800-624-4347**	847-455-4500	530
Magikist Monarch Drapery & Carpet Cleaners Inc 16619 S						
Kilbourn St	Oak Forest	IL	60452	**800-244-4336**	773-378-8600	150
Magla Products LLC 159 South St	Morristown	NJ	07960	**800-247-5281**	973-984-7998	566
Magline Inc 503 S Mercer St	Pinconning	MI	48650	**800-624-5463**	989-879-2411	462
Magna Carta Co 1 Park Ave	New York	NY	10016	**888-663-7275**	212-591-9500	384-4
Magna Chek Inc						
32701 Edward Ave	Madison Heights	MI	48071	**800-582-8947**	248-597-0089	728
Magna Design Inc						
5804 204th St SW	Lynnwood	WA	98046	**800-233-2304**	425-776-2181	314-1
Magna Solutions						
1220 Lebourgneuf Blvd Suite 250	Quebec	QC	G2K2G4	**800-361-0528**	418-622-8003	176-1
Magna Visual Inc 9400 Watson Rd	Saint Louis	MO	63126	**800-843-3399**	314-843-9000	523
Magnasync Corp						
1135 N Mansfield Ave	Hollywood	CA	90038	**800-366-3564**	323-962-0382	720
Magnat Rolls Inc						
52 O'Neil St PO Box 1310	Easthampton	MA	01027	**800-370-4256**	413-527-4256	476
Magnesium Elektron 1001 College St	Madison	IL	62060	**800-851-3145***	618-452-5190	476
*Sales						
Magnet Schultz of America Inc						
401 Plaza Dr	Westmont	IL	60559	**800-635-3778***	630-789-0600	202
*Cust Svc						
Magnetic Component Engineering Inc						
2830 Lomita Blvd	Torrance	CA	90505	**800-989-5656**		450
Magnetic Metals Corp						
1900 Hayes Ave	Camden	NJ	08105	**800-257-8174**	856-964-7842	472
Magnetics Society. IEEE						
IEEE Operations Ctr 445 Hoes Ln	Piscataway	NJ	08854	**800-678-4333**	732-981-0060	49-19
Magnetrol International Inc						
5300 Belmont Rd	Downers Grove	IL	60515	**800-624-8765**	630-969-4000	200
Magnifying Center						
10086 W McNab Rd	Tamarac	FL	33321	**800-364-1612**	954-722-1580	533
Magnivision 3700 Commerce Pkwy	Miramar	FL	33025	**800-237-4231**	954-986-9000	531
Magnolia Bible College						
822 S Huntington St	Kosciusko	MS	39090	**800-748-8655**	662-289-2896	163
Magnolia Brush Mfg Inc						
1001 N Cedar PO Box 932	Clarksville	TX	75426	**800-248-2261**	903-427-2261	104
Magnolia-Columbia County Chamber of Commerce 202 N Pine St	Magnolia	AR	71753	**800-482-3330**	870-234-4352	137
Magnolia Hotel Dallas						
1401 Commerce St	Dallas	TX	75201	**888-915-1110**	214-915-6500	373
Magnolia Hotel Denver 818 17th St	Denver	CO	80202	**888-915-1110**	303-607-9000	373
Magnolia Hotel & Spa						
623 Courtney St	Victoria	BC	V8W1B8	**877-624-6654**	250-381-0999	372
Magnolia Marketing						
809 Jefferson Hwy	Jefferson	LA	70121	**800-899-6056**	504-837-1500	82-3
Magnolia Metal Corp 6161 Abbott	Omaha	NE	68119	**800-228-4043**	402-455-8760	303
Magnolia Plantation & Gardens						
3550 Ashley River Rd	Charleston	SC	29414	**800-367-3517**	843-571-1266	98
Magnum Integrated Technologies						
4 Thomas Dr Unit 5	Westbrook	ME	04092	**800-830-0642**	207-854-9791	448
Magruder Color Co Inc						
1029 Newark Ave	Elizabeth	NJ	07208	**800-631-4461**	973-242-1300	142
MagStar Technologies						
410 11th Ave S	Hopkins	MN	55343	**800-473-8837**	952-935-6921	610
Magtrol Inc 70 Gardenville Pkwy W	Buffalo	NY	14224	**800-828-7844**	716-668-5555	609
Maguire Oil Co 1201 Elm St Suite 4000	Dallas	TX	75270	**800-969-6248**	214-741-5137	525
Mahaffey Theater for the Performing Arts 400 1st						
St S	Saint Petersburg	FL	33701	**800-874-9015**	727-892-5798	562
Maharam 45 Rasons Ct	Hauppauge	NY	11788	**800-645-3943**	631-582-3434	583
Maharishi University of Management						
1000 N 4th St	Fairfield	IA	52557	**800-369-6480**	641-472-7000	163
Mahr Federal Inc 1144 Eddy St	Providence	RI	02905	**800-343-2050***	401-784-3100	200
*Orders						
Maid Brigade USA/Minimaid Canada						
4 Concourse Pkwy Suite 200	Atlanta	GA	30328	**800-722-6243**	770-551-9630	150
Maid-Rite Steak Co Inc						
105 Keystone Industrial Pk	Dunmore	PA	18512	**800-233-4259**	570-343-4748	291-26
Maids International The						
4820 Dodge St	Omaha	NE	68132	**800-843-6243**	402-558-5555	150
Mail Advertising Supply Co Inc						
1450 S West Ave	Waukesha	WI	53189	**800-558-2126**	262-549-1730	544
Mail Boxes Etc						
6060 Cornerstone Ct W	San Diego	CA	92121	**800-456-0414**	858-455-8800	114
Mail Center Management Report						
3 Park Ave 30th Fl	New York	NY	10016	**800-401-5937**	212-244-0360	521-2
Mail Contractors of America						
100 Morgan Keegan Dr						
Suite 200	Little Rock	AR	72202	**800-294-7743**	501-280-0500	769
Mail-Well Envelope Co						
8310 S Valley Hwy Suite 400	Englewood	CO	80112	**888-543-5439**	303-566-4500	260
Mailbox Bookbag Magazine						
3515 W Market St Suite 200	Greensboro	NC	27403	**800-714-7991**	336-854-0309	449-8
Mailing & Fulfillment Service Assn (MFSA) 1421 Prince St Suite 410	Alexandria	VA	22314	**800-333-6272**	703-836-9200	49-18
Main Street America Group 55 West St	Keene	NH	03431	**800-258-5310**	603-352-4000	384-4
Main Street Gourmet Inc						
170 Muffin Ln	Cuyahoga Falls	OH	44223	**800-678-6246**	330-929-0000	291-2
Main Street Inn						
2200 Main St	Hilton Head Island	SC	29926	**800-471-3001**	843-681-3001	373
Main Street Restaurant Group Inc						
5050 N 40th St Suite 200	Phoenix	AZ	85018	**888-677-5080**	602-852-9000	656
NASDAQ: MAIN						
Main Street Station Hotel & Casino						
200 N Main St	Las Vegas	NV	89101	**800-713-8933**	702-387-1896	373
Mainco Elevator Services Inc						
5-25 51st Ave	Long Island City	NY	11101	**800-464-6487**	718-786-3301	188-1
MainControl Inc						
7900 Westpark Dr Suite T500	McLean	VA	22102	**800-981-3328**	703-749-2308	176-1
Maine						
Bill Status						
State House 100 State						
House Station	Augusta	ME	04333	**800-301-3178**	207-287-1692	425
Economic & Community Development						
Dept 59 State House Stn	Augusta	ME	04333	**800-541-5872**	207-287-2656	335
Emergency Management Agency						
72 State House Stn	Augusta	ME	04333	**800-452-8735**	207-626-4503	335
Environmental Protection Dept						
17 State House Stn	Augusta	ME	04333	**800-452-1942**	207-287-7688	335
Finance Authority of Maine (FAME)						
PO Box 949	Augusta	ME	04332	**800-228-3734**	207-623-3263	711
Parks & Land Bureau						
22 State House Stn	Augusta	ME	04333	**800-332-1501***	207-287-3821	335
*Campground Resv						
Rehabilitation Services Bureau						
150 State House Stn	Augusta	ME	04333	**800-760-1573**	207-624-5950	335
Tourism Office 59 State House Stn	Augusta	ME	04333	**888-624-6345**	207-287-5711	335
Maine Aviation Corp						
1001 Westbrook St	Portland	ME	04102	**888-359-7600**	207-780-1811	14
Maine Biotechnology Services Inc						
1037 R Forest Ave	Portland	ME	04103	**800-925-9476**	207-797-5454	229
Maine College of Art 97 Spring St	Portland	ME	04101	**800-639-4808**	207-775-3052	163
Maine Educator Magazine						
35 Community Dr	Augusta	ME	04330	**800-452-8709**	207-622-5866	449-8
Maine Industrial Tires Ltd						
9 Laurence Rd	Gorham	ME	04038	**800-782-2371***	207-856-6381	739
*Sales						
Maine Instrument Flight						
Augusta State Airport PO Box 2	Augusta	ME	04332	**888-643-3597**	207-622-1211	63
Maine Maritime Academy	Castine	ME	04420	**800-227-8465**	207-326-4311	163
Maine & Maritimes Corp						
209 State St	Presque Isle	ME	04769	**877-655-4448**	207-768-5811	774
AMEX: MAM						
Maine Medical Assn						
30 Associate Dr	Manchester	ME	04351	**800-772-0815**	207-622-3374	466
Maine Public Broadcasting Corp (MPBC)						
65 Texas Ave	Bangor	ME	04401	**800-884-1717**	207-941-1010	620
Maine Veterans Home-Bangor						
44 Hogan Rd	Bangor	ME	04401	**888-684-4665**	207-942-2333	780
Maine Veterans Home-Scarborough						
290 US Rt 1	Scarborough	ME	04074	**888-684-4666**	207-883-7184	780
Maine Veterans Home-South Paris						
477 High St	South Paris	ME	04281	**888-684-4668**	207-743-6300	780
Maine Windjammer Assn						
251 Jefferson St MS-06	Waldoboro	ME	04572	**800-807-9463**		760
Maine Windjammer Cruises						
PO Box 617	Camden	ME	04843	**800-736-7981**	207-236-2938	217
Maines Equipment & Supply Co						
PO Box 450	Conklin	NY	13748	**800-800-4825**	607-772-0055	295
Maines Paper & Food Service Co						
101 Broome Corporate Pkwy	Conklin	NY	13748	**800-366-3669**	607-772-1936	292-8
Mainland Nursery Inc J50 W Turner Rd	Lodi	CA	95242	**800-366-4048**	209-334-1680	363
Mainline Information Systems Inc						
1700 Summit Lake Dr	Tallahassee	FL	32317	**800-811-4429**	850-219-5000	178
Mainliner Motor Express Inc						
PO Box 7439	Omaha	NE	68107	**800-228-9887**	402-734-3500	769
Mainship Corp 255 Diesel Rd	Saint Augustine	FL	32084	**800-829-5847**	904-829-0500	91
Mainsoft Corp						
224 Airport Pkwy Suite 300	San Jose	CA	95110	**800-624-6946**	408-200-4000	176-12
Mainstay 1320 Flynn Rd Suite 401	Camarillo	CA	93012	**800-362-2605***	805-484-9400	176-12
*Orders						
MainStay Funds						
169 Lackawanna Ave	Parsippany	NJ	07054	**800-695-9950**		517
MainStay Suites						
10750 Columbia Pike	Silver Spring	MD	20901	**800-424-6423**	301-592-5000	369
Maintech Div Volt Information Sciences Inc 39 Paterson Ave	Wallington	NJ	07057	**800-426-8324**	973-614-1700	178
Maintenance Management Newsletter						
7201 McKinney Cir	Frederick	MD	21704	**800-243-0876**	301-698-7100	521-2
Mainzer Alfred Inc						
27-08 40th Ave	Long Island City	NY	11101	**800-222-2737**	718-392-4200	130
Mainzer Minton Co Inc						
144 Main St	Hackettstown	NJ	07840	**800-944-7632**	908-979-0800	34
Mairs & Power Funds						
332 Minnesota St Suite W-1520	Saint Paul	MN	55101	**800-304-7404**	651-222-8478	517
Maison Dupuy Hotel						
1001 Toulouse St	New Orleans	LA	70112	**800-535-9177**	504-586-8000	373
Maison Orleans - A Ritz-Carlton Hotel 904 Rue Iberville	New Orleans	LA	70112	**800-241-3333**	504-670-2900	373
Majestic 60 Cherry St	Bridgeport	CT	06605	**800-673-2543**	203-367-7900	596
Majestic Hotel 528 W Brompton	Chicago	IL	60657	**800-727-5108**	773-404-3499	373
Majestic Investor Holdings LLC						
1 Buffington Harbor Dr	Gary	IN	46406	**888-225-8258**	219-977-7777	132
Majestic Resort & Spa						
101 Park Ave	Hot Springs	AR	71901	**800-643-1504**	501-623-5511	373
Majestic Theatre 245 W 44th St	New York	NY	10036	**800-432-7250**	212-239-6200	732
Major Brands						
550 E 13th Ave	North Kansas City	MO	64116	**800-467-1070**	816-221-1070	82-3
Major Brands-Columbia						
1502 Business 70 W	Columbia	MO	65202	**800-264-9988**	573-443-3169	82-3
Major Electric Supply Inc						
123 High St	Pawtucket	RI	02860	**800-444-1660**	401-724-7100	245
Major Hagen & Africa						
500 Washington St 5th Fl	San Francisco	CA	94111	**877-482-1010**	415-956-1010	262
Major Indoor Soccer League (MISL)						
1175 Post Rd E	Westport	CT	06880	**866-647-5638**	203-222-4900	48-22
Major League Baseball (Office of the Commissioner) 245 Park Ave						
31st Fl	New York	NY	10167	**800-704-2937***	212-931-7800	703
*Cust Svc						
Major Pharmaceutical Co						
31778 Enterprise Dr	Livonia	MI	48150	**800-521-5098**	734-525-8700	572
Majors JA Co 1401 Lakeway Dr	Lewisville	TX	75057	**800-633-1851**	972-353-1100	97

Name / Address	City	State	ZIP	Toll-Free	Phone	Class
Make-A-Wish Foundation of America 3550 N Central Ave Suite 300	Phoenix	AZ	85012	**800-722-9474**	602-279-9474	48-5
Make Today Count 1235 E Cherokee St	Springfield	MO	65804	**800-432-2273**	417-885-3324	48-17
MakeMusic! Inc 6210 Bury Dr	Eden Prairie	MN	55346	**800-843-2066**	952-937-9611	176-6
NASDAQ: MMUS						
Makena Resort Maui Prince Hotel 5400 Makena Alanui	Makena	HI	96753	**800-321-6248**	808-874-1111	655
MakeUpMania! of New York 154 Orchard St	New York	NY	10002	**800-711-7182**	212-533-5900	211
Makino Inc 7680 Innovation Way	Mason	OH	45040	**888-625-4661**	513-573-7200	447
Makita USA Inc 14930 Northam St Suite C	La Mirada	CA	90638	**800-462-5482**	714-522-8088	747
Malaco Music Group Inc 3023 W Northside Dr	Jackson	MS	39213	**800-272-7936***	601-982-4522	643
*Cust Svc						
Malaga Inn 359 Church St	Mobile	AL	36602	**800-235-1586**	251-438-4701	373
Malahide Design & Mfg Inc 209 Griffith Rd	Stratford	ON	N5A6S4	**800-867-5077**	519-273-0603	545
Malarkey Roofing Co 3131 N Columbia Blvd	Portland	OR	97217	**800-545-1191**	503-283-1191	46
Malaysia Airlines 100 N Sepulveda Blvd Suite 400	El Segundo	CA	90245	**800-552-9264**	310-535-9288	26
Malbor Vicion Center 409 N 78th St	Omaha	NE	68114	**800-701-3937**	402-393-4500	533
Malco Products Inc 14080 State Hwy 55 NW	Annandale	MN	55302	**800-328-3530**	320-274-8246	746
Malco Products Inc PO Box 892	Barberton	OH	44203	**800-253-2526**	330-753-0361	149
Malcolm Pirnie Inc 104 Corporate Park Dr	White Plains	NY	10602	**800-759-5020**	914-694-2100	258
Malden Mills Industries Inc 46 Stafford St	Lawrence	MA	01841	**800-252-6688**	978-685-6341	730-1
Male Survivor 5505 Connecticut Ave NW PMB 103	Washington	DC	20015	**800-738-4181**		48-17
Malev-Hungarian Airlines 90 John St Suite 312	New York	NY	10038	**800-223-6884**	212-566-9944	26
Malev Hungarian Airlines Duna Club 90 John St Suite 312	New York	NY	10038	**800-223-6884**	212-566-9944	27
Malibu Beach Inn 22878 Pacific Coast Hwy	Malibu	CA	90265	**800-462-5428**	310-456-6444	373
Malibu Hills Vineyards 29000 Newton Canyon Rd	Malibu	CA	90265	**800-814-0733**	310-463-9532	81-3
Mallet & Co Inc 51 Arch St Ext	Carnegie	PA	15106	**800-245-2757**	412-276-9000	291-23
Malleys Chocolates 13400 Brookpark Rd	Cleveland	OH	44135	**800-275-6255**	216-226-8300	291-8
Mallin Casual Furniture 1441 Peerless Way	Montebello	CA	90640	**800-251-6537**	323-513-1041	314-4
Mallinckrodt Baker Inc 222 Red School Ln	Phillipsburg	NJ	08865	**800-582-2537**	908-859-2151	470
Mallinckrodt Inc 675 McDonnell Blvd	Hazelwood	MO	63042	**888-744-1414**	314-654-2000	229
Mallinckrodt Pharmaceutical Group 675 McDonnell Blvd	Hazelwood	MO	63042	**800-554-5343**	314-654-2000	470
Mallory & Church LLC 676 S Industrial Way	Seattle	WA	98108	**800-255-8437**	206-587-2100	153-13
Mallory Hotel 729 SW 15th Ave	Portland	OR	97205	**800-228-8657**	503-223-6311	373
Malloy Air East Inc Francis S Gabreski Airport	Westhampton Beach	NY	11978	**888-673-9888**	631-288-5410	63
Malloy Lithographing Inc PO Box 1124	Ann Arbor	MI	48106	**800-722-3231**	734-665-6113	614
Malnati Organization Inc 3685 Woodhead Dr	Northbrook	IL	60062	**800-568-8646**	847-562-1814	656
Malnove Inc 13434 F St	Omaha	NE	68137	**800-228-9877**	402-330-1100	102
Malone College 515 25th St NW	Canton	OH	44709	**800-521-1146**	330-471-8100	163
Malone Freight Lines 1901 Floyd Bradford Rd	Trussville	AL	35173	**800-366-6350**	205-951-1900	769
Maloney Technical Products 1300 E Berry St	Fort Worth	TX	76119	**800-231-7236**	817-923-3344	585
Maloof Joe G & Co Inc 701 Comanche Rd NE	Albuquerque	NM	87107	**800-760-2293**	505-243-2293	82-1
Malt-O-Meal Inc 80 S 8th St Suite 2600	Minneapolis	MN	55402	**800-328-4452**	612-338-8551	291-4
Malt Products Corp 88 Market St	Saddle Brook	NJ	07663	**800-526-0180**	201-845-4420	103
Maltby Electric Supply Co Inc 336 7th St	San Francisco	CA	94103	**800-339-0668**	415-863-5000	245
Maltz Jupiter Theatre 1001 E Indiantown Rd	Jupiter	FL	33477	**800-445-1666**	561-743-2666	734
Malvern Daily Record 219 Locust St	Malvern	AR	72104	**800-582-5794**	501-337-7523	522-2
Malvern Institute 940 King Rd	Malvern	PA	19355	**800-486-0017**	610-647-0330	712
Malvern Systems Inc 81 Lancaster Ave Suite 216	Malvern	PA	19355	**800-296-9642**	610-296-9642	176-1
Mama Kayer's Baltimore Bakery Inc 1140 Kingwood Ave	Norfolk	VA	23502	**800-627-7850**	757-855-4731	291-1
Mamma.com Inc 384 Saint Jacques St W Suite 100	Montreal	QC	H2Y1S1	**888-841-2372**	514-844-2700	677
NASDAQ: MAMA						
Mammoth Inc 101 W 82nd St	Chaska	MN	55318	**800-328-3321**	952-361-2711	15
Mammoth Mountain Resort 1 Minaret Rd PO Box 24	Mammoth Lakes	CA	93546	**800-626-6684**	760-934-2571	655
MAMSI Life & Health Insurance Co 4 Taft Ct	Rockville	MD	20850	**800-544-2853**	301-762-8205	384-3
MAN Roland Inc 800 E Oak Hill Dr	Westmont	IL	60559	**800-700-2344**	630-920-2000	617
MANA (Manufacturers' Agents National Assn) 1 Spectrum Pointe Dr Suite 150	Lake Forest	CA	92630	**877-626-2776**	949-859-4040	49-18
Mana Products Inc 32-02 Queens Blvd	Long Island City	NY	11101	**800-221-3071***	718-361-2550	211
*Cust Svc						
Managed Care Pharmacy. Academy of 100 N Pitt St Suite 400	Alexandria	VA	22314	**800-827-2627**	703-683-8416	49-8
Managed Care Physicians. National Assn of 4435 Waterfront Dr Suite 101 PO Box 4765	Glen Allen	VA	23058	**800-722-0376**	804-527-1905	49-8
Managed Health Network Inc 1600 Los Gamos Dr Suite 300	San Rafael	CA	94903	**800-327-2133**		454
Management Accounting Quarterly 10 Paragon Dr	Montvale	NJ	07645	**800-638-4427***	201-573-9000	449-5
*Cust Svc						
Management Assn. American 1601 Broadway	New York	NY	10019	**800-262-9699**	212-586-8100	753
Management Assn. Christian 635 Camino De Los Mares Suite 205	San Clemente	CA	92673	**800-727-4262**	949-487-0900	49-12
Management Consultants USA Inc. Institute of 2025 M St NW Suite 800	Washington	DC	20036	**800-221-2557**	202-367-1134	49-12
Management Information Control Systems Inc (MICS) 2025 9th St	Los Osos	CA	93402	**800-838-6427**	805-543-7000	176-10
Management Network Group Inc 7300 College Blvd Suite 302	Overland Park	KS	66210	**888-480-8664**	913-345-9315	195
NASDAQ: TMNG						
Management Recruiters International Worldwide Inc 200 Public Sq 31st Fl	Cleveland	OH	44114	**800-875-4000**	216-696-1122	262
Management Science Assoc Inc 6565 Penn Ave	Pittsburgh	PA	15206	**800-672-4636**	412-362-2000	176-12
Management. Society for Advancement of Texas A&M Univ Corpus Christi College of Business 6300 Ocean Dr FC111	Corpus Christi	TX	78412	**888-827-6077**	361-825-6045	49-12
Management Technology America Ltd 8233 Via Paseo del Norte Bldg C Suite 100	Scottsdale	AZ	85258	**800-366-6633**	480-998-0200	176-11
Managers. Institute of Certified Professional James Madison University MSC 5504	Harrisonburg	VA	22807	**800-568-4120**	540-568-3247	49-12
Manager's Intelligence Report 316 N Michigan Ave Suite 300	Chicago	IL	60601	**800-878-5331**	312-960-4100	521-2
ManageSoft Corp 10 Post Office Sq Suite 600N	Boston	MA	02109	**800-441-4330**	617-532-1600	176-1
Managing 401K Plans Newsletter 30 Park Ave 30th Fl	New York	NY	10016	**800-401-5937**	212-244-0360	521-1
Managing Accounts Payable Newsletter 3 Park Ave 30th Fl	New York	NY	10016	**800-401-5937**	212-244-0360	521-1
Managing Benefits Plans Newsletter 3 Park Ave 30th Fl	New York	NY	10016	**800-401-5937**	212-244-0360	521-1
Managing Credit Receivables & Collections Newsletter 3 Park Ave 30th Fl	New York	NY	10016	**800-401-5937**	212-244-0360	521-1
Managing Customer Service Newsletter 3 Park Ave 30th Fl	New York	NY	10016	**800-401-5937**	212-244-0360	521-2
Managing International Credit & Collections Newsletter 3 Park Ave 30th Fl	New York	NY	10016	**800-401-5937**	212-244-0360	521-2
Managing Logistics Newsletter 3 Park Ave 30th Fl	New York	NY	10016	**800-401-5937**	212-244-0360	521-2
Manan Medical Products Inc 241 W Palatine Rd	Wheeling	IL	60090	**800-424-6779**	847-637-3333	468
Manatee Club. Save the 500 N Maitland Ave	Maitland	FL	32751	**800-432-5646**	407-539-0990	48-3
Manatee Cortez Floral Co 1320 33rd St W	Palmetto	FL	34221	**800-752-9845**	941-722-3279	288
Manatron Inc 510 E Milham Ave	Portage	MI	49002	**800-666-5300***	269-567-2900	176-11
NASDAQ: MANA ■ *Cust Svc						
Manatt's Inc 1775 Old Six Rd	Brooklyn	IA	52211	**800-877-1258**	641-522-9206	187-4
Manchester College 604 E College Ave	North Manchester	IN	46962	**800-852-3648**	260-982-5000	163
Manchester East Hotel & Suites 7065 N Port Washington Rd	Milwaukee	WI	53217	**800-723-8280**	414-351-6960	373
Manchester Technologies Inc 160 Oser Ave	Hauppauge	NY	11788	**800-378-1231**	631-435-1199	172
NASDAQ: MANC						
Manchester Tool Co 5142 Manchester Rd	Akron	OH	44319	**800-237-8789***	330-644-8853	447
*Cust Svc						
Manchu Wok 85 Citizen Ct Unit 9	Markham	ON	L6G1A8	**800-361-8864**	905-946-7200	657
Manchu Wok Canada Inc 85 Citizen Ct Unit 9	Markham	ON	L6G1A8	**800-361-8864**	905-946-7200	656
Mancini BT Co Inc 876 S Milpitas Blvd	Milpitas	CA	95036	**800-488-4286**	408-942-7900	188-12
Mancini BT Co Inc Brookman Div 876 S Milpitas Blvd Suite 81	Milpitas	CA	95035	**800-488-4286**	408-942-7900	185
Mancini Henry Institute 10811 Washington Blvd Suite 250	Culver City	CA	90232	**888-464-1903**	310-845-1900	563-3
Manda Fine Meats 2445 Sorrel Ave	Baton Rouge	LA	70802	**800-343-2642**	225-344-7636	292-9
Mandalay Bay Resort & Casino 3950 Las Vegas Blvd S	Las Vegas	NV	89119	**877-632-7800**	702-632-7777	655
Mandarin Library Automation Inc 1060 Holland Dr Suite 36	Boca Raton	FL	33487	**800-426-7477**	561-995-4010	176-12
Mandarin Oriental Hotel Group 9841 Airport Blvd Suite 822	Los Angeles	CA	90045	**800-526-6566**	310-670-6422	369
Mandarin Oriental Miami 500 Brickell Key Dr	Miami	FL	33131	**800-526-6566**	305-913-8288	373
Mandarin Oriental San Francisco 222 Sansome St	San Francisco	CA	94104	**800-526-6566**	415-276-9888	373
Mandarin Oriental Washington DC 1330 Maryland Ave SW	Washington	DC	20024	**888-888-1778**	202-554-8588	373
Mandee Shop 12 Vreeland Ave	Totowa	NJ	07512	**800-969-2446**	973-890-0021	155-6
Mandel Scientific Co Ltd 2 Admiral Pl	Guelph	ON	N1G4N4	**800-265-8356**	519-763-2145	410
MANDEX Inc 12500 Fair Lakes Cir Suite 125	Fairfax	VA	22033	**888-662-6339**	703-227-0900	178
Maneely John Co 900 Haddon Ave	Collingswood	NJ	08108	**800-257-8182**	856-854-5400	481
Manele Bay Hotel 1 Manele Rd	Lanai City	HI	96763	**800-321-4666**	808-565-7700	655
Mangosoft Inc 12 Pine St Ext	Nashua	NH	03060	**888-886-2646**	603-324-0400	176-12
Manhasset Specialty Co 3505 Fruitvale Blvd	Yakima	WA	98902	**800-795-0965**	509-248-3810	516
Manhattan Area Chamber of Commerce 501 Poyntz Ave	Manhattan	KS	66502	**800-759-0134**	785-776-8829	137
Manhattan Bagel Co Inc 100 Horizon Ctr Blvd	Hamilton	NJ	08691	**800-308-2457**	609-631-7000	69
Manhattan Beachwear Inc 6560 Bandini Blvd	Los Angeles	CA	90040	**800-279-2987**	323-887-7448	153-17

Name / Address	City	State	ZIP	Toll-Free	Phone	Class
Manhattan College 4513 Manhattan College Pkwy	Bronx	NY	10471	**800-622-9235**	718-862-8000	163
Manhattan Convention & Visitors Bureau 501 Poyntz Ave	Manhattan	KS	66502	**800-759-0134**	785-776-8829	205
Manhattan Public Library 629 Poyntz Ave.	Manhattan	KS	66502	**800-432-2796**	785-776-4741	426
Manhattanville College 2900 Purchase St.	Purchase	NY	10577	**800-328-4553**	914-323-5464	163
Manistee News-Advocate PO Box 317	Manistee	MI	49660	**888-723-3592**	231-723-3592	522-2
Manistique Papers Inc 453 S Mackinac Ave.	Manistique	MI	49854	**800-743-2389**	906-341-2175	547
Manitoba Telecom Services Inc 333 Main St *TSE: MBT*	Winnipeg	MB	R3C3V6	**800-565-1936**	204-941-8244	721
Manitou Cliff Dwellings Museum Hwy 24 W	Manitou Springs	CO	80829	**800-354-9971**	719-685-5242	509
Manitou North America 6401 Imperial Dr *Cust Svc	Waco	TX	76712	**800-433-3304***	254-799-0232	462
Manitowoc Ice Inc 2110 S 26th St	Manitowoc	WI	54220	**800-545-5720**	920-682-0161	650
Manitowoc-Two Rivers Area Chamber of Commerce 1515 Memorial Dr PO Box 903	Manitowoc	WI	54221	**800-262-7892**	920-684-5575	137
Manitowoc Visitor & Convention Bureau 4221 Calumet Ave PO Box 966	Manitowoc	WI	54221	**800-627-4896**	920-683-4388	205
Mankato-Kasota Stone Inc 818 N Willow St	Mankato	MN	56001	**800-437-7059**	507-625-2746	710
Mankato State University 122 Taylor Ctr.	Mankato	MN	56001	**800-722-0544**	507-389-1822	163
Manke Lumber Co Inc 1717 Marine View Dr NE	Tacoma	WA	98422	**800-426-8488**	253-572-6252	671
Mann Barbara B Performing Arts Hall 8099 College Pkwy SW	Fort Myers	FL	33919	**800-440-7469**	239-489-3033	562
Mann Edge Tool Co PO Box 351 *Sales	Lewistown	PA	17044	**800-248-8303***	717-248-9628	746
Mann Horace Educators Corp 1 Horace Mann Plaza *NYSE: HMN*	Springfield	IL	62715	**800-999-1030**	217-789-2500	355-4
Mann Horace Insurance Co 1 Horace Mann Plaza	Springfield	IL	62715	**800-999-1030**	217-789-2500	384-2
Mann Horace Life Insurance Co 1 Horace Mann Plaza	Springfield	IL	62715	**800-999-1030**	217-789-2500	384-2
Mann Packing Co Inc PO Box 690	Salinas	CA	93902	**800-285-1002**	831-422-7405	12-1
Manna Pro Corp 707 Spirit 40 Pk Dr Suite 150	Chesterfield	MO	63005	**800-690-9908**	636-681-1700	438
Mannatech Inc 600 S Royal Ln Suite 200 *NASDAQ: MTEX*	Coppell	TX	75019	**800-281-4469**	972-471-7400	361
Mannes College of Music 150 W 85th St	New York	NY	10024	**800-292-3040**	212-580-0210	163
Manning Greg Auctions Inc 775 Passaic Ave *NASDAQ: GMAI*	West Caldwell	NJ	07006	**800-221-0243**	973-882-0004	51
Mannington Carpets Inc PO Box 12281	Calhoun	GA	30701	**800-241-2262**	706-629-7301	131
Mannington Mills Inc 75 Mannington Mills Rd *Cust Svc	Salem	NJ	08079	**800-356-6787***	856-935-3000	286
Mannix Architectural Window Products 345 Crooked Hill Rd	Brentwood	NY	11717	**800-752-6483**	631-231-0800	232
Manny's Sanitary Supplies Inc 4866 Tchoupitoulas St	New Orleans	LA	70115	**800-256-2398**	504-899-2358	398
Manoir du Lac Delage 40 ave du Lac	Lac Delage	QC	G0A4P0	**888-202-3242**	418-848-2551	655
Manor House Inn 106 West St	Bar Harbor	ME	04609	**800-437-0088**	207-288-3759	373
Manor Park Inc 2208 North Loop 250 W	Midland	TX	79707	**800-523-9898**	432-689-9898	659
Manor Vail Lodge 595 E Vail Valley Dr	Vail	CO	81657	**800-950-8245**	970-476-5651	655
ManorCare Health Services - Arlington Heights 715 W Central Rd	Arlington Heights	IL	60005	**888-427-8020**	847-392-2020	441
ManorCare Health Services - Oak Lawn East 9401 S Kostner Ave	Oak Lawn	IL	60453	**800-427-1902**	708-423-7882	441
Manpower Demonstration Research Corp 16 E 34th St 19th Fl	New York	NY	10016	**800-221-3165**	212-532-3200	654
Mansfield University Alumni Hall	Mansfield	PA	16933	**800-577-6826**	570-662-4000	163
Mansfield/Richland County Convention & Visitors Bureau 124 N Main St	Mansfield	OH	44902	**800-642-8282**	419-525-1300	205
Mansion on Forsyth Park 700 Drayton St	Savannah	GA	31401	**888-711-5114**	912-238-5158	373
Mansion on Turtle Creek 2821 Turtle Creek Blvd	Dallas	TX	75219	**800-527-5432**	214-559-2100	373
Mansion View Inn & Suites 529 S 4th St	Springfield	IL	62701	**800-252-1083**	217-544-7411	373
Manson Construction Co 5209 E Marginal Way S	Seattle	WA	98134	**800-262-6766**	206-762-0850	187-5
Mansours Department Store Inc 26 W Lafayette Sq	LaGrange	GA	30240	**888-311-2289**	706-884-7305	227
Mantaline Corp 4754 E High St	Mantua	OH	44255	**800-321-0948**	330-274-2264	664
Mantas Inc 13650 Dulles Technology Dr	Herndon	VA	20171	**866-462-6827**	703-673-0577	247
Mantex Corp 611 Industrial Pkwy	Imlay City	MI	48444	**800-666-2689**	810-721-2100	591
Manton Industrial Cork Products Inc 415 Oser Ave Unit U	Hauppauge	NY	11788	**800-663-1921**	631-273-0700	208
Mantros-Haeuser & Co Inc 1175 Post Rd E	Westport	CT	06880	**800-344-4229**	203-454-1800	540
Mantua Mfg Co 7900 Northfield Rd *Orders	Walton Hills	OH	44146	**800-333-8333***	440-232-8865	314-2
Manual Woodworkers & Weavers Inc 3737 Howard Gap Rd	Hendersonville	NC	28792	**800-542-3139**	828-692-7333	731
Manuel Lujan Insurance Inc PO Box 3727	Albuquerque	NM	87190	**888-652-7771**	505-758-2206	384-4
Manufactured Housing Enterprises Inc 09302 US SR 6	Bryan	OH	43506	**800-821-0220**	419-636-4511	495
Manufactured Housing Institute (MHI) 2101 Wilson Blvd Suite 610	Arlington	VA	22201	**800-505-5500**	703-558-0400	49-3
Manufactured Housing Institute PAC (MHI PAC) 2101 Wilson Blvd Suite 610	Arlington	VA	22201	**800-505-5500**	703-558-0400	604
Manufactured Structures Corp 3089 E Fort Wayne Rd PO Box 350	Rochester	IN	46975	**800-662-5344**	574-223-4794	107
Manufacturers' Agents National Assn (MANA) 1 Spectrum Pointe Dr Suite 150	Lake Forest	CA	92630	**877-626-2776**	949-859-4040	49-18
Manufacturers Assn International. Fabricators & 833 Featherstone Rd	Rockford	IL	61107	**800-432-2832**	815-399-8700	49-13
Manufacturers Council. Nail 401 N Michigan Ave	Chicago	IL	60611	**800-868-4265**	312-245-1575	49-19
Manufacturers Group Inc 1084 Wellington Way PO Box 4310	Lexington	KY	40544	**800-264-3303**	859-223-6703	623-6
Manufacturers Life Insurance Co of New York 100 Summit Lake Dr 2nd Fl	Valhalla	NY	10595	**800-551-2078**	914-773-0708	384-2
Manufacturers Life Insurance Co USA 38500 N Woodward Ave Suite 325	Bloomfield Hills	MI	48304	**800-968-8761**	248-644-1444	384-2
Manufacturers. National Assn of 1331 Pennsylvania Ave NW Suite 600	Washington	DC	20004	**800-814-8468**	202-637-3000	49-12
Manufacturers & Traders Trust Co 1 M & T Plaza	Buffalo	NY	14203	**800-724-2440**	716-842-4470	71
Manufacturing & Consulting Services Inc 7633 E Acoma Dr Suite 104	Scottsdale	AZ	85260	**800-932-9329**	480-991-8700	176-5
Manufacturing Engineering Magazine 1 SME Dr	Dearborn	MI	48128	**800-733-4763**	313-271-1500	449-21
Manufacturing Engineers. Society of 1 SME Dr	Dearborn	MI	48121	**800-733-4763**	313-271-1500	49-13
Manufacturing Jewelers & Suppliers of America (MJSA) 45 Royal Little Dr.	Providence	RI	02904	**800-444-6572**	401-274-3840	49-4
Manufacturing Sciences. National Center for 3025 Boardwalk	Ann Arbor	MI	48108	**800-222-6267**	734-995-0300	654
Manufacturing Systems Magazine 2000 Clearwater Dr.	Oak Brook	IL	60523	**800-662-7776**	630-320-7000	449-7
Manufacturing Technology. Association for 7901 Westpark Dr	McLean	VA	22102	**800-524-0475**	703-893-2900	49-12
Manulife Financial Corp 200 Bloor St E *NYSE: MFC*	Toronto	ON	M4W1E5	**800-795-9767**	416-926-3000	355-4
Manulife New York 100 Summit Lake Dr 2nd Fl	Valhalla	NY	10595	**800-551-2078**	914-773-0708	384-2
Manzella Productions 80 Sonwil Dr	Buffalo	NY	14225	**800-645-6837**	716-681-8880	153-8
MAP International PO Box 215000	Brunswick	GA	31521	**800-225-8550**	912-265-6010	48-5
MAPA Spontex Inc 100 Spontex Dr *Cust Svc	Columbia	TN	38401	**800-537-2897***	931-388-5632	566
MAPEI Corp 1851 NW 22nd St	Fort Lauderdale	FL	33311	**800-426-2734**	954-485-8575	3
Mapes Industries Inc 2929 Cornhusker Hwy	Lincoln	NE	68504	**800-228-2391**	402-466-1985	688
MAPICS Inc 1000 Windward Concourse Pkwy Suite 100 *NASDAQ: MAPX*	Alpharetta	GA	30005	**888-362-7427**	678-319-8000	176-5
MapInfo Corp 1 Global View *NASDAQ: MAPS*	Troy	NY	12180	**800-552-2511**	518-285-6000	176-8
Maple City Ice Co Inc 371 Cleveland Rd *Cust Svc	Norwalk	OH	44857	**800-736-6091***	419-668-2531	82-1
Maple City Rubber Co 55 Newton St	Norwalk	OH	44857	**800-841-9434**	419-668-8261	750
Maple Donuts Inc 3455 E Market St	York	PA	17402	**800-627-5348**	717-757-7826	69
Maple Grove Farms of Vermont Inc 1052 Portland St	Saint Johnsbury	VT	05819	**800-525-2540**	802-748-5141	291-39
Maple Hill Farm Bed & Breakfast Inn 11 Inn Rd	Hallowell	ME	04330	**800-622-2708**	207-622-2708	373
Maple Hill Farms Inc 12 Burr Rd PO Box 767	Bloomfield	CT	06002	**800-243-0067**	860-242-9689	291-27
Maple Island Inc 2497 7th Ave E Suite 105	North Saint Paul	MN	55109	**800-369-1022**	651-773-1000	291-10
Maple Knoll Village 11100 Springfield Pike	Cincinnati	OH	45246	**800-789-6008**	513-782-2717	659
Maple Lee Flowers Inc 615 High St	Worthington	OH	43085	**800-414-0000**	614-885-5350	287
Maplehurst Inc 50 Maplehurst Dr	Brownsburg	IN	46112	**800-428-3200**	317-858-9000	291-2
Maples Industries Inc 2210 Moody Ridge Rd	Scottsboro	AL	35768	**800-537-3304**	256-259-1327	131
Maquoketa Valley Rural Electric Co-op PO Box 370	Anamosa	IA	52205	**800-927-6068**	319-462-3542	244
Mar-El Aviation Inc DBA Jet Air Jet Charter 547 Perimeter Rd Hanger 2 PO Box 178207	Nashville	TN	37217	**888-812-6604**	615-361-1007	14
Mar-Jac Poultry Inc PO Box 1017	Gainesville	GA	30503	**800-226-0561**	770-536-0561	608
Maradyne Corp 4540 W 160th St	Cleveland	OH	44135	**800-537-7444**	216-362-0755	15
Marakon Assoc 245 Park Ave 44th Fl	New York	NY	10167	**800-264-3000**	212-377-5000	193
Maranatha Baptist Bible College Inc 745 W Main St	Watertown	WI	53094	**800-622-2947**	920-261-9300	163
Marasco Newton Group Ltd 2801 Clarendon Blvd	Arlington	VA	22201	**800-486-0220**	703-516-9100	193
Marathon Enterprises Inc 66 E Union Ave	East Rutherford	NJ	07073	**800-722-7388**	201-935-3330	291-26
Marathon Equipment Co 909 County Hwy 9 S PO Box 1798	Vernon	AL	35592	**800-269-7237**	205-695-9105	379
Marathon (Greater) Chamber of Commerce 12222 Overseas Hwy	Marathon	FL	33050	**800-262-7284**	305-743-5417	137
Marathon Technologies Corp 295 Foster St	Littleton	MA	01460	**800-884-6425**	978-489-1100	174
Maravia Corp of Idaho 602 E 45th St	Boise	ID	83714	**800-223-7238**	208-322-4949	701
Marblelife Inc 805 W North Carrier Pkwy Suite 220	Grand Prairie	TX	75050	**800-627-4569**	972-623-0500	188-15
Marburger Farm Dairy Inc 1506 Mars Evans City Rd	Evans City	PA	16033	**800-331-1295**	724-538-4752	11-3
Marburn Stores Inc 225 Walker St *Cust Svc	Cliffside Park	NJ	07010	**888-627-2876***	201-943-0222	357

Name / Address	City	State	Zip	Toll-Free	Phone	Class
Marc Climatic Inc 1611 Elmview Dr	Houston	TX	77080	**800-397-0131**	713-464-8587	15
M/A/R/C Group 1660 NW Ridge Cir	Irving	TX	75038	**800-527-2680**	972-983-0400	458
MARC Promotions 7172 Lakeview Pkwy W Dr	Indianapolis	IN	46268	**800-422-8851**	317-290-3516	10
Marc Publishing Co 600 Germantown Pike Suite B	Lafayette Hill	PA	19444	**800-432-5478**	610-834-8585	623-6
Marc Resorts Hawaii 2155 Kalakaua Ave Suite 318	Honolulu	HI	96815	**800-535-0085**	808-926-5900	369
Marcal Paper Mills Inc 1 Market St	Elmwood Park	NJ	07407	**800-631-8451**	201-796-4000	547
MarCap Corp 20 N Wacker Dr Suite 2150	Chicago	IL	60606	**800-621-1677**	312-641-0233	214
Marcel Dekker Inc 270 Madison Ave *Sales	New York	NY	10016	**800-228-1160***	212-696-9000	623-2
Marcel Watch Corp/Oleg Cassini Watch Co 200 Meadowland Pkwy	Secaucus	NJ	07094	**800-422-6053**	201-330-5600	403
Marchon Eyewear Inc 35 Hub Dr	Melville	NY	11747	**800-645-1300**	631-755-2020	531
Marco 2640 Commerce Dr	Harrisburg	PA	17110	**800-232-1121**	717-545-1060	10
Marco Beach Ocean Resort 480 S Collier Blvd	Marco Island	FL	34145	**800-715-8517**	239-393-1400	655
Marco Crane & Rigging Co 221 S 35th Ave	Phoenix	AZ	85009	**800-668-2671**	602-272-2671	261-2
Marco Island Beach Resort. Hilton 560 S Collier Blvd	Marco Island	FL	34145	**800-443-4550**	239-394-5000	666
Marco Island Chamber of Commerce 1102 N Collier Blvd	Marco Island	FL	34145	**800-788-6272**	239-394-7549	137
MARCOA Publishing Inc 9955 Black Mountain Rd	San Diego	CA	92126	**800-854-2935**	858-695-9600	623-1
Marcone Appliance Parts Inc 2300 Clark Ave	Saint Louis	MO	63103	**800-325-7588**	314-231-7141	245
MARCOR Remediation Inc 246 Cockeysville Rd Suite 1	Hunt Valley	MD	21030	**800-547-0128**	410-785-0001	653
Marco's Pizza 5252 Monroe St	Toledo	OH	43623	**800-262-7267**	419-885-4844	657
Marcum & Kliegman LLP 130 Crossways Park Dr	Woodbury	NY	11797	**800-921-0777**	516-921-6000	2
Marcus Brothers Textiles Inc 980 Ave of the Americas	New York	NY	10018	**800-548-8295**	212-354-8700	583
Marcus Dairy Inc 3 Sugar Hollow Rd	Danbury	CT	06810	**800-243-2511**	203-748-5611	291-27
Marcus Theatres Corp 100 E Wisconsin Ave Suite 19 *Cust Svc	Milwaukee	WI	53202	**800-274-0099***	414-905-1000	733
Marden's Inc 184 College Ave	Waterville	ME	04901	**800-564-3337**	207-873-6111	778
Mares America Corp 1 Selleck St	Norwalk	CT	06855	**800-874-3236**	203-855-0631	701
Marfan Foundation. National 22 Manhasset Ave	Port Washington	NY	11050	**800-862-7326**	516-883-8712	48-17
Margaritaville Inc 424-A Fleming St	Key West	FL	33040	**800-262-6835**	305-296-9089	657
Margate on Winnipesaukee 76 Lake St	Laconia	NH	03246	**800-627-4283**	603-524-5210	655
Marglen Industries Inc 1748 Ward Mountain Rd NE	Rome	GA	30161	**800-627-4536**	706-295-5621	131
Mariah Foods 1333 Indiana Ave	Columbus	IN	47201	**800-227-6328**	812-378-3366	465
Marian College 3200 Cold Spring Rd	Indianapolis	IN	46222	**800-772-7264**	317-955-6000	163
Marian College of Fond du Lac 45 S National Ave	Fond du Lac	WI	54935	**800-262-7426**	920-923-7650	163
Marian Court College 35 Littles Pt Rd	Swampscott	MA	01907	**800-418-9868**	781-595-6768	160
Marian Heath Greeting Cards Inc 9 Kendrick Rd *Sales	Wareham	MA	02571	**800-338-3740***	508-291-0766	130
Mariani Ernest F Co Inc 614 W 600 South	Salt Lake City	UT	84104	**800-453-2927**	801-359-3744	651
Mariani Packing Co Inc 500 Crocker Dr	Vacaville	CA	95688	**800-231-1287**	707-452-2800	12-1
Marianjoy Rehabilitation Hospital & Clinics 26 W 171 Roosevelt Rd	Wheaton	IL	60187	**800-462-2371**	630-462-4000	366-4
Marie Callender Inc 27081 Aliso Creek Rd Suite 200	Aliso Viejo	CA	92656	**800-776-7437**	949-448-5300	657
Marie Claire Magazine 1790 Broadway 3rd Fl	New York	NY	10019	**800-777-3287**	212-649-5000	449-11
Marietta College 215 5th St	Marietta	OH	45750	**800-331-7896**	740-376-4643	163
Marietta Conference Center & Resort 500 Powder Springs St	Marietta	GA	30064	**888-685-2500**	770-427-2500	370
Marietta Corp 37 Huntington St	Cortland	NY	13045	**800-431-3023**	607-753-6746	10
Marietta Drapery & Window Coverings Co 22 Trammel St	Marietta	GA	30064	**800-241-7974**	770-428-3335	731
Marietta Memorial Hospital 401 Matthew St	Marietta	OH	45750	**800-523-3977**	740-374-1400	366-2
Marietta Structures Corp PO Box 653	Marietta	OH	45750	**800-633-9969**	740-373-3211	181
Marietta Times 700 Channel Ln	Marietta	OH	45750	**800-531-1215**	740-373-2121	522-2
Marijuana Anonymous World Services (MA) PO Box 2912	Van Nuys	CA	91404	**800-766-6779**		48-21
Marijuana Laws. National Organization for the Reform of 1600 K St NW Suite 501	Washington	DC	20006	**888-676-6765**	202-483-5500	48-8
Marimba Inc 440 Clyde Ave	Mountain View	CA	94043	**888-930-5282**	650-930-5282	176-1
Marin County Visitors Bureau 1013 Larkspur Landing Cir	Larkspur	CA	94939	**866-925-2060**	415-925-2060	205
Marin Independent Journal PO Box 6150	Novato	CA	94948	**800-782-5277**	415-883-8600	522-2
Marina Del Mar Resort & Marina 527 Caribbean Dr	Key Largo	FL	33037	**800-451-3483**	305-451-4107	373
Marina Dunes Resort 3295 Dunes Dr	Marina	CA	93933	**877-944-3863**	831-883-9478	373
Marina Suites 1117 Hwy 1	Dewey Beach	DE	19971	**888-777-3613**	302-227-1700	373
Marine Corps Assn (MCA) PO Box 1775	Quantico	VA	22134	**800-336-0291**	703-640-6161	48-19
Marine Corps League (MCL) PO Box 3070	Merrifield	VA	22116	**800-625-1775**	703-207-9588	48-19
Marine Corps Relief Society. Navy- 4015 Wilson Blvd 10th Fl	Arlington	VA	22203	**800-654-8364**	703-696-4904	48-19
Marine Corps Reserve Assn (MCRA) 337 Potomac Ave	Quantico	VA	22134	**800-927-6270**	703-630-3772	48-19
Marine Petroleum Trust 901 Main St Bank of America Plaza 17th Fl *NASDAQ: MARPS*	Dallas	TX	75202	**800-985-0794**	214-209-2310	662
Marine Surf Waikiki Hotel 364 Seaside Ave	Honolulu	HI	96815	**888-456-7873**	808-931-2424	373
Marine Surveyors. National Assn of PO Box 9306	Chesapeake	VA	23321	**800-822-6267**	757-638-9638	49-21
Marineland of Florida 9600 Ocean Shore Blvd	Marineland	FL	32080	**888-279-9194**	904-460-1275	40
Mariner Health Care Inc 1 Ravinia Dr Suite 1500	Atlanta	GA	30346	**800-929-4762**	678-443-7000	442
Mariners' Museum 100 Museum Dr	Newport News	VA	23606	**800-581-7245**	757-596-2222	509
Mario Industries Inc 2490 Paterson Ave SW	Roanoke	VA	24016	**800-458-1244**	540-342-1111	431
Marion Area (Greater) Chamber of Commerce 2305 W Main St	Marion	IL	62959	**800-699-1760**	618-997-6311	137
Marion Ceramics Inc Hwy 301 N	Marion	SC	29571	**800-845-4010**	843-423-1311	148
Marion County Chamber of Commerce 110 Adams St	Fairmont	WV	26554	**800-296-3379**	304-363-0442	137
Marion County International Raceway 2303 Richwood-LaRue Rd	La Rue	OH	43332	**800-422-6247**	740-499-3666	504
Marion Daily Republican PO Box 490	Marion	IL	62959	**800-238-3853**	618-993-2626	522-2
Marion-Grant County Convention & Visitors Bureau 217 S Adams St	Marion	IN	46952	**800-662-9474**	765-668-5435	205
Marion Military Institute 1101 Washington St	Marion	AL	36756	**800-664-1842**	334-683-2306	160
Marion Steel Co 912 Cheney Ave	Marion	OH	43302	**800-333-4011**	740-383-4011	709
Marisol Inc 213 W Union Ave	Bound Brook	NJ	08805	**877-627-4765**	732-469-5100	653
Maritime Administration 400 7th St SW *Hotline	Washington	DC	20590	**800-996-2723***	202-366-5812	336-13
Maritz Research Inc 1355 N Highway Dr	Fenton	MO	63099	**800-446-1690**	636-827-4000	458
Maritz Travel Co 1395 N Highway Dr	Fenton	MO	63099	**800-253-7562**	636-827-4000	377
MarJam Supply Co Inc 20 Rewe St	Brooklyn	NY	11211	**800-462-7526**	718-388-6465	359
Mark The 25 E 77th St	New York	NY	10021	**800-843-6275**	212-744-4300	373
Mark Andy Inc 18081 Chesterfield Airport Rd	Chesterfield	MO	63005	**800-700-6275**	636-532-4433	617
Mark Fore & Strike Inc 6500 Park of Commerce Blvd *Orders	Boca Raton	FL	33487	**800-327-3627***	561-241-1700	155-4
Mark Hershey Farms Inc 479 Horseshoe Pike	Lebanon	PA	17042	**888-801-3301**	717-867-4624	438
Mark Hopkins San Francisco. InterContinental 1 Nob Hill	San Francisco	CA	94108	**800-662-4455**	415-392-3434	373
Mark Master Inc 11111 N 46th St	Tampa	FL	33617	**800-441-6275**	813-988-6000	459
Mark Sand & Gravel Co PO Box 458	Fergus Falls	MN	56538	**800-427-8316**	218-736-7523	493-4
Mark Shale 10441 Beaudin Blvd Suite 100	Woodridge	IL	60517	**800-488-2686**	630-427-1100	155-4
Mark Spencer Hotel 409 SW 11th Ave	Portland	OR	97205	**800-548-3934**	503-224-3293	373
Mark Travel Corp 8907 N Port Washington Rd	Milwaukee	WI	53217	**800-558-3060**	414-228-7472	760
Mark Trece Inc 112 Connolly Rd	Fallston	MD	21047	**800-638-1464**	410-893-3903	770
Mark Twain Hotel 225 NE Adams St	Peoria	IL	61602	**866-325-6351**	309-676-3600	373
Mark Window Products Inc 2900 S Fairview St	Santa Ana	CA	92704	**800-427-4127**	714-641-1411	88
Markel Corp 435 School Ln	Plymouth Meeting	PA	19462	**800-462-4479**	610-272-8960	594-2
Markel Corp 4521 Highwoods Pkwy *NYSE: MKL*	Glen Allen	VA	23060	**800-446-6671**	804-747-0136	355-4
Markel Insurance Co 4600 Cox Rd	Glen Allen	VA	23060	**800-431-1270**	804-527-2700	384-4
Markel Insurance Co 4521 Highwoods Pkwy	Glen Allen	VA	23060	**800-446-6671**	804-747-0136	384-4
Markem Corp 150 Congress St PO Box 2100	Keene	NH	03431	**800-462-7536**	603-352-1130	459
Marker International 1070 W 2300 S	Salt Lake City	UT	84119	**800-453-3862**	801-972-2100	153-1
Market Central Inc 1650 Gum Branch Rd Suite A	Jacksonville	NC	28540	**888-773-3501**	910-937-0725	176-7
Market Data Retrieval 1 Forest Pkwy	Shelton	CT	06484	**800-333-8802**	203-926-4800	5
Market Decisions 50 W Rivercenter Blvd Suite 600	Covington	KY	41011	**800-248-2770**	859-905-4800	458
Market Scan Information Systems Inc 31416 Agoura Rd Suite 110	Westlake Village	CA	91361	**800-658-7226**	818-575-2000	176-10
Market Street Mortgage Corp PO Box 22128	Tampa	FL	33622	**800-669-3210**	727-724-7000	498
Market Transport Ltd 110 N Marine Dr	Portland	OR	97217	**800-547-0781**	503-283-2405	769
Market Wire Inc 5757 W Century Blvd 2nd Fl	Los Angeles	CA	90045	**800-774-9473**	310-846-3600	520
MarketAxess Holdings Inc 140 Broadway 42nd Fl *NASDAQ: MKTX*	New York	NY	10005	**877-638-0037**	212-813-6000	176-4
Marketers Assn. American Wholesale 2750 Prosperity Ave Suite 550	Fairfax	VA	22031	**800-482-2962**	703-208-3358	49-18
Marketing Analysts Inc 176 Croghan Spur Rd Suite 100	Charleston	SC	29407	**800-513-4247**	843-797-8900	458
Marketing Assn. American 311 S Wacker Dr Suite 5800	Chicago	IL	60606	**800-262-1150**	312-542-9000	49-18
Marketing Assn. Business 400 N Michigan Ave 15th Fl	Chicago	IL	60611	**800-664-4262**	312-822-0005	49-18
Marketing Assn. Livestock 10510 NW Ambassador Dr	Kansas City	MO	64153	**800-821-2048**	816-891-0502	48-2
Marketing Assn. Medical 74 New Montgomery St Suite 230	San Francisco	CA	94105	**800-551-2173**	415-764-4807	49-18
Marketing Assn. Retail Advertising & 325 7th St NW Suite 1100	Washington	DC	20004	**800-673-4692**	202-661-3052	49-18
Marketing. Association for Interactive 1430 Broadway 8th Fl	New York	NY	10018	**888-337-0008**	212-790-1406	48-9
Marketing Displays International 38271 W 12-Mile Rd *Sales	Farmington Hills	MI	48331	**800-228-8925***	248-553-1900	692
Marketing Innovators International Inc 9701 W Higgins Rd Suite 400	Rosemont	IL	60018	**800-633-8747**	847-696-1111	377
Marketing for Lawyers Newsletter 345 Park Ave S	New York	NY	10010	**800-888-8300**	212-779-9200	521-10
Marketing Library Services Newsletter 143 Old Marlton Pike	Medford	NJ	08055	**800-300-9868**	609-654-6266	521-10
Marketing Network. ABA 1120 Connecticut Ave NW	Washington	DC	20036	**800-226-5377**	202-663-5268	49-2

				Toll-Free	Phone	Class
Marketing News 311 S Wacker Dr Suite 5800	Chicago	IL	60606	800-262-1150	312-542-9000	449-5
Marketing & Planning Systems 201 Jones Rd	Waltham	MA	02451	800-696-6605	781-642-6277	458
Marketing Professional Services. Society for 99 Canal Center Plaza Suite 330	Alexandria	VA	22314	800-292-7677	703-549-6117	49-18
Marketing Research Services Inc 720 Pete Rose Way Suite 200	Cincinnati	OH	45202	800-729-6774	513-579-1555	458
Marketing Services. Association of Retail 10 Drs James Parker Blvd Suite 103	Red Bank	NJ	07701	866-231-6310	732-842-5070	49-18
Marketing Services Inc DBA Adventures Out West 15001 N 74th St	Scottsdale	AZ	85260	800-755-0935*	602-996-6100	748
*Resv						
Marketing Services. National Assn for Retail PO Box 906	Plover	WI	54467	888-526-2767	715-342-0948	49-18
Marketing Workshop Inc 3725 Da Vinci Ct Suite 200	Norcross	GA	30092	800-284-7707	770-449-6767	458
MarketingJobs.com 15275 Collier Blvd Suite 201	Naples	FL	34119	877-348-5627		257
Markhurd Corp 13400 68th Ave N	Minneapolis	MN	55311	800-627-4873	763-420-9606	713
MarkMonitor Inc 391 N Ancestor Pl	Boise	ID	83704	800-337-7520*	208-389-5740	389
*Cust Svc						
Mark's Work Warehouse 30-1035 64th Ave SE	Calgary	AB	T2H2J7	800-663-6275	403-692-7793	155-5
Marksman Products Inc 5482 Argosy Dr	Huntington Beach	CA	92649	800-822-8005	714-898-7535	279
Mark/Space Softworks 654 N Santa Cruz Ave Suite 300	Los Gatos	CA	95030	800-799-1718	408-293-7299	176-7
MarkWest Energy Partners LP 155 Inverness Dr W Suite 200	Englewood	CO	80112	800-730-8388	303-290-8700	586
AMEX: MWE						
MarkWest Hydrocarbon Inc 155 Inverness Dr W Suite 200	Englewood	CO	80112	800-730-8388	303-290-8700	527
AMEX: MWP						
Marlboro College 2582 South Rd PO Box A	Marlboro	VT	05344	800-343-0049	802-257-4333	163
Marlboro Electric Co-op Inc PO Box 1057	Bennettsville	SC	29512	800-922-9174	843-479-3855	244
Marley Cooling Technologies 7401 W 129th St	Overland Park	KS	66213	800-462-7539	913-664-7400	92
Marley Engineered Products 470 Beauty Spot Rd E	Bennettsville	SC	29512	800-452-4179	843-479-4006	37
Marley Mouldings Ltd Hwy 11 W Bearcreek Rd	Marion	VA	24354	800-368-3117	276-783-8161	304
Marlin Business Services Inc DBA Marlin Leasing Corp 124 Gaither Dr Suite 170	Mount Laurel	NJ	08054	888-479-9123	856-727-9526	261-3
NASDAQ: MRLN						
Marlin Firearms Co 100 Kenna Dr	North Haven	CT	06473	800-544-8892*	203-239-5621	279
*Cust Svc						
Marlin Hotel 1200 Collins Ave	Miami Beach	FL	33139	800-688-7678	305-604-5063	373
Marlin Leasing Corp 124 Gaither Dr Suite 170	Mount Laurel	NJ	08054	888-479-9123	856-727-9526	261-3
NASDAQ: MRLN						
Marlin Ralph & Co 1814 Dolphin Dr Suite A	Waukesha	WI	53186	800-922-8437	262-549-5100	153-13
Marmon Group Inc 225 W Washington St 19th Fl	Chicago	IL	60606	800-621-0386	312-372-9500	184
Marmon-Herrington Co 13001 Magisterial Dr	Louisville	KY	40223	800-227-0727	502-253-0277	60
Marmon/Keystone Corp PO Box 992	Butler	PA	16003	800-544-1748	724-283-3000	483
Marotta Controls Inc 78 Boonton Ave	Montville	NJ	07045	888-627-6882	973-334-7800	776
MarQueen Hotel 600 Queen Anne Ave N	Seattle	WA	98109	888-445-3076	206-282-7407	373
Marquesa Hotel 600 Fleming St	Key West	FL	33040	800-869-4631	305-292-1919	373
Marquette Country Convention & Visitors Bureau 2552 US Hwy 41 W Suite 300	Marquette	MI	49855	800-544-4321	906-228-7749	205
Marquette General Hospital 580 College Ave	Marquette	MI	49855	800-652-9752	906-228-9440	366-2
Marquette Hotel 710 Marquette Ave	Minneapolis	MN	55402	800-328-4782	612-333-4545	373
Marquette University 1442 W Wisconsin Ave	Milwaukee	WI	53233	800-222-6544	414-288-7700	163
Marquis Corp 596 Hoffman Rd	Independence	OR	97351	800-275-0888	503-838-0888	367
Marquis Theatre 211 W 45th St	New York	NY	10036	800-755-4000	212-307-4100	732
Marquis Who's Who 562 Central Ave	New Providence	NJ	07974	800-473-7020		623-2
Marriage Enrichment. Association for Couples in PO Box 10596	Winston-Salem	NC	27108	800-634-8325	336-724-1526	48-6
Marriage & Family Counselors. International Assn of c/o American Counseling Assn 5999 Stevenson Ave	Alexandria	VA	22304	800-545-2223	703-823-9800	49-15
Marriott Beach Resort. Key Largo Bay 103800 Overseas Hwy	Key Largo	FL	33037	866-849-3753	305-453-0000	655
Marriott Conference Centers 1 Marriott Dr	Washington	DC	20058	800-453-0309	301-380-3000	369
Marriott Conference Hotel. Ashman Court 111 W Main St	Midland	MI	48642	877-645-3643	989-839-0500	370
Marriott Conference Hotel. Hickory Ridge 1195 Summerhill Dr	Lisle	IL	60532	800-334-0344	630-971-5000	370
Marriott Conference Hotel. Lafayette Yard 1 W Lafayette St	Trenton	NJ	08608	800-228-9290	609-421-4000	370
Marriott Conference Hotel at the University of Cincinnati. Kingsgate 151 Goodman Dr	Cincinnati	OH	45219	800-228-9290	513-487-3800	370
Marriott Conference Resort. Evergreen 4021 Lakeview Dr	Stone Mountain	GA	30083	800-228-9290	770-879-9900	370
Marriott Coronado Island Resort 2000 2nd St	Coronado	CA	92118	800-228-9290	619-435-3000	655
Marriott Golf & Yacht Club Bay Point Resort Village 4200 Marriott Dr	Panama City Beach	FL	32408	800-874-7105	850-236-6000	655
Marriott Harbor Beach Resort & Spa 3030 Holiday Dr	Fort Lauderdale	FL	33316	800-228-9290	954-525-4000	655
Marriott Hotels Resorts & Suites 1 Marriott Dr	Washington	DC	20058	800-228-9290	301-380-3000	369
Marriott Hotels Rewards Program 310 Bearcat Dr	Salt Lake City	UT	84115	800-450-4442*	800-249-0800	371
*Sales						
Marriott Hutchinson Island Beach Resort & Marina 555 NE Ocean Blvd	Stuart	FL	34996	800-775-5936	772-225-3700	655
Marriott International Inc 1 Marriott Dr	Washington	DC	20058	800-228-9290	301-380-3000	369
NYSE: MAR						
Courtyard by Marriott 1 Marriott Dr	Washington	DC	20058	800-321-2211	301-380-3000	369
ExecuStay Corp 7595 Rickenbacker Dr	Gaithersburg	MD	20879	888-840-7829	301-212-9660	209
Fairfield Inn by Marriott 1 Marriott Dr	Washington	DC	20058	800-228-9290	301-380-3000	369
Marriott Conference Centers 1 Marriott Dr	Washington	DC	20058	800-453-0309	301-380-3000	369
Marriott Hotels Resorts & Suites 1 Marriott Dr	Washington	DC	20058	800-228-9290	301-380-3000	369
Renaissance Hotels 1 Marriott Dr	Washington	DC	20058	800-638-8108	301-380-3000	369
Residence Inn by Marriott 1 Marriott Dr	Washington	DC	20058	800-638-8108	301-380-3000	369
SpringHill Suites by Marriott 1 Marriott Dr	Washington	DC	20058	800-228-9290	301-380-3000	369
TownePlace Suites by Marriott 1 Marriott Dr	Washington	DC	20058	800-228-9290	301-380-3000	369
Marriott International PAC 1 Marriott Dr	Washington	DC	20058	800-228-9290	301-380-3000	604
Marriott Kaua'i Resort & Beach Club 3610 Rice St	Lihue	HI	96766	800-220-2925	808-245-5050	655
Marriott Kingsgate Conference Hotel at University of Cincinnati 151 Goodman Dr	Cincinnati	OH	45219	800-228-9290	513-487-3800	370
Marriott Marco Island Resort Golf Club & Spa 400 S Collier Blvd	Marco Island	FL	34145	800-438-4373	239-394-2511	655
Marriott Maui Resort 100 Nohea Kai Dr	Lahaina	HI	96761	800-763-1333	808-667-1200	655
Marriott MeadowView Conference Resort & Convention Center 1901 Meadowview Pkwy	Kingsport	TN	37660	800-820-5055	423-578-6600	370
Marriott Mountain Resort at Vail 715 W Lionshead Cir	Vail	CO	81657	800-648-0720	970-476-4444	655
Marriott Resort & Beach Club. Sawgrass 1000 PGA Tour Blvd	Ponte Vedra Beach	FL	32082	800-457-4653	904-285-7777	655
Marriott Resort & Convention Center. Orlando World Center 8701 World Ctr Dr	Orlando	FL	32821	800-621-0638	407-239-4200	655
Marriott Resort Ihilani. JW 92-1001 Olani St	Kapolei	HI	96707	800-626-4446	808-679-0079	655
Marriott Resort. Laguna Cliffs 25135 Park Lantern	Dana Point	CA	92629	800-228-9290	949-661-5000	655
Marriott Resort & Spa. Desert Springs 74855 Country Club Dr	Palm Desert	CA	92260	800-331-3112	760-341-2211	655
Marriott Resort & Spa. Rancho Las Palmas 41000 Bob Hope Dr	Rancho Mirage	CA	92270	800-458-8786	760-568-2727	655
Marriott Resort & Spa. Seaview 401 S New York Rd	Galloway	NJ	08205	800-228-9290	609-652-1800	655
Marriott San Jose 301 S Market St	San Jose	CA	95113	800-314-0928	408-280-1300	373
Marriott Vacation Club International 10400 Fernwood Rd	Bethesda	MD	20817	800-845-5279	301-380-3000	738
Marriott West Palm Beach 1001 Okeechobee Blvd	West Palm Beach	FL	33401	800-376-2292	561-833-1234	373
Marriott Westfields Resort & Conference Center 14750 Conference Center Dr	Chantilly	VA	20151	800-635-5666	703-818-0300	370
Marriott's Beachplace Towers 21 S Fort Lauderdale Beach Blvd	Fort Lauderdale	FL	33316	800-854-5279	954-525-4440	373
Marriott's Grand Hotel Resort & Golf Club 1 Grand Blvd	Point Clear	AL	36564	800-544-9933	251-928-9201	655
Marriott's Griffin Gate Resort 1800 Newtown Pike	Lexington	KY	40511	800-228-9290	859-231-5100	655
Marriott's Lincolnshire Resort 10 Marriott Dr	Lincolnshire	IL	60069	800-228-9290	847-634-0100	655
Marriton Limousine 13900 N IH-35 Suite J	Austin	TX	78728	800-940-7007	512-329-7007	433
Marrow Donor Program. National 3001 Broadway St NE Suite 500	Minneapolis	MN	55413	800-526-7809	612-627-5800	48-17
Mars Advertising Co Inc 2377 Southfield Rd	Southfield	MI	48075	800-521-9317	248-936-2200	4
Mars Electric Co 38868 Mentor Ave	Willoughby	OH	44094	800-288-6277	440-946-2250	245
Mars Electronics International (MEI) 1301 Wilson Dr	West Chester	PA	19380	800-345-8215*	610-430-2500	55
*Cust Svc						
Mars Hill College 100 Athletics St	Mars Hill	NC	28754	866-642-4968	828-689-1201	163
Mars Supermarkets Inc 3401 E Federal St	Baltimore	MD	21213	888-284-7773	410-342-0197	339
Marseilles Hotel 1741 Collins Ave	Miami Beach	FL	33139	800-327-4739	305-538-5711	373
Marsh Bellofram Corp SR 2 PO Box 305	Newell	WV	26050	800-727-5646	304-387-1200	321
Marsh Electronics Inc 1563 S 101st St	Milwaukee	WI	53214	800-558-1238*	414-475-6000	245
*Cust Svc						
Marsh Furniture Co Inc 1001 S Centennial St	High Point	NC	27260	800-756-2774	336-884-7363	116
Marsh Ridge Resort 4815 Old US Hwy 27 S	Gaylord	MI	49735	800-743-7529	989-732-5552	655
Marshall AW Co PO Box 16127	Salt Lake City	UT	84116	800-273-4713	801-328-4713	744
Marshall Concrete Products Inc 1088 Industrial Ave	Danville	VA	24541	800-537-5884	434-792-1233	181

Name / Address	City	State	ZIP	Toll-Free	Phone	Class
Marshall DeKalb Electric Co-op PO Box 724	Boaz	AL	35957	**800-239-3692**	256-593-4262	244
Marshall Durbin Food Corp 2830 Commerce Blvd	Irondale	AL	35210	**800-768-2456**	205-956-3505	11-8
Marshall Field's Travel Service 700 Nicollet Mall	Minneapolis	MN	55402	**800-316-6166**	612-375-2884	760
Marshall Funds PO Box 1348	Milwaukee	WI	53201	**800-236-3863**		517
Marshall Gas Controls Inc 1000 Civic Center Loop	San Marcos	TX	78666	**800-447-9513**	512-396-2257	776
Marshall (Greater) Chamber of Commerce 213 W Austin St	Marshall	TX	75670	**800-953-7868**	903-935-7868	137
Marshall & Ilsley Corp 770 N Water St *NYSE: MI*	Milwaukee	WI	53202	**800-342-2265**	414-765-7801	355-2
Marshall Independent PO Box 411	Marshall	MN	56258	**800-640-6148**	507-537-1551	522-2
Marshall Miller & Schroeder Inc 150 S 5th St Suite 3000	Minneapolis	MN	55402	**800-328-6122**	612-376-1500	679
Marshall Pottery 4901 Elysian Fields Rd	Marshall	TX	75670	**888-768-8721**	903-927-5400	330
Marshall & Sterling Inc 110 Main St	Poughkeepsie	NY	12601	**800-333-3766**	845-454-0800	383
Marshall & Swift 911 Wilshire Blvd Suite 1600	Los Angeles	CA	90017	**800-544-2678**	213-683-9000	176-10
Marshall & Swift/Boeckh 2885 S Calhoun Rd	New Berlin	WI	53151	**800-205-1288**	262-780-2800	380
Marshalltown Co 104 S 8th Ave	Marshalltown	IA	50158	**800-888-0127**	641-753-5999	746
Marshfield Convention & Visitors Bureau 700 S Central Ave	Marshfield	WI	54449	**800-422-4541**	715-384-3454	205
Marshfield News-Herald PO Box 70	Marshfield	WI	54449	**800-967-2087**	715-384-3131	522-2
Marshmallow Cone Co 5141 Fischer Pl	Cincinnati	OH	45217	**800-641-8551**	513-641-2345	291-8
Marsico Funds PO Box 3210	Milwaukee	WI	53201	**888-860-8686**		517
Marta Track Constructors Inc 4390 Imeson Rd	Jacksonville	FL	32219	**888-250-5746**		187-8
Martec Pharmaceutical Inc 1800 N Topping	Kansas City	MO	64120	**800-822-6782**	816-241-4144	573
Martek Biosciences Corp 6480 Dobbin Rd *NASDAQ: MATK*	Columbia	MD	21045	**888-652-7246**	410-740-0081	86
Marten House Hotel & Lilly Conference Center 1801 W 86th St	Indianapolis	IN	46260	**800-736-5634**	317-872-4111	370
Marten Transport Ltd 129 Marten St *NASDAQ: MRTN*	Mondovi	WI	54755	**800-395-3000**	715-926-4216	769
Martha Stewart Living Magazine 11 W 42nd St	New York	NY	10036	**800-999-6518**	212-827-8000	449-11
Martha Washington Inn 150 W Main St	Abingdon	VA	24210	**800-555-8000**	276-628-3161	373
Martha's Vineyard & Nantucket Reservations 73 Lagoon Pond Rd	Vineyard Haven	MA	02568	**800-649-5671**	508-693-7200	368
Martin Archery Inc 3134 W Hwy 12	Walla Walla	WA	99362	**800-541-8902**	509-529-2554	701
Martin Aviation 19300 Ike Jones Rd	Santa Ana	CA	92707	**800-793-9191**	714-210-2945	25
Martin Brothers Container & Timber Products Corp 747 Lindell St PO Box 87	Martin	TN	38237	**800-426-6984**	731-587-3171	199
Martin Color-Fi Inc 320 Neeley St	Sumter	SC	29150	**800-843-6382**	803-436-4200	594-1
Martin County Travel & Tourism Authority 100 E Church St	Williamston	NC	27892	**800-776-8566**	252-792-6605	205
Martin Engineering 1 Martin Pl	Neponset	IL	61345	**800-544-2947**	309-594-2384	206
Martin Fireproofing Corp PO Box 27 Kenmore Stn	Buffalo	NY	14217	**800-766-3969**	716-692-3680	181
Martin Furniture 7757 St Andrews Ave	San Diego	CA	92154	**800-268-5669**	619-671-5100	314-1
Martin Glass Co Inc 25 Center Plaza	Belleville	IL	62220	**800-325-1946**	618-277-1946	62-2
Martin Guitar Co 510 Sycamore St	Nazareth	PA	18064	**800-345-3103**	610-759-2837	516
Martin Howard Inc 4315 Meyer Rd	Fort Wayne	IN	46806	**800-348-4759**	260-447-5591	769
Martin JB Co 10 E 53rd St	New York	NY	10022	**800-223-0525**	212-421-2020	730-1
Martin LP Gas Inc 2606 N Longview St	Kilgore	TX	75662	**800-441-8569**	903-984-0781	311
Martin Marietta Magnesia Specialties Inc 195 Chesapeake Pk Plaza Suite 200	Baltimore	MD	21220	**800-648-7400**	410-780-5500	141
Martin Methodist College 433 W Madison St	Pulaski	TN	38478	**800-467-1273**	931-363-9804	160
Martin Petersen Co Inc 9800 55th St	Kenosha	WI	53144	**800-677-1326**	262-658-1326	188-10
Martin-Senour Paints 101 Prospect Ave NW	Cleveland	OH	44115	**800-542-8468**	216-566-2000	540
Martin Stanley Cos Inc 1881 Campus Commons Dr Suite 101	Reston	VA	20191	**800-446-4807**	703-715-7800	639
Martin Supply Co 200 Appleton Ave	Sheffield	AL	35660	**800-828-8116**		378
Martin Tractor Co Inc 1737 SW 42nd St	Topeka	KS	66609	**800-666-5770**	785-266-5770	353
Martin Trucking Inc PO Box M	Hugoton	KS	67951	**800-737-0047**	620-544-4920	769
Martin University 2171 Avondale Pl	Indianapolis	IN	46218	**866-344-3114**	317-543-3235	163
Martin Wells Industries PO Box 01406	Los Angeles	CA	90001	**800-421-6000**	323-581-6266	128
Martin Wheel Co Inc 342 West Ave	Tallmadge	OH	44278	**800-462-7846**	330-633-3278	739
Martin-Williams Advertising 60 S 6th St Suite 2800	Minneapolis	MN	55402	**800-632-1388**	612-340-0800	4
Martinair 5550 Glades Rd Suite 600	Boca Raton	FL	33431	**800-627-8462**	561-391-6165	26
Martinair Holland Cargo 5550 Glades Rd Suite 600	Boca Raton	FL	33431	**800-366-3734**	561-391-1313	13
MartinAire Partners LP 4745 Frank Luke Dr	Addison	TX	75001	**800-282-3828**	972-349-5700	13
Martina's Flowers & Gifts 3830 Washington Rd West Town Market Sq	Martinez	GA	30907	**800-927-1204**	706-863-7172	287
Martin/Decker Totco Instrumentation Inc 1200 Cypress Creek Rd	Cedar Park	TX	78613	**800-423-3319**	512-340-5000	526
Martinique Promotion Bureau 444 Madison Ave 16th Fl	New York	NY	10022	**800-391-4909**		764
Martin's Herend Imports Inc 21440 Pacific Blvd	Sterling	VA	20167	**800-643-7363**	703-450-1601	716
Martin's Pastry Shop Inc 1000 Potato Roll Ln *Cust Svc	Chambersburg	PA	17201	**800-548-1200***	717-263-9580	291-35
Martin's Potato Chips Inc 5847 Lincoln Hwy W	Thomasville	PA	17364	**800-272-4477**	717-792-3565	291-35
Martins Run 11 Martins Run	Media	PA	19063	**800-327-3875**	610-353-7660	659
Martinsburg-Berkeley County Chamber of Commerce 198 Viking Way	Martinsburg	WV	25401	**800-332-9007**	304-267-4841	137
Martinsville Bulletin PO Box 3711	Martinsville	VA	24115	**800-234-6575**	276-638-8801	522-2
Martinsville-Henry County Chamber of Commerce 115 Broad St	Martinsville	VA	24112	**866-632-3378**	276-632-6401	137
Martori Farms 7332 E Butherus Dr	Scottsdale	AZ	85260	**800-627-8674**	480-998-1444	310-4
Martrex Inc 14525 Hwy 7	Minnetonka	MN	55345	**800-328-3627**	952-933-5000	272
Marty's Shoes Inc 60 Enterprise Ave N *Cust Svc	Secaucus	NJ	07094	**800-262-7897***	201-319-0500	296
Marvel Abrasive Products Inc 6230 S Oak Park Ave	Chicago	IL	60638	**800-621-0673**	773-586-8700	1
Marvel Enterprises Inc 417 5th Ave *NYSE: MVL*	New York	NY	10016	**800-217-9158**	212-576-4000	750
Marvel Group Corp 3843 W 43rd St *Cust Svc	Chicago	IL	60632	**800-621-8846***	773-523-4804	314-1
Marvel Screw Machine Products 58 Lafayette St	Waterbury	CT	06708	**800-394-6767**	203-756-7058	610
Marvell Semiconductor Inc 700 1st Ave	Sunnyvale	CA	94089	**800-752-3334**	408-222-2500	174
Marvelwood School 476 Skiff Mountain Rd PO Box 3001	Kent	CT	06757	**800-440-9107**	860-927-0047	611
Marvin & Palmer Assoc Inc 1201 N Market St Suite 2300	Wilmington	DE	19801	**800-775-4259**	302-573-3570	393
Marvin WB Mfg Co 211 Glenn Ave	Urbana	OH	43078	**800-733-1706**	937-653-7131	37
Marvin Windows & Doors 104 State Ave N	Warroad	MN	56763	**800-346-5044**	218-386-1430	234
Marvy William Co Inc 1540 St Clair Ave	Saint Paul	MN	55105	**800-874-2651**	651-698-0726	78
Marwas Steel Co DBA Laurel Steel Products Co 1 Mount Pleasant Rd	Scottdale	PA	15683	**800-426-1983**	724-887-8090	482
Marx Hotel & Conference Center 701 E Genesee St	Syracuse	NY	13210	**877-843-6279**	315-479-7000	373
MARX International Inc 2900 Chamblee-Tucker Rd Bldg 9 Suite 100	Atlanta	GA	30341	**800-627-9468**	770-986-8887	176-12
Mary Ann Liebert Publishers Inc 140 Huguenot St 3rd Fl	New Rochelle	NY	10801	**800-654-3237**	914-740-2100	623-9
Mary Baldwin College PO Box 1500	Staunton	VA	24402	**800-468-2262**	540-887-7019	163
Mary Free Bed Hospital & Rehabilitation Center 235 Wealthy St SE	Grand Rapids	MI	49503	**800-528-8989**	616-242-0300	366-4
Mary Imogene Bassett Hospital 1 Atwell Rd	Cooperstown	NY	13326	**800-227-7388**	607-547-3456	366-2
Mary Kay Inc 16251 Dallas Pkwy *Cust Svc	Addison	TX	75001	**800-627-9529***	972-687-6300	211
Mary Kay Inc Mfg Group 1330 Regal Row *Cust Svc	Dallas	TX	75247	**800-627-9529***	972-687-6300	211
Mary Maxim Inc 2001 Holland Ave PO Box 5019	Port Huron	MI	48061	**800-962-9504**	810-987-2000	451
Mary of Puddin Hill Inc 201 E I-30 *Orders	Greenville	TX	75403	**800-545-8889***	903-455-2651	291-1
Marygrove College 8425 W McNichols Rd	Detroit	MI	48221	**866-313-1927**	313-927-1200	163
Maryland						
Aging Dept 301 W Preston St Rm 1007	Baltimore	MD	21201	**800-243-3425**	410-767-1100	335
Bill Status 90 State Cir	Annapolis	MD	21401	**800-492-7122**	410-946-5400	425
Chief Medical Examiner 111 Penn St	Baltimore	MD	21201	**800-833-6263**	410-333-3250	335
Child Support Enforcement Administration 311 W Saratoga St	Baltimore	MD	21201	**800-332-6347**	410-767-7674	335
Criminal Injuries Compensation Board 6776 Reisterstown Rd Suite 312	Baltimore	MD	21215	**888-679-9347**	410-585-3010	335
Emergency Management Agency 5401 Rue Saint Lo Dr	Reisterstown	MD	21136	**877-636-2872**	410-517-3600	335
Health & Mental Hygiene Dept 201 W Preston St 5th Fl	Baltimore	MD	21201	**877-463-3464**	410-767-6500	335
Higher Education Commision 839 Bestgate Rd Suite 400	Annapolis	MD	21401	**800-974-0203**	410-260-4500	335
Public Service Commission 6 Saint Paul St 16th Fl	Baltimore	MD	21202	**800-492-0474**	410-767-8000	335
Rehabilitation Services Div 2301 Argonne Dr	Baltimore	MD	21218	**888-554-0334**	410-554-9385	335
State Forest & Park Service 580 Taylor Ave Rm E-3 *Campground Resv	Annapolis	MD	21401	**888-432-2267***	410-260-8186	335
Student Financial Assistance Office 839 Bestgate Rd Suite 400	Annapolis	MD	21401	**800-974-1024**	410-260-4565	711
Tourism Development Office 217 E Redwood St 9th Fl	Baltimore	MD	21202	**800-543-1036**	410-767-3400	335
Treasurer 80 Calvert St Rm 109	Annapolis	MD	21401	**800-974-0468**	410-260-7533	335
Veterans Affairs Dept 31 Hopkins Plaza Rm 110	Baltimore	MD	21201	**800-446-4926**	410-333-4428	335
Vital Records Div 6550 Reisterstown Rd	Baltimore	MD	21215	**800-832-3277**	410-764-3038	335
Maryland Assn of Realtors 2594 Riva Rd	Annapolis	MD	21401	**800-638-6425**	410-841-6080	642
Maryland Bar Journal 520 W Fayette St	Baltimore	MD	21201	**800-492-1964**	410-685-7878	449-15
Maryland Cork Co Inc PO Box 126	Elkton	MD	21922	**800-662-2675**	410-398-2955	208
Maryland Inn 58 State Cir	Annapolis	MD	21401	**800-847-8882**	410-263-2641	373
Maryland Match Corp 605 Alluvion St	Baltimore	MD	21230	**800-423-0013**	410-752-8164	461
Maryland Plastics Inc 251 E Central Ave *Cust Svc	Federalsburg	MD	21632	**800-544-5582***	410-754-5566	596
Maryland Public Television (MPT) 11767 Owings Mills Blvd	Owings Mills	MD	21117	**800-223-3678**	410-356-5600	620

Listing	Toll-Free	Phone	Class
Maryland Quality Meats Inc 701 W Hamburg St, Baltimore MD 21230	**800-368-2579**	410-539-7055	292-9
Maryland State Bar Assn Inc 520 W Fayette St, Baltimore MD 21201	**800-492-1964**	410-685-7878	73
Maryland State Medical Society 1211 Cathedral St, Baltimore MD 21201	**800-492-1056**	410-539-0872	466
Maryland Veterinary Medical Assn 8015 Corporate Dr Suite A, Baltimore MD 21236	**888-884-6862**	410-931-3332	782
Maryland & Virginia Milk Producers Co-op Assn Inc 1985 Isaac Newton Sq W, Reston VA 20190	**800-552-1976**	703-742-6800	292-4
Marylhurst University 17600 Pacific Hwy PO Box 261, Marylhurst OR 97036	**800-634-9982**	503-636-8141	163
Marymount College 100 Marymount Ave, Tarrytown NY 10591	**800-724-4312**	914-332-8295	163
Marymount Manhattan College 221 E 71st St, New York NY 10021	**800-627-9668**	212-517-0400	163
Marymount University 2807 N Glebe Rd, Arlington VA 22207	**800-548-7638**	703-522-5600	163
Maryville College 502 E Lamar Alexander Pkwy, Maryville TN 37804	**800-597-2687**	865-981-8000	163
Maryville Daily Forum PO Box 188, Maryville MO 64468	**800-582-7863**	660-562-2424	522-2
Maryville University of Saint Louis 13550 Conway Rd, Saint Louis MO 63141	**800-627-9855**	314-529-9300	163
Marywood University 2300 Adams Ave, Scranton PA 18509	**866-279-9663**	570-348-6234	163
MAS Funds 100 Front St Suite 1100, West Conshohocken PA 19428	**800-354-8185**	610-940-5000	517
Mashantucket Pequot Gaming Enterprise Inc PO Box 3777, Mashantucket CT 06338	**800-752-9244**	860-312-3000	132
Masland Carpets Inc 716 Bill Myles Dr, Saraland AL 36571	**800-633-0468**	251-675-9080	131
Mason Candlelight Co 8729 Aviation Blvd, Inglewood CA 90301	**800-556-2766**		122
Mason City Convention & Visitors Bureau PO Box 1128, Mason City IA 50402	**800-423-5724**	641-422-1663	205
Mason Contractors Assn of America (MCAA) 33 S Roselle Rd, Schaumburg IL 60193	**800-536-2225**	847-301-0001	49-3
Mason Controls 13955 Balboa Blvd, Sylmar CA 91342	**800-232-7700**	818-361-3366	494
Mason & Hanger Group Inc 300 W Vine St Suite 1300, Lexington KY 40507	**800-586-2766**	859-252-9980	258
Mason Wells 770 N Water St 11th Fl, Milwaukee WI 53202	**800-342-2265**	414-765-7800	394
Masonite Holdings Inc 1 N Dale Mabry Hwy Suite 950, Tampa FL 33609	**800-895-2723**	813-877-2726	234
Masonry Institute. International James Brice House 42 East St, Annapolis MD 21401	**800-803-0295**	410-280-1305	49-3
Mass Electric Construction Co 180 Guest St, Boston MA 02135	**800-933-6322**	617-254-1015	188-4
Mass Marketing Inc 401 Isom Bldg 100, San Antonio TX 78216	**800-279-1149**	210-344-1960	339
Massachusetts			
Bill Status 1 Ashburton Pl Rm 1611, Boston MA 02108	**800-392-6090**	617-727-7030	425
Child Support Enforcement Div 51 Sleeper St 3rd Fl, Boston MA 02205	**800-332-2733**	617-626-4170	335
Educational Financing Authority 125 Summer St, Boston MA 02110	**800-449-6332**	617-261-9760	711
Elder Affairs Office 1 Ashburton Pl 5th Fl, Boston MA 02108	**800-243-4636**	617-727-7750	335
State Government Information, MA	**866-888-2808**		335
Travel & Tourism Office 10 Park Plaza Suite 4510, Boston MA 02116	**800-227-6277**	617-973-8500	335
Massachusetts Assn of Realtors 256 2nd Ave, Waltham MA 02451	**800-725-6272**	781-890-3700	642
Massachusetts Bar Assn 20 West St, Boston MA 02111	**866-627-7577**	617-338-0500	73
Massachusetts College of Pharmacy & Health Sciences 179 Longwood Ave, Boston MA 02115	**800-225-5506**	617-732-2800	163
Massachusetts Dental Society 2 Willow St Suite 200, Southborough MA 01745	**800-943-9200**	508-480-9797	225
Massachusetts Electric Co 25 Research Dr, Westborough MA 01582	**800-322-3223**	508-389-2000	774
Massachusetts Maritime Academy 101 Academy Dr, Buzzards Bay MA 02532	**800-544-3411**	508-830-5000	163
Massachusetts Medical Society 860 Winter St, Waltham MA 02451	**800-322-2303**	781-893-4610	466
Massachusetts Mutual Life Insurance Co 1295 State St, Springfield MA 01111	**800-272-2216**	413-788-8411	384-2
Massage Center at Mohonk Mountain House 1000 Mountain Rest Rd, New Paltz NY 12561	**800-772-6646**	845-256-2751	698
Massage Professionals. Associated Bodywork & 1271 Sugarbush Dr, Evergreen CO 80439	**800-458-2267**	303-674-8478	48-17
Massanutten Regional Library 174 S Main St, Harrisonburg VA 22801	**877-695-4272**	540-434-4475	426
MASSBANK 123 Haven St, Reading MA 01867	**800-447-1052**	781-662-0100	71
MASSBANK Corp 123 Haven St, Reading MA 01867 *NASDAQ: MASB*	**800-447-1052**	781-662-0100	355-2
Massey Services Inc 610 N Wymore Rd, Maitland FL 32751	**800-432-1820**	407-645-2500	567
Massillon Community Hospital 875 8th St NE, Massillon OH 44646	**800-346-4869**	330-832-8761	366-2
MassMutual Funds 1295 State St, Springfield MA 01111	**800-542-6767**	413-788-8411	517
MassMutual PAC 1295 State St, Springfield MA 01111	**800-272-2216**	413-788-8411	604
Masson Alex R Inc 12819 198th St, Linwood KS 66052	**800-444-6210**	913-301-3281	363
MAST (MAST Vacation Partners Inc) 17 W 635 Butterfield Rd Suite 150, Oakbrook Terrace IL 60181	**888-305-3951**	630-889-9817	761
MAST Vacation Partners Inc (MAST) 17 W 635 Butterfield Rd Suite 150, Oakbrook Terrace IL 60181	**888-305-3951**	630-889-9817	761
MasTec Energy Services Inc 209 Art Bryan Dr PO Box 1, Asheboro NC 27204	**800-672-5853**	336-672-1244	187-10
Master Appliance Corp 2420 18th St, Racine WI 53403	**800-558-9413**	262-633-7791	747
Master-Bilt Products 908 Hwy 15 N, New Albany MS 38652	**800-647-1284**	662-534-9061	15
Master Builders 23700 Chagrin Blvd, Beachwood OH 44122	**800-628-9990**	216-839-7500	143
Master Chemical Corp PO Box 10001, Perrysburg OH 43552 *Sales	**800-874-6329***	419-874-7902	530

Listing	Toll-Free	Phone	Class
Master Distributors Inc 1220 Olympic Blvd, Santa Monica CA 90404	**800-421-8153**	310-452-1229	245
Master Finish Co 2020 Nelson Ave SE, Grand Rapids MI 49507	**888-372-2913**	616-245-1228	472
Master Hosts Inns & Resorts 1726 Montreal Cir, Tucker GA 30084	**800-247-4677**	770-270-1180	369
Master Industries Inc 14420 Myford Rd, Irvine CA 92606 *Cust Svc	**800-854-3794***	949-660-0644	701
Master Lock Co 137 W Forest Hills Ave, Oak Creek WI 53154	**800-308-9242**	414-571-5625	345
Master Mark Plastic Products Inc PO Box 662, Albany MN 56307 *Cust Svc	**800-535-4838***	320-845-2111	420
Master Nursery Garden Centers Inc 2211 Olympic Blvd, Walnut Creek CA 94595	**800-576-5102**	925-934-1144	318
Master Pitching Machine 4200 NE Birmingham Rd, Kansas City MO 64117	**800-878-8228**	816-452-0228	701
Masterack-Crown Inc 4171 B Lincolnway E, Wooster OH 44691 *Cust Svc	**800-321-4934***	330-262-6010	60
MasterCard International Inc 2000 Purchase St, Purchase NY 10577	**800-247-4623**	914-249-2000	213
Mastercard/Cirrus ATM Network 2200 Mastercard Blvd, O'Fallon MO 63366	**800-300-3069**	636-722-6100	70
Masterchem Industries 3135 Hwy M, Imperial MO 63052	**800-325-3552**	636-942-2510	540
MasterCraft Boat Co 100 Cherokee Cove Dr, Vonore TN 37885	**800-443-8774**	423-884-2221	91
Mastercraft Inc PO Box 326, Shipshewana IN 46565	**800-522-5652**	260-768-4101	315
MasterCuts Div Regis Corp 7201 Metro Blvd, Minneapolis MN 55439	**888-888-7778**	952-947-7777	79
Masterfit Golf Ltd 4128 S 3rd St, Jacksonville Beach FL 32250	**888-501-7834**	904-246-3100	701
Masterfoods USA 800 High St, Hackettstown NJ 07840	**800-222-0293**	908-852-1000	291-8
Masterpiece Studios 2080 Lookout Dr Box 8240, North Mankato MN 56002	**800-447-0219**	507-388-8788	130
Master's College 21726 Placerita Canyon Rd, Santa Clarita CA 91321	**800-568-6248**	661-259-3540	163
Masters of Design 81 John Dietsch Blvd PO Box 2719, Attleboro Falls MA 02763	**800-542-3728**	508-695-0201	401
Masters Gallery Foods Inc 328 County Hwy PP, Plymouth WI 53073	**800-236-8431**	920-893-8431	292-4
Masters Inc 7891 Beechcraft Ave, Gaithersburg MD 20879	**800-257-2871**	301-948-8950	188-10
Masters Inn Preferred Guest Program PO Box 13069, Savannah GA 31416 *Resv	**800-633-3434***	912-352-4493	371
Masters Inns PO Box 13069, Savannah GA 31416	**800-633-3434**	912-352-4493	369
Masterson Co Inc 4023 W National Ave, Milwaukee WI 53215	**800-558-0990**	414-647-1132	291-8
Mastodon State Historic Site 1050 Museum Dr, Imperial MO 63052	**800-334-6946**	636-464-2976	554
Matanuska Maid Dairy 814 W Northern Lights Blvd, Anchorage AK 99503	**800-478-5223**	907-561-5223	292-4
Match Frame 8531 Fairhaven, San Antonio TX 78229	**800-929-2790**	210-614-5678	501
Match.com Inc 3001 George Bush Hwy Suite 100, Richardson TX 75082	**800-926-2824**	214-827-2262	224
Matco Tools 4403 Allen Rd, Stow OH 44224	**800-368-6651**	330-929-4949	746
Mate Precision Tooling Inc 1295 Lund Blvd, Anoka MN 55303	**800-328-4492**	763-421-0230	745
Material Handling Industry of America (MHIA) 8720 Red Oak Blvd Suite 201, Charlotte NC 28217	**800-345-1815**	704-676-1190	49-13
Material & Process Engineering. Society for the Advancement of 1161 Park View Dr, Covina CA 91724	**800-562-7360**	626-331-0616	49-19
Material Sciences Corp 2200 E Pratt Blvd, Elk Grove Village IL 60007 *NYSE: MSC*	**800-877-9078**	847-439-8270	472
Material Service Corp 222 N LaSalle St Suite 1200, Chicago IL 60601	**800-642-8936**	312-372-3600	493-5
Materials Management in Health Care Magazine 1 N Franklin St Suite 2700, Chicago IL 60606	**800-621-6902**	312-893-6800	449-5
Mathematical Assn of America (MAA) 1529 18th St NW, Washington DC 20036	**800-741-9415**	202-387-5200	49-19
Mathematical Society. American 201 Charles St PO Box 6248, Providence RI 02940 *Cust Svc	**800-321-4267***	401-455-4000	49-19
Mathematics. National Council of Teachers of 1906 Association Dr, Reston VA 20191 *Orders	**800-235-7566***	703-620-9840	49-5
Mathematics. Society for Industrial & Applied 3600 Market St 6th Fl, Philadelphia PA 19104	**800-447-7426**	215-382-9800	49-19
Matheson Trucking Inc 10519 E Stockton Blvd Suite 125, Elk Grove CA 95624	**800-455-7678**	916-685-2330	769
Mathews Brothers Co PO Box 345, Belfast ME 04915	**800-639-7203**	207-338-3360	234
Mathews Co 500 Industrial Ave, Crystal Lake IL 60039	**800-323-7045**	815-459-2210	269
Mathias Ham House Historic Site 2241 Lincoln Ave, Dubuque IA 52001	**800-226-3369**	563-557-9545	50
Mathis-Akins Concrete Block Co Inc 130 Lower Elm St, Macon GA 31202	**888-469-0680**	478-746-5154	181
Mathis Brothers Furniture Inc 3434 W Reno Ave, Oklahoma City OK 73107	**800-329-3434**	405-943-3434	316
Matlaw's Food Products Inc 135 Front Ave, West Haven CT 06516 *Cust Svc	**800-934-8266***	203-934-5233	291-14
Matol Botanical International Ltd 290 La Brosse Ave, Pointe-Claire QC H9R6R6	**800-363-1890**	514-426-2865	786
Matot DA Inc 2501 Van Buren St, Bellwood IL 60104	**800-369-1070**	708-547-1888	255
Matria Healthcare Inc 1850 Parkway Pl 12th Fl, Marietta GA 33067 *NASDAQ: MATR*	**800-456-4060**	770-767-4500	455
Matrix Bancorp Inc 700 17th St Suite 2100, Denver CO 80202 *NASDAQ: MTXC*	**800-594-2079**	303-595-9898	355-2
Matrix Capital Bank 277 E Amador Ave, Las Cruces NM 88001	**800-511-5081**	505-524-7748	71

Name / Address	City	State	Zip	Toll-Free	Phone	Class
Matrix Essentials Inc 30601 Carter St	Solon	OH	44139	**800-282-2822**	440-248-3700	211
Matrix Security Systems LLC 109 S Old Dupont Rd	Wilmington	DE	19805	**800-498-5581**	302-683-9101	683
Matrix Service Co 10701 E Ute St *NASDAQ: MTRX*	Tulsa	OK	74116	**800-866-8822**	918-838-8822	528
Matson Integrated Logistics Inc 17 W 635 Butterfield Rd Suite 600	Villa Park	IL	60181	**800-325-0325**	630-203-3500	440
Matson Navigation Co 555 12th St *Cust Svc	Oakland	CA	94607	**800-462-8766***	510-628-4000	307
Matsui Nursery Inc 1645 Old Stage Rd	Salinas	CA	93908	**800-793-6433**	831-422-6433	363
Matsushita Avionics Systems 22333 29th Dr SE	Bothell	WA	98021	**800-755-2684**	425-415-9000	52
Matsushita Electric Corp of America 1 Panasonic Way	Secaucus	NJ	07094	**888-275-2595**	201-348-7000	52
Mattel Inc 333 Continental Blvd *NYSE: MAT* ■ *Cust Svc	El Segundo	CA	90245	**800-524-8697***	310-252-2000	750
Matthew Bender & Co (now LexisNexis Matthew Bender) 744 Broad St	Newark	NJ	07102	**800-252-9257**	973-820-2000	623-2
Matthews Book Co Inc 11559 Rock Island Ct	Maryland Heights	MO	63043	**800-633-2665**	314-432-1400	96
Matthews International Corp 2 Northshore Ctr Suite 200 *NASDAQ: MATW*	Pittsburgh	PA	15212	**800-223-4964**	412-442-8200	303
Matthews International Corp Bronze Div 1315 W Liberty Ave	Pittsburgh	PA	15226	**888-838-8890**	412-571-5500	303
Matthews International Corp Graphics Systems Div 252 Park West Dr	Pittsburgh	PA	15275	**800-245-1129**	412-788-2111	537
Matthews Medical & Scientific Book Inc 11559 Rock Island Ct	Maryland Heights	MO	63043	**800-633-2665**	314-432-1400	96
Matthijssen Inc 14 Rt 10	East Hanover	NJ	07936	**800-845-2200**	973-887-1100	173
Mattson Spray Equipment 230 W Coleman St	Rice Lake	WI	54868	**800-877-4857**	715-234-1617	170
Mattson Technology Inc 47131 Bayside Pkwy *NASDAQ: MTSN*	Fremont	CA	94538	**800-628-8766**	510-657-5900	685
Maui Community College 310 W Kaahumanu Ave	Kahului	HI	96732	**800-479-6692**	808-984-3267	160
Maui Divers of Hawaii Ltd 1520 Liona St	Honolulu	HI	96814	**800-462-4454**	808-946-7979	401
Maui Jim Inc 721 Wainee St	Lahaina	HI	96761	**800-848-3644**	808-661-8841	531
Maui-Molokai Sea Cruises 831 Eha St Suite 101	Wailuku	HI	96793	**800-468-1287**	808-242-8777	217
Maui News PO Box 550	Wailuku	HI	96793	**800-827-0347**	808-244-3981	522-2
Maui Ocean Center 192 Maalaea Rd	Wailuku	HI	96793	**800-350-5634**	808-270-7000	40
Maui Prince Hotel 5400 Makena Alanui	Makena	HI	96753	**800-321-6248**	808-874-1111	655
Maui Resort & Spa. Hyatt Regency 200 Nohea Kai Dr	Lahaina	HI	96761	**800-233-1234**	808-661-1234	655
Maui Tacos International Inc 180 Interstate N Pkwy SE Suite 500	Atlanta	GA	30339	**888-628-4822**	770-226-8226	657
Maumee Bay Resort & Conference Center 1750 Park Rd 2	Oregon	OH	43618	**800-282-7275**	419-836-1466	373
Mauna Kea Beach Hotel 62-100 Maunakea Beach Dr	Kohala Coast	HI	96743	**800-882-6060**	808-882-7222	655
Mauna Lani Bay Hotel & Bungalows 68-1400 Mauna Lani Dr	Kohala Coast	HI	96743	**800-367-2323**	808-885-6622	655
Mauna Lani Spa at Mauna Lani Resort 68-1365 Pauoa Rd	Kohala Coast	HI	96743	**866-877-6982**	808-881-7922	698
Mauna Loa Macadamia Nut Corp HC01 Box 3 *Cust Svc	Hilo	HI	96720	**800-832-9993***	808-982-6562	11-10
Maupintour Inc 10650 W Charleston Blvd	Las Vegas	NV	89135	**800-255-4266**	702-260-3600	748
Maurice Abravanel Hall 123 W South Temple	Salt Lake City	UT	84101	**888-451-2787**	801-533-5626	562
Maurice Lenell Cooky Co 4474 N Harlem Ave	Norridge	IL	60706	**800-323-1760**	708-456-6500	291-1
Maurice's Gourmet Barbeque PO Box 6847	West Columbia	SC	29171	**800-628-7423**	803-791-5887	291-19
Mauritzon Inc 3939 W Belden Ave	Chicago	IL	60647	**800-621-4352**	773-235-6000	718
Maury Regional Hospital 1224 Trotwood Ave	Columbia	TN	38401	**800-799-5053**	931-381-1111	366-2
Maust Transportation 21848 76th Ave S	Kent	WA	98032	**800-446-2878**	253-479-0261	769
Mautino Distributing Co 500 N Richards St *Cust Svc	Spring Valley	IL	61362	**800-851-2756***	815-664-4311	82-1
Mautner Enterprises 155 E 76 St	New York	NY	10021	**800-628-8637**	212-452-1871	199
Maverick Boat Co Inc 3207 Industrial 29th St	Fort Pierce	FL	34946	**888-742-5569**	772-465-0631	91
Maverick Coach Lines Ltd 7984 Webster Rd	Delta	BC	V4G1G6	**888-842-2448**	604-940-2332	108
Maverick Media Inc 123 W 17th St	Syracuse	NE	68446	**800-742-7662**	402-269-2135	623-8
Maverick Transportation Inc PO Box 15428	Little Rock	AR	72231	**800-289-6600**	501-945-6130	769
Maverick Tube Corp 16401 Swingley Ridge Rd Suite 700 *NYSE: MVK*	Chesterfield	MO	63017	**888-628-8823**	636-733-1600	481
Max Factor 1 Procter & Gamble Plaza	Cincinnati	OH	45202	**800-526-8787**	513-983-1100	211
Max Group Corp 17011 Green Dr	City of Industry	CA	91745	**800-256-9040**	626-935-0050	172
Max Katz Inc 235 S LaSalle St	Indianapolis	IN	46201	**800-225-3729**	317-635-9561	68
Max & Lucy 5444 E Washington St Suite 3	Phoenix	AZ	85034	**877-975-5050**	602-275-5050	130
Max Rouse & Sons Inc 361 S Robertson Blvd	Beverly Hills	CA	90211	**800-421-0816**	310-360-9200	51
Maxell Corp of America 22-08 Rt 208	Fair Lawn	NJ	07410	**800-533-2836**	201-794-5900	644
Maxfield Candy Co 1050 S 200 West	Salt Lake City	UT	84101	**800-288-8002**	801-355-5321	291-8
Maxillofacial Surgeons. American Assn of Oral & 9700 W Bryn Mawr Ave	Rosemont	IL	60018	**800-822-6637**	847-678-6200	49-8
Maxim Crane Works 800 Waterfront Dr	Pittsburgh	PA	15222	**866-629-4648**	412-320-4900	261-2
Maxim Healthcare Services 7080 Samuel Morse Dr	Columbia	MD	21046	**800-796-2946**	410-910-1500	358
Maxim Integrated Products Inc 120 San Gabriel Dr *NASDAQ: MXIM*	Sunnyvale	CA	94086	**800-659-5909**	408-737-7600	686
Maxim Magazine 1040 Avenue of the Americas 16th Fl	New York	NY	10018	**800-829-5572**	212-302-2626	449-11
Maxim Mary Inc 2001 Holland Ave PO Box 5019	Port Huron	MI	48061	**800-962-9504**	810-987-2000	451
Maxim Mfg Co PO Box 110	Sebastopol	MS	39359	**800-621-2789**	601-625-7471	420
Maximum Human Performance Inc (MHP Inc) 1376 Pompton Ave	Cedar Grove	NJ	07009	**888-783-8844**	973-785-9055	786
Maxis Inc 2121 N California Blvd Suite 600	Walnut Creek	CA	94596	**800-245-4525**	925-933-5630	176-6
Maxon Furniture Inc 21606 86th Pl S *Cust Svc	Kent	WA	98031	**800-876-4274***	253-872-0396	314-1
Maxon Industries Inc 11921 Slauson Ave	Santa Fe Springs	CA	90670	**800-227-4116**	562-464-0099	462
Maxor National Pharmacy Services Corp 320 S Polk St Suite 100	Amarillo	TX	79101	**800-658-6146**	806-324-5400	575
Maxtor Corp 500 McCarthy Blvd *NYSE: MXO*	Milpitas	CA	95035	**800-262-9867**	408-894-5000	171-8
Maxum Development Corp PO Box 316	Crystal Lake	IL	60039	**800-813-3410**	815-444-0100	176-12
MaxVision Corp 495 Production Ave	Madison	AL	35758	**800-533-5805**	256-772-3058	171-3
Maxwell House Hotel Nashville. Millennium 2025 Metro Center Blvd	Nashville	TN	37228	**866-866-8086**	615-259-4343	373
Maxxam Analytics Inc 335 Laird Rd Unit 2	Guelph	ON	N1H6J3	**888-266-7889**	519-836-2400	408
MAXxess Systems Inc 1515 S Manchester Ave	Anaheim	CA	92802	**800-842-0221**	714-772-1000	681
Maxygen Inc 515 Galveston Dr *NASDAQ: MAXY*	Redwood City	CA	94063	**888-629-9436**	650-298-5300	86
MaxYield Cooperative PO Box 49	West Bend	IA	50597	**800-383-0003**	515-887-7211	271
May Advertising International Ltd 1200 Forum Way S	Fort Worth	TX	76140	**800-800-4629**	817-336-5671	8
May Earl Seed & Nursery 208 N Elm St	Shenandoah	IA	51603	**800-831-4193**	712-246-1020	318
May George S International Co 303 S Northwest Hwy	Park Ridge	IL	60068	**800-999-3020**	847-825-8806	193
May Natural History Museum & Museum of Space Exploration 710 Rock Creek Canyon Rd	Colorado Springs	CO	80926	**800-666-3841**	719-576-0450	509
May Trucking Co 4185 Brooklake Rd PO Box 9039	Salem	OR	97305	**800-547-9169**	503-393-7030	769
Maybelline New York 575 5th Ave	New York	NY	10017	**800-944-0730**	212-818-1500	211
Mayborn Frank W Civic & Convention Center 3303 N 3rd St	Temple	TX	76501	**800-478-0338**	254-298-5720	204
Mayco Industries LLC 18 W Oxmoor Rd	Birmingham	AL	35209	**800-749-6061**	205-942-4242	688
Mayco Oil Co 775 Louis Dr	Warminster	PA	18974	**800-523-3903**	215-672-6600	530
Mayer Berkshire Corp 25 Edison Dr	Wayne	NJ	07470	**800-245-6789**	973-696-6200	153-10
Mayer Electric Supply Co 3405 4th Ave S	Birmingham	AL	35222	**800-444-8524**	205-583-3500	245
Mayer Frank & Assoc Inc 1975 Wisconsin Ave	Grafton	WI	53024	**800-225-3987**	262-377-4700	231
Mayer Motivations Inc 2434 E Las Olas Blvd	Fort Lauderdale	FL	33301	**888-611-4376**	954-523-0074	377
Mayer Pollock Steel Corp PO Box 759	Pottstown	PA	19464	**800-323-5502**	610-323-5500	674
Mayfair The - A Wyndham Historic Hotel 806 Saint Charles St	Saint Louis	MO	63101	**800-996-3426**	314-421-2500	373
Mayfair Hotel & Spa 3000 Florida Ave	Coconut Grove	FL	33133	**800-433-4555**	305-441-0000	373
Mayfield Dairy Farms Inc PO Box 310	Athens	TN	37371	**800-362-9546**	423-745-2151	291-27
Mayfield Inn & Suites 16615 109th Ave	Edmonton	AB	T5P4K8	**800-661-9804**	780-484-0821	372
Mayfield Paper Co 1115 S Hill St	San Angelo	TX	76903	**800-725-1441**	325-653-1444	549
Mayfield Transfer Co Inc 3200 W Lake St	Melrose Park	IL	60160	**800-222-2959**	708-681-4440	769
Mayflower Co-operative Bank 30 S Main St *NASDAQ: MFLR*	Middleboro	MA	02346	**800-552-4344**	508-947-4343	71
Mayflower Park Hotel 405 Olive Way	Seattle	WA	98101	**800-426-5100**	206-623-8700	373
Mayflower Retirement Community 1620 Mayflower Ct	Winter Park	FL	32792	**800-228-6518**	407-672-1620	659
Mayflower Tours Inc 1225 Warren Ave PO Box 490	Downers Grove	IL	60515	**800-323-7604**	630-435-8500	748
Mayflower Transit Inc 1 Mayflower Dr	Fenton	MO	63026	**800-428-1234**	636-305-4000	508
Mayfran International 6650 Beta Dr	Mayfield Village	OH	44143	**800-321-6988**	440-461-4100	206
Mayhew Steel Products Inc 199 Industrial Blvd	Turners Falls	MA	01376	**800-872-0037**	413-863-4860	746
Mayland Community College PO Box 547	Spruce Pine	NC	28777	**800-462-9526**	828-765-7351	160
Mayline Group 619 N Commerce St	Sheboygan	WI	53081	**800-822-8037**	920-457-5537	314-1
Maynard HB & Co Inc 8 Parkway Ctr	Pittsburgh	PA	15220	**888-629-6273**	412-921-2400	193
Mayo Aviation Inc 7735 S Peoria St	Englewood	CO	80112	**800-525-0194**	303-790-9777	14
Mayo Civic Center 30 Civic Center Dr SE	Rochester	MN	55904	**800-422-2199**	507-281-6184	204
Mayo Clinic Proceedings Magazine 200 1st St SW Siebens Bldg 770	Rochester	MN	55905	**800-707-7040**	507-284-2094	449-16
Mayor's Jewelers Inc 14051 NW 14th St Suite 200 *AMEX: MYR*	Sunrise	FL	33323	**800-223-6964**	954-846-8000	402
Mays Chemical Co Inc 5611 E 71st St	Indianapolis	IN	46220	**800-525-4803**	317-842-8722	144
Maysteel LLC N89 W14700 Patrita Dr PO Box 1240	Menomonee Falls	WI	53052	**800-255-1247**	262-255-2400	688
Maytag Appliances 403 W 4th St N *Cust Svc	Newton	IA	50208	**800-688-9900***	641-792-7000	36

Name / Address	City	State	Zip	Toll-Free	Phone	Class
Maytag-Cleveland Cooking Products 740 King Edward Ave	Cleveland	TN	37320	**800-688-1120**	423-472-3371	36
Maytag Corp 403 W 4th St N *NYSE: MYG*	Newton	IA	50208	**800-688-9900**	641-792-7000	36
Maytag Dairy Farms Inc 2282 E 8th N	Newton	IA	50208	**800-247-2458**	641-792-1133	11-3
Maytag-Newton Laundry Products 403 West 4th St N	Newton	IA	50208	**800-866-9900**	641-792-7000	36
Mayville State University 330 3rd St NE	Mayville	ND	58257	**800-437-4104**	701-788-2301	163
Maywood Park 8600 W North Ave	Melrose Park	IL	60160	**800-748-5782**	708-343-4800	628
Mazda North American Operations 7755 Irvine Ctr Dr *Cust Svc	Irvine	CA	92618	**800-222-5500***	949-727-1990	59
Mazon Assoc Inc 600 W Airport Fwy	Irving	TX	75062	**800-442-2740**	972-554-6967	268
Mazza Vineyards & Winery 11815 E Lake Rd	North East	PA	16428	**800-796-9463**	814-725-8695	50
Mazzella Lifting Technologies 21000 Aerospace Pkwy	Cleveland	OH	44142	**800-362-4601**	440-239-7000	462
MBA (Military Benefit Assn) PO Box 221110	Chantilly	VA	20153	**800-336-0100**	703-968-6200	48-19
MBA (Mortgage Bankers Assn) 1919 Pennsylvania Ave NW	Washington	DC	20006	**800-793-6222**	202-557-2700	49-2
MBI Inc 47 Richards Ave	Norwalk	CT	06857	**800-243-5160**	203-853-2000	451
MBIA Insurance Corp 113 King St	Armonk	NY	10504	**800-765-6242**	914-273-4545	384-5
MBNA (Monument Builders of North America) 401 N Michigan Ave Suite 2200	Chicago	IL	60611	**800-233-4472**	312-321-5143	49-3
MBNA America Bank NA	Wilmington	DE	19884	**800-441-7048**		71
MBNA Corp 1100 N King St *NYSE: KRB*	Wilmington	DE	19884	**800-441-7048**	302-456-8588	355-2
MBS Textbook Exchange Inc 2711 W Ash St	Columbia	MO	65203	**800-325-0530**	573-445-2243	97
MC & A Inc 615 Piikoi St Suite 1000	Honolulu	HI	96814	**877-589-5501**	808-589-5500	760
MC Sports 3070 Shaffer Ave SE	Grand Rapids	MI	49512	**800-626-1762**	616-942-2600	702
MC2 10601 Baur Blvd	Saint Louis	MO	63132	**800-826-3977**	314-569-0333	183
MCA (Marine Corps Assn) PO Box 1775	Quantico	VA	22134	**800-336-0291**	703-640-6161	48-19
MCAA (Mason Contractors Assn of America) 33 S Roselle Rd	Schaumburg	IL	60193	**800-536-2225**	847-301-0001	49-3
MCAA (Mechanical Contractors Assn of America) 1385 Piccard Dr	Rockville	MD	20850	**800-556-3653**	301-869-5800	49-3
McAfee Inc 3965 Freedom Cir *NYSE: MFE*	Santa Clara	CA	95054	**888-847-8766**	408-988-3832	176-12
McAlester News-Capital & Democrat PO Box 987	McAlester	OK	74502	**877-307-4237**	918-423-1700	522-2
McAlister's Corp 731 S Pear Orchard Rd Suite 51	Ridgeland	MS	39157	**888-855-3354**	601-952-1100	657
McAllen Chamber of Commerce 120 Ash Ave	McAllen	TX	78505	**877-622-5536**	956-682-2871	137
McAllen Convention & Visitors Bureau 1200 Ash St	McAllen	TX	78501	**877-622-5536**	956-682-2871	205
McAninch Corp 6800 Lake Dr Suite 125	West Des Moines	IA	50266	**800-383-3201**	515-267-2500	188-5
McArthur Dairy Inc 500 Sawgrass Corporate Pkwy	Sunrise	FL	33325	**877-803-6565**	954-846-1234	291-27
MCC (Mennonite Central Committee) 21 S 12th St PO Box 500	Akron	PA	17501	**888-563-4676**	717-859-1151	48-5
MCC Inc PO Box 1137	Appleton	WI	54912	**800-236-8132**	920-749-3360	187-4
McCabe & Assoc Inc 9700 Patuxent Dr Suite 103	Columbia	MD	21045	**800-638-6316**	410-381-3710	176-12
McCadam Cheese Co Inc 14 Annette St	Heuvelton	NY	13654	**800-724-3373**	315-344-2441	291-5
McCain Bindery Systems Inc 3802 W 128th St *Cust Svc	Alsip	IL	60803	**800-225-9363***	708-824-9600	93
McCain Foods USA Inc 2905 Butterfield Rd	Oak Brook	IL	60523	**800-938-7799**	630-472-0420	291-21
McCain Snack Foods 555 N Hickory Farm Ln PO Box 2518	Appleton	WI	54913	**800-767-7377**	920-997-2828	291-21
McCall Aviation PO Box 771	McCall	ID	83638	**800-992-6559**	208-634-7137	63
McCall Pattern Co 615 McCall Rd	Manhattan	KS	66502	**800-255-2762**	785-776-4041	557
McCall Service Inc 2861 College St	Jacksonville	FL	32205	**800-342-6948**	904-389-5561	567
McCallie School 500 Dodds Rd	Chattanooga	TN	37404	**800-234-2163**	423-624-8300	611
McCamly Plaza Hotel 50 Capital Ave SW	Battle Creek	MI	49017	**888-622-2659**	269-963-7050	373
McCann's Engineering & Mfg Co 4570 W Colorado Blvd	Los Angeles	CA	90039	**800-423-2429**	818-637-7200	650
McCarl's Inc 1413 9th Ave	Beaver Falls	PA	15010	**800-643-5660**	724-843-5660	188-10
McCarthy Improvement Co Inc 5401 Victoria Ave	Davenport	IA	52807	**800-728-0322**	563-359-0321	187-4
McCartin McAuliffe Mechanical Contractors Inc 4508 Columbia Ave	Hammond	IN	46327	**866-998-6600**	219-931-6600	188-10
McClarin Plastics Inc 600 Linden Ave PO Box 486	Hanover	PA	17331	**800-233-3189**	717-637-2241	595
McClendon Transportation Group PO Box 641	Lafayette	AL	36862	**800-633-7710**	334-864-9311	769
McClintock Jessica Inc 1400 16th St	San Francisco	CA	94103	**800-333-5301**	415-553-8200	153-21
McCloud WB & Co 2500 W Higgins Rd Suite 850 *Cust Svc	Hoffman Estates	IL	60195	**800-332-7805***	847-585-0650	567
McClure Co 4101 N 6th St	Harrisburg	PA	17110	**800-382-1319**	717-232-9743	188-10
McClure-Johnston Co 201 Corey Ave	Braddock	PA	15104	**800-232-0018**	412-351-4300	190-4
McCollister & Co 2200 South Ave	Council Bluffs	IA	51503	**800-798-6457**	712-322-4038	530
McCollister's Transportation Group Inc 1800 Rt 130 N	Burlington	NJ	08016	**800-257-9595**	609-386-0600	508
McCombs Enterprises 755 E Mulberry Ave Suite 600	San Antonio	TX	78212	**800-460-4883**	210-821-6523	57
McCone Electric Co-op Inc PO Box 368	Circle	MT	59215	**800-684-3605**	406-485-3430	244
McConnell Cabinets Inc 13110 Louden Ln	City of Industry	CA	91746	**800-794-7895**	626-937-2200	116
McCook Community College 1205 E 3rd St	McCook	NE	69001	**800-658-4348**	308-345-8100	160
McCook Daily Gazette PO Box 1268	McCook	NE	69001	**800-269-1426**	308-345-4500	522-2
McCook Electric Co-op Inc PO Box 250	Salem	SD	57058	**800-942-3113**	605-425-2661	244
McCook Public Power District PO Box 1147	McCook	NE	69001	**800-658-4285**	308-345-2500	244
McCormick & Co Inc 1201 3rd St	Alexandria	LA	71301	**800-523-8391**	318-487-6397	623-8
McCormick & Co Inc 18 Loveton Cir *NYSE: MKC*	Sparks	MD	21152	**800-632-5847**	410-771-7301	291-37
McCormick & Co Inc Food Service Div 226 Schilling Cir	Hunt Valley	MD	21031	**800-327-6838**	410-771-7500	291-37
McCormick & Co Inc McCormick Flavor Div 226 Schilling Cir	Hunt Valley	MD	21031	**800-327-6838**	410-771-7500	291-37
McCormick & Co Inc US Consumer Products Div 211 Schilling Cir	Hunt Valley	MD	21031	**800-292-5300**	410-527-6000	291-37
McCormick Ingredients 10901 Gilroy Rd	Hunt Valley	MD	21031	**800-632-5847**	410-771-5008	291-37
McCormick Place 2301 S Lake Shore Dr	Chicago	IL	60616	**800-263-9170**	312-791-7000	204
McCormick Ranch. Millennium Resort Scottsdale 7401 N Scottsdale Rd	Scottsdale	AZ	85253	**800-243-1332**	480-948-5050	655
McCorvey Sheet Metal Works Inc PO Box 405	Galena Park	TX	77547	**800-580-7545**	713-672-7545	688
McCourt Label Co 20 Egbert Ln	Lewis Run	PA	16738	**800-458-2390**	814-362-3851	404
McCoy-Ellison Inc PO Box 967	Monroe	NC	28111	**800-811-5348**	704-289-5413	729
McCranie Implement Co PO Box 628	Hawkinsville	GA	31036	**800-245-9046**	478-892-9046	270
McCranie Motors & Tractors Inc PO Box 770	Unadilla	GA	31091	**800-841-4050**	478-627-3291	270
McCrea Equipment Co Inc 4463 Beech Rd	Temple Hills	MD	20748	**800-597-0091**	301-423-4585	188-10
McCrometer Inc 3255 W Stetson Ave	Hemet	CA	92545	**800-220-2279**	951-652-6811	200
McCullagh SJ Inc 245 Swan St	Buffalo	NY	14204	**800-753-3473**	716-856-3473	291-7
McCullough & Assoc PO Box 29803	Atlanta	GA	30359	**800-969-1606**	404-325-1606	144
McDaniel College 2 College Hill	Westminster	MD	21157	**800-638-5005**	410-848-7000	163
McDaniel Fire Systems 1055 W Joliet Rd	Valparaiso	IN	46385	**800-348-2632**	219-462-0571	188-13
McDATA Corp 380 Interlocken Crescent Suite 600 *NASDAQ: MCDTA*	Broomfield	CO	80021	**800-545-5773**	720-558-8000	174
McDonald AY Mfg Co 4800 Chavenelle Rd *Cust Svc	Dubuque	IA	52002	**800-292-2737***	563-583-7311	584
McDonald Candy Co 2350 W Broadway St	Eugene	OR	97402	**877-722-5503**	541-345-8421	292-3
McDonald ML Co PO Box 315	Watertown	MA	02471	**800-733-6243**	617-923-0900	188-8
McDonald Publishing 567 Hanley Industrial Ct	Saint Louis	MO	63144	**800-722-8080**	314-781-7400	242
McDonald Technologies International Inc 1920 Diplomat Dr	Farmers Branch	TX	75234	**800-678-7046**	972-243-6767	613
McDonald's Corp 1 McDonald's Plaza *NYSE: MCD*	Oak Brook	IL	60523	**800-234-6227**	630-623-3000	657
McDougal Littell PO Box 1667	Evanston	IL	60204	**800-323-5435**	847-869-2300	623-2
McDougall John W Co Inc 3731 Amy Lynn Dr	Nashville	TN	37218	**800-264-1122**	615-321-3900	688
McDowell County Tourism Development Authority 1170 W Tate St	Marion	NC	28752	**888-233-6111**	828-652-1103	205
McDowell-Craig Office Furniture 13146 Firestone Blvd	Norwalk	CA	90650	**877-921-2100**	562-921-4441	314-1
McElroy Metal Mill Inc 1500 Hamilton Rd	Bossier City	LA	71111	**800-950-6531**	318-747-8000	471
McFarland Cascade 1640 E Marc St *Cust Svc	Tacoma	WA	98421	**800-426-8430***	253-572-3033	806
McFarlane Mfg Co Inc 1259 Water St	Sauk City	WI	53583	**800-627-8569**	608-643-3321	272
McGean 2910 Harvard Ave *Orders	Cleveland	OH	44105	**800-932-7006***	216-441-4900	143
McGean-Rohco Inc DBA McGean 2910 Harvard Ave *Orders	Cleveland	OH	44105	**800-932-7006***	216-441-4900	143
McGill Electrical Product Group 9377 W Higgins Rd	Rosemont	IL	60018	**888-832-0660**	800-722-8515	803
McGill Inc 131 E Prairie St	Marengo	IL	60152	**800-982-9884**	815-568-7244	523
McGlinn Capital Management 850 N Wyomissing Blvd	Wyomissing	PA	19610	**800-783-1478**	610-374-5125	393
McGoldrick Oil Co 8808 McGoldrick Dr	Shreveport	LA	71129	**800-844-6490**	318-687-6490	525
McGraphics Inc 601 Hagan St	Nashville	TN	37203	**888-280-8200**	615-242-8779	545
McGrath RentCorp DBA Mobile Modular Management Corp 5700 Las Positas Rd *NASDAQ: MGRC*	Livermore	CA	94551	**800-352-2900**	925-606-9200	495
McGraw-Hill Construction 2 Penn Plaza	New York	NY	10121	**800-221-0088**		623-9
McGraw-Hill Cos Inc CTB/McGraw-Hill Div 20 Ryan Ranch Rd	Monterey	CA	93940	**800-538-9547**	831-393-0700	243
McGraw-Hill Cos Inc Macmillan/McGraw-Hill Div 2 Pennsylvania Plaza	New York	NY	10121	**800-442-9685**	212-512-2000	242
McGraw-Hill Cos Inc SRA/McGraw-Hill Div 8787 Orion Pl	Columbus	OH	43240	**800-468-4850**	614-430-6600	242
McGraw-Hill Higher Education Group 1333 Burr Ridge Pkwy	Burr Ridge	IL	60527	**800-634-3963**	630-789-4000	623-2
McGraw-Hill Osborne 2100 Powell St 10th Fl	Emeryville	CA	94608	**800-227-0900**	510-420-7700	623-11
McGraw-Hill Professional Publishing Group 2 Penn Plaza 11th Fl	New York	NY	10121	**800-262-4729**	212-512-2000	623-2
McGregor Industries Inc 46 Line St Keystone Industrial Pk	Dunmore	PA	18512	**800-326-6786**	570-343-2436	482
McGriff Seibels & Williams Inc 2211 7th Ave S PO Box 10265	Birmingham	AL	35202	**800-476-2211**	205-252-9871	383
McGuire Furniture Co 1201 Bryant St	San Francisco	CA	94103	**800-662-4847**	415-626-1414	314-2
McGuire Hunter Holmes Veterans Affairs Medical Center 1201 Broad Rock Blvd	Richmond	VA	23249	**800-784-8381**	804-675-5000	366-6
McGuire WB Co 1 Hudson Ave	Hudson	NY	12534	**800-624-8473**	518-828-7652	462

Name / Address	City	State	Zip	Toll-Free	Phone	Class
McGuire's Resort 7880 Mackinaw Trail	Cadillac	MI	49601	**800-632-7302**	231-775-9947	655
McHenry Metals Golf Corp 4502 Marquette Ave	Jacksonville	FL	32210	**866-410-2544**		701
MCI Inc 22001 Loudoun County Pkwy *NASDAQ: MCIP*	Ashburn	VA	20147	**877-624-1000**	703-886-5600	721
McIlhenny Co Hwy 329 *Orders	Avery Island	LA	70513	**800-634-9599***	337-365-8173	291-19
McIntire Co 745 Clark Ave	Bristol	CT	06010	**800-437-9247**	860-585-0050	19
McIntosh College 23 Cataract Ave	Dover	NH	03820	**800-624-6867**	603-742-1234	158
McIntosh Inns 440 Feheley Dr McIntosh Bldg.	King of Prussia	PA	19406	**800-444-2775**	610-279-6000	369
McIntosh Laboratory Inc 2 Chambers St	Binghamton	NY	13903	**800-538-6576**	607-723-3512	52
McJunkin Corp 835 Hillcrest Dr E	Charleston	WV	25311	**800-624-8603**	304-348-5211	378
McKay Nursery Co Inc 750 S Monroe St	Waterloo	WI	53594	**800-236-4242**	920-478-2121	318
McKee Button Co Inc PO Box 230 *Cust Svc	Muscatine	IA	52761	**800-553-9662***	563-263-2421	583
McKee Floor Covering Inc 2785 Hwy 55	Eagan	MN	55121	**800-328-2020**	651-454-1700	356
McKee Foods Corp PO Box 750 *Cust Svc	Collegedale	TN	37315	**800-522-4499***	423-238-7111	291-1
McKees Rocks Forgings Inc 75 Nichol Ave	McKees Rocks	PA	15136	**800-223-2818**	412-778-2020	474
McKelligon Canyon 3 McKelligon Rd	El Paso	TX	79930	**800-915-8482**	915-581-0700	50
McKendree College 701 College Rd	Lebanon	IL	62254	**800-232-7228**	618-537-4481	163
McKenna Professional Imaging Inc 2815 Falls Ave	Waterloo	IA	50701	**800-238-3456**	319-235-6265	577
McKenney's Inc 1056 Moreland Industrial Blvd SE	Atlanta	GA	30316	**800-489-5000**	404-622-5000	188-10
McKeon Door Corp 95 29th St	Brooklyn	NY	11232	**800-266-9392**	718-965-0700	232
McKesson Automated Prescription Systems 4333 Shreveport Hwy	Pineville	LA	71360	**800-551-6578**	318-640-8114	486
McKesson Corp 1 Post St *NYSE: MCK*	San Francisco	CA	94104	**800-482-3784**	415-983-8300	355-3
McKesson Health Systems 1 Post St	San Francisco	CA	94104	**800-571-2889**	415-983-8300	576
McKesson Information Solutions 5995 Windward Pkwy	Alpharetta	GA	30005	**800-981-8601**	404-338-6000	176-10
McKesson Medical Group Extended Care 8121 10th Ave N	Golden Valley	MN	55427	**800-328-8111**	763-595-6000	467
McKesson Medical-Surgical 8741 Landmark Rd	Richmond	VA	23228	**800-446-3008**	804-264-7500	467
McKesson Medication Management 7115 Northland Terr Suite 500	Brooklyn Park	MN	55428	**877-806-7888**	763-354-1200	576
McKesson Pharmacy Systems 30881 Schoolcraft Rd	Livonia	MI	48150	**800-521-1758**	734-427-2000	176-11
McKesson Specialty Pharmaceuticals 5712 Jarvis St	New Orleans	LA	70123	**888-456-7274**	504-736-7827	237
McKinley Air Transport Inc PO Box 2406	North Canton	OH	44720	**800-225-6446**	330-499-3316	25
McKinley Medical LLP 4080 Youngfield St	Wheat Ridge	CO	80033	**800-578-0555**	303-420-9569	468
McKinney Products Inc 820 Davis St	Scranton	PA	18505	**800-346-7707**	570-346-7551	345
McKinsey & Co Inc 55 E 52nd St	New York	NY	10022	**800-221-1026**	212-446-7000	193
McKinstry Co 5005 3rd Ave S	Seattle	WA	98134	**800-669-6223**	206-762-3311	188-10
McKnight Plywood Inc 201 N 1st St	West Helena	AR	72390	**800-566-2145**	870-572-2501	602
MCL Cafeterias Inc 2730 E 62nd St	Indianapolis	IN	46220	**800-530-9625**	317-257-5425	657
MCL Inc 501 S Woodcreek Rd *Support	Bolingbrook	IL	60440	**800-743-4625***	630-759-9500	633
McLane Co Inc 4747 McLane Pkwy	Temple	TX	76504	**800-299-1401**	254-771-7500	292-8
McLaren Hospice Service 1515 Cal Dr	Davison	MI	48423	**800-206-4806**	810-496-8855	365
McLaren Regional Medical Center 401 S Ballenger Hwy	Flint	MI	48532	**800-821-6517**	810-342-2000	366-2
McLaughlin & Moran Inc 40 Slater Rd	Cranston	RI	02920	**800-423-0156**	401-463-5454	82-1
McLaughlin Research Corp 132 Johnnycake Hill Rd	Middletown	RI	02842	**800-556-7154**	401-849-4010	258
McLean Electric Co-op Inc PO Box 399	Garrison	ND	58540	**800-263-4922**	701-463-2291	244
McLean Inc 3409 E Miraloma Ave *Cust Svc	Anaheim	CA	92806	**800-451-2424***	714-996-5451	447
McLellan Equipment Inc 251 Shaw Rd	South San Francisco	CA	94080	**800-848-8449**	650-873-8100	189
McLellan Rod Co 159 Homer Ave	Palo Alto	CA	94301	**800-467-2443**	650-330-8990	363
McLennan County Electric Co-op PO Box 357	McGregor	TX	76657	**800-840-2957**	254-840-2871	244
McLeod Co-op Power Assn 1231 Ford Ave N	Glencoe	MN	55336	**800-494-6272**	320-864-3148	244
McLeod Hospice 555 E Cheves St	Florence	SC	29506	**800-768-4556**	843-777-2564	365
McLeod Trucking & Rigging PO Box 790376	Charlotte	NC	28206	**800-438-0330**	704-372-3611	769
McLoone Metal Graphics Co 75 Sumner St	La Crosse	WI	54602	**800-624-6641**	608-784-1260	692
MCM Inc 707 N Main St	Leominster	MA	01453	**800-270-0707**	978-537-0704	35
McMoRan Exploration Co 1615 Poydras St *NYSE: MMR*	New Orleans	LA	70112	**800-535-7094**	504-582-4000	527
McMoRan Oil & Gas Co 1615 Poydras St	New Orleans	LA	70112	**800-535-7094**	504-582-4000	525
McMurry University S 14 St & Sayles Blvd	Abilene	TX	79697	**800-460-2392**	325-793-3800	163
McNally Industries LLC 340 W Benson Ave PO Box 129	Grantsburg	WI	54840	**800-473-0053**	715-463-8300	627
McNaughton-McKay Electric Co Inc 1357 E Lincoln Ave	Madison Heights	MI	48071	**800-527-5033**	248-399-7500	245
McNeal Enterprises Inc 2031 Ringwood Ave	San Jose	CA	95131	**800-562-6325**	408-922-7290	591
McNear Brick & Block 1 McNear Brickyard Rd	San Rafael	CA	94901	**888-442-6811**	415-454-6811	148
McNeese State University 4205 Ryan St	Lake Charles	LA	70609	**800-622-3352**	337-475-5000	163
Frazar Library PO Box 91415	Lake Charles	LA	70609	**800-622-3352**	337-475-5723	426
McNeil Consumer & Specialty Pharmaceuticals 7050 Camp Hill Rd	Fort Washington	PA	19034	**800-962-5357**	215-273-7000	572
McNeil & NRM Inc 96 E Crosier St	Akron	OH	44311	**800-669-2525**	330-253-2525	379
McNichols Co 5505 W Gray St	Tampa	FL	33609	**800-237-3828**	813-282-3828	483
McNish Corp 840 N Russell Ave	Aurora	IL	60506	**800-992-5537**	630-892-7921	793
McNulty's Tea & Coffee Co Inc 109 Christopher St	New York	NY	10014	**800-356-5200**	212-242-5351	156
MCP Industries Inc Mission Clay Products Div 1655 E 6th St	Corona	CA	92879	**800-795-6067**	951-736-1881	148
McPherson College PO Box 1402	McPherson	KS	67460	**800-365-7402**	620-241-0731	163
McPhillips Mfg Co Inc PO Box 169	Mobile	AL	36601	**800-348-6274**	251-438-1681	234
McQuaide WC Inc 153 Macridge Ave	Johnstown	PA	15904	**800-456-0292**	814-269-6000	769
McQuesten Co 600 Iron Horse Pk	North Billerica	MA	01862	**800-752-0129**	978-663-3435	190-3
MCR Safety 5321 E Shelby Dr	Memphis	TN	38118	**800-955-6887**	901-795-5810	153-8
MCRA (Marine Corps Reserve Assn) 337 Potomac Ave	Quantico	VA	22134	**800-927-6270**	703-630-3772	48-19
McRae Industries Inc PO Box 1239 *AMEX: MRI/A*	Mount Gilead	NC	27306	**800-768-5248**	910-439-6147	184
McSweeney Joseph & Sons Inc PO Box 26409	Richmond	VA	23260	**800-552-6927**	804-359-6024	291-26
MCT Wholesale 575 12th St	Macon	GA	31201	**800-637-0190**	478-743-2236	744
McWane Center Science Museum 200 19th St N	Birmingham	AL	35203	**877-462-9263**	205-714-8300	509
MD-Both Industries 40 Nickerson Rd	Ashland	MA	01721	**800-288-2684**	508-881-4100	476
MD IPA 4 Taft Ct	Rockville	MD	20850	**800-638-8898**	301-762-8205	384-3
MDA (Muscular Dystrophy Assn) 3300 E Sunrise Dr	Tucson	AZ	85718	**800-572-1717**	520-529-2000	48-17
MDBS Inc 1305 Cumberland Ave	West Lafayette	IN	47906	**800-445-6327**	765-463-7200	176-2
MDI Security Systems Inc 9725 Datapoint Dr Suite 200 *NASDAQ: MDII*	San Antonio	TX	78229	**866-435-7634**	210-477-5400	681
MDL Capital Management Inc 309 Smithville St 5th Fl	Pittsburgh	PA	15222	**877-635-3863**	215-893-8800	393
MDL Information Systems Inc 14600 Catalina St *Cust Svc	San Leandro	CA	94577	**800-326-3002***	510-895-1313	176-11
MDNA (Machinery Dealers National Assn) 315 S Patrick St	Alexandria	VA	22314	**800-872-7807**	703-836-9300	49-18
MDRT (Million Dollar Round Table) 325 W Touhy Ave	Park Ridge	IL	60068	**800-879-6378**	847-692-6378	49-9
MDS Matrx 145 Mid County Dr	Orchard Park	NY	14127	**800-847-1000**	716-662-6650	226
MDS Pharma Services Inc 2350 Cohen St	Saint-Laurent	QC	H4R2N6	**800-724-5941**	514-333-0033	409
ME Global 3901 University Ave NE	Minneapolis	MN	55421	**800-328-3858**	763-788-1651	302
ME Heuck Co Inc 3274 Beekman St *Cust Svc	Cincinnati	OH	45223	**800-359-3200***	513-681-1774	477
Me-N-Ed's Pizzerias 5701 N West Ave	Fresno	CA	93711	**888-636-3373**	559-432-0399	657
ME Sharpe Inc 80 Business Park Dr Suite 202 *Orders	Armonk	NY	10504	**800-541-6563***	914-273-1800	623-2
MEA Voice Magazine PO Box 2573	East Lansing	MI	48826	**800-292-1934**	517-332-6551	449-8
Meade County Times-Tribune PO Box 129	Sturgis	SD	57785	**800-253-3656**	605-347-2503	522-4
Meade Instruments Corp 6001 Oak Canyon *NASDAQ: MEAD*	Irvine	CA	92618	**800-626-3233**	949-451-1450	534
Meadow Lake Resort 100 St Andrews Dr	Columbia Falls	MT	59912	**800-321-4653**	406-892-8700	655
Meadowbrook Insurance Group Inc 26600 Telegraph Rd Suite 300 *NYSE: MIG*	Southfield	MI	48034	**800-482-2726**	248-358-1100	355-4
Meadowlakes 300 Meadow Lakes	Hightstown	NJ	08520	**800-222-0609**	609-448-4100	659
Meadowland Farmers Co-op 101 1st Ave E	Lamberton	MN	56152	**800-527-5824**	507-752-7352	272
Meadowlands Exposition Center 355 Plaza Dr	Secaucus	NJ	07094	**888-400-3976**	201-330-7773	204
Meadowood Napa Valley 900 Meadowood Ln	Saint Helena	CA	94574	**800-458-8080**	707-963-3646	655
Meadows Foundation Inc 3003 Swiss Ave	Dallas	TX	75204	**800-826-9431**	214-826-9431	300
Meadows Psychiatric Center 132 Meadows Dr	Centre Hall	PA	16828	**800-641-7529**	814-364-2161	366-3
Meadowvale Resort & Conference Centre, Delta 6750 Mississauga Rd	Mississauga	ON	L5N2L3	**800-268-1133**	905-821-1981	655
MeadowView Conference Resort & Convention Center, Marriott 1901 Meadowview Pkwy	Kingsport	TN	37660	**800-820-5055**	423-578-6600	370
Meadville Tribune 947 Federal Ct	Meadville	PA	16335	**800-879-0006**	814-724-6370	522-2
MeadWestvaco Consumer & Office Products 10 W 2nd St	Dayton	OH	45402	**800-648-6323**	937-495-6323	542-3
MeadWestvaco Corp Envelope Div 2001 Roosevelt Ave	Springfield	MA	01104	**800-628-9265**	413-736-7211	260
MeadWestvaco Fiber Sales Courthouse Plaza NE	Dayton	OH	45463	**800-345-6323**	937-495-3379	624
Mean Gene's Burgers 2930 W Maple St	Sioux Falls	SD	57107	**800-648-6227**	605-336-6961	657
Means Industries Inc 1860 S Jefferson Ave	Saginaw	MI	48601	**800-869-1433**	989-754-3300	480
Means RS Co Inc 63 Smiths Ln	Kingston	MA	02364	**800-334-3509**	781-585-7880	623-2
MeansBusiness Inc 374 Congress St Suite 603	Boston	MA	02210	**800-231-8338**	617-956-9921	623-10
Mears Transportation Group 324 W Gore St	Orlando	FL	32806	**800-759-5219**	407-422-4561	433
Measurement Group, Computer 151 Fries Mill Rd Suite 104	Turnersville	NJ	08012	**800-436-7264**	856-401-1700	48-9
Measurement Society, IEEE Instrumentation & IEEE Operations Ctr 445 Hoes Ln	Piscataway	NJ	08854	**800-678-4333**	732-981-0060	49-19
Measurement Specialties Inc 710 Rt 46 E Suite 206 *AMEX: MSS*	Fairfield	NJ	07004	**800-236-6746**	973-808-3020	672

Entry	Toll-Free	Phone	Class
MeasureUp Inc 2325 Lakeview Pkwy Suite 175 ..... Alpharetta GA 30004	**800-649-1687**	678-356-5000	752
Meat Industry Suppliers Assn (MISA) Food Processing Machinery Assn 200 Dangerfield Rd 1st Fl .... Alexandria VA 22314	**800-331-8816**	703-684-1080	49-6
MECA Sportswear Inc 4225 White Bear Suite 400 ... Vadnais Heights MN 55110	**800-729-6322**	651-638-3800	153-5
MECCO Marking & Traceability PO Box 307 .... Ingomar PA 15127	**888-369-9199**	412-369-9199	459
Mechanical Contractors Assn of America (MCAA) 1385 Piccard Dr ... Rockville MD 20850	**800-556-3653**	301-869-5800	49-3
Mechanical Contractors Assn of America PAC 1385 Piccard Dr ...... Rockville MD 20850	**800-556-3653**	301-869-5800	604
Mechanical Engineering Magazine 3 Park Ave .... New York NY 10016 *Cust Svc	**800-843-2763***	212-591-7000	449-21
Mechanical Engineers. American Society of 3 Park Ave .... New York NY 10016 *Cust Svc	**800-843-2763***	212-591-7722	49-19
Mechanical Equipment Co Inc 1615 Poydras St Suite 1400 .... New Orleans LA 70112	**800-599-2152**	504-599-4000	793
Mechanical Inc 2279 Rt 20 E .... Freeport IL 61032	**800-747-1955**	815-962-8050	188-10
Mechanical Officials. International Assn of Plumbing & 5001 E Philadelphia St .... Ontario CA 91761	**800-854-2766**	909-472-4100	49-7
Mechanical Technology Inc 431 New Karner Rd .... Albany NY 12205 *NASDAQ: MKTY*	**800-828-8210**	518-533-2200	654
Mechanicsville Local PO Box 1118 .... Mechanicsville VA 23111	**800-476-0197**	804-746-1235	522-4
Mecklenburg Electric Co-op PO Box 2451 .... Chase City VA 23924	**800-989-4161**	434-372-6100	244
Meco Corp 1500 Industrial Rd .... Greeneville TN 37745	**800-251-7558**	423-639-1171	314-3
MecStat Laboratories 1700 S Mt Prospect Rd .... Des Plaines IL 60018	**800-235-2367**	847-375-0770	407
Med Diversified Inc 100 Brickstone Sq 5th Fl .... Andover MA 01810	**888-656-9903**	978-323-2500	176-10
Med-Emerg International Inc 6711 Mississauga Rd Suite 404 ... Mississauga ON L5N2W3	**800-265-3429**	905-858-1368	707
Med-Employ.com Inc 3905 E Martin Way Suite D .... Olympia WA 98506	**800-942-2480**		257
Med-Eng Systems Inc 2400 St Laurent Blvd .... Ottawa ON K1G6C4	**800-644-9078**	613-739-9646	566
Med Tech 135 NW 100 Ave .... Plantation FL 33324	**800-786-9555**	954-434-4341	347
MED-TECH Resource Inc 2053 Franklin Way .... Marietta GA 30067	**800-538-7498**	770-955-7292	755
Medaille College 18 Agassiz Cir .... Buffalo NY 14214	**800-292-1582**	716-884-3281	163
Medallion Financial Corp 437 Madison Ave 38th Fl .... New York NY 10022 *NASDAQ: TAXI*	**877-633-2554**	212-328-2100	214
Medart Inc 126 Manufacturers Dr .... Arnold MO 63010	**800-888-7181**	636-282-2300	378
Medco Health Solutions Inc 100 Parsons Pond Dr .... Franklin Lakes NJ 07417 *NYSE: MHS* ■ *Cust Svc	**800-248-2268***	201-269-3400	575
Medcom Trainex 6060 Phyllis Dr ...... Cypress CA 90630 *Cust Svc	**800-877-1443***	714-891-1443	502
Medea Corp 5525 Oakdale Ave .... Woodland Hills CA 91364	**888-296-3332**	818-880-0303	174
Medecins Sans Frontieres 333 7th Ave 2nd Fl .... New York NY 10001	**888-392-0392**	212-679-6800	48-5
Medeco Security Locks Inc PO Box 3075 .... Salem VA 24153	**800-839-3157**	540-380-5000	345
Medegen Medical Products 209 Medegen Dr .... Gallaway TN 38036 *Cust Svc	**800-233-1987***	901-867-2951	469
Medex Inc 2231 Rutherford Rd .... Carlsbad CA 92008	**800-848-1757**	760-602-4400	468
Medex Inc 6250 Shier Rings Rd .... Dublin OH 43016 *Cust Svc	**800-848-1757***	614-889-2220	468
MedExpress Pharmacy Ltd 1431 W Innes St .... Salisbury NC 28144	**800-808-8060**	704-633-3113	576
Medford Leas 1 Medford Leas Way .... Medford NJ 08055	**800-331-4302**	609-654-3000	659
Medford Mail Tribune PO Box 1108 .... Medford OR 97501	**800-366-2527**	541-776-4411	522-2
Media 100 Inc 450 Donald Lynch Blvd .... Marlborough MA 01752	**800-773-1770**	508-460-1600	176-8
Media Arts Group Inc 900 Lightpost Way .... Morgan Hill CA 95037	**800-366-3733**	408-201-5000	330
Media Bypass Magazine 4900 Tippecanoe Dr .... Evansville IN 47715	**800-429-7277**	812-477-8670	449-17
Media Cybernetics LP 8484 Georgia Ave Suite 200 .... Silver Spring MD 20910 *Sales	**800-992-4256***	301-495-3305	176-10
Media Factory Inc 48873 Kato Rd ..... Fremont CA 94539	**800-879-9536**	510-438-0373	239
Media Inc. Accuracy in 4455 Connecticut Ave NW Suite 330 .... Washington DC 20008	**800-787-4567**	202-364-4401	49-14
Media & Methods Magazine 1429 Walnut St 10th Fl .... Philadelphia PA 19102	**800-555-5657**	215-563-6005	449-8
Media Networks Inc 1 Station Pl 5th Fl .... Stamford CT 06902	**800-225-3457**	203-967-3100	6
Media Play 10400 Yellow Circle Dr ... Minnetonka MN 55343 *Cust Svc	**800-371-4425***	952-932-7700	514
Media Relations Newsletter 316 N Michigan Ave Suite 300 ...... Chicago IL 60601	**800-878-5331**	312-960-4100	521-11
Media Sciences International Inc 40 Boroline Rd .... Allendale NJ 07401 *AMEX: GFX*	**888-376-8378**	201-236-4311	172
Media Services 500 S Sepulveda Blvd 4th Fl ..... Los Angeles CA 90049	**800-333-7518**	310-440-9600	559
Media Watch PO Box 618 .... Santa Cruz CA 95061	**800-631-6355**	831-423-6355	48-8
Media3 Technologies LLC 33 Riverside Dr N River Commerce Pk .... Pembroke MA 02359	**800-903-9327**	781-826-1213	795
MediaBay Inc 2 Ridgedale Ave Suite 300 ...... Cedar Knolls NJ 07927 *NASDAQ: MBAY*	**800-688-4442**	973-539-9528	451
Mediacom Communications Corp 100 Crystal Run Rd .... Middletown NY 10941 *NASDAQ: MCCC*	**888-692-9090**	845-695-2600	117
Medialink Worldwide Inc 708 3rd Ave 8th Fl .... New York NY 10017 *NASDAQ: MDLK*	**800-843-0677**	212-682-8300	502
Medic Aid Response Systems Ltd 167 Village Rd .... Harring Cove NS B3V1H2	**800-565-9135**	902-454-8877	565
MEDICA PO Box 9310 .... Minneapolis MN 55440 *Cust Svc	**800-952-3455***	952-992-2900	384-3
Medical Action Industries Inc 800 Prime Pl .... Hauppauge NY 11788 *NASDAQ: MDCI*	**800-645-7042**	631-231-4600	469
Medical Analysis Systems Inc 46360 Fremont Blvd .... Fremont CA 94538	**800-582-3095**	800-232-3342	229
Medical Assistants. American Assn of 20 N Wacker Dr Suite 1575 .... Chicago IL 60606	**800-228-2262**	312-899-1500	49-8
Medical Assn. Alabama 19 S Jackson St .... Montgomery AL 36104	**800-239-6272**	334-263-6441	466
Medical Assn. American 515 N State St .... Chicago IL 60610	**800-621-8335**	312-464-5000	49-8
Medical Assn. American Podiatric 9312 Old Georgetown Rd .... Bethesda MD 20814	**800-275-2762**	301-571-9200	49-8
Medical Assn. Arizona 810 W Bethany Home Rd .... Phoenix AZ 85013	**800-482-3480**	602-246-8901	466
Medical Assn. Florida 123 S Adams St .... Tallahassee FL 32301	**800-762-0233**	850-224-6496	466
Medical Assn. Georgia 1330 W Peachtree St NW Suite 500 ... Atlanta GA 30309	**800-282-0224**	404-876-7535	466
Medical Assn. Hawaii 1360 S Beretania St Suite 200 ...... Honolulu HI 96814	**866-536-8666**	808-536-7702	466
Medical Assn. Indiana State 322 Canal Walk .... Indianapolis IN 46202	**800-257-4762**	317-261-2060	466
Medical Assn. Kentucky 4965 US Hwy 42 KMA Bldg Suite 2000 .... Louisville KY 40222	**800-686-9923**	502-426-6200	466
Medical Assn. Maine 30 Associate Dr .... Manchester ME 04351	**800-772-0815**	207-622-3374	466
Medical Assn. Minnesota 1300 Godward St NE Suite 2500 .... Minneapolis MN 55413	**800-342-5662**	612-378-1875	466
Medical Assn. Mississippi State 408 W Parkway Pl .... Ridgeland MS 39157	**800-898-0251**	601-853-6733	466
Medical Assn. Missouri State 113 Madison St .... Jefferson City MO 65101	**800-869-6762**	573-636-5151	466
Medical Assn. Montana 2021 11th Ave Suite 1 .... Helena MT 59601	**877-443-4000**	406-443-4000	466
Medical Assn. National 1012 10th St NW .... Washington DC 20001	**800-662-0554**	202-347-1895	49-8
Medical Assn. Ohio State 3401 Mill Run Dr .... Hilliard OH 43026	**800-766-6762**	614-527-6762	466
Medical Assn. Oklahoma State 601 NW Grand Blvd .... Oklahoma City OK 73118	**800-522-9452**	405-843-9571	466
Medical Assn. South Carolina 132 W Park Blvd .... Columbia SC 29210	**800-327-1021**	803-798-6207	466
Medical Assn. Southern 35 Lakeshore Dr .... Birmingham AL 35209	**800-423-4992**	205-945-1840	49-8
Medical Assn. Tennessee 2301 21st Ave A .... Nashville TN 37212	**800-659-1862**	615-385-2100	466
Medical Assn. Texas 401 W 15th St ..... Austin TX 78701	**800-880-1300**	512-370-1300	466
Medical Assn. Washington State 2033 6th Ave Suite 1100 .... Seattle WA 98121	**800-552-0612**	206-441-9762	466
Medical Assn. West Virginia State 4301 MacCorkle Ave .... Charleston WV 25364	**800-257-4747**	304-925-0342	466
Medical Assurance 20 Allen Ave Suite 420 .... Saint Louis MO 63119	**800-492-7212**	314-961-7700	384-5
Medical Assurance Inc 100 Brookwood Pl Suite 300 ..... Birmingham AL 35209	**800-282-6242**	205-877-4400	384-5
Medical Boards of the US Inc. Federation of State 400 Fuller Wiser Rd Suite 300 .... Euless TX 76039	**800-876-5396**	817-868-4000	49-8
Medical Center Enterprise 400 N Edwards St .... Enterprise AL 36330	**800-993-6837**	334-347-0584	366-2
Medical Center at Princeton Home Care 208 Bunn Dr .... Princeton NJ 08540	**800-584-4153**	609-497-4900	358
Medical City Hospital Transplant Center 7777 Forest Ln Bldg A 12 S .... Dallas TX 75230	**800-348-4318**	972-566-6547	758
Medical College of Georgia 1120 15th St .... Augusta GA 30912	**800-736-2273**	706-721-0211	163
Medical Corps. International 1919 Santa Monica Blvd Suite 300 .... Santa Monica CA 90404	**800-481-4462**	310-826-7800	48-5
Medical Device Technologies Inc 3600 SW 47th Ave .... Gainesville FL 32608	**800-338-0440**	352-338-0440	468
Medical Directions Inc 410 Saw Mill River Rd Suite 1005 ..... Ardsley NY 10502	**800-647-0573**	914-478-8500	262
Medical Directors Assn. American 10480 Little Patuxent Pkwy Suite 760 .... Columbia MD 21044	**800-876-2632**	410-740-9743	49-8
Medical Doctor Assoc Inc 145 Technology Pkwy NW .... Norcross GA 30092	**800-780-3500**	770-246-9191	193
Medical Economics Magazine 5 Paragon Dr .... Montvale NJ 07645	**888-581-8052**	973-944-7777	449-16
Medical Eye Bank of Maryland 815 Park Ave .... Baltimore MD 21201	**800-756-4824**	410-752-2020	265
Medical Genetics Consultants 910 Washington Ave .... Ocean Springs MS 39564	**800-362-4363**	228-872-3680	408
Medical Graphics Corp 350 Oak Grove Pkwy .... Saint Paul MN 55127	**800-333-4137**	651-484-4874	249
Medical Group Management Assn (MGMA) 104 Inverness Terr E ..... Englewood CO 80112	**877-275-6462**	303-799-1111	49-8
Medical Instrumentation. Association for the Advancement of 1110 N Glebe Rd Suite 220 .... Arlington VA 22201	**800-332-2264**	703-525-4890	49-8
Medical Liability Mutual Insurance Co (MLMIC) 2 Park Ave 25th Fl .... New York NY 10016	**800-275-6564**	212-576-9800	384-5
Medical Liability Mutual Insurance Co HUM Div 8 British-American Blvd ...... Latham NY 12110	**800-635-0666**	518-786-2700	384-5
Medical Malpractice Law & Strategy Newsletter 345 Park Ave S .... New York NY 10010	**800-888-8300**	212-779-9200	521-7
Medical Manager Health Systems 3001 N Rocky Point Dr E Suite 400 ... Tampa FL 33607	**800-330-3612**	813-287-2990	176-10
Medical Manager MacHealth 210 Gateway Mall Suite 102 .... Lincoln NE 68505	**800-888-4344**	402-466-8100	176-11

Name / Address	City	State	ZIP	Toll-Free	Phone	Class
Medical Marketing Assn (MMA) 74 New Montgomery St Suite 230	San Francisco	CA	94105	**800-551-2173**	415-764-4807	49-18
Medical Mission Board. Catholic 10 W 17th St	New York	NY	10011	**800-678-5659**	212-242-7757	48-5
Medical Mutual Insurance Co of Maine PO Box 15275	Portland	ME	04112	**800-942-2791**		384-5
Medical Mutual Liability Insurance Society of Maryland 225 International Cir	Hunt Valley	MD	21030	**800-492-0193**	410-785-0050	384-5
Medical Protective Co PO Box 15021	Fort Wayne	IN	46885	**800-463-3776**	260-485-9622	384-5
Medical Rehabilitation Providers Assn. American 1710 'N' St NW	Washington	DC	20036	**888-346-4624**	202-223-1920	49-8
Medical Research Foundation. Dystonia 1 E Wacker Dr Suite 2430	Chicago	IL	60601	**800-377-3978**	312-755-0198	48-17
Medical Resources Inc 125 State St	Hackensack	NJ	07601	**800-537-7272**	201-488-6230	376
Medical Review Officers. American Assn of PO Box 12873	Research Triangle Park	NC	27709	**800-489-1839**	919-489-5407	49-8
Medical Services of America Inc 171 Monroe Ln	Lexington	SC	29072	**800-845-5850**	803-957-0500	358
Medical Society. Arkansas PO Box 55088	Little Rock	AR	72215	**800-542-1058**	501-224-8967	466
Medical Society. Colorado 7351 Lowry Blvd	Denver	CO	80230	**800-654-5653**	720-859-1001	466
Medical Society. Connecticut State 160 Saint Ronan St	New Haven	CT	06511	**800-635-7740**	203-865-0587	466
Medical Society. Delaware 131 Continental Dr Suite 405	Newark	DE	19713	**800-348-6800**	302-658-7596	466
Medical Society. Iowa 1001 Grand Ave	West Des Moines	IA	50265	**800-747-3070**	515-223-1401	466
Medical Society. Kansas 623 SW 10th Ave	Topeka	KS	66612	**800-332-0156**	785-235-2383	466
Medical Society. Louisiana State 6767 Perkins Rd Suite 100	Baton Rouge	LA	70808	**800-375-9508**	225-763-8500	466
Medical Society. Maryland State 1211 Cathedral St	Baltimore	MD	21201	**800-492-1056**	410-539-0872	466
Medical Society. Massachusetts 860 Winter St	Waltham	MA	02451	**800-322-2303**	781-893-4610	466
Medical Society. New Hampshire 7 N State St	Concord	NH	03301	**800-564-1909**	603-224-1909	466
Medical Society. New Jersey 2 Princess Rd	Lawrenceville	NJ	08648	**800-322-6765**	609-896-1766	466
Medical Society. New Mexico 7770 Jefferson NE Suite 400	Albuquerque	NM	87109	**800-748-1596**	505-828-0237	466
Medical Society. New York State 420 Lakeville Rd PO Box 5404	Lake Success	NY	11042	**800-523-4405**	516-488-6100	466
Medical Society. North Carolina 222 N Person St	Raleigh	NC	27601	**800-722-1350**	919-833-3836	466
Medical Society. Vermont 134 Main St	Montpelier	VT	05601	**800-640-8767**	802-223-7898	466
Medical Society. Virginia 4205 Dover Rd	Richmond	VA	23221	**800-746-6768**	804-353-2721	466
Medical Society. Wisconsin State 330 E Lakeside St	Madison	WI	53701	**866-442-3800**	608-257-6781	466
Medical Sonographers. American Registry of Diagnostic 51 Monroe St Plaza East 1	Rockville	MD	20850	**800-541-9754**	301-738-8401	49-8
Medical Sonography. Society of Diagnostic 2745 N Dallas Pkwy Suite 350	Plano	TX	75093	**800-229-9506**	214-473-8057	49-8
Medical Staffing Assoc Inc 6731 Whittier Ave Suite A300	McLean	VA	22101	**800-235-5105**	703-893-1773	707
Medical Student Assn. American 1902 Association Dr	Reston	VA	20191	**800-767-2266**	703-620-6600	49-5
Medical Teams International. Northwest PO Box 10	Portland	OR	97207	**800-959-4325**	503-624-1000	48-5
Medical Technologists. American 710 Higgins Rd	Park Ridge	IL	60068	**800-275-1268**	847-823-5169	49-8
Medical Technology Systems Inc 2003 Gandy Blvd N Suite 800 *AMEX: MPP*	Saint Petersburg	FL	33702	**800-334-6663**	727-571-1616	537
Medical Transcription. American Assn for 100 Sycamore Ave	Modesto	CA	95354	**800-982-2182**	209-527-9620	49-8
Medical University of South Carolina 171 Ashley Ave	Charleston	SC	29425	**800-424-6872**	843-792-9241	163
MedicAlert Foundation International 2323 Colorado Ave *Cust Svc	Turlock	CA	95382	**800-432-5378***	209-668-3333	48-17
Medicap Pharmacies Inc 4350 Westown Pkwy Suite 400 *Cust Svc	West Des Moines	IA	50266	**800-445-2244***	515-224-8400	236
Medicare Compliance Alert Newsletter 11300 Rockville Pike Suite 1100	Rockville	MD	20852	**800-929-4824**	301-287-2700	521-7
Medicare Hotline	Baltimore	MD	21207	**800-633-4227**		336-6
Medicare. National Committee to Preserve Social Security & 10 G St NE Suite 600	Washington	DC	20002	**800-966-1935**	202-216-0420	48-7
Medicare Rights Center (MRC) 1460 Broadway 17th Fl *hotline	New York	NY	10036	**800-333-4114***	212-869-3850	48-17
Medicine. American College for Advancement in 23121 Verdugo Dr Suite 204	Laguna Hills	CA	92653	**800-532-3688**	949-583-7666	49-8
Medicine. American Institute of Ultrasound in 14750 Sweitzer Ln Suite 100	Laurel	MD	20707	**800-638-5352**	301-498-4100	49-8
Medicine. American Orthopaedic Society for Sports 6300 N River Rd Suite 500	Rosemont	IL	60018	**877-321-3500**	847-292-4900	49-8
Medicine. Association of Program Directors in Internal 2501 M St NW Suite 550	Washington	DC	20037	**800-622-4558**	202-887-9450	49-8

Name / Address	City	State	ZIP	Toll-Free	Phone	Class
Medicine. Canadian Academy of Sport 1010 Polytek St Unit 14 Suite 100	Ottawa	ON	K1J9H9	**877-585-2394**	613-748-5851	49-8
Medicine Online Inc 18800 Delaware St Suite 650	Huntington Beach	CA	92648	**888-666-5638**	714-848-0444	351
Medicine. Physicians' Committee for Responsible 5100 Wisconsin Ave NW Suite 400	Washington	DC	20016	**866-416-7276**	202-686-2210	49-8
Medicine Shoppe International Inc 1100 N Lindbergh Blvd *Cust Svc	Saint Louis	MO	63132	**800-325-1397***	314-993-6000	236
Medicine Surgery & Ophthalmology. American Society of Contemporary 820 N Orleans St Suite 208	Chicago	IL	60610	**800-621-4002**	312-440-0699	49-8
MedicineNet Inc 903 Calle Amanecer Suite 300	San Clemente	CA	92673	**800-221-5698**	949-940-6500	351
Medicines Co 200 5th Ave *NASDAQ: MDCO*	Waltham	MA	02451	**800-656-4662**	781-464-1500	86
Medicis Pharmaceutical Corp 8125 N Hayden Rd *NYSE: MRX* ■ *Cust Svc	Scottsdale	AZ	85258	**800-550-5115***	602-808-8800	572
Medico Industries Inc 1500 Hwy 315	Wilkes-Barre	PA	18711	**800-633-0027**	570-825-7711	261-2
Medico Life Insurance Co 1515 S 75th St	Omaha	NE	68124	**800-228-6080**	402-391-6900	384-2
Medicore Inc 2337 W 76th St *NASDAQ: MDKI*	Hialeah	FL	33016	**800-327-8894**	305-558-4000	467
Medifast Inc 11445 Cronhill Dr *AMEX: MED*	Owings Mills	MD	21117	**866-463-3432**	410-581-8042	291-11
MediGrafix Inc 11205 Wright Cir Suite 120	Omaha	NE	68144	**877-284-5147**	402-333-3323	755
MedImmune Inc 1 MedImmune Way *NASDAQ: MEDI*	Gaithersburg	MD	20878	**877-633-4411**	301-398-0000	86
MedImpact Healthcare Systems Inc 10680 Treena St Suite 500	San Diego	CA	92131	**800-788-2949**	858-566-2727	575
Medina Electric Co-op Inc PO Box 370	Hondo	TX	78861	**800-381-3334**	830-741-4384	244
Medina Gazette 805 W Liberty St	Medina	OH	44256	**800-633-4623**	330-725-4166	522-2
MEDIQ Inc 1 MEDIQ Plaza	Pennsauken	NJ	08110	**800-222-4776**	856-665-9300	261-5
Mediterranean Shipping Co Cruises 6700 N Andrews Ave Suite 605	Fort Lauderdale	FL	33309	**800-666-9333**	954-772-6262	217
Mediware Information Systems Inc 11711 W 79th St *NASDAQ: MEDW*	Lenexa	KS	66214	**800-255-0026**	913-307-1000	176-11
MEDjet International Inc 1000 Urban Ctr Dr	Birmingham	AL	35242	**800-356-2161**	205-592-4460	31
Medline Industries Inc 1 Medline Pl. *Cust Svc	Mundelein	IL	60060	**800-323-6284***	847-949-5500	566
MedlinePlus National Library of Medicine 8600 Rockville Pike	Bethesda	MD	20894	**888-346-3656**	301-594-5983	351
Mednik Riverbend 4245 Forest Pk Blvd	Saint Louis	MO	63108	**800-325-7193**	314-535-9090	497
MedPlus Inc 4690 Parkway Dr	Mason	OH	45040	**800-444-6235**	513-229-5500	176-10
MedQuist Inc 5 Greentree Ctr Suite 311	Marlton	NJ	08053	**800-233-3030**	856-596-8877	755
Medrad Inc 1 Medrad Dr *Cust Svc	Indianola	PA	15051	**800-633-7237***	412-767-2400	468
Medstaff National Medical Staffing Inc 1000 Pk 40 Plaza	Durham	NC	27713	**800-476-3275**		707
MedStar Health 5565 Sterrett Pl 5th Fl	Columbia	MD	21044	**877-772-6505**	410-772-6500	348
Medstone International Inc 100 Columbia Suite 100	Aliso Viejo	CA	92656	**800-633-7866**	949-448-7700	347
Medtech Products Inc PO Box 1108	Jackson	WY	83001	**800-443-4908**	307-733-1680	237
MedTech USA 6310 San Vicente Blvd Suite 404	Los Angeles	CA	90048	**800-640-8000**	323-964-1000	176-3
MEDTOX Diagnostics Inc 1238 Anthony Rd	Burlington	NC	27215	**800-334-1116**	336-226-6311	229
MEDTOX Scientific Inc 402 W County Rd D *AMEX: TOX*	Saint Paul	MN	55112	**800-832-3244**	651-636-7466	407
Medtronic Arterial Vascular Engineering 3576 Unocal Pl	Santa Rosa	CA	95403	**800-308-7868**	707-525-0111	468
Medtronic of Canada Ltd 6733 Kitimat Rd	Mississauga	ON	L5N1W3	**800-268-5346**	905-826-6020	249
Medtronic Emergency Response Systems 11811 Willows Rd NE	Redmond	WA	98052	**800-442-1142**	425-867-4000	249
Medtronic Energy & Component Center (MECC) 6700 Shingle Creek Pkwy	Brooklyn Center	MN	55430	**800-328-2518**	763-514-1000	76
Medtronic Inc 710 Medtronic Pkwy NE *NYSE: MDT* ■ *Cust Svc	Minneapolis	MN	55432	**800-328-2518***	763-574-4000	249
Medtronic Inc Heart Valve Div 1851 E Deere Ave	Santa Ana	CA	92705	**800-326-3330**	949-474-3943	469
Medtronic Microelectronics Center 2343 W Medtronic Way	Tempe	AZ	85281	**800-633-8766**	480-929-5507	686
Medtronic MiniMed Inc 18000 Devonshire St	Northridge	CA	91325	**800-933-3322**	818-362-5958	469
Medtronic Neurosurgery 125 Cremona Dr *Cust Svc	Goleta	CA	93117	**800-468-9710***	805-968-1546	468
Medtronic Perfusion Systems 7611 Northland Dr	Brooklyn Park	MN	55428	**800-328-3320**	763-391-9000	249
Medtronic Powered Surgical Solutions 4620 N Beach St	Fort Worth	TX	76137	**800-433-7639**	817-788-6400	469
Medtronic Sofamor Danek Inc 1800 Pyramid Pl	Memphis	TN	38132	**800-763-2667**	901-396-2695	469
Medtronic Xomed Inc 6743 Southpoint Dr N	Jacksonville	FL	32216	**800-874-5797**	904-296-9600	469
MedWatch 5600 Fishers Ln HFD-410	Rockville	MD	20857	**888-463-6332**	301-827-7240	336-6
Medwave Inc 4382 Round Lake Rd W *NASDAQ: MDWV*	Arden Hills	MN	55112	**800-894-7601**	651-639-1227	468
MEE Material Handling Equipment 11721 W Carmen Ave	Milwaukee	WI	53225	**800-992-0292**	414-353-3300	378

Name / Address	City	State	Zip	Toll-Free	Phone	Class
Meeder Equipment Co 12323 6th St	Rancho Cucamonga	CA	91739	**800-423-3711**	909-463-0600	352
Meeker Co-op Light & Power Assn PO Box 522	Litchfield	MN	55355	**800-232-6257**	320-693-3231	244
MEEMIC Holdings Inc 691 N Squirrel Rd Suite 100	Auburn Hills	MI	48326	**888-463-3642**	248-373-5700	355-4
Meese Inc 1745 Cragmont St	Madison	IN	47250	**800-829-4535**	812-273-3232	596
Meese Orbitron Dunne Co 535 N Midland Ave	Saddle Brook	NJ	07663	**800-829-3230**	201-796-4667	198
Meeting News 770 Broadway	New York	NY	10003	**800-950-1314**	646-654-4420	449-5
Meeting Street Inn 173 Meeting St	Charleston	SC	29401	**800-842-8022**	843-723-1882	373
Meetings & Conventions Magazine 500 Plaza Dr	Secaucus	NJ	07094	**800-446-6551**	201-902-2000	449-5
Meetings & Incentives Group 21760 Stevens Creek Blvd	Cupertino	CA	95014	**800-752-9202**	408-973-1915	183
MEG Div SteelWorks Inc 502 S Green St *Cust Svc	Cambridge City	IN	47327	**800-645-3315***	765-478-3141	281
MEGA Life & Health Insurance Co 9151 Grapevine Hwy	North Richland Hills	TX	76180	**800-527-2845**	817-255-3100	384-2
Mega-Pro International Inc 251 W Hilton Dr	Saint George	UT	84770	**800-541-9469**	435-673-1001	786
MegaPath Networks Inc 6691 Owens Dr	Pleasanton	CA	94588	**877-634-2728**	925-201-2500	390
Megatech Corp 555 Woburn St	Tewksbury	MA	01876	**800-767-6342**	978-937-9600	754
Megger 4271 Bronze Way	Dallas	TX	75237	**800-723-2861**	214-333-3201	247
Meggitt/S-TEC 1 S-Tec Way	Mineral Wells	TX	76067	**800-872-7832**	940-325-9406	519
MEGTEC Systems Co 830 Prosper Rd *Cust Svc	De Pere	WI	54115	**800-558-5535***	920-336-5715	379
Meguiar's Inc 17991 Mitchell S *Cust Svc	Irvine	CA	92614	**800-347-5700***	949-752-8000	149
Meherrin Agricultural & Chemical Co Inc PO Box 200	Severn	NC	27877	**800-775-0333**	252-585-1744	272
MEI (Mars Electronics International) 1301 Wilson Dr *Cust Svc	West Chester	PA	19380	**800-345-8215***	610-430-2500	55
Meier's Wine Cellars Inc 6955 Plainfield Rd	Silverton	OH	45236	**800-346-2941**	513-891-2900	81-3
Meijer Frederik Gardens & Sculpture Park 1000 East Beltline Ave NE	Grand Rapids	MI	49525	**888-974-1580**	616-957-1580	98
Meijer Inc 2929 Walker Ave NW	Grand Rapids	MI	49544	**800-543-3704**	616-453-6711	339
Meineke Car Care Centers 128 S Tryon St Suite 900	Charlotte	NC	28202	**800-275-5200**	704-377-8855	62-3
Meininger HR Co 499 Broadway	Denver	CO	80203	**800-950-2787**	303-698-3838	45
Meisel Music Inc PO Box 90	Springfield	NJ	07081	**800-634-7350**	973-379-5000	516
Meisel Visual Imaging 433 Regal Row	Dallas	TX	75247	**800-527-5186**	214-688-4900	577
Meissner Tractors Inc Hwy 2 & 87 PO Box 1111	Havre	MT	59501	**800-800-3113**	406-265-5887	270
Meister Publishing Co 37733 Euclid Ave *Orders	Willoughby	OH	44094	**800-572-7740***	440-942-2000	623-9
Mel Bay Publications Inc 4 Industrial Dr	Pacific	MO	63069	**800-863-5229**	636-257-3970	623-2
Melaleuca Inc 3910 S Yellowstone Hwy *Sales	Idaho Falls	ID	83402	**800-282-3000***	208-522-0700	361
Melbourne-Palm Bay Area Chamber of Commerce 1005 E Strawbridge Ave	Melbourne	FL	32901	**800-771-9922**	321-724-5400	137
Melbourne/Palm Bay Area Convention & Visitor Bureau 1005 E Strawbridge Ave	Melbourne	FL	32901	**800-771-9922**	321-724-5400	205
Meldisco 933 MacArthur Blvd	Mahwah	NJ	07430	**800-777-1330**	201-934-2000	296
Mele Enterprises Inc 2007 Beechgrove Pl	Utica	NY	13501	**800-635-6353**	315-733-4600	199
Melhado George & Co 10 Merchant St	Sharon	MA	02067	**800-635-4236**	781-784-5550	744
Melhana - The Grand Plantation 301 Showboat Ln	Thomasville	GA	31792	**888-920-3030**	229-226-2290	373
Melin Tool Co 5565 Venture Dr Unit C	Cleveland	OH	44130	**800-521-1078**	216-362-4200	484
Melissa's/World Variety Produce Inc 5325 S Soto St	Vernon	CA	90058	**800-468-7111**	323-588-0151	292-7
Melitta Canada Inc 1 Greensboro Dr Suite 202	Rexdale	ON	M9W1C8	**800-565-4882**	416-243-8979	291-7
Melles Griot Inc 2051 Palomar Airport Rd Suite 200 *Cust Svc	Carlsbad	CA	92009	**800-645-2737***	760-268-5131	534
Melling Tool Co PO Box 1188	Jackson	MI	49204	**800-777-8172**	517-787-8172	60
Mellon Bank NA 500 Grant St 1 Mellon Bank Ctr	Pittsburgh	PA	15258	**800-635-5662**	412-234-5000	71
Melo-Tone Vending Inc 130 Broadway	Somerville	MA	02145	**800-322-7741**	617-666-4900	55
Melody Farms/Stroh's Ice Cream Co 1000 Maple St	Detroit	MI	48207	**800-234-8871**	313-568-5100	291-25
Melrath Gasket Inc 2901 W Hunting Pk Ave	Philadelphia	PA	19129	**800-635-7284**	215-223-6000	321
Melrose Hotel 140 E 63rd St	New York	NY	10021	**800-223-1020**	212-838-5700	373
Melrose Hotel Dallas 3015 Oak Lawn Ave	Dallas	TX	75219	**800-635-7673**	214-521-5151	373
Melrose Hotel Washington DC 2430 Pennsylvania Ave NW	Washington	DC	20037	**800-635-7673**	202-955-6400	373
Melster Candy Co 500 E Madison St	Cambridge	WI	53523	**800-535-4401**	608-423-3221	291-8
Melting Pot Restaurants Inc 8810 Twin Lakes Blvd	Tampa	FL	33614	**800-783-0867**	813-881-0055	657
Melton Truck Lines Inc 808 N 161 East Ave	Tulsa	OK	74116	**800-545-6651**	918-234-8000	769
Membership Group Inc. North American 12301 Whitewater Dr Suite 260	Minnetonka	MN	55343	**800-634-8598**	952-936-9333	361
MemberWorks Inc 680 Washington Blvd *NASDAQ: MBRS*	Stamford	CT	06901	**800-374-6135**	203-324-7635	9
MEMCO Barge Line 16090 Wingley Ridge Rd	Chesterfield	MO	63017	**800-207-8011**	636-530-2100	457
Memec Inc 3721 Valley Centre Dr	San Diego	CA	92130	**888-882-2444**	858-314-8800	245
Memorial Healthcare Center 826 W King St	Owosso	MI	48867	**800-206-8706**	989-723-5211	366-2
Memorial Hermann Memorial City Hospital 921 Gessner Rd	Houston	TX	77024	**800-392-6370**	713-932-3000	366-2
Memorial Hospital 1101 Michigan Ave	Logansport	IN	46947	**800-243-4512**	574-753-7541	366-2
Memorial Hospital 325 South Belmont St PO Box 15118	York	PA	17405	**800-436-4326**	717-843-8623	366-2
Memorial Hospital of Sweetwater County 1200 College Dr	Rock Springs	WY	82901	**800-307-3711**	307-362-3711	366-2
Memorial Medical Center of East Texas PO Box 1447	Lufkin	TX	75902	**800-348-5969**	936-634-8111	366-2
Memphis College of Art Overton Park 1930 Poplar Ave	Memphis	TN	38104	**800-727-1088**	901-272-5151	163
Memphis Convention & Visitors Bureau 47 Union Ave	Memphis	TN	38103	**800-873-6282**	901-543-5300	205
Memphis Cook Convention Center 255 N Main St	Memphis	TN	38103	**800-726-0915**	901-576-1200	204
Memphis Engraving Co 5120 Elmore Rd	Memphis	TN	38134	**800-426-6803**	901-388-8200	770
Memphis Hardwood Flooring Co 1551 N Thomas St	Memphis	TN	38107	**800-346-3010**	901-526-7306	671
Memphis Machinery & Supply Co Inc 2881 Directors Cove	Memphis	TN	38131	**800-388-4485**	901-527-4443	809
Memphis Motorsports Park 5500 Taylor-Forge DR	Millington	TN	38053	**866-407-7333**	901-358-7223	504
Memphis Publishing Co 495 Union Ave *Cust Svc	Memphis	TN	38103	**800-444-6397***	901-529-2211	623-8
Memry Corp 3 Berkshire Blvd *AMEX: MRY*	Bethel	CT	06801	**866-466-3679**	203-739-1100	476
Memtron Technologies Inc 530 N Franklin St *Cust Svc	Frankenmuth	MI	48734	**800-234-7525***	989-652-2656	171-1
Menard Electric Co-op PO Box 200	Petersburg	IL	62675	**800-872-1203**	217-632-7746	244
Menardi 1 Maxwell Dr	Trenton	SC	29847	**800-321-3218**	803-663-6551	68
Menasha Corp 1645 Bergstrom Rd	Neenah	WI	54956	**800-558-5073**	920-751-1000	101
Menasha Packaging Co 1645 Bergstrom Rd	Neenah	WI	54956	**800-558-5073**	920-751-1000	101
MENC: National Assn for Music Education 1806 Robert Fulton Dr	Reston	VA	20191	**800-336-3768**	703-860-4000	49-5
Mended Hearts 7272 Greenville Ave	Dallas	TX	75231	**888-432-1899**	214-706-1442	48-17
Mendelson & Assoc 2615 S Hill St	Los Angeles	CA	90007	**800-421-8250**	213-746-0745	401
Mendocino Coast Chamber of Commerce 332 N Main St PO Box 1141	Fort Bragg	CA	95437	**800-726-2780**	707-961-6300	137
Mendocino Hotel & Garden Suites 45080 Main St	Mendocino	CA	95460	**800-548-0513**	707-937-0511	373
Mendocino Wine Co 501 Parducci Rd	Ukiah	CA	95482	**888-362-9463**	707-463-5350	81-3
Mendota Insurance Co 1285 Northland Dr	Mendota Heights	MN	55120	**800-422-0792**	651-688-4100	384-4
Menger Hotel 204 Alamo Plaza	San Antonio	TX	78205	**800-345-9285**	210-223-4361	373
Menke Marking Devices PO Box 2986	Santa Fe Springs	CA	90670	**800-231-6023**	562-921-1380	459
Menlo College 1000 El Camino Real	Atherton	CA	94027	**800-556-3656**	650-543-3753	163
Menlo Worldwide Inc 1 Lagoon Dr Suite 400	Redwood City	CA	94065	**800-227-1981**	650-596-4000	440
Mennel Milling Co 128 W Crocker St	Fostoria	OH	44830	**800-688-8151**	419-435-8151	291-23
Mennen Medical Corp 2540 Metropolitan Dr	Trevose	PA	19053	**800-223-2201**	215-322-9997	249
Menninger Clinic PO Box 809045	Houston	TX	77280	**800-351-9058**	713-275-5000	366-3
Menno Travel Service Inc DBA MTS Travel Inc 124 E Main St 4th Fl	Ephrata	PA	17522	**800-642-8315**	717-733-4131	760
Mennonite Brethren Biblical Seminary 4824 E Butler Ave	Fresno	CA	93727	**800-251-6227**	559-251-8628	164-3
Mennonite Central Committee (MCC) 21 S 12th St PO Box 500	Akron	PA	17501	**888-563-4676**	717-859-1151	48-5
Mennonite Publishing House 616 Walnut Ave *Sales	Scottdale	PA	15683	**800-245-7894***	724-887-8500	623-4
Menominee Paper 144 1st St	Menominee	MI	49858	**800-258-3781**	906-863-5595	551
Menomonie Area (Greater) Chamber of Commerce 342 E Main St	Menomonie	WI	54751	**800-283-1862**	715-235-9087	137
Menopause Society. North American 5900 Landerbrook Dr Suite 195	Mayfield Heights	OH	44124	**800-774-5342**	440-442-7550	49-8
Men's Fitness Magazine 21100 Erwin St *Orders	Woodland Hills	CA	91367	**800-340-8958***	818-884-6800	449-13
Men's Health Magazine 33 E Minor St	Emmaus	PA	18098	**800-666-2303**	610-967-5171	449-13
Men's Wearhouse Inc 40650 Encyclopedia Cir *NYSE: MW*	Fremont	CA	94538	**800-777-8580**	510-723-8200	155-3
Mensa Ltd. American 1229 Corporate Dr W	Arlington	TX	76006	**800-666-3672**	817-607-0060	48-15
Mental Health Assn. National 2001 N Beauregard St 12th Fl *Help Line	Alexandria	VA	22311	**800-969-6642***	703-684-7722	48-17
Mental Health Counselors Assn. American 801 N Fairfax St Suite 304	Alexandria	VA	22314	**800-326-2642**	703-548-6002	49-15
Mental Health Law Reporter Newsletter 8737 Colesville Rd Suite 1100	Silver Spring	MD	20910	**800-274-6737**	301-587-6300	521-8
Mental Health Report 8737 Colesville Rd Suite 1100	Silver Spring	MD	20910	**800-274-6737**	301-587-6300	521-8
Mental Illness. National Resource Center on Homelessness & 345 Delaware Ave	Delmar	NY	12054	**800-444-7415**	518-439-7415	49-15
Mental Retardation. American Assn on 444 N Capitol St NW Suite 846	Washington	DC	20001	**800-424-3688**	202-387-1968	48-17
Mentally Ill. National Alliance for the 2107 Wilson Blvd Suite 300	Arlington	VA	22201	**800-950-6264**	703-524-7600	48-17
Mentholatum Co Inc 707 Sterling Dr	Orchard Park	NY	14127	**800-688-7660**	716-677-2500	572

	Toll-Free	Phone	Class
MENTOR 313 Congress St ... Boston MA 02210	**800-388-5150**	617-790-4800	454
Mentor Corp 201 Mentor Dr ... Santa Barbara CA 93111 *NYSE: MNT*	**800-525-0245**	805-681-6000	469
Mentor Graphics Corp 8005 SW Boeckman Rd ... Wilsonville OR 97070 *NASDAQ: MENT*	**800-592-2210**	503-685-7000	176-5
Mepco Label Systems PO Box 932 ... Stockton CA 95201	**800-975-2235**	209-946-0201	404
Mer-Kote Products Inc 501 S Van Ness Ave ... Torrance CA 90501	**800-851-6303**	323-775-2461	594-2
Mercantile Bank Corp 216 N Division Ave ... Grand Rapids MI 49503 *NASDAQ: MBWM*	**888-345-6296**	616-406-3000	355-2
Mercantile Mortgage Corp 2 Hopkins Plaza Suite 900 ... Baltimore MD 21201	**800-874-7880**	410-347-8940	498
Mercantile-Safe Deposit & Trust Co 2 Hopkins Plaza ... Baltimore MD 21201	**888-212-0100**	410-237-5569	71
Merced Conference & Visitors Bureau 690 W 16th St ... Merced CA 95340	**800-446-5353**	209-384-7092	205
Mercedes-Benz Credit Corp PO Box 685 ... Roanoke TX 76262	**800-654-6222**		215
Mercedes-Benz USA 1 Mercedes Dr ... Montvale NJ 07645 *Cust Svc	**800-222-0100***	201-573-0600	59
Mercedes Electric Supply Inc 8550 NW South River Dr ... Miami FL 33166	**800-636-5550**	305-887-5550	245
Mercer County Community College PO Box B ... Trenton NJ 08690	**800-392-6222**	609-586-4800	160
James Kerney Campus N Broad & Academy St ... Trenton NJ 08608	**800-392-6222**	609-586-4800	160
West Windsor Campus 1200 Old Trenton Rd ... West Windsor NJ 08550	**800-392-6222**	609-586-4800	160
Mercer County Convention & Visitors Bureau 50 N Water Ave ... Sharon PA 16146	**800-637-2370**	724-346-3771	205
Mercer County Convention & Visitors Bureau 500 Bland St PO Box 4088 ... Bluefield WV 24701	**800-221-3206**	304-325-8438	205
Mercer Hotel 147 Mercer St ... New York NY 10012	**888-918-6060**	212-966-6060	373
Mercer Human Resource Consulting 777 S Figueroa St ... Los Angeles CA 90017	**866-879-3384**	213-346-2200	192
Mercer Industries Inc 10760 SW Denney Rd ... Beaverton OR 97008	**800-962-7860**	503-526-3650	232
Mercer Insurance Group Inc 10 N Hwy 31 ... Pennington NJ 08534 *NASDAQ: MIGP*	**800-223-0534**	609-737-0426	384-4
Mercer Management Consulting 1166 Ave of the Americas 32 Fl ... New York NY 10036	**800-532-6888**	212-345-8000	193
Mercer Transportation Co Inc PO Box 35610 ... Louisville KY 40232	**800-626-5375**	502-584-2301	769
Mercer University 1400 Coleman Ave ... Macon GA 31207	**800-637-2378**	478-301-2700	163
Mercer University Press 1400 Coleman Ave ... Macon GA 31207	**800-637-2378**	478-301-2880	623-5
Mercer University Walter F George School of Law 1021 Georgia Ave ... Macon GA 31207	**800-637-2378**	478-301-2605	164-1
Merchandise Mart 470 Merchandise Mart ... Chicago IL 60654	**800-677-6278**	312-527-7902	204
Merchant Factors Corp 1430 Broadway 18th Fl ... New York NY 10018	**800-929-3293**	212-840-7575	268
Merchants Bancshares Inc PO Box 1009 ... Burlington VT 05402 *NASDAQ: MBVT*	**800-322-5222**	802-658-3400	355-2
Merchants Credit Bureau PO Box 458 ... Augusta GA 30903	**800-426-5265**	706-823-6246	212
Merchant's Inc 9073 Euclid Ave ... Manassas VA 20110	**800-368-3130**	703-368-3171	62-5
Merchants Insurance Group PO Box 903 ... Buffalo NY 14240	**800-462-1077**	716-849-3333	384-4
Merchants Metals Inc 3838 N Sam Houston Pkwy E Suite 600 ... Houston TX 77032	**800-254-0080**	281-372-3800	275
Merchants Solutions Co 4422 Roosevelt Rd ... Hillside IL 60162	**800-244-1160**	708-449-6650	113
Merck & Co Inc 1 Merck Dr PO Box 100 ... Whitehouse Station NJ 08889 *NYSE: MRK* ■ *Cust Svc	**800-672-6372***	908-423-1000	572
Merco-Savory Inc 1111 N Hadley Rd ... Fort Wayne IN 46804 *Cust Svc	**800-547-2513***	260-459-8200	293
Mercury Computer Systems Inc 199 Riverneck Rd ... Chelmsford MA 01824 *NASDAQ: MRCY*	**800-229-2006**	978-256-1300	171-3
Mercury General Corp 4484 Wilshire Blvd ... Los Angeles CA 90010 *NYSE: MCY*	**800-431-6654**	323-937-1060	384-4
Mercury Instruments Inc 3940 Virginia Ave ... Cincinnati OH 45227	**800-642-4629**	513-272-1111	200
Mercury Interactive Corp 379 N Whisman Rd ... Mountain View CA 94043 *NASDAQ: MERQ*	**800-837-8911**	650-603-5200	176-12
Mercury Lighting Products Co Inc 20 Audrey Pl ... Fairfield NJ 07004	**800-637-2879**	973-244-9444	431
Mercury Luggage Mfg Co DBA Mercury Luggage/Seward Trunk 4843 Victor St ... Jacksonville FL 32207	**800-874-1885**	904-733-9595	444
Mercury Luggage/Seward Trunk 4843 Victor St ... Jacksonville FL 32207	**800-874-1885**	904-733-9595	444
Mercury Marine Ltd 2395 Meadowpine Blvd ... Mississauga ON L5N7W6	**800-388-2166**	905-567-6372	259
Mercury Online Solutions Inc 600 Ericksen Ave NE Suite 200 ... Bainbridge Island WA 98110	**888-460-8866**	206-285-0347	603
Mercury Plastics Inc 14825 Salt Lake Ave ... City of Industry CA 91746	**800-831-2517**	626-961-0165	67
Mercury Plastics Inc 123 Willamette Ln ... Bowling Green KY 42101	**800-347-0338**	270-782-8026	67
Mercury Resort 100 Collins Ave ... Miami Beach FL 33139	**877-786-2732**	305-398-3000	373
Mercy College 555 Broadway ... Dobbs Ferry NY 10522	**800-637-2969**	914-693-4500	163
Bronx Campus 1200 Water Pl ... Bronx NY 10461	**800-637-2969**	718-518-7710	163
White Plains Campus 277 Martine Ave ... White Plains NY 10601	**800-637-2969**	914-948-3666	163
Yorktown Heights Campus 2651 Strang Blvd ... Yorktown Heights NY 10598	**800-637-2969**	914-245-6100	163
Mercy Corps 3015 SW 1st Ave ... Portland OR 97201	**800-292-3355**	503-796-6800	48-5

	Toll-Free	Phone	Class
Mercy Hospital of Kansas 401 Woodland Hills Blvd ... Fort Scott KS 66701	**877-336-3729**	620-223-2200	366-2
Mercy Hospital Medical Center 1111 6th Ave ... Des Moines IA 50314	**800-637-2993**	515-247-3121	366-2
Mercy Medical Center 375 E Park Ave ... Durango CO 81301	**800-345-2516**	970-247-4311	366-2
Mercy Medical Center 301 St Paul Pl ... Baltimore MD 21202	**800-636-3729**	410-332-9000	366-2
Mercy Medical Center 1301 15th Ave W ... Williston ND 58801	**800-544-3579**	701-774-7400	366-2
Mercy Medical Center 1320 Mercy Dr ... Canton OH 44708	**800-999-8662**	330-489-1000	366-2
Mercy Medical Center North Iowa 1000 4th St SW ... Mason City IA 50401	**800-433-3883**	641-422-7000	366-2
Mercy Medical Center Redding 2175 Rosaline Ave ... Redding CA 96001	**800-521-6377**	530-225-6000	366-2
Mercy-USA for Aid & Development Inc (M-USA) 44450 Pinetree Dr Suite 201 ... Plymouth MI 48170	**800-556-3729**	734-454-0011	48-5
Mercyhurst College 501 E 38th St ... Erie PA 16546	**800-825-1926**	814-824-2202	163
Meredith Collection 1201 Millerton St SE ... Canton OH 44707	**877-497-4273**	330-484-1656	736
Meredith College 3800 Hillsborough St ... Raleigh NC 27607	**800-637-3348**	919-760-8581	163
Mereen-Johnson Machine Co 4401 Lyndale Ave N ... Minneapolis MN 55412	**888-465-7297**	612-529-7791	809
Merge Technologies Inc 1126 S 70th St Suite S-107B ... Milwaukee WI 53214 *NASDAQ: MRGE*	**877-446-3743**	414-977-4000	375
Mergent FIS Inc 60 Madison Ave 6th Fl ... New York NY 10010	**800-342-5647**	212-413-7700	623-10
Mergent Inc 60 Madison Ave 6th Fl ... New York NY 10010	**888-411-0893**	212-413-7700	623-9
Merger Fund PO Box 701 ... Milwaukee WI 53201	**800-343-8959**	414-765-4124	517
Mergers & Acquisitions Magazine 1 State Street Plaza ... New York NY 10004 *Cust Svc	**800-455-5844***	212-803-6051	449-5
Meri Meri 525 Harbor Blvd ... Bwlmont CA 94002	**800-733-4770**	650-508-2300	130
Mericon Industries Inc 8819 N Pioneer Rd ... Peoria IL 61615	**800-242-6464**	309-693-2150	573
Meridian Aerospace Group Ltd 3796 Vest Mill Rd ... Winston-Salem NC 27103	**800-538-7767**	336-765-5454	759
Meridian Bioscience Inc 3471 River Hills Dr ... Cincinnati OH 45244 *NASDAQ: VIVO* ■ *Cust Svc	**800-543-1980***	513-271-3700	229
Meridian Community College 910 Hwy 19 N ... Meridian MS 39307	**800-622-8431**	601-483-8241	160
Meridian Gold Co 9670 Gateway Dr Suite 200 ... Reno NV 89521 *NYSE: MDG*	**800-557-4699**	775-850-3777	492
Meridian Group 9 Parkway N Suite 500 ... Deerfield IL 60015	**800-811-2674**	847-940-1200	178
Meridian Inc 4805 G St ... Omaha NE 68117	**800-733-7765**	402-733-6400	770
Meridian Mattress Factory Inc PO Box 5127 ... Meridian MS 39302	**800-844-3875**	601-693-3875	463
Meridian Medical Technologies Inc 6350 Stevens Forest Rd Suite 301 ... Columbia MD 21046	**800-638-8093**	443-259-7800	468
Meridian Order Buyers Inc 5125 Hwy 45 N PO Box 1566 ... Meridian MS 39301	**800-833-4566**	601-483-8207	437
Meridian Plaza Resort 2310 N Ocean Blvd ... Myrtle Beach SC 29577	**800-323-3011**	843-626-4734	373
Meridian Project Systems 1180 Iron Point Rd Suite 300 ... Folsom CA 95630	**800-850-2660**	916-294-2000	176-1
Meridian Star PO Box 1591 ... Meridian MS 39302	**800-232-2525**	601-693-1551	522-2
Meridian Star Inc 814 22nd Ave ... Meridian MS 39301	**800-232-2525**	601-693-1551	623-8
Meridian Technology Leasing Services 570 Lake Cook Rd Suite 300 ... Deerfield IL 60015 *Cust Svc	**800-426-3090***	847-940-1200	261-1
Meridian/Lauderdale County Tourism Bureau 212 21st Ave PO Box 5313 ... Meridian MS 39301	**888-868-7720**	601-482-8001	205
Merillat Industries Inc PO Box 1946 ... Adrian MI 49221	**800-575-8763**	517-263-0771	116
Merisel Inc 200 Continental Blvd ... El Segundo CA 90245 *NASDAQ: MSEL* ■ *Sales	**800-637-4735***	310-615-3080	172
Merit Abrasive Products Inc 7301 Orangewood Ave PO Box 3195 ... Garden Grove CA 92842	**800-421-1936**	714-677-1144	1
Merit Electric Co Inc 6520 125th Ave N ... Largo FL 33773	**800-539-3900**	727-536-5945	188-4
Merit Medical Systems Inc 1600 W Merit Pkwy ... South Jordan UT 84095 *NASDAQ: MMSI*	**800-356-3748**	801-253-1600	468
Merit Resources Inc 4165 120th St ... Des Moines IA 50323	**800-336-1931**	515-278-1931	619
Merit Systems Protection Board (MSPB) 1615 M St NW ... Washington DC 20419	**800-209-8960**	202-653-7200	336-16
Merit Travel Group Inc 145 King St W Suite 2020 ... Toronto ON M5H1J8	**800-268-5940**	416-364-3775	760
Merit USA 620 Clark Ave ... Pittsburg CA 94565	**800-445-6374**	925-432-6900	483
Meritus Consulting Services LLC 1899 Powers Ferry Rd Suite 205 ... Atlanta GA 30339	**800-637-4887**	770-988-2600	193
Merle Norman Cosmetics Inc 9130 Bellanca Ave ... Los Angeles CA 90045	**800-421-2060**	310-641-3000	211
Merlin Information Services 215 S Complex Dr ... Kalispell MT 59901	**800-367-6646**	406-755-8550	621
Merrell Footwear 9341 Courtland Dr NE ... Rockford MI 49351 *Cust Svc	**888-637-7001***	616-866-5500	296
Merriam-Webster Inc PO Box 281 ... Springfield MA 01102	**800-828-1880**	413-734-3134	623-2
Merrick & Co 2450 S Peoria St ... Aurora CO 80014	**800-544-1714**	303-751-0741	258
Merrick Industries Inc 10 Arthur Dr ... Lynn Haven FL 32444	**800-345-8440**	850-265-3611	672
Merrick Pet Foods PO Box 2257 ... Hereford TX 79045	**800-664-7387**	806-364-2565	568
Merrick Systems Inc 4801 Woodway Suite 100E ... Houston TX 77056	**800-842-8389**	713-355-6800	176-10
Merrick's Inc 2415 Parview Rd PO Box 620307 ... Middleton WI 53562	**800-637-7425**	608-831-3440	438
Merrill Area Chamber of Commerce 120 S Mill St ... Merrill WI 54452	**877-907-2757**	715-536-9474	137
Merrill Blueberry Farms Inc PO Box 149 ... Ellsworth ME 04605	**800-711-6551**	207-667-2541	310-1
Merrill Corp 1 Merrill Cir ... Saint Paul MN 55108	**800-688-4400**	651-646-4501	615

Name / Address	City	State	ZIP	Toll-Free	Phone	Class
Merrill Lynch Commodities 20 E Greenway Plaza Suite 700	Houston	TX	77046	866-820-6000	713-544-6222	774
Merrill Lynch Family of Funds PO Box 45289	Jacksonville	FL	32232	800-637-3863		517
Merrill Lynch Life Insurance Co 4804 Deer Lake Dr E	Jacksonville	FL	32246	800-535-5549	904-218-7000	384-2
Merrill Mfg Corp PO Box 566	Merrill	WI	54452	800-826-5300	715-536-5533	798
Merrill & Ring Inc 813 E 8th St PO Box 1058	Port Angeles	WA	98362	800-827-2367	360-452-2367	297
Merrill-Sharpe Ltd 250 Clearbrook Rd	Elmsford	NY	10523	800-832-0159	914-347-8686	153-12
Merrill/Daniels Printing Co 40 Commercial St	Everett	MA	02149	800-553-7733	617-389-7900	615
Merrimack Valley Distributing Co 50 Prince St	Danvers	MA	01923	800-698-0250	978-777-2213	82-1
Merrimack Valley Hospice 360 Merrimack St Bldg 9	Lawrence	MA	01843	800-933-5593	978-552-4000	365
Merrimack Valley Wood Products Co B St Derry Industrial Park	Derry	NH	03038	800-955-0702	603-432-2581	489
Merritt Center PO Box 2087	Payson	AZ	85547	800-414-9880	928-474-4268	660
Merritt Equipment Co 9339 Hwy 85	Henderson	CO	80640	800-634-3036	303-289-2286	768
Merritt Joseph & Co 650 Franklin Ave	Hartford	CT	06114	800-344-4477	860-296-2500	580
Merry Maids 3839 Forrest Hill-Irene Rd	Memphis	TN	38125	800-798-8000	901-597-8100	150
Merrygro Farms Inc 34135 Cardinal Ln	Eustis	FL	32736	888-637-7947	352-589-0868	318
Mertz Inc 1701 N Waverly	Ponca City	OK	74601	800-654-6433	580-762-5646	269
Mervis Industries Inc 3295 E Main St	Danville	IL	61834	800-637-3016	217-442-5300	674
MerX City 7600 Wayzata Blvd	Golden Valley	MN	55426	800-356-6826	763-253-6500	239
Merz Pharmaceuticals Inc 4215 Tudor Ln	Greensboro	NC	27410	800-334-0514	336-856-2003	572
Mesa Air Group Inc 410 N 44th St Suite 700 *NASDAQ: MESA*	Phoenix	AZ	85008	800-637-2247	602-685-4000	355-1
Mesa Airlines 410 N 44th St Suite 700	Phoenix	AZ	85008	800-637-2247	602-685-4000	26
Mesa Community College 1833 W Southern Ave	Mesa	AZ	85202	866-532-4983	480-461-7000	160
Mesa Convention & Visitors Bureau 120 N Center St	Mesa	AZ	85201	800-283-6372	480-827-4700	205
Mesa Distributing Co Inc 8870 Liquid Ct	San Diego	CA	92121	800-275-1071	858-452-2300	82-1
Mesa Laboratories Inc 12100 W 6th Ave *NASDAQ: MLAB* ■ *Sales	Lakewood	CO	80228	800-992-6372*	303-987-8000	467
Mesa Rubber Co 1726 S Magnolia Ave	Monrovia	CA	91016	888-393-8635	626-359-9361	321
Mesa State College 1100 North Ave	Grand Junction	CO	81501	800-982-6372	970-248-1020	163
Mesabi Range Community & Technical College 1100 Industrial Pk Dr PO Box 648	Eveleth	MN	55734	800-657-3860	218-741-3095	160
Mesco Metal Buildings 400 N Kimball Ave PO Box 93629	Southlake	TX	76092	800-556-3726	817-488-8511	106
Mesirow Financial Inc 350 N Clark St	Chicago	IL	60610	800-453-0600	312-595-6000	679
Mesirow Financial Private Equity 350 N Clark St	Chicago	IL	60610	800-453-0600	312-595-6099	779
Mesirow Insurance Services Inc 350 N Clark St	Chicago	IL	60610	888-973-2323	312-595-6200	383
Meskwaki Bingo Hotel Casino 1504 305th St	Tama	IA	52339	800-728-4263	641-484-2108	133
Mesquite Chamber of Commerce 617 N Ebrite St	Mesquite	TX	75149	800-541-2355	972-285-0211	137
Messenger The 713 Central Ave	Fort Dodge	IA	50501	800-622-6613	515-573-2141	522-2
Messenger The PO Box 529	Madisonville	KY	42431	800-726-6397	270-821-6833	522-2
Messenger The PO Box 1190	Hillsboro	NH	03244	800-281-2859	603-464-3388	522-4
Messenger Publishing Co 9300 Johnson Rd	Athens	OH	45701	800-233-6611	740-592-6612	623-8
Messiah College 1 College Ave	Grantham	PA	17027	800-233-4220	717-766-2511	163
Messianic Museum 1928 Hamill Rd	Hixson	TN	37343	888-876-8150	423-876-8150	509
Messinger Bearings Corp 10385 Drummond Rd	Philadelphia	PA	19154	800-203-2729	215-739-6880	77
Met-Pro Corp PO Box 144 *NYSE: MPR*	Harleysville	PA	19438	800-722-3267	215-723-6751	379
Met-Pro Corp Flex-Kleen Div 955 Hawthorn Dr	Itasca	IL	60143	800-621-0734	630-775-0707	19
Met-Pro Corp Fybroc Div 700 Emlen Way	Telford	PA	18969	800-392-7621	215-723-8155	627
Met-Pro Corp Keystone Filter Div 2485 N Penn Rd	Hatfield	PA	19440	800-811-4424	215-822-1963	793
Met-Pro Corp Sethco Div 70 Arkay Dr	Hauppauge	NY	11788	800-645-0500	631-435-0530	627
Met-Pro Corp Stiles-Kem Div 1570 S Lakeside Dr	Waukegan	IL	60085	800-562-1537	847-689-1100	143
MET-Rx Nutrition Inc 851 Broken Sound Pkwy NW	Boca Raton	FL	33487	800-926-3879	561-999-1337	786
Meta Financial Group Inc 121 E 5th PO Box 1307 *NASDAQ: CASH*	Storm Lake	IA	50588	800-792-6815	712-732-4117	355-2
META Group Inc 208 Harbor Dr 4th Fl	Stamford	CT	06912	800-756-6382	203-973-6700	178
Meta Health Technology Inc 330 7th Ave 14th Fl	New York	NY	10001	800-334-6840	212-695-5870	176-11
Metabolife International Inc 5643 Copley Dr *Cust Svc	San Diego	CA	92111	800-962-3438*	858-490-5222	786
Metacom Inc 251 1st Ave N 2nd Fl	Minneapolis	MN	55401	800-236-0289		239
MetaCrawler 601 108th Ave NE Suite 1200	Bellevue	WA	98004	866-438-4677	425-201-6100	677
MetaEdge Corp 1257 Tasman Dr Suite C	Sunnyvale	CA	94089	888-755-9100	408-752-9977	176-1
Metafile Information Systems Inc 2900 43rd St NW *Sales	Rochester	MN	55901	800-638-2445*	507-286-9232	176-11
Metal Box International 11600 W King St	Franklin Park	IL	60131	800-622-2697	847-455-8500	479
Metal Building Components Inc 10943 Sam Houston Pkwy W	Houston	TX	77064	877-713-6224	281-445-8555	106
Metal Bulletin Inc 1250 Broadway 26th Fl	New York	NY	10001	800-638-2525	212-213-6202	623-9
Metal Cladding Inc 230 S Niagara St	Lockport	NY	14094	800-432-5513	716-434-5513	472
Metal Edge Magazine 333 7th Ave 11th Fl	New York	NY	10001	800-741-1289	212-780-3500	449-9
Metal Equipment Co 875 Crocker Rd	Westlake	OH	44145	800-700-6326	440-835-3100	206
Metal-Fab Inc 3025 May St	Wichita	KS	67213	800-835-2830	316-943-2351	688
Metal Management Inc 500 N Dearborn St Suite 400 *NASDAQ: MTLM*	Chicago	IL	60610	888-645-0700	312-645-0700	674
Metal Sales Mfg Corp 7800 State Rd 60	Sellersburg	IN	47172	800-406-7387	812-246-1935	106
Metal Ware Corp 1700 Monroe St *Cust Svc	Two Rivers	WI	54241	800-288-4545*	920-793-1368	37
MetalCenter Inc 12034 S Greenstone Ave	Santa Fe Springs	CA	90670	800-448-0001	562-944-3322	483
Metalcrete Industries Inc 10330 Brecksville Rd	Cleveland	OH	44141	800-526-5602	440-526-5600	3
Metalex Corp 1530 Artaius Pkwy	Libertyville	IL	60048	800-323-0792	847-362-8300	709
Metallic Arts Inc 914 N Lake Rd	Spokane	WA	99212	800-541-3200	509-489-7173	766
Metallurgical Products Co 810 Lincoln Ave PO Box 598	West Chester	PA	19381	800-659-4672	610-696-6770	476
Metallurgy & Exploration Inc. Society for Mining 8307 Shaffer Pkwy	Littleton	CO	80127	800-763-3132	303-973-9550	49-13
Metals USA Inc 3 Riverway Suite 600 *NASDAQ: MUSA*	Houston	TX	77056	888-871-8701	713-965-0990	483
Metals Week Newsletter 55 Water St	New York	NY	10041	800-223-6180	212-438-2000	521-13
Metaltech Inc 206 Prospect Ave	Kirkwood	MO	63122	800-325-9886	314-965-4550	688
Metalworking Lubricants Co 25 W Silverdome Industrial Pk	Pontiac	MI	48342	800-394-5494	248-332-3500	530
MetaSolv Inc 5556 Tennyson Pkwy *NASDAQ: MSLV*	Plano	TX	75024	800-925-2940	972-403-8300	176-10
Metaullics Systems 31935 Aurora Rd	Solon	OH	44139	800-638-2859	440-349-8800	490
Metavante Corp 4900 W Brown Deer Rd	Brown Deer	WI	53223	800-236-3282	414-357-2290	250
Metco Mfg Co Inc 1993 County Line Rd	Warrington	PA	18976	888-343-1993	215-343-1993	745
Metcut Research Inc 3980 Rosslyn Dr	Cincinnati	OH	45209	800-966-2888	513-271-5100	728
Meteor Crater & Museum of Astrogeology Exit 233 off I-40 Meteor Crater Rd	Winslow	AZ	86047	800-289-5898	928-289-2362	509
Meteorlogix LLC 11400 Rupp Dr	Burnsville	MN	55337	800-328-2278	952-890-0609	464
Meter Devices Co Inc 3359 Bruening Ave SW PO Box 6382 Stn B	Canton	OH	44706	888-367-6383	330-455-0301	715
Metglas Inc 440 Allied Dr	Conway	SC	29526	800-581-7654	843-349-7319	476
Methanex Corp 200 Burrard St Suite 1800 *NASDAQ: MEOH*	Vancouver	BC	V6C3M1	800-900-6384	604-661-2600	142
Methanol Institute (MI) 4100 N Fairfax Dr Suite 740	Arlington	VA	22203	888-275-0768	703-248-3636	48-12
Methodist Alliance Hospice 6423 Shelby View Dr Suite 103	Memphis	TN	38134	800-968-8326	901-380-8169	365
Methodist College 5400 Ramsey St	Fayetteville	NC	28311	800-488-7110	910-630-7000	163
Methodist Committee on Relief. United 475 Riverside Dr Suite 330	New York	NY	10115	800-554-8583	212-870-3814	48-5
Methodist Manor House 1001 Middleford Rd	Seaford	DE	19973	800-775-4593	302-629-4593	659
Methodist Rehabilitation Center 1350 E Woodrow Wilson Dr	Jackson	MS	39216	800-223-6672	601-981-2611	366-4
Metier Ltd 3222 'N' St NW 5th Fl	Washington	DC	20007	877-965-9501	202-965-9500	39
MetLife Auto & Home Insurance Co 700 Quaker Ln	Warwick	RI	02886	800-422-4272	401-827-2400	384-4
MetLife Inc 27-01 Queens Plaza North 1 MetLife Plaza *NYSE: MET*	Long Island City	NY	11101	800-638-5433	212-578-2211	384-2
MetLife Investors Insurance Co 22 Corporate Plaza Dr	Newport Beach	CA	92660	800-848-3854	949-629-1300	384-2
Metpar Corp 95 State St	Westbury	NY	11590	888-638-7271	516-333-2600	281
Metra Electronics Corp 460 Walker St *Sales	Holly Hill	FL	32117	800-221-0932*	386-257-1186	52
MetraPark 308 6th Ave N PO Box 2514	Billings	MT	59103	800-366-8538	406-256-2422	204
MetraPark Arena 308 6th Ave N	Billings	MT	59101	800-366-8538	406-256-2400	706
Metretek Inc 300 North Dr	Melbourne	FL	32934	800-327-8559	321-259-9700	486
Metretek Technologies Inc 303 E 17th Ave Suite 660	Denver	CO	80203	800-394-8169	303-785-8080	774
Metric Products Inc 4671 Leahy St	Culver City	CA	90232	800-763-8742	310-815-9000	34
Metrix Instrument Co 1711 Townhurst Dr	Houston	TX	77043	800-638-7494	713-461-2131	464
Metro Creative Graphics Inc 519 8th Ave	New York	NY	10018	800-223-1600	212-947-5100	338
Metro Financial Services PO Box 970817	Dallas	TX	75397	800-327-2274	214-363-4557	214
Metro Flag 47 Bassett Hwy	Dover	NJ	07802	800-666-3524	973-366-1776	282
Metro Group Inc PO Box 211	Buffalo	NY	14225	800-836-7262	716-668-5223	623-8
Metro Jackson Convention & Visitors Bureau 921 N President St	Jackson	MS	39202	800-354-7695	601-960-1891	205
Metro Label Corp 1395 Chattahoochee Ave NW	Atlanta	GA	30318	800-235-8814	404-351-5044	404
Metro One Telecommunications Inc 11200 Murray Scholls Pl *NASDAQ: INFO*	Beaverton	OR	97007	800-933-4034	503-643-9500	222
Metro Restoration Inc PO Box 115	Thornton	IL	60476	877-570-1315	708-339-6300	84
Metro-Tel Corp 11422 Miracle Hills Dr	Omaha	NE	68154	888-998-8300	402-498-2964	720
MetroHealth Medical Center 2500 MetroHealth Dr	Cleveland	OH	44109	800-554-5251	216-778-7800	366-2
Metrolina Greenhouses Inc 16400 Huntersville-Concord Rd	Huntersville	NC	28078	800-222-2905	704-875-1371	363
Metrolina Steel Inc PO Box 790465	Charlotte	NC	28206	800-849-7835	704-598-7007	483
Metrolink 700 S Flower St Suite 2600	Los Angeles	CA	90017	800-371-5465	213-347-2800	460
Metrologic Instruments Inc 90 Coles Rd *NASDAQ: MTLG* ■ *Sales	Blackwood	NJ	08012	800-436-3876*	856-228-8100	171-7

Name / Address	City	State	ZIP	Toll-Free	Phone	Class
Metromedia Energy Inc 6 Industrial Way W Suite F	Eatontown	NJ	07724	**800-828-9427**	732-542-7575	774
Metromont Prestress PO Box 2486	Greenville	SC	29602	**888-295-0383**	864-295-0295	181
MetroPCS Communications Inc 8144 Walnut Hill Ln Suite 800 *Cust Svc	Dallas	TX	75231	**888-863-8768***	214-265-2550	721
Metropolis Magazine 61 W 23rd St 4th Fl	New York	NY	10010	**800-344-3046**	212-627-9977	449-2
Metropolitan Ceramics 1201 Millerton St SE	Canton	OH	44707	**800-325-3945**	330-484-4887	736
Metropolitan College of New York 75 Varick St	New York	NY	10013	**800-338-4465**	212-343-1234	163
Metropolitan Community College PO Box 3777	Omaha	NE	68103	**800-228-9553**	402-457-2400	160
Metropolitan Health Networks Inc 250 Australian Ave S Suite 400	West Palm Beach	FL	33401	**888-663-8227**	561-805-8500	455
Metropolitan Home Magazine 1633 Broadway 44th Fl	New York	NY	10019	**800-374-4638**	212-767-4500	449-11
Metropolitan Hotel 569 Lexington Ave	New York	NY	10022	**800-836-6471**	212-752-7000	373
Metropolitan Hotel Toronto 108 Chestnut St	Toronto	ON	M5G1R3	**800-668-6600**	416-977-5000	372
Metropolitan Hotel Vancouver 645 Howe St	Vancouver	BC	V6C2Y9	**800-667-2300**	604-687-1122	372
Metropolitan Indianapolis Public Broadcasting Corp 1401 N Meridian St	Indianapolis	IN	46202	**800-633-7419**	317-636-2020	620
Metropolitan Library System 125 Tower Dr	Burr Ridge	IL	60527	**866-734-2004**	630-734-5000	426
Metropolitan Life Insurance Co 1 Madison Ave	New York	NY	10010	**800-638-5433**	212-578-2211	384-2
Metropolitan Opera Guild 70 Lincoln Ctr Plaza 6th Fl	New York	NY	10023	**800-829-2525**	212-769-7000	48-4
Metropolitan Plant & Flower Exchange 459 Main St	Fort Lee	NJ	07024	**800-942-1050**	201-944-1050	287
Metropolitan Poultry & Seafood Co 1920 Stanford Ct	Landover	MD	20785	**800-522-0060**	301-772-0060	292-10
Metropolitan Radio Group Inc 2010 S Stewart Ave	Springfield	MO	65804	**800-961-5595**	417-862-0852	629
Metropolitan Transportation Authority (MTA) PO Box 194	Los Angeles	CA	90001	**800-266-6883**	213-922-2000	460
Metropolitan Tucson Convention & Visitors Bureau 100 S Church Ave	Tucson	AZ	85701	**800-638-8350**	520-624-1817	205
Metropolitan Utilities District 1723 Harney St	Omaha	NE	68102	**800-732-5864**	402-449-8155	774
Metropolitan Vacuum Cleaner Co Inc 1 Ramapo Ave	Suffern	NY	10901	**800-822-1602**	845-357-1600	775
Metrosonics 1060 Corporate Center Dr	Oconomowoc	WI	53066	**800-245-0779**	262-567-9157	464
MetroStars 1 Harmon Plaza 3rd Fl	Secaucus	NJ	07094	**800-638-7684**	201-583-7000	703
Metrotech Corp 488 Tasman Dr	Sunnyvale	CA	94089	**800-446-3392**	408-734-1400	464
Metrowerks 7700 W Parmer Ln	Austin	TX	78729	**800-377-5416**	512-996-5300	176-12
Metso Dynapac Inc PO Box 615	Schertz	TX	78154	**800-867-6060**	210-474-5770	189
Metters Industries Inc 8200 Greensboro Dr Suite 500	McLean	VA	22102	**800-638-8377**	703-821-3300	178
Metz Beverage Co Inc 302 N Custer St	Sheridan	WY	82801	**800-821-4010**	307-672-5848	82-2
Metzger Packing Co Inc 520 S 2nd St	Paducah	KY	42002	**800-347-9630**	270-442-3503	291-26
Mexican Restaurants Inc 1135 Edgebrook St *NASDAQ: CASA*	Houston	TX	77034	**800-741-7574**	713-943-7574	656
Mexicana Airlines 6151 W Century Blvd Suite 1124	Los Angeles	CA	90045	**800-531-7923**	310-646-0401	26
Mexicana Airlines Frecuenta 482 W San Ysidro Blvd Suite 754	San Ysidro	CA	92173	**800-531-7901**		27
Mexico Ledger PO Box 8	Mexico	MO	65265	**800-246-0050**	573-581-1111	522-2
Mexico Tourism Board 5975 Sunset Dr Suite 305	Miami	FL	33143	**800-446-3942**	786-621-2909	764
Mexico Tourism Board 225 N Michigan Ave Suite 1850	Chicago	IL	60601	**800-446-3942**	312-228-0517	764
Mexico Tourism Board 400 Madison Ave Suite 11-C	New York	NY	10017	**800-446-3942**	212-308-2110	764
Mexico Tourism Board 4507 San Jacinto Suite 308	Houston	TX	77004	**800-446-3942**	713-772-2581	764
Meyer Corp 525 Curtola Pkwy *Cust Svc	Vallejo	CA	94590	**800-388-3872***	707-551-2800	477
Meyer Crest Ltd 2051 Hilltop Dr Suite A-26	Redding	CA	96002	**800-626-1900**	530-221-8250	369
Meyer Fred Inc 3800 SE 22nd Ave	Portland	OR	97202	**800-858-9202**	503-232-8844	339
Meyer Fred Jewelers Inc 3800 SE 22nd Ave	Portland	OR	97202	**800-858-9202**	503-797-5550	402
Meyer H Dairy Co 415 John St	Cincinnati	OH	45215	**800-347-6455**	513-948-8811	291-27
Meyer Plastics Inc 5167 E 65th St	Indianapolis	IN	46220	**800-968-4131**	317-259-4131	591
Meyer Robert R Planetarium 900 Arkadelphia Rd Birmingham Southern College PO Box 549036	Birmingham	AL	35254	**800-523-5793**	205-226-4770	587
Meyer Tool Inc 3055 Colerain Ave	Cincinnati	OH	45225	**800-286-7362**	513-681-7362	446
Meyer Truck Equipment Inc 196 W State Rd 56	Jasper	IN	47546	**800-456-3451**	812-695-3451	505
Meyercord Revenue 475 Village Dr	Carol Stream	IL	60188	**800-223-6269**	630-682-6200	459
Meyerhoff Joseph Symphony Hall 1212 Cathedral St	Baltimore	MD	21201	**800-442-1198**	410-783-8100	562
Meyers A & Sons Corp 325 W 38th St	New York	NY	10018	**800-666-5577**	212-279-6632	583
Meyer's Bakeries Inc 2700 E 3rd St	Hope	AR	71802	**800-643-1542**	870-777-9031	291-1
Meyers Co Inc 7277 Boone Ave N	Brooklyn Park	MN	55428	**800-927-9709**	763-533-9730	615
Meyers WF Co 1017 14th St PO Box 426	Bedford	IN	47421	**800-457-4055**	812-275-4485	447
MF Cachat Co 14600 Detroit Ave Suite 600	Lakewood	OH	44107	**800-729-8900**	216-228-8900	144
MFB Corp 4100 Edison Lakes Pkwy *NASDAQ: MFBC*	Mishawaka	IN	46545	**800-400-0433**	574-277-4200	355-2
MFJ Enterprises Inc 300 Industrial Park Rd	Starkville	MS	39759	**800-647-1800**	662-323-5869	633
MFM Industries Inc 3951 NW County Rd 329 *Cust Svc	Reddick	FL	32686	**800-922-6369***	352-854-0070	568
MFS Investment Management 500 Boylston St	Boston	MA	02116	**800-637-2929**	617-954-5000	393
MG Design Assoc Corp 8778 100th St	Pleasant Prairie	WI	53158	**800-643-9442**	262-947-8890	230
MGE UPS Systems 1660 Scenic Ave	Costa Mesa	CA	92626	**800-438-7373**	714-557-1636	252
MGFA (Myasthenia Gravis Foundation of America) 1821 University Ave W Suite S256	Saint Paul	MN	55104	**800-541-5454**	651-917-6256	48-17
MGI Pharma Inc 5775 W Old Shakopee Rd Suite 100 *NASDAQ: MOGN* ■ *Orders	Bloomington	MN	55437	**800-562-4531***	952-346-4700	572
MGIC Investment Corp 250 E Kilbourn Ave *NYSE: MTG*	Milwaukee	WI	53202	**800-558-9900**	414-347-6480	355-4
MGM Brakes Div Indian Head Industries Inc 8530 Cliff Cameron Dr	Charlotte	NC	28269	**800-527-1534**	704-547-7411	60
MGM Grand Detroit Casino 1300 John C Lodge	Detroit	MI	48226	**877-888-2121**	313-393-7777	133
MGM Grand Hotel & Casino 3799 Las Vegas Blvd S	Las Vegas	NV	89109	**800-929-1111**	702-891-1111	655
MGM Mirage Design Group Inc 3260 Industrial Rd	Las Vegas	NV	89109	**800-477-5110**	702-792-4600	185
MGM Transformer Co 5701 Smithway St	Commerce	CA	90040	**800-423-4366**	323-726-0888	756
MGM Transport Corp 1 Railroad Ave	Ridgefield	NJ	07657	**800-646-8726**	201-840-1340	769
MGMA (Medical Group Management Assn) 104 Inverness Terr E	Englewood	CO	80112	**877-275-6462**	303-799-1111	49-8
MGP Ingredients Inc 1300 Main St *NASDAQ: MGPI*	Atchison	KS	66002	**800-255-0302**	913-367-1480	291-23
MH Fogel & Co Inc 2839 Liberty Ave	Pittsburgh	PA	15222	**800-245-2954**	412-261-3921	38
MH Zeigler & Sons Inc 1513 N Broad St	Lansdale	PA	19446	**800-854-6123**	215-855-5161	291-20
MHF Logistical Solutions Inc 800 Cranberry Woods Dr Suite 450	Cranberry Township	PA	16066	**877-452-9300**	724-772-9800	440
MHI (Manufactured Housing Institute) 2101 Wilson Blvd Suite 610	Arlington	VA	22201	**800-505-5500**	703-558-0400	49-3
MHI PAC (Manufactured Housing Institute PAC) 2101 Wilson Blvd Suite 610	Arlington	VA	22201	**800-505-5500**	703-558-0400	604
MHIA (Material Handling Industry of America) 8720 Red Oak Blvd Suite 201	Charlotte	NC	28217	**800-345-1815**	704-676-1190	49-13
MHM Services Inc 1593 Spring Hill Rd Suite 610	Vienna	VA	22182	**800-416-3649**	703-749-4600	455
MHP Inc (Maximum Human Performance Inc) 1376 Pompton Ave	Cedar Grove	NJ	07009	**888-783-8844**	973-785-9055	786
MHSS Enterprises 4200 N 29th Ave	Hollywood	FL	33020	**800-990-6696**	954-894-9494	153-21
MI Windows & Doors Inc 650 W Market St	Gratz	PA	17030	**800-949-3818**	717-365-3300	232
Mi8 Corp 601 W 26th St 11th Fl	New York	NY	10001	**800-965-4648**	212-727-0911	39
Mia Bambini Inc 360 Merrimack St Riverwalk Building 9	Lawrence	MA	01843	**800-766-1254**	978-682-3600	155-1
Miami-Cass County Rural Electric Membership Corp PO Box 168	Peru	IN	46970	**800-844-6668**	765-473-6668	244
Miami Children's Hospital 3100 SW 62nd Ave	Miami	FL	33155	**800-432-6837**	305-666-6511	366-1
Miami Clay Co 270 NE 183rd St	Miami	FL	33179	**800-651-4695**	305-651-4695	45
Miami Executive Aviation Inc 15001 NW 42 Ave	Miami	FL	33054	**800-861-1343**	305-687-8410	63
Miami (Greater) Chamber of Commerce 1601 Biscayne Blvd	Miami	FL	33132	**888-660-5955**	305-350-7700	137
Miami (Greater) Convention & Visitors Bureau 701 Brickell Ave Suite 2700	Miami	FL	33131	**800-933-8448**	305-539-3000	205
Miami Herald 1 Herald Plaza	Miami	FL	33132	**800-437-2535**	305-350-2111	522-2
Miami Herald Broward Edition 1520 E Sunrise Blvd	Fort Lauderdale	FL	33304	**800-441-0444**	954-462-3000	522-2
Miami International Airport Hotel NW 20th St & Le Jeune Rd	Miami	FL	33122	**800-327-1276**	305-871-4100	373
Miami News-Record PO Box 940	Miami	OK	74355	**800-611-1032**	918-542-5533	522-2
Miami Project to Cure Paralysis PO Box 016960 Mail Locator R-48	Miami	FL	33101	**800-782-6387**	305-243-6001	654
Miami Systems Corp 10001 Alliance Rd	Cincinnati	OH	45242	**800-543-4540**	513-793-0110	111
Miami University Middletown Campus 4200 E University Blvd	Middletown	OH	45042	**800-662-2262**	513-727-3200	163
Miami Valley Hospital 1 Wyoming St	Dayton	OH	45409	**800-544-0630**	937-223-6192	366-2
Micato Safaris 15 W 26th St 11th Fl	New York	NY	10010	**800-642-2861**	212-545-7111	748
Miccosukee Resort & Convention Center 500 SW 177th Ave	Miami	FL	33194	**877-242-6464**	305-925-2555	655
Miceli Dairy Products Co 2721 E 90th St	Cleveland	OH	44104	**800-551-7196**	216-791-6222	291-5
Michael Angelo's Gourmet Foods Inc 200 Michael Angelo Way	Austin	TX	78728	**800-526-4918**	512-218-3500	291-36
Michael Anthony Jewelers Inc 124 S Terrace Ave	Mount Vernon	NY	10550	**800-966-8800**	914-699-0000	401
Michael Baker Corp 100 Airsite Dr Airsite Business Pk *AMEX: BKR*	Moon Township	PA	15108	**800-553-1153**	412-269-6300	258
Michael Bondanza Inc 10 W 46th St 12th Fl	New York	NY	10036	**800-835-0041**	212-869-0043	401
Michael Business Machines Corp 3134 Industry Dr *Cust Svc	North Charleston	SC	29418	**800-223-2508***	843-552-2700	112

Company / Address	City	State	ZIP	Toll-Free	Phone	Class
Michael C Fina Inc 545 5th Ave	New York	NY	10017	**800-289-3462**	212-557-2500	357
Michael David & Co Inc 10801 Decatur Rd	Philadelphia	PA	19154	**800-523-3806**	215-632-3100	291-15
Michael-David Vineyards 4580 W Hwy 12	Lodi	CA	95242	**888-707-9463**	209-368-7384	50
Michael Day Enterprises Inc PO Box 179	Wadsworth	OH	44282	**800-758-0960**	330-336-7611	594-2
Michael Foods Inc 301 Carlson Pkwy Suite 400	Minnetonka	MN	55305	**800-325-4270**	952-258-4000	608
Michael J Fox Foundation for Parkinson's Research PO Box 4777 Grand Central Stn	New York	NY	10163	**800-708-7644**		300
Michael JJ Inc 74 Industrial Ave	Little Ferry	NJ	07643	**800-879-0470**	201-641-3600	770
Michael Lewis Simon Products Co Inc 201 Mittel Dr	Wood Dale	IL	60191	**800-323-8808**	630-350-1060	87
Michael Ramey & Assoc Inc PO Box 744	Danville	CA	94526	**800-321-0505**	925-820-8900	392
Michael's Cooperage Co Inc 363 W Pershing Rd	Chicago	IL	60609	**800-262-6281**	773-268-6281	125
Michael's Finer Meats & Seafoods 3775 Zane Trace Dr	Columbus	OH	43228	**800-282-0518**	614-527-4900	292-9
Michaels of Oregon 1710 Redsoils Ct	Oregon City	OR	97045	**800-962-5757**	503-557-0536	701
Michaels Stores Inc 8000 Bent Branch Dr *NYSE: MIK* ■ *Cust Svc	Irving	TX	75063	**800-642-4235***	972-409-1300	45
Michael's Transportation Service Inc 140 Yolano Dr	Vallejo	CA	94589	**800-295-2448**	707-643-2099	110
Michel & Co PO Box 85515	San Diego	CA	92186	**800-533-7263**		330
Michel RE Co Inc 1 RE Michel Dr	Glen Burnie	MD	21060	**800-283-7362**	410-760-4000	601
Michelangelo Hotel 152 W 51st St	New York	NY	10019	**800-237-0990**	212-765-1900	373
Michelin North America PO Box 19001 *Cust Svc	Greenville	SC	29602	**800-847-3435***	864-458-5000	739
Michelman Inc 9080 Shell Rd	Cincinnati	OH	45236	**800-477-0498**	513-793-7766	540
Michiana College 1030 E Jefferson Blvd	South Bend	IN	46617	**800-743-2447**	574-237-0774	158
Michigan						
Education Trust PO Box 30198	Lansing	MI	48909	**800-638-4543**	517-335-4767	711
Parks & Recreation Bureau PO Box 30257 *Campground Resv	Lansing	MI	48909	**800-447-2757***	517-373-9900	335
Rehabilitation Services PO Box 30010	Lansing	MI	48909	**800-605-6722**	517-373-3390	335
Student Financial Services Bureau PO Box 30047	Lansing	MI	48909	**800-642-5626**	517-373-4897	711
Travel Michigan 300 N Washington Sq	Lansing	MI	48913	**888-784-7328**	517-373-0670	335
Michigan Assn of Realtors 720 N Washington Ave	Lansing	MI	48906	**800-454-7842**	517-372-8890	642
Michigan Chamber of Commerce 600 S Walnut St	Lansing	MI	48933	**800-748-0266**	517-371-2100	138
Michigan Community Blood Centers 1036 Fuller Ave NE	Grand Rapids	MI	49503	**866-642-5663**	616-774-2300	90
Michigan Community Blood Centers Northwest 2575 Aero Pk Dr	Traverse City	MI	49686	**800-935-5311**	231-935-3030	90
Michigan Consolidated Gas Co 2000 2nd Ave *Cust Svc	Detroit	MI	48226	**800-477-4747***	313-235-4000	774
Michigan Eye Bank & Transplantation Center 1000 Wall St	Ann Arbor	MI	48105	**800-247-7250**	734-764-3262	265
Michigan International Speedway 12626 US 12	Brooklyn	MI	49230	**800-354-1010**	517-592-6666	504
Michigan Manufacturing Technology Center 47911 Halyard Dr	Plymouth	MI	48170	**888-414-6682**		654
Michigan Millers Mutual Insurance Co PO Box 30060	Lansing	MI	48909	**800-888-1914**	517-482-6211	384-4
Michigan Out-of-Doors Magazine PO Box 30235	Lansing	MI	48909	**800-777-6720**	517-371-1041	449-22
Michigan Republican State Committee 2121 E Grand River Ave	Lansing	MI	48912	**877-644-6704**	517-487-5413	605-2
Michigan. State Bar of 306 Townsend St	Lansing	MI	48933	**800-968-1442**	517-372-9030	73
Michigan State University DCL College of Law 368 Law College Bldg	East Lansing	MI	48824	**800-844-9352**	517-432-6810	164-1
Michigan State University Press 1405 S Harrison Rd Suite 25	East Lansing	MI	48823	**800-678-2120**	517-355-9543	623-5
Michigan Technological University 1400 Townsend Dr	Houghton	MI	49931	**888-688-1885**	906-487-2335	163
Michigan Theological Seminary 41550 E Ann Arbor Trail	Plymouth	MI	48170	**888-687-2737**	734-207-9581	164-3
MichTel Communications LLC 10 W Huron St	Pontiac	MI	48343	**888-244-6381**	248-771-5000	390
Mickey Truck Bodies Inc 1305 Trinity Ave PO Box 2044	High Point	NC	27261	**800-334-9061**	336-882-6806	768
Micrel Inc 1849 Fortune Dr *NASDAQ: MCRL*	San Jose	CA	95131	**800-800-2045**	408-944-0800	686
Micro 2000 Inc 1100 E Broadway Suite 301	Glendale	CA	91205	**800-864-8008**	818-547-0125	176-12
Micro Bio-Medics Inc 846 Pelham Pkwy	Pelham Manor	NY	10803	**800-431-2743**	914-738-8400	467
Micro Care Corp 595 John Downey Dr	New Britain	CT	06051	**800-638-0125**	860-827-0626	149
Micro Component Technology Inc 2340 W County Rd C	Saint Paul	MN	55113	**800-628-1628**	651-697-4000	685
Micro Design International Inc 45 Skyline Dr Suite 1017	Lake Mary	FL	32746	**800-228-0891**	407-472-6000	174
Micro Electronics Inc 4119 Leap Rd	Hilliard	OH	43026	**800-634-3478**	614-850-3000	171-3
Micro Express Inc 8 Hammond Dr Suite 105	Irvine	CA	92618	**800-989-9900**		171-3
Micro Group Inc 7 Industrial Pk Rd	Medway	MA	02053	**800-255-8823**	508-533-4925	584
Micro Industries Corp 8399 Green Meadow Dr N	Westerville	OH	43081	**800-722-1845**	740-548-7878	613
Micro Industries Inc 2990 S Main St	Salt Lake City	UT	84115	**800-446-3902**	801-466-2232	688
Micro Instrument Corp 1199 Emerson St	Rochester	NY	14606	**800-200-3150**	585-458-3150	446
Micro Linear Corp 2050 Concourse Dr *NASDAQ: MLIN*	San Jose	CA	95131	**800-998-5200**	408-433-5200	686
Micro Matic USA Inc 10726 N 2nd St	Machesney Park	IL	61115	**800-435-6950**	815-968-7557	650
Micro Networks Corp 324 Clark St	Worcester	MA	01606	**800-544-0052**	508-852-5400	247
Micro Planning International Inc 2225 Buchtel Blvd Suite 505	Denver	CO	80210	**800-852-7526**		176-1
Micro Solutions Enterprises 9111 Mason Ave	Chatsworth	CA	91311	**800-673-4968**	818-407-7500	616
Micro Solutions Inc 132 W Lincoln Hwy	DeKalb	IL	60115	**800-890-7227**	815-756-3411	171-8
Micro Therapeutics Inc 2 Goodyear Bldg A *NASDAQ: MTIX*	Irvine	CA	92618	**800-684-6733**	949-837-3700	468
MicroAire Surgical Instruments Inc 1641 Edlich Dr	Charlottesville	VA	22911	**800-538-5561**	434-975-8000	468
MicroBilt Corp 1640 Airport Rd Suite 115	Kennesaw	GA	30144	**800-884-4747**		176-10
Microbix Biosystems Inc 341 Bering Ave	Toronto	ON	M8Z3A8	**800-794-6694**	416-234-1624	86
MicroBiz Corp 1 Park Way	Upper Saddle River	NJ	07458	**800-385-0072**	201-785-1311	176-1
Microboards Technology LLC 8150 Mallory Ct PO Box 846	Chanhassen	MN	55317	**800-646-8881**	952-556-1600	171-8
Microchip Technology Inc 2355 W Chandler Blvd *NASDAQ: MCHP*	Chandler	AZ	85224	**800-437-2767**	480-792-7200	686
Microelectronics Technology Alert Newsletter 7550 W 1-10 Suite 400	San Antonio	TX	77220	**877-463-7678**	210-348-1000	521-12
MicroFilm Products Co 157 Avalon Gardens Dr	Nanuet	NY	10954	**800-642-7668**	845-371-3780	487
MicroFinancial Inc 10-M Commerce Way *NYSE: MFI*	Woburn	MA	01801	**800-843-5327**	781-994-4800	214
Microfluidics International Corp PO Box 9101	Newton	MA	02464	**800-370-5452**	617-969-5452	293
Micromanipulator Co Inc 1555 Forrest Way *Cust Svc	Carson City	NV	89706	**800-654-5659***	775-882-7377	247
MicroMarine Ltd 7 Industrial Pk Rd	Medway	MA	02053	**800-451-8746**	508-634-0205	701
MicroMetl Corp 3035 N Shadeland Ave	Indianapolis	IN	46226	**800-662-4822**	317-524-5400	650
Micromuse Inc 139 Townsend St 5th Fl *NASDAQ: MUSE*	San Francisco	CA	94107	**800-638-2665**	415-538-9090	176-7
MicronPC LLC 906 E Karcher Rd	Nampa	ID	83687	**888-464-2766**	208-893-3434	171-3
MicroPass Rewards Program 900 Skyline Dr Suite 100	Marion	IL	62959	**888-222-2142**	800-373-0092	371
MicroPatent LLC 250 Dodge Ave	East Haven	CT	06512	**800-648-6787**	203-466-5055	621
Microphor Inc 452 E Hill Rd *Orders	Willits	CA	95490	**800-358-8280***	707-459-5563	600
Microprocessor Report 298 S Sunnyvale Ave Suite 101	Sunnyvale	CA	94086	**800-527-0288**	408-328-3900	521-3
Micropump Inc 1402 NE 136th Ave *Sales	Vancouver	WA	98684	**800-671-6269***	360-253-2008	627
Micros Systems Inc 7031 Columbia Gateway Dr *NASDAQ: MCRS*	Columbia	MD	21046	**800-937-2211**	443-285-6000	603
Microscopy Society of America (MSA) 230 E Ohio St Suite 400	Chicago	IL	60611	**800-538-3672**	312-644-1527	49-19
Microsemi Corp 2381 Morse Ave *NASDAQ: MSCC*	Irvine	CA	92614	**800-713-4113**	949-221-7100	686
Microsoft Corp 1 Microsoft Way *NASDAQ: MSFT* ■ *Sales	Redmond	WA	98052	**800-426-9400***	425-882-8080	176-1
Microsoft Great Plains Business Solutions 1 Lone Tree Rd	Fargo	ND	58104	**888-477-7877**	701-281-6500	176-1
Microsoft Network (MSN) 1 Microsoft Way *Sales	Redmond	WA	98052	**800-426-9400***	425-882-8080	390
Microsoft Press 1 Microsoft Way *Cust Svc	Redmond	WA	98052	**800-426-9400***	425-882-8080	623-2
MicroStrategy Inc 1861 International Dr *NASDAQ: MSTR*	McLean	VA	22102	**800-927-1868**	703-848-8600	176-11
Microtech Computers Inc 4921 Legends Dr *Tech Supp	Lawrence	KS	66049	**800-828-9533***	785-841-9513	171-3
Microtek Medical Holdings Inc 1850 Beaver Ridge Cir Suite E *NASDAQ: MTMD*	Norcross	GA	30071	**800-777-7977**	770-806-9898	469
Microtek Medical Inc 512 Lehmberg Rd	Columbus	MS	39702	**800-824-3027**	662-327-1863	469
Microtel Inns & Suites 13 Corporate Sq Suite 250	Atlanta	GA	30329	**888-222-2142**	404-321-4045	369
MicroVision Development Inc 5541 Fermi Ct Suite 120	Carlsbad	CA	92008	**800-998-4555**	760-438-7781	176-8
Microvision Inc 19910 N Creek Pkwy *NASDAQ: MVIS*	Bothell	WA	98011	**888-822-6847**	425-415-6847	534
MicroVote General Corp 6366 Guilford Ave	Indianapolis	IN	46220	**800-257-4901**	317-257-4900	788
Microwave Radio Communications 101 Billerica Ave Bldg 6	North Billerica	MA	01862	**800-490-5700**	978-671-5700	633
Microwave Theory & Techniques Society. IEEE IEEE Operations Ctr 445 Hoes Ln	Piscataway	NJ	08854	**800-678-4333**	732-981-0060	49-19
MICS (Management Information Control Systems Inc) 2025 9th St	Los Osos	CA	93402	**800-838-6427**	805-543-7000	176-10
Mid-America Building Products Co 29797 Beck Rd	Wixom	MI	48393	**800-521-8486**		690
Mid-America Charter Lines 2513 E Higgins Rd	Elk Grove Village	IL	60007	**800-323-0312**	847-437-3779	108
Mid-America Merchandising Inc 204 W 3rd St	Kansas City	MO	64105	**800-333-6737**	816-471-5600	10
Mid-America Packaging LLC 3501 Jefferson Pkwy	Pine Bluff	AR	71602	**800-469-5120**	870-541-5120	68
Mid-America Science Museum 500 Mid-America Blvd	Hot Springs	AR	71913	**800-632-0583**	501-767-3461	509

Name / Address	City	State	ZIP	Toll-Free	Phone	Class
Mid-America Transplant Services 1139 Olivette Executive Pkwy	Saint Louis	MO	63132	**888-376-4854**	314-991-1661	535
Mid-American Coaches Inc PO Box 1609	Washington	MO	63090	**800-365-8687**	636-239-4700	108
Mid American Growers Inc RR 1 Box 36	Granville	IL	61326	**800-892-6888**	815-339-6831	363
Mid-Carolina Electric Co-op Inc PO Box 669 *Cust Svc	Lexington	SC	29071	**888-813-8000***	803-749-6555	244
Mid-Century Insurance Co 4680 Wilshire Blvd	Los Angeles	CA	90010	**888-516-5656**	323-932-3200	384-4
Mid Coast Hospital 123 Medical Center Dr	Brunswick	ME	04011	**877-729-0181**	207-729-0181	366-2
Mid-Columbia Bus Co 73458 Bus Barn Ln	Pendleton	OR	97801	**888-291-7513**	541-276-5621	110
Mid-Continent Casualty Co PO Box 1409	Tulsa	OK	74101	**800-722-4994**	918-587-7221	384-4
Mid-Continent Eye Bank 3306 E Central Ave	Wichita	KS	67208	**800-366-6791**	316-688-3937	265
Mid-Continent Regional Technology Transfer Center 301 Tarrow MS 8000	College Station	TX	77840	**800-472-6785**	979-845-2907	654
Mid-Continental Restoration Co Inc PO Box 429	Fort Scott	KS	66701	**800-835-3700**	620-223-3700	188-7
Mid-Iowa Co-op PO Box 160	Conrad	IA	50621	**800-458-9753**	641-366-2040	271
Mid-Island Electrical Supply 59 Mall Dr	Commack	NY	11725	**877-324-2636**	631-864-4242	245
Mid-Lakes Distributing Inc 1029 W Adams St	Chicago	IL	60607	**888-733-2700**	312-733-1033	601
Mid Louisiana Gas Co 1100 Louisiana St Suite 2950	Houston	TX	77002	**888-650-8900**	713-650-8900	320
Mid Michigan Hospice 3007 N Saginaw Rd	Midland	MI	48640	**800-852-9350**	989-633-1400	365
Mid-Ohio Aviation 6020 N Honeytown Rd	Smithville	OH	44677	**800-669-4243**	330-669-2671	63
Mid Ohio Energy Co-op Inc PO Box 224	Kenton	OH	43326	**888-382-6732**	419-673-7289	244
Mid-Ohio Sports Car Course 7721 Steam Corners Rd PO Box 3108	Lexington	OH	44904	**800-643-6446**	419-884-4000	504
Mid Penn Bancorp Inc 349 Union St *AMEX: MBP*	Millersburg	PA	17601	**800-672-6843**	717-692-2133	355-2
Mid Pines Inn & Golf Club 1010 Midland Rd	Southern Pines	NC	28387	**800-323-2114**	910-692-2114	655
Mid-Plains Community College McDonald-Belton Campus 601 W State Farm Rd	North Platte	NE	69101	**800-658-4308**	308-535-3700	160
Mid-South Electric Co-op Assn PO Box 970	Navasota	TX	77868	**888-525-6677**	936-825-5100	244
Mid-South Mfg Co 338 Commerce St	Jackson	TN	38301	**800-824-1622**	731-424-2525	34
Mid-South Tissue Bank 5600 Pleasant View Rd Suite 107	Memphis	TN	38134	**888-366-6775**	901-683-6566	535
Mid-South Wire Co Inc 1070 Visco Dr	Nashville	TN	37210	**800-714-7800**	615-244-5258	800
Mid-State Bancshares PO Box 6002 *NASDAQ: MDST*	Arroyo Grande	CA	93421	**800-473-7788**	805-473-6829	355-2
Mid-State Bank 1026 Grand Ave PO Box 6002	Arroyo Grande	CA	93421	**800-473-7788**	805-489-4293	71
Mid-State Machine Products Inc 83 Verti Dr	Winslow	ME	04901	**800-341-4672**	207-873-6136	745
Mid-State Mfg Corp 1115 Aldrich Ave N *Cust Svc	Minneapolis	MN	55411	**800-328-7144***	612-522-3631	803
Mid-State Technical College 500 32nd St N	Wisconsin Rapids	WI	54494	**888-575-6782**	715-422-5444	787
Mid States Dairy Co 6040 N Lindbergh Blvd	Saint Louis	MO	63042	**800-473-1150**	314-731-1150	291-27
Mid-States Supply Co 1716 Guinotte Ave	Kansas City	MO	64120	**800-825-1410**	816-842-4290	601
Mid-West Metallic Building Co 7301 Fairview St	Houston	TX	77041	**800-777-9378**	713-466-7788	106
Mid-West National Life Ins Co of Tennessee 9151 Grapevine Hwy	North Richland Hills	TX	76182	**800-733-1110**		384-2
Mid-West Spring & Stamping Co 1404 Joliet Rd Unit C	Romeoville	IL	60446	**800-838-7812**	630-739-3800	705
Midamar Corp PO Box 218	Cedar Rapids	IA	52406	**800-362-3711**	319-362-3711	292-9
Midamerica Hotels Corp 105 S Mt Auburn Rd PO Box 1570	Cape Girardeau	MO	63702	**888-866-4326**	573-334-0546	369
MidAmerica Nazarene University 2030 E College Way	Olathe	KS	66062	**800-800-8887**	913-782-3750	163
MidAmerican Energy Co 666 Grand Ave	Des Moines	IA	50309	**800-338-8007**	515-242-4300	774
Midas International Corp 1300 Arlington Heights Rd	Itasca	IL	60143	**800-621-0144**	630-438-3000	62-3
Midco Call Center Services 4901 E 26th St	Sioux Falls	SD	57110	**800-843-8800**	605-330-4125	722
MidCoast Credit Corp 1926 10th Ave N Suite 400	Lake Worth	FL	33461	**800-218-5919**	561-540-6224	498
Midcom Inc 121 Airport Dr	Watertown	SD	57201	**800-643-2661**	605-886-4385	720
Midcontinent Communications PO Box 5010	Sioux Falls	SD	57117	**800-888-1300**	605-229-1775	117
Middendorf Meat Co Inc 3737 N Broadway	Saint Louis	MO	63147	**800-949-6328**	314-241-4800	292-9
Middle Georgia Electric Membership Corp PO Box 190	Vienna	GA	31092	**800-342-0144**	229-268-2671	244
Middle River Aircraft Systems 103 Chesapeake Pk Plaza	Baltimore	MD	21220	**800-880-9975**	410-682-1000	23
Middle School Assn. National 4151 Executive Pkwy Suite 300	Westerville	OH	43081	**800-528-6672**	614-895-4730	49-5
Middle States Assn of Colleges & Schools 3624 Market St	Philadelphia	PA	19104	**800-355-1258**	215-662-5600	49-5
Middle Tennessee Medical Center 400 N Highland Ave	Murfreesboro	TN	37130	**800-596-3455**	615-849-4100	366-2
Middle Tennessee Mental Health Institute 221 Stewarts Ferry Pike	Nashville	TN	37214	**800-575-3506**	615-902-7400	366-3
Middle Tennessee Natural Gas Utility District 1036 W Broad	Smithville	TN	37166	**800-880-6373**	615-597-4300	774
Middle Tennessee State University 1301 E Main St	Murfreesboro	TN	37132	**800-433-6878**	615-898-2300	163
Middlebury Inn 14 Courthouse Sq	Middlebury	VT	05753	**800-842-4666**	802-388-4961	373
Middleby Corp 1400 Toastmaster Dr *NASDAQ: MIDD* ■ *Cust Svc	Elgin	IL	60120	**800-323-2210***	847-741-3300	293
Middlesex Hospital 28 Crescent St	Middletown	CT	06457	**800-664-5031**	860-344-6110	366-2
Middlesex Insurance Co 3 Carlisle Rd	Westford	MA	01886	**800-225-1390**	978-392-7000	384-4
Middlesex Mutual Assurance Co 213 Court St PO Box 891	Middletown	CT	06457	**800-899-0032**	860-347-4621	384-4
Middlesex Savings Bank 6 Main St	Natick	MA	01760	**800-438-6797**	508-653-0300	71
Middlesex Water Co 1500 Ronson Rd *NASDAQ: MSEX*	Iselin	NJ	08830	**800-729-4030**	732-634-1500	774
Middleton Building Supply Inc 5 Kings Hwy	Middleton	NH	03887	**800-647-8989**	603-473-2314	671
Middleton John Inc 418 W Church Rd	King of Prussia	PA	19406	**800-523-1126**	610-265-1400	741-3
Middleton Village Nursing & Rehabilitation Center 6201 Elmwood Ave	Middleton	WI	53562	**877-836-2676**	608-831-8300	441
Middletown Journal PO Box 490	Middletown	OH	45042	**888-397-6397**	513-422-3611	522-2
Middletown Regional Hospital 105 McKnight Dr	Middletown	OH	45044	**800-338-4057**	513-424-2111	366-2
Middletowne Hotel. Helmsley 148 E 48th St	New York	NY	10017	**800-221-4982**	212-755-3000	373
MidFirst Bank PO Box 76149	Oklahoma City	OK	73147	**888-643-3477**	405-943-8002	71
Midian Electronics Inc 2302 E 22nd St *Orders	Tucson	AZ	85713	**800-643-4267***	520-884-7981	252
Midland Asphalt Corp 640 Young St	Tonawanda	NY	14150	**800-573-0400**	716-692-0730	46
Midland Chamber of Commerce 109 N Main St	Midland	TX	79701	**800-624-6435**	432-683-3381	137
Midland Co PO Box 1256 *NASDAQ: MLAN*	Cincinnati	OH	45201	**800-543-2644**	513-943-7100	355-4
Midland County Convention & Visitors Bureau 300 Rodd St Suite 101	Midland	MI	48640	**888-464-3526**	989-839-9901	205
Midland Daily News 124 S McDonald St	Midland	MI	48640	**800-835-6679**	989-835-7171	522-2
Midland Financial Co 501 NW Grand Blvd	Oklahoma City	OK	73118	**800-851-5041**	405-840-7600	355-2
Midland Hospice Care 200 SW Frazier Cir	Topeka	KS	66606	**800-491-3691**	785-232-2044	365
Midland Hospital Supply Inc 2011 Great Northern Dr	Fargo	ND	58102	**800-747-4450**	701-235-4451	467
Midland-Impact LLC 103 Lincoln St	Danville	IN	46122	**800-525-0272**	317-745-4491	438
Midland Industries Inc 1424 N Halsted St	Chicago	IL	60622	**800-662-8228**	312-664-7300	476
Midland Iron & Steel Co 3301 4th Ave	Moline	IL	61265	**800-223-5942**	309-764-6723	674
Midland Loan Services Inc 10851 Mastin	Overland Park	KS	66210	**800-327-8083**	913-253-9000	498
Midland Lutheran College 900 N Clarkson St	Fremont	NE	68025	**800-642-8382**	402-721-5480	163
Midland Memorial Hospital 2200 W Illinois Ave	Midland	TX	79701	**800-833-2916**	432-685-1111	366-2
Midland Mortgage Co PO Box 26648	Oklahoma City	OK	73126	**800-654-4566**		498
Midland Paper 101 E Palatine Rd	Wheeling	IL	60090	**800-523-7477**	847-777-2700	543
Midland Reporter-Telegram PO Box 1650	Midland	TX	79702	**800-542-3952**	432-682-5311	522-2
Midlands Carrier Transicold Inc 10707 S 149th St	Omaha	NE	68138	**800-655-9382**	402-895-5500	651
Midlands Technical College PO Box 2408	Columbia	SC	29202	**800-922-8038**	803-738-1400	160
Midnight Rose Hotel & Casino 256 E Bennett Ave	Cripple Creek	CO	80813	**888-461-7529**	719-689-2446	133
Midnight Sun Adventure Travel 1845-B Fort St	Victoria	BC	V8R1J6	**800-255-5057**	250-480-9409	748
Midpeninsula Pathways Hospice 585 N Mary Ave	Sunnyvale	CA	94085	**800-900-0811**	408-773-5900	365
Midsouth Aviation Alliance Corp 2432 Winchester Rd	Memphis	TN	38116	**800-893-6222**	901-396-7318	14
MidSouth Bancorp Inc 102 Versailles Blvd *AMEX: MSL*	Lafayette	LA	70501	**800-213-2265**	337-237-8343	355-2
Midstate College 411 W Northmoor Rd	Peoria	IL	61614	**800-251-4299**	309-692-4092	787
Midstate Electric Co-op Inc PO Box 127	La Pine	OR	97739	**800-722-7219**	541-536-2126	244
Midstate Mills Inc 324 E 'A' St	Newton	NC	28658	**800-222-1032**	828-464-1611	291-23
Midstate Raceway Inc 14 Ruth St PO Box 860	Vernon	NY	13476	**877-777-8559**	315-829-2201	628
Midstream Fuel Service LLC 5900 Memorial Dr Suite 305	Houston	TX	77007	**800-368-5990**	713-350-6800	319
Midtown Hotel 220 Huntington Ave	Boston	MA	02115	**800-343-1177**	617-262-1000	373
Midway College 512 E Stephens St	Midway	KY	40347	**800-755-0031**	859-846-4421	163
Midway Hospital Medical Center 5925 San Vincente Blvd	Los Angeles	CA	90019	**800-827-8599**	323-938-3161	366-2
Midwesco Filter Resources Inc 385 Battaile Dr	Winchester	VA	22601	**800-336-7300**	540-667-8500	19
Midwest Air Group Inc 6744 S Howell Ave *NYSE: MEH*	Oak Creek	WI	53154	**800-452-2022**	414-570-4000	355-1
Midwest Airlines Inc 6744 S Howell Ave	Oak Creek	WI	53154	**800-452-2022**	414-570-4000	26
Midwest Airlines Midwest Miles 6744 S Howell Ave Dept 16	Oak Creek	WI	53154	**800-452-2022**	414-570-4000	27
Midwest Canvas Corp 4635 W Lake St	Chicago	IL	60644	**800-433-4701**	773-287-4400	718
Midwest Coast Transport 1600 E Benson Rd *Cust Svc	Sioux Falls	SD	57104	**800-843-6699***	605-339-8400	769
Midwest Communications Inc 904 Grand Ave	Wausau	WI	54403	**877-903-2171**	715-842-1437	629
Midwest Corporate Aviation 3512 N Webb Rd	Wichita	KS	67226	**800-435-9622**	316-636-9700	63

Listing	Toll-Free	Phone	Class
Midwest Crisis Cleaning Inc 1011 Burgess Ave .... Crystal City MO 63019	**877-937-4862**	636-937-4862	84
Midwest Dental Products Corp 901 W Oakton St .... Des Plaines IL 60018	**800-800-2888***	847-640-4800	226
*Cust Svc			
Midwest Drywall Co Inc 1351 S Reca Ct ....Wichita KS 67209	**888-722-9559**	316-722-9559	188-9
Midwest EAP Solutions Inc 1010 W Saint Germain St Suite 580 .... Saint Cloud MN 56301	**800-383-1908**	320-253-1909	454
Midwest Elastomers Inc PO Box 412 ....Wapakoneta OH 45895	**800-786-3539**	419-738-8844	594-3
Midwest Electric Co-op Corp PO Box 970 .... Grant NE 69140	**800-451-3691**	308-352-4356	244
Midwest Electric Inc PO Box 10.... Saint Marys OH 45885	**800-962-3830**	419-394-4110	244
Midwest Employers Casualty Co 14755 N Outer 40 Dr Suite 300... Chesterfield MO 63017	**877-632-2474**	636-449-7000	384-4
Midwest Energy Co-op PO Box 127 ... Cassopolis MI 49031	**800-492-5989**	269-445-1000	244
Midwest Energy Inc PO Box 898 ....Hays KS 67601	**800-222-3121**	785-625-3437	244
Midwest Eye Banks & Transplantation Center 800 S Wells St Suite 185..... Chicago IL 60607	**800-548-4703**	312-706-9650	265
Midwest Folding Products Inc 1414 S Western Ave............... Chicago IL 60608	**800-621-4716**	312-666-3366	314-3
Midwest Helicopter Airways Inc 525 Executive Dr ....Willowbrook IL 60527	**800-323-7609**	630-325-7860	354
Midwest Industries Inc PO Box 235... Ida Grove IA 51445	**800-859-3028**	712-364-3365	751
Midwest Library Service Inc 11443 St Charles Rock Rd......... Bridgeton MO 63044	**800-325-8833**	314-739-3100	97
Midwest Living Magazine 1716 Locust St................ Des Moines IA 50309	**800-678-8093**	515-284-2662	449-22
Midwest Marketing Inc 239 Hwy 61 PO Box 125........ Bloomsdale MO 63627	**800-662-7538**	573-483-2577	361
Midwest Mechanical Group 540 Executive Dr ....Willowbrook IL 60527	**800-600-4047***	630-655-4200	188-10
*Svc			
Midwest Medical Services 4280 Bluestem Rd .... Charleston IL 61920	**888-850-7377**		347
Midwest Motor Express Inc 5015 E Main Ave .... Bismarck ND 58502	**800-741-4097**	701-223-1880	769
Midwest Motorist Magazine 12901 N 40th Dr ....Saint Louis MO 63141	**800-222-7623**	314-523-7350	449-22
Midwest Office Furniture & Supply Co 987 S West Temple ....Salt Lake City UT 84101	**800-351-4553**	801-359-7681	524
Midwest Paper Tube & Can Corp PO Box 510006 ....New Berlin WI 53151	**800-577-1400***	262-782-7300	125
*Cust Svc			
Midwest Payment Systems 38 Fountain Sq Plaza ....Cincinnati OH 45263	**800-972-3030**	513-579-5300	70
Midwest Products Co Inc 400 S Indiana St.................... Hobart IN 46342	**800-348-3497***	219-942-1134	750
*Orders			
Midwest Quality Gloves Inc 835 Industrial Rd .... Chillicothe MO 64601	**800-821-3028**	660-646-2165	153-8
Midwest Sales & Service Inc 917 S Chapin St............... South Bend IN 46601	**800-772-7262**	574-287-3365	38
Midwest Steel Inc 2525 E Grand Blvd ... Detroit MI 48211	**800-578-7880**	313-873-2220	188-14
Midwest Tile & Concrete Products Inc 4309 Webster Rd .... Woodburn IN 46797	**800-359-4701**	260-749-5173	181
Midwest Tool & Cutlery Co Inc 1210 Progress St PO Box 160........Sturgis MI 49091	**800-782-4659**	269-651-2476	219
Midwest Truck & Auto Parts 4200 S Morgan St .... Chicago IL 60609	**800-934-2727**	312-225-1550	61
Midwest Veterinary Supply Inc 11965 Larc Industrial Blvd.........Burnsville MN 55337	**800-328-2975**	952-894-4350	467
Midwest Walnut Co 1914 Postevin St .... Council Bluffs IA 51503	**800-592-5688**	712-325-9191	439
Midwest Wire Products Inc 800 Woodward Heights ....Ferndale MI 48220	**800-989-9881**	248-399-5100	75
Midwest Wire Products LLC PO Box 770 ....Sturgeon Bay WI 54235	**800-445-0225**	920-743-6591	479
Midwestern Industries Inc 915 Oberlin Rd SW .... Massillon OH 44647	**877-474-9464**	330-837-4203	189
Midwestern Regional Medical Center 2520 Elisha Ave ....Zion IL 60099	**800-322-9183**	847-872-4561	366-5
Midwestern State University 3410 Taft Blvd .... Wichita Falls TX 76308	**800-842-1922**	940-397-4000	163
Midwestock 9218 Metcalf Suite 145 .... Overland Park KS 66212	**800-474-9974**	816-474-0229	582
MidWestOne Financial Group Inc 222 1st Ave E............................ Oskaloosa IA 52577	**800-303-6740**	641-673-8448	355-2
NASDAQ: OSKY			
Miele Inc 9 Independence Way....... Princeton NJ 08540	**800-843-7231**	609-419-9898	36
Mighty Distributing System of America Inc 650 Engineering Dr .... Norcross GA 30092	**800-829-3900**	770-448-3900	61
Mighty Ducks of Anaheim 2695 Katella Ave Arrowhead Pond of Anaheim.......................Anaheim CA 92806	**877-945-3946**	714-704-2700	703
Migration Ministries. Episcopal 815 2nd Ave....................New York NY 10017	**800-334-7626**	212-716-6252	48-5
Mii Amo at Enchantment Resort 525 Boynton Canyon Rd ....Sedona AZ 86336	**888-749-2137**	928-282-2900	698
MII Inc Lundia Div 600 Capitol Way...............Jacksonville IL 62650	**800-726-9663**	217-243-8585	281
MIIX Group Inc 2 Princess Rd..... Lawrenceville NJ 08648	**800-257-6288**	609-896-2404	355-4
MIIX Insurance Co of New York 2 Princess Rd................Lawrenceville NJ 08648	**800-234-6449**	609-896-2404	384-5
MIIX Insurance Cos 2 Princess Rd................Lawrenceville NJ 08648	**800-234-6449**	609-896-2404	384-5
Mikasa Inc 1 Mikasa Dr .... Secaucus NJ 07096	**800-833-4681***	201-867-9210	716
*Cust Svc			
Mike-Sell's Potato Chip Co 333 Leo St ... Dayton OH 45404	**800-257-4742**	937-228-9400	291-35
Mike Shaw Chevrolet Buick Saab 1080 S Colorado Blvd ....Denver CO 80246	**800-223-1615**	303-757-6161	57
Mikes Restaurants Inc 8250 Decarie Blvd Suite 310 ....Montreal QC H4P2P5	**866-346-4537**	514-341-5544	657
Mikohn Gaming Corp 920 Pilot Rd ... Las Vegas NV 89119	**800-336-8449**	702-896-3890	317
NASDAQ: MIKN			
Mikron Industries Inc 1034 6th Ave N..... Kent WA 98032	**800-456-8020**	253-854-8020	233
Mikron Infrared Inc 16 Thornton Rd.... Oakland NJ 07436	**800-631-0176**	201-405-0900	200
NASDAQ: MIKR			
Milaeger's Inc 4838 Douglas Ave....... Racine WI 53402	**800-669-1229**	262-639-2040	318
Milan Express Co Inc 1091 Kefauver Dr PO Box 699......... Milan TN 38358	**800-231-7303**	731-686-7428	769
MiLAN Technology 1329 Moffett Pk Dr............. Sunnyvale CA 94089	**800-466-4526**	408-744-2775	174
Milastar Corp 7317 W Lake St ..... Minneapolis MN 55426	**877-888-8874**	952-929-7815	475
Milbar Div Stride Tool Inc 530 E Washington St.......... Chagrin Falls OH 44022	**877-225-8858**	440-247-4600	746
Milbar Hydro-Test Inc 651 Aero Dr... Shreveport LA 71107	**800-259-8210**	318-227-8210	528
Milberg Weiss Bershad & Schulman LLP 1 Pennsylvania Plaza 49th Fl.... New York NY 10119	**800-320-5081**	212-594-5300	419
Milco Industries Inc 550 E 5th St... Bloomsburg PA 17815	**800-867-0288**	570-784-0400	153-15
Milco Mfg Co 2147 E 10-Mile Rd....... Warren MI 48091	**800-697-6452**	586-755-7320	798
MILCOM Systems Corp 532 Viking Dr............... Virginia Beach VA 23452	**800-967-0966**	757-463-2800	681
Milcor Inc 1150 N Cable Rd ....Lima OH 45805	**800-528-1411**		688
Miles City Star PO Box 1216 ....Miles City MT 59301	**800-323-6505**	406-234-0450	522-2
Miles College 5500 Myron Massey Blvd........... Fairfield AL 35064	**800-445-0708**	205-929-1000	163
Miles Community College 2715 Dickinson St ....Miles City MT 59301	**800-541-9281**	406-874-6100	160
Miles Farm Supplies LLC 1401 B Spring Bank Dr ....Owensboro KY 42303	**800-666-4537**	270-926-2420	272
Miles Kimball Co 41 W 8th Ave ....Oshkosh WI 54901	**800-546-2255**	920-231-3800	451
Miles Media Group Inc 6751 Professional Pkwy W Suite 200 ....Sarasota FL 34240	**800-683-0010**	941-342-2300	623-9
Miles & More PO Box 946 .... Santa Clarita CA 91380	**800-581-6400**		27
Miles & Stockbridge PC 10 Light St... Baltimore MD 21202	**800-344-2532**	410-727-6464	419
Milestone Contractors LP 3410 S-650 E...................Columbus IN 47203	**800-559-7910**	812-579-5248	187-4
Milford Mirror 1000 Bridgeport Ave .....Shelton CT 06484	**800-843-6791**	203-926-2080	522-4
Milgard Mfg 1010 54th Ave E......... Tacoma WA 98424	**800-562-8444**	253-922-2030	232
Milgro Nursery LLC 340 Rosewood Ave Suite J .... Camarillo CA 93010	**800-645-4769**	805-383-3616	363
Military Active Retired Travel Club. Special 600 University Office Blvd Suite 1A ....Pensacola FL 32504	**800-354-7681**		48-23
Military & Aerospace Electronics Magazine 98 Spit Brook Rd..........Nashua NH 03062	**800-225-0556**	603-891-0123	449-12
Military Benefit Assn (MBA) PO Box 221110 ....Chantilly VA 20153	**800-336-0100**	703-968-6200	48-19
Military Book Club Doubleday Direct Inc 1225 S Market St .... Mechanicsburg PA 17055	**800-688-4442**		94
Military Comptrollers. American Society of 415 N Alfred.......... Alexandria VA 22314	**800-462-5637**	703-549-0360	48-19
Military Engineer Magazine 607 Prince St.................. Alexandria VA 22314	**800-336-3097**	703-549-3800	449-12
Military Engineers. Society of American 607 Prince St.......... Alexandria VA 22314	**800-336-3097**	703-549-3800	48-19
Military History Magazine 741 Miller Dr SE Suite D2 .... Leesburg VA 20175	**800-829-3340**	703-771-9400	449-10
Military Officer Magazine 201 N Washington St............ Alexandria VA 22314	**800-245-8762**	703-549-2311	449-12
Military Officers Assn of America (MOAA) 201 N Washington St ..... Alexandria VA 22314	**800-234-6622**	703-549-2311	48-19
Military Service for America Memorial Foundation. Women in Dept 560.................. Washington DC 20042	**800-222-2294**	703-533-1155	48-19
Military Service for America Memorial. Women in Memorial Dr Arlington National Cemetery................ Arlington VA 22211	**800-222-2294**	703-533-1155	50
Military Service Co Div EBSCO Industries Inc PO Box 1943 ..... Birmingham AL 35201	**800-255-3722**	205-991-6600	322
Military Surgeons of the US. Association of 9320 Old Georgetown Rd................. Bethesda MD 20814	**800-761-9320**	301-897-8800	49-8
Military Widows. Society of 5535 Hempstead Way .... Springfield VA 22151	**800-842-3451**	703-750-1342	48-19
Milk Producers Federation. National 2101 Wilson Blvd Suite 400........ Arlington VA 22201	**888-549-7600**	703-243-6111	49-6
Milk Specialties Co PO Box 278........Dundee IL 60118	**800-323-5424**	847-426-3411	438
Milkco Inc 220 Deaverview Rd ....Asheville NC 28806	**800-842-8021**	828-254-9560	291-27
Mill Creek Lumber & Supply 6201 S 129th East Ave PO Box 4770 ... Tulsa OK 74159	**800-364-6455**	918-747-2000	190-3
Mill-Max Mfg Corp 190 Pine Hollow Rd............. Oyster Bay NY 11771	**800-294-8027**	516-922-6000	803
Mill Mountain Theatre 1 Market Sq 2nd Fl................Roanoke VA 24011	**800-317-6455**	540-342-5740	562
Mill-Rose Co 7995 Tyler Blvd .... Mentor OH 44060	**800-321-3533**	440-255-9171	104
Mill Run Tours Inc 424 Madison Ave 11th Fl ....New York NY 10017	**800-645-5786**	212-486-9840	17
Mill Steel Co 5116 36th St SE ....Grand Rapids MI 49512	**800-247-6455**	616-949-6700	709
Mill Street Inn 75 Mill St ....Newport RI 02840	**800-392-1316**	401-849-9500	373
Mill Supply Div 264 Morse St......... Hamden CT 06517	**800-243-6648**	203-777-7668	88
Mill Valley Inn 165 Throckmorton Ave........... Mill Valley CA 94941	**800-595-2100**	415-389-6608	373
Millbrook Distribution Services 88 Huntoon Memorial Hwy .... Leicester MA 01524	**800-225-7398**	508-892-8171	237
Millbrook Press Inc 2 Old New Milford Rd ....Brookfield CT 06804	**800-462-4703**	203-740-2220	623-2
Millcraft Paper Co 6800 Grant Ave.... Cleveland OH 44105	**800-826-4444**	216-441-5500	543
Millcraft SMS Services LLC PO Box 1107 ....Oil City PA 16301	**800-394-4862**	814-677-9400	745
Mille Lacs Band of Ojibwe 43408 Oodena Dr..................Onamia MN 56359	**800-709-6445**	320-532-4181	132
Mille Lacs Electric Co-op PO Box 230.... Aitkin MN 56431	**800-450-2191**	218-927-2191	244
Milledgeville-Baldwin County Convention & Visitors Bureau 200 W Hancock St............. Milledgeville GA 31061	**800-653-1804**	478-452-4687	205
Millenicom 1735 SW Miles St Suite 2000 .... Portland OR 97219	**888-925-4221**	503-768-3063	390
Millenium Aviation 2365 Bernville Rd Reading Regional Airport .... Reading PA 19605	**800-366-9419**	610-374-0100	63

Name / Address	City	State	ZIP	Toll-Free	Phone	Class
Millennium Biltmore Hotel Los Angeles 506 S Grand Ave	Los Angeles	CA	90071	**800-245-8673**	213-624-1011	373
Millennium Bostonian Hotel 26 North St Faneuil Hall Marketplace	Boston	MA	02109	**800-343-0922**	617-523-3600	373
Millennium Chemicals Inc 20 Wight Ave Suite 100	Hunt Valley	MD	21030	**866-225-5642**	410-229-4400	142
Millennium Hotel Anchorage 4800 Spenard Rd	Anchorage	AK	99517	**800-544-0553**	907-243-2300	373
Millennium Hotel Boulder 1345 28th St	Boulder	CO	80302	**866-866-8086**	303-443-3850	373
Millennium Hotel Cincinnati 141 W 6th St	Cincinnati	OH	45202	**800-876-2100**	513-352-2100	373
Millennium Hotel Durham 2800 Campus Walk Ave	Durham	NC	27705	**800-633-5379**	919-383-8575	373
Millennium Hotel Minneapolis 1313 Nicollet Mall	Minneapolis	MN	55403	**866-866-8086**	612-332-6000	373
Millennium Hotel New York Broadway 145 W 44th St	New York	NY	10036	**800-622-5569**	212-768-4400	370
Millennium Knickerbocker Hotel Chicago 163 E Walton Pl	Chicago	IL	60611	**800-621-8140**	312-751-8100	373
Millennium Laser Eye Centers 1750 Tysons Blvd Suite 120	McLean	VA	22102	**888-565-2737**	703-761-4999	785
Millennium Maxwell House Hotel Nashville 2025 Metro Center Blvd	Nashville	TN	37228	**866-866-8086**	615-259-4343	373
Millennium Resort Scottsdale McCormick Ranch 7401 N Scottsdale Rd	Scottsdale	AZ	85253	**800-243-1332**	480-948-5050	655
Millennium Specialty Chemicals 601 Crestwood St	Jacksonville	FL	32208	**800-231-6728**	904-768-5800	143
Millennium Telecom LLC 310 60th St NW	Sauk Rapids	MN	56379	**877-720-6249**	320-253-5489	168
Millennium Teleservices LLC 425 Raritan Ctr Pkwy	Edison	NJ	08837	**877-877-7698**		722
Miller AC Concrete Products Inc PO Box 199	Spring City	PA	19475	**800-229-2922**	610-948-4600	181
Miller Architects & Builders Inc 3335 W Saint Germain St	Saint Cloud	MN	56301	**800-772-1758**	320-251-4109	258
Miller Bill Bar-B-Q 430 S Santa Rosa St	San Antonio	TX	78207	**800-339-3111**	210-225-4461	657
Miller BK Co Inc 4501 B Auth Place	Suitland	MD	20746	**800-801-7632**	301-423-6200	435
Miller Building Systems Inc 58120 CR 3 S	Elkhart	IN	46517	**800-423-2559**	574-295-1214	107
Miller Chemical & Fertilizer Corp 120 Radio Rd	Hanover	PA	17331	**800-233-2040**	717-632-8921	276
Miller & Co LLC 9700 W Higgins Rd Suite 1000	Rosemont	IL	60018	**800-727-9847**	847-696-2400	490
Miller Consolidated Industries Inc 2221 Arbor Blvd	Dayton	OH	45439	**800-589-4133**	937-294-2681	475
Miller-Cooper Co 5187 Merriam Dr	Merriam	KS	66203	**800-289-6246**	913-312-5020	381
Miller Curtain Co Inc PO Box 240790	San Antonio	TX	78224	**800-741-9020**	210-483-1000	731
Miller EA Inc 410 N 200 West	Hyrum	UT	84319	**800-873-0939**	435-245-6456	465
Miller Electric Co 2251 Rosselle St *Sales	Jacksonville	FL	32204	**800-554-4761***	904-388-8000	188-4
Miller Fluid Power Corp 800 N York Rd	Bensenville	IL	60106	**800-323-8207**	630-766-3400	220
Miller Frank & Sons Inc 13831 S Emerald Ave	Riverdale	IL	60827	**800-423-6358**	708-201-7200	149
Miller Golf Inc 835 Bill Jones Industrial Dr	Springfield	TN	37172	**800-343-1000**	615-384-1286	701
Miller Harry Canvas Co Inc 850 Albany St	Boston	MA	02119	**800-225-5598**	617-427-2300	718
Miller HC Co 3030 Lowell Dr	Green Bay	WI	54311	**800-829-6555**		87
Miller Herman for Health Care 855 E Main Ave PO Box 302	Zeeland	MI	49464	**888-443-4357**		314-3
Miller Herman Inc 855 E Main Ave *NASDAQ: MLHR*	Zeeland	MI	49464	**888-443-4357**	616-654-3000	314-1
Miller Industries Inc 8503 Hilltop Dr *NYSE: MLR*	Ooltewah	TN	37363	**800-292-0330**	423-238-4171	505
Miller International Inc Rocky Mountain Clothing Co Div 8500 Zuni St	Denver	CO	80260	**800-688-4449**	303-428-5696	153-20
Miller Johnson Steichen Kinnard Inc 60 S 6th St Suite 3000	Minneapolis	MN	55402	**800-444-7884**	612-455-5555	679
Miller Machinery & Supply Co 127 NE 27th St	Miami	FL	33137	**800-273-3030**	305-573-1300	270
Miller Multiplex Inc 512 Stockton St	Richmond	VA	23224	**800-757-1112**	804-232-4551	231
Miller Office Furniture 1212 Lincoln Dr	High Point	NC	27260	**800-438-4324**	336-819-6400	314-1
Miller Oil Co PO Box 1858	Norfolk	VA	23501	**800-333-4645**	757-623-6600	569
Miller Packing Co PO Box 1390	Lodi	CA	95241	**800-624-2328**	209-339-2310	291-26
Miller Pipeline Corp 8850 Crawfordsville Rd	Indianapolis	IN	46234	**800-428-3742**	317-293-0278	187-10
Miller Products Co Inc 2220 91st St	North Bergen	NJ	07047	**800-782-7437**	201-662-2010	566
Miller RA Industries Inc 14500 168th Ave	Grand Haven	MI	49417	**888-845-9450**	616-842-9450	633
Miller Saint Nazianz Inc 511 E Main St	Saint Nazianz	WI	54232	**800-247-5557**	920-773-2121	269
Miller-Stephenson Chemical Co 55 Backus Ave *Tech Supp	Danbury	CT	06810	**800-992-2424***	203-743-4447	143
Miller TR Mill Co Inc PO Box 708	Brewton	AL	36427	**800-633-6740**	251-867-4331	671
Miller Transporters Inc 5500 Hwy 80 W *Cust Svc	Jackson	MS	39209	**800-645-5378***	601-922-8331	769
Miller WC & AN Cos 4701 Sangamore Rd	Bethesda	MD	20816	**800-599-4711**	301-229-4000	186
Miller WC & AN Realtors 4910 Massachusetts Ave NW Suite 119	Washington	DC	20016	**877-362-1300**	202-362-1300	638
Miller Wire Works Inc 7429 Georgia Rd	Birmingham	AL	35212	**800-783-0341**	205-592-0341	275
Millers First Insurance Co 111 E 4th St	Alton	IL	62002	**800-558-0500**	618-463-3636	384-4
Millers Forge Inc 1411 Capital Ave	Plano	TX	75074	**800-527-3474**	972-422-2145	219
Millers Mutual Insurance Assn 111 E 4th St	Alton	IL	62002	**800-558-0500**	618-463-3636	384-4
Millhaven Co Inc 1705 Millhaven Rd	Sylvania	GA	30467	**800-421-8043**	912-829-4742	11-4
Milliken & Co KEX Div 201 Lukken Industrial Dr W MS 801	LaGrange	GA	30240	**800-342-5539**		131
Milliken Millwork Inc 6361 Sterling Dr N	Sterling Heights	MI	48312	**800-686-9218**	586-264-0950	489
Milliken Publishing Co Inc 11643 Lilburn Park Dr	Saint Louis	MO	63146	**800-325-4136**	314-991-4220	242
Millikin University 1184 W Main St	Decatur	IL	62522	**800-373-7733**	217-424-6211	163
Millin Publishing Group Inc 1150 Connecticut Ave NW Suite 900	Washington	DC	20036	**888-739-8500**	202-862-4375	623-9
Million Air 4300 Westgrove Dr	Addison	TX	75001	**800-248-1602**	972-248-1600	63
Million Air Interlink Inc 8501 Telephone Rd	Houston	TX	77061	**888-589-9059**	713-640-4000	25
Million Dollar Round Table (MDRT) 325 W Touhy Ave	Park Ridge	IL	60068	**800-879-6378**	847-692-6378	49-9
Millipore Corp 80 Ashby Rd *NYSE: MIL*	Bedford	MA	01730	**800-221-1975**	781-533-6000	411
Millrock Inc 67 Federal Ave	Quincy	MA	02169	**800-645-7625**	617-890-1090	281
Mills College 5000 MacArthur Blvd	Oakland	CA	94613	**800-876-4557**	510-430-2135	163
Mills Cos Inc 5215 Gershwin Ave N	Saint Paul	MN	55128	**800-367-9045**	651-770-6660	472
Mills House Hotel 115 Meeting St	Charleston	SC	29401	**800-874-9600**	843-577-2400	373
Mills Iron Works Inc 14834 Maple St	Gardena	CA	90247	**800-421-2281**	323-321-6520	584
Millsaps College 1701 N State St	Jackson	MS	39210	**800-352-1050**	601-974-1000	163
MillSource PO Box 170	Montevallo	AL	35115	**800-756-0199**	205-665-2546	304
Millwork Distributors. Association of 10047 Robert Trent Jones Pkwy	New Port Richey	FL	34655	**800-786-7274**	727-372-3665	49-3
Millwork Producers Assn. Wood Moulding & 507 First St	Woodland	CA	95695	**800-550-7889**	530-661-9591	49-3
Milne Travel 40 Patchen Rd	South Burlington	VT	05403	**800-698-1415**	802-864-0204	748
Milner Hotels Inc 1526 Centre St	Detroit	MI	48226	**800-521-0592**	313-962-5400	369
Milnot Co 100 S 4th St Suite 1010 *Sales	Saint Louis	MO	63102	**800-877-6455***	314-436-7667	291-10
Milsco Mfg Co 9009 N 51st St	Brown Deer	WI	53223	**800-645-7261**	414-354-0500	678
Milson & Louis 83 Ames St	Brockton	MA	02302	**877-835-6457**	508-559-0770	356
Milton Hershey School PO Box 830	Hershey	PA	17033	**800-322-3248**	717-520-2100	611
Miltons Inc 250 Granite St	Braintree	MA	02184	**800-645-8667**	781-848-1880	155-3
Miltope Corp 500 Richardson Rd S	Hope Hull	AL	36043	**800-645-8673**	334-284-8665	171-3
Milwaukee Area Technical College 700 W State St	Milwaukee	WI	53233	**800-720-6282**	414-297-6600	787
Milwaukee Dustless Brush Co 10930 W Lapham St	Milwaukee	WI	53214	**800-632-3220**	414-476-1147	104
Milwaukee Electric Tool Corp 13135 W Lisbon Rd	Brookfield	WI	53005	**800-729-3878**	262-781-3600	747
Milwaukee Envelope Inc 1880 Executive Dr	Oconomowoc	WI	53006	**800-236-1980**	262-569-5555	260
Milwaukee (Greater) Convention & Visitors Bureau 101 W Wisconsin Ave Suite 425	Milwaukee	WI	53203	**800-231-0903**	414-273-3950	205
Milwaukee Institute of Art & Design 273 E Erie St	Milwaukee	WI	53202	**888-749-6423**	414-276-7889	163
Milwaukee Journal Sentinel 333 W State St	Milwaukee	WI	53203	**800-456-5943**	414-224-2318	522-2
Milwaukee Magazine 417 E Chicago St	Milwaukee	WI	53202	**800-662-4818**	414-273-1101	449-22
Milwaukee Marble & Granite Co Inc 4535 W Mitchell St	Milwaukee	WI	53214	**877-645-6272**	414-645-0305	710
Milwaukee Mutual Insurance Co 400 S Executive Dr Suite 200	Brookfield	WI	50005	**800-733-7366**	262-207-8500	384-4
Milwaukee School of Engineering 1025 N Broadway St	Milwaukee	WI	53202	**800-332-6763**	414-277-6763	163
Milwaukee Stove & Furnace Supply Co 5070 W State St	Milwaukee	WI	53208	**800-677-0213**	414-258-0300	601
Milwaukee Symphony Orchestra 700 N Water St Suite 700	Milwaukee	WI	53202	**800-291-7605**	414-291-6010	563-3
Milwaukee Valve Co Inc 2375 S Burrell St	Milwaukee	WI	53207	**800-348-6544**	414-744-5240	776
Milwhite Inc 5487 South Padre Island Hwy	Brownsville	TX	78521	**800-442-0082**	956-547-1970	493-2
Minarik Corp 905 E Thompson Ave	Glendale	CA	91201	**800-427-2757**	818-637-7500	507
MindBranch Inc 160 Water St	Williamstown	MA	01267	**800-774-4410**	413-458-7600	97
MindLeaders.com Inc 851 W 3rd Ave Bldg 3	Columbus	OH	43212	**800-223-3732**	614-781-7300	752
Mindmaker Inc 100 Century Center Ct Suite 800	San Jose	CA	95112	**877-277-4786**	408-467-9200	176-7
MindPlay Educational Software 440 S Williams Blvd Suite 206	Tucson	AZ	85711	**800-221-7911**	520-888-1800	176-3
Mine Safety Appliances Co (MSA) 121 Gamma Dr *NYSE: MSA*	Pittsburgh	PA	15238	**800-672-2222**	412-967-3000	566
Mine Safety & Health Administration (MSHA) 1100 Wilson Blvd	Arlington	VA	22209	**800-746-1554**	202-693-9419	336-11
Mineral Daily News Tribune Inc 24 Armstrong St	Keyser	WV	26726	**800-788-4026**	304-788-3333	623-8
Mineral & Pigment Solutions Inc 1000 Coolidge St	South Plainfield	NJ	07080	**800-732-0562**	908-561-6100	483
Mineral Springs Resort 11000 Palm Dr	Desert Hot Springs	CA	92240	**800-635-8660**	760-329-6484	697
Mineral Wells Area Chamber of Commerce 511 E Hubbard St	Mineral Wells	TX	76067	**800-252-6989**	940-325-2557	137
Minerva Networks Inc 2111 Tasman Dr	Santa Clara	CA	95054	**800-806-9594**	408-567-9400	633
Mingledorffs Inc 6675 Jones Mill Ct	Norcross	GA	30092	**800-282-4911**	770-446-6311	601
Mini Maid Services 2727 Canton Rd Suite 550	Marietta	GA	30066	**800-627-6464**	770-422-3565	150
Mini Togs Inc 3030 Aurora Ave	Monroe	LA	71211	**800-588-6227**	318-388-4916	153-4
Mining Metallurgy & Exploration Inc. Society for 8307 Shaffer Pkwy	Littleton	CO	80127	**800-763-3132**	303-973-9550	49-13
Ministries. Wheat Ridge 1 Pierce Pl Suite 250E	Itasca	IL	60143	**800-762-6748**	630-766-9066	48-20
Ministries. Wider Church 700 Prospect Ave NE 7th Fl	Cleveland	OH	44115	**866-822-8224**	216-736-3200	48-20
Ministry Home Care Hospice Services 611 Saint Joseph Ave Saint Joseph's Hospital	Marshfield	WI	54449	**800-397-4216**	715-387-7052	365

Name / Address	City	State	ZIP	Toll-Free	Phone	Class
Minka Group 1151 W Bradford Ct.	Corona	CA	92882	**800-221-7977**	951-735-9220	431
Minn-Dak Yeast Co Inc 18175 Red River Rd W	Wahpeton	ND	58075	**800-348-0991**	701-642-3300	291-42
MINNCOR Industries 1450 Energy Park Dr Suite 110	Saint Paul	MN	55108	**800-646-6267**	651-603-0118	618
Minneapolis College of Art & Design 2501 Stevens Ave S	Minneapolis	MN	55404	**800-874-6223**	612-874-3760	163
Minneapolis Community & Technical College 1501 Hennepin Ave.	Minneapolis	MN	55403	**800-247-0911**	612-659-6200	160
Minneapolis Grain Exchange 400 S 4th St Rm 130	Minneapolis	MN	55415	**800-827-4746**	612-321-7101	680
Minneapolis (Greater) Convention & Visitors Assn 250 Marquette Ave Suite 1300	Minneapolis	MN	55401	**800-445-7412**	612-767-8000	205
Minneapolis Institute of Arts 2400 3rd Ave S	Minneapolis	MN	55404	**888-642-2787**	612-870-3000	509
Minneapolis Metro North Convention & Visitors Bureau 6200 Shingle Creek Pkwy Suite 248	Brooklyn Center	MN	55430	**800-541-4364**	763-566-7722	205
Minneapolis-Saint Paul CityBusiness 527 Marquette Ave Suite 300	Minneapolis	MN	55402	**800-704-3757**	612-288-2141	449-5
Minneapolis-Saint Paul Magazine 220 S 6th St Suite 500	Minneapolis	MN	55402	**800-788-0204**	612-339-7571	449-22
Minnesota						
Aging Board 444 Lafayette Rd N	Saint Paul	MN	55155	**800-657-3889**	651-296-1531	335
Arts Board 400 Sibley St Suite 200	Saint Paul	MN	55101	**800-866-2787**	651-215-1600	335
Consumer Protection Office 445 Minnesota St Suite 1400	Saint Paul	MN	55101	**800-657-3787**	651-296-3353	335
Crime Victims Reparations Board 445 Minnesota St Suite 2300	Saint Paul	MN	55101	**888-622-8799**	651-282-6256	335
Higher Education Services Office 1450 Energy Park Dr Suite 350	Saint Paul	MN	55108	**800-657-3866**	651-642-0567	711
Historical Society 345 Kellogg Blvd W	Saint Paul	MN	55102	**888-727-8386**	651-296-6126	335
Licensing Div 85 7th Pl E Suite 600	Saint Paul	MN	55101	**800-657-3978**	651-296-6319	335
Natural Resources Dept 500 Lafayette Rd	Saint Paul	MN	55155	**888-646-6367**	651-296-2549	335
Rehabilitation Services Branch 390 N Robert St 1st Fl	Saint Paul	MN	55101	**800-328-9095**	651-296-5616	335
Tourism Office 121 7th Pl E Suite 100	Saint Paul	MN	55101	**800-657-3700**	651-296-5029	335
Minnesota Assn of Realtors 5750 Lincoln Dr	Edina	MN	55436	**800-862-6097**	952-935-8313	642
Minnesota Chamber of Commerce 400 Robert St N Suite 1500	Saint Paul	MN	55101	**800-821-2230**	651-292-4650	138
Minnesota Chamber of Commerce 400 Robert St N Suite 1500	Saint Paul	MN	55101	**800-821-2230**	651-292-4650	137
Minnesota Chemical Co 2285 Hampden Ave	Saint Paul	MN	55114	**800-328-5689**	651-646-7521	418
Minnesota Conway 314 W 86th St Suite 101	Bloomington	MN	55420	**800-223-2587**	952-345-3473	667
Minnesota Corn Processors Inc 400 W Erie Rd	Marshall	MN	56258	**800-328-4150**	507-537-2676	291-23
Minnesota Democratic Farmer Labor Party 255 E Plato Blvd	Saint Paul	MN	55107	**800-999-7457**	651-293-1200	605-1
Minnesota Dental Assn 2236 Marshall Ave	Saint Paul	MN	55104	**800-950-3368**	651-646-7454	225
Minnesota Diversified Products Inc DBA Diversifoam Products 9091 County Rd 50	Rockford	MN	55373	**800-669-0100**	763-477-5854	590
Minnesota Educator Magazine 41 Sherburne Ave.	Saint Paul	MN	55103	**800-652-9073**	651-227-9541	449-8
Minnesota Electric Supply Co 1209 E Hwy 12	Willmar	MN	56201	**800-992-8830**	320-235-2255	245
Minnesota Eye Consultants PA 710 E 24th St Suite 106	Minneapolis	MN	55404	**800-526-7632**	612-813-3600	785
Minnesota Fire & Casualty Co 7900 W 78th St	Edina	MN	55439	**800-727-5353**	952-829-1400	384-4
Minnesota Historical Society History Center Museum 345 Kellogg Blvd W	Saint Paul	MN	55102	**800-657-3773**	651-296-6126	509
Minnesota Library Assn (MLA) 1619 Dayton Ave Suite 314	Saint Paul	MN	55104	**877-867-0982**	651-641-0982	427
Minnesota Life Insurance Co 400 Robert St N	Saint Paul	MN	55101	**800-328-6124**	651-665-3500	384-2
Minnesota Lions Eye Bank 420 Delaware St SE MMC 493	Minneapolis	MN	55455	**866-887-4448**	612-625-5159	265
Minnesota Medical Assn 1300 Godward St NE Suite 2500	Minneapolis	MN	55413	**800-342-5662**	612-378-1875	466
Minnesota Medicine Magazine 1300 Godward St NE Suite 2500	Minneapolis	MN	55413	**800-342-5662**	612-378-1875	449-16
Minnesota Opera 620 N 1st St	Minneapolis	MN	55401	**800-676-6737**	612-333-2700	563-2
Minnesota Power Inc 30 W Superior St	Duluth	MN	55802	**800-228-4966**	218-722-2641	774
Minnesota Public Radio (MPR) 45 E 7th St	Saint Paul	MN	55101	**800-228-7123**	651-290-1212	620
Minnesota State Bar Assn 600 Nicollet Mall Suite 380	Minneapolis	MN	55402	**800-882-6722**	612-333-1183	73
Minnesota State Community & Technical College Fergus Falls 1414 College Way	Fergus Falls	MN	56537	**877-450-3322**	218-739-7500	160
Minnesota State University Moorhead 1104 7th Ave S	Moorhead	MN	56563	**800-593-7246**	218-477-2161	163
Minnesota Supply Co Inc 6470 Flying Cloud Dr	Eden Prairie	MN	55344	**800-869-1058**	952-828-7300	378
Minnesota Technology Inc 111 3rd Ave S	Minneapolis	MN	55401	**800-325-3073**	612-373-2900	654
Minnesota Twins Hubert H Humphrey Metrodome 34 Kirby Puckett Pl	Minneapolis	MN	55415	**800-338-9467**	612-375-1366	703
Minnesota Valley Co-op Light & Power Assn PO Box 717	Montevideo	MN	56265	**800-247-5051**	320-269-2163	244
Minnesota Valley Electric Co-op 125 Minnesota Valley Electric Dr	Jordan	MN	55352	**800-282-6832**	952-492-2313	244
Minnesota Veterans Home-Minneapolis 5101 Minnehaha Ave S	Minneapolis	MN	55407	**877-838-6757**	612-721-0600	780
Minnesota Veterans Home-Silver Bay 45 Banks Blvd	Silver Bay	MN	55614	**877-729-8387**	218-226-6300	780
Minnesota West Community & Technical College 1450 Collegeway	Worthington	MN	56187	**800-657-3966**	507-372-3400	160
Minnesota Zoo 13000 Zoo Blvd.	Apple Valley	MN	55124	**800-366-7811**	952-431-9200	811
Minntech Corp 14605 28th Ave N	Minneapolis	MN	55447	**800-328-3345**	763-553-3300	468
Minor PW & Son Inc PO Box 678	Batavia	NY	14020	**800-524-1084**	585-343-1500	296
Minor Rubber Co Inc 49 Ackerman St	Bloomfield	NJ	07003	**800-433-6886**	973-338-6800	664
Minorities in Business Insider Newsletter 8204 Fenton St	Silver Spring	MD	20910	**800-666-6380**	301-588-6380	521-2
Minority Contractors. National Assn of 666 11th St NW Suite 520	Washington	DC	20001	**866-688-6262**	202-347-8259	49-3
Minority Supplier Development Council. National 1040 Ave of the Americas 2nd Fl	New York	NY	10018	**888-396-1110**	212-944-2430	49-18
Minot Convention & Visitors Bureau 1020 S Broadway	Minot	ND	58701	**800-264-2626**	701-857-8206	205
Minot Daily News 301 4th St SE	Minot	ND	58701	**800-735-3119**	701-857-1900	522-2
Minot State University 500 University Ave W	Minot	ND	58707	**800-777-0750**	701-858-3000	163
Bottineau 105 Simrall Blvd.	Bottineau	ND	58318	**800-542-6866**	701-228-5451	160
Minova USA Inc 150 Carley Ct.	Georgetown	KY	40324	**800-626-2948**	502-863-6800	594-2
Minskoff Theatre 200 W 45th St	New York	NY	10036	**800-755-4000**	212-307-4100	732
Minto Builders 4400 W Sample Rd Suite 200	Coconut Creek	FL	33073	**800-767-4490**	954-973-4490	639
Minute Maid Co 2000 St James Pl	Houston	TX	77056	**800-888-6488**	713-888-5000	291-20
Minuteman International Inc 111 S Rohlwing Rd	Addison	IL	60101	**800-323-9420**	630-627-6900	379
Minuteman Press International Inc 61 Executive Blvd	Farmingdale	NY	11735	**800-645-3006**	631-249-1370	305
Minwax Co 10 Mountainview Rd.	Upper Saddle River	NJ	07458	**800-526-0495**	201-818-7500	540
Mira Monte Inn & Suites 69 Mt Desert St	Bar Harbor	ME	04609	**800-553-5109**	207-288-4263	373
Mirabito Fuel Group 44 Grand St	Sidney	NY	13838	**800-934-9480**	607-561-2700	311
Miracle-Ear Inc 5000 Cheshire Ln N	Plymouth	MN	55446	**800-234-7714**	763-268-4000	469
Miracle Method US Corp 4239 N Nevada Ave Suite 115	Colorado Springs	CO	80907	**800-444-8827**	719-594-9091	188-11
Miracle Recreation Equipment Co 878 Hwy 60	Monett	MO	65708	**800-523-4202**	417-235-6917	340
Miracle Steel Corp 600 Oakwood Rd PO Box 1266	Watertown	SD	57201	**888-508-4545**	605-886-7885	106
MiraCosta College 1 Barnard Dr.	Oceanside	CA	92056	**888-201-8480**	760-757-2121	160
Mirage The 3400 Las Vegas Blvd S	Las Vegas	NV	89109	**800-627-6667**	702-791-7111	655
Miramar Hotel at Waikiki 2345 Kuhio Ave	Honolulu	HI	96815	**800-367-2303**	808-922-2077	373
Miramar Mining Corp 889 Harbourside Dr Suite 300 *AMEX: MNG*	North Vancouver	BC	V7P3S1	**800-663-8780**	604-985-2572	492
Miramont Castle Museum 9 Capitol Hill Ave	Manitou Springs	CO	80829	**888-685-1011**	719-685-1011	509
Miramonte Resort & Spa 45000 Indian Wells Ln	Indian Wells	CA	92210	**800-237-2926**	760-341-2200	655
Mirant Corp 1155 Perimeter Ctr W	Atlanta	GA	30338	**800-334-2726**	678-579-7000	774
Mirassou Vineyards 3000 Aborn Rd	San Jose	CA	95135	**800-775-1936**	408-274-4000	81-3
Miraval Life in Balance 5000 E Via Estancia Miraval	Catalina	AZ	85739	**800-825-4000**	520-825-4000	697
Miravant Medical Technologies 336 Bollay Dr	Santa Barbara	CA	93117	**800-685-2959**	805-685-9880	86
Mirbeau Inn & Spa 851 W Genesee St	Skaneateles	NY	13152	**877-647-2328**	315-685-5006	373
Miroil Div Oil Process Systems Inc 602 N Tacoma St	Allentown	PA	18109	**800-523-9844**	610-437-4618	293
Mirror Image Internet Inc 49 Dragon Ct	Woburn	MA	01801	**866-374-4113**	781-376-1100	176-7
Miscellaneous Metals Inc 5719 Industry Ln PO Box 3818	Frederick	MD	21705	**800-492-7828**	301-695-8820	482
Misener Marine Construction Inc 5600 W Commerce St	Tampa	FL	33616	**866-211-9742**	813-839-8441	187-5
MISL (Major Indoor Soccer League) 1175 Post Rd E	Westport	CT	06880	**866-647-5638**	203-222-4900	48-22
Miss America Organization 2 Miss America Way Suite 1000	Atlantic City	NJ	08401	**800-282-6477**	609-345-7571	179
Miss Elaine Inc 8430 Valcour Ave	Saint Louis	MO	63123	**800-458-1422**	314-631-1900	153-15
Miss Laura's Visitor Center 2 N 'B' St	Fort Smith	AR	72901	**800-637-1477**	479-783-8888	50
Missco Corp 2510 Lakeland Terr Suite 100	Jackson	MS	39216	**800-647-5333**	601-987-8600	315
Missing Children Assn Inc. North America 136 Rt 420 Hwy	South Esk	NB	E1V4N8	**800-260-0753**	506-627-1209	48-6
Missing & Exploited Children. National Center for 699 Prince St	Alexandria	VA	22314	**800-843-5678**	703-274-3900	48-6
Mission Aviation Fellowship (MAF) 1849 N Wabash Ave.	Redlands	CA	92374	**800-359-7623**	909-794-1151	48-20
Mission Board. Catholic Medical 10 W 17th St	New York	NY	10011	**800-678-5659**	212-242-7757	48-5
Mission Chamber of Commerce 220 E 9th St	Mission	TX	78572	**800-580-2700**	956-585-2727	137
Mission Clay Products Div MCP Industries Inc 1655 E 6th St	Corona	CA	92879	**800-795-6067**	951-736-1881	148
Mission Federal Credit Union 5785 Oberlin Dr Suite 333	San Diego	CA	92121	**800-640-5463**	858-524-2850	216
Mission Foods 2110 Santa Fe Dr	Pueblo	CO	81006	**800-821-3187**	719-543-4350	291-35
Mission Inn 3649 Mission Inn Ave	Riverside	CA	92501	**800-843-7755**	951-784-0300	373
Mission Inn Golf & Tennis Resort 10400 CR 48	Howey in the Hills	FL	34737	**800-874-9053**	352-324-3101	655
Mission Kleensweep Products Inc 2433 Birkdale St	Los Angeles	CA	90031	**888-201-8866**	323-223-1405	149
Mission Linen Supply 702 E Montecito St *Hum Res	Santa Barbara	CA	93103	**877-641-3626***	805-682-8588	434

Name / Address	City	State	Zip	Toll-Free	Phone	Class
Mission Pharmacal PO Box 786099	San Antonio	TX	78278	**800-531-3333**	210-696-8400	572
Mission Point Resort 1 Lake Shore Dr PO Box 430	Mackinac Island	MI	49757	**800-833-7711**	906-847-3312	655
Mission Resources Corp 1331 Lamar St Suite 1455 *NASDAQ: MSSN*	Houston	TX	77010	**888-454-4105**	713-495-3000	525
Mission West Properties 10050 Bandley Dr *AMEX: MSW*	Cupertino	CA	95014	**800-222-5401**	408-725-0700	639
MissionAir 704 Southgate Rd	Saint Andrews	MB	R1A3P8	**877-231-2992**	204-231-2992	14
Missionary Union. Gospel 10000 N Oak Trafficway	Kansas City	MO	64155	**800-468-1892**	816-734-8500	48-20
Missionary Union. Woman's 100 Missionary Ridge	Birmingham	AL	35242	**800-968-7301**	205-991-8100	48-20
Mississippi						
Banking & Consumer Finance Dept PO Box 23729	Jackson	MS	39225	**800-844-2499**	601-359-1031	335
Child Support Enforcement Div PO Box 352	Jackson	MS	39205	**800-948-4010**	601-359-4861	335
Consumer Protection Div PO Box 1609	Jackson	MS	39215	**800-551-1830**	601-359-1111	335
Contractors Board PO Box 320279	Jackson	MS	39232	**800-880-6161**	601-354-6161	335
Crime Victim Compensation Program PO Box 267	Jackson	MS	39205	**800-829-6766**	601-359-6766	335
Emergency Management Agency PO Box 4501	Jackson	MS	39296	**800-222-6362**	601-352-9100	335
Parks & Recreation Div PO Box 451	Jackson	MS	39205	**800-467-2757**	601-432-2266	335
Prepaid Affordable College Tuition Program (MPACT) PO Box 120	Jackson	MS	39205	**800-987-4450**	601-359-5255	711
Rehabilitation Services Dept PO Box 1698	Jackson	MS	39215	**800-443-1000**	601-853-5100	335
Tourism Development Div PO Box 849	Jackson	MS	39205	**866-733-6477**	601-359-3297	335
Mississippi Agriculture & Forestry Museum/National Agricultural Aviation Museum 1150 Lakeland Dr	Jackson	MS	39216	**800-844-8687**	601-354-6113	509
Mississippi Assn of Realtors PO Box 321000	Jackson	MS	39232	**800-747-1103**	601-932-9325	642
Mississippi Business Journal 5120 Galaxie Dr	Jackson	MS	39206	**800-283-4625**	601-364-1000	449-5
Mississippi Chemical Corp 3622 Hwy 49 E PO Box 388	Yazoo City	MS	39194	**800-433-1351**	662-746-4131	276
Mississippi Coast Coliseum & Convention Center 2350 Beach Blvd	Biloxi	MS	39531	**800-726-2781**	228-594-3700	204
Mississippi College 200 S Capitol St	Clinton	MS	39058	**800-738-1236**	601-925-3000	163
Mississippi County Electric Co-op PO Box 7	Blytheville	AR	72316	**800-439-4563**	870-763-4563	244
Mississippi Democratic Party PO Box 1583	Jackson	MS	39215	**888-674-3367**	601-969-2913	605-1
Mississippi Economic Council PO Box 23276	Jackson	MS	39225	**800-748-7626**	601-969-0022	138
Mississippi Educator Magazine 775 N State St	Jackson	MS	39202	**800-530-7998**	601-354-4463	449-8
Mississippi Export Railroad Co 4519 McInnis Ave	Moss Point	MS	39563	**866-353-3322**	228-475-3322	634
Mississippi Gulf Coast Community College PO Box 548	Perkinston	MS	39573	**866-735-1122**	601-928-5211	160
Mississippi Gulf Coast Convention & Visitors Bureau 942 Beach Dr	Gulfport	MS	39507	**888-467-4853**	228-896-6699	205
Mississippi Library Commission 1221 Ellis Ave	Jackson	MS	39209	**800-647-7542**	601-961-4111	426
Mississippi Lime Co 7 Alby St	Alton	IL	62002	**800-437-5463**	618-465-7741	432
Mississippi Music Inc 222 S Main St	Hattiesburg	MS	39401	**800-844-5821**	601-544-5821	514
Mississippi Opera PO Box 1551	Jackson	MS	39215	**877-676-7372**	601-960-1528	563-2
Mississippi Power Co Inc 2992 W Beach Blvd	Gulfport	MS	39501	**800-353-9777**	228-864-1211	774
Mississippi Public Broadcasting 3825 Ridgewood Rd	Jackson	MS	39211	**800-922-9698**	601-432-6565	620
Mississippi River Museum 101 Mud Island Dr	Memphis	TN	38103	**800-507-6507**	901-576-7230	509
Mississippi River Museum. National Rivers Hall of Fame & 550 E 3rd St Ice Harbor	Dubuque	IA	52001	**800-226-3369**	563-557-9545	509
Mississippi River Transmission Inc 9900 Clayton Rd *Cust Svc	Saint Louis	MO	63124	**800-325-4005***	314-991-9900	320
Mississippi Sports Hall of Fame & Museum 1152 Lakeland Dr	Jackson	MS	39216	**800-280-3263**	601-982-8264	511
Mississippi State Medical Assn 408 W Parkway Pl	Ridgeland	MS	39157	**800-898-0251**	601-853-6733	466
Mississippi State Port Authority at Gulfport 1 Hancock Plaza Suite 1401	Gulfport	MS	39503	**877-881-4367**	228-865-4300	607
Mississippi Symphony Orchestra 201 E Pascagoula St	Jackson	MS	39201	**800-898-5050**	601-960-1565	563-3
Mississippi University for Women 1100 College St W-Box 1613	Columbus	MS	39701	**877-462-8439**	662-329-4750	163
Mississippi Valley Equipment Co Inc 1198 Pershall Rd	Saint Louis	MO	63137	**800-325-8001**	314-869-8600	353
Mississippi Valley Regional Blood Center 5500 Lakeview Pkwy	Davenport	IA	52807	**800-747-5401**	563-359-5401	90
Mississippi Valley Title Insurance Co 315 Tom Bigbee St	Jackson	MS	39201	**800-647-2124**	601-969-0222	384-6
Missoula Convention & Visitors Bureau 1121 E Broadway Suite 103	Missoula	MT	59802	**800-526-3465**	406-543-6623	205
Missoula Electric Co-op Inc 1700 W Broadway	Missoula	MT	59808	**800-352-5200**	406-541-4433	244
Missoulian PO Box 8029	Missoula	MT	59807	**800-366-7102**	406-523-5200	522-2
Missouri						
Child Support Enforcement Div PO Box 1527	Jefferson City	MO	65102	**800-859-7999**	573-751-4301	335
Higher Education Dept 3515 Amazonas Dr	Jefferson City	MO	65109	**800-473-6757**	573-751-2361	335
State Parks Div PO Box 176	Jefferson City	MO	65102	**800-334-6946**	573-751-2479	335
Student Assistance Resource Services (MOSTARS) 3515 Amazonas Dr	Jefferson City	MO	65109	**800-473-6757**	573-751-2361	711
Tourism Div PO Box 1055	Jefferson City	MO	65102	**800-877-1234**	573-526-5900	335
Transportation Dept PO Box 270	Jefferson City	MO	65102	**888-275-6636**	573-751-2551	335
Missouri Assn of Realtors 2601 Bernadette Pl	Columbia	MO	65203	**800-403-0101**	573-445-8400	642
Missouri Gas Energy 3420 Broadway	Kansas City	MO	64111	**800-582-1234**	816-360-5500	774
Missouri Repertory Theatre 4949 Cherry St	Kansas City	MO	64110	**888-502-2700**	816-235-2727	563-4
Missouri Southern State University 3950 E Newman Rd	Joplin	MO	64801	**800-606-6772**	417-625-9300	163
Missouri Sports Hall of Fame 3861 E Stan Musial Dr	Springfield	MO	65809	**800-498-5678**	417-889-3100	511
Missouri State Medical Assn 113 Madison St	Jefferson City	MO	65101	**800-869-6762**	573-636-5151	466
Missouri State Museum Capitol Bldg Room B2	Jefferson City	MO	65101	**800-336-6946**	573-751-2854	509
Missouri Synod. Lutheran Church 1333 S Kirkwood Rd	Saint Louis	MO	63122	**888-843-5267**	314-965-9000	48-20
Missouri Vocational Enterprises PO Box 1898 *Sales	Jefferson City	MO	65102	**800-392-8486***	573-751-6663	618
Missouri Western State College 4525 Downs Dr	Saint Joseph	MO	64507	**800-662-7041**	816-271-4266	163
Missourian Publishing Co 14 W Main St	Washington	MO	63090	**888-239-7701**	636-239-7701	623-8
Mister Money USA 2057 Vermont Dr	Fort Collins	CO	80525	**800-827-7296**	970-493-0574	139
Mister Twister LLC 1401 Commerce St	Minden	LA	71055	**800-344-6331**	318-377-8818	701
Misty Harbor & Barefoot Beach Resort Rt 11B	Gilford	NH	03246	**800-336-4789**	603-293-4500	373
Misys Healthcare Systems LLC 8529 Six Forks Rd	Raleigh	NC	27615	**800-334-8534**	919-847-8102	176-11
MIT Press 55 Hayward St *Sales	Cambridge	MA	02142	**800-356-0343***	617-253-5646	623-5
Mitchell 1 14145 Danielson St	Poway	CA	92064	**888-724-6742**	858-391-5000	623-11
Mitchell College 437 Pequot Ave	New London	CT	06320	**800-443-2811**	860-701-5000	160
Mitchell E Stewart Inc PO Box 2799	Baltimore	MD	21225	**800-870-6365**	410-354-0600	190-1
Mitchell Electric Membership Corp PO Box 409	Camilla	GA	31730	**800-479-6034**	229-336-5221	244
Mitchell Furniture Systems Inc 1700 W St Paul Ave	Milwaukee	WI	53201	**800-290-5960**	414-342-3111	314-3
Mitchell Gold Co 135 One Comfortable Pl	Taylorsville	NC	28681	**800-789-5401**	828-632-9200	314-2
Mitchell Industrial Tire Co PO Box 71839	Chattanooga	TN	37407	**800-251-7226**	423-698-4442	739
Mitchell International Inc 9889 Willow Creek Rd	San Diego	CA	92131	**800-854-7030**	858-578-6550	623-11
Mitchell Metal Products Inc PO Box 789	Kosciusko	MS	39090	**800-258-6137**	662-289-7110	688
Mitchell Supreme Fuel 532 Freeman St	Orange	NJ	07050	**800-832-7090**	973-678-1800	311
Mitchell W 12014 W 54th Dr Suite 100	Arvada	CO	80002	**800-421-4840**	303-425-1800	561
Mitchellace Inc 830 Murray St	Portsmouth	OH	45662	**800-848-8696**	740-354-2813	730-5
MiTek Industries Inc 14515 N Outer 40 Rd Suite 300	Chesterfield	MO	63017	**800-325-8075**	314-434-1200	92
Mitek Products 249 Vanderbilt Ave	Norwood	MA	02062	**800-356-4835**		469
Mitel Networks Corp 350 Legget Dr	Kanata	ON	K2K2W7	**800-267-6244**	613-592-2122	720
Mitem Corp 640 Menlo Ave *Sales	Menlo Park	CA	94025	**800-826-4836***	650-323-1500	176-12
Mitsubishi Canada Ltd 200 Granville St Suite 2800	Vancouver	BC	V6C1G6	**877-348-9988**	604-654-8000	59
Mitsubishi Digital Electronics America Inc 9351 Jeronimo Rd	Irvine	CA	92618	**800-332-2119**	949-465-6000	52
Mitsubishi Electric & Electronics USA Inc 5665 Plaza Dr	Cypress	CA	90630	**800-843-2515**	714-220-2500	252
Mitsubishi Polyester Film LLC 2001 Hood Rd	Greer	SC	29650	**800-845-2009**	864-879-5000	589
Mitsui Chemicals America Inc 2500 Westchester Ave Suite 110	Purchase	NY	10577	**800-682-2377**	914-253-0777	142
Mitsui Foods Inc 35 Maple St	Norwood	NJ	07648	**800-777-2322**	201-750-0500	292-11
Mitsumi Electronics Corp 5808 W Campus Circle Dr *Tech Supp	Irving	TX	75063	**800-648-7864***	972-550-7300	171-8
MITY Enterprises Inc 1301 W 400 North *NASDAQ: MITY*	Orem	UT	84057	**800-327-1692**	801-224-0589	314-3
Mix Software Inc 1203 Berkeley Dr	Richardson	TX	75081	**800-333-0330**	972-238-8554	176-2
Miyako Inn & Spa 328 E 1st St	Los Angeles	CA	90012	**800-228-6596**	213-617-2000	373
Mizuno USA 4925 Avalon Ridge Pkwy	Norcross	GA	30071	**800-333-7888**	770-441-5553	701
MJ Daly & Sons Inc 110 Mattatuck Heights	Waterbury	CT	06705	**800-992-3603**	203-753-5131	188-13
MJ Flaherty Co 1 Gateway Ctr Suite 450	Newton	MA	02458	**800-370-2280**	617-969-1492	188-10
MJ Soffe Co 1 Soffe Dr	Fayetteville	NC	28312	**800-723-4223**	910-483-2500	153-1
MJM Electric Co-op Inc 264 N East St PO Box 80	Carlinville	IL	62626	**800-648-4729**	217-854-3137	244
MJSA (Manufacturing Jewelers & Suppliers of America) 45 Royal Little Dr	Providence	RI	02904	**800-444-6572**	401-274-3840	49-4
MK Diamond Products Inc 1315 Storm Pkwy	Torrance	CA	90501	**800-421-5830**	310-539-5221	670
MK Morse Co 1101 11th St SE	Canton	OH	44707	**800-733-3377**	330-453-8187	670
MK Resources Co 60 E South Temple St Suite 1225	Salt Lake City	UT	84111	**800-664-6528**	801-297-6900	492
MKG Cartridge Systems Inc 1090 Lorimar Dr	Mississauga	ON	L5S1R8	**800-881-7545**	905-564-9218	616
MKS Inc 410 Albert St *Sales	Waterloo	ON	N2L3V3	**800-265-2797***	519-884-2251	176-2
MKS Instruments Inc 90 Industrial Way *NASDAQ: MKSI*	Wilmington	MA	01887	**800-227-8766**	978-284-4000	200
ML McDonald Co PO Box 315	Watertown	MA	02471	**800-733-6243**	617-923-0900	188-8
MLA (Minnesota Library Assn) 1619 Dayton Ave Suite 314	Saint Paul	MN	55104	**877-867-0982**	651-641-0982	427
MLMIC (Medical Liability Mutual Insurance Co) 2 Park Ave 25th Fl	New York	NY	10016	**800-275-6564**	212-576-9800	384-5
MLP Seating Corp 2125 Lively Blvd	Elk Grove Village	IL	60007	**800-723-3030**	847-956-1700	314-3

Name / Address	City	State	ZIP	Toll-Free	Phone	Class
MLQ Attorney Services 2110 Powers Ferry Rd Suite 305	Atlanta	GA	30339	**800-446-8794**	770-984-7007	621
MLT Vacations 4660 W 77th St	Edina	MN	55435	**800-362-3520**	952-474-2540	760
MLW Services Inc 100 William St	New York	NY	10038	**800-962-5524**	212-797-9600	383
MM Fowler Inc 4220 Neal Rd	Durham	NC	27705	**800-313-6635**	919-309-2925	319
MM Systems Corp 50 MM Way	Pendergrass	GA	30567	**800-241-3460**	706-824-7500	232
MMA (Medical Marketing Assn) 74 New Montgomery St Suite 230	San Francisco	CA	94105	**800-551-2173**	415-764-4807	49-18
MMF Industries Inc 370 Alice St	Wheeling	IL	60090	**800-445-8293***	847-537-7890	665
*Cust Svc						
MMG Corp 1717 Olive St	Saint Louis	MO	63103	**800-264-8437**	314-421-2182	153-13
MMG North America 126 Pennsylvania Ave	Paterson	NJ	07503	**800-664-7712**	973-345-8900	252
MMG Works/Status Promotions 106 W 11th St Suite 500	Kansas City	MO	64105	**800-945-4044**	816-472-5988	10
MML Bay State Life Insurance Co 1295 State St	Springfield	MA	01111	**800-767-1000***	413-788-8411	384-2
*Cust Svc						
MML Investors Services Inc 1414 Main St	Springfield	MA	01144	**800-542-6767**	413-737-8400	397
MMM Carpets Unlimited Inc 3100 Molinaro St	Santa Clara	CA	95054	**800-355-4666**	408-988-4661	285
MNM Group Inc 3235 Sunset Ln	Hatboro	PA	19040	**800-645-3477**		801
Mo-Kan Livestock Markets Inc RR 2 Box 152	Butler	MO	64730	**800-887-8156**	660-679-6535	437
MOAA (Military Officers Assn of America) 201 N Washington St	Alexandria	VA	22314	**800-234-6622**	703-549-2311	48-19
Moai Technologies Inc 100 1st Ave Suite 900	Pittsburgh	PA	15222	**800-814-1548**	412-454-5550	176-7
Moana Surfrider. Sheraton 2365 Kalakaua Ave	Honolulu	HI	96815	**800-325-3535**	808-922-3111	655
Moberly Area Community College 101 College Ave	Moberly	MO	65270	**800-622-2070**	660-263-4110	160
Mobile Area Chamber of Commerce 451 Government St	Mobile	AL	36602	**800-422-6951**	251-433-6951	137
Mobile Bay Convention & Visitors Bureau 1 S Water St	Mobile	AL	36602	**800-566-2453**	251-208-2000	205
Mobile Mini Inc 7420 S Kyrene Rd Suite 101	Tempe	AZ	85283	**800-288-5669**	480-894-6311	106
NASDAQ: MINI						
Mobile Modular Management Corp 5700 Las Positas Rd	Livermore	CA	94551	**800-352-2900**	925-606-9200	495
NASDAQ: MGRC						
Mobile Paint Mfg Co 4775 Hamilton Blvd	Theodore	AL	36582	**800-621-6952**	251-443-6110	540
Mobile Press Register Inc PO Box 2488	Mobile	AL	36652	**800-239-1340**	251-433-1551	623-8
Mobile Regional Airport (MOB)	Mobile	AL	36608	**800-357-5373**	251-633-0313	28
Mobile Register 401 N Water St	Mobile	AL	36602	**800-239-1340**	251-219-5400	522-2
Mobile/Modular Express Inc 1301 Trimble Rd	Edgewood	MD	21040	**800-321-7971**	410-676-3700	495
Mobility. AIM Inc - Assn for Automatic Identification & 125 Warrendale-Bayne Rd	Warrendale	PA	15086	**800-338-0206**	724-934-4470	49-19
MOCA Div Arrow Enterprise Computing Solutions 5230 Pacific Concourse Dr Bldg 2 4th Fl	Los Angeles	CA	90045	**800-786-3425***	310-643-1400	172
*Sales						
MOCAP Inc 13100 Manchester Rd	Saint Louis	MO	63131	**800-633-6775**	314-543-4000	597
MOD-PAC Corp 1801 Elmwood Ave	Buffalo	NY	14207	**800-666-3722***	716-873-0640	102
NASDAQ: MPAC ■ *Cust Svc						
Mod-Systems Inc 2172-B River Rd PO Box 585	Greer	SC	29652	**800-637-2937**	864-879-3850	523
MODCOMP Inc 1650 W McNab Rd	Fort Lauderdale	FL	33309	**800-327-3287**	954-974-1380	176-7
Model Aeronautics. Academy of 5161 E Memorial Dr	Muncie	IN	47302	**800-435-9262**	765-287-1256	48-18
Model Airplane News PO Box 428	Mount Morris	IL	61054	**800-877-5160**	815-734-1243	449-14
Model Coverall Service Inc 100 28th St SE	Grand Rapids	MI	49548	**800-968-6491**	616-241-6491	434
Model Railroader Magazine 21027 Crossroads Cir	Waukesha	WI	53186	**888-350-2413**	262-796-8776	449-14
Modell's Sporting Goods 498 7th Ave 20th Fl	New York	NY	10018	**800-250-7405**	212-822-1000	155-5
Modern Bride Magazine 4 Times Square	New York	NY	10036	**800-777-5786***	212-286-2860	449-11
*Cust Svc						
Modern Builders Supply Inc 302 McClurg Rd	Youngstown	OH	44512	**800-783-4117**	330-729-2690	190-3
Modern Building Materials Inc 8011 Green Bay Rd	Kenosha	WI	53142	**800-622-3166***	262-694-3166	181
*Cust Svc						
Modern Continental Construction Co 600 Memorial Dr	Cambridge	MA	02139	**800-833-6307**	617-864-6300	187-4
Modern Corp 4746 Model City Rd	Model City	NY	14107	**800-662-0012**	716-754-8226	791
Modern Dispersions Inc 78 Marguerite Ave	Leominster	MA	01453	**800-633-6434**	978-534-3370	594-2
Modern Engineering Inc 633 South Blvd Suite 200	Rochester Hills	MI	48307	**800-875-6423**	248-606-6100	258
Modern Equipment Sales & Rental Co 24 Brookside Dr	Wilmington	DE	19804	**800-227-2525**	302-658-5257	261-4
Modern Group Ltd 2501 Durham Rd	Bristol	PA	19007	**800-223-3827**	215-943-9100	378
Modern Group Ltd 1655 Louisiana St	Beaumont	TX	77701	**800-231-8198***	409-833-2665	269
*Cust Svc						
Modern Healthcare Magazine 360 N Michigan Ave	Chicago	IL	60601	**800-678-9595**	312-649-5200	449-5
Modern Ice Equipment & Supply Co DBA Modern Tour Inc 109 May Dr	Harrison	OH	45030	**800-543-1581**	513-367-2101	651
Modern Library 1745 Broadway	New York	NY	10019	**800-726-0600***	212-751-2600	623-2
*Cust Svc						
Modern Machine & Engineering Corp 1707 Jefferson St NE	Minneapolis	MN	55413	**800-218-8838**	612-781-3347	610
Modern Machine Shop Magazine 6915 Valley Ave	Cincinnati	OH	45244	**800-950-8020**	513-527-8800	449-21
Modern Management Inc 253 Commerce Dr Suite 105	Grayslake	IL	60030	**800-323-1331**	847-945-7400	192
Modern Medical Modalities Corp PO Box 957	Union	NJ	07083	**800-367-3926**		261-5
Modern Metals Industries Inc PO Box 888	El Segundo	CA	90245	**800-437-6633**	310-516-0851	281
Modern Mind Software Inc 801 1st Ave S Suite 200	Seattle	WA	98134	**888-784-2929**		176-1
Modern Plastics Magazine 110 William St 11th Fl	New York	NY	10038	**800-257-9402**	212-621-4900	449-21
Modern Salon Magazine 400 Knightsbridge Pkwy	Lincolnshire	IL	60069	**800-621-2845**	847-634-2600	449-21
Modern Tour Inc 109 May Dr	Harrison	OH	45030	**800-543-1581**	513-367-2101	651
Modern Welding Co Inc 2880 New Hartford Rd	Owensboro	KY	42303	**800-922-1932**	270-685-4404	92
Modern Woodmen Co of America 1701 1st Ave	Rock Island	IL	61201	**800-447-9811**	309-786-6481	384-2
Modernage Photo Service Inc 1381 E 6th St	Los Angeles	CA	90021	**800-974-3686**	213-628-8194	581
Modernfold Inc 215 W New Rd	Greenfield	IN	46140	**800-869-9685**	317-468-6700	281
Modesto Bee 1325 H St PO Box 5256	Modesto	CA	95354	**800-776-4233**	209-578-2000	522-2
Modesto Convention & Visitors Bureau 1150 9th St Suite C	Modesto	CA	95354	**888-640-8467**	209-526-5588	205
Modis Inc 1 Independent Dr Suite 215	Jacksonville	FL	32202	**800-372-2788**	904-360-2300	455
Moeller Electric Corp USA 15311 Vantage Pkwy Suite 190	Houston	TX	77032	**800-451-5110**	713-933-0999	202
Moeller Mfg Co Inc Punch & Die Div 43938 Plymouth Oaks Blvd	Plymouth	MI	48170	**800-521-7613**	734-416-0000	745
Moen Inc 25300 Al Moen Dr	North Olmsted	OH	44070	**800-289-6636***	440-962-2000	598
*Cust Svc						
Moen Inc CSI Bath Accessories Div 25300 Al Moen Dr	North Olmsted	OH	44070	**800-321-8809**	440-962-2000	598
Moen Industries 12333 E Los Nietos Rd	Santa Fe Springs	CA	90670	**800-423-4747**	562-946-6381	537
Moews Seed Co Inc Rt 89 S	Granville	IL	61326	**800-663-9795**	815-339-2201	11-5
Moffitt H Lee Cancer Center & Research Institute 12902 Magnolia Dr	Tampa	FL	33612	**800-456-3434**	813-972-4673	366-5
Mohair Council of America 233 W Twohig Rd PO Box 5337	San Angelo	TX	76902	**800-583-3161**	325-655-3161	48-2
Mohave Community College 1971 Jagerson Ave	Kingman	AZ	86401	**800-678-3695**	928-757-0879	160
Lake Havasu Campus 1977 W Acoma Blvd	Lake Havasu City	AZ	86403	**888-203-4394**	928-855-7812	160
Mohave Valley Campus 3400 Hwy 95	Bullhead City	AZ	86442	**888-203-4395**	928-758-3926	160
North Mohave Campus PO Box 980	Colorado City	AZ	86021	**800-678-3992**	928-875-2799	160
Mohave Electric Co-op Inc 1999 Arena Dr	Bullhead City	AZ	86442	**800-685-4251**	928-763-4115	244
Mohave Valley Daily News PO Box 21209	Bullhead City	AZ	86439	**800-571-3835**	928-763-2505	522-2
Mohawk Canoes 963 County Rd 427N	Longwood	FL	32750	**800-686-6429**	407-834-3233	701
Mohawk Carpet Corp 160 S Industrial Blvd	Calhoun	GA	30703	**800-241-4494**	706-629-7721	131
Mohawk Commercial Business 443 Nathaniel Dr	East Dublin	GA	31027	**800-554-6637**	478-272-7711	131
Mohawk Finishing Products Inc 22 S Center St	Hickory	NC	28603	**800-545-0047**	828-261-0325	540
Mohawk Home 3090 Sugar Valley Rd NW	Sugar Valley	GA	30746	**800-843-4473**	706-629-7916	131
Mohawk Industries Inc 160 S Industrial Blvd	Calhoun	GA	30703	**800-241-4494**	706-629-7721	131
NYSE: MHK						
Mohawk Industries Inc Bigelow Commercial Div 160 S Industrial Blvd	Calhoun	GA	30703	**800-233-4490***	706-629-7721	131
*Cust Svc						
Mohawk Industries Inc Karastan Div 335 Summit Rd	Eden	NC	27288	**800-845-8877***	336-627-7200	131
*Cust Svc						
Mohawk Industries Inc Lees Carpets Div 706 Green Valley Rd	Greensboro	NC	27408	**800-523-5647**	336-378-9162	131
Mohawk Mfg Inc 2175 Beechgrove Pl	Utica	NY	13501	**800-765-3110**	315-793-3000	92
Mohawk Paper Mills Inc 465 Saratoga St	Cohoes	NY	12047	**800-843-6455**	518-237-1740	547
Mohawk/CDT 9 Mohawk Dr	Leominster	MA	01453	**800-422-9961**	978-537-9961	801
Mohegan Sun Resort & Casino 1 Mohegan Sun Blvd	Uncasville	CT	06382	**888-226-7711**	860-862-8000	133
Mohonk Mountain House 1000 Mountain Rest Rd	New Paltz	NY	12561	**800-772-6646**	845-255-1000	655
Mohr Microfilm Corp 20 S Linden Ave Bldg 2-B	South San Francisco	CA	94080	**800-373-1834**	650-244-9911	487
Mojave A Desert Resort 73721 Shadow Mountain Dr	Palm Desert	CA	92260	**866-846-8357**	760-346-6121	373
Mokry-Tesmer Inc 707 Maryetta St	Middletown	OH	45042	**800-383-5135**	513-424-5135	546
Mold-A-Matic Corp DBA MAMCO 147 River St	Oneonta	NY	13820	**800-486-8611**	607-433-2121	745
Mold Base Industries Inc 7501 Derry St	Harrisburg	PA	17111	**800-241-6656**	717-564-7960	745
Molded Fiber Glass Tray Co 6175 US Hwy 6	Linesville	PA	16424	**800-458-6050***	814-683-4500	198
*Sales						
Molded Rubber & Plastic Corp 13161 W Glendale Ave	Butler	WI	53007	**888-781-7122**	262-781-7122	664
Moldex Metric Inc 10111 W Jefferson Blvd	Culver City	CA	90232	**800-421-0668**	310-837-6500	566
Moldflow Corp 430 Boston Post Rd	Wayland	MA	01778	**800-284-6653**	508-358-5848	176-5
NASDAQ: MFLO						
Molding Corp of America 2701 N Ontario St	Burbank	CA	91504	**800-634-3991**	818-840-9288	593
Mole Hollow Candles Ltd 3 Deerfield Ave	Shelburne Falls	MA	01370	**800-445-6653***	413-625-6337	322
*Cust Svc						
Molecular Devices Corp 1311 Orleans Dr Suite 408	Sunnyvale	CA	94089	**800-635-5577**	408-747-1700	410
NASDAQ: MDCC						

Name / Address	City	State	Zip	Toll-Free	Phone	Class
Molecular Pathology Laboratory						
250 E Broadway	Maryville	TN	37804	**800-932-2943**	865-380-9746	408
Molex Inc 2222 Wellington Ct	Lisle	IL	60532	**800-786-6539***	630-969-4550	252
NASDAQ: MOLX ■ *Cust Svc						
Molex Premise Networks						
8 Executive Dr	Hudson	NH	03051	**800-866-3827**	603-324-0200	720
Molin Concrete Products Co						
415 Lilac St	Lino Lakes	MN	55014	**800-336-6546**	651-786-7722	181
Molina Healthcare Inc						
1 Golden Shore Dr	Long Beach	CA	90802	**800-526-8196**	562-435-3666	384-3
NYSE: MOH						
Mollenberg-Betz Inc 300 Scott St	Buffalo	NY	14204	**800-368-4998**	716-614-7473	188-10
Molloy College						
1000 Hempstead Ave PO						
Box 5002	Rockville Centre	NY	11571	**888-466-5569**	516-678-5000	163
Molly Maid Inc 3948 Ranchero Dr	Ann Arbor	MI	48108	**800-665-5962**	734-822-6800	150
Molon Motor & Coil Corp						
3737 Industrial Ave	Rolling Meadows	IL	60008	**800-526-6867**	847-253-6000	507
Molson Coors Brewing Co						
1225 17th St Suite 1875	Denver	CO	80202	**800-642-6116**	303-277-6661	103
NYSE: TAP						
Moltech Power Systems						
12801 NW Hwy 441	Alachua	FL	32615	**800-677-6937**	386-462-3911	76
Momeni Inc 36 E 31st St 2nd Fl	New York	NY	10016	**800-536-6778**	212-532-9577	356
Momentum Systems Ltd						
41 Twosome Dr Suite 9	Moorestown	NJ	08057	**800-279-1384**	856-727-0777	176-7
Momentum Technologies Inc						
1507 Boettler Rd	Uniontown	OH	44685	**800-720-0261**	330-896-5900	592
Mon River Towing Inc						
200 Speers St	Belle Vernon	PA	15012	**800-245-8051**	724-483-8051	457
Mona Electrical Co						
7915 Malcolm Rd Suite 102	Clinton	MD	20735	**800-438-6662**	301-868-8400	188-4
Monaco Coach Corp						
91320 Coburg Industrial Way	Coburg	OR	97408	**800-634-0855**	541-686-8011	120
NYSE: MNC						
Monaco Coach Corp Holiday Rambler						
Div 606 Nelson's Pkwy	Wakarusa	IN	46573	**800-650-7337**	574-862-7211	120
Monaco Government Tourist Office						
565 5th Ave	New York	NY	10017	**800-753-9696**	212-286-3330	764
Monadnock Paper Mills Inc						
117 Antrim Rd	Bennington	NH	03442	**800-221-2159***	603-588-3311	547
*Orders						
Monahan Thomas Co Inc 202 N Oak St	Arcola	IL	61910	**800-637-7739**	217-268-4955	291-23
Monarch Beverage Co						
3424 Peachtree Rd Suite 1450	Atlanta	GA	30326	**800-241-3732**	404-262-4040	81-2
Monarch Cement Co						
449 1200 St PO Box 1000	Humboldt	KS	66748	**800-362-0570**	620-473-2223	135
Monarch Ceramic Tile						
4321 Bryson Blvd	Florence	AL	35630	**800-289-8453***	256-764-6181	736
*Cust Svc						
Monarch Grand Vacations						
23091 Mill Creek Dr	Laguna Hills	CA	92653	**800-828-4200**	949-609-2400	738
Monarch Hotel & Conference Center						
12566 SE 93rd Ave	Clackamas	OR	97015	**800-492-8700**	503-652-1515	373
Monarch Industries Inc 99 Main St	Warren	RI	02885	**800-669-9663**	401-247-5200	304
Monarch Luggage Co Inc						
2580 Prospect Ct	Aurora	IL	60504	**800-747-2802**	630-585-6030	444
Monarch Machine Corp Vanguard						
Supreme Machine Div PO Box 5009	Monroe	NC	28111	**800-222-1971**	704-283-8171	729
Monarch Mountain Lodge						
22720 W US Hwy 50	Monarch	CO	81227	**888-996-7669**	719-539-2581	655
Monarch Pharmaceuticals Inc						
501 5th St	Bristol	TN	37620	**800-776-3637**	423-989-8000	572
Monarch Rubber Co						
3500 Pulaski Hwy	Baltimore	MD	21224	**800-638-6312**	410-342-8510	663
Mondavi Robert Co						
7801 St Helena Hwy PO Box 106	Oakville	CA	94562	**888-766-6328**	707-259-9463	81-3
Monday Magazine 818 Broughton St	Victoria	BC	V8W1E4	**800-661-6335**	250-382-6188	522-4
Monday Morning Books						
150 Bayview Dr PO Box 1134	Palo Alto	CA	94301	**800-255-6049**		242
Mondera.com 45 W 45th St 15th Fl	New York	NY	10036	**800-666-3372**	212-997-9350	402
Mondrian Hotel						
8440 Sunset Blvd	West Hollywood	CA	90069	**800-525-8029**	323-650-8999	373
Money Control Inc						
34099 Melinz Pkwy	Eastlake	OH	44095	**800-321-0765**	440-946-3000	55
Money Magazine						
Rockefeller Ctr Time & Life Bldg	New York	NY	10020	**800-633-9970**	212-522-1212	449-11
Money Mailer Inc						
14271 Corporate Dr	Garden Grove	CA	92843	**800-234-2771**	714-265-4100	5
MoneyGram International Inc						
1550 Utica Ave S Suite 100	Saint Louis Park	MN	55416	**800-328-5678**	952-591-3000	70
NYSE: MGI						
Money's Mushrooms Ltd						
24 Duncan St 5th Fl	Toronto	ON	M5V2B8	**800-661-8623**	416-977-1400	11-7
Mongolia Casing Corp						
4706 Grand Ave	Maspeth	NY	11378	**800-221-4887**	718-628-4500	291-26
Monical Pizza Corp 530 N Kinzie Ave	Bradley	IL	60915	**800-929-3227**	815-937-1890	657
MonierLifetile Inc						
7575 Irvine Ctr Dr Suite 100	Irvine	CA	92618	**800-224-2024**	949-756-1605	181
Monitor The 1400 E Nolana Loop	McAllen	TX	78504	**800-366-4343**	956-683-4000	522-2
Monitor Sugar Co Inc						
2600 S Euclid Ave	Bay City	MI	48706	**800-227-9110**	989-686-0161	291-38
Monitronics International Inc						
12801 Stemmons Fwy Suite 821	Dallas	TX	75234	**800-447-9239***	972-243-7443	683
*Cust Svc						
Monmouth Medical Center						
300 2nd Ave	Long Branch	NJ	07740	**888-661-7484**	732-222-5200	366-2
Monmouth Plantation 36 Melrose Ave	Natchez	MS	39120	**800-828-4531**	601-442-5852	373
Monmouth University						
400 Cedar Ave	West Long Branch	NJ	07764	**800-543-9671**	732-571-3456	163
Monobind Inc 100 N Point Dr	Lake Forest	CA	92630	**800-854-6265**	949-951-2665	229
Monro Muffler Brake Inc						
200 Holleder Pkwy	Rochester	NY	14615	**800-876-6676**	585-647-6400	62-3
NASDAQ: MNRO						
Monroe Bancorp						
210 E Kirkwood Ave	Bloomington	IN	47408	**800-319-2664**	812-336-0201	355-2
NASDAQ: MROE						
Monroe Chamber of Commerce						
212 Walnut St Suite 100	Monroe	LA	71201	**888-531-9535**	318-323-3461	137
Monroe Clinic Hospital 515 22nd Ave	Monroe	WI	53566	**800-338-0568**	608-324-1000	366-2
Monroe College 2501 Jerome Ave	Bronx	NY	10468	**800-556-6676**	718-933-6700	158
Monroe County Community College						
1555 S Raisinville Rd	Monroe	MI	48161	**877-937-6222**	734-242-7300	160
Monroe County Library System						
3700 S Custer Rd	Monroe	MI	48161	**800-462-2050**	734-241-5277	426
Monroe County Tourist Development						
Council 1201 White St Suite 102	Key West	FL	33040	**800-352-5397**	305-296-1552	205
Monroe Electronics Inc						
100 Housel Ave	Lyndonville	NY	14098	**800-821-6001**	585-765-2254	247
Monroe Fluid Technology Inc						
36 Draffin Rd Box 810	Hilton	NY	14468	**800-828-6351**	585-392-3434	143
Monroe Hardware Co PO Box 5015	Monroe	NC	28111	**800-222-1974**	704-289-3121	346
Monroe Table Co 316 N Walnut St	Colfax	IA	50054	**800-247-2488**	515-674-3511	314-3
Monroe Times PO Box 230	Monroe	WI	53566	**800-236-2240**	608-328-4202	522-2
Monroe Title Insurance Corp						
47 W Main St	Rochester	NY	14614	**800-966-6763**	585-232-4950	384-6
Monroe Truck Equipment Inc						
1051 W 7th St	Monroe	WI	53566	**800-356-8134**	608-328-8127	505
Monroe Village						
1 David Brainerd Dr	Monroe Township	NJ	08831	**800-833-4447**	732-521-6400	659
Monroe-West Monroe Convention &						
Visitors Bureau						
601 Constitution Dr	West Monroe	LA	71292	**800-843-1872**	318-387-5691	205
Monroeville Area Chamber of						
Commerce 4268 Northern Pike	Monroeville	PA	15146	**888-753-5522**	412-856-0622	137
Monrovia Nursery Growers						
18331 E Foothill Blvd	Azusa	CA	91702	**800-999-9321**	626-334-9321	363
Monsanto Enviro-Chem Systems Inc						
14522 S Outer 40 Rd	Chesterfield	MO	63017	**800-567-8858**	314-275-5700	187-7
Monster Muscle Magazine						
PO Box 2561	Spokane	WA	99220	**800-268-2248**	509-534-4489	449-13
Monster Worldwide Inc						
622 3rd Ave 39th Fl	New York	NY	10017	**800-867-2001**	212-351-7000	262
NASDAQ: MNST						
Monster.com						
5 Clock Tower Pl Suite 500	Maynard	MA	01754	**800-666-7837**	978-461-8000	257
MonsterTRAK						
1964 Westwood Blvd 3rd Fl	Los Angeles	CA	90025	**800-999-8725**	310-474-3377	257
Montage Resort & Spa						
30801 S Coast Hwy	Laguna Beach	CA	92651	**866-271-6953**	949-715-6001	655
Montague Industrial Inc						
PO Box 6016	Florence	SC	29502	**800-922-7820**	803-775-1102	206
Montague Machine Co						
15 Rastallis St	Turners Falls	MA	01376	**800-555-6891**	413-863-4301	546
Montana						
Arts Council PO Box 202201	Helena	MT	59620	**800-282-3092**	406-444-6430	335
Consumer Protection Office						
PO Box 200501	Helena	MT	59620	**800-322-2272**	406-444-4311	335
Historical Society 225 N Roberts St	Helena	MT	59620	**800-243-9900**	406-444-2694	335
Promotion Div (Travel Montana)						
PO Box 200533	Helena	MT	59620	**800-847-4868**	406-444-2654	335
Public Instruction Office						
PO Box 202501	Helena	MT	59620	**888-231-9393**	406-444-3095	335
Montana Assn of Realtors						
208 N Montana Ave Suite 203	Helena	MT	59601	**800-477-1864**	406-443-4032	642
Montana Correctional Enterprises						
300 Conley Lake Rd	Deer Lodge	MT	59722	**800-815-6252**	406-846-1320	618
Montana-Dakota Utilities Co						
918 E Divide Ave	Bismarck	ND	58506	**800-638-3278**	701-222-7600	774
Montana Dental Assn						
17 1/2 S Last Chance Gulch St	Helena	MT	59601	**800-257-4988**	406-443-2061	225
Montana Historical Society Museum						
225 N Roberts St	Helena	MT	59620	**800-243-9900**	406-444-2694	509
Montana Medical Assn						
2021 11th Ave Suite 1	Helena	MT	59601	**877-443-4000**	406-443-4000	466
Montana Mills Bread Co Inc						
2171 Monroe Ave Suite 205A	Rochester	NY	14618	**877-662-7323**	585-242-7540	291-1
Montana Public Radio						
32 Campus Dr University						
of Montana	Missoula	MT	59812	**800-325-1565**	406-243-4931	620
Montana Public Television						
PO Box 10715	Bozeman	MT	59715	**800-426-8243**	406-994-3437	620
Montana Rail Link Inc						
101 International Way	Missoula	MT	59808	**800-338-4750**	406-523-1500	634
Montana River Outfitters						
923 10th Ave N	Great Falls	MT	59401	**800-800-8218**	406-761-1677	748
Montana Standard PO Box 627	Butte	MT	59703	**800-877-1074**	406-496-5500	522-2
Montana State University						
Bozeman PO Box 172180	Bozeman	MT	59717	**888-678-2287**	406-994-2452	163
Northern PO Box 7751	Havre	MT	59501	**800-662-6132**	406-265-3700	163
Montana Tech of the University of Montana						
1300 W Park St	Butte	MT	59701	**800-445-8324**	406-496-4101	163
Montana's Cookhouse Saloon						
6303 Airport Rd	Mississauga	ON	L4V1R8	**800-860-4082**	905-405-6500	657
Montauk Yacht Club Resort & Marina						
32 Star Island Rd	Montauk	NY	11954	**888-692-8668**	631-668-3100	655
Montblanc North America						
430 Mountain Ave	Murray Hill	NJ	07974	**800-995-4810**	908-508-2300	560
Montcap Financial Corp						
3500 de Maisonneuve Blvd W						
Suite 1510	Montreal	QC	H3Z3C1	**800-231-2977**	514-932-8223	268
Montclair State University						
1 Normal Ave	Upper Montclair	NJ	07043	**800-331-9205**	973-655-4000	163
Monte Carlo Inn-Airport Suites						
5 Derry Rd	Mississauga	ON	L5T2H8	**800-363-6400**	905-564-8500	372
Monte Carlo Resort & Casino						
3770 Las Vegas Blvd S	Las Vegas	NV	89109	**800-311-8999**	702-730-7777	655
Monte Package Co Inc						
3752 Riverside Rd	Riverside	MI	49084	**800-653-2807**	269-849-1722	199
Monte Vista Hotel & Spa						
414 N Palm Canyon Dr	Palm Springs	CA	92262	**800-789-3188**	760-325-5641	373
Montello Heel Mfg Inc						
13 Emerson Ave	Brockton	MA	02305	**800-245-4335**	508-586-0603	296
Montello Inc 6106 E 32nd Pl Suite 100	Tulsa	OK	74135	**800-331-4628**	918-665-1170	143
Monterey Bay Aquarium						
886 Cannery Row	Monterey	CA	93940	**800-555-3656**	831-648-4800	40
Monterey Bay Inn 242 Cannery Row	Monterey	CA	93940	**800-424-6242**	831-373-6242	373

Company / Address	City	State	ZIP	Toll-Free	Phone	Class
Monterey Conference Center 1 Portola Plaza	Monterey	CA	93940	**800-742-8091**	831-646-3770	204
Monterey County Convention & Visitors Bureau PO Box 1770	Monterey	CA	93942	**888-221-1010**	831-649-1770	205
Monterey County Herald 8 Upper Ragsdale	Monterey	CA	93940	**888-646-4422**	831-372-3311	522-2
Monterey Hotel 406 Alvarado St	Monterey	CA	93940	**800-727-0960**	831-375-3184	373
Monterey Inn Resort 2259 Prince of Wales Dr	Ottawa	ON	K2E6Z8	**800-565-1311**	613-226-5813	372
Monterey Institute of International Studies 460 Pierce St	Monterey	CA	93940	**800-824-7235**	831-647-4123	163
Monterey Mills Inc 1725 E Delavan Dr	Janesville	WI	53546	**800-255-9665**	608-754-2866	730-4
Monterey Mushrooms Inc 60 Westgate Dr	Watsonville	CA	95076	**800-333-6874**	831-763-5300	11-7
Monterey Pasta Co 1528 Moffett St *NASDAQ: PSTA*	Salinas	CA	93905	**800-588-7782**	831-753-6262	291-31
Monterey Plaza Hotel & Spa 400 Cannery Row	Monterey	CA	93940	**800-334-3999**	831-646-1700	373
Monterey's Little Mexico 1135 Edgebrook St	Houston	TX	77034	**800-741-7574**	713-943-7574	657
Monterey's Tex-Mex Cafe 1135 Edgebrook St	Houston	TX	77034	**800-741-7574**	713-943-7574	657
Montfort Bros Inc 44 Elm St	Fishkill	NY	12524	**800-724-1777**	845-896-6225	181
Montfort Group The 44 Elm St	Fishkill	NY	12524	**800-724-1777**	845-896-6225	181
Montgomery Area Chamber of Commerce Convention & Visitor Bureau 300 Water St Union Stn	Montgomery	AL	36104	**800-240-9452**	334-261-1100	205
Montgomery Aviation Corp 4525 Selma Hwy	Montgomery	AL	36108	**800-392-8044**	334-288-7334	63
Montgomery Community College 1011 Page St	Troy	NC	27371	**800-839-6222**	910-576-6222	160
Montgomery County Chamber of Commerce 366 W Main St PO Box 309	Amsterdam	NY	12010	**800-743-7337**	518-842-8200	137
Montgomery County Visitors & Convention Bureau 218 E Pike St	Crawfordsville	IN	47933	**800-866-3973**	765-362-5200	205
Montgomery Mutual Insurance Co 17810 Meeting House Rd	Sandy Spring	MD	20860	**800-638-8933**	301-924-4700	384-4
Montgomery Theater 271 S Market St	San Jose	CA	95113	**800-533-2345**	408-277-3900	562
Montgomery Truss & Panel Inc 803 W Main St	Grove City	PA	16127	**800-245-0334**	724-458-7500	805
Monticello Inn 127 Ellis St	San Francisco	CA	94102	**800-669-7777**	415-392-8800	373
Montour Oil Service Co 112 Broad St PO Box 128	Montoursville	PA	17754	**800-332-8915**	570-368-8611	569
Montpelier Glove & Safety Co Inc 129 N Main St PO Box 7	Montpelier	IN	47359	**800-645-3931**	765-728-2481	153-8
Montreal Exchange 800 Victoria Sq PO Box 61	Montreal	QC	H4Z1A9	**800-361-5353**	514-871-2424	680
Montreal (Greater) Convention & Tourism Bureau 1555 rue Peel Bureau 600	Montreal	QC	H3A3L8	**800-363-7777**	514-844-5400	205
Montreal Inn Beach Dr & Madison Ave	Cape May	NJ	08204	**800-525-7011**	609-884-7011	655
Montreal Museum of Decorative Arts 1379 rue Sherbrook O	Montreal	QC	H3G1J5	**800-899-6873**	514-285-1600	509
Montreal Science Centre Saint-Laurent Blvd & de la Commune St King-Edward Pier	Montreal	QC	H2Y2E2	**877-496-4724**	514-496-4724	509
Montreat College 310 Gaither Cir	Montreat	NC	28757	**800-622-6968**	828-669-8011	163
Montrose Chamber of Commerce 1519 E Main St	Montrose	CO	81401	**800-923-5515**	970-249-5000	137
Montrose Hanger Co PO Box 1149	Wilson	NC	27894	**800-849-8038**	252-237-8038	344
Montrose Travel 2355 Honolulu Ave	Montrose	CA	91020	**800-766-4687**	818-553-3210	760
Montrose Visitor & Convention Bureau 1519 E Main St	Montrose	CO	81401	**800-873-0244**	970-240-1414	205
Montrose/CDT 28 Sword St	Auburn	MA	01501	**800-346-6626**	508-791-3161	801
Montserrat College of Art 23 Essex St	Beverly	MA	01915	**800-836-0487**	978-922-8222	163
Monument Builders of North America (MBNA) 401 N Michigan Ave Suite 2200	Chicago	IL	60611	**800-233-4472**	312-321-5143	49-3
Monumental General Insurance Co 520 Park Ave	Baltimore	MD	21201	**800-233-4624**	410-685-5500	384-5
Monumental Life Insurance Co 2 E Chase St	Baltimore	MD	21202	**800-638-3080**	410-685-2900	384-2
MONY Life Insurance Co of America 1290 Ave of the Americas	New York	NY	10104	**800-487-6669**	212-544-1234	384-2
Moodie Implement Inc 3701 E Hwy 14	Pierre	SD	57501	**800-742-8110**	605-224-1631	270
Moody Bible Institute 820 N La Salle St	Chicago	IL	60610	**800-356-6639**	312-329-4400	163
Moody Dunbar Inc 3202 Hwy 107	Chuckey	TN	37641	**800-251-8202**	423-257-4712	291-20
Moody Gardens 1 Hope Blvd	Galveston	TX	77554	**800-582-4673**	409-744-4673	40
Moody Gardens Convention Center 1 Hope Blvd	Galveston	TX	77554	**800-582-4673**	409-744-4673	204
Moody Gardens Hotel 7 Hope Blvd	Galveston	TX	77554	**888-388-8484**	409-741-8484	373
Moody Magazine 820 N La Salle Blvd *Cust Svc	Chicago	IL	60610	**800-284-9551***	312-329-2164	449-18
Moody Nolan Inc 300 Spruce St Suite 300	Columbus	OH	43215	**877-530-4984**	614-461-4664	258
Moog Inc Seneca & Jamison Rd *NYSE: MOG/A*	East Aurora	NY	14052	**800-664-6664**	716-652-2000	202
Moon Products Inc 1150 5th Ave N PO Box 1309	Lewisburg	TN	37091	**800-541-3758**	931-359-1501	560
Mooney Aircraft Corp Louis Schreiner Field	Kerrville	TX	78028	**800-456-3033**	830-896-6000	21
Moonlight Spa at Moonlight Lodge 1 Mountain Loop Rd	Big Sky	MT	59716	**800-845-4428**	406-995-7700	698
Moore Benjamin & Co 51 Chestnut Ridge Rd	Montvale	NJ	07645	**800-344-0400**	201-573-9600	540
Moore College of Art & Design 20th & The Pkwy	Philadelphia	PA	19103	**800-523-2025**	215-965-4014	163
Moore Food Distributors Co 9910 Page Ave	Saint Louis	MO	63132	**800-467-7878**	314-426-1300	292-7
Moore-Handley Inc 3140 Pelham Pkwy	Birmingham	AL	35124	**800-633-3848**	205-663-8011	346
Moore Industries International Inc 16650 Schoenborn St	North Hills	CA	91343	**800-999-2900**	818-894-7111	200
Moore Medical Corp 389 John Downey Dr *Sales	New Britain	CT	06050	**800-234-1464***	860-826-3600	467
Moore North America 1200 S Lakeside Dr	Bannockburn	IL	60015	**800-745-0780**	847-607-6000	111
Moore Regional Hospital 155 Memorial Dr	Pinehurst	NC	28374	**800-672-6072**	910-215-1000	366-2
Moore Wallace Response Marketing Services 1200 S Lakeside Dr	Bannockburn	IL	60015	**800-745-0780**	847-607-6000	5
Moorfeed Corp 6996 E 32nd St	Indianapolis	IN	46226	**888-545-7171**	317-545-7171	269
Moorpark Hotel 4241 Moorpark Ave	San Jose	CA	95129	**877-740-6622**	408-864-0300	373
Moose Creek Ranch 219 E Moose Creek Rd	Victor	ID	83455	**800-676-0075**	208-787-2784	238
MOPS International 2370 S Trenton Way	Denver	CO	80231	**800-929-1287**	303-733-5353	48-6
Mor-Gran-Sou Electric Co-op Inc PO Box 297	Flasher	ND	58535	**800-750-8212**	701-597-3301	244
Morabito Baking Co Inc 757 Kohn St	Norristown	PA	19401	**800-525-7747**	610-275-5419	291-1
Moraine Materials Co Inc 1400 Commerce Center Dr	Franklin	OH	45005	**888-667-2463**	937-743-0650	180
Moraine Park Technical College 235 N National Ave	Fond du Lac	WI	54936	**800-472-4554**	920-922-8611	787
Moran Printing Inc 5425 Florida Blvd	Baton Rouge	LA	70806	**800-211-8335**	225-923-2550	614
Morco Inc 125 High St	Cochranton	PA	16314	**800-247-4093**	814-425-7476	10
More Hawaii for Less Inc 1200 Quail St Suite 290	Newport Beach	CA	92660	**800-967-6687**	949-724-5050	760
More Magazine 125 Park Ave	New York	NY	10017	**888-699-4036**	212-557-6600	449-11
Morehead State University 150 University Blvd	Morehead	KY	40351	**800-585-6781**	606-783-2221	163
Morehouse College 830 Westview Dr SW *Admissions	Atlanta	GA	30314	**800-851-1254***	404-681-2800	163
Morehouse Foods Inc 760 Epperson Dr	City of Industry	CA	91748	**888-297-9800**	626-854-1655	291-19
Moreland & Altobelli Assoc Inc 2211 Beaver Ruin Rd Suite 190	Norcross	GA	30071	**800-899-4689**	770-263-5945	258
Moreno Arturo Owner Anaheim Angels 2000 Gene Autry Way	Anaheim	CA	92806	**888-796-4256**	714-634-2000	561
Moresource Inc 401 Vandiver Dr	Columbia	MO	65202	**800-495-5678**	573-814-1234	619
Moreton Fred A & Co 709 E South Temple	Salt Lake City	UT	84102	**800-594-8949**	801-531-1234	383
Moretrench American Corp 100 Stickle Ave PO Box 316	Rockaway	NJ	07866	**800-394-6673**	973-627-2100	188-5
Moretz Inc 514 W 21st St	Newton	NC	28658	**800-438-9127**	828-464-0751	153-10
Morgan Adhesives Co DBA MACtac 4560 Darrow Rd	Stow	OH	44224	**800-762-2822**	330-688-1111	3
Morgan Brothers Bag Co Inc PO Box 25577	Richmond	VA	23260	**800-368-2247**	804-355-9107	68
Morgan Building Systems Inc 2800 McCree Rd	Garland	TX	75041	**800-935-0321**	972-864-7300	107
Morgan Coach Lines Inc 236 Greenfield Rd PO Box 259	South Deerfield	MA	01373	**800-344-3979**	413-665-8036	748
Morgan Corp 35 Thousand Oaks Blvd	Morgantown	PA	19543	**800-666-7426**	610-286-5025	505
Morgan Foods Inc 90 W Morgan St	Austin	IN	47102	**888-430-1780**	812-794-1170	291-20
Morgan Grain & Feed Co 260 Front St PO Box 248	Morgan	MN	56266	**800-449-3157**	507-249-3157	438
Morgan Hill Plastics Inc 640 E Dunne Ave	Morgan Hill	CA	95037	**800-449-0322**	408-779-2118	591
Morgan Hotel & Suites 315 E Woodlawn Rd	Charlotte	NC	28217	**800-522-1994**	704-522-0852	373
Morgan JE Knitting Mills Inc 143 Mahanoy Ave PO Box 390	Tamaqua	PA	18252	**800-448-8240**	570-668-3330	153-18
Morgan Keegan & Co Inc 50 N Front St 17th Fl	Memphis	TN	38103	**800-366-7426**	901-524-4100	679
Morgan Keegan Inc 50 N Front St 17th Fl	Memphis	TN	38103	**800-366-7426**	901-524-4100	355-3
Morgan Olson Corp 1801 S Nottawa Rd	Sturgis	MI	49091	**800-624-9005**	269-659-0200	505
Morgan Run Resort & Club 5690 Cancha de Golf	Rancho Santa Fe	CA	92091	**800-378-4653**	858-756-2471	655
Morgan Services Inc 323 N Michigan Ave	Chicago	IL	60601	**888-966-7426**	312-346-3181	434
Morgan Stanley 1585 Broadway *NYSE: MWD*	New York	NY	10036	**800-223-2440**	212-761-4000	679
Morgan Stanley Family of Funds 1585 Broadway	New York	NY	10036	**800-869-6397**	212-761-4000	517
Morgan Stanley Institutional Funds 73 Tremont St	Boston	MA	02108	**800-548-7786**	617-557-8000	517
Morgan Stanley Investment Management 1221 Ave of the Americas 22nd Fl	New York	NY	10020	**800-419-2861**	212-762-7400	679
Morgan Tire & Auto Inc 2021 Sunnydale Blvd	Clearwater	FL	33765	**800-269-4424**	727-442-8388	62-5
Morganite Crucible Inc 22 N Plains Industrial Rd Suite 1	Wallingford	CT	06492	**800-936-7550**	203-697-0808	649
Morgan's Foods Inc 24200 Chagrin Blvd Suite 126 *AMEX: MR*	Beachwood	OH	44122	**800-869-8691**	216-360-7500	656
Morgans Hotel 237 Madison Ave	New York	NY	10016	**800-334-3408**	212-686-0300	373
Morgantown Area Chamber of Commerce 1009 University Ave	Morgantown	WV	26507	**800-618-2525**	304-292-3311	137
Morgantown (Greater) Convention & Visitors Bureau 201 High St Suite 3	Morgantown	WV	26505	**800-458-7373**	304-292-5081	205
Morgenstern Julie Julie Morgenstern's Professional Organizers 300 W 53rd St Suite 1L	New York	NY	10019	**866-742-6473**	212-544-8722	561
Morinda Inc PO Box 4000	Orem	UT	84059	**800-445-2969**	801-431-6000	291-11
Moritz Embroidery Works Inc PO Box 187	Mount Pocono	PA	18344	**800-533-4183**	570-839-9600	256

Name / Address	City	State	Zip	Toll-Free	Phone	Class
Morley Candy Makers Inc 23770 Hall Rd	Clinton Township	MI	48036	**800-651-7263**	586-468-4300	291-8
Morley-Murphy Co 200 S Washington St Suite 305	Green Bay	WI	54301	**877-499-3171**	920-499-3171	601
Morley Sales Co Inc 809 W Madison St	Chicago	IL	60607	**800-828-0424**	312-829-1125	292-5
Mormac Marine Group Inc 1 Landmark Sq Suite 710	Stamford	CT	06901	**800-669-8903**	203-977-8900	307
Morning Call 101 N 6th St	Allentown	PA	18101	**800-666-5492**	610-820-6500	522-2
Morning Call Inc 101 N 6th St	Allentown	PA	18101	**800-666-5492**	610-820-6500	623-8
Morning Journal 308 W Maple St	Lisbon	OH	44432	**800-862-6224**	330-424-9541	522-2
Morning Journal 1657 Broadway Ave	Lorain	OH	44052	**800-765-6901**	440-245-6901	522-2
Morning News of Northwest Arkansas PO Box 7	Springdale	AR	72765	**888-692-1222**	479-751-6200	522-2
Morning Sentinel 31 Front St	Waterville	ME	04901	**800-452-4666**	207-873-3341	522-2
Morning Song Wild Bird Food 4824 Tazer Dr	Lafayette	IN	47905	**800-552-2516**	765-446-1466	568
Morning Star Publishing Co 711 W Pickard St	Mount Pleasant	MI	48858	**800-616-6397**	989-772-2971	623-8
Morning Sun PO Drawer H	Pittsburg	KS	66762	**800-794-6536**	620-231-2600	522-2
Morning Times 201 N Lehigh Ave	Sayre	PA	18840	**800-459-6397**	570-888-9643	522-2
Morningside of Fullerton 800 Morningside Dr	Fullerton	CA	92835	**800-499-6010**	714-529-2952	659
Morningstar Inc 225 W Wacker Dr *NASDAQ: MORN* ■ *Orders	Chicago	IL	60606	**800-735-0700***	312-696-6000	623-9
Moroch Partners 3625 N Hall St Suite 1100	Dallas	TX	75219	**800-916-4327**	214-520-9700	4
Morongo Casino Resort & Spa 49500 Seminole Dr PO Box 366	Cabazon	CA	92230	**800-252-4499**	951-849-3080	133
MORPACE International Inc 31700 Middlebelt Rd Suite 200	Farmington Hills	MI	48334	**800-878-7223**	248-737-5300	458
Morrilton Packing Co Inc 51 Blue Diamond Dr	Morrilton	AR	72110	**800-264-2475**	501-354-2474	465
Morris-Butler House 1204 N Park Ave	Indianapolis	IN	46202	**800-450-4534**	317-636-5409	50
Morris Communications Co LLC 725 Broad St	Augusta	GA	30901	**800-622-6358**	706-724-0851	623-8
Morris Coupling Co 2240 W 15th St	Erie	PA	16505	**800-426-1579**	814-459-1741	481
Morris Daily Herald PO Box 749	Morris	IL	60450	**800-215-9778**	815-942-3221	522-2
Morris & Dickson Co Ltd PO Box 51367	Shreveport	LA	71135	**800-388-3833**	318-797-7900	237
Morris Industries Inc 777 Rt 23 PO Box 278	Pompton Plains	NJ	07444	**800-835-0777**	973-835-6600	526
Morris Kirschman Co Inc 5050 Almonaster St	New Orleans	LA	70126	**800-289-9430**	504-947-6673	316
Morris Murdock Travel 240 E Morris Ave Suite 400	Salt Lake City	UT	84115	**800-888-6699**	801-487-9731	760
Morris Performing Arts Center 211 N Michigan St	South Bend	IN	46601	**800-537-6415**	574-235-9190	562
Morris Robert E Co Inc 17 Talcott Notch Rd	Farmington	CT	06032	**800-223-0785**	860-678-0200	378
Morris Scrap Metal Inc PO Box 460	Sherman	MS	38869	**800-467-5865**	662-844-6441	674
Morrison Brothers Co PO Box 238 *Cust Svc	Dubuque	IA	52004	**800-553-4840***	563-583-5701	526
Morrison-Clark Inn 1101 11th St NW	Washington	DC	20001	**800-222-8474**	202-898-1200	373
Morrison County Record 216 SE 1st St	Little Falls	MN	56345	**888-637-2345**	320-632-2345	522-4
Morrison House 116 S Alfred St	Alexandria	VA	22314	**800-367-0800**	703-838-8000	373
Morrison Management Specialists Inc 5801 Peachtree Dunwoody Rd	Atlanta	GA	30342	**800-622-1035**	404-845-3330	294
Morrison Milling Co 319 E Prairie St	Denton	TX	76201	**800-866-5487**	940-387-6111	291-23
Morrisville State College PO Box 901	Morrisville	NY	13408	**800-258-0111**	315-684-6000	160
Morrow Equipment Co Inc 3218 Pringle Rd SE	Salem	OR	97302	**800-505-7766**	503-585-5721	261-2
Morrow William & Co 10 E 53rd St *Cust Svc	New York	NY	10022	**800-242-7737***	212-207-7000	623-2
Morse Automotive East 101 Friction Dr	Cartersville	GA	30120	**800-746-6773**	770-607-2222	636
Morse Ed Automotive Group Inc 6363 NW 6th Way Suite 400	Fort Lauderdale	FL	33309	**800-336-6773**	954-351-0055	57
Morse MK Co 1101 11th St SE	Canton	OH	44707	**800-733-3377**	330-453-8187	670
Mortara Instrument Inc 7865 N 86th St	Milwaukee	WI	53224	**800-231-7437**	414-354-1600	249
Mortgage Assn. National Home Equity 1301 Pennsylvania Ave NW Suite 500	Washington	DC	20004	**800-342-1121**	202-347-1210	49-2
Mortgage Bankers Assn (MBA) 1919 Pennsylvania Ave NW	Washington	DC	20006	**800-793-6222**	202-557-2700	49-2
Mortgage Computer Applications Inc 2650 Washington Blvd Suite 203 *Cust Svc	Ogden	UT	84401	**800-421-3277***	801-621-3900	176-11
Mortgage Guaranty Insurance Corp 270 E Kilbourn Ave	Milwaukee	WI	53202	**800-558-9900**	414-347-6480	384-5
Mortgage Market Information Services Inc 53 E Saint Charles Rd	Villa Park	IL	60181	**800-509-4636**	630-834-7555	520
MortgageIT Holdings Inc 33 Maiden Ln *NYSE: MHL*	New York	NY	10038	**877-684-4826**	212-651-7700	498
Morticians Assn. National Funeral Directors & 3951 Snapfinger Pkwy Suite 570	Decatur	GA	30035	**800-434-0958**	404-286-6680	49-4
Morton Buildings Inc 252 W Adams St	Morton	IL	61550	**800-426-6686**	309-263-7474	106
Morton Grove Pharmaceuticals Inc 6451 Main St	Morton Grove	IL	60053	**800-346-6854**	847-967-5600	573
Morton Salt Group PO Box 1496	New Iberia	LA	70562	**800-551-9086**	337-867-4231	668
Mosaic Co 12800 Whitewater Dr MS 190 *NYSE: MOS*	Minnetonka	MN	55343	**800-918-8270**		276
Mosaic Hotel 125 S Spalding Dr	Beverly Hills	CA	90212	**800-463-4466**	310-278-0303	373
Moscow Chamber of Commerce 411 S Main St	Moscow	ID	83843	**800-380-1801**	208-882-1800	137
Moses Lake Area Chamber of Commerce 324 S Pioneer Way	Moses Lake	WA	98837	**800-992-6234**	509-765-7888	137
Moss Adams LLP 1001 4th Ave 31st Fl	Seattle	WA	98154	**800-243-4936**	206-223-1820	2
Moss Ben Jewellers 300-201 Portage Ave	Winnipeg	MB	R3B3K6	**888-236-6677**	204-947-6682	402
Moss Inc 2605 Cab Over Dr Suite 11	Hanover	MD	21076	**800-932-6677**	410-768-3442	229
Moss Supply Co Inc PO Box 26338	Charlotte	NC	28221	**800-438-0770**	704-596-8717	232
Mossberg OF & Sons Inc 7 Grasso Ave	North Haven	CT	06473	**800-989-4867**	203-230-5300	279
Mosser Victorian Hotel 54 4th St	San Francisco	CA	94103	**800-227-3804**	415-986-4400	373
Mote Marine Laboratory 1600 Ken Thompson Pkwy	Sarasota	FL	34236	**800-690-6083**	941-388-4441	654
Motel 6 LP 4001 International Pkwy	Carrollton	TX	75007	**800-466-8356**	972-360-9000	369
Motel Rochambeau 929 Capitol Landing Rd	Williamsburg	VA	23185	**800-368-1055**	757-229-2851	373
Mother Jones Magazine 731 Market St Suite 600	San Francisco	CA	94103	**800-438-6656**	415-665-6637	449-17
Mother Murphy's Labs Inc PO Box 16846	Greensboro	NC	27416	**800-849-1277**	336-273-1737	291-15
Motherhood Maternity 456 N 5th St	Philadelphia	PA	19123	**800-291-7800**	215-873-2200	155-6
Mothers Against Drunk Driving (MADD) 511 E John Carpenter Fwy Suite 700	Irving	TX	75062	**800-438-6233**	214-744-6233	48-6
Mother's Polishes Waxes & Cleaners 5456 Industrial Dr	Huntington Beach	CA	92649	**800-221-8257**	714-891-3364	149
Mothers of Twins Clubs Inc. National Organization of PO Box 438	Thompsons Station	TN	37179	**877-540-2200**	615-595-0936	48-6
Mothers Work Inc 456 N 5th St *NASDAQ: MWRK*	Philadelphia	PA	19123	**800-291-7800**	215-873-2200	155-6
Motient Corp 300 Knightsbridge Pkwy	Lincolnshire	IL	60069	**800-872-6222**	847-478-4200	669
Motion Industries Inc 1605 Alton Rd	Birmingham	AL	35210	**800-526-9328**	205-956-1122	378
Motion Picture Assn (MPA) 15503 Ventura Blvd	Encino	CA	91436	**800-662-6797**	818-995-6600	48-4
Motion Picture Assn of America (MPAA) 15503 Ventura Blvd	Encino	CA	91436	**800-662-6797**	818-995-6600	48-4
MotivAction 16355 36th Ave N Suite 100	Minneapolis	MN	55446	**800-326-2226**	763-525-5200	377
Motivation Through Incentives Inc PO Box 481097	Kansas City	MO	64148	**800-826-3464**	816-942-0122	377
Motivational Manager Newsletter 316 N Michigan Ave Suite 300	Chicago	IL	60601	**800-878-5331**	312-960-4100	521-2
MotivePower 4600 Apple St	Boise	ID	83716	**800-272-7702**	208-947-4800	636
Motlow State Community College PO Box 8500	Lynchburg	TN	37352	**800-654-4877**	931-393-1500	160
Moto Photo Inc 4444 Lake Center Dr	Dayton	OH	45426	**800-733-6686**	937-854-6686	577
Motor Age Magazine 859 Williamette St	Eugene	OR	97401	**800-822-6678**	541-984-5299	449-3
Motor Appliance Corp 555 Spirit of St Louis Blvd	Chesterfield	MO	63005	**800-622-3406**	636-532-3406	507
Motor Boating Magazine 18 Marshall St Suite 114	South Norwalk	CT	06834	**800-888-9123**	203-299-5950	449-4
Motor Cargo Industries Inc 845 W Center St	North Salt Lake	UT	84054	**800-922-4099**	801-936-1111	769
Motor City Electric Co Inc 9446 Grinnell St	Detroit	MI	48213	**800-860-8020**	248-585-8200	188-4
Motor Club of America Enterprises Inc 3200 Wilshire Blvd	Oklahoma City	OK	73156	**800-288-2889**		53
Motor Coach Assn. Family 8291 Clough Pike	Cincinnati	OH	45244	**800-543-3622**	513-474-3622	48-23
Motor Coach Group Inc. International 8645 College Blvd Suite 220	Overland Park	KS	66210	**888-447-3466**	913-906-0111	49-21
Motor Coach Industries International Co 1700 E Golf Rd	Schaumburg	IL	60173	**800-743-3624**	847-285-2000	505
Motor Products Owosso Corp 201 S Delaney Rd	Owosso	MI	48867	**800-248-3841**	989-725-5151	507
Motor Trend Magazine 6420 Wilshire Blvd 7th Fl	Los Angeles	CA	90048	**800-800-6848**	323-782-2000	449-3
Motor Vehicle Administrators. American Assn of 4301 Wilson Blvd Suite 400	Arlington	VA	22203	**800-515-8881**	703-522-4200	49-7
Motor Vehicle Regulation Newsletter PO Box 7376	Alexandria	VA	22307	**800-876-2545**	703-768-9600	521-7
MotorCity Casino 2901 Grand River Ave	Detroit	MI	48201	**877-777-0711**	313-237-7711	133
Motorcoach Assn. United 113 S West St 4th Fl	Alexandria	VA	22314	**800-424-8262**	703-838-2929	49-21
Motorcycle Hall of Fame Museum 13515 Yarmouth Dr	Pickerington	OH	43147	**800-262-5646**	614-856-1900	511
Motorcycle Industry Magazine 1521 Church St	Gardnerville	NV	89410	**800-576-4624**	775-782-0222	449-21
Motorcyclist Assn. American 13515 Yarmouth Dr	Pickerington	OH	43147	**800-262-5646**	614-856-1900	48-22
Motorcyclist Magazine 6420 Wilshire Blvd	Los Angeles	CA	90048	**800-800-7433**	323-782-2000	449-3
MotorHome Magazine 2575 Vista Del Mar Dr *Cust Svc	Ventura	CA	93001	**800-678-1201***	805-667-4100	449-22
Motorists Assn. National 402 W 2nd St	Waunakee	WI	53597	**800-882-2785**	608-849-6000	49-21
Motorlease Corp 1506 New Britain Ave	Farmington	CT	06032	**800-243-0182**	860-677-9711	284
Motorola Canada Ltd 8133 Warden Ave	Markham	ON	L6G1B3	**800-268-3395**	905-948-5200	720
Motorola Computer Group 2900 S Diablo Way	Tempe	AZ	85282	**800-759-1107**	602-438-3000	613
Motorola Inc 1301 E Algonquin Rd *NYSE: MOT*	Schaumburg	IL	60196	**800-331-6456**	847-576-5000	686
Motorola Inc Broadband Communications Sector 101 Tournament Dr	Horsham	PA	19044	**800-523-6678**	215-323-1000	633
Motorola Inc Cellular Subscriber Sector 600 N US Hwy 45	Libertyville	IL	60048	**800-331-6456**	847-523-5000	720
Motorola Inc Land Mobile Products Sector 1301 E Algonquin Rd	Schaumburg	IL	60196	**800-247-2346**	847-576-5000	720

Name / Address	City	State	ZIP	Toll-Free	Phone	Class
Motors Insurance Corp 1 GMAC Insurance Plaza	Saint Louis	MO	63045	**800-642-6464**	314-492-8000	384-4
Motorsports Hall of Fame of America 43700 Expo Center Dr	Novi	MI	48375	**800-250-7223**	248-349-7223	511
Motorsports Museum. Hendrick 4411 Papa Joe Hendrick Blvd	Charlotte	NC	28262	**877-467-4890**	704-455-3400	511
Motricity 2800 Meridian Pkwy Suite 150	Durham	NC	27713	**800-746-7646**	919-287-7400	222
Motson Graphics Inc 1717 Bethlehem Pike	Flourtown	PA	19031	**800-972-1986**	215-233-0500	675
Mott CS Children's Hospital 1500 E Medical Center Dr	Ann Arbor	MI	48109	**800-211-8181**	734-936-4000	366-1
Mottahedeh & Co 225 5th Ave	New York	NY	10010	**800-242-3050**	212-685-3050	356
Mott's Inc 900 King St	Rye Brook	NY	10573	**800-426-4891**	914-612-4000	291-20
Moulding & Millwork Producers Assn. Wood 507 First St	Woodland	CA	95695	**800-550-7889**	530-661-9591	49-3
Moultrie-Colquitt County Chamber of Commerce 116 1st Ave SE	Moultrie	GA	31768	**888-408-4748**	229-985-2131	137
Moultrie Feeders 150 Industrial Rd	Alabaster	AL	35007	**800-653-3334**	205-664-6700	701
Moultrie Mfg Co PO Box 2948	Moultrie	GA	31776	**800-841-8674**	229-985-1312	482
Mound City Industries Inc 1315 Cherokee St	Saint Louis	MO	63118	**800-727-1548**	314-773-5200	292-3
Mount Airy (Greater) Chamber of Commerce 200 N Main St	Mount Airy	NC	27030	**800-948-0949**	336-786-6116	137
Mount Airy News PO Box 808	Mount Airy	NC	27030	**800-826-6397**	336-786-4141	522-2
Mount Aloysius College 7373 Admiral Perry Hwy	Cresson	PA	16630	**888-823-2220**	814-886-6383	163
Mount Arbor Nurseries 201 E Ferguson Rd *Sales	Shenandoah	IA	51601	**800-831-4125***	712-246-4250	363
Mount Bachelor Village Resort & Conference Center 19717 Mt Bachelor Dr	Bend	OR	97702	**800-452-9846**	541-389-5900	655
Mount Marty College 1105 W 8th St	Yankton	SD	57078	**800-658-4552**	605-668-1011	163
Mount Mary College 2900 N Menomonee River Pkwy	Milwaukee	WI	53222	**800-321-6265**	414-256-1219	163
Mount Mercy College 1330 Elmhurst Dr NE	Cedar Rapids	IA	52402	**800-248-4504**	319-368-6460	163
Mount Olive College 634 Henderson St	Mount Olive	NC	28365	**800-653-0854**	919-658-2502	163
Mount Olive Pickle Co PO Box 609	Mount Olive	NC	28365	**800-672-5041**	919-658-2535	291-19
Mount Pleasant News PO Box 240	Mount Pleasant	IA	52641	**800-373-2411**	319-385-3131	522-2
Mount Pulaski Products Inc 908 N Vine St	Mount Pulaski	IL	62548	**800-577-2627**	217-792-3211	143
Mount Regis Center 405 Kimball Ave	Salem	VA	24153	**800-477-3447**	540-389-4761	712
Mount Saint Mary College 330 Powell Ave	Newburgh	NY	12550	**888-937-6762**	845-569-3248	163
Mount Saint Mary's College 12001 Chalon Rd	Los Angeles	CA	90049	**800-999-9893**	310-954-4250	163
Doheny Campus 10 Chester Pl *Admissions	Los Angeles	CA	90007	**800-999-9893***	213-477-2561	160
Mount Saint Mary's University 16300 Old Emmitsburg Rd	Emmitsburg	MD	21727	**800-448-4347**	301-447-5214	163
Mount Savage Specialty Refractories Co 736 W Ingomar Rd	Ingomar	PA	15127	**800-437-6777**	412-367-9100	648
Mount Shasta Resort 1000 Siskiyou Lake Blvd	Mount Shasta	CA	96067	**800-958-3363**	530-926-3030	655
Mount Snow Resort Rt 100	West Dover	VT	05356	**800-451-4211**	802-464-3333	655
Mount Union College 1972 Clark Ave	Alliance	OH	44601	**800-334-6682**	330-823-2590	163
Mount Vernon College 2100 Foxhall Rd NW	Washington	DC	20007	**800-447-3765**	202-242-6672	163
Mount Vernon Convention & Visitors Bureau 200 Potomac Blvd	Mount Vernon	IL	62864	**800-252-5464**	618-242-3151	205
Mount Vernon Hotel 24 W Franklin St	Baltimore	MD	21201	**800-245-5256**	410-727-2000	373
Mount Vernon Mills Inc PO Box 3478	Greenville	SC	29602	**800-845-8857**	864-233-4151	730-1
Mount Vernon Mills Inc La France Industries Div 290 Old Anderson Hwy	La France	SC	29656	**800-845-9728**	864-646-3213	730-1
Mount Vernon Nazarene University 800 Martinsburg Rd	Mount Vernon	OH	43050	**800-782-2435**	740-397-1244	163
Mount Vernon Screw Products Inc PO Box 250	Mount Vernon	IN	47620	**800-880-5502**	812-838-5501	610
Mount View Hotel & Spa 1457 Lincoln Ave	Calistoga	CA	94515	**800-772-8838**	707-942-6877	373
Mount Washington Hotel & Resort Rt 302	Bretton Woods	NH	03575	**800-314-1752**	603-278-1000	655
Mount Wheeler Power Inc PO Box 15000	Ely	NV	89315	**800-977-6937**	775-289-8981	244
Mountain America Credit Union PO Box 9001	West Jordan	UT	84084	**800-748-4302**	801-325-6228	216
Mountain Bicycling Assn. International 207 Canyon Blvd Suite 301 PO Box 7578	Boulder	CO	80306	**888-442-4622**	303-545-9011	48-23
Mountain Bike Magazine 33 E Minor St	Emmaus	PA	18098	**800-666-1817**	610-967-5171	449-14
Mountain Club. Appalachian 5 Joy St *Orders	Boston	MA	02108	**800-262-4455***	617-523-0636	48-13
Mountain Electric Co-op Inc PO Box 180	Mountain City	TN	37683	**888-721-9111**	423-727-1800	244
Mountain Haus 292 E Meadow Dr	Vail	CO	81657	**800-237-0922**	970-476-2434	373
Mountain High Hosiery Ltd 675 Gateway Center Dr	San Diego	CA	92102	**800-528-5355**	619-262-9202	153-10
Mountain Home Area Chamber of Commerce 1023 Hwy 62 E	Mountain Home	AR	72653	**800-822-3536**	870-425-5111	137
Mountain Jack 10200 Willow Creek Rd	San Diego	CA	92131	**800-570-9159**	858-689-2333	657
Mountain Lake Hotel 115 Hotel Cir	Pembroke	VA	24136	**800-346-3334**	540-626-7121	373
Mountain Laurel Resort & Spa Rt 940 PO Box 9	White Haven	PA	18661	**800-255-7625**	570-443-8411	655
Mountain Laurel Spa at Stonewall Resort 940 Resort Dr	Roanoke	WV	26447	**888-278-8150**	304-269-8881	698
Mountain Lodge at Telluride 457 Mountain Village Blvd	Telluride	CO	81435	**866-368-6867**	970-369-5000	655
Mountain Manor Inn & Golf Club Creek Rd PO Box 1067	Marshalls Creek	PA	18335	**800-626-6747**	570-223-8098	655
Mountain Manor Treatment Center Rt 15 PO Box 136	Emmitsburg	MD	21727	**800-537-3422**	301-447-2361	712
Mountain Parks Electric Inc PO Box 170	Granby	CO	80446	**877-887-3378**	970-887-3378	244
Mountain People's Warehouse Inc 12745 Earhart Ave	Auburn	CA	95602	**800-679-8735**	530-889-9531	292-8
Mountain Sky Guest Ranch PO Box 1219	Emigrant	MT	59027	**800-548-3392**	406-333-4911	238
Mountain State Blue Cross & Blue Shield 700 Market St	Parkersburg	WV	26102	**800-344-5514**	304-424-7700	384-3
Mountain State University 609 S Kanawha St	Beckley	WV	25801	**800-766-6067**	304-253-7351	163
Mountain States Plants Corp 1421 W Gentile St	Layton	UT	84041	**800-326-4490**	801-544-8878	363
Mountain Travel Sobek 1266 66th St Suite 4	Emeryville	CA	94608	**888-687-6235**	510-594-6000	748
Mountain Trek Fitness Retreat & Health Spa Ltd 4952 North St	Ainsworth Hot Springs	BC	V0G1A0	**800-661-5161**	250-229-5636	697
Mountain Valley Spring Co 150 Central Ave	Hot Springs	AR	71901	**800-643-1501**	501-623-6671	792
Mountain View Electric Assn Inc PO Box 1600	Limon	CO	80828	**800-388-9881**	719-775-2861	244
Mountain View Inn 1001 Village Dr	Greensburg	PA	15601	**800-537-8709**	724-834-5300	373
Mountain Villas 9525 W Skyline Pkwy	Duluth	MN	55810	**800-642-6377**	218-624-5784	373
Mountainbird Inc DBA Salmon Air 29 Hamner Dr	Salmon	ID	83467	**800-448-3413**	208-756-6211	14
Mountaineer Racetrack Rt 2 PO Box 358	Chester	WV	26034	**800-804-0468**	304-387-2400	628
Mountainland Supply Co 1505 W 130 South	Orem	UT	84058	**800-666-5434**	801-224-6050	601
Mountaire Farms 17269 NC Hwy 71 N	Lumber Bridge	NC	28357	**800-962-0720**	910-843-5942	608
Mountaire Farms of North Carolina 203 Morris Farm Rd	Candor	NC	27229	**800-284-4528**	910-974-3232	438
Mountrail-Williams Electric Co-op PO Box 1346	Williston	ND	58802	**800-279-2667**	701-577-3765	244
Mouser Custom Cabinetry PO Box 2527	Elizabethtown	KY	42702	**800-345-7537**	270-737-7477	116
Mouser Electronics Corp 1000 N Main St	Mansfield	TX	76063	**800-346-6873**	817-804-3888	245
Movie Gallery Inc 900 W Main St *NASDAQ: MOVI* ■ *Cust Svc	Dothan	AL	36301	**866-209-5533***	334-677-2108	784
Moviefone Inc 333 Westchester Ave 2nd Fl *Cust Svc	White Plains	NY	10604	**800-745-0009***	914-872-0333	735
Movies Unlimited Inc 3015 Darnell Rd	Philadelphia	PA	19154	**800-668-4344**	215-637-4444	451
Moving Comfort Inc 4500 Southgate Pl Suite 800	Chantilly	VA	20151	**800-763-6000**	703-631-1000	153-1
Moving Express 9180 Kelvin Ave	Chatsworth	CA	91311	**800-844-3977**	818-591-8579	508
Moving Picture Technicians. International Alliance of Theatrical Stage Employees 1430 Broadway 20th Fl	New York	NY	10018	**800-223-6872**	212-730-1770	405
Movsovitz & Sons of Florida Inc 3100 Hilton St	Jacksonville	FL	32209	**800-393-3663**	904-764-7681	292-7
Moxie Java International LLC 199 E 52nd St Suite 100	Boise	ID	83714	**800-659-6963**	208-322-7773	156
Moyco Technologies Inc 200 Commerce Dr	Montgomeryville	PA	18936	**800-331-8837**	215-855-4300	1
Moyer Packing Co PO Box 64395	Souderton	PA	18964	**800-876-6722**	215-723-5555	465
Moyer & Son Inc 113 E Reliance Rd	Souderton	PA	18964	**800-345-0419**	215-723-6000	438
Moyno Inc 1895 W Jefferson St	Springfield	OH	45506	**800-325-1331**	937-327-3111	627
Mozel Inc 1900 W Gate Dr	Columbia	IL	62236	**800-260-5348**	618-281-3040	144
Mozilla Foundation 1350 Villa St Suite C *Tech Supp	Mountain View	CA	94041	**888-586-4539***	650-903-0888	48-9
Mozzarella's Cafe 150 W Church Ave	Maryville	TN	37801	**800-325-0755**	865-379-5700	657
MP Husky Corp PO Box 16749	Greenville	SC	29606	**800-277-4810**	864-234-4800	804
MP Pumps Inc 34800 Bennett Dr	Fraser	MI	48026	**800-563-8006**	586-293-8240	627
MPA (Magazine Publishers of America) 810 7th Ave 24th Fl	New York	NY	10019	**888-567-3228**	212-872-3700	49-16
MPA (Motion Picture Assn) 15503 Ventura Blvd	Encino	CA	91436	**800-662-6797**	818-995-6600	48-4
MPAA (Motion Picture Assn of America) 15503 Ventura Blvd	Encino	CA	91436	**800-662-6797**	818-995-6600	48-4
MPBC (Maine Public Broadcasting Corp) 65 Texas Ave	Bangor	ME	04401	**800-884-1717**	207-941-1010	620
MPC Promotions Inc 2026 Shepherdsville Rd	Louisville	KY	40218	**800-331-0989**	502-451-4900	153-9
MPD Inc 316 E 9th St	Owensboro	KY	42303	**866-225-5673**	270-685-6200	410
MPEC (Multi-Purpose Events Center) 1000 5th St	Wichita Falls	TX	76301	**800-799-6732**	940-716-5500	204
MPI Label Systems Inc 450 Courtney Rd	Sebring	OH	44672	**800-837-2134**	330-938-2134	404
MPI Media Group 16101 S 108th Ave	Orland Park	IL	60467	**800-777-2223**	708-460-0555	500
MPI Technologies 37 East St	Winchester	MA	01890	**888-674-8088**	781-729-8300	589
MPL Technologies 9400 King St *Cust Svc	Franklin Park	IL	60131	**800-323-0970***	847-678-7555	469
Mpower Communications Corp 175 Sully's Trail Suite 300	Pittsford	NY	14534	**888-777-5802**	585-218-6550	721
MPR (Minnesota Public Radio) 45 E 7th St	Saint Paul	MN	55101	**800-228-7123**	651-290-1212	620
MPS Group Inc 2920 Scotten St	Detroit	MI	48210	**800-741-8779**	313-841-7588	191
MPSI Systems Inc 4343 S 118th East Ave *Cust Svc	Tulsa	OK	74146	**800-727-6774***	918-877-6774	176-11
MPT (Maryland Public Television) 11767 Owings Mills Blvd	Owings Mills	MD	21117	**800-223-3678**	410-356-5600	620
MPW Industrial Services Group Inc 9711 Lancaster Rd SE *NASDAQ: MPWG*	Hebron	OH	43025	**800-827-8790**	740-927-8790	150
Mr Goodcents Franchise Systems Inc 8997 Commerce Dr	DeSoto	KS	66018	**800-648-2368**	913-583-8400	657

Name / Address	City	State	ZIP	Toll-Free	Phone	Class
Mr Hero 5755 Granger Rd Suite 200	Independence	OH	44131	**800-837-9599**	216-398-1101	657
Mr Jim's Pizza Inc 4276 Kellway Cir.	Addison	TX	75001	**800-583-5960**	972-267-5467	657
Mr Rooter Corp 1010 N University Pk Dr.	Waco	TX	76707	**800-583-8003**	254-745-2444	188-10
Mr Sub 4576 Yonge St.	Toronto	ON	M2N6P1	**800-668-7827**	416-225-5545	657
Mr Subb Franchise Corp 601 Columbia St.	Cohoes	NY	12047	**800-267-7822**	518-783-0276	657
Mr Transmission 9675 Yonge St 2nd Fl	Richmond Hill	ON	L4C1V7	**800-373-8432**	905-884-1511	62-6
Mr Winter Inc 8085 W 26th Ct	Hialeah	FL	33016	**800-327-3371**	305-556-6741	650
MRC (Medicare Rights Center) 1460 Broadway 17th Fl *hotline	New York	NY	10036	**800-333-4114***	212-869-3850	48-17
MRC Bearings Inc 402 Chandler St. *Cust Svc	Jamestown	NY	14701	**800-672-7000***	716-661-2600	77
MRO Software Inc 100 Crosby Dr. *NASDAQ: MROI* ■ *Cust Svc	Bedford	MA	01730	**800-243-7734***	781-280-2000	176-1
Mrs Alison's Cookie Co Inc 1600 Pk 370 Pl Suite 2	Hazelwood	MO	63042	**800-878-6772**	314-298-2595	291-9
Mrs Baird's Bakeries Inc 7301 South Fwy	Fort Worth	TX	76134	**800-366-7921**	817-293-6230	291-1
Mrs Clark's Foods LLC 740 SE Dalby Dr.	Ankeny	IA	50021	**866-971-6500**	515-964-8100	291-21
Mrs Crockett's Kitchens Inc 8021-G Forum Way	Fort Worth	TX	76140	[illegible]	[illegible]	[illegible]
Mrs Fields Original Cookies Inc 2855 E Cottonwood Pkwy Suite 400	Salt Lake City	UT	84121	**800-348-6311**	801-736-5600	69
Mrs T's Pierogies 600 E Center St PO Box 606	Shenandoah	PA	17976	**800-233-3170**	570-462-2745	291-36
Mrs Winner's Chicken & Biscuits 6055 Barfield Rd.	Atlanta	GA	30328	**877-733-5577**	404-459-5805	657
MRV Communications Inc 20415 Nordhoff St *NASDAQ: MRVC* ■ *Sales	Chatsworth	CA	91311	**800-858-7815***	818-773-0900	779
MS Co PO Box 480	Attleboro	MA	02703	**800-675-4657**	508-222-1700	399
Ms Magazine 1600 Wilson Blvd Suite 801	Arlington	VA	22209	**866-672-6363**	703-522-4201	449-11
MSA (Microscopy Society of America) 230 E Ohio St Suite 400	Chicago	IL	60611	**800-538-3672**	312-644-1527	49-19
MSA (Mine Safety Appliances Co) 121 Gamma Dr. *NYSE: MSA*	Pittsburgh	PA	15238	**800-672-2222**	412-967-3000	566
MSC 3900 E Sprague Ave	Spokane	WA	99202	**800-835-3510**	509-536-4700	384-3
MSC Cruises USA Inc 6700 N Andrews Ave Suite 605	Fort Lauderdale	FL	33309	**800-666-9333**	954-772-6262	217
MSC Industrial Direct Co 75 Maxess Rd. *NYSE: MSM*	Melville	NY	11747	**800-645-7270**	516-812-2000	378
MSC Liquid Filtration Corp 198 Freshwater Blvd. *Cust Svc	Enfield	CT	06082	**800-237-7359***	860-745-7475	793
MSC.Software Corp 2 MacArthur Pl	Santa Ana	CA	92707	**800-345-2078**	714-444-5112	176-5
MSF (Multiple Sclerosis Foundation) 6350 N Andrews Ave.	Fort Lauderdale	FL	33309	**800-225-6495**	954-776-6805	48-17
MSHA (Mine Safety & Health Administration) 1100 Wilson Blvd.	Arlington	VA	22209	**800-746-1554**	202-693-9419	336-11
MSI Entran Devices Inc 10 Washington Ave	Fairfield	NJ	07004	**888-836-8726**	973-227-1002	464
MSI International Inc 245 Peachtree Ctr Ave Suite 2500	Atlanta	GA	30303	**800-801-1820**	404-659-5236	262
MSI Inventory Service Corp PO Box 230129	Flowood	MS	39232	**800-820-1460**	601-939-0130	391
MSI/Canterbury Inc 200 Lanidex Plaza	Parsippany	NJ	07054	**800-638-2252**		753
MSK Precision Parts Inc 4100 NW 10th Ave.	Fort Lauderdale	FL	33309	**800-992-5018**	954-776-0770	610
MSM Industries Inc 802 Swan Dr.	Smyrna	TN	37167	**800-648-6648**	615-355-4355	663
MSN (Microsoft Network) 1 Microsoft Way *Sales	Redmond	WA	98052	**800-426-9400***	425-882-8080	390
MSN Encarta 1 Microsoft Way	Redmond	WA	98052	**800-426-9400**	425-882-8080	677
MSN House & Home 1 Microsoft Way	Redmond	WA	98052	**800-642-7676**	425-882-8080	498
MSN Search 1 Microsoft Way	Redmond	WA	98052	**800-386-5550**	425-882-8080	677
MSPB (Merit Systems Protection Board) 1615 M St NW	Washington	DC	20419	**800-209-8960**	202-653-7200	336-16
MSS* Group Inc 960 I-25 S Suite F	Castle Rock	CO	80104	**800-873-5790**	303-814-6774	455
Mt Hood Beverage Co 3601 NW Yeon Ave	Portland	OR	97210	**800-788-9992**	503-274-9990	82-1
MTA (Metropolitan Transportation Authority) PO Box 194	Los Angeles	CA	90001	**800-266-6883**	213-922-2000	460
MTA Today Magazine 20 Ashburton Pl.	Boston	MA	02108	**800-392-6175**	617-742-7950	449-8
MTD Products Inc PO Box 368022	Cleveland	OH	44136	**800-800-7310**	330-225-2600	420
MTE Corp PO Box 9013	Menomonee Falls	WI	53051	**800-253-8210**	262-253-8200	756
MTH Industries 1 MTH Plaza	Hillside	IL	60162	**800-231-9711**	708-498-1100	188-6
MTI Inc 1050 NW 229th Ave.	Hillsboro	OR	97124	**800-426-6844**	503-648-6500	603
MTI Technology Corp 14661 Franklin Ave. *NASDAQ: MTIC*	Tustin	CA	92780	**800-999-9684**	714-481-7800	174
MTM Technologies Inc 850 Canal St 3rd Fl *NASDAQ: MTMC*	Stamford	CT	06902	**800-468-6782**	203-975-3700	174
MTNA (Music Teachers National Assn) 441 Vine St Suite 505	Cincinnati	OH	45202	**888-512-5278**	513-421-1420	49-5
MTN/ATC Teleports 3044 N Commerce Pkwy	Miramar	FL	33025	**877-464-4686**	954-538-4000	669
MTR Gaming Group Inc PO Box 358 *NASDAQ: MNTG*	Chester	WV	26034	**800-804-0468**	304-387-8300	628
MTS Inc 2500 Del Monte St	West Sacramento	CA	95691	**800-225-0880**	916-373-2500	658
MTS Safety Products Inc 150 2nd St	Belmont	MS	38827	**800-647-8168**	662-454-9245	566
MTS Systems Corp 14000 Technology Dr. *NASDAQ: MTSC* ■ *Cust Svc	Eden Prairie	MN	55344	**800-328-2255***	952-937-4000	464
MTS Travel Inc 124 E Main St 4th Fl	Ephrata	PA	17522	**800-642-8315**	717-733-4131	760
MTX Corp 4545 E Baseline Rd.	Phoenix	AZ	85042	**800-225-5689**	602-438-4545	52
Mu Phi Epsilon International Music Fraternity 4705 N Sonora Ave Suite 114	Fresno	CA	93722	**888-259-1471**	559-227-1898	48-16
Muckleshoot Indian Casino 2402 Auburn Way S.	Auburn	WA	98002	**800-804-4944**	253-804-4444	133
Muehlstein H & Co Inc 800 Connecticut Ave.	Norwalk	CT	06854	**800-257-3746**	203-855-6000	592
Mueller Brass Co 2199 Lapeer Ave.	Port Huron	MI	48060	**800-553-3336**	810-987-7770	476
Mueller Co 500 W Eldorado St	Decatur	IL	62522	**800-432-4471**	217-423-4471	776
Mueller Industries Inc 8285 Tournament Dr Suite 150 *NYSE: MLI*	Memphis	TN	38125	**800-348-8464**	901-753-3200	476
Mueller Paul Co 1600 W Phelps St. *NASDAQ: MUEL*	Springfield	MO	65802	**800-641-2830**	417-831-3000	379
Mueller Refrigeration Co Inc 121 Rogers St PO Box 239 *Cust Svc	Hartsville	TN	37074	**800-251-8983***	615-374-2124	776
Mueller Steam Specialty 1491 NC Hwy 20 W	Saint Pauls	NC	28384	**800-334-6259**	910-865-8241	379
Muench-Kreuzer Candle Co 617 E Hiawatha Blvd	Syracuse	NY	13208	**800-448-7884**	315-471-4515	122
Muir Glen Organic Tomato Products 719 Metcalf St	Sedro Woolley	WA	98284	**800-832-6345**	360-855-0100	291-20
Muir-Roberts Co Inc 68 S Main St Suite 900	Salt Lake City	UT	84101	**877-268-2002**	801-363-7695	292-7
Mulberry Inn. Fort Collins 4333 E Mulberry St	Fort Collins	CO	80524	**800-234-5548**	970-493-9000	373
Mule Lighting Inc 46 Baker St	Providence	RI	02905	**800-556-7690**	401-941-4446	431
Mulhern Belting Inc 148 Bauer Dr	Oakland	NJ	07436	**800-253-6300**	201-337-5700	364
Mulholland Harper Co Inc 24778 Meeting House Rd PO Box C	Denton	MD	21629	**800-882-3052**	410-479-1300	692
Mullen 36 Essex St	Wenham	MA	01984	**800-363-6010**	978-468-1155	4
Multi-Ad Services Inc 1720 W Detweiller Dr.	Peoria	IL	61615	**800-348-6485**	309-692-1530	176-1
Multi-Link Communications Inc 4704 Harlan St Suite 420	Denver	CO	80212	**888-968-5465**	303-831-1977	721
Multi-Pak Corp 180 Atlantic St	Hackensack	NJ	07601	**800-234-7441**	201-342-7474	36
Multi-Tech Systems 2205 Woodale Dr. *Cust Svc	Mounds View	MN	55112	**800-328-9717***	763-785-3500	496
Multi-Wall Corp Div Real Reel Corp 50 Taylor Dr. *Cust Svc	East Providence	RI	02916	**800-992-4166***	401-434-1070	125
Multiband Corp 9449 Science Ctr Dr. *NASDAQ: MBND*	New Hope	MN	55428	**800-475-7135**	763-504-3000	721
Multichannel News 360 Park Ave S *Cust Svc	New York	NY	10010	**888-343-5563***	646-746-6400	449-9
Multicoat Corp 23331 Antonio Pkwy	Rancho Santa Margarita	CA	92688	**877-685-8426**	949-888-7100	490
Multifilm Packaging Corp 1040 N McLean Blvd	Elgin	IL	60123	**800-837-9727**	847-695-7600	538
Multimatic Products Inc 390 Oser Ave	Hauppauge	NY	11788	**800-767-7633**	631-231-1515	610
Multimax Inc 1441 McCormick Dr	Largo	MD	20774	**800-339-8828**	301-925-8222	178
MultiMedia Schools Magazine 143 Old Marlton Pike	Medford	NJ	08055	**800-300-9868**	609-654-6266	449-7
Multipet International Inc 265 W Commercial Ave	Moonachie	NJ	07074	**800-900-6738**	201-438-6600	568
Multiple Sclerosis Foundation (MSF) 6350 N Andrews Ave.	Fort Lauderdale	FL	33309	**800-225-6495**	954-776-6805	48-17
Multiple Sclerosis Society. National 733 3rd Ave	New York	NY	10017	**800-344-4867**	212-986-3240	48-17
Multiquip Inc 18910 Wilmington Ave	Carson	CA	90746	**800-421-1244**	310-537-3700	378
Multisorb Technologies Inc 325 Harlem Rd. *Cust Svc	West Seneca	NY	14224	**800-445-9890***	716-824-8900	143
Multiton MIC Corp 5701 Eastport Blvd	Richmond	VA	23231	**800-229-7400**	804-737-7400	462
Multnomah Greyhound Park PO Box 9	Fairview	OR	97024	**800-888-7576**	503-667-7700	628
Multnomah Publishers PO Box 1720	Sisters	OR	97759	**800-929-0910**	541-549-1144	623-4
Muncie-Delaware County Chamber of Commerce 401 S High St	Muncie	IN	47305	**800-336-1373**	765-288-6681	137
Muncie Star-Press PO Box 2408	Muncie	IN	47307	**800-783-7827**	765-213-5700	522-2
Muncie Visitors Bureau 425 N High St	Muncie	IN	47305	**800-568-6862**	765-284-2700	205
Muncy Homes Inc 1567 Rt 442	Muncy	PA	17756	**800-788-1555**	570-546-2261	107
Munder Funds 480 Pierce St	Birmingham	MI	48009	**800-468-6337**	248-647-9200	517
Municipal Auditorium Arena 301 W 13th St Suite 100	Kansas City	MO	64105	**800-821-7060**	816-513-5000	706
Municipal Clerks. International Institute of 8331 Utica Ave Suite 200	Rancho Cucamonga	CA	91730	**800-251-1639**	909-944-4162	49-7
Municipal Credit Union PO Box 3205	New York	NY	10007	**800-843-1867**	212-693-4900	216
Municipal Litigation Reporter 590 Dutch Valley Rd NE	Atlanta	GA	30324	**800-926-7926**	404-881-1141	521-7
Municipal Mortgage & Equity LLC (MuniMae) 621 E Pratt St Suite 300 *NYSE: MMA*	Baltimore	MD	21202	**888-788-3863**		498
Municipal Signal Assn. International 165 E Union St PO Box 539	Newark	NY	14513	**800-723-4672**	315-331-2182	49-7
MuniMae (Municipal Mortgage & Equity LLC) 621 E Pratt St Suite 300 *NYSE: MMA*	Baltimore	MD	21202	**888-788-3863**		498
Munk Peter Fndr/Chm Barrick Gold Corp Canada Trust Tower 161 Bay St Suite 3700	Toronto	ON	M5J2S1	**800-720-7415**		561
Munro & Co PO Box 1157	Hot Springs	AR	71902	**800-826-8676**	501-262-6000	296
Munson Hospice 1105 6th St	Traverse City	MI	49684	**800-252-2065**	231-935-6520	365
Munson's Candy Kitchen Inc DBA Munson's Chocolates PO Box 9217	Bolton	CT	06043	**888-868-6766**	860-649-4332	291-8
Munters Corp PO Box 6428	Fort Myers	FL	33911	**800-446-6868**	239-936-1555	15
Munters Corp Cargocaire Div PO Box 640 *Sales	Amesbury	MA	01913	**800-843-5360***	978-388-0600	15

Name / Address	City	State	ZIP	Toll-Free	Phone	Class
Muralo Co Inc 148 E 5th St	Bayonne	NJ	07002	**800-631-3440**	201-437-0770	540
Murata Electronics North America Inc 2200 Lake Pk Dr	Smyrna	GA	30080	**800-241-6574**	770-436-1300	252
Murata Machinery USA Inc 2120 I-85 S	Charlotte	NC	28208	**800-428-8469**	704-875-9280	448
Murdered Children. Parents of 100 E 8th St Suite B-41	Cincinnati	OH	45202	**888-818-7662**	513-721-5683	48-6
Murdock Webbing Co 27 Foundry St	Central Falls	RI	02863	**800-375-2052**	401-724-3000	730-5
Muriel Siebert & Co Inc 885 3rd Ave Suite 1720 *Cust Svc	New York	NY	10022	**800-872-0444***	212-644-2400	679
Murphy Brown LLC PO Box 759	Rose Hill	NC	28458	**800-311-9458**	910-289-2111	11-6
Murphy Co Mechanical Contractors & Engineers 1233 N Price Rd	Saint Louis	MO	63132	**800-992-6601**	314-997-6600	188-10
Murphy Exploration & Production Co 131 S Robertson St	New Orleans	LA	70161	**800-765-9501**	504-561-2811	525
Murphy Harry L Inc 42 Bonaventura Dr	San Jose	CA	95134	**800-439-6777**	408-955-1100	285
Murphy James A & Son Inc PO Box 3006	South Attleboro	MA	02703	**800-422-3237**	508-761-5060	399
Murphy Oil Corp 200 Peach St *NYSE: MUR*	El Dorado	AR	71730	**800-643-2364**	870-862-6411	525
Murphy Oil USA Inc 200 Peach St	El Dorado	AR	71730	**800-643-2364**	870-862-6411	570
Murray-Calloway County Chamber of Commerce 805 N 12th St	Murray	KY	42071	**800-900-5171**	270-753-5171	137
Murray Guard Inc 58 Murray Guard Dr	Jackson	TN	38305	**800-238-3830**	731-668-3400	682
Murray Sheet Metal Co Inc 3112 7th St	Parkersburg	WV	26101	**800-464-8801**	304-422-5431	688
Murray State University PO Box 9	Murray	KY	42071	**800-272-4678**	270-762-3741	163
Murray's Discount Auto Stores 8080 Hagerty Rd	Belleville	MI	48111	**800-946-8772**	734-957-8080	54
Murrey International USA 14150 S Figueroa St	Los Angeles	CA	90061	**800-421-1022**	310-532-6091	701
Murrows Transfer Inc PO Box 4095 *Cust Svc	High Point	NC	27263	**800-669-2928***	336-475-6101	769
Murry's Inc 8300 Pennsylvania Ave	Upper Marlboro	MD	20772	**800-638-5806**	301-420-6400	291-26
Muscatine Community College 152 Colorado St	Muscatine	IA	52761	**888-336-3907**	563-288-6001	160
Muscatine Journal 301 E 3rd St	Muscatine	IA	52761	**800-383-3198**	563-263-2331	522-2
Muscle & Fitness Magazine 21100 Erwin St *Orders	Woodland Hills	CA	91367	**800-423-5590***	818-884-6800	449-13
Musco Lighting 100 1st Ave W	Oskaloosa	IA	52577	**800-825-6030**	641-673-0411	431
Musco Olive Products Inc 17950 Via Nicolo	Tracy	CA	95376	**800-523-9828**	209-836-4600	291-19
Muscular Dystrophy Assn (MDA) 3300 E Sunrise Dr	Tucson	AZ	85718	**800-572-1717**	520-529-2000	48-17
Musculoskeletal Transplant Foundation 125 May St Suite 300	Edison	NJ	08837	**800-433-6576**	732-661-0202	535
Muse The 130 W 46th St	New York	NY	10036	**877-692-6873**	212-485-2400	373
Muse Magazine 30 Grove St Suite C	Peterborough	NH	03458	**800-821-0115**	603-924-7209	449-6
Musee Conti-Wax Museum of Louisiana Legends 917 Rue Conti French Quarter	New Orleans	LA	70112	**800-233-5405**	504-525-2605	509
Musee de l'Amerique Francaise 2 cote de la Fabrique	Quebec	QC	G1R4R7	**866-710-8031**	418-692-2843	509
Musee du Quebec Parc des Champs-de-Bataille	Quebec	QC	G1R5H3	**866-220-2150**	418-643-2150	509
Museum of American Financial History 28 Broadway	New York	NY	10004	**877-983-4626**	212-908-4110	509
Museum of American Illustration 128 E 63rd St	New York	NY	10021	**800-746-8738**	212-838-2560	509
Museum of Beverage Containers & Advertising 1055 Ridgecrest Dr	Millersville	TN	37072	**800-826-4929**	615-859-5236	509
Museum of the Cherokee Indian PO Box 1599	Cherokee	NC	28719	**888-665-7249**	828-497-3481	509
Museum of Early Southern Decorative Arts 924 S Main St	Winston-Salem	NC	27101	**800-441-5305**	336-721-7360	509
Museum Facsimilies 117 4th St	Pittsfield	MA	01201	**800-499-0020**	413-499-0020	130
Museum of Fine Arts 220 State St	Springfield	MA	01103	**800-625-7738**	413-263-6800	509
Museum of Fine Arts 1001 Bissonnet St	Houston	TX	77005	**888-733-6324**	713-639-7300	509
Museum of Geology 501 E Saint Joseph St South Dakota School of Mines & Technology	Rapid City	SD	57701	**800-544-8162**	605-394-2467	509
Museum of Glass 1801 E Dock St	Tacoma	WA	98402	**866-468-7386**	253-284-4750	509
Museum of Making Music 5790 Armada Dr	Carlsbad	CA	92008	**877-551-9976**	760-438-5996	509
Museum of the Mountain Man 700 E Hennick St	Pinedale	WY	82941	**877-686-6266**	307-367-4101	509
Museum of Natural History & Science 1301 Western Ave Cincinnati Museum Ctr	Cincinnati	OH	45203	**800-733-2077**	513-287-7000	509
Museum of Nebraska History 131 Centennial Mall N	Lincoln	NE	68508	**800-833-6747**	402-471-4754	509
Museum of Northern Arizona 3101 N Fort Valley Rd	Flagstaff	AZ	86001	**800-423-1069**	928-774-5211	509
Museum of Science Science Pk	Boston	MA	02114	**866-770-4363**	617-589-0100	509
Museum of Science & Industry 4801 E Fowler Ave	Tampa	FL	33617	**800-995-6674**	813-987-6300	509
Museum of Science & Industry 5700 S Lake Shore Dr	Chicago	IL	60637	**800-468-6674**	773-684-1414	509
Musgrave Pencil Co Inc PO Box 290	Shelbyville	TN	37162	**800-736-2450**	931-684-3611	560
Music123 1 Cherry Hill Suite 800	Cherry Hill	NJ	08002	**888-590-9700**	856-779-6300	515
Music & Arts Centers Inc 4626 Wedgewood Blvd	Frederick	MD	21703	**800-237-7760**	301-620-4040	515
Music Assn. Country 1 Music Cir S	Nashville	TN	37203	**800-998-4636**	615-244-2840	48-4
Music Box Theatre 239 W 45th St	New York	NY	10036	**800-432-7250**	212-239-6200	732
Music City Record Distributors Inc 25 Lincoln St	Nashville	TN	37210	**800-467-1050**	615-255-7315	512
Music Education. MENC: National Assn for 1806 Robert Fulton Dr	Reston	VA	20191	**800-336-3768**	703-860-4000	49-5
Music Fraternity. Mu Phi Epsilon International 4705 N Sonora Ave Suite 114	Fresno	CA	93722	**888-259-1471**	559-227-1898	48-16
Music Industries Corp 625 Locust St *Orders	Garden City	NY	11530	**800-431-6699***	516-794-1888	516
Music Operators Assn. Amusement & 33 W Higgins Rd Suite 830	South Barrington	IL	60010	**800-937-2662**	847-428-7699	48-23
Music Products Assn. NAMM - International 5790 Armada Dr	Carlsbad	CA	92008	**800-767-6266**	760-438-8001	49-18
Music Teachers National Assn (MTNA) 441 Vine St Suite 505	Cincinnati	OH	45202	**888-512-5278**	513-421-1420	49-5
Music Telecom Inc 580 Howard Ave	Somerset	NJ	08873	**800-648-3647**	732-469-0880	496
Musica Obscura PO Box 1571	Longmont	CO	80502	**800-655-8563**	303-702-0482	514
Musical Artists. American Guild of 1430 Broadway 14th Fl	New York	NY	10018	**800-543-2462**	212-265-3687	48-4
Musical Heritage Society 1710 Hwy 35 *Cust Svc	Oakhurst	NJ	07755	**800-333-4647***	732-531-7000	94
Musician's Friend Inc PO Box 4370	Medford	OR	97501	**800-391-8762**	541-772-5173	515
Musicians of the US & Canada. American Federation of 1501 Broadway Suite 600	New York	NY	10036	**800-762-3444**	212-869-1330	405
Musiciansbuy.com Inc 11-7830 Byron Dr	West Palm Beach	FL	33404	**877-778-7845**	561-842-7451	515
Musicland Group Inc 10400 Yellow Circle Dr *Cust Svc	Minnetonka	MN	55343	**800-371-4425***	952-932-7700	514
Musicnotes Inc 8020 Excelsior Dr Suite 201	Madison	WI	53717	**800-944-4667**	608-662-1680	514
Musicorp PO Box 30819	Charleston	SC	29417	**800-845-1922**	843-763-9083	516
Musiker Discovery Programs Inc 1326 Old Northern Blvd	Roslyn	NY	11576	**888-878-6637**	516-621-3939	748
Muskegon Chronicle PO Box 59	Muskegon	MI	49443	**800-783-3161**	231-722-3161	522-2
Muskegon Community College 221 S Quarterline Rd	Muskegon	MI	49442	**866-711-4622**	231-773-9131	160
Muskegon County Convention & Visitors Bureau 610 W Western Ave	Muskegon	MI	49440	**800-250-9283**	231-724-3100	205
Muskingum College 163 Stormont St	New Concord	OH	43762	**800-752-6082**	740-826-8211	163
Muskogee Daily Phoenix PO Box 1968	Muskogee	OK	74402	**800-730-3649**	918-684-2828	522-2
Musson RC Rubber Co Inc 1320 E Archwood Ave *Cust Svc	Akron	OH	44306	**800-321-2381***	330-773-7651	663
Musson Theatrical Inc 890 Walsh Ave	Santa Clara	CA	95050	**800-843-2837**	408-986-0210	708
Mustang Dynamometer 2300 Pinnacle Pkwy	Twinsburg	OH	44087	**888-468-7826**	330-963-5400	464
Mustang Tractor & Equipment Co 12800 NW Fwy	Houston	TX	77040	**800-256-1001**	713-460-2000	353
Mutiny Hotel 2951 S Bayshore Dr	Miami	FL	33133	**888-868-8469**	305-441-2100	373
Mutual of America Life Insurance Co 320 Park Ave	New York	NY	10022	**800-468-3785**	212-224-1600	384-2
Mutual Benefit Assn. Armed Services PO Box 160384	Nashville	TN	37216	**800-251-8434**	615-851-0800	48-19
Mutual of Enumclaw Insurance Co 1460 Wells St	Enumclaw	WA	98022	**800-366-5551**	360-825-2591	384-4
Mutual Industries Inc 707 W Grange St	Philadelphia	PA	19120	**800-523-0888**	215-927-6000	730-3
Mutual Insurance Companies. National Assn of 3601 Vincennes Rd PO Box 875525	Indianapolis	IN	46268	**800-336-2642**	317-875-5250	49-9
Mutual Materials Co 605 119th Ave NE	Bellevue	WA	98005	**800-477-3008**	425-452-2300	148
Mutual of Omaha Cos Mutual of Omaha Plaza	Omaha	NE	68175	**800-775-6000**	402-342-7600	355-4
Mutual of Omaha Insurance Co Mutual of Omaha Plaza	Omaha	NE	68175	**800-775-6000**	402-342-7600	384-2
Mutual Protective Insurance Co 1515 S 75th St	Omaha	NE	68124	**800-228-6080**	402-391-6900	384-2
Mutual Savings Bank 4949 W Brown Deer Rd *Cust Svc	Milwaukee	WI	53223	**800-261-6888***	414-354-1500	71
Mutual Savings Life Insurance Co 2801 Hwy 31 S *Cust Svc	Decatur	AL	35603	**800-239-6754***	256-552-7011	384-2
Mutual Trust Life Insurance Co 1200 Jorie Blvd	Oak Brook	IL	60522	**800-323-7320**	630-990-1000	384-2
MutualFirst Financial Inc 110 E Charles St *NASDAQ: MFSF*	Muncie	IN	47305	**800-382-8031**	765-747-2800	355-2
Muvico Theaters 3101 N Federal Hwy 6th Fl	Ft Lauderdale	FL	33306	**800-294-6585**	954-564-6550	733
Muzak LLC 3318 Lakemont Blvd	Fort Mill	SC	29708	**800-331-3340**	803-396-3000	513
Muze Inc 304 Hudson St 8th Fl	New York	NY	10013	**800-935-4848**	212-824-0300	176-7
MVM Inc 1593 Spring Hill Rd Suite 700	Vienna	VA	22182	**800-727-1949**	703-790-3138	682
MVP Health Plan 625 State St	Schenectady	NY	12305	**800-777-4793**	518-370-4793	384-3
MVP Laboratories Inc 5510 Miller Ave	Ralston	NE	68127	**800-856-4648**	402-331-5106	574
MW Manufacturers Inc 433 N Main St	Rocky Mount	VA	24151	**888-999-8400**	540-483-0211	489
MWA Direct Inc 8600 109th Ave N Suite 100	Champlin	MN	55316	**800-967-9154**	763-576-4111	5
MWW Group 1 Meadowlands Plaza 6th Fl	East Rutherford	NJ	07073	**800-724-7602**	201-507-9500	622
MXL Industries Inc 1764 Rohrerstown Rd	Lancaster	PA	17601	**800-233-0159**	717-569-8711	593
My EMatch.com LLC PO Box 66535	Saint Pete Beach	FL	33736	**800-215-7560**	727-866-1583	224
My Favorite Muffin 500 Lake Cook Rd Suite 475	Deerfield	IL	60015	**800-251-6101**	847-948-7520	305
My Friend's Place 106 Hammond Dr	Atlanta	GA	30328	**800-882-9436**	404-843-2803	657
Myakka River State Park 13207 State Rd 72	Sarasota	FL	34241	**800-326-3521**	941-361-6511	554

Name	City	State	ZIP	Toll-Free	Phone	Class
Myasthenia Gravis Foundation of America (MGFA) 1821 University Ave W Suite S256	Saint Paul	MN	55104	**800-541-5454**	651-917-6256	48-17
myCFO Inc 1700 Seaport Blvd 4th Fl	Redwood City	CA	94063	**877-692-3609**	650-210-5000	396
Myers Container Corp 5801 Christie Ave Suite 255	Emeryville	CA	94608	**800-228-7269**	510-652-6847	197
Myers D & Sons Inc 4311 Erdman Ave	Baltimore	MD	21213	**800-367-7463**	410-522-7500	296
Myers University 112 Prospect Ave E	Cleveland	OH	44115	**877-366-9377**	216-696-9000	163
Myerson Ben Candy Co Inc 928 Towne Ave	Los Angeles	CA	90021	**800-421-8448**	213-623-6266	291-8
MyFamily.com Inc 360 W 4800 North	Provo	UT	84606	**800-262-3787**	801-705-7000	677
Mykrolis Corp 129 Concord Rd Bldg 2 *NYSE: MYK*	Billerica	MA	01821	**877-695-7654**	978-436-6500	685
Myles Lee Transmissions 140 Rt 17 N	Paramus	NJ	07652	**800-426-5114**	201-262-0555	62-6
MYOB US Inc 300 Roundhill Dr *Cust Svc	Rockaway	NJ	07866	**800-322-6962***	973-586-2200	176-1
Myogen Inc 7575 W 103rd Ave Suite 102 *NASDAQ: MYOG*	Westminster	CO	80021	**877-696-4361**	303-410-6666	86
MyPoints.com Inc 188 The Embarcadero 5th Fl	San Francisco	CA	94105	**888-262-4528**	415-615-1100	7
Myriad Genetics Inc 320 Wakara Way *NASDAQ: MYGN*	Salt Lake City	UT	84108	**800-469-7423**	801-582-3400	86
Myrmo & Sons Inc PO Box 3215	Eugene	OR	97403	**800-683-7040**	541-747-4561	446
Myron Corp 205 Maywood Ave	Maywood	NJ	07607	**800-526-9766**	201-843-6464	10
Myrtle Beach Area Chamber of Commerce 1200 N Oak St	Myrtle Beach	SC	29577	**800-356-3016**	843-626-7444	137
Myrtle Beach Area Convention Bureau 1200 N Oak St	Myrtle Beach	SC	29577	**800-356-3016**	843-626-7444	205
Myrtle Beach Convention Center 2101 N Oak St	Myrtle Beach	SC	29577	**800-537-1690**	843-918-1225	204
Myrtle Beach Reservation Service 1551 21st Ave N Suite 20	Myrtle Beach	SC	29577	**800-626-7477**	843-626-7477	368
Myrtle Beach Resort 5905 S Kings Hwy	Myrtle Beach	SC	29578	**888-627-3767**	843-238-1559	373
Mystery Guild Doubleday Direct Inc 1225 S Market St	Mechanicsburg	PA	17055	**800-688-4442**		94
Mystic Chamber of Commerce 14 Holmes St	Mystic	CT	06355	**866-572-9578**	860-572-9578	137
Mystic Color Lab Inc Masons Island Rd PO Box 144	Mystic	CT	06355	**800-367-6061**		577
Mystic Lake Casino 2400 Mystic Lake Blvd	Prior Lake	MN	55372	**800-262-7799**	952-445-9000	133
Mystic Sea Resort 2105 S Ocean Blvd	Myrtle Beach	SC	29577	**800-443-7050**	843-448-8446	655
Mystic Seaport Museum Inc 75 Greenmanville Ave PO Box 6000	Mystic	CT	06355	**888-973-2767**	860-572-0711	509
MyTravel Canada Inc 130 Merton St	Toronto	ON	M4S1A4	**800-668-1743**	416-485-1700	760
Myvesta.org Inc 6 Taft Ct Suite 200	Rockville	MD	20850	**800-698-3782**	301-762-5270	48-10
MZ Berger & Co Inc 33-00 Northern Blvd	Long Island City	NY	11101	**800-221-0131**		151

N

Name	City	State	ZIP	Toll-Free	Phone	Class
N-Viro International Corp 3450 W Central Ave Suite 328	Toledo	OH	43606	**800-666-8476**	419-535-6374	791
N Wasserstrom & Sons Inc 2300 Lockbourne Rd	Columbus	OH	43207	**800-444-4697**	614-228-5550	295
Na-Churs/Alpine Solutions 421 Leader St	Marion	OH	43302	**800-622-4877**	740-382-5701	276
NA Degerstrom Inc 3303 N Sullivan Rd	Spokane	WA	99216	**800-637-3773**	509-928-3333	492
Na Hoola Spa at Hyatt Regency Waikiki Resort 2424 Kalakaua Ave	Honolulu	HI	96815	**800-233-1234**	808-921-6097	698
NAA (National Aeronautic Assn) 1815 N Fort Myer Dr Suite 500	Arlington	VA	22209	**800-644-9777**	703-527-0226	48-22
NAA (National Auctioneers Assn) 8880 Ballentine St	Overland Park	KS	66214	**888-541-8084**	913-541-8084	49-18
NAACP (National Assn for the Advancement of Colored People) 4805 Mount Hope Dr	Baltimore	MD	21215	**877-622-2798**	410-358-8900	48-8
NAADAC - Assn for Addiction Professionals 901 N Washington St Suite 600	Alexandria	VA	22314	**800-548-0497**	703-741-7686	49-15
NAADAC PAC 901 N Washington St Suite 600	Alexandria	VA	22314	**800-548-0497**	703-741-7686	604
NAAG (National Assn of Attorneys General) 750 1st St NE Suite 1100	Washington	DC	20002	**888-245-6224**	202-326-6000	49-7
Nabi Biopharmaceuticals 5800 Pk of Commerce Blvd NW *NASDAQ: NABI*	Boca Raton	FL	33487	**800-635-1766**	561-989-5800	229
Nabors Drilling International Ltd 515 W Greens Rd Suite 1000	Houston	TX	77067	**877-622-6777**	281-874-0035	529
Nabors Drilling USA Inc 515 W Greens Rd Suite 1000	Houston	TX	77067	**888-622-6777**	281-874-0035	529
Nabors Industries Ltd 515 W Greens Rd Suite 1200 *AMEX: NBR*	Houston	TX	77067	**888-622-6777**	281-874-0035	529
NABT (National Assn of Biology Teachers) 12030 Sunrise Valley Dr Suite 110	Reston	VA	20191	**800-406-0775**	703-264-9696	49-5
NACA (National Assn for Campus Activities) 13 Harbison Way	Columbia	SC	29212	**800-845-2338**	803-732-6222	49-5
NACAC (National Assn for College Admission Counseling) 1631 Prince St	Alexandria	VA	22314	**800-822-6285**	703-836-2222	49-5
NACCC (National Assn of Congregational Christian Churches) 8473 S Howell Ave	Oak Creek	WI	53154	**800-262-1620**	414-764-1620	48-20
NACCO Industries Inc 5875 Landerbrook Dr Suite 300 *NYSE: NC*	Cleveland	OH	44124	**800-531-3964**	440-449-9600	184
NACCP (National Assn of Child Care Professionals) 7610 Hwy 71 W Suite E	Austin	TX	78735	**800-537-1118**	512-301-5557	48-6
NACCRRA (National Assn of Child Care Resource & Referral Agencies) 1319 F St NW Suite 500	Washington	DC	20004	**800-424-2246**	202-393-5501	48-6
NACDA (National Assn of Collegiate Directors of Athletics) 24651 Detroit Rd	Westlake	OH	44145	**800-996-2232**	440-892-4000	48-22
NACDS (National Assn of Chain Drug Stores) 413 N Lee St	Alexandria	VA	22314	**800-678-6223**	703-549-3001	49-18
NACDS PAC (National Assn of Chain Drug Stores PAC) 413 N Lee St	Alexandria	VA	22314	**800-678-6223**	703-549-3001	604
NACE (National Assn of Colleges & Employers) 62 Highland Ave	Bethlehem	PA	18017	**800-544-5272**	610-868-1421	49-5
NACHA - Electronic Payments Assn (NACHA) 13665 Dulles Technology Dr Suite 300	Herndon	VA	20171	**800-487-9180**	703-561-1100	49-2
Nachi America Inc 5022 W 79th St	Indianapolis	IN	46268	**888-340-2747**	317-334-9993	77
Nackard Beverage Inc 5660 E Pensdock Ave	Flagstaff	AZ	86004	**800-622-5273**	928-526-2229	82-3
NACM (National Assn for Court Management) National Ctr for State Courts 300 Newport Ave	Williamsburg	VA	23185	**800-616-6165**	757-259-1841	49-10
NACM (National Assn of Credit Management) 8840 Columbia 100 Pkwy	Columbia	MD	21045	**800-955-8815**	410-740-5560	49-2
Nacogdoches Convention & Visitors Bureau 200 E Main St	Nacogdoches	TX	75961	**888-653-3788**	936-564-7351	205
Nacogdoches Medical Center 4920 Stallings Dr	Nacogdoches	TX	75961	**800-539-2772**	936-569-9481	366-2
NACS (National Assn of College Stores) 500 E Lorain St	Oberlin	OH	44074	**800-622-7498**	440-775-7777	49-18
NACS (National Assn of Convenience Stores) 1600 Duke St *Cust Svc	Alexandria	VA	22314	**800-966-6227***	703-684-3600	49-18
NACST (National Assn of Catholic School Teachers) 1700 Sansom St Suite 903	Philadelphia	PA	19103	**800-996-2278**	215-665-0993	49-5
NACVA (National Assn of Certified Valuation Analysts) 1111 E Brickyard Rd Suite 200	Salt Lake City	UT	84106	**800-677-2009**	801-486-0600	49-12
NADA (National Automobile Dealers Assn) 8400 Westpark Dr	McLean	VA	22102	**800-252-6232**	703-821-7000	49-18
NADONA/LTC (National Assn of Directors of Nursing Administration in Long Term Care) 10101 Alliance Rd Suite 140	Cincinnati	OH	45242	**800-222-0539**	513-791-3679	49-8
NADSA (National Adult Day Services Assn) 8201 Greensboro Dr Suite 300	McLean	VA	22102	**800-424-9046**	703-610-9000	48-6
NAEA (National Assn of Enrolled Agents) 1120 Connecticut Ave NW Suite 460	Washington	DC	20036	**800-424-4339**	202-822-6232	49-10
NAED (National Assn of Electrical Distributors Inc) 1100 Corporate Sq Dr Suite 100	Saint Louis	MO	63132	**888-791-2512**	314-991-9000	49-18
NAEPC (National Assn of Estate Planners & Councils) 1120 Chester Ave Suite 470	Cleveland	OH	44114	**866-226-2224**		49-10
NAESP (National Assn of Elementary School Principals) 1615 Duke St	Alexandria	VA	22314	**800-386-2377**	703-684-3345	49-5
NAEYC (National Assn for the Education of Young Children) 1509 16th St NW	Washington	DC	20036	**800-424-2460**	202-232-8777	49-5
NAF (National Abortion Federation) 1755 Massachusetts Ave NW Suite 600	Washington	DC	20036	**800-772-9100**	202-667-5881	49-8
NAFC (National Assn for Continence) 62 Columbus St	Charleston	SC	29403	**800-252-3337**	843-377-0900	48-17
NAFCC (National Assn for Family Child Care) 5202 Pinemont Dr	Salt Lake City	UT	84123	**800-359-3817**	801-269-9338	48-6
NAFCO 3907 Aero Pl Suite 1	Lakeland	FL	33811	**800-999-3712**	863-644-8463	214
NAFCU (National Assn of Federal Credit Unions) 3138 10th St N	Arlington	VA	22201	**800-336-4644**	703-522-4770	49-2
NAFE (National Assn for Female Executives) 60 E 42nd St 27th Fl	New York	NY	10165	**800-927-6233**	212-351-6400	49-12
Nagelbush Mechanical Inc 5385 Nob Hill Rd	Sunrise	FL	33351	**800-354-3111**	954-748-7893	188-10
NAGWS (National Assn for Girls & Women in Sport) 1900 Association Dr	Reston	VA	20191	**800-213-7193**	703-476-3400	48-22
NAHA (National Assn for Holistic Aromatherapy) 3327 W Indian Trail Rd	Spokane	WA	99208	**888-275-6242**	509-325-3419	48-17
NAHB (National Assn of Home Builders) 1201 15th St NW	Washington	DC	20005	**800-368-5242**	202-266-8200	49-3
NAHB Research Center 400 Prince Georges Blvd	Upper Marlboro	MD	20774	**800-638-8556**	301-249-4000	654
NAHI (National Assn of Home Inspectors Inc) 4248 Park Glen Rd	Minneapolis	MN	55416	**800-448-3942**	952-928-4641	49-3
NAHJ (National Assn of Hispanic Journalists) 529 14th St NW National Press Bldg Suite 1000	Washington	DC	20045	**888-346-6245**	202-662-7145	49-14
NAHQ (National Assn for Healthcare Quality) 4700 W Lake Ave	Glenview	IL	60025	**800-966-9392**	847-375-4720	49-8
NAHRO (National Assn of Housing & Redevelopment Officials) 630 'I' St NW	Washington	DC	20001	**877-866-2476**	202-289-3500	49-7
Nai-Ni Chen Dance Co PO Box 1121	Fort Lee	NJ	07024	**800-650-0246**		563-1
NAIC (National Adoption Information Clearinghouse) 330 C St SW	Washington	DC	20447	**888-251-0075**	703-352-3488	336-6
NAIC (National Assn of Investors Corp) PO Box 220	Royal Oak	MI	48068	**877-275-6242**	248-583-6242	49-2

Entry	Toll-Free	Phone	Class
NAICS (North American Industry Classification System) US Census Bureau 4700 Silver Hill Rd .... Washington DC 20333	**888-756-2427**	301-763-4636	336-2
NAIFA (National Assn of Insurance & Financial Advisors) 2901 Telestar Ct .... Falls Church VA 22042	**877-866-2432***	703-770-8100	49-9
*Sales			
NAIHC (National American Indian Housing Council) 900 2nd St NE Suite 305 .... Washington DC 20002	**800-284-9165**	202-789-1754	49-7
Nail Manufacturers Council (NMC) 401 N Michigan Ave .... Chicago IL 60611	**800-868-4265**	312-245-1575	49-19
NAILM (National Assn of Institutional Linen Management) 2130 Lexington Rd Suite H .... Richmond KY 40475	**800-669-0863**	859-624-0177	49-4
Nailpro Magazine 7628 Densmore Ave .... Van Nuys CA 91406	**800-442-5667**	818-782-7328	449-21
NAIOP (National Assn of Industrial & Office Properties) 2201 Cooperative Way 3rd Fl .... Herndon VA 20171	**800-666-6780**	703-904-7100	49-17
Naismith Memorial Basketball Hall of Fame 1000 W Columbus Ave ..... Springfield MA 01105	**877-446-6752**	413-231-5490	511
Nakano Foods Inc 55 E Euclid Ave .... Mount Prospect IL 60056	**800-323-4358**	847-590-0059	291-41
Naked Juice Co 935 W 8th St .... Azusa CA 91702	**800-745-8423**	626-852-2500	291-20
Nakoma Group 16795 Von Karman Ave Suite 240 ...... Irvine CA 92606	**877-891-2811**	949-222-0244	176-1
Nalco Co 1601 W Diehl Rd .... Naperville IL 60563	**877-813-3523**	630-305-1000	143
NYSE: NLC			
Nalge Nunc International 75 Panorama Creek Dr .... Rochester NY 14625	**800-625-4327**	585-586-8800	411
NAM (National Assn of Manufacturers) 1331 Pennsylvania Ave NW Suite 600 .... Washington DC 20004	**800-814-8468**	202-637-3000	49-12
NAMA (National Agri-Marketing Assn) 11020 King St Suite 205 .... Overland Park KS 66210	**800-530-5646**	913-491-6500	49-18
Namco Controls Corp 6095 Parkland Blvd Suite 310 .... Mayfield Heights OH 44124	**800-626-8324***	440-460-1360	681
*Cust Svc			
NAMCP (National Assn of Managed Care Physicians) 4435 Waterfront Dr Suite 101 PO Box 4765 .... Glen Allen VA 23058	**800-722-0376**	804-527-1905	49-8
Name Maker Inc PO Box 43821 .... Atlanta GA 30336	**800-241-2890**		730-5
Names4ever.com 10350 Barnes Canyon Rd .... San Diego CA 92121	**877-275-8763***	858-410-6929	389
*Sales			
NameSecure LLC PO Box 27096 .... Concord CA 94527	**800-299-1288**	925-609-1111	389
NAMIC (National Assn of Mutual Insurance Companies) 3601 Vincennes Rd PO Box 875525 .... Indianapolis IN 46268	**800-336-2642**	317-875-5250	49-9
NAMM - International Music Products Assn 5790 Armada Dr .... Carlsbad CA 92008	**800-767-6266**	760-438-8001	49-18
NAMS (National Assn of Marine Surveyors Inc) PO Box 9306 ..... Chesapeake VA 23321	**800-822-6267**	757-638-9638	49-21
NAMS (North American Menopause Society) 5900 Landerbrook Dr Suite 195 .... Mayfield Heights OH 44124	**800-774-5342**	440-442-7550	49-8
Nancy's Pizzeria 8200 W 185th St Suite J .... Tinley Park IL 60477	**800-626-2977**	708-444-4411	657
NANN (National Assn of Neonatal Nurses) 4700 W Lake Ave .... Glenview IL 60025	**800-451-3795**	847-375-3660	49-8
Nanogen Inc 10398 Pacific Ctr Ct .... San Diego CA 92121	**877-626-6436**	858-410-4600	410
NASDAQ: NGEN			
Nanometrics Inc 1550 Buckeye Dr ..... Milpitas CA 95035	**800-955-6266**	408-435-9600	464
NASDAQ: NANO			
Nanophase Technologies Corp 1319 Marquette Dr .... Romeoville IL 60446	**877-653-8100**	630-771-6708	478
NASDAQ: NANX			
Nanotech Alert Newsletter 7550 W I-10 Suite 400 .... San Antonio TX 77229	**877-463-7678**	210-348-1000	521-12
Nantucket Electric Co 2 Fairgrounds Rd .... Nantucket MA 02554	**800-322-3223***	508-325-8000	774
*Cust Svc			
Nanz & Kraft Florists Inc 141 Breckenridge Ln .... Louisville KY 40207	**800-897-6551**	502-897-6551	287
NAO Inc 1284 E Sedgley Ave .... Philadelphia PA 19134	**800-523-3495***	215-743-5300	19
*Cust Svc			
NAON (National Assn of Orthopaedic Nurses) 401 N Michigan Ave Suite 2200 .... Chicago IL 60611	**800-289-6266**		49-8
NAP (National Assn of Parliamentarians) 213 S Main St .... Independence MO 64050	**888-627-2929**	816-833-3892	49-12
Napa River Inn 500 Main St .... Napa CA 94559	**877-251-8500**	707-251-8500	373
Napa Valley College 2277 Napa-Vallejo Hwy .... Napa CA 94558	**800-826-1077**	707-253-3005	160
Napa Valley Grill 2200 Powell St Suite 750 .... Emeryville CA 94608	**800-294-9323**	510-594-4262	657
Napa Valley Register PO Box 150 .... Napa CA 94559	**800-504-6397**	707-226-3711	522-2
NAPCO Inc 535 Napco Rd .... Sparta NC 28675	**800-854-8621**	336-372-5228	87
Napco Inc 125 McFann Rd .... Valencia PA 16059	**800-786-2726**	724-898-1511	688
NAPCO Security Systems Inc 333 Bayview Ave .... Amityville NY 11701	**800-645-9445**	631-842-9400	681
NASDAQ: NSSC			
NAPFA (National Assn of Personal Financial Advisors) 3250 N Arlington Suite 109 ... Arlington Heights IL 60004	**800-366-2732**	847-537-7722	49-2
Napili Kai Beach Club 5900 Honoapiilani Rd .... Lahaina HI 96761	**800-367-5030**	808-669-6271	655
NAPL (National Assn for Printing Leadership) 75 W Century Rd .... Paramus NJ 07652	**800-642-6275***	201-634-9600	49-16
*Cust Svc			
Naples Beach Hotel & Golf Club 851 Gulf Shore Blvd N .... Naples FL 34102	**800-237-7600**	239-261-2222	655
Naples Philharmonic Orchestra 5833 Pelican Bay Blvd Philharmonic Center for the Arts .... Naples FL 34108	**800-597-1900**	239-597-1900	563-3
Napoleon/Lynx 111 Weires Dr .... Archbold OH 43502	**800-338-5399**	419-445-1010	232
Napp Systems Inc 260 S Pacific St .... San Marcos CA 92078	**800-854-2860**	760-510-6277	770
NAPPS (National Assn of Professional Process Servers) PO Box 4547 ...... Portland OR 97208	**800-477-8211**	503-222-4180	49-10
NAPR (National Assn of Physician Recruiters) PO Box 150127 .... Altamonte Springs FL 32715	**800-726-5613**	407-774-7880	49-8
Napster LLC 9044 Melrose Ave ..... Los Angeles CA 90069	**800-839-4210**	310-281-5000	39
NARA (National Archives & Records Administration) 8601 Adelphi Rd .... College Park MD 20740	**866-272-6272**	301-837-0482	336-16
Narada Productions Inc 4650 N Port Washington Rd ...... Milwaukee WI 53212	**800-966-3699**	414-961-8350	643
Narco Avionics 270 Commerce Dr .... Fort Washington PA 19034	**800-223-3636***	215-643-2900	633
*Sales			
NARDA (North American Retail Dealers Assn) 10 E 22nd St Suite 310 ...... Lombard IL 60148	**800-621-0298**	630-953-8950	49-18
Nardini Fire Equipment Co Inc 405 County Rd 'E' W .... Saint Paul MN 55126	**888-627-3464**	651-483-6631	667
NAREIT (National Assn of Real Estate Investment Trusts) 1875 'I' St NW Suite 600 .... Washington DC 20006	**800-362-7348**	202-739-9400	49-17
NARI (National Assn of the Remodeling Industry) 780 Lee St Suite 200 .... Des Plaines IL 60016	**800-611-6274**	847-298-9200	49-3
NARIC (National Rehabilitation Information Center) 4200 Forbes Blvd Suite 202 .... Lanham MD 20706	**800-346-2742**	301-459-5900	48-17
NARMS (National Assn for Retail Marketing Services) PO Box 906 ...... Plover WI 54467	**888-526-2767**	715-342-0948	49-18
NARO (National Assn of Royalty Owners) PO Box 5779 .... Norman OK 73070	**800-558-0557**	405-573-2972	49-17
NARPM (National Assn of Residential Property Managers) 8317 Cross Pk Dr Suite 150 .... Austin TX 78754	**800-782-3452**	512-381-6091	49-17
Narragansett Electric Co 280 Melrose St .... Providence RI 02907	**800-322-3223***	401-784-7000	774
*Cust Svc			
Narrow Fabric Industries Inc 7th & W Reading Ave PO Box 6948 .... West Reading PA 19611	**800-523-8118**	610-376-2891	730-5
NARSA (National Automotive Radiator Service Assn) 15000 Commerce Pkwy Suite C .... Mount Laurel NJ 08054	**800-551-3232**	856-439-1575	49-21
NARTE (National Assn of Radio & Telecommunications Engineers) 167 Village St .... Medway MA 02053	**800-896-2783**	508-533-8333	49-19
NAS Recruitment Communications 1 Infinity Corporate Ctr Dr .... Cleveland OH 44125	**866-627-7327**	216-478-0300	4
NASA (National Aeronautics & Space Administration) 300 'E' St SW ... Washington DC 20546	**800-424-9183**	202-358-0000	336-16
NASA John F Kennedy Space Center Public Inquiries .... Kennedy Space Center FL 32899	**800-561-8618**	321-867-5000	654
NASA Tech Briefs 317 Madison Ave Suite 1900 .... New York NY 10017	**800-944-6272**	212-490-3999	449-19
NASAA (North American Securities Administrators Assn) 10 G St NE Suite 710 .... Washington DC 20002	**888-846-2722**	202-737-0900	49-2
NASB Financial Inc 12498 S 71st Hwy .... Grandview MO 64030	**800-677-6272**	816-765-2200	355-2
NASDAQ: NASB			
NASBA (National Assn of State Boards of Accountancy) 150 4th Ave N Suite 700 .... Nashville TN 37219	**800-272-3926**	615-880-4200	49-1
NASBE (National Assn of State Boards of Education) 277 S Washington St Suite 100 .... Alexandria VA 22314	**800-368-5023**	703-684-4000	49-5
NASCAR Winston Cup Illustrated Magazine 120 W Morehead St Suite 320 .... Charlotte NC 28202	**800-883-7323**	704-371-3966	449-3
NASCC (National Assn of Service & Conservation Corps) 666 11th St NW Suite 1000 .... Washington DC 20001	**800-666-2722**	202-737-6272	48-6
NASCO International Inc 901 Janesville Ave .... Fort Atkinson WI 53538	**800-558-9595***	920-563-2446	451
*Orders			
NASD (National Assn of Securities Dealers Inc) 1735 K St NW ..... Washington DC 20006	**800-289-9999**	202-728-8000	49-2
Nasdaq Stock Market Inc 9600 Blackwell Rd .... Rockville MD 20850	**877-536-2737**	301-978-8008	680
Nasdaq Trader 9513 Key West Ave .... Rockville MD 20850	**800-777-5606**		396
NASFM (National Assn of State Fire Marshals) PO Box 4137 .... Clifton Park NY 12065	**877-996-2736**	518-371-0018	49-7
NASFT (National Assn for the Specialty Food Trade Inc) 120 Wall St 27th Fl .... New York NY 10005	**800-627-3869**	212-482-6440	49-6
Nash County Visitors Bureau PO Box 392 .... Rocky Mount NC 27802	**800-849-6825**	252-972-5080	205
Nash Elmo Industries 9 Trefoil Dr ..... Trumbull CT 06611	**800-553-6274**	203-459-3900	170
Nash Mfg Inc 315 W Ripy St .... Fort Worth TX 76110	**800-433-2901**	817-926-5223	701
Nash Produce Co 6160 S North Carolina 58 .... Nashville NC 27856	**800-334-3032**	252-443-6011	11-11
Nashua Corp 11 Trafalgar Sq 2nd Fl ..... Nashua NH 03063	**800-258-1370**	603-880-2323	542-1
NYSE: NSH			
Nashua Corp Label Products Div 3838 S 108th St .... Omaha NE 68144	**800-533-8806**	402-397-3600	404
Nashville Chamber of Commerce 211 Commerce St Suite 100 .... Nashville TN 37201	**800-657-6910**	615-743-3000	137
Nashville Convention & Visitors Bureau 211 Commerce St Suite 100 .... Nashville TN 37201	**800-657-6910**	615-259-4700	205

Listing	City	State	ZIP	Toll-Free	Phone	Class
Nashville Jet 110 Tune Airport Dr	Nashville	TN	37209	**800-824-4778**	615-350-8400	14
Nashville State Community College 120 White Bridge Rd	Nashville	TN	37209	**800-272-7363**	615-353-3333	787
Nashville Wire Products Mfg Co 199 Polk Ave	Nashville	TN	37210	**888-743-2595**	615-743-2500	75
NASN (National Assn of School Nurses) PO Box 1300	Scarborough	ME	04070	**877-627-6476**	207-883-2117	49-8
NASO (National Assn of Sports Officials) 2017 Lathrop Ave	Racine	WI	53405	**800-733-6100**	262-632-5448	48-22
NASS (National Agricultural Statistics Service) 1400 Independence Ave SW Rm 4117	Washington	DC	20250	**800-727-9540**	202-720-2707	336-1
Nassau Inn The 10 Palmer Square	Princeton	NJ	08542	**800-862-7728**	609-921-7500	373
Nassau World Wide Movers Inc 63 Lamar St	West Babylon	NY	11704	**800-327-9343**	631-420-8340	508
Nastasi & Assoc Inc 147 Herricks Rd	Garden City Park	NY	11040	**800-353-0990**	516-746-1800	188-9
Nastech Pharmaceutical Co Inc 3450 Monte Villa Pkwy *NASDAQ: NSTK*	Bothell	WA	98021	**888-627-2579**	425-908-3600	86
NASW (National Assn of Social Workers) 750 1st St NE Suite 700	Washington	DC	20002	**800-638-8799**	202-408-8600	49-7
NASW News 750 1st St NE Suite 700	Washington	DC	20002	**800-638-8799**	202-408-8600	449-16
NAT-COM Inc 2622 Audubon Rd	Audubon	PA	19403	**800-486-7947**	610-666-7947	187-1
NATA (National Air Transportation Assn) 4226 King St	Alexandria	VA	22302	**800-808-6282**	703-845-9000	49-21
NATA (National Athletic Trainers Assn) 2952 Stemmons Fwy Suite 200	Dallas	TX	75247	**800-879-6282**	214-637-6282	48-22
NATCA (National Air Traffic Controllers Assn) 1325 Massachusetts Ave NW	Washington	DC	20005	**800-266-0895**	202-628-5451	405
Natchez Convention Center 211 Main St	Natchez	MS	39120	**888-475-9744**	601-442-5881	204
Natchez Convention & Visitors Bureau 640 S Canal St Box C	Natchez	MS	39120	**800-647-6724**	601-446-6345	205
Natchez Democrat PO Box 1447	Natchez	MS	39121	**888-878-9101**	601-442-9101	522-2
Natchez Newspapers Inc 503 N Canal St	Natchez	MS	39120	**888-878-9101**	601-442-9101	623-8
Natchez Trace Parkway 2680 Natchez Trace Pkwy	Tupelo	MS	38804	**800-305-7417**	662-680-4025	554
NATE (National Assn of Tower Erectors) 8 2nd St SE	Watertown	SD	57201	**888-882-5865**	605-882-5865	49-3
Natexis Bleichroeder Inc 1345 Ave of the Americas	New York	NY	10105	**800-435-0336**	212-698-3000	679
Nathan Adelson Hospice 4141 S Swenson St	Las Vegas	NV	89119	**888-281-8646**	702-733-0320	365
Nathan's Famous Inc 1400 Old Country Rd Suite 400 *NASDAQ: NATH*	Westbury	NY	11590	**800-628-4267**	516-338-8500	657
Nation Magazine 33 Irving Pl 8th Fl *Cust Svc	New York	NY	10003	**800-333-8536***	212-209-5400	449-17
National Abortion Federation (NAF) 1755 Massachusetts Ave NW Suite 600	Washington	DC	20036	**800-772-9100**	202-667-5881	49-8
National Academy Press 2101 Constitution Ave NW PO Box 285	Washington	DC	20055	**800-624-6242**	202-334-3313	623-2
National Academy of Public Administration 1100 New York Ave NW Suite 1090 E	Washington	DC	20005	**800-883-3190**	202-347-3190	49-7
National Academy of Recording Arts & Sciences 3402 Pico Blvd	Santa Monica	CA	90405	**800-423-2017**	310-392-3777	48-4
National Academy of Sciences (NAS) 500 5th St NW	Washington	DC	20001	**800-624-6242**	202-334-2138	49-19
National Action Financial Services Inc 3587 Parkway Ln	Norcross	GA	30092	**800-452-2411**	770-248-9909	157
National Administration Co DBA eGroupManager 1819 Clarkson Rd Suite 301	Chesterfield	MO	63017	**800-992-8044**	636-530-7700	47
National Adoption Center 1500 Walnut St Suite 701	Philadelphia	PA	19102	**800-862-3678**	215-735-9988	48-6
National Adoption Information Clearinghouse (NAIC) 330 C St SW	Washington	DC	20447	**888-251-0075**	703-352-3488	336-6
National Adult Day Services Assn (NADSA) 8201 Greensboro Dr Suite 300	McLean	VA	22102	**800-424-9046**	703-610-9000	48-6
National Aeronautic Assn (NAA) 1815 N Fort Myer Dr Suite 500	Arlington	VA	22209	**800-644-9777**	703-527-0226	48-22
National Aeronautics & Space Administration (NASA) 300 'E' St SW	Washington	DC	20546	**800-424-9183**	202-358-0000	336-16
National Afro-American Museum & Cultural Center 1350 Brush Row Rd PO Box 578	Wilberforce	OH	45384	**800-752-2603**	937-376-4944	509
National Agri-Marketing Assn (NAMA) 11020 King St Suite 205	Overland Park	KS	66210	**800-530-5646**	913-491-6500	49-18
National Agricultural Statistics Service (NASS) 1400 Independence Ave SW Rm 4117	Washington	DC	20250	**800-727-9540**	202-720-2707	336-1
National AIDS Hotline	Washington	DC	20201	**800-342-2437**		336-6
National Air Ambulance 3495 SW 9th Ave	Fort Lauderdale	FL	33315	**800-525-0166**	954-359-9400	31
National Air Traffic Controllers Assn (NATCA) 1325 Massachusetts Ave NW	Washington	DC	20005	**800-266-0895**	202-628-5451	405
National Air Transportation Assn (NATA) 4226 King St	Alexandria	VA	22302	**800-808-6282**	703-845-9000	49-21
National Alliance of Blind Students Inc 1155 15th St NW Suite 1004	Washington	DC	20005	**800-424-8666**	202-467-5081	48-11
National Alliance for the Mentally Ill (NAMI) 2107 Wilson Blvd Suite 300	Arlington	VA	22201	**800-950-6264**	703-524-7600	48-17
National Alliance for Youth Sports 2050 Vista Pkwy	West Palm Beach	FL	33411	**800-729-2057**	561-684-1141	48-22
National American Indian Housing Council (NAIHC) 900 2nd St NE Suite 305	Washington	DC	20002	**800-284-9165**	202-789-1754	49-7
National American University 321 Kansas City St	Rapid City	SD	57701	**800-843-8892**	605-394-4800	163
Albuquerque Campus 4775 Indian School Rd NE Suite 200	Albuquerque	NM	87110	**800-843-8892**	505-265-7517	163
Roseville Campus 1550 W Hwy 36	Roseville	MN	55113	**800-843-8892**	651-644-1265	163
Sioux Falls Campus 2801 S Kiwanis Ave Suite 100	Sioux Falls	SD	57105	**800-388-5430**	605-334-5430	163
National Anti-Vivisection Society (NAVS) 53 W Jackson Blvd Suite 1552	Chicago	IL	60604	**800-888-6287**	312-427-6065	48-3
National Arbitration & Mediation 1010 Northern Blvd Suite 336	Great Neck	NY	11021	**877-373-8853**	516-829-4343	41
National Arbor Day Foundation 211 N 12th St	Lincoln	NE	68508	**888-448-7337**	402-474-5655	48-13
National Archives & Records Administration (NARA) 8601 Adelphi Rd	College Park	MD	20740	**866-272-6272**	301-837-0482	336-16
Archival Research Catalog 8601 Adelphi Rd	College Park	MD	20740	**866-272-6272**		336-16
National Artcraft Supply Co 7996 Darrow Rd *Orders	Twinsburg	OH	44087	**800-526-7419***	330-963-6011	43
National Assn for the Advancement of Colored People (NAACP) 4805 Mount Hope Dr	Baltimore	MD	21215	**877-622-2798**	410-358-8900	48-8
National Assn of Attorneys General (NAAG) 750 1st St NE Suite 1100	Washington	DC	20002	**888-245-6224**	202-326-6000	49-7
National Assn of Biology Teachers (NABT) 12030 Sunrise Valley Dr Suite 110	Reston	VA	20191	**800-406-0775**	703-264-9696	49-5
National Assn for Campus Activities (NACA) 13 Harbison Way	Columbia	SC	29212	**800-845-2338**	803-732-6222	49-5
National Assn of Catholic School Teachers (NACST) 1700 Sansom St Suite 903	Philadelphia	PA	19103	**800-996-2278**	215-665-0993	49-5
National Assn of Certified Natural Health Professionals 714 E Winona Ave	Warsaw	IN	46580	**800-321-1005**		48-17
National Assn of Certified Valuation Analysts (NACVA) 1111 E Brickyard Rd Suite 200	Salt Lake City	UT	84106	**800-677-2009**	801-486-0600	49-12
National Assn of Chain Drug Stores (NACDS) 413 N Lee St	Alexandria	VA	22314	**800-678-6223**	703-549-3001	49-18
National Assn of Chain Drug Stores PAC (NACDS PAC) 413 N Lee St	Alexandria	VA	22314	**800-678-6223**	703-549-3001	604
National Assn of Child Care Professionals (NACCP) 7610 Hwy 71 W Suite E	Austin	TX	78735	**800-537-1118**	512-301-5557	48-6
National Assn of Child Care Resource & Referral Agencies (NACCRRA) 1319 F St NW Suite 500	Washington	DC	20004	**800-424-2246**	202-393-5501	48-6
National Assn for College Admission Counseling (NACAC) 1631 Prince St	Alexandria	VA	22314	**800-822-6285**	703-836-2222	49-5
National Assn of College Stores (NACS) 500 E Lorain St	Oberlin	OH	44074	**800-622-7498**	440-775-7777	49-18
National Assn of Colleges & Employers (NACE) 62 Highland Ave	Bethlehem	PA	18017	**800-544-5272**	610-868-1421	49-5
National Assn of Collegiate Directors of Athletics (NACDA) 24651 Detroit Rd	Westlake	OH	44145	**800-996-2232**	440-892-4000	48-22
National Assn of Congregational Christian Churches (NACCC) 8473 S Howell Ave	Oak Creek	WI	53154	**800-262-1620**	414-764-1620	48-20
National Assn for Continence (NAFC) 62 Columbus St	Charleston	SC	29403	**800-252-3337**	843-377-0900	48-17
National Assn of Convenience Stores (NACS) 1600 Duke St *Cust Svc	Alexandria	VA	22314	**800-966-6227***	703-684-3600	49-18
National Assn for Court Management (NACM) National Ctr for State Courts 300 Newport Ave	Williamsburg	VA	23185	**800-616-6165**	757-259-1841	49-10
National Assn of Credit Management (NACM) 8840 Columbia 100 Pkwy	Columbia	MD	21045	**800-955-8815**	410-740-5560	49-2
National Assn of Dental Laboratories (NADL) 325 John Knox Rd Suite L-103	Tallahassee	FL	32303	**800-950-1150**	850-205-5626	49-8
National Assn of Directors of Nursing Administration in Long Term Care (NADONA/LTC) 10101 Alliance Rd Suite 140	Cincinnati	OH	45242	**800-222-0539**	513-791-3679	49-8
National Assn for the Education of Young Children (NAEYC) 1509 16th St NW	Washington	DC	20036	**800-424-2460**	202-232-8777	49-5
National Assn of Electrical Distributors Inc (NAED) 1100 Corporate Sq Dr Suite 100	Saint Louis	MO	63132	**888-791-2512**	314-991-9000	49-18
National Assn of Elementary School Principals (NAESP) 1615 Duke St	Alexandria	VA	22314	**800-386-2377**	703-684-3345	49-5
National Assn of Enrolled Agents (NAEA) 1120 Connecticut Ave NW Suite 460	Washington	DC	20036	**800-424-4339**	202-822-6232	49-10
National Assn of Estate Planners & Councils (NAEPC) 1120 Chester Ave Suite 470	Cleveland	OH	44114	**866-226-2224**		49-10
National Assn for the Exchange of Industrial Resources (NAEIR) 560 McClure St	Galesburg	IL	61401	**800-562-0955**	309-343-0704	48-5
National Assn for Family Child Care (NAFCC) 5202 Pinemont Dr	Salt Lake City	UT	84123	**800-359-3817**	801-269-9338	48-6

Listing	City	State	ZIP	Toll-Free	Phone	Class
National Assn of Federal Credit Unions (NAFCU) 3138 10th St N	Arlington	VA	22201	**800-336-4644**	703-522-4770	49-2
National Assn for Female Executives (NAFE) 60 E 42nd St 27th Fl	New York	NY	10165	**800-927-6233**	212-351-6400	49-12
National Assn of Free Will Baptists (NAFWB) 5233 Mt View Rd	Antioch	TN	37013	**877-767-7659**	615-731-6812	48-20
National Assn for Girls & Women in Sport (NAGWS) 1900 Association Dr	Reston	VA	20191	**800-213-7193**	703-476-3400	48-22
National Assn for Healthcare Quality (NAHQ) 4700 W Lake Ave	Glenview	IL	60025	**800-966-9392**	847-375-4720	49-8
National Assn of Hispanic Journalists (NAHJ) 529 14th St NW National Press Bldg Suite 1000	Washington	DC	20045	**888-346-6245**	202-662-7145	49-14
National Assn for Holistic Aromatherapy (NAHA) 3327 W Indian Trail Rd	Spokane	WA	99208	**888-275-6242**	509-325-3419	48-17
National Assn of Home Builders (NAHB) 1201 15th St NW	Washington	DC	20005	**800-368-5242**	202-266-8200	49-3
National Assn of Home Builders Research Center 400 Prince Georges Blvd	Upper Marlboro	MD	20774	**800-638-8556**	301-249-4000	654
National Assn of Home Inspectors Inc (NAHI) 4248 Park Glen Rd	Minneapolis	MN	55416	**800-448-3942**	952-928-4641	49-3
National Assn of Housing & Redevelopment Officials (NAHRO) 630 'I' St NW	Washington	DC	20001	**877-866-2476**	202-289-3500	49-7
National Assn of Industrial & Office Properties (NAIOP) 2201 Cooperative Way 3rd Fl	Herndon	VA	20171	**800-666-6780**	703-904-7100	49-17
National Assn of Institutional Linen Management (NAILM) 2130 Lexington Rd Suite H	Richmond	KY	40475	**800-669-0863**	859-624-0177	49-4
National Assn of Insurance & Financial Advisors (NAIFA) 2901 Telestar Ct	Falls Church	VA	22042	**877-866-2432***	703-770-8100	49-9
*Sales						
National Assn of Insurance Women (International) 1847 E 15th St	Tulsa	OK	74104	**800-766-6249**	918-744-5195	49-9
National Assn of Investors Corp (NAIC) PO Box 220	Royal Oak	MI	48068	**877-275-6242**	248-583-6242	49-2
National Assn of Managed Care Physicians (NAMCP) 4435 Waterfront Dr Suite 101 PO Box 4765	Glen Allen	VA	23058	**800-722-0376**	804-527-1905	49-8
National Assn of Manufacturers (NAM) 1331 Pennsylvania Ave NW Suite 600	Washington	DC	20004	**800-814-8468**	202-637-3000	49-12
National Assn of Marine Surveyors Inc (NAMS) PO Box 9306	Chesapeake	VA	23321	**800-822-6267**	757-638-9638	49-21
National Assn of Master Appraisers 303 W Cypress St	San Antonio	TX	78212	**800-229-6262**	210-271-0781	49-17
National Assn of Minority Contractors 666 11th St NW Suite 520	Washington	DC	20001	**866-688-6262**	202-347-8259	49-3
National Assn of Mutual Insurance Companies (NAMIC) 3601 Vincennes Rd PO Box 875525	Indianapolis	IN	46268	**800-336-2642**	317-875-5250	49-9
National Assn of Neonatal Nurses (NANN) 4700 W Lake Ave	Glenview	IL	60025	**800-451-3795**	847-375-3660	49-8
National Assn for Olmsted Parks 733 15th St NW Suite 700	Washington	DC	20005	**866-666-6905**	202-783-6606	48-13
National Assn of Orthopaedic Nurses (NAON) 401 N Michigan Ave Suite 2200	Chicago	IL	60611	**800-289-6266**		49-8
National Assn for Parents of Children with Visual Impairments (NAPVI) PO Box 317	Watertown	MA	02471	**800-562-6265**	617-972-7441	48-17
National Assn of Parliamentarians (NAP) 213 S Main St	Independence	MO	64050	**888-627-2929**	816-833-3892	49-12
National Assn of Personal Financial Advisors (NAPFA) 3250 N Arlington Suite 109	Arlington Heights	IL	60004	**800-366-2732**	847-537-7722	49-2
National Assn of Physician Recruiters (NAPR) PO Box 150127	Altamonte Springs	FL	32715	**800-726-5613**	407-774-7880	49-8
National Assn of Pizzeria Operators 908 S 8th St Suite 200	Louisville	KY	40203	**800-489-8324**	502-736-9500	49-6
National Assn of Police Athletic Leagues (PAL) 618 US Hwy 1 Suite 201	North Palm Beach	FL	33408	**800-725-7743**	561-844-1823	48-22
National Assn for Printing Leadership (NAPL) 75 W Century Rd	Paramus	NJ	07652	**800-642-6275***	201-634-9600	49-16
*Cust Svc						
National Assn of Professional Insurance Agents (PIA) 400 N Washington St	Alexandria	VA	22314	**800-742-6900**	703-836-9340	49-9
National Assn of Professional Process Servers (NAPPS) PO Box 4547	Portland	OR	97208	**800-477-8211**	503-222-4180	49-10
National Assn of Radio & Telecommunications Engineers (NARTE) 167 Village St	Medway	MA	02053	**800-896-2783**	508-533-8333	49-19
National Assn of Real Estate Investment Trusts (NAREIT) 1875 'I' St NW Suite 600	Washington	DC	20006	**800-362-7348**	202-739-9400	49-17
National Assn of REALTORS 430 N Michigan Ave	Chicago	IL	60611	**800-874-6500**	312-329-8200	49-17
National Assn of the Remodeling Industry (NARI) 780 Lee St Suite 200	Des Plaines	IL	60016	**800-611-6274**	847-298-9200	49-3
National Assn of Residential Property Managers (NARPM) 8317 Cross Pk Dr Suite 150	Austin	TX	78754	**800-782-3452**	512-381-6091	49-17
National Assn for Retail Marketing Services (NARMS) PO Box 906	Plover	WI	54467	**888-526-2767**	715-342-0948	49-18
National Assn of Retired Federal Employees 606 N Washington St	Alexandria	VA	22314	**800-627-3394**	703-838-7760	604
National Assn of Royalty Owners (NARO) PO Box 5779	Norman	OK	73070	**800-558-0557**	405-573-2972	49-17
National Assn of School Nurses (NASN) PO Box 1300	Scarborough	ME	04070	**877-627-6476**	207-883-2117	49-8
National Assn of Securities Dealers Inc (NASD) 1735 K St NW	Washington	DC	20006	**800-289-9999**	202-728-8000	49-2
National Assn for the Self-Employed (NASE) PO Box 612067 DFW Airport	Dallas	TX	75261	**800-232-6273**		49-12
National Assn of Service & Conservation Corps (NASCC) 666 11th St NW Suite 1000	Washington	DC	20001	**800-666-2722**	202-737-6272	48-6
National Assn of Social Workers (NASW) 750 1st St NE Suite 700	Washington	DC	20002	**800-638-8799**	202-408-8600	49-7
National Assn for the Specialty Food Trade Inc (NASFT) 120 Wall St 27th Fl	New York	NY	10005	**800-627-3869**	212-482-6440	49-6
National Assn of Sports Officials (NASO) 2017 Lathrop Ave	Racine	WI	53405	**800-733-6100**	262-632-5448	48-22
National Assn of State Boards of Accountancy (NASBA) 150 4th Ave N Suite 700	Nashville	TN	37219	**800-272-3926**	615-880-4200	49-1
National Assn of State Boards of Education (NASBE) 277 S Washington St Suite 100	Alexandria	VA	22314	**800-368-5023**	703-684-4000	49-5
National Assn of State Fire Marshals (NASFM) PO Box 4137	Clifton Park	NY	12065	**877-996-2736**	518-371-0018	49-7
National Assn of Tax Professionals (NATP) 720 Association Dr	Appleton	WI	54914	**800-558-3402**	920-749-1040	49-1
National Assn of Tower Erectors (NATE) 8 2nd St SE	Watertown	SD	57201	**888-882-5865**	605-882-5865	49-3
National Assn of Town Watch (NATW) 1 E Wynnewood Rd Suite 102	Wynnewood	PA	19096	**800-648-3688**	610-649-7055	48-7
National Assn of Underwater Instructors (NAUI) 1232 Tech Blvd	Tampa	FL	33619	**800-553-6284**	813-628-6284	48-22
National Assn for Uniformed Services (NAUS) 5535 Hempstead Way	Springfield	VA	22151	**800-842-3451**	703-750-1342	48-19
National Assn of Vascular Access Networks (NAVAN) 11441 S State St Suite A113	Draper	UT	84020	**888-576-2826**	801-576-1824	49-8
National Assn of Women Business Owners (NAWBO) 8405 Greensboro Dr Suite 800	McLean	VA	22102	**800-556-2926**	703-506-3268	49-12
National Assn of Women in Construction (NAWIC) 327 S Adams St	Fort Worth	TX	76104	**800-552-3506**	817-877-5551	49-3
National Athletic Trainers Assn (NATA) 2952 Stemmons Fwy Suite 200	Dallas	TX	75247	**800-879-6282**	214-637-6282	48-22
National Atlas of America 508 National Ctr 12201 Sunrise Valley Dr	Reston	VA	20192	**888-275-8747**		336-9
National Auctioneers Assn (NAA) 8880 Ballentine St	Overland Park	KS	66214	**888-541-8084**	913-541-8084	49-18
National Automated Clearing House Assn 13665 Dulles Technology Dr Suite 300	Herndon	VA	20171	**800-487-9180**	703-561-1100	49-2
National Automatic Sprinkler Industries 8000 Corporate Dr	Landover	MD	20785	**800-638-2603**	301-577-1700	188-13
National Automobile Dealers Assn (NADA) 8400 Westpark Dr	McLean	VA	22102	**800-252-6232**	703-821-7000	49-18
National Automotive Radiator Service Assn (NARSA) 15000 Commerce Pkwy Suite C	Mount Laurel	NJ	08054	**800-551-3232**	856-439-1575	49-21
National Bank of South Carolina 1 Broad St	Sumter	SC	29150	**800-708-5687**	803-778-8259	71
National Bankcard Systems 2600 Via Fortuna Suite 240	Austin	TX	78749	**800-823-6835**	512-494-9200	254
National Banner Co 11938 Harry Hines Blvd	Dallas	TX	75234	**800-527-0860**	972-241-2131	282
National Baptist Convention USA Inc 1700 Baptist World Ctr Dr	Nashville	TN	37207	**866-531-3054**	615-228-6292	48-20
National Bar Assn (NBA) 1225 11th St NW	Washington	DC	20001	**800-621-2988**	202-842-3900	49-10
National Baseball Hall of Fame & Museum 25 Main St	Cooperstown	NY	13326	**888-425-5633**	607-547-7200	511
National Bedding Co 61 Leona Dr	Middleboro	MA	02346	**800-343-1006**	508-946-4700	463
National Bedding Co Div Serta Inc 1500 Lee Lane	Beloit	WI	53511	**800-767-6267**	608-365-6266	463
National Beef Packing Co Inc PO Box 20046	Kansas City	MO	64195	**800-449-2333**		465
National Beer Wholesalers Assn (NBWA) 1101 King St Suite 600	Alexandria	VA	22314	**800-300-6417**	703-683-4300	49-6
National Benefit Life Insurance Co 333 W 34th St 10th Fl	New York	NY	10001	**800-222-2062**	212-615-7500	384-2
National Beverage Corp 1 N University Dr	Plantation	FL	33324	**888-462-2349**	954-581-0922	81-2
AMEX: FIZ						
National Book Festival Library of Congress 101 Independence Ave SE	Washington	DC	20540	**888-714-4696**		277
National Border Patrol Museum 4315 Transmountain Rd	El Paso	TX	79924	**877-276-8738**	915-759-6060	509
National Braille Press Inc 88 Saint Stephens St	Boston	MA	02115	**888-965-8965**	617-266-6160	623-2
National Breast Cancer Coalition (NBCC) 1101 17th St NW Suite 1300	Washington	DC	20036	**800-622-2838**	202-296-7477	48-17
National Business Assn (NBA) 5151 Beltline Rd Suite 1150	Dallas	TX	75254	**800-456-0440**	972-458-0900	49-12
National Business Forms Inc 100 Pennsylvania Ave	Greeneville	TN	37743	**800-722-8544***	423-638-7691	111
*Cust Svc						
National Business Furniture Inc PO Box 514052	Milwaukee	WI	53203	**800-558-1010***	414-276-8511	315
*Sales						
National Business Services 1601 Magoffin Ave	El Paso	TX	79901	**800-777-7807***	915-544-1271	314-1
*Sales						
National Businesswomen's Leadership Assn PO Box 419107	Kansas City	MO	64141	**800-258-7246**	913-432-7755	753

Name / Address	City	State	ZIP	Toll-Free	Phone	Class
National Cable Television Cooperative Inc (NCTC) 11200 Corporate Ave	Lenexa	KS	66219	**800-825-0357**	913-599-5900	49-14
National Cancer Institute (NCI) 6116 Executive Blvd MSC 8322	Bethesda	MD	20892	**800-422-6237**	301-435-3848	654
National Car Rental 6929 N Lakewood Ave Suite 100	Tulsa	OK	74117	**800-227-7368**	918-401-6000	126
National Caregiving Foundation 801 N Pitt St Suite 116	Alexandria	VA	22314	**800-930-1357**	703-299-9300	48-6
National Carriers Inc PO Box 1358	Liberal	KS	67905	**800-835-9180**	620-624-1621	769
National Catholic Reporter Publishing Co 115 E Armour Blvd	Kansas City	MO	64111	**800-333-7373**	816-531-0538	623-9
National Caves Assn PO Box 280	Park City	KY	42160	**866-552-2837**	270-749-2228	48-23
National Center for Assault Prevention (NCAP) 606 Delsea Dr	Sewell	NJ	08080	**800-258-3189**	856-582-7000	48-17
National Center for Complementary & Alternative Medicine (NCCAM) National Institutes of Health 31 Center Dr Bldg 31	Bethesda	MD	20892	**888-644-6226**	301-435-5042	336-6
National Center of Continuing Education 1100 Lakeway Dr Suite 200 PO Box 342588	Lakeway	TX	78734	**800-824-1254**	512-261-1937	787
National Center for Employee Development 2801 E State Hwy 9	Norman	OK	73071	**866-278-4434**	405-447-9100	370
National Center for Environmental Health 4770 Buford Hwy Bldg 101	Chamblee	GA	30341	**888-232-6789**	770-488-7000	336-6
National Center for Family Literacy (NCFL) 325 W Main St Suite 300	Louisville	KY	40202	**877-326-5481**	502-584-1133	48-11
National Center for Genome Resources 2935 Rodeo Pk Dr E	Santa Fe	NM	87505	**800-450-4854**	505-982-7840	654
National Center for Homeopathy (NCH) 801 N Fairfax St Suite 306	Alexandria	VA	22314	**877-624-0613**	703-548-7790	48-17
National Center for Infectious Diseases Travelers' Health Centers for Disease Control & Prevention 1600 Clifton Rd NE	Atlanta	GA	30333	**877-394-8747**		336-6
National Center for Juvenile Justice (NCJJ) 3700 S Water St Suite 200	Pittsburgh	PA	15203	**800-577-6903**	412-227-6950	48-8
National Center for Manufacturing Sciences (NCMS) 3025 Boardwalk	Ann Arbor	MI	48108	**800-222-6267**	734-995-0300	654
National Center for Missing & Exploited Children (NCMEC) 699 Prince St	Alexandria	VA	22314	**800-843-5678**	703-274-3900	48-6
National Center for Retirement Benefits Inc 666 Dundee Rd Suite 1200	Northbrook	IL	60062	**800-666-1000**	847-564-1111	192
National Center for State Courts (NCSC) 300 Newport Ave	Williamsburg	VA	23185	**800-616-6164**	757-253-2000	49-7
National Center for Stuttering (NCS) 200 E 33rd St	New York	NY	10016	**800-221-2483**	212-532-1460	48-17
National Center for Toxicological Research 3900 NCTR Rd	Jefferson	AR	72079	**800-638-3321**	870-543-7000	336-6
National Center for Victims of Crime (NCVC) 2000 M St NW Suite 480	Washington	DC	20036	**800-394-2255**	202-467-8700	48-8
National Center on Women & Aging Brandeis University Heller Graduate School MS 035	Waltham	MA	02454	**800-929-1995**	781-736-3866	48-6
National Chemicals Inc PO Box 32 *Cust Svc	Winona	MN	55987	**800-533-0027***	507-454-5640	149
National Child Abuse Hotline 15757 N 78th St	Scottsdale	AZ	85260	**800-422-4453**	480-922-8212	48-6
National Child Care Assn (NCCA) 1016 Rosser St	Conyers	GA	30012	**800-543-7161**	770-922-8198	48-6
National Child Care Information Center (NCCIC) 243 Church St NW 2nd Fl	Vienna	VA	22180	**800-616-2242**		336-6
National Child Safety Council (NCSC) 4065 Page Ave	Jackson	MI	49204	**800-327-5107**	517-764-6070	48-6
National Children's Cancer Society (NCCS) 1015 Locust St Suite 600	Saint Louis	MO	63101	**800-532-6459**	314-241-1600	48-17
National Church Furnishings Co 2600 Commercial Blvd	Centralia	WA	98531	**800-225-4599**	360-736-9323	314-3
National Cigar Corp PO Box 97	Frankfort	IN	46041	**800-321-0247**	765-659-3326	741-2
National City Bank 1900 E 9th St	Cleveland	OH	44114	**888-622-4932**	216-575-2000	71
National City Bank of Kentucky 101 S 5th St	Louisville	KY	40202	**800-727-8686**	502-581-4200	71
National City Bank of Michigan/Illinois 2595 Waukegan Rd *Cust Svc	Bannockburn	IL	60015	**800-925-9259***	847-317-2350	71
National City Chamber of Commerce 901 National City Blvd	National City	CA	91950	**800-292-4624**	619-477-9339	137
National City Corp 1900 E 9th St *NYSE: NCC*	Cleveland	OH	44114	**800-622-8100**	216-575-2000	355-2
National City Mortgage Co 3232 Newmark Dr *Cust Svc	Miamisburg	OH	45342	**800-253-7313***	937-297-3600	498
National Clearinghouse for Alcohol & Drug Information PO Box 2345	Rockville	MD	20847	**800-729-6686**	301-468-2600	336-6
National Clearinghouse on Child Abuse & Neglect Information 330 C St SW	Washington	DC	20447	**800-394-3366**	703-385-7565	336-6
National Cleveland-Style Polka Hall of Fame 605 E 22nd St	Euclid	OH	44123	**866-667-6552**	216-261-3263	509
National Club Assn (NCA) 1201 15th St NW Suite 450	Washington	DC	20005	**800-625-6221**	202-822-9822	48-23
National Coalition to Abolish the Death Penalty (NCADP) 920 Pennsylvania Ave SE	Washington	DC	20003	**888-286-2237**	202-543-9577	48-8
National College of Business & Technology 1813 E Main St	Salem	VA	24153	**800-664-1886**	540-986-1800	158
Bluefield 100 Logan St	Bluefield	VA	24605	**800-664-1886**	276-326-3621	158
Pikeville 288 S Mayo Trail Suite 2	Pikeville	KY	41501	**800-664-1886**	606-432-5477	158
Roanoke Valley 1813 E Main St	Salem	VA	24153	**800-664-1886**	540-986-1800	158
National Committee for Employer Support of the Guard & Reserve (ESGR) 1555 Wilson Blvd Suite 200	Arlington	VA	22209	**800-336-4590**	703-696-1386	48-19
National Committee to Preserve Social Security & Medicare (NCPSSM) 10 G St NE Suite 600	Washington	DC	20002	**800-966-1935**	202-216-0420	48-7
National Committee for Quality Assurance (NCQA) 2000 L St NW Suite 500	Washington	DC	20036	**800-236-5903**	202-955-3500	48-10
National Community Pharmacists Assn (NCPA) 100 Daingerfield Rd	Alexandria	VA	22314	**800-544-7447**	703-683-8200	49-8
National Confectioners Assn (NCA) 8320 Old Courthouse Rd Suite 300	Vienna	VA	22182	**800-433-1200**	703-790-5750	49-6
National Confectioners Assn PAC 8320 Old Courthouse Rd Suite 300	Vienna	VA	22182	**800-433-1200**	703-790-5750	604
National Conference for Community & Justice (NCCJ) 475 Park Ave S 19th Fl	New York	NY	10016	**800-352-6225**	212-545-1300	48-8
National Conference of States on Building Codes & Standards (NCSBCS) 505 Huntmar Park Dr Suite 210	Herndon	VA	20170	**800-362-2633**	703-437-0100	49-7
National Congress of Parents & Teachers 541 N Fairbanks Ct Suite 1300	Chicago	IL	60611	**800-307-4782**	312-670-6782	48-11
National Constitution Center 525 Arch St Independence Mall	Philadelphia	PA	19106	**866-917-1787**	215-409-6600	509
National Construction Rentals Inc 15319 Chatsworth St	Mission Hills	CA	91345	**800-874-6285**	818-221-6000	261-2
National Consumers League (NCL) 1701 K St NW Suite 1200	Washington	DC	20006	**800-876-7060**	202-835-3323	48-10
National Contract Management Assn (NCMA) 8260 Greensboro Dr Suite 200	McLean	VA	22102	**800-344-8096**	571-382-0082	49-12
National Corvette Museum 350 Corvette Dr	Bowling Green	KY	42101	**800-538-3883**	270-781-7973	509
National Cotton Council of America 1918 North Pkwy	Memphis	TN	38112	**800-377-9030**	901-274-9030	49-18
National Council for Adoption (NCFA) 225 N Washington St	Alexandria	VA	22314	**866-212-3678**	703-299-6633	48-6
National Council on the Aging (NCOA) 300 D St SW Suite 801	Washington	DC	20024	**800-424-9046**	202-479-1200	48-6
National Council on Alcoholism & Drug Dependence (NCADD) 20 Exchange Pl Suite 2902	New York	NY	10005	**800-622-2255**	212-269-7797	48-17
National Council on Compensation Insurance 901 Peninsula Corporate Cir *Cust Svc	Boca Raton	FL	33487	**800-622-4123***	561-893-1000	383
National Council on Economic Education (NCEE) 1140 6th Ave 2nd Fl	New York	NY	10036	**800-338-1192**	212-730-7007	49-5
National Council of Examiners for Engineering & Surveying (NCEES) 280 Seneca Creek Rd	Clemson	SC	29631	**800-250-3196**	864-654-6824	49-3
National Council of Exchangors (NCE) 630 Quintana Rd Suite 150	Morro Bay	CA	93442	**800-324-1031**		49-17
National Council on Family Relations (NCFR) 3989 Central Ave NE Suite 550	Minneapolis	MN	55421	**888-781-9331**	763-781-9331	48-6
National Council of Jewish Women (NCJW) 53 W 23rd St 6th Fl	New York	NY	10010	**800-829-6259**	212-645-4048	48-24
National Council on Problem Gambling Inc 208 G St NE 1st Fl	Washington	DC	20002	**800-522-4700**	202-547-9204	49-8
National Council on Radiation Protection & Measurements (NCRP) 7910 Woodmont Ave Suite 400	Bethesda	MD	20814	**800-229-2652**	301-657-2652	49-19
National Council of La Raza (NCLR) 1111 19th St NW Suite 1000	Washington	DC	20036	**800-311-6257**	202-785-1670	48-14
National Council for the Social Studies (NCSS) 8555 16th St Suite 500	Silver Spring	MD	20910	**800-296-7840**	301-588-1800	49-5
National Council of Teachers of English (NCTE) 1111 W Kenyon Rd	Urbana	IL	61801	**800-369-6283**	217-328-3870	49-5
National Council of Teachers of Mathematics (NCTM) 1906 Association Dr *Orders	Reston	VA	20191	**800-235-7566***	703-620-9840	49-5
National Court Appointed Special Advocate Assn (CASA) 100 W Harrison St North Tower Suite 500	Seattle	WA	98119	**800-628-3233**	206-270-0072	48-6
National Court Reporters Assn (NCRA) 8224 Old Courthouse Rd	Vienna	VA	22182	**800-272-6272**	703-556-6272	49-10
National Court Reporters Assn PAC 8224 Old Courthouse Rd	Vienna	VA	22182	**800-272-6272**	703-556-6272	604
National Cowgirl Museum & Hall of Fame 1720 Gendy St	Fort Worth	TX	76107	**800-476-3263**	817-336-4475	509
National CPA Health Care Advisors Assn (HCAA) 10831 Old Mill Rd Suite 400	Omaha	NE	68154	**888-475-4476**	402-778-7922	49-1
National Craft Assn (NCA) 2012 Ridge Rd E Suite 120	Rochester	NY	14622	**800-715-9594**	585-266-5472	48-18
National Credit Union Administration 1775 Duke St *Fraud Hotline	Alexandria	VA	22314	**800-827-9650***	703-518-6300	336-16
National Criminal Justice Reference Service PO Box 6000	Rockville	MD	20849	**800-851-3420**	301-519-5500	336-10
National Crop Insurance Services (NCIS) 7201 W 129th St Suite 200	Overland Park	KS	66213	**800-951-6247**	913-685-2767	48-2
National Cycle Inc 2200 Maywood Dr	Maywood	IL	60153	**877-972-7336**	708-343-0400	506
National Dart Assn (NDA) 5613 W 74th St	Indianapolis	IN	46278	**800-808-9884**	317-387-1299	48-22
National Data Access Corp 2 Office Park Ct Suite 103	Columbia	SC	29223	**800-528-8790**	803-699-6130	621

Name / Address	City	State	ZIP	Toll-Free	Phone	Class
National Diagnostics Inc 305 Patton Dr	Atlanta	GA	30336	**800-526-3867**	404-699-2121	229
National Diecasting Machinery & Kard Trim Presses 33 Plan Way Bldg 7	Warwick	RI	02886	**800-242-1253**	401-737-3005	448
National Disaster Medical System 500 C Street SW Suite 713	Washington	DC	20472	**800-872-6967**		336-7
National Discount Cruise Co 1401 N Cedar Crest Blvd Suite 56	Allentown	PA	18104	**800-788-8108**	610-439-4883	760
National Disease Research Interchange (NDRI) 1628 John F Kennedy Blvd 8 Penn Ctr 8th Fl	Philadelphia	PA	19103	**800-222-6374**	215-557-7361	265
National Dissemination Center for Children with Disabilities 1825 Connecticut Ave	Washington	DC	20009	**800-695-0285**	202-884-8200	48-17
National Distributing Co Inc 1 National Dr SW	Atlanta	GA	30336	**800-282-3548**	404-696-9440	82-3
National Diversity Newspaper Job Bank c/o Morris Communications PO Box 936	Augusta	GA	30903	**800-622-6358**		257
National Do Not Call Registry	Washington	DC	20580	**888-382-1222**		336-16
National Dog Registry (NDR) PO Box 116	Woodstock	NY	12498	**800-637-3647**	845-679-2355	48-3
National Domestic Violence Hotline (NDVH) PO Box 161810	Austin	TX	78716	**800-799-7233**	512-794-1133	48-6
National Down Syndrome Congress (NDSC) 1370 Center Dr Suite 102	Atlanta	GA	30338	**800-232-6372**	770-604-9500	48-17
National Down Syndrome Society (NDSS) 666 Broadway 8th Fl	New York	NY	10012	**800-221-4602**	212-460-9330	48-17
National Eating Disorders Assn 603 Stewart St Suite 803	Seattle	WA	98101	**800-931-2237**	206-382-3587	48-17
National Electrical Carbon Products Inc 251 Forrester Dr	Greenville	SC	29607	**800-543-6322**	864-458-7700	127
National Electronic Distributors Assn (NEDA) 1111 Alderman Dr Suite 400	Alpharetta	GA	30005	**800-347-6332**	678-393-9990	49-18
National Electronics Service Dealers Assn (NESDA) 3608 Pershing Ave	Fort Worth	TX	76107	**800-946-0201**	817-921-9061	49-18
National Emblem Inc 17036 S Avalon Blvd	Carson	CA	90746	**800-877-6185**	310-515-5055	256
National Employee Assistance Services Inc N 17 W 24100 Riverwood Dr Suite 300	Waukesha	WI	53188	**800-634-6433**	262-798-3900	454
National Endowment for the Humanities (NEH) 1100 Pennsylvania Ave NW	Washington	DC	20506	**800-634-1121**	202-606-8400	336-16
National Energy & Gas Transmission 7600 Wisconsin Ave	Bethesda	MD	20814	**888-874-3677**	301-280-6800	774
National Energy Research Scientific Computing Center (NERSC) Lawrence Berkeley National Laboratory 1 Cyclotron Rd MS 50C3396	Berkeley	CA	94720	**800-847-6070**	510-486-5849	654
National Energy Technology Laboratory (NETL) US Dept of Energy 3610 Collins Ferry Rd PO Box 880	Morgantown	WV	26507	**800-432-8330**	304-285-4764	654
National Engineering Service Corp 72 Mirona Rd	Portsmouth	NH	03801	**800-562-3463**	603-431-9740	707
National Engraving Co 248 Oxmoor Ct	Birmingham	AL	35209	**800-633-8613**	205-942-2809	770
National Envelope Corp 29-10 Hunters Pt Ave	Long Island City	NY	11101	**800-877-9551**	718-786-0300	260
National Examiner Magazine 1000 American Media Way	Boca Raton	FL	33467	**800-749-7733**	561-997-7733	449-11
National Exchange Club 3050 W Central Ave	Toledo	OH	43606	**800-924-2643**	419-535-3232	48-15
National Family Caregivers Assn (NFCA) 10400 Connecticut Ave Suite 500	Kensington	MD	20895	**800-896-3650**	301-942-6430	48-6
National Family Farm Coalition (NFFC) 110 Maryland Ave NE Suite 307	Washington	DC	20002	**800-639-3276**	202-543-5675	48-2
National Farmers Organization (NFO) 528 Billy Sunday Rd Suite 100	Ames	IA	50010	**800-247-2110**	515-292-2000	48-2
National Farmers Union 11900 E Cornell Ave	Aurora	CO	80014	**800-347-1961**	303-337-5500	48-2
National Farmers Union News 11900 E Cornell Ave	Aurora	CO	80014	**800-347-1961**	303-337-5500	521-13
National Farmers Union Property & Casualty Co 11900 E Cornell Ave	Aurora	CO	80014	**800-669-0622**	303-337-5500	384-4
National Federation of Community Broadcasters (NFCB) 970 Broadway Suite 1000	Oakland	CA	94612	**888-280-6322**	510-451-8200	49-14
National Federation of Community Development Credit Unions (NFCDCU) 120 Wall St 10th Fl	New York	NY	10005	**800-437-8711**	212-809-1850	49-2
National Federation of Independent Business (NFIB) 1201 F St NW Suite 200	Washington	DC	20004	**800-552-6342**	202-554-9000	49-12
National Federation of Independent Business SAFE Trust 1201 F St NW Suite 200	Washington	DC	20004	**800-552-6342**	202-554-9000	604
National Federation of State High School Assns (NFHS) PO Box 690 *Cust Svc	Indianapolis	IN	46206	**800-776-3462***	317-972-6900	48-22
National FFA Organization 6060 FFA Dr	Indianapolis	IN	46268	**800-772-0939**	317-802-6060	48-2
National Fiber Technology LLC 300 Canal St	Lawrence	MA	01840	**800-842-2751**	978-686-2964	342
National Fibromyalgia Partnership Inc (NFP) 140 Zinn Way PO Box 160	Linden	VA	22642	**866-725-4404**		48-17
National Film Board of Canada PO Box 6100 Station Centre-Ville	Montreal	QC	H3C3H5	**800-267-7710**	514-283-9000	502
National Filter Media Corp 691 N 400 West	Salt Lake City	UT	84103	**800-777-4248**	801-363-6736	19
National Fire Protection Assn (NFPA) 1 Batterymarch Pk	Quincy	MA	02169	**800-344-3555**	617-770-3000	48-17
National Flange & Fitting Co 4420 Creekmont Dr	Houston	TX	77091	**800-231-1424**	713-688-2515	474
National Flood Insurance Program 500 C St SW	Washington	DC	20472	**800-427-4661**	202-646-2500	336-7
National Flood Services Inc 451 Hungerford Dr Suite 408	Rockville	MD	20850	**800-251-6274**	301-251-1880	455
National Football League Players Assn (NFLPA) 2021 L St NW Suite 600	Washington	DC	20036	**800-372-2000**	202-463-2200	48-22
National Forest Foundation Fort Missoula Rd Bldg 27 Suite 3	Missoula	MT	59804	**866-733-4633**	406-542-2805	48-13
National Foster Parent Assn (NFPA) 7512 Stanich Ave Suite 6	Gig Harbor	WA	98335	**800-557-5238**	253-853-4000	48-6
National Foundation for Cancer Research (NFCR) 4600 East West Hwy Suite 525	Bethesda	MD	20814	**800-321-2873**	301-654-1250	654
National Foundation for Credit Counseling (NFCC) 801 Roeder Rd Suite 900	Silver Spring	MD	20910	**800-388-2227**	301-589-5600	48-10
National Foundation of Dentistry for the Handicapped (NFDH) 1800 15th St Unit 100	Denver	CO	80202	**888-471-6334**	303-534-5360	48-17
National Frame Builders Assn (NFBA) 4840 Bob Billings Pkwy Suite 1000	Lawrence	KS	66049	**800-557-6957**	785-843-2444	49-3
National Fraternity of Kappa Delta Rho 331 S Main St	Greensburg	PA	15601	**800-536-5371**	724-838-7100	48-16
National Fraud Information Center (NFIC) 1701 K St NW Suite 1200	Washington	DC	20006	**800-876-7060**	202-835-3323	48-10
National Freight Inc 71 W Park Ave	Vineland	NJ	08360	**800-922-5088**	856-691-7000	440
National Fresh Water Fishing Hall of Fame 10360 Hall of Fame Dr	Hayward	WI	54843	**866-268-4333**	715-634-4440	511
National Fruit Product Co Inc PO Box 2040	Winchester	VA	22604	**800-551-5167**	540-662-3401	310-3
National Fuel Gas Co 6363 Main St *NYSE: NFG* ■ *Cust Svc	Williamsville	NY	14221	**800-365-3234***	716-857-7000	355-5
National Fuel Gas Distribution Corp 6363 Main St	Williamsville	NY	14221	**800-365-3234**	716-857-7000	774
National Fuel Gas Supply Corp 6363 Main St *Cust Svc	Williamsville	NY	14221	**800-365-3234***	716-857-7000	774
National Fuel Resources Inc 165 Lawrence Bell Dr Suite 120	Williamsville	NY	14221	**800-839-9993**	716-630-6786	774
National Funeral Directors Assn (NFDA) 13625 Bishop's Dr	Brookfield	WI	53005	**800-228-6332**	262-789-1880	49-4
National Funeral Directors & Morticians Assn (NFDMA) 3951 Snapfinger Pkwy Suite 570	Decatur	GA	30035	**800-434-0958**	404-286-6680	49-4
National Futures Assn (NFA) 200 W Madison St	Chicago	IL	60606	**800-366-6321**	312-781-1300	49-2
National Garden Clubs Inc (NGC) 4401 Magnolia Ave Suite 1600	Saint Louis	MO	63110	**800-550-6007**	314-776-7574	48-18
National Gardening Assn (NGA) 1100 Dorset St	South Burlington	VT	05403	**800-538-7476**	802-863-5251	48-18
National Gaucher Foundation (NGF) 5410 Edson Ln Suite 260	Rockville	MD	20852	**800-428-2437**	301-816-1515	48-17
National Genealogical Society (NGS) 3108 Columbia Pike Suite 300	Arlington	VA	22204	**800-473-0060**	703-525-0050	48-18
National General Insurance Co 1 GMAC Plaza	Saint Louis	MO	63045	**800-847-6442**	314-493-8000	384-4
National Geographic Adventure Magazine 1145 17th St NW	Washington	DC	20036	**800-647-5463**	202-857-7000	449-11
National Geographic Magazine 1145 17th St NW	Washington	DC	20036	**800-647-5463**	202-857-7000	449-11
National Geographic Society 1145 17th St NW *Orders	Washington	DC	20036	**800-647-5463***	202-857-7000	49-19
National Geographic Society Explorers Hall 1145 17th St NW	Washington	DC	20036	**800-647-5463**	202-857-7589	509
National Geographic Traveler Magazine 1145 17th St NW	Washington	DC	20036	**800-647-5463**	202-857-7000	449-22
National Geographic World Magazine 1145 17th St NW	Washington	DC	20036	**800-647-5463**	202-857-7000	449-6
National Glass Assn (NGA) 8200 Greensboro Dr Suite 302	McLean	VA	22102	**866-342-5642**	703-442-4890	49-13
National Golf Course Owners Assn (NGCOA) 291 Seven Farms Dr 2nd Fl	Charleston	SC	29492	**800-933-4262**	843-881-9956	48-23
National Golf Foundation (NGF) 1150 S US Hwy 1 Suite 401	Jupiter	FL	33477	**800-733-6006**	561-744-6006	48-22
National Grain & Feed Assn (NGFA) 1250 I St NW Suite 1003	Washington	DC	20005	**800-680-9223**	202-289-0873	48-2
National Grange 1616 H St NW	Washington	DC	20006	**888-447-2643**	202-628-3507	48-2
National Grange Mutual Insurance Co 55 West St	Keene	NH	03431	**800-258-5310**	603-352-4000	384-4
National Greenhouse Co 6 Industrial Dr	Pana	IL	62557	**800-826-9314**	217-562-9333	106
National Grid USA 25 Research Dr	Westborough	MA	01582	**888-424-2113**	508-389-2000	355-5
National Ground Water Assn (NGWA) 601 Dempsey Rd	Westerville	OH	43081	**800-551-7379**	614-898-7791	48-12
National Ground Water Assn PAC 601 Dempsey Rd	Westerville	OH	43081	**800-551-7379**	614-898-7791	604
National Guard Assn of the US (NGAUS) 1 Massachusetts Ave NW Suite 200	Washington	DC	20001	**888-226-4287**	202-789-0031	48-19
National Guard Products Inc 4985 E Raines Rd	Memphis	TN	38118	**800-647-7874**	901-795-6900	232
National Guard of the US. Enlisted Assn of the 3133 Mt Vernon Ave	Alexandria	VA	22305	**800-234-3264**	703-519-3846	48-19
National Guardian Life Insurance Co PO Box 1191	Madison	WI	53701	**800-548-2962**	608-257-5611	384-2
National Gypsum Co 2001 Rexford Rd	Charlotte	NC	28211	**800-628-4662**	704-365-7300	341
National Hansen's Disease Programs (NHDP) 1770 Physicians Park Dr	Baton Rouge	LA	70816	**800-642-2477**	225-756-3773	654

Name / Address	City	State	ZIP	Toll-Free	Phone	Class
National Hardwood Lumber Assn (NHLA) 6830 Raleigh-LaGrange Rd	Memphis	TN	38134	**800-933-0318**	901-377-1818	49-3
National Headache Foundation (NHF) 820 N Orleans St Suite 217	Chicago	IL	60610	**888-643-5552**		48-17
National Health Care Affiliates Inc 651 Delaware Ave	Buffalo	NY	14202	**800-999-6422**	716-881-4425	358
National Health Club Assn 640 Plaza Dr Suite 300	Highlands Ranch	CO	80129	**800-765-6422**	303-753-6422	48-22
National Health Council (NHC) 1730 M St NW Suite 500	Washington	DC	20036	**800-684-6814**	202-785-3910	48-17
National Health Information Center (NHIC) PO Box 1133	Washington	DC	20013	**800-336-4797**	301-565-4167	336-6
National Health Insurance Co PO Box 619999	Dallas	TX	75261	**800-237-1900**	817-640-1900	384-2
National Hemophilia Foundation (NHF) 116 W 32nd St 11th Fl	New York	NY	10001	**800-424-2634**	212-328-3700	48-17
National Heritage Academies 3850 Broadmoor Ave SE Suite 201	Grand Rapids	MI	49512	**800-699-9235**	616-222-1700	241
National Herpes Resource Center (HRC) PO Box 13827	Research Triangle Park	NC	27709	**800-227-8922**	919-361-8488	48-17
National Highway Institute 4600 N Fairfax Dr	Arlington	VA	22203	**877-558-6873**	703-235-0500	336-13
National Highway Traffic Safety Administration (NHTSA)						
Auto Safety Hotline	Washington	DC	20590	**888-327-4236**		336-13
National Center for Statistics & Analysis 400 7th St SW Rm 6125	Washington	DC	20590	**800-934-8517**	202-366-1503	336-13
National Hockey League Players Assn (NHLPA) 777 Bay St Suite 2400	Toronto	ON	M5G2C8	**800-363-4625**	416-408-4040	48-22
National Home Centers Inc 1106 N Old Missouri Rd	Springdale	AR	72765	**800-540-0529**	479-756-1700	359
National Home Equity Mortgage Assn (NHEMA) 1301 Pennsylvania Ave NW Suite 500	Washington	DC	20004	**800-342-1121**	202-347-1210	49-2
National Home Furnishings Assn (NHFA) 3010 Tinsley Dr Suite 101	High Point	NC	27265	**800-888-9590**	336-886-6100	49-4
National Home Infusion Assn (NHIA) 205 Daingerfield Rd	Alexandria	VA	22314	**800-544-7447**	703-549-3740	49-8
National Honor Society (NHS) 1904 Association Dr	Reston	VA	20191	**800-253-7746**	703-860-0200	48-11
National Hopeline Network 2001 N Beauregard St 12th Fl	Alexandria	VA	22311	**800-784-2433**	703-684-7722	48-17
National Hospice & Palliative Care Organization (NHPCO) 1700 Diagonal Rd Suite 625 *Help Line	Alexandria	VA	22314	**800-658-8898***	703-837-1500	49-8
National Hotel 1677 Collins Ave	Miami Beach	FL	33139	**800-327-8370**	305-532-2311	373
National HPV & Cervical Cancer Prevention Resource Center PO Box 13827	Research Triangle Park	NC	27709	**800-277-8922**	919-361-8400	48-17
National Hunger Clearinghouse 505 8th Ave Suite 2100	New York	NY	10018	**800-453-2648**	212-629-8850	48-5
National Imagery & Mapping Agency 4600 Sangamore Rd	Bethesda	MD	20816	**800-455-0899**	301-227-3785	336-3
National Immunization Program 1600 Clifton Rd NE MS E05	Atlanta	GA	30333	**800-232-2522**	404-639-8200	336-6
National Independent Automobile Dealers Assn (NIADA) 2521 Brown Blvd	Arlington	TX	76006	**800-682-3837**	817-640-3838	49-18
National Independent Flag Dealers Assn (NIFDA) 214 N Hale St	Wheaton	IL	60187	**877-544-3524**	630-510-4500	49-18
National Indian Gaming Assn (NIGA) 224 2nd St SE	Washington	DC	20003	**800-286-6442**	202-546-7711	48-23
National Industries for the Blind (NIB) 1901 N Beauregard St Suite 200 *Cust Svc	Alexandria	VA	22311	**800-433-2304***	703-998-0770	48-17
National Inhalant Prevention Coalition (NIPC) 2904 Kerbey Ln	Austin	TX	78703	**800-269-4237**	512-480-8953	48-17
National Institute of Corrections 1860 Industrial Cir Suite A	Longmont	CO	80501	**800-877-1461**	303-682-0213	336-10
National Institute of Governmental Purchasing (NIGP) 151 Spring St Suite 300	Herndon	VA	20170	**800-367-6447**	703-736-8900	49-7
National Institute of Neurological Disorders & Stroke (NINDS) 31 Center Dr Bldg 31 Rm 8A52	Bethesda	MD	20892	**800-352-9424**	301-496-9746	336-6
National Institute for Occupational Safety & Health 200 Independence Ave SW	Washington	DC	20201	**800-356-4674**	202-401-6997	336-6
National Institute for Rehabilitation Engineering (NIRE) PO Box T	Hewitt	NJ	07421	**800-736-2216**	973-853-6585	48-17
National Institutes of Health (NIH) Osteoporosis & Related Bone Diseases - National Resource Center 1232 22nd St NW	Washington	DC	20037	**800-624-2663**	202-223-0344	336-6
National Instrument Co Inc 4119 Fordleigh Rd	Baltimore	MD	21215	**800-526-1301**	410-764-0900	537
National Instruments Corp 11500 N Mopac Expy *NASDAQ: NATI* ■ *Cust Svc	Austin	TX	78759	**800-433-3488***	512-794-0100	176-5
National Insulation Assn (NIA) 99 Canal Center Plaza Suite 222	Alexandria	VA	22314	**877-968-7642**	703-683-6422	49-3
National Insurance Crime Bureau (NICB) 10330 S Roberts Rd	Palos Hills	IL	60465	**800-447-6282**	708-430-2430	49-9
National InterBank PO Box 1245	Indianapolis	IN	46206	**877-468-7265**		71
National Interfaith Coalition on Aging (NICA) 300 D St SW	Washington	DC	20024	**800-424-9046**	202-479-1200	48-6
National International Roofing Corp 11317 Smith Dr	Huntley	IL	60142	**800-221-7663**	847-669-3444	188-12
National Interstate Corp 3250 Interstate Dr *NASDAQ: NATL*	Richfield	OH	44286	**800-929-1500**	330-659-8900	384-4
National Inventors Hall of Fame 221 S Broadway St Inventure Place	Akron	OH	44308	**800-968-4332**	330-762-4463	509
National Jets Air Center 3495 SW 9th Ave	Fort Lauderdale	FL	33315	**800-525-0166**	954-359-9400	63
National Jeweler Magazine 770 Broadway	New York	NY	10003	**800-250-2430**	646-654-4500	449-21
National Jewish Medical & Research Center 1400 Jackson St	Denver	CO	80206	**800-222-5864**	303-388-4461	654
National Journal 600 New Hampshire Ave NW	Washington	DC	20037	**800-356-4838**	202-266-7230	449-17
National Journal Group Inc 600 New Hampshire Ave NW 4th Fl	Washington	DC	20037	**800-207-8001**	202-739-8400	623-9
National Jousting Hall of Fame 94 Natural Chimneys Ln	Mount Solon	VA	22843	**888-430-2267**	540-350-2510	511
National Jurist Magazine PO Box 939039	San Diego	CA	92913	**800-465-3462**	858-503-7572	449-15
National Kidney Foundation (NKF) 30 E 33rd St Suite 1100	New York	NY	10016	**800-622-9010**	212-889-2210	48-17
National Kitchen & Bath Assn (NKBA) 687 Willow Grove St	Hackettstown	NJ	07840	**800-843-6522**	908-852-0033	49-3
National Label Co Inc 2025 Joshua Rd	Lafayette Hill	PA	19444	**800-872-5223**	610-825-3250	404
National Labor College 10000 New Hampshire Ave	Silver Spring	MD	20903	**800-462-4237**	301-431-6400	158
National Labor Relations Board (NLRB) 1099 14th St NW	Washington	DC	20570	**800-736-2983**	202-273-1991	336-16
National Law Journal 345 Park Ave S	New York	NY	10010	**800-888-8300**	212-779-9200	449-15
National Lead Information Center 422 S Clinton Ave	Rochester	NY	14620	**800-424-5323**		336-16
National League for Nursing (NLN) 61 Broadway	New York	NY	10006	**800-669-1656**	212-363-5555	49-8
National League for Nursing Accrediting Commission Inc (NLNAC) 61 Broadway 33rd Fl	New York	NY	10006	**800-669-1656**	212-363-5555	48-1
National Library Bindery Co 100 Hembree Park Dr	Roswell	GA	30076	**800-422-7908**	770-442-5490	93
National Library of Education 400 Maryland Ave SW	Washington	DC	20202	**800-424-1616**	202-205-5015	336-4
National Library of Medicine 8600 Rockville Pike	Bethesda	MD	20894	**888-346-3656**	301-594-5983	336-6
National Life Insurance Co 1 National Life Dr	Montpelier	VT	05604	**800-732-8939**	802-229-3333	384-2
National Lighting Co Inc 522 Cortlandt St	Belleville	NJ	07109	**800-969-6285**	973-751-1600	431
National Linen Service 1420 Peachtree St NE Suite 200	Atlanta	GA	30309	**800-225-4636**	404-853-6000	434
National Little Britches Rodeo Assn (NLBRA) 1045 W Rio Grande St	Colorado Springs	CO	80906	**800-763-3694**	719-389-0333	48-22
National Logistics Services LLC 11445 G Cronridge Dr	Owings Mills	MD	21117	**800-638-8672**	410-581-1800	467
National-Louis University 2840 Sheridan Rd	Evanston	IL	60201	**800-443-5522**	847-475-1100	163
Chicago Campus 122 S Michigan Ave	Chicago	IL	60603	**800-443-5522**	312-621-9650	163
Wheaton Campus 200 S Naperville Rd	Wheaton	IL	60187	**800-443-5522**	630-668-3838	163
National Luggage Dealers Assn (NLDA) 1817 Elmdale Ave	Glenview	IL	60026	**866-998-6869**	847-998-6869	49-18
National Lumber 71 Maple St	Mansfield	MA	02048	**800-370-9663**	508-339-8020	359
National Lumber & Building Material Dealers Assn (NLBMDA) 40 Ivy St SE	Washington	DC	20003	**800-634-8645**	202-547-2230	49-18
National Lumber Co 24595 Groesbeck Hwy	Warren	MI	48089	**800-462-9712**	586-775-8200	190-3
National Marfan Foundation (NMF) 22 Manhasset Ave	Port Washington	NY	11050	**800-862-7326**	516-883-8712	48-17
National Marrow Donor Program (NMDP) 3001 Broadway St NE Suite 500	Minneapolis	MN	55413	**800-526-7809**	612-627-5800	48-17
National Medical Assn (NMA) 1012 10th St NW	Washington	DC	20001	**800-662-0554**	202-347-1895	49-8
National Medical Health Card Systems Inc DBA NMHCrx Pharmacy Benefits Manager 26 Harbor Park Dr *NASDAQ: NMHC*	Port Washington	NY	11050	**800-645-3332**	516-626-0007	575
National Medical Services Inc 3701 Welsh Rd	Willow Grove	PA	19090	**800-522-6671**	215-657-4900	407
National Mental Health Assn (NMHA) 2001 N Beauregard St 12th Fl *Help Line	Alexandria	VA	22311	**800-969-6642***	703-684-7722	48-17
National Mental Health Information Center PO Box 42557	Washington	DC	20015	**800-789-2647**	301-443-1805	336-6
National MENTOR Inc DBA MENTOR 313 Congress St	Boston	MA	02210	**800-388-5150**	617-790-4800	454
National Metal Abrasive Inc PO Box 150	Wadsworth	OH	44282	**800-837-8505**	330-334-1566	1
National Metal Fabricators 2395 Greenleaf Ave	Elk Grove Village	IL	60007	**800-323-8849**	847-439-5321	688
National Mfg Co 1 1st Ave *Cust Svc	Sterling	IL	61081	**800-346-9445***	815-625-1320	345
National Middle School Assn (NMSA) 4151 Executive Pkwy Suite 300	Westerville	OH	43081	**800-528-6672**	614-895-4730	49-5
National Milk Producers Federation (NMPF) 2101 Wilson Blvd Suite 400	Arlington	VA	22201	**888-549-7600**	703-243-6111	49-6
National Minority Supplier Development Council (NMSDC) 1040 Ave of the Americas 2nd Fl	New York	NY	10018	**888-396-1110**	212-944-2430	49-18
National Mississippi River Museum & Aquarium 550 E 3rd St Ice Harbor	Dubuque	IA	52001	**800-226-3369**	563-557-9545	509
National Molding Corp 5 Dubon Ct	Farmingdale	NY	11735	**800-544-7162**	631-293-8696	593
National Molding Corp Security Plastics Div 14427 NW 60th Ave	Miami Lakes	FL	33014	**800-327-3787**	305-823-5440	593
National Motor Club of America Inc 6500 Beltline Rd Suite 200	Irving	TX	75063	**800-523-4582**	972-999-4400	53

Listing	Toll-Free	Phone	Class
National Motorists Assn (NMA) 402 W 2nd St.................. Waunakee WI 53597	**800-882-2785**	608-849-6000	49-21
National Multiple Sclerosis Society 733 3rd Ave....................New York NY 10017	**800-344-4867**	212-986-3240	48-17
National Museum of the American Indian (Smithsonian Institution) 1 Bowling Green.................New York NY 10004	**800-242-6624**	212-514-3700	509
National Museum of Naval Aviation 1750 Radford Blvd Suite C.........Pensacola FL 32508	**800-327-5002**	850-452-3604	509
National Museum of Patriotism 1405 Spring St NW................ Atlanta GA 30309	**877-276-1692**	404-875-0691	509
National Museum of Racing & Hall of Fame 191 Union Ave............Saratoga Springs NY 12866	**800-562-5394**	518-584-0400	511
National Museum of Wildlife Art 2820 Rungius Rd PO Box 6825...... Jackson WY 83002	**800-313-9553**	307-733-5771	509
National Museum of Women in the Arts 1250 New York Ave NW..... Washington DC 20005	**800-222-7270**	202-783-5000	509
National Mutual Benefit Inc 6522 Grand Teton Plaza............Madison WI 53719	**800-779-1936**	608-833-1936	384-2
National Native American AIDS Prevention Center (NNAAPC) 436 14th St Suite 1020............ Oakland CA 94612	**800-283-6880**	510-444-2051	48-17
National Needlework Assn (TNNA) 1100-H Brandywine Blvd PO Box 3388......................Zanesville OH 43702	**800-889-8662**	740-455-6773	48-18
National Network of Estate Planning Attorneys Inc (NNEPA) 1 Valmont Plaza 4th Fl.......................Omaha NE 68154	**888-837-4090**	402-964-3700	49-10
National Neurofibromatosis Foundation 95 Pine St 16th Fl...............New York NY 10005	**800-323-7938**	212-344-6633	48-17
National Newspaper Assn (NNA) Univ of Missouri 127 Neff Annex PO Box 7540..................Columbia MO 65205	**800-829-4662**	573-882-5800	49-14
National Niemann-Pick Disease Foundation (NNPDF) 415 Madison Ave.............Fort Atkinson WI 53538	**877-287-3672**	920-563-0930	48-17
National Nonwovens 180 Pleasant St.............. Easthampton MA 01027	**800-333-3469**	413-527-3445	730-6
National Notary Assn (NNA) 9350 DeSoto Ave...............Chatsworth CA 91313	**800-876-6827**	818-739-4000	49-12
National Notary Magazine 9350 DeSoto Ave...............Chatsworth CA 91311 *Cust Svc	**800-876-6827***	818-739-4000	449-5
National Nursing Staff Development Organization (NNSDO) 7794 Grow Dr..................Pensacola FL 32514	**800-489-1995**	850-474-0995	49-8
National Nutritional Foods Assn (NNFA) 3931 MacArthur Blvd Suite 101................. Newport Beach CA 92660	**800-966-6632**	949-622-6272	49-6
National O-Ring Div Hutchinson Seal Corp 11634 Patton Rd............. Downey CA 90241	**800-421-3837**	562-862-8163	321
National Office Furniture 1205 Kimball Blvd................. Jasper IN 47549	**800-482-1717**		314-1
National Oil & Gas Inc PO Box 476.... Bluffton IN 46714	**800-322-8454**	260-824-2220	569
National Oilwell Varco Inc 10000 Richmond Ave Suite 400...... Houston TX 77042 *NYSE: NOV*	**888-262-8645**	713-346-7500	526
National Organization for Albinism & Hypopigmentation (NOAH) PO Box 959..............East Hampstead NH 03826	**800-473-2310**	603-887-2310	48-17
National Organization of Mothers of Twins Clubs Inc (NOMOTC) PO Box 438............Thompsons Station TN 37179	**877-540-2200**	615-595-0936	48-6
National Organization for Rare Disorders (NORD) 55 Kenosia Ave PO Box 1968.......................Danbury CT 06813	**800-999-6673**	203-744-0100	48-17
National Organization for the Reform of Marijuana Laws (NORML) 1600 K St NW Suite 501........ Washington DC 20006	**888-676-6765**	202-483-5500	48-8
National Organization for Victim Assistance (NOVA) 1730 Park Rd NW...................... Washington DC 20010	**800-879-6682**	202-232-6682	48-8
National Osteoporosis Foundation (NOF) 1232 22nd St NW......... Washington DC 20037	**800-223-9994**	202-223-2226	48-17
National Ovarian Cancer Coalition (NOCC) 500 NE Spanish River Blvd Suite 8.................. Boca Raton FL 33431	**888-682-7426**	561-393-0005	48-17
National Packaging Cos Display Group 105 Ave L.......................Newark NJ 07105	**800-589-5808**	973-589-2155	101
National Paper & Sanitary Supply 2511 S 156th Cir..................Omaha NE 68130	**800-647-2737**	402-330-5507	549
National Park Community College 101 College Dr................Hot Springs AR 71913	**800-760-1825**	501-760-4222	160
National Park Service Reservation Center 12501 Willowbrook Rd.... Cumberland MD 21502	**800-365-2267**		762
National Parking Assn (NPA) 1112 16th St NW Suite 300...... Washington DC 20036	**800-647-7275**	202-296-4336	49-3
National Parkinson Foundation (NPF) 1501 NW 9th Ave..................Miami FL 33136	**800-327-4545**	305-547-6666	48-17
National Parks Conservation Assn (NPCA) 1300 19th St NW Suite 300.................... Washington DC 20036	**800-628-7275**	202-223-6722	48-13
National Parks Magazine 1300 19th St NW Suite 300...... Washington DC 20036	**800-628-7275**	202-223-6722	449-19
National Partitions & Interiors Inc 340 W 78th Rd....................Hialeah FL 33014	**866-528-4616**	305-822-3721	281
National Passport Information Center...................... Washington DC 20520	**877-487-2778**		336-12
National Peace Corps Assn (NPCA) 1900 L St NW Suite 205........ Washington DC 20036	**800-424-8580**	202-293-7728	48-5
National Peace Foundation (NPF) 666 11th St NW Suite 202....... Washington DC 20001	**800-237-3223**	202-783-7030	48-5
National Pen Corp 16885 Via Del Compo Ct Suite 100..................... San Diego CA 92127	**800-854-1000**	858-675-3000	10
National Penn Bancshares Inc PO Box 547................... Boyertown PA 19512 *NASDAQ: NPBC*	**800-822-3321**	610-367-6001	355-2
National Penn Bank PO Box 547.... Boyertown PA 19512	**800-822-3321**	610-367-6001	71
National Pesticide Information Center (NPIC) 333 Weniger Hall...........Corvallis OR 97331	**800-858-7378**		48-17
National PetCare Centers (NPC) 3540 JFK Pkwy................ Fort Collins CO 80525	**877-738-4677**	970-226-6632	781
National Pharmacy Technicians Assn (NPTA) 3920 FM 1960 W Suite 380... Houston TX 77068	**888-247-8700**	281-866-7900	49-8
National Pipe & Plastics Inc 3421 Old Vestal Rd................Vestal NY 13850	**800-836-4350**	607-729-9381	585
National Polytechnic College of Engineering & Oceaneering 272 S Fries Ave.............. Wilmington CA 90744	**800-432-3483**	310-834-2501	787
National Pork Producers Council PAC 122 C St NW Suite 875......... Washington DC 20001	**866-701-6388**	202-347-3600	604
National Precast Concrete Assn (NPCA) 10333 N Meridian St Suite 272....................Indianapolis IN 46290	**800-366-7731**	317-571-9500	49-3
National Prescription Administrators Inc 711 Ridgedale Ave............East Hanover NJ 07936	**800-526-7813**	973-503-1000	575
National Presto Industries Inc 3925 N Hastings Way.............Eau Claire WI 54703 *NYSE: NPK*	**800-877-0441**	715-839-2121	37
National Prevention Information Network (NPIN) PO Box 6003...... Rockville MD 20849	**800-458-5231**	301-562-1098	336-6
National Print Group Inc PO Box 5968................Chattanooga TN 37406	**800-624-0408**	423-622-2254	692
National Print Group Inc National Posters Div 1001 Latta St.......Chattanooga TN 37406	**800-624-0408**	423-622-1106	8
National Printing Converters Inc 18 S Murphy Ave..................... Brazil IN 47834	**800-877-6724**	812-448-2555	404
National Property Inspections Inc 11620 Arbor St Suite 100........... Omaha NE 68144	**800-333-9807**	402-333-9807	360
National Psoriasis Foundation (NPF) 6600 SW 92nd Ave Suite 300.......Portland OR 97223	**800-723-9166**	503-244-7404	48-17
National PTA 541 N Fairbanks Ct Suite 1300...... Chicago IL 60611	**800-307-4782**	312-670-6782	48-11
National Public Records Inc 4426 Hugh Howell Rd Suite B314..... Tucker GA 30084	**800-343-6641**	770-938-1050	621
National Publishing Co 11311 Roosevelt Blvd........... Philadelphia PA 19154	**800-333-1863**	215-676-1863	614
National Railroad Passenger Corp DBA Amtrak 60 Massachusetts Ave NE...................... Washington DC 20002	**800-872-7245**	202-906-3000	635
National Railway Equipment Co (NREC) 14400 S Robey St................Dixmoor IL 60426	**800-253-2905**	708-388-6002	636
National Raisin Co PO Box 219........ Fowler CA 93625	**800-874-3726**	559-834-5981	310-5
National Recreation & Park Assn (NRPA) 22377 Belmont Ridge Rd...........Ashburn VA 20148	**800-626-6772**	703-858-0784	48-23
National Recreation Reservation Service PO Box 140...........Ballston Spa NY 12020	**877-444-6777**		762
National Recreational Vehicle Owners Club PO Box 520................Gonzalez FL 32560	**800-281-9186**	850-937-8354	48-23
National Register Publishing Co 562 Central Ave............New Providence NJ 07974	**800-473-7020**		623-2
National Rehabilitation Assn (NRA) 633 S Washington St............. Alexandria VA 22314	**888-258-4295**	703-836-0850	48-17
National Rehabilitation Information Center (NARIC) 4200 Forbes Blvd Suite 202....................... Lanham MD 20706	**800-346-2742**	301-459-5900	48-17
National Research Center for Coal & Energy PO Box 6064...........Morgantown WV 26506	**800-624-8301**	304-293-2867	654
National Reservation Bureau 3100 W Sahara Ave Suite 207..... Las Vegas NV 89109	**800-831-2754**	702-794-2820	368
National Resource Center on Domestic Violence (NRCDV) 6400 Flank Dr Suite 1300.................... Harrisburg PA 17112	**800-537-2238**	717-545-6400	48-6
National Resource Center on Homelessness & Mental Illness (NRC) 345 Delaware Ave.............Delmar NY 12054	**800-444-7415**	518-439-7415	49-15
National Resource Center on Native American Aging (NRCNAA) 501 N Columbia Rd Rm 4531....Grand Forks ND 58202	**800-896-7628**	701-777-3437	48-6
National Resource Center for Special Needs Adoptions 16250 Northland Dr Suite 120......................Southfield MI 48075	**877-767-5437**	248-443-7080	48-6
National Restaurant Assn (NRA) 1200 17th St NW.............. Washington DC 20036	**800-424-5156**	202-331-5900	49-6
National Restaurant Assn PAC 1200 17th St NW.............. Washington DC 20036	**800-424-5156**	202-331-5900	604
National Retail Federation (NRF) 325 7th St NW Suite 1100....... Washington DC 20004	**800-673-4692**	202-783-7971	49-18
National Retail Hardware Assn (NRHA) 5822 W 74th St......... Indianapolis IN 46278 *Cust Svc	**800-772-4424***	317-290-0338	49-18
National Revenue Center 550 Main St....................Cincinnati OH 45202	**800-937-8864**	513-684-3334	336-14
National Revenue Corp 4000 E 5th Ave.................Columbus OH 43219	**800-789-7862**	614-864-3377	157
National Reye's Syndrome Foundation (NRSF) 426 N Lewis St............... Bryan OH 43506	**800-233-7393**	419-636-2679	48-17
National Rifle Assn of America (NRA) 11250 Waples Mill Rd.............. Fairfax VA 22030 *Membership	**800-672-3888***	703-267-1000	48-22
National Right to Work Committee (NRTWC) 8001 Braddock Rd Suite 500.....................Springfield VA 22160	**800-325-7892**	703-321-8510	49-12
National Rivet & Mfg Co 21 E Jefferson St.................Waupun WI 53963	**888-324-5511**	920-324-5511	274
National Roofing Contractors Assn (NRCA) 10255 W Higgins Rd Suite 600..................... Rosemont IL 60018 *Cust Svc	**800-323-9545***	847-299-9070	49-3
National Rosacea Society 800 S Northwest Hwy Suite 200... Barrington IL 60010	**888-662-5874**	847-382-8971	48-17

Alphabetical Section

Name / Address	City	State	ZIP	Toll-Free	Phone	Class
National Runaway Switchboard (NRS) 3080 N Lincoln Ave	Chicago	IL	60657	**800-621-4000**	773-880-9860	48-6
National Rural Electric Cooperative Assn (NRECA) 4301 Wilson Blvd	Arlington	VA	22203	**866-673-2299**	703-907-5500	48-12
National Rural Utilities Cooperative Finance Corp 2201 Cooperative Way Woodland Pk	Herndon	VA	20171	**800-424-2954**	703-709-6700	498
National RV Holdings Inc 3411 N Perris Blvd	Perris	CA	92571	**800-322-6007**	951-943-6007	120
NYSE: NVH						
National Safe Corp 4400 34th St N Unit G	Saint Petersburg	FL	33714	**800-634-8174**	727-525-7800	665
National Safety Apparel Inc 3865 W 150th St	Cleveland	OH	44111	**800-553-0672**	216-941-1111	566
National Safety Council (NSC) 1121 Spring Lake Dr	Itasca	IL	60143	**800-621-7619**	630-285-1121	48-17
National Salon Resources Inc 3109 Louisiana Ave N	Minneapolis	MN	55427	**800-622-0003**	763-546-9500	78
National Salvage & Service Corp 417 S Walnut St	Bloomington	IN	47401	**800-769-8437**	812-339-9000	759
National School Products 101 E Broadway	Maryville	TN	37804	**800-627-9393**	865-984-3960	673
National School Supply & Equipment Assn (NSSEA) 8380 Colesville Rd Suite 250	Silver Spring	MD	20910	**800-395-5550**	301-495-0240	49-18
National Science Center Fort Discovery 1 7th St	Augusta	GA	30901	**800-325-5445**	706-821-0200	509
National Science Teachers Assn (NSTA) 1840 Wilson Blvd	Arlington	VA	22201	**800-722-6782***	703-243-7100	49-5
*Sales						
National Seating Co 200 National Dr	Vonore	TN	37885	**800-222-7328**	423-884-6651	678
National Security. Business Executives for 1717 Pennsylvania Ave NW Suite 350	Washington	DC	20006	**800-296-2125**	202-296-2125	49-12
National Security Life & Accident Insurance Co PO Box 149151	Austin	TX	78714	**800-880-5044**	512-837-7100	384-2
National Seminars Group 6901 W 63rd St	Shawnee Mission	KS	66202	**800-258-7246**	913-432-7755	753
National Senior Golf Assn (NSGA) 3672 Nottingham Way	Hamilton Square	NJ	08690	**800-282-6772**	609-631-8145	48-22
National Serv-All Inc 6231 McBeth Rd	Fort Wayne	IN	46809	**800-876-9001**	260-747-4117	791
National Sheriffs' Assn (NSA) 1450 Duke St	Alexandria	VA	22314	**800-424-7827**	703-836-7827	49-7
National Shoe Retailers Assn (NSRA) 7150 Columbia Gateway Dr Suite G	Columbia	MD	21046	**800-673-8446**	410-381-8282	49-18
National Shrine of Saint John Neumann 1019 N 5th St	Philadelphia	PA	19123	**888-315-1860**	215-627-3080	50
National Slovak Society of the USA (NSS) 351 Valley Brook Rd	McMurray	PA	15317	**800-488-1890**	724-731-0094	48-14
National Small Business Assn (NSBA) 1156 15th St NW Suite 1100	Washington	DC	20005	**800-345-6728**	202-393-8830	49-12
National Soccer Coaches Assn of America (NSCAA) 6700 Squibb Rd Suite 215	Mission	KS	66202	**800-458-0678**	913-362-1747	48-22
National Society of Accountants (NSA) 1010 N Fairfax St	Alexandria	VA	22314	**800-966-6679**	703-549-6400	49-1
National Society for Experiential Education (NSEE) 515 King St Suite 240	Alexandria	VA	22314	**800-803-4170**	703-706-9552	48-11
National Society for Park Resources (NSPR) c/o National Recreation & Park Assn 22377 Belmont Ridge Rd	Ashburn	VA	20148	**800-626-6772**	703-858-0784	48-23
National Society of Professional Engineers (NSPE) 1420 King St	Alexandria	VA	22314	**800-285-6773**	703-684-2800	49-19
National Softball Hall of Fame & Museum 2801 NE 50th St	Oklahoma City	OK	73111	**800-654-8337**	405-424-5266	511
National Speakers Bureau 1663 W 7th Ave	Vancouver	BC	V6J1S4	**800-661-4110**	604-734-3663	699
National Speakers Bureau Inc 14047 W Petronalla Dr Suite 102	Libertyville	IL	60048	**800-323-9442**	847-295-1122	699
National Speed Sport News Magazine PO Box 1210	Harrisburg	NC	28075	**866-455-2531**	704-455-2531	449-3
National Spinal Cord Injury Assn (NSCIA) 6701 Democracy Blvd Suite 300-9	Bethesda	MD	20817	**800-962-9629**		48-17
National Spinning Co Inc 111 W 40th St 28th Fl	New York	NY	10018	**800-868-7764**	212-382-6400	730-9
National Spirit Group Ltd 2010 Merritt Dr	Garland	TX	75041	**800-527-4366**	972-840-1233	153-19
National Sporting Goods Assn (NSGA) 1601 Feehanville Dr Suite 300	Mount Prospect	IL	60056	**800-815-5422**	847-296-6742	49-4
National Sprint Car Hall of Fame & Museum 1 Sprint Capital Pl	Knoxville	IA	50138	**800-874-4488**	641-842-6176	511
National Staff Development Council (NSDC) 5995 Fairfield Rd Suite 4	Oxford	OH	45056	**800-727-7288**	513-523-6029	49-5
National-Standard Co 1631 Lake St	Niles	MI	49120	**800-777-1618**	269-683-8100	676
National Starch & Chemical Co 10 Finderne Ave	Bridgewater	NJ	08807	**800-797-4992**	908-685-5000	143
National Stock Exchange (NSX) 440 S LaSalle St Suite 2600	Chicago	IL	60605	**800-843-3924**	312-786-8803	680
National Stock Sign Co 1040 El Dorado Ave	Santa Cruz	CA	95062	**800-462-7726**	831-476-2020	692
National Stone Sand & Gravel Assn (NSSGA) 1605 King St	Alexandria	VA	22314	**800-342-1415**	703-525-8788	49-3
National Strength & Conditioning Assn (NSCA) 1885 Bob Johnson Dr	Colorado Springs	CO	80906	**800-815-6826**	719-632-6722	48-22
National Stroke Assn (NSA) 9707 E Easter Ln	Englewood	CO	80112	**800-787-6537**	303-649-9299	48-17
National Student Campaign Against Hunger & Homelessness (NSCAHH) 233 N Pleasant St Suite 32	Amherst	MA	01002	**800-664-8647**	413-253-6417	48-5
National Stuttering Assn (NSA) 119 W 40th St 14th Fl	New York	NY	10018	**800-364-1677**	212-944-4050	48-17
National Sunflower Assn PAC 4023 State St	Bismarck	ND	58503	**888-718-7033**	701-328-5100	604
National Super Service Co Inc 3115 Frenchman Rd	Toledo	OH	43607	**800-677-1663***	419-531-2121	379
*Cust Svc						
National System of Garage Ventilation Inc 714 N Church St	Decatur	IL	62521	**800-728-8368**	217-423-7314	16
National Systems Contractors Assn (NSCA) 625 1st St SE Suite 420	Cedar Rapids	IA	52401	**800-446-6722**	319-366-6722	49-20
National Taxpayer Advocate 1111 Constitution Ave NW	Washington	DC	20224	**877-777-4778**	202-622-6100	336-14
National Taxpayers Union (NTU) 108 N Alfred St	Alexandria	VA	22314	**800-829-4258**	703-683-5700	48-7
National Tay-Sachs & Allied Diseases Assn (NTSAD) 2001 Beacon St Suite 204	Brighton	MA	02135	**800-906-8723**	617-277-4463	48-17
National Teaching Aids Div American Educational Products LLC 401 Hickory St	Fort Collins	CO	80522	**800-289-9299***	970-484-7445	242
*Cust Svc						
National Technical Information Service (NTIS) 5285 Port Royal Rd	Springfield	VA	22161	**800-553-6847***	703-605-6000	336-2
*Orders						
FedWorld.gov US Dept of Commerce 5285 Port Royal Rd	Springfield	VA	22161	**800-553-6847**	703-605-6000	336-2
FLITE US Supreme Court Database US Dept of Commerce 5285 Port Royal Rd	Springfield	VA	22161	**800-553-6847**	703-605-6000	336-2
National Technical Systems Inc 24007 Ventura Blvd Suite 200	Calabasas	CA	91302	**800-759-2687**	818-591-0776	728
NASDAQ: NTSC						
National Technological University 155 5th Ave S Suite 600	Minneapolis	MN	55401	**800-582-9976**	866-688-6797	163
National Technology Transfer Center 316 Washington Ave	Wheeling	WV	26003	**800-678-6882**	304-243-2455	654
National Theatre 1321 Pennsylvania Ave NW	Washington	DC	20004	**800-447-7400**	202-628-6161	562
National Thoroughbred Racing Assn (NTRA) 2525 Harrodsburg Rd	Lexington	KY	40504	**800-722-3287**	859-223-5444	48-22
National Tobacco Co LP 3029 W Muhammad Ali Blvd	Louisville	KY	40212	**800-331-5964***	502-778-4421	741-3
*Cust Svc						
National Tool & Mfg Co Inc 100-124 N 12th St	Kenilworth	NJ	07033	**800-223-0926**	908-276-1600	745
National Tooling & Machining Assn (NTMA) 9300 Livingston Rd	Fort Washington	MD	20744	**800-248-6862**	301-248-6200	49-13
National Trade Productions Inc 313 S Patrick St	Alexandria	VA	22314	**800-687-7469**	703-683-8500	183
National Truck Equipment Assn (NTEA) 37400 Hills Tech Dr	Farmington Hills	MI	48331	**800-441-6832**	248-489-7090	49-21
National Truck Leasing System DBA NationaLease 1 S 450 Summit Ave Suite 300	Oakbrook Terrace	IL	60181	**800-729-6857**	630-953-8878	767
National Trust for Historic Preservation 1785 Massachusetts Ave NW	Washington	DC	20036	**800-944-6847**	202-588-6000	48-13
National Tube Form Inc 3405 Engle Rd	Fort Wayne	IN	46809	**800-752-1458**	260-478-2363	584
National Underground Railroad Freedom Center 50 E Freedom Way	Cincinnati	OH	45202	**877-648-4838**	513-333-7500	509
National Underwriter Co 5081 Olympic Blvd	Erlanger	KY	41018	**800-543-0874**	859-692-2100	623-2
National Underwriter Magazine 3341 Newark St	Hoboken	NJ	07030	**800-543-0874**	201-963-2300	449-5
National University 11255 N Torrey Pines Rd	La Jolla	CA	92037	**800-628-8648**	858-642-8000	163
National University of Health Sciences 200 E Roosevelt Rd	Lombard	IL	60148	**800-826-6285**	630-629-2000	163
National Urban Technology Center 55 John St Suite 300	New York	NY	10038	**800-998-3212**	212-528-7350	48-6
National Utility Contractors Assn (NUCA) 4301 N Fairfax Dr Suite 360	Arlington	VA	22203	**800-662-6822**	703-358-9300	49-3
National Vaccine Information Center (NVIC) 421-E Church St	Vienna	VA	22180	**800-909-7468**	703-938-3783	48-17
National Van Lines Inc 2800 W Roosevelt Rd	Broadview	IL	60155	**800-323-1962**	708-450-2900	508
National Vessel Movement Center 408 Coast Guard Dr	Kearneysville	WV	25430	**800-708-9823**	304-264-2502	336-7
National Vision Inc 296 Grayson Hwy	Lawrenceville	GA	30045	**800-571-5202**	770-822-3600	658
AMEX: NVI						
National Vitamin Co 2075 W Scranton Ave	Porterville	CA	93257	**800-538-5828**	559-781-8871	786
National Volunteer Fire Council (NVFC) 1050 17th St NW Suite 490	Washington	DC	20036	**888-275-6832**	202-887-5700	49-4
National Waterworks Inc 200 W Hwy 6 Suite 620	Waco	TX	76712	**800-817-5355**	254-772-5355	378
National Welders Supply Co Inc 810 Gesco St	Charlotte	NC	28208	**800-866-4422**	704-333-5475	378
National Wellness Institute (NWI) 1300 College Ct PO Box 827	Stevens Point	WI	54481	**800-243-8694**	715-342-2969	48-17
National Western Life Insurance Co 850 E Anderson Ln	Austin	TX	78752	**800-531-5442**	512-836-1010	384-2
NASDAQ: NWLIA						
National Wholesale Co Inc 400 National Blvd	Lexington	NC	27292	**800-480-4673**	336-248-5904	451
National Wild Horse & Burro Program PO Box 3270	Sparks	NV	89432	**866-468-7826**	775-475-2222	336-9
National Wild Turkey Federation (NWTF) 770 Augusta Rd PO Box 530	Edgefield	SC	29824	**800-843-6983***	803-637-3106	48-3
*Cust Svc						

Listing	City	State	ZIP	Toll-Free	Phone	Class
National Wildlife Federation (NWF) 11100 Wildlife Center Dr *Cust Svc	Reston	VA	20190	**800-822-9919***	703-438-6000	48-3
National Wildlife Magazine 11100 Wildlife Ctr Dr *Cust Svc	Reston	VA	22090	**800-822-9919***	703-438-6000	449-19
National Wildlife Refuge Assn (NWRA) 1010 Wisconsin Ave NW Suite 200	Washington	DC	20007	**877-396-6972**	202-333-9075	48-13
National Wine & Spirits Inc PO Box 1602	Indianapolis	IN	46206	**800-562-7359**	317-636-6092	82-3
National Wire Fabric 701 Arkansas St	Star City	AR	71667	**800-643-1558**	870-628-4201	676
National Women's Health Information Center 8550 Arlington Blvd Suite 300	Fairfax	VA	22031	**800-994-9662**		336-6
National Wood Flooring Assn (NWFA) 111 Chesterfield Industrial Blvd	Chesterfield	MO	63005	**800-422-4556**	636-519-9663	49-3
National Woodland Owners Assn (NWOA) 374 Maple Ave E Suite 310	Vienna	VA	22180	**800-476-8733**	703-255-2700	48-2
National Youth Advocacy Coalition (NYAC) 1638 R St NW Suite 300	Washington	DC	20009	**800-541-6922**	202-319-7596	48-6
National Youth Sports Coaches Assn (NYSCA) 2050 Vista Pkwy	West Palm Beach	FL	33411	**800-729-2057**	561-684-1141	48-22
NationaLease 1 S 450 Summit Ave Suite 300	Oakbrook Terrace	IL	60181	**800-729-6857**	630-953-8878	767
NationJob Inc 601 SW 9th St Suites J & K	Des Moines	IA	50309	**800-292-7731**	515-280-3672	257
NationLink Wireless 342 Cool Springs Blvd Suite 200	Franklin	TN	37067	**800-496-2355**	615-567-2224	35
Nations Funds PO Box 34602	Charlotte	NC	28254	**800-321-7854**		517
NationsRent Inc 450 E Las Olas Blvd Suite 1400	Fort Lauderdale	FL	33301	**800-667-9328**	954-760-6550	261-2
Nationwide Credit Inc 2015 Vaughn Rd Bldg 300	Kennesaw	GA	30144	**800-456-4729**	770-644-7400	157
Nationwide Custom Homes 1100 Rives Rd	Martinsville	VA	24115	**800-216-7001**	276-632-7101	107
Nationwide Financial Services Inc 5100 Rings Rd *NYSE: NFS*	Dublin	OH	43017	**800-321-9332**		355-4
Nationwide Foods/Brookfield Farms 700 E 107th St	Chicago	IL	60628	**800-243-1014**	773-787-4900	292-9
Nationwide Health Plans 5525 Parkcenter Cir	Dublin	OH	43017	**800-259-4458**	614-854-3001	384-3
Nationwide Information Services Inc 52 James St 5th Fl	Albany	NY	12207	**800-873-3482**	518-449-8429	621
Nationwide Insurance Enterprise 1 Nationwide Plaza	Columbus	OH	43215	**800-882-2822**	614-249-7111	355-4
Nationwide Life & Annuity Insurance Co 5100 Rings Rd	Dublin	OH	43017	**800-882-2822**	614-249-7111	384-2
Nationwide Life Insurance Co 5100 Rings Rd	Dublin	OH	43017	**800-882-2822**	614-249-7111	384-2
Nationwide Mutual Fire Insurance Co 1 Nationwide Plaza	Columbus	OH	43215	**800-882-2822**	614-249-7111	384-4
Nationwide Property & Casualty Insurance Co 1 Nationwide Plaza	Columbus	OH	43215	**800-882-2822**	614-249-7111	384-4
Nationwide Provident 1000 Chesterbrook Blvd	Berwyn	PA	19312	**800-523-4681**	610-889-1717	384-2
Nationwide Recovery Systems Inc 2304 Tarpley Rd Suite 134	Carrollton	TX	75006	**800-458-6357**	972-798-1000	157
Nationwide Van Lines Inc 5450 S State Rd 7 Suite 39	Hollywood	FL	33314	**800-310-0056**	954-585-3945	508
Native American Aging. National Resource Center on 501 N Columbia Rd Rm 4531	Grand Forks	ND	58202	**800-896-7628**	701-777-3437	48-6
Native American AIDS Prevention Center. National 436 14th St Suite 1020	Oakland	CA	94612	**800-283-6880**	510-444-2051	48-17
Native American Report 8737 Colesville Rd Suite 1100	Silver Spring	MD	20910	**800-274-6737**	301-587-6300	521-7
NATP (National Assn of Tax Professionals) 720 Association Dr	Appleton	WI	54914	**800-558-3402**	920-749-1040	49-1
Natrol Inc 21411 Prairie St *NASDAQ: NTOL*	Chatsworth	CA	91311	**800-262-8765**	818-739-6000	786
NATSO Inc 1737 King St Suite 200	Alexandria	VA	22314	**888-275-2876**	703-549-2100	49-21
Naturade Products Inc 14370 Myford Rd Suite 100	Irvine	CA	92606	**800-367-2880**	714-573-4800	786
Natural Alternatives International Inc 1185 Linda Vista Dr Suite D *NASDAQ: NAII*	San Marcos	CA	92069	**800-848-2646**	760-744-7340	786
Natural Factors Nutritional Products Inc 1111 80th St Suite 100	Everett	WA	98203	**800-322-8704**	425-513-8800	786
Natural Factors Nutritional Products Ltd 1550 United Blvd	Coquitlam	BC	V3K6Y7	**800-663-8900**	604-420-4229	786
Natural Gas Services Group Inc 2911 S CR 1260 *AMEX: NGS*	Midland	TX	79706	**888-891-6275**	432-563-3947	526
Natural Golf Corp 1200 E Business Center Dr Suite 400	Mount Prospect	IL	60056	**888-628-4653**	847-321-4000	754
Natural Health Professionals. National Assn of Certified 714 E Winona Ave	Warsaw	IN	46580	**800-321-1005**		48-17
Natural History Magazine American Museum of Natural History 175-208 Central Pk W	New York	NY	10024	**800-234-5252**	212-769-5500	449-19
Natural Life Pet Products Inc 412 W Saint John St PO Box 159	Girard	KS	66743	**800-367-2391**	620-724-8012	568
Natural Organics Inc 548 Broadhollow Rd	Melville	NY	11747	**800-645-9500**	631-293-0030	786
NaturaLawn of America Inc 1 E Church St	Frederick	MD	21701	**800-989-5444**	301-694-5440	421
Naturally Vitamin Supplements Inc 4404 E Elwood St	Phoenix	AZ	85040	**800-899-4499**	480-991-0200	786
NaturalPoint Inc 33872 Eastgate Cir SE	Corvallis	OR	97333	**888-865-5535**	541-753-6645	171-1
Nature National Press Bldg 529 14th St NW Suite 968	Washington	DC	20045	**800-524-0384**	202-737-2355	449-19
Nature Canada 1 Nicholas St Suite 606	Ottawa	ON	K1N7B7	**800-267-4088**	613-562-3447	48-13
Nature Conservancy 4245 N Fairfax Dr Suite 100 *Cust Svc	Arlington	VA	22203	**800-628-6860***	703-841-5300	48-13
Nature Conservancy of Canada 110 Eglinton Ave W Suite 400	Toronto	ON	M4R1A3	**800-465-0029**	416-932-3202	48-13
Nature Store Roger Tory Peterson Institute 311 Curtis St	Jamestown	NY	14701	**800-758-6841**	716-665-2473	518
Nature's Life 900 Larkspur Landing Cir Suite 105	Larkspur	CA	94939	**800-247-6997**	435-655-6790	786
Nature's Sunshine Products Inc 75 E 1700 South *NASDAQ: NATR* ■ *Cust Svc	Provo	UT	84606	**800-223-8225***	801-342-4300	786
Nature's Table Franchise Co 800 N Magnolia Ave	Orlando	FL	32803	**800-222-6090**	407-481-2544	657
Nature's Way 10 Mountain Springs Pkwy	Springville	UT	84663	**800-962-8873**	801-489-1500	786
Naturopathic Physicians. American Assn of 3201 New Mexico Ave NW Suite 350	Washington	DC	20016	**866-538-2267**	202-895-1392	48-17
Natus Medical Inc 1501 Industrial Rd *NASDAQ: BABY*	San Carlos	CA	94070	**800-255-3901**	650-802-0400	249
Natvar 8720 US 70 W	Clayton	NC	27520	**800-395-6288**	919-553-4151	589
NATW (National Assn of Town Watch) 1 E Wynnewood Rd Suite 102	Wynnewood	PA	19096	**800-648-3688**	610-649-7055	48-7
Naugatuck Glass Co PO Box 71	Naugatuck	CT	06770	**800-533-3513**	203-729-5227	328
NAUI (National Assn of Underwater Instructors) 1232 Tech Blvd	Tampa	FL	33619	**800-553-6284**	813-628-6284	48-22
NAUS (National Assn for Uniformed Services) 5535 Hempstead Way	Springfield	VA	22151	**800-842-3451**	703-750-1342	48-19
Nautilus Insurance Co 7273 E Butherus Dr	Scottsdale	AZ	85260	**800-842-8972**	480-951-0905	384-4
NAV CANADA 77 Metcalfe St	Ottawa	ON	K1P5L6	**800-876-4693**	613-563-5588	20
NAV Canada Training & Conference Center 1950 Montreal Rd	Cornwall	ON	K6H6L2	**877-832-6416**	613-936-5000	370
Navajo Express Inc PO Box 1780	Denver	CO	80217	**800-525-1969**	303-287-3800	769
Naval Affairs Magazine 125 N West St	Alexandria	VA	22314	**800-372-1924**	703-683-1400	449-12
Naval Enlisted Reserve Assn (NERA) 6703 Farragut Ave	Falls Church	VA	22042	**800-776-9020**	703-534-1329	48-19
Naval Facilities Engineering Service Center (NFESC) 1100 23rd Ave	Port Hueneme	CA	93043	**888-484-3372**	805-982-1393	654
Naval Heritage Center. US Navy Memorial & 701 Pennsylvania Ave NW Suite 123	Washington	DC	20004	**800-821-8892**	202-737-2300	50
Naval Home 1800 Beach Dr	Gulfport	MS	39507	**800-332-3527**	228-897-4026	659
Naval Institute Press 2062 Generals Hwy	Annapolis	MD	21401	**800-233-8764**	410-224-3378	623-5
Naval Institute. US 291 Wood Rd	Annapolis	MD	21402	**800-233-8764**	410-268-6110	48-19
Naval Reserve Assn (NRA) 1619 King St	Alexandria	VA	22314	**866-672-4968**	703-548-5800	48-19
NAVAN (National Assn of Vascular Access Networks) 11441 S State St Suite A113	Draper	UT	84020	**888-576-2826**	801-576-1824	49-8
Navarre Corp 7400 49th Ave N *NASDAQ: NAVR*	New Hope	MN	55428	**800-728-4000**	763-535-8333	172
Navarro College 3200 W 7th Ave	Corsicana	TX	75110	**800-628-2776**	903-874-6501	160
Navarro County Electric Co-op Inc PO Drawer 616	Corsicana	TX	75151	**800-771-9095**	903-874-7411	244
NavCom Defense Electronics Inc 4323 Arden Dr	El Monte	CA	91731	**800-729-8191**	626-442-0123	519
Navellier Securities Corp 1 E Liberty St 3rd Fl	Reno	NV	89501	**800-887-8671**	775-785-2300	393
Navico Inc DBA Navy Brand Mfg Co 3670 Scarlet Oak Blvd	Saint Louis	MO	63122	**800-325-3312**	636-861-5500	149
Navigant Consulting Inc 615 N Wabash Ave *NYSE: NCI*	Chicago	IL	60611	**800-621-8390**	312-573-5600	193
Navigant International Canada 2810 Matheson Blvd E 3rd FL	Mississauga	ON	L4W4X7	**800-668-1116**	905-629-9975	760
Navigant International Inc 84 Inverness Cir E *NASDAQ: FLYR*	Englewood	CO	80112	**877-628-4426**	303-706-0800	761
Navigators Group Inc 1 Penn Plaza 55th Fl *NASDAQ: NAVG*	New York	NY	10119	**800-496-2901**	212-244-2333	355-4
Navis Logistics Network 5675 DTC Blvd Suite 280	Greenwood Village	CO	80111	**800-525-6309**	303-741-6626	539
Navis Pack & Ship Centers 5675 DTC Blvd Suite 280	Greenwood Village	CO	80111	**800-525-6309**	303-741-6626	114
NaviSite Inc 400 Minuteman Rd *NASDAQ: NAVI*	Andover	MA	01810	**888-298-8222**	978-682-8300	39
Navistar Financial Corp 2850 W Golf Rd	Rolling Meadows	IL	60008	**800-233-9121**	847-734-4000	214
NaviSys Inc 499 Thornall St	Edison	NJ	08837	**800-775-3592**	732-549-3663	176-10
Navitar Inc 200 Commerce Dr *Cust Svc	Rochester	NY	14623	**800-828-6778***	585-359-4000	580
Navopache Electric Co-op Inc 1878 W White Mountain Blvd	Lakeside	AZ	85929	**800-543-6324**	928-368-5118	244
NavPress PO Box 35001 *Cust Svc	Colorado Springs	CO	80935	**800-366-7788***	719-548-9222	623-4
NAVS (National Anti-Vivisection Society) 53 W Jackson Blvd Suite 1552	Chicago	IL	60604	**800-888-6287**	312-427-6065	48-3
NAVTEQ Corp 222 Merchandise Mart Suite 900 *NYSE: NVT*	Chicago	IL	60654	**888-628-6277**	312-894-7000	222
Navy Brand Mfg Co 3670 Scarlet Oak Blvd	Saint Louis	MO	63122	**800-325-3312**	636-861-5500	149
Navy Exchange Service Command (NEXCOM) 3280 Virginia Beach Blvd	Virginia Beach	VA	23452	**800-628-3924**	757-463-6200	778

Name / Address	City	State	ZIP	Toll-Free	Phone	Class
Navy Federal Credit Union PO Box 3000	Merrifield	VA	22119	**800-914-9494**	703-255-8500	216
Navy League of the US 2300 Wilson Blvd	Arlington	VA	22201	**800-356-5760**	703-528-1775	48-19
Navy-Marine Corps Relief Society (NMCRS) 4015 Wilson Blvd 10th Fl	Arlington	VA	22203	**800-654-8364**	703-696-4904	48-19
Navy Times Magazine 6883 Commercial Dr	Springfield	VA	22159	**800-424-9335**	703-750-9000	449-12
Nawas International Travel Service Inc 777 Post Rd 3rd Fl	Darien	CT	06820	**800-221-4984**	203-656-3033	748
NAWBO (National Assn of Women Business Owners) 8405 Greensboro Dr Suite 800	McLean	VA	22102	**800-556-2926**	703-506-3268	49-12
NAWIC (National Assn of Women in Construction) 327 S Adams St	Fort Worth	TX	76104	**800-552-3506**	817-877-5551	49-3
NAWLA (North American Wholesale Lumber Assn) 3601 Algonquin Rd Suite 400	Rolling Meadows	IL	60008	**800-527-8258**	847-870-7470	49-18
NAYSI (North American Youth Sport Institute) 4985 Oak Garden Dr	Kernersville	NC	27284	**800-767-4916**	336-784-4926	48-22
Nazarene Publishing House Inc PO Box 419527	Kansas City	MO	64141	**800-877-0700**	816-931-1900	623-4
Nazarene Theological Seminary 1700 E Meyer Blvd	Kansas City	MO	64131	**800-831-3011**	816-333-6254	161-3
Nazareth College of Rochester 4245 East Ave	Rochester	NY	14618	**800-462-3944**	585-586-2525	163
Nazareth Speedway Hwy 191	Nazareth	PA	18064	**888-629-7223**	610-759-8000	504
Nazdar 8501 Hedge Lane Terr	Shawnee	KS	66227	**800-767-9942**	913-422-1888	381
NB Handy Co 65 10th St	Lynchburg	VA	24504	**800-284-6242**	434-847-4495	601
NBA (National Bar Assn) 1225 11th St NW	Washington	DC	20001	**800-621-2988**	202-842-3900	49-10
NBA (National Business Assn) 5151 Beltline Rd Suite 1150	Dallas	TX	75254	**800-456-0440**	972-458-0900	49-12
NBC Capital Corp NBC Plaza 301 E Main St *AMEX: NBY*	Starkville	MS	39759	**888-622-7341**	662-323-1341	355-2
NBC Capital Markets Group Inc 850 Ridge Lake Blvd Suite 400	Memphis	TN	38120	**800-795-2421**	901-842-3700	679
NBCC (National Breast Cancer Coalition) 1101 17th St NW Suite 1300	Washington	DC	20036	**800-622-2838**	202-296-7477	48-17
NBMDA (North American Building Material Distribution Assn) 401 N Michigan Ave Suite 2400	Chicago	IL	60611	**888-747-7862**	312-644-6610	49-18
NBT Bancorp Inc 52 S Broad St *NASDAQ: NBTB*	Norwich	NY	13815	**800-628-2265**	607-337-2265	355-2
NBT Bank NA 52 S Broad St	Norwich	NY	13815	**800-628-2265**		71
NBTY Inc 90 Orville Dr *NYSE: NTY*	Bohemia	NY	11716	**800-645-5412**	631-567-9500	786
NBWA (National Beer Wholesalers Assn) 1101 King St Suite 600	Alexandria	VA	22314	**800-300-6417**	703-683-4300	49-6
NC Machinery Co 17035 W Valley Hwy	Tukwila	WA	98188	**800-562-4735**	425-251-9800	378
NC Plus Hybrids 3820 N 56th St	Lincoln	NE	68504	**800-279-7999**	402-467-2517	272
NC Products Corp PO Box 27077	Raleigh	NC	27611	**800-662-1983**	919-772-6301	181
NCA (National Club Assn) 1201 15th St NW Suite 450	Washington	DC	20005	**800-625-6221**	202-822-9822	48-23
NCA (National Confectioners Assn) 8320 Old Courthouse Rd Suite 300	Vienna	VA	22182	**800-433-1200**	703-790-5750	49-6
NCA (National Craft Assn) 2012 Ridge Rd E Suite 120	Rochester	NY	14622	**800-715-9594**	585-266-5472	48-18
NCAA Hall of Champions 1 NCAA Plaza 700 W Washington St	Indianapolis	IN	46204	**800-735-6222**	317-916-4255	511
NCADD (National Council on Alcoholism & Drug Dependence) 20 Exchange Pl Suite 2902	New York	NY	10005	**800-622-2255**	212-269-7797	48-17
NCADP (National Coalition to Abolish the Death Penalty) 920 Pennsylvania Ave SE	Washington	DC	20003	**888-286-2237**	202-543-9577	48-8
NCAE News Bulletin PO Box 27347	Raleigh	NC	27611	**800-662-7924**	919-832-3000	449-8
NCAP (National Center for Assault Prevention) 606 Delsea Dr	Sewell	NJ	08080	**800-258-3189**	856-582-7000	48-17
NCCA (National Child Care Assn) 1016 Rosser St	Conyers	GA	30012	**800-543-7161**	770-922-8198	48-6
NCCAM (National Center for Complementary & Alternative Medicine) National Institutes of Health 31 Center Dr Bldg 31	Bethesda	MD	20892	**888-644-6226**	301-435-5042	336-6
NCCI Holdings Inc 901 Peninsula Corporate Cir *Cust Svc	Boca Raton	FL	33487	**800-622-4123***	561-893-1000	383
NCCIC (National Child Care Information Center) 243 Church St NW 2nd Fl	Vienna	VA	22180	**800-616-2242**		336-6
NCCJ (National Conference for Community & Justice) 475 Park Ave S 19th Fl	New York	NY	10016	**800-352-6225**	212-545-1300	48-8
NCCS (National Children's Cancer Society) 1015 Locust St Suite 600	Saint Louis	MO	63101	**800-532-6459**	314-241-1600	48-17
NCE (National Council of Exchangors) 630 Quintana Rd Suite 150	Morro Bay	CA	93442	**800-324-1031**		49-17
NCE Computer Group 1973 Friendship Dr Suite B *Cust Svc	El Cajon	CA	92020	**800-767-2587***	619-212-3000	173
NCEE (National Council on Economic Education) 1140 6th Ave 2nd Fl	New York	NY	10036	**800-338-1192**	212-730-7007	49-5
NCEES (National Council of Examiners for Engineering & Surveying) 280 Seneca Creek Rd	Clemson	SC	29631	**800-250-3196**	864-654-6824	49-3
NCFA (National Council for Adoption) 225 N Washington St	Alexandria	VA	22314	**866-212-3678**	703-299-6633	48-6
NCFL (National Center for Family Literacy) 325 W Main St Suite 300	Louisville	KY	40202	**877-326-5481**	502-584-1133	48-11
NCFR (National Council on Family Relations) 3989 Central Ave NE Suite 550	Minneapolis	MN	55421	**888-781-9331**	763-781-9331	48-6
NCH (National Center for Homeopathy) 801 N Fairfax St Suite 306	Alexandria	VA	22314	**877-624-0613**	703-548-7790	48-17
NCH Corp 2727 Chemsearch Blvd	Irving	TX	75062	**800-243-6835**	972-438-0226	149
NCI (National Cancer Institute) 6116 Executive Blvd MSC 8322	Bethesda	MD	20892	**800-422-6237**	301-435-3848	654
NCI Building Systems Inc 7301 Fairview St *NYSE: NCS*	Houston	TX	77041	**800-777-9378**	713-466-7788	106
NCI Information Systems Inc 11730 Plaza America Dr	Reston	VA	20190	**888-409-5457**	703-707-6900	178
NCIS (National Crop Insurance Services) 7201 W 129th St Suite 200	Overland Park	KS	66213	**800-951-6247**	913-685-2767	48-2
NCJJ (National Center for Juvenile Justice) 3700 S Water St Suite 200	Pittsburgh	PA	15203	**800-577-6903**	412-227-6950	48-8
NCJW (National Council of Jewish Women) 53 W 23rd St 6th Fl	New York	NY	10010	**800-829-6259**	212-645-4048	48-24
NCL (National Consumers League) 1701 K St NW Suite 1200	Washington	DC	20006	**800-876-7060**	202-835-3323	48-10
NCLR (National Council of La Raza) 1111 19th St NW Suite 1000	Washington	DC	20036	**800-311-6257**	202-785-1670	48-14
NCMA (National Contract Management Assn) 8260 Greensboro Dr Suite 200	McLean	VA	22102	**800-344-8096**	571-382-0082	49-12
NCMEC (National Center for Missing & Exploited Children) 699 Prince St	Alexandria	VA	22314	**800-843-5678**	703-274-3900	48-6
NCMIC Insurance Co 14001 University Ave	Clive	IA	50325	**800-769-2000**	515-313-4500	384-5
NCMS (National Center for Manufacturing Sciences) 3025 Boardwalk	Ann Arbor	MI	48108	**800-222-6267**	734-995-0300	654
NCMS Bulletin 222 N Person St	Raleigh	NC	27601	**800-722-1350**	919-833-3836	449-16
NCO Financial Systems Inc 507 Prudential Rd	Horsham	PA	19044	**800-220-2274**	215-441-3000	157
NCO Group Inc 507 Prudential Rd *NASDAQ: NCOG*	Horsham	PA	19044	**800-220-2274**	215-441-3000	157
NCO Group Inc Commercial Services Div 3850 N Causeway Blvd 2nd Fl	Metairie	LA	70002	**800-745-6007**	504-834-8800	157
NCO Portfolio Management Inc 507 Prudential Rd	Horsham	PA	19044	**800-220-2274**	215-441-3000	157
NCOA (National Council on the Aging) 300 D St SW Suite 801	Washington	DC	20024	**800-424-9046**	202-479-1200	48-6
NCOA (Non-Commissioned Officers Assn) 10635 IH-35 N *Cust Svc	San Antonio	TX	78233	**800-662-2620***	210-653-6161	48-19
NCPA (National Community Pharmacists Assn) 100 Daingerfield Rd	Alexandria	VA	22314	**800-544-7447**	703-683-8200	49-8
NCPL Inc DBA Northern Cards 5694 Ambler Dr	Mississauga	ON	L4W2K9	**877-627-7444**	905-625-4944	130
NCQA (National Committee for Quality Assurance) 2000 L St NW Suite 500	Washington	DC	20036	**800-236-5903**	202-955-3500	48-10
NCR Corp 1700 S Patterson Blvd *NYSE: NCR* ■ *Cust Svc	Dayton	OH	45479	**800-531-2222***	937-445-5000	603
NCRA (National Court Reporters Assn) 8224 Old Courthouse Rd	Vienna	VA	22182	**800-272-6272**	703-556-6272	49-10
NCREL (North Central Regional Educational Laboratory) 1120 E Diehl Rd Suite 200	Naperville	IL	60563	**800-356-2735**	630-649-6500	654
NCRIC Group Inc 1115 30th St NW *NASDAQ: NCRI*	Washington	DC	20007	**800-613-3615**	202-969-1866	355-4
NCRIC Inc 1115 30th St NW	Washington	DC	20007	**800-613-3615**	202-969-1866	384-5
NCRIC Insurance Agency Inc 1115 30th St NW	Washington	DC	20007	**800-613-3615**	202-969-1866	384-2
NCRP (National Council on Radiation Protection & Measurements) 7910 Woodmont Ave Suite 400	Bethesda	MD	20814	**800-229-2652**	301-657-2652	49-19
NCS Pearson Inc 5601 Green Valley Dr Suite 220	Bloomington	MN	55437	**800-431-1421**	952-681-3000	176-3
NCSBCS (National Conference of States on Building Codes & Standards) 505 Huntmar Park Dr Suite 210	Herndon	VA	20170	**800-362-2633**	703-437-0100	49-7
NCSC (National Center for State Courts) 300 Newport Ave	Williamsburg	VA	23185	**800-616-6164**	757-253-2000	49-7
NCSS (National Council for the Social Studies) 8555 16th St Suite 500	Silver Spring	MD	20910	**800-296-7840**	301-588-1800	49-5
NCTC (National Cable Television Cooperative Inc) 11200 Corporate Ave	Lenexa	KS	66219	**800-825-0357**	913-599-5900	49-14
NCTE (National Council of Teachers of English) 1111 W Kenyon Rd	Urbana	IL	61801	**800-369-6283**	217-328-3870	49-5
NCTM (National Council of Teachers of Mathematics) 1906 Association Dr *Orders	Reston	VA	20191	**800-235-7566***	703-620-9840	49-5
nCube Corp 1825 NW 167th Pl	Beaverton	OR	97006	**800-654-2823**	503-629-5088	633
NDA (National Dart Assn) 5613 W 74th St	Indianapolis	IN	46278	**800-808-9884**	317-387-1299	48-22
NDCHealth Corp 1 National Data Plaza *NYSE: NDC*	Atlanta	GA	30329	**800-225-5632**	404-728-2000	223
NDR (National Dog Registry) PO Box 116	Woodstock	NY	12498	**800-637-3647**	845-679-2355	48-3
NDRI (National Disease Research Interchange) 1628 John F Kennedy Blvd 8 Penn Ctr 8th Fl	Philadelphia	PA	19103	**800-222-6374**	215-557-7361	265
NDS Americas 3501 Jamboree Rd Suite 200 *NASDAQ: NNDS*	Newport Beach	CA	92660	**866-398-8749**	949-725-2500	720
NDSC (National Down Syndrome Congress) 1370 Center Dr Suite 102	Atlanta	GA	30338	**800-232-6372**	770-604-9500	48-17
NDSS (National Down Syndrome Society) 666 Broadway 8th Fl	New York	NY	10012	**800-221-4602**	212-460-9330	48-17
NEA Medical Center 3024 Stadium Blvd	Jonesboro	AR	72401	**800-999-4486**	870-972-7000	366-2
NEA Today Magazine 1201 16th St NW	Washington	DC	20036	**800-229-4200**	202-822-7207	449-8

Listing	Toll-Free	Phone	Class
NEAC Compressor Service USA Inc 191 Howard St, Franklin PA 16323	**800-458-0453**	814-437-3711	170
Neal Robinson Wholesale Greenhouses 975 Robindale Rd, Brownsville TX 78523	**800-874-2740**	956-831-4656	363
Neapco Inc PO Box 399, Pottstown PA 19464	**800-821-2374**	610-323-6000	60
Near North Insurance Brokerage Inc 875 N Michigan Ave Suite 1900, Chicago IL 60611	**800-859-6719**	312-280-5600	383
Neas Ralph G Pres People for the American Way 2000 M St NW Suite 400, Washington DC 20036	**800-326-7329**	202-467-4999	561
Nebraska			
Arts Council 3838 Davenport St, Omaha NE 68131	**800-341-4067**	402-595-2122	335
Bill Status 2018 State Capitol Bldg, Lincoln NE 68509	**800-724-7456**	402-471-2877	425
Child Support Enforcement Div PO Box 94728, Lincoln NE 68509	**877-631-9973**	402-471-8715	335
Consumer Protection Div 2115 State Capitol Bldg, Lincoln NE 68509	**800-727-6432**	402-471-2682	335
Economic Development Dept PO Box 94666, Lincoln NE 68509	**800-426-6505**	402-471-3747	335
Public Accountancy Board PO Box 94725, Lincoln NE 68509	**800-564-6111**	402-471-3595	335
Travel & Tourism Div PO Box 98907, Lincoln NE 68509	**877-632-7275**	402-471-3796	335
Vocational Rehabilitation Services Div PO Box 94987, Lincoln NE 68509	**877-637-3422**	402-471-3644	335
Workers' Compensation Court PO Box 98908, Lincoln NE 68509	**800-599-5155**	402-471-6468	335
Nebraska Book Co Inc 4700 S 19th St, Lincoln NE 68512	**800-869-0366**	402-421-7300	97
Nebraska City News-Press PO Box 757, Nebraska City NE 68410	**877-269-3358**	402-873-3334	522-2
Nebraska College of Technical Agriculture RR 3 Box 23A, Curtis NE 69025	**800-328-7847**	308-367-4124	787
Nebraska Democratic Party 633 S 9th St Suite 201, Lincoln NE 68508	**800-677-7068**	402-434-2180	605-1
Nebraska Educational Telecommunications (NET) 1800 N 33rd St, Lincoln NE 68503	**800-228-4630**	402-472-3611	620
Nebraska Furniture Mart Inc 700 S 72nd St, Omaha NE 68114	**800-359-1200**	402-397-6100	316
Nebraska Machinery Co Inc PO Box 809, North Platte NE 69103	**800-494-9560**	308-532-3100	378
Nebraska Plastics Inc PO Box 45, Cozad NE 69130	**800-445-2887**	308-784-2500	585
Nebraska Realtors Assn 145 S 56th St Suite 100, Lincoln NE 68510	**800-777-5231**	402-323-6500	642
Nebraska Republican Party 1610 N St, Lincoln NE 68508	**800-829-3459**	402-475-2122	605-2
Nebraska State Bar Assn 635 S 14th St, Lincoln NE 68501	**800-927-0117**	402-475-7091	73
Nebraska Wesleyan University 5000 St Paul Ave, Lincoln NE 68504	**800-541-3818**	402-466-2371	163
NEBS (New England Business Service Inc) 500 Main St, Groton MA 01471	**800-225-6380*** *Sales	978-448-6111	111
NEC Computers International 10850 Gold Center Dr Suite 200, Rancho Cordova CA 95670	**800-632-4525**	916-763-7000	171-3
NEC Electronics Inc 2880 Scott Blvd, Santa Clara CA 95052	**800-366-9782**	408-588-6000	686
NEC Inc 1504 Elm Hill Pike, Nashville TN 37210	**800-666-8243**	615-367-9110	770
NEC-Mitsubishi Electronics Display of America Inc 500 Park Blvd Suite 1100, Itasca IL 60143	**888-632-6487*** *Sales	630-467-3000	171-4
NEC Research Institute Inc 4 Independence Way, Princeton NJ 08540	**888-777-6324**	609-520-1555	654
NEC Solutions (America) Inc 1250 N Arlington Heights Rd Suite 400, Itasca IL 60143	**800-632-4636**	630-467-5000	171-4
NEC USA Inc 8 Corporate Ctr Dr, Melville NY 11747	**800-338-9549**	631-753-7000	720
NECCO (New England Confectionery Co) 135 American Legion Hwy, Revere MA 02151	**800-225-5508**	781-485-4500	291-8
Necco Ed & Assoc 804 Solida Rd, South Point OH 45680	**877-506-3226**	740-894-1520	754
NED Corp 18 Grafton St 2nd Fl, Worcester MA 01604	**800-343-6086**	508-798-8546	484
NEDA (National Electronic Distributors Assn) 1111 Alderman Dr Suite 400, Alpharetta GA 30005	**800-347-6332**	678-393-9990	49-18
Nedco Electronics 594 American Way, Payson UT 84651	**800-605-2323**	801-465-1790	245
Nederlander Theatre 208 W 41st St, New York NY 10036	**800-755-4000**	212-307-4100	732
Needham & Co Inc 445 Park Ave 3rd Fl, New York NY 10022	**800-903-3268**	212-371-8300	679
Needletrades Industrial & Textile Employees. Union of 275 7th Ave, New York NY 10001	**800-238-6483**	212-265-7000	405
Needlework Assn. National 1100-H Brandywine Blvd PO Box 3388, Zanesville OH 43702	**800-889-8662**	740-455-6773	48-18
Neely Mfg Inc 2178 Hwy 2, Corydon IA 50060	**800-247-1785**	641-872-1100	10
Neenah Foundry Co 2121 Brooks Ave, Neenah WI 54956	**800-558-5075**	920-725-7000	302
Neenah Paper Inc 1400 Holcomb Bridge Rd, Roswell GA 30076	**800-558-5061*** *Cust Svc	770-587-8000	542-3
Neff Athletic Lettering Co 645 Pine St PO Box 218, Greenville OH 45331	**800-232-6333*** *Cust Svc	937-548-3194	766
Neff Corp 3750 NW 87th Ave Suite 400, Miami FL 33178	**888-709-6333**	305-513-3350	261-2
Neff Packaging Solutions 2001 Kuntz Rd, Dayton OH 45404	**800-445-4383**	937-233-3333	539
Negro College Fund Inc. United 8260 Willow Oaks Corporate Dr Suite 400, Fairfax VA 22031	**800-331-2244**	703-205-3400	48-11
Negro Leagues Baseball Museum 1616 E 18th St, Kansas City MO 64108	**888-221-6526**	816-221-1920	511
NEH (National Endowment for the Humanities) 1100 Pennsylvania Ave NW, Washington DC 20506	**800-634-1121**	202-606-8400	336-16
Nehi Royal Crown Bottling & Distributing Co Inc PO Box 1687, Bowling Green KY 42102	**800-626-5255**	270-842-8106	82-2
Nehring Electric Works Inc 813 E Locust St, DeKalb IL 60115	**800-435-4481**	815-756-2741	801
NeighborCare Inc 7 E Lee St, Baltimore MD 21202 *NASDAQ: NCRX*	**888-872-3030**	410-752-2600	576
Neighborhood Health Partnership Inc 7600 Corporate Ctr Dr, Miami FL 33126	**800-354-0222**	305-715-2200	384-3
Neighborhood Hospice 795 E Marshall St Suite 204, West Chester PA 19380	**800-848-1155**	610-696-6511	365
Neighborhood Reinvestment Corp Regional Offices North Central District 1111 W 39th St Suite 100W, Kansas City MO 64111	**800-823-1428**	816-931-4176	336-16
Neighbors Inc. World 4127 NW 122nd St, Oklahoma City OK 73120	**800-242-6387**	405-752-9700	48-5
Neil Simon Theatre 250 W 52nd St, New York NY 10019	**800-755-4000**	212-307-4100	732
Neilsen Mfg Inc 3501 Portland Rd NE, Salem OR 97303	**800-292-2495**	503-585-0040	709
Nektar Therapeutics 150 Industrial Rd, San Carlos CA 94070 *NASDAQ: NKTR*	**800-438-1985**	650-631-3100	86
Nekton Diving Cruises 520 SE 32nd St, Fort Lauderdale FL 33316	**800-899-6753**	954-463-9324	217
NELCO Inc 98 Baldwin Ave, Woburn MA 01801	**800-635-2613**	781-933-1940	469
Nellie Mae Corp 50 Braintree Hill Park Suite 300, Braintree MA 02184	**800-367-8848*** *Cust Svc	781-849-1325	215
Nellie Mae Education Foundation 1250 Hancock St Suite 205N, Quincy MA 02169	**877-635-5436**	781-348-4200	300
Nelnet Inc 121 S 13th St Suite 201, Lincoln NE 68508 *NYSE: NNI*	**888-486-4722**	402-458-2370	215
Nelson & Belding Contractors Corp 17626 S Broadway, Gardena CA 90248	**800-464-9969**	310-527-6200	188-5
Nelson Bibles PO Box 141000, Nashville TN 37214	**800-251-4000**	615-889-9000	623-4
Nelson Crab Inc PO Box 520, Tokeland WA 98590	**800-262-0069**	360-267-2911	291-13
Nelson Electric Supply Co Inc 926 State St, Racine WI 53404	**800-994-5666**	262-637-7661	245
Nelson Information 195 Broadway, New York NY 10007	**800-333-6357**	646-822-6499	623-6
Nelson-Jameson Inc 2400 E 5th St, Marshfield WI 54449	**800-826-8302**	715-387-1151	378
Nelson Laboratories Ltd 4001 N Lewis Ave, Sioux Falls SD 57104	**800-843-3322**	605-336-2451	574
Nelson LR Corp 1 Sprinkler Ln, Peoria IL 61615	**800-635-7668*** *Sales	309-690-2200	420
Nelson Motivation Inc 12245 World Trade Dr Suite C, San Diego CA 92128	**800-575-5521**	858-487-1046	753
Nelson Mullins Riley & Scarborough LLP 1320 Main St 17th Fl, Columbia SC 29201	**800-237-2000**	803-799-2000	419
Nelson & Small Inc 212 Canco Rd, Portland ME 04103	**800-341-0780**	207-775-5666	38
Nelson Thomas Inc PO Box 141000, Nashville TN 37214 *NYSE: TNM*	**800-251-4000**	615-889-9000	623-4
Nelson Tommy 402 BNA Dr Bldg 100 Suite 600, Nashville TN 37217	**800-251-4000**	615-889-9000	623-4
Nelson Tree Service Inc 3300 Office Park Dr, Dayton OH 45439	**800-522-4311**	937-294-1313	765
Nelson Westerberg Inc 1500 Arthur Ave Suite 200, Elk Grove Village IL 60007	**800-245-2080**	847-437-2080	508
Nemacolin Woodlands Resort & Spa 1001 Lafayette Dr, Farmington PA 15437	**800-422-2736**	724-329-8555	655
Nemaha-Marshall Electric Co-op PO Box 0, Axtell KS 66403	**866-736-2347**	785-736-2345	244
Nemetschek North America 7150 Riverwood Dr, Columbia MD 21046	**888-646-4223**	410-290-5114	176-8
Nemschoff Chairs Inc 909 N 8th St, Sheboygan WI 53081	**800-203-8916*** *Cust Svc	920-457-7726	314-3
Neogen Corp 620 Lesher Pl, Lansing MI 48912 *NASDAQ: NEOG*	**800-234-5333**	517-372-9200	229
NEON Communications Inc 2200 W Park Dr Suite 200, Westborough MA 01581	**800-891-5080**	508-616-7800	387
Neon Software Inc 244 Lafayette Cir, Lafayette CA 94549	**800-334-6366*** *Sales	925-283-9771	176-12
Neon Systems Inc 14100 SW Fwy Suite 500, Sugar Land TX 77478 *NASDAQ: NEON*	**800-505-6366**	281-491-4200	176-1
Neonatal Nurses. Association of Women's Health Obstetric & 2000 L St NW Suite 740, Washington DC 20036	**800-673-8499**	202-261-2400	49-8
Neonatal Nurses. National Assn of 4700 W Lake Ave, Glenview IL 60025	**800-451-3795**	847-375-3660	49-8
NeoPhotonics Corp 2911 Zanker Rd, San Jose CA 95134	**800-499-7519**	408-232-9200	686
Neopost Inc 30955 Huntwood Ave, Hayward CA 94544	**800-827-4543*** *Cust Svc	510-489-6800	112
Neopost Inc Canada 150 Steelcase Rd W, Markham ON L3R3J9	**800-636-7678**	905-475-3722	112
Neoprobe Corp 425 Metro Place N Suite 300, Dublin OH 43017	**800-793-0079**	614-793-7500	375
NeoResins 730 Main St, Wilmington MA 01887	**800-225-0947**	978-658-6600	594-2
NeoRx Corp 300 Elliott Ave W Suite 500, Seattle WA 98119 *NASDAQ: NERX*	**800-736-3679**	206-281-7001	86
Neostyle Eyewear Corp 2605 State St, San Diego CA 92103	**800-854-2782**	619-299-0755	532
Neoware Systems Inc 400 Feheley Dr, King of Prussia PA 19406 *NASDAQ: NWRE*	**800-437-1551**	610-277-8300	171-3
NEPA (Newsletter & Electronic Publishers Assn) 1501 Wilson Blvd Suite 509, Arlington VA 22209	**800-356-9302**	703-527-2333	49-14
Nepa Pallet & Container Co Inc PO Box 399, Snohomish WA 98291	**800-562-3932**	360-568-3185	541
Nepera Inc 41 Arden House Rd, Harriman NY 10926	**800-963-7372**	845-782-1200	470
Nephrology Nurses' Assn. American 200 E Holly Ave, Pitman NJ 08080	**888-600-2662**	856-256-2320	49-8
Nephron Pharmaceuticals Corp 4121 SW 34th St, Orlando FL 32811	**800-443-4313**	407-246-1389	573
Neptco Inc 30 Hamlet St, Pawtucket RI 02861	**800-354-5445**	401-722-5500	717
Neptune Society 4312 Woodman Ave 3rd Fl, Sherman Oaks CA 91423	**888-637-8863**	818-953-9995	499
NER Data Products Inc 307 S Delsea Dr, Glassboro NJ 08028	**800-257-5235**	856-881-5524	616
NERA (Naval Enlisted Reserve Assn) 6703 Farragut Ave, Falls Church VA 22042	**800-776-9020**	703-534-1329	48-19
Nerdy Books 135 Main St, Flemington NJ 08822	**866-843-8477**	908-788-4676	623-2
Nesbitt Contracting Co Inc 100 S Price Rd, Tempe AZ 85281	**800-966-4188**	480-894-2831	187-4

Name / Address	City	State	Zip	Toll-Free	Phone	Class
NESC Williams Inc 18 Harrison St.	Zanesville	OH	43701	**800-453-4644**	740-453-0375	62-5
NESDA (National Electronics Service Dealers Assn) 3608 Pershing Ave	Fort Worth	TX	76107	**800-946-0201**	817-921-9061	49-18
Nestle Purina PetCare Co Checkerboard Sq	Saint Louis	MO	63164	**800-835-6369**	314-982-1000	568
Nestle Waters North America Inc 2767 E Imperial Hwy	Brea	CA	92821	**800-877-7775**	714-792-2100	792
NET (Nebraska Educational Telecommunications) 1800 N 33rd St	Lincoln	NE	68503	**800-228-4630**	402-472-3611	620
net-linx Publishing Solutions Inc 1740 N Market Blvd	Sacramento	CA	95834	**800-445-4744**	916-830-2400	176-10
Net2Phone Inc 520 Broad St. *NASDAQ: NTOP*	Newark	NJ	07102	**800-225-5438**	973-438-3111	721
NetBank Inc 11475 Great Oaks Way Royal Ctr Three Suite 100 *NASDAQ: NTBK*	Alpharetta	GA	30022	**888-256-6932**	770-343-6006	71
NetBank Payment Systems Inc 200 Briarwood W Dr	Jackson	MS	39206	**800-523-2104**	601-956-1222	70
NetBase Corp 4443 Brookfield Corporate Dr Suite 200 *Cust Svc	Chantilly	VA	20151	**888-456-6528***	703-814-4040	39
NetByTel Inc 1141 S Rogers Cir Suite 9	Boca Raton	FL	33487	**800-638-2983**	561-988-5050	606
Netegrity Inc 201 Jones Rd. *NASDAQ: NETE*	Waltham	MA	02451	**800-325-9870**	781-890-1700	176-12
NetFlix Inc 970 University Ave *NASDAQ: NFLX* ■ *Cust Svc	Los Gatos	CA	95032	**888-638-3549***	408-399-3700	784
NetFutures 150 S Wacker Dr Suite 2350	Chicago	IL	60606	**888-449-6784**	312-277-0051	167
NETg Inc 1751 W Diehl Rd 2nd Fl. *Cust Svc	Naperville	IL	60563	**800-265-1900***	630-369-3000	752
NETGEAR Inc 4500 Great America Pkwy *NASDAQ: NTGR* ■ *Cust Svc	Santa Clara	CA	95054	**888-638-4327***	408-907-8000	174
NETGROCER.com Inc 14 Post Rd	Oakland	NJ	07436	**888-638-4762**	201-337-3900	339
Netherland Rubber Co 2931 Exon Ave	Cincinnati	OH	45241	**800-582-1877**	513-733-0883	321
Netherlands Board of Tourism & Conventions 355 Lexington Ave 19th Fl	New York	NY	10017	**888-464-6552**	212-370-7360	764
NetIQ Corp 3553 N 1st St *NASDAQ: NTIQ* ■ *Sales	San Jose	CA	95134	**888-323-6768***	408-856-3000	176-12
NETL (National Energy Technology Laboratory) US Dept of Energy 3610 Collins Ferry Rd PO Box 880	Morgantown	WV	26507	**800-432-8330**	304-285-4764	654
NetLibrary Inc 4888 Pearl East Cir Suite 103	Boulder	CO	80301	**800-413-4557**	303-415-2548	97
NetManage Inc 20883 Stevens Creek Blvd *NASDAQ: NETM*	Cupertino	CA	95014	**800-558-7656**	408-973-7171	176-12
NetNation Communications Inc 555 W Hastings St Suite 1410	Vancouver	BC	V6B4N6	**888-277-0000**	604-684-6892	795
Neto Sausage Co Inc PO Box 578	Santa Clara	CA	95052	**888-482-6386**	408-296-0818	291-26
NetPro Computing Inc 4747 N 22 St Suite 400	Phoenix	AZ	85016	**800-998-5090**	602-346-3600	176-12
NetRatings Inc 890 Hillview Ct Suite 300 *NASDAQ: NTRT*	Milpitas	CA	95035	**888-634-1222**	408-941-2900	458
Netrition Inc 20 Petra Ln.	Albany	NY	12205	**888-817-2411**	518-464-0765	350
Netscape Communications Corp 466 Ellis St *Tech Supp	Mountain View	CA	94043	**800-411-0707***	650-254-1900	176-7
NetScout Systems Inc 310 Littleton Rd *NASDAQ: NTCT*	Westford	MA	01886	**800-999-5946**	978-614-4000	176-7
NetSilicon Inc 411 Waverly Oaks Rd Suite 304	Waltham	MA	02452	**800-243-2333**	781-647-1234	686
NetSolve Inc 9500 Amberglen Blvd *NASDAQ: NTSL*	Austin	TX	78729	**800-638-7658**	512-340-3000	178
NetSuite Inc 2955 Campus Dr Suite 100	San Mateo	CA	94403	**800-762-5524**	650-627-1000	39
NetTest North America Inc 6 Rhoads Dr	Utica	NY	13502	**800-443-6154**	315-266-5000	247
netViz Corp 12 S Summit Ave Suite 300	Gaithersburg	MD	20877	**800-827-1856**	301-258-5087	176-7
Network Appliance Inc 495 E Java Dr. *NASDAQ: NTAP* ■ *Sales	Sunnyvale	CA	94089	**800-443-4537***	408-822-6000	174
Network Communications Inc 2305 New Point Pkwy	Lawrenceville	GA	30043	**800-841-3401**	770-962-7220	615
Network Communications International Corp 1809 Judson Rd	Longview	TX	75605	**888-686-3699**	903-757-4455	721
Network Computing Devices Inc 10795 SW Cascade Blvd	Portland	OR	97223	**800-800-9599**	503-431-8600	171-3
Network Courier Service Corp 9010 Bellanca Ave	Los Angeles	CA	90045	**800-938-1801**	310-410-7700	536
Network Equipment Technologies Inc 6900 Paseo Padre Pkwy. *NYSE: NWK*	Fremont	CA	94555	**888-828-8080**	510-713-7300	720
Network Information Center 7990 Science Applications Ct MS CV-50	Vienna	VA	22183	**800-365-3642**	703-676-1051	336-3
Network Services LLC 525 S Douglas St.	El Segundo	CA	90245	**800-536-0700**		721
Network Solutions LLC 13200 Woodland Pk Rd	Herndon	VA	20171	**800-638-9759**	703-742-0400	389
Network Telephone Corp 3300 N Pace Blvd.	Pensacola	FL	32505	**888-432-4855**	850-432-4855	721
Network World Magazine 118 Turnpike Rd.	Southborough	MA	01772	**800-622-1108**	508-875-6400	449-7
Networking. Consortium for School 1710 Rhode Island Ave NW Suite 900	Washington	DC	20036	**866-267-8747**	202-861-2676	48-9
Networld Communications 3221 20th St. *Cust Svc	San Francisco	CA	94110	**800-284-9519***	415-276-8000	720
NetZero Inc 21301 Burbank Blvd.	Woodland Hills	CA	91367	**877-638-3117**	818-287-3000	390
Neuberger Berman Funds PO Box 8403	Boston	MA	02266	**800-877-9700**	212-476-8800	517
Neuberger Berman LLC 605 3rd Ave	New York	NY	10158	**800-223-6448**	212-476-9000	393
Neumade Products Corp 30-40 Pecks Ln	Newtown	CT	06470	**800-645-6687**	203-270-1100	580
Neumade Products Corp Xetron Div 30-40 Pecks Ln	Newtown	CT	06470	**800-526-0722**	203-270-1100	580
Neumann College 1 Neumann Dr	Aston	PA	19014	**800-963-8626**	610-459-0905	163
Neun HP Co Inc 75 N Main St.	Fairport	NY	14450	**800-724-2641**	585-388-1360	102
Neural Networks Society. IEEE IEEE Operations Ctr 445 Hoes Ln	Piscataway	NJ	08854	**800-678-4333**	732-981-0060	49-19
Neurochem Inc 275 Armand Frappier *NASDAQ: NRMX*	Laval	QC	H7V4A7	**877-680-4500**	450-680-4500	86
Neurocrine Biosciences Inc 12790 El Camino Real *NASDAQ: NBIX*	San Diego	CA	92130	**800-876-3522**	858-617-7600	86
Neurofibromatosis Foundation. National 95 Pine St 16th Fl	New York	NY	10005	**800-323-7938**	212-344-6633	48-17
Neurological Surgeons. American Assn of 5550 Meadowbrook Dr.	Rolling Meadows	IL	60068	**888-566-2267**	847-378-0500	49-8
Neurology. American Academy of 1080 Montreal Ave	Saint Paul	MN	55116	**800-879-1960**	651-695-2717	49-8
NeuroMetrix 62 4th Ave. *NASDAQ: NURO*	Waltham	MA	02451	**888-786-7287**	781-890-9989	249
Neuroscience Nurses. American Assn of 4700 W Lake Ave	Glenview	IL	60025	**888-557-2266**	847-375-4733	49-8
Neutral Posture Inc 3904 N Texas Ave	Bryan	TX	77803	**800-446-3746**	979-778-0502	314-1
Neutrogena Corp 5760 W 96th St *Cust Svc	Los Angeles	CA	90045	**800-217-1136***	310-642-1150	211
Neuville Industries Inc 9451 Neuville Ave PO Box 286	Hildebran	NC	28637	**800-334-2587**	828-397-5566	153-10
Nevada *Bill Status* 401 S Carson St	Carson City	NV	89701	**800-992-6761**	775-684-6800	425
Child Support Enforcement Office 2527 N Carson St.	Carson City	NV	89706	**800-992-0900**	775-687-4744	335
Consumer Affairs Div 1850 E Sahara Ave Suite 101	Las Vegas	NV	89104	**800-326-5202**	702-486-7355	335
Economic Development Commission 108 E Proctor St.	Carson City	NV	89701	**800-336-1600**	775-687-4325	335
Insurance Div 788 Fairview Dr Suite 300	Carson City	NV	89701	**800-992-0900**	775-687-4270	335
Motor Vehicles Dept 555 Wright Way	Carson City	NV	89711	**877-368-7828**	775-684-4368	335
Securities Div 555 E Washington Ave Suite 5200	Las Vegas	NV	89101	**800-758-6440**	702-486-2440	335
Tourism Commission 401 N Carson St.	Carson City	NV	89701	**800-237-0774**	775-687-4322	335
Nevada Appeal 580 Mallory Way	Carson City	NV	89701	**800-221-8013**	775-882-2111	522-2
Nevada Assn of Realtors 760 Margrave Dr Suite 200	Reno	NV	89502	**800-748-5526**	775-829-5911	642
Nevada Dental Assn 8863 W Flamingo Rd Suite 102	Las Vegas	NV	89147	**800-962-6710**	702-255-4211	225
Nevada Landing Hotel & Casino 2 Goodsprings Rd	Jean	NV	89019	**800-628-6682**	702-387-5000	133
Nevada Magazine 401 N Carson St	Carson City	NV	89701	**800-495-3281**	775-687-5416	449-22
Nevada Power Co 6226 W Sahara Ave *Cust Svc	Las Vegas	NV	89146	**800-331-3103***	702-367-5000	774
Nevada State Bank PO Box 990	Las Vegas	NV	89125	**800-727-4743**	702-383-0009	71
Nevada. State Bar of 600 E Charleston Blvd	Las Vegas	NV	89104	**800-254-2797**	702-382-2200	73
Nevele Grande Resort & Country Club 1 Nevele Rd	Ellenville	NY	12428	**800-647-6000**	845-647-6000	655
Neville Chemical Co 2800 Neville Rd *Cust Svc	Pittsburgh	PA	15225	**877-704-4200***	412-331-4200	594-2
Nevo Corp 50 Haynes Ct	Ronkonkoma	NY	11779	**800-955-6836**	631-585-8787	313
New Age Electronics Inc 21950 Arnold Ctr Rd	Carson	CA	90810	**800-234-0300**	310-549-0000	113
New Age Health Spa 7491 SR 55	Neversink	NY	12765	**800-682-4348**	845-985-7601	697
New Amsterdam Theatre 214 W 42nd St.	New York	NY	10036	**800-755-4000**	212-307-4100	732
New Balance Athletic Shoe Inc 20 Guest St Brighton Landing	Boston	MA	02135	**800-622-1218**	617-783-4000	296
New Belgium Brewing Co 500 Linden St.	Fort Collins	CO	80524	**888-622-4044**	970-221-0524	103
New Braunfels Chamber of Commerce 390 S Seguin St.	New Braunfels	TX	78130	**800-572-2626**	830-625-2385	137
New Braunfels Herald-Zeitung 707 Landa St	New Braunfels	TX	78130	**877-409-9860**	830-625-9144	522-2
New Britain Candy Co 24 Maple St	Wethersfield	CT	06129	**800-382-0515**	860-257-7058	292-3
New Brunswick Scientific Co Inc 44 Talmadge Rd *NASDAQ: NBSC* ■ *Cust Svc	Edison	NJ	08818	**800-631-5417***	732-287-1200	411
New Brunswick Theological Seminary 17 Seminary Pl.	New Brunswick	NJ	08901	**800-445-6287**	732-247-5241	164-3
New Castle Industries Inc PO Box 7359	New Castle	PA	16107	**800-897-2830**	724-656-5600	610
New Centennial Inc 420 10th Ave PO Box 708	Columbus	GA	31902	**800-241-7541**	706-323-6446	92
New Century Financial Corp 18400 Von Karman Ave Suite 1000 *NYSE: NEW*	Irvine	CA	92612	**800-967-7623**	949-440-7030	498
New City Packing & Provision 2600 Church Rd	Aurora	IL	60504	**800-621-0397**	630-851-8800	465
New College of California 50 Fell St	San Francisco	CA	94102	**800-335-6262**	415-241-1300	163
New Columbia Joist Co 2093 Old Hwy 15	New Columbia	PA	17856	**800-233-3199**	570-568-6761	688
NEW Cooperative Inc 2626 1st Ave S	Fort Dodge	IA	50501	**800-362-2233**	515-955-2040	271
New Dimensions Radio Broadcasting Network PO Box 569	Ukiah	CA	95482	**800-935-8273**	707-468-5215	632

	Toll-Free	Phone	Class
New Dimensions Research Corp 260 Spagnoli Rd. Melville NY 11747	800-637-8870	631-694-1356	231
New Directions Behavioral Health LLC PO Box 6729 Leawood KS 66206	800-528-5763	913-982-8200	454
New Directions Inc 30800 Chagrin Blvd Cleveland OH 44124	800-750-6709	216-591-0324	712
New Edge Networks 3000 Columbia House Blvd Suite 106 Vancouver WA 98661	877-725-3343	360-693-9009	390
New England Airlines Inc 56 Airport Rd Westerly RI 02891	800-243-2460	401-596-2460	26
New England Art Publisher Inc DBA Birchcraft Studios Inc PO Box 328 Rockland MA 02370	800-333-0405	781-878-5151	130
New England Baptist Hospital 125 Parker Hill Ave. Boston MA 02120	800-340-6324	617-754-5214	366-2
New England Bible College 879 Sawyer St South Portland ME 04116	800-286-1859	207-799-5979	163
New England Business Service Inc (NEBS) 500 Main St Groton MA 01471 *Sales	800-225-6380*	978-448-6111	111
New England Center 15 Strafford Ave University of New Hampshire Durham NH 03824	800-590-4334	603-862-2712	370
New England Central Railway Inc 2 Federal St Suite 201 Saint Albans VT 05478 *Cust Svc	800-800-3450*	802-527-3450	634
New England Coffee Co 100 Charles St Malden MA 02149	800-225-3537	781-324-8094	291-7
New England College 26 Bridge St Henniker NH 03242	800-521-7642	603-428-2211	163
New England College of Finance 89 South St 1 Lincoln Plaza Boston MA 02111	888-696-6323	617-951-2350	158
New England Computer Services Inc 168 Boston Post Rd Suites 6 & 7 Madison CT 06443 *Sales	800-766-6327*	203-245-3999	176-10
New England Confectionery Co (NECCO) 135 American Legion Hwy Revere MA 02151	800-225-5508	781-485-4500	291-8
New England Container Co Inc 455 George Washington Hwy Smithfield RI 02917	800-333-3109	401-231-2100	197
New England Culinary Institute 250 Main St Montpelier VT 05602	877-223-6324	802-223-6324	787
New England Door Corp 15 Campanelli Cir Canton MA 02021	800-969-5151	781-821-2737	489
New England Financial 501 Boylston St Boston MA 02116 *Cust Svc	800-388-4000*	617-578-2000	384-2
New England Gas Co 100 Weybosset St Providence RI 02903	800-227-8000	401-272-5040	774
New England Homes Inc 270 Ocean Rd Greenland NH 03840	800-800-8831	603-436-8830	107
New England Institute of Technology 2410 Metro Centre Blvd West Palm Beach FL 33407	800-826-9986	561-842-8324	787
New England Institute of Technology 2500 Post Rd Warwick RI 02886	800-736-7744	401-467-7744	787
New England Insulation Co 55 North St. Canton MA 02021	800-346-6307	781-828-6600	188-10
New England Journal of Medicine 10 Shattuck St Boston MA 02115	800-843-6356	617-734-9800	449-16
New England Life Insurance Co 501 Boylston St Boston MA 02116	800-388-4000	617-578-2000	384-2
New England Newsclip Agency Inc 5 Auburn St Framingham MA 01701	800-235-3879	508-879-4460	612
New England Newspaper Supply Co 9 Railroad Ave Millbury MA 01527	800-347-7377	508-865-0800	523
New England Organ Bank 1 Gateway Ctr Suite 202 Newton MA 02458	800-446-6362	617-244-8000	535
New England Plastics Corp 126 Duchaine Blvd New Bedford MA 02745 *Cust Svc	800-292-3500*	508-998-3111	593
New England Revolution 1 Patriot Pl Gillette Stadium Foxboro MA 02035	877-438-7387	508-543-5001	703
New England Ropes Inc 848 Airport Rd Fall River MA 02720	800-333-6679	508-678-8200	207
New England Securities Corp 485 E Rt 1 S 4th Fl Iselin NJ 08830	800-472-7227		679
New England Security Inc 10 Industrial Dr PO Box 562 Westerly RI 02891	800-556-7395	401-596-0660	683
New Enterprise Rural Electric Co-op Inc PO Box 75 New Enterprise PA 16664	800-270-3177	814-766-3221	244
New Era Cap Co Inc 8061 Erie Rd Derby NY 14047	800-989-0445	716-549-0445	153-9
New Focus Inc 2584 Junction Ave San Jose CA 95134 *Sales	866-683-6287*	408-919-1500	534
New Frontier The 3120 Las Vegas Blvd S Las Vegas NV 89109	800-634-6966	702-794-8200	133
New Hampshire			
Housing Finance Authority PO Box 5087 Manchester NH 03108	800-439-7247	603-472-8623	335
Travel & Tourism Development Office PO Box 1856 Concord NH 03302	800-386-4664	603-271-2665	335
Victims' Assistance Commission 33 Capitol St. Concord NH 03301	800-300-4500	603-271-1284	335
Worker's Compensation Div 95 Pleasant St Concord NH 03301	800-272-4353	603-271-3176	335
New Hampshire Business & Industry Assn 122 N Main St 3rd Fl Concord NH 03301	800-540-5388	603-224-5388	138
New Hampshire Community Technical College			
Berlin Campus 2020 Riverside Dr Berlin NH 03570	800-445-4525	603-752-1113	787
Laconia Campus 379 Belmont Rd Laconia NH 03246	800-357-2992	603-524-3207	787
New Hampshire Distributors Inc 65 Regional Dr Concord NH 03301	800-852-3781	603-224-9991	82-1
New Hampshire Electric Co-op 579 Tenney Mountain Hwy Plymouth NH 03264	800-698-2007	603-536-1800	244
New Hampshire Institute of Art 148 Concord St Manchester NH 03104	866-241-4918	603-623-0313	509
New Hampshire Medical Society 7 N State St Concord NH 03301	800-564-1909	603-224-1909	466
New Hampshire Office of Travel & Tourism 172 Pembroke Rd PO Box 1856 Concord NH 03302	800-386-4664	603-271-2666	205
New Hampshire Plastics Inc 1 Bouchard St. Manchester NH 03103	800-258-3036	603-669-8523	589
New Hampshire Public Television (NHPTV) 268 Mast Rd Durham NH 03824	800-639-8408	603-868-1100	620
New Hampshire Technical Institute 31 College Dr Concord NH 03301	800-247-0179	603-271-6484	787
New Hampshire Thrift Bancshares Inc 9 Main St Newport NH 03773 *NASDAQ: NHTB*	800-281-5772	603-863-5772	355-2
New Hanover Regional Medical Center 2131 S 17th St. Wilmington NC 28401	877-228-8135	910-343-7000	366-2
New Haven (Greater) Convention & Visitors Bureau 59 Elm St. New Haven CT 06510	800-332-7829	203-777-8550	205
New Haven Hotel 229 George St. New Haven CT 06510	800-644-6835	203-498-3100	373
New Haven Register 40 Sargent Dr. New Haven CT 06511	800-925-2509	203-789-5200	522-2
New High Glass Inc 12713 SW 125th Ave Miami FL 33186	800-452-7787	305-232-0840	538
New Holland Church Furniture 313 Prospect St New Holland PA 17557	800-648-9663	717-354-4521	314-3
New Holland Concrete 828 E Earl Rd PO Box 218 New Holland PA 17557	800-543-3860	717-354-1200	181
New Holland Construction North America 245 E North Ave Carol Stream IL 60188	888-290-7377	630-260-4000	269
New Horizon Kids Quest Inc 16355 36th Ave N Suite 700 Plymouth MN 55446	800-941-1007	763-557-1111	146
New Horizons Computer Learning Centers Inc 1900 S State College Blvd Suite 100 Anaheim CA 92806	888-222-3380	714-712-1000	752
New Horizons Diagnostics Corp 9110 Red Branch Rd Columbia MD 21045	800-888-5015	410-992-9357	229
New Horizons Tour & Travel Inc 2727 Spring Arbor Rd Jackson MI 49203	800-327-4695	517-788-6822	748
New Horizons Worldwide Inc 1900 S State College Blvd Suite 200 Anaheim CA 92806 *NASDAQ: NEWH*	800-725-3276	714-940-8000	752
New Jersey			
Bill Status State House Annex PO Box 068 Trenton NJ 08625	800-792-8630	609-292-4840	425
Child Support Office PO Box 716 Trenton NJ 08625	800-621-5437	609-588-2385	335
Higher Education Student Assistance Authority 4 Quakerbridge Plaza PO Box 540 Trenton NJ 08625	800-792-8670	609-588-7944	711
Mental Health Services Div PO Box 272 Trenton NJ 08625	800-382-9717	609-777-0700	335
Military & Veterans' Affairs Dept 101 Eggert Crossing Rd Lawrenceville NJ 08648	800-624-0508	609-530-4600	335
Motor Vehicle Commission 225 E State St PO Box 160 Trenton NJ 08666	888-486-3339	609-292-6500	335
Travel & Tourism Div PO Box 820 Trenton NJ 08625	800-847-4865	609-777-0885	335
New Jersey Bureau of State Use Industries PO Box 863 Trenton NJ 08625	800-321-6524	609-292-4036	618
New Jersey Business Forms Mfg Co 55 W Sheffield Ave Englewood NJ 07631	800-466-6523	201-569-4500	111
New Jersey City University 2039 JFK Blvd Jersey City NJ 07305	888-441-6528	201-200-2000	163
New Jersey Clipping Service 75 E Northfield Rd Livingston NJ 07039	800-631-1160	973-994-3333	612
New Jersey Devils Continental Airlines Arena 50 Rt 120N East Rutherford NJ 07073	800-653-3845	201-935-6050	703
New Jersey Education Law Report PO Box 241 Burtonsville MD 20866	800-359-6049	301-384-1573	521-4
New Jersey Institute of Technology 323 ML King Jr Blvd Newark NJ 07102	800-926-6548	973-596-3000	163
New Jersey Machine Inc 56 Etna Rd Lebanon NH 03766 *Sales	800-432-2990*	603-448-0300	537
New Jersey Manufacturers Insurance Co 301 Sullivan Way West Trenton NJ 08628	800-232-6600	609-883-1300	384-4
New Jersey Medical Society 2 Princess Rd Lawrenceville NJ 08648	800-322-6765	609-896-1766	466
New Jersey Monthly Magazine 55 Park Pl Box 920 Morristown NJ 07963 *Cust Svc	888-419-0419*	973-539-8230	449-22
New Jersey Natural Gas Co 1415 Wyckoff Rd Wall NJ 07719	800-221-0051	732-938-1480	527
New Jersey Nets 390 Murray Hill Pkwy Nets Champion Ctr East Rutherford NJ 07073	800-765-6387	201-935-8888	703
New Jersey Performing Arts Center 1 Center St Newark NJ 07102	888-466-5722	973-642-8989	562
New Jersey Public Broadcasting PO Box 777 Trenton NJ 08625	800-792-8645	609-777-5000	620
New Jersey Symphony Orchestra 2 Central Ave Newark NJ 07102	888-255-3476	973-624-3713	563-3
New Jersey Transit Corp 1 Penn Plaza E Newark NJ 07105 *Cust Svc	800-772-3606*	973-491-7000	460
New Leaf Press PO Box 726 Green Forest AR 72638	800-999-3777	870-438-5288	623-4
New Life Hiking Spa 2617 Killington Rd Killington VT 05751	800-228-4676	802-422-4302	697
New Life Hospice 5255 N Abbe Rd Elyria OH 44035	800-770-5767	440-934-1458	365
New London Energy 410 Bank St New London CT 06320	800-944-8803	860-271-2020	311
New Method Steel Stamps Inc 31313 Kendall Ave Fraser MI 48026	888-318-6677	586-293-0200	459
New Mexico			
Arts Div 228 E Palace Ave Santa Fe NM 87501	800-879-4278	505-827-6490	335
Children Youth & Families Dept PO Drawer 5160 Santa Fe NM 87502	800-610-7610	505-827-7610	335
Consumer Protection Div PO Drawer 1508 Santa Fe NM 87504	800-300-2020	505-827-6060	335
Environment Dept 1190 St Francis Dr Santa Fe NM 87503	800-219-6157	505-827-2855	335
Ethics Administration 325 Don Gaspar St Suite 300 Santa Fe NM 87503	800-477-3632	505-827-3895	335
Higher Education Commission 1068 Cerrillos Rd Santa Fe NM 87501	800-279-9777	505-827-7383	335

Name / Address	City	State	Zip	Toll-Free	Phone	Class
Highway & Transportation Dept PO Box 1149	Santa Fe	NM	87504	**877-887-7094**	505-827-5100	335
Human Services Dept PO Box 2348	Santa Fe	NM	87504	**800-432-6217**	505-827-7750	335
Lieutenant Governor State Capitol Bldg 4th Fl	Santa Fe	NM	87503	**800-432-4406**	505-827-3050	335
Mortgage Finance Authority 344 4th St SW	Albuquerque	NM	87102	**800-444-6880**	505-843-6880	335
Secretary of State 325 Don Gaspar Ave Suite 300	Santa Fe	NM	87501	**800-477-3632**	505-827-3600	335
State Parks Div PO Box 1147	Santa Fe	NM	87504	**888-667-2757**	505-476-3355	335
Tourism Dept 491 Old Santa Fe Trail	Santa Fe	NM	87503	**800-545-2070**	505-827-7400	335
Vocational Rehabilitation Div 435 St Michaels Dr Bldg D	Santa Fe	NM	87505	**800-235-5387**	505-954-8500	335
New Mexico Central Reservations 800 20th St NW Suite B	Albuquerque	NM	87104	**800-466-7829**	505-766-9770	368
New Mexico Correctional Industries 4337 SR 14	Santa Fe	NM	87505	**800-568-8789**	505-827-8838	618
New Mexico Highlands University 1005 University St	Las Vegas	NM	87701	**877-850-9064**	505-425-7511	163
New Mexico Institute of Mining & Technology Campus Stn	Socorro	NM	87801	**800-428-8324**	505-835-5614	163
New Mexico Junior College 5317 Lovington Hwy	Hobbs	NM	88240	**800-657-6260**	505-392-4510	160
New Mexico Lions Eye Bank 2501 Yale Blvd SE Suite 100	Albuquerque	NM	87106	**888-616-3937**	505-266-3937	265
New Mexico Magazine 495 Old Santa Fe Trail	Santa Fe	NM	87501	**800-898-6639**	505-476-0202	449-22
New Mexico Medical Society 7770 Jefferson NE Suite 400	Albuquerque	NM	87109	**800-748-1596**	505-828-0237	466
New Mexico Military Institute 101 W College Blvd	Roswell	NM	88201	**800-421-5376***	505-624-8050	160
*Admitting						
New Mexico Museum of Space History PO Box 5430	Alamogordo	NM	88311	**877-333-6589**	505-437-2840	509
New Mexico Newspapers Inc PO Box 450	Farmington	NM	87499	**800-395-6397**	505-325-4545	623-8
New Mexico. Realtors Assn of 2201 Brothers Rd	Santa Fe	NM	87505	**800-224-2282**	505-982-2442	642
New Mexico. State Bar of 5121 Masthead St NE	Albuquerque	NM	87109	**800-876-6227**	505-797-6000	73
New Mexico State University PO Box 30001 MSC-3A	Las Cruces	NM	88003	**800-662-6678**	505-646-3121	163
Carlsbad Campus 1500 University Dr	Carlsbad	NM	88220	**888-888-2199**	505-234-9200	160
New Mexico State Veterans Center 992 S Broadway St	Truth or Consequences	NM	87901	**800-964-3976**	505-894-9081	780
New Mexico Symphony Orchestra 4407 Menaul Blvd NE	Albuquerque	NM	87110	**800-251-6676**	505-881-9590	563-3
New Moon Magazine 34 E Superior St Suite 200	Duluth	MN	55802	**800-381-4743**	218-728-5507	449-6
New Orleans Accommodations Bed & Breakfast Service 828 Rue Royal Suite 259	New Orleans	LA	70116	**888-240-0070**	504-561-0447	368
New Orleans Cold Storage & Warehouse Co Inc 3411 Jourdan Rd Terminal	New Orleans	LA	70126	**800-782-2653**	504-944-4400	790-2
New Orleans Hospitality Enterprises Inc 610 S Peter St	New Orleans	LA	70130	**800-543-6332**	504-587-1600	748
New Orleans Magazine 111 Veterans Memorial Blvd Suite 1800	Metairie	LA	70005	**877-221-3512***	504-831-3731	449-22
*Edit						
New Orleans Metropolitan Convention & Visitors Bureau 2020 St Charles Ave	New Orleans	LA	70130	**800-672-6124**	504-566-5011	205
New Orleans Opera Assn 305 Baronne St Suite 500	New Orleans	LA	70112	**800-881-4459**	504-529-2278	563-2
New Otani Hotel & Garden 120 S Los Angeles St	Los Angeles	CA	90012	**800-639-6826**	213-629-1200	373
New Otani Kaimana Beach Hotel 2863 Kalakaua Ave	Honolulu	HI	96815	**800-356-8264**	808-923-1555	373
New Otani North America Reservation Center 120 S Los Angeles St	Los Angeles	CA	90012	**800-421-8795**	213-629-1114	368
New Penn Motor Express Inc 625 S 5th Ave	Lebanon	PA	17042	**800-285-5000***	717-274-2521	769
*Cust Svc						
New Pig Corp 1 Pork Ave	Tipton	PA	16684	**800-468-4647**	814-684-0101	149
New Plan Excel Realty Trust Inc 420 Lexington Ave 7th Fl	New York	NY	10170	**800-468-7526**	646-344-8600	641
NYSE: NXL						
NEW Plastics Corp 112 4th St	Luxemburg	WI	54217	**800-666-5207**	920-845-2326	99
NEW Plastics Corp Renew Plastics Div PO Box 480	Luxemburg	WI	54217	**800-666-5207**	920-845-2326	647
New Process Steel Corp 5800 Westview Dr	Houston	TX	77055	**800-392-4989**	713-686-9631	483
New Readers Press 1320 Jamesville Ave	Syracuse	NY	13210	**800-448-8878**	315-422-9121	623-2
New Republic Magazine 1331 H St Suite 700	Washington	DC	20005	**800-827-1289***	202-508-4444	449-17
*Cust Svc						
New River Community College PO Box 1127	Dublin	VA	24084	**866-462-6722**	540-674-3600	160
New Riverside Ochre Co Inc PO Box 460	Cartersville	GA	30120	**800-248-0176***	770-382-4568	493-1
*Orders						
New Seabury Resort 20 Red Brook Rd	Mashpee	MA	02649	**800-999-9033**	508-477-9111	655
New South Cos Inc 3700 Clay Pond Rd	Myrtle Beach	SC	29579	**800-346-8675**	843-236-9399	671
New South Federal Savings Bank 1900 Crestwood Blvd	Irondale	AL	35210	**800-366-3030**	205-951-4000	71
New Technology Week Newsletter 1325 G St Suite 1003	Washington	DC	20005	**800-926-5464**	202-638-4260	521-12
New Tribes Mission (NTM) 1000 E 1st St	Sanford	FL	32771	**866-547-2460**	407-323-3430	48-20
New West Symphony 2100 E Thousand Oaks Blvd Suite D	Thousand Oaks	CA	91362	**866-776-8400**	805-497-5800	563-3
New World Coffee 100 Horizon Ctr Blvd	Hamilton	NJ	08691	**800-308-2457**	609-631-7000	156
New World Inn 265 33rd Ave	Columbus	NE	68601	**800-433-1492**	402-564-1492	373
New World Library 14 Pamaron Way	Novato	CA	94949	**800-972-6657**	415-884-2100	623-4
New World Pasta Co 85 Shannon Rd	Harrisburg	PA	17112	**800-227-2782***	717-526-2200	291-31
*Sales						
New World Restaurant Group Inc 100 Horizon Center Blvd	Hamilton	NJ	08691	**800-859-3090**	609-631-7000	656
New World Symphony 541 Lincoln Rd	Miami Beach	FL	33139	**800-597-3331**	305-673-3330	563-3
New World Tours Inc 7920 Gainsford Ct	Bristow	VA	20136	**800-322-7733**	703-643-9800	748
New York Academy of Sciences 2 E 63rd St	New York	NY	10021	**800-843-6927**	212-838-0230	49-19
New York Accessories Group Inc 411 5th Ave 4th Fl	New York	NY	10016	**800-366-7254**	212-532-7911	153-13
New York Air Brake Co 748 Starbuck Ave	Watertown	NY	13601	**888-836-6922**	315-786-5200	636
New York Arm Wrestling Assn (NYAWA) PO Box 670062	Flushing	NY	11367	**877-692-2767**	718-544-4592	48-22
New York Barbells 160 Home St	Elmira	NY	14904	**800-446-1833**	607-733-8038	263
New York Board of Trade 1 N End Ave 13th Fl	New York	NY	10282	**800-433-4348**	212-748-4000	680
New York Business Development Corp 50 Beaver St 6th Fl	Albany	NY	12207	**800-923-2504**	518-463-2268	214
New York Central Art Supply 62 3rd Ave	New York	NY	10003	**800-950-6111**	212-473-7705	45
New York Central Mutual Fire Insurance Co 1899 Central Plaza E	Edmeston	NY	13335	**800-234-6926**	607-965-8321	384-4
New York City Ballet Inc 20 Lincoln Center New York State Theatre	New York	NY	10023	**800-580-8730**	212-870-5656	563-1
New York & Co 450 W 33rd St 5th Fl	New York	NY	10001	**800-723-5333**	212-736-1222	155-6
NYSE: NWY						
New York Community Bancorp Inc 615 Merrick Ave	Westbury	NY	11590	**888-550-9888**	516-683-4100	355-2
NYSE: NYB						
New York Dragons 1535 Old Country Rd	Plainview	NY	11803	**800-882-4753**	516-501-6700	703
New York Education Law Report 360 Hiatt Dr	Palm Beach	FL	33418	**800-341-7874**	561-622-6520	521-4
New York Envelope Corp 29-10 Hunters Pt Ave	Long Island City	NY	11101	**800-877-9551**	718-786-0300	260
New York Graphic Society Ltd 129 Glover Ave	Norwalk	CT	06850	**800-677-6947**	203-847-2000	623-10
New York Harbor Watch 1733 Sheepshead Bay Rd	Brooklyn	NY	11235	**800-564-5433**	718-615-2500	522-4
New York Health & Racquet Club Inc 3 New York Plaza 18th Fl	New York	NY	10004	**800-472-2378**	212-797-1500	349
New York Helmsley Hotel 212 E 42nd St	New York	NY	10017	**800-221-4982**	212-490-8900	373
New York Historical Society 170 Central Park W	New York	NY	10024	**888-860-6947**	212-873-3400	509
New York Institute of Technology New York Institute of Technology Northern Blvd	Old Westbury	NY	11568	**800-345-6948**	516-686-1015	163
Islip Campus Carlton Ave	Central Islip	NY	11722	**800-873-6948**	631-348-3200	163
Manhattan Campus 1855 Broadway	New York	NY	10023	**800-345-6948**	212-261-1500	163
New York Law Journal 345 Park Ave S	New York	NY	10010	**800-888-8300**	212-779-9200	449-15
New York Library Assn (NYLA) 252 Hudson Ave	Albany	NY	12210	**800-252-6952**	518-432-6952	427
New York Life Foundation 51 Madison Ave Suite 1600	New York	NY	10010	**800-710-7945**	212-576-7341	299
New York Life Insurance & Annuity Corp 51 Madison Ave	New York	NY	10010	**800-598-2019**	212-576-7000	384-2
New York Magazine 444 Madison Ave	New York	NY	10022	**800-678-0900***	212-508-0700	449-22
*Circ						
New York Marine & General Insurance Co 913 3rd Ave 10th Fl	New York	NY	10022	**800-367-0224**	212-551-0600	384-4
New York Mets Shea Stadium 123-01 Roosevelt Ave	Flushing	NY	11368	**800-221-1155**	718-507-6387	703
New York Military Academy 78 Academy Ave	Cornwall-on-Hudson	NY	12520	**888-275-6962**	845-534-3710	611
New York New York Hotel & Casino 3790 Las Vegas Blvd S	Las Vegas	NV	89109	**800-693-6763**	702-740-6969	133
New York Palace Hotel 455 Madison Ave	New York	NY	10022	**800-697-2522**	212-888-7000	373
New York Post 1211 Ave of the Americas	New York	NY	10036	**800-552-7678**	212-930-8000	522-2
New York-Presbyterian Healthcare System 622 W 168th St	New York	NY	10032	**877-697-9355**	212-305-2500	348
New York Review of Books 1755 Broadway 5th Fl	New York	NY	10019	**800-829-5088**	212-757-8070	449-11
New York School of Interior Design 170 E 70th St	New York	NY	10021	**800-336-9743**	212-472-1500	163
New York (State)						
Agriculture & Markets Dept 10A Airline Dr	Albany	NY	12235	**800-554-4501**	518-457-3880	335
Bill Status 55 Elk St	Albany	NY	12210	**800-342-9860**	518-455-7545	425
Consumer Protection Board 5 Empire State Plaza Suite 2101	Albany	NY	12223	**800-697-1220**	518-474-3514	335
Empire State Development 30 S Pearl St	Albany	NY	12245	**800-782-8369**	518-292-5100	335
Higher Education Services Corp 99 Washington Ave	Albany	NY	12255	**888-697-4372**	518-473-1574	711
Parks Recreation & Historic Preservation Office 1 Empire State Plaza	Albany	NY	12238	**800-456-2267***	518-474-0456	335
*Campground Resv						

Name / Address	City	State	ZIP	Toll-Free	Phone	Class
Taxation & Finance Dept WA Harriman Campus Bldg 8	Albany	NY	12227	**800-225-5829**	518-457-2244	335
Tourism Div PO Box 2603	Albany	NY	12220	**800-225-5697**	518-474-4116	335
New York State Assn of Realtors 130 Washington Ave	Albany	NY	12210	**800-422-2501**	518-463-0300	642
New York State Bar Assn 1 Elk St	Albany	NY	12207	**800-342-3661**	518-463-3200	73
New York State Canal Corp 200 Southern Blvd	Albany	NY	12201	**800-422-6254**	518-471-5010	457
New York State Clipping Service 200 Central Park Ave N	Hartsdale	NY	10530	**800-772-5477**	914-948-2525	612
New York State Electric & Gas Corp Corporate Dr PO Box 5240	Binghamton	NY	13902	**800-572-1111**		774
New York State Medical Society 420 Lakeville Rd PO Box 5404	Lake Success	NY	11042	**800-523-4405**	516-488-6100	466
New York State Veterinary Medical Society 9 Highland Ave	Albany	NY	12205	**800-876-9867**	518-437-0787	782
New York Sun 105 Chambers St 2nd Fl	New York	NY	10007	**866-692-7861**	212-406-2000	522-2
New York Susquehanna & Western Railway Corp 1 Railroad Ave	Cooperstown	NY	13326	**800-366-6979**	607-547-2555	634
New York Testing Group Inc 47 Hudson St	Ossining	NY	10562	**800-282-8701**	631-952-7300	728
New York Tours 1414 Grand St	Hoboken	NJ	07030	**800-735-8530**		748
New York Wire Co 152 Main St	Mount Wolf	PA	17347	**800-699-4732**	717-266-5626	676
New Yorker Boiler Co Inc 21 E Lincoln Ave Suite 100	Hatfield	PA	19440	**800-535-4679**	215-855-8055	352
New Yorker Magazine 4 Times Sq	New York	NY	10036	**800-825-2510**	212-286-5400	449-11
New Yorker Magazine Cartoon Bank Div 145 Palisade St Suite 373	Dobbs Ferry	NY	10522	**800-897-8666**	914-478-5527	520
New York/New Jersey MetroStars 1 Harmon Plaza 3rd Fl	Secaucus	NJ	07094	**800-638-7684**	201-583-7000	703
New Zealand Tourism Board 501 Santa Monica Blvd Suite 300	Santa Monica	CA	90401	**866-639-9325**	310-395-7480	764
NewAge Industries Inc Plastics Technology Group 145 James Way	Southampton	PA	18966	**800-506-3924**	215-526-2300	364
NewAgeSys Inc 5 Vaughn Dr Suite 310	Princeton	NJ	08540	**888-863-9243**	609-919-9800	178
Newall Mfg Co 30 E Adams St	Chicago	IL	60603	**800-621-6296**	312-236-2789	399
Newark Group 20 Jackson Dr	Cranford	NJ	07016	**800-777-7890**	908-276-4000	551
Newark & Licking County Chamber of Commerce 50 W Locust St	Newark	OH	43055	**800-589-8224**	740-345-9757	137
Newark Museum 49 Washington St	Newark	NJ	07102	**800-768-7386**	973-596-6550	509
Newark In One 4801 N Ravenswood Ave	Chicago	IL	60640	**800-463-9275**		245
Newark Paperboard Products Inc 20 Jackson Dr	Cranford	NJ	07016	**800-777-7890**	908-276-4000	544
Newark Wire Cloth Co 160 Verona Ave	Newark	NJ	07013	**800-221-0392**	973-483-7700	676
Newberry Area Tourism Assn 4947 E County Rd 460	Newberry	MI	49868	**800-831-7292**	906-293-5739	205
Newberry College 2100 College St	Newberry	SC	29108	**800-845-4955**	803-276-5010	163
Newberry Electric Co-op Inc PO Box 477	Newberry	SC	29108	**800-479-8838**	803-276-1121	244
Newbury College 129 Fisher Ave	Brookline	MA	02445	**800-639-2879**	617-730-7000	163
Newcomb College 108 Newcomb Hall	New Orleans	LA	70118	**800-873-9283**	504-865-5422	163
Newcomer Products Inc PO Box 272	Latrobe	PA	15650	**800-245-6880**	724-537-5531	484
Newell Coach Corp PO Box 511	Miami	OK	74354	**888-363-9355**	918-542-3344	120
Newell Paper Co 1212 Grand Ave PO Box 631	Meridian	MS	39301	**800-844-8894**	601-693-1783	543
Newell Rubbermaid Inc Home & Family Group 10B Glenlake Pkwy Suite 600	Atlanta	GA	30328	**800-434-4314**	770-407-3800	477
Newell Rubbermaid Inc Kirsch Div 916 S Arcade Ave	Freeport	IL	61032	**800-328-7290**	815-235-4171	88
Newell Rubbermaid Inc Levolor Div 4110 Premier Dr	High Point	NC	27265	**800-232-2028**	336-812-8181	88
Newell Rubbermaid Inc Shur-Line Div 4051 S Iowa Ave	Saint Francis	WI	53235	**800-558-3958**	414-481-4500	104
Newfield Exploration Co 363 N Sam Houston Pkwy Suite 2020 *NYSE: NFX*	Houston	TX	77060	**800-419-4789**	281-847-6000	525
Newfound Technology Corp 330 Codman Hill Rd	Boxborough	MA	01719	**800-225-0228**	508-303-8200	633
Newfoundland & Labrador Tourism PO Box 8730	Saint John's	NL	A1B4K2	**800-563-6353**	709-729-2830	763
Newgen Results Corp 10243 Genetic Center Dr	San Diego	CA	92121	**800-763-9436**	858-346-5000	5
Newhall Land & Farming Co 23823 Valencia Blvd	Valencia	CA	91355	**800-342-3612**	661-255-4000	639
Newly Weds Foods Inc 4140 W Fullerton Ave *Cust Svc	Chicago	IL	60639	**800-621-7521***	773-489-7000	291-37
Newman & Co Inc 6101 Tacony St	Philadelphia	PA	19135	**800-523-3256**	215-333-8700	551
Newman JC Cigar Co 2701 16th St *Orders	Tampa	FL	33605	**800-477-1884***	813-248-2124	741-2
Newman Theological College 15611 St Albert Trail	Edmonton	AB	T6V1H3	**800-386-7231**	780-447-2993	164-3
Newman University 3100 McCormick Ave	Wichita	KS	67213	**877-639-6268**	316-942-4291	163
Newman's Inc 1300 Gazin St	Houston	TX	77020	**800-231-3505**	713-675-8631	378
NewMarket Corp 330 S 4th St *NYSE: NEU*	Richmond	VA	23219	**800-625-5191**	804-788-5000	355-3
NewMech Cos Inc 1633 Eustis St	Saint Paul	MN	55108	**800-942-4444**	651-645-0451	188-10
NewMil Bancorp Inc 19 Main St *NASDAQ: NMIL*	New Milford	CT	06776	**800-525-6672**	860-355-7600	355-2
Newpark Drilling Fluids LLC 5560B NW 72nd St	Oklahoma City	OK	73132	**800-444-0682**	405-721-0207	586
Newpoint Div Fiskars Brands Inc 17300 Medina Rd Suite 800	Plymouth	MN	55447	**800-639-7646**	763-557-8889	803
Newport Beach Conference & Visitors Bureau 110 Newport Ctr Dr Suite 120	Newport Beach	CA	92660	**800-942-6278**	949-719-6100	205
Newport Beachside Hotel & Resort 16701 Collins Ave	Miami Beach	FL	33160	**800-327-5476**	305-949-1300	373
Newport Business Institute 945 Greensburg Rd	Lower Burrell	PA	15068	**800-752-7695**	724-339-7542	158
Newport Business Institute 941 W 3rd St	Williamsport	PA	17701	**800-962-6971**	570-326-2869	158
Newport Corp 1791 Deere Ave *NASDAQ: NEWP* ■ *Sales	Irvine	CA	92606	**800-222-6440***	949-863-3144	534
Newport County Convention & Visitors Bureau 23 America's Cup Ave	Newport	RI	02840	**800-326-6030**	401-849-8048	205
Newport Daily Express PO Box 347	Newport	VT	05855	**800-464-6568**	802-334-6568	522-2
Newport Electronics Inc 2229 S Yale St *Cust Svc	Santa Ana	CA	92704	**800-639-7678***	714-540-4914	247
Newport Gateway Hotel 31 W Main Rd	Middletown	RI	02842	**800-427-9444**	401-847-2735	373
Newport (Greater) Chamber of Commerce 555 SW Coast Hwy	Newport	OR	97365	**800-262-7844**	541-265-8801	137
Newport Harbor Hotel & Marina 49 America's Cup Ave	Newport	RI	02840	**800-955-2558**	401-847-9000	373
Newport Jet Center 19711 Campus Dr Suite 100	Santa Ana	CA	92707	**800-500-5061**	949-851-5061	63
Newport Layton Home Fashions Inc 14546 N Lombard St	Portland	OR	97203	**800-752-2225**	503-283-4864	731
Newport Leasing Inc 4750 Von Karman Ave *Cust Svc	Newport Beach	CA	92660	**800-678-9426***	949-476-8476	261-1
Newport News Inc 711 3rd Ave 4th Fl *Sales	New York	NY	10017	**800-894-9639***	212-986-2585	451
Newport News Industrial Corp 182 Enterprise Dr	Newport News	VA	23603	**800-627-0353**	757-380-7053	776
Newport News Shipbuilding Employees Credit Union 3711 Huntington Ave	Newport News	VA	23607	**800-928-8801**	757-928-8850	216
Newport News Tourism Development Office 700 Town Ctr Dr Suite 320	Newport News	VA	23606	**888-493-7386**	757-926-1400	205
Newport Printing Systems 4120 Birch St Suite 108	Newport Beach	CA	92660	**800-660-1988**	949-261-8248	111
Newport Reservations 174 Bellevue Ave Suite 203	Newport	RI	02840	**800-842-0102**	401-842-0102	368
Newport Steel Corp 530 W 9th St	Newport	KY	41071	**800-348-7751**	859-292-6000	481
Newport Wave Inc 15 McLean	Irvine	CA	92620	**800-999-2611**	949-651-1099	176-1
News & Advance PO Box 10129	Lynchburg	VA	24506	**800-275-8831**	434-385-5512	522-2
News America Marketing 1211 Ave of the Americas 5th Fl	New York	NY	10036	**800-462-0852**	212-782-8000	5
News-Banner PO Box 436	Bluffton	IN	46714	**800-579-7476**	260-824-0224	522-2
News Courier PO Box 670	Athens	AL	35612	**800-844-5480**	256-232-2720	522-2
News Directors Assn. Radio-Television 1600 K St NW Suite 700	Washington	DC	20006	**800-807-8632**	202-659-6510	49-14
News-Dispatch 121 W Michigan Blvd	Michigan City	IN	46360	**800-489-9292**	219-874-7211	522-2
News-Enterprise 408 W Dixie Ave	Elizabethtown	KY	42701	**800-653-6344**	270-769-1200	522-2
News-Herald 501 W 11th St	Panama City	FL	32401	**800-345-8688**	850-747-5000	522-2
News-Herald 7085 Mentor Ave	Willoughby	OH	44094	**800-947-2737**	440-951-0000	522-2
News-Herald PO Box 928	Oil City	PA	16301	**800-352-1002**	814-676-7444	522-2
News Journal 950 W Basin Rd	New Castle	DE	19720	**800-235-9100**	302-324-2500	522-2
News Journal 70 W 4th St	Mansfield	OH	44902	**800-472-5547**	419-522-3311	522-2
News Journal Co PO Box 15505	Wilmington	DE	19850	**800-235-9100**	302-324-2500	623-8
News Leader 11 N Central Ave	Staunton	VA	24402	**800-793-2459**	540-885-7281	522-2
News-Messenger 1700 Cedar St	Fremont	OH	43420	**800-766-6397**	419-332-5511	522-2
News & Observer 215 S McDowell St	Raleigh	NC	27601	**800-365-3115**	919-829-4500	522-2
News-Press 2442 Dr ML King Jr Blvd *News Rm	Fort Myers	FL	33901	**800-468-0350***	239-335-0200	522-2
News & Record 200 E Market St	Greensboro	NC	27401	**800-553-6880**	336-373-7000	522-2
News-Review 345 NE Winchester St	Roseburg	OR	97470	**800-683-3321**	541-672-3321	522-2
News-Sentinel 600 W Main St	Fort Wayne	IN	46802	**800-444-3303**	260-461-8222	522-2
News-Star 411 N 4th St	Monroe	LA	71201	**800-259-7788**	318-322-5161	522-2
News-Sun The PO Box 39	Kendallville	IN	46755	**800-717-4679**	260-347-0400	522-2
News Sun 32 Park St	Berea	OH	44017	**800-362-8008**	216-986-7550	522-4
News-Tribune 426 2nd St	La Salle	IL	61301	**800-892-6452**	815-223-3200	522-2
News-Virginian The PO Box 1027	Waynesboro	VA	22980	**800-368-0509**	540-949-8213	522-2
Newsbank Inc 5020 Tamiami Trail N Suite 110 *Cust Svc	Naples	FL	34103	**800-243-7694***	239-263-6004	380
Newsclip 363 W Erie St 7th Fl	Chicago	IL	60610	**800-544-8433**	312-751-7300	612
Newsday Inc 235 Pinelawn Rd	Melville	NY	11747	**800-639-7329**	631-843-4000	522-2
NewsHub 96 Mowat Ave	Toronto	ON	M6K3M1	**800-371-6992**	416-535-0123	677
Newsletter & Electronic Publishers Assn (NEPA) 1501 Wilson Blvd Suite 509	Arlington	VA	22209	**800-356-9302**	703-527-2333	49-14
Newspaper Assn. National Univ of Missouri 127 Neff Annex PO Box 7540	Columbia	MO	65205	**800-829-4662**	573-882-5800	49-14
Newspaper Enterprise Assn 200 Madison Ave 4th Fl	New York	NY	10016	**800-221-4816**	212-293-8500	520
Newspaper Guild CWA 501 3rd St NW Suite 250	Washington	DC	20001	**800-585-5864**	202-434-7177	405
Newsweek Inc 251 W 57th St *Cust Svc	New York	NY	10019	**800-634-6842***	212-445-4000	623-9
Newsweek Magazine 251 W 57th St *Cust Svc	New York	NY	10019	**800-631-1040***	212-445-4000	449-17
NewTek Inc 5131 Beckwith Blvd *Cust Svc	San Antonio	TX	78249	**800-862-7837***	210-370-8000	176-8
Newtex Industries Inc 8050 Victor Mendon Rd	Victor	NY	14564	**800-836-1001**	585-924-9135	730-3
Newton Convention & Visitor Bureau 113 1st Ave W	Newton	IA	50208	**800-798-0299**	641-792-5545	205
Newton Kansan PO Box 268	Newton	KS	67114	**888-526-7261**	316-283-1500	522-2
Newton Medical Center 600 Medical Ctr Dr	Newton	KS	67114	**800-811-3183**	316-283-2700	366-2
Newton Mfg Co 1123 1st Ave E	Newton	IA	50208	**800-500-7227**	641-792-4121	10
Newtron Group Inc 8183 W El Cajon Dr	Baton Rouge	LA	70815	**800-644-2752**	225-927-8921	188-4
NEXCOM (Navy Exchange Service Command) 3280 Virginia Beach Blvd	Virginia Beach	VA	23452	**800-628-3924**	757-463-6200	778

Name / Address	City	State	ZIP	Toll-Free	Phone	Class
Nexgenix Inc 320 Commerce	Irvine	CA	92602	**800-663-9436**	714-665-6200	176-7
Nexion 1625 The Alameda 9th Fl	San Jose	CA	95126	**800-747-6813**	408-280-6410	761
Nexity Bank 3500 Blue Lake Dr Suite 330	Birmingham	AL	35243	**877-738-6391**	205-298-6391	71
NEXPAK Corp 3475 Forest Lake Dr Suite 200	Uniontown	OH	44685	**800-442-5742**	330-896-3050	597
NexPress Solutions LLC 1447 Saint Paul St	Rochester	NY	14653	**877-446-3977**	585-253-5224	617
Nexstar Financial Corp 19 Research Pk Ct	Saint Charles	MO	63304	**877-706-7382**	636-685-9100	498
Next Proteins International PO Box 2469	Carlsbad	CA	92018	**800-468-6398**	760-431-8152	786
Nextel Communications Inc 2001 Edmund Halley Dr *NASDAQ: NXTL*	Reston	VA	20191	**800-639-8352**	703-433-4000	721
Nextel Partners Inc 4500 Carillon Point Rd *NASDAQ: NXTP*	Kirkland	WA	98033	**888-566-6111**	425-576-3600	721
NextHealth Inc 16600 N Lago del Oro Pkwy	Tucson	AZ	85739	**888-792-5800**		355-3
Nextira One Federal 510 Spring St Suite 200 *Cust Svc	Herndon	VA	20170	**800-822-8374***	703-885-7900	178
NextiraOne LLC 2800 Post Oak Blvd	Houston	TX	77056	**800-510-0561**	713-307-4000	720
Nexxus Products Co 82 Coromar Dr	Goleta	CA	93117	**800-444-6399**	805-968-6900	211
Neyer Al Inc 10151 Carver Rd Suite 100	Cincinnati	OH	45242	**877-271-6400**	513-271-6400	639
Neyra Industries 10700 Evendale Dr	Cincinnati	OH	45241	**800-543-7077**	513-733-1000	46
NF Smith & Assoc LP 5306 Hollister Rd	Houston	TX	77040	**800-468-7866**	713-430-3000	245
NFA (National Futures Assn) 200 W Madison St	Chicago	IL	60606	**800-366-6321**	312-781-1300	49-2
NFBA (National Frame Builders Assn) 4840 Bob Billings Pkwy Suite 1000	Lawrence	KS	66049	**800-557-6957**	785-843-2444	49-3
NFC (Nissan Forklift Corp North America) 240 N Prospect St	Marengo	IL	60152	**800-871-5438**	815-568-0061	462
NFCA (National Family Caregivers Assn) 10400 Connecticut Ave Suite 500	Kensington	MD	20895	**800-896-3650**	301-942-6430	48-6
NFCB (National Federation of Community Broadcasters) 970 Broadway Suite 1000	Oakland	CA	94612	**888-280-6322**	510-451-8200	49-14
NFCC (National Foundation for Credit Counseling) 801 Roeder Rd Suite 900	Silver Spring	MD	20910	**800-388-2227**	301-589-5600	48-10
NFCR (National Foundation for Cancer Research) 4600 East West Hwy Suite 525	Bethesda	MD	20814	**800-321-2873**	301-654-1250	654
NFDA (National Funeral Directors Assn) 13625 Bishop's Dr	Brookfield	WI	53005	**800-228-6332**	262-789-1880	49-4
NFDMA (National Funeral Directors & Morticians Assn) 3951 Snapfinger Pkwy Suite 570	Decatur	GA	30035	**800-434-0958**	404-286-6680	49-4
NFESC (Naval Facilities Engineering Service Center) 1100 23rd Ave	Port Hueneme	CA	93043	**888-484-3372**	805-982-1393	654
NFFC (National Family Farm Coalition) 110 Maryland Ave NE Suite 307	Washington	DC	20002	**800-639-3276**	202-543-5675	48-2
NFHS (National Federation of State High School Assns) PO Box 690 *Cust Svc	Indianapolis	IN	46206	**800-776-3462***	317-972-6900	48-22
NFIB (National Federation of Independent Business) 1201 F St NW Suite 200	Washington	DC	20004	**800-552-6342**	202-554-9000	49-12
NFIC (National Fraud Information Center) 1701 K St NW Suite 1200	Washington	DC	20006	**800-876-7060**	202-835-3323	48-10
NFO (National Farmers Organization) 528 Billy Sunday Rd Suite 100	Ames	IA	50010	**800-247-2110**	515-292-2000	48-2
NFPA (National Fire Protection Assn) 1 Batterymarch Pk	Quincy	MA	02169	**800-344-3555**	617-770-3000	48-17
NFPA (National Foster Parent Assn) 7512 Stanich Ave Suite 6	Gig Harbor	WA	98335	**800-557-5238**	253-853-4000	48-6
NGA (National Glass Assn) 8200 Greensboro Dr Suite 302	McLean	VA	22102	**866-342-5642**	703-442-4890	49-13
NGAS Resources Inc 120 Prosperous Pl Suite 201 *NASDAQ: NGAS*	Lexington	KY	40509	**800-977-2363**	859-263-3948	525
NGAUS (National Guard Assn of the US) 1 Massachusetts Ave NW Suite 200	Washington	DC	20001	**888-226-4287**	202-789-0031	48-19
NGCOA (National Golf Course Owners Assn) 291 Seven Farms Dr 2nd Fl	Charleston	SC	29492	**800-933-4262**	843-881-9956	48-23
NGF (National Gaucher Foundation) 5410 Edson Ln Suite 260	Rockville	MD	20852	**800-428-2437**	301-816-1515	48-17
NGF (National Golf Foundation) 1150 S US Hwy 1 Suite 401	Jupiter	FL	33477	**800-733-6006**	561-744-6006	48-22
NGFA (National Grain & Feed Assn) 1250 I St NW Suite 1003	Washington	DC	20005	**800-680-9223**	202-289-0873	48-2
NGK Metals Corp 917 US Hwy 11 S *Sales	Sweetwater	TN	37874	**800-523-8268***	423-337-5500	303
NGS (National Genealogical Society) 3108 Columbia Pike Suite 300	Arlington	VA	22204	**800-473-0060**	703-525-0050	48-18
NGWA (National Ground Water Assn) 601 Dempsey Rd	Westerville	OH	43081	**800-551-7379**	614-898-7791	48-12
NHDP (National Hansen's Disease Programs) 1770 Physicians Park Dr	Baton Rouge	LA	70816	**800-642-2477**	225-756-3773	654
NHEMA (National Home Equity Mortgage Assn) 1301 Pennsylvania Ave NW Suite 500	Washington	DC	20004	**800-342-1121**	202-347-1210	49-2
NHF (National Headache Foundation) 820 N Orleans St Suite 217	Chicago	IL	60610	**888-643-5552**		48-17
NHF (National Hemophilia Foundation) 116 W 32nd St 11th Fl	New York	NY	10001	**800-424-2634**	212-328-3700	48-17
NHFA (National Home Furnishings Assn) 3010 Tinsley Dr Suite 101	High Point	NC	27265	**800-888-9590**	336-886-6100	49-4
NHIA (National Home Infusion Assn) 205 Daingerfield Rd	Alexandria	VA	22314	**800-544-7447**	703-549-3740	49-8
NHIC (National Health Information Center) PO Box 1133	Washington	DC	20013	**800-336-4797**	301-565-4167	336-6
NHLA (National Hardwood Lumber Assn) 6830 Raleigh-LaGrange Rd	Memphis	TN	38134	**800-933-0318**	901-377-1818	49-3
NHLPA (National Hockey League Players Assn) 777 Bay St Suite 2400	Toronto	ON	M5G2C8	**800-363-4625**	416-408-4040	48-22
NHPCO (National Hospice & Palliative Care Organization) 1700 Diagonal Rd Suite 625 *Help Line	Alexandria	VA	22314	**800-658-8898***	703-837-1500	49-8
NHPTV (New Hampshire Public Television) 268 Mast Rd	Durham	NH	03824	**800-639-8408**	603-868-1100	620
NHS University Hospital 985230 Nebraska Medical Ctr	Omaha	NE	68198	**800-642-1095**	402-559-4000	366-2
NIA (National Insulation Assn) 99 Canal Center Plaza Suite 222	Alexandria	VA	22314	**877-968-7642**	703-683-6422	49-3
NIA Group Inc 66 Rt 17 N	Paramus	NJ	07652	**800-321-2122**	201-845-6600	383
Niacet Corp 400 47th St	Niagara Falls	NY	14304	**800-828-1207**	716-285-1474	142
Niagara Blower Co Inc 673 Ontario St	Buffalo	NY	14207	**800-426-5169**	716-875-2000	15
Niagara Cutter Inc 200 John James Audubon Pkwy	Amherst	NY	14228	**888-689-8400**	716-689-8400	484
Niagara Duty Free Shop 5726 Falls Ave	Niagara Falls	ON	L2G7T5	**877-612-4337**	905-374-3700	240
Niagara Frontier Hockey LP HSBC Arena 1 Seymour H Knox III Plaza	Buffalo	NY	14203	**888-467-2273**	716-855-4100	703
Niagara LaSalle Corp 1412 150th St	Hammond	IN	46327	**877-289-2277**	219-853-6000	709
Niagara Mohawk A National Grid Co 300 Erie Blvd W	Syracuse	NY	13202	**888-424-2113**	315-474-1511	355-5
Niagara Parks Botanical Gardens 2565 Niagara Pkwy N PO box 150	Niagara Falls	ON	L2E6T2	**877-642-7275**	905-356-8554	98
Niagara Plastics Co 7090 Edinboro Rd *Sales	Erie	PA	16509	**800-458-0465***	814-868-3671	152
Niagara Tourism & Convention Corp 345 3rd St Suite 605	Niagara Falls	NY	14303	**800-338-7890**	716-282-8992	205
Niagara Transformer Corp 1747 Dale Rd	Buffalo	NY	14225	**800-817-5652**	716-896-6500	756
Niagara University	Niagara University	NY	14109	**800-462-2111**	716-286-8700	163
NIB (National Industries for the Blind) 1901 N Beauregard St Suite 200 *Cust Svc	Alexandria	VA	22311	**800-433-2304***	703-998-0770	48-17
NIBCO Inc 1516 Middlebury St	Elkhart	IN	46515	**800-234-0227**	574-295-3000	584
NIC Inc 10540 S Ridgeview Rd *NASDAQ: EGOV*	Olathe	KS	66061	**877-234-3468**	913-498-3468	176-10
NICA (National Interfaith Coalition on Aging) 300 D St SW	Washington	DC	20024	**800-424-9046**	202-479-1200	48-6
NICB (National Insurance Crime Bureau) 10330 S Roberts Rd	Palos Hills	IL	60465	**800-447-6282**	708-430-2430	49-9
Nice Ball Bearings Inc 2060 Detwiler Rd	Kulpsville	PA	19443	**800-321-6423**	215-256-6681	77
Nice-Pak Products Inc 2 Nice-Pak Pk	Orangeburg	NY	10962	**800-999-6423**	845-365-1700	548-2
NICE Systems Inc 301 Rt 17 N 10th Fl	Rutherford	NJ	07070	**888-577-6423**	201-964-2600	720
Nicholas-Applegate Capital Management 600 W Broadway 30th Fl	San Diego	CA	92101	**800-551-8045**	619-687-8100	393
Nicholas Family of Funds 700 N Water St Suite 1010	Milwaukee	WI	53202	**800-227-5987**	414-272-6133	517
Nicholas Financial Inc 2454 McMullen-Booth Rd Bldg C *NASDAQ: NICK*	Clearwater	FL	33759	**800-237-2721**	727-726-0763	215
Nicholls State University 906 E 1st St	Thibodaux	LA	70310	**877-642-4655**	985-446-8111	163
Nichols Aluminum 1725 Rockingham Rd	Davenport	IA	52802	**800-553-5508**	563-336-4801	476
Nichols College PO Box 5000	Dudley	MA	01571	**800-470-3379**	508-943-1560	163
Nichols Five Star Charters & Tours PO Box 709	Fond du Lac	WI	54936	**877-373-6456**	920-929-8030	748
Nichols Institute Diagnostics 1311 Calle Batido	San Clemente	CA	92673	**800-286-4643**	949-940-7200	375
Nichols Wire Co 1547 Helton Dr	Florence	AL	35630	**800-633-3156**	256-764-4271	800
Nicholson Construction Co 12 McClane St	Cuddy	PA	15031	**800-388-2340**	412-221-4500	188-5
Nicholson HR Co 6320 Oakleaf Ave *Cust Svc	Baltimore	MD	21215	**800-638-3514***	410-764-2323	291-20
Nick Strimbu Inc 3500 Parkway Rd	Brookfield	OH	44403	**800-446-8785**	330-448-4071	769
Nickelodeon Family Suites by Holiday Inn 14500 Continental Gateway	Orlando	FL	32821	**877-387-5437**	407-387-5437	655
Nickers International Ltd PO Box 50066	Staten Island	NY	10305	**800-642-5377**	718-448-6283	786
Nickerson State Park 3488 Main St	Brewster	MA	02631	**877-422-6762**	508-896-3491	554
Nickles Alfred Bakery Inc 26 N Main St	Navarre	OH	44662	**800-635-1110**	330-879-5635	291-1
Nicol Scales Inc 7239 Envoy Ct	Dallas	TX	75247	**800-225-8181**	214-428-8181	672
Nicolet Area Technical College PO Box 518	Rhinelander	WI	54501	**800-544-3039**	715-365-4410	160
Nicolet Forest Bottling Co Inc 39 S Barrington Rd	Barrington	IL	60010	**888-928-3756**	847-382-2950	792
Nicor Gas 1844 Ferry Rd	Naperville	IL	60563	**888-642-6748**	630-983-8888	774
Nida Corp 300 S John Rodes Blvd	Melbourne	FL	32904	**800-327-6432**	321-727-2265	694
Niedner Ltd 675 Merrill St	Coaticook	QC	J1A2S2	**800-567-2703**	514-637-5572	666
Niehoff CE & Co 2021 Lee St *Tech Supp	Evanston	IL	60202	**800-643-4633***	847-866-6030	246
Nielsen Co 7405 Industrial Rd	Florence	KY	41042	**800-877-7405**	859-525-7405	615
Nielsen-Massey Vanillas Inc 1550 Shields Dr	Waukegan	IL	60085	**800-525-7873**	847-578-1550	291-15
Nielsons Skanska Inc 22419 County Rd G	Cortez	CO	81321	**800-638-5545**	970-565-8000	187-8
Niemann Foods Inc 1501 N 12th St	Quincy	IL	62301	**800-800-3916**	217-221-5600	339

Name / Address	City	State	ZIP	Toll-Free	Phone	Class
Niemann-Pick Disease Foundation. National 415 Madison Ave	Fort Atkinson	WI	53538	877-287-3672	920-563-0930	48-17
NIFDA (National Independent Flag Dealers Assn) 214 N Hale St	Wheaton	IL	60187	877-544-3524	630-510-4500	49-18
NIGA (National Indian Gaming Assn) 224 2nd St SE	Washington	DC	20003	800-286-6442	202-546-7711	48-23
NightHawk Systems Inc 8200 E Pacific Pl Suite 204 *Sales	Denver	CO	80231	800-735-3650*	303-337-4811	720
Nightingale-Conant Corp 6245 W Howard St *Cust Svc	Niles	IL	60714	800-323-3938*	847-647-0300	502
Nightscaping 1705 E Colton Ave	Redlands	CA	92374	800-544-4840	909-794-2121	431
NIGP (National Institute of Governmental Purchasing) 151 Spring St Suite 300	Herndon	VA	20170	800-367-6447	703-736-8900	49-7
Nike Inc 1 Bowerman Dr *NYSE: NKE* ■ *Cust Svc	Beaverton	OR	97005	800-344-6453*	503-671-6453	296
Nikko Hotels International 222 Mason St	San Francisco	CA	94102	800-645-5687	415-394-1111	369
Nikon Inc 1300 Walt Whitman Rd *Cust Svc	Melville	NY	11747	800-645-6687*	631-547-4200	580
Niles Daily Star 217 N 4th St	Niles	MI	49120	888-725-0108	269-683-2100	522-2
Nilfisk-Advance Group 14600 21st Ave N *Cust Svc	Plymouth	MN	55447	800-989-2235*	763-745-3500	379
Nim-Cor Inc 575 Amherst St	Nashua	NH	03061	888-464-6267	603-889-2153	206
Nina Enterprises 1350 S Leavitt St	Chicago	IL	60608	800-886-8688	312-733-6400	523
Nina Footwear Co Inc 730 5th Ave 8th Fl	New York	NY	10019	800-233-6462	212-399-2323	296
NINDS (National Institute of Neurological Disorders & Stroke) 31 Center Dr Bldg 31 Rm 8A52	Bethesda	MD	20892	800-352-9424	301-496-9746	336-6
Nine West Group Inc 1129 Westchester Ave Nine West Plaza	White Plains	NY	10604	800-260-2227	914-640-6400	296
Ninety-Nines Inc 4300 Amelia Earhart Rd	Oklahoma City	OK	73159	800-944-1929	405-685-7969	48-24
Nintendo of America Inc 4822 150th Ave NE *Cust Svc	Redmond	WA	98052	800-255-3700*	425-882-2040	750
Niobrara Electric Assn Inc PO Box 697	Lusk	WY	82225	800-322-0544	307-334-3221	244
NIPC (National Inhalant Prevention Coalition) 2904 Kerbey Ln	Austin	TX	78703	800-269-4237	512-480-8953	48-17
Nippon Express Travel USA 22 Center Point Dr Suite 110	La Palma	CA	90623	800-654-8228	714-521-2050	760
Nippon Life Insurance Co of America 521 5th Ave 5th Fl	New York	NY	10175	800-252-7174	212-682-3000	384-2
Nippon Steel USA Inc 80 3rd Ave 34th Fl	New York	NY	10017	800-345-6477	212-486-7150	483
NIPSCO (Northern Indiana Public Service Co) 801 E 86th Ave *Cust Svc	Merrillville	IN	46410	800-464-7726*	219-853-5200	774
NIRE (National Institute for Rehabilitation Engineering) PO Box T	Hewitt	NJ	07421	800-736-2216	973-853-6585	48-17
Nishnabotna Valley Rural Electric Co-op PO Box 714	Harlan	IA	51537	800-234-5122	712-755-2166	244
NiSource Inc 801 E 86th Ave *NYSE: NI*	Merrillville	IN	46410	800-464-7726	219-853-5200	355-5
Nissan Canada Inc 5290 Orbitor Dr	Mississauga	ON	L4W4Z5	800-387-0122	905-629-2888	59
Nissan Forklift Corp North America (NFC) 240 N Prospect St	Marengo	IL	60152	800-871-5438	815-568-0061	462
Nissan Motor Corp USA Infiniti Div PO Box 191	Gardena	CA	90248	800-647-7263	310-532-3111	59
Nissin Foods USA Co Inc 2001 W Rosecrans Ave *Cust Svc	Gardena	CA	90249	800-664-3537*	310-327-8478	291-31
Niteo Partners Inc 379 Thornall St 5th Fl	Edison	NJ	08837	888-406-5033	732-767-0400	178
Nitro USA 5 Commerce Ave	Lebanon	NH	03784	877-648-7666	603-298-9867	701
Nitta Casings Inc PO Box 858 *Cust Svc	Somerville	NJ	08876	800-526-3970*	908-218-4400	293
Nitta Gelatin Inc 201 W Passaic St	Rochelle Park	NJ	07662	800-278-7680	201-368-0071	291-22
Nittany Lion Inn 200 W Park Ave	State College	PA	16803	800-233-7505	814-865-8500	373
Nittany Printing & Publishing Co 3400 E College Ave	State College	PA	16801	800-327-5500	814-238-5000	623-8
Nitto Denko America Inc 48500 Fremont Blvd	Fremont	CA	94538	800-356-4880	510-445-5400	686
Niver Western Wear Inc PO Box 10122	Fort Worth	TX	76185	800-433-5752	817-924-4299	153-20
Nixon Uniform Service Inc 2925 Northeast Blvd *Sales	Wilmington	DE	19802	888-649-6687*	302-764-7550	434
NJN Public Television & Radio PO Box 777	Trenton	NJ	08625	800-792-8645	609-777-5000	620
NKBA (National Kitchen & Bath Assn) 687 Willow Grove St	Hackettstown	NJ	07840	800-843-6522	908-852-0033	49-3
NKC of America Inc 1584 E Brooks Rd	Memphis	TN	38116	800-532-6727	901-396-5353	206
NKF (National Kidney Foundation) 30 E 33rd St Suite 1100	New York	NY	10016	800-622-9010	212-889-2210	48-17
NKS Distributors Inc 399 New Churchmans Rd	New Castle	DE	19720	800-292-9509	302-322-1811	82-3
NLBMDA (National Lumber & Building Material Dealers Assn) 40 Ivy St SE	Washington	DC	20003	800-634-8645	202-547-2230	49-18
NLBRA (National Little Britches Rodeo Assn) 1045 W Rio Grande St	Colorado Springs	CO	80906	800-763-3694	719-389-0333	48-22
NLC Inc PO Box 348	Jackson	MO	63755	800-747-4743	573-243-3141	798
NLDA (National Luggage Dealers Assn) 1817 Elmdale Ave	Glenview	IL	60026	866-998-6869	847-998-6869	49-18
NLN (National League for Nursing) 61 Broadway	New York	NY	10006	800-669-1656	212-363-5555	49-8
NLNAC (National League for Nursing Accrediting Commission Inc) 61 Broadway 33rd Fl	New York	NY	10006	800-669-1656	212-363-5555	48-1
NLP Enterprises Inc PO Box 349	Owings Mills	MD	21117	800-962-9380	410-356-7500	188-8
NLRB (National Labor Relations Board) 1099 14th St NW	Washington	DC	20570	800-736-2983	202-273-1991	336-16
NLS Animal Health 11445 G Cronridge Dr	Owings Mills	MD	21117	800-638-8674	410-581-1800	467
NLynx Technologies Inc 8313 Hwy 71 W *Tech Supp	Austin	TX	78735	888-659-6967*	512-301-8000	174
NMA (National Medical Assn) 1012 10th St NW	Washington	DC	20001	800-662-0554	202-347-1895	49-8
NMA (National Motorists Assn) 402 W 2nd St	Waunakee	WI	53597	800-882-2785	608-849-6000	49-21
NMC-Wollard Inc 2021 Truax Blvd	Eau Claire	WI	54703	800-656-6867	715-835-3151	462
NMDP (National Marrow Donor Program) 3001 Broadway St NE Suite 500	Minneapolis	MN	55413	800-526-7809	612-627-5800	48-17
NMF (National Marfan Foundation) 22 Manhasset Ave	Port Washington	NY	11050	800-862-7326	516-883-8712	48-17
NMHA (National Mental Health Assn) 2001 N Beauregard St 12th Fl *Help Line	Alexandria	VA	22311	800-969-6642*	703-684-7722	48-17
NMHCrx Pharmacy Benefits Manager 26 Harbor Park Dr *NASDAQ: NMHC*	Port Washington	NY	11050	800-645-3332	516-626-0007	575
NMPF (National Milk Producers Federation) 2101 Wilson Blvd Suite 400	Arlington	VA	22201	888-549-7600	703-243-6111	49-6
NMS Communications 100 Crossing Blvd *NASDAQ: NMSS* ■ *Sales	Framingham	MA	01702	800-533-6120*	508-271-1000	720
NMSA (National Middle School Assn) 4151 Executive Pkwy Suite 300	Westerville	OH	43081	800-528-6672	614-895-4730	49-5
NMSDC (National Minority Supplier Development Council) 1040 Ave of the Americas 2nd Fl	New York	NY	10018	888-396-1110	212-944-2430	49-18
NMT Medical Inc 27 Wormwood St *NASDAQ: NMTI*	Boston	MA	02210	800-666-6484	617-737-0930	469
NNA (National Newspaper Assn) Univ of Missouri 127 Neff Annex PO Box 7540	Columbia	MO	65205	800-829-4662	573-882-5800	49-14
NNA (National Notary Assn) 9350 DeSoto Ave	Chatsworth	CA	91313	800-876-6827	818-739-4000	49-12
NNAAPC (National Native American AIDS Prevention Center) 436 14th St Suite 1020	Oakland	CA	94612	800-283-6880	510-444-2051	48-17
NNFA (National Nutritional Foods Assn) 3931 MacArthur Blvd Suite 101	Newport Beach	CA	92660	800-966-6632	949-622-6272	49-6
NNSDO (National Nursing Staff Development Organization) 7794 Grow Dr	Pensacola	FL	32514	800-489-1995	850-474-0995	49-8
NNT Corp 1320 Norwood Ave	Itasca	IL	60143	800-556-9999	630-875-9600	447
No Fear 2251 Faraday Ave	Carlsbad	CA	92008	800-266-3327	760-931-9550	153-1
No-Sag Products Corp 2225 Production Rd	Kendallville	IN	46755	800-345-0775	260-347-2600	345
NOAH (National Organization for Albinism & Hypopigmentation) PO Box 959	East Hampstead	NH	03826	800-473-2310	603-887-2310	48-17
Noah's New York Bagels Inc 255 Ygnacio Valley Rd Suite 200	Walnut Creek	CA	90601	800-936-6247	925-979-6000	69
Nob Hill Lambourne 725 Pine St	San Francisco	CA	94108	800-274-8466	415-433-2287	373
Nob Hill Spa at the Huntington Hotel 1075 California St	San Francisco	CA	94108	800-227-4683	415-345-2888	698
Nob Hill Spa. Huntington Hotel & 1075 California St	San Francisco	CA	94108	800-227-4683	415-474-5400	373
Nobel 5759 Fleet St	Carlsbad	CA	92008	800-986-6235	760-405-0105	721
Nobel Biocare USA Inc 22715 Savi Ranch Pkwy	Yorba Linda	CA	92887	800-993-8100	714-282-4800	226
Nobel Insurance 12225 Greenville Ave Suite 750	Dallas	TX	75243	800-766-6235	972-644-0434	384-4
Nobel/Sysco Food Services Inc 1101 W 48th Ave	Denver	CO	80221	800-366-6696	303-458-4000	292-8
Nobility Homes Inc 3741 SW 7th St *NASDAQ: NOBH*	Ocala	FL	34474	800-476-6624	352-732-5157	495
Noble Corp 13135 S Dairy Ashford Rd Suite 800 *NYSE: NE*	Sugar Land	TX	77478	800-231-6326	281-276-6100	529
Noble Fiber Technologies 300 Palm St	Scranton	PA	18505	877-978-2842	570-558-5309	594-1
Noble Planetarium 1501 Montgomery St Museum of Science & History	Fort Worth	TX	76107	888-255-9300	817-732-1631	587
Noble Roman's Pizza Inc 1 Virginia Ave Suite 800	Indianapolis	IN	46204	800-585-0669	317-634-3377	657
Noble Rural Electric Membership Corp PO Box 137	Albion	IN	46701	800-933-7362	260-636-2113	244
Nobles Co-op Electric PO Box 788	Worthington	MN	56187	800-776-0517	507-372-7331	244
NobleWorks Inc 123 Grand St *Sales	Hoboken	NJ	07030	800-346-6253*	201-420-0095	130
NOCC (National Ovarian Cancer Coalition) 500 NE Spanish River Blvd Suite 8	Boca Raton	FL	33431	888-682-7426	561-393-0005	48-17
NOCO Energy Corp 2440 Sheridan Dr	Tonawanda	NY	14150	800-500-6626	716-874-6200	569
Nocona Athletic Goods Co 208 W Walnut St	Nocona	TX	76255	800-433-0957	940-825-3326	701
Nocona Boot Co 610 W Daggett St	Fort Worth	TX	76104	800-545-8707	817-332-4385	296
Nodak Electric Co-op Inc PO Box 13000	Grand Forks	ND	58208	800-732-4373	701-746-4461	244
Noell Crane & Service Inc 2030 Ponderosa St	Portsmouth	VA	23701	800-996-6355	757-405-0311	462
Noevir USA Inc 1095 SE Main St	Irvine	CA	92614	800-872-8817	949-660-1111	361
NOF (National Osteoporosis Foundation) 1232 22nd St NW	Washington	DC	20037	800-223-9994	202-223-2226	48-17

Name / Address	City	State	Zip	Toll-Free	Phone	Class
Noise Regulation Report 8737 Colesville Rd Suite 1100	Silver Spring	MD	20910	**800-274-6737**	301-587-6300	521-5
Nokia Inc 6000 Connection Dr. *NYSE: NOK*	Irving	TX	75039	**800-547-9810**	972-894-5000	720
Nolan Robert E Co Inc 90 Hopmeadow St	Simsbury	CT	06070	**800-653-1941**	860-658-1941	193
Nolan Ryan Exhibit Center 2925 S Hwy 35	Alvin	TX	77511	**800-350-7926**	281-388-1134	511
Noland Co 80 29th St *NASDAQ: NOLD*	Newport News	VA	23607	**800-446-8960**	757-928-9000	601
Nolo.com 950 Parker St. *Cust Svc	Berkeley	CA	94710	**800-728-3555***	510-549-1976	176-9
Nolte Assoc Inc 1750 Creekside Oaks Dr Suite 200	Sacramento	CA	95833	**800-216-6583**	916-641-1500	258
NOMOTC (National Organization of Mothers of Twins Clubs Inc) PO Box 438	Thompsons Station	TN	37179	**877-540-2200**	615-595-0936	48-6
Non-Commissioned Officers Assn (NCOA) 10635 IH-35 N *Cust Svc	San Antonio	TX	78233	**800-662-2620***	210-653-6161	48-19
Non-Profit Career Network PO Box 241	Haddam	CT	06438	**888-844-4870**	860-345-3255	257
Nondestructive Testing Inc. American Society for 1711 Arlingate Ln *Orders	Columbus	OH	43228	**800-222-2768***	614-274-6003	49-19
Nonferrous Products Inc PO Box 349	Franklin	IN	46131	**800-423-5612**	317-738-2558	474
Nonpareil Corp 40 N 400 W	Blackfoot	ID	83221	**800-522-2223**	208-785-5880	291-18
Nook Industries 4950 E 49th St	Cuyahoga Heights	OH	44125	**800-321-7800**	216-271-7900	609
Noon Hour Food Products Inc 215 N Des Plaines *Cust Svc	Chicago	IL	60661	**800-621-6636***	312-382-1177	291-13
Nor-Cal Products Inc 1967 S Oregon St	Yreka	CA	96097	**800-824-4166**	530-842-4458	584
Nor-Cote International Inc 506 Lafayette Ave	Crawfordsville	IN	47933	**800-488-9180**	765-362-9180	381
Nor-Lake Inc PO Box 248	Hudson	WI	54016	**800-388-5253**	715-386-2323	650
NOR PAC (North Pacific Group Inc) 815 NE Davis St	Portland	OR	97232	**800-547-8440**	503-231-1166	190-3
Noranda Aluminum Inc 801 Crescent Ctr Dr Suite 600	Franklin	TN	37067	**800-344-7522**	615-771-5700	476
Norben Import Corp 99 S Newman St	Hackensack	NJ	07601	**800-526-4652**	201-487-0855	288
Norbest Inc 6875 S 900 East	Midvale	UT	84047	**800-453-5327**	801-566-5656	292-10
Norbord Industries Inc 1 Toronto St 6th Fl *TSE: NBD*	Toronto	ON	M5C2W4	**877-263-9367**	416-643-8820	602
Norbord Industries Inc 1 Toronto St Suite 600	Toronto	ON	M5C2W4	**800-387-1740**	416-365-0710	602
Norcal Mutual Insurance Co Inc 560 Davis St	San Francisco	CA	94111	**800-652-1051**	415-397-9700	384-5
Norcal Waste Systems Inc 160 Pacific Ave Suite 200	San Francisco	CA	94111	**800-652-1275**	415-875-1000	791
Norco Windows Inc 811 Factory St PO Box 140	Hawkins	WI	54530	**800-826-6793**	715-585-6311	234
Norcraft Cos LLC 3020 Denmark Ave Suite 100	Eagan	MN	55121	**800-297-0661**	651-234-3300	116
Norcross Safety Products LLC 1136 2nd St *Cust Svc	Rock Island	IL	61201	**800-777-9021***	309-786-7741	566
NORD (National Organization for Rare Disorders) 55 Kenosia Ave PO Box 1968	Danbury	CT	06813	**800-999-6673**	203-744-0100	48-17
Nord Resources Corp 3048 N Seven Dash Rd PO Box 384	Dragoon	AZ	85609	**800-543-2599**	520-586-2241	492
Nord-Viscount Corp 50 Lawrence Ave	Brooklyn	NY	11230	**866-278-7674**	718-854-5586	149
Nordaas American Homes Co Inc 10091 State Hwy 22 PO Box 116	Minnesota Lake	MN	56068	**800-658-7076**	507-462-3331	186
Nordic Products Inc DBA NORPRO 2215 Merrill Creek Pkwy	Everett	WA	98203	**800-722-0202**	425-261-1000	477
Nordic Software Inc PO Box 83499	Lincoln	NE	68501	**800-306-6502**	402-489-1557	176-3
Nordic Ware Inc 5005 Hwy 7	Minneapolis	MN	55416	**800-328-4310**	952-920-2888	477
Nordson Corp 28601 Clemens Rd *NASDAQ: NDSN*	Westlake	OH	44145	**800-321-2881**	440-892-1580	379
Nordstrom Inc 1617 6th Ave Suite 500 *NYSE: JWN*	Seattle	WA	98101	**800-285-5800**	206-628-2111	227
Nordyne Inc 8000 Phoenix Pkwy	O'Fallon	MO	63366	**888-667-4822**	636-561-7300	15
Norelco Consumer Products Co 1010 Washington Blvd	Stamford	CT	06912	**800-243-7884**	203-973-0200	211
Norfolk Convention & Visitors Bureau 232 E Main St	Norfolk	VA	23510	**800-368-3097**	757-664-6620	205
Norfolk Daily News PO Box 977	Norfolk	NE	68702	**877-371-1020**	402-371-1020	522-2
Norfolk Southern Corp 3 Commercial Pl *NYSE: NSC* ■ *Cust Svc	Norfolk	VA	23510	**800-635-5768***	757-629-2600	184
Norfolk Southern Railway Co 3 Commercial Pl	Norfolk	VA	23510	**800-635-5768**	757-629-2600	634
Norforge & Machining Inc 195 N Dean St	Bushnell	IL	61422	**800-457-7699**	309-772-3124	474
Norit Americas Inc 3200 W University Ave PO Box 790	Marshall	TX	75671	**800-641-9245**	903-923-1000	141
Noritake Co Inc 15-22 Fair Lawn Ave	Fair Lawn	NJ	07410	**888-296-3423**		716
Norkus Enterprises Inc 505 Richmond Ave	Point Pleasant Beach	NJ	08742	**800-281-4047**	732-899-4040	203
Norlen Inc 900 Grossman Dr	Schofield	WI	54476	**800-648-6594**	715-359-0506	471
Norm Thompson Outfitters Inc 3188 NW Aloclek Dr	Hillsboro	OR	97124	**800-547-1160**	503-614-4600	451
Norman Convention & Visitors Bureau 224 W Gray St Suite 104	Norman	OK	73069	**800-767-7260**	405-366-8095	205
Norman Data Defense Systems Inc 9302 Lee Hwy Suite 950A	Fairfax	VA	22031	**888-466-6762**	703-267-6109	176-12
Norman Supply Co 825 SW 5th St	Oklahoma City	OK	73109	**800-375-3457**	405-235-9511	598
Norman W Paschall Co Inc 1 Paschall Rd	Peachtree City	GA	30269	**800-849-1820**	770-487-7945	730-8
Normandale Community College 9700 France Ave S	Bloomington	MN	55431	**866-880-8740**	952-487-8200	160
Normandy Industries Inc PO Box 40	Verona	PA	15147	**800-322-9463**	412-826-1825	585
NorMed 4310 S 131 Pl	Seattle	WA	98168	**800-288-8200**	206-242-8228	469
Norment Security Group Inc 3224 Mobile Hwy	Montgomery	AL	36108	**800-633-1968**	334-281-8440	683
NORML (National Organization for the Reform of Marijuana Laws) 1600 K St NW Suite 501	Washington	DC	20006	**888-676-6765**	202-483-5500	48-8
Noro-Moseley Partners 4200 Northside Pkwy NW Bldg 9	Atlanta	GA	30327	**800-648-0520**	404-233-1966	779
NORPAC Foods Inc 930 W Washington St *Sales	Stayton	OR	97383	**800-733-9311***	503-769-2101	291-21
NORPRO 2215 Merrill Creek Pkwy	Everett	WA	98203	**800-722-0202**	425-261-1000	477
Norris Comprehensive Cancer Center & Hospital 1441 Eastlake Ave	Los Angeles	CA	90033	**800-522-6237**	323-865-3000	366-5
Norris Cylinder Co 1535 FM 1845	Longview	TX	75603	**800-527-8418**	903-757-7633	220
Norris Electric Co-op PO Box 6000	Newton	IL	62448	**877-783-8765**	618-783-8765	244
Norris Garland C Co 1101 Terry Rd	Apex	NC	27502	**800-331-8920**	919-387-1059	549
Norris Public Power District PO Box 399	Beatrice	NE	68310	**800-858-4707**	402-223-4038	244
Norsat International Inc 4401 Still Creek Dr Suite 300	Burnaby	BC	V5C6G9	**888-830-4223**	604-292-9000	720
Norscot Group Inc 1000 W Donges Bay Rd	Mequon	WI	53092	**800-653-3313**	262-241-3313	10
Norse Dairy Systems PO Box 1869	Columbus	OH	43216	**800-338-7465**	614-294-4931	291-9
Norstan Inc 5101 Shady Oak Rd	Minnetonka	MN	55343	**800-667-7826**	952-352-4000	720
Nortel Networks Corp 8200 Dixie Rd Suite 100 *NYSE: NT*	Brampton	ON	L6T5P6	**800-666-7835**	905-863-0000	720
North Adams Common Nursing Home 175 Franklin St	North Adams	MA	01247	**800-278-0021**	413-664-4041	441
North Alabama Electric Co-op PO Box 628	Stevenson	AL	35772	**800-572-2900**	256-437-2281	244
North America Missing Children Assn Inc 136 Rt 420 Hwy	South Esk	NB	E1V4N8	**800-260-0753**	506-627-1209	48-6
North American Air Charter Inc 90 Arrival Ave Long Island MacArthur Airport	Ronkonkoma	NY	11779	**800-516-4430**	631-737-4430	14
North American Black Historical Museum Inc 277 King St	Amherstburg	ON	N9V2C7	**800-713-6336**	519-736-5433	509
North American Building Material Distribution Assn (NBMDA) 401 N Michigan Ave Suite 2400	Chicago	IL	60611	**888-747-7862**	312-644-6610	49-18
North American Co for Life & Health Insurance 525 W Van Buren St	Chicago	IL	60607	**800-800-3656**	312-648-7600	384-2
North American Container Corp 5851 Riverview Rd	Mableton	GA	30126	**800-929-3468**	404-691-0611	101
North American Enclosures Inc 65 Jetson Ln	Central Islip	NY	11722	**800-645-9209**	631-234-9500	304
North American Fisherman Magazine 12301 Whitewater Dr Suite 260	Minnetonka	MN	55343	**800-843-6232**	952-936-9333	449-20
North American Hunter Magazine 12301 Whitewater Dr Suite 260	Minnetonka	MN	55343	**800-922-4868**	952-936-9333	449-20
North American Industries Inc 80 Holton St	Woburn	MA	01801	**800-847-8470**	781-721-4446	462
North American Industry Classification System (NAICS) US Census Bureau 4700 Silver Hill Rd	Washington	DC	20333	**888-756-2427**	301-763-4636	336-2
North American Membership Group Inc 12301 Whitewater Dr Suite 260	Minnetonka	MN	55343	**800-634-8598**	952-936-9333	361
North American Menopause Society (NAMS) 5900 Landerbrook Dr Suite 195	Mayfield Heights	OH	44124	**800-774-5342**	440-442-7550	49-8
North American Mfg Co Ltd 4455 E 71st St	Cleveland	OH	44105	**800-626-3477**	216-271-6000	352
North American Plywood Corp 12343 Hawkins St *Sales	Santa Fe Springs	CA	90670	**800-421-1372***	562-941-7575	602
North American Products Corp 1180 Wernsing Rd *Cust Svc	Jasper	IN	47546	**800-634-8665***	812-482-2000	447
North American Publishing Co 1500 Springarden St Suite 1200	Philadelphia	PA	19130	**800-627-2689**	215-238-5482	623-9
North American Retail Dealers Assn (NARDA) 10 E 22nd St Suite 310	Lombard	IL	60148	**800-621-0298**	630-953-8950	49-18
North American Roofing Services Inc 6151 W 80th St	Indianapolis	IN	46278	**800-876-5602**	317-875-5434	188-12
North American Savings Bank FSB 12498 S 71 Hwy	Grandview	MO	64030	**800-677-6272**	816-765-2200	71
North American Scientific Inc 20200 Sunburst St *NASDAQ: NASI*	Chatsworth	CA	91311	**800-992-6274**	818-734-8600	229
North American Securities Administrators Assn (NASAA) 10 G St NE Suite 710	Washington	DC	20002	**888-846-2722**	202-737-0900	49-2
North American Specialty Insurance Co 650 Elm St 6th Fl	Manchester	NH	03101	**800-542-9200**	603-644-6600	384-4
North American Spine Society (NASS) 22 Calendar Ct 2nd Fl	La Grange	IL	60525	**877-774-6337**	708-588-8080	49-8
North American Title Co 2185 N California Blvd Suite 575	Walnut Creek	CA	94596	**800-869-3434**	925-935-5599	384-6
North American Tool Corp 215 Elmwood Ave	South Beloit	IL	61080	**800-872-8277**	815-389-2300	484
North American Wholesale Lumber Assn (NAWLA) 3601 Algonquin Rd Suite 400	Rolling Meadows	IL	60008	**800-527-8258**	847-870-7470	49-18
North American Youth Sport Institute (NAYSI) 4985 Oak Garden Dr	Kernersville	NC	27284	**800-767-4916**	336-784-4926	48-22

Name / Address	City	State	ZIP	Toll-Free	Phone	Class
North Arkansas College 1515 Pioneer Dr	Harrison	AR	72601	**800-679-6622**	870-743-3000	160
North Bay & District Chamber of Commerce 1375 Seymour St PO Box 747	North Bay	ON	P1B8J8	**888-249-8998**	705-472-8480	136
North of Boston Convention & Visitors Bureau 17 Peabody Sq	Peabody	MA	01960	**877-662-9299**	978-977-7760	205
North Carolina						
Marine Fisheries Div PO Box 769	Morehead City	NC	28557	**800-682-2632**	252-726-7021	335
State Education Assistance Authority PO Box 14103	Research Triangle Park	NC	27709	**800-700-1775**	919-549-8614	711
State Ports Authority 2202 Burnett Blvd PO Box 9002	Wilmington	NC	28402	**800-334-0682**	910-763-1621	607
Tourism Div 301 N Wilmington St	Raleigh	NC	27601	**800-847-4862**	919-733-4171	335
North Carolina A & T State University 1601 E Market St *Admissions	Greensboro	NC	27411	**800-443-8964***	336-334-7500	163
North Carolina Aquarium at Fort Fisher 900 Loggerhead Rd	Kure Beach	NC	28449	**866-301-3476**	910-458-8257	40
North Carolina Aquarium on Roanoke Island PO Box 967 Airport Rd	Manteo	NC	27954	**866-332-3475**	252-473-3493	40
North Carolina Assn of Realtors Inc 4511 Weybridge Ln	Greensboro	NC	27407	**800-443-9956**	336-294-1415	642
North Carolina Democratic Party 220 Hillsborough St	Raleigh	NC	27603	**800-229-3367**	919-821-2777	605-1
North Carolina Eye Bank Inc 3622 Lyckan Pkwy	Durham	NC	27707	**800-552-9956**		265
North Carolina Eye Bank Inc 3900 Westpoint Blvd Suite F	Winston-Salem	NC	27103	**800-552-9956**	336-765-0932	265
North Carolina Foam Industries Inc 1515 Carter St	Mount Airy	NC	27030	**800-346-8229**	336-789-9161	190-4
North Carolina Granite Corp PO Box 151 *Sales	Mount Airy	NC	27030	**800-227-6242***	336-786-5141	710
North Carolina High Country Host 1700 Blowing Rock Rd	Boone	NC	28607	**800-438-7500**	828-264-1299	205
North Carolina Medical Society 222 N Person St	Raleigh	NC	27601	**800-722-1350**	919-833-3836	466
North Carolina Mutual Life Insurance Co 411 W Chapel Hill St	Durham	NC	27701	**800-626-1899**	919-682-9201	384-2
North Carolina Mutual Wholesale Drug Co PO Box 411	Durham	NC	27702	**800-800-8551**	919-596-2151	237
North Carolina State Bar 208 Fayetteville St Mall	Raleigh	NC	27601	**800-662-7407**	919-828-4620	73
North Carolina Veterinary Medical Assn 1611 Jones Franklin Rd Suite 108	Raleigh	NC	27606	**800-446-2862**	919-851-5850	782
North Carolina Wesleyan College 3400 N Wesleyan Blvd	Rocky Mount	NC	27804	**800-488-6292**	252-985-5100	163
North Carolina Zoological Park 4401 Zoo Pkwy	Asheboro	NC	27205	**800-488-0444**	336-879-7000	811
North Central Assn Higher Learning Commission 30 N La Salle St Suite 2400	Chicago	IL	60602	**800-621-7440**	312-263-0456	49-5
North Central Bancshares Inc 825 Central Ave *NASDAQ: FFFD*	Fort Dodge	IA	50501	**800-272-3445**	515-576-7531	355-2
North Central College 30 N Brainard St	Naperville	IL	60540	**800-411-1861**	630-637-5800	163
North Central Electric Co-op Inc PO Box 475	Attica	OH	44807	**800-426-3072**	419-426-3072	244
North Central Michigan College 1515 Howard St	Petoskey	MI	49770	**888-298-6605**	231-348-6605	160
North Central Missouri College 1301 Main St	Trenton	MO	64683	**800-880-6180**	660-359-3948	160
North Central Missouri Electric Co-op Inc 1098 Hwy E PO Box 220	Milan	MO	63556	**800-279-2264**	660-265-4404	244
North Central Public Power District 1409 Main St	Creighton	NE	68729	**800-578-1060**	402-358-5112	244
North Central Regional Educational Laboratory (NCREL) 1120 E Diehl Rd Suite 200	Naperville	IL	60563	**800-356-2735**	630-649-6500	654
North Central State College 2441 Kenwood Circle	Mansfield	OH	44906	**888-755-4899**	419-755-4800	787
North Central University 910 Elliot Ave S	Minneapolis	MN	55404	**800-289-6222**	612-343-4480	163
North Coast Energy Inc 1993 Case Pkwy	Twinsburg	OH	44087	**800-645-6427**	330-425-2330	525
North Country Community College 23 Santanoni Ave	Saranac Lake	NY	12983	**888-879-6222**	518-891-2915	160
North Country Free Press PO Box 330	Granville	NY	12832	**800-354-4232**	518-642-1234	522-4
North Country Trail Assn (NCTA) 229 E Main St	Lowell	MI	49331	**866-445-3628**	616-897-5987	48-23
North County Journal 7751 N Lindbergh Blvd	Hazelwood	MO	63042	**866-440-4500**	314-972-1111	522-4
North County Times 207 E Pennsylvania Ave *News Rm	Escondido	CA	92025	**800-200-0704***	760-745-6611	522-2
North Dakota						
Accountancy Board 2701 S Columbia Rd	Grand Forks	ND	58201	**800-532-5904**	701-775-7100	335
Children & Family Services Div 600 E Boulevard Ave	Bismarck	ND	58505	**800-245-3736**	701-328-2316	335
Consumer Protection Div 600 E Boulevard Ave Dept 125	Bismarck	ND	58505	**800-472-2600**	701-328-3404	335
Human Services Dept 600 E Boulevard Ave Dept 325	Bismarck	ND	58505	**800-472-2622**	701-328-2310	335
Insurance Dept 600 E Boulevard Ave Dept 401	Bismarck	ND	58505	**800-247-0560**	701-328-2440	335
Parks & Recreation Dept 1835 E Bismarck Expy *Campground Resv	Bismarck	ND	58504	**800-807-4723***	701-328-5357	335
Secretary of State 600 E Boulevard Ave Dept 108	Bismarck	ND	58505	**800-352-0867**	701-328-2900	335
Tourism Div 604 E Boulevard Ave	Bismarck	ND	58505	**800-435-5663**	701-328-2525	335
Vocational Rehabilitation Div 600 S 2nd St Suite 1B	Bismarck	ND	58504	**800-755-2745**	701-328-8950	335
North Dakota Assn of Realtors 318 W Apollo Ave	Bismarck	ND	58503	**800-279-2361**	701-355-1010	642
North Dakota (Greater) Assn PO Box 2639	Bismarck	ND	58502	**800-382-1405**	701-222-0929	138
North Dakota Mill PO Box 13078	Grand Forks	ND	58208	**800-538-7721**	701-795-7000	291-23
North Dakota State College of Science 800 6th St N	Wahpeton	ND	58076	**800-342-4325**	701-671-2401	160
North Dakota State University 1301 12th Ave N	Fargo	ND	58105	**800-488-6378**	701-231-8011	163
North Dakota Veterinary Medical Assn 921 S 9th St Suite 120	Bismarck	ND	58504	**877-637-6386**	701-221-7740	782
North East Mississippi Electric Power Assn 10 County Rd 2050	Oxford	MS	38655	**877-234-6331**	662-234-6331	244
North Face Inc 2013 Farallon Dr	San Leandro	CA	94577	**800-535-3331**	510-618-3500	701
North Fork Bancorp Inc 275 Broad Hollow Rd *NYSE: NFB*	Melville	NY	11747	**877-694-9111**	631-844-1000	355-2
North Fork Ranch 555395 Hwy 285	Shawnee	CO	80475	**800-843-7895**	303-838-9873	238
North Georgia College & State University	Dahlonega	GA	30597	**800-498-9581**	706-864-1800	163
North Georgia Electric Membership Corp 1850 Cleveland Hwy	Dalton	GA	30722	**800-282-4022**	706-259-9441	244
North Greenville College PO Box 1892	Tigerville	SC	29688	**800-468-6642**	864-977-7000	160
North Haven Gardens Inc 7700 Northaven Rd	Dallas	TX	75230	**800-347-2342**	214-363-6715	318
North Hennepin Community College 7411 85th Ave N	Brooklyn Park	MN	55445	**800-818-0395**	763-424-0702	160
North Idaho College 1000 W Garden Ave	Coeur d'Alene	ID	83814	**877-404-4536**	208-769-3300	160
North Iowa Area Community College 500 College Dr	Mason City	IA	50401	**888-466-4222**	641-423-1264	160
North Island Financial Credit Union 2300 Boswell Rd *Cust Svc	Chula Vista	CA	91914	**800-752-4419***	619-656-1600	216
North Itasca Electric Co-op 301 Main Ave	Bigfork	MN	56628	**800-762-4048**	218-743-3131	244
North Lake Tahoe Resort Assn 3000 N Lake Blvd Suite 10	Tahoe City	CA	96145	**800-824-6348**	530-583-3494	205
North Light Magazine 4700 E Galbraith Rd *Orders	Cincinnati	OH	45236	**800-289-0963***	513-531-2690	449-11
North Maple Inn at Basking Ridge 300 N Maple Ave	Basking Ridge	NJ	07920	**800-288-2687**	908-953-3000	370
North Mississippi Medical Center Hospice 422-A E President St	Tupelo	MS	38801	**800-852-1610**	662-377-3612	365
North Olympic Peninsula Visitor & Convention Bureau 338 W 1st St Suite 104	Port Angeles	WA	98362	**800-942-4042**	360-452-8552	205
North Pacific 2419 Science Pkwy	Okemos	MI	48864	**800-942-8220**	517-349-8220	190-3
North Pacific Group Inc (NOR PAC) 815 NE Davis St	Portland	OR	97232	**800-547-8440**	503-231-1166	190-3
North Park University 3225 W Foster Ave	Chicago	IL	60625	**800-888-6728**	773-244-5500	163
North Pittsburgh Systems Inc 4008 Gibsonia Rd *NASDAQ: NPSI*	Gibsonia	PA	15044	**800-541-9225**	724-443-9600	355-3
North Plains Electric Co-op Inc 14585 Hwy 83 N	Perryton	TX	79070	**800-272-5482**	806-435-5482	244
North Platte Telegraph PO Box 370	North Platte	NE	69103	**800-753-7092**	308-532-6000	522-2
North Platte/Lincoln County Convention & Visitors Bureau 219 S Dewey St	North Platte	NE	69103	**800-955-4528**	308-532-4729	205
North Safety Products 2000 Plainfield Pike *Cust Svc	Cranston	RI	02921	**800-430-4110***	401-943-4400	566
North Shore Bank FSB 15700 W Bluemound Rd	Brookfield	WI	53005	**800-236-4672**	262-785-1600	71
North Shore Gas Co 3001 Grand Ave	Waukegan	IL	60085	**866-556-6004**		774
North Side Journal 7751 N Lindbergh Blvd	Hazelwood	MO	63042	**866-440-4500**	314-972-1111	522-4
North Star Communications Group Inc 1900 International Pk Dr	Birmingham	AL	35243	**888-836-6784**	877-862-8682	707
North Star Electric Co-op Inc 441 State Hwy 172 NW	Baudette	MN	56623	**888-634-2202**	218-634-2202	244
North Star Glove Co 2916 S Steele St	Tacoma	WA	98409	**800-423-1616**	253-627-7107	153-8
North Star Lighting Inc 2150 Parkes Dr	Broadview	IL	60155	**800-229-4330**	708-681-4330	431
North States Industries Inc 1507 92nd Ln NE	Blaine	MN	55449	**800-848-8421**	763-486-1754	568
North Suburban Library System 200 W Dundee Rd	Wheeling	IL	60090	**800-374-7134**	847-459-1300	426
North Vancouver Chamber of Commerce 124 W 1st St Suite 102	North Vancouver	BC	V7M3N3	**877-880-4699**	604-987-4488	136
North West Rural Electric Co-op 1505 Albany Pl SE	Orange City	IA	51041	**800-383-0476**	712-707-4935	244
North Western Electric Co-op Inc 04125 SR 576	Bryan	OH	43506	**800-647-6932**	419-636-5051	244
North Winds Investigations Inc PO Box 1654	Rogers	AR	72757	**800-530-4514**	479-925-1612	392
Northampton Community College 3835 Green Pond Rd	Bethlehem	PA	18020	**877-543-0998**	610-861-5300	160
Northbay Medical Center 1200 B Gale Wilson Blvd	Fairfield	CA	94533	**888-294-3600**	707-429-3600	366-2
Northcentral Technical College 1000 W Campus Dr	Wausau	WI	54401	**888-682-7144**	715-675-3331	787
Northeast Bancorp 158 Court St *AMEX: NBN*	Auburn	ME	04210	**800-284-5989**	207-777-6411	355-2
Northeast Construction Inc 100 Hwy 70	Lakewood	NJ	08701	**800-879-8204**	732-364-8200	187-10
Northeast Delta Dental PO Box 2002	Concord	NH	03302	**800-537-1715**	603-223-1000	384-3
Northeast Indiana Bancorp Inc 648 N Jefferson St *NASDAQ: NEIB*	Huntington	IN	46750	**800-550-3372**	260-356-3311	355-2

Name / Address	City	State	ZIP	Toll-Free	Phone	Class
Northeast Investors Funds 150 Federal St	Boston	MA	02110	**800-225-6704**	617-523-3588	517
Northeast Iowa Community College						
Calmar Campus PO Box 400	Calmar	IA	52132	**800-728-2256**	563-562-3263	160
Dubuque Campus 700 Main St	Dubuque	IA	52001	**800-728-7367**	563-557-8271	160
Peosta Campus 10250 Sundown Rd	Peosta	IA	52068	**800-728-7367**	563-556-5110	160
Northeast Kingdom Chamber of Commerce 51 Depot Sq Suite 3	Saint Johnsbury	VT	05819	**800-639-6379**	802-748-3678	137
NorthEast Medical Center 920 Church St N	Concord	NC	28025	**800-842-6868**	704-783-3000	366-2
Northeast Mississippi Community College 101 Cunningham Blvd	Booneville	MS	38829	**800-555-2154**	662-728-7751	160
Northeast Mississippi Daily Journal 1242 S Green St	Tupelo	MS	38804	**800-264-6397**	662-842-2611	522-2
Northeast Nebraska Public Power District 303 Logan St	Wayne	NE	68787	**800-750-9277**	402-375-1360	244
Northeast Oklahoma Electric Co-op Inc 443857 E Hwy 60 PO Box 948	Vinita	OK	74301	**800-256-6405**	918-256-6405	244
Northeast Pennsylvania Convention & Visitors Bureau 99 Glenmaura National Blvd	Scranton	PA	18507	**800-229-3526**	570-963-6363	205
Northeast Pennsylvania Financial Corp 12 E Broad St	Hazleton	PA	18201	**888-466-6745**	570-459-3700	355-2
Northeast Power Report 2 Penn Plaza 25th FL	New York	NY	10121	**800-223-6180**	800-752-8872	521-5
Northeast State Technical Community College PO Box 696	Elizabethton	TN	37644	**800-836-7822**	423-547-8450	787
Northeast Texas Community College 1735 Chapel Hill Rd	Mount Pleasant	TX	75455	**800-870-0142**	903-572-1911	160
Northeast Times Booster 409 Washington Ave	Towson	MD	21204	**877-696-0660**	410-337-2400	522-4
Northeast Times Reporter 409 Washington Ave	Towson	MD	21204	**877-696-0660**	410-337-2400	522-4
Northeast Utilities 197 Selden St	Berlin	CT	06037	**800-286-5000**	860-665-5000	355-5
NYSE: NU						
Northeast Wisconsin Technical College 2740 W Mason St	Green Bay	WI	54307	**800-422-6982**	920-498-5400	787
Northeastern Junior College 100 College Ave	Sterling	CO	80751	**800-626-4637**	970-521-6600	160
Northeastern Log Homes Inc 492 Scott Hwy	Groton	VT	05046	**800-992-6526**	802-584-3336	107
Northeastern Pennsylvania Philharmonic 957 Broadcast Ctr	Avoca	PA	18641	**800-836-3413**	570-457-8301	563-3
Northeastern State University 601 N Grand Ave	Tahlequah	OK	74464	**800-722-9614**	918-456-5511	163
Tahlequah 600 N Grand Ave	Tahlequah	OK	74464	**800-722-9614**	918-456-5511	163
Northern Air Cargo Inc 3900 W International Airport Rd	Anchorage	AK	99502	**800-727-2141**	907-243-3331	13
Northern Air Inc 5500 44th St SE	Grand Rapids	MI	49512	**800-262-4953**	616-336-4700	25
Northern Alleghenies Vacation Region 2883 Pennsylvania Ave W Ext	Warren	PA	16365	**800-624-7802**	814-726-1222	205
Northern Arizona University PO Box 4084	Flagstaff	AZ	86011	**888-667-3628**	928-523-5511	163
Cline Library PO Box 6022	Flagstaff	AZ	86011	**800-247-3380**	928-523-6802	426
Northern Cards 5694 Ambler Dr	Mississauga	ON	L4W2K9	**877-627-7444**	905-625-4944	130
Northern Cards 5694 Ambler Dr	Mississauga	ON	L4W2K9	**877-627-7444**	905-625-4944	130
Northern Colorado Business Report 141 S College Ave	Fort Collins	CO	80524	**800-440-3506**	970-221-5400	449-5
Northern Cross Industries Inc 92 Hardwood Way	Brattleboro	VT	05301	**800-257-4501**	802-257-4501	88
Northern Distributing Co Inc 319 Corinth Rd	Glens Falls	NY	12804	**800-342-9565**	518-792-3112	82-1
Northern Electric Co-op Inc 39456 133nd St	Bath	SD	57427	**800-529-0310**	605-225-0310	244
Northern Exposure Greeting Cards 461 Sebastopol Ave	Santa Rosa	CA	95401	**800-237-3524**	707-546-2153	130
Northern Fruit Co Inc 220 3rd St NE	East Wenatchee	WA	98802	**800-234-6651**	509-884-6651	12-1
Northern Funds PO Box 75986	Chicago	IL	60675	**800-595-9111**	312-557-2790	517
Northern Hotel Billings 19 N Broadway	Billings	MT	59101	**800-542-5121**	406-245-5121	373
Northern Illinois University PO Box 3001	DeKalb	IL	60115	**800-892-3050**	815-753-1000	163
Northern Illinois University College of Law 1425 W Lincoln Hwy	DeKalb	IL	60115	**800-892-3050**	815-753-8559	164-1
Northern Indiana Commuter Transportation District 33 E US Hwy 12	Chesterton	IN	46304	**800-356-2079**	219-926-5744	460
Northern Indiana Public Service Co (NIPSCO) 801 E 86th Ave	Merrillville	IN	46410	**800-464-7726***	219-853-5200	774
*Cust Svc						
Northern Institutional Funds 801 S Canal St C5S	Chicago	IL	60607	**800-637-1380**		517
Northern Isles 300 Manley St	Brockton	MA	02303	**800-666-5105**	508-513-3013	153-12
Northern Kentucky Convention & Visitors Bureau 50 E RiverCenter Blvd Suite 100	Covington	KY	41011	**800-447-8489**	859-261-4677	205
Northern Kentucky University Nunn Dr	Highland Heights	KY	41099	**800-637-9948**	859-572-5100	163
Northern Labs Inc PO Box 850	Manitowoc	WI	54221	**800-558-7621**	920-684-7137	149
Northern Light Balloon Expeditions PO Box 1695	Sedona	AZ	86339	**800-230-6222**	928-282-2274	748
Northern Lights Inc 421 Cherry St	Sagle	ID	83860	**800-326-9594**	208-263-5141	244
Northern Log Homes Inc 300 Bomarc Rd	Bangor	ME	04401	**800-553-7311**	207-942-6869	107
Northern Maine Community College 33 Edgemont Dr	Presque Isle	ME	04769	**800-535-6682***	207-768-2700	787
*Admissions						
Northern Michigan University 1401 Presque Isle Ave	Marquette	MI	49855	**800-682-9797**	906-227-2650	163
Northern Montana Hospital 30 13th St	Havre	MT	59501	**800-352-5097**	406-265-2211	366-2
Northern Navajo Medical Center PO Box 160	Shiprock	NM	87420	**800-549-5644**	505-368-6001	366-2
Northern Neck Electric Co-op Inc 85 Saint Johns St PO Box 288	Warsaw	VA	22572	**800-243-2860**	804-333-3621	244
Northern Oklahoma College 1220 E Grand St PO Box 310	Tonkawa	OK	74653	**888-429-5715**	580-628-6200	160
Northern Plains Electric Co-op 1515 W Main St	Carrington	ND	58421	**800-882-2500**	701-652-3156	244
Northern Plastic Lumber 164 Needham St Unit 1	Lindsay	ON	K9V5R7	**888-255-1222**	705-878-5700	647
Northern Precision Casting Co Inc PO Box 580	Lake Geneva	WI	53147	**800-934-4903**	262-248-4461	301
Northern Security Insurance Co PO Box 188	Montpelier	VT	05601	**800-451-5000**	802-223-2341	384-4
Northern Star Broadcasting LLC 1356 Mackinaw Ave	Cheboygan	MI	49721	**888-847-2346**	231-627-2341	629
Northern State University 1200 S Jay St	Aberdeen	SD	57401	**800-678-5330**	605-626-3011	163
Northern States Financial Corp 1601 N Lewis Ave	Waukegan	IL	60085	**800-339-4432**	847-244-6000	355-2
NASDAQ: NSFC						
Northern Technologies Corp 23123 E Mission Ave	Liberty Lake	WA	99019	**800-456-1875**	509-927-0401	252
Northern Technologies International Corp (NTIC) 6680 N Hwy 49	Lino Lakes	MN	55014	**800-328-2433**	651-784-1250	143
AMEX: NTI						
Northern Tool & Equipment Co 2800 Southcross Dr W	Burnsville	MN	55306	**800-221-0516**	952-894-9510	359
Northern Tours 2740 Bauer St	Eau Claire	WI	54701	**800-735-8687**	715-834-1463	108
Northern Trust Bank of Florida NA 700 Brickell Ave	Miami	FL	33131	**800-468-2352**	305-372-1000	71
Northern Trust Co 50 S LaSalle St	Chicago	IL	60675	**888-289-6542**	312-630-6000	71
Northern Trust Co of Connecticut 300 Atlantic St Suite 400	Stamford	CT	06901	**800-722-4609**	203-977-7000	393
Northern Trust Securities 50 S La Salle St 12th Fl	Chicago	IL	60675	**800-621-2253**	312-557-2000	679
Northern Utilities Inc 300 Friberg Pkwy	Westborough	MA	01581	**800-882-5454**	508-836-7000	774
Northern Video Systems Inc 4465 Granite Dr Suite 700	Rocklin	CA	95677	**800-366-4472**	916-630-4700	245
Northern Virginia Daily 152 N Holliday St	Strasburg	VA	22657	**800-296-5137**	540-465-5137	522-2
Northern Virginia Electric Co-op PO Box 2710	Manassas	VA	22110	**888-335-0500**	703-335-0500	244
Northern Waters Library Service 3200 E Lakeshore Dr	Ashland	WI	54806	**800-228-5684**	715-682-2365	426
Northern Wyoming Daily News PO Box 508	Worland	WY	82401	**800-788-4679**	307-347-3241	522-2
Northfield Lines Inc 32611 Northfield Blvd	Northfield	MN	55057	**888-670-8068**	507-645-5267	108
Northland Aluminum Products Inc DBA Nordic Ware Inc 5005 Hwy 7	Minneapolis	MN	55416	**800-328-4310**	952-920-2888	477
Northland Baptist Bible College W10085 Pike Plains Rd	Dunbar	WI	54119	**888-466-7845**	715-324-5245	163
Northland College 1411 Ellis Ave	Ashland	WI	54806	**800-753-1840**	715-682-1699	163
Northland Communications Corp 101 Stewart St Suite 700	Seattle	WA	98101	**800-448-0273**	206-674-3900	117
Northland Community & Technical College 1101 US Hwy 1 E	Thief River Falls	MN	56701	**800-959-6282**	218-681-0701	160
Northland Corp 701 Ranney Dr	Greenville	MI	48838	**800-223-3900**	616-754-5601	36
Northland Inn & Executive Conference Center 7025 Northland Dr	Minneapolis	MN	55428	**800-441-6422**	763-536-8300	370
Northland Insurance Co PO Box 64816	Saint Paul	MN	55164	**800-237-9334**	651-688-4100	384-4
Northland Pioneer College PO Box 610	Holbrook	AZ	86025	**800-266-7845**	928-532-6111	160
Northland Plastics Inc PO Box 290	Sheboygan	WI	53082	**800-776-7163**	920-458-0732	589
Northland Products Co PO Box 418	Waterloo	IA	50704	**800-772-1724**	319-234-5585	530
Northland Services Inc 6700 W Marginal Way SW Suite 600	Seattle	WA	98106	**800-426-3113**	206-763-3000	307
Northrim BanCorp Inc 3111 C St	Anchorage	AK	99503	**800-478-3311**	907-562-0062	71
NASDAQ: NRIM						
Northrop Grumman Information Technology 4800 Hampden Ln Suite 200	Bethesda	MD	20814	**800-366-4822**	301-961-0500	519
Northshire Bookstore 4869 Main St	Manchester Center	VT	05255	**800-437-3700**	802-362-2200	96
Northside Aviation Inc McCollum Airport PO Box 490	Kennesaw	GA	30156	**800-754-4300**	770-422-4300	63
Northstar Computer Forms Inc 7130 Northland Cir N	Brooklyn Park	MN	55428	**800-765-6787**	763-531-7340	111
Northstar Cruises 80 Bloomfield Ave Suite 102	Caldwell	NJ	07006	**800-249-9360**	973-228-5005	760
Northstar Hotel, Crowne Plaza Minneapolis 618 2nd Ave S	Minneapolis	MN	55402	**800-556-7827**	612-338-2288	373
NorthStar Moving Corp 9324 Corbin Ave	Northridge	CA	91324	**800-275-7767**	818-727-0128	508
Northstar-at-Tahoe PO Box 129	Truckee	CA	96160	**800-466-6784**	530-562-1010	655
NORTHSTAR Travel Media LLC 500 Plaza Dr	Secaucus	NJ	07094	**800-742-7076**	201-902-2000	623-9
Northway Financial Inc PO Box 9	Berlin	NH	03570	**800-442-6666**	603-752-1171	355-2
NASDAQ: NWFI						
Northwest Administrators Inc 2323 Eastlake Ave E	Seattle	WA	98102	**800-552-7334**	206-329-4900	383
Northwest Airlines Cargo Div 5101 Northwest Dr	Saint Paul	MN	55111	**800-692-2746**		13
Northwest Airlines Corp 2700 Lone Oak Pkwy	Eagan	MN	55121	**800-225-2525**	612-726-2111	355-1
NASDAQ: NWAC						
Northwest Airlines Inc (NWA) 2700 Lone Oak Pkwy	Eagan	MN	55121	**800-225-2525**	612-726-2111	26
Northwest Airlines WorldPerks 601 Oak St	Chisholm	MN	55719	**800-447-3757**		27
Northwest Area Foundation 60 Plato Blvd E Suite 400	Saint Paul	MN	55107	**888-904-9821**	651-224-9635	298
NorthWest Arkansas Community College 1 College Dr	Bentonville	AR	72712	**800-995-6922**	479-636-9222	160
Northwest Arkansas Paper Co 2400 Cantrell Rd Suite 116	Little Rock	AR	72202	**800-643-3068**	501-374-5884	549
Northwest Arkansas Times PO Box 1607	Fayetteville	AR	72702	**800-498-1991**	479-571-6400	522-2

Alphabetical Section

Name / Address	City	State	ZIP	Toll-Free	Phone	Class
Northwest Bancorp Inc 301 2nd Ave *NASDAQ: NWSB*	Warren	PA	16365	**877-672-5678**	814-726-2140	355-2
Northwest Bedding Co 6102 S Hayford Rd	Spokane	WA	99224	**800-456-7686**	509-244-3000	463
Northwest Christian College 828 E 11th Ave	Eugene	OR	97401	**877-463-6622**	541-343-1641	163
Northwest College 231 W 6th St	Powell	WY	82435	**800-560-4692**	307-754-6000	160
Northwest Connecticut Convention & Visitors Bureau 21 Church St	Waterbury	CT	06702	**888-588-7880**	203-597-9527	205
Northwest Controls 188 Fox Run Dr	Defiance	OH	43512	**800-888-6932**	419-782-9479	245
Northwest Federal Credit Union 200 Spring St	Herndon	VA	20170	**800-336-3384**	703-709-8900	216
Northwest Florida Daily News PO Box 2949	Fort Walton Beach	FL	32549	**800-755-1185**	850-863-1111	522-2
Northwest Georgia Trade & Convention Center 2211 Dug Gap Battle Rd	Dalton	GA	30720	**800-824-7469**	706-272-7676	204
Northwest Grain Growers Inc 850 N 4th Ave	Walla Walla	WA	99362	**800-994-4290**	509-525-6510	271
Northwest Herald PO Box 250	Crystal Lake	IL	60039	**800-589-8910**	815-459-4122	522-2
Northwest Herald Inc PO Box 250	Crystal Lake	IL	60039	**800-589-8910**	815-459-4040	623-8
Northwest Indian College 2522 Kwina Rd	Bellingham	WA	98226	**866-676-2772**	360-676-2772	161
Northwest Iowa Community College 603 W Park St	Sheldon	IA	51201	**800-352-4907**	712-324-5061	160
Northwest Iowa Transportation Inc 2755 200th St	Fort Dodge	IA	50501	**877-776-1700**	515-576-5519	108
Northwest Lions Eye Bank 901 Boren Ave Suite 810	Seattle	WA	98104	**800-847-5786**	206-682-8500	265
Northwest Location Services Inc DBA Legal Locate Services PO Box 1345	Puyallup	WA	98371	**800-916-3724**	253-848-7767	392
Northwest Medical Teams International (NWMTI) PO Box 10	Portland	OR	97207	**800-959-4325**	503-624-1000	48-5
Northwest Missouri State University 800 University Dr	Maryville	MO	64468	**800-633-1175**	660-562-1212	163
Northwest Natural Gas Co DBA NW Natural 220 NW 2nd Ave *NYSE: NWN*	Portland	OR	97209	**800-422-4012**	503-226-4211	774
Northwest Natural Gas Development Corp 220 NW 2nd Ave	Portland	OR	97209	**800-422-4012**	503-226-4211	525
Northwest Nazarene University 623 Holly St *Admissions	Nampa	ID	83686	**877-668-4968***	208-467-8011	163
Northwest Pennsylvania's Great Outdoors Visitors Bureau 175 Main St	Brookville	PA	15825	**800-348-9393**	814-849-5197	205
Northwest Physicians Mutual Insurance Co 2965 Ryan Dr SE	Salem	OR	97301	**800-243-3503**	503-371-8228	384-5
Northwest Pipe Co 200 SW Market St Suite 1800 *NASDAQ: NWPX*	Portland	OR	97201	**800-989-9631**	503-946-1200	481
Northwest Plaza 650-A Northwest Plaza	Saint Ann	MO	63074	**800-264-7841**	314-298-0071	452
Northwest Protective Service Inc 2700 Elliott Ave	Seattle	WA	98121	**888-981-4040**	206-448-4040	682
Northwest Publications 99 E State St	Rockford	IL	61104	**800-383-7827**	815-987-1200	623-8
Northwest Rural Public Power District PO Box 249	Hay Springs	NE	69347	**800-847-0492**	308-638-4445	244
Northwest Savings Bank 301 2nd Ave	Warren	PA	16365	**800-822-2009**	814-726-2140	71
Northwest Signal PO Box 567	Napoleon	OH	43545	**800-559-6779**	419-592-5055	522-2
Northwest Technical Institute 11995 Singletree Ln	Eden Prairie	MN	55344	**800-443-4223**	952-944-0080	787
Northwest Tissue Center 921 Terry Ave	Seattle	WA	98104	**800-858-2282**	206-292-1879	535
Northwest University 5520 108th Ave NE *Admissions	Kirkland	WA	98033	**800-669-3781***	425-822-8266	163
Northwestern Business College 4829 N Lipps Ave	Chicago	IL	60630	**800-396-5613**	773-777-4220	158
Northwestern College 101 7th St SW	Orange City	IA	51041	**800-747-4757**	712-707-7000	163
Northwestern College 3003 Snelling Ave N *Admissions	Saint Paul	MN	55113	**800-827-6827***	651-631-5100	163
Northwestern Corp PO Box 490	Morris	IL	60450	**800-942-1316**	815-942-1300	55
Northwestern Electric Co-op Inc 2925 William Ave	Woodward	OK	73802	**800-375-7423**	580-256-7425	244
NorthWestern Energy 600 Market St W	Huron	SD	57350	**800-245-6977**	605-352-8411	774
Northwestern Industries Inc 2500 W Jameson St	Seattle	WA	98199	**800-426-2771**	206-285-3140	325
Northwestern Michigan College 1701 E Front St	Traverse City	MI	49686	**800-748-0566**	231-995-1000	160
Northwestern Pacific Indemnity Co 15 Mountain View Rd *Claims	Warren	NJ	07059	**800-252-4670***	908-903-2000	384-4
Northwestern Products Inc 721 Industrial Park Rd	Ashland	WI	54806	**800-328-7317**	715-685-9500	323
Northwestern Publishing House 1250 N 113th St *Orders	Milwaukee	WI	53226	**800-662-6022***	414-475-6600	623-4
Northwestern Rural Electric Co-op Assn Inc PO Box 207	Cambridge Springs	PA	16403	**800-472-7910**		244
Northwestern Supply Co Inc 525 Progress Rd	Waite Park	MN	56387	**800-397-6972**	320-251-0812	272
Northwestern University Center for Public Safety (NUCPS) 600 Foster	Evanston	IL	60204	**800-323-4011**	847-491-5476	49-7
Northwest/KLM 2700 Lone Oak Pkwy	Eagan	MN	55121	**800-225-2525**	612-726-2111	26
Northwood University *Florida Campus* 2600 N Military Trail	West Palm Beach	FL	33409	**800-458-8325**	561-478-5500	163
Michigan Campus 4000 Whiting Dr	Midland	MI	48640	**800-457-7878**	989-837-4200	163
Texas Campus 1114 W FM 1382	Cedar Hill	TX	75104	**800-927-9663**	972-291-1541	163
Norton Co 1 New Bond St	Worcester	MA	01606	**800-543-4335**	508-795-5000	1
Norton Co Diamond Tool Div 65 Beale Rd *Cust Svc	Arden	NC	28704	**800-438-4773***	828-684-2500	484
Norton Co Refractories Div 1 New Bond St Box 15008	Worcester	MA	01615	**800-543-4335**	508-795-5000	649
Norton & Son Inc 148 E 5th St	Bayonne	NJ	07002	**800-631-3440**	201-437-0770	540
Norton WW & Co Inc 500 5th Ave	New York	NY	10110	**800-223-2584**	212-354-5500	623-2
Norton's Flowers & Gifts 2900 Washtenaw Ave *Sales	Ypsilanti	MI	48197	**800-682-8667***	734-434-2700	287
Nortrak Inc DBA VAE Nortrak North America Inc 3422 1st Ave S	Seattle	WA	98134	**800-638-4657**	206-622-0125	474
Nortrax Equipment Co 310 Industrial Park Dr	Ashland	WI	54806	**800-472-6685**	715-682-5522	353
Norvell Electronics Inc PO Box 701027	Dallas	TX	75370	**800-477-0021**	972-858-3713	245
Norwalk Co Inc 20 N Water St	Norwalk	CT	06854	**800-556-5001**	203-838-4766	170
Norwalk Furniture Corp 100 Furniture Pkwy *Orders	Norwalk	OH	44857	**800-837-2565***	419-668-4461	314-2
Norwalk Reflector 61 E Monroe St PO Box 71	Norwalk	OH	44857	**800-589-3771**	419-668-3771	522-2
Norwalk-Wilbert Vault Co 425 Harral Ave	Bridgeport	CT	06604	**800-826-9406**	203-366-5678	134
Norway. Sons of 1455 W Lake St	Minneapolis	MN	55408	**800-945-8851**	612-827-3611	48-14
Norwegian Coastal Voyage Inc 405 Park Ave	New York	NY	10022	**800-323-7436**	212-319-1300	217
Norwegian Cruise Line Ltd 7665 Corporate Ctr Dr	Miami	FL	33126	**800-327-7030**	305-436-4000	217
Norwich University 158 Harmon Dr	Northfield	VT	05663	**800-468-6679**	802-485-2000	163
Norwood Financial Corp 717 Main St *NASDAQ: NWFL*	Honesdale	PA	18431	**800-598-5002**	570-253-1455	355-2
Norwood Hotel 112 Marion St	Winnipeg	MB	R2H0T1	**888-888-1878**	204-233-4475	372
Norwood Kingsley Machine Co 2538 Wisconsin Ave	Downers Grove	IL	60515	**800-421-0995**	630-968-0647	379
Norwood Marking Systems Kingsley Div 2538 Wisconsin Ave	Downers Grove	IL	60515	**800-626-3464**	630-968-0646	459
Norwood Promotional Products Inc 318 E 7th St	Auburn	IN	46706	**800-827-5151**	260-925-1700	10
Norwood Sash & Door Mfg Co 4953 Section Ave	Norwood	OH	45212	**800-599-5043**	513-531-5700	489
Norwood Souvenir 202 F Ave NW	Cedar Rapids	IA	52405	**800-413-8371**	319-366-7831	10
Not-for-Profit Services Assn (NSA) 10831 Old Mill Rd Suite 400	Omaha	NE	68154	**888-475-4476**	402-778-7922	49-1
Notary Assn. National 9350 DeSoto Ave	Chatsworth	CA	91313	**800-876-6827**	818-739-4000	49-12
Notini Albert H & Sons Inc 225 Aiken St	Lowell	MA	01854	**800-366-8464**	978-459-7151	744
Notre Dame College of Ohio 4545 College Rd	South Euclid	OH	44121	**877-632-6446**	216-381-1680	163
Notre Dame de Namur University 1500 Ralston Ave	Belmont	CA	94002	**800-263-0545**	650-508-3600	163
Nott-Atwater Co 1309 N Bradley Rd	Spokane	WA	99212	**800-288-7278**	509-922-4522	321
Nottoway Plantation 30970 Hwy 405	White Castle	LA	70788	**866-428-4748**	225-346-8263	509
Nouvelles Images Inc 22 Eagle Rd	Danbury	CT	06810	**800-345-1383**	203-730-1004	130
NOVA (National Organization for Victim Assistance) 1730 Park Rd NW	Washington	DC	20010	**800-879-6682**	202-232-6682	48-8
Nova Biomedical Corp 200 Prospect St Suite 3	Waltham	MA	02454	**800-458-5813**	781-894-0800	410
Nova Fisheries 2532 Yale Ave E	Seattle	WA	98102	**888-458-6682**	206-781-2000	280
NOVA Information Systems 1 Concourse Pkwy Suite 300	Atlanta	GA	30328	**800-725-1243**	770-396-1456	176-4
Nova Internet Services Inc 12225 Greenville Ave SUite 230	Dallas	TX	75243	**877-668-2663**	214-904-9600	390
NOVA Savings Bank 1535 Locust St	Philadelphia	PA	19102	**877-322-6511**	215-545-6500	71
Nova Scotia Dept of Tourism & Culture PO Box 456	Halifax	NS	B3J2R5	**800-565-0000**	902-424-5000	763
Nova Scotia Power Inc PO Box 910	Halifax	NS	B3J2W5	**800-428-6230**	902-428-6230	774
Nova Solutions Inc 421 W Industrial Ave	Effingham	IL	62401	**800-730-6682**	217-342-7070	314-1
Nova Southeastern University 3301 College Ave	Fort Lauderdale	FL	33314	**800-541-6682**	954-262-8000	163
Nova Southeastern University Shepard Broad Law Center 3305 College Ave	Fort Lauderdale	FL	33314	**800-986-6529**	954-262-6100	164-1
Novacap Inc 25136 Anza Dr	Valencia	CA	91355	**800-227-2447**	661-295-5920	252
NovaCare Inc 680 American Ave	King of Prussia	PA	19406	**800-331-8840**	610-992-7200	347
Novacel 55 Tower Rd	Newton	MA	02464	**800-561-7906**	617-527-4980	538
Novaflex Hose Inc 449 Trollingwood Rd *Cust Svc	Haw River	NC	27258	**800-334-4270***	336-578-2161	364
NovaGold Resources Inc 1055 Dunsmuir St Suite 3454 *AMEX: NG*	Vancouver	BC	V7X1K8	**866-699-6227**	604-663-6227	492
Novalek Inc 2242 Davis Ct	Hayward	CA	94545	**800-877-7387**	510-782-4058	568
NovaMed Inc 980 N Michigan Ave Suite 1620 *NASDAQ: NOVA*	Chicago	IL	60611	**800-388-4133**	312-664-4100	785
Novapak Corp 370 Stevers Crossing Rd	Philmont	NY	12565	**800-672-7721**	518-672-7721	99
Novar Controls Corp 3333 Copley Rd	Copley	OH	44321	**800-348-1235**	330-670-1010	201
Novartis Animal Vaccine 1447 140th St	Larchwood	IA	51241	**800-843-3386**	712-477-2811	574
Novartis Nutrition 1600 Utica Ave S Suite 600	Saint Louis Park	MN	55416	**800-999-9978**	952-925-2100	786
Novartis Pharmaceuticals Canada Inc 385 boul Bouchard	Dorval	QC	H9S1A9	**800-465-2244**	514-631-6775	572
Novartis Pharmaceuticals Corp 1 Health Plaza *Cust Svc	East Hanover	NJ	07936	**888-669-6682***	862-778-8300	572
NovaSoft Information Technology Corp 3705 Quakerbridge Rd Suite 112	Mercerville	NJ	08619	**888-668-2763**	609-588-5500	176-1
Novastar Financial Inc 8140 Ward Pkwy Suite 300 *NYSE: NFI*	Kansas City	MO	64114	**800-469-4270**	816-237-7000	640
NovaStor Corp 80-B W Cochran St	Simi Valley	CA	93065	**800-668-2786**	805-579-6700	176-12

Name / Address	City	State	ZIP	Toll-Free	Phone	Class
Novatec Inc 222 E Thomas Ave	Baltimore	MD	21225	**800-237-8379**	410-789-4811	313
Novatel Wireless Inc 9255 Towne Centre Dr Suite 225 *NASDAQ: NVTL*	San Diego	CA	92121	**888-888-9231**	858-320-8800	496
Novations Group Inc 745 Boylston St Suite 300	Boston	MA	02116	**888-652-9975**	617-247-0214	753
Novations Training Solutions 4621 121st St	Urbandale	IA	50323	**888-776-8268**	515-224-0919	502
Novato Chamber of Commerce 807 DeLong Ave	Novato	CA	94945	**800-897-1164**	415-897-1164	137
Novavax Inc 508 Lapp Rd *NASDAQ: NVAX*	Malvern	PA	19355	**888-669-9111**	484-913-1200	86
Novell Design Studio Inc 129 Chestnut St	Roselle	NJ	07203	**888-916-6835**	908-245-4200	401
Novell Inc 1800 S Novell Pl *NASDAQ: NOVL*	Provo	UT	84606	**800-453-1267**	801-861-7000	176-1
Novellus Systems Inc 4000 N 1st St *NASDAQ: NVLS*	San Jose	CA	95134	**800-800-3079**	408-943-9700	685
Novelties Trade Assn. Souvenirs Gifts & 10 E Athens Ave Suite 208	Ardmore	PA	19003	**800-284-5451**	610-645-6940	49-18
Novelty Advertising Co PO Box 250	Coshocton	OH	43812	**800-848-9163**	740-622-3113	323
Noven Pharmaceuticals Inc 11960 SW 144th St *NASDAQ: NOVN*	Miami	FL	33186	**800-253-5099**	305-253-5099	572
Noveon Hilton-Davis Inc 2235 Langdon Farm Rd *Cust Svc	Cincinnati	OH	45237	**800-477-1022***	513-841-4000	141
Noveon Inc 9911 Brecksville Rd	Cleveland	OH	44141	**800-380-5397**	216-447-5000	143
Noville Essential Oil Co 124 Case Dr	South Plainfield	NJ	07080	**888-668-4553**	908-754-2222	564
Novo Nordisk of North America Inc 100 College Rd W	Princeton	NJ	08540	**800-727-6500**		572
Novo Nordisk Pharmaceuticals Inc 100 College Rd W *Cust Svc	Princeton	NJ	08540	**800-727-6500***	609-987-5800	572
Novogen Inc 1 Landmark Sq Suite 240 *NASDAQ: NVGN*	Stamford	CT	06901	**888-480-8529**	203-327-1188	86
Novosci 2828 N Crescent Ridge Dr	The Woodlands	TX	77381	**800-322-2273**	281-363-4950	468
Novoste Corp 4350 International Blvd Suite E *NASDAQ: NOVT*	Norcross	GA	30093	**800-668-6783**	770-717-0904	468
Novotel Montreal Centre 1180 rue de la Montagne	Montreal	QC	H3G1Z1	**800-668-6835**	514-861-6000	372
Novotel New York 226 W 52nd St	New York	NY	10019	**800-221-3185**	212-315-0100	373
Novotel Ottawa 33 Nicholas St	Ottawa	ON	K1N9M7	**800-668-6835**	613-230-3033	372
Novotel Toronto Centre 45 The Esplanade	Toronto	ON	M5E1W2	**800-668-6835**	416-367-8900	372
Novotel Toronto North York Hotel 3 Park Home Ave	North York	ON	M2N6L3	**800-668-6835**	416-733-2929	372
NOVUS Auto Glass Repair & Replacement 12800 Hwy 13 S	Minneapolis	MN	55378	**800-328-1137**	952-944-8000	62-2
Novus International Inc 530 Maryville Center Dr	Saint Louis	MO	63141	**888-906-6887**	314-576-8886	438
Nox-Crete Inc 1444 S 20th St	Omaha	NE	68108	**800-369-9800**	402-341-2080	143
NP Dodge Real Estate 8701 W Dodge Rd Suite 300	Omaha	NE	68114	**800-642-5008**	402-397-4900	638
NPA (National Parking Assn) 1112 16th St NW Suite 300	Washington	DC	20036	**800-647-7275**	202-296-4336	49-3
nPassage Inc 2505 2nd Ave Suite 405	Seattle	WA	98121	**888-486-7447**	206-441-8782	176-10
NPC (National PetCare Centers) 3540 JFK Pkwy	Fort Collins	CO	80525	**877-738-4677**	970-226-6632	781
NPC Inc 250 Elm St	Milford	NH	03055	**800-626-2180**	603-673-8680	584
NPCA (National Parks Conservation Assn) 1300 19th St NW Suite 300	Washington	DC	20036	**800-628-7275**	202-223-6722	48-13
NPCA (National Peace Corps Assn) 1900 L St NW Suite 205	Washington	DC	20036	**800-424-8580**	202-293-7728	48-5
NPCA (National Precast Concrete Assn) 10333 N Meridian St Suite 272	Indianapolis	IN	46290	**800-366-7731**	317-571-9500	49-3
NPF (National Parkinson Foundation) 1501 NW 9th Ave	Miami	FL	33136	**800-327-4545**	305-547-6666	48-17
NPF (National Psoriasis Foundation) 6600 SW 92nd Ave Suite 300	Portland	OR	97223	**800-723-9166**	503-244-7404	48-17
NPIC (National Pesticide Information Center) 333 Weniger Hall	Corvallis	OR	97331	**800-858-7378**		48-17
NPIN (National Prevention Information Network) PO Box 6003	Rockville	MD	20849	**800-458-5231**	301-562-1098	336-6
NPTA (National Pharmacy Technicians Assn) 3920 FM 1960 W Suite 380	Houston	TX	77068	**888-247-8700**	281-866-7900	49-8
NPTA Alliance 500 Bi-County Blvd Suite 200E	Farmingdale	NY	11735	**800-355-6782**	631-777-2223	49-18
NR Hamm Quarry Inc PO Box 17	Perry	KS	66073	**888-597-5464**	785-597-5111	493-5
NRA (National Rehabilitation Assn) 633 S Washington St	Alexandria	VA	22314	**888-258-4295**	703-836-0850	48-17
NRA (National Rifle Assn of America) 11250 Waples Mill Rd *Membership	Fairfax	VA	22030	**800-672-3888***	703-267-1000	48-22
NRA (Naval Reserve Assn) 1619 King St	Alexandria	VA	22314	**866-672-4968**	703-548-5800	48-19
NRA Institute for Legislative Action 11250 Waples Mill Rd	Fairfax	VA	22030	**800-672-3888**	703-267-1000	604
NRC (Nuclear Regulatory Commission)	Washington	DC	20555	**800-368-5642**	301-415-8200	336-16
NRC Sports Inc 603 Pleasant St	Paxton	MA	01612	**800-243-5033**	508-852-8206	451
NRCA (National Roofing Contractors Assn) 10255 W Higgins Rd Suite 600 *Cust Svc	Rosemont	IL	60018	**800-323-9545***	847-299-9070	49-3
NRD LLC 2937 Alt Blvd PO Box 310	Grand Island	NY	14072	**800-525-8076**	716-773-7634	200
NREC (National Railway Equipment Co) 14400 S Robey St	Dixmoor	IL	60426	**800-253-2905**	708-388-6002	636
NREC Power Systems 5222 Hwy 311	Houma	LA	70360	**800-851-6732**	985-872-5480	259
NRECA (National Rural Electric Cooperative Assn) 4301 Wilson Blvd	Arlington	VA	22203	**866-673-2299**	703-907-5500	48-12
NRF (National Retail Federation) 325 7th St NW Suite 1100	Washington	DC	20004	**800-673-4692**	202-783-7971	49-18
NRG Energy Inc 901 Marquette Ave Suite 2300 *NYSE: NRG*	Minneapolis	MN	55402	**800-241-4674**	612-373-5300	774
NRI Industries Inc 394 Symington Ave	Toronto	ON	M6N2W3	**800-387-8501**	416-657-1111	663
NRN Designs 5142 Argosy Ave	Huntington Beach	CA	92649	**800-421-6958**	714-898-6363	130
NRPA (National Recreation & Park Assn) 22377 Belmont Ridge Rd	Ashburn	VA	20148	**800-626-6772**	703-858-0784	48-23
NRS (National Runaway Switchboard) 3080 N Lincoln Ave	Chicago	IL	60657	**800-621-4000**	773-880-9860	48-6
NRTWC (National Right to Work Committee) 8001 Braddock Rd Suite 500	Springfield	VA	22160	**800-325-7892**	703-321-8510	49-12
NS Group Inc 530 W 9th St *NYSE: NSS*	Newport	KY	41071	**800-348-7751**	859-292-6809	709
NSA (National Sheriffs' Assn) 1450 Duke St	Alexandria	VA	22314	**800-424-7827**	703-836-7827	49-7
NSA (National Society of Accountants) 1010 N Fairfax St	Alexandria	VA	22314	**800-966-6679**	703-549-6400	49-1
NSA (National Stroke Assn) 9707 E Easter Ln	Englewood	CO	80112	**800-787-6537**	303-649-9299	48-17
NSA (National Stuttering Assn) 119 W 40th St 14th Fl	New York	NY	10018	**800-364-1677**	212-944-4050	48-17
NSA (Not-for-Profit Services Assn) 10831 Old Mill Rd Suite 400	Omaha	NE	68154	**888-475-4476**	402-778-7922	49-1
NSBA (National Small Business Assn) 1156 15th St NW Suite 1100	Washington	DC	20005	**800-345-6728**	202-393-8830	49-12
NSC International 7090 Central Ave	Hot Springs	AR	71913	**800-643-1520**	501-525-0133	378
NSCA (National Strength & Conditioning Assn) 1885 Bob Johnson Dr	Colorado Springs	CO	80906	**800-815-6826**	719-632-6722	48-22
NSCA (National Systems Contractors Assn) 625 1st St SE Suite 420	Cedar Rapids	IA	52401	**800-446-6722**	319-366-6722	49-20
NSCAA (National Soccer Coaches Assn of America) 6700 Squibb Rd Suite 215	Mission	KS	66202	**800-458-0678**	913-362-1747	48-22
NSCIA (National Spinal Cord Injury Assn) 6701 Democracy Blvd Suite 300-9	Bethesda	MD	20817	**800-962-9629**		48-17
NSEA Voice Magazine 605 S 14th St	Lincoln	NE	68508	**800-742-0047**	402-475-7611	449-8
NSEE (National Society for Experiential Education) 515 King St Suite 240	Alexandria	VA	22314	**800-803-4170**	703-706-9552	48-11
NSGA (National Senior Golf Assn) 3672 Nottingham Way	Hamilton Square	NJ	08690	**800-282-6772**	609-631-8145	48-22
NSGA (National Sporting Goods Assn) 1601 Feehanville Dr Suite 300	Mount Prospect	IL	60056	**800-815-5422**	847-296-6742	49-4
NSI Software 2 Hudson Pl Suite 700	Hoboken	NJ	07030	**800-775-4674**	201-656-2121	176-12
NSK Corp 4200 Goss Rd	Ann Arbor	MI	48105	**800-521-0605**	734-761-9500	609
NSPE (National Society of Professional Engineers) 1420 King St	Alexandria	VA	22314	**800-285-6773**	703-684-2800	49-19
NSPR (National Society for Park Resources) c/o National Recreation & Park Assn 22377 Belmont Ridge Rd	Ashburn	VA	20148	**800-626-6772**	703-858-0784	48-23
NSRA (National Shoe Retailers Assn) 7150 Columbia Gateway Dr Suite G	Columbia	MD	21046	**800-673-8446**	410-381-8282	49-18
NSSEA (National School Supply & Equipment Assn) 8380 Colesville Rd Suite 250	Silver Spring	MD	20910	**800-395-5550**	301-495-0240	49-18
NSSGA (National Stone Sand & Gravel Assn) 1605 King St	Alexandria	VA	22314	**800-342-1415**	703-525-8788	49-3
NSTA (National Science Teachers Assn) 1840 Wilson Blvd *Sales	Arlington	VA	22201	**800-722-6782***	703-243-7100	49-5
NSTAR 800 Boylston St *NYSE: NST*	Boston	MA	02199	**800-592-2000**	617-424-2000	355-5
NSTAR Communications Inc 800 Boylston St	Boston	MA	02199	**800-592-2000**	617-424-2000	721
NSTAR Electric 1 Nstar Way *Cust Svc	Westwood	MA	02090	**800-592-2000***	781-441-8000	774
NSTAR Gas 1 NSTAR Way	Westwood	MA	02090	**800-592-2000**		774
NSX (National Stock Exchange) 440 S LaSalle St Suite 2600	Chicago	IL	60605	**800-843-3924**	312-786-8803	680
NTEA (National Truck Equipment Assn) 37400 Hills Tech Dr	Farmington Hills	MI	48331	**800-441-6832**	248-489-7090	49-21
NTELOS Inc 401 Spring Ln Suite 300 PO Box 1990	Waynesboro	VA	22980	**800-482-1133**	540-946-3500	721
NTIC (Northern Technologies International Corp) 6680 N Hwy 49 *AMEX: NTI*	Lino Lakes	MN	55014	**800-328-2433**	651-784-1250	143
NTIS (National Technical Information Service) 5285 Port Royal Rd *Orders	Springfield	VA	22161	**800-553-6847***	703-605-6000	336-2
NTL Institute for Applied Behavioral Science 300 N Lee St Suite 300	Alexandria	VA	22314	**800-777-5227**	703-548-8840	753
NTM (New Tribes Mission) 1000 E 1st St	Sanford	FL	32771	**866-547-2460**	407-323-3430	48-20
NTMA (National Tooling & Machining Assn) 9300 Livingston Rd	Fort Washington	MD	20744	**800-248-6862**	301-248-6200	49-13
NTN Bearing Corp of America 1600 E Bishop Ct Suite 100	Mount Prospect	IL	60056	**800-468-6528**	847-298-7500	609
NTN Communications Inc 5966 La Place Ct Suite 100 *AMEX: NTN*	Carlsbad	CA	92008	**888-752-9686**	760-438-7400	502
NTP Republic PO Box 2448	Holyoke	MA	01041	**800-739-1129**	413-493-6800	538
NTP Software 427-3 Amherst St Suite 381	Nashua	NH	03063	**800-226-2755**	603-622-4400	176-12
NTRA (National Thoroughbred Racing Assn) 2525 Harrodsburg Rd	Lexington	KY	40504	**800-722-3287**	859-223-5444	48-22
NTSAD (National Tay-Sachs & Allied Diseases Assn) 2001 Beacon St Suite 204	Brighton	MA	02135	**800-906-8723**	617-277-4463	48-17

Name / Address	City	State	Zip	Toll-Free	Phone	Class
NTU (National Taxpayers Union) 108 N Alfred St	Alexandria	VA	22314	**800-829-4258**	703-683-5700	48-7
Nu-Air Mfg Co 8105 Anderson Rd	Tampa	FL	33634	**800-282-6627**	813-885-1654	232
Nu-Art Publishers Inc 6247 W 74th St	Bedford Park	IL	60638	**800-323-0398**	708-496-4900	130
Nu Horizons Electronics Corp 70 Maxess Rd *NASDAQ: NUHC*	Melville	NY	11747	**888-747-6846**	631-396-5000	245
Nu-Lite Electrical Wholesalers 850 Edwards Ave	Harahan	LA	70123	**800-256-1603**	504-733-3300	245
Nu-Look Fashions Inc 5080 Sinclair Rd Suite 200	Columbus	OH	43229	**800-800-4500**	614-885-4936	153-12
Nu Med Technologies Inc 7225 S 85th E Ave Suite 200	Tulsa	OK	74133	**800-640-3131**	918-249-2697	535
Nu Van Technology Inc 2155 Hwy 1187 PO Box 759	Mansfield	TX	76063	**800-487-1734**	817-477-1734	768
Nu-Ventures Inc 1324 W Milham St	Portage	MI	49024	**888-432-8379**	269-226-4400	656
Nu-Wa Industries Inc 3701 Johnson Rd	Chanute	KS	66720	**800-835-0676**	620-431-2088	120
Nu-Wool Co Inc 2472 Port Sheldon St	Jenison	MI	49428	**800-748-0128**	616-669-0100	382
Nu-Yale Cleaners 6300 Hwy 62	Jeffersonville	IN	47130	**888-644-7400**	812-285-7400	417
NUCA (National Utility Contractors Assn) 4301 N Fairfax Dr Suite 360	Arlington	VA	22203	**800-662-6822**	703-358-9300	49-3
Nuclear Insurers. American 95 Glastonbury Blvd	Glastonbury	CT	06033	**888-561-3433**	860-682-1301	49-9
Nuclear News PO Box 97781	Chicago	IL	60678	**800-323-3044**	708-352-6611	521-5
Nuclear & Plasma Sciences Society. IEEE IEEE Operations Ctr 445 Hoes Ln	Piscataway	NJ	08854	**800-678-4333**	732-981-0060	49-19
Nuclear Regulatory Commission (NRC)	Washington	DC	20555	**800-368-5642**	301-415-8200	336-16
Nuclear Regulatory Commission Regional Offices						
Region 1 475 Allendale Rd	King of Prussia	PA	19406	**800-432-1156**	610-337-5000	336-16
Region 2 61 Forsyth St SW Suite 23T85	Atlanta	GA	30303	**800-577-8510**	404-562-4400	336-16
Region 3 2443 Warrenville Rd	Lisle	IL	60532	**800-522-3025**	630-829-9500	336-16
Region 4 611 Ryan Plaza Dr Suite 4005	Arlington	TX	76011	**800-952-9677**	817-860-8100	336-16
Nuclear Society. American 555 N Kensington Ave	La Grange Park	IL	60526	**800-323-3044**	708-352-6611	49-19
Nuclear Waste News 8737 Colesville Rd Suite 1100	Silver Spring	MD	20910	**800-274-6737**	301-589-5103	521-5
Nuclearfuel Newsletter 1200 G St NW Suite 1000	Washington	DC	20005	**800-223-6180**	202-383-2100	521-5
Nucleonics Week Newsletter 1200 G St NW Suite 1100	Washington	DC	20005	**800-223-6180**	202-383-2100	521-5
Nucor Corp Cold Finish Div 2800 N Governor Williams Hwy	Darlington	SC	29540	**800-333-0590**	843-395-8689	709
Nucor Corp Fastener Div PO Box 6100	Saint Joe	IN	46785	**800-955-6826**	260-337-1600	345
Nucor Corp Steel Div 1455 Hagan Ave	Huger	SC	29450	**888-466-8267**	843-336-6000	709
Nucor-Yamato Steel Co PO Box 1228	Blytheville	AR	72316	**800-289-6977**	870-762-5500	709
NUCPS (Northwestern University Center for Public Safety) 600 Foster	Evanston	IL	60204	**800-323-4011**	847-491-5476	49-7
Nueces Electric Co-op 709 E Main St	Robstown	TX	78380	**800-632-9288**	361-387-2581	244
Nufarm America Co 1333 Burr Ridge Pkwy Suite 125A	Burr Ridge	IL	60521	**800-345-3330**	708-754-3330	276
Nukote International Inc 200 Beasley Dr	Franklin	TN	37064	**800-251-1910**	615-794-9000	616
Nulaid Foods Inc 200 W 5th St	Ripon	CA	95366	**800-788-8871**	209-599-2121	292-10
Nulco Lighting PO Box 1328	Pawtucket	RI	02862	**800-668-5269**	401-728-5200	431
Numark Laboratories Inc 164 Northfield Ave	Edison	NJ	08837	**800-338-8079**	732-417-1870	572
Numerex Corp 1600 Parkwood Cir Suite 200 *NASDAQ: NMRX*	Atlanta	GA	30339	**800-665-5686**	770-693-5950	720
Numeridex Inc 632 Wheeling Rd	Wheeling	IL	60090	**800-323-7737**	847-541-8840	113
Numismatic Assn. American 818 N Cascade Ave	Colorado Springs	CO	80903	**800-367-9723**	719-632-2646	48-18
Numo Mfg Co 1072 E Hwy 175	Kaufman	TX	75142	**800-253-0434**	972-962-5400	10
Numonics Corp 101 Commerce Dr	Montgomeryville	PA	18936	**800-523-6716**	215-362-2766	171-1
Nunavut Tourism PO Box 1450	Iqaluit	NU	X0A0H0	**800-491-7910**	867-979-6551	763
Nunhems USA Inc 1200 Anderson Corner Rd *Cust Svc	Parma	ID	83660	**800-733-9505***	208-674-4000	684
Nuprecon Inc 35131 SE Center St	Snoqualmie	WA	98065	**800-442-2072**	425-881-0623	188-17
Nurse Assns of America. Visiting 99 Summer St Suite 1700	Boston	MA	02110	**800-426-2547**	617-737-3200	49-8
Nursefinders Inc 1701 E Lamar Blvd Suite 200	Arlington	TX	76006	**800-445-0459**	817-460-1181	707
Nurserymen's Exchange 475 6th St	San Francisco	CA	94103	**800-227-5630**	415-392-0078	363
Nurses in AIDS Care. Association of 3538 Ridgewood Rd	Akron	OH	44333	**800-260-6780**	330-670-0101	49-8
Nurses. American Assn of Critical-Care 101 Columbia	Aliso Viejo	CA	92656	**800-809-2273**	949-362-2000	49-8
Nurses. American Assn of Neuroscience 4700 W Lake Ave	Glenview	IL	60025	**888-557-2266**	847-375-4733	49-8
Nurses. American Assn of Occupational Health 2920 Brandywine Rd Suite 100	Atlanta	GA	30341	**888-646-4631**	770-455-7757	49-8
Nurses. American Society of PeriAnesthesia 10 Melrose Ave Suite 110	Cherry Hill	NJ	08003	**877-737-9696**	856-616-9600	49-8
Nurses Assn. American 8515 Georgia Ave Suite 400	Silver Spring	MD	20910	**800-274-4262**	301-628-5000	49-8
Nurses' Assn. American Holistic 2733 E Lakin Dr Suite 2	Flagstaff	AZ	86004	**800-278-2462**	928-526-2196	48-17
Nurses Assn. Emergency 915 Lee St	Des Plaines	IL	60016	**800-900-9659**	847-460-4000	49-8
Nurses & Associates Inc. Society of Gastroenterology 401 N Michigan Ave	Chicago	IL	60611	**800-245-7462**	312-321-5165	49-8
Nurses. Association of Women's Health Obstetric & Neonatal 2000 L St NW Suite 740	Washington	DC	20036	**800-673-8499**	202-261-2400	49-8
Nurse's Book Society Doubleday Select Inc 101 Park Ave 2nd Fl	New York	NY	10178	**800-321-7323**		94
Nurses. National Assn of Neonatal 4700 W Lake Ave	Glenview	IL	60025	**800-451-3795**	847-375-3660	49-8
Nurses. National Assn of Orthopaedic 401 N Michigan Ave Suite 2200	Chicago	IL	60611	**800-289-6266**		49-8
Nurses. National Assn of School PO Box 1300	Scarborough	ME	04070	**877-627-6476**	207-883-2117	49-8
Nurses Society. Wound Ostomy & Continence 4700 W Lake Ave	Glenview	IL	60025	**888-224-9626**		49-8
Nurseweek Magazine 1156 Aster Ave Suite C	Sunnyvale	CA	94086	**800-859-2091**	408-249-5877	449-16
Nursing 2004 Magazine 323 Norristown Rd Suite 200	Ambler	PA	19002	**800-346-7844**	215-646-8700	449-16
Nursing Accrediting Commission Inc. National League for 61 Broadway 33rd Fl	New York	NY	10006	**800-669-1656**	212-363-5555	48-1
Nursing Administration in Long Term Care. National Assn of Directors of 10101 Alliance Rd Suite 140	Cincinnati	OH	45242	**800-222-0539**	513-791-3679	49-8
Nursing. American Academy of Ambulatory Care 200 E Holly Ave Box 56	Pitman	NJ	08080	**800-262-6877**	856-256-2350	49-8
Nursing Center 323 Norristown Rd Suite 200	Ambler	PA	19002	**800-346-7844**	215-646-8700	677
Nursing Management Magazine 323 Norristown Rd Suite 200	Ambler	PA	19002	**800-346-7844**	215-646-8700	449-16
Nursing. National League for 61 Broadway	New York	NY	10006	**800-669-1656**	212-363-5555	49-8
Nursing Society. Oncology 125 Enterprise Dr	Pittsburgh	PA	15275	**866-257-4667**	412-859-6100	49-8
Nursing Staff Development Organization. National 7794 Grow Dr	Pensacola	FL	32514	**800-489-1995**	850-474-0995	49-8
Nussbaum Trucking Inc 2200 N Main St	Normal	IL	61761	**800-322-7305**	309-452-4426	769
Nutcracker Brands Inc PO Box 420	Billerica	MA	01821	**800-638-6887**	978-663-5400	291-28
Nutra-Blend Inc 3200 E 2nd St	Neosho	MO	64850	**800-657-5657**	417-451-6111	574
Nutraceutical International Corp 1400 Kearns Blvd 2nd Fl *NASDAQ: NUTR*	Park City	UT	84060	**800-669-8877**	435-655-6000	786
Nutraceutix Inc 9609 153rd Ave NE	Redmond	WA	98052	**800-548-3222**	425-883-9518	470
NutraSweet Co 200 World Trade Ctr Merchandise Mart *Cust Svc	Chicago	IL	60654	**800-323-5321***	312-873-5000	291-38
Nutrilawn Inc 5397 Eglinton Ave W Suite 110	Toronto	ON	M9C5K6	**800-396-6096**	416-620-7100	421
NutriSystem Inc 200 Welsh Rd *AMEX: NSI*	Horsham	PA	19044	**800-321-8446**	215-706-5300	797
Nutrition 21 Inc 4 Manhattanville Rd *NASDAQ: NXXI*	Purchase	NY	10577	**800-699-3533**	914-701-4500	470
Nutrition. American Society for Parenteral & Enteral 8630 Fenton St Suite 412	Silver Spring	MD	20910	**800-727-4567**	301-587-6315	49-8
Nutrition for Life International 10235 W Little York Suite 300	Houston	TX	77040	**800-800-7377**	713-460-1976	361
Nutrition Research Newsletter 605 3rd Ave	New York	NY	10158	**800-825-7550**	201-748-6000	521-8
Nutritional Consultants. American Assn of 401 Kings Hwy	Winona Lake	IN	46590	**888-828-2262**	574-269-6165	49-8
Nutritional Foods Assn. National 3931 MacArthur Blvd Suite 101	Newport Beach	CA	92660	**800-966-6632**	949-622-6272	49-6
Nutro Products Inc 445 Wilson Way	City of Industry	CA	91744	**800-833-5330**	626-968-0532	568
Nuts & Volts Magazine 430 Princeland Ct *Orders	Corona	CA	92879	**800-783-4624***	951-371-8497	449-14
Nuttall Gear LLC PO Box 1032	Niagara Falls	NY	14302	**800-432-0121**	716-731-5180	700
NuVasive Inc 10065 Old Grove Rd *NASDAQ: NUVA*	San Diego	CA	92131	**800-455-1476**	858-271-7070	468
Nuveen Investments Inc 333 W Wacker Dr *NYSE: JNC*	Chicago	IL	60606	**800-257-8787**	312-917-7700	679
Nuveen Mutual Funds PO Box 463	East Syracuse	NY	13057	**800-257-8787**		517
NuView Systems Inc 155 West Street Suite 7	Wilmington	MA	01887	**800-244-7654**	978-988-7884	176-1
Nuvite Chemical Compounds Corp 213 Freeman St	Brooklyn	NY	11222	**800-394-8351**	718-383-8351	149
NuVox Communications Inc 16090 Swingley Ridge Rd Suite 500	Chesterfield	MO	63017	**800-800-9681**	636-537-5700	721
NuWare Technology Corp Inc 100 Wood Ave S Suite 306	Iselin	NJ	08830	**800-688-9273**	732-494-0550	178
NVFC (National Volunteer Fire Council) 1050 17th St NW Suite 490	Washington	DC	20036	**888-275-6832**	202-887-5700	49-4
NVIC (National Vaccine Information Center) 421-E Church St	Vienna	VA	22180	**800-909-7468**	703-938-3783	48-17
NVIDIA Corp 2701 San Tomas Expy *NASDAQ: NVDA*	Santa Clara	CA	95050	**877-768-4342**	408-486-2000	613
NW Natural 220 NW 2nd Ave *NYSE: NWN*	Portland	OR	97209	**800-422-4012**	503-226-4211	774
NWA (Northwest Airlines Inc) 2700 Lone Oak Pkwy	Eagan	MN	55121	**800-225-2525**	612-726-2111	26
NWA WorldVacations 2915 N Broadway	Minot	ND	58703	**800-727-1111**	701-839-5555	760
NWF (National Wildlife Federation) 11100 Wildlife Center Dr *Cust Svc	Reston	VA	20190	**800-822-9919***	703-438-6000	48-3
NWFA (National Wood Flooring Assn) 111 Chesterfield Industrial Blvd	Chesterfield	MO	63005	**800-422-4556**	636-519-9663	49-3
NWL Transformers Inc 312 Rising Sun Rd	Bordentown	NJ	08505	**800-742-5695**	609-298-7300	252
NWMTI (Northwest Medical Teams International) PO Box 10	Portland	OR	97207	**800-959-4325**	503-624-1000	48-5

Listing	City	State	ZIP	Toll-Free	Phone	Class
NWT Tourism Box 610	Yellowknife	NT	X1A2N5	**800-661-0788**	867-873-7200	763
NYAC (National Youth Advocacy Coalition) 1638 R St NW Suite 300	Washington	DC	20009	**800-541-6922**	202-319-7596	48-6
Nyack College 1 South Blvd *Admissions	Nyack	NY	10960	**800-336-9225***	845-358-1710	163
NYC & Co 810 7th Ave 3rd Fl	New York	NY	10019	**800-692-8474**	212-484-1200	205
NYLA (New York Library Assn) 252 Hudson Ave	Albany	NY	12210	**800-252-6952**	518-432-6952	427
NYLIFE Securities Inc 335 Madison Ave Suite 200	New York	NY	10017	**800-695-4785**	212-351-6000	679
Nylok Corp 15260 Hallmark Dr	Macomb	MI	48042	**800-826-5161**	586-786-0100	3
Nylon Corp of America 333 Sundial Ave	Manchester	NH	03103	**800-851-2001**	603-627-5150	594-1
NYMAGIC Inc 919 3rd Ave 10th Fl. *NYSE: NYM*	New York	NY	10022	**800-367-0224**	212-551-0600	355-4
Nymox Pharmaceutical Corp 9900 Cavendish Blvd Suite 306 *NASDAQ: NYMX*	Saint-Laurent	QC	H4M2V2	**800-936-9669**	514-332-3222	86
NYP Corp 805 E Grand St	Elizabeth	NJ	07201	**800-524-1052**	908-351-6550	68
NYSCA (National Youth Sports Coaches Assn) 2050 Vista Pkwy	West Palm Beach	FL	33411	**800-729-2057**	561-684-1141	48-22
NYSCO Products Inc 2350 Lafayette Ave	Bronx	NY	10473	**800-227-8685**	718-792-9000	125
Nystrom 3333 Elston Ave	Chicago	IL	60618	**800-621-8086**	773-463-1144	623-1
Nystrom Inc 9300 73rd Ave N	Brooklyn Park	MN	55428	**800-547-2635**	763-488-9200	232
NZMP Inc 635 N 12th St Suite 101	Lemoyne	PA	17043	**800-358-9096**	717-920-4000	292-4
n|Frame Inc 701 Congressional Blvd Suite 100	Carmel	IN	46032	**888-223-8633**	317-805-3759	387

O

Listing	City	State	ZIP	Toll-Free	Phone	Class
O Berk Co 3 Milltown Ct	Union	NJ	07083	**800-631-7392**	908-851-9500	378
O-Cedar Brands Inc 505 N Railroad Ave	North Lake	IL	60164	**800-332-8690**		497
O Henry Hotel 624 Green Valley Rd	Greensboro	NC	27408	**800-965-8259**	336-854-2000	373
O-AT-KA Milk Products Co-op Inc PO Box 718	Batavia	NY	14021	**800-828-8152**	585-343-0536	291-3
O The Oprah Magazine PO Box 7831	Red Oak	IA	51591	**888-446-4438**		449-11
O & S Cattle Co 100 Stockyards Rd Suite 106	South Saint Paul	MN	55075	**800-328-0124**	651-455-1102	437
O-Z/Gedney 7770 N Frontage Rd	Skokie	IL	60077	**877-999-7652**	847-679-7800	804
OAA (Opticians Assn of America) 12100 Sunset Hills Rd Suite 130	Reston	VA	20190	**800-443-8997**	703-437-4377	49-8
OAG Worldwide 3025 Highland Pkwy Suite 200	Downers Grove	IL	60515	**800-323-3537**	630-515-5300	623-10
Oahe Electric Co-op Inc 102 S Cranford St PO Box 216	Blunt	SD	57522	**800-640-6243**	605-962-6243	244
Oak Assoc Funds PO Box 219441	Kansas City	MO	64121	**888-462-5386**		517
Oak Bay Beach Hotel & Marine Resort 1175 Beach Dr	Victoria	BC	V8S2N2	**800-668-7758**	250-598-4556	655
Oak Brook Bank 1400 16th St.	Oak Brook	IL	60523	**800-536-3000**	630-571-1050	71
Oak Brook Hills Resort & Conference Center 3500 Midwest Rd	Oak Brook	IL	60523	**800-445-3315**	630-850-5555	370
Oak Hall Industries 840 Union St	Salem	VA	24153	**800-456-7623**	540-387-0000	153-14
Oak Hills Christian College 1600 Oak Hills Rd SW	Bemidji	MN	56601	**888-751-8670**	218-751-8670	163
Oak Island Resort & Spa PO Box 6	Western Shore	NS	B0J3M0	**800-565-5075**	902-627-2600	655
Oak Meadow Lodge 11503 Browning Rd	Evansville	IN	47725	**800-933-1920**	812-867-6431	373
Oak Park Area Convention and Visitors Bureau 158 N Forest Ave	Oak Park	IL	60301	**888-625-7275**	708-524-7800	205
Oak Ridge Conference Center 1 Oak Ridge Dr. *Sales	Chaska	MN	55318	**800-737-9588***	952-368-3100	370
Oak Ridge Convention & Visitors Bureau 302 S Tulane Ave	Oak Ridge	TN	37830	**800-887-3429**	865-482-7821	205
Oakdale Electric Co-op 489 N Oakwood St	Oakdale	WI	54660	**800-241-2468**	608-372-4131	244
Oakhurst Dairy 364 Forest Ave	Portland	ME	04101	**800-482-0718**	207-772-7468	291-27
Oakland City University 138 N Lucretia St	Oakland City	IN	47660	**800-737-5125**	812-749-4781	163
Oakland Convention Center 1001 Broadway	Oakland	CA	94607	**800-262-5526**	510-451-4000	204
Oakland Press Co 48 W Huron St	Pontiac	MI	48342	**800-686-2236**	248-332-8181	623-8
Oakland University Walton Blvd & Squirrel Rd	Rochester	MI	48309	**800-625-8648**	248-370-2100	163
Oaklawn Park 2705 Central Ave	Hot Springs	AR	71901	**800-625-5296**	501-623-4411	628
Oakleaf Waste Management LLC 800 Connecticut Blvd 1 Oakleaf Ctr	East Hartford	CT	06108	**888-625-5323**	860-290-1250	791
Oakley Inc 1 Icon *NYSE: OO* ■ *Cust Svc	Foothill Ranch	CA	92610	**800-403-7449***	949-951-0991	531
Oakley-Lindsay Center 300 Civic Center Plaza Suite 237	Quincy	IL	62301	**800-978-4748**	217-223-1000	204
Oakmark Family of Funds 2 N La Salle St Suite 500	Chicago	IL	60602	**800-625-6275**	312-621-0600	517
Oaks Group 11451 Katy Fwy Suite 505	Houston	TX	77079	**800-277-9373**	713-722-8080	355-3
Oaks Hotel & Convention Center 3300 W Russell St	Sioux Falls	SD	57107	**800-326-4656**	605-336-9000	373
Oaks at Ojai 122 E Ojai Ave	Ojai	CA	93023	**800-753-6257**	805-646-5573	697
Oaks Treatment Center 1407 W Stassney Ln	Austin	TX	78745	**800-843-6257**	512-464-0200	366-5
Oakton Distributors Inc 125 E Oakton St	Des Plaines	IL	60018	**800-262-5866**	847-294-5858	38
Oakwood College 7000 Adventist Blvd	Huntsville	AL	35896	**800-824-5312**	256-726-7356	163
Oakwood Friends School 22 Spackenkill Rd	Poughkeepsie	NY	12603	**800-843-3341**	845-462-4200	611
Oakwood Health Services Corp PO Box 2500	Dearborn	MI	48123	**800-543-9355**	313-593-7000	348
Oakwood Hospital & Medical Center 18101 Oakwood Blvd	Dearborn	MI	48124	**800-543-9355**	313-593-7000	366-2
Oakwood Laboratories LLC 7670 1st Pl Suite A	Oakwood	OH	44146	**888-625-9352**	440-359-0000	86
Oakwood Worldwide 2222 Corinth Ave	Los Angeles	CA	90064	**800-888-0808**	310-478-1021	209
Oakworks Inc 923 E Wellspring Rd	New Freedom	PA	17349	**800-558-8850**	717-235-6807	467
OAO Technology Solutions Inc 7500 Greenway Ctr Dr 16th Fl	Greenbelt	MD	20770	**800-720-9030**	301-486-0400	178
Oasis Corp 265 N Hamilton Rd	Columbus	OH	43213	**800-950-3226**	614-861-1350	15
Oasis Imaging Products Inc 460 Amherst St	Nashua	NH	03063	**888-627-6555**	603-880-3991	616
Oasis Industries Inc 1600 Mountain St.	Aurora	IL	60505	**800-323-2748**	630-898-3500	367
Oasis Outsourcing Inc 4400 N Congress Ave Suite 250	West Palm Beach	FL	33407	**800-627-4735**	561-627-4735	619
Oasis Resort Casino Golf & Spa 897 W Mesquite Blvd.	Mesquite	NV	89027	**800-621-0187**	702-346-5232	655
Oasis Villa Resort Hotel 4190 E Palm Canyon Dr.	Palm Springs	CA	92264	**800-247-4664**	760-328-1499	655
Oatey Co 4700 W 160th St *Cust Svc	Cleveland	OH	44135	**800-321-9532***	216-267-7100	598
Oatmeal Studios Inc 35 Town Rd *Cust Svc	Rochester	VT	05767	**800-628-6325***	802-767-3171	130
OB Macaroni Co PO Box 53 *Orders	Fort Worth	TX	76101	**800-553-4336***	817-335-4629	291-31
Obagi Medical Products Inc 310 Golden Shore	Long Beach	CA	90802	**800-636-7546**	562-628-1007	211
Oberbeck Feed Co 700 Walnut St	Highland	IL	62249	**800-632-2012**	618-654-2387	438
Oberg Industries Inc 2301 Silverville Rd	Freeport	PA	16229	**800-286-1275**	724-295-2121	745
Oberlin Farms Dairy Inc DBA Dairymen's Milk Co 3068 W 106th St	Cleveland	OH	44111	**800-944-2301**	216-671-2300	291-27
Oberlin Inn 7 N Main St.	Oberlin	OH	44074	**800-376-4173**	440-775-1111	373
Oberto Sausage Co 7060 S 238th St	Kent	WA	98032	**877-234-7902**	253-437-6100	291-26
Oberweis Securities Inc 951 Ice Cream Dr Suite 200	North Aurora	IL	60542	**800-323-6166**	630-801-6000	679
Obesity Assn. American 1250 24th St NW Suite 300	Washington	DC	20037	**800-986-2373**	202-776-7711	48-17
Obici Louise Memorial Hospital 2800 Godwin Blvd	Suffolk	VA	23434	**800-237-5788**	757-934-4000	366-2
Obie Media Corp 4211 W 11th Ave. *NASDAQ: OBIE*	Eugene	OR	97402	**800-233-6243**	541-686-8400	8
Object/FX Corp 10 2nd St NE Suite 400	Minneapolis	MN	55413	**800-762-7748**	612-312-2002	176-1
Objectivity Inc 640 W California Ave Suite 210	Sunnyvale	CA	94086	**800-767-6259**	408-992-7100	176-1
O'Brien International 14615 NE 91st St	Redmond	WA	98052	**800-662-7436**	425-202-2100	701
O'Brien RJ & Assoc 222 S Riverside Plaza Suite 900	Chicago	IL	60606	**800-621-0757**	312-373-5000	167
O'Bryan Brothers Inc 4220 W Belmont Ave	Chicago	IL	60641	**800-627-9262**	773-283-3000	153-15
Observer The 1406 5th St	La Grande	OR	97850	**800-422-3110**	541-963-3161	522-2
Observer-Dispatch 221 Oriskany Plaza	Utica	NY	13501	**800-765-5303**	315-792-5000	522-2
Observer Publishing Co 122 S Main St	Washington	PA	15301	**800-222-6397**	724-222-2200	623-8
Observer-Reporter 122 S Main St	Washington	PA	15301	**800-222-6397**	724-222-2200	522-2
Obstetric & Neonatal Nurses. Association of Women's Health 2000 L St NW Suite 740	Washington	DC	20036	**800-673-8499**	202-261-2400	49-8
OC Tanner Co 1930 S State St	Salt Lake City	UT	84115	**800-453-7490**	801-486-2430	401
OCA Inc 3850 N Causeway Blvd Suite 1040 *NYSE: OCA*	Metairie	LA	70031	**800-626-8666**		455
Ocala-Marion County Chamber of Commerce 110 E Silver Springs Blvd	Ocala	FL	34470	**888-629-8051**	352-629-8051	137
Ocala Star-Banner PO Box 490	Ocala	FL	34478	**800-541-2171**	352-867-4010	522-2
Occidental-Allegro Hotels & Resorts 6303 Blue Lagoon Dr Suite 250	Miami	FL	33126	**800-858-2258**	305-262-5909	369
Occidental Chemical Corp 5005 LBJ Fwy	Dallas	TX	75244	**800-570-8880**	972-404-3300	141
Occidental College 1600 Campus Rd	Los Angeles	CA	90041	**800-825-5262**	323-259-2700	163
Occupational Education. Council on 41 Perimeter Ctr East NE Suite 640	Atlanta	GA	30346	**800-917-2081**	770-396-3898	48-1
Occupational Health Nurses. American Assn of 2920 Brandywine Rd Suite 100	Atlanta	GA	30341	**888-646-4631**	770-455-7757	49-8
Occupational Health & Rehabilitation Inc 175 Derby St Suite 36	Hingham	MA	02043	**800-622-4584**	781-741-5175	455
Occupational Safety & Health Administration (OSHA) 200 Constitution Ave NW	Washington	DC	20210	**800-321-6742**	202-693-1999	336-11
Oce-USA Inc 5450 N Cumberland Ave 6th Fl	Chicago	IL	60656	**800-877-6232**	773-714-8500	578
Ocean Beauty Seafoods Inc 1100 W Ewing St	Seattle	WA	98119	**800-877-0185**	206-285-6800	291-14
Ocean Bio-Chem Inc 4041 SW 47th Ave *NASDAQ: OBCI*	Fort Lauderdale	FL	33314	**800-327-8583**	954-587-6280	149
Ocean Breeze International 3910 N Via Real	Carpinteria	CA	93013	**888-715-8888**	805-684-1747	363
Ocean Center 101 N Atlantic Ave	Daytona Beach	FL	32118	**800-858-6444**	386-254-4500	204
Ocean City Chamber of Commerce 12320 Ocean Gateway	Ocean City	MD	21842	**888-626-3386**	410-213-0144	137
Ocean City Convention & Visitors Bureau 4001 Coastal Hwy	Ocean City	MD	21842	**800-626-2326**	410-289-8181	205
Ocean City Hotel-Motel-Restaurant Assn PO Box 340	Ocean City	MD	21843	**800-626-2326**	410-289-6733	368
Ocean Conservancy 1725 DeSales St NW Suite 600	Washington	DC	20036	**800-519-1541**	202-429-5609	48-13

Name / Address	City	State	Zip	Toll-Free	Phone	Class
Ocean County College PO Box 2001	Toms River	NJ	08753	**877-622-3477**	732-255-0400	160
Ocean Dunes Resort & Villas 201 75th Ave N	Myrtle Beach	SC	29578	**800-845-0635**	843-449-7441	373
Ocean Edge Resort & Golf Club 2907 Main St	Brewster	MA	02631	**800-343-6074**	508-896-9000	655
Ocean Five Hotel 436 Ocean Dr	Miami Beach	FL	33139	**888-531-8122**	305-532-7093	373
Ocean Forest Villa Resort 5601 N Ocean Blvd	Myrtle Beach	SC	29577	**800-845-0347**	843-449-9661	373
Ocean Hammock Resort 300 Clubhouse Dr	Palm Coast	FL	32137	**800-654-6538**	386-445-3000	655
Ocean Kayak 2460 Salashan Loop	Ferndale	WA	98248	**800-852-9257**	360-366-4003	701
Ocean Key - A Noble House Resort Zero Duval St	Key West	FL	33040	**800-328-9815**	305-296-7701	655
Ocean Key Resort 424 Atlantic Ave	Virginia Beach	VA	23451	**800-955-9700**	757-425-2200	373
Ocean Manor Resort 4040 Galt Ocean Dr	Fort Lauderdale	FL	33308	**800-955-0444**	954-566-7500	373
Ocean One Cruise Outlet 3264 Marilynn St	Lancaster	CA	93536	**877-362-7770**	661-949-2873	760
Ocean Pacific Apparel Corp 3 Studebaker	Irvine	CA	92618	**800-562-3269**	949-580-1888	153-3
Ocean Place Resort & Spa 1 Ocean Blvd	Long Branch	NJ	07740	**800-411-6493**	732-571-4000	655
Ocean Pointe Resort Hotel & Spa. Delta Victoria 45 Songhees Rd	Victoria	BC	V9A6T3	**800-667-4677**	250-360-2999	655
Ocean Pointe Suites at Key Largo 500 Burton Dr	Tavernier	FL	33070	**800-882-9464**	305-853-3000	373
Ocean Reef Resort 7100 N Ocean Blvd	Myrtle Beach	SC	29572	**800-542-0048**	843-449-4441	373
Ocean Resort Hotel Waikiki 175 Paoakalani Ave	Honolulu	HI	96815	**800-367-2317**	808-922-3861	373
Ocean Shores Convention Center 120 Chance ala Mer	Ocean Shores	WA	98569	**800-874-6737**	360-289-4411	204
Ocean Spray Cranberries Inc 1 Ocean Spray Dr	Lakeville-Middleboro	MA	02349	**800-662-3263**	508-946-1000	291-20
Ocean Walk Shoppes at the Village 250 N Atlantic Ave	Daytona Beach	FL	32118	**877-845-9255**		50
Ocean Waters Spa 600 N Atlantic Ave	Daytona Beach	FL	32118	**800-767-4471**	386-267-1660	697
Oceana Publications Inc 75 Main St *Orders	Dobbs Ferry	NY	10522	**800-831-0758***	914-693-8100	623-2
Oceaneering International Inc 11911 FM 529 *NYSE: OII*	Houston	TX	77041	**800-527-1865**	713-329-4500	528
OceanFirst Bank 975 Hooper Ave	Toms River	NJ	08753	**888-623-2633**	732-240-4500	71
OceanFirst Financial Corp 975 Hooper Ave *NASDAQ: OCFC*	Toms River	NJ	08754	**888-623-2633**	732-240-4500	355-2
Oceania Cruises Inc 8120 NW 53rd St Suite 100	Miami	FL	33166	**800-531-5619**	305-514-2300	217
Oceanic Engineering Society. IEEE IEEE Operations Ctr 445 Hoes Ln	Piscataway	NJ	08854	**800-678-4333**	732-981-0060	49-19
Oceanic USA 2002 Davis St	San Leandro	CA	94577	**800-435-3483**	510-562-0500	701
Oceanography. American Society of Limnology & 5400 Bosque Blvd Suite 680	Waco	TX	76710	**800-929-2756**	254-399-9635	49-19
Oceans Resorts Inc 2025 S Atlantic Ave	Daytona Beach Shores	FL	32118	**800-874-7420**	386-257-1950	369
Oceanus Motel 6 2nd St	Rehoboth Beach	DE	19971	**800-852-5011**	302-227-8200	373
Ocenco Inc 10225 82nd Ave	Pleasant Prairie	WI	53158	**800-932-2293**	262-947-9000	666
Ochsner Clinic Foundation 1514 Jefferson Hwy	New Orleans	LA	70121	**800-928-6247**	504-842-3000	366-2
OCI Chemical Corp 2 Corporate Dr Suite 440	Shelton	CT	06484	**800-865-1774**	203-225-3100	493-1
OCLC (Online Computer Library Center Inc) 6565 Frantz Rd	Dublin	OH	43017	**800-848-5878**	614-764-6000	49-11
Ocmulgee Electric Membership Corp 5722 Eastman St	Eastman	GA	31023	**800-342-5509**	478-374-7001	244
Oconee Electric Membership Corp 3453 Hwy 80 W	Dudley	GA	31022	**800-522-2930**	478-676-3191	244
O'Connor Woods 3400 Wagner Heights Rd	Stockton	CA	95209	**800-249-6637**	209-956-3400	659
Oconomowoc Convention & Visitors Bureau 174 E Wisconsin Ave	Oconomowoc	WI	53066	**800-524-3744**	262-569-2185	205
Oconto Electric Co-op 7478 Rea Rd PO Box 168	Oconto Falls	WI	54154	**800-472-8410**	920-846-2816	244
Octave Chanute Aerospace Museum 1011 Pacesetter Dr	Rantoul	IL	61866	**877-726-8685**	217-893-1613	509
October Co Inc PO Box 71	Easthampton	MA	01027	**800-628-9346**	413-527-9380	281
Ocular Sciences Inc 475 Eccles Ave	South San Francisco	CA	94080	**800-628-5367**	650-583-1400	531
Ocular Surgeons. International Assn of 820 N Orleans St Suite 208	Chicago	IL	60610	**800-621-4002**	312-440-0699	49-8
Ocwen Financial Corp 1665 Palm Beach Lakes Blvd *NYSE: OCN*	West Palm Beach	FL	33401	**800-746-2936**	561-681-8000	355-2
O'Day Equipment Inc 1301 40th St NW	Fargo	ND	58102	**800-654-6329**	701-282-9260	625
Odd Fellows. Independent Order of 422 Trade St	Winston-Salem	NC	27101	**800-235-8358**	336-725-5955	48-15
Odell Brewing Co 800 E Lincoln Ave	Fort Collins	CO	80524	**888-887-2797**	970-498-9070	103
Odell Simms & Assoc 7704 Leesburg Pike	Falls Church	VA	22043	**800-662-7400**	703-903-9797	5
Odessa American PO Box 2952	Odessa	TX	79760	**888-375-6262**	432-337-4661	522-2
Odessa Chamber of Commerce 700 N Grant Suite 200	Odessa	TX	79761	**800-780-4678**	432-332-9111	137
Odessa Convention & Visitors Bureau 700 N Grant Ave Suite 200	Odessa	TX	79761	**800-780-4678**	432-333-7871	205
Odessa Trading Co 9 W 1st Ave	Odessa	WA	99159	**800-726-2661**	509-982-2661	270
Odimo Inc 14001 NW 4th St *NASDAQ: ODMO*	Sunrise	FL	33325	**888-342-6663**	954-835-2233	402
ODL Inc 215 E Roosevelt Ave	Zeeland	MI	49464	**800-288-1800**	616-772-9111	325
Odom Corp 20415 72 Ave S Suite 210	Kent	WA	98032	**800-767-6366**	253-437-3000	82-1
Odom's Tennessee Pride Sausage Inc 1201 Neelys Bend Rd	Madison	TN	37115	**800-327-6269**	615-868-1360	291-26
Odon Wagner Gallery 196 Davenport Rd	Toronto	ON	M5R1J2	**800-551-2465**	416-962-0438	42
ODS Health Plans Inc 601 SW 2nd Ave	Portland	OR	97204	**800-852-5195**	503-228-6554	384-3
Odwalla Inc 120 Stone Pine Rd	Half Moon Bay	CA	94019	**800-639-2552**	650-726-1888	291-20
Odyssey Magazine 30 Grove St Suite C	Peterborough	NH	03458	**800-821-0115**	603-924-7209	449-6
Odyssey OneSource Inc 204 N Ector Dr	Euless	TX	76039	**800-580-3090**	817-267-6090	619
Odyssey Re Holdings Corp 300 1st Stamford Pl *NYSE: ORH*	Stamford	CT	06902	**866-246-9945**	203-977-8000	384-4
Oelwein Daily Register PO Box 511	Oelwein	IA	50662	**800-211-1076**	319-283-2144	522-2
OEM Worldwide Inc 2920 Kelly Ave PO Box 430	Watertown	SD	57201	**800-258-7989**	605-886-2519	252
OETA (Oklahoma Educational TV Authority) 7403 N Kelley St	Oklahoma City	OK	73111	**800-879-6382**	405-848-8501	620
OF Mossberg & Sons Inc 7 Grasso Ave	North Haven	CT	06473	**800-989-4867**	203-230-5300	279
Off the Beaten Path 7 E Beall St	Bozeman	MT	59715	**800-445-2995**	406-586-1311	748
Office Beer Bar & Grill 1450 Rt 22 W	Mountainside	NJ	07092	**800-518-1855**	908-518-1800	657
Office Depot Inc 2200 Old Germantown Rd *NYSE: ODP*	Delray Beach	FL	33445	**800-937-3600**	561-278-4800	524
Office Furnishings Ltd 725 S 25th Ave	Bellwood	IL	60104	**800-728-8550**	708-547-8550	315
Office Laboratory Accreditation. Commission on 9881 Broken Land Pkwy Suite 200	Columbia	MD	21046	**800-981-9883**	410-381-6581	49-8
Office Products Assn. School Home & 3131 Elbee Rd	Dayton	OH	45439	**800-854-7467**	937-297-2250	49-4
Office & Professional Employees International Union 265 W 14th St Suite 610	New York	NY	10011	**800-346-7348**	212-675-3210	405
Office Properties. National Assn of Industrial & 2201 Cooperative Way 3rd Fl	Herndon	VA	20171	**800-666-6780**	703-904-7100	49-17
Office of Special Counsel 1730 M St NW Suite 300	Washington	DC	20036	**800-872-9855**	202-653-1800	336-16
Office Suppliers Inc 13716 Crayton Blvd	Hagerstown	MD	21742	**800-225-2723**	301-797-3120	524
OfficeMax Inc 150 E Pierce Rd *NYSE: OMX*	Itasca	IL	60143	**800-472-6473**	630-773-5000	523
Officers Assn. Non-Commissioned 10635 IH-35 N *Cust Svc	San Antonio	TX	78233	**800-662-2620***	210-653-6161	48-19
Offutt RD Co PO Box 7160	Fargo	ND	58106	**877-444-7363**	701-237-6062	11-11
Ofoto Inc 1480 64th St Suite 300	Emeryville	CA	94608	**800-360-9098**	510-229-1200	577
OG & E Electric Services 3220 S High	Oklahoma City	OK	73124	**800-272-9741**	405-553-3000	774
Ogden Eccles Conference Center 2415 Washington Blvd	Ogden	UT	84401	**800-337-2690**	801-395-3200	204
Ogden Regional Medical Center 5475 S 500 East	Ogden	UT	84405	**800-237-9194**	801-479-2111	366-2
Ogden/Weber Convention & Visitors Bureau 2501 Wall Ave Union Stn Suite 201	Ogden	UT	84401	**800-255-8824**	801-627-8288	205
OGE Energy Corp 321 N Harvey St *NYSE: OGE*	Oklahoma City	OK	73102	**800-272-9741**	405-553-3000	355-5
Oglebay Institute's Mansion & Glass Museums The Burton Center Oglebay Pk	Wheeling	WV	26003	**800-624-6988**	304-242-7272	509
Oglebay Norton Co 1001 Lakeside Ave 15th Fl	Cleveland	OH	44114	**800-321-4230**	216-861-3300	492
Oglebay Resort & Conference Center Rt 88 N Oglebay Pk	Wheeling	WV	26003	**800-624-6988**	304-243-4000	655
Oglethorpe University 4484 Peachtree Rd NE	Atlanta	GA	30319	**800-428-4484**	404-261-1441	163
Oglevee Ltd 152 Oglevee Ln	Connellsville	PA	15425	**800-437-4733**	724-628-8360	363
Ogontz Corp 2835 Terwood Rd	Willow Grove	PA	19090	**800-523-2478**	215-657-4770	776
OGR (International Order of the Golden Rule) 13523 Lakefront Dr	Bridgeton	MO	63045	**800-637-8030**	314-209-7142	49-4
OHANA Hotels of Hawaii 2375 Kuhio Ave	Honolulu	HI	96815	**800-462-6262**	808-921-6600	369
Ohaus Corp 19-A Chapin Rd PO Box 2033	Pine Brook	NJ	07058	**800-672-7722**	973-377-9000	672
OHIC Insurance Co 155 E Broad St 4th Fl	Columbus	OH	43215	**800-666-6442**	614-221-7777	384-5
Ohio						
Agriculture Dept 8995 E Main St	Reynoldsburg	OH	43068	**800-282-1955**	614-728-6200	335
Child Support Office 30 E Broad St 32nd Fl	Columbus	OH	43215	**800-686-1556**	614-752-6561	335
Crime Victim Services 150 E Gay St 25th Fl	Columbus	OH	43215	**800-582-2877**	614-466-5610	335
Development Dept 77 S High St	Columbus	OH	43215	**800-848-1300**	614-466-2480	335
Education Dept 25 S Front St	Columbus	OH	43215	**877-644-6338**	614-466-3641	335
Insurance Dept 2100 Stella Ct	Columbus	OH	43215	**800-686-1526**	614-644-2658	335
Parks & Recreation Div 2045 Morse Rd Bldg C-3	Columbus	OH	43229	**800-282-7275**	614-265-6561	335
Rehabilitation Services Commission 400 E Campus View Blvd	Columbus	OH	43235	**800-282-4536**	614-438-1200	335
State Grants & Scholarships Office PO Box 182452	Columbus	OH	43218	**888-833-1133**	614-466-7420	711
Travel & Tourism Div PO Box 1001	Columbus	OH	43216	**800-282-5393**	614-466-8844	335
Tuition Trust Authority 580 S High St Suite 208 *Cust Svc	Columbus	OH	43215	**800-233-6734***	614-752-9400	711
Wildlife Div 2045 Morse Rd Bldg G	Columbus	OH	43229	**800-945-3543**	614-265-6300	335
Workers' Compensation Bureau 30 W Spring St	Columbus	OH	43215	**800-644-6292**	614-644-6292	335
Ohio Art Co 1 Toy St	Bryan	OH	43506	**800-641-6226**	419-636-3141	750
Ohio Associated Enterprises LLC 1359 W Jackson St	Painesville	OH	44077	**800-863-9014**	440-354-3148	803
Ohio Bar Title Insurance Co 8425 Pulsar Pl Suite 210	Columbus	OH	43240	**800-628-4853**	614-825-4029	384-6

Name / Address	City	State	ZIP	Toll-Free	Phone	Class
Ohio Brush Co 2680 Lisbon Rd	Cleveland	OH	44104	**888-411-3265**	216-791-3265	104
Ohio Cast Products Inc 2408 13th St NE	Canton	OH	44705	**800-909-2278**	330-456-4784	302
Ohio Casualty Corp 9450 Seward Rd *NASDAQ: OCAS*	Fairfield	OH	45014	**800-843-6446**	513-603-2400	355-4
Ohio Casualty Insurance Co 9450 Seward Rd	Fairfield	OH	45014	**800-843-6446**	513-603-2400	384-4
Ohio Chamber of Commerce 230 E Town St	Columbus	OH	43215	**800-622-1893**	614-228-4201	138
Ohio Desk Co 1122 Prospect Ave E	Cleveland	OH	44115	**800-326-0601**	216-623-0600	315
Ohio Dominican University 1216 Sunbury Rd	Columbus	OH	43219	**800-955-6446**	614-253-2741	163
Ohio Drilling Co 2405 Bostic Blvd SW	Massillon	OH	44647	**800-860-2285**	330-832-1521	188-16
Ohio Edison Co 76 S Main St PO Box 3637 *Cust Svc	Akron	OH	44309	**800-633-4766***	800-646-0400	774
Ohio Farmers Insurance Co 1 Park Cir	Westfield Center	OH	44251	**800-243-0210**	330-887-0101	384-4
Ohio Gasket & Shim Co Inc 976 Evans Ave	Akron	OH	44305	**800-321-2438**	330-630-2030	321
Ohio Historical Center 1982 Velma Ave	Columbus	OH	43211	**800-686-6124**	614-297-2300	509
Ohio Institute of Photography & Technology 2029 Edgefield Rd	Dayton	OH	45439	**800-932-9698**	937-294-6155	787
Ohio Lawyer Magazine PO Box 16562	Columbus	OH	43216	**800-282-6556**	614-487-2050	449-15
Ohio Legacy Corp 305 W Liberty St *NASDAQ: OLCB*	Wooster	OH	44691	**866-674-5301**	330-263-1955	71
Ohio Library Council (OLC) 2 Easton Oval Suite 525	Columbus	OH	43215	**800-436-5423**	614-416-2258	427
Ohio Life Insurance Co PO Box 410288	Kansas City	MO	64141	**800-456-6446**	816-391-2000	384-2
Ohio Machinery Co 3993 E Royalton Rd	Broadview Heights	OH	44147	**800-837-6200**	440-526-6200	353
Ohio Magazine 1422 Euclid Ave Suite 730	Cleveland	OH	44115	**800-210-7293**	216-771-2833	449-22
Ohio Magnetics Inc 5400 Dunham Rd	Maple Heights	OH	44137	**800-486-6446**	216-662-8484	462
Ohio Medicine Magazine 3401 Mill Run Dr	Hilliard	OH	43026	**800-766-6762**	614-527-6762	449-16
Ohio Motorists Assn 5700 Brecksville Rd	Independence	OH	44131	**800-711-5370**	216-606-6100	53
Ohio National Financial Services Inc 1 Financial Way Suite 100	Cincinnati	OH	45242	**800-366-6654**	513-794-6100	355-4
Ohio National Life Insurance Co 1 Financial Way Suite 100	Cincinnati	OH	45242	**800-366-6654**	513-794-6100	384-2
Ohio Northern University 525 S Main St	Ada	OH	45810	**888-408-4668**	419-772-2000	163
Ohio Nut & Bolt Co 33 Lou Groza Blvd	Berea	OH	44017	**800-362-0291**	440-243-0200	274
Ohio Packing Co PO Box 30961	Columbus	OH	43230	**800-282-6403**	614-239-1600	465
Ohio Penal Industries 1221 McKinley Ave	Columbus	OH	43222	**800-237-3454**	614-752-0287	618
Ohio Savings Bank FSB 1801 E 9th St	Cleveland	OH	44114	**800-860-2025**	216-622-4100	71
Ohio Savings Financial Corp 1801 E 9th St Suite 200	Cleveland	OH	44114	**800-696-2222**	216-622-4100	355-2
Ohio Sealants Inc 7405 Production Dr	Mentor	OH	44060	**800-321-3578**	440-255-8900	3
Ohio Security Insurance Co 9450 Seward Rd	Fairfield	OH	45014	**800-843-6446**	513-867-3000	384-4
Ohio State Bar Assn 1700 Lake Shore Dr	Columbus	OH	43204	**800-282-6556**	614-487-2050	73
Ohio State Medical Assn 3401 Mill Run Dr	Hilliard	OH	43026	**800-766-6762**	614-527-6762	466
Ohio Transmission & Pump Co 1900 Jetway Blvd	Columbus	OH	43219	**800-837-6827**	614-342-6123	378
Ohio University						
Chillicothe Campus 101 University Dr	Chillicothe	OH	45601	**877-462-6824**	740-774-7200	163
Eastern Campus 45425 National Rd	Saint Clairsville	OH	43950	**800-648-3331**	740-695-1720	163
Southern Campus 1804 Liberty Ave	Ironton	OH	45638	**800-626-0513**	740-533-4600	163
Ohio University Press Scott Quadrangle *Sales	Athens	OH	45701	**800-621-2736***	740-593-1155	623-5
Ohio Valley AFM Inc 3955 Alexandria Pike	Cold Spring	KY	41076	**800-359-3971**	859-781-3800	203
Ohio Valley Banc Corp 420 3rd Ave *NASDAQ: OVBC*	Gallipolis	OH	45631	**800-468-6682**	740-446-2631	355-2
Ohio Valley College 1 Campus View Dr	Vienna	WV	26105	**877-446-8668**	304-865-6000	163
Ohio Veterans Home 3416 Columbus Ave *Admissions	Sandusky	OH	44870	**800-572-7934***	419-625-2454	780
Ohio Veterinary Medical Assn 3168 Riverside Dr	Columbus	OH	43221	**800-662-6862**	614-486-7253	782
Ohio Wesleyan University 61 S Sandusky St University Hall	Delaware	OH	43015	**800-862-0612**	740-369-4431	163
Ohline Corp 1930 W 139th St	Gardena	CA	90249	**800-585-3197**	310-327-4630	489
Ohmart/VEGA Corp 4241 Allendorf Dr	Cincinnati	OH	45209	**800-543-8668**	513-272-0131	464
Ohmite Mfg Co 1600 Golf Rd Suite 850	Rolling Meadows	IL	60008	**866-964-6483**	847-258-0300	252
Ohmstede Ltd 895 N Main St	Beaumont	TX	77701	**800-568-2328**	409-833-6375	92
OI Analytical 151 Graham Rd *NASDAQ: OICO*	College Station	TX	77845	**800-653-1711**	979-690-1711	410
OI Corp DBA OI Analytical 151 Graham Rd *NASDAQ: OICO*	College Station	TX	77845	**800-653-1711**	979-690-1711	410
OIC International 240 W Tulpehocken St	Philadelphia	PA	19144	**800-653-6424**	215-842-0860	48-5
Oil Center Research Inc 106 Montrose Ave	Lafayette	LA	70503	**800-256-8977**	337-232-2496	530
Oil Change Assn. Automotive 12810 Hillcrest Rd Suite 221	Dallas	TX	75230	**800-331-0329**	972-458-9468	49-21
Oil Chemists Society. American 2211 W Bradley Ave	Champaign	IL	61821	**800-336-2627**	217-359-2344	48-12
Oil Creek District Library Center 2 Central Ave	Oil City	PA	16301	**888-645-2489**	814-678-3054	426
Oil Creek Plastics Inc PO Box 385	Titusville	PA	16354	**800-537-3661**	814-827-3661	585
Oil Express Newsletter 11300 Rockville Pike Suite 1100	Rockville	MD	20852	**800-929-4824**	301-816-8950	521-5
Oil & Gas Compact Commission. Interstate 900 NE 23rd St PO Box 53127	Oklahoma City	OK	73152	**800-822-4015**	405-525-3556	48-12
Oil & Gas Journal PO Box 1260	Tulsa	OK	74101	**800-331-4463**	918-835-3161	449-21
Oil Price Information Service Newsletter 3349 Hwy 138 Bldg D Suite D *Cust Svc	Wall	NJ	07719	**888-301-2645***	732-901-8800	521-5
Oil Process Systems Inc Miroil Div 602 N Tacoma St	Allentown	PA	18109	**800-523-9844**	610-437-4618	293
Oiles America Corp 44099 Plymouth Oaks Blvd Suite 109	Plymouth	MI	48170	**888-645-3726**	734-414-7400	77
Oilgear Co PO Box 343924 *NASDAQ: OLGR* ■ *Sales	Milwaukee	WI	53234	**800-276-5356***	414-327-1700	626
Ojai Valley Inn & Spa 905 Country Club Rd	Ojai	CA	93023	**800-422-6524**	805-646-5511	655
Ojai Valley School 723 El Paseo Rd	Ojai	CA	93023	**800-433-4687**	805-646-1423	611
Ojo Caliente Mineral Springs Resort 50 Los Banos Dr PO Box 68	Ojo Caliente	NM	87549	**800-222-9162**	505-583-2233	697
OK Corral 308 E Allen St	Tombstone	AZ	85638	**800-518-1566**	520-457-3456	50
OK Foods Inc PO Box 1119	Fort Smith	AR	72902	**800-635-9441**	479-783-0244	608
Okay Food Co Inc 500 Abney Ave	Lufkin	TX	75902	**800-256-6455**	936-634-4648	203
O'Keeffe's Inc 325 Newhall St	San Francisco	CA	94124	**888-653-3333**	415-822-4222	232
Okefenoke Rural Electric Membership Corp 174 E Cleveland St	Nahunta	GA	31553	**800-262-5131**	912-462-5131	244
Oki America Inc 785 N Mary Ave	Sunnyvale	CA	94085	**800-654-3282**	408-720-1900	171-6
Oki Data Americas Inc 2000 Bishops Gate Blvd *Cust Svc	Mount Laurel	NJ	08054	**800-654-3282***	856-235-2600	171-6
Oki Network Technologies 785 N Mary Ave	Sunnyvale	CA	94085	**800-641-8909**	408-737-6477	720
Oklahoma						
Commerce Dept 900 N Stiles Ave	Oklahoma City	OK	73104	**800-879-6552**	405-815-6552	335
Environmental Quality Dept 707 N Robinson Ave PO Box 1677	Oklahoma City	OK	73101	**800-869-1400**	405-702-1000	335
Housing Finance Agency 1140 NW 63rd St Suite 200	Oklahoma City	OK	73116	**800-256-1489**	405-848-1144	335
Parks Div PO Box 52002	Oklahoma City	OK	73152	**800-654-8240**	405-521-3411	335
Rehabilitative Services Dept 3535 NW 58th St Suite 500	Oklahoma City	OK	73112	**800-845-8476**	405-951-3400	335
Tourism & Recreation Dept 15 N Robinson St Suite 100	Oklahoma City	OK	73105	**800-652-6552**	405-521-2406	335
Workers' Compensation Div 4001 N Lincoln Blvd	Oklahoma City	OK	73105	**888-269-5353**	405-528-1500	335
Oklahoma Assn of Realtors 9807 N Broadway	Oklahoma City	OK	73114	**800-375-9944**	405-848-9944	642
Oklahoma Bar Assn PO Box 53036	Oklahoma City	OK	73152	**800-522-8065**	405-416-7000	73
Oklahoma Christian University PO Box 11000	Oklahoma City	OK	73136	**800-877-5010**	405-425-5000	163
Oklahoma City Convention & Visitors Bureau 189 W Sheridan St	Oklahoma City	OK	73102	**800-225-5652**	405-297-8912	205
Oklahoma City Museum of Art 415 Couch Dr	Oklahoma City	OK	73102	**800-579-9278**	405-236-3100	509
Oklahoma City National Memorial PO Box 323	Oklahoma City	OK	73101	**888-542-4673**	405-235-3313	554
Oklahoma City University 2501 N Blackwelder Ave	Oklahoma City	OK	73106	**800-633-7242**	405-521-5000	163
Oklahoma Correctional Industries 3402 ML King Blvd	Oklahoma City	OK	73111	**800-522-3565**	405-425-7500	618
Oklahoma Dental Assn 629 NW Grand Blvd	Oklahoma City	OK	73118	**800-876-8890**	405-848-8873	225
Oklahoma Dept of Libraries 200 NE 18th St	Oklahoma City	OK	73105	**800-522-8116**	405-521-2502	426
Oklahoma Educational TV Authority (OETA) 7403 N Kelley St	Oklahoma City	OK	73111	**800-879-6382**	405-848-8501	620
Oklahoma Fixture Co DBA Penloyd/OFC 2900 E Apache St	Tulsa	OK	74110	**800-233-3794**	918-836-3794	281
Oklahoma Heritage Center 201 NW 14th St	Oklahoma City	OK	73103	**888-501-2059**	405-235-4458	50
Oklahoma Jazz Hall of Fame 322 N Greenwood Ave	Tulsa	OK	74120	**800-348-9336**	918-596-1001	509
Oklahoma Medical Research Foundation (OMRF) 825 NE 13th St	Oklahoma City	OK	73104	**800-522-0211**	405-271-6673	654
Oklahoma Natural Gas Co 401 N Harvey	Oklahoma City	OK	73101	**800-664-5463**	405-551-6500	774
Oklahoma Panhandle State University 323 Eagle Blvd	Goodwell	OK	73939	**800-664-6778**	580-349-2611	163
Oklahoma Publishing Co 9000 N Broadway Ext	Oklahoma City	OK	73114	**800-375-3450**	405-475-3311	623-8
Oklahoma State Chamber 330 NE 10th St	Oklahoma City	OK	73104	**800-364-6465**	405-235-3669	138
Oklahoma State Medical Assn 601 NW Grand Blvd	Oklahoma City	OK	73118	**800-522-9452**	405-843-9571	466
Oklahoma State University						
Oklahoma City 900 N Portland Ave	Oklahoma City	OK	73107	**800-560-4099**	405-947-4421	160
Tulsa 700 N Greenwood Ave	Tulsa	OK	74106	**800-364-0710**	918-594-8000	163
Oklahoma State University Okmulgee 1801 E 4th St	Okmulgee	OK	74447	**800-722-4471**	918-293-4678	787
Oklahoma Surety Co 1437 S Boulder Ave Suite 200	Tulsa	OK	74119	**800-722-4994**	918-587-7221	384-4
Oklahoma Waste & Wiping Rag Co Inc 2013 SE 18th St *Cust Svc	Oklahoma City	OK	73129	**800-232-4433***	405-670-3100	730-8
Oklahoman The 9000 N Broadway	Oklahoma City	OK	73114	**800-375-6397**	405-475-3311	522-2
O'Krent Floor Covering Co 2075 N Loop 1604 E	San Antonio	TX	78232	**800-369-7387**	210-227-7387	285
OKS-Ameridial Inc 4535 Strausser St NW	North Canton	OH	44720	**800-445-7128**	330-497-4888	722

Listing	City	State	ZIP	Toll-Free	Phone	Class
OLA (Ontario Library Assn) 100 Lombard St Suite 303	Toronto	ON	M5CIM3	**866-873-9867**	416-363-3388	427
OLA (Optical Laboratories Assn) 11096-A Lee Hwy Suite 101	Fairfax	VA	22030	**800-477-5652**	703-359-2830	49-8
Olan Mills Inc Box 23456	Chattanooga	TN	37422	**800-251-6320**	423-622-5141	579
Olathe Chamber of Commerce 142 N Cherry St	Olathe	KS	66061	**800-921-5678**	913-764-1050	137
OLC (Ohio Library Council) 2 Easton Oval Suite 525	Columbus	OH	43215	**800-436-5423**	614-416-2258	427
Old Alabama Town 301 Columbus St	Montgomery	AL	36104	**888-240-1850**	334-240-4500	50
Old American Insurance Co 3520 Broadway	Kansas City	MO	64111	**800-733-6242**	816-753-4900	384-2
Old Barracks Museum Barrack St	Trenton	NJ	08608	**888-227-7225**	609-396-1776	509
Old Chicago Restaurants 248 Centennial Pkwy	Louisville	CO	80027	**800-273-9827**	303-664-4000	657
Old Colony Envelope Co 70 Tpke Industrial Rd *Cust Svc	Westfield	MA	01085	**800-343-1273***	413-568-2431	260
Old Colony Hospice 14 Page Terr	Stoughton	MA	02072	**800-370-1322**	781-341-4145	365
Old Crows. Association of 1000 N Payne St Suite 300	Alexandria	VA	22314	**888-653-2769**	703-549-1600	48-19
Old Dominion Freight Line Inc 500 Old Dominion Way *NASDAQ: ODFL*	Thomasville	NC	27360	**800-432-6335**	336-889-5000	769
Old Dominion Insurance Co 4601 Touchton Rd E Suite 330 PO Box 16100	Jacksonville	FL	32245	**800-226-0875**	904-642-3000	384-4
Old Dominion Peanut Corp 208 W 24th St	Norfolk	VA	23517	**800-368-6887**	757-622-1633	291-28
Old Dominion University	Norfolk	VA	23529	**800-348-7926**	757-683-3000	163
Old Dutch Foods Inc 2375 Terminal Rd	Roseville	MN	55113	**800-989-2447**	651-633-8810	292-3
Old Florida Museum 254-D San Marco Ave	Saint Augustine	FL	32084	**800-813-3208**	904-824-8874	509
Old German Free School Building 507 E 10th St	Austin	TX	78701	**866-482-4847**	512-482-0927	50
Old Jail Museum 167 San Marco Ave	Saint Augustine	FL	32084	**800-397-4071**	904-829-3800	509
Old London Foods 1776 Eastchester Rd	Bronx	NY	10461	**888-266-4445**	718-409-1776	291-1
Old Mansion Foods Inc 1558 W Washington St PO Box 2026	Petersburg	VA	23803	**800-476-1877**	804-862-9889	291-7
Old National Bancorp 1 Main St *NYSE: ONB*	Evansville	IN	47708	**800-731-2265**	812-464-1494	355-2
Old National Bank 420 Main St	Evansville	IN	47708	**800-731-2265**	812-464-1200	71
Old Navy Clothing Co 1 Harrison St *Cust Svc	San Francisco	CA	94105	**800-653-6289***	650-952-4400	155-2
Old Neighborhood Foods 37 Waterhill St	Lynn	MA	01905	**800-628-3529**	781-595-1557	465
Old Newbury Crafters Inc 36 Main St	Amesbury	MA	01913	**800-343-1388**	978-388-0983	693
Old Republic International Corp 307 N Michigan Ave *NYSE: ORI*	Chicago	IL	60601	**800-621-0365**	312-346-8100	355-4
Old Republic Minnehoma Insurance Co 8282 S Memorial Dr	Tulsa	OK	74133	**800-331-4065**	918-307-1000	384-5
Old Republic National Title Insurance Co 400 2nd Ave S	Minneapolis	MN	55401	**800-328-4441**	612-371-1111	384-6
Old Republic Surety 445 S Moorlands Rd Suite 301	Brookfield	WI	53005	**800-217-1792**	262-797-2640	384-5
Old Second Bancorp Inc 37 S River St *NASDAQ: OSBC*	Aurora	IL	60506	**888-892-6565**	630-892-0202	355-2
Old State Capitol Museum 100 W Broadway	Frankfort	KY	40601	**877-444-7867**	502-564-3016	509
Old Town Canoe Co PO Box 548	Old Town	ME	04468	**800-343-1555**	207-827-5514	701
Old Virginia Brick Co 2500 W Main St	Salem	VA	24153	**800-879-8227**	540-389-2357	148
Old West Tours 3432 Limestone Dr	Rosamond	CA	93560	**800-868-7777**	661-256-4091	748
Old Wisconsin Sausage Co 2107 S 17th St	Sheboygan	WI	53081	**800-558-7840**	920-458-4304	291-26
Oldcastle Glass Group 2425 Olympic Blvd Suite 525E	Santa Monica	CA	90404	**866-653-2278**	310-264-4700	190-2
Oldcastle Inc 375 N Ridge Rd Suite 350	Atlanta	GA	30350	**800-899-8455**	770-804-3363	181
Oldcastle Precast Building Systems Div 1014 Cromwell Bridge Rd	Towson	MD	21286	**800-523-9144**	410-296-1200	188-3
Olde Country Reproductions Inc 722 W Market St *Cust Svc	York	PA	17405	**800-358-3997***	717-848-1859	693
Older Americans Report 8737 Colesville Rd Suite 1100	Silver Spring	MD	20910	**800-274-6737**	301-587-6300	521-6
Older Women's League (OWL) 1750 New York Ave NW Suite 350	Washington	DC	20006	**800-825-3695**	202-783-6686	48-6
Oldest Wooden School House 14 Saint George St	Saint Augustine	FL	32084	**888-653-7245**	904-824-0192	50
Oldham County Chamber of Commerce 412 E Main ST	LaGrange	KY	40031	**800-813-9953**	502-222-1635	137
Olds Products Co 10700 88th Ave	Pleasant Prairie	WI	53158	**800-233-8064**	262-947-3500	291-19
Olds Seed Solutions 2901 Tackers Ave	Madison	WI	53707	**800-356-7333**	608-249-9291	684
Olean Times-Herald 639 Norton Dr	Olean	NY	14760	**800-722-8812**	716-372-3121	522-2
O'Leary Paint 300 E Oakland	Lansing	MI	48906	**800-477-2066**	517-487-2066	540
Oles Envelope Corp 532 E 25th St	Baltimore	MD	21218	**800-822-6537**	410-243-1520	260
Oleta River State Park 3400 NE 163rd St	North Miami Beach	FL	33160	**800-326-3521**	305-919-1846	554
Oley Foundation Albany Medical Ctr 214 Hun Memorial MC A-28	Albany	NY	12208	**800-776-6539**	518-262-5079	48-17
Olga's Kitchen Inc 1940 Northwood Dr	Troy	MI	48084	**800-336-5427**	248-362-0001	657
Olin Center 342 Newbury St	Boston	MA	02115	**800-778-7669**	617-247-3033	414
Olin Corp Winchester Div 427 N Shamrock St	East Alton	IL	62024	**800-356-2666**	618-258-2000	279
Olin Skis 19215 Vashon Hwy SW	Vashon	WA	98070	**800-522-7547**	206-463-3631	701
Olinger Distributing Co 5337 W 78th St	Indianapolis	IN	46268	**800-366-1090**	317-876-1188	82-3
Olis Inc 130 Conway Dr Suite A	Bogart	GA	30622	**800-852-3504**	706-353-6547	410
Olive View Medical Center 14445 Olive View Dr	Sylmar	CA	91342	**800-970-5478**	818-364-1555	366-2
Oliver Instrument Co 831 Division St PO Box 189	Adrian	MI	49221	**877-668-0885**	517-263-2132	447
Oliver Machinery Co 1210 Andover Park E	Tukwila	WA	98188	**800-559-5065**	206-575-2722	809
Oliver-Mercer Electric Co-op Inc 800 Highway Dr	Hazen	ND	58545	**800-748-5533**	701-748-2293	244
Oliver Oil Co Inc PO Box 248	Chambersburg	PA	17201	**800-634-8729**	717-264-5165	311
Oliver Products Co 445 6th St NW	Grand Rapids	MI	49504	**800-253-3893**	616-456-7711	293
Oliver Trucking Co Inc PO Box 53	Winchester	KY	40392	**800-354-7421**	859-744-6373	769
Oliver Winery 8024 N SR-37	Bloomington	IN	47404	**800-258-2783**	812-876-5800	50
Olivet College 320 S Main St	Olivet	MI	49076	**800-456-7189**	269-749-7000	163
Olivet Nazarene University 1 University Ave	Bourbonnais	IL	60914	**800-648-1463**	815-939-5011	163
Olivetti Office USA Inc 379 Campus Dr 2nd Fl	Somerset	NJ	08875	**888-261-4555**	732-627-9977	112
Olivia Cruises & Resorts 434 Brannan St	San Francisco	CA	94107	**800-631-6277**	415-962-5700	748
OLM LLC 4 Trefoil Dr	Trumbull	CT	06611	**877-265-6638**	203-445-7700	795
Olmsted Parks. National Assn for 733 15th St NW Suite 700	Washington	DC	20005	**866-666-6905**	202-783-6606	48-13
Olney Central College 305 N West St	Olney	IL	62450	**866-622-4322**	618-395-4351	160
Olney Daily Mail PO Box 340	Olney	IL	62450	**800-804-9383**	618-393-2931	522-2
Olney Friends School 61830 Sandy Ridge Rd	Barnesville	OH	43713	**800-303-4291**	740-425-3655	611
Olon Industries Inc 42 Armstrong Ave	Georgetown	ON	L7G4R9	**800-387-2319**	905-877-7300	588
Olsen Implement Inc 2025 US Hwy 14 W	Huron	SD	57350	**800-627-5469**	605-352-7100	270
Olsen Thielen & Co Ltd 223 Little Canada Rd	Saint Paul	MN	55117	**800-866-4521**	651-483-4521	2
Olsonite Corp 25 Dart Rd	Newnan	GA	30265	**800-521-8266**	770-253-3930	599
Olsson Roofing Co Inc 740 S Lake St	Aurora	IL	60506	**800-445-9655**	630-892-0449	188-12
Olsson's Books & Records 106 S Union St	Alexandria	VA	22314	**800-989-8084**	703-684-0032	96
Olsun Electrics Corp 10901 Commercial St	Richmond	IL	60071	**800-336-5786**	815-678-2421	756
Olum's of Binghamton Inc 3701 Vestal Pkwy E *Cust Svc	Vestal	NY	13850	**800-247-0533***	607-729-5775	316
Olympia Group Inc 505 S 7th Ave	City of Industry	CA	91746	**800-888-8782**	626-336-4999	746
Olympia Resort & Spa 1350 Royale Mile Rd	Oconomowoc	WI	53066	**800-558-9573**	262-567-0311	655
Olympian Oil Co 999 Bayhill Dr Suite 135	San Bruno	CA	94066	**800-899-4659**	650-873-8200	319
Olympia/Thurston County Visitor & Convention Bureau PO Box 7338	Olympia	WA	98507	**877-704-7500**	360-704-7544	205
Olympic Airways 7000 Austin St	Forest Hills	NY	11375	**800-736-5717**	718-269-2200	26
Olympic Center Arena 2634 Main St	Lake Placid	NY	12946	**800-462-6236**	518-523-1655	706
Olympic College 1600 Chester Ave	Bremerton	WA	98337	**800-259-6718**	360-792-6050	160
Shelton 937 W Alpine Way	Shelton	WA	98584	**800-259-6718**	360-427-2119	160
Olympic Corporate Suites 400 Village Gardens SW	Calgary	AB	T3H2L1	**800-791-8788**	403-246-1040	372
Olympic Hall of Fame. US 1750 E Boulder St	Colorado Springs	CO	80909	**888-659-8687**	719-866-4500	511
Olympic Limousine Service Inc 5005 Rts 33 & 34	Farmingdale	NJ	07727	**800-822-9797**	732-938-6666	433
Olympic Pipeline Co 2319 Lind Ave SW	Renton	WA	98055	**877-659-7473**	425-235-7736	586
Olympic Stadium 4549 Pierre-de-Coubertin Ave	Montreal	QC	H1V3N7	**800-463-9767**	514-252-4679	706
Olympic Steel Inc 5080 Richmond Rd *NASDAQ: ZEUS*	Bedford Heights	OH	44146	**800-321-6290**	216-292-3800	483
Olympic Structures Inc 1850 93rd Ave SW	Olympia	WA	98512	**800-562-6066**	360-943-5433	805
Olympics Inc. Special 1133 19th St NW 11th Fl	Washington	DC	20036	**800-700-8585**	202-628-3630	48-22
Olympus America Inc 2 Corporate Ctr Dr	Melville	NY	11747	**800-446-5967**	631-844-5000	580
Olympus Flag & Banner 9000 W Heather Ave	Milwaukee	WI	53224	**800-558-9620**	414-355-2010	282
OM Group Inc 811 Sharon Dr *NYSE: OMG*	Westlake	OH	44145	**800-321-9696**	440-899-2950	143
Omaha Community Playhouse 6915 Cass St	Omaha	NE	68132	**888-782-4338**	402-553-0800	563-4
Omaha (Greater) Convention & Visitors Bureau 1001 Farnam St Suite 200	Omaha	NE	68102	**800-332-1819**	402-444-4660	205
Omaha Property & Casualty Insurance Co 3102 Farnam St	Omaha	NE	68131	**800-788-9488**	402-342-3326	384-4
Omaha Steaks International Inc 10909 John Galt Blvd	Omaha	NE	68137	**800-960-8400**	402-597-8370	333
Omaha World-Herald 1334 Dodge St	Omaha	NE	68102	**800-284-6397**	402-444-1000	522-2
OMCO Inc 214 E Mill St	Odon	IN	47562	**800-274-0203**	812-636-7362	438
Omega Communications Inc 29 E Maryland SE	Indianapolis	IN	46204	**800-622-6728**	317-264-4010	117
Omega Engineering Inc 1 Omega Dr PO Box 4047	Stamford	CT	06907	**800-826-6342**	203-359-1660	200
Omega Financial Corp 366 Walker Dr *NASDAQ: OMEF*	State College	PA	16801	**800-494-1810**	814-231-7680	355-2
Omega Institute for Holistic Studies 150 Lake Dr	Rhinebeck	NY	12572	**800-944-1001**	845-266-4444	660
Omega Optical Co Inc 13515 N Stemmons Fwy	Dallas	TX	75234	**800-366-6342**	972-241-4141	531
Omega Shielding Products 1384 Pompton Ave	Cedar Grove	NJ	07009	**800-828-5784**	973-890-7455	321
Omega World Travel Inc 3102 Omega Office Pk Dr Suite 100	Fairfax	VA	22031	**800-756-6342**	703-359-8888	760
OMI Corp 1 Station Pl Metro Ctr *NYSE: OMM*	Stamford	CT	06902	**800-344-9711**	203-602-6700	308
Omicron Delta Epsilon PO Box 1486	Hattiesburg	MS	39403	**800-584-5514**	601-264-3115	48-16
Omnetics Connector Corp 7260 Commerce Cir E *Cust Svc	Minneapolis	MN	55432	**800-343-0025***	763-572-0656	803

Name / Address	City	State	ZIP	Toll-Free	Phone	Class
Omni American Federal Credit Union PO Box 150098	Fort Worth	TX	76108	**800-695-2328**	817-246-0111	216
Omni Cable Corp 905 Airport Rd Suite C	West Chester	PA	19380	**800-292-6664**	610-701-0100	245
OMNI Fitness Equipment Inc 2344 Summer St	Stamford	CT	06902	**877-875-6664**	203-978-5200	702
Omni Hotels 420 Decker Dr Suite 200	Irving	TX	75062	**800-843-6664**	972-730-6664	369
Omni Hotels Select Guest Program 11819 Miami St 3rd Fl *Cust Svc	Omaha	NE	68164	**877-440-6664***	800-367-6664	371
Omni Interlocken Resort 500 Interlocken Blvd	Broomfield	CO	80021	**800-843-6664**	303-438-6600	655
Omni International Inc 435 12th St SW PO Box 1409	Vernon	AL	35592	**800-844-6664**	205-695-9173	314-1
Omni Limousine Inc 4440 E Cheyenne Ave Suite A	Las Vegas	NV	89115	**800-325-8003**	702-367-1000	433
Omni Orlando Resort at Championsgate 1500 Masters Blvd	Orlando	FL	33896	**800-843-6664**	407-390-6664	655
Omnicare Clinical Research 630 Alledale Rd	King of Prussia	PA	19406	**800-290-5766**	484-679-2400	654
OmniCare Health Plan 1155 Brewery Pk Blvd Suite 250 *Cust Svc	Detroit	MI	48207	**800-477-6664***	313-393-0200	384-3
Omnicare Inc 100 E RiverCenter Blvd Suite 1600 *NYSE: OCR*	Covington	KY	41011	**800-342-5627**	859-392-3300	576
Omnicell Inc 1201 Charleston Rd *NASDAQ: OMCL*	Mountain View	CA	94043	**800-850-6664**	650-843-6100	411
Omnicom Group Inc 437 Madison Ave *NYSE: OMC*	New York	NY	10022	**800-332-3336**	212-415-3600	355-3
Omniflight Helicopters Inc 4650 Airport Pkwy	Addison	TX	75001	**800-727-4644**	972-776-0130	31
Omniglow Corp 96 Windsor St *Cust Svc	West Springfield	MA	01089	**800-762-7548***	413-739-8252	431
Omnigraphics Inc 615 Griswold St Ford Bldg Suite 1400 *Orders	Detroit	MI	48226	**800-234-1340***	313-961-1340	623-2
Omniplex 2100 NE 52nd St	Oklahoma City	OK	73111	**800-532-7652**	405-602-6664	509
OMNIPLEX World Services Corp 14840 Conference Ctr Dr	Chantilly	VA	20151	**800-356-3406**	703-652-3100	267
Omniprint 9700 Philadelphia Ct	Lanham	MD	20706	**800-774-6809**	301-731-5200	623-9
OmniSource Corp 1610 N Calhoun St	Fort Wayne	IN	46808	**800-666-4789**	260-422-5541	674
Omnitronics LLC 341 Harbor St PO Box 120	Conneaut	OH	44030	**888-872-3104**	440-593-1111	52
OMNOVA Solutions Inc Performance Chemicals Div 165 S Cleveland Ave *Cust Svc	Mogadore	OH	44260	**888-353-4173***	330-628-9925	143
OMRF (Oklahoma Medical Research Foundation) 825 NE 13th St	Oklahoma City	OK	73104	**800-522-0211**	405-271-6673	654
Omron Electronics Inc 1 Commerce Dr	Schaumburg	IL	60173	**800-556-6766**	847-843-7900	202
Omron Healthcare Inc 300 Lakeview Pkwy	Vernon Hills	IL	60061	**800-323-1482**	847-680-6200	467
Omron Systems Inc 55 E Commerce Dr *Tech Supp	Schaumburg	IL	60173	**800-706-6766***	847-884-0322	603
Omsco ShawCor 6418 Esperson St	Houston	TX	77011	**800-426-6726**	713-844-3700	526
OmTool Ltd 8A Industrial Way *NASDAQ: OMTL*	Salem	NH	03079	**800-886-7845**	603-898-8900	176-7
OMYA Inc 100 North Point Ctr E Suite 310	Alpharetta	GA	30022	**800-749-6692**	770-751-7030	141
On Assignment Inc 26651 W Agoura Rd *NASDAQ: ASGN*	Calabasas	CA	91302	**800-995-7378**	818-878-7900	707
On the Border Mexican Cafe 6820 LBJ Fwy	Dallas	TX	75240	**800-983-4637**	972-980-9917	657
On Campus Magazine 555 New Jersey Ave NW	Washington	DC	20001	**800-238-1133**	202-879-4400	449-8
On Command Corp 4610 S Ulster St 6th Fl	Denver	CO	80237	**800-797-7654**	720-873-3200	117
On the Scene 54 W Illinois St Suite 550	Chicago	IL	60610	**800-621-5327**	312-661-1440	183
ON Semiconductor Corp 5005 E McDowell Rd *NASDAQ: ONNN*	Phoenix	AZ	85008	**800-282-9855**	602-244-6600	686
Onalaska Center for Commerce & Tourism 800 Oak Forest Dr	Onalaska	WI	54650	**800-873-1901**	608-781-9570	205
Onamac Industries Inc 11504 Airport Rd Bldg G	Everett	WA	98204	**877-742-2718**	425-743-6676	446
Once Upon A Child 4200 Dahlberg Dr Suite 100	Minneapolis	MN	55422	**800-433-2540**	763-520-8500	155-1
Oncogene Science 80 Rogers St *Sales	Cambridge	MA	02142	**888-674-3424***	617-492-7289	229
Oncology. American Society of Clinical 1900 Duke St Suite 200	Alexandria	VA	22314	**888-282-2552**	703-299-0150	49-8
Oncology. American Society for Therapeutic Radiology & 12500 Fair Lakes Cir Suite 375	Fairfax	VA	22033	**800-962-7876**	703-502-1550	49-8
Oncology Group. Gynecologic 1600 JFK Blvd Suite 1020	Philadelphia	PA	19103	**800-225-3053**	215-854-0770	49-8
Oncology Nursing Society (ONS) 125 Enterprise Dr	Pittsburgh	PA	15275	**866-257-4667**	412-859-6100	49-8
Ondeo Degremont Inc 2924 Emerywood Pkwy	Richmond	VA	23294	**800-446-1150**	804-756-7600	793
One Liberty Properties Inc 60 Cutter Mill Rd Suite 303 *NYSE: OLP*	Great Neck	NY	11021	**800-450-5816**	516-466-3100	641
One Napili Way 5355 Lower Honoapiilani Hwy	Lahaina	HI	96761	**800-841-6284**	808-669-2007	738
One Touch Systems Inc 40 Airport Pkwy	San Jose	CA	95110	**888-777-9677**	408-436-4600	176-7
One Washington Circle Hotel 1 Washington Cir NW	Washington	DC	20037	**800-424-9671**	202-872-1680	373
ONEAC Corp 27944 N Bradley Rd	Libertyville	IL	60048	**800-327-8801**	847-816-6000	252
O'Neal Steel Inc 744 41st St N	Birmingham	AL	35222	**800-292-4090**	205-599-8000	483
OneBeacon Insurance Group 1 Beacon St	Boston	MA	02108	**800-327-6286**	617-725-6000	384-4
Oneida Bingo & Casino 2020 Airport Dr	Oneida	WI	54155	**800-238-4263**	920-497-8118	133
Oneida County Convention & Visitors Bureau PO Box 551	Utica	NY	13503	**800-426-3132**	315-724-7221	205
Oneida Financial Corp 182 Main St *NASDAQ: ONFC*	Oneida	NY	13421	**800-211-0564**	315-363-2000	355-2
Oneida Ltd 163-181 Kenwood Ave	Oneida	NY	13421	**800-877-6667**	315-361-3000	716
Oneida Nation Museum W892 County Rd EE PO Box 365	De Pere	WI	54155	**800-236-2214**	920-869-2768	509
O'Neill Eugene Theatre 230 W 49th St	New York	NY	10019	**800-432-7250**	212-239-6200	732
O'Neill Inc 1071 41st Ave PO Box 6300	Santa Cruz	CA	95063	**800-538-0764**	831-475-7500	701
OneMind Connect Inc 2 Corporate Plaza Suite 100	Newport Beach	CA	92660	**877-658-5022**	949-640-0701	39
Oneonta Trading Corp 1 Oneonta Way	Wenatchee	WA	98804	**800-688-2191**	509-663-2631	292-7
OneSource 1600 Parkwood Cir Suite 400	Atlanta	GA	30339	**800-424-4477**	770-436-9900	105
OneSource Distributors Inc 3951 Oceanic Dr	Oceanside	CA	92056	**800-521-5092**	760-966-4500	245
OneSource Information Services Inc 300 Baker Ave	Concord	MA	01742	**800-333-8036**	978-318-4300	623-10
OneTravel Inc 258 Main St 3rd Fl	East Greenville	PA	18041	**800-929-2523**	215-541-1030	762
OneUnited Bank 133 Federal St	Boston	MA	02110	**877-663-8648**	617-457-4400	71
OneWorkplace 475 Brannan St	San Francisco	CA	94107	**800-899-4324**	415-357-2200	315
Onfield Apparel Group LLC 8677 LogoAthletic Ct	Indianapolis	IN	46219	**800-955-6467**	317-895-7000	153-1
ONGUARD Industries 1850 Clark Rd	Havre de Grace	MD	21078	**800-365-2282**	410-272-2000	296
ONIX Systems Inc 9303 W Sam Houston Pkwy S	Houston	TX	77099	**877-290-7422**	713-272-0404	410
Online Computer Library Center Inc (OCLC) 6565 Frantz Rd	Dublin	OH	43017	**800-848-5878**	614-764-6000	49-11
Online Copy Corp 48815 Kato Rd	Fremont	CA	94539	**800-833-4460**	510-226-6810	239
Online Inc 88 Danbury Rd Suite D	Wilton	CT	06897	**800-248-8466**	203-761-1466	623-9
Online Magazine 143 Old Marlton Pike	Medford	NJ	08055	**800-300-9868**	609-654-6266	449-7
OnlineCityGuide.com LLC 1940 Elm Hill Pike	Nashville	TN	37210	**800-467-1218**	615-259-4500	762
Onondaga Coach Corp PO Box 277	Auburn	NY	13021	**800-451-1570**	315-255-2216	108
OnPoint LP 4301 Cambridge Rd	Fort Worth	TX	76155	**800-325-2580**	817-355-8200	722
onProject Inc 3 Wing Dr Suite 225	Cedar Knolls	NJ	07927	**877-936-6776**	973-971-9970	39
ONS (Oncology Nursing Society) 125 Enterprise Dr	Pittsburgh	PA	15275	**866-257-4667**	412-859-6100	49-8
Onsat Magazine PO Box 2347 *Cust Svc	Shelby	NC	28151	**800-234-0021***	704-482-9673	449-9
Onslow County Tourism 1099 Gum Branch Rd	Jacksonville	NC	28541	**800-932-2144**	910-455-1113	205
Onsrud Cutter Inc 800 Liberty Dr	Libertyville	IL	60048	**800-234-1560**	847-362-1560	484
Ontario Convention Center 2000 Convention Center Way	Ontario	CA	91764	**800-455-5755**	909-937-3000	204
Ontario Convention & Visitors Bureau 2000 Convention Ctr Way	Ontario	CA	91764	**800-455-5755**	909-937-3000	205
Ontario Convention & Visitors Bureau 676 SW 5th Ave	Ontario	OR	97914	**888-889-8012**	541-889-8012	205
Ontario Knife Co 26 Empire St	Franklinville	NY	14737	**800-222-5233**	716-676-5527	219
Ontario Library Assn (OLA) 100 Lombard St Suite 303	Toronto	ON	M5CIM3	**866-873-9867**	416-363-3388	427
Ontario Library Service North - Kirkland Lake 11 Station Rd S	Kirkland Lake	ON	P2N3H2	**800-461-6348**	705-567-3341	428
Ontario Mills 1 Mills Cir Suite 1	Ontario	CA	91764	**888-526-4557**	909-484-8300	452
Ontario Tourism Marketing Partnership Corp 900 Bay St Hearst Block 10th Fl	Toronto	ON	M7A2E1	**800-668-2746**	905-282-1721	763
Ontonagon County Rural Electric Assn 500 James K Paul St	Ontonagon	MI	49953	**800-562-7128**	906-884-4151	244
Onyx Industrial Services Inc 1980 N Hwy 146	La Porte	TX	77571	**877-719-5086**	713-307-2100	791
Onyx Software Corp 1100 112th Ave NE Suite 100 *NASDAQ: ONXS*	Bellevue	WA	98004	**888-275-6699**	425-451-8060	176-1
Ooh La La! 1377 N Trail Creek Way	Eagle	ID	83616	**866-664-5258**	208-939-8940	130
OOIDA (Owner-Operator Independent Drivers Assn) 1 NW OOIDA Dr	Grain Valley	MO	64029	**800-444-5791**	816-229-5791	49-21
OPCO Inc PO Box 101	Latrobe	PA	15650	**800-229-6726**	724-537-9300	590
Open Kitchen Inc 1161 W 21st St	Chicago	IL	60608	**800-339-5334**	312-666-5334	294
Open Plan Systems Inc 14140 N Washington Hwy PO Box 1810	Ashland	VA	23005	**800-849-7239**	804-228-5600	314-1
Open Solutions RDS Technologies 7820 Innovation Blvd Suite 100	Indianapolis	IN	46278	**800-888-2112**	317-610-3500	176-4
Open Systems Inc 1157 Valley Park Dr Suite 105 *Sales	Shakopee	MN	55379	**800-328-2276***	952-496-2465	176-1
Open Systems Management Inc 1511 3rd Ave Suite 905	Seattle	WA	98101	**866-601-8011**	206-583-8373	176-12
Open Systems Solutions Inc 710 Floral Vale Blvd	Yardley	PA	19067	**800-898-6774**	215-579-8111	178
Open Text Corp 185 Columbia St W *NASDAQ: OTEX* ■ *Sales	Waterloo	ON	N2L5Z5	**888-450-2547***	519-888-7111	176-7
Open Text Corp (USA) 100 Tri-State International Pkwy 3rd Fl *Sales	Lincolnshire	IL	60069	**800-507-5777***	847-267-9330	176-7
OpenAir Inc 80 Lincoln St 6th Fl *Sales	Boston	MA	02111	**888-367-1715***	617-351-0230	39
OpenConnect Systems Inc 2711 LBJ Fwy Suite 700	Dallas	TX	75234	**800-551-5881**	972-484-5200	176-7

Listing	City	State	ZIP	Toll-Free	Phone	Class
OPENFIELD Solutions 5800 Ambler Dr Suite 215	Mississauga	ON	L4W4J4	**800-387-3262**	905-507-4333	113
TSE: SYS						
OpenNetwork Technologies Inc 13577 Feather Sound Dr	Clearwater	FL	33762	**877-561-9500**	727-561-9500	176-12
OPENonline 1650 Lake Shore Dr Suite 350	Columbus	OH	43204	**888-381-5656**	614-481-6999	621
OpenTable Inc 799 Market St 4th Fl	San Francisco	CA	94103	**800-673-6822**	415-344-4200	176-10
OpenWorks 4742 N 24th St Suite 300	Phoenix	AZ	85016	**800-777-6736**	602-224-0440	305
Opera Guild. Metropolitan 70 Lincoln Ctr Plaza 6th Fl	New York	NY	10023	**800-829-2525**	212-769-7000	48-4
Opera Omaha 1625 Farnam St Suite 100	Omaha	NE	68102	**877-346-7372**	402-346-0357	563-2
Opera Pacific 600 W Warner Ave	Santa Ana	CA	92707	**800-346-7372**	714-546-6000	563-2
Opera Santa Barbara 123 W Padre St Suite A	Santa Barbara	CA	93105	**800-563-7181**	805-898-3890	563-2
Opera Theatre at Wildwood 20919 Denny Rd	Little Rock	AR	72223	**888-278-7727**	501-821-7275	563-2
Operation USA 8320 Melrose Ave Suite 200	Los Angeles	CA	90069	**800-678-7255**	323-658-8876	48-5
Operational Technologies Corp 4100 NW Loop 410 Suite 230	San Antonio	TX	78229	**800-677-8072**	210-731-0000	258
Operations Management. APICS - Assn for 5301 Shawnee Rd	Alexandria	VA	22312	**800-444-2742**	703-354-8851	49-13
Operations Research & the Management Sciences. Institute for 7240 Parkway Dr Suite 310	Hanover	MD	21076	**800-446-3676**	443-757-3500	49-19
Operator Service Co 5302 Ave Q	Lubbock	TX	79412	**800-658-6041**	806-747-2474	721
Ophthalmology. American Academy of 655 Beach St	San Francisco	CA	94109	**800-222-3937**	415-561-8500	49-8
Ophthalmology. American Society of Contemporary Medicine Surgery & 820 N Orleans St Suite 208	Chicago	IL	60610	**800-621-4002**	312-440-0699	49-8
Ophthalmology Consultants The Center for LASIK 5800 Colonial Dr Suite 100	Margate	FL	33063	**800-448-8770**	954-977-8770	785
Oppenheimer Cos Inc 877 W Main St Suite 700	Boise	ID	83702	**800-727-9939**	208-343-4883	292-8
OppenheimerFunds Inc PO Box 5270	Denver	CO	80217	**800-525-7048**	303-671-3200	517
Optek Technology Inc 1645 Wallace Dr	Carrollton	TX	75006	**800-341-4747**	972-323-2200	686
Optelecom Inc 12920 Cloverleaf Ctr Dr	Germantown	MD	20874	**800-293-4237**	301-444-2200	720
NASDAQ: OPTC						
Optex America Inc 1845 W 205th St	Torrance	CA	90501	**800-966-7839**	310-533-1500	681
Opti-Com Mfg Network Co Inc 259 Plauche St	Harahan	LA	70123	**800-345-8774**	504-736-0331	804
Optical Cable Corp 5290 Concourse Dr	Roanoke	VA	24019	**800-622-7711**	540-265-0690	801
NASDAQ: OCCF						
Optical Laboratories Assn (OLA) 11096-A Lee Hwy Suite 101	Fairfax	VA	22030	**800-477-5652**	703-359-2830	49-8
Optical Laser Inc 5702 Bolsa Ave Suite 100	Huntington Beach	CA	92649	**800-776-9215**	714-379-4400	172
Optical Shop of Aspen International 25 Brookline	Aliso Viejo	CA	92656	**800-647-2345**	949-360-1010	533
Optical Society of America (OSA) 2010 Massachusetts Ave NW	Washington	DC	20036	**800-762-6960**	202-223-8130	49-8
OptiCare Health Systems Inc 87 Grandview Ave	Waterbury	CT	06708	**800-225-5393**	203-574-2020	658
AMEX: OPT						
Opticians Assn of America (OAA) 12100 Sunset Hills Rd Suite 130	Reston	VA	20190	**800-443-8997**	703-437-4377	49-8
Optimal Hospice 4800 Stockdale Hwy Suite 215	Bakersfield	CA	93309	**888-597-6115**	661-387-1527	365
Optimal Nutrients 1163 Chess Dr Unit F	Foster City	CA	94404	**800-966-8874**	650-525-0112	291-11
Optimist International 4494 Lindell Blvd	Saint Louis	MO	63108	**800-500-8130**	314-371-6000	48-15
Optimist Magazine 4494 Lindell Blvd	Saint Louis	MO	63108	**800-500-8130**	314-371-6000	449-10
Optimum Choice Inc 4 Taft Ct	Rockville	MD	20850	**800-544-2853**	301-545-5900	384-3
Optimum Health Institute 6970 Central Ave	Lemon Grove	CA	91945	**800-993-4325**	619-464-3346	697
Optimum Health Services Inc 707 60th St Ct E Suite A	Bradenton	FL	34208	**800-841-1585**	941-747-1585	384-3
Optimum Resource Inc 18 Hunter Rd	Hilton Head Island	SC	29926	**888-784-2592**	843-689-8000	176-3
Option Advisor Newsletter 1259 Kemper Meadow Dr	Cincinnati	OH	45240	**800-448-2080**	513-589-3800	521-9
Option Care Inc 485 Half Day Rd Suite 300	Buffalo Grove	IL	60089	**800-879-6137**	847-465-2100	358
NASDAQ: OPTN						
Option One Mortgage Corp 3 Ada	Irvine	CA	92618	**800-704-0800**	949-790-3600	498
optionsXpress Inc 39 S LaSalle St Suite 220	Chicago	IL	60603	**888-280-8020**	312-630-3300	167
NASDAQ: OXPS						
OPW Engineered Systems Inc 2726 Henkle Dr	Lebanon	OH	45036	**800-547-9393***	513-932-9114	609
*Cust Svc						
OPW Fueling Components PO Box 405003	Cincinnati	OH	45240	**800-422-2525**	513-870-3100	777
ORA Corp DBA Delimex 7878 Airway Rd	San Diego	CA	92154	**800-382-6253**	619-661-5440	291-36
Oracle Corp 500 Oracle Pkwy	Redwood Shores	CA	94065	**800-672-2531***	650-506-7000	176-1
NASDAQ: ORCL ■ *Sales						
Oral Health America 410 N Michigan Ave Suite 352	Chicago	IL	60611	**800-523-3438**	312-836-9900	48-17
Oral Implantologists. International Congress of 248 Lorraine Ave 3rd Fl	Upper Montclair	NJ	07043	**800-442-0525**	973-783-6300	49-8
Oral & Maxillofacial Surgeons. American Assn of 9700 W Bryn Mawr Ave	Rosemont	IL	60018	**800-822-6637**	847-678-6200	49-8
Oral Roberts University 7777 S Lewis Ave	Tulsa	OK	74171	**800-678-8876**	918-495-6161	163
Orange 21 Inc 2070 Las Palmas Dr	Carlsbad	CA	92009	**800-779-3937**	760-804-8420	531
NASDAQ: ORNG						
Orange Bakery Inc 17751 Cowan Ave	Irvine	CA	92614	**800-576-6836**	949-863-1377	291-2
Orange Belt Stages 2134 E Mineral King Ave	Visalia	CA	93292	**800-266-7433**	559-733-4408	748
Orange Chamber of Commerce 439 E Chapman Ave	Orange	CA	92866	**800-938-0073**	714-538-3581	137
Orange Convention & Visitors Bureau 803 W Green Ave	Orange	TX	77630	**800-528-4906**	409-883-1010	205
Orange County Convention Center 9800 International Dr	Orlando	FL	32819	**800-345-9845**	407-685-9800	204
Orange County Regional History Center 65 E Central Blvd	Orlando	FL	32801	**800-965-2030**	407-836-8500	509
Orange County Register 625 N Grand Ave	Santa Ana	CA	92701	**877-469-7344**	714-796-7000	522-2
Orange County Rural Electric Membership Corp PO Box 208	Orleans	IN	47452	**888-337-5900**	812-865-2229	244
Orange County Teachers Federal Credit Union 2115 N Broadway	Santa Ana	CA	92706	**800-462-8328**	714-258-4000	216
Orange Cove-Sanger Citrus Assn 180 South Ave	Orange Cove	CA	93646	**800-533-8871**	559-626-4453	310-2
Orange Glo International 8200 E Maplewood Ave Suite 703	Greenwood Village	CO	80111	**800-781-7529**	303-740-1909	149
Orange Julius of America 7505 Metro Blvd	Minneapolis	MN	55439	**800-679-6556**	952-830-0200	657
Orange & Rockland Utilities Inc 1 Blue Hill Plaza	Pearl River	NY	10965	**877-434-4100**	845-352-6000	774
Orange Tree Golf & Conference Resort 10601 N 56th St	Scottsdale	AZ	85254	**800-228-0386**	480-948-6100	655
Orangeburg County Chamber of Commerce 155 Riverside Dr	Orangeburg	SC	29116	**800-545-6153**	803-534-6821	137
OraPharma Inc 732 Louis Dr	Warminster	PA	18974	**888-553-6010**	215-956-2200	86
OraSure Technologies Inc 220 1st St	Bethlehem	PA	18015	**800-869-3538**	610-882-1820	229
NASDAQ: OSUR						
ORBCOMM LLC 21700 Atlantic Blvd	Dulles	VA	20166	**800-672-2666**	703-433-6300	669
ORBIS Corp 1055 Corporate Ctr Dr	Oconomowoc	WI	53066	**800-999-8683**	262-560-5000	198
ORBIS International Inc 520 8th Ave 11th Fl	New York	NY	10018	**800-672-4787**	646-674-5500	48-5
Orbit International Corp 80 Cabot Ct	Hauppauge	NY	11788	**800-663-5366**	631-435-8300	519
NASDAQ: ORBT						
Orbital Sciences Corp 21839 Atlantic Blvd	Dulles	VA	20166	**877-672-4825**	703-406-5000	494
NYSE: ORB						
Orbitz LLC 200 S Wacker Dr Suite 1900	Chicago	IL	60606	**888-656-4546**	312-894-5000	762
ORC Plastics 920 E Raleigh St	Siler City	NC	27344	**800-214-0942**		593
Orchard Hotel 665 Bush St	San Francisco	CA	94108	**888-717-2881**	415-362-8878	373
Orchard-Rite Ltd Inc PO Box 9308	Yakima	WA	98909	**800-676-4460**	509-457-9196	269
Orchards Hotel 222 Adams Rd	Williamstown	MA	01267	**800-225-1517**	413-458-9611	373
Orchestra New England College & Elm Sts Battell Chapel Yale University	New Haven	CT	06510	**800-476-9040**		563-3
Orchid Cellmark Inc 4390 Rt 1	Princeton	NJ	08540	**888-398-9352**	609-750-2200	86
NASDAQ: ORCH						
Orchid GeneScreen 2600 Stemmons Fwy Suite 133	Dallas	TX	75207	**800-362-8378**	214-631-8152	408
Orchids Paper Products Co 4826 Hunt St	Pryor	OK	74361	**800-832-4908**	918-825-0616	548-2
Orco Block Co Inc 8042 Katella Ave	Stanton	CA	90680	**800-473-6726**	714-527-2239	181
Orcon Corp 1570 Atlantic St	Union City	CA	94587	**800-227-0505**	510-489-8100	589
Order of the Sons of Italy in America (OSIA) 219 'E' St NE	Washington	DC	20002	**800-547-6742**	202-547-2900	48-14
Orders Distributing Co Inc 1 Whitlee Ct	Greenville	SC	29607	**888-867-3377***	864-288-4220	356
*Cust Svc						
Ore-Cal Corp 634 S Crocker St	Los Angeles	CA	90021	**800-827-7474**	213-680-9540	292-5
Oreck Corp 100 Plantation Rd	New Orleans	LA	70123	**800-535-8810***	504-733-8761	775
*Orders						
Oregon						
Fish & Wildlife Dept 3406 Cherry Ave NE	Salem	OR	97303	**800-720-6339**	503-947-6000	335
Parks & Recreation Dept 725 Summer St NE Suite C	Salem	OR	97301	**800-551-6949**	503-986-0667	335
Seniors & People with Disabilities Div 500 Summer St NE 2nd Fl	Salem	OR	97310	**800-282-2096**	503-945-5811	335
Student Assistance Commission 1500 Valley River Dr Suite 100	Eugene	OR	97401	**800-452-8807**	541-687-7400	711
Tourism Commission 670 Hawthorne Ave SE Suite 240	Salem	OR	97301	**800-547-7842**	503-378-8850	335
Transportation Dept 355 Capitol St NE Suite 135	Salem	OR	97301	**888-275-6368**	503-986-3200	335
Vocational Rehabilitation Services Office 500 Summer St NE	Salem	OR	97310	**800-452-2147**	503-945-5880	335
Oregon Assn of Realtors 693 Chemeketa St NE	Salem	OR	97308	**800-252-9115**	503-362-3645	642
Oregon-California Trails Assn PO Box 1019	Independence	MO	64051	**888-811-6282**	816-252-2276	48-23
Oregon Catholic Press 5536 NE Hassalo St	Portland	OR	97213	**800-548-8749**	503-281-1191	623-4
Oregon Chai Inc 1745 NW Marshall St	Portland	OR	97209	**888-874-2424**		291-40
Oregon Coast Magazine 4969 Hwy 101 Suite 2	Florence	OR	97439	**800-348-8401**	541-997-8401	449-22
Oregon Connection 1125 S 1st St	Coos Bay	OR	97420	**800-255-5318**	541-267-7804	322
Oregon Convention Center 777 NE ML King Jr Blvd	Portland	OR	97232	**800-791-2250**	503-235-7575	204
Oregon Cutting Systems Div Blount Inc 4909 SE International Way	Portland	OR	97222	**800-223-5168**	503-653-8881	747
Oregon Freeze Dry Inc PO Box 1048	Albany	OR	97321	**800-547-4060**	541-926-6001	291-18
Oregon Garden 879 W Main St PO Box 155	Iverton	OR	97381	**877-674-2733**	503-874-8100	98
Oregon Glass Co 10450 SW Ridder Rd	Wilsonville	OR	97070	**800-547-0217**	503-682-3846	325
Oregon Health & Science University School of Medicine 3181 SW Sam Jackson Park Rd L-109	Portland	OR	97239	**800-775-5460**	503-494-7800	164-2

Alphabetical Section

Name / Address	City	ST	ZIP	Toll-Free	Phone	Class
Oregon Institute of Technology						
3201 Campus Dr	Klamath Falls	OR	97601	**800-422-2017**	541-885-1155	163
Oregon Museum of Science & Industry						
1945 SE Water Ave	Portland	OR	97214	**800-955-6674**	503-797-4000	509
Oregon Mutual Insurance Co						
PO Box 808	McMinnville	OR	97128	**800-888-2141**	503-565-2141	384-4
Oregon Mutual Insurance Group						
PO Box 808	McMinnville	OR	97128	**800-888-2141**	503-565-2141	384-4
Oregon State Bar Bulletin						
5200 SW Meadows Rd	Lake Oswego	OR	97035	**800-452-8260**	503-620-0222	449-15
Oregon State University	Corvallis	OR	97331	**800-291-4192**	541-737-0123	163
Oregon State University Press						
500 Kerr Administration Bldg	Corvallis	OR	97331	**800-426-3797***	541-737-3166	623-5
*Orders						
Oregon Steel Mills Inc						
1000 SW Broadway Suite 2200	Portland	OR	97205	**800-547-9451**	503-223-9228	709
NYSE: OS						
Oregon Symphony Orchestra						
921 SW Washington St Suite 200	Portland	OR	97205	**800-228-7343**	503-228-4294	563-3
Oregon Veterans' Home						
700 Veterans Dr	The Dalles	OR	97058	**800-846-8460**	541-296-7190	780
Oregon Veterinary Medical Assn						
1880 Lancaster Dr NE Suite 118	Salem	OR	97305	**800-235-3502**	503-399-0311	782
O'Reilly & Assoc Inc						
1005 Gravenstein Hwy N	Sebastopol	CA	95472	**800-998-9938**	707-829-0515	623-11
Orelube Corp 201 E Bethpage Rd	Plainview	NY	11803	**800-645-9124**	516-249-6500	530
Orfila Vineyards & Winery						
13455 San Pasqual Rd	Escondido	CA	92025	**800-868-9463**	760-738-6500	50
Organ Recovery & Education. Center						
for 204 Sigma Dr RIDC Park	Pittsburgh	PA	15238	**800-366-6777**	412-366-6777	265
Organ Sharing. United Network for						
700 N 4th St	Richmond	VA	23219	**888-894-6361**	804-330-8500	48-17
Organ Supply Industries Inc						
2320 W 50th St	Erie	PA	16506	**800-458-0289**	814-835-2244	516
Organ Transplant Assn. Children's						
2501 Cota Dr	Bloomington	IN	47403	**800-366-2682**	812-336-8872	48-17
Organic Chemical Manufacturers						
Assn. Synthetic 1850 M St NW						
Suite 700	Washington	DC	20036	**888-377-0778**	202-721-4100	49-19
Organic Gardening Magazine						
33 E Minor St	Emmaus	PA	18098	**800-666-2206***	610-967-5171	449-14
*Circ						
Organic Milling Co						
505 W Allen Ave	San Dimas	CA	91773	**800-638-8686**	909-599-0961	291-4
Organic Style Magazine 33 Minor St	Emmaus	PA	18098	**800-848-4735**	610-967-8154	449-13
Organic Valley Family of Farms						
1 Organic Way	LaFarge	WI	54639	**888-444-6455**	608-625-2602	292-7
Organists. American Guild of						
475 Riverside Dr Suite 1260	New York	NY	10115	**800-246-5115**	212-870-2310	48-4
Organizational Dynamics Inc						
790 Boston Rd Suite 201	Billerica	MA	01821	**800-634-4636**	978-671-5454	193
Organon Inc 375 Mt Pleasant Ave	West Orange	NJ	07052	**800-631-1253**	973-325-4500	572
Orica USA Inc 33101 E Quincy Ave	Watkins	CO	80137	**877-336-7422**	303-268-5000	264
Oriel Instruments Corp						
150 Long Beach Blvd	Stratford	CT	06615	**800-714-5393**	203-377-8282	534
Orient Express Hotels Inc						
1155 Ave of the Americas 30th Fl	New York	NY	10036	**800-237-1236**	212-302-5055	369
NYSE: OEH						
Orient Lines Inc 7665 Corporate Ctr Dr	Miami	FL	33126	**800-333-7300**	305-468-2000	217
Oriental Medicine. American Assn of						
PO Box 162340	Sacramento	CA	95816	**866-455-7999**	916-443-4770	48-17
Oriental Trading Co Inc 5455 S						
90th St	Omaha	NE	68127	**800-225-6440**	402-596-1200	451
Oriental Weavers Group Sphinx Div						
3252 Lower Dug Gap Rd SW	Dalton	GA	30720	**800-832-8020**	706-277-9666	131
Origen Financial Inc						
27777 Franklin Rd Suite 1700	Southfield	MI	48034	**866-467-4436**	248-746-7000	498
NASDAQ: ORGN						
Original Designs/Famor Inc						
44-40 11th St	Long Island City	NY	11101	**800-458-4300**	718-706-8989	401
Original Italian Pasta Products Co Inc						
6 ConAgra Dr	Omaha	NE	68102	**800-563-9786**	402-595-6935	291-31
Original Lincoln Logs Ltd						
5 Riverside Dr	Chestertown	NY	12817	**800-833-2461**	518-494-5500	107
Original Parts Group Inc						
5252 Bolsa Ave	Huntington Beach	CA	92649	**800-243-8355**	714-230-6000	54
Origins Natural Resources Inc						
767 5th Ave	New York	NY	10153	**800-723-7310***	212-572-4200	211
*Cust Svc						
Oriole Homes Corp						
6400S Congress Ave Suite 2000	Boca Raton	FL	33487	**800-964-6631**	561-999-1860	639
Oriole Park at Camden Yards						
333 W Camden St	Baltimore	MD	21201	**888-848-2473**	410-576-0300	706
Orion Auto PO Box 118090	Charleston	SC	29423	**800-462-6342**	843-561-0510	384-4
Orion Futures 1905 W Busch Blvd	Tampa	FL	33612	**888-769-9399**	813-876-9662	167
Orion International Consulting Group Inc						
1250 Capital of Texas Hwy S Bldg 1						
Suite 270	Austin	TX	78746	**800-336-7466**	512-327-7111	707
Orion Magazine 187 Main St	Great Barrington	MA	01230	**888-909-6568**	413-528-4422	449-19
Orion Pacific Inc 8682 N Olive Ave	Orange	CA	92865	**800-827-7890**	714-283-8687	748
Orix Financial Services Inc						
600 Town Park Ln	Kennesaw	GA	30144	**866-674-9112**	770-970-6000	214
Orkin Exterminating Co Inc						
2170 Piedmont Rd NE	Atlanta	GA	30324	**800-346-7546**	404-888-2000	567
Orlando The 8384 W 3rd St	Los Angeles	CA	90048	**800-624-6835**	323-658-6600	373
Orlando Baking Co Inc						
7777 Grand Ave	Cleveland	OH	44104	**800-362-5504**	216-361-1872	291-1
Orlando Business Journal						
315 E Robinson St Suite 250	Orlando	FL	32801	**888-649-6251**	407-649-8470	449-5
Orlando Magazine						
11900 Biscayne Blvd Suite 300	Miami	FL	33181	**800-243-0609**	305-892-6644	449-22
Orlando Opera 1111 N Orange Ave	Orlando	FL	32804	**800-336-7372**	407-426-1717	563-2
Orlando Science Center						
777 E Princeton St	Orlando	FL	32803	**888-672-4386**	407-514-2000	509
Orlando Sentinel 633 N Orange Ave	Orlando	FL	32801	**800-347-6868**	407-420-5000	522-2
Orlando World Center Marriott Resort &						
Convention Center 8701 World						
Ctr Dr	Orlando	FL	32821	**800-621-0638**	407-239-4200	655

Name / Address	City	ST	ZIP	Toll-Free	Phone	Class
Orlando/Orange County Convention &						
Visitors Bureau 6700 Forum Dr						
Suite 100	Orlando	FL	32821	**800-551-0181**	407-363-5800	205
Orleans Las Vegas Hotel & Casino						
4500 W Tropicana Ave	Las Vegas	NV	89103	**888-365-7111**	702-365-7111	133
Orlimar Golf Equipment Co						
1385 Park Center Dr	Vista	CA	92081	**877-675-4627***	760-305-0013	701
*Cust Svc						
ORMCO Corp 1717 W Collins Ave	Orange	CA	92867	**800-854-1741**	714-516-7400	226
Ormec Systems Corp 19 Linden Pk	Rochester	NY	14625	**800-656-7632**	585-385-3520	202
Ormet Primary Aluminum Corp						
43840 State Rd 7 PO Box 176	Hannibal	OH	43931	**800-282-9701**	740-483-1381	476
Oro-Cal Mfg Co Inc 1720 Bird St	Oroville	CA	95965	**800-367-6225**	530-533-5085	401
O'Rourke Bros Distributing Inc						
3885 Elmore Ave Suite 100	Davenport	IA	52807	**800-523-4730**	563-823-1501	38
O'Rourke Wrecking Co						
660 Lunken Park Dr	Cincinnati	OH	45226	**800-354-9850**	513-871-1400	188-17
Oroville Area Chamber of Commerce						
1789 Montgomery St	Oroville	CA	95965	**800-655-4653**	530-538-2542	137
Oroville Mercury Register PO Box 651	Oroville	CA	95965	**800-827-1421**	530-533-3131	522-2
Orphan Foundation of America (OFA)						
12020-D N Shore Dr	Reston	VA	20190	**800-950-4673**	571-203-0270	48-6
Orphan Medical Inc						
13911 Ridgedale Dr Suite 250	Minnetonka	MN	55305	**888-867-7426**	952-513-6900	86
NASDAQ: ORPH						
Orr Safety Corp						
11601 Interchange Dr	Louisville	KY	40229	**800-726-6789**	502-774-5791	667
Orrco Inc 228 W Chestnut St	Orrville	OH	44667	**800-321-3085**	330-683-5015	568
ORT. American						
817 Broadway 10th Fl	New York	NY	10003	**800-364-9678**	212-353-5800	48-5
Orthman Mfg Inc PO Box B	Lexington	NE	68850	**800-658-3270**	308-324-4654	269
Ortho BioTech Products LP						
PO Box 6914	Bridgewater	NJ	08807	**800-325-7504***	908-541-4000	86
*Cust Svc						
Ortho-Clinical Diagnostics Inc						
1001 US Rt 202 N PO Box 350	Raritan	NJ	08869	**800-828-6316**	908-218-1300	468
Orthodontists. American Assn of						
401 N Lindbergh Blvd	Saint Louis	MO	63141	**800-424-2841**	314-993-1700	49-8
Orthodontists PAC. American Assn of						
401 N Lindbergh Blvd	Saint Louis	MO	63141	**800-424-2841**	314-993-1700	604
Orthodox Christian Charities.						
International 110 West Rd						
Suite 360	Baltimore	MD	21204	**877-803-4622**	410-243-9820	48-5
Orthofix Inc 1720 Bray Central Dr	McKinney	TX	75069	**800-527-0404**	469-742-2500	469
OrthoLogic Corp						
1275 W Washington St	Tempe	AZ	85281	**800-937-5520**	602-286-5520	469
NASDAQ: OLGC						
Orthopaedic Nurses. National Assn of						
401 N Michigan Ave Suite 2200	Chicago	IL	60611	**800-289-6266**		49-8
Orthopaedic Society for Sports						
Medicine. American 6300 N						
River Rd Suite 500	Rosemont	IL	60018	**877-321-3500**	847-292-4900	49-8
Orthovita Inc 45 Great Valley Pkwy	Malvern	PA	19355	**800-676-8482**	610-640-1775	469
NASDAQ: VITA						
Ortloff Engineers Ltd						
415 W Wall Ave Suite 2000	Midland	TX	79701	**888-367-0020**	432-685-0277	258
Orvis Co Inc PO Box 798	Manchester	VT	05254	**800-541-3541**	802-362-3622	701
OSA (Optical Society of America)						
2010 Massachusetts Ave NW	Washington	DC	20036	**800-762-6960**	202-223-8130	49-8
Osage Valley Electric Co-op Assn						
1321 N Orange	Butler	MO	64730	**800-889-6832**	660-679-3131	244
Osborn International						
5401 Hamilton Ave	Cleveland	OH	44114	**800-720-3358***	216-361-1900	104
*Cust Svc						
Osborne Construction Co Inc						
PO Box 97010	Kirkland	WA	98083	**888-270-8221**	425-827-4221	185
Osborne Industries Inc						
120 N Industrial Ave	Osborne	KS	67473	**800-255-0316**	785-346-2192	269
Osborne Innovative Products Inc						
2221 2nd St	Enumclaw	WA	98022	**800-325-7238**	360-825-4299	701
Oscar G Carlstedt Co						
577 College St	Jacksonville	FL	32204	**800-654-5739**	904-354-8474	288
Osceola Electric Co-op Inc 204 8th St	Sibley	IA	51249	**888-754-2519**	712-754-2519	244
Osceola News-Gazette						
PO Box 422068	Kissimmee	FL	34742	**800-327-2166**	407-846-7600	522-4
Osco Drugs 250 E Park Ctr Blvd	Boise	ID	83706	**800-541-2863**	208-395-6200	236
Oscor Inc 3816 DeSoto Blvd	Palm Harbor	FL	34683	**800-726-7267**	727-937-2511	249
OSF Saint Francis Medical Center						
530 NE Glen Oak Ave	Peoria	IL	61637	**888-627-5673**	309-655-2000	366-2
OSG Ivers-Lee Ltd 31 Hansen Rd S	Brampton	ON	L6W3H7	**800-387-1188**	905-451-5535	86
OSG Tap & Die Inc						
676 E Fullerton Ave	Glendale Heights	IL	60139	**800-837-2223**	630-790-1400	484
OSHA (Occupational Safety & Health						
Administration) 200 Constitution						
Ave NW	Washington	DC	20210	**800-321-6742**	202-693-1999	336-11
OSHA Up-to-Date Newsletter						
1121 Spring Lake Dr	Itasca	IL	60143	**800-621-7619***	630-285-1121	521-8
*Cust Svc						
OshKosh B'Gosh Inc 112 Otter Ave	Oshkosh	WI	54901	**800-282-4674**	920-231-8800	153-4
NASDAQ: GOSHA						
Oshkosh Northwestern PO Box 2926	Oshkosh	WI	54903	**800-924-6168**	920-235-7700	522-2
Oshkosh Northwestern Co						
224 State St	Oshkosh	WI	54901	**800-924-6168**	920-235-7700	623-8
OSIA (Order of the Sons of Italy in						
America) 219 'E' St NE	Washington	DC	20002	**800-547-6742**	202-547-2900	48-14
Oskaloosa Herald PO Box 530	Oskaloosa	IA	52577	**888-672-2581**	641-672-2581	522-2
Osmonics Inc 5951 Clearwater Dr	Minnetonka	MN	55343	**800-328-0992**	952-933-2277	793
Osmose Inc 980 Ellicott St	Buffalo	NY	14209	**800-877-7653**	716-882-5905	806
OSRAM Sylvania Automotive Lighting						
Div 275 W Main St	Hillsboro	NH	03244	**800-729-3777**	603-464-5533	430
OSRAM Sylvania Electronic Components						
& Materials 100 Endicott St	Danvers	MA	01923	**800-544-4828**	978-777-1900	479
OSRAM Sylvania Glass Technologies						
131 Portsmouth Ave	Exeter	NH	03833	**800-258-8290**	603-772-4331	429
Osseointegration. Academy of						
85 W Algonquin Rd						
Suite 550	Arlington Heights	IL	60005	**800-656-7736**	847-439-1919	49-8
Ostbye & Anderson Inc						
10055 51st Ave N	Minneapolis	MN	55442	**800-328-4368**	763-553-1515	401

Name / Address	City	State	ZIP	Toll-Free	Phone	Class
Osteomed Corp 3885 Arapaho Rd *Cust Svc	Addison	TX	75001	**800-456-7779***	972-677-4600	468
Osteometer MediTech Inc 12515 Chadron Ave	Hawthorne	CA	90250	**866-421-7762**	310-978-3073	468
Osteopathic Assn. American 142 E Ontario St	Chicago	IL	60611	**800-621-1773**	312-202-8000	49-8
Osteopathic Family Physicians. American College of 330 E Algonquin Rd Suite 1	Arlington Heights	IL	60005	**800-323-0794**	847-228-6090	49-8
Osteoporosis Foundation. National 1232 22nd St NW	Washington	DC	20037	**800-223-9994**	202-223-2226	48-17
Osteoporosis & Related Bone Diseases - National Resource Center 1232 22nd St NW	Washington	DC	20037	**800-624-2663**	202-223-0344	336-6
Osteotech Inc 51 James Way *NASDAQ: OSTE*	Eatontown	NJ	07724	**800-537-9842**	732-542-2800	86
Osterman Jewelers 375 Ghent Rd	Akron	OH	44333	**800-681-8796**	330-668-5000	402
Osthoff Resort 101 Osthoff Ave	Elkhart Lake	WI	53020	**800-876-3399**	920-876-3366	655
Ostomy Assn. United 19772 MacArthur Blvd Suite 200	Irvine	CA	92612	**800-826-0826**	949-660-8624	48-17
Ostomy & Continence Nurses Society. Wound 4700 W Lake Ave	Glenview	IL	60025	**888-224-9626**		49-8
Ostrom Mushroom Farms 8323 Steilacoom Rd SE	Olympia	WA	98513	**800-640-7408**	360-491-1410	11-7
O'Sullivan Furniture 1900 Gulf St *Cust Svc	Lamar	MO	64759	**800-327-9782***	417-682-3322	314-2
Osvold HC Co 2828 University Ave SE	Minneapolis	MN	55414	**800-328-4827**	612-331-1581	281
Oswald James B Co 1360 E 9th St Suite 600	Cleveland	OH	44114	**800-466-0468**	216-241-0468	383
Otari Corp 9420 Lurline Ave Unit C	Chatsworth	CA	91311	**800-735-1786**	818-734-1785	52
OTC Div SPX Corp 655 Eisenhower Dr	Owatonna	MN	55060	**800-533-6127**	507-455-7000	745
Otelco Inc 5050 3rd Ave E *AMEX: OTT*	Oneonta	AL	35121	**800-286-4600**	205-625-3591	721
Otero County Electric Co-op Inc 202 Burro Ave PO Box 227	Cloudcroft	NM	88317	**800-548-4660**	505-682-2521	244
Otesaga The PO Box 311	Cooperstown	NY	13326	**800-348-6222**	607-547-9931	655
Otis College of Art & Design 9045 Lincoln Blvd	Los Angeles	CA	90045	**800-527-6847**	310-665-6820	163
Otomix 3691 Lenawee Ave	Los Angeles	CA	90016	**800-701-7867**	310-815-4700	296
Otsego Club 696 M-32 E Main St PO Box 556	Gaylord	MI	49734	**800-752-5510**	989-732-5181	655
Otsego County Chamber 12 Carbon St	Oneonta	NY	13820	**877-568-7346**	607-432-4500	137
Ottawa Citizen 1101 Baxter Rd PO Box 5020	Ottawa	ON	K2C3M4	**800-267-6100**	613-829-9100	522-1
Ottawa County Visitors Bureau 770 SE Catawba Rd	Port Clinton	OH	43452	**800-441-1271**	419-734-4386	205
Ottawa Herald 104 S Cedar St	Ottawa	KS	66067	**800-467-8383**	785-242-4700	522-2
Ottawa Senators Corel Ctr 1000 Palladium Dr *Orders	Kanata	ON	K2V1A5	**888-688-7367***	613-599-0250	703
Ottawa Tourism & Convention Authority 130 Albert St Suite 1800	Ottawa	ON	K1P5G4	**800-363-4465**	613-237-5150	205
Ottawa Truck Inc 415 E Dundee St	Ottawa	KS	66067	**888-229-6300**	785-242-2200	505
Ottawa University 10020 N 25th Ave	Phoenix	AZ	85021	**800-235-9586**	602-371-1188	163
Ottawa University 10020 N 25th Ave	Phoenix	AZ	85021	**800-235-9586**	602-371-1188	163
Ottawa University 13402 N Scottsdale Rd Suite B170	Scottsdale	AZ	85254	**800-235-9586**	602-749-5184	163
Ottawa University 1001 S Cedar St	Ottawa	KS	66067	**800-755-5200**	785-242-5200	163
Ottawa Visitors Center 100 W Lafayette St	Ottawa	IL	61350	**888-688-2924**	815-434-2737	205
Ottenberg's Bakery Inc 655 Taylor St NE	Washington	DC	20017	**800-334-7264**	202-529-5800	291-1
Ottens Flavors 7800 Holstein Ave	Philadelphia	PA	19153	**800-523-0767**	215-365-7800	291-15
Otter Tail Corp 215 S Cascade St *NASDAQ: OTTR*	Fergus Falls	MN	56537	**877-688-9288**	218-739-8200	355-3
Otter Tail Power Co 215 S Cascade St	Fergus Falls	MN	56537	**800-551-3593**	218-739-8200	774
Otterbein College 1 Otterbein College	Westerville	OH	43081	**800-488-8144**	614-823-1500	163
Otto Candies Inc 17271 Hwy 90	Des Allemands	LA	70030	**800-535-4563**	504-469-7700	457
Ottosen Propeller & Accessories Inc 105 S 28th St	Phoenix	AZ	85034	**800-528-7551**	602-275-8514	759
Ottumwa Area Chamber of Commerce 217 E Mian St	Ottumwa	IA	52501	**800-564-5274**	641-682-3465	137
Ottumwa Courier 213 E 2nd St	Ottumwa	IA	52501	**800-532-1504**	641-684-4611	522-2
Ottumwa Regional Health Center 1001 Pennsylvania Ave	Ottumwa	IA	52501	**800-933-6742**	641-682-7511	366-2
Ouachita Baptist University 410 Ouachita St	Arkadelphia	AR	71998	**800-342-5628**	870-245-5000	163
Our Lady of Holy Cross College 4123 Woodland Dr	New Orleans	LA	70131	**800-259-7744**	504-394-7744	163
Our Lady of the Lake University 411 SW 24th St	San Antonio	TX	78207	**800-436-6558**	210-434-6711	163
Our Sunday Visitor Inc 200 Noll Plaza	Huntington	IN	46750	**800-348-2440**	260-356-8400	623-8
Outdoor Ethics Inc. Leave No Trace Center for PO Box 997	Boulder	CO	80306	**800-332-4100**	303-442-8222	48-23
Outdoor JobNet c/o Outdoor Network PO Box 1928	Boulder	CO	80306	**800-688-6387**	303-444-7117	257
Outdoor Life Magazine 2 Park Ave	New York	NY	10016	**800-227-2224**	212-779-5000	449-14
Outdoor Photographer Magazine 12121 Wilshire Blvd Suite 1200 *Cust Svc	Los Angeles	CA	90025	**800-283-4410***	310-820-1500	449-14
Outdoor Resorts of America Inc 79-687 Country Club Rd Suite 201	Bermuda Dunes	CA	92201	**800-541-2582**	760-345-2046	121
Outdoors. America 5816 Kingston Pike	Knoxville	TN	37919	**800-524-4814**	865-558-3595	48-23
Outdoorsman's Edge Doubleday Direct Inc 1225 S Market St	Mechanicsburg	PA	17055	**800-688-4442**		94
Outer Banks Sportswear 1000 E Hanes Mill Rd PO Box 15901	Winston-Salem	NC	27105	**800-438-2029**		153-21
Outer Banks Visitors Bureau 1 Visitor Center Cir	Manteo	NC	27954	**800-446-6262**	252-473-2138	205
Outlook from the State Capitals Newsletter PO Box 7376	Alexandria	VA	22307	**800-876-2545**	703-768-9600	521-7
Outokumpu American Brass Inc 70 Sayre St *Sales	Buffalo	NY	14207	**800-642-7277***	716-879-6700	476
Outokumpu Livernois Engineering Co 25315 Kean St	Dearborn	MI	48124	**800-900-0200**	313-278-0200	258
Outokumpu Stainless 425 N Martingale Rd Suite 1600	Schaumburg	IL	60173	**800-833-8703**	847-517-4050	709
Outpost.com 25 N Main St	Kent	CT	06757	**877-688-7678**	860-927-2050	177
Outreach International PO Box 210	Independence	MO	64051	**888-833-1235**	816-833-0883	48-5
Outrigger Hotels & Resorts 2375 Kuhio Ave	Honolulu	HI	96815	**800-688-7444**	808-921-6600	369
Outrigger Luana Waikiki 2045 Kalakaua Ave	Honolulu	HI	96815	**800-445-8811**	808-955-6000	373
Outside Magazine 400 Market St	Santa Fe	NM	87501	**800-688-7433**	505-989-7100	449-14
Outsourcing Solutions Inc 390 S Woods Mill Rd Suite 350	Chesterfield	MO	63017	**800-962-5191**	314-576-0022	157
Outtask Inc 209 Madison St Suite 400	Alexandria	VA	22314	**888-662-6248**	703-837-6100	39
Outward Bound USA 100 Mystery Point Rd	Garrison	NY	10524	**866-467-7651**	845-424-4000	754
Ovarian Cancer Coalition. National 500 NE Spanish River Blvd Suite 8	Boca Raton	FL	33431	**888-682-7426**	561-393-0005	48-17
Ovarian Cancer Registry. Gilda Radner Familial Roswell Park Cancer Institute Elm & Carlton Sts	Buffalo	NY	14263	**800-682-7426**	716-845-4503	48-17
Ovation The Arts Network 5801 Duke St Suite D-112	Alexandria	VA	22304	**800-682-8466**	703-813-6310	725
Ovation Guitars 37 Greenwoods Rd *Cust Svc	New Hartford	CT	06057	**800-552-4681***	860-379-7575	516
Ovation Travel Group 71 5th Ave 11th Fl	New York	NY	10003	**800-431-1112**	212-679-1600	760
Overall Laundry Service Inc 7200 Hardeson Rd	Everett	WA	98203	**800-683-7255**	425-353-0800	434
Overcomers Outreach PO Box 2208	Oakhurst	CA	93644	**800-310-3001**	559-692-2630	48-21
Overcoming Objections Newsletter 360 Hiatt Dr	Palm Beach Gardens	FL	33418	**800-621-5463**	561-622-9914	521-10
Overdrive Magazine 3200 Rice Mine Rd NE	Tuscaloosa	AL	35406	**800-633-5953**	205-349-2990	449-21
Overhead Conveyor Co 1330 Hilton Rd	Ferndale	MI	48220	**800-396-2554**	248-547-3800	206
Overhead Door Co of Sacramento Inc 6756 Franklin Blvd	Sacramento	CA	95823	**800-929-3667**	916-421-3747	188-2
Overhead Door Corp 1900 Crown Dr	Farmers Branch	TX	75234	**800-275-3290**	972-233-6611	232
Overholtzer Church Furniture Inc 626 Kearney Ave *Sales	Modesto	CA	95352	**800-366-1716***	209-529-1716	314-3
Overland Park Convention & Visitors Bureau 9001 W 110th St Suite 100	Overland Park	KS	66210	**800-262-7275**	913-491-0123	205
Overland Storage Inc 4820 Overland Ave *NASDAQ: OVRL*	San Diego	CA	92123	**800-729-8725**	858-571-5555	174
Overly Mfg Co 574 W Otterman St	Greensburg	PA	15601	**800-979-7300**	724-834-7300	482
Overnite Corp PO Box 1216 *NASDAQ: OVNT*	Richmond	VA	23218	**800-334-3343**	804-231-8000	769
Overseas Adventure Travel 347 Congress St	Boston	MA	02210	**800-493-6824**		748
Overseas Shipholding Group Inc 511 5th Ave *NYSE: OSG*	New York	NY	10017	**800-223-1722**	212-953-4100	308
Overstock.com Inc 6322 S 3000 East Suite 100 *NASDAQ: OSTK* ■ *Cust Svc	Salt Lake City	UT	84121	**800-843-2446***	801-947-3100	778
Overstreet Paving Co 17728 US Hwy 41	Spring Hill	FL	34610	**800-741-1631**	352-796-1631	187-4
Overton Brooks Veterans Affairs Medical Center 510 E Stoner Ave	Shreveport	LA	71101	**800-863-7441**	318-221-8411	366-6
Overton Power District # 5 615 N Moapa Valley Blvd PO Box 395	Overton	NV	89040	**800-393-2512**	702-397-2512	244
Ovid Technologies Inc 333 7th Ave 4th Fl	New York	NY	10001	**800-950-2035**	646-674-6300	380
OvisLink Technologies Corp 1301 John Reed Ct	City of Industry	CA	91745	**888-605-6847**	626-854-1805	174
OW Houts & Sons Inc 120 N Buckhout St *Cust Svc	State College	PA	16801	**800-252-3583***	814-238-6701	227
Owatonna Area Chamber of Commerce & Tourism 320 Hoffman Dr	Owatonna	MN	55060	**800-423-6466**	507-451-7970	137
Owatonna Granite Rock of Ages 1300 Hoffman Dr	Owatonna	MN	55060	**800-422-2397**	507-451-4882	710
Owen Electric Co-op Inc 510 S Main St PO Box 400	Owenton	KY	40359	**800-372-7612**	502-484-3471	244
Owen Industries Inc 501 Ave H	Carter Lake	IA	51510	**800-831-9252**	712-347-5500	483
Owen Mfg Inc PO Box 398	Owen	WI	54460	**800-524-0105**	715-229-2123	580
Owen Pacific Inc 1236 S Compton Ave	Los Angeles	CA	90021	**877-693-6722**	213-747-7125	188-12
Owens & Assoc Investigations 2245 San Diego Ave Suite 225	San Diego	CA	92110	**800-297-1343**	619-297-1343	392
Owens Community College *Findlay* 300 Davis St	Findlay	OH	45840	**800-346-3529**	419-429-3500	160
Owens Community College *Toledo* 30335 Oregon Rd	Perrysburg	OH	43551	**800-466-9367**	419-661-7000	160
Owens Corning Fabricating Solutions 426 N Main St	Elkhart	IN	46516	**877-632-2935**	574-522-8473	688
Owens Country Sausage Inc 1403 E Lookout Dr	Richardson	TX	75082	**800-966-9367**	972-235-7181	291-26
Owens RC Co 310 N Blythe St	Gallatin	TN	37066	**800-821-2933**	615-452-5658	741-3

Name / Address	City	State	Zip	Toll-Free	Phone	Class
Owens RS & Co 5535 N Lynch Ave	Chicago	IL	60630	**800-282-6200**	773-282-6000	766
Owensboro Community & Technical College 4800 New Hartford Rd	Owensboro	KY	42303	**866-755-6282**	270-686-4400	158
Owensboro-Davies County Tourist Commission 215 E 2nd St	Owensboro	KY	42303	**800-489-1131**	270-926-1100	205
Owensboro Grain Co 719 E 2nd St	Owensboro	KY	42303	**800-874-0305**	270-926-2032	291-29
Owensby & Kritikos Inc 671 Whitney Ave Bldg B	Gretna	LA	70056	**800-749-3122**	504-368-3122	728
OWL (Older Women's League) 1750 New York Ave NW Suite 350	Washington	DC	20006	**800-825-3695**	202-783-6686	48-6
Owner-Operator Independent Drivers Assn (OOIDA) 1 NW OOIDA Dr	Grain Valley	MO	64029	**800-444-5791**	816-229-5791	49-21
Owyhee Plaza Hotel 1109 Main St	Boise	ID	83702	**800-233-4611**	208-343-4611	373
Ox Paper Tube & Core Inc 331 Maple Ave	Hanover	PA	17331	**800-414-2476**	717-630-0230	125
Oxfam America 26 West St	Boston	MA	02111	**800-776-9326**	617-482-1211	48-5
Oxford Biomedical Research Inc 2165 Avon Industrial Dr	Rochester Hills	MI	48309	**800-692-4633**	248-852-8815	229
Oxford Capital Partners LLC PO Box 61585	Potomac	MD	20859	**888-224-3035**	301-983-8000	268
Oxford College PO Box 1418	Oxford	GA	30054	**800-723-8328**	770-784-8328	160
Oxford Global Resources Inc 100 Cummings Ctr Suite 206L	Beverly	MA	01915	**800-426-9196**	978-236-1182	707
Oxford Health Insurance Inc 48 Monroe Tpk	Trumbull	CT	06611	**800-889-7546**	203-459-9100	384-3
Oxford Health Plans (CT) Inc 48 Monroe Tpk	Trumbull	CT	06611	**800-889-7546**	203-459-9100	384-3
Oxford Health Plans Inc 48 Monroe Tpke	Trumbull	CT	06611	**800-444-6222**	203-459-9100	384-3
Oxford Health Plans (NH) Inc 10 Tara Blvd	Nashua	NH	03062	**800-889-7630**	603-891-7000	384-3
Oxford Health Plans (NJ) Inc 111 Wood Ave 2nd Fl	Iselin	NJ	08830	**800-201-6920**	732-623-1000	384-3
Oxford Health Plans (NY) Inc 1133 Ave of the Americas	New York	NY	10036	**800-889-7622**	212-805-3400	384-3
Oxford Homes Inc PO Box 679	Oxford	ME	04270	**800-341-0436**		495
Oxford Hotel 1600 17th St	Denver	CO	80202	**800-228-5838**	303-628-5400	373
Oxford Instruments Measurement Systems 945 Busse Rd	Elk Grove Village	IL	60007	**800-678-1117**	847-439-4404	464
Oxford-Lafayette County Chamber of Commerce 299 W Jackson Ave	Oxford	MS	38655	**800-880-6967**	662-234-4651	137
Oxford Life Insurance Co 2721 N Central Ave	Phoenix	AZ	85004	**800-528-0463**	602-263-6666	384-2
Oxford Palace 745 S Oxford Ave	Los Angeles	CA	90005	**800-532-7887**	213-389-8000	373
Oxford Tourism Council 107 Courthouse Sq Suite 1	Oxford	MS	38655	**800-758-9177**	662-234-4680	205
Oxford University Press 198 Madison Ave	New York	NY	10016	**800-334-4249**	212-726-6000	623-5
Oxis International Inc 6040 N Cutter Cir Suite 317	Portland	OR	97217	**800-547-3686**	503-283-3911	86
Oxmoor House Inc 2100 Lakeshore Dr	Birmingham	AL	35209	**800-633-4910**	205-445-6000	623-2
Oxnard Convention & Visitors Bureau 200 W 7th St	Oxnard	CA	93030	**800-269-6273**	805-385-7545	205
OXO International 75 9th Ave 5th Fl	New York	NY	10011	**800-545-4411**	212-242-3333	477
Oxxford Clothes Inc 1220 W Van Buren St	Chicago	IL	60607	**888-469-9367**	312-829-3600	153-12
Oyster Point Hotel Marina & Conference Center 146 Bodman Pl	Red Bank	NJ	07701	**800-345-3484**	732-530-8200	373
Ozark Area Chamber of Commerce 294 Painter Ave	Ozark	AL	36360	**800-582-8497**	334-774-9321	137
Ozark Border Electric Co-op 3281 S Westwood Blvd	Poplar Bluff	MO	63902	**800-392-0567**	573-785-4631	244
Ozark Christian College 1111 N Main St	Joplin	MO	64801	**800-299-4622**	417-624-2518	163
Ozark Electric Co-op N Hwy 39 PO Box 420	Mount Vernon	MO	65712	**800-947-6393**	417-466-2144	244
Ozark Motor Lines Inc 3934 Homewood Rd	Memphis	TN	38118	**800-264-4100**	901-251-9711	769
Ozark Regional Transit 2423 E Robinson Ave	Springdale	AR	72764	**800-865-5901**	479-756-5901	109
Ozarks Electric Co-op Corp PO Box 848	Fayetteville	AR	72702	**800-521-6144**	479-521-2900	244

P

Name / Address	City	State	Zip	Toll-Free	Phone	Class
P & B Mfg Co Inc 655 Waterman Ave	East Providence	RI	02914	**800-556-7462**	401-438-0550	400
P & C Foods 1200 State Fair Blvd *Cust Svc	Syracuse	NY	13209	**800-724-0205***	315-457-9460	339
P-Com Inc 3175 S Winchester Blvd	Campbell	CA	95008	**800-646-7266**	408-866-3666	720
P & G Steel Products Co Inc 54 Gruner Rd	Buffalo	NY	14227	**800-952-3696**	716-896-7900	479
P & H Mfg Co PO Box 349 *Sales	Shelbyville	IL	62565	**800-879-2123***	217-774-2123	269
P-W Industries Inc 9415 Kruse Rd	Pico Rivera	CA	90660	**800-452-3023**	562-463-9055	804
Paasche Airbrush Co 4311 N Normandy *Sales	Chicago	IL	60634	**800-621-1907***	773-867-9191	43
PAB Bankshares Inc 3250 Valdosta Rd *AMEX: PAB*	Valdosta	GA	31602	**800-394-2321**	229-241-2775	355-2
Pabco Fluid Power Co Inc 5750 Hillside Ave	Cincinnati	OH	45233	**800-727-2226**	513-941-6200	378
PABCO Gypsum 37849 Cherry St	Newark	CA	94560	**800-829-1577**	510-792-1577	341
Pabst Brewing Co 121 Interpark Blvd Suite 300	San Antonio	TX	78216	**800-935-2337**	210-226-0231	103
Pabst Theater 144 E Wells St	Milwaukee	WI	53202	**800-511-1552**	414-286-3665	562
PAC Paper Inc 6416 NW Whitney Rd	Vancouver	WA	98665	**800-223-4981**	360-695-7771	544
Pac-West Telecomm Inc 4210 Coronado Ave *NASDAQ: PACW*	Stockton	CA	95204	**800-399-3389**	209-926-3300	721
Paca William House & Garden 186 Prince George St	Annapolis	MD	21401	**800-603-4020**	410-263-5553	50
Pacal LLC 2500 W County Rd B	Roseville	MN	55113	**800-328-9836**	651-631-1111	476
PACCAR Leasing Corp 777 106th Ave NE PO Box 1518	Bellevue	WA	98009	**800-426-1420**	425-468-7400	767
PACCAR Parts 750 Houser Way N	Renton	WA	98055	**800-477-0251**	425-254-4400	61
Pace American Inc 11550 Harter Dr	Middlebury	IN	46540	**800-247-5767**	574-825-7223	768
Pace Dairy Foods Co 2700 Valleyhigh Dr NW	Rochester	MN	55901	**800-533-1687**	507-288-6315	291-5
Pace International LLC 1011 Western Ave Suite 807	Seattle	WA	98104	**800-247-8711**	206-264-7599	276
Pace Prints 32 E 57th St 3rd Fl	New York	NY	10022	**877-440-7223**	212-421-3237	42
Pace Products Inc 8950 Bond St	Overland Park	KS	66214	**888-389-8203**	913-469-5588	46
Pace Resources Inc 40 S Richland Ave	York	PA	17404	**800-274-2224**	717-852-1300	258
Pace Stone Inc 663 Washington St	Eden	NC	27288	**800-789-0236**	336-623-2158	285
Pace University 1 Pace Plaza	New York	NY	10038	**866-722-3338**	212-346-1200	163
Pacer Global Logistics 6805 Perimeter Dr	Dublin	OH	43016	**800-837-7584**	614-923-1400	440
Pacer International Inc 2300 Clayton Rd Suite 1200 *NASDAQ: PACR*	Concord	CA	94520	**877-917-2237**	925-887-1400	355-3
Pacer Pumps Div ASM Industries Inc 41 Industrial Cir *Cust Svc	Lancaster	PA	17601	**[illegible]***	717-[illegible]	[illegible]
Pacer Technology 9420 Santa Anita Ave	Rancho Cucamonga	CA	91730	**800-538-3091**	909-987-0550	3
Pacesetter Steel Service Inc 3300 Town Point Dr	Kennesaw	GA	30144	**800-749-6505**	770-919-8000	483
Pacific Bag Inc 2045 120th Ave NE Suite 100	Bellevue	WA	98005	**800-562-2247**	425-455-1128	66
Pacific Beach Hotel 2490 Kalakaua Ave	Honolulu	HI	96815	**800-367-6060**	808-922-1233	373
Pacific Beverage Co 5305 Ekwill St *Cust Svc	Santa Barbara	CA	93111	**800-325-2278***	805-964-0611	82-1
Pacific Biometrics Inc 220 W Harrison St	Seattle	WA	98119	**800-767-9151**	206-298-0068	229
Pacific Building Systems 2100 N Pacific Hwy	Woodburn	OR	97071	**800-727-7844**	503-981-9581	106
Pacific Capital Bancorp 1 S Los Carneros Rd *NASDAQ: PCBC*	Goleta	CA	93117	**888-400-7228**	805-564-6300	355-2
Pacific Capital Bank 30343 Canwood St Suite 100	Agoura Hills	CA	91301	**800-272-7200**	818-865-3300	71
Pacific Cataract & Laser Institute 2517 NE Kresky Ave	Chehalis	WA	98532	**800-224-7254**	360-748-8632	785
Pacific Coast Jet Charter Inc PO Box 419074	Rancho Cordova	CA	95741	**800-655-3599**	916-631-6507	14
Pacific Combustion Engineering Co 2107 Border Ave	Torrance	CA	90501	**800-342-4442**	310-212-6300	411
Pacific Corporate & Title Services 914 S St	Sacramento	CA	95814	**800-230-4988**	916-558-4988	621
Pacific Crest Trail Assn (PCTA) 5325 Elkhorn Blvd PMB 256	Sacramento	CA	95842	**888-728-7245**	916-349-2109	48-23
Pacific Delight Tours Inc 3 Park Ave 38th Fl	New York	NY	10016	**800-221-7179**	212-818-1781	748
Pacific Detroit Diesel Allison 600 S 56th Pl	Ridgefield	WA	98642	**800-882-3860**	360-887-7400	378
Pacific Exchange 115 Samsone St 3rd Fl	San Francisco	CA	94104	**877-729-7291**	415-393-4000	680
Pacific Fibre & Rope Co Inc 903 Flint Ave Suite 27	Wilmington	CA	90748	**800-825-7673**	310-834-4567	207
Pacific Fixture Co Inc 9725 Variel Ave	Chatsworth	CA	91311	**800-272-2349**	818-727-1545	281
Pacific Grain Products International Inc PO Box 2060 *Cust Svc	Woodland	CA	95776	**800-747-0161***	530-662-5056	291-23
Pacific Grinding Wheel Co 13120 State Ave	Marysville	WA	98271	**800-688-9328**	360-659-6201	1
Pacific Handy Cutter Inc 2968 Randolph Ave *Cust Svc	Costa Mesa	CA	92626	**800-229-2233***	714-662-1033	219
Pacific Hoe Co 2700 SE Tacoma St	Portland	OR	97202	**800-547-5537**	503-234-9501	809
Pacific Indemnity Co 801 S Figueroa St 24th Fl	Los Angeles	CA	90017	**800-262-4459**	213-612-0880	384-4
Pacific Institute 1709 Harbor Ave SW	Seattle	WA	98126	**800-426-3660**	206-628-4800	753
Pacific International Rice Mills Inc PO Box 652	Woodland	CA	95776	**800-747-4764**	530-666-1691	291-23
Pacific Internet 105 W Clay St *NASDAQ: PCNTF*	Ukiah	CA	95482	**888-722-8638**	707-468-1005	795
Pacific Life Insurance Co 700 Newport Ctr Dr	Newport Beach	CA	92660	**800-347-7787**	949-219-3011	384-2
Pacific Lutheran Theological Seminary 2770 Marin Ave	Berkeley	CA	94708	**800-235-7587**	510-524-5264	164-3
Pacific Lutheran University 1010 122nd St S	Tacoma	WA	98447	**800-274-6758**	253-531-6900	163
Pacific Magtron International Corp 1600 California Cir	Milpitas	CA	95035	**800-998-2822**	408-956-8888	172
Pacific Mercantile Bancorp 949 South Coast Dr *NASDAQ: PMBC*	Costa Mesa	CA	92626	**877-450-2265**	714-438-2500	355-2
Pacific Modern Homes Inc 9723 Railroad St *Sales	Elk Grove	CA	95624	**800-395-1011***	916-685-9514	107
Pacific Mutual Holding Co 700 Newport Ctr Dr	Newport Beach	CA	92660	**800-347-7787**		355-4
Pacific Northwest Bank 275 SE Pioneer Way	Oak Harbor	WA	98277	**800-869-7114**	360-679-4181	71
Pacific Northwest National Laboratory (PNNL) 902 Battelle Blvd PO Box 999	Richland	WA	99352	**888-375-7665**	509-375-2121	654
Pacific Northwest Ticket Service 2864 77th Ave SE	Mercer Island	WA	98040	**800-281-0753**	206-232-0150	735
Pacific Northwest Title Co of Washington Inc 215 Columbia St	Seattle	WA	98104	**877-285-6423**	206-622-1040	384-6
Pacific Packaging Products Inc 24 Industrial Way	Wilmington	MA	01887	**800-777-0300**	978-657-9100	549

Name / Address	City	State	Zip	Toll-Free	Phone	Class
Pacific Palisades Hotel 1277 Robson St	Vancouver	BC	V6E1C4	**800-663-1815**	604-688-0461	372
Pacific Palms Conference Resort 1 Industry Hills Pkwy	City of Industry	CA	91744	**800-524-4557**	626-810-4455	655
Pacific Paper Tube Inc 1025 98th Ave	Oakland	CA	94603	**888-377-8823**	510-562-8823	125
Pacific Plaza Hotel 400 Spring St	Seattle	WA	98104	**800-426-1165**	206-623-3900	373
Pacific Power & Light 825 NE Multnomah St *Cust Svc	Portland	OR	97232	**888-221-7070***	503-813-5000	774
Pacific Premier Bancorp Inc 1600 Sunflower Ave 2nd Fl *NASDAQ: PPBI*	Costa Mesa	CA	92626	**888-388-5433**	714-431-4000	355-2
Pacific Press Publishing Assn 1350 N Kings Rd *Cust Svc	Nampa	ID	83687	**800-545-2449***	208-465-2500	623-9
Pacific Press Technologies 714 Walnut St	Mount Carmel	IL	62863	**800-851-3586**	618-262-8666	448
Pacific Racing Assn Inc 1100 Eastshore Hwy	Albany	CA	94706	**800-675-7001**	510-559-7300	628
Pacific Reservation Service 2520 Westlake Ave N	Seattle	WA	98109	**800-684-2932**	206-439-7677	368
Pacific Rim Mining Co 625 Howe St Suite 410 *AMEX: PMU*	Vancouver	BC	V6C2T6	**888-775-7097**	604-689-1976	492
Pacific Roller Die Co 1321 W Winton Ave	Hayward	CA	94545	**800-253-6463**	510-782-7242	448
Pacific Seafood Co PO Box 97	Clackamas	OR	97015	**800-388-1101**	503-657-1101	291-13
Pacific Service Federal Credit Union 2850 Shadelands Dr	Walnut Creek	CA	94598	**888-858-6878**	925-296-6200	216
Pacific States Felt & Mfg Co Inc 23850 Clawiter Rd	Hayward	CA	94545	**800-566-8866**	510-783-0277	321
Pacific Steel & Recycling 1401 3rd St NW	Great Falls	MT	59404	**800-889-6264**	406-727-6222	483
Pacific Sunwear of California Inc 3450 E Miraloma Ave *NASDAQ: PSUN*	Anaheim	CA	92806	**800-444-6770**	714-414-4000	155-4
Pacific Terrace Hotel 610 Diamond St	San Diego	CA	92109	**800-344-3370**	858-581-3500	373
Pacific Trail Inc 1700 Westlake Ave N Suite 200	Seattle	WA	98109	**800-877-8878**	206-270-5300	153-1
Pacific Union College 1 Angwin Ave	Angwin	CA	94508	**800-862-7080**	707-965-6311	163
Pacific Union Dental 1390 Willow Pass Rd Suite 800	Concord	CA	94520	**800-999-3367**	925-363-6000	384-3
Pacific University 2043 College Way	Forest Grove	OR	97116	**877-722-8648**	503-357-6151	163
Pacific Western University 1650 Westwood Blvd Suite 205	Los Angeles	CA	90024	**800-423-3244**	310-446-5503	163
Pacific Wings Kahului Airport Commuter Terminal 1 Kahului Airport Rd	Kahului	HI	96732	**888-575-4547**	808-873-0877	26
PacifiCare of Arizona PO Box 52078	Phoenix	AZ	85072	**800-347-8600**	602-244-8200	384-3
PacifiCare Behavioral Health Inc 3120 Lake Ctr Dr	Santa Ana	CA	92704	**800-357-5850**	714-445-0300	454
PacifiCare of California 5701 Katella Ave	Cypress	CA	90630	**800-624-8822**	714-952-1121	384-3
PacifiCare of Colorado 6455 S Yosemite St	Greenwood Village	CO	80111	**800-877-9777**	303-220-5800	384-3
PacifiCare Dental PO Box 25187	Santa Ana	CA	92704	**800-622-6388**		384-3
PacifiCare Health Systems Inc 5995 Plaza Dr *NYSE: PHS* ■ *Cust Svc	Cypress	CA	90630	**800-624-8822***	714-952-1121	384-3
PacifiCare of Nevada 700 E Warm Spring	Las Vegas	NV	89119	**800-826-4347**	702-269-7500	384-3
PacifiCare of Oklahoma 7666 E 61st St Suite 500	Tulsa	OK	74133	**800-459-8890**	918-459-1100	384-3
PacifiCare of Oregon 5 Centerpointe Dr Suite 600	Lake Oswego	OR	97035	**800-922-1444**		384-3
Pacificare of Texas 6200 NW Pkwy	San Antonio	TX	78249	**800-624-7272**	210-474-5000	384-3
PacifiCare Vision PO Box 66033	Anaheim	CA	92816	**800-622-6388**		384-3
PacifiCare of Washington 7525 SE 24th St Suite 200	Mercer Island	WA	98040	**800-829-2925**	206-236-2500	384-3
PacifiCorp 825 NE Multnomah St	Portland	OR	97232	**877-722-5001**	503-813-5000	774
Package Industries Inc 15 Harback Rd	Sutton	MA	01590	**800-225-7242**	508-865-5871	106
Package Pavement Co Inc PO Box 408	Stormville	NY	12582	**800-724-8193**	845-221-2224	46
Packaging Assn. Reusable Industrial 8401 Corporate Dr Suite 450	Landover	MD	20785	**800-533-3786**	301-577-3786	49-13
Packaging Corp of America 1900 W Field Ct *NYSE: PKG*	Lake Forest	IL	60045	**888-828-2850**	847-482-2000	101
Packaging Distribution Services Inc (PDS) 2308 Sunset Rd	Des Moines	IA	50321	**800-747-2699**	515-243-3156	549
Packaging Machinery Manufacturers Institute (PMMI) 4350 N Fairfax Dr Suite 600	Arlington	VA	22203	**800-275-7664**	703-243-8555	49-13
Packaging Professionals. Institute of 1601 N Bond St Suite 101	Naperville	IL	60563	**800-432-4085**	630-544-5050	49-13
Packaging & Shipping Specialists 5211 85th St Suite 104	Lubbock	TX	79424	**800-877-8884**		114
Packaging Store The 5675 DTC Blvd Suite 280	Greenwood Village	CO	80111	**800-525-6309**	303-741-6626	114
Packaging Systems International Inc 4990 Acoma St *Parts	Denver	CO	80216	**800-525-6110***	303-296-4445	537
Packaging Technologies 807 W Kimberly Rd *Sales	Davenport	IA	52806	**800-257-5622***	563-391-1100	537
Packard Industries Inc 1515 US 31 N *Orders	Niles	MI	49120	**800-253-0866***	269-684-2550	281
Packer Country Regional Tourism Office 1901 S Oneida St	Green Bay	WI	54304	**888-867-3342**	920-494-9507	205
Packerland Inc PO Box 247	Plainwell	MI	49080	**800-841-2961**	269-685-6886	465
Packerland Packing Co Inc PO Box 23000	Green Bay	WI	54305	**800-753-7724**	920-468-4000	465
Packeteer Inc 10201 N De Anza Blvd *NASDAQ: PKTR*	Cupertino	CA	95014	**800-697-2253**	408-873-4400	174
PacketVideo Corp 10350 Science Center Dr Suite 210	San Diego	CA	92121	**877-308-2500**	858-731-5300	222
Packing Material Co 27280 Haggerty Rd Suite C-16	Farmington Hills	MI	48331	**888-927-4797**	248-489-7000	541
Packless Industries PO Box 20668 *Cust Svc	Waco	TX	76702	**800-347-4859***	254-666-7700	15
Packless Metal Hose Inc DBA Packless Industries PO Box 20668 *Cust Svc	Waco	TX	76702	**800-347-4859***	254-666-7700	15
Paco Feed Yard Inc PO Box 956	Friona	TX	79035	**800-725-3433**	806-265-3281	11-1
PACO Pumps Inc 800 Koomey Rd	Brookshire	TX	77423	**800-926-6688**	281-934-6014	627
Pacon Corp 2525 N Casaloma Dr	Appleton	WI	54912	**800-333-2545**	920-830-5050	544
Pactiv Corp 1900 W Field Ct *NYSE: PTV*	Lake Forest	IL	60045	**888-828-2850**	847-482-2000	551
Padco Inc 2220 Elm St SE	Minneapolis	MN	55414	**800-328-5513**	612-378-7270	104
Paddock Laboratories Inc 3940 Quebec Ave N *Orders	Minneapolis	MN	55427	**800-328-5113***	763-546-4676	470
Padgett Business Services Inc 160 Hawthorne Park	Athens	GA	30606	**800-723-4388**	706-548-1040	2
PADI (Professional Assn of Diving Instructors International) 30151 Tomas St *Sales	Rancho Santa Margarita	CA	92688	**800-729-7234***	949-858-7234	48-22
PADIC Inc 1609 E Broadway	Gainesville	TX	76240	**800-679-5727**	940-665-6130	392
Padnos Louis Iron & Metal Co PO Box 1979	Holland	MI	49422	**800-442-3509**	616-396-6521	674
Paducah Newspapers Inc PO Box 2300	Paducah	KY	42002	**800-959-1771**	270-575-8600	623-8
Paducah Sun PO Box 2300	Paducah	KY	42002	**800-959-1771**	270-575-8600	522-2
Paducah Technology College 509 S 30th St	Paducah	KY	42001	**800-995-4438**	270-444-9676	787
PaeTec Communications Inc 1 PaeTec Plaza 600 Willowbrook Office Pk	Fairport	NY	14450	**877-472-3832**	585-340-2500	721
Page & Assoc Inc DBA Lifeline Program 1979 Lakeside Pkwy Suite 925	Tucker	GA	30084	**800-572-4346**	800-252-5282	783
Page Belting Co 24 Chenell Dr	Concord	NH	03301	**800-258-3654**	603-225-5523	423
Page One Bookstore 11018 Montgomery Blvd NE	Albuquerque	NM	87111	**800-521-4122**	505-294-2026	96
Paget Foundation for Paget's Disease of Bone & Related Disorders 120 Wall St Suite 1602	New York	NY	10005	**800-237-2438**	212-509-5335	48-17
Pagoda Hotel 1525 Rycroft St	Honolulu	HI	96814	**800-367-6060**	808-941-6611	373
Paige Electric Corp 1160 Springfield Rd	Union	NJ	07083	**800-327-2443**	908-687-7810	245
Pain Assn. American Chronic PO Box 850	Rocklin	CA	95677	**800-533-3231**	916-632-0922	48-17
Pain.com Dannemiller Memorial Educational Foundation 5711 NW Parkway Suite 100	San Antonio	TX	78249	**800-328-2308**	210-641-8311	351
Paine College 1235 15th St	Augusta	GA	30901	**800-476-7703**	706-821-8200	163
Paint & Decorating Retailers Assn (PDRA) 403 Axminister Dr	Fenton	MO	63026	**800-737-0107**	636-326-2636	49-18
Painted Buffalo Inn 400 W Broadway	Jackson	WY	83001	**800-288-3866**	307-733-4340	373
Painter Bus Lines Inc 1 N Main St	Del Rio	TX	78840	**800-256-2757**	830-775-7515	108
Painting & Decorating Contractors of America (PDCA) 11960 Westline Industrial Dr Suite 201	Saint Louis	MO	63146	**800-332-7322**	314-514-7322	49-3
Paisano Publications 28210 Dorothy Dr	Agoura Hills	CA	91301	**800-247-6246**	818-889-8740	623-9
Pajaro Valley Greenhouses Inc 214 Lewis Rd *Cust Svc	Watsonville	CA	95077	**800-538-5922***	831-722-2773	363
Pak Mail Centers of America Inc 7173 S Havana St Suite 600	Englewood	CO	80112	**800-778-6665**	303-957-1000	114
Pakistan International Airlines Corp 505 8th Ave 14th Fl	New York	NY	10018	**800-221-2552**	212-760-8484	26
PAL (National Assn of Police Athletic Leagues) 618 US Hwy 1 Suite 201	North Palm Beach	FL	33408	**800-725-7743**	561-844-1823	48-22
Pala Casino Resort & Spa 11154 Hwy 76 PO Box 40	Pala	CA	92059	**877-946-7252**	760-510-5100	655
Pala Mesa Resort 2001 Old Hwy 395	Fallbrook	CA	92028	**800-722-4700**	760-728-5881	655
Palace Hotel 2 New Montgomery St	San Francisco	CA	94105	**800-325-3535**	415-512-1111	373
Palace Resort & Spa in the Walt Disney World Resort. Wyndham 1900 Buena Vista Dr	Lake Buena Vista	FL	32830	**800-996-3426**	407-827-2727	655
Palace Station Hotel & Casino 2411 W Sahara Ave	Las Vegas	NV	89102	**800-634-3101**	702-367-2411	133
Palace Theater 1420 Celebrity Cir Broadway at the Beach	Myrtle Beach	SC	29577	**800-905-4228**	843-448-9224	562
Palace Theatre 1564 Broadway	New York	NY	10036	**800-755-4000**	212-307-4100	732
Palace Theatre & Saloon Airport Way & Peger Rd	Fairbanks	AK	99709	**800-354-7274**	907-452-7274	562
Paladin Data Systems Corp 19362 Powder Hill Pl NE	Poulsbo	WA	98370	**800-532-8448**	360-779-2400	175
Palais des Congres de Montreal-Convention Centre 159 rue Saint-Antoine O 9e étage	Montreal	QC	H2Z1H2	**800-268-8122**	514-871-8122	204
Palais Royal 10201 S Main St	Houston	TX	77025	**800-324-3244**	713-667-5601	155-2
Palatka Daily News 1825 St Johns Ave	Palatka	FL	32178	**800-881-7355**	386-328-2721	522-2
Palisade Corp 31 Decker Rd	Newfield	NY	14867	**800-432-7475**	607-277-8000	176-1
Pall Corp 2200 Northern Blvd *NYSE: PLL*	East Hills	NY	11548	**800-645-6532**	516-484-5400	379
Pall Life Sciences Inc 600 S Wagner Rd	Ann Arbor	MI	48103	**800-521-1520**	734-665-0651	410
Pallet Masters Inc 655 E Florence Ave	Los Angeles	CA	90001	**800-675-2571**	323-758-6559	541
PalletOne Inc 1470 US Hwy 17 S	Bartow	FL	33831	**800-771-1148**	863-533-1147	541

Name / Address	City	State	ZIP	Toll-Free	Phone	Class
Palliative Care Organization. National Hospice & 1700 Diagonal Rd Suite 625 *Help Line	Alexandria	VA	22314	**800-658-8898***	703-837-1500	49-8
Palm Beach Atlantic University PO Box 24708	West Palm Beach	FL	33416	**888-468-6722**	561-803-2000	163
Palm Beach Casino Line 1 E 11th St Suite 500	Riviera Beach	FL	33404	**800-841-7447**	561-845-2101	133
Palm Beach Co 2020 Elmwood Ave	Buffalo	NY	14207	**800-543-1919**	716-874-5000	153-12
Palm Beach Community College *Central Campus* 4200 Congress Ave	Lake Worth	FL	33461	**866-576-7222**	561-868-3350	160
Palm Beach Gardens Campus 3160 PGA Blvd	Palm Beach Gardens	FL	33410	**866-576-7222**	561-207-5300	160
Palm Beach County Convention Center 650 Okeechobee Blvd	West Palm Beach	FL	33401	**800-833-5733**	561-366-3019	204
Palm Beach County Convention & Visitors Bureau 1555 Palm Beach Lakes Blvd Suite 800	West Palm Beach	FL	33401	**800-833-5733**	561-471-3995	205
Palm Beach Daily Business Review 324 Datura St Suite 140	West Palm Beach	FL	33401	**800-777-7300**	561-820-2060	449-5
Palm Beach Illustrated Magazine 1000 N Dixie Hwy Suite C	West Palm Beach	FL	33401	**800-308-7346**	561-659-0210	449-22
Palm Beach Newspapers Inc PO Box 24700	West Palm Beach	FL	33416	**800-432-7597**	561-820-4100	623-8
Palm Beach Post 2751 S Dixie Hwy	West Palm Beach	FL	33405	**800-432-7595**	561-820-4100	522-2
Palm Management Corp 1730 Rhode Island Ave NW Suite 900	Washington	DC	20036	**800-388-7256**	202-775-7256	656
Palm Mortuary Inc 1325 N Main St	Las Vegas	NV	89101	**800-542-2902**	702-464-8300	499
Palm Mountain Resort & Spa 155 S Belardo Rd	Palm Springs	CA	92262	**800-622-9451**	760-325-1301	373
Palm Mountain Resort & Spa. 155 S Belardo Rd	Palm Springs	CA	92262	**800-622-9451**	760-325-1301	373
Palm Plaza Oceanfront Resort 3301 S Atlantic Ave	Daytona Beach Shores	FL	32118	**800-329-8662**	386-767-1711	373
Palm Press Inc 1442A Walnut St PMB 120	Berkeley	CA	94709	**800-322-7256**	510-486-0502	130
Palm Restaurant 1730 Rhode Island Ave NW Suite 900	Washington	DC	20036	**800-795-7256**	202-775-7256	657
Palm Springs Air Museum 745 N Gene Autry Trail	Palm Springs	CA	92262	**800-562-2604**	760-778-6262	509
Palm Springs Convention Center 277 N Avenida Caballeros	Palm Springs	CA	92262	**800-333-7535**	760-325-6611	204
Palm Springs Desert Resorts Convention & Visitors Authority 70-100 Hwy 111	Rancho Mirage	CA	92270	**800-967-3767**	760-770-9000	205
Palm Springs Disposal Co 4690 E Mesquite Ave	Palm Springs	CA	92264	**800-973-3873**	760-327-1351	791
Palm Springs Riviera Resort & Racket Club 1600 N Indian Canyon Dr	Palm Springs	CA	92262	**800-444-8311**	760-327-8311	655
Palmer Asphalt Co Inc PO Box 58	Bayonne	NJ	07002	**800-352-9898**	201-339-0855	46
Palmer Candy Co 311 Bluff St	Sioux City	IA	51103	**800-831-0828**	712-258-5543	291-8
Palmer & Cay Inc 25 Bull St	Savannah	GA	31401	**800-755-9594**	912-234-6621	383
Palmer-Donavin Mfg Co 1200 Steelwood Rd	Columbus	OH	43212	**800-589-4412**	614-486-9657	190-3
Palmer Holland Inc 25000 Country Club Blvd Suite 400	North Olmsted	OH	44070	**800-635-4822**	440-686-2300	144
Palmer House Hilton 17 E Monroe St	Chicago	IL	60603	**800-445-8667**	312-726-7500	373
Palmer Investigative Services 624 W Gurley St Suite A	Prescott	AZ	86305	**800-280-2951**	928-778-2951	392
Palmer Moving & Storage Co 24660 Dequindre Rd	Warren	MI	48091	**800-521-3954**	586-834-3400	508
Palmetto Brick Co 3501 Brickyard Rd	Wallace	SC	29596	**800-922-4423**	843-537-7861	148
Palmetto Dunes Resort 4 Queen Folly Rd	Hilton Head Island	SC	29938	**800-845-6130**	843-785-1161	655
Palmetto Electric Co-op 4063 Grays Hwy PO Box 820	Ridgeland	SC	29936	**800-922-5551**	843-726-5551	244
Palmetto General Hospital 2001 W 68th St	Hialeah	FL	33016	**888-222-2020**	305-823-5000	366-2
Palmetto Health Home Care & Hospice 1400 Pickens St	Columbia	SC	29202	**800-238-1884**	803-296-3100	365
Palmetto Optical 1727 Laurel St	Columbia	SC	29201	**800-845-2231**	803-799-8168	533
palmOne Inc 400 N McCarthy Blvd *NASDAQ: PLMO*	Milpitas	CA	95035	**800-881-7256**	408-503-7000	171-2
Palms The 3025 Collins Ave	Miami Beach	FL	33140	**800-550-0505**	305-534-0505	373
Palms at Palm Springs 572 N Indian Canyon Dr	Palm Springs	CA	92262	**800-753-7256**	760-325-1111	697
Palms Resort 2500 N Ocean Blvd	Myrtle Beach	SC	29578	**800-528-0451**	843-626-8334	655
Palms West Chamber of Commerce PO Box 1062	Loxahatchee	FL	33470	**800-790-2364**	561-790-6200	137
Palms West Hospital 13001 Southern Blvd	Loxahatchee	FL	33470	**866-857-3936**	561-798-3300	366-2
Palmyra Bologna Co Inc DBA Seltzer's Smokehouse Meats PO Box 111	Palmyra	PA	17078	**800-282-6336**	717-838-6336	291-26
Palo Duro Meat PO Box 31117	Amarillo	TX	79120	**800-625-4785**	806-372-5781	465
Palomar Medical Technologies Inc 82 Cambridge St *NASDAQ: PMTI*	Burlington	MA	01803	**800-725-6627**	781-993-2300	415
Palomar Pomerado Health System 15615 Pomerado Rd	Poway	CA	92064	**800-628-2880**	858-613-4000	348
Palomar Technologies Inc 2230 Oak Ridge Way	Vista	CA	92083	**800-854-3467**	760-931-3600	798
Palos Verdes Inn 1700 S Pacific Coast Hwy	Redondo Beach	CA	90277	**800-421-9241**	310-316-4211	373
Paltier Div Lyon Metal Products Inc 1701 Kentucky St	Michigan City	IN	46360	**800-348-3201**	219-872-7238	462
Pam Cos 200 S Petro Ave	Sioux Falls	SD	57107	**800-456-2660**	605-336-1788	61
PAM Transportation Services Inc PO Box 188 *NASDAQ: PTSI*	Tontitown	AR	72770	**800-879-7261**	479-361-9111	769
PAMA (Professional Aviation Maintenance Assn) 717 Princess St	Alexandria	VA	22314	**866-865-7262**	703-683-3171	49-21
Pamarco Global Graphics 209 E 11th Ave	Roselle	NJ	07203	**800-526-2180**	908-665-8500	617
Pampa Regional Medical Center 1 Medical Plaza	Pampa	TX	79065	**800-896-3684**	806-665-3721	366-2
Pampered Chef Ltd 1 Pampered Chef Ln	Addison	IL	60101	**800-266-5562**	630-261-8900	361
Pamplin Communications Corp 10209 SE Division St	Portland	OR	97266	**866-233-7102**	503-251-1597	629
Pamrapo Bancorp Inc 611 Ave C PO Box 98 *NASDAQ: PBCI*	Bayonne	NJ	07002	**800-680-6872**	201-339-4600	355-2
Pan Abode Cedar Homes Inc 4350 Lake Washington Blvd N	Renton	WA	98056	**800-782-2633**	425-255-8260	107
Pan-American Life Insurance Co 601 Poydras St *Life Ins	New Orleans	LA	70130	**800-999-0514***	504-566-1300	384-2
Pan American Screw Inc 630 Reese Dr SW	Conover	NC	28613	**800-951-2222**	828-466-0060	274
Pan-O-Gold Baking Co 44 E Saint Germain St	Saint Cloud	MN	56304	**800-444-7005**	320-251-9361	291-1
Pan-Osten Co 6944 Louisville Rd	Bowling Green	KY	42101	**800-472-6678**	270-783-3900	281
Pan Pacific Hotels & Resorts 500 Post St	San Francisco	CA	94102	**800-327-8585**	415-732-7747	369
Pan Pacific Lodge Whistler 4320 Sundial Crescent	Whistler	BC	V0N1B4	**888-905-9995**	604-905-2999	655
Pan Pacific Retail Properties Inc 1631-B S Melrose Dr *NYSE: PNP*	Vista	CA	92081	**800-776-1002**	760-727-1002	641
Panalarm Div AMETEK Power Instruments 1725 Western Dr	West Chicago	IL	60185	**800-213-9568**	630-231-5900	200
Panalaytical 12 Michigan Dr	Natick	MA	01760	**800-279-7297**	508-647-1100	410
Panalpina Inc 1776 On-the-Green 67 E Park Pl	Morristown	NJ	07960	**866-202-0377**	973-683-9000	440
Panama City Beach Convention & Visitors Bureau 17001 Panama City Beach Pkwy	Panama City Beach	FL	32413	**800-722-3224**	850-233-5070	205
Panasonic Computer Solutions Co 1 Panasonic Way	Secaucus	NJ	07094	**800-662-3537**	201-348-7000	171-3
Panasonic Consumer Electronics Co 1 Panasonic Way	Secaucus	NJ	07094	**888-275-2595**	201-348-7000	52
Panavision Inc 6219 DeSoto Ave	Woodland Hills	CA	91367	**800-367-7262**	818-316-1000	580
Panbio Inc 9075 Guilford Rd	Columbia	MD	21046	**800-962-6790**	410-381-8550	229
Panchero's Mexican Grill 2475 Coral Ct Suite B	Coraville	IA	52241	**888-639-2378**	319-545-6565	657
Pancho's Mexican Buffet Inc 3500 Noble Ave	Fort Worth	TX	76111	**800-433-7670**	817-831-0081	657
Panda Express 1683 Walnut Grove Ave	Rosemead	CA	91770	**800-487-2632**	626-799-9898	657
Panda Inn 1683 Walnut Grove Ave	Rosemead	CA	91770	**800-487-2632**	626-799-9898	657
Panda Restaurant Group 1683 Walnut Grove Ave	Rosemead	CA	91770	**800-877-8988**	626-799-9898	656
Pandjiris Inc 5151 Northrup Ave	Saint Louis	MO	63110	**800-237-2006**	314-776-6893	798
Panduit Corp 17301 S Ridgeland Ave	Tinley Park	IL	60477	**888-506-5400**	708-532-1800	803
Panel Prints Inc 1001 Moosic Rd	Old Forge	PA	18518	**800-557-2635**	570-457-8334	615
Panel Processing Inc 120 N Industrial Hwy	Alpena	MI	49707	**800-433-7142**	989-356-9007	807
Panera Bread Co 6710 Clayton Rd *NASDAQ: PNRA*	Richmond Heights	MO	63117	**800-301-5566**	314-633-7100	69
Panhandle Co-op Assn 401 S Beltline Hwy W *Cust Svc	Scottsbluff	NE	69363	**800-732-4546***	308-632-5301	272
Panhandle Telecommunication Systems Inc 2224 NW Hwy 64	Guymon	OK	73942	**800-327-7525**	580-338-7525	721
Pannier Corp 207 Sandusky St	Pittsburgh	PA	15212	**800-233-2009**	412-323-4900	485
Pannier Graphics 345 Oak Rd	Gibsonia	PA	15044	**800-544-8428**	724-265-4900	692
Pannikin Coffee & Tea 675 G St	San Diego	CA	92101	**800-232-6482**	619-239-7891	156
Panola-Harrison Electric Co-op 410 E Houston St	Marshall	TX	75670	**800-972-1093**	903-935-7936	244
Panola Partnership Inc 150-A Public Sq	Batesville	MS	38606	**888-872-6652**	662-563-3126	137
Panolam Industries International Inc 20 Progress Dr	Shelton	CT	06484	**800-672-6652**	203-925-1556	807
Panorama Balloon Tours PO Box 218	Del Mar	CA	92014	**800-455-3592**	760-271-3467	748
Panorama Flight Service Inc 67 Tower Rd	White Plains	NY	10604	**888-359-7266**	914-328-9800	63
Panoramic Inc 1500 N Parker Dr	Janesville	WI	53545	**800-333-1394**	608-754-8850	102
Pantages Theater 901 Broadway	Tacoma	WA	98402	**800-291-7593**	253-591-5890	562
Pantagraph PO Box 2907	Bloomington	IL	61702	**800-747-7323**	309-829-9411	522-2
Panther Industries Inc 600 N Beach St	Fort Worth	TX	76111	**800-433-7664**	817-834-7164	149
Pantry Inc 1801 Douglas Dr *NASDAQ: PTRY*	Sanford	NC	27330	**800-476-7574**	919-774-6700	203
Panzer Nursery Inc 17980 SW Baseline Rd	Beaverton	OR	97006	**888-212-5327**	503-645-1185	363
Paoli Inc 201 E Martin St	Orleans	IN	47452	**800-457-7415**	812-723-2791	314-1
Papa Gino's Inc 600 Providence Hwy	Dedham	MA	02026	**800-727-2446**	781-461-1200	657
Papa John's International Inc 2002 Papa John's Blvd *NASDAQ: PZZA*	Louisville	KY	40299	**877-547-7272**	502-261-7272	657
Papa Razzi 284 Newbury St	Boston	MA	02115	**800-424-2753**	617-536-2800	657
Paper Assn. American Forest & 1111 19th St NW Suite 800	Washington	DC	20036	**800-878-8878**	202-463-2700	48-2
Paper Bag Players 225 W 99th St	New York	NY	10025	**800-777-2247**	212-663-0390	563-4
Paper Conversions Inc 6761 Thompson Rd N	Syracuse	NY	13211	**800-729-2823**	315-437-1641	542-3
Paper Industry. Technical Assn of the Pulp & 15 Technology Pkwy S *Sales	Norcross	GA	30092	**800-332-8686***	770-446-1400	49-13
Paper Magic Group Inc 401 Adams Ave Suite 501 *Cust Svc	Scranton	PA	18510	**800-258-1044***	570-961-3863	130

Name / Address	City	State	ZIP	Toll-Free	Phone	Class
Paper Magic Group Inc Eureka School Div 401 Adams Ave *Cust Svc	Scranton	PA	18510	**800-258-1044***	570-961-3863	242
Paper-Pak Products Inc 545 Terrace Dr	San Dimas	CA	91773	**800-635-4560**	909-971-5000	548-2
Paper Prince 2001 Kennedy St NE	Minneapolis	MN	55413	**800-717-1574**	612-378-4691	130
Paper Products Co Inc 36 Terminal Way	Pittsburgh	PA	15219	**800-837-2702**	412-481-6200	549
Paper Science & Technology. Institute of 500 10th St NW	Atlanta	GA	30332	**800-558-6611**	404-894-5700	49-13
Paper Systems Inc 185 S Pioneer Blvd	Springboro	OH	45066	**888-564-6774**	937-746-6841	544
Paper Tigers Inc 2121 Waukegan Rd Suite 130	Bannockburn	IL	60015	**800-621-1774**	847-919-6500	646
Paperclip Software Inc 611 US Rte 46	Hasbrouck Heights	NJ	07604	**800-929-3503**	201-329-6300	176-1
Papercon Inc 2700 Apple Valley Rd NE	Atlanta	GA	30319	**800-241-0619**	404-261-7205	538
Papercone Corp 3200 Fern Valley Rd	Louisville	KY	40213	**800-626-5308**	502-961-9493	260
PaperDirect Inc 1005 E Woodmen Rd	Colorado Springs	CO	80920	**800-272-7377**	719-594-4100	543
Paperdoll Co 4944 Encino Ave	Encino	CA	91316	**866-223-1145**	818-906-8411	130
PaperTroupe Ltd 2975 W Soffel Ave	Melrose Park	IL	60160	**888-338-9244**	708-338-3838	130
Pappadeaux Seafood Kitchen 642 Yale St	Houston	TX	77007	**877-277-2748**	713-869-0151	657
Pappas Clement & Co Inc 1045 N Parsonage Rd	Seabrook	NJ	08302	**800-257-7019**	856-455-1000	291-20
Pappas Restaurants Inc 642 Yale St	Houston	TX	77007	**877-277-2748**	713-869-0151	657
Pappas Seafood House 642 Yale St	Houston	TX	77077	**877-277-2748**	713-869-0151	657
Pappasito's Cantina 642 Yale St	Houston	TX	77007	**877-277-2748**	713-869-0151	657
Pappy's Golf Shop 4030 N Sinton Rd	Colorado Springs	CO	80907	**800-530-2345**	719-633-2064	701
Papyrus Franchise Corp 500 Chadbourne Rd	Fairfield	CA	94533	**800-333-6724**	707-425-8006	129
Par-A-Dice Hotel 7 Blackjack Blvd	East Peoria	IL	61611	**800-727-2342**	309-699-7711	373
Par-A-Dice Riverboat Casino 21 Blackjack Blvd	East Peoria	IL	61611	**800-727-2342**	309-698-7711	133
Par Pharmaceutical Inc 1 Ram Ridge Rd	Spring Valley	NY	10977	**800-828-9393**	845-425-7100	573
PAR Technology Corp 8383 Seneca Tpke *NYSE: PTC*	New Hartford	NY	13413	**800-448-6505**	315-738-0600	603
Par-Way Tryson Co 107 Bolte Ln	Saint Clair	MO	63077	**800-844-4554**	636-629-4545	291-30
Para-Chem Southern Inc PO Box 127	Simpsonville	SC	29681	**800-763-7272**	864-967-7691	3
Para Laboratories Inc 100 Rose Ave	Hempstead	NY	11550	**800-645-3752**	516-538-4600	211
Para Systems Inc 1455 LeMay Dr	Carrollton	TX	75007	**800-238-7272**	972-446-7363	252
Parable Christian Stores 3563 Empleo St	San Luis Obispo	CA	93401	**888-644-0500**	805-543-2644	96
Parachute Assn. US 1440 Duke St	Alexandria	VA	22314	**800-371-8772**	703-836-3495	48-22
Paradigm Health Corp 1001 Galaxy Way Suite 300	Concord	CA	94520	**800-676-6777**	925-676-2300	455
Paradigm Medical Industries Inc 2355 S 1070 West	Salt Lake City	UT	84119	**800-742-0671**	801-977-8970	534
Paradise Chamber of Commerce 5550 Sky Way Suite 1	Paradise	CA	95969	**888-845-2769**	530-877-9356	137
Paradise Inc PO Drawer Y	Plant City	FL	33564	**800-330-8952**	813-752-1155	291-8
Paradise Inn 819 Simonton St	Key West	FL	33040	**800-888-9648**	305-293-8007	373
Paradise Island Vacations 1000 S Pine Island Rd Suite 800	Plantation	FL	33324	**800-722-7466**	954-809-2000	760
Paradise Point Resort & Spa 1404 W Vacation Rd	San Diego	CA	92109	**800-344-2626**	858-274-4630	655
Paradise Post PO Drawer 70	Paradise	CA	95967	**800-924-0908**	530-877-4413	522-4
Paradise Valley Resort. Doubletree 5401 N Scottsdale Rd	Scottsdale	AZ	85250	**800-222-8733**	480-947-5400	655
Paradyne Networks Inc 8545 126th Ave N *NASDAQ: PDYN* ■ *Cust Svc	Largo	FL	33773	**800-805-9493***	727-530-2000	720
Paragon Air Kahului Airport Commuter Airline Terminal PO Box 575	Kahului	HI	96733	**800-428-1231**	808-244-3356	14
Paragon Casino Resort 711 Paragon Pl	Marksville	LA	71351	**800-946-1946**	318-253-1946	133
Paragon Computer Professionals Inc 25 Commerce Dr 2nd Fl	Cranford	NJ	07016	**800-462-5582**	908-709-6767	178
Paragon Engineering Services Inc 10777 Clay Rd	Houston	TX	77041	**800-324-7272**	713-570-1000	258
Paragon Imaging Inc 400 W Cummings Pk Suite 2050	Woburn	MA	01801	**800-937-6881**	781-937-9800	176-8
Paragon Industries Inc 2011 South Town E Blvd	Mesquite	TX	75149	**800-876-4328**	972-288-7557	313
Paragon Investments 9941 NW Hwy 24 Suite 3	Silver Lake	KS	66539	**888-452-8751**		167
Paragon Laboratories 20433 Earl St	Torrance	CA	90503	**800-228-6965**	310-370-1563	786
Paragon Life Insurance Co 190 Carondelet Plaza	Saint Louis	MO	63105	**800-685-0124**		384-2
Paragon Packaging Inc 49-B Sherwood Terr	Lake Bluff	IL	60044	**888-615-0065**	847-615-0065	102
Paragon Tours 25 Market St	Swansea	MA	02777	**800-999-5050**	508-379-1976	748
Parallax Inc 599 Menlo Dr Suite 100	Rocklin	CA	95765	**888-512-1024**	916-624-8333	613
Parallel Petroleum Corp 1004 N Big Spring St Suite 400 *NASDAQ: PLLL*	Midland	TX	79701	**800-299-3727**	432-684-3727	525
Paralysis Foundation. Christopher Reeve 500 Morris Ave	Springfield	NJ	07081	**800-225-0292**	973-379-2690	48-17
Paralyzed Veterans of America (PVA) 801 18th St NW	Washington	DC	20006	**800-424-8200**	202-872-1300	48-19
Paramount Apparel International Inc 1 Paramount Dr PO Box 98	Bourbon	MO	65441	**800-255-4287**	573-732-4411	153-9
Paramount Cards Inc 400 Pine St	Pawtucket	RI	02860	**800-554-5017**	401-726-0800	130
Paramount Coffee Co 130 N Larch Ave	Lansing	MI	48912	**800-968-1222**	517-372-5500	292-2
Paramount Cosmetics Inc 93 Entin Rd Suite 4	Clifton	NJ	07014	**800-522-9880**	973-472-2323	211
Paramount Distillers Inc 3116 Berea Rd	Cleveland	OH	44111	**800-821-2989**	216-671-6300	81-1
Paramount Export Co 175 Filbert St Suite 201	Oakland	CA	94607	**800-869-0150**	510-839-0150	292-7
Paramount Fitness Corp 6450 E Bandini Blvd	Los Angeles	CA	90040	**800-721-2121**	323-721-2121	263
Paramount Health Care PO Box 928	Toledo	OH	43697	**800-462-3589**	419-887-2525	384-3
Paramount Industrial Cos Inc 1112 Kingwood Ave	Norfolk	VA	23502	**800-777-5337**	757-855-3321	463
Paramount Industries Inc 304 N Howard St	Croswell	MI	48422	**800-521-5405**	810-679-2551	431
Paramount Paper Ltd 953 Alma Rd *Cust Svc	Maxton	NC	28364	**800-727-9444***	910-844-5293	538
Paramount Ready Mix Concrete Inc 13949 E Stage Rd PO Box 2823	Santa Fe Springs	CA	90670	**888-404-4125**	562-404-4125	180
Paramount Sales Co Inc 10140 Gallows Point Dr *Cust Svc	Knoxville	TN	37931	**800-251-9183***	865-470-9977	403
Paramount Technologies Inc 2075 E West Maple Rd Suite B-203	Commerce Township	MI	48390	**800-725-4408**	248-960-0909	39
Paramount's Carowinds 14523 Carowinds Blvd	Charlotte	NC	28273	**800-888-4386**	704-588-2606	32
Paramount's Kings Island 6300 Kings Island Dr	Kings Island	OH	45034	**800-288-0808**	513-754-5700	32
Parasec Inc 640 Bercut Dr Suite A	Sacramento	CA	95814	**800-533-7272**	916-441-1001	621
Parcel Plus Inc 12715 Telge Rd	Cypress	TX	77429	**888-662-5553**	281-256-4100	114
Parco Foods LLC 2200 W 138th St	Blue Island	IL	60406	**888-371-9200**	708-371-9200	291-1
Parco-Hesse Corp 1060 Andre-Line Rd	Granby	QC	J2J1J9	**800-363-5975**	450-378-4696	768
Parent Assn. National Foster 7512 Stanich Ave Suite 6	Gig Harbor	WA	98335	**800-557-5238**	253-853-4000	48-6
Parenteral & Enteral Nutrition. American Society for 8630 Fenton St Suite 412	Silver Spring	MD	20910	**800-727-4567**	301-587-6315	49-8
Parenthood Federation of America. Planned 434 W 33rd St	New York	NY	10001	**800-829-7732**	212-541-7800	48-6
Parenting Magazine 530 5th Ave 4th Fl *Circ	New York	NY	10036	**800-234-0847***	212-522-8989	449-11
Parents of America. College 8300 Boone Blvd Suite 500	Vienna	VA	22182	**888-256-4627**	703-761-6702	48-11
Parents of Children Who Are Deaf or Hard of Hearing Inc. BEGINNINGS for 3714 A Benson Dr	Raleigh	NC	27619	**800-541-4327**	919-850-2746	48-17
Parents of Children with Visual Impairments. National Assn for PO Box 317	Watertown	MA	02471	**800-562-6265**	617-972-7441	48-17
Parents Magazine 375 Lexington Ave 10th Fl	New York	NY	10017	**800-727-3682**	212-499-2000	449-11
Parents of Murdered Children (POMC) 100 E 8th St Suite B-41	Cincinnati	OH	45202	**888-818-7662**	513-721-5683	48-6
Parents & Teachers. National Congress of 541 N Fairbanks Ct Suite 1300	Chicago	IL	60611	**800-307-4782**	312-670-6782	48-11
Parents Without Partners (PWP) 1650 S Dixie Hwy Suite 510	Boca Raton	FL	33432	**800-637-7974**	561-391-8833	48-6
ParentWatch Inc 49 W 37th St 14th Fl	New York	NY	10018	**800-696-2664**	212-869-8282	145
PAREXEL International Corp 195 West St *NASDAQ: PRXL*	Waltham	MA	02451	**800-727-3935**	781-487-9900	654
Parfums de Coeur Ltd 85 Old Kings Hwy N	Darien	CT	06820	**800-887-2738**	203-655-8807	564
Parfums Givenchy Inc 19 E 57th St	New York	NY	10022	**800-479-6427**	212-931-2600	564
Paris Accessories Inc 350 5th Ave 70th Fl	New York	NY	10118	**800-223-7557**	212-868-0500	153-13
Paris Business Products 122 Kissel Rd *Cust Svc	Burlington	NJ	08016	**800-523-6454***	609-387-7300	111
Paris Co Inc 822 Main St	Oxford	ME	04271	**800-678-5112**	207-539-8221	750
Paris Convention & Visitors Bureau 1125 Bonham St	Paris	TX	75460	**800-727-4789**	903-784-2501	205
Paris Daily Beacon News PO Box 100	Paris	IL	61944	**800-587-5955**	217-465-6424	522-2
Paris-Henry County Chamber of Commerce 2508 Eastwood St	Paris	TN	38242	**800-345-1103**	731-642-3431	137
Paris Junior College 2400 Clarksville St	Paris	TX	75460	**800-232-5804**	903-785-7661	160
Paris Lace Inc 1500 Main Ave	Clifton	NJ	07011	**800-533-5223**	973-478-9035	730-4
Paris Las Vegas 3655 Las Vegas Blvd S	Las Vegas	NV	89109	**888-266-5687**	702-946-7000	373
Paris Mountain State Park 2401 State Park Rd	Greenville	SC	29609	**866-345-7275**	864-244-5565	554
Paris News PO Box 1078	Paris	TX	75461	**800-683-1929**	903-785-8744	522-2
Parish International Inc PO Box 468	Hempstead	TX	77445	**877-496-8378**	979-826-8222	474
Parish Publications Inc 6503 19 1/2 Mile Rd	Sterling Heights	MI	48314	**800-521-4486**	586-997-4241	623-10
Park Air Express 18931 Snow Rd	Cleveland	OH	44142	**800-522-0750**	216-362-7275	552
Park Assn. National Recreation & 22377 Belmont Ridge Rd	Ashburn	VA	20148	**800-626-6772**	703-858-0784	48-23
Park Bancorp Inc 5400 S Pulaski Rd *NASDAQ: PFED*	Chicago	IL	60632	**888-727-5333**	773-582-8616	355-2
Park Central The 640 Ocean Dr	Miami Beach	FL	33139	**800-727-5236**	305-538-1611	373
Park Central Hotel 1010 Houston St	Fort Worth	TX	76102	**800-848-7275**	817-336-2011	373
Park Central New York 870 7th Ave	New York	NY	10019	**800-346-1359**	212-247-8000	373
Park City Chamber of Commerce/Convention & Visitors Bureau 1910 Prospector Ave Suite 103	Park City	UT	84060	**800-453-1360**	435-649-6100	205
Park City Mountain Resort 1310 Lowell Ave PO Box 39	Park City	UT	84060	**800-222-7275**	435-649-8111	655
Park Construction Co Inc 500 73rd St NE Suite 123	Minneapolis	MN	55432	**800-328-2556**	763-786-9800	188-5
Park County Travel Council 836 Sheridan Ave	Cody	WY	82414	**800-393-2639**	307-587-2297	205
Park East Hotel 916 E State St	Milwaukee	WI	53202	**800-328-7275**	414-276-8800	373
Park Electric Co-op Inc 5706 US Hwy 89 S PO Box 1119	Livingston	MT	59047	**888-298-0657**	406-222-3100	244
Park Entrance Oceanfront Motel RR2 Box 180B 15 Ocean Dr	Bar Harbor	ME	04609	**800-288-9703**	207-288-9703	373
Park Farms Inc 1925 30th St NE	Canton	OH	44705	**800-683-6511**	330-455-0241	608
Park To Fly Inc 7855 N Frontage Rd	Orlando	FL	32812	**888-851-8875**	407-851-8044	552

Name / Address	City	State	ZIP	Toll-Free	Phone	Class
Park Hotel 2200 Rexford Rd	Charlotte	NC	28211	**800-334-0331**	704-364-8220	373
Park Hyatt Beaver Creek Resort & Spa 136 E Thomas Pl	Beaver Creek	CO	81620	**800-233-1234**	970-949-1234	655
Park Hyatt Hotels 71 S Walker Dr	Chicago	IL	60606	**800-233-1234**	312-750-1234	369
Park Industries Inc 6600 Saukview Dr	Saint Cloud	MN	56303	**800-328-2309**	320-251-5077	379
Park Inn PO Box 59159	Minneapolis	MN	55459	**800-670-7275***	763-212-1000	369
*Resv						
Park International Corp 1401 Freeman Ave PO Box 4189	Long Beach	CA	90804	**800-624-9118**	562-494-7002	92
Park Lane Classic Residence by Hyatt 200 Glenwood Cir	Monterey	CA	93940	**800-782-5730**	831-373-6126	659
Park Lane Hotel at Four Seasons 3005 High Point Rd	Greensboro	NC	27403	**800-942-6556**	336-294-4565	373
Park Lane Hotel. Helmsley 36 Central Park S	New York	NY	10019	**800-221-4982**	212-371-4000	373
Park Lane Hotels International 55 Cyril Magnin St	San Francisco	CA	94102	**800-650-7272**	415-398-4491	369
Park 'N Fly 2060 Mt Paran Rd Suite 207	Atlanta	GA	30327	**800-325-4863**	404-264-1000	552
Park National Corp 50 N 3rd St	Newark	OH	43055	**800-762-2616**	740-349-8451	355-2
AMEX: PRK						
Park Plaza Hotel Oakland 150 Hegenberger Rd	Oakland	CA	94621	**800-635-5301**	510-635-5300	373
Park & Recreation Educators. Society of c/o National Recreation & Park Assn 22377 Belmont Ridge Rd	Ashburn	VA	20148	**800-626-6772**	703-858-0784	48-23
Park & Recreation Society. American c/o National Recreation & Park Assn 22377 Belmont Ridge Rd	Ashburn	VA	20148	**800-626-6772**	703-858-4741	48-23
Park Resources. National Society for c/o National Recreation & Park Assn 22377 Belmont Ridge Rd	Ashburn	VA	20148	**800-626-6772**	703-858-0784	48-23
Park Seed Co 1 Parkton Ave	Greenwood	SC	29647	**800-845-3369***	864-223-8555	684
*Orders						
Park Shore Resort 600 Neapolitan Way	Naples	FL	34103	**888-627-1595**	239-263-2222	655
Park Shore Waikiki 2586 Kalakaua Ave	Honolulu	HI	96815	**800-367-2377**	808-923-0411	373
Park South Hotel 122 E 28th St	New York	NY	10016	**800-315-4642**	212-448-0888	373
Park & Trail Foundation. Ice Age 207 E Buffalo St Suite 515	Milwaukee	WI	53202	**800-227-0046**	414-278-8518	48-23
Park University 8700 NW River Pk Dr	Parkville	MO	64152	**800-745-7275**	816-741-2000	163
Park Vista Memphis 939 Ridge Lake Blvd	Memphis	TN	38120	**800-371-8065**	901-684-6664	373
Park Vista Resort Hotel 705 Cherokee Orchard Rd PO Box 30	Gatlinburg	TN	37738	**800-421-7275**	865-436-9211	373
Park Water Co 9750 Washburn Rd	Downey	CA	90241	**800-727-5987**	562-923-0711	774
Parkdale Mills Inc 531 Cotton Blossom Cir	Gastonia	NC	28054	**800-331-1843**	704-864-8761	730-9
Parke County Rural Electric Membership Corp 119 W High St	Rockville	IN	47872	**800-537-3913**	765-569-3133	244
ParkEast Tours 100 Environs Pk	Helena	AL	35080	**800-223-6078**	205-428-1700	748
Parkedale Pharmaceuticals Inc 870 Parkdale Rd	Rochester	MI	48307	**800-615-5464***	248-651-9081	572
*Sales						
Parker Brothers Div Hasbro Inc 200 Narragansett Park Dr	Pawtucket	RI	02862	**888-836-7025**		750
Parker County Transportation Service Inc PO Box 1055	Mineral Wells	TX	76068	**866-521-1391**		109
Parker Drilling Co 1401 Enclave Pkwy Suite 600	Houston	TX	77077	**800-545-3645**	281-406-2000	529
NYSE: PKD						
Parker Fluid Connectors Group 6035 Parkland Blvd	Cleveland	OH	44124	**800-272-7537**	216-896-3000	364
Parker Hannifin Corp 6035 Parkland Blvd	Cleveland	OH	44124	**800-272-7537***	216-896-3000	220
NYSE: PH ■ *Cust Svc						
Parker Hannifin Corp Aircraft Wheel & Brake Div 1160 Center Rd	Avon	OH	44011	**800-272-5464**	440-937-6211	759
Parker Hannifin Corp Brass Products Div 300 Parker Dr	Otsego	MI	49078	**800-272-7537**	269-694-9411	777
Parker Hannifin Corp Composite Sealing Systems Div 7664 Panasonic Way	San Diego	CA	92154	**800-272-7537**	619-661-7000	321
Parker Hannifin Corp Daedal Div 1140 Sandy Hill Rd	Irwin	PA	15642	**800-245-6903**	724-861-8200	534
Parker Hannifin Corp Electromechanical Automation Div 5500 Business Park Dr	Rohnert Park	CA	94928	**800-358-9068**	707-584-7558	202
Parker Hannifin Corp Finite Filtratio & Separation Div 500 Glaspie St	Oxford	MI	48371	**800-521-4357**	248-628-6400	19
Parker Hannifin Corp Fluid Power Systems Div 595 Shelter Rd	Lincolnshire	IL	60069	**800-401-5015**	847-821-9478	777
Parker Hannifin Corp General Valve Div 19 Gloria Ln	Fairfield	NJ	07004	**800-482-8258**	973-575-4844	777
Parker Hannifin Corp Skinner Valve Div 95 Edgewood Ave	New Britain	CT	06051	**800-825-8305**	860-827-2300	777
Parker Hannifin Corp Veriflo Div 250 Canal Blvd	Richmond	CA	94804	**800-962-4074**	510-235-9590	200
Parker Instrumentation Group 6035 Parkland Blvd	Cleveland	OH	44124	**800-272-7537**	216-896-3000	220
Parker McCrory Mfg Co 2000 Forest Ave	Kansas City	MO	64108	**800-662-1038**	816-221-2000	202
Parker Metal Corp 243 Stafford St	Worcester	MA	01603	**800-225-9011**	508-791-7131	345
Parker Paint Mfg Co Inc 3003 S Tacoma Way	Tacoma	WA	98409	**800-826-4308**	253-473-1122	540
Parker Publications Inc PO Box 483	North Salem	NY	10560	**866-968-7872**	914-763-6933	130
Parker Smith & Feek Inc 2233 112th Ave NE	Bellevue	WA	98004	**800-457-0220**	425-709-3600	383
Parker Towing Co Inc 100 1/2 Greensboro Ave PO Box 20908	Tuscaloosa	AL	35402	**800-329-1677**	205-349-1677	457
Parkersburg News PO Box 1787	Parkersburg	WV	26102	**800-642-1997**	304-485-1891	522-2
Parkersburg/Wood County Convention & Visitors Bureau 350 7th St	Parkersburg	WV	26101	**800-752-4982**	304-428-1130	205
ParkerVision Inc 8493 Baymeadows Way	Jacksonville	FL	32256	**800-532-8034**	904-737-1367	633
NASDAQ: PRKR						
Parkhurst Mfg Co 18997 Hwy Y	Sedalia	MO	65302	**800-821-7380**	660-826-8685	505
Parking Assn. National 1112 16th St NW Suite 300	Washington	DC	20036	**800-647-7275**	202-296-4336	49-3
Parking Co of America 11101 Lakewood Blvd	Downey	CA	90241	**866-727-5728**	562-862-2118	552
Parkinson Disease Assn. American 1250 Hyland Blvd Suite 4D	Staten Island	NY	10305	**800-223-2732**	718-981-8001	48-17
Parkinson Foundation. National 1501 NW 9th Ave	Miami	FL	33136	**800-327-4545**	305-547-6666	48-17
Parkinson's Disease Foundation (PDF) 710 W 168th St	New York	NY	10032	**800-457-6676**	212-923-4700	48-17
Parkinson's Research. Michael J Fox Foundation for PO Box 4777 Grand Central Stn	New York	NY	10163	**800-708-7644**		300
Parkland Plastics Inc PO Box 339	Middlebury	IN	46540	**800-835-4110**	574-825-4336	647
Parkland Regional Library 5404 56th Ave	Lacombe	AB	T4L1G1	**800-567-9024**	403-782-3850	428
Parkline Inc PO Box 65	Winfield	WV	25213	**800-786-4855**	304-586-2113	106
Parks Brothers Farm Inc 6733 Parks Rd	Van Buren	AR	72956	**800-334-5770**	479-474-1125	363
Parks Canada 25 Eddy St MC 25-7 N 7th Fl	Gatineau	QC	K1A0M5	**888-773-8888**	819-997-0055	553
Parks Conservation Assn. National 1300 19th St NW Suite 300	Washington	DC	20036	**800-628-7275**	202-223-6722	48-13
Parks Corp 1 West St	Fall River	MA	02720	**800-225-8543**	508-679-5938	540
Parks. National Assn for Olmsted 733 15th St NW Suite 700	Washington	DC	20005	**866-666-6905**	202-783-6606	48-13
Parkview Hospital 2200 Randallia Dr	Fort Wayne	IN	46805	**888-856-2522**	260-373-4000	366-2
Parkview Medical Center 400 W 16th St	Pueblo	CO	81003	**800-543-8984**	719-584-4000	366-2
Parkway Inn 125 N Jackson St PO Box 494	Jackson	WY	83001	**800-247-8390**	307-733-3143	373
Parkway Plaza Hotel 123 W 'E' St	Casper	WY	82601	**800-270-7829**	307-235-1777	373
Parkway Properties Inc 188 E Capitol St Suite 1000	Jackson	MS	39201	**800-748-1667**	601-948-4091	641
NYSE: PKY						
Parkway Regional Medical Center 160 NW 170th St	North Miami Beach	FL	33169	**888-651-1100**	305-654-5050	366-2
Parliament Building (Hotel du Parlement) 1045 rue des Parlementaires	Quebec	QC	G1A1A3	**866-337-8837**	418-641-2638	50
Parliamentarians. National Assn of 213 S Main St	Independence	MO	64050	**888-627-2929**	816-833-3892	49-12
Parma Community General Hospital 7007 Powers Blvd	Parma	OH	44129	**866-699-7244**	440-743-3000	366-2
Parmed Pharmaceuticals Inc 4220 Hyde Park Blvd	Niagara Falls	NY	14305	**800-727-6331**	716-284-5666	237
Parmelee Industries Inc 8101 Lenexa Dr	Lenexa	KS	66214	**800-821-5218**	913-599-5555	566
Parmelee Industries Inc US Safety Div 8101 Lenexa Dr	Lenexa	KS	66214	**800-821-5218**	913-599-5555	566
Parnell-Martin Co Inc 1315 N Graham St	Charlotte	NC	28206	**800-849-2443**	704-375-8651	601
Parr Instrument Co 211 53rd St	Moline	IL	61265	**800-872-7720**	309-762-7716	411
Parr Lumber 5630 NW 5 Oaks Dr	Hillsboro	OR	97124	**877-849-7277**	503-614-2500	190-3
Parrish Tire Co Inc 5130 Indiana Ave	Winston-Salem	NC	27106	**800-849-8473**	336-767-0202	62-5
Parson Group 333 W Wacker Dr Suite 1620	Chicago	IL	60606	**800-389-8686**	312-578-1170	193
Parson Jack B Cos 2350 S 1900 West	Ogden	UT	84401	**888-672-7766**	801-731-1111	187-4
Parsons Brinckerhoff Inc 1 Penn Plaza 2nd Fl	New York	NY	10119	**800-877-7754**	212-465-5000	258
Parsons Corp 100 W Walnut St	Pasadena	CA	91124	**800-883-7300**	626-440-2000	258
Parsons Frank Paper Co Inc 2270 Beaver Rd	Landover	MD	20785	**800-944-9940**	301-386-4700	543
Parsons Infrastructure & Technology 100 W Walnut St	Pasadena	CA	91124	**800-883-7300**	626-440-4000	258
Parsons Mfg Corp 1055 O'Brien Dr	Menlo Park	CA	94025	**800-221-0823**	650-324-4726	591
Parsons Paper Co PO Box 309	Holyoke	MA	01041	**800-842-9029**	413-532-3222	547
Parsons PFI 150 Federal St	Boston	MA	02110	**800-555-0532**	617-946-9400	258
Parsons School of Design 2 W 13th St	New York	NY	10011	**800-252-0852**	212-229-8900	163
Parsons Sun PO Box 836	Parsons	KS	67357	**800-530-5723**	620-421-2000	522-2
Particle Measuring Systems Inc 5475 Airport Blvd	Boulder	CO	80301	**800-238-1801***	303-443-7100	410
*Cust Svc						
Partition Specialties Inc 714 C St Suite 3	San Rafael	CA	94901	**800-982-9255**	415-721-1040	188-9
Partners of the Americas 1424 K St NW Suite 700	Washington	DC	20005	**800-322-7844**	202-628-3300	48-5
Partners National Health Plans of North Carolina Inc PO Box 24907	Winston-Salem	NC	27114	**800-942-5695**	336-760-4822	384-3
Partners Trust Bank 233 Genesee St	Utica	NY	13501	**800-765-4968**	315-768-3000	71
Partnership for a Drug-Free America 405 Lexington Ave Suite 1601	New York	NY	10174	**888-575-3115**	212-922-1560	48-17
Parton Lumber Co Inc 251 Parton Rd	Rutherfordton	NC	28139	**800-624-1510**	828-287-4257	671
Partridge Inn 2110 Walton Way	Augusta	GA	30904	**800-476-6888**	706-737-8888	373
Parts Assoc Inc 12420 Plaza Dr	Parma	OH	44130	**800-321-1128**	216-433-7700	346
Parts Central Inc 3243 Whitfield St	Macon	GA	31204	**800-226-9396**	478-745-0878	61
Parts Plus 5050 Poplar Ave Suite 2020	Memphis	TN	38157	**800-727-8112**	901-682-9090	49-18
PartsBase Inc 905 Clint Moore Rd	Boca Raton	FL	33487	**888-322-6896**	561-953-0700	759
Party City Corp 400 Commons Way	Rockaway	NJ	07866	**800-883-2100**	973-983-0888	555
NASDAQ: PCTY						
Party Concepts Inc 5730 Technology Cir	Appleton	WI	54914	**800-296-2160**	920-738-3600	555
Party Land Inc 5215 Militia Hill Rd	Plymouth Meeting	PA	19462	**800-778-9563**	610-941-6200	555
Party Line Cruise Co 301 Broadway Suite 142	Riviera Beach	FL	33404	**866-463-3779**	561-472-9860	217
Pasadena Convention & Visitors Bureau 171 S Los Robles Ave	Pasadena	CA	91101	**800-307-7977**	626-795-9311	205
Pasadena Star-News 911 E Colorado Blvd	Pasadena	CA	91109	**800-788-1200**	626-578-6300	522-2

Company / Address	Toll-Free	Phone	Class
Paschall Norman W Co Inc 1 Paschall Rd . . . . . Peachtree City GA 30269	**800-849-1820**	770-487-7945	730-8
Pasco-Hernando Community College 10230 Ridge Rd . . . . New Port Richey FL 34654	**877-879-7422**	727-847-2727	160
Paslin Co 25411 Ryan Rd . . . . . Warren MI 48091	**877-972-7546**	586-758-0200	745
Paslode 888 Forest Edge Dr . . . . . Vernon Hills IL 60061	**800-682-3428**	847-634-1900	747
Paso Robles Inn 1103 Spring St . . . . Paso Robles CA 93446	**800-676-1713**	805-238-2660	373
Pass & Seymour/Legrand PO Box 4822 . . . . . Syracuse NY 13221	**800-223-4185**	315-468-6211	803
Passenger Vessel Assn (PVA) 801 N Quincy St Suite 200 . . . . . Arlington VA 22203	**800-807-8360**	703-807-0100	49-21
Passkey.com Inc 180 Old Colony Ave . . . Quincy MA 02170 *Sales	**800-211-4234***	617-237-8200	39
Passport Corp 140 E Ridgewood Ave Mack Ctr III . . . Paramus NJ 07652	**800-926-6736**	201-634-1100	176-1
Passport Inn 1726 Montreal Cir . . . . . Tucker GA 30084	**800-251-1962**	770-270-1180	369
Passport Newsletter 5315 N Clark St PMB 501 . . . . . Chicago IL 60640	**800-542-6670**	773-769-6760	521-6
Pasta Connections 1000 Corporate Dr . . . . . Fort Lauderdale FL 33334	**800-487-2729**	954-351-5100	657
Pasta House Co 1143 Macklind Ave . . . . . Saint Louis MO 63110	**800-467-2782**	314-535-6644	657
Pasta USA Inc PO Box 7399 . . . . . Spokane WA 99207	**800-456-2084**	509-489-7219	291-31
Pastel Journal 4700 E Galbraith Rd . . . Cincinnati OH 45236	**800-283-0963**	513-531-2690	449-2
Pastorelli Food Products Inc 162 N Sangamon St . . . . . Chicago IL 60607	**800-767-2829**	312-666-2041	291-36
Pat Catan's Craft Centers 13000 Darice Pkwy . . . . . Strongsville OH 44149	**800-321-1494**	440-238-9150	45
Pat & Mario's 10 Kingsbridge Garden Cir Suite 600 . . . . . Mississauga ON L5R3K6	**800-361-3111**	905-568-0000	657
Pat O'Brien's International Inc 718 Saint Peter St . . . . . New Orleans LA 70116	**800-597-4823**	504-525-4823	657
Patagonia Inc 259 W Santa Clara Dr PO Box 150 . . . Ventura CA 93001 *Cust Svc	**800-638-6464***	805-643-8616	155-4
Pataula Electric Membership Corp 925 Barkley St PO Box 289 . . . . . Cuthbert GA 31740	**888-631-9757**	229-732-3171	244
Patch Products Inc 1400 E Inman Pkwy . . . . Beloit WI 53511	**800-524-4263**	608-362-6896	750
Patco Corp 51 Ballou Blvd . . . . . Bristol RI 02809 *Cust Svc	**800-343-7875***	401-254-0600	717
Patcraft Commercial Div Queen Carpet Co 616 Duvall Rd . . . . . Chatsworth GA 30705	**800-241-4014**	706-279-4000	131
Patelco Credit Union 156 2nd St . . . . . San Francisco CA 94105	**800-358-8228**	415-442-6200	216
Patent Construction Systems 1 Mack Centre Dr . . . . . Paramus NJ 07652	**800-969-5600**	201-261-5600	482
Paternity Testing Corp 300 Portland St . . . . . Columbia MO 65201	**888-837-8323**	573-442-9948	408
Paterno Wines International 900 Armour Dr . . . . . Lake Bluff IL 60044	**800-950-7676**	847-604-8900	82-3
Paterson Pacific Parchment Co 625 Greg St . . . . . Sparks NV 89431	**800-678-8104**	775-353-3000	549
Paterson Stamp Works PO Box 1677 . . . . Clifton NJ 07015	**800-782-6766**	973-478-5600	459
Path 1 Network Technologies Inc 6215 Ferris Sq Suite 140 . . . . . San Diego CA 92121 *AMEX: PNO*	**877-663-7284**	858-450-4220	176-7
Patheon Inc 2100 Syntex Ct . . . . . Mississauga ON L5N7K9	**888-728-4366**	905-821-4001	470
Pathfinder Bancorp Inc 214 W 1st St . . . . Oswego NY 13126 *NASDAQ: PBHC*	**800-811-5620**	315-343-0057	355-2
Pathfinder Group 6009 Quinpool Rd Suite 700 . . . . . Halifax NS B3K5J7	**800-200-7284**	902-425-2445	47
Pathologists. College of American 325 Waukegan Rd . . . . . Northfield IL 60093	**800-323-4040**	847-832-7000	49-8
Pathology. American Society for Clinical 2100 W Harrison St . . . . . Chicago IL 60612 *Cust Svc	**800-621-4142***	312-738-1336	49-8
Pathology. American Society for Colposcopy & Cervical 20 W Washington St Suite 1 . . . . . Hagerstown MD 21740	**800-787-7227**	301-733-3640	49-8
Pathology Center 8303 Dodge St . . . . . Omaha NE 68114	**888-432-8980**	402-354-4540	409
Pathway Press 1080 Montgomery Ave NE . . . . . Cleveland TN 37311 *Sales	**800-553-8506***	423-476-4512	623-2
Pathways Home Health & Hospice 585 N Mary Ave . . . . . Sunnyvale CA 94085	**888-755-7855**	408-773-5900	365
Pathways to Peace Inc PO Box 259 . . . . . Cassadaga NY 14718	**800-775-4212**	716-595-3884	48-21
Patient Care Magazine 5 Paragon Dr . . . Montvale NJ 07645	**888-581-8052**	973-944-7777	449-16
Patient Infosystems Inc 46 Prince St 1st Fl . . . . . Rochester NY 14607	**800-276-2575**	585-242-7200	176-10
Patina Oil & Gas Corp 1625 Broadway Suite 2000 . . . . . Denver CO 80202 *NYSE: POG*	**866-404-8161**	303-389-3600	525
Patricia Grand Resort 2710 N Ocean Blvd . . . . . Myrtle Beach SC 29577	**800-255-4763**	843-448-8453	655
Patricia Seybold Group 210 Commercial St . . . . . Boston MA 02109	**800-826-2424**	617-742-5200	455
Patrick & Co 611 Mission St . . . . San Francisco CA 94520	**800-792-0755**	415-392-2640	524
Patrick Industries Inc 1800 S 14th St . . . Elkhart IN 46516 *NASDAQ: PATK*	**800-331-2151**	574-294-7511	116
Patrick Industries Inc Patrick Metals Div 5020 Lincolnway E . . . . . Mishawaka IN 46544	**800-922-9692**	574-255-9692	476
Patrick James Inc 3457 W Shaw Ave . . . . Fresno CA 93711	**888-427-6003**	559-275-4300	155-3
Patrick Metals Div Patrick Industries Inc 5020 Lincolnway E . . . . . Mishawaka IN 46544	**800-922-9692**	574-255-9692	476
Patriot Forge Co 1802 Cranberry St . . . . . Erie PA 16502	**877-495-9542**	814-456-2088	474
Patriot National Bancorp Inc 900 Bedford St . . . . . Stamford CT 06901 *NASDAQ: PNBK*	**800-762-7620**	203-324-7500	355-2
Patriot-News 812 Market St . . . . . Harrisburg PA 17101	**800-692-7207**	717-255-8100	522-2
Patriot Transportation Holding Inc 1801 Art Museum Dr 3rd Fl . . . . . Jacksonville FL 32207 *NASDAQ: PATR*	**877-704-1776**	904-396-5733	769
Patriots Point Naval & Maritime Museum Charleston Harbor 40 Patriots Point Rd . . . . . Mount Pleasant SC 29464	**800-248-3508**	843-884-2727	509
Patten University 2433 Coolidge Ave . . . Oakland CA 94601	**877-472-8836**	510-261-8500	163
Patterson Cos Inc 1031 Mendota Heights Rd . . . . . Saint Paul MN 55120 *NASDAQ: PDCO*	**800-328-5536**	651-686-1600	467
Patterson Drilling Co PO Box 1416 . . . . . Snyder TX 79550	**800-245-0167**	325-574-6300	529
Patterson Frozen Foods Inc PO Box 114 . . . . . Patterson CA 95363	**800-821-1007**	209-892-2611	291-21
Patterson-Schwartz & Assoc Inc 913 Delaware Ave . . . . . Wilmington DE 19806	**800-438-2961**	302-656-3141	638
Patterson TravelStore 855 Howe Ave Suite 5 . . . . . Sacramento CA 95825	**800-283-2772**	916-929-5555	760
Patterson-UTI Energy Inc 4510 Lamesa Hwy . . . . . Snyder TX 79549 *NASDAQ: PTEN*	**800-245-0167**	325-573-1104	529
Patton Harris Rust & Assoc PC 14532 Lee Rd . . . . . Chantilly VA 20151	**800-550-7472**	703-449-6700	258
Patton & Patton Software Corp 3815 N Oracle Rd . . . . . Tucson AZ 85705	**800-525-0082**	520-888-6500	176-8
Patuxent Publishing Co 10750 Little Patuxent Pkwy . . . . . Columbia MD 21044	**800-884-8797**	410-730-3620	623-8
Paul Arpin Van Lines 99 James P Murphy Hwy . . . . . West Warwick RI 02893	**800-343-3500**	401-828-8111	508
Paul Casket Co 505 S Green St . . . . . Cambridge City IN 47327	**800-521-8202**	765-478-3991	134
Paul Davis Restoration Inc 1 Independence Dr Suite 2300 . . . . Jacksonville FL 32202	**800-722-1818**	904-737-2779	305
Paul deLima Co Inc PO Box 4813 . . . . . Syracuse NY 13221	**800-962-8864**	315-699-5282	291-7
Paul Ecke Ranch Inc 441 Saxony Rd . . . Encinitas CA 92024	**800-468-3253**	760-753-1134	363
Paul Frederick Inc 223 W Poplar St . . . Fleetwood PA 19522	**800-247-1417**	610-944-0909	155-3
Paul H Gesswein & Co 255 Hancock Ave . . . . . Bridgeport CT 06605	**800-544-2043**	203-366-5400	399
Paul Hastings Janofsky & Walker LLP 515 S Flower St 25th Fl . . . . . Los Angeles CA 90071	**888-745-9557**	213-683-6000	419
Paul Laurence Dunbar House 219 N Paul Laurence Dunbar St . . . . . Dayton OH 45407	**800-860-0148**	937-224-7061	50
Paul Lavitt Mills Inc 1517 'F' Ave SE . . . . Hickory NC 28602	**800-825-7285**	828-328-2463	153-10
Paul Lois & Partners 150 Presidential Way . . . . . Woburn MA 01801	**800-989-1550**	781-782-5000	622
Paul Mueller Co 1600 W Phelps St . . . . Springfield MO 65802 *NASDAQ: MUEL*	**800-641-2830**	417-831-3000	379
Paul Quinn College 3837 Simpson Stuart Rd . . . . . Dallas TX 75241	**800-237-2648**	214-376-1000	163
Paul Revere Life Insurance Co 18 Chestnut St . . . . . Worcester MA 01608	**800-799-0990**	508-799-4441	384-2
Paul Smith's College of Arts & Sciences Rt 30 & 86 PO box 265 . . . . . Paul Smiths NY 12970	**800-421-2605**	518-327-6227	160
Paul Stuart Inc Madison Ave & 45th St . . . . . New York NY 10017 *Orders	**800-678-8278***	212-682-0320	155-4
Paul W Bryant Museum 300 Paul W Bryant Dr . . . . . Tuscaloosa AL 35487	**866-772-2327**	205-348-4668	511
Paula CM Co 6049 Hi-Tek Ct . . . . . Mason OH 45040	**800-543-4464**	513-336-3100	322
Paulding-Putman Electric Co-op 910 N Williams St . . . . . Paulding OH 45879	**800-686-2357**	419-399-5015	244
Pauline Books & Media 50 Saint Paul's Ave . . . . . Boston MA 02130 *Sales	**800-876-4463***	617-522-8911	623-4
Paulson Capital Corp 811 SW Naito Pkwy Suite 200 . . . . . Portland OR 97204 *NASDAQ: PLCC* ■ *Cust Svc	**800-458-5667***	503-243-6000	679
Paulson Investment Co Inc 811 SW Naito Pkwy Suite 200 . . . . . Portland OR 97204 *Cust Svc	**800-458-5667***	503-243-6000	679
Pauwels Transformers 1 Pauwels Dr . . . . . Washington MO 63090	**800-833-6582**	636-239-6783	756
Pavco Inc 4450 Cranwood Pkwy . . . . Warrensville Heights OH 44128 *Orders	**800-321-7735***	216-332-1000	143
Pavco Industries Inc PO Box 612 . . . . Pascagoula MS 39568	**800-346-7206**	228-762-3172	602
Pavement Institute. Interlocking Concrete 1444 'I' St NW Suite 700 . . . . . Washington DC 20005	**800-241-3652**	202-712-9036	49-3
Pavestone Plus Inc RR 1 1081 Rife Rd . . . . . Cambridge ON N1R5S3	**800-265-6496**	519-740-6000	181
Pawleys Plantation 70 Tanglewood Dr . . . . . Pawleys Island SC 29585	**800-367-9959**	843-237-6009	655
Pawling Corp 157 Charles Colman Blvd . . . . . Pawling NY 12564	**800-431-0101**	845-855-1000	663
PawnMart Inc 6400 Atlantic Blvd Suite 190 . . . . . Norcross GA 30071	**800-729-6261**	678-720-0660	558
PAX TV 601 Clearwater Park Rd . . . . West Palm Beach FL 33401	**800-646-7296**	561-659-4122	725
Pax World Fund Family 222 State St . . . . . Portsmouth NH 03801	**800-767-1729**	603-431-8022	517
Paxar Corp 105 Corporate Park Dr . . . . . White Plains NY 10604 *NYSE: PXR*	**888-447-2927**	914-697-6800	171-6
Paxar Corp Systems Group 1 Wilcox St . . . Sayre PA 18840	**800-947-2927**	570-888-6641	404
Paxson Communications Corp 601 Clearwater Park Rd . . . . West Palm Beach FL 33401 *AMEX: PAX*	**800-646-7296**	561-659-4122	724
Paxton Co 1111 Ingleside Rd . . . . . Norfolk VA 23502	**800-234-7290**	757-853-6781	759
Paxton Products Corp 10125 Carver Rd . . . . . Cincinnati OH 45242	**800-441-7475**	513-891-7474	19
Paxton Van Lines Inc 5300 Port Royal Rd . . . . . Springfield VA 22151	**800-336-4536**	703-321-7600	508
Paxton & Vierling Steel Co 501 Ave H . . . . . Carter Lake IA 51510	**800-831-9252**	712-347-5500	471
Pay-O-Matic Corp 160 Oak Dr . . . . . Syosset NY 11791	**888-729-3773**	516-496-4900	139
Pay for Performance Newsletter 3 Park Ave 30th Fl . . . . . New York NY 10016	**800-401-5937**	212-244-0360	521-2
Pay Plus Benefits Inc 1110 N Center Pkwy Suite B . . . . . Kennewick WA 99336	**888-531-5781**	509-735-1143	619
Paychex Business Solutions 10105 Dr Martin Luthur King Jr St N . . . . . Saint Petersburg FL 33716	**800-741-6277**	727-579-0505	619
Paychex Inc 911 Panorama Trail S . . . . Rochester NY 14625 *NASDAQ: PAYX*	**800-828-4411**	585-385-6666	559

Name / Address	City	State	Zip	Toll-Free	Phone	Class
Payden & Rygel 333 S Grand Ave	Los Angeles	CA	90071	**800-572-9336**	213-625-1900	393
Payless Car Rental System Inc 2350 N 34th St N	Saint Petersburg	FL	33713	**800-729-5377**	727-321-6352	126
Payless ShoeSource Inc 3231 SE 6th St *NYSE: PSS* ■ *Cust Svc	Topeka	KS	66607	**800-444-7463***	785-233-5171	296
Paymaster Technologies Inc 900 Pratt Blvd	Elk Grove Village	IL	60007	**800-462-4477**	847-758-1234	112
Paymaster Technology Corp 1 Cotton Row	Scott	MO	00772	**000-321-0909**	002-742-3331	11-2
PayMaxx Inc 302 S Royal Oaks Blvd	Franklin	TN	37064	**877-729-6299**	615-791-4000	559
Payne Engineering Co Rt 29 Rocky Step Rd *Orders	Scott Depot	WV	25560	**800-331-1345***	304-757-7353	202
Payne Printery Inc 1101 Dallas Memorial Hwy	Dallas	PA	18612	**800-724-3188**	570-675-1147	338
PayNet Merchant Services Inc 2000 Town Center Suite 2260	Southfield	MI	48075	**888-855-8644**	248-354-1111	254
Payroll 1 Inc 333 W 7th St	Royal Oak	MI	48067	**888-999-7291**	248-548-7020	559
Payroll Manager's Report 3 Park Ave 30th Fl	New York	NY	10016	**800-401-5937**	212-244-0360	521-2
Payson Casters Inc 2323 N Delaney Rd	Gurnee	IL	60031	**800-323-4552**	847-336-6200	345
PaySource Inc 251 New Karner Rd	Albany	NY	12205	**888-452-9743**	518-452-9743	619
PayTech 640 E Purdue Dr Suite 102	Phoenix	AZ	85020	**000-072-0064**	002-700-1017	019
Paytrust Inc 4900 W Brown Deer Rd	Milwaukee	WI	53223	**800-729-8787**		250
Paywise Inc 122 E 42nd St Suite 520	New York	NY	10168	**800-975-8607**	212-953-1287	559
PB & H Moulding Corp 124 Pickard Dr E	Syracuse	NY	13211	**800-746-9724**	315-455-5602	304
PBHG Funds Inc 1400 Liberty Ridge Dr	Wayne	PA	19087	**800-433-0051**	610-647-4100	517
PBI Market Equipment Inc 2667 Gundry Ave	Signal Hill	CA	90755	**800-421-3753**	562-595-4785	295
PBI/Gordon Corp PO Box 014090	Kansas City	MO	64101	**800-821-7925**	816-421-4070	276
PBM Corp 20600 Chagrin Blvd Suite 450	Cleveland	OH	44122	**800-341-5809**	216-283-7999	39
PBM Graphics Inc PO Box 13603	Durham	NC	27709	**800-849-8100**	919-544-6222	615
PBM Inc 1070 Sandy Hill Rd	Irwin	PA	15642	**800-967-4726**	724-863-0550	777
PC Connection Inc 730 Milford Rd Rt 101A *NASDAQ: PCCC*	Merrimack	NH	03054	**800-800-1111**	603-683-2000	177
PC Connection Inc MacConnection Div DBA MacConnection 730 Milford Rd Rt 101A	Merrimack	NH	03054	**800-800-0014**	603-683-2000	177
PC Gamer Magazine 150 N Hill Dr	Brisbane	CA	94005	**800-898-7159**	415-468-4684	449-14
PC Magazine 28 E 28th St	New York	NY	10016	**800-289-0429**	212-503-5100	449-7
PC Mall Inc 2555 W 190th St *NASDAQ: MALL*	Torrance	CA	90504	**800-413-3833**	310-354-5600	177
PC Wholesale 444 Scott Dr	Bloomingdale	IL	60108	**800-525-4727**	630-307-1700	172
PC World Communications Inc 501 2nd St	San Francisco	CA	94107	**800-997-2967**	415-243-0500	623-9
PC World Magazine 501 2nd St Suite 600	San Francisco	CA	94107	**800-234-3498**	415-243-0500	449-7
PCA International Inc 815 Mathews Mint Hill Rd *Cust Svc	Matthews	NC	28105	**877-763-4456***	704-847-8011	579
PCC Specialty Products Inc Reed-Rico Div 18 Industrial Dr *Cust Svc	Holden	MA	01520	**800-343-6068***	508-829-4491	448
PCI Energy Services 1 Energy Dr	Lake Bluff	IL	60044	**800-345-6108**	847-680-8100	446
PCI Services Inc 30 Winter St 12th Fl	Boston	MA	02108	**800-261-3111**	617-535-3000	176-10
PCIA - Wireless Infrastructure Assn 500 Montgomery St Suite 700	Alexandria	VA	22314	**800-759-0300**	703-739-0300	49-20
PCMA (Professional Convention Management Assn) 2301 S Lake Shore Dr Suite 1001	Chicago	IL	60616	**877-827-7262**	312-423-7262	49-12
PC/Nametag 124 Horizon Dr	Verona	WI	53593	**800-233-9767**	877-626-3824	176-8
PCRM (Physicians' Committee for Responsible Medicine) 5100 Wisconsin Ave NW Suite 400	Washington	DC	20016	**866-416-7276**	202-686-2210	49-8
PCS Co 34488 Doreka Dr	Fraser	MI	48026	**800-521-0546**	586-294-7780	745
PD George Co Inc 5200 N 2nd St	Saint Louis	MO	63147	**800-325-7492**	314-621-5700	540
PDCA (Painting & Decorating Contractors of America) 11960 Westline Industrial Dr Suite 201	Saint Louis	MO	63146	**800-332-7322**	314-514-7322	49-3
PDF (Parkinson's Disease Foundation) 710 W 168th St	New York	NY	10032	**800-457-6676**	212-923-4700	48-17
PDG Environmental Inc 1386 Beulah Rd Bldg 801	Pittsburgh	PA	15235	**800-972-7341**	412-243-3200	653
PDI Financial Group 601 N Lynndale Dr	Appleton	WI	54914	**800-234-7341**	920-739-2303	679
PDI Inc 10 Mountainview Rd *NASDAQ: PDII*	Upper Saddle River	NJ	07458	**800-242-7494**	201-258-8450	194
PDK (Phi Delta Kappa International) 408 N Union St PO Box 789	Bloomington	IN	47402	**800-766-1156**	812-339-1156	48-16
PDK Labs Inc 145 Ricefield Ln	Hauppauge	NY	11788	**800-221-0855**	631-273-2630	572
PDQ Mfg Inc 1698 Scheuring Rd	De Pere	WI	54115	**800-227-3373**	920-983-8333	379
PDRA (Paint & Decorating Retailers Assn) 403 Axminister Dr	Fenton	MO	63026	**800-737-0107**	636-326-2636	49-18
PDS (Packaging Distribution Services Inc) 2308 Sunset Rd	Des Moines	IA	50321	**800-747-2699**	515-243-3156	549
PDS Gaming Corp 6171 McLeod Dr Suite L *NASDAQ: PDSG*	Las Vegas	NV	89120	**800-479-3612**	702-736-0700	214
PDS Technical Services 1320 Greenway Dr Suite 550	Dallas	TX	75038	**800-270-4737**	972-550-1212	707
Pea River Electric Co-op 1311 W Roy Parker Rd	Ozark	AL	36360	**800-264-7732**	334-774-2545	244
Peabody Auditorium 600 Auditorium Blvd	Daytona Beach	FL	32118	**866-605-4276**	386-671-3460	562
Peabody Conservatory of Music 1 E Mt Vernon Pl	Baltimore	MD	21202	**800-368-2521**	410-659-8110	163
Peabody Institute of the Johns Hopkins University Peabody Conservatory of Music 1 E Mt Vernon Pl	Baltimore	MD	21202	**800-368-2521**	410-659-8110	163
Peabody Little Rock 3 Statehouse Plaza	Little Rock	AR	72201	**800-527-1745**	501-906-4000	373
Peabody Memphis 149 Union Ave	Memphis	TN	38103	**800-833-2548**	901-529-4000	373
Peabody Orlando 9801 International Dr	Orlando	FL	32819	**800-732-2639**	407-352-4000	373
Peace Arch Entertainment Group Inc 150 W 1st Ave Suite 200 *AMEX: PAE*	Vancouver	BC	V5Y1A4	**888-588-3608**	604-681-9308	503
Peace Bridge Duty Free Inc Peace Bridge Plaza PO Box 339	Fort Erie	ON	L2A5N1	**800-361-1302**	905-871-5400	240
Peace College 15 E Peace St	Raleigh	NC	27604	**800-732-2347**	919-508-2000	160
Peace Corps 1111 20th St NW	Washington	DC	20526	**800-424-8580**	202-692-2100	336-16
Peace Corps Assn. National 1900 L St NW Suite 205	Washington	DC	20036	**800-424-8580**	202-293-7728	48-5
Peace Foundation. National 666 11th St NW Suite 202	Washington	DC	20001	**800-237-3223**	202-783-7030	48-5
Peace. Hoover Institution on War Revolution & Stanford University 434 Galvez Mall	Stanford	CA	94305	**877-466-8374**	650-723-1754	654
Peace River Electric Co-op Inc 1499 US Hwy 17 N PO Box 1310	Wauchula	FL	33873	**800-282-3824**	863-773-4116	244
Peace River Regional Medical Center 2500 Harbor Blvd	Port Charlotte	FL	33952	**800-226-4122**	941-766-4122	366-2
Peace Software Inc 6205 Blue Lagoon Dr Suite 500	Miami	FL	33126	**888-407-3223**	305-341-2400	176-10
Peaceable Kingdom Press 950 Gilman St	Berkeley	CA	94710	**800-444-7778**	510-558-2051	130
Peaceful Valley Ranch 475 Peaceful Valley Rd	Lyons	CO	80540	**800-955-6343**	303-747-2881	238
Peach State Labs Inc 180 Burlington Rd PO Box 5424	Rome	GA	30162	**800-634-1653**	706-291-8743	143
Peachpit Press 1249 8th St	Berkeley	CA	94710	**800-283-9444**	510-524-2178	623-2
Peachtree Doors & Windows Inc 2744 Ramsey Rd	Gainesville	GA	30501	**800-443-5692**	770-534-8070	232
Peachtree Fabrics Inc 1400 English St	Atlanta	GA	30318	**800-732-2437**	404-351-5400	583
Peachtree Hospice 4300 Rogers Ave Suuite 33	Fort Smith	AR	72903	**800-752-0444**	479-494-0100	365
Peachtree Life Settlements 6501 Park of Commerce Blvd Suite 140-B	Boca Raton	FL	33487	**866-730-4411**	561-962-3900	783
Peacock Crate Factory 225 Cash St *Orders	Jacksonville	TX	75766	**800-666-5647***	903-586-5321	199
Peacock Hislop Staley & Given Inc 2999 N 44th St Suite 100	Phoenix	AZ	85018	**800-999-1818**	602-952-6800	397
Peacock Suites Resort 1745 S Anaheim Blvd	Anaheim	CA	92805	**800-522-6401**	714-535-8255	373
Peak of the Market 1200 King Edward St	Winnipeg	MB	R3H0R5	**888-289-7325**	204-633-7325	292-7
Peak Nutrition 1097 11th St	Syracuse	NE	68446	**800-600-2069**	402-269-2825	786
Peak Technical Services Inc 300 Penn Ctr Blvd Suite 800	Pittsburgh	PA	15235	**800-825-8088**	412-824-2000	707
Peak Technologies Inc 9200 Berger Rd	Columbia	MD	21046	**800-950-6372**	410-312-6000	172
Peaks Resort & Golden Door Spa. Wyndham 136 Country Club Dr	Telluride	CO	81435	**800-789-2220**	970-728-6800	655
Peanut Processors Inc PO Box 160	Dublin	NC	28332	**800-334-8383**	910-862-2136	291-28
Peapack-Gladstone Financial Corp PO Box 178 *AMEX: PGC*	Gladstone	NJ	07934	**800-742-7595**	908-234-0700	355-2
Peapod LLC 9933 Woods Dr	Skokie	IL	60077	**800-573-2763**	847-583-9400	339
Pearl Meat Packing Co Inc 196 Quincy St	Boston	MA	02121	**800-462-3022**	617-445-6020	465
Pearl Paint Co Inc 308 Canal St	New York	NY	10013	**800-221-6845**	212-431-7932	45
Pearl River Resort 13541 Hwy 16 W	Choctaw	MS	39350	**800-557-0711**	601-650-1234	133
Pearl River Valley Electric Power Assn 1422 Hwy 13 N	Columbia	MS	39429	**800-320-0312**	601-736-2666	244
Pearle Vision Inc 1925 Enterprise Pkwy	Twinsburg	OH	44087	**800-282-3931**	330-486-3000	533
Pearson Drew Marketing Inc 15006 Beltway Dr	Addison	TX	75001	**800-879-0880**	972-702-8055	153-9
Pearson Education Inc 1 Lake St *Cust Svc	Upper Saddle River	NJ	07458	**800-922-0579***	201-236-7000	623-2
Pearson Education Inc Allyn & Bacon/Longman Publishers 75 Arlington St Suite 300 *Orders	Boston	MA	02116	**800-852-8024***	617-848-7090	623-2
Pearson RA Co 8120 W Sunset Hwy	Spokane	WA	99224	**800-732-7766**	509-838-6226	537
Pearson's Candy Co 2140 W 7th St *Cust Svc	Saint Paul	MN	55116	**800-328-6507***	651-698-0356	291-8
Pechanga Resort & Casino 45000 Pechanga Pkwy	Temecula	CA	92592	**877-711-2946**	951-693-1819	655
Pechters Baking 840 Jersey St	Harrison	NJ	07029	**800-525-5779**	973-483-3374	291-1
Peck & Hale LLC 180 Division Ave	West Sayville	NY	11796	**800-448-7325**	631-589-2510	666
Peck's Products Co 1220 Switzer Ave	Saint Louis	MO	63147	**800-325-8891**	314-385-5454	149
Pecora Corp 165 Wambold Rd	Harleysville	PA	19438	**800-523-6688**	215-723-6051	3
Pedernales Electric Co-op Inc 300 Haley Rd	Johnson City	TX	78636	**888-554-4732**	830-868-7155	244
Pediatric AIDS Foundation. Elizabeth Glaser 2950 31st St Suite 125	Santa Monica	CA	90405	**888-499-4673**	310-314-1459	48-17
Pediatric Services of America Inc 310 Technology Pkwy *NASDAQ: PSAI*	Norcross	GA	30092	**800-950-1580**	770-441-1580	358
Pediatrics. American Academy of 141 Northwest Point Blvd	Elk Grove Village	IL	60007	**800-433-9016**	847-434-4000	49-8
Pediatrix Medical Group Inc PO Box 559001 *NYSE: PDX*	Fort Lauderdale	FL	33355	**800-243-3839**	954-384-0175	455
Pediatrix Screening PO Box 219	Bridgeville	PA	15017	**866-463-6436**	412-220-2300	408
Pedinol Pharmacal Inc 30 Banfi Plaza N	Farmingdale	NY	11735	**800-733-4665**	631-293-9500	573
Pedorthic Footwear Assn (PFA) 7150 Columbia Gateway Dr Suite G	Columbia	MD	21046	**800-673-8447**	410-381-7278	48-17

Name / Address	City	State	Zip	Toll-Free	Phone	Class
Pedro Companies 106 E 10th St	Saint Paul	MN	55101	**800-328-9284**	651-224-9491	444
Pee Dee Electric Membership Corp PO Box 859	Wadesboro	NC	28170	**800-992-1626**	704-694-2114	244
Peebles Inc 1 Peebles St	South Hill	VA	23970	**800-723-4548**	434-447-5200	227
Peelle Co 34 Central Ave	Hauppauge	NY	11788	**800-645-1056**	631-231-6000	255
Peer Bearing Co 2200 Norman Dr S	Waukegan	IL	60085	**800-433-7337**	847-578-1000	77
Peer Food Products Co 4631 S McDowell Ave	Chicago	IL	60609	**800-365-5644**	773-927-1440	291-26
Peerless Chain Co 1416 E Sanborn St	Winona	MN	55987	**800-533-8056**	507-457-9100	802
Peerless Cleaners Inc 519 N Monroe St	Decatur	IL	62522	**800-879-7056**	217-423-7703	84
Peerless Electronics Inc 19 Wilbur St	Lynbrook	NY	11563	**800-285-2121**	516-594-3500	245
Peerless Group 823 Main St	Little Rock	AR	72201	**800-880-7671**	501-375-8266	770
Peerless Importers Inc 16 Bridgewater St	Brooklyn	NY	11222	**800-338-3880**	718-383-5500	82-3
Peerless Industries Inc 1980 Hawthorne Ave	Melrose Park	IL	60160	**800-729-0307**	708-865-8870	479
Peerless Machinery Corp PO Box 769	Sidney	OH	45365	**800-999-3327**	937-492-4158	293
Peerless Mattress & Furniture Co PO Box 7650	Flint	MI	48507	**800-253-0937**	810-230-7440	316
Peerless Mfg Co US Hwy 82 E	Shellman	GA	39886	**800-225-4617**	229-679-5353	269
Peerless Pottery Inc PO Box 145	Rockport	IN	47635	**800-457-5785**	812-649-6430	600
Peerless Premier Appliance Co 119 S 14th St	Belleville	IL	62222	**800-858-5844**	618-233-0475	36
Peerless Products Inc 2403 S Main St	Fort Scott	KS	66701	**800-279-9999**	620-223-4610	232
Peerless Systems Corp 2381 Rosecrans Ave *NASDAQ: PRLS*	El Segundo	CA	90245	**800-362-5738**	310-536-0908	176-8
Peerless Tyre Co 5000 Kingston St	Denver	CO	80239	**800-999-7810**	303-371-4300	54
Peerless-Winsmith Inc 1401 W Market St	Warren	OH	44485	**800-676-3651**	330-399-3651	700
Peery Hotel 110 W 300 South	Salt Lake City	UT	84101	**800-331-0073**	801-521-4300	373
Peet Frate Line Inc 650 S Eastwood Dr PO Box 1129	Woodstock	IL	60098	**800-435-6909**	815-338-5500	769
Peet's Coffee & Tea Inc 1400 Park Ave *NASDAQ: PEET ■ *Orders*	Emeryville	CA	94608	**800-999-2132***	510-594-2100	156
Peg-Perego USA Inc 3625 Independence Dr *Cust Svc	Fort Wayne	IN	46808	**800-728-2108***	260-482-8191	64
Pegasus Communications Corp 225 E City Line Ave	Bala Cynwyd	PA	19004	**888-438-7488**	610-934-7000	724
Pegasus Imaging Corp 4522 Spruce St Suite 200 *Sales	Tampa	FL	33607	**800-875-7009***	813-875-7575	176-8
Pegasus International Hotel 501 Southard St	Key West	FL	33040	**800-397-8148**	305-294-9323	373
Pegasus Solutions Inc 8350 N Central Expy Suite 1900 *NASDAQ: PEGS*	Dallas	TX	75206	**800-528-2422**	214-234-4000	332
Pegasus Web Technologies Inc Rt 10 E 17-19B Suite 220	Parsippany	NJ	07054	**888-734-9320**	973-267-4707	795
Peggy Knight Solutions Inc 180 Harbor Dr Suite 221	Sausalito	CA	94965	**800-997-7753**	415-289-1777	342
Pegler-Sysco Food Services Co 1700 Center Park Rd	Lincoln	NE	68512	**800-366-1031**	402-423-1031	292-8
PEI-Genesis 2180 Hornig Rd	Philadelphia	PA	19116	**800-523-0727**	215-673-0400	245
Peirce College 1420 Pine St	Philadelphia	PA	19102	**888-467-3472**	215-545-6400	163
Peirce-Phelps Inc 2000 N 59th St	Philadelphia	PA	19131	**800-222-2742**	215-879-7000	38
Peirone Produce Co 524 E Trent Ave	Spokane	WA	99202	**800-552-5837**	509-838-3515	292-7
Pekin Insurance Co 2505 Court St	Pekin	IL	61558	**800-322-0160**	309-346-1161	384-4
Pekin Life Insurance Co 2505 Court St	Pekin	IL	61558	**800-322-0160**	309-346-1161	384-2
Peking Handicraft Inc 1388 San Mateo Ave	South San Francisco	CA	94080	**800-872-6888**	650-871-3788	356
Pelco 3500 Pelco Way	Clovis	CA	93612	**800-289-9100**	559-292-1981	633
Pelham Hotel 444 Common St	New Orleans	LA	70130	**888-211-3447**	504-522-4444	373
Pelican Financial Inc 811 Anchor Rode Dr *AMEX: PFI*	Naples	FL	34103	**800-219-4777**	239-403-0076	355-2
Pelican Rope Works Inc 4001 W Carriage Dr	Santa Ana	CA	92704	**800-464-7673**	714-545-0116	207
Pelivan Transit 333 S Oak St PO Drawer B	Big Cabin	OK	74332	**800-482-4594**	918-783-5793	109
Pella Co-op Electric Assn 2615 Washington St	Pella	IA	50219	**800-619-1040**	641-628-1040	244
Pella Corp 102 Main St *Cust Svc	Pella	IA	50219	**800-288-7281***	641-628-1000	234
Pelletier Ray Pelletier Management Group PO Box 810	Zionsville	IN	46077	**800-662-4625**		561
Pelouze Scale Co 7400 W 100 Pl	Bridgeview	IL	60455	**800-654-8330**	708-598-9100	672
Pelstar LLC 7400 W 100th Pl	Bridgeview	IL	60455	**800-638-3722**	708-598-9100	672
Pelton & Crane A DCI Co 11727 Fruehauf Dr *Cust Svc	Charlotte	NC	28273	**800-659-6560***	704-588-2126	226
Pemberton Fabricators Inc 30 Indel Ave	Rancocas	NJ	08073	**800-573-6322**	609-267-0922	688
Pembina Pipeline Income Fund 700 9th Ave SW Suite 2000 *TSE: PIF.UN*	Calgary	AB	T2P3V4	**888-428-3222**	403-231-7500	397
Pembroke Hospital 199 Oak St *Admissions	Pembroke	MA	02359	**800-222-2237***	781-826-8161	366-3
Pemiscot-Dunklin Electric Co-op PO Box 657	Hayti	MO	63851	**800-558-6641**	573-757-6641	244
Pemko Mfg Co Inc 4226 Transport St	Ventura	CA	93003	**800-283-9988**	805-642-2600	321
PEMSTAR Inc 3535 Technology Dr NW *NASDAQ: PMTR*	Rochester	MN	55901	**888-736-7827**	507-288-6720	613
Penco Products Inc 99 Brower Ave	Oaks	PA	19456	**800-562-1000**	610-666-0500	314-1
Pencoa Mfg Corp 117 State St *Cust Svc	Westbury	NY	11590	**800-989-7527***	516-997-2330	560
Pencor Services Inc 613 3rd St	Palmerton	PA	18071	**800-634-6572**	610-826-2552	117
Penda Corp 2344 W Wisconsin St	Portage	WI	53901	**800-356-7704**	608-742-5301	60
Pendle Hill 338 Plush Mill Rd	Wallingford	PA	19086	**800-742-3150**	610-566-4507	660
Pendleton Convention Center 1601 Westgate Ave	Pendleton	OR	97801	**800-863-9358**	541-276-6569	204
Pendleton Grain Growers Inc PO Box 1248	Pendleton	OR	97801	**800-422-7611**	541-276-7611	271
Pendleton Woolen Mills Inc 2516 SE Mailwell Dr	Portland	OR	97222	**800-760-4844**	503-226-4801	153-5
Pendu Mfg Inc 718 N Shirk Rd	New Holland	PA	17557	**800-233-0471**	717-354-4348	809
Penfield Mfg Co 1710 N Salina St	Syracuse	NY	13208	**800-724-1868**	315-471-7145	463
Penford Corp 7094 S Revere Pkwy *NASDAQ: PENX*	Englewood	CO	80112	**800-204-7369**	303-649-1900	143
Penford Products Co PO Box 428	Cedar Rapids	IA	52406	**800-553-7294**	319-398-3700	291-23
Pengo Corp 500 E Hwy 10 *Cust Svc	Laurens	IA	50554	**800-599-0211***	712-845-2540	189
Pengrowth Energy Trust 111 5th Ave SW 29th Fl *NYSE: PGH*	Calgary	AB	T2P3Y6	**800-223-4122**	403-233-0224	662
Penguin Books Canada Ltd 10 Alcorn Ave Suite 300	Toronto	ON	M4V3B2	**800-810-3104**	416-925-2249	623-2
Penguin Group (USA) Inc 375 Hudson St *Cust Svc	New York	NY	10014	**800-631-8571***	212-366-2000	623-2
Penguin Hotel 1418 Ocean Dr	Miami Beach	FL	33139	**800-235-3296**	305-534-9334	373
Penguin Point Franchise Systems Inc 2691 E US 30	Warsaw	IN	46580	**800-577-5755**	574-267-3107	657
Penhall International Inc 1801 Penhall Way	Anaheim	CA	92803	**800-736-4255**	714-778-6677	188-17
Peninsula Airways Inc 6100 Boeing Ave	Anchorage	AK	99502	**800-448-4226**	907-243-2485	26
Peninsula Asset Management Inc 1111 3rd Ave W Suite 340	Bradenton	FL	34205	**800-269-6417**	941-748-8680	393
Peninsula Beverly Hills 9882 S Santa Monica Blvd	Beverly Hills	CA	90212	**800-462-7899**	310-551-2888	373
Peninsula Chicago 108 E Superior St	Chicago	IL	60611	**866-288-8889**	312-337-2888	373
Peninsula Daily News PO Box 1330	Port Angeles	WA	98362	**800-826-7714**	360-452-2345	522-2
Peninsula Hospital 2347 Jones Bend Rd	Louisville	TN	37777	**800-526-8215**	865-970-9800	366-3
Peninsula Light Co PO Box 78	Gig Harbor	WA	98335	**888-809-8021**	253-857-5950	244
Peninsula New York 700 5th Ave	New York	NY	10019	**800-262-9467**	212-956-2888	373
Peninsula Regional Medical Center 100 E Carroll St	Salisbury	MD	21801	**800-543-7780**	410-546-6400	366-2
Penloyd/OFC 2900 E Apache St	Tulsa	OK	74110	**800-233-3794**	918-836-3794	281
Penmar Inc PO Box 299	Haverstraw	NY	10927	**800-431-7890**	845-429-2600	422
Penn Aluminum International Inc 1117 N 2nd St PO Box 490	Murphysboro	IL	62966	**800-445-7366**	618-684-2146	476
Penn Color Inc 400 Old Dublin Pike	Doylestown	PA	18901	**800-523-6032**	215-345-6550	540
Penn Commercial Inc 242 Oak Spring Rd	Washington	PA	15301	**888-309-7484**	724-222-5330	158
Penn Emblem Co 10909 Dutton Rd	Philadelphia	PA	19154	**800-793-7366**	215-632-7800	256
Penn Federal Savings Bank 36 Ferry St	Newark	NJ	07105	**800-722-0351**	973-589-8616	71
Penn Fibre Plastics 2434 Bristol Rd *Cust Svc	Bensalem	PA	19020	**800-662-7366***	215-702-9551	589
Penn Hills Resort Rt 447 & 191 PO Box 309	Analomink	PA	18320	**800-233-8240**	570-421-6464	655
Penn Insurance & Annuity Co 600 Dresher Rd *Cust Svc	Horsham	PA	19044	**800-523-0650***	215-956-8000	384-2
Penn Line Service Inc PO Box 462	Scottdale	PA	15683	**800-448-9110**	724-887-9110	187-10
Penn Machine Co 106 Station St	Johnstown	PA	15905	**800-763-0406**	814-288-1547	584
Penn Maid Foods Inc 10975 Dutton Rd	Philadelphia	PA	19154	**800-220-7063**	215-824-2800	291-27
Penn Mutual Life Insurance Co 600 Dresher Rd *Cust Svc	Horsham	PA	19044	**800-523-0650***	215-956-8000	384-2
Penn National Insurance Co 2 N 2nd St Penn National Plaza	Harrisburg	PA	17101	**800-388-4764**	717-234-4941	384-4
Penn Octane Corp 77-530 Enfield Ln Bldg D *NASDAQ: POCC*	Palm Desert	CA	92211	**877-419-6265**	760-772-9080	320
Penn State Dickinson School of Law 150 S College St	Carlisle	PA	17013	**800-840-1122**	717-240-5000	164-1
Penn State DuBois 1 College Pl	Du Bois	PA	15801	**800-346-7627**	814-375-4700	160
Penn State Fayette Rt 119 N	Uniontown	PA	15401	**877-568-4130**	724-430-4100	160
Penn State Harrisburg 777 W Harrisburg Pike	Middletown	PA	17057	**800-222-2056**	717-948-6000	163
Penn State Mont Alto 1 Campus Dr	Mont Alto	PA	17237	**800-392-6173**	717-749-6000	160
Penn State York 1031 Edgecomb Ave	York	PA	17403	**800-778-6227**	717-771-4000	160
Penn Stater Conference Center Hotel 215 Innovation Blvd	State College	PA	16803	**800-233-7505**	814-863-5000	370
Penn Treaty American Corp 3440 Lehigh St *NYSE: PTA*	Allentown	PA	18103	**800-222-3469**	610-965-2222	355-4
Penn Treaty Network America Insurance Co 3440 Lehigh St	Allentown	PA	18103	**800-362-0700**	610-965-2222	384-2
Penn-Wheeling Metal Closure & Caps 1701 Wheeling Ave	Glen Dale	WV	26038	**800-999-2567**	304-845-3402	152
Pennco Tech 3815 Otter St	Bristol	PA	19007	**800-575-9399**	215-824-3200	787
Penncorp Servicegroup Inc 600 N 2nd St Suite 500	Harrisburg	PA	17101	**800-544-9050**	717-234-2300	621
PennEngineering & Mfg Corp 5190 Old Easton Rd	Danboro	PA	18916	**800-237-4736**	215-766-8853	274
Penney JC Co Inc PO Box 10001 *NYSE: JCP ■ *Orders*	Dallas	TX	75301	**800-222-6161***	972-431-1000	227
Penney JC Optical Co 1 Harmon Dr Glen Oaks Industrial Park	Glendora	NJ	08012	**800-524-0789**	856-228-1000	533
PennFed Financial Service Inc 622 Eagle Rock Ave *NASDAQ: PFSB*	West Orange	NJ	07052	**800-722-0351**	973-669-7366	355-2
Pennfield Corp 711 Rohrerstown Rd	Lancaster	PA	17604	**800-732-0467**	717-299-2561	438
Pennichuck Corp 25 Manchester St *NASDAQ: PNNW*	Merrimack	NH	03054	**800-553-5191**	603-882-5191	774
Pennington Seed Inc 1280 Atlantic Hwy	Madison	GA	30650	**800-277-1412**	706-342-1234	684
Pennland Insurance Co 355 Maple Ave	Harleysville	PA	19438	**800-523-6344**	215-256-5000	384-4

Name / Address	City	State	ZIP	Toll-Free	Phone	Class
Pennock Co 4700 Wissahickon Ave	Philadelphia	PA	19144	**800-473-1222**	215-844-6600	288
PennRock Financial Services Corp 1060 Main St *NASDAQ: PRFS*	Blue Ball	PA	17506	**800-346-3437**	717-354-4541	355-2
Penn's View Hotel 14 N Front St	Philadelphia	PA	19106	**800-331-7634**	215-922-7600	373
Pennsylvania						
Higher Education Assistance Agency 1200 N 7th St	Harrisburg	PA	17102	**800-692-7392**	717-720-2860	711
State Lottery 2850 Turnpike Industrial Dr	Middletown	PA	17057	**800-692-7481**	717-986-4699	443
State Parks Bureau PO Box 8551	Harrisburg	PA	17105	**888-727-2757**	717-787-6640	335
Tourism Office 404 North St 4th Fl	Harrisburg	PA	17120	**800-847-4872**	717-720-1301	335
Transportation Dept 400 North St	Harrisburg	PA	17120	**800-932-4600**	717-787-2838	335
Tuition Account Plan (TAP 529) PO Box 42529	Philadelphia	PA	19101	**800-440-4000**		711
Vocational Rehabilitation Office 909 Green St	Harrisburg	PA	17120	**800-442-6351**	717-787-5244	335
Pennsylvania Bar Assn 100 South St	Harrisburg	PA	17101	**800-932-0311**	717-238-6715	73
Pennsylvania Bureau of Correctional Industries DBA Big House Products & Services PO Box 47	Camp Hill	PA	17001	**877-673-3724**	717-731-7132	618
Pennsylvania Chamber of Business & Industry 417 Walnut St	Harrisburg	PA	17101	**800-225-7224**	717-255-3252	138
Pennsylvania College of Technology 1 College Ave *Admissions	Williamsport	PA	17701	**800-367-9222***	570-326-3761	787
Pennsylvania Commerce Bancorp Inc 100 Senate Ave *NASDAQ: COBH*	Camp Hill	PA	17011	**800-937-2003**	717-975-5630	355-2
Pennsylvania Convention Center 1101 Arch St	Philadelphia	PA	19107	**800-428-9000**	215-418-4700	204
Pennsylvania Dutch Candies 1250 Slate Hill Rd	Camp Hill	PA	17011	**800-233-7082**	717-761-5440	291-8
Pennsylvania Dutch Convention & Visitors Bureau 501 Greenfield Rd	Lancaster	PA	17601	**800-723-8824**	717-299-8901	205
Pennsylvania House Co 137 10th St N *Cust Svc	Lewisburg	PA	17837	**800-782-9663***	570-523-1285	314-2
Pennsylvania Institute of Technology 800 Manchester Ave	Media	PA	19063	**800-422-0025**	610-565-7900	787
Pennsylvania Manufacturers Assn Insurance Co 380 Sentry Pkwy	Blue Bell	PA	19422	**800-222-2749**	610-397-5000	384-4
Pennsylvania Medical Society Liability Insurance Co 777 E Park Dr	Harrisburg	PA	17111	**800-445-1212**	717-558-7500	384-5
Pennsylvania Power Co 76 S Main St *Cust Svc	Akron	OH	44308	**800-720-3600***	800-646-0400	774
Pennsylvania Scale Co 1042 New Holland Ave	Lancaster	PA	17601	**800-233-0473**	717-295-6935	672
Pennsylvania State Employees Credit Union 1 Credit Union Pl	Harrisburg	PA	17110	**800-237-7328**	717-234-8484	216
Pennsylvania State University						
Altoona College 3000 Ivyside Pk	Altoona	PA	16601	**800-848-9843**	814-949-5466	160
Beaver Campus of the Commonwealth College 100 University Dr	Monaca	PA	15061	**877-564-6778**	724-773-3500	160
DuBois Campus of Commonwealth College 1 College Pl	Du Bois	PA	15801	**800-346-7627**	814-375-4700	160
Fayette Campus of Commonwealth College Rt 119 N	Uniontown	PA	15401	**877-568-4130**	724-430-4100	160
Harrisburg Campus of Capital College 777 W Harrisburg Pike	Middletown	PA	17057	**800-222-2056**	717-948-6000	163
Mont Alto Campus of Commonwealth College 1 Campus Dr	Mont Alto	PA	17237	**800-392-6173**	717-749-6000	160
York Campus 1031 Edgecomb Ave	York	PA	17403	**800-778-6227**	717-771-4000	160
Pennsylvania State University Dickinson School of Law 150 S College St	Carlisle	PA	17013	**800-840-1122**	717-240-5000	164-1
Pennsylvania State University Press 820 N University Dr USBI Suite C	University Park	PA	16802	**800-326-9180**	814-865-1327	623-5
Pennsylvania Tool & Gages Inc PO Box 534	Meadville	PA	16335	**877-827-8285**	814-336-3136	745
Pennsylvania Veterinary Medical Assn 905 W Governor Rd Suite 320	Hershey	PA	17033	**888-550-7862**	717-533-7934	782
PennWell Publishing Co 1421 S Sheridan Rd	Tulsa	OK	74112	**800-331-4463**	918-835-3161	623-9
Penny Laine Papers 2211 Century Ctr Blvd Suite 110	Irving	TX	75062	**800-456-6484**	972-812-3000	130
Pennyrile Rural Electric Co-op Corp PO Box 2900 *Cust Svc	Hopkinsville	KY	42241	**800-297-4710***	270-886-2555	244
Pennysaver 27101 Puerto Real Suite 250	Mission Viejo	CA	92691	**800-873-5548**	949-614-2600	623-8
Penray Cos Inc 440 Denniston Ct	Wheeling	IL	60090	**800-373-6729**	847-459-5000	143
Pensacola Aviation Center Inc 4145 Jerry L Maygarden Rd	Pensacola	FL	32504	**800-874-6580**	850-434-0636	63
Pensacola Christian College 250 Brent Ln	Pensacola	FL	32503	**800-722-4636**	850-478-8496	163
Pensacola Convention & Visitors Bureau 1401 E Gregory St	Pensacola	FL	32502	**800-874-1234**	850-434-1234	205
Pensacola Junior College 1000 College Blvd	Pensacola	FL	32504	**888-897-3605**	850-484-1000	160
Pensacola News Journal 101 E Romana St	Pensacola	FL	32508	**800-288-2021**	850-435-8500	522-2
Pension Benefit Guaranty Corp 1200 K St NW *Cust Svc	Washington	DC	20005	**800-400-7242***	202-326-4000	336-16
Pensions & Investments Magazine 711 3rd Ave *Cust Svc	New York	NY	10017	**888-446-1422***	212-210-0115	449-5
Penske Automotive Group 3534 N Peck Rd	El Monte	CA	91731	**800-355-6646**	626-580-6000	57
Penske Corp Rt 10 Green Hills PO Box 563	Reading	PA	19603	**800-222-0277**	610-775-6000	259
Penske Truck Leasing Co LP Rt 10 Green Hills PO Box 563	Reading	PA	19603	**800-222-0277**	610-775-6000	767
Penson Financial Services Inc 1700 Pacific Ave Suite 1400	Dallas	TX	75201	**800-696-3585**	214-765-1100	679

Name / Address	City	State	ZIP	Toll-Free	Phone	Class
Pentagon Federal Credit Union 1001 N Fairfax St	Alexandria	VA	22314	**800-247-5626**		216
Pentair Pool Products Inc 1620 Hawkins Ave	Sanford	NC	27330	**800-831-7133**	919-566-8000	627
Pentastar Aviation 7310 Highland Rd	Waterford	MI	48327	**800-662-9612**	248-666-3630	14
Pentax Imaging Co 600 12th St Suite 300	Golden	CO	80401	**800-543-6144**	303-799-8000	171-6
Pentel of America Ltd 2005 Columbia St	Torrance	CA	90503	**800-262-1127**	310-320-3831	560
Penthouse Magazine 2 Penn Plaza Suite 1125	New York	NY	10121	**800-289-7368**	212-702-6000	449-11
Penticton & Wine Country Chamber of Commerce 888 Westminster Ave W	Penticton	BC	V2A8S2	**800-663-5052**	250-492-4103	136
Pentwater Wire Products Inc PO Box 947	Pentwater	MI	49449	**800-437-2871**	231-869-6911	281
Penwest Pharmaceuticals Co 2981 Rt 22 *NASDAQ: PPCO*	Patterson	NY	12563	**800-431-2457**	845-878-8400	86
People for the American Way (PFAW) 2000 M St NW Suite 400	Washington	DC	20036	**800-326-7329**	202-467-4999	48-7
People en Espanol Magazine Rockefeller Ctr Time & Life Bldg	New York	NY	10020	**800-950-8100**	212-522-1212	449-11
People for the Ethical Treatment of Animals (PETA) 501 Front St *Orders	Norfolk	VA	23510	**800-483-4366***	757-622-7382	48-3
People Magazine Rockefeller Ctr Time & Life Bldg	New York	NY	10020	**800-541-9000**	212-522-1212	449-11
People-to-People Health Foundation 255 Carter Hall Ln	Millwood	VA	22646	**800-544-4673**	540-837-2100	48-5
PeopleClick.com Inc 2 Hannover Sq 7th Fl	Raleigh	NC	27601	**877-820-4400**	919-645-2800	176-1
PeoplePC Inc 100 Pine St Suite 1100	San Francisco	CA	94111	**800-736-7537**	415-732-4400	390
Peoples Bancorp Inc 138 Putnam St *NASDAQ: PEBO*	Marietta	OH	45750	**800-374-6123**	740-373-3155	355-2
Peoples Bancorp of North Carolina Inc 518 W 'C' St *NASDAQ: PEBK*	Newton	NC	28658	**800-948-7195**	828-464-5620	355-2
Peoples BancTrust Co Inc 310 Broad St *NASDAQ: PBTC*	Selma	AL	36701	**800-278-8725**	334-875-1000	355-2
People's Bank 850 Main St Bridgeport Ctr *NASDAQ: PBCT*	Bridgeport	CT	06604	**800-894-0300**	203-338-7171	71
People's Co-op Services 3935 Hwy 14 PO Box 339	Rochester	MN	55903	**800-214-2694**	507-288-4004	244
Peoples Community Bancorp Inc 11 S Broadway *NASDAQ: PCBI*	Lebanon	OH	45036	**888-815-3530**	513-932-3876	355-2
People's Electric Co-op 1130 W Main St	Ada	OK	74821	**877-455-3031**	580-332-3031	244
Peoples Electrical Contractors Inc 277 E Fillmore Ave	Saint Paul	MN	55107	**888-777-3409**	651-227-7711	188-4
Peoples Energy Corp 130 E Randolph Dr *NYSE: PGL* ■ *Cust Svc	Chicago	IL	60601	**866-556-6001***	312-240-4000	355-5
Peoples First Community Bank 2305 Hwy 77	Panama City	FL	32405	**800-624-9699**	850-769-5261	71
People's First Properties Inc 1022 W 23rd St Suite 400	Panama City	FL	32405	**800-624-9699**	850-769-1111	355-2
Peoples Gas Light & Coke Co 130 E Randolph Dr	Chicago	IL	60601	**866-556-6001**	312-240-4000	774
Peoples Heritage Bank 1 Portland Sq PO Box 9540 *Cust Svc	Portland	ME	04112	**800-462-3666***	207-761-8500	71
People's Mutual Holdings 850 Main St	Bridgeport	CT	06604	**800-392-3009**	203-338-7171	355-2
People's Securities Inc 1000 Lafayette Blvd	Bridgeport	CT	06601	**800-772-4400**	203-338-0800	679
Peoplesmith Software Inc 50 Cole Pkwy Suite 34 *Sales	Scituate	MA	02066	**800-777-2460***	781-545-7300	176-12
PeopleSoft Inc 4460 Hacienda Dr	Pleasanton	CA	94588	**800-380-7638**	925-225-3000	176-1
PeopleSupport Inc 1100 Glendon Ave Suite 1250 *NASDAQ: PSPT*	Los Angeles	CA	90024	**877-914-5999**	310-824-6200	39
Peopleware Inc 110 110th Ave NE Suite 590	Bellevue	WA	98004	**800-869-7166**	425-454-6444	176-10
Peoria Area Convention & Visitors Bureau 456 Fulton St Suite 300	Peoria	IL	61602	**800-747-0302**	309-676-0303	205
Peoria Chamber of Commerce 10601 N 83rd Dr	Peoria	AZ	85385	**800-580-2645**	623-979-3601	137
Peoria Charter Coach Co 2600 NE Adams St	Peoria	IL	61603	**800-448-0572**	309-688-9523	108
Peoria Disposal Co PO Box 9071	Peoria	IL	61612	**888-988-0760**	309-688-0760	791
Peoria Journal Star 1 News Plaza	Peoria	IL	61643	**800-225-5757**	309-686-3000	522-2
Peoria Journal-Star Inc 1 News Plaza	Peoria	IL	61643	**800-225-5757**	309-686-3000	623-8
Pep Boys - Manny Moe & Jack 3111 W Allegheny Ave *NYSE: PBY*	Philadelphia	PA	19132	**800-737-2697**	215-227-9000	54
PEP Direct Inc 19 Stoney Brook Dr	Wilton	NH	03086	**877-782-3782**	603-654-6141	312
Pepco Energy Services Inc 1300 N 17th St Suite 1600	Arlington	VA	22209	**800-363-7499**	703-253-1800	774
Pepperidge Farm Inc 595 Westport Ave *PR	Norwalk	CT	06851	**888-737-7374***	203-846-7000	291-1
Peppermill Hotel & Casino 2707 S Virginia St	Reno	NV	89502	**800-282-2444**	775-826-2121	133
Pepperoni Grill 1220 S Santa Fe Ave	Edmond	OK	73003	**800-679-3607**	405-705-5000	657
Pepsi Bottling Group Inc 1 Pepsi Way *NYSE: PBG* ■ *PR	Somers	NY	10589	**800-433-2652***	914-767-6000	81-2
PepsiCo Inc 700 Anderson Hill Rd *NYSE: PEP* ■ *PR	Purchase	NY	10577	**800-433-2652***	914-253-2000	184
Peptides International Inc 11621 Electron Dr	Louisville	KY	40299	**800-777-4779**	502-266-8787	229
Per Mar Security 1910 E Kimberly Rd	Davenport	IA	52807	**800-473-7627**	563-326-6291	683
Per-Se Technologies Inc 1145 Sanctuary Pkwy Suite 200 *NASDAQ: PSTI*	Alpharetta	GA	30004	**877-736-3773**	770-237-4300	455

Company / Address	City	State	ZIP	Toll-Free	Phone	Class
Perceptics Corp 9737 Cogdill Rd Suite 200	Knoxville	TN	37932	**800-448-8544**	865-966-9200	176-12
Perception Inc 111 Kayaker Way	Easley	SC	29642	**800-595-2925**	864-859-7518	701
Perceptron Inc 47827 Halyard Dr — *NASDAQ: PRCP*	Plymouth	MI	48170	**800-333-7753**	734-414-6100	464
Perclose Inc 400 Saginaw Dr	Redwood City	CA	94063	**800-587-7965**	650-474-3000	469
Percussion Software Inc 92 Montvale Ave Suite 2100	Stoneham	MA	02180	**800-283-0800**	781-438-9900	176-1
Perdido Beach Resort 27200 Perdido Beach Blvd	Orange Beach	AL	36561	**800-634-8001**	251-981-9811	655
Perdue Farms Inc PO Box 1537	Salisbury	MD	21802	**800-457-3738**	410-543-3000	608
Peregrine Foundation. Canadian 250 Merton St Suite 104	Toronto	ON	M4S1B1	**888-709-3944**	416-481-1233	48-3
Peregrine Pharmaceuticals Inc 14272 Franklin Ave Suite 100 — *NASDAQ: PPHM*	Tustin	CA	92780	**800-694-5334**	714-508-6000	86
Peregrine Systems Inc 3611 Valley Center Dr	San Diego	CA	92130	**800-638-5231**	858-481-5000	176-1
Perennial Public Power District 2122 S Lincoln Ave	York	NE	68467	**800-289-0288**	402-362-3355	244
Perez Trading Co Inc 3490 NW 125th St	Miami	FL	33167	**800-999-7599**	305-769-0761	549
PERF (Police Executive Research Forum) 1120 Connecticut Ave NW Suite 930	Washington	DC	20036	**888-202-4563**	202-466-7820	49-7
Perfecopy Co 103 W 61st St — *Cust Svc	Westmont	IL	60559	**800-323-4030***	630-769-9901	616
Perfecseal Inc 9800 Bustleton Ave	Philadelphia	PA	19115	**888-673-4100**	215-673-4500	538
Perfect Commerce Inc 850 NW Chipman Rd Suite 5050	Lees Summit	MO	64063	**888-726-8848**	816-448-4444	39
Perfect Fit Glove Co Inc 85 Innsbruck Dr	Buffalo	NY	14227	**800-245-6837**	716-668-2000	153-8
Perfect Fit Industries Inc 261 5th Ave — *Cust Svc	New York	NY	10016	**800-438-1516***	212-679-6656	731
Perfect Look Salons DBA Beauty Management Inc 270 Beavercreek Rd Suite 100	Oregon City	OR	97405	**888-268-7577**	503-723-3200	79
Perfect Shutters Inc 12213 Hwy 173	Hebron	IL	60034	**800-548-3336**	815-648-2401	690
Perfect Thread Co Inc 10 E Merrick Rd	Valley Stream	NY	11580	**800-645-3500**	516-825-6565	730-9
PerfectData Corp 110 W Easy St	Simi Valley	CA	93065	**800-973-7332**	805-581-4000	523
Perfection Clutch Co 100 Perfection Way	Timmonsville	SC	29161	**800-258-8312**	843-326-5544	60
Perfection Gear Inc 9 N Bear Creek Rd	Asheville	NC	28806	**800-532-5314**	828-253-0000	700
Performance Contracting Group Inc 16047 W 110th St	Lenexa	KS	66219	**800-255-6866**	913-888-8600	188-10
Performance Contracting Inc 6621 E Mission Ave	Spokane	WA	99212	**800-541-4323**	509-535-4814	185
Performance Fibers 15801 Woods Edge Rd	Colonial Heights	VA	23834	**800-486-0148**		594-1
Performance Inc 1 Performance Way — *Cust Svc	Chapel Hill	NC	27514	**800-727-2433***	919-933-9113	702
Performance Office Papers 21673 Cedar Ave	Lakeville	MN	55044	**800-458-7189**	952-469-1400	111
Performance Validation LLC 2601 Fortune Cir Suite 200C	Indianapolis	IN	46241	**800-875-8897**	317-248-8848	728
Perfumania Inc 251 International Pkwy	Sunrise	FL	33325	**866-600-3600**	954-335-9100	564
Perfume Originals Products Div Eagle Marketing Inc 2412 Sequoia Pk	Yukon	OK	73099	**800-233-7424**	405-354-1027	564
Pergo Inc 3128 Highwoods Blvd Suite 100	Raleigh	NC	27604	**800-222-1827**	919-773-6000	286
PeriAnesthesia Nurses. American Society of 10 Melrose Ave Suite 110	Cherry Hill	NJ	08003	**877-737-9696**	856-616-9600	49-8
Pericom Semiconductor Corp 3545 N 1st St — *NASDAQ: PSEM*	San Jose	CA	95134	**800-435-2336**	408-435-0800	686
Perillo Tours 577 Chestnut Ridge Rd	Woodcliff Lake	NJ	07677	**800-431-1515**	201-307-1234	748
Perimeter Technology Inc 540 N Commercial St	Manchester	NH	03101	**800-645-1650**	603-645-1616	39
Periodical Publishers Service Bureau 1 N Superior St	Sandusky	OH	44870	**800-654-9204**	419-626-0623	361
Periodontology. American Academy of 737 N Michigan Ave Suite 800	Chicago	IL	60611	**800-282-4867**	312-787-5518	49-8
Peripheral Dynamics Inc 5150 Campus Dr Whitemarsh Industrial Pk	Plymouth Meeting	PA	19462	**800-523-0253**	610-825-7090	171-7
Peripheral Mfg Inc 4775 Paris St	Denver	CO	80239	**800-468-6888**	303-371-8651	644
Periscope 921 Washington Ave S	Minneapolis	MN	55415	**800-339-2103**	612-339-2100	4
Peritoneal Dialysis. International Society for 66 Martin St	Milton	ON	L9T2R2	**888-834-1001**	905-875-2456	49-8
Perkasie Industries Corp PO Box 179 — *Sales	Perkasie	PA	18944	**800-523-6747***	215-257-6581	591
PerkinElmer Fluid Sciences Inc 11642 Old Baltimore Pike	Beltsville	MD	20705	**800-691-4666**	301-937-4010	321
PerkinElmer Fluid Sciences Inc Pressure Science 11642 Old Baltimore Pike	Beltsville	MD	20705	**800-691-4666**	301-937-4010	609
PerkinElmer Instruments Inc 710 Bridgeport Ave	Shelton	CT	06484	**800-762-4000**	203-925-4600	410
PerkinElmer Life & Analytical Sciences Inc 549 Albany St	Boston	MA	02118	**800-446-0035**	617-482-9595	229
PerkinElmer Optoelectronics Inc 2175 Mission College Blvd	Santa Clara	CA	95054	**800-775-6786**	408-565-0850	686
Perkins Coie LLP 1201 3rd Ave 40th Fl Suite 4800	Seattle	WA	98101	**800-829-1177**	206-583-8888	419
Perkins Restaurant & Bakery 6075 Poplar Ave Suite 800	Memphis	TN	38119	**800-877-7375**	901-766-6400	657
Perkins Specialized Transportation Inc 5502 W 73rd St	Indianapolis	IN	46268	**800-428-3762**	317-297-3550	769
Perkins & Will 330 N Wabash Ave Suite 3600	Chicago	IL	60611	**800-837-9455**	312-755-0770	258
Perko's Cafe 2246 E Date Ave	Fresno	CA	93706	**800-230-4985**	559-485-8520	657
Perley-Halladay Assoc Inc 1442 Phoenixville Pike	West Chester	PA	19380	**800-248-5800**	610-296-5800	790-2
Perlick Corp 8300 W Good Hope Rd	Milwaukee	WI	53223	**800-558-5592**	414-353-7060	650
Perma-Bound 617 E Vandalia Rd	Jacksonville	IL	62650	**800-637-6581**	217-243-5451	93
Perma-Fix Environmental Services Inc 1940 NW 67th Pl — *NASDAQ: PESI*	Gainesville	FL	32653	**800-365-6066**	352-373-4200	653
Perma Glas-Mesh Inc 345 3rd St Suite 615	Niagara Falls	NY	14303	**800-762-6694**	716-285-0731	46
Perma-Glaze Inc 1638 Research Loop Rd Suite 160	Tucson	AZ	85710	**800-332-7397**	520-722-9718	188-11
Perma-Type Co Inc 83 Northwest Dr	Plainville	CT	06062	**800-243-4234**	860-747-9999	469
Permacel US Hwy 1 S Box 671	North Brunswick	NJ	08902	**800-755-8273**	732-418-2400	717
Permalin Products Corp 205 W 39th St 16th Fl	New York	NY	10018	**800-417-3762**	212-768-7400	542-1
Permanent General Cos Inc 2636 Elm Hill Pike	Nashville	TN	37214	**800-280-1466**	615-242-1961	384-4
Permanent Magnet Co Inc 4437 Bragdon St	Indianapolis	IN	46226	**800-547-1336**	317-547-1336	450
PermaTreat Pest Control Inc 10745 Courthouse Rd	Fredericksburg	VA	22408	**800-944-8592**	540-891-7811	567
Permatron Group 1180 Pratt Blvd	Elk Grove Village	IL	60007	**800-882-8012**	847-434-1421	18
Permco Inc 1500 Frost Rd	Streetsboro	OH	44241	**800-628-2801**	330-626-2801	626
Pernod Ricard USA 777 Westchester Ave	White Plains	NY	10604	**800-488-7539**	914-539-4500	82-3
Perona Farms Food Specialties 350 Andover Sparta Rd	Andover	NJ	07821	**800-762-8569**	973-729-7878	291-14
Perot Systems Corp 2300 W Plano Pkwy — *NYSE: PER*	Plano	TX	75075	**888-407-3768**	972-577-0000	178
Perot Systems Corp Government Services Group 8550 Arlington Blvd Suite 300	Fairfax	VA	22031	**888-560-9477**	703-560-9477	193
Perreca Electric Co 520 Broadway	Newburgh	NY	12550	**800-973-7732**	845-562-4080	188-4
Perrigo Co 515 Eastern Ave — *NASDAQ: PRGO*	Allegan	MI	49010	**800-253-3606**	269-673-8451	573
Perrigo International Inc 515 Eastern Ave	Allegan	MI	49010	**800-827-2296**	269-673-8451	573
Perry Chemical & Mfg Co Inc PO Box 6419	Lafayette	IN	47903	**800-592-6614**	765-474-3404	590
Perry Daily Journal PO Box 311	Perry	OK	73077	**888-709-2197**	580-336-2222	522-2
Perry Ellis International Inc 3000 NW 107th Ave — *NASDAQ: PERY*	Miami	FL	33172	**800-327-7587**	305-592-2830	153-12
Perry Engineering Co Inc 1945 Millwood Pike	Winchester	VA	22602	**800-272-4310**	540-667-4310	188-5
Perry Equipment Corp 118 Washington Walters Industrial Pk	Mineral Wells	TX	76067	**800-877-7326**	940-325-2575	526
Perry Judd's Inc 575 W Madison St	Waterloo	WI	53594	**800-737-7948**	920-478-3551	615
Perry Mfg Co 100 Woltz St	Mount Airy	NC	27030	**800-922-8384**	336-786-6171	153-21
Perry Mfg Co Inc 1233 W 18th St	Indianapolis	IN	46202	**800-428-7200**	317-231-9037	482
Perrygraf Co 25 W 550 Geneva Rd Suite 1934	Carol Stream	IL	60188	**800-423-5329**	630-784-0100	10
Perry's Ice Cream Co Inc 1 Ice Cream Plaza	Akron	NY	14001	**800-873-7797**	716-542-5492	291-25
Perseus Inc 387 Park Ave S	New York	NY	10016	**800-386-5656**	212-340-8100	623-2
Persidion Solutions 1 Harbison Way Suite 114	Columbia	SC	29212	**800-948-8524**	803-781-7810	619
Persimmon Press PO Box 297	Belmont	CA	94002	**800-910-5080**		130
Persistence Software Inc 1720 S Amphlett Blvd 3rd Fl — *Sales	San Mateo	CA	94402	**800-803-8491***	650-372-3600	176-12
Person & Covey Inc 616 Allen Ave	Glendale	CA	91201	**800-423-2341**	818-240-1030	211
Persona Inc 17 Duffy Pl PO Box 12155 Station A	Saint John's	NL	A1B4L1	**866-737-7662**	709-754-3775	117
Personal Excellence Magazine 1366 East 1120 South	Provo	UT	84606	**800-304-9782**	801-375-4060	449-11
Personal Finance Newsletter 1750 Old Meadow Rd Suite 300	McLean	VA	22102	**800-832-2330**	703-905-8000	521-9
Personal Jet Charter Inc 5401 E Perimeter Rd	Fort Lauderdale	FL	33309	**800-432-1538**	954-776-4515	63
Personal-Touch Home Care Inc 22215 Northern Blvd	Bayside	NY	11361	**800-937-4747**	718-468-4747	358
Personnel Data Systems Inc (PDS) 650 Sentry Pkwy Suite 200	Blue Bell	PA	19422	**800-243-8737**	610-828-4294	176-1
Personnel Management Inc 1499 Windhorst Way Suite 220	Greenwood	IN	46143	**888-967-5764**	317-888-4400	707
Personnel Management Inc PO Box 6657	Shreveport	LA	71136	**800-259-4126**	318-869-4555	619
Personnel One Div Career Blazers Inc 222 W Las Colinas Blvd Suite 1250E	Irving	TX	75039	**800-787-6750**	214-296-6700	707
Perspectives Ltd 20 N Clark Suite 2650	Chicago	IL	60602	**800-456-6327**	312-558-1560	454
Perstorp Polyols Inc 600 Matzinger Rd — *Cust Svc	Toledo	OH	43612	**800-537-0280***	419-729-5448	142
Peru State College 600 Hoyt St	Peru	NE	68421	**800-742-4412**	402-872-3815	163
Peru Tourist Office 495 Biltmore Way Suite 404	Coral Gables	FL	33134	**866-661-7378**	305-476-1220	764
Peru Tribune 26 W 3rd St	Peru	IN	46970	**800-737-4488**	765-473-6641	522-2
Perugina Brands of America 800 N Brand Blvd 8th Fl	Glendale	CA	91203	**800-544-1672**	818-551-3530	292-3
Pervasive Software Inc 12365 Riata Trace Pkwy Bldg B — *NASDAQ: PVSW*	Austin	TX	78727	**800-287-4383**	512-231-6000	176-12
Pesticide Information Center. National 333 Weniger Hall	Corvallis	OR	97331	**800-858-7378**		48-17
Pesticide & Toxic Chemical News 1725 K St NW Suite 506	Washington	DC	20006	**888-732-7070**	202-887-6320	521-5
Pet Food Express 2131 Williams St	San Leandro	CA	94577	**877-472-7777**	510-346-7777	568
Pet Industry Joint Advisory Council (PIJAC) 1220 19th St NW Suite 400	Washington	DC	20036	**800-553-7387**	202-452-1525	49-4

Name / Address	City	State	ZIP	Toll-Free	Phone	Class
Pet Products Manufacturers Assn. American 255 Glenville Rd	Greenwich	CT	06831	**800-452-1225**	203-532-0000	49-4
Pet Supermarket Inc 13700 NW 2nd St	Sunrise	FL	33325	**800-361-0049**	954-351-0834	568
Pet Supplies 'Plus' Inc 22670 Haggerty Rd Suite 200	Farmington Hills	MI	48335	**866-477-7747**	248-374-1900	568
Pet Supply Assn Inc. World Wide 406 S 1st Ave	Arcadia	CA	91006	**800-999-7295**	626-447-2222	49-18
PETA (People for the Ethical Treatment of Animals) 501 Front St *Orders	Norfolk	VA	23510	**800-483-4366***	757-622-7382	48-3
Petaluma Poultry Processors PO Box 7368	Petaluma	CA	94955	**800-556-6789**	707-763-1904	608
Petcare Insurance Brokers Ltd 710 Dorval Dr Suite 400	Oakville	ON	L6K3V7	**877-738-4584**	905-842-2615	384-1
PETCO Animal Supplies Inc 9125 Rehco Rd *NASDAQ: PETC*	San Diego	CA	92121	**877-738-6742**	858-453-7845	568
Petco Inc 3050 Walkent Ave NW	Grand Rapids	MI	49544	**800-437-3826**	616-784-5868	423
Peter Deilmann Cruises 1800 Diagonal Rd Suite 170	Alexandria	VA	22314	**800-348-8287**	703-549-1741	217
Peter Glenn Ski & Sports 2901 W Oakland Pk Blvd	Fort Lauderdale	FL	33311	**800-818-0946**	954-484-7800	702
Peter Harris Clothes 952 Troy-Schenectady Rd	Latham	NY	12110	**800-444-1650**	518-785-1650	155-2
Peter Pan Bus Lines Inc 1776 Main St	Springfield	MA	01102	**800-237-8747**	413-781-2900	109
Peter Piper Inc 14635 N Kierland Blvd Suite 160	Scottsdale	AZ	85254	**800-899-3425**	480-609-6400	657
Peters Machinery Inc 500 S Vandemark Rd	Sidney	OH	45365	**800-999-3327**	937-492-4158	293
Petersen Aluminum Corp 1005 Tonne Rd	Elk Grove Village	IL	60007	**800-323-1960**	847-228-7150	688
Petersen Aviation 7155 Valjean Ave	Van Nuys	CA	91406	**800-451-7270**	818-989-2300	14
Petersen Martin Co Inc 9800 55th St	Kenosha	WI	53144	**800-677-1326**	262-658-1326	188-10
Petersen's Hunting Magazine 6420 Wilshire Blvd	Los Angeles	CA	90048	**800-800-8326**	323-782-2000	449-20
Petersen's Photographic Magazine 6420 Wilshire Blvd *Cust Svc	Los Angeles	CA	90048	**800-800-3686***	323-782-2000	449-14
Peterson Industries Inc 616 E Hwy 36	Smith Center	KS	66967	**800-368-3759**	785-282-6825	120
Peterson Machine Tool Inc 5425 Antioch Dr	Merriam	KS	66202	**800-255-6308**	913-432-7500	379
Peterson Mfg Co 4200 E 135th St	Grandview	MO	64030	**800-821-3490**	816-765-2000	430
Peterson Picture Frame Co Inc 2720 W Belmont Ave	Chicago	IL	60641	**800-293-7011**	773-463-8888	304
Peterson Steel Corp 61 W Mountain St	Worcester	MA	01606	**800-325-3245**	508-853-3630	483
Peterson Tractor Co 955 Marina Blvd	San Leandro	CA	94577	**888-738-3776**	510-357-6200	270
Peterson William R Oil Co 276 Main St Suite 1 PO box 31	Portland	CT	06480	**800-622-6971**	860-342-3560	311
Peterson's Guides Inc Princeton Pike Corporate Ctr 2000 Lenox Dr	Lawrenceville	NJ	08648	**800-338-3282**	609-896-1800	623-2
PetFoodDirect.com 203 Progress Dr *Cust Svc	Montgomeryville	PA	18936	**800-865-1333***	215-699-4535	568
Petit Jean Electric Co-op 270 Quality Dr	Clinton	AR	72031	**800-786-7618**	501-745-2493	244
Petite Auberge 863 Bush St	San Francisco	CA	94108	**800-365-3004**	415-928-6000	373
Petite Sophisticate 100 Phoenix Ave	Enfield	CT	06082	**800-662-8042**	860-741-0771	155-6
Petland Inc 250 Riverside St	Chillicothe	OH	45601	**800-221-5935**	740-775-2464	568
PetMed Express Inc 1441 SW 26th Ave *NASDAQ: PETS*	Pompano Beach	FL	33069	**800-738-6337**	954-979-5995	568
Petoskey News-Review PO Box 528	Petoskey	MI	49770	**800-968-2544**	231-347-2544	522-2
Petoskey/Harbor Springs/Boyne Country Visitors Bureau 401 E Mitchell St	Petoskey	MI	49770	**800-845-2828**	231-348-2755	205
Petro-Canada 150 6th Ave SW *NYSE: PCZ*	Calgary	AB	T2P3E3	**800-668-0220**	403-296-8000	570
Petro Heat & Power Corp 28 Southfield Ave	Stamford	CT	06902	**800-775-4645**	203-323-2121	311
Petro Plastics Co Inc 450 South Ave	Garwood	NJ	07027	**800-486-4738**	908-789-1200	588
Petro Stopping Centers 6080 Surety Dr	El Paso	TX	79905	**800-331-8809**	915-779-4711	319
Petrocco Farms 14110 Brighton Rd	Brighton	CO	80601	**888-876-2207**	303-659-6498	11-11
Petrocelli Electric Co Inc 2209 Queens Plaza N	Long Island City	NY	11101	**800-253-2721**	718-752-2200	188-4
Petroclean Inc PO Box 92	Carnegie	PA	15106	**800-247-3592**	412-279-9556	653
Petrocon Engineering Inc PO Box 20397	Beaumont	TX	77720	**800-256-5710**	409-840-2100	258
Petrofund Energy Trust 444 7th Ave SW Suite 600 *TSE: PTF.UN*	Calgary	AB	T2P0X8	**888-318-1457**	403-218-8625	662
Petroleum Assn of America. Independent 1201 15th St NW Suite 300	Washington	DC	20005	**800-433-2851**	202-857-4722	48-12
Petroleum Development Corp 103 E Main St *NASDAQ: PETD*	Bridgeport	WV	26330	**800-624-3821**	304-842-6256	525
Petroleum Engineers. Society of 222 Palisades Creek Dr	Richardson	TX	75080	**800-456-6863**	972-952-9393	48-12
Petroleum Geologists. American Assn of 1444 S Boulder Ave	Tulsa	OK	74119	**800-364-2274**	918-584-2555	48-12
Petroleum Helicopters Inc 2001 SE Evangeline Thwy *NASDAQ: PHEL*	Lafayette	LA	70508	**800-235-2452**	337-235-2452	354
Petroleum & Industrial Workers. International Union of 8131 E Rosecrans Ave	Paramount	CA	90723	**800-624-5842**	562-630-6232	405
Petroleum Marketers Assn of America (PMAA) 1901 N Fort Myer Dr Suite 500	Arlington	VA	22209	**800-300-7622**	703-351-8000	49-18
Petroleum Marketers Assn of America's Small Business Community 1901 N Fort Myer Dr Suite 500	Arlington	VA	22209	**800-300-7622**	703-351-8000	604
Petroleum & Resources Corp 7 Saint Paul St Suite 1140 *NYSE: PEO*	Baltimore	MD	21202	**800-638-2479**	410-752-5900	397
Petroleum Technology Transfer Council (PTTC) 16010 Barkers Point Ln Suite 220	Houston	TX	77079	**888-843-7882**	281-921-1720	48-12
Petron Inc PO Box 8718	Alexandria	LA	71306	**800-551-6678**	318-445-5685	769
PetroQuest Energy Inc 400 E Kaliste Saloom Rd Suite 6000 *NASDAQ: PQUE*	Lafayette	LA	70508	**800-755-8381**	337-232-7028	527
Petro's Chili & Chips 5614 Kingston Pike 2nd Fl	Knoxville	TN	37919	**800-738-7639**	865-588-1076	657
Pet's Health Plan PO Box 2847	North Canton	OH	44720	**877-592-7387**	330-305-1352	384-1
Petsche AE Co Inc 2112 W Division St	Arlington	TX	76012	**800-777-9280**	817-461-9473	245
PETsMART Direct 1989 Transit Way	Brockport	NY	14420	**800-785-0504**	585-637-7508	451
PETsMART Inc 19601 N 27th Ave *NASDAQ: PETM* ■ *Cust Svc	Phoenix	AZ	85027	**800-738-1385***	623-580-6100	568
Pettis Jerry L Memorial Veterans Affairs Medical Center 11201 Benton St *Mail Rm	Loma Linda	CA	92357	**800-741-8387***	909-825-7084	366-6
Petty Machine Co Inc 2403 Forbes Rd	Gastonia	NC	28056	**800-343-0960**	704-864-3254	729
Peugeot Motors of America Inc 150 Clove Rd Overlook at Great Notch	Little Falls	NJ	07424	**800-223-0587**	973-812-4444	59
Pevely Dairy Co 1001 S Grand Blvd	Saint Louis	MO	63104	**800-727-4407**	314-771-4400	292-4
Pew Charitable Trusts 2005 Market St 1 Commerce Sq Suite 1700	Philadelphia	PA	19103	**800-634-4850**	215-575-9050	300
Peyser David Sportswear Inc 8890 Spence St	Bay Shore	NY	11706	**800-367-7900**	631-231-7788	153-12
Peyton Meats Inc 3 Butterfield Trail Suite 101	El Paso	TX	79906	**800-351-1024**	915-751-6632	292-9
Pez Candy Inc 35 Prindle Hill Rd	Orange	CT	06477	**800-243-6087**	203-795-0531	291-8
PFA (Pedorthic Footwear Assn) 7150 Columbia Gateway Dr Suite G	Columbia	MD	21046	**800-673-8447**	410-381-7278	48-17
Pfaltzgraff Co 140 E Market St	York	PA	17401	**800-999-2811**	717-848-5500	716
Pfeiffer University 48380 Hwy 52 N	Misenheimer	NC	28109	**800-338-2060**	704-463-1360	163
Pfeiffer Vacuum Inc 24 Trafalgar Sq *Orders	Nashua	NH	03063	**800-248-8254***	603-578-6500	411
PFERD Milwaukee Brush Co Inc 30 Jytek Dr	Leominster	MA	01453	**800-336-3444**	978-840-6420	104
PFF Bancorp Inc PO Box 1520 *NYSE: PFB*	Pomona	CA	91769	**888-733-5465**	909-623-2323	355-2
PFF Bank & Trust 350 S Garey Ave	Pomona	CA	91767	**888-733-5465**		71
PFG/AFI Foodservice 1 Center Dr	Elizabeth	NJ	07207	**800-275-0155**	908-629-1800	292-8
Pfister Hotel 424 E Wisconsin Ave	Milwaukee	WI	53202	**800-558-8222**	414-273-8222	373
Pfister Hybrid Corn Co 187 N Fayette St	El Paso	IL	61738	**888-647-3478**	309-527-6010	11-5
Pfizer Canada Inc 17300 TransCanada Hwy	Kirkland	QC	H9J2M5	**800-463-6001**	514-695-0500	572
Pfizer Canada Inc Consumer Healthcare 2200 Eglinton Ave E	Toronto	ON	M1L2N3	**800-387-6577**	416-288-2200	572
Pfizer Inc 235 E 42nd St *NYSE: PFE* ■ *Prod Info	New York	NY	10017	**800-733-4717***	212-573-2323	572
PFL Life Insurance Co 4333 Edgewood Rd NE	Cedar Rapids	IA	52499	**800-247-3615**	319-398-8511	384-2
PFSweb Inc 500 N Central Expwy Suite 500 *NASDAQ: PFSW*	Plano	TX	75074	**888-330-5504**	972-881-2900	455
PG & E Corp 1 Market St *NYSE: PCG*	San Francisco	CA	94105	**800-743-5000**	415-267-7000	355-5
PG Energy Co 1 PEI Ctr *Cust Svc	Wilkes-Barre	PA	18711	**800-432-8017***	570-829-8600	320
PG Publishing Co 34 Blvd of the Allies *Cust Svc	Pittsburgh	PA	15222	**800-228-6397***	412-263-1100	623-8
PGA of America 100 Ave of the Champions	Palm Beach Gardens	FL	33418	**800-477-6465**	561-624-8400	48-22
PGA National Resort & Spa 400 Ave of the Champions	Palm Beach Gardens	FL	33418	**800-633-9150**	561-627-2000	655
PGI Inc 44 Canal Ctr Plaza 2nd Fl	Alexandria	VA	22314	**888-744-8326**	703-528-8484	183
PGI International Ltd 16101 Vallen Dr	Houston	TX	77041	**800-231-0233**	713-466-0056	776
PGI Nonwovens/Chicopee Inc 1203 S Chicopee Rd	Benson	NC	27504	**800-631-5594**	919-894-4111	730-6
PGT Industries Inc 1070 Technology Dr	Nokomis	FL	34275	**877-550-6006**	941-480-1600	232
PharmaCare Management Services Inc 695 George Washington Hwy	Lincoln	RI	02865	**800-237-6184**	401-334-0069	575
Pharmaceutical Care Network 9343 Tech Center Dr Suite 200	Sacramento	CA	95826	**800-777-9216**	916-361-4400	575
Pharmaceutical Representative Magazine 2 Northfield Plaza Suite 300	Northfield	IL	60093	**800-451-7838**	847-441-3700	449-5
Pharmaceutical Scientists. American Assn of 2107 Wilson Blvd Suite 700	Arlington	VA	22201	**877-998-2277**	703-243-2800	49-19
Pharmacists. American Society of Consultant 1321 Duke St	Alexandria	VA	22314	**800-355-2727**	703-739-1300	49-8
Pharmacists Assn. American 2215 Constitution Ave NW	Washington	DC	20037	**800-237-2742**	202-628-4410	49-8
Pharmacists Assn. National Community 100 Daingerfield Rd	Alexandria	VA	22314	**800-544-7447**	703-683-8200	49-8
Pharmacists. International Academy of Compounding PO Box 1365	Sugar Land	TX	77487	**800-927-4227**	281-933-8400	49-8
Pharmacists Mutual Insurance Co 808 US Hwy 18 W	Algona	IA	50511	**800-247-5930**	515-295-2461	384-4
Pharmacopeia. US 12601 Twinbrook Pkwy	Rockville	MD	20852	**800-877-6209**	301-881-0666	49-8
Pharmacy. Academy of Managed Care 100 N Pitt St Suite 400	Alexandria	VA	22314	**800-827-2627**	703-683-8416	49-8

Name / Address	City	State	Zip	Toll-Free	Phone	Class
Pharmacy. Academy of Students of American Pharmacists Assn 2215 Constitution Ave NW	Washington	DC	20037	**800-237-2742**	202-628-4410	49-8
Pharmacy Technicians Assn. National 3920 FM 1960 W Suite 380	Houston	TX	77068	**888-247-8700**	281-866-7900	49-8
Pharmacy Today Magazine 2215 Constitution Ave NW	Washington	DC	20037	**800-327-2742**	202-429-7557	449-16
Pharmacyclics Inc 995 E Arques Ave *NASDAQ: PCYC*	Sunnyvale	CA	94085	**800-458-0330**	408-774-0330	86
Pharmanex Inc 75 W Ctr	Provo	UT	84601	**888-742-7626**	801-345-9800	786
Pharmaton Natural Health Products Div Boehringer Ingelheim Pharmaceuticals Inc 900 Ridgebury Rd	Ridgefield	CT	06877	**800-451-6688**	203-798-9988	786
Pharmavite Corp 8510 Balboa Ave Suite 300 PO Box 9609	Northridge	CA	91325	**800-423-2405**	818-221-6200	786
PharmChem Inc 4600 N Beach St	Haltom City	TX	76137	**800-446-5177**	817-605-5300	407
Pharmed Group Corp 3075 NW 107th Ave	Miami	FL	33172	**800-683-7342**	305-592-2324	237
PharMerica Inc 175 Kelsey Ln	Tampa	FL	33619	**800-237-7676**	877-975-2273	576
Pharmics Inc PO Box 27554	Salt Lake City	UT	84127	**800-456-4138**	801-966-4138	573
PharMingen Inc 10975 Torreyana Rd	San Diego	CA	92121	**800-848-6227**	858-812-8800	86
Pharmion Corp 2525 28th St Suite 200 *NASDAQ: PHRM*	Boulder	CO	80301	**866-742-7646**	720-564-9100	572
Pharmos Corp 99 Wood Ave S Suite 311 *NASDAQ: PARS*	Iselin	NJ	08830	**888-308-5520**	732-452-9556	572
Pharos-Tribune PO Box 210	Logansport	IN	46947	**800-676-4125**	574-722-5000	522-2
Phase Forward Inc 880 Winter St *NASDAQ: PFWD*	Waltham	MA	02451	**888-703-1122**	781-890-7878	176-10
Phase One Inc 200 Broadhollow Rd Suite 312	Melville	NY	11747	**888-742-7366**	631-757-0400	580
PHCC (Plumbing-Heating-Cooling Contractors National Assn) 180 S Washington St	Falls Church	VA	22040	**800-533-7694**	703-237-8100	49-3
PHD Inc 9009 Clubridge Dr	Fort Wayne	IN	46809	**800-624-8511**	260-747-6151	220
PhDx Systems Inc 1001 University Blvd SE Suite 103	Albuquerque	NM	87106	**888-999-7439**	505-764-0174	39
Pheasant Run Resort & Spa 4051 E Main St	Saint Charles	IL	60174	**800-999-3319**	630-584-6300	655
Phelps County Regional Medical Center 1000 W 10th St	Rolla	MO	65401	**877-311-8899**	573-364-3100	366-2
Phelps Dodge Corp 1 N Central Ave *NYSE: PD*	Phoenix	AZ	85004	**800-528-1182**	602-366-8100	492
Phelps Dodge Magnet Wire Co 2131 S Coliseum Blvd	Fort Wayne	IN	46803	**800-255-2542**	260-421-5400	800
Phelps Dodge Mining Co 1 N Central Ave	Phoenix	AZ	85004	**800-528-1182**	602-366-8100	492
Phelps Fan Mfg Co Inc 10701 I-30	Little Rock	AR	72209	**800-742-6899**	501-568-5550	15
Phenix City-Russell County Chamber of Commerce 1107 Broad St	Phenix City	AL	36867	**800-892-2248**	334-298-3639	137
Phenix Supply Co 5330 Dividend Dr	Decatur	GA	30035	**800-688-3032**	770-981-2800	378
PHH Arval 940 Ridgebrook Rd	Sparks	MD	21152	**800-665-9744**	410-771-1900	284
Phi Alpha Theta Univ of South Florida 4202 E Fowler Ave SOC 107	Tampa	FL	33620	**800-394-8195**	813-974-8212	48-16
Phi Beta Lambda Inc. Future Business Leaders of America - 1912 Association Dr	Reston	VA	20191	**800-325-2946**	703-860-3334	48-11
Phi Delta Kappa International (PDK) 408 N Union St PO Box 789	Bloomington	IN	47402	**800-766-1156**	812-339-1156	48-16
Phi Delta Kappan Magazine PO Box 789	Bloomington	IN	47402	**800-766-1156**	812-339-1156	449-10
Phi Delta Phi International Legal Fraternity 1426 21st St NW	Washington	DC	20036	**800-368-5606**	202-223-6801	48-16
Phi Kappa Psi 510 Lockerbie St	Indianapolis	IN	46202	**800-486-1852**	317-632-1852	48-16
Phi Kappa Tau 5221 Morning Sun Rd	Oxford	OH	45056	**800-758-1906**	513-523-4193	48-16
Phi Mu Fraternity 3558 Habersham at Northlake	Tucker	GA	30084	**888-744-6836**	770-496-5582	48-16
Phibro Animal Health Corp 400 Kelby St 1 Parker Plaza	Fort Lee	NJ	07024	**800-223-0434**	201-944-6020	141
Phil Long Dealerships 1212 Motor City Dr	Colorado Springs	CO	80906	**800-685-5664**	719-575-7100	57
Philadelphia Baking Co 9400 Bluegrass Rd	Philadelphia	PA	19114	**800-775-5623**	215-464-4242	291-1
Philadelphia Biblical University 200 Manor Ave	Langhorne	PA	19047	**800-366-0049**	215-752-5800	163
Philadelphia Business Journal 400 Market St Suite 1200	Philadelphia	PA	19106	**800-220-3202**	215-238-1450	449-5
Philadelphia Chewing Gum Corp N Eagle & Lawrence Rds	Havertown	PA	19083	**800-793-5548**	610-449-1700	291-6
Philadelphia Consolidated Holding Corp 1 Bala Plaza Suite 100 *NASDAQ: PHLY*	Bala Cynwyd	PA	19004	**877-438-7459**	610-617-7900	355-4
Philadelphia Convention & Visitors Bureau 1700 Market St Suite 3000	Philadelphia	PA	19103	**800-225-5745**	215-636-3300	205
Philadelphia Insurance Cos 1 Bala Plaza Suite 100	Bala Cynwyd	PA	19004	**800-525-7662**	610-617-7900	384-4
Philadelphia Life Insurance Co 11815 N Pennsylvania St	Carmel	IN	46032	**800-525-7662**	317-817-6100	384-2
Philadelphia Magazine 1818 Market St 36th Fl	Philadelphia	PA	19103	**800-777-1003**	215-564-7700	449-22
Philadelphia Mixers Corp 1221 E Main St *Cust Svc	Palmyra	PA	17078	**800-733-1341***	717-832-2800	189
Philadelphia-Neshoba County Chamber of Commerce 410 Poplar Ave PO Box 330	Philadelphia	MS	39350	**877-752-2643**	601-656-1000	137
Philadelphia Orchestra 260 S Broad St Suite 1600	Philadelphia	PA	19102	**800-457-8354**	215-893-1900	563-3
Philadelphia Reserve Supply Co 400 Mack Dr	Croydon	PA	19021	**800-347-7726**	215-785-3141	190-4
Philadelphia Sign Co Inc 707 W Spring Garden St	Palmyra	NJ	08065	**800-355-1460**	856-829-1460	692
Philadelphia Stock Exchange 1900 Market St	Philadelphia	PA	19103	**800-843-7459**	215-496-5404	680
Philadelphia Tramrail Co 2207 E Ontario St	Philadelphia	PA	19134	**800-523-3654**	215-533-5100	462
Philadelphia University 4201 Henry Ave	Philadelphia	PA	19144	**800-951-7287**	215-951-2800	163
Philander Smith College 1 Trudie Kibbe Reed Dr	Little Rock	AR	72202	**800-446-6772**	501-375-9845	163
Philanthropic Research Inc 427 Scotland St	Williamsburg	VA	23185	**800-784-9378**	757-229-4631	48-10
Philbrook Museum of Art & Gardens 2727 S Rockford Rd	Tulsa	OK	74114	**800-324-7941**	918-749-7941	509
Philip Crosby Assoc II Inc PO Box 2687	Winter Park	FL	32790	**800-223-3932**	407-679-7796	193
Philip Morris USA 615 Maury St *Cust Svc	Richmond	VA	23224	**800-343-0975***	804-274-2000	741-1
Philippine Airlines Inc 116 McDonnell Rd *Resv	San Francisco	CA	94128	**800-435-9725***	650-877-4818	26
Philips Consumer Electronics PO Box 467300 *Cust Svc	Atlanta	GA	31146	**800-531-0039***	770-821-2400	52
Philips Lighting Co 200 Franklin Sq Dr	Somerset	NJ	08875	**800-555-0050**	732-563-3000	429
Philips Medical Systems 3000 Minuteman Rd	Andover	MA	01810	**866-246-7306**	978-687-1501	375
Philips Oral Healthcare Inc 35301 SE Center St	Snoqualmie	WA	98065	**800-957-9310**	425-396-2000	211
Philips Semiconductors 1109 McKay Dr	San Jose	CA	95131	**800-447-1500**	408-434-3000	686
Philips Ultrasound 22100 Bothell Everett Hwy *Cust Svc	Bothell	WA	98021	**800-433-3246***	425-487-7000	375
Phillips Beach Plaza Hotel 1301 Atlantic Ave	Ocean City	MD	21842	**800-492-5834**	410-289-9121	373
Phillips Brothers Inc 1555 W Jefferson St	Springfield	IL	62702	**800-637-9327**	217-787-3014	614
Phillips Distributing Corp 3010 Nob Hill Rd	Madison	WI	53713	**800-236-7269**	608-222-9177	82-3
Phillips Distribution Inc 3000 E Houston St PO Box 200067	San Antonio	TX	78220	**800-580-2397**	210-227-2397	549
Phillip's Flower Shops Inc 524 N Cass Ave	Westmont	IL	60559	**800-356-7257**	630-719-5200	287
Phillips Group 501 Fulling Mill Rd	Middletown	PA	17057	**800-538-7500**	717-944-0400	524
Phillips & Jordan Inc 6621 Wilbanks Rd	Knoxville	TN	37912	**800-955-0876**	865-688-8342	188-5
Phillips Mushroom Farms Inc 1011 Kaolin Rd	Kennett Square	PA	19348	**800-722-8818**	610-444-4492	11-7
Phillips Plywood Co Inc 13599 Desmond St	Pacoima	CA	91331	**800-649-6410**	818-897-7736	602
Phillips Seafood Restaurants 1215 E Fort Ave	Baltimore	MD	21230	**800-648-7067**	443-263-1200	657
Phillips-Van Heusen Corp 200 Madison Ave *NYSE: PVH*	New York	NY	10016	**800-777-1726**	212-381-3500	153-12
Phillips Victor L Co 4100 Gardner Ave	Kansas City	MO	64120	**800-878-9290**	816-241-9290	353
Philly Franchising Co 120 Interstate N Pkwy E Suite 112	Atlanta	GA	30339	**800-886-8826**	770-952-6152	657
philosophy inc 4602 E Hammond Ln	Phoenix	AZ	85034	**800-568-3151**	480-736-8200	211
PHL Limousine 101 Rt 130 Suite 6	Cinnaminson	NJ	08077	**866-264-5466**	856-786-7151	433
Phoebe Putney Memorial Hospital 417 W 3rd Ave	Albany	GA	31702	**877-312-1167**	229-312-1000	366-2
Phoenician The 6000 E Camelback Rd	Scottsdale	AZ	85251	**800-888-8234**	480-941-8200	655
Phoenix American Inc 2401 Kerner Blvd	San Rafael	CA	94901	**800-266-2344**	415-485-4500	214
Phoenix Civic Plaza Convention Center 111 N 3rd St	Phoenix	AZ	85004	**800-282-4842**	602-262-6225	204
Phoenix Color Corp 540 Western Maryland Pkwy	Hagerstown	MD	21740	**800-632-4111**	301-733-0018	614
Phoenix Computer Assoc Inc 10 Sasco Hill Rd	Fairfield	CT	06824	**800-432-1815**	203-319-3060	172
Phoenix Down Corp 85 Rt 46 W	Totowa	NJ	07512	**800-255-3696**	973-812-8100	731
Phoenix Flower Shops 5012 E Thomas Rd Suite 4	Phoenix	AZ	85018	**888-311-0404**	602-840-1200	287
Phoenix Footwear Group Inc 107 Main St *AMEX: PXG*	Old Town	ME	04468	**800-341-1550**	207-827-4431	296
Phoenix Forging Co Inc 800 Front St	Catasauqua	PA	18032	**800-444-3674**	610-264-2861	474
Phoenix Fuel Co Inc 2502 N Black Canyon Hwy	Phoenix	AZ	85009	**800-444-5823**	602-278-6271	569
Phoenix Gold International Inc 9300 N Decatur St	Portland	OR	97203	**800-950-1449**	503-286-9300	52
Phoenix Growth Capital Corp 2401 Kerner Blvd	San Rafael	CA	94901	**800-227-2626**	415-485-4500	214
Phoenix Hotel 601 Eddy St	San Francisco	CA	94109	**800-248-9466**	415-776-1380	373
Phoenix House Foundation Inc 164 W 74th St	New York	NY	10023	**800-262-2463**	212-595-5810	712
Phoenix Inn Eugene 850 Franklin Blvd	Eugene	OR	97403	**800-344-0131**	541-344-0001	373
Phoenix Inn Salem North 1590 Weston Ct NE	Salem	OR	97301	**888-239-9593**	503-581-7004	373
Phoenix Inn Salem South 4370 Commercial St SE	Salem	OR	97302	**800-445-4498**	503-588-9220	373
Phoenix Inn Vancouver 12712 SE 2nd Cir	Vancouver	WA	98684	**888-988-8100**	360-891-9777	373
Phoenix International 812 W Southern Ave	Orange	CA	92865	**800-203-4800**	714-283-4800	171-8
Phoenix International Freight Services Ltd 712 N Central Ave	Wood Dale	IL	60191	**800-959-9590**	630-766-9444	306
Phoenix Leasing Inc 2401 Kerner Blvd	San Rafael	CA	94901	**800-266-2344**	415-485-4500	214
Phoenix Life Insurance Co 1 American Row *Cust Svc	Hartford	CT	06102	**800-628-1936***	860-403-5000	384-2

Name / Address	City	State	ZIP	Toll-Free	Phone	Class
Phoenix Magazine 8501 E Princess Dr Suite 190	Scottsdale	AZ	85255	**800-228-6540**	480-664-3960	449-22
Phoenix Mfg Inc 3655 E Roeser Rd	Phoenix	AZ	85040	**800-325-6952**	602-437-1034	15
Phoenix Mutual Funds PO Box 8301	Boston	MA	02266	**800-243-1574**		517
Phoenix Newspapers Inc 200 E Van Buren St	Phoenix	AZ	85004	**800-331-9303**	602-444-8000	623-8
Phoenix Park Hotel 520 North Capitol St NW	Washington	DC	20001	**800-824-5419**	202-638-6900	373
Phoenix Society for Burn Survivors 2153 Wealthy St SE Suite 215	East Grand Rapids	MI	49506	**800-888-2876**	616-458-2773	48-17
Phoenix Symphony 455 N 3rd St Suite 390	Phoenix	AZ	85004	**800-776-9080**	602-495-1999	563-3
Phoenix Technologies Ltd 915 Murphy Ranch Rd *NASDAQ: PTEC*	Milpitas	CA	95035	**800-677-7305**	408-570-1000	176-12
Phoenix Technologies Ltd Award Software International Div 411 E Plumeria Dr	San Jose	CA	95134	**800-677-7305**	408-570-1000	176-12
Phoenix Wire Cloth Inc 585 Stephenson Hwy	Troy	MI	48083	**800-458-3286**	248-585-6350	676
Phonic Ear Inc 3880 Cypress Dr	Petaluma	CA	94954	**800-227-0735**	707-769-1110	469
Photo Control Corp 4800 Quebec Ave N *NASDAQ: PHOC*	Minneapolis	MN	55428	**800-787-8078**	763-537-3601	580
Photo Insider Magazine 11 Vreeland Rd	Florham Park	NJ	07932	**800-631-0300**	973-377-1003	449-21
Photo Marketing Assn International (PMA) 3000 Picture Pl	Jackson	MI	49201	**800-762-9287**	517-788-8100	49-18
Photo Researchers Inc 60 E 56th St	New York	NY	10022	**800-833-9033**	212-758-3420	582
Photo Resource Hawaii 111 Hekili St Suite 241	Kailua	HI	96734	**888-599-7773**	808-599-7773	582
Photo USA 3736 Franklin Rd	Roanoke	VA	24014	**888-234-6320**	540-344-0961	577
Photobiology. American Society for 810 E 10th St	Lawrence	KS	66044	**800-627-0629**	785-843-1235	49-19
PhotoFun.com Inc 10201 E Cholla St	Scottsdale	AZ	85260	**888-746-8638**		577
Photographers of America Inc. Professional 229 Peachtree St NE Suite 2200	Atlanta	GA	30303	**800-786-6277**	404-522-8600	48-4
PhotoLetter 1910 35th Ave Pine Lake Farm	Osceola	WI	54020	**800-624-0266**	715-248-3800	521-13
PhotoMedex Inc 147 Keystone Dr *NASDAQ: PHMD*	Montgomeryville	PA	18936	**800-366-4758**	215-619-3600	415
Photosource International 1910 35th Rd Pine Lake Farm	Osceola	WI	54020	**800-624-0266**	715-248-3800	623-9
PhotoSpin Inc 4030 Palos Verdes Dr N Suite 200	Rolling Hills Estates	CA	90274	**888-246-1313**	310-265-1313	176-9
PhotoWorks Inc 1260 16th Ave W	Seattle	WA	98119	**800-345-6967**	206-281-1390	577
Photri 3701 S George Mason Dr Suite C-2N	Falls Church	VA	22041	**800-544-0385**	703-931-8600	582
Physical Education Recreation & Dance. American Alliance for Health 1900 Association Dr	Reston	VA	20191	**800-213-7193**	703-476-3400	48-22
Physical Electronics Inc 18725 Lake Dr E	Chanhassen	MN	55317	**800-328-7515**	952-828-6100	410
Physical Therapy Assn. American 1111 N Fairfax St	Alexandria	VA	22314	**800-999-2782**	703-684-2782	49-8
Physician Computer Network Inc 180 Passaic Ave	Fairfield	NJ	07004	**800-844-2131**	973-808-0088	455
Physician Executives. American College of 4890 W Kennedy Blvd Suite 200	Tampa	FL	33609	**800-562-8088**	813-287-2000	49-8
Physician Office Lab News 11300 Rockville Pike Suite 1100	Rockville	MD	20852	**800-929-4824**	301-287-2700	521-8
Physician Practice Coder Newsletter 11300 Rockville Pike Suite 1100	Rockville	MD	20852	**800-929-4824**	301-287-2700	521-8
Physician Recruiters. Association of Staff 1711 W County Rd B Suite 300N	Roseville	MN	55113	**800-830-2777**	651-635-0359	49-8
Physician Recruiters. National Assn of PO Box 150127	Altamonte Springs	FL	32715	**800-726-5613**	407-774-7880	49-8
Physician Specialists Inc. American Assn of 2296 Henderson Mill Rd Suite 206	Atlanta	GA	30345	**800-447-9397**	770-939-8555	49-8
Physician & Sportsmedicine Magazine 4530 W 77th St	Minneapolis	MN	55435	**800-525-5003**	952-835-3222	449-16
Physicians. American Academy of Disability Evaluating 150 N Wacker Dr Suite 1420	Chicago	IL	60606	**800-456-6095**	312-658-1171	49-8
Physicians. American Academy of Family 11400 Tomahawk Creek Pkwy	Leawood	KS	66211	**800-274-2237**	913-906-6000	49-8
Physicians. American Assn of Naturopathic 3201 New Mexico Ave NW Suite 350	Washington	DC	20016	**866-538-2267**	202-895-1392	48-17
Physicians. American College of 190 N Independence Mall W	Philadelphia	PA	19106	**800-523-1546**	215-351-2400	49-8
Physicians. American College of Emergency PO Box 619911	Dallas	TX	75261	**800-798-1822**	972-550-0911	49-8
Physicians. American College of Osteopathic Family 330 E Algonquin Rd Suite 1	Arlington Heights	IL	60005	**800-323-0794**	847-228-6090	49-8
Physicians. Association of Emergency 911 Whitewater Dr	Mars	PA	16046	**866-772-1818**	724-772-1818	49-8
Physicians. Canadian Assn of Emergency 1785 Alta Vista Dr Suite 104	Ottawa	ON	K1G3Y6	**800-463-1158**	613-523-3343	49-8
Physicians' Committee for Responsible Medicine (PCRM) 5100 Wisconsin Ave NW Suite 400	Washington	DC	20016	**866-416-7276**	202-686-2210	49-8
Physicians Health Plan Inc PO Box 30377	Lansing	MI	48909	**800-832-9186**	517-364-8400	384-3
Physicians Healthcare Plans Inc 55 Alhambra Plaza 7th Fl	Coral Gables	FL	33134	**800-577-1072**	305-441-9400	384-3
Physicians Life Insurance Co 2600 Dodge St	Omaha	NE	68131	**800-228-9100**	402-633-1000	384-2
Physicians Mutual Insurance Co 2600 Dodge St	Omaha	NE	68131	**800-228-9100**	402-633-1000	384-2
Physicians. National Assn of Managed Care 4435 Waterfront Dr Suite 101 PO Box 4765	Glen Allen	VA	23058	**800-722-0376**	804-527-1905	49-8
Physicians Plus Insurance Corp 22 E Mifflin St Suite 200	Madison	WI	53703	**800-545-5015**	608-282-8900	384-3
Physicians' Reciprocal Insurers 111 E Shore Rd	Manhasset	NY	11030	**800-632-6040**	516-365-6690	384-5
Physicians Search 5581 E Stetson Ct	Anaheim	CA	92807	**800-748-6320**	714-685-1047	262
Physicians Weight Loss Centers of America Inc 395 Springside Dr	Akron	OH	44333	**800-205-7887**	330-666-7952	797
Physics Today Magazine 1 Physics Ellipse	College Park	MD	20740	**800-344-6902**	301-209-3040	449-19
Physiometrix Inc 101 Billerica Ave 5 Billerica Pk *NASDAQ: PHYX*	North Billerica	MA	01862	**800-474-9746**	978-670-2422	468
Phytron Inc 1347 Main St	Waltham	MA	02451	**800-967-4987**	781-647-3581	507
PI Inc PO Box 669 *Cust Svc	Athens	TN	37371	**800-951-3542***	423-745-6213	597
PI & Information Services LLC PO Box 157	Beaverton	OR	97075	**800-649-7530**	503-643-4274	392
Pi Lambda Phi Fraternity Inc 304 Federal Rd Suite 113	Brookfield	CT	06804	**800-394-7573**	203-740-1044	48-16
Pi Lambda Theta PO Box 6626	Bloomington	IN	47407	**800-487-3411**		48-16
Pi Sigma Epsilon (PSE) 3747 Howell Ave	Milwaukee	WI	53207	**800-761-9350**	414-328-1952	48-16
PIA (National Assn of Professional Insurance Agents) 400 N Washington St	Alexandria	VA	22314	**800-742-6900**	703-836-9340	49-9
Piad Precision Casting Corp RD 12 Box 38	Greensburg	PA	15601	**800-441-9858**	724-838-5500	303
PIA/GATF (Printing Industries of America/Graphic Arts Technical Foundation) 200 Deer Run Rd	Sewickley	PA	15143	**800-910-4283**	412-741-6860	49-16
PianoDisc 4111 N Freeway Blvd	Sacramento	CA	95834	**800-566-3472**	916-567-9999	516
Piantedosi Baking Co Inc 240 Commercial St	Malden	MA	02148	**800-339-0080**	781-321-3400	291-1
Pibbs Industries 133-15 32nd Ave	Flushing	NY	11354	**800-551-5020**	718-445-8046	78
Pic Design Corp 86 Benson Rd PO Box 1004	Middlebury	CT	06762	**800-243-6125**	203-758-8272	609
Pic-Mount Imaging Corp 2300 Arrowhead Dr	Carson City	NV	89706	**800-458-6875**	775-887-5100	580
PIC USA 3033 Nashville Rd PO Box 348	Franklin	KY	42135	**800-325-3398**	270-586-9224	11-6
Picasso Travel 350 5th Ave Suite 1417	New York	NY	10118	**800-525-3632**	212-244-5454	17
Piccadilly Cafeterias Inc 3232 Sherwood Forest Blvd	Baton Rouge	LA	70816	**800-535-9974**	225-293-9440	657
Piccadilly Circus Pizza 1007 Okoboji Ave	Milford	IA	51351	**800-338-4340**	712-338-2771	657
Piccadilly Inn Airport 5115 E McKinley Ave	Fresno	CA	93727	**800-468-3587**	559-251-6000	373
Piccadilly Inn Shaw 2305 W Shaw Ave	Fresno	CA	93711	**800-468-3587**	559-226-3850	373
Piccadilly Inn University 4961 N Cedar Ave	Fresno	CA	93726	**800-468-3587**	559-224-4200	373
Pick Up Stix Inc 1330 Calle Avanzado	San Clemente	CA	92673	**800-400-7849**	949-361-3189	657
Pickaway County Chamber of Commerce 135 W Main	Circleville	OH	43113	**800-897-9420**	740-474-4923	137
Pickaway County District Public Library 1160 N Court St	Circleville	OH	43113	**888-268-3756**	740-477-1644	426
Pickaway County Visitors Bureau 135 W Main St	Circleville	OH	43113	**888-770-7425**	740-474-4923	205
Pickens-Kane Moving Co 410 N Milwaukee Ave	Chicago	IL	60610	**800-853-6462**	312-942-0330	508
Pickwick Electric Co-op 530 Mulberry Ave	Selmer	TN	38375	**800-372-8258**	731-645-3411	244
Pickwick Grand Heritage Hotel 85 5th St	San Francisco	CA	94103	**800-437-4824**	415-421-7500	373
Pickwick Hotel 1023 20th St S	Birmingham	AL	35205	**800-255-7304**	205-933-9555	373
Pickwick Hotel 132 W Broadway	San Diego	CA	92101	**800-826-0009**	619-234-9200	373
PICO Holdings Inc 875 Prospect St Suite 301 *NASDAQ: PICO*	La Jolla	CA	92037	**888-389-3222**	858-456-6022	355-4
Pico Macom Inc 355 Parkside Dr	San Fernando	CA	91340	**800-421-6511**	818-493-4300	633
Pictorvision 7701 Haskel Ave Suite B	Van Nuys	CA	91406	**800-876-5583**	818-785-9881	580
Picture Arts 99 Pasadena Ave	South Pasadena	CA	91030	**800-720-9755**	323-257-4400	582
Picture People 1157 Triton Dr Suite B	Foster City	CA	94404	**800-827-4686**	650-578-9291	579
PictureQuest 8280 Greensboro Dr Suite 520	McLean	VA	22102	**800-764-7427**		582
Picturesque Stock Photo Agency 1520-3 Brookside Dr	Raleigh	NC	27604	**800-450-3377**	919-828-0023	582
Pied Piper Mills Inc 423 E Lake Dr	Hamlin	TX	79520	**800-338-4610**	325-576-3684	438
Piedmont Airlines Inc DBA US Airways Express 5443 Airport Terminal Rd	Salisbury	MD	21804	**800-354-3394**	410-742-2996	26
Piedmont College 165 Central Ave	Demorest	GA	30535	**800-277-7020**	706-778-8033	163
Piedmont Hawthorne Aerocentre 4360 Agar Dr	Richmond	BC	V7B1A3	**888-298-7326**	604-279-9922	63
Piedmont Hawthorne Aviation 3821 N Liberty St *Sales	Winston-Salem	NC	27105	**800-259-1940***	336-776-6060	63
Piedmont Home Textile Inc PO Box 267	Walhalla	SC	29691	**800-334-9033**	864-638-3636	731
Piedmont Mechanical Inc 116 John Dodd Rd	Spartanburg	SC	29303	**800-849-5724**	864-578-9114	188-10
Piedmont Natural Gas 1915 Rexford Rd *NYSE: PNY*	Charlotte	NC	28211	**800-752-7504**	704-364-3120	774
Piedmont Technical College 620 N Emerald Rd	Greenwood	SC	29646	**800-868-5528**	864-941-8324	787
Pier 5 Hotel 711 Eastern Ave	Baltimore	MD	21202	**866-583-4162**	410-539-2000	373

Toll-Free | Phone | Class

Pier 39
Beach & Embarcadero Sts ..... San Francisco CA 94133 **800-325-7437** 415-981-7437 50
Pier 39 LP Inc
Beach & Embarcadero Sts
Stairway 2 Level 3 .... San Francisco CA 94133 **800-325-7437** 415-705-5500 641
Pier 66. Hyatt Regency
2301 SE 17th St Cswy
Pier 66 .... Fort Lauderdale FL 33316 **800-233-1234** 954-525-6666 655
Pier House Resort & Caribbean Spa
1 Duval St...................... Key West FL 33040 **800-327-8340** 305-296-4600 655
Pier Pointe Resort
4320 El Mar Dr........ Lauderdale-by-the-Sea FL 33308 **800-331-6384** 954-776-5121 373
Pierburg Instruments Inc
47519 Halyard Dr................ Plymouth MI 48170 **800-394-3569** 734-446-8360 486
Pierce Art Center
9801 Nicollet Ave............. Bloomington MN 55420 **800-338-9801** 952-884-1991 45
Pierce Biotechnology Inc
3747 N Meridian Rd.............. Rockford IL 61101 **800-874-3723** 815-968-0747 229
Pierce Distribution Services Inc
PO Box 15600 ....Loves Park IL 61132 **800-466-7397** 815-636-5650 539
Pierce Mfg Inc 2600 American Dr .....Appleton WI 54914 **888-974-3723*** 920-832-3000 505
*Cust Svc
Pierce Pacific Mfg Inc
PO Box 30509 ....Portland OR 97294 **800-760-3270** 503-808-9110 189
Pierce-Pepin Electric Co-op
7725 US Hwy 10 .... Ellsworth WI 54011 **800-924-2133** 715-273-4355 244
Pierce Transit
3701 96th St SW PO Box 99070....Lakewood WA 98499 **800-562-8109** 253-581-8000 460
Pierpont Inn 550 Sanjon Rd .... Ventura CA 93001 **800-285-4667** 805-643-6144 373
Pierpont Morgan Library
29 E 36th St....................New York NY 10016 **800-861-0001*** 212-685-0008 509
*Orders
Pierre Area Chamber of Commerce
800 W Dakota Ave .... Pierre SD 57501 **800-962-2034** 605-224-7361 137
Pierre Convention & Visitors Bureau
800 W Dakota Ave PO Box 548........ Pierre SD 57501 **800-962-2034** 605-224-7361 205
Pierre Native Plant Arboretum
Izaak Walton Rd .... Pierre SD 57501 **800-228-5254** 605-773-3594 98
Pigeon Forge Dept of Tourism
2450 Parkway................ Pigeon Forge TN 37863 **800-251-9100** 865-453-8574 205
Piggly Wiggly Carolina Co Inc
PO Box 118047 .... Charleston SC 29423 **800-243-9880** 843-554-9880 339
Piggly Wiggly Corp
2605 Sagebrush Dr Suite 200 .. Flower Mound TX 75028 **800-800-8215** 972-410-2901 339
PIJAC (Pet Industry Joint Advisory Council) 1220 19th St NW
Suite 400 .... Washington DC 20036 **800-553-7387** 202-452-1525 49-4
Pike County Chamber of Commerce & Economic Development District
112 N Railroad Blvd.............. McComb MS 39648 **800-399-4404** 601-684-2291 137
Pike Electric Inc 100 Pike Way .....Mount Airy NC 27030 **800-343-7453** 336-789-2171 188-4
Pike & Fischer Inc
1010 Wayne Ave Suite 1400 .... Silver Spring MD 20910 **800-255-8131** 301-562-1530 623-9
Pike Industries Inc
3 Eastgate Park Rd................ Belmont NH 03220 **800-283-7453** 603-527-5100 187-4
Pike Lumber Co Inc PO Box 247......... Akron IN 46910 **800-356-4554** 574-893-4511 671
Pikes Peak Community College
5675 S Academy Blvd ......Colorado Springs CO 80906 **800-456-6847** 719-576-7711 160
Pikeville College 147 Sycamore St..... Pikeville KY 41501 **866-232-7700** 606-218-5250 163
Piknik Products Co Inc
3806 Day St .... Montgomery AL 36108 **800-300-8557*** 334-265-1567 291-19
*Cust Svc
Pilgrim Haven 373 Pine Ln .... Los Altos CA 94022 **877-284-7635** 650-948-8291 659
Pilgrim Plastic Products Co
1200 W Chestnut St.............. Brockton MA 02301 **877-343-7810** 508-436-6300 10
Pilgrim Tours & Travel Inc
3821 Main St PO Box 268.......Morgantown PA 19543 **800-322-0788** 610-286-0788 748
Pill Ralph Electrical Supply Co
307 Dorchester Ave .... Boston MA 02127 **800-879-7455** 617-269-8200 245
Pillar Industries 21905 Gateway Rd ...Brookfield WI 53045 **800-558-7733** 262-317-5300 313
Pillar to Post Inc
13902 N Dale Mabry Hwy Suite 300 ... Tampa FL 33618 **800-294-5591** 813-962-4461 360
Pillars Hotel 125 High St .... Buffalo NY 14203 **877-633-4667** 716-845-0112 373
Pillars Hotel at New River Sound
111 N Birch Rd............. Fort Lauderdale FL 33304 **800-800-7666** 954-467-9639 373
Piller Inc 334 CR 49 .... Middletown NY 10940 **800-597-6937** 845-355-5000 507
Pilling Surgical
200 Precision Rd Suite 200........ Horsham PA 19044 **800-523-6507*** 215-442-8700 468
*Cust Svc
Pillsbury Baptist Bible College
315 S Grove Ave ....Owatonna MN 55060 **800-747-4557** 507-451-2710 163
Pillsbury Winthrop LLP
50 Fremont St.............. San Francisco CA 94105 **800-477-0770** 415-983-1000 419
Pilot Air Freight Corp
314 N Middletown Rd ....Lima PA 19037 **800-447-4568*** 610-891-8100 440
*Cust Svc
Pilot Chemical Co
11756 Burke St............Santa Fe Springs CA 90670 **800-707-4568** 562-698-6778 143
Pilot-News PO Box 220 .... Plymouth IN 46563 **800-933-0356** 574-936-3101 522-2
Pilot Software Inc 1 Canal Pk....... Cambridge MA 02141 **800-944-0094** 617-374-9400 176-1
Pilot Travel Centers LLC
PO Box 10146 .... Knoxville TN 37939 **800-562-6210** 865-588-7487 319
Pilot Tribune PO Box 1187 .... Storm Lake IA 50588 **800-798-6397** 712-732-3130 522-2
Pilots Assn. Air Line
535 Herndon Pkwy................Herndon VA 20170 **800-359-2572** 703-689-2270 405
Pilots Assn. Aircraft Owners &
421 Aviation Way .... Frederick MD 21701 **800-872-2672** 301-695-2000 49-21
Pilots Assn. American
499 S Capitol St SW Suite 409 ... Washington DC 20003 **800-527-4568** 202-484-0700 49-21
Pima Community College
4905 E Broadway Blvd..............Tucson AZ 85709 **800-860-7462** 520-206-4500 160
West Campus 2202 W Anklam Rd.....Tucson AZ 85709 **800-860-7462** 520-206-6600 160
PIMCO Funds 2187 Atlantic St........ Stamford CT 06902 **800-628-1237** 517
PIMCO Institutional Funds
PO Box 219024 .... Kansas City MO 64121 **800-927-4648** 517
Pine Bluff Commercial
PO Box 6469 ....Pine Bluff AR 71611 **800-669-3110** 870-534-3400 522-2
Pine Bluff Convention Center
1 Convention Ctr Plaza............Pine Bluff AR 71601 **800-536-7660** 870-536-7600 204
Pine Bluff Convention & Visitors Bureau 1 Convention Ctr Plaza .....Pine Bluff AR 71601 **800-536-7660** 870-536-7600 205
Pine Crest Inn 85 Pine Crest Ln .... Tryon NC 28782 **800-633-3001** 828-859-9135 373
Pine Hall Brick Co
2701 Shorefair Dr........... Winston-Salem NC 27105 **800-952-7425** 336-721-7536 148
Pine Manor College
400 Heath St................. Chestnut Hill MA 02467 **800-762-1357** 617-731-7000 163
Pine Needles Lodge & Golf Club
PO Box 88 .... Southern Pines NC 28388 **800-747-7272** 910-692-7111 655
Pine Rest Christian Mental Health Services PO Box 165..........Grand Rapids MI 49508 **800-678-5500** 616-455-5000 366-3
Pine State Knitwear Co Inc
630 Independence Blvd ....Mount Airy NC 27030 **800-542-1533** 336-789-9121 153-16
Pine State Trading Co 8 Ellis Ave...... Augusta ME 04330 **800-873-3825** 207-622-3741 82-1
Pine Tree Point Resort
70 Anthony St PO Box 99 .....Alexandria Bay NY 13607 **888-746-3229** 315-482-9911 655
Pinehurst Resort & Country Club
80 Carolina Vista Dr.............. Pinehurst NC 28374 **800-487-4653** 910-295-6811 655
PineIsle Resort. Renaissance
9000 Holiday Rd......... Lake Lanier Islands GA 30518 **800-468-3571** 770-945-8921 655
Pines Lodge 141 Scott Hill Rd ....Avon CO 81620 **800-859-8242** 970-845-7900 373
Pines Mfg Inc 30505 Clemens Rd...... Westlake OH 44145 **800-207-2840** 440-835-5553 485
Pines Resort The 103 Shore Rd .... Digby NS B0V1A0 **800-667-4637** 902-245-2511 655
Pinestone Resort PO Box 809....... Haliburton ON K0M1S0 **800-461-0357** 705-457-1800 655
Pinkerton's Inc
4330 Park Terrace Dr........Westlake Village CA 91361 **800-232-7465** 818-706-6800 682
Pinnacle Air 802 Airport Rd .... Springdale AR 72764 **800-828-4462** 479-751-4462 24
Pinnacle Airlines Inc
1689 Nonconnah Blvd Suite 111 .... Memphis TN 38132 **800-603-4594** 901-348-4100 26
NASDAQ: PNCL
Pinnacle Consulting Group Inc
71 Moore Rd ....Wayland MA 01778 **800-693-7466** 508-358-8070 193
Pinnacle Data Systems Inc
6600 Port Rd Suite 100...........Groveport OH 43125 **800-882-8282** 614-748-1150 171-3
AMEX: PNS
Pinnacle Fitness
12440 E Imperial Hwy Suite 300..... Norwalk CA 90651 **800-447-7457** 562-484-2000 349
Pinnacle Frames & Accents Inc
2606 Hwy 67 S PO Box 507 ..... Pocahontas AR 72455 **800-231-9974** 870-892-5227 304
Pinnacle Health Hospice
3705 Elmwood Dr............... Harrisburg PA 17110 **800-889-1098** 717-671-3700 365
Pinnacle Inn Resort
301 Pinnacle Inn Rd............. Banner Elk NC 28604 **800-405-7888** 828-387-2231 655
Pinnacle Motor Club
3801 William D Tate St Suite 800 ...Grapevine TX 76051 **800-446-1289** 53
Pinnacle Systems Inc
280 N Bernardo Ave..........Mountain View CA 94043 **800-522-8783*** 650-526-1600 171-5
NASDAQ: PCLE ■ *Sales
Pinnacle West Capital Corp
400 N 5th St..................... Phoenix AZ 85004 **800-457-2983** 602-250-1000 355-5
NYSE: PNW
Pioneer The 502 N State St......... Big Rapids MI 49307 **800-968-1114** 231-796-4831 522-2
Pioneer Broach Co
6434 Telegraph Rd.............Los Angeles CA 90040 **800-621-1945** 323-728-1263 447
Pioneer Cos Inc
700 Louisiana St Suite 4300 .... Houston TX 77002 **800-423-4117** 713-570-3200 141
NASDAQ: PONR
Pioneer Electric Co-op
300 Herbert St ....Greenville AL 36037 **800-239-3092** 334-382-6636 244
Pioneer Electric Co-op Inc
1850 W Oklahoma St.............. Ulysses KS 67880 **800-794-9302** 620-356-1211 244
Pioneer Electronics (USA) Inc
2265 E 220th St............... Long Beach CA 90810 **800-421-1404*** 310-952-2000 52
*Cust Svc
Pioneer Funds 60 State St............. Boston MA 02109 **800-225-6292** 617-742-7825 517
Pioneer Hi-Bred International Inc
400 Locust St Capital Sq
Suite 800 .... Des Moines IA 50309 **800-247-6803** 515-248-4800 11-5
Pioneer Inc 5184 Pioneer Rd ....Meridian MS 39301 **800-647-6272** 601-483-5211 61
Pioneer Investment Management Inc
60 State St 4th Fl.................. Boston MA 02109 **800-225-6292** 617-742-7825 679
Pioneer Life Insurance Co
11815 N Pennsylvania St............ Carmel IN 46032 **800-759-7007** 317-817-6100 384-2
Pioneer Limousine Service
15643 Sherman Way ....Van Nuys CA 91406 **800-640-0700** 818-609-1566 433
Pioneer Machinery Co
3239 Sunset Blvd PO
Box 3079 .... West Columbia SC 29171 **888-983-9990** 803-936-9990 353
Pioneer Medical Systems
37 Washington St................. Melrose MA 02176 **800-338-2303** 781-662-2222 565
Pioneer Mfg 4529 Industrial Pkwy .... Cleveland OH 44135 **800-877-1500** 216-671-5500 540
Pioneer Mutual Life Insurance Co
PO Box 2546 .... Fargo ND 58108 **800-437-4692** 701-297-5700 384-2
Pioneer National Latex Co
246 E 4th St.................... Ashland OH 44805 **800-537-6723** 419-289-3300 750
Pioneer Natural Resources Co
303 W Wall St Suite 101 .... Midland TX 79701 **800-532-5291** 432-683-4768 525
NYSE: PXD
Pioneer Photo Albums Inc
9801 Deering Ave..............Chatsworth CA 91311 **800-366-3686** 818-882-2161 87
Pioneer Railcorp 1318 S Johanson Rd....Peoria IL 61607 **800-914-3810** 309-697-1400 634
NASDAQ: PRRR
Pioneer Resort & Marina
1000 Pioneer Dr.................Oshkosh WI 54902 **800-683-1980** 920-233-1980 373
Pioneer Rural Electric Co-op Inc
344 W US Rt 36 PO Box 604 .... Piqua OH 45356 **800-762-0997** 937-773-2523 244
Pioneer Telephone Co-op
1304 Main St PO Box 631.........Philomath OR 97370 **888-929-1014** 541-929-3135 721
Pioneer Telephone Co-op Inc
108 E Roberts Ave PO Box 539.....Kingfisher OK 73750 **800-992-0234** 405-375-4111 721
Pioneer Tool & Forge Inc
101 6th St ....New Kensington PA 15068 **800-359-6408** 724-337-4700 747
Pioneer Wholesale Co 500 W Bagley Rd ... Berea OH 44017 **888-234-5400** 440-234-5400 44
Pioneer/Eclipse Corp 1 Eclipse Rd ...... Sparta NC 28675 **800-367-3550*** 336-372-8080 379
*Cust Svc
Pipe Distributors Inc 5400 Mesa Dr.... Houston TX 77028 **800-989-7473** 713-635-4200 483
Piper Jaffray Cos
800 Nicollet Mall Suite 800 ...... Minneapolis MN 55402 **800-333-6000** 612-303-6000 679
NYSE: PJC

Name / Address	City	State	ZIP	Toll-Free	Phone	Class
Piper Jaffray Ventures 800 Nicollet Mall Suite 800	Minneapolis	MN	55402	**800-333-6000**	612-303-6000	779
Piper Products Inc 300 S 84th Ave	Wausau	WI	54401	**800-558-5880**	715-842-2724	293
Pipestem Resort State Park PO Box 150	Pipestem	WV	25979	**800-225-5982**	304-466-1800	554
Pipestone Publishing Co PO Box 277	Pipestone	MN	56164	**800-325-6440**	507-825-3333	623-8
Pipin Industries Inc 6500 W 65th St Suite 200	Chicago	IL	60638	**888-706-8646**	708-458-3440	232
Piqua Materials Inc 1750 W Statler Rd	Piqua	OH	45356	**800 338 3062**	937-773-4824	710
Pirelli Cables & Systems 700 Industrial Dr *Cust Svc	Lexington	SC	29072	**800-845-8507***	803-951-4800	801
Pirelli Tire North America 100 Pirelli Dr PO Box 700	Rome	GA	30161	**800-747-3554**		739
Pitcher Inn 275 Main St	Warren	VT	05674	**888-867-4824**	802-496-6350	373
Pitco Frialator Inc PO Box 501	Concord	NH	03302	**800-258-3708**	603-225-6684	293
Pitney Bowes Credit Corp 27 Waterview Dr	Shelton	CT	06484	**800-243-9506**	203-922-4000	214
Pitney Bowes Inc 1 Elmcroft Rd *NYSE: PBI*	Stamford	CT	06926	**800-672-6937**	203-356-5000	112
Pitney Bowes Management Services 220 E 42 St 4th Fl	New York	NY	10017	**800-669-0800**	917-351-2900	455
Pitney Hardin Kipp & Szuch LLP 200 Campus Dr	Florham Park	NJ	07932	**800-343-7457**	973-966-6300	419
Pitt & Greene Electric Membership Corp 3989 W Wilson St	Farmville	NC	27828	**800-622-1362**	252-753-3128	244
Pitt Ohio Express 15 27th St *Cust Svc	Pittsburgh	PA	15222	**800-366-7488***	412-281-9883	769
Pitt Plastics Inc 1400 Atkinson Ave	Pittsburg	KS	66762	**800-835-0366**	620-231-4030	67
Pittsburg Area Chamber of Commerce 117 W 4th St	Pittsburg	KS	66762	**800-879-1112**	620-231-1000	137
Pittsburg State University 1701 S Broadway St	Pittsburg	KS	66762	**800-854-7488**	620-231-7000	163
Pittsburg Tank & Tower Co Inc 1 Watertank Pl	Henderson	KY	42420	**800-499-8265**	270-826-9000	188-14
Pittsburgh Corning Corp 800 Presque Isle Dr	Pittsburgh	PA	15239	**800-245-1217**	724-327-6100	382
Pittsburgh Cut Flower Co 1901 Liberty Ave	Pittsburgh	PA	15222	**800-837-2837**	412-355-7000	288
Pittsburgh (Greater) Chamber of Commerce 425 6th Ave 11th Fl	Pittsburgh	PA	15219	**800-843-8772**	412-392-4500	137
Pittsburgh (Greater) Convention & Visitors Bureau 425 6th Ave 30th Fl	Pittsburgh	PA	15219	**800-359-0758**	412-281-7711	205
Pittsburgh Institute of Aeronautics PO Box 10897	Pittsburgh	PA	15236	**800-444-1440**	412-462-9011	787
Pittsburgh Institute of Mortuary Science Inc 5808 Baum Blvd	Pittsburgh	PA	15206	**800-933-5808**	412-362-8500	787
Pittsburgh Magazine 4802 5th Ave *Sales	Pittsburgh	PA	15213	**800-495-7323***	412-622-6440	449-22
Pittsburgh Penguins 1 Chatham Ctr Suite 400	Pittsburgh	PA	15219	**800-642-7366**	412-642-1300	703
Pittsburgh Supercomputing Center 4400 5th Ave	Pittsburgh	PA	15213	**800-221-1641**	412-268-4960	654
Pittsburgh Technical Institute 1111 McKee Rd	Oakdale	PA	15071	**800-905-9985**	412-809-5100	787
Pittsburgh Testing Lab Div Professional Service Industries Inc 850 Poplar St	Pittsburgh	PA	15220	**866-842-9637**	412-922-4000	728
Pittsburgh Tribune-Review 503 Martindale St 3rd Fl	Pittsburgh	PA	15212	**800-433-3045**	412-321-6460	522-2
Pittsburgh Zoo & PPG Aquarium 1 Wild Pl	Pittsburgh	PA	15206	**800-474-4966**	412-665-3639	811
Pittsville Homes Inc PO Box C	Pittsville	WI	54466	**888-248-8371**	715-884-2511	107
Pitzer College 1050 N Mills Ave	Claremont	CA	91711	**800-748-9371**	909-621-8129	163
Pivot Interiors 2740 Zanker Rd Suite 100	San Jose	CA	95134	**800-350-7135**	408-432-5600	315
Pivotal Corp 858 Beatty St Suite 700	Vancouver	BC	V6B1C1	**877-797-4595**	604-699-8000	39
Pixar Animation Studios 1200 Park Ave *NASDAQ: PIXR*	Emeryville	CA	94608	**800-888-9856**	510-752-3000	33
Pizza Boli's 5725 Falls Rd	Baltimore	MD	21209	**800-234-2654**		657
Pizza Factory Inc 49430 Rd 426	Oakhurst	CA	93644	**800-654-4840**	559-683-3377	657
Pizza Hut Inc 14841 N Dallas Pkwy	Dallas	TX	75254	**800-948-8488**	972-338-7700	657
Pizza Inn Inc 3551 Plano Pkwy *NASDAQ: PZZI*	The Colony	TX	75056	**800-880-9955**	469-384-5000	657
Pizza Pizza Ltd 580 Jarvis St	Toronto	ON	M4Y2H9	**800-265-9762**	416-967-1010	657
Pizza Plus Pizza Inc 1816 Volunteer Pkwy	Bristol	TN	37620	**800-675-1220**	423-652-2336	657
Pizza Pro Inc 2107 N 2nd St PO Box 1285	Cabot	AR	72023	**800-777-7554**	501-605-1175	657
Pizza Ranch Inc 1121 Main St	Hull	IA	51239	**800-321-3401**	712-439-1150	657
Pizzagalli Construction Co 50 Joy Dr	South Burlington	VT	05403	**800-760-7607**	802-658-4100	185
Pizzeria Operators. National Assn of 908 S 8th St Suite 200	Louisville	KY	40203	**800-489-8324**	502-736-9500	49-6
PJ Keating Co 998 Reservoir Rd	Lunenburg	MA	01462	**800-441-4119**	978-582-9931	187-4
PJ's Coffee Franchises LLC 2800 Hessmer Ave Suite C	Metairie	LA	70002	**800-749-5547**	504-454-9459	156
PK Safety Supply 2005 Clement Ave Bldg 9	Alameda	CA	94501	**800-829-9580**	510-337-8880	667
PKM Electric Co-op Inc 406 N Minnesota St	Warren	MN	56762	**800-552-7366**	218-745-4711	244
PLA (Public Library Assn) 50 E Huron St	Chicago	IL	60611	**800-545-2433**	312-280-5752	49-11
Place D'Armes Hotel 625 Saint Ann St	New Orleans	LA	70116	**800-366-2743**	504-524-4531	373
Place Louis Riel All-Suite Hotel 190 Smith St	Winnipeg	MB	R3C1J8	**800-665-0569**	204-947-6961	372
Place WB LLC 368 W Sumner St	Hartford	WI	53027	**800-826-4433**	262-673-3130	424
PlaceWare Inc 295 N Bernardo Ave *Sales	Mountain View	CA	94043	**888-526-6170***	650-526-6100	176-7
Placon Corp 6096 McKee Rd	Madison	WI	53719	**800-541-1535**	608-271-5634	591
Plaid Enterprises Inc 3225 Westech Dr	Norcross	GA	30092	**800-842-4197**	678-291-8100	43
Plaid Pantries Inc 10025 SW Allen Blvd	Beaverton	OR	97005	**800-677-5243**	503-646-4246	203
Plain Dealer 1801 Superior Ave	Cleveland	OH	44114	**800-688-4802**	216-999-4800	522-2
Plains All American Pipeline LP 333 Clay St Suite 1600 *NYSE: PAA* ■ *Mktg	Houston	TX	77002	**800-564-3036***	713-646-4100	586
Plains Cotton Co-op Assn PO Box 2827	Lubbock	TX	79408	**800-333-8011**	806-763-8011	271
Plains Dairy Products 300 N Taylor St	Amarillo	TX	79107	**800-365-5608**	806-374-0385	292-4
Plains Exploration & Production Co 700 Milam St Suite 3100 *NYSE: PXP*	Houston	TX	77002	**800-934-6083**	832-239-6000	525
Plains Hotel 1600 Central Ave	Cheyenne	WY	82001	**866-275-2467**	307-638-3311	373
Plain's Regional Medical Center 2100 ML King Blvd	Clovis	NM	88101	**800-221-3706**	505-769-2141	366-2
Plains Reporter PO Box 1447	Williston	ND	58802	**800-950-2165**	701-572-2165	522-4
Plaintree Systems Inc 110 Decosta St	Arnprior	ON	K7S3X1	**800-461-0062**	613-623-3434	174
Plainview Chamber of Commerce 710 W 5th St	Plainview	TX	79072	**800-658-2685**	806-296-7431	137
Plan 21 2000 W Loop S Suite 600	Houston	TX	77027	**800-622-7276**	713-621-6500	454
Plan USA 155 Plan Way	Warwick	RI	02886	**800-556-7918**	401-738-5600	48-6
Planar Systems Inc 1195 NW Compton Dr *NASDAQ: PLNR*	Beaverton	OR	97006	**866-475-2627**	503-748-1100	171-4
Plane & Pilot Magazine 12121 Wilshire Blvd Suite 1200	Los Angeles	CA	90025	**800-283-4330**	310-820-1500	449-14
Planemasters Ltd 32 W 611 Tower Rd DuPage Airport	West Chicago	IL	60185	**800-994-6400**	630-513-2100	14
PLANET (Professional Landcare Network) 950 Herndon Pkwy Suite 450	Herndon	VA	20170	**800-395-2522**	703-736-9666	48-2
Planit Solutions Inc 3800 Palisades Dr	Tuscaloosa	AL	35405	**800-280-6932**	205-556-9199	176-5
Planned Parenthood Federation of America 434 W 33rd St	New York	NY	10001	**800-829-7732**	212-541-7800	48-6
Plano Centre 2000 E Springcreek Pkwy	Plano	TX	75074	**800-817-5266**	972-422-0296	204
Plano Convention & Visitors Bureau 2000 E Spring Creek Pkwy	Plano	TX	75074	**800-817-5266**	972-422-0296	205
Plano Molding Co 431 E South St	Plano	IL	60545	**800-451-2122**	630-552-3111	198
Plant City (Greater) Chamber of Commerce 106 N Evers St	Plant City	FL	33563	**800-760-2315**	813-754-3707	137
Plant Maintenance Service Corp 3000 Fite Rd	Memphis	TN	38127	**800-514-9701**	901-353-9880	92
Plant Reclamation 912 Harbour Way S	Richmond	CA	94804	**800-637-0339**	510-233-6552	188-17
Plantation at Fall Creek Resort 1-A Fall Creek Dr	Branson	MO	65616	**800-510-7472**	417-334-6404	655
Plantation Inn 3470 Keeter St	Branson	MO	65616	**800-324-8748**	417-334-3600	373
Plantation Inn & Golf Resort 9301 W Fort Island Trail	Crystal River	FL	34429	**800-632-6262**	352-795-4211	655
Plantation Inn of New England 295 Burnett Rd	Chicopee	MA	01020	**800-248-8495**	413-592-8200	373
Plante & Moran LLP 27400 Northwestern Hwy	Southfield	MI	48034	**800-827-1280**	248-352-2500	2
Planters Electric Membership Corp 1740 Hwy 25 N	Millen	GA	30442	**800-324-4722**	478-982-4722	244
Planters Inn 29 Abercorn St	Savannah	GA	31401	**800-554-1187**	912-232-5678	373
Planters Inn 112 N Market St	Charleston	SC	29401	**800-845-7082**	843-722-2345	373
Plantronics Inc PO Box 635 *NYSE: PLT*	Santa Cruz	CA	95061	**800-544-4660**	831-426-5858	720
Plants Sites & Parks Magazine PO Box 2754	High Point	NC	27261	**800-561-5681**	336-605-1055	449-5
Plants of the Southwest 3095 Agua Fria Rd	Santa Fe	NM	87507	**800-788-7333**	505-438-8888	318
PlanVista Corp 4010 Boy Scout Blvd Suite 200	Tampa	FL	33607	**866-318-6564**	813-353-2300	384-3
Plaquemine Lock Museum 57730 Main St	Plaquemine	LA	70764	**877-987-7158**	225-687-7158	509
Plaskolite Inc 1770 Joyce Ave	Columbus	OH	43219	**800-848-9124**	614-294-3281	589
Plasmon Plc 400 Inverness Pkwy Suite 310	Englewood	CO	80112	**800-451-6845**	720-873-2500	171-8
PlasTEAK PO Box 4290	Akron	OH	44321	**800-320-1841**	330-668-2587	647
Plastech Corp 56 E Broadway Ave Suite 210	Forest Lake	MN	55025	**800-223-0462**	651-407-5700	593
Plasti-Kote Co Inc 1000 Lake Rd	Medina	OH	44256	**800-431-5928**	330-725-4511	540
Plastic Card Systems Inc 31 Pierce St PO Box 1070	Northborough	MA	01532	**800-742-2273**	508-351-6210	171-6
Plastic Development Co Inc PO Box 4007	Williamsport	PA	17701	**800-451-1420**	570-323-3060	367
Plastic Dress-Up Co 11077 E Rush St	South El Monte	CA	91733	**800-800-7711**	626-442-7711	766
Plastic Forming Co Inc 20 S Bradley Rd	Woodbridge	CT	06525	**800-732-2060**	203-397-1338	198
Plastic Lumber Co Inc 115 W Bartges St	Akron	OH	44311	**800-886-8990**	330-762-8989	647
Plastic Packaging Corp 1227 Union St *Cust Svc	West Springfield	MA	01090	**800-342-2011***	413-785-1553	198
Plastic & Reconstructive Surgery. American Academy of Facial 310 S Henry St	Alexandria	VA	22314	**800-332-3223**	703-299-9291	49-8
Plastic Safety Systems Inc 2444 Baldwin Rd	Cleveland	OH	44104	**800-662-6338**	216-231-8590	666
Plastic Sales Southern Inc 6490 Fleet St	Los Angeles	CA	90040	**800-257-7747**	323-728-8309	592
Plastic Surgeons. American Society of 444 E Algonquin Rd	Arlington Heights	IL	60005	**888-475-2784**	847-228-9900	49-8
Plastic Surgery. American Society for Aesthetic 11081 Winners Cir	Los Alamitos	CA	90720	**800-364-2147**	562-799-2356	49-8
Plasticoid Co 249 W High St	Elkton	MD	21921	**800-398-2806**	410-398-2800	663
Plastics Color & Compounding Inc 349 Lake Rd	Dayville	CT	06241	**888-549-7820**	860-774-3770	594-2
Plastics Mfg Inc 7301 Caldwell Rd	Harrisburg	NC	28075	**800-446-5191**	704-455-5191	590
Plastival 1685 Holmes Rd	Elgin	IL	60123	**800-231-9721**	847-931-4771	647
Plastomer Technologies 23 Friends Ln	Newtown	PA	18940	**800-798-1288**	215-968-5011	597

Name / Address	City	State	ZIP	Toll-Free	Phone	Class
Plastpro Inc 9 Peach Tree Hill Rd	Livingston	NJ	07039	**800-779-0561**	973-994-7708	597
Plastronics Socket Co Inc 2601 Texas Dr *Cust Svc	Irving	TX	75062	**800-582-5822***	972-258-1906	252
Platform Computing Corp 3760 14th Ave	Markham	ON	L3R3T7	**877-528-3676**	905-948-8448	176-1
PLATO Learning Inc 10801 Nesbitt Ave S *NASDAQ: TUTR*	Bloomington	MN	55437	**800-869-2000**	952-832-1000	176-3
Plato Woodwork Inc PO Box 98	Plato	MN	55370	**800-328-5924**	320-238-2193	116
Platt Electric Supply 10605 SW Allen Blvd	Beaverton	OR	97005	**800-257-5288**	503-641-6121	245
Platt & Labonia Co 70 Stoddard Ave	North Haven	CT	06473	**800-505-9099**	203-239-5681	688
Platt Luggage Inc 4051 W 51st St	Chicago	IL	60632	**800-222-1555**	773-838-2000	444
Plattco Corp 7 White St	Plattsburgh	NY	12901	**800-352-1731**	518-563-4640	776
Platte-Clay Electric Co-op Inc 1000 W Hwy 92 PO Box 100	Kearney	MO	64060	**800-431-2131**	816-628-3121	244
Platte Valley Bible College PO Box 1227	Scottsbluff	NE	69363	**888-305-8083**	308-632-6933	163
Platts 2 Penn Plaza 25th Fl	New York	NY	10121	**800-752-8878**	212-904-3070	623-9
Plattsburgh Free Trader PO Box 338	Elizabethtown	NY	12932	**800-277-6567**	518-873-6368	522-4
Plattsburgh State 101 Broad St	Plattsburgh	NY	12901	**888-673-0012**	518-564-2040	163
Platz Flowers & Supply Inc 8501 Frontage Rd	Morton Grove	IL	60053	**888-752-8048**	847-966-3100	288
Play It Again Sports 4200 Dahlberg Dr Suite 100	Minneapolis	MN	55422	**800-433-2540**	763-520-8500	305
Playbill Magazine 525 7th Ave Suite 1801	New York	NY	10018	**800-533-4330**	212-557-5757	449-9
Playboy Magazine 680 N Lake Shore Dr	Chicago	IL	60611	**800-999-4438**	312-751-8000	449-11
Playbuoy Pontoon Mfg Inc 903 Michigan Ave PO Box 698	Alma	MI	48801	**800-334-2913**	989-463-2112	91
PlayCore Inc 430 Chestnut St Suite 300	Chattanooga	TN	37402	**888-404-5737**	423-756-0015	340
Players Assn. National Football League 2021 L St NW Suite 600	Washington	DC	20036	**800-372-2000**	202-463-2200	48-22
Players Assn. National Hockey League 777 Bay St Suite 2400	Toronto	ON	M5G2C8	**800-363-4625**	416-408-4040	48-22
Playgirl Magazine 801 2nd Ave 9th Fl	New York	NY	10017	**800-877-6139**	212-661-7878	449-11
Playground Environments 82 Modular Ave	Commack	NY	11725	**800-777-6596**	631-231-1300	340
Playhouse Square Center 1501 Euclid Ave Suite 200	Cleveland	OH	44115	**800-888-9941**	216-771-4444	562
Playmobil USA Inc 26 Commerce Dr	Cranbury	NJ	08512	**800-752-9662**	609-395-5566	750
PlayNetwork Inc 8727 148th Ave NE *Sales	Redmond	WA	98052	**888-567-7529***	425-497-8100	513
Playskool Div Hasbro Inc 1027 Newport Ave	Pawtucket	RI	02861	**800-242-7276**	401-431-8697	750
Playtex Products Inc 300 Nyala Farms Rd *NYSE: PYX*	Westport	CT	06880	**800-999-9700**	203-341-4000	548-2
Playworld Systems Inc 1000 Buffalo Rd	Lewisburg	PA	17837	**800-233-8404**	570-522-9800	340
Plaza 500 Hotel 500 W 12th Ave	Vancouver	BC	V5Z1M2	**800-473-1811**	604-873-1811	372
Plaza Artists Materials 173 Madison Ave	New York	NY	10016	**800-327-3200**	212-689-2870	45
Plaza Fifty 155 E 50th St	New York	NY	10022	**866-233-4642**	212-751-5710	373
Plaza Fleet Parts Inc 1520 S Broadway	Saint Louis	MO	63104	**800-325-7618**	314-231-5047	61
Plaza Group Inc 10375 Richmond Ave Suite 1620	Houston	TX	77042	**800-876-3738**	713-266-0707	144
Plaza Hotel & Apartments 1007 N Cass St	Milwaukee	WI	53202	**800-340-9590**	414-276-2101	373
Plaza Inn 215 Brazilian Ave *Resv	Palm Beach	FL	33480	**800-233-2632***	561-832-8666	373
Plaza Inn 900 Medical Arts NE	Albuquerque	NM	87102	**800-237-1307**	505-243-5693	373
Plaza Resort & Spa 600 N Atlantic Ave	Daytona Beach	FL	32118	**800-874-7420**	386-255-4471	655
Plaza Suite Hotel 409 S Cole Rd	Boise	ID	83709	**800-376-3608**	208-375-7666	373
Plaza Suite Hotel Resort 620 S Peters St	New Orleans	LA	70130	**800-770-6721**	504-524-9500	373
Plaza Suites Silicon Valley 3100 Lakeside Dr	Santa Clara	CA	95054	**800-345-1554**	408-748-9800	373
PLC Medical Systems Inc 10 Forge Pk	Franklin	MA	02038	**800-232-8422**	508-541-8800	415
PLC Systems Inc 10 Forge Pk *AMEX: PLC*	Franklin	MA	02038	**800-232-8422**	508-541-8800	415
Pleasant Excavating Co Inc 24024 Frederick Rd Suite 200	Clarksburg	MD	20871	**800-842-1180**	301-428-0800	188-5
Pleasant Holidays LLC 2404 Townsgate Rd	Westlake Village	CA	91361	**800-242-9244**	818-991-3390	760
Pleasant Valley Potato Inc 275 E Elmore St PO Box 538	Aberdeen	ID	83210	**888-867-7783**	208-397-4194	12-1
Plej's Linen Supermarket 454 S Anderson Rd Suite 600	Rock Hill	SC	29730	**800-838-4599**	803-324-4284	357
Plextor Corp 48383 Fremont Blvd Suite 120	Fremont	CA	94538	**800-886-3935**	510-440-2000	171-8
Plezall Wipers Inc 9869 NW 79th Ave	Hialeah Gardens	FL	33016	**800-237-8724**	305-556-3744	497
PLI (Practising Law Institute) 810 7th Ave 26th Fl	New York	NY	10019	**800-260-4754**	212-824-5700	49-10
Plibrico Co 1010 N Hooker St	Chicago	IL	60622	**800-511-6203**	312-337-9000	649
Plim Plaza Hotel 2nd St & Boardwalk PO Box 160	Ocean City	MD	21843	**800-837-3587**	410-289-6181	373
Pliva Inc 72 Eagle Rock Ave	East Hanover	NJ	10736	**800-922-0547**	973-386-5566	573
PLM International Inc 3988 N Central Expy Bldg 5 6th Fl	Dallas	TX	75204	**800-626-7549**		393
Plumas County Visitors Bureau 550 Crescent St	Quincy	CA	95971	**800-326-2247**	530-283-6345	205
Plumas-Sierra Rural Electric Co-op 73233 Hwy 70 Suite A	Portola	CA	96122	**800-555-2207**	530-832-4261	244
Plumb Supply Co 1622 NE 51st Ave	Des Moines	IA	50313	**800-483-9511**	515-262-9511	601
Plumbers Supply Co 1000 E Main St	Louisville	KY	40206	**800-626-5133**	502-582-2261	601
Plumbing Distributors Inc 20 Collins Industrial Way	Lawrenceville	GA	30046	**800-262-9231**	770-963-9231	601
Plumbing-Heating-Cooling Contractors National Assn (PHCC) 180 S Washington St	Falls Church	VA	22040	**800-533-7694**	703-237-8100	49-3
Plumbing & Mechanical Officials. International Assn of 5001 E Philadelphia St	Ontario	CA	91761	**800-854-2766**	909-472-4100	49-7
Plump Jack's Squaw Valley Inn 1920 Squaw Valley Rd	Olympic Valley	CA	96146	**800-323-7666**	530-583-1576	373
Plumrose USA Inc 7 Lexington Ave	East Brunswick	NJ	08816	**800-526-4909**	732-257-6600	465
Plumtree Software Inc 500 Sansome St *NASDAQ: PLUM*	San Francisco	CA	94111	**800-810-7586**	415-263-8900	39
Plus Group Inc 555 E Butterfield Rd Suite 330	Lombard	IL	60148	**800-782-3346**	630-515-0500	707
PLX Technology Inc 870 W Maude Ave *NASDAQ: PLXT*	Sunnyvale	CA	94085	**800-759-3735**	408-774-9060	686
Plymold Seating 615 Centennial Dr	Kenyon	MN	55946	**800-759-6653**	507-789-5111	314-1
Plymouth Bancorp Inc 151 Campanelli Dr	Middleboro	MA	02346	**800-882-4994**	508-946-3000	355-2
Plymouth Div DaimlerChrysler Corp 800 Chrysler Dr E *Cust Svc	Auburn Hills	MI	48326	**800-992-1997***	248-576-5741	59
Plymouth Products Inc 502 Indiana Ave	Sheboygan	WI	53082	**800-222-7558**	920-457-9435	793
Plymouth Savings Bank 226 Main St	Wareham	MA	02571	**800-426-7937**	508-295-3800	71
Plymouth State University 17 High St	Plymouth	NH	03264	**800-842-6900**	603-535-2237	163
Plymouth Theatre 236 W 45th St	New York	NY	10036	**800-432-7250**	212-239-6200	732
Plymouth Tube Co 29 W 150 Warrenville Rd	Warrenville	IL	60555	**800-323-9506**	630-393-3550	481
Plywood Supply Inc 7036 NE 175th St	Kenmore	WA	98028	**800-683-9663**	425-485-8585	602
PM Co 1500 Kemper Meadow Dr	Cincinnati	OH	45240	**800-327-4359**	513-825-7626	544
PM Lattner Mfg Co PO Box 1527	Cedar Rapids	IA	52406	**800-345-1527**	319-366-0778	352
PM Resources Inc 13001 St Charles Rock Rd *Cust Svc	Bridgeton	MO	63044	**800-447-5463***	314-291-6720	574
PMA (Photo Marketing Assn International) 3000 Picture Pl	Jackson	MI	49201	**800-762-9287**	517-788-8100	49-18
PMAA (Petroleum Marketers Assn of America) 1901 N Fort Myer Dr Suite 500	Arlington	VA	22209	**800-300-7622**	703-351-8000	49-18
PMC Capital Inc 17950 Preston Rd Suite 600	Dallas	TX	75252	**800-486-3223**	972-349-3200	214
PMC Commercial Trust 17950 Preston Rd Suite 600 *AMEX: PCC*	Dallas	TX	75252	**800-486-3223**	972-349-3200	214
PMC Global Inc 12243 Branford St	Sun Valley	CA	91352	**800-423-5632**	818-896-1101	143
PMC Specialties Group Inc 501 Murray Rd	Cincinnati	OH	45217	**800-543-2466**	513-242-3300	142
PMI (Project Management Institute) 4 Campus Blvd	Newtown Square	PA	19073	**866-276-4764**	610-356-4600	49-12
PMI Dental Health Plan 12898 Towne Ctr Dr	Cerritos	CA	90703	**800-422-4234**	562-924-8311	384-3
PMI Group Inc 3003 Oak Rd *NYSE: PMI*	Walnut Creek	CA	94597	**800-288-1970**	925-658-7878	355-4
PMI Mortgage Insurance Co 3003 Oak Rd	Walnut Creek	CA	94597	**800-288-1970**	925-658-7878	384-5
PML Microbiologicals Inc 27120 SW 95th Ave *Cust Svc	Wilsonville	OR	97070	**800-628-7014***	503-570-2500	229
PMMI (Packaging Machinery Manufacturers Institute) 4350 N Fairfax Dr Suite 600	Arlington	VA	22203	**800-275-7664**	703-243-8555	49-13
PMP Corp 25 Security Dr *Cust Svc	Avon	CT	06001	**800-243-6628***	860-677-9656	486
PNC Bank Advisors NA 99 High St 27th Fl	Boston	MA	02110	**800-762-3374**		71
PNC Bank Delaware 300 Delaware Ave	Wilmington	DE	19899	**800-722-1172**	302-429-1011	71
PNC Bank NA 249 5th Ave 1 PNC Plaza	Pittsburgh	PA	15222	**888-762-2265**	412-762-2000	71
PNC Equipment Leasing Corp 620 Liberty Ave 2 PNC Plaza 13th Fl	Pittsburgh	PA	15222	**800-762-6260**	412-762-4848	214
PNC Financial Services Group Inc 249 5th Ave 1 PNC Plaza *NYSE: PNC*	Pittsburgh	PA	15222	**877-762-2000**	412-762-2000	355-2
PNC Park 115 Federal St	Pittsburgh	PA	15212	**800-289-2827**	412-321-2827	706
PNE Inc 7482 Presidents Dr	Orlando	FL	32809	**800-998-2525**	407-857-3888	198
Pneutek Inc 17 Friars Dr	Hudson	NH	03051	**800-431-8665**	603-883-1660	747
PNM Resources Inc Alvarado Sq *NYSE: PNM* ■ *Cust Svc	Albuquerque	NM	87158	**800-687-7854***	505-848-2700	774
PNNL (Pacific Northwest National Laboratory) 902 Battelle Blvd PO Box 999	Richland	WA	99352	**888-375-7665**	509-375-2121	654
PNS Inc 581 Dado St	San Jose	CA	95131	**800-537-4767**	408-944-0500	245
PNY Technologies Inc 299 Webro Rd	Parsippany	NJ	07054	**800-769-7079**	973-515-9700	283
Poblocki Sign Co LLC 922 S 70th St	West Allis	WI	53214	**800-776-7064**	414-453-4010	692
Pocket Books 1230 Ave of the Americas 13th Fl *Cust Svc	New York	NY	10020	**800-223-2336***	212-698-7000	623-2
Pocono Manor Golf Resort & Spa Rt 314	Pocono Manor	PA	18349	**800-233-8150**	570-839-7111	655
Pocono Mountains Vacation Bureau 1004 Main St	Stroudsburg	PA	18360	**800-722-9199**	570-421-5791	205
Pocono Raceway Long Pond Rd PO Box 500	Long Pond	PA	18334	**800-722-3929**	570-646-2300	504
Pocono Record 511 Lenox St	Stroudsburg	PA	18360	**800-756-4237**	570-421-3000	522-2
Podiatric Medical Assn. American 9312 Old Georgetown Rd	Bethesda	MD	20814	**800-275-2762**	301-571-9200	49-8
Podiatric Medicine. American Assn of Colleges of 1350 Piccard Dr Suite 322	Rockville	MD	20850	**800-922-9266**	301-990-7400	49-8

Name / Address	City	State	ZIP	Toll-Free	Phone	Class
Podiatry Insurance Co of America DBA PICA Group 110 Westwood Pl Suite 100	Brentwood	TN	37027	**866-742-2477**	615-371-8776	384-5
Poe Edgar Allan Museum 1914-16 E Main St	Richmond	VA	23223	**888-213-2763**	804-648-5523	509
PoFolks Restaurants 500 Harmon Ave	Panama City	FL	32401	**888-870-3055**	850-763-0501	657
pogo.com Inc 300 California St 8th Fl	San Francisco	CA	94104	**800-804-0836**	415-778-3500	443
Pohly & Partners Inc 27 Melcher St 2nd Fl	Boston	MA	02210	**877-687-6459**	617-451-1700	623-9
Point The PO Box 1327	Saranac Lake	NY	12983	**800-255-3530**	518-891-5674	655
Point Park University 201 Wood St	Pittsburgh	PA	15222	**800-321-0129**	412-391-4100	163
Point Plaza Suites & Conference Hotel 950 J Clyde Morris Blvd	Newport News	VA	23601	**800-841-1112**	757-599-4460	373
Point-of-Purchase Advertising International (POPAI) 1660 L St NW 10th Fl	Washington	DC	20036	**888-407-6724**	202-530-3000	49-18
Pointe Coupee Electric Membership Corp PO Box 160	New Roads	LA	70760	**800-738-7232**	225-638-3751	244
Pointe Hilton Resort at Tapatio Cliffs 11111 N 7th St	Phoenix	AZ	85020	**800-876-4683**	602-866-7500	655
Pointe Hilton at Squaw Peak Resort 7677 N 16th St	Phoenix	AZ	85020	**800-685-0550**	602-997-2626	655
Pointe Scientific Inc 5449 Research Dr	Canton	MI	48188	**800-445-9853**	734-487-8300	229
Pointe South Mountain Resort 7777 S Pointe Pkwy	Phoenix	AZ	85044	**877-800-4888**	602-438-9000	655
Pointe Technology Group Inc 8201 Corporate Dr Suite 700	Landover	MD	20785	**800-730-6171**	301-306-4400	178
Points of Light Foundation & Volunteer Center National Network 1400 'I' St NW Suite 800	Washington	DC	20005	**800-750-7653**	202-729-8000	48-5
Poison Control Center. ASPCA Animal 1717 S Philo Rd Suite 36	Urbana	IL	61802	**888-426-4435**	217-337-5030	48-3
Poison Control Centers. American Assn of 3201 New Mexico Ave Suite 330	Washington	DC	20016	**800-222-1222**	202-362-7217	49-8
Poisoned Pen Bookstore 4014 N Goldwater Blvd	Scottsdale	AZ	85251	**888-560-9919**	480-947-2974	96
Poker Chips Online LLC 380 Warren Ave	Portland	ME	04103	**888-797-2200**	506-575-8827	317
Pola USA Inc 251 E Victoria St	Carson	CA	90746	**800-222-6564**	310-527-9696	361
Polar Air Cargo 2000 Westchester Ave	Purchase	NY	10577	**800-462-2012**		13
Polar Beverages Inc 1001 Southbridge St *Cust Svc	Worcester	MA	01610	**800-225-7410***	508-753-4300	81-2
Polar Service Centers 7600 E Sam Houston Pkwy N	Houston	TX	77049	**800-955-8558**	281-459-6400	768
Polar Tank Trailer Inc 12810 CR 17	Holdingford	MN	56340	**800-826-6589**	320-746-2255	768
Polar Ware Co Inc PO Box 211 *Cust Svc	Sheboygan	WI	53082	**800-237-3655***	920-458-3561	478
Polaris Pool Systems Inc 2620 Commerce Way *Cust Svc	Vista	CA	92081	**800-822-7933***	760-599-9600	793
Polarity Therapy Assn. American PO Box 19858	Boulder	CO	80308	**800-359-5620**	303-545-2080	48-17
Polaroid Corp 1265 Main St Suite W-7 *Cust Svc	Waltham	MA	02451	**800-343-5000***	781-386-2000	580
Polep J Distribution Services Inc 705 Meadow St	Chicopee	MA	01013	**800-447-6537**	413-592-4141	744
Police Associations. International Union of 1421 Prince St Suite 400	Alexandria	VA	22314	**800-247-4872**	703-549-7473	405
Police Athletic Leagues. National Assn of 618 US Hwy 1 Suite 201	North Palm Beach	FL	33408	**800-725-7743**	561-844-1823	48-22
Police Executive Research Forum (PERF) 1120 Connecticut Ave NW Suite 930	Washington	DC	20036	**888-202-4563**	202-466-7820	49-7
Police & Fire Federal Credit Union 901 Arch St	Philadelphia	PA	19107	**800-228-8801**	215-931-0300	216
Police & Fire Professionals of America. International Union Security 25510 Kelly Rd	Roseville	MI	48066	**800-228-7492**	586-772-7250	405
Police. Fraternal Order of 1410 Donelson Pike Suite A-17	Nashville	TN	37217	**800-451-2711**	615-399-0900	48-15
Police. International Assn of Chiefs of 515 N Washington St	Alexandria	VA	22314	**800-843-4227**	703-836-6767	49-7
Policy Assn. Foreign 470 Park Ave S 2nd Fl	New York	NY	10016	**800-628-5754**	212-481-8100	48-7
Policy Institute. Progressive 600 Pennsylvania Ave SE Suite 400	Washington	DC	20003	**800-546-0027**	202-547-0001	654
Polish & Slavic Federal Credit Union 140 Greenpoint Ave	Brooklyn	NY	11222	**800-297-2181**	718-383-6268	216
Political Education. American Federation of Teachers Committee on 555 New Jersey Ave NW	Washington	DC	20001	**800-238-1133**	202-879-4400	604
Politics. Institute of World 1521 16th St NW	Washington	DC	20036	**888-566-9497**	202-462-2101	654
Politics & Prose Bookstore 5015 Connecticut Ave	Washington	DC	20008	**800-722-0790**	202-364-1919	96
Polk Audio Inc 5601 Metro Dr	Baltimore	MD	21215	**800-377-7655**	410-358-3600	52
Polk-Burnett Electric Co-op 1001 SR 35	Centuria	WI	54824	**800-421-0283**	715-646-2191	244
Polk County Chamber of Commerce/Development Authority 604 Goodyear St	Rockmart	GA	30153	**800-226-2517**	770-684-8760	137
Polk County Farmers Co-op DBA Ag West Supply 9055 Rickreall Rd	Rickreall	OR	97371	**800-842-2224**	503-363-2332	270
Polk County Rural Public Power District 120 W 4th St	Stromsburg	NE	68666	**888-242-5265**	402-764-4381	244
Polk County Travel & Tourism 317 N Trade St	Tryon	NC	28782	**800-440-7848**	828-859-8300	205
Polkton Mfg Co Inc 6713 E Marshville Blvd PO Box 220	Marshville	NC	28103	**800-445-0044**	704-624-3200	153-19
Pollard The 2 N Broadway PO Box 650	Red Lodge	MT	59068	**800-765-5273**	406-446-0001	373
Pollo Tropical Inc 7300 N Kendall Dr 8th Fl	Miami	FL	33156	**888-778-7696**	305-670-7696	657
Pollock Paper & Packaging 1 Pollock Pl	Grand Prairie	TX	75050	**800-843-7320**	972-263-2126	549
Pollstar 4697 W Jacquelyn Ave	Fresno	CA	93722	**800-344-7383**	559-271-7900	449-9
Polo Ralph Lauren Corp 650 Madison Ave *NYSE: RL*	New York	NY	10022	**888-475-7674**	212-318-7000	153-21
Polsinello Fuels Inc 41 Riverside Ave	Rensselaer	NY	12144	**800-334-5823**	518-463-0084	311
Poly-America Inc 2000 W Marshall Dr	Grand Prairie	TX	75051	**800-527-3322**	972-647-4374	67
Poly Hi Solidur Inc 2710 American Way	Fort Wayne	IN	46809	**877-476-5944**	260-479-4100	594-2
Poly Molding Corp 96 4th Ave	Haskell	NJ	07420	**800-229-7161**	973-835-7161	590
Poly-Pak Industries Inc 125 Spagnoli Rd	Melville	NY	11747	**800-969-1995**	631-293-6767	67
Polyair Inter Pack Inc 258 Attwell Dr *AMEX: PPK*	Toronto	ON	M9W5B2	**800-456-4348**	416-740-2687	538
Polycom Inc 4750 Willow Rd *NASDAQ: PLCM*	Pleasanton	CA	94588	**866-476-5926**	925-924-6000	720
PolyConversions Inc 505 Condit Dr	Rantoul	IL	61866	**888-893-3330**	217-893-3330	566
Polygon Co 103 Industrial Pk Dr PO Box 176	Walkerton	IN	46574	**800-918-9261**	574-586-3145	591
Polygon Northwest Co 11624 SE 5th St Suite 200	Bellevue	WA	98005	**800-765-9466**	425-586-7700	639
PolyMask Corp 500 Thornburg Dr	Conover	NC	28613	**800-624-4772**	828 465 3053	717
Polymedco Inc 510 Furnace Dock Rd	Cortlandt Manor	NY	10567	**800-431-2123**	914-739-5400	229
PolyMedica Corp 11 State St *NASDAQ: PLMD*	Woburn	MA	01801	**800-886-4050**	781-933-2020	467
Polymer Group Inc 4055 Saber Pl Suite 201	North Charleston	SC	29405	**800-631-5594**		730-1
Polymer Plastics Corp 645 National Ave	Mountain View	CA	94043	**800-369-2213**	650-968-2212	592
Polynesian Adventure Tours Inc 1049 Kikowaena Pl	Honolulu	HI	96819	**800-622-3011**	808-833-3000	748
Polynesian Cultural Center 55-370 Kamehameha Hwy	Laie	HI	96762	**800-367-7060**	808-293-3000	509
Polynesian Resort The 615 Ocean Shores Blvd NW	Ocean Shores	WA	98569	**800-562-4836**	360-289-3361	655
PolyOne Corp 33587 Walker Rd *NYSE: POL*	Avon Lake	OH	44012	**866-765-9663**	440-930-1000	594-2
PolyPhaser Corp 2225 Park Pl *Cust Svc	Minden	NV	89423	**800-325-7170***	775-782-2511	803
Polysciences Inc 400 Valley Rd *Cust Svc	Warrington	PA	18976	**800-523-2575***	215-343-6484	229
Polytechnic University 6 Metrotech Ctr	Brooklyn	NY	11201	**800-765-9832**	718-260-3600	163
Polytron Corp 4400 Wyland Dr	Elkhart	IN	46516	**888-228-0246**	574-522-0246	202
PolyVision Corp 3970 Johns Creek Ct Suite 325	Suwanee	GA	30024	**800-620-7659**	678-542-3100	171-1
Polywood Inc 125 National Rd	Edison	NJ	08817	**800-915-0043**	732-248-8810	647
POM Inc 200 S Elmira Ave PO Box 430	Russellville	AR	72802	**800-331-7275**	479-968-2880	486
Pomare Ltd 700 N Nimitz Hwy	Honolulu	HI	96817	**800-272-5282**	808-524-3966	153-3
POMC (Parents of Murdered Children) 100 E 8th St Suite B-41	Cincinnati	OH	45202	**888-818-7662**	513-721-5683	48-6
POMCO 2425 James St	Syracuse	NY	13206	**800-766-2687**	315-432-9171	383
Pomerantz A & Co 701 Market St Suite 7000	Philadelphia	PA	19106	**800-344-9135**	215-408-2100	315
Pomeroy IT Solutions Inc 1020 Petersburg Rd *NASDAQ: PMRY*	Hebron	KY	41048	**800-846-8727**	859-586-1515	178
Pompano Masonry Corp 880 S Andrews Ave	Pompano Beach	FL	33069	**800-762-7425**	954-946-3033	188-7
Pomps Tire Service Inc 1123 Cedar St	Green Bay	WI	54302	**800-236-8911**	920-435-8301	740
Ponca City News PO Box 191	Ponca City	OK	74602	**866-765-3311**	580-765-3311	522-2
Ponca City Tourism 516 E Grand Ave	Ponca City	OK	74601	**866-763-8092**		205
Ponce de Leon's Fountain of Youth 11 Magnolia Ave	Saint Augustine	FL	32084	**800-356-8222**	904-829-3168	50
Ponderosa Steakhouses 6500 International Pkwy Suite 1000	Plano	TX	75093	**800-727-8355**	972-588-5000	657
Pontarelli Limousine Service 2225 W Hubbard St	Chicago	IL	60612	**800-322-5466**	312-226-5466	433
Pontchartrain Hotel 2031 St Charles Ave	New Orleans	LA	70140	**800-777-6193**	504-524-0581	373
Pontchartrain. Hotel 2 Washington Blvd	Detroit	MI	48226	**800-227-6963**	313-965-0200	373
Pontchartrain Materials Corp 3819 France Rd	New Orleans	LA	70126	**800-255-9848**	504-949-7571	181
Ponte Vedra Beach. Lodge & Club at 607 Ponte Vedra Blvd	Ponte Vedra Beach	FL	32082	**800-243-4304**	904-273-9500	655
Ponte Vedra Inn & Club 200 Ponte Vedra Blvd	Ponte Vedra Beach	FL	32082	**800-234-7842**	904-285-1111	655
Pontiac Div General Motors Corp 300 Renaissance Ctr *Cust Svc	Detroit	MI	48265	**800-762-2737***	313-556-5000	59
Pontiac-GMC Div General Motors Corp 300 Renaissance Ctr *Cust Svc	Detroit	MI	48265	**800-762-2737***	313-556-5000	59
Pony Express National Memorial 914 Penn St	Saint Joseph	MO	64503	**800-530-5930**	816-279-5059	509
Poof-Slinky Inc 45400 Helm St PO Box 701394	Plymouth	MI	48170	**800-829-9502**	734-454-9552	750
Pool Co Texas Ltd PO Box 2545	Hobbs	NM	88241	**800-299-1388**	505-392-6591	528
Pool & Spa Professionals. Association of 2111 Eisenhower Ave	Alexandria	VA	22314	**800-323-3996**	703-838-0083	49-4

Name / Address	City	State	ZIP	Toll-Free	Phone	Class
Poolmaster Inc 770 W Del Paso Rd Suite W	Sacramento	CA	95834	**800-854-1776**	916-567-9800	701
Poolplayers Assn. American 1000 Lake St Louis Blvd Suite 325	Lake Saint Louis	MO	63367	**800-372-2536**	636-625-8611	48-22
Pop Rocket Inc 6330 San Vicente Blvd	Los Angeles	CA	90048	**800-238-0798**	323-932-4300	750
POPAI (Point-of-Purchase Advertising International) 1660 L St NW 10th Fl	Washington	DC	20036	**888-407-6724**	202-530-3000	49-18
Popeyes Chicken & Biscuits 5555 Glenridge Connector NE Suite 300	Atlanta	GA	30342	**866-232-4403**	404-459-4450	657
Popular Club 22 Lincoln Pl	Garfield	NJ	07026	**800-767-2582**	973-470-3800	451
Popular Ford Sales Inc 2505 Coney Island Ave	Brooklyn	NY	11223	**888-622-9122**	718-376-5600	57
Popular Inc 209 Ponce de Leon Ave *NASDAQ: BPOP*	San Juan	PR	00919	**888-724-3650**	787-765-9800	355-2
Popular Mechanics Magazine 224 W 57th St	New York	NY	10019	**800-333-4948**	212-649-2000	449-14
Popular Science Magazine Time Life Bldg Rockefeller Ctr *Cust Svc	New York	NY	10020	**800-289-9399***	212-779-5000	449-19
Population Connection 1400 16th St NW Suite 320	Washington	DC	20036	**800-767-1956**	202-332-2200	48-5
Population-Environment Balance Inc 2000 P St NW Suite 600	Washington	DC	20036	**800-866-6269**	202-955-5700	48-7
Population Reference Bureau (PRB) 1875 Connecticut Ave NW Suite 520	Washington	DC	20009	**800-877-9881**	202-483-1100	48-7
Porex Technologies Corp 500 Bohannon Rd *Cust Svc	Fairburn	GA	30213	**800-241-0195***	770-964-1421	597
Pork Report PO Box 9114	Des Moines	IA	50306	**800-456-7675**	515-223-2600	449-1
Porky Products Corp 400 Port Carteret Dr	Carteret	NJ	07008	**800-952-0265**	732-541-0200	292-9
Porsche Cars North America Inc 980 Hammond Dr Suite 1000	Atlanta	GA	30328	**800-545-8039**	770-290-3500	59
Port Arthur Convention & Visitors Bureau 3401 Cultural Ctr Dr	Port Arthur	TX	77642	**800-235-7822**	409-985-7822	205
Port of Astoria 1 Portway St	Astoria	OR	97103	**800-860-4093**	503-325-4521	607
Port of Baltimore Maryland Port Administration 401 E Pratt St World Trade Ctr	Baltimore	MD	21202	**800-638-7519**	410-385-4484	607
Port of Brownsville 1000 Foust Rd	Brownsville	TX	78521	**800-378-5395**	956-831-4592	607
Port Canaveral 200 George King Blvd	Cape Canaveral	FL	32920	**888-767-8226**	321-783-7831	607
Port City Press Div Cadmus Communications 1323 Greenwood Rd	Baltimore	MD	21208	**800-858-7678**	410-486-3000	614
Port of Corpus Christi 222 Power St	Corpus Christi	TX	78401	**800-580-7110**	361-882-5633	607
Port of Duluth Duluth Seaway Port Authority 1200 Port Terminal Dr	Duluth	MN	55802	**800-232-0703**	218-727-8525	607
Port of Everett 2911 Bond St Suite 202	Everett	WA	98201	**800-729-7678**	425-259-3164	607
Port Freeport PO Box 615	Freeport	TX	77542	**800-362-5473**	979-233-2667	607
Port of Houston 111 E Loop N *Cust Svc	Houston	TX	77029	**800-688-3625***	713-670-2400	607
Port Huron Area (Greater) Chamber of Commerce 920 Pine Grove Ave	Port Huron	MI	48060	**800-361-0526**	810-985-7101	137
Port of Lake Charles 150 Marine St	Lake Charles	LA	70601	**800-845-7678**	337-439-3661	607
Port of New Orleans 1350 Port of New Orleans Pl *Mktg	New Orleans	LA	70130	**800-776-6652***	504-522-2551	607
Port of Norfolk Virginia Port Authority 600 World Trade Ctr	Norfolk	VA	23510	**800-446-8098**	757-683-8000	607
Port-O-Call Hotel 1510 Boardwalk	Ocean City	NJ	08226	**800-334-4546**	609-399-8812	373
Port Orchard Chamber of Commerce 1014 Bay St Suite 8	Port Orchard	WA	98366	**800-982-8139**	360-876-3505	137
Port of Pittsburgh 425 6th Ave Suite 2990	Pittsburgh	PA	15219	**877-609-9870**	412-201-7330	607
Port Plastics Inc 16750 Chestnut St	City of Industry	CA	91748	**800-800-0039**	626-333-7678	592
Port of Portland 121 NW Everett St	Portland	OR	97209	**800-547-8411**	503-944-7000	607
Port of Sacramento 3251 Beacon Blvd Suite 210	West Sacramento	CA	95691	**888-258-7969**	916-371-8000	607
Port of Saint Petersburg 300 2nd Ave SE	Saint Petersburg	FL	33701	**800-782-8350**	727-893-7329	607
Port of San Diego PO Box 120488	San Diego	CA	92112	**800-854-2757**	619-686-6200	607
Port of Seattle PO Box 1209	Seattle	WA	98111	**800-426-7817**	206-728-3000	607
Port of South Louisiana 171 Belle Terre Blvd Suite 100	LaPlace	LA	70069	**888-752-7678**	985-652-9278	607
Port of Stockton 2201 W Washington St	Stockton	CA	95203	**800-344-3213**	209-946-0246	607
Port Townsend Marine Science Center 532 Battery Way	Port Townsend	WA	98368	**800-566-3932**	360-385-5582	509
Porta-Fab Corp 18080 Chesterfield Airport Rd	Chesterfield	MO	63005	**800-325-3781**	636-537-5555	106
Porta Systems Corp 6851 Jericho Tpke Suite 170	Syosset	NY	11791	**800-937-6782**	516-364-9300	720
Portage County District Library 10482 South St	Garrettsville	OH	44231	**800-500-5179**	330-527-4378	426
Portage Electric Products Inc 7700 Freedom Ave NW	North Canton	OH	44720	**888-464-7374**	330-499-2727	201
Portal Inc 10 Tracy Dr	Avon	MA	02322	**800-966-3030**	508-588-3030	232
Portal Publications Ltd PO Box 6172	Novato	CA	94948	**800-227-1720**	415-884-6200	130
Portal Software Inc 10200 S De Anza Blvd *NASDAQ: PRSF*	Cupertino	CA	95014	**888-767-8259**	408-572-2000	176-1
Portales News-Tribune PO Box 848	Portales	NM	88130	**800-658-6944**	505-356-4481	522-2
Portco Corp 3601 SE Columbia Way Suite 260	Vancouver	WA	98661	**800-676-8666**	360-696-1641	66
Portec Rail Products Inc PO Box 38250 *NASDAQ: PRPX*	Pittsburgh	PA	15238	**800-722-9960**	412-782-6000	636
Porteous Fastener Co 1300 Morse Ave	Elk Grove Village	IL	60007	**800-935-2002**	847-228-6313	346
Porter Athletic Equipment Co 2500 S 25th Ave	Broadview	IL	60155	**800-947-6783**	708-338-2000	701
Porter-Cable Corp 4825 Hwy 45 N	Jackson	TN	38305	**800-321-9443**	731-668-8600	747
Porter Capital Corp 2112 1st Ave N	Birmingham	AL	35203	**800-737-7344**	205-322-5442	268
Porter Instrument Co Inc 245 Township Line Rd PO Box 907	Hatfield	PA	19440	**800-457-2001**	215-723-4000	200
Porter International 388 Newburyport Tpke	Rowley	MA	01969	**800-343-8138**	978-922-2611	379
Porter Paints Inc 400 S 13th St	Louisville	KY	40203	**800-332-6270**	502-588-9200	540
Porter Precision Products Inc 2734 Banning Rd	Cincinnati	OH	45239	**800-543-7041**	513-923-3777	745
Porter Wright Morris & Arthur LLP 41 S High St 29th Fl	Columbus	OH	43215	**800-533-2794**	614-227-2000	419
PorterCorp 4240 N 136th Ave	Holland	MI	49424	**800-354-7721**	616-399-1963	106
Porter's Camera Store PO Box 628	Cedar Falls	IA	50613	**800-553-2001**	319-268-0104	119
Porters of Racine 301 6th St	Racine	WI	53403	**800-558-3245**	262-633-6363	316
Portfolio Recovery Assoc LLC 120 Corporate Blvd *NASDAQ: PRAA*	Norfolk	VA	23502	**888-772-7326**	757-519-9300	157
Porthole Cruise Magazine 4517 NW 31st Ave	Fort Lauderdale	FL	33309	**888-774-4768**	954-377-7777	449-22
Portion Pac Inc 7325 Snider Rd	Mason	OH	45040	**800-232-4829**	513-398-0400	291-19
Portland General Electric 121 SW Salmon St *Cust Svc	Portland	OR	97204	**800-548-8818***	503-464-8000	774
Portland Meadows Horse Track 1001 N Schmeer Rd	Portland	OR	97217	**800-944-3127**	503-285-9144	628
Portland Oregon Visitors Assn 1000 SW Broadway Suite 2300	Portland	OR	97204	**800-962-3700**	503-275-9750	205
Portland Regency Hotel 20 Milk St	Portland	ME	04101	**800-727-3436**	207-774-4200	373
Portland State University 724 SW Harrison St	Portland	OR	97201	**800-547-8887**	503-725-3000	163
Portland Teachers Credit Union PO Box 3750	Portland	OR	97208	**800-527-3932**	503-228-7077	216
Portofino Hotel & Yacht Club 260 Portofino Way	Redondo Beach	CA	90277	**800-468-4292**	310-379-8481	373
Portofino Inn & Suites 1831 South Harbor Blvd	Anaheim	CA	92802	**888-297-7143**	714-782-7600	373
Portola Packaging Inc 898 Faulstich Ct	San Jose	CA	95112	**800-767-8652**	408-573-2000	152
Portola Plaza Hotel 2 Portola Plaza	Monterey	CA	93940	**888-222-5851**	831-649-4511	373
Portola Tech International Inc 85 Fairmount St	Woonsocket	RI	02895	**800-556-7630**	401-765-0600	152
Portsmouth Area Chamber of Commerce 324 Chillicothe St PO Box 509	Portsmouth	OH	45662	**800-648-2574**	740-353-7647	137
Portsmouth Convention & Visitors Bureau 505 Crawford St Suite 2	Portsmouth	VA	23704	**800-767-8782**	757-393-5327	205
Portsmouth Daily Times PO Box 581	Portsmouth	OH	45662	**800-298-5232**	740-353-3101	522-2
Portsmouth Herald 111 Maplewood Ave	Portsmouth	NH	03801	**800-439-0303**	603-436-1800	522-2
Portsmouth Regional Hospital 333 Borthwick Ave	Portsmouth	NH	03801	**800-685-8282**	603-436-5110	366-2
Portuguese Trade & Tourism Office 590 5th Ave 4th Fl	New York	NY	10036	**800-767-8842**	646-723-0200	764
Posca Brothers Dental Laboratory Inc 641 W Willow St	Long Beach	CA	90806	**800-537-672.**	562-427-1811	406
Poses Frederic M 1 Centennial Ave Chm/CEO American Standard Cos Inc	Piscataway	NJ	08854	**800-223-0068**	732-980-6000	561
Posey Co 5635 Peck Rd	Arcadia	CA	91006	**800-767-3933**	626-443-3143	469
Positech Corp 191 N Rush Lake Rd	Laurens	IA	50554	**800-831-6026**	712-841-4548	462
Positron Corp 1304 Langham Creek Dr Suite 300	Houston	TX	77084	**800-766-2984**	281-492-7100	375
Positronic Industries Inc PO Box 8247	Springfield	MO	65801	**800-641-4054**	417-866-2322	252
Possis Medical Inc 9055 Evergreen Blvd NW *NASDAQ: POSS*	Minneapolis	MN	55433	**800-810-7677**	763-780-4555	468
Post Buckley Schuh & Jernigan 2001 NW 107th Ave	Miami	FL	33172	**800-597-7275**	305-592-7275	258
Post-Bulletin 18 1st Ave SE	Rochester	MN	55903	**800-562-1758**	507-285-7600	522-2
Post-Crescent 306 W Washington St	Appleton	WI	54912	**800-236-6397**	920-733-4411	522-2
Post Glover LifeLink Inc 4750 Olympic Blvd Bldg B	Erlanger	KY	41018	**800-287-4123**	859-283-5900	252
Post Glover Resistors Inc 4750 Olympic Blvd *Cust Svc	Erlanger	KY	41018	**800-537-6144***	859-283-0778	252
Post Group Inc 6335 Homewood Ave	Hollywood	CA	90028	**800-827-7896**	323-462-2300	501
Post Hotel 200 Pipestone Rd PO Box 69	Lake Louise	AB	T0L1E0	**800-661-1586**	403-522-3989	372
Post-Journal PO Box 190	Jamestown	NY	14702	**866-756-9600**	716-487-1111	522-2
Post-Newsweek Tech Media Group 10 G St NE Suite 500	Washington	DC	20002	**866-447-6864**	202-772-2500	623-9
Post Properties Inc 4401 Northside Pkwy Suite 800 *NYSE: PPS*	Atlanta	GA	30327	**877-644-7678**	404-846-5000	639
Post Publishing Co PO Box 4639	Salisbury	NC	28145	**800-633-8957**	704-633-8950	623-8
Post Ranch Inn Hwy 1	Big Sur	CA	93920	**800-527-2200**	831-667-2200	655
Post-Register PO Box 1800	Idaho Falls	ID	83403	**800-574-6397**	208-522-1800	522-2
Post-Standard PO Box 4915	Syracuse	NY	13221	**800-765-4569**	315-470-0011	522-2
Post-Star PO Box 2157	Glens Falls	NY	12801	**800-724-2543**	518-792-3131	522-2
Post-Tribune 1433 E 83rd Ave	Merrillville	IN	46410	**800-876-8974**	219-648-3055	522-2
Postal World Newsletter 11300 Rockville Pike Suite 1100	Rockville	MD	20852	**800-929-4824**	301-287-2700	521-7
PostalAnnex+ Inc 7580 Metropolitan Dr Suite 200	San Diego	CA	92108	**800-456-1525**	619-563-4800	114
Postcards from the Moon 1525 Summit Ave	Seattle	WA	98122	**800-872-1410**	206-861-1971	130
Postgraduate Medicine Magazine 4530 W 77th St	Minneapolis	MN	55435	**800-525-5003**	952-835-3222	449-16
Postler & Jaeckle Corp 615 South Ave	Rochester	NY	14620	**800-724-4252**	585-546-7450	188-10

Name / Address	City	State	Zip	Toll-Free	Phone	Class
PostMark Press Inc 16 Spruce St	Watertown	MA	02472	**888-924-3520**	617-924-3520	130
PostNet Postal & Business Centers 181 N Arroyo Grande Blvd Suite 100-A	Henderson	NV	89074	**800-841-7171**	702-792-7100	114
Posty Cards Inc 1600 Olive St *Sales	Kansas City	MO	64127	**800-554-5018***	816-231-2323	130
Potash Corp 1101 Skokie Blvd	Northbrook	IL	60062	**800-645-2183**	847-849-4200	276
Potash Corp of Saskatchewan Inc 122 1st Ave S Suite 500 *NYSE: POT*	Saskatoon	SK	S7K7G3	**800-667-3930**	306-933-8500	276
Potawatomi Inn Pokagan State Park 6 Lane 100A Lake James	Angola	IN	46703	**877-768-2928**	260-833-1077	655
Potentials Magazine 50 S 9th St *Cust Svc	Minneapolis	MN	55402	**800-328-4329***	612-333-0471	449-5
Potluck Press 1229 21st Ave E	Seattle	WA	98112	**877-818-5500**	206-323-8310	130
Potomac Ridge Behavioral Health 14901 Broschart Rd	Rockville	MD	20850	**800-204-8600**	301-251-4500	366-3
Potomac State College 101 Fort Ave	Keyser	WV	26726	**800-262-7332**	304-788-6800	160
Potomac Supply Corp 1398 Kinsale Rd *Sales	Kinsale	VA	22488	**800-365-3900***	804-472-2527	541
Potter Electric Signal Co Inc 2081 Craig Rd	Saint Louis	MO	63146	**800-325-3936**	314-878-4321	681
Potter JC Sausage Co 1914 Hwy 70 E	Durant	OK	74702	**800-321-8549**	580-924-2414	291-26
Potter-Roemer PO Box 3527	City of Industry	CA	91744	**800-366-3473**	626-855-4890	666
Potter's Wax Museum 17 King St	Saint Augustine	FL	32084	**800-584-4781**	904-829-9056	509
Pottsville Republican 111 Mahantongo St	Pottsville	PA	17901	**800-622-1737**	570-622-3456	522-2
Poudre Valley Rural Electric Assn Inc 7649 Rea Pkwy	Fort Collins	CO	80528	**800-432-1012**	970-226-1234	244
Poughkeepsie Journal 85 Civic Ctr Plaza	Poughkeepsie	NY	12601	**800-765-1120**	845-437-4800	522-2
Pounding Mill Quarry Corp 171 St Clair's Crossing	Bluefield	VA	24605	**888-661-7625**	276-326-1145	493-5
Poverty Point National Monument c/o Poverty Point State Historic Site 6859 Hwy 577	Pioneer	LA	71226	**888-926-5492**	318-926-5492	554
Powder River Energy Corp 221 Main St	Sundance	WY	82729	**800-442-3630**	307-283-3531	244
Powder River Transportation 1700 E Hwy 14-16 PO Box 218	Gillette	WY	82717	**800-442-3682**	307-682-0960	109
Powderhorn Guest Ranch 1525 County Rd 27	Powderhorn	CO	81243	**800-786-1220**	970-641-0220	238
Powell Electronics Inc 4848 S Island Ave	Philadelphia	PA	19153	**800-235-7880**	215-365-1900	245
Powell Goldstein LLP 1201 W Peachtree St NW 14th Fl	Atlanta	GA	30309	**800-769-3552**	404-572-6600	419
Powell Skate One Corp 30 S La Patera Ln	Santa Barbara	CA	93117	**800-884-3813**	805-964-1330	701
Powell Structural Systems Inc 130 Johnson Dr	Delaware	OH	43015	**800-351-7176**	740-549-0465	805
Powell Symphony Hall 718 N Grand Blvd	Saint Louis	MO	63103	**800-232-1880**	314-533-2500	562
Powell William Co 2503 Spring Grove Ave	Cincinnati	OH	45214	**800-888-2583**	513-852-2000	776
Powell's Books Inc 7 NW 9th Ave	Portland	OR	97209	**800-878-7323**	503-228-0540	96
Powell's City of Books 1005 W Burnside St	Portland	OR	97209	**800-878-7323**	503-228-4651	96
Power Battery Co Inc 25 McLean Blvd	Paterson	NJ	07514	**800-783-7697**	973-523-8630	76
Power City Electric Inc 3327 E Olive Ave	Spokane	WA	99202	**800-877-8549**	509-535-8500	188-4
Power Construction Co LLC 2360 N Palmer Dr	Schaumburg	IL	60173	**800-307-4048**	847-925-1300	185
Power Corp of Canada 751 Victoria Sq *TSE: POW*	Montreal	QC	H2Y2J3	**800-890-7440**	514-286-7400	184
Power Electronics Society. IEEE IEEE Operations Ctr 445 Hoes Ln	Piscataway	NJ	08854	**800-678-4333**	732-981-0060	49-19
Power Engineering Corp PO Box 766	Wilkes-Barre	PA	18703	**800-626-0903**	570-823-8822	258
Power Engineering & Equipment Co 20009 S Rancho Way	Rancho Dominguez	CA	90220	**800-231-6906**	310-886-1133	321
Power Engineering Society. IEEE IEEE Operations Ctr 445 Hoes Ln	Piscataway	NJ	08854	**800-678-4333**	732-981-0060	49-19
Power Financial Corp 751 Victoria Sq	Montreal	QC	H2Y2J3	**800-890-7440**	514-286-7400	355-4
Power Marketing Administrations Bonneville Power Administration 905 NE 11th Ave	Portland	OR	97232	**800-282-3713**	503-230-3000	336-5
Power Measurement Ltd 2195 Keating Cross Rd	Saanichton	BC	V8M2A5	**866-466-7627**	250-652-7100	247
Power Motive Corp 5000 Vasquez Blvd	Denver	CO	80216	**800-627-0087**	303-355-5900	353
Power & Motoryacht Magazine 260 Madison Ave 8th Fl	New York	NY	10016	**800-284-8036**	917-256-2200	449-4
Power-One Inc 740 Calle Plano *NASDAQ: PWER*	Camarillo	CA	93012	**800-678-9445**	805-987-8741	252
Power Sentry Div Fiskars Brands Inc 17300 Medina Rd Suite 800	Plymouth	MN	55447	**800-852-4312**	763-557-8889	803
Power Squadrons. US PO Box 30423	Raleigh	NC	27622	**888-367-8777**	919-821-0281	48-22
Power Surge Technologies Inc 2349 Jamestown Ave	Independence	IA	50644	**800-867-5055**	319-334-4229	795
Power Technologies Inc 1482 Erie Blvd	Schenectady	NY	12305	**800-395-4784**	518-374-1220	193
Power & Telephone Supply Co Inc 2673 Yale Ave *Cust Svc	Memphis	TN	38112	**800-238-7514***	901-324-6116	245
PowerBar Inc 2150 Shattuck Ave	Berkeley	CA	94704	**800-587-6937**	510-843-1330	291-11
Powercom Corp 1807 N Center St *Cust Svc	Beaver Dam	WI	53916	**800-444-4014***	920-887-3148	721
Powerex Inc 200 Hillis St	Youngwood	PA	15697	**800-451-1415**	724-925-7272	686
Powernail Co 1300 Rose Rd	Lake Zurich	IL	60047	**800-323-1653**	847-634-3000	747
Powers Distributing Co Inc 3700 Giddings Rd	Orion	MI	48359	**800-498-4008**	248-393-3700	82-1
Powers Process Controls 3400 Oakton St	Skokie	IL	60076	**800-669-4217**	847-673-6700	201
Powers Transportation Systems Inc PO Box 103	Savannah	GA	31402	**888-673-1287**	912-966-2198	769
Powerware Corp 8609 Six Forks Rd	Raleigh	NC	27615	**800-554-3448**	919-872-3020	252
Powerwave Technologies Inc 1801 E Saint Andrew Pl *NASDAQ: PWAV*	Santa Ana	CA	92705	**888-797-9283**	714-466-1000	633
Powerway Inc 6919 Hillsdale Ct	Indianapolis	IN	46250	**800-964-9004**	317-598-1760	176-1
Powrmatic Inc PO Box 439	Finksburg	MD	21048	**800-966-9100**	410-833-9100	352
Pozas Brothers Trucking Co Inc 8130 Enterprise Dr	Newark	CA	94560	**800-874-8383**	510-742-9939	769
Pozen Inc 1414 Raleigh Rd Suite 400 *NASDAQ: POZN*	Chapel Hill	NC	27517	**888-264-1828**	919-913-1030	86
PPA (Professional Photographers of America Inc) 229 Peachtree St NE Suite 2200	Atlanta	GA	30303	**800-786-6277**	404-522-8600	48-4
PPAI (Promotional Products Assn International) 3125 Skyway Cir N	Irving	TX	75038	**888-492-6891**	972-252-0404	49-18
PPC Mechanical Seals 2769 Mission Dr	Baton Rouge	LA	70805	**800-731-7325**	225-356-4333	321
PPL Corp 2 N 9th St *NYSE: PPL*	Allentown	PA	18101	**800-342-5775**	610-774-5151	355-5
PPL Electric Utilities Corp 2 N 9th St *Cust Svc	Allentown	PA	18101	**800-342-5775***	610-774-5151	774
PPL EnergyPlus LLC 2 N 9th St *Cust Svc	Allentown	PA	18101	**800-342-5775***	610-774-5151	774
PPL Gas Utilities Corp 57 S 3rd St	Oxford	PA	19363	**800-959-7366**	610-932-2000	774
PPL Generation LLC 2 N 9th St *Cust Svc	Allentown	PA	18101	**800-342-5775***	610-774-5151	774
PPOM LLC 28588 Northwestern Hwy	Southfield	MI	48034	**800-831-1166**	248-357-7766	384-3
ppoNEXT Inc 1501 Hughes Way Suite 400	Long Beach	CA	90802	**866-776-6398**		384-3
PQ Corp 1200 W Swedes Ford Rd *Cust Svc	Berwyn	PA	19312	**800-944-7411***	610-651-4200	141
PR Intelligence Newsletter 316 N Michigan Ave Suite 300	Chicago	IL	60601	**800-878-5331**	312-960-4100	521-11
PR Newswire 810 7th Ave 35th Fl	New York	NY	10019	**800-832-5522**	212-596-1500	520
PR Reporter Newsletter 316 N Michigan Ave Suite 300	Chicago	IL	60601	**800-493-4867**	312-960-4140	521-11
Prab Inc 5944 E Kilgore Rd	Kalamazoo	MI	49048	**800-968-7722**	269-382-8200	206
Practical Accountant Magazine PO Box 408	Congers	NY	10920	**800-260-2793**		449-5
Practical Allergy Research Foundation 1421 Colvin Blvd	Buffalo	NY	14223	**800-787-8780**	716-875-5578	48-17
Practical Horseman Magazine 665 Quince Orchard Rd Suite 600 *Cust Svc	Gaithersburg	MD	20878	**877-717-8929***	301-977-3900	449-14
Practical Lawyer Magazine 4025 Chestnut St	Philadelphia	PA	19104	**800-253-6397**	215-243-1600	449-15
Practical Real Estate Lawyer Magazine 4025 Chestnut St	Philadelphia	PA	19104	**800-253-6397**	215-243-1600	449-15
PracticeWares Dental Supply 11291 Sunrise Pk Dr	Rancho Cordova	CA	95742	**800-800-4939**	916-638-8020	467
Practising Law Institute (PLI) 810 7th Ave 26th Fl	New York	NY	10019	**800-260-4754**	212-824-5700	49-10
PRADCO Outdoor Brands Div EBSCO Industries Inc 3601 Jenny Lind Rd	Fort Smith	AR	72901	**800-531-1201**	479-782-8971	701
Prader-Willi Syndrome Assn (USA) 5700 Midnight Pass Rd Suite 6	Sarasota	FL	34242	**800-926-4797**	941-312-0400	48-17
Prado Vision Center 7522 N Himes Ave	Tampa	FL	33614	**877-455-2745**	813-931-0500	785
Praeger Publishers 88 Post Rd W *Sales	Westport	CT	06881	**800-225-5800***	203-226-3571	623-2
Prager Brush Co Inc 730 Echo St NW	Atlanta	GA	30318	**800-241-5696**	404-875-9292	104
Pragma Systems Inc 3700 W Parmer Ln Suite 100 *Sales	Austin	TX	78727	**800-224-1675***	512-219-7270	176-12
Pragmatech Software Inc 15 Trafalgar Sq	Nashua	NH	03063	**800-401-9580**	603-249-1400	176-7
Prairie Area Library System 4021 Morsay Dr	Rockford	IL	61107	**877-542-7257**	815-229-0330	426
Prairie Farms Dairy Inc 1100 N Broadway St	Carlinville	IL	62626	**800-654-2547**	217-854-2547	291-27
Prairie Group Inc 7601 W 79th St *Sales	Bridgeview	IL	60455	**800-649-3690***	708-458-0400	180
Prairie Lakes Co-op 524 Pulp St PO Box 580	Starbuck	MN	56381	**800-808-1626**	320-239-2226	438
Prairie Lakes Hospital & Care Center 401 9th Ave NW	Watertown	SD	57201	**877-917-7547**	605-882-7000	366-2
Prairie Land Electric Co-op Inc 1101 W Hwy 36	Norton	KS	67654	**800-577-3323**	785-877-3323	244
Prairie Lights Bookstore 15 S Dubuque St	Iowa City	IA	52240	**800-295-2665**	319-337-2681	96
Prairie Livestock Inc Barton Ferry Rd	West Point	MS	39773	**800-647-6350**	662-494-5651	437
Prairie Public Broadcasting Inc 207 N 5th St	Fargo	ND	58102	**800-359-6900**	701-241-6900	620
Prairie View A & M University PO Box 3089	Prairie View	TX	77446	**800-787-7826**	936-857-2626	163
Prairie Waste Service Inc 6449 Valley Dr	Bettendorf	IA	52722	**800-233-9634**	563-332-0050	791
Pratesi Linens Inc 381 Park Ave S Suite 1223	New York	NY	10016	**800-332-6925**	212-689-3150	357
Pratt AS & Sons 1901 Fort Myer Dr Suite 501 *Cust Svc	Arlington	VA	22209	**800-572-2797***	703-528-0145	623-9
Pratt & Austin Co Inc 1 Cabot St	Holyoke	MA	01040	**800-848-8020**	413-532-0106	542-3
Pratt Henry Co 401 S Highland Ave	Aurora	IL	60506	**877-436-7728**	630-844-4000	777
Pratt Institute 200 Willoughby Ave	Brooklyn	NY	11205	**800-331-0834**	718-636-3600	163
Pratt & Whitney Canada Inc 1000 Marie-Victorin Blvd	Longueuil	QC	J4G1A1	**800-268-8000**	450-677-9411	22
Pratt & Whitney Government Engines & Space Propulsion Div PO Box 109600	West Palm Beach	FL	33410	**800-327-3246**	561-796-2000	494
Pratt & Whitney Power Systems Inc 80 Lamberton Rd	Windsor	CT	06095	**800-525-8199**	860-565-5776	259

Name / Address	City	State	ZIP	Toll-Free	Phone	Class
Praxair Inc 39 Old Ridgebury Rd *NYSE: PX*	Danbury	CT	06810	**800-772-9247**	203-837-2000	141
Praxair MRC 542 Rt 303	Orangeburg	NY	10962	**800-827-4387**	845-359-4200	686
Praxis Series Online Educational Testing Service Teaching & Learning Div Rosedale Rd	Princeton	NJ	08541	**800-772-9476**	609-771-7395	243
PRB (Population Reference Bureau) 1875 Connecticut Ave NW Suite 520	Washington	DC	20009	**800-877-9881**	202-483-1100	48-7
Pre-Paid Legal Services Inc 1 Pre-Paid Way *AMEX: PPD*	Ada	OK	74820	**800-654-7757**	580-436-1234	384-5
Preble Feed & Grain Inc Werling Dr PO Box 52	Preble	IN	46782	**800-566-4452**	260-547-4452	438
Precast Concrete Assn. National 10333 N Meridian St Suite 272	Indianapolis	IN	46290	**800-366-7731**	317-571-9500	49-3
Precept Medical Products Inc 370 Airport Rd	Arden	NC	28704	**800-851-4431**	828-681-0209	566
Precious Metals Institute. International 4400 Bayou Blvd Suite 18	Pensacola	FL	32503	**866-289-8484**	850-476-1156	49-4
Precipitator Services Group Inc 1625 Broad St	Elizabethton	TN	37643	**800-345-0484**	423-543-7331	19
Precise Technology Inc 501 Mosside Blvd	North Versailles	PA	15137	**800-949-2101**	412-823-2100	593
Precision Assoc Inc 740 Washington Ave N *Cust Svc	Minneapolis	MN	55401	**800-394-6590***	612-333-7464	664
Precision Auto Care Inc 748 Miller Dr SE	Leesburg	VA	20175	**800-438-8863**	703-777-9095	62-5
Precision Brand Products Inc 2250 Curtiss St	Downers Grove	IL	60515	**800-535-3727**	630-969-7200	345
Precision Devices Inc 8840 N Greenview Dr	Middleton	WI	53562	**800-274-9825**	608-831-4445	252
Precision Dynamics Corp 13880 Del Sur St	San Fernando	CA	91340	**800-847-0670**	818-897-1111	469
Precision Dynamics Inc 60 Production Ct	New Britain	CT	06051	**888-840-1230**	860-229-3753	777
Precision Electronic Glass Inc 1013 Hendee Rd	Vineland	NJ	08360	**800-982-4734**	856-691-2234	328
Precision Energy Services 500 Winscott Rd	Fort Worth	TX	76126	**800-669-9326**	817-249-7200	200
Precision Fabrics Group Inc 301 N Elm St Suite 600	Greensboro	NC	27401	**800-284-8001**	336-510-8000	730-1
Precision Foods Inc 11457 Olde Cabin Rd	Saint Louis	MO	63141	**800-442-5242**	314-567-7400	291-37
Precision Industries Inc 4611 S 96th St	Omaha	NE	68127	**800-373-7777**	402-593-7000	378
Precision Optics Corp Inc 22 E Broadway *NASDAQ: POCI*	Gardner	MA	01440	**800-447-2812**	978-630-1800	375
Precision Pallet Co 721 Parkwood Ave	Romeoville	IL	60446	**800-255-8532**	815-886-1061	541
Precision Parts & Remanufacturing Co 4411 SW 19th St	Oklahoma City	OK	73108	**800-654-3846**	405-681-2592	246
Precision Pattern Inc 1643 S Maize Rd	Wichita	KS	67209	**800-448-5127**	316-721-3100	678
Precision Products Inc 316 Limit St *Cust Svc	Lincoln	IL	62656	**800-225-5891***	217-735-1590	420
Precision Response Corp 8151 Peters Rd Suite 3000	Plantation	FL	33324	**800-866-4443**	954-693-3700	722
Precision Rolled Products Inc 306 Columbia Tpke	Florham Park	NJ	07932	**800-321-0135**	973-822-9100	709
Precision Scientific Inc 170 Marcel Dr *Cust Svc	Winchester	VA	22602	**800-621-8820***	540-869-9892	411
Precision Screw Thread Corp S 82 W 19275 Apollo Dr	Muskego	WI	53150	**800-828-3431**	262-679-9000	446
Precision Solar Controls Inc 2985 Market St	Garland	TX	75041	**800-686-7414**	972-278-0553	692
Precision Steel Warehouse Inc 3500 N Wolf Rd	Franklin Park	IL	60131	**800-323-0740**	847-455-7000	483
Precision Tank & Equipment Co Inc 3503 Conover Rd	Virginia	IL	62691	**800-258-4197**	217-452-7228	269
Precision Technology Inc 39 Sheep Davis Rd	Pembroke	NH	03275	**800-362-7717**	603-224-9989	93
Precision Tune Auto Care Inc PO Box 5000	Leesburg	VA	20177	**800-438-8863**	703-777-9095	62-5
Precision Twist Drill Co 301 Industrial Ave	Crystal Lake	IL	60012	**800-877-3745**	815-459-2040	747
Precision Valve Corp PO Box 309	Yonkers	NY	10702	**800-431-2697**	914-969-6500	478
Precision Walls Inc 4501 Beryl Rd	Raleigh	NC	27606	**800-849-9255**	919-832-0380	188-9
Precision Wood Products Inc PO Box 529	Vancouver	WA	98660	**877-743-9663**	360-694-8322	541
Precisionform Inc 148 W Airport Rd	Lititz	PA	17543	**800-233-3821**	717-560-7610	610
Precitech Precision Inc 44 Blackbrook Rd	Keene	NH	03431	**800-295-2510**	603-357-2511	484
Precor Inc 20031 142nd Ave NE	Woodinville	WA	98072	**800-786-8404**	425-486-9292	263
Preferred Care Inc 259 Monroe Ave	Rochester	NY	14607	**800-950-3224**	585-325-3920	384-3
Preferred CommunityChoice PPO 218 W 6th St	Tulsa	OK	74119	**800-278-7563**	918-594-5200	384-3
Preferred Employers Group Inc 10800 Biscayne Blvd 10th Fl	Miami	FL	33161	**800-433-5755**	305-893-4040	384-4
Preferred Employers Insurance Co PO Box 85478	San Diego	CA	92186	**888-472-9224**	619-688-3900	384-4
Preferred Group of Mutual Funds PO Box 8320	Boston	MA	02266	**800-662-4769**		517
Preferred Health Systems Inc 8535 E 21st St N	Wichita	KS	67206	**800-990-0345**	316-609-2345	384-3
Preferred Hotels & Resorts Worldwide Inc 311 S Wacker Dr Suite 1900	Chicago	IL	60606	**800-323-7500**	312-913-0400	368
Preferred Living 88 Upham St	Malden	MA	02148	**800-343-2177**	781-321-5793	209
Preferred Meal Systems Inc 5240 Saint Charles Rd *Cust Svc	Berkeley	IL	60163	**800-886-6325***	708-318-2500	291-36
Preferred Mental Health Management Inc 401 E Douglas Ave Suite 300	Wichita	KS	67202	**800-776-4357**	316-262-0444	454
Preferred Mutual Insurance Co 1 Preferred Way	New Berlin	NY	13411	**800-333-7642**	607-847-6161	384-4
Pregnancy & Infant Loss Support Inc. SHARE St Joseph's Health Ctr 300 1st Capitol Dr	Saint Charles	MO	63301	**800-821-6819**	636-947-6164	48-21
Premera Blue Cross DBA Blue Cross & Blue Shield of Alaska PO Box 91080	Seattle	WA	98111	**800-345-6784**	425-670-4000	384-3
Premera Blue Cross DBA MSC 3900 E Sprague Ave	Spokane	WA	99202	**800-835-3510**	509-536-4700	384-3
Premera HealthPlus PO Box 2113 *Cust Svc	Seattle	WA	98111	**800-527-6675***	425-918-4700	384-3
Premier Beverage Co of Florida 9801 Premier Pkwy	Miramar	FL	33025	**800-432-2002**	954-436-9200	82-3
Premier Coach Co Inc 67 Champlain Dr	Colchester	VT	05446	**800-532-1811**	802-655-4456	108
Premier Community Bankshares Inc 4095 Valley Pike *NASDAQ: PREM*	Winchester	VA	22602	**800-526-2265**	540-869-6600	355-2
Premier Dental Products Co Inc 1710 Romano Dr Box 4500	Plymouth Meeting	PA	19462	**888-773-6872**	610-239-6000	226
Premier Die Casting Co 1177 Rahway Ave	Avenel	NJ	07001	**800-394-3006**	732-634-3000	303
Premier Financial Bancorp Inc 2883 5th Ave *NASDAQ: PFBI*	Huntington	WV	25702	**866-269-0298**	304-525-1600	355-2
Premier Gateway Inc 320 SW Stark St Suite 315	Portland	OR	97204	**800-777-8369**	503-294-6478	17
Premier Golf 4355 River Green Pkwy	Duluth	GA	30096	**800-283-4653**	770-291-4100	760
Premier Incentives Inc 2 Market Sq	Marblehead	MA	01945	**888-255-0000**	781-639-4444	377
Premier Industries Inc 1320 Russell St	Covington	KY	41011	**800-354-9817**	859-581-1390	548-1
Premier Jets 2140 NE 25th Ave Hillsboro Airport	Hillsboro	OR	97124	**800-635-8583**	503-640-2927	14
Premier Malt Products Inc 25760 Groesbeck Hwy Suite 103 *Cust Svc	Warren	MI	48089	**800-521-1057***	586-443-3355	453
Premier Meetings & Incentives 2150 S Washburn St	Oshkosh	WI	54903	**800-236-5095**	920-236-8030	377
Premier Pet Insurance PO Box 96	Minneapolis	MN	55440	**877-774-2273**		384-1
Premier Plastics 635 E 15th St	Tacoma	WA	98421	**800-422-6864**	253-627-2151	99
Premier Resorts & Hotels 2600 SW 3rd Ave 6th Fl	Miami	FL	33129	**800-877-3643**	305-856-7083	369
Premier Resorts International PO Box 4800	Park City	UT	84060	**888-774-3533**	435-655-4800	369
Premier Resorts Sun Valley PO Box 659	Sun Valley	ID	83353	**800-635-4444**	208-727-4000	655
Premier Suites 11601 W Markham Rd Suite D	Little Rock	AR	72211	**800-735-2955**	501-221-7378	373
Premier Tool & Die Cast Corp 9886 N Tudor Rd	Berrien Springs	MI	49103	**800-417-8717**	269-471-7715	303
Premier Tours 1430 Walnut St 2nd Fl	Philadelphia	PA	19102	**800-545-1910**	215-893-9966	748
Premier Wine & Spirits DBA Gallo Wine Distributors Inc 345 Underhill Blvd	Syosset	NY	11791	**800-272-4255**	516-921-9005	82-3
Premiere Direct/Legwear Express 227 Avery Ave *Orders	Morganton	NC	28655	**800-280-1222***	828-439-8724	153-10
Premiere Magazine 1633 Broadway *Cust Svc	New York	NY	10019	**800-274-4027***	212-767-6000	449-9
Premiere Radio Networks Inc 15260 Ventura Blvd Suite 500	Sherman Oaks	CA	91403	**800-533-8686**	818-377-5300	632
Premiere Tickets & Tours Inc 201 Shannon Oaks Cir	Cary	NC	27512	**800-775-1617**	919-481-4868	735
Premio Foods Inc 50 Utter Ave	Hawthorne	NJ	07506	**800-864-7622**	973-427-1106	291-26
PremiumWear Inc 5500 Feltl Rd *Cust Svc	Minnetonka	MN	55343	**800-347-6098***	952-979-1700	153-12
Prentice-Hall Inc 1 Lake St	Upper Saddle River	NJ	07458	**800-947-7700**	201-236-7000	623-2
Prentice Hall-Professional Technical Reference 1 Lake St	Upper Saddle River	NJ	07458	**800-947-7700**	201-236-7000	623-2
Presbyterian Church (USA) 100 Witherspoon St	Louisville	KY	40202	**888-728-7228**	502-569-5000	48-20
Presbyterian College 503 S Broad St	Clinton	SC	29325	**800-476-7272**	864-833-2820	163
Presbyterian Disaster Assistance (PDA) 100 Witherspoon St	Louisville	KY	40202	**888-728-7228**	502-569-5839	48-5
Presbyterian Healthcare Services 1100 Central Ave SE	Albuquerque	NM	87106	**800-545-4030**	505-841-1234	348
Presbyterian Hospital of Greenville PO Box 1059	Greenville	TX	75403	**800-984-9223**	903-408-5000	366-2
Presbyterian-Saint Luke's Medical Center Blood & Marrow Transplant Program 1719 E 19th Ave	Denver	CO	80218	**877-268-9300**	303-839-6953	758
Presbyterian SeniorCare-Westminster Place 1215 Hulton Rd	Oakmont	PA	15139	**877-772-6500**	412-828-5600	441
Presbyterians Today Magazine 100 Witherspoon St	Louisville	KY	40202	**800-227-2872**	502-569-5637	449-18
Presco Food Seasonings Inc PO Box 152	Flemington	NJ	08822	**800-526-1713**	908-782-4919	291-37
Prescott Chamber of Commerce 117 W Goodwin St	Prescott	AZ	86303	**800-266-7534**	928-445-2000	137
Prescott College 220 Grove Ave	Prescott	AZ	86301	**877-350-2100**	928-778-2090	163
Prescott Everett J Inc 32 Prescott St	Gardiner	ME	04345	**800-876-1357**	207-582-1851	601
Prescott Hotel 545 Post St	San Francisco	CA	94102	**800-271-3632**	415-563-0303	373
Prescription Solutions 3515 Harbor Blvd	Costa Mesa	CA	92626	**800-562-6223**	714-825-3600	575
Presearch Inc 8500 Executive Park Ave Suite 400	Fairfax	VA	22031	**800-922-9259**	703-876-6400	178
Presentation College 1500 N Main St	Aberdeen	SD	57401	**800-437-6060**	605-225-1634	160
Preservation Hall 726 Saint Peter St	New Orleans	LA	70116	**888-946-5299**	504-522-2841	562
Preservation Magazine 1785 Massachusetts Ave NW	Washington	DC	20036	**800-944-6847**	202-588-6000	449-2

Name / Address	City	State	ZIP	Toll-Free	Phone	Class
Preserver Group Inc 95 Rt 17 S	Paramus	NJ	07653	**800-242-0332**	201-291-2000	355-4
Preserver Insurance Co 95 Rt 17 S	Paramus	NJ	07653	**800-242-0332**	201-291-2000	384-4
President Casino on the Admiral 802 N 1st St	Saint Louis	MO	63102	**800-772-3647**	314-622-1111	133
President Casino Broadwater Resort 2110 Beach Blvd	Biloxi	MS	39531	**800-843-7737**	228-388-2211	655
President Casinos Inc 800 N 1st St	Saint Louis	MO	63102	**800-772-3647**	314-622-3000	132
President Hotel 1423 Collins Ave	Miami Beach	FL	33139	**800-235-3296**	305-538-2882	373
Presidential Aviation 1725 NW 51st Pl Fort Lauderdale Executive Airport Hangar 71	Fort Lauderdale	FL	33309	**888-772-8622**	954-772-8622	14
Presidential Life Corp 69 Lydecker St *NASDAQ: PLFE*	Nyack	NY	10960	**800-926-7599**	845-358-2300	355-4
Presidential Life Insurance Co 69 Lydecker St	Nyack	NY	10960	**800-926-7599**	845-358-2300	384-2
Presidential Online Bank 4520 East-West Hwy	Bethesda	MD	20814	**800-383-6266**	301-652-0700	71
Presidential Realty Corp 180 S Broadway *AMEX: PDL/A*	White Plains	NY	10605	**800-948-2977**	914-948-1300	214
Presidents' Organization. Young 451 S Decker Dr Suite 200	Irving	TX	75062	**800-773-7976**	972-650-4600	49-12
Presidio Corp 7601 Ora Glen Dr Suite 100	Greenbelt	MD	20770	**800-452-6926**	301-313-2000	178
Presley Tours Inc 16 Presley Park Dr PO Box 58	Makanda	IL	62958	**800-621-6100**	618-549-0704	748
Presque Isle Electric & Gas Co-op PO Box 308	Onaway	MI	49765	**800-423-6634**	989-733-8515	244
Press Assn. Independent 2729 Mission St Suite 201	San Francisco	CA	94110	**877-463-9624**	415-643-4401	49-16
Press Assn. Inter American 1801 SW 3rd Ave 7th Fl	Miami	FL	33129	**877-747-4272**	305-634-2465	49-14
Press Democrat PO Box 569	Santa Rosa	CA	95402	**800-675-5056**	707-546-2020	522-2
Press-Enterprise 3512 14th St	Riverside	CA	92501	**800-933-1400**	951-684-1200	522-2
Press-Enterprise Co PO Box 792	Riverside	CA	92502	**800-933-1400**	951-684-1200	623-8
Press-Enterprise Inc 3185 Lackawanna Ave	Bloomsburg	PA	17815	**800-228-3483**	570-784-2121	623-8
Press Journal 14522 S Outer 40 Dr	Chesterfield	MO	63017	**866-440-4500**	314-821-1110	522-4
Press-Republican 170 Margaret St	Plattsburgh	NY	12901	**800-288-7323**	518-561-2300	522-2
Press-Seal Gasket Corp 6932 Gettysburg Pike	Fort Wayne	IN	46804	**800-348-7325**	260-436-0521	321
Press & Sun Bulletin PO box 1270	Binghamton	NY	13902	**800-365-0077**	607-798-1234	522-2
Presscut Industries Inc 1540 Selene Dr Suite 100	Carrollton	TX	75006	**800-442-4924**	972-389-0615	321
Pressed4Time Inc 8 Clock Tower Pl Suite 110	Maynard	MA	01754	**800-423-8711**	978-823-8300	417
Presstek Inc 55 Executive Dr *NASDAQ: PRST*	Hudson	NH	03051	**877-862-2227**	603-595-7000	770
Pressure BioSciences Inc 375 West St *NASDAQ: PBIO*	West Bridgewater	MA	02379	**800-676-1881**	508-580-1900	86
Pressure Concrete Inc PO Box 1303	Florence	AL	35631	**800-633-3141**	256-764-5941	188-3
Pressure Systems Inc 34 Research Dr	Hampton	VA	23666	**800-678-7226**	757-865-1243	200
Prestera Trucking PO Box 399	South Point	OH	45680	**800-759-9555**	740-894-4770	769
Prestige Cosmetics Corp 1441 W Newport Center Dr	Deerfield Beach	FL	33442	**800-722-7488**	954-480-9202	211
Prestige Financial 1420 S 500 West	Salt Lake City	UT	84115	**866-737-2733**	801-844-2100	215
Prestige Inc 101 S 8th St	Neodesha	KS	66757	**800-328-4006**	620-325-8500	116
Prestige Travel & Cruises Inc 6175 Spring Mountain Rd	Las Vegas	NV	89146	**800-553-0204**	702-251-5552	760
Prestigeline Inc 5 Inez Dr	Bay Shore	NY	11706	**800-776-5483**	631-273-3636	431
Prestini Musical Instruments Inc 2020 N Aurora Dr	Nogales	AZ	85628	**800-528-6569**	520-287-4931	516
Presto Food Stores Inc 2009 N Airport Rd	Plant City	FL	33563	**800-881-3511**	813-754-3511	203
Presto Products Co 670 N Perkins St	Appleton	WI	54912	**800-558-3525**	920-739-9471	67
Presto Tape Inc 1626 Bridgewater Rd	Bensalem	PA	19020	**800-331-1373**	215-245-8555	717
Presto-X Co PO Box 2578	Omaha	NE	68103	**800-759-1942**	402-554-1942	567
Prestolite Electric Inc 2311 Green Rd Suite B *Cust Svc	Ann Arbor	MI	48105	**800-354-0560***	734-913-6600	246
Prestolite Wire Corp 200 Galleria Officentre Suite 212	Southfield	MI	48034	**800-498-3132**	248-355-4422	801
Preston County Convention & Visitors Bureau 200 1/2 W Main St	Kingwood	WV	26537	**800-571-0912**	304-329-4660	205
Preston Gates & Ellis LLP 925 4th Ave Suite 2900	Seattle	WA	98104	**800-551-4613**	206-623-7580	419
Preston Refrigeration Co Inc 3200 Fiberglass Rd	Kansas City	KS	66115	**800-621-1813**	913-621-1813	651
Pretty Products Inc 437 Cambridge Rd	Coshocton	OH	43812	**800-837-9160**	740-622-3522	60
Pretzelmaker 2855 E Cottonwood Pkwy Suite 400	Salt Lake City	UT	84121	**800-266-5437**	801-736-5600	657
Pretzels Inc 123 Harvest Rd PO Box 503	Bluffton	IN	46714	**800-456-4838**	260-824-4838	291-9
Preuss Alan Florists 17680-E W Bluemound Rd	Brookfield	WI	53045	**800-839-8400**	262-786-7900	287
Prevent Blindness America 211 W Wacker Dr Suite 1700	Chicago	IL	60606	**800-331-2020**	312-363-6001	48-17
Prevent Child Abuse America 200 S Michigan Ave 17th Fl	Chicago	IL	60604	**800-244-5373**	312-663-3520	48-6
Preventing Business Fraud Newsletter 3 Park Ave 30th Fl	New York	NY	10016	**800-401-5937**	212-244-0360	521-2
Prevention Book Club 33 E Minor St *Cust Svc	Emmaus	PA	18098	**800-914-9363***	610-967-5171	94
Prevention Information Network. National PO Box 6003	Rockville	MD	20849	**800-458-5231**	301-562-1098	336-6
Prevention Magazine 33 E Minor St	Emmaus	PA	18098	**800-813-8070**	610-967-5171	449-13
Prevost Car Inc 35 boul Gagnon	Sainte-Claire	QC	G0R2V0	**800-463-8876**	418-883-3391	505
Prevue Pet Products Inc 224 N Maplewood Ave	Chicago	IL	60612	**800-243-3624**	312-243-3624	568
PRG-Schultz International Inc 600 Galleria Pkwy Suite 100 *NASDAQ: PRGX*	Atlanta	GA	30339	**800-752-5894**	770-779-3900	2
Price Books & Forms Inc 751 N Coney Ave	Azusa	CA	91702	**800-423-8961**	626-334-0348	623-2
Price Brothers Co PO Box 825	Dayton	OH	45401	**800-543-5147**	937-226-8700	181
Price Canyon Ranch PO Box 1065	Douglas	AZ	85608	**800-727-0065**	520-558-2383	238
Price Edwards & Co 210 Park Ave Suite 1000	Oklahoma City	OK	73102	**800-316-7811**	405-843-7171	641
Price Electric Co-op Inc 508 N Lake Ave	Phillips	WI	54555	**800-884-0881**	715-339-2155	244
Price Esther Candies Inc 1709 Wayne Ave	Dayton	OH	45410	**800-782-0326**	937-253-2121	291-8
Price Perceptions Newsletter 3030 NW Expy Suite 725	Oklahoma City	OK	73112	**800-231-0477**	405-604-8726	521-1
Price Pfister Inc 19701 Da Vinci St	Lake Forest	CA	92610	**800-732-8238**	949-672-4000	598
Price T Rowe Group Inc 100 E Pratt St *NASDAQ: TROW*	Baltimore	MD	21202	**800-638-7890**	410-345-2000	355-3
Price T Rowe Mutual Funds 100 E Pratt St	Baltimore	MD	21202	**800-638-5660**	410-345-2000	517
Priceline.com Inc 800 Connecticut Ave *NASDAQ: PCLN*	Norwalk	CT	06854	**800-774-2354**	203-299-8000	51
PRIDE (Prison Rehabilitative Industries & Diversified Enterprises Inc) 12425 28th St N Suite 103	Saint Petersburg	FL	33716	**800-643-8495**	727-572-1987	618
Pride Feeders I Ltd RR 2 Box 67	Hooker	OK	73945	**800-872-7251**	580-253-6381	11-1
Pride International Inc 5847 San Felipe Suite 3300 *NYSE: PDE*	Houston	TX	77057	**800-645-2067**	713-789-1400	528
Pride Offshore Inc 410 S Van Ave	Houma	LA	70363	**800-624-1106**	985-872-4700	529
Priester Aviation 1061 S Wolf Rd	Wheeling	IL	60090	**888-323-7887**	847-537-1133	25
Priester Pecan Co Inc PO Box 381	Fort Deposit	AL	36032	**800-277-3226**	334-227-4301	291-28
Priests. Survivors Network of Those Abused by PO Box 6416	Chicago	IL	60680	**877-409-2720**	312-409-2720	48-21
PRIMA North America Inc 711 E Main St *Cust Svc	Chicopee	MA	01020	**800-722-1133***	413-598-5200	416
Primary Health 800 Park Blvd Suite 760	Boise	ID	83712	**800-688-5008**	208-344-1811	384-3
Primary Teachers' Book Club Doubleday Select Inc 101 Park Ave 2nd Fl	New York	NY	10178	**800-321-7323**		94
Primavera Systems Inc 3 Bala Plaza W Suite 700 *Sales	Bala Cynwyd	PA	19004	**800-423-0245***	610-667-8600	176-1
Prime Hospitality Corp 700 Rt 46 E *NYSE: PDQ*	Fairfield	NJ	07004	**800-444-8888**	973-882-1010	369
AmeriSuites 700 Rt 46 E	Fairfield	NJ	07004	**800-833-1516**	973-882-1010	369
Prime Hotels & Resorts 700 Rt 46 E *Resv	Fairfield	NJ	07004	**866-864-3649***	973-882-1010	369
Wellesley Inn & Suites 700 Rt 46 E	Fairfield	NJ	07004	**800-444-8888**	973-882-1010	369
PRIME Hotel & Suites San Diego/Sorrento Mesa 5975 Lusk Blvd	San Diego	CA	92121	**800-996-3426**	858-558-1818	373
Prime Hotels & Resorts 700 Rt 46 E *Resv	Fairfield	NJ	07004	**866-864-3649***	973-882-1010	369
Prime Inc PO Box 4208 *Cust Svc	Springfield	MO	65808	**800-848-4560***	417-866-0001	769
Prime Leather Finishes Co Inc 205 S 2nd St	Milwaukee	WI	53204	**800-558-7285**	414-276-1668	143
Prime Mfg Corp 1619 Kuntz Rd	Dayton	OH	45404	**800-657-0707**	937-496-3807	636
Prime Office Products 7500 Lindbergh Dr	Gaithersburg	MD	20879	**800-478-7782**	301-721-4300	524
Prime Outlets Ellenton 5461 Factory Shops Blvd	Ellenton	FL	34222	**888-260-7608**	941-723-1150	452
Prime Pubs Inc 10 Kingsbridge Garden Cir Suite 600	Mississauga	ON	L5R3K6	**800-361-3111**	905-568-0000	657
Prime Rate Premium Finance Corp 2141 Enterprise Dr PO Box 100507 *Cust Svc	Florence	SC	29501	**800-777-7458***	843-669-0937	215
Prime Resources Corp 1100 Boston Ave	Bridgeport	CT	06610	**800-873-7746**	203-331-9100	10
Prime Restaurant Group Inc 10 Kingsbridge Garden Cir Suite 600	Mississauga	ON	L5R3K6	**800-613-1111**	905-568-0000	656
Prime Retail LP 217 E Redwood St 20th Fl	Baltimore	MD	21202	**800-980-7467**	410-234-0782	641
Prime Rewards 10 Kingsbridge Rd	Fairfield	NJ	07007	**800-982-6374**		371
Prime Sirloin Steak House 129 Fast Ln	Mooresville	NC	28117	**877-704-5939**	704-660-5939	657
Prime Therapeutics Inc 1020 Discovery Rd Suite 100	Eagan	MN	55121	**800-858-0723**	651-286-4000	575
PrimeArray Systems Inc 127 Riverneck Rd	Chelmsford	MA	01824	**800-433-5133**	978-654-6250	174
PRIMEDIA Productions 4101 International Pkwy	Carrollton	TX	75007	**800-761-4386**	972-309-4700	503
Primera Technology Inc 2 Carlson Pkwy Suite 375	Plymouth	MN	55447	**800-797-2772**	763-475-6676	171-6
Primerica Financial Services 3120 Breckinridge Blvd	Duluth	GA	30099	**800-257-4725**	770-381-1000	393
PrimeSource Building Products Inc 2115 E Beltline	Carrollton	TX	75006	**800-745-3341**	972-416-1976	190-3
PrimeSource Healthcare Inc 3708 E Columbia St	Tucson	AZ	85714	**888-842-6999**	520-512-1100	467
PrimeWest Energy Trust 150 6th Ave SW Suite 5100	Calgary	AB	T2P3Y7	**877-968-7878**	403-234-6600	662
Primex Plastics Corp 1235 N 'F' St	Richmond	IN	47374	**800-222-5116**	765-966-7774	589
Primm Valley Resort & Casino 31900 S Las Vegas Blvd	Primm	NV	89019	**800-386-7867**	702-382-1212	655
Primm Valley Resorts 31900 S Las Vegas Blvd	Primm	NV	89019	**800-386-7867**	702-382-1212	132
Primo Microphones Inc 1805 Couch Dr	McKinney	TX	75069	**800-767-7466**	972-548-9807	52

Company / Address	City	State	ZIP	Toll-Free	Phone	Class
Primrose Oil Co Inc PO Box 29665	Dallas	TX	75229	**800-275-2772**	972-241-1100	530
Primrose School Franchising Co 3660 Cedarcrest Rd	Acworth	GA	30101	**800-745-0677**	770-529-4100	146
Primus Knowledge Solutions Inc 1601 5th Ave Suite 1900 *NASDAQ: PKSI*	Seattle	WA	98101	**800-277-4427**	206-292-1000	176-1
Primus Telecommunications 7901 Jones Ranch Dr Suite 900 *NASDAQ: PRTL*	McLean	VA	22102	**800-226-4884**	703-902-2800	721
Prince Albert National Park PO Box 100	Waskesiu Lake	SK	S0J2Y0	**877-255-7267**	306-663-4522	553
Prince Castle Inc 355 E Kehoe Blvd	Carol Stream	IL	60188	**800-722-7853**	630-462-8800	293
Prince Conti Hotel 830 Conti St	New Orleans	LA	70112	**800-366-2743**	504-529-4172	373
Prince Corp 8351 County Rd H	Marshfield	WI	54449	**800-777-2486**	715-384-3105	568
Prince Edward Island Tourism PO Box 2000	Charlottetown	PE	C1A7N8	**888-734-7529**	902-368-4000	763
Prince George Hotel 1725 Market St	Halifax	NS	B3J3N9	**800-565-1567**	902-425-1986	372
Prince George's County Conference & Visitors Bureau 9200 Basil Ct Suite 101	Largo	MD	20774	**888-925-8300**	301-925-8300	205
Prince Music Theater 100 S Broad St Suite 650	Philadelphia	PA	19110	**800-964-6895**	215-972-1000	734
Prince Preferred Guest Program 100 Holomoana St	Honolulu	HI	96815	**800-774-6234**		371
Prince Resorts Hawaii 100 Holomoana St	Honolulu	HI	96815	**800-774-6234**	808-956-1111	369
Prince Rubber & Plastics Co Inc 137 Arthur St	Buffalo	NY	14207	**800-225-8505**	716-877-7400	664
Prince Rupert Daily News 801 2nd Ave W	Prince Rupert	BC	V8J1H6	**800-343-0022**	250-624-6781	522-1
Prince Sports Inc 1 Advantage Ct	Bordentown	NJ	08505	**800-283-6647**	609-291-5800	701
Prince Street Technologies Ltd 14641 E Don Jillian Rd	City of Industry	CA	91746	**800-221-3684**	626-333-4585	131
Princess Anne The 1350 Richmond Rd	Williamsburg	VA	23185	**800-552-5571**	757-229-2455	373
Princess Bayside Beach Hotel & Golf Center 4801 Coastal Hwy	Ocean City	MD	21842	**800-854-9785**	410-723-2900	373
Princess Cruise Line Ltd 24200 Town Ctr Dr	Santa Clarita	CA	91355	**800-421-0522**	661-753-0000	217
Princess House Inc 470 Miles Standish Blvd *Sales	Taunton	MA	02780	**800-622-0039***	508-823-0711	361
Princess Royale Oceanfront Hotel & Conference Center 9100 Coastal Hwy	Ocean City	MD	21842	**800-476-9253**	410-524-7777	373
Princess Soft Toys 7664 W 78th St	Minneapolis	MN	55439	**800-252-7638**	952-829-5772	750
Princess Tours 2815 2nd Ave Suite 400	Seattle	WA	98121	**800-426-0442**	206-336-6000	748
Princeton Daily Clarion 100 N Gibson St PO Box 30	Princeton	IN	47670	**800-467-5130**	812-385-2525	522-2
Princeton eCom Corp 650 College Rd E 2nd Fl	Princeton	NJ	08540	**866-606-3000**	609-606-3000	250
Princeton Excess & Surplus Lines Insurance Co 555 College Rd E	Princeton	NJ	08543	**800-255-5676**	609-243-4200	384-4
Princeton Gamma-Tech Inc 1026 Rt 518	Rocky Hill	NJ	08553	**800-229-7484**	609-924-7310	464
Princeton Graphics Systems Inc 3300 Irvine Ave Suite 120 *Cust Svc	Newport Beach	CA	92660	**800-747-6249***	949-777-3379	171-4
Princeton Insurance Cos 746 Alexander Rd	Princeton	NJ	08540	**800-433-0157**	800-334-0588	384-4
Princeton National Bancorp Inc 606 S Main St *NASDAQ: PNBC*	Princeton	IL	61356	**800-293-0451**	815-875-4444	355-2
Princeton Review 2315 Broadway *NASDAQ: REVU*	New York	NY	10024	**800-333-0369**	212-874-8282	243
Princeton Softech Inc 111 Campus Dr	Princeton	NJ	08540	**800-457-7060**	609-627-5500	176-1
Princeton University Press 41 William St *Sales	Princeton	NJ	08540	**800-777-4726***	609-258-4900	623-5
Princeville Resort 5520 Ka Haku Rd	Princeville	HI	96722	**800-826-1260**	808-826-9644	655
Principal Financial Group Inc 711 High St *NYSE: PFG*	Des Moines	IA	50392	**800-986-3343**	515-247-5111	355-4
Principal Life Insurance Co 711 High St	Des Moines	IA	50392	**800-986-3343**	515-247-5111	384-2
Principal Technical Services Inc 24102 Brookfield Cir	Lake Forest	CA	92630	**888-787-3711**	949-457-9035	707
Principals. National Assn of Elementary School 1615 Duke St	Alexandria	VA	22314	**800-386-2377**	703-684-3345	49-5
Principia College 1 Maybeck Pl	Elsah	IL	62028	**800-277-4648**	618-374-2131	163
Principle Business Enterprises Inc PO Box 129 *Cust Svc	Dunbridge	OH	43414	**800-467-3224***	419-352-1551	548-2
Princor Financial Services Corp PO Box 10423	Des Moines	IA	50306	**800-247-4123**	515-247-5111	393
Pringle Development Inc 26600 Ace Ave	Leesburg	FL	34748	**800-325-4471**	352-365-2303	639
Prinsco Inc 108 W Hwy 7 PO Box 265	Prinsburg	MN	56281	**800-992-1725**	320-978-4116	589
Print Magazine 700 E State St	Iola	WI	54990	**800-258-0929**	715-445-2214	449-5
Print-O-Tape Inc 755 Tower Rd	Mundelein	IL	60060	**800-346-6311**	847-362-1476	404
Print PAC 100 Daingerfield Rd 4th Fl	Alexandria	VA	22314	**800-742-2666**	703-519-8113	604
Printed Systems 1271 Gillingham Rd *Sales	Neenah	WI	54956	**800-352-2332***	920-886-2000	404
PrintEdd Products of North America 2641 Forum Dr	Grand Prairie	TX	75052	**800-367-6728**	972-988-3133	111
Printegra Inc 403 Westpark Ct Suite A	Peachtree City	GA	30269	**800-422-6070**	770-631-6070	111
Printek Inc 1517 Townline Rd	Benton Harbor	MI	49022	**800-368-4636**	269-925-3200	171-6
Printers & Stationers Inc 113 N Court St	Florence	AL	35630	**800-233-5514**	256-764-8061	524
Printgraphics Inc 1170 Industrial Park Dr	Vandalia	OH	45377	**800-543-7510**	937-898-3008	111
PrintImage International 70 E Lake St Suite 333	Chicago	IL	60601	**800-234-0040**	312-726-8015	49-16
Printing Developments Inc 2010 Indiana St	Racine	WI	53405	**800-558-9425**	262-554-1030	770
Printing House for the Blind. American 1839 Frankfort Ave PO Box 6085	Louisville	KY	40206	**800-223-1839**	502-895-2405	623-10
Printing House Craftsmen. International Assn of 7042 Brooklyn Blvd	Minneapolis	MN	55429	**800-466-4274**	763-560-1620	49-16
Printing & Imaging Assn. Digital 10015 Main St	Fairfax	VA	22031	**888-385-3588**	703-385-1339	49-16
Printing Industries of America/Graphic Arts Technical Foundation (PIA/GATF) 200 Deer Run Rd	Sewickley	PA	15143	**800-910-4283**	412-741-6860	49-16
Printing Leadership. National Assn for 75 W Century Rd *Cust Svc	Paramus	NJ	07652	**800-642-6275***	201-634-9600	49-16
Printpack Inc 4335 Wendell Dr	Atlanta	GA	30336	**800-241-9984**	404-691-5830	538
Printpack Inc Film Products Div PO Box 110	New Castle	DE	19720	**800-572-4345**	302-323-0900	538
Printronix Inc 14600 Myford Rd *NASDAQ: PTNX*	Irvine	CA	92606	**800-665-6210**	714-368-2300	171-6
Priority Club Rewards PO Box 30320	Salt Lake City	UT	84130	**888-211-9874**	800-272-9273	371
Priority Express Courier Service 5 Chelsea Pkwy	Boothwyn	PA	19061	**800-526-4646**	610-364-3300	536
Priority Health 1231 E Beltline Ave NE	Grand Rapids	MI	49525	**800-942-0954**	616-942-0954	384-3
Priority Health Managed Benefits Inc 1231 E Beltline NE	Grand Rapids	MI	49525	**800-942-0954**	616-942-0954	384-3
Priority Healthcare Corp 250 Technology Pk Suite 124 *NASDAQ: PHCC*	Lake Mary	FL	32746	**800-942-5999**	407-804-6700	576
Priority Management Systems Inc 13251 Delf Pl Suite 420	Richmond	BC	V6V2A2	**800-221-9031**	604-214-7772	753
Priority Publications 6700 France Ave S Suite 200	Edina	MN	55435	**800-727-6397**	952-920-9928	5
Priority Wire & Cable Inc 8200 E Roosevelt Rd	North Little Rock	AR	72206	**800-945-5542**	501-372-5444	245
PRISM International 605 Benson Rd Suite B	Garner	NC	27529	**800-336-9793**	919-771-0657	49-12
Prism Studios Inc 2505 Kennedy St NE	Minneapolis	MN	55413	**800-659-2001**	612-331-1000	338
Prismaflex Inc 1645 Queens Way E	Mississauga	ON	L4X3A3	**800-526-1488**	905-279-9793	692
Prison Fellowship Ministries (PF) PO Box 1550	Merrifield	VA	22116	**877-498-0100**	703-478-0100	48-8
Prison Health Services 105 Westpark Dr Suite 200	Brentwood	TN	37027	**800-729-0069**	615-373-3100	384-3
Prison Rehabilitative Industries & Diversified Enterprises Inc (PRIDE) 12425 28th St N Suite 103	Saint Petersburg	FL	33716	**800-643-8495**	727-572-1987	618
Pritchard Electric Co Inc PO Box 2503	Huntington	WV	25725	**877-457-8904**	304-529-2566	188-4
Pritchett LLC 5800 Granite Pkwy Suite 455	Plano	TX	75024	**800-992-5922**	972-731-1500	193
Pritikin Longevity Center & Spa 19735 Turnberry Way	Aventura	FL	33180	**800-327-4914**	305-935-7131	697
Priva Sport 8505 Devonshire Rd	Montreal	QC	H4P2L3	**877-568-8662**	514-341-9548	701
PrivatAir Inc 611 Access Rd	Stratford	CT	06615	**800-380-4009**	203-337-4600	14
Private Business Inc 9020 Overlook Blvd PO Box 1603 *NASDAQ: PBIZ*	Brentwood	TN	37024	**800-235-5584**		176-11
Private Citizen Inc PO Box 233	Naperville	IL	60566	**800-288-5865**	630-393-2370	48-10
Private Security Case Law Reporter 590 Dutch Valley Rd NE	Atlanta	GA	30324	**800-926-7926**	404-881-1141	521-7
PrivateBancorp Inc 10 N Dearborn St Suite 900 *NASDAQ: PVTB*	Chicago	IL	60602	**800-662-7748**	312-683-7100	355-2
Pro-Dex Inc 151 E Columbine Ave *NASDAQ: PDEX*	Santa Ana	CA	92707	**800-562-6204**	714-241-4411	355-3
Pro-Fac Co-op Inc 350 Linden Oaks *NASDAQ: PFACP*	Rochester	NY	14625	**800-999-5044**	585-218-4210	291-20
Pro Farmer Newsletter 6612 Chancellor Dr Suite 300 *Cust Svc	Cedar Falls	IA	50613	**800-772-0023***	319-277-1278	521-13
Pro Golf of America Inc 32751 Middlebelt Rd	Farmington Hills	MI	48334	**800-521-6388**	248-737-0553	702
Pro Golf Travel 515 Madison Ave 10th Fl	New York	NY	10022	**888-685-4426**	212-409-9585	760
Pro Image Corp 1805 Loucks Rd	York	PA	17404	**800-245-7259**	717-764-5880	770
Pro Image Franchise LLC 233 N 1250 West Suite 200	Centerville	UT	84014	**888-477-6326**	801-296-9999	155-5
Pro Insurance Co 2600 Professionals Dr	Okemos	MI	48864	**800-292-1036**	517-349-6500	384-5
Pro-Kennex Inc 5122 Avenida Encinas Suite 120	Carlsbad	CA	92008	**800-854-1908**	760-804-8322	701
Pro-Line Boats Inc PO Box 1348	Crystal River	FL	34423	**800-344-1281**	352-795-4111	91
Pro-Line Cap Co 1332 N Main St	Fort Worth	TX	76106	**800-227-2456**	817-246-1978	153-9
Pro-Line International Inc 2121 Panoramic Cir	Dallas	TX	75212	**800-527-5879**	214-631-4247	211
Pro-Pet LLC 1400 McKinley Rd	Saint Marys	OH	45885	**800-245-4125**	419-394-3374	568
Pro Staff Personnel Services 50 S 10th St Suite 500	Minneapolis	MN	55403	**800-829-5369**	612-373-2600	707
Pro Star Sports Inc 1133 Winchester Ave	Kansas City	MO	64126	**800-821-8482**	816-241-9737	263
Pro Tapes & Specialties 100 Northfield Ave	Edison	NJ	08837	**800-345-0234**	732-346-0900	717
ProAssurance Corp 100 Brookwood Pl *NYSE: PRA*	Birmingham	AL	35209	**800-282-6242**	205-877-4400	355-4
ProCard Inc 1819 Denver W Dr Bldg 26 Suite 265	Golden	CO	80401	**800-469-6578**	303-279-2255	176-10
ProCare Vision Centers Inc 1949 Newark-Granville Rd	Granville	OH	43023	**800-837-5569**	740-587-3937	533

Name / Address	City	State	ZIP	Toll-Free	Phone	Class
Proceedings of the IEEE Magazine 445 Hoes Ln	Piscataway	NJ	08855	**800-678-4333**	732-562-5478	449-21
Process Construction Inc 1421 Queen City Ave	Cincinnati	OH	45214	**888-251-2211**	513-251-2211	188-10
Process Efficiency Products Inc 322 Rolling Hills Rd	Mooresville	NC	28117	**800-243-4586**	704-662-3133	793
Process Engineering. Society for the Advancement of Material & 1161 Park View Dr	Covina	CA	91724	**800-562-7360**	626-331-0616	49-19
Process Equipment Co 6555 S SR-202	Tipp City	OH	45371	**800-424-0325**	937-667-4451	446
Process Equipment Inc 2770 Welborn St	Pelham	AL	35124	**800-765-9863**	205-663-5330	19
Process Industries 3860 N River Rd	Schiller Park	IL	60176	**800-860-1631**	847-671-1631	446
Process Servers. National Assn of Professional PO Box 4547	Portland	OR	97208	**800-477-8211**	503-222-4180	49-10
Process Software Corp 959 Concord St	Framingham	MA	01701	**800-722-7770**	508-879-6994	176-12
Processed Plastic Co 1001 Aucutt Rd	Montgomery	IL	60538	**800-323-6165**	630-892-7981	750
ProCom Inc PO Box 27	Lamoni	IA	50140	**800-433-9893**	641-784-8841	722
Procom Technology Inc 58 Discovery	Irvine	CA	92618	**800-800-8600**	949-852-1000	171-8
Procter & Gamble Co Clairol Div 1 Blachley Rd	Stamford	CT	06922	**800-223-5800**	203-357-5000	211
Procter & Gamble Cosmetics 11050 York Rd *Cust Svc	Hunt Valley	MD	21030	**800-638-6204***	800-851-8262	211
Procter & Gamble Pharmaceuticals Canada Inc PO Box 355 Station A	Toronto	ON	M5W1C5	**800-668-0150**	416-730-4711	572
Proctor Financial Insurance Corp 295 Kirts Blvd Suite 100	Troy	MI	48084	**800-521-6800**	248-269-5700	383
Proctor Stanley Co 2016 Midway Dr	Twinsburg	OH	44087	**800-352-0123**	330-425-7814	378
Procyon BioPharma Inc 1650 Transcanada Hwy Suite 200	Dorval	QC	H9P1H7	**877-776-2966**	514-685-9283	86
ProCyte Corp PO Box 808 *Cust Svc	Redmond	WA	98073	**888-966-1010***	425-869-1239	572
Prodata Systems Inc 3855 Monte Villa Pkwy Suite 105	Bothell	WA	98021	**866-487-8346**	425-487-8300	39
ProDrivers Div Career Blazers Inc 222 W Las Colinas Blvd Suite 1250E	Irving	TX	75039	**800-787-6750**	214-296-6700	707
Producers Co-op Assoc 300 E Buffalo PO Box 323	Girard	KS	66743	**800-442-2809**	620-724-8241	438
Producers Inc. United 5909 Cleveland Ave	Columbus	OH	43231	**800-456-3276**	614-890-6666	437
Producers Livestock Marketing Assn 4809 S 114th St	Omaha	NE	68137	**800-257-4046**	402-597-9189	437
Producers Peanut Co Inc 337 Moore Ave	Suffolk	VA	23434	**800-847-5491**	757-539-7496	291-32
Producers & Quantity Photos Inc 6660 Santa Monica Blvd *Cust Svc	Hollywood	CA	90038	**800-843-9259***	323-467-6178	239
Product Design & Development Magazine 301 Gilbraltar Dr	Morris Plains	NJ	07950	**800-547-7377**	973-292-5100	449-21
Product Development Technologies Inc 600 Heathrow Dr	Lincolnshire	IL	60069	**800-747-6600**	847-821-3000	258
Product Information Network 9697 E Mineral Ave	Englewood	CO	80112	**800-525-7002**	303-792-3111	725
Product Liability Law & Strategy Newsletter 345 Park Ave S	New York	NY	10010	**800-888-8300**	212-779-9200	521-7
Product Safety Engineering Society. IEEE IEEE Operations Ctr 445 Hoes Ln	Piscataway	NJ	08854	**800-678-4333**	732-981-0060	49-19
Production Equipment Co 401 Liberty St	Meriden	CT	06450	**800-758-5697**	203-235-5795	462
Production Management Industries LLC 9761 Hwy 90 E	Morgan City	LA	70380	**800-229-3837**	985-631-3837	528
Production Products Co 6176 E Molloy Rd	East Syracuse	NY	13057	**800-800-6652**	315-431-7200	610
Production Tool Supply 8655 E Eight Mile Rd	Warren	MI	48089	**800-366-3600**	586-755-7770	378
Productive Alternatives Inc 1205 N Tower Rd	Fergus Falls	MN	56537	**800-477-7246**	218-736-5668	228
Productive Data Systems Inc 6160 S Syracuse Way Suite 300	Greenwood Village	CO	80111	**800-404-7165**	303-220-7165	707
Productivity Inc 100 Commerce Dr Suite 120	Shelton	CT	06484	**800-966-5423**	203-225-0451	753
Productivity Point International Inc 2950 Gateway Center Blvd	Morrisville	NC	27560	**800-774-2727**	919-379-5611	752
Productivity & Quality Center. American 123 Post Oak Ln 3rd Fl	Houston	TX	77024	**800-776-9676**	713-681-4020	49-12
Producto Machine Co 800 Union Ave *Cust Svc	Bridgeport	CT	06607	**800-243-9898***	203-367-8675	745
Proferas Inc 1136 Moosic St	Scranton	PA	18505	**800-360-7763**	570-342-4181	291-36
Professional Apartment Management Newsletter 149 5th Ave 16th Fl	New York	NY	10010	**800-643-8095**	800-519-3692	521-2
Professional Assessment for Beginning Teachers Educational Testing Service Teaching & Learning Div Rosedale Rd	Princeton	NJ	08541	**800-772-9476**	609-771-7395	243
Professional Assn of Diving Instructors International (PADI) 30151 Tomas St *Sales	Rancho Santa Margarita	CA	92688	**800-729-7234***	949-858-7234	48-22
Professional Aviation Maintenance Assn (PAMA) 717 Princess St	Alexandria	VA	22314	**866-865-7262**	703-683-3171	49-21
Professional Bank Services Inc 6200 Dutchmans Ln Suite 305	Louisville	KY	40205	**800-523-4778**	502-451-6633	193
Professional Carpet Systems Inc 4211 Atlantic Ave	Raleigh	NC	27604	**800-925-5055**	919-875-8871	150
Professional Communication Society. IEEE IEEE Operations Ctr 445 Hoes Ln	Piscataway	NJ	08854	**800-678-4333**	732-981-0060	49-19
Professional Community Management Inc 23726 Birtcher Dr	Lake Forest	CA	92630	**800-369-7260**	949-768-7261	641
Professional Construction Services Inc 8001 Downman Rd	New Orleans	LA	70126	**800-562-4318**	504-241-8001	187-4
Professional Convention Management Assn (PCMA) 2301 S Lake Shore Dr Suite 1001	Chicago	IL	60616	**877-827-7262**	312-423-7262	49-12
Professional Cutlery Direct LLC 242 Branford Rd	North Branford	CT	06471	**800-859-6994**	203-871-1000	451
Professional Dental Technologies 267 E Main St	Batesville	AR	72501	**800-228-5595**	870-698-2300	226
Professional Electric Products Co 33210 Lakeland Blvd	Eastlake	OH	44095	**800-872-7000**	440-946-3790	245
Professional Employees International Union. Office & 265 W 14th St Suite 610	New York	NY	10011	**800-346-7348**	212-675-3210	405
Professional Golfer's Assn 100 Ave of the Champions	Palm Beach Gardens	FL	33418	**800-477-6465**	561-624-8400	48-22
Professional Information Management 600 Meadowland Pkwy Suite 131	Secaucus	NJ	07094	**800-237-5241**	201-866-2625	183
Professional Landcare Network (PLANET) 950 Herndon Pkwy Suite 450	Herndon	VA	20170	**800-395-2522**	703-736-9666	48-2
Professional Liability Underwriting Society 5353 Wayzata Blvd Suite 600	Minneapolis	MN	55416	**800-845-0778**	952-746-2580	49-9
Professional Photographers of America Inc (PPA) 229 Peachtree St NE Suite 2200	Atlanta	GA	30303	**800-786-6277**	404-522-8600	48-4
Professional Placement Resources 333 1st St N Suite 200	Jacksonville Beach	FL	32250	**888-909-5038**		707
Professional Practice Assn. American 350 Fairway Dr Suite 200	Deerfield Beach	FL	33441	**800-221-2168**	954-571-1877	49-8
Professional Recognition. Council for 2460 16th St NW	Washington	DC	20009	**800-424-4310**	202-265-9090	49-5
Professional Records & Information Services Management International 605 Benson Rd Suite B	Garner	NC	27529	**800-336-9793**	919-771-0657	49-12
Professional Research Services Inc 4901 W 77th St Suite 135	Minneapolis	MN	55435	**800-886-4777**	952-941-9040	621
Professional Service Industries Inc 1901 S Meyers Rd Suite 400	Oakbrook Terrace	IL	60181	**800-426-2897**	630-691-1490	258
Professional Service Industries Inc Pittsburgh Testing Lab Div 850 Poplar St	Pittsburgh	PA	15220	**866-842-9637**	412-922-4000	728
Professional Shorthand Reporters Inc 601 Poydras St Suite 1615	New Orleans	LA	70130	**800-536-5255**	504-529-5255	436
Professional Speakers Network 10436 Oak Ridge Dr	Zionsville	IN	46077	**800-222-1556**	317-873-9840	699
Professional Staff Management Inc 224 S 5th St Suite C	Richmond	IN	47374	**800-967-5515**	765-935-1515	619
Professional Tennis Registry PO Box 4739	Hilton Head Island	SC	29938	**800-421-6289**	843-785-7244	48-22
Professional Travel Inc 25000 Country Club Blvd Suite 170	North Olmsted	OH	44070	**800-247-0060**	440-734-8800	760
Proflowers.com 5005 Wateridge Vista Dr 2nd Fl	San Diego	CA	92121	**800-776-3569**	858-454-9850	287
ProForma 8800 E Pleasant Valley Rd	Independence	OH	44131	**800-825-1525**	216-520-8400	615
Proformance Insurance Co 4 Paragon Way	Freehold	NJ	07728	**800-298-5742**	732-665-1100	384-4
Progeny Marketing Innovations 801 Crescent Ctr Dr Suite 200	Franklin	TN	37067	**800-251-2148**		193
Progistix-Solutions Inc 20 Norelco Dr	North York	ON	M9L1S2	**800-277-6447**	416-401-7000	440
Program Directors in Internal Medicine. Association of 2501 M St NW Suite 550	Washington	DC	20037	**800-622-4558**	202-887-9450	49-8
Program Planning Professionals 3923 Ranchero Dr	Ann Arbor	MI	48108	**888-364-1182**	734-741-7770	193
Programmer's Paradise Inc 1157 Shrewsbury Ave Suite C *NASDAQ: PROG*	Shrewsbury	NJ	07702	**800-445-7899**	732-389-8950	172
Progress Bank 4 Sentry Pkwy Suite 200 *Cust Svc	Blue Bell	PA	19422	**800-945-9905***	610-825-8800	71
Progress Casting Group Inc 2600 Niagara Ln N	Plymouth	MN	55447	**800-866-3025**	763-557-1000	303
Progress Energy Florida Inc 100 Central Ave *Cust Svc	Saint Petersburg	FL	33733	**800-700-8744***	727-820-5151	774
Progress Energy Inc 411 Fayetteville St *NYSE: PGN*	Raleigh	NC	27602	**800-452-2777**	919-546-6111	355-5
Progress Linen Inc LLC 711 E Vermont St Suite 200	Indianapolis	IN	46202	**888-297-8049**	317-263-5260	434
Progress Paint Co Inc 201 E Market St	Louisville	KY	40202	**800-626-6407**	502-584-0151	540
Progress Printing Co 2677 Waterlick Rd	Lynchburg	VA	24502	**800-572-7804**	434-239-9213	615
Progress Rail Services 1600 Progress Dr	Albertville	AL	35950	**800-476-8769**	256-593-1260	674
Progress Software Corp 14 Oak Pk *NASDAQ: PRGS*	Bedford	MA	01730	**800-477-6473**	781-280-4000	176-1
Progressive Casualty Insurance Co 6300 Wilson Mills Rd Campus E	Mayfield Village	OH	44143	**800-321-9843**	440-461-5000	384-4
Progressive Corp 6300 Wilson Mills Rd *NYSE: PGR*	Mayfield Village	OH	44143	**800-321-9843**	440-461-5000	355-4
Progressive Crane Inc 13721 Bennington Ave	Cleveland	OH	44135	**800-832-7263**	216-251-6126	462
Progressive Employer Services 2469 Enterprise Rd Suite B	Clearwater	FL	33763	**800-741-7848**	727-712-9121	619
Progressive Farmer Magazine 2100 Lakeshore Dr	Birmingham	AL	35209	**800-366-4712**	205-445-6000	449-1

Alphabetical Section

Company / Address	City	State	ZIP	Toll-Free	Phone	Class
Progressive Information Technologies 315 Busser Rd	Emigsville	PA	17318	**800-673-2500**	717-764-5908	770
Progressive National Baptist Convention Inc (PNBC) 601 50th St NE	Washington	DC	20019	**800-876-7622**	202-396-0558	48-20
Progressive Plastics Inc 14801 Emery Ave	Cleveland	OH	44135	**800-252-0053**	216-252-5595	99
Progressive Policy Institute (PPI) 600 Pennsylvania Ave SE Suite 400	Washington	DC	20003	**800-546-0027**	202-547-0001	654
Progresso Quality Foods Co 500 W Elmer Rd	Vineland	NJ	08360	**800-200-9377**	856-691-1565	291-36
Project HOPE 255 Carter Hall Ln	Millwood	VA	22646	**800-544-4673**	540-837-2100	48-5
Project Management Institute (PMI) 4 Campus Blvd	Newtown Square	PA	19073	**866-276-4764**	610-356-4600	49-12
Project Safe Neighborhoods Office of Justice Programs 810 7th St NW	Washington	DC	20531	**800-458-0786**		196
Project Vote 6805 Oak Creek Dr	Columbus	OH	43229	**800-546-8683**	614-523-2560	48-7
Project Vote Smart 1 Common Ground	Philipsburg	MT	59858	**888-868-3762**	406-859-8683	48-7
Projections Unlimited Inc 14831 Myford Rd	Tustin	CA	92780	**800-551-4405**	714-544-2700	245
Projector Solution 181 Avenida La Pata Suite 100	San Clemente	CA	92673	**800-701-9869**	949-940-2400	119
Prolab Nutrition 11 Britton Dr	Bloomfield	CT	06002	**800-776-5221**	860-769-5550	786
Prolab Visual Imaging Services Inc 123 NW 36th St	Seattle	WA	98107	**800-426-6770**	206-547-5447	577
Prolifics 116 John St 20th Fl	New York	NY	10038	**800-458-3313**	212-267-7722	176-2
ProLiteracy Worldwide 1320 Jamesville Ave	Syracuse	NY	13210	**800-448-8878**	315-422-9121	48-5
ProLogis 14100 E 35th Pl *NYSE: PLD*	Aurora	CO	80011	**800-566-2706**	303-375-9292	641
Prolon Inc PO Box 568	Port Gibson	MS	39150	**800-628-7749**	601-437-4211	596
Promedia Computer Supplies Ltd Co 12806 Schabarum Ave Unit C-D	Irwindale	CA	91706	**800-583-5833**	626-960-5778	523
Promega Corp 2800 Woods Hollow Rd	Madison	WI	53711	**800-356-9526**	608-274-4330	229
Prometheus Laboratories Inc 5739 Pacific Center Blvd	San Diego	CA	92121	**888-423-5227**	858-824-0895	572
Promise Keepers 4045 Pecos St PO Box 11798	Denver	CO	80211	**800-888-7595**	303-964-7600	48-20
Promise Technology Inc 1745 McCandless Dr *Sales	Milpitas	CA	95035	**800-888-0245***	408-228-6300	613
Promissor Inc 1007 Church St Suite 314	Evanston	IL	60201	**800-255-1312**	847-866-2001	243
Promissor Inc 3 Bala Plaza W Suite 300	Bala Cynwyd	PA	19004	**888-204-6231**	610-617-5093	243
Promotional Products Assn International (PPAI) 3125 Skyway Cir N	Irving	TX	75038	**888-492-6891**	972-252-0404	49-18
Promotions Unlimited Corp DBA Ben Franklin Stores 7601 Durand Ave	Racine	WI	53408	**800-992-9307**	262-681-7000	305
ProMutual Group 101 Arch St 4th Fl	Boston	MA	02110	**800-225-6168**	617-330-1755	384-5
Properties. National Assn of Industrial & Office 2201 Cooperative Way 3rd Fl	Herndon	VA	20171	**800-666-6780**	703-904-7100	49-17
Property Damage Appraisers Inc PO Box 9230	Fort Worth	TX	76147	**800-749-7324**	817-731-5555	383
Property Managers. National Assn of Residential 8317 Cross Pk Dr Suite 150	Austin	TX	78754	**800-782-3452**	512-381-6091	49-17
Property Owners Exchange Inc 6630 Baltimore National Pike Suite 208	Baltimore	MD	21228	**800-869-3200**	410-719-0100	621
Property-Owners Insurance Co PO Box 30660	Lansing	MI	48909	**800-288-8740**	517-323-1200	384-2
Propet USA Inc 25612 74th Ave S	Kent	WA	98032	**800-877-6738**	253-854-7600	296
Prophet Financial Systems Inc 115 Everett Ave	Palo Alto	CA	94301	**800-772-8040**	650-322-4183	396
Propper Mfg Co Inc 36-04 Skillman Ave *Cust Svc	Long Island City	NY	11101	**800-832-4300***	718-392-6650	468
ProQuest Information & Learning Co 300 N Zeeb Rd	Ann Arbor	MI	48106	**800-521-0600**	734-761-4700	380
Proscape Technologies Inc 1155 Business Ctr Dr	Horsham	PA	19044	**800-459-9300**	215-441-0300	176-11
ProSight Inc 9600 SW Barnes Rd Suite 300	POrtland	OR	97255	**877-531-9121**	503-889-4800	176-10
ProsoftTraining 410 N 44th St Suite 600 *NASDAQ: POSO*	Phoenix	AZ	85008	**888-776-7638**	602-794-4199	752
Prospect Mold Inc 1100 Main St	Cuyahoga Falls	OH	44221	**800-683-3312**	330-929-3311	745
Prospector Hotel 375 Whittier St	Juneau	AK	99801	**800-331-2711**	907-586-3737	373
Prospector Square Hotel & Conference Center 2200 Sidewinder Dr	Park City	UT	84060	**800-453-3812**	435-649-7100	373
Prostate Society. American 7188 Ridge Rd PO Box 870	Hanover	MD	21076	**800-308-1106**	410-859-3735	48-17
ProSteel 1400 S State St	Provo	UT	84606	**877-501-7233**	801-373-2385	665
Prosthodontic Society. American 426 Hudson St	Hackensack	NJ	07601	**877-499-3500**	201-440-7699	49-8
Protech Armored Products 13386 International Pkwy	Jacksonville	FL	32218	**800-428-0588**	904-741-5400	566
Protection One Inc 1035 N 3rd St Suite 101	Lawrence	KS	66044	**800-438-4357**	785-856-5500	683
Protection Services Inc 635 Lucknow Rd	Harrisburg	PA	17110	**866-489-1234**	717-236-9307	692
Protective Insurance Co 1099 N Meridian St Suite 700	Indianapolis	IN	46204	**800-231-6024**	317-636-9800	384-5
Protective Life & Annuity Insurance Co 2801 Hwy 280 S	Birmingham	AL	35223	**800-866-3555**	205-879-9230	384-2
Protective Life Corp PO Box 2606 *NYSE: PL*	Birmingham	AL	35202	**800-333-3418**	205-879-9230	355-4
Protective Life Insurance Co 2801 Hwy 280 S	Birmingham	AL	35223	**800-866-3555**	205-879-9230	384-2
Protector Corp 337 S Arthur Ave	Louisville	CO	80027	**800-438-1012**	303-926-5400	523
Protectoseal Co 225 W Foster Ave	Bensenville	IL	60106	**800-323-2268**	630-595-0800	124
Protegrity Services Inc PO Box 914700	Longwood	FL	32791	**800-883-4000**	407-788-1717	383
Protel Inc 4150 Kidron Rd	Lakeland	FL	33811	**800-925-8882**	863-644-5558	720
Protexall Inc 77 S Henderson St PO Box 1287	Galesburg	IL	61402	**800-334-8939**	309-342-3106	153-19
Protide Pharmaceuticals Inc 1311 Helmo Ave	Saint Paul	MN	55128	**800-552-3569**	651-730-1500	229
Protocol Marketing Group 1751 Lake Cook Rd Suite 400	Deerfield	IL	60015	**800-867-7892**	847-236-3400	722
ProtoNet PO Box 8781	Calabasas	CA	91372	**800-551-0636**	818-876-0636	176-7
ProtoSource Network 2511 W Shaw Ave Suite 102	Fresno	CA	93711	**866-490-8600**	559-486-8638	390
Protravel International Inc 515 Madison Ave 10th Fl	New York	NY	10022	**800-227-1059**	212-755-4550	760
Provantage Corp 7249 Whipple Ave NW	North Canton	OH	44720	**800-336-1166**	330-494-3781	172
Proven Direct W165 N5761 Ridgewood Dr	Menomonee Falls	WI	53051	**866-890-6245**	262-703-0760	5
Provena Covenant Medical Center 1400 W Park St	Urbana	IL	61801	**800-245-6697**	217-337-2000	366-2
Provia Software Inc 5460 Corporate Grove Blvd SE	Grand Rapids	MI	49512	**877-776-8421**	616-285-3311	176-1
Provide Commerce Inc 5005 Wateridge Vista Dr Suite 200 *NASDAQ: PRVD* ■ *Cust Svc	San Diego	CA	92121	**888-373-7437***	858-638-4900	658
Providence Behavioral Health Hospital 1233 Main St	Holyoke	MA	01040	**800-274-7724**	413-539-2400	712
Providence Biltmore Hotel Kennedy Plaza 11 Dorrance St	Providence	RI	02903	**800-294-7709**	401-421-0700	373
Providence Casket Co 1 Industrial Cir	Lincoln	RI	02865	**800-848-2999**	401-726-1700	134
Providence Chain 225 Carolina Ave	Providence	RI	02905	**800-783-1499**	401-781-1330	399
Providence College 549 River Ave	Providence	RI	02918	**800-721-6444**	401-865-1000	163
Providence Hospice & Home Care of Snohomish County 2731 Wetmore Ave Suite 500	Everett	WA	98201	**800-825-0045**	425-261-4800	365
Providence Hospital 914 S Scheuber Rd	Centralia	WA	98531	**877-736-2803**	360-736-2803	366-2
Providence Journal 75 Fountain St	Providence	RI	02902	**888-697-7656**	401-277-7000	522-2
Providence Medford Medical Center 1111 Crater Lake Ave	Medford	OR	97504	**877-541-0588**	541-773-6611	366-2
Providence Mutual Fire Insurance Co 340 East Ave	Warwick	RI	02886	**877-763-1800**	401-827-1800	384-4
Providence Saint Peter Hospital 413 Lilly Rd NE	Olympia	WA	98506	**888-492-9480**	360-491-9480	366-2
Providence Service Corp 620 N Craycroft Rd *NASDAQ: PRSC*	Tucson	AZ	85711	**800-489-0064**	520-748-7108	454
Providence Sound Home Care & Hospice PO Box 5008	Olympia	WA	98509	**800-869-7062**	360-459-8311	365
Providence Warwick Convention & Visitors Bureau 1 W Exchange St	Providence	RI	02903	**800-233-1636**	401-274-1636	205
Providence Washington Insurance Co 88 Boyd Ave	East Providence	RI	02914	**800-752-4549**	401-453-7000	384-4
Providence & Worcester Railroad Co 75 Hammond St *AMEX: PWX*	Worcester	MA	01610	**800-447-2003**	508-755-4000	634
Provident American Insurance Co Inc 10501 N Central Expy Suite 200	Dallas	TX	75231	**800-933-9456**	214-696-9091	384-2
Provident Bank 830 Bergen Ave	Jersey City	NJ	07306	**800-448-7768**	201-333-1000	71
Provident Central Credit Union 303 Twin Dolphin Dr	Redwood Shores	CA	94065	**800-632-4600**	650-508-0300	216
Provident Financial Holdings Inc 3756 Central Ave *NASDAQ: PROV*	Riverside	CA	92506	**800-442-5201**	951-686-6060	355-2
Provident-Integrity Distribution 741 Cool Springs Blvd *Sales	Franklin	TN	37067	**800-333-9000***	615-261-6500	512
Provident Savings Bank FSB 3756 Central Ave	Riverside	CA	92506	**800-686-3756**	951-686-6060	71
Provident Travel Corp 11309 Montgomery Rd	Cincinnati	OH	45249	**800-543-2120**	513-247-1100	760
Provider Networks of America Inc PO Box 101387	Fort Worth	TX	76185	**800-462-7554**		384-3
Providian Financial Corp 201 Mission St *NYSE: PVN*	San Francisco	CA	94105	**800-525-7557**	415-543-0404	215
Providian National Bank 295 Main St *Cust Svc	Tilton	NH	03276	**800-537-4332***	603-286-4346	71
Proview Technology 7372 Doig Dr	Garden Grove	CA	92841	**800-776-8439**	714-799-3899	171-4
Provo International Inc 1 Bluehill Plaza PO Box 1548	Pearl River	NY	10965	**888-559-5550**	845-623-8553	390
Provue Development Corp 18411 Gothard St Unit A	Huntington Beach	CA	92648	**800-966-7878**	714-841-7779	176-1
Proxim Corp 510 DeGuigne Dr *NASDAQ: PROX*	Sunnyvale	CA	94085	**800-229-1630**	408-731-2700	720
Proximity Inc 99 Swift St Suite 200	South Burlington	VT	05403	**800-433-2900**	802-264-2900	721
ProxyMed Inc 2555 Davie Rd Suite 110 *NASDAQ: PILL*	Fort Lauderdale	FL	33317	**800-997-7699**	954-473-1001	39
Prozyme Inc 1933 Davis St Suite 207	San Leandro	CA	94577	**800-457-9444**	510-638-6900	229
PRSA (Public Relations Society of America) 33 Maiden Ln 11th Fl	New York	NY	10038	**800-937-7772**	212-995-2230	49-18
Prudent Speculator Newsletter 32392 Coast Hwy Suite 260	Laguna Beach	CA	92651	**800-258-7786**	949-497-7657	521-9
Prudential Distributors Inc PO Box 3088	Spokane	WA	99220	**800-767-5567**	509-535-2401	38
Prudential Financial Inc 751 Broad St *NYSE: PRU*	Newark	NJ	07102	**800-843-7625**	973-802-6000	393
Prudential Northwest Real Estate 2497 Bethel Rd SE	Port Orchard	WA	98366	**800-463-7768**	360-876-5522	638

Name / Address	City	State	ZIP	Toll-Free	Phone	Class
Prudential Real Estate Affiliates Inc 3333 Michelson Dr Suite 1000	Irvine	CA	92612	**800-999-1120**	949-794-7900	638
Prudential Steel Ltd 140 4th Ave SW Suite 1800	Calgary	AB	T2P3N3	**800-661-1050**	403-267-0300	709
Prym-Dritz Corp 950 Brisack Rd	Spartanburg	SC	29303	**800-255-7796***	864-576-5050	583
*Cust Svc						
Pryor Fred Seminars 9757 Metcalf Ave	Overland Park	KS	66212	**800-780-8476**	913-967-8599	753
PS Energy Group Inc 2987 Clairmont Rd Suite 450	Atlanta	GA	30329	**800-334-7548**	404-321-5711	774
PS Greetings Inc 5730 N Tripp Ave	Chicago	IL	60646	**800-621-8823***	773-267-6069	130
*Sales						
PSA Airlines Inc DBA US Airways Express 3400 Terminal Dr	Vandalia	OH	45377	**800-235-0986**	937-454-1116	26
PSB Bancorp Inc 1835 Market St 11 Penn Ctr Suite 2601	Philadelphia	PA	19103	**866-437-2265**	215-979-7900	355-2
NASDAQ: PSBI						
PSC Inc 959 Terry St	Eugene	OR	97402	**800-695-5700**	541-683-5700	171-7
PSE (Pi Sigma Epsilon) 3747 Howell Ave	Milwaukee	WI	53207	**800-761-9350**	414-328-1952	48-16
PSEG Power LLC 80 Park Plaza	Newark	NJ	07101	**800-436-7734**	973-430-7000	774
PSF Industries Inc 65 S Horton St	Seattle	WA	98134	**800-426-1204**	206-622-1252	188-10
PSI Inc 10630 Marina Dr	Olive Branch	MS	38654	**866-638-7926**	662-895-8777	597
Psi Upsilon Fraternity 3003 E 96th St	Indianapolis	IN	46240	**800-394-1833**	317-571-1833	48-16
PSNC Energy 800 Gaston Rd	Gastonia	NC	28056	**800-222-1034**	704-864-6731	774
Psoriasis Foundation. National 6600 SW 92nd Ave Suite 300	Portland	OR	97223	**800-723-9166**	503-244-7404	48-17
Psychemedics Corp 1280 Massachusetts Ave	Cambridge	MA	02138	**800-628-8073**	617-868-7455	407
AMEX: PMD						
Psychiatric Assn. American 1000 Wilson Blvd Suite 1825	Arlington	VA	22209	**888-357-7924**	703-907-7300	49-15
Psychiatric Institute of Washington 4228 Wisconsin Ave NW	Washington	DC	20016	**800-369-2273**	202-885-5600	366-3
Psychiatry. American Academy of Child & Adolescent 3615 Wisconsin Ave NW	Washington	DC	20016	**800-333-7636**	202-966-7300	49-15
Psychiatry & the Law. American Academy of 1 Regency Dr PO Box 30	Bloomfield	CT	06002	**800-331-1389**	860-242-5450	49-15
Psychological Assn. American 750 1st St NE	Washington	DC	20002	**800-374-2721**	202-336-5500	49-15
Psychological Corp 19500 Bulverdy Rd	San Antonio	TX	78259	**800-228-0752**	210-339-5000	623-10
Psychology Boards. Association of State & Provincial 7177 Halcyon Summit Dr	Montgomery	AL	36117	**800-448-4069**	334-832-4580	49-7
Psychology Today Magazine 115 E 23 St 9th Fl	New York	NY	10010	**800-234-8361***	212-260-7210	449-11
*Sales						
Psychophysiology & Biofeedback. Association for Applied 10200 W 44th Ave Suite 304	Wheat Ridge	CO	80033	**800-477-8892**	303-422-8436	49-8
Psychotherapy Assn. American Group 25 E 21st St 6th Fl	New York	NY	10010	**877-668-2472**	212-477-2677	49-15
Psychotherapy Networker 7705 13th St NW	Washington	DC	20012	**888-883-3782**	202-829-2452	449-16
PT-1 Long Distance Inc 30-50 Whitestone Expwy	Flushing	NY	11354	**888-660-5377***	718-939-9000	721
*Cust Svc						
PT Freeport Indonesia Co 1615 Poydras St	New Orleans	LA	70112	**800-535-7094**	504-582-4000	492
PTC Alliance Copperleaf Corporate Ctr 6051 Wallace Rd Ext Sutie 200	Wexford	PA	15090	**888-299-8823**	412-299-7900	481
PTI Technologies Inc 501 Del Norte Blvd	Oxnard	CA	93030	**800-331-2701**	805-604-3700	379
PTMW Inc 3501 NW US Hwy 24	Topeka	KS	66618	**800-842-1546**	785-232-7792	759
PTR-Precision Technologies Inc 120 Post Rd	Enfield	CT	06082	**888-478-7832**	860-741-2281	416
PTS Corp 5233 Hwy 37 S	Bloomington	IN	47401	**800-844-3291**	812-824-9331	633
PTTC (Petroleum Technology Transfer Council) 16010 Barkers Point Ln Suite 220	Houston	TX	77079	**888-843-7882**	281-921-1720	48-12
Public Administration. National Academy of 1100 New York Ave NW Suite 1090 E	Washington	DC	20005	**800-883-3190**	202-347-3190	49-7
Public Assistance & Welfare Trends Newsletter PO Box 7376	Alexandria	VA	22307	**800-876-2545**	703-768-9600	521-8
Public Belt Railroad Commission 4822 Tchoupitulas St	New Orleans	LA	70115	**800-524-3421***	504-896-7410	637
*Cust Svc						
Public Broadcasting. Corporation for 401 9th St NW	Washington	DC	20004	**800-272-2190**	202-879-9600	300
Public Broadcasting Council of Central New York PO Box 2400	Syracuse	NY	13220	**800-451-9269**	315-453-2424	620
Public Broadcasting Northwest Pennsylvania 8425 Peach St	Erie	PA	16509	**800-727-8854**	814-864-3001	620
Public Gas Assn. American 201 Massachusetts Ave NE Suite C-4	Washington	DC	20002	**800-927-4204**	202-464-2742	48-12
Public Information on the Environment. American 316 Oak St PO Box 676	Northfield	MN	55057	**800-320-2743**	507-645-5613	48-13
Public Land. Trust for 116 New Montgomery St 4th Fl	San Francisco	CA	94105	**800-729-6428**	415-495-4014	48-13
Public Library Assn (PLA) 50 E Huron St	Chicago	IL	60611	**800-545-2433**	312-280-5752	49-11
Public Management Assn for Human Resources. International 1617 Duke St	Alexandria	VA	22314	**800-220-4762**	703-549-7100	49-12
Public Museum of Grand Rapids 272 Pearl St NW Van Andel Museum Ctr	Grand Rapids	MI	49504	**800-459-4253**	616-456-3977	509
Public Policy Institute. AARP 601 'E' St NW	Washington	DC	20049	**888-687-2277**	202-434-2277	654
Public Policy Research. American Enterprise Institute for 1150 17th St NW Suite 1100	Washington	DC	20036	**800-862-5801**	202-862-5800	654
Public Relations Society of America (PRSA) 33 Maiden Ln 11th Fl	New York	NY	10038	**800-937-7772**	212-995-2230	49-18
Public-Safety Communications Officials International Inc. Association of 351 N Williamson Blvd	Daytona Beach	FL	32114	**888-272-6911**	386-322-2500	49-7
Public Safety & Justice Policies Newsletter PO Box 7376	Alexandria	VA	22307	**800-876-2545**	703-768-9600	521-7
Public Safety. Northwestern University Center for 600 Foster	Evanston	IL	60204	**800-323-4011**	847-491-5476	49-7
Public Service Electric & Gas Co 80 Park Plaza	Newark	NJ	07102	**800-436-7734***	973-430-7000	774
*Cust Svc						
Public Service of New Hampshire 780 N Commercial St	Manchester	NH	03105	**800-662-7764**	603-669-4000	774
Public Storage Inc 701 Western Ave	Glendale	CA	91201	**800-567-0759***	818-244-8080	790-3
NYSE: PSA ■ *Cust Svc						
Public Supply Co Inc 1236 NW 4th St	Oklahoma City	OK	73106	**800-259-6355**	405-272-9621	232
Public Technology Inc 1301 Pennsylvania Ave NW Suite 800	Washington	DC	20004	**800-852-4934**	202-626-2400	49-7
Public Welfare Foundation Inc 1200 U St NW	Washington	DC	20009	**800-275-7934**	202-965-1800	300
Publications & Communications Inc 11675 Jollyville Rd Suite 150	Austin	TX	78759	**800-678-9724**	512-250-9023	623-9
Publications International Ltd 7373 N Cicero Ave	Lincolnwood	IL	60712	**800-745-9299**	847-676-3470	623-2
Publick House Historic Resort 295 Main St Rt 131	Sturbridge	MA	01566	**800-782-5425**	508-347-3313	373
Publishers of America. Magazine 810 7th Ave 24th Fl	New York	NY	10019	**888-567-3228**	212-872-3700	49-16
Publishers. American Society of Composers Authors & 1 Lincoln Plaza	New York	NY	10023	**800-952-7227**	212-621-6000	48-4
Publishers Assn. Newsletter & Electronic 1501 Wilson Blvd Suite 509	Arlington	VA	22209	**800-356-9302**	703-527-2333	49-14
Publishers. Association of Directory 116 Cass St	Traverse City	MI	49684	**800-267-9002**		49-16
Publishers. Association of Test 1201 Pennsylvania Ave Suite 300	Washington	DC	20004	**866-240-7909**		49-5
Publishers Clearing House 101 Channel Dr	Port Washington	NY	11050	**800-645-9242**	516-883-5432	451
Publishers Group Inc 1400 65th St Suite 250	Emeryville	CA	94608	**800-788-3123**	510-595-3664	97
Publishers Group West 1400 65th St Suite250	Emeryville	CA	94608	**800-788-3123**	510-595-3664	97
Publishers Press Inc 100 Frank E Simon Ave	Shepherdsville	KY	40165	**800-627-5801**	502-955-6526	614
Publishers Printing Co 100 Frank E Simon Ave	Shepherdsville	KY	40165	**800-627-5801**	502-543-2251	615
Publishers Weekly Magazine 360 Park Ave S	New York	NY	10010	**800-278-2991***	646-746-6758	449-21
*Cust Svc						
Publishing Group of America Inc 341 Cool Springs Blvd Suite 400	Franklin	TN	37067	**800-720-6323**	615-468-6000	623-9
Publix Super Markets Inc 3300 Airport Rd	Lakeland	FL	33811	**800-342-1227***	863-688-1188	339
*PR						
Pucel Enterprises Inc 1440 E 36th St	Cleveland	OH	44114	**800-336-4986**	216-881-4604	462
Puck Implement Co 402 6th St	Manning	IA	51455	**800-458-4431**	712-653-2574	270
Pueblo Chieftain 825 W 6th St PO Box 440	Pueblo	CO	81003	**800-279-6397**	719-544-3520	522-2
Pueblo Community College 900 W Orman Ave	Pueblo	CO	81004	**888-642-6017**	719-549-3200	160
Pueblo Grande Museum & Archaeological Park 4619 E Washington St	Phoenix	AZ	85034	**877-706-4408**	602-495-0901	509
Puerto Rico Convention Bureau 1730 Rhode Island Ave NW Suite 601	Washington	DC	20036	**800-875-4765**	202-457-9262	205
Puerto Rico Telephone Co PO Box 360998	San Juan	PR	00936	**800-981-2050**	787-782-8282	721
Puerto Rico Tourism Co 3575 W Cahuenga Blvd Suite 405	Los Angeles	CA	90068	**800-874-1230**	323-874-5991	764
Puerto Rico Tourism Co 901 Ponce de Leon Blvd Suite 101	Coral Gables	FL	33134	**800-815-7391**	305-445-9112	764
Puerto Rico Tourism Co 666 5th Ave 15th Fl	New York	NY	10103	**800-223-6530**	212-586-6262	764
Puffin Inn 4400 Spenard Rd	Anchorage	AK	99517	**800-478-3346**	907-243-4044	373
Puget Sound Blood Center 921 Terry Ave	Seattle	WA	98104	**800-366-2831**	206-292-6500	90
Puget Sound Christian College 1618 Hewitt Ave	Everett	WA	98201	**888-775-8699**	425-257-3090	163
Puget Sound Energy Inc 10608 NE 4th St	Bellevue	WA	98009	**888-225-5773**	425-454-6363	774
Puget Sound Rope Corp 1012 2nd St	Anacortes	WA	98221	**800-366-8480**	360-293-8488	207
Puget Sound Truck Lines Inc 3720 Airport Way S	Seattle	WA	98134	**800-638-2254**	206-623-1600	769
Pulaski Financial Corp 12300 Olive Blvd	Saint Louis	MO	63141	**800-261-0113**	314-878-2210	355-2
NASDAQ: PULB						
Pulitzer Inc 900 N Tucker Blvd	Saint Louis	MO	63101	**800-365-0820**	314-340-8000	623-8
NYSE: PTZ						
Pullman Chamber of Commerce 415 N Grand Ave	Pullman	WA	99163	**800-365-6948**	509-334-3565	137
Pullman/Holt Corp 10702 N 46th St	Tampa	FL	33617	**800-237-7582**	813-971-2223	379
Pulp Couture 230 W Huron St Suite 2E	Chicago	IL	60610	**800-404-6968**	312-420-2139	130

Name / Address	City	State	Zip	Toll-Free	Phone	Class
Pulp & Paper Industry. Technical Assn of the 15 Technology Pkwy S *Sales	Norcross	GA	30092	**800-332-8686***	770-446-1400	49-13
Pulse Communications Inc 2900 Towerview Rd *Cust Svc	Herndon	VA	20171	**800-381-1997***	703-471-2900	720
Pulte Home Corp 100 Bloomfield Hills Pkwy Suite 300	Bloomfield Hills	MI	48304	**800-777-8583**	248-644-7300	639
Pulte Homes Inc 100 Bloomfield Hills Pkwy Suite 300 *NYSE: PHM*	Bloomfield Hills	MI	48304	**800-777-8583**	248-647-2750	355-3
Pulte Mortgage LLC 7475 S Joliet St	Englewood	CO	80112	**800-488-0053**	303-740-8800	498
Puma North America Inc 5 Lyberty Way	Westford	MA	01886	**800-662-7862**	978-698-1000	296
Pummill Business Forms Inc 903 Chicago Dr	Grand Rapids	MI	49509	**888-786-6455**	616-475-9000	111
Pumpkin Hollow Farm 1184 Rt 11	Craryville	NY	12521	**877-325-3583**	518-325-3583	660
Punch Networks Corp 100 4th Ave N 6th Fl	Seattle	WA	98101	**877-467-8624**	206-404-6000	39
PunchStock 8517 Excelsior Dr Suite 200	Madison	WI	53717	**800-390-0461**	608-828-2700	582
PUR Water Purification Products 9300 N 75th Ave	Minneapolis	MN	55428	**800-787-5463**	763-315-5500	793
Purafil Inc 2654 Weaver Way	Doraville	GA	30340	**800-222-6367**	770-662-8545	19
Puratos Corp 1941 Old Cuthbert Rd	Cherry Hill	NJ	08034	**800-654-0036**	856-428-4300	291-16
Purcell Construction Co 1550 Starkey Rd	Largo	FL	33771	**888-568-1555**		186
Purcell Tire & Rubber Co 301 N Hall St	Potosi	MO	63664	**800-326-8410**	573-438-2133	739
Purchasing Magazine 275 Washington St *Cust Svc	Newton	MA	02458	**800-446-6551***	617-964-3030	449-5
Purchasing. National Institute of Governmental 151 Spring St Suite 300	Herndon	VA	20170	**800-367-6447**	703-736-8900	49-7
Purdue Pharma LP 1 Stamford Forum *Cust Svc	Stamford	CT	06901	**800-877-5666***	203-588-8000	572
Purdue University Press 1407 Campus Courts Bldg E *Orders	West Lafayette	IN	47907	**800-247-6553***	765-494-2038	623-5
Pure Fishing America 1900 18th St	Spirit Lake	IA	51360	**877-777-3850**	712-336-1520	701
Pure-Flo Solutions Group 110-B W Cochran St	Simi Valley	CA	93065	**800-926-8884**	805-520-7200	584
Pure-Flo Water Co 7737 Mission Gorge Rd *Cust Svc	Santee	CA	92071	**800-787-3356***	619-448-5120	792
Pure Resources 500 W Illinois Ave	Midland	TX	79701	**800-725-6612**	432-498-8600	525
Pure Water Inc 3725 Touzalin Ave *Cust Svc	Lincoln	NE	68507	**800-875-5915***	402-467-9300	793
PureEdge Solutions 4396 W Saanich Rd	Victoria	BC	V8Z3E9	**888-517-2675**	250-708-8000	176-7
PureSafety 1321 Murfreesboro Rd Suite 200	Nashville	TN	37217	**888-202-3016**	615-367-4404	39
PureWorks Inc DBA PureSafety 1321 Murfreesboro Rd Suite 200	Nashville	TN	37217	**888-202-3016**	615-367-4404	39
Puritan of Cape Cod 408 Main St	Hyannis	MA	02601	**800-924-0606**	508-775-2400	155-2
PuriTec 7251 W Lake Mead Blvd Suite 300	Las Vegas	NV	89128	**888-491-4100**	702-562-8802	18
Purity Dairies Inc 360 Murfreesboro Rd	Nashville	TN	37210	**800-947-6455**	615-244-1900	291-27
Purity Products Inc 1800 NW 70th Ave	Miami	FL	33126	**800-654-0235**	305-592-3600	291-41
Purity Wholesale Grocers Inc 5400 Broken Sound Blvd NW Suite 100	Boca Raton	FL	33487	**800-323-6838**	561-994-9360	292-8
Purolator Courier Ltd 5995 Avebury Rd	Mississauga	ON	L5R3T8	**888-744-7123**	905-712-1084	536
Purolator Products Air Filtration Co 880 Facet Rd	Henderson	NC	27536	**800-334-6659**	252-492-1141	19
Pursley Inc 9115 58th Dr E Suite A	Bradenton	FL	34202	**800-683-7584**	941-753-7851	318
Pursuit Boats 3901 St Lucie Blvd	Fort Pierce	FL	34946	**800-947-8778**	772-465-6006	91
Putman Media Inc 555 W Pierce Rd Suite 301	Itasca	IL	60143	**800-984-7644**	630-467-1300	623-9
Putnam County Convention & Visitors Bureau 12 W Washington St	Greencastle	IN	46135	**800-829-4639**	765-653-8743	205
Putnam County Library System 601 College Rd	Palatka	FL	32177	**800-231-4045**	386-329-0126	426
Putnam Family of Funds PO Box 41203	Providence	RI	02940	**800-225-1581**		517
Putnam Investments 1 Post Office Sq	Boston	MA	02109	**888-478-8626**	617-292-1000	393
Putnam Lovell NBF 65 E 55th St Park Ave Tower 34th Fl	New York	NY	10022	**800-531-5190**	212-546-7500	393
Putnam Plastics Inc 255 S Alex Rd	West Carrollton	OH	45449	**800-457-3099**	937-866-6261	67
Putnam Precision Molding Inc 11 Danco Rd	Putnam	CT	06260	**800-752-7865**	860-928-7911	593
Putt-Putt Golf Courses of America Inc 6350 Quadrangle Dr Suite 210	Chapel Hill	NC	27517	**888-788-8788**	910-401-9759	645
Putterman M & Co Inc 4834 S Oakley St	Chicago	IL	60609	**800-621-0146**	773-927-4120	718
Putumayo World Music 411 Lafayette St 4th Fl	New York	NY	10003	**888-788-8629**	212-995-9400	643
Putzmeister America 1733 90th St	Sturtevant	WI	53177	**800-884-7210**	262-886-3200	189
PVA (Paralyzed Veterans of America) 801 18th St NW	Washington	DC	20006	**800-424-8200**	202-872-1300	48-19
PVA (Passenger Vessel Assn) 801 N Quincy St Suite 200	Arlington	VA	22203	**800-807-8360**	703-807-0100	49-21
PVC Container Corp 2 Industrial Way W	Eatontown	NJ	07724	**800-975-2784**	732-542-0060	99
PVF Capital Corp 30000 Aurora Rd *NASDAQ: PVFC*	Solon	OH	44139	**800-676-2572**	440-248-7171	355-2
PVG Asset Management Corp 24918 Genesee Trail Rd	Golden	CO	80401	**800-777-0818**	303-526-0548	393
PVI Industries Inc 3209 Galvez Ave PO Box 7124	Fort Worth	TX	76111	**800-784-8326**	817-335-9531	92
PVS Chemicals Inc 10900 Harper Ave	Detroit	MI	48213	**800-787-6659**	313-921-1200	143
PVT Networks Inc 1311 Main St	Artesia	NM	88210	**866-746-9844**	505-746-9844	721
PW Athletic Mfg Co 140 N Gilbert Rd	Mesa	AZ	85203	**800-687-5768**	928-778-4232	340
PW Minor & Son Inc PO Box 678	Batavia	NY	14020	**800-524-1084**	585-343-1500	296
PW Stephens Inc 15201 Pipeline Ln Unit B	Huntington Beach	CA	92649	**800-937-1521**	714-892-2028	653
PWP (Parents Without Partners) 1650 S Dixie Hwy Suite 510	Boca Raton	FL	33432	**800-637-7974**	561-391-8833	48-6
Pyle A Dule Distribution & Warehousing Inc 650 Westtown Rd	West Chester	PA	19381	**800-523-5020**	610-696-5800	790-1
Pyle A Dule Inc PO Box 564	West Chester	PA	19381	**800-523-5020**	610-696-5800	440
Pyramid Breweries Inc 91 S Royal Brougham Way *NASDAQ: PMID*	Seattle	WA	98134	**800-603-3336**	206-682-8322	103
Pyramid Life Insurance Co PO Box 12922	Pensacola	FL	32591	**800-777-1126**		384-2
Pyramid Masonry Contractors Inc 2330 Mellon Ct	Decatur	GA	30035	**800-345-4750**	770-987-4750	188-7
Pyramid Media PO Box 1048	Santa Monica	CA	90406	**800-421-2303**	310-828-7577	500
Pyramid Technologies Inc 48 Elm St	Meriden	CT	06450	**888-479-7264**	203-238-0550	151
Pyromation Inc 5211 Industrial Rd	Fort Wayne	IN	46825	**800-837-6805**	260-484-2580	200
Pyrotek Inc 9503 E Montgomery Ave	Spokane	WA	99206	**800-797-6835**	509-926-6212	127

Q

Name / Address	City	State	Zip	Toll-Free	Phone	Class
Q Comm International Inc 510 E Technology Ave Bldg C *AMEX: QMM*	Orem	UT	84097	**800-626-9941**	801-226-4222	721
Q3 JMC Inc 605 Miami St	Urbana	OH	43078	**800-767-1422**	937-652-2181	92
QAD Inc 6450 Via Real *NASDAQ: QADI* ■ *Sales	Carpinteria	CA	93013	**800-373-1144***	805-684-6614	176-1
Qantas Airways Cargo 6555 W Imperial Hwy	Los Angeles	CA	90045	**800-227-0290**	310-665-2280	13
Qantas Airways Frequent Flyer Program 6080 Center Dr	Los Angeles	CA	90045	**800-227-4220**	310-726-1400	27
Qantas Airways Ltd 6080 Center Dr Suite 400	Los Angeles	CA	90045	**800-227-4500**	310-726-1400	26
Qantas Vacations 300 Continental Blvd Suite 350	El Segundo	CA	90245	**800-348-8145**	310-322-6359	760
Qatar Airways 399 Thornall St	Edison	NJ	08837	**877-777-2827**	732-321-1701	26
Qatar Airways Privilege Club 399 Thornall St	Edison	NJ	08837	**877-777-2827**	732-321-1701	27
Qdoba Restaurant Corp 4865 Ward Rd Suite 500	Wheat Ridge	CO	80033	**877-261-4783**	720-898-2300	657
QED Inc 1661 W 3rd Ave	Denver	CO	80223	**800-700-5011**	303-825-5011	245
QEP Co Inc 1081 Holland Dr *NASDAQ: QEPC*	Boca Raton	FL	33487	**800-777-8665**	561-994-5550	746
QLogic Corp 26650 Aliso Viejo Pkwy *NASDAQ: QLGC*	Aliso Viejo	CA	92656	**800-662-4471**	949-389-6000	686
QLT Inc 887 Great Northern Way *TSE: QLT*	Vancouver	BC	V5T4T5	**800-663-5486**	604-707-7000	86
QNX Software Sytems Ltd 175 Terence Matthews Crescent	Kanata	ON	K2M1W8	**800-363-9001**	613-591-0931	176-1
Qore Property Science 11420 Johns Creek Pkwy	Duluth	GA	30097	**877-767-3462**	770-476-3555	728
QRCA (Qualitative Research Consultants Assn Inc) PO Box 967	Camden	TN	38320	**888-674-7722**	731-584-8080	49-18
QRS Corp 1400 Marina Way S	Richmond	CA	94804	**800-872-8255**	510-215-5000	223
QS/1 Data Systems PO Box 6052	Spartanburg	SC	29304	**800-845-7558**	864-503-9455	176-10
QSA ToolWorks LLC 64 W 48th St 9th Fl	New York	NY	10036	**800-784-7018**	516-935-9151	176-7
QSC Audio Products Inc 1675 MacArthur Blvd	Costa Mesa	CA	92626	**800-854-4079**	714-754-6175	52
Quabaug Corp 18 School St	North Brookfield	MA	01535	**800-325-5022**	508-867-7731	296
Quad Cities Convention & Visitors Bureau 2021 River Dr	Moline	IL	61265	**800-747-7800**	563-322-3911	205
Quad-City Times 500 E 3rd St	Davenport	IA	52801	**800-437-4641**	563-383-2200	522-2
QuadraMed Corp 22 Pelican Way *AMEX: QD*	San Rafael	CA	94901	**800-473-7633**	415-482-2100	176-10
Quadrant Engineering Plastic Products PO Box 14235	Reading	PA	19612	**800-366-0300**	610-320-6600	591
Quadrex Corp PO Box 3881 *Sales	Woodbridge	CT	06525	**800-275-7033***	203-393-3112	329
Quadstone Inc 286 Congress St 6th Fl	Boston	MA	02210	**800-821-8031**	617-457-5200	176-1
Quail Hollow Resort. Renaissance 11080 Concord-Hambden Rd	Painesville	OH	44077	**800-792-0258**	440-497-1100	655
Quail Lodge Resort & Golf Club 8205 Valley Greens Dr	Carmel	CA	93923	**800-538-9516**	831-624-2888	655
Quail Ridge Inn Taos Ski Valley Rd PO Box 707	Taos	NM	87571	**800-624-4448**	505-776-2211	655
Quail Run Lodge 1130 Bob Harman Rd	Savannah	GA	31408	**800-627-7035**	912-964-1421	373
Quaker Chemical Corp 901 Hector St *NYSE: KWR*	Conshohocken	PA	19428	**800-523-7010**	610-832-4000	143
Quaker City Castings Inc 310 Euclid St	Salem	OH	44460	**800-445-8853**	330-332-1566	302
Quaker City Motor Parts Co 680 N Broad St	Middletown	DE	19709	**800-538-6272**	302-378-9862	61
Quaker Furniture Inc 3060 Main Ave SE	Hickory	NC	28602	**800-356-5732**	828-322-1794	314-1
Quaker Oats Co 555 W Monroe St	Chicago	IL	60661	**800-555-6287**	312-821-1000	291-36
Quaker Square Hotel. Crowne Plaza 135 S Broadway St	Akron	OH	44308	**866-668-6689**	330-253-5970	373
Quaker Window Products Inc PO Box 128	Freeburg	MO	65035	**800-347-0438**	573-744-5211	232
Qual-Craft Industries PO Box 559	Stoughton	MA	02072	**800-231-5647**	781-344-1000	345
QualChoice Health Plan Inc 6000 Parkland Blvd	Cleveland	OH	44124	**800-208-1232**	440-460-0093	384-3
Qualified Remodeler Magazine 1233 Janesville Ave	Fort Atkinson	WI	53538	**800-547-7377**	920-563-6388	449-21
Qualis Inc 4600 Park Ave	Des Moines	IA	50321	**800-334-4514**	515-243-3000	574

Name / Address	City	State	ZIP	Toll-Free	Phone	Class
Qualitative Research Consultants Assn Inc (QRCA) PO Box 967	Camden	TN	38320	**888-674-7722**	731-584-8080	49-18
Quality. American Society for 600 N Plankinton Ave	Milwaukee	WI	53201	**800-248-1946**	414-272-8575	49-13
Quality Assurance. National Committee for 2000 L St NW Suite 500	Washington	DC	20036	**800-238-5903**	202-955-3500	48-10
Quality Biological Inc 7581 Lindbergh Dr	Gaithersburg	MD	20879	**800-443-9331**	301-840-9331	229
Quality Books Inc 1003 West Pines Rd *Cust Svc	Oregon	IL	61061	**800-323-4241***	815-732-4450	97
Quality Cabinets 515 Big Stone Gap Rd	Duncanville	TX	75137	**800-284-3888**	972-298-6103	116
Quality Candy Shoppes Inc PO Box 070581	Milwaukee	WI	53207	**800-972-2658**	414-483-4500	123
Quality Center. American Productivity & 123 Post Oak Ln 3rd Fl	Houston	TX	77024	**800-776-9676**	713-681-4020	49-12
Quality Containers of New England 247 Portland St Suite 300	Yarmouth	ME	04096	**800-639-1550**	207-846-5420	99
Quality Dining Inc 4220 Edison Lakes Pkwy	Mishawaka	IN	46545	**800-589-3820**	574-271-4600	656
Quality Distribution Inc 3802 Corporex Pk Dr Suite 200 *NASDAQ: QLTY*	Tampa	FL	33619	**800-282-2031**	813-630-5826	769
Quality Films Inc 321 Duncan St PO Box 459	Schoolcraft	MI	49087	**800-306-5263**	269-679-5263	589
Quality First Newsletter 360 Hiatt Dr	Palm Beach Gardens	FL	33418	**800-621-5463**	561-622-6520	521-2
Quality Hotel on Broadway 215 W 94th St	New York	NY	10025	**800-228-5151**	212-866-6400	373
Quality Hotel & Conference Center 2261 N Causeway Blvd	Metairie	LA	70001	**800-228-5151**	504-833-8211	373
Quality Hotel Downtown 1335 Howe St	Vancouver	BC	V6Z1R7	**800-663-8474**	604-682-0229	372
Quality Hotel Times Square 157 W 47th St	New York	NY	10036	**800-424-6423**	212-768-3700	373
Quality Inn & Suites Los Alamos 2201 Trinity Dr	Los Alamos	NM	87544	**800-279-9279**	505-662-7211	373
Quality Inn & Suites Naples Golf Resort 4100 Golden Gate Pkwy	Naples	FL	34116	**800-277-0017**	239-455-1010	655
Quality Inn & Suites Seattle 225 Aurora Ave N	Seattle	WA	98109	**800-255-7932**	206-728-7666	373
Quality Inns Hotels & Suites 10750 Columbia Pike	Silver Spring	MD	20901	**800-424-6423**	301-592-5000	369
Quality King Distributors Inc 2060 9th Ave	Ronkonkoma	NY	11779	**800-676-5554**	631-439-2000	237
Quality Lighting 11500 Melrose Ave	Franklin Park	IL	60131	**800-545-1326**	847-451-0040	431
Quality Meats & Seafoods 700 Center St	West Fargo	ND	58078	**800-959-4250**	701-282-0202	465
Quality Metal Products Inc 11500 W 13th Ave	Lakewood	CO	80215	**800-700-4730**	303-232-4242	688
Quality Mfg Inc 969 Labore Industrial Ct	Saint Paul	MN	55110	**800-243-5473**	651-483-5473	692
Quality Park 2520 Como Ave	Saint Paul	MN	55108	**800-328-2990**	651-645-0251	260
Quality Perforating Inc 166 Dundaff St	Carbondale	PA	18407	**800-872-7373**	570-282-4344	479
Quality-PFG 4901 Asher Ave	Little Rock	AR	72204	**800-568-3141**	501-568-3141	292-8
Quality Progress Magazine PO Box 3005	Milwaukee	WI	53201	**800-248-1946**	414-272-8575	449-21
Quality S Mfg Inc 3801 N 43rd Ave	Phoenix	AZ	85019	**800-521-8181**	602-233-3499	751
Quality Systems Inc 18191 Von Karman Ave Suite 450 *NASDAQ: QSII* ■ *Cust Svc	Irvine	CA	92612	**800-888-7955***	949-255-2600	176-10
Qualstar Corp 3990-B Heritage Oak Ct *NASDAQ: QBAK*	Simi Valley	CA	93063	**800-468-0680**	805-583-7744	171-8
QualTeq Inc 800 Montros Ave MS CN1037	South Plainfield	NJ	07080	**800-257-5347**	908-668-0999	695
Quanex Corp 1900 West Loop S Suite 1500 *NYSE: NX*	Houston	TX	77027	**800-231-8176**	713-961-4600	709
Quantimetrix Corp 2005 Manhattan Beach Blvd	Redondo Beach	CA	90278	**800-624-8380**	310-536-0006	229
Quantum Analytics 363 Vintage Park Dr	Foster City	CA	94404	**800-992-4199**	650-312-0900	261-4
Quantum Corp 501 Sycamore Dr *NYSE: DSS* ■ *Tech Supp	Milpitas	CA	95035	**800-826-8022***	408-944-4000	171-8
Quantum Corporate Funding Ltd 1140 Ave of the Americas 16th Fl	New York	NY	10036	**800-352-2535**	212-768-1200	268
Quantum Resources 300 Arboretum Pl Suite 500	Richmond	VA	23236	**800-446-9852**	804-320-4800	707
Quantum/ATL PO Box 57100	Irvine	CA	92619	**800-677-6268**	949-856-7800	171-8
Quark Expeditions Inc 1019 Post Rd	Darien	CT	06820	**800-356-5699**	203-656-0499	217
Quark Inc 1800 Grant St *Cust Svc	Denver	CO	80203	**800-676-4575***	303-894-8888	176-8
Quarter Horse Assn. American PO Box 200	Amarillo	TX	79168	**800-414-7433**	806-376-4811	48-3
Quarterage Hotel 560 Westport Rd	Kansas City	MO	64111	**800-942-4233**	816-931-0001	373
Quarterpath Inn 620 York St	Williamsburg	VA	23185	**800-446-9222**	757-220-0960	373
Quartz Mountain Resort & Conference Center 22469 Lodge Rd	Lone Wolf	OK	73655	**877-999-5567**	580-563-2424	655
Quartzdyne Inc 1020 W Atherton Dr	Salt Lake City	UT	84123	**888-353-7956**	801-266-6958	252
Quatech Inc 5675 Hudson Industrial Pkwy	Hudson	OH	44236	**800-553-1170**	330-655-9000	613
Qubein Nido Creative Services Inc PO Box 6008	High Point	NC	27262	**800-989-3010**	336-889-3010	561
Quebec Inn 7175 boul Hamel	Sainte-Foy	QC	G2G1B6	**800-567-5276**	418-872-9831	372
Quebecor World Inc 612 rue Saint-Jacques *NYSE: IQW*	Montreal	QC	H3C4M8	**800-567-7070**	514-954-0101	615
Queen Anne Hotel 1590 Sutter St	San Francisco	CA	94109	**800-227-3970**	415-441-2828	373
Queen of Cards 10008 S 67th E Pl	Tulsa	OK	74133	**888-899-2508**	918-299-1850	130
Queen Carpet Co Patcraft Commercial Div 616 Duvall Rd	Chatsworth	GA	30705	**800-241-4014**	706-279-4000	131
Queen City TV & Appliance Co Inc 2430 I-85 S	Charlotte	NC	28208	**800-365-6665**	704-391-6000	35
Queen & Crescent Hotel 344 Camp St	New Orleans	LA	70130	**800-975-6652**	504-587-9700	373
Queen Cutlery Co 507 Chestnut St *Sales	Titusville	PA	16354	**800-222-5233***	814-827-3673	219
Queen Helene 100 Rose Ave	Hempstead	NY	11550	**800-645-3752**	516-538-4600	211
Queen Kapiolani Hotel 150 Kapahulu Ave	Honolulu	HI	96815	**800-367-2317**	808-922-1941	373
Queen Mary Seaport 1126 Queens Hwy	Long Beach	CA	90802	**800-437-2934**	562-435-3511	509
Queens University of Charlotte 1900 Selwyn Ave	Charlotte	NC	28274	**800-849-0202**	704-337-2212	163
Queensboro Farm Products Inc 156-02 Liberty Ave	Jamaica	NY	11433	**800-696-8970**	718-658-5000	292-4
Quest Diagnostics Inc 1 Malcolm Ave *NYSE: DGX*	Teterboro	NJ	07608	**800-631-1390**		409
Quest Diagnostics at Nichols Institute 33608 Ortega Hwy	San Juan Capistrano	CA	92690	**800-642-4657**	949-728-4000	409
Quest International Flavors USA Inc 10 Painters Mill Rd	Owings Mills	MD	21117	**800-743-1399**	410-363-2550	291-15
Quest International Fragrances USA Inc 400 International Dr	Mount Olive	NJ	07828	**800-598-5986**	973-691-7100	564
Quest Software Inc 8001 Irvine Center Dr Suite 600 *NASDAQ: QSFT*	Irvine	CA	92618	**800-306-9329**	949-754-8000	176-1
Quest Technologies Inc 1060 Corporate Center Dr	Oconomowoc	WI	53066	**800-245-0779**	262-567-9101	200
Questar Corp 180 E 100 South PO Box 45360 *NYSE: STR*	Salt Lake City	UT	84145	**800-323-5517**	801-324-5000	355-5
Questar Gas Co PO Box 45360	Salt Lake City	UT	84145	**800-323-5517**	801-324-5111	774
Questar Gas Management Co PO Box 45601	Salt Lake City	UT	84145	**800-323-5517**	801-324-2400	320
Questar Inc 680 N Lake Shore Dr Suite 900	Chicago	IL	60611	**800-544-8422**	312-266-9400	500
Questar InfoComm Inc 180 E 100 South PO Box 45433	Salt Lake City	UT	84145	**800-729-6790**	801-324-5856	721
Questcor Pharmaceuticals Inc 3260 Whipple Rd *AMEX: QSC*	Union City	CA	94587	**800-411-3065**	510-400-0700	86
Questel Orbit 7925 Jones Branch Dr	McLean	VA	22102	**800-456-7248**	703-873-4700	621
Questia Media America Inc 24 Greenway Plaza Suite 450	Houston	TX	77046	**888-950-2580**	713-358-2500	380
Queue Inc 1450 Barnum Ave Suite 207	Bridgeport	CT	06610	**800-232-2224**	203-335-0906	176-3
Quick Center for the Arts Fairfield University 1073 Benson Rd	Fairfield	CT	06430	**877-278-7396**	203-254-4242	562
Quick Cooking Magazine 5400 S 60th St	Greendale	WI	53129	**800-344-6913**	414-423-0100	449-11
Quick Eagle Networks Inc 217 Humboldt Ct	Sunnyvale	CA	94089	**888-280-5465**	408-745-6200	176-12
Quick International Courier 212 5th Ave 18th Fl	New York	NY	10010	**800-488-4400**	212-689-4151	536
Quick & Reilly Inc 26 Broadway 14th Fl	New York	NY	10004	**800-672-7220**	212-747-1200	679
Quick Search 4155 Buena Vista	Dallas	TX	75204	**800-473-2840**	214-358-2840	621
QuickArrow Inc 11675 Jollyville Rd Suite 200	Austin	TX	78759	**800-914-7638**	512-381-0600	39
Quicken PO Box 7850 *NASDAQ: INTU* ■ *Cust Svc	Mountain View	CA	94039	**800-446-8848***	650-944-6000	176-9
Quicken Loans 20555 Victor Pkwy	Livonia	MI	48152	**888-565-2488**	734-805-7285	498
QuickenMortgage PO Box 7850	Mountain View	CA	94039	**888-565-2488**	650-944-6000	498
QuickSet International Inc 3650 Woodhead Dr *Orders	Northbrook	IL	60062	**800-247-6563***	847-498-0700	580
Quidel Corp 10165 McKellar Ct *NASDAQ: QDEL*	San Diego	CA	92121	**800-874-1517**	858-552-1100	229
Quigley Corp 621 Shady Retreat Rd *NASDAQ: QGLY*	Doylestown	PA	18091	**877-265-3339**	215-345-0919	572
Quigo Technologies Inc 377 5th Ave 6th Fl	New York	NY	10016	**866-333-7932**	212-213-2363	176-7
Quikbook 381 Park Ave S 3rd Fl	New York	NY	10016	**800-789-9887**	212-779-7666	368
Quikey Mfg Co 1500 Industrial Pkwy	Akron	OH	44310	**877-901-1200**	330-633-8106	10
QUIKRETE Cos 3490 Piedmont Rd Suite 1300	Atlanta	GA	30305	**800-282-5828**	404-634-9100	181
Quiksilver Inc 15202 Graham St *NYSE: ZQK*	Huntington Beach	CA	92649	**800-576-4004**	714-889-2200	153-3
Quikstik Label Mfg Co 210 Broadway	Everett	MA	02149	**800-225-3496**	617-389-7570	404
QuikTrip Corp 4705 S 129th East Ave	Tulsa	OK	74134	**800-544-5749**	918-615-7700	203
Quill Corp PO Box 94081 *Orders	Palatine	IL	60094	**800-789-1331***	847-634-4800	523
Quimby House Inn 109 Cottage St	Bar Harbor	ME	04609	**800-344-5811**	207-288-5811	373
Quimby-Walstrom Paper Co PO Box 1806	Grand Rapids	MI	49501	**800-632-5930**	616-784-4700	543
Quinco Tool Products Co 21000 Hubbell Rd	Oak Park	MI	48237	**800-521-1910**	248-968-5000	484
Quincy College 34 Coddington St	Quincy	MA	02169	**800-698-1700**	617-984-1600	160
Quincy Convention & Visitors Bureau 300 Civic Ctr Plaza Suite 237	Quincy	IL	62301	**800-978-4748**	217-223-1000	205
Quincy Herald-Whig PO Box 909	Quincy	IL	62306	**800-373-9444**	217-223-5100	522-2
Quincy Mutual Fire Insurance Co 57 Washington St	Quincy	MA	02169	**800-899-1116**	617-472-8770	384-4
Quincy Newspapers Inc 130 S 5th St	Quincy	IL	62301	**800-373-9444**	217-223-5100	623-8
Quincy University 1800 College Ave	Quincy	IL	62301	**800-688-4295**	217-228-5210	163
Quinlan Karen Ann Hospice 99 Sparta Ave	Newton	NJ	07860	**800-882-1117**	973-383-0115	365

Name / Address	City	State	ZIP	Toll-Free	Phone	Class
Quinnipiac University 275 Mt Carmel Ave	Hamden	CT	06518	**800-462-1944**	203-582-8200	163
Quintiles Canada Inc 100 Alexis-Nihon Suite 800	Saint Laurent	QC	H4M2P4	**800-799-6166**	514-855-0888	572
Quintiles Transnational Corp PO Box 13979	Research Triangle Park	NC	27709	**800-875-2888**	919-998-2000	572
Quinton Cardiology Systems Inc 3303 Monte Villa Pkwy *NASDAQ: QUIN*	Bothell	WA	98021	**800-426-0337**	425-402-2000	249
Quinzani's Bakery 380 Harrison Ave	Boston	MA	02118	**800-999-1062**	617-426-2114	291-1
Quip Industries Inc 191 Methodist St	Carlyle	IL	62231	**800-851-4013**	618-594-2437	731
Quipp Inc 4800 NW 157th St *NASDAQ: QUIP*	Miami	FL	33014	**800-345-9680**	305-623-8700	379
Quirch Foods Co 7600 NW 82nd Pl	Miami	FL	33166	**800-458-5252**	305-691-3535	292-9
Quixote Corp 35 E Wacker Dr Suite 1100 *NASDAQ: QUIX*	Chicago	IL	60601	**888-323-6374**	312-467-6755	666
Quorum A Lanier Co 950 Blue Gentian Rd Suite 100	Eagan	MN	55121	**800-328-4454**	651-234-5678	436
Quorum Hotel Tampa-Westshore 700 N Westshore Blvd	Tampa	FL	33609	**877-478-6786**	813-289-8200	373
Quotesmith.com Inc 8205 S Cass Ave Suite 102 *NASDAQ: QUOT*	Darien	IL	60561	**800-556-9393**	630-515-0170	383
Quovadx Inc 6400 S Fiddler's Green Cir Suite 1000 *NASDAQ: QVDX*	Englewood	CO	80111	**800-723-3033**	303-488-2019	176-10
QVC Inc 1200 Wilson Dr	West Chester	PA	19380	**800-367-9444**		725

R

Name / Address	City	State	ZIP	Toll-Free	Phone	Class
R-Anell Custom Homes Inc 35439 Hwy 16 N	Denver	NC	28037	**800-951-5511**	704-483-5511	495
R & B Inc 3400 E Walnut St *NASDAQ: RBIN*	Colmar	PA	18915	**800-523-2492**	215-997-1800	60
R & D Magazine 100 Enterprise Dr Suite 600 Box 912	Rockaway	NJ	07866	**800-222-0289**	973-920-7000	449-19
R & D Systems Inc 614 McKinley Pl NE	Minneapolis	MN	55413	**800-343-7475**	612-379-2956	229
R Johns Ltd PO Box 149107	Austin	TX	78714	**800-521-9493**		401
R & K Industrial Products Co 1945 N 7th St *Cust Svc	Richmond	CA	94801	**800-842-7655***	510-234-7212	663
R & M Energy Systems PO Box 2871 *Sales	Borger	TX	79008	**800-858-4158***	806-274-5293	378
R & M Office Furniture Inc 9615 Oates Dr	Sacramento	CA	95827	**800-660-1756**	916-362-1756	315
R & O Elevator Co Inc 8310 Pillsbury Ave S	Bloomington	MN	55420	**800-735-3046**	952-888-9255	188-1
R & R Marketing LLC 10 Patton Dr	West Caldwell	NJ	07006	**800-772-2096**	973-228-5100	82-3
R & S/Godwin Truck Body Co LLC 5168 S US Hwy 23	Ivel	KY	41642	**800-826-7413**	606-874-2151	505
R & W Supply Inc 2210 Hall Ave	Littlefield	TX	79339	**800-477-1191**	806-385-4447	270
R2 Technology Inc 1195 W Fremont Ave	Sunnyvale	CA	94087	**866-243-2533**	408-481-5600	249
RA Bloch Cancer Foundation 4400 Main St	Kansas City	MO	64111	**800-433-0464**	816-932-8453	48-17
RA Miller Industries Inc 14500 168th Ave	Grand Haven	MI	49417	**888-845-9450**	616-842-9450	633
RA Pearson Co 8120 W Sunset Hwy	Spokane	WA	99224	**800-732-7766**	509-838-6226	537
R/A Performance Group 135 Main St Suite 1120	San Francisco	CA	94105	**800-235-1446**	415-869-6500	183
RAA (Reinsurance Assn of America) 1301 Pennsylvania Ave NW Suite 900	Washington	DC	20004	**800-638-3651**	202-638-3690	49-9
RAB (Radio Advertising Bureau) 261 Madison Ave 23rd Fl	New York	NY	10016	**800-252-7234**	212-681-7200	49-18
RAB Electric Mfg Inc 170 Ludlow Ave	Northvale	NJ	07647	**800-938-1010**	201-784-8600	431
Rabbis. Central Conference of American 355 Lexington Ave 18th Fl	New York	NY	10017	**800-935-2227**	212-972-3636	48-20
Rabbit Hill Inn Lower Waterford Rd	Lower Waterford	VT	05848	**800-762-8669**	802-748-5168	373
rabbittransit 1230 Roosevelt Ave	York	PA	17404	**800-632-9063**	717-846-5562	460
Raben Tire Co Inc 400 NW 4th St	Evansville	IN	47708	**800-322-6247**	812-465-5566	740
Raber Packing Co 1413 N Raber Rd	Peoria	IL	61604	**800-331-0545**	309-673-0721	465
Rabjohn LE Inc 1833 N Daly St	Los Angeles	CA	90031	**800-559-3737**	323-221-9163	15
Rabo AG Services PO Box 668	Cedar Falls	IA	50613	**800-395-8505**	319-277-0261	272
Rabun Gap-Nacoochee School 339 Nacoochee Dr	Rabun Gap	GA	30568	**800-543-7467**	706-746-7467	611
Racal Instruments Inc 4 Goodyear *Cust Svc	Irvine	CA	92618	**800-722-3262***	949-859-8999	247
Raccoon Mountain Caverns 319 W Hills Dr	Chattanooga	TN	37419	**800-823-2267**	423-821-9403	50
Race Face Components Inc 100 Braid St Unit 100	New Westminster	BC	V3L3P4	**800-527-9244**	604-527-9996	153-1
RaceTrac Petroleum Inc 300 Technology Ct	Smyrna	GA	30082	**888-636-5589**	770-431-7600	319
Racine County Convention & Visitors Bureau 14015 Washington Ave	Sturtevant	WI	53177	**800-272-2463**	262-884-6400	205
Racine Federated Inc Hedland Div 2200 South St	Racine	WI	53404	**800-433-5263**	262-639-6770	486
Racing Assn. National Thoroughbred 2525 Harrodsburg Rd	Lexington	KY	40504	**800-722-3287**	859-223-5444	48-22

Name / Address	City	State	ZIP	Toll-Free	Phone	Class
Racing & Hall of Fame. National Museum of 191 Union Ave	Saratoga Springs	NY	12866	**800-562-5394**	518-584-0400	511
Rackspace Ltd 9725 Datapoint Dr Suite 100	San Antonio	TX	78229	**800-961-2888**	210-447-4000	795
Racore Technology Corp 4125 S 6000 West	West Valley City	UT	84128	**877-252-9779**	801-973-9779	174
Racquet & Sportsclub Assn. International Health 263 Summer St 8th Fl	Boston	MA	02210	**800-228-4772**	617-951-0055	48-22
Racquet Stringers Assn. US 330 Main St	Vista	CA	92084	**888-900-3545**	760-536-1177	48-22
Racquetball Assn. US 1685 W Uintah St	Colorado Springs	CO	80904	**800-234-5396**	719-635-5396	48-22
RAD Data Communications Ltd 900 Corporate Dr	Mahwah	NJ	07430	**800-444-7234**	201-529-1100	720
Rada Mfg Co 905 Industrial St	Waverly	IA	50677	**800-311-9691**	319-352-5454	219
Raddison Inn Manchester 700 Elm St	Manchester	NH	03101	**800-333-3333**	603-625-1000	373
Radford University Norwood St & Rt 11	Radford	VA	24142	**800-890-4265**	540-831-5000	163
Radiac Abrasives Inc 1015 S College Ave	Salem	IL	62881	**800-851-1095**	618-548-4200	1
Radian Asset Assurance Inc 335 Madison Ave 25th Fl	New York	NY	10017	**800-523-1988**	212-983-3100	384-5
Radian Communications Services Corp 2700 Matheson Blvd E West Tower Suite 800	Mississauga	ON	L4W4V9	**866-472-3126**	905-212-8200	720
Radian Group Inc 1601 Market St *NYSE: RDN*	Philadelphia	PA	19103	**800-523-1988**	215-564-6600	384-5
Radian Guaranty Inc 1601 Market St	Philadelphia	PA	19103	**800-523-1988**	215-564-6600	384-5
Radiant Communications Corp 1050 W Pender St Suite 1600	Vancouver	BC	V6E4T3	**888-219-2111**	604-257-0500	795
Radiant Electric Co-op Inc 100 N 15th St	Fredonia	KS	66736	**800-821-0956**	620-378-2161	244
Radiant Systems Inc 3925 Brookside Pkwy *NASDAQ: RADS*	Alpharetta	GA	30022	**800-229-0991**	770-576-6000	603
Radiation Management Consultants 3019 Darnell Rd	Philadelphia	PA	19154	**800-793-1304**	215-824-1300	455
Radiation Monitoring Devices 44 Hunt St Suite 2	Watertown	MA	02472	**800-532-3763**	617-926-1167	464
Radiation Protection & Measurements. National Council on 7910 Woodmont Ave Suite 400	Bethesda	MD	20814	**800-229-2652**	301-657-2652	49-19
Radiation Therapy Services Inc 2234 Colonial Blvd *NASDAQ: RTSX*	Fort Myers	FL	33907	**888-376-9729**	239-931-7275	347
Radiator Service Assn. National Automotive 15000 Commerce Pkwy Suite C	Mount Laurel	NJ	08054	**800-551-3232**	856-439-1575	49-21
Radiator Specialty Co 1900 Wilkinson Blvd	Charlotte	NC	28208	**800-438-4532**	704-377-6555	143
Radica USA Ltd 13628-A Beta Rd *NASDAQ: RADA*	Dallas	TX	75244	**800-803-9611**	972-490-4247	750
Radio Advertising Bureau (RAB) 261 Madison Ave 23rd Fl	New York	NY	10016	**800-252-7234**	212-681-7200	49-18
Radio America 1030 15th St NW Suite 1040	Washington	DC	20005	**800-807-4703**	202-408-0944	630
Radio Control Boat Modeler PO Box 433	Mount Morris	IL	61054	**800-877-5160**	815-734-1243	449-14
Radio Distributing Co Inc 27015 Trolley Industrial Dr	Taylor	MI	48180	**800-462-1544**	313-295-4500	38
Radio Flyer Inc 6515 W Grand Ave	Chicago	IL	60707	**800-621-7613**	773-637-7100	750
Radio Systems Corp 10427 Electric Ave *Cust Svc	Knoxville	TN	37932	**800-732-2677***	865-777-5404	568
Radio & Telecommunications Engineers. National Assn of 167 Village St	Medway	MA	02053	**800-896-2783**	508-533-8333	49-19
Radio-Television News Directors Assn (RTNDA) 1600 K St NW Suite 700	Washington	DC	20006	**800-807-8632**	202-659-6510	49-14
Radiocat 32-A Mellor Ave	Baltimore	MD	21228	**800-323-9729**	410-788-5200	781
Radiodetection Corp RR 2 Box 756	Bridgton	ME	04009	**800-524-1739**	207-647-3185	247
Radiologic Technologists. American Society of 15000 Central Ave SE	Albuquerque	NM	87123	**800-444-2778**	505-298-4500	49-8
Radiologix Inc 2200 Ross Ave Suite 3600 *AMEX: RGX*	Dallas	TX	75201	**800-908-9302**	214-303-2776	455
Radiology Administrators. American Healthcare 490-B Boston Post Rd Suite 101	Sudbury	MA	01776	**800-334-2472**	978-443-7591	49-8
Radiology. American College of 1891 Preston White Dr	Reston	VA	20191	**800-227-5463**	703-648-8900	49-8
Radiology Business Management Assn (RBMA) 8001 Irvine Center Dr Suite 1060	Irvine	CA	92618	**888-224-7262**	949-340-5000	49-8
Radiology & Oncology. American Society for Therapeutic 12500 Fair Lakes Cir Suite 375	Fairfax	VA	22033	**800-962-7876**	703-502-1550	49-8
Radiology. Society of Interventional 10201 Lee Hwy Suite 500	Fairfax	VA	22030	**800-488-7284**	703-691-1805	49-8
Radiometer America Inc 810 Sharon Dr	Westlake	OH	44145	**800-736-0600**	440-871-8900	467
RadioShack 100 Throckmorton St Suite 1800	Fort Worth	TX	76102	**800-843-7422**	817-415-3011	35
RadioShack Corp 300 RadioShack Cir *NYSE: RSH*	Fort Worth	TX	76102	**800-843-7422**	817-415-3700	658
Radisson Hotel Hyannis 287 Iyannough Rd	Hyannis	MA	02601	**800-333-3333**	508-771-1700	373
Radisson Hotel Miami Downtown 1601 Biscayne Blvd	Miami	FL	33132	**800-333-3333**	305-374-0000	373
Radisson Hotel Palm Beach Airport 1808 S Australian Ave	West Palm Beach	FL	33409	**800-333-3333**	561-689-6888	373
Radisson Hotels & Resorts PO Box 59159	Minneapolis	MN	55459	**800-333-3333**	763-212-5526	369

Name / Address	City	State	ZIP	Toll-Free	Phone	Class
Radisson Resort Parkway 2900 Parkway Blvd	Kissimmee	FL	34747	800-333-3333	407-396-7000	655
Radisson Resort South Padre Island 500 Padre Blvd	South Padre Island	TX	78597	800-333-3333	956-761-6511	655
Radisson Resort & Spa Scottsdale 7171 N Scottsdale Rd	Scottsdale	AZ	85253	800-333-3333	480-991-3800	655
Radisson Seven Seas Cruises 600 Corporate Dr Suite 410	Fort Lauderdale	FL	33334	800-477-7500	954-776-6123	217
RadiSys Corp 5445 NE Dawson Creek Dr *NASDAQ: RSYS*	Hillsboro	OR	97124	800-950-0044	503-615-1100	613
Radix International Corp 4855 Wiley Post Way	Salt Lake City	UT	84116	800-367-9256	801-537-1717	171-2
Radner Gilda Familial Ovarian Cancer Registry Roswell Park Cancer Institute Elm & Carlton Sts	Buffalo	NY	14263	800-682-7426	716-845-4503	48-17
Radnor Hotel 591 E Lancaster Ave	Saint Davids	PA	19087	800-537-3000	610-688-5800	373
RADO USA 1200 Harbor Blvd	Weehawken	NJ	07086	877-839-5223	201-271-1400	151
RadView Software Inc 7 New England Executive Pk *NASDAQ: RDVW*	Burlington	MA	01803	888-723-8439	781-238-1111	176-12
Radyne Corp 211 W Boden St	Milwaukee	WI	53207	800-236-8360	414-481-8360	313
RAE Corp 4615 W Prime Pkwy	McHenry	IL	60050	800-323-7049	815-385-3500	507
RAE Corp Technical Systems Div PO Box 1206	Pryor	OK	74361	888-498-8922	918-825-7222	15
RAE Systems Inc 3775 N 1st St *AMEX: RAE*	San Jose	CA	95134	877-723-2878	408-952-8200	200
Raffles L'Ermitage Beverly Hills 9291 Burton Way	Beverly Hills	CA	90210	800-800-2113	310-278-3344	373
Raft River Rural Electric Co-op Inc 155 N Main St PO Box 617	Malta	ID	83342	800-342-7732	208-645-2211	244
Ragan Lawrence Communications Inc 316 N Michigan Ave Suite 300	Chicago	IL	60601	800-878-5331	312-960-4140	623-9
Ragan Report Newsletter 316 N Michigan Ave Suite 300 *Cust Svc	Chicago	IL	60601	800-878-5331*	312-960-4100	521-2
Ragen Mackenzie Group Inc 999 3rd Ave Suite 4000	Seattle	WA	98104	800-456-4457	206-343-5000	679
Ragland CB Co 2720 Eugenia Ave	Nashville	TN	37211	800-234-4455	615-259-4622	292-8
Rail Europe Group 44 S Broadway 11th Fl	White Plains	NY	10601	800-438-7245	914-682-2999	748
Rail Link Inc 4337 Pablo Oaks Ct Suite 104	Jacksonville	FL	32224	888-902-7245	904-223-1110	637
RailAmerica Inc 5300 Broken Sound Blvd NW 2nd Fl *NYSE: RRA*	Boca Raton	FL	33487	800-211-7245	561-994-6015	634
Railex Corp 89-02 Atlantic Ave	Ozone Park	NY	11416	800-352-3244	718-845-5454	206
Railglide Systems 12995 Hillview St	Detroit	MI	48227	800-451-5262	313-834-0100	206
Railroad Pass Hotel & Casino 2800 S Boulder Hwy	Henderson	NV	89015	800-654-0877	702-294-5000	133
Railroad Retirement Board 844 N Rush St	Chicago	IL	60611	800-808-0772	312-751-4500	336-16
Railroads. Association of American 50 F St NW *Cust Svc	Washington	DC	20001	800-544-7245*	202-639-2100	49-21
Rails Co 101 Newark Way	Maplewood	NJ	07040	800-217-2457	973-763-4320	759
Rails-to-Trails Conservancy (RTC) 1100 17th St NW 10th Fl *Orders	Washington	DC	20036	800-888-7747*	202-331-9696	48-13
Railserve Inc 1691 Phoenix Blvd Suite 110	Atlanta	GA	30349	800-345-7245	770-996-6838	637
Rain or Shine LandscapeUSA 13126 NE Airport Way	Portland	OR	97230	800-966-1033	503-255-1981	318
Rainbow 61 Entrada	Santa Fe	NM	87507	800-810-3686	505-820-3434	582
Rainbow Art Glass Inc 1761 Rt 34 S	Wall	NJ	07727	800-526-2356	732-681-6003	325
Rainbow International 1010 N University Park Dr	Waco	TX	76707	800-583-9100	254-745-2444	150
Rainbow Magnetics Inc 3221 W MacArthur Blvd *Sales	Santa Ana	CA	92704	800-248-6200*	714-540-4777	10
Rainbow Mfg Co 1 Rainbow Dr *Cust Svc	Fitzgerald	GA	31750	800-841-0323*	229-423-4341	269
Rainbow Trout Ranch 1484 FDR 250	Antonito	CO	81120	800-633-3397	719-376-5659	238
Rainbows 2100 Golf Rd Suite 370	Rolling Meadows	IL	60008	800-266-3206	847-952-1770	48-6
Raindance Communications Inc 1157 Century Dr *NASDAQ: RNDC*	Louisville	CO	80027	800-878-7326	303-928-2400	176-7
Raindance Spa at the Lodge at Sonoma Renaissance Resort 1325 Broadway	Sonoma	CA	95476	888-710-8008	707-931-2034	698
RAINfinity 2740 Zanker Rd Suite 200	San Jose	CA	95134	877-724-6333	408-382-5000	176-7
Rainforest Action Network (RAN) 221 Pine St Suite 500	San Francisco	CA	94104	800-989-7246	415-398-4404	48-13
Rainforest Cafe 1510 W Loop South	Houston	TX	77027	800-552-6379	713-850-1010	657
Rainier Industries Ltd 18435 Olympic Ave S	Tukwila	WA	98188	800-869-7162	425-251-1800	718
Rainier Investment Management Mutual Funds 601 Union St Suite 2801	Seattle	WA	98101	800-248-6314	206-464-0400	517
Rainier Pacific Financial Group Inc 1498 Pacific Ave *NASDAQ: RPFG*	Tacoma	WA	98402	800-228-2858	253-926-4000	355-2
Raining Data Corp 17500 Cartwright Rd *NASDAQ: RDTA*	Irvine	CA	92614	800-367-7425	949-442-4400	176-12
Rainmaker LP 50 W 2nd Ave	Vancouver	BC	V5Y1B3	800-616-4433	604-874-8700	501
RainMaker Software Inc 475 Sentry Pkwy Suite 4000 *Cust Svc	Blue Bell	PA	19422	800-341-4012*	610-567-3400	176-10
Rainmaker Systems Inc 1800 Green Hills Rd *NASDAQ: RMKR*	Scotts Valley	CA	95066	800-631-1545	831-430-3800	194
RAINN (Rape Abuse & Incest National Network) 635-B Pennsylvania Ave SE	Washington	DC	20003	800-656-4673	202-544-1034	48-6
Rainsoft Water Conditioning Co Inc 2080 E Lunt Ave	Elk Grove Village	IL	60007	800-860-7638	847-437-9400	793
Rainstar University 8370 E Via De Ventura St Suite K-100	Scottsdale	AZ	85258	888-724-6782	480-423-0375	787
Rainy River Community College 1501 Hwy 71	International Falls	MN	56649	800-456-3996	218-285-7722	160
Raj The 1734 Jasmine Ave	Fairfield	IA	52556	800-248-9050	641-472-9580	697
Ralco-Mix Products Inc 1600 Hahn Rd	Marshall	MN	56258	800-533-5308	507-532-5740	430
Raleigh America Inc Diamondback Div 6004 S 190th St Suite 101	Kent	WA	98032	800-222-5527	253-395-1100	83
Raleigh General Hospital 1710 Harper Rd	Beckley	WV	25801	800-368-8016	304-256-4100	366-2
Raleigh (Greater) Convention & Visitors Bureau 421 Fayetteville St Mall Suite 1505	Raleigh	NC	27602	800-849-8499	919-834-5900	205
Raleigh USA 6004 S 190th St Suite 101	Kent	WA	98032	800-222-5527	253-395-1100	83
Raley's PO Box 15618	Sacramento	CA	95852	800-925-9989	916-373-3333	339
Ralls County Electric Co-op 17594 Hwy 19	New London	MO	63459	877-985-8711	573-985-8711	244
Rally's Hamburgers Inc 4300 W Cypress St Suite 600	Tampa	FL	33607	800-800-8072	813-283-7000	657
Ralph Friedland & Brothers Inc 17 Industrial Dr	Cliffwood Beach	NJ	07735	800-631-2162	732-290-9800	88
Ralph Lauren 650 Madison Ave	New York	NY	10022	888-475-7674	212-318-7000	273
Ralph Maltby's GolfWorks 4820 Jacksontown Rd	Newark	OH	43055	800-848-8358	740-328-4193	701
Ralph Marlin & Co 1814 Dolphin Dr Suite A	Waukesha	WI	53186	800-922-8437	262-549-5100	153-13
Ralph Pill Electrical Supply Co 307 Dorchester Ave	Boston	MA	02127	800-879-7455	617-269-8200	245
Ralph Sechler & Son Inc 5686 State Rd 1	Saint Joe	IN	46785	800-332-5461	260-337-5461	291-19
Ralphs Grocery Co 1100 W Artesia Blvd *Cust Svc	Compton	CA	90220	888-437-3496*	310-884-9000	339
Ram The 10013 59th Ave SW	Lakewood	WA	98499	888-898-4050	253-588-1788	657
Ram Building Components Co 9500 Henry Ct	Zeeland	MI	49464	800-827-5434	616-875-8157	805
Ram Graphics Inc 2408 S Park Ave	Alexandria	IN	46001	800-531-4656		675
Ram International Inc 4664 World Pkwy Cir	Saint Louis	MO	63134	800-884-4726	314-427-3000	306
Ram Tool & Supply Co PO Box 320979	Birmingham	AL	35232	800-292-6027	205-591-2527	346
RAMA (Retail Advertising & Marketing Assn) 325 7th St NW Suite 1100	Washington	DC	20004	800-673-4692	202-661-3052	49-18
Rama Corp 600 W Esplanade Ave	San Jacinto	CA	92583	800-472-5670	951-654-7351	15
Ramada Franchise Systems Inc 1 Sylvan Way	Parsippany	NJ	07054	800-932-6726	973-428-9700	369
Ramada Inn & Conference Center Bossier 4000 Industrial Dr	Bossier City	LA	71111	800-272-6232	318-747-0711	373
Rambus Inc 4440 El Camino Real *NASDAQ: RMBS*	Los Altos	CA	94022	800-726-2879	650-947-5000	686
Ramco-Gershenson Properties Trust 31500 Northwestern Hwy Suite 300 *NYSE: RPT*	Farmington Hills	MI	48334	800-225-6765	248-350-9900	641
Ramesys Hospitality Inc 1 Cragwood Rd Suite 202	South Plainfield	NJ	07080	800-888-8819	908-941-1300	176-10
Ramey Farmers Co-op Creamery 5139 345th Ave	Foley	MN	56329	888-219-1768	320-355-2313	291-3
Ramey Michael & Assoc Inc PO Box 744	Danville	CA	94526	800-321-0505	925-820-8900	392
Ramona VNA & Hospice 890 W Stetson Ave Suite A	Hemet	CA	92543	800-588-7862	951-658-9288	365
Ramos Oil Co Inc 1515 S River Rd	West Sacramento	CA	95691	800-477-7266	916-371-2570	569
Ramp 66 2800 Terminal St	North Myrtle Beach	SC	29582	800-433-8918	843-272-5337	63
Ramsey Outdoor Store 240 SR 17 N	Paramus	NJ	07652	800-699-5874	201-261-5000	702
Ramsey Winch Co Inc 1600 N Garnett Rd	Tulsa	OK	74116	800-777-2760	918-438-2760	189
Ramtron International Corp 1850 Ramtron Dr *NASDAQ: RMTR*	Colorado Springs	CO	80921	800-545-3726	719-481-7000	686
RAN (Rainforest Action Network) 221 Pine St Suite 500	San Francisco	CA	94104	800-989-7246	415-398-4404	48-13
Ranch Inn 45 E Pearl St	Jackson	WY	83001	800-348-5599	307-733-6363	373
Ranch at Steamboat 1 Ranch Rd	Steamboat Springs	CO	80487	800-525-2002	970-879-3000	373
Rancho Bernardo Inn 17550 Bernardo Oaks Dr	San Diego	CA	92128	877-517-9342	858-675-8500	655
Rancho Las Palmas Marriott Resort & Spa 41000 Bob Hope Dr	Rancho Mirage	CA	92270	800-458-8786	760-568-2727	655
Rancho Los Amigos National Rehabilitation Center 7601 E Imperial Hwy	Downey	CA	90242	877-726-2461	562-401-7111	366-4
Rancho de los Caballeros 1551 S Vulture Mine Rd	Wickenburg	AZ	85390	800-684-5030	928-684-5484	655
Rancho de la Osa Guest Ranch PO Box 1	Sasabe	AZ	85633	800-872-6240	520-823-4257	238
Rancho Valencia Resort 5921 Valencia Cir PO Box 9126	Rancho Santa Fe	CA	92067	800-548-3664	858-756-1123	655
Rancho Viejo Resort & Country Club 1 Rancho Viejo Dr	Rancho Viejo	TX	78575	800-531-7400	956-350-4000	655
Rancocas Metals Corp 35 Indel Ave	Rancocas	NJ	08073	800-762-6382	609-267-4120	483
Rand Financial Services Inc 141 W Jackson Blvd Suite 1950	Chicago	IL	60604	800-842-7263	312-559-8800	167
Rand McNally & Co 8255 N Central Park Ave	Skokie	IL	60076	800-333-0136	847-329-8100	623-1
Rand-Whitney Container Corp 1 Agrand St	Worcester	MA	01607	800-370-9111	508-791-2301	101
Randa Corp 120 W 45th St 38th Fl	New York	NY	10036	800-632-5843	212-768-8800	153-13
Randal Nutritional Products Inc 1595 Hampston Way PO Box 7328	Santa Rosa	CA	95407	800-221-1697	707-528-1800	786
Randall Brothers Inc 665 Marietta St NW *Cust Svc	Atlanta	GA	30313	800-476-4539*	404-892-6666	489

Name / Address	City	State	ZIP	Toll-Free	Phone	Class
Randall County Feedyard 15000 FM 2219	Amarillo	TX	79119	**800-658-6063**	806-499-3701	11-1
Randall Foods Inc 2905 E 50th St	Vernon	CA	90058	**800-372-6581**	323-587-2383	608
Randall Publishing Co 3200 Rice Mine Rd NE *Cust Svc	Tuscaloosa	AL	35406	**800-633-5953***	205-349-2990	623-9
Randalls Food Markets Inc PO Box 4506 *PR	Houston	TX	77210	**800-420-5385***	713-268-3500	339
Randell Mfg Inc 520 S Coldwater Rd	Weidman	MI	48893	**800-621-8560**	989-644-3331	379
Randolph-Brooks Federal Credit Union PO Box 2097	Universal City	TX	78148	**800-580-3300**	210-945-3300	216
Randolph Electric Membership Corp 879 McDowell Rd	Asheboro	NC	27204	**800-672-8212**	336-625-5177	244
Randolph-Macon Academy 200 Academy Dr	Front Royal	VA	22630	**800-272-1172**	540-636-5200	611
Randolph-Macon College PO Box 5005	Ashland	VA	23005	**800-888-1762**	804-798-8372	163
Randolph-Macon Woman's College 2500 Rivermont Ave	Lynchburg	VA	24503	**800-745-7692**	434-947-8000	163
Random Acts of Kindness Foundation 1727 Tremont Pl	Denver	CO	80202	**800-660-2811**	303-297-1964	48-5
Random House Inc 1745 Broadway *Cust Svc	New York	NY	10019	**800-733-3000***	212-782-9000	623-2
Random House Reference & Information Publishing 1745 Broadway *Orders	New York	NY	10019	**800-733-3000***	212-751-2600	623-2
Range Co-op Inc 102 S Hoover Rd	Virginia	MN	55792	**800-862-8628**	218-741-7393	311
Rangen Inc 115 13th Ave S	Buhl	ID	83316	**800-657-6446**	208-543-6421	438
Ranger Construction Industries Inc 101 Sansbury's Way	West Palm Beach	FL	33411	**800-969-9402**	561-793-9400	187-4
Ranger Creek Guest Ranch PO Box 47	Shell	WY	82441	**888-817-7787**	307-272-5107	238
Ranger Insurance Co 10777 Westheimer Rd Suite 500	Houston	TX	77042	**800-392-1970**	713-954-8100	384-4
Ranger Rick Magazine 11100 Wildlife Ctr Dr	Reston	VA	20190	**800-822-9919**		449-6
Ranor Inc 1 Bella Dr	Westminster	MA	01473	**800-225-9552**	978-874-0591	471
Ransco Industries 1801 Solar Dr Suite 190	Oxnard	CA	93030	**800-828-9903**	805-981-1518	379
Ransohoff Inc 4933 Provident Dr	Cincinnati	OH	45246	**800-248-9274**	513-870-0100	206
Ransom & Randolph Co 3535 Briarfield Blvd	Maumee	OH	43537	**800-800-7496**	419-865-9497	649
Ransome Engine Power Div Giles & Ransome Inc 2975 Galloway Rd	Bensalem	PA	19020	**800-753-4228**	215-639-4300	270
Rape Abuse & Incest National Network (RAINN) 635-B Pennsylvania Ave SE	Washington	DC	20003	**800-656-4673**	202-544-1034	48-6
Raphael Hotel Group 200 W 12th St	Kansas City	MO	64105	**800-821-5343**	816-421-6100	369
Raphael Kansas City 325 Ward Pkwy	Kansas City	MO	64112	**800-821-5343**	816-756-3800	373
Rapid City Convention & Visitors Bureau 444 Mt Rushmore Rd N	Rapid City	SD	57701	**800-487-3223**	605-343-1744	205
Rapid City Journal 507 Main St	Rapid City	SD	57701	**800-843-2300**	605-394-8300	522-2
Rapid Displays Inc 4300 W 47th St	Chicago	IL	60632	**800-356-5775**	773-927-5000	231
Rapid Industries Inc 4003 Oaklawn Dr	Louisville	KY	40219	**800-727-4381**	502-968-3645	206
Rapid Rack Industries Inc 14421 Bonelli St	City of Industry	CA	91746	**800-736-7225**	626-333-7225	281
Rapid Ways Truck Leasing Inc 3940 Great Midwest Dr	Kansas City	MO	64161	**800-962-7322**	816-455-7262	767
Rapidforms Inc 301 Grove Rd *Cust Svc	Thorofare	NJ	08086	**800-257-8354***	856-384-1144	111
Rapidigm Inc 4400 Campbells Run Rd	Pittsburgh	PA	15205	**800-944-6055**	412-494-9898	193
RAPIDS Wholesale Equipment Co 6201 S Gateway Dr	Marion	IA	52302	**800-899-6610**	319-364-5186	295
Rapiscan Security Products Inc 3232 El Segundo Blvd	Hawthorne	CA	90250	**800-318-7226**	310-978-1457	681
Rappahannock Electric Co-op 247 Industrial Ct	Fredericksburg	VA	22408	**800-552-3904**	540-898-8500	244
Rare Disorders. National Organization for 55 Kenosia Ave PO Box 1968	Danbury	CT	06813	**800-999-6673**	203-744-0100	48-17
Rare Hospitality International Inc 8215 Roswell Rd Bldg 600 *NASDAQ: RARE*	Atlanta	GA	30350	**800-434-6245**	770-399-9595	656
Raritan Computer Inc 400 Cottontail Ln	Somerset	NJ	08873	**800-724-8090**	732-764-8886	252
Rasmussen CA Inc 2360 Shasta Way	Simi Valley	CA	93065	**800-479-2888**	805-527-9330	187-4
Rath & Strong Inc 45 Hayden Ave	Lexington	MA	02421	**800-622-2025**	781-861-1700	193
Rational Recovery PO Box 800	Lotus	CA	95651	**800-303-2873**	530-621-2667	48-21
Ratner Cos 1577 Spring Hill Rd Suite 500	Vienna	VA	22182	**800-874-6288**	703-698-7090	79
Rauland-Borg Corp 3450 W Oakton St	Skokie	IL	60076	**800-621-0087**	847-679-0900	385
Raven Biological Laboratories Inc 8607 Park Dr	Omaha	NE	68127	**800-728-5702**	402-593-0781	86
Raven Industries Inc 205 E 6th St *NASDAQ: RAVN*	Sioux Falls	SD	57104	**800-227-2836**	605-336-2750	589
Rawah Ranch 11447 N County Rd 103	Jelm	WY	82063	**800-820-3152**		238
Rawhide Motel 75 S Millward St PO Box 4800	Jackson	WY	83001	**800-835-2999**	307-733-1216	373
Rawlings Sporting Goods Co PO Box 22000	Saint Louis	MO	63126	**800-729-5464**	636-349-3500	701
Rawlins Daily Times 522 W Buffalo St PO Box 370	Rawlins	WY	82301	**800-541-3411**	307-324-3411	522-2
Rawson & Co Inc PO Box 924288	Houston	TX	77292	**800-779-1414**	713-684-1400	245
Raxco Software Inc 6 Montgomery Village Ave Suite 500 *Tech Supp	Gaithersburg	MD	20879	**800-546-9728***	301-527-0803	176-12
Ray Burner/RD Miners Co 401 Parr Blvd	Richmond	CA	94801	**800-729-2876**	510-236-4972	313
Ray Mart Inc PO Box 5548	Beaumont	TX	77726	**800-341-7788**	409-835-4744	359
Ray Products Co Inc 1700 Chablis Ave	Ontario	CA	91761	**800-423-7859**	909-390-9906	591
Raybestos Products Co 1204 Darlington Ave	Crawfordsville	IN	47933	**800-428-0825**	765-362-3500	60
Raybourn Group International Inc 7150 Winton Dr Suite 300	Indianapolis	IN	46268	**800-362-2546**	317-328-4636	47
Rayburn Sam Memorial Veterans Center 1201 E 9th St	Bonham	TX	75418	**800-924-8387**	903-583-2111	366-6
Raychem Corp 300 Constitution Dr	Menlo Park	CA	94025	**800-729-2436**	650-361-3333	800
Rayfo Inc 15629 Clayton Ave	Rosemount	MN	55068	**800-624-4764**	651-437-4441	197
Raymarine Inc 21 Manchester St	Merrimack	NH	03054	**800-539-5539**	603-881-5200	519
Raymond Building Supply Corp 7751 Bayshore Rd	North Fort Myers	FL	33917	**877-731-7272**	239-731-8300	190-3
Raymond Corp 8-20 S Canal St	Greene	NY	13778	**800-235-7200**	607-656-2311	462
Raymond Excavating Co Inc 800 Gratiot Blvd	Marysville	MI	48040	**888-837-6770**	810-364-6881	188-5
Raymond F Kravis Center for the Performing Arts 701 Okeechobee Blvd	West Palm Beach	FL	33401	**800-572-8471**	561-832-7469	562
Raymond James Financial Inc 880 Carillon Pkwy *NYSE: RJF*	Saint Petersburg	FL	33716	**800-248-8863**	727-573-3800	679
Raymond Vineyard & Cellar Inc 849 Zinfandel Ln	Saint Helena	CA	94574	**800-525-2659**	707-963-3141	81-3
Raynor Garage Doors 1101 E River Rd	Dixon	IL	61021	**800-472-9667**	815-288-1431	232
Rayovac Corp 601 Rayovac Dr *NYSE: ROV*	Madison	WI	53711	**800-237-7000**	608-275-3340	76
Raypak Inc 2151 Eastman Ave	Oxnard	CA	93030	**800-947-2975**	805-278-5300	352
Raytech Industries 475 Smith St *Cust Svc	Middletown	CT	06457	**800-225-9626***	860-632-2020	1
Raytek Inc 1201 Shaffer Rd Bldg 2	Santa Cruz	CA	95060	**800-227-8074**	831-458-1110	686
Raytel Medical Corp 7 Waterside Crossing	Windsor	CT	06095	**800-367-1095**	860-298-6100	376
Raytheon Aircraft Charter & Management 10225 E Kellogg	Wichita	KS	67201	**800-519-6283**		14
Raytheon Commercial Infrared 13532 N Central Expy MS 37	Dallas	TX	75243	**800-990-3275**	972-344-4000	200
Raytheon Intelligence & Information Systems 1200 S Jupiter Rd	Garland	TX	75042	**800-752-6163**	972-205-5409	519
Rayven Inc 431 Griggs St N *Cust Svc	Saint Paul	MN	55104	**800-878-3776***	651-642-1112	616
Raz Transportation 11655 SW Pacific Hwy	Portland	OR	97223	**888-684-3322**	503-684-3322	748
RBA - Retailer's Bakery Assn 14239 Park Center Dr	Laurel	MD	20707	**800-638-0924**	301-725-2149	49-6
RBC Capital Markets 1 Liberty Plaza	New York	NY	10006	**888-886-8296**	212-428-6200	679
RBC Centura 1417 Centura Hwy	Rocky Mount	NC	27804	**800-236-8872**	252-454-4400	71
RBC Centura Banks Inc 134 N Church St	Rocky Mount	NC	27804	**800-236-8872**	252-454-4400	355-2
RBC Insurance 2300 Main St Suite 450	Kansas City	MO	64108	**800-262-5433**	816-218-6500	384-2
RBC Prism 222 Merchandise Mart Plaza Suite 550	Chicago	IL	60654	**877-217-9988**	312-494-0020	498
RBC Transport Dynamics Corp 3131 W Segerstrom Ave PO Box 1953	Santa Ana	CA	92704	**800-854-3922**	714-546-3131	609
RBF Consulting 14725 Alton Pkwy	Irvine	CA	92618	**800-479-3808**	949-472-3505	258
RBMA (Radiology Business Management Assn) 8001 Irvine Center Dr Suite 1060	Irvine	CA	92618	**888-224-7262**	949-340-5000	49-8
RC Fine Foods PO Box 236	Belle Mead	NJ	08502	**800-526-3953**	908-359-5500	291-11
RC Knox & Co Inc 1 Goodwin Sq 24th Fl	Hartford	CT	06103	**800-742-2765**	860-524-7600	383
R/C Modeler Magazine 144 W Sierra Madre Blvd	Sierra Madre	CA	91024	**800-523-1736**	626-355-1476	449-14
RC Musson Rubber Co Inc 1320 E Archwood Ave *Cust Svc	Akron	OH	44306	**800-321-2381***	330-773-7651	663
RC Owens Co 310 N Blythe St	Gallatin	TN	37066	**800-821-2933**	615-452-5658	741-3
RC Smith Co 14200 Southcross Dr W	Burnsville	MN	55306	**800-747-7648**	952-854-0711	281
RC Willey & Son Inc 2601 S 300 W	Salt Lake City	UT	84115	**800-444-3876**	801-461-3900	316
RCA Rubber Co 1833 E Market St	Akron	OH	44305	**800-321-2340**	330-784-1291	286
RCG Information Technology Inc 379 Thornall St 14th Fl	Edison	NJ	08837	**800-333-7816**	732-744-3500	178
RCI (Resort Condominiums International) 9998 N Michigan Rd	Carmel	IN	46032	**800-481-5738**	317-805-9000	738
RCI (Retail Confectioners International) 1807 Glenview Rd Suite 204	Glenview	IL	60025	**800-545-5381**	847-724-6120	49-6
RCI Environmental Inc PO Box 1668	Sumner	WA	98390	**800-848-3777**	253-863-5300	187-10
RCL Enterprises 200 E Bethany Dr	Allen	TX	75002	**877-275-4725**	972-390-6400	614
RCN Corp 105 Carnegie Ctr *NASDAQ: RCNI*	Princeton	NJ	08540	**800-746-4726**	609-734-3700	721
RCP Block & Brick Inc 8240 Broadway	Lemon Grove	CA	91945	**800-732-7425**	619-460-7250	181
RCR: Radio Communications Report 777 E Speer Blvd	Denver	CO	80203	**800-678-9595**	303-733-2500	449-21
RD Offutt Co PO Box 7160	Fargo	ND	58106	**877-444-7363**	701-237-6062	11-11
RDA Group 450 Enterprise Ct	Bloomfield Hills	MI	48302	**800-669-7324**	248-332-5000	458
RDI Marketing Services 9920 Carver Rd	Cincinnati	OH	45242	**800-388-7636**	513-984-5927	5
Re-Bath Corp 1055 S Country Club Dr Bldg 2	Mesa	AZ	85210	**800-426-4573**	480-844-1575	188-11
RE Chapman Co 30 N Main St	West Boylston	MA	01583	**800-727-6231**	508-835-6231	188-16
RE Lewis Refrigeration Inc 803 S Lincoln St PO Box 92	Creston	IA	50801	**800-264-0767**	641-782-8183	651
RE Michel Co Inc 1 RE Michel Dr	Glen Burnie	MD	21060	**800-283-7362**	410-760-4000	601
REA Energy Co-op Inc 75 Airport Rd	Indiana	PA	15701	**800-211-5667**	724-349-4800	244
Rea Magnet Wire Co Inc 3600 E Pontiac St	Fort Wayne	IN	46803	**800-732-9473**	260-421-7321	800
Reach Resort. Wyndham 1435 Simonton St	Key West	FL	33040	**800-996-3426**	305-296-5000	655
Reaco Battery Service Corp 17217 Rt 37	Johnston City	IL	62951	**800-957-3226**	618-983-5441	76
Read House Hotel & Suites 827 Broad St	Chattanooga	TN	37402	**800-691-1255**	423-266-4121	373
Reader's Digest Assn Inc Reader's Digest Rd *NYSE: RDA*	Pleasantville	NY	10570	**800-635-5006**	914-238-1000	623-9
Reader's Digest Magazine Reader's Digest Rd *Cust Svc	Pleasantville	NY	10570	**800-234-9000***	914-238-1000	449-11

Name / Address	City	State	Zip	Toll-Free	Phone	Class
Reader's Subscription Doubleday Select Inc 101 Park Ave 2nd Fl	New York	NY	10178	**800-321-7323**		94
Readers Wholesale Distributors Inc 1201 Naylor St	Houston	TX	77002	**800-766-0001**	713-224-8300	356
Readi-Bake Inc 361 Benigno Blvd	Bellmawr	NJ	08031	**800-852-2253**	440-237-3712	291-36
Reading Area Community College 10 S 2nd St PO Box 1706	Reading	PA	19603	**800-626-1665**	610-372-4721	160
Reading Bakery Systems 380 Old West Penn Ave	Robesonia	PA	19551	**800-693-5816**	610-693-5816	293
Reading & Berks County Visitors Bureau 352 Penn St	Reading	PA	19602	**800-443-6610**	610-375-4085	205
Reading Eagle 345 Penn St	Reading	PA	19601	**800-633-7222**	610-371-5000	522-2
Reading Is Fundamental Inc (RIF) 1825 Connecticut Ave NW Suite 400	Washington	DC	20009	**877-743-7323**	202-673-0020	48-11
Reading Rock Inc 4600 Devitt Dr	Cincinnati	OH	45246	**800-482-6466**	513-874-2345	181
Reading Truck Body Inc 10 Hancock Blvd	Reading	PA	19611	**800-458-2226**	610-775-3301	505
Reading Tube Corp PO Box 14026	Reading	PA	19612	**800-523-8263**	610-926-4141	481
Readington Farms Inc 12 Mill Rd	Whitehouse	NJ	08888	**800-426-1707**	908-534-2121	291-27
ReadMe.Doc Discount Computer Books Inc PO Box 21450	Lehigh Valley	PA	18002	**800-678-1473**	610-317-8800	96
Ready Electric Co Inc 2030 Frankfort Ave	Louisville	KY	40206	**800-536-2512**	502-893-2511	188-4
Ready Metal Mfg Co Inc 4500 W 47th St	Chicago	IL	60632	**800-638-7334**	773-376-9700	688
Ready Metal Mfg Co Inc Ready Fixtures Div 4500 W 47th St	Chicago	IL	60632	**800-638-7334**	773-376-9700	281
Ready Mix Concrete Co PO Box 27326	Raleigh	NC	27611	**800-849-0668**	919-790-1520	180
Ready.gov Naval Security Stn	Washington	DC	20528	**800-237-3239**		336-7
Reagan Ronald Presidential Library & Museum 40 Presidential Dr	Simi Valley	CA	93065	**800-410-8354**	805-577-4000	426
Real Cities Network 35 S Market St	San Jose	CA	95113	**877-732-5248**	408-938-6000	795
Real Estate Brokerage Managers. Council of 430 N Michigan Ave Suite 300	Chicago	IL	60611	**800-621-8738**	312-321-4400	49-17
Real Estate Buyer's Agent Council (REBAC) 430 N Michigan Ave	Chicago	IL	60611	**800-648-6224**	312-329-8656	49-17
Real Estate Investment Trusts. National Assn of 1875 'I' St NW Suite 600	Washington	DC	20006	**800-362-7348**	202-739-9400	49-17
Real Estate Law Report 610 Opperman Dr *Cust Svc	Eagan	MN	55123	**800-328-4880***	651-687-7000	521-7
Real Estate Management. Institute of 430 N Michigan Ave	Chicago	IL	60611	**800-837-0706**	312-329-6000	49-17
Real Estate One Inc 29630 Orchard Lake Rd	Farmington Hills	MI	48334	**800-521-0508**	248-851-2600	638
Real Goods Trading Corp 360 Interlocken Blvd Suite 300	Broomfield	CO	80021	**800-762-7325**	303-222-3600	451
Real Reel Corp Multi-Wall Corp Div 50 Taylor Dr *Cust Svc	East Providence	RI	02916	**800-992-4166***	401-434-1070	125
Real Yellow Pages Online 754 Peachtree St	Atlanta	GA	30308	**888-935-8818**	877-573-2597	623-6
Realen Homes LP 1040 Stoney Hill Rd Suite 100	Yardley	PA	19067	**800-732-5368**	215-497-0600	186
Realigent Inc 2800 Saturn Ave Suite 200	Brea	CA	92821	**800-704-9302**	714-993-4295	176-10
RealLegal.com 3025 S Parker Rd 12th Fl	Aurora	CO	80014	**888-584-9988**	303-584-9988	176-10
Realm Business Solutions Inc 13727 Noel Rd Suite 800	Dallas	TX	75240	**866-697-3256**	469-791-1000	39
RealNetworks Inc 2601 Elliott Ave Suite 1000 *NASDAQ: RNWK* ■ *Cust Svc	Seattle	WA	98121	**888-768-3248***	206-674-2700	176-8
Realtime Software Corp 950 Lee St Suite 200	Des Plaines	IL	60016	**800-323-1143**	847-803-1100	176-1
Realtor Magazine 430 N Michigan Ave 9th Fl	Chicago	IL	60610	**800-874-6500**	312-329-8458	449-5
Realtors. Arizona Assn of 255 E Osborne Rd Suite 200	Phoenix	AZ	85012	**800-426-7274**	602-248-7787	642
Realtors Assn. Arkansas 204 Executive Ct Suite 300	Little Rock	AR	72205	**888-333-2206**	501-225-2020	642
Realtors Assn. Louisiana 4639 Bennington Ave	Baton Rouge	LA	70808	**800-266-8538**	225-923-2210	642
Realtors Assn. Nebraska 145 S 56th St Suite 100	Lincoln	NE	68510	**800-777-5231**	402-323-6500	642
Realtors Assn of New Mexico 2201 Brothers Rd	Santa Fe	NM	87505	**800-224-2282**	505-982-2442	642
Realtors. Colorado Assn of 309 Inverness Way S	Englewood	CO	80112	**800-944-6550**	303-790-7099	642
Realtors. Connecticut Assn of 111 Founders Plaza 11th Fl	East Hartford	CT	06108	**800-335-4862**	860-290-6601	642
Realtors. Delaware Assn of 9 E Loockerman St Suite 315	Dover	DE	19901	**800-305-4445**	302-734-4444	642
Realtors. Idaho Assn of 1450 W Bannock St	Boise	ID	83702	**800-621-7553**	208-342-3585	642
Realtors Inc. North Carolina Assn of 4511 Weybridge Ln	Greensboro	NC	27407	**800-443-9956**	336-294-1415	642
Realtors. Iowa Assn of 1370 NW 114th St Suite 100	Clive	IA	50325	**800-532-1515**	515-453-1064	642
Realtors. Kansas Assn of 3644 SW Burlingame Rd	Topeka	KS	66611	**800-366-0069**	785-267-3610	642
Realtors. Kentucky Assn of 161 Prosperous Pl	Lexington	KY	40509	**800-264-2185**	859-263-7377	642
Realtors Land Institute 430 N Michigan Ave	Chicago	IL	60611	**800-441-5263**	312-329-8440	49-17
Realtors. Maryland Assn of 2594 Riva Rd	Annapolis	MD	21401	**800-638-6425**	410-841-6080	642
Realtors. Massachusetts Assn of 256 2nd Ave	Waltham	MA	02451	**800-725-6272**	781-890-3700	642
Realtors. Michigan Assn of 720 N Washington Ave	Lansing	MI	48906	**800-454-7842**	517-372-8890	642
Realtors. Minnesota Assn of 5750 Lincoln Dr	Edina	MN	55436	**800-862-6097**	952-935-8313	642
Realtors. Mississippi Assn of PO Box 321000	Jackson	MS	39232	**800-747-1103**	601-932-9325	642
Realtors. Missouri Assn of 2601 Bernadette Pl	Columbia	MO	65203	**800-403-0101**	573-445-8400	642
Realtors. Montana Assn of 208 N Montana Ave Suite 203	Helena	MT	59601	**800-477-1864**	406-443-4032	642
REALTORS. National Assn of 430 N Michigan Ave	Chicago	IL	60611	**800-874-6500**	312-329-8200	49-17
Realtors. Nevada Assn of 760 Margrave Dr Suite 200	Reno	NV	89502	**800-748-5526**	775-829-5911	642
Realtors. New York State Assn of 130 Washington Ave	Albany	NY	12210	**800-422-2501**	518-463-0300	642
Realtors. North Dakota Assn of 318 W Apollo Ave	Bismarck	ND	58503	**800-279-2361**	701-355-1010	642
Realtors. Oklahoma Assn of 9807 N Broadway	Oklahoma City	OK	73114	**800-375-9944**	405-848-9944	642
Realtors. Oregon Assn of 693 Chemeketa St NE	Salem	OR	97308	**800-252-9115**	503-362-3645	642
Realtors. South Carolina Assn of 3780 Fernandina Rd	Columbia	SC	29210	**800-233-6381**	803-772-5206	642
Realtors. Texas Assn of 1115 San Jacinto Blvd Suite 200	Austin	TX	78701	**800-873-9155**	512-480-8200	642
Realtors. Utah Assn of 5710 S Green St	Murray	UT	84123	**800-594-8933**	801-268-4747	642
Realtors. Vermont Assn of 148 State St	Montpelier	VT	05602	**866-248-6182**	802-229-0513	642
Realtors. Virginia Assn of 10231 Telegraph Rd	Glen Allen	VA	23059	**800-755-8271**	804-264-5033	642
Realtors. Washington Assn of 504 E 14th Ave Suite 200	Olympia	WA	98501	**800-562-6024**	360-943-3100	642
Realtors. Wyoming Assn of PO Box 2312	Casper	WY	82602	**800-676-4085**	307-237-4085	642
Realty Executives International 2398 E Camelback Rd Suite 900	Phoenix	AZ	85016	**800-252-3366**	602-957-0747	638
Realty One 6000 Rockside Woods Blvd	Cleveland	OH	44131	**877-328-2500**	216-328-2500	638
Reames Foods Inc PO Box 71159	Des Moines	IA	50325	**800-247-4194**	515-967-4254	291-31
Reason Magazine 3415 S Sepulveda Blvd Suite 400 *Cust Svc	Los Angeles	CA	90034	**888-732-7668***	310-391-2245	449-17
Reassure America Life Insurance Co PO box 360	Hartford	CT	06141	**800-323-8764**		384-2
REBAC (Real Estate Buyer's Agent Council) 430 N Michigan Ave	Chicago	IL	60611	**800-648-6224**	312-329-8656	49-17
Rebar Engineering Inc 10706 Painter Ave	Santa Fe Springs	CA	90670	**800-555-9807**	562-946-2461	188-14
Rebco Inc 1171-1225 Madison Ave	Paterson	NJ	07509	**800-777-0787**	973-684-0200	232
Rebsamen Insurance Inc 1500 Riverfront Dr	Little Rock	AR	72202	**800-542-0226**	501-661-4800	383
Rebuilding Together 1536 16th St NW	Washington	DC	20036	**800-473-4229**	202-483-9083	48-5
Recall Corp 1 Recall Ctr 180 Technology Pkwy	Norcross	GA	30092	**888-732-2556**	770-776-1200	790-1
Reciprocal of America 4200 Innslake Dr	Glen Allen	VA	23060	**800-284-8847**	804-747-8600	384-5
Recital Corp 100 Cummings Ctr Suite 318J	Beverly	MA	01915	**800-873-7443**	978-921-5594	176-2
Reckitt Benckiser Inc PO Box 225 *Cust Svc	Parsippany	NJ	07054	**800-888-0192***	973-633-3600	149
Reckson Assoc Realty Corp 225 Broadhollow Rd Suite 212 *NYSE: RA*	Melville	NY	11747	**888-732-5766**	631-694-6900	641
Reconditioned Systems Inc 444 W Fairmont Dr	Tempe	AZ	85282	**800-280-5000**	480-968-1772	314-1
Reconstructive Surgery. American Academy of Facial Plastic & 310 S Henry St	Alexandria	VA	22314	**800-332-3223**	703-299-9291	49-8
Record The 530 E Market St	Stockton	CA	95201	**800-606-9741**	209-943-6397	522-2
Record-Argus 10 Penn Ave	Greenville	PA	16125	**800-542-3100**	724-588-5000	522-2
Record-Courier 126 N Chestnut St PO Box 1201	Ravenna	OH	44266	**800-560-9657**	330-296-9657	522-2
Record Herald 138 S Fayette St	Washington Court House	OH	43160	**800-200-4968**	740-335-3611	522-2
Record Search America Inc 5527 Kendall St	Boise	ID	83706	**866-865-8003**	208-375-1906	621
Recorder & Times 1600 California Ave	Brockville	ON	K6V5T8	**800-267-4434**	613-342-4441	522-1
Recording Academy 3402 Pico Blvd	Santa Monica	CA	90405	**800-423-2017**	310-392-3777	48-4
Recording Arts & Sciences. National Academy of 3402 Pico Blvd	Santa Monica	CA	90405	**800-423-2017**	310-392-3777	48-4
Recording for the Blind & Dyslexic (RFB&D) 20 Roszel Rd	Princeton	NJ	08540	**800-221-4792**	609-452-0606	48-17
Recording Industry Assn of America Inc (RIAA) 1330 Connecticut Ave NW Suite 300	Washington	DC	20036	**800-223-2328**	202-775-0101	48-4
Records & Information Services Management International. Professional 605 Benson Rd Suite B	Garner	NC	27529	**800-336-9793**	919-771-0657	49-12
Recortec Inc 1620 Berryessa Rd Suite A	San Jose	CA	95133	**888-732-6783**	408-928-1480	171-3
Recovery. Rational PO Box 800	Lotus	CA	95651	**800-303-2873**	530-621-2667	48-21
Recovery's Unlimited Inc PO Box 1349	Melville	NY	11747	**800-507-4275**	516-222-1200	157
Recreation. American Assn for Leisure & 1900 Association Dr	Reston	VA	20191	**800-213-7193**	703-476-3400	48-23
Recreation Creation Inc 215 W Mechanic St *Cust Svc	Hillsdale	MI	49242	**800-766-9458***	517-439-1591	340
Recreation & Park Assn. National 22377 Belmont Ridge Rd	Ashburn	VA	20148	**800-626-6772**	703-858-0784	48-23
Recreation Society. American Park & c/o National Recreation & Park Assn 22377 Belmont Ridge Rd	Ashburn	VA	20148	**800-626-6772**	703-858-4741	48-23
Recreation Vehicle Industry Assn (RVIA) 1896 Preston White Dr	Reston	VA	20191	**800-336-0154**	703-620-6003	49-21
Recreational Equipment Inc (REI) 6750 S 228th St *Orders	Kent	WA	98032	**800-426-4840***	253-395-3780	702

Name / Address	City	State	ZIP	Toll-Free	Phone	Class
Recreational Vehicle Club. Good Sam PO Box 6888	Englewood	CO	80155	**800-234-3450**		48-23
Recreational Vehicle Owners Club. National PO Box 520	Gonzalez	FL	32560	**800-281-9186**	850-937-8354	48-23
Recreatives Industries Inc 60 Depot St	Buffalo	NY	14206	**800-255-2511**	716-855-2226	30
Recruiters. Association of Staff Physician 1711 W County Rd B Suite 300N	Roseville	MN	55113	**800-830-2777**	651-635-0359	49-8
Recruiters. National Assn of Physician PO Box 150127	Altamonte Springs	FL	32715	**800-726-5613**	407-774-7880	49-8
Recruiters OnLine Network Inc (RON) 947 Essex Ln	Medina	OH	44256	**888-364-4667**		257
Recruiting Trends Newsletter 1 Phoenix Mill Ln 3rd FL	Peterborough	NH	03458	**800-531-0007**	603-924-0900	521-2
Recycled Paper Greetings Inc 3636 N Broadway *Cust Svc	Chicago	IL	60613	**800-777-9494***	773-348-6410	130
Recycled Plastic Products Inc 1600 W Evans Ave Unit J	Englewood	CO	80110	**800-235-7940**	303-975-0033	647
Red Alert Bio-Response Service Inc PO Box 941629	Houston	TX	77094	**800-570-1833**	281-993-0016	84
Red Bluff Daily News 545 Diamond Ave	Red Bluff	CA	96080	**800-497-6397**	530-527-2151	522-2
Red Bridge Interactive Inc 2 Richmond Sq Suite 113K	Providence	RI	02906	**877-367-4676**	401-223-1141	176-7
Red Bud Industries 200 B & E Industrial Dr	Red Bud	IL	62278	**800-851-4612**	618-282-3801	485
Red Carpet Charters PO Box 94626	Oklahoma City	OK	73143	**888-878-5100**	405-672-5100	108
Red Carpet Inn 1726 Montreal Cir.	Tucker	GA	30084	**800-251-1962**	770-270-1180	369
Red Devil Inc 2400 Vauxhall Rd	Union	NJ	07083	**800-423-3845**	908-688-6900	3
Red Diamond Inc PO Box 2168	Birmingham	AL	35201	**800-292-4651**	205-254-3138	291-7
RED Distribution 79 5th Ave 15th Fl	New York	NY	10003	**800-733-1966**	212-404-0600	512
Red Dot Corp 1209 W Corsicana St *Cust Svc	Athens	TX	75751	**800-657-2234***	903-675-9181	106
Red Farm Studio Co Inc 1135 Roosevelt Ave	Pawtucket	RI	02862	**800-556-7090**	401-728-9300	130
Red Hat Inc 1801 Varsity Dr *NASDAQ: RHAT*	Raleigh	NC	27606	**888-733-4281**	919-754-3700	176-12
Red Hot & Blue Restaurants Inc 1701 Clarendon Blvd Suite 105	Arlington	VA	22209	**800-723-0745**	703-276-8833	657
Red Jacket Div Veeder-Root 125 Powder Forest Dr	Simsbury	CT	06070	**800-873-3313**	860-651-2700	627
Red Kap Industries Inc 545 Marriott Dr Suite 200	Nashville	TN	37214	**800-733-5271**	615-565-5000	153-19
Red Lake Electric Co-op Inc 412 International Dr SW PO Box 43	Red Lake Falls	MN	56750	**800-245-6068**	218-253-2168	244
Red Lake Gaming Enterprises Inc PO Box 543	Red Lake	MN	56671	**800-568-6649**	218-679-2111	132
Red Lion Hotels Inc 201 W North River Dr Suite 100	Spokane	WA	99201	**800-325-4000**	509-459-6100	369
Red Lion Templin's Hotel on the River 414 E 1st Ave	Post Falls	ID	83854	**800-733-5466**	208-773-1611	655
Red Mountain Spa 1275 E Red Mountain Cir.	Ivins	UT	84738	**800-407-3002**	435-673-4905	697
Red River Commodities Inc 501 42nd St NW	Fargo	ND	58102	**800-437-5539**	701-282-2600	684
Red River Mfg Inc 202 8th St W	West Fargo	ND	58078	**800-762-5557**	701-282-3013	768
Red River Valley Rural Electric Assn 1003 Memorial Dr	Marietta	OK	73448	**800-749-3364**	580-276-3364	244
Red Roof Inns Inc 4001 International Pkwy	Carrollton	TX	75007	**800-733-7663**	972-360-9000	369
Red Sail Sports Inc 1 Ferry Bldg Suite 255	San Francisco	CA	94111	**877-733-7245**	415-981-4411	748
Red Simpson Inc PO Box 12120	Alexandria	LA	71315	**800-737-4733**	318-487-1074	188-4
Red Star Bioproducts 5600 W Raymond St	Indianapolis	IN	46241	**800-445-0073**	317-243-3521	291-42
Red Wing Shoe Co Inc 314 Main St *Cust Svc	Red Wing	MN	55066	**800-733-9464***	651-388-8211	296
Red Wing Software Inc 491 Hwy 19	Red Wing	MN	55066	**800-732-9464**	651-388-1106	176-1
REDA PO Box 1181	Bartlesville	OK	74005	**800-331-0970**	918-661-2000	627
Redback Networks Inc 300 Holger Way *NASDAQ: RBAK*	San Jose	CA	95134	**866-727-5400**	408-750-5000	720
Redback Networks Systems Canada Inc 4190 Still Creek Dr Suite 200	Burnaby	BC	V5C6C6	**877-922-2847**	604-629-7000	720
Redbook Magazine 224 W 57th St	New York	NY	10019	**800-888-0008**	212-649-2000	449-11
Redco Foods Inc 1 Hansen Island	Little Falls	NY	13365	**800-556-6674**	315-823-1300	291-40
Redding Civic Auditorium 777 Auditorium Dr	Redding	CA	96001	**888-225-4130**	530-225-4130	562
Redding Convention & Visitors Bureau 777 Auditorium Dr	Redding	CA	96001	**800-874-7562**	530-225-4100	205
Reddy Ice & Cassco Refrigerated Services PO Box 548	Harrisonburg	VA	22801	**800-999-4231**	540-433-2751	790-2
Reddy Ice Ltd 8450 N Central Expy Suite 1800	Dallas	TX	75231	**800-683-4423**	214-526-6740	374
Redeemer University College 777 Garner Rd E	Ancaster	ON	L9K1J4	**877-779-0913**	905-648-2131	773
RedEnvelope Inc 149 New Montgomery St *NASDAQ: REDE*	San Francisco	CA	94105	**877-733-3683**	415-371-9100	322
Redevelopment Officials. National Assn of Housing & 630 'I' St NW	Washington	DC	20001	**877-866-2476**	202-289-3500	49-7
Redfish America LLC 5050 N 40th St Suite 200	Phoenix	AZ	85018	**888-677-5080**	602-852-9000	657
Redico Inc 943 Buford Hwy	Buford	GA	30518	**800-242-3920**	770-614-1401	651
Redken Laboratories Inc 575 5th Ave *Cust Svc	New York	NY	10017	**800-423-5280***	212-818-1500	211
Redlake MASD Inc 5295 Ferris Sq Suite A	San Diego	CA	92121	**800-453-1223**	858-481-8182	580
Redland Brick Inc 15718 Clear Spring Rd	Williamsport	MD	21795	**800-366-2742**	301-223-7700	148
Redlands Community College 1300 S Country Club Rd	El Reno	OK	73036	**866-415-6367**	405-262-2552	160
Redlands Daily Facts 700 Brookside Ave	Redlands	CA	92373	**800-922-0922**	909-793-3221	522-2
Redlon & Johnson 172-174 Saint John St	Portland	ME	04102	**800-905-5250**	207-773-4755	601
Redmont. Crowne Plaza Hotel Birmingham-The 2101 5th Ave N	Birmingham	AL	35203	**800-227-6963**	205-324-2101	373
RedPrairie Corp 20700 Swenson Dr Suite 200	Waukesha	WI	53186	**800-990-2632**	262-317-2000	176-1
Red's Market Inc 8801 Exchange Dr	Orlando	FL	32809	**800-226-3930**	407-857-3930	292-7
RedSiren Inc 650 Smithfield St Suite 910	Pittsburgh	PA	15222	**877-360-7602**	412-281-4427	174
Redstone Federal Credit Union 220 Wynn Dr NW	Huntsville	AL	35893	**800-234-1234**	256-837-6110	216
Redstone Inn 82 Redstone Blvd	Redstone	CO	81623	**800-748-2524**	970-963-2526	373
Redwood Assn. California 405 Enfrente Dr Suite 200	Novato	CA	94949	**888-225-7339**	415-382-0662	48-2
Redwood Electric Co-op 60 Pine St	Clements	MN	56224	**888-251-5100**	507-692-2214	244
Redwood Painting Co Inc 620 W 10th St	Pittsburg	CA	94565	**800-227-0622**	925-432-4500	188-8
Redwood Terrace 710 W 13th Ave *Mktg	Escondido	CA	92025	**800-842-6775***	760-747-4306	659
Redwoods League. Save-the- 114 Sansome St Rm 1200	San Francisco	CA	94104	**888-836-0005**	415-362-2352	48-13
Reebok International Ltd 1895 JW Foster Blvd *NYSE: RBK*	Canton	MA	02021	**800-843-4444**	781-401-5000	296
Reed & Barton Silversmiths Corp 144 W Britannia St	Taunton	MA	02780	**800-822-1824**	508-824-6611	693
Reed Business Information 100 Enterprise Dr Suite 600	Rockaway	NJ	07866	**800-446-6551**	973-920-7000	623-9
Reed College 3203 SE Woodstock Blvd	Portland	OR	97202	**800-547-4750**	503-771-1112	163
Reed Conner & Birdwell Inc 11111 Santa Monica Blvd Suite 1700	Los Angeles	CA	90025	**877-478-4722**	310-478-4005	393
Reed Elsevier Inc 121 Chanlon Rd	New Providence	NJ	07974	**800-526-4902**	908-464-6800	623-2
Reed Exhibitions 275 Washington St	Newton	MA	02458	**800-732-2914**	617-630-2260	183
Reed Mfg Co 1425 W 8th St	Erie	PA	16502	**800-666-3691**	814-452-3691	746
Reed Mfg Co Inc 1321 S Veterans Blvd	Tupelo	MS	38801	**800-647-1280**	662-842-4472	153-11
Reed-Rico Div PCC Specialty Products Inc 18 Industrial Dr *Cust Svc	Holden	MA	01520	**800-343-6068***	508-829-4491	448
Reed's 129-131 W Main St	Tupelo	MS	38804	**800-627-3337**	662-842-6453	227
Reeds Jewelers Inc 2525 S 17th St *Orders	Wilmington	NC	28401	**877-406-3266***	910-350-3100	402
Reef Brazil 9660 Chesapeake Dr	San Diego	CA	92123	**800-423-6855**	858-514-3600	296
Reef Resort 2101 S Ocean Blvd	Myrtle Beach	SC	29577	**800-845-1212**	843-448-1765	655
Reelcraft Industries Inc 1 Reelcraft Ctr PO Box 248	Columbia City	IN	46725	**800-444-3134**	260-248-8188	118
Reese Enterprises Inc 16350 Asher Ave	Rosemount	MN	55068	**800-328-0953**	651-423-1126	232
Reese HB Candy Co 925 Reese Ave *Cust Svc	Hershey	PA	17033	**800-468-1714***	717-534-4106	291-8
Reese Pharmaceutical Co PO Box 1957	Cleveland	OH	44106	**800-321-7178**	216-231-6441	237
Reese Products Inc 2602 College Ave	Goshen	IN	46528	**800-326-1090**	574-537-6800	751
Reese Teleservices Inc 925 Penn Ave	Pittsburgh	PA	15222	**800-365-3500**	412-355-0800	722
Reeve Store Equipment Co 9131 Bermudez St PO Box 276	Pico Rivera	CA	90660	**800-927-3383**	562-949-2535	281
Refco Inc 550 W Jackson Blvd Suite 1300	Chicago	IL	60661	**800-365-9310**	312-788-2000	167
Reference & User Services Assn (RUSA) 50 E Huron St	Chicago	IL	60611	**800-545-2433**	312-280-4398	49-11
Referral Agencies. National Assn of Child Care Resource & 1319 F St NW Suite 500	Washington	DC	20004	**800-424-2246**	202-393-5501	48-6
Reflexite North America 315 South St	New Britain	CT	06051	**800-654-7570**	860-223-9297	666
Reform Now. Association of Community Organizations for 739 8th St SE	Washington	DC	20003	**877-552-2676**	202-547-2500	48-7
Reformed Bible College 3333 East Beltline Ave NE	Grand Rapids	MI	49525	**800-511-3749**	616-222-3000	163
Reformed Church in America 475 Riverside Dr 18th Fl	New York	NY	10115	**800-722-9977**	212-870-3071	48-20
Reformed Theological Seminary 5422 Clinton Blvd	Jackson	MS	39209	**800-543-2703**	601-923-1600	164-3
Refractive Surgery. American Society of Cataract & 4000 Legato Rd Suite 850	Fairfax	VA	22033	**800-451-1339**	703-591-2220	49-8
Refrigerated Food Express Inc PO Box 347	Avon	MA	02322	**800-225-2350**	508-587-4600	769
Refrigerating & Air-Conditioning Engineers Inc. American Society of Heating 1791 Tullie Cir NE *Cust Svc	Atlanta	GA	30329	**800-527-4723***	404-636-8400	49-3
Refrigeration Distributors International. Heating Airconditioning & 1389 Dublin Rd	Columbus	OH	43215	**888-253-2128**	614-488-1835	49-18
Refrigeration Research Inc 525 N 5th St	Brighton	MI	48116	**800-311-8469**	810-227-1151	15
Refrigeration Service Engineers Society (RSES) 1666 Rand Rd	Des Plaines	IL	60016	**800-297-5660**	847-297-6464	49-3
RefrigiWear Inc 54 Breakstone Dr *Cust Svc	Dahlonega	GA	30533	**800-645-3744***	706-864-5757	153-5
Refron Inc 38-18 33rd St	Long Island City	NY	11101	**800-473-3766**	718-392-8002	651
Reftech Div RENO Refractories Inc 601 Reno Dr	Morris	AL	35116	**800-741-7366**		649
Refugee Committee. American 430 Oak Grove St Suite 204	Minneapolis	MN	55403	**800-875-7060**	612-872-7060	48-5
Refugees International (RI) 1705 'N' St NW	Washington	DC	20036	**800-733-8433**	202-828-0110	48-5
Regal-Beloit Corp Electra-Gear Div 1110 N Anaheim Blvd	Anaheim	CA	92801	**800-877-4327**	714-535-6061	700

Name / Address	City	State	ZIP	Toll-Free	Phone	Class
Regal Entertainment Group 7132 Regal Ln *NYSE: RGC*	Knoxville	TN	37918	**877-835-5734**	865-922-1123	733
Regal Kitchens Inc 8600 NW South River Dr	Miami	FL	33166	**800-432-0731**	305-885-0111	116
Regal Marine Industries Inc 2300 Jetport Dr	Orlando	FL	32809	**800-877-3425**	407-851-4360	91
Regal Mfg Co 900 S Ajax Ave	City of Industry	CA	91748	**800-582-3092**	626-964-6534	804
Regal Plastic Supply Co 111 E 10th Ave	North Kansas City	MO	64116	**800-627-2102**	816-421-6290	592
Regal Plastic Supply Co Southern Div 2356 Merrell Rd	Dallas	TX	75229	**800-441-1553**	972-484-0741	592
Regal Travel 720 Iwilei Rd Suite 101	Honolulu	HI	96817	**800-817-9920**	808-566-7000	760
Regalia Mfg Co PO Box 4448	Rock Island	IL	61204	**800-798-7471**	309-788-7471	766
Regence Blue Cross Blue Shield of Oregon PO Box 1271	Portland	OR	97207	**800-547-0939**	503-225-5364	384-3
Regence Blue Shield 1800 9th Ave	Seattle	WA	98101	**800-544-4246**	206-464-3600	384-3
Regence Blue Shield of Idaho 1602 21st Ave	Lewiston	ID	83501	**800-632-2022**	208-746-2671	384-3
Regence BlueCross BlueShield of Utah 2890 E Cottonwood Pkwy **Cust Svc*	Salt Lake City	UT	84121	**800-624-6519***	801-333-2100	384-3
Regency Centers 121 W Forsyth St Suite 200 *NYSE: REG*	Jacksonville	FL	32202	**800-950-6333**	904-356-7000	641
Regency Electric 4348 Southpoint Blvd Suite 400	Jacksonville	FL	32216	**877-309-0204**	904-281-0600	188-4
Regency Fairbanks Hotel 95 10th Ave	Fairbanks	AK	99701	**800-348-1340**	907-452-3200	373
Regency House Hotel 140 Rt 23 N	Pompton Plains	NJ	07444	**800-696-0304**	973-696-0900	373
Regency House Natural Health Spa 2000 S Ocean Dr	Hallandale Beach	FL	33009	**800-454-0003**	954-454-2220	697
Regency Inn & Suites 3450 S Clack St	Abilene	TX	79606	**800-676-7262**	325-695-7700	373
Regency Lighting Co 16665 Arminta St	Van Nuys	CA	91406	**800-284-2024**	818-901-0255	245
Regency Limousine International 23-57 83rd St	East Elmhurst	NY	11370	**866-754-5466**	718-507-4000	433
Regency Savings Bank 24 N Washington St	Naperville	IL	60540	**800-933-0298**	630-357-4500	71
Regency Suites Calgary 610 4th Ave SW	Calgary	AB	T2P0K1	**800-468-4044**	403-231-1000	372
Regency Suites Green Bay 333 Main St	Green Bay	WI	54301	**800-236-3330**	920-432-4555	373
Regency Suites Hotel Midtown Atlanta 975 W Peachtree St	Atlanta	GA	30309	**800-642-3629**	404-876-5003	373
Regeneration Technologies Inc 11621 Research Cir *NASDAQ: RTIX*	Alachua	FL	32615	**877-343-6832**	386-418-8888	86
Regeneron Pharmaceuticals Inc 777 Old Saw Mill River Rd *NASDAQ: REGN*	Tarrytown	NY	10591	**800-637-8322**	914-347-7000	86
Regent Assisted Living Inc 121 SW Morrison St Suite 1000	Portland	OR	97204	**888-853-7468**	503-227-4000	442
Regent College 5800 University Blvd	Vancouver	BC	V6T2E4	**800-663-8664**	604-224-3245	164-3
Regional Hospital of Jackson 367 Hospital Blvd	Jackson	TN	38305	**800-454-9970**	731-661-2000	366-2
Regional Information & Communication Exchange Rice University Library 6100 S Main St MS 240	Houston	TX	77005	**800-359-7030**	713-348-3553	380
Regional Jet Center 12344 Tower Dr	Bentonville	AR	72712	**866-962-3835**	479-205-1100	63
Regional Medical Center 900 Hospital Dr	Madisonville	KY	42431	**800-998-5100**	270-825-5100	366-2
Regional Medical Center of Orangeburg & Calhoun Counties 3000 Saint Matthews Rd	Orangeburg	SC	29118	**800-476-3377**	803-395-2200	366-2
Regional Recycling LLC 897 Adamson St SW **Cust Svc*	Atlanta	GA	30315	**800-800-6733***	404-332-1750	674
Regional Tissue Bank QEII Health Sciences 5788 University Ave Rm 431 McKenzie Bldg Ctr	Halifax	NS	B3H1V7	**800-314-6515**	902-473-7360	535
Regional Transportation District (RTD) 1600 Blake St	Denver	CO	80202	**800-877-7433**	303-628-9000	460
Regions Bank 417 20th St N	Birmingham	AL	35202	**800-765-6530**	205-326-7100	71
Regions Financial Corp 417 N 20th St *NYSE: RF*	Birmingham	AL	35203	**800-734-4667**	205-326-7100	355-2
Regions Hospital 640 Jackson St	Saint Paul	MN	55101	**800-332-5720**	651-254-3456	366-2
Regions Mortgage Inc 605 S Perry St	Montgomery	AL	36104	**800-392-5669**	334-223-3701	498
Regis College 235 Wellesley St	Weston	MA	02493	**866-438-7344**	781-768-7000	163
Regis Corp 7201 Metro Blvd *NYSE: RGS*	Minneapolis	MN	55439	**888-888-7778**	952-947-7777	79
Regis Corp Cost Cutters Family Hair Care Div 7201 Metro Blvd	Minneapolis	MN	55439	**888-888-7778**	952-947-7777	79
Regis Corp MasterCuts Div 7201 Metro Blvd	Minneapolis	MN	55439	**888-888-7778**	952-947-7777	79
Regis Corp Regis Hairstylists Div 7201 Metro Blvd	Minneapolis	MN	55439	**888-888-7778**	952-947-7777	79
Regis Corp SmartStyle Div 7201 Metro Blvd	Minneapolis	MN	55439	**888-888-7778**	952-947-7777	79
Regis Corp Supercuts Div 7201 Metro Blvd	Minneapolis	MN	55439	**888-888-7778**	952-947-7777	79
Regis Corp Trade Secret Div 7201 Metro Blvd	Minneapolis	MN	55439	**888-888-7778**	952-947-7777	79
Regis Hairstylists Div Regis Corp 7201 Metro Blvd	Minneapolis	MN	55439	**888-888-7778**	952-947-7777	79
Regis University 3333 Regis Blvd	Denver	CO	80221	**800-568-8932**	303-458-4100	163
Regis University 1501 Academy Ct	Fort Collins	CO	80524	**800-390-0891**	970-472-2200	163
Colorado Springs 7450 Campus Dr	Colorado Springs	CO	80920	**800-568-8932**		163
Register-Herald 801 N Kanawha St	Beckley	WV	25801	**800-950-0250**	304-255-4400	522-2
Register-Mail 140 S Prairie St PO Box 310	Galesburg	IL	61401	**800-747-7181**	309-343-7181	522-2
Register-Star 364 Warren St	Hudson	NY	12534	**800-836-4069**	518-828-1616	522-2
Register.com Inc 575 8th Ave 11th Fl *NASDAQ: RCOM*	New York	NY	10018	**800-899-9703**	212-798-9100	389
Registry Resort 475 Seagate Dr	Naples	FL	34103	**800-247-9810**	239-597-3232	655
Regnery Publishing Inc 1 Massachusetts Ave NW	Washington	DC	20001	**800-462-6420**	202-216-0600	623-2
Regulations.gov Government Printing Office	Washington	DC	20401	**888-293-6498**		196
Regulatory Risk Monitor 11300 Rockville Pike Suite 1100	Rockville	MD	20852	**800-929-4824**	301-816-8950	521-1
Rehab Plus Therapeutics Products Inc 105 Industrial Dr	Levelland	TX	79336	**800-288-8059**	806-791-2288	469
RehabCare Group Inc 7733 Forsyth Blvd Suite 2300 *NYSE: RHB*	Saint Louis	MO	63105	**800-677-1238**	314-863-7422	347
Rehabilitation Assn. National 633 S Washington St	Alexandria	VA	22314	**888-258-4295**	703-836-0850	48-17
Rehabilitation Engineering. National Institute for PO Box T	Hewitt	NJ	07421	**800-736-2216**	973-853-6585	48-17
Rehabilitation Facilities. Commission on Accreditation of 4891 E Grant Rd	Tucson	AZ	85712	**888-281-6531**	520-325-1044	48-1
Rehabilitation Hospital of Indiana 4141 Shore Dr	Indianapolis	IN	46254	**800-933-0123**	317-329-2000	366-4
Rehabilitation Hospital of the Pacific Inc 226 N Kuakini St	Honolulu	HI	96817	**800-973-4226**	808-531-3511	366-4
Rehabilitation Information Center. National 4200 Forbes Blvd Suite 202	Lanham	MD	20706	**800-346-2742**	301-459-5900	48-17
Rehabilitation Institute of Chicago 345 E Superior St **Admitting*	Chicago	IL	60611	**800-354-7342***	312-238-1000	366-4
Rehabilitation Providers Assn. American Medical 1710 'N' St NW	Washington	DC	20036	**888-346-4624**	202-223-1920	49-8
RehabWorks Inc 103 Corporate Dr E	Langhorne	PA	19047	**800-563-1103**	215-504-5100	707
Rehau Inc PO Box 1706	Leesburg	VA	20177	**800-247-9445**	703-777-5255	233
Rehoboth Beach-Dewey Beach Chamber of Commerce 501 Rehoboth Ave	Rehoboth Beach	DE	19971	**800-441-1329**	302-227-2233	137
Rehrig Pacific Co 4010 E 26th St	Los Angeles	CA	90023	**800-421-6244**	323-262-5145	198
REI (Recreational Equipment Inc) 6750 S 228th St **Orders*	Kent	WA	98032	**800-426-4840***	253-395-3780	702
REI Adventures PO Box 1938	Sumner	WA	98390	**800-622-2236**	253-437-1100	748
Reichhold Inc 2400 Ellis Rd	Durham	NC	27703	**800-448-3482**	919-990-7500	594-2
Reid State Technical College I-65 & Hwy 83 PO Box 588	Evergreen	AL	36401	**866-578-1313**	251-578-1313	787
Reid Tool Supply Co Inc 2265 Black Creek Rd **Sales*	Muskegon	MI	49444	**800-253-0421***	231-777-3951	346
Reidler Decal Corp 1 Reidler Rd	Saint Clair	PA	17970	**800-628-7770**	570-429-1812	404
Reiff & Nestor Co PO Box 147	Lykens	PA	17048	**800-521-3422**	717-453-7113	484
Reilly Industries Inc 300 N Meridian St **Admitting*	Indianapolis	IN	46204	**800-888-3536***	317-247-8141	142
Reilly Mortgage Group Inc 2010 Corporate Ridge Suite 1000	McLean	VA	22102	**877-724-7792**	703-760-4700	498
Reily Electric Supply Inc 3011 Lausat St	Metairie	LA	70001	**800-662-1906**	504-835-8888	245
Reily William B & Co Inc 640 Magazine St	New Orleans	LA	70130	**800-535-1961**	504-524-6131	291-19
Reiman Publications 5400 S 60th St	Greendale	WI	53129	**800-344-6913**	414-423-0100	623-9
Reimers Electra Steam Inc PO Box 37	Clear Brook	VA	22624	**800-872-7562**	540-662-3811	352
Reindl Bindery Co Inc 111 E Reindl Way	Glendale	WI	53212	**800-878-1121**	414-906-1111	93
Reinhardt College 7300 Reinhardt College Cir	Waleska	GA	30183	**877-346-4273**	770-720-5600	163
Reinhart Boerner Van Deuren SC 1000 N Water St Suite 2100	Milwaukee	WI	53202	**800-553-6215**	414-298-1000	419
Reinhart FoodService Inc 1500 Saint James St	La Crosse	WI	54603	**800-827-4010**	608-782-2660	292-8
Reinsurance Assn of America (RAA) 1301 Pennsylvania Ave NW Suite 900	Washington	DC	20004	**800-638-3651**	202-638-3690	49-9
Reinsurance Group of America Inc 1370 Timberlake Manor Pkwy *NYSE: RGA*	Chesterfield	MO	63017	**888-736-5445**	636-736-7000	355-4
Reis Inc 5 W 37th St 12th Fl	New York	NY	10018	**800-366-7347**	212-921-1122	458
Reiter Dairy Inc 1415 W Waterloo Rd	Akron	OH	44314	**800-362-0825**	330-745-1123	292-4
Rejuvenation Inc 1100 SE Grand	Portland	OR	97214	**888-401-1900**	503-231-1900	431
Relais & Chateaux Assn 148 E 63 St	New York	NY	10012	**800-735-2478**	212-319-4880	48-23
Relais International 1690 Woodward Dr Suite 215	Ottawa	ON	K2C3R8	**888-294-5244**	613-226-5571	176-12
Relational Technology Services 7720 Rivers Edge Dr Suite 200	Columbus	OH	43235	**866-999-4787**	614-431-4433	261-1
Relax The Back Corp 15901 Hawthorne Blvd Suite 401	Lawndale	CA	90260	**800-222-5728**		305
Relco Locomotives Inc 113 Industrial Dr	Minooka	IL	60447	**800-435-6091**	815-467-3030	261-6
Reliability Society. IEEE IEEE Operations Ctr 445 Hoes Ln	Piscataway	NJ	08854	**800-678-4333**	732-981-0060	49-19
Reliable Automotive 10600 Mastin St **Cust Svc*	Overland Park	KS	66212	**800-521-9901***	913-894-9090	61
Reliable Corp 150 E Pierce Rd **Cust Svc*	Itasca	IL	60143	**800-359-5000***	630-438-8888	523
Reliable of Milwaukee Inc 233 E Chicago St PO Box 563	Milwaukee	WI	53201	**800-336-6876**	414-272-5084	153-18
Reliable Tire Co 805 N Blackhorse Pike PO Box 39	Blackwood	NJ	08012	**800-342-3426**	856-232-0700	740
Reliable Tractor Inc PO Box 808	Tifton	GA	31793	**800-255-4401**	229-382-4400	270
Reliable Trucking Inc 5141 Commercial Cir	Concord	CA	94520	**800-952-3344**	925-681-6500	769

Name / Address	City	State	Zip	Toll-Free	Phone	Class
RELIAGENE Technologies Inc 5525 Mounes St Suite 101	New Orleans	LA	70123	**800-256-4106**	504-734-9700	408
Reliance Color Labs Inc PO Box 3640	Hampton Park	MD	20791	**800-332-6567**		577
Reliance Medical Products Inc 3535 Kings Mills Rd	Mason	OH	45040	**800-735-0357**	513-398-3937	314-3
Reliance Standard Life Insurance 2001 Market St Suite 1500	Philadelphia	PA	19103	**800-351-7500**	267-256-3500	384-2
Reliance Steel & Aluminum Co Bralco Metals Div 15090 Northam St	La Mirada	CA	90638	**800-628-1864**	714-736-4800	483
Reliance Trading Corp of America 2222 W 138th St	Blue Island	IL	60406	**800-782-7673**	708-597-2300	288
Reliance Trailer Mfg Co 7911 Redwood Dr	Cotati	CA	94931	**800-339-7911**	707-795-0081	768
Reliance Upholstery Supply Co 15902 S Main St	Gardena	CA	90248	**800-522-5252**	323-321-2300	730-6
Reliance Well Service PO Box 787	Magnolia	AR	71754	**800-458-6451**	870-234-2700	529
Reliant Energy Inc PO Box 4932 *NYSE: RRI*	Houston	TX	77210	**866-872-6646**	713-497-3000	774
Reliant Glass & Door Systems LLC 3208 Washington Ave	Sheboygan	WI	53081	**800-234-7432**	920-458-4611	188-6
Relief Agency International. Adventist Development & 12501 Old Columbia Pike	Silver Spring	MD	20904	**800-424-2372**	301-680-6380	48-5
Relief Committee. Christian Reformed World 2850 Kalamazoo Ave SE	Grand Rapids	MI	49560	**800-552-7972**	616-224-0740	48-5
Relief & Development. Episcopal 815 2nd Ave	New York	NY	10017	**800-334-7626**		48-5
Relief International. Direct 27 S La Patera Ln	Santa Barbara	CA	93117	**800-676-1638**	805-964-4767	48-5
Relief. Lutheran World 700 Light St	Baltimore	MD	21230	**800-597-5972**	410-230-2700	48-5
Relief Services. Catholic 209 W Fayette St	Baltimore	MD	21201	**800-235-2772**	410-625-2220	48-5
Relief Services. Christian 2550 Huntington Ave Suite 200	Alexandria	VA	22303	**800-337-3543**	703-317-9086	48-5
Relief Society. Navy-Marine Corps 4015 Wilson Blvd 10th Fl	Arlington	VA	22203	**800-654-8364**	703-696-4904	48-19
Relief. United Methodist Committee on 475 Riverside Dr Suite 330	New York	NY	10115	**800-554-8583**	212-870-3814	48-5
Religion News Service 1101 Connecticut Ave NW Suite 350	Washington	DC	20036	**800-767-6781**	202-463-8777	520
Religious Liberty. Becket Fund for 1350 Connecticut Ave NW Suite 605	Washington	DC	20036	**800-232-5385**	202-955-0095	48-8
Religious Science International (RSI) 901 E 2nd Ave Suite 301	Spokane	WA	99202	**800-662-1348**	509-624-7000	48-20
Reliv International Inc 136 Chesterfield Industrial Blvd *NASDAQ: RELV*	Chesterfield	MO	63005	**800-735-4887**	636-537-9715	361
Relizon Co 220 E Monument Ave	Dayton	OH	45402	**866-789-8999**	937-228-5000	111
RELM Wireless Corp 7100 Technology Dr *Cust Svc	West Melbourne	FL	32904	**800-422-6281***	321-984-1414	633
Relo & Mobility Management 161 N Clark St Suite 1250	Chicago	IL	60601	**800-621-6510**	312-424-0400	652
Relocation America 25800 Northwestern Hwy Suite 210 *Cust Svc	Southfield	MI	48075	**800-521-0508***	248-208-2900	652
Relocation Council. Employee 1717 Pennsylvania Ave NW Suite 800	Washington	DC	20006	**888-372-2255**	202-857-0857	49-12
Relton Corp PO Box 60019 *Cust Svc	Arcadia	CA	91066	**800-423-1505***	626-446-8201	746
Rem Sales Inc 34 Bradley Park Rd	East Granby	CT	06026	**800-808-1020**	860-653-0071	378
Remacor Inc PO Box 366 Rt 168	West Pittsburg	PA	16160	**800-422-2366**	724-535-4357	476
Re/MAX Equity Group Inc 84505 SW Nimbus Ave	Beaverton	OR	97008	**800-283-3358**	503-670-3000	638
RE/MAX International Inc 8390 E Crescent Pkwy Suite 500 *Cust Svc	Greenwood Village	CO	80111	**800-525-7452***	303-770-5531	638
Re/MAX International Relocation Services Inc 8390 E Crescent Pkwy Suite 500	Greenwood Village	CO	80111	**800-442-3501**	303-770-5531	652
RE/MAX Ontario-Atlantic 7101 Syntex Dr	Mississauga	ON	L5N6H5	**888-542-2499**	905-542-2400	638
RE/MAX of Western Canada Inc 1664 Richter St Suite 213	Kelowna	BC	V1Y8N3	**800-563-3622**	250-860-3628	638
Remedy Temp Inc 101 Enterprise Suite 100 *NASDAQ: REMX*	Aliso Viejo	CA	92656	**800-828-3726**	949-425-7600	707
Remel Inc 12076 Santa Fe Dr	Lenexa	KS	66215	**800-255-6730**	913-888-0939	229
Remet Corp 210 Commons Rd	Utica	NY	13502	**800-445-2424**	315-797-8700	301
Reminder The PO Box 210	Vernon	CT	06066	**888-456-2211**	860-875-3366	522-4
Reminder Press Inc 130 Old Town Rd	Vernon	CT	06066	**888-456-2211**	860-875-3366	623-8
Remington Arms Co Inc 870 Remington Dr PO Box 700	Madison	NC	27025	**800-243-9700**	336-548-8700	279
Remington Arms Co Inc Stren Fishing Lines Div PO Box 700	Madison	NC	27025	**800-243-9700**	336-548-8700	701
Remington Oil & Gas Corp 8201 Preston Rd Suite 600 *NYSE: REM*	Dallas	TX	75225	**800-521-5481**	214-210-2650	525
Remington Products Co LLC 601 Rayovac Dr *Cust Svc	Madison	WI	53711	**800-736-4648***	608-275-3340	211
Remington Suite Hotel 220 Travis St	Shreveport	LA	71101	**800-444-6750**	318-425-5000	373
Remington Theatre 3701 W Hwy 76	Branson	MO	65616	**800-884-4536**	417-336-1220	562
Reminisce Magazine 5400 S 60th St	Greendale	WI	53129	**800-344-6913**	414-423-0100	449-11
Remmele Engineering Inc 10 Old Hwy 8 SW	New Brighton	MN	55112	**800-222-7737**	651-635-4100	745
Remmey the Pallet Co PO Box 558	Willow Grove	PA	19090	**800-725-5385**	267-913-0002	541
Remo Inc 28101 Industry Dr	Valencia	CA	91355	**800-525-5134**	661-294-5600	516
Remodeling Industry. National Assn of the 780 Lee St Suite 200	Des Plaines	IL	60016	**800-611-6274**	847-298-9200	49-3
Remodeling Magazine 1 Thomas Cir NW Suite 600	Washington	DC	20005	**888-269-8410**	202-452-0800	449-21
Remote Dynamics Inc 1155 Kas Dr Suite 100 *NASDAQ: REDI*	Richardson	TX	75081	**800-828-4696**	972-301-2000	222
Remy Amerique Inc 1350 6th Ave 7th Fl	New York	NY	10019	**800-858-9898**	212-399-4200	82-3
Renaissance Esmeralda Resort 44-400 Indian Wells Ln	Indian Wells	CA	92210	**800-552-4386**	760-773-4444	655
Renaissance Fort Lauderdale-Plantation Hotel 1230 S Pine Island Rd	Plantation	FL	33324	**800-316-7708**	954-472-2252	373
Renaissance Grand Hotel 800 Washington Ave	Saint Louis	MO	63101	**800-468-3571**	314-621-9600	373
Renaissance Greeting Cards Inc 10 Renaissance Way	Sanford	ME	04073	**800-688-9998**	207-324-4153	130
Renaissance Hotel Savery 401 Locust St	Des Moines	IA	50309	**800-798-2151**	515-244-2151	373
Renaissance Hotels 1 Marriott Dr	Washington	DC	20058	**800-638-8108**	301-380-3000	369
Renaissance Learning Inc 2911 Peach St *NASDAQ: RLRN*	Wisconsin Rapids	WI	54494	**800-338-4204**	715-424-3636	176-3
Renaissance Orlando Resort 6677 Sea Harbor Dr	Orlando	FL	32821	**800-380-7917**	407-351-5555	655
Renaissance Pinelsle Resort 9000 Holiday Rd	Lake Lanier Islands	GA	30518	**800-468-3571**	770-945-8921	655
Renaissance Portsmouth Hotel & Waterfront Conference Center 425 Water St	Portsmouth	VA	23704	**888-839-1775**	757-673-3000	370
Renaissance Quail Hollow Resort 11080 Concord-Hambden Rd	Painesville	OH	44077	**800-792-0258**	440-497-1100	655
Renaissance Resort & Spa. Eden Roc - A 4525 Collins Ave	Miami Beach	FL	33140	**800-327-8337**	305-531-0000	655
Renaissance Tampa Hotel International Plaza 4200 Jim Walter Blvd	Tampa	FL	33607	**800-644-2685**	813-877-9200	373
Renaissance Vinoy Resort & Golf Club 501 5th Ave NE	Saint Petersburg	FL	33701	**800-468-3571**	727-894-1000	655
Renaissance Wailea Beach Resort 3550 Wailea Alanui Dr	Kihei	HI	96753	**800-992-4532**	808-879-4900	655
Renaissance World Golf Village Resort 500 S Legacy Trail	Saint Augustine	FL	32092	**888-740-7020**	904-940-8000	655
Renasant Corp 209 Troy St *AMEX: PHC*	Tupelo	MS	38802	**800-680-1601**	662-680-1001	355-2
Renco Encoders Inc 26 Coromar Dr	Goleta	CA	93117	**800-248-6044**	805-968-1525	200
Rene Of Paris 15551 Cabrito Rd	Van Nuys	CA	91406	**800-353-7363**	818-908-3100	342
Renee's Garden Seeds Inc 7389 W Zayante Rd	Felton	CA	95018	**888-880-7228**	831-335-7228	684
Renegade Center for the Arts 404 W Superior St	Duluth	MN	55802	**888-722-6627**	218-722-6775	562
Reneson Hotel Group 121 7th St	San Francisco	CA	94103	**800-444-5816**	415-626-0200	369
Renew Plastics Div NEW Plastics Corp PO Box 480	Luxemburg	WI	54217	**800-666-5207**	920-845-2326	647
Renewable Energy Clearinghouse. Energy Efficiency & PO Box 43165	Olympia	WA	98504	**877-337-3463**		196
Renfro Corp 661 Linville Rd	Mount Airy	NC	27030	**800-334-9091**	336-719-8000	153-10
Renk William F & Sons Inc 6800 Wilburn Rd	Sun Prairie	WI	53590	**800-289-7365**	608-837-7351	11-5
Rennoc Corp 3501 Southeast Blvd *Cust Svc	Vineland	NJ	08360	**800-372-7100***	856-327-5400	153-5
Reno Gazette-Journal 955 Kuenzli St	Reno	NV	89502	**800-648-5048**	775-788-6200	522-2
RENO Refractories Inc 601 Reno Dr	Morris	AL	35116	**800-741-7366**	205-647-0240	649
RENO Refractories Inc Reftech Div 601 Reno Dr	Morris	AL	35116	**800-741-7366**		649
Reno-Sparks Convention & Visitors Authority PO Box 837	Reno	NV	89504	**800-443-1482**	775-827-7600	205
Renold Ajax Inc 100 Bourne St *Cust Svc	Westfield	NY	14787	**800-879-2529***	716-326-3121	609
Renova Lighting Systems Inc 300 High Point Ave	Portsmouth	RI	02871	**800-635-6682**	401-682-1850	431
Rensselaer Polytechnic Institute 275 Windsor St	Hartford	CT	06120	**800-433-4723**	860-548-2400	787
Rensselaer Polytechnic Institute 110 8th St	Troy	NY	12180	**800-448-6562**	518-276-6216	163
Rent-A-Center Inc 5700 Tennyson Pkwy 3rd Fl *NASDAQ: RCII*	Plano	TX	75024	**800-275-2696**	972-801-1100	261-3
Rent-A-PC Inc 265 Oser Ave	Hauppauge	NY	11788	**877-736-8272**	631-273-8888	261-1
Rent-A-Wreck of America LLC 10324 S Dolfield Rd	Owings Mills	MD	21117	**800-535-1391**	410-581-5755	126
Rental Assn. American 1900 19th St	Moline	IL	61265	**800-334-2177**	309-764-2475	49-4
Rental Organizations. Association of Progressive 1504 Robin Hood Trail	Austin	TX	78703	**800-204-2776**	512-794-0095	49-18
Rental Research Services Inc 11300 Minnetonka Mills Rd	Minnetonka	MN	55305	**800-328-0333**	952-935-5700	621
Rental Service Corp 6929 E Greenway Pkwy Suite 200	Scottsdale	AZ	85254	**888-736-8772**	480-905-3300	261-2
Rental Services Assn. Textile 1800 Diagonal Rd Suite 200	Alexandria	VA	22314	**800-868-8772**	703-519-0029	49-4
Rental Uniform Co Inc 2117 Berry St	Kingsport	TN	37664	**800-214-5614**	423-247-4101	434
Rentenbach Engineering Co 2400 Sutherland Ave	Knoxville	TN	37919	**800-621-4941**	865-546-2440	258
Rentrak Corp 7700 NE Ambassador Pl 1 Airport Ctr *NASDAQ: RENT*	Portland	OR	97220	**800-929-5656**	503-284-7581	176-1
Rentway Inc 1 Rentway Pl *NYSE: RWY*	Erie	PA	16505	**800-736-8929**	814-455-5378	261-3
Renville-Sibley Co-op Power Assn 103 Oak St	Danube	MN	56230	**800-826-2593**	320-826-2593	244
Repair Equality. Coalition for Auto 119 Oronoco St Suite 300	Alexandria	VA	22314	**800-229-5380**	703-519-7555	49-21

Alphabetical Section

Listing	City	State	ZIP	Toll-Free	Phone	Class
Repeat-O-Type Mfg Corp 665 State Hwy 23 *Cust Svc	Wayne	NJ	07470	**800-288-3330***	973-696-3330	616
Replacement Parts Inc 1901 E Roosevelt Rd	Little Rock	AR	72206	**877-282-6591**	501-375-1215	61
Replacements Ltd PO Box 26029	Greensboro	NC	27420	**800-737-5223**	336-697-3000	357
Repligen Corp 41 Seyon St *NASDAQ: RGEN* ■ *Sales	Waltham	MA	02453	**800-622-2259***	781-449-9560	86
Replogle Globes Inc 2801 S 25th Ave	Broadview	IL	60155	**800-275-4452**	708-343-0900	242
Report on Disability Programs Newsletter 8737 Colesville Rd Suite 1100	Silver Spring	MD	20910	**800-274-6737**	301-587-6300	521-8
Report on Literacy Programs Newsletter 8737 Colesville Rd Suite 1100	Silver Spring	MD	20910	**800-274-6737**	301-587-6300	521-4
Report on Preschool Programs Newsletter 8737 Colesville Rd Suite 1100	Silver Spring	MD	20910	**800-274-6737**	301-587-6300	521-4
Report on Salary Surveys 3 Park Ave 30th Fl	New York	NY	10016	**800-401-5937**	212-244-0360	521-2
Reporter The PO Box 630	Fond du Lac	WI	54936	**800-261-7323**	920-922-4600	522-2
Repository 500 Market Ave S	Canton	OH	44702	**877-580-8300**	330-580-8300	522-2
Repp Ltd Big & Tall Stores 555 Turnpike St	Canton	MA	02021	**000-690-7377**	781 828-9300	155-3
Reproduction Enterprises Inc 908 N Prairie Rd	Stillwater	OK	74075	**866-734-2855**	405-377-8037	12-2
Reproduction Systems Inc 1828 Walnut St Suite 900	Kansas City	MO	64108	**800-633-6125**	816-471-1414	239
Reproductive Rights. Center for 120 Wall St 14th Fl	New York	NY	10005	**800-786-9711**	917-637-3600	48-8
Reprographic Assn. International 401 N Michigan Ave	Chicago	IL	60611	**800-833-4742**	312-245-1026	49-16
Reprogrphics Once Inc 36060 Industrial Rd	Livonia	MI	48150	**800-968-7788**	734-542-8800	580
ReproTech Ltd 1944 Lexington Ave N	Roseville	MN	55113	**888-489-8944**	651-489-0827	535
Reptiles Magazine 3 Burroughs	Irvine	CA	92618	**800-365-4421**	949-855-8822	449-14
Reptron Electronics Inc 13700 Reptron Blvd	Tampa	FL	33626	**800-800-5441**	813-854-2000	613
Republic The 333 2nd St	Columbus	IN	47201	**800-876-7811**	812-372-7811	522-2
Republic Bancorp Inc 601 W Market St *NASDAQ: RBCAA*	Louisville	KY	40202	**888-540-5363**	502-584-3600	355-2
Republic Bancorp Inc 1070 E Main St *NASDAQ: RBNC*	Owosso	MI	48867	**888-722-7377**	989-725-7337	355-2
Republic Bank 2425 E Grand River Ave	Lansing	MI	48912	**888-722-7377**	517-483-6700	71
Republic Beverage 8045 Northcourt Rd	Houston	TX	77040	**800-292-3303**	832-782-1000	82-3
Republic Engineered Products Inc 3770 Embassy Pkwy	Akron	OH	44333	**800-232-7157**	330-670-3000	709
Republic Indemnity Co of America 15821 Ventura Blvd Suite 370	Encino	CA	91436	**800-821-4520**	818-990-9860	384-4
Republic Insurance Co Inc 2727 Turtle Creek Blvd	Dallas	TX	75219	**800-344-2275**	214-559-1222	384-4
Republic-Lagun Machine Tool Co 1000 E Carson St	Carson	CA	90745	**800-421-2105**	310-518-1100	447
Republic Mortgage Insurance Co 190 Oak Plaza Blvd	Winston-Salem	NC	27105	**800-999-7642**	336-661-0015	384-5
Republic Powdered Metals Inc 2628 Pearl Rd	Medina	OH	44256	**800-551-7081**	330-225-3192	540
Republic Services Inc 110 SE 6th St Suite 2800 *NYSE: RSG*	Fort Lauderdale	FL	33301	**877-241-8396**	954-769-2400	791
Republic Storage Systems Co Inc 1038 Belden Ave NE *Sales	Canton	OH	44705	**800-477-1255***	330-438-5800	281
Republic Tobacco 2301 Ravine Way	Glenview	IL	60025	**800-288-8888**	847-832-9700	744
Republic Western Insurance Co 2721 N Central Ave *Claims	Phoenix	AZ	85004	**800-528-7134***	602-263-6755	384-4
Republic Windows & Doors Inc 930 W Evergreen Ave	Chicago	IL	60622	**800-248-1775**	312-932-8000	232
Republican-American 389 Meadow St	Waterbury	CT	06702	**800-992-3232**	203-574-3636	522-2
Republican-American Inc 389 Meadow St	Waterbury	CT	06702	**800-992-3232**	203-574-3636	623-8
Republican Eagle PO Box 15	Red Wing	MN	55066	**800-535-1660**	651-388-8235	522-2
Republican National Committee 310 1st St SE	Washington	DC	20003	**800-445-5768**	202-863-8500	605
Request Foods Inc PO Box 2577 *Sales	Holland	MI	49422	**800-748-0378***	616-786-0900	291-36
ReQuest Inc 100 Saratoga Village Blvd Suite 44 *Cust Svc	Ballston Spa	NY	12020	**800-236-2812***	518-899-1254	52
Res-Care Inc 10140 Linn Station Rd *NASDAQ: RSCR*	Louisville	KY	40223	**800-866-0860**	502-394-2100	754
RES Mfg Co Inc 7801 N 73rd St	Milwaukee	WI	53223	**800-334-8044**	414-354-4530	479
Rescar Inc 1101 31st St Suite 250	Downers Grove	IL	60515	**800-851-5196**	630-963-1114	637
Resco Plastics Inc 93783 Newport Ln	Coos Bay	OR	97420	**800-266-5097**	541-269-5485	647
Resco Products Inc 2 Penn Ctr W Suite 430	Pittsburgh	PA	15276	**888-283-5505**	412-494-4491	648
Rescue Missions. Association of Gospel 1045 Swift Ave	Kansas City	MO	64116	**800-624-5156**	816-471-8020	48-20
Research Assoc Inc 27999 Clemens Rd	Westlake	OH	44145	**800-255-9693**	440-892-1000	392
Research Consultants Assn Inc. Qualitative PO Box 967	Camden	TN	38320	**888-674-7722**	731-584-8080	49-18
Research on Demand Inc PO Box 479	Santa Barbara	CA	93102	**800-227-0750**	005-900-4095	380
Research & Diagnostic Antibodies 4872 E 2nd St	Benicia	CA	94510	**800-858-7322**	707-746-6800	229
Research & Enlightenment. Association for 215 67th St	Virginia Beach	VA	23451	**800-333-4499**	757-428-3588	48-17
Research Libraries. Association of College & 50 E Huron St	Chicago	IL	60611	**800-545-2433**	312-280-2519	49-11
Research Libraries Group Inc (RLG) 2029 Stierlin Ct Suite 100	Mountain View	CA	94043	**800-537-7546**	650-962-9951	49-5
Research Libraries Group News 1200 Villa St	Mountain View	CA	94041	**800-537-7546**	650-962-9951	521-4
Research Organics Inc 4353 E 49th St	Cleveland	OH	44125	**800-321-0570**	216-883-8025	229
Research Pharmaceutical Services Inc 610 W Germantown Pike Suite 200	Plymouth Meeting	PA	19462	**866-777-1151**	215-540-0700	707
Research to Prevent Blindness Inc (RPB) 645 Madison Ave 21st Fl	New York	NY	10022	**800-621-0026**	212-752-4333	48-17
Research Products Corp 1015 E Washington Ave	Madison	WI	53703	**800-334-6011**	608-257-8801	18
Research & Special Programs Administration Hazardous Materials Safety Office 400 7th St SW Rm 8321	Washington	DC	20590	**800-467-4922**	202-366-0656	336-13
Research Technology International Inc 4700 W Chase Ave *Sales	Lincolnwood	IL	60712	**800-323-7520***	847-677-3000	580
Research Triangle Institute 3040 Cornwallis Rd PO Box 12194	Research Triangle Park	NC	27709	**800-334-8571**	919-541-6000	654
Research!America 1101 King St Suite 520	Alexandria	VA	22314	**800-366-2873**	703-739-2577	48-5
Reser's Fine Foods Inc PO Box 8	Beaverton	OR	97075	**800-333-6431**	503-643-6431	291-33
Reservations USA 3171 North Pkwy	Pigeon Forge	TN	37863	**800-251-4444**	865-453-1000	368
Reserve Assn. Naval 1619 King St	Alexandria	VA	22314	**866-672-4968**	703-548-5800	48-19
Reserve Assn. Naval Enlisted 6703 Farragut Ave	Falls Church	VA	22042	**800-776-9020**	703-534-1329	48-19
Reserve National Insurance Co Inc PO Box 18448	Oklahoma City	OK	73154	**800-654-9106**	405-848-7931	384-2
Reserve Officers Assn of the US (ROA) 1 Constitution Ave NE	Washington	DC	20002	**800-809-9448**	202-479-2200	48-19
ReserveAmerica 2480 Meadowvale Blvd Suite 120	Mississauga	ON	L5N8M6	**800-695-4636**	905-286-6600	762
Reserves Network The 22021 Brookpark Rd	Fairview Park	OH	44126	**866-876-2020**	440-779-1400	619
Residence Inn by Marriott 1 Marriott Dr	Washington	DC	20058	**800-638-8108**	301-380-3000	369
ResidenSea 5200 Blue Lagoon Dr Suite 790	Miami	FL	33139	**800-970-6601**	305-264-9090	217
Residential Property Managers. National Assn of 8317 Cross Pk Dr Suite 150	Austin	TX	78754	**800-782-3452**	512-381-6091	49-17
Residential Specialists. Council of 430 N Michigan Ave Suite 300	Chicago	IL	60611	**800-462-8841**	312-321-4400	49-17
Resilite Sports Products PO Box 764	Sunbury	PA	17801	**800-326-9307**	570-473-3529	701
Resinall Corp 3065 High Ridge Rd *Cust Svc	Stamford	CT	06905	**800-421-0561***	203-329-7100	594-2
ResMed Inc 14040 Danielson St *NYSE: RMD*	Poway	CA	92064	**800-424-0737**	858-746-2400	468
Resolute Systems Inc 1550 N Prospect Ave	Milwaukee	WI	53202	**800-776-6060**	414-276-4774	41
Resolution Inc 19 Gregory Dr	South Burlington	VT	05403	**800-862-8900**	802-862-8881	501
Resolution Packaging Inc 3 Borinski Dr Suite E	Lincoln Park	NJ	07035	**800-556-1321**	973-633-7795	102
Resolution Specialty Materials 200 Railroad St	Roebuck	SC	29376	**800-476-4476**	864-253-8400	143
Resonate Inc 385 Moffett Park Dr	Sunnyvale	CA	94089	**877-737-6628**	408-548-5600	176-7
Resort 2 Me 2600 Garden Rd Suite 111	Monterey	CA	93940	**800-757-5646**	831-642-6622	368
Resort Condominiums International (RCI) 9998 N Michigan Rd	Carmel	IN	46032	**800-481-5738**	317-805-9000	738
Resort at Deer Harbor 31 Jack & Jill Ln PO Box 200	Deer Harbor	WA	98243	**888-376-4480**	360-376-4420	655
Resort at Ludlow Bay 1 Heron Rd	Port Ludlow	WA	98365	**800-732-1239**	360-437-0411	373
Resort at Ludlow Bay 1 Heron Rd	Port Ludlow	WA	98365	**877-805-0868**	360-437-2222	655
Resort at the Mountain 68010 E Fairway Ave	Welches	OR	97067	**800-669-7666**	503-622-3101	655
Resort at Seabrook Island 3772 Seabrook Island Rd	Seabrook Island	SC	29455	**800-845-2475**	843-768-2500	655
Resort Semiahmoo 9565 Semiahmoo Pkwy	Blaine	WA	98230	**800-770-7992**	360-318-2000	655
Resort Sports Network PO Box 7528	Portland	ME	04112	**800-653-0697**	207-772-5000	725
Resort at Squaw Creek 400 Squaw Creek Rd	Olympic Valley	CA	96146	**800-327-3353**	530-583-6300	655
Resort Suites 7677 E Princess Blvd	Scottsdale	AZ	85255	**800-541-5203**	480-585-1234	373
Resort World. Clarion Suites 2800 N Poinciana Blvd	Kissimmee	FL	34746	**800-423-8604**	407-997-5000	373
Resorts Atlantic City 1133 Boardwalk	Atlantic City	NJ	08401	**800-336-6378**	609-344-6000	655
Resorts East Chicago 777 Harrah's Blvd	East Chicago	IN	46312	**877-496-1777**	219-378-3000	133
Resorts Tunica 1100 Casino Strip Blvd PO Box 750 *Resv	Robinsonville	MS	38664	**866-797-7111***	662-363-7777	133
Resorts Worldwide Inc. Preferred Hotels & 311 S Wacker Dr Suite 1900	Chicago	IL	60606	**800-323-7500**	312-913-0400	368
Resource Action Center. Southeast Asia 1628 16th St NW 3rd Fl	Washington	DC	20009	**800-600-9188**	202-667-4690	48-5
Resource Bancshares Mortgage Group Inc 9710 Two Notch Rd	Columbia	SC	29223	**800-627-1991**	803-462-8000	498
Resource Careers 343 W Bagley Rd Suite 302 *Cust Svc	Berea	OH	44017	**800-899-1770***	440-243-2810	652
Resource Connection Inc 161 S Main St	Middleton	MA	01949	**800-649-5228**	978-777-9333	183
Resource Development Corp 280 Daines St Suite 200	Birmingham	MI	48009	**800-360-7222**	248-646-2300	39
Resource Dynamics International Inc 3350 Boca Raton Blvd Suite A38	Boca Raton	FL	33431	**888-999-1623**		193
Resource Interactive 343 N Front St	Columbus	OH	43215	**800-550-5815**		4

Company / Address	City	State	ZIP	Toll-Free	Phone	Class
Resource Management Plus Inc 1211 Locust St	Philadelphia	PA	19107	**800-408-8951**	215-545-7222	47
Resource Management Service Inc 100 Corporate Ridge Suite 200	Birmingham	AL	35242	**800-995-9516**	205-991-9516	297
Resource One Computer Systems Inc 1159 Dublin Rd	Columbus	OH	43215	**800-393-7627**	614-485-4800	178
ResourceMFG Div Career Blazers Inc 222 W Las Colinas Blvd Suite 1250E	Irving	TX	75039	**800-787-6750**	214-296-6700	707
Resources Global Professionals 695 Town Center Dr Suite 600 *NASDAQ: RECN*	Costa Mesa	CA	92626	**800-900-1131**	714-430-6400	707
Respiratory Distributors Inc 110 E Azalea Ave	Foley	AL	36535	**800-872-8672**	251-943-5844	237
Respironics Inc 1010 Murry Ridge Ln *NASDAQ: RESP*	Murrysville	PA	15668	**800-345-6443**	724-387-5200	249
Respironics Novametrix Medical Systems Inc 5 Technology Dr	Wallingford	CT	06492	**800-243-3444**	203-265-7701	249
Response Biomedical Corp 8081 Lougheed Hwy	Burnaby	BC	V5A1W9	**888-591-5577**	604-681-4101	410
Response Envelope Inc 1340 S Baker Ave	Ontario	CA	91761	**800-750-0046**	909-923-5855	260
Response USA Inc 535 Rt 38 Suite 500	Cherry Hill	NJ	08002	**800-777-9807**	856-661-0700	683
Responsible Medicine. Physicians' Committee for 5100 Wisconsin Ave NW Suite 400	Washington	DC	20016	**866-416-7276**	202-686-2210	49-8
Responsys Inc 3 Lagwood Dr Suite 300	Redwood City	CA	94065	**800-624-5356**	650-801-7400	39
Rest Ministries Inc PO Box 502928	San Diego	CA	92150	**888-751-7378**	858-486-4685	48-21
RESTAT 724 Elm St *Cust Svc	West Bend	WI	53095	**800-248-1062***	262-338-5760	575
Restaurant Assn. National 1200 17th St NW	Washington	DC	20036	**800-424-5156**	202-331-5900	49-6
Restaurant Developers Corp 5755 Granger Rd Suite 200	Independence	OH	44131	**800-837-9599**	216-398-1101	656
Restaurant & Stores Equipment Co 230 W 700 South	Salt Lake City	UT	84101	**800-877-0087**	801-364-1981	295
Restaurants Unlimited Inc 1818 N Northlake Way	Seattle	WA	98103	**877-855-6106**	206-634-0550	656
Restland Funeral Home & Cemetary 13005 Greenville Ave	Dallas	TX	75243	**800-749-7379**	972-238-7111	499
Restless Legs Syndrome Foundation Inc 819 2nd St SW	Rochester	MN	55902	**877-463-6757**	507-287-6465	48-17
Reston Hospital Center 1850 Town Ctr Pkwy	Reston	VA	20190	**800-695-9426**	703-689-9000	366-2
Restonic Mattress Corp 385 Court St Suite 210	Plymouth	MA	02360	**800-898-6075**	508-732-9805	463
Restoration. Association of Specialists in Cleaning & 8229 Cloverleaf Dr Suite 460	Millersville	MD	21108	**800-272-7012**	410-729-9900	49-4
Results Telemarketing Inc 499 Sheridan St 4th Fl	Dania Beach	FL	33004	**800-284-5318**	954-921-2400	722
RESUMate Inc 135 E Bennett St Suite 5 *Cust Svc	Saline	MI	48176	**800-530-9310***	734-429-8510	176-10
Resun Leasing Inc 22810 Quicksilver Dr	Dulles	VA	20166	**800-554-6506**	703-709-8880	495
Retail Advertising & Marketing Assn (RAMA) 325 7th St NW Suite 1100	Washington	DC	20004	**800-673-4692**	202-661-3052	49-18
Retail Confectioners International (RCI) 1807 Glenview Rd Suite 204	Glenview	IL	60025	**800-545-5381**	847-724-6120	49-6
Retail Dealers Assn. North American 10 E 22nd St Suite 310	Lombard	IL	60148	**800-621-0298**	630-953-8950	49-18
Retail Federation. National 325 7th St NW Suite 1100	Washington	DC	20004	**800-673-4692**	202-783-7971	49-18
Retail Marketing Services. Association of 10 Drs James Parker Blvd Suite 103	Red Bank	NJ	07701	**866-231-6310**	732-842-5070	49-18
Retail Marketing Services. National Assn for PO Box 906	Plover	WI	54467	**888-526-2767**	715-342-0948	49-18
Retailing Assn. Electronic 2000 N 14th St Suite 300	Arlington	VA	22201	**800-987-6462**	703-841-1751	49-18
Retardation. American Assn on Mental 444 N Capitol St NW Suite 846	Washington	DC	20001	**800-424-3688**	202-387-1968	48-17
Retec Group 300 Baker Ave Suite 302	Concord	MA	01742	**877-222-2260**	978-371-3200	191
Retek Inc 950 Nicollet Mall	Minneapolis	MN	55403	**877-517-3835**	612-587-5000	176-10
Retired Americans. Alliance for 888 16th St NW Ste 520	Washington	DC	20006	**888-373-6497**	202-974-8222	48-6
Retired Federal Employees. National Assn of 606 N Washington St	Alexandria	VA	22314	**800-627-3394**	703-838-7760	604
Retired Persons. Canadian Assn of 1304-27 Queen St E	Toronto	ON	M5C2M6	**800-363-9736**	416-363-8748	48-6
Retired & Senior Volunteer Program (RSVP) PO Box 70675	Washington	DC	20024	**800-424-8867**		196
Retired Travel Club. Special Military Active 600 University Office Blvd Suite 1A	Pensacola	FL	32504	**800-354-7681**		48-23
Retirement Letter 7811 Montrose Rd *Cust Svc	Potomac	MD	20854	**800-804-0940***	301-340-2100	521-6
Retirement System Group Inc 150 E 42nd St 27th Fl	New York	NY	10017	**800-446-7774**	212-503-0100	393
Retractable Technologies Inc 511 Lobo Ln *AMEX: RVP*	Little Elm	TX	75068	**888-806-2626**	972-294-1010	469
Retreat Healthcare PO Box 803	Brattleboro	VT	05302	**800-345-5550**	802-257-7785	366-3
RETS Institute of Technology 300 Highrise Dr	Louisville	KY	40213	**800-999-7387**	502-968-7191	787
RETS Tech Center 555 E Alex Bell Rd	Centerville	OH	45459	**800-837-7387**	937-433-3410	787
Rettew Assoc Inc 3020 Columbia Ave	Lancaster	PA	17603	**800-738-8395**	717-394-3721	258
Reusable Industrial Packaging Assn (RIPA) 8401 Corporate Dr Suite 450	Landover	MD	20785	**800-533-3786**	301-577-3786	49-13
Revcor Inc 251 Edwards Ave	Carpentersville	IL	60110	**800-323-8261**	847-428-4411	19
Revelation Software 99 Kinderkamack Rd	Westwood	NJ	07675	**800-262-4747**	201-594-1422	176-2
Revell-Monogram LLC 725 Landwehr Rd	Northbrook	IL	60062	**800-833-3570**	847-770-6100	750
Revels Tractor Co Inc 2217 N Main St	Fuquay-Varina	NC	27526	**800-849-5469**	919-552-5697	270
Revere Copper Products Inc 1 Revere Pk	Rome	NY	13440	**800-448-1776**	315-338-2022	476
Revere Group 1285 Baxter Pkwy Suite 15	Deerfield	IL	60015	**888-473-8373**	847-790-9800	193
Revere Mills Inc 3000 S River Rd	Des Plaines	IL	60018	**800-367-8258**	847-759-6800	356
Review & Herald Publishing Assn 55 W Oak Ridge Dr	Hagerstown	MD	21740	**800-456-3991**	301-393-3000	623-9
Review Times PO Box 947	Fostoria	OH	44830	**800-457-2796**	419-435-6641	522-2
Revive Spa at the JW Marriott Desert Ridge Resort Phoenix 5350 E Marriott Dr	Phoenix	AZ	85054	**866-738-4834**	480-293-3700	698
Revlon Consumer Products Corp 237 Park Ave	New York	NY	10017	**800-473-8566**	212-527-4000	211
Revlon Inc 237 Park Ave *NYSE: REV*	New York	NY	10017	**800-473-8566**	212-527-4000	355-3
Revolution & Peace. Hoover Institution on War Stanford University 434 Galvez Mall	Stanford	CA	94305	**877-466-8374**	650-723-1754	654
Rewards Network 2 N Riverside Plaza Suite 950 *AMEX: IRN*	Chicago	IL	60606	**800-841-7102**	312-521-6767	213
Rex Artist Supplies 2263 SW 37th Ave	Miami	FL	33145	**800-739-2782**	305-445-1413	45
Rex-Buckeye Co Inc 1230A W 58th St	Cleveland	OH	44102	**800-932-0011**	216-939-9000	447
REX Fine Foods 4100 Howard Ave	New Orleans	LA	70153	**800-344-8314**	504-822-4141	291-41
Rex Heat Treat 8th St & Valley Forge Rd PO Box 270	Lansdale	PA	19446	**800-220-6053**	215-855-1131	475
Rex-Hide Inc 705 S Lyons Ave	Tyler	TX	75702	**800-527-8403**	903-593-7387	663
Rex Moore Electrical Contractors & Engineers 3601 Parkway Pl	West Sacramento	CA	95691	**800-266-1922**	916-372-1300	188-4
Rex Packaging 136 Eastport Rd	Jacksonville	FL	32218	**800-821-0798**	904-757-5210	102
Rex Ranch Resort & Spa 131 Alamo Rd	Amado	AZ	85645	**800-547-2696**	520-398-2914	697
REX Stores Corp 2875 Needmore Rd *NYSE: RSC*	Dayton	OH	45414	**800-528-9739**	937-276-3931	35
Rex Supply Co 3715 Harrisburg Blvd	Houston	TX	77003	**800-369-0669**	713-222-2251	378
Rexall Sundown Inc 6111 Broken Sound Pkwy NW	Boca Raton	FL	33487	**800-327-0908**	561-241-9400	786
Rexam Inc 4201 Congress St Suite 340	Charlotte	NC	28209	**800-289-2800**	704-551-1500	538
Rexam Medical Packaging 1919 S Butterfield Rd	Mundelein	IL	60060	**800-543-8604**	847-362-9000	538
Rexel Ryall Electrical Supplies 2627 W 6th Ave	Denver	CO	80204	**800-759-2728**	303-629-7721	245
Rexhall Industries Inc 46147 7th St W	Lancaster	CA	93534	**800-929-5280**	661-726-0565	120
Rexius Forest By-Products Inc 1275 Bailey Hill Rd	Eugene	OR	97402	**800-285-7227**	541-342-1835	288
Reye's Syndrome Foundation. National 426 N Lewis St	Bryan	OH	43506	**800-233-7393**	419-636-2679	48-17
Reynaldo's Mexican Food Co Inc 4911 Mason St	South Gate	CA	90280	**800-686-4911**		291-36
Reynolda House Museum of American Art 2250 Reynolda Rd	Winston-Salem	NC	27106	**888-663-1149**	336-725-5325	509
Reynolds-Alberta Museum PO Box 6360	Wetaskiwin	AB	T9A2G1	**800-661-4726**	780-361-1351	509
Reynolds Co 140-B Regal Row	Dallas	TX	75247	**800-851-0304**	214-630-9000	245
Reynolds International LP 5000 N 29th St	McAllen	TX	78504	**800-441-8161**	956-687-7500	269
Reynolds Plantation 100 Linger Longer Rd	Greensboro	GA	30642	**800-852-5885**	706-467-3151	655
Reynolds Russell Assoc Inc 200 Park Ave 23rd Fl	New York	NY	10166	**888-772-6200**	212-351-2000	262
Reynolds Smith & Hills Inc PO Box 4850 Suite 400	Jacksonville	FL	32201	**800-741-2014**	904-296-2000	258
RF Knox Co Inc PO Box 1337	Smyrna	GA	30081	**800-989-7401**	770-434-7401	688
RF Monolithics Inc 4441 Sigma Rd *NASDAQ: RFMI*	Dallas	TX	75244	**800-704-6079**	972-233-2903	245
RF Scientific Inc 5644 Commerce Dr	Orlando	FL	32839	**800-741-5465**	407-856-1050	633
RFB&D (Recording for the Blind & Dyslexic) 20 Roszel Rd	Princeton	NJ	08540	**800-221-4792**	609-452-0606	48-17
RFK Transportation 5650 6th St SW	Cedar Rapids	IA	52404	**800-322-8412**	319-364-8102	769
RG Barry Corp 13405 Yarmouth Dr NW	Pickerington	OH	43147	**800-848-7560**	614-864-6400	296
RG Group 258 W Market St	York	PA	17405	**866-744-7687**	717-849-0320	626
RG Shakour Inc 254 Turnpike Rd	Westborough	MA	01581	**800-262-9090**	508-366-8282	237
RG Vanderweil Engineers Inc 274 Summer St	Boston	MA	02210	**800-726-2840**	617-423-7423	258
RGA Accessories Inc 350 5th Ave Suite 2101	New York	NY	10118	**800-221-8828**	212-273-9200	154
RGIS Inventory Specialists 2000 E Taylor Rd	Auburn Hills	MI	48326	**800-521-3102**	248-651-2511	391
RGS (Ruffed Grouse Society) 451 McCormick Rd	Coraopolis	PA	15108	**888-564-6747**	412-262-4044	48-3
RGS Energy Group Inc 89 East Ave	Rochester	NY	14649	**888-253-8888**	585-546-2700	355-5
RH Barringer Distributing Co Inc 1620 Fairfax Rd	Greensboro	NC	27407	**800-273-0555**	336-854-0555	82-1
RH Kuhn Co DBA Roomful Express 55th St & AVRR	Pittsburgh	PA	15201	**888-696-7378**	412-784-1250	316
RH Kyle Furniture Co 1352 Hansford St	Charleston	WV	25301	**800-624-9170**	304-346-0671	315
RH Macy & Co Inc DBA Macy's 151 W 34th St *Cust Svc	New York	NY	10001	**800-526-1202***	212-695-4400	227
RH White Construction Co Inc 41 Central St	Auburn	MA	01501	**800-922-8182**	508-832-3295	187-10
Rhapsody.com 2012 16th St	San Francisco	CA	94103	**866-311-0228**	415-934-2000	677
Rhe Tech Inc 1500 E North Territorial Rd	Whitmore Lake	MI	48189	**800-837-4921**	734-769-0585	594-2

Name / Address	City	State	ZIP	Toll-Free	Phone	Class
Rheem Mfg Co 405 Lexington Ave 22nd Fl *Cust Svc	New York	NY	10174	**800-432-8373***	212-916-8100	16
Rheem Mfg Co Water Heater Div 2600 Gunter Park Dr E	Montgomery	AL	36109	**800-621-5622**	334-260-1500	36
Rhein Chemie Corp 1014 Whitehead Rd Ext *Cust Svc	Trenton	NJ	08638	**800-289-2436***	609-771-9100	143
Rhett House Inn 1009 Craven St	Beaufort	SC	29902	**888-480-9530**	843-524-9030	373
RHIMR (Robert Half Management Resources) 2884 Sand Hill Rd Suite 200	Menlo Park	CA	94025	**888-400-7474**	650-234-6000	193
Rhino Foods Inc 79 Industrial Pkwy	Burlington	VT	05401	**800-639-3350**	802-862-0252	291-2
Rhino Records 3400 W Olive Ave	Burbank	CA	91505	**800-827-4466**	818-238-6100	643
Rhode Island						
Higher Education Assistance Authority 560 Jefferson Blvd	Warwick	RI	02886	**800-922-9855**	401-736-1100	711
Tourism Div 1 W Exchange St	Providence	RI	02903	**800-556-2484**	401-222-2601	335
Rhode Island Blood Center 405 Promenade St	Providence	RI	02908	**800-283-8385**	401-453-8360	90
Rhode Island PBS 50 Park Lane	Providence	RI	02907	**800-613-8836**	401-222-3636	620
Rhode Island School of Design 2 College St	Providence	RI	02903	**800-364-7473**	401-454-6100	163
Rhode Island Textile Co 211 Columbus Ave	Pawtucket	RI	02861	**800-556-6488**	401-722-3700	730-5
Rhode Island Veterinary Medical Assn 11 S Angell St Suite 347	Providence	RI	02906	**877-521-0103**		782
Rhodes College 2000 North Pkwy	Memphis	TN	38112	**800-844-5969**	901-843-3000	163
Rhodes Colleges Inc 6 Hutton Ctr Dr Suite 400	Santa Ana	CA	92707	**888-741-4271**	714-427-3000	241
Rhodes Furniture Co 1800 E 5th Ave	Columbus	OH	43219	**877-274-6337**	614-253-7441	316
Rhodes International Inc PO Box 25487	Salt Lake City	UT	84125	**800-876-7333**	801-972-0122	291-16
Rhodia Inc 259 Prospect Plains Rd CN 7500 *Cust Svc	Cranbury	NJ	08512	**888-776-7337***	609-860-4000	142
RHR International Co 220 Gerry Dr	Wood Dale	IL	60191	**800-892-4496**	630-766-7007	193
Rhythm City Casino 101 W River Dr	Davenport	IA	52801	**800-262-8711**	563-322-2628	133
RI Lampus Co 816 RI Lampus Ave	Springdale	PA	15144	**800-872-7310**	724-274-5035	181
RIA Group 395 Hudson St *Cust Svc	New York	NY	10014	**800-950-1205***	212-367-6300	623-2
RIAA (Recording Industry Assn of America Inc) 1330 Connecticut Ave NW Suite 300	Washington	DC	20036	**800-223-2328**	202-775-0101	48-4
Rialto Theater 310 S 9th St	Tacoma	WA	98402	**800-291-7593**	253-591-5890	562
Riande Continental Miami Bayside Hotel 146 Biscayne Blvd	Miami	FL	33132	**800-742-6331**	305-358-4555	373
Rib Crib Corp 4535 S Harvard St	Tulsa	OK	74135	**800-275-9677**	918-712-7427	657
Ribbon Technology Corp PO Box 30758	Gahanna	OH	43230	**800-848-0477**	614-864-5444	800
Ribelin Sales Inc 3857 Miller Pk Dr	Garland	TX	75042	**800-374-1594**	972-272-1594	144
Rice AH Corp 55 Spring St *Sales	Pittsfield	MA	01201	**800-765-7423***	413-443-6477	730-5
Rice Barton Corp 25 Southgate St	Worcester	MA	01610	**800-225-9415**	508-752-2821	546
Rice Fruit Co 2760 Carlisle Rd PO Box 66	Gardners	PA	17324	**800-627-3359**	717-677-8131	310-3
Rice Hospice 301 SW Becker Ave	Willmar	MN	56201	**800-336-7423**	320-231-4450	365
Rice I & Co Inc 11500 Roosevelt Blvd Bldg D	Philadelphia	PA	19116	**800-232-6022**	215-673-7423	291-15
Rice Lake Weighing Systems 230 W Coleman St	Rice Lake	WI	54868	**800-472-6703**	715-234-9171	672
Rice Packaging Inc 356 Somers Rd	Ellington	CT	06029	**800-367-6725**	860-872-8341	102
Rice University 6100 Main St	Houston	TX	77005	**800-527-6957**	713-348-0000	163
Ricerca Biosciences 7528 Auburn Rd	Painesville	OH	44077	**888-742-3722**	440-357-3300	654
Rich Benjamin F Co PO Box 6031	Newark	DE	19714	**800-237-4241**	302-894-0498	233
Rich Maid Kabinetry Inc 633 W Lincoln Ave	Myerstown	PA	17067	**800-295-2912**	717-866-2112	116
Rich Mountain Electric Co-op Inc PO Box 897	Mena	AR	71953	**877-828-4074**	479-394-4140	244
Rich Products Corp 1 Robert Rich Way	Buffalo	NY	14213	**800-828-2021**	716-878-8000	291-36
Rich Ranch PO Box 495	Seeley Lake	MT	59868	**800-532-4350**	406-677-2317	238
Rich-SeaPak Corp PO Box 20670	Saint Simons Island	GA	31522	**800-654-9731**	912-638-5000	291-13
Rich Worldwide Travel Inc 500 Mamaroneck Ave	Harrison	NY	10528	**800-431-1130**	914-835-7600	760
Richard Band's Profitable Investing Newsletter 7811 Montrose Rd	Potomac	MD	20854	**800-211-8565**	301-340-2100	521-9
Richard Chang Assoc 15265 Alton Pkwy Suite 300	Irvine	CA	92618	**800-756-8096**	949-727-7477	193
Richard E Jacobs Group Inc 25425 Center Ridge Rd	Cleveland	OH	44145	**800-852-9558**	440-871-4800	641
Richard Rodgers Theatre 226 W 46th St	New York	NY	10036	**800-755-4000**	212-307-4100	732
Richard Young's Intelligence Report 7811 Montrose Rd	Potomac	MD	20854	**800-301-8969**	301-340-2100	521-9
Richards Brush Co 5200 4th Ave S *Cust Svc	Seattle	WA	98108	**800-732-1110***	206-623-3720	104
Richards Industries Inc 3170 Wasson Rd *Cust Svc	Cincinnati	OH	45209	**800-543-7311***	513-533-5600	584
Richards JA Co 903 N Pitcher St	Kalamazoo	MI	49007	**800-253-3288**	269-343-4684	448
Richards Maple Products Inc 545 Water St	Chardon	OH	44024	**800-352-4052**	440-286-4160	291-39
Richards SP Co 6300 Highlands Pkwy	Smyrna	GA	30082	**888-436-6881**	770-436-6881	523
Richards-Wilcox Inc 600 S Lake St	Aurora	IL	60506	**800-253-5668**	630-897-6951	206
Richardson Chamber of Commerce 411 Belle Grove Dr	Richardson	TX	75080	**800-777-8001**	972-234-4141	137
Richardson Convention & Visitors Services 411 W Arapaho Rd Suite 105	Richardson	TX	75080	**888-690-7287**	972-744-4034	205
Richardson Electronics Ltd 40 W 267 Keslinger Rd PO Box 393 *NASDAQ: RELL* ■ *Sales	LaFox	IL	60147	**800-348-5580***	630-208-2200	245
Richco Inc 8145 River Dr	Morton Grove	IL	60053	**800-466-8301**	773-539-4060	597
Richeson Jack & Co Inc 557 Marcella Dr	Kimberly	WI	54136	**800-233-2404**	920-738-0744	43
Richland Chamber of Commerce 710-A George Washington Way	Richland	WA	99352	**877-218-7729**	509-946-1651	137
Richland Glass Co Inc 1640 Southwest Blvd	Vineland	NJ	08360	**800-959-0312**		328
Richman Group of Cos 599 W Putnam Ave	Greenwich	CT	06830	**800-333-3509**	203-869-0900	639
Richman Ice Cream Co 91 18th Ave	Paterson	NJ	07513	**800-883-3332**	973-684-8935	291-25
Richman SD Sons Inc 2435 Wheatsheaf Ln	Philadelphia	PA	19137	**800-648-3576**	215-535-5100	674
Richmond The 1757 Collins Ave	Miami Beach	FL	33139	**800-327-3163**	305-538-2331	373
Richmond American Homes Inc 6550 S Greenwood Plaza Blvd	Centennial	CO	80111	**888-402-4663**	303-773-2727	639
Richmond County Chamber of Commerce 505 Rockingham Rd	Rockingham	NC	28380	**800-858-1688**	910-895-9058	137
Richmond Eye & Ear Surgical Specialty Center 8700 Stony Point Pkwy	Richmond	VA	23235	**800-328-7334**	804-775-4500	366-5
Richmond Gear PO Box 238 *Sales	Liberty	SC	29657	**800-476-6446***	864-843-9231	700
Richmond Hill Inn 87 Richmond Hill Dr	Asheville	NC	28806	**888-742-4554**	828-252-7313	373
Richmond International Forest Products Inc 4050 Innslake Dr Suite 100	Glen Allen	VA	23060	**800-767-0111**	804-747-0111	190-3
Richmond Metropolitan Convention & Visitors Bureau 401 N 3rd St	Richmond	VA	23219	**800-370-9004**	804-782-2777	205
Richmond Newspapers Inc PO Box 85333	Richmond	VA	23293	**800-468-3383**	804-649-6000	623-8
Richmond Times-Dispatch 333 E Franklin St	Richmond	VA	23219	**800-468-3382**	804-649-6990	522-2
Richmond/Wayne County Convention & Tourism Bureau 5701 National Rd E	Richmond	IN	47374	**800-828-8414**	765-935-8687	205
Richmor Aviation Inc 1142 Rt 94 Columbia County Airport	Hudson	NY	12534	**800-331-6101**	518-828-9461	63
Rich's Business Directories Inc 2551 Casey Ave Suite A	Mountain View	CA	94043	**800-969-7424**	650-564-9464	623-6
Rick Johnson & Assoc of Colorado 1649 Downing St	Denver	CO	80218	**800-530-2300**	303-296-2200	392
Rickeys - A Hyatt Hotel 4219 El Camino Real	Palo Alto	CA	94306	**800-233-1234**	650-493-8000	373
Ricklin-Echikson Assoc 374 Millburn Ave	Millburn	NJ	07041	**800-544-2317**	973-376-2020	192
Ricoh Corp 5 Dedrick Pl	West Caldwell	NJ	07006	**800-637-4264**	973-882-2000	578
Ricoh Printing Systems America Inc 2635-A Park Center Dr *Cust Svc	Simi Valley	CA	93065	**800-887-8848***	805-578-4000	171-6
Riddell Footwear 11426 Moog Dr	Saint Louis	MO	63146	**800-367-6822**	314-432-7171	296
Ride Snowboards 19215 Vashon Hwy SW	Vashon	WA	98070	**800-757-5806**	206-463-3631	701
Rider University 2083 Lawrenceville Rd	Lawrenceville	NJ	08648	**800-257-9026**	609-896-5000	163
Rides Mass Transit District (RMTD) PO Box 190	Rosiclare	IL	62982	**877-667-6122**	618-285-3342	109
Ridge Behavioral Health System 3050 Rio Dosa Dr	Lexington	KY	40509	**800-753-4673**	859-269-2325	366-3
Ridge Co Inc 1535 S Main St	South Bend	IN	46613	**800-348-2409**	574-234-3143	61
Ridge Road Express Inc 5355 Junction Rd	Lockport	NY	14094	**800-847-4887**	716-625-9211	110
Ridge Tahoe 400 Ridge Club Dr PO Box 5790	Stateline	NV	89449	**800-334-1600**	775-588-3553	655
Ridgecrest Area Convention & Visitors Bureau 139 Balsam St	Ridgecrest	CA	93555	**800-847-4830**	760-375-8202	205
Ridgeview Medical Center 500 S Maple St	Waconia	MN	55387	**800-967-4620**	952-442-2191	366-2
Ridgewater College						
Hutchinson Campus 2 Century Ave SE PO Box 1097	Hutchinson	MN	55350	**800-222-4424**	320-587-3636	160
Willmar Campus 2101 15th Ave NW	Willmar	MN	56201	**800-722-1151**	320-235-5114	160
Ridgeway Clock Co 1131 Mica Rd PO Box 407 *Cust Svc	Ridgeway	VA	24148	**800-828-4441***	276-956-3111	151
Ridgewood Corp 270 Rt 17 S *Cust Svc	Mahwah	NJ	07430	**800-562-0214***	201-529-5500	601
Ridgways Inc 5711 Hillcroft St	Houston	TX	77036	**800-777-1623**	713-782-8580	770
Riding Mountain National Park General Delivery *Campground Resv	Wasagaming	MB	R0J2H0	**800-707-8480***	204-848-7272	553
Riedell Shoes Inc 122 Cannon River Ave	Red Wing	MN	55066	**800-698-6893**	651-388-8251	701
Riegel Consumer Products PO Box E	Johnston	SC	29832	**800-845-3251**	803-275-2541	731
RIF (Reading Is Fundamental Inc) 1825 Connecticut Ave NW Suite 400	Washington	DC	20009	**877-743-7323**	202-673-0020	48-11
Rifkin A Co 1400 Sans Souci Pkwy *Cust Svc	Wilkes-Barre	PA	18706	**800-458-7300***	570-825-9551	68
Rifle Assn of America. National 11250 Waples Mill Rd *Membership	Fairfax	VA	22030	**800-672-3888***	703-267-1000	48-22
Rigg William Co 777 Main St Suite C-50	Fort Worth	TX	76102	**800-275-4449**	817-335-4444	383
Riggs Bank 800 17th St NW	Washington	DC	20006	**800-368-5800**	202-835-5240	71
Riggs National Corp 1503 Pennsylvania Ave NW	Washington	DC	20005	**800-368-5800**	301-887-6000	355-2
Right-Gard Corp 531 N 4th St PO Box 286	Denver	PA	17517	**800-535-1122**		566
Right Management Consultants Inc 1818 Market St 33rd Fl	Philadelphia	PA	19103	**800-237-4448**	215-988-1588	192
Right to Work Committee. National 8001 Braddock Rd Suite 500	Springfield	VA	22160	**800-325-7892**	703-321-8510	49-12
RightCHOICE Managed Care Inc DBA Alliance Blue Cross Blue Shield 1831 Chestnut St	Saint Louis	MO	63103	**800-366-2583**	314-923-4444	384-3
Righteous Babe Records PO Box 95 Ellicott Station	Buffalo	NY	14205	**800-664-3769**	716-852-8020	643

Name / Address	City	State	Zip	Toll-Free	Phone	Class
RightNow Technologies Inc 40 Enterprise Blvd; *NASDAQ: RNOW*	Bozeman	MT	59718	**877-363-5678**	406-522-4200	39
Rights. Center for Individual 1233 20th St NW Suite 300	Washington	DC	20036	**877-426-2665**	202-833-8400	48-8
Rigid Building Systems Ltd 18933 Aldine Westfield Rd	Houston	TX	77073	**888-467-4443**	281-443-9065	106
Rigid Hitch Inc 3301 W Burnsville Pkwy; *Cust Svc	Burnsville	MN	55337	**800-624-7630***	952-895-5001	751
Rim Country Regional Chamber of Commerce 100 W Main St	Payson	AZ	85547	**800-672-9766**	928-474-4515	137
Rim & Wheel Service Inc 1014 Gest St	Cincinnati	OH	45203	**800-783-6940**	513-721-6940	61
Rimage Corp 7725 Washington Ave S; *NASDAQ: RIMG*	Minneapolis	MN	55439	**800-445-8288**	952-944-8144	171-8
Rimex Metals (USA) Inc 2850 Woodbridge Ave	Edison	NJ	08837	**800-526-7600**	732-549-3800	472
Rimrock Foundation 1231 N 29th St	Billings	MT	59101	**800-227-3953**	406-248-3175	712
Rimrock Resort Hotel 300 Mountain Ave PO Box 1110	Banff	AB	T1L1J2	**800-661-1587**	403-762-3356	655
Rimrock Stages Inc PO Box 988	Billings	MT	59103	**800-255-7655**	406-245-5392	109
RIMS (Risk & Insurance Management Society Inc) 655 3rd Ave 2nd Fl	New York	NY	10017	**800-711-0317**	212-286-9292	49-9
Rinalli Boats Ltd 1600 N King St	Seguin	TX	78155	**866-746-2554**	830-372-3300	91
Ring Container Technology 1 Industrial Pk Dr	Oakland	TN	38060	**800-280-7464**	901-465-3607	124
Ring Specialty Co 2691 30th St	Boulder	CO	80301	**800-328-6330**	303-440-5507	401
Ringling School of Art & Design 2700 N Tamiami Trail	Sarasota	FL	34234	**800-255-7695**	941-351-5100	163
Rink Systems Inc 1103 Hershey St	Albert Lea	MN	56007	**800-944-7930**	507-373-9175	15
Rinker Materials Corp 1501 Belvedere Rd	West Palm Beach	FL	33406	**800-226-5521**	561-833-5555	181
Rinker Materials Corp Hydro Conduit Div 6560 Langfield Rd Bldg 3	Houston	TX	77092	**800-909-7763**	832-590-5300	181
Rinn Div Dentsply International Inc 1212 Abbott Dr	Elgin	IL	60123	**800-323-0970**	847-742-1115	226
Rio All-Suite Hotel & Casino 3700 W Flamingo Rd	Las Vegas	NV	89103	**888-746-7482**	702-777-7777	655
Rio Bravo Resort 11200 Lake Ming Rd	Bakersfield	CA	93306	**888-517-5500**	661-872-5000	655
Rio Delmar Enterprises PO Box 1409	Easton	MD	21601	**800-638-4402**	410-822-8866	420
Rio Grande Co 201 Santa Fe Dr	Denver	CO	80223	**800-864-4280**	303-825-2211	190-1
Rio Grande Electric Co-op Inc Hwy 90 & State Hwy 131 PO Box 1509	Brackettville	TX	78832	**800-749-1509**	830-563-2444	244
Rio Grande Portland Cement Co 4253 Montgomery Blvd NE Suite 210	Albuquerque	NM	87109	**800-234-2266**	505-881-5303	135
Rio Grande Valley Business Journal 1300 Wild Rose Ln	Brownsville	TX	78520	**800-556-9876**	956-546-5113	449-5
Rio Products Inc 5050 S Yellowstone Hwy	Idaho Falls	ID	83402	**800-553-0838**	208-524-7760	701
Rio Rico Resort & Country Club 1069 Camino Caralampi	Rio Rico	AZ	85648	**800-288-4746**	520-281-1901	655
Rio Salado College 2323 W 14th St	Tempe	AZ	85281	**800-729-1197**	480-517-8540	160
Rio Verde Development Inc 18815 E Four Peaks Blvd	Rio Verde	AZ	85263	**800-233-7103**	480-471-3350	186
Rio Vista Rehabilitation Hospital 1740 Curie Dr	El Paso	TX	79902	**800-999-8392**	915-544-3399	366-4
Rip Griffin Truck Travel Center Inc PO Box 10128	Lubbock	TX	79408	**800-333-9330**	806-763-9349	319
RIPA (Reusable Industrial Packaging Assn) 8401 Corporate Dr Suite 450	Landover	MD	20785	**800-533-3786**	301-577-3786	49-13
Ripley Co 46 Nooks Hill Rd	Cromwell	CT	06416	**800-528-8665**	860-635-2200	746
Ripley's Aquarium 1110 Celebrity Cir Broadway at the Beach	Myrtle Beach	SC	29577	**800-734-8888**	843-916-0888	40
Ripley's Believe It or Not! Museum 3326 W Hwy 76	Branson	MO	65616	**800-998-4418**	417-337-5300	509
Ripley's Believe It or Not! Museum New York Ave & Boardwalk	Atlantic City	NJ	08401	**877-713-4233**	609-347-2001	509
Ripon College 300 Seward St	Ripon	WI	54971	**800-947-4766**	920-748-8337	163
Risdall Advertising Agency 550 Main St	New Brighton	MN	55112	**888-747-3255**	651-631-1098	4
Rising Sun/Ohio County Convention & Tourism Bureau 120 N Walnut St	Rising Sun	IN	47040	**888-776-4786**	812-438-4933	205
Risk & Insurance Management Society Inc (RIMS) 655 3rd Ave 2nd Fl	New York	NY	10017	**800-711-0317**	212-286-9292	49-9
Risk Management Alternatives Inc 2675 Breckinridge Blvd	Duluth	GA	30096	**800-275-7075**	770-925-5000	157
Risk Management Assn. RMA - 1650 Market St 1 Liberty Pl Suite 2300; *Cust Svc	Philadelphia	PA	19103	**800-677-7621***	215-446-4000	49-2
Risk Planners Inc PO Box 240	Minneapolis	MN	55440	**800-328-7475**	952-914-5777	384-4
RiskWatch Inc 2568A Riva Rd Suite 300	Annapolis	MD	21401	**800-448-4666**	410-224-4773	176-10
RISO Inc 300 Rosewood Dr Suite 210	Danvers	MA	01923	**800-876-7476**	978-777-7377	171-6
Risser Oil Corp 2865 Executive Dr	Clearwater	FL	33762	**800-572-0075**	727-573-4000	569
Rita Blanca Electric Co-op Inc PO Box 1947	Dalhart	TX	79022	**800-299-4506**	806-249-4506	244
Rita's Water Ice Franchise Corp 1525 Ford Rd	Bensalem	PA	19020	**800-677-7482**	215-633-9899	221
Ritchey Alan Inc 740 S I-35 E Frontage Rd	Valley View	TX	76272	**800-877-0273**	940-726-3276	769
Ritchie Bros Auctioneers Inc 6500 River Rd; *NYSE: RBA*	Richmond	BC	V6X4G5	**800-663-1739**	604-273-7564	51
Ritchie & Page Distributing Co Inc 292 3rd St	Trenton	NJ	08611	**800-257-9360**	609-392-1146	82-1
Rite-Hite Corp 4343 Chavenelle Dr	Dubuque	IA	52004	**800-456-0600**	563-556-2020	469
Rite-Style Optical Co PO Box 3068	Omaha	NE	68103	**800-373-3200**	402-492-8822	533
Rite Way Oil & Gas Co Inc PO Box 27049	Omaha	NE	68127	**800-279-6401**	402-331-6400	569
RiteMade Paper Converters 1015 Tyler St; *Cust Svc	Fredericksburg	VA	22401	**800-368-3485***	540-371-8626	544
Riteway Bus Service Inc Motorcoach Div W201 N13900 Fond du Lac Ave	Richfield	WI	53076	**800-776-7026**	414-677-3282	108
Rittal Corp 1 Rittal Pl	Springfield	OH	45504	**800-477-4000**	937-399-0500	804
Rittenhouse Book Distributors Inc 511 Feheley Dr; *Cust Svc	King of Prussia	PA	19406	**800-345-6425***	610-277-1414	97
Rittenhouse Financial Services Inc 5 Radnor Corporate Ctr Suite 300	Radnor	PA	19087	**800-847-6369**	610-254-9600	393
Rittenhouse Hotel 210 W Rittenhouse Sq	Philadelphia	PA	19103	**800-635-1042**	215-546-9000	373
Ritter E & Co Inc 106 Frisco St	Marked Tree	AR	72365	**800-323-0355**	870-358-2200	11-2
Ritter Technology LLC 100 Williams Dr	Zelienople	PA	16063	**800-374-8837**	724-452-6000	777
Ritz Camera Centers Inc 6711 Ritz Way; *Orders	Beltsville	MD	20705	**877-690-0099***	301-419-0000	119
Ritz-Carlton Amelia Island 4750 Amelia Island Pkwy	Amelia Island	FL	32034	**800-241-3333**	904-277-1100	655
Ritz-Carlton Georgetown 3100 South St NW	Washington	DC	20007	**800-241-3333**	202-912-4100	373
Ritz-Carlton Half Moon Bay 1 Miramontes Pt Rd	Half Moon Bay	CA	94019	**800-244-3333**	650-712-7000	655
Ritz-Carlton Hotel Co LLC 4445 Willard Ave Suite 800	Chevy Chase	MD	20815	**800-241-3333**	301-547-4700	369
Ritz-Carlton Hotel. Maison Orleans - A 904 Rue Iberville	New Orleans	LA	70112	**800-241-3333**	504-670-2900	373
Ritz-Carlton Key Biscayne 455 Grand Bay Dr	Key Biscayne	FL	33149	**800-241-3333**	305-365-9575	655
Ritz-Carlton Laguna Niguel 1 Ritz Carlton Dr	Dana Point	CA	92629	**800-241-3333**	949-240-2000	655
Ritz-Carlton Lake Las Vegas 1610 Lake Las Vegas Pkwy	Henderson	NV	89011	**800-241-3333**	702-567-4700	373
Ritz-Carlton Naples 280 Vanderbilt Beach Rd	Naples	FL	34108	**800-241-3333**	239-598-3300	655
Ritz-Carlton Naples Golf Resort 2600 Tiburon Dr	Naples	FL	34109	**888-856-2164**	239-593-2000	655
Ritz-Carlton Orlando Grande Lakes 4012 Central Florida Pkwy	Orlando	FL	32837	**800-241-3333**	407-206-2400	373
Ritz-Carlton Palm Beach 100 S Ocean Blvd	Manalapan	FL	33462	**800-241-3333**	561-533-6000	655
Ritz-Carlton Reynolds Plantation 1 Lake Oconee Trail	Greensboro	GA	30642	**800-826-1945**	706-467-0600	655
Ritz-Craft Corp of Pennsylvania Inc 15 Industrial Pk Rd	Mifflinburg	PA	17844	**800-326-9836**	570-966-1053	495
Ritz Plaza Hotel 1701 Collins Ave	Miami Beach	FL	33139	**800-522-6400**	305-534-3500	373
Riu Hotel Florida Beach 3101 Collins Ave	Miami	FL	33140	**888-666-8816**	305-673-5333	373
Rival Co 32B Spur Dr	El Paso	TX	79906	**800-557-4825**		37
Rivard's Quality Seeds Inc 103 Main St	Argyle	MN	56713	**888-543-6638**	218-437-6638	438
Rivco Products Inc 440 S Pine St	Burlington	WI	53105	**888-801-8222**	262-763-8222	506
River Bend Industries 2421 16th Ave S	Moorhead	MN	56560	**800-365-3070**	218-236-1818	198
River City Brass Band 885 Progress St	Pittsburgh	PA	15212	**800-292-7222**	412-322-7222	563-3
River City Petroleum Inc PO Box 235	West Sacramento	CA	95691	**800-441-2108**	916-371-4960	569
River Country Tourism Bureau 316 E Charlotte PO Box 579	Centreville	MI	49032	**800-447-2821**	269-467-4452	205
River. Friends of the 915 20th St	Sacramento	CA	95814	**888-464-2477**	916-442-3155	48-13
River Inn 924 25th St NW	Washington	DC	20037	**800-424-2741**	202-337-7600	373
River Palms Resort & Casino 2700 S Casino Dr	Laughlin	NV	89029	**800-835-7904**	702-298-2242	133
River Park Hospital 1230 6th Ave	Huntington	WV	25701	**800-992-9101**	304-526-9111	366-3
River Ranch Fresh Foods 1156 Abbott St	Salinas	CA	93901	**800-538-5868**	831-758-1390	12-1
River Region West Campus 1111 N Frontage Rd	Vicksburg	MS	39180	**800-548-2419**	601-636-2611	366-2
River Street Inn 115 E River St	Savannah	GA	31401	**800-253-4229**	912-234-6400	373
River Valley Bancorp 430 Clifty Dr; *NASDAQ: RIVR*	Madison	IN	47250	**800-994-4849**	812-273-4949	355-2
RiverBarge Excursion Lines Inc 201 Opelousas Ave	New Orleans	LA	70114	**888-462-2743**	504-365-0022	218
Riverdeep Inc 500 Redwood Blvd	Novato	CA	94947	**800-825-4420**	415-763-4700	176-3
Riveredge Nature Center 4458 W Hawthorne Dr Box 26	Newburg	WI	53060	**800-287-8098**	262-375-2715	50
Riveredge Resort Hotel 17 Holland St	Alexandria Bay	NY	13607	**800-365-6987**	315-482-9917	373
Riverhead Building Supply Corp 1093 Pulaski St	Riverhead	NY	11901	**800-378-3650**	631-727-3650	190-3
Riverland Community College 1900 8th Ave NW	Austin	MN	55912	**800-247-5039**	507-433-0600	160
Riverland Energy Co-op 625 W Main St	Arcadia	WI	54612	**800-411-9115**	608-323-3381	244
RiverMead Retirement Community 150 RiverMead Rd	Peterborough	NH	03458	**800-200-5433**	603-924-0062	659
RiverPoint Group LLC 9450 W Bryn Mawr Ave Suite 700	Rosemont	IL	60018	**800-297-5601**	847-233-9600	178
Rivers. American 1025 Vermont Ave NW Suite 720	Washington	DC	20005	**800-296-6900**	202-347-7550	48-13
River's Edge Resort Cottages 4200 Boat St	Fairbanks	AK	99709	**800-770-3343**	907-474-0286	373
Rivers Oceans & Mountains Adventures Inc (ROAM) 7025 Beggs Rd	Nelson	BC	V1L5P6	**877-271-7626**	250-354-2056	748
Riverside Art Shop 1600 Grand Army Hwy	Somerset	MA	02726	**800-354-9899**	508-672-6735	45
Riverside Brick & Supply Co 12th & Maury St	Richmond	VA	23224	**800-666-0444**	804-232-6786	148
Riverside Clay Co Inc 201 Truss Ferry Rd	Pell City	AL	35128	**800-226-4542**	205-338-3366	493-2
Riverside Convention & Visitors Bureau 3750 University Ave Suite 175	Riverside	CA	92501	**888-913-4636**	951-222-4700	205
Riverside Distributors 636 S Oak St	Iowa Falls	IA	50126	**800-247-5111**	641-648-4271	97

Name / Address	City	State	ZIP	Toll-Free	Phone	Class
Riverside Hotel 620 E Las Olas Blvd	Fort Lauderdale	FL	33301	**800-325-3280**	954-467-0671	373
Riverside Inn 1 Fountain Ave	Cambridge Springs	PA	16403	**800-964-5173**	814-398-4645	373
Riverside Mattress Co Inc 225 Dunn Rd	Fayetteville	NC	28312	**888-288-5195**	910-483-0461	463
Riverside Mfg Co 301 Riverside Dr	Moultrie	GA	31768	**800-841-8677**	229-985-5210	153-19
Riverside Military Academy 2001 Riverside Dr	Gainsville	GA	30501	**800-462-2338**	770-532-6251	611
Riverside Paper Co 110 N Kensington Dr *Cust Svc	Appleton	WI	54915	**800-443-6326***	920-991-2212	544
Riverside Paper Corp 800 S Lawe St *Cust Svc	Appleton	WI	54915	**800-443-6326***	920-991-2200	547
Riverside Publishing Co 425 Spring Lake Dr	Itasca	IL	60143	**800-323-9540**	630-467-7000	243
Riverside Resort & Casino. Don Laughlin's 1650 Casino Dr	Laughlin	NV	89029	**800-227-3849**	702-298-2535	133
Riverside Scrap Iron PO Box 5288	Riverside	CA	92517	**800-399-4766**	951-686-2120	674
Riverside Transit Agency (RTA) 1825 3rd St PO Box 59968	Riverside	CA	92517	**800-800-7821**	951-682-1234	460
Riverside Travel Group Inc 13343 SE Stark St Suite 200	Portland	OR	97233	**800-772-2228**	503-255-2950	761
Riverside Visitors Center 3750 University Ave Suite 175	Riverside	CA	92501	**888-913-4636**	951-684-4636	205
Riverstone Networks Inc 5200 Great America Pkwy	Santa Clara	CA	95054	**888-924-6797**	408-878-6500	720
Riverton Ranger PO Box 993	Riverton	WY	82501	**800-428-7229**	307-856-2244	522-2
Rivertown Newspaper Group 2760 N Service Dr PO Box 15	Red Wing	MN	55066	**800-535-1660**	651-388-8235	623-8
Rivervalley Behavioral Health Hospital 1000 Industrial Dr	Owensboro	KY	42301	**800-755-8477**	270-686-8477	712
Riverview Hospital 395 Westfield Rd	Noblesville	IN	46060	**800-523-6001**	317-773-0760	366-2
Riviana Foods Inc PO Box 2636	Houston	TX	77252	**800-626-9522**	713-529-3251	291-23
Rivier College 420 Main St	Nashua	NH	03060	**800-447-4843**	603-888-1311	163
Riviera Finance 220 Ave I	Redondo Beach	CA	90277	**800-872-7484**		268
Riviera Holdings Corp 2901 Las Vegas Blvd S *AMEX: RIV*	Las Vegas	NV	89109	**800-634-6753**	702-734-5110	369
Riviera Hotel 1431 Robson St	Vancouver	BC	V6G1C1	**888-699-5222**	604-685-1301	372
Riviera Hotel & Casino 2901 Las Vegas Blvd S *Resv	Las Vegas	NV	89109	**800-634-6753***	702-734-5110	655
Riviera Resort & Racket Club. Palm Springs 1600 N Indian Canyon Dr	Palm Springs	CA	92262	**800-444-8311**	760-327-8311	655
Rivio Inc 2500 Augustine Dr	Santa Clara	CA	95054	**888-777-7077**	408-653-4400	39
RJ Boar's Franchising Corp 3127 Brady St Suite 3	Davenport	IA	52803	**877-395-8910**	563-322-2627	657
RJ Gator's Hometown Grill & Bar 609 Hepburn Ave Suite 103	Jupiter	FL	33458	**800-438-4286**	561-575-0326	657
Rj Gordon & Co 8730 W Sunset Blvd Suite 290	West Hollywood	CA	90069	**800-746-7366**	310-734-3500	193
RJ O'Brien & Assoc 222 S Riverside Plaza Suite 900	Chicago	IL	60606	**800-621-0757**	312-373-5000	167
RJ Singer International Inc 4801 W Jefferson Blvd *Sales	Los Angeles	CA	90016	**800-824-9035***	323-735-1717	444
RJ Thomas Mfg Co Inc PO Box 946	Cherokee	IA	51012	**800-725-5115**	712-225-5115	314-4
RJN Group Inc 200 W Front St	Wheaton	IL	60187	**800-227-7838**	630-682-4700	191
RK Mechanical Inc 9300 E Smith Rd	Denver	CO	80207	**800-783-0075**	303-355-9696	188-10
RKA Petroleum 28340 Wick Rd	Romulus	MI	48174	**800-875-3835**	734-946-2199	571
RL Adams Plastics Inc 5955 Crossroads Commerce Pkwy	Wyoming	MI	49517	**800-968-2241**	616-261-4400	590
RL Winston Rod Co 500 S Main St	Twin Bridges	MT	59754	**800-237-8763**	406-684-5674	701
RL Ziegler Co Inc PO Box 1640	Tuscaloosa	AL	35403	**800-392-6328**	205-758-3621	465
RLG (Research Libraries Group Inc) 2029 Stierlin Ct Suite 100	Mountain View	CA	94043	**800-537-7546**	650-962-9951	49-5
RLI Corp 9025 N Lindbergh Dr *NYSE: RLI*	Peoria	IL	61615	**800-331-4929**	309-692-1000	355-4
RLI Insurance Co 9025 N Lindbergh Dr	Peoria	IL	61615	**800-331-4929**	309-692-1000	384-4
RMA - Risk Management Assn 1650 Market St 1 Liberty Pl Suite 2300 *Cust Svc	Philadelphia	PA	19103	**800-677-7621***	215-446-4000	49-2
RMC Carolina Materials Inc PO Box 19178	Greensboro	NC	27419	**800-849-6894**	336-294-1124	181
RMC Florida Materials 801 McCue Rd	Lakeland	FL	33815	**800-282-4657**	863-688-5787	180
RMC Inc 1040 S High St	Harrisonburg	VA	22801	**800-726-7625**	540-434-5333	438
RMC Pacific Materials Inc 6601 Koll Center Pkwy PO box 5252	Pleasanton	CA	94566	**800-227-5186**	925-462-7181	180
RMH Teleservices Inc 15 Campus Blvd	Newtown Square	PA	19073	**800-325-3100**	610-352-3100	722
RMPB (Rocky Mountain Public Broadcasting Network) 1089 Bannock St	Denver	CO	80204	**800-274-6666**	303-892-6666	620
RMT Inc 744 Heartland Trail	Madison	WI	53717	**800-283-3443**	608-831-4444	258
RMT Technology 435 Eastern Ave	Bellwood	IL	60104	**800-228-9949**	708-544-1017	484
RMTD (Rides Mass Transit District) PO Box 190	Rosiclare	IL	62982	**877-667-6122**	618-285-3342	109
RN Magazine 5 Paragon Dr	Montvale	NJ	07645	**888-581-8052**	973-944-7777	449-16
RNC Capital Management LLC 11601 Wilshire Blvd 25th Fl	Los Angeles	CA	90025	**800-877-7624**	310-477-6543	393
Ro-An Industries Corp 64-20 Admiral Ave	Middle Village	NY	11379	**800-255-7626**	718-821-1115	537
Ro-Lab American Rubber Co Inc 8830 W Linne Rd	Tracy	CA	95304	**888-276-2993**	209-836-0965	364
ROA (Reserve Officers Assn of the US) 1 Constitution Ave NE	Washington	DC	20002	**800-809-9448**	202-479-2200	48-19
ROACO Logistics Services 970 N Oaklawn Ave	Elmhurst	IL	60126	**877-941-0400**	630-941-0400	440
Road America PO Box P	Elkhart Lake	WI	53020	**800-365-7223**	920-892-4576	504

Name / Address	City	State	ZIP	Toll-Free	Phone	Class
Road America Motor Club 7300 Corporate Ctr Dr Suite 601	Miami	FL	33126	**800-262-7262**	305-392-4300	53
Road Atlanta Raceway 5300 Winder Hwy	Braselton	GA	30517	**800-849-7223**	770-967-6143	504
Road King Inn Columbia Mall 3300 30th Ave S	Grand Forks	ND	58201	**800-707-1391**	701-746-1391	373
Road King Magazine 28 Whitebridge Rd Suite 209	Nashville	TN	37205	**800-385-9745**	615-627-2200	449-21
Road Rescue Inc 2914 Spartan Pl	Marion	SC	29571	**800-328-3804**	843-676-2900	505
Road & Track Magazine 1499 Monrovia Ave *Cust Svc	Newport Beach	CA	92663	**800-876-8316***	949-720-5300	449-3
Roadgard Motor Club 11222 Quail Roost Dr	Miami	FL	33157	**800-432-8603**		53
Roadhouse Grill Inc 2703-A Gateway Dr	Pompano Beach	FL	33069	**800-680-2279**	954-957-2600	657
Roadway Express Inc 1077 Gorge Blvd	Akron	OH	44310	**800-762-3929**	330-384-1717	769
ROAM (Rivers Oceans & Mountains Adventures Inc) 7025 Beggs Rd	Nelson	BC	V1L5P6	**877-271-7626**	250-354-2056	748
Roaman's 2300 Southeastern Ave	Indianapolis	IN	46283	**800-459-1025**		451
Roane State Community College 276 Patton Ln	Harriman	TN	37748	**800-343-9104**	865-354-3000	160
Roanoke Bible College 715 N Poindexter St	Elizabeth City	NC	27909	**800-722-8980**	252-334-2070	163
Roanoke Chowan Publishing PO Box 1325	Ahoskie	NC	27910	**888-639-7437**	252 332 2123	623-8
Roanoke College 221 College Ln	Salem	VA	24153	**800-388-2276**	540-375-2500	163
Roanoke Electric Co-op 401 N Main St	Rich Square	NC	27869	**800-433-2236**	252-539-2236	244
Roanoke Electric Steel Corp 102 Westside Blvd NW *NASDAQ: RESC*	Roanoke	VA	24017	**800-765-6567**	540-342-1831	709
Roanoke Gas Co 519 Kimball Rd	Roanoke	VA	24030	**800-552-6514**	540-777-3800	774
Roanoke Symphony 541 Luck Ave Suite 200	Roanoke	VA	24016	**866-277-9127**	540-343-6221	563-3
Roanoke Times 201 W Campbell Ave SW	Roanoke	VA	24011	**800-346-1234**	540-981-3100	522-2
Roanoke Valley Convention & Visitors Bureau 101 Shenandoah Ave NE	Roanoke	VA	24016	**800-635-5535**	540-342-6025	205
Roanwell Corp 2564 Park Ave	Bronx	NY	10451	**866-292-3301**	718-401-0288	52
Roaring Spring Blank Book Co 740 Spang St *Cust Svc	Roaring Spring	PA	16673	**800-441-1653***	814-224-5141	87
Robbie Mfg Inc 10810 Mid America Ave	Lenexa	KS	66219	**800-255-6328**	913-492-3400	590
Robbins Anthony 9888 Carroll Centre Rd	San Diego	CA	92126	**800-445-8183**	858-535-9900	561
Robbins Co 400 O'Neil Blvd	Attleboro	MA	02703	**800-343-3970**	508-222-2900	377
Robbins Inc 4777 Eastern Ave	Cincinnati	OH	45226	**800-543-1913**	513-871-8988	671
Robbins LLC PO Box 60	Tuscumbia	AL	35674	**800-633-3312**	256-383-5441	739
Robbins Lumber Inc PO Box 9	Searsmont	ME	04973	**800-287-5067**	207-342-5221	671
Robbins LW Assoc 201 Summer St	Holliston	MA	01746	**800-229-5972**	508-893-0210	312
Robbins Mfg Co PO Box 17939	Tampa	FL	33682	**800-282-9336**	813-971-3030	806
Robbins Sabin Paper Co 497 Circle Freeway Dr Suite 490	Cincinnati	OH	45246	**800-424-5574**	513-874-5270	547
Robern Inc 701 N Wilson Ave	Bristol	PA	19007	**800-877-2376**	215-826-9800	314-2
Roberson Museum & Science Center 30 Front St	Binghamton	NY	13905	**888-269-5325**	607-772-0660	509
Robert Allen Fabrics Inc 55 Cabot Blvd	Mansfield	MA	02048	**800-333-3777**	508-339-9151	583
Robert Arranaga & Co Inc 216 S Alameda St	Los Angeles	CA	90012	**800-639-0059**	213-622-1261	295
Robert Bosch Corp Blaupunkt Div 2800 S 25th Ave *Sales	Broadview	IL	60155	**800-323-1943***	708-865-5200	52
Robert Bosch Corp Packaging Technology Div 9890 Red Arrow Hwy	Bridgman	MI	49106	**800-292-6724**	269-466-4000	537
Robert Bosch Tool Corp 4300 W Peterson Ave1800 W Central Rd	Mount Prospect	IL	60056	**800-301-8255**	224-223-2000	747
Robert C Williams American Museum of Papermaking 500 10th St NW	Atlanta	GA	30318	**800-558-6611**	404-894-7840	509
Robert E Morris Co Inc 17 Talcott Notch Rd	Farmington	CT	06032	**800-223-0785**	860-678-0200	378
Robert E Nolan Co Inc 90 Hopmeadow St	Simsbury	CT	06070	**800-653-1941**	860-658-1941	193
Robert Gaspard Co Inc 200 N Janacek Rd	Brookfield	WI	53045	**800-784-6868**	262-784-6800	153-14
Robert Gibb & Sons Inc 205 SW 40th St	Fargo	ND	58103	**800-842-7366**	701-282-5900	188-10
Robert H Wager Co 570 Montroyal Rd	Rural Hall	NC	27045	**800-562-7024**	336-969-6909	776
Robert Half Management Resources (RHIMR) 2884 Sand Hill Rd Suite 200	Menlo Park	CA	94025	**888-400-7474**	650-234-6000	193
Robert J Hanafin Inc PO Box 509	Endicott	NY	13761	**800-448-4826**	607-754-3500	383
Robert and Margrit Mondavi Center for the Performing Arts 1 Shields Ave	Davis	CA	95616	**866-754-2787**	530-754-2787	562
Robert Mfg Co Inc 10667 Jersey Blvd	Rancho Cucamonga	CA	91730	**800-877-6237**	909-987-4654	584
Robert Mfg Co Inc 4000 E 10th Ct	Hialeah	FL	33013	**800-780-3684**	305-691-5311	444
Robert Mondavi Co 7801 St Helena Hwy PO Box 106	Oakville	CA	94562	**888-766-6328**	707-259-9463	81-3
Robert Morris College						
Chicago Campus 401 S State St	Chicago	IL	60605	**800-225-1520**	312-935-6800	163
DuPage Campus 905 Meridian Lake Dr	Aurora	IL	60504	**800-762-5960**		160
Orland Park Campus 43 Orland Sq Dr	Orland Park	IL	60462	**800-225-1520**	708-460-8000	163
Springfield Campus 3101 Montvale Dr	Springfield	IL	62704	**800-868-9300**	217-793-2500	163
Robert Morris University 6001 University Blvd	Moon Township	PA	15108	**800-762-0097**	412-262-8200	163
Robert Packer Hospital 1 Guthrie Sq	Sayre	PA	18840	**888-448-8474**	570-888-6666	366-2
Robert R Meyer Planetarium 900 Arkadelphia Rd Birmingham Southern College PO Box 549036	Birmingham	AL	35254	**800-523-5793**	205-226-4770	587

				Toll-Free	Phone	Class
Robert S Fisher & Co Inc 19 Liberty St	Newark	NJ	07102	**800-526-8052**	973-622-2658	401
Robert W Baird & Co Inc PO Box 672	Milwaukee	WI	53201	**800-792-2473**	414-765-3500	679
Robert Wholey & Co Inc 1501 Penn Ave	Pittsburgh	PA	15222	**800-248-0568**	412-261-3693	292-5
Roberts Automatic Products Inc 880 Lake Dr	Chanhassen	MN	55317	**800-879-9837**	952-949-1000	610
Roberts Dairy 3805 S Emanuel Cleaver II Blvd	Kansas City	MO	64128	**800-279-1692**	816-921-7370	291-27
Roberts Dairy Co PO Box 3825	Omaha	NE	68103	**800-779-4321**	402-344-4321	292-4
Roberts FL & Co Inc 93 W Broad St PO Box 1964	Springfield	MA	01102	**800-628-4004**	413-781-7444	319
Roberts-Gordon Inc PO Box 44	Buffalo	NY	14240	**800-828-7450**	716-852-4400	352
Roberts Hawaii Inc 680 Iwilei Rd Dole Office Bldg Suite 700	Honolulu	HI	96817	**800-831-5541**	808-523-7750	748
Roberts John Co 9687 E River Rd	Coon Rapids	MN	55433	**800-551-1534**	763-755-5500	615
Roberts JR Corp 7745 Greenback Ln Suite 300	Citrus Heights	CA	95610	**800-551-1534**	916-729-5600	185
Roberts Wesleyan College 2301 Westside Dr	Rochester	NY	14624	**800-777-4792***	585-594-6000	163
*Admissions						
Robertshaw Industrial Products 1602 Mustang Dr	Maryville	TN	37801	**800-228-7429**	865-981-3100	200
Robertson Furniture Co Inc 720 Elberton St PO Box 847	Toccoa	GA	30577	**800-241-0713**	706-886-1494	314-1
Robertson Inc 97 Bronte St N	Milton	ON	L9T2N8	**800-268-5090**	905-878-2866	274
Robertson Mfg Inc 112 Woodland Ave	West Grove	PA	19390	**800-260-5423**	610-869-9600	718
Robinair Div SPX Corp 655 Eisenhower Dr	Owatonna	MN	55060	**800-628-6496**	507-455-7000	201
Robins GS & Co 126 Chouteau Ave	Saint Louis	MO	63102	**800-777-5155**	314-621-5165	144
Robins Kaplan Miller & Ciresi LLP 800 LaSalle Ave 2800 LaSalle Plaza	Minneapolis	MN	55402	**800-553-9910**	612-349-8500	419
Robinson Brick Co 1845 W Dartmouth Ave	Denver	CO	80110	**800-477-9002**	303-783-3000	148
Robinson Center 426 W Markham St 7 Statehouse Plaza	Little Rock	AR	72201	**800-844-4781**	501-376-4781	562
Robinson CH Worldwide Inc 8100 Mitchell Rd Suite 200	Eden Prairie	MN	55344	**800-247-5644**	952-937-8500	440
NASDAQ: CHRW						
Robinson & Cole LLP 280 Trumbull St	Hartford	CT	06103	**800-826-3579**	860-275-8200	419
Robinson Geo M & Co 852 85th Ave	Oakland	CA	94621	**800-894-8942**	510-632-7017	188-13
Robinson Industries Inc 3051 Curtis Rd	Coleman	MI	48618	**800-525-0391**	989-465-6111	538
Robinson Mfg Co Inc 798 Market St PO Box 338	Dayton	TN	37321	**800-251-7286**	423-775-2212	153-18
Robinson Neal Wholesale Greenhouses 975 Robindale Rd	Brownsville	TX	78523	**800-874-2740**	956-831-4656	363
Robinson Terminal Warehouse Corp 2 Duke St	Alexandria	VA	22314	**800-331-6593**	703-836-8300	790-1
Robotics & Automation Society. IEEE IEEE Operations Ctr 445 Hoes Ln	Piscataway	NJ	08854	**800-678-4333**	732-981-0060	49-19
Robson Communities 9532 E Riggs Rd	Sun Lakes	AZ	85248	**800-732-9949**	480-895-9200	639
Robustelli Event Services 30 Spring St	Stamford	CT	06902	**888-258-9398**		183
Robustelli World Travel Inc 460 Summer St	Stamford	CT	06901	**800-243-2654**	203-352-0500	760
Roche Bioscience 3431 Hillview Ave	Palo Alto	CA	94304	**800-796-8395**	650-855-5050	86
Roche Diagnostics Corp 9115 Hague Rd PO Box 50457	Indianapolis	IN	46256	**800-428-5076***	317-521-2000	229
*Cust Svc						
Roche Diagnostics North America 9115 Hague Rd PO Box 50457	Indianapolis	IN	46256	**800-428-5076***	317-521-2000	229
*Cust Svc						
Roche Mfg Co Inc PO Box 4156	Dublin	GA	31040	**800-515-3251**	478-272-3340	276
Rocher Yves Inc 50 Briarhollow Rd Suite 500-W	Houston	TX	77027	**800-222-6222**	713-626-2255	361
Rochester Big & Tall 700 Mission St	San Francisco	CA	94103	**800-282-8200**	415-982-6455	155-3
Rochester College 800 W Avon Rd	Rochester Hills	MI	48307	**800-521-6010**	248-218-2011	163
Rochester Community & Technical College 851 30th Ave SE	Rochester	MN	55904	**800-247-1296**	507-285-7210	160
Rochester Convention & Visitors Bureau 111 S Broadway Suite 301	Rochester	MN	55904	**800-634-8277**	507-288-4331	205
Rochester Drug Co-op Inc PO Box 24389	Rochester	NY	14624	**800-333-0538**	585-271-7220	237
Rochester Eye & Human Parts Bank DBA Rochester/Finger Lakes Eye & Tissue Bank 524 White Spruce Blvd	Rochester	NY	14623	**800-568-4321**	585-272-7890	265
Rochester Gas & Electric Corp 89 East Ave	Rochester	NY	14649	**888-253-8888**	585-546-2700	774
Rochester Gauges Inc of Texas 11616 Harry Hines Blvd	Dallas	TX	75229	**800-821-1829**	972-241-2161	200
Rochester (Greater) Visitors Assn 45 East Ave Suite 400	Rochester	NY	14604	**800-677-7282**	585-546-3070	205
Rochester Medical Corp 1 Rochester Medical Dr	Stewartville	MN	55976	**800-243-3315**	507-533-9600	468
NASDAQ: ROCM						
Rochester Midland Corp 333 Hollenbeck St PO Box 31515	Rochester	NY	14603	**800-836-1627**	585-336-2200	143
Rochester Orchestra & Chorale 301 N Broadway	Rochester	MN	55906	**877-286-8742**	507-286-8742	563-3
Rochester Sentinel PO Box 260	Rochester	IN	46975	**800-686-2112**	574-223-2111	522-2
Rochester Shoe Tree Co Inc PO Box 746	Ashland	NH	03217	**800-692-3300***	603-968-3301	344
*Cust Svc						
Rochester/Finger Lakes Eye & Tissue Bank 524 White Spruce Blvd	Rochester	NY	14623	**800-568-4321**	585-272-7890	265
Rochling Engineered Plastics 120 Rochling St PO Box 2729	Gastonia	NC	28053	**800-541-4419***	704-922-7814	588
*Cust Svc						
Rock of Ages Corp RR 1 Box 1140	Graniteville	VT	05654	**800-421-0166**	802-476-3115	710
NASDAQ: ROAC						
Rock Bottom Restaurants Inc 248 Centennial Pkwy	Louisville	CO	80027	**800-273-9827**	303-664-4000	656
Rock City Gardens 1400 Patten Rd	Lookout Mountain	GA	30750	**800-854-0675**	706-820-2531	50
Rock County Electric Co-op Assn 2815 Kennedy Rd	Janesville	WI	53547	**888-236-0665**	608-752-4550	244
Rock Creek Resort HC 49 Box 3500	Red Lodge	MT	59068	**800-667-1119**	406-446-1111	655
Rock Island Corp 530 Oak Court Dr Suite 260	Memphis	TN	38117	**800-529-5701**	901-529-5700	346
Rock 'N Learn Inc 105 Commercial Cir	Conroe	TX	77304	**800-348-8445**	936-539-2731	242
Rock River Valley Blood Center 419 N 6th St	Rockford	IL	61107	**866-889-9073**	815-965-8751	90
Rock & Roll Hall of Fame & Museum 1 Key Plaza	Cleveland	OH	44114	**800-349-7625**	216-781-7625	509
Rock Springs Chamber of Commerce 1897 Dewar Dr	Rock Springs	WY	82901	**800-463-8637**	307-362-3771	137
Rock Springs Guest Ranch 64201 Tyler Rd	Bend	OR	97701	**800-225-3833**	541-382-1957	238
Rock-Tenn Co 504 Thrasher St	Norcross	GA	30071	**800-762-5836**	770-448-2193	551
NYSE: RKT						
Rock-Tenn Co Corrugated Packaging & Display Div 504 Thrasher St	Norcross	GA	30071	**800-762-5836**	770-448-2193	101
Rock-Tenn Co Folding Carton Div PO Box 4098	Norcross	GA	30091	**800-762-5836**	770-448-2193	102
Rock-Tenn Co Recycled Fiber Div 504 Thrasher St	Norcross	GA	30071	**800-762-5836**	770-448-2193	646
Rock-Tred Corp 3415 W Howard St	Skokie	IL	60076	**800-762-8733**	847-673-8200	188-2
Rock Valley College 3301 N Mulford Rd	Rockford	IL	61114	**800-973-7821**	815-921-7821	160
Rock View Resort 1049 Parkview Dr	Hollister	MO	65672	**800-375-9530**	417-334-4678	373
Rock & Waterscape Systems Inc 11 Whatney	Irvine	CA	92618	**800-328-9762**	949-770-1936	188-7
Rock Wool Mfg Co PO Box 506	Leeds	AL	35094	**800-874-7625***	205-699-6121	382
*Sales						
Rockefeller Foundation 420 5th Ave	New York	NY	10018	**800-645-1133**	212-869-8500	300
Rocket Box Inc 125 E 144th St	Bronx	NY	10451	**800-762-5521**	718-292-5370	198
Rocket Supply Corp 404 N Hwy 115	Roberts	IL	60962	**800-252-6871**	217-395-2278	505
Rockford Area Convention & Visitors Bureau 102 N Main St	Rockford	IL	61101	**800-521-0849**	815-963-8111	205
Rockford College 5050 E State St	Rockford	IL	61108	**800-892-2984**	815-226-4000	163
Rockford Corp 600 S Rockford Dr	Tempe	AZ	85281	**800-669-9899**	480-967-3565	52
NASDAQ: ROFO						
Rockford Institute 928 N Main St	Rockford	IL	61103	**800-383-0680**	815-964-5053	654
Rockford Medical & Safety Co 2420 Harrison Ave	Rockford	IL	61108	**800-541-2528**	815-394-4809	469
Rockford Motors Inc DBA Emery Air Charter Inc 1 Airport Cir	Rockford	IL	61125	**800-435-8090**	815-968-8287	25
Rockford Register Star 99 E State St	Rockford	IL	61104	**800-383-7827**	815-987-1200	522-2
Rockford Systems Inc 4620 Hydraulic Rd	Rockford	IL	61109	**800-922-7533***	815-874-7891	202
*Cust Svc						
Rockhurst University 1100 Rockhurst Rd	Kansas City	MO	64110	**800-842-6776**	816-501-4000	163
Rockhurst University Continuing Education Center Inc PO Box 419107	Kansas City	MO	64141	**800-258-7246**	913-432-7755	753
Rocking Horse Ranch Resort 600 Rt 44-55	Highland	NY	12528	**800-647-2624**	845-691-2927	655
Rockingham Electrical Supply Co Inc 187 River Rd	Newington	NH	03801	**800-727-2310**	603-436-2310	245
Rockingham Memorial Hospital 235 Cantrell Ave	Harrisonburg	VA	22801	**800-543-2201**	540-433-4100	366-2
Rockingham New Holland Inc 600 W Market St	Harrisonburg	VA	22802	**800-360-5313**	540-434-6791	270
Rockland Community College 145 College Rd	Suffern	NY	10901	**800-722-7666**	845-574-4000	160
Rockland Credit Finance LLC 6 Park Center Ct Suite 212	Owings Mills	MD	21117	**866-725-5263**	410-902-0393	268
Rockland Electric Co 1 Blue Hill Plaza	Pearl River	NY	10965	**877-434-4100**	845-352-6000	774
Rockland Inc 650 Englesville Rd	Boyertown	PA	19512	**800-656-7625**	610-369-1008	229
Rockland Industries Inc PO Box 17293	Baltimore	MD	21297	**800-876-2566***	410-522-2505	730-7
*Cust Svc						
Rockland Journal-News PO Box 300	West Nyack	NY	10994	**800-942-1010**	845-358-2200	522-2
Rockland Trust Co 288 Union St	Rockland	MA	02370	**800-826-6100**	781-878-6100	71
Rocklin Park Hotel 5450 China Garden Rd	Rocklin	CA	95677	**888-630-9400**	916-630-9400	373
Rockmount Ranch Wear Mfg Co 1626 Wazee St	Denver	CO	80202	**800-776-2566**	303-629-7777	153-20
Rockport Co Inc 1895 SW Foster Blvd	Canton	MA	02021	**800-762-5767**	781-401-5000	296
Rockport Schooner Cruises PO Box 987	Rockport	ME	04856	**866-732-2473**	207-230-1049	217
Rockview Dairies Inc PO Box 668	Downey	CA	90241	**800-423-2479**	562-927-5511	292-4
Rockwell Collins Inc 400 Collins Rd NE	Cedar Rapids	IA	52498	**888-265-5467**	319-295-1000	519
NYSE: COL						
Rockwell Farms Inc 332 Rockwell Farms Rd	Rockwell	NC	28138	**800-635-6576**	704-279-5589	363
Rockwell Lime Co Inc 4110 Rockwood Rd	Manitowoc	WI	54220	**800-558-7711**	920-682-7771	432
Rockwood Retaining Walls Inc 7200 Hwy 63 N	Rochester	MN	55906	**800-535-2375**	507-288-8850	181
Rocky Mount Cord Co 381 N Grace St	Rocky Mount	NC	27804	**800-342-9130***	252-977-9130	207
*Orders						
Rocky Mount Museum 200 Hyder Hill Rd	Piney Flats	TN	37686	**888-538-1791**	423-538-7396	509
Rocky Mountain Clothing Co Div Miller International Inc 8500 Zuni St	Denver	CO	80260	**800-688-4449**	303-428-5696	153-20
Rocky Mountain College 1511 Poly Dr	Billings	MT	59102	**800-877-6259**	406-657-1000	163
Rocky Mountain Growers 14095 Peyton Hwy	Peyton	CO	80831	**800-687-3001**	719-749-2510	363
Rocky Mountain Health Plans PO Box 10600	Grand Junction	CO	81502	**800-843-0719**	970-244-7760	384-3

Company / Address	City	State	ZIP	Toll-Free	Phone	Class
Rocky Mountain Lions Eye Bank PO Box 6026	Aurora	CO	80045	800-444-7479	720-848-3937	265
Rocky Mountain Milling LLC 400 Platte St	Platteville	CO	80651	888-785-7636	970-785-2794	291-23
Rocky Mountain News 400 W Colfax Ave	Denver	CO	80204	800-933-1990	303-892-5000	522-2
Rocky Mountain Orthodontics Inc (RMO Inc) 650 W Colfax Ave	Denver	CO	80204	800-525-6044	303-592-8200	226
Rocky Mountain Public Broadcasting Network (RMPB) 1089 Bannock St	Denver	CO	80204	800-274-6666	303-892-6666	620
Rocky Mountain Tissue Bank 2993 S Peoria St Suite 390	Aurora	CO	80014	800-424-5169	303-337-3330	535
Rocky Rococo 105 E Wisconsin Ave	Oconomowoc	WI	53066	800-888-7625	262-569-5580	657
Rocky Shoes & Boots Inc 39 E Canal St	Nelsonville	OH	45764	800-421-5151	740-753-1951	296
NASDAQ: RCKY						
Rod McLellan Co 159 Homer Ave	Palo Alto	CA	94301	800-467-2443	650-330-8990	363
Rodale Inc 33 E Minor St	Emmaus	PA	18098	800-848-4735*	610-967-8154	623-9
*Cust Svc						
Roden Electrical Supply Co 170 Mabry Hood Rd	Knoxville	TN	37922	800-532-8742	865-546-8755	245
Rodeo Assn. National Little Britches 1045 W Rio Grande St	Colorado Springs	CO	80906	800-763-3694	719-389-0333	48-22
Rodes Apparel 4938 Brownsboro Rd	Louisville	KY	40222	800-950-7633	502-584-3112	155-4
Rodeway Inns 10750 Columbia Pike	Silver Spring	MD	20901	800-424-6423	301-592-5000	369
Rodgers Richard Theatre 226 W 46th St	New York	NY	10036	800-755-4000	212-307-4100	732
Rodney Hunt Co Inc 46 Mill St	Orange	MA	01364	800-448-8860	978-544-2511	471
Rodney Strong Vineyards 1145 Old Redwood Hwy	Healdsburg	CA	95448	800-474-9463	707-433-6511	81-3
Roe Dental Laboratory Inc 9565 Midwest Ave	Garfield Heights	OH	44125	800-228-6663	216-663-2233	406
Roeder Implement Co Inc 1010 Skyline Dr	Hopkinsville	KY	42240	800-844-3994	270-886-3994	420
Roeder Implement Inc 2550 Rockdale Rd	Dubuque	IA	52003	800-557-1184	563-557-1184	270
Roehl Transport Inc 1916 E 29th St PO Box 750	Marshfield	WI	54449	800-826-8367	715-387-3795	769
Roel Construction Co Inc 3366 Kurtz St	San Diego	CA	92110	800-662-7635	619-297-4156	185
Roentgen Ray Society. American 44211 Slatestone Ct	Leesburg	VA	20176	800-438-2777	703-729-3353	49-8
Roesch Inc 100 N 24th St	Belleville	IL	62222	800-423-6243	618-233-2760	472
Roetzel & Andress 222 S Main St	Akron	OH	44308	800-837-2701	330-376-2700	419
Rogan Corp 3455 Woodhead Dr	Northbrook	IL	60062	800-423-1543	847-498-2300	597
Roger Smith Hotel 501 Lexington Ave	New York	NY	10017	800-445-0277	212-755-1400	373
Roger Williams The 131 Madison Ave	New York	NY	10016	877-847-4444*	212-448-7000	373
*Resv						
Roger Williams Mint 79 Walton St	Attleboro	MA	02703	800-225-2734	508-226-3310	479
Roger Williams University 1 Old Ferry Rd	Bristol	RI	02809	800-458-7144	401-253-1040	163
Rogers 519 W Avalon Ave Suite 7	Muscle Shoals	AL	35661	800-219-8245	256-383-1828	227
Rogers & Assoc 1875 Century Park E Suite 300	Los Angeles	CA	90067	800-554-6901	310-552-6922	622
Rogers Brothers Corp 100 Orchard St	Albion	PA	16401	800-441-9880	814-756-4121	768
Rogers Buddy Music Inc 6891 Simpson Ave	Cincinnati	OH	45239	888-276-8742	513-729-1950	515
Rogers Communications Inc 333 Bloor St E	Toronto	ON	M4W1G9	888-620-7777	416-935-7777	721
NYSE: RG						
Rogers Corp 1 Technology Dr	Rogers	CT	06263	800-227-6437	860-774-9605	594-2
NYSE: ROG						
Rogers Department Store Inc 1001 28th St SW	Grand Rapids	MI	49509	800-727-7643	616-538-6000	155-2
Rogers Julie Theatre 765 Pearl St	Beaumont	TX	77701	800-782-3081	409-838-3435	562
Rogers-Lowell Area Chamber of Commerce 317 W Walnut St	Rogers	AR	72756	800-364-1240	479-636-1240	137
Rogers Ltd 1050 Central Ave	Middletown	OH	45044	800-888-8805	513-422-5407	402
Rogers Lunt & Bowlen Co DBA Lunt Silversmiths 298 Federal St	Greenfield	MA	01301	800-242-2774	413-774-2774	693
Rogers State University 1701 W Will Rogers Blvd	Claremore	OK	74017	800-256-7511	918-343-7546	163
Bartlesville Campus 4001 E Adams Rd	Bartlesville	OK	74006	800-256-7511	918-335-3500	160
Rogers Supply Co Inc PO Box 740	Champaign	IL	61824	800-252-0406	217-356-0166	651
Rogers Tool Works Inc PO Box 9	Rogers	AR	72757	800-525-9855	479-636-1515	447
Rogers Wireless Communications Inc 1 Mount Pleasant Rd	Toronto	ON	M4Y2Y5	800-268-7347	416-935-1100	721
Rogue Ales Co 2320 OSU Dr	Newport	OR	97365	800-850-1115	541-867-3660	103
Rogue Community College 3345 Redwood Hwy	Grants Pass	OR	97527	800-411-6508	541-956-7500	160
Rogue Valley Manor 1200 Mira Mar Ave	Medford	OR	97504	800-848-7868	541-857-7777	659
Rogue Valley Medical Center 2825 E Barnett Rd	Medford	OR	97504	800-944-7073	541-789-7000	366-2
Rogue Wave Software Inc 5500 Flatiron Pkwy	Boulder	CO	80301	800-487-3217	303-473-9118	176-2
Rohm Electronics USA LLC 10145 Pacific Heights Blvd Suite 1000	San Diego	CA	92121	800-955-7646	858-625-3600	245
Rohm & Haas Electronic Materials 455 Forest St	Marlborough	MA	01752	800-832-6200	508-481-7950	143
Rohn Industries Inc 6718 W Plank Rd	Peoria	IL	61604	800-862-4849	309-697-4400	462
Rohn Jim Jim Rohn International 2835 Exchange Blvd Suite 200	Southlake	TX	76092	800-929-0434	817-442-5407	561
Rohrer Bus Service 190 Pic Rite Ln	Lewisburg	PA	17837	800-487-8687	570-524-5800	108
Rohrman Bob Auto Group 701 Sagamore Pkwy S	Lafayette	IN	47905	800-488-3534	765-448-1000	57
Roland DGA Corp 15363 Barranca Pkwy	Irvine	CA	92618	800-542-2307	949-727-2100	171-6
Roland E Powell Convention Center 4001 Coastal Hwy	Ocean City	MD	21842	800-626-2326	410-289-8311	204
Roland Machinery Co 816 N Dirksen Pkwy	Springfield	IL	62702	800-252-2926	217-789-7711	353
Rolf Institute of Structural Integration 5055 Chaparral Ct Suite 103	Boulder	CO	80301	800-530-8875	303-449-5903	48-17
Roll-A-Way Inc 10601 Oak St NE	Saint Petersburg	FL	33716	800-683-9505	727-576-1143	690
Roll Shutter Systems Inc 21633 N 14th Ave	Phoenix	AZ	85027	800-551-7655	623-869-7057	690
Rolla Area Chamber of Commerce 1301 Kingshighway St	Rolla	MO	65401	888-809-3817	573-364-3577	137
Rolladen Inc 550 Ansin Blvd	Hallandale	FL	33009	800-748-8837	954-921-1522	690
Rolled Alloys Inc 125 W Sterns Rd	Temperance	MI	48182	800-521-0332	734-847-0561	483
Rollerblade Inc 1 Advantage Ct	Bordentown	NJ	08505	800-232-7655	609-291-5800	701
Rollette Oil Co 2104 Beloit Ave	Janesville	WI	53546	800-362-0888	608-754-0035	319
Rollex Aluminum 1100 Richmond St	Jackson	TN	38301	800-238-3953	731-424-2000	476
Rollex Corp 2001 Lunt Ave	Elk Grove Village	IL	60007	800-251-3300*	847-437-3000	688
*Cust Svc						
Rolling Hills Electric Co 122 W Main St	Mankato	KS	66956	877-906-5903	785-378-3151	244
Rolling Hills Farm Service Inc 421 N 10th St	Winterset	IA	50273	800-352-3276	515-462-2644	272
Rolling Shield Inc 2500 NW 74th Ave	Miami	FL	33122	800-474-9404	305-470-9404	690
Rollprint Packaging Products Inc 320 Stewart Ave	Addison	IL	60101	800-276-7629	630-628-1700	538
Rolls-Royce Energy System Inc 105 N Sandusky St	Mount Vernon	OH	43050	800-284-8782	740-393-8888	259
Rolls-Royce Engine Services Inc 7200 Earhart Rd	Oakland	CA	94621	800-622-2677	510-613-1000	25
Rolls-Royce North America 14850 Conference Ctr Dr Suite 100	Chantilly	VA	20151	800-274-5387	703-834-1700	22
Rollsource Papers 2392 S Wolf Rd	Des Plaines	IL	60018	800-525-7785	847-699-3100	544
Rolsafe 5845 Corporation Cir	Fort Myers	FL	33905	800-833-5486	239-694-5400	690
Rolyn Inc 189 Macklin St	Cranston	RI	02920	800-824-2683	401-944-0844	401
Roma Food Enterprises Inc 45 Stanford Rd	Piscataway	NJ	08854	800-526-7662	732-463-7662	292-11
Romac Industries Inc 21919 20th Ave SE Suite 100	Bothell	WA	98021	800-426-9341	425-951-6200	584
Romacorp Inc 9304 Forest Ln Suite 200	Dallas	TX	75243	800-286-7662	214-343-7800	656
Roman Corp 1810 Richard Ave	Santa Clara	CA	95050	800-497-7462	408-988-1222	291-26
Roman Meal Co 2101 S Tacoma Way	Tacoma	WA	98409	800-426-3600	253-475-0964	291-16
Roman Research Inc 430 Court St	Plymouth	MA	02362	800-225-8652	508-747-8220	400
Romano Bros Beverage Co 300 E Crossroads Pkwy Bolingbrook Corp Ctr	Bolingbrook	IL	60440	800-776-0180	630-685-3000	82-3
Romanoff Electric Corp 5055 Enterprise Blvd	Toledo	OH	43612	800-866-2627	419-726-2627	188-4
Romanoff International Supply Corp 9 Deforest St	Amityville	NY	11701	800-221-7448*	631-842-2400	399
*Cust Svc						
Romano's Macaroni Grill 6820 LBJ Fwy	Dallas	TX	75240	800-983-4637	972-980-9917	657
Romano's School Bus Service 1065 Belvoir Rd	Plymouth Meeting	PA	19462	800-877-2871	610-272-7671	110
Rome Bancorp Inc 100 W Dominick St	Rome	NY	13440	800-280-9315	315-336-7300	355-2
NASDAQ: ROMED						
Rome (Greater) Chamber of Commerce 1 Riverside Pkwy	Rome	GA	30161	800-234-3154	706-291-7663	137
Rome Specialty Co Inc Rosco Div 501 W Embargo St	Rome	NY	13440	800-794-8357	315-337-8200	701
Rome Tool & Die Co Inc 113 Hemlock St	Rome	GA	30161	800-241-3369	706-234-6743	745
Romerovski Corp 450 W Westfield Ave	Roselle Park	NJ	07204	800-852-9944	908-241-3000	154
Romic Environmental Technologies Corp 2081 Bay Rd	East Palo Alto	CA	94303	800-766-4248	650-324-1638	653
RON (Recruiters OnLine Network Inc) 947 Essex Ln	Medina	OH	44256	888-364-4667		257
Ron Foth Advertising 8100 N High St	Columbus	OH	43235	888-766-3684	614-888-7771	4
Ron Tonkin Dealerships 122 NE 122nd Ave	Portland	OR	97230	800-460-5328	503-255-4100	57
Ron Weber & Assoc Inc 185 Plains Rd Suite 302 E	Milford	CT	06460	800-835-6584	203-799-0000	722
Ronald Reagan Building & International Trade Center 1300 Pennsylvania Ave NW	Washington	DC	20004	888-393-3306	202-312-1300	810
Ronald Reagan Presidential Library & Museum 40 Presidential Dr	Simi Valley	CA	93065	800-410-8354	805-577-4000	426
Ronan Engineering Co 21200 Oxnard St	Woodland Hills	CA	91367	800-327-6626	818-883-5211	200
Ronco Communications & Electronics Inc 595 Sheridan Dr	Tonawanda	NY	14150	888-879-8011	716-873-0760	188-4
Ronin Corp 2 Research Way 2nd Fl	Princeton	NJ	08540	800-352-2926	609-452-0060	194
Ronpak Inc 4301 New Brunswick Ave	South Plainfield	NJ	07080	888-766-7251*	732-968-8000	67
*Cust Svc						
Ronson Corp Campus Dr Corporate Pk 3	Somerset	NJ	08875	800-526-4281	732-469-8300	143
NASDAQ: RONC						
Roode Packing Co Inc PO Box 510	Fairbury	NE	68352	800-245-5808	402-729-2253	465
Roofing Contractors Assn. National 10255 W Higgins Rd Suite 600	Rosemont	IL	60018	800-323-9545*	847-299-9070	49-3
*Cust Svc						
Roofing Wholesale Co Inc 1918 W Grant St	Phoenix	AZ	85009	800-782-2116	602-258-3794	190-4
Roomful Express 55th St & AVRR	Pittsburgh	PA	15201	888-696-7378	412-784-1250	316
Rooms To Go Inc 11540 US Hwy 92 E	Seffner	FL	33584	800-766-6786*	813-623-5400	316
*Cust Svc						
Roosevelt Franklin D Library & Museum 4079 Albany Post Rd	Hyde Park	NY	12538	800-337-8474	845-229-8114	426
Roosevelt Hotel 45 E 45th St	New York	NY	10017	888-833-3969	212-661-9600	373
Roosevelt Paper Co 1 Roosevelt Dr	Mount Laurel	NJ	08054	800-523-3470	856-303-4100	543
Roosevelt University 430 S Michigan Ave	Chicago	IL	60605	877-277-5978	312-341-3500	163
Roosevelt WA Co 2727 Commerce St	La Crosse	WI	54603	800-279-2726	608-781-2000	601

Listing	City	State	Zip	Toll-Free	Phone	Class
Root Candles Co 623 W Liberty St	Medina	OH	44256	**800-289-7668**	330-725-6677	122
Root Studios Inc 1131 W Sheridan Rd	Chicago	IL	60660	**800-962-8089**	773-761-5500	579
RootsWeb.com 360 W 4800 North	Provo	UT	84606	**800-262-3787**	801-705-7000	677
Ropak Corp 660 S State College Blvd	Fullerton	CA	92831	**800-367-3779**	714-870-9757	198
Roper Pump Co PO Box 269 *Sales	Commerce	GA	30529	**800-944-6769***	706-335-5551	627
Ropkey Graphics Inc 4923 W 78th St	Indianapolis	IN	46268	**800-783-8265**	317-632-5446	770
Roppe Corp 1602 N Union St	Fostoria	OH	44830	**800-537-9527**	419-435-8546	286
Roquette America Inc 1417 Exchange St	Keokuk	IA	52632	**800-553-7030**	319-524-5757	291-23
Rosacea Society, National 800 S Northwest Hwy Suite 200	Barrington	IL	60010	**888-662-5874**	847-382-8971	48-17
Rosario Resort & Spa 1400 Rosario Rd	Eastsound	WA	98245	**800-562-8820**	360-376-2222	655
Rosback Co 125 Hawthorne Ave	Saint Joseph	MI	49085	**800-542-2420**	269-983-2582	617
Rosco Div Rome Specialty Co Inc 501 W Embargo St	Rome	NY	13440	**800-794-8357**	315-337-8200	701
Rosco Laboratories Inc 52 Harbor View Ave	Stamford	CT	06902	**800-767-2669**	203-708-8900	708
Roscoe Co 3535 W Harrison St *Cust Svc	Chicago	IL	60624	**800-722-5010***	773-722-5000	434
Roscoe Moss Co 4360 Worth St	Los Angeles	CA	90063	**800-767-2634**	323-261-4185	584
Roscoe Village 381 Hill St	Coshocton	OH	43812	**800-877-1830**	740-622-9310	509
Rose Art Industries Inc 6 Regent St	Livingston	NJ	07039	**800-272-9667**	973-535-1313	750
Rose Garden 1 Center Ct	Portland	OR	97227	**800-231-8750**	503-797-9619	706
Rose Hills Co 3888 S Workman Mill Rd	Whittier	CA	90601	**800-328-7526**	562-699-0921	499
Rose Hotel 807 Main St	Pleasanton	CA	94566	**800-843-9540**	925-846-8802	373
Rose-Hulman Institute of Technology 5500 Wabash Ave	Terre Haute	IN	47803	**800-248-7448**	812-877-1511	163
Rose Packing Co Inc 65 S Barrington Rd	South Barrington	IL	60010	**800-323-7363**	847-381-5700	465
Rose Printing Co Inc 2503 Jackson Bluff Rd	Tallahassee	FL	32304	**800-227-3725**	850-576-4151	614
Rose Products & Services Inc 545 Stimmel Rd	Columbus	OH	43223	**800-264-1568**	614-443-7647	398
Rose Society, American 8877 Jefferson Paige Rd	Shreveport	LA	71119	**800-637-6534**	318-938-5402	48-18
Roseau Electric Co-op Inc 903 3rd St NE	Roseau	MN	56751	**888-847-8840**	218-463-1543	244
Roseburg Forest Products Co PO Box 1088	Roseburg	OR	97470	**800-245-1115**	541-679-3311	671
Rosecroft Raceway 6336 Rosecroft Dr	Fort Washington	MD	20744	**877-818-9467**	301-567-4000	628
Rosedale on Robson Suite Hotel 838 Hamilton St	Vancouver	BC	V6B6A2	**800-661-8870**	604-689-8033	372
Rosedown Plantation & Gardens 12501 Hwy 10	Saint Francisville	LA	70775	**888-376-1867**	225-635-3332	50
Rosellen Suites at Stanley Park 2030 Barclay St	Vancouver	BC	V6G1L5	**888-317-6648**	604-689-4807	372
Rosemont College 1400 Montgomery Ave	Rosemont	PA	19010	**800-331-0708**	610-527-0200	163
Rosemont Industries Inc 1700 West St	Cincinnati	OH	45215	**800-782-9958**	513-733-4277	661
Rosemount Analytical Inc Process Analytical Div 6565 P Davis Industrial Pkwy	Solon	OH	44139	**800-433-6076**	330-682-9010	200
Rosemount Analytical Inc Uniloc Div 2400 Barranca Pkwy	Irvine	CA	92606	**800-854-8257**	949-863-1181	200
Rosemount Inc 8200 Market Blvd *Cust Svc	Chanhassen	MN	55317	**800-999-9307***	952-941-5560	200
Rosen Centre Hotel 9840 International Dr	Orlando	FL	32819	**800-800-9840**	407-996-9840	373
Rosen Hotels & Resorts Inc 9840 International Dr	Orlando	FL	32819	**800-204-7234**	407-996-9840	369
Rosen Plaza Hotel 9700 International Dr	Orlando	FL	32819	**800-366-9700**	407-996-9700	373
Rosenberger's Dairies Inc 847 Forty Foot Rd PO Box 901	Hatfield	PA	19440	**800-355-9074**	215-855-9074	203
Rosencrantz-Bemis Enterprises Inc 1105 281 Bypass	Great Bend	KS	67530	**800-466-2467**	620-793-5512	188-16
Rosendin Electric Inc 880 N Mabury Rd	San Jose	CA	95133	**800-540-4734**	408-286-2800	188-4
Rosen's Inc 1120 Lake Ave	Fairmont	MN	56031	**800-798-2000**	507-238-4201	144
Rosenthal & Rosenthal Inc 1370 Broadway	New York	NY	10018	**800-999-4800**	212-356-1400	268
Rosewood Hotels & Resorts 500 Crescent Ct Suite 300	Dallas	TX	75201	**888-767-3966**	214-880-4200	369
Roslyn Claremont Hotel 1221 Old Northern Blvd	Roslyn	NY	11576	**800-626-9005**	516-625-2700	373
Ross Breeders Inc 5015 Bradford Dr NW	Huntsville	AL	35805	**800-826-9685**	256-890-3800	11-8
Ross Brothers Construction Co Inc PO Box 767	Ashland	KY	41105	**800-910-7222**	606-739-5139	188-10
Ross Industries Inc 5321 Midland Rd	Midland	VA	22728	**800-336-6010**	540-439-3271	293
Ross Island Sand & Gravel Co PO Box 82249	Portland	OR	97282	**800-543-0230**	503-239-5504	190-1
Ross Matthews Mills Inc 657 Quarry St	Fall River	MA	02723	**800-753-7677**	508-677-0601	730-5
Ross Metals Corp 54 W 47th St	New York	NY	10036	**800-654-7677**	212-869-4433	476
Ross Optical Industries Inc 1410 Gail Borden Pl Suite A-3	El Paso	TX	79935	**800-880-5417**	915-595-5417	534
Ross Products Div Abbott Laboratories 625 Cleveland Ave *PR	Columbus	OH	43215	**800-227-5767***	614-624-7677	291-10
Ross Reels 1 Ponderosa Ct	Montrose	CO	81401	**800-336-1050**	970-249-1212	701
Ross & Roberts Inc 1299 W Broad St	Stratford	CT	06615	**800-822-4220**	203-378-9363	589
Ross Simons Jewelers Inc 9 Ross Simons Dr	Cranston	RI	02920	**800-835-0919**	401-463-3100	402
Ross Stores Inc 8333 Central Ave *NASDAQ: ROST*	Newark	CA	94560	**800-289-7677**	510-505-4400	155-2
Ross Systems Inc 2 Concourse Pkwy Suite 800	Atlanta	GA	30328	**877-767-7462**	770-351-9600	176-1
Ross Technology Corp 104 N Maple Ave	Leola	PA	17540	**800-345-8170**	717-656-2095	92
Rostra Precision Controls Inc 2519 Dana Dr *Cust Svc	Laurinburg	NC	28352	**800-782-3379***	910-276-4853	519
Roswell Chamber of Commerce 131 W 2nd St	Roswell	NM	88202	**877-849-7679**	505-623-5695	137
Roswell Convention & Visitors Bureau 617 Atlanta St	Roswell	GA	30075	**800-776-7935**	770-640-3253	205
Roswell Park Cancer Institute Elm & Carlton Sts	Buffalo	NY	14263	**800-685-6825**	716-845-2300	366-5
Blood & Marrow Transplantation Program Elm & Carlton Sts	Buffalo	NY	14263	**800-685-6825**	716-845-3516	758
Rotary Corp PO Box 747	Glennville	GA	30427	**800-841-3989**	912-654-3433	420
Rotary Forms Press Inc 835 S High St	Hillsboro	OH	45133	**800-654-2876**	937-393-3426	111
Rotary Lift 2700 Lanier Dr	Madison	IN	47250	**800-640-5438**	812-273-1622	379
RoTech Medical Corp 4506 LB McLeod Rd Suite F	Orlando	FL	32811	**800-357-3835**	407-841-2115	358
Rotek Inc 1400 S Chillicothe Rd	Aurora	OH	44202	**800-221-8043**	330-562-4000	77
Rotella's Italian Bakery Inc 6949 S 108th St	La Vista	NE	68128	**800-759-0360**	402-592-6600	69
Roth Distributing Co 11300 W 47th St	Minnetonka	MN	55343	**800-642-3227**	952-933-4428	38
Roth Pump Co PO Box 4330	Rock Island	IL	61204	**888-444-7684**	309-787-1791	627
Roth Staffing Cos Inc 333 City Blvd W Suite 100	Orange	CA	92868	**888-304-4684**	714-939-8600	707
Rothe Development Inc 4614 Sinclair Rd	San Antonio	TX	78222	**800-229-5209**	210-648-3131	654
Rotmans Furniture & Carpet 725 Southbridge St	Worcester	MA	01610	**800-768-6267**	508-755-5276	316
RotoMetrics Group 800 Howerton Ln	Eureka	MO	63025	**800-325-3851**	636-587-3600	745
Rotor Clip Co Inc 187 Davidson Ave *Cust Svc	Somerset	NJ	08873	**800-631-5857***	732-469-7333	321
Rott-Keller Supply Co Inc PO Box 390	Fargo	ND	58107	**800-342-4709**	701-235-0563	740
Rottler Mfg 8029 S 200th St	Kent	WA	98032	**800-452-0534**	253-872-7050	447
Rough Creek Lodge PO Box 2400 *Resv	Glen Rose	TX	76043	**800-864-4705***	254-965-3700	373
Rough Notes Co Inc 11690 Technology Dr	Carmel	IN	46032	**800-428-4384**	317-582-1600	623-9
Rough Notes Magazine 11690 Technology Dr	Carmel	IN	46032	**800-428-4384**	317-582-1600	449-5
Rough Rider Industries 3303 E Main Ave	Bismarck	ND	58506	**800-732-0557**	701-328-6161	618
Round Hill Vineyards & Cellars 1680 Silverado Trail	Saint Helena	CA	94574	**800-778-0424**	707-963-5251	81-3
Round Rock Chamber of Commerce 212 E Main St	Round Rock	TX	78664	**800-747-3479**	512-255-5805	137
Rounder Records 1 Camp St	Cambridge	MA	02140	**800-768-6337**	617-354-0700	643
Rountree Transport & Rigging Inc 2640 N Lane Ave	Jacksonville	FL	32254	**800-342-5036**	904-781-1033	769
Rouse Max & Sons Inc 361 S Robertson Blvd	Beverly Hills	CA	90211	**800-421-0816**	310-360-9200	51
Routh JH Packing Co Inc 4413 W Bogart Rd	Sandusky	OH	44870	**800-446-6759**	419-626-2251	465
Routzahn's PO Box 663	Frederick	MD	21705	**800-132-1177**	301-662-2141	316
Rovanco Piping Systems Inc 20535 SE Frontage Rd	Joliet	IL	60431	**800-289-7473**	815-741-6700	584
ROW Window Co 612 Moen Ave	Joliet	IL	60434	**800-966-3769**	815-725-5491	489
Rowan County Convention & Visitors Bureau 204 E Innes St Suite 120	Salisbury	NC	28144	**800-332-2343**	704-638-3100	205
Rowan Regional Home Health & Hospice 825A W Henderson St	Salisbury	NC	28144	**888-279-0304**	704-637-7645	365
Rowan University 201 Mullica Hill Rd	Glassboro	NJ	08028	**800-447-1165**	856-256-4000	163
Rowe Cindy Auto Glass 4750 Lindle Rd	Harrisburg	PA	17111	**800-882-4639**	717-939-7551	62-2
Rowe Cos 1650 Tysons Blvd Suite 710 *AMEX: ROW*	McLean	VA	22102	**800-340-7693**	703-847-8670	314-2
Rowe Furniture Inc 1650 Tysons Blvd Suite 710	McLean	VA	22102	**800-334-7693**	703-847-8670	314-2
Rowe International Inc 1500 Union Ave SE	Grand Rapids	MI	49507	**800-636-2787**	616-243-3633	55
Rowe Machinery & Automation Inc 76 Hinckley Rd	Clinton	ME	04927	**800-247-2645**	207-426-2351	485
Rowenta Inc 196 Boston Ave	Medford	MA	02155	**800-769-3682**	781-396-0600	37
Rowing Assn. US 201 S Capitol Ave Suite 400	Indianapolis	IN	46225	**800-314-4769**	317-237-5656	48-22
Rowland Coffee Roasters Inc 5605 NW 82 Ave	Miami	FL	33166	**800-990-9039**	305-594-9039	291-7
Rowlett Chamber of Commerce 3910 Main St	Rowlett	TX	75088	**800-796-8644**	972-475-3200	137
Rowmark Inc 2040 Industrial Dr	Findlay	OH	45840	**800-243-3339**	419-425-2407	588
Roxane Laboratories Inc 1809 Wilson Rd *Cust Svc	Columbus	OH	43228	**800-520-1631***	614-276-4000	572
Roxio Inc 455 El Camino Real *NASDAQ: ROXI* ■ *Cust Svc	Santa Clara	CA	95050	**866-279-7694***	408-367-3100	176-8
Roy Anderson Corp 11400 Reichold Rd	Gulfport	MS	39503	**800-688-4003**	228-896-4000	185
Roy Bros Inc 764 Boston Rd *Cust Svc	Billerica	MA	01821	**800-225-0830***	978-667-1921	769
Roy E Hanson Jr Mfg 1924 Compton Ave	Los Angeles	CA	90011	**800-421-9395**	213-747-7514	92
Roy Houff Co 6200 S Oak Park Ave	Chicago	IL	60638	**800-366-1769**	773-586-8118	288
Royal Air Maroc 55 E 59th St Suite 17B	New York	NY	10022	**800-344-6726**	212-750-5115	26
Royal Alliance Assoc Inc 733 3rd Ave 4th Fl	New York	NY	10017	**800-821-5100**	212-551-5100	679
Royal Aloha Vacation Club 1505 Dillingham Blvd Suite 212	Honolulu	HI	96817	**800-367-5212**	808-847-8050	738
Royal American Charter Lines Inc 17725 Volbrecht Rd	Lansing	IL	60438	**800-323-5281**	708-474-7474	108
Royal Appliance Mfg Co 7005 Cochran Rd	Glenwillow	OH	44139	**888-321-1134**	440-996-2000	775
Royal Assn. American 1701 American Royal Ct	Kansas City	MO	64102	**800-821-5857**	816-221-9800	48-2
Royal Bancshares of Pennsylvania Inc 732 Montgomery Ave *NASDAQ: RBPAA*	Narberth	PA	19072	**800-417-5198**	610-668-4700	355-2
Royal Bank of Pennsylvania 732 Montgomery Ave	Narberth	PA	19072	**800-417-5198**	610-668-4700	71
Royal Bank of Scotland 101 Park Ave 10th Fl	New York	NY	10178	**800-741-9607**	212-401-3200	71

Alphabetical Section

Name / Address	City	State	ZIP	Toll-Free	Phone	Class
Royal Baths Mfg Co 14635 Chrisman Rd	Houston	TX	77039	**800-826-0074**	281-442-3400	367
Royal British Columbia Museum 675 Belleville St	Victoria	BC	V8W9W2	**888-447-7977**	250-356-7226	509
Royal Brush Mfg Inc 6707 Broadway	Merrillville	IN	46410	**800-247-2211**	219-660-4170	43
Royal Business Forms Inc 3301 Ave 'E' East	Arlington	TX	76011	**800-255-9303**	817-640-5248	111
Royal Cake Co Inc 315 Cassell St	Winston-Salem	NC	27107	**800-334-5260**	336-785-8700	291-1
Royal Canadian Military Institute 426 University Ave	Toronto	ON	M5G1S9	**800-585-1072**	416-597-0286	509
Royal Canadian Mounted Police Centennial Museum 6101 Dewdney Ave	Regina	SK	S4P3J7	**877-526-0585**	306-780-5838	509
Royal Canin USA Inc 500 Fountain Lakes Blvd Suite 100	Saint Charles	MO	63301	**800-592-6687**	636-926-0003	568
Royal Caribbean Cruises Ltd 1050 Caribbean Way *NYSE: RCL*	Miami	FL	33132	**800-398-9819**	305-539-6000	217
Royal Caribbean International 1050 Caribbean Way	Miami	FL	33132	**800-327-6700**	305-539-6000	217
Royal China & Porcelain Cos Inc 1265 Glen Ave *Orders	Moorestown	NJ	08057	**800-631-7120***	856-866-2900	716
Royal Coach Tours 630 Stockton Ave	San Jose	CA	95126	**800-927-6925**	408-279-4801	748
Royal Coachman Inn 5805 Pacific Hwy E	Tacoma	WA	98424	**800-422-3051**	253-922-2500	373
Royal Coachman Worldwide 540 Thomas Blvd	Orange	NJ	07050	**800-472-7433**	973-676-0200	433
Royal Consumer Information Products Inc 379 Campus Dr *Sales	Somerset	NJ	08875	**888-261-4555***	732-627-9977	112
Royal Doulton USA Inc 200 Cottontail Ln	Somerset	NJ	08873	**800-682-4462**	732-356-7880	716
Royal Floor Mats Div Fiskars Brands Inc 3000 W Orange Ave	Apopka	FL	32703	**800-621-4253**	407-889-5533	663
Royal Garden at Waikiki Hotel 440 Olohana St	Honolulu	HI	96815	**800-367-5666**	808-943-0202	373
Royal Glass Co 9241 Hampton Overlook	Capital Heights	MD	20743	**800-509-4495**	301-808-2855	62-2
Royal HM Inc 689 Pennington Ave	Trenton	NJ	08618	**800-257-9452**	609-396-9176	144
Royal Holiday Beach Resort 1980 Beach Blvd	Biloxi	MS	39531	**800-874-0402**	228-388-7553	373
Royal Host Real Estate Investment Trust 5940 Macleod Trail S Suite 500 *TSE: RYL* ■ *Cust Svc	Calgary	AB	T2H2G4	**877-626-4004***	403-259-9800	640
Royal Hotel South Beach 758 Washington Ave	Miami Beach	FL	33139	**888-394-6835**	305-673-9009	373
Royal Jordanian Airlines 6 E 43rd St 27th Fl	New York	NY	10017	**800-223-0470**	212-949-0060	26
Royal Lahaina Resort 2780 Kekaa Dr	Lahaina	HI	96761	**800-447-6925**	808-661-3611	655
Royal Melrose Granite Co 202 S 3rd Ave	Cold Spring	MN	56320	**800-328-7021**	320-685-5101	710
Royal Nepal Airlines North America 16250 Ventura Blvd Suite 115	Encino	CA	91436	**800-266-3725**		26
Royal Oak Foundation 26 Broadway Suite 950	New York	NY	10004	**800-913-6565**	212-480-2889	48-13
Royal Oil & Gas Corp 1 Indian Spring Rd	Indiana	PA	15701	**800-346-0246**	724-463-0246	525
Royal Palms Resort & Spa 5200 E Camelback Rd	Phoenix	AZ	85018	**800-672-6011**	602-840-3610	655
Royal Plastics Inc 9410 Pineneedle Dr	Mentor	OH	44060	**800-533-2163**	440-352-1357	593
Royal Plaza Hotel 425 E Main Rd	Middletown	RI	02842	**800-825-7072**	401-846-3555	373
Royal Precision Inc 535 Migeon Ave	Torrington	CT	06790	**800-920-4848**	860-489-9254	701
Royal Regency Hotel 165 Tuckahoe Rd	Yonkers	NY	10710	**800-215-3858**	914-476-6200	373
Royal Roads University 2005 Sooke Rd	Victoria	BC	V9B5Y2	**800-788-8028**	250-391-2550	773
Royal Seating Ltd 1110 Industrial Blvd *Cust Svc	Cameron	TX	76520	**800-460-4916***	254-697-6421	314-3
Royal Sonesta Hotel Boston 5 Cambridge Pkwy	Cambridge	MA	02142	**800-766-3782**	617-806-4200	373
Royal Sonesta Hotel New Orleans 300 Bourbon St	New Orleans	LA	70130	**800-766-3782**	504-586-0300	373
Royal Suite Lodge 3811 Minnesota Dr	Anchorage	AK	99503	**800-282-3114**	907-563-3114	373
Royal Sun Inn 1700 S Palm Canyon Dr	Palm Springs	CA	92264	**800-619-4786**	760-327-1564	373
Royal & SunAlliance Insurance Co of Canada 10 Wellington St E	Toronto	ON	M5E1L5	**800-268-8406**	416-366-7511	384-4
Royal & SunAlliance USA 9300 Arrowpoint Blvd	Charlotte	NC	28273	**800-523-5451**	704-522-2000	384-4
Royal Textile Mills Inc 929 Firetower Rd	Yanceyville	NC	27379	**800-334-9361**	336-694-4121	153-1
Royal Tours Inc PO Box 998	Randleman	NC	27317	**800-997-6925**	336-629-9080	748
Royal Towers Hotel & Casino 140 6th St	New Westminster	BC	V3M1J4	**800-663-0202**	604-524-3777	372
Royal Tyrrell Museum of Palaeontology Hwy 838 Midland Provincial Pk	Drumheller	AB	T0J0Y0	**888-440-4240**	403-823-7707	509
Royal Wine Corp 63 Le Fante Ln	Bayonne	NJ	07002	**800-382-8299**	718-384-2400	81-3
Royale Coach 1330 Wade Dr	Elkhart	IN	46514	**877-466-6226**		62-7
Royale Theatre 242 W 45th St	New York	NY	10036	**800-432-7250**	212-239-6200	732
Royalton Hotel 44 W 44th St	New York	NY	10036	**800-606-6090**	212-869-4400	373
Royalty Carpet Mills Inc 17111 Red Hill Ave	Irvine	CA	92614	**800-854-8331**	949-474-4000	131
Royalty Owners. National Assn of PO Box 5779	Norman	OK	73070	**800-558-0557**	405-573-2972	49-17
Royce & Assoc LLC 1414 Ave of the Americas 9th Fl	New York	NY	10019	**800-348-1414**	212-486-1445	393
Royce Funds 1414 Ave of the Americas	New York	NY	10019	**800-337-6923**		517
Royer's Flower Shops 810 S 12th St	Lebanon	PA	17042	**888-276-9377**	717-273-2683	287
Roylco Inc 3251 Abbeville Hwy	Anderson	SC	29624	**800-362-8656**	864-296-0043	242
Royster-Clark Inc 6 Executive Dr	Collinsville	IL	62234	**800-767-2855**	618-346-7300	272
Rozelle Cosmetics PO Box 70	Westfield	VT	05874	**800-451-4216**	802-744-2270	211
RP Fedder Corp 1237 E Main St	Rochester	NY	14609	**800-288-1660**	585-288-1600	19
RPA Process Technologies 9151 Shaver Rd	Portage	MI	49024	**800-525-4214**	269-323-1313	379
RPB (Research to Prevent Blindness Inc) 645 Madison Ave 21st Fl	New York	NY	10022	**800-621-0026**	212-752-4333	48-17
RPM International Inc 2628 Pearl Rd *NYSE: RPM*	Medina	OH	44256	**800-776-4488**	330-273-5090	540
RPM Pizza LLC 15384 5th St	Gulfport	MS	39503	**800-622-6000**	228-832-4000	656
RPS Products Inc 281 Keyes Ave	Hampshire	IL	60140	**800-683-7030**	847-683-3400	19
RR Bowker LLC 630 Central Ave	New Providence	NJ	07974	**800-521-8110**	908-286-1090	623-2
RR Donnelley Logistics 7501 S Quincy St	Willowbrook	IL	60527	**800-800-7447**		5
RREEF 101 California St 26th Fl	San Francisco	CA	94111	**800-222-5885**	415-781-3300	393
RS Bacon Veneer Co 6951 High Grove Blvd	Burr Ridge	IL	60527	**800-443-7995**	630-323-1414	602
RS Corcoran Co 500 N Vine St	New Lenox	IL	60451	**800-637-1067**	815-485-2156	627
RS Electronics Inc 34443 Schoolcraft Rd	Livonia	MI	48150	**800-366-7750**	734-525-1155	245
RS Hughes Co Inc 10639 Glenoaks Blvd	Pacoima	CA	91331	**877-774-8443**	818-686-9111	378
RS Investments PO Box 219717	Kansas City	MO	64121	**800-766-3863**		517
RS Means Co Inc 63 Smiths Ln	Kingston	MA	02364	**800-334-3509**	781-585-7880	623-2
RS Owens & Co 5535 N Lynch Ave	Chicago	IL	60630	**800-282-6200**	773-282-6000	766
RSA Security Inc 174 Middlesex Tpke *NASDAQ: RSAS*	Bedford	MA	01730	**800-301-5000**	781-515-5000	176-12
RSES (Refrigeration Service Engineers Society) 1666 Rand Rd	Des Plaines	IL	60016	**800-297-5660**	847-297-6464	49-3
RSI (Religious Science International) 901 E 2nd Ave Suite 301	Spokane	WA	99202	**800-662-1348**	509-624-7000	48-20
RSI Home Products Inc 400 E Orangethorpe Ave	Anaheim	CA	92801	**888-774-8062**	714-449-2200	116
RSM McGladrey Inc 3600 American Blvd W 3rd Fl	Bloomington	MN	55431	**800-274-3978**	952-835-9930	2
RSVP (Retired & Senior Volunteer Program) PO Box 70675	Washington	DC	20024	**800-424-8867**		196
RSVP Martha's Vineyard PO Box 2042	Oak Bluffs	MA	02557	**866-778-7689**	508-693-9371	368
RSVP Vacations 2535 25th Ave S	Minneapolis	MN	55406	**800-328-7787**		748
RT Mfg 1186 N Industrial Park Dr	Orem	UT	84057	**800-524-9607**		314-2
RT Technologies 2000 L St NW Suite B-1	Washington	DC	20036	**800-231-5758**	202-331-0576	239
RT Vanderbilt Co Inc 30 Winfield St *Cust Svc	Norwalk	CT	06855	**800-243-6064***	203-853-1400	142
RTA (Riverside Transit Agency) 1825 3rd St PO Box 59968	Riverside	CA	92517	**800-800-7821**	951-682-1234	460
RTA Hospice 511 S Mudsprings Rd	Payson	AZ	85541	**800-450-9558**	928-472-6340	365
RTC (Rails-to-Trails Conservancy) 1100 17th St NW 10th Fl *Orders	Washington	DC	20036	**800-888-7747***	202-331-9696	48-13
RTD (Regional Transportation District) 1600 Blake St	Denver	CO	80202	**800-877-7433**	303-628-9000	460
RTEC (Rural Transit Enterprises Coordinated Inc) 100 Main St PO Box 746	Mount Vernon	KY	40456	**800-321-7832**	606-256-9835	109
RTI International 3040 Cornwallis Rd PO Box 12194	Research Triangle Park	NC	27709	**800-334-8571**	919-541-6000	654
RTI Shelving Systems Inc 339 Kingsland Ave	Brooklyn	NY	11222	**800-746-5846**	212-279-0435	281
RTI Transport Inc 5635 Clay Ave SW	Grand Rapids	MI	49548	**800-666-0701**	616-531-1467	769
RTKL Assoc Inc 901 S Bond St	Baltimore	MD	21231	**800-345-7855**	410-537-6000	258
RTNDA (Radio-Television News Directors Assn) 1600 K St NW Suite 700	Washington	DC	20006	**800-807-8632**	202-659-6510	49-14
RTP Co 580 E Front St	Winona	MN	55987	**800-433-4787**	507-454-6900	594-2
RTS Financial Service 8601 Monrovia	Lenexa	KS	66215	**800-860-7926**	913-492-6351	268
RTS Packaging LLC 504 Thrasher St	Norcross	GA	30071	**800-822-1914**	770-448-2244	101
RTS Wright Industries LLC PO Box 17914	Nashville	TN	37217	**800-782-4202**	615-361-6600	379
RTW Inc 8500 Normandale Lake Blvd Suite 1400 *NASDAQ: RTWI*	Bloomington	MN	55437	**800-789-2242**	952-893-0403	384-4
RUAN Transportation Management Systems 666 Grand Ave Suite 3100	Des Moines	IA	50309	**800-997-7826**	515-245-2500	767
RubbAir Door Div Eckel Industries Inc 100 Groton Shirley Rd	Ayer	MA	01432	**800-966-7822**	978-772-0480	233
Rubber Engineering PO Box 26188 *Cust Svc	Salt Lake City	UT	84126	**800-453-6403***	801-530-7887	664
Rubber Stamper Magazine 207 Commercial Ct	Morganville	NJ	07751	**800-969-7176**	732-536-5160	449-14
Rubbercraft Corp of California 15627 S Broadway	Gardena	CA	90248	**800-782-2379**	310-328-5402	321
Rubbermaid Commercial Products 3124 Valley Ave	Winchester	VA	22601	**800-347-9800**	540-667-8700	597
Rubbermaid Home Products 1147 Akron Rd	Wooster	OH	44691	**888-895-2110**	330-264-6464	64
Rubenstein Brothers Inc 102 St Charles Ave	New Orleans	LA	70130	**800-725-7823**	504-581-6666	155-3
Rubin Brothers Inc 2241 S Halsted St	Chicago	IL	60608	**800-632-2308**	312-942-1111	153-19
Ruby Falls 1720 S Scenic Hwy	Chattanooga	TN	37409	**800-755-7105**	423-821-2544	50
Ruby Tuesday Inc 150 W Church Ave *NYSE: RI*	Maryville	TN	37801	**800-325-0755**	865-379-5700	657
Ruby's Diner Inc 660 Newport Ctr Dr Suite 850	Newport Beach	CA	92660	**800-439-7829**	949-644-7829	657
Rudd Equipment Co 4344 Poplar Level Rd	Louisville	KY	40213	**800-283-7833**	502-456-4050	353
Rudolf Steiner College 9200 Fair Oaks Blvd	Fair Oaks	CA	95628	**800-515-8203**	916-961-8727	163
Rudolph Foods Co Inc 6575 Bellefontaine Rd	Lima	OH	45804	**800-241-7675**	419-648-3611	291-9

Company / Address	City	State	ZIP	Toll-Free	Phone	Class
Ruff Thomas W & Co Inc 1114 Dublin Rd	Columbus	OH	43215	**800-828-0234**	614-487-4000	315
Ruffed Grouse Society (RGS) 451 McCormick Rd	Coraopolis	PA	15108	**888-564-6747**	412-262-4044	48-3
Ruffin Building Systems Inc 6914 Hwy 2 *Sales	Oak Grove	LA	71263	**800-421-4232***	318-428-2305	106
Rug Barn Inc 234 Industrial Park Rd PO Box 1187	Abbeville	SC	29620	**800-784-2276**	800-626-7033	131
Rug Doctor LP 4701 Old Shepard Pl	Plano	TX	75093	**800-234-6286**	972-673-1400	261-3
Rug Hooking Magazine 1300 Market St Suite 202	Lemoyne	PA	17043	**800-233-9055**	717-234-5091	449-14
Rug Institute. Carpet & 310 S Holiday Ave	Dalton	GA	30720	**800-882-8846**	706-278-3176	49-4
Rugg Mfg Co Inc PO Box 428	Greenfield	MA	01302	**800-633-8772**	413-773-5471	420
Ruiz Food Products Inc 501 S Alta Ave	Dinuba	CA	93618	**800-477-6474**	559-591-5510	291-36
RuleSpace Inc 111 SW 5th Ave Suite 2100	Portland	OR	97204	**800-387-8373**	503-290-5100	176-7
Rummel Klepper & Kahl LLP 81 Mosher St	Baltimore	MD	21217	**800-787-3755**	410-728-2900	258
Rumpke Consolidated Cos Inc 10795 Hughes Rd	Cincinnati	OH	45251	**800-582-3107**	513-851-0122	791
Rumsey Electric Co 15 Colwell Ln	Conshohocken	PA	19428	**800-462-2402**	610-832-9000	245
Runaway Switchboard. National 3080 N Lincoln Ave	Chicago	IL	60657	**800-621-4000**	773-880-9860	48-6
Runaway Tours Inc 1040 Vannes Ave	San Francisco	CA	94109	**800-622-0723**	415-268-8200	748
Runner's World Magazine 33 E Minor St *Cust Svc	Emmaus	PA	18098	**800-666-2828***	610-967-5171	449-13
Running Assn. American 4405 East-West Hwy Suite 405	Bethesda	MD	20814	**800-776-2732**	301-913-9517	48-22
Running Press Book Publishers 125 S 22nd St	Philadelphia	PA	19103	**800-345-5359**	215-567-5080	623-2
Runza Drive-Ins of America Inc 5931 S 58th St Suite D	Lincoln	NE	68516	**800-929-2394**	402-423-2394	657
Runzheimer International Runzheimer Pk	Rochester	WI	53167	**800-558-1702**	262-971-2200	192
Ruotolo Assoc Inc 29 Broadway Suite 210	Cresskill	NJ	07626	**800-786-8656**	201-568-3898	312
Rural Cellular Corp 3905 Dakota St SW PO Box 2000 *NASDAQ: RCCC* ■ *Cust Svc	Alexandria	MN	56308	**800-450-2000***	320-762-2000	721
Rural Electric Co-op Inc PO Box 609	Lindsay	OK	73052	**800-259-3504**	405-756-3104	244
Rural Electric Convenience Co-op Co 3973 W SR 104 PO Box 19	Auburn	IL	62615	**800-245-7322**	217-438-6197	244
Rural Electric Cooperative Assn. National 4301 Wilson Blvd	Arlington	VA	22203	**866-673-2299**	703-907-5500	48-12
Rural Transit Enterprises Coordinated Inc (RTEC) 100 Main St PO Box 746	Mount Vernon	KY	40456	**800-321-7832**	606-256-9835	109
Rural Utilities Cooperative Finance Corp. National 2201 Cooperative Way Woodland Pk	Herndon	VA	20171	**800-424-2954**	703-709-6700	498
Rural/Metro Corp 8401 E Indian School Rd *NASDAQ: RURL*	Scottsdale	AZ	85251	**800-421-5718**	480-994-3886	31
Ruritan National PO Box 487 *Orders	Dublin	VA	24084	**877-787-8727***	540-674-5431	48-15
RUSA (Reference & User Services Assn) 50 E Huron St	Chicago	IL	60611	**800-545-2433**	312-280-4398	49-11
Rusch Inc 2450 Meadowbrook Pkwy	Duluth	GA	30096	**800-553-5214**	770-623-0816	469
Rush Computer Rentals 29 North Plains Rd	Wallingford	CT	06492	**800-526-7368**	203-284-8277	261-1
Rush Enterprises Inc 555 IH 35 S Suite 500 *NASDAQ: RUSHA*	New Braunfels	TX	78130	**800-973-7874**	830-626-5200	261-2
Rush Gears Inc 550 Virginia Dr	Fort Washington	PA	19034	**800-523-2576**	215-542-9000	700
Rush Shelby Energy Inc 1504 S Harrison St	Shelbyville	IN	46176	**800-427-0497**	317-398-6621	244
Rushmore View Inn 610 Hwy 16A	Keystone	SD	57751	**800-888-2603**	605-666-4466	373
Russ Bassett Co 8189 Byron Rd	Whittier	CA	90606	**800-350-2445**	562-945-2445	281
Russ Berrie & Co Inc 111 Bauer Dr *NYSE: RUS*	Oakland	NJ	07436	**800-272-7877**	201-337-9000	750
Russ Darrow Group W133 N8569 Executive Pkwy	Menomonee Falls	WI	53051	**800-732-7769**	262-250-9600	57
Russ' Restaurants Inc 390 E 8th St	Holland	MI	49423	**800-521-1778**	616-396-6571	657
Russel Metals Bahcall Group PO Box 1054 *Sales	Appleton	WI	54912	**800-236-0500***	920-734-9271	483
Russel Metals Inc 1900 Minnesota Ct Suite 210 *TSE: RUS*	Mississauga	ON	L5N3C9	**800-268-0750**	905-819-7777	483
Russelectric Inc 99 Industrial Park Rd	Hingham	MA	02043	**800-225-5250**	781-749-6000	715
Russell Athletic Div Russell Corp 755 Lee St	Alexander City	AL	35010	**800-729-2905**	256-500-4000	153-1
Russell Corp 755 Lee St *NYSE: RML*	Alexander City	AL	35010	**800-729-2905**	256-500-4000	153-1
Russell Corp Jerzees Div 755 Lee St	Alexander City	AL	35010	**800-729-2905**	256-500-4000	153-3
Russell Corp Russell Athletic Div 755 Lee St	Alexander City	AL	35010	**800-729-2905**	256-500-4000	153-1
Russell Florist Inc 5001 Gravois Blvd	Saint Louis	MO	63116	**800-351-9003**	314-351-4676	287
Russell Frank Co PO Box 1616	Tacoma	WA	98402	**800-426-7969**	253-572-9500	393
Russell Investment Group 909 A St	Tacoma	WA	98402	**800-787-7354**		393
Russell Pipe & Foundry Co Inc Hwy 22 W	Alexander City	AL	35010	**800-824-4513**	256-234-2514	302
Russell Reynolds Assoc Inc 200 Park Ave 23rd Fl	New York	NY	10166	**888-772-6200**	212-351-2000	262
Russell Sage College 45 Ferry St	Troy	NY	12180	**888-837-9724**	518-244-2217	163
Russell Standard Corp PO Box 479	Bridgeville	PA	15017	**800-323-3053**	412-221-7300	46
Russell Stover Candies Inc 4900 Oak St	Kansas City	MO	64112	**800-477-8683**	816-842-9240	291-8
Russell T Gilman Inc 1230 Cheyenne Ave	Grafton	WI	53024	**800-445-6267**	262-377-2434	484
Russell William Ltd 1710 Midway Rd	Odenton	MD	21113	**800-638-9667**	410-551-3600	281
Russer Foods Inc 665 Perry St	Buffalo	NY	14210	**800-828-1885**	716-826-6400	291-26
Russian National Group 130 W 42nd St Suite 1804	New York	NY	10036	**877-221-7120**	212-575-3431	764
Russian National Tourist Office 130 W 42nd St Suite 1804	New York	NY	10036	**877-221-7120**	212-575-3431	764
Rust College 150 E Rust Ave	Holly Springs	MS	38635	**888-886-8492**	662-252-8000	163
Rust-Oleum Corp 11 Hawthorn Pkwy *Cust Svc	Vernon Hills	IL	60061	**800-323-3584***	847-367-7700	540
Rustler Lodge Hwy 210 PO Box 8030	Alta	UT	84092	**888-532-2582**	801-742-2200	655
Ruston/Lincoln Chamber of Commerce 104 E Mississippi Ave	Ruston	LA	71270	**800-392-9032**	318-255-2031	137
Rusty Parrot Lodge & Spa PO Box 1657	Jackson	WY	83001	**800-458-2004**	307-733-2000	655
Rusty Pelican 940 Calle Negocio Suite 250	San Clemente	CA	92673	**877-729-4867**	949-366-6260	657
Rutenberg Arthur Homes Inc 13922 58th St N	Clearwater	FL	33760	**800-274-6637**	727-536-5900	186
Rutgers Organics Corp 201 Struble Rd	State College	PA	16801	**800-458-3434**	814-238-2424	141
Rutgers University Press 100 Joyce Kilmer Ave *Orders	Piscataway	NJ	08854	**800-446-9323***	732-445-7762	623-5
Ruth Eckerd Hall 1111 McMullen Booth Rd	Clearwater	FL	33759	**800-875-8682**	727-791-7060	562
Rutherfoord Thomas Inc 1 S Jefferson St	Roanoke	VA	24011	**800-283-1478**	540-982-3511	383
Rutherford B Hayes Presidential Center Spiegel Grove	Fremont	OH	43420	**800-998-7737**	419-332-2081	426
Rutherford County Chamber of Commerce 501 Memorial Blvd	Murfreesboro	TN	37129	**800-716-7560**	615-893-6565	137
Rutherford County Tourism Development Authority 1990 US Hwy 221 S	South Forest City	NC	28043	**800-849-5998**	828-245-1492	205
Rutherford Electric Membership Corp 186 Hudlow Rd PO Box 1569	Forest City	NC	28043	**800-521-0920**	828-245-1621	244
Rutherford Institute PO Box 7482	Charlottesville	VA	22906	**800-225-1791**	434-978-3888	48-8
Ruth's Chris Steak House 3321 Hessmer Ave	Metairie	LA	70002	**800-487-4785**	504-454-6560	657
Rutland Herald PO Box 668	Rutland	VT	05702	**800-776-5512**	802-775-5511	522-2
Rutland Plastic Technologies 10021 Rodney St	Pineville	NC	28134	**800-438-5134**	704-553-0046	594-2
Rutland Plywood 1 Ripley Rd	Rutland	VT	05701	**800-457-0023**	802-747-4000	602
Rutland Products 86 Center St PO Box 340	Rutland	VT	05702	**800-544-1307**	802-775-5519	104
Rutland Regional Medical Center 160 Allen St	Rutland	VT	05701	**800-649-2187**	802-775-7111	366-2
Rutledge Hill Press PO Box 141000	Nashville	TN	37214	**800-251-4000**	615-889-9000	623-2
Rutt HandCrafted Cabinetry 215 Diller Ave *Cust Svc	New Holland	PA	17557	**800-220-7888***	717-351-1700	116
Ruttger's Bay Lake Lodge 25039 Tame Fish Lake Rd Box 400	Deerwood	MN	56444	**800-450-4545**	218-678-2885	655
Ruud Mfg Co 405 Lexington Ave 22nd Fl *Cust Svc	New York	NY	10174	**800-432-8373***	212-916-8100	15
RV Club. Escapees 100 Rainbow Dr	Livingston	TX	77351	**888-757-2582**	936-327-8873	48-23
RVers. Family Campers & 4804 Transit Rd Bldg 2	Depew	NY	14043	**800-245-9755**	716-668-6242	48-23
RVIA (Recreation Vehicle Industry Assn) 1896 Preston White Dr	Reston	VA	20191	**800-336-0154**	703-620-6003	49-21
RVing Coalition. Go 1896 Preston White Dr	Reston	VA	20191	**888-467-8464**	703-620-6003	48-23
RVing Women PO Box 1940	Apache Junction	AZ	85217	**888-557-8464**	480-671-6226	48-23
RVSI Inspection LLC 425 Rabro Dr E	Hauppauge	NY	11788	**800-669-5234**	631-273-9700	685
RW Beck Inc 1001 4th Ave Suite 2500	Seattle	WA	98154	**800-285-2325**	206-695-4700	191
RW Beckett Corp PO Box 1289	Elyria	OH	44036	**800-645-2876**	440-327-1060	352
RW Reed Co DBA Reed's 129-131 W Main St	Tupelo	MS	38804	**800-627-3337**	662-842-6453	227
RWD Technologies Inc 5521 Research Park Dr	Baltimore	MD	21228	**877-952-8301**	410-869-1000	178
RWM Casters Co PO Box 668	Gastonia	NC	28053	**800-253-6634**	704-866-8533	345
Rx Optical 1700 S Park St	Kalamazoo	MI	49001	**800-792-2737**	269-342-0003	533
Rx Worldwide Meetings Inc 3060 Communications Pkwy Suite 200	Plano	TX	75093	**800-562-1713**	214-291-2920	183
RxAmerica LLC 221 N Charles Lindbergh Dr	Salt Lake City	UT	84116	**800-770-8014**	801-961-6000	575
Ryan Beck & Co 18 Columbia Tpke	Florham Park	NJ	07932	**800-342-2325**	973-549-4000	679
Ryan Charles Assoc Inc 300 Summer St Suite 1100	Charleston	WV	25301	**877-342-0161**	304-342-0161	622
Ryan Herco Products Corp 3010 N San Fernando Blvd	Burbank	CA	91504	**800-848-1141**	818-841-1141	592
Ryan Inc Eastern 786 S Military Trail	Deerfield Beach	FL	33442	**800-433-1476**	954-427-5599	187-4
Ryan International Airlines Inc 266 N Main St	Wichita	KS	67202	**800-727-0457**	316-265-7400	13
Ryan Kelly Equipment Co 900 Kelly Ryan Dr	Blair	NE	68008	**800-640-6967**	402-426-2151	269
Ryan Rope Works 953 Benton Ave	Winslow	ME	04901	**800-848-4495**	207-872-0031	207
Ryce Jimmy Center For Victims of Predatory Abduction 908 Coquina Ln	Vero Beach	FL	32963	**800-546-7923**	772-492-0200	48-6
Rycenga Homes Inc 17127 Hickory St *Sales	Spring Lake	MI	49456	**800-424-8040***	616-842-8040	107
Rycoline Products Inc 5540 N Northwest Hwy	Chicago	IL	60630	**800-621-1003**	773-775-6755	143
Ryder System Inc 3600 NW 82nd Ave *NYSE: R*	Miami	FL	33166	**800-327-3399**	305-593-3726	767

Name / Address	City	State	ZIP	Toll-Free	Phone	Class
Rydex Funds 9601 Blackwell Rd Suite 500	Rockville	MD	20850	**800-820-0888**	301-296-5100	517
Rydin Decal Co 660 Pond Dr	Wood Dale	IL	60191	**800-448-1991**	630-766-8410	404
Ryland Group Inc 24025 Park Sorrento Suite 400 *NYSE: RYL*	Calabasas	CA	91302	**800-267-0998**	818-223-7500	639
Ryobi Technologies Inc 1428 Pearman Dairy Rd	Anderson	SC	29625	**800-525-2579**	864-226-6511	346
Rytex Co 100 N Park Ave	Peru	IN	46970	**800-277-5458**		542-3

S

Name / Address	City	State	ZIP	Toll-Free	Phone	Class
S & D Coffee Inc PO Box 1628 *Cust Svc	Concord	NC	28026	**800-933-2210***	704-782-3121	291-7
S Howes Co Inc 25 Howard St	Silver Creek	NY	14136	**888-255-2611**	716-934-2611	293
S Lichtenberg & Co Inc 295 5th Ave Rm 918 *Cust Svc	New York	NY	10010	**800-6[illegible]2-1060***	212-689-4510	731
S & M Machine Service Inc 206 E Highland Dr	Oconto Falls	WI	54154	**800-323-1579**	920-846-8130	447
S & M Moving Systems Inc 12128 Burke St	Santa Fe Springs	CA	90670	**800-336-5556**	562-567-2100	508
S & ME Inc 3109 Spring Forest Rd *Cust Svc	Raleigh	NC	27616	**800-849-2517***	919-872-2660	191
S & O Coach Lines Inc 6630 Fly Rd	East Syracuse	NY	13057	**800-242-4244**	315-431-4462	108
S Parker Hardware Mfg Corp PO Box 9882	Englewood	NJ	07631	**800-772-7537**	201-569-1600	345
S & R Uniforms Inc 1833 14th St W	Bradenton	FL	34205	**800-553-4065**	941-748-1245	434
S & S Cafeterias 2124 Riverside Dr	Macon	GA	31204	**800-841-5385**	478-745-4759	657
S & S Industries Inc 32-00 Skillman Ave	Long Island City	NY	11101	**800-543-9154**	718-585-1333	800
S & S Machinery Co 140 53rd St	Brooklyn	NY	11232	**800-540-9723**	718-492-7400	447
S & S Mills Inc 205 Boring Dr	Dalton	GA	30721	**800-392-6890**	706-277-3677	131
S & S Worldwide Inc 75 Mill St *Orders	Colchester	CT	06415	**800-243-9232***	860-537-3451	451
S & S X-Ray Products Inc 10625 Telge Rd	Houston	TX	77095	**800-347-9729**	800-231-1747	375
S Schwab Co Inc 12101 Upper Potomac Industrial Pk	Cumberland	MD	21502	**800-533-5437**	301-729-4488	153-4
S & T Bancorp Inc 43 S 9th St *NASDAQ: STBA*	Indiana	PA	15701	**800-325-2265**	724-349-1800	355-2
S & T Bank 800 Philadelphia St *Cust Svc	Indiana	PA	15701	**800-325-2265***	724-349-1800	71
S-T Industries Inc 301 Armstrong Blvd N	Saint James	MN	56081	**800-326-2039**	507-375-3211	484
S1 Corp 3500 Lenox Rd Suite 200 *NASDAQ: SONE*	Atlanta	GA	30326	**888-457-2237**	404-923-3500	176-10
S2 Systems Inc 4965 Preston Pk Blvd Suite 100	Plano	TX	75093	**800-527-4131**	972-599-5600	176-1
SA Comunale Co Inc 2900 Newpark Dr	Barberton	OH	44203	**800-776-7181**	330-706-3040	188-13
SA Healy Co 1910 S Highland Ave Suite 300	Lombard	IL	60148	**888-724-3259**	630-678-3110	258
SA-SO Co PO Box 67484	Saint Paul	MN	55164	**800-527-2450**		692
SAA (Sex Addicts Anonymous) PO Box 70949	Houston	TX	77270	**800-477-8191**	713-869-4902	48-21
SAA (Stepfamily Assn of America) 650 J St Suite 205	Lincoln	NE	68508	**800-735-0329**	402-477-7837	48-6
Saab Cars USA Inc 300 Renaissance Ctr	Detroit	MI	48265	**800-722-2872**	313-556-5000	59
Saags Products Inc 1799 Factor Ave	San Leandro	CA	94577	**800-352-7224**	510-352-8000	291-26
Saba Software Inc 2400 Bridge Pkwy *NASDAQ: SABA*	Redwood Shores	CA	94065	**877-803-1900**	650-696-3840	176-3
Sabel Steel Industries Inc PO Box 4747 *Sales	Montgomery	AL	36103	**800-392-5754***	334-265-6771	483
Sabin Corp 3800 Constitution Ave	Bloomington	IN	47402	**800-264-4510**	812-323-4500	588
Sabin Robbins Paper Co 497 Circle Freeway Dr Suite 490	Cincinnati	OH	45246	**800-424-5574**	513-874-5270	547
Sabine Royalty Trust 901 Main St 17th Fl Bank of America Plaza *NYSE: SBR*	Dallas	TX	75202	**800-365-6541**	214-209-2400	662
Sabine Universal Products Inc PO Box 295	Port Arthur	TX	77641	**800-482-9446**	409-982-9446	759
Sabreliner Corp 7733 Forsyth Blvd Suite 1500	Clayton	MO	63105	**800-325-4663**	314-863-6880	25
Sabreliner Corp 3551 Doniphan Dr	Neosho	MO	64850	**800-325-4663**	417-451-1810	21
Sabrett Food Products Corp 66 E Union Ave	East Rutherford	NJ	07073	**800-722-7388**	201-935-3330	291-26
Sac County Rural Electric Co-op 601 E Main St PO Box 397	Sac City	IA	50583	**866-722-6732**	712-662-4275	244
Sac Osage Electric Co-op Inc 4815 E Hwy 54	El Dorado Springs	MO	64744	**800-876-2701**	417-876-2721	244
Sacks Ann Tile & Stone Inc 8120 NE 33rd Dr	Portland	OR	97211	**800-278-8453**	503-281-7751	736
Sacramento Bag Mfg Co 530 Q St	Sacramento	CA	95814	**800-287-2247**	916-441-6121	68
Sacramento Bee 2100 Q St *Cust Svc	Sacramento	CA	95816	**800-284-3233***	916-321-1000	522-2
Sacramento Convention & Visitors Bureau 1608 'I' St	Sacramento	CA	95814	**800-292-2334**	916-808-7777	205
Sacramento Medical Foundation Blood Center 1625 Stockton Blvd	Sacramento	CA	95816	**800-995-4420**	916-456-1500	90
Sacred Heart Hospital 900 W Clairemont Ave	Eau Claire	WI	54701	**888-445-4554**	715-839-4121	366-2
Sacred Heart Hospital of Pensacola 5151 N 9th Ave	Pensacola	FL	32504	**800-874-1026**	850-416-7000	366-2
Sacred Heart Medical Center 1255 Hilyard St	Eugene	OR	97401	**800-288-7444**	541-686-7300	366-2
SADD (Students Against Destructive Decisions) 255 Main St	Marlborough	MA	01752	**877-723-3462**	508-481-3568	48-6
Saddlebrook Resort 5700 Saddlebrook Way	Wesley Chapel	FL	33543	**800-729-8383**	813-973-1111	655
Saddleridge 44 Meadows Ln	Beaver Creek	CO	81620	**800-859-8242**	970-845-5450	373
Sadlier William H Inc 9 Pine St 2nd Fl	New York	NY	10005	**800-582-5437**	212-227-2120	623-2
Sadoff & Rudoy Industries LLP 240 W Arndt St	Fond du Lac	WI	54935	**800-236-5700**	920-921-2070	674
SAE (Sigma Alpha Epsilon Fraternity) 1856 Sheridan Rd	Evanston	IL	60201	**800-233-1856**	847-475-1856	48-16
SAE (Society of Automotive Engineers Inc) 400 Commonwealth Dr	Warrendale	PA	15096	**877-606-7323**	724-776-4841	49-21
SAF (Society of American Florists) 1601 Duke St	Alexandria	VA	22314	**800-336-4743**	703-836-8700	49-4
Saf-T-Cab Inc 3241 S Parkway Dr	Fresno	CA	93725	**800-344-7491**	559-268-5541	505
Saf-T-Gard International Inc 205 Huehl Rd	Northbrook	IL	60062	**800-548-4273**	847-291-1600	667
Safari Motor Inn 345 N Hwy 99 West	McMinnville	OR	97128	**800-321-5543**	503-472-5187	373
Safari Technologies Inc 411 Washington St	Otsego	MI	49078	**888-694-7230**	269-694-9471	174
Safari West Wildlife Preserve & Tent Camp 3115 Porter Creek Rd	Santa Rosa	CA	95404	**800-616-2695**	707-579-2551	811
Safariland Ltd Inc 3120 E Mission Blvd	Ontario	CA	91761	**800-347-1200**	909-923-7300	566
Safco Products Co 9300 W Research Ctr Rd	New Hope	MN	55428	**800-328-3020**	763-536-6700	314-1
Safe Auto Insurance Co 3883 E Broad St	Columbus	OH	43213	**800-723-3288**	614-231-0200	384-4
SAFE Credit Union 3720 Madison Ave	North Highlands	CA	95660	**800-733-7233**	916-979-7233	216
Safe-T-Gard Corp 12105 W Cedar Dr *Cust Svc	Lakewood	CO	80228	**800-356-9026***	303-763-8900	566
Safe Tables Our Priority (STOP) PO Box 4352	Burlington	VT	05406	**800-350-7867**	802-863-0555	48-17
Safe Tables Our Priority. STOP - PO Box 4352	Burlington	VT	05406	**800-350-7867**	802-863-0555	48-17
Safe Transit Assn. International 1400 Abbott Rd Suite 160	East Lansing	MI	48823	**888-367-4782**	517-333-3437	49-21
SafeBrowse.com Inc 315 Northpoint Pkwy Suite F	Acworth	GA	30102	**877-944-7070**		390
SAFECO Corp 4333 Brooklyn Ave NE *NASDAQ: SAFC*	Seattle	WA	98185	**800-562-1018**	206-545-5000	355-4
SAFECO Mutual Funds PO Box 34890	Seattle	WA	98124	**800-624-5711**		517
Safeguard Business Systems Inc 8585 N Stemmons Fwy Suite 600 N	Dallas	TX	75247	**800-338-0636**	214-905-3935	140
Safeguard Chemical Corp 411 Wales Ave	Bronx	NY	10454	**800-536-3170**	718-585-3170	276
SafeGuard Health Enterprises Inc 95 Enterprise Suite 100	Aliso Viejo	CA	92656	**800-880-1800**	949-425-4300	384-3
Safeguard Scientifics Inc 435 Devon Park Dr Suite 800 *NYSE: SFE*	Wayne	PA	19087	**888-733-1200**	610-293-0600	779
Safelite Glass Corp 2400 Farmers Dr 5th Fl	Columbus	OH	43235	**800-835-2257**	614-210-9465	62-2
SafeNet Inc 4690 Millennium Dr *NASDAQ: SFNT* ■ *Sales	Belcamp	MD	21017	**800-533-3958***	410-931-7500	174
Safetran Systems Corp 2400 Nelson Miller Pkwy	Louisville	KY	40223	**800-626-2710**	502-244-7400	691
Safety 1st Inc 45 Dan Rd	Canton	MA	02021	**800-962-7233**	781-364-3100	64
Safety Bus Service 7200 Park Ave	Pennsauken	NJ	08109	**800-367-7233**	856-665-2662	110
Safety Communications Officials International Inc. Association of Public- 351 N Williamson Blvd	Daytona Beach	FL	32114	**888-272-6911**	386-322-2500	49-7
Safety Council. National 1121 Spring Lake Dr	Itasca	IL	60143	**800-621-7619**	630-285-1121	48-17
Safety Council. National Child 4065 Page Ave	Jackson	MI	49204	**800-327-5107**	517-764-6070	48-6
Safety Engineering Society. IEEE Product IEEE Operations Ctr 445 Hoes Ln	Piscataway	NJ	08854	**800-678-4333**	732-981-0060	49-19
Safety Harbor Resort & Spa 105 N Bayshore Dr	Safety Harbor	FL	34695	**888-237-8772**	727-726-1161	655
Safety. Institute for Business & Home 4775 E Fowler Ave	Tampa	FL	33617	**866-675-4247**	813-286-3400	49-9
Safety-Kleen Corp 5400 Legacy Dr Cluster 2 Bldg 3	Plano	TX	75024	**800-669-5740**	972-265-2000	653
Safety National Casualty Corp 2043 Woodland Pkwy	Saint Louis	MO	63146	**800-289-7224**	314-995-5300	384-4
Safety. Northwestern University Center for Public 600 Foster	Evanston	IL	60204	**800-323-4011**	847-491-5476	49-7
Safety Products Inc 3517 Craftsman Blvd	Lakeland	FL	33803	**800-248-6860**	863-665-3601	667
Safety Seal Piston Ring Co 4000 Airport Rd *Sales	Marshall	TX	75672	**800-962-3631***	903-938-9241	128
Safety Services Assn. American Traffic 15 Riverside Pkwy Suite 100	Fredericksburg	VA	22406	**800-272-8772**	540-368-1701	49-21
Safety Solutions Inc 6161 Shamrock Ct PO Box 8100	Dublin	OH	43016	**800-232-7463**	614-799-9900	667
Safety Speed Cut Mfg Co Inc 13943 Lincoln St NE	Ham Lake	MN	55304	**800-772-2327**	763-755-1600	809
Safety Supply South Inc 100 Centrum Dr	Irmo	SC	29063	**800-522-8344**	803-732-1500	667
Safety Today 2425 Speigel Dr Suite A	Groveport	OH	43125	**800-837-5900**	614-409-7200	667
Safeware Inc 3200 Hubbard Rd	Landover	MD	20785	**800-331-6707**	301-683-1234	667
SafeWay Hydraulics Inc 4040 Norex Dr *Cust Svc	Chaska	MN	55318	**800-222-1169***	952-448-2600	777
Safeway Insurance Group 790 Pasquinelli Dr	Westmont	IL	60559	**800-273-0300**	630-887-8300	384-4

Name / Address	City	State	ZIP	Toll-Free	Phone	Class
Safeway Sign Co 9875 Yucca Rd	Adelanto	CA	92301	800-637-7233	760-246-7070	692
SAFLINK Corp 777 108th Ave NE Suite 2100	Bellevue	WA	98004	800-762-9595	425-278-1100	176-12
Safway Services Inc PO Box 1991	Milwaukee	WI	53201	800-558-4772	262-523-6500	261-4
Saga Communications Inc 73 Kercheval Ave *NYSE: SGA*	Grosse Pointe Farms	MI	48236	888-886-7070	313-886-7070	629
Sagamore The 110 Sagamore Rd	Bolton Landing	NY	12814	800-358-3585	518-644-9400	655
Sagamore Health Network 11555 N Meridian St Suite 400	Carmel	IN	46032	800-364-3469	317-573-2886	384-3
Sagamore Insurance Co 1099 N Meridian St Suite 700	Indianapolis	IN	46204	800-231-6024	317-636-9800	384-4
Sage College of Albany 140 New Scotland Ave	Albany	NY	12208	888-837-9724	518-292-1730	160
Sage Mfg Corp 8500 NE Day Rd	Bainbridge Island	WA	98110	800-533-3004	206-842-6608	701
Sage Publications Inc 2455 Teller Rd	Thousand Oaks	CA	91320	800-818-7243	805-499-9774	623-2
Sagebrush Education Resources 2101 N Topeka Blvd	Topeka	KS	66608	800-255-3502	785-233-4252	93
Sagebrush Steakhouse 129 Fast Ln	Mooresville	NC	28117	877-704-5939	704-660-5939	657
Sagem Morpho Inc 1145 Broadway Suite 200	Tacoma	WA	98402	800-346-2674	253-383-3617	85
Sager Electronics Inc 97 Libbey Industrial Pkwy	Weymouth	MA	02189	800-541-9371	781-682-4844	245
Saginaw Control & Engineering Inc 95 Midland Rd	Saginaw	MI	48603	800-234-6871	989-799-6871	804
Saginaw County Convention & Visitors Bureau 515 N Washington Ave 3rd Fl	Saginaw	MI	48607	800-444-9979	989-752-7164	205
Saginaw Harness Raceway 2701 E Genesee St	Saginaw	MI	48601	800-636-7223	989-755-3451	628
Saginaw News 203 S Washington Ave	Saginaw	MI	48607	800-875-6397	989-752-7171	522-2
Saginaw Valley State University 7400 Bay Rd	University Center	MI	48710	800-968-9500	989-964-4000	163
Sahara Hotel & Casino 2535 Las Vegas Blvd S	Las Vegas	NV	89109	888-696-2121	702-737-2111	133
SAIA-Burgess Inc PO Box 427	Vandalia	OH	45377	800-888-9765	937-898-3621	202
Saia Motor Freight Line Inc 11465 Johns Creek Pkwy Suite 400	Duluth	GA	30097	800-950-7242	770-232-4050	769
SAIL Magazine 98 N Washington St 2nd Fl	Boston	MA	02114	800-745-7245	617-720-8600	449-4
Sailing Assn. US 15 Maritime Dr PO Box 1260	Portsmouth	RI	02871	800-877-2451	401-683-0800	48-22
Sailing World Magazine 5 John Clarke Rd *Cust Svc	Newport	RI	02840	866-436-2460*	401-847-1588	449-4
SailNet 3864 Leeds Ave *Cust Svc	Charleston	SC	29405	866-724-5638*	843-972-2010	702
Sailport Resort 2506 Rocky Point Dr	Tampa	FL	33607	800-255-9599	813-281-9599	373
Saint Agnes HealthCare 900 Caton Ave	Baltimore	MD	21229	800-875-8750	410-368-6000	366-2
Saint Agnes Home Care Hospice 239 Trowbridge Dr	Fond du Lac	WI	54936	800-236-4156	920-923-7950	365
Saint Agnes Hospital 430 E Division St	Fond du Lac	WI	54935	800-922-3400	920-929-2300	366-2
Saint Alphonsus Regional Medical Center 1055 N Curtis Rd	Boise	ID	83706	877-341-2121	208-367-2121	366-2
Saint Ambrose University 518 W Locust St	Davenport	IA	52803	800-383-2627	563-333-6000	163
Saint Andrew. Society of 3383 Sweet Hollow Rd	Big Island	VA	24526	800-333-4597	434-299-5956	48-5
Saint Andrew's College 15800 Yonge St	Aurora	ON	L4G3H7	877-378-1899	905-727-3178	611
Saint Andrew's College 1121 College Dr	Saskatoon	SK	S7N0W3	877-664-8970	306-966-8970	164-3
Saint Andrews Estates 6152 Verde Trail N *Mktg	Boca Raton	FL	33433	800-850-2287*	561-487-5500	659
Saint Andrews Presbyterian College 1700 Dogwood Mile	Laurinburg	NC	28352	800-763-0198	910-277-5000	163
Saint Ann/Marie Antoinette Hotel 717 Conti St	New Orleans	LA	70130	888-535-3603	504-581-1881	373
Saint Anselm College 100 St Anselm Dr	Manchester	NH	03102	888-426-7356	603-641-7500	163
Saint Anthony Hospital 1000 N Lee St	Oklahoma City	OK	73101	800-227-6964	405-272-7000	366-2
Saint Anthony Medical Center 5666 E State St	Rockford	IL	61108	800-343-3185	815-226-2000	366-2
Saint Anthony Messenger Magazine 28 W Liberty St	Cincinnati	OH	45202	800-488-0488	513-241-5616	449-18
Saint Augustine's College 1315 Oakwood Ave *Admissions	Raleigh	NC	27610	800-948-1126*	919-516-4016	163
Saint Barnabas Medical Center 94 Old Short Hills Rd	Livingston	NJ	07039	888-724-7123	973-533-5000	366-2
Saint Bernard Preparatory School 1600 Saint Bernard Dr SE	Cullman	AL	35055	800-722-0999	256-739-6682	611
Saint Bonaventure University Rt 417 PO Box D	Saint Bonaventure	NY	14778	800-462-5050	716-375-2400	163
Saint Catherine's School 6001 Grove Ave	Richmond	VA	23226	800-648-4982	804-288-2804	611
Saint Charles Mercy Hospital 2600 Navarre Ave	Oregon	OH	43616	800-692-6363	419-696-7200	366-2
Saint Clair Die Casting LLC 225 St Clair Industrial Park Dr	Saint Clair	MO	63077	800-367-7232	636-629-2550	303
Saint Clair Inn 500 N Riverside Ave	Saint Clair	MI	48079	800-482-8327	810-329-2222	373
Saint Clair Pakwell Div Field Container Co LP 120 25th Ave *Cust Svc	Bellwood	IL	60104	800-323-1922*	708-547-7500	542-2
Saint Cloud Area Chamber of Commerce 110 6th Ave S	Saint Cloud	MN	56301	800-264-2040	320-251-2940	137
Saint Cloud Area Convention & Visitors Bureau 525 Hwy 10 S Suite 1	Saint Cloud	MN	56304	800-264-2940	320-251-4170	205
Saint Cloud Civic Center 10 4th Ave S	Saint Cloud	MN	56301	800-450-7272	320-255-7272	204
Saint Cloud Hospital 1406 6th Ave N	Saint Cloud	MN	56303	800-835-6652	320-251-2700	366-2
Saint Cloud State University 720 4th Ave S	Saint Cloud	MN	56301	800-369-4260	320-255-3822	163
Saint Cloud Technical College 1540 Northway Dr	Saint Cloud	MN	56303	800-222-1009	320-308-5089	787
Saint Cloud Times PO Box 768	Saint Cloud	MN	56302	800-272-8770	320-255-8700	522-2
Saint Croix Casino & Hotel 777 US Hwys 8 & 63	Turtle Lake	WI	54889	800-846-8946	715-986-4777	133
Saint Croix Chippewa Tribe of Wisconsin 24663 Angeline Ave	Webster	WI	54893	800-236-2195	715-349-2195	132
Saint Croix Electric Co-op 1925 Ridgeway St	Hammond	WI	54015	800-924-3407	715-796-7000	244
Saint Croix Forge Inc 5195 Scandia Trail	Forest Lake	MN	55025	800-966-3668	651-464-8967	474
Saint Croix of Park Falls Ltd PO Box 279	Park Falls	WI	54552	800-826-7042	715-762-3226	701
Saint Croix Press Inc 1185 S Knowles Ave	New Richmond	WI	54017	800-826-6622	715-246-5811	623-9
Saint David's Rehabilitation Hospital 1005 E 32nd St	Austin	TX	78705	800-533-8545	512-867-5100	366-4
Saint Edward's University 3001 S Congress Ave	Austin	TX	78704	800-555-0164	512-448-8500	163
Saint Elizabeth Hospital 1506 S Oneida St	Appleton	WI	54915	800-223-7332	920-738-2000	366-2
Saint Elizabeth Hospital Medical Center 1501 Hartford St	Lafayette	IN	47904	800-371-6011	765-423-6011	366-2
Saint Elizabeth Medical Center-North 401 E 20th St	Covington	KY	41014	800-888-7362	859-292-4000	366-2
Saint Francis Health Care Center 401 N Broadway	Green Springs	OH	44836	800-248-2552	419-639-2626	366-5
Saint Francis Health Center 1700 SW 7th St	Topeka	KS	66606	800-444-2954	785-295-8000	366-2
Saint Francis Hospice 414-A Pettigru St	Greenville	SC	29601	800-277-2273	864-233-5300	365
Saint Francis Hospital 6161 S Yale Ave	Tulsa	OK	74136	800-888-9599	918-494-2200	366-2
Saint Francis Medical Center 2620 W Faidley Ave	Grand Island	NE	68803	800-353-4896	308-384-4600	366-2
Saint Francis University 169 Lakeview Dr	Loretto	PA	15940	866-342-5738	814-472-3000	163
Saint-Gobain Advanced Ceramics Latrobe 4702 Rt 982	Latrobe	PA	15650	800-438-7237	724-539-6000	248
Saint-Gobain Calmar Inc 333 S Turnbull Canyon Rd	City of Industry	CA	91745	800-841-4112	626-937-2600	152
Saint-Gobain Containers Inc 1509 S Macedonia Ave	Muncie	IN	47302	800-428-8642	765-741-7000	327
Saint-Gobain Corp 750 E Swedesford Rd	Valley Forge	PA	19482	800-274-8530	610-341-7000	325
Saint Gregory Luxury Hotel & Suites 2033 M Street NW	Washington	DC	20036	800-829-5034	202-530-3600	373
Saint Gregory's University 1900 W MacArthur Dr	Shawnee	OK	74873	888-784-7347	405-878-5100	163
Saint Ives Cleveland Inc 4437 E 49th St	Cleveland	OH	44125	800-634-1262	216-271-5300	615
Saint Ives Laboratories Inc 2525 Armitage Ave	Melrose Park	IL	60160	800-333-6666	708-450-3000	211
Saint James Hotel 330 Magazine St	New Orleans	LA	70130	800-273-1889	504-304-4000	373
Saint James Hotel 406 Main St	Red Wing	MN	55066	800-252-1875	651-388-2846	373
Saint James Theatre 246 W 44th St	New York	NY	10036	800-432-7250	212-239-6200	732
Saint Joe Distributing 5808 Corporate Dr	Saint Joseph	MO	64507	800-892-9072	816-233-8213	744
Saint Joe Towns & Resorts 7900 Glades Rd Suite 200	Boca Raton	FL	33434	800-527-8432	561-479-1100	639
Saint John Fisher College 3690 East Ave	Rochester	NY	14618	800-444-4640	585-385-8000	163
Saint John Knits Inc 17522 Armstrong Ave	Irvine	CA	92614	877-755-8463	949-863-1171	153-21
Saint John & Partners Advertising & Public Relations 5220 Belfort Rd Suite 400	Jacksonville	FL	32256	800-642-2828	904-281-2500	4
Saint John's College Santa Fe Campus 1160 Camino Cruz Blanca	Santa Fe	NM	87505	800-331-5232	505-984-6060	163
Saint Johns County Convention & Visitors Bureau 88 Riberia St Suite 400	Saint Augustine	FL	32084	800-653-2489	904-829-1711	205
Saint John's Hospice Care 1378 E Republic Rd	Springfield	MO	65804	800-330-8304	417-820-7550	365
Saint John's Medical Center 1615 Delaware St	Longview	WA	98632	800-438-7562	360-423-1530	366-2
Saint John's Medical Center 625 E Broadway	Jackson	WY	83001	800-877-7078	307-733-3636	366-2
Saint John's Military School 110 E Otis Ave PO Box 827	Salina	KS	67402	866-704-5294	785-823-7231	611
Saint John's Northwestern Military Academy 1101 N Genesee St	Delafield	WI	53018	800-752-2338	262-646-7115	611
Saint John's Preparatory School 1857 Watertower Rd PO Box 4000	Collegeville	MN	56321	800-525-7737	320-363-3321	611
Saint John's University	Collegeville	MN	56321	800-245-6467	320-363-2196	163
Saint John's University School of Law 8000 Utopia Pkwy	Jamaica	NY	11439	888-978-5647	718-990-6611	164-1
Saint John's=Ravenscourt School 400 South Dr	Winnipeg	MB	R3T3K5	800-437-0040	204-477-2400	611
Saint Joseph Area Chamber of Commerce 3003 Frederick Ave	Saint Joseph	MO	64506	800-748-7856	816-232-4461	137
Saint Joseph Convention & Visitors Bureau 109 S 4th St	Saint Joseph	MO	64501	800-785-0360	816-233-6688	205
Saint Joseph Corp 50 MacIntosh Blvd	Concord	ON	L4K4P3	877-660-3111	905-660-3111	615
Saint Joseph Hospital 172 Kinsley St	Nashua	NH	03060	877-899-6345	603-882-3000	366-2
Saint Joseph Hospital 2901 Squalicum Pkwy	Bellingham	WA	98225	800-541-7209	360-734-5400	366-2
Saint Joseph Mercy Home Care & Hospice 806 Airport Blvd	Ann Arbor	MI	48108	888-884-6569	734-327-3400	365
Saint Joseph News-Press PO Box 29	Saint Joseph	MO	64502	800-779-6397	816-271-8500	522-2
Saint Joseph News Press & Gazette Co PO Box 29	Saint Joseph	MO	64502	800-779-6397	816-271-8500	623-8

Name	Address	City	State	ZIP	Toll-Free	Phone	Class
Saint Joseph Packaging Inc	4515 Easton Rd	Saint Joseph	MO	64503	**800-383-3000**	816-233-3181	102
Saint Joseph Tobacco Co Inc DBA Saint Joe Distributing	5808 Corporate Dr	Saint Joseph	MO	64507	**800-892-9072**	816-233-8213	744
Saint Joseph's College	278 Whites Bridge Rd	Standish	ME	04084	**800-338-7057**	207-893-7746	163
Saint Joseph's Hospital of Atlanta	5665 Peachtree Dunwoody Rd NE	Atlanta	GA	30342	**800-678-5637**	404-851-7001	366-2
Saint Joseph's Hospital Health Center	301 Prospect Ave	Syracuse	NY	13203	**888-785-6371**	315-448-5111	366-2
Saint Joseph's Hospital & Health Center	30 7th St W	Dickinson	ND	58601	**800-446-6215**	701-456-4000	366-2
Saint Joseph's Medical Center	523 N 3rd St	Brainerd	MN	56401	**888-829-2861**	218-829-2861	366-2
Saint Jude Medical Inc	1 Lillehei Plaza *NYSE: STJ*	Saint Paul	MN	55117	**800-328-9634**	651-483-2000	469
Saint Jude Medical Inc Heart Valve Div	1 Lillehei Plaza	Saint Paul	MN	55117	**800-328-9634**	651-483-2000	249
Saint Julien Hotel & Spa	900 Walnut St	Boulder	CO	80302	**877-303-0900**	720-406-9696	373
Saint Kitts Tourism Authority	414 E 75th St Suite 5	New York	NY	10021	**800-582-6208**	212-535-1234	764
Saint Lawrence County Chamber of Commerce	101 Main St	Canton	NY	13617	**877-228-7810**	315-386-4000	137
Saint Lawrence University	23 Romoda Dr	Canton	NY	13617	**800-285-1856**	315-229-5261	163
Saint Louis Bread Co	6710 Clayton Rd	Richmond Heights	MO	63117	**800-301-5566**	314-633-7100	69
Saint Louis Children's Hospital	1 Children's Pl	Saint Louis	MO	63110	**800-678-5437**	314-454-6000	366-1
Saint Louis Christian College	1360 Grandview Dr	Florissant	MO	63033	**800-887-7522**	314-837-6777	163
Saint Louis College of Pharmacy	4588 Parkview Pl	Saint Louis	MO	63110	**800-278-5267**	314-367-8700	163
Saint Louis Convention & Visitors Commission	1 Metropolitan Sq Suite 1100	Saint Louis	MO	63102	**800-325-7962**	314-421-1023	205
Saint Louis Embroidery	1759 Scherer Pkwy	Saint Charles	MO	63303	**800-423-0450**	636-724-2200	256
Saint Louis Helicopter LLC	18004 Edison Ave	Chesterfield	MO	63005	**800-325-4046**	636-532-1177	354
Saint Louis Hotel	730 Bienville St	New Orleans	LA	70130	**800-535-9111**	504-581-7300	373
Saint Louis Music Inc	1400 Ferguson Ave	Saint Louis	MO	63133	**800-727-4512**	314-727-4512	516
Saint Louis Paper & Box Co	3843 Garfield Ave	Saint Louis	MO	63113	**800-779-7901**	314-531-7900	549
Saint Louis Post-Dispatch	900 N Tucker Blvd	Saint Louis	MO	63101	**800-365-0820**	314-340-8000	522-2
Saint Louis Rams	1 Rams Way	Earth City	MO	63045	**800-246-7267*** *Cust Svc	314-982-7267	703
Saint Louis Regional Commerce & Growth Assn	1 Metropolitan Sq Suite 1300	Saint Louis	MO	63102	**877-785-7242**	314-231-5555	137
Saint Louis Science Center	5050 Oakland Ave	Saint Louis	MO	63110	**800-456-7572**	314-289-4400	509
Saint Louis Symphony Orchestra	718 N Grand Blvd	Saint Louis	MO	63103	**800-232-1880**	314-533-2500	563-3
Saint Louis Trimming Div Trimtex	400 Park Ave	Williamsport	PA	17701	**800-326-9135**	570-326-9135	583
Saint Louis University	221 N Grand Blvd	Saint Louis	MO	63103	**800-758-3678**	314-977-2222	163
Saint Lucia Tourist Board	800 2nd Ave 9th Fl	New York	NY	10017	**800-456-3984**	212-867-2950	764
Saint Lucie County Tourist Development Council	2300 Virginia Ave	Fort Pierce	FL	34982	**800-344-8443**	772-462-1535	205
Saint Luke Hospital East	85 N Grand Ave	Fort Thomas	KY	41075	**800-345-7151**	859-572-3100	366-2
Saint Luke Hospital West	7380 Turfway Rd	Florence	KY	41042	**800-345-7151**	859-962-5200	366-2
Saint Luke's Hospital of New Bedford	101 Page St	New Bedford	MA	02740	**800-245-8537**	508-997-1515	366-2
Saint Luke's Hospital & Regional Trauma Center	915 E 1st St	Duluth	MN	55805	**800-321-3790**	218-249-5555	366-2
Saint Luke's Regional Medical Center	2720 Stone Park Blvd	Sioux City	IA	51104	**800-352-4660**	712-279-3500	366-2
Saint Maarten Tourist Office	675 3rd Ave Suite 1807	New York	NY	10017	**800-786-2278**	212-953-2084	764
Saint Marie's Gopher News Co	9000 10th Ave N	Minneapolis	MN	55427	**800-279-2665**	763-546-5300	97
Saint Marks Historic Railroad State Trail	W of 363 S of 319 (Capital Circle)	Tallahassee	FL	32301	**877-822-5208**	850-245-2052	50
Saint Martin Tourist Office	675 3rd Ave Suite 1807	New York	NY	10017	**877-956-1234**	212-475-8970	764
Saint Martin's College	5300 Pacific Ave SE	Lacey	WA	98503	**800-368-8803**	360-438-4311	163
Saint Martin's Press Inc	175 5th Ave	New York	NY	10010	**888-330-8477*** *Cust Svc	212-674-5151	623-2
Saint Mary-Corwin Medical Center	1008 Minnequa Ave	Pueblo	CO	81004	**800-228-4039**	719-560-4000	366-2
Saint Mary Medical Center	401 W Poplar St	Walla Walla	WA	99362	**800-452-3320**	509-525-3320	366-2
Saint Mary Mercy Hospital	36475 Five-Mile Rd	Livonia	MI	48154	**800-464-7492**	734-655-4800	366-2
Saint Mary Parish Library	206 Iberia St	Franklin	LA	70538	**800-732-8698**	337-828-1624	426
Saint Mary-of-the-Woods College	3301 St Mary Rd	Saint Mary-of-the-Woods	IN	47876	**800-926-7692**	812-535-5106	163
Saint Mary's College		Notre Dame	IN	46556	**800-551-7621**	574-284-4587	163
Saint Mary's College of California	1928 St Mary's Rd	Moraga	CA	94575	**800-800-4762**	925-631-4000	163
Saint Mary's College of Maryland	18952 E Fisher Rd	Saint Mary's City	MD	20686	**800-492-7181**	240-895-5000	163
Saint Mary's Good Samaritan Inc	605 N 12th St	Mount Vernon	IL	62864	**800-310-0484**	618-242-4600	348
Saint Mary's Health Care System	1230 Baxter St	Athens	GA	30606	**800-233-7864**	706-548-7581	366-2
Saint Mary's Health Center	6420 Clayton Rd	Richmond Heights	MO	63117	**800-284-2854**	314-768-8000	366-2
Saint Mary's Hospital	25500 Point Lookout Rd PO Box 527	Leonardtown	MD	20650	**800-222-1764**	301-475-8981	366-2
Saint Mary's Hospital	2251 N Shore Dr	Rhinelander	WI	54501	**800-578-0840**	715-361-2000	366-2
Saint Mary's Hospital & Medical Center	2635 N 7th St PO Box 1628	Grand Junction	CO	81502	**800-458-3888**	970-244-2273	366-2
Saint Mary's Hospital Ozaukee	13111 N Port Washington Rd	Mequon	WI	53097	**800-848-2844**	262-243-7300	366-2
Saint Mary's Medical Center	2900 1st Ave	Huntington	WV	25702	**800-978-6279**	304-526-1234	366-2
Saint Mary's Medical Center	1726 Shawano Ave	Green Bay	WI	54303	**800-666-5606**	920-498-4200	366-2
Saint Mary's School	900 Hillsborough St	Raleigh	NC	27603	**800-948-2557**	919-424-4100	611
Saint Mary's University	1 Camino Santa Maria	San Antonio	TX	78228	**800-367-7868**	210-436-3126	163
Saint Mary's University of Minnesota	700 Terrace Heights	Winona	MN	55987	**800-635-5987**	507-452-4430	163
Saint Mary's University School of Law	1 Camino Santa Maria	San Antonio	TX	78228	**800-367-7868**	210-436-3523	164-1
Saint Michael's College	1 Winooski Pk	Colchester	VT	05439	**800-762-8000**	802-654-2000	163
Saint Michaels Harbour Inn & Marina	101 N Harbor Rd	Saint Michaels	MD	21663	**800-955-9001**	410-745-9001	373
Saint Michael's University School	3400 Richmond Rd	Victoria	BC	V8P4P5	**800-661-5199**	250-592-2411	611
Saint Nicholas Hospital	1601 N Taylor Dr	Sheboygan	WI	53081	**800-472-6710**	920-459-8300	366-2
Saint Norbert College	100 Grant St	De Pere	WI	54115	**800-236-4878**	920-403-3005	163
Saint Olaf College	1520 St Olaf Ave	Northfield	MN	55057	**800-800-3025**	507-646-2222	163
Saint Paul College	235 Marshall Ave	Saint Paul	MN	55102	**800-227-6029**	651-846-1600	787
Saint Paul Convention & Visitors Bureau	175 W Kellogg Blvd Suite 502	Saint Paul	MN	55102	**800-627-6101**	651-265-4900	205
Saint Paul Fire & Marine Insurance Co	385 Washington St	Saint Paul	MN	55102	**800-328-2189**	651-310-7911	384-4
Saint Paul Flight Center	270 Airport Rd	Saint Paul	MN	55107	**800-368-0107**	651-227-8108	63
Saint Paul Hotel	350 Market St	Saint Paul	MN	55102	**800-292-9292**	651-292-9292	373
Saint Paul Pioneer Press	345 Cedar St	Saint Paul	MN	55101	**800-950-9080**	651-222-1111	522-2
Saint Paul Travelers Cos Inc	385 Washington St *NYSE: STA*	Saint Paul	MN	55102	**800-328-2189**	651-310-7911	355-4
Saint Paul's College	115 College Dr	Lawrenceville	VA	23868	**800-678-7071**	434-848-3111	163
Saint Peter's College	2641 JFK Blvd	Jersey City	NJ	07306	**888-772-9933**	201-915-9000	163
Saint Petersburg Times	490 1st Ave S	Saint Petersburg	FL	33701	**800-333-7505**	727-893-8111	522-2
Saint Petersburg/Clearwater Area Convention & Visitors Bureau	14450 46th St N Suite 108	Clearwater	FL	33762	**800-345-6710**	727-464-7200	205
Saint Philip's College	1801 ML King Dr	San Antonio	TX	78203	**866-493-3940**	210-531-3200	160
Saint Regis Aspen	315 E Dean St	Aspen	CO	81611	**888-454-9005**	970-920-3300	373
Saint Regis Culvert Inc	202 Morrell St	Charlotte	MI	48813	**800-527-4604**	517-543-3430	688
Saint Regis Detroit. Hotel	3071 W Grand Blvd	Detroit	MI	48202	**800-848-4810**	313-873-3000	373
Saint Regis Hotel	602 Dunsmuir St	Vancouver	BC	V6B1Y6	**800-770-7929**	604-681-1135	372
Saint Regis Hotel Winnipeg	285 Smith St	Winnipeg	MB	R3C1K9	**800-663-7344**	204-942-0171	372
Saint Regis Houston	1919 Briar Oaks Ln	Houston	TX	77027	**800-325-3589**	713-840-7600	373
Saint Regis Los Angeles Hotel & Spa	2055 Ave of the Stars	Los Angeles	CA	90067	**877-787-3452**	310-277-6111	373
Saint Regis Monarch Beach Resort & Spa	1 Monarch Beach Resort	Dana Point	CA	92629	**800-722-1543**	949-234-3200	655
Saint Regis New York	2 E 55th St	New York	NY	10022	**800-759-7550**	212-753-4500	373
Saint Regis Washington DC	923 16th St NW	Washington	DC	20006	**800-325-3535**	202-638-2626	373
Saint Stanislaus College	304 S Beach Blvd	Bay Saint Louis	MS	39520	**800-517-6257**	228-467-9057	611
Saint Stephen's Episcopal School	2900 Bunny Run	Austin	TX	78746	**888-377-7937**	512-327-1213	611
Saint Tammany Parish Tourist & Convention Commission	68099 Hwy 59	Mandeville	LA	70471	**800-634-9443**	985-892-0520	205
Saint Thomas Aquinas College	125 Rt 340	Sparkill	NY	10976	**800-999-7822**	845-398-4000	163
Saint Thomas University	16401 NW 37th Ave	Miami	FL	33054	**800-367-9010**	305-628-6546	163
Saint Timothy's School	8400 Greenspring Ave	Stevenson	MD	21153	**800-467-8846**	410-486-7400	611
Saint Tropez Hotel	455 E Harmon Ave	Las Vegas	NV	89109	**800-666-5400**	702-369-5400	373
Saint Vincent Charity Hospital	2351 E 22nd St	Cleveland	OH	44115	**800-451-8128**	216-861-6200	366-2
Saint Vincent College	300 Fraser Purchase Rd	Latrobe	PA	15650	**800-782-5549**	724-532-6600	163
Saint Vincent & the Grenadines Tourist Information Office	801 2nd Ave 21st Fl	New York	NY	10017	**800-729-1726**	212-687-4981	764
Saint Vincent Hospice	8450 N Payne Rd Suite 100	Indianapolis	IN	46268	**888-780-7284**	317-338-4040	365
Saint Vincent Hospital	835 S Van Buren St	Green Bay	WI	54301	**800-236-3030**	920-433-0111	366-2
Saint Xavier University	3700 W 103rd St	Chicago	IL	60655	**800-462-9288**	773-298-3000	163

Name / Address	City	State	ZIP	Toll-Free	Phone	Class
Sakonnet Vineyards 162 W Main Rd	Little Compton	RI	02837	**800-919-4637**	401-635-8486	50
Saks Inc 3455 Hwy 80 W	Jackson	MS	39209	**800-443-6856**	601-968-4400	213
Saladmaster Inc 230 Westway Pl Suite 101	Arlington	TX	76018	**800-765-5795**	817-633-3555	477
Salamanca Press PO Box 111	Salamanca	NY	14779	**800-474-9874**	716-945-1644	522-2
Salco Products Inc 20W201 101st St Suite A	Lemont	IL	60439	**800-535-8990**	630-783-2570	636
Salem Academy 500 Salem Ave	Winston-Salem	NC	27101	**877-407-2536**	336-721-2643	611
Salem College 601 S Church St	Winston-Salem	NC	27101	**800-327-2536**	336-721-2600	163
Salem Conference Center 200 Commercial St SE *Sales	Salem	OR	97301	**877-589-1700***	503-589-1700	204
Salem Convention & Visitors Assn 1313 Mill St SE	Salem	OR	97301	**800-874-7012**	503-581-4325	205
Salem Five & Savings Bank 210 Essex St	Salem	MA	01970	**888-666-5500**		71
Salem International University 223 W Main St	Salem	WV	26426	**800-283-4562**	304-782-5011	163
Salem Label Co 1472 Salem Pkwy	Salem	OH	44460	**888-274-7465**	330-332-1591	404
Salem Leasing Corp PO Box 24788	Winston-Salem	NC	27114	**800-877-2536**	336-768-6800	767
Salem News PO Box 268	Salem	OH	44460	**877-332-4601**	330-332-4601	522-2
Salem-Republic Rubber Co 475 W California Ave	Sebring	OH	44672	**800-686-4199**	330-938-9801	364
Salem Witch Museum 19 1/2 Washington Sq N	Salem	MA	01970	**800-544-1692**	978-744-1692	509
Sales Management Report 316 N Michigan Ave Suite 300	Chicago	IL	60601	**800-878-5331**	312-960-4100	521-10
Salesforce.com Inc 1 Market St The Landmark Suite 300 *NYSE: CRM*	San Francisco	CA	94105	**800-667-6389**	415-901-7000	39
SalesLink Corp 425 Medford St	Charlestown	MA	02129	**888-231-2568**	617-886-4800	176-10
Salesmanship Newsletter 360 Hiatt Dr	Palm Beach Gardens	FL	33418	**800-621-5463**	561-622-9914	521-10
Salesnet Inc 580 Harrison Ave 2nd Fl	Boston	MA	02118	**877-350-0160**	617-350-0160	39
Salinas Valley Memorial Hospital 450 E Romie Ln	Salinas	CA	93901	**888-755-7864**	831-757-4333	366-2
Salisbury Hotel 123 W 57th St	New York	NY	10019	**888-692-5757**	212-246-1300	373
Salisbury Pewter Co 29085 Airpark Dr	Easton	MD	21601	**800-824-4708**	410-770-4901	693
Salisbury Post 131 W Innes St	Salisbury	NC	28144	**800-633-8957**	704-633-8950	522-2
Salisbury University 1101 Camden Ave	Salisbury	MD	21801	**888-543-0148**	410-543-6000	163
Salisbury WH & Co 7520 N Long Ave	Skokie	IL	60077	**877-406-4501**	847-679-6700	566
Salish Kootenai Community College PO Box 70	Pablo	MT	59855	**877-752-6553**	406-275-4800	161
Salish Lodge & Spa 6501 Railroad Ave PO Box 1109	Snoqualmie	WA	98065	**800-272-5474**	425-888-2556	373
Salishan Lodge & Golf Resort PO Box 118	Gleneden Beach	OR	97388	**800-452-2300**	541-764-2371	655
Salishan Lodge & Golf Resort. PO Box 118	Gleneden Beach	OR	97388	**800-452-2300**	541-764-2371	655
Sallie Mae Inc 12061 Bluemont Way *Cust Svc	Reston	VA	20190	**888-272-5543***	703-810-3000	215
Sally Beauty Co Inc 3001 Colorado Blvd	Denton	TX	76210	**800-275-7255**	940-898-7500	78
Sally Lou Fashions Corp 1400 Broadway 6th Fl	New York	NY	10018	**800-258-1540**	212-354-9670	153-21
Salmon Air 29 Hamner Dr	Salmon	ID	83467	**800-448-3413**	208-756-6211	14
Salmon Federation. Atlantic PO Box 5200	Saint Andrews	NB	E5B3S8	**800-565-5666**	506-529-1033	48-3
Salmon River Electric Co-op Inc 1130 Main St PO Box 384	Challis	ID	83226	**877-806-2283**	208-879-2283	244
Salomon Brothers Investment Series 100 First Stamford Pl	Stamford	CT	06902	**866-811-7256**		517
Salomon North America 5055 N Greeley Ave	Portland	OR	97217	**877-272-5666**	971-234-2300	296
Salon Assn (TSA) 15825 N 71st St Suite 100	Scottsdale	AZ	85254	**800-211-4872**	480-281-0429	49-4
Salt Lake Convention & Visitors Bureau 90 S West Temple	Salt Lake City	UT	84101	**800-541-4955**	801-521-2822	205
Salt Lake County Center for the Arts 50 W 200 South	Salt Lake City	UT	84101	**888-451-2787**	801-323-6800	562
Salt Palace Convention Center 100 S West Temple	Salt Lake City	UT	84101	**877-547-4656**	801-534-4777	204
Salt River Electric Co-op Corp 111 W Brashear Ave	Bardstown	KY	40004	**800-221-7465**	502-348-3931	244
Salt River Project (SRP) 1521 N Project Dr	Tempe	AZ	85281	**800-258-4777**	602-236-5900	774
Salt Water Sportsman Magazine 263 Summer St 3rd Fl	Boston	MA	02210	**888-888-3217**	617-303-3660	449-20
Saltbox Illustrations 75 Green St Box 299	Clinton	MA	01510	**800-322-3866**	978-368-8711	130
Salter Bus Lines Inc 212 Hudson Ave	Jonesboro	LA	71251	**800-223-8056**	318-259-2522	108
Saltgrass Steak House Corp 1510 W Loop South	Houston	TX	77027	**800-552-6379**	713-850-1010	657
Salton Inc 1955 W Field Ct *NYSE: SFP*	Lake Forest	IL	60045	**800-272-5629**	847-803-4600	37
Salvador Dali Museum 1000 3rd St S	Saint Petersburg	FL	33701	**800-442-3254**	727-823-3767	509
Salvation Army PO Box 269	Alexandria	VA	22313	**800-725-2769**	703-684-5500	48-5
Salve Regina University 100 Ochre Point Ave	Newport	RI	02840	**888-467-2583**	401-847-6650	163
SAM (Society for Advancement of Management) Texas A&M Univ Corpus Christi College of Business 6300 Ocean Dr FC111	Corpus Christi	TX	78412	**888-827-6077**	361-825-6045	49-12
Sam Ash Music Corp PO Box 9047	Hicksville	NY	11802	**888-615-5904**	516-932-6400	515
Sam Goody 10400 Yellow Circle Dr *Cust Svc	Minnetonka	MN	55343	**800-371-4225***	952-932-7700	514
Sam Hausman Meat Packer Inc PO Box 2422	Corpus Christi	TX	78403	**800-364-5521**	361-883-5521	465
Sam Houston Electric Co-op Inc 150 E Church St PO Box 1121	Livingston	TX	77351	**800-458-0381**	936-327-5711	244
Sam Houston Race Park 7575 N Sam Houston Pkwy W	Houston	TX	77064	**800-807-7223**	281-807-7223	628
Sam Houston State University 1903 University Ave	Huntsville	TX	77340	**866-232-7528**	936-294-1111	163
Sam Kane Beef Processors Inc 9001 Leopard St	Corpus Christi	TX	78409	**800-242-4142**	361-241-5000	465
Sam Rayburn Memorial Veterans Center 1201 E 9th St	Bonham	TX	75418	**800-924-8387**	903-583-2111	366-6
Sam S Accursio & Sons Farms PO Box 901767	Homestead	FL	33090	**800-233-6826**	305-246-3455	11-11
Sam Swope Auto Group LLC 10 Swope Auto Ctr	Louisville	KY	40299	**800-228-9086**	502-499-5000	57
Samaritan Care Hospice 24445 Northwestern Hwy Suite 105	Southfield	MI	48075	**800-397-9360**	248-355-9900	365
Samaritan Care Hospice 653 Skippack Pike	Blue Bell	PA	19422	**800-764-6878**	215-653-7310	365
Samaritan Care Hospice 9535 Forest Ln Suite 229	Dallas	TX	75243	**800-473-2430**	972-690-6632	365
Samaritan Hospice 5 Eves Dr Suite 300	Marlton	NJ	08053	**800-229-8183**	856-596-1600	365
Samaritan Medical Center 830 Washington St	Watertown	NY	13601	**877-888-6138**	315-785-4000	366-2
Samco Scientific Corp 1050 Arroyo Ave	San Fernando	CA	91340	**800-522-3359**	818-838-2400	411
SAME (Society of American Military Engineers) 607 Prince St	Alexandria	VA	22314	**800-336-3097**	703-549-3800	48-19
SameDayMusic 65 Greenwood Ave	Midland Park	NJ	07432	**866-744-7736**		515
Samford University 800 Lakeshore Dr	Birmingham	AL	35229	**800-888-7218**	205-726-3673	163
Sammons Preston Inc 4 Sammons Ct	Bolingbrook	IL	60440	**800-323-5547**	630-226-1300	467
Sammons Trucking 3665 W Broadway	Missoula	MT	59808	**800-548-9276**	406-728-2600	769
Samoset Resort 220 Warrenton St	Rockport	ME	04856	**800-341-1650**	207-594-2511	655
Sampco Inc 651 W Washington Blvd Suite 300	Chicago	IL	60661	**800-767-0689**	312-346-1506	292-9
SAMPE (Society for the Advancement of Material & Process Engineering) 1161 Park View Dr	Covina	CA	91724	**800-562-7360**	626-331-0616	49-19
Sample Case Magazine 632 N Park St	Columbus	OH	43215	**800-848-0123**	614-228-3276	449-10
Sam's Cheesecake Inc 7666 Miramar Rd	San Diego	CA	92126	**800-833-8835**	858-578-3460	291-2
Sams LL Inc 1203 Industrial Blvd	Cameron	TX	76520	**800-537-4723**	254-697-6754	314-3
Sams Technical Publishing 9850 E 30th St *Cust Svc	Indianapolis	IN	46229	**800-428-7267***	317-396-9850	623-2
Sam's Town Hotel & Casino Shreveport 315 Clyde Fant Pkwy	Shreveport	LA	71101	**877-429-0711**	318-424-7777	133
Sam's Town Hotel & Gambling Hall 1477 Casino Strip Blvd	Robinsonville	MS	38664	**800-456-0711**	662-363-0700	133
Sam's Town Hotel & Gambling Hall 5111 Boulder Hwy	Las Vegas	NV	89122	**800-634-6371**	702-456-7777	133
Samsill Corp 5740 Hartman Rd	Fort Worth	TX	76119	**800-255-1100**	817-536-1906	87
Samson Energy Co LP 2 W 2nd St Samson Plaza	Tulsa	OK	74103	**800-283-1791**	918-583-1791	525
Samson Investment Co 2 W 2nd St Samson Plaza	Tulsa	OK	74103	**800-283-1791**	918-583-1791	525
Samson Mfg Co PO Box 807	Waynesboro	GA	30830	**800-682-1959**	706-554-2129	731
Samson Rope Technologies Inc 2090 Thornton Rd *Cust Svc	Ferndale	WA	98248	**800-227-7673***	360-384-4669	207
Samsonite Corp 11200 E 45th Ave	Denver	CO	80239	**800-223-7267**	303-373-2000	444
Samsung Electronics America Inc 105 Challenger Rd	Ridgefield Park	NJ	07660	**800-726-7864**	201-229-4000	52
Samsung Semiconductors Inc 3655 N 1st St	San Jose	CA	95134	**800-726-7864**	408-544-4000	686
Samtec Inc 520 Parkeast Blvd	New Albany	IN	47150	**800-726-8329**	812-944-6733	252
Samuel Adams Boston Beer Co 30 Germania St	Boston	MA	02130	**800-372-1131**	617-522-9080	103
Samuel Cabot Inc 100 Hale St	Newburyport	MA	01950	**800-877-8246**	978-465-1900	540
Samuel Mancino's Italian Eatery 1324 W Milham St	Portage	MI	49024	**888-432-8379**	269-226-4400	657
Samuel Merritt College 370 Hawthorne Ave	Oakland	CA	94609	**800-607-6377**	510-869-6576	163
Samuel Son & Co Ltd 20001 Sherwood St	Detroit	MI	48234	**800-521-0870**	313-893-5000	709
Samueli Susan Owner Mighty Ducks of Anaheim 2695 Katella Ave Arrowhead Pond of Anaheim	Anaheim	CA	92806	**877-945-3946**	714-704-2700	561
Samuels Allen Auto Group 301 Owen Ln	Waco	TX	76710	**800-762-8850**	254-761-6800	57
Samuels Jewelers Inc 2914 Montopolis Dr Suite 200	Austin	TX	78741	**877-726-8357**	512-369-1400	402
Samy's Camera Inc 431 S Fairfax Ave	Los Angeles	CA	90036	**800-321-4726**	323-938-2420	119
San Angelo Chamber of Commerce 418 W Avenue B	San Angelo	TX	76903	**800-375-1206**	325-655-4136	137
San Angelo Convention & Visitors Bureau 418 West Ave B	San Angelo	TX	76903	**800-375-1206**	325-653-1206	205
San Angelo Standard Times Inc PO Box 5111	San Angelo	TX	76902	**800-588-1884**	325-653-1221	623-8
San Antonio Convention & Visitors Bureau 203 S Saint Marys St 2nd Fl	San Antonio	TX	78205	**800-447-3372**	210-207-6700	205
San Antonio Express-News Ave 'E' & 3rd St	San Antonio	TX	78205	**800-555-1551**	210-250-3000	522-2
San Antonio Federal Credit Union 6061 IH 10W	San Antonio	TX	78201	**800-234-7228**	210-258-1414	216
San Bernard Electric Co-op Inc 309 W Main St	Bellville	TX	77418	**800-364-3171**	979-865-3171	244
San Bernardino Convention & Visitors Bureau 201 N 'E' St Suite 103	San Bernardino	CA	92401	**800-867-8366**	909-889-3980	205
San Bernardino County Museum 2024 Orange Tree Ln	Redlands	CA	92374	**888-247-3344**	909-307-2669	509

Name / Address	City	State	Zip	Toll-Free	Phone	Class
San Carlos Hotel 150 E 50th St	New York	NY	10022	**800-722-2012**	212-755-1800	373
San Diego Blood Bank 440 Upas St	San Diego	CA	92103	**800-479-3902**	619-296-6393	90
San Diego Business Journal 4909 Murphy Canyon Rd Suite 200	San Diego	CA	92123	**888-425-7325**	858-277-6359	449-5
San Diego Chargers 4020 Murphy Canyon Rd	San Diego	CA	92123	**877-242-7437**	858-874-4500	703
San Diego Concierge 4379 30th St Suite 4	San Diego	CA	92104	**800-979-9091**	619-280-4121	368
San Diego Convention Center 111 W Harbor Dr	San Diego	CA	92101	**800-525-7322**	619-525-5000	204
San Diego County Credit Union 6545 Sequence Dr	San Diego	CA	92121	**877-732-2848**		216
San Diego Daily Transcript 2131 3rd Ave	San Diego	CA	92101	**800-697-6397**	619-232-4381	522-2
San Diego Eye Bank 9444 Balboa Ave Suite 100	San Diego	CA	92123	**800-393-2265**	858-694-0444	265
San Diego Gas & Electric Co 101 Ash St	San Diego	CA	92101	**800-411-7343**	619-696-2000	774
San Diego Hospice 4311 3rd Ave	San Diego	CA	92103	**800-696-9474**	619-688-1600	365
San Diego Magazine 1450 Front St	San Diego	CA	92101	**800-600-2489**	619-230-9292	449-22
San Diego National Bank 1420 Kettner Blvd	San Diego	CA	92101	**888-724-7362**	619-231-4989	71
San Diego Union-Tribune 350 Camino De La Reina	San Diego	CA	92112	**800-244-6397**	619-299-3131	522-2
San Dieguito Printers 1880 Diamond St	San Marcos	CA	92069	**800-321-5794**	760-744-0910	623-10
San Francisco Art Institute 800 Chestnut St	San Francisco	CA	94133	**800-345-7324**	415-771-7020	163
San Francisco Chronicle 901 Mission St	San Francisco	CA	94103	**866-732-4766**	415-777-7100	522-2
San Francisco Elevator Co Inc 1940 Oakdale Ave	San Francisco	CA	94124	**800-310-1397**	415-821-1402	188-1
San Francisco Examiner 450 Mission St	San Francisco	CA	94105	**866-733-7232**	415-826-1100	522-2
San Francisco French Bread Co 580 Julie Ann Way	Oakland	CA	94621	**888-661-7687**	510-729-6232	291-1
San Francisco Music Box Co 3113 Woodcreek Dr	Downers Grove	IL	60515	**800-227-2190**		322
San Francisco Reservations 360 22nd St Suite 300	Oakland	CA	94612	**800-677-1550**	510-628-4444	368
San Gabriel Valley Tribune 1210 N Azusa Canyon Rd	West Covina	CA	91790	**800-788-1200**	626-962-8811	522-2
San Isabel Electric Assn 893 E Enterprise Dr	Pueblo	CO	81002	**800-279-7432**	719-547-2160	244
San Joaquin Hotel 1309 W Shaw Ave	Fresno	CA	93711	**800-775-1309**	559-225-1309	373
San Jose Center for the Performing Arts 408 Almaden Ave	San Jose	CA	95110	**800-533-2345**	408-277-5277	562
San Jose Convention & Cultural Facilities 408 Almaden Blvd	San Jose	CA	95110	**800-533-2345**	408-277-5277	204
San Jose Convention & Visitors Bureau 408 Almaden Blvd	San Jose	CA	95110	**800-726-5673**	408-295-9600	205
San Jose Delta Assoc Inc 482 Sapena Ct	Santa Clara	CA	95054	**800-809-4308**	408-727-1448	490
San Jose McEnery Convention Center 150 W San Carlos St	San Jose	CA	95113	**800-533-2345**	408-277-3900	204
San Juan Airlines Co 4000 Airport Rd Suite A	Anacortes	WA	98221	**800-874-4434**	360-293-4691	14
San Juan Basin Royalty Trust 2525 Ridgmar Blvd Suite 100 *NYSE: SJT*	Fort Worth	TX	76116	**866-809-4553**		662
San Juan College 4601 College Blvd	Farmington	NM	87402	**800-864-4871**	505-326-3311	160
San Luis Obispo New Times 505 Higuera St	San Luis Obispo	CA	93401	**800-215-0300**	805-546-8208	522-4
San Luis Resort Spa & Conference Center 5222 Seawall Blvd	Galveston Island	TX	77551	**800-445-0090**	409-744-1500	655
San Luis Tallow Co Inc PO Box 3835	San Luis Obispo	CA	93403	**800-281-8660**	805-543-8660	291-12
San Luis Valley Rural Electric Co-op 3625 US Hwy 160 W	Monte Vista	CO	81144	**800-332-7634**	719-852-3538	244
San Manuel Indian Bingo & Casino 777 San Manuel Blvd	Highland	CA	92346	**800-359-2464**	909-864-5050	133
San Marcos Area Chamber of Commerce 202 N CM Allen Pkwy	San Marcos	TX	78667	**888-200-5620**	512-393-5900	137
San Marcos Baptist Academy 2801 Ranch Rd 12	San Marcos	TX	78666	**800-428-5120**	512-753-8000	611
San Marcos Golf Resort & Conference Center. Sheraton 1 San Marcos Pl	Chandler	AZ	85225	**800-528-8071**	480-812-0900	655
San Mateo County Convention & Visitors Bureau 111 Anza Blvd Suite 410	Burlingame	CA	94010	**800-288-4748**	650-348-7600	205
San Mateo County Expo Center 2495 S Delaware St	San Mateo	CA	94403	**800-338-3976**	650-574-3247	204
San Mateo County Times 1080 S Amphlett Blvd	San Mateo	CA	94402	**800-595-9595**	650-348-4321	522-2
San Mateo County Transit District 1250 San Carlos Ave	San Carlos	CA	94070	**800-660-4287**	650-508-6200	460
San Mateo Times Group Newspapers 1080 S Amphlett Blvd	San Mateo	CA	94402	**800-843-6397**	650-348-4321	623-8
San Miguel Power Assn Inc PO Box 817	Nucla	CO	81424	**800-864-7256**	970-864-7311	244
San Miguel Produce Inc 4444 Naval Air Rd	Oxnard	CA	93033	**888-347-3367**	805-488-0981	11-11
San Patricio Electric Co-op Inc 402 E Sinton St	Sinton	TX	78387	**888-740-2220**	361-364-2220	244
San Pedro Peninsula Chamber of Commerce 390 W 7th St	San Pedro	CA	90731	**888-447-3376**	310-832-7272	137
San Rafael Chamber of Commerce 817 Mission Ave	San Rafael	CA	94901	**800-454-4163**	415-454-4163	137
San Ramon Valley Conference Center 3301 Crow Canyon Rd	San Ramon	CA	94583	**800-521-4335**	925-866-7500	370
San Sebastian Winery 157 King St	Saint Augustine	FL	32084	**888-352-9463**	904-826-1594	50
San Vicente Inn & Golf Course 24157 San Vicente Rd	Ramona	CA	92065	**800-776-1289**	760-789-8290	655
San Ysidro Ranch 900 San Ysidro Ln	Montecito	CA	93108	**800-368-6788**	805-969-5046	655
Sanborn Map Co 629 5th Ave	Pelham	NY	10803	**800-930-3298**	914-738-1649	623-1
Sanborn Mark Sanborn & Associates Inc 818 Summer Dr	Highlands Ranch	CO	80126	**800-650-3343**	303-683-0714	561
Sanborn Tours Inc 2015 S 10th St	McAllen	TX	78503	**800-395-8482**	956-682-9872	748
Sancap Abrasives 16123 Armour St NE	Alliance	OH	44601	**800-433-6663**	330-821-3510	1
Sanchez Oil & Gas Corp 1920 Sandman St	Laredo	TX	78041	**800-292-7699**	956-722-8092	527
Sanctuary on Camelback Mountain 5700 E McDonald Dr	Paradise Valley	AZ	85253	**800-245-2051**	480-948-2100	655
Sand Dollar Inn 755 Abrego St	Monterey	CA	93940	**800-982-1986**	831-372-7551	373
Sand Dunes Resort Hotel 201 74th Ave N	Myrtle Beach	SC	29572	**800-845-6701**	843-449-3313	373
Sand & Gravel Assn. National Stone 1605 King St	Alexandria	VA	22314	**800-342-1415**	703-525-8788	49-3
Sand Seed Service Inc 4765 Hwy 143	Marcus	IA	51035	**800-352-2228**	712-376-4135	684
Sandals Resorts International 4950 SW 72nd Ave	Miami	FL	33155	**888-726-3257**	305-284-1300	369
Sandals Signature Guest Program 4950 SW 72nd Ave	Miami	FL	33155	**800-726-3257**	305-284-1300	371
Sandalwood Hotel & Suites 5050 Orbitor Dr	Mississauga	ON	L4W4X2	**800-387-3355**	905-238-9600	372
Sandata Technologies Inc 26 Harbor Park Dr *Sales	Port Washington	NY	11050	**800-544-7263***	516-484-4400	176-11
Sandberg Sikorski Jaffe 37 W 26th St 11th Fl	New York	NY	10010	**800-223-0553**	212-843-7464	401
Sandcastle Hotel. Helmsley 1540 Ben Franklin Dr	Sarasota	FL	34236	**800-225-2181**	941-388-2181	373
Sandcastle Motel 123 2nd St	Rehoboth Beach	DE	19971	**800-372-2112**	302-227-0400	373
Sandella's LLC 9 Brookside Pl	West Redding	CT	06896	**888-544-9984**	203-544-9984	657
Sanderling Resort & Spa 1461 Duck Rd	Duck	NC	27949	**800-701-4111**	252-261-4111	655
Sanders Brothers Inc 1709 Old Georgia Hwy	Gaffney	SC	29342	**800-527-1684**	864-489-1144	188-10
Sanders Lead Co 1 Sanders Rd PO Box 707	Troy	AL	36081	**800-633-8744**	334-566-1563	476
Sanders Mfg Co 1422 Lebanon Rd	Nashville	TN	37210	**866-254-6611**	615-254-6611	10
Sanders Morris Harris Group Inc 600 Travis St Suite 3100 *NASDAQ: SMHG*	Houston	TX	77002	**800-538-0020**	713-993-4610	355-3
Sanderson Farms Inc Foods Div 4418 Mangum Dr	Flowood	MS	39208	**800-844-8291**	601-939-9790	291-36
Sanderson-MacLeod Inc 1199 S Main St	Palmer	MA	01069	**866-522-3481**	413-283-3481	104
Sanderson Plumbing Products Inc PO Box 1367	Columbus	MS	39705	**800-647-1042**	662-328-4000	599
Sanderson Safety Supply Co 1101 SE 3rd Ave	Portland	OR	97214	**800-547-0927**	503-238-5700	667
Sanderson & Sons Ltd 285 Grand Ave 3 Patriot Ctr	Englewood	NJ	07631	**800-894-6185**	201-894-8400	583
Sandestin Beach Golf Resort & Spa. Hilton 4000 Sandestin Blvd S	Destin	FL	32550	**800-367-1271**	850-267-9500	655
Sandestin Golf & Beach Resort 9300 Emerald Coast Pkwy W	Sandestin	FL	32550	**800-277-0800**	850-267-8000	655
Sandhills Community College 3395 Airport Rd	Pinehurst	NC	28374	**800-338-3944**	910-692-6185	160
Sandhills Publishing 120 W Harvest Dr	Lincoln	NE	68521	**800-544-1382**	402-479-2181	623-9
Sandia Casino 30 Rainbow Rd NE	Albuquerque	NM	87113	**800-526-9366**	505-796-7500	133
Sandler Sales Institute 10411 Stevenson Rd	Stevenson	MD	21153	**800-638-5686**	410-653-1993	753
Sandman Hotel Calgary 888 7th Ave SW	Calgary	AB	T2P3J3	**800-726-3626**	403-237-8626	372
Sandman Hotel Vancouver 180 W Georgia St	Vancouver	BC	V6B4P4	**800-726-3626**	604-681-2211	372
Sandman Hotel West Edmonton 17635 Stony Plain Rd	Edmonton	AB	T5S1E3	**800-726-3626**	780-483-1385	372
Sandmeyer Steel Co 1 Sandmeyer Ln	Philadelphia	PA	19116	**800-523-3663**	215-464-7100	709
Sandoz Inc 506 Carnegie Ctr Suite 400	Princeton	NJ	08540	**800-525-8747**	609-627-8500	573
Sandpiper Beach Resort. TradeWinds 6000 Gulf Blvd	Saint Pete Beach	FL	33705	**800-237-0707**	727-360-5551	655
Sandpiper. Club Med 3500 SE Morningside Blvd	Port Saint Lucie	FL	34952	**800-258-2633**	772-335-4400	655
Sandridge Food Corp 133 Commerce Dr	Medina	OH	44256	**800-280-7951**	330-725-2348	291-33
Sands Beach Club All-Suite Resort Hotel 9400 Shore Dr	Myrtle Beach	SC	29572	**800-845-6999**	843-449-1531	373
Sands Hotel & Casino 136 S Kentucky Ave	Atlantic City	NJ	08401	**800-227-2637**	609-441-4000	133
Sands Ocean Club Resort 9550 Shore Dr	Myrtle Beach	SC	29572	**800-845-6701**	843-449-6461	373
Sands Regency Hotel & Casino 345 N Arlington Ave *Resv	Reno	NV	89501	**800-648-3553***	775-348-2200	373
Sands Regent 345 N Arlington Ave *NASDAQ: SNDS*	Reno	NV	89501	**800-648-3553**	775-348-2200	369
Sandusky Cabinets Inc PO Box 517	Arvin	CA	93203	**800-336-0674**	661-854-5551	281
Sandusky-Chicago Abrasive Wheel Co 1100 W Barker Ave	Michigan City	IN	46360	**800-843-4980**	219-879-6601	1
Sandusky Register 314 W Market St	Sandusky	OH	44870	**800-466-1243**	419-625-5500	522-2
SanduskyAthol International 100 22nd St PO Box 105	Butner	NC	27509	**800-282-6523**	919-575-6523	730-2
Sandvik Coromant Co 1702 Nevins Rd *Cust Svc	Fair Lawn	NJ	07410	**800-726-3845***	201-794-5000	447
Sandvik Inc 1702 Nevins Rd	Fair Lawn	NJ	07410	**800-726-3845**	201-794-5000	355-3
Sandvik Sorting Systems Inc 500 E Burnett Ave	Louisville	KY	40217	**800-926-6839**	502-636-1414	206
Sandy Corp 1500 W Big Beaver Rd	Troy	MI	48084	**800-733-4739**	248-649-0800	193
Sandy Point Inn 6485 Twin Lakes Rd	Boulder	CO	80301	**800-322-2939**	303-530-2939	373
Sandy Spring Bancorp Inc 17801 Georgia Ave *NASDAQ: SASR*	Olney	MD	20832	**800-399-5919**	301-774-6400	355-2

Company / Address	City	State	ZIP	Toll-Free	Phone	Class
Sane Solutions LLC 35 Belver Ave Suite 230	North Kingstown	RI	02852	**800-407-3570**	401-295-4809	176-7
Sanese Services Inc 6465 Busch Blvd	Columbus	OH	43229	**800-589-3410**	614-436-1234	294
Sanfilippo John B & Son Inc 2299 Busse Rd *NASDAQ: JBSS*	Elk Grove Village	IL	60007	**800-323-6887**	847-593-2300	291-28
Sanford Corp 2707 Butterfield Rd *Cust Svc	Oak Brook	IL	60523	**800-438-3703***	800-323-0749	560
Sanford Rose Assoc 3737 Embassy Pkwy Suite 200	Akron	OH	44333	**800-731-7724**	330-670-9797	262
Sangre de Cristo Electric Assn 2978 N US Hwy 24	Buena Vista	CO	81211	**800-933-3823**	719-395-2412	244
Sanibel Harbour Resort & Spa 17260 Harbour Pointe Dr	Fort Myers	FL	33908	**800-767-7777**	239-466-4000	655
Sanibel Inn 937 E Gulf Dr	Sanibel	FL	33957	**800-237-1491**	239-472-3181	655
SaniServ Inc 451 E County Line Rd	Mooresville	IN	46158	**800-733-8073**	317-831-7030	293
Sanitary Mattress Co Inc 5808 Berry Brook Dr	Houston	TX	77017	**800-603-3375**	713-227-0121	463
Sanitary Supply Assn. International 7373 N Lincoln Ave	Lincolnwood	IL	60712	**800-225-4772**	847-982-0800	49-18
Sanofi-Synthelabo Canada Inc 15 Allstate Pkwy	Markham	ON	L3R5B4	**800-668-7401**	905-513-4444	86
Sanovo Engineering 4225 SW Kirklawn Ave *Sales	Topeka	KS	66609	**800-255-2463***	785-266-5511	293
Sanrio Inc 570 Eccles Ave	South San Francisco	CA	94080	**800-325-8316**	650-952-2880	323
Santa Barbara Bank & Trust 20 E Carrillo St	Santa Barbara	CA	93102	**800-320-5353**	805-564-6300	71
Santa Barbara Inn 901 E Cabrillo Blvd	Santa Barbara	CA	93103	**800-231-0431**	805-966-2285	373
Santa Barbara News-Press 715 Anacapa St	Santa Barbara	CA	93101	**800-654-3292**	805-564-5200	522-2
Santa Barbara News-Press Publishing Co 715 Anacapa St	Santa Barbara	CA	93101	**800-654-3292**	805-564-5200	623-8
Santa Barbara Visitors Bureau & Film Commission 1601 Anacapa St	Santa Barbara	CA	93101	**800-927-4688**	805-966-9222	205
Santa Clara Chamber of Commerce 1850 Warburton Ave	Santa Clara	CA	95050	**800-272-6822**	408-244-8244	137
Santa Clara Convention/Visitors Bureau 1850 Warburton Ave	Santa Clara	CA	95050	**800-272-6822**	408-244-9660	205
Santa Clara Valley Transportation Authority (VTA) 3331 N 1st St	San Jose	CA	95134	**800-894-9908**	408-321-5555	460
Santa Clarita Conference Center. Hyatt Valencia & 24500 Town Center Dr	Valencia	CA	91355	**800-233-1234**	661-799-1234	373
Santa Cruz County Conference & Visitors Council 1211 Ocean St	Santa Cruz	CA	95060	**800-833-3494**	831-425-1234	205
Santa Fe Accommodations 320 Artist Rd	Santa Fe	NM	87501	**800-745-9910**	505-988-2800	368
Santa Fe Convention & Visitors Bureau 201 W Marcy St	Santa Fe	NM	87504	**800-777-2489**	505-955-6200	205
Santa Fe County 102 Grant Ave	Santa Fe	NM	87504	**800-894-7028**	505-986-6200	334
Santa Fe Jet Center Inc 121 Aviation Dr Bldg 3005	Santa Fe	NM	87507	**800-263-7695**	505-471-2525	63
Santa Fe Opera PO Box 2408	Santa Fe	NM	87504	**800-280-4654**	505-986-5900	563-2
Santa Fe Southern Railway 410 S Guadalupe St	Santa Fe	NM	87501	**888-989-8600**	505-989-8600	50
Santa Fe Stages 422 W San Francisco St	Santa Fe	NM	87501	**877-222-3022**	505-982-6683	563-4
Santa Fe Station 4949 N Rancho Dr	Las Vegas	NV	89130	**866-767-7771**	702-658-4900	133
Santa Fe Symphony 211 W San Francisco St	Santa Fe	NM	87501	**800-480-1319**	505-983-1414	563-3
Santa Maria Inn 801 S Broadway	Santa Maria	CA	93454	**800-462-4276**	805-928-7777	373
Santa Maria Valley Chamber of Commerce 614 S Broadway	Santa Maria	CA	93454	**800-331-3779**	805-925-2403	137
Santa Maria Valley Convention & Visitors Bureau 614 S Broadway	Santa Maria	CA	93454	**800-331-3779**	805-925-2403	205
Santa Monica Convention & Visitors Bureau 520 Broadway Suite 250	Santa Monica	CA	90401	**800-544-5319**	310-319-6263	205
Santa Rosa Junior College 1501 Mendocino Ave	Santa Rosa	CA	95401	**800-564-7752**	707-527-4011	160
Santee Electric Co-op Inc 424 Sumter Hwy	Kingstree	SC	29556	**800-922-1604**	843-355-6187	244
Sanyo Laser Products 1767 Sheridan St	Richmond	IN	47374	**800-704-7648**	765-935-7574	644
Sanyo Mfg Corp 3333 Sanyo Rd	Forrest City	AR	72335	**800-877-5032**	870-633-5030	52
SAP America Inc 3999 W Chester Pike	Newtown Square	PA	19073	**800-727-5872**	610-661-1000	176-1
Sapa Inc 7933 NE 21st Ave	Portland	OR	97211	**800-547-0790**	503-972-1404	472
Sapp Brothers Petroleum Inc 660 S Main St	West Point	NE	68788	**800-922-0382**	402-372-5485	569
Sapporo USA Inc 11 E 44 St Suite 708	New York	NY	10017	**800-827-8234**	212-922-9165	82-1
Saputo Cheese USA 325 Tompkins St	Fond du Lac	WI	54935	**800-345-9714**	920-922-0600	291-10
Sara Lee Bakery Group Gardner Div 3401 E Washington Ave	Madison	WI	53704	**800-676-4395**	608-244-4747	291-1
Sara Lee Branded Apparel 1000 E Hanes Mill Rd	Winston-Salem	NC	27105	**800-685-7557**	336-519-4400	153-18
Sara Lee Corp 70 W Madison St *NYSE: SLE*	Chicago	IL	60602	**800-621-5235**	312-726-2600	355-3
Sara Lee Direct 450 W Hanes Mill Rd *Cust Svc	Winston-Salem	NC	27105	**800-522-1151***	336-519-8360	451
Sara Lee Food & Beverage 10151 Carver Rd	Cincinnati	OH	45242	**800-351-7111**	513-936-2000	291-2
Sara Lee Foundation 3 First National Plaza 47th Fl	Chicago	IL	60602	**800-727-2533**	312-558-8448	299
Sara Lee Household Products 707 Eagle View Blvd	Exton	PA	19341	**800-879-5494**	610-321-1220	211
Sarah Lawrence College 1 Meadway	Bronxville	NY	10708	**800-888-2858**	914-337-0700	163
Saranac Glove Co 999 LOmbardi Ave	Green Bay	WI	54304	**800-727-2622**	920-435-3737	153-8
Sarasota Ballet of Florida 5555 N Tamiami Trail	Sarasota	FL	34243	**866-269-6334**	941-359-0099	563-1
Sarasota Convention & Visitors Bureau 655 N Tamiami Trail	Sarasota	FL	34236	**800-522-9799**	941-957-1877	205
Sarasota Herald-Tribune 801 S Tamiami Trail	Sarasota	FL	34236	**866-284-7102**	941-953-7755	522-2
Sarasota Jungle Gardens 3701 Bay Shore Dr	Sarasota	FL	34234	**877-861-6547**	941-355-5305	811
Sarasota Memorial Hospital 1700 S Tamiami Trail	Sarasota	FL	34239	**800-764-8255**	941-917-9000	366-2
Sarasota Opera 61 N Pineapple Ave	Sarasota	FL	34236	**888-673-7212**	941-366-8450	563-2
Saratoga County Chamber of Commerce 28 Clinton St	Saratoga Springs	NY	12866	**800-526-8970**	518-584-3255	137
SARCOM Inc 8337 Green Meadows Dr N Suite A	Lewis Center	OH	43035	**800-326-3962**	614-854-1300	174
SARCOM Inc AEP Colloids Div 393 Church St PO Box 3425	Saratoga Springs	NY	12866	**800-848-0658**	518-584-4105	144
Sardelli T & Sons Inc 195 Dupont Dr	Providence	RI	02907	**800-327-4641**	401-944-8510	401
Sargent Art Inc 100 E Diamond Ave	Hazleton	PA	18201	**800-424-3596**	570-454-3596	43
Sargent Controls & Aerospace 5675 W Burlingame Rd	Tucson	AZ	85743	**800-932-5273**	520-744-1000	220
Sargent Fletcher Inc 9400 E Flair Dr	El Monte	CA	91731	**800-504-0101**	626-443-7171	23
Sargent Mfg Co 100 Sargent Dr *Sales	New Haven	CT	06511	**800-906-6606***	203-562-2151	345
Sargent-Welch 911 Commerce Ct	Buffalo Grove	IL	60089	**800-727-4368**		411
Sargento Foods Inc 1 Persnickety Pl	Plymouth	WI	53073	**800-558-5802**	920-893-8484	291-5
Sarnafil Inc 100 Dan Rd	Canton	MA	02021	**800-451-2504**	781-828-5400	46
Sarofim Fayez & Co 2 Houston Ctr Suite 2907	Houston	TX	77010	**800-288-7125**	713-654-4484	393
Sartomer Co 502 Thomas Jones Way	Exton	PA	19341	**800-345-8247**	610-363-4100	594-2
Sartori Food Corp 107 Pleasant View Rd *Cust Svc	Plymouth	WI	53073	**800-558-5888***	920-893-6061	291-5
SASCO Electric 12900 Alondra Blvd	Cerritos	CA	90703	**800-477-4422**	562-926-0900	188-4
Sashco Inc 720 S Rochester Ave Suite D	Ontario	CA	91761	**800-600-3232**	909-937-8222	188-6
Saskatchewan Roughriders 2940 10th Ave Taylor Field * Box 1277	Regina	SK	S4P3B8	**888-474-3377**	306-569-2323	703
Sasol Wax Americas Inc 2 Corporate Dr Suite 434	Shelton	CT	06484	**800-423-7071**	203-925-4300	144
Satellink Communications Inc 1100 Northmeadow Pkwy Suite 100	Roswell	GA	30076	**800-426-2283**	770-625-2599	721
Satellite Broadcasting & Communications Assn (SBCA) 1730 M St NW Suite 600	Washington	DC	20036	**800-541-5981**	202-349-3620	49-14
Satellite Direct Magazine PO Box 310156	Newington	CT	06131	**800-234-4220**	206-262-8183	449-9
Satellite Hotel 411 Lakewood Cir	Colorado Springs	CO	80910	**800-423-8409**	719-596-6800	373
Satellite Industries Inc 2530 Xenium Ln N	Minneapolis	MN	55441	**800-328-3332**	763-553-1900	495
Satellite Orbit Magazine 701 5th Ave 42nd Fl	Seattle	WA	98104	**800-234-4220**	206-262-8183	449-9
Satilla Rural Electric Membership Corp 101 W 17th St PO Box 906	Alma	GA	31510	**888-738-6926**	912-632-7222	244
Satin American Corp 40 Oliver Terr	Shelton	CT	06484	**800-272-7711**	203-929-6363	715
Satori Software Inc 2815 2nd Ave Suite 500	Seattle	WA	98121	**800-553-6477**	206-443-0765	176-1
SatoTravel 511 Shaw Rd	Sterling	VA	20166	**800-776-7286**	703-708-9400	760
Saturday Evening Post Magazine 1100 Waterway Blvd	Indianapolis	IN	46202	**800-558-2376**	317-634-1100	449-11
Saturday Evening Post Society 1100 Waterway Blvd	Indianapolis	IN	46202	**800-558-2376**	317-636-8881	623-9
Saturn Corp Div General Motors Corp 100 Saturn Pkwy MD 371-999-S24 *Cust Svc	Spring Hill	TN	37174	**800-553-6000***	931-486-5000	59
Saturn Industries Inc 157 Union Tpke	Hudson	NY	12534	**800-775-1651**	518-828-9956	127
Satyam Computer Services Ltd 1 Gatehall Dr Suite 301	Parsippany	NJ	07054	**800-450-7605**	973-656-0650	178
Saucony Inc 13 Centennial Dr *NASDAQ: SCNYA*	Peabody	MA	01960	**800-365-4933**	978-532-9000	296
Sauder & Rippel Inc 1450 SR 251	Minonk	IL	61760	**800-825-6983**	309-432-2531	270
Sauder Woodworking Co 502 Middle St PO Box 156 *Cust Svc	Archbold	OH	43502	**800-523-3987***	419-446-2711	314-2
Saudi Arabian Airlines 12555 N Burrough Dr	Houston	TX	77067	**800-472-8342**	281-873-1000	26
Saudi Arabian Airlines Alfursan Program 12555 N Burrough Dr	Houston	TX	77067	**800-472-8342**	281-873-1000	27
Sauer LE Machine Co 3535 Tree Ct Industrial Blvd	Saint Louis	MO	63122	**800-745-4107**	636-225-5358	546
Saul Ewing LLP 1500 Market St Centre Sq W 38th Fl	Philadelphia	PA	19102	**800-355-7777**	215-972-7777	419
Saul Zaentz Co 2600 10th St	Berkeley	CA	94710	**800-227-0466**	510-549-1528	501
Saul Zaentz Film Center 2600 10th St	Berkeley	CA	94710	**800-227-0466**	510-549-1528	501
Sault Convention & Visitors Bureau 536 Ashman St	Sault Sainte Marie	MI	49783	**800-647-2858**	906-632-3366	205
Sauna Warehouse Inc 20902 Bake Pkwy Suite 110	Lake Forest	CA	92630	**800-906-2242**	949-699-0820	601
Saunders Archery Co 1874 14th Ave PO Box 1707 *Cust Svc	Columbus	NE	68601	**800-228-1408***	402-564-7176	701
Saunders Brothers Inc 170 Forest St	Westbrook	ME	04092	**800-343-0675**	207-854-2551	808
Saunders Div RS Hughes Co Inc 905 Allen Ave *Sales	Glendale	CA	91201	**800-845-6500***	818-953-3000	446
Saunders Mfg Co Inc 61 Nickerson Hill Rd *Cust Svc	Readfield	ME	04355	**800-341-4674***	207-685-3385	479

Name / Address	City	State	ZIP	Toll-Free	Phone	Class
Sauquoit Industries LLC 300 Palm St	Scranton	PA	18505	**800-858-5552**	570-348-2751	730-2
Sause Brothers Ocean Towing Co Inc 3710 NW Front Ave	Portland	OR	97210	**800-488-4167**	503-222-1811	457
Sav-On Discount Office Supplies 6601 Will Rogers Blvd Suite B	Fort Worth	TX	76140	**866-571-8177**	817-568-5200	524
Savage Industries Inc 100 Springdale Rd	Westfield	MA	01085	**800-370-0712**	413-568-7001	279
Savage Laboratories Div Altana Inc 60 Baylis Rd	Melville	NY	11747	**800-231-0206**	631-454-7677	572
Savage WJ Co Inc 100 Indel Ave PO Box 156	Rancocas	NJ	08073	**877-779-8763**	609-267-8000	447
Savane International Div 4902 W Waters Ave	Tampa	FL	33634	**800-327-2464**	813-249-4900	153-12
Savanna Pallets Co PO Box 308	McGregor	MN	55760	**800-348-5708**	218-768-2077	541
Savannah Area Chamber of Commerce 101 E Bay St	Savannah	GA	31401	**877-728-2662**	912-644-6400	137
Savannah Area Convention & Visitors Bureau 101 E Bay St	Savannah	GA	31401	**877-728-2662**	912-644-6401	205
Savannah College of Art & Design PO Box 2072	Savannah	GA	31402	**800-869-7223**	912-525-5100	163
Savannah Distributing Co PO Box 1388	Savannah	GA	31402	**800-551-0777**	912-233-1167	82-1
Savannah Electric & Power Co 600 E Bay St	Savannah	GA	31401	**800-437-3890**		774
Save the Children Federation Inc 54 Wilton Rd	Westport	CT	06880	**800-728-3843**	203-221-4000	48-5
Save the Manatee Club (SMC) 500 N Maitland Ave	Maitland	FL	32751	**800-432-5646**	407-539-0990	48-3
Save-the-Redwoods League 114 Sansome St Rm 1200	San Francisco	CA	94104	**888-836-0005**	415-362-2352	48-13
SAVE - Suicide Awareness Voices of Education 9001 Bloomington Fwy Suite 150	Bloomington	MN	55420	**888-511-7283**	952-946-7998	49-15
Savers Property & Casualty Insurance Co 11880 College Blvd Suite 500	Overland Park	KS	66210	**800-351-1411**	913-339-5000	384-4
Savient Pharmaceuticals Inc 1 Tower Center Blvd 14th Fl *NASDAQ: SVNT*	East Brunswick	NJ	08816	**800-284-2480**	732-418-9300	470
Savoy Hotel 580 Geary St	San Francisco	CA	94102	**800-227-4223**	415-441-2700	373
Savoy on South Beach 425 Ocean Dr	Miami Beach	FL	33139	**800-237-2869**	305-532-0200	373
Savoy Suites Georgetown 2505 Wisconsin Ave NW	Washington	DC	20007	**800-944-5377**	202-337-9700	373
SAVVIS Inc 12851 Worldgate Dr *NASDAQ: SVVS*	Herndon	VA	20170	**800-728-8471**	703-234-8000	387
Sawgrass Marriott Resort & Beach Club 1000 PGA Tour Blvd	Ponte Vedra Beach	FL	32082	**800-457-4653**	904-285-7777	655
Sawgrass Mills 12801 W Sunrise Blvd	Sunrise	FL	33323	**800-356-4557**	954-846-2300	452
Sawmill Creek Resort 400 Sawmill Creek	Huron	OH	44839	**800-729-6455**	419-433-3800	655
Sawnee Electric Membership Corp 543 Atlantic Hwy	Cumming	GA	30028	**800-635-9131**	770-887-2363	244
Sawtooth Group 100 Woodbridge Ctr Dr Suite 102	Woodbridge	NJ	07095	**800-636-6365**	732-636-6600	4
Sax Arts & Crafts Inc 2725 S Moorland Rd *Cust Svc	New Berlin	WI	53151	**800-558-6696***	262-784-6880	44
SAX North Atlantic Services Inc 432 Fairfield Ave	Stamford	CT	06902	**800-223-5127**	203-348-3645	532
Saxon Mortgage Inc 4880 Cox Rd	Glen Allen	VA	23060	**800-538-8202**	804-967-7400	498
Saxonburg Ceramics Inc PO Box 688	Saxonburg	PA	16056	**800-245-1270**	724-352-1561	248
Saxonville USA 96 Springfield Rd	Charlestown	NH	03603	**800-882-2106**	603-826-4024	190-3
Saybrook Point Inn & Spa 2 Bridge St	Old Saybrook	CT	06475	**800-243-0212**	860-395-2000	655
Saydah Cecil Co 2935 E 12th St	Los Angeles	CA	90023	**800-221-4617**	323-263-9321	731
Sayers Group LLC 1150 Feehanville Dr	Mount Prospect	IL	60056	**800-323-5357**	847-391-4040	178
Saylor Beall Mfg Co Inc 400 N Kibbee St	Saint Johns	MI	48879	**800-248-9001**	989-224-2371	170
Saztec International 900 Middlesex Tpke	Billerica	MA	01821	**800-888-4664**	978-901-9614	176-12
SB Ballard Construction Co 2828 Shipps Corner Rd	Virginia Beach	VA	23453	**800-296-0209**	757-440-5555	188-3
SB Whistler & Sons Inc PO Box 207	Akron	NY	14001	**800-828-1010**	716-542-4141	745
SBA (Small Business Administration) 409 3rd St SW	Washington	DC	20416	**800-827-5722**	202-205-6600	336-16
SBA Communications Corp 5900 Broken Sound Pkwy NW *NASDAQ: SBAC*	Boca Raton	FL	33487	**800-487-7483**	561-995-7670	168
SBAA (Spina Bifida Assn of America) 4590 MacArthur Blvd NW Suite 250	Washington	DC	20007	**800-621-3141**	202-944-3285	48-17
Sbarro Inc 401 Broadhollow Rd *Cust Svc	Melville	NY	11747	**800-766-4949***	631-715-4100	657
Sbar's Inc 14 Sbar Blvd	Moorestown	NJ	08057	**800-989-7227**	856-234-8220	44
SBC Capital Services 2000 W SBC Center Dr	Hoffman Estates	IL	60196	**800-346-8082**	847-290-5000	214
SBC Communications Inc 175 E Houston St *NYSE: SBC*	San Antonio	TX	78205	**888-875-6388**	210-821-4105	721
SBC Foundation 130 E Travis St Suite 350	San Antonio	TX	78205	**800-591-9663**	210-351-2210	299
SBC Prodigy 6500 River Place Blvd Bldg 3 *Cust Svc	Austin	TX	78730	**800-776-3449***	512-527-1500	390
SBC Smart Yellow Pages 100 E Big Beaver Rd	Troy	MI	48083	**800-434-7778**	248-524-7300	623-6
SBCA (Satellite Broadcasting & Communications Assn) 1730 M St NW Suite 600	Washington	DC	20036	**800-541-5981**	202-349-3620	49-14
SBC/Sporto Corp 1100 Massachusetts Ave *Cust Svc	Boston	MA	02125	**888-277-6786***	617-442-9778	296
SBE Inc 2305 Camino Ramon Suite 200 *NASDAQ: SBEI*	San Ramon	CA	94583	**800-925-2666**	925-355-2000	202
SBM Div Arrow Electronics 11455 Lakefield Dr	Duluth	GA	30097	**888-228-2101**	770-623-3430	172
SBS Technologies Inc 2400 Louisiana Blvd NE AFC Bldg 5 Suite 600 *NASDAQ: SBSE*	Albuquerque	NM	87110	**800-727-1553**	505-875-0600	171-3
SBS Transit Inc 3747 Colorado Ave	Sheffield Village	OH	44054	**800-548-5304**	440-949-8121	108
SC Johnson & Son Inc 1525 Howe St	Racine	WI	53403	**800-494-4855**	262-260-2000	149
SC Loveland Co Inc PO Box 368	Pennsville	NJ	08070	**800-523-2687**	856-935-8100	307
SCA (Student Conservation Assn) 689 River Rd PO Box 550	Charlestown	NH	03603	**888-722-9675**	603-543-1700	48-13
SCA Consumer Packaging 1401 Pleasant St	DeKalb	IL	60115	**800-756-7638**	815-756-8451	537
SCA North America Inc 500 Baldwin Tower *Cust Svc	Eddystone	PA	19022	**800-992-9939***	610-499-3700	548-2
SCA Packaging North America 800 5th Ave	New Brighton	PA	15066	**800-887-2276**	724-843-8200	538
SCA Tissue North America 1451 McMahon Dr PO Box 2400	Neenah	WI	54957	**866-722-6659**	920-725-7031	548-2
Scala North America Inc 300 International Pkwy Suite 230	Heathrow	FL	32746	**888-722-5241**	407-333-8829	176-1
Scale-Tronix Inc 200 E Post Rd	White Plains	NY	10601	**800-873-2001**	914-948-8117	672
Scales Air Compressor Corp 110 Voice Rd	Carle Place	NY	11514	**800-777-9096**	516-248-9096	170
Scan International Inc 1800-I Rockville Pike	Rockville	MD	20852	**800-386-0989**	301-984-2960	316
Scan-Optics Inc 169 Progress Dr	Manchester	CT	06040	**800-543-8681**	860-645-7878	176-8
SCANA Communications Inc 1426 Main St MC 107 *Cust Svc	Columbia	SC	29201	**800-679-5463***	803-217-7383	168
SCANA Corp 1426 Main St *NYSE: SCG*	Columbia	SC	29218	**800-251-7234**	803-748-3000	355-5
SCANA Energy Marketing Inc 1426 Main St MC 092	Columbia	SC	29201	**800-472-1051**	803-217-1300	774
Scandinavian Airlines System 9 Polito Ave	Lyndhurst	NJ	07071	**800-221-2350**	201-896-3600	26
Scandinavian Airlines System EuroBonus (SAS) 9 Polito Ave	Lyndhurst	NJ	07071	**800-437-5807**		27
Scania USA Inc 121 Interpark Blvd Suite 601	San Antonio	TX	78216	**800-272-2642**	210-403-0007	505
ScanSoft Inc 9 Centennial Dr *NASDAQ: SSFT* ■ *Cust Svc	Peabody	MA	01960	**800-248-6550***	978-977-2000	176-12
ScanSource Inc 6 Logue Ct *NASDAQ: SCSC*	Greenville	SC	29615	**800-944-2432**	864-288-2432	172
Scanticon Hotel & Conference Center. Valley Forge 1210 1st Ave	King of Prussia	PA	19406	**800-333-3333**	610-265-1500	370
Scantron Corp 34 Parker	Irvine	CA	92618	**800-722-6876**	949-639-7500	171-7
Scantron Service Group 2020 S 156th Cir	Omaha	NE	68130	**800-228-3628**	402-697-3000	173
Scapa Tapes North America 746 Gotham Pkwy	Carlstadt	NJ	07072	**800-801-0323**	201-939-0565	717
Scattergood Friends School 1951 Delta Ave	West Branch	IA	52358	**888-737-4636**	319-643-7628	611
Scavuzzo's Inc 2840 Gwinnot St	Kansas City	MO	64120	**800-800-4707**	816-231-1517	292-9
SCBT Financial Corp 950 John C Calhoun Dr *NASDAQ: SCBT*	Orangeburg	SC	29115	**800-277-2175**	803-534-2175	355-2
SCCA (Sports Car Club of America) PO Box 19400	Topeka	KS	66619	**800-770-2055**	785-357-7222	48-18
SCDAA (Sickle Cell Disease Assn of America) 16 S Calvert St Suite 600	Baltimore	MD	21202	**800-421-8453**	410-528-1555	48-17
Scenic Airlines Inc 2705 Airport Dr	North Las Vegas	NV	89032	**800-634-6801**	702-638-3300	748
Scenic Rivers Energy Co-op 231 N Sheridan St	Lancaster	WI	53813	**800-236-2141**	608-723-2121	244
Schaedler Yesco Distribution Inc 951 S 13th St	Harrisburg	PA	17104	**800-998-1621**	717-233-1621	245
Schaefer Systems International Inc 10021 Westlake Dr	Charlotte	NC	28273	**800-876-6000**	704-944-4500	198
Schaeffer Mfg Co Inc 102 Barton St *Cust Svc	Saint Louis	MO	63104	**800-325-9962***	314-865-4100	530
Schaeffer's Investment Research Inc 5151 Pfeiffer Dr Suite 250	Cincinnati	OH	45242	**800-448-2080**	513-589-3800	623-9
Schafers Bakery Inc 5085 W Grand River Ave	Lansing	MI	48906	**800-347-7373**	517-886-3842	291-1
Schaffner Mfg Co Inc 21 Herron Ave Schaffner Ctr	Pittsburgh	PA	15202	**800-292-9903**	412-761-9902	1
Schaller & Weber Inc 22-35 46th St *Orders	Astoria	NY	11105	**800-847-4115***	718-721-5480	291-26
Schantz Dan Farm & Greenhouses LLC 8025 Spinnerstown Rd	Zionsville	PA	18092	**800-451-3064**	610-967-2181	363
Schatten Properties Management Co Inc 1514 South St	Nashville	TN	37212	**800-892-1315**	615-329-3011	639
Schatz Bearing Corp 10 Fairview Ave	Poughkeepsie	NY	12601	**800-554-1406**	845-452-6000	77
Schawk Inc 1695 S River Rd *NYSE: SGK*	Des Plaines	IL	60018	**800-621-1909**	847-827-9494	615
Schawkgraphics Inc 1600 E Sherwin Ave	Des Plaines	IL	60018	**800-621-1909**	847-296-6000	770
Scheduled Airlines Traffic Offices Inc DBA SatoTravel 511 Shaw Rd	Sterling	VA	20166	**800-776-7286**	703-708-9400	760
Scheib Earl Inc 15206 Ventura Blvd Suite 200	Sherman Oaks	CA	91403	**800-639-3275**	818-981-9992	62-4
Scheid Vineyards Inc 305 Hilltown Rd *NASDAQ: SVIN*	Salinas	CA	93908	**888-772-4343**	831-455-9990	310-5
Schein Henry Inc 135 Duryea Rd *NASDAQ: HSIC*	Melville	NY	11747	**800-582-2702**	631-843-5500	467
Scheirer Machine Co Inc 3200 Industrial Blvd	Bethel Park	PA	15102	**800-448-4590**	412-833-6500	446
Schenck Business Solutions 200 E Washington St	Appleton	WI	54911	**800-236-2246**	920-731-8111	2
Schenck EE Co PO Box 5200	Portland	OR	97208	**800-433-0722**	503-284-4124	583
Schenck Pegasus Corp 2890 John R Rd	Troy	MI	48083	**800-899-5119**	248-689-9000	464

Listing	Toll-Free	Phone	Class
Schenck Trebel Corp 535 Acorn St....Deer Park NY 11729	800-873-2357	631-242-4010	672
Schendel Pest Services 1824 S Kansas Ave ....Topeka KS 66612	800-233-3956	785-232-9357	567
Schenkel's Dairy 1019 Flax Mill Rd ..Huntington IN 46750	800-862-6455	260-356-4225	292-4
Scherer Labs Inc 84 Church St Suite C.............. Marietta GA 33063	800-310-5357	770-514-1333	572
Schering-Plough Corp 2000 Galloping Hill Rd........... Kenilworth NJ 07033 *NYSE: SGP* ■ *Mktg	888-793-7253*	908-298-4000	572
Schering-Plough Corp Animal Health Div 1095 Morris Ave.................... Union NJ 07083 *Cust Svc	800-521-5767*	908-298-4000	574
Schering-Plough HealthCare Products Corp PO Box 377................ Memphis TN 38151 *Cust Svc	800-842-4090*	901-320-2011	572
Schering-Plough Pharmaceuticals 2000 Galloping Hill Rd........... Kenilworth NJ 07033 *Mktg	888-793-7253*	908-298-4000	572
Schering-Plough Research Institute 2015 Galloping Hill Rd........... Kenilworth NJ 07033	800-222-7579	908-298-4000	654
Schetky Northwest Sales Inc 8430 NE Killingsworth St........... Portland OR 97220	800-255-8341	503-287-4141	505
Scheu & Kniss Inc PO Box 2947...... Louisville KY 40201	800-635-6303	502-635-6303	446
Schick Shadel Hospital 12101 Ambaum Blvd SW............ Seattle WA 98146	800-272-8464	206-244-8100	712
Schiff Hardin & Waite LLP 233 S Wacker Dr 6600 Sears Tower...................... Chicago IL 60606	800-258-7799	312-258-5500	419
Schiffmayer Plastics Corp 1201 Armstrong St...............Algonquin IL 60102	800-621-1092	847-658-8140	593
Schildwachter Fred M & Sons Inc 1400 Ferris Pl...................... Bronx NY 10461	800-642-3646	718-828-2500	311
Schilli Transportation Services Inc 6358 W US 24 ....Remington IN 47977	800-759-2101	219-261-2101	769
Schindler Elevator Corp 20 Whippany Rd............... Morristown NJ 07960	800-225-3123	973-397-6500	255
Schinner AD Co Inc 4901 W State St.................. Milwaukee WI 53208	800-776-4709	414-771-4300	549
Schisa Brothers Inc PO Box 3350..... Syracuse NY 13220	800-676-3287	315-463-0213	292-9
Schlegel Systems Inc 1555 Jefferson Rd ....Rochester NY 14623	800-828-6237	585-427-7200	321
Schleicher & Schuell Bioscience Inc 10 Optical Ave ....Keene NH 03431 *Cust Svc	800-245-4024*	603-352-3810	410
Schlessman Seed Co 11513 US Rt 250 ... Milan OH 44846	888-534-7333	419-499-2572	684
Schlotzsky's Ltd 203 Colorado St........Austin TX 78701 *Sales	800-846-2867*	512-236-3600	657
Schlueter Co PO Box 548 ....Janesville WI 53547	800-359-1700	608-755-5455	293
Schmidt Baking Co Inc 7801 Fitch Ln................... Baltimore MD 21236	800-456-2253	410-668-8200	291-1
Schmidt CG Inc 11777 W Lake Pk Dr .... Milwaukee WI 53224	800-248-1254	414-577-1177	185
Schmidt Charles GG & Co Inc 301 W Grand Ave................. Montvale NJ 07645	800-724-6438	201-391-5300	746
Schmidt Machine Co 7013 State Hwy 199 N...... Upper Sandusky OH 43351	800-589-3814	419-294-3814	270
Schmiede Corp 1865 Riley Creek Rd PO Box 1630 .... Tullahoma TN 37388	800-535-1851	931-455-4801	446
Schmieding HC Produce Co PO Box 369 .... Springdale AR 72765	800-643-3607	479-751-4517	292-7
Schmitt Music Co 100 N 6th St Suite 850B .... Minneapolis MN 55403	800-767-3434	612-339-4811	515
Schmitt Sales Inc 2101 St Rita's Ln..... Buffalo NY 14221	800-873-8080	716-639-1500	319
Schnader Harrison Segal & Lewis LLP 1600 Market St Suite 3600... Philadelphia PA 19103	800-541-5997	215-751-2000	419
Schnadig Corp 1111 E Touhy Ave Suite 500..... Des Plaines IL 60018	800-468-8730	847-803-6000	314-2
Schneider Automation Inc 1 High St ....North Andover MA 01845	800-468-5342	978-794-0800	200
Schneider Charles Furniture 518 N 10th St............... Council Bluffs IA 51503	800-831-5878	712-328-1587	314-2
Schneider Corp 8901 Otis Ave...... Indianapolis IN 46216	800-898-0332	317-826-7100	258
Schneider Group 5400 Bosque Blvd Suite 680 .... Waco TX 76710	800-375-7363	254-776-3550	183
Schneider Logistics Inc 3101 S Packerland Dr .... Green Bay WI 54313	800-525-9358	920-592-2000	440
Schneider National Inc 3101 S Packerland Dr PO Box 2545 .... Green Bay WI 54306 *Cust Svc	800-558-6767*	920-592-2000	769
Schneider Valley Farms Dairy 1860 E 3rd St.................Williamsport PA 17701	800-332-8563	570-326-2021	291-27
Schnitzer Steel Industries Inc 3200 NW Yeon Ave .... Portland OR 97210 *NASDAQ: SCHN*	800-666-2992	503-224-9900	709
Schnuck Markets Inc 11420 Lackland Rd..............Saint Louis MO 63146	800-264-4400	314-994-9900	339
Schoharie County Chamber of Commerce 315 Main St PO Box 400 ....Schoharie NY 12157	800-418-4748	518-295-7033	137
Scholarcraft Inc PO Box 170748 ... Birmingham AL 35217 *Cust Svc	888-765-5200*	205-841-1922	314-3
Scholars. Dollars for Scholarship America 1 Scholarship Way................Saint Peter MN 56082	800-537-4180	507-931-1682	711
Scholarship America 1 Scholarship Way ....Saint Peter MN 56082	800-537-4180	507-931-1682	48-11
Scholarship Fund. Hispanic 55 2nd St Suite 1500......... San Francisco CA 94105	877-473-4636	415-808-2300	711
Scholastic Arrow Book Club Scholastic Inc 557 Broadway.......New York NY 10012 *Orders	800-724-6527*	212-343-6100	94
Scholastic Book Fairs Inc 1080 Greenwood Blvd .... Lake Mary FL 32746	800-874-4809	407-829-7300	97
Scholastic Coach & Athletic Director Magazine 557 Broadway ....New York NY 10012	800-724-6527	212-343-6100	449-8
Scholastic Corp 557 Broadway ....New York NY 10012 *NASDAQ: SCHL* ■ *Cust Svc	800-724-6527*	212-343-6100	623-9
Scholastic Firefly Book Club Scholastic Inc 557 Broadway.......New York NY 10012 *Orders	800-724-6527*	212-343-6100	94
Scholastic Lucky Book Club Scholastic Inc 557 Broadway.......New York NY 10012 *Orders	800-724-6527*	212-343-6100	94
Scholastic News 557 Broadway ......New York NY 10012 *Orders	800-724-6527*	212-343-6100	242
Scholastic Parent & Child Magazine 557 Broadway...................New York NY 10012	800-724-6527	212-343-6100	449-11
Scholastic Seesaw Book Club PO Box 7503 ....Jefferson City MO 65102	800-724-2424		94
Scholastic TAB Book Club Scholastic Inc 557 Broadway.......New York NY 10012 *Orders	800-724-6527*	212-343-6100	94
Scholastic Tours Inc 3841 Nostrand Ave................Brooklyn NY 11235	800-221-6209	718-934-9400	748
Scholle Custom Packaging Inc 201 W Glocheski Dr.............. Manistee MI 49660	800-968-5211	231-723-5211	68
Scholler Inc 95 James Way Suite 100.......Southampton PA 18966	800-220-1504	215-942-0200	143
School Administrators. American Assn of 801 N Quincy St Suite 700 ...... Arlington VA 22203	800-771-1162	703-528-0700	49-5
School Administrators. American Federation of 1729 21st St NW .. Washington DC 20009	800-354-2372	202-986-4209	49-5
School Annual Publishing Co 500 Science Pk Rd Suite B ..... State College PA 16803	800-436-6030		623-2
School Apparel Inc 1099 Sneath Ln ... San Bruno CA 94066	800-227-3215	650-827-7400	153-19
School of the Art Institute of Chicago 37 S Wabash Ave................. Chicago IL 60603	800-232-7242	312-899-5219	163
School Assn. National Middle 4151 Executive Pkwy Suite 300.... Westerville OH 43081	800-528-6672	614-895-4730	49-5
School & Community Magazine PO Box 458 .... Columbia MO 65205	800-392-0532	573-442-3127	449-8
School Counselor Assn. American 1101 King St Suite 625 .... Alexandria VA 22314	800-306-4722	703-683-2722	49-5
School Health Assn. American 7263 State Rt 43 PO Box 708.......... Kent OH 44240	800-445-2742	330-678-1601	49-5
School Home & Office Products Assn (SHOPA) 3131 Elbee Rd .... Dayton OH 45439	800-854-7467	937-297-2250	49-4
School Law News Newsletter 360 Hiatt Dr .... Palm Beach Gardens FL 33418	800-638-8437	800-341-7874	521-4
School Librarians. American Assn of 50 E Huron St................... Chicago IL 60611	800-545-2433	312-280-4386	49-11
School Mate Inc 77 Conalco Dr .... Jackson TN 38302	800-264-4108	731-935-2000	242
School of the Museum of Fine Arts 230 The Fenway .... Boston MA 02115	800-643-6078	617-267-6100	163
School Networking. Consortium for 1710 Rhode Island Ave NW Suite 900 .... Washington DC 20036	866-267-8747	202-861-2676	48-9
School Nurses. National Assn of PO Box 1300 .... Scarborough ME 04070	877-627-6476	207-883-2117	49-8
School & Preschool Inc DBA Learning How 8895 McGaw Rd............ Columbia MD 21045	800-675-7627	410-381-0828	673
School Principals. National Assn of Elementary 1615 Duke St .... Alexandria VA 22314	800-386-2377	703-684-3345	49-5
School Specialty Inc PO Box 1579.....Appleton WI 54912 *NASDAQ: SCHS*	888-388-3224	920-734-5712	673
School Supply & Equipment Assn. National 8380 Colesville Rd Suite 250 .... Silver Spring MD 20910	800-395-5550	301-495-0240	49-18
School Teachers. National Assn of Catholic 1700 Sansom St Suite 903 .... Philadelphia PA 19103	800-996-2278	215-665-0993	49-5
School-Tech Inc 745 State Cir Box 1941 .... Ann Arbor MI 48106	800-521-2832	734-761-5072	340
School of Visual Arts 209 E 23rd St. . . New York NY 10010	800-436-4204	212-592-2000	163
School-to-Work Report 8737 Colesville Rd Suite 1100... Silver Spring MD 20910	800-274-6737	301-587-6300	521-4
Schools of Allied Health Professions. Association of 1730 M St NW Suite 500 .... Washington DC 20036	800-497-8080	202-293-4848	49-8
Schools. Association of Boarding 4455 Connecticut Ave NW Suite A-200................. Washington DC 20008	800-541-5908	202-966-8705	48-11
Schools Federal Credit Union 5210 Madison Ave .... Sacramento CA 95841	800-962-0990	916-569-5400	216
Schools Inc. Communities in 277 S Washington St Suite 210.... Alexandria VA 22314	800-247-4543	703-519-8999	48-6
Schools International. Association of Christian 731 Chapel Hills Dr ....Colorado Springs CO 80920 *Cust Svc	800-367-0798*	719-528-6906	49-5
Schools International. Christian 3350 E Paris Ave SE ....Grand Rapids MI 49512	800-635-8288	616-957-1070	49-5
Schools & Libraries Div. Universal Service Administrative Co 2000 L St NW................ Washington DC 20036	888-203-8100		721
Schools. Middle States Assn of Colleges & 3624 Market St...... Philadelphia PA 19104	800-355-1258	215-662-5600	49-5
Schools. Southern Assn of Colleges & 1866 Southern Ln................. Decatur GA 30033	800-248-7701	404-679-4500	49-5
Schott Corp 3 Odell Plaza .... Yonkers NY 10701	800-633-4505	914-968-8900	328
Schott Fiber Optics Inc 122 Charlton St ....Southbridge MA 01550	800-343-6120	508-765-9744	534
Schott International Inc 2850 Gilchrist Rd..................Akron OH 44305	800-321-2178	330-773-7851	583
Schottenstein Stores Corp 1800 Moler Rd ....Columbus OH 43207	800-743-4577	614-221-9200	658
Schreiber AH Co 460 W 34th St 10th Fl............New York NY 10001	800-724-1612	212-564-2700	153-17
Schreiber Corp 100 Schreiber Dr ..... Trussville AL 35173	800-535-0944	205-655-7466	793
Schreiber Corp 2239 Fenkell St......... Detroit MI 48238	800-275-3024	313-864-4900	188-12
Schreiber Foods Inc 425 Pine St .... Green Bay WI 54301	800-344-0333	920-437-7601	291-5
Schreiner University 2100 Memorial Blvd............... Kerrville TX 78028	800-343-4919	830-792-7217	163
Schreiner's Iris Gardens 3625 Quinaby Rd NE ....Salem OR 97303	800-525-2367	503-393-3232	98

Company / Address	City	State	ZIP	Toll-Free	Phone	Class
Schroeder Industries 580 W Park Rd	Leetsdale	PA	15056	**800-722-4810**	724-318-1100	206
Schroeder Milk Co Inc 2080 Rice St	Maplewood	MN	55113	**800-354-6775**	651-487-1471	291-27
Schroeder's Cosmopolitan Bakery Inc PO Box 183	Buffalo	NY	14213	**800-850-7763**	716-885-4894	291-2
Schroeder's Flowerland Inc 1530 S Webster Ave	Green Bay	WI	54301	**800-236-4769**	920-436-6363	287
Schuck Component Systems Inc 8205 N 67th Ave	Glendale	AZ	85302	**800-666-3661**	623-931-3661	188-2
Schuessler Knitting Mills 1523 N Fremont St	Chicago	IL	60622	**800-227-5648**	312-642-1490	153-16
Schuff International Inc 420 S 19th Ave	Phoenix	AZ	85009	**800-528-0513**	602-252-7787	355-3
Schuff Steel Co 420 S 19th Ave	Phoenix	AZ	85009	**800-528-0513**	602-252-7787	188-14
Schulman A Inc 3550 W Market St	Akron	OH	44333	**800-662-3751**	330-666-3751	594-2
NASDAQ: SHLM						
Schulmerich Carillons Inc 35 Carillon Hill Rd	Sellersville	PA	18960	**800-772-3557**	215-257-2771	516
Schult Homes Corp 221 US 20 W	Middlebury	IN	46540	**800-516-7392**	574-825-5881	495
Schulte Corp 12115 Ellington Ct	Cincinnati	OH	45249	**800-669-3225**	513-489-9300	281
Schumacher Electric Corp 801 Business Ctr Dr	Mount Prospect	IL	60056	**800-621-5485**	847-385-1600	252
Schumacher F & Co 79 Madison Ave	New York	NY	10016	**800-556-0040**	212-213-7900	731
Schurman Fine Papers 500 Chadbourne Rd Box 6030	Fairfield	CA	94533	**800-333-6724***	707-428-0200	542-3
*Sales						
Schuster Electronics Inc 11320 Grooms Rd	Cincinnati	OH	45242	**800-877-6875**	513-489-1400	245
Schuster's Building Products Inc 901 E Troy Ave	Indianapolis	IN	46203	**800-424-0190**	317-787-3201	181
Schutt Sports 1200 E Union Ave PO Box 426	Litchfield	IL	62056	**800-637-2047**	217-324-2712	566
Schutte & Koerting LLC 2233 State Rd	Bensalem	PA	19020	**800-752-8558**	215-639-0900	379
Schuylkill Chamber of Commerce 91 S Progress Ave	Pottsville	PA	17901	**800-755-1942**	570-622-1942	137
Schuylkill Products Inc 121 River St	Cressona	PA	17929	**800-631-1591**	570-385-2352	181
Schwaab Inc 11415 W Burleigh St	Milwaukee	WI	53222	**800-935-9877**	414-771-4150	459
Schwab Charles & Co Inc 101 Montgomery St	San Francisco	CA	94104	**800-435-4000***	415-627-7000	679
*Cust Svc						
Schwab Charles Corp 101 Montgomery St	San Francisco	CA	94104	**800-648-5300**	415-627-7000	355-3
NYSE: SCH						
Schwab & Co Inc 1111 Linwood Blvd	Oklahoma City	OK	73106	**800-364-6328***	405-235-2377	465
*Cust Svc						
Schwab Corp PO Box 5088	Lafayette	IN	47903	**800-428-7678**	765-447-9470	665
Schwab Mutual Funds 101 Montgomery St	San Francisco	CA	94104	**800-435-4000**	415-627-7000	517
Schwank Inc 2 Schwank Way at Hwy 56N	Waynesboro	GA	30830	**800-776-8459**	706-554-6191	352
Schwan's Bakery 1651 Montreal Cir	Tucker	GA	30084	**800-241-4166**	770-449-4900	291-2
Schwan's Minh Foods 1251 Scarborough Ln	Pasadena	TX	77506	**888-724-9267**	713-740-7200	291-36
Schwan's Sales Enterprises Inc 115 W College Dr	Marshall	MN	56258	**800-533-5290**	507-532-3274	291-36
Schwartz Pickle Co 4401 W 44th Pl	Chicago	IL	60632	**800-621-4273**	773-927-7700	291-19
Schwarz 8338 Austin Ave	Morton Grove	IL	60053	**800-323-4903**	847-966-2550	549
Schwarz Pharma Inc PO Box 2038	Milwaukee	WI	53201	**800-558-5114**	262-238-5400	572
Schwarzkopf & Henkel Div Henkel Corp 1063 McGraw Ave Suite 100	Irvine	CA	92614	**800-326-2855**	949-794-5500	211
Schwebel Baking Co 965 E Midlothian Blvd PO Box 6018	Youngstown	OH	44501	**800-860-2867**	330-783-2860	291-1
Schweitzer-Mauduit International Inc 100 North Point Ctr E Suite 600	Alpharetta	GA	30022	**800-514-0186**	770-569-4272	547
NYSE: SWM						
Schweizer Emblem Co 1022 Busse Hwy	Park Ridge	IL	60068	**800-942-5215***	847-292-1022	256
*Cust Svc						
Schwerdtle Inc 166 Elm St	Bridgeport	CT	06604	**800-535-0004**	203-330-2750	459
Sci-Port Discovery Center 820 Clyde Fant Pkwy	Shreveport	LA	71101	**877-724-7678**	318-424-3466	509
SciClone Pharmaceuticals Inc 901 Mariners Island Blvd Suite 205	San Mateo	CA	94404	**800-724-2566**	650-358-3456	572
NASDAQ: SCLN						
Scicom Data Services Ltd 10101 Bren Rd E	Minnetonka	MN	55343	**800-488-9087**	952-933-4200	223
Science. American Assn for the Advancement of 1200 New York Ave NW	Washington	DC	20005	**800-731-4939**	202-326-6400	49-19
Science Central 1950 N Clinton St	Fort Wayne	IN	46805	**800-442-6376**	260-424-2400	509
Science Fiction Book Club Doubleday Direct Inc 1225 S Market St	Mechanicsburg	PA	17055	**800-688-4442**		94
Science Inc. Association for Women in 1200 New York Ave NW Suite 650	Washington	DC	20005	**800-886-2947**	202-326-8940	49-19
Science Magazine 1200 New York Ave NW	Washington	DC	20005	**800-731-4939**	202-326-6500	449-19
Science Museum of Virginia 2500 W Broad St	Richmond	VA	23220	**800-659-1727**	804-864-1400	509
Science News 1719 'N' St NW	Washington	DC	20036	**800-552-4412***	202-785-2255	449-19
*Sales						
Science Teachers Assn. National 1840 Wilson Blvd	Arlington	VA	22201	**800-722-6782***	703-243-7100	49-5
*Sales						
ScienceCare Anatomical Inc 2020 W Melinda Ln	Phoenix	AZ	85027	**800-417-3747**	602-331-3641	535
Sciences. National Academy of 500 5th St NW	Washington	DC	20001	**800-624-6242**	202-334-2138	49-19
Sciences. New York Academy of 2 E 63rd St	New York	NY	10021	**800-843-6927**	212-838-0230	49-19
Scientech Inc 5649 Arapahoe Ave	Boulder	CO	80303	**800-525-0522**	303-444-1361	672
Scientech Inc 200 S Woodruff Ave	Idaho Falls	ID	83401	**800-247-8818**	208-529-1000	258
Scientific American Inc 415 Madison Ave	New York	NY	10017	**800-333-1199***	212-451-8550	623-9
*Cust Svc						
Scientific American Magazine 415 Madison Ave	New York	NY	10017	**800-333-1199***	212-754-8550	449-19
*Orders						
Scientific-Atlanta Inc 5030 Sugarloaf Pkwy	Lawrenceville	GA	30044	**800-433-6222***	770-236-5000	633
NYSE: SFA ■ *Sales						
Scientific Computing & Instrumentation Magazine 100 Enterprise Dr Suite 600	Rockaway	NJ	07866	**800-662-7776**	973-920-7000	449-7
Scientific Games Corp 750 Lexington Ave 25th Fl	New York	NY	10022	**800-367-9345**	212-754-2233	317
NASDAQ: SGMS						
Scientific Learning Corp 300 Frank H Ogawa Plaza Suite 500	Oakland	CA	94612	**888-665-9707**	510-444-3500	176-3
NASDAQ: SCIL						
Scientific Protein Laboratories Inc PO Box 158	Waunakee	WI	53597	**800-334-4775**	608-849-5944	470
Scientific Research Society. Sigma Xi PO Box 13975	Research Triangle Park	NC	27709	**800-243-6534**	919-549-4691	48-16
Scientific Technologies Inc 6550 Dumbarton Cir	Fremont	CA	94555	**800-221-7060**	510-608-3400	202
NASDAQ: STIZ						
Scientist. First Church of Christ 175 Huntington Ave	Boston	MA	02115	**800-288-7090**	617-450-2000	48-20
Scientists. Union of Concerned 2 Brattle Sq	Cambridge	MA	02238	**800-664-8276**	617-547-5552	48-13
Sciforma Corp 985 University Ave	Los Gatos	CA	95032	**800-533-9876***	408-354-0144	176-1
*Sales						
SCIMEDX Corp 100 Ford Rd	Denville	NJ	07834	**800-221-5598**	973-625-8822	229
Scion Steel Inc 23800 Blackstone St	Warren	MI	48089	**800-288-2127**	586-755-4000	709
Scios Inc 6500 Paseo Padre Pkwy	Fremont	CA	94555	**800-972-4670**	510-248-2500	86
Scioto Sign Co Inc 6047 US Rt 68 N	Kenton	OH	43326	**800-572-4686**	419-673-1261	692
SciQuest Inc 5151 McCrimmon Pkwy Suite 216	Morrisville	NC	27560	**800-233-1121**	919-659-2100	176-4
Scleroderma Foundation 12 Kent Way Suite 101	Byfield	MA	01922	**800-722-4673**	978-463-5843	48-17
SCO Group Inc 355 S 520 West Suite 100	Lindon	UT	84042	**888-553-3305**	801-765-4999	176-1
NASDAQ: SCOX						
Scolding Locks Corp 1520 W Rogers Ave	Appleton	WI	54914	**800-537-9707**	920-733-5561	211
Scoliosis Assn Inc 2500 N Military Trail	Boca Raton	FL	33431	**800-800-0669**	561-994-4435	48-17
SCOOTER Store Inc 1650 Independence Dr	New Braunfels	TX	78132	**800-723-4535**	830-626-5600	469
SCORE American Soccer Co Inc 726 E Anaheim St	Wilmington	CA	90744	**800-626-7774**	310-830-6161	153-19
SCORE Assn 409 3rd St SW 6th Fl	Washington	DC	20024	**800-634-0245**	202-205-6762	49-12
SCORE! Educational Centers 66 Franklin St Suite 300	Oakland	CA	94607	**800-497-2673**	510-817-3700	146
Scot Forge Co PO Box 8	Spring Grove	IL	60081	**800-435-6621**	815-675-1000	474
Scot Laboratories Div Scott Fetzer Co 16841 Park Circle Dr	Chagrin Falls	OH	44023	**800-486-7268**	440-543-3033	149
Scot Pump 6437 Pioneer Rd	Cedarburg	WI	53012	**888-835-0600**	262-377-7000	627
Scotch Lumber Co PO Box 38	Fulton	AL	36446	**800-936-4424**	334-636-4424	671
Scotchman Industries Inc 180 E Hwy 14	Philip	SD	57567	**800-843-8844**	605-859-2542	484
Scotia Capital Markets 1 Liberty Plaza	New York	NY	10006	**800-472-6842**	212-225-5000	679
Scotia Prince Cruises Ltd 468 Commercial St	Portland	ME	04101	**800-341-7540**	207-775-5611	217
Scotsman Ice Systems 775 Corporate Woods Pkwy	Vernon Hills	IL	60061	**800-726-8762**	847-215-4500	650
Scotsman Inn East 465 S Webb Rd	Wichita	KS	67207	**800-477-7268**	316-684-6363	373
Scotsman Inn West 5922 W Kellogg St	Wichita	KS	67209	**800-950-7268**	316-943-3800	373
Scotsman Publishing Co PO Box 352	Cambridge	MN	55008	**800-473-1981**	763-689-1981	623-8
Scott Community College 500 Belmont Rd	Bettendorf	IA	52722	**888-336-3907**	563-441-4001	160
Scott Construction Inc PO Box 340	Lake Delton	WI	53940	**800-843-1556**	608-254-2555	187-4
Scott Electric 1000 S Main St PO Box S	Greensburg	PA	15601	**800-442-8045**	724-834-4321	245
Scott Fetzer Co Scot Laboratories Div 16841 Park Circle Dr	Chagrin Falls	OH	44023	**800-486-7268**	440-543-3033	149
Scott Fly Rod Co 2355 Air Park Way	Montrose	CO	81401	**800-728-7208**	970-249-3180	701
Scott Foresman 1900 E Lake Ave	Glenview	IL	60025	**800-554-4411***	847-729-3000	623-2
*Cust Svc						
Scott Health & Safety PO Box 569	Monroe	NC	28111	**800-247-7257**	704-291-8300	566
Scott Industries Inc PO Box 7	Henderson	KY	42419	**800-951-9276**	270-831-2037	382
Scott Machinery Co 4055 S 500 West	Salt Lake City	UT	84123	**800-734-7441**	801-262-7441	353
Scott Madden & Assoc Inc 2626 Glenwood Ave Suite 480	Raleigh	NC	27608	**800-321-9774**	919-781-4191	193
Scott Resources Div American Educational Products LLC 401 Hickory St	Fort Collins	CO	80522	**800-289-9299***	970-484-7445	242
*Cust Svc						
Scott Sign Systems Inc 7524 Commerce Pl	Sarasota	FL	34243	**800-237-9447**	941-355-5171	692
Scott & Stringfellow Inc 909 E Main St	Richmond	VA	23219	**800-552-7757**	804-643-1811	679
Scott Studios Corp 13375 Stemmons Fwy	Dallas	TX	75234	**888-438-7268**	972-620-2211	176-10
Scott USA Inc PO Box 2030	Sun Valley	ID	83353	**800-292-5874**	208-622-1000	701
Scott Valley Resort & Guest Ranch 223 Scott Valley Trail	Mountain Home	AR	72653	**888-855-7747**	870-425-5136	238
Scott & White Health Plan 2401 S 31st St	Temple	TX	76508	**800-321-7947**	254-298-3000	384-3
Scott & White Memorial Hospital 2401 S 31st St	Temple	TX	76508	**800-792-3710**	254-724-2111	366-2
Scottish Inns 1726 Montreal Cir	Tucker	GA	30084	**800-251-1962**	770-270-1180	369

Company	Address	City	State	ZIP	Toll-Free	Phone	Class
Scotts Lawn Service	14111 Scottslawn Rd	Marysville	OH	43041	**888-872-6887**	937-644-0011	421
Scott's Liquid Gold Inc	4880 Havana St	Denver	CO	80239	**800-447-1919**	303-373-4860	149
Scotts Miracle-Gro Co	14111 Scottslawn Rd *NYSE: SMG* ■ *Cust Svc	Marysville	OH	43041	**800-543-8873***	937-644-0011	276
Scottsdale Camelback Resort	6302 E Camelback Rd	Scottsdale	AZ	85251	**800-891-8585**	480-947-3300	655
Scottsdale Convention & Visitors Bureau	4343 N Scottsdale Rd Suite 170	Scottsdale	AZ	85251	**800-782-1117**	480-421-1004	205
Scottsdale Insurance Co	8877 N Gainey Ctr Dr	Scottsdale	AZ	85258	**800-423-7675**	480-365-4000	384-4
Scottsdale Plaza Resort	7200 N Scottsdale Rd	Scottsdale	AZ	85253	**800-832-2025**	480-948-5000	655
Scottsdale Resort Accommodations	14505 N Hayden Rd Suite 341	Scottsdale	AZ	85260	**888-868-4378**	480-515-2300	368
Scottsdale Resort & Conference Center	7700 E McCormick Pkwy	Scottsdale	AZ	85258	**800-528-0293**	480-991-9000	370
Scottsdale Resort at Gainey Ranch. Hyatt Regency	7500 E Doubletree Ranch Rd	Scottsdale	AZ	85258	**800-233-1234**	480-991-3388	655
Scoular Co	2027 Dodge St	Omaha	NE	68102	**800-488-3500**	402-342-3500	271
Scovill Fasteners Inc	1802 Scovill Dr *Cust Svc	Clarkesville	GA	30523	**800-756-4734***	706-754-1000	583
SCPIE Holdings Inc	1888 Century Park E Suite 800 *NYSE: SKP*	Los Angeles	CA	90067	**800-962-5549**	310-551-5900	355-4
SCPIE Indemnity Co	1888 Century Pk E Suite 800 *Sales	Los Angeles	CA	90067	**800-962-5549***	310-551-5900	384-5
Scranton Times Co	149 Penn Ave	Scranton	PA	18503	**800-228-4637**	570-348-9100	623-8
Scranton Times-Tribune	149 Penn Ave	Scranton	PA	18503	**800-228-4637**	570-348-9100	522-2
Scribbles & Giggles	1 American Rd *Cust Svc	Cleveland	OH	44144	**800-527-9560***	216-252-8800	129
Scribes Online	21670 Ridgetop Cir Suite 100	Sterling	VA	20166	**800-873-4710**		755
Scripps College	1030 Columbia Ave	Claremont	CA	91711	**800-770-1333**	909-621-8000	163
Scripps EW Co	312 Walnut St Suite 2800 *NYSE: SSP*	Cincinnati	OH	45202	**800-888-3000**	513-977-3000	623-8
Scripps Green Hospital	10666 N Torrey Pines Rd	La Jolla	CA	92037	**800-727-4777**	858-455-9100	366-2
Scripps Health	4275 Campus Point Ct	San Diego	CA	92121	**800-727-4777**	858-678-6111	348
Scripps Howard Inc	PO Box 5380	Cincinnati	OH	45201	**800-888-3000**	513-977-3000	623-8
Scripps Memorial Hospital-La Jolla	9888 Genesee Ave	La Jolla	CA	92037	**800-727-4777**	858-457-4123	366-2
Script Care Inc	6380 Folsom Dr	Beaumont	TX	77706	**800-880-9902**	409-833-9061	575
ScriptSave	333 E Wetmore Rd 4th Fl	Tucson	AZ	85705	**800-347-5985**	520-888-8070	575
Scruggs Co Inc	PO Box 2065	Valdosta	GA	31604	**800-230-7263**	229-242-2388	187-4
SCS Engineers	3711 Long Beach Blvd 9th Fl	Long Beach	CA	90807	**800-326-9544**	562-426-9544	258
SCS Transportation Inc	4435 Main St Suite 930 *NASDAQ: SCST*	Kansas City	MO	64111	**800-533-9643**	816-960-3664	769
SCTE (Society of Cable Telecommunications Engineers)	140 Philips Rd	Exton	PA	19341	**800-542-5040**	610-363-6888	49-19
Scudder Funds	PO Box 219669	Kansas City	MO	64121	**800-728-3337**		517
Scully-Jones Corp	1901 S Rockwell St	Chicago	IL	60608	**800-752-8665**	773-247-5900	484
Scully Signal Co	70 Industrial Way	Wilmington	MA	01887	**800-272-8559**	617-692-8600	200
SD Richman Sons Inc	2435 Wheatsheaf Ln	Philadelphia	PA	19137	**800-648-3576**	215-535-5100	674
SDF Realty Corp	1650 Hotel Circle N Suite 215	San Diego	CA	92108	**800-809-1952**	619-209-4777	498
SDI Technologies Inc	1299 Main St *Cust Svc	Rahway	NJ	07065	**800-888-4491***	732-574-9000	52
SDMS (Society of Diagnostic Medical Sonography)	2745 N Dallas Pkwy Suite 350	Plano	TX	75093	**800-229-9506**	214-473-8057	49-8
SDPB (South Dakota Public Broadcasting)	555 N Dakota St PO Box 5000	Vermillion	SD	57069	**800-456-0766**	605-677-5861	620
SE Technologies Inc	98 Vanadium Rd Bldg D 2nd Fl	Coraopolis	PA	15108	**800-685-0354**	412-221-1100	258
Sea Breeze Fruit Flavors Inc	441 Rt 202	Towaco	NJ	07082	**800-732-2733**	973-334-7777	291-15
Sea Cloud Cruises Inc	32-40 N Dean St	Englewood	NJ	07631	**888-732-2568**	201-227-9404	217
Sea Crest Resort & Conference Center	350 Quaker Rd	North Falmouth	MA	02556	**800-225-3110**	508-540-9400	655
Sea-Esta II Motel	713 Rehoboth Ave	Rehoboth Beach	DE	19971	**800-436-6591**	302-227-8199	373
Sea Gate Travel LLC	16 E 34th St 3rd Fl	New York	NY	10016	**800-622-6622**	212-689-9525	760
Sea Gull Lighting Products Inc	301 W Washington St	Riverside	NJ	08075	**800-347-5483**	856-764-0500	431
Sea Gull Motel on the Beach	2613 Atlantic Ave	Virginia Beach	VA	23451	**800-426-4855**	757-425-5711	373
Sea Harvest Packing Co	PO Box 818	Brunswick	GA	31521	**800-627-4300**	912-264-3212	291-14
Sea Island Co	100 1st St	Sea Island	GA	31561	**800-732-4752**	912-638-3611	641
Sea Island Spa at the Cloister	100 Hudson Pl	Sea Island	GA	31561	**800-732-4752**	912-638-5148	698
Sea Life Park	41-202 Kalanianaole Hwy	Waimanalo	HI	96795	**866-365-7446**	808-259-7933	40
Sea Mist Resort	1200 S Ocean Blvd	Myrtle Beach	SC	29577	**800-732-6478**	843-448-1551	655
Sea Palms Golf & Tennis Resort	5445 Frederica Rd	Saint Simons Island	GA	31522	**800-841-6268**	912-638-3351	655
Sea Pines Plantation Co Inc	32 Greenwood Dr	Hilton Head Island	SC	29928	**800-925-4653**	843-785-3333	639
Sea Pines Resort	32 Greenwood Dr	Hilton Head Island	SC	29928	**800-732-7463**	843-785-3333	655
Sea Ranch Lodge	PO Box 44	The Sea Ranch	CA	95497	**800-732-7262**	707-785-2371	373
Sea Star Line LLC	100 Bell Tel Way Suite 300	Jacksonville	FL	32216	**877-775-7447**	904-855-1260	307
Sea Tow Services International Inc	1560 Youngs Ave	Southold	NY	11971	**800-473-2869**	631-765-3660	457
Sea Turtle Inn	1 Ocean Blvd	Atlantic Beach	FL	32233	**800-874-6000**	904-249-7402	373
Sea Venture Resort	100 Ocean View Ave	Pismo Beach	CA	93449	**800-662-5545**	805-773-4994	655
Sea View Hotel	9909 Collins Ave	Bal Harbour	FL	33154	**800-447-1010**	305-866-4441	373
Sea Watch International Ltd	8978 Glebe Pk Dr	Easton	MD	21601	**800-732-2526**	410-822-7500	291-14
Seaboard Asphalt Products Co	3601 Fairfield Rd	Baltimore	MD	21226	**800-536-0332**	410-355-0330	46
Seaboard Corp	9000 W 67th St *AMEX: SEB*	Shawnee Mission	KS	66202	**800-388-4647**	913-676-8800	184
Seaboard Folding Box Corp	35 Daniels St	Fitchburg	MA	01420	**800-225-6313**	978-342-8921	102
Seaboard International Forest Products LLC	22 Cotton Rd Suite F PO Box 6059	Nashua	NH	03063	**800-669-6800**	603-881-3700	190-3
Seaboard Marine Ltd	8001 NW 79th Ave	Miami	FL	33166	**800-753-0681**	305-863-4444	308
Seaboard Tank Lines Inc	124 Monahan Ave	Dunmore	PA	18512	**800-338-4221**	570-343-2491	769
Seabonay Beach Resort	1159 Hillsboro Mile	Hillsboro Beach	FL	33062	**800-777-1961**	954-427-2525	655
Seabourn Cruise Line	6100 Blue Lagoon Dr Suite 400	Miami	FL	33126	**800-929-9595**	305-463-3000	217
Seabrook Wallcoverings Inc	1325 Farmville Rd	Memphis	TN	38122	**800-238-9152**	901-320-3500	789
SeaChange International Inc	124 Acton St *NASDAQ: SEAC*	Maynard	MA	01754	**888-732-2641**	978-897-0100	633
Seacoast Banking Corp of Florida	PO Box 9012 *NASDAQ: SBCF*	Stuart	FL	34995	**800-706-9991**	772-287-4000	355-2
Seacoast Hospice	10 Hampton Rd	Exeter	NH	03833	**800-416-9207**	603-778-7391	365
Seacoast Suites Hotel	5101 Collins Ave	Miami Beach	FL	33140	**800-969-6329**	305-865-5152	373
Seacomm Erectors Inc	32527 SR 2	Sultan	WA	98294	**800-497-8320**	360-793-6564	187-1
SEACOR Marine Inc	5005 Railroad Ave	Morgan City	LA	70380	**800-989-7062**	985-385-3475	308
Seacrest Oceanfront Resort on the South Beach	803 S Ocean Blvd	Myrtle Beach	SC	29577	**800-845-1112**	843-913-5800	373
SEA/Datamarine Inc	7030 220th St SW	Mountlake Terrace	WA	98043	**800-426-1330**	425-771-2182	633
SeaDream Yacht Club	2601 S Bayshore Dr PH 1B	Coconut Grove	FL	33133	**800-707-4911**	305-631-6100	217
SeaEscape Entertainment Inc	3045 N Federal Hwy	Fort Lauderdale	FL	33306	**877-732-3722**	954-453-2200	133
SeaEurope Holidays Inc	6801 Lake Worth Rd Suite 103	Lake Worth	FL	33467	**800-533-3755**	561-432-4100	748
SeaFab	9561 Satellite Blvd Suite 350	Orlando	FL	32837	**877-265-1491**	407-852-6170	469
Seafarer of Chatham	2079 Main St	Chatham	MA	02633	**800-786-2772**	508-432-1739	373
Seafarers International Union	5201 Auth Way	Camp Springs	MD	20746	**800-252-4674**	301-899-0675	405
SeaGate Convention Centre	401 Jefferson Ave	Toledo	OH	43604	**800-243-4667**	419-255-3300	204
Seagate Hotel & Beach Club	400 S Ocean Blvd	Delray Beach	FL	33483	**800-233-3581**	561-276-2421	373
Seal Glove Mfg Inc	525 North St	Millersburg	PA	17061	**800-992-5444**	717-692-4747	153-8
Seal Methods Inc	11915 Shoemaker Ave	Santa Fe Springs	CA	90670	**800-423-4777**	562-944-0291	321
Seald-Sweet Growers Inc	1991 74th Ave *Sales	Vero Beach	FL	32966	**800-336-2926***	772-569-2244	310-2
Sealed Air Corp Cryovac Div	100 Rogers Bridge Rd Bldg A	Duncan	SC	29334	**800-845-7551**	864-433-2000	538
Sealed Air Corp Packaging Products Div	301 Mayhill St	Saddle Brook	NJ	07663	**800-346-5855**	201-712-7000	538
Sealed Unit Parts Co Inc	2230 Landmark Pl	Allenwood	NJ	08720	**800-333-9125**	732-223-6644	15
Sealing Devices Inc	4400 Walden Ave *Cust Svc	Lancaster	NY	14086	**800-727-3257***	716-684-7600	321
Sealing Equipment Products Co Inc	123 Airpark Industrial Rd *Cust Svc	Alabaster	AL	35007	**800-633-4770***	205-403-7500	321
Sealy Corp	1 Office Pkwy at Sealy Dr *Cust Svc	Trinity	NC	27370	**800-697-3259***	336-861-3500	463
Seaman Corp	1000 Venture Blvd	Wooster	OH	44691	**800-927-8578**	330-262-1111	730-2
Seaman Furniture Co Inc	300 Crossways Pk Dr	Woodbury	NY	11797	**800-445-2403**	516-496-9560	316
Seaman Timber Co Inc	PO Box 372	Montevallo	AL	35115	**800-782-8155**	205-665-2536	806
SeamCraft Inc	932 W Dakin St	Chicago	IL	60613	**800-322-2441**	773-281-5150	343
Seaport Hotel	1 Seaport Ln	Boston	MA	02210	**877-732-7678**	617-385-4000	373
Sear-Brown Group	85 Metro Park	Rochester	NY	14623	**800-724-4131**	585-272-1814	258
SEARAC (Southeast Asia Resource Action Center)	1628 16th St NW 3rd Fl	Washington	DC	20009	**800-600-9188**	202-667-4690	48-5
Search Co International	1535 Grant St Suite 140	Denver	CO	80203	**800-727-2120**	303-863-1800	621
Search Network Ltd	1501 42nd St 2 Corporate Pl Suite 210	West Des Moines	IA	50266	**800-383-5050**	515-223-1153	621
Searcher: The Magazine for Database Professionals	143 Old Marlton Pike	Medford	NJ	08055	**800-300-9868**	609-654-6266	449-7
SearchTec Inc	211 N 13th St 6th Fl	Philadelphia	PA	19107	**800-762-5018**	215-963-0888	621
Sears Home Improvement Products	1024 Florida Central Pkwy	Longwood	FL	32750	**800-222-5030**	407-767-0990	232
Sears Mfg Co	1718 S Concord St PO Box 3667 *Cust Svc	Davenport	IA	52808	**800-553-3013***	563-383-2800	678
Sears Roebuck Acceptance Corp	3711 Kennett Pike	Greenville	DE	19807	**800-729-7722**	302-434-3100	215
Sears Tower	233 S Wacker Dr	Chicago	IL	60606	**877-759-3325**	312-875-9449	50

Name / Address	City	State	ZIP	Toll-Free	Phone	Class
Seascape Resort 100 Seascape Dr	Destin	FL	32550	**800-874-9106**	850-837-9181	655
Seaside Civic & Convention Center 415 1st Ave	Seaside	OR	97138	**800-394-3303**	503-738-8585	204
Seaside Music Theater 176 Northbeach St	Daytona Beach	FL	32114	**800-854-5592**	386-252-6200	562
Seasongood & Mayer LLC 414 Walnut St Suite 300	Cincinnati	OH	45202	**800-767-7207**	513-621-2000	679
Seasons' Enterprises Ltd 1790 W Cortland Ct Suite B PO Box 965	Addison	IL	60101	**800-789-0211**	630-628-0211	291-11
Seasons Hospice 7008 Security Blvd Suite 300	Baltimore	MD	21244	**888-523-6000**	410-594-9100	365
SeaSpecialties Inc 1111 NW 159th Dr	Miami	FL	33169	**800-654-6682**	305-625-5112	292-5
SeaSpecialties Inc Florida Smoked Fish Div 1111 NW 159th Dr	Miami	FL	33169	**800-654-6682**	305-625-5112	291-13
Seat of the Soul Foundation 1257 Siskiyou Blvd Suite 57	Ashland	OR	97520	**888-440-7685**	541-482-8999	48-20
Seats Inc 1515 Industrial St PO Box 60	Reedsburg	WI	53959	**800-443-0615**	608-524-4316	678
Seattle Art Supply Inc 2108 Western Ave	Seattle	WA	98121	**800-223-2787**	206-223-2787	45
Seattle Bible College 2363 NW 80th St	Seattle	WA	98117	**877-722-9673**	206-784-1888	163
Seattle Cancer Care Alliance 825 Eastlake Ave E PO Box 19023	Seattle	WA	98109	**800-804-8824**	206-288-1024	758
Seattle Lighting Fixture Co 222 2nd Ave Ext S *Cust Svc	Seattle	WA	98104	**800-689-1000***	206-622-1962	357
Seattle Limousine Service PO Box 80205	Seattle	WA	98108	**800-274-3339**	206-762-3339	433
Seattle Mfg Corp 6930 Salashan Pkwy	Ferndale	WA	98248	**800-426-6251**	360-366-5534	566
Seattle Opera PO Box 9248 *Sales	Seattle	WA	98109	**800-426-1619***	206-389-7600	563-2
Seattle Pacific Industries 21216 72nd Ave S	Kent	WA	98032	**800-777-1145**	206-282-8889	153-3
Seattle Pacific University 3307 3rd Ave W	Seattle	WA	98119	**800-366-3344**	206-281-2000	163
Seattle Refrigeration & Mfg Co 1057 S Director St	Seattle	WA	98108	**800-228-8881**	206-762-7740	650
Seattle Repertory Theatre 155 Mercer St PO Box 900923	Seattle	WA	98109	**877-900-9285**	206-443-2210	563-4
Seattle Seahawks 11220 NE 53rd St	Kirkland	WA	98033	**888-635-4295**	425-827-9777	703
Seattle Storm 351 Elliott Ave W Suite 500	Seattle	WA	98119	**800-743-7021**	206-281-5800	703
Seattle Super Saver 701 Pike St Suite 800	Seattle	WA	98101	**800-535-7071**	206-461-5800	368
Seattle SuperSonics 351 Elliott Ave W Suite 500	Seattle	WA	98119	**800-743-7021**	206-281-5800	703
Seattle Systems Inc 26296 Twelve Trees Ln NW	Poulsbo	WA	98370	**800-248-6463**	360-697-5656	469
Seattle University 901 12th Ave	Seattle	WA	98122	**800-542-0833**	206-296-6000	163
Seattle's Best Coffee Co 2401 Utah Ave S	Seattle	WA	98134	**800-611-7793**		156
Seaview Industries Inc 4595 NW 37th Ct	Miami	FL	33142	**800-282-8688**	305-633-9650	690
SeaView Inn 240 Aquidneck Ave	Newport	RI	02842	**800-495-2046**	401-846-5000	373
Seaview Marriott Resort & Spa 401 S New York Rd	Galloway	NJ	08205	**800-228-9290**	609-652-1800	655
Seaway Food Town Inc 1020 Ford St	Maumee	OH	43537	**800-221-8816**	419-893-9401	339
SeaWorld Orlando 7007 Sea World Dr	Orlando	FL	32821	**800-327-2424**	407-351-3600	32
SeaWorld San Antonio 10500 SeaWorld Dr	San Antonio	TX	78251	**800-722-2762**	210-523-3000	32
SeaWorld San Diego 500 SeaWorld Dr	San Diego	CA	92109	**800-257-4268**	619-226-3901	32
Sebago Inc 55 Hutcherson Dr	Gorham	ME	04038	**800-365-5505**	207-854-8474	296
Sebasco Harbor Resort 27 Keynon Rd	Phippsburg	ME	04562	**800-225-3819**	207-389-1161	655
Sebastian International Inc 6109 DeSoto Ave *Cust Svc	Woodland Hills	CA	91367	**800-347-4424***	818-999-5112	211
Sebastiani Vineyards Inc 389 4th St E	Sonoma	CA	95476	**800-888-5532**	707-938-5532	81-3
Sebastopol Area Chamber of Commerce 265 S Main St	Sebastopol	CA	95472	**877-828-4748**	707-823-3032	137
Sebring (Greater) Chamber of Commerce 309 Circle Park Dr	Sebring	FL	33870	**877-844-6007**	863-385-8448	137
SEC (Securities & Exchange Commission) 450 5th St NW	Washington	DC	20549	**800-732-0330**	202-942-0020	336-16
SEC Accounting Report 395 Hudson St 4th Fl	New York	NY	10014	**800-431-9025**	212-367-6300	521-1
Secap USA Inc 10 Clipper Rd	West Conshohocken	PA	19428	**800-523-0320**	610-825-6205	113
Sechler Ralph & Son Inc 5686 State Rd 1	Saint Joe	IN	46785	**800-332-5461**	260-337-5461	291-19
Seco-Larm USA Inc 16842 Millikan Ave	Irvine	CA	92606	**800-662-0800**	949-261-2999	681
Secoa Inc 8650 109th Ave N	Champlin	MN	55316	**800-328-5519**	763-506-8800	708
Second Amendment Foundation 12500 NE 10th Pl	Bellevue	WA	98005	**800-426-4302**	425-454-7012	48-8
Second City Chicago 1616 N Wells St	Chicago	IL	60614	**877-778-4707**	312-664-4032	563-4
Second Cup Ltd 6303 Airport Rd	Mississauga	ON	L4V1R8	**800-338-2610**	905-405-6700	156
Second Harvest. America's 35 E Wacker Dr Suite 2000	Chicago	IL	60601	**800-771-2303**	312-263-2303	48-5
Second Millennium Equity Services Inc 796 Deer Park Ave	Babylon	NY	11703	**877-227-4466**		157
SECO/Warwick Corp 180 Mercer St	Meadville	PA	16335	**800-458-6071**	814-724-1400	313
Secret Garden Spa at the Prince of Wales Hotel 6 Picton St PO Box 46	Niagara-on-the-Lake	ON	L0S1J0	**888-669-5566**	905-468-0515	698
Secretary of Agriculture Fraud Waste & Abuse Hotline	Washington	DC	20250	**800-424-9121**		336-1
Secretary of Commerce Fraud Hotline	Washington	DC	20230	**800-424-5197**		336-2
Secretary of Defense Defense Hotline for Fraud Waste & Abuse	Washington	DC	20301	**800-424-9098**		336-3
Secretary of the Interior Fraud Hotline	Washington	DC	20240	**800-424-5081**		336-9
Secretary of Veterans Affairs Fraud Hotline	Washington	DC	20420	**800-488-8244**		336-15

Name / Address	City	State	ZIP	Toll-Free	Phone	Class
SecuGen Corp 2356 Walsh Ave	Santa Clara	CA	95051	**866-942-8800**	408-727-7787	85
Secura Insurance Cos PO Box 819	Appleton	WI	54912	**800-558-3405**	920-739-3161	384-4
Secure Computing Corp 4810 Hardwood Rd *NASDAQ: SCUR*	San Jose	CA	95124	**800-692-5625**	408-979-6100	176-12
SecureInfo Corp 211 North Loop 1604 E Suite 200	San Antonio	TX	78232	**888-677-9351**	210-403-5600	178
Securitech Inc 8230 E Broadway Suite E-10	Tucson	AZ	85710	**800-805-4473**	520-721-0305	621
Securities Administrators Assn. North American 10 G St NE Suite 710	Washington	DC	20002	**888-846-2722**	202-737-0900	49-2
Securities Dealers Inc. National Assn of 1735 K St NW	Washington	DC	20006	**800-289-9999**	202-728-8000	49-2
Securities & Exchange Commission (SEC) 450 5th St NW	Washington	DC	20549	**800-732-0330**	202-942-0020	336-16
Office of Investor Education & Assistance 450 5th St NW	Washington	DC	20549	**800-732-0330**	202-942-7040	336-16
Securitron Magnalock Corp 550 Vista Blvd *Sales	Sparks	NV	89434	**800-624-5625***	775-355-5625	345
Security Assoc International Inc 2101 S Arlington Heights Rd Suite 150	Arlington Heights	IL	60005	**800-323-7601**	847-956-8650	683
Security Benefit Group of Cos 1 Security Benefit Pl	Topeka	KS	66636	**800-888-2461**	785-438-3000	384-2
Security Benefit Life Insurance Co 1 Security Benefit Pl	Topeka	KS	66636	**800-888-2461**	785-438-3000	384-2
Security. Business Executives for National 1717 Pennsylvania Ave NW Suite 350	Washington	DC	20006	**800-296-2125**	202-296-2125	49-12
Security Chain Co PO Box 949	Clackamas	OR	97015	**800-547-6806**	503-656-5400	666
Security Check PO Box 1211	Oxford	MS	38655	**800-634-4484**	662-234-0440	112
Security Corp 22325 Roethel Dr	Novi	MI	48375	**888-374-5789**	248-374-5700	683
Security Defense Systems Corp 160 Park Ave	Nutley	NJ	07110	**800-325-6339**	973-235-0606	681
Security Engineered Machinery Co Inc PO Box 1045 *Sales	Westborough	MA	01581	**800-225-9293***	508-366-1488	112
Security Financial Life Insurance Co 4000 Pine Lake Rd	Lincoln	NE	68516	**800-284-8575**	402-434-9500	384-2
Security Funds 1 Security Benefit Pl	Topeka	KS	66636	**800-888-2461**	785-438-3000	517
Security Health Plan of Wisconsin Inc 1515 St Joseph Ave	Marshfield	WI	54449	**800-472-2363**	715-387-5621	384-3
Security. International Assn of Personnel in Employment 1801 Louisville Rd	Frankfort	KY	40601	**888-898-9960**	502-223-4459	49-12
Security Life Insurance Co of America 10901 Red Circle Dr	Minnetonka	MN	55343	**800-328-4667**	952-544-2121	384-2
Security Mutual Life Insurance Co of New York PO Box 1625	Binghamton	NY	13902	**800-346-7171**	607-723-3551	384-2
Security Officers. International Union of 2201 Broadway Suite 101	San Leandro	CA	94612	**800-772-3326**	510-625-9913	405
Security Police & Fire Professionals of America. International Union 25510 Kelly Rd	Roseville	MI	48066	**800-228-7492**	586-772-7250	405
Security Savings Mortgage Corp 217 2nd St NW Suite 1000	Canton	OH	44702	**800-421-8059**	330-455-5600	498
Security Search & Abstract Co 201 N Presidential Blvd Suite 102	Bala Cynwyd	PA	19004	**800-345-9494**	610-664-5912	621
Security Service Federal Credit Union 16211 La Cantera Pkwy	San Antonio	TX	78256	**800-527-7328**	210-476-4000	216
Security Services & Technologies 2450 Blvd of the Generals Valley Forge Business Ctr	Norristown	PA	19403	**888-446-7781**	610-630-6790	681
Security Software Systems Inc 1998 Bucktail Ln	Sugar Grove	IL	60554	**888-835-7278**	630-466-1038	176-7
Security Solutions Inc 3224 Lake Woodard Dr	Raleigh	NC	27604	**888-531-1018**	919-828-1018	683
Security Storage Co 1701 Florida Ave NW	Washington	DC	20009	**800-736-6825**	202-234-5600	508
Security Supply Corp 196 Maple Ave	Selkirk	NY	12158	**800-333-2226**	518-767-2226	601
SED International Inc 4916 N Royal Atlanta Dr *Sales	Tucker	GA	30084	**800-444-8962***	770-491-8962	172
SED Medical Laboratories 5601 Office Blvd	Albuquerque	NM	87109	**800-999-5227**	505-727-6300	409
Sedalia Area Chamber of Commerce 600 E 3rd St	Sedalia	MO	65301	**800-827-5295**	660-826-2222	137
Sedalia Implement Co 2205 S Limit Ave	Sedalia	MO	65301	**800-752-5476**	660-826-0466	270
Sedgwick County Electric Co-op 1355 S 383rd St W PO Box 220	Cheney	KS	67025	**866-542-4732**	316-542-3131	244
Sedgwick Detert Moran & Arnold LLP 1 Embarcadero Ctr 16th Fl	San Francisco	CA	94111	**800-826-3262**	415-781-7900	419
Sedimentary Geology. Society for 6128 E 38th St Suite 308	Tulsa	OK	74135	**800-865-9765**	918-610-3361	49-19
Sedlak Interiors Inc 34300 Solon Rd	Solon	OH	44139	**800-260-2949**	440-248-2424	316
See Ltd 8806 Beverly Blvd	Los Angeles	CA	90048	**800-258-8292**	310-385-1919	316
SeeBeyond Technology Corp 181 W Huntington Dr *NASDAQ: SBYN*	Monrovia	CA	91016	**800-425-0541**	626-471-6000	176-1
SEEC Inc Park West 1 Suite 200 Cliff Mine Rd	Pittsburgh	PA	15275	**800-682-7332**	412-893-0300	176-1
Seed Trade Assn. American 225 Reinekers Ln Suite 650	Alexandria	VA	22314	**888-890-7333**	703-837-8140	48-2
Seedburo Equipment Co 1022 W Jackson Blvd	Chicago	IL	60607	**800-284-5779**	312-738-3700	270
Seedway Inc 1734 Railroad Pl	Hall	NY	14463	**800-836-3710**	585-526-6391	684
Seeker Rod Co Inc 1340 W Cowles St	Long Beach	CA	90813	**800-373-3537**	562-491-0076	701
Seelye Plastics Inc 9700 Newton Ave S	Bloomington	MN	55431	**800-328-2728**	952-881-2658	592
seepex Inc 511 Speedway Dr	Enon	OH	45323	**800-695-3659**	937-864-7150	627

Name / Address	City	State	ZIP	Toll-Free	Phone	Class
See's Candies Inc 210 El Camino Real	South San Francisco	CA	94080	**800-951-7337***	650-761-2490	291-8
*Cust Svc						
Sefar America Inc 120 Mt Holly Bypass	Lumberton	NJ	08048	**800-289-8385**	609-613-5000	730-3
Segel & Son Inc 107 S South St	Warren	PA	16365	**800-252-1215**	814-723-4900	674
segNET Technologies Inc 9 Landing Rd PO Box 369	Enfield	NH	03748	**800-763-5556**	603-643-5883	174
Segue Software Inc 201 Spring St	Lexington	MA	02421	**800-287-1329**	781-402-1000	176-1
NASDAQ: SEGU						
Segway LLC 14 Technology Dr	Bedford	NH	03110	**866-473-4929**	603-222-6000	505
Sehman Tire Service Inc 814 Atlantic Ave PO Box 889	Franklin	PA	16323	**800-895-8663**	814-437-7878	740
SEI Information Technology 1420 Kensington Rd Suite 102	Oak Brook	IL	60523	**888-734-7343**	630-413-5050	175
SEI Investments Co 1 Freedom Valley Dr	Oaks	PA	19456	**800-610-1114**	610-676-1000	393
NASDAQ: SEIC						
SEI Mutual Funds Services PO Box 1098	Oaks	PA	19456	**800-342-5734**		517
Seibels Bruce Group Inc 1501 Lady St	Columbia	SC	29201	**800-525-8835**	803-748-2000	384-4
Seibert Inc 1901 S Rockwell St	Chicago	IL	60608	**800-435-4530***	815-945-2411	484
*Sales						
Seidler Cos Inc 515 S Figueroa St Suite 1100	Los Angeles	CA	90071	**800-840-1090**	213-683-4500	679
Seiko Corp of America 1111 MacArthur Blvd	Mahwah	NJ	07430	**800-782-2510***	201-529-5730	403
*Cust Svc						
Seiko Instruments USA Inc 2990 W Lomita Blvd	Torrance	CA	90505	**800-358-0880**	310-517-7050	151
Seiko Instruments USA Inc Business & Home Office Products Div 2990 W Lomita Blvd	Torrance	CA	90505	**800-358-0880**	310-517-7050	171-6
Seiko Instruments USA Inc Micro Printer Div 2990 W Lomita Blvd	Torrance	CA	90505	**800-553-6570**	310-517-7778	171-6
Seiler Instrument & Mfg Co Inc 170 E Kirkham Ave	Saint Louis	MO	63119	**800-489-2282**	314-968-2282	534
Seismic Energy Products LP 518 Progress Way	Athens	TX	75751	**800-603-8766**	903-675-8571	663
Seitchik Industries Inc 1843 W Allegheny Ave	Philadelphia	PA	19132	**800-523-0814**	215-226-0200	153-12
Seitlin 9800 NW 41st St Suite 300	Miami	FL	33178	**800-677-7348**	305-591-0090	383
SEK Genetics 9305 70th Rd	Galesburg	KS	66740	**800-443-6389**	620-763-2211	12-2
Sekisui America Corp 666 5th Ave 12th Fl	New York	NY	10103	**800-866-4005**	212-489-3500	592
Sekisui America Corp Voltek Div 100 Shepard St	Lawrence	MA	01843	**800-225-0668***	978-685-2557	590
*Cust Svc						
Seko Worldwide Inc 1100 Arlington Heights Rd	Itasca	IL	60143	**800-323-1235**	630-919-4800	440
Selby Furniture Hardware Co 321 Rider Ave	Bronx	NY	10451	**800-224-0058**	718-993-3700	345
Selden's Home Furnishings & Interior Design 1802 62nd Ave E	Tacoma	WA	98424	**800-870-7880**	253-922-5700	316
Select-A-Ticket Inc 25 Rt 23 S	Riverdale	NJ	07457	**800-735-3288**	973-839-6100	735
Select Business Solutions 6260 Lookout Rd	Boulder	CO	80301	**888-472-7347**	303-305-4115	176-1
Select Comfort Corp 6105 Trenton Ln N	Plymouth	MN	55442	**800-472-7185**	763-551-7000	463
NASDAQ: SCSS						
Select Energy Services Inc 24 Prime Pkwy	Natick	MA	01760	**800-325-4432**	508-653-0456	191
Select Medical Corp 4716 Old Gettysburg Rd	Mechanicsburg	PA	17055	**888-735-6332**	717-972-1100	455
Select-O-Hits Inc 1981 Fletcher Creek Dr	Memphis	TN	38133	**800-346-0723**	901-388-1190	512
Select Portfolio Servicing Inc PO Box 65250	Salt Lake City	UT	84165	**800-258-8602**	801-293-1883	215
Select Suites Airport Center 4221 E McDowell Rd	Phoenix	AZ	85008	**800-845-3020**	602-267-7917	373
Select Suites Biltmore Center 4341 N 24th St	Phoenix	AZ	85016	**800-821-8005**	602-954-8049	373
Select Suites Fiesta Mall 960 W Southern Ave	Mesa	AZ	85210	**800-633-5972**	480-962-8343	373
Select Suites North Mesa-Sierra Madre 900 N Country Club Dr	Mesa	AZ	85201	**800-821-8005**	480-962-7940	373
Select Suites South Mesa-Peppertree 1318 S Vineyard St	Mesa	AZ	85210	**800-354-0893**	480-833-2959	373
Select Tool & Die Corp 60 Heid Ave	Dayton	OH	45404	**800-797-4150**	937-233-9191	745
Selected Funds PO Box 8243	Boston	MA	02266	**800-243-1575**		517
Selected Independent Funeral Homes 500 Lake Cook Rd Suite 205	Deerfield	IL	60015	**800-323-4219**	847-236-9401	49-4
Selectica Inc 3 W Plumeria Dr	San Jose	CA	95134	**877-712-9560**	408-570-9700	176-1
NASDAQ: SLTC						
Selective Insurance Co of America 40 Wantage Ave	Branchville	NJ	07890	**800-777-9656**	973-948-3000	384-4
Selective Insurance Group Inc 40 Wantage Ave	Branchville	NJ	07890	**800-777-9656**	973-948-3000	355-4
NASDAQ: SIGI						
Selective Way Insurance Co 40 Wantage Ave	Branchville	NJ	07890	**800-777-9656**	973-948-3000	384-4
Self-Employed. National Assn for the PO Box 612067 DFW Airport	Dallas	TX	75261	**800-232-6273**		49-12
Self-Insurance Institute of America Inc (SIIA) PO Box 1237	Simpsonville	SC	29681	**800-851-7789**	864-962-2208	49-9
Self Magazine 4 Times Sq	New York	NY	10036	**800-274-6111**	212-286-2860	449-11
Self-Seal Container Corp 401 E 4th St	Bridgeport	PA	19405	**800-334-1428**	610-275-2300	125
Self Storage Assn (SSA) 6506 Louisdale Rd Suite 315	Springfield	VA	22150	**888-735-3784**	703-921-9123	49-21
Selig Chemical Industries Inc 115 Kendall Park Ln	Atlanta	GA	30336	**800-447-3544**		149
Selig Enterprises Inc 1100 Spring St NW Suite 550	Atlanta	GA	30309	**800-830-9965**	404-876-5511	641
Seligman & Assoc 1 Town Sq Suite 1913	Southfield	MI	48076	**866-864-9824**	248-862-8000	641
Seligman Group of Funds 100 Park Avenue	New York	NY	10017	**800-221-7844**	212-850-1864	517
Seligman J & W & Co Inc 100 Park Ave	New York	NY	10017	**800-221-7844**	212-850-1864	393
Sellers & Josephson Inc 86 Rt 4 E	Englewood	NJ	07631	**800-274-3385**	201-567-1353	789
Selling Power Magazine 1140 International Pkwy	Fredericksburg	VA	22406	**800-752-7355**	540-752-7000	449-5
Selling to Seniors Newsletter 8204 Fenton St	Silver Spring	MD	20910	**800-666-6380**	301-588-6380	521-10
Sellmore Industries Inc 815 Smith St	Buffalo	NY	14206	**800-783-1900**	716-854-1600	232
Sellstrom Mfg Co 1 Sellstrom Dr	Palatine	IL	60067	**800-323-7402**	847-358-2000	566
Selma-Dallas County Chamber of Commerce 912 Selma Ave	Selma	AL	36701	**800-457-3562**	334-875-7241	137
Selma Times-Journal PO Box 611	Selma	AL	36702	**800-522-1681**	334-875-2110	522-2
Selmer Co Inc 600 Industrial Pkwy	Elkhart	IN	46515	**800-348-7426**	574-522-1675	516
Seltzer's Smokehouse Meats PO Box 111	Palmyra	PA	17078	**800-282-6336**	717-838-6336	291-26
SEMA Equipment Inc 11555 Hwy 60 Blvd	Wanamingo	MN	55983	**800-569-1377**	507-824-2256	270
Semasys Inc 702 Ashland St	Houston	TX	77007	**800-231-1425***	713-869-8331	281
*Cust Svc						
SEMCO Energy Gas Co 1411 3rd St Suite A	Port Huron	MI	48060	**800-624-2019**	810-987-2200	774
SEMI (Semiconductor Equipment & Materials International) 3081 Zenker Rd	San Jose	CA	95134	**800-974-7364**	408-943-6900	49-19
Semiconductor Circuits Inc 49 Range Rd	Windham	NH	03087	**800-448-4724***	603-893-2330	252
*Cust Svc						
Semiconductor Equipment & Materials International (SEMI) 3081 Zenker Rd	San Jose	CA	95134	**800-974-7364**	408-943-6900	49-19
Seminar Leaders Assn. American 2405 E Washington Blvd	Pasadena	CA	91104	**800-735-0511**	626-791-1211	49-12
Seminis Inc 2700 Camino del Sol	Oxnard	CA	93030	**800-647-7386**	805-647-1572	684
Seminole Casino Hollywood 4150 N State Rd 7	Hollywood	FL	33021	**866-222-7466**	954-961-3220	133
Seminole Casino Immokalee 506 S 1st St	Immokalee	FL	34143	**800-218-0007**		133
Seminole Coconut Creek Casino 5550 NW 40th St	Coconut Creek	FL	33073	**866-222-2466**	954-977-6700	133
Seminole County Convention & Visitors Bureau 1230 Douglas Ave Suite 116	Longwood	FL	32779	**800-800-7832**	407-665-2900	205
Seminole Hard Rock Hotel & Casino Hollywood 1 Seminole Way	Hollywood	FL	33314	**800-937-0010**	954-327-7625	655
Seminole Hard Rock Hotel & Casino Tampa 5223 N Orient Rd	Tampa	FL	33610	**800-282-7016**	813-621-1302	133
Seminole Stores Inc PO Box 940	Ocala	FL	34478	**800-683-1881**	352-732-4143	438
Semitool Inc 655 W Reserve Dr	Kalispell	MT	59901	**800-548-8495**	406-752-2107	685
NASDAQ: SMTL						
Semling-Menke Co Inc PO Box 378	Merrill	WI	54452	**800-333-2206**	715-536-9411	234
Semo Electric Co-op 505 S Main St	Sikeston	MO	63801	**800-813-5230**	573-471-5821	244
Semonin Realtors 4967 US Hwy 42 Suite 200	Louisville	KY	40222	**800-548-1650**	502-425-4760	638
Semotus Solutions Inc 16400 Lark Ave Suite 230	Los Gatos	CA	95032	**800-775-1377**	408-358-7100	222
AMEX: DLK						
Sempra Energy Corp 101 Ash St	San Diego	CA	92101	**800-411-7343**	619-696-2000	355-5
NYSE: SRE						
SemWare Corp 730 Elk Cove Ct	Kennesaw	GA	30152	**800-467-3692**	678-355-9810	176-2
Sen Plex Corp 938 Kohou St	Honolulu	HI	96817	**800-552-4553**	808-848-0111	641
Senate Luxury Suites 900 SW Tyler St	Topeka	KS	66612	**800-488-3188**	785-233-5050	373
Senator Inn and Spa of Augusta 284 Western Ave	Augusta	ME	04330	**877-772-2224**	207-622-8800	698
SENCO Products Inc 8485 Broadwell Rd	Cincinnati	OH	45244	**800-543-4596***	513-388-2000	747
*Tech Supp						
Sencore Inc 3200 Sencore Dr	Sioux Falls	SD	57107	**800-736-2673***	605-339-0100	247
*Cust Svc						
Senderex Cargo Inc 10425 S La Cienega Blvd	Los Angeles	CA	90045	**800-421-5846**	310-342-2900	306
Sendmail Inc 6425 Christie Ave 4th Fl	Emeryville	CA	94608	**888-594-3150**	510-594-5400	176-7
Seneca Beverage Corp 388 Upper Oakwood Ave	Elmira	NY	14903	**800-724-0350**	607-734-6111	82-1
Seneca Capital Management LLC 909 Montgomery St Suite 500	San Francisco	CA	94133	**800-828-1212**	415-486-6500	393
Seneca College Residence & Conference Centre 1760 Finch Ave E	Toronto	ON	M2J5G3	**877-225-8664**	416-491-8811	372
Seneca County Convention & Visitors Bureau 114 S Washington St	Tiffin	OH	44883	**888-736-3221**	419-447-5866	205
Seneca Hotel 200 E Chestnut St	Chicago	IL	60611	**800-800-6261**	312-787-8900	373
Seneca Pharmaceutical Inc 8621 Barefoot Industrial Rd	Raleigh	NC	27617	**800-545-3701**	919-783-6936	573
Seneca Resources Corp 1201 Louisiana St Suite 400	Houston	TX	77002	**800-622-6695**	713-654-2650	525
Seneca Wire & Mfg Co 319 S Vine St	Fostoria	OH	44830	**800-537-9537***	419-435-9261	800
*Sales						
Senior Corps 1201 New York Ave NW	Washington	DC	20525	**800-424-8867**	202-606-5000	336-16
Senior Fitness Assn. American PO Box 2575	New Smyrna Beach	FL	32170	**800-243-1478**	386-423-6634	48-6
Senior Gleaners Inc 1951 Bell Ave	Sacramento	CA	95838	**800-585-1530**	916-925-3240	48-5
Senior Golf Assn. National 3672 Nottingham Way	Hamilton Square	NJ	08690	**800-282-6772**	609-631-8145	48-22
Senior Tours Canada Inc 225 Eglinton Ave W	Toronto	ON	M4R1A9	**800-268-3492**	416-322-1529	748
Senior Volunteer Program. Retired & PO Box 70675	Washington	DC	20024	**800-424-8867**		196
SeniorNet 121 2nd St 7th Fl	San Francisco	CA	94105	**800-747-6848**	415-495-4990	169
Seniors Coalition 4401 Fair Lakes Ct Suite 210	Fairfax	VA	22033	**800-325-9891**	703-631-4211	48-6
Seniors Coalition. 4401 Fair Lakes Ct Suite 210	Fairfax	VA	22033	**800-325-9891**	703-631-4211	48-6
Seniors Unlimited LLC 53 W Huron St	Pontiac	MI	48342	**800-837-1333**	248-338-1333	748
Sennheiser Electronics Corp 1 Enterprise Dr	Old Lyme	CT	06371	**877-736-6434**	860-434-9190	245
Sensible Car Rental Inc 96 Freneau Ave Suite 2	Matawan	NJ	07747	**800-367-5159**	732-583-8500	126
Sensidyne Inc 16333 Bay Vista Dr	Clearwater	FL	33760	**800-451-9444**	727-530-3602	200
Sensient Colors Inc 2526 Baldwin St	Saint Louis	MO	63106	**800-325-8110**	314-889-7600	141

Name / Address	City	State	ZIP	Toll-Free	Phone	Class
Sensient Technologies Corp 777 E Wisconsin Ave 11th Fl *NYSE: SXT*	Milwaukee	WI	53202	800-558-9892	414-271-6755	291-15
Sensor Systems LLC 2800 Anvil St	Saint Petersburg	FL	33710	800-688-2181	727-347-2181	464
Sensor Technology Newsletter 7550 W I-10 Suite 400	San Antonio	TX	77229	877-463-7678	210-348-1000	521-12
Sensormatic Electronics Corp 6600 Congress Ave	Boca Raton	FL	33487	800-327-1765	561-912-6000	681
SensorMedics Corp 22745 Savi Ranch Pkwy	Yorba Linda	CA	92887	800-231-2466	714-283-2228	249
Sentara Careplex Hospital 3000 Colliseum Dr	Hampton	VA	23616	800-736-8272	757-736-1000	366-2
Sentara Home Care Services 535 Independence Pkwy Suite 200	Chesapeake	VA	23320	888-461-5649	757-382-4980	358
Sentient Jet Inc 600 Cordwainer Dr Executive Jet Corporate Ctr	Norwell	MA	02061	877-324-9538	781-763-0200	14
Sentinel The 300 W 6th St	Hanford	CA	93230	800-582-0471	559-582-0471	522-2
Sentinel PO Box 681	Fairmont	MN	56031	800-598-5597	507-235-3303	522-2
Sentinel The 457 E North St	Carlisle	PA	17013	800-829-5570	717-243-2611	522-2
Sentinel Funds PO Box 1499	Montpelier	VT	05601	800-282-3863	802-229-7355	517
Sentinel Lubricants Corp PO Box 694240	Miami	FL	33269	800-842-6400	305-625-6400	530
Sento Corp 808 E Utah Valley Dr *NASDAQ: SNTO*	American Fork	UT	84003	800-868-8448	801-492-2000	752
Sentry Group 900 Linden Ave	Rochester	NY	14625	800-828-1438	585-381-4900	665
Sentry Insurance Group 1800 N Point Dr	Stevens Point	WI	54481	800-227-0201	715-346-6000	355-4
Sentry Life Insurance Co 1800 N Point Dr *Cust Svc	Stevens Point	WI	54481	800-533-7827*	715-346-6000	384-2
Sentry Technology Corp 1881 Lakeland Ave	Ronkonkoma	NY	11779	800-645-4224	631-739-2100	681
Separation of Church & State. Americans United for 518 C St NE	Washington	DC	20002	800-875-3707	202-466-3234	48-7
sephora.com Inc 525 Market St First Market Tower 3rd Fl *Cust Svc	San Francisco	CA	94105	877-737-4672*	415-977-4300	211
SEPM (Society for Sedimentary Geology) 6128 E 38th St Suite 308	Tulsa	OK	74135	800-865-9765	918-610-3361	49-19
Sepp Leaf Products Inc 381 Park Ave S Suite 1301	New York	NY	10016	800-971-7377	212-683-2840	44
Sepulveda Veterans Affairs Medical Center 16111 Plummer St	North Hills	CA	91343	800-516-4567	818-891-7711	366-6
Sequachee Valley Electric Co-op 512 Cedar Ave PO Box 31	South Pittsburg	TN	37380	800-923-2203	423-837-8605	244
Sequatchie Concrete Service Inc 406 Cedar Ave	South Pittsburg	TN	37380	800-824-0824	423-837-7913	181
Sequatchie Handle Works 219 Handle St	Sequatchie	TN	37374	800-221-3419	423-942-5901	808
Sequenom Inc 3595 John Hopkins Ct *NASDAQ: SQNM*	San Diego	CA	92121	877-443-6663	858-202-9000	86
Sequent Inc 222 E Campus View Blvd	Columbus	OH	43235	888-456-3627	614-436-5880	619
Sequoia Fund Inc 767 5th Ave Suite 4701	New York	NY	10153	800-686-6884	212-832-5280	517
Sequoia Vacuum Systems Inc 164 Jefferson Dr	Menlo Park	CA	94025	800-994-0494	650-322-7281	775
SER - Jobs for Progress National Inc 5215 N O'Connor Blvd Suite 2550	Irving	TX	75039	800-427-2306	972-506-7815	48-6
SER Solutions Inc 21680 Ridgetop Cir *Sales	Sterling	VA	20166	800-274-5676*	703-948-5500	176-7
Seradyn Inc 7998 Georgetown Rd Suite 1000	Indianapolis	IN	46268	800-428-4072	317-610-3800	229
Sercomp Corp 21050 Lassen St	Chatsworth	CA	91311	800-477-7372	818-341-1680	616
Seren Innovations Inc 15 S 5th St Suite 500	Minneapolis	MN	55402	800-427-8686	612-395-3500	117
Serene Hotel & Suites 12004 Coastal Hwy	Ocean City	MD	21842	800-542-4444	410-250-4000	373
Serengeti Eyewear Inc 9200 Cody St *Cust Svc	Overland Park	KS	66214	888-838-1449*	913-752-3400	531
Serengeti Systems Inc 812 W 11th St 3rd Fl	Austin	TX	78701	800-634-3122	512-345-2211	176-12
Serenity Lane 616 E 16th St	Eugene	OR	97401	800-543-9905	541-687-1110	712
Serfilco Ltd 2900 MacArthur Blvd	Northbrook	IL	60062	800-323-5431	847-559-1777	627
Sergeants Assn. Air Force 5211 Auth Rd	Suitland	MD	20746	800-638-0594	301-899-3500	48-19
Sergeant's Pet Care Products 2637 S 158th Plaza Suite 100	Omaha	NE	68130	800-224-7387	402-938-7000	568
Sericol Inc 1101 W Cambridge Dr	Kansas City	KS	66103	800-737-4265	913-342-4060	381
Serigraph Inc 3801 E Decorah Road	West Bend	WI	53095	800-279-6060	262-335-7200	675
Serologicals Corp 5655 Spalding Dr *NASDAQ: SERO*	Norcross	GA	30092	800-842-9099	678-728-2000	86
Serono Inc 1 Technology Pl	Rockland	MA	02370	800-283-8088	781-982-9000	86
Serrano Hotel 405 Taylor St	San Francisco	CA	94102	877-294-9709	415-885-2500	373
Serta Inc 325 Spring Lake Dr	Itasca	IL	60143	888-557-3782	630-285-9300	463
Serta Inc Herr Mfg Div 18 Prestige Ln	Lancaster	PA	17603	800-626-6249	717-392-4168	463
Serta Inc National Bedding Co Div 1500 Lee Lane	Beloit	WI	53511	800-767-6267	608-365-6266	463
Serta Mattress/AW Inc 8415 Ardmore Rd	Landover	MD	20785	800-638-0520	301-322-1000	463
Sertoma International 1912 E Meyer Blvd	Kansas City	MO	64132	800-593-5646	816-333-8300	48-5
Servall Co 6761 E Ten Mile Rd	Center Line	MI	48015	800-989-7378	586-754-1818	38
Serve You Custom Prescription Management 9051 W Heather Ave	Milwaukee	WI	53224	888-243-6890	414-410-8100	575
Server Products Inc PO Box 98	Richfield	WI	53076	800-558-8722	262-628-5600	293
Server Technology Inc 1040 Sandhill Dr	Reno	NV	89521	800-835-1515	775-284-2000	174
Service by Air Inc 222 Crossways Pk Dr	Woodbury	NY	11797	800-243-5545	516-921-4101	13
Service & Conservation Corps. National Assn of 666 11th St NW Suite 1000	Washington	DC	20001	800-666-2722	202-737-6272	48-6
Service Electric Cable TV & Communications 2260 Ave A	Bethlehem	PA	18017	800-232-9100	610-865-9100	117
Service Employees International Union 1313 L St NW	Washington	DC	20005	800-424-8592	202-898-3200	405
Service Experts Inc 2140 Lake Pk Blvd Fl 4T	Richardson	TX	75080	877-536-8580	972-497-5000	188-10
Service Ideas Inc 2354 Ventura Dr	Woodbury	MN	55125	800-328-4493	651-730-8800	295
Service Mfg Corp 5414 W Roosevelt Rd	Chicago	IL	60644	800-338-7082	773-287-5500	343
Service Oil Inc 1718 E Main Ave	West Fargo	ND	58078	800-726-0133	701-277-1050	319
Service One Cleaning Consultants & Management 5104 N Orange Blossom Trail Suite 220	Orlando	FL	32810	800-522-7111		150
Service Steel & Pipe Inc 1130 Fullerton St	Shreveport	LA	71107	800-256-8598	318-222-9462	483
ServiceCare 3680 Leeds Ave	Charleston	SC	29405	800-796-8889		687
ServiceMagic Inc 14023 Denver W Pkwy Bldg 64 Suite 200	Golden	CO	80401	800-474-1596	303-963-7200	677
ServiceMaster Clean 3839 Forrest Hill Irene Rd	Memphis	TN	38125	800-242-0442	901-597-7500	150
ServiceMaster Co 3250 Lacey Rd Suite 600 *NYSE: SVM*	Downers Grove	IL	60515	866-782-6787	630-663-2000	184
Services Management International. Association for 1342 Colonial Blvd Suite 25	Fort Myers	FL	33907	800-333-9786	239-275-7887	49-12
ServiceWare Technologies Inc 333 Allegheny Ave Suite 301	Oakmont	PA	15139	800-572-5748	412-826-1158	176-1
ServInt Internet Services 6861 Elm St Suite 2B	McLean	VA	22101	800-573-7846	703-847-1381	387
Servo Products Co 34940 Lakeland Blvd	East Lake	OH	44095	800-521-7359	440-975-9684	447
Servpro Industries Inc 575 Airport Rd	Gallatin	TN	37066	800-826-9586	615-451-0600	150
ServUsa Internet PO Box 745 *Tech Supp	Laurinburg	NC	28353	877-467-3788*	910-276-1633	390
SES Americom Inc 4 Research Way *Sales	Princeton	NJ	08540	800-273-0329*	609-987-4000	669
SESAC Inc 55 Music Sq E	Nashville	TN	37203	800-826-9996	615-320-0055	48-4
SETA Corp 6862 Elm St Suite 600	McLean	VA	22101	888-753-6240	703-821-8178	178
SETAC (Society of Environmental Toxicology & Chemistry) 1010 N 12th Ave	Pensacola	FL	32501	888-899-2088	850-469-1500	49-19
Setco Sales Co 5880 Hillside Ave	Cincinnati	OH	45233	800-543-0470	513-941-5110	447
Sethco Div Met-Pro Corp 70 Arkay Dr	Hauppauge	NY	11788	800-645-0500	631-435-0530	627
Sethness Products Co 3422 W Touhy Ave	Chicago	IL	60645	888-772-1880	847-329-2080	291-15
Seton Hall University 400 S Orange Ave	South Orange	NJ	07079	800-738-6648	973-761-9332	163
Seton Hall University School of Law 1 Newark Ctr	Newark	NJ	07102	888-415-7271	973-642-8747	164-1
Seton Hill University 1 Seton Hill Dr	Greensburg	PA	15601	800-826-6234	724-838-4255	163
Setra Systems Inc 159 Swanson Rd	Boxborough	MA	01719	800-257-3872	978-263-1400	464
Settle Inn Airport 2620 S Packerland Dr	Green Bay	WI	54313	800-688-9052	920-499-1900	373
Settle Inn Resort & Conference Center 3050 Green Mountain Dr	Branson	MO	65616	800-677-6906	417-335-4700	373
Settlement Assn of America. Viatical & Life 800 Mayfair Cir	Orlando	FL	32803	800-842-9811	407-894-3797	49-9
Settlement Services Corp 1004 W Taft Ave *Sales	Orange	CA	92865	800-767-7832*	714-998-1111	176-11
Settlers Life Insurance Co PO Box 8600	Bristol	VA	24203	800-523-2650	276-645-4300	384-2
Seven Gables Inn 26 N Meramec Ave	Saint Louis	MO	63105	800-433-6590	314-863-8400	373
Seven Oaks Capital 5745 Essen Ln Suite 102	Baton Rouge	LA	70810	800-511-4588	225-757-1919	268
Seven Springs Mountain Resort 777 Waterwheel Dr	Champion	PA	15622	800-452-2223	814-352-7777	655
Seven Up Bottling Group of Kansas 2900 S Hydraulic St	Wichita	KS	67216	800-540-0001	316-529-3777	82-2
Seven Worldwide Inc 225 W Superior Ave	Chicago	IL	60610	877-777-7934	312-943-0400	338
Sevenson Environmental Services Inc 2749 Lockport Rd	Niagara Falls	NY	14305	800-777-3836	716-284-0431	653
SevenSpace/Nuclio Corp 20098 Ashbrook Pl	Ashburn	VA	20147	866-977-7223	703-726-6777	39
Seventeen Magazine 1440 Broadway 13th Fl	New York	NY	10018	800-388-1749	917-934-6500	449-6
Seventh Generation Inc 212 Battery St Suite A	Burlington	VT	05401	800-456-1191	802-658-3773	149
Severn Trent Systems 20405 State Hwy 249 Suite 600	Houston	TX	77070	800-231-4611	281-320-7100	176-10
Sevylor USA Inc 4398 Corporate Center Dr	Los Alamitos	CA	90720	800-821-4645	714-503-6300	701
Sewanee 735 University Ave	Sewanee	TN	37383	800-522-2234	931-598-1238	163
Seward County Community College PO Box 1137	Liberal	KS	67905	800-373-9951	620-624-1951	160
Sewell Clothing Co Inc 115 Pacific Ave	Bremen	GA	30110	800-241-1221	770-537-3862	153-12
Sewell Warren Clothing Co 126 Hamilton Ave	Bremen	GA	30110	800-876-9722	770-537-2391	153-12
Sewn Products Equipment Suppliers Assn (SPESA) 5107 Falls of the Neuse Suite B15	Raleigh	NC	27609	888-447-7372	919-872-8909	49-13
Sex Addicts Anonymous (SAA) PO Box 70949	Houston	TX	77270	800-477-8191	713-869-4902	48-21
Sexton Can Co Inc 23 E St	Cambridge	MA	02141	888-739-8662	617-577-8999	124
Seybold Patricia Group 210 Commercial St	Boston	MA	02109	800-826-2424	617-742-5200	455

Name / Address	City	State	Zip	Toll-Free	Phone	Class
Seyfarth Shaw LLP 55 E Monroe St Suite 4200	Chicago	IL	60603	**800-342-4432**	312-346-8000	419
Seyforth Roofing Co Inc 2601 Wood Dr	Garland	TX	75041	**866-870-2800**	972-864-8591	188-12
Seymour Mfg Co Inc 500 N Broadway St	Seymour	IN	47274	**800-457-1909**	812-522-2900	746
SFA (American Senior Fitness Assn) PO Box 2575	New Smyrna Beach	FL	32170	**800-243-1478**	386-423-6634	48-6
SFA Inc 9315 Largo Dr W Suite 200	Largo	MD	20774	**800-787-2732**	301-350-0938	258
SFI Inc 225 W Olney Rd	Norfolk	VA	23510	**800-899-8713**	757-622-8001	111
SG Cowen Securities Corp 1221 Ave of the Americas	New York	NY	10020	**800-942-7575**	212-278-6000	679
SG Supply Co 12900 S Throop St	Calumet Park	IL	60827	**800-626-9130**	708-371-8800	601
SG Wholesale Roofing Supplies Inc 1000 E 6th St	Santa Ana	CA	92701	**888-747-8500**	714-568-1906	190-4
SGH Golf Inc 9403 Kenwood Rd Suite C110	Cincinnati	OH	45242	**800-284-8884**	513-984-0414	760
SGIA (Specialty Graphic Imaging Assn) 10015 Main St	Fairfax	VA	22031	**888-385-3588**	703-385-1335	49-16
SGL Carbon Corp 307 Jamestown Rd	Morganton	NC	28655	**800-828-6601**	828-437-3221	127
SGNA (Society of Gastroenterology Nurses & Associates Inc) 401 N Michigan Ave	Chicago	IL	60611	**800-245-7462**	312-321-5165	49-8
SGS Canada Inc 6275 Northam Dr Unit 2	Mississauga	ON	L4V1Y8	**800-636-0847**	905-676-9595	728
SGS US Testing Co Inc 291 Fairfield Ave *Cust Svc	Fairfield	NJ	07004	**800-777-8378***	973-575-5252	728
Shadow Mountain Resort & Club 45-750 San Luis Rey	Palm Desert	CA	92260	**800-472-3713**	760-346-6123	655
Shadowbrook Inn & Resort 615 SR 6 E	Tunkhannock	PA	18657	**800-955-0295**	570-836-2151	655
Shafer Valve Co 2500 Park Ave W	Mansfield	OH	44906	**800-876-4311**	419-529-4311	220
Shafer's Bus Lines Div Southern Bus Stages Inc 750 Harry L Dr	Johnson City	NY	13790	**800-287-8986**	607-797-2006	108
Shaffer Communications Group Inc 8584 Katy Fwy Suite 300	Houston	TX	77024	**800-243-7525**	713-463-0022	168
Shaffer Sportswear Mfg Inc 224 N Washington St *Orders	Neosho	MO	64850	**800-643-3300***	417-451-9444	153-1
Shaffer Trucking Inc 49 E Main St PO Box 418 *Cust Svc	New Kingstown	PA	17072	**800-742-3337***	717-766-4708	769
Shaffstall Corp 8531 Bash St	Indianapolis	IN	46250	**800-923-8439**	317-842-2077	171-8
Shake & Shingle Bureau. Cedar 7101 Horne St Suite 2	Mission	BC	V2V7A2	**800-843-3578**	604-820-7700	49-3
Shaker Recruitment Advertising & Communications 1100 Lake St	Oak Park	IL	60301	**800-323-5170**	708-383-5320	4
Shaker Village of Pleasant Hill 3501 Lexington Rd	Harrodsburg	KY	40330	**800-734-5611**	859-734-5411	509
Shakespeare Composites & Electronics 19845 US Hwy 76	Newberry	SC	29108	**800-800-9008**	803-276-5504	597
Shakespeare Fishing Tackle Co 3801 Westmore Dr *Cust Svc	Columbia	SC	29223	**800-347-3759***	803-754-7000	701
Shakespeare Monofilaments & Specialty Polymers PO Box 4060	Columbia	SC	29240	**800-845-2110**	803-754-7011	597
Shakespeare Theatre 516 8th St SE	Washington	DC	20003	**877-487-8849**	202-547-3230	562
Shakey's USA 2200 W Valley Blvd	Alhambra	CA	91803	**888-444-6686**	626-537-0737	657
Shaklee Corp 4747 Willow Rd	Pleasanton	CA	94588	**800-742-5533**	925-924-2000	361
Shakopee Valley Printing 5101 Valley Industrial Blvd S	Shakopee	MN	55379	**800-752-9906**	952-445-8260	615
Shakour RG Inc 254 Turnpike Rd	Westborough	MA	01581	**800-262-9090**	508-366-8282	237
Shale Mark Co 10441 Beaudin Blvd Suite 100	Woodridge	IL	60517	**800-488-2686**	630-427-1100	155-4
Shalmet Corp 116 Pinedale Industrial Rd	Orwigsburg	PA	17961	**888-278-1414**	570-366-1414	709
Shaman Drum Bookshop 311-315 S State St	Ann Arbor	MI	48104	**800-490-7023**	734-662-7407	96
Shambaugh & Son LP 7614 Opportunity Dr	Fort Wayne	IN	46825	**800-234-9988**	260-487-7777	188-10
Shambhala Mountain Center 4921 County Rd 68C	Red Feather Lakes	CO	80545	**888-788-7221**	970-881-2184	660
Shamrock Communications Inc 149 Penn Ave	Scranton	PA	18503	**800-228-4637**	570-348-9108	629
Shamrock Food Service 3055 Prosperity Ave	Fairfax	VA	22031	**800-345-7534**	703-849-9300	294
Shamrock Foods Co Inc 2540 N 29th Ave	Phoenix	AZ	85009	**800-388-3247**	602-233-6400	291-27
Shamrock Scientific Specialty Systems Inc 34 Davis Dr	Bellwood	IL	60104	**800-323-0249**	708-547-9005	404
Shamrock Steel Sales Inc 238 W County Rd S	Odessa	TX	79763	**800-299-2317**	432-337-2317	483
ShaNah Spa at the Bishop's Lodge 1297 Bishop's Lodge Rd	Santa Fe	NM	87504	**800-974-2624**	505-819-4000	698
Shands Hospital at the University of Florida 1600 SW Archer Rd	Gainesville	FL	32610	**800-749-7424**	352-265-0111	366-2
Blood & Bone Marrow Transplant Program 1600 SW Archer Rd Box 100403	Gainesville	FL	32610	**800-749-7424**	352-265-0062	758
Shangri-La International Hotels Inc 1501 Broadway Suite 502	New York	NY	10036	**800-942-5050**	212-768-3190	369
Shangri-La Resort 57401 E Hwy 125	Afton	OK	74331	**800-331-4060**	918-257-4204	655
Shank Services 9000 Emmott Rd Suite A	Houston	TX	77040	**800-406-3835**	713-896-4300	569
Shanken M Communications Inc 387 Park Ave S 8th Fl	New York	NY	10016	**800-866-0775**	212-684-4224	623-9
Shannon Medical Center 120 E Harris Ave	San Angelo	TX	76903	**888-653-6741**	325-653-6741	366-2
Shannon & Wilson Inc PO Box 300303	Seattle	WA	98103	**800-633-6800**	206-632-8020	258
Shanty Creek Resort 1 Shanty Creek Rd	Bellaire	MI	49615	**800-678-4111**	231-533-8621	655
Shape Global Technology Inc 90 Community Dr *Cust Svc	Sanford	ME	04073	**800-627-5836***	207-324-5200	593
Shape LLC 2105 Corporate Dr	Addison	IL	60101	**800-367-5811**	630-620-8394	756
Shapell Industries Inc 8383 Wilshire Blvd Suite 700	Beverly Hills	CA	90211	**800-655-9502**	323-655-7330	639
Share Corp 7821 N Faulkner Rd	Milwaukee	WI	53224	**800-776-7192**	414-355-4000	149
Share Our Strength 1730 'M' St NW Suite 700	Washington	DC	20036	**800-969-4767**	202-393-2925	48-5
SHARE Pregnancy & Infant Loss Support Inc St Joseph's Health Ctr 300 1st Capitol Dr	Saint Charles	MO	63301	**800-821-6819**	636-947-6164	48-21
ShareBuilder Corp 1445 120th Ave NE	Bellevue	WA	98005	**866-747-2537**	425-451-4440	679
Shared Technologies Inc 1405 S Beltline Rd	Coppell	TX	75019	**888-835-4444**	972-462-5800	720
Shareholder.com 12 Clock Tower Pl Suite 300	Maynard	MA	01754	**800-990-6397**	978-461-3111	39
Shari's Restaurants 9400 SW Gemini Dr	Beaverton	OR	97008	**800-433-5334**	503-605-4299	657
Sharon Regional Health System 740 E State St	Sharon	PA	16146	**866-228-1055**	724-983-3911	366-2
Sharon Tube Co 134 Mill St	Sharon	PA	16146	**800-245-8115**	724-981-5200	481
Sharp Brothers Seed Co 2005 S Sycamore	Healy	KS	67850	**800-462-8483**	620-398-2231	684
Sharp Corp 23 Carland Rd	Conshohocken	PA	19428	**800-892-6197**	610-279-3550	89
Sharp Electronics Corp 1 Sharp Plaza	Mahwah	NJ	07430	**800-237-4277**	201-529-8200	52
Sharpe Dry Goods Co Inc 200 N Broadway St	Checotah	OK	74426	**800-238-6491**	918-473-2233	155-2
Sharpe ME Inc 80 Business Park Dr Suite 202 *Orders	Armonk	NY	10504	**800-541-6563***	914-273-1800	623-2
Sharpe Mfg Co 8750 Pioneer Blvd	Santa Fe Springs	CA	90670	**800-742-7731**	562-908-6800	170
Sharper Image Corp 650 Davis St *NASDAQ: SHRP*	San Francisco	CA	94111	**800-344-4444**	415-445-6000	35
Shasta Beverages Inc 26901 Industrial Blvd	Hayward	CA	94545	**800-326-8640**	510-783-3200	81-2
Shasta Industries PO Box 30 *Cust Svc	Middlebury	IN	46540	**800-233-5571***	574-825-8555	120
Shattuck-Saint Mary's School 1000 Shumway Ave PO Box 218	Faribault	MN	55021	**800-421-2724**	507-333-1616	611
Shaver Transportation Co Inc 4900 NW Front Ave	Portland	OR	97210	**888-228-8850**	503-228-8850	309
Shaw-Clayton Corp 123 Carlos Dr *Cust Svc	San Rafael	CA	94903	**800-537-6712***	415-472-1522	198
Shaw Communications Inc 630 3rd Ave SW Suite 900 *NYSE: SJR*	Calgary	AB	T2P4L4	**888-750-7429**	403-750-4500	117
Shaw Environmental & Infrastructure Inc 4171 Essen Ln	Baton Rouge	LA	70809	**800-444-9586**	225-932-2500	791
Shaw Group Inc 4171 Essen Ln *NYSE: SGR*	Baton Rouge	LA	70809	**800-747-3322**	225-932-2500	584
Shaw Industries Inc 616 E Walnut Ave	Dalton	GA	30721	**800-742-9872**	706-278-3812	131
Shaw Mike Chevrolet Buick Saab 1080 S Colorado Blvd	Denver	CO	80246	**800-223-1615**	303-757-6161	57
Shaw & Shaw 2421 N Glassell St	Orange	CA	92865	**800-933-6756**	714-921-5442	619
Shaw & Slavsky Inc 13821 Elmira Ave	Detroit	MI	48227	**800-521-7527**	313-834-3990	10
Shaw Trucking Inc 7804 Belvedere Rd	West Palm Beach	FL	33411	**800-930-7263**		769
Shaw University 118 E South St *Admissions	Raleigh	NC	27601	**800-214-6683***	919-546-8275	163
Shaw Willis Express Inc 201 N Elm St	Elm Springs	AR	72728	**800-643-3540**	479-248-7261	769
Shawano Country Chamber of Commerce 213 E Green Bay St	Shawano	WI	54166	**800-235-8528**	715-524-2139	137
Shawano Leader 1464 E Green Bay St	Shawano	WI	54166	**800-236-2105**	715-526-2121	522-2
Shawmut Inn 280 Friend St	Boston	MA	02114	**800-350-7784**	617-720-5544	373
Shawnee Area Chamber of Commerce 15100 W 67th St Suite 202	Shawnee	KS	66217	**888-550-7282**	913-631-6545	137
Shawnee Inn & Golf Resort PO Box 67 1 River Rd	Shawnee on Delaware	PA	18356	**800-742-9633**	570-424-4000	655
Shawnee News-Star PO Box 1688	Shawnee	OK	74802	**800-332-2305**	405-273-4200	522-2
Shawnee State University 940 2nd St	Portsmouth	OH	45662	**800-959-2778**	740-351-3221	163
Shawver & Assoc PO Box 1592	Corpus Christi	TX	78403	**800-364-2333**	361-880-8968	392
Shawver & Son Inc 144 NE 44th St	Oklahoma City	OK	73105	**800-320-5121**	405-525-9451	188-4
Shea JF Co Inc 655 Brea Canyon Rd	Walnut	CA	91789	**800-755-7432**	909-594-9500	187-4
Sheaffer Pen Corp 301 Ave H	Fort Madison	IA	52627	**800-346-3736**	319-372-3300	560
Shealy's Truck Center Inc 1340 Bluff Rd	Columbia	SC	29201	**800-951-8580**	803-771-0176	505
Shearman & Sterling LLP 599 Lexington Ave	New York	NY	10022	**800-521-2918**	212-848-4000	419
Shea's Performing Arts Center 646 Main St	Buffalo	NY	14202	**800-217-4327**	716-847-1410	562
Sheboygan County Chamber of Commerce 712 Riverfront Dr Suite 101	Sheboygan	WI	53081	**800-457-9497**	920-457-9491	137
Sheboygan Press PO Box 358	Sheboygan	WI	53082	**800-686-3900**	920-457-7711	522-2
Sheedy Drayage Co Inc 1215 Michigan St	San Francisco	CA	94107	**800-792-2984**	415-648-7171	769
Sheehan Hotel 620 Sutter St	San Francisco	CA	94102	**800-848-1529**	415-775-6500	373
Sheet Metal Workers International Assn (SMWIA) 1750 New York Ave NW 6th Fl	Washington	DC	20006	**800-457-7694**	202-783-5880	49-3
Sheet Music Magazine 2 Depot Plaza Suite 301 *Claims	Bedford Hills	NY	10507	**800-759-3036***	914-244-8500	449-9
Sheetz Inc 5700 6th Ave	Altoona	PA	16602	**800-487-5444**	814-946-3611	203
Sheffer Corp 6990 Cornell Rd *Sales	Cincinnati	OH	45242	**800-387-2191***	513-489-9770	220
Sheffield Laboratories 170 Broad St	New London	CT	06320	**800-222-1087**	860-442-4451	211
Sheffield Measurement Inc 660 S Military Rd PO Box 1658 *Cust Svc	Fond du Lac	WI	54936	**800-535-1236***	920-921-7100	202

Company	Address	City	State	ZIP	Toll-Free	Phone	Class
Sheffield Plastics Inc *Cust Svc	119 Salisbury Rd	Sheffield	MA	01257	**800-254-1707***	413-229-8711	589
Sheffield Steel Corp	2300 Hwy S 97	Sand Springs	OK	74063	**800-331-3304**	918-245-1335	709
Sheftel A & Sons Inc *Cust Svc	2121 31st St SW	Allentown	PA	18103	**800-542-2426***	610-797-9420	730-8
Shelborne Beach Resort	1801 Collins Ave	Miami Beach	FL	33139	**800-327-8757**	305-531-1271	373
Shelburne Murray Hill	303 Lexington Ave	New York	NY	10016	**866-233-4642**	212-689-5200	373
Shelby Chamber of Commerce	142 N Gamble St Suite A	Shelby	OH	44875	**888-245-2426**	419-342-2426	137
Shelby County Chamber of Commerce	501 N Harrison St	Shelbyville	IN	46176	**800-318-4083**	317-398-6647	137
Shelby County Office of Tourism	315 E Main St	Shelbyville	IL	62565	**800-874-3529**	217-774-2244	205
Shelby Cullom Davis & Co	609 5th Ave 11th Fl	New York	NY	10017	**800-232-0303**	212-207-3500	679
Shelby Elastics Inc	639 N Post Rd	Shelby	NC	28150	**800-562-4507**	704-487-4301	730-5
Shelby Electric Co-op	Rt 128 N 6th St PO Box 560	Shelbyville	IL	62565	**800-677-2612**	217-774-3986	244
Shelby Energy Co-op Inc	620 Old Finchville Rd	Shelbyville	KY	40065	**800-292-6585**	502-633-4420	244
Shelby Materials Inc	PO Box 280	Shelbyville	IN	46176	**800-548-9516**	317-398-4485	180
Shelbyville-Bedford County Chamber of Commerce	100 N Cannon Blvd	Shelbyville	TN	37160	**888-662-2525**	931-684-3482	137
Shelbyville News	PO Box 750	Shelbyville	IN	46176	**800-362-0114**	317-398-6631	522-2
Sheldahl Inc	1150 Sheldahl Rd	Northfield	MN	55057	**800-533-0505**	507-663-8000	686
Sheldon Jackson College	801 Lincoln St	Sitka	AK	99835	**800-478-4556**	907-747-5221	163
Shell Chemicals Canada Ltd	400 4th Ave	Calgary	AB	T2P0J4	**888-791-4314**		142
Shell Credit Card	4300 Westown Pkwy	West Des Moines	IA	50266	**877-236-5153**		213
Shell Lubricants	5700 S Lee Rd	Cleveland	OH	44137	**800-321-8577**	216-332-4200	530
Shell Oil Co	PO Box 2463	Houston	TX	77252	**888-467-4355**	713-241-6161	525
Shell Point Village *Mktg	15000 Shell Point Blvd	Fort Myers	FL	33908	**800-780-1131***	239-466-1111	659
Shelly Inc	17171 Murphy Ave	Irvine	CA	92614	**888-669-9850**	949-417-8070	252
Shelter Life Insurance Co *Claims	1817 W Broadway	Columbia	MO	65218	**800-743-5837***	573-445-8441	384-2
Shelter Mutual Insurance Co	1817 W Broadway	Columbia	MO	65218	**800-743-5837**	573-445-8441	384-4
Shelter Pointe Hotel	1551 Shelter Island Dr	San Diego	CA	92106	**800-566-2524**	619-221-8000	373
Shelton-Mason County Chamber of Commerce	221 W Railroad Ave	Shelton	WA	98584	**800-576-2021**	360-426-2021	137
Shenandoah Life Insurance Co	2301 Brambleton Ave	Roanoke	VA	24015	**800-848-5433**	540-985-4400	384-2
Shenandoah University	1460 University Dr	Winchester	VA	22601	**800-432-2266**	540-665-4581	163
Shenandoah Valley Electric Co-op	PO Box 236	Mount Crawford	VA	22841	**800-234-7832**	540-434-2200	244
Shenandoah Valley Westminster-Canterbury	300 Westminster-Canterbury Dr	Winchester	VA	22603	**800-492-9463**	540-665-5914	659
Shenandoah's Pride Dairy Inc	168 Dinkel Ave PO Box 120	Mount Crawford	VA	22841	**888-840-6001**	540-442-6000	291-27
Shenvalee Golf Resort	9660 Fairway Dr PO Box 930	New Market	VA	22844	**888-339-3181**	540-740-3181	655
Shepard Niles Inc	220 N Genesee St	Montour Falls	NY	14865	**800-481-2260**	607-535-7111	462
Shephard's Beach Resort	619 S Gulfview Blvd	Clearwater Beach	FL	33767	**800-237-8477**	727-442-5107	373
Shepherd CE Co Inc	2221 Canada Dry St	Houston	TX	77023	**800-324-6733**	713-928-3763	589
Shepherd Construction Co Inc	1800 Briarcliff Rd NE	Atlanta	GA	30329	**800-282-0806**	404-325-9350	187-4
Shepherd Electric Supply *Sales	7401 Pulaski Hwy	Baltimore	MD	21237	**800-253-1777***	410-866-6000	245
Shepherd of the Hills Homestead & Outdoor Theatre	5586 W Hwy 76	Branson	MO	65616	**800-653-6288**	417-334-4191	562
Shepherd University	301 King St	Shepherdstown	WV	25443	**800-344-5231**	304-876-5000	163
Shepherdsville-Bullitt County Tourism Commission	395 Paraquet Springs Dr	Shepherdsville	KY	40165	**800-526-2068**	502-543-8687	205
Sheplar's	9103 E Almeda Rd	Houston	TX	77054	**800-729-1150**	713-799-1150	378
Sheppard Pratt at Ellicott City	4100 College Ave	Ellicott City	MD	21043	**800-883-3322**	410-465-3322	366-3
Sheppard Pratt Health System	6501 N Charles St	Baltimore	MD	21204	**800-627-0330**	410-938-3000	366-3
Sheraton Bal Harbour Beach Resort	9701 Collins Ave	Miami Beach	FL	33154	**800-325-3535**	305-865-7511	655
Sheraton Casino & Hotel	1107 Casino Center Dr	Robinsonville	MS	38664	**800-391-3777**	662-363-4900	133
Sheraton Ferncroft Resort	50 Ferncroft Rd	Danvers	MA	01923	**800-325-3535**	978-777-2500	655
Sheraton Hotels & Resorts	1111 Westchester Ave	White Plains	NY	10604	**800-325-3535**	914-640-8100	369
Sheraton Hyannis Resort	West End Cir	Hyannis	MA	02601	**800-325-3535**	508-775-7775	655
Sheraton Kauai Resort	2440 Hoonani Rd	Koloa	HI	96756	**888-847-0208**	808-742-1661	655
Sheraton Meadowlands Hotel & Conference Center	2 Meadowlands Plaza	East Rutherford	NJ	07073	**800-325-3535**	201-896-0500	370
Sheraton Moana Surfrider	2365 Kalakaua Ave	Honolulu	HI	96815	**800-325-3535**	808-922-3111	655
Sheraton New York Hotel & Towers	811 7th Ave	New York	NY	10019	**800-223-6550**	212-581-1000	370
Sheraton San Marcos Golf Resort & Conference Center	1 San Marcos Pl	Chandler	AZ	85225	**800-528-8071**	480-812-0900	655
Sheraton Sand Key Resort	1160 Gulf Blvd	Clearwater Beach	FL	33767	**800-325-3535**	727-595-1611	655
Sheraton Steamboat Resort & Conference Center	2200 Village Inn Ct	Steamboat Springs	CO	80487	**800-325-3535**	970-879-2220	655
Sheraton Waikiki	2255 Kalakaua Ave	Honolulu	HI	96815	**800-325-3535**	808-922-4422	655
Sheraton Wild Horse Pass Resort & Spa	5594 W Wild Horse Pass Blvd	Chandler	AZ	85226	**888-218-8989**	602-225-0100	655
Sheridan Books Inc	613 E Industrial Dr	Chelsea	MI	48118	**800-999-2665**	734-475-9145	614
Sheridan College	PO Box 1500	Sheridan	WY	82801	**800-913-9139**	307-674-6446	160
Sheridan County Chamber of Commerce	PO Box 707	Sheridan	WY	82801	**800-453-3650**	307-672-2485	137
Sheridan Healthcare Inc	1613 N Harrison Pkwy Bldg C Suite 200	Sunrise	FL	33323	**800-437-2672**	954-838-2371	455
Sheriffs' Assn. National	1450 Duke St	Alexandria	VA	22314	**800-424-7827**	703-836-7827	49-7
Shermag Inc *Sales	2171 King St W	Sherbrooke	QC	J1J2G1	**800-363-2635***	819-566-1515	314-2
Sherman Area Chamber of Commerce	307 W Washington St Suite 100	Sherman	TX	75090	**888-893-1188**	903-893-1184	137
Sherman Convention & Visitors Council	307 W Washington St Suite 100	Sherman	TX	75090	**888-893-1188**	903-893-1184	206
Sherman Edward A Publishing Co	101 Malbone Rd	Newport	RI	02840	**800-320-2378**	401-849-3300	623-8
Sherman Industries	PO Box 646	Madison	AL	35758	**800-239-7490**	256-772-7490	181
Sherman International Corp	1400 Urban Ctr Dr Suite 200	Birmingham	AL	35242	**800-277-6920**	205-970-7500	181
Sherman & Reilly Inc *Sales	PO Box 11267	Chattanooga	TN	37401	**800-251-7780***	423-756-5300	462
Sherman Wire Co	428 Gibbons Rd	Sherman	TX	75092	**800-527-4637**	903-893-0191	676
Sherrod Vans Inc	6464 Greenland Rd	Jacksonville	FL	32258	**800-824-6333**	904-268-3321	62-7
Sherry Mfg Co Inc	3287 NW 65th St	Miami	FL	33147	**800-741-4750**	305-693-7000	153-3
Sherry-Netherland Hotel	781 5th Ave	New York	NY	10022	**800-247-4377**	212-355-2800	373
Sherwin-Williams Co *NYSE: SHW*	101 Prospect Ave NW	Cleveland	OH	44115	**800-996-7566**	216-566-2000	540
Sherwood	2111 Liberty Dr	Niagara Falls	NY	14304	**800-438-2916**	716-283-1010	776
Sherwood America	13101 Moore St	Cerritos	CA	90703	**800-777-8755**	562-741-0960	52
Sherwood Construction Co Inc	3219 W May St	Wichita	KS	67213	**800-852-6038**	316-943-0211	187-4
Sherwood Tool Inc	10 Main St	Kensington	CT	06037	**888-313-0954**	860-828-4161	546
Shield Security	150 W Wardlow Rd	Long Beach	CA	90807	**800-793-3354**	562-283-1100	682
Shieldalloy Metallurgical Corp	545 Beckett Rd Suite 201	Swedesboro	NJ	08085	**800-762-2020**	856-692-4200	476
Shields Bag & Printing Co	1009 Rock Ave	Yakima	WA	98902	**800-541-8630**	509-248-7500	67
Shilo Inns	11600 SW Shilo Ln	Portland	OR	97225	**800-222-2244**	503-641-6565	369
Shimadzu Medical Systems	20101 S Vermont Ave	Torrance	CA	90502	**800-228-1429**	310-217-8855	375
Shimadzu Scientific Instruments Inc	7102 Riverwood Dr	Columbia	MD	21046	**800-477-1227**	410-381-1227	410
Shimer College	PO Box 500	Waukegan	IL	60079	**800-215-7173**	847-623-8400	163
Shin-Etsu Silicones of America	1150 Damar Dr	Akron	OH	44305	**800-544-1745**	330-630-9860	142
Shingle Bureau. Cedar Shake &	7101 Horne St Suite 2	Mission	BC	V2V7A2	**800-843-3578**	604-820-7700	49-3
Shionogi Qualicaps Inc	6505 Franz Warner Pkwy	Whitsett	NC	27377	**800-227-7853**	336-449-3900	572
Ship N Shore *Cust Svc	100 Sylvan Rd Suite 600	Woburn	MA	01801	**866-711-7447***	800-892-5537	760
Shipley Energy Co	550 E King St	York	PA	17405	**800-839-1849**	717-848-4100	311
Shipowners Claims Bureau (SCB)	60 Broad St 37th Fl	New York	NY	10004	**800-730-2535**	212-847-4500	49-21
Shippers Express Co	1651 Kerr Dr	Jackson	MS	39204	**800-647-2480**	601-948-4251	769
Shipping Assn. Jewelers	125 Carlsbad St	Cranston	RI	02920	**800-688-4572**	401-943-6490	49-21
Shirley Plantation	501 Shirley Plantation Rd	Charles City	VA	23030	**800-232-1613**	804-829-5121	50
Shive-Hattery Inc	PO Box 1803	Cedar Rapids	IA	52406	**800-798-0227**	319-364-0227	258
Shively Labs	PO Box 389	Bridgton	ME	04009	**888-744-8359**	207-647-3327	633
Shivvers Inc	614 W English St	Corydon	IA	50060	**800-245-9093**	641-872-1005	269
Sho-Air International	50 Corporate Park	Irvine	CA	92606	**800-227-9111**	949-476-9111	306
Shoals Chamber of Commerce	612 S Court St	Florence	AL	35630	**877-764-4661**	256-764-4661	137
Shoe Carnival Inc *NASDAQ: SCVL* ■ *Cust Svc	8233 Baumgart Rd	Evansville	IN	47725	**800-430-7463***	812-867-6471	296
Shoe Pavilion Inc *NASDAQ: SHOE*	1380 Fitzgerald Dr	Pinole	CA	94564	**800-736-5523**	510-222-4405	296
Shoe Retailers Assn. National	7150 Columbia Gateway Dr Suite G	Columbia	MD	21046	**800-673-8446**	410-381-8282	49-18
Shoe Show of Rocky Mountain Inc *Cust Svc	2201 Trinity Church Rd	Concord	NC	28027	**888-557-4637***	704-782-4143	296
Shoemaker Tex & Son Inc	714 W Cienega Ave	San Dimas	CA	91773	**800-345-9959**	909-592-2071	423
Shoes.com Inc *Cust Svc	11965 Venice Blvd Suite 404	Los Angeles	CA	90066	**888-233-6743***	310-566-7911	296
Shoffner Industries Inc	5631 S NC 62	Burlington	NC	27215	**800-476-9356**	336-226-9356	805
Shogren Hosiery Mfg Co	225 Wilshire Ave SW	Concord	NC	28025	**888-206-0002**	704-786-5617	153-10
ShoLodge Inc	130 Maple Dr N	Hendersonville	TN	37075	**800-222-2222**	615-264-8000	369
Shoney's Inn Inc	130 Maple Dr N	Hendersonville	TN	37075	**800-552-4667**	615-264-8000	369
Shoney's Inc	1717 Elm Hill Pike Suite B1	Nashville	TN	37202	**877-474-6639**	615-391-5395	656
Shoney's Inn Inc	130 Maple Dr N	Hendersonville	TN	37075	**800-552-4667**	615-264-8000	369

Name / Address	City	State	Zip	Toll-Free	Phone	Class
Shonfeld's USA Inc 3100 S Susan St	Santa Ana	CA	92704	**877-447-8933**	714-429-1922	292-11
Shook Hardy & Bacon LLP 2555 Grand Blvd	Kansas City	MO	64108	**800-821-7962**	816-474-6550	419
Shook National Corp 4977 Northcutt Pl	Dayton	OH	45414	**800-664-1844**	937-276-6666	187-7
Shooting Times Magazine PO Box 1790 *Orders	Peoria	IL	61656	**800-727-4353***	309-682-6626	449-20
Shop at Home LLC 5388 Hickory Hollow Pkwy	Antioch	TN	37013	**800-224-9739**	615-263-8000	725
Shop 'n Save Inc 10461 Manchester Rd	Kirkwood	MO	63122	**800-368-7052**	314-984-0900	339
Shop 'n Save Massachusetts Inc 145 Pleasant Hill Rd	Scarborough	ME	04074	**800-341-6393**	207-883-2911	339
Shop-Rite Supermarkets Inc PO Box 2328	Fort Oglethorpe	GA	30742	**800-742-3347**	706-861-3347	339
SHOPA (School Home & Office Products Assn) 3131 Elbee Rd	Dayton	OH	45439	**800-854-7467**	937-297-2250	49-4
ShopNBC 6740 Shady Oak Rd	Eden Prairie	MN	55344	**800-676-5523**	952-943-6000	725
Shoppers Food Warehouse Corp 4600 Forbes Blvd	Lanham	MD	20706	**800-775-9888**	301-306-8600	339
Shoppers Guide PO Box 328	Everett	PA	15537	**800-596-5428**	814-652-5191	522-4
ShopRite Supermarkets Inc PO Box 7812	Edison	NJ	08818	**800-746-7748**	732-417-0850	339
Shops at Carolina Furniture 5425 Richmond Rd	Williamsburg	VA	23188	**800-582-8916**	757-565-3000	316
Shopsmith Inc 6530 Poe Ave *Cust Svc	Dayton	OH	45414	**800-543-7586***	937-898-6070	809
Shore Financial Corp 25020 Shore Pkwy *NASDAQ: SHBK*	Onley	VA	23418	**800-852-8176**	757-787-1335	355-2
Shore Line Newspapers 1100 Boston Post Rd	Guilford	CT	06437	**800-922-7066**	203-453-2711	623-8
Shore Memorial Hospital 9507 Hospital Ave PO Box 17	Nassawadox	VA	23413	**800-834-7035**	757-414-8000	366-2
Shoreham Hotel 33 W 55th St	New York	NY	10019	**800-553-3347**	212-247-6700	373
Shorewood CenTrust Mortgage Corp 1926 10th Ave N Suite 400	Lake Worth	FL	33461	**800-218-5919**	561-540-6224	498
Shorr Packaging Inc 800 N Commerce St	Aurora	IL	60504	**888-978-1122**	630-978-1000	549
Short-Elliott-Hendrickson Inc 3535 Vadnais Ctr Dr	Saint Paul	MN	55110	**800-325-2055**	651-490-2000	258
Short Freight Lines Inc 459 S River Rd	Bay City	MI	48708	**800-248-0625**	989-893-3505	769
Short Hills Tours PO Box 310	Short Hills	NJ	07078	**800-348-6871**	973-467-2113	748
Short JR Milling Co 150 S Wacker Dr	Chicago	IL	60606	**800-544-8734**	312-559-5450	291-23
Shorter College 315 Shorter Ave	Rome	GA	30165	**800-868-6980**	706-233-7319	163
Shorty's Truck & Railroad Car Parts Inc 7744 Alabama Hwy 144 PO Box 270	Alexandria	AL	36250	**800-227-7995**	256-892-3131	759
Showalter Flying Services Orlando Executive Airport PO Box 140753	Orlando	FL	32814	**800-894-7331**	407-894-7331	63
Showbiz Magazine 2290 Corporate Circle Suite 250	Henderson	NV	89074	**800-746-9484**	702-383-7185	449-9
Showboat Atlantic City 801 Boardwalk	Atlantic City	NJ	08401	**800-427-7247**	609-343-4000	133
Showboats International Magazine 1600 SE 17th St Suite 200 *Cust Svc	Fort Lauderdale	FL	33316	**800-876-6976***	954-525-8626	449-4
ShowCase Div SPSS Inc 233 S Wacker Dr 11th Fl	Chicago	IL	60606	**800-259-1028**		176-12
Shower Rite Inc 7519 S Greenwood Ave	Chicago	IL	60619	**800-925-9131**	773-483-5400	325
Shred First LLC 160 Discovery Dr	Roebuck	SC	29376	**800-387-2009**	864-577-9645	455
Shreiner Co 1 Taylor Dr PO Box 347	Killbuck	OH	44637	**800-722-9915**	330-276-6135	546
Shreve Crump & Low Co Inc 330 Boylston St	Boston	MA	02116	**800-225-7088**	617-267-9100	357
Shreve Land Co Inc 666 Travis St Suite 100	Shreveport	LA	71101	**800-259-0056**	318-226-0056	186
Shreveport-Bossier Convention & Tourist Bureau 629 Spring St	Shreveport	LA	71101	**800-551-8682**	318-222-9391	205
Shriners Hospitals for Children Chicago 2211 N Oak Park Ave	Chicago	IL	60707	**800-237-5055**	773-622-5400	366-1
Shriners Hospitals for Children Cincinnati 3229 Burnet Ave	Cincinnati	OH	45229	**800-875-8580**	513-872-6000	366-1
Shriners Hospitals for Children Galveston 815 Market St	Galveston	TX	77550	**800-292-3938**	409-621-1366	366-1
Shriners Hospitals for Children Greenville 950 W Faris Rd	Greenville	SC	29605	**800-591-7564**	864-271-3444	366-1
Shriners Hospitals for Children Honolulu 1310 Punahou St	Honolulu	HI	96826	**888-888-6314**	808-941-4466	366-1
Shriners Hospitals for Children Lexington 1900 Richmond Rd	Lexington	KY	40502	**800-668-4634**	859-266-2101	366-1
Shriners Hospitals for Children Los Angeles 3160 Geneva St	Los Angeles	CA	90020	**800-237-5055**	213-388-3151	366-1
Shriners Hospitals for Children Philadelphia 3551 N Broad St	Philadelphia	PA	19140	**800-281-4050**	215-430-4000	366-1
Shriners Hospitals for Children Saint Louis 2001 S Lindbergh Blvd	Saint Louis	MO	63131	**800-237-5055**	314-432-3600	366-1
Shriners Hospitals for Children Twin Cities 2025 E River Pkwy	Minneapolis	MN	55414	**888-293-2832**	612-596-6100	366-1
SHRM (Society for Human Resource Management) 1800 Duke St	Alexandria	VA	22314	**800-283-7476**	703-548-3440	49-12
SHRM Global Forum 1800 Duke St	Alexandria	VA	22314	**800-283-7476**	703-548-3440	169
Shubert Theatre 225 W 44th St	New York	NY	10036	**800-432-7250**	212-239-6200	732
Shubert Ticketing Services 234 W 44th St	New York	NY	10036	**800-545-2559**	212-944-3700	735
Shuford Mills Inc 1985 Tate Blvd SE	Hickory	NC	28601	**800-633-7649**	828-328-2131	730-9
Shugart Studios Inc 812 College Ave	Levelland	TX	79336	**800-888-4322**	806-894-4322	579
Shula's Hotel & Golf Club. Don 6842 Main St	Miami Lakes	FL	33014	**800-247-4852**	305-821-1150	655
Shula's Steak House 7601 Miami Lakes Dr	Miami Lakes	FL	33014	**800-247-4852**	305-820-8102	657
Shur-Co Inc 2309 Shur-Lok St PO Box 713	Yankton	SD	57078	**800-437-4172**	605-665-6000	718
Shur-Line Div Newell Rubbermaid Inc 4051 S Iowa Ave	Saint Francis	WI	53235	**800-558-3958**	414-481-4500	104
Shure Inc 5800 W Touhy Ave	Niles	IL	60714	**800-257-4873**	847-866-2200	52

Name / Address	City	State	Zip	Toll-Free	Phone	Class
Shure Mfg Corp 1901 W Main St	Washington	MO	63090	**800-227-4873**	636-390-7100	314-1
SHURflo Pump Mfg Co Inc 5900 Katella Ave Suite A	Cypress	CA	90630	**800-854-3218**	562-795-5200	627
Shurgard Storage Centers Inc 1155 Valley St Suite 400 *NYSE: SHU*	Seattle	WA	98109	**800-748-7427**	206-624-8100	790-3
Shurtape Technologies Inc 1506 Highland Ave NE	Hickory	NC	28601	**800-438-5779**	828-322-2700	717
Shuster Barry Information Services 1157 Tucker Rd	North Dartmouth	MA	02747	**877-852-2507**	508-999-5436	621
Shuster Laboratories Inc 85 John Rd	Canton	MA	02021	**800-444-8705**	781-821-2200	654
Shuster's Building Components 2920 Clay Pike	Irwin	PA	15642	**800-366-6733**	724-446-7000	489
Shutter Mill Inc 8517 S Perkins Rd	Stillwater	OK	74074	**800-416-6455**	405-377-6455	690
Shutterbug Magazine 1419 Chaffee Dr Suite 1	Titusville	FL	32780	**800-829-3340**	386-447-6318	449-14
Shutters on the Beach 1 Pico Blvd	Santa Monica	CA	90405	**800-334-9000**	310-458-0030	373
Shuttleworth Inc 10 Commercial Rd	Huntington	IN	46750	**800-444-7412**	260-356-8500	206
SI Jacobson Mfg Co 1414 Jacobson Dr	Waukegan	IL	60085	**800-621-5492**	847-623-1414	538
Si Tanka University *Eagle Butte* 435 N Elm St	Eagle Butte	SD	57625	**800-710-7159**	605-964-8011	161
Huron 333 9th St SW	Huron	SD	57350	**800-710-7159**	605-352-8721	161
SI Technologies Inc 14192 Franklin Ave *Cust Svc	Tustin	CA	92780	**800-872-4784***	714-731-1234	672
SIAM (Society for Industrial & Applied Mathematics) 3600 Market St 6th Fl	Philadelphia	PA	19104	**800-447-7426**	215-382-9800	49-19
Siboney Corp PO Box 221029	Saint Louis	MO	63122	**888-726-8100**	314-822-3163	176-3
Sibson Consulting 600 Alexander Pk Suite 208	Princeton	NJ	08540	**800-257-0486**	609-520-2700	192
Sickle Cell Disease Assn of America (SCDAA) 16 S Calvert St Suite 600	Baltimore	MD	21202	**800-421-8453**	410-528-1555	48-17
Sico North America Inc 7525 Cahill Rd	Minneapolis	MN	55439	**800-328-6138**	952-941-1700	314-3
SICOR Inc 19 Hughes	Irvine	CA	92618	**800-729-9991**	949-455-4700	470
Sidewinder Conversions 45681Yale Rd W	Chilliwack	BC	V2P2N1	**888-266-2299**	604-792-2082	62-7
Siding Institute. Vinyl 1667 K St NW Suite 1000	Washington	DC	20006	**888-367-8741**	202-974-5200	49-13
Sidney Daily News PO Box 4099	Sidney	OH	45365	**800-688-4820**	937-498-8088	522-2
Sidney Sun-Telegraph PO Box 193	Sidney	NE	69162	**888-254-2818**	308-254-2818	522-2
Sidran Inc 14280 Gillis Rd *Cust Svc	Farmers Branch	TX	75244	**800-969-5015***	214-352-7979	153-20
SIDS Alliance. First Candle/ 1314 Bedford Ave Suite 210	Baltimore	MD	21208	**800-221-7437**	410-653-8226	48-17
SIDS Institute. American 509 Augusta Dr	Marietta	GA	30067	**800-232-7437**	770-426-8746	48-6
Siebel Systems Inc 2207 Bridgepointe Pkwy *NASDAQ: SEBL*	San Mateo	CA	94404	**800-647-4300**	650-295-5000	39
Siebert Financial Corp 885 3rd Ave Suite 1720 *NASDAQ: SIEB*	New York	NY	10022	**877-327-8379**	212-644-2400	355-3
Siebert Muriel & Co Inc 885 3rd Ave Suite 1720 *Cust Svc	New York	NY	10022	**800-872-0444***	212-644-2400	679
Siegel Display Products 300 6th Ave N	Minneapolis	MN	55401	**800-626-0322**	612-340-1493	230
Siegel-Robert Inc 8645 S Broadway	Saint Louis	MO	63111	**800-433-1030**	314-638-8300	472
Siegel & Stockman Inc 126 W 25th St	New York	NY	10001	**888-515-8949**	212-633-1508	456
Siegfried USA Inc 33 Industrial Pk Rd *Cust Svc	Pennsville	NJ	08070	**877-763-8630***	856-678-3601	470
Siemens Airfield Solutions Inc 977 Gahanna Pkwy	Columbus	OH	43230	**800-545-4157**	614-861-1304	431
Siemens Building Technologies Inc Fire Safety Div 8 Fernwood Rd	Florham Park	NJ	07932	**800-222-0108**	973-593-2600	681
Siemens Corp 153 E 53rd St 56th Fl	New York	NY	10022	**800-743-6367**	212-258-4000	184
Siemens Dematic Electronics Assembly Systems Inc 3140 Northwoods Pkwy Suite 300	Norcross	GA	30071	**888-768-4357**	770-797-3000	685
Siemens Dematic Material Handling Automation Div 507 Plymouth Ave NE *Cust Svc	Grand Rapids	MI	49505	**800-530-9153***	616-913-6200	462
Siemens Financial Services Inc 170 Wood Ave S	Iselin	NJ	08830	**800-327-4443**	732-590-6500	214
Siemens Foundation 170 Wood Ave S	Iselin	NJ	08830	**877-822-5233**	732-603-5886	299
Siemens Health Services 51 Valley Stream Pkwy	Malvern	PA	19355	**888-767-8326**	610-219-6300	39
Siemens Hearing Instruments Inc 10 Constitution Ave	Piscataway	NJ	08855	**800-766-4500**	732-562-6600	469
Siemens Home Appliances 5551 McFadden Ave	Huntington Beach	CA	92649	**888-474-3636**		36
Siemens ITS 8004 Cameron Rd	Austin	TX	78754	**800-388-6882**	512-837-8310	691
Siemens Logistics & Assembly Systems 507 Plymouth Ave	Grand Rapids	MI	49505	**877-725-7500**	616-913-6200	176-10
Siemens Logistics & Assembly Systems Inc Postal Automation Div 1401 Nolan Ryan Expy	Arlington	TX	76011	**800-433-5175**	817-436-7000	171-7
Siemens Medical Solutions Health Services Corp 51 Valley Stream Pkwy	Malvern	PA	19355	**888-767-8326**	610-219-6300	39
Siemens Medical Solutions Inc 51 Valley Stream Pkwy	Malvern	PA	19355	**866-872-9745**	610-448-6300	375
Siemens Medical Solutions Ultrasound Div 1230 Shorebird Way	Mountain View	CA	94043	**800-422-8766**	650-969-9112	375
Siemens Power Transmission & Distribution Inc 7000 Siemens Rd	Wendell	NC	27591	**800-347-6659**	919-365-2200	609
Siemens Transportation Systems Inc 7464 French Rd	Sacramento	CA	95828	**800-722-8044**	916-681-3000	636

Alphabetical Section

Name / Address	City	State	ZIP	Toll-Free	Phone	Class
Siemer Milling Co 111 W Main St	Teutopolis	IL	62467	**800-826-1065**	217-857-3131	291-23
Siemon Co 101 Siemon Co Dr	Watertown	CT	06795	**866-548-5814**	860-945-4200	801
Siena College 515 Loudon Rd	Loudonville	NY	12211	**800-457-4362**	518-783-2423	163
Siena Heights University 1247 E Siena Heights Dr	Adrian	MI	49221	**800-521-0009**	517-263-0731	163
Siena Hotel 1505 E Franklin St	Chapel Hill	NC	27514	**800-223-7379**	919-929-4000	373
Sierra Club of Canada 1 Nicholas St Suite 412	Ottawa	ON	K1N7B7	**888-810-4204**	613-241-4611	48-13
Sierra Club Foundation 85 2nd St Suite 750	San Francisco	CA	94105	**800-216-2110**	415-995-1780	48-13
Sierra Designs Inc 2011 Cherry St Suite 202	Louisville	CO	80027	**800-635-0461**		701
Sierra Energy 1020 Winding Creek Rd Suite 100	Roseville	CA	95678	**800-552-0748**	916-218-1600	569
Sierra Eye & Tissue Donor Services 1700 Alhambra Blvd Suite 112	Sacramento	CA	95816	**800-762-8819**	916-456-1450	535
Sierra Health & Life Insurance Co PO Box 15645	Las Vegas	NV	89114	**800-888-2264**	702-242-7000	384-2
Sierra Inc 2635 Golf Ave	Racine	WI	53404	**800-722-7263**	262-638-1851	173
Sierra Industries Inc Garner Municipal Airport 122 Howard Langford Dr	Uvalde	TX	78802	**888-835-9377**	830-278-4381	25
Sierra Instruments Inc 5 Harris Ct Bldg L	Monterey	CA	93940	**800-866-0200**	831-373-0200	200
Sierra Insurance Group 2716 N Tenaya Way 6th Fl	Las Vegas	NV	89128	**800-230-3904**	702-838-8244	384-4
Sierra Legal Defense Fund 131 Water St Suite 214	Vancouver	BC	V6B4M3	**800-926-7744**	604-685-5618	48-13
Sierra Nevada Stage Lines 2050 Glendale Ave	Sparks	NV	89431	**800-822-6009**	775-331-2877	108
Sierra NV Healthcare Systems (VA Medical Center) 1000 Locust St	Reno	NV	89502	**888-838-6256**	775-786-7200	366-6
Sierra Office Supply & Printing 4007 Transport St	Palo Alto	CA	94303	**800-433-0282**	650-845-2091	523
Sierra Pacific Power Co 6100 Neil Rd	Reno	NV	89511	**800-962-0399**	775-834-4011	774
Sierra Pacific Resources 6226 W Sahara Ave *NYSE: SRP*	Las Vegas	NV	89146	**800-331-3134**	702-367-5000	355-5
Sierra Royale All Suite Hotel 6300 Rue Marielyne	San Antonio	TX	78238	**800-289-2444**	210-647-0041	373
Sierra Tucson Inc 39580 S Lago Del Oro Pkwy	Tucson	AZ	85739	**800-842-4487**	520-624-4000	712
Sierra Ventures 2884 Sand Hill Rd Suite 100	Menlo Park	CA	94025	**800-819-9665**	650-854-1000	779
SIG Mfg Co Inc 401 S Front St *Sales	Montezuma	IA	50171	**800-247-5008***	641-623-5154	750
SIGARMS Inc 18 Industrial Dr *Orders	Exeter	NH	03833	**800-325-3693***	603-772-2302	279
Sigco Sun Products Inc PO Box 331	Breckenridge	MN	56520	**800-654-4145**	218-643-8467	291-11
SIGCOM 4230 Beechwood Dr	Greensboro	NC	27410	**877-474-4266**	336-547-9700	174
Sigma-Aldrich Chemical Co 3050 Spruce St *Sales	Saint Louis	MO	63103	**800-325-3010***	314-771-5765	142
Sigma-Aldrich Corp 3050 Spruce St *NASDAQ: SIAL*	Saint Louis	MO	63103	**800-325-3010**	314-771-5765	143
Sigma Alpha Epsilon Fraternity (SAE) 1856 Sheridan Rd	Evanston	IL	60201	**800-233-1856**	847-475-1856	48-16
Sigma Alpha Mu Fraternity 9245 N Meridian St Suite 105	Indianapolis	IN	46260	**888-369-9361**	317-846-0600	48-16
Sigma Coatings USA 1401 Destrehan Ave	Harvey	LA	70058	**800-221-7978**	504-347-4321	540
Sigma Design 5521 Jackson St *Sales	Alexandria	LA	71303	**888-990-0900***	318-449-9900	176-8
Sigma Designs Inc 1221 California Cir *NASDAQ: SIGM* ■ *Sales	Milpitas	CA	95035	**800-845-8086***	408-262-9003	686
Sigma Electronics Inc 1027 Commercial Ave	East Petersburg	PA	17520	**866-569-2681**	717-569-2681	252
Sigma Environmental Services Inc 1300 W Canal St	Milwaukee	WI	53233	**800-732-4671**	414-643-4200	653
Sigma Phi Epsilon Fraternity 310 S Boulevard	Richmond	VA	23220	**800-313-1901**	804-353-1901	48-16
Sigma Pi Fraternity PO Box 1897	Brentwood	TN	37024	**888-744-6274**		48-16
Sigma Systems Inc 201 Boston Post Rd Suite 201	Marlborough	MA	01752	**888-867-4462**	508-357-6300	707
Sigma Theta Tau International 550 W North St	Indianapolis	IN	46202	**888-634-7575**	317-634-8171	48-16
Sigma Xi Scientific Research Society PO Box 13975	Research Triangle Park	NC	27709	**800-243-6534**	919-549-4691	48-16
Sign Assn. International 707 N Saint Asaph St	Alexandria	VA	22314	**888-472-7446**	703-836-4012	49-4
Sign Builders Inc 4800 Jefferson Ave PO Box 28380	Birmingham	AL	35221	**800-222-7330**		692
Sign Designs Inc 204 Campus Way	Modesto	CA	95350	**800-421-7446**	209-524-4484	692
Sign Resource Inc 6135 District Blvd	Maywood	CA	90270	**800-423-4283**	323-771-2098	692
Sign*A*Rama 1801 S Australian Ave	West Palm Beach	FL	33409	**800-286-8671**	561-640-5570	692
Signal Assn. International Municipal 165 E Union St PO Box 539	Newark	NY	14513	**800-723-4672**	315-331-2182	49-7
Signal Communications Inc 6555 NW 9th Ave Suite 108	Fort Lauderdale	FL	33309	**800-400-3220**	954-493-6363	691
Signal Magazine 4400 Fair Lakes Ct	Fairfax	VA	22033	**800-336-4583**	703-631-6100	449-5
Signal Processing Society. IEEE IEEE Operations Ctr 445 Hoes Ln	Piscataway	NJ	08854	**800-678-4333**	732-981-0060	49-19
Signalert Corp 150 Great Neck Rd Suite 301	Great Neck	NY	11021	**800-829-6229**	516-829-6444	393
Signature Bank 565 5th Ave *NYSE: SBNY*	New York	NY	10017	**866-744-5463**	646-822-1500	71
Signature Flight Support 201 S Orange Ave Suite 1100	Orlando	FL	32801	**800-428-5597**	407-648-7200	63
Signature Graphics Inc 1000 Signature Dr	Porter	IN	46304	**800-356-3235**	219-926-4994	338
Signature Group 200 N Martingale Rd	Schaumburg	IL	60173	**800-621-0393**	847-605-3000	384-4
Signature Inn 8 Perimeter Ctr E Suite 8050	Atlanta	GA	30346	**800-822-5252**	770-901-9020	369
Signature Services Corp 2705 Hawes Ave	Dallas	TX	75235	**800-929-5519**	214-353-2661	294
Signature Works Inc 1 Signature Dr	Hazlehurst	MS	39083	**800-647-2468**	601-894-1771	497
Signet Armorlite Inc 130 N Bingham Dr	San Marcos	CA	92069	**800-950-5367**	760-744-4000	531
Signet Marking Devices 3121 Red Hill Ave	Costa Mesa	CA	92626	**800-421-5150**	714-549-0341	459
Signore Inc 55-57 Jefferson St	Ellicottville	NY	14731	**800-828-2808**	716-699-2361	314-1
Signs First PO Box 11569	Memphis	TN	38111	**800-852-2163**	901-682-2264	692
Signs & More in 24 1739 St Marys Ave	Parkersburg	WV	26101	**800-358-2358**	304-424-7446	692
Signs Now Corp 4900 Manatee Ave W Suite 201	Bradenton	FL	34209	**800-356-3373**	941-747-7747	692
Signs by Tomorrow-USA Inc 6460 Dobbin Rd	Columbia	MD	21045	**800-765-7446**	410-992-7192	692
Signtronix Inc 1445 W Sepulveda Blvd	Torrance	CA	90501	**800-729-4853**		692
SIIA (Self-Insurance Institute of America Inc) PO Box 1237	Simpsonville	SC	29681	**800-851-7789**	864-962-2208	49-9
Sika Corp 201 Polito Ave	Lyndhurst	NJ	07071	**800-933-7452**	201-933-8800	143
Silberline Mfg Co Inc 130 Lincoln Dr PO Box B	Tamaqua	PA	18252	**800-348-4824**	570-668-6050	141
Silbrico Corp 6300 River Rd	Hodgkins	IL	60525	**800-323-4287**	708-354-3350	490
Silco Oil Co Inc 181 E 56th Ave Suite 600	Denver	CO	80216	**800-707-4526**	303-292-0500	569
Silent Knight 7550 Meridian Cir Suite 100	Maple Grove	MN	55369	**800-328-0103**	763-493-6400	681
Silgan Plastics Corp 14515 N Outer Forty Suite 210	Chesterfield	MO	63017	**800-274-5426**	314-542-9223	99
Silicon Laboratories Inc 4635 Boston Ln *NASDAQ: SLAB*	Austin	TX	78735	**877-444-3032**	512-416-8500	686
Silicon Valley Staffing 2200 Powell St Suite 510	Emeryville	CA	94608	**877-660-6000**	510-923-9898	707
Sillies Greeting Card Co 14551 Judicial Rd Suite 130	Burnsville	MN	55306	**800-355-9148**	952-892-5666	130
Silver City-Grant County Chamber of Commerce 201 N Hudson St	Silver City	NM	88061	**800-548-9378**	505-538-3785	137
Silver Cloud Inn Seattle-Lake Union 1150 Fairview Ave N	Seattle	WA	98109	**800-330-5812**	206-447-9500	373
Silver Eagle Refining 2355 S 1100 W	Woods Cross	UT	84087	**800-927-9736**	801-298-3211	570
Silver Fox Tours & Motorcoaches 3 Silver Fox Dr	Millbury	MA	01527	**800-342-5998**	508-865-6000	748
Silver King Hotel 1485 Empire Ave	Park City	UT	84060	**800-331-8652**	435-649-5500	373
Silver King Refrigeration Inc 1600 Xenium Ln N	Minneapolis	MN	55441	**800-328-3329**	763-923-2441	650
Silver Lake College 2406 S Alverno Rd	Manitowoc	WI	54220	**800-236-4752**	920-686-6175	163
Silver Lake Cookie Co Inc 141 Freeman Ave	Islip	NY	11751	**800-645-9048**	631-581-4000	291-9
Silver Legacy Resort & Casino 407 N Virginia St	Reno	NV	89501	**800-687-8733**	775-329-4777	133
Silver Line Building Products 1 Silver Line Dr *Sales	North Brunswick	NJ	08902	**800-234-4228***	732-435-1000	232
Silver Palate PO Box 512	Cresskill	NJ	07626	**800-872-5283**	201-568-0110	291-41
Silver Springs 5656 E Silver Springs Blvd	Silver Springs	FL	34488	**888-422-8727**	352-236-2121	32
Silver Springs Citrus Inc 25411 N Mare Ave	Howey in the Hills	FL	34737	**800-940-2277**	352-324-2101	310-2
Silver Star Automotive Group 3905 Auto Mall Dr	Thousand Oaks	CA	91362	**800-995-5175**	805-371-5400	57
Silver Star Meats Inc PO Box 393	McKees Rocks	PA	15136	**800-548-1321**	412-771-5539	291-26
Silver State Industries PO Box 7011	Carson City	NV	89702	**800-648-7578**	775-887-3303	618
Silver State Liquor & Wine Inc 325 E Nugget Ave	Sparks	NV	89431	**800-543-3867**	775-331-3400	82-3
Silver Terrace Nurseries Inc 501 North St	Pescadero	CA	94060	**800-323-5977**	650-879-2110	363
Silverado Resort 1600 Atlas Peak Rd	Napa	CA	94558	**800-532-0500**	707-257-0200	655
Silverado Tours Inc 241 Prado Rd	San Luis Obispo	CA	93401	**800-478-4287**	805-544-7658	748
Silverhawk Aviation Inc 1751 W Kearney Ave	Lincoln	NE	68524	**800-479-5851**	402-475-8600	63
Silverleaf Resorts Inc 1221 Riverbend Dr	Dallas	TX	75247	**800-613-0310**	214-631-1166	738
SilverPlume 4775 Walnut St Suite 2-B	Boulder	CO	80301	**800-677-4442**	303-444-0695	380
Silversea Cruises 110 E Broward Blvd	Fort Lauderdale	FL	33301	**800-722-9955**	954-522-4477	217
SilverStone Group 11516 Miracle Hills Dr Suite 102	Omaha	NE	68154	**800-288-5501**	402-964-5400	383
Silverton Hotel & Casino 3333 Blue Diamond Rd	Las Vegas	NV	89139	**800-588-7711**	702-263-7777	133
Silvertree Hotel 100 Elbert Ln	Snowmass Village	CO	81615	**800-525-9402**	970-923-3520	373
Silvestri Studio Inc 8125 Beach St	Los Angeles	CA	90001	**800-647-8874**	323-277-4420	456
Silvi Concrete Inc 355 Newbold Rd	Fairless Hills	PA	19030	**800-426-6273**	215-295-0777	180
Silvon Software Inc 900 Oakmont Lane Suite 400	Westmont	IL	60559	**800-874-5866**	630-655-3313	176-1
Sima Products Corp 140 Pennsylvania Ave Bldg 5	Oakmont	PA	15139	**800-345-7462**	412-828-3700	52
Simcala Inc PO Box 68	Mount Meigs	AL	36057	**800-321-9828**	334-215-7560	476
Simco Longhorn Leather Co Inc 1800 Daisy St *Cust Svc	Chattanooga	TN	37406	**800-251-6294***	423-624-3331	423
Simco Sales Service of Pennsylvania Inc DBA Jack & Jill Ice Cream Co 3100 Marwin Ave	Bensalem	PA	19020	**800-220-2300**	215-639-2300	292-4
Simi Winery 16275 Healdsburg Ave	Healdsburg	CA	95448	**800-746-4880**	707-433-6981	81-3
SIMKAR Corp 700 Ramona Ave	Philadelphia	PA	19120	**800-523-3602**	215-831-7700	431
Simmons Allied Pet Foods Inc 1450 Hills Pl	Atlanta	GA	30318	**800-241-8504**	404-351-2400	568

Name / Address	City	State	ZIP	Toll-Free	Phone	Class
Simmons-Boardman Publishing Corp 345 Hudson St 12th Fl	New York	NY	10014	**800-895-4389**	212-620-7200	623-9
Simmons College 300 The Fenway	Boston	MA	02115	**800-345-8468**	617-521-2000	163
Simmons First National Corp 501 Main St *NASDAQ: SFNCA*	Pine Bluff	AR	71601	**800-272-2102**	870-541-1000	355-2
Simmons Industries Inc 601 N Hico St	Siloam Springs	AR	72761	**888-831-7007**	479-524-8151	608
Simmons Market Research Bureau Inc 700 W Hillsboro Blvd Bldg 4 Suite 201	Deerfield Beach	FL	33441	**800-999-7672**	954-427-4104	458
Simms Capital Management Inc 55 Railroad Ave	Greenwich	CT	06830	**888-258-6365**	203-252-5700	393
Simon Candy Co 31 N Spruce St	Elizabethtown	PA	17022	**800-367-2441**	717-367-2441	291-8
Simon Foundation for Incontinence PO Box 815	Wilmette	IL	60091	**800-237-4666**	847-864-3913	48-17
Simon Joseph & Sons 2202 E River St	Tacoma	WA	98421	**800-562-8464**	253-272-9364	674
Simon Neil Theatre 250 W 52nd St	New York	NY	10019	**800-755-4000**	212-307-4100	732
Simon Resources Inc 2525 Trenton Ave	Williamsport	PA	17701	**800-822-2001**	570-326-9041	674
Simon & Schuster Inc 1230 Ave of the Americas *Cust Svc	New York	NY	10020	**800-223-2336***	212-698-7000	623-2
Simon & Schuster Interactive 1230 Ave of the Americas	New York	NY	10020	**800-223-2348**	212-698-7000	176-6
Simon Wiesenthal Center 1399 S Roxbury Dr	Los Angeles	CA	90035	**800-900-9036**	310-553-9036	48-8
Simonds International 135 Intervale Rd	Fitchburg	MA	01420	**800-343-1616**	978-343-3731	670
Simoniz USA 201 Boston Tpke	Bolton	CT	06043	**800-227-5536**	860-646-0172	149
Simonsen Industries Inc 500 Hwy 31 E	Quimby	IA	51049	**800-831-4860**	712-445-2211	269
Simonton Court Historic Inn & Cottages 320 Simonton St	Key West	FL	33040	**800-944-2687**	305-294-6386	373
Simple Simon's Pizza 6650 S Lewis St	Tulsa	OK	74136	**800-261-6375**	918-496-1272	657
SimpleTech Inc 3001 Daimler St *NASDAQ: STEC*	Santa Ana	CA	92705	**800-367-7330**	949-476-1180	283
Simplex Inc 1139 N MacArthur Blvd	Springfield	IL	62702	**800-637-8603**	217-525-6995	252
Simplex Industries Inc 1 Simplex Dr	Scranton	PA	18504	**800-233-4233**	570-346-5113	107
SimplexGrinnell Ltd 50 Technology Dr	Westminster	MA	01441	**800-746-7539**	978-731-2500	681
Simplicity Pattern Co Inc 2 Park Ave 12th Fl	New York	NY	10016	**888-588-2700**	212-372-0500	557
Simplot JR Co 999 Main St	Boise	ID	83702	**800-635-5008**	208-336-2110	291-21
Simplot JR Co AgriBusiness Group PO Box 70013	Boise	ID	83707	**800-635-9444**	208-672-2700	276
Simplot JR Co Food Group 6360 S Federal Way	Boise	ID	83716	**800-635-0408**	208-384-8000	291-21
Simply Cruises Inc 3814 Hampton Ave	Saint Louis	MO	63109	**888-367-9398**	314-832-8880	760
Simply Orange Juice Co 2659 Orange Ave	Apopka	FL	32703	**800-871-2653**		291-20
Simpson College 701 N 'C' St	Indianola	IA	50125	**800-362-2454**	515-961-6251	163
Simpson Dura-Vent Inc 877 Cotting Ct	Vacaville	CA	95688	**800-227-7374**	707-446-1786	688
Simpson Housing LP 8110 E Union Ave Suite 200	Denver	CO	80237	**888-330-5951**		639
Simpson Mfg Co Inc 4120 Dublin Blvd Suite 400 *NYSE: SSD*	Dublin	CA	94568	**800-925-5099**	925-560-9000	16
Simpson Strong-Tie Co Inc 4120 Dublin Blvd Suite 400	Dublin	CA	94568	**800-925-5099**	925-560-9000	345
Simpson University 2211 College View Dr	Redding	CA	96003	**800-598-2493**	530-226-4606	163
Sims Bros Inc PO Box 1170	Marion	OH	43301	**800-536-7461**	740-387-9041	674
SIMS Respiratory Support Products 9255 Custom House Plaza Suite L	San Diego	CA	92154	**800-258-5361**	619-710-1000	469
Simtrol Inc 2200 Norcross Pkwy Suite 255	Norcross	GA	30071	**800-423-0769**	770-242-7566	176-12
Simulation Sciences Inc 26561 Rancho Pkwy S	Lake Forest	CA	92630	**800-746-7241**	949-455-8150	176-5
Sinai Hospital of Baltimore 2401 W Belvedere Ave	Baltimore	MD	21215	**800-444-8233**	410-601-9000	366-2
Sinai Samaritan Medical Center 945 N 12th St	Milwaukee	WI	53201	**888-414-7762**	414-219-2000	366-2
Sinclair Marketing 550 E South Temple	Salt Lake City	UT	84102	**800-325-3265**	801-524-2700	569
Sinclair Oil Corp 550 E South Temple	Salt Lake City	UT	84102	**800-552-8695**	801-524-2700	570
Sinclair & Rush Inc 123 Manufacturers Dr	Arnold	MO	63010	**800-827-2277**	636-282-6800	589
Sinco Inc 701 Middle St *Cust Svc	Middletown	CT	06457	**800-243-6753***	860-632-0500	207
Singapore Airlines KrisFlyer 5670 Wilshire Blvd Suite 1900	Los Angeles	CA	90036	**800-742-3333**		27
Singapore Airlines Ltd 5670 Wilshire Blvd 18th Fl	Los Angeles	CA	90036	**800-742-3333**	323-934-8833	26
Singapore Tourism Board 4929 Wilshire Blvd Suite 510	Beverly Hills	CA	90010	**800-283-9595**	323-677-0808	764
Singer Equipment Co Inc 3030 Kutztown Rd	Reading	PA	19605	**800-422-8126**	610-929-8000	295
Singer RJ International Inc 4801 W Jefferson Blvd *Sales	Los Angeles	CA	90016	**800-824-9035***	323-735-1717	444
Singer Sewing Co PO Box 7017	La Vergne	TN	37086	**877-738-9869**	615-213-0880	37
Singing in America. Society for the Preservation & Encouragement of Barber Shop Quartet 7930 Sheridan Rd	Kenosha	WI	53143	**800-876-7464**	262-653-8440	48-18
Singing Hills Resort at Sycuan 3007 Dehesa Rd	El Cajon	CA	92019	**800-457-5568**	619-442-3425	655
Singing News Magazine 330 University Hall Dr	Boone	NC	28607	**800-255-2810**	828-264-3700	449-9
SingleSource Roofing Corp 1200 McKee Ave	McKees Rocks	PA	15136	**800-777-6610**	412-771-8866	188-12
Singleton Seafood Co 5024 Uceta Rd	Tampa	FL	33619	**800-732-3663**	813-241-1500	291-14
Sinton Dairy Foods Co LLC 3801 N Sinton Rd	Colorado Springs	CO	80907	**800-388-4970**	719-633-3821	291-10
Sioux City Convention Center 801 4th St	Sioux City	IA	51101	**800-593-2228**	712-279-4800	204
Sioux City Convention Center/Auditorium/Tourism Bureau 801 4th St	Sioux City	IA	51101	**800-593-2228**	712-279-4800	205
Sioux City Foundry Co 801 Division St	Sioux City	IA	51102	**800-831-0874**	712-252-4181	302
Sioux City Journal 515 Pavonia St	Sioux City	IA	51102	**800-397-3530**	712-293-4300	522-2
Sioux Falls Arena 1201 West Ave N	Sioux Falls	SD	57104	**800-338-3177**	605-367-7288	706
Sioux Falls Construction Co Inc PO Drawer F	Sioux Falls	SD	57101	**800-888-1640**	605-336-1640	187-4
Sioux Falls Convention & Visitors Bureau 200 N Phillips Ave Suite 102	Sioux Falls	SD	57104	**800-333-2072**	605-336-1620	205
Sioux Honey Assn Co-op PO Box 388	Sioux City	IA	51102	**888-270-6956**	712-258-0638	291-24
Sioux-Preme Packing Co PO Box 255	Sioux Center	IA	51250	**800-735-7675**	712-722-2555	465
Sioux Steel Co 196 1/2 E 6th St	Sioux Falls	SD	57104	**800-557-4689**	605-336-1750	269
Sioux Tools Inc 250 Snap-on Dr *Orders	Murphy	NC	28906	**800-722-7290***	828-835-9765	747
Sioux Valley-Southwestern Electric Co-op Inc 47092 SD Hwy 34	Colman	SD	57017	**800-234-1960**	605-534-3535	244
Siouxland Community Blood Bank 1019 Jones St	Sioux City	IA	51102	**800-798-4208**	712-252-4208	90
Sipi Metals Corp 1720 N Elston Ave	Chicago	IL	60622	**800-621-8013**	773-276-0070	476
SIR (Society of Interventional Radiology) 10201 Lee Hwy Suite 500	Fairfax	VA	22030	**800-488-7284**	703-691-1805	49-8
Sir Francis Drake Hotel 450 Powell St	San Francisco	CA	94102	**800-227-5480**	415-392-7755	373
Sir Speedy Inc 26722 Plaza Dr	Mission Viejo	CA	92691	**800-854-8297**	949-348-5000	615
Sirach Capital Management Inc 520 Pike St Suite 2800	Seattle	WA	98101	**800-788-9078**	206-624-3800	393
Sirata Beach Resort & Conference Center 5300 Gulf Blvd	Saint Pete Beach	FL	33706	**866-587-8538**	727-363-5100	655
SIRCHIE Finger Print Laboratories Inc 100 Hunter Pl	Youngsville	NC	27596	**800-356-7311**	919-554-2244	85
Sirenza Microdevices Inc 303 S Technology Ct *NASDAQ: SMDI*	Broomfield	CO	80021	**800-764-6642**	303-327-3030	686
Siris AJ Corp Inc PO Box AV	Paterson	NJ	07509	**800-526-5300**	973-684-7700	597
Sirius Satellite Radio Inc 1221 Ave of the Americas *NASDAQ: SIRI*	New York	NY	10020	**888-539-7474**	212-584-5100	630
Sirius Solution LLC 3700 Buffalo Speedway Suite 1100	Houston	TX	77098	**800-585-1085**	713-888-0488	193
Sirsi Corp 101 Washington St SE *Sales	Huntsville	AL	35801	**800-917-4774***	256-704-7000	176-10
SIRVA Inc 700 Oakmont Ln *NYSE: SIR*	Westmont	IL	60559	**800-234-2788**	630-570-3000	652
SISCOM 100 Arapahoe Ave Suite 2	Boulder	CO	80302	**800-325-6307**	303-449-0442	176-10
Sise Inn 40 Court St	Portsmouth	NH	03801	**877-747-3466**	603-433-1200	373
Siskin Hospital for Physical Rehabilitation 1 Siskin Plaza	Chattanooga	TN	37403	**800-474-7546**	423-634-1200	366-4
Siskin Steel & Supply Co Inc PO Box 1191 *Sales	Chattanooga	TN	37401	**800-756-3671***	423-756-3671	483
Siskiyou Daily News PO Box 129	Yreka	CA	96097	**800-540-5905**	530-842-5777	522-2
Sit 'n Sleep 3853 Overland Ave	Culver City	CA	90232	**800-675-3536**	310-842-6850	316
SITEL Corp 7277 World Communication Dr *NYSE: SWW*	Omaha	NE	68122	**800-225-4858**	402-963-6810	722
Sitex Corp 705 Pennel St	Henderson	KY	42420	**800-278-3537**	270-827-3537	434
Sitka Convention & Visitors Bureau 303 Lincoln St Suite 4	Sitka	AK	99835	**800-557-4852**	907-747-5940	205
Sivaco Wire Group 800 rue Ouellette	Marieville	QC	J3M1P5	**800-876-9473**	450-658-8741	800
Sivananda Ashram Yoga Ranch Budd Rd Box 195	Woodbourne	NY	12788	**800-783-9642**	845-436-6492	697
Sivyer Steel Corp 225 S 33rd St	Bettendorf	IA	52722	**800-474-8937**	563-355-1811	302
Six Flags Fiesta Texas 17000 IH-10 W	San Antonio	TX	78257	**800-473-4378**	210-697-5000	32
Six Flags Kentucky Kingdom 937 Phillips Ln	Louisville	KY	40209	**800-727-3267**	502-366-2231	32
Six Flags New England Route 159 1623 Main St	Agawam	MA	01001	**800-370-7488**	413-786-9300	32
Six L's Packing Co Inc 315 E New Market Rd	Immokalee	FL	34142	**800-554-6606**	239-657-4221	11-11
Six Robblees' Inc 11010 Tukwila International Blvd	Tukwila	WA	98168	**800-275-7499**	206-767-7970	61
Six States Distributors Inc 247 W 1700 South	Salt Lake City	UT	84115	**800-453-5703**	801-488-4666	61
Sixth Avenue Inn 2000 6th Ave	Seattle	WA	98121	**800-648-6440**	206-441-8300	373
Sixth Floor Museum 411 Elm St Dealey Plaza	Dallas	TX	75202	**888-485-4854**	214-747-6660	509
SJ McCullagh Inc 245 Swan St	Buffalo	NY	14204	**800-753-3473**	716-856-3473	291-7
SJE-Rhombus 22650 County Hwy 6 PO Box 1708	Detroit Lakes	MN	56502	**800-746-6287**	218-847-1317	200
SK Hand Tool Corp 3535 W 47th St	Chicago	IL	60632	**800-822-5575**	773-523-1300	746
Skagen Designs Inc 640 Maestro Dr Suite 100	Reno	NV	89511	**800-937-3576**	775-850-5500	151
Skaggs Cos 3828 S Main St	Murray	UT	84115	**800-879-1787**	801-261-4400	667
Skagit Valley Casino Resort 5984 N Darrk Ln	Bow	WA	98232	**877-275-2448**	360-724-7777	133
Skagit Valley College 2405 E College Way	Mount Vernon	WA	98273	**877-385-5360**	360-416-7600	160
Skagit Valley Herald PO Box 578	Mount Vernon	WA	98273	**800-683-3300**	360-424-3251	522-2
Skagway Convention & Visitors Bureau 245 Broadway PO Box 1025	Skagway	AK	99840	**888-762-1898**	907-983-2854	205
Skandia US Holding Corp 1 Corporate Dr Tower 1	Shelton	CT	06484	**800-628-6039**	203-926-1888	355-4
Skate Canada Hall of Fame 865 Shefford Rd	Ottowa	ON	K1J1H9	**877-211-2372**	613-747-1007	511

Name / Address	City	State	ZIP	Toll-Free	Phone	Class
SKB Corp 434 W Levers Pl	Orange	CA	92867	**800-410-2024**	714-637-1252	444
Skechers USA Inc 228 Manhattan Beach Blvd Suite 200 *NYSE: SKX*	Manhattan Beach	CA	90266	**800-456-3627**	310-318-3100	296
Skeeter Products Inc 1 Skeeter Rd	Kilgore	TX	75662	**800-753-3837**	903-984-0541	91
Skeleton Federation. US Bobsled & 196 Old Military Rd	Lake Placid	NY	12946	**800-262-7533**	518-523-1842	48-22
SKF USA Inc 1111 Adams Ave	Norristown	PA	19403	**800-440-4753**	610-630-2800	609
Ski Areas Assn. Cross Country 259 Bolton Rd	Winchester	NH	03470	**877-779-2754**	603-239-4341	48-22
Ski Magazine 2 Park Ave	New York	NY	10016	**800-227-2224**	212-779-5000	449-20
Ski-Pak Inc PO Box 30085	Seattle	WA	98113	**800-446-4688**	206-729-8200	760
Skiing Magazine 2 Park Ave	New York	NY	10016	**800-227-2224**	212-779-5000	449-20
SkillPath Seminars 6900 Squibb Rd	Shawnee Mission	KS	66202	**800-873-7545**	913-362-3900	753
SkillSoft PLC 107 Northeastern Blvd *NASDAQ: SKIL*	Nashua	NH	03062	**877-545-5763**	603-324-3000	753
SkillsUSA-VICA Inc PO Box 3000 *Orders	Leesburg	VA	20177	**800-321-8422***	703-777-8810	48-11
Skin Cancer Foundation 245 5th Ave Suite 1403	New York	NY	10016	**800-754-6490**	212-725-5176	48-17
Skinner Valve Div Parker Hannifin Corp 95 Edgewood Ave	New Britain	CT	06051	**800-825-8305**	860-827-2300	777
SklarPeppler Furniture Corp 617 Victoria St E	Whitby	ON	L1N5S7	**800-263-2607**	905-619-6523	314-2
Skuttle Mfg Co 101 Margaret St	Marietta	OH	45750	**800-848-9786**	740-373-9169	15
Sky Bright Inc 65 Aviation Dr	Gilford	NH	03246	**800-639-6012**	603-528-6818	63
Sky High Red Rock Balloon Adventures 105 Canyon Diablo	Sedona	AZ	86351	**800-258-3754**	928-284-0040	748
Sky Hotel 709 E Durant Ave	Aspen	CO	81611	**800-882-2582**	970-925-6760	373
Sky Publishing Corp 49 Bay State Rd	Cambridge	MA	02138	**800-253-0245**	617-864-7360	623-9
Sky & Telescope Magazine 49 Bay State Rd	Cambridge	MA	02138	**800-253-0245**	617-864-7360	449-19
Sky Ute Casino 14826 Hwy 172 N	Ignacio	CO	81137	**888-842-4180**	970-563-3000	133
Sky Valley Golf Course Resort 696 Sky Valley Way	Sky Valley	GA	30537	**800-437-2416**	706-746-5302	655
Skydance Helicopters 2207 Bellanca St Suite B	Minden	NV	89423	**800-882-1651**	775-782-4040	354
Skylark Meats Inc 4430 S 110th St	Omaha	NE	68137	**800-228-2248**	402-592-0300	465
Skyline Chili Inc 4180 Thunderbird Ln	Fairfield	OH	45014	**800-443-4371**	513-874-1188	657
Skyline Corp 2520 By-Pass Rd *NYSE: SKY*	Elkhart	IN	46514	**800-348-7469**	574-294-6521	120
Skyline Displays Inc 3355 Discovery Rd	Eagan	MN	55121	**800-328-2725**	651-234-6000	230
Skyline Exhibits 3355 Discovery Rd	Eagan	MN	55121	**800-328-2725**	651-234-6000	230
Skyline Hotel 725 10th Ave	New York	NY	10019	**800-433-1982**	212-586-3400	373
SkyMall Inc 1520 E Pima St	Phoenix	AZ	85034	**800-759-6255**	602-254-9777	451
Skyo Industries Inc 171 Brook Ave	Deer Park	NY	11729	**800-645-5535**	631-586-4702	746
Skyservice Airlines Inc 31 Fasken Dr	Etobicoke	ON	M9W1K6	**800-701-9448**	416-679-5700	14
SkyStream Networks Inc 455 DeGuigne Dr *Cust Svc	Sunnyvale	CA	94085	**877-475-9787***	408-616-3300	633
SkyTech Inc Martin State Airport 701 Wilson Point Rd Hanger 3	Baltimore	MD	21220	**888-386-3596**	410-574-4144	759
SkyTech Inc 550 Airport Rd	Rock Hill	SC	29732	**888-386-3596**	803-366-5108	63
SkyTel Communications Inc 550 Clinton Ctr Dr *Cust Svc	Clinton	MS	39056	**800-759-8737***	601-944-1300	721
Skytop Lodge 1 Skytop	Skytop	PA	18357	**800-345-7759**	570-595-7401	655
Skyworks Solutions Inc 20 Sylvan Rd *NASDAQ: SWKS* ■ *Sales	Woburn	MA	01801	**800-411-3619***	781-935-5150	686
Skyy Spirits Inc 1 Beach St Suite 300	San Francisco	CA	94133	**800-367-7599**	415-315-8000	81-1
Slack Inc 6900 Grove Rd	Thorofare	NJ	08086	**800-257-8290**	856-848-1000	623-9
Slade Gorton Co Inc 4433 W 42nd Pl	Chicago	IL	60632	**800-524-8237**	773-927-2400	292-5
Slade's Ferry Bancorp 100 Slade's Ferry Ave *NASDAQ: SFBC*	Somerset	MA	02726	**800-643-7537**	508-675-2121	355-2
Slant Fin Corp 100 Forest Dr	Greenvale	NY	11548	**800-775-4552**	516-484-2600	15
Slavery Group Inc. American Anti- 198 Tremont St Suite 421	Boston	MA	02116	**800-884-0719**	617-426-8161	48-5
Sledd Charles M Co 100 E Cove Ext	Wheeling	WV	26003	**800-333-0374**	304-243-1820	744
Sleep Inn & Suites 10750 Columbia Pike	Silver Spring	MD	20901	**800-424-6423**	301-592-5000	369
Sleepmaster Products Co LP 2001 Lower Rd	Linden	NJ	07036	**800-524-0856**	908-986-5000	463
Sleepy's Inc 175 Central Ave S	Bethpage	NY	11714	**800-753-3797**	516-844-8800	316
Slender Lady Inc 45 NE Loop 410 Suite 500	San Antonio	TX	78216	**888-227-8187**	210-877-1500	797
Slickbar Products Corp 18 Beach St	Seymour	CT	06483	**800-322-2666**	203-888-7700	793
SlickEdit Inc 3000 Aerial Center Pkwy Suite 120	Morrisville	NC	27560	**800-934-3348**	919-473-0070	176-2
Slidell Area (Greater) Chamber of Commerce 118 W Hall Ave	Slidell	LA	70460	**800-471-3758**	985-643-5678	137
Slidell Inc 2355 Lemond Rd PO Box 710	Owatonna	MN	55060	**800-298-3990**	507-451-0365	537
Slim-Fast Foods Co 777 S Flagler Dr Suite 1400	West Palm Beach	FL	33401	**877-375-4632**	561-833-9920	291-11
Slippery Rock University	Slippery Rock	PA	16057	**800-020-4778**	724-730-9000	103
SLM Corp 12061 Bluemont Way *NYSE: SLM*	Reston	VA	20190	**888-272-5543**	703-810-3000	215
SLM Mfg Corp 215 Davidson Ave	Somerset	NJ	08873	**800-526-3708**	732-469-7500	589
Sloan Implement Co 120 N Business 51	Assumption	IL	62510	**800-745-4020**	217-226-4411	270
Sloan Management Review 77 Massachusetts Ave E60-100	Cambridge	MA	02139	**800-876-5764**	617-253-7170	449-5
Sloan Valve Co 10500 Seymour Ave	Franklin Park	IL	60131	**800-982-5839**	847-671-4300	598
Sloans Lake Managed Care Inc 6501 S Fiddler's Green Cir Suite 300	Greenwood Village	CO	80111	**800-850-2249**	303-691-2200	384-3
Slocomb Industries Inc 801 Pencader Dr	Newark	DE	19702	**800-348-6233**	302-266-7101	233
Slope Electric Co-op Inc 116 E 12th St	New England	ND	58647	**800-559-4191**	701-579-4191	244
Slosman Corp 100 Fairview Rd	Asheville	NC	28803	**800-544-9387**	828-274-2100	730-8
Slovak Society of the USA. National 351 Valley Brook Rd	McMurray	PA	15317	**800-488-1890**	724-731-0094	48-14
SLS (Society of Laparoendoscopic Surgeons) 7330 SW 62nd Pl Suite 410	South Miami	FL	33143	**800-446-2659**	305-665-9959	49-8
Sludge Newsletter 8737 Colesville Rd Suite 1100	Silver Spring	MD	20910	**800-274-6737**	301-587-6300	521-5
Slush Puppie Frozen Drink Div of Dr Pepper/Seven-Up Inc PO Box 869077	Plano	TX	75086	**800-527-7096**		291-15
Slutsky Jeff Street Fighter Marketing Inc 467 Waterbury Ct	Gahanna	OH	43230	**800-758-8759**	614-337-7474	561
Sly Inc 8300 Dow Cir	Strongsville	OH	44136	**800-334-2957**	440-891-3200	19
SM Arnold Inc 7901 Michigan Ave *Cust Svc	Saint Louis	MO	63111	**800-325-7865***	314-544-4103	104
SM Consulting Inc 1306 Concourse Dr Suite 200	Linthicum	MD	21090	**888-476-2937**	410-691-5200	178
SMA (Southern Medical Assn) 35 Lakeshore Dr	Birmingham	AL	35209	**800-423-4992**	205-945-1840	49-8
Small Business Administration (SBA) 409 3rd St SW	Washington	DC	20416	**800-827-5722**	202-205-6600	336-16
Small Business Assn. National 1156 15th St NW Suite 1100	Washington	DC	20005	**800-345-6720**	202-393-0030	49-12
Small Businesses Assn. American 206 E College St Suite 201B	Grapevine	TX	76051	**800-942-2722**	817-488-8770	49-12
Small Planet Foods 719 Metcalf St	Sedro Woolley	WA	98284	**800-624-4123**	360-855-0100	291-18
Small Precision Tools Inc 1330 Clegg St	Petaluma	CA	94954	**800-346-4927**	707-765-4545	685
SMART (Special Military Active Retired Travel Club) 600 University Office Blvd Suite 1A	Pensacola	FL	32504	**800-354-7681**		48-23
Smart Card Alert Newsletter 300 S Wacker Dr Suite 1800	Chicago	IL	60606	**800-535-8403**	312-913-1334	521-1
Smart Card Alliance Inc 191 Clarkville Rd	Princeton Junction	NJ	08550	**800-556-6828**	609-799-5654	49-2
Smart Card Solutions LLC 229 E Capitol Dr	Hartland	WI	53029	**888-225-6442**	262-369-3400	176-12
Smart City Networks 3720 Howard Hughes Pkwy Suite 190	Las Vegas	NV	89109	**888-446-6911**	702-943-6000	721
Smart Document Solutions 120 Bluegrass Valley Pkwy	Alpharetta	GA	30005	**800-367-1500**	770-360-1700	239
Smart & Final Foodservice Distributors Inc 4343 E Fremont St	Stockton	CA	95215	**800-336-6200**	209-948-1814	292-8
Smart & Final Inc 600 Citadel Dr *NYSE: SMF*	Commerce	CA	90040	**800-894-0511**	323-869-7500	339
Smart Industries Corp 1626 Delaware Ave	Des Moines	IA	50317	**800-553-2442**	515-265-9900	317
SMART Modular Technologies Inc 4211 Starboard Dr	Fremont	CA	94538	**800-956-7627**	510-623-1231	613
Smart Online Inc PO Box 12794	Research Triangle Park	NC	27709	**800-578-9000**	919-765-5000	39
SMART Technologies Inc 1207 11th Ave SW Suite 300	Calgary	AB	T3C0M5	**888-427-6278**	403-245-0333	171-1
SmartCertify Direct 25400 US Hwy 19N Suite 285 *Orders	Clearwater	FL	33763	**800-653-4933***	727-724-8994	176-3
SmartDM Inc 822 Airpark Ctr Dr	Nashville	TN	37217	**888-816-0925**	615-850-3000	5
SmarterKids.com Inc 2 Lower Ragsdale Rd Suite 200	Monterey	CA	93940	**800-293-9314**	831-333-2000	749
SmarTire Systems Inc 13151 Vanier Pl Suite 150 *NASDAQ: SMTR*	Richmond	BC	V5V2J1	**888-982-3001**	604-276-9884	60
SmartMoney Magazine 250 W 55th St	New York	NY	10019	**800-444-4204**	212-765-7323	449-11
SMARTpages.com PO Box 567	Saint Louis	MO	63188	**877-647-6278**		677
SmarTrunk Systems Inc 401 W 35th St Bldg B	National City	CA	91950	**866-870-9052**	619-426-6440	720
SMARTS (System Management ARTS Inc) 44 S Broadway	White Plains	NY	10601	**877-276-2787**	914-948-6200	176-1
SmartStyle Div Regis Corp 7201 Metro Blvd	Minneapolis	MN	55439	**888-888-7778**	952-947-7777	79
Smash Hit Subs 2930 W Maple St	Sioux Falls	SD	57107	**800-648-6227**	605-336-6961	657
SMC (Save the Manatee Club) 500 N Maitland Ave	Maitland	FL	32751	**800-432-5646**	407-539-0990	48-3
SMC Networks Inc 38 Tesla	Irvine	CA	92618	**800-762-4968**	949-679-8000	174
SMC Pneumatics Inc 3011 N Franklin Rd	Indianapolis	IN	46226	**800-762-7621**	317-899-4440	777
SME (Society of Manufacturing Engineers) 1 SME Dr	Dearborn	MI	48121	**800-733-4763**	313-271-1500	49-13
SME (Society for Mining Metallurgy & Exploration Inc) 8307 Shaffer Pkwy	Littleton	CO	80127	**800-763-3132**	303-973-9550	49-13
Smead Mfg Co 600 Smead Blvd *Cust Svc	Hastings	MN	55033	**888-737-6323***	651-437-4111	550
SMI Rebar of North Carolina 2528 N Chester St	Gastonia	NC	28052	**800-476-6975**	704-865-8571	471
SMI Steel Alabama 101 S 50th St	Birmingham	AL	35212	**800-621-0262**	205-592-8981	709
Smidth FL Inc 2040 Ave C	Bethlehem	PA	18017	**800-523-9482**	610-264-6011	462
Smile Train Inc 245 5th Ave Suite 2201	New York	NY	10016	**877-543-7645**	212-689-9199	48-5
Smith Air Compressors 1761 Genesis Dr	La Porte	IN	46350	**800-635-6587**	219-324-7776	170
Smith AO Corp 11270 W Park Pl Suite 170 *NYSE: AOS*	Milwaukee	WI	53224	**800-359-4065**	414-359-4000	507
Smith AO Water Products Co 500 Lindahl Pkwy	Ashland City	TN	37015	**800-365-8170**	615-792-4371	36
Smith Barney 388 Greenwich St 16th Fl	New York	NY	10013	**800-221-3636**		679
Smith Barney Asset Management 300 1st Stamford Pl	Stamford	CT	06902	**888-772-9996**		397
Smith Barney Family of Funds PO Box 9699	Providence	RI	02940	**800-451-2010**		517
Smith & Butterfield Co Inc 2800 Lynch Rd	Evansville	IN	47711	**800-321-6543**	812-422-3261	524
Smith Charles E Corporate Living 400 15th St S	Arlington	VA	22202	**888-234-7829**	703-920-9550	209

Name / Address	City	State	ZIP	Toll-Free	Phone	Class
Smith Co 4455 Connecticut Ave NW Suite 600B	Washington	DC	20008	**800-895-0999**	202-895-0900	722
Smith Dairy 1381 Dairy Ln	Orrville	OH	44667	**800-776-7076**	330-683-8710	291-27
Smith Dairy Wayne Div 1590 NW 11th St	Richmond	IN	47375	**800-875-9296**	765-935-7521	291-27
Smith Dray Line 320 Frontage Rd	Greenville	SC	29611	**800-327-5673**	864-269-3696	508
Smith ED & Sons Ltd 944 Hwy 8	Winona	ON	L8E5S3	**800-263-9246**	905-643-1211	291-20
Smith-Edwards-Dunlap Co 2867 E Allegheny Ave	Philadelphia	PA	19134	**800-829-0020**	215-425-8800	614
Smith Equipment Mfg Co 2601 Lockheed Ave *Cust Svc	Watertown	SD	57201	**800-328-3363***	605-882-3200	798
Smith LE Glass Co 1900 Liberty St	Mount Pleasant	PA	15666	**800-537-6484**	724-547-3544	330
Smith Graham & Co 600 Travis St Suite 6900	Houston	TX	77002	**800-739-4470**	713-227-1100	393
Smith & Hawken Inc 4 Hamilton Landing Suite 100	Novato	CA	94949	**800-776-5558**	415-506-3700	318
Smith HC Ltd 20600 Chagrin Blvd Tower East Suite 200	Shaker Heights	OH	44122	**800-442-7583**	216-752-9966	262
Smith HD Wholesale Drug Co 4650 Industrial Dr	Springfield	IL	62703	**800-252-8090**	217-529-0211	237
Smith International Inc PO Box 60068 *NYSE: SII*	Houston	TX	77205	**800-877-6484**	281-443-3370	526
Smith-Lee Co Inc 537 Fitch St	Oneida	NY	13421	**800-448-3363**	315-363-2500	544
Smith Litho 1029 E Gude Dr	Rockville	MD	20850	**800-622-2577**	301-424-1400	615
Smith McDonald Corp 304 Sonwil Dr	Buffalo	NY	14225	**800-753-8548**	716-684-7200	597
Smith Mfg Co DBA Aero-Fast Bicycle Co PO Box 3812	Jacksonville	FL	32206	**800-656-2376**	904-354-3339	83
Smith Micro Software Inc 51 Columbia Suite 200 *NASDAQ: SMSI*	Aliso Viejo	CA	92656	**800-964-7674**	949-362-5800	176-7
Smith & Nephew Inc 1450 E Brooks Rd *Cust Svc	Memphis	TN	38116	**800-238-7538***	901-396-2121	469
Smith & Nephew Inc Endoscopy Div 150 Minuteman Rd	Andover	MA	01810	**800-343-8386**	978-749-1000	468
Smith & Nephew Inc Orthopaedic Div 1450 Brooks Rd	Memphis	TN	38116	**800-821-5700**	901-396-2121	469
Smith & Nephew Inc Wound Management Div 11775 Starkey Rd *Cust Svc	Largo	FL	33773	**800-876-1261***	727-392-1261	469
Smith NF & Assoc LP 5306 Hollister Rd	Houston	TX	77040	**800-468-7866**	713-430-3000	245
Smith Pipe & Steel Inc 735 N 19th Ave *Cust Svc	Phoenix	AZ	85009	**800-352-4596***	602-257-9494	483
Smith Protective Services Inc 8918 John W Carpenter Fwy	Dallas	TX	75247	**800-634-1381**	214-631-4444	682
Smith Ranch Homes 500 Deer Valley Rd *Mktg	San Rafael	CA	94903	**800-772-6264***	415-492-4900	659
Smith RC Co 14200 Southcross Dr W	Burnsville	MN	55306	**800-747-7648**	952-854-0711	281
Smith & Sons Foods Inc 2124 Riverside Dr	Macon	GA	31204	**800-841-5385**	478-745-4759	656
Smith TM Tool International Corp PO Box 1065	Mount Clemens	MI	48046	**800-521-4894**	586-468-1465	484
Smith & Wesson Academy 299 Page Blvd	Springfield	MA	01104	**800-331-0852**	413-846-6461	754
Smith & Wesson Corp 2100 Roosevelt Ave *Cust Svc	Springfield	MA	01104	**800-331-0852***	413-781-8300	279
Smith & Wesson Holding Corp 2100 Roosevelt Ave *AMEX: SWB*	Springfield	MA	01104	**800-331-0852**	413-781-8300	279
Smith William A Construction Co Inc 6060 Armour Dr	Houston	TX	77020	**800-925-5011**	713-673-6208	187-8
Smith XS Inc PO Box X	Red Bank	NJ	07701	**800-631-2226**	732-222-4600	106
Smithereen Exterminators Inc 3451 Church St	Evanston	IL	60203	**800-336-3500**	847-675-0010	567
Smithfield Foods Inc 200 Commerce St *NYSE: SFD*	Smithfield	VA	23430	**800-276-6158**	757-365-3000	465
Smithfield Ham & Products Co Inc 401 N Church St	Smithfield	VA	23430	**800-628-2242**	757-357-2121	291-26
Smithfield Packing Co Inc 501 N Church St	Smithfield	VA	23430	**800-444-9180**	757-357-4321	465
Smiths Detection 30 Hook Mountain Rd	Pine Brook	NJ	07058	**800-536-2277**	973-830-2100	410
Smith's Food & Drug Centers Inc 1550 S Redwood Rd	Salt Lake City	UT	84104	**800-444-8081**	801-974-1400	339
Smiths Medical ASD Inc 160 Weymouth St	Rockland	MA	02370	**800-553-8351**	781-878-8011	469
Smiths Medical ASD Inc 10 Bowman Dr	Keene	NH	03431	**800-258-5361**	603-352-3812	469
Smiths Medical PM Inc N7 W22025 Johnson Rd *Cust Svc	Waukesha	WI	53186	**800-558-2345***	262-542-3100	249
Smithsonian Air & Space Magazine 750 9th St NW Suite 7100 *Cust Svc	Washington	DC	20560	**800-766-2149***	202-275-1230	449-19
Smithsonian Folkways Recordings 750 9th St NW Suite 4100	Washington	DC	20560	**800-410-9815**	202-275-1143	643
Smithsonian Institution 1000 Jefferson Dr SW	Washington	DC	20560	**800-766-2149**	202-357-2700	509
Smithsonian Magazine 750 9th St NW Suite 7100	Washington	DC	20001	**800-766-2149**	202-275-2000	449-11
Smithway Motor Xpress Inc 2031 Quail Ave *NASDAQ: SMXC*	Fort Dodge	IA	50501	**800-247-4972**	515-576-7418	769
SMO (Southern Maryland Oil Co Inc) 6355 Crain Hwy	La Plata	MD	20646	**800-492-3420**	301-932-3600	569
Smock Fansler Corp 2910 W Minnesota St	Indianapolis	IN	46241	**800-281-6605**	317-248-8371	188-3
Smokeless Tobacco Council 1627 K St NW Suite 700	Washington	DC	20006	**800-272-7144**	202-452-1252	48-2
Smokey Bones BBQ 5900 Lake Ellenor Dr	Orlando	FL	32809	**800-421-3035**	407-245-4000	657
Smoky Mountain Visitors Bureau 7906 E Lamar Alexander Pkwy	Townsend	TN	37882	**800-525-6834**	865-448-6134	205
Smoky Shadows Motel 4215 Parkway	Pigeon Forge	TN	37863	**800-282-2121**	865-453-7155	373
Smooth-On Inc 2000 Saint John St	Easton	PA	18042	**800-766-6841**	610-252-5800	43
Smoothie King Franchises Inc 2400 Veterans Blvd Suite 110	Kenner	LA	70062	**800-577-4200**	504-467-4006	350
SMPS (Society for Marketing Professional Services) 99 Canal Center Plaza Suite 330	Alexandria	VA	22314	**800-292-7677**	703-549-6117	49-18
SMR Technologies Inc 93 Nettie Fenwick Rd	Fenwick	WV	26202	**800-767-6899**	304-846-2554	663
SMS Data Products Group Inc 1501 Farm Credit Dr	McLean	VA	22102	**800-331-1767**	703-709-9898	178
Smucker JM Co 1 Strawberry Ln *NYSE: SJM*	Orrville	OH	44667	**888-550-9555**	330-682-3000	291-20
Smuggler's Inn 6350 E Speedway Blvd	Tucson	AZ	85710	**800-525-8852**	520-296-3292	373
Smugglers' Notch Resort 4323 Vermont Rt 108 S	Jeffersonville	VT	05464	**800-451-8752**	802-644-8851	655
Smulekoff's Fine Home Furnishings PO Box 74090	Cedar Rapids	IA	52407	**888-384-6995**	319-362-2181	316
Smurfit-Stone Container Corp 150 N Michigan Ave 17th Fl *NASDAQ: SSCC*	Chicago	IL	60601	**877-772-2999**	312-346-6600	101
SMW (Society of Military Widows) 5535 Hempstead Way	Springfield	VA	22151	**800-842-3451**	703-750-1342	48-19
Smyth Cos Inc 1085 Snelling Ave N	Saint Paul	MN	55180	**800-642-4544**	651-646-4544	404
Smyth Jewelers 29 Greenmeadow Dr	Timonium	MD	21093	**800-638-3333**	410-252-6666	402
Smyth Systems Inc 7100 Whipple Ave NW	North Canton	OH	44720	**800-767-6984**	330-499-6392	176-9
Snack Food Assn 1711 King St Suite 1	Alexandria	VA	22314	**800-628-1334**	703-836-4500	49-6
Snake River Lodge & Spa 7710 Granite Loop Rd	Teton Village	WY	83025	**800-445-4655**	307-733-3657	655
SNAP (Survivors Network of Those Abused by Priests) PO Box 6416	Chicago	IL	60680	**877-409-2720**	312-409-2720	48-21
Snap-on Credit Corp 1125 Tri-State Pkwy Suite 700	Gurnee	IL	60031	**877-777-8455**	847-782-7700	214
Snap-on Diagnostics 420 Barclay Blvd	Lincolnshire	IL	60069	**800-967-8030**	847-478-0700	247
Snap-on Inc ATI Tools Div 2425 Vineyard Ave	Escondido	CA	92029	**800-284-4460**	760-746-8301	746
Snap-Tite Autoclave Engineers Div 8325 Hessinger Dr	Erie	PA	16509	**800-458-0409**	814-838-5700	92
Snap-Tite Inc 8325 Hessinger Dr	Erie	PA	16509	**800-458-0409**	814-838-5700	584
Snapper Inc 535 Macon St *Cust Svc	McDonough	GA	30253	**800-935-2967***	770-957-9141	420
Snapple Beverage Corp 709 Westchester Ave	White Plains	NY	10604	**800-964-7842**		81-2
Snappy Air Distribution Products 1011 11th Ave SE	Detroit Lakes	MN	56501	**800-328-2044**	218-847-9258	447
Snappy Tomato Pizza Co 7230 Turfway Rd	Florence	KY	41042	**888-463-7627**	859-525-4680	657
SNC Mfg Co Inc 101 W Waukau Ave	Oshkosh	WI	54902	**800-558-3325**	920-231-7370	252
SNE Enterprises Inc 888 Southview Dr	Mosinee	WI	54455	**800-826-1707**	715-693-7000	234
Snell House 21 Atlantic Ave	Bar Harbor	ME	04609	**866-763-5524**	207-288-8004	373
Snell & Wilmer LLP 400 E Van Buren St 1 Arizona Ctr	Phoenix	AZ	85004	**800-322-0430**	602-382-6000	419
Snelling Personnel Services 12801 N Central Expy Suite 700	Dallas	TX	75243	**800-766-5556**	972-239-7575	707
Snelson Co Inc 601 W State St	Sedro Woolley	WA	98284	**800-624-6536**	360-856-6511	187-10
Snokist Growers Co-op PO Box 1587	Yakima	WA	98907	**800-258-0470**	509-453-5631	292-7
Snow College 150 E College Ave *PR	Ephraim	UT	84627	**800-848-3399***	435-283-7000	160
Snow King Resort 400 E Snow King Ave PO Box SKI	Jackson	WY	83001	**800-522-5464**	307-733-5200	655
Snow & Nealley Co PO Box 876	Bangor	ME	04402	**800-933-6642**	207-947-6642	746
Snowbird Mountain Lodge 4633 Santeetlah Rd	Robbinsville	NC	28771	**800-941-9290**	828-479-3433	373
Snowbird Ski & Summer Resort Hwy 210 PO Box 929000	Snowbird	UT	84092	**800-453-3000**	801-742-2222	655
Snowboarder Magazine PO Box 1028 *Orders	Dana Point	CA	92629	**800-955-9120***	949-496-5922	449-20
Snowdance LLC PO Box 699	Brownsville	VT	05037	**800-243-0011**	802-484-7000	369
Snowmass Club PO Box G-2	Snowmass Village	CO	81615	**800-525-0710**	970-923-5600	655
Snowmass Conference Center 76 Elbert Ln	Snowmass Village	CO	81615	**800-598-2006**	970-923-2000	370
Snowmass Resort Assn & Convention Center 38 Snowmass Village Upper Mall PO Box 5566	Snowmass Village	CO	81615	**800-598-2006**	970-923-2000	205
Snowmobile Magazine 6420 Sycamore Ln Suite 100 *Cust Svc	Maple Grove	MN	55369	**800-848-6247***	763-383-4400	449-20
Snow's Cards & Gifts 1609 1st Ave S	Birmingham	AL	35233	**800-937-6697**	205-322-1397	129
Snow's/Doxsee Inc 994 Ocean Dr	Cape May	NJ	08204	**800-459-0396**	609-884-0440	291-13
Snowshoe Mountain Resort 10 Snowshoe Dr	Snowshoe	WV	26209	**877-441-4386**	304-572-1000	655
Snowy Owl Inn 4 Village Rd	Waterville Valley	NH	03215	**800-766-9969**	603-236-8383	373
Snyder of Berlin 1313 Stadium Dr	Berlin	PA	15530	**800-374-7949**	814-267-4641	291-35
Snyder Paper Corp 250 26th St Dr SE	Hickory	NC	28602	**800-222-8562**	828-328-2501	549
Snyder Tom Productions Inc 80 Coolidge Hill Rd	Watertown	MA	02472	**800-342-0236**	617-926-6000	176-3
Snyder Wholesale Tire Co 401 Cadiz Rd	Wintersville	OH	43953	**800-967-8473**	740-264-5543	740
Snyder's of Hanover 1350 York St	Hanover	PA	17331	**800-233-7125**	717-632-4477	291-9
Soap Opera Digest 261 Madison Ave 10th Fl	New York	NY	10016	**800-829-9095**	212-716-2700	449-9
Soap Opera Weekly Magazine 261 Madison Ave 9th Fl	New York	NY	10016	**800-829-9096**	212-716-8400	449-9
SOAR (Sound of America Records) 5200 Constitution NE	Albuquerque	NM	87110	**800-890-7627**	505-268-6110	643

				Toll-Free	Phone	Class
Soaring Eagle Casino & Resort 6800 E Soaring Eagle Blvd	Mount Pleasant	MI	48858	**877-232-4532**	989-775-5777	133
Sobel Westex Inc 2670 Southwestern Ave	Las Vegas	NV	89109	**800-282-3041**	702-735-4973	356
Sobeys Inc 115 King St	Stellarton	NS	B0K1S0	**888-944-0442***	902-752-8371	339
*Cust Svc						
Sobieski Bancorp Inc 105 E Jefferson Blvd Suite 800	South Bend	IN	46601	**888-321-8961**	574-239-7047	355-2
NASDAQ: SOBI						
Soccer Coaches Assn of America. National 6700 Squibb Rd Suite 215	Mission	KS	66202	**800-458-0678**	913-362-1747	48-22
Soccer Federation. US 1801 S Prairie Ave	Chicago	IL	60616	**800-759-9636**	312-808-1300	48-22
Soccer League. Major Indoor 1175 Post Rd E	Westport	CT	06880	**866-647-5638**	203-222-4900	48-22
Soccer Organization. American Youth 12501 S Isis Ave	Hawthorne	CA	90250	**800-872-2976***	310-643-6455	48-22
*Cust Svc						
Social Action. Evangelicals for 10 E Lancaster Ave	Wynnewood	PA	19096	**800-650-6600**	610-645-9390	48-7
Social & Economic Sciences Research Center Washington State University Wilson Hall Rm 133 PO Box 644014	Pullman	WA	99164	**800-833-0867**	509-335-1511	654
Social Health Assn. American PO Box 13827	Research Triangle Park	NC	27709	**800-277-8922**	919-361-8400	48-17
Social Implications of Technology. IEEE Society on IEEE Operations Ctr 445 Hoes Ln	Piscataway	NJ	08854	**800-678-4333**	732-981-0060	49-19
Social Security Administration (SSA) 6401 Security Blvd	Baltimore	MD	21235	**800-772-1213**	410-965-3120	336-16
Social Security & Medicare. National Committee to Preserve 10 G St NE Suite 600	Washington	DC	20002	**800-966-1935**	202-216-0420	48-7
Social Studies. National Council for the 8555 16th St Suite 500	Silver Spring	MD	20910	**800-296-7840**	301-588-1800	49-5
Social Studies School Service 10200 Jefferson Blvd Box 802	Culver City	CA	90232	**800-421-4246**	310-839-2436	96
Social Work Boards. Association of 400 Southridge Pkwy Suite B	Culpeper	VA	22701	**800-225-6880**	540-829-6880	49-7
Social Work Leadership in Health Care. Society for 1211 Locust St	Philadelphia	PA	19107	**866-237-9542**	215-599-6134	49-15
Social Work Magazine 750 1st St NE Suite 700	Washington	DC	20002	**800-638-8799**	202-408-8600	449-16
Social Workers. National Assn of 750 1st St NE Suite 700	Washington	DC	20002	**800-638-8799**	202-408-8600	49-7
SocialPlus.com Inc 356 W 40th St 3rd Fl	New York	NY	10018	**888-701-2004**	212-244-7723	176-10
Societe Generale USA 1221 Ave of the Americas	New York	NY	10020	**800-942-7575**	212-278-6000	71
Society for Advancement of Management (SAM) Texas A&M Univ Corpus Christi College of Business 6300 Ocean Dr FC111	Corpus Christi	TX	78412	**888-827-6077**	361-825-6045	49-12
Society for the Advancement of Material & Process Engineering (SAMPE) 1161 Park View Dr	Covina	CA	91724	**800-562-7360**	626-331-0616	49-19
Society of American Florists (SAF) 1601 Duke St	Alexandria	VA	22314	**800-336-4743**	703-836-8700	49-4
Society of American Florists PAC 1601 Duke St	Alexandria	VA	22314	**800-336-4743**	703-836-8700	604
Society of American Military Engineers (SAME) 607 Prince St	Alexandria	VA	22314	**800-336-3097**	703-549-3800	48-19
Society of Automotive Engineers Inc (SAE) 400 Commonwealth Dr	Warrendale	PA	15096	**877-606-7323**	724-776-4841	49-21
Society of Cable Telecommunications Engineers (SCTE) 140 Philips Rd	Exton	PA	19341	**800-542-5040**	610-363-6888	49-19
Society of Certified Insurance Counselors PO Box 27027	Austin	TX	78755	**800-633-2165**	512-345-7932	49-9
Society of Diagnostic Medical Sonography (SDMS) 2745 N Dallas Pkwy Suite 350	Plano	TX	75093	**800-229-9506**	214-473-8057	49-8
Society of Environmental Toxicology & Chemistry (SETAC) 1010 N 12th Ave	Pensacola	FL	32501	**888-899-2088**	850-469-1500	49-19
Society of Financial Service Professionals (SFSP) 270 S Bryn Mawr Ave	Bryn Mawr	PA	19010	**800-392-6900**	610-526-2500	49-9
Society of Gastroenterology Nurses & Associates Inc (SGNA) 401 N Michigan Ave	Chicago	IL	60611	**800-245-7462**	312-321-5165	49-8
Society for Healthcare Strategy & Market Development American Hospital Assn 1 N Franklin St 28th Fl	Chicago	IL	60606	**800-242-2626**	312-422-3888	49-8
Society for Human Resource Management (SHRM) 1800 Duke St	Alexandria	VA	22314	**800-283-7476**	703-548-3440	49-12
Society for Industrial & Applied Mathematics (SIAM) 3600 Market St 6th Fl	Philadelphia	PA	19104	**800-447-7426**	215-382-9800	49-19
Society of Interventional Radiology (SIR) 10201 Lee Hwy Suite 500	Fairfax	VA	22030	**800-488-7284**	703-691-1805	49-8
Society of Laparoendoscopic Surgeons (SLS) 7330 SW 62nd Pl Suite 410	South Miami	FL	33143	**800-446-2659**	305-665-9959	49-8
Society of Manufacturing Engineers (SME) 1 SME Dr	Dearborn	MI	48121	**800-733-4763**	313-271-1500	49-13
Society for Marketing Professional Services (SMPS) 99 Canal Center Plaza Suite 330	Alexandria	VA	22314	**800-292-7677**	703-549-6117	49-18
Society of Military Widows (SMW) 5535 Hempstead Way	Springfield	VA	22151	**800-842-3451**	703-750-1342	48-19
Society for Mining Metallurgy & Exploration Inc (SME) 8307 Shaffer Pkwy	Littleton	CO	80127	**800-763-3132**	303-973-9550	49-13
Society of Park & Recreation Educators (SPRE) c/o National Recreation & Park Assn 22377 Belmont Ridge Rd	Ashburn	VA	20148	**800-626-6772**	703-858-0784	48-23
Society of Petroleum Engineers (SPE) 222 Palisades Creek Dr	Richardson	TX	75080	**800-456-6863**	972-952-9393	48-12
Society for the Preservation & Encouragement of Barber Shop Quartet Singing in America 7930 Sheridan Rd	Kenosha	WI	53143	**800-876-7464**	262-653-8440	48-18
Society of Saint Andrew 3383 Sweet Hollow Rd	Big Island	VA	24526	**800-333-4597**	434-299-5956	48-5
Society for Sedimentary Geology (SEPM) 6128 E 38th St Suite 308	Tulsa	OK	74135	**800-865-9765**	918-610-3361	49-19
Society for Social Work Leadership in Health Care 1211 Locust St	Philadelphia	PA	19107	**866-237-9542**	215-599-6134	49-15
Society of Telecommunications Consultants (STC) PO Box 416	Fall River Mills	CA	96028	**800-782-7670**	530-336-7070	49-20
Socket Communications Inc 37400 Central Ct	Newark	CA	94560	**800-552-3300**	510-744-2700	613
NASDAQ: SCKT						
SOCMA (Synthetic Organic Chemical Manufacturers Assn) 1850 M St NW Suite 700	Washington	DC	20036	**888-377-0778**	202-721-4100	49-19
Socorro Electric Co-op Inc 215 E Manazannez St	Socorro	NM	87801	**800-351-7575**	505-835-0560	244
Socrates Media LLC DBA Made E-Z Products LLC 227 W Monroe St Suite 500	Chicago	IL	60606	**800-822-4566**	312-762-5600	111
Sodak Gaming Inc 5301 S Hwy 16	Rapid City	SD	57701	**800-711-7322**	605-341-5400	317
Soderberg Inc 230 Eva St	Saint Paul	MN	55107	**800-755-5655**	651-291-1400	531
Sodexho Inc 9801 Washingtonian Blvd	Gaithersburg	MD	20878	**800-763-3946**	301-987-4000	294
Sofco Div US Foodservice Inc 3366 Walden Ave	Depew	NY	14043	**800-724-2571***	716-685-6001	295
*Cust Svc						
Sofco Div US Foodservice Inc 702 Potential Pkwy	Scotia	NY	12302	**800-836-7632***	518-374-7810	295
*Orders						
Sofec Inc 14741 Yorktown Plaza	Houston	TX	77070	**800-462-6003**	713-510-6600	258
Soffe MJ Co 1 Soffe Dr	Fayetteville	NC	28312	**800-723-4223**	910-483-2500	153-1
Soft Drink Letter 313 South Ave Suite 202	Fanwood	NJ	07023	**800-359-6049**	908-889-6336	521-13
Soft-Lite LLC 10250 Philipp Pkwy	Streetsboro	OH	44241	**800-551-1953**	330-528-3400	233
Soft Sheen/Carson Products Div L'Oreal USA Inc 8522 S LaFayette	Chicago	IL	60620	**800-342-7661**	800-621-6143	211
Softball Assn of America Inc. Amateur 2801 NE 50th St	Oklahoma City	OK	73111	**800-654-8337**	405-424-5266	48-22
Softball Assn National Hall of Fame. Amateur 2801 NE 50th St	Oklahoma City	OK	73111	**800-654-8337**	405-424-5266	511
SofTech Inc 2 Highwood Dr Suite 200	Tewksbury	MA	01876	**800-800-3702**	978-640-6222	176-5
Softmart Inc 450 Acorn Ln	Downingtown	PA	19335	**800-328-1319***	610-518-4000	172
*Cust Svc						
SoftPress Systems Ltd 3020 Bridgeway Suite 310	Sausalito	CA	94965	**800-853-6454**	415-331-4820	176-8
Softrax Corp 45 Shawmut Rd	Canton	MA	02021	**888-476-3872**	781-830-9200	176-10
Softub Inc 27615 Ave Hopkins	Valencia	CA	91355	**800-554-1120***	661-702-1401	599
*Sales						
Software 602 Inc 8833 Perimeter Pk Blvd Suite 702	Jacksonville	FL	32216	**888-468-6602**	904-642-5400	176-7
Software AG USA 11190 Sunrise Valley Dr	Reston	VA	20191	**800-525-7859**	703-860-5050	176-1
Software Alliance. Business 1150 18th St Suite 700	Washington	DC	20036	**888-667-4722**	202-872-5500	48-9
Software Dealers Assn. Video 16530 Ventura Blvd Suite 400	Encino	CA	91436	**800-955-8732**	818-385-1500	49-18
Software Engineering of America Inc 1230 Hempstead Tpke	Franklin Square	NY	11010	**800-272-7322**	516-328-7000	176-12
Software Etc Stores Inc 2250 William D Tate Ave	Grapevine	TX	76051	**800-288-9020**	817-424-2000	177
Software House 70 Westview St	Lexington	MA	02421	**800-550-6660**	781-466-6660	681
Software Industry Report 1150 Connecticut Ave NW Suite 900	Washington	DC	20036	**888-739-8500**	202-862-4375	521-3
Software Labs Inc PO Box 6064	Bellevue	WA	98008	**800-569-7900**	425-653-2432	176-7
Software Pursuits Inc 1500 Fashion Island Blvd Suite 205	San Mateo	CA	94404	**800-367-4823**	650-372-0900	176-12
Software Spectrum Inc 2140 Merritt Dr	Garland	TX	75041	**800-624-0503**	972-840-6600	172
Software Success Newsletter 990 Washington St Suite 308	Dedham	MA	02026	**888-479-6663**	781-320-9460	521-3
Software Technology Group 2455 Parleys Way Suite 150	Salt Lake City	UT	84109	**888-595-1001**	801-595-1000	178
Softworld Inc 395 Totten Pond Rd Suite 201	Waltham	MA	02451	**877-899-1166**	781-466-8882	707
SoHo Grand Hotel 310 W Broadway	New York	NY	10013	**800-965-3000**	212-965-3000	373
SOHOware Inc 3050 Coronado Dr	Santa Clara	CA	95054	**800-632-1118**	408-565-9888	174
Soil & Water Conservation Society (SWCS) 945 SW Ankeny Rd	Ankeny	IA	50021	**800-843-7645**	515-289-2331	48-13
Sojourner-Douglass College 500 N Caroline St	Baltimore	MD	21205	**800-732-2630**	410-276-0306	163
Sokol & Co 5315 Dansher Rd	Countryside	IL	60525	**800-328-7656***	708-482-8250	291-1
*Cust Svc						
Sola Communications Inc 113 N Patch St	Scott	LA	70583	**800-458-8301**	337-235-1515	681
SOLA Optical USA Inc 2277 Pine View Way	Petaluma	CA	94954	**800-533-5368**	707-763-9911	531
Solae Co PO Box 88940	Saint Louis	MO	63188	**800-325-7136**		786
Solar Communications Inc 1120 Frontenac Rd	Naperville	IL	60563	**800-323-2751**	630-983-1400	615
Solar Tours 1629 'K' St NW Suite 604	Washington	DC	20006	**800-388-7652**	202-861-5864	17
Solarcom Holdings Inc 1 Sun Ct	Norcross	GA	30092	**888-786-3282**	770-449-6116	172
Soldier of Fortune Magazine 5735 Arapahoe Ave Suite A-5	Boulder	CO	80303	**800-800-7630**	303-449-3750	449-12
Sole Source Inc 63820 Clausen Dr	Bend	OR	97701	**800-285-1657**	541-389-0360	130
Solectek Corp 6370 Nancy Ridge Dr Suite 109	San Diego	CA	92121	**800-437-1518**	858-450-1220	174

Name / Address	City	State	ZIP	Toll-Free	Phone	Class
Solgar Vitamin Co Inc 500 Willow Tree Rd	Leonia	NJ	07605	**800-645-2246**	201-944-2311	786
Soliant LLC 1872 Hwy 9 Bypass	Lancaster	SC	29720	**800-288-9401**		589
Solid State Circuits Society. IEEE IEEE Operations Ctr 445 Hoes Ln	Piscataway	NJ	08854	**800-678-4333**	732-981-0060	49-19
Solid Waste Assn of North America (SWANA) 100 Wayne Ave Suite 700	Silver Spring	MD	20910	**800-467-9262**	301-585-2898	48-12
Solid Waste Report 8737 Colesville Rd Suite 1100	Silver Spring	MD	20910	**800-274-6737**	301-587-6300	521-5
Solid Waste Services Inc DBA JP Mascaro Inc 600 W Neversink Rd	Reading	PA	19606	**800-334-3403**	610-779-8807	791
SolidWorks Corp 300 Baker Ave	Concord	MA	01742	**800-693-9000**	978-371-5011	176-10
Solite LLC 3900 Shannon St	Chesapeake	VA	23324	**888-854-9634**	757-494-5200	490
Solitec Wafer Processing Inc 685 River Oaks Pkwy	San Jose	CA	95134	**800-648-4040**	408-955-9939	685
Soliton Inc 99 Wall St 17th Fl	New York	NY	10005	**800-201-0569**	212-344-3988	176-12
Solitude Mountain Ski Resort 12000 Big Cottonwood Canyon	Solitude	UT	84121	**800-748-4754**	801-534-1400	655
Solo Cup Co 1505 E Main St *Cust Svc	Urbana	IL	61802	**800-367-2877***	217-384-1800	548-1
Solo Web Hosting 10350 Barnes Canyon Rd *Sales	San Diego	CA	92121	**877-275-8763***	858-410-6929	795
Soloflex Inc 570 NE 53rd Ave	Hillsboro	OR	97124	**800-547-8802**	503-640-8891	263
Solomon Howard 909 3rd Ave 23rd Fl Chm/CEO Forest Laboratories Inc.	New York	NY	10022	**800-947-5227**	212-421-7850	561
Solomon Metal Co 580 Lynnway	Lynn	MA	01905	**800-326-8959**	781-581-7000	674
Solomon-Page Group LLC 1140 Ave of the Americas 9th Fl	New York	NY	10036	**800-296-7646**	212-403-6100	707
Solucient 1007 Church St Suite 700	Evanston	IL	60201	**800-366-7526**	847-424-4400	176-10
Solunet Inc 1571 Robert J Conlan Blvd Suite 110	Palm Bay	FL	32905	**888-765-8638**	321-676-7947	720
Solus Industrial Innovations LLC 30152 Aventura *Cust Svc	Rancho Santa Margarita	CA	92688	**800-825-8364***	949-589-3900	345
Solutek Corp 94 Shirley St	Boston	MA	02119	**800-403-0770**	617-445-5335	143
Solution 6 North America 3525 Piedmont Rd Bldg 8 Suite 500	Atlanta	GA	30305	**877-608-4369**	404-720-3600	176-1
Solvay America Inc 3333 Richmond Ave	Houston	TX	77098	**800-231-6313**	713-525-6000	572
Solvay Interox Inc 3333 Richmond Ave	Houston	TX	77098	**800-468-3769**	713-525-6500	141
Solvay Minerals Inc 3333 Richmond Ave	Houston	TX	77098	**800-443-2785**	713-525-6800	493-1
Solvay Pharma Inc 60 Columbia Way Suite 102	Markham	ON	L3R0C9	**800-268-4276**	905-944-2480	572
Solvay Pharmaceuticals Inc 901 Sawyer Rd	Marietta	GA	30062	**800-241-1643**	770-578-9000	572
Solvents & Chemicals Inc 4704 Shank Rd PO Box 490	Pearland	TX	77581	**800-622-3990**	281-485-5377	144
Somagen Diagnostics Inc 9220 25th Ave	Edmonton	AB	T6N1E1	**800-661-9993**	780-702-9500	467
Somera Communications Inc 5383 Hollister Ave Suite 100 *NASDAQ: SMRA*	Santa Barbara	CA	93111	**800-761-1206**	805-681-3322	245
Somerset Community College 808 Monticello St	Somerset	KY	42501	**877-629-9722**	606-679-8501	160
Somerset Door & Column Co 174 Sagamore St	Somerset	PA	15501	**800-242-7916**	814-444-9427	489
Somerset Hills Hotel 200 Liberty Corner Rd	Warren	NJ	07059	**800-688-0700**	908-647-6700	373
Somerset House Publishing 10688 Haddington *Sales	Houston	TX	77043	**800-444-2540***	713-932-6847	623-10
Somerset Industries Inc 68 Harrison St	Gloversville	NY	12078	**800-262-0606**	518-773-7383	730-1
Somerset Inn 2601 W Big Beaver Rd	Troy	MI	48084	**800-228-8769**	248-643-7800	373
Somerset Pharmaceuticals Inc 2202 NW Shore Blvd Suite 450	Tampa	FL	33607	**800-892-8889**	813-288-0040	572
Somerset Rural Electric Co-op Inc 223 Industrial Pk Rd PO Box 270	Somerset	PA	15501	**800-443-4255**	814-445-4106	244
Somerset Tire Services Inc 400 W Main St	Bound Brook	NJ	08805	**800-445-1434**	732-356-8500	62-5
Somerset Welding & Steel Inc 10558 Somerset Pike *Sales	Somerset	PA	15501	**800-598-8552***	814-445-9312	505
Sommer Brothers Seed Co PO Box 248	Pekin	IL	61555	**800-747-2127**	309-346-2127	11-5
Sommer Electric Corp 818 3rd St NE	Canton	OH	44704	**800-766-6373**	330-455-9454	245
Sommer Metalcraft Corp 315 Poston Dr	Crawfordsville	IN	47933	**800-654-3124**	765-362-6200	478
Sompo Japan Insurance Co of America 2 World Financial Ctr 225 Liberty St 43rd Fl	New York	NY	10281	**800-444-6870**	212-416-1200	384-4
Sonalysts Inc 215 Parkway N	Waterford	CT	06385	**800-526-8091**	860-442-4355	258
Sonesta Beach Resort & Spa Key Biscayne 350 Ocean Dr	Key Biscayne	FL	33149	**800-766-3782**	305-361-2021	655
Sonesta Hotel & Suites Coconut Grove 2889 McFarlane Rd	Coconut Grove	FL	33133	**800-766-3782**	305-529-2828	373
Sonesta International Hotels Corp 116 Huntington Ave 9th Fl *NASDAQ: SNSTA*	Boston	MA	02116	**800-766-3782**	617-421-5400	369
Sonex Enterprises Inc 9990 Lee Hwy Suite 500	Fairfax	VA	22030	**888-766-3972**	703-691-8122	195
Song Airways LLC PO Box 20504	Atlanta	GA	30320	**800-359-7664**		26
Soniat House 1133 Chartres St	New Orleans	LA	70116	**800-544-8808**	504-522-0570	373
Sonic Air Systems Inc 1050 Beacon St	Brea	CA	92821	**800-827-6642**	714-255-0124	19
Sonic Corp 300 Johnny Bench Dr *NASDAQ: SONC*	Oklahoma City	OK	73104	**800-569-6656**	405-280-7654	656
Sonic Drive-in Restaurants 101 Park Ave Suite 1400	Oklahoma City	OK	73102	**800-569-6656**	405-280-7654	657
Sonic Foundry Inc 1617 Sherman Ave *NASDAQ: SOFO*	Madison	WI	53704	**800-577-6642**	608-256-3133	176-9
Sonic Innovations Inc 2795 E Cottonwood Pkwy Suite 660 *NASDAQ: SNCI* ■ *Cust Svc	Salt Lake City	UT	84121	**888-423-7834***	801-365-2800	469

Name / Address	City	State	ZIP	Toll-Free	Phone	Class
Sonic Solutions 101 Rowland Way *NASDAQ: SNIC*	Novato	CA	94945	**888-766-4248**	415-893-8000	176-8
Sonicor Instrument Corp 100 Wartburg Ave	Copiague	NY	11726	**800-864-5022**	631-842-3344	771
Sonics & Materials Inc 53 Church Hill Rd	Newtown	CT	06470	**800-745-1105**	203-270-4600	771
SonicWALL Inc 1143 Borregas Ave *NASDAQ: SNWL*	Sunnyvale	CA	94089	**888-222-6563**	408-745-9600	174
Sonnenalp Resort of Vail 20 Vail Rd	Vail	CO	81657	**800-654-8312**	970-476-5656	655
Sonobond Ultrasonics Inc 1191 McDermott Dr	West Chester	PA	19380	**800-323-1269**	610-696-4710	798
Sonoco Corrflex Display 701 Rickert St	Statesville	NC	28677	**800-334-8384**	704-872-7777	231
Sonoco Products Co 1 N 2nd St *NYSE: SON*	Hartsville	SC	29550	**800-377-2692**	843-383-7000	538
Sonographers. American Registry of Diagnostic Medical 51 Monroe St Plaza East 1	Rockville	MD	20850	**800-541-9754**	301-738-8401	49-8
Sonography. Society of Diagnostic Medical 2745 N Dallas Pkwy Suite 350	Plano	TX	75093	**800-229-9506**	214-473-8057	49-8
Sonoma County Transit 355 W Robles Ave	Santa Rosa	CA	95407	**800-345-7433**	707-585-7516	460
Sonora Regional Medical Center 1000 Greenly Rd	Sonora	CA	95370	**800-235-7203**	209-532-3161	366-2
SonoSite Inc 21919 30th Dr SE *NASDAQ: SONO*	Bothell	WA	98021	**888-482-9449**	425-951-1200	375
Sons of Italy in America. Order of the 219 'E' St NE	Washington	DC	20002	**800-547-6742**	202-547-2900	48-14
Sons of Norway 1455 W Lake St	Minneapolis	MN	55408	**800-945-8851**	612-827-3611	48-14
Sonstegard Foods Inc 707 E 41st St Suite 222	Sioux Falls	SD	57105	**800-533-3184**	605-338-4642	608
Sonus Corp 5000 Cheshire Ln N	Plymouth	MN	55446	**888-447-0443**		347
Sonwai Spa at the Hyatt Regency Scottsdale Resort at Gainey Ranch 7500 E Doubletree Ranch Rd	Scottsdale	AZ	85258	**800-233-1234**	480-483-5558	698
Sony Corp of America 550 Madison Ave	New York	NY	10022	**800-282-2848**	212-833-6800	52
Sony Electronics Inc 1 Sony Dr *Cust Svc	Park Ridge	NJ	07656	**800-222-7669***	201-930-1000	52
Sooner Micro Systems Inc PO Box 470666	Tulsa	OK	74147	**800-324-9393**	918-664-8383	176-1
Sooner Pipe Inc 1331 Lamar St 4 Houston Ctr Suite 970	Houston	TX	77010	**800-888-9161**	713-759-1200	378
Sopheon Corp 2850 Metro Dr Suite 600	Minneapolis	MN	55425	**800-367-8358**	952-851-7581	380
Sophie Station Hotel 1717 University Ave	Fairbanks	AK	99709	**800-528-4916**	907-479-3650	373
Sophos Inc 6 Kimball Ln Suite 400	Lynnfield	MA	01940	**888-767-4679**	781-973-0110	176-12
SOR Inc 14685 W 105th St	Lenexa	KS	66215	**800-676-6794**	913-888-2630	200
Sorbee International Ltd 9990 Global Rd	Philadelphia	PA	19115	**800-654-3997**	215-677-5200	291-8
Sorrento Electronics Inc 4949 Greencraig Ln	San Diego	CA	92123	**800-252-1180**	858-522-8300	464
Sorrento Hotel 900 Madison St	Seattle	WA	98104	**800-426-1265**	206-622-6400	373
SOS (Store Opening Solutions) 800 Middle Tennessee Blvd	Murfreesboro	TN	37129	**877-388-9262**	615-867-0858	440
SOS Children's Villages-USA 1317 F St NW Suite 550	Washington	DC	20004	**800-886-5767**	202-347-7920	48-6
SOS Staffing Services Inc 2650 Decker Lake Blvd Suite 500	Salt Lake City	UT	84119	**800-474-1722**	801-484-4400	707
Sosnick J & Sons Inc 258 Littlefield Ave	South San Francisco	CA	94080	**800-443-6737**	650-952-2226	292-11
Sotheby's International Realty 38 E 61st St	New York	NY	10021	**800-848-2541**	212-606-4100	638
Soules Luke Acosta 1920 Westridge Dr	Irving	TX	75038	**800-486-0928**	972-518-1442	292-8
Sound Advice Inc 2501 SW 32nd Terr *Cust Svc	Pembroke Park	FL	33023	**800-749-1897***	954-922-4434	35
Sound of America Records (SOAR) 5200 Constitution NE	Albuquerque	NM	87110	**800-890-7627**	505-268-6110	643
Sound Casket Inc 20350 71st Ave NE Suite F	Arlington	WA	98223	**800-735-7274**	425-259-6012	134
Sound Enhancements Inc 185 Detroit St	Cary	IL	60013	**800-284-5172**	847-639-4646	516
Sound Floor Coverings Inc 18375 Olympic Ave S *Orders	Tukwila	WA	98188	**800-288-2289***	206-575-1181	356
Sound Shore Fund PO Box 1810	Greenwich	CT	06836	**800-551-1980**	203-629-1980	517
Souper Salad Inc 140 Heimer Rd Suite 400	San Antonio	TX	78232	**800-346-7687**	210-495-9644	657
Souplantation 15822 Bernardo Ctr Dr Suite A	San Diego	CA	92127	**800-874-1600**	858-675-1600	657
Source Northwest Inc 8329 216th St SE *Cust Svc	Woodinville	WA	98072	**800-426-1321***	360-512-3535	356
Source Resources PO Box 88	Cookeville	TN	38503	**800-678-8774**	931-537-3641	392
Source Technologies Inc 2910 Whitehall Pk Dr	Charlotte	NC	28273	**800-922-8501**	704-969-7500	176-1
Sourcecorp Inc 3232 McKinney Ave Suite 1000 *NASDAQ: SRCP*	Dallas	TX	75204	**888-339-4462**	214-740-6500	455
SourcingLink.net Inc 16870 W Bernardo Dr Suite 400 *NASDAQ: SNET*	San Diego	CA	92127	**800-717-4565**	858-385-8900	39
South African Airways 515 E Las Olas Blvd 16th Fl	Fort Lauderdale	FL	33301	**800-722-9675**	954-769-5000	26
South African Airways Voyager 515 E Las Olas Blvd Sun Trust Bldg 16th Fl	Fort Lauderdale	FL	33301	**800-359-7220**	954-769-5000	27
South African Tourism Board 500 5th Ave 20th Fl Suite 2040	New York	NY	10110	**800-822-5368**	212-730-2929	764
South Alabama Electric Co-op 13192 Hwy 231 S	Troy	AL	36081	**800-556-2060**	334-566-2060	244
South Arkansas Community College PO Box 7010	El Dorado	AR	71731	**800-955-2289**	870-862-8131	160
South Baldwin Regional Medical Center 1613 N McKenzie St	Foley	AL	36535	**800-580-3627**	251-949-3400	366-2

				Toll-Free	Phone	Class
South Baylo University 1126 N Brookhurst St	Anaheim	CA	92801	**888-642-2956**	714-533-1495	163
South Beach Beverage Co 40 Richards Ave *Cust Svc	Norwalk	CT	06854	**800-588-0548***	203-899-7111	81-2
South Beach Marina Inn & Vacation Rentals 232 South Sea Pines Dr	Hilton Head Island	SC	29928	**800-367-3909**	843-671-6498	373
South Beloit Water Gas & Electric Co 4902 N Biltmore Ln	Madison	WI	53718	**800-862-6222**	608-458-3311	774
South Bend Lathe 3300 W Sample St Suite 1200	South Bend	IN	46619	**800-245-2843**	574-289-7771	447
South Bend Medical Foundation 530 N Lafayette Blvd	South Bend	IN	46601	**800-544-0925**	574-234-4176	409
South Bend Scrap & Processing Div Sturgis Iron & Metal Co 1305 Prairie Ave	South Bend	IN	46613	**800-232-2441**	574-287-3311	674
South Bend Tribune 225 W Colfax Ave	South Bend	IN	46626	**800-220-7378**	574-235-6161	522-2
South Bend/Mishawaka Convention & Visitors Bureau 401 E Colfax Ave Suite 310	South Bend	IN	46617	**800-828-7881**	574-234-0051	205
South Carolina						
Child Support Enforcement Office PO Box 1409	Columbia	SC	29202	**800-768-5858**	803-898-9210	335
Consumer Affairs Dept PO Box 5757	Columbia	SC	29250	**800-922-1594**	803-734-4200	335
Disabilities & Special Needs Dept 3440 Harden St Ext PO Box 4706	Columbia	SC	29240	**888-376-4636**	803-898-9600	335
Motor Vehicles Div PO Box 1498	Blythewood	SC	29016	**800-422-1368**	803-896-5000	335
Securities Div PO Box 11549	Columbia	SC	29211	**877-232-5378**	803-734-9916	335
State Ports Authority 176 Concord St	Charleston	SC	29401	**800-845-7106**	843-723-8651	607
South Carolina Aquarium PO Box 130001	Charleston	SC	29413	**800-722-6455**	843-720-1990	40
South Carolina Assn of Realtors 3780 Fernandina Rd	Columbia	SC	29210	**800-233-6381**	803-772-5206	642
South Carolina Assn of Veterinarians 1226 Pickens St Suite 203	Columbia	SC	29201	**800-441-7228**		782
South Carolina Chamber of Commerce 1201 Main St Suite 1700	Columbia	SC	29201	**800-799-4601**	803-799-4601	138
South Carolina Democratic Party PO Box 5965	Columbia	SC	29250	**800-841-1817**	803-799-7798	605-1
South Carolina Educational Television Commission PO Box 11000	Columbia	SC	29211	**800-922-5437**	803-737-3200	620
South Carolina Elastic Co 201 South Carolina Elastic Rd	Landrum	SC	29356	**800-845-6700**	864-457-3388	730-5
South Carolina Federal Credit Union PO Box 190012	North Charleston	SC	29419	**800-845-0432**	843-797-8300	216
South Carolina Medical Assn 132 W Park Blvd	Columbia	SC	29210	**800-327-1021**	803-798-6207	466
South Carolina Press Services Inc PO Box 11429	Columbia	SC	29211	**888-727-7377**	803-750-9561	612
South Carolina State University 300 College St NE *Admissions	Orangeburg	SC	29117	**800-260-5956***	803-536-7000	163
South Carolina Tees Inc PO Box 66	Columbia	SC	29202	**800-829-5000**	803-256-1393	154
South Central Arkansas Electric Co-op PO Box 476	Arkadelphia	AR	71923	**800-814-2931**	870-246-6701	244
South Central Co-op 40 W Park Dr	Gibbon	MN	55335	**800-690-6534**	507-834-6534	272
South Central Electric Assn 71176 Tiell Dr PO Box 150	Saint James	MN	56081	**888-805-7232**	507-375-3164	244
South Central Indiana Rural Electric Membership Corp 300 Morton Ave PO Box 3100	Martinsville	IN	46151	**800-264-7362**	765-342-3344	244
South Central Power Co Inc 2780 Coon Path Rd	Lancaster	OH	43130	**800-282-5064**	740-653-4422	244
South Central Public Power District 275 S Main St	Nelson	NE	68961	**800-557-5254**	402-225-2351	244
South Cone Inc DBA Reef Brazil 9660 Chesapeake Dr	San Diego	CA	92123	**800-423-6855**	858-514-3600	296
South Dakota						
Child Support Div 700 Governors Dr	Pierre	SD	57501	**800-286-9145**	605-773-3641	335
Crime Victims' Compensation Program 700 Governors Dr	Pierre	SD	57501	**800-696-9476**	605-773-6317	335
Economic Development Office 711 E Wells Ave	Pierre	SD	57501	**800-872-6190**	605-773-3301	335
Parks & Recreation Div 523 E Capitol Ave *Campground Resv	Pierre	SD	57501	**800-710-2267***	605-773-3391	335
Rehabilitation Services Div 500 E Capitol Ave	Pierre	SD	57501	**800-265-9684**	605-773-3195	335
Tourism Office 711 E Wells Ave	Pierre	SD	57501	**800-732-5682**	605-773-3301	335
Vital Records 600 E Capitol Ave	Pierre	SD	57501	**800-738-2301**	605-773-4961	335
South Dakota Lions Eye Bank 1321 W 22nd St	Sioux Falls	SD	57105	**800-245-7846**	605-373-1008	265
South Dakota Newspaper Services 527 Main Ave Suite 202	Brookings	SD	57006	**800-658-3697**	605-692-4300	612
South Dakota Public Broadcasting (SDPB) 555 N Dakota St PO Box 5000	Vermillion	SD	57069	**800-456-0766**	605-677-5861	620
South Dakota School of Mines & Technology 501 E Saint Joseph St	Rapid City	SD	57701	**800-544-8162**	605-394-2414	163
South Dakota State Library 800 Governors Dr	Pierre	SD	57501	**800-423-6665**	605-773-3131	426
South Dakota State University PO Box 2201	Brookings	SD	57007	**800-952-3541**	605-688-4121	163
South Dakota Symphony Orchestra 300 N Dakota Ave Suite 116	Sioux Falls	SD	57104	**866-681-7376**	605-335-7933	563-3
South Dakota Wheat Growers Assn 110 6th Ave SE	Aberdeen	SD	57401	**888-429-4902**	605-225-5500	271
South Davis Community Hospital 401 South 400 E	Bountiful	UT	84010	**877-913-2847**	801-295-2361	441
South Financial Group Inc 104 S Main St *NASDAQ: TSFG* ■ *Cust Svc	Greenville	SC	29601	**800-476-6400***	864-255-7900	355-2
South Florida Air Cargo 1801 NW 66 Ave Bldg 709 Tower 1	Miami	FL	33122	**800-327-2578**	305-871-7780	13
South Florida Sun-Sentinel 200 E Las Olas Blvd *Cust Svc	Fort Lauderdale	FL	33301	**800-548-6397***	954-356-4000	522-2
South Georgia College 100 W College Pk Dr	Douglas	GA	31533	**800-342-6364**	912-389-4510	160
South Georgia Pecan Co 309 S Lee St	Valdosta	GA	31601	**800-627-6630**	229-244-1321	291-28
South Idaho Press 230 E Main St	Burley	ID	83318	**800-817-5480**	208-678-2201	522-2
South Jersey Gas Co 1 S Jersey Plaza Rt 54	Folsom	NJ	08037	**888-766-9900**	609-561-9000	774
South Jersey Industries Inc Rt 54 1 S Jersey Plaza *NYSE: SJI* ■ *Cust Svc	Folsom	NJ	08037	**888-766-9900***	609-561-9000	355-5
South Jersey Shopper's Guide Inc 8 Ranoldo Terr	Cherry Hill	NJ	08034	**800-229-8775**	856-616-4900	623-8
South Kentucky Rural Electrical Co-op 925 N Main St PO Box 910	Somerset	KY	42502	**800-264-5112**	606-678-4121	244
South Mountain Restoration Center 10058 S Mountain Rd	South Mountain	PA	17261	**877-765-0331**	717-749-3121	441
South Padre Island Convention Centre 7355 Padre Blvd	South Padre Island	TX	78597	**800-657-2373**	956-761-3000	204
South Padre Island Convention & Visitors Bureau 600 Padre Blvd	South Padre Island	TX	78597	**800-767-2373**	956-761-6433	205
South Piedmont Community College PO Box 126	Polkton	NC	28135	**800-766-0319**	704-272-7635	160
South Plains Electric Co-op Inc 4727 S Loop 289 Suite 200	Lubbock	TX	79408	**800-658-2655**	806-775-7732	244
South River Electric Membership Corp 17494 US 421 S PO Box 931	Dunn	NC	28335	**800-338-5530**	910-892-8071	244
South Seas Hotel 1751 Collins Ave	Miami Beach	FL	33139	**800-345-2678**	305-538-1411	373
South Seas Resort 5400 Plantation Rd	Captiva	FL	33924	**800-965-7772**	239-472-5111	655
South Shore Hospital 55 Fogg Rd	South Weymouth	MA	02190	**800-472-3434**	781-340-8000	366-2
South Shore Transportation Inc 4010 Columbus Ave	Sandusky	OH	44870	**800-418-9726**	419-626-6267	769
South Sioux City Convention & Visitors Bureau 3900 Dakota Ave Suite 11	South Sioux City	NE	68776	**800-793-6327**	402-494-1307	205
South Sound Business Examiner 1517 S Fawcett St Suite 350	Tacoma	WA	98402	**800-540-6899**	253-404-0891	449-5
South Texas Blood & Tissue Center 6211 IH-10 W	San Antonio	TX	78201	**800-292-5534**	210-731-5555	90
South Texas Can Co Inc 103 E Benge Rd	Fort Gibson	OK	74434	**800-776-2107**	918-478-2117	124
South Texas Public Broadcasting System Inc 4455 S Padre Island Dr Suite 38	Corpus Christi	TX	78411	**800-307-5338**	361-855-2213	620
South Texas Vocational Technical Institute 2419 E Haggar Ave	Weslaco	TX	78596	**888-279-3556**	956-969-1564	787
South University						
Montgomery Campus 5355 Vaughn Rd	Montgomery	AL	36116	**866-629-2901**	334-395-8800	158
West Palm Beach Campus 1760 N Congress Ave	West Palm Beach	FL	33409	**866-629-2902**	561-697-9200	160
South-Western Thomson Learning 5191 Natorp Blvd	Mason	OH	45040	**800-543-0487**	513-543-0487	623-2
Southampton Inn 91 Hill St	Southampton	NY	11968	**800-832-6500**	631-283-6500	373
Southaven Chamber of Commerce 8700 Northwest Dr Suite 100	Southaven	MS	38671	**800-272-6551**	662-342-6114	137
Southbend Co Inc 1100 Old Honeycutt Rd	Fuquay-Varina	NC	27526	**800-348-2558**	919-552-9161	293
Southco Distributing Co 701 Patetown Rd	Goldsboro	NC	27530	**800-969-3172**	919-735-8012	292-8
Southeast Asia Resource Action Center (SEARAC) 1628 16th St NW 3rd Fl	Washington	DC	20009	**800-600-9188**	202-667-4690	48-5
Southeast-Atlantic Corp 6001 Bowdendale Ave	Jacksonville	FL	32216	**800-329-2067**	904-739-1000	82-2
Southeast Colorado Power Assn 901 W 3rd	La Junta	CO	81050	**800-332-8634**	719-384-2551	244
Southeast Community College 700 College Rd	Cumberland	KY	40823	**888-274-7322**	606-589-2145	160
Middlesboro Campus 1300 Chichester Ave	Middlesboro	KY	40965	**888-274-7322**	606-242-2145	160
Whitesburg Campus 2 Long Ave	Whitesburg	KY	41858	**888-274-7322**	606-633-0279	160
Southeast Community College-Beatrice 4771 W Scott St	Beatrice	NE	68310	**800-233-5027**	402-228-3468	160
Southeast Community College-Lincoln 8800 'O' St	Lincoln	NE	68520	**800-642-4075**	402-471-3333	160
Southeast Community College-Milford 600 State St	Milford	NE	68405	**800-933-7223**	402-761-2131	787
Southeast Electric Co-op Inc 110 S Main St	Ekalaka	MT	59324	**888-485-8762**	406-775-8762	244
Southeast Iowa Blood Center 1007 Pennsylvania Ave	Ottumwa	IA	52501	**800-452-1097**	641-682-8149	90
Southeast Milk Inc 1950 SE Hwy 484	Belleview	FL	34420	**800-598-7866**	352-245-2437	291-27
Southeast Missourian PO Box 699	Cape Girardeau	MO	63702	**800-879-1210**	573-335-6611	522-2
Southeast Volusia Chamber of Commerce 115 Canal St	New Smyrna Beach	FL	32168	**877-460-8410**	386-428-2449	137
Southeastern Aluminum Products Inc 6701 Suemac Pl *Sales	Jacksonville	FL	32254	**800-243-8200***	904-781-8200	232
Southeastern Community Blood Center 1731 Riggins Rd	Tallahassee	FL	32308	**800-722-2218**	850-877-7181	90
Southeastern Construction & Maintenance Co Inc 1150 Pebbledale Rd PO Box 1055	Mulberry	FL	33860	**800-511-1600**	863-428-1511	188-14
Southeastern Electric Co-op Inc 501 S Broadway Ave	Marion	SD	57043	**800-333-2859**	605-648-3619	244

Name / Address	City	State	Zip	Toll-Free	Phone	Class
Southeastern Equipment Co Inc 10874 E Pike Rd	Cambridge	OH	43725	**800-798-5438**	740-432-6303	353
Southeastern Freight Lines Inc 420 Davega Rd	Lexington	SC	29073	**800-637-7335**	803-794-7300	769
Southeastern Illinois College 3575 College Rd	Harrisburg	IL	62946	**866-338-2742**	618-252-6376	160
SouthEastern Illinois Electric Co-op 585 Hwy 142 S	Eldorado	IL	62930	**800-833-2611**	618-273-2611	244
Southeastern Indiana Rural Electric Membership Corp 712 Buckeye St	Osgood	IN	47037	**800-737-4111**	812-689-4111	244
Southeastern Library Network 1438 W Peachtree St NW Suite 200	Atlanta	GA	30309	**800-999-8558**	404-892-0943	426
Southeastern Louisiana University 752 University Stn	Hammond	LA	70402	**800-222-7358**	985-549-2000	163
Southeastern Metals Mfg Co Inc 11801 Industry Dr	Jacksonville	FL	32218	**800-874-2335**	904-757-4200	232
Southeastern Oklahoma State University 1405 N 4th St	Durant	OK	74701	**800-435-1327**	580-745-2000	163
Southeastern Plastics Corp 15 Home News Row	New Brunswick	NJ	08901	**800-966-2247**	732-846-8500	67
Southeastern Steel Co 211 N Koppers Rd	Florence	SC	29506	**800-476-7372**	843-662-5236	471
Southeastern University 1000 Longfellow Blvd	Lakeland	FL	33801	**800-500-8760**	863-667-5000	163
Southeastern Wholesale Tire Co 4721 Trademark Dr	Raleigh	NC	27610	**800-849-9215**	919-832-3900	740
Southerland Inc 1973 Southerland Dr	Nashville	TN	37207	**888-226-9009**	615-226-9650	463
Southern Accents Magazine 2100 Lakeshore Dr	Birmingham	AL	35209	**800-366-4712**	205-445-6000	449-22
Southern Adventist University 4881 Taylor Cir	Collegedale	TN	37315	**800-768-8437**	423-238-2111	163
Southern Air Inc PO Box 4205	Lynchburg	VA	24502	**800-743-1214**	434-385-6200	188-10
Southern Arkansas University 100 E University St	Magnolia	AR	71753	**800-332-7286**	870-235-4000	163
Southern Assn of Colleges & Schools 1866 Southern Ln	Decatur	GA	30033	**800-248-7701**	404-679-4500	49-5
Southern Audio Services 15049 Florida Blvd	Baton Rouge	LA	70819	**800-843-8823**	225-272-7135	52
Southern Baptist Theological Seminary 2825 Lexington Rd	Louisville	KY	40280	**800-626-5525**	502-897-4011	164-3
Southern Belle Dairy Co Inc PO Box 1020	Somerset	KY	42502	**800-468-4798**	606-679-1131	291-27
Southern Biotechnology Assoc Inc 160A Oxmoor Blvd	Birmingham	AL	35209	**800-722-2255**	205-945-1774	229
Southern Bus Stages Inc Shafer's Bus Lines Div 750 Harry L Dr	Johnson City	NY	13790	**800-287-8986**	607-797-2006	108
Southern California Edison Co 2244 Walnut Grove Ave	Rosemead	CA	91770	**800-655-4555**	626-302-1212	774
Southern California Gas Co 555 W 5th St	Los Angeles	CA	90013	**800-427-2200**	213-244-1200	774
Southern California Regional Rail Authority 700 S Flower St Suite 2600	Los Angeles	CA	90017	**800-371-5465**	213-347-2800	460
Southern Centrifugal Inc 4180 S Creek Rd	Chattanooga	TN	37406	**800-722-7277**	423-622-4131	303
Southern Christian University 1200 Taylor Rd	Montgomery	AL	36117	**800-351-4040**	334-387-3877	163
Southern Clay Products Inc 1212 Church St	Gonzales	TX	78629	**800-324-2891**	830-672-2891	493-2
Southern Co Inc 3101 Carrier St	Memphis	TN	38116	**800-264-7626**	901-345-2531	526
Southern Coach Co 1300 E Pettigrew St	Durham	NC	27701	**800-222-4793**	919-688-1230	108
Southern Communications Services Inc DBA Southern LINC 5555 Glenridge Connector Suite 500	Atlanta	GA	30342	**800-406-0151**	678-443-1500	721
Southern Components Inc 7360 Julie Frances Rd	Shreveport	LA	71129	**800-256-2144**	318-687-3330	805
Southern Concrete Construction Co Inc PO Box 711	Albany	GA	31702	**800-768-6888**	229-435-0786	181
Southern Concrete Materials Inc 35 Meadow Rd	Asheville	NC	28803	**800-288-6421**	828-253-6421	180
Southern Cotton Oil Co PO Box 1470	Decatur	IL	62525	**800-637-5824**	217-424-5526	291-29
Southern Elevator Co Inc 130 O'Connor St	Greensboro	NC	27416	**800-373-0058**	336-274-2401	188-1
Southern Farm Bureau Casualty Insurance Co 1800 E County Line Rd Suite 400	Ridgeland	MS	39157	**800-272-7977**	601-957-7777	384-4
Southern Film Extruders Inc 1829 Eastchester Dr Suite 100	High Point	NC	27265	**800-334-6101**	336-885-8091	589
Southern Folder & Index Co 475 Bailey Rd	El Dorado	AR	71730	**888-368-6432**	870-863-5184	550
Southern Foods Inc 3500 Old Battleground Rd	Greensboro	NC	27410	**800-441-3663**	336-545-3800	292-9
Southern FS Inc 1900 E Main St	Marion	IL	62959	**800-492-7684**	618-993-2833	272
Southern Glove Mfg Co Inc 749 AC Little Dr *Cust Svc	Newton	NC	28658	**800-222-1113***	828-464-4884	153-8
Southern Graphic Systems Inc 2823 S Floyd St	Louisville	KY	40209	**800-228-3720**	502-637-5443	770
Southern Guaranty Insurance Co PO Box 235004	Montgomery	AL	36123	**800-633-5606**	334-270-6000	384-4
Southern Health Services Inc 9881 Mayland Dr	Richmond	VA	23233	**800-424-0077**	804-747-3700	384-3
Southern Holdings Inc 4801 Florida Ave	New Orleans	LA	70117	**800-467-2727**	504-944-3371	674
Southern Illinois Electric Co-op 7420 US Hwy 51 S	Dongola	IL	62926	**800-762-1400**	618-827-3555	244
Southern Illinois Healthcare 1239 E Main St	Carbondale	IL	62902	**866-744-2468**	618-457-5200	348
Southern Illinois University Press 1915 University Press Dr	Carbondale	IL	62901	**800-346-2680**	618-453-2281	623-5
Southern Illinoisan PO Box 2108	Carbondale	IL	62902	**800-228-0429**	618-529-5454	522-2
Southern Imperial Inc 1400 Eddy Ave *Cust Svc	Rockford	IL	61103	**800-747-4665***	815-877-7041	281
Southern Importers Inc 3859 Battleground Ave Suite 300 *Cust Svc	Greensboro	NC	27410	**800-334-9658***	336-292-4521	288
Southern Indiana Convention & Tourism Bureau 315 Southern Indiana Ave	Jeffersonville	IN	47130	**800-552-3842**	812-282-6654	205
Southern Indiana Rehabilitation Hospital 3104 Blackiston Blvd	New Albany	IN	47150	**800-737-7090**	812-941-8300	366-4
Southern Indiana Rural Electric Co-op Inc 1776 10th St	Tell City	IN	47586	**800-323-2316**	812-547-2316	244
Southern Industrial Constructors Inc 6101 Triangle Dr	Raleigh	NC	27617	**800-851-0868**	919-782-4600	188-10
Southern Iowa Electric Co-op Inc 800 E Franklin St	Bloomfield	IA	52537	**800-607-2027**	641-664-2277	244
Southern Kentucky Rehab 1300 Campbell Ln	Bowling Green	KY	42104	**800-989-5775**	270-782-6900	366-4
Southern LINC 5555 Glenridge Connector Suite 500	Atlanta	GA	30342	**800-406-0151**	678-443-1500	721
Southern Living Magazine 2100 Lakeshore Dr	Birmingham	AL	35209	**800-366-6700**	205-445-6000	449-22
Southern Maid Donut Flour Co 3615 Cavalier Dr	Garland	TX	75042	**800-936-6887**	972-272-6425	69
Southern Maine Community College 2 Fort Rd	South Portland	ME	04106	**877-282-2182**	207-741-5500	787
Southern Maryland Electric Co-op PO Box 1937	Hughesville	MD	20637	**888-440-3311**	301-274-3111	244
Southern Maryland Oil Co Inc (SMO) 6355 Crain Hwy	La Plata	MD	20646	**800-492-3420**	301-932-3600	569
Southern Medical Assn (SMA) 35 Lakeshore Dr	Birmingham	AL	35209	**800-423-4992**	205-945-1840	49-8
Southern Medical Journal 35 Lakeshore Dr	Birmingham	AL	35209	**800-423-4992**	205-945-1840	449-16
Southern Metal Industries Inc PO Box 219	Ringgold	GA	30736	**800-241-5246**	706-935-4486	281
Southern Metals Co 111 N Raleigh Ave PO Box 471	Sheffield	AL	35660	**800-843-2771**	256-383-3261	481
Southern Methodist University 6425 Boaz Ln	Dallas	TX	75205	**800-323-0672**	214-768-2000	163
Southern Methodist University Press 6404 Hilltop Ln 314 Fondren Library W	Dallas	TX	75275	**800-826-8911**	214-768-1432	623-5
Southern Midcoast Maine Chamber 59 Pleasant St	Brunswick	ME	04011	**800-725-8797**	207-725-8797	137
Southern Mills Inc 6501 Mall Blvd	Union City	GA	30291	**800-241-8630**	770-969-1000	730-3
Southern Natural Gas Co PO Box 2563	Birmingham	AL	35202	**800-633-8570**	205-325-7410	320
Southern Nazarene University 6729 NW 39th Expy	Bethany	OK	73008	**800-648-9899**	405-789-6400	163
Southern New Hampshire University 2500 N River Rd	Manchester	NH	03106	**800-642-4968**	603-668-2211	163
Southern Ocean County Chamber of Commerce 265 W 9th St	Ship Bottom	NJ	08008	**800-292-6372**	609-494-7211	137
Southern Office Furniture Distributors Inc 719 N Regional Rd	Greensboro	NC	27409	**800-933-6369**	336-668-4192	315
Southern Ontario Library Service 151 Bloor St W 5th Fl	Toronto	ON	M5S1T6	**800-387-5765**	416-961-1669	428
Southern Optical 501 Merritt Ave	Nashville	TN	37203	**800-333-8498**	615-256-6631	533
Southern Optical Co Inc 1909 N Church St	Greensboro	NC	27405	**800-888-8842**	336-272-8146	531
Southern Orchard Supply Co DBA Lane Packing Inc Hwy 96 & 50 Ln Rd PO Box 1087	Fort Valley	GA	31030	**800-277-3224**	478-825-3592	310-3
Southern Petroleum Lab Inc 8880 Interchange Dr	Houston	TX	77054	**800-969-6775**	713-660-0901	728
Southern Pine Electric Power Assn 110 Risher St	Taylorsville	MS	39168	**800-231-5240**	601-785-6511	244
Southern Polytechnic State University 1100 S Marietta Pkwy	Marietta	GA	30060	**800-635-3204**	678-915-4188	163
Southern Progress Corp 2100 Lakeshore Dr	Birmingham	AL	35209	**800-366-4712**	205-445-6000	623-9
Southern Prosthetic Supply Co 6025 Shiloh Rd Suite A *Cust Svc	Alpharetta	GA	30005	**800-767-7776***	678-455-8888	467
Southern Public Power District PO Box 1687	Grand Island	NE	68802	**800-652-2013**	308-384-2350	244
Southern Pump & Tank Co 4800 N Graham St *Cust Svc	Charlotte	NC	28269	**800-477-2826***	704-596-4373	378
Southern Refrigeration Corp 2026 Salem Ave SW	Roanoke	VA	24016	**800-763-4433**	540-342-3493	651
Southern Research Co Inc 2850 Centenary Blvd	Shreveport	LA	71104	**888-772-6952**	318-227-9700	392
Southern Research Institute 2000 9th Ave S	Birmingham	AL	35205	**800-967-6774**	205-581-2000	654
Southern Scrap Material Co Inc 6847 Scenic Hwy	Baton Rouge	LA	70807	**800-355-4453**	225-355-4453	674
Southern Security Life Insurance Co 755 Rinehart Rd Suite 200 *NASDAQ: SSLI*	Lake Mary	FL	32746	**800-336-9558**	407-321-7113	384-2
Southern Spring & Stamping Inc 401 Sub Station Rd	Venice	FL	34292	**800-450-5882**	941-488-2276	704
Southern States Phosphate & Fertilizer Co PO Box 546	Savannah	GA	31402	**888-337-8922**	912-232-1101	276
Southern Structures Inc 918 Young St PO Box 52005	Lafayette	LA	70505	**800-264-5981**	337-856-5981	106
Southern Tool Mfg Co Inc PO Box 12008	Winston-Salem	NC	27117	**800-334-5262**	336-788-6321	345
Southern University Shreveport 3050 ML King Jr Dr	Shreveport	LA	71107	**800-458-1472**	318-674-3300	160
Southern University & A & M College Branch Post Office	Baton Rouge	LA	70813	**800-256-1531**	225-771-4500	163
Southern University Law Center PO Box 9294	Baton Rouge	LA	70813	**800-537-1135**	225-771-6297	164-1
Southern University Museum of Art 610 Texas St Suite 110	Shreveport	LA	71101	**800-458-1472**	318-678-4631	509
Southern Vermont College 982 Manison Dr	Bennington	VT	05201	**800-378-2782**	802-442-5427	163
Southern Virginia University 1 University Hill Dr	Buena Vista	VA	24416	**800-229-8420**	540-261-8400	163
Southern Weaving Co 1005 W Bramlett Rd	Greenville	SC	29611	**800-849-8962**	864-233-1635	730-5

Name / Address	City	State	ZIP	Toll-Free	Phone	Class
Southern Wesleyan University 907 Wesleyan Dr	Central	SC	29630	**800-282-8798**	864-644-5000	163
Southern West Virginia Convention & Visitors Bureau 200 Main St	Beckley	WV	25801	**800-847-4898**	304-252-2244	205
Southern Wine & Spirits Co PO Box 5603	Denver	CO	80217	**800-332-9956**	303-292-1711	82-3
Southern Wine & Spirits Inc 1600 NW 163rd St	Miami	FL	33169	**800-432-6431**	305-625-4171	82-3
Southern Wipers 100 Fairview Rd	Asheville	NC	28803	**800-544-9387**	828-274-2100	497
Southernmost On the Beach 508 South St	Key West	FL	33040	**800-354-4455**	305-296-5611	373
Southernmost Illinois Tourism Bureau PO Box 378	Anna	IL	62906	**800-248-4373**	618-833-9928	205
Southernmost Motel 1319 Duval St	Key West	FL	33040	**800-354-4455**	305-296-6577	373
SouthFirst Bancshares Inc 126 N Norton Ave. *AMEX: SZB*	Sylacauga	AL	35150	**800-239-1492**	256-245-4365	355-2
Southfork Hotel 1600 N Central Expy	Plano	TX	75074	**866-665-2680**	972-578-8555	373
Southgate Tower 371 7th Ave	New York	NY	10001	**800-637-8483**	212-563-1800	373
Southland Athletic Mfg Co 714 E Grove	Terrell	TX	75160	**800-527-7637**	972-563-3321	153-1
Southland Micro Systems 7 Morgan	Irvine	CA	92618	**800-255-4200**	949-380-1958	686
Southland Oil Co 5170 Galaxie Dr	Jackson	MS	39206	**800-222-7630**	601-981-4151	570
Southland Racing Corp 1550 N Ingram Blvd	West Memphis	AR	72301	**800-467-0102**	870-735-3670	628
Southland Title Co 7530 N Glenoaks Blvd	Burbank	CA	91504	**800-747-7777**	818-767-2000	384-6
Southland Window Fashions 408 Arlington St	Houston	TX	77007	**800-299-9030**	713-863-7761	88
SouthPark Mall 4400 Sharon Rd	Charlotte	NC	28211	**888-364-4411**	704-364-4411	452
Southside Bancshares Inc 1201 S Beckham Ave *NASDAQ: SBSI*	Tyler	TX	75701	**800-962-4284**	903-531-7111	355-2
Southside Electric Co-op Inc 2000 W Virgina Ave	Crewe	VA	23930	**800-552-2118**	434-645-7721	244
Southside Virginia Community College 109 Campus Dr	Alberta	VA	23821	**888-220-7822**	434-949-1000	160
SouthStar Energy Services LLC 817 W Peachtree St NW Suite 1000	Atlanta	GA	30308	**888-442-7288**	404-685-4000	774
SouthTrust Bank 420 20th St N	Birmingham	AL	35203	**800-239-2300**	205-254-5000	71
SouthTrust Corp PO Box 2554 *NASDAQ: SOTR*	Birmingham	AL	35290	**800-239-2300**	205-254-5000	355-2
SouthTrust Mortgage Corp 210 Wildwood Pkwy Suite 200	Birmingham	AL	35209	**800-239-2322**	205-667-8100	498
Southwark Metal Mfg Co Inc 2800 Red Lion Rd	Philadelphia	PA	19114	**800-523-1052**	215-735-3401	688
Southway Inn 2431 Bank St	Ottawa	ON	K1V8R9	**877-688-4929**	613-737-0811	372
Southwest Airlines Air Cargo 8028 Aviation Pl	Dallas	TX	75235	**800-533-1222**	214-792-5534	13
Southwest Airlines Co 2702 Love Field Dr *NYSE: LUV* ■ *Resv	Dallas	TX	75235	**800-435-9792***	214-792-4000	26
Southwest Airlines PAC 2702 Love Field Fr	Dallas	TX	75235	**800-435-9792**	214-792-4000	604
Southwest Airlines Rapid Rewards PO Box 36657	Dallas	TX	75235	**800-445-9267**		27
Southwest Airport Services Inc 11811 N Brantly St Ellington Field Bldg 500	Houston	TX	77034	**800-426-5237**	281-484-6551	63
Southwest Arkansas Electric Co-op Corp PO Box 1807	Texarkana	AR	75504	**800-782-2743**	870-772-2743	244
Southwest Art Magazine 5444 Westheimer St Suite 1440	Houston	TX	77056	**800-621-3963**	713-296-7900	449-2
Southwest Bancorp Inc 608 S Main St *NASDAQ: OKSB*	Stillwater	OK	74074	**800-727-2230**	405-372-2230	355-2
Southwest Baptist University 1600 University Ave	Bolivar	MO	65613	**800-526-5859**	417-326-5281	163
Southwest Canners Inc PO Box 809	Portales	NM	88130	**800-658-2085**	505-356-6623	82-2
Southwest Daily Times PO Box 889	Liberal	KS	67905	**800-279-5826**	620-624-2541	522-2
Southwest Gas Corp 4300 W Tropicana Ave *NYSE: SWX*	Las Vegas	NV	89103	**800-748-5539**	702-365-1555	774
Southwest Gas Corp Northern Nevada Div 400 Eagle Station Ln	Carson City	NV	89701	**800-832-2555**	775-887-2706	774
Southwest Gas Corp Southern Arizona Div 3401 E Gas Rd	Tucson	AZ	85714	**800-428-7324**	520-794-6596	774
Southwest Gas Corp Southern California Div 13471 Mariposa Rd	Victorville	CA	92395	**800-443-8093**	760-951-4021	774
Southwest Georgia Financial Corp 201 1st St SE *AMEX: SGB*	Moultrie	GA	31768	**888-683-2265**	229-985-1120	355-2
Southwest Institute of Healing Arts 1100 E Apache Blvd	Tempe	AZ	85281	**888-504-9106**	480-994-9244	787
Southwest Iowa Rural Electric Cooperative 626 Davis Ave	Corning	IA	50841	**888-591-1261**	641-322-3165	244
Southwest Jet Aviation Ltd 14988 N 78th Way Scottsdale Municipal Airport	Scottsdale	AZ	85260	**800-991-7076**	480-991-7076	14
Southwest King County Chamber of Commerce 14220 Interurban Ave S	Tukwila	WA	98168	**800-638-8613**	206-575-1633	137
Southwest Louisiana Convention & Visitors Bureau 1205 N Lakeshore Dr	Lake Charles	LA	70601	**800-456-7952**	337-436-9588	205
Southwest Louisiana Electric Membership Corp 3420 Hwy 167 N	Lafayette	LA	70509	**888-275-3626**	337-896-5384	244
Southwest Medical Assoc Inc PO Box 2168	Rockport	TX	78382	**800-929-4854**	361-729-0646	707
Southwest Minnesota State University 1501 State St	Marshall	MN	56258	**800-642-0684**	507-537-7021	163
Southwest Mississippi Electric Power Assn 18671 Hwy 61	Lorman	MS	39096	**800-287-8564**	601-437-3611	244
Southwest Missouri State University 901 S National Ave	Springfield	MO	65804	**800-492-7900**	417-836-5000	163
Southwest Oilfield Products 10340 Wallisville Rd	Houston	TX	77013	**800-392-4600**	713-675-7541	526
Southwest Plastic Binding Co Inc 109 Millwell Ct	Maryland Heights	MO	63043	**800-325-3628**	314-739-4400	87
Southwest Public Power District 221 N Main St	Palisade	NE	69040	**800-379-7977**	308-285-3295	244
Southwest Rural Electric Assn 700 N Broadway	Tipton	OK	73570	**800-256-7973**	580-667-5281	244
Southwest Tennessee Community College PO Box 780	Memphis	TN	38101	**877-717-7822**	901-333-5000	160
Southwest Tennessee Electric Membership Corp PO Box 989	Brownsville	TN	38012	**800-772-0472**	731-772-1322	244
Southwest Texas Electric Co-op Inc 101 E Gillis St	Eldorado	TX	76936	**800-643-3980**	325-853-2544	244
Southwest Wisconsin Technical College 1800 Bronson Blvd	Fennimore	WI	53809	**800-362-3322**	608-822-3262	787
Southwestern Adventist University 100 W Hillcrest Dr	Keene	TX	76059	**800-433-2240**	817-645-3921	163
Southwestern Assemblies of God University 1200 Sycamore St	Waxahachie	TX	75165	**888-937-7248**	972-937-4010	163
Southwestern Christian College PO Box 10	Terrell	TX	75160	**800-925-9357**	972-524-3341	163
Southwestern College 2625 E Cactus Rd	Phoenix	AZ	85032	**800-247-2697**	602-992-6101	163
Southwestern College 100 College St	Winfield	KS	67156	**800-846-1543**	620-221-4150	163
Southwestern Community College 1501 W Townline St	Creston	IA	50801	**800-247-4023**	641-782-7081	160
Southwestern Community College 447 College Dr	Sylva	NC	28779	**800-447-4091**	828-586-4091	160
Southwestern Electric Co-op Inc PO Box 549	Greenville	IL	62246	**800-637-8667**	618-664-1025	244
Southwestern Eye Center 2610 E University Dr	Mesa	AZ	85213	**800-425-8404**	480-892-8400	785
Southwestern Indian Polytechnic Institute 9169 Coors Rd	Albuquerque	NM	87184	**800-586-7474**	505-346-2346	161
Southwestern Industries Inc 2615 Homestead Pl	Rancho Dominguez	CA	90220	**800-421-6875**	310-608-4422	447
Southwestern Life Holdings Inc 8710 Freeport Pkwy Suite 150	Irving	TX	75063	**800-792-4368**		355-4
Southwestern Life Insurance Co 8710 Freeport Pkwy Suite 150	Irving	TX	75063	**800-792-4368**		384-2
Southwestern Michigan College 58900 Cherry Grove Rd	Dowagiac	MI	49047	**800-456-8675**	269-782-1000	160
Niles Area Campus 2229 US 12 E	Niles	MI	49120	**800-456-8675**	269-687-1600	160
Southwestern Motor Transport Inc 4600 Goldfield	San Antonio	TX	78218	**800-531-1071**	210-661-6791	769
Southwestern Oregon Community College 1988 Newmark Ave	Coos Bay	OR	97420	**800-962-2838**	541-888-2525	160
Southwestern Petroleum Corp 534 N Main St	Fort Worth	TX	76106	**800-877-9372**	817-332-2336	530
Southwestern University PO Box 770	Georgetown	TX	78627	**800-252-3166**	512-863-1200	163
Southwestern Vermont Medical Center 100 Hospital Dr	Bennington	VT	05201	**800-543-1624**	802-442-6361	366-2
Southwestern/Great American 2451 Atrium Way *Cust Svc	Nashville	TN	37214	**800-251-1542***	615-391-2500	97
Southwire Co 1 Southwire Dr	Carrollton	GA	30119	**800-444-1700**	770-832-4242	476
Southwire Co Machinery Div 401 Fertilla St	Carrollton	GA	30117	**800-444-1700**	770-832-4900	473
Southworth Co 265 Main St	Agawam	MA	01001	**800-225-1839**	413-789-1200	542-3
Souvenirs Gifts & Novelties Trade Assn 10 E Athens Ave Suite 208	Ardmore	PA	19003	**800-284-5451**	610-645-6940	49-18
Sovereign Bancorp Inc PO Box 12646 *NYSE: SOV*	Reading	PA	19612	**800-683-4663**	610-320-8400	355-2
Sovereign Bank FSB PO Box 12646 *Cust Svc	Reading	PA	19612	**800-683-4663***	610-320-8400	71
Sovereign Bank Wholesale Lending Div 1022 E Lancaster Ave	Rosemont	PA	19010	**888-696-8879**	610-525-1860	498
Sovereign Packaging Group PO Box 1092	Buffalo	NY	14240	**800-888-4910**	716-856-4910	3
Sovereign Specialty Chemicals 6315 Wiehe Rd	Cincinnati	OH	45237	**800-365-1301**	513-351-1300	3
Sovex Foods PO Box 2178	Collegedale	TN	37315	**877-396-3145**	423-396-3145	291-4
Sowles Co 3045 Hwy 13 Suite 100	Eagan	MN	55121	**888-376-9537**	651-287-9700	188-14
Soybean Assn. American 12125 Woodcrest Executive Dr Suite 100	Saint Louis	MO	63141	**800-688-7692**	314-576-1770	48-2
Soybean Board. United 16640 Chesterfield Grove Rd Suite 130	Chesterfield	MO	63005	**800-989-8721**	636-530-1777	48-2
Soybean Digest 7900 International Dr Suite 300 *Cust Svc	Minneapolis	MN	55425	**800-441-0294***	952-851-4677	449-1
SP Richards Co 6300 Highlands Pkwy	Smyrna	GA	30082	**888-436-6881**	770-436-6881	523
Spa at the Amelia Island Plantation 60 Amelia Village	Amelia Island	FL	32034	**877-843-7722**	904-432-2220	698
Spa at the Arizona Biltmore Resort 2400 E Missouri Ave	Phoenix	AZ	85016	**800-950-0086**	602-955-6600	698
Spa & Athletic Club at the Lodge at Breckinridge 112 Overlook Dr	Breckenridge	CO	80424	**800-736-1607**	970-453-4274	698
Spa-Atlantis 1350 N Ocean Blvd	Pompano Beach	FL	33062	**800-583-3500**	954-941-6688	697
Spa at the Bacara Resort 8103 Hollister Ave	Santa Barbara	CA	93117	**877-422-4245**	805-571-4210	698
Spa at the Beau Rivage Resort & Casino 875 Beach Blvd	Biloxi	MS	39530	**888-750-7111**	228-386-7474	698
Spa at Bernardus Lodge 415 Carmel Valley Rd PO Box 80	Carmel Valley	CA	93924	**888-648-9463**	831-658-3514	698
Spa at the Bodega Bay Lodge 103 Coast Hwy 1	Bodega Bay	CA	94923	**800-368-2468**	707-875-3525	698
Spa at Bonaventure Resort & Spa 250 Racquet Club Rd	Weston	FL	33326	**800-787-7248**	954-349-5515	698
Spa at the Breakers 1 S County Rd	Palm Beach	FL	33480	**888-273-2537**	561-653-6656	698
Spa at the Broadmoor 1 Lake Ave	Colorado Springs	CO	80906	**800-634-7711**	719-577-5770	698
Spa at the Camelback Inn JW Marriott Resort Golf Club & Spa 5402 E Lincoln Dr	Scottsdale	AZ	85253	**800-922-2635**	480-596-7040	698
Spa at Carefree Resort & Villas 37220 Mule Train Rd	Carefree	AZ	85377	**888-488-9034**	480-595-3853	698

Name / Address	City	State	ZIP	Toll-Free	Phone	Class
Spa at the Chattanoogan 1201 S Broad St	Chattanooga	TN	37402	**800-619-0018**	423-424-3779	698
Spa at the Chrysalis Inn 804 10th St	Bellingham	WA	98225	**888-808-0005**	360-392-5515	698
Spa Claremont at the Claremont Resort 41 Tunnel Rd	Berkeley	CA	94705	**800-551-7266**	510-549-8566	698
Spa at Coeur d'Alene 115 S 2nd St	Coeur d'Alene	ID	83814	**800-688-5253**	208-765-4000	697
Spa Concept Bromont 90 Stanstead St	Bromont	QC	J2L1K6	**800-567-7727**	450-534-2717	697
Spa at the CopperWynd Resort & Club 13225 N Eagle Ridge Dr	Fountain Hills	AZ	85268	**877-707-7760**	480-333-1835	698
Spa at Cordillera 2206 Cordillera Way	Edwards	CO	81623	**800-877-6419**	800-877-3529	698
Spa at La Costa 2100 Costa del Mar Rd	Carlsbad	CA	92009	**800-729-4772**	760-931-7570	698
Spa at the Delta Victoria Ocean Pointe Resort 45 Songhees Rd	Victoria	BC	V9A6T3	**800-575-8882**	250-360-5858	698
Spa at the Diplomat Country Club 501 Diplomat Pkwy	Hallandale	FL	33009	**800-327-1212**	954-883-4905	698
Spa at the Don CeSar Beach Resort 3400 Gulf Blvd	Saint Pete Beach	FL	33706	**800-282-1116**	727-360-1883	698
Spa at Eagle Crest Resort 1522 Cline Falls Hwy PO Box 1215	Redmond	OR	97756	**800-682-4786**	541-923-9647	698
Spa at Eden Roc A Renaissance Resort & Spa 4525 Collins Ave	Miami Beach	FL	33140	**800-327-8337**	305-674-5585	698
Spa Esmeralda at the Renaissance Esmeralda Resort 44-400 Indian Wells Ln	Indian Wells	CA	92210	**800-468-3571**	760-836-1265	698
Spa at the Fairmont Inn Sonoma Mission Inn 100 Boyes Blvd	Sonoma	CA	95476	**877-289-7354**		698
Spa & Fitness Club at the Four Seasons Hotel Washington 2800 Pennsylvania Ave NW	Washington	DC	20007	**800-819-5053**	202-944-2022	698
Spa at Fox Harb'r 1337 Fox Harbour Rd	Wallace	NS	B0K1Y0	**866-257-1801**	902-257-4307	698
Spa Fusion at the Hilton San Francisco 333 O'Farrell St	San Francisco	CA	94102	**800-445-8667**	415-923-5014	698
Spa Gaucin at the Saint Regis Monarch Beach 1 Monarch Beach Resort	Dana Point	CA	92629	**800-722-1543**	949-234-3367	698
Spa at Grand Lake 1667 Exeter Rd	Lebanon	CT	06249	**800-843-7721**	860-642-4306	697
Spa Grande at the Grand Wailea Resort Maui 3850 Wailea Alanui Dr	Wailea	HI	96753	**800-772-1933**	808-875-1234	698
Spa at Gurney's Inn Resort 290 Old Montauk Hwy	Montauk	NY	11954	**800-848-7639**	631-668-1892	698
Spa at the Hilton Sedona Resort 10 Ridge View Dr	Sedona	AZ	86351	**877-273-3762**	928-284-6975	698
Spa at the Hilton Short Hills Hotel 41 JFK Pkwy	Short Hills	NJ	07078	**800-445-8667**	973-912-7956	698
Spa at the Homestead Rt 220 Main St PO Box 2000	Hot Springs	VA	24445	**800-838-1766**	540-839-7547	698
Spa Hotel & Casino 100 N Indian Canyon Dr	Palm Springs	CA	92262	**800-854-1279**	760-325-1461	133
Spa at the Hotel Hershey 100 Hotel Rd	Hershey	PA	17033	**877-772-9988**	717-520-5888	698
Spa Internazionale at Fisher Island Hotel & Resort 1 Fisher Island Dr	Miami	FL	33109	**800-537-3708**	305-535-6030	698
Spa at the JW Marriott Denver at Cherry Creek 150 Clayton Ln	Denver	CO	80206	**800-228-9290**	303-316-2700	698
Spa at the JW Marriott Desert Springs Resort Palm Desert 74855 Country Club Dr	Palm Desert	CA	92260	**800-331-3112**	760-341-1856	698
Spa at the JW Marriott Ihilani Resort 92-1001 Olani St	Kapolei	HI	96707	**800-626-4446**	808-679-3321	698
Spa at the Kauai Marriott Resort & Beach Club 3610 Rice St	Lihue	HI	96766	**800-220-2925**	808-246-4918	698
Spa at Kingsmill Resort 1010 Kingsmill Rd	Williamsburg	VA	23185	**800-965-4772**	757-253-8230	698
Spa at the Laguna Cliffs Marriott Resort 25135 Park Lantern	Dana Point	CA	92629	**800-228-9290**	949-487-7576	698
Spa at the Lansdowne Resort 44050 Woodridge Pkwy	Leesburg	VA	20176	**800-541-4801**	703-729-4036	698
Spa Las Palmas at the Marriott Rancho Las Palmas Resort 41000 Bob Hope Dr	Rancho Mirage	CA	92270	**877-843-7720**	760-836-3106	698
Spa Las Palmas at Marriott's Rancho Las Palmas Resort 41000 Bob Hope Dr	Rancho Mirage	CA	92270	**800-932-2198**	760-836-3106	698
Spa at the Loews Santa Monica Beach Hotel 1700 Ocean Ave	Santa Monica	CA	90401	**800-325-6397**	310-899-4040	698
Spa at the Loews Ventana Canyon Resort 7000 N Resort Dr	Tucson	AZ	85750	**800-235-6397**	520-529-7830	698
Spa Luana at Turtle Bay Resort 57-091 Kamehameha Hwy	Kahuku	HI	96731	**800-203-3650**	808-447-6868	698
Spa at the Mandarin Oriental Miami 500 Brickell Key Dr	Miami	FL	33131	**800-526-6566**	305-913-8332	698
Spa at the Marriott Harbor Beach Resort 3030 Holiday Dr	Fort Lauderdale	FL	33316	**800-222-6543**	954-765-3032	698
Spa at the Marriott Marco Island Resort Golf Club & Spa 400 S Collier Blvd	Marco Island	FL	34145	**800-438-4373**	239-642-2686	698
Spa at the Marriott Tampa Waterside 700 S Florida Ave	Tampa	FL	33602	**888-268-1616**	813-204-6300	698
Spa at the Marriott's Grand Hotel & Resort 1 Grand Blvd PO Box 639	Point Clear	AL	36564	**800-544-9933**	251-928-9201	698
Spa at Le Merigot JW Marriott Beach Hotel Santa Monica 1740 Ocean Ave	Santa Monica	CA	90401	**877-637-4468**	310-395-9700	698
Spa Moana at the Hyatt Regency Maui Resort 200 Nohea Kai Dr	Lahaina	HI	96761	**800-233-1234**	808-667-4725	698
Spa at Montage Resort 30801 S Coast Hwy	Laguna Beach	CA	92651	**866-271-6953**	949-715-6010	698
Spa at Monterey Plaza Hotel 400 Cannery Row	Monterey	CA	93940	**800-334-3999**	831-645-4098	698
Spa at the Moody Gardens Hotel 7 Hope Blvd	Galveston	TX	77554	**888-388-8484**	409-683-4440	698
Spa Moulay at the Hyatt Regency Lake Las Vegas Resort 101 Montelago Blvd	Henderson	NV	89011	**800-233-1234**	702-567-6049	698
Spa Mystique at the Westin Century Plaza Hotel 10220 Constellation Ave	Los Angeles	CA	90067	**800-937-8461**	310-551-3251	698
Spa at Nemacolin Woodlands Resort 1001 Lafayette Dr	Farmington	PA	15437	**800-422-2736**	724-329-6772	698
Spa at the Norwich Inn 607 W Thames St	Norwich	CT	06360	**800-275-4772**	860-886-2401	698
Spa Olakino at the Waikiki Beach Marriott Resort 2552 Kalakaua Ave	Honolulu	HI	96815	**800-367-5370**	808-924-2121	698
Spa at the Omni Orlando Resort at Championsgate 1500 Masters Blvd	Champions Gate	FL	33896	**800-843-6664**	407-390-6664	698
Spa at the Omni Tucson National Golf Resort & Spa 2727 W Club Dr	Tucson	AZ	85742	**800-297-2000**	520-877-2367	698
Spa at the Orlando World Center Marriott Resort & Convention Center 8701 World Ctr Dr	Orlando	FL	32821	**800-621-0638**	407-238-8705	698
Spa Pallazo at the Boca Raton Resort & Club 501 E Camino Real	Boca Raton	FL	33432	**888-491-2622**	561-347-4772	698
Spa at Pebble Beach 17 Mile Dr PO Box 1128	Pebble Beach	CA	93953	**888-565-7615**	831-649-7615	698
Spa at Pechanga Resort & Casino 45000 Pechanga Pkwy	Temecula	CA	92592	**888-732-4264**	951-719-8501	698
Spa at the PGA National Resort 450 Avenue of the Champions	Palm Beach Gardens	FL	33418	**800-633-9150**	561-627-3111	698
Spa at Pinehurst Resort 180 Barrett Rd E	Pinehurst	NC	28374	**800-487-4653**	910-235-8320	698
Spa at the Ponte Vedra Inn & Club 200 Ponte Vedra Blvd	Ponte Vedra Beach	FL	32082	**800-234-7842**	904-273-7700	698
Spa Professionals. Association of Pool & 2111 Eisenhower Ave	Alexandria	VA	22314	**800-323-3996**	703-838-0083	49-4
Spa La Quinta at La Quinta Resort 49-499 Eisenhower Dr PO Box 69	La Quinta	CA	92253	**800-598-3828**	760-777-4800	698
Spa Resort The 100 N Indian Canyon Dr	Palm Springs	CA	92262	**800-854-1279**	760-325-1461	655
Spa Resort Casino 401 E Amado Rd	Palm Springs	CA	92262	**800-854-1279**	760-883-1000	655
Spa at the Ritz-Carlton Amelia Island 4750 Amelia Island Pkwy	Amelia Island	FL	32034	**800-241-3333**	904-277-1087	698
Spa at the Ritz-Carlton Bachelor Gulch 0130 Daybreak Ridge	Avon	CO	81620	**800-241-3333**	970-343-1138	698
Spa at the Ritz-Carlton Coconut Grove 3300 SW 27th Ave	Coconut Grove	FL	33133	**800-241-3333**	305-644-4680	698
Spa at the Ritz-Carlton Half Moon Bay 1 Miramontes Pt Rd	Half Moon Bay	CA	94019	**800-241-3333**	650-712-7091	698
Spa at the Ritz-Carlton Huntington Hotel 1401 S Oak Knoll Ave	Pasadena	CA	91106	**800-241-3333**	626-585-6414	698
Spa at the Ritz-Carlton Key Biscayne 455 Grand Bay Dr	Key Biscayne	FL	33149	**800-241-3333**	305-365-4158	698
Spa at the Ritz-Carlton Naples 280 Vanderbilt Beach Rd	Naples	FL	34108	**800-241-3333**	239-514-6100	698
Spa at the Ritz-Carlton New Orleans 921 Canal St	New Orleans	LA	70112	**800-241-3333**	504-670-2929	698
Spa at the Ritz-Carlton Orlando Grande Lakes 4012 Central Florida Pkwy	Orlando	FL	32837	**800-241-3333**	407-393-4200	698
Spa at the Ritz-Carlton Reynolds Plantation 1 Lake Oconee Tr	Greensboro	GA	30642	**800-241-3333**	706-467-7181	698
Spa at the Ritz-Carlton Sarasota 1111 Ritz-Carlton Dr	Sarasota	FL	34236	**800-241-3333**	941-309-2000	698
Spa at the Ritz-Carlton South Beach 1 Lincoln Rd	Miami Beach	FL	33139	**800-241-3333**	786-276-4090	698
Spa at the Ritz-Carlton Tysons Corner 1700 Tysons Blvd	McLean	VA	22102	**800-241-3333**	703-744-3924	698
Spa at the Saddlebrook Resort 5700 Saddlebrook Way	Wesley Chapel	FL	33543	**800-729-8383**	813-907-4419	698
Spa at the Sagamore 110 Sagamore Rd	Bolton Landing	NY	12814	**800-358-3585**	518-743-6081	698
Spa at the Saint Regis Aspen 315 E Dean St	Aspen	CO	81611	**888-625-5144**	970-920-3300	698
Spa at the Salish Lodge 6501 Railroad Ave PO Box 1109	Snoqualmie	WA	98065	**800-272-5474**	425-831-6535	698
Spa Samadhi at Inn at Sunrise Springs 242 Los Pinos Rd	Santa Fe	NM	87507	**800-955-0028**	505-428-3614	698
Spa at the Sanctuary on Camelback Mountain 5700 E McDonald Dr	Paradise Valley	AZ	85253	**800-245-2051**	480-948-2100	698
Spa at the Sanderling Resort 1461 Duck Rd	Duck	NC	27949	**800-701-4111**	252-261-7744	698
Spa at Sanibel Harbour Resort 17260 Harbour Pointe Dr	Fort Myers	FL	33908	**800-676-7777**	239-466-2156	698
Spa at Saybrook Point Inn 2 Bridge St	Old Saybrook	CT	06475	**800-243-0212**	860-395-3245	698
Spa Shiki at the Lodge of Four Seasons Horseshoe Bend Pkwy PO Box 215	Lake Ozark	MO	65049	**800-843-5253**	573-365-8108	698
Spa du Soleil at the Auberge du Soleil 180 Rutherford Hill Rd	Rutherford	CA	94573	**800-348-5406**	707-967-3159	698
Spa at the Sonesta Beach Resort Key Biscayne 350 Ocean Dr	Key Biscayne	FL	33149	**800-766-3782**	305-365-2949	698
Spa at the Stoweflake Mountain Resort 1746 Mountain Rd PO Box 369	Stowe	VT	05672	**800-253-2232**	802-760-1083	698
Spa Suites at Kahala Mandarin Oriental Hawaii Resort 5000 Kahala Ave	Honolulu	HI	96816	**800-367-2525**	808-739-8938	698
Spa Terre at the Hotel Viking 1 Bellevue Ave	Newport	RI	02840	**800-556-7126**	401-848-4848	698
Spa Terre at the Inn & Spa at Loretto 211 Old Santa Fe Trail	Santa Fe	NM	87501	**800-727-5531**	505-984-7997	698
Spa Terre at the Little Palm Island Resort 28500 Overseas Hwy	Little Torch Key	FL	33042	**800-343-8567**	305-515-3028	698
Spa Terre at Paradise Point Resort 1404 Vacation Rd	San Diego	CA	92109	**800-344-2626**	858-581-5998	698

Name / Address	City	State	Zip	Toll-Free	Phone	Class
Spa Terre at SunBurst Resort 4925 N Scottsdale Rd	Scottsdale	AZ	85251	**800-528-7867**	480-424-6072	698
Spa Toccare at Borgata Hotel Casino 1 Borgata Way	Atlantic City	NJ	08401	**866-692-6742**	609-317-7555	698
Spa at Topnotch at Stowe Resort 4000 Mountain Rd	Stowe	VT	05672	**800-451-8686**	802-253-6463	698
Spa Torrey Pines at the Lodge at Torrey Pines 11480 N Torrey Pines Rd	La Jolla	CA	92037	**800-656-0087**	858-777-6690	698
Spa at the Vail Marriott Mountain Resort 715 W Lionshead Cir	Vail	CO	81657	**800-648-0720**	970-479-5004	698
Spa at the Vail Mountain Lodge 352 E Meadow Dr	Vail	CO	81657	**866-476-0700**	970-476-7721	698
Spa at the Villagio Inn 6481 Washington St	Yountville	CA	94599	**800-351-1133**	707-948-5050	698
Spa Vita di Lago at The Ritz Carlton Lake Las Vegas 1610 Lake Las Vegas Pkwy	Henderson	NV	89011	**800-241-3333**	702-567-4600	698
Spa at the Watermark Hotel 212 W Crockett St	San Antonio	TX	78205	**866-605-1212**	210-396-5840	698
Spa at the Westin Maui Resort 2365 Kaanapali Pkwy	Lahaina	HI	96761	**866-500-8313**	808-661-2588	698
Spa at White Oaks Conference Resort 253 Taylor Rd	Niagara-on-the-Lake	ON	L0S1J0	**800-263-5766**	905-641-2599	698
Spa Without Walls at the Fairmont Orchid Hawaii 1 N Kaniku Dr	Kohala Coast	HI	96743	**800-845-9905**	808-885-2000	698
Space Center Inc 2501 Rosegate	Saint Paul	MN	55113	**800-548-9737**	651-604-4200	639
Space Coast Credit Union PO Box 419001	Melbourne	FL	32941	**800-447-7228**	321-752-2222	216
Space Imaging Inc 12076 Grant St	Thornton	CO	80241	**800-697-4454**	303-254-2000	713
Space Institute. University of Tennessee 411 BH Goethert Pkwy	Tullahoma	TN	37388	**888-822-8874**	931-393-7100	654
Space Needle 400 Broad St *Resv	Seattle	WA	98109	**800-937-9582***	206-905-2200	50
Space Science Education. Challenger Center for 1250 N Pitt St	Alexandria	VA	22314	**800-987-8277**	703-683-9740	48-11
Space Systems/Loral 3825 Fabian Way	Palo Alto	CA	94303	**800-332-6490**	650-852-4000	633
SpaceCom Systems Inc 1950 E 71st St	Tulsa	OK	74136	**800-950-6690**		669
SpaceGuard Products 711 S Commerce Dr	Seymour	IN	47274	**800-841-0680**	812-523-3044	281
Spacelabs Medical Inc 5150 220th Ave SE	Issaquah	WA	98029	**800-287-7108**	425-657-7200	249
Spacesaver Corp 1450 Janesville Ave	Fort Atkinson	WI	53538	**800-492-3434**	920-563-6362	281
Spaghetti Warehouse Inc 12200 Stemmons Fwy Suite 100 *Cust Svc	Dallas	TX	75234	**800-929-4000***	972-241-5500	657
SpaHalekulani at the Halekulani Hotel 2199 Kalia Rd	Honolulu	HI	96815	**800-367-2343**	808-931-5322	698
Spalding 150 Brookdale Dr *Cust Svc	Springfield	MA	01104	**800-772-5346***	413-735-1400	701
Spalding Rehabilitation Hospital 900 Potomac St	Aurora	CO	80011	**800-367-3309**	303-367-1166	366-4
Spalding University 851 S 4th St	Louisville	KY	40203	**800-896-8941**	502-585-9911	163
Span-America Medical Systems Inc 70 Commerce Ctr *NASDAQ: SPAN*	Greenville	SC	29615	**800-888-6752**	864-288-8877	469
Spandeck Inc 129 Confederate Dr	Franklin	TN	37064	**800-272-3325**	615-794-4556	462
Spangler Candy Co 400 N Portland St PO Box 71 *Sales	Bryan	OH	43506	**800-653-8638***	419-636-4221	291-8
Spanish Military Hospital Museum 3 Aviles St	Saint Augustine	FL	32084	**800-597-7177**	904-827-0807	509
Sparkle International Inc 26851 Richmond Rd	Cleveland	OH	44146	**800-321-0770**	216-464-4212	150
Sparkletts Drinking Water Corp 3280 E Foothill Blvd Suite 400	Pasadena	CA	91107	**800-492-8377**	626-585-1000	792
Sparks Belting Co 3800 Stahl Dr SE	Grand Rapids	MI	49546	**800-451-4537**	616-949-2750	364
Sparks Exhibits & Environments 10232 Palm Dr	Santa Fe Springs	CA	90670	**800-925-7727**	562-941-0101	230
Sparling Instruments Co Inc 4097 N Temple City Blvd *Sales	El Monte	CA	91731	**800-800-3569***	626-444-0571	486
Sparrer Sausage Co Inc 4320 W Ogden Ave	Chicago	IL	60623	**800-666-3287**	773-762-3334	291-26
Sparrow Label Group PO Box 5010	Brentwood	TN	37024	**800-347-4777**	615-371-6800	643
Spartan Chemical Co Inc 1110 Spartan Dr	Maumee	OH	43537	**800-537-8990**	419-531-5551	143
Spartan Distributors Inc 487 W Division St	Sparta	MI	49345	**800-822-2216**	616-887-7301	270
Spartan School of Aeronautics 8820 E Pine St *Admissions	Tulsa	OK	74115	**800-331-1204***	918-836-6886	787
Spartanburg Herald-Journal 189 W Main St	Spartanburg	SC	29304	**800-922-4158**	864-582-4511	522-2
Spartanburg Regional Medical Center 101 E Wood St	Spartanburg	SC	29303	**800-868-8784**	864-560-6000	366-2
Spartanburg Steel Products Inc PO Box 6428	Spartanburg	SC	29304	**800-334-6318**	864-585-5216	124
Spartanburg Technical College PO Box 4386	Spartanburg	SC	29305	**800-922-3679**	864-591-3600	787
Spartech Corp 120 S Central Ave Suite 1700 *NYSE: SEH*	Clayton	MO	63105	**888-721-4242**	314-721-4242	594-2
Sparton Corp 2400 E Ganson St *NYSE: SPA*	Jackson	MI	49202	**800-248-9579**	517-787-8600	681
Sparton Electronics 8500 Bluewater Rd NW	Albuquerque	NM	87121	**800-772-7866**	505-892-5300	200
Spaulding for Children 16250 Northland Dr Suite 120	Southfield	MI	48075	**877-767-5437**	248-443-7080	48-6
Spaulding Composites Co 55 Nadeau Dr	Rochester	NH	03867	**800-964-0555**	603-332-0555	588
Spaulding Composites Co Fab Div 55 Nadeau Dr	Rochester	NH	03867	**800-964-0555**	603-332-0555	591
Spaulding Lighting Inc 1736 Dreman Ave *Cust Svc	Cincinnati	OH	45223	**800-221-5666***	513-541-3486	431
SPD Technologies 13500 Roosevelt Blvd	Philadelphia	PA	19116	**800-832-4773**	215-677-4900	715
SPE (Society of Petroleum Engineers) 222 Palisades Creek Dr	Richardson	TX	75080	**800-456-6863**	972-952-9393	48-12
Speakeasy Inc 2222 2nd Ave	Seattle	WA	98121	**800-556-5829**	206-728-9770	390
Speaker JW Corp PO Box 489	Germantown	WI	53022	**800-558-7288**	262-251-6660	430
Speakers Guild Inc PO Box 1540	Sandwich	MA	02563	**800-343-4530**	508-888-6702	699
Speaking Rock Casino & Entertainment Centre 122 S Old Pueblo Rd	El Paso	TX	79907	**800-772-2646**	915-860-7777	133
Speakman Co 400 Anchor Mill Rd	New Castle	DE	19720	**800-537-2107**	302-764-9100	598
Spear-O-Wigwam Guest Ranch PO Box 1081	Sheridan	WY	82801	**888-818-3833**		238
Spearfish Canyon Resort 10619 Roughlock Falls Rd	Lead	SD	57754	**877-975-6343**	605-584-3435	655
Spec Building Materials Inc 4300 West Ave	San Antonio	TX	78213	**800-588-3892**	210-342-2727	190-4
Spec Print Inc 1710 N Mt Juliet Rd	Mount Juliet	TN	37122	**800-989-3325**	615-758-5913	404
Specco Industries Inc 13087 Main St	Lemont	IL	60439	**800-441-6646**	630-257-5060	143
Special Counsel 1 Independent Dr Suite 112	Jacksonville	FL	32202	**800-737-3436**	904-737-3436	707
Special Education Report 360 Hiatt Dr *Sales	Palm Beach Gardens	FL	33418	**800-621-5463***	561-622-6520	521-4
Special Interest Autos Magazine PO Box 196	Bennington	VT	05201	**800-227-4373**	802-442-3101	449-3
Special Metals Corp 4317 Middle Settlement Rd	New Hartford	NY	13413	**800-334-8351**	315-798-2900	476
Special Military Active Retired Travel Club (SMART) 600 University Office Blvd Suite 1A	Pensacola	FL	32504	**800-354-7681**		48-23
Special Olympics Inc 1133 19th St NW 11th Fl	Washington	DC	20036	**800-700-8585**	202-628-3630	48-22
Special Plastics Systems Inc 385 W Valley St	San Bernardino	CA	92401	**800-423-4422**	909-888-2531	585
Special Projects Mfg Co 7601 Wyatt Dr	Fort Worth	TX	76108	**800-342-7458**	817-246-2461	446
Special Wish Foundation Inc 5340 E Main St Suite 208	Columbus	OH	43213	**800-486-9474**	614-575-9474	48-5
Specialists Inc. American Assn of Physician 2296 Henderson Mill Rd Suite 206	Atlanta	GA	30345	**800-447-9397**	770-939-8555	49-8
Specialized Bicycle Components 15130 Concord Cir	Morgan Hill	CA	95037	**877-808-8154**	408-779-6229	83
Specialized Investigations 14530 Delano St	Van Nuys	CA	91411	**800-714-3728**	818-909-9607	392
Specialized Printed Forms Inc 352 Center St	Caledonia	NY	14423	**800-688-2381**	585-538-2381	111
Specialized Services Inc 23077 Greenfield Rd Suite 470	Southfield	MI	48075	**866-774-2004**	248-557-1030	455
Specialized Vehicles Corp 400 Hackney Ave	Washington	NC	97889	**800-763-0700**	252-946-6521	505
Specialty Bakers Inc 450 S State Rd	Marysville	PA	17053	**800-233-0778**	717-957-2131	291-1
Specialty Brands Inc 4200 E Concours Dr *Cust Svc	Ontario	CA	91764	**800-782-1180***	909-477-4700	291-36
Specialty Catalog Corp 21 Bristol Dr	South Easton	MA	02375	**800-472-4017**	508-238-0199	451
Specialty Filaments Inc 1 Howard St	Burlington	VT	05401	**800-451-3448**	802-863-6333	594-1
Specialty Food Trade Inc. National Assn for the 120 Wall St 27th Fl	New York	NY	10005	**800-627-3869**	212-482-6440	49-6
Specialty Graphic Imaging Assn (SGIA) 10015 Main St	Fairfax	VA	22031	**888-385-3588**	703-385-1335	49-16
Specialty Hospital Jacksonville 4901 Richard St	Jacksonville	FL	32207	**800-378-9497**	904-737-3120	366-5
Specialty Laboratories Inc 2211 Michigan Ave *NYSE: SP* ■ *Sales	Santa Monica	CA	90404	**800-421-7110***	310-828-6543	409
Specialty Merchandise Corp 9447 De Soto Ave *Orders	Chatsworth	CA	91311	**800-877-7621***	818-998-3300	361
Specialty Motors Inc 25060 Ave Tibbitts	Valencia	CA	91355	**800-232-2612**	661-257-7388	507
Specialty Plastic Fabricators Inc 9658 W 196th St	Mokena	IL	60448	**800-747-9509**	708-479-5501	198
Specialty Products & Insulation Co 1097 Commercial Ave	East Petersburg	PA	17520	**800-788-7764**	717-519-4000	190-4
Specialty Rental Tools & Supply Inc 1131 E FM 517	Alvin	TX	77511	**800-253-1085**	281-331-1800	261-2
Specialty Tires of America Inc 1600 Washington St	Indiana	PA	15701	**800-622-7327**	724-349-9010	739
Specialty Tools & Fasteners Distributors Assn (STAFDA) 500 Elm Grove Rd	Elm Grove	WI	53122	**800-352-2981**	262-784-4774	49-18
Specialty Tours Inc 3095 S Parker Rd Suite 150	Aurora	CO	80014	**800-342-4299**	303-337-7488	748
Specialty Vehicle Institute of America (SVIA) 2 Jenner St Suite 150	Irvine	CA	92618	**800-887-2887**	949-727-3727	49-21
Specification Rubber Products Inc 1568 1st St N	Alabaster	AL	35007	**800-633-3415**	205-663-2521	321
Speck Plastics Inc PO Box 421	Nazareth	PA	18064	**800-755-2922**	610-759-1807	591
Spec's Liquor Warehouse 2410 Smith St	Houston	TX	77006	**888-526-8787**	713-526-8787	435
Spec's Music Inc 501 Collins Ave	Miami Beach	FL	33139	**800-540-1242**	305-534-3667	514
Spectacular Sport Specials Inc 5813 Citrus Blvd	New Orleans	LA	70123	**800-451-5772**	504-734-9511	760
Spectator The 44 Frid St	Hamilton	ON	L8N3G3	**800-263-6902**	905-526-3333	522-1
Spectera Inc 2811 Lord Baltimore Dr	Baltimore	MD	21244	**800-638-3120**	410-265-6084	384-3
Spectera Vision 100 Corporate Pt Suite 285	Culver City	CA	90230	**800-305-0230**	310-242-6200	384-3
Spectra Fund Alger Shareholder Services 30 Montgomery St	Jersey City	NJ	07302	**800-711-6141**		517
Spectra-Physics Inc 1335 Terra Bella Ave	Mountain View	CA	94043	**800-456-2552**	650-961-2550	416

Company	City	State	ZIP	Toll-Free	Phone	Class
Spectrachem Corp 10 Dell Glen Ave Suite 3A	Lodi	NJ	07644	**800-524-2806**	973-253-3553	381
SpectraLink Corp 5755 Central Ave. *NASDAQ: SLNK*	Boulder	CO	80301	**800-676-5465**	303-440-5330	720
Spectranetics Corp 96 Talamine Ct *NASDAQ: SPNC*	Colorado Springs	CO	80907	**800-633-0960**	719-633-8333	415
Spectraserv Inc 75 Jacobus Ave.	South Kearny	NJ	07032	**800-445-4436**	973-589-0277	769
SpectraSite Inc 100 Regency Forest Dr Suite 400 *NYSE: SSI*	Cary	NC	27511	**888-468-0112**	919-468-0112	168
Spectro Alloys Corp 13220 Doyle Path	Rosemount	MN	55068	**800-328-9321**	651-437-2815	476
SPECTRO Analytical Instruments Inc 1515 N Hwy 281	Marble Falls	TX	78654	**800-580-6608**	830-798-8786	464
Spectronics Corp 956 Brush Hollow Rd	Westbury	NY	11590	**800-274-8888**		200
Spectrum Brands 2150 Schultz Rd	Saint Louis	MO	63146	**800-341-0020**	314-427-4886	276
Spectrum Communications Cabling Services Inc 226 N Lincoln Ave	Corona	CA	92882	**800-319-8711**	951-371-0549	174
Spectrum Corp 10048 Easthaven Blvd.	Houston	TX	77075	**800-392-5050**	713-944-6200	692
Spectrum Dyed Yarns Inc 136 Patterson Rd	Kings Mountain	NC	28086	**800-221-9456**	704-739-7401	730-9
Spectrum Glass Co PO Box 646	Woodinville	WA	98072	**800-426-3120**	425-483-6699	325
Spectrum Healthcare Resources Inc 12647 Olive Blvd Suite 600	Saint Louis	MO	63141	**800-325-3982**	314-744-4100	455
Spectrum Industries Inc 1600 Johnson St	Chippewa Falls	WI	54729	**800-235-1262**	715-723-6750	281
Spectrum Interiors Inc 2652 Crescent Springs Pike	Crescent Springs	KY	41017	**888-353-2696**	859-331-2696	188-9
Spectrum Label Corp 30803 San Clemente St	Hayward	CA	94544	**800-545-2235**	510-477-0707	404
Spectrum Laboratories Inc 18617 Broadwick St	Rancho Dominguez	CA	90220	**800-634-3300**	310-885-4600	410
Spectrum Organic Products Inc 5341 Old Redwood Hwy	Petaluma	CA	94952	**800-995-2705**	707-778-8900	291-19
Spectrum Resources Tower LP 6400 Arlington Blvd Suite 1000	Falls Church	VA	22042	**888-508-6937**	703-533-1312	168
Spectrum Signal Processing Inc 2700 Production Way Suite 200 *NASDAQ: SSPI*	Burnaby	BC	V5A4X1	**800-663-8986**	604-421-5422	613
Spectrum Site Management Corp 6060 N Central Expy Suite 642	Dallas	TX	75206	**800-966-8885**	214-540-0359	168
Spectrum Systems Inc 3410 W Nine-Mile Rd	Pensacola	FL	32526	**877-837-6644**	850-944-3392	410
Spedecut Abrasives 10042 Rancho Rd	Adelanto	CA	92301	**800-423-4836**	760-246-6850	1
Speech-Language-Hearing Assn. American 10801 Rockville Pike	Rockville	MD	20852	**800-498-2071**	301-897-5700	49-8
Speechwriter's Newsletter 316 N Michigan Ave Suite 300	Chicago	IL	60601	**800-878-5331**	312-960-4100	521-11
Speedee Oil Change & Tune-Up Inc PO Box 1350	Madisonville	LA	70447	**800-451-7461**	985-845-1919	62-5
Speedling Inc 4300 Old 41 Hwy S PO box 7238	Sun City	FL	33586	**800-771-2543**	813-645-3221	363
Speedskating. US PO Box 450639	Westlake	OH	44145	**800-634-4766**	440-899-0128	48-22
Speedware Corp 9999 Cavendish Blvd Suite 100	Saint-Laurent	QC	H4M2X5	**800-361-6782**	514-747-7007	176-1
Speedway of Southern New Mexico 3590 W Picacho Ave	Las Cruces	NM	88005	**800-658-9650**	505-524-7913	504
Speedway SuperAmerica LLC 500 Speedway Dr **Cust Svc*	Enon	OH	45323	**800-643-1948***	937-864-3000	319
Speedy Auto & Glass Inc 9675 SE 36th St	Mercer Island	WA	98040	**800-533-6545**	206-232-9500	62-2
Speer Mechanical Inc 600 Oakland Park Ave	Columbus	OH	43214	**800-282-6017**	614-261-6331	188-10
Speidel Corp 25 Fairmount Ave	East Providence	RI	02914	**800-441-2200**	401-519-2000	400
Spelman College 350 Spelman Ln SW **Admissions*	Atlanta	GA	30314	**800-982-2411***	404-681-3643	163
Spenard Builders Supply Inc 840 K St Suite 200	Anchorage	AK	99501	**800-478-3141**	907-261-9120	359
Spencer Conference Centre 551 Windermere Rd	London	ON	N5X2T1	**800-983-6523**	519-679-4546	370
Spencer Cos Inc 120 Woodson St NW	Huntsville	AL	35801	**800-633-2910**	256-533-1150	569
Spencer Gifts Inc 6826 Black Horse Pike	Egg Harbor Township	NJ	08234	**800-762-0419**	609-645-3300	322
Spencer Industries Inc 19308 68th Ave S	Kent	WA	98032	**800-367-5646**	253-796-1100	759
Spencer Oil Co Inc 16410 Common Rd	Roseville	MI	48066	**800-445-7562**	586-775-5022	311
Spencer Press Inc 90 Spencer Dr.	Wells	ME	04090	**800-765-0039**	207-646-9926	615
Spencer Recovery Centers Inc 1316 S Coast Hwy	Laguna Beach	CA	92651	**800-252-6465**	949-376-3705	712
Spencer Turbine Co 600 Day Hill Rd	Windsor	CT	06095	**800-232-4321**	860-688-8361	19
Spencers Inc 238 Willow St	Mount Airy	NC	27030	**800-633-9111**	336-789-9111	153-18
Spenco Medical Corp PO Box 2501	Waco	TX	76702	**800-877-3626**	254-772-6000	469
Sperry Automatics Co Inc PO Box 717	Naugatuck	CT	06770	**800-923-3709**	203-729-4589	610
Sperry DR & Co 112 N Grant St	North Aurora	IL	60542	**888-997-9297**	630-892-4361	448
Sperry & Hutchinson Co Inc 45 Congress St Bldg L	Salem	MA	01970	**800-435-5674**	978-740-5600	9
Sperry Marine 1070 Seminole Trail **Cust Svc*	Charlottesville	VA	22901	**800-368-2010***	434-974-2000	519
Sperry & Rice Mfg Co LLC 9146 US Hwy 52	Brookville	IN	47012	**800-541-9277**	765-647-4141	664
Sperry Top-Sider 191 Spring St. **Cust Svc*	Lexington	MA	02421	**800-666-5689***	617-824-6000	296
SPESA (Sewn Products Equipment Suppliers Assn) 5107 Falls of the Neuse Suite B15	Raleigh	NC	27609	**888-447-7372**	919-872-8909	49-13
Spescom Software Inc 10052 Mesa Ridge Ct Suite 100	San Diego	CA	92121	**800-992-6784**	858-625-3000	176-1
Spherion Corp 2050 Spectrum Blvd. *NYSE: SFN*	Fort Lauderdale	FL	33309	**866-435-7456**	954-308-7600	707
Spheris 720 Cool Springs Blvd Suite 200	Franklin	TN	37067	**800-368-1717**	615-261-1500	755
Spherix Inc 12051 Indian Creek Ct *NASDAQ: SPEX ■ *Mktg*	Beltsville	MD	20705	**800-727-0602***	301-419-3900	191
SPI Pharma 321 Cherry Ln	New Castle	DE	19720	**800-789-9755**	302-576-8554	470
Spice Hunter Inc 184 Suburban Rd	San Luis Obispo	CA	93403	**800-444-3061**	805-544-4466	291-37
Spice World Inc 8101 Presidents Dr.	Orlando	FL	32809	**800-433-4979**	407-851-9432	291-37
Spicers Paper Inc 12310 E Slauson Ave	Santa Fe Springs	CA	90670	**800-774-2377**	562-698-1199	543
Spider Magazine 30 Grove St Suite C	Peterborough	NH	03458	**800-821-0115**	603-924-7209	449-6
Spider Staging Corp 365 Upland Dr	Tukwila	WA	98188	**800-428-7887**	206-575-6445	482
Spiegel Inc 3500 Lacey Rd **Orders*	Downers Grove	IL	60515	**800-345-4500***	630-986-8800	451
Spiewak I & Sons Inc 469 7th Ave 10th Fl **Cust Svc*	New York	NY	10018	**800-223-6850***	212-695-1620	153-19
Spillis Candela DMJM 800 Douglas Entrance North Tower 2nd Fl.	Coral Gables	FL	33134	**800-999-4727**	305-444-4691	258
Spin Magazine 205 Lexington Ave 3rd Fl. **Cust Svc*	New York	NY	10016	**800-274-7597***	212-231-7400	449-9
Spin Master Ltd 450 Front St W	Toronto	ON	M5V1B6	**800-622-8339**	416-364-6002	750
Spina Bifida Assn of America (SBAA) 4590 MacArthur Blvd NW Suite 250	Washington	DC	20007	**800-621-3141**	202-944-3285	48-17
Spinal Cord Injury Assn. National 6701 Democracy Blvd Suite 300-9	Bethesda	MD	20817	**800-962-9629**		48-17
Spindrift Inn 652 Cannery Row	Monterey	CA	93940	**800-841-1879**	831-646-8900	373
Spine Society. North American 22 Calendar Ct 2nd Fl.	La Grange	IL	60525	**877-774-6337**	708-588-8080	49-8
Spiniello Cos 12 E Daniel Rd	Fairfield	NJ	07004	**800-227-8384**	973-808-8383	187-10
Spinnaker Coating Inc 518 E Water St.	Troy	OH	45373	**800-543-9452**	937-332-6500	544
Spinnaker Industries Inc 4846 Jennings Ln.	Louisville	KY	40218	**800-932-6210**		404
Spir-It Inc 159 Rangeway Rd.	North Billerica	MA	01862	**800-321-7667**	978-964-1551	597
Spiral Binding Co Inc 1 Maltese Dr.	Totowa	NJ	07511	**800-631-3572**	973-256-0666	87
Spiralock Corp 25235 Dequindre Rd Madison Tech Ctr	Madison Heights	MI	48071	**800-521-2688**	248-543-7800	484
SpiralWest Inc 325 Pine St	Sausalito	CA	94965	**888-774-7259**	415-332-6797	4
Spirax Sarco Inc 1150 Northpoint Blvd	Blythewood	SC	29016	**800-883-4411**	803-714-2000	200
Spire Communications Inc PO Box 1989	Apopka	FL	32704	**877-797-7473**		390
Spire Corp 1 Patriots Pk *NASDAQ: SPIR*	Bedford	MA	01730	**800-510-4815**	781-275-6000	685
Spire Inc 65 Bay St	Dorchester	MA	02125	**800-653-3323**	617-426-3323	338
Spirent Communications 15200 Omega Dr	Rockville	MD	20850	**800-385-0110**	301-590-3600	247
Spirit Airlines Inc 2800 Executive Way	Miramar	FL	33025	**800-772-7117**	954-447-7965	26
Spirit Aviation Inc 16233 Vanowen St Hangar 1	Van Nuys	CA	91406	**800-995-1865**	818-989-4642	14
Spirit of Dubuque 400 3rd St Ice Harbor	Dubuque	IA	52001	**800-747-8093**	563-583-8093	218
Spirit Inspired PO Box 7904	Atlanta	GA	30357	**877-474-8460**	404-792-3664	130
Spirit Manufacturing Inc 5702 Krueger Dr.	Jonesboro	AR	72401	**800-258-4555**	870-935-1107	263
Spirit Services 1021 Ware St	Albany	GA	31705	**888-774-7484**	229-436-1811	434
Spirite Industries Inc 150 S Dean St	Englewood	NJ	07631	**800-272-6897**	201-871-4910	153-18
Spirits Council of the US Inc. Distilled 1250 'I' St NW Suite 400	Washington	DC	20005	**888-862-7597**	202-628-3544	49-6
SPL Integrated Solutions 9180 Rumsey Rd Suite D-4	Columbia	MD	21045	**800-292-4125**	410-992-0998	720
Split Rock Resort 1 Lake Dr	Lake Harmony	PA	18624	**800-255-7625**	570-722-9111	655
Spokane Art Supply Inc N 1303 Monroe St	Spokane	WA	99201	**800-556-5568**	509-327-6622	45
Spokane Civic Theatre 1020 N Howard St	Spokane	WA	99205	**800-446-9576**	509-325-1413	562
Spokane Community College 1810 N Greene St.	Spokane	WA	99217	**800-248-5644**	509-533-7000	160
Spokane Convention & Visitors Bureau 201 W Main Suite 301	Spokane	WA	99201	**888-776-5263**	509-747-3230	205
Spokane Falls Community College 3410 W Fort George Wright Dr	Spokane	WA	99224	**888-509-7944**	509-533-3500	160
Spokane Steel Foundry Co 3808 N Sullivan Rd Bldg 1	Spokane	WA	99220	**800-541-3601**	509-924-0440	302
Spokesman Review 999 W Riverside Ave	Spokane	WA	99201	**800-338-8801**	509-459-5000	522-2
Sponaugle GR & Sons Inc 4391 Chambers Hill Rd	Harrisburg	PA	17111	**800-866-7036**	717-564-1515	188-10
Spongex Corp 6 Bridge St	Shelton	CT	06484	**800-782-7749**	203-924-9335	590
Spontex Inc 100 Spontex Dr	Columbia	TN	38401	**800-251-4222**	931-388-5632	497
Spoon River Electric Co-op Inc PO Box 340	Canton	IL	61520	**877-404-2572**	309-647-2700	244
Sport Aviation Magazine 3000 Poberezny Rd	Oshkosh	WI	54902	**800-843-3612**	920-426-4800	449-20
Sport Chalet Inc 1 Sport Chalet Dr *NASDAQ: SPCH*	La Canada	CA	91011	**888-801-9162**	818-790-2717	702
Sport-Haley Inc 4600 E 48th Ave *NASDAQ: SPOR*	Denver	CO	80216	**800-627-9211**	303-320-8800	153-3
Sport Institute. North American Youth 4985 Oak Garden Dr.	Kernersville	NC	27284	**800-767-4916**	336-784-4926	48-22
Sport It Inc 12041 World Trade Dr Suite 2	San Diego	CA	92128	**888-233-2659**	858-592-6532	10
Sport Medicine. Canadian Academy of 1010 Polytek St Unit 14 Suite 100	Ottawa	ON	K1J9H9	**877-585-2394**	613-748-5851	49-8
Sport. National Assn for Girls & Women in 1900 Association Dr.	Reston	VA	20191	**800-213-7193**	703-476-3400	48-22
Sport Obermeyer Ltd USA Inc 115 AABC	Aspen	CO	81611	**800-525-4203**	970-925-5060	153-5
Sport Supply Group Inc 1901 Diplomat Dr.	Dallas	TX	75234	**800-527-7510**	972-484-9484	701
Sporting Classics Magazine PO Box 23707	Columbia	SC	29224	**800-849-1004**	803-736-2424	449-20

Name / Address	City	State	ZIP	Toll-Free	Phone	Class
Sporting Goods Assn. National 1601 Feehanville Dr Suite 300	Mount Prospect	IL	60056	**800-815-5422**	847-296-6742	49-4
Sporting News 10176 Corporate Sq Dr Suite 200	Saint Louis	MO	63132	**800-443-1886**	314-997-7111	449-20
SportPharma USA Inc 111 Speen St	Framingham	MA	01701	**800-654-4246**	508-620-1500	786
Sports Assn. Diabetes Exercise & 8001 Montcastle Dr	Nashville	TN	37221	**800-898-4322**		48-17
Sports Belle Inc 6723 Pleasant Ridge Rd *Sales	Knoxville	TN	37921	**800-888-2063***	865-938-2063	153-1
Sports Car Club of America (SCCA) PO Box 19400	Topeka	KS	66619	**800-770-2055**	785-357-7222	48-18
Sports Car Magazine 16842 Von Karman Ave Suite 125	Irvine	CA	92706	**800-722-7140**	949-417-6700	449-3
Sports Clubs of Canada 2 Sheppard Ave E Suite 200	Willowdale	ON	M2N5Y7	**800-967-5688**	416-221-6900	349
Sports Coaches Assn. National Youth 2050 Vista Pkwy	West Palm Beach	FL	33411	**800-729-2057**	561-684-1141	48-22
Sports Empire PO Box 6169	Lakewood	CA	90714	**800-255-5258**	562-920-2350	760
Sports Endeavors Inc 431 US Hwy 70-A E	Hillsborough	NC	27278	**800-934-3876**	919-644-6800	702
Sports Foundation. Women's Eisenhower Pk	East Meadow	NY	11554	**800-227-3988**	516-542-4700	48-22
Sports Hall of Fame. Missouri 3861 E Stan Musial Dr	Springfield	MO	65809	**800-498-5678**	417-889-3100	511
Sports Hall of Fame & Museum. Mississippi 1152 Lakeland Dr	Jackson	MS	39216	**800-280-3263**	601-982-8264	511
Sports Hall of Fame. Texas 1108 S University Parks Dr	Waco	TX	76706	**800-567-9561**	254-756-1633	511
Sports Illustrated for Kids Magazine 135 W 50th St *Cust Svc	New York	NY	10020	**800-992-0196***	212-522-1212	449-6
Sports Illustrated Magazine 135 W 50th St Time & Life Bldg	New York	NY	10020	**800-541-1000**	212-522-4044	449-20
Sports Leisure Vacations 9521-H Folsom Blvd	Sacramento	CA	95827	**800-951-5556**	916-361-2051	748
Sports Medicine. American Orthopaedic Society for 6300 N River Rd Suite 500	Rosemont	IL	60018	**877-321-3500**	847-292-4900	49-8
Sports. National Alliance for Youth 2050 Vista Pkwy	West Palm Beach	FL	33411	**800-729-2057**	561-684-1141	48-22
Sports Network 2200 Byberry Rd	Hatboro	PA	19040	**800-583-5499**	215-441-8444	520
Sports Officials. National Assn of 2017 Lathrop Ave	Racine	WI	53405	**800-733-6100**	262-632-5448	48-22
Sports Science Institute. Gatorade 617 W Main St	Barrington	IL	60010	**800-616-4774**	847-381-1980	654
Sports Sciences Assn. International 400 E Gutierrez St	Santa Barbara	CA	93101	**800-892-4772**	805-884-8111	48-22
Sports Section Inc 2150 Boggs Rd Suite 200	Duluth	GA	30096	**800-321-9127**	770-622-4900	581
Sports Spectrum Magazine PO Box 2037	Indian Trail	NC	28709	**866-821-2971**		449-20
Sports Travel Inc 60 Main St PO Box 50	Hatfield	MA	01038	**800-662-4424**	413-247-7678	748
Sports Turf Managers Assn 805 New Hampshire St Suite E	Lawrence	KS	66044	**800-323-3875**	785-843-2549	48-22
Sportsclub Assn. International Health Racquet & 263 Summer St 8th Fl	Boston	MA	02210	**800-228-4772**	617-951-0055	48-22
Sportservice Corp 40 Fountain Plaza	Buffalo	NY	14202	**800-828-7240**	716-858-5000	294
Sportsman's Guide Inc 411 Farwell Ave *NASDAQ: SGDE* ■ *Cust Svc	South Saint Paul	MN	55075	**800-888-5222***	651-451-3030	451
SportsPlay Equipment Inc 5642 Natural Bridge Ave	Saint Louis	MO	63120	**800-727-8180**	314-389-4140	340
SportsTicker Enterprises ESPN Plaza Bldg B 4th Fl	Bristol	CT	06010	**800-367-8935**	860-766-1899	520
Spot Image Corp 14595 Avion Pkwy Suite 500	Chantilly	VA	20151	**800-275-7768**	703-715-3100	713
Spot-Not Car Washes Inc PO Box 1269	Joplin	MO	64802	**800-682-7629**	417-781-6233	62-1
Spotlight 29 Casino 46-200 Harrison Pl	Coachella	CA	92236	**866-878-6729**	760-775-5566	133
Spouse Foundation. Well 63 W Main St Suite H	Freehold	NJ	07728	**800-838-0879**	732-577-8899	48-6
Spradling International Inc 200 Cahaba Valley Pkwy PO Box 1668	Pelham	AL	35124	**800-333-0955**	205-985-4206	583
Sprague Energy 2 International Dr Suite 200	Portsmouth	NH	03801	**800-225-1560**	603-431-1000	569
Spraying Systems Co PO Box 7900	Wheaton	IL	60189	**800-957-7729**	630-665-5000	478
Sprayway Inc 500 S Vista Ave	Addison	IL	60101	**800-332-9000**	630-628-3000	143
SPRE (Society of Park & Recreation Educators) c/o National Recreation & Park Assn 22377 Belmont Ridge Rd	Ashburn	VA	20148	**800-626-6772**	703-858-0784	48-23
Spreitzer Inc 3145 16th Ave SW	Cedar Rapids	IA	52404	**800-823-0399**	319-365-9155	353
Spring Arbor Distributors 1 Ingram Blvd	La Vergne	TN	37086	**800-395-4340**		97
Spring Arbor University 106 E Main St	Spring Arbor	MI	49283	**800-968-0011**	517-750-1200	163
Spring Creek Ranch 1800 Spirit Dance Rd	Jackson	WY	83001	**800-443-6139**	307-733-8833	373
Spring Crest Window Fashions 4375 Prado Rd Unit 104	Corona	CA	92880	**800-552-5523**	951-340-2293	357
Spring Engineers Inc 9740 Tanner Rd	Houston	TX	77041	**800-899-9488**	713-690-9488	705
Spring Glen Fresh Foods Inc 314 Spring Glen Dr PO Box 518	Ephrata	PA	17522	**800-641-2853**	717-733-2201	291-19
Spring-Green Lawn Care Corp 11909 Spaulding School Dr	Plainfield	IL	60544	**800-435-4051**	815-436-8777	421
Spring Grove Cemetery 4521 Spring Grove Ave	Cincinnati	OH	45232	**888-853-2230**	513-681-6680	499
Spring Grove Hospital Center 55 Wade Ave	Catonsville	MD	21228	**866-734-3337**	410-402-6000	366-3
Spring Harbor Hospital 123 Andover Rd	Westbrook	ME	04092	**888-524-0080**	207-761-2200	366-3
Spring Hill College 4000 Dauphin St	Mobile	AL	36608	**800-742-6704**	251-380-4000	163
Spring Lake Village 5555 Montgomery Dr	Santa Rosa	CA	95409	**800-795-1267**	707-538-8400	659
Springdale Chamber of Commerce 202 W Emma	Springdale	AR	72765	**800-972-7261**	479-872-2222	137
Springer Electric Co-op Inc PO Box 698	Springer	NM	87747	**800-288-1353**	505-483-2421	244
Springer Penguin Inc 460 Grand Blvd	Westbury	NY	11590	**800-529-4375**	516-333-4400	650
Springer-Verlag New York Inc 233 Spring St	New York	NY	10013	**800-777-4643**	212-460-1500	623-2
Springfield Area Chamber of Commerce 202 S John Q Hammons Pkwy	Springfield	MO	65806	**800-879-7504**	417-862-5567	137
Springfield Area Convention & Visitors Bureau 333 N Limestone St Suite 201	Springfield	OH	45503	**800-803-1553**	937-325-7621	205
Springfield Armory 420 W Main St	Geneseo	IL	61254	**800-680-6866**	309-944-5631	279
Springfield Chamber of Commerce 101 S 'A' St PO Box 155	Springfield	OR	97477	**866-346-1651**	541-746-1651	137
Springfield-Clark County Chamber of Commerce 333 N Limestone St Suite 201	Springfield	OH	45503	**800-803-1553**	937-325-7621	137
Springfield College 263 Alden St	Springfield	MA	01109	**800-343-1257**	413-748-3000	163
Springfield College 1010 W Sunshine St	Springfield	MO	65807	**800-475-2669**	417-864-7220	158
Springfield College in Illinois 1500 N 5th St	Springfield	IL	62702	**800-635-7289**	217-525-1420	160
Springfield Convention & Visitors Bureau 109 N 7th St	Springfield	IL	62701	**800-545-7300**	217-789-2360	205
Springfield Electric Supply Co 700 N 9th St	Springfield	IL	62708	**800-757-2101**	217-788-2100	245
Springfield (Greater) Convention & Visitors Bureau 1441 Main St Suite 136	Springfield	MA	01103	**800-723-1548**	413-787-1548	205
Springfield Hospital Center 6655 Sykesville Rd	Sykesville	MD	21784	**800-333-7564**	410-795-2100	366-3
Springfield Missouri Convention & Visitors Bureau 3315 E Battlefield Rd	Springfield	MO	65804	**800-678-8767**	417-881-5300	205
Springfield News Leader 651 Boonville Ave *Circ	Springfield	MO	65806	**800-695-2005***	417-836-1100	522-2
Springfield News-Sun 202 N Limestone St	Springfield	OH	45503	**888-890-7323**	937-328-0300	522-2
Springfield ReManufacturing Corp 650 N Broadview Pl	Springfield	MO	65802	**800-772-7733**	417-862-3501	259
SpringHill Suites by Marriott 1 Marriott Dr	Washington	DC	20058	**800-228-9290**	301-380-3000	369
Springs Industries Inc 205 N White St	Fort Mill	SC	29715	**800-438-6709**	803-547-1500	731
Springs Inn 2020 Harrodsburg Rd	Lexington	KY	40503	**800-354-9503**	859-277-5751	373
Springs Memorial Hospital 800 W Meeting St	Lancaster	SC	29720	**800-488-2567**	803-286-1481	366-2
Sprint Canada Inc 2235 Sheppard Ave E Suite 600 *Cust Svc	North York	ON	M2J5G1	**800-980-5464***	416-496-1644	721
Sprint Car Hall of Fame & Museum. National 1 Sprint Capital Pl	Knoxville	IA	50138	**800-874-4488**	641-842-6176	511
Sprint Corp 6200 Sprint Pkwy	Overland Park	KS	66251	**800-829-0965**		355-5
Sprint North Supply Co Inc 600 New Century Pkwy	New Century	KS	66031	**800-755-3004**	913-791-7000	245
Sprint PCS Group 6991 Sprint Pkwy	Overland Park	KS	66251	**800-829-0965**		721
Spruce Point Inn 88 Grandview Ave PO Box 237	Boothbay Harbor	ME	04538	**800-553-0289**	207-633-4152	655
SPSS Inc 233 S Wacker Dr 11th Fl *NASDAQ: SPSS*	Chicago	IL	60606	**800-543-2185**	312-651-3000	176-1
SPSS Inc ShowCase Div 233 S Wacker Dr 11th Fl	Chicago	IL	60606	**800-259-1028**		176-12
Spurlin Industries Inc PO Box 707	Palmetto	GA	30268	**800-749-4475**	770-463-1644	367
Sputtered Films Inc 320 Nopal St	Santa Barbara	CA	93103	**888-734-3456**	805-963-9651	685
SPX Corp 13515 Ballantyne Corporate Pl *NYSE: SPW*	Charlotte	NC	28277	**800-446-2617**	704-752-4400	184
SPX Corp Lindberg Div 304 Hart St	Watertown	WI	53094	**800-873-4468**	920-261-7000	313
SPX Corp OTC Div 655 Eisenhower Dr	Owatonna	MN	55060	**800-533-6127**	507-455-7000	745
SPX Corp Robinair Div 655 Eisenhower Dr	Owatonna	MN	55060	**800-628-6496**	507-455-7000	201
SPX Dock Products 1612 Hutton Dr Suite 140	Carrollton	TX	75006	**866-691-1377**	972-466-0707	462
SPX Process Equipment 611 Sugar Creek Rd	Delavan	WI	53115	**800-252-5200**	262-728-1900	379
Spyre Infostructure Inc 25 Imperial St Suite 210	Toronto	ON	M5P1B9	**888-467-7973**	416-487-7797	39
SPYRUS Inc 2355 Oakland Rd Suite 1	San Jose	CA	95131	**800-277-9787**	408-953-0700	176-12
SQN Signature Systems 65 Indel Ave 2nd Fl	Rancocas	NJ	08073	**888-744-7226**	609-261-5500	176-10
Square Books 160 Courthouse Sq	Oxford	MS	38655	**800-648-4001**	662-236-2262	96
Square H Brands 2731 S Soto St *Cust Svc	Los Angeles	CA	90023	**800-424-6339***	323-267-4600	465
Squaw Peak Resort. Pointe Hilton at 7677 N 16th St	Phoenix	AZ	85020	**800-685-0550**	602-997-2626	655
Squaw Valley USA PO Box 2007	Olympic Valley	CA	96146	**800-545-4350**	530-583-6985	655
Squire Cogswell/Aeros Instruments Inc 1111 Lakeside Dr	Gurnee	IL	60031	**800-448-0770**	847-855-0500	170
Squire Sanders & Dempsey LLP 127 Public Sq 4900 Key Tower	Cleveland	OH	44114	**800-743-2773**	216-479-8500	419
SRA/McGraw-Hill Div McGraw-Hill Cos Inc 8787 Orion Pl	Columbus	OH	43240	**800-468-4850**	614-430-6600	242
SRC (Syracuse Research Corp) 6225 Running Ridge Rd	North Syracuse	NY	13212	**800-724-0451**	315-452-8000	654
SRC Devices Inc 888 Prospect St Suite 201	San Diego	CA	92037	**866-772-8668**	858-292-8770	202

Company / Address	City	State	ZIP	Toll-Free	Phone	Class
SRC Software Inc 13190 SW 68th Pkwy	Portland	OR	97223	**800-544-3477**	503-608-3300	176-1
SRDS 1700 Higgins Rd	Des Plaines	IL	60018	**800-851-7737**	847-375-5000	623-2
SRI Sports Inc 701 Leander Dr	Leander	TX	78641	**800-233-5714**	512-259-0080	286
SriLankan Airlines 1936 Wilshire Blvd	Los Angeles	CA	90057	**877-915-2652**	213-483-8808	26
SriLankan Airlines Skywards 1936 Wilshire Blvd	Los Angeles	CA	90057	**877-915-2652**	213-483-8808	27
SRP (Salt River Project) 1521 N Project Dr	Tempe	AZ	85281	**800-258-4777**	602-236-5900	774
SS White Medical Products Inc 151 Old New Brunswick Rd *Cust Svc	Piscataway	NJ	08854	**888-779-4483***	732-752-8300	468
SS White Technologies Inc 151 Old New Brunswick Rd	Piscataway	NJ	08854	**800-872-2673**	732-752-8300	609
SSA (Self Storage Assn) 6506 Louisdale Rd Suite 315	Springfield	VA	22150	**888-735-3784**	703-921-9123	49-21
SSA (Social Security Administration) 6401 Security Blvd	Baltimore	MD	21235	**800-772-1213**	410-965-3120	336-16
SSA Marine 1131 SW Klickitat Way	Seattle	WA	98134	**800-422-3505**	206-623-0304	457
SSgA funds 1 Lincoln St	Boston	MA	02111	**800-997-7327**	617-664-6089	517
SSL Americas Inc 3585 Engineering Dr Suite 200	Norcross	GA	30092	**888-387-3927**	770-582-2222	566
SSM Hospice 2 Harbor Bend Ct	Lake Saint Louis	MO	63367	**800-835-1212**	636-695-2050	365
SSM Rehab 6420 Clayton Rd Executive Offices	Saint Louis	MO	63117	**800-818-9494**	314-768-5300	366-4
SSP Litronic 17861 Cartwright Rd	Irvine	CA	92614	**800-454-8766**	949-851-1085	176-12
SST Corp 635 Brighton Rd	Clifton	NJ	07012	**800-222-0921**	973-473-4300	470
ST Griswold & Co Inc PO Box 849	Williston	VT	05495	**800-339-4565**	802-658-0201	181
ST Media Group International Inc 407 Gilbert Ave	Cincinnati	OH	45202	**800-925-1110**	513-421-2050	623-9
Sta-Home Health Agency Inc 406 Briarwood Dr Bldg 200	Jackson	MS	39206	**800-782-4663**	601-956-5100	358
Sta-Home Hospice 406 Briarwood Dr Suite 500	Jackson	MS	39206	**800-336-6557**	601-991-1933	365
STAAR Surgical Co 1911 Walker Ave *NASDAQ: STAA*	Monrovia	CA	91016	**800-292-7902**	626-303-7902	531
Stabila Inc 332 Industrial Dr	South Elgin	IL	60177	**800-869-7460**	847-488-0050	746
Stabile Cos Inc 21 Manchester St	Merrimack	NH	03054	**800-432-4892**	603-889-0318	186
Stacey's 581 Market St	San Francisco	CA	94105	**800-233-8467**	415-421-4687	96
Stack-On Products Co PO Box 489	Wauconda	IL	60084	**800-323-9601**	847-526-1611	479
Stackbin Corp 29 Powderhill Rd *Sales	Lincoln	RI	02865	**800-333-1603***	401-333-1600	197
Stackpole Books 5067 Ritter Rd *Sales	Mechanicsburg	PA	17055	**800-732-3669***	717-796-0411	623-2
Stada Pharmaceuticals Inc 5 Cedar Brook Dr	Cranbury	NJ	08512	**800-542-6682**	609-409-5999	573
Stadler's Country Hams Inc PO Box 397	Elon	NC	27244	**800-262-1795**	336-584-1396	292-9
Stadt Corp 2 Cumberland St	Brooklyn	NY	11205	**800-221-1763**	718-858-4200	291-38
Staedtler Inc 21900 Plummer St	Chatsworth	CA	91311	**800-800-3691**	818-882-6000	560
Stafast Products Inc 505 Lake Shore Blvd	Painesville	OH	44077	**800-782-3278**	440-357-5546	274
STAFDA (Specialty Tools & Fasteners Distributors Assn) 500 Elm Grove Rd	Elm Grove	WI	53122	**800-352-2981**	262-784-4774	49-18
Staff Development Council. National 5995 Fairfield Rd Suite 4	Oxford	OH	45056	**800-727-7288**	513-523-6029	49-5
Staff Management Inc 5919 Spring Creek Rd	Rockford	IL	61114	**800-535-3518**	815-282-3900	619
Staff One Inc 1100 W Main St	Durant	OK	74701	**800-771-7823**	580-920-1212	619
Staff Resources Inc 870 Manzanita Ct Suite A *Sales	Chico	CA	95926	**888-835-5774***	530-345-2487	619
Staffdigest Magazine 7474 S Kirkwood Suite 108	Houston	TX	77072	**800-444-0674**	281-498-2913	449-5
Staffing Plus 555 E Butterfield Rd Suite 330	Lombard	IL	60148	**800-782-3346**	630-515-0500	619
StaffingSolutions Div Career Blazers Inc 222 W Las Colinas Blvd Suite 1250E	Irving	TX	75039	**800-787-6750**	214-296-6700	707
Stafford County Flour Mills Co PO Box 7	Hudson	KS	67545	**800-530-5640**	620-458-4121	291-23
Stafford Jim Theatre 3440 W Hwy 76	Branson	MO	65616	**800-677-8533**	417-335-8080	562
Stafford-Smith Inc 3414 S Burdick St	Kalamazoo	MI	49001	**800-968-2442**	269-343-1240	651
Stage Neck Inn 8 Stage Neck Rd Rt 1A Box 70	York Harbor	ME	03911	**800-222-3238**	207-363-3850	655
Stage & Screen BOOKSPAN 1225 S Market St	Mechanicsburg	PA	17055	**800-688-4442**		94
Stage Stores Inc 10201 S Main St *NASDAQ: STGS*	Houston	TX	77025	**800-315-7257**	713-667-5601	658
STAHL A Scott Fetzer Co 3201 W Old Lincoln Way	Wooster	OH	44691	**800-392-7251**	330-264-7441	505
Stahl Soap Corp 1 Branca Rd	East Rutherford	NJ	07073	**800-527-5115**	201-507-5770	211
Stahly Cartage Co 119 S Main St	Edwardsville	IL	62025	**800-851-5553**	618-656-5070	769
Stained Glass Overlay Inc 1827 N Case St	Orange	CA	92865	**800-944-4746**	714-974-6124	330
Stainmaster 175 Townmark Dr	Kennesaw	GA	30144	**800-438-7668**	877-446-8478	131
Staker & Parson Cos 2350 S 1900 W	Ogden	UT	84401	**800-748-4100**	801-731-1111	187-4
Stalker Software Inc 655 Redwood Hwy Suite 275	Mill Valley	CA	94941	**800-262-4722**	415-383-7164	176-12
Stamas Yacht Inc 300 Pampas Ave *Sales	Tarpon Springs	FL	34689	**800-782-6271***	727-937-4118	91
Stamats Communications Inc 615 5th St SE	Cedar Rapids	IA	52401	**800-553-8878**	319-364-6167	623-9
Stambaugh Henry H Auditorium 1000 5th Ave	Youngstown	OH	44504	**866-582-8963**	330-747-5175	562
Stamford Suites 720 Bedford St	Stamford	CT	06901	**866-394-4365**	203-359-7300	373
Stamp-Rite Inc 154 S Larch St	Lansing	MI	48912	**800-328-1988**	517-487-5071	459
Stampede Technologies Inc 80 Rhoades Ctr Dr	Dayton	OH	45458	**800-763-3423**	937-291-5035	174
Stamper Black Hills Gold Jewelry 7201 S Hwy 16 *Cust Svc	Rapid City	SD	57702	**800-523-7515***	605-342-0751	401

Company / Address	City	State	ZIP	Toll-Free	Phone	Class
Stamps.com Inc 3420 Ocean Park Blvd Suite 1040 *NASDAQ: STMP*	Santa Monica	CA	90405	**888-434-0055**	310-581-7200	176-1
Stan Hywet Hall & Gardens 714 N Portage Path	Akron	OH	44403	**888-836-5533**	330-836-5533	509
Stanadyne Corp 92 Deerfield Rd	Windsor	CT	06095	**800-929-0919**	860-525-0821	60
Stanbury Uniforms Inc 108 Stanbury Industrial Dr PO Box 100	Brookfield	MO	64628	**800-826-2246**	660-258-2246	153-19
Stancil Corp 2644 S Croddy Way	Santa Ana	CA	92704	**800-782-6245**	714-546-2002	52
Stanco Metal Products Inc 2101 168th Ave	Grand Haven	MI	49417	**800-530-9655**	616-842-5000	479
Stand For Children 516 SE Morrison St Suite 206	Portland	OR	97214	**800-663-4032**	503-235-2305	48-6
Standard The 40 Island Ave	Miami Beach	FL	33139	**800-327-8363**	305-673-1717	655
Standard Abrasives Inc 4201 Guardian St	Simi Valley	CA	93063	**800-423-5444**	805-520-5800	1
Standard Aero Ltd 33 Allen Dyne Rd	Winnipeg	MB	R3H1A1	**888-836-4433**	204-775-9711	25
Standard Air & Lite Corp 2406 Woodmere Dr	Pittsburgh	PA	15205	**800-472-2458**	412-920-6505	601
Standard Alloys & Mfg PO Box 969	Port Arthur	TX	77640	**800-231-8240**	409-983-3201	627
Standard Beverage Corp 2416 E 37th St N	Wichita	KS	67219	**800-999-7707**	316-838-7707	82-3
Standard Candy Co Inc 715 Massman Dr	Nashville	TN	37210	**800-226-4340**	615-889-6360	291-8
Standard Casing Co Inc 60 Amity St	Jersey City	NJ	07304	**800-847-4141**	201-434-6300	291-26
Standard Chartered Bank 1 Madison Ave	New York	NY	10010	**800-269-3101**	212-667-0700	71
Standard Digital Imaging 4426 S 108th St	Omaha	NE	68137	**800-642-8062**	402-592-1292	239
Standard Drug Co 1 Westbury Sq Bldg B	Saint Charles	MO	63301	**877-482-5874**	636-946-6557	237
Standard Duplicating Machines Corp 10 Connector Rd	Andover	MA	01810	**800-526-4774**	978-470-1920	113
Standard Educational Corp 900 Northshore Dr Suite 252 *Cust Svc	Lake Bluff	IL	60044	**800-332-8755***	847-283-0301	623-2
Standard Electric Co 2650 Trautner Dr PO Box 5289	Saginaw	MI	48603	**800-322-0215**	989-497-2100	245
Standard Examiner 2072 Layton Hills Mall	Layton	UT	84041	**800-651-2105**	801-629-5220	522-4
Standard-Examiner 332 Standard Way	Ogden	UT	84412	**800-234-5505**	801-625-4200	522-2
Standard Federal Bank 2600 W Big Beaver Rd	Troy	MI	48084	**800-643-9600**	248-643-9600	71
Standard Furniture Mfg Co Inc 801 Hwy 31 S	Bay Minette	AL	36507	**800-827-7866**	251-937-6741	314-2
Standard Golf Co 6620 Nordic Dr	Cedar Falls	IA	50613	**800-553-1707**	319-266-2638	701
Standard Knapp Inc 63 Pickering St *Cust Svc	Portland	CT	06480	**800-628-9565***	860-342-1100	537
Standard Labs Inc 147 11th Ave Suite 100	South Charleston	WV	25303	**888-216-0239**	304-744-6800	728
Standard Life & Accident Insurance Co PO Box 1800	Galveston	TX	77553	**888-350-1488**		384-2
Standard Life Insurance Co of Indiana 10689 N Pennsylvania St *Mktg	Indianapolis	IN	46280	**800-767-7749***	317-574-6200	384-2
Standard Locknut Inc 1045 E 169th St	Westfield	IN	46074	**800-783-6887**	317-867-0100	446
Standard Mattress Co Inc 261 Weston St	Hartford	CT	06120	**800-873-8498**	860-549-2000	463
Standard Mfg Co Inc 750 2nd Ave *Cust Svc	Troy	NY	12182	**800-227-1056***	518-235-2200	153-5
Standard Paper Box Machine Co Inc 347 Coster St	Bronx	NY	10474	**800-367-8755**	718-328-3300	546
Standard Parking Corp 900 N Michigan Ave Suite 1600 *NASDAQ: STAN*	Chicago	IL	60611	**888-700-7275**	312-274-2000	552
Standard Perforating & Mfg 3636 S Kedzie Ave	Chicago	IL	60632	**800-621-0273**	773-254-3232	92
Standard & Poor's 55 Water St 45th Fl *Cust Svc	New York	NY	10041	**800-344-3014***	212-438-2000	393
Standard & Poor's Corp 55 Water St	New York	NY	10041	**800-289-8000**	212-438-2000	623-2
Standard & Poor's Outlook Newsletter 55 Water St	New York	NY	10041	**800-221-5277**	212-438-2000	521-9
Standard & Poor's Stock Reports 55 Water St	New York	NY	10041	**800-221-5277**	212-438-2000	521-9
Standard Publishing Co 8121 Hamilton Ave *Orders	Cincinnati	OH	45231	**800-543-1353***	513-931-4050	623-9
Standard Register Co PO Box 1167 *NYSE: SR*	Dayton	OH	45401	**800-755-6405**	937-221-1000	111
Standard Roofing Co 516 N McDonough St PO Box 1309	Montgomery	AL	36102	**800-239-5705**	334-834-3000	188-12
Standard Roofings Inc 100 Park Rd	Tinton Falls	NJ	07724	**800-624-0036**	732-542-3300	190-4
Standard Sand & Silica Co PO Box 1059	Davenport	FL	33836	**877-444-7263**	863-422-7100	493-4
Standard Structures Inc 340 Standard Ave	Windsor	CA	95492	**800-862-4936**	707-836-8100	805
Standard Swiss Embroidery Co 5900 S Eastern Ave Suite 166	Commerce	CA	90040	**800-443-8357**	323-582-8057	256
Standard Tar Products Co 2456 W Cornell St	Milwaukee	WI	53209	**800-825-7650**	414-873-7650	143
Standard Textile Co Inc 1 Knollcrest	Cincinnati	OH	45237	**800-888-5000**	513-761-9255	469
Standard Textile Co Inc Fantagraph Div One Knollcrest Dr	Cincinnati	OH	45237	**800-888-5000**	513-761-9255	731
Standards Inc. Certified Financial Planner Board of 1670 Broadway Suite 600	Denver	CO	80202	**888-237-6275**	303-830-7500	49-2
Standards. National Conference of States on Building Codes & 505 Huntmar Park Dr Suite 210	Herndon	VA	20170	**800-362-2633**	703-437-0100	49-7

Name / Address	City	State	ZIP	Toll-Free	Phone	Class
Standco Industries Inc 2701 Clinton Dr	Houston	TX	77020	**800-231-6018**	713-224-6311	321
Standco Industries Inc Oilfield Products Div 2701 Clinton Dr	Houston	TX	77020	**800-231-6018**	713-224-6311	526
Standex Corp Federal industries Div 215 Federal Ave PO Box 290	Belleville	WI	53508	**800-356-4206**	608-424-3331	650
Standex International Corp Air Distribution Products Group 7601 State Rd.	Philadelphia	PA	19136	**800-899-2850**	215-338-2850	688
Standex International Corp Custom Hoists Div PO Box 98	Hayesville	OH	44838	**800-837-4668**	419-368-4721	220
Stanford Shopping Center 180 El Camino Real	Palo Alto	CA	94304	**800-772-9332**	650-617-8585	452
Stanford University Press 1450 Page Mill Rd	Palo Alto	CA	94304	**800-621-2736**	650-723-9434	623-5
Stanion Wholesale Electric Co 812 S Main St PO Box F	Pratt	KS	67124	**800-880-2008**	620-672-5678	245
Stanislaus Farm Supply Co 624 E Service Rd	Modesto	CA	95358	**800-323-0725**	209-538-7070	272
Stanislaus Food Products Co 1202 D St	Modesto	CA	95354	**800-327-7201**	209-522-7201	291-20
Stanley Access Technologies 65 Scott Swamp Rd	Farmington	CT	06032	**800-722-2377**	860-677-2861	232
Stanley Assoc Inc 300 N Washington St Suite 400	Alexandria	VA	22314	**866-774-0577**	703-684-1125	178
Stanley Creations Inc 1414 Willow Ave.	Melrose Park	PA	19027	**800-220-1414**	215-635-6200	401
Stanley Furniture Co Inc 1641 Fairystone Pk Hwy. *NASDAQ: STLY*	Stanleytown	VA	24168	**800-216-6888**	276-627-2000	314-2
Stanley Hardware 480 Myrtle St *Cust Svc	New Britain	CT	06053	**800-337-4393***	860-225-5111	181
Stanley Home Decor 480 Myrtle St	New Britain	CT	06053	**800-782-6539**	860-225-5111	232
Stanley Home Products 1 Fuller Way *Cust Svc	Great Bend	KS	67530	**800-628-9032***	620-792-1711	361
Stanley Hotel 333 Wonderview Ave	Estes Park	CO	80517	**800-976-1377**	970-586-3371	373
Stanley Korshak 500 Crescent Ct Suite 100	Dallas	TX	75201	**800-972-5959**	214-871-3600	155-4
Stanley M Proctor Co 2016 Midway Dr	Twinsburg	OH	44087	**800-352-0123**	330-425-7814	378
Stanley Martin Cos Inc 1881 Campus Commons Dr Suite 101	Reston	VA	20191	**800-446-4807**	703-715-7800	639
Stanley Mechanics Tools 12827 Valley Branch Ln *Orders	Dallas	TX	75234	**800-505-4648***	972-247-1367	746
Stanley Steemer International Inc 5500 Stanley Steemer Pkwy	Dublin	OH	43016	**800-848-7496**	614-764-2007	150
Stanley TK Inc PO Box 31	Waynesboro	MS	39367	**800-477-2855**	601-735-2855	528
Stanley Tools Inc 480 Myrtle St *Cust Svc	New Britain	CT	06053	**800-262-2161***	860-225-5111	746
Stanley Tools Worldwide 480 Myrtle St *Cust Svc	New Britain	CT	06053	**800-262-2161***	860-225-5111	746
Stanley Vidmar Storage Technologies 11 Grammes Rd PO Box 1151	Allentown	PA	18105	**800-523-9462**	610-797-6600	281
Stanley Works 1000 Stanley Dr *NYSE: SWK* ■ *Cust Svc	New Britain	CT	06053	**800-262-2161***	860-225-5111	746
Stanmar Inc 130 Boston Post Rd	Sudbury	MA	01776	**800-617-3607**	978-443-9922	641
Stanton County Public Power District PO Box 319	Stanton	NE	68779	**877-439-2300**	402-439-2228	244
Stanton Group 3405 Annapolis Ln N Suite 100	Plymouth	MN	55447	**800-754-9867**	763-278-4000	192
Stanton's Sheet Music 330 S 4th St	Columbus	OH	43215	**800-426-8742**	614-224-4257	515
Staplcotn Co-op Assn Inc 214 W Market St	Greenwood	MS	38930	**800-293-6231**	662-453-6231	271
Staples Business Advantage 45 E Wesley St *Orders	South Hackensack	NJ	07606	**888-333-6494***	201-488-2900	523
Staples Inc 500 Staples Dr *NASDAQ: SPLS*	Framingham	MA	01702	**877-235-9088**	508-253-5000	524
Staples National Advantage 45 E Wesley St	South Hackensack	NJ	07606	**800-999-9077**	201-488-2900	523
Stapleton-Spence Packing Co 1530 The Alameda Suite 320	San Jose	CA	95126	**800-297-8815**	408-297-8815	291-20
Stapleton Technologies Inc 1350 W 12th St	Long Beach	CA	90813	**800-266-0541**	562-437-0541	143
Staplex Co 777 5th Ave *Cust Svc	Brooklyn	NY	11232	**800-221-0822***	718-768-3333	112
Star Beacon PO Box 2100	Ashtabula	OH	44005	**800-554-6768**	440-998-2323	522-2
Star Binding & Trimming Corp 1109 Grand Ave	North Bergen	NJ	07047	**800-782-7150**	201-864-2220	730-5
Star Building Systems 8600 S I-35	Oklahoma City	OK	73149	**800-879-7827**	405-636-2010	106
Star Cellular 1371 S Bascom Ave	San Jose	CA	95128	**800-969-0023**	408-288-8500	35
Star Clippers Inc 4101 Salzedo St	Coral Gables	FL	33146	**800-442-0551**	305-442-0550	217
Star-Courier PO Box A	Kewanee	IL	61443	**800-397-7827**	309-852-2181	522-2
Star Cruises 7665 Corporate Ctr Dr	Miami	FL	33126	**800-327-9020**	305-436-4000	217
Star Distributors Inc 10 Eder Rd	West Haven	CT	06516	**800-922-3501**	203-932-3636	82-1
Star Fine Foods 4652 E Date Ave	Fresno	CA	93725	**800-694-4872**	559-498-2900	291-30
Star Food Products Inc PO Box 1479	Burlington	NC	27216	**800-672-5310**	336-227-4079	291-33
Star Furniture Co Inc 16666 Barker Springs Rd	Houston	TX	77084	**800-364-6661**	281-492-6661	316
Star Gas Partners LP 2187 Atlantic St *NYSE: SGU*	Stamford	CT	06902	**800-966-9827**	203-328-7300	311
Star-Gazette 201 Baldwin St	Elmira	NY	14902	**800-836-8970**	607-734-5151	522-2
Star-Herald PO Box 1709	Scottsbluff	NE	69363	**800-846-6102**	308-632-9000	522-2
STAR Human Resources Group Inc 2222 W Dunlap Ave Suite 350	Phoenix	AZ	85021	**800-308-5948**	602-956-4200	384-3
Star of Indiana Charter Services Inc 8111 N SR 37	Bloomington	IN	47404	**800-933-0097**	812-876-7851	108
Star Insurance Co 26600 Telegraph Rd	Southfield	MI	48034	**800-482-2726**	248-358-1100	384-4
Star Island Resort 5000 Avenue of the Stars	Kissimmee	FL	34746	**800-513-2820**	407-997-8000	373
Star-Ledger The 1 Star Ledger Plaza	Newark	NJ	07102	**800-501-2100**	973-877-4141	522-2
Star The Marion 150 Court St	Marion	OH	43302	**800-626-1331**	740-387-0400	522-2
Star Meetings & Events 301 N Morton St	Bloomington	IN	47404	**866-546-1687**	812-331-8800	183
Star Micronics America Inc 1150 King George's Post Rd	Edison	NJ	08837	**800-782-7636**	732-623-5500	171-6
Star Milling Co 24067 Water St	Perris	CA	92570	**800-733-6455**	951-657-3143	438
Star Nail Products Inc 29120 Ave Paine	Valencia	CA	91355	**800-762-6245**	661-257-7827	211
Star-News PO Box 840	Wilmington	NC	28402	**800-272-1277**	910-343-2000	522-2
Star-News Newspapers PO Box 840	Wilmington	NC	28402	**800-222-2385**	910-343-2296	623-8
Star Nursery Inc 125 Cassia Way	Henderson	NV	89014	**866-584-7827**	702-568-7000	318
Star Observers. American Assn of Variable 25 Birch St	Cambridge	MA	02138	**800-223-0138**	617-354-0484	49-19
Star One Federal Credit Union 166 8th Ave Bldg 166	Sunnyvale	CA	94089	**800-552-1455**	408-742-2801	216
Star Packaging Corp 453 85th Cir	College Park	GA	30349	**800-252-5414**	404-763-2800	67
Star Rentals Inc 1919 4th Ave S	Seattle	WA	98134	**800-825-7880**	206-622-7880	261-2
Star Sales Co Inc 1803 N Central St	Knoxville	TN	37917	**800-347-9494**	865-524-0771	323
Star Scientific Inc 801 Liberty Way *NASDAQ: STSI*	Chester	VA	23836	**800-867-6663**	804-530-0535	741-1
Star Stainless Screw Co 30 West End Rd	Totowa	NJ	07512	**800-631-3540**	973-256-2300	346
Star Systems Inc 495 N Keller Rd Suite 500	Maitland	FL	32751	**888-233-7337**	321-263-3000	70
Star Trac by Unisen Inc 14410 Myford Rd	Irvine	CA	92606	**800-228-6635**	714-669-1660	263
Star Transportation Inc 1116 Polk Ave	Nashville	TN	37210	**800-333-3060**	615-256-4336	769
Star Tribune 425 Portland Ave	Minneapolis	MN	55488	**800-827-8742**	612-673-4000	522-2
Star Truck Rentals Inc 3940 Eastern Ave SE	Grand Rapids	MI	49508	**800-748-0468**	616-243-7033	767
StarBand Communciations Inc 1760 Old Meadow Rd *Cust Svc	McLean	VA	22102	**800-478-2722***	703-287-3000	669
Starbucks Corp 2401 Utah Ave S *NASDAQ: SBUX*	Seattle	WA	98134	**800-782-7282**	206-447-1575	156
Starcraft Corp 2703 College Ave	Goshen	IN	46528	**800-348-7440**	574-533-1105	62-7
Starcraft Marine LLC 201 Starcraft Dr PO Box 517	Topeka	IN	46571	**800-535-5722**	260-593-2500	91
Stardust Resort & Casino 3000 Las Vegas Blvd S	Las Vegas	NV	89109	**800-634-6757**	702-732-6111	133
Starflo Corp 940 Crosscreek Rd SE	Orangeburg	SC	29115	**800-888-2583**	803-536-9660	776
Stargate Holdings Corp 2805 Butterfield Rd Suite 100	Oak Brook	IL	60523	**800-282-6541**	630-572-2242	389
Stark Carpet Corp 979 3rd Ave 11th Fl	New York	NY	10022	**800-223-1224**	212-752-9000	356
Stark Ceramics Inc 600 W Church St	East Canton	OH	44730	**800-321-0662**	330-488-1211	148
Stark State College of Technology 6200 Frank Ave NW	Canton	OH	44720	**800-797-8275**	330-494-6170	787
Stark Truss Co 109 Miles Ave SW	Canton	OH	44710	**800-933-2258**	330-478-2100	805
Starkey Laboratories Inc 6700 Washington Ave S	Eden Prairie	MN	55344	**800-328-8602**	952-941-6401	469
Starkville Area Chamber of Commerce 1 Research Blvd Suite 204	Starkville	MS	39759	**800-649-8687**	662-323-3322	137
Starkweather & Shepley Inc 60 Catamore Blvd	East Providence	RI	02914	**800-854-4625**	401-435-3600	383
Starlight Starbright Children's Foundation 5900 Wilshire Blvd Suite 2530	Los Angeles	CA	90036	**800-274-7827**	323-634-0080	48-17
Starlite Limousines LLC 15111 N Hayden Rd Suite 300	Scottsdale	AZ	85260	**800-875-4104**	480-905-1234	433
Starlite Recovery Center PO Box 317	Center Point	TX	78010	**800-292-0148**	830-634-2212	712
Starr Electric Co Inc PO Box 9298	Greensboro	NC	27429	**800-732-0241**	336-275-0241	188-4
Starr Litigation Services Inc 1201 Grand Ave	West Des Moines	IA	50265	**800-627-8277**	515-224-1616	436
Starr Tours 2531 E State St	Trenton	NJ	08619	**800-782-7703**	609-587-0626	108
Starrett Corp 6203 Johns Rd Suite 8	Tampa	FL	33634	**800-237-8350**	813-882-3616	650
Stars of David International Inc 3175 Commercial Ave Suite 100	Northbrook	IL	60062	**800-782-7349**	847-509-9929	48-6
Startel Corp 17661 Cowan Ave	Irvine	CA	92614	**800-782-7835**	949-863-8700	720
Starvin' Artist Supplies 757 W Golf Rd	Schaumburg	IL	60194	**800-427-8478**	847-843-3600	45
Starving Students Moving & Storage Co 1850 Sawtelle Blvd 3rd Fl	Los Angeles	CA	90025	**800-441-6683**	310-854-4464	508
Starwood Hotels Preferred Guest Program 111 Westchester Ave	White Plains	NY	10604	**888-625-4988**	512-834-2426	371
Starwood Hotels & Resorts Worldwide Inc 1111 Westchester Ave *NYSE: HOT* ■ *Cust Svc	White Plains	NY	10604	**877-443-4585***	914-640-8100	369
Four Points by Sheraton Hotels 1111 Westchester Ave *Cust Svc	White Plains	NY	10604	**877-443-4585***	914-640-8100	369
Luxury Collection 1111 Westchester Ave *Cust Svc	White Plains	NY	10604	**877-443-4585***	914-640-8100	369
Sheraton Hotels & Resorts 1111 Westchester Ave	White Plains	NY	10604	**800-325-3535**	914-640-8100	369
W Hotels 1111 Westchester Ave	White Plains	NY	10604	**877-443-4585**	914-640-8100	369
Westin Hotels & Resorts 1111 Westchester Ave	White Plains	NY	10604	**877-443-4585**	914-640-8100	369
Starwood Vacation Ownership Inc 8800 Vistana Center Dr	Orlando	FL	32821	**800-847-8262**	407-239-3000	738
Stash Tea Co Inc PO Box 910	Portland	OR	97207	**800-547-1514**	503-684-4482	291-40
State The 1401 Shop Rd	Columbia	SC	29201	**800-888-5353**	803-771-6161	522-2
State. Americans United for Separation of Church & 518 C St NE	Washington	DC	20002	**800-875-3707**	202-466-3234	48-7
State Auto Financial Corp 518 E Broad St *NASDAQ: STFC*	Columbus	OH	43215	**800-444-9950**	614-464-5000	355-4

Name / Address	City	State	ZIP	Toll-Free	Phone	Class
State Auto National Insurance Co 518 E Broad St	Columbus	OH	43215	**800-444-9950**	614-464-5000	384-4
State Auto Property & Casualty Insurance Co 518 E Broad St	Columbus	OH	43215	**800-444-9950**	614-464-5000	384-4
State Automobile Mutual Insurance Co 518 E Broad St	Columbus	OH	43215	**800-444-9950**	614-464-5000	384-4
State Bank Supervisors. Conference of 1155 Connecticut Ave NW 5th Fl	Washington	DC	20036	**800-886-2727**	202-296-2840	49-7
State Bar of Arizona 4201 N 24th St Suite 200	Phoenix	AZ	85016	**866-482-9227**	602-252-4804	73
State Bar of Georgia 104 Marietta St NW Suite 100	Atlanta	GA	30303	**800-334-6865**	404-527-8700	73
State Bar of Michigan 306 Townsend St	Lansing	MI	48933	**800-968-1442**	517-372-9030	73
State Bar of Nevada 600 E Charleston Blvd	Las Vegas	NV	89104	**800-254-2797**	702-382-2200	73
State Bar of New Mexico 5121 Masthead St NE	Albuquerque	NM	87109	**800-876-6227**	505-797-6000	73
State Bar of Texas 1414 Colorado St	Austin	TX	78701	**800-204-2222**	512-463-1463	73
State Bar of Wisconsin 5302 Eastpark Blvd	Madison	WI	53718	**800-728-7788**	608-257-3838	73
State Courts. National Center for 300 Newport Ave	Williamsburg	VA	23185	**800-616-6164**	757-253-2000	49-7
State Electric Supply Co Inc 2010 2nd Ave *Cust Svc	Huntington	WV	25703	**800-624-3417***	304-523-7491	245
State Employees Credit Union 501 S Capitol Ave	Lansing	MI	48933	**800-937-7328**	517-267-7328	216
State Employees' Credit Union 1000 Wade Ave	Raleigh	NC	27605	**888-732-8562**	919-839-5000	216
State Employees Credit Union of Maryland Inc 971 Corporate Blvd	Linthicum	MD	21090	**800-879-7328**	410-487-7328	216
State Employees Federal Credit Union 1239 Washington Ave	Albany	NY	12206	**800-727-3328**	518-452-8234	216
State Fair Foods 3900 Meacham Blvd	Haltom City	TX	76117	**800-641-6412**	817-427-7700	291-36
State Farm Financial Services FSB PO Box 2316	Bloomington	IL	61702	**877-734-2265**		71
State Farm Mutual Funds PO Box 219548	Kansas City	MO	64121	**800-447-4930**		517
State Governments. Council of 2760 Research Park Dr PO Box 11910 *Sales	Lexington	KY	40578	**800-800-1910***	859-244-8000	49-7
State of the Heart Home Health & Hospice 1350 N Broadway	Greenville	OH	45331	**800-417-7535**	937-548-2999	365
State Industrial Products 3100 Hamilton Ave	Cleveland	OH	44114	**800-782-2436**	216-861-7114	149
State Information Bureau 842 E Park Ave	Tallahassee	FL	32301	**800-881-1742**	850-561-3990	392
State Journal-Register 1 Copley Plaza	Springfield	IL	62701	**800-397-6397**	217-788-1300	522-2
State Library of Ohio 274 E 1st Ave	Columbus	OH	43201	**800-686-1532**	614-644-7061	426
State Life Insurance Co 1 American Sq PO Box 368	Indianapolis	IN	46206	**800-428-9198**	317-285-2300	384-2
State Narrow Fabrics Inc 2902 Borden Ave	Long Island City	NY	11101	**800-221-7288**	718-392-8787	730-5
State-O-Maine 1372 Broadway Suite 1800	New York	NY	10018	**866-456-6843**	212-302-1070	153-12
State Pipe & Supply Co 9615 S Norwalk Blvd	Santa Fe Springs	CA	90670	**800-733-6410**	562-695-5555	483
State Plating 450 N 9th St	Elwood	IN	46036	**800-428-6340**	765-552-5047	472
State Plaza Hotel 2117 'E' St NW	Washington	DC	20037	**800-424-2859**	202-861-8200	373
State Street Research Funds PO Box 8408	Boston	MA	02266	**800-882-3302**	617-357-7800	517
State Street Research & Management 1 Financial Ctr 31st Fl	Boston	MA	02111	**800-882-0052**	617-357-7800	393
State Theatre 15 Livingston Ave	New Brunswick	NJ	08901	**877-782-8311**	732-247-7200	562
State University of New York College of Agriculture & Technology at Cobleskill Rt 7	Cobleskill	NY	12043	**800-295-8988**	518-255-5525	163
State University of New York College of Environmental Science & Forestry 1 Forestry Dr	Syracuse	NY	13210	**800-777-7373**	315-470-6500	163
State University of New York College at Fredonia 178 Central Ave	Fredonia	NY	14063	**800-252-1212**	716-673-3251	163
State University of New York College at Geneseo 1 College Cir	Geneseo	NY	14454	**866-245-5211**	585-245-5211	163
State University of New York College at Oneonta Ravine Pkwy	Oneonta	NY	13820	**800-786-9123**	607-436-3500	163
State University of New York College of Technology at Alfred 10 Upper College Dr	Alfred	NY	14802	**800-425-3733**	607-587-4215	160
State University of New York College of Technology at Canton 34 Cornell Dr	Canton	NY	13617	**800-388-7123**	315-386-7011	160
State University of New York College of Technology at Delhi 2 Main St	Delhi	NY	13753	**800-963-3544**	607-746-4000	160
State University of New York Institute of Technology (SUNYIT) PO Box 3050	Utica	NY	13504	**800-786-9832**	315-792-7500	163
State University of New York at New Paltz 75 S Manheim Blvd	New Paltz	NY	12561	**888-639-7589**	845-257-2121	163
State University of New York at Plattsburgh 101 Broad St	Plattsburgh	NY	12901	**888-673-0012**	518-564-2040	163
State University of New York at Potsdam 44 Pierrpont Ave	Potsdam	NY	13676	**877-768-7326**	315-267-2000	163
State University of New York Press 194 Washington Ave Suite 305 *Orders	Albany	NY	12210	**800-666-2211***	518-472-5000	623-5
State University of New York Upstate Medical University 766 Irving Ave	Syracuse	NY	13210	**800-736-2171**	315-464-4570	164-2
State Volunteer Mutual Insurance Co 101 W Park Dr Suite 300	Brentwood	TN	37027	**800-342-2239**	615-377-1999	384-5
State Wide Aluminum 23601 CR 6 E PO Box 987	Elkhart	IN	46515	**800-860-2594**	574-262-2594	232
Statehouse Convention Center Markham & Main #1 1 Statehouse Plaza	Little Rock	AR	72201	**800-844-4781**	501-376-4781	204
Statehouse Inn 981 Grove St	Boise	ID	83702	**800-243-4622**	208-342-4622	373
Staten Island Hotel 1415 Richmond Ave	Staten Island	NY	10314	**800-532-3532**	718-698-5000	373
States Industries Inc PO Box 7037	Eugene	OR	97401	**800-626-1981**	541-688-7871	602
Statesville Brick Co 391 Brickyard Rd	Statesville	NC	28677	**800-522-4716**	704-872-4123	148
Statex Petroleum Inc 1801 Royal Ln Suite 606	Dallas	TX	75229	**800-989-3427**	972-869-2800	525
Station Casinos Inc 2411 W Sahara Ave *NYSE: STN*	Las Vegas	NV	89102	**800-544-2411**	702-367-2411	132
Stationers Inc 1945 5th Ave	Huntington	WV	25703	**800-862-7200**	304-528-2780	524
Statistical Assn. American 1429 Duke St	Alexandria	VA	22314	**888-231-3473**	703-684-1221	49-19
Stats Inc 8130 Lehigh Ave *Orders	Morton Grove	IL	60053	**800-637-8287***	847-677-3322	520
StatSpin Inc 85 Morse St	Norwood	MA	02062	**800-782-8774**	781-551-0100	410
Staub Metals Corp PO Box 1425	Paramount	CA	90723	**800-447-8282**	562-602-2200	483
Staubach Co 15601 Dallas Pkwy Suite 400	Addison	TX	75001	**800-944-0012**	972-361-5000	638
Stauffer DF Biscuit Co PO Box 1426 Belmont & 6th Ave	York	PA	17405	**800-673-2473**	717-843-9016	291-9
Stavis Seafoods Inc 212 Northern Ave Suite 305	Boston	MA	02210	**800-390-5103**	617-482-6349	292-5
Stay Aspen Snowmass 425 Rio Grande Pl	Aspen	CO	81611	**800-670-0792**	970-925-9000	368
Staybridge Suites by Holiday Inn 3 Ravinia Dr Suite 100	Atlanta	GA	30346	**800-465-4329**	770-604-2000	369
STC (Society of Telecommunications Consultants) PO Box 416	Fall River Mills	CA	96028	**800-782-7670**	530-336-7070	49-20
Steak & Ale 6500 International Pkwy Suite 1000	Plano	TX	75093	**800-727-8355**	972-588-5000	657
Steak n Shake Co 36 S Pennsylvania St Suite 500 *NYSE: SNS*	Indianapolis	IN	46204	**800-437-2406**	317-633-4100	657
Steak-Out Franchising Inc 6801 Governors Lake Pkwy Suite 100	Norcross	GA	30071	**877-878-3257**	678-533-6000	657
Steak-Umm Co LLC 153 Searles Rd	Pomfret Center	CT	06259	**800-394-7427**	860-928-5900	291-36
Stealth Computer Corp 530 Rowntree Dairy Rd Unit 5	Woodbridge	ON	L4L8H2	**888-783-2584**	905-264-9000	171-3
Steam Brothers Inc 2124 E Sweet Ave	Bismarck	ND	58504	**800-767-5064**	701-222-1263	150
Steamatic Inc 303 Arthur St	Fort Worth	TX	76107	**800-544-1303**	817-332-1575	150
Steamboat Grand Resort Hotel & Conference Center 2300 Mt Werner Cir	Steamboat Springs	CO	80487	**877-269-2628**	970-871-5500	655
Steamboat Resort & Conference Center. Sheraton 2200 Village Inn Ct	Steamboat Springs	CO	80487	**800-325-3535**	970-879-2220	655
Steamboat Resorts PO Box 772995	Steamboat Springs	CO	80477	**800-525-5502**	970-879-8000	369
Steamboat Ski & Resort Corp 2305 Mt Werner Cir	Steamboat Springs	CO	80487	**877-237-2628**	970-879-6111	655
Steamtown National Historic Site 150 S Washington Ave	Scranton	PA	18503	**888-693-9391**	570-340-5200	554
Stearns Co-op Electric Assn 900 E Kraft Dr	Melrose	MN	56352	**800-962-0655**	320-256-4241	244
Stearns & Foster Bedding Co 1 Office Pkwy at Sealy Dr	Trinity	NC	27370	**800-867-3259**	336-861-3500	463
Stearns Inc 1100 Stearns Dr	Sauk Rapids	MN	56379	**800-333-1179**	320-252-1642	701
Stearns Packaging Corp 4200 Sycamore Ave	Madison	WI	53714	**800-655-5008**	608-246-5150	149
Stearnswood Inc PO Box 50	Hutchinson	MN	55350	**800-657-0144**	320-587-2137	199
Steck-Vaughn Co 10801 N MoPac Expy Bldg 3	Austin	TX	78759	**800-531-5015**	512-343-8227	623-2
Steco Mfg 2215 S Van Buren St	Enid	OK	73703	**800-627-8326**	580-237-7433	768
Steel Ceilings Inc 500 N 3rd St	Coshocton	OH	43812	**800-848-0496**	740-622-4655	482
Steel City Corp 190 N Meridian Rd	Youngstown	OH	44501	**800-321-0350**	330-792-7663	479
Steel City Inc 3441 Parkwood Rd SE	Bessemer	AL	35022	**800-264-5075**	205-426-3807	188-14
Steel Engineers Inc 716 W Mesquite Ave	Las Vegas	NV	89106	**800-838-4043**	702-386-0023	483
Steel Grip Inc 700 Garfield St	Danville	IL	61832	**800-223-1595**	217-442-6240	566
Steel Industries Inc 12600 Beech-Daly Rd	Redford	MI	48239	**877-783-3599**	313-535-8505	474
Steel & Pipe Supply Co 555 Poyntz Ave	Manhattan	KS	66502	**800-521-2345**	785-537-2222	483
Steel Tank Institute (STI) 570 Oakwood Rd	Lake Zurich	IL	60047	**800-275-1300**	847-438-8265	49-13
Steel Technologies Inc 15415 Shelbyville Rd *NASDAQ: STTX*	Louisville	KY	40245	**800-828-2170**	502-245-2110	709
Steel Warehouse Co Inc 2722 W Tucker Dr	South Bend	IN	46619	**800-348-2529**	574-236-5100	483
Steel of West Virginia Inc 17th St & 2nd Ave	Huntington	WV	25703	**800-624-3492**	304-696-8200	709
Steelcase Inc PO Box 1967 *NYSE: SCS*	Grand Rapids	MI	49501	**888-783-3522**	616-247-2710	314-1
SteelCloud Co 1306 Squire Ct *NASDAQ: SCLD*	Dulles	VA	20166	**800-296-3866**	703-450-0400	174
Steelcraft Corp 2700 Jackson Ave	Memphis	TN	38108	**800-238-4012**	901-452-5200	19
Steelcraft Mfg Co 9017 Blue Ash Rd *Cust Svc	Cincinnati	OH	45242	**800-930-8585***	513-745-6400	232
Steele Canvas Basket Corp 201 William St PO Box 6267 IMCN	Chelsea	MA	02150	**800-541-8929**	617-889-0202	718
Steele-Waseca Co-op Electric PO Box 485	Owatonna	MN	55060	**800-526-3514**	507-451-7340	244
Steere Enterprises Inc 285 Commerce St	Tallmadge	OH	44278	**800-875-4926**	330-633-4926	593
Steiff North America 425 Paramont Dr	Raynham	MA	02767	**800-830-0429**	508-828-2377	750
Stein Eriksen Lodge 7700 Stein Way	Park City	UT	84060	**800-453-1302**	435-649-3700	655

Company / Address	City	State	ZIP	Toll-Free	Phone	Class
Stein Fibers Ltd						
4 Computer Dr W Suite 200	Albany	NY	12205	**888-489-2790**	518-489-5700	594-1
Stein Hospice Service						
1200 Sycamore Line	Sandusky	OH	44870	**800-625-5269**	419-625-5269	365
Steinen William Mfg Co						
29 E Halsey Rd	Parsippany	NJ	07054	**800-724-3343**	973-887-6400	598
Steiner Corp						
505 E South Temple	Salt Lake City	UT	84102	**800-408-0208**	801-328-8831	184
Steiner Electric Co Inc						
1250 Touhy Ave	Elk Grove Village	IL	60007	**800-783-4637**	847-228-0400	245
Steiner Industries 5801 N Tripp Ave	Chicago	IL	60646	**800-621-4515**	773-588-3444	566
Steinhafels 16250 W Rogers Dr	New Berlin	WI	53151	**800-813-2358**	262-784-0500	316
Steinway & Sons						
1 Steinway Pl	Long Island City	NY	11105	**800-366-1853**	718-721-2600	516
Steiny & Co Inc						
221 N Ardmore Ave PO						
Box 74901	Los Angeles	CA	90004	**800-350-2331**	213-382-2331	188-4
Stelco Inc PO Box 2030	Hamilton	ON	L8N3T1	**800-263-9305**	905-528-2511	709
TSE: STE.a						
Stella FD Products Co 7000 Fenkell St	Detroit	MI	48238	**800-447-7356**	313-341-6400	378
Stellar Group 2900 Hartley Rd	Jacksonville	FL	32257	**800-488-2900**	904-260-2900	185
StellArt 2012 Waltzer Rd	Santa Rosa	CA	95403	**866-621-1987**	707-569-1378	130
Stellent Inc						
7777 Golden Triangle Dr	Eden Prairie	MN	55344	**800-909-0774**	952-903-2000	176-7
NASDAQ: STEL						
Stemco LP						
300 Industrial Blvd PO Box 1989	Longview	TX	75606	**800-527-8492**	903-758-9981	60
Sten Corp 13828 Lincoln St NE	Ham Lake	MN	55304	**800-328-7958**	763-755-9516	467
NASDAQ: STEN						
Stens Corp PO Box 490	Jasper	IN	47547	**800-457-7444**	812-482-2526	420
Stentor Inc						
5000 Marina Blvd Suite 100	Brisbane	CA	94005	**877-328-2808***	650-866-4100	375
*Cust Svc						
Step Inside Design Magazine						
6000 N Forest Park Dr	Peoria	IL	61614	**800-255-8800**	309-688-8800	449-2
Stepan Co 22 W Frontage Rd	Northfield	IL	60093	**800-745-7837***	847-446-7500	143
NYSE: SCL ■ *Tech Supp						
Stepfamily Assn of America (SAA)						
650 J St Suite 205	Lincoln	NE	68508	**800-735-0329**	402-477-7837	48-6
Stepfamily Foundation						
333 West End Ave Suite 11C	New York	NY	10023	**800-759-7837**	212-877-3244	48-6
Stephan Co						
1850 W McNab Rd	Fort Lauderdale	FL	33309	**800-327-4963**	954-971-0600	211
AMEX: TSC						
Stephen F Austin. InterContinental						
701 Congress Ave	Austin	TX	78701	**800-327-0200**	512-457-8800	373
Stephens College 1200 E Broadway	Columbia	MO	65215	**800-876-7207**	573-442-2211	163
Stephens Inc 111 Center St	Little Rock	AR	72201	**800-643-9691**	501-377-2000	679
Stephens Media Group Washington News Bureau 666 11th St NW						
Rm 535	Washington	DC	20001	**800-366-7390**	202-783-1760	520
Stephens PW Inc						
15201 Pipeline Ln Unit B	Huntington Beach	CA	92649	**800-937-1521**	714-892-2028	653
Stephenson & Lawyer Inc						
3831 Patterson Ave SE	Grand Rapids	MI	49512	**800-968-5535**	616-949-8100	590
Stephenson's Flower Shops						
145 S Locust St	Camp Hill	PA	17011	**800-735-6937**	717-761-5990	287
Stepping Stone Falls 5161 Branch Rd	Flint	MI	48506	**800-648-4242**	810-736-7100	50
Stereo Review						
1633 Broadway 45th Fl	New York	NY	10019	**800-876-9011***	212-767-6000	449-9
*Cust Svc						
Stericycle Inc 28161 N Keith Dr	Lake Forest	IL	60045	**800-355-8773**	800-643-0240	791
NASDAQ: SRCL						
Sterigenics						
2015 Spring Rd Suite 650	Oak Brook	IL	60523	**800-472-4508**	630-928-1700	771
Sterilite Corp PO Box 524	Townsend	MA	01469	**800-225-1046**	978-597-8702	596
Sterilone						
2125 Biscayne Blvd Suite 580	Miami Beach	FL	33137	**877-271-1057**	305-572-0660	18
STERIS Corp 5960 Heisley Rd	Mentor	OH	44060	**800-548-4873**	440-354-2600	468
NYSE: STE						
Steris Laboratories Inc						
620 N 51st Ave	Phoenix	AZ	85043	**800-272-5525***	602-278-1400	573
*Cust Svc						
Sterling Art Supply 18871 Teller Ave	Irvine	CA	92612	**800-953-2953**	949-553-0101	45
Sterling Bancshares Inc						
2550 N Loop W Suite 200	Houston	TX	77092	**888-777-8735**	713-466-8300	355-2
NASDAQ: SBIB						
Sterling Bank 15000 North-West Fwy	Houston	TX	77040	**888-777-8735**	713-466-8300	71
Sterling Business Forms						
5300 Crater Lake Ave	Central Point	OR	97502	**800-759-3676***	541-779-3173	111
*Cust Svc						
Sterling Capital Corp						
635 Madison Ave 18th Fl	New York	NY	10022	**800-949-3456**	212-980-3360	397
AMEX: SPR						
Sterling China USA LLC 511 12th St	Wellsville	OH	43968	**800-682-7628**	330-532-1544	716
Sterling-Clark-Lurton Corp						
184 Commercial St	Malden	MA	02148	**800-225-4444**	781-322-0163	540
Sterling College 125 W Cooper	Sterling	KS	67579	**800-346-1017**	620-278-2173	163
Sterling College						
PO Box 72	Craftsbury Common	VT	05827	**800-648-3591**	802-586-7711	787
Sterling Commerce Inc						
4600 Lakehurst Ct	Dublin	OH	43016	**800-876-9772**	614-793-7000	176-1
Sterling Communications Inc						
221 Sun Valley Blvd Suite G	Lincoln	NE	68528	**888-438-0316**	402-438-0316	622
Sterling Courier Systems Inc						
1110 Herndon Pkwy 2nd Fl	Herndon	VA	20170	**800-633-6666**	703-471-4488	536
Sterling Cruises & Travel						
8700 W Flagler St Suite 105	Miami	FL	33174	**800-435-7967**	305-592-2522	760
Sterling Die Div Goodrich Corp						
5565 Venture Dr Suite D	Parma	OH	44130	**800-533-1300**	216-267-1300	745
Sterling Electric Inc						
16752 Armstrong Ave	Irvine	CA	92606	**800-654-6220***	949-474-0520	507
*Cust Svc						
Sterling Fibers Inc 5005 Sterling Way	Pace	FL	32571	**800-874-8593***	850-994-5311	594-2
*Cust Svc						
Sterling Financial Corp						
111 N Wall St	Spokane	WA	99201	**800-772-7791**	509-624-4114	355-2
NASDAQ: STSA						
Sterling Healthcare						
1000 Park Forty Plaza Suite 500	Durham	NC	27713	**800-476-4587**	919-383-0355	455
Sterling Hotel 1300 H St	Sacramento	CA	95814	**800-365-7660**	916-448-1300	373
Sterling Inc 5200 W Clinton Ave	Milwaukee	WI	53223	**800-783-7835***	414-354-0970	200
*Cust Svc						
Sterling John Corp PO Box 469	Richmond	IL	60071	**800-367-5726**	815-678-2031	345
Sterling Optical						
100 Quentin Roosevelt Blvd	Garden City	NY	11530	**800-332-6302**	516-390-2100	533
Sterling Paper Co						
2155 E Castor Ave	Philadelphia	PA	19134	**800-745-5350**	215-744-5350	102
Sterling Phillips & Assoc Inc						
4739 Utica St Suite 212	Metairie	LA	70006	**800-375-5773**	504-887-0202	157
Sterling Plumbing Group Inc						
444 Highland Dr	Kohler	WI	53044	**888-783-7546***	920-457-4441	598
*Cust Svc						
Sterling Production Control Units						
2280 W Dorothy Ln	Dayton	OH	45439	**800-968-7728**	937-299-5594	379
Sterling Publishing Co Inc						
387 Park Ave S 5th Fl	New York	NY	10016	**800-367-9692***	212-532-7160	623-2
*Cust Svc						
Sterling Savings Bank 111 N Wall St	Spokane	WA	99201	**800-772-7791**	509-624-4114	71
Sterling Scale Co Inc						
20950 Boening Dr	Southfield	MI	48075	**800-331-0031**	248-358-0590	672
Sterling Spring Corp 5432 W 54th St	Chicago	IL	60638	**800-969-7884**	773-582-6464	705
Sterling Testing Systems Inc						
249 W 17th St 6th Fl	New York	NY	10011	**800-899-2272**	212-736-5100	621
Sterling Textile Services						
5909 Blair Rd NW	Washington	DC	20011	**800-626-9280**	202-723-9535	434
Sterling Truck Corp						
4420 Sherwin Rd	Willoughby	OH	44094	**888-785-4357***	440-269-5500	505
*Cust Svc						
Sterling/MacFadden Partnership						
333 7th Ave 11th Fl	New York	NY	10001	**800-741-1289**	212-979-4800	623-9
Stern H Jewelers Inc 645 5th Ave	New York	NY	10022	**800-747-8376**	212-688-0300	402
Stern Jacob & Sons Inc						
1464 E Valley Rd	Santa Barbara	CA	93108	**800-223-7054**	805-565-1411	291-12
Sterne Agee & Leach Inc						
800 Shades Creek Pkwy						
Suite 700	Birmingham	AL	35209	**800-240-1438**	205-949-3500	679
Sterner Lighting Systems Inc						
351 Lewis Ave W PO Box 805	Winsted	MN	55395	**800-328-7480**		431
Stetson University						
421 N Woodland Blvd	DeLand	FL	32723	**800-688-0101**	386-822-7000	163
Steuben County Rural Electric Membership Corp PO Box 359	Angola	IN	46703	**888-233-9088**	260-665-3563	244
Steuben County Tourism Bureau						
207 S Wayne St	Angola	IN	46703	**800-525-3101**	260-665-5386	205
Steuben Glass 1 Steuben Way	Corning	NY	14830	**800-424-4240**	607-974-8584	330
Steuben Rural Electric Co-op Inc						
9 Wilson Ave	Bath	NY	14810	**800-843-3414**	607-776-4161	244
Steven Barclay Agency						
12 Western Ave	Petaluma	CA	94952	**888-965-7323**	707-773-0654	699
Steven Engineering Inc						
230 Ryan Way	South San Francisco	CA	94080	**800-258-9200**	650-588-9200	245
Steven Fabrics Co						
1400 Van Buren St NE	Minneapolis	MN	55413	**800-328-2558**	612-781-6671	731
Steven Madden Ltd						
52-16 Barnett Ave	Long Island City	NY	11104	**800-747-6233**	718-446-1800	296
NASDAQ: SHOO						
Steven Windsor Inc						
6535 Arlington Blvd	Falls Church	VA	22042	**800-765-3487**	703-533-9784	155-3
Stevens Aviation Inc						
600 Delaware St Donaldson						
Industrial Pk	Greenville	SC	29605	**800-359-7838**	864-879-6000	63
Stevens Creek Software LLC						
PO Box 2126	Cupertino	CA	95015	**800-823-4279**	408-725-0424	176-9
Stevens Institute of Technology						
Castle Point on the Hudson	Hoboken	NJ	07030	**800-458-5323**	201-216-5194	163
Stevens Transport PO Box 279010	Dallas	TX	75227	**800-233-9369**	972-216-9000	769
Stevens Travel Management Inc						
55 Broad St 17th Fl	New York	NY	10004	**800-275-7400**	212-696-4300	760
Stevens Water Monitoring Systems						
5465 SW Western Ave Suite F	Beaverton	OR	97005	**800-452-5272**	503-469-8000	534
Stevens Worldwide Van Lines						
527 Morley Dr	Saginaw	MI	48601	**800-678-3836**	989-755-3000	508
Stevenson Lumber						
1585 Monroe Tpke PO Box 123	Stevenson	CT	06491	**800-972-4260**	203-261-2555	190-3
Steve's Books & Magazines						
2612 S Harvard	Tulsa	OK	74114	**888-743-0989**	918-743-3544	96
Steves & Sons Inc						
203 Humble Ave	San Antonio	TX	78225	**800-627-5111***	210-924-5111	234
*Sales						
Stew Leonard's 100 Westport Ave	Norwalk	CT	06851	**800-729-7839**	203-847-9088	333
Steward Inc 1200 E 36th St	Chattanooga	TN	37407	**800-634-2673***	423-867-4100	248
*Cust Svc						
Steward Machine Co Inc						
3911 13th Ave N	Birmingham	AL	35234	**800-394-6461**	205-841-6461	446
Stewart & Assoc Inc						
50 W Douglas St Suite 1200	Freeport	IL	61032	**800-442-3807**	815-235-3807	392
Stewart Directories Inc						
10540 J York Rd	Cockeysville	MD	21030	**800-311-0786**	410-628-5988	623-6
Stewart Douglas Co						
2402 Advance Rd	Madison	WI	53718	**800-279-2795**	608-221-1155	673
Stewart EFI LLC						
45 Old Waterbury Rd	Thomaston	CT	06787	**800-393-5387**	860-283-8213	480
Stewart Engineering Supply Inc						
3221 E Pioneer Pkwy	Arlington	TX	76010	**800-533-1265**	817-640-1767	113
Stewart Enterprises Inc						
1333 S Clearview Pkwy	Jefferson	LA	70121	**800-257-1610**	504-729-1400	499
NASDAQ: STEI						
Stewart Filmscreen Corp						
1161 W Sepulveda Blvd	Torrance	CA	90502	**800-762-4999**	310-326-1422	580
Stewart Information Services Corp						
1980 Post Oak Blvd Suite 800	Houston	TX	77056	**800-729-1900**	713-625-8100	384-6
NYSE: STC						
Stewart Regional Blood Center						
815 S Baxter Ave	Tyler	TX	75701	**800-252-5584**	903-535-5400	90
Stewart & Stevenson Services Inc						
2707 North Loop W	Houston	TX	77008	**800-527-3246**	713-868-7700	259
NYSE: SVC						

Name / Address	City	State	ZIP	Toll-Free	Phone	Class
Stewart & Stevenson Services Inc						
Power Products Div						
5840 Dahlia St	Commerce City	CO	80022	**800-727-7441**	303-287-7441	379
Stewart Sutherland Inc						
5411 E 'V' Ave	Vicksburg	MI	49097	**800-253-1034**	269-649-0530	66
Stewart Systems 808 Stewart Ave.	Plano	TX	75074	**800-966-5808**	972-422-5808	206
Stewart Title Co						
1980 Post Oak Blvd Suite 800	Houston	TX	77056	**800-729-1900**	713-625-8100	384-6
Stewart Title Guaranty Co						
1980 Post Oak Blvd Suite 800	Houston	TX	77056	**800-729-1900**	713-625-8100	384-6
Stewart's Inc 604 N West Ave	Sioux Falls	SD	57104	**800-537-2625**	605-336-2775	79
Stewarts Private Blend Food Inc						
4110 W Wrightwood Ave	Chicago	IL	60639	**800-654-2862**	773-489-2500	291-7
STI (Steel Tank Institute)						
570 Oakwood Rd	Lake Zurich	IL	60047	**800-275-1300**	847-438-8265	49-13
STI Automation Sensors						
1025 W 1700 N	Logan	UT	84321	**888-525-7300**	435-753-7300	200
STI Classic Funds						
PO Box 4418 MC 712	Atlanta	GA	30302	**800-428-6970**		517
STI Knowledge Inc						
4 Concourse Pkwy Suite 290	Atlanta	GA	30328	**888-243-5733**	770-280-2630	455
Sticht Herman H Co Inc						
45 Main St Suite 701	Brooklyn	NY	11201	**800-221-3203**	718-852-7602	464
Stiefel Laboratories Inc						
255 Alhambra Cir Suite 1000	Coral Gables	FL	33134	**888-784-3335**	305-443-3807	572
Stifel Financial Corp						
501 N Broadway	Saint Louis	MO	63102	**800-488-0970**	314-342-2000	679
NYSE: SF						
Stifel Nicolaus & Co Inc						
501 N Broadway	Saint Louis	MO	63102	**800-488-0970**	314-342-2000	679
Stihl Inc 536 Viking Dr	Virginia Beach	VA	23452	**800-467-8445***	757-486-9100	747
*Cust Svc						
Stik-II Products Inc 41 O'Neill St	Easthampton	MA	01027	**800-356-3572**	413-527-7120	717
Stila Cosmetics						
551 Madison Ave 12th Fl	New York	NY	10022	**877-565-1299**	646-282-1000	211
Stiles-Kem Div Met-Pro Corp						
1570 S Lakeside Dr.	Waukegan	IL	60085	**800-562-1537**	847-689-1100	143
Stiles Landscape Co						
1080 SW 12 Ave	Pompano Beach	FL	33069	**866-250-4074**	954-781-0247	413
Still Life Retreat						
394591 Concession 2 RR1	Durham	ON	N0G1R0	**877-584-8880**	519-369-3663	660
Stillman College PO Box 1430	Tuscaloosa	AL	35403	**800-841-5722***	205-349-4240	163
*Admissions						
Stillwater Chamber of Commerce						
409 S Main St	Stillwater	OK	74076	**800-593-5573**	405-372-5573	137
Stillwater Milling Co 512 E 6th St	Stillwater	OK	74074	**800-364-6804**	405-372-3445	438
Stillwater Spa at the Hyatt Regency						
Newport 1 Goat Island	Newport	RI	02840	**800-233-1234**	401-851-3225	698
StillWaters Resort						
797 Moonbrook Dr	Dadeville	AL	36853	**800-687-3732**	256-825-7021	655
Stillwell Hotel 838 S Grand Ave	Los Angeles	CA	90017	**800-553-4774**	213-627-1151	373
Stilson Die-Draulic Div Stocker Yale Inc						
15935 Sturgeon St	Roseville	MI	48066	**877-784-5766**	586-778-1100	484
Stimple & Ward Co						
3400 Babcock Blvd	Pittsburgh	PA	15237	**800-792-6457**	412-364-5200	507
Stimson Lane Ltd						
14111 NE 145th St	Woodinville	WA	98072	**800-267-6793**	425-488-1133	310-5
Stimson Lumber Co						
520 SW Yamhill St Suite 700	Portland	OR	97204	**800-445-9758**	503-222-1676	671
Stinehour Press 853 Lancaster Rd	Lunenburg	VT	05906	**800-331-7753**	802-328-2507	614
Stirling Properties						
109 Northpark Blvd Suite 300	Covington	LA	70433	**888-261-2022**	985-898-2022	641
Sto-Cote Products Inc						
218 South Rd	Genoa City	WI	53128	**800-435-2621**	262-279-6000	589
Stock Building Supply 4403 Bland Rd	Raleigh	NC	27609	**877-734-6365**	919-431-1000	190-3
Stock Car Racing Magazine						
5555 Concord Pkwy S Suite 326	Concord	NC	28075	**800-333-2633**	863-644-0449	449-3
Stock Drive Products/Sterling						
Instrument						
2101 Jericho Tpke	New Hyde Park	NY	11040	**800-354-1144**	516-328-3300	609
Stock Equipment Co						
16490 Chillicothe Rd	Chagrin Falls	OH	44023	**800-289-7326**	440-543-6000	269
Stock Seed Farms 28008 Mill Rd	Murdock	NE	68407	**800-759-1520**	402-867-3771	684
Stock Yards Packing Co Inc						
PO Box 12450	Chicago	IL	60612	**800-621-3687**	312-733-6050	291-26
StockCap 123 Manufacturers Dr	Arnold	MO	63010	**800-827-2277**	636-282-6800	152
Stocker Yale Inc Stilson Die-Draulic Div						
15935 Sturgeon St	Roseville	MI	48066	**877-784-5766**	586-778-1100	484
StockerYale Inc 32 Hampshire Rd	Salem	NH	03079	**800-843-8011**	603-893-8778	534
NASDAQ: STKR						
Stockham Div Crane Co						
2129 3rd Ave SE	Cullman	AL	35055	**800-786-2542**	256-775-3800	776
Stockli Ski USA Inc PO Box 370206	Denver	CO	80237	**800-638-6284**	303-220-9737	701
Stockmen's Livestock Market Inc						
E Hwy 50 PO Box 280	Yankton	SD	57078	**800-532-0952**	605-665-9641	437
Stockpot Inc 22505 SR 9	Woodinville	WA	98072	**800-468-1611**	425-415-2000	291-36
Stockyard Photos 1410 Hutchins St	Houston	TX	77003	**800-238-4105**	713-520-0898	582
Stockyards Hotel						
109 E Exchange Ave	Fort Worth	TX	76106	**800-423-8471**	817-625-6427	373
Stoel Rives LLP						
900 SW 5th Ave Suite 2600	Portland	OR	97204	**800-887-8635**	503-224-3380	419
Stok Software Inc						
373 Nesconset Hwy Suite 287	Hauppauge	NY	11788	**888-448-8668**	631-232-2228	176-10
Stokes Electric Co Inc						
1701 McCalla Ave	Knoxville	TN	37915	**800-999-0351**	865-525-0351	245
Stoller Enterprises Inc						
4001 W Sam Houston Pkwy N						
Suite 100	Houston	TX	77043	**800-539-5283**	713-461-1493	276
Stoller Fisheries Inc PO Box B	Spirit Lake	IA	51360	**800-831-5174**	712-336-1750	291-14
Stoller's W Honey Inc PO Box 97	Latty	OH	45855	**888-233-6446**	419-399-5786	291-24
Stolt Offshore Inc						
10787 Clay Rd Suite 110	Houston	TX	77041	**800-299-3483**	713-430-1100	528
NASDAQ: SOSA						
Stone Construction Equipment Inc						
8662 Main St	Honeoye	NY	14471	**800-888-9926**	585-229-5141	189
Stone Energy Corp						
625 E Kaliste Saloom Rd	Lafayette	LA	70508	**800-551-3340**	337-237-0410	525
NYSE: SGY						

Name / Address	City	State	ZIP	Toll-Free	Phone	Class
Stone Hill Winery 601 State Hwy 165	Branson	MO	65616	**888-926-9463**	417-334-1897	50
Stone International LLC						
317 Neely Ferry Rd Suite 3	Mauldin	SC	29662	**800-762-2637***	864-288-4822	153-1
*Cust Svc						
Stone Legacy Corp						
S1075 Westland Ct E	Spring Valley	WI	54767	**877-563-6465***	715-778-5079	701
*Sales						
Stone Legal Resources Group						
100 Summer St 10th Fl	Boston	MA	02110	**877-529-5627**	617-482-4100	707
Stone Mountain Accessories						
10 W 33rd St Suite 728	New York	NY	10001	**866-865-0786***	212-563-2500	422
*Cust Svc						
Stone Mountain Park						
Hwy 78 PO Box 689	Stone Mountain	GA	30086	**800-317-2006**	770-498-5690	50
Stone Sand & Gravel Assn. National						
1605 King St	Alexandria	VA	22314	**800-342-1415**	703-525-8788	49-3
Stone Soup Magazine PO Box 83	Santa Cruz	CA	95063	**800-447-4569**	831-426-5557	449-6
Stone Street Capital						
7316 Wisconsin Ave 5th Fl	Bethesda	MD	20814	**800-586-7786**		783
Stonebriar Resort. Westin						
1549 Legacy Dr	Frisco	TX	75034	**800-937-8461**	972-668-8000	655
Stonebridge Bank PO Box 2425	West Chester	PA	19380	**800-807-1666**	610-280-4700	71
Stonebridge Inn						
300 Carriage Way PO						
Box 5008	Snowmass Village	CO	81615	**800-922-7242**	970-923-2420	373
Stonebridge Life Insurance Co						
2700 W Plano Pkwy	Plano	TX	75075	**800-527-9027**	972-881-6000	384-2
Stonebridge Press Inc 25 Elm St	Southbridge	MA	01550	**800-536-5836**	508-764-4325	623-8
Stonehedge Inn						
160 Pawtucket Blvd	Tyngsboro	MA	01879	**800-648-7070**	978-649-4400	373
Stoneleigh Hotel 2927 Maple Ave	Dallas	TX	75201	**800-255-9299**	214-871-7111	373
StoneMor Partners LP DBA Cornerstone						
Family Services 155 Rittenhouse Cir	Bristol	PA	19007	**877-857-8890**	215-826-2800	499
NASDAQ: STON						
Stoner Inc 1070 Robert Fulton Hwy	Quarryville	PA	17566	**800-227-5538**	717-786-7355	143
Stonewall Resort 940 Resort Dr	Roanoke	WV	26447	**888-278-8150**	304-269-7400	655
Stoneway Electric Supply Co						
402 N Perry St	Spokane	WA	99202	**800-841-1408**	509-535-2933	245
Stoney Creek Inn						
101 Mariner's Way	East Peoria	IL	61611	**800-659-2220**	309-694-1300	373
Stonhard Inc 1 Park Ave	Maple Shade	NJ	08052	**800-854-0310***	856-779-7500	286
*Cust Svc						
Stonington Corp 111 Mosher St	Holyoke	MA	01040	**800-370-2673***	413-493-1500	125
*Cust Svc						
Stonyfield Farm Inc 10 Burton Dr.	Londonderry	NH	03053	**800-776-2697**	603-437-4040	291-25
STOP (Safe Tables Our Priority)						
PO Box 4352	Burlington	VT	05406	**800-350-7867**	802-863-0555	48-17
Stop-N-Go Inc 1 Valero Way	San Antonio	TX	78249	**800-333-3377**	210-592-2000	203
Stopka & Assoc						
975 Weiland Rd Suite 100	Buffalo Grove	IL	60089	**800-984-7031**	847-215-3900	178
STOPS Inc 8855 Grissom Pkwy	Titusville	FL	32780	**800-487-0521**	321-383-0499	384-4
Stor-All Systems Inc						
1375 W Hillsboro Blvd	Deerfield Beach	FL	33442	**800-937-8673**	954-421-7888	790-3
Stora Enso North America Corp						
2 Landmark Sq 3rd Fl	Stamford	CT	06901	**888-807-8672**	203-356-2300	547
NYSE: SEO						
Storage Assn. Self						
6506 Louisdale Rd Suite 315	Springfield	VA	22150	**888-735-3784**	703-921-9123	49-21
Storage Engine Inc						
1 Sheila Dr Bldg 6A	Tinton Falls	NJ	07724	**866-734-8899**	732-747-6995	174
Storage Equipment Co Inc						
1258 Titan Dr	Dallas	TX	75247	**800-443-1791**	214-630-9221	315
Storage Technology Corp						
1 StorageTek Dr	Louisville	CO	80028	**800-877-9220**	303-673-5151	171-8
NYSE: STK						
StorageASP Inc						
515 Consumers Rd Suite 405	Toronto	ON	M2J4Z2	**877-747-0330**	416-750-4002	39
Storck USA LP						
325 N LaSalle St Suite 400	Chicago	IL	60610	**800-621-7772**	312-467-5700	291-8
Store Opening Solutions (SOS)						
800 Middle Tennessee Blvd	Murfreesboro	TN	37129	**877-388-9262**	615-867-0858	440
Storer Coachways						
3519 McDonald Ave	Modesto	CA	95358	**800-621-3383**	209-521-8250	108
Storer Meats Co Inc						
3007 Clinton Ave	Cleveland	OH	44113	**800-355-7537**	216-621-7538	291-26
Storey Communications Inc						
210 Mass Moca Way	North Adams	MA	01247	**800-335-3432**	413-346-2100	623-2
Stork Gamco Inc PO Box 1258	Gainesville	GA	30503	**800-347-8675**	770-532-7041	293
Stork News of America Inc						
1305 Hope Mills Rd Suite A	Fayetteville	NC	28304	**800-633-6395**	910-426-1357	129
Storm King School						
314 Mountain Rd	Cornwall-on-Hudson	NY	12520	**800-225-9144**	845-534-9860	611
Storm Mfg Group Inc						
23201 Normandie Ave	Torrance	CA	90501	**800-210-2525**	310-326-8287	776
Storm Products Inc						
165 S 800 West	Brigham City	UT	84302	**800-369-4402**	435-723-0403	701
Storm Safe Shutters						
3593 Veronica Shoemaker Blvd	Fort Myers	FL	33916	**800-257-8676**	239-432-9181	690
Stormont-Vail Regional Health Center						
1500 SW 10th St	Topeka	KS	66604	**800-432-2951**	785-354-6000	366-2
Stornoway Diamond Corp						
625 Howe St Suite 860	Vancouver	BC	V6C2T6	**888-338-2200**	604-331-2259	493-3
TSE: SWY						
Storopack Inc 12007 S Woodruff Ave.	Downey	CA	90241	**800-829-1491**	562-803-1584	590
Stout Marketing Inc						
6425 W Florissant Ave	Saint Louis	MO	63136	**800-325-8530**	314-385-4600	692
Stowe Mountain Resort						
5781 Mountain Rd	Stowe	VT	05672	**800-253-4754**	802-253-3000	655
Stoweflake Mountain Resort & Spa						
1746 Mountain Rd PO Box 369	Stowe	VT	05672	**800-253-2232**	802-253-7355	655
Strafford Publications Inc						
PO Box 13729	Atlanta	GA	30324	**800-926-7926**	404-881-1141	623-9
Straight A Tours & Travel						
715 N Ferncreek Ave	Orlando	FL	32803	**800-237-5440**	407-896-1242	748
Straight Line Sports LLC						
19011 Woodinville-Snohomish						
Rd Suite 130	Woodinville	WA	98072	**800-248-5564**	425-527-1148	701

Alphabetical Section

Company / Address	City	State	ZIP	Toll-Free	Phone	Class
Strait Music Co 2428 W Ben White Blvd	Austin	TX	78704	**800-725-8877**	512-476-6927	515
Strand Lighting Inc 6603 Darin Way	Cypress	CA	90630	**800-733-0564**	714-230-8200	431
Strand Theatre 619 Louisiana Ave	Shreveport	LA	71101	**800-313-6373**	318-226-1481	562
Strang Communications 600 Rinehart Rd *Sales	Lake Mary	FL	32746	**800-451-4598***	407-333-0600	623-9
Strange's Florist Inc 3313 Mechanicsville Pike	Richmond	VA	23223	**800-421-4070**	804-321-2200	287
Strata Inc 567 S Valley View Suite 1 *Sales	Saint George	UT	84770	**800-678-7282***	435-628-5218	176-8
Stratagene Inc 11011 N Torrey Pines Rd *NASDAQ: STGN*	La Jolla	CA	92037	**800-894-1304**	858-535-5400	229
Stratasys Inc 14950 Martin Dr *NASDAQ: SSYS*	Eden Prairie	MN	55344	**888-480-3548**	952-937-3000	258
Stratcor Inc 4955 Steubenville Pike Suite 305	Pittsburgh	PA	15205	**800-573-6052**	412-787-4500	492
Stratecom Graphics 235 Conway Dr	Bogart	GA	30622	**800-205-9159**	706-546-8840	675
Strategic Air & Space Museum 28210 W Park Hwy	Ashland	NE	68003	**800-358-5029**	402-944-3100	509
Strategic Diagnostics Inc 111 Pencader Dr *NASDAQ: SDIX*	Newark	DE	19702	**800-544-8881**	302-456-6789	229
Strategic Employee Publications Newsletter 316 N Michigan Ave Suite 300	Chicago	IL	60601	**800-878-5331**	312-960-4100	521-11
Strategic Equipment & Supply Corp 1031 Madeira Ave	Minneapolis	MN	55405	**800-328-5133**	612-381-3100	295
Strategic Management Group Inc 3624 Market St	Philadelphia	PA	19104	**866-874-4899**	215-387-4000	193
Strategic Outsourcing Inc 5260 Parkway Plaza Blvd Suite 140	Charlotte	NC	28217	**800-572-2412**	704-523-2191	619
Strater Hotel 699 Main Ave	Durango	CO	81301	**800-247-4431**	970-247-4431	373
Stratex Networks Inc 120 Rose Orchard Way *NASDAQ: STXN*	San Jose	CA	95134	**800-362-9283**	408-943-0777	720
Stratford Court 45 Katherine Blvd	Palm Harbor	FL	34684	**800-772-2622**	727-787-1500	659
Stratford Homes LP 402 S Weber Ave	Stratford	WI	54484	**800-448-1524**	715-687-3133	107
Stratford Hotel 242 Powell St	San Francisco	CA	94102	**888-504-6835**	415-397-7080	373
Stratford Publishing Services 70 Landmark Hill Dr	Brattleboro	VT	05301	**800-451-4328**	802-254-6073	770
Stratford Star 1000 Bridgeport Ave	Shelton	CT	06484	**800-843-6791**	203-926-2080	522-4
Strathallan Hotel 550 East Ave	Rochester	NY	14607	**800-678-7284**	585-461-5010	373
Stratham Tire Inc 355 Rt 125	Brentwood	NH	03833	**800-427-7217**	603-679-5840	739
Strathcona Hotel 919 Douglas St	Victoria	BC	V8W2C2	**800-663-7476**	250-383-7137	372
Strathcona Hotel 60 York St	Toronto	ON	M5J1S8	**800-268-8304**	416-363-3321	372
Stratix Corp 4920 Avalon Ridge Pkwy Suite 600	Norcross	GA	30071	**800-343-0343**	770-326-7580	171-7
Stratosphere Tower Hotel & Casino 2000 S Las Vegas Blvd	Las Vegas	NV	89104	**800-998-6937**	702-380-7777	133
Strattec Security Corp 3333 W Good Hope Rd *NASDAQ: STRT*	Milwaukee	WI	53209	**888-710-5770**	414-247-3333	60
Stratton Equity Co-op Co Inc PO Box 25	Stratton	CO	80836	**800-752-2068**	719-348-5347	271
Stratton Seed Co 1530 Hwy 79 S PO box 1088	Stuttgart	AR	72160	**800-264-4433**	870-673-4433	684
Stratton Travel Management 860 Wyckoff Ave	Mahwah	NJ	07430	**800-223-0599**	201-405-1999	760
Stratton Veterans Affairs Medical Center 113 Holland Ave	Albany	NY	12208	**800-223-4810**	518-626-5000	366-6
Stratus Pharmaceuticals Inc 14377 SW 142nd St	Miami	FL	33186	**800-442-7882**	305-254-6793	573
Stratus Properties Inc 98 San Jacinto Blvd Suite 220 *NASDAQ: STRS*	Austin	TX	78701	**800-690-0315**	512-478-5788	639
Stratus Services Group Inc 500 Craig Rd Suite 201	Manalapan	NJ	07726	**800-777-1557**	732-866-0300	707
Stratus Technologies 111 Powdermill Rd	Maynard	MA	01754	**800-787-2887**	978-461-7000	176-12
Strauss Inc 648 E 1100 N PO Box 149	North Manchester	IN	46962	**800-982-7172**	260-982-2181	438
Strauss Levi & Co 1155 Battery St	San Francisco	CA	94111	**800-872-5384**	415-501-6000	153-11
Strawberries Music & Video 38 Corporate Cir	Albany	NY	12203	**800-540-1242**	518-452-1242	514
Strayer Education Inc 2121 15th St N *NASDAQ: STRA*	Arlington	VA	22201	**877-892-5100**	703-892-5100	241
Strayer University 1133 15th St NW	Washington	DC	20005	**888-360-1588**	202-408-2400	163
Alexandria Campus 2730 Eisenhower Ave	Alexandria	VA	22314	**888-478-7293**	703-329-9100	163
Arlington Campus 2121 15th St N	Arlington	VA	22201	**888-478-7293**	703-892-5100	163
Fredericksburg Campus 4500 Plank Rd	Fredericksburg	VA	22407	**800-765-8680**	540-785-8800	163
Takoma Park Campus 6830 Laurel St NW	Washington	DC	20012	**877-722-8100**	202-722-8100	163
Streater Inc 411 S 1st Ave	Albert Lea	MN	56007	**800-527-4197**	507-373-0611	281
Streator Dependable Mfg Co 410 W Broadway St	Streator	IL	61364	**800-795-0551**	815-672-0551	462
Streett JD & Co Inc 144 Weldon Pkwy	Maryland Heights	MO	63043	**800-678-6600**	314-432-6600	530
Streicher Mobile Fueling Inc 800 W Cypress Creek Rd Suite 580 *NASDAQ: FUEL*	Fort Lauderdale	FL	33309	**800-383-5734**	954-308-4200	311
Stren Fishing Lines Div Remington Arms Co Inc PO Box 700	Madison	NC	27025	**800-243-9700**	336-548-8700	701
Strength & Conditioning Assn. National 1885 Bob Johnson Dr	Colorado Springs	CO	80906	**800-815-6826**	719-632-6722	48-22
StressGen Biotechnologies Corp 4243 Glanford Ave Suite 350	Victoria	BC	V8Z4B9	**800-661-4978**	250-744-2811	86
Stretch & Sew Inc PO Box 25306	Tempe	AZ	85282	**800-547-7717**	480-966-1462	557
Stride Rite Corp 191 Spring St *NYSE: SRR* ■ *Cust Svc	Lexington	MA	02421	**800-666-5689***	617-824-6000	296
Stride Tool Inc Milbar Div 530 E Washington St	Chagrin Falls	OH	44022	**877-225-8858**	440-247-4600	746
Strimbu Nick Inc 3500 Parkway Rd	Brookfield	OH	44403	**800-446-8785**	330-448-4071	769
Strine Printing Co Inc 30 Grumbacher Rd	York	PA	17402	**800-477-8746**	717-767-6602	615
Strippit/LVD 12975 Clarence Ctr Rd	Akron	NY	14001	**800-828-1527**	585-542-4511	448
Stroehmann Bakeries Inc 255 Business Center Dr Suite 200	Horsham	PA	19044	**800-355-1260**	215-672-8010	291-1
Stroh Die Casting Co Inc 11123 W Burleigh St *Cust Svc	Milwaukee	WI	53222	**800-843-2871***	414-771-7100	303
Stroheim & Romann Inc 31-11 Thomson Ave	Long Island City	NY	11101	**800-974-8444**	718-706-7000	583
Stroke Assn. National 9707 E Easter Ln	Englewood	CO	80112	**800-787-6537**	303-649-9299	48-17
Stromberg Consulting 711 3rd Ave	New York	NY	10017	**800-662-5889**	646-935-4300	193
Stromberg Sheet Metal Works Inc 6701 Distribution Dr	Beltsville	MD	20705	**800-348-5778**	301-931-1000	188-10
Strong Enterprises Inc 11236 Satellite Blvd	Orlando	FL	32837	**800-344-6319**	407-859-9317	566
Strong Financial Corp PO Box 2936	Milwaukee	WI	53201	**800-368-1030**	414-359-1400	393
Strong Group Inc 39 Grove St *Orders	Gloucester	MA	01930	**800-225-0724***	978-281-3300	423
Strong Rodney Vineyards 1145 Old Redwood Hwy	Healdsburg	CA	95448	**800-474-9463**	707-433-6511	81-3
Strong Tool Co 1251 E 286th St	Cleveland	OH	44132	**800-362-0293**	216-289-2450	484
Stronghaven Inc 5090 MacDougall Dr SW	Atlanta	GA	30336	**800-233-2487**	404-699-9680	101
Structural Concepts Corp 888 Porter Rd	Muskegon	MI	49441	**800-433-9489**	231-798-8888	281
Structural Integration. Rolf Institute of 5055 Chaparral Ct Suite 103	Boulder	CO	80301	**800-530-8875**	303-449-5903	48-17
Structural Metals Inc 1 Steel Mill Dr *Sales	Seguin	TX	78156	**800-227-6489***	830-372-8200	471
Structural Wood Corp 4000 Labore Rd	Saint Paul	MN	55110	**800-652-9058**	651-426-8111	805
Structure House 3017 Pickett Rd	Durham	NC	27705	**800-553-0052**	919-493-4205	697
Structures Unlimited Inc 88 Pine St	Manchester	NH	03103	**800-225-3895**	603-645-6539	688
Stry-Lenkoff Co Inc 1100 W Broadway St	Louisville	KY	40232	**800-626-8247**	502-587-6804	111
Stryker Corp 2725 Fairfield Rd *NYSE: SYK*	Kalamazoo	MI	49002	**800-726-2725**	269-385-2600	468
Stryker Instruments 4100 E Milham Ave *Cust Svc	Kalamazoo	MI	49001	**800-253-3210***	269-323-7700	468
STS Consultants Ltd 750 Corporate Woods Pkwy	Vernon Hills	IL	60061	**800-859-7871**	847-279-2500	258
Stuart Anderson's Black Angus 4410 El Camino Real Suite 201	Los Altos	CA	94022	**800-750-0211**	650-949-6400	657
Stuart C Irby Co 815 S State St PO Box 1819	Jackson	MS	39215	**800-844-1811**	601-969-1811	245
Stuart DA Co 4580 Weaver Pkwy	Warrenville	IL	60555	**800-323-1438**	630-393-0833	530
Stuart Hall 235 E Frederick St PO Box 210	Staunton	VA	24402	**888-306-8926**	540-885-0356	611
Stuart News PO Box 9009	Stuart	FL	34995	**800-381-6397**	772-287-1550	522-2
Stuart Paul Inc Madison Ave & 45th St *Orders	New York	NY	10017	**800-678-8278***	212-682-0320	155-4
Stubbs HB Co 27027 Mound Rd	Warren	MI	48092	**800-968-2132**	586-574-9700	230
Stuckey's Corp 8555 16th St Suite 850	Silver Spring	MD	20910	**800-423-6171**	301-585-8222	657
Stucki A Co 2600 Neville Rd	Pittsburgh	PA	15225	**800-771-7302**	412-771-7300	636
Studebaker National Museum 525 S Main St	South Bend	IN	46601	**888-391-5600**	574-235-9714	509
Student Advantage Inc 280 Summer St	Boston	MA	02210	**800-333-2920**	617-912-2011	9
Student Aid News Newsletter 360 Hiatt Dr	Palm Beach Gardens	FL	33418	**800-638-8437**	800-341-7874	521-4
Student Assn. US 1413 K St NW 9th Fl	Washington	DC	20005	**877-877-2669**	202-347-8772	48-11
Student Campaign Against Hunger & Homelessness. National 233 N Pleasant St Suite 32	Amherst	MA	01002	**800-664-8647**	413-253-6417	48-5
Student Conservation Assn (SCA) 689 River Rd PO Box 550	Charlestown	NH	03603	**888-722-9675**	603-543-1700	48-13
Student Lawyer Magazine 750 N Lake Shore Dr	Chicago	IL	60611	**800-285-2221**	312-988-5000	449-15
Student Loan Corp PO Box 6191 *NYSE: STU*	Sioux Falls	SD	57117	**800-967-2400**	605-331-0821	215
Student Tours Inc 2 Webaqua Rd	Vineyard Haven	MA	02568	**800-331-7093**	508-693-5078	748
Student Transportation of America Inc 3349 Hwy 138 Bldg B Suite D	Wall	NJ	07719	**888-942-2250**	732-280-4200	110
Student Travel Services Inc 1413 Madison Pk Dr	Glen Burnie	MD	21061	**800-648-4849**	410-859-4200	748
Students Against Destructive Decisions (SADD) 255 Main St	Marlborough	MA	01752	**877-723-3462**	508-481-3568	48-6
Students of Pharmacy. Academy of American Pharmacists Assn 2215 Constitution Ave NW	Washington	DC	20037	**800-237-2742**	202-628-4410	49-8
Studio 6 4001 International Pkwy	Carrollton	TX	75007	**800-466-8356**	972-360-9000	369
Studio Arena Theatre 710 Main St	Buffalo	NY	14202	**800-777-8243**	716-856-8025	563-4
StudioPLUS 100 Dunbar St	Spartanburg	SC	29306	**888-788-3467**	864-573-1600	369
Stuecker & Assoc Inc 1169 Eastern Pkwy Suite 2243	Louisville	KY	40217	**800-799-9327**	502-452-9227	454
Stuller Settings Inc 302 Rue Louis XIV	Lafayette	LA	70598	**800-877-7777**		399
Stulz-Sickles Steel Co PO Box 273	Elizabeth	NJ	07207	**800-351-1776**	908-351-1776	798
Stumps Inc 1 Party Pl PO Box 305	South Whitley	IN	46787	**800-348-5084**	260-723-5171	555

Name / Address	City	State	ZIP	Toll-Free	Phone	Class
Stupp Brothers Inc 3800 Weber Rd	Saint Louis	MO	63125	**800-899-1856**	314-638-5000	471
Stupp Corp 12555 Ronaldson Rd	Baton Rouge	LA	70807	**800-535-9999**	225-775-8800	481
Stuppy Greenhouse Mfg Inc 120 E 12th Ave	North Kansas City	MO	64116	**800-877-5025**	816-842-3071	106
Sturbridge Host Hotel & Conference Center 366 Main St	Sturbridge	MA	01566	**800-582-3232**	508-347-7393	373
Sturdisteel Co 131 Ava Dr	Hewitt	TX	76643	**800-433-3116**	254-666-5155	314-3
Sturdy Corp 1822 Carolina Beach Rd	Wilmington	NC	28401	**800-721-3282**	910-763-8261	202
Sturgeon Electric Co Inc 12150 E 112th Ave	Henderson	CO	80640	**800-288-5155**	303-286-8000	188-4
Sturgis Foundry Corp PO Box 568	Sturgis	MI	49091	**800-809-7203**	269-651-8544	302
Sturgis Iron & Metal Co PO Box 579	Sturgis	MI	49091	**800-446-0794**	269-651-7851	674
Sturgis Iron & Metal Co South Bend Scrap & Processing Div 1305 Prairie Ave	South Bend	IN	46613	**800-232-2441**	574-287-3311	674
Sturgis Journal PO Box 660	Sturgis	MI	49091	**800-686-5653**	269-651-5407	522-2
Sturgis Tom Pretzels Inc 2267 Lancaster Pike	Reading	PA	19607	**800-817-3834**	610-775-0335	291-9
Sturm Foods Inc PO Box 287	Manawa	WI	54949	**800-347-8876**	920-596-2511	292-11
Sturm Rapid Response Center 1305 Main St	Barboursville	WV	25504	**800-624-3485**	304-736-3476	627
Stuttering Assn. National 119 W 40th St 14th Fl	New York	NY	10018	**800-364-1677**	212-944-4050	48-17
Stuttering Foundation of America 3100 Walnut Grove Rd Suite 603	Memphis	TN	38111	**800-992-9392**	901-452-7343	48-17
Stuttering. National Center for 200 E 33rd St	New York	NY	10016	**800-221-2483**	212-532-1460	48-17
Styles for Less 12728 S Shoemaker Ave	Santa Fe Springs	CA	90670	**800-929-3466**	562-229-3400	155-6
Stylex Inc Tungsten Rd PO Box 5038	Delanco	NJ	08075	**800-257-5742**	856-461-5600	314-1
Styline Industries Inc PO Box 100	Huntingburg	IN	47542	**800-521-5381**	812-683-4848	314-1
StyroChem International 3607 N Sylvania Ave	Fort Worth	TX	76111	**800-448-6232**	817-759-4400	590
Styrotek Inc PO Box 1180	Delano	CA	93216	**800-936-2611**	661-725-4957	590
Sub Station II Inc 425 N Main St	Sumter	SC	29150	**800-779-2970**	803-773-4711	657
Sub-Zero Freezer Co Inc 4717 Hammersley Rd *Prod Info	Madison	WI	53711	**800-222-7820***	608-271-2233	36
Subaru of America Inc PO Box 6000 *Cust Svc	Cherry Hill	NJ	08034	**800-782-2783***	856-488-8500	59
Subco Foods Inc 4350 S Taylor Dr	Sheboygan	WI	53081	**800-473-0757**	920-457-7761	291-16
Subiaco Academy 405 N Subiaco Ave	Subiaco	AR	72865	**800-364-7824**	479-934-1025	611
Substance Abuse Foundation 3125 E 7th St	Long Beach	CA	90804	**888-476-2743**	562-439-7755	712
Substance Abuse Funding Week 8204 Fenton St	Silver Spring	MD	20910	**800-666-6380**	301-588-6384	521-8
Suburban Press & Metro Press PO Box 169	Millbury	OH	43447	**800-300-6158**	419-836-2221	522-4
Suburban Propane Partners LP 240 Rt 10 W PO Box 206 *NYSE: SPH*	Whippany	NJ	07981	**800-526-0620**	973-887-5300	311
Suburban Review PO Box 912	Athens	GA	30603	**800-533-4252**	706-549-0123	522-4
Suburban Transit Corp 750 Somerset St	New Brunswick	NJ	08901	**800-222-0492**	732-249-1100	109
Subway Restaurants 325 Bic Dr	Milford	CT	06460	**800-888-4848**	203-877-4281	657
Suby Von Haden & Assoc SC 1221 John Q Hammons Dr PO Box 44966	Madison	WI	53744	**800-279-2616**	608-831-8181	2
Success Motivation International Inc 5000 Lakeshore Dr *Sales	Waco	TX	76710	**888-391-0050***	254-776-9966	361
Successful Closing Techniques Newsletter 360 Hiatt Dr	Palm Beach Gardens	FL	33418	**800-621-5463**	561-622-9914	521-10
Successful Farming Magazine 1716 Locust St *Cust Svc	Des Moines	IA	50309	**800-374-3276***	515-284-3000	449-1
Successful Supervisor Newsletter 360 Hiatt Dr	Palm Beach Gardens	FL	33418	**800-621-5463**	561-622-9914	521-2
Successories Inc 2520 Diehl Rd	Aurora	IL	60504	**800-621-1423**	630-820-7200	305
Sud-Chemie Inc 1600 W Hill St	Louisville	KY	40210	**800-626-5355**	502-634-7200	141
Suddath Cos 815 S Main St	Jacksonville	FL	32207	**800-395-7100**	904-390-7100	508
Sudenga Industries Inc 2002 Kingbird Ave	George	IA	51237	**800-314-3908**	712-475-3301	269
Suffolk News-Herald PO Box 1220	Suffolk	VA	23439	**866-828-9237**	757-539-3437	522-2
Suffolk University 8 Ashburton Pl	Boston	MA	02108	**800-678-3365**	617-573-8000	163
Sugar Creek Foods Inc 301 N El Paso St	Russellville	AR	72810	**800-445-2715**	479-968-1005	291-25
Sugar Creek Scrap Inc PO Box 208	West Terre Haute	IN	47885	**800-466-7462**	812-533-2147	674
Sugar Foods Corp 950 3rd Ave 21st Fl	New York	NY	10022	**800-666-3285**	212-753-6900	292-11
Sugar Hill Records 501-A Washington St	Durham	NC	27701	**800-996-4455**	919-489-4349	643
Sugarbush Resort & Inn 1840 Sugarbush Access Rd	Warren	VT	05674	**800-537-8427**	802-583-6300	655
Sugarloaf/USA 5092 Access Rd	Carrabassett Valley	ME	04947	**800-843-5623**	207-237-2000	655
Suhner Mfg Inc PO Box 1234	Rome	GA	30162	**800-323-6886**	706-235-8047	747
Suicide Awareness Voices of Education. SAVE - 9001 Bloomington Fwy Suite 150	Bloomington	MN	55420	**888-511-7283**	952-946-7998	49-15
Suicide. International Task Force on Euthanasia & Assisted PO Box 760	Steubenville	OH	43952	**800-958-5678**	740-282-3810	48-8
Suicide Prevention. American Foundation for 120 Wall St 22nd Fl	New York	NY	10005	**888-333-2377**	212-363-3500	48-17
Suit-Kote Corp 1911 Lorings Crossing Rd	Cortland	NY	13045	**800-622-5636**	607-753-1100	46
SuiteAmerica 4970 Windplay Dr Suite C-1	El Dorado Hills	CA	95762	**800-363-9779**	916-367-9501	209
Suites at Fisherman's Wharf 2655 Hyde St	San Francisco	CA	94109	**800-227-3608**	415-771-0200	373
Suites at Waterfront Plaza 325 Lake Ave S	Duluth	MN	55802	**877-766-2665**	218-722-2143	373
Suitt Construction Co Inc 201 E McBee Ave Suite 300	Greenville	SC	29601	**800-388-2724**	864-250-5000	185
Sul Ross State University E Hwy 90	Alpine	TX	79832	**888-722-7778**	432-837-8011	163
Sullair Corp 3700 E Michigan Blvd	Michigan City	IN	46360	**800-785-5247**	219-879-5451	170
Sullivan & Brampton Inc 1688 Abram Ct	San Leandro	CA	94577	**800-257-5900**	510-483-7771	718
Sullivan County Rural Electric Co-op Inc PO Box 65	Forksville	PA	18616	**800-570-5081**	570-924-3381	244
Sullivan Curtis Monroe 2100 Main St Suite 350	Irvine	CA	92614	**800-427-3253**	949-250-7172	383
Sullivan International Group Inc 409 Camino Real Rio S Suite 204	San Diego	CA	92108	**888-744-1432**	619-260-1432	258
Sullivan-Palatek Inc River Rd	Claremont	NH	03743	**800-334-5022**	603-543-3131	170
Sullivan RM Transportation 649 Cottage St	Springfield	MA	01104	**800-628-1064**	413-739-2558	769
Sullivan-Schein Dental 10920 W Lincoln Ave	West Allis	WI	53227	**800-648-6684**	414-321-8881	467
Sullivan Tire Co Inc 41 Accord Park Dr	Norwell	MA	02061	**800-892-1955**	781-982-1550	62-5
Sullivan University 3101 Bardstown Rd	Louisville	KY	40205	**800-844-1354**	502-456-6504	163
Sullivan's 224 E Douglas Ave	Wichita	KS	67227	**800-234-0888**	316-264-8899	657
Sulphur Springs New Telegram 401 Church St	Sulphur Springs	TX	75482	**800-245-2149**	903-885-8663	522-2
Sulphur Springs Valley Electric Co-op Inc PO Box 820	Willcox	AZ	85644	**800-422-9288**	520-384-2221	244
Sultan & Sons 650 SW 9th Terr	Pompano Beach	FL	33069	**800-299-6601**	954-782-6600	357
Sulzer Metco US Inc 1101 Prospect Ave	Westbury	NY	11590	**800-638-2699**	516-334-1300	170
Sumaria Systems Inc 99 Rosewood Dr Suite 140	Danvers	MA	01923	**888-245-9810**	978-739-4200	178
Sumerel Bob Tires & Service Inc 3646 E Broad St	Columbus	OH	43213	**800-858-0421**	614-237-6325	740
Sumitomo Machinery Corp of America 4200 Holland Blvd	Chesapeake	VA	23323	**800-762-9256**	757-485-3355	700
Summer Beach Resort 5456 First Coast Hwy	Amelia Island	FL	32034	**800-862-9297**	904-277-0905	655
Summerfield Suites by Wyndham 1950 Stemmons Fwy Suite 6001	Dallas	TX	75207	**800-833-4353**	214-863-1000	369
Summers Mfg Co Inc 338 Railway Ave	Maddock	ND	58348	**800-732-4347**	701-438-2855	269
Summit Aviation Inc PO Box 258	Middletown	DE	19709	**800-441-9343**	302-834-5400	25
Summit Bank Corp 4360 Chamblee Dunwoody Rd Suite 300 *NASDAQ: SBGA*	Atlanta	GA	30341	**800-752-4343**	770-454-0400	355-2
Summit Chemical Co 7657 Canton Ctr Dr	Baltimore	MD	21224	**800-227-8664**	410-282-5200	276
Summit Corp of America 1430 Waterbury Rd	Thomaston	CT	06787	**800-854-0176**	860-283-4391	472
Summit Electric Supply Co 2900 Stanford NE	Albuquerque	NM	87107	**800-824-4400**	505-884-4400	245
Summit Food Service Distributors Inc 580 Industrial Rd	London	ON	N5V1V1	**800-265-9267**	519-453-3410	294
Summit Global Partners Inc 1445 Ross Ave Suite 4200	Dallas	TX	75202	**800-494-9418**	214-443-3500	383
Summit Holding Southeast Inc PO Box 988	Lakeland	FL	33802	**800-282-7648**	863-665-6060	355-4
Summit Hotels & Resorts 311 S Wacker Dr Suite 1900	Chicago	IL	60606	**800-457-4000**	312-913-0400	369
Summit Industries Inc 1220 W Railroad St	Corona	CA	92882	**800-347-8664**	951-371-1744	506
Summit Industries Inc 839 Pickens Industrial Dr	Marietta	GA	30062	**800-241-6996**	770-590-0600	149
Summit Lodge 4359 Main St	Whistler	BC	V0N1B4	**888-913-8811**	604-932-2778	372
Summit Plastics Inc 107 Laurel St	Summit	MS	39666	**800-790-7117**	601-276-7500	589
Summit R & D Group 8515 Blue Jacket	Lenexa	KS	66214	**800-843-7347**	913-888-6222	5
Summit Trailer Sales Inc 1 Summit Plaza	Summit Station	PA	17979	**800-437-3729**	570-754-3511	768
Sumner-Cowley Electric Co-op Inc PO Box 220	Wellington	KS	67152	**888-326-3356**	620-326-3356	244
Sumner Regional Medical Center 555 Hartsville Pike	Gallatin	TN	37066	**800-728-4217**	615-452-4210	366-2
Sumter Electric Membership Corp PO Box 1048	Americus	GA	31709	**800-342-6978**	229-924-8041	244
Sumter Utilities Inc PO Box 579	Sumter	SC	29151	**800-678-8665**	803-469-8585	187-10
SumTotal Systems Inc 2444 Charleston Rd *NASDAQ: SUMT*	Mountain View	CA	94043	**866-768-6825**	650-934-9500	176-3
Sun The 399 N 'D' St	San Bernardino	CA	92401	**800-922-0922**	909-889-9666	522-2
Sun The PO Box 259	Bremerton	WA	98337	**888-377-3711**	360-377-3711	522-2
Sun Bancorp Inc 226 Landis Ave *NASDAQ: SNBC*	Vineland	NJ	08360	**800-691-7701**	856-691-7700	355-2
Sun Building Systems 9 Stauffer Industrial Pk	Taylor	PA	18517	**888-740-8218**	570-562-0110	107
Sun Co 399 N 'D' St	San Bernardino	CA	92401	**800-548-5448**	909-889-9666	623-8
Sun Coast Resources Inc 6922 Cavalcade St	Houston	TX	77028	**800-677-3835**	713-844-9600	569
Sun Control Products Inc 11 E Veterans Memorial Hwy	Kasson	MN	55944	**800-533-0010**	507-634-2081	88
Sun Country Airlines Inc 1300 Mendota Heights Rd	Mendota Heights	MN	55120	**800-359-6786**	651-681-3900	26
Sun-Delta Capital Access Center Inc 819 Main St	Greenville	MS	38701	**800-829-5338**	662-335-5291	395
Sun Devil Fire Equipment Inc 2211 S 3rd Dr	Phoenix	AZ	85003	**800-536-3845**	623-245-0636	667
Sun Drilling Products Corp PO Box 129	Belle Chasse	LA	70037	**800-962-6490**	504-393-2778	530
Sun Ergoline Inc 1 Walter Kratz Dr	Jonesboro	AR	72401	**800-643-0086**	870-935-1130	429
Sun Health Hospice Care Services & Residence 12740 N Plaza del Rio Blvd	Peoria	AZ	85381	**800-858-9428**	623-815-2800	365

Name / Address	City	State	Zip	Toll-Free	Phone	Class
Sun Healthcare Group Inc 101 Sun Ave NE (*NASDAQ: SUNH*)	Albuquerque	NM	87109	**800-856-2512**	505-821-3355	442
Sun Healthcare Group Inc Pharmaceutical Services 101 Sun Ave NE	Albuquerque	NM	87109	**800-729-6600**	505-468-4168	237
Sun Herald 23170 Harborview Rd	Charlotte Harbor	FL	33980	**800-830-7861**	941-206-1000	522-2
Sun Herald 205 DeBuys Rd	Gulfport	MS	39507	**800-346-5022**	228-896-2100	522-2
Sun Herald 28895 Lorain Rd	North Olmsted	OH	44070	**800-466-7861**	216-986-6070	522-4
Sun Holidays Inc 7208 Sand Lake Rd Suite 207	Orlando	FL	32819	**800-422-8000**		760
SUN Home Health Services & Hospice 61 Duke St	Northumberland	PA	17857	**888-478-6227**	570-473-8320	365
Sun Islands Hawaii Inc 2299 Kuhio Ave 1st Fl	Honolulu	HI	96815	**800-560-3338**	808-926-3888	760
Sun-Journal PO Box 4400	Lewiston	ME	04243	**800-482-0759**	207-784-5411	522-2
Sun Land Beef Co 651 S 91st Ave PO Box 99	Tolleson	AZ	85353	**888-573-2038**	623-936-7177	465
Sun Life Financial Inc 150 King St W (*NYSE: SLF*)	Toronto	ON	M5H1J9	**800-786-5433**	416-979-9966	355-4
Sun Life Insurance & Annuity Co of New York PO Box 9133	Wellesley Hills	MA	02481	**800-447-7569**		384-2
Sun Magazine 1000 American Media Way	Boca Raton	FL	33467	**800-749-7733**	561-997-7733	449-11
Sun-Maid Growers of California 13525 S Bethel Ave (*Sales)	Kingsburg	CA	93631	**800-272-4746***	559-896-8000	291-18
Sun Microsystems Inc 4150 Network Cir (*NASDAQ: SUNW*)	Santa Clara	CA	95054	**800-786-0404**	650-960-1300	174
Sun Mountain Lodge 604 Patterson Lake Rd PO Box 1000	Winthrop	WA	98862	**800-572-0493**	509-996-2211	655
Sun National Bank 226 Landis Ave	Vineland	NJ	08360	**800-293-7701**	856-691-7700	71
Sun News 914 Frontage Rd E	Myrtle Beach	SC	29578	**800-568-1800**	843-626-8555	522-2
Sun Newspapers 5510 Cloverleaf Pkwy	Cleveland	OH	44125	**800-362-8008**	216-986-2600	623-8
Sun Orchard of Florida Inc PO Box 2008	Haines City	FL	33844	**877-875-8423**	863-422-5062	291-21
Sun Orchard Inc 1198 W Fairmont Dr	Tempe	AZ	85282	**800-505-8423**	480-966-1770	291-20
Sun Post Newspaper Group 1688 Meridian Ave Suite 404	Miami Beach	FL	33139	**888-769-7678**	305-538-9700	623-8
Sun Publishing Corp 201 N Thorp St	Hobbs	NM	88240	**800-993-2123**	505-393-2123	623-8
Sun Rams Products Inc 8736 Lion St	Rancho Cucamonga	CA	91730	**800-866-7267**	909-980-1160	531
Sun River Electric Co-op Inc PO Box 309	Fairfield	MT	59436	**800-452-7516**	406-467-2526	244
Sun-Sentinel Co 200 E Las Olas Blvd	Fort Lauderdale	FL	33301	**800-548-6397**	954-356-4000	623-8
Sun Solution Consulting 101 Sun Ave NE	Albuquerque	NM	87109	**800-729-6600**	505-821-3355	455
Sun Steel Treating Inc 55 N Mill St	South Lyon	MI	48178	**877-471-0844**	248-471-0844	475
Sun Valley Floral Farms Inc 3160 Upper Bay Rd	Arcata	CA	95521	**800-747-0396**	707-826-8700	363
Sun Valley Resort 1 Sun Valley Rd	Sun Valley	ID	83353	**800-786-8259**	208-622-2001	655
Sun Valley Stages Inc PO Box 936	Twin Falls	ID	83303	**800-574-8661**	208-733-3921	108
Sun Valley Technical Repair Inc 15555 Concord Cir	Morgan Hill	CA	95037	**800-250-5858**	408-779-4115	173
Sun Valley/Ketchum Chamber & Visitors Bureau PO Box 2420	Sun Valley	ID	83353	**800-634-3347**	208-726-3423	137
Sun Viking Lodge 2411 S Atlantic Ave	Daytona Beach Shores	FL	32118	**800-874-4469**	386-252-6252	373
Sun Wheels & Ramps 2156 N Detroit St	Warsaw	IN	46580	**888-478-6746**	574-267-3281	83
SunAmerica Life Insurance Co 1 SunAmerica Ctr	Los Angeles	CA	90067	**800-445-7862**	310-772-6000	384-2
SunAmerica Mutual Funds 733 3rd Ave 4th Fl	New York	NY	10017	**800-858-8850**	212-551-5100	517
Sunbeam Television Corp 1401 79th Street Cswy	Miami	FL	33141	**800-845-7777**	305-751-6692	724
Sunbelt Computer Systems Inc 13090 Swan Lake Rd CR 468 (*Sales)	Tyler	TX	75704	**800-359-5907***	903-881-0400	176-2
Sunbelt Furniture Express Inc PO Box 487	Hickory	NC	28603	**800-766-1117**	828-464-7240	769
Sunbelt Rentals Inc 1337 Hundred Oaks Dr (*Mktg)	Charlotte	NC	28217	**800-452-1963***	704-348-2676	261-4
Sunbelt Software USA 101 N Garden Ave	Clearwater	FL	33755	**888-688-8457**	727-562-0101	176-12
Sunbird Air Services Inc 1251 W Blee Rd	Springfield	OH	45502	**800-537-2711**	937-322-2711	14
Sunburst Foods Inc 1002 Sunburst Dr	Goldsboro	NC	27534	**800-849-3196**	919-778-2151	291-34
SunBurst Resort 4925 N Scottsdale Rd	Scottsdale	AZ	85251	**800-528-7867**	480-945-7666	655
Sunburst Technology 101 Castleton St	Pleasantville	NY	10570	**800-321-7511**	914-747-3310	176-3
Sunburst Vacations 310 1st Ave	Needham Heights	MA	02494	**800-786-2877**	781-707-2668	760
Sunco Carriers Inc 1025 N Chestnut Rd	Lakeland	FL	33805	**800-237-8288**	863-688-1948	769
Suncoast News 6214 US Hwy 19	New Port Richey	FL	34652	**800-376-4786**	727-815-1000	522-4
Suncoast Schools Federal Credit Union 6804 E Hillsborough Ave	Tampa	FL	33610	**800-999-5887**	813-621-7511	216
SunCom Wireless Holdings Inc 1100 Cassatt Rd (*NYSE: TPC* ■ *Cust Svc)	Berwyn	PA	19312	**800-786-7378***	610-651-5900	721
SunCruz Casino 647 E Dania Beach Blvd	Dania Beach	FL	33004	**800-474-3423**	954-929-3880	133
SunCruz Casino - Port Canaveral 610 Glen Cheek Dr	Cape Canaveral	FL	32920	**800-474-3423**	321-783-2770	133
SunDance Rehabilitation Corp 101 Sun Ave NE	Albuquerque	NM	87109	**800-729-6600**	505-821-3355	347
Sundance Ski Resort North Fork Provo Canyon	Provo	UT	84604	**800-892-1600**	801-225-4107	655
Sundance Trail Guest Ranch 17931 Red Feather Lakes Rd	Red Feather Lakes	CO	80545	**800-357-4930**	970-224-1222	238
Sunday River Ski Resort 15 S Ridge Rd	Newry	ME	04261	**800-543-2754**	207-824-3000	655
Sundial Beach & Tennis Resort 1451 Middle Gulf Dr	Sanibel	FL	33957	**800-237-4184**	239-472-4151	655
Sundial Special Vacations Inc 2609 Hwy 101 N Suite 103	Seaside	OR	97138	**800-547-9198**	503-738-3324	748
Sundowner Hotel Casino 450 N Arlington Ave	Reno	NV	89503	**800-648-5490**	775-786-7050	373
Sundowner Trailers Inc 9805 S State Hwy 48	Coleman	OK	73432	**800-654-3879**	580-937-4255	751
Sundt Construction Inc 4101 E Irvington Rd	Tucson	AZ	85714	**800-467-5544**	520-748-7555	185
Sunflower Carriers Inc PO Box 9 (*Cust Svc)	York	NE	68467	**800-775-5000***	402-362-7491	769
Sunflower Racing Inc 9700 Leavenworth Rd	Kansas City	KS	66109	**800-695-7223**	913-299-9797	628
SunGard Availability Services 550 E 84th Ave Suite E5	Thornton	CO	80229	**877-246-3569**	303-942-2800	387
SunGard Collegis Inc 2300 Maitland Center Pkwy Suite 340	Maitland	FL	32751	**800-800-1874**	407-660-1199	176-10
SunGard Data Systems Inc 680 E Swedesford Rd (*NYSE: SDS*)	Wayne	PA	19087	**800-523-4970**	650-377-3897	223
SunGard Energy Systems 825 3rd Ave 28th Fl	New York	NY	10022	**877-230-6551**	212-888-3600	176-10
SunGard HTE Inc 1000 Business Center Dr	Lake Mary	FL	32746	**800-727-8088**	407-304-3235	176-10
SunGard Insurance Systems 2000 S Dixie Hwy	Miami	FL	33133	**800-669-3372**	305-858-8200	176-11
SunGard Pentamation Inc 3 W Broad St Suite 1 (*Cust Svc)	Bethlehem	PA	18018	**800-333-3619***	610-691-3616	176-11
SunGard SCT Inc 4 Country View Rd	Malvern	PA	19355	**800-223-7036**	610-647-5930	176-10
Sunglass Hut International Inc 4000 Luxottica Pl	Mason	OH	45040	**800-767-0990**	513-765-6000	533
Sunline Coach Co Inc 245 S Muddy Creek Rd	Denver	PA	17517	**800-827-6406**	717-336-2858	120
Sunlow Inc 1071 Howell Mill Rd NW	Atlanta	GA	30318	**800-678-6569**	404-872-8135	295
Sunmar Inc 500 108th Ave NE Suite 1710	Bellevue	WA	98004	**800-443-4127**	425-577-1870	308
Sunmar Shipping Inc 500 108th Ave NE Suite 1710	Bellevue	WA	98004	**800-443-4127**	425-577-1870	308
Sunnen Products Co 7910 Manchester Ave	Saint Louis	MO	63143	**800-325-3670**	314-781-2100	447
Sunniland Corp PO Box 8001	Sanford	FL	32772	**800-432-1130**	407-322-2421	276
Sunny Fresh Foods Inc 206 W 4th St	Monticello	MN	55362	**800-872-3447**	763-271-5600	608
Sunny Land Tours Inc 166 Main St	Hackensack	NJ	07601	**800-783-7839**	201-487-2150	748
Sunnyland Div Ventura Foods LLC 3900 Vanderbilt Rd	Birmingham	AL	35217	**800-338-8682**	205-808-3514	291-30
Sunnyvale Seafood Corp 1651 Pomona Ave	San Jose	CA	95110	**800-726-2326**	408-289-9198	292-5
Sunoco Chemicals 1801 Market St 10 Penn Ctr	Philadelphia	PA	19103	**800-786-6261**	215-977-3321	142
Sunoco Inc 1801 Market St (*NYSE: SUN*)	Philadelphia	PA	19103	**800-786-6261**	215-977-3000	525
SunPark Inc 6 Fountain Plaza	Buffalo	NY	14202	**866-400-7275**	716-332-4200	552
SunQuesT Systems 7170 Zionsville Rd	Indianapolis	IN	46268	**800-808-4774**	317-299-3391	656
SunQuest Vacations 77-6435 Kuakini Hwy	Kailua-Kona	HI	96740	**800-367-5168**	808-329-6438	760
Sunrider International 1625 Abalone Ave (*Orders)	Torrance	CA	90501	**888-278-6743***	310-781-3808	361
Sunrise Greetings 1145 Sunrise Greetings Ct (*Sales)	Bloomington	IN	47404	**800-457-4045***	812-336-9900	130
Sunrise Medical Continuing Care Group 5001 Joerns Dr	Stevens Point	WI	54481	**800-972-7581**	715-341-3600	314-3
Sunrise Medical Inc 2382 Faraday Ave Suite 200	Carlsbad	CA	92008	**800-278-6747**	760-930-1500	469
Sunrise Senior Living Inc 7902 Westpark Dr (*NYSE: SRZ*)	McLean	VA	22102	**800-929-4124**	703-273-7500	442
Sunrise Specialty Co 930 98th Ave	Oakland	CA	94603	**800-646-9117**	510-729-7277	600
Sunrise Suites Resort 3685 Seaside Dr	Key West	FL	33040	**800-723-5200**	305-296-6661	373
Sunrise Technologies International Inc 3400 W Warren AVe	Fremont	CA	94538	**800-789-4949**	510-623-9001	415
Sunriver Resort 1 Center Dr PO Box 3609	Sunriver	OR	97707	**800-547-3922**	541-593-1000	655
Sunroc Corp 60 Starlifter Ave Kent County Aero Pk	Dover	DE	19901	**800-478-6762**	302-678-7800	650
Sunsational Cruises 710 W Elliot Rd	Tempe	AZ	85284	**800-239-6252**	480-491-6248	760
Sunset Aviation 351 Airport Rd	Novato	CA	94945	**800-359-7861**	415-897-4522	14
Sunset Inn Travel Apartments 1111 Burnaby St	Vancouver	BC	V6E1P4	**800-786-1997**	604-688-2474	372
Sunset Key Guest Cottages at Hilton Key West Resort 245 Front St	Key West	FL	33040	**888-477-7786**	305-292-5300	655
Sunset Life Insurance Co of America PO Box 219139	Kansas City	MO	64121	**800-678-6898**		384-2
Sunset Magazine 80 Willow Rd	Menlo Park	CA	94025	**800-777-0117**	650-321-3600	449-11
Sunset Marquis Hotel & Villas 1200 N Alta Loma Rd	West Hollywood	CA	90069	**800-858-9758**	310-657-1333	373
Sunset Moulding Co Inc 2231 Paseo Ave	Live Oak	CA	95953	**800-824-5888**	530-695-1801	304
Sunset Publishing Corp 80 Willow Rd	Menlo Park	CA	94025	**800-227-7346**	650-321-3600	623-9
Sunshine Art Studios Inc 270 Main St	Agawam	MA	01001	**800-873-7681**	413-821-8700	130
SunShine Cafe Restaurants 7112 Zionsville Rd	Indianapolis	IN	46268	**800-808-4774**	317-299-3391	657
Sunshine Dairy Foods Inc 801 NE 21st Ave	Portland	OR	97232	**800-544-0554**	503-234-7526	292-4
Sunshine Foliage World 2060 Steve Roberts Special	Zolfo Springs	FL	33890	**800-872-0607**	863-735-0501	363

Company	City	State	ZIP	Toll-Free	Phone	Class
Sunshine Girl Creations Inc 11115 Excelsior Blvd	Hopkins	MN	55343	866-899-3632	952-931-2464	130
Sunshine Makers Inc 15922 Pacific Coast Hwy	Huntington Harbour	CA	92649	800-228-0709	714-840-1319	149
Sunshine Mills Inc 500 6th St SW	Red Bay	AL	35582	800-633-3349	256-356-9541	568
SunShine Pages 3445 N Causeway Blvd Suite 1000	Metairie	LA	70002	800-259-9835	504-832-9835	623-6
SunSpots International 1918 NE 181st Ave	Portland	OR	97230	800-334-5623	503-666-3893	760
Sunsweet Growers Inc 901 N Walton Ave	Yuba City	CA	95993	800-417-2253	530-674-5010	291-18
Sunterra Corp 3865 W Cheyenne Ave *NASDAQ: SNRR*	North Las Vegas	NV	89032	800-411-9922	702-804-8600	738
Suntory Water Group Inc 5660 New Northside Dr Suite 500	Atlanta	GA	30328	800-444-7873	770-933-1400	792
SunTrips Inc 2350 Paragon Dr *Resv	San Jose	CA	95131	800-786-8747*	408-432-1101	760
Suntron Corp 2401 W Grandview Rd Suite 1 *NASDAQ: SUNN*	Phoenix	AZ	85023	866-554-1223	602-789-6600	613
SunTrust Banks Inc 303 Peachtree St NE *NYSE: STI*	Atlanta	GA	30308	800-688-7878	404-588-7711	355-2
SunTrust Mortgage Inc 1001 Semmes Ave	Richmond	VA	23224	800-634-7928	804-291-0740	498
SunTrust Robinson Humphrey Capital Markets 3333 Peachtree Rd NE Atlanta Financial Ctr	Atlanta	GA	30326	877-266-6501	404-926-5000	679
SUNY Canton 34 Cornell Dr	Canton	NY	13617	800-388-7123	315-386-7011	160
SUNY Cobleskill Rt 7	Cobleskill	NY	12043	800-295-8988	518-255-5525	163
SUNY Delhi 2 Main St	Delhi	NY	13753	800-963-3544	607-746-4000	160
SUNY-ESF 1 Forestry Dr	Syracuse	NY	13210	800-777-7373	315-470-6500	163
SUNY Fredonia 178 Central Ave	Fredonia	NY	14063	800-252-1212	716-673-3251	163
SUNY Geneseo 1 College Cir	Geneseo	NY	14454	866-245-5211	585-245-5211	163
SUNY Institute of Technology PO Box 3050	Utica	NY	13504	800-786-9832	315-792-7500	163
SUNY New Paltz 75 S Manheim Blvd	New Paltz	NY	12561	888-639-7589	845-257-2121	163
SUNY Oneonta Ravine Pkwy	Oneonta	NY	13820	800-786-9123	607-436-3500	163
SUNY Potsdam 44 Pierrpont Ave	Potsdam	NY	13676	877-768-7326	315-267-2000	163
SUNY Rockland 145 College Rd	Suffern	NY	10901	800-722-7666	845-574-4000	160
SUNY Ulster Cottekill Rd	Stone Ridge	NY	12484	800-724-0833	845-687-5000	160
SUNY Upstate Medical University 766 Irving Ave	Syracuse	NY	13210	800-736-2171	315-464-4570	164-2
SUNYIT (State University of New York Institute of Technology) PO Box 3050	Utica	NY	13504	800-786-9832	315-792-7500	163
Supelco Inc 595 N Harrison Rd Supelco Pk	Bellefonte	PA	16823	800-247-6628	814-359-3441	410
Super 8 Motels Inc 1910 8th Ave NE	Aberdeen	SD	57401	800-800-8000	605-225-2272	369
Super Brush Co 165 Front St Suite 4	Chicopee	MA	01013	800-272-0591	413-592-4195	104
Super Coups Inc 350 Revolutionary Dr	East Taunton	MA	02718	800-626-2620	508-977-2000	5
Super Dollar Stores 3401 Gresham Lake Rd	Raleigh	NC	27615	800-366-9144	919-876-6000	778
Super Electric Construction Co 4300 W Chicago Ave	Chicago	IL	60651	800-344-1936	773-489-4400	188-4
Super Glass Corp 1020 E 48th St	Brooklyn	NY	11203	800-237-2211	718-469-9300	329
Super Holiday Tours 116 Gatlin Ave	Orlando	FL	32806	800-327-2116	407-851-0060	748
Super Products Corp 17000 W Cleveland Ave	New Berlin	WI	53151	800-837-9711	262-784-7100	379
Super Sack Mfg Corp 11510 Data Dr	Dallas	TX	75218	800-331-9200	214-340-7060	68
Super Secur Mfg Co 15125 Proctor Ave	City of Industry	CA	91746	800-591-9880	626-333-2543	106
Super Shoe Stores Inc 601 Dual Hwy	Hagerstown	MD	21740	888-392-2204	301-766-7513	296
Super Sky Products Inc 10301 N Enterprise Dr	Mequon	WI	53092	800-558-0467	262-242-2000	232
Superb Internet Corp 700 W Pender St Suite 1400	Vancouver	BC	V6C1G8	888-354-6128	604-638-2525	795
SuperComm Inc 5001 LBJ Fwy Suite 550	Dallas	TX	75244	800-252-9556	972-726-2000	223
Supercomputing Center. Pittsburgh 4400 5th Ave	Pittsburgh	PA	15213	800-221-1641	412-268-4960	654
Supercuts Div Regis Corp 7201 Metro Blvd	Minneapolis	MN	55439	888-888-7778	952-947-7777	79
Superdome 1500 Poydras PO Box 52439	New Orleans	LA	70152	800-756-7074	504-587-3663	706
SuperFlow Corp 3512 N Tejon St	Colorado Springs	CO	80907	800-471-7701	719-471-1746	464
Superfund Week Newsletter 8737 Colesville Rd Suite 1100 *Cust Svc	Silver Spring	MD	20910	800-274-6737*	301-587-6300	521-7
SuperGen Inc 4140 Dublin Blvd Suite 200 *NASDAQ: SUPG*	Dublin	CA	94568	800-353-1075	925-560-0100	86
SuperGlass Windshield Repair 6101 Chancellor Dr Suite 200	Orlando	FL	32809	888-771-2700	407-240-1920	62-2
Superior Air Charter Inc 3650 Biddle Rd Suite 16	Medford	OR	97504	800-793-1030	541-772-5660	14
Superior Boiler Works Inc 3524 E 4th St PO Box 1527	Hutchinson	KS	67504	800-444-6693	620-662-6693	92
Superior Carriers Inc 2122 York Rd Suite 150	Oak Brook	IL	60523	800-654-7707	630-573-2555	769
Superior Clay Corp 6566 Superior Rd SE	Uhrichsville	OH	44683	800-848-6166	740-922-4122	148
Superior Consultant Holdings Corp 17570 W 12-Mile Rd	Southfield	MI	48076	800-781-0960	248-386-8300	193
Superior Dairy Inc 4719 Navarre Rd SW	Canton	OH	44706	800-683-2479	330-477-4515	291-27
Superior Design International Inc 6365 NW 6th Way Suite 360	Fort Lauderdale	FL	33309	800-850-4222	954-938-5400	707
Superior Die Set Corp 900 W Drexel Ave	Oak Creek	WI	53154	800-558-6040	414-764-4900	745
Superior Die Tool & Machine Co 2301 Fairwood Ave	Columbus	OH	43207	800-292-2181	614-444-2181	745
Superior Energy Services Inc 1105 Peters Rd *NYSE: SPN*	Harvey	LA	70058	800-259-7774	504-362-4321	527
Superior Essex Communications LLC 150 Interstate North Pkwy	Atlanta	GA	30339	800-685-4887	770-657-6000	720
Superior Essex Inc 150 Interstate North Pkwy *NASDAQ: SPSX*	Atlanta	GA	30339	800-685-6543	770-657-6000	801
Superior Essex Inc Magnet Wire/Winding Wire Div PO Box 1601 *Cust Svc	Fort Wayne	IN	46802	800-551-8948*	260-461-4633	800
Superior Fabricators Inc PO Box 0539	Baldwin	LA	70514	800-960-7271	337-923-7271	92
Superior Foods Inc 275 Westgate Dr	Watsonville	CA	95076	888-373-7871	831-728-3691	292-7
Superior Graphite Co 10 S Riverside Plaza Suite 1470 *Orders	Chicago	IL	60606	800-325-0337*	312-559-2999	127
Superior Industries International Inc 7800 Woodley Ave *NYSE: SUP*	Van Nuys	CA	91406	800-545-9882	818-781-4973	60
Superior Information Services Inc 300 Phillips Blvd Suite 500	Trenton	NJ	08618	800-848-0489	609-883-7000	621
Superior Machine Co of South Carolina Inc 692 N Cashua Rd	Florence	SC	29502	800-736-9898	843-664-3001	485
Superior Mfg Group 7171 W 65th St	Chicago	IL	60638	800-621-2802	708-458-4600	286
Superior Oil Co Inc 400 W Regent St	Indianapolis	IN	46225	800-553-5480	317-781-4400	592
Superior Packing Co 1477 Drew Ave Suite 101	Davis	CA	95616	800-228-5262	530-758-3091	465
Superior Pharmaceutical Co 1385 Kemper Meadow Dr	Cincinnati	OH	45240	800-826-5035	513-851-3600	237
Superior Plus Income Fund 605 5th Ave SW Suite 2820 *TSE: SPF.UN*	Calgary	AB	T2P3H5	866-490-7587	403-218-2970	397
Superior Press Inc 11930 Hamden Pl	Santa Fe Springs	CA	90670	888-590-7998	562-948-1866	87
Superior Products Catalog Co 510 W County Rd D *Sales	Saint Paul	MN	55112	800-328-9800*	651-636-1110	295
Superior Shade & Blind Co Inc 1541 N Powerline Rd	Pompano Beach	FL	33069	800-325-9018	954-975-8122	88
Superior Solvents & Chemicals 400 W Regent St	Indianapolis	IN	46225	800-553-5480	317-781-4400	144
Superior Technical Resources Inc 250 International Dr	Williamsville	NY	14231	800-568-8310	716-631-8310	707
Superior Tire & Rubber Corp PO Box 308 *Cust Svc	Warren	PA	16365	800-289-1456*	814-723-2370	739
Superior Tool Co 100 Hayes Dr Unit C	Brooklyn Heights	OH	44131	800-533-3244	216-398-8600	746
Superior Uniform Group Inc 10055Seminole Blvd *AMEX: SGC* ■ *Cust Svc	Seminole	FL	33772	800-727-8643*	727-397-9611	153-19
Superior/Douglas County Convention & Visitors Bureau 205 Belknap St	Superior	WI	54880	800-942-5313	715-394-7716	205
Superlite Block Co Inc 4150 W Turney Ave	Phoenix	AZ	85019	800-366-7877	602-269-3561	181
Supermall of the Great Northwest 1101 SuperMall Way	Auburn	WA	98001	800-729-8258	253-833-9500	452
Supermarket Systems Inc PO Box 472513	Charlotte	NC	28247	800-553-1905	704-542-6000	651
SuperPawn 3021 Business Ln	Las Vegas	NV	89103	800-511-2568	702-735-4444	558
Superscape Inc 131 Calle Iglesia Suite 200	San Clemente	CA	92672	800-965-7411		176-8
Superstar Dept 1142	Tulsa	OK	74182	800-642-8080		117
Superstar Satellite Entertainment 7140 S Lewis Ave	Tulsa	OK	74136	800-225-5772	918-488-4100	117
Supertex Inc 1235 Bordeaux Dr *NASDAQ: SUPX*	Sunnyvale	CA	94089	800-487-8737	408-744-0100	686
SUPERVALU Inc 11840 Valley View Rd *NYSE: SVU* ■ *Cust Svc	Eden Prairie	MN	55344	888-256-2800*	952-828-4000	292-8
Supervision & Curriculum Development. Association for 1703 N Beauregard St	Alexandria	VA	22311	800-933-2723	703-578-9600	49-5
Supplier Development Council. National Minority 1040 Ave of the Americas 2nd Fl	New York	NY	10018	888-396-1110	212-944-2430	49-18
Supplier Selection & Management Report 3 Park Ave 30th Fl	New York	NY	10016	800-401-5937	212-244-0360	521-2
Supply Management. Institute for 2055 Centennial Cir *Cust Svc	Tempe	AZ	85284	800-888-6276*	480-752-6275	49-12
Supply Room Cos Inc 14140 N Washington Hwy	Ashland	VA	23005	800-849-7239	804-412-1200	524
Support Net Inc 4400 W 96th St	Indianapolis	IN	46268	800-255-3390	317-735-0200	172
SupportSoft Inc 575 Broadway *NASDAQ: SPRT*	Redwood City	CA	94063	877-493-2778	650-556-9440	176-7
Supra Telecom Inc 7795 W Flagler St Suite 39	Miami	FL	33144	888-317-8772	305-447-5401	721
Supra Telecommunications & Information Systems DBA Supra Telecom Inc 7795 W Flagler St Suite 39	Miami	FL	33144	888-317-8772	305-447-5401	721
Supreme Beverage 2100-A Jackson Ave	Huntsville	AL	35804	800-281-1482	256-534-1482	82-1
Supreme Corp 2581 E Kerchen Rd PO Box 463	Goshen	IN	46527	800-642-4889	574-642-4888	505
Supreme Corp 325 Spence Rd	Conover	NC	28613	888-604-6975	828-322-6975	730-9
Supreme Industries Inc 2581 E Kerchen Rd PO Box 463 *AMEX: STS*	Goshen	IN	46527	800-642-4889	574-642-3070	505
Sur-Seal Gasket & Packing Inc 6156 Wesselman Rd	Cincinnati	OH	45248	800-345-8966	513-574-8500	321
Sur La Table 5701 6th Ave S Suite 486	Seattle	WA	98108	800-243-0852	206-682-7175	357
Sure Power Industries Inc 10189 SW Avery St *Tech Supp	Tualatin	OR	97062	800-845-6269*	503-692-5360	246
Sure Winner Foods Inc PO Box 430	Saco	ME	04072	800-640-6447	207-282-1258	292-4
Surefit 939 Marcon Blvd	Allentown	PA	18109	888-754-7166	610-264-7300	731
SurePayroll 4709 Golf Rd Suite 900	Skokie	IL	60076	877-954-7873	847-676-8420	559

Name / Address	City	State	ZIP	Toll-Free	Phone	Class
Surety Assoc 120 Grace Dr	Easley	SC	29640	**800-922-0445**	864-220-9884	384-5
Surety Group Inc 1900 Emery St NW Suite 120	Atlanta	GA	30318	**800-486-8211**	404-352-8211	384-5
Surety LLC 12950 Worldgate Dr Suite 150	Herndon	VA	20170	**800-298-3115**	703-707-9901	176-7
SureWest Communications 211 Lincoln St *NASDAQ: SURW*	Roseville	CA	95678	**877-686-6141**	916-786-6141	721
Surf & Sand Resort 1555 South Coast Hwy	Laguna Beach	CA	92651	**888-869-7569**	949-497-4477	373
Surface Combustion Inc 1700 Indian Wood Cir	Maumee	OH	43537	**800-537-8980**	419-891-7150	313
Surface Mount Distribution Inc 1 Oldfield	Irvine	CA	92618	**800-229-7634**	949-470-7700	245
Surface Protection Industries Inc Zolatone Div 3360 E Pico Blvd	Los Angeles	CA	90023	**800-372-6292**	323-269-9231	540
SurfControl USA 5550 Scotts Valley Dr	Scotts Valley	CA	95066	**800-368-3366**	831-440-2500	176-7
Surfer Magazine PO Box 420235	Palm Coast	FL	32142	**800-289-0636**	386-447-6383	449-20
Surfing Magazine 950 Calle Amanecer Suite C	San Clemente	CA	92673	**800-879-0484**	949-492-7873	449-20
Surfsand Resort 148 W Gower Rd	Cannon Beach	OR	97110	**800-547-6100**	503-436-2274	373
Surfside Inn 1211 Atlantic Ave	Virginia Beach	VA	23451	**800-437-2497**	757-428-1183	373
Surftides Beach Resort 2945 NW Jetty Ave	Lincoln City	OR	97367	**800-452-2159**	541-994-2191	373
Surgeons. American Assn of Neurological 5550 Meadowbrook Dr	Rolling Meadows	IL	60068	**888-566-2267**	847-378-0500	49-8
Surgeons. American Assn of Oral & Maxillofacial 9700 W Bryn Mawr Ave	Rosemont	IL	60018	**800-822-6637**	847-678-6200	49-8
Surgeons. American College of 633 N Saint Clair St	Chicago	IL	60611	**800-621-4111**	312-202-5000	49-8
Surgeons. American College of Eye 334 E Lake Rd Suite 135	Palm Lake Harbor	FL	34685	**888-335-0077**	727-480-8542	49-8
Surgeons. American College of Foot & Ankle 8725 W Higgins Rd Suite 555	Chicago	IL	60631	**800-421-2237**	773-693-9300	49-8
Surgeons. American Society of Plastic 444 E Algonquin Rd	Arlington Heights	IL	60005	**888-475-2784**	847-228-9900	49-8
Surgeons. International Assn of Ocular 820 N Orleans St Suite 208	Chicago	IL	60610	**800-621-4002**	312-440-0699	49-8
Surgeons. Society of Laparoendoscopic 7330 SW 62nd Pl Suite 410	South Miami	FL	33143	**800-446-2659**	305-665-9959	49-8
Surgeons of the US. Association of Military 9320 Old Georgetown Rd	Bethesda	MD	20814	**800-761-9320**	301-897-8800	49-8
Surgery. American Society of Cataract & Refractive 4000 Legato Rd Suite 850	Fairfax	VA	22033	**800-451-1339**	703-591-2220	49-8
Surgery of the Hand. American Society for 6300 N River Rd Suite 600	Rosemont	IL	60018	**888-576-2774**	847-384-8300	49-8
Surgery & Ophthalmology. American Society of Contemporary Medicine 820 N Orleans St Suite 208	Chicago	IL	60610	**800-621-4002**	312-440-0699	49-8
Surgical Appliance Industries Inc 3960 Rosslyn Dr	Cincinnati	OH	45209	**800-888-0458**	513-271-4594	469
Surgical Services Inc 5776 Hoffner Ave Suite 200	Orlando	FL	32822	**800-349-4374**	407-249-1946	455
Surgical Specialties Corp 100 Dennis Dr	Reading	PA	19606	**800-523-3332**	610-404-1000	468
Surgical Staff Inc PO Box 192	San Mateo	CA	94401	**800-339-9599**	650-558-3999	707
Surinam Airways Ltd 7270 NW 12th St Suite 255	Miami	FL	33126	**800-327-6864**	305-599-1196	26
Surpas Resource Corp 3120 Hayes Rd Suite 200	Houston	TX	77082	**800-934-1240**	281-529-3140	157
Surprise Valley Electric Co-op PO Box 691	Alturas	CA	96101	**866-843-2667**	530-233-3511	244
Surrey Hotel 20 E 76th St	New York	NY	10021	**800-637-8483**	212-288-3700	373
Surry-Yadkin Electric Membership Corp PO Box 305	Dobson	NC	27017	**800-682-5903**	336-386-8241	244
Surveying. National Council of Examiners for Engineering & 280 Seneca Creek Rd	Clemson	SC	29631	**800-250-3196**	864-654-6824	49-3
Surveyors. National Assn of Marine PO Box 9306	Chesapeake	VA	23321	**800-822-6267**	757-638-9638	49-21
Survivors Network of Those Abused by Priests (SNAP) PO Box 6416	Chicago	IL	60680	**877-409-2720**	312-409-2720	48-21
Susan G Komen Breast Cancer Foundation 5005 LBJ Fwy Suite 250	Dallas	TX	75244	**800-462-9273**	972-855-1600	48-17
Sushi Doraku 8685 NW 53rd Terr Suite 201	Miami	FL	33166	**800-327-3369**	305-593-0770	657
SusQtech 600 Pegasus Ct Suite 100	Winchester	VA	22602	**888-603-0304**	540-723-8700	175
Susquehanna Bancshares Inc 24 N Cedar St PO Box 1000 *NASDAQ: SUSQ*	Lititz	PA	17543	**800-311-3182**	717-626-4721	355-2
Susquehanna Bank 100 West Rd	Baltimore	MD	21204	**800-619-0334**	410-938-8610	71
Susquehanna Pfaltzgraff Co 140 E Market St	York	PA	17401	**800-999-2811**	717-848-5500	184
Susquehanna Radio Corp 140 E Market St	York	PA	17401	**800-367-8261**	717-848-5500	629
Susquehanna Technologies DBA SusQtech 600 Pegasus Ct Suite 100	Winchester	VA	22602	**888-603-0304**	540-723-8700	175
Susquehanna University 514 University Ave	Selinsgrove	PA	17870	**800-326-9672**	570-374-0101	163
Suss Consulting 801 Old York Rd Noble Plaza Suite 305	Jenkintown	PA	19046	**888-984-5900**	215-884-5900	194
Sussex Bancorp 399 Rt 23 S *AMEX: SBB*	Franklin	NJ	07416	**800-511-9900**	973-827-2914	355-2
Sussex Co Inc PO Box 749	Milford	DE	19963	**800-537-5995**	302-422-8037	154
Sussex Post PO Box 737	Dover	DE	19903	**800-282-8586**	302-934-9261	522-4
Sussex Rural Electric Co-op PO Box 346	Sussex	NJ	07461	**877-504-6463**	973-875-5101	244

Name / Address	City	State	ZIP	Toll-Free	Phone	Class
Sussman Automatic Corp 43-20 34th St	Long Island City	NY	11101	**800-238-3535**	718-937-4500	92
Suter Co Inc 258 May St	Sycamore	IL	60178	**800-435-6942**	815-895-9186	291-36
Sutherland Lumber Co 4000 Main St	Kansas City	MO	64111	**800-821-2252**	816-756-3000	359
Sutherland Stewart Inc 5411 E 'V' Ave	Vicksburg	MI	49097	**800-253-1034**	269-649-0530	66
Sutphen Corp 7000 Columbus-Marysville Rd	Amlin	OH	43002	**800-726-7030**	614-889-1005	505
Sutter Davis Hospital 2000 Sutter Pl	Davis	CA	95616	**800-745-0227**	530-756-6440	366-2
Sutter Health 2200 River Plaza	Sacramento	CA	95833	**800-606-7070**	916-733-8800	348
Suttle PO Box 548	Hector	MN	55342	**800-852-8662**	320-848-6711	720
Sutton Place Hotel Chicago 21 E Bellevue Pl	Chicago	IL	60611	**866-378-8866**	312-266-2100	373
Sutton Place Hotel Newport Beach 4500 MacArthur Blvd	Newport Beach	CA	92660	**800-243-4141**	949-476-2001	373
Sutton Place Hotel Toronto 955 Bay St	Toronto	ON	M5S2A2	**800-268-3790**	416-924-9221	372
Sutton Place Hotel Vancouver 845 Burrard St	Vancouver	BC	V6Z2K6	**800-961-7555**	604-682-5511	372
Suzanna's Kitchen Inc 4025 Buford Hwy	Duluth	GA	30096	**800-241-2455**	770-476-9900	291-26
Suzio L Concrete Co Inc PO Box 748	Meriden	CT	06450	**888-789-4626**	203-237-8421	180
Suzuki Musical Instrument Corp PO Box 261030 *Cust Svc	San Diego	CA	92196	**800-854-1594***	858 566 9710	516
Suzy's Zoo Corp 2355 Northside Dr Suite 202 *Cust Svc	San Diego	CA	92108	**800-780-9066***	619-282-9401	130
Svenhard's Swedish Bakery Inc 335 Adeline St	Oakland	CA	94607	**800-333-7836**	510-834-5035	291-1
SVIA (Specialty Vehicle Institute of America) 2 Jenner St Suite 150	Irvine	CA	92618	**800-887-2887**	949-727-3727	49-21
SVS Vision 140 Macomb Pl	Mount Clemens	MI	48043	**800-225-3095**	586-468-7370	533
Swag The 2300 Swag Rd	Waynesville	NC	28785	**800-789-7672**	828-926-0430	373
Swager Communications Inc 501 E Swager Dr	Fremont	IN	46737	**800-968-5601**	260-495-5165	187-1
Swaggart Jimmy Ministries 8919 World Ministry Blvd *Orders	Baton Rouge	LA	70810	**800-288-8350***	225-768-8300	48-20
Swan Hellenic Cruises 631 Commack Rd Suite 1A	Commack	NY	11725	**877-800-7926**	631-858-1263	217
Swan Legal Search 11500 Olympic Blvd Suite 370	Los Angeles	CA	90064	**888-860-1154**	310-445-5010	262
SWANA (Solid Waste Assn of North America) 100 Wayne Ave Suite 700	Silver Spring	MD	20910	**800-467-9262**	301-585-2898	48-12
SWANA-Solid Waste Assn of North America Newsletter 1100 Wayne Ave Suite 700	Silver Spring	MD	20910	**800-467-9262**	301-585-2898	521-5
Swaner Hardwood Co Inc PO Box 4200	Burbank	CA	91503	**800-368-1108**	818-953-5350	671
Swank JM Co 520 W Penn St	North Liberty	IA	52317	**800-593-6375**	319-626-3683	292-8
Swank Motion Pictures Inc 201 S Jefferson Ave	Saint Louis	MO	63103	**800-876-5577**	314-534-6300	500
Swans Candles 8933 Gravelly Lake Dr SW	Lakewood	WA	98499	**888-848-7926**	253-584-4666	322
Swanson Contracting Co 11701 S Mayfield Ave	Alsip	IL	60803	**800-622-6850**	708-388-0623	187-8
Swanson Engineering & Mfg Co 1133 E Redondo Blvd	Inglewood	CA	90302	**800-633-1158**	310-671-6915	688
Swanson & Youngdale Inc 6565 W 23rd St	Saint Louis Park	MN	55426	**800-486-7824**	952-545-2541	188-8
Swany America Corp 109 Balzano Dr	Johnstown	NY	12095	**800-237-9269**	518-725-2000	153-8
Swarovski Consumer Goods Ltd 1 Kenney Dr	Cranston	RI	02920	**800-289-4900**	401-463-6400	400
Swarthmore College 500 College Ave	Swarthmore	PA	19081	**800-667-3110**	610-328-8300	163
Swarthout Coaches Inc 115 Graham Rd	Ithaca	NY	14850	**800-772-7267**	607-257-2277	108
Swatch Group 1200 Harbor Blvd 7th Fl	Weehawken	NJ	07087	**800-456-5354**	201-271-1400	151
SWCA Inc 2120 N Central Ave Suite 130	Phoenix	AZ	85004	**800-828-8517**	602-274-3831	191
SWCS (Soil & Water Conservation Society) 945 SW Ankeny Rd	Ankeny	IA	50021	**800-843-7645**	515-289-2331	48-13
Sweden House 4605 E State St	Rockford	IL	61108	**800-886-4138**	815-398-4130	373
Sweed Machinery Inc 653 2nd Ave PO Box 228 *Sales	Gold Hill	OR	97525	**800-888-1352***	541-855-1512	485
Sweeney Convention Center 201 W Marcy St	Santa Fe	NM	87504	**800-777-2489**	505-955-6200	204
Sweepster Inc 2800 N Zeeb Rd	Dexter	MI	48130	**800-456-7100**	734-996-9116	104
Sweet Adelines International 9110 S Toledo Ave	Tulsa	OK	74137	**800-992-7464**	918-622-1444	48-18
Sweet Briar College 134 Chappel Rd	Sweet Briar	VA	24595	**800-381-6142**	434-381-6100	163
Sweet Candy Co Inc 3780 W Directors Row	Salt Lake City	UT	84104	**800-669-8669**	801-886-1444	291-8
Sweet Mfg Co Inc 200 E Leffel Ln *Cust Svc	Springfield	OH	45505	**800-334-7254***	937-325-1511	206
Sweet Street Desserts PO Box 15127 *Orders	Reading	PA	19612	**800-793-3897***	610-921-8113	291-9
Sweet Tomatoes 15822 Bernardo Ctr Dr Suite A	San Diego	CA	92127	**800-874-1600**	858-675-1600	657
Sweetwater Reporter PO Box 750	Sweetwater	TX	79556	**800-401-3763**	325-236-6677	522-2
Sweetwater Technologies PO Box 1473	Temecula	CA	92593	**888-711-7575**	951-303-0999	143
Swensen's Ice Cream Co 4175 Veterans Memorial Hwy	Ronkonkoma	NY	11779	**800-423-2763**	631-737-9898	221
Swenson Spreader Co 127 Walnut St	Lindenwood	IL	61049	**888-825-7323**	815-393-4455	189
SWEPCo 1 Riverside Plaza	Columbus	OH	43215	**888-216-3523**		774
SWH Corp 17852 E 17th St South Bldg Suite 108	Tustin	CA	92780	**866-566-6464**	714-544-4826	656
SWH Supply Co 242 E Main St	Louisville	KY	40202	**800-866-6672**	502-589-9287	651
Swibco Inc 4810 Venture Rd	Lisle	IL	60532	**877-794-2261**	630-968-8900	750

Company / Address	City	State	ZIP	Toll-Free	Phone	Class
Swift & Co 1770 Promontory Cir.	Greeley	CO	80634	**800-555-2588**	970-506-8000	291-26
Swift Energy Co 16825 Northchase Dr Suite 400 *NYSE: SFY*	Houston	TX	77060	**800-777-2412**	281-874-2700	525
Swift Glass Co Inc 131 W 22nd St.	Elmira Heights	NY	14903	**800-537-9438**	607-733-7166	328
Swift Instruments Inc 952 Dorchester Ave	Boston	MA	02125	**800-446-1116**	617-436-2960	532
Swift M & Sons Inc 10 Love Ln	Hartford	CT	06112	**800-628-0380**	860-522-1181	290
Swift Transportation Co Inc 2200 S 75th Ave. *NASDAQ: SWFT*	Phoenix	AZ	85043	**800-800-2200**	602-269-9700	769
Swifty Oil Co Inc PO Box 1002	Seymour	IN	47274	**800-742-8497**	812-522-1640	319
Swiger Coils Systems Inc 4677 Manufacturing Rd	Cleveland	OH	44135	**800-321-3310**	216-362-7500	507
Swim 'n Sport Retail Inc 2396 NW 96th Ave.	Miami	FL	33172	**800-497-2111**	305-593-5071	155-6
Swindal-Powell Co 7750 Phillips Hwy.	Jacksonville	FL	32256	**800-422-8903**	904-739-0100	315
Swing-N-Slide Corp 1212 Barberry Dr	Janesville	WI	53545	**800-888-1232**	608-755-4777	340
Swintec Corp 320 W Commercial Ave	Moonachie	NJ	07074	**800-225-0867**	201-935-0115	112
Swisher County Cattle Co PO Box 129	Tulia	TX	79088	**800-658-6064**	806-627-4231	11-1
Swisher Electric Co-op Inc 401 SW 2nd St.	Tulia	TX	79088	**800-530-4344**	806-995-3567	244
Swisher Hygiene Co 6849 Fairview Rd	Charlotte	NC	28210	**800-444-4138**	704-364-7707	150
Swisher International Group Inc PO Box 2230	Jacksonville	FL	32203	**800-843-3731**	904-353-4311	741-2
Swisher International Inc 6849 Fairview Rd	Charlotte	NC	28210	**800-444-4138**	704-364-7707	150
Swiss Army Brands Inc 1 Research Dr PO Box 874 *Cust Svc	Shelton	CT	06484	**800-243-4057***	203-929-6391	346
Swiss Chalet Rotisserie & Grill 6303 Airport Rd	Mississauga	ON	L4V1R8	**800-860-4082**	905-405-6500	657
Swiss International Airlines Ltd 10 E 53rd St.	New York	NY	10022	**877-359-7947**		26
Swiss Re America Corp 175 King St.	Armonk	NY	10504	**877-794-7773**	914-828-8000	384-4
Swiss Re Life & Health America Inc 175 King St	Armonk	NY	10504	**877-794-7773**	914-828-8500	355-4
Swiss TravelClub 10 E 53rd St	New York	NY	10022	**877-359-7947**		27
Swiss Valley Farms Co 21100 Holden Dr	Davenport	IA	52806	**800-747-6113**	563-391-3341	291-5
Swisscom North America 2001 L St NW Suite 750	Washington	DC	20036	**800-966-1145**	202-785-1145	721
Swisslog Translogic 10825 E 47th Ave.	Denver	CO	80239	**800-525-1841**	303-371-7770	206
Swissotel Chicago 323 E Wacker Dr.	Chicago	IL	60601	**800-654-7263**	312-565-0565	373
Swissotel New York - The Drake 440 Park Ave	New York	NY	10022	**800-372-5369**	212-421-0900	373
Switchboard Inc 120 Flanders Rd	Westborough	MA	01581	**800-343-1511**	508-898-8000	677
Switlik Parachute Co Inc PO Box 1328	Trenton	NJ	08607	**800-525-2747**	609-587-3300	566
Switzerland Tourism 608 5th Ave Suite 202	New York	NY	10020	**800-794-7795**	212-757-5944	764
Swope Sam Auto Group LLC 10 Swope Auto Ctr.	Louisville	KY	40299	**800-228-9086**	502-499-5000	57
SY Bancorp Inc 1040 E Main St *AMEX: SYI*	Louisville	KY	40206	**800-625-9066**	502-582-2571	355-2
Sybase Inc 1 Sybase Dr. *NYSE: SY*	Dublin	CA	94568	**800-879-2273**	925-236-5000	176-1
Sybex Inc 1151 Marina Village Pkwy.	Alameda	CA	94501	**800-227-2346**	510-523-8233	623-2
Sybron Chemicals Inc PO Box 66	Birmingham	NJ	08011	**800-678-0020**	609-893-1100	143
Sycamore Networks Inc 220 Mill Rd. *NASDAQ: SCMR*	Chelmsford	MA	01824	**877-792-2667**	978-250-2900	174
Sycuan Casino & Resort 5469 Casino Way	El Cajon	CA	92019	**800-279-2826**	619-445-6002	133
SYGMA Network Inc 2000 Westbelt Dr	Columbus	OH	43228	**800-347-7344**	614-771-3801	292-8
Sykes Enterprises Inc 400 N Ashley Dr Suite 2800 *NASDAQ: SYKE*	Tampa	FL	33602	**800-867-9537**	813-274-1000	178
Sykes HealthPlan Services Inc 11405 Bluegrass Pkwy.	Louisville	KY	40299	**888-421-7477**	502-267-4900	455
Sylvan Dale Guest Ranch 2939 N County Rd 31 D.	Loveland	CO	80538	**877-667-3999**	970-667-3915	238
Sylvan Inc PO Box 249	Saxonburg	PA	16056	**866-352-7520**	724-352-7520	11-7
Sylvan Learning Centers 1001 Fleet St	Baltimore	MD	21202	**800-627-4276**	410-843-8000	241
Sylvest Farms Inc 3500 Western Blvd	Montgomery	AL	36108	**800-277-2473**	334-281-0400	608
Symantec Corp 20330 Stevens Creek Blvd *NASDAQ: SYMC* ■ *Cust Svc	Cupertino	CA	95014	**800-441-7234***	408-517-8000	176-12
Symark Software 30401 Agoura Rd Suite 200	Agoura Hills	CA	91301	**800-234-9072**	818-575-4000	176-12
Symbol Mattress Co 1814 High Point Ave	Richmond	VA	23230	**800-446-2791**	804-353-8965	463
Symbol Technologies Inc 1 Symbol Plaza *NYSE: SBL*	Holtsville	NY	11742	**800-722-6234**	631-738-2400	171-7
Symmetricom Inc 2300 Orchard Pkwy *NASDAQ: SYMM*	San Jose	CA	95131	**888-367-7966**	408-433-0910	720
Symmons Industries Inc 31 Brooks Dr	Braintree	MA	02184	**800-796-6667**	781-848-2250	598
Symon Communications Inc 500 N Central Expy Suite 175	Plano	TX	75074	**800-827-9666**	972-578-8484	174
Symons Corp 200 E Touhy Ave	Des Plaines	IL	60018	**800-800-7601**	847-298-3200	189
Symons International Group Inc 4720 Kingsway Dr	Indianapolis	IN	46205	**800-342-5243**	317-259-6300	355-4
Symphony Center 220 S Michigan Ave	Chicago	IL	60604	**800-223-7114**	312-294-3333	562
Symphony Health Services 11350 McCormick Rd Executive Plaza IV Suite 600	Hunt Valley	MD	21031	**800-359-5971**	443-886-2200	707
Symrise Inc 300 North St	Teterboro	NJ	07608	**800-422-1559**	201-288-3200	143
Syms Corp 1 Syms Way *NYSE: SYM*	Secaucus	NJ	07094	**800-322-7967**	201-902-9600	155-2
SYN-X Pharma Inc 1 Marmac Dr	Toronto	ON	M9W1E7	**877-246-7593**	416-798-3445	86
Synagro Technologies Inc 1800 Bering Dr Suite 1000 *NASDAQ: SYGR*	Houston	TX	77057	**800-370-0035**	713-369-1700	791
Synalloy Corp 2155 W Croft Cir *NASDAQ: SYNL* ■ *Orders	Spartanburg	SC	29302	**800-763-1001***	864-585-3605	584
Synbiotics Corp 11011 Via Frontera	San Diego	CA	92127	**800-228-4305**	858-451-3771	574
Syncor International Corp 6464 Canoga Ave	Woodland Hills	CA	91367	**800-999-9098**	818-737-4000	237
Syncroflo Inc 6700 Best Friend Rd	Norcross	GA	30071	**800-886-4443**	770-447-4443	627
Syndicate Store Fixtures Inc 402 N Main St	Middlebury	IN	46540	**800-626-3407**	574-825-9561	281
Synergent Biochem Inc 12038 Centralia Rd Suite C	Hawaiian Gardens	CA	90716	**800-585-8580**	562-809-3389	229
SYNERGI Global Travel Management 16 E 34th St 3rd Fl.	New York	NY	10016	**800-622-6622**	212-404-8814	761
Synergistic International Inc DBA Glass Doctor 1020 N University Parks Dr	Waco	TX	76707	**800-280-9959**	254-745-2480	62-2
Synergy Resource Group Inc 3131 Fernbrook Ln Suite 111	Plymouth	MN	55447	**888-990-9959**	763-566-5999	47
Syngenta Corp 2200 Concord Pike	Wilmington	DE	19803	**800-759-4500**	302-425-2000	276
Syngenta Crop Protection Inc PO Box 18300	Greensboro	NC	27419	**800-334-9481**	336-632-6000	276
Syngenta Seeds Inc 7500 Olson Memorial Hwy.	Golden Valley	MN	55427	**800-445-0956**	763-593-7333	684
Syngenta Seeds Inc Flowers Div 5300 Katrine Ave	Downers Grove	IL	60515	**800-323-7253**	630-969-6300	684
Synkoloid Co 148 E 5th St	Bayonne	NJ	07002	**800-631-3440**	201-437-0770	3
SYNNEX Corp 839 Pellham Ridge Dr *NYSE: SNX*	Greenville	SC	29615	**800-756-9888**		172
Synopsys Inc 700 E Middlefield Rd *NASDAQ: SNPS*	Mountain View	CA	94043	**800-541-7737**	650-584-5000	176-10
Synovis Life Technologies Inc 2575 University Ave W Suite 180 *NASDAQ: SYNO*	Saint Paul	MN	55114	**800-487-9627**	651-603-3700	469
Synrad Inc 4600 Campus Pl	Mukilteo	WA	98275	**800-796-7231**	425-349-3500	416
Syntegra USA 4201 Lexington Ave N	Arden Hills	MN	55126	**800-257-6736**	651-415-2999	178
Syntellect Inc 16610 N Black Canyon Hwy Suite 100	Phoenix	AZ	85053	**800-788-9733**	602-789-2800	720
Synthes USA 1690 Russell Rd	Paoli	PA	19301	**800-523-0322**	610-647-9700	469
Synthetic Industries Inc 309 LaFayette Rd	Chickamauga	GA	30707	**800-258-3121**	706-375-3121	131
Synthetic Organic Chemical Manufacturers Assn (SOCMA) 1850 M St NW Suite 700	Washington	DC	20036	**888-377-0778**	202-721-4100	49-19
Syntrio 555 Howard St Suite 100	San Francisco	CA	94105	**888-858-2887**	415-951-7913	39
Synventive Molding Solutions Inc 10 Centennial Dr.	Peabody	MA	01960	**800-367-5662**	978-750-8065	379
Sypris Technologies PO Box 32160	Louisville	KY	40232	**800-626-5655**	502-774-6011	474
Sypris Test & Measurement 6120 Hanging Moss Rd	Orlando	FL	32807	**800-775-2550**	407-678-6900	728
Syracuse China Co 2900 Court St.	Syracuse	NY	13208	**800-448-5711**	315-455-5671	716
Syracuse Convention & Visitors Bureau 572 S Salina St.	Syracuse	NY	13202	**800-234-4797**	315-470-1910	205
Syracuse Research Corp (SRC) 6225 Running Ridge Rd	North Syracuse	NY	13212	**800-724-0451**	315-452-8000	654
Syracuse Scenery & Stage Lighting Co Inc 101 Monarch Dr.	Liverpool	NY	13088	**800-453-7775**	315-453-8096	708
Syracuse Stamping Co Inc 1054 S Clinton St.	Syracuse	NY	13202	**800-581-5555**	315-476-5306	480
Syracuse Symphony Orchestra 411 Montgomery St Suite 40	Syracuse	NY	13202	**800-724-3810**	315-424-8222	563-3
Syrian Associated Charities. American Lebanese 501 St Jude Pl.	Memphis	TN	38105	**800-822-6344**	901-578-2000	48-5
Syroco Inc 7528 State Fair Blvd	Baldwinsville	NY	13027	**800-853-9272**	315-635-9911	314-4
Sys Technology Inc 17358 Railroad St.	City of Industry	CA	91748	**866-834-9155**	626-810-2345	171-3
Syska & Hennessy Group 11 W 42nd St.	New York	NY	10036	**800-328-1600**	212-921-2300	258
SYSPRO 959 S Coast Dr Suite 100	Costa Mesa	CA	92626	**800-369-8649**	714-437-1000	176-1
Systech Corp 16510 Via Esprillo	San Diego	CA	92127	**800-800-8970**	858-674-6500	174
Systech Retail Systems Inc DBA OPENFIELD Solutions 5800 Ambler Dr Suite 215 *TSE: SYS*	Mississauga	ON	L4W4J4	**800-387-3262**	905-507-4333	113
System Innovators Inc 10550 Deerwood Park Blvd Suite 700	Jacksonville	FL	32256	**800-963-5000**	904-281-9090	176-10
System Management ARTS Inc (SMARTS) 44 S Broadway	White Plains	NY	10601	**877-276-2787**	914-948-6200	176-1
Systema Corp 633 Skokie Blvd Suite 240	Northbrook	IL	60062	**800-270-9530**	847-498-9530	192
Systematic Financial Management LP 300 Frank W Burr Blvd 7th Fl Glenpoint Ctr E	Teaneck	NJ	07666	**800-258-0497**	201-928-1982	393
Systemax Inc 11 Harbor Pk Dr *NYSE: SYX*	Port Washington	NY	11050	**800-845-6225**	516-625-1555	171-3
Systems Contractors Assn. National 625 1st St SE Suite 420	Cedar Rapids	IA	52401	**800-446-6722**	319-366-6722	49-20
Systems Man & Cybernetics Society. IEEE IEEE Operations Ctr 445 Hoes Ln	Piscataway	NJ	08854	**800-678-4333**	732-981-0060	49-19
Systems Mfg Corp 1037 Powers Rd *Cust Svc	Conklin	NY	13748	**800-762-7587***	607-775-1100	281
SystemSoft Corp 275 Grove St Suite I-300	Newton	MA	02466	**800-796-0088**	617-614-4315	176-12
Systran Financial Services Corp 4949 SW Meadows Rd Suite 500	Oswego	OR	97035	**800-824-2075**	503-675-5700	214
Systron Donner Inertial Div BEI Technologies Inc 2700 Systron Dr	Concord	CA	94518	**800-227-1625**	925-671-6400	519

Company	City	State	ZIP	Toll-Free	Phone	Class
Sytel Inc 6430 Rockledge Dr Suite 400	Bethesda	MD	20817	**888-866-0881**	301-530-1000	178
SyVox 1850 I-30	Rockwall	TX	75087	**866-436-3782**	972-938-1653	176-7

T

Company	City	State	ZIP	Toll-Free	Phone	Class
T & D Metal Products Co 602 E Walnut St	Watseka	IL	60970	**800-634-7267**	815-432-4938	479
T & E Industries Inc 215 Watchung Ave *Sales	Orange	NJ	07050	**800-245-7080***	973-672-5454	321
T & F Informa 6000 NW Broken Sound Pkwy Suite 300	Boca Raton	FL	33487	**800-272-7737**	561-994-0555	623-6
T-Fal Corp 1 Boland Dr Suite 101	West Orange	NJ	07052	**800-395-8325**	973-736-0300	477
T & L Golf Magazine 1120 6th Ave	New York	NY	10036	**800-947-7961**	212-382-5600	449-20
T Marzotti Co Chatham Village Foods Div 15 Kendrick Rd	Wareham	MA	02571	**800-771-3888**	508-291-2304	291-9
T-Mobile USA Inc 12920 SE 38th St	Bellevue	WA	98006	**800-318-9270**		721
T & R Electric Supply Co Inc PO Box 180	Colman	SD	57017	**800-843-7994**	605-534-3555	756
T & R Graphic Imaging Inc 2535 17th St	Denver	CO	80211	**800-525-2497**	303-458-0626	770
T Rowe Price Assoc Inc 100 E Pratt St	Baltimore	MD	21202	**800-638-7890**	410-345-2000	393
T Rowe Price Group Inc 100 E Pratt St *NASDAQ: TROW*	Baltimore	MD	21202	**800-638-7890**	410-345-2000	355-3
T Rowe Price Mutual Funds 100 E Pratt St	Baltimore	MD	21202	**800-638-5660**	410-345-2000	517
T & S Brass & Bronze Works Inc PO Box 1088 *Cust Svc	Travelers Rest	SC	29690	**800-476-4103***	864-834-4102	598
T Sardelli & Sons Inc 195 Dupont Dr	Providence	RI	02907	**800-327-4641**	401-944-8510	401
T-Square Miami Blueprint Co 998 W Flagler St	Miami	FL	33130	**800-432-3360**	305-324-1234	239
T & T Truck & Crane Service Inc 1375 N Olive St	Ventura	CA	93001	**800-655-3348**	805-488-4475	261-2
T & T Trucking Inc 11396 N Hwy 99	Lodi	CA	95240	**800-692-3457**	209-368-3629	769
T2 Systems Inc 7835 Woodland Dr Suite 250	Indianapolis	IN	46278	**800-434-1502**	317-524-5500	176-10
TA Assoc 125 High St High St Tower Suite 2500	Boston	MA	02110	**800-836-8873**	617-574-6700	779
TAB Products Co 605 4th St	Mayville	WI	53050	**888-822-9777**	920-387-3131	523
TABB Inc PO Box 10	Chester	NJ	07930	**800-887-8222**	908-879-2323	621
Tabbies Div Xertrex International Inc 1530 W Glenlake Ave	Itasca	IL	60143	**800-822-2437**	630-773-4020	550
Taber Bushnell Inc 7709 Winpark Dr	Minneapolis	MN	55427	**800-811-9362**	763-546-0994	480
Tabor College 400 S Jefferson St	Hillsboro	KS	67063	**800-822-6799**	620-947-3121	163
TABS (Association of Boarding Schools) 4455 Connecticut Ave NW Suite A-200	Washington	DC	20008	**800-541-5908**	202-966-8705	48-11
TAC Air Inc 701 S Robison Rd	Texarkana	TX	75504	**800-772-0077**	903-794-3835	63
TAC Americas 1650 W Crosby Rd	Carrollton	TX	75006	**800-274-5551**	972-323-1111	201
TAC Worldwide Cos 888 Washington St	Dedham	MA	02026	**800-588-0707**	781-251-8000	707
TACA International Airlines 6824 Veterans Blvd Suite 100-A	Metairie	LA	70003	**800-535-8780**	504-887-7847	26
TACC Div Illinois Tool Works Inc 56 Air Station Industrial Pk	Rockland	MA	02370	**800-503-6991**	781-878-7015	3
Taco Bueno Restaurants Inc 3033 Kellway Dr Suite 122	Carrollton	TX	75006	**800-440-0778**	972-417-4800	657
Taco Cabana Inc 8918 Tesoro Dr Suite 200	San Antonio	TX	78217	**800-357-9924**	210-804-0990	657
Taco Inc 1160 Cranston St	Cranston	RI	02920	**800-822-6007**	401-942-8000	352
Taco John's International Inc 808 W 20th St	Cheyenne	WY	82001	**800-854-0819**	307-635-0101	657
Taco Maker Inc 4605 Harrison Blvd	Ogden	UT	84403	**800-207-5804**	801-476-9780	657
Taco Mayo Inc 10405 Greenbriar Pl	Oklahoma City	OK	73159	**800-291-8226**	405-691-8226	657
Taco Tico Inc 2118 N Tyler St Suite B-100	Wichita	KS	67212	**877-681-0220**	316-681-0220	657
Taco Time International Inc 7730 E Greenway Rd Suite 104	Scottsdale	AZ	85260	**800-547-8907**	480-443-0200	657
Tacoma Regional Convention & Visitor Bureau 1119 Pacific Ave 5th Fl	Tacoma	WA	98402	**800-272-2662**	253-627-2836	205
Tacoma Rubber Stamp Co 919 Market St	Tacoma	WA	98402	**800-544-7281**	253-383-5433	459
Tacone 950 S Flower St Suite 105	Los Angeles	CA	90015	**877-482-2663**	213-236-0950	657
Taconic Inc 136 Coonbrook Rd PO Box 69	Petersburgh	NY	12138	**800-833-1805**	518-658-3202	730-2
Tacony Corp 1760 Gilsinn Ln	Fenton	MO	63026	**800-482-2669**	636-349-3000	38
Tadiran US Battery Div 2 Seaview Blvd Suite 102	Port Washington	NY	11050	**800-537-1368**	516-621-4980	76
Tadpole Computer Inc 20450 Stevens Creek Blvd 3rd Fl	Cupertino	CA	95014	**800-734-5483**	408-973-9944	171-3
TAF (Taxpayers Against Fraud Education Fund) 1220 19th St NW Suite 501	Washington	DC	20036	**800-873-2573**	202-296-4826	49-10
Tafco Equipment Co Inc 1304 W 1st St *Sales	Blue Earth	MN	56013	**800-328-3189***	507-526-3247	505
Taft College 29 Emmons Park Dr	Taft	CA	93268	**800-379-6784**	661-763-4282	160
Taft Contracting Co Inc 9000 W 67th St	Hodgkins	IL	60525	**800-942-9385**	708-656-7500	188-1
Tag-A-Long Expeditions 452 N Main St	Moab	UT	84532	**800-453-3292**	435-259-8946	748
TAG Aviation Inc 6855 34th Ave S	Minneapolis	MN	55450	**800-726-1673**	612-726-1673	25
Tag Aviation USA Inc 111 Anza Blvd Suite 200	Burlingame	CA	94010	**800-331-1930**	650-342-1717	14
Tag Heuer USA 966 S Springfield Ave	Springfield	NJ	07081	**800-321-4832**	973-467-1890	151
Tag-It Pacific Inc 21900 Burbank Blvd Suite 270 *AMEX: TAG*	Woodland Hills	CA	91367	**800-335-4443**	818-444-4100	404
Tagline Greetings 1100 Irvine Blvd Suite 123	Tustin	CA	92780	**800-782-4546**	714-662-5807	130
Tahera Diamond Corp 121 Richmond St W Suite 803 *TSE: TAH*	Toronto	ON	M5H2K1	**877-777-2004**	416-777-1998	493-3
Tahiti Tourisme 300 Continental Blvd Suite 160	El Segundo	CA	90245	**800-365-4949**	310-414-8484	764
Tahlequah Daily Press PO Box 888	Tahlequah	OK	74465	**800-725-8866**	918-456-8833	522-2
Tahoe Seasons Resort 3901 Saddle Rd	South Lake Tahoe	CA	96150	**800-540-4874**	530-541-6700	373
Tailhook Assn 9696 Businesspark Ave	San Diego	CA	92131	**800-322-4665**	858-689-9223	48-19
Taisho Pharmaceutical California Inc 3878 Carson St Suite 216	Torrance	CA	90503	**877-531-4559**	310-543-2035	572
Taitron Components Inc 28040 W Harrison Pkwy *NASDAQ: TAIT*	Valencia	CA	91355	**800-247-2232**	661-257-6060	245
Taiyo Yuden (USA) Inc 1930 N Thoreau Dr Suite 190	Schaumburg	IL	60173	**800-348-2496**	847-925-0888	252
Takashimaya Inc 693 5th Ave	New York	NY	10022	**800-753-2038**	212-350-0100	227
Take 3 Trailers Inc 2007 Longwood Dr	Brenham	TX	77833	**866-428-2533**	979-337-9568	751
Take One Magazine 86 Elm St	Peterborough	NH	03458	**800-677-8847**	603-924-7271	449-9
Take Pounds Off Sensibly 4575 S 5th St	Milwaukee	WI	53207	**800-932-8677**	414-482-4620	48-17
Take Root PO Box 930	Kalama	WA	98625	**888-766-8674**	360-673-3720	48-21
Talbert Mfg Inc 1628 W SR-114 *Cust Svc	Rensselaer	IN	47978	**800-348-5232***	219-866-7141	768
Talbot Financial Corp 7770 Jefferson St NE Suite 200	Albuquerque	NM	87109	**800-800-5661**	505-828-4000	383
Talbot Tours Inc 1952 Camden Ave	San Jose	CA	95124	**800-662-9933**	408-879-0101	748
Talbots Inc 1 Talbots Dr *NYSE: TLB*	Hingham	MA	02043	**800-225-8200**	781-749-7600	155-6
Talbott Hotel 20 E Delaware Pl	Chicago	IL	60611	**800-825-2688**	312-944-4970	373
Talbott Recovery Campus 5448 Yorktowne Dr	Atlanta	GA	30349	**800-445-4232**	770-994-0185	712
Talent Tree 9703 Richmond Ave	Houston	TX	77042	**800-999-1515**	713-789-1818	707
Taleo Corp 575 Market St 8th Fl *NASDAQ: TLEO*	San Francisco	CA	94105	**888-836-3669**	415-538-9068	176-1
Talisma Corp 10900 NE 4th St Suite 1510	Bellevue	WA	98004	**877-934-3276**	425-688-3800	39
Talk O'Texas Brands Inc 1610 Roosevelt St	San Angelo	TX	76905	**800-749-6572**	325-655-6077	291-20
Talk Radio Network PO Box 3755	Central Point	OR	97502	**888-383-3733**	541-664-8827	632
Talking Rain Beverage Co 30520 SE 84th St *Cust Svc	Preston	WA	98050	**800-734-0748***	425-222-4900	792
Talladega Castings & Machine Co Inc 228 N Court St	Talladega	AL	35160	**800-766-6708**	256-362-5550	302
Talladega Machinery & Supply Co Inc PO Box 736 *Cust Svc	Talladega	AL	35161	**800-289-8672***	256-362-4124	302
Tallahassee Area Convention & Visitors Bureau 106 E Jefferson St	Tallahassee	FL	32301	**800-628-2866**	850-413-9200	205
Tallahassee Democrat 277 N Magnolia Dr	Tallahassee	FL	32301	**800-777-2154**	850-599-2100	522-2
Tallahassee-Leon County Civic Center 505 W Pensacola St	Tallahassee	FL	32301	**800-322-3602**	850-487-1691	204
Tallan Inc 628 Hebron Ave Bldg 2 Suite 502	Glastonbury	CT	06033	**800-677-3693**	860-633-3693	175
Tallant Industries Inc 4900 Ondura Dr	Fredericksburg	VA	22407	**800-777-7663**	540-898-7000	190-4
Tallapoosa River Electric Co-op PO Box 675	Lafayette	AL	36862	**800-332-8732**	334-864-9331	244
Talley Defense Systems Inc 4153 N Higley Rd	Mesa	AZ	85277	**800-444-8837**	480-898-2200	379
Talley Management Group Inc 19 Mantua Rd	Mount Royal	NJ	08061	**888-423-4233**	856-423-7222	47
Tally Systems Corp PO Box 70	Hanover	NH	03755	**800-262-3877**	603-643-1300	176-12
TallyGenicom 4500 Daly Dr Suite 100	Chantilly	VA	20151	**800-436-4266**	703-633-8700	171-6
TALX Corp 1850 Borman Ct *NASDAQ: TALX*	Saint Louis	MO	63146	**800-888-8277**	314-214-7000	39
Tamarack Forestry Service Inc PO Box 769	Canton	NY	13617	**800-858-0437**	315-386-2010	765
Tamarack Funds PO Box 219757	Kansas City	MO	64121	**800-422-2766**		517
Tamaya Resort & Spa. Hyatt Regency 1300 Tuyuna Trail	Santa Ana Pueblo	NM	87004	**800-233-1234**	505-867-1234	655
Tamco Inc PO Box 371	Monongahela	PA	15063	**800-826-2672**	724-258-6622	746
Tamiami Automotive Group 8250 SW 8th St	Miami	FL	33144	**800-845-2886**	305-266-5500	57
Tamiment Resort & Conference Center Bush Kills Fall Rd	Tamiment	PA	18371	**800-532-8280**	570-588-6652	655
Tamko Roofing Products Inc PO Box 1404	Joplin	MO	64802	**800-641-4691**	417-624-6644	46
Tampa Airlines Cargo 1650 NW 66th Ave Bldg 708 Suite 206	Miami	FL	33122	**800-327-1520**	305-526-6720	13
Tampa Bay Convention & Visitors Bureau 400 N Tampa St Suite 2800	Tampa	FL	33602	**800-826-8358**	813-223-1111	205
Tampa Bay Devil Rays Tropicana Field 1 Tropicana Dr	Saint Petersburg	FL	33705	**888-697-2373**	727-825-3137	703
Tampa Bay Downs Inc 11225 Racetrack Rd	Tampa	FL	33626	**800-200-4434**	813-855-4401	628
Tampa Bay Fisheries Inc 3060 Gallagher Rd	Dover	FL	33527	**800-234-2561**	813-752-8883	291-14
Tampa Bay Performing Arts Center 1010 N WC MacInnes Pl	Tampa	FL	33602	**800-955-1045**	813-222-1000	562

Name / Address	City	State	ZIP	Toll-Free	Phone	Class
Tampa Convention Center 333 S Franklin St	Tampa	FL	33602	**800-426-5630**	813-274-8511	204
Tampa Farm Service Inc 14425 Haynes Rd	Dover	FL	33527	**800-441-3447**	813-659-0605	11-8
Tampa G Mfg Co 5105 S Lois Ave	Tampa	FL	33611	**800-365-1559**	813-229-1559	701
Tampa (Greater) Chamber of Commerce 615 Channelside Dr Suite 108	Tampa	FL	33602	**800-298-2672**	813-228-7777	137
Tampa International Airport (TPA)	Tampa	FL	33607	**800-767-8882**	813-870-8700	28
Tampa Maid Foods Inc 1600 Kathleen Rd	Lakeland	FL	33805	**800-237-7637**	863-687-4411	291-14
Tampa Port Authority 1101 Channelside Dr	Tampa	FL	33602	**800-741-2297**	813-905-7678	607
Tampa Technical Institute 2410 E Bush Blvd	Tampa	FL	33612	**800-992-4850**	813-935-5700	163
Tampa Tribune 202 S Parker St	Tampa	FL	33606	**800-282-5588**	813-259-7600	522-2
TAMSCO (Technical & Management Services Corp) 4041 Powder Mill Rd Suite 700	Calverton	MD	20705	**800-282-6727**	301-595-0710	178
Tan-Tar-A Resort Golf Club & Spa PO Box 188 TT *Resv	Osage Beach	MO	65065	**800-826-8272***	573-348-3131	655
Tanagraphics Inc 263 9th Ave	New York	NY	10001	**800-606-6876**	212-255-6876	615
Tandem Staffing Solutions Inc 1690 S Congress Ave Suite 210	Delray Beach	FL	33445	**800-275-5000**	561-454-3500	707
Tandem Users' Group. International 401 N Michigan	Chicago	IL	60611	**800-845-4884**	312-321-6851	48-9
Tandy Brands Accessories Inc 690 E Lamar Blvd Suite 200 *NASDAQ: TBAC*	Arlington	TX	76011	**800-570-7443**	817-548-0090	153-2
Tandy Leather Co 3847 E Loop 820 S	Fort Worth	TX	76119	**888-890-1611**	817-451-1480	45
Tangent Computer Inc 197 Airport Blvd	Burlingame	CA	94010	**800-342-9388**	650-342-9388	171-3
Tanger Factory Outlet Centers Inc 3200 Northline Ave Suite 360 *NYSE: SKT*	Greensboro	NC	27408	**800-438-8474**	336-292-3010	641
Tanglewood Resort Hotel & Conference Center 290 Tanglewood Cir	Pottsboro	TX	75076	**800-833-6569**	903-786-2968	655
Tangram Enterprise Solutions Inc 11000 Regency Pkwy Suite 301	Cary	NC	27511	**800-482-6472**	919-653-6000	176-1
Tangram Interiors Inc 9200 Sorensen Ave	Santa Fe Springs	CA	90670	**800-700-1377**	562-365-5000	315
Tanimura & Antle Inc PO Box 4070	Salinas	CA	93912	**800-772-4542**	831-455-2950	11-11
Tanita Corp of America Inc 2625 S Clearbrook Dr	Arlington Heights	IL	60005	**800-826-4828**	847-640-9241	672
Tank Lines Inc 1357 Diamond Springs Rd	Virginia Beach	VA	23455	**800-969-1357**	757-464-9349	769
Tankstar USA Inc PO Box 736	Milwaukee	WI	53201	**800-338-5699**	414-671-1600	769
Tanner Cos LLC 581Rock Rd	Rutherfordton	NC	28139	**800-669-3662**	828-287-4205	153-21
Tanner Electric Co PO Box 1426	North Bend	WA	98045	**800-472-0208**	425-888-0623	244
Tanner Industries Inc 735 Davisville Rd 3rd Fl	Southampton	PA	18966	**800-643-6226**	215-322-1238	144
Tanner OC Co 1930 S State St	Salt Lake City	UT	84115	**800-453-7490**	801-486-2430	401
Tanning Research Labs Inc DBA Hawaiian Tropic 1190 US Hwy 1 N	Ormond Beach	FL	32174	**800-874-4844**	386-677-9559	211
Tanque Verde Guest Ranch 14301 E Speedway Blvd	Tucson	AZ	85748	**800-234-3833**	520-296-6275	655
Tantalus Lodge 4200 Whistler Way	Whistler	BC	V0N1B4	**888-633-4046**	604-932-4146	655
Taos Moccasins PO Box 708	Taos	NM	87571	**800-662-8267**	505-758-4276	296
TAP Air Portugal 399 Market St *Resv	Newark	NJ	07105	**800-221-7370***	973-344-4490	26
TAP Plastics Inc 6475 Sierra Ln	Dublin	CA	94568	**800-894-0827**	925-829-4889	596
Tapatio Springs Golf Resort & Conference Center PO Box 550	Boerne	TX	78006	**800-999-3299**	830-537-4611	655
Tapco International 11307 W Little York Rd	Houston	TX	77041	**866-827-2660**	713-466-0300	776
Tape Craft Corp 200 Tape Craft Dr *Cust Svc	Oxford	AL	36203	**800-521-1783***	256-236-2535	730-5
Tape & Label Converters Inc 8231 Allport Ave	Santa Fe Springs	CA	90670	**888-285-2462**	562-945-3486	404
Tapecon Inc 10 Latta Rd	Rochester	NY	14612	**800-333-2408**	585-621-8400	404
TAPEMARK Co 150 E Marie Ave	West Saint Paul	MN	55118	**800-535-1998**	651-455-1611	404
Tapestry Pharmaceuticals Inc 4840 Pearl E Cir Suite 300W *NASDAQ: TPPH*	Boulder	CO	80301	**800-976-2776**	303-516-8500	470
Tapeswitch Corp 100 Schmitt Blvd	Farmingdale	NY	11735	**800-234-8273**	631-630-0442	715
Tapmatic Corp 802 Clearwater Loop	Post Falls	ID	83854	**800-854-6019**	208-773-8048	484
TAPPI (Technical Assn of the Pulp & Paper Industry) 15 Technology Pkwy S *Sales	Norcross	GA	30092	**800-332-8686***	770-446-1400	49-13
Taprell Loomis Div Chilcote Co 2160 Superior Ave	Cleveland	OH	44114	**800-827-5679**	216-781-6000	550
Tapscott's 1403 E 18th St	Owensboro	KY	42303	**800-626-1922**	270-684-2308	288
Tara Materials Inc PO Box 646	Lawrenceville	GA	30046	**800-241-8129**	770-963-5256	43
Tara Picture Frames 7615 Siempre Viva Rd	San Diego	CA	92154	**800-788-9969**	619-671-1018	304
Tara Toy Corp 40 Adams Ave	Hauppauge	NY	11788	**800-899-8272**	631-273-8697	750
Tarantella Inc 425 Encinal St *NASDAQ: TTLA* ■ *Sales	Santa Cruz	CA	95060	**800-995-9806***	831-427-7222	176-12
Target Corp 33 S 6th St *NYSE: TGT* ■ *Cust Svc	Minneapolis	MN	55402	**800-440-0680***	612-304-6073	658
TARGET Funds PO Box 8098	Philadelphia	PA	19101	**800-225-1852**		517
Target Logistic Services Inc 201 W Carob St	Compton	CA	90220	**800-283-8888**	310-900-1974	306
Target Products Inc 17400 W 119th St	Olathe	KS	66061	**800-288-5040**	913-928-1000	484
Target Stores 1000 Nicollet Mall	Minneapolis	MN	55403	**800-440-0680**	612-304-6073	227
Targeted Genetics Corp 1100 Olive Way Suite 100 *NASDAQ: TGEN*	Seattle	WA	98101	**800-828-6022**	206-623-7612	86
Targus Inc 1211 N Miller St	Anaheim	CA	92806	**800-950-5122**	714-765-5555	444
Tarkett Inc 1001 Yamaska St E	Farnham	QC	J2N1J7	**800-363-9276**	450-293-3173	286
Tarleton State University PO Box T-0030	Stephenville	TX	76402	**800-687-8236**	254-968-9125	163

Name / Address	City	State	ZIP	Toll-Free	Phone	Class
Tarlton Corp 5500 W Park Ave	Saint Louis	MO	63110	**888-827-5866**	314-633-3300	185
Taro Pharmaceuticals Inc 130 East Dr	Brampton	ON	L6T1C1	**800-268-1975**	905-791-8276	572
Taro Pharmaceuticals USA Inc 5 Skyline Dr *NASDAQ: TARO*	Hawthorne	NY	10532	**800-544-1449**	914-345-9001	573
Tarr LLC 2429 N Borthwick	Portland	OR	97227	**800-422-5069**	503-288-5294	144
Tarrant Apparel Group 3151 E Washington Blvd *NASDAQ: TAGS*	Los Angeles	CA	90023	**800-780-8250**	323-780-8250	153-21
Tarryall River Ranch 27001.5 County Rd 77	Lake George	CO	80827	**800-408-8407**	719-748-1214	238
Tartan Yachts 1920 Fairport Nursery Rd	Fairport Harbor	OH	44077	**888-330-3484**	440-354-3111	91
TAS Construction Inc 20105 Krahn Rd	Spring	TX	77388	**800-652-2227**	281-350-0832	188-3
Tas Group Inc DBA Air Charter Team 10015 NW Ambassador Dr Suite 202	Kansas City	MO	64153	**800-205-6610**	816-283-3280	14
TASER International Inc 17800 N 85th St *NASDAQ: TASR*	Scottsdale	AZ	85255	**800-978-2737**	480-905-2000	566
Task Industries Inc 1325 E Franklin Ave	Pomona	CA	91766	**800-961-9377**	909-629-1600	263
Taste of Home Magazine 5400 S 60th St	Greendale	WI	53129	**800-344-6913**	414-423-0100	449-11
Taste of Nature Inc 400 S Beverly Dr Suite 214 *Cust Svc	Beverly Hills	CA	90212	**800-898-2783***	310-396-4433	292-3
Tasty Baking Co 2801 W Hunting Park Ave *NYSE: TBC*	Philadelphia	PA	19129	**800-330-8677**	215-221-8500	291-1
Tate Access Floors Inc 7510 Montevideo Rd	Jessup	MD	20794	**800-231-7788**	410-799-4200	482
Tate Engineering Systems Inc 1560 Caton Ctr Dr	Baltimore	MD	21227	**800-800-8283**	410-242-8800	378
Tate & Lyle North America 2200 E Eldorado St *Cust Svc	Decatur	IL	62525	**800-782-7248***	217-423-4411	291-38
Tatnuck Bookseller & Sons 335 Chandler St	Worcester	MA	01602	**800-642-6657**	508-756-7644	96
Tattered Cover Book Store Inc 1628 16th St	Denver	CO	80202	**800-833-9327**	303-436-1070	96
Tatung Co of America Inc 2850 El Presidio St	Long Beach	CA	90810	**800-827-2850**	310-637-2105	171-4
Tau Beta Pi Assn PO Box 2697	Knoxville	TN	37901	**800-828-2382**	865-546-4578	48-16
Tau Beta Sigma National Honorary Band Sorority PO Box 849	Stillwater	OK	74076	**800-543-6505**	405-372-2333	48-16
Tauck World Discovery 10 Norden Pl	Norwalk	CT	06855	**800-468-2825**	203-899-6500	748
Taunton Press Inc 63 S Main St	Newtown	CT	06470	**800-243-7252**	203-426-8171	623-9
Tauro Brothers Trucking Co 1775 N State St	Girard	OH	44420	**800-860-9763**	330-545-9763	769
Taurus Service Inc Grift Flat Rd PO Box 164	Mehoopany	PA	18629	**800-836-5123**	570-833-5123	12-2
Tavaero Jet Charter 7930 Airport Blvd	Houston	TX	77061	**800-343-3771**	713-643-6043	14
Tawas Area Tourism & Convention Bureau PO Box 10	Tawas City	MI	48764	**877-868-2927**		205
Tax Management Inc 1231 25th St NW	Washington	DC	20037	**800-372-1033**	202-452-4200	623-9
Tax Management Inc BNA Software Div 1250 23rd St NW	Washington	DC	20037	**800-424-2938**	202-728-7962	176-10
Tax Professionals. National Assn of 720 Association Dr	Appleton	WI	54914	**800-558-3402**	920-749-1040	49-1
Taxation. Accreditation Council for Accountancy & 1010 N Fairfax St	Alexandria	VA	22314	**888-289-7763**	703-549-2228	48-1
Taxation. Americans for Fair PO Box 27487	Houston	TX	77227	**800-324-7829**	713-963-9023	48-7
Taxation & Revenue Policies Newsletter PO Box 7376	Alexandria	VA	22307	**800-876-2545**	703-768-9600	521-7
Taxes-Property Newsletter PO Box 7376	Alexandria	VA	22307	**800-876-2545**	703-768-9600	521-7
Taxpayers Against Fraud Education Fund (TAF) 1220 19th St NW Suite 501	Washington	DC	20036	**800-873-2573**	202-296-4826	49-10
Taxpayers Union. National 108 N Alfred St	Alexandria	VA	22314	**800-829-4258**	703-683-5700	48-7
TaxPro Inc DBA EconoTax Inc 5846 Ridgewood Rd Suite B-101	Jackson	MS	39211	**800-748-9106**	601-956-0500	719
Tay-Sachs & Allied Diseases Assn. National 2001 Beacon St Suite 204	Brighton	MA	02135	**800-906-8723**	617-277-4463	48-17
Tayloe Paper Co Inc 6717 E 13th St	Tulsa	OK	74112	**800-825-6911**	918-835-6911	549
Taylor Ball Inc 6100 Thornton Ave Suite 200	Des Moines	IA	50321	**800-373-0330**	515-471-4700	185
Taylor Bedding Inc 1133 MacArthur Ave	New Orleans	LA	70058	**800-826-2839**	504-341-0059	463
Taylor Brothers Inc PO Box 11198	Lynchburg	VA	24506	**800-288-6767**	434-237-8100	489
Taylor Building Products PO Box 457	West Branch	MI	48661	**800-248-3600**	989-345-5110	232
Taylor Business Institute 23 W 17th St 7th Fl	New York	NY	10011	**800-959-9999**	212-229-1963	158
Taylor Capital Group Inc 9550 W Higgins Rd 5th Fl *NASDAQ: TAYC*	Rosemont	IL	60018	**800-727-2265**	847-537-0020	355-2
Taylor Co 750 N Blackhawk Blvd	Rockton	IL	61072	**800-255-0626**	815-624-8333	293
Taylor Corp 1725 Roe Crest Dr	North Mankato	MN	56003	**800-545-6620**	507-625-2828	355-3
Taylor Cos 75 Taylor St	Bedford	OH	44146	**888-758-2956**	440-232-0700	314-1
Taylor Cutlery 1736 N Eastman Rd	Kingsport	TN	37664	**800-251-0254**	423-247-2406	219
Taylor DC Co 312 29th St NE	Cedar Rapids	IA	52402	**800-333-7763**	319-363-2073	188-12
Taylor-Dunn Mfg Co Inc 2114 W Ball Rd	Anaheim	CA	92804	**800-688-8680**	714-956-4040	462
Taylor Electric Co-op Inc PO Box 250	Merkel	TX	79536	**800-992-0086**	325-928-4715	244
Taylor Excel PO Box 188	Wyalusing	PA	18853	**800-828-9527**	570-746-3000	465
Taylor & Francis Group LLC DBA T & F Informa 6000 NW Broken Sound Pkwy Suite 300	Boca Raton	FL	33487	**800-272-7737**	561-994-0555	623-6
Taylor & Francis Routledge Publishers Inc 270 Madison Ave	New York	NY	10016	**800-634-7064**	917-351-7100	623-2
Taylor Freezer Sales Co Inc 2032 Atlantic Ave	Chesapeake	VA	23324	**800-768-6945**	757-545-7900	651

Name / Address	City	State	ZIP	Toll-Free	Phone	Class
Taylor & Fulton Inc 932 5th Ave W	Palmetto	FL	34221	**800-457-5577**	941-729-3883	11-11
Taylor Hobson Inc 2100 Golf Rd Suite 350	Rolling Meadows	IL	60008	**800-872-7265**	847-290-8090	464
Taylor Industries Inc 1533 E Euclid Ave	Des Moines	IA	50313	**800-362-2500**	515-262-8221	651
Taylor Made Golf Co 5545 Fermi Ct *Cust Svc	Carlsbad	CA	92008	**800-456-8633***	760-918-6000	701
Taylor-Morley Homes 17107 Chesterfield Airport Rd Suite 200	Chesterfield	MO	63005	**888-297-3155**	314-434-9000	639
Taylor Pittsburgh Manufacturing 7 Rocky Mount Rd	Athens	TN	37303	**800-456-7929**	423-745-3110	269
Taylor Provision Co PO Box 5108	Trenton	NJ	08638	**800-772-7126**	609-392-1113	291-26
Taylor Publishing Co 1550 W Mockingbird Ln	Dallas	TX	75235	**800-677-2800**	214-637-2800	623-2
Taylor Rental 203 Jandus Rd	Cary	IL	60013	**800-833-3004**	847-462-5440	261-3
Taylor Technologies Inc 31 Loveton Cir *Cust Svc	Sparks	MD	21152	**800-837-8548***	410-472-4340	793
Taylor University 236 W Reade Ave	Upland	IN	46989	**800-882-3456**	765-998-2751	163
Fort Wayne Campus 1025 W Rudisill Blvd	Fort Wayne	IN	46807	**800-233-3922**	260-456-2111	163
Taylor University College & Seminary 11525 23rd Ave	Edmonton	AB	T0J4T0	**800-507-4900**	780-431-5200	104-0
Tayloreel Corp PO Box 476	Oakwood	GA	30566	**877-503-1612**	770-503-1612	118
TB Butler Publishing Co 410 W Erwin St	Tyler	TX	75702	**800-333-9141**	903-597-8111	623-8
TB Wood's Inc 440 N 5th Ave *NASDAQ: TBWC*	Chambersburg	PA	17201	**888-829-6637**	717-264-7161	609
TBC Corp 4770 Hickory Hill Rd *NASDAQ: TBCC*	Memphis	TN	38141	**800-238-6469**	901-363-8030	740
TBI (Tissue Banks International) 815 Park Ave	Baltimore	MD	21201	**800-756-4824**	410-752-3800	535
TBWA Chiat/Day Inc 488 Madison Ave 7th Fl	New York	NY	10022	**877-666-2347**	212-804-1000	4
TC Pipelines LP 450 1st St SW *NASDAQ: TCLP*	Calgary	AB	T2P5H1	**800-361-6522**	403-920-2000	320
TC Thiolon USA Corp 1131 Broadway St	Dayton	TN	37321	**800-251-1033**	423-775-0792	594-1
TCBY Enterprises Inc 2855 E Cottonwood Pkwy Suite 400	Salt Lake City	UT	84121	**888-900-8229**	801-736-5600	221
TCE Capital Corp 505 Consumers Rd Suite 707	Toronto	ON	M2J4V8	**800-465-0400**	416-497-7400	268
TCF Financial Corp 801 Marquette Ave *NYSE: TCB*	Minneapolis	MN	55402	**800-533-1723**	612-661-6500	355-2
TCF National Bank 801 Marquette Ave	Minneapolis	MN	55402	**800-328-0728**	612-661-6500	71
TCI College of Technology 320 W 31st St	New York	NY	10001	**800-878-8246**	212-594-4000	158
TCI Powder Coatings Inc 4036 Dixon Dr	Ellaville	GA	31806	**800-533-9067**	229-937-5411	540
TCI Scales 4208 Russell Rd Unit E	Mukilteo	WA	98275	**800-522-2206**	425-353-4384	672
TCI Solutions Inc 17752 Skypark Cir Suite 160	Irvine	CA	92614	**800-621-7452**	949-476-1122	176-11
TCIA (Tree Care Industry Assn) 3 Perimeter Rd Unit 1	Manchester	NH	03103	**800-733-2622**	603-314-5380	48-13
TCIM Services Inc 1013 Centre Rd Suite 400	Wilmington	DE	19805	**800-333-2255**	302-633-3000	722
TCR Corp 1600 67th Ave N *Cust Svc	Minneapolis	MN	55430	**800-328-8961***	763-560-2200	610
TCS Expeditions 710 2nd Ave Suite 840	Seattle	WA	98104	**800-727-7477**	206-727-7300	748
TCU (TRUST for Credit Unions) 4900 Sears Tower 51st Fl	Chicago	IL	60606	**800-621-2550**	312-655-4400	517
TCW Galileo Funds PO Box 9821	Providence	RI	02940	**800-386-3829**		517
TD Waterhouse Bank NA 1 Harborside Financial Plaza 4A 8th Fl	Jersey City	NJ	07310	**888-327-9962**		71
TD Waterhouse Group Inc 100 Wall St	New York	NY	10005	**800-835-0245**	212-806-3500	679
TD Williamson Inc 5725 S Lewis St Suite 300	Tulsa	OK	74105	**888-839-6766**	918-447-5001	526
TDEC Inc 7735 Old Georgetown Rd Suite 1010	Bethesda	MD	20814	**800-424-8332**	301-718-0703	223
TDK Electronics Corp 901 Franklin Ave	Garden City	NY	11530	**800-835-8273**	516-535-2600	644
TDK USA Corp 901 Franklin Ave	Garden City	NY	11530	**800-835-8273**	516-535-2600	52
TDM Inc DBA Colgan Air Services 2709 Fanta Reed Rd	La Crosse	WI	54603	**800-658-9498**	608-783-8359	14
TDS Telecommunications Corp 525 Junction Rd	Madison	WI	53717	**800-358-3648**	608-664-4000	721
Teacher Created Resources Inc 6421 Industry Way	Westminster	CA	92683	**888-343-4335**	714-891-7895	242
Teachers. American Federation of 555 New Jersey Ave NW	Washington	DC	20001	**800-238-1133**	202-879-4400	405
Teachers Assn. National Science 1840 Wilson Blvd *Sales	Arlington	VA	22201	**800-722-6782***	703-243-7100	49-5
Teachers Committee on Political Education. American Federation of 555 New Jersey Ave NW	Washington	DC	20001	**800-238-1133**	202-879-4400	604
Teachers Credit Union 110 S Main St	South Bend	IN	46601	**800-333-3828**	574-232-8011	216
Teachers of English. National Council of 1111 W Kenyon Rd	Urbana	IL	61801	**800-369-6283**	217-328-3870	49-5
Teachers Federal Credit Union 2410 N Ocean Ave	Farmingville	NY	11738	**800-341-4333**	631-698-7000	216
Teachers of Mathematics. National Council of 1906 Association Dr. *Orders	Reston	VA	20191	**800-235-7566***	703-620-9840	49-5
Teachers. National Assn of Biology 12030 Sunrise Valley Dr Suite 110	Reston	VA	20191	**800-406-0775**	703-264-9696	49-5
Teachers. National Assn of Catholic School 1700 Sansom St Suite 903	Philadelphia	PA	19103	**800-996-2278**	215-665-0993	49-5
Teachers National Assn. Music 441 Vine St Suite 505	Cincinnati	OH	45202	**888-512-5278**	513-421-1420	49-5
Teachers. National Congress of Parents & 541 N Fairbanks Ct Suite 1300	Chicago	IL	60611	**800-307-4782**	312-670-6782	48-11
Teaching Exceptional Children Magazine 1110 N Glebe Rd Suite 300	Arlington	VA	22201	**888-232-7733**	703-620-3660	449-8
Teaching K-8 Magazine 40 Richards Ave *Cust Svc	Norwalk	CT	06854	**800-678-8793***	203-855-2650	449-8
Teaching & Learning Co 1204 Buchanan St	Carthage	IL	62321	**800-852-1234**	217-357-2591	242
Team Cobra Products 7240 W Erie St Suite 3	Chandler	AZ	85226	**800-336-7784**	480-889-1035	701
Team Financial Inc 8 W Peoria St Suite 200 PO Box 402 *NASDAQ: TFIN*	Paola	KS	66071	**800-880-6262**	913-294-9667	355-2
Team Health Inc 1900 Winston Rd Suite 300	Knoxville	TN	37919	**800-342-2898**	865-693-1000	707
Team Inc DBA Team Industrial Services Inc 200 Hermann Dr *AMEX: TMI*	Alvin	TX	77511	**800-662-8326**	281-331-6154	191
Team Industrial Services Inc 200 Hermann Dr *AMEX: TMI*	Alvin	TX	77511	**800-662-8326**	281-331-6154	191
Team Leader Newsletter 360 Hiatt Dr	Palm Beach Gardens	FL	33418	**800-621-5463**	561-622-9914	521-2
Team Losi Inc 4710 E Guasti Rd	Ontario	CA	91761	**800-338-4639**	909-390-9595	750
TeamQuest Corp 1 TeamQuest Way	Clear Lake	IA	50428	**800-551-8326**	641-357-2700	176-12
TeamSource Technical Services 800 Paloma Dr Suite 230	Round Rock	TX	78664	**800-489-0585**	512-275-0941	753
TeamStaff Inc 300 Atrium Dr *NASDAQ: TSTF*	Somerset	NJ	08873	**800-374-1001**	732-748-1700	707
TeamStaff Rx 1901 Ulmerton Rd Suite 800	Clearwater	FL	33762	**800-345-9642**		707
Teamwork Newsletter 360 Hiatt Dr	Palm Beach Gardens	FL	33418	**800-621-5463**	561-622-6520	521-2
TEC Corp PO Box 207	Sioux City	IA	51102	**800-832-2936**	712-252-4275	188-4
TEC International Inc 11452 El Camino Real Suite 400	San Diego	CA	92130	**800-274-2367**	858-627-4050	49-12
Tec Minerals Inc Hwy 787	Cleveland	TX	77327	**800-833-5442**	281-592-6428	490
TEC Products Co Inc 100 Middlesex Ave PO Box 309	Carteret	NJ	07008	**800-922-1998**	732-969-8700	549
TEC Specialty Products Inc 315 S Hicks Rd *Cust Svc	Palatine	IL	60067	**800-832-9002***	847-358-9500	3
Tech Data Corp 5350 Tech Data Dr *NASDAQ: TECD*	Clearwater	FL	33760	**800-237-8931**	727-539-7429	172
Tech International 200 E Coshocton St	Johnstown	OH	43031	**800-336-8324**	740-967-9015	739
Tech Lighting LLC 7401 N Hamlin	Skokie	IL	60076	**800-522-5315**	847-410-4400	431
Tech Supply PO Box 56747	Hayward	CA	94545	**800-245-8324**	510-783-7085	739
Tech-Tran Corp 50 Indel Ave PO Box 232	Rancocas	NJ	08073	**800-257-9420**	609-267-6750	756
Tech.logix Group of Bell Industries Inc 3502 Woodview Trace Suite 100	Indianapolis	IN	46268	**800-722-1599**	317-227-6700	178
Techalloy Co Inc 370 Franklin Tpke	Mahwah	NJ	07430	**800-882-1006**	201-529-0900	800
Techalloy Co Inc Baltimore Wire Div 2310 Chesapeake Ave	Baltimore	MD	21222	**800-638-1458**	410-633-9300	800
Teche Holding Co 211 Willow St *AMEX: TSH*	Franklin	LA	70538	**800-256-1500**	337-828-3212	355-2
Techline USA LLC 500 S Division St	Waunakee	WI	53597	**800-356-8400**		314-1
Techmar Communications Inc 45 Dan Rd	Canton	MA	02021	**800-832-4627**	781-821-8324	455
Techne Corp 614 McKinley Pl NE *NASDAQ: TECH*	Minneapolis	MN	55413	**800-328-2400**	612-379-8854	229
Techni-Tool Inc 1547 N Trooper Rd PO Box 1117 *Cust Svc	Worcester	PA	19490	**800-832-4866***	610-941-2400	346
Technibilt Corp PO Box 310 *Cust Svc	Newton	NC	28658	**800-351-2278***	828-464-7388	75
Technical Assn of the Pulp & Paper Industry (TAPPI) 15 Technology Pkwy S *Sales	Norcross	GA	30092	**800-332-8686***	770-446-1400	49-13
Technical Chemical Co 3327 Pipeline Rd	Cleburne	TX	76033	**800-527-0885**	817-645-6088	143
Technical Coatings Laboratory LLC 205 Old Farms Rd	Avon	CT	06001	**800-782-8704**	860-673-3245	540
Technical College of the Lowcountry 921 Ribaut Rd	Beaufort	SC	29901	**800-768-8252**	843-525-8324	787
Technical Consumer Products Inc 300 Lena Dr	Aurora	OH	44202	**800-324-1496**	330-995-6111	429
Technical Education. Association for Career & 1410 King St	Alexandria	VA	22314	**800-826-9972**	703-683-3111	49-5
Technical Information Service. National 5285 Port Royal Rd. *Orders	Springfield	VA	22161	**800-553-6847***	703-605-6000	336-2
Technical & Management Services Corp (TAMSCO) 4041 Powder Mill Rd Suite 700	Calverton	MD	20705	**800-282-6727**	301-595-0710	178
Technical Resource Connection Inc 12320 Racetrack Rd	Tampa	FL	33626	**800-872-2992**	813-891-6084	178
Technical Services Assoc Inc (TSA) 2 Kacey Ct	Mechanicsburg	PA	17055	**800-388-1415**	717-691-5691	176-11
Technical Sourcing International Inc 7168 Expy	Missoula	MT	59808	**877-549-9123**	406-549-9123	470
Technidrill Systems Inc 429 Portage Blvd	Kent	OH	44240	**800-914-5863**	330-724-5516	447
Technisource Inc 2300 Cottondale Ln Suite 250	Little Rock	AR	72202	**877-664-1101**	501-664-1100	707
Technologists. American Society of Radiologic 15000 Central Ave SE	Albuquerque	NM	87123	**800-444-2778**	505-298-4500	49-8
Technology. AeA: Advancing the Business of 5201 Great America Pkwy Suite 520	Santa Clara	CA	95054	**800-284-4232**	408-987-4200	49-4
Technology Assessment. International Center for 660 Pennsylvania Ave SE Suite 302	Washington	DC	20003	**800-600-6664**	202-547-9359	49-19

Name / Address	City	State	ZIP	Toll-Free	Phone	Class
Technology Assn. Business 12411 Wornall Rd	Kansas City	MO	64145	**800-316-9721**	816-941-3100	49-18
Technology. Association for Educational Communications & 1800 N Stonelake Dr Suite 2	Bloomington	IN	47404	**877-677-2328**	812-335-7675	49-5
Technology & Business Integrators 50 Tice Blvd	Woodcliff Lake	NJ	07677	**800-676-9470**	201-573-0400	193
Technology Commercialization. Center for 1400 Computer Dr	Westborough	MA	01581	**800-472-6785**	508-870-0042	654
Technology in Education. International Society for 480 Charnelton St	Eugene	OR	97401	**800-336-5191**	541-302-3777	49-5
Technology Flavors & Fragrances Inc 10 Edison St E *AMEX: TFF*	Amityville	NY	11701	**800-427-3908**	631-842-7600	291-15
Technology Funding Inc 460 St Michael's Dr Suite 1000	Santa Fe	NM	87505	**800-821-5323**	505-982-2200	779
Technology Futures Inc 13740 N Research Blvd Bldg C	Austin	TX	78750	**800-835-3887**	512-258-8898	195
Technology. IEEE Society on Social Implications of IEEE Operations Ctr 445 Hoes Ln	Piscataway	NJ	08854	**800-678-4333**	732-981-0060	49-19
Technology Inc. Public 1301 Pennsylvania Ave NW Suite 800	Washington	DC	20004	**800-852-4934**	202-626-2400	49-7
Technology Innovations Inc 555 E Easy St	Simi Valley	CA	93065	**800-286-0651**	805-426-1000	173
Technology International. Women in 13351 Riverside Dr Suite 441	Sherman Oaks	CA	91423	**800-334-9484**	818-788-9484	49-19
Technology Marketing Corp 1 Technology Plaza *Cust Svc	Norwalk	CT	06854	**800-243-6002***	203-852-6800	623-2
Technology Research Corp 5250 140th Ave N *NASDAQ: TRCI* ■ *Mktg	Clearwater	FL	33760	**800-780-4324***	727-535-0572	803
Technology Society. IEEE Vehicular IEEE Operations Ctr 445 Hoes Ln	Piscataway	NJ	08854	**800-678-4333**	732-981-0060	49-19
Technology Solutions Co (TSC) 205 N Michigan Ave Suite 1500 *NASDAQ: TSCC*	Chicago	IL	60601	**800-819-2250**	312-228-4500	178
Technology Transfer Center. Far West Regional South Hope St Research Annex 3716 Rm 200	Los Angeles	CA	90007	**800-642-2872**	213-743-2353	654
Technology Transfer Center. Mid-Continent Regional 301 Tarrow MS 8000	College Station	TX	77840	**800-472-6785**	979-845-2907	654
Technology Transfer Center. National 316 Washington Ave	Wheeling	WV	26003	**800-678-6882**	304-243-2455	654
Technology Transfer Council. Petroleum 16010 Barkers Point Ln Suite 220	Houston	TX	77079	**888-843-7882**	281-921-1720	48-12
TechnoServe 49 Day St	Norwalk	CT	06854	**800-999-6757**	203-852-0377	48-5
TechSmith Corp 2405 Woodlake Dr	Okemos	MI	48864	**800-517-3001**	517-381-2300	176-8
TechTarget 117 Kendrick St Suite 800	Needham	MA	02111	**888-274-4111**	781-657-1000	623-10
TechTeam Global Inc 27335 W Eleven-Mile Rd *NASDAQ: TEAM*	Southfield	MI	48034	**800-522-4451**	248-357-2866	178
TechWorks 4030 W Braker Ln Suite 120 *Cust Svc	Austin	TX	78759	**800-688-7466***	512-794-8533	613
Tecnica USA 19 Technology Dr	West Lebanon	NH	03784	**800-258-3897**	603-298-8032	701
Tecnico Corp 831 Industrial Ave	Chesapeake	VA	23324	**800-786-2207**	757-545-4013	689
Tecnomatix Technologies Inc 21500 Haggerty Rd Suite 300	Northville	MI	48167	**800-304-8326**	248-699-2500	176-5
Teco Barge Line PO Box 790	Metropolis	IL	62960	**800-455-5731**	618-524-3100	457
Teco Diagnostics 1268 N Lakeview Ave	Anaheim	CA	92807	**800-222-9880**	714-693-7788	229
TECO Ocean Shipping 1300 E 8th Ave Suite F-300	Tampa	FL	33605	**800-835-4161**	813-209-4200	307
Tecom Industries Inc 375 Conejo Ridge Ave	Thousand Oaks	CA	91361	**800-959-0495**	805-267-0100	633
Tecot Electric Supply Co 55 Lukens Dr	New Castle	DE	19720	**800-344-9905**	302-421-3900	245
TECSYS Inc 87 Prince St 5th Fl	Montreal	QC	H3C2M7	**800-922-8649**	514-866-0001	176-1
Tectum Inc 105 S 6th St	Newark	OH	43055	**888-977-9691**	740-345-9691	807
Tecumseh Corrugated Box Co 707 S Evans	Tecumseh	MI	49286	**800-837-8374**	517-423-2126	101
Tecumseh Products Co Engine & Transmission Group 900 North St *Cust Svc	Grafton	WI	53024	**800-477-1277***	262-377-2700	259
Ted PO Box 66100 *Resv	Chicago	IL	60666	**800-225-5833***	877-228-1327	26
Teddy Bear Museum 2511 Pine Ridge Rd	Naples	FL	34109	**866-365-2327**	239-598-2711	509
Teel Plastics Inc 426 Hitchcock St	Baraboo	WI	53913	**800-322-8335**	608-355-3080	585
Teen People Magazine 1271 6th Ave Time & Life Bldg	New York	NY	10020	**800-284-0200**	212-522-1212	449-6
Teeter Irrigation Inc 2295 S Old Hwy 83	Garden City	KS	67846	**800-834-7481**	620-276-8257	270
Tefron USA Inc 201 St Germain Ave SW	Valdese	NC	28690	**800-554-5541**	828-879-6500	153-10
TEGAM Inc 10 Tegam Way	Geneva	OH	44041	**800-666-1010**	440-466-6100	247
Tehachapi (Greater) Chamber of Commerce PO Box 401	Tehachapi	CA	93581	**866-822-4180**	661-822-4180	137
Teikyo Post University 800 Country Club Rd	Waterbury	CT	06723	**800-345-2562**	203-596-4500	163
Tejas Warehouse System 324 Pleasant St	Waco	TX	76704	**800-535-9786**	254-752-9241	790-1
Tekelec 26580 W Agoura Rd *NASDAQ: TKLC*	Calabasas	CA	91302	**800-835-3532**	818-880-5656	720
Teknor Apex Co 505 Central Ave	Pawtucket	RI	02861	**800-556-3864**	401-725-8000	594-3
Teknowledge Corp 1800 Embarcadero Rd *NASDAQ: TEKC*	Palo Alto	CA	94303	**800-285-0500**	650-424-0500	176-7
TEKPAK Inc 1410 S Washington St	Marion	AL	36756	**800-876-8841**	334-683-6121	125
Tekra Corp 16700 W Lincoln Ave	New Berlin	WI	53151	**800-448-3572**	262-784-5533	592
Tektronix Inc 14200 SW Karl Braun Dr PO Box 500 *NYSE: TEK*	Beaverton	OR	97077	**800-833-9200**	503-627-7111	247
Tel Electronics Inc 705 E Main St	American Fork	UT	84003	**800-564-9424**	801-756-9606	720
Telair International Inc 4175 Guardian St	Simi Valley	CA	93063	**800-989-4827**	805-306-8066	519
Telarc International Corp 23307 Commerce Pk Rd	Cleveland	OH	44122	**800-801-5810**	216-464-2313	643
Telco Systems Inc 2 Hampshire St Suite 3A	Foxboro	MA	02035	**800-221-2849**	781-551-0300	720
Telcordia Technologies Inc 1 Telcordia Dr *Sales	Piscataway	NJ	08854	**800-521-2673***	732-699-2000	176-10
TelCove 712 N Main St	Coudersport	PA	16915	**866-835-2683**	814-260-2000	721
Tele-Serve 409 Main St *Cust Svc	Eau Claire	WI	54701	**800-428-8159***	715-834-3442	723
Tele-Track 155 Technology Pkwy Suite 800	Norcross	GA	30092	**800-729-6981**	770-449-8809	212
Telebyte Inc 270 Pulaski Rd	Greenlawn	NY	11740	**800-835-3298**	631-423-3232	174
TeleCheck International Inc 5251 Westheimer Rd	Houston	TX	77056	**800-835-3243**	713-331-7600	139
Teleco Inc 430 Woodruff Rd Suite 300	Greenville	SC	29607	**800-800-6159**	864-297-4400	245
TeleCommunication Systems Inc 275 West St Suite 400 *NASDAQ: TSYS*	Annapolis	MD	21401	**800-810-0827**	410-263-7616	222
Telecommunications Assn Inc. Industrial 1110 N Glebe Rd Suite 500	Arlington	VA	22201	**800-482-8282**	703-528-5115	49-20
Telecommunications Consultants. Society of PO Box 416	Fall River Mills	CA	96028	**800-782-7670**	530-336-7070	49-20
Telecommunications Engineers. National Assn of Radio & 167 Village St	Medway	MA	02053	**800-896-2783**	508-533-8333	49-19
Telecommunications Engineers. Society of Cable 140 Philips Rd	Exton	PA	19341	**800-542-5040**	610-363-6888	49-19
Telecommunications Industry Assn (TIA) 2500 Wilson Blvd Suite 300	Arlington	VA	22201	**800-799-6682**	703-907-7700	49-20
Telecommunications Magazine 685 Canton St	Norwood	MA	02062	**800-225-9978**	781-769-9750	449-21
Telecommunications Report 7201 McKinney Cir *Cust Svc	Frederick	MD	21704	**800-822-6338***	301-698-7100	521-11
Telect Inc 2111 N Molter Rd	Liberty Lake	WA	99019	**800-551-4567**	509-926-6000	720
Teledyne Advanced Pollution Instrumentation 6565 Nancy Ridge Dr	San Diego	CA	92121	**800-324-5190**	858-657-9800	200
Teledyne Brown Engineering PO Box 070007	Huntsville	AL	35807	**800-933-2091**	256-726-1000	258
Teledyne Brown Engineering Environmental Services PO Box 070007	Huntsville	AL	35807	**800-933-2091**	256-726-1000	728
Teledyne Monitor Labs 35 Inverness Dr E	Englewood	CO	80112	**800-422-1499**	303-792-3300	200
Teleflex Fluid Systems Inc One Firestone Dr	Suffield	CT	06078	**800-225-9077**	860-668-1285	777
Teleflex Medical Group 2917 Weck Dr	Research Triangle Park	NC	27709	**800-334-9751**	919-544-8000	468
TeleflexGFI Control Systems LP 100 Hollinger Crescent	Kitchener	ON	N2K2Z3	**800-667-4275**	519-576-4270	60
Teleflora Inc 11444 W Olympic Blvd 4th Fl	Los Angeles	CA	90064	**800-321-2654**	310-231-9199	289
Telefonica Data USA 1221 Brickell Ave Suite 600 *NYSE: TEF*	Miami	FL	33131	**866-839-0926**	305-925-5473	721
Telegenix Inc 1930 Olney Ave Bldg 32	Cherry Hill	NJ	08034	**800-424-5220**	856-424-5220	720
Teleglobe International Holdings Ltd 1000 de la Gauchetiere St W *NASDAQ: TLGB*	Montreal	QC	H3B4X5	**800-465-7551**	514-868-7272	387
Telegram & Gazette 20 Franklin St PO Box 15012	Worcester	MA	01615	**800-678-6680**	508-793-9100	522-2
Telegraph The PO Box 278	Alton	IL	62002	**800-477-1447**	618-463-2500	522-2
Telegraph-Forum 119 W Rensselaer St	Bucyrus	OH	44820	**877-838-6329**	419-562-3333	522-2
Telegraph Herald 801 Bluff St	Dubuque	IA	52001	**800-553-4801**	563-588-5611	522-2
Telelatino Network Inc (TLN) 5125 Steeles Ave W	Toronto	ON	M9L1R5	**800-551-8401**	416-744-8200	725
Telelogic North America Inc 9401 Jeronimo Rd *Sales	Irvine	CA	92618	**877-275-4777***	949-830-8022	176-1
Telemarketing Co DBA TTC Marketing Solutions 3945 N Neenah Ave	Chicago	IL	60634	**800-777-6340**	773-545-0407	722
Telemarketing Concepts 80 Triangle Ctr	Yorktown Heights	NY	10598	**800-666-0858**	914-245-0701	722
Telemechanics Inc 6791-A Whitfield Industrial Ave	Sarasota	FL	34243	**800-227-7485**	941-751-3452	173
Telemundo Communications Group Inc 2290 W 8th Ave	Hialeah	FL	33010	**800-688-8851**	305-884-8200	724
TeleNational Marketing 2918 N 72nd St *Cust Svc	Omaha	NE	68134	**800-333-6106***	402-548-1100	722
Teleperformance USA 200 N 2200 W	Salt Lake City	UT	84116	**800-938-7872**	801-359-6843	722
Telephonics Corp 815 Broad Hollow Rd	Farmingdale	NY	11735	**877-755-7700**	631-755-7000	633
Telephony Magazine 330 N Wabash Ave Suite 2300	Chicago	IL	60611	**800-458-0479**	312-595-1080	449-21
Telerx 723 Dresher Rd	Horsham	PA	19044	**800-283-5379**	215-347-5700	722
Telesensory Inc 520 Almanor Ave *Cust Svc	Sunnyvale	CA	94085	**800-804-8004***	408-616-8700	176-12
TeleServices Direct 6050 Corporate Way	Indianapolis	IN	46278	**800-736-6072**	317-216-2240	722
TeleSight Inc 820 N Franklin St	Chicago	IL	60610	**800-608-3651**	312-640-2532	458
Telesis Technologies Inc 740 Welch Rd *Sales	Commerce Township	MI	48390	**800-654-5696***	248-624-4249	459
Telesource Div Career Blazers Inc 222 W Las Colinas Blvd Suite 1250E	Irving	TX	75039	**800-787-6750**	214-296-6700	707
TeleSpectrum Worldwide Inc 443 S Gulph Rd	King of Prussia	PA	19406	**888-878-7400**	610-878-7400	722

Name / Address	City	State	ZIP	Toll-Free	Phone	Class
TeleSystems Marketing Inc 3600 S Gessner St Suite 259	Houston	TX	77063	**800-622-0190**	713-784-3439	722
TeleTech Holdings Inc 9197 S Peoria St *NASDAQ: TTEC*	Englewood	CO	80112	**800-835-3832**	303-397-8100	722
Teletouch Communications Inc 1913 Deerbrook Dr	Tyler	TX	75703	**888-800-0232**	903-595-8889	721
Television Cooperative Inc. National Cable 11200 Corporate Ave	Lenexa	KS	66219	**800-825-0357**	913-599-5900	49-14
Television News Directors Assn. Radio- 1600 K St NW Suite 700	Washington	DC	20006	**800-807-8632**	202-659-6510	49-14
Telex Communications Inc 12000 Portland Ave S *Sales	Burnsville	MN	55337	**800-828-6107***	952-884-4051	52
Telfer Oil Co 211 Foster St	Martinez	CA	94553	**800-624-9917**	925-228-1515	769
Telford Aviation Inc 154 Maine St	Bangor	ME	04401	**800-639-4809**	207-262-6098	63
Teligent Inc PO Box 341210	Bethesda	MD	20827	**888-411-1175**		721
Telkonet Inc 20374 Seneca Meadows Pkwy *AMEX: TKO*	Germantown	MD	20876	**866-375-8446**	240-912-1800	174
Tellme Networks Inc 1310 Villa St	Mountain View	CA	94041	**800-555-8355**	650-930-9000	606
Telogy 3200 Whipple Rd	Union City	CA	94587	**800-835-6494**	510-675-9500	261-4
Telonic Berkeley Inc 2825 Laguna Canyon Rd	Laguna Beach	CA	92651	**800-854-2436**	949-494-9401	252
Telpar Inc 1550 Lakeway Dr Suite 500	Lewisville	TX	75057	**800-872-4886**	972-420-4700	171-6
Telrad Connegy Inc 10 Executive Blvd *Cust Svc	Farmingdale	NY	11735	**800-628-3038***	631-420-8800	720
Telsco Industries Inc Weathermatic 3301 W Kingsley Rd	Garland	TX	75041	**888-484-3776**	972-278-6131	420
Telsmith Inc 10910 N Industrial Dr	Mequon	WI	53092	**800-765-6601**	262-242-6600	189
Telstra Inc 575 5th Ave 39th Fl	New York	NY	10017	**877-835-7872**	212-231-7744	721
Teltone Corp PO Box 945	Bothell	WA	98041	**800-426-3926**	425-487-1515	720
Teltronics Inc 2150 Whitfield Industrial Way	Sarasota	FL	34243	**800-486-7685**	941-753-5000	720
Telum International Corp 175 Commerce Valley Dr W Suite 230	Woodbridge	ON	L3T3A2	**888-278-9211**	905-882-4784	176-10
TELUS Corp 3777 Kingsway Ave *NYSE: TU*	Burnaby	BC	V5H3Z7	**888-811-2323**	604-432-2151	721
Telwares Inc 4471 Legendary Dr Suite 100	Destin	FL	32541	**888-835-9273**	850-650-9800	195
Temecula Creek Inn 44501 Rainbow Canyon Rd	Temecula	CA	92592	**800-962-7335**	951-694-1000	655
Temo Sunrooms Inc 20400 Hall Rd	Clinton Township	MI	48038	**800-344-8366**	586-286-0410	106
Tempco Electric Heater Mfg 607 N Central Ave	Wood Dale	IL	60191	**800-323-6859**	630-350-2252	313
Tempe Convention & Visitors Bureau 51 W 3rd St Suite 105	Tempe	AZ	85281	**800-283-6734**	480-894-8158	205
Tempe Mission Palms Hotel & Conference Center 60 E 5th St	Tempe	AZ	85281	**800-547-8705**	480-894-1400	370
Tempel Steel Co 5500 N Wolcott Ave	Chicago	IL	60640	**800-621-7700**	773-250-8000	709
Temperature Systems Inc 5001 Voges Rd	Madison	WI	53718	**800-366-0930**	608-271-7500	601
Temple Chamber of Commerce 2 N 5th St	Temple	TX	76501	**800-374-9123**	254-773-2105	137
Temple College 2600 S 1st St	Temple	TX	76504	**800-460-4636**	254-298-8300	160
Temple Daily Telegram PO Box 6114	Temple	TX	76503	**800-460-6397**	254-778-4444	522-2
Temple-Inland Financial Services Inc 1300 S Mopac Expy	Austin	TX	78746	**800-964-9420**	512-434-8000	355-2
Temple-Inland Forest Products Corp 303 S Temple Dr	Diboll	TX	75941	**800-262-5512**	936-829-5511	807
Temple-Inland Inc 1300 S Mopac Expy *NYSE: TIN*	Austin	TX	78746	**800-826-8807**	512-434-8000	184
Temple Square 50 W North Temple St	Salt Lake City	UT	84150	**800-453-3860**	801-240-1245	50
Temple University Press 1601 N Broad St USB 305	Philadelphia	PA	19122	**800-447-1656**	215-204-8787	623-5
Templin's Resort on the River. Red Lion 414 E 1st Ave	Post Falls	ID	83854	**800-733-5466**	208-773-1611	655
Tempo Research Corp 1390 Aspen Way	Vista	CA	92083	**888-860-8535**	760-598-8900	252
Temporary Solutions Inc 10515 Crestwood Dr	Manassas	VA	20109	**888-874-5627**	703-368-3800	707
Temporary VIP Suites 43000 W Nine-Mile Rd Suite 305	Novi	MI	48375	**888-847-7848**	248-347-1551	209
Temptronic Corp 4 Commercial St *Cust Svc	Sharon	MA	02067	**800-558-5080***	781-688-2300	410
Tempus Resorts International 7380 Sand Lake Rd Suite 600	Orlando	FL	32819	**800-463-7256**	407-226-1000	738
Ten Cate Nicolon USA 365 S Holland Dr	Pendergrass	GA	30567	**888-795-0808**	706-693-2226	730-3
Ten Speed Press PO Box 7123	Berkeley	CA	94707	**800-841-2665**	510-559-1600	623-2
Ten-Tec Inc 1185 Dolly Parton Pkwy *Cust Svc	Sevierville	TN	37862	**800-833-7373***	865-453-7172	633
Ten United Pittsburgh 420 Fort Duquesne Blvd Suite 1900 1Gateway Ctr	Pittsburgh	PA	15222	**800-937-3657**	412-471-5300	4
Tender Loving Care Staff Builders 1983 Marcus Ave Suite 200	Lake Success	NY	11042	**800-444-4633**	516-358-1000	358
Tenebril Inc 75 Federal St 6th Fl	Boston	MA	02110	**800-790-9060**	617-912-6600	176-12
Tenenbaum's Vacation Stores Inc 300 Market St	Kingston	PA	18704	**800-545-7099**	570-288-8747	760
Tenera Inc 100 Bush St Suite 850	San Francisco	CA	94104	**800-447-9388**	415-445-3200	193
TenFold Corp 698 W 10000 S Suite 200	South Jordan	UT	84095	**800-836-3653**	801-495-1010	176-1
Tenke Mining Corp 885 W Georgia St Suite 2101 *TSE: TNK*	Vancouver	BC	V6C3E8	**888-689-7842**	604-689-7842	492
Tennant Co 701 N Lilac Dr *NYSE: TNC* ■ *Cust Svc	Minneapolis	MN	55422	**800-553-8033***	763-540-1200	379
Tenneco Automotive Inc 500 N Field Dr *NYSE: TEN*	Lake Forest	IL	60045	**800-777-9564**	847-482-5000	60
Tennessean 1100 Broadway	Nashville	TN	37203	**800-342-8237**	615-259-8800	522-2
Tennessee						
Baccalaureate Education System Trust (BEST) PO Box 198786	Nashville	TN	37219	**888-486-2378**	615-532-8056	711
Child Support Services Div 400 Deaderick St 12th Fl	Nashville	TN	37248	**800-838-6911**	615-313-4880	335
Mental Health & Developmental Disabilities Dept 425 5th Ave N 3rd Fl	Nashville	TN	37243	**800-669-1851**	615-532-6500	335
Real Estate Commission 500 James Robertson Pkwy Suite 180	Nashville	TN	37243	**800-342-4031**	615-741-2273	335
State Parks Div 401 Church St 7th Fl	Nashville	TN	37243	**888-867-2757**	615-532-0001	335
Student Assistance Corp 404 James Robertson Pkwy Suite 1950	Nashville	TN	37243	**800-257-6526**	615-741-1346	711
Tennessee Aquarium 1 Broad St	Chattanooga	TN	37401	**800-262-0695**	423-265-0695	40
Tennessee Bar Assn 221 4th Ave N Suite 400	Nashville	TN	37219	**800-899-6993**	615-383-7421	73
Tennessee Fitness Spa 299 Natural Bridge Pk Rd	Waynesboro	TN	38485	**800-235-8365**	931-722-5589	697
Tennessee Florist Supply Inc 2713 John Deere Dr	Knoxville	TN	37917	**800-951-7451**	865-524-7451	288
Tennessee Mat Co Inc 1414 4th Ave S	Nashville	TN	37210	**800-264-3030**	615-254-8381	663
Tennessee Medical Assn 2301 21st Ave A	Nashville	TN	37212	**800-659-1862**	615-385-2100	466
Tennessee Rehabilitative Initiative in Correction (TRICOR) 240 Great Circle Rd Suite 310	Nashville	TN	37228	**800-958-7426**	615-741-5705	618
Tennessee State Museum 505 Deaderick St	Nashville	TN	37243	**800-407-4324**	615-741-2692	509
Tennessee State University 3500 John A Merritt Blvd PO Box 9609 *Admissions	Nashville	TN	37209	**888-463-6878***	615-963-5000	163
Tennessee Technological University PO Box 5006	Cookeville	TN	38505	**800-255-8881**	931-372-3101	163
Tennessee Temple University 1815 Union Ave	Chattanooga	TN	37404	**800-553-4050**	423-493-4100	163
Tennessee Valley Electric Co-op 515 Florence Rd	Savannah	TN	38372	**866-925-4916**	731-925-4916	244
Tennessee Valley Printing Co Inc PO Box 2213	Decatur	AL	35609	**888-353-4612**	256-353-4612	623-8
Tennessee Veterinary Medical Assn 618 Church St Suite 220	Nashville	TN	37219	**800-697-3587**	615-254-3687	782
Tennessee Walking Horse Breeders' & Exhibitors' Assn (TWHBEA) PO Box 286	Lewisburg	TN	37091	**800-359-1574**	931-359-1574	48-3
Tennessee Wesleyan College PO Box 40	Athens	TN	37371	**800-742-5892**	423-745-7504	163
Tennessee/DCI Donor Services 1714 Hayes St	Nashville	TN	37203	**800-969-4438**	615-234-5200	535
Tennis Assn. US 70 W Red Oak Ln	White Plains	NY	10604	**800-990-8782**	914-696-7000	48-22
Tennis Assn. US Professional 3535 Briarpark Dr Suite 1	Houston	TX	77042	**800-877-8248**	713-978-7782	48-22
Tennis Hall of Fame & Museum. International 194 Bellevue Ave	Newport	RI	02840	**800-457-1144**	401-849-3990	511
Tennis Registry. Professional PO Box 4739	Hilton Head Island	SC	29938	**800-421-6289**	843-785-7244	48-22
Tennsco Corp 201 Tennsco Dr PO Box 1888 *Cust Svc	Dickson	TN	37056	**800-251-8184***	615-446-8000	314-1
Tension Envelope Corp 819 E 19th St	Kansas City	MO	64108	**800-388-5122**	816-471-3800	260
Tensolite Co 100 Tensolite Dr	Saint Augustine	FL	32092	**800-458-9960**	904-829-5600	801
Tensor Corp 285 Commandants Way Suite 10	Chelsea	MA	02150	**800-872-5267**	617-884-7744	431
TEOCO Corp 12701 Fair Lakes Cir Suite 350	Fairfax	VA	22033	**888-868-3626**	703-322-9200	779
TEPPCO (Texas Eastern Products Pipeline Co) 2929 Allen Pkwy	Houston	TX	77019	**800-877-3636**	713-759-3636	586
TEPPCO Partners LP 2929 Allen Pkwy *NYSE: TPP*	Houston	TX	77019	**800-877-3636**	713-759-3636	320
Terabeam Wireless 8000 Lee Hwy	Falls Church	VA	22042	**888-297-9090**	703-205-0600	720
Terasen Inc 1111 W Georgia St *TSE: TER*	Vancouver	BC	V6E4M4	**800-224-9376**	604-576-7000	774
Terayon Communication Systems Inc 4988 Great America Pkwy *NASDAQ: TERN*	Santa Clara	CA	95054	**888-783-7296**	408-235-5500	496
Teresi Trucking Inc PO Box 1270	Lodi	CA	95241	**800-692-3431**	209-368-2472	769
Terex Corp Crane Div 202 Raleigh St	Wilmington	NC	28412	**800-250-2726**	910-395-8500	462
Terex Corp Load King Div 701 E Rose St PO Box 427	Elk Point	SD	57025	**800-264-5522**	605-356-3301	768
Terlato Wine Group 900 Armour Dr	Lake Bluff	IL	60044	**800-950-7676**	847-604-8900	82-3
Term Limits Foundation. US 240 Waukegan Rd Suite 200	Glenview	IL	60025	**800-733-6440**	202-379-3000	48-7
Terminix International Co 860 Ridge Lake Blvd	Memphis	TN	38120	**800-654-7848**	901-766-1333	567
Terner's of Miami Inc 3050 NW 40th St	Miami	FL	33142	**800-662-4395**	305-638-7778	422
Terra Community College 2830 Napoleon Rd	Fremont	OH	43420	**800-334-3886**	419-334-8400	160
Terra Entertainment 12335 Santa Monica Blvd Suite 336	Los Angeles	CA	90025	**877-788-3772**	310-268-1210	500
Terra Tek Inc 400 Wakara Way	Salt Lake City	UT	84108	**800-372-2522**	801-584-2400	728
Terra Universal Inc 165 Freedom Ave	Anaheim	CA	92801	**800-767-0100**	714-526-0100	19
Terraces of Phoenix 7550 N 16th St	Phoenix	AZ	85020	**877-279-6207**	602-944-4455	659
Terre Haute Convention & Visitors Bureau 643 Wabash Ave	Terre Haute	IN	47807	**800-366-3043**	812-234-5555	205
Terre Haute First National Bank 1 First Financial Plaza	Terre Haute	IN	47807	**800-511-0045**	812-238-6000	71
Terre Haute Regional Hospital 3901 S 7th St	Terre Haute	IN	47802	**800-678-8474**	812-232-0021	366-2

				Toll-Free	Phone	Class
Terrebonne General Medical Center						
8166 Main St	Houma	LA	70360	**800-456-9121**	985-873-4141	366-2
Terrian Transportation Inc DBA King Ward Coach Lines 110 N Bridge St	Holyoke	MA	01040	**800-639-4805**	413-539-5858	108
Terry-Durin Co 409 7th Ave SE	Cedar Rapids	IA	52401	**800-332-8114**	319-364-4106	245
Terry Laboratories Inc						
390 N Wickham Rd Suite F	Melbourne	FL	32935	**800-367-2563**	321-259-1630	470
Terry Newspapers Inc 108 W 1st St	Geneseo	IL	61254	**888-422-3837**	309-944-2119	623-8
Terry Precision Bicycles for Women Inc						
1657 E Park Dr	Macedon	NY	14502	**800-289-8379***	315-986-2103	83
*Orders						
Terryberry Co						
2033 Oak Industrial Dr NE	Grand Rapids	MI	49505	**800-253-0882**	616-458-1391	401
Terry's Tire Town Inc						
2360 W Main St	Alliance	OH	44601	**800-235-2921**	330-821-5022	740
Terumo Cardiovascular Systems Corp						
6200 Jackson Rd	Ann Arbor	MI	48103	**800-262-3304**	734-663-4145	468
Terumo Medical Corp						
2101 Cottontail Ln	Somerset	NJ	08873	**800-283-7866**	732-302-4900	468
Terwilliger Plaza						
2545 SW Terwilliger Blvd	Portland	OR	97201	**800-875-4211**	503-226-4911	659
Tesa Tape Inc 5825 Carnegie Blvd	Charlotte	NC	28209	**800-873-8825**	704-554-0707	717
Tesco Williamsen Inc						
1925 W Indiana Ave	Salt Lake City	UT	84104	**800-828-9847**	801-973-9400	505
Tescom Corp 12616 Industrial Blvd	Elk River	MN	55330	**800-447-1204**	763-241-3349	200
Tesko Welding & Mfg Co						
7350 W Montrose Ave	Norridge	IL	60706	**800-621-4514**	708-452-0045	281
Tesoro Alaska Petroleum Co						
2700 Gambell St Suite 500	Anchorage	AK	99503	**800-478-4447**	907-561-5521	570
Tesoro Refining & Marketing Co						
3450 S 344th Way Suite 201	Auburn	WA	98001	**800-473-1123**	253-896-8700	569
TESSCO Technologies Inc						
11126 McCormick Rd	Hunt Valley	MD	21031	**800-472-7373**	410-229-1000	245
NASDAQ: TESS						
Test Automation & Controls						
1036 Destrehan Ave	Harvey	LA	70058	**800-861-6792**	504-371-3000	200
Test Publishers, Association of						
1201 Pennsylvania Ave						
Suite 300	Washington	DC	20004	**866-240-7909**		49-5
Testa Communications						
25 Willowdale Ave	Port Washington	NY	11050	**800-937-7678**	516-767-2500	623-9
TestAmerica Inc 122 Lyman St	Asheville	NC	28801	**800-344-5759**	828-258-3746	728
Testing Inc, American Society for Nondestructive 1711 Arlingate Ln	Columbus	OH	43228	**800-222-2768***	614-274-6003	49-19
*Orders						
Testing Machines Inc						
2 Fleetwood Ct	Ronkonkoma	NY	11749	**800-678-3221**	631-439-5400	464
Testor Corp 440 Blackhawk Park Ave	Rockford	IL	61104	**800-962-3741**	815-962-6654	750
Testwell Laboratories Inc						
47 Hudson St	Ossining	NY	10562	**800-444-9013**	914-762-9000	258
Teters Floral Products Inc						
1425 S Lillian Ave	Bolivar	MO	65613	**800-999-5996**	417-326-7654	288
Teton Pines Resort & Country Club						
3450 N Clubhouse Dr	Wilson	WY	83014	**800-238-2223**	307-733-1005	655
Tetra Holdings US Inc						
3001 Commerce St	Blacksburg	VA	24060	**800-526-0650**	540-951-5400	568
Tetra Medical Supply Corp						
6364 W Gross Pt Rd	Niles	IL	60714	**800-621-4041***	847-647-0590	467
*Cust Svc						
Tetra Pak Inc						
101 Corporate Woods Pkwy	Vernon Hills	IL	60061	**800-358-3872**	847-955-6000	102
Tetra Tech FW Inc						
1000 The American Rd	Morris Plains	NJ	07950	**800-580-3765**	973-630-8000	258
TETRA Technologies Inc						
25025 I-45 N	The Woodlands	TX	77380	**800-327-7817**	281-367-1983	141
NYSE: TTI						
Tetrahedron Assoc Inc						
PO Box 710157	San Diego	CA	92171	**800-958-3872**	619-661-0552	448
Teufel Nursery Inc						
12345 NW Barnes Rd	Portland	OR	97229	**800-483-8335**	503-646-1111	288
Teufel Nursery Inc Landscape Div						
12345 NW Barnes Rd	Portland	OR	97229	**800-483-8335**	503-646-1111	421
Teva Pharmaceutical USA						
1090 Horsham Rd	North Wales	PA	19454	**800-545-8800**	215-591-3000	573
NASDAQ: TEVA						
Teva Sport Sandals PO Box 968	Flagstaff	AZ	86002	**800-367-8382***	928-779-5938	296
*Orders						
Tex Shoemaker & Son Inc						
714 W Cienega Ave	San Dimas	CA	91773	**800-345-9959**	909-592-2071	423
Tex Tan Western Leather Co						
808 S US Hwy 77A	Yoakum	TX	77995	**800-531-3608***	361-293-2314	423
*Cust Svc						
Tex-Tech Industries Inc						
105 N Main St PO Box 8	North Monmouth	ME	04265	**800-441-7089**	207-933-4404	730-3
Texace Corp						
402 W Nueva St PO Box 7429	San Antonio	TX	78207	**800-835-8973**	210-227-7551	153-9
Texacraft Inc 603 SE 14th St	Ocala	FL	34471	**800-231-9790**		314-4
Texans Credit Union						
777 E Campbell Rd	Richardson	TX	75081	**800-843-5295**	972-348-2000	216
Texarkana Chamber of Commerce						
819 State Line Ave	Texarkana	TX	75501	**877-275-5289**	903-792-7191	137
Texarkana Gazette PO Box 621	Texarkana	TX	75504	**800-955-8518**	903-794-3311	522-2
Texas						
Assistive & Rehabilitation Services Dept						
4800 N Lamar Blvd 3rd Fl	Austin	TX	78756	**800-252-5204**	512-377-0500	335
Bill Status						
State Capitol 1100 Congress Ave						
Rm 2N-3	Austin	TX	78711	**877-824-7038**	512-463-2182	425
Child Support Div						
MC 040 PO Box 12017	Austin	TX	78711	**800-252-8014**	512-460-6000	335
Comptroller of Public Accounts						
111 E 17th St	Austin	TX	78774	**800-531-5441**	512-463-4600	335
Consumer Protection Div						
PO Box 12548	Austin	TX	78711	**800-621-0508**	512-463-2185	335
Crime Victims Services Div						
PO Box 12198	Austin	TX	78711	**800-983-9933**	512-936-1200	335
Ethics Commission						
201 E 14th St 10th Fl	Austin	TX	78701	**800-325-8506**	512-463-5800	335

				Toll-Free	Phone	Class
Lottery Commission PO Box 16630	Austin	TX	78761	**800-375-6886**	512-344-5000	443
Parks & Wildlife Dept						
4200 Smith School Rd	Austin	TX	78744	**800-792-1112**	512-389-4800	335
Public Utility Commission						
PO Box 13326	Austin	TX	78711	**888-782-8477**	512-936-7000	335
Tourism Div PO Box 12728	Austin	TX	78711	**800-888-8839**	512-462-9191	335
Vital Statistics Bureau PO Box 12040	Austin	TX	78711	**888-963-7111**		335
Workers Compensation Commission						
7551 Metro Center Dr	Austin	TX	78744	**800-372-7713**	512-804-4000	335
Texas A & M University - Commerce						
PO Box 3011	Commerce	TX	75428	**888-868-2682**	903-886-5081	163
Texas A & M University - Corpus Christi 6300 Ocean Dr	Corpus Christi	TX	78412	**800-482-6822**	361-825-2624	163
Texas A & M University at Galveston						
200 Seawolf Pkwy Bldg 3026	Galveston	TX	77553	**877-322-4443**	409-740-4428	163
Texas A & M University Press						
John H Lindsey Bldg						
4354 TAMUS	College Station	TX	77843	**800-826-8911***	979-845-1436	623-5
*Orders						
Texas Aluminum Industries Inc						
2900 Patio Dr	Houston	TX	77017	**800-231-4009**	713-946-9000	688
Texas Art Supply 2001 Montrose Blvd	Houston	TX	77006	**800-888-9278**	713-526-5221	45
Texas Assn of Business & Chamber of Commerce 1209 Nueces St	Austin	TX	78701	**800-856-6721**	512-477-6721	138
Texas Assn of Realtors						
1115 San Jacinto Blvd Suite 200	Austin	TX	78701	**800-873-9155**	512-480-8200	642
Texas Basket Co 100 Myrtle Dr	Jacksonville	TX	75766	**800-657-2200**	903-586-8014	199
Texas Book Co 8501 Technology Cir	Greenville	TX	75403	**800-527-1016**	903-455-6937	97
Texas Boot Co PO Box 17307	Nashville	TN	37217	**800-628-2668**	615-695-2000	296
Texas Center for Infectious Diseases						
2303 SE Military Dr	San Antonio	TX	78223	**800-839-5864**	210-534-8857	366-5
Texas Children's Hospital						
6621 Fannin St	Houston	TX	77030	**800-364-5437**	832-824-1000	366-1
Texas Christian University						
TCU Box 297013	Fort Worth	TX	76129	**800-828-3764**	817-257-7490	163
Texas Coffee Co Inc PO Box 31	Beaumont	TX	77704	**800-259-3400**	409-835-3434	291-7
Texas Concrete Co 4702 N Vine St	Victoria	TX	77904	**800-242-3511**	361-573-9145	181
Texas Crushed Stone Co						
5300 S IH-35	Georgetown	TX	78628	**800-772-8272**	512-863-5511	493-5
Texas Disposal Systems Inc						
12200 Carl Rd	Creedmoor	TX	78610	**800-375-8375**	512-392-1515	791
Texas Dow Employees Credit Union						
1001 FM 2004	Lake Jackson	TX	77566	**800-839-1154**	979-297-1154	216
Texas Drug Co						
1101 W Vickery Blvd	Fort Worth	TX	76104	**888-378-4668**	817-335-5761	237
Texas Eastern Products Pipeline Co (TEPPCO) 2929 Allen Pkwy	Houston	TX	77019	**800-877-3636**	713-759-3636	586
Texas Farm Products Co						
915 S Fredonia St	Nacogdoches	TX	75961	**800-392-3110**	936-564-3711	568
Texas Fiber-Poly Foam Inc						
1200 Rink St	Brenham	TX	77833	**800-798-6729**	979-836-6625	590
Texas Gas Service Co						
1301 South MoPac Expwy Suite 400	Austin	TX	78746	**800-700-2443**	512-477-5852	774
Texas Granite Div Cold Spring Granite Inc 2400 Hwy 1431 W	Marble Falls	TX	78654	**800-247-2637**	830-693-4316	710
Texas Hospital Insurance Exchange						
6300 La Calma Dr Suite 550	Austin	TX	78752	**800-792-0060**	512-451-5775	384-5
Texas Instruments Inc 12500 TI Blvd	Dallas	TX	75243	**800-336-5236***	972-995-2011	686
NYSE: TXN ■ *Cust Svc						
Texas-Lehigh Cement Co PO Box 610	Buda	TX	78610	**800-388-5408**	512-295-6111	135
Texas Library Assn (TLA)						
3355 Bee Cave Rd Suite 401	Austin	TX	78746	**800-580-2852**	512-328-1518	427
Texas Life Insurance Co PO Box 830	Waco	TX	76703	**800-283-9233**	254-752-6521	384-2
Texas Lime Co PO Box 851	Cleburne	TX	76033	**800-772-8000***	817-641-4433	432
*Orders						
Texas Lutheran University						
1000 W Court St	Seguin	TX	78155	**800-771-8521**	830-372-8000	163
Texas Maritime Museum						
1202 Navigation Cir	Rockport	TX	78382	**866-729-2469**	361-729-1271	509
Texas Meat Purveyor						
4241 Director Dr	San Antonio	TX	78219	**800-552-3234**	210-337-1011	291-26
Texas Medical Assn 401 W 15th St	Austin	TX	78701	**800-880-1300**	512-370-1300	466
Texas Medicine Magazine						
401 W 15th St	Austin	TX	78701	**800-880-1300**	512-370-1300	449-16
Texas Mexican Railway Co						
5810 San Bernardo Ave Suite 350	Laredo	TX	78041	**800-283-9639**	956-728-6700	634
Texas Monthly Magazine 701 Brazos St	Austin	TX	78701	**800-759-2000**	512-320-6900	449-22
Texas Motorplex PO Box 1439	Ennis	TX	75120	**800-668-6775**	972-878-2641	504
Texas-New Mexico Power Co						
4100 International Plaza Tower 2						
9th Fl	Fort Worth	TX	76109	**800-435-2822**	817-731-0099	774
Texas Observer 307 W 7th St	Austin	TX	78701	**800-939-6620**	512-477-0746	522-4
Texas Oil & Chemical Co						
7752 FM 418	Silsbee	TX	77656	**800-324-1123**	409-385-1400	570
Texas Orthopedic Hospital						
7401 S Main St	Houston	TX	77030	**800-678-4501**	713-799-8600	366-5
Texas Pacific Indemnity Co						
15 Mountain View Rd	Warren	NJ	07059	**800-252-4670**	908-903-2000	384-4
Texas Petrochemicals LP						
3 Riverway Suite 1500	Houston	TX	77056	**877-584-3256**	713-627-7474	142
Texas Pipe & Supply Co Inc						
2330 Holmes Rd	Houston	TX	77051	**800-233-8736**	713-799-9235	483
Texas Process Equipment Co						
5880 Bingle Rd	Houston	TX	77092	**800-828-4114**	713-460-5555	378
Texas Public Radio (TPR)						
8401 Datapoint Dr Suite 800	San Antonio	TX	78229	**800-622-8977**	210-614-8977	620
Texas Rangers						
Ameriquest Field in Arlington 1000						
Ballpark Way	Arlington	TX	76011	**888-968-3927**	817-273-5222	703
Texas Refinery Corp						
840 N Main St	Fort Worth	TX	76106	**800-827-0711**	817-332-1161	530
Texas Roadhouse Inc						
6040 Dutchmans Ln Suite 400	Louisville	KY	40205	**800-839-7623**	502-426-9984	657
NASDAQ: TXRH						
Texas Scottish Rite Hospital for Children						
2222 Welborn St	Dallas	TX	75219	**800-421-1121**	214-521-3168	366-1
Texas Southmost College						
80 Fort Brown St	Brownsville	TX	78520	**800-850-0160**	956-544-8200	160

Entry	Toll-Free	Phone	Class
Texas Sports Hall of Fame 1108 S University Parks Dr........... Waco TX 76706	**800-567-9561**	254-756-1633	511
Texas State Aquarium 2710 N Shoreline Blvd........ Corpus Christi TX 78402	**800-477-4853**	361-881-1200	40
Texas. State Bar of 1414 Colorado St....Austin TX 78701	**800-204-2222**	512-463-1463	73
Texas State Technical College			
Harlingen Campus 1902 N Loop 499.............. Harlingen TX 78550	**800-852-8784**	956-364-4000	160
Sweetwater Campus 300 College Dr.............. Sweetwater TX 79556	**800-592-8784**	325-235-7300	787
Waco Campus 3801 Campus Dr....... Waco TX 76705	**800-792-8784**	254-799-3611	787
Texas State University-San Marcos 601 University Dr.............. San Marcos TX 78666	**866-798-2287**	512-245-2111	163
Texas Station Gambling Hall & Hotel 2101 Texas Star Ln... North Las Vegas NV 89032	**800-654-8888***	702-631-1000	133
*Resv			
Texas Tech University PO Box 45005...Lubbock TX 79409	**888-270-3369**	806-742-1480	163
Texas Tech University Press 2903 4th St.....................Lubbock TX 79409	**800-832-4042**	806-742-2982	623-5
Texas Transplant Institute 7700 Floyd Curl Dr.............San Antonio TX 78229	**800-298-7824**	210-575-3817	758
Texas United Corp 4800 San Felipe....Houston TX 77056	**800-554-8658**	713-877-1793	141
Texas United Pipe Inc 11627 N Houston Rosslyn Rd.......Houston TX 77086	**800-966-8741***	281-448-3276	585
*Sales			
Texas Vet Lab Inc 1702 N Bell St... San Angelo TX 76903	**800-284-8403**	325-653-4505	574
Texas Wesleyan University 1201 Wesleyan St...............Fort Worth TX 76105	**800-580-8980**	817-531-4444	163
Texas Wesleyan University School of Law 1515 Commerce St..........Fort Worth TX 76102	**800-733-9529**	817-212-4000	164-1
Texas Woman's University PO Box 425589...................Denton TX 76204	**888-948-9984**	940-898-2000	163
Texmate Inc 995 Park Ctr Dr............Vista CA 92081	**800-839-6283**	760-598-9899	247
TexStyle Inc 5555 Murray Ave Suite A..........Cincinnati OH 45227	**800-875-8001**	513-272-1800	731
Textile Employees. Union of Needletrades Industrial & 275 7th Ave....................New York NY 10001	**800-238-6483**	212-265-7000	405
Textile & Garment Council. UFCW 4207 Lebanon Pike Suite 200..... Hermitage TN 37076	**888-462-4892**	615-889-9221	405
Textile Rental Services Assn (TRSA) 1800 Diagonal Rd Suite 200...... Alexandria VA 22314	**800-868-8772**	703-519-0029	49-4
Textile Rubber & Chemical Co Inc 1300 Tiarco Dr SW................. Dalton GA 30721	**800-727-8453**	706-277-1300	594-3
Textile Service Assn. Uniform & 1300 N 17th St Suite 750......... Arlington VA 22209	**800-486-6745**	703-247-2600	49-4
Textilease Corp 10733 Tucker St......Beltsville MD 20705	**800-299-9708**	301-937-4555	434
Textron Power Transmission 240 E 12th St................ Traverse City MI 49685	**888-994-2663***	231-946-8410	700
*Sales			
Texwood Furniture Corp 1353 W 2nd St..Taylor TX 76574	**888-878-0000**	512-352-3000	314-3
TF Financial Corp 3 Penns Trail...... Newtown PA 18940	**888-918-4473**	215-579-4000	355-2
NASDAQ: THRD			
TFA (Thyroid Foundation of America Inc) 1 Longfellow Pl Suite 1518.......... Boston MA 02114	**800-832-8321**	617-534-1500	48-17
TFH Publications Inc 3rd & Union Aves 1 TFH Plaza...... Neptune NJ 07753	**800-631-2188**	732-988-8400	623-2
TFT (Trees for Tomorrow) 519 Sheridan St E PO Box 609....Eagle River WI 54521	**800-838-9472**	715-479-6456	49-5
TFX Medical Inc 50 Plantation Dr....... Jaffrey NH 03452	**800-548-6600**	603-532-7706	468
TGF Precision Haircutters 8280 Westpark Dr................Houston TX 77063	**800-622-1330**	713-952-8080	79
TGI Friday's Worldwide Inc 4201 Marsh Ln..................Carrollton TX 75007	**800-374-3297**	972-662-5400	657
TGL 300 Wilson Ave................Norwalk CT 06854	**800-587-1584**	203-853-4747	444
TH Properties 345 Main St.........Harleysville PA 19438	**800-225-5847***	215-513-4270	186
*Sales			
Thaddeus Stevens College of Technology 750 E King St.........Lancaster PA 17602	**800-842-3832**	717-299-7701	787
Thai Airways International Cargo 6501 W Imperial Hwy...........Los Angeles CA 90045	**800-426-8678**	310-670-8592	13
Thai Airways International Ltd 222 N Sepulveda Blvd Suite 1950................... El Segundo CA 90245	**800-426-5204**	310-640-0097	26
Thai Airways Royal Orchid Plus 222 N Sepulveda Blvd Suite 1950.................... El Segundo CA 90245	**800-426-5204**		27
Thales ATM 23501 W 84th St........ Shawnee KS 66227	**800-526-3433**	913-422-2600	519
Thales Broadcast & Multimedia Inc 104 Feeding Hills Rd............ Southwick MA 01077	**800-266-9283**	413-569-0116	633
Thales Communications Inc 22605 Gateway Center Dr........ Clarksburg MD 20871	**800-258-4420**	240-864-7000	633
Thales e-Security Inc 2200 N Commerce Pkwy Suite 200....Weston FL 33326	**888-744-4976**	954-888-6200	176-12
Thalner Electronics Laboratory Inc 7235 Jackson Rd............... Ann Arbor MI 48103	**800-686-7235**	734-761-4506	245
Tharco Inc 2222 Grant Ave........San Lorenzo CA 94580	**800-772-2332**	510-276-8600	101
Thatcher Co PO Box 27407.......Salt Lake City UT 84127	**800-348-0034**	801-972-4587	143
Thatcher Tubes LLC 1005 Courtaulds Dr.............Woodstock IL 60098	**888-842-8243**	815-334-1200	589
Thayer Hotel 674 Thayer Rd........West Point NY 10996	**800-247-5047**	845-446-4731	373
Thayer Scale Corp 91 Schoosett St...Pembroke MA 02359	**800-225-0450**	781-826-8101	672
The Plaza 5th Ave & Central Park S...New York NY 10019	**800-759-3000**	212-759-3000	373
The Registry at Info Avenue LLC PO Box 698.....................Fort Mill SC 29716	**800-950-4726**	803-802-4600	389
Theatre. American Assn of Community 8402 BriarWood Cir............. Lago Vista TX 78645	**866-687-2228**	512-267-0711	48-4
Theatre Under the Stars 800 Bagby Suite 200..............Houston TX 77002	**800-678-5440**	713-558-2600	563-4
Theatrical Stage Employees Moving Picture Technicians. International Alliance of 1430 Broadway 20th Fl...........New York NY 10018	**800-223-6872**	212-730-1770	405
Thebault LP Co 249 Pomeroy Rd PO Box 169.....Parsippany NJ 07054	**800-843-2285**	973-884-1300	615
Theda Care at Home 201 E Bell St......Neenah WI 54956	**800-984-5554**	920-969-0919	365
Theda Clark Medical Center 130 2nd St.......................Neenah WI 54956	**800-236-3122**	920-729-3100	366-2

Entry	Toll-Free	Phone	Class
Thelen Sand & Gravel Inc 28955 W SR-173..................Antioch IL 60002	**800-537-2324**	847-395-3313	493-4
Theodore Francis Green State Airport (PVD).........................Warwick RI 02886	**888-268-7222**	401-737-4000	28
Theological Library Assn. American 250 S Wacker Dr Suite 1600........ Chicago IL 60606	**888-665-2852**	312-454-5100	48-20
Ther-A-Pedic Midwest Inc 2350 5th St.................. Rock Island IL 61201	**800-322-1054**	309-788-0401	463
Theragenics Corp 5203 Bristol Industrial Way.......... Buford GA 30518	**800-458-4372**	770-271-0233	229
NYSE: TGX			
Therapy Assn. American Physical 1111 N Fairfax St............... Alexandria VA 22314	**800-999-2782**	703-684-2782	49-8
Therapy Assn. American Polarity PO Box 19858................... Boulder CO 80308	**800-359-5620**	303-545-2080	48-17
Theriault's PO Box 151.............Annapolis MD 21404	**800-966-3655**	410-224-3655	51
Therics Inc 115 Campus Dr......... Princeton NJ 08540	**888-784-3742**	609-514-7200	86
Therma-Tru Corp 1687 Woodlands Dr...Maumee OH 43537	**800-537-8827**	419-891-7400	232
Therma-Wave Inc 1250 Reliance Way... Fremont CA 94539	**800-238-4376**	510-668-2200	247
NASDAQ: TWAV			
Thermador 5551 McFadden Ave....... Huntington Beach CA 92649	**800-735-4328**	714-901-6600	36
Thermafiber Inc 3711 W Mill St........ Wabash IN 46992	**888-834-2371**	260-563-2111	382
Thermagon Inc 4707 Detroit Ave...... Cleveland OH 44102	**888-246-9050**	216-939-2300	594-2
Thermal Circuits Inc 1 Technology Way...Salem MA 01970	**800-808-4328**	978-745-1162	313
Thermal Dynamics Corp 82 Benning St............... West Lebanon NH 03784	**800-752-7621**	603-298-5711	447
Thermal Engineering Corp 2741 The Boulevard.............. Columbia SC 29209	**800-331-0097**	803-783-0750	313
Thermal Industries Inc 301 Brushton Ave............... Pittsburgh PA 15221	**800-245-1540**	412-244-6400	233
Thermasys Heat Transfer 2760 Gunter Park Dr W........ Montgomery AL 36109	**800-233-3201**	334-277-1810	92
Thermo CRS 5344 John Lucas Dr.... Burlington ON L7L6A6	**800-365-7587**	905-332-2000	176-12
Thermo Electric Co Inc 109 N 5th St................. Saddle Brook NJ 07663	**800-766-4020***	201-843-5800	200
*Sales			
Thermo Electron Corp 81 Wyman St PO Box 9056.........Waltham MA 02454	**800-678-5599**	781-622-1000	464
NYSE: TMO			
Thermo Elemental 27 Forge Pkwy...... Franklin MA 02038	**800-229-4087**	508-520-1880	410
Thermo Environmental Instruments Inc 27 Forge Pkwy.................. Franklin MA 02038	**866-282-0430**	508-520-0430	200
Thermo Finnigan 355 River Oaks Pkwy............. San Jose CA 95134	**800-456-4552**	408-965-6000	410
Thermo Flow Automation 9303 W Sam Houston Pkwy S....... Houston TX 77099	**800-437-7979**	713-272-0404	200
Thermo Forma 401 Millcreek Rd....... Marietta OH 45750	**800-848-3080**	740-373-4763	411
Thermo LabSystems 100 Cummings Ctr Suite 407J........Beverly MA 01915	**888-888-8173**	978-524-1400	410
Thermo Mattson 5225 Verona Rd Bldg 5............Madison WI 53711	**800-423-6641**	608-276-6100	410
Thermo MeasureTech Inc 2555 N I-35.................Round Rock TX 78664	**800-736-0801**	512-388-9100	200
Thermo Nicolet 5225 Verona Rd.......Madison WI 53711	**800-642-6538**	608-276-6100	410
Thermo Orion 166 Cummings Ctr.......Beverly MA 01915	**800-225-1480**	978-922-4400	410
Thermo Radiometrie Corp 10010 Mesa Rim Rd............ San Diego CA 92121	**800-488-4399**		464
Thermo-Serv Inc 3901 Pipestone Rd......Dallas TX 75212	**800-527-2648**	214-631-0307	590
Thermo Shandon 171 Industry Dr.... Pittsburgh PA 15275	**800-547-7429**	412-788-1133	410
Thermo Spas Inc 155 East St...... Wallingford CT 06492	**800-876-0158**	203-265-6133	367
Thermo-Twin Industries Inc 1155 Allegheny Ave.............. Oakmont PA 15139	**800-641-2211**	412-826-1000	232
Thermodyn Corp 3550 Silica Rd....... Sylvania OH 43560	**800-654-6518**	419-841-7782	664
ThermoElectric Cooling America Corp 4048 W Schubert Ave............ Chicago IL 60639	**888-832-2872**	773-342-4900	15
ThermoGenesis Corp 2711 Citrus Rd............ Rancho Cordova CA 95742	**800-783-8357**	916-858-5100	411
NASDAQ: KOOL			
Thermoguard Insulation Co N 125 Dyer Rd...................Spokane WA 99212	**800-541-0579**	509-535-4600	382
Thermometrics Inc 808 US Hwy 1...... Edison NJ 08817	**800-246-7019**	732-287-2870	200
Thermopatch Corp 2204 Erie Blvd E... Syracuse NY 13224	**800-252-6555***	315-446-8110	729
*Cust Svc			
Thermoplastic Processes Inc 1268 Valley Rd.....................Stirling NJ 07980	**888-554-6400**	908-561-3000	589
Thermos Co 2550 W Golf Rd Suite 800...Rolling Meadows IL 60008	**800-243-0745***	847-439-7821	596
*Cust Svc			
ThermoSafe Brands 3930 Ventura Dr Suite 450... Arlington Heights IL 60004	**800-323-7442**	847-398-0110	590
Thermoseal Glass Corp 400 Water St.................. Gloucester NJ 08130	**800-456-7788**	856-456-3109	325
Thermwell Products Co 420 Rt 17 S... Mahwah NJ 07430	**800-526-5265**	201-684-4400	382
Thermwood Corp 904 Buffaloville Rd...... Dale IN 47523	**800-533-6901***	812-937-4476	809
*Mktg			
Thern Inc 5712 Industrial Park Rd......Winona MN 55987	**800-843-7648**	507-454-2996	462
TheStreet.com Inc 14 Wall St 15th Fl...............New York NY 10005	**800-562-9571**	212-321-5000	396
NASDAQ: TSCM			
Theta Delta Chi Inc 214 Lewis Wharf.... Boston MA 02110	**800-999-1847**	617-742-8886	48-16
Theta Phi Alpha Fraternity Inc 27025 Knickerbocker Rd.........Bay Village OH 44140	**877-843-8274**	440-899-9282	48-16
Theta Tau Professional Engineering Fraternity 815 Brazos St Suite 710.....Austin TX 78701	**800-264-1904**	512-472-1904	48-16
Theta Xi Fraternity PO Box 411134...............Saint Louis MO 63141	**800-783-6294**	314-993-6294	48-16
Thetford Corp PO Box 1285........ Ann Arbor MI 48106	**800-521-3032**	734-769-6000	599
Thibaut Inc 480 Frelinghuysen Ave......Newark NJ 07114	**800-223-0704**	973-643-1118	789
Thibodaux Regional Medical Center PO Box 1118................. Thibodaux LA 70302	**800-822-8442**	985-447-5500	366-2
Thief River Falls Convention & Visitors Bureau 2017 Hwy 59 SE....................Thief River Falls MN 56701	**800-827-1629**	218-681-3720	205
Thiel College 75 College Ave.........Greenville PA 16125	**800-248-4435**	724-589-2000	163
Things Remembered Inc 5500 Avion Park Dr........Highland Heights OH 44143	**800-874-2653**	440-473-2000	322
Think Federal Credit Union 5200 Members Pkwy NW..........Rochester MN 55901	**800-288-3425**	507-288-3425	216

Name / Address	City	State	ZIP	Toll-Free	Phone	Class
think3 Inc 312 Walnut St Suite 2470	Cincinnati	OH	45202	**800-323-6770**	513-263-6770	176-8
Thinkpath Inc 201 W Creek Blvd.	Brampton	ON	L6T5S6	**800-334-3911**	905-460-3040	707
Third Avenue Funds PO Box 9802	Providence	RI	02940	**800-443-1021**	212-888-6685	517
Third Federal Savings Bank 3 Penns Trail	Newtown	PA	18940	**800-844-7345**	215-579-4600	71
Third Federal Savings & Loan Assn of Cleveland 7007 Broadway Ave	Cleveland	OH	44105	**800-944-7828**	216-441-6000	71
Third Wave Technologies Inc 502 S Rosa Rd. *NASDAQ: TWTI*	Madison	WI	53719	**888-898-2357**	608-273-8933	86
Thoele Dental Laboratories Inc 540 Progress Dr.	Waite Park	MN	56387	**800-899-1115**	320-252-2070	406
Thomas Aquinas College 10000 N Ojai Rd.	Santa Paula	CA	93060	**800-634-9797**	805-525-4417	163
Thomas B Finan Center 10102 Country Club Rd SE PO Box 1722	Cumberland	MD	21501	**888-854-0035**	301-777-2405	366-3
Thomas & Betts Corp 8155 T & B Blvd. *NYSE: TNB*	Memphis	TN	38125	**800-888-0211**	901-252-8000	804
Thomas C Wilson Inc 21-11 44th Ave.	Long Island City	NY	11101	**800-230-2636**	718-729-3360	747
Thomas Cattle Co Inc 14451 NE 20 St	Williston	FL	32696	**800-654-1871**	352-528-4518	437
Thomas Charles C Publisher 2600 S 1st St. *Sales	Springfield	IL	62704	**800-258-8980***	217-789-8980	623-2
Thomas College 180 W River Rd	Waterville	ME	04901	**800-339-7001**	207-859-1111	163
Thomas Concrete Inc 2500 Cumberland Pkwy Suite 200	Atlanta	GA	30339	**800-633-4661**	770-431-3300	180
Thomas Conveyor Co 555 Burleson Blvd	Burleson	TX	76028	**800-433-2217**	817-295-7151	206
Thomas County Feeders Inc 1762 US Hwy 83	Colby	KS	67701	**800-257-2409**	785-462-3947	11-1
Thomas Creative Apparel 1 Harmony Pl	New London	OH	44851	**800-537-2575**	419-929-1506	153-14
Thomas Dave Foundation for Adoption 4288 W Dublin Granville Rd.	Dublin	OH	43017	**800-275-3832**	614-764-8454	300
Thomas Edison State College 101 W State St.	Trenton	NJ	08608	**888-442-8372**	609-984-1102	163
Thomas Engineering Inc 575 W Central Rd.	Hoffman Estates	IL	60195	**800-634-9910**	847-358-5800	379
Thomas G Faria Corp 385 Norwich-New London Tpke	Uncasville	CT	06382	**800-473-2742**	860-848-9271	486
Thomas Group Inc 5221 N O'Connor Blvd Suite 500	Irving	TX	75039	**800-826-2057**	972-869-3400	193
Thomas H Lee Co 100 Federal St Suite 3500	Boston	MA	02110	**800-227-1050**	617-227-1050	397
Thomas Industries Inc 4360 Brownsboro Rd Suite 300 *NYSE: TII*	Louisville	KY	40207	**800-626-2847**	502-893-4600	170
Thomas Monahan Co Inc 202 N Oak St	Arcola	IL	61910	**800-637-7739**	217-268-4955	291-23
Thomas More College 333 Thomas More Pkwy	Crestview Hills	KY	41017	**800-825-4557**	859-344-3332	163
Thomas Nelson Inc PO Box 141000 *NYSE: TNM*	Nashville	TN	37214	**800-251-4000**	615-889-9000	623-4
Thomas Publishing Co 5 Penn Plaza	New York	NY	10001	**800-699-9822**	212-695-0500	623-2
Thomas Reprographics 600 N Central Expy.	Richardson	TX	75080	**800-877-3776**	972-231-7227	239
Thomas RJ Mfg Co Inc PO Box 946	Cherokee	IA	51012	**800-725-5115**	712-225-5115	314-4
Thomas Scientific 99 Highville Rd	Swedesboro	NJ	08085	**800-345-2100**	856-467-2000	411
Thomas Steel Strip Corp Delaware Ave NW	Warren	OH	44485	**800-321-7778**	330-841-6111	709
Thomas Technology & Solutions Inc 1 Progress Dr.	Horsham	PA	19044	**800-872-2828**	215-682-5000	770
Thomas Transcription Services Inc 550 Balmoral Cir Suite 305	Jacksonville	FL	32218	**888-878-2889**	904-751-5058	755
Thomas Veterinary Drug 9165 W VanBuren St	Tolleson	AZ	85353	**800-359-8387**	623-936-3363	574
Thomas W Ruff & Co Inc 1114 Dublin Rd	Columbus	OH	43215	**800-828-0234**	614-487-4000	315
Thomas WS Transfer Inc 1854 Morgantown Ave	Fairmont	WV	26554	**800-624-8062**	304-363-8050	769
Thomasville Medical Center 207 Old Lexington Rd	Thomasville	NC	27360	**800-880-0110**	336-472-2000	366-2
Thomasville Times-Enterprise PO Box 650	Thomasville	GA	31799	**888-224-2402**	229-226-2400	522-2
Thombert Inc 316 E 7th St N	Newton	IA	50208	**800-433-3572**	641-792-4449	597
Thompson American Health Consultants Inc 3525 Piedmont Rd NE Bldg 6 Suite 400 *Cust Svc	Atlanta	GA	30305	**800-688-2421***	404-262-7436	623-9
Thompson Hospitality 505 Huntmar Pk Dr Suite 350	Herndon	VA	20170	**800-842-2737**	703-709-0145	656
Thompson Institute 5650 Derry St	Harrisburg	PA	17111	**800-272-4632**	717-564-4112	158
Thompson ISI ResearchSoft 2141 Palomar Airport Rd Suite 350	Carlsbad	CA	92009	**800-722-1227**	760-438-5526	176-3
Thompson Norm Outfitters Inc 3188 NW Aloclek Dr.	Hillsboro	OR	97124	**800-547-1160**	503-614-4600	451
Thompson Packers Inc 550 Carnation St.	Slidell	LA	70460	**800-989-6328**	985-641-6640	465
Thompson Publishing Group Inc 1725 K St NW Suite 700 *Cust Svc	Washington	DC	20006	**800-677-3789***	202-872-4000	623-9
Thompson Pump & Mfg Co Inc 4620 City Ctr Dr.	Port Orange	FL	32129	**800-767-7310**	386-767-7310	627
Thompson Siegel & Walmsley Inc 5000 Monument Ave	Richmond	VA	23230	**800-697-1056**	804-353-4500	393
Thompson Technologies Inc 114 Townpark Dr Suite 100	Kennesaw	GA	30144	**888-794-7947**	770-794-8380	707
Thoms Proestler Co 8001 TPC Rd	Rock Island	IL	61204	**800-747-1234**	309-787-1234	292-8
Thoms Rehabilitation Hospital 68 Sweeten Creek Rd.	Asheville	NC	28803	**800-627-1533**	828-274-2400	366-4
Thomson CenterWatch Inc 22 Thomson Pl 47th Fl. *Cust Svc	Boston	MA	02210	**800-765-9647***	617-856-5900	623-10
Thomson Corp 1 Station Pl Metro Ctr	Stamford	CT	06902	**800-354-9706**	203-539-8000	355-3
Thomson Elite 5100 W Goldleaf Cir Suite 100 *Cust Svc	Los Angeles	CA	90056	**800-274-9287***	323-642-5200	176-10
Thomson Financial 22 Thomson Pl.	Boston	MA	02210	**888-837-4636**	617-345-2000	380
Thomson Financial Publishing Inc 4709 W Golf Rd 6th Fl.	Skokie	IL	60076	**800-321-3373**	847-676-9600	623-2
Thomson-Hood Veterans Center 100 Veterans Dr	Wilmore	KY	40390	**800-928-4838**	859-858-2814	780
Thomson Learning 10650 Tobben Dr	Independence	KY	41051	**800-354-9706**		623-2
Thomson Learning Wadsworth PO Box 6904	Florence	KY	41022	**800-354-9706**		623-2
Thomson Media 1 State Street Plaza 27th Fl	New York	NY	10004	**800-535-8403**	212-803-8200	623-9
Thomson Prometric 1000 Lancaster St	Baltimore	MD	21202	**866-776-6387**	443-923-8668	243
Thomson Scientific 3501 Market St.	Philadelphia	PA	19104	**800-523-1850**	215-386-0100	623-9
Thomson & Thomson 500 Victory Rd	North Quincy	MA	02171	**800-692-8833**	617-479-1600	621
Thomson's Art Store 184 Mamaroneck Ave.	White Plains	NY	10601	**800-287-4885**	914-949-4885	45
Thor Inc 382 S Arthur Ave.	Louisville	CO	80027	**800-862-2111**	303-876-4100	761
Thor-Lo Inc 2210 Newton Dr	Statesville	NC	28677	**888-846-7567**	704-872-6522	153-10
Thor-Shackel Horseradish Co 16 W 224th Shore Ct.	Burr Ridge	IL	60527	**800-951-9696**	630-986-1333	291-19
Thor Tool Corp 865 Estabrook St	San Leandro	CA	94577	**800-222-8467**	510-357-6777	745
Thoratec Corp 6035 Stoneridge Dr *NASDAQ: THOR*	Pleasanton	CA	94588	**800-528-2577**	925-847-8600	249
Thorco Industries Inc 1300 E 12th St.	Lamar	MO	64759	**800-445-3375**	417-682-3375	231
Thorn L Co Inc PO Box 198.	New Albany	IN	47151	**800-662-4594**	812-246-4461	190-1
Thornburg Investment Management Funds 119 E Marcy St Suite 202	Santa Fe	NM	87501	**800-533-9337**	505-984-0200	517
Thorndike Press 295 Kennedy Memorial Dr	Waterville	ME	04901	**800-223-1244**	207-859-1000	623-2
Thornton Oil Corp 10101 Linn Station Rd Suite 200	Louisville	KY	40223	**800-928-8022**	502-425-8022	319
Thoro'Bred Inc 5020 E La Palma Ave	Anaheim	CA	92807	**800-854-6059**	714-779-2581	474
Thoroughbred Direct Intermodal Services 2260 Butler Pike Suite 400	Plymouth Meeting	PA	19462	**877-250-2902**	610-567-3360	440
Thoroughbred Owners & Breeders Assn (TOBA) PO Box 4367	Lexington	KY	40544	**888-606-8622**	859-276-2291	48-3
Thoroughbred Racing Assn. National 2525 Harrodsburg Rd.	Lexington	KY	40504	**800-722-3287**	859-223-5444	48-22
Thoroughbred Software International Inc 285 Davidson Ave Suite 302	Somerset	NJ	08873	**800-524-0430**	732-560-1377	176-2
Thorp Seed Co RR 3 Box 257	Clinton	IL	61727	**800-648-2676**	217-935-2171	684
Thorpe JT & Son Inc 1060 Hensley St.	Richmond	CA	94801	**800-577-1755**	510-233-2500	313
Thousand Hills Golf Resort 245 S Wildwood Dr	Branson	MO	65616	**800-864-4145**	417-336-5873	373
Thousand Oaks Inn 75 W Thousand Oaks Blvd.	Thousand Oaks	CA	91360	**800-600-6878**	805-497-3701	373
Thousand Trails Inc 3801 Parkwood Blvd Suite 100	Frisco	TX	75034	**800-328-6226**	214-618-7200	121
Thread Check Inc 390 Oser Ave	Hauppauge	NY	11788	**800-767-7633**	631-231-1515	484
Threaded Rod Co Inc 1929 Columbia Ave	Indianapolis	IN	46202	**800-354-3330**	317-921-3000	448
Three Bars Cattle & Guest Ranch 9500 Wycliffe Perry Creek Rd	Cranbrook	BC	V1C7C7	**877-426-5230**	250-426-5230	238
Three Chimneys Inn 1201 Chapel St.	New Haven	CT	06511	**800-443-1554**	203-789-1201	373
Three D Graphics Inc 11340 W Olympic Blvd Suite 352	Los Angeles	CA	90064	**800-913-0008**	310-231-3330	176-8
Three Lakes Information Bureau 1704 Superior St PO Box 262	Three Lakes	WI	54562	**800-972-6103**	715-546-3344	205
Three Notch Electric Membership Corp PO Box 367	Donalsonville	GA	39845	**800-239-5377**	229-524-5377	244
Three Rivers Community College 2080 Three Rivers Blvd	Poplar Bluff	MO	63901	**877-879-8722**	573-840-9600	160
Three States Supply Co LLC 666 EH Crump Blvd	Memphis	TN	38101	**800-666-1565**	901-948-8651	601
Thriftlodge 1 Sylvan Way	Parsippany	NJ	07054	**800-578-7878**	973-428-9700	369
Thrifty Car Rental 5310 E 31st St.	Tulsa	OK	74135	**800-367-2277**	918-665-3930	126
Thrifty White Stores 6901 E Fish Lake Rd Suite 118	Maple Grove	MN	55369	**800-816-2887**	763-513-4300	236
Thrivent Financial for Lutherans 4321 N Ballard Rd	Appleton	WI	54919	**800-847-4836**	920-734-5721	384-2
Thruway Fasteners Inc 2910 Niagara Falls Blvd	North Tonawanda	NY	14120	**800-201-1619**	716-694-1434	346
Thunderbird Forest Products 8180 Industrial Pkwy	Sacramento	CA	95824	**800-824-5104**	916-381-4200	304
Thunderbird Products Inc 2200 W Monroe St.	Decatur	IN	46733	**800-736-7685**		91
Thunderbird Rural Public Transportation System 4860 Knickerbocker St PO Box 60050	San Angelo	TX	76906	**800-728-2592**	325-944-9666	109
Thundercloud Subs 1102 W 6th St.	Austin	TX	78703	**800-256-7895**	512-479-8805	657
Thuro Metal Products Inc 21-25 Grand Blvd N	Brentwood	NY	11717	**800-238-3929**	631-435-0444	610
Thurston CE & Sons Inc 3335 Croft St *Cust Svc	Norfolk	VA	23513	**800-444-7713***	757-855-7700	188-9
Thybar Corp 913 S Kay Ave.	Addison	IL	60101	**800-666-2872**	630-543-5300	688
Thyroid Foundation of America Inc (TFA) 1 Longfellow Pl Suite 1518	Boston	MA	02114	**800-832-8321**	617-534-1500	48-17
Thyssen Elevator Co 15141 E Whittier Blvd Suite 505	Whittier	CA	90603	**800-288-3538**	562-693-9491	188-1
ThyssenKrupp Elevator 6266 Hurt Rd	Horn Lake	MS	38637	**877-230-0303**	662-393-2110	255
ThyssenKrupp Stahl Co 11 E Pacific PO Box 6	Kingsville	MO	64061	**888-395-1042**	816-597-3322	303
TI Automotive 12345 E Nine-Mile Rd	Warren	MI	48090	**800-521-2500**	586-758-6500	60
TIA (Telecommunications Industry Assn) 2500 Wilson Blvd Suite 300	Arlington	VA	22201	**800-799-6682**	703-907-7700	49-20
TIA (Tire Industry Assn) 1532 Pointer Ridge Pl Suite E	Bowie	MD	20716	**800-876-8372**	301-430-7280	49-4
TIAA-CREF 730 3rd Ave	New York	NY	10017	**800-842-2776**	212-490-9000	384-2

Name / Address	City	State	ZIP	Toll-Free	Phone	Class
TIAA-CREF Mutual Funds PO Box 8009	Boston	MA	02266	**800-223-1200**		517
Tiara Corp 2425 Oakton St	Evanston	IL	60202	**800-323-6510**	847-570-4700	401
Tia's Tex Mex						
1101 N Union Bower Rd Suite 160	Irving	TX	75061	**800-486-5322**	972-554-6886	657
TIB Financial Corp						
99451 Overseas Hwy	Key Largo	FL	33037	**800-233-6330**	305-451-4660	355-2
NASDAQ: TIBB						
Ticket Box Inc						
2125 Center Ave Suite 509	Fort Lee	NJ	07024	**800-842-5440**	201-461-8771	735
Ticket Heaven						
600 S County Farm Rd Suite 144	Wheaton	IL	60187	**800-260-6616**	630-260-0626	735
Ticket Pros USA						
245 Peachtree Ctr Ave Suite M-39	Atlanta	GA	30303	**800-962-2985**	404-524-8491	735
Ticket Source Inc						
5516 E Mockingbird Ln Suite 100	Dallas	TX	75206	**800-557-6872**	214-821-9011	735
Ticketfinder.com						
236 W Portal Ave Suite 360	San Francisco	CA	94127	**800-523-1515**	650-757-3514	735
Ticketmall.com						
245 Peachtree Ctr Ave Suite M-39	Atlanta	GA	30303	**800-962-2985**	404-524-8491	735
Ticketmaster						
3701 Wilshire Blvd 7th Fl	Los Angeles	CA	90010	**800-366-8652**	213-381-2000	735
Ticketmonster Inc						
303 Frederick Rd	Catonsville	MD	21228	**800-637-3719**	410-719-0030	735
Tickets Galore Inc 33 Haddon Ave	Westmont	NJ	08108	**888-849-9663**	856-869-8499	735
Tickets.com Inc						
555 Anton Blvd 11th Fl	Costa Mesa	CA	92626	**800-352-0212**	714-327-5400	735
TicketWeb Inc PO Box 77250	San Francisco	CA	94103	**866-468-7630***	800-965-4827	735
*Cust Svc						
Tickle Pink Inn at Carmel Highlands						
155 Highland Dr	Carmel	CA	93923	**800-635-4774**	831-624-1244	373
Ticona LLC 8040 Dixie Hwy	Florence	KY	41042	**800-833-4882**	859-525-4740	594-2
Ticor Title Insurance Co						
203 N LaSalle St Suite 2200	Chicago	IL	60601	**800-879-1167**	312-621-5000	384-6
Tidel Engineering Inc						
2310 McDaniel Dr	Carrollton	TX	75006	**800-678-7577**	972-484-3358	56
Tideland Electric Membership Corp						
PO Box 159	Pantego	NC	27860	**800-637-1079**	252-943-3046	244
Tidelands Royalty Trust PO Box 830650	Dallas	TX	75202	**800-985-0794**	214-209-2400	662
Tides The 1220 Ocean Dr	Miami Beach	FL	33139	**800-688-7678**	305-604-5070	373
Tides Resort 480 King Carter Dr	Irvington	VA	22480	**800-843-3746**	804-438-5000	655
Tidewater Community College						
Chesapeake Campus						
1428 Cedar Rd	Chesapeake	VA	23322	**800-371-0898**	757-822-5100	160
Portsmouth Campus						
7000 College Dr	Portsmouth	VA	23703	**800-371-0898**	757-822-2124	160
Virginia Beach Campus						
1700 College Crescent	Virginia Beach	VA	23453	**800-371-0898**	757-822-7100	160
Tidewater Inc						
601 Poydras St Suite 1900	New Orleans	LA	70130	**800-678-8433**	504-568-1010	457
NYSE: TDW						
Tidewater Inn & Conference Center						
101 E Dover St	Easton	MD	21601	**800-237-8775**	410-822-1300	373
TIDI Products LLC 570 Enterprise Dr	Neenah	WI	54956	**800-215-5464**	920-751-4300	469
Tidland Corp 2305 SE 8th Ave	Camas	WA	98607	**800-426-1000**	360-834-2345	729
Tie King Inc 243 44th St	Brooklyn	NY	11232	**800-852-9261**	718-768-8484	153-13
Tier Technologies Inc						
10780 Parkridge Blvd Suite 400	Reston	VA	20191	**800-789-8437**	571-382-1000	178
NASDAQ: TIER						
Tierra Verde Island Resort						
200 Madonna Blvd	Tierra Verde	FL	33715	**800-934-0549**	727-867-8611	373
TierraNet Inc						
9573 Chesapeake Dr 1st Fl	San Diego	CA	92123	**877-843-7721**	858-560-9416	795
Tietex International						
3010 N Blackstock Rd	Spartanburg	SC	29301	**800-843-8390**	864-574-0500	730-6
Tiffany & Co 727 5th Ave	New York	NY	10022	**800-526-0649***	212-755-8000	402
NYSE: TIF ■ *Orders						
Tiffen Mfg Corp 90 Oser Ave	Hauppauge	NY	11788	**800-645-2522**	631-273-2500	580
Tiffin Area Chamber of Commerce						
62 S Washington St	Tiffin	OH	44883	**800-253-3314**	419-447-4141	137
Tiffin Parts 235 Miami St	Tiffin	OH	44883	**800-219-6354**	419-447-6545	462
Tiffin University 155 Miami St	Tiffin	OH	44883	**800-968-6446**	419-447-6442	163
Tift Regional Medical Center						
901 E 18th St	Tifton	GA	31794	**800-648-1935**	229-382-7120	366-2
Tifton Aluminum Co Inc						
250 Southwell Blvd	Tifton	GA	31794	**800-841-2030***	229-382-7330	476
*Sales						
Tifton Gazette PO Box 708	Tifton	GA	31793	**888-382-4321**	229-382-4321	522-2
Tifton-Tift County Chamber of Commerce						
100 Central Ave	Tifton	GA	31794	**800-550-8438**	229-382-6200	137
TIG Specialty Insurance Solutions						
5205 N O'Connor Blvd	Irving	TX	75039	**800-472-7583**	972-831-5000	384-4
Tiger Aircraft LLC 226 Pilot Way	Martinsburg	WV	25401	**877-808-4437**	304-260-0038	21
Tiger Button Co Inc						
307 W 38th St 4th Fl	New York	NY	10018	**800-223-2754**	212-594-0570	583
Tiger Electronics Div Hasbro Inc						
1027 Newport Ave	Pawtucket	RI	02861	**800-844-3733**	401-431-8697	750
Tiger Financial News Network						
2401 W Bay Dr Suite 126	Largo	FL	33770	**877-518-9190**	727-518-9190	630
TigerDirect Inc						
7795 W Flagler St Suite 35	Miami	FL	33144	**800-955-1888**	305-415-2200	177
Tighe Industries Inc 333 E 7th Ave	York	PA	17404	**800-839-1039**	717-252-1578	153-1
TIGHITCO Inc 2300 Marietta Blvd NW	Atlanta	GA	30318	**800-223-1205**	404-355-1205	382
TII Network Technologies Inc						
1385 Akron St	Copiague	NY	11726	**888-844-4720**	631-789-5000	626
NASDAQ: TIII						
Tillamook People's Utility District						
PO Box 433	Tillamook	OR	97141	**800-422-2535**	503-842-2535	244
Tilley Chemical Co Inc						
501 Chesapeake Pk Plaza	Baltimore	MD	21220	**800-638-6968**	410-574-4500	144
Tillotson Healthcare Corp						
8025 S Willow St Suite 203	Manchester	NH	03103	**800-445-6830**	603-472-6600	469
Tilson HR Inc						
1499 Windhorst Way Suite 100	Greenwood	IN	46143	**800-276-3976**	317-885-3838	619
Tim Hortons 4150 Tuller Rd Suite 236	Dublin	OH	43017	**888-376-4835**	614-791-4200	69
TimBar Packaging & Display						
148 N Penn St PO Box 449	Hanover	PA	17331	**800-572-6061**	717-632-4727	101
Timber Products Co 305 S 4th St	Springfield	OR	97477	**800-547-9520**	541-747-4577	190-3
Timber Truss Housing Systems Inc						
PO Box 996	Salem	VA	24153	**800-766-9072**	540-387-0273	805

Name / Address	City	State	ZIP	Toll-Free	Phone	Class
Timberland Bancorp Inc PO Box 697	Hoquiam	WA	98550	**800-562-8761**	360-533-4747	355-2
NASDAQ: TSBK						
Timberland Co 200 Domain Dr	Stratham	NH	03885	**800-258-0855**	603-772-9500	296
NYSE: TBL						
Timberland Homes Inc						
1201 37th St NW	Auburn	WA	98001	**800-488-5036**	253-735-3435	107
Timberland Management Services Inc						
PO Box 819	Centreville	MS	39631	**800-306-6439**	601-645-6440	297
Timberlawn Mental Health System						
4600 Samuell Blvd	Dallas	TX	75228	**800-426-4944**	214-381-7181	366-3
Timberline Lodge						
88 Hwy 150	Timberline Lodge	OR	97028	**800-547-1406**	503-272-3311	655
Timberline Software Corp						
15195 NW Greenbriar Pkwy	Beaverton	OR	97006	**800-628-6583**	503-690-6775	176-11
Timberwolf Tours Ltd						
51404 RR 264 Suite 34	Spruce Grove	AB	T7Y1E4	**888-467-9697**	780-470-4966	748
Time The 224 W 49th St	New York	NY	10019	**877-846-3692**	212-246-5252	373
Time Magazine						
Rockefeller Ctr Time & Life Bldg	New York	NY	10020	**800-541-2000**	212-522-1212	449-17
Time Mark Corp 11440 E Pine St	Tulsa	OK	74116	**800-862-2875**	918-438-1220	202
Time-O-Matic Inc 1015 Maple St	Danville	IL	61832	**800-637-2645**	217-442-0611	202
Time Oil Co 2737 W Commodore Way	Seattle	WA	98199	**800-552-0748**	206-285-2400	569
Time Warner Book Group Inc						
1271 Ave of the Americas	New York	NY	10020	**800-759-0190**	212-522-7200	623-2
Time Warner Cable 290 Harbor Dr	Stamford	CT	06902	**800-950-2266**	203-328-0600	117
Time Warner Communications Inc						
1266 Dublin Rd	Columbus	OH	43215	**800-492-9324**	614-481-5050	117
Time Warner Telecom Inc						
10475 Park Meadow Dr	Littleton	CO	80124	**800-565-8982**	303-566-1000	721
NASDAQ: TWTC						
Timecruiser Computing Corp						
9 Law Dr 3rd Fl	Fairfield	NJ	07004	**877-450-9482**	973-244-7856	176-7
Timely Inc 10241 Norris Ave	Pacoima	CA	91331	**800-247-6242**	818-896-3094	281
TimeMed Labeling Systems Inc						
144 Tower Dr	Burr Ridge	IL	60527	**800-323-4840***	630-986-1800	544
*Cust Svc						
Timer Digest Newsletter						
PO Box 1688	Greenwich	CT	06836	**800-356-2527**	203-629-3503	521-9
Times The 601 45th Ave	Munster	IN	46321	**800-837-3232**	219-933-3200	522-2
Times 222 Lake St	Shreveport	LA	71130	**800-551-8892**	318-459-3200	522-2
Times-Bulletin PO Box 271	Van Wert	OH	45891	**800-727-2036**	419-238-2285	522-2
Times & Democrat PO Box 1766	Orangeburg	SC	29116	**877-534-1060**	803-533-5500	522-2
Times Festival of Reading						
PO Box 1121	Saint Petersburg	FL	33731	**800-333-7505**	727-445-4142	277
Times Fiber Communications Inc						
358 Hall Ave	Wallingford	CT	06492	**800-677-2288**	203-265-8500	800
Times Herald Inc						
410 Markley St PO Box 591	Norristown	PA	19404	**800-887-2501**	610-272-2500	623-8
Times Herald-Record						
40 Mulberry St PO Box 2046	Middletown	NY	10940	**800-295-2181**	845-341-1100	522-2
Times Journal PO Box 680349	Fort Payne	AL	35968	**800-348-4637**	256-845-2550	522-2
Times Leader 200 S 4th St	Martins Ferry	OH	43935	**800-244-5671**	740-633-1131	522-2
Times Mirror Magazines Inc						
2Park Ave	New York	NY	10016	**800-227-2224**	212-779-5000	623-9
Times-News PO Box 548	Twin Falls	ID	83303	**800-658-3883**	208-733-0931	522-2
Times-News PO Box 481	Burlington	NC	27216	**800-488-0085**	336-227-0131	522-2
Times-News PO Box 490	Hendersonville	NC	28793	**800-849-8050**	828-692-0505	522-2
Times News						
594 Blakeslee Blvd Dr W	Lehighton	PA	18235	**800-443-0377**	610-377-2051	522-2
Times News Publishing Co						
707 S Main St	Burlington	NC	27215	**800-488-0085**	336-227-0131	623-8
Times-Picayune						
3800 Howard Ave	New Orleans	LA	70125	**800-925-0000**	504-826-3279	522-2
Times Publishing Co 222 Lake St	Shreveport	LA	71101	**800-525-4335**	318-459-3200	623-8
Times Record 3600 Wheeler Ave	Fort Smith	AR	72901	**888-274-4051**	479-785-7700	522-2
Times Record 219 S College Ave	Aledo	IL	61231	**800-582-4373**	309-582-5112	522-4
Times Record PO Box 10	Brunswick	ME	04011	**800-879-3311**	207-729-3311	522-2
Times Record News PO Box 120	Wichita Falls	TX	76307	**800-627-1646**	940-767-8341	522-2
Times Recorder 34 S 4th St	Zanesville	OH	43701	**800-886-7326**	740-452-4561	522-2
Times Reporter						
629 Wabash Ave NW	New Philadelphia	OH	44663	**800-837-8666**	330-364-5577	522-2
Times-Republican PO Box 1300	Marshalltown	IA	50158	**800-542-7893**	641-753-6611	522-2
Times-West Virginian PO Box 2530	Fairmont	WV	26555	**800-846-3798**	304-367-2500	522-2
Timesavers Inc						
11123 89th Ave N	Maple Grove	MN	55369	**800-537-3611**	763-488-6600	379
TimeValue Software						
4 Jenner St Suite 100	Irvine	CA	92618	**800-426-4741***	949-727-1800	176-11
*Sales						
Timex Corp 555 Christian Rd	Middlebury	CT	06762	**800-367-8463**	203-346-5000	151
Timken Co 1835 Dueber Ave SW	Canton	OH	44706	**800-223-1954**	330-438-3000	77
NYSE: TKR						
Timken Latrobe Steel Co						
2626 Ligonier St PO Box 31	Latrobe	PA	15650	**800-245-7856**	724-537-7711	709
Timpte Inc 1827 Industrial Dr	David City	NE	68632	**888-256-4884**	402-367-3056	768
Tim's Cascade Style Potato Chips						
PO Box 2302	Auburn	WA	98071	**800-533-8467**	253-833-0255	291-35
Tindall Corp PO Box 1778	Spartanburg	SC	29304	**800-849-4521**	864-576-3230	181
Tinder Box International Ltd						
3 Bala Plaza E Suite 102	Bala Cynwyd	PA	19004	**800-846-3372**	610-668-4220	743
Tingley Rubber Corp						
1 Cragwood Rd	South Plainfield	NJ	07080	**800-631-5498***	908-757-7474	566
*Cust Svc						
Tingue Brown & Co						
535 N Midland Ave	Saddle Brook	NJ	07663	**800-829-4536***	201-796-4490	583
*Sales						
Tinker Federal Credit Union						
PO Box 45750	Tinker AFB	OK	73145	**800-456-4828**	405-732-0324	216
Tinnitus Assn. American						
65 SW Yamhill	Portland	OR	97205	**800-634-8978**	503-248-9985	48-17
Tioga County Visitors Bureau						
114 Main St	Wellsboro	PA	16901	**888-846-4228**	570-724-0635	205
Tioga Pipe Supply Co Inc						
2450 Wheatsheaf Ln	Philadelphia	PA	19137	**800-523-3678**	215-831-0700	483
Tiona Truck Line Inc PO Box 90	Butler	MO	64730	**800-821-3046**	660-679-4197	769
Tip Inc. We PO Box 1296	Rancho Cucamonga	CA	91729	**800-782-7463**	909-987-5005	48-8
TIP Rural Electric Co-op PO Box 534	Brooklyn	IA	52211	**800-934-7976**	641-522-9221	244
Tipmont Rural Electric Membership Corp						
PO Box 20	Linden	IN	47955	**800-726-3953**	765-339-7211	244

Name / Address	City	State	Zip	Toll-Free	Phone	Class
Tipper Tie Inc 2000 Lufkin Rd	Apex	NC	27502	**800-331-2905**	919-362-8811	152
TippingPoint Technologies Inc 7501-B N Capital of Texas Hwy	Austin	TX	78731	**888-648-9663**	512-681-8000	721
TIPS (Tobacco Information & Prevention Source) National Ctr for Chronic Disease Prevention & Health Promotion 2900 Woodcock Blvd	Atlanta	GA	30341	**800-311-3435**		196
Tipton & Hurst Inc 1801 N Grant St	Little Rock	AR	72207	**800-633-3036**	501-666-3333	322
TIR Systems Ltd 7700 Riverfront Gate *TSE: TIR*	Burnaby	BC	V5J5M4	**800-663-2036**	604-294-8477	431
Tire Centers LLC 310 Inglesby Pkwy	Duncan	SC	29334	**800-603-2430**	864-329-2700	740
Tire Distribution Systems Inc 11900 W 44th Ave	Wheat Ridge	CO	80033	**800-541-8473**	303-422-2300	62-5
Tire Industry Assn (TIA) 1532 Pointer Ridge Pl Suite E	Bowie	MD	20716	**800-876-8372**	301-430-7280	49-4
Tire Kingdom Inc 823 Donald Ross Rd	Juno Beach	FL	33408	**800-383-3040**	561-842-4290	62-5
Tire Rack 7101 Vorden Pkwy	South Bend	IN	46628	**800-428-8359**	574-287-2345	740
Tire-Rama Inc PO Box 23509	Billings	MT	59104	**800-828-1642**	406-245-4006	740
Tires Plus 2021 Sunnydale Blvd	Clearwater	FL	33765	**800-269-4424**	727-441-3727	62-5
Tires Plus Total Car Care 2021 Sunnydale Blvd	Clearwater	FL	33765	**800-269-4424**	727-441-3727	62-5
Tishcon Corp 30 New York Ave	Westbury	NY	11590	**800-848-8442**	516-333-3050	786
Tishman Realty & Construction Co Inc 666 5th Ave	New York	NY	10103	**800-609-8474**	212-399-3600	186
Tissue Banks International 815 Park Ave	Baltimore	MD	21201	**800-756-4824**	410-752-2020	265
Tissue Banks International (TBI) 815 Park Ave	Baltimore	MD	21201	**800-756-4824**	410-752-3800	535
Titan America Inc 1151 Azalea Garden Rd	Norfolk	VA	23502	**800-468-7622**	757-858-6500	180
Titan Completion Products Ltd 1266 Lakeview Dr FM 661	Mansfield	TX	79088	**800-320-5110**	817-473-9321	264
Titan Corp 3033 Science Park Rd *NYSE: TTN*	San Diego	CA	92121	**800-359-4404**	858-552-9500	654
Titan Farms 5 RW Du Bose Rd	Ridge Spring	SC	29129	**888-848-2672**	803-685-5381	310-3
Titan International Inc 2701 Spruce St *NYSE: TWI*	Quincy	IL	62301	**800-872-2327**	217-228-6011	60
Titan Machinery Inc PO Box 310	Wahpeton	ND	58074	**800-654-4313**	701-642-8424	270
Titan Pharmaceuticals Inc 400 Oyster Point Blvd Suite 505 *AMEX: TTP*	South San Francisco	CA	94080	**800-500-6608**	650-244-4990	86
Titan Specialties Inc PO Box 2316 *Sales	Pampa	TX	79066	**800-692-4486***	806-665-3781	526
Titan Steel Corp 2500-B Broening Hwy	Baltimore	MD	21224	**800-359-4678**	410-631-5200	483
Titan Tire Co 2345 E Market St	Des Moines	IA	50317	**800-872-2327**	515-265-9200	739
Titan Wheel Corp 2701 Spruce St	Quincy	IL	62301	**800-518-4826**	217-228-6011	60
Titan Wireless Inc 3033 Science Park Rd	San Diego	CA	92121	**800-359-4404**	858-552-9500	721
Titanium Industries Inc 181 E Halsey Rd	Parsippany	NJ	07054	**888-482-6486**	973-428-1900	483
Titeflex Corp 603 Hendee St	Springfield	MA	01139	**800-765-2525**	413-739-5631	364
Title Assn. American Land 1828 L St NW Suite 705	Washington	DC	20036	**800-787-2582**	202-296-3671	49-10
Title First Agency Inc 555 S Front St Suite 400	Columbus	OH	43215	**800-837-4032**	614-224-9207	621
Title Guaranty of Hawaii Inc 235 Queen St	Honolulu	HI	96813	**888-352-7389**	808-533-6261	384-6
Title Industry PAC 1828 L St NW Suite 705	Washington	DC	20036	**800-787-2582**	202-296-3671	604
Title Resources Guaranty Co 8111 LBJ Fwy Suite 1200	Dallas	TX	75251	**800-526-8018**	972-644-6500	384-6
Titmus Optical Inc 3811 Corporate Dr *Cust Svc	Petersburg	VA	23805	**800-446-1802***	804-732-6121	531
TiVo Inc 2160 Gold St *NASDAQ: TIVO*	Alviso	CA	95002	**877-367-8486**	408-519-9100	117
Tivoli Lodge 386 Hanson Ranch Rd	Vail	CO	81657	**800-451-4756**	970-476-5615	373
Tivoli Systems Inc 9442 Capital of Texas Hwy N Plaza 1 Suite 100	Austin	TX	78759	**877-848-6541**	512-436-8000	176-1
Tix Travel & Ticket Agency Inc 201 Main St	Nyack	NY	10960	**800-269-6849**		761
TJ Cinnamons 1000 Corporate Dr	Fort Lauderdale	FL	33334	**800-487-2729**	954-351-5100	291-1
TJ Cope Inc 11500 Norcom Rd	Philadelphia	PA	19154	**800-426-4293**	215-961-2570	804
TJ Hale Co W 139 N 9499 Hwy 145 PO Box 250	Menomonee Falls	WI	53051	**800-236-4253**	262-255-5555	281
TJ Maxx 770 Cochituate Rd *Cust Svc	Framingham	MA	01701	**800-926-6299***	508-390-1000	155-2
TJ Samson Community Hospital 1301 N Race St	Glasgow	KY	42141	**800-651-5635**	270-651-4444	366-2
Tjernlund Products Inc 1601 9th St	White Bear Lake	MN	55110	**800-255-4208**	651-426-2993	19
TK Stanley Inc PO Box 31	Waynesboro	MS	39367	**800-477-2855**	601-735-2855	528
TKGA (Knitting Guild of America) 1100-H Brandywine Blvd PO Box 3388	Zanesville	OH	43702	**800-969-6069**	740-452-4541	48-18
TKO Dock Doors N56 W24701 N Corporate Cir	Sussex	WI	53089	**800-575-3366**	262-820-1217	232
TL Enterprises Inc 2575 Vista Del Mar Dr	Ventura	CA	93001	**800-765-1912**	805-667-4100	623-9
TLA (Texas Library Assn) 3355 Bee Cave Rd Suite 401	Austin	TX	78746	**800-580-2852**	512-328-1518	427
TLC (Learning Channel The) 8516 Georgia Ave	Silver Spring	MD	20910	**888-404-5969**	240-662-2000	725
TLC Vision Corp 5280 Solar Dr Suite 300 *NASDAQ: TLCV*	Mississauga	ON	L4W5M8	**888-225-5852**	905-602-2020	785
TLN (Telelatino Network Inc) 5125 Steeles Ave W	Toronto	ON	M9L1R5	**800-551-8401**	416-744-8200	725
TM Smith Tool International Corp PO Box 1065	Mount Clemens	MI	48046	**800-521-4894**	586-468-1465	484
TM Window & Door 601 NW 12th Ave	Pompano Beach	FL	33069	**800-511-1746**	954-781-4430	232
TMI Coatings Inc 2805 Dodd Rd	Saint Paul	MN	55121	**800-328-0229**	651-452-6100	188-8
TMI Systems Design Corp 50 S 3rd Ave West	Dickinson	ND	58601	**800-456-6716**	701-456-6716	314-3
TML Information Services Inc 116-55 Queens Blvd Suite 210	Forest Hills	NY	11375	**800-733-9777**	718-793-3737	621
TNNA (National Needlework Assn) 1100-H Brandywine Blvd PO Box 3388	Zanesville	OH	43702	**800-889-8662**	740-455-6773	48-18
TNP Enterprises Inc 4100 International Plaza 9th Fl Tower 2	Fort Worth	TX	76109	**800-435-2822**	817-731-0099	355-5
TNR Technical Inc 301 Central Park Dr	Sanford	FL	32771	**800-346-0601**	407-321-3011	76
TNS Inc DBA Transaction Network Services 1939 Roland Clarke Pl *NYSE: TNS*	Reston	VA	20191	**800-240-2824**	703-453-8300	721
TNS Merchant & Credit Card Services 1939 Roland Clarke Pl	Reston	VA	20191	**800-240-2824**	703-453-8338	213
TNT Express Worldwide Corp 3 Huntington Quadrangle Suite 201S *Cust Svc	Melville	NY	11747	**800-558-5555***	631-760-0700	536
TNT Logistics North America 10751 Deerwood Park Blvd Suite 200	Jacksonville	FL	32256	**888-564-4789**	904-928-1400	440
TNT Tickets Inc 23881 Via Fabricante Suite 505	Mission Viejo	CA	92691	**800-425-5849**	949-458-5744	735
Toa Reinsurance Co of America 177 Madison Ave PO Box 1930	Morristown	NJ	07962	**800-898-7977**	973-898-9480	384-4
TOAST.net 4841 Monroe St Suite 307	Toledo	OH	43623	**888-862-7863**	419-292-2200	390
TOBA (Thoroughbred Owners & Breeders Assn) PO Box 4367	Lexington	KY	40544	**888-606-8622**	859-276-2291	48-3
Tobacco Council. Smokeless 1627 K St NW Suite 700	Washington	DC	20006	**800-272-7144**	202-452-1252	48-2
Tobacco Exporters International USA Ltd 2280 Mountain Industrial Blvd	Tucker	GA	30084	**800-221-4134**	770-934-8540	744
Tobacco-Free Kids. National Center for 1400 'I' St NW Suite 1200	Washington	DC	20005	**800-284-5437**	202-296-5469	48-17
Tobacco Information & Prevention Source (TIPS) National Ctr for Chronic Disease Prevention & Health Promotion 2900 Woodcock Blvd	Atlanta	GA	30341	**800-311-3435**		196
Toccoa Falls College 328 Chappel Dr	Toccoa Falls	GA	30598	**800-868-3257**	706-886-6831	163
Todai Franchising LLC 3700 Wilshire Blvd Suite 560	Los Angeles	CA	90010	**888-558-6324**	213-628-1858	657
Today's Christian Woman Magazine 465 Gundersen Dr *Orders	Carol Stream	IL	60188	**800-365-9484***	630-260-6200	449-18
Today's News-Herald 2225 W Acoma Blvd	Lake Havasu City	AZ	86403	**800-894-2109**	928-453-4237	522-2
Today's Vision 6970 FM 1960 W Suite A	Houston	TX	77069	**800-733-8632**	281-469-2020	533
Todd AM Co 1717 Douglas Ave	Kalamazoo	MI	49005	**800-968-2603**	269-343-2603	470
Todd Combustion Group 2 Armstrong Rd 3rd Fl	Shelton	CT	06484	**800-225-0085**	203-925-0380	313
Todd Investment Advisors Inc 101 S 5th St Suite 3160	Louisville	KY	40202	**888-544-8633**	502-585-3121	393
Todd-Wadena Electric Co-op PO Box 431	Wadena	MN	56482	**800-321-8932**	218-631-3120	244
TODDS Enterprises Inc 610 S 56th Ave	Phoenix	AZ	85043	**800-242-7687**	602-484-9584	291-36
Tofias Fleishman Shapiro & Co PC 350 Massachusetts Ave	Cambridge	MA	02139	**888-761-8835**	617-761-0600	2
Toftrees Resort & Conference Center 1 Country Club Ln	State College	PA	16803	**800-252-3551**	814-234-8000	655
Tog Shop Inc Lester Sq *Orders	Americus	GA	31710	**800-367-8647***	229-924-8800	451
Togo's Eateries Inc 130 Royal St	Canton	MA	02021	**800-859-5339**	781-737-3000	657
Tokio Marine Life 230 Park Ave	New York	NY	10169	**800-628-2796**	212-297-6600	384-4
Tokyo Electron America Inc 2400 Grove Blvd	Austin	TX	78741	**800-828-6596**	512-424-1000	685
Tol-O-Matic Inc 3800 County Rd 116	Hamel	MN	55340	**800-328-2174**	763-478-8000	220
Toland CE & Son 5300 Industrial Way	Benicia	CA	94510	**800-675-1166**	707-747-1000	188-14
Tolco Inc 1375 Sampson Ave	Corona	CA	92879	**800-786-5266**	951-737-5599	584
Toledo Edison Co 76 S Main St *Cust Svc	Akron	OH	44308	**800-447-3333***	800-646-0400	774
Toledo (Greater) Convention & Visitors Bureau 401 Jefferson Ave	Toledo	OH	43604	**800-243-4667**	419-321-6404	205
Toledo Molding & Die Inc 4 E Laskey Rd	Toledo	OH	43612	**800-437-5116**	419-476-0581	593
Toledo Museum of Art 2445 Monroe St	Toledo	OH	43620	**800-644-6862**	419-255-8000	509
Toledo Opera 425 Jefferson Ave Suite 415	Toledo	OH	43604	**866-860-9048**	419-255-7464	563-2
Toledo Symphony 1838 Parkwood Ave Suite 310	Toledo	OH	43624	**800-348-1253**	419-246-8000	563-3
Toll Brothers Inc 250 Gibraltar Rd *NYSE: TOL*	Horsham	PA	19044	**800-289-8655**	215-938-8000	639
Toll Robert I 250 Gibraltar Rd Chm/CEO Toll Brothers Inc	Horsham	PA	19044	**800-289-8655**	215-938-8000	561
Tolleson Lumber Co Inc 903 Jernigan St	Perry	GA	31069	**800-768-2105**	478-988-3800	671
Tollgrade Communications Inc 493 Nixon Rd *NASDAQ: TLGD* ■ *Cust Svc	Cheswick	PA	15024	**800-878-3399***	412-820-1400	720
Tolz King Duvall Anderson & Assoc Inc 444 Cedar St Suite 1500	Saint Paul	MN	55101	**800-247-1714**	651-292-4400	258
Tom Bengard Ranch Inc PO Box 80090	Salinas	CA	93912	**800-546-3517**	831-422-9021	11-11
Tom Hassenfritz Equipment Co 1300 W Washington St	Mount Pleasant	IA	52641	**800-634-4885**	319-385-3114	270
Tom James Co 424 S Lynn Riggs Blvd	Claremore	OK	74017	**800-237-2140**	918-341-3773	153-12
Tom Snyder Productions Inc 80 Coolidge Hill Rd	Watertown	MA	02472	**800-342-0236**	617-926-6000	176-3
Tom Sturgis Pretzels Inc 2267 Lancaster Pike	Reading	PA	19607	**800-817-3834**	610-775-0335	291-9

Alphabetical Section

Name / Address	City	State	ZIP	Toll-Free	Phone	Class
Tom Thumb 619 8th Ave	Crestview	FL	32536	**800-682-8486**	850-682-5171	203
Tomah Convention & Visitors Bureau 805 Superior Ave PO Box 625	Tomah	WI	54660	**800-948-6624**	608-372-2166	205
Tomax Corp 224 S 200 West	Salt Lake City	UT	84101	**800-255-8120**	801-990-0909	176-1
Tombigbee Electric Co-op Inc PO Box 610	Guin	AL	35563	**800-621-8069**	205-468-3325	244
Tomco Auto Products Co Inc 4330 E 26th St	Los Angeles	CA	90023	**800-858-3458**	323-268-4830	128
Tomkins Industries Inc LASCO Products Group 151 Industrial St	Lancaster	TX	75134	**800-876-3044**	972-227-6692	599
Tommy Armour Golf Co 36 Dufflaw Rd *Cust Svc	Toronto	ON	M6A2W1	**800-723-4653***	416-630-4996	701
Tommy Hilfiger USA Inc 25 W 39th St	New York	NY	10018	**800-888-8802**	212-840-8888	153-3
Tommy Nelson 402 BNA Dr Bldg 100 Suite 600	Nashville	TN	37217	**800-251-4000**	615-889-9000	623-4
Tommy Tape Mfg Inc 135 Redstone St	Southington	CT	06489	**800-866-8273**	860-378-0111	717
Tompkins Assoc 8970 Southall Rd	Raleigh	NC	27616	**800-789-1257**	919-876-3667	193
Tompkins Cortland Community College 170 North St	Dryden	NY	13053	**888-567-8211**	607-844-8211	160
Tompkins Trustco Inc 110 N Tioga St Ithaca Commons *AMEX: TMP*	Ithaca	NY	14850	**800-273-3210**	607-273-3210	71
Tom's of Maine Inc PO Box 710	Kennebunk	ME	04043	**800-367-8667**	207-985-2944	211
Tone Commander Systems Inc 11609 49th Pl W	Mukilteo	WA	98275	**800-524-0024**	425-349-1000	720
Tongass Trading Co 201 Dock St	Ketchikan	AK	99901	**800-235-5102**	907-225-5101	227
Toni & Guy USA Inc 2311 Midway Rd	Carrollton	TX	75006	**800-256-9391**	972-931-1567	79
Tonkin Ron Dealerships 122 NE 122nd Ave	Portland	OR	97230	**800-460-5328**	503-255-4100	57
Tony Lama Boot Co Inc 1137 Tony Lama St	El Paso	TX	79915	**800-866-9526**	915-778-8311	296
Tony Roma's Famous for Ribs 9304 Forest Ln Suite 200	Dallas	TX	75243	**800-286-7662**	214-343-7800	657
Too Inc 8323 Walton Pkwy *NYSE: TOO*	New Albany	OH	43054	**800-934-4496**	614-775-3500	658
Toobs Inc 349 B Quintana Rd	Morro Bay	CA	93442	**800-795-8662**	805-772-5742	701
Tooele County Chamber of Commerce 201 N Main PO Box 460	Tooele	UT	84074	**800-378-0690**	435-882-0690	137
Tooling & Machining Assn. National 9300 Livingston Rd	Fort Washington	MD	20744	**800-248-6862**	301-248-6200	49-13
Tools for Bending Inc 194 W Dakota Ave *Cust Svc	Denver	CO	80223	**800-873-3305***	303-777-7170	448
Tools & Fasteners Distributors Assn. Specialty 500 Elm Grove Rd	Elm Grove	WI	53122	**800-352-2981**	262-784-4774	49-18
Toolwire Inc 6120 Stoneridge Mall Rd Suite 110	Pleasanton	CA	94588	**866-935-8665**	925-227-8500	39
Tootsie Roll Industries Inc 7401 S Cicero Ave *NYSE: TR*	Chicago	IL	60629	**800-877-7655**	773-838-3400	291-8
Tootsies 4045 Westheimer Rd	Houston	TX	77027	**800-580-2220**	713-629-9990	155-6
Top Concepts Co 13436 McGrath Rd	Houston	TX	77047	**800-856-0696**	713-434-0696	188-12
Top Flight Paper Products Inc 1300 Central Ave	Chattanooga	TN	37408	**800-777-3740**	423-266-8171	260
Top-Flite Golf Co 425 Meadow St	Chicopee	MA	01021	**866-834-6532**	413-536-1200	701
Top-Seal Corp 2236 E University Dr	Phoenix	AZ	85034	**800-452-8677**	602-629-9000	152
Topa Insurance Corp 1800 Ave of the Stars 12th Fl	Los Angeles	CA	90067	**800-949-6505**	310-201-0451	384-4
Topcon Medical Systems Inc 37 W Century Rd	Paramus	NJ	07652	**800-223-1130**	201-261-9450	375
Topeka Capital-Journal 616 SE Jefferson St	Topeka	KS	66607	**800-777-7171**	785-295-1111	522-2
Topeka Convention & Visitors Bureau 1275 SW Topeka Blvd	Topeka	KS	66612	**800-235-1030**	785-234-1030	205
Topnotch at Stowe Resort & Spa 4000 Mountain Rd	Stowe	VT	05672	**800-451-8686**	802-253-8585	655
Topps Safety Apparel Inc 2516 E State Rd 14	Rochester	IN	46975	**800-348-2990**	574-223-4311	153-19
TOPS 2275 Cabot Dr	Lisle	IL	60532	**800-444-4660**	630-588-6000	111
TOPS Club Inc 4575 S 5th St	Milwaukee	WI	53207	**800-932-8677**	414-482-4620	48-17
Tops Markets Inc 6363 Main St	Williamsville	NY	14221	**800-522-2522**	716-635-5000	339
TopWorx Inc 3300 Fern Valley Rd	Louisville	KY	40213	**800-969-9020**	502-969-8000	715
Tor Books 175 5th Ave 14th Fl *Cust Svc	New York	NY	10010	**800-221-7945***	212-388-0100	623-2
TOR Minerals International Inc 722 Burleson St *NASDAQ: TORM*	Corpus Christi	TX	78302	**888-464-0147**	361-882-5175	141
Torch Energy Advisors Inc 1221 Lamar St Suite 1600	Houston	TX	77010	**800-324-8672**	713-650-1246	393
Torch Energy Royalty Trust 1221 Lamar Suite 1600 *NYSE: TRU*	Houston	TX	77010	**800-536-7453**		662
Torch Offshore Inc 401 Whitney Ave Suite 400	Gretna	LA	70056	**800-878-6724**	504-367-7030	187-5
Toreador Resources Corp 4809 Cole Ave Suite 108 *NASDAQ: TRGL*	Dallas	TX	75205	**800-966-2141**	214-559-3933	525
Torian Plum Condo Resort 1855 Ski Time Square Dr	Steamboat Springs	CO	80487	**800-228-2458**	970-879-8811	655
Torke Coffee Roasting Co Inc 3455 Paine Ave PO Box 694	Sheboygan	WI	53081	**800-242-7671**	920-458-4114	291-7
Tornos Technologies US Corp 70 Pocono Rd	Brookfield	CT	06804	**800-243-5027**	203-775-4319	447
Toro Co 8111 Lyndale Ave *NYSE: TTC*	Bloomington	MN	55420	**800-595-6841**	952-888-8801	420
Toro Co Irrigation Div 5825 Jasmine St	Riverside	CA	92502	**800-664-4740**	951-688-9221	269
Toronto Blue Jays 1 Blue Jays Way	Toronto	ON	M5V1J1	**888-654-6529**	416-341-1000	703
Toronto Convention & Visitors Assn 207 Queen's Quay W Suite 590	Toronto	ON	M5J1A7	**800-363-1990**	416-203-2600	205
Toronto Stock Exchange 130 King St W	Toronto	ON	M5X1J2	**888-873-8392**	416-947-4700	680
Torray Fund 7501 Wisconsin Ave Suite 1100	Bethesda	MD	20814	**800-443-3036**	301-493-4600	517
Torrington Supply Co Inc 100 N Elm St	Waterbury	CT	06723	**800-445-9936**	203-756-3641	601
Tortuga Coastal Cantina 1135 Edgebrook St	Houston	TX	77034	**800-741-7574**	713-943-7574	657
Tosh Farms 1586 Atlantic Ave	Henry	TN	38231	**888-243-4885**	731-243-4861	11-4
Toshiba America Electronic Components Inc 19900 MacArthur Blvd Suite 400 *Cust Svc	Irvine	CA	92612	**800-879-4963***	949-455-2000	686
Toshiba America Inc 1251 Ave of the Americas 41st Fl	New York	NY	10020	**800-457-7777**	212-596-0600	52
Toshiba America Information Systems Inc 9740 Irvine Blvd *Cust Svc	Irvine	CA	92618	**800-457-7777***	949-583-3000	171-3
Toshiba America Medical Systems Inc 2441 Michelle Dr	Tustin	CA	92780	**800-421-1968**	714-730-5000	375
Toshiba America MRI Inc 300 Utah Ave Suite 100	South San Francisco	CA	94080	**800-477-4674**	650-872-2722	375
Toshiba International Corp 13131 W Little York Rd	Houston	TX	77041	**800-231-1412**	713-466-0277	507
Tosoh SMD Inc 3600 Gantz Rd	Grove City	OH	43123	**800-678-8942**	614-875-7912	686
Total Control Products Inc 2500 Austin Dr	Charlottesville	VA	22911	**800-263-6041**	434-978-5000	171-3
Total Energy Services Ltd 520 5th Ave SW Suite 2410 *TSE: TOT*	Calgary	AB	T2P3R7	**877-818-6825**	403-216-3939	529
Total Image Specialists 1877 E 17th Ave	Columbus	OH	43219	**800-366-7446**	614-564-1300	692
Total Logistic Control Inc 8300 Logistic Dr	Zeeland	MI	49464	**800-333-5599**	616-772-9009	790-2
Total Lubricants USA 5 N Stiles St	Linden	NJ	07036	**800-344-2241**	908-862-9300	530
Total Meeting Resources Inc 1435A McLendon Dr	Decatur	GA	30033	**800-783-5881**	770-496-8580	183
Total Plastics Inc 3316 Pagosa Ct	Indianapolis	IN	46226	**800-382-4635**	317-543-3540	591
Total System Services Inc 1600 1st Ave *NYSE: TSS*	Columbus	GA	31901	**800-241-0912**	706-649-2310	254
Total Technologies Ltd 9 Studebaker	Irvine	CA	92618	**800-669-4885**	949-465-0200	252
Total Travel & Tickets Inc 6250 N Andrews Ave Suite 205	Fort Lauderdale	FL	33309	**800-493-8499**	954-493-9151	735
Totality Corp 44 Montgomery St Suite 500	San Francisco	CA	94104	**888-486-8254**	415-402-3000	39
TOTE (Totem Ocean Trailer Express Inc) 32001 32nd Ave S Suite 200	Federal Way	WA	98001	**800-426-0074**		307
Tote Cart Co Inc 1802 Preston St	Rockford	IL	61102	**800-435-5709**	815-963-3414	75
Totem Electric of Tacoma 2332 S Jefferson Ave	Tacoma	WA	98402	**800-562-8478**	253-383-5022	188-4
Totem Ocean Trailer Express Inc (TOTE) 32001 32nd Ave S Suite 200	Federal Way	WA	98001	**800-426-0074**		307
Toter Inc PO Box 5338	Statesville	NC	28677	**800-424-0422**	704-872-8171	198
Totes Isotoner Corp 9655 International Blvd	Cincinnati	OH	45246	**800-762-8712**	513-682-8200	772
Toto Tours Ltd 1326 W Albion Ave	Chicago	IL	60626	**800-565-1241**	773-274-8686	748
TOTO USA Inc 1155 Southern Rd	Morrow	GA	30260	**888-295-8134**	770-282-8686	600
Touch for Health Kinesiology Assn PO Box 392	New Carlisle	OH	45344	**800-466-8342**	937-845-3404	48-17
TouchAmerica PO Box 1304	Hillsborough	NC	27278	**800-678-6824**	919-732-6968	78
Touchstone Applied Science Assoc Inc 4 Hardscrabble Heights PO Box 382 *Cust Svc	Brewster	NY	10509	**800-800-2598***	845-277-8100	242
TouchSystems Corp 220 Tradesmen Dr	Hutto	TX	78634	**800-320-5944**	512-846-2424	603
Tougaloo College 500 W County Line Rd *Admissions	Tougaloo	MS	39174	**888-424-2566***	601-977-7700	163
Tougher Industries Inc 175 Broadway	Albany	NY	12204	**800-836-0752**	518-465-3426	188-10
TOUGHLOVE International 100 Mechanics St	Doylestown	PA	18901	**800-333-1069**	215-348-7090	48-6
Tour Assn Inc. National 546 E Main St	Lexington	KY	40508	**800-682-8886**	859-226-4444	48-23
Tourco Inc 16 E Pond Rd	Nobleboro	ME	04555	**800-537-5378**	207-563-2288	748
Tourette Syndrome Assn Inc 42-40 Bell Blvd Suite 205	Bayside	NY	11361	**888-486-8738**	718-224-2999	48-17
Touring & Tasting 207 E Victoria St	Santa Barbara	CA	93101	**800-850-4370**	805-965-2813	435
Tourism Assn of the Dickinson County Area 600 S Stephenson Ave	Iron Mountain	MI	49801	**800-236-2447**	906-774-2945	205
Tourism Australia 6100 Center Dr Suite 1150	Los Angeles	CA	90045	**800-369-6863**	310-695-3200	764
Tourism Authority of Thailand 611 N Larchmont Blvd 1st Fl	Los Angeles	CA	90004	**800-842-4526**	323-461-9814	764
Tourism Bureau Southwestern Illinois 10950 Lincoln Trail	Fairview Heights	IL	62208	**800-442-1488**	618-397-1488	205
Tourism Calgary 238 11th Ave SE Suite 200	Calgary	AB	T2G0X8	**800-661-1678**	403-263-8510	205
Tourism Grays Harbor PO Box 1229	Elma	WA	98541	**800-621-9625**	360-482-2651	205
Tourism Lewis County 500 NW Chamber of Commerce Way	Chehalis	WA	98532	**800-525-3323**	360-748-8885	205
Tourism Malaysia 818 W 7th St Suite 970	Los Angeles	CA	90017	**800-336-6842**	213-689-9702	764
Tourism Malaysia 120 E 56th St Suite 810	New York	NY	10022	**800-336-6842**	212-754-1113	764
Tourism New Brunswick 26 Roseberry St	Campbellton	NB	E3N2G4	**800-561-0123**	506-789-4982	763
Tourism New Zealand 501 Santa Monica Blvd Suite 300	Santa Monica	CA	90401	**866-639-9325**	310-395-7480	764
Tourism Saskatchewan 1922 Park St	Regina	SK	S4N7M4	**877-237-2273**	306-787-9600	763
Tourism Vancouver 200 Burrard St	Vancouver	BC	V6C3L6	**800-663-6000**	604-683-2000	205
Tourism Yukon PO Box 2703	Whitehorse	YT	Y1A2C6	**800-661-0494**	867-667-5036	763
Tourisme Montréal 1555 rue Peel Bureau 600	Montreal	QC	H3A3L8	**800-363-7777**	514-844-5400	205

Name / Address	City	State	ZIP	Toll-Free	Phone	Class
Tourisme Quebec 1010 Saint Catherines W 4th Fl	Montreal	QC	H3B1G2	800-363-7777		763
Tower 2000 Inc 310 60th St NW	Sauk Rapids	MN	56379	877-720-6249	320-253-5489	187-1
Tower Erectors. National Assn of 8 2nd St SE	Watertown	SD	57201	888-882-5865	605-882-5865	49-3
Tower Federal Credit Union 7901 Sandy Spring Rd	Laurel	MD	20707	800-787-8328	301-497-7000	216
Tower Financial Corp 116 E Berry St *NASDAQ: TOFC*	Fort Wayne	IN	46802	877-427-7220	260-427-7000	355-2
Tower on the Park Hotel 9715 110th St	Edmonton	AB	T5K2M1	800-720-2179	780-488-1626	372
Tower Records 2500 Del Monte St Bldg C	West Sacramento	CA	95691	800-225-0880	916-373-2500	514
Tower Travel Management 1 Tower Ln Suite 2520	Oakbrook Terrace	IL	60181	800-542-9700	630-954-3000	760
Towing & Recovery Assn of America (TRAA) 2121 Eisenhower Ave Suite 200	Alexandria	VA	22314	800-728-0136	703-684-7734	49-21
Towmaster Inc 61381 US Hwy 12	Litchfield	MN	55355	800-462-4517	320-693-7900	768
Town & Country Cedar Homes Co 4772 US Hwy 131 S	Petoskey	MI	49770	800-968-3178	231-347-4360	107
Town & Country Electric 2662 American Dr	Appleton	WI	54915	800-274-2345	920-738-1500	188-4
Town & Country Furniture 6545 Airline Hwy	Baton Rouge	LA	70805	800-375-6660	225-355-6666	316
Town & Country Inn & Conference Center 2008 Savannah Hwy	Charleston	SC	29407	800-334-6660	843-571-1000	373
Town & Country Magazine 1700 Broadway	New York	NY	10019	800-289-8696	212-903-5000	449-11
Town & Country Motor Inn Rt 2 PO Box 220	Gorham	NH	03581	800-325-4386	603-466-3315	373
Town & Country Resort & Convention Center 500 Hotel Cir N	San Diego	CA	92108	800-772-8527	619-291-7131	655
Town & Country Trust 300 E Lombard St Suite 1700 *NYSE: TCT*	Baltimore	MD	21202	800-735-2468	410-539-7600	641
Town Fair Tire Co Inc 460 Coe Ave	East Haven	CT	06512	800-972-2245	203-467-8600	54
Town Food Service Equipment Co 351 Bowery	New York	NY	10003	800-221-5032	212-473-8355	293
Town Inn Suites 620 Church St	Toronto	ON	M4Y2G2	800-387-2755	416-964-3311	372
Town Talk Inc 6310 Cane Run Rd PO Box 58157	Louisville	KY	40268	800-626-2220	502-933-7575	153-9
Town Watch. National Assn of 1 E Wynnewood Rd Suite 102	Wynnewood	PA	19096	800-648-3688	610-649-7055	48-7
Towne Realty Inc 710 N Plankinton Ave 12th Fl	Milwaukee	WI	53203	800-945-4450	414-273-2200	638
Towne Square 2000 Inc 402 Hawkins St	Hillsboro	TX	76645	800-356-1663	254-582-7444	314-2
TownePlace Suites by Marriott 1 Marriott Dr	Washington	DC	20058	800-228-9290	301-380-3000	369
TownHouse Inn 1411 10th Ave S	Great Falls	MT	59405	800-442-4667	406-761-4600	373
Townsend Engineering Co PO Box 1433	Des Moines	IA	50305	800-247-8609	515-265-8181	293
Townsend Hotel 100 Townsend St	Birmingham	MI	48009	800-548-4172	248-642-7900	373
Townsend Industries Inc 6650 NE 41st Ave	Altoona	IA	50009	877-868-3544	515-967-4261	617
Towson University 8000 York Rd	Towson	MD	21252	800-225-5878	410-704-2000	163
Toxic Substances & Disease Registry. Agency for Centers for Disease Control & Prevention 1600 Clifton Rd NE Bldg 37 MS E-29	Atlanta	GA	30333	888-422-8737	404-498-0110	654
Toxicology & Chemistry. Society of Environmental 1010 N 12th Ave	Pensacola	FL	32501	888-899-2088	850-469-1500	49-19
Toyo Ink America LLC 710 W Belden	Addison	IL	60101	800-227-8696	630-930-5100	381
Toyo Tire USA Corp 6261 Katella Ave Suite 2B	Cypress	CA	90630	800-678-3250	714-236-2080	739
Toyoda Machinery USA Inc 316 W University Dr	Arlington Heights	IL	60004	800-257-2985	847-253-0340	447
Toyoshima Special Steel USA 735 S Saint Paul St	Indianapolis	IN	46203	800-428-4599	317-638-3511	462
Toyota Canada Inc 1 Toyota Pl *Cust Svc	Scarborough	ON	M1H1H9	888-869-6828*	416-438-6320	59
Toyota Motor Credit Corp 19001 S Western Ave *Cust Svc	Torrance	CA	90509	800-392-2968*	310-787-1310	215
Toyota Motor North America Inc 9 W 57th St Suite 4900	New York	NY	10019	800-331-4331	212-223-0303	355-3
Toyota Motor Sales USA Inc 19001 S Western Ave *Cust Svc	Torrance	CA	90509	800-331-4331*	310-468-4000	59
Toyota Motor Sales USA Inc Lexus Div 19001 S Western Ave *Cust Svc	Torrance	CA	90509	800-331-4331*	310-468-4000	59
Toyota Tsusho America Inc 437 Madison Ave 29th Fl	New York	NY	10022	800-883-0100	212-418-0100	483
Toys 'R' Us Inc 1 Geoffrey Way *NYSE: TOY*	Wayne	NJ	07470	800-869-7787	973-617-3500	749
TP Orthodontics Inc 100 Center Plaza	La Porte	IN	46350	800-348-8856	219-785-2591	226
TPi Billing Solutions PO Box 472330	Tulsa	OK	74147	800-332-0023	918-664-0144	250
TPI Corp PO Box 4973	Johnson City	TN	37602	800-251-0382	423-477-4131	16
TPL (Trust for Public Land) 116 New Montgomery St 4th Fl	San Francisco	CA	94105	800-729-6428	415-495-4014	48-13
TPL Communications 3370 San Fernando Rd Unit 206	Los Angeles	CA	90065	800-447-6937	323-256-3000	633
TPR (Texas Public Radio) 8401 Datapoint Dr Suite 800	San Antonio	TX	78229	800-622-8977	210-614-8977	620
TQ3 Travel Solutions 84 Inverness Cir E	Englewood	CO	80112	877-628-4426	303-706-0800	761
TQ3Navigant 84 Inverness Cir E	Englewood	CO	80112	877-628-4426	303-706-0800	760
TQ3NavigantVacations.com 84 Inverness Cir E	Englewood	CO	80112	800-783-9200	303-706-0800	760
TR Miller Mill Co Inc PO Box 708	Brewton	AL	36427	800-633-6740	251-867-4331	671
TRAA (Towing & Recovery Assn of America) 2121 Eisenhower Ave Suite 200	Alexandria	VA	22314	800-728-0136	703-684-7734	49-21
TRAC Media Services 4380 N Campbell Ave Suite 205	Tucson	AZ	85718	888-299-1866	520-299-1866	620
Trachte Building Systems Inc 314 Wilburn Rd	Sun Prairie	WI	53590	800-356-5824	608-837-7899	106
Track Data Corp 56 Pine St *NASDAQ: TRAC*	New York	NY	10005	800-223-0113	212-943-4555	176-10
TRACO 71 Progress Ave	Cranberry Township	PA	16066	800-468-7226	724-776-7000	232
Tract Society. American 1624 N 1st St	Garland	TX	75040	800-548-7228	972-276-9408	48-20
Tractech Inc 11445 Stephens Dr	Warren	MI	48090	800-328-3850	586-759-3850	60
Traction Wholesale Center Inc 1515 Parkway Ave	Trenton	NJ	08628	800-846-8847	609-771-9383	740
Trade Secret Div Regis Corp 7201 Metro Blvd	Minneapolis	MN	55439	888-888-7778	952-947-7777	79
Trade-Winds Environmental Restoration Inc 100 Sweeneydale Ave	Bay Shore	NY	11706	800-282-8701	631-435-8900	84
Trader Publications Inc 185 Kisco Ave	Mount Kisco	NY	10549	800-689-5933	914-666-6222	623-8
Trader Vic's Inc 2 Fifer Ave Suite 130	Corte Madera	CA	94925	877-762-4824	415-927-9788	657
Tradeshow Week Newsletter 5700 Wilshire Blvd Suite 120	Los Angeles	CA	90036	800-375-4212	323-965-5300	521-2
TradeStation Group Inc 8050 SW 10th St Suite 2000 *NASDAQ: TRAD*	Plantation	FL	33324	800-871-3577	954-652-7000	176-10
TradeStation Securities Inc 8050 SW 10th St Suite 2000	Plantation	FL	33324	800-515-3238	954-652-7000	679
TradeWinds Island Grand Beach Resort 5500 Gulf Blvd	Saint Pete Beach	FL	33705	800-360-4016	727-367-6461	655
TradeWinds Sandpiper Beach Resort 6000 Gulf Blvd	Saint Pete Beach	FL	33705	800-237-0707	727-360-5551	655
Trading Direct 160 Broadway E Bldg 7th Fl	New York	NY	10038	800-925-8566	212-766-0230	679
Traditional Home Magazine 1716 Locust St *Circ	Des Moines	IA	50309	800-374-8791*	515-284-3000	449-11
Trados Inc 1292 Hammerwood Ave	Sunnyvale	CA	94089	888-487-2367	408-743-3500	176-1
Traex Co 101 Traex Plaza	Dane	WI	53529	800-356-8006	608-849-2500	295
Trafalgar Ghurka Ltd 300 Wilson Ave	Norwalk	CT	06854	800-587-1584	203-853-4747	444
Trafalgar Tours 801 E Katella Ave	Anaheim	CA	92805	866-544-4434		748
Traffic Control Corp 780 W Belden Ave Suite D	Addison	IL	60101	800-996-6511	630-543-1300	691
Traffic Control Service Inc 1881 Betmor Ln	Anaheim	CA	92805	800-222-8274	714-937-0422	261-4
Traffic Safety Services Assn. American 15 Riverside Pkwy Suite 100	Fredericksburg	VA	22406	800-272-8772	540-368-1701	49-21
Trail Assn. North Country 229 E Main St	Lowell	MI	49331	866-445-3628	616-897-5987	48-23
Trail Assn. Pacific Crest 5325 Elkhorn Blvd PMB 256	Sacramento	CA	95842	888-728-7245	916-349-2109	48-23
Trail Foundation. Ice Age Park & 207 E Buffalo St Suite 515	Milwaukee	WI	53202	800-227-0046	414-278-8518	48-23
Trail Heritage Foundation. Lewis & Clark PO Box 3434	Great Falls	MT	59404	888-701-3434	406-454-1234	48-23
Trail King Industries Inc 147 Industrial Pk Rd	Brookville	PA	15825	800-545-1549	814-849-2342	768
Trailer Bridge Inc 10405 New Berlin Rd E *NASDAQ: TRBR*	Jacksonville	FL	32226	800-554-1589	904-751-7100	307
Trailer Life Magazine 2575 Vista Del Mar Dr	Ventura	CA	93001	800-765-7070	805-667-4100	449-22
Trailmobile Corp 1101 Skokie Blvd Suite 350	Northbrook	IL	60062	800-877-4990	847-504-2000	768
Trailmobile Trailer LLC 1101 Skokie Blvd Suite 350	Northbrook	IL	60062	800-877-4990	847-504-2000	768
Trails Assn. Oregon-California PO Box 1019	Independence	MO	64051	888-811-6282	816-252-2276	48-23
Trailstar Mfg Corp 20700 Harrisburg-Westville Rd	Alliance	OH	44601	800-235-5635	330-821-9900	768
Trainers Assn. National Athletic 2952 Stemmons Fwy Suite 200	Dallas	TX	75247	800-879-6282	214-637-6282	48-22
Training in the Behavioral Sciences. Association for Advanced 5126 Ralston St	Ventura	CA	93003	800-472-1931	805-676-3030	49-5
Training & Development. American Society for 1640 King St Box 1443	Alexandria	VA	22313	800-628-2783	703-683-8100	49-5
Training Magazine 50 S 9th St *Cust Svc	Minneapolis	MN	55402	800-328-4329*	612-333-0471	449-5
Trains Magazine 21027 Crossroads Cir	Waukesha	WI	53186	888-350-2413	262-796-8776	449-14
Trajen Inc 10510 Superfortress Ave	Mather	CA	95655	800-565-2647	916-368-1455	63
Tramco Pump Co 1500 W Adams St	Chicago	IL	60607	877-872-6260	312-243-5800	627
Tranax Technologies Inc 44320 Nobel Dr	Fremont	CA	94538	888-340-2484	510-770-2227	56
Trandes Corp 4601 Presidents Dr Suite 360	Lanham	MD	20706	800-878-0201	301-459-0200	258
Trans Am Travel Inc 4300 King St Suite 130	Alexandria	VA	22302	800-822-7600	703-998-7676	17
Trans-Bridge Lines Inc 2012 Industrial Dr	Bethlehem	PA	18017	800-962-9135	610-868-6001	109
Trans-Bridge Tours 1155 MacArthur Rd	Whitehall	PA	18052	800-962-9135	610-776-8687	748
Trans-Lux Corp 110 Richards Ave *AMEX: TLX*	Norwalk	CT	06854	800-243-5544	203-853-4321	171-4
Trans-Lux Fair-Play Inc 1700 Delaware Ave	Des Moines	IA	50317	800-247-0265	515-265-5305	171-4
Trans National Communications International Inc 2 Charlesgate W Suite 500	Boston	MA	02215	800-900-5210	617-369-1000	721
Trans Technology Corp Breeze-Eastern Div 700 Liberty Ave *Sales	Union	NJ	07083	800-929-1919*	908-686-4000	462
Trans World Entertainment Corp 38 Corporate Cir *NASDAQ: TWMC*	Albany	NY	12203	800-540-1242	518-452-1242	514

Name / Address	City	State	ZIP	Toll-Free	Phone	Class
TransAct Technologies Inc 7 Laser Ln — *NASDAQ: TACT*	Wallingford	CT	06492	**800-243-8941**	203-269-1198	171-6
Transaction Network Services 1939 Roland Clarke Pl — *NYSE: TNS*	Reston	VA	20191	**800-240-2824**	703-453-8300	721
TransAm Trucking Inc 15910 S 169th Hwy	Olathe	KS	66051	**800-573-0588**	913-782-5300	769
Transamerica Commercial Finance Corp 11121 Carmel Commons Blvd Suite 350	Charlotte	NC	28226	**800-932-0999**	704-542-5134	214
Transamerica Financial Life Insurance Co 4 Manhattanville Rd Mail Drop 2-50	Purchase	NY	10577	**888-617-6781**	914-697-8000	384-2
Transamerica IDEX Mutual Funds PO Box 9015 — *Cust Svc	Clearwater	FL	33758	**800-233-4339***	727-299-1800	517
Transamerica Investment Management 1150 S Olive St Suite 2700	Los Angeles	CA	90015	**866-846-1800**	720-941-9124	393
Transamerica Life Insurance & Annuity Co 1150 S Olive St	Los Angeles	CA	90015	**800-346-1608**	213-742-3111	384-2
Transamerica Occidental Life Insurance Co 1150 S Olive St — *Cust Svc	Los Angeles	CA	90015	**800-852-4678***	213-742-2111	384-2
Transat Holidays USA Inc 140 S Federal Hwy	Dania	FL	33004	**866-828-4872**	954-920-0090	760
Transat AT Inc 1160 Cargo A-1 Rd Montreal International Airport — *TSE: TRZ*	Mirabel	QC	J7N1G9	**877-470-1011**	450-476-1011	760
TransCanada Pipelines Ltd 450 1st St SW — *NYSE: TRP*	Calgary	AB	T2P5H1	**800-661-3805**	403-920-2000	320
Transcat Inc 35 Vantage Point Dr — *NASDAQ: TRNS*	Rochester	NY	14624	**800-828-1470**	585-352-7777	200
Transcend Services Inc 945 E Paces Ferry Rd NE Suite 1475 — *NASDAQ: TRCR*	Atlanta	GA	30326	**800-225-7552**	404-836-8000	455
Transcentive Inc 2 Enterprise Dr	Shelton	CT	06484	**888-340-4267**	203-944-7300	176-1
TransChemical Inc 419 E DeSoto Ave	Saint Louis	MO	63147	**888-873-6481**	314-231-6905	144
Transco Industries Inc 5534 NE 122nd Ave	Portland	OR	97230	**800-545-9991**	503-256-1955	206
Transco Products Corp PO Box 1025	Linden	NJ	07036	**800-876-0039**	908-862-0030	644
TransCon Builders Inc 25250 Rockside Rd	Bedford Heights	OH	44146	**800-362-0371**	440-439-3400	639
Transcontinent Record Sales Inc DBA Record Theatre 1762 Main St	Buffalo	NY	14208	**800-836-0751**	716-883-9520	514
Transcontinental Insurance Co 333 S Wabash Ave CNA Ctr	Chicago	IL	60685	**800-262-2000**	312-822-5000	384-4
Transcontinental Media 1100 Rene-Levesque Blvd W 24th fl	Montreal	QC	H3B4X9	**800-461-3773**	514-392-9000	623-9
Transcontinental Printing Inc 395 Lebeau Blvd	Saint-Laurent	QC	H4N1S2	**800-337-8560**	514-337-8560	614
Transcontinental Realty Investors Inc 1800 Valley View Ln 1 Hickory Ctr — *NYSE: TCI*	Dallas	TX	75234	**800-400-6407**	469-522-4200	640
TransCore Holdings Inc 8158 Adams Dr Bldg 200	Hummelstown	PA	17036	**800-233-2172**	717-561-2400	258
Transcraft Corp 110 Florsheim Dr	Anna	IL	62906	**800-950-2995**	618-833-5151	768
Transcript International 3900 NW 12th St Suite 200	Lincoln	NE	68521	**800-228-0226**	402-474-4800	633
Transcription. American Assn for Medical 100 Sycamore Ave	Modesto	CA	95354	**800-982-2182**	209-527-9620	49-8
Transeastern Properties Inc 3300 N University Dr Suite 001	Coral Springs	FL	33065	**877-352-4635**	954-346-9700	639
Transervice Lease Corp 5 Dakota Dr Suite 209	Lake Success	NY	11042	**800-645-8018**	516-488-3400	284
Transgenomic Inc 12325 Emmet St — *NASDAQ: TBIO*	Omaha	NE	68164	**888-233-9283**	402-452-5400	410
TransGlobal Vacations 8907 N Port Washington Rd	Milwaukee	WI	53217	**800-699-2080**	414-228-7472	760
Transicoil 2560 General Armistead Ave	Norristown	PA	19403	**800-323-7115**	610-539-4400	507
Transilwrap Co Inc 9201 W Belmont Ave	Franklin Park	IL	60131	**800-745-5802**	847-678-1800	589
Transit Assn. International Safe 1400 Abbott Rd Suite 160	East Lansing	MI	48823	**888-367-4782**	517-333-3437	49-21
Transit Mix Concrete & Materials Co PO Box 5187	Beaumont	TX	77726	**800-835-4933**	409-835-4933	180
Transit Union. Amalgamated 5025 Wisconsin Ave NW 3rd Fl	Washington	DC	20016	**888-240-1196**	202-537-1645	405
Transitions Optical Inc 9251 Belcher Rd	Pinellas Park	FL	33782	**800-848-1506**	727-545-0400	531
Translators. Wycliffe Bible PO Box 628200	Orlando	FL	32862	**800-992-5433**	407-852-3611	48-20
Translite Sonoma 22678 Broadway Suite 1	Sonoma	CA	95476	**800-473-3242**	707-996-6906	431
Transmedia Productions Inc 719 Battery St	San Francisco	CA	94111	**800-229-7234**	415-956-3118	632
Transmission USA 4444 W 147th St	Midlothian	IL	60445	**800-377-9247**	708-389-5922	305
Transnation Title Insurance Co 101 Gateway Ctr Pkwy Gateway 1	Richmond	VA	23205	**800-388-8822**	804-267-8000	384-6
Transnational Financial Network Inc 401 Taraval St 2nd Fl — *AMEX: TFN*	San Francisco	CA	94116	**888-229-2344**	415-242-7800	498
TransNet Corp 45 Columbia Rd	Somerville	NJ	08876	**800-526-4965**	908-253-0500	174
Transocean Inc 4 Greenway Plaza — *NYSE: RIG*	Houston	TX	77046	**888-748-6334**	713-232-7500	529
Transora 10 S Riverside Plaza Suite 2000	Chicago	IL	60606	**877-872-5984**	312-463-4000	176-4
Transource Computers Corp 10850 N 24th Ave Suite 102	Phoenix	AZ	85029	**800-486-3715**	602-997-8101	171-3
Transparent Language Inc 9 Executive Park Dr	Merrimack	NH	03054	**800-730-2230**	603-262-6300	176-3
Transplant Assn. Children's Organ 2501 Cota Dr	Bloomington	IN	47403	**800-366-2682**	812-336-8872	48-17
Transplant Services Center University of Texas 5323 Harry Hines Blvd MC 9074	Dallas	TX	75390	**800-433-6667**	214-648-2609	535
Transpo Electronics Inc 2150 Brengle Ave	Orlando	FL	32808	**800-327-7792**	407-298-4563	246
Transport Assn of America. Air 1301 Pennsylvania Ave NW Suite 1100	Washington	DC	20004	**800-319-2463**	202-626-4000	49-21
Transport Corp of America Inc 1715 Yankee Doodle Rd — *NASDAQ: TCAM*	Eagan	MN	55121	**800-328-3927**	651-686-2500	769
Transport Health Employees. International Union of Industrial Service 254 W 31st St	New York	NY	10001	**800-331-1070**	212-696-5545	405
Transport Inc PO Box 400	Moorhead	MN	56561	**800-949-7678**	218-236-6300	769
Transport International Pool 426 W Lancaster Ave	Devon	PA	19333	**800-333-2030**	610-647-4900	767
Transport Service Co 908 N Elm St Suite 101 — *Sales	Hinsdale	IL	60521	**800-323-5561***	630-920-5800	769
Transportation Assn of America. Community 1341 G St NW Suite 1000	Washington	DC	20005	**800-527-8279**	202-628-1480	49-21
Transportation Assn. National Air 4226 King St	Alexandria	VA	22302	**800-808-6282**	703-845-9000	49-21
Transportation Capital Corp 437 Madison Ave 38th Fl	New York	NY	10022	**800-829-4867**	212-328-2100	395
Transportation Insurance Co 333 S Wabash Ave	Chicago	IL	60604	**800-262-2000**	312-822-5000	384-4
Transportation Research Board (TRB) 500 5th St NW	Washington	DC	20001	**800-424-9818**	202-334-2934	49-21
Transportation Research Center Inc Ohio State University 10820 Rt 347 PO Box B 67	East Liberty	OH	43319	**800-837-7872**	937-666-2011	654
Transportation Society of America. Intelligent 1100 17th St NW Suite 1200	Washington	DC	20036	**800-374-8472**	202-484-4847	49-21
Transportation Union. United 14600 Detroit Ave	Lakewood	OH	44107	**800-558-8842**	216-228-9400	405
TransPro Inc 100 Gando Dr — *AMEX: TPR*	New Haven	CT	06513	**800-755-2160**	203-401-6450	16
Transtar Metals 14400 S Figueroa St	Gardena	CA	90248	**800-344-4972**	323-321-1700	483
Transtector Systems Inc 10701 Airport Dr	Hayden Lake	ID	83835	**800-882-9110**	208-772-8515	803
Transtek Inc PO Box 4174	Harrisburg	PA	17111	**800-871-1935**	717-564-6151	62-5
TransUnion LLC 555 W Adams St	Chicago	IL	60661	**800-916-8800**	312-258-1717	212
Transwall Div Kimball International Inc 1220 Wilson Dr	West Chester	PA	19380	**800-441-9255**	610-429-1400	281
TransWestern Publishing Co LLC 8344 Clairemont Mesa Blvd	San Diego	CA	92111	**800-333-1111**	858-467-2800	623-6
TransWorks 9910 Dupont Circle Dr E Suite 200	Fort Wayne	IN	46825	**800-435-4691**	260-487-4400	176-10
TransWorld Media 353 Airport Rd	Oceanside	CA	92054	**800-788-7072**	760-722-7777	623-9
TransWorld SNOWboarding Magazine 353 Airport Rd	Oceanside	CA	92054	**800-788-7072**	760-722-7777	449-20
TransWorld Surf Magazine 353 Airport Rd	Oceanside	CA	92054	**800-788-7072**	760-722-7777	449-20
Transworld Systems Inc 5880 Commerce Blvd	Rohnert Park	CA	94928	**800-435-1526**	707-584-4225	157
Transylvania University 300 N Broadway	Lexington	KY	40508	**800-872-6798**	859-233-8300	163
Tranter Inc 1900 Old Burk Hwy	Wichita Falls	TX	76307	**800-414-6908**	940-723-7125	92
Tranter Inc Texas Div 1900 Old Burk Hwy	Wichita Falls	TX	76306	**800-414-6908**	940-723-7125	92
Tranzonic Cos 670 Alpha Dr	Highland Heights	OH	44143	**800-553-7979**	440-449-6550	548-2
Trapp Family Lodge 700 Trapp Hill Rd PO Box 1428	Stowe	VT	05672	**800-826-7000**	802-253-8511	655
Trau & Loevner Inc 5817 Centre Ave	Pittsburgh	PA	15206	**800-245-6207**	412-361-7700	675
Traulsen & Co Inc 4401 Blue Mound Rd	Fort Worth	TX	76106	**800-825-8220**	817-625-9671	15
Trauma Society. American 8903 Presidential Pkwy Suite 512	Upper Marlboro	MD	20772	**800-556-7890**	301-420-4189	49-8
Trauth Louis Dairy Inc 16 E 11th St	Newport	KY	41071	**800-544-6455**	859-431-7553	291-25
Travcoa 2424 SE Bristol Suite 310	Newport Beach	CA	92660	**800-992-2003**	949-476-2800	748
Travel + Leisure Magazine 1120 Ave of the Americas 10th Fl	New York	NY	10036	**800-888-8728**	212-382-5600	449-22
Travel Adventures Inc 1175 S Lapeer Rd	Lapeer	MI	48446	**800-356-2737**	810-664-1777	748
Travel Advisors 7930 Lee Blvd	Leawood	KS	66206	**800-745-6260**	913-649-6266	760
Travel Agent Magazine 1 Park Ave 2nd Fl	New York	NY	10016	**800-342-8244**	212-951-6600	449-22
Travel Agent Network. International Airlines 300 Garden City Plaza Suite 342	Garden City	NY	11530	**800-294-2826**	516-663-6000	49-21
Travel Agents. American Society of 1101 King St Suite 200	Alexandria	VA	22314	**800-440-2782**	703-739-2782	48-23
Travel Agents. Association of Retail 73 White Bridge Rd Box 238	Nashville	TN	37205	**800-969-6069**		49-21
Travel Agents. Institute of Certified 148 Linden St Suite 305	Wellesley	MA	02482	**800-542-4282**	781-237-0280	48-23
Travel Alberta 10123 99th St Suite 1600 Sun Life Pl	Edmonton	AB	T5J3H1	**800-252-3782**	780-427-4321	763
Travel Assn. International Gay & Lesbian 4331 N Federal Hwy Suite 304	Fort Lauderdale	FL	33308	**800-448-8550**	954-776-2626	48-23
Travel Authority Inc 702 N Shore Dr Suite 300	Jeffersonville	IN	47130	**800-626-2717**	812-206-5100	760
Travel Bound Inc 599 Broadway 12th Fl	New York	NY	10012	**800-808-9541**	212-334-1350	748
Travel Channel 8516 Georgia Ave	Silver Spring	MD	20910	**888-404-5969**	240-662-2000	725
Travel Club. Special Military Active Retired 600 University Office Blvd Suite 1A	Pensacola	FL	32504	**800-354-7681**		48-23

Name / Address	City	State	ZIP	Toll-Free	Phone	Class
Travel Destinations Management Group Inc 110 Painters Mill Rd Suite 36	Owings Mills	MD	21117	800-635-7307	410-363-3111	760
Travel Dynamics International 132 E 70th St	New York	NY	10021	800-257-5767	212-517-7555	217
Travel Executives. Association of Corporate 515 King St Suite 340	Alexandria	VA	22314	800-228-3669	703-683-5322	48-23
Travel Guard International 1145 Clark St	Stevens Point	WI	54481	800-826-1300	715-345-0505	384-7
Travel Holiday Magazine 1633 Broadway *Circ	New York	NY	10019	800-937-9241*	212-767-6000	449-22
Travel Impressions Ltd 465 Smith St	Farmingdale	NY	11735	800-284-0044	631-845-8000	760
Travel Inc 4355 River Green Pkwy	Duluth	GA	30096	800-452-6575	770-291-4100	760
Travel Inn Biloxi 2010 Beach Blvd	Biloxi	MS	39531	800-676-4465	228-388-5531	373
Travel Institute 148 Linden St Suite 305	Wellesley	MA	02482	800-542-4282	781-237-0280	48-23
Travel Insured International 52-S Oakland Ave PO Box 280568	East Hartford	CT	06128	800-243-3174	860-528-7663	384-7
Travel Manitoba 155 Carlton St 7th Fl	Winnipeg	MB	R3C3H8	800-665-0040	204-945-3777	763
Travel Marketing Inc PO Box 69629	Portland	OR	97239	800-283-1022	503-222-1020	377
Travel Mates of Virginia Inc PO Box 2	Harrisonburg	VA	22803	888-262-4863	540-434-4155	748
Travel Planners Inc 381 Park Ave S	New York	NY	10016	800-221-3531	212-532-1660	368
Travel-Rite International 3000 Dundee Rd Suite 309	North Brooke	IL	60062	877-880-3033	847-412-1420	760
Travel Services. Greater Independent Assn of National 29 W 36th St 8th Fl	New York	NY	10018	800-442-6871	212-545-7460	761
Travel Team Inc 2495 Main St	Buffalo	NY	14214	800-633-6782	716-862-7600	760
Travel Tours Inc 2111 W Hwy 51 PO Box 40	Wagoner	OK	74477	800-331-3192	918-485-4595	748
Travel & Transport Inc 2120 S 72nd St	Omaha	NE	68124	800-228-2545	402-399-4500	760
Travel Weekly Crossroads Magazine 500 Plaza Dr	Secaucus	NJ	07094	800-742-7076	201-902-2000	449-21
travel.bc.ca 4252 Commerce Cir	Victoria	BC	V8Z4M2	800-663-6000	866-810-6645	763
TravelAge West Magazine 9911 W Pico Blvd 11th Fl	Los Angeles	CA	90035	800-585-7321	310-772-7430	449-22
Traveland 1055 Wilshire Blvd Suite 1705	Los Angeles	CA	90017	800-321-6336	213-482-2323	748
TravelCenters of America 24601 Center Ridge Rd Suite 200	Westlake	OH	44145	800-872-7024	440-808-9100	319
Travelcorp 917 Duke St	Alexandria	VA	22314	800-770-6910	703-299-9003	377
TraveLeaders Group Inc 1701 Ponce de Leon Blvd	Coral Gables	FL	33134	800-327-0180	305-445-2999	760
Travelennium Inc 5050 Poplar Ave Suite 115	Memphis	TN	38157	800-844-4924	901-767-0761	760
Travelers Express Co Inc 1550 Utica Ave S Suite 100	Minneapolis	MN	55416	800-542-3590	952-591-3000	70
Travelers Life & Annuity Co 1 Cityplace	Hartford	CT	06103	800-334-4298	860-308-1000	384-2
Travelers Motor Club 720 NW 50th St	Oklahoma City	OK	73154	800-654-9208	405-848-1711	53
Travelex Insurance Services Inc 2121 N 117th Ave Suite 300	Omaha	NE	68164	888-457-4602	402-491-3200	384-7
Travelex International Inc 2500 W Higgins Rd Suite 1065	Hoffman Estates	IL	60195	800-882-0499	847-882-0400	761
Travelex Worldwide Money 29 Broadway	New York	NY	10006	800-815-1795	212-363-6206	70
Travelhost Inc 10701 N Stemmons Fwy	Dallas	TX	75220	800-527-1782	972-556-0541	623-9
Travelhost Magazine 10701 N Stemmons Fwy	Dallas	TX	75220	800-527-1782	972-556-0541	449-22
Traveline Travel Agencies Inc 4074 Erie St	Willoughby	OH	44094	888-700-8747	440-946-4040	760
Travellers Rest Plantation & Museum 636 Farrell Pkwy	Nashville	TN	37220	866-832-8197	615-832-8197	50
Travelmore/Carlson-Wagonlit Travel 212 W Colfax Ave	South Bend	IN	46601	877-543-5752	574-232-3061	760
TravelNow.com Inc 4124 S McCann Ct	Springfield	MO	65804	800-568-1972	417-864-3600	762
Travelocity 3150 Sabre Dr	Southlake	TX	76092	888-709-5983	682-605-3000	762
Travelodge Hotels Inc 1 Sylvan Way	Parsippany	NJ	07054	800-578-7878	973-428-9700	369
Thriftlodge 1 Sylvan Way	Parsippany	NJ	07054	800-578-7878	973-428-9700	369
Travelong Inc 225 W 35th St Suite 1501	New York	NY	10001	800-537-6043	212-736-2166	760
Travelpro USA 700 Banyan Trail	Boca Raton	FL	33431	888-741-7471	561-998-2824	444
TravelQuest International 305 Double D Dr	Prescott	AZ	86303	800-830-1998	928-445-7754	748
Travelsavers Inc 71 Audrey Ave	Oyster Bay	NY	11771	800-726-7283	516-624-0500	761
TravelSmith Outfitters Inc 60 Leveroni Ct	Novato	CA	94949	800-950-1600	415-382-1855	451
TravelStore Inc 11601 Wilshire Blvd	Los Angeles	CA	90025	800-343-9779	310-575-5540	760
TravelVisions 1000 Heritage Ctr Cir	Round Rock	TX	78664	800-452-2256	512-238-3166	760
Travelweb.com 2777 Stemmons Fwy Suite 675	Dallas	TX	75207	800-818-0033		368
Travers Tool Co Inc 128-15 26th Ave *Cust Svc	Flushing	NY	11354	800-221-0270*	718-886-7200	378
Traverse City Convention & Visitors Bureau 101 W Grandview Pkwy	Traverse City	MI	49684	800-940-1120	231-947-1120	205
Traverse Electric Co-op Inc PO Box 66	Wheaton	MN	56296	800-927-5443	320-563-8616	244
Travis Body & Trailer Inc 13955 Furman Rd FM 529	Houston	TX	77041	800-535-4372	713-466-5888	768
Travis Federal Credit Union 1 Travis Way	Vacaville	CA	95687	800-877-8328	707-449-4000	216
Travis Meats Inc PO Box 670	Powell	TN	37849	800-247-7606	865-938-9051	465
TRAVIZON Inc 10 State St 2nd Fl	Woburn	MA	01801	888-781-5200	781-994-1200	760
Traymore Hotel 2445 Collins Ave	Miami Beach	FL	33140	800-445-1512	305-534-7111	373
TRB (Transportation Research Board) 500 5th St NW	Washington	DC	20001	800-424-9818	202-334-2934	49-21
TRC Cos Inc 5 Waterside Crossing *NYSE: TRR*	Windsor	CT	06095	800-365-8254	860-289-8631	191
TRC Staffing Services Inc 100 Ashford Ctr N Suite 500	Atlanta	GA	30338	800-488-8008	770-392-1411	707
Tread Corp PO Box 13207	Roanoke	VA	24032	800-900-6881	540-982-6881	665
Treasure Bay Casino Resort 1980 Beach Blvd	Biloxi	MS	39531	800-747-2839	228-388-6610	655
Treasure Chest Casino 5050 Williams Blvd	Kenner	LA	70065	800-298-0711	504-443-8000	133
Treasure Island Hotel & Casino 3300 Las Vegas Blvd S	Las Vegas	NV	89109	800-944-7444	702-894-7111	655
Treasure Island Resort 2025 S Atlantic Ave	Daytona Beach Shores	FL	32118	800-543-5070	386-255-8371	373
Treasure Island Resort & Casino 5734 Sturgeon Lake Rd	Welch	MN	55089	800-222-7077	651-388-6300	133
Treats International Franchise Corp 418 Preston St	Ottawa	ON	K1S4N2	800-461-4003	613-563-4073	156
Trebor Enterprises Ltd PO Box 88	Freeport	IL	61032	800-552-6470	815-235-1700	401
Trece Mark Inc 112 Connolly Rd	Fallston	MD	21047	800-638-1464	410-893-3903	770
Tredegar Corp 1100 Boulders Pkwy Suite 200 *NYSE: TG*	Richmond	VA	23225	800-411-7441	804-330-1000	355-3
Tredegar Corp Film Products Div 1100 Boulders Pkwy	Richmond	VA	23225	800-411-7441	804-330-1222	589
Tree Care Industry Assn (TCIA) 3 Perimeter Rd Unit 1	Manchester	NH	03103	800-733-2622	603-314-5380	48-13
Tree of Life Inc 405 Golfway W Dr *Cust Svc	Saint Augustine	FL	32095	800-223-2910*	904-824-1846	292-8
Tree Preservation Co 708 Blair Mill Rd	Willow Grove	PA	19090	800-248-8733	215-784-4200	765
TreeAge Software Inc 1075 Main St	Williamstown	MA	01267	800-254-1911	413-458-0104	176-1
Trees Inc 650 N Sam Houston Pkwy E Suite 209	Houston	TX	77060	800-676-7712	281-447-1327	765
Trees for Tomorrow (TFT) 519 Sheridan St E PO Box 609	Eagle River	WI	54521	800-838-9472	715-479-6456	49-5
Treetops Resort 3962 Wilkinson Rd	Treetops Village	MI	49735	800-444-6711	989-732-6711	655
TREEV Inc 13454 Sunrise Valley Dr Suite 400	Herndon	VA	20171	800-254-0994	703-478-2260	176-1
Trek Inc 11601 Maple Ridge Rd	Medina	NY	14103	800-367-8735	585-798-3140	247
TrekAmerica PO Box 189	Rockaway	NJ	07866	800-221-0596	973-983-1144	748
Trelleborg Wheel Systems America Inc 61 State Rt 43 N	Hartville	OH	44632	800-666-8473	330-877-1211	739
Tremco Inc Roofing Div 3735 Green Rd	Beachwood	OH	44122	800-852-6013	216-292-5000	3
Tremont Boston - A Wyndham Historic Hotel 275 Tremont St	Boston	MA	02116	888-223-7220	617-426-1400	373
Tremont Chicago 100 E Chestnut St	Chicago	IL	60611	800-621-8133	312-751-1900	373
Tremont Hotel Baltimore 8 E Pleasant St	Baltimore	MD	21202	800-873-6668	410-576-1200	373
Tremont Plaza Hotel Baltimore 222 Saint Paul Pl	Baltimore	MD	21202	800-873-6668	410-727-2222	373
Trencor Inc 9600 Corporate Pk Dr	Loudon	TN	37774	800-527-6020	865-408-2100	189
TREND enterprises Inc 300 9th Ave SW *Cust Svc	New Brighton	MN	55112	800-328-0818*	651-631-2850	242
Trendex Inc 240 E Maryland Ave Suite 100	Saint Paul	MN	55117	800-328-9200	651-489-4655	87
TrendMicro Inc 10101 N De Anza Blvd Suite 200	Cupertino	CA	95014	800-228-5651	408-257-1500	176-12
Trendware International Inc 3135 Kashiwa St	Torrance	CA	90505	888-326-6061	310-891-1100	174
Trendway Corp PO Box 9016	Holland	MI	49422	800-968-5344	616-399-3900	314-1
Trendwest Resorts Inc 9805 Willows Rd NE	Redmond	WA	98052	800-722-3487	425-498-2500	738
Trent Inc 201 Leverington Ave	Philadelphia	PA	19127	800-544-8736	215-482-5000	313
Trent University 1600 W Bank Dr	Peterborough	ON	K9J7B8	888-739-8885	705-748-1011	773
Trenwick America Re Corp 1 Canterbury Green	Stamford	CT	06901	866-330-6719	203-353-5500	384-4
Trenwick Group Ltd 1 Canterbury Green	Stamford	CT	06901	866-330-6719	203-353-5500	355-4
Trenwyth Industries Inc PO Box 438 *Cust Svc	Emigsville	PA	17318	800-233-1924*	717-767-6868	181
Trerice HO Co 12950 W Eight-Mile Rd	Oak Park	MI	48237	888-873-7423	248-399-8000	200
TressAllure/General Wig 5800 NW 163rd St	Miami Lakes	FL	33014	800-777-9447	305-823-0600	342
Trevecca Nazarene University 333 Murfreesboro Rd	Nashville	TN	37210	888-210-4868	615-248-1200	163
Trex Co Inc 160 Exeter Dr *NYSE: TWP*	Winchester	VA	22603	800-289-8739	540-678-4070	647
Trex Enterprises 10455 Pacific Center Ct	San Diego	CA	92121	800-626-5885	858-646-5300	375
Tri-Campbell Farms 15111 Hwy 17	Grafton	ND	58237	877-999-7783	701-352-3116	11-11
Tri-Cities Convention & Visitors Bureau 6951 W Grandridge Blvd	Kennewick	WA	99336	800-254-5824	509-735-8486	205
Tri-City Herald PO Box 2608	Tri-Cities	WA	99302	800-411-5085	509-582-1500	522-2
Tri-Community Area Chamber of Commerce 380 Main St	Sturbridge	MA	01566	888-788-7274	508-347-2761	137
Tri-Continental Corp 100 Park Ave 3rd Fl *NYSE: TY*	New York	NY	10017	800-221-7844	212-850-1864	397
TRI-COR Industries Inc 4600 Forbes Blvd Suite 205	Lanham	MD	20706	800-764-7275	301-731-6140	178
Tri-County Electric Co-op PO Box 626	Rushford	MN	55971	800-432-2285	507-864-7783	244
Tri-County Electric Co-op Assn PO Box 159	Lancaster	MO	63548	888-457-3734	660-457-3733	244
Tri-County Electric Co-op Inc PO Box 208	Madison	FL	32341	800-999-2285	850-973-2285	244
Tri-County Electric Co-op Inc PO Drawer 309	Mount Vernon	IL	62864	800-244-5151	618-244-5151	244
Tri-County Electric Co-op Inc 302 E Glaydas St PO Box 880	Hooker	OK	73945	800-522-3315	580-652-2418	244

Name / Address	City	State	ZIP	Toll-Free	Phone	Class
Tri-County Electric Co-op Inc PO Box 217	Saint Matthews	SC	29135	**877-874-1215**	803-874-1215	244
Tri-County Electric Co-op Inc 600 Northwest Pkwy	Azle	TX	76020	**800-367-8232**	817-444-3201	244
Tri-County Electric Membership Corp PO Box 487	Gray	GA	31032	**800-342-3812**	478-986-3134	244
Tri-County Electric Membership Corp PO Box 40	Lafayette	TN	37083	**800-369-2111**	615-666-2111	244
Tri-County Rural Electric Co-op Inc PO Box 526	Mansfield	PA	16933	**800-343-2559**	570-662-2175	244
Tri-Dim Filter Corp 93 Industrial Dr Bldg 2	Louisa	VA	23093	**800-458-9835**	540-967-2600	19
Tri-K Industries Inc 151 Veterans Dr	Northvale	NJ	07647	**800-526-0372**	201-750-1055	470
Tri-Lite Inc 1642 Besley Ct	Chicago	IL	60622	**800-322-5250**	773-384-7765	431
TRI MAP International Inc 111 Val Dervin Pkwy	Stockton	CA	95206	**888-687-4627**	209-234-0100	253
Tri-Mer Corp 1400 Monroe St	Owosso	MI	48867	**800-688-7838**	989-723-7838	19
Tri-Pak Machinery Inc 1102 N Commerce St	Harlingen	TX	78550	**800-531-7343**	956-423-5140	537
Tri-Rentals Inc 3103 E Broadway Suite 400	Phoenix	AZ	85040	**800-678-3854**	602-232-9900	261-3
Tri-State Brick & Tile Co Inc 2050 Forest Ave	Jackson	MS	39286	**800-962-2101**	601-981-1410	148
Tri-State Coach Lines Inc 2101 W 37th Ave	Gary	IN	46408	**800-248-8747**	219-884-0054	109
Tri-State Distributors 1104 W Pullman Rd	Moscow	ID	83843	**877-878-2835**	208-882-4555	702
Tri-State Drilling Inc 16940 Hwy 55 W	Plymouth	MN	55446	**800-383-1033**	763-553-1234	188-16
Tri-State Envelope Corp 20th & Market Sts 1 Orgler Pl	Ashland	PA	17921	**800-233-3102**	570-875-0433	260
Tri-State Hospital Supply Corp 301 Catrell Dr	Howell	MI	48843	**800-248-4058**	517-546-5400	469
Tri-State Insurance Co of Minnesota 10 Roundwind Rd PO Box 500	Luverne	MN	56156	**800-533-0303**	507-283-9561	384-4
Tri-State Iron & Metal Co PO Box 775	Texarkana	AR	75504	**800-773-8409**	870-773-8409	674
Tri-State Livestock News 1022 Main St PO Box 129	Sturgis	SD	57785	**800-253-3656**	605-347-2585	623-8
Tri-State Travel Inc PO Box 307	Galena	IL	61036	**800-779-4869**	815-777-0820	748
Tri-State Truck & Equipment Inc 1124 Main St	Billings	MT	59103	**800-227-1132**	406-245-3188	353
Tri-State University 1 University Blvd	Angola	IN	46703	**800-347-4878**	260-665-4100	163
Tri-State Utility Products Inc 1030 Atlanta Industrial Dr	Marietta	GA	30065	**800-282-7985**	770-427-3119	245
Tri-Wall 2626 County Rd 71	Butler	IN	46721	**888-874-9255**	260-868-2151	539
Triad Guaranty Inc 101 S Stratford Rd *NASDAQ: TGIC*	Winston-Salem	NC	27104	**800-451-4872**	336-723-1282	355-4
Triad Guaranty Insurance Corp 101 S Stratford Rd *Cust Svc	Winston-Salem	NC	27104	**888-691-8074***	336-723-1282	384-5
Triad Hospitals Inc 5800 Tennyson Pkwy *NYSE: TRI*	Plano	TX	75024	**800-238-6006**	214-473-7000	348
Triad Products Co 1801 W 'B' St	Hastings	NE	68901	**800-241-3704**	402-462-2181	597
Trial Lawyers of America. Association of 1050 31st St NW	Washington	DC	20007	**800-424-2725**	202-965-3500	49-10
Trial Magazine 1050 31st St NW	Washington	DC	20007	**800-424-2725**	202-965-3500	449-15
TrialGraphix Inc 155 NE 40th St	Miami	FL	33137	**800-334-5403**	305-576-5400	436
Triangle Blueprint Co 2721 Brunswick Pike	Lawrenceville	NJ	08648	**800-792-8800**	609-883-3600	239
Triangle Brick Co 6523 Hwy 55	Durham	NC	27713	**800-672-8547**	919-544-1796	148
Triangle C Ranch 3737 Hwy 26	Dubois	WY	82513	**800-661-4928**	307-455-2225	238
Triangle Package Machinery Co 6655 W Diversey Ave	Chicago	IL	60707	**800-621-4170**	773-889-0200	537
Triangle Rent A Car Co 4226A South Blvd	Charlotte	NC	28209	**800-643-7368**	704-527-1900	126
Triangle Suspension Systems Inc Maloney Rd	Du Bois	PA	15801	**800-458-6077**	814-375-7211	60
Triangle Tech Inc 1940 Perrysville Ave	Pittsburgh	PA	15214	**800-874-8324**	412-359-1000	787
Du Bois School PO Box 551	Du Bois	PA	15801	**800-874-8324**	814-371-2090	787
Erie School 2000 Liberty St	Erie	PA	16502	**800-874-8324**	814-453-6016	787
Greensburg 222 E Pittsburgh St	Greensburg	PA	15601	**800-533-4224**	724-832-1050	787
Triangle Textiles Ltd 1320 E Division St	Slaton	TX	79364	**800-622-8299**	806-828-6573	730-8
Triangle X Ranch 2 Triangle X Ranch Rd	Moose	WY	83012	**888-860-0005**	307-733-2183	238
Trianon Old Naples 955 7th Ave S	Naples	FL	34102	**877-482-5228**	239-435-9600	373
Triarc Cos Inc 280 Park Ave 41st Fl *NYSE: TRY*	New York	NY	10017	**800-787-4272**	212-451-3000	355-3
Triarc Restaurant Group 1000 Corporate Dr	Fort Lauderdale	FL	33334	**800-487-2729**	954-351-5100	656
Triboro Quilt Mfg Inc 172 S Broadway	White Plains	NY	10605	**800-227-2077**	914-428-7551	64
Tribune The PO Box 112	San Luis Obispo	CA	93406	**800-477-8799**	805-781-7800	522-2
Tribune 600 Edwards Rd	Fort Pierce	FL	34982	**800-444-8742**	772-461-2050	522-2
Tribune PO Box 419000	Melbourne	FL	32941	**800-633-8449**	321-242-3801	522-4
Tribune The PO Box 447	Seymour	IN	47274	**800-800-8212**	812-522-4871	522-2
Tribune The 317 5th St PO Box 380	Ames	IA	50010	**800-234-8742**	515-232-2160	522-2
Tribune Chronicle 240 Franklin St SE	Warren	OH	44482	**888-550-8742**	330-841-1600	522-2
Tribune-Democrat 425 Locust St	Johnstown	PA	15907	**800-473-0998**	814-532-5050	522-2
Tribune Media Services Inc 435 N Michigan Ave Suite 1500	Chicago	IL	60611	**800-245-6536**	312-222-4444	520
Tribune Radio Network 435 N Michigan Ave	Chicago	IL	60611	**800-654-8597**	312-222-3342	630
Tribune Review Publishing Co 622 Cabin Hill Dr	Greensburg	PA	15601	**800-433-3045**	724-834-1151	623-8
Tribune-Star PO Box 149	Terre Haute	IN	47808	**800-783-8742**	812-231-4200	522-2
Tricare Home Health & Hospice 205 E Palmer Ave	Bellefontaine	OH	43311	**800-886-5936**	937-593-6333	365
Trickle Up Program Inc 104 W 27th St 12th Fl	New York	NY	10001	**866-246-9980**	212-255-9980	48-5
TriCo Bancshares 63 Constitution Dr *NASDAQ: TCBK*	Chico	CA	95973	**800-922-8742**	530-898-0300	355-2
Trico Products Corp 3255 W Hamlin Rd	Rochester Hills	MI	48309	**888-565-9632**	248-371-1700	60
TRICOR (Tennessee Rehabilitative Initiative in Correction) 240 Great Circle Rd Suite 310	Nashville	TN	37228	**800-958-7426**	615-741-5705	618
Tricor America Inc 717 Airport Blvd	South San Francisco	CA	94080	**800-669-7631**	650-877-3650	536
Tricorbraun Inc 10330 Old Olive St Rd	Saint Louis	MO	63141	**800-325-7782**	314-569-3633	549
Tridan International Inc 130 N Jackson St	Danville	IL	61832	**800-369-3544**	217-443-3592	485
Trident Seafood Corp 5303 Shilshole Ave NW	Seattle	WA	98107	**800-367-6065**	206-783-3818	291-14
Trident Technical College 7000 Rivers Ave PO Box 118067	Charleston	SC	29423	**877-349-6184**	843-574-6111	787
Trikon Technologies Inc 17835 New Hope St Suite A *NASDAQ: TRKN*	Fountain Valley	CA	92708	**800-727-5585**	714-968-4299	685
Trilegiant Corp DBA AutoVantage 100 Connecticut Ave	Norwalk	CT	06850	**800-876-7787**		53
Trilithic Inc 9710 Park Davis Dr	Indianapolis	IN	46235	**800-344-2412**	317-895-3600	247
Trilla-Nesco Corp 2391 Cassens Dr	Fenton	MO	63026	**800-966-3786**	636-343-7333	197
Trilogy Communications Inc 2910 Hwy 80 E	Pearl	MS	39208	**800-874-5649**	601-932-4461	801
Trilogy Software Inc 5001 Plaza on the Lake	Austin	TX	78746	**877-292-3266**	512-874-3100	176-1
Trimac Transportation System PO Box 3000	Rapid City	SD	57709	**800-843-4012**	605-348-1063	769
Trimaco LLC 2800 Meridian Pkwy Suite 185	Durham	NC	27713	**866-874-6226**	919-433-4010	718
Trimble Engineering & Construction Div 5475 Kellenburger Rd	Dayton	OH	45424	**800-538-7800**	937-233-8921	416
Trimble Navigation Ltd 749 N Mary Ave *NASDAQ: TRMB*	Sunnyvale	CA	94085	**800-827-8000**	408-481-8000	519
Trimco/Builders Brass Works PO Box 23277	Los Angeles	CA	90023	**877-786-8387**	323-262-4191	345
Trimedyne Inc 15091 Bake Pkwy	Irvine	CA	92618	**800-733-5273**	949-559-5300	415
Trimfit Inc 1900 Frost Rd Suite 111	Bristol	PA	19007	**800-347-7697**	215-781-0600	153-10
Trimfoot Shoe Co 115 Trimfoot Terr	Farmington	MO	63640	**800-325-6116**	573-756-6616	296
TrimMaster 4860 N 5th St Hwy	Temple	PA	19560	**800-356-4237**	610-921-0203	729
Trimtex Co Inc 400 Park Ave	Williamsport	PA	17701	**800-326-9135**	570-326-9135	730-5
Trimtex Saint Louis Trimming Div 400 Park Ave	Williamsport	PA	17701	**800-326-9135**	570-326-9135	583
Trine Products Corp 1430 Ferris Pl	Bronx	NY	10461	**800-858-8501**	718-829-4796	385
Triner Scale & Mfg Co 2842 Sanderwood Dr	Memphis	TN	38118	**800-238-0152**	901-795-0746	672
TriNet Group Inc 1100 San Leandro Blvd Suite 300	San Leandro	CA	94577	**800-638-0461**	510-352-5000	619
Trinidad State Junior College 600 Prospect St	Trinidad	CO	81082	**800-621-8752**	719-846-5011	160
Trinity Bible College 50 S 6th Ave	Ellendale	ND	58436	**800-523-1603**	701-349-3621	163
Trinity Biotech PLC 5919 Farnsworth Ct	Carlsbad	CA	92008	**800-331-2291**	760-929-0500	229
Trinity Christian College 6601 W College Dr	Palos Heights	IL	60463	**800-748-0085**	708-597-3000	163
Trinity Episcopal School for Ministry 311 11th St	Ambridge	PA	15003	**800-874-8754**	724-266-3838	164-3
Trinity Fitting Group Inc 2525 Stemmons Fwy	Dallas	TX	75207	**800-527-4500**	214-589-8177	584
Trinity Furniture Mfg 2885 Lorraine Ave	Temple	TX	76501	**800-256-7397**	254-778-4727	314-3
Trinity Home Care 114-02 15th Ave	College Point	NY	11356	**877-687-7369**	718-961-1634	358
Trinity Hospice 1049 Cresthaven Rd	Memphis	TN	38119	**800-727-6416**	901-767-6767	365
Trinity Hospice LLC 1437 S Boulder Ave Suite 1080	Tulsa	OK	74119	**800-473-4368**	918-742-7559	365
Trinity Industries Inc 2525 Stemmons Fwy *NYSE: TRN*	Dallas	TX	75207	**800-631-4420**	214-631-4420	184
Trinity Industries Inc Highway Safety Products Div 2525 N Stemmons Fwy	Dallas	TX	75207	**800-527-6050**	214-589-8814	688
Trinity Industries Inc LPG Containers Div 2525 N Stemmons Fwy	Dallas	TX	75207	**888-558-8265**	214-589-8213	92
Trinity International University 2065 Half Day Rd	Deerfield	IL	60015	**800-822-3225**	847-317-7000	163
South Florida Campus 111 NW 183rd St Suite 500	Miami	FL	33169	**877-392-3586**	305-770-5100	163
Trinity Investment Management Corp 10 St James Ave	Boston	MA	02116	**800-422-1854**	617-728-7200	393
Trinity Mining Service 109 48th St	Pittsburgh	PA	15201	**800-245-6206**	412-682-4700	636
Trinity Public Utility District PO Box 1216	Weaverville	CA	96093	**800-968-7783**	530-623-5536	244
Trinity Rail Group Inc 2525 Stemmons Fwy	Dallas	TX	75207	**800-631-4420**	214-631-4420	636
Trinity Universal Insurance Co 10000 N Central Expy	Dallas	TX	75231	**800-777-2249**	214-360-8000	384-4
Trinity University 1 Trinity Pl	San Antonio	TX	78212	**800-874-6489**	210-999-7207	163
Trinity Valley Community College Athens 100 Cardinal Dr	Athens	TX	75751	**866-882-2937**	903-675-6200	160
Trinity Valley Electric Co-op Inc PO Box 888	Kaufman	TX	75142	**800-766-9576**	972-932-2214	244
Trinity Western University 7600 Glover Rd	Langley	BC	V2Y1Y1	**888-468-6898**	604-888-7511	773
Trinity Workplace Learning 4101 International Pkwy	Carrollton	TX	75007	**800-624-2272**	972-309-4000	502
TrinityCare Hospice 18331 Gridley Rd Suite F	Cerritos	CA	90703	**866-210-1055**	562-809-2150	365
Trinsic Inc 601 S Harbour Island Blvd Suite 220 *NASDAQ: TRIN*	Tampa	FL	33602	**800-511-4572**	813-273-6261	721
Trion Inc 101 McNeill Rd	Sanford	NC	27330	**866-829-2440**	919-775-2201	19
Trion Industries Inc 297 Laird St	Wilkes-Barre	PA	18702	**800-444-4665**	570-824-1000	281
TriPath Imaging Inc 780 Plantation Dr *NASDAQ: TPTH*	Burlington	NC	27215	**800-426-2176**	336-222-9707	375
Tripath Technology Inc 2560 Orchard Pkwy *NASDAQ: TRPH*	San Jose	CA	95131	**877-874-7284**	408-750-3000	686

Name / Address	City	State	Zip	Toll-Free	Phone	Class
Tripifoods Inc 1427 William St	Buffalo	NY	14240	**800-851-7400**	716-853-7400	292-8
Triple A Oil 12342 Inwood Rd	Dallas	TX	75244	**800-657-9595**	972-503-3333	319
Triple Crown Nutrition Inc 319 Barry Ave S Suite 303	Wayzata	MN	55391	**800-451-9916**	952-473-6330	438
Triple Crown Services 2720 Dupont Commerce Ct	Fort Wayne	IN	46825	**800-325-6510**	260-416-3600	634
Triple R Ranch PO Box 124	Keystone	SD	57751	**888-777-2624**	605-666-4605	238
TripleInk 60 S 6th St Suite 2600	Minneapolis	MN	55402	**800-632-1388**	612-342-9800	757
Triple/S Dynamics Inc PO Box 151027	Dallas	TX	75315	**800-527-2116**	214-828-8600	462
Triplett Corp 1 Triplett Dr	Bluffton	OH	45817	**800-874-7538**	419-358-5015	247
Triplett Office Essentials Corp 3553 109th St	Des Moines	IA	50322	**800-437-5034**	515-270-9150	524
Tripos Inc 1699 S Hanley Rd *NASDAQ: TRPS*	Saint Louis	MO	63144	**800-323-2960**	314-647-1099	176-5
TripQuest Inc 786 N Beal Pkwy Suite 7A	Fort Walton Beach	FL	32548	**888-459-8747**	850-862-8999	760
TripRewards PO Box 19807	Knoxville	TN	37939	**800-367-8747**		371
Tripwire Inc 326 SW Broadway 3rd Fl	Portland	OR	97205	**800-874-7947**	503-276-7500	176-12
TriQuint Semiconductor Inc 2300 NE Brookwood Pkwy *NASDAQ: TQNT*	Hillsboro	OR	97124	**888-258-5873**	503-615-9000	686
Triton College 2000 N 5th Ave	River Grove	IL	60171	**800-942-7404**	708-456-0300	160
Triton Systems Inc 522 E Railroad St	Long Beach	MS	39560	**800-259-6672**	228-868-1317	56
Triumph Boats 100 Golden Dr	Durham	NC	27705	**800-564-4225**	919-382-3149	91
Triumph Industries 8687 S 77th Ave	Bridgeview	IL	60455	**800-752-9957**	708-598-5100	472
Triumph Instruments & Avionics 1425 Grand Central Ave	Glendale	CA	91201	**800-525-6696**	818-246-8431	25
Triumph Learning 136 Madison Ave	New York	NY	10016	**800-221-9372**	212-652-0200	623-2
Triumph Pet Industries Inc 7 Lake Station Rd	Warwick	NY	10990	**800-331-5144**	845-469-5125	568
Triumph Seed Co Hwy 62 Bypass PO Box 1050	Ralls	TX	79357	**800-530-4789**	806-253-2584	684
Triversity Inc 3550 Victoria Pk Ave Suite 400	Toronto	ON	M2H2N5	**888-287-4629**	416-791-7100	176-1
Trizec Canada Inc 181 Bay St Suite 3820 *TSE: TZC.SV*	Toronto	ON	M5J2T3	**877-239-7200**	416-361-7200	517
TriZetto Group Inc 567 San Nicolas Dr Suite 360 *NASDAQ: TZIX*	Newport Beach	CA	92660	**800-569-1222**	949-719-2200	39
TRM Corp 5208 NE 122nd Ave *NASDAQ: TRMM*	Portland	OR	97230	**800-877-8762**	503-257-8766	114
Troika International Inc 1555 Los Palos St	Los Angeles	CA	90023	**800-787-6452**	323-415-0199	342
Trojan Battery Co 12380 Clark St *Cust Svc	Santa Fe Springs	CA	90670	**800-423-6569***	562-946-8381	76
Trojan Inc PO Box 850	Mount Sterling	KY	40353	**800-264-0526**	859-498-0526	429
TrollCarnival Book Club PO Box 7504	Jefferson City	MO	65102	**800-654-3037**		94
Trompeter Electronics Inc 31186 La Baya Dr	Westlake Village	CA	91362	**800-982-2629**	818-707-2020	252
Trone Advertising 4035 Piedmont Pkwy	High Point	NC	27265	**877-493-3043**	336-886-1622	4
Trophy Nut Co Inc 320 N 2nd St	Tipp City	OH	45371	**800-729-6887**	937-667-8478	291-28
Trophyland USA Inc 7001 W 20th Ave	Hialeah	FL	33014	**800-327-5820**		766
Tropical Everglades Visitor Assn 160 US 1	Florida City	FL	33034	**800-388-9669**	305-245-9180	205
Tropical Shipping PO Box 10683	Riviera Beach	FL	33419	**800-367-6200**	561-881-3900	308
Tropical Winds 705 S Ocean Blvd	Myrtle Beach	SC	29578	**800-843-3466**	843-448-4304	655
Tropical Winds Oceanfront Hotel 1398 N Atlantic Ave	Daytona Beach	FL	32118	**800-245-6099**	386-258-1016	373
Tropicana Casino & Resort 2831 Boardwalk	Atlantic City	NJ	08401	**800-843-8767**	609-340-4000	373
Tropicana Field 1 Tropicana Dr	Saint Petersburg	FL	33705	**888-326-7297**	727-825-3120	706
Tropicana Inn & Suites 1540 S Harbor Blvd	Anaheim	CA	92802	**800-828-4898**	714-635-4082	373
Tropicana Resort & Casino 3801 Las Vegas Blvd S *Resv	Las Vegas	NV	89109	**888-826-8767***	702-739-2222	655
Tropitone Furniture Co Inc 5 Marconi *Cust Svc	Irvine	CA	92618	**800-654-7000***	949-951-2010	314-4
Trotting Assn. US 750 Michigan Ave	Columbus	OH	43215	**800-887-8782**	614-224-2291	48-22
Trout Unlimited (TU) 1300 N 17th St Suite 500	Arlington	VA	22209	**800-834-2419**	703-522-0200	48-3
Troutman Sanders LLP 600 Peachtree St NE Suite 5200	Atlanta	GA	30308	**800-255-8752**	404-885-3000	419
Trouw Nutrition 115 Executive Dr	Highland	IL	62249	**800-870-9233**	618-654-2070	438
Trover Solutions Inc 1930 Bishop Ln Suite 1500	Louisville	KY	40218	**800-456-7318**	502-454-1340	383
Trowelon Inc 973 Haven Pl Suite D	Green Bay	WI	54313	**800-975-8778**	920-499-8778	540
Troxler Electronic Laboratories Inc 3008 Cornwallis Rd PO Box 12057	Research Triangle Park	NC	27709	**877-876-9537**	919-549-8661	200
Troy-CSL Lighting Inc 14625 E Clark Ave	City of Industry	CA	91745	**800-533-8769**	626-336-4511	431
TROY Group Inc 2331 S Pullman St	Santa Ana	CA	92705	**877-324-3254**	949-250-3280	171-6
Troy Publishing Co 501 Broadway	Troy	NY	12180	**800-934-4304**	518-270-1200	623-8
Troy State University 600 University Ave	Troy	AL	36082	**800-551-9716**	334-670-3100	163
Montgomery PO Drawer 4419	Montgomery	AL	36103	**800-355-8786**	334-834-1400	163
Phenix City Campus 1 University Pl	Phenix City	AL	36869	**888-876-9787**	334-297-1007	163
Troy Sunshade Co 607 Riffle Ave	Greenville	OH	45331	**800-833-8769**	937-548-2466	718
Troyer Foods Inc PO Box 608	Goshen	IN	46527	**800-876-9377**	574-533-0302	292-10
Troyer Potato Products Inc 810 Rt 97S	Waterford	PA	16441	**800-458-0485**	814-796-2611	291-35
TR's Last-Mile Telecom Report 7201 McKinney Cir	Frederick	MD	21704	**800-822-6338**	301-698-7100	521-11
TRSA (Textile Rental Services Assn) 1800 Diagonal Rd Suite 200	Alexandria	VA	22314	**800-868-8772**	703-519-0029	49-4
Tru-Flex Metal Hose Corp PO Box 247	West Lebanon	IN	47991	**800-255-6291**	765-893-4403	584
Tru-Kay Mfg Co 2 Carol Dr	Lincoln	RI	02865	**800-795-2105**	401-333-2105	401
Tru-Link Fence Co 5440 W Touhy Ave	Skokie	IL	60077	**888-568-9300**	847-568-9300	275
Tru-Stone Technologies PO Box 430	Waite Park	MN	56387	**800-959-0517**	320-251-7171	710
Tru-Vue Glass & Artboard Co 9400 W 55th St *Cust Svc	McCook	IL	60525	**800-621-8339***	708-485-5080	325
Tru-Weld Grating Inc 2000 Corporate Dr	Wexford	PA	15090	**800-445-7093**	724-934-5320	482
TRUARC Co LLC 70 E Willow St *Cust Svc	Millburn	NJ	07041	**800-228-4460***	973-926-5000	321
Truck Equipment Assn. National 37400 Hills Tech Dr	Farmington Hills	MI	48331	**800-441-6832**	248-489-7090	49-21
Truck Equipment Service Co 800 Oak St	Lincoln	NE	68521	**800-869-0363**	402-476-3225	768
Truck-Lite Co Inc 310 E Elmwood Ave *Cust Svc	Falconer	NY	14733	**800-562-5012***	716-665-6214	430
Truck Transport Inc 2280 Cassens Dr	Fenton	MO	63026	**800-274-5995**	636-343-1877	769
Truck Utilities Inc 2370 English St	Saint Paul	MN	55109	**800-869-1075**	651-484-3305	505
Truckin Movers Corp 1031 Harvest St	Durham	NC	27704	**800-334-1651**	919-682-2300	508
Trucking Assns. American 2200 Mill Rd	Alexandria	VA	22314	**800-282-5463**	703-838-1700	49-21
Trucks. Coalition Against Bigger 901 N Pitt St Suite 310	Alexandria	VA	22314	**888-222-8123**	703-535-3131	49-21
True BASIC Inc 1523 Maple St	Hartford	VT	05047	**800-436-2111**	802-296-2711	176-3
True Fitness Technology Inc 865 Hoff Rd	O'Fallon	MO	63366	**800-426-6570**	636-272-7100	263
True Mfg Co 301 Cannonball Ln	O'Fallon	MO	63366	**800-325-6152**	636-240-2400	650
True Temper Sports 8275 Tournament Dr Suite 200	Memphis	TN	38125	**800-355-8783**	901-746-2000	701
True Vine Online 50 Damsite Rd	Center Barnstead	NH	03225	**877-878-3846**		390
True2Form Collision Repair Centers 4853 Galaxy Pkwy Suite E	Cleveland	OH	44128	**888-223-8783**	216-591-0730	62-4
TrueCareers Inc 12061 Bluemont Way	Reston	VA	20190	**800-441-4062**		257
Truett-McConnell College 100 Alumni Dr	Cleveland	GA	30528	**800-226-8621**	706-865-2134	160
TruGreen ChemLawn 860 Ridge Lake Blvd	Memphis	TN	38120	**800-878-4733**	901-681-1800	421
Truheat Corp 700 Grand St	Allegan	MI	49010	**800-879-6199**	269-673-2145	313
Truitt Brothers Inc 1105 Front St NE	Salem	OR	97301	**800-547-8712**	503-362-3674	291-20
Truliant Federal Credit Union 3200 Truliant Way	Winston-Salem	NC	27103	**800-822-0382**	336-659-1955	216
Truly Nolen of America Inc 3636 E Speedway Blvd	Tucson	AZ	85716	**800-528-3442**	520-327-3447	567
Truman Arnold Cos 701 S Robison Rd	Texarkana	TX	75504	**800-243-5343**	903-794-3835	569
Truman Harry S Presidential Library & Museum 500 W Hwy 24	Independence	MO	64050	**800-833-1225**	816-833-1400	426
Truman State University 100 E Normal St	Kirksville	MO	63501	**800-892-7792**	660-785-4000	163
Trumbull County Convention & Visitors Bureau 650 Youngstown-Warren Rd	Niles	OH	44446	**800-672-9555**	330-544-3468	205
Trump Casino Hotel 1 Buffington Harbor Dr	Gary	IN	46406	**888-218-7867**	219-977-7000	133
Trump International Hotel & Tower 1 Central Park W	New York	NY	10023	**888-448-7867**	212-299-1000	373
Trump International Sonesta Beach Resort 18101 Collins Ave	Sunny Isles Beach	FL	33160	**800-766-3782**	305-692-5600	373
Trump Marina Hotel & Casino Huron Ave & Brigantine Blvd *Resv	Atlantic City	NJ	08401	**800-777-8477***	609-441-2000	133
Trump Plaza Hotel & Casino 2225 Mississippi Ave	Atlantic City	NJ	08401	**800-677-7378**	609-441-6000	133
Trump Taj Mahal Casino Resort 1000 Boardwalk & Virginia Ave *Resv	Atlantic City	NJ	08401	**800-825-8786***	609-449-1000	655
Trus Joist MacMillan LP 200 E Mallard Dr *Cust Svc	Boise	ID	83706	**800-338-0515***	208-364-1200	805
TruSecure Corp 13650 Dulles Technology Dr Suite 500	Herndon	VA	20171	**888-627-2281**	703-480-8200	176-12
Truss Mfg Co Inc 17317 Westfield Pk Rd	Westfield	IN	46074	**800-467-4525**	317-896-2571	805
Truss-T Structures Inc DBA Pacific Building Systems 2100 N Pacific Hwy	Woodburn	OR	97071	**800-727-7844**	503-981-9581	106
TRUST for Credit Unions (TCU) 4900 Sears Tower 51st Fl	Chicago	IL	60606	**800-621-2550**	312-655-4400	517
Trust Digital Inc 7900 W Park Dr Suite A50	McLean	VA	22102	**888-760-9401**	703-760-9400	176-12
Trust for Public Land (TPL) 116 New Montgomery St 4th Fl	San Francisco	CA	94105	**800-729-6428**	415-495-4014	48-13
TruStar Solutions Inc 10029 E 126th St Suite D	Fishers	IN	46038	**888-547-4472**	317-813-0500	176-11
Trustmark Corp PO Box 291 *NASDAQ: TRMK*	Jackson	MS	39205	**800-844-2000**	601-208-5111	355-2
Trustmark Insurance Co 400 Field Dr	Lake Forest	IL	60045	**800-877-9077**	847-615-1500	384-2
Trustmark National Bank 248 E Capitol St	Jackson	MS	39201	**800-844-2000**	601-208-5111	71
Trustreet Properties Inc 450 S Orange Ave *NYSE: TSY*	Orlando	FL	32801	**877-667-4769**	407-540-2000	640
Trutec Industries Inc 4700 Gateway Blvd	Springfield	OH	45502	**800-933-8832**	937-323-8833	475
Truth The PO Box 487	Elkhart	IN	46515	**800-585-5416**	574-294-1661	522-2
Truth Hardware Inc 700 W Bridge St *Cust Svc	Owatonna	MN	55060	**800-866-7884***	507-451-5620	345
Truth Publishing Co Inc 421 S 2nd St	Elkhart	IN	46516	**800-585-5416**	574-294-1661	623-8
Tryon Palace Historic Sites & Gardens 610 Pollock St	New Bern	NC	28562	**800-767-1560**	252-514-4900	98
TSA (Salon Assn) 15825 N 71st St Suite 100	Scottsdale	AZ	85254	**800-211-4872**	480-281-0429	49-4

Name / Address	City	State	ZIP	Toll-Free	Phone	Class
TSA (Technical Services Assoc Inc) 2 Kacey Ct	Mechanicsburg	PA	17055	**800-388-1415**	717-691-5691	176-11
TSC (Technology Solutions Co) 205 N Michigan Ave Suite 1500 *NASDAQ: TSCC*	Chicago	IL	60601	**800-819-2250**	312-228-4500	178
TSC Apparel LLC 12080 Mosteller Rd	Cincinnati	OH	45241	**800-543-7230**	513-771-1138	154
TSI Inc 500 Cardigan Rd	Shoreview	MN	55126	**800-234-8822**	651-483-0900	200
TSN Inc 4001 Salazar Way PO Box 679	Frederick	CO	80530	**800-800-4131**	303-530-0600	549
TSN Labs Inc PO Box 38	Midvale	UT	84047	**800-769-7290**	801-261-2252	786
TSTA Advocate Magazine 316 W 12th St	Austin	TX	78701	**800-324-5355**	512-476-5355	449-8
TST/Impreso Inc 652 Southwestern Blvd	Coppell	TX	75019	**800-527-2878**	972-462-0100	542-1
TT Group Inc 702 Carnation Dr	Aurora	MO	65605	**800-445-0886**	417-678-2181	296
TTB (Alcohol & Tobacco Tax & Trade Bureau) 650 Massachusetts Ave NW	Washington	DC	20226	**877-882-3277**	202-927-8100	336-14
National Revenue Center 550 Main St	Cincinnati	OH	45202	**800-937-8864**	513-684-3334	336-14
TTI Inc 2441 Northeast Pkwy *Sales	Fort Worth	TX	76106	**800-845-5119***	817-740-9000	245
TTS Payrolls Inc 21 Penn Plaza Suite 1008	New York	NY	10001	**866-887-4749**		559
TTSG (Twinless Twins Support Group International) PO Box 980481	Ypsilanti	MI	48198	**888-205-8962**		48-21
TTX Co 101 N Wacker Dr	Chicago	IL	60606	**800-621-5854**	312-853-3223	261-6
TU (Trout Unlimited) 1300 N 17th St Suite 500	Arlington	VA	22209	**800-834-2419**	703-522-0200	48-3
Tubby's Inc 35807 Moravian	Clinton Township	MI	48035	**800-752-0644**	586-792-2369	657
Tube Art Displays Inc 2730 Occidental Ave S	Seattle	WA	98134	**800-562-2854**	206-223-1122	692
Tube Forming Inc 2101 W Belt Line Rd	Carrollton	TX	75006	**800-513-0022**	972-512-2400	584
Tube Processing Corp 604 E Le Grande Ave	Indianapolis	IN	46203	**800-776-4119**	317-787-1321	481
Tubelite Inc 4878 Mackinaw Trail	Reed City	MI	49677	**800-866-2227**	231-832-2211	232
Tubular Steel Inc 1031 Executive Pkwy Dr	Saint Louis	MO	63141	**800-882-8527**	314-851-9200	483
Tucker County Convention & Visitors Bureau William Ave & 4th St PO Box 565	Davis	WV	26260	**800-782-2775**	304-259-5315	205
Tucker Rocky Distributing Inc 4900 Alliance Gateway Fwy	Fort Worth	TX	76177	**800-283-8787**	817-258-9000	61
TUCOWS Inc 96 Mowat Ave	Toronto	ON	M6K3M1	**800-371-6992**	416-535-0123	389
TUCOWS Inc Domain Direct Div 96 Mowat Ave	Toronto	ON	M6K3M1	**800-371-6992**	416-531-2697	389
Tucson Citizen 4850 S Park Ave	Tucson	AZ	85714	**800-695-4492**	520-573-4560	522-2
Tucson Electric Power Co PO Box 711 *Cust Svc	Tucson	AZ	85702	**800-328-8853***	520-571-4000	774
Tucson Medical Center 5301 E Grant Rd	Tucson	AZ	85712	**800-526-5353**	520-327-5461	366-2
Tucson Medical Center Hospice 5301 E Grant Rd	Tucson	AZ	85712	**800-526-5353**	520-324-2438	365
Tucson Realty & Trust Co 335 N Wilmont Rd Suite 505	Tucson	AZ	85711	**877-254-5740**	520-577-7000	641
Tuesday Morning Corp 6250 LBJ Fwy *NASDAQ: TUES*	Dallas	TX	75240	**800-457-0099**	972-387-3562	322
Tuf-Wear USA 1001 Industrial Ave	North Platte	NE	69101	**800-445-5210**	308-532-0187	701
Tufco Technologies Inc PO Box 23500 *NASDAQ: TFCO*	Green Bay	WI	54305	**800-558-8145**	920-336-0054	544
Tuff-Weld Wood Specialties 7569 Woodman Pl *Cust Svc	Van Nuys	CA	91405	**800-223-2955***	818-988-0991	766
Tuffaloy Products Inc 601 High Tech Ct	Greer	SC	29650	**800-521-3722**	864-879-0763	798
Tuffy Auto Service Centers 1414 Baronial Plaza Dr	Toledo	OH	43615	**800-228-8339**	419-865-6900	62-5
Tuftco Corp 2318 S Holtzclaw Ave	Chattanooga	TN	37408	**800-288-3826**	423-698-8601	729
Tuftex Carpet Mills 15305 Valley View Ave	Santa Fe Springs	CA	90670	**877-224-7429**	562-921-0951	131
Tufts Associated Health Plans Inc 333 Wyman St	Waltham	MA	02451	**800-462-0224**	781-466-9400	384-3
Tufts-New England Medical Center Bone Marrow Transplant Program 750 Washington St Box 542	Boston	MA	02111	**866-636-5001**	617-636-0154	758
Tugboat Inn 80 Commercial St PO Box 267	Boothbay Harbor	ME	04538	**800-248-2628**	207-633-4434	373
Tulalip Casino 10200 Quil Ceda Blvd	Tulalip	WA	98271	**888-272-1111**	360-651-1111	133
Tulane University 6823 St Charles Ave	New Orleans	LA	70118	**800-873-9283**	504-865-5000	163
Tulane University Hospital & Clinic 1415 Tulane Ave	New Orleans	LA	70112	**800-588-5800**	504-588-5263	366-2
Tulip City Air Service Inc 1581 S Washington Ave	Holland	MI	49423	**800-748-0515**	616-392-7831	14
Tulkoff Products Co Inc 1101 S Conkling St	Baltimore	MD	21224	**800-638-7343**	410-327-6585	291-19
Tull JM Metals Co Inc PO Box 4725	Norcross	GA	30091	**800-243-8855**	770-368-4311	483
Tully's Coffee Corp 3100 Airport Way S	Seattle	WA	98134	**800-968-8559**	206-233-2070	156
Tulox Plastics Corp 401 S Miller Ave *Cust Svc	Marion	IN	46953	**800-234-1118***	765-664-5155	589
Tulsa Convention Center 100 Civic Ctr	Tulsa	OK	74103	**800-678-7177**	918-596-7177	204
Tulsa Convention & Visitors Bureau 2 W 2nd St Suite 150 Williams Ctr Tower II	Tulsa	OK	74103	**800-558-3311**	918-585-1201	205
Tulsa Dental Div Dentsply International Inc 5100 E Skelly Dr Suite 300	Tulsa	OK	74135	**800-662-1202**	918-493-6598	226
Tulsa Performing Arts Center 110 E 2nd St	Tulsa	OK	74103	**800-364-7122**	918-596-7122	562
Tulsa World 315 S Boulder Ave	Tulsa	OK	74103	**800-897-3557**	918-583-2161	522-2
Tulsair Beechcraft Inc PO Box 582470	Tulsa	OK	74158	**800-331-4071**	918-835-7651	25
Tumbleweed Communications Corp 700 Saginaw Dr *NASDAQ: TMWD*	Redwood City	CA	94063	**800-696-1978**	650-216-2000	176-7

Name / Address	City	State	ZIP	Toll-Free	Phone	Class
Tumbling River Ranch 3715 Park County Rd 62 Box 30	Grant	CO	80448	**800-654-8770**	303-838-5981	238
Tumlare Corp 2128 Bellmore Ave	Bellmore	NY	11710	**800-223-4664**	516-781-0322	760
Tumor Assn. American Brain 2720 River Rd	Des Plaines	IL	60018	**800-886-2282**	847-827-9910	48-17
Tundra Semiconductor Corp 603 March Rd *TSE: TUN*	Ottawa	ON	K2K2M5	**800-267-7231**	613-592-0714	686
Tunica County Convention & Visitors Bureau 13625 Hwy 61 N	Robinsonville	MS	38664	**888-488-6422**	662-363-3800	205
Tunnell KW Co Inc 900 E 8th Ave Suite 106	King of Prussia	PA	19406	**800-532-2483**	610-337-0820	193
Tuohy Furniture Corp 42 St Albans Pl *Cust Svc	Chatfield	MN	55923	**800-533-1696***	507-867-4280	314-1
Tupelo Convention & Visitors Bureau 399 E Main St	Tupelo	MS	38804	**800-533-0611**	662-841-6521	205
Tupelo National Battlefield c/o Natchez Trace Pkwy 2680 Natchez Trace Pkwy	Tupelo	MS	38804	**800-305-7417**	662-680-4027	554
Tupperware Corp PO Box 2353 *NYSE: TUP* ■ *Cust Svc	Orlando	FL	32802	**800-772-4001***	407-847-3111	596
Turano Baking Co 6501 W Roosevelt Rd	Berwyn	IL	60402	**800-458-5662**	708-788-9220	291-1
Turbo Refrigerating LLC 1815 Shady Oaks Dr	Denton	TX	76205	**800-775-8648**	940-387-4301	650
TurboCare Chicopee 2140 Westover Rd	Chicopee	MA	01022	**800-887-2622**	413-593-0500	446
Turbosonic Technologies Inc 239 New Rd Bldg B-205	Parsippany	NJ	07054	**800-882-9280**	973-244-9544	19
Turbotrip.com 4124 S McCann Ct	Springfield	MO	65804	**800-473-7829**		368
Turf Managers Assn. Sports 805 New Hampshire St Suite E	Lawrence	KS	66044	**800-323-3875**	785-843-2549	48-22
Turf Professionals Equipment Co 13899 W 101st St	Lenexa	KS	66215	**800-299-3245**	913-599-0333	270
Turf Valley Resort & Conference Center 2700 Turf Valley Rd	Ellicott City	MD	21042	**800-666-8873**	410-465-1500	655
Turkey Federation. National Wild 770 Augusta Rd PO Box 530 *Cust Svc	Edgefield	SC	29824	**800-843-6983***	803-637-3106	48-3
Turkey Hill Dairy Inc 2601 River Rd	Conestoga	PA	17516	**800-688-7539**	717-872-5461	291-25
Turkish Airlines 437 Madison Ave	New York	NY	10022	**800-874-8875**		26
Turkish Airlines Miles & Miles 437 Madison Ave	New York	NY	10022	**800-874-8875**		27
Turkish Tourist Office 821 UN Plaza 1st Fl	New York	NY	10017	**877-367-8875**	212-687-2194	764
Turks & Caicos Islands Tourism Office 2715 E Oakland Park Blvd Suite 101	Fort Lauderdale	FL	33306	**800-241-0824**	954-568-6588	764
Turmatic Systems Inc 11600 Adie Rd	Saint Louis	MO	63043	**888-432-0070**	314-993-0600	447
Turner-Brooks Inc 28811 John R Rd	Madison Heights	MI	48071	**800-560-7003**	248-548-3400	188-2
Turner Funds 1205 Westlakes Dr Suite 100	Berwyn	PA	19312	**800-424-4865**	610-251-0268	517
Turner Industries Ltd 8687 United Plaza Blvd Suite 500	Baton Rouge	LA	70809	**800-288-6503**	225-922-5050	187-9
Turner Syndrome Society of the US 14450 TC Jester Suite 260	Houston	TX	77014	**800-365-9944**	832-249-9988	48-17
Turning Point Hospital 3015 Veterans Pkwy	Moultrie	GA	31788	**800-342-1075**	229-985-4815	712
Turning Point of Tampa 6227 Sheldon Rd	Tampa	FL	33615	**800-397-3006**	813-882-3003	712
Turning Stone Casino Resort 5218 Patrick Rd	Verona	NY	13478	**800-771-7711**	315-361-7711	133
Turtle Bay Resort 57-091 Kamehameha Hwy	Kahuku	HI	96731	**800-203-3650**	808-293-8811	655
Turtle Cove Spa at Mountain Harbor Resort 994 Mountain Harbor Rd PO Box 1268	Mount Ida	AR	71957	**800-832-2276**	870-867-1220	698
Turtle Magazine 1100 Waterway Blvd	Indianapolis	IN	46202	**800-558-2376**	317-636-8881	449-6
Turtle Wax Inc 5655 W 73rd St	Chicago	IL	60638	**800-323-9883**	708-563-3600	149
Turtleback Books 5701 Manufacturers Dr	Madison	WI	53704	**800-448-8939**		97
Tuscaloosa Convention & Visitors Bureau 1305 Greensboro Ave	Tuscaloosa	AL	35401	**800-538-8696**	205-391-9200	205
Tuscaloosa News 315 28th Ave	Tuscaloosa	AL	35401	**800-888-8639**	205-345-0505	522-2
Tuscan Dairy Farms Inc 750 Union Ave	Union	NJ	07083	**800-672-1137**	908-686-1500	291-27
Tuscarora Yarns Inc 8760 E Franklin St	Mount Pleasant	NC	28124	**800-849-6527**	704-436-6527	730-9
Tusculum College 60 Shiloh Rd Hwy 107	Greeneville	TN	37743	**800-729-0256**	423-636-7300	163
Tuskegee University *Admissions	Tuskegee	AL	36088	**800-622-6531***	334-727-8011	163
Tut Systems Inc 6000 SW Meadows Rd Suite 200 *NASDAQ: TUTS*	Lake Oswego	OR	97035	**877-225-7255**	971-217-0400	720
Tuthill Corp 8500 S Madison St	Burr Ridge	IL	60527	**800-888-4455**	630-382-4900	627
Tuthill Corp M-D Pneumatics Div 4840 W Kearney St	Springfield	MO	65803	**800-825-6937**	417-865-8715	19
Tuthill Corp Plastics Group 2050 Sunnydale Blvd	Clearwater	FL	33765	**800-447-5278**	727-446-8593	593
Tuthill Linkage Group 2110 Summit St	New Haven	IN	46774	**800-233-6213**	260-749-5105	609
Tuthill Transport Technologies 1205 Industrial Pk Dr *Cust Svc	Mount Vernon	MO	65712	**800-753-0050***	417-466-2178	60
Tuthill Vacuum Systems 4840 W Kearney St	Springfield	MO	65803	**800-225-3810**	417-865-8115	170
Tutor Time Learning Systems Inc 621 NW 53rd St Suite 115	Boca Raton	FL	33487	**800-275-1235**	561-237-2200	146
Tuttle-Click Automotive Group 41 Auto Center Dr	Irvine	CA	92618	**800-926-8253**	949-598-4800	57
Tuttle Publishing 364 Innovation Dr Airport Industrial Pk *Sales	North Clarendon	VT	05759	**800-526-2778***	802-773-8930	623-2

Name / Address	City	State	Zip	Toll-Free	Phone	Class
Tutwiler The - A Wyndham Historic Hotel 2021 Park Pl N	Birmingham	AL	35203	**800-996-3426**	205-322-2100	373
.TV Corp International 21345 Ridge Top Cir	Dulles	VA	20166	**800-255-2218**	703-948-3200	389
TV Guide 100 Matsonford Rd 4 Radnor Corp Ctr *Cust Svc	Radnor	PA	19088	**800-866-1400***	610-293-8500	449-9
TV Guide Channel 7140 S Lewis Ave	Tulsa	OK	74136	**800-447-7388**	918-488-4450	725
TV Japan 100 Broadway 15th Fl *Cust Svc	New York	NY	10005	**800-518-8576***	212-262-3377	727
TV Jobs c/o Broadcast Employment Services PO Box 4116	Oceanside	CA	92052	**800-374-0119**	760-754-8177	257
TW Medical Veterinary Supply 3610 Lohman Ford Rd	Lago Vista	TX	78645	**888-787-4483**	512-267-8800	574
Tweedy Browne Funds 350 Park Ave 9th Fl	New York	NY	10022	**800-432-4789**	212-916-0600	517
Tweeter Home Entertainment Group Inc 40 Pequot Way *NASDAQ: TWTR*	Canton	MA	02021	**800-893-3837**	781-821-2900	35
Twentieth Century Plastics Inc 205 S Puente St	Brea	CA	92821	**800-767-0777**	714-441-4500	87
TWHBEA (Tennessee Walking Horse Breeders' & Exhibitors' Assn) PO Box 286	Lewisburg	TN	37091	**800-359-1574**	931-359-1574	48-3
Twin Cities Air Service 81 Airport Dr	Auburn	ME	04210	**800-564-3882**	207-782-3882	14
Twin City EDM 7940 Rancher Rd	Fridley	MN	55432	**800-269-8919**	763-783-7808	446
Twin City Knitting Co Inc 104 Rock Barn Rd NE PO Box 1179 *Cust Svc	Conover	NC	28613	**800-438-6884***	828-464-4830	153-10
Twin City Testing 662 Cromwell Ave	Saint Paul	MN	55114	**888-645-8378**	651-645-3601	728
Twin County Regional Hospital 200 Hospital Dr	Galax	VA	24333	**800-295-3342**	276-236-8181	366-2
Twin Falls Area Chamber of Commerce 858 Blue Lakes Blvd N	Twin Falls	ID	83301	**866-894-6325**	208-733-3974	137
Twin Farms Stage Rd PO box 115	Barnard	VT	05031	**800-894-6327**	802-234-9999	373
Twin Hills Collectables LLC 70 Hickory Rd	Hickory	KY	42051	**800-210-8230**	270-856-2277	750
Twin Lakes Telephone Co-op 201 W Gore Ave *Cust Svc	Gainesboro	TN	38562	**800-644-8582***	931-268-2151	721
Twin Oaks Hammocks 138 Twin Oaks Rd	Louisa	VA	23093	**800-688-8946**	540-894-5125	314-4
Twin Palms Hotel 225 E Apache Blvd	Tempe	AZ	85281	**800-367-0835**	480-967-9431	373
Twin Peaks Ranch PO Box 774	Salmon	ID	83467	**800-659-4899**	208-894-2290	238
Twin Sisters Productions LLC 2680 W Market St	Akron	OH	44333	**800-248-8946**	330-864-3000	242
Twin Town Treatment Center 1706 University Ave	Saint Paul	MN	55104	**800-645-3662**	651-645-3661	712
Twin Valley Electric Co-op PO Box 385	Altamont	KS	67330	**866-784-5500**	620-784-5500	244
Twin Valleys Public Power District PO Box 160	Cambridge	NE	69022	**800-658-4266**	308-697-3315	244
Twinbrook Medical Center 3805 Field St	Erie	PA	16511	**800-427-9149**	814-898-5600	441
Twinco Romax 4635 Willow Dr	Medina	MN	55340	**800-682-3800**	763-478-2360	61
Twinhead Corp 48303 Fremont Blvd *Sales	Fremont	CA	94538	**800-995-8946***	510-492-0828	171-3
Twinlab Corp 150 Motor Pkwy Suite 210	Hauppauge	NY	11788	**800-645-5626**	631-467-3140	786
Twinless Twins Support Group International (TTSG) PO Box 980481	Ypsilanti	MI	48198	**888-205-8962**		48-21
Twins Clubs Inc. National Organization of Mothers of PO Box 438	Thompsons Station	TN	37179	**877-540-2200**	615-595-0936	48-6
Twins Magazine 11211 E Arapahoe Rd Suite 101	Centennial	CO	80112	**888-558-9467**	303-290-8500	449-10
Twirl Jet Spas Inc 3990 Industrial Ave	Hemet	CA	92545	**800-854-4890**	951-766-4306	367
Twist Magazine 270 Sylvan Ave *Cust Svc	Englewood Cliffs	NJ	07632	**800-757-7053***	201-569-6699	449-6
Twitchell Corp 4031 Ross Clark Cir NW	Dothan	AL	36303	**800-633-7550**	334-792-0002	730-2
Two Bunch Palms Resort & Spa 67425 Two Bunch Palms Trail	Desert Hot Springs	CA	92240	**800-472-4334**	760-329-8791	655
Two Men & A Truck International Inc 3400 Belle Chase Way	Lansing	MI	48911	**800-345-1070**	517-394-7210	508
TWP Inc 2831 10th St	Berkeley	CA	94710	**800-227-1570**	510-548-4434	676
TxF Products PO Box 1118	Brownwood	TX	76804	**800-441-7894**	325-646-1504	497
TXI Operations LP DBA Louisiana Industries PO Box 5396	Bossier City	LA	71171	**800-894-5422**	318-742-3111	181
TXU Electric & Gas 1601 Bryan St	Dallas	TX	75201	**800-242-9113**	214-812-4600	774
Ty Inc 280 Chestnut Ave *Cust Svc	Westmont	IL	60559	**800-876-8000***	630-920-1515	750
Tyco Adhesives 25 Forge Pkwy	Franklin	MA	02038	**800-248-7659**	508-918-1600	717
Tyco Electronics Corp Corcom Div 844 E Rockland Rd	Libertyville	IL	60048	**800-643-8391**	847-680-7400	247
Tyco Healthcare Retail Group Inc 601 Allendale Rd PO Box 61930	King of Prussia	PA	19406	**800-262-0042**	610-265-5000	548-2
Tyco Healthcare/Mallinckrodt 3600 N 2nd St PO Box 5840	Saint Louis	MO	63134	**888-744-1414**	314-654-2000	468
Tyco International Ltd 9 Roszel Rd *NYSE: TYC*	Princeton	NJ	08540	**800-320-2350**	609-720-4200	184
Tyco Plastics Inc 1401 W 94th St	Bloomington	MN	55431	**800-873-3941**	952-884-7281	589
Tyden Brammall Inc 409 Hoosier Dr	Angola	IN	46703	**800-348-4777**	260-665-3176	321
Tyler Area Chamber of Commerce 315 N Broadway Ave	Tyler	TX	75702	**800-235-5712**	903-592-1661	137
Tyler Building Systems LP 3535 Shiloh Rd	Tyler	TX	75707	**800-442-8979**	903-561-3000	106
Tyler Convention & Visitors Bureau 315 N Broadway	Tyler	TX	75702	**800-235-5712**	903-592-1661	205
Tyler Equipment Corp 251 Shaker Rd	East Longmeadow	MA	01028	**800-292-6351**	413-525-6351	353
Tyler Junior College PO Box 9020	Tyler	TX	75711	**800-687-5680**	903-510-2523	160
Tyler Morning Telegraph PO Box 2030	Tyler	TX	75710	**800-333-8411**	903-597-8111	522-2
Tyler Refrigeration 1329 Lake St	Niles	MI	49120	**800-992-3744**	269-683-2000	650
Tymco Inc 225 E Industrial Blvd	Waco	TX	76705	**800-258-9626**	254-799-5546	505
Tyndale House Publishers Inc 351 Executive Dr	Carol Stream	IL	60188	**800-323-9400**	630-668-8300	623-4
Tyndale University College & Seminary 25 Ballyconnor Ct	Toronto	ON	M2M4B3	**877-896-3253**	416-226-6380	164-3
Typesetting Inc 1144 S Robertson Blvd	Los Angeles	CA	90035	**800-794-8973**	310-273-3330	770
TYR Sport 15391 Springdale St	Huntington Beach	CA	92649	**800-252-7878**	714-897-0799	153-17
Tyres International Inc 619 E Tallmadge Ave	Akron	OH	44310	**800-321-0941**	330-374-1000	740
Tyson Events Center 401 Gordon Dr	Sioux City	IA	51101	**800-593-2228**	712-279-4850	204
Tyson Foods Inc 2210 W Oaklawn Dr *NYSE: TSN*	Springdale	AR	72762	**800-643-3410**	479-290-4000	608
Tyson Prepared Foods Inc 5701 McNutt Rd	Santa Teresa	NM	88008	**800-351-8184**	505-589-0100	291-26
Tysons Corner Center 1961 Chain Bridge Rd Suite 105	McLean	VA	22102	**888-289-7667**	703-893-9400	452
Tzetzo Brothers Inc 1100 Military Rd	Buffalo	NY	14217	**800-248-2881**	716-877-0800	292-3

U

Name / Address	City	State	Zip	Toll-Free	Phone	Class
U-Haul International Inc PO Box 21502	Phoenix	AZ	85036	**800-468-4285**	602-263-6011	767
U & LC Magazine 200 Ballardvale Rd	Wilmington	MA	01887	**800-424-8973**		449-21
U-Save Auto Rental of America Inc 4780 I-55 N Suite 300	Jackson	MS	39211	**800-438-2300**	601-713-4333	126
U-Store-It Trust 6745 Engle Rd Suite 300 *NYSE: YSI*	Middleburg Heights	OH	44130	**800-234-4494**	440-234-0700	790-3
UAB Medical West PO Box 847	Bessemer	AL	35021	**877-481-7001**	205-481-7000	366-2
UAL Corp 1200 E Algonquin Rd	Elk Grove Township	IL	60007	**800-241-6522**	847-700-4000	355-1
UAP Timberland LLC 140 Arkansas St	Monticello	AR	71655	**800-752-7009**	870-367-8561	297
uBid Inc 8550 W Bryn Mawr Ave Suite 200	Chicago	IL	60631	**888-900-8243**	773-272-5000	51
UBS Capital Markets 111 Pavonia Ave E Newport Financial Ctr	Jersey City	NJ	07310	**800-543-7995**	201-963-9100	679
UBS Financial Services Inc 1285 Ave of the Americas	New York	NY	10019	**800-221-3260**	212-713-2000	679
UBS Global Asset Management Mutual Funds PO Box 9786	Providence	RI	02940	**800-647-1568**		517
UBS Warburg LLC 677 Washington Blvd	Stamford	CT	06901	**800-221-3260**	203-719-3000	679
UC Davis Cancer Center 4501 X St	Sacramento	CA	95817	**800-362-5566**	916-734-5800	366-5
UC Milk Co Inc 234 N Scott St	Madisonville	KY	42431	**800-462-2354**	270-821-7221	291-27
UCB Pharma Inc 1950 Lake Park Dr	Smyrna	GA	30080	**800-477-7877**	770-970-7500	572
UCBH Holdings Inc 555 Montgomery St *NASDAQ: UCBH*	San Francisco	CA	94111	**800-288-3899**	415-928-0700	355-2
UCC (United Church of Christ) 700 Prospect Ave	Cleveland	OH	44115	**866-822-8224**	216-736-2100	48-20
UCC Direct Services 2727 Allen Pkwy Suite 1000	Houston	TX	77019	**800-833-5778**	713-533-4600	621
UCC Filing & Search Services Inc 526 E Park Ave	Tallahassee	FL	32302	**800-822-5436**	850-681-6528	621
UCD Hospice 3630 Business Dr Suite G	Sacramento	CA	95820	**800-268-9232**	916-734-2458	365
UCI Medical Center University of California Irvine 101 City Dr S	Orange	CA	92868	**877-824-3627**	714-456-6011	366-2
UCP National 1660 L St NW Suite 700	Washington	DC	20036	**800-872-5827**	202-776-0406	48-17
UCS (Union of Concerned Scientists) 2 Brattle Sq	Cambridge	MA	02238	**800-664-8276**	617-547-5552	48-13
UDL Laboratories Inc 1718 Northrock Ct	Rockford	IL	61103	**800-435-5272**	815-282-1201	573
UDWI Rural Electric Membership Corp PO Box 427	Bloomfield	IN	47424	**800-489-7362**	812-384-4446	244
UEC Technologies LLC 600 Grant St Rm 1644	Pittsburgh	PA	15219	**800-245-4450**	412-433-6527	258
UFCW Textile & Garment Council 4207 Lebanon Pike Suite 200	Hermitage	TN	37076	**888-462-4892**	615-889-9221	405
UGI Utilities Inc 100 Kachel Blvd Green Hills Corporate Ctr Suite 400	Reading	PA	19607	**800-276-2722**	610-796-3400	774
Uhe George Co Inc 12 Rt 17 N	Paramus	NJ	07653	**800-850-4075**	201-843-4000	470
Uhlmann Co 1009 Central St	Kansas City	MO	64105	**800-383-8201**	816-221-8200	291-23
UHP Healthcare 3405 W Imperial Hwy	Inglewood	CA	90303	**800-544-0088**	310-671-3465	384-3
UICI 9151 Grapevine Hwy *NYSE: UCI*	North Richland Hills	TX	76180	**800-527-5504**	817-255-5200	355-4
UIL Holdings Corp 157 Church St *NYSE: UIL*	New Haven	CT	06510	**800-722-5584**	203-499-2000	355-5
Uintah County 147 E Main St	Vernal	UT	84078	**800-966-4680**	435-781-0770	334
Ukiah Daily Journal PO Box 749	Ukiah	CA	95482	**800-729-0123**	707-468-3500	522-2
Ukraine International Airlines 1643-A W Henderson	Cleburne	TX	76033	**800-876-0114**	817-641-3478	26
Ukraine International Airlines Panorama Club 1643-A W Henderson	Cleburne	TX	76033	**800-876-0114**	817-641-3478	27

Name / Address	City	State	ZIP	Toll-Free	Phone	Class
Ukrainian National Assn PO Box 280	Parsippany	NJ	07054	**800-253-9862**	973-292-9800	48-14
Ukrop's Super Markets Inc 600 Southlake Blvd.	Richmond	VA	23236	**800-868-2270**	804-379-7300	339
Ulbrich Stainless Steels & Special Metals Inc 57 Dodge Ave	North Haven	CT	06473	**800-243-1676**	203-239-4481	709
Ulead Systems Inc 20000 Mariner Ave Suite 200	Torrance	CA	90503	**800-858-5323**	310-896-6388	176-8
Ulery Greenhouse Co 2625 Old Clifton Rd *Cust Svc	Springfield	OH	45501	**800-722-5143***	937-325-5543	363
ULI (Urban Land Institute) 1025 Thomas Jefferson St NW Suite 500W *Orders	Washington	DC	20007	**800-321-5011***	202-624-7000	48-8
Ulico Casualty Co 8403 Colesville Rd	Silver Springs	MD	20910	**800-431-5425**	202-682-0900	384-5
ULLICO Inc 8403 Colesville Rd.	Silver Springs	MD	20910	**800-431-5425**	202-682-0900	355-4
Ulrich Chemical Inc 3111 N Post Rd	Indianapolis	IN	46226	**800-844-8632**	317-898-8632	144
Ulrich Planfiling Equipment Corp 2120 4th Ave PO Box 135	Lakewood	NY	14750	**800-346-2875**	716-763-1815	314-1
Ulster County Community College Cottekill Rd	Stone Ridge	NY	12484	**800-724-0833**	845-687-5000	160
Ulta3 Inc 1135 Arbor Dr	Romeoville	IL	60446	**866-858-2266**	630-226-0020	211
Ulticom Inc 1020 Briggs Rd *NASDAQ: ULCM* ■ *Sales	Mount Laurel	NJ	08054	**888-295-6664***	856-787-2700	176-10
Ultimate Electronics Inc 321-A W 84th Ave	Thornton	CO	80260	**800-260-2660**	303-412-2500	35
Ultimate Software Group Inc 2000 Ultimate Way *NASDAQ: ULTI*	Weston	FL	33326	**800-432-1729**	954-331-7000	176-1
Ultimate Support Systems Inc 2506 Zurich Dr	Fort Collins	CO	80524	**800-525-5628**	970-493-4488	516
Ultimate Technology Corp 100 Rawson Rd	Victor	NY	14564	**800-349-0546**	585-924-9500	603
Ultra Care Home Medical 2001 Janice Ave	Melrose Park	IL	60160	**800-222-9444**	773-804-7400	358
Ultra Electronics-DNE Technologies Inc 50 Barnes Park N	Wallingford	CT	06492	**800-370-4485**	203-265-7151	633
Ultra Hardware Products LLC 1777 Hylton Rd	Pennsauken	NJ	08110	**800-426-6379**	856-663-5050	345
Ultra-Lab Nutrition Inc 7491 N Federal Hwy Suite 148	Boca Raton	FL	33487	**800-800-0267**	561-367-1474	786
Ultra Play Systems Inc 1675 Locust St	Red Bud	IL	62278	**800-458-5872**	618-282-8200	340
Ultracraft Co 6163 Old 421 Rd	Liberty	NC	27298	**800-262-4046**	336-622-4281	116
Ultradata Systems Inc 1240 Dielman Industrial Dr	Saint Louis	MO	63132	**800-274-0971**	314-997-2250	171-2
UltraDNS Corp 1000 Marina Blvd Suite 600	Brisbane	CA	94005	**888-367-4812**	650-228-2300	39
Ultrafabrics LLC 400 Executive Blvd	Elmsford	NY	10523	**888-361-9216**	914-460-1730	730-3
Ultrafryer Systems 302 Spencer Ln	San Antonio	TX	78201	**800-545-9189**	210-731-5000	293
Ultralife Batteries Inc 2000 Technology Pkwy *NASDAQ: ULBI*	Newark	NY	14513	**800-332-5000**	315-332-7100	76
Ultramar Diamond Shamrock Corp 2200 ave McGill College	Montreal	QC	H3A3L3	**800-361-4253**	514-499-6111	570
Ultramar Travel Management International 14 E 47th St 5th Fl	New York	NY	10017	**888-856-2929**	212-856-5600	760
Ultrasonics Ferroelectrics & Frequency Control Society. IEEE IEEE Operations Ctr 445 Hoes Ln	Piscataway	NJ	08854	**800-678-4333**	732-981-0060	49-19
Ultrasound in Medicine. American Institute of 14750 Sweitzer Ln Suite 100	Laurel	MD	20707	**800-638-5352**	301-498-4100	49-8
UltraStaff 3730 Kirby Dr Suite 900	Houston	TX	77098	**800-522-7707**	713-522-7100	707
Ultratech Inc 3050 Zanker Rd *NASDAQ: UTEK*	San Jose	CA	95134	**800-222-1213**	408-321-8835	685
UMA (United Motorcoach Assn) 113 S West St 4th Fl	Alexandria	VA	22314	**800-424-8262**	703-838-2929	49-21
UMB Bank NA 1010 Grand Blvd.	Kansas City	MO	64106	**800-821-2171**	816-860-7000	71
UMB Capital Corp 1010 Grand Blvd.	Kansas City	MO	64106	**800-821-2171**	816-860-7914	394
UMB Financial Corp 1010 Grand Blvd. *NASDAQ: UMBF*	Kansas City	MO	64106	**800-821-2171**	816-860-7000	355-2
UMCOR (United Methodist Committee on Relief) 475 Riverside Dr Suite 330	New York	NY	10115	**800-554-8583**	212-870-3814	48-5
Una Mas Restaurants Inc 25064 Viking St	Hayward	CA	94545	**888-862-2627**	408-747-7000	657
Unaflex Inc 3901 NE 12th Ave	Pompano Beach	FL	33064	**800-327-1286**	954-943-5002	364
Unarco Material Handling Inc 701 16th Ave E	Springfield	TN	37172	**800-862-7261**	615-384-3531	281
UNC-TV (University of North Carolina Center for Public Television) 10 TW Alexander Dr PO Box 14900	Research Triangle Park	NC	27709	**800-906-5050**	919-549-7060	620
Uncas Mfg Co 150 Niantic Ave *Cust Svc	Providence	RI	02907	**800-776-0980***	401-944-4700	401
UNCF (United Negro College Fund Inc) 8260 Willow Oaks Corporate Dr Suite 400	Fairfax	VA	22031	**800-331-2244**	703-205-3400	48-11
Uncle Milton Industries Inc 5717 Corsa Ave	Westlake Village	CA	91362	**800-869-7555**	818-707-0800	750
Under Armour Performance Apparel 1020 Hull St	Baltimore	MD	21230	**888-427-6687**	410-468-2512	153-18
UndercoverWear Inc 30 Commerce Way Suite 2	Tewksbury	MA	01876	**800-733-0007**	978-851-8580	361
Underground Construction Co Inc PO Box 2000	Benicia	CA	94510	**800-227-2314**	707-746-8800	187-10
Underwater Instructors. National Assn of 1232 Tech Blvd.	Tampa	FL	33619	**800-553-6284**	813-628-6284	48-22
Underwater Kinetics 13400 Danielson St	Poway	CA	92064	**800-852-7483**	858-513-9100	701
Underwood Machinery Transport Inc 940 W Troy Ave	Indianapolis	IN	46225	**800-428-2372**	317-783-9235	769
Underwriters MGA Inc PO Box 5488	McAllen	TX	78502	**888-560-3240**	956-364-3066	384-4
Underwriters Reinsurance Co 26050 Mureau Rd	Calabasas	CA	91302	**800-332-2801**	818-878-9500	384-4
Underwriting. Association for Advanced Life 2901 Telestar Ct.	Falls Church	VA	22042	**888-275-0092**	703-641-9400	49-9
Underwriting Society. Professional Liability 5353 Wayzata Blvd Suite 600	Minneapolis	MN	55416	**800-845-0778**	952-746-2580	49-9
Unex Conveying Systems Inc 50 Progress Pl *Cust Svc	Jackson	NJ	08527	**800-695-7726***	732-928-2800	206
UNext.com 500 Lake Cook Rd Suite 150	Deerfield	IL	60015	**877-405-4500**	847-405-5000	241
Unger Co 12401 Berea Rd	Cleveland	OH	44111	**800-321-1418**	216-252-1400	538
UNHCR. USA for 1775 K St NW Suite 290	Washington	DC	20006	**800-770-1100**	202-296-1115	48-5
Uni-Form Components Co 16969 Old Beaumont Hwy 90	Houston	TX	77049	**800-231-3272**	281-456-9310	478
Uni-Marts LLC 477 E Beaver Ave *AMEX: UNI*	State College	PA	16801	**800-494-1500**	814-234-6000	203
Unibilt Industries Inc PO Box 373	Vandalia	OH	45377	**800-777-9942**	937-890-7570	107
Unical Aviation Inc 4775 Irwindale Ave	Irwindale	CA	91706	**800-813-1901**	626-813-1901	759
Unicapital Leasing 433 New Park Ave	West Hartford	CT	06110	**800-444-8333**	860-233-3663	214
UNICCO Service Co 275 Grove St Suite 3-200	Auburndale	MA	02466	**800-283-9222**	617-527-5222	267
Unicell Body Co 571 Howard St *Cust Svc	Buffalo	NY	14206	**800-628-8914***	716-853-8628	505
Unicity Network Inc 1201 N 800 East	Orem	UT	84097	**800-748-4334**	801-226-2224	361
Unico Inc 3725 Nicholson Rd	Franksville	WI	53126	**800-245-1859**	262-886-5678	507
UNICOM Electric Inc 907 S Canada Ct	City of Industry	CA	91748	**800-346-6668**	626-964-7873	174
UnicornHRO 25B Hanover Rd	Florham Park	NJ	07932	**800-343-6844**	973-360-0688	39
Unicorp 291 Cleveland St	Orange	NJ	07050	**800-526-1389**	973-674-1700	345
Unicorr Connecticut Container Corp 455 Sackett Point Rd	North Haven	CT	06473	**800-229-4269**	203-248-2161	101
Unicover Corp 1 Unicover Ctr *Cust Svc	Cheyenne	WY	82008	**800-443-4225***	307-771-3000	451
Unicru Inc 9525 SW Gemini Dr	Beaverton	OR	97008	**800-933-6321**	503-596-3100	176-11
Uniden America Corp 4700 Amon Carter Blvd *Cust Svc	Fort Worth	TX	76155	**800-297-1023***	817-858-3300	720
Uniek Inc 805 Uniek Dr	Waunakee	WI	53597	**800-248-6435**	608-849-9999	304
Unified Foodservice Purchasing Co-op LLC 950 Breckenridge Ln	Louisville	KY	40207	**800-444-4144**	502-896-5900	295
Unified Western Grocers Inc 6433 S E Lake Rd	Portland	OR	97222	**800-777-3305**	503-833-1000	292-8
UniFirst Corp 68 Jonspin Rd *NYSE: UNF*	Wilmington	MA	01887	**800-347-7888**	978-658-8888	434
Uniflex Inc 383 W John St	Hicksville	NY	11802	**800-223-0564**	516-932-2000	67
Uniform Commercial Code Law Letter 610 Opperman Dr *Cust Svc	Eagan	MN	55123	**800-328-4880***	651-687-7000	521-13
Uniform & Textile Service Assn (UTSA) 1300 N 17th St Suite 750	Arlington	VA	22209	**800-486-6745**	703-247-2600	49-4
Uniformed Services. National Assn for 5535 Hempstead Way	Springfield	VA	22151	**800-842-3451**	703-750-1342	48-19
Uniformed Services University of the Health Sciences 4301 Jones Bridge Rd	Bethesda	MD	20814	**800-772-1743**		164-2
Uniformed Services University of the Health Sciences (USUHS) 4301 Jones Bridge Rd *Admissions	Bethesda	MD	20814	**800-772-1743***	301-295-3103	336-3
UniForum Assn PO Box 3177	Annapolis	MD	21043	**800-333-8649**	410-715-9500	48-9
Unify Corp 2101 Arena Blvd Suite 100	Sacramento	CA	95834	**800-248-6439**	916-928-6400	176-7
Unigard Security Insurance Co 15805 NE 24th St	Bellevue	WA	98008	**800-777-1757**	425-641-4321	384-4
Unigen Corp 45388 Warm Springs Blvd	Fremont	CA	94539	**800-826-0808**	510-657-2680	613
UNIGLOBE Travel USA LLC 18662 MacArthur Blvd Suite 100	Irvine	CA	92612	**800-863-1606**	949-623-9000	761
UniGroup Inc 1 Premier Dr	Fenton	MO	63026	**800-325-3924**	636-305-5000	508
UniGroup Worldwide UTS 1 Worldwide Dr	Saint Louis	MO	63026	**800-325-3924**	636-349-3600	508
Unilab Corp 18408 Oxnard St	Tarzana	CA	91356	**800-696-7502**	818-996-7300	409
Unilever Home & Personal Care North America 800 Sylvan Ave 1st Fl	Englewood Cliffs	NJ	07632	**800-745-9595**	201-862-2000	211
Unilever of Puerto Rico Inc PO Box 599	Bayamon	PR	00960	**800-981-3405**	787-740-3400	211
UniLink Software Inc 7322 Newman Blvd *Cust Svc	Dexter	MI	48130	**800-968-0600***	734-426-5860	176-1
Uniloc Div Rosemount Analytical Inc 2400 Barranca Pkwy	Irvine	CA	92606	**800-854-8257**	949-863-1181	200
Uniloy Milacron Inc 5550 Occidental Hwy	Tecumseh	MI	49286	**800-419-7771**	734-428-8371	745
Unilux Inc 59 N 5th St	Saddle Brook	NJ	07663	**800-522-0801**	201-712-1266	464
Unimark Inc 9910 Widmer Rd *Cust Svc	Lenexa	KS	66215	**800-255-6356***	913-649-2424	174
Unimin Corp 258 Elm St	New Canaan	CT	06840	**800-223-2236**	203-966-8880	493-4
Union The 464 Sutton Way	Grass Valley	CA	95945	**800-899-9561**	530-273-9561	522-2
Union Acceptance Corp 250 N Shadeland Ave	Indianapolis	IN	46219	**800-221-6809**	317-231-6400	215
Union Bankshares Corp 212 N Main St *NASDAQ: UBSH*	Bowling Green	VA	22427	**800-546-5031**	804-633-5031	355-2
Union Beverage Co 2600 W 35th St	Chicago	IL	60632	**800-685-6868**	773-254-9000	82-3
Union Butterfield Corp PO Box 9000	Crystal Lake	IL	60039	**800-222-8665**		484
Union Central Life Insurance Co 1876 Waycross Rd	Cincinnati	OH	45240	**800-825-1551**	513-595-2200	384-2

Listing	Toll-Free	Phone	Class
Union City Body Co			
301 S Jackson Pike ..... Union City IN 47390	888-990-8222	765-964-3121	505
Union City Daily Messenger			
PO Box 430 ..... Union City TN 38281	866-885-0744	731-885-0744	522-2
Union College 310 College St ..... Barbourville KY 40906	800-489-8646	606-546-4151	163
Union College 3800 S 48th St ..... Lincoln NE 68506	800-228-4600	402-488-2331	163
Union College 807 Union St ..... Schenectady NY 12308	888-843-6688	518-388-6000	163
Union of Concerned Scientists (UCS)			
2 Brattle Sq ..... Cambridge MA 02238	800-664-8276	617-547-5552	48-13
Union County Chamber of Commerce			
227 E 5th St ..... Marysville OH 43040	800-642-0087	937-642-6279	137
Union County Chamber of Commerce			
135 W Main St ..... Union SC 29379	877-202-8755	864-427-9039	137
Union Drilling Inc PO Drawer 40 ..... Buckhannon WV 26201	800-352-3839	304-472-4610	529
Union Eyecare Centers			
9700 Rockside Rd Suite 190 ..... Valley View OH 44125	800-443-9699	216-986-9700	533
Union Federal Bank of Indianapolis			
45 N Pennsylvania St ..... Indianapolis IN 46204	800-284-8585	317-269-4700	71
Union Fidelity Life Insurance Co			
500 Virginia Dr ..... Fort Washington PA 19034	800-523-5758		384-2
Union Financial Bancshares Inc			
203 W Main St ..... Union SC 29379	888-427-9002	864-427-9000	355-2
NASDAQ: UFBS			
Union Group 649 Alden St ..... Fall River MA 02722	800-289-3523	508-676-8580	87
Union Industries Inc 10 Admiral St ..... Providence RI 02908	800-556-6454	401-274-7000	538
Union Institute & University			
440 E McMillan St ..... Cincinnati OH 45206	800-486-3116	513-861-6400	163
Vermont College 36 College St ..... Montpelier VT 05602	800-336-6794	802-828-8500	163
Union Labor Life Insurance Co			
8403 Colesville Rd ..... Silver Spring MD 20910	800-431-5425	202-682-0900	384-2
Union Leader 100 William Loeb Dr ..... Manchester NH 03109	800-562-8218	603-668-4321	522-2
Union Line Inc 2241 S Halsted St ..... Chicago IL 60608	800-632-2308	312-942-1111	153-19
Union National Fire Insurance Co			
8282 Goodwood Blvd ..... Baton Rouge LA 70806	800-765-0550	225-927-3430	384-4
Union National Life Insurance Co			
8282 Goodwood Blvd ..... Baton Rouge LA 70806	800-765-0550	225-927-3430	384-2
Union Pacific Corp 1400 Douglas St ..... Omaha NE 68179	888-870-8777	402-544-5000	355-3
NYSE: UNP			
Union Pacific Railroad Co			
1416 Dodge St ..... Omaha NE 68179	888-870-8777	402-271-5000	634
Union Pacific Railroad Employees' Health Systems 795 N			
400 West ..... Salt Lake City UT 84103	800-547-0421	801-595-4300	384-3
Union Pen Co PO Box 220 ..... Hagaman NY 12086	800-846-6600		560
Union Power Co-op PO Box 5014 ..... Monroe NC 28111	800-922-6840	704-289-3145	244
Union Rural Electric Co-op Inc			
15461 US 36E ..... Marysville OH 43040	800-642-1826	937-642-1826	244
Union Standard Equipment Co			
801 E 141st St ..... Bronx NY 10454	800-237-8873	718-585-0200	293
Union Standard Insurance Co			
122 W Carpenter Fwy Suite 350 ..... Irving TX 75039	800-444-0049	972-719-2400	384-4
Union Station - A Wyndham Historic Hotel 1001 Broadway ..... Nashville TN 37203	800-996-3426	615-726-1001	373
Union Switch & Signal Inc			
1000 Technology Dr ..... Pittsburgh PA 15219	800-351-1520	412-688-2400	691
Union Tank Car Co			
175 W Jackson Blvd Suite 2100 ..... Chicago IL 60604	800-635-3770	312-431-3111	636
Union Theological Seminary & Presbyterian School of Christian Education 3401 Brook Rd ..... Richmond VA 23227	800-229-2990	804-355-0671	164-3
Union-Tribune Publishing Co			
PO Box 120191 ..... San Diego CA 92112	800-244-6397	619-299-3131	623-8
Union University			
1050 Union University Dr ..... Jackson TN 38305	800-338-6466	731-661-5210	163
UnionTools Inc			
390 W Nationwide Blvd ..... Columbus OH 43215	800-848-6657	614-222-4400	746
Uniontown Newspapers Inc			
8-18 E Church St ..... Uniontown PA 15401	800-342-8254	724-439-7500	623-8
UniPress Software Inc			
2025 Lincoln Hwy ..... Edison NJ 08817	800-222-0550	732-287-2100	176-12
UniPro Foodservice Inc			
2500 Cumberland Pkwy Suite 600 ..... Atlanta GA 30339	800-366-7723	770-952-0871	292-8
Unipunch Products Inc 370 Babcock St ..... Buffalo NY 14206	800-828-7061*	716-825-7960	745
*Sales			
Unique Carpets Ltd 7360 Jurupa Ave ..... Riverside CA 92504	800-547-8266	951-352-8125	131
Unique Functional Products Corp			
135 Sunshine Ln ..... San Marcos CA 92069	800-854-1905	760-744-1610	751
Unique Industries Inc			
2400 S Weccacoe Ave ..... Philadelphia PA 19148	800-888-1705	215-336-4300	323
Unique Photo Inc			
11 Vreeland Rd ..... Florham Park NJ 07932	800-631-0300	973-377-5555	119
Unirex Inc 9310 E 37th St N ..... Wichita KS 67226	800-397-1257	316-636-1228	759
Uniroyal Engineered Products LLC			
501 S Water St ..... Stoughton WI 53589	800-873-8800	608-873-6631	730-2
UniSea Inc			
15400 NE 90th St PO Box 97019 ..... Redmond WA 98073	800-535-8509	425-881-8181	291-14
Uniseal Inc PO Box 6288 ..... Evansville IN 47719	800-443-6297	812-425-1361	3
Unisearch Inc 1780 Barnes Blvd SW ..... Tumwater WA 98512	800-722-0708	360-956-9500	621
Unisec Inc 2555 Nicholson St ..... San Leandro CA 94577	800-982-4587	510-352-5610	681
Unishippers Assn			
746 E Winchester Suite 200 ..... Salt Lake City UT 84107	800-999-8721	801-487-0600	536
UniSource Energy Corp			
1 S Church Ave ..... Tucson AZ 85701	800-328-8853	520-571-4000	355-5
NYSE: UNS			
Unisource Maintenance Supply Systems Inc 13217 S			
Figueroa St ..... Los Angeles CA 90061	888-242-1827	310-527-3000	398
Unisource Worldwide Inc			
6600 Governors Lake Pkwy ..... Norcross GA 30071	800-282-7958	770-447-9000	543
Unistrut Corp 4205 Elizabeth St ..... Wayne MI 48184	800-521-7730*	734-721-4040	471
*Cust Svc			
Unit Chemical Corp			
4161 Redwood Ave ..... Los Angeles CA 90066	800-879-8648	323-870-1923	149
Unit Corp 7130 S Lewis Ave Suite 1000 ..... Tulsa OK 74136	800-722-3612	918-493-7700	529
NYSE: UNT			
Unitarian Universalist Service Committee (UUSC)			
130 Prospect St ..... Cambridge MA 02139	800-388-3920	617-868-6600	48-5

Listing	Toll-Free	Phone	Class
UNITE HERE 275 7th Ave ..... New York NY 10001	800-238-6483	212-265-7000	405
United Ad Label Inc			
30 Hazelwood Dr Suite 100 ..... Amherst NY 14228	800-992-5755		404
United Air Specialists Inc			
4440 Creek Rd ..... Cincinnati OH 45242	800-252-4647	513-891-0400	19
United Airlines Cargo Services Div			
PO Box 66100 ..... Chicago IL 60666	800-822-2746	847-700-5004	13
United Airlines Inc PO Box 66100 ..... Chicago IL 60666	800-241-6522	847-700-4000	26
United Airlines Mileage Plus			
PO Box 28870 ..... Tucson AZ 85726	800-421-4655		27
United American Insurance Co Inc			
PO Box 8080 ..... McKinney TX 75070	800-331-2512	972-529-5085	384-2
United Bancorp Inc 201 S 4th St ..... Martins Ferry OH 43935	888-275-5566	740-633-0445	355-2
NASDAQ: UBCP			
United Bancshares Inc			
100 S High St ..... Columbus Grove OH 45830	800-837-8111	419-659-2141	355-2
NASDAQ: UBOH			
United Bank 11185 Main St ..... Fairfax VA 22030	800-730-6169	703-219-4850	71
United Bankshares Inc			
514 Market St ..... Parkersburg WV 26101	800-345-4862	304-424-8800	355-2
NASDAQ: UBSI			
United Behavioral Health Inc			
425 Market St 27th Fl ..... San Francisco CA 94105	800-888-2998	415-547-5000	454
United Beverage Co 624 N 44th Ave ..... Phoenix AZ 85043	888-340-4962	602-233-1900	82-1
United-Bilt Homes Inc			
PO Box 4346 ..... Shreveport LA 71134	800-551-8955	318-861-4572	186
United Blood Services of Arkansas			
Fort Smith 5300 S 'U' St ..... Fort Smith AR 72903	800-934-9415	479-452-5880	90
Hot Springs			
1635 Higdon Ferry Rd ..... Hot Springs AR 71913	800-286-2116	501-624-0667	90
United Blood Services of Mississippi			
Meridian 1115 25th Ave ..... Meridian MS 39301	877-582-2482	601-482-2482	90
Tupelo 4326 S Eason Blvd ..... Tupelo MS 38803	800-844-8870	662-842-8870	90
United Blood Services of Montana			
Billings 1444 Grand Ave ..... Billings MT 59102	800-365-4450	406-248-9168	90
United Blood Services of Nevada Reno			
1125 Terminal Way ..... Reno NV 89502	800-627-4928	775-329-6451	90
United Blood Services of New Mexico Albuquerque			
1515 University Blvd NE ..... Albuquerque NM 87102	800-333-8037	505-843-6227	90
United Blood Services of North Dakota			
Bismarck 517 S 7th St ..... Bismarck ND 58502	800-456-6159	701-258-4512	90
Fargo 1320 1st Ave N ..... Fargo ND 58102	800-293-8203	701-293-9453	90
United Blood Services of Texas			
El Paso 2325 Pershing Dr ..... El Paso TX 79903	800-333-7128	915-544-5422	90
McAllen 1312 Pecan Blvd ..... McAllen TX 78501	888-827-4376	956-682-1314	90
San Angelo			
2020 W Beauregard St ..... San Angelo TX 76901	800-756-0024	325-223-7500	90
United Brass Works Inc			
714 S Main St ..... Randleman NC 27317	800-334-3035	336-498-2661	776
United Building Centers Masonry Products Div PO Box 599 ..... Garden City KS 67846	800-545-7411	620-276-8294	181
United Business Forms Inc			
8482 W Allens Bridge Rd ..... Greeneville TN 37743	800-547-5351	423-639-5551	111
United California Discount Corp			
2035 S Myrtle Ave ..... Monrovia CA 91017	800-228-7151	626-303-3551	268
United Casualty Insurance Co			
1 E Wacker Dr Suite 1313 ..... Chicago IL 60601	800-777-8467	312-661-4600	384-4
United Cerebral Palsy			
1660 L St NW Suite 700 ..... Washington DC 20036	800-872-5827	202-776-0406	48-17
United Chair Co 147 St-Pierre St ..... Sainte-Pie QC J0H1W0	800-723-5181	450-772-2495	314-1
United Church of Christ (UCC)			
700 Prospect Ave ..... Cleveland OH 44115	866-822-8224	216-736-2100	48-20
United Communications Group			
11300 Rockville Pike Suite 1100 ..... Rockville MD 20852	800-929-4824	301-816-8950	623-6
United Community Banks Inc			
63 Hwy 515 ..... Blairsville GA 30512	866-270-7200	706-781-2265	355-2
NASDAQ: UCBI			
United Community Financial Corp			
275 Federal Plaza W ..... Youngstown OH 44503	888-822-4751	330-742-0500	355-2
NASDAQ: UCFC			
United Community Hospital			
631 N Broad St Ext ..... Grove City PA 16127	877-459-5455	724-450-7000	366-2
United Concordia Cos Inc			
2000 Town Ctr Suite 2200 ..... Southfield MI 48075	800-944-6432	248-353-6410	384-3
United Crane Rentals Inc			
111 N Michigan Ave ..... Kenilworth NJ 07033	800-356-6260	908-245-6260	261-2
United Dairy Farmers			
3955 Montgomery Rd ..... Cincinnati OH 45212	800-654-2809	513-396-8700	291-27
United Dairy Inc 300 N 5th St ..... Martins Ferry OH 43935	800-252-1542	740-633-1451	291-27
United Data Systems 959 Broad St ..... Augusta GA 30901	800-241-2404*	706-823-9723	176-11
*Sales			
United Defense Steel Products Div			
2101 W 10th St ..... Anniston AL 36201	800-468-9731	256-237-2841	794
United Design Corp PO Box 1200 ..... Noble OK 73068	800-527-4883	405-872-3468	330
United Distillers Products Co			
4320 S 94th St ..... Omaha NE 68127	800-572-3664	402-339-9100	82-3
United Distributors Inc PO Box 1077 ..... Macon GA 31202	800-749-7694	478-746-7694	82-3
United Dominion Realty Trust Inc			
400 E Cary St ..... Richmond VA 23219	800-800-2691	804-780-2691	641
NYSE: UDR			
United Drill Bushing Corp			
12200 Woodruff Ave ..... Downey CA 90241	800-486-3466	562-803-1521	484
United Electric Co-op Inc			
PO Box 319 ..... Savannah MO 64485	800-748-1488	816-324-3155	244
United Electric Co-op Inc			
PO Box 688 ..... Du Bois PA 15801	888-581-8969	814-371-8570	244
United Electric Controls Co			
180 Dexter Ave ..... Watertown MA 02472	800-545-1416	617-926-1000	200
United Energy Inc			
8040 NE Sandy Blvd Suite 300 ..... Portland OR 97213	800-291-1793	503-287-4000	569
United Engine & Machine Co Inc			
4909 Goni Rd ..... Carson City NV 89706	800-648-7970	775-882-7790	128
United Executive Jet Inc DBA JetCorp			
18152 Edison Ave ..... Chesterfield MO 63005	800-325-4811	636-530-7000	14
United Express			
1200 E Algonquin Rd ..... Elk Grove Township IL 60007	800-241-6522	847-700-4000	26
United Farmers Co-op PO Box 310 ..... Shelby NE 68662	800-742-7813	402-527-5511	271

	Toll-Free	Phone	Class
United Feather & Down Inc 414 E Golf Rd. . . . Des Plaines IL 60016	**800-932-3696**	847-296-6500	731
United Feature Syndicate Inc 200 Madison Ave 4th Fl . . . . New York NY 10016	**800-221-4816**	212-293-8500	520
United Fire & Casualty Co PO Box 73909 . . . . Cedar Rapids IA 52407 *NASDAQ: UFCS*	**800-332-7977**	319-399-5700	384-4
United Fire Equipment Co 335 N 4th Ave . . . . Tucson AZ 85705	**800-362-0150**	520-622-3639	667
United Fire Group 118 2nd Ave SE . . . . Cedar Rapids IA 52401	**800-332-7977**	319-399-5700	355-4
United Fixtures Co 601 N 8th St. . . . Niles MI 49120	**800-468-8447**	269-683-0311	345
United Food & Commercial Workers International Union (UFCW) 1775 K St NW . . . . Washington DC 20006	**800-551-4010**	202-223-3111	405
United Foods Inc 10 Pictsweet Dr. . . . Bells TN 38006	**800-367-7412**	731-422-7600	291-21
United Gilsonite Laboratories PO Box 70 . . . . Scranton PA 18501	**800-272-3235**	570-344-1202	540
United Guaranty Corp 230 N Elm St . . . . Greensboro NC 27401	**800-334-8966**	336-373-0232	384-5
United-Guardian Inc PO Box 18050 . . Hauppauge NY 11788 *AMEX: UG*	**800-645-5566**	631-273-0900	470
United Hardware Distributing Co PO Box 410 . . . . Minneapolis MN 55440	**800-835-6560**	763-559-1800	346
United Healthcare Insurance Co 9900 Bren Rd E . . . . Minnetonka MN 55343	**800-328-5979**	952-936-1300	384-2
United Heartland Inc PO Box 3026. . . Milwaukee WI 53201	**800-258-2667**	262-787-7700	384-4
United Heritage Mutual Life Insurance Co PO Box 7777. . . . Meridian ID 83680	**800-657-6351**	208-466-7856	384-2
United Hospice-Lilburn 3945 Lawrenceville Hwy. . . . Lilburn GA 30047	**800-544-4788**	770-925-1143	365
United Illuminating Co 157 Church St . . . . New Haven CT 06510 *Cust Svc	**800-722-5584***	203-499-2000	774
United Industrial Piping Inc 9740 Near Dr . . . . Cincinnati OH 45246	**800-633-9690**	513-874-2004	188-10
United Investors Life Insurance Co 2001 3rd Ave S . . . . Birmingham AL 35233	**800-318-4542**	205-325-4300	384-2
United Laboratories Inc 320 37th Ave . . . . Saint Charles IL 60174	**800-323-2594**	630-377-0900	143
United Life Insurance Co PO Box 73909 . . . . Cedar Rapids IA 52407	**800-332-7977**	319-399-5700	384-2
United Liquors Ltd 175 Campanelli Dr . . . . Braintree MA 02185	**800-323-9666**	781-348-8000	82-3
United Marine Inc 490 NW South River Dr. . . . Miami FL 33128	**800-432-8575**	305-545-8445	759
United Marketing Solutions 7644 Dynatech Ct. . . . Springfield VA 22153	**800-368-3501**	703-644-0200	5
United Media 200 Madison Ave 4th Fl . . . . New York NY 10016	**800-221-4816**	212-293-8500	520
United Metal Fabricators Inc 1316 Eisenhower Blvd . . . . Johnstown PA 15904 *Sales	**800-638-5322***	814-266-8726	314-3
United Methodist Committee on Relief (UMCOR) 475 Riverside Dr Suite 330 . . . . New York NY 10115	**800-554-8583**	212-870-3814	48-5
United Methodist Publishing House PO Box 801 . . . . Nashville TN 37202 *Cust Svc	**800-672-1789***	615-749-6000	623-4
United Mineral & Chemical Corp 1100 Valley Brook Ave . . . . Lyndhurst NJ 07071	**800-777-0505**	201-507-3300	144
United Motorcoach Assn (UMA) 113 S West St 4th Fl . . . . Alexandria VA 22314	**800-424-8262**	703-838-2929	49-21
United National Group 3 Bala Plaza E Suite 300 . . . . Bala Cynwyd PA 19004	**800-333-0352**	610-664-1500	384-4
United National Insurance Co 3 Bala Plaza E Suite 300 . . . . Bala Cynwyd PA 19004	**800-333-0352**	610-664-1500	384-4
United Nations Federal Credit Union 820 2nd Ave 12th Fl. . . . New York NY 10017	**800-891-2471**	212-338-8100	216
United Nations Publications 2 UN Plaza Suite DC2-853 . . . . New York NY 10017	**800-253-9646**	212-963-8302	623-2
United Natural Foods Inc 260 Lake Rd PO Box 999. . . . Dayville CT 06241 *NASDAQ: UNFI*	**800-877-8898**	860-779-2800	292-8
United Negro College Fund Inc (UNCF) 8260 Willow Oaks Corporate Dr Suite 400 . . . . Fairfax VA 22031	**800-331-2244**	703-205-3400	48-11
United Network for Organ Sharing (UNOS) 700 N 4th St. . . . Richmond VA 23219	**888-894-6361**	804-330-8500	48-17
United Notions Inc 13800 Hutton St. . . . Dallas TX 75234	**800-527-9447**	972-484-8901	583
United Oil Recovery Inc 14-16 W Main St . . . . Meriden CT 06451	**800-631-2099**	203-238-6745	653
United of Omaha Life Insurance Co Mutual of Omaha Plaza . . . . Omaha NE 68175	**800-775-6000**	402-342-7600	384-2
United Ostomy Assn (UOA) 19772 MacArthur Blvd Suite 200. . . . Irvine CA 92612	**800-826-0826**	949-660-8624	48-17
United PanAm Financial Corp 3990 Westerly Pl Suite 200 . . . Newport Beach CA 92660 *NASDAQ: UPFC*	**800-833-1940**	949-224-1917	355-2
United Parcel Service Inc (UPS) 55 Glenlake Pkwy NE . . . . Atlanta GA 30328 *NYSE: UPS* ■ *Cust Svc	**800-742-5877***	404-828-6000	536
United Pioneer Co 10 W 33rd St . . . . New York NY 10001	**800-466-9823**	212-279-3931	566
United Pipe & Supply Co Inc 90099 Prairie Rd . . . . Eugene OR 97402	**800-288-6511**	541-688-6511	601
United Plywood & Lumber Inc 1640 Mims Ave SW . . . . Birmingham AL 35211	**800-272-6486**	205-925-7601	602
United Power Inc PO Box 929 . . . . Brighton CO 80601	**800-468-8809**	303-659-0551	244
United Press International (UPI) 1510 H St NW . . . . Washington DC 20005	**800-783-4874**	202-898-8000	520
United Producers Inc 5909 Cleveland Ave . . . . Columbus OH 43231	**800-456-3276**	614-890-6666	437
United Receptacle Inc PO Box 870 . . . Pottsville PA 17901	**800-233-0314**	570-622-7715	480
United Recovery Systems Inc 5800 N Course Dr . . . . Houston TX 77072	**800-568-0399**	713-977-1234	157
United Refining Co Inc 15 Bradley St. . . . Warren PA 16365	**800-458-6097**	814-723-1500	570
United Refrigeration Inc 11401 Roosevelt Blvd. . . . Philadelphia PA 19154	**800-852-5132**	215-698-9100	651
United Rental Highway Technology 880 N Addison Rd . . . . Villa Park IL 60181 *Cust Svc	**800-323-2462***	630-932-4600	261-6
United Rentals Inc 5 Greenwich Office Pk . . . . Greenwich CT 06830 *NYSE: URI*	**800-877-3687**	203-622-3131	261-2
United Resource Systems Inc 10075 W Colfax Ave. . . . Lakewood CO 80215	**800-441-7364**	303-205-0152	157
United Retail Group Inc 365 W Passaic St. . . . Rochelle Park NJ 07662 *NASDAQ: URGI*	**877-708-8740**	201-845-0880	658
United Road Services Inc 17 Computer Dr W. . . . Albany NY 12205	**888-730-7797**	518-446-0140	769
United Rural Electric Membership Corp PO Box 605 . . . . Markle IN 46770	**800-542-6339**	260-758-3155	244
United Salt Corp 4800 San Felipe St. . . . Houston TX 77056	**800-554-8658**	713-877-2600	493-1
United Services Automobile Assn (USAA) 9800 Fredericksburg Rd . . . San Antonio TX 78288	**800-531-8222**	210-498-2211	184
United Silicone Inc 4471 Walden Ave . . . . Lancaster NY 14086	**800-365-8222**	716-681-8222	379
United Sleep Products Inc 412 Oak St. . . Denver PA 17517	**800-447-2119**	717-336-2846	463
United Soybean Board (USB) 16640 Chesterfield Grove Rd Suite 130 . . . . Chesterfield MO 63005	**800-989-8721**	636-530-1777	48-2
United Space Alliance 1150 Gemini Ave . . . . Houston TX 77058	**800-329-4036**	281-212-6200	267
United Stationers Inc 2200 E Golf Rd. . . . Des Plaines IL 60016 *NASDAQ: USTR*	**800-424-4003**	847-699-5000	523
United Steel & Wire Co 4909 Wayne Rd . . . . Battle Creek MI 49015	**800-227-7887**	269-962-5571	75
United Student Aid Funds Inc DBA USA Funds 11100 USA Pkwy. . . . Fishers IN 46038	**800-824-7044**	317-849-6510	215
United Suppliers Inc 30473 260th St . . . . Eldora IA 50627	**800-782-5123**	641-858-2341	272
United Systems Access Inc 5 Bragdon Ln Suite 200. . . . Kennebunk ME 04043	**877-872-2800**	207-467-8000	721
United Taconite LLC PO Box 180 . . . . Eveleth MN 55734	**800-560-4532**	218-744-7800	492
United Textile Co Inc 2225 Grant Ave. . . . San Lorenzo CA 94580	**800-233-0077**	510-276-2288	497
United Tote Co 11505 Susquehanna Trail. . . . Glen Rock PA 17327	**800-238-8683**	717-227-4350	317
United Transportation Union 14600 Detroit Ave. . . . Lakewood OH 44107	**800-558-8842**	216-228-9400	405
United Trust Group Inc 5250 S 6th St. . . . Springfield IL 62703	**800-323-0050**	217-241-6300	355-4
United Utility Supply Co-op Inc 4515 Bishop Ln . . . . Louisville KY 40218	**800-357-5232**	502-459-4011	245
United Vacations 8907 N Port Washington Rd . . . . Milwaukee WI 53217	**800-377-1816**	414-351-8470	760
United Van Lines Inc 1 United Dr. . . . Fenton MO 63026	**800-325-3924**	636-326-3100	508
United Way of America 701 N Fairfax St. . . . Alexandria VA 22314	**800-892-2757**	703-836-7100	48-5
United Wholesale Lumber Co 8009 Doe Ave. . . . Visalia CA 93291	**800-651-2037**	559-651-2037	541
United World Life Insurance Co Mutual of Omaha Plaza . . . . Omaha NE 68175	**800-775-6000**	402-342-7600	384-2
United Yellow Pages Inc 12442 Knott St 2nd Fl . . . . Garden Grove CA 92841	**800-343-2046**	714-889-5200	623-6
United/Anco Industries Inc 15981 Airline Hwy . . . . Baton Rouge LA 70817	**800-999-8479**	225-752-2000	188-9
UnitedHealth Group Inc 9900 Bren Rd East. . . . Minnetonka MN 55343 *NYSE: UNH*	**800-328-5979**	952-936-1300	384-3
UnitedHealthcare PO Box 1459. . . . Minneapolis MN 55440	**800-328-5979**	952-936-1300	384-3
Unitrin Inc 1 E Wacker Dr. . . . Chicago IL 60601 *NYSE: UTR*	**800-990-0546**	312-661-4600	355-4
Unitrol 1108 Raymond Way. . . . Anaheim CA 92801	**800-854-3375**	714-871-3336	691
Unitron Inc PO Box 38902. . . . Dallas TX 75238	**800-527-1279**	214-340-8600	507
Unity Bancorp Inc 64 Old Hwy 22. . . . Clinton NJ 08809 *NASDAQ: UNTY*	**800-540-4790**	908-730-7630	355-2
Unity Health Plans 840 Carolina St. . . . Sauk City WI 53583	**800-362-3308**	608-643-2491	384-3
Unity Hospice 439 E 31st St Suite 213. . . . Chicago IL 60616	**888-949-1188**	312-949-1188	365
Unity Hospice 916 Willard Dr Suite 100 . . . . Green Bay WI 54304	**800-990-9249**	920-494-0225	365
Unity Mutual Life Insurance Co PO Box 5000 . . . . Syracuse NY 13250	**800-836-7100**	315-448-7000	384-2
Univar USA Inc PO Box 34325 . . . . Seattle WA 98124	**800-234-4588**	425-889-3400	144
Univera Healthcare 205 Park Club Ln. . . . Buffalo NY 14221	**800-628-8451**	716-847-1480	384-3
Universal Access Inc 200 S Wacker Dr Suite 1200. . . . Chicago IL 60606	**888-482-4669**	312-660-5000	721
Universal American Financial Corp 6 International Dr Suite 190. . . . Rye Brook NY 10573 *NASDAQ: UHCO*	**800-332-3377**	914-934-8300	355-4
Universal American Mortgage Co 311 Park Place Blvd Suite 500. . . . Clearwater FL 33759	**800-696-4619**	727-791-2111	498
Universal Automotive Industries Inc 11859 S Central Ave. . . . Alsip IL 60803 *NASDAQ: UVSL*	**800-301-2725**	708-293-4050	60
Universal Battery 1702 Hayden Dr . . . . Carrollton TX 75006	**800-749-0222**	972-387-0850	245
Universal Beverages PO Box 448 . . . . Ponte Vedra Beach FL 32004	**888-426-7936**	904-280-7795	792
Universal Brush Mfg Co 16200 Dixie Hwy . . . . Markham IL 60428	**800-323-3474**	708-331-1700	104
Universal Builders Supply Inc 216 S Terrace Ave . . . . Mount Vernon NY 10550	**800-582-0070**	914-699-2400	482
Universal Care Inc 1600 E Hill St . . . . Signal Hill CA 90755	**800-635-6668**	562-424-6200	384-3
Universal Compression Holdings Inc 4444 Brittmoore Rd . . . . Houston TX 77041 *NYSE: UCO*	**800-234-4650**	713-335-7000	261-4
Universal Convention Photography Inc 7121 Grand National Dr Suite 104. . . . Orlando FL 32819	**800-553-5499**	407-352-5302	581
Universal Display & Fixtures Co 726 E Hwy 121. . . . Lewisville TX 75057	**800-235-0701**	972-221-5022	75
Universal Ensco Inc 1811 Bering Dr. . . . Houston TX 77057	**800-966-1811**	713-977-7770	258
Universal Fabric Structures Inc 2200 Kumry Rd . . . . Quakertown PA 18951	**800-634-8368**	215-529-9921	718

Name / Address	City	State	ZIP	Toll-Free	Phone	Class
Universal Fasteners Inc PO Box 240	Lawrenceburg	KY	40342	800-786-2561	502-839-6971	583
Universal Fibers Inc PO Box 8930 *Cust Svc	Bristol	VA	24203	800-457-4759*	276-669-1161	730-9
Universal Forest Products Inc 2801 E Beltline Ave NE *NASDAQ: UFPI*	Grand Rapids	MI	49525	800-598-9663	616-364-6161	671
Universal Health Services Inc 367 S Gulph Rd *NYSE: UHS*	King of Prussia	PA	19406	800-347-7750	610-768-3300	348
Universal Hospital Services Inc 3800 W 80th St Suite 1250	Bloomington	MN	55431	800-847-7368	952-893-3200	261-5
Universal Industries Inc 5800 Nordic Dr	Cedar Falls	IA	50613	800-553-4446	319-277-7501	206
Universal Instruments Corp 90 Bevier St	Binghamton	NY	13904	800-842-9732	607-779-7522	685
Universal Map 795 Progress Ct	Williamston	MI	48895	800-829-6277	517-655-5641	623-1
Universal Mfg Co 405 Diagonal St PO Box 190	Algona	IA	50511	800-545-9350	515-295-3557	60
Universal Mfg Co Inc 5450 Deramus Ave	Kansas City	MO	64120	800-821-2724	816-231-2771	750
Universal Mfg Corp 318 Gidney St	Shelby	NC	28150	800-553-8648	704-487-4359	153-15
Universal Mfg Corp PO Box 220	Zelienople	PA	16063	800-836-8780	724-452-8300	482
Universal Molding Co Inc 10807 Stanford Ave	Lynwood	CA	90262	888-437-1750	310-886-1750	476
Universal Money Centers Inc 6800 Squibb Rd	Shawnee Mission	KS	66202	800-234-6860	913-831-2055	70
Universal Overall Co 1060 W Van Buren St *Cust Svc	Chicago	IL	60607	800-621-3344*	312-226-3336	153-19
Universal Polymer & Rubber Ltd 15730 S Madison Rd	Middlefield	OH	44062	800-782-2375	440-632-1691	664
Universal Premium Acceptance Corp 8245 Nieman Rd Suite 100	Lenexa	KS	66214	800-877-7848	913-894-6150	214
Universal Press Syndicate 4520 Main St Suite 700	Kansas City	MO	64111	800-255-6734	816-932-6600	520
Universal Security Instruments Inc 7-A Gwynns Mill Ct	Owings Mills	MD	21117	800-390-4321	410-363-3000	681
Universal Service Administrative Co 2000 L St NW Suite 200	Washington	DC	20036	888-641-8722	202-776-0200	721
Universal Service Administrative Co Rural Health Care Div 80 S Jefferson Rd	Whippany	NJ	07981	800-229-5476	973-581-6706	721
Universal Service Administrative Co Schools & Libraries Div 2000 L St NW	Washington	DC	20036	888-203-8100		721
Universal Sodexho 5749 Susitna Dr	Harahan	LA	70123	800-535-1946	504-733-5761	294
Universal Solutions Inc 100 Business Park Dr Suite C	Ridgeland	MS	39157	800-611-7093	601-899-5000	721
Universal Steel Buildings Inc 2472 Sunset Dr	Grenada	MS	38902	800-748-9967	662-226-4512	188-14
Universal Steel Co 6600 Grant Ave	Cleveland	OH	44105	800-927-2659	216-883-4972	483
Universal Studios Florida 1000 Universal Studios Plaza	Orlando	FL	32819	888-837-2237	407-363-8000	32
Universal Studios Hollywood 100 Universal City Plaza	Universal City	CA	91608	800-864-8377	818-622-3801	32
Universal SuperAbrasives 84 O'Leary Dr	Bensenville	IL	60106	800-323-6676	630-238-3300	1
Universal Surety of America 950 Echo Ln Suite 250	Houston	TX	77024	888-736-9704	713-722-4600	384-5
Universal Tax Systems 6 Mathis Dr *Sales	Rome	GA	30165	800-755-9473*	706-232-7757	176-10
Universal Truckload Services Inc 11355 Stephens Rd *NASDAQ: UACL*	Warren	MI	48089	800-233-9445	586-920-0100	769
Universal Underwriters Group 7045 College Blvd	Overland Park	KS	66211	800-821-7803	913-339-1000	384-4
Universal Wire Cloth Co 16 N Steel Rd	Morrisville	PA	19067	800-523-0575	215-736-8981	676
Universal's Islands of Adventure 1000 Universal Studios Plaza	Orlando	FL	32819	888-837-2273	407-363-8000	32
Universal/Univis Inc 23 W Bacon St	Plainville	MA	02762	800-899-5432	508-695-3584	531
Universite Laval Pavillion Bonensant	Quebec	QC	G1K7P4	877-785-2825	418-656-2131	773
Universite de Moncton 165 Massey Ave	Moncton	NB	E1A3E9	800-363-8336	506-858-4000	773
Universities & Colleges. Association of Governing Boards of 1 Dupont Cir NW Suite 400	Washington	DC	20036	800-356-6317	202-296-8400	49-5
Universities. Hispanic Assn of Colleges & 8415 Datapoint Dr Suite 400	San Antonio	TX	78229	800-780-4228	210-692-3805	49-5
University of Akron 381 Buchtel Mall *Admissions	Akron	OH	44325	800-655-4884*	330-972-7077	163
Wayne College 1901 Smucker Rd	Orrville	OH	44667	800-221-8308	330-683-2010	160
University of Alabama Box 870132	Tuscaloosa	AL	35487	800-933-2262	205-348-6010	163
University of Alabama at Birmingham 1530 3rd Ave S HUC260	Birmingham	AL	35294	800-421-8743	205-934-4011	163
Bone Marrow Transplant Program 619 S 19th St P302 West Pavilion	Birmingham	AL	35249	800-822-6478	205-934-1911	758
University of Alabama in Huntsville 301 Sparkman Dr	Huntsville	AL	35899	800-824-2255	256-824-6070	163
University of Alabama Press 20 Research Dr Rm 201 McMillan Bldg *Orders	Tuscaloosa	AL	35487	800-621-2736*	205-348-5180	623-5
University of Alaska Anchorage Kodiak College 117 Benny Benson Dr	Kodiak	AK	99615	800-486-7660	907-486-4161	160
University of Alaska Fairbanks PO Box 757480	Fairbanks	AK	99775	800-478-1823	907-474-7500	163
Northwest Campus 400 E Front St Pouch 400	Nome	AK	99762	800-478-2202	907-443-2201	163
University of Alaska Press Box 756240	Fairbanks	AK	99775	888-252-6657	907-474-5831	623-5
University of Alaska Southeast						
Juneau Campus 11120 Glacier Hwy	Juneau	AK	99801	877-465-4827	907-465-6457	163
Sitka Campus 1332 Seward Ave	Sitka	AK	99835	800-478-6653	907-747-6653	160
University at Albany 1400 Washington Ave	Albany	NY	12222	800-293-7869	518-442-3300	163
University at Albany 1400 Washington Ave	Albany	NY	12222	800-293-7869	518-443-5555	163
University of Arizona Press 355 S Euclid Ave Suite 103 *Orders	Tucson	AZ	85719	800-426-3797*	520-621-1441	623-5
University of Arkansas 232 Hunt Hall	Fayetteville	AR	72701	800-377-8632	479-575-5346	163
University of Arkansas at Fort Smith PO Box 3649	Fort Smith	AR	72913	888-512-5466	479-788-7000	160
University of Arkansas - Monticello PO Box 3600	Monticello	AR	71656	800-844-1826	870-367-6811	163
University of Arkansas Pine Bluff 1200 N University Dr *Admissions	Pine Bluff	AR	71601	800-264-6585*	870-575-8000	163
University of Arkansas Press McIlroy House 201 Ozark Ave	Fayetteville	AR	72701	800-626-0090	479-575-3246	623-5
University of the Arts 320 S Broad St	Philadelphia	PA	19102	800-616-2787	215-717-6000	163
University of Baltimore 1420 N Charles St	Baltimore	MD	21201	877-277-5982	410-837-4200	163
University Bancorp Inc 959 Maiden Ln *NASDAQ: UNIB*	Ann Arbor	MI	48105	888-944-5004	734-741-5858	355-2
University of Bridgeport 126 Park Ave	Bridgeport	CT	06604	800-392-3582	203-576-4000	163
University of British Columbia 2329 West Mall	Vancouver	BC	V6T1Z4	877-272-1422	604-822-9836	773
University at Buffalo 15 Capen Hall	Buffalo	NY	14260	888-822-3648	716-645-2450	163
University of California Irvine College of Medicine Medical Education Bldg 802	Irvine	CA	92697	800-824-5388	949-824-5388	164-2
University of California Press 2120 Berkeley Way	Berkeley	CA	94704	800-822-6657	510-642-4247	623-5
University of Charleston 2300 MacCorkle Ave SE	Charleston	WV	25304	800-995-4682	304-357-4800	163
University of Chicago Hospitals 5841 S Maryland Ave	Chicago	IL	60637	800-289-6333	773-702-1000	366-2
University of Chicago Press 1427 E 60th St *Sales	Chicago	IL	60637	800-621-2736*	773-702-7700	623-5
University of Chicago Press Journals Div PO Box 37005	Chicago	IL	60637	877-705-1878	773-753-3347	623-9
University of Colorado at Colorado Springs PO Box 7150	Colorado Springs	CO	80933	800-990-8227	719-262-3000	163
University of Connecticut Health Center John Dempsey Hospital 263 Farmington Ave	Farmington	CT	06030	800-535-6232	860-679-2000	366-2
University of Dallas 1845 E Northgate Dr	Irving	TX	75062	800-628-6999	972-721-5000	163
University of Dayton 300 College Pk	Dayton	OH	45469	800-837-7433	937-229-1000	163
University of Denver 2199 S University Blvd	Denver	CO	80208	800-525-9495	303-871-2036	163
University of Detroit Mercy 4001 W McNichols Rd *Admissions	Detroit	MI	48219	800-635-5020*	313-993-1000	163
University of Detroit Mercy School of Law 651 E Jefferson Ave	Detroit	MI	48226	866-428-1610	313-596-0264	164-1
University of Dubuque 2000 University Ave	Dubuque	IA	52001	800-722-5583	563-589-3000	163
University of Evansville 1800 Lincoln Ave	Evansville	IN	47722	800-423-8633	812-479-2000	163
University of Findlay 1000 N Main St	Findlay	OH	45840	800-548-0932	419-422-8313	163
University Games Corp 2030 Harrison St	San Francisco	CA	94110	800-347-4818	415-503-1600	750
University of Georgia Press 330 Research Dr Suite B-100 *Orders	Athens	GA	30602	800-266-5842*	706-369-6163	623-5
University of Great Falls 1301 20th St S	Great Falls	MT	59405	800-856-9544	406-761-8210	163
University of Hartford 200 Bloomfield Ave	West Hartford	CT	06117	800-947-4303	860-768-4296	163
University of Hawaii						
Hilo 200 W Kawili St	Hilo	HI	96720	800-897-4456	808-974-7414	163
Manoa 2600 Campus Rd Rm 001	Honolulu	HI	96822	800-823-9771	808-956-8975	163
West Oahu 96-129 Ala Ike	Pearl City	HI	96782	866-299-8656	808-454-4742	163
University of Hawaii Press 2840 Kolowalu St	Honolulu	HI	96822	888-847-7377	808-956-8255	623-5
University Hospital SUNY Health Center at Syracuse 750 E Adams St	Syracuse	NY	13210	877-464-5540	315-464-5540	366-2
University of Houston Victoria 3007 N Ben Wilson St	Victoria	TX	77901	877-970-4848	361-570-4848	163
University of Idaho PO Box 444264	Moscow	ID	83844	888-884-3246	208-885-6111	163
Boise 322 E Front St	Boise	ID	83702	866-264-7384	208-334-2999	163
University of Idaho College of Law University of Idaho College of Law PO Box 442321	Moscow	ID	83844	888-884-3246	208-885-4977	164-1
University of Illinois Springfield 1 University Plaza	Springfield	IL	62703	800-252-8533	217-206-6174	163
University of Illinois Press 1325 S Oak St *Orders	Champaign	IL	61820	800-545-4703*	217-333-0950	623-5
University of the Incarnate Word 4301 Broadway St	San Antonio	TX	78209	800-749-9673	210-829-6000	163
University of Indianapolis 1400 E Hanna Ave	Indianapolis	IN	46227	800-232-8634	317-788-3368	163
University Inn 2360 University Dr	Boise	ID	83706	800-345-7170	208-345-7170	373
University Inn & Conference Center 2401 N Forest Rd	Amherst	NY	14226	800-537-8483	716-636-7500	370
University of Iowa Athletics Hall of Fame KHF Bldg 446	Iowa City	IA	52242	866-469-2326	319-384-1031	511
University of Iowa Hospitals & Clinics Blood & Marrow Transplantation Program 200 Hawkins Dr C332 General Hospital	Iowa City	IA	52242	800-944-8220	319-356-3337	758
University of Judaism 15600 Mulholland Dr	Los Angeles	CA	90077	888-853-6763	310-476-9777	163
University of Kentucky 100 Funkhouser Bldg	Lexington	KY	40536	866-900-4685	859-257-9000	163

Name / Address	City	State	ZIP	Toll-Free	Phone	Class
University of Louisiana at Lafayette						
104 University Cir	Lafayette	LA	70503	**800-752-6553**	337-482-1000	163
University of Louisiana at Monroe						
700 University Ave	Monroe	LA	71209	**800-372-5127**	318-342-5430	163
University of Louisville						
2301 S 3rd St	Louisville	KY	40292	**800-334-8635**	502-852-5555	163
University of Maine						
5713 Chadbourne Hall	Orono	ME	04469	**877-486-2364**	207-581-1110	163
Fort Kent 23 University Dr	Fort Kent	ME	04743	**888-879-8635**	207-834-7500	163
Machias 9 O'Brien Ave	Machias	ME	04654	**888-468-6866**	207-255-1200	163
University of Manitoba						
66 Chancellors Cir	Winnipeg	MB	R3T2N2	**800-224-7713***	204-474-8880	773
*Admissions						
University of Mary Hardin-Baylor						
900 College St UMHB Box 8004	Belton	TX	76513	**800-727-8642**	254-295-8642	163
University of Mary Washington						
1301 College Ave	Fredericksburg	VA	22401	**800-468-5614**	540-654-1000	163
University of Maryland Baltimore County 1000 Hilltop Cir	Baltimore	MD	21250	**800-862-2482**	410-455-2902	163
University of Maryland Medical System						
22 S Greene St	Baltimore	MD	21201	**800-492-5538**	410-328-8667	348
University of Maryland University College						
3501 University Blvd E	Adelphi	MD	20783	**800-888-8682**	301-985-7000	163
University of Maryland University College Marriott Conference Center Hotel						
3501 University Blvd E	Adelphi	MD	20783	**800-727-8622**	301-985-7303	370
University Medical Center Blood & Marrow Transplantation Program						
1501 N Campbell Ave PO Box 24-5176	Tucson	AZ	85724	**800-831-9205**	520-694-6172	758
University Medical Center-Mesabi						
750 E 34th St	Hibbing	MN	55746	**888-870-8626**	218-262-4881	366-2
University of Memphis	Memphis	TN	38152	**800-669-2678**	901-678-2040	163
University of Miami Dept of Orthopedic Rehabilitation Tissue Bank 1600 NW 10th Ave Rm 8080	Miami	FL	33136	**888-684-7783**	305-243-6465	535
University of Miami Sylvester Comprehensive Cancer Center Blood & Marrow Transplant Program						
PO Box 016960	Miami	FL	33101	**800-545-2292**	305-243-1000	758
University of Minnesota Crookston						
2900 University Ave Selvig Hall	Crookston	MN	56716	**800-232-6466**	218-281-6510	163
University of Minnesota Duluth						
10 University Dr	Duluth	MN	55812	**800-232-1339**	218-726-8000	163
University of Minnesota Morris						
600 E 4th St	Morris	MN	56267	**800-992-8863**	320-589-6035	163
University of Minnesota Press						
111 3rd Ave S Suite 290	Minneapolis	MN	55401	**800-621-2736**	612-627-1942	623-5
University of Minnesota Rochester						
855 30th Ave SE	Rochester	MN	55904	**800-947-0117**	507-280-2838	163
University of Minnesota Twin Cities						
231 Pillsbury Dr SE Williamson Hall	Minneapolis	MN	55455	**800-752-1000**	612-625-5000	163
University of Missouri Kansas City						
5100 Rockhill Rd	Kansas City	MO	64110	**800-775-8652**	816-235-1000	163
University of Missouri Press						
2910 LeMone Blvd	Columbia	MO	65201	**800-828-1894**	573-882-7641	623-5
University of Missouri Rolla						
1870 Miner Cir G2 Parker Hall	Rolla	MO	65409	**800-522-0938**	573-341-4111	163
University of Missouri Saint Louis						
1 University Blvd	Saint Louis	MO	63121	**888-462-8675**	314-516-5000	163
University of Mobile						
5735 College Pkwy	Mobile	AL	36613	**800-946-7267**	251-675-5990	163
University of Montana						
32 Campus Dr	Missoula	MT	59812	**800-462-8636**	406-243-6266	163
University of Montevallo						
Station 6030	Montevallo	AL	35115	**800-292-4349**	205-665-6030	163
University of Nebraska						
Kearney 905 W 25th St	Kearney	NE	68849	**800-532-7639**	308-865-8441	163
Lincoln 501 N 14th St	Lincoln	NE	68588	**800-742-8800**	402-472-7211	163
University of Nebraska Medical Center						
985230 Nebraska Medical Ctr	Omaha	NE	68198	**800-642-1095**	402-559-4000	366-2
University of Nebraska Press						
1111 Lincoln Mall	Lincoln	NE	68588	**800-755-1105***	402-472-3581	623-5
*Orders						
University of Nevada Press MS 166	Reno	NV	89557	**877-682-6657***	775-784-6573	623-5
*Orders						
University of New England						
11 Hills Beach Rd	Biddeford	ME	04005	**800-477-4863**	207-283-0171	163
Westbrook College 716 Stevens Ave	Portland	ME	04103	**800-477-4863**	207-797-7261	163
University of New Haven						
300 Boston Post Rd	West Haven	CT	06516	**800-342-5864**	203-932-7000	163
University of New Mexico						
University Hill NE	Albuquerque	NM	87131	**800-225-5866**	505-277-0111	163
Gallup 200 College Rd	Gallup	NM	87301	**800-225-5866**	505-863-7500	163
University of New Mexico Press						
3721 Spirit Dr SE	Albuquerque	NM	87106	**800-249-7737***	505-277-4810	623-5
*Orders						
University of New Orleans						
Administrative Bldg Rm 103 Lakefront	New Orleans	LA	70148	**800-256-5866**	504-280-6000	163
University of North Alabama						
1 Harrison Plaza	Florence	AL	35632	**800-825-5862**	256-765-4100	163
University of North Carolina Asheville						
1 University Heights	Asheville	NC	28804	**800-531-9842**	828-251-6600	163
University of North Carolina Center for Public Television (UNC-TV) 10 TW Alexander Dr PO Box 14900	Research Triangle Park	NC	27709	**800-906-5050**	919-549-7060	620
University of North Carolina Pembroke						
PO Box 1510	Pembroke	NC	28372	**800-949-8627**	910-521-6000	163
University of North Carolina Press						
116 S Boundary St	Chapel Hill	NC	27514	**800-848-6224**	919-966-3561	623-5
University of North Carolina Wilmington 601 S College Rd	Wilmington	NC	28403	**800-228-5571**	910-962-3000	163
University of North Dakota						
PO Box 8357	Grand Forks	ND	58202	**800-225-5863**	701-777-2011	163
University of North Texas						
PO Box 311277	Denton	TX	76203	**800-868-8211**	940-565-2681	163
DNA Identity Laboratory Health Science Ctr 3500 Camp Bowie Blvd	Fort Worth	TX	76107	**800-687-5301**	817-735-5015	408
University of North Texas Press						
1820 Highland Ave Bain Hall Rm 101	Denton	TX	76201	**800-826-8911***	940-565-2142	623-5
*Sales						
University of Northern Colorado						
501 20th St	Greeley	CO	80639	**888-700-4862**	970-351-2881	163
University of Northern Iowa						
1222 W 27th St	Cedar Falls	IA	50614	**800-772-2037**	319-273-2281	163
University of Oklahoma 1000 Asp Ave	Norman	OK	73019	**877-488-1674**	405-325-0311	163
University of Oklahoma Press						
2800 Venture Dr	Norman	OK	73069	**800-627-7377***	405-325-2000	623-5
*Orders						
University of Ottawa						
550 Cumberland St	Ottawa	ON	K1N6N5	**877-868-8292**	613-562-5800	773
University of Ottawa Faculty of Medicine						
75 Laurier Ave E Tabaret Hall	Ottawa	ON	K1N6N5	**877-868-8292**	613-562-5700	164-2
University of the Ozarks						
415 N College Ave	Clarksville	AR	72830	**800-264-8636**	479-754-3839	163
University of the Pacific						
3001 Pacific Ave	Stockton	CA	95211	**800-959-2867**	209-946-2011	163
University of Pennsylvania Press						
4200 Pine St	Philadelphia	PA	19104	**800-537-5487***	215-898-6261	623-5
*Cust Svc						
University of Phoenix						
4605 E Elwood St	Phoenix	AZ	85040	**800-776-4867**	480-966-7400	163
University of Pittsburgh						
Bradford 300 Campus Dr	Bradford	PA	16701	**800-872-1787**	814-362-7500	163
Johnstown 157 Blackington Hall	Johnstown	PA	15904	**800-765-4875**	814-269-7050	163
University of Pittsburgh Medical Center Health System						
200 Lothrop St	Pittsburgh	PA	15213	**800-533-8762**	412-647-2345	348
University of Pittsburgh Press						
3400 Forbes Ave 5th Fl	Pittsburgh	PA	15261	**800-666-2211***	412-383-2456	623-5
*Sales						
University of Pittsburgh at Titusville						
504 E Main St	Titusville	PA	16354	**888-878-0462**	814-827-5668	160
University Place Conference Center & Hotel-Indianapolis 850 W Michigan St	Indianapolis	IN	46202	**800-627-2700**	317-269-9000	370
University Plaza Hotel & Conference Center 3110 Olentangy River Rd	Columbus	OH	43202	**877-677-5292**	614-267-7461	373
University Plaza Hotel & Convention Center 333 S John Q Hammons Pkwy	Springfield	MO	65806	**800-465-4329**	417-864-7333	373
University of Portland						
5000 N Willamette Blvd	Portland	OR	97203	**800-227-4568**	503-943-7911	163
University Press of America						
4501 Forbes Blvd Suite 200	Lanham	MD	20706	**800-462-6420**	301-459-3366	623-2
University Press Books						
2430 Bancroft Way	Berkeley	CA	94704	**800-676-8722**	510-548-0585	96
University Press of Colorado						
5589 Arapahoe Ave Suite 206C	Boulder	CO	80303	**800-627-7377***	720-406-8849	623-5
*Mktg						
University Press of Florida						
15 NW 15th St	Gainesville	FL	32611	**800-226-3822***	352-392-1351	623-5
*Sales						
University Press of Kentucky						
663 S Limestone St	Lexington	KY	40508	**800-839-6855***	859-257-8400	623-5
*Sales						
University Press of Mississippi						
3825 Ridgewood Rd	Jackson	MS	39211	**800-737-7788**	601-432-6205	623-5
University Press of New England						
37 Lafayette St	Lebanon	NH	03766	**800-421-1561***	603-643-5585	623-5
*Orders						
University Press of Virginia						
210 Sprigg Ln	Charlottesville	VA	22903	**800-831-3406***	434-924-3469	623-5
*Sales						
University of Prince Edward Island						
550 University Ave	Charlottetown	PE	C1A4P3	**800-606-8734**	902-566-0400	773
University Products Inc PO Box 101	Holyoke	MA	01041	**800-628-1912***	413-532-3372	550
*Cust Svc						
University Professors. American Assn of 1012 14th St NW Suite 500	Washington	DC	20005	**800-424-2973**	202-737-5900	49-5
University of Puget Sound						
1500 N Warner St	Tacoma	WA	98416	**800-396-7191**	253-879-3611	163
University of Redlands						
1200 E Colton Ave PO Box 3080	Redlands	CA	92374	**800-455-5064**	909-335-4074	163
University of Richmond	Richmond	VA	23173	**800-700-1662**	804-289-8000	163
University of Saint Augustine						
1 University Blvd	Saint Augustine	FL	32086	**800-241-1027**	904-826-0084	163
University of Saint Francis						
2701 Spring St	Fort Wayne	IN	46808	**800-729-4732**	260-434-3100	163
University of Saint Mary						
4100 S 4th St Trafficway	Leavenworth	KS	66048	**800-752-7043**	913-682-5151	163
University of Saint Thomas						
2115 Summit Ave	Saint Paul	MN	55105	**800-328-6819**	651-962-5000	163
University of Saint Thomas						
3800 Montrose Blvd	Houston	TX	77006	**800-856-8565**	713-522-7911	163
University of San Diego						
5998 Alcala Pk	San Diego	CA	92110	**800-248-4873**	619-260-4600	163
University of San Francisco						
2130 Fulton St	San Francisco	CA	94117	**800-225-5873***	415-422-5555	163
*Admissions						
University of the Sciences						
600 S 43rd St	Philadelphia	PA	19104	**866-304-8747**	215-596-8800	163
University of Sciences & Arts of Oklahoma 1727 W Alabama Ave	Chickasha	OK	73018	**800-933-8726**	405-224-3140	163
University of Scranton						
800 Linden St St Thomas Hall	Scranton	PA	18510	**888-727-2686**	570-941-7400	163
University of Sioux Falls						
1101 W 22nd St	Sioux Falls	SD	57105	**800-888-1047**	605-331-5000	163
University of the South						
735 University Ave	Sewanee	TN	37383	**800-522-2234**	931-598-1238	163

	Toll-Free	Phone	Class
University of South Alabama 307 University Blvd, Mobile AL 36688	**800-872-5247**	251-460-6101	163
University of South Carolina, Columbia SC 29208	**800-922-9755**	803-777-7000	163
Aiken 471 University Pkwy, Aiken SC 29801	**888-969-8722**	803-648-6851	163
Sumter 200 Miller Rd, Sumter SC 29150	**888-872-7868**	803-775-8727	163
Upstate 800 University Way, Spartanburg SC 29303	**800-277-8727**	864-503-5246	163
University of South Carolina Press 1600 Hampton St 5th Fl, Columbia SC 29208 *Orders	**800-768-2500***	803-777-5243	623-5
University of South Carolina Salkehatchie PO Box 617, Allendale SC 29810	**800-922-5500**	803-584-3446	160
University of South Carolina Union PO Box 729, Union SC 29379	**800-768-5566**	864-429-8728	160
University of South Dakota 414 E Clark St, Vermillion SD 57069	**877-269-6837**	605-677-5341	163
University of South Dakota School of Law 414 E Clark St, Vermillion SD 57069	**877-269-6837**	605-677-5443	164-1
University of South Florida			
Lakeland Campus 3433 Winter Lake Rd, Lakeland FL 33803	**800-873-5636**	863-667-7000	163
Tampa Campus 4202 E Fowler Ave, Tampa FL 33620	**877-873-2855**	813-974-2011	163
University of the South Press 735 University Ave Fulford Hall, Sewanee TN 37383	**800-289-4919**	931-598-1286	623-5
University of Southern Indiana 8600 University Blvd, Evansville IN 47712	**800-467-1965**	812-464-8600	163
University of Southern Maine PO Box 9300, Portland ME 04104	**800-800-4876**	207-780-4141	163
University Subscription Service 1213 Butterfield Rd, Downers Grove IL 60515	**800-876-1213**	630-960-3233	361
University of Tampa 401 W Kennedy Blvd, Tampa FL 33606	**800-733-4773**	813-253-6228	163
University of Tennessee, Knoxville TN 37996	**800-221-8657**	865-974-1000	163
University of Tennessee Chattanooga 615 McCallie Ave, Chattanooga TN 37403	**800-882-6627**	423-425-4662	163
University of Tennessee Martin 554 University St, Martin TN 38238	**800-829-8861**	731-881-7020	163
University of Tennessee Space Institute 411 BH Goethert Pkwy, Tullahoma TN 37388	**888-822-8874**	931-393-7100	654
University of Texas Arlington 701 S Nedderman Dr, Arlington TX 76019	**800-687-2882**	817-272-6287	163
University of Texas at Austin Performing Arts Center E 23rd St & E Robert Dedman Dr, Austin TX 78705	**800-687-6010**	512-471-1444	562
University of Texas Brownsville 80 Fort Brown St, Brownsville TX 78520	**800-850-0160**	956-544-8200	163
University of Texas Medical Branch at Galveston 301 University Blvd, Galveston TX 77555	**800-228-1841**	409-772-2618	164-2
University of Texas Permian Basin 4901 E University Blvd, Odessa TX 79762	**866-552-8872**	432-552-2605	163
University of Texas Press 2100 Comal St, Austin TX 78722 *Sales	**800-252-3206***	512-471-7233	623-5
University of Texas San Antonio 6900 North Loop 1604 W, San Antonio TX 78249	**800-669-0919**	210-458-4011	163
University of Texas Tyler 3900 University Blvd, Tyler TX 75799	**800-888-9537**	903-566-7000	163
University of Toledo 2801 W Bancroft St, Toledo OH 43606	**800-586-5336**	419-530-4636	163
University of Tulsa 600 S College Ave, Tulsa OK 74104	**800-331-3050**	918-631-2307	163
University of Utah 201 S 1460 East, Salt Lake City UT 84112	**800-868-5618**	801-581-7200	163
University of Utah Hospital & Clinics Blood & Marrow Transplant Program 50 N Medical Dr, Salt Lake City UT 84132	**800-664-8268**	801-585-2044	758
University of La Verne 1950 3rd St, La Verne CA 91750	**800-876-4858**	909-593-3511	163
University of Virginia's College at Wise 1 College Ave, Wise VA 24293	**888-282-9324**	276-328-0102	163
University of Washington Tacoma 1900 Commerce St, Tacoma WA 98402	**800-736-7750**	253-692-4400	163
University of Washington Press 1326 5th Ave Suite 555, Seattle WA 98101	**800-441-4115**	206-543-4050	623-5
University of West Alabama Station 4 UWA, Livingston AL 35470	**800-621-8044**	205-652-3400	163
University of West Florida 11000 University Pkwy, Pensacola FL 32514	**800-263-1074**	850-474-2000	163
University Wholesalers Inc 1945 Main St, Colchester VT 05446	**800-852-5222**	802-655-8030	740
University of Wisconsin Colleges 780 Regent St, Madison WI 53715	**888-463-6892**	608-262-1783	160
Marathon County 518 S 7th Ave, Wausau WI 54401	**888-367-8962**	715-261-6100	160
University of Wisconsin Eau Claire 105 Garfield Ave PO Box 4004, Eau Claire WI 54701	**888-463-6893**	715-836-2637	163
McIntyre Library 105 Garfield Ave, Eau Claire WI 54702	**877-267-1384**	715-836-3715	426
University of Wisconsin Platteville 1 University Plaza, Platteville WI 53818	**800-362-5515**	608-342-1125	163
University of Wisconsin Stout 802 S Broadway, Menomonie WI 54751	**800-447-8688**	715-232-1232	163
Library 315 10th Ave E, Menomonie WI 54751	**800-787-8688**	715-232-1215	426
University Women. American Assn of 1111 16th St NW, Washington DC 20036	**800-326-2289**	202-785-7700	49-5
University of Wyoming 1000 E University Ave Dept 3435, Laramie WY 82071	**800-342-5996**	307-766-5160	163
Univex Corp 3 Old Rockingham Rd, Salem NH 03079	**800-258-6358**	603-893-6191	293
Uniweld Products Inc 2850 Ravenswood Rd, Fort Lauderdale FL 33312	**800-323-2111**	954-584-2000	798
Uniworld 17323 Ventura Blvd, Encino CA 91316	**800-733-7820**	818-382-7820	218
UniWorld Group Inc 100 Ave of the Americas 15th Fl, New York NY 10013	**800-900-2958**	212-219-1600	4
Unizan Bank NA 422 Main St, Zanesville OH 43701 *Cust Svc	**800-346-2011***	740-452-8444	71
Unizan Financial Corp 220 Market Ave S, Canton OH 44702 *NASDAQ: UNIZ*	**866-235-7203**	330-438-1118	355-2
Unlimited Systems Corp Inc DBA Konexx 5550 Oberlin Dr, San Diego CA 92121	**800-275-6354**	858-622-1400	496
Uno Chicago Grill 100 Charles Park Rd, Boston MA 02132	**866-600-8667**	617-323-9200	657
UNOS (United Network for Organ Sharing) 700 N 4th St, Richmond VA 23219	**888-894-6361**	804-330-8500	48-17
UNOVA Inc 6001 36th Ave W, Everett WA 98203 *NYSE: UNA*	**800-829-8959**	425-265-2400	184
UNR-Leavitt 1717 W 115th St, Chicago IL 60643	**800-532-8488**	773-239-7700	481
Unruh-Foster Inc 501 E Texcoco St, Montezuma KS 67867	**800-279-7283**	620-846-2215	270
Unverferth Mfg Co Inc 18107 US 224 W, Kalida OH 45853	**800-322-6301**	419-532-3121	269
Unwin Scheben Korynta Huettl Inc 2515 A St, Anchorage AK 99503	**888-706-8754**	907-276-4245	258
Unz & Co 8 Easy St, Bound Brook NJ 08805	**800-631-3098**	732-868-0706	111
UOA (United Ostomy Assn) 19772 MacArthur Blvd Suite 200, Irvine CA 92612	**800-826-0826**	949-660-8624	48-17
UOP LLC 25 E Algonquin Rd, Des Plaines IL 60017	**800-877-6184**	847-391-2000	141
UP Electric/Wittock Supply Co 2201 E Industrial Dr, Iron Mountain MI 49801	**800-562-7102**	906-774-4455	601
Up With Paper 3255 Fairfield Ave PO Box 3962, Bridgeport CT 06605	**800-852-7677**	203-337-4540	130
Up With People 1675 Broadway Suite 1460, Denver CO 80202	**877-264-8856**	303-460-7100	48-15
UPI (United Press International) 1510 H St NW, Washington DC 20005	**800-783-4874**	202-898-8000	520
Uponor Aldyl Co 7901 N Kickapoo St, Shawnee OK 74804	**800-454-0480**	405-273-0900	585
Upper Cumberland Electric Membership Corp 138 Gordonsville Hwy, South Carthage TN 37030	**800-261-2940**	615-735-2940	244
Upper Iowa University PO Box 1859, Fayette IA 52142	**800-553-4150**	563-425-5200	163
Upper Peninsula Power Co 600 E Lakeshore Dr, Houghton MI 49931	**800-562-7680**		774
Upper Room Chapel & Museum 1908 Grand Ave, Nashville TN 37212	**800-972-0433**	615-340-7207	509
UpRight Inc 2686 S Maple Ave, Fresno CA 93725 *Cust Svc	**800-926-5438***	559-443-6600	462
UPS (United Parcel Service Inc) 55 Glenlake Pkwy NE, Atlanta GA 30328 *NYSE: UPS* ■ *Cust Svc	**800-742-5877***	404-828-6000	536
UPS Supply Chain Solutions 12380 Morris Rd, Alpharetta GA 30005	**866-822-5336**	678-746-4365	440
Upshaw Gene Exec Dir National Football League Players Assn 2021 L St NW Suite 600, Washington DC 20036	**800-372-2000**	202-463-2200	561
Upsher-Smith Laboratories Inc 6701 Evenstad Dr, Maple Grove MN 55369	**800-328-3344**	763-473-4412	572
Upstate Farms Co-op 25 Anderson Rd, Buffalo NY 14225	**800-724-6455**	716-892-3156	291-27
Upstate New York Transplant Services Inc 165 Genesee St, Buffalo NY 14203	**800-227-4771**	716-853-6667	265
Upstate Tours & Travel 207 Geyser Rd, Saratoga Springs NY 12866	**800-237-5252**	518-584-5252	748
Urban Alternative PO Box 4000, Dallas TX 75208	**800-800-3222**	214-943-3868	48-20
Urban Decay 729 Farad St, Costa Mesa CA 92627	**800-784-8722**	949-631-4504	211
Urban Land Institute (ULI) 1025 Thomas Jefferson St NW Suite 500W, Washington DC 20007 *Orders	**800-321-5011***	202-624-7000	48-8
Urban Services Systems Inc 2041 ML King Ave SE, Washington DC 20020	**800-766-0635**	202-678-7393	791
Urban Technology Center. National 55 John St Suite 300, New York NY 10038	**800-998-3212**	212-528-7350	48-6
Urban Transport News 8737 Colesville Rd Suite 1100, Silver Spring MD 20910	**800-274-6737**	301-589-5103	521-13
Urbana University 579 College Way, Urbana OH 43078	**800-787-2262**	937-484-1301	163
Urchin Software Corp 2165 India St, San Diego CA 92101 *Sales	**888-887-2446***	619-233-1400	176-10
Urologic Disease. American Foundation for 1000 Corporate Blvd Suite 410, Linthicum MD 21090	**800-828-7866**	410-689-3990	48-17
Urological Assn. American 1000 Corporate Blvd, Linthicum MD 21090	**866-746-4282**	410-689-3700	49-8
Urologix Inc 14405 21st Ave N, Minneapolis MN 55447 *NASDAQ: ULGX*	**800-475-1403**	763-475-1400	468
Ursa Farmers Co-op Inc 202 Maple Ave PO Box 8, Ursa IL 62376	**800-964-2115**	217-964-2111	438
Urstadt Biddle Properties Inc 321 Railroad Ave, Greenwich CT 06830 *NYSE: UBP*	**800-323-8216**	203-863-8200	641
Ursula of Switzerland Inc 31 Mohawk Ave, Waterford NY 12188	**800-826-4041**	518-237-2580	153-21
Ursuline College 2550 Lander Rd, Pepper Pike OH 44124	**888-877-8546**	440-449-4200	163
URW America Inc 93 Canaan Back Rd, Barrington NH 03825	**800-229-8791**	603-664-2130	176-8
US Air Force Academy Dept of the Air Force Headquarters USAFA, USAF Academy CO 80840	**800-379-1455**	719-333-1110	488
US Airconditioning Distributors 16900 Chestnut St, City of Industry CA 91748	**800-937-7222**	626-854-4500	601
US Airways Express 2203 Air Cargo Rd, Wichita KS 67209	**800-428-4322**	316-942-8137	26
US Airways Express 5443 Airport Terminal Rd, Salisbury MD 21804	**800-354-3394**	410-742-2996	26
US Airways Express 3400 Terminal Dr, Vandalia OH 45377	**800-235-0986**	937-454-1116	26
US Airways Express 2345 Crystal Dr Crystal Pk 4, Arlington VA 22227	**800-428-4322**	703-872-7000	26
US Airways Group Inc 2345 Crystal Dr Crystal Pk 4, Arlington VA 22227	**800-428-4322**	703-872-7000	355-1
US Airways Inc 2345 Crystal Dr Crystal Pk 4, Arlington VA 22227	**800-428-4322**	703-872-7000	26
US Airways Shuttle Inc La Guardia Airport, Flushing NY 11371	**800-428-4322**	718-397-6200	26
US Allegiance Inc 63004 Layton Ave, Bend OR 97701	**800-327-1402**	541-330-6282	130
US Alliance Federal Credit Union 600 Midland Ave, Rye NY 10580 *Cust Svc	**800-431-2754***	914-921-0500	216
US Apple Assn 8233 Old Courthouse Rd Suite 200, Vienna VA 22182	**800-781-4443**	703-442-8850	48-2
US Army Engineer Research & Development Center (ERDC) 3909 Halls Ferry Rd ATTN: CEERD-PA-Z, Vicksburg MS 39180	**800-522-6937**	601-634-2502	654

Name / Address	City	State	ZIP	Toll-Free	Phone	Class
Centrifuge Research Center ATTN: CEERD-PA-Z 3909 Halls Ferry Rd	Vicksburg	MS	39180	**800-522-6937**	601-634-2502	654
Coastal & Hydraulics Laboratory ATTN: CEERD-PA-Z 3909 Halls Ferry Rd	Vicksburg	MS	39180	**800-522-6937**	601-634-2502	654
Construction Engineering Research Laboratory PO Box 9005	Champaign	IL	61826	**800-872-2375**	217-352-6511	654
Geotechnical & Structures Laboratory ATTN: CEERD-PA-Z 3909 Halls Ferry Rd	Vicksburg	MS	39180	**800-522-6937**	601-634-2502	654
Information Technology Laboratory 3909 Halls Ferry Rd ATTN: CEERD-IV-Z	Vicksburg	MS	39180	**800-522-6937**	601-634-2502	654
US Army Research Laboratory (ARL) ATTN: AMSRL-CS-PA 2800 Powder Mill Rd	Adelphi	MD	20783	**800-276-9522**	301-394-1178	654
US Auto Club Motoring Div Inc PO Box 660460	Dallas	TX	75226	**800-348-2761**		53
US Bakery DBA Franz Bakery 340 NE 11th Ave	Portland	OR	97232	**800-935-5679**	503-232-2191	291-1
US Bancorp 800 Nicollet Mall *NYSE: USB*	Minneapolis	MN	55402	**800-872-2657**	651-466-3000	355-2
US Bancorp 8534 E Kemper Rd	Cincinnati	OH	45249	**800-582-9702**	513-247-0300	355-2
US Bancorp Leasing & Financial Inc 13010 SW 68th Pkwy	Portland	OR	97223	**800-253-3468**	503-797-0200	214
US Bank NA 800 Nicollet Mall	Minneapolis	MN	55402	**800-872-2657**	651-466-3000	71
US Banker Magazine 1 State St 27th Fl	New York	NY	10004	**800-221-1809**	212-967-7000	449-5
US Battery Mfg Corp 1675 Sampson Ave	Corona	CA	92879	**800-695-0945**	951-371-8090	76
US Biathlon Assn 29 Ethan Allen Ave	Colchester	VT	05446	**800-242-8456**	802-654-7833	48-22
US Biosystems Inc 3231 NW 7th Ave	Boca Raton	FL	33431	**888-862-5227**	561-447-7373	728
US Bobsled & Skeleton Federation (USBSF) 196 Old Military Rd	Lake Placid	NY	12946	**800-262-7533**	518-523-1842	48-22
US Borax Inc 26877 Tourney Rd	Valencia	CA	91355	**800-533-4872**	661-287-5400	141
US Bronze Powders Inc 408 Rt 202 N PO Box 31	Flemington	NJ	08822	**800-544-0186**	908-782-5454	476
US Bronze Sign Co 811 2nd Ave	New Hyde Park	NY	11040	**800-872-5155**	516-352-5155	766
US Button Corp 328 Kennedy Dr	Putnam	CT	06260	**800-243-1842**	860-928-2707	583
US Can Co 98 Amlajack Blvd	Newnan	GA	30265	**800-929-4274**	770-253-7176	596
US Cargo & Courier Service 900 Williams Ave	Columbus	OH	43212	**800-234-8608**	614-552-2746	769
US Catholic Magazine 205 W Monroe *Cust Svc	Chicago	IL	60606	**800-328-6515***	312-236-7782	449-18
US Census Bureau Regional Offices						
Charlotte 901 Center Park Dr Suite 106	Charlotte	NC	28217	**800-331-7360**	704-344-6100	336-2
Dallas 8585 N Stemmons Fwy Suite 800-S	Dallas	TX	75247	**800-835-9952**	214-253-4400	336-2
Detroit 1395 Brewery Park Blvd	Detroit	MI	48207	**800-432-1495**	313-259-0056	336-2
Kansas City 1211 N 8th St	Kansas City	KS	66101	**800-728-4748**	913-551-6728	336-2
US Central Credit Union 9701 Renner Blvd	Lenexa	KS	66219	**888-872-0440**	913-227-6000	216
US Ceramic Tile Co 4244 Mt Pleasant St NW Suite 720	North Canton	OH	44720	**800-321-0684**	330-649-5000	736
US Chamber of Commerce 1615 H St NW	Washington	DC	20062	**800-638-6582**	202-659-6000	138
US Chemical & Plastics PO Box 709	Massillon	OH	44648	**800-321-0672**	330-830-6000	60
US Chemical Safety & Hazard Investigation Board 2175 K St NW Suite 400	Washington	DC	20037	**800-424-8802**	202-261-7600	336-16
US Chess Federation 3068 US Rt 9 W Suite 100 *Sales	New Windsor	NY	12553	**800-388-5464***	845-562-8350	48-18
US Chrome Corp 175 Garfield Ave	Stratford	CT	06615	**800-637-9019**	203-378-9622	472
US Citizenship & Immigration Services (USCIS) 20 Massachusetts Ave NW	Washington	DC	20536	**800-870-3676**	202-514-4600	336-7
US Coachways Inc 36 Richmond Terr Suite 304	Staten Island	NY	10301	**800-359-5991**	718-477-4242	433
US Coast Guard (USCG) National Vessel Movement Center 408 Coast Guard Dr	Kearneysville	WV	25430	**800-708-9823**	304-264-2502	336-7
US Coast Guard Academy 15 Mohegan Ave	New London	CT	06320	**800-883-8724**	860-444-8444	163
US Coast Guard Regional Offices Atlantic Area District 1 408 Atlantic Ave	Boston	MA	02110	**800-848-3942**	617-223-8515	336-7
US Commission on Civil Rights 624 9th St NW	Washington	DC	20425	**800-552-6843**	202-376-7700	336-16
US Computer Emergency Readiness Team Naval Security Stn	Washington	DC	20535	**888-282-0870**	202-401-4600	336-7
US Contractors Inc 622 Commerce St	Clute	TX	77531	**800-897-9882**	979-265-7451	187-7
US Corporate Services 380 Jackson St Suite 418	Saint Paul	MN	55101	**800-327-1186**	651-227-7575	621
US Curling Assn PO Box 866	Stevens Point	WI	54481	**888-287-5377**	715-344-1199	48-22
US Datalink Inc 6711 Bayway Dr	Baytown	TX	77520	**800-527-7930**	281-424-7223	621
US Diamond Wheel Co 101 Kendall Point Dr	Oswego	IL	60543	**800-223-0457**	630-898-9000	490
US Digital Corp 11100 NE 34th Cir	Vancouver	WA	98682	**800-736-0194**	360-260-2468	176-10
US Dismantlement LLC 2600 S Throop St	Chicago	IL	60608	**800-648-3801**	312-328-1400	188-17
US Drug Testing Laboratories DBA MecStat Laboratories 1700 S Mt Prospect Rd	Des Plaines	IL	60018	**800-235-2367**	847-375-0770	407
US Elastomer 161 Marble Mill Rd	Marietta	GA	30060	**800-394-8735**	770-424-4850	594-3
US Electrical Motors 8100 W Florissant Ave Bldg K	Saint Louis	MO	63136	**888-637-7333**	314-553-2000	507
US Fish & Wildlife Service (USFWS) 1849 C St NW	Washington	DC	20240	**800-344-9453**	202-208-4717	336-9
US Foodservice Inc Sofco Div 3366 Walden Ave *Cust Svc	Depew	NY	14043	**800-724-2571***	716-685-6001	295
US Foodservice Inc Sofco Div 702 Potential Pkwy *Orders	Scotia	NY	12302	**800-836-7632***	518-374-7810	295
US Franchise Systems Inc 13 Corporate Sq Suite 250	Atlanta	GA	30329	**888-225-5151**	404-321-4045	369
Best Inns & Suites 13 Corporate Sq Suite 250	Atlanta	GA	30329	**800-237-8466**	404-321-4045	369
Hawthorn Suites 13 Corporate Sq Suite 250	Atlanta	GA	30329	**800-527-1133**	404-321-4045	369
Microtel Inns & Suites 13 Corporate Sq Suite 250	Atlanta	GA	30329	**888-222-2142**	404-321-4045	369
US Geological Survey (USGS) 12201 Sunrise Valley Dr	Reston	VA	20192	**888-275-8747**	703-648-4000	336-9
Ask USGS 12201 Sunrise Valley Dr	Reston	VA	20192	**888-275-8747**		336-9
National Atlas of America 508 National Ctr 12201 Sunrise Valley Dr	Reston	VA	20192	**888-275-8747**		336-9
US Global Investors Inc PO Box 781234 *NASDAQ: GROW*	San Antonio	TX	78278	**800-873-8637**	210-308-1234	393
US Golf Assn (USGA) PO Box 708 *Orders	Far Hills	NJ	07931	**800-336-4446***	908-234-2300	48-22
US Golf Assn Museum 77 Liberty Corner Rd	Far Hills	NJ	07931	**800-222-8742**	908-234-2300	511
US Government Printing Office (GPO) 732 N Capitol St NW	Washington	DC	20401	**866-512-1800**	202-512-0000	623-2
Federal Register Online 732 N Capitol St NW	Washington	DC	20401	**888-293-6498**	202-512-1530	337
US Grant Hotel - A Wyndham Historic Hotel 326 Broadway	San Diego	CA	92101	**800-237-5029**	619-232-3121	373
US Gypsum Co 125 S Franklin St	Chicago	IL	60606	**800-621-9622**	312-606-4000	341
US Hispanic Chamber of Commerce 2175 K St NW Suite 100	Washington	DC	20037	**800-874-2286**	202-842-1212	48-14
US Hockey Hall of Fame PO Box 657	Eveleth	MN	55734	**800-443-7825**	218-744-5167	511
US Immigration & Customs Enforcement (ICE) 425 'I' St NW	Washington	DC	20536	**866-347-2423**	202-514-1900	336-7
US Industries Inc 1701 1st Ave	Evansville	IN	47710	**800-264-1501**	812-425-2428	188-12
US Ink Corp 651 Garden St	Carlstadt	NJ	07072	**800-423-8838**	201-935-8666	381
US Intec Inc PO Box 2845 *Tech Supp	Port Arthur	TX	77643	**800-624-6832***	409-724-7024	46
US Investigations Services Inc 1137 Branchton Rd	Annandale	PA	16018	**888-794-8747**	724-794-5612	621
US Junior Chamber of Commerce PO Box 7	Tulsa	OK	74102	**800-529-2337**	918-584-2481	48-7
US Kids Magazine 1100 Waterway Blvd	Indianapolis	IN	46202	**800-558-2376**	317-636-8881	449-6
US Laboratories Inc 7895 Convoy Ct Suite 18	San Diego	CA	92111	**800-487-0355**	858-715-5800	258
US Learning Inc 516 Tennessee St Suite 219	Memphis	TN	38103	**800-647-9166**	901-767-5700	753
US LEC Corp 6801 Morrison Blvd 3 Morrocroft Ctr *NASDAQ: CLEC*	Charlotte	NC	28211	**800-588-7380**	704-319-1000	721
US Legal Support Inc 519 N Sam Houston Pkwy E Suite 200	Houston	TX	77060	**800-622-1107**	713-653-7100	436
US Liability Insurance Group 190 S Warner Rd	Wayne	PA	19087	**800-523-5545**	610-688-2535	384-5
US Lime & Minerals Inc 13800 Montfort Dr Suite 330 *NASDAQ: USLM*	Dallas	TX	75240	**800-991-5463**	972-991-8400	432
US Line Co 16 Union Ave	Westfield	MA	01085	**800-456-4665**	413-562-3629	207
US Machine Tools Corp 94 Custer St	West Hartford	CT	06110	**800-664-0013**	860-953-8306	448
US Marshals Service 1735 Jefferson Davis Hwy	Arlington	VA	22202	**800-336-0102**	202-307-9100	336-10
US Merchant Marine Academy 300 Steamboat Rd	Kings Point	NY	11024	**866-546-4778**	516-773-5000	163
US Military Academy Admissions Bldg 606	West Point	NY	10996	**800-822-8762**	845-938-5746	488
US Mills Inc 200 Reservoir St Suite 202	Needham	MA	02494	**800-422-1125**	781-444-0440	291-4
US Mint 801 9th St NW *Cust Svc	Washington	DC	20220	**800-872-6468***	202-354-7200	336-14
US Music Corp 444 E Courtland St	Mundelein	IL	60060	**800-877-6863**	847-949-0444	516
US National Response Team 1200 Pennsylvania Ave NW MC 5104A	Washington	DC	20460	**800-424-8802**	202-267-2675	336-16
US Natural Resources Inc 8000 NE Parkway Dr Suite 100	Vancouver	WA	98662	**800-289-8767**	360-892-2650	809
US Naval Academy 117 Decatur Rd	Annapolis	MD	21402	**888-249-7707**	410-293-1000	488
US Naval Institute 291 Wood Rd	Annapolis	MD	21402	**800-233-8764**	410-268-6110	48-19
US Navy Memorial & Naval Heritage Center 701 Pennsylvania Ave NW Suite 123	Washington	DC	20004	**800-821-8892**	202-737-2300	50
US News & World Report 1050 Thomas Jefferson St NW	Washington	DC	20007	**800-436-6520**	202-955-2000	449-17
US Oil Co Inc 425 S Washington St	Combined Locks	WI	54113	**800-444-0202**	920-739-6101	569
US Oil & Refining Co 3001 Marshall Ave	Tacoma	WA	98421	**800-424-2012**	253-383-1651	570
US Olympic Hall of Fame 1750 E Boulder St	Colorado Springs	CO	80909	**888-659-8687**	719-866-4500	511
US Oncology Inc 16825 Northchase Dr Suite 1300 *NASDAQ: USON*	Houston	TX	77060	**800-381-2637**	832-601-8766	455
US Optical Disc Inc 1 Eagle Dr	Sanford	ME	04073	**800-743-1124**	207-324-1124	644
US Parachute Assn (USPA) 1440 Duke St	Alexandria	VA	22314	**800-371-8772**	703-836-3495	48-22
US Patent & Trademark Office	Washington	DC	20231	**800-786-9199**	703-308-4357	336-2
US Pharmacist Magazine 100 Ave of the Americas 9th Fl	New York	NY	10013	**877-529-1746**	212-274-7000	449-16
US Pharmacopeia (USP) 12601 Twinbrook Pkwy	Rockville	MD	20852	**800-877-6209**	301-881-0666	49-8
US Physical Therapy 1300 W Sam Houston Pkwy Suite 300 *NASDAQ: USPH*	Houston	TX	77042	**800-580-6285**	713-297-7000	347

Company / Address	City	State	ZIP	Toll-Free	Phone	Class
US Plastic Corp 1390 Newbrecht Rd.	Lima	OH	45801	**800-537-9724**	419-228-2242	198
US Plastic Lumber Corp 2300 Glades Rd Suite 440W *NASDAQ: USPL*	Boca Raton	FL	33431	**866-272-8775**	561-394-3511	647
US Playing Card Co 4590 Beech St.	Cincinnati	OH	45212	**800-863-1333**	513-396-5700	750
US Postal Service (USPS) 475 L'Enfant Plaza West SW *Cust Svc	Washington	DC	20260	**800-275-8777***	202-268-2284	336-16
US Power Squadrons (USPS) PO Box 30423	Raleigh	NC	27622	**888-367-8777**	919-821-0281	48-22
US Professional Tennis Assn (USPTA) 3535 Briarpark Dr Suite 1	Houston	TX	77042	**800-877-8248**	713-978-7782	48-22
US Racquet Stringers Assn (USRSA) 330 Main St	Vista	CA	92084	**888-900-3545**	760-536-1177	48-22
US Racquetball Assn (USRA) 1685 W Uintah St.	Colorado Springs	CO	80904	**800-234-5396**	719-635-5396	48-22
US Rail News 8737 Colesville Rd Suite 1100	Silver Spring	MD	20910	**800-274-6737**	301-589-5103	521-13
US Repeating Arms Co 344 Winchester Ave	New Haven	CT	06511	**800-322-4626**	203-789-5000	279
US Robotics Corp 935 National Pkwy	Schaumburg	IL	60173	**877-710-0884**	847-874-2000	496
US Rowing Assn 201 S Capitol Ave Suite 400	Indianapolis	IN	46225	**800-314-4769**	317-237-5656	48-22
US Rubber Reclaiming Inc 2000 Rubber Way Dr	Vicksburg	MS	39810	**800-842-6043**	601-636-7071	646
US Safety Div Parmelee Industries Inc 8101 Lenexa Dr	Lenexa	KS	66214	**800-821-5218**	913-599-5555	566
US Sailing Assn 15 Maritime Dr PO Box 1260	Portsmouth	RI	02871	**800-877-2451**	401-683-0800	48-22
US Samica Inc PO Box 848	Rutland	VT	05702	**800-248-5528**	802-775-5528	804
US Seamless Inc 2001 1st Ave N	Fargo	ND	58102	**888-743-3632**	701-241-8888	188-12
US Search.com Inc 5401 Beethoven St	Los Angeles	CA	90066	**877-327-2450**	310-302-6300	621
US Security Assoc Inc 200 Mansell Ct 5th Fl	Roswell	GA	30076	**800-241-0267**	770-625-1400	682
US Silica Co PO Box 187	Berkeley Springs	WV	25411	**800-243-7500**	304-258-2500	493-4
US Soccer Federation 1801 S Prairie Ave	Chicago	IL	60616	**800-759-9636**	312-808-1300	48-22
US Space & Rocket Center 1 Tranquility Base	Huntsville	AL	35805	**800-637-7223**	256-837-3400	509
US Speedskating PO Box 450639	Westlake	OH	44145	**800-634-4766**	440-899-0128	48-22
US Stove Co Inc PO Box 151	South Pittsburg	TN	37380	**800-750-2723**	423-837-2100	352
US Student Assn (USSA) 1413 K St NW 9th Fl	Washington	DC	20005	**877-877-2669**	202-347-8772	48-11
US Suites Portland 10220 SW Nimbus St.	Portland	OR	97223	**800-877-8483**	503-443-2033	373
US Surgical Corp 150 Glover Ave	Norwalk	CT	06856	**800-722-8772**	203-845-1000	468
US Tennis Assn (USTA) 70 W Red Oak Ln.	White Plains	NY	10604	**800-990-8782**	914-696-7000	48-22
US Term Limits (USTL) 240 Waukegan Rd Suite 200	Glenview	IL	60025	**800-733-6440**	202-379-3000	48-7
US Tile Co Inc 909 W Railroad St.	Corona	CA	92882	**800-252-9548**	951-737-0200	148
US Tissue & Cell Inc (East Div) 2925 Vernon Pl Suite 301	Cincinnati	OH	45219	**800-558-5004**	513-558-6400	535
US Trade Representative Office of the 600 17th St NW	Washington	DC	20508	**888-473-8787**	202-395-3230	336
US Traffic Corp 9603 S John St	Santa Fe Springs	CA	90670	**800-733-7872**	562-923-9600	691
US Trotting Assn (USTA) 750 Michigan Ave.	Columbus	OH	43215	**800-887-8782**	614-224-2291	48-22
US Trust Corp 114 W 47th St	New York	NY	10036	**800-878-7878**	212-852-1000	393
US Tsubaki Inc 301 E Marquardt Dr	Wheeling	IL	60090	**800-323-7790**	847-459-9500	609
US Unwired Inc 901 Lakeshore Dr.	Lake Charles	LA	70601	**800-673-2200**	337-436-9000	721
US Venture Partners 2735 Sand Hill Rd Suite 300	Menlo Park	CA	94025	**877-773-8787**	650-854-9080	779
US Virgin Islands Dept of Tourism 444 N Capitol St NW Suite 305	Washington	DC	20001	**800-372-8784**	202-624-3590	764
US Virgin Islands Dept of Tourism 2655 S LeJeune Rd Suite 907	Coral Gables	FL	33134	**800-372-8784**	305-442-7200	764
US Virgin Islands Dept of Tourism 500 N Michigan Ave Suite 2030	Chicago	IL	60611	**888-656-8784**		764
US Vision Inc 1 Harmon Dr Glen Oaks Industrial Pk	Glendora	NJ	08012	**800-524-0789**	856-228-1000	658
Us Weekly Magazine 1290 Ave of the Americas 2nd Fl. *Cust Svc	New York	NY	10104	**800-283-3956***	212-484-1616	449-11
US Xpress Enterprises Inc 4080 Jenkins Rd. *NASDAQ: XPRSA*	Chattanooga	TN	37421	**800-251-6291**	423-510-3000	769
USA 800 Inc PO Box 16795	Raytown	MO	64133	**800-821-7539**	816-358-1303	722
USA 3000 Airlines 335 Bishop Hollow Rd Suite 100	Newtown Square	PA	19073	**877-872-3000**	610-325-1280	26
USA Baby 793 Springer Dr.	Lombard	IL	60148	**800-323-4108**	630-652-0600	316
USA Diagnostics Inc 4630 N University Dr PMB 310	Coral Springs	FL	33067	**800-273-8798**	954-970-3934	376
USA Direct Inc 2901 Blackbridge Rd.	York	PA	17402	**800-441-1850**	717-852-1000	5
USA Dubs 29 W 38th St.	New York	NY	10018	**800-872-3821**	212-398-6400	644
USA Freedom Corps 1600 Pennsylvania Ave NW West Wing	Washington	DC	20500	**877-872-2677**		336
USA Funds 11100 USA Pkwy.	Fishers	IN	46038	**800-824-7044**	317-849-6510	215
USA Hotel Guide 630 US 1 Suite 200	North Palm Beach	FL	33408	**888-729-7705**	561-845-8899	368
USA Hotels 860 Wyckoff Ave.	Mahwah	NJ	07430	**800-343-8861**	201-847-9000	368
USA Lending Group 10542 S Jordan Gateway Suite 300	Salt lake City	UT	84095	**877-434-8042**	801-676-1200	498
USA Managed Care Organization 7301 N 16th St Suite 201	Phoenix	AZ	85020	**800-872-0020**	602-371-3860	384-3
USA Mobility Inc 6910 Richmond Hwy *NASDAQ: USMO*	Alexandria	VA	22306	**800-344-1004**	703-660-6677	721
USA Student Travel 5080 Robert J Mathews Pkwy	El Dorado Hills	CA	95762	**888-949-0650**	916-939-6805	748
USA Today 7950 Jones Branch Dr. *Cust Svc	McLean	VA	22108	**800-872-0001***	703-854-3400	522-3
USA Truck Inc 3200 Industrial Pk Rd *NASDAQ: USAK*	Van Buren	AR	72956	**800-872-8782**	479-471-2500	769
USA for UNHCR 1775 K St NW Suite 290	Washington	DC	20006	**800-770-1100**	202-296-1115	48-5
USA Water Ski 1251 Holy Cow Rd	Polk City	FL	33868	**800-533-2972**	863-324-4341	48-22
USA Weekend Magazine 535 Madison Ave 21st Fl *Edit	New York	NY	10022	**800-487-2956***	212-715-2100	449-11
USA Workers' Injury Network 916 S Capital of Texas Hwy	Austin	TX	78746	**800-872-0820**	512-306-0201	384-4
USA Wrestling 6155 Lehman Dr.	Colorado Springs	CO	80918	**800-999-8531**	719-598-8181	48-22
USA.NET Inc 1155 Kelly Johnson Blvd Suite 400	Colorado Springs	CO	80920	**800-653-0179**	719-265-2930	39
USAA (United Services Automobile Assn) 9800 Fredericksburg Rd	San Antonio	TX	78288	**800-531-8222**	210-498-2211	184
USAA FSB 9800 Fredericksburg Rd	San Antonio	TX	78288	**800-531-8022**	210-498-1289	71
USAA Funds 9800 Fredericksburg Rd USAA Bldg	San Antonio	TX	78288	**800-531-8448**	210-498-7290	517
USAA Life Insurance Co 9800 Fredericksburg Rd	San Antonio	TX	78288	**800-531-8000**	210-498-8000	384-2
USAA Property & Casualty Insurance Group 9800 Fredericksburg Rd	San Antonio	TX	78288	**800-531-8111**		384-4
USAA Real Estate Co 9830 Colonnade Blvd Suite 600	San Antonio	TX	78230	**800-531-8182**	210-498-3222	641
USANA Health Sciences Inc 3838 W Parkway Blvd *NASDAQ: USNA*	Salt Lake City	UT	84120	**888-950-9595**	801-954-7100	786
USB (United Soybean Board) 16640 Chesterfield Grove Rd Suite 130	Chesterfield	MO	63005	**800-989-8721**	636-530-1777	48-2
USB Holding Co Inc 100 Dutch Hill Rd. *AMEX: UBH*	Orangeburg	NY	10962	**800-616-3491**	845-365-4600	355-2
USBSF (US Bobsled & Skeleton Federation) 196 Old Military Rd	Lake Placid	NY	12946	**800-262-7533**	518-523-1842	48-22
USCIS (US Citizenship & Immigration Services) 20 Massachusetts Ave NW	Washington	DC	20536	**800-870-3676**	202-514-4600	336-7
USDA Graduate School 600 Maryland Ave SW	Washington	DC	20024	**888-744-4723**	202-314-3400	336-1
USDA Meat & Poultry Hotline	Washington	DC	20250	**800-535-4555**	202-720-3333	336-1
USEC Inc 6903 Rockledge Dr 4th Fl *NYSE: USU*	Bethesda	MD	20817	**800-273-7754**	301-564-3200	141
User-Friendly Group Inc DBA Friendly Cruises Inc 3081 S Sycamore Village Dr	Superstition Mountain	AZ	85218	**800-842-1786**	888-842-1786	760
User Services Assn. Reference & 50 E Huron St.	Chicago	IL	60611	**800-545-2433**	312-280-4398	49-11
Users Inc 1250 Drummers Ln	Valley Forge	PA	19482	**800-523-7282**	610-687-9400	223
USF Bestway Inc 17200 N Perimeter Dr	Scottsdale	AZ	85255	**800-274-1250**	480-760-1675	769
USF Corp 8550 W Bryn Mawr Ave Suite 700	Chicago	IL	60631	**800-873-8680**	773-824-1000	355-3
USF Dugan Inc 2015 S Meridian Ave.	Wichita	KS	67213	**800-888-4151**	316-941-3000	769
USF Holland Inc 750 E 40th St	Holland	MI	49423	**800-456-6322**	616-395-5000	769
USF Logistics Inc 2122 York Rd Suite 300	Oak Brook	IL	60523	**800-723-9100**	630-754-3000	440
USF Reddaway Inc PO Box 1035	Clackamas	OR	97015	**800-395-1360**	503-650-1286	769
USFilter Corp 40-004 Cook St.	Palm Desert	CA	92211	**800-994-4811**	760-340-0098	793
USFilter/Zimpro 301 W Military Rd	Rothschild	WI	54474	**800-826-1476**	715-359-7211	793
USFWS (US Fish & Wildlife Service) 1849 C St NW	Washington	DC	20240	**800-344-9453**	202-208-4717	336-9
USG Annuity & Life Co 909 Locust St.	Des Moines	IA	50309	**800-369-3690**	515-698-7100	384-2
USG Corp 125 S Franklin St. *NYSE: USG*	Chicago	IL	60606	**800-621-9622**	312-606-4000	341
USG Interiors Inc 125 S Franklin St	Chicago	IL	60606	**800-621-9622**	312-606-4000	382
USGA (US Golf Assn) PO Box 708 *Orders	Far Hills	NJ	07931	**800-336-4446***	908-234-2300	48-22
USGS (US Geological Survey) 12201 Sunrise Valley Dr.	Reston	VA	20192	**888-275-8747**	703-648-4000	336-9
Ushio America Inc 5440 Cerritos Ave	Cypress	CA	90630	**800-326-1960**	714-236-8600	429
USI Inc (USinternetworking Inc) 1 USi Plaza	Annapolis	MD	21401	**800-839-4874**	410-897-4400	39
uSight 727 N 1550 E	Orem	UT	84097	**800-544-9459**	801-356-3131	796
Usinger Fred Inc 1030 N Old World 3rd St.	Milwaukee	WI	53203	**800-558-9997**	414-276-9100	291-26
USinternetworking Inc (USI Inc) 1 USi Plaza	Annapolis	MD	21401	**800-839-4874**	410-897-4400	39
USIS Commercial Services 6365 Taft St Suite 2000	Hollywood	FL	33024	**800-881-5993**	954-989-9965	621
USL Pharma 301 S Cherokee St.	Denver	CO	80223	**800-445-8091**	303-607-4500	573
USM Corp 32 Stevens St	Haverhill	MA	01830	**800-343-0772**	978-374-0303	379
USMotivation 7840 Roswell Rd Bldg 100 Suite 300	Atlanta	GA	30350	**800-476-0496**	770-290-4700	377
USNR Corp Irvington-Moore Div PO Box 40666	Jacksonville	FL	32203	**800-289-8767**	904-354-2301	462
USNR Inc 2727 E Grand Ave	Hot Springs	AR	71901	**800-289-8767**	501-262-1010	809
USP (US Pharmacopeia) 12601 Twinbrook Pkwy	Rockville	MD	20852	**800-877-6209**	301-881-0666	49-8
USPA (US Parachute Assn) 1440 Duke St	Alexandria	VA	22314	**800-371-8772**	703-836-3495	48-22
Uspar Enterprises Inc 13404 S Monte Vista Ave.	Chino	CA	91710	**800-251-4612**	909-591-7506	431
USPersonnel 2300 Valley View Ln Suite 300	Irving	TX	75062	**888-506-7785**	972-871-0400	619
USPS (US Postal Service) 475 L'Enfant Plaza West SW *Cust Svc	Washington	DC	20260	**800-275-8777***	202-268-2284	336-16

Name / Address	City	State	Zip	Toll-Free	Phone	Class
USPTA (US Professional Tennis Assn) 3535 Briarpark Dr Suite 1	Houston	TX	77042	**800-877-8248**	713-978-7782	48-22
USRA (US Racquetball Assn) 1685 W Uintah St	Colorado Springs	CO	80904	**800-234-5396**	719-635-5396	48-22
USRSA (US Racquet Stringers Assn) 330 Main St	Vista	CA	92084	**888-900-3545**	760-536-1177	48-22
USS Alabama Battleship Memorial Park 2703 Battleship Pkwy	Mobile	AL	36602	**800-426-4929**	251-433-2703	50
USS Lexington Museum on the Bay 2914 N Shoreline Blvd	Corpus Christi	TX	78403	**800-523-9539**	361-888-4873	509
USS Missouri Memorial 1 Arizona Memorial Pl USS Bowfin Submarine Museum	Honolulu	HI	96818	**888-877-6477**	808-423-2263	50
USS-POSCO Industries PO Box 471	Pittsburg	CA	94565	**800-877-7672**	925-439-6000	709
USSA (US Student Assn) 1413 K St NW 9th Fl	Washington	DC	20005	**877-877-2669**	202-347-8772	48-11
UST Inc 100 W Putnam Ave *NYSE: UST*	Greenwich	CT	06830	**800-243-8536**	203-661-1100	355-3
USTA (US Tennis Assn) 70 W Red Oak Ln	White Plains	NY	10604	**800-990-8782**	914-696-7000	48-22
USTA (US Trotting Assn) 750 Michigan Ave	Columbus	OH	43215	**800-887-8782**	614-224-2291	48-22
USTL (US Term Limits) 240 Waukegan Rd Suite 200	Glenview	IL	60025	**800-733-6440**	202-379-3000	48-7
USUHS (Uniformed Services University of the Health Sciences) 4301 Jones Bridge Rd *Admissions	Bethesda	MD	20814	**800-772-1743***	301-295-3103	336-3
Utah						
Higher Education Assistance Authority 60 S 400 West	Salt Lake City	UT	84101	**877-336-7378**	801-321-7294	711
Parks & Recreation Div PO Box 146001 *Campground Resv	Salt Lake City	UT	84114	**800-322-3770***	801-538-7220	335
Rehabilitation Office 250 E 500 South	Salt Lake City	UT	84111	**800-473-7530**	801-538-7530	335
Travel Development Div 300 N State St	Salt Lake City	UT	84114	**800-200-1160**	801-538-1900	335
Utah Assn of Realtors 5710 S Green St	Murray	UT	84123	**800-594-8933**	801-268-4747	642
Utah Business Magazine 1245 E Brickyard Rd Suite 90	Salt Lake City	UT	84106	**800-823-0038**	801-568-0114	449-5
Utah Jazz 301 W South Temple St Delta Ctr	Salt Lake City	UT	84101	**800-358-7328**	801-325-2500	703
Utah Medical Products Inc 7043 S 300 West *NASDAQ: UTMD*	Midvale	UT	84047	**800-533-4984**	801-566-1200	468
Utah Power & Light 825 NE Multnomah St *Cust Svc	Portland	OR	97232	**888-221-7070***	503-813-5000	774
Utah Refractories Corp 2200 North 1100 W	Lehi	UT	84043	**800-345-6808**	801-768-3591	648
Utah Republican Party 117 E South Temple St	Salt Lake City	UT	84111	**800-230-8824**	801-533-9777	605-2
Utah Transit Authority 3600 South 700 W PO Box 30810	Salt Lake City	UT	84130	**800-743-3882**	801-262-5626	460
Utah Valley Convention & Visitors Bureau 111 S University Ave	Provo	UT	84601	**800-222-8824**	801-851-2100	205
Utak Laboratories Inc 25020 Ave Tibbitts	Valencia	CA	91355	**800-235-3442**	661-294-3935	229
UTC Fire & Security 5201 Explorer Dr	Mississauga	ON	L4W4H1	**800-661-4149**	905-629-2600	681
UTC Fuel Cells 195 Governors Hwy	South Windsor	CT	06074	**866-383-5235**	860-727-2200	252
Ute Mountain Casino 3 Weeminuche Dr	Towaoc	CO	81334	**800-258-8007**	970-565-8800	133
Utell International Resorts 8350 N Central Expy Suite 1900	Dallas	TX	75206	**800-223-6510**	214-234-4000	368
Utendahl Capital Management LP 30 Broad St 21st Fl	New York	NY	10004	**877-941-4900**	212-797-2688	679
UTEX Industries Inc 10810 Old Katy Rd	Houston	TX	77043	**800-359-9230**	713-467-1000	321
Utica Boilers Inc PO Box 4729	Utica	NY	13504	**800-325-5479**	315-797-1310	352
Utica College of Syracuse University 1600 Burrstone Rd	Utica	NY	13502	**800-782-8884**	315-792-3111	163
Utica Cutlery Co 820 Noyes St	Utica	NY	13502	**800-888-4223**	315-733-4663	693
Utica Mutual Insurance Co PO Box 530	Utica	NY	13503	**800-274-1914**	315-734-2000	355-4
Utica National Insurance Group 180 Genesee St	New Hartford	NY	13413	**800-274-1914**	315-734-2000	384-2
Utica National Life Insurance Co 180 Genesee St	New Hartford	NY	13413	**800-274-1914**	315-734-2000	384-2
Utica School of Commerce 201 Bleecker St	Utica	NY	13501	**800-321-4872**	315-733-2307	158
Utilities Cooperative Finance Corp. National Rural 2201 Cooperative Way Woodland Pk	Herndon	VA	20171	**800-424-2954**	703-709-6700	498
Utility Contractors Assn. National 4301 N Fairfax Dr Suite 360	Arlington	VA	22203	**800-662-6822**	703-358-9300	49-3
Utility Contractors Inc PO Box 2079	Wichita	KS	67201	**888-766-2576**	316-265-9506	187-4
Utility Environment Report 2 Penn Plaza 25th Fl	New York	NY	10121	**800-223-6180**	800-752-8872	521-5
Utility Equipment Leasing Corp N4 W22610 Bluemound Rd	Waukesha	WI	53186	**800-558-0999**	262-547-1600	261-2
Utility Forecaster Newsletter 1750 Old Meadow Rd Suite 300	McLean	VA	22102	**800-832-2330**	703-905-8000	521-9
Utne Reader Magazine 1624 Harmon Pl Suite 330 *Cust Svc	Minneapolis	MN	55403	**800-736-8863***	612-338-5040	449-11
Utrecht 6 Corporate Dr	Cranbury	NJ	08512	**800-223-9132**	609-409-8001	43
UTSA (Uniform & Textile Service Assn) 1300 N 17th St Suite 750	Arlington	VA	22209	**800-486-6745**	703-247-2600	49-4
Utz Quality Foods Co 900 High St	Hanover	PA	17331	**800-367-7629**	717-637-6644	291-35
UUSC (Unitarian Universalist Service Committee) 130 Prospect St	Cambridge	MA	02139	**800-388-3920**	617-868-6600	48-5
Uvex Safety Inc 10 Thurber Blvd	Smithfield	RI	02917	**800-343-3411**	401-232-1200	566
UVP Inc 2066 W 11th St	Upland	CA	91786	**800-452-6788**	909-946-3197	429
UXB International Inc 1715 Pratt Dr Suite 1300	Blacksburg	VA	24060	**800-422-4892**	540-443-3700	653
UXU Ranch 1710 Yellowstone Hwy	Wapiti	WY	82450	**800-373-9027**	307-587-2143	238

V

Name / Address	City	State	Zip	Toll-Free	Phone	Class
V Communications Inc 2290 N 1st St Suite 101	San Jose	CA	95131	**800-648-8266**	408-965-4000	176-12
V & E Kohnstamm Inc 882 3rd Ave	Brooklyn	NY	11232	**800-847-4500**	718-788-6320	291-15
V-ONE Corp 20300 Century Blvd Suite 200	Germantown	MD	20874	**800-495-8663**	301-515-5200	176-12
V-T Industries Inc 1000 Industrial Pk	Holstein	IA	51025	**800-827-1615**	712-368-4381	588
V Western Textile Cos 3400 Treecourt Industrial Blvd	Saint Louis	MO	63122	**800-624-8731**	636-225-9400	34
VA (Department of Veterans Affairs) 810 Vermont Ave NW	Washington	DC	20420	**800-827-1000**	202-273-6000	336-15
VA Central Alabama Veterans Health Care System 215 Perry Hill Rd	Montgomery	AL	36109	**800-214-8387**	334-272-4670	366-6
VA Hudson Valley Health Care System Franklin Delano Roosevelt Campus PO Box 100	Montrose	NY	10548	**800-269-8749**	914-737-4400	366-6
Vacation Co 42 New Orleans Rd	Hilton Head Island	SC	29928	**800-845-7018**	843-686-6100	368
Vacation Express Inc 301 Perimeter Center N NE Suite 500	Atlanta	GA	30346	**800-309-4717**	404-315-4848	760
Vacation Internationale 1417 116th Ave NE	Bellevue	WA	98004	**800-444-6633**	425-454-3065	738
Vacation Rental Managers Assn (VRMA) PO Box 1202	Santa Cruz	CA	95061	**800-871-8762**	831-426-8762	49-17
Vacation Village Hotel 647 S Coast Hwy	Laguna Beach	CA	92651	**800-843-6895**	949-494-8566	373
Vacation.com 1650 King St Suite 450	Alexandria	VA	22314	**800-843-0733**	703-535-5505	761
Vacations by Adventure Tours 10670 N Central Expy	Dallas	TX	75231	**800-642-8872**	214-210-6100	760
Vaccine Information Center. National 421-E Church St	Vienna	VA	22180	**800-909-7468**	703-938-3783	48-17
Vacudyne Inc 375 E Joe Orr Rd	Chicago Heights	IL	60411	**800-459-9591**	708-757-5200	379
VAE Nortrak North America Inc 3422 1st Ave S	Seattle	WA	98134	**800-638-4657**	206-622-0125	474
Vagabond Inns Inc 5933 W Century Blvd Suite 200	Los Angeles	CA	90045	**800-522-1555**	310-410-5700	369
Vail Cascade Resort & Spa 1300 Westhaven Dr	Vail	CO	81657	**800-420-2424**	970-476-7111	655
Vail Valley Chamber of Commerce 100 E Meadow Dr Suite 34	Vail	CO	81657	**800-525-3875**	970-476-1000	137
Vail Valley Tourism Bureau 100 E Meadow Dr Suite 34	Vail	CO	81657	**800-525-3875**	970-476-1000	205
Vaisala-GAI 2705 E Medina Rd Suite 111	Tucson	AZ	85706	**800-283-4557**	520-741-2838	464
Vaisala Inc 10-D Gill St	Woburn	MA	01801	**888-824-7252**	781-933-4500	464
Val Ltd Inc 2601 S 70th St	Lincoln	NE	68506	**800-556-8150**	402-434-9350	656
Val-Pak Direct Marketing System Inc 8605 Largo Lakes Dr	Largo	FL	33773	**800-237-6266**	727-393-1270	5
Val Surf Inc 4810 Whitsett Ave	Valley Village	CA	91607	**888-825-7873**	818-769-6977	702
Val-U Inn Motels 16100 NW Cornell Rd Suite 100	Beaverton	OR	97006	**800-443-7777**	503-531-4000	369
Valassis Communications Inc 19975 Victor Pkwy *NYSE: VCI*	Livonia	MI	48152	**800-437-0479**	734-591-3000	615
Valberg LLD 14792 172nd Dr SE	Monroe	WA	98272	**800-487-2206**	360-794-9885	252
Valco Inc 210 E Main St	Coldwater	OH	45828	**800-531-1064**	419-678-8731	269
Valdosta Daily Times PO Box 968	Valdosta	GA	31603	**800-600-4838**	229-244-1880	522-2
Valdosta State University 1500 N Patterson St	Valdosta	GA	31698	**800-618-1878**	229-333-5800	163
Valeant Pharmaceuticals International 3300 Hyland Ave *NYSE: VRX*	Costa Mesa	CA	92626	**800-548-5100**	714-545-0100	572
Valence Technology Inc 301 Conestoga Way *NASDAQ: VLNC*	Henderson	NV	89015	**888-825-3623**	702-558-1000	76
Valenite Inc 1675 Whitcomb Ave *Cust Svc	Madison Heights	MI	48071	**800-488-9112***	248-589-1000	447
Valent USA Corp 1333 N California Blvd Suite 600	Walnut Creek	CA	94596	**800-624-6094**	925-256-2700	276
Valentino's 2601 S 70th St	Lincoln	NE	68506	**888-240-8257**	402-434-9350	657
Valerie Wilson Travel Inc 475 Park Ave S	New York	NY	10016	**800-776-1116**	212-532-3400	760
Valero Energy Corp 1 Valero Way *NYSE: VLO*	San Antonio	TX	78249	**800-531-7911**	210-370-2000	570
Valhalla Inn Toronto 1 Valhalla Inn Rd	Etobicoke	ON	M9B1S9	**800-268-2500**	416-239-2391	372
Valiant 110 Crossways Park Dr	Woodbury	NY	11797	**800-521-4555**	516-390-1100	176-1
Valiant Products Corp 2727 5th Ave W *Cust Svc	Denver	CO	80204	**800-347-2727***	303-892-1234	434
VALIC (Variable Annuity Life Insurance Co) 2929 Allen Pkwy	Houston	TX	77019	**800-633-8960**	713-522-1111	384-2
Vallejo Convention & Visitors Bureau 495 Mare Island Way	Vallejo	CA	94590	**800-482-5535**	707-642-3653	205
Vallejo Times Herald 440 Curtola Pkwy	Vallejo	CA	94590	**800-600-1141**	707-644-1141	522-2
Vallen Corp 521 N Sam Houston Pkwy E Suite 300	Houston	TX	77060	**800-372-3389**	281-500-4500	667
Valley Asphalt Corp 11641 Mosteller Rd	Cincinnati	OH	45241	**800-686-9725**	513-771-0820	187-4
Valley Automotive Inc 32501 Dequindre Rd *Cust Svc	Madison Heights	MI	48071	**800-344-3112***	248-588-6900	751
Valley Barber & Beauty Supply 413 W Harrison St	Harlingen	TX	78550	**800-292-7548**	956-423-0727	78

	Toll-Free	Phone	Class
Valley Best-Way Building Supply 118 S Union Rd .... Spokane WA 99206	800-722-4491	509-924-1250	805
Valley Blox Inc 210 Stone Spring Rd .... Harrisonburg VA 22801	800-648-6725	540-434-6725	181
Valley Blox Inc Americast Div 11352 Virginia Precast Rd .... Ashland VA 23005	800-999-2279	804-798-6068	181
Valley Cabinet Inc 845 Prosper Rd .... De Pere WI 54115	800-236-8981	920-336-3174	116
Valley City State University 101 College St SW.............. Valley City ND 58072	800-532-8641	701-845-7990	163
Valley City Times-Record PO Box 697 .... Valley City ND 58072	800-254-0674	701-845-0463	522-2
Valley Co-op Oil Mill PO Box 533609 .... Harlingen TX 78553	800-775-3382	956-425-4545	291-29
Valley Craft Inc 2001 S Hwy 61...... Lake City MN 55041 *Cust Svc	800-328-1480*	651-345-3386	462
Valley Decorating Co 2829 E Hamilton Ave .... Fresno CA 93721	800-245-2817	559-495-1100	589
Valley-Dynamo 2525 Handley Ederville Rd......Richland Hills TX 76118	800-248-2837	817-299-3070	317
Valley Electric Assn PO Box 237..... Pahrump NV 89041	800-742-3330	775-727-5312	244
Valley Fertilizer & Chemical Co Inc PO Box 816 .... Mount Jackson VA 22842	800-571-3121	540-477-3121	276
Valley Forge Christian College 1401 Charlestown Rd........... Phoenixville PA 19460	800-432-8322	610-935-0450	163
Valley Forge Convention Center 1160 1st Ave .... King of Prussia PA 19406	888-267-1500	610-337-4000	204
Valley Forge Convention & Visitors Bureau 600 W Germantown Pike Suite 130 .... Plymouth Meeting PA 19462	800-441-3549	610-834-1550	205
Valley Forge Flag Co Inc 1700 Conrad Weiser Pkwy....... Womelsdorf PA 19567 *Cust Svc	800-743-5247*	610-589-5888	282
Valley Forge Insurance Co 100 CNA Dr .... Nashville TN 37214	800-437-8854	615-871-1400	384-4
Valley Forge Military Academy & College 1001 Eagle Rd .... Wayne PA 19087	800-234-8362	610-989-1300	160
Valley Forge Scanticon Hotel & Conference Center 1210 1st Ave .... King of Prussia PA 19406	800-333-3333	610-265-1500	370
Valley Fresh Inc 680 D St............Turlock CA 95380	800-526-3189	209-668-3695	608
Valley Fruit Inc PO Box 770............ Pharr TX 78577	800-255-1486	956-787-3241	310-2
Valley Group Inc PO Box 1119......... Albany OR 97321	800-456-6343	541-928-2344	384-4
Valley Health Plan Inc 2270 Eastridge Ctr ....Eau Claire WI 54701	800-472-5411	715-836-1254	384-3
Valley Hospice 380 Summit Ave.... Steubenville OH 43952	877-467-7423	740-283-7487	365
Valley Inc 4400 Mangum Dr.......... Flowood MS 39232	800-748-9985	601-664-3100	294
Valley Inn Tecumseh Rd PO Box 1..... Waterville Valley NH 03215	800-343-0969	603-236-8336	655
Valley Joist 3019 Gault Ave N....... Fort Payne AL 35967	800-633-2258	256-845-2330	688
Valley Lea Laboratories 4609 Grape Rd Suite D-4.........Mishawaka IN 46545	800-822-1283	574-272-8484	728
Valley Morning Star PO Box 511 ..... Harlingen TX 78551	866-578-7827	956-430-6212	522-2
Valley National Bancorp 1455 Valley Rd.................... Wayne NJ 07470 *NYSE: VLY*	800-522-4100	973-305-8800	355-2
Valley News PO Box 877... White River Junction VT 05001	800-874-2226	603-298-8711	522-2
Valley News Dispatch 210 4th Ave.... Tarentum PA 15084	877-698-2553	724-226-1006	522-2
Valley News Today PO Box 369 .... Shenandoah IA 51601	800-369-3097	712-246-3097	522-2
Valley Park Hotel 2404 Stevens Creek Blvd .... San Jose CA 95128	800-954-6835	408-293-5000	373
Valley Power Systems Inc 425 S Hacienda Blvd .... City of Industry CA 91745	800-924-4265	626-333-1243	759
Valley Rural Electric Co-op Inc PO Box 477 .... Huntingdon PA 16652	800-432-0680	814-643-2650	244
Valley Town Crier 1811 N 23rd St ..... McAllen TX 78501	800-556-9876	956-682-2423	522-4
Valley Transit Co Inc 215 N 'A' St.... Harlingen TX 78550	800-580-4710	956-423-4710	109
Valley View Mall 4802 Valley View Blvd ....Roanoke VA 24012	800-321-1711	540-563-4400	452
Valley Welders Supply 320 N 11th St.... Billings MT 59101	800-821-9470	406-256-3330	378
Valley Yellow Pages 1850 N Gateway Blvd Suite 132 ...... Fresno CA 93727	800-350-8887	559-251-8888	623-6
Valleycast Inc 553 Carter Ct..........Kimberly WI 54136	800-747-2912	920-749-3820	476
Valleyfair 1 Valleyfair Dr............Shakopee MN 55379	800-386-7433	952-445-7600	32
Valleylab 5920 Longbow Dr .... Boulder CO 80301	800-255-8522	303-530-2300	249
Vallis Form Service Inc 1966 Quincy Ct........... Glendale Heights IL 60139	800-323-0246	630-893-2940	111
Valmont Industries Inc 1 Valmont Plaza................... Omaha NE 68154 *NYSE: VMI*	800-825-6668	402-963-1000	269
Valparaiso University 1700 Chapel Dr................. Valparaiso IN 46383	888-468-2576	219-464-5000	163
Valparaiso University School of Law 656 S Greenwich St............. Valparaiso IN 46383	888-825-7652	219-465-7829	164-1
Valpey Fisher Corp 75 South St..... Hopkinton MA 01748 *AMEX: VPF*	800-982-5737	508-435-6831	252
Valspar Corp 1101 S 3rd St .... Minneapolis MN 55415 *NYSE: VAL*	800-328-8044	612-332-7371	540
Valspar Refinish Inc 210 Crosby St ... Picayune MS 39466 *Cust Svc	800-556-1347*	601-798-4731	540
Valtec International Inc PO Box 747... Ivoryton CT 06442	800-825-8321	860-767-8211	759
Valuation Analysts. National Assn of Certified 1111 E Brickyard Rd Suite 200................Salt Lake City UT 84106	800-677-2009	801-486-0600	49-12
Value City Furniture 1800 Moler Rd...Columbus OH 43207	800-743-4577	614-221-9200	316
Value Line Asset Management 220 E 42nd St 6th Fl ....New York NY 10017	800-634-3583	212-907-1500	393
Value Line Funds PO Box 219729... Kansas City MO 64121	800-223-0818		517
Value Line Inc 220 E 42nd St 6th Fl...New York NY 10017 *NASDAQ: VALU* ■ *Cust Svc	800-634-3583*	212-907-1500	623-9
Value In Pharmaceuticals (VIP) 3000 Alt Blvd .... Grand Island NY 14072	800-724-3784	716-773-4600	237
Value Plastics Inc 3325 Timberline Rd .... Fort Collins CO 80525	888-404-5837	970-223-8306	597
ValueClick Inc 4353 Park Terrace Dr........Westlake Village CA 91361 *NASDAQ: VCLK*	877-825-8323	818-575-4500	7
ValueOptions Inc 12369 Sunrise Valley Dr Suite C ...... Reston VA 20191	800-236-4648	703-390-6800	454
ValueVision Media Inc 6740 Shady Oak Rd............ Eden Prairie MN 55344 *NASDAQ: VVTV*	800-788-2454	952-943-6000	725
ValueWeb 3250 W Commercial Blvd Suite 200 .... Fort Lauderdale FL 33309	800-934-6788	954-429-3449	795
Valvoline Co 3499 Blazer Pkwy....... Lexington KY 40509	800-354-9061	859-357-7777	530
Vamac Inc 4201 Jacque St......... Richmond VA 23230	800-768-2622	804-353-7811	601
Van Air Systems Inc 2950 Mechanic St................ Lake City PA 16423	800-840-9906	814-774-2631	379
Van Ausdall & Farrar Inc 1214 N Meridian St .... Indianapolis IN 46204	800-467-7474	317-634-2913	523
Van Bergen & Greener Inc 1818 Madison St .... Maywood IL 60153	800-621-3889	708-343-4700	246
Van Bloem Gardens 500 Pirkle Ferry Rd Suite D....... Cummings GA 30130	800-683-2852	770-667-3344	288
Van Bortel Aircraft Inc 4900 S Collins St................ Arlington TX 76018	800-759-4295	817-468-7788	759
Van Bourgondien & Sons Inc 245 Rt 109.....................West Babylon NY 11704	800-622-9997	631-669-3500	318
Van Cleef & Arpels Inc 744 5th Ave... New York NY 10019	800-822-5797	212-644-9500	402
Van Den Bosch John A Co 4511 Holland Ave..................Holland MI 49422 *Cust Svc	800-968-6477*	616-848-2000	438
Van Diest Supply Co PO Box 610.. Webster City IA 50595	800-779-2424	515-832-2366	276
Van Dusen & Meyer Inc 50 Parrott Dr...Shelton CT 06484	800-760-6242	203-929-6355	446
Van Dyke Supply Co 39771 Hwy 34 E...............Woonsocket SD 57385	800-843-3320	605-796-4425	451
Van Dyne Crotty Inc 3233 Newmark Dr .... Miamisburg OH 45342	800-236-9555	937-236-1500	434
Van Enterprises 8500 W Shawnee Mission Pkwy Suite 200............Shawnee Mission KS 66202	800-747-4400	913-432-6400	57
Van Galder Bus Co 715 S Pearl St .... Janesville WI 53548	800-747-7407	608-752-5407	108
Van Gilder Insurance Corp 700 Broadway Suite 1000 .... Denver CO 80203	800-873-8500	303-837-8500	383
Van Horn Metz & Co 201 E Elm St ....Conshohocken PA 19428	800-523-0424	610-828-4500	144
Van Kampen Funds 2800 Post Oak Blvd ....Houston TX 77056	800-341-2911	713-438-4000	517
Van Kampen Investments Inc 1 Parkview Plaza...........Oakbrook Terrace IL 60181	800-225-2222	630-684-6000	393
Van Meter Industrial Inc 240 33rd Ave SW............. Cedar Rapids IA 52404	800-332-8468	319-366-5301	245
Van Meter Insurance 1240 Fair Way St ....Bowling Green KY 42103	800-960-3560	270-781-2020	383
Van Rooy Coffee Co 4569 Spring Rd .. Cleveland OH 44131	877-826-7669	216-749-7069	291-7
Van Ru Credit Corp 1350 E Touhy Ave Suite 300E.... Des Plaines IL 60018	800-468-2678	847-824-2414	157
Van San Corp 16735 E Johnson Dr .... City of Industry CA 91745	800-423-1829	626-961-7211	314-1
Van Son Holland Ink Corp of America 185 Oval Dr .... Islandia NY 11749	800-645-4182		381
Van Wagoner Funds PO Box 9682 ... Providence RI 02940	800-228-2121		517
Van Well Nursery 2821 Grant Rd .... East Wenatchee WA 98802	800-572-1553	509-886-8189	288
Van Wezel Performing Arts Center 777 N Tamiami Trail...............Sarasota FL 34236	800-826-9303	941-953-3368	562
Van Wingerden International Inc 1856 Jeffress Rd .... Fletcher NC 28732	800-226-3597	828-891-4116	363
Van Zandt James E Veterans Affairs Medical Center 2907 Pleasant Valley Blvd ....Altoona PA 16602	877-626-2500	814-943-8164	366-6
Van Zyverden Inc 8079 Van Zyverden Rd.............Meridian MS 39305	800-332-2852	601-679-8274	288
Vanadium Group Corp 400 Rouser Rd Bldg 2.......Moon Township PA 15108	800-685-0354	412-264-2030	258
Vance 10467 White Granite Dr Suite 210..... Oakton VA 22124	800-533-6754	703-592-1400	682
Vance Bros Inc PO Box 300107 .... Kansas City MO 64130	800-821-8549	816-923-4325	46
Vance Publishing Corp 400 Knightsbridge Pkwy......... Lincolnshire IL 60069	800-621-2845	847-634-2600	623-9
Vancouver Aquarium Marine Science Center PO Box 3232 .... Vancouver BC V6B3X8	800-931-1186	604-659-3474	40
Vancouver Canucks General Motors Pl 800 Griffiths Way................. Vancouver BC V6B6G1	888-672-2229	604-899-4600	703
Vancouver Door Co Inc PO Box 1418... Puyallup WA 98371	800-999-3667	253-845-9581	234
Vancouver (Greater) Convention & Visitors Bureau 200 Burrard St.... Vancouver BC V6C3L6	800-663-6000	604-683-2000	205
Vancouver Island Helicopters Ltd 1962 Canso Rd.............. North Saanich BC V8L5V5	866-844-4354	250-656-3987	354
Vancouver Port Authority 100 The Point 999 Canada Pl ..... Vancouver BC V6C3T4	888-767-8826	604-665-9000	607
Vanderbilt Beach Resort 9225 Gulf Shore Dr N .... Naples FL 34108	800-243-9076	239-597-3144	655
Vanderbilt Chemical Corp 30 Winfield St.................... Norwalk CT 06855	800-243-6064	203-853-1400	142
Vanderbilt Hall Hotel 41 Mary St ...... Newport RI 02840	888-826-4255	401-846-6200	373
Vanderbilt Inn on the Gulf 11000 Gulf Shore Dr N .... Naples FL 34108	800-643-8654	239-597-3151	373
Vanderbilt Mortgage & Finance Inc 500 Alcoa Trail .... Maryville TN 37804	800-970-7250	865-380-3000	498
Vanderbilt RT Co Inc 30 Winfield St.... Norwalk CT 06855 *Cust Svc	800-243-6064*	203-853-1400	142
Vanderbilt University 2201 W End Ave................. Nashville TN 37235	800-288-0432	615-322-7311	163
Vanderbilt University Medical Center 1211 22nd Ave S .... Nashville TN 37232	800-288-7777	615-322-5000	366-2
VanderCook College of Music 3140 S Federal St................. Chicago IL 60616	800-448-2655	312-225-6288	163
Vanderweil RG Engineers Inc 274 Summer St .... Boston MA 02210	800-726-2840	617-423-7423	258
Vanee Foods Co Inc 5418 McDermott Dr.............. Berkeley IL 60163 *Cust Svc	800-654-6647*	708-449-7300	291-36
Vanguard Brokerage Services PO Box 2600 ....Valley Forge PA 19482	800-992-8327	610-669-1000	679

Listing	City	State	ZIP	Toll-Free	Phone	Class
Vanguard Car Rental USA 6929 N Lakewood Ave Suite 100	Tulsa	OK	74117	**800-837-0032**	918-401-6000	126
Vanguard Cleaning Systems Inc 655 Mariners Island Blvd Suite 303	San Mateo	CA	94404	**800-564-6422**	650-594-1500	150
Vanguard East 1172 Azalea Garden Rd	Norfolk	VA	23502	**800-221-1264**	757-857-3600	10
Vanguard Funds PO Box 1110	Valley Forge	PA	19482	**800-871-3879**		517
Vanguard Furniture Co Inc 109 Simpson St	Conover	NC	28613	**800-968-1702**	828-328-5631	314-2
Vanguard Group 455 Devon Park Dr	Wayne	PA	19087	**800-662-7447**	610-669-1000	393
Vanguard Supreme Machine Div Monarch Machine Corp PO Box 5009	Monroe	NC	28111	**800-222-1971**	704-283-8171	729
Vanguard University of Southern California 55 Fair Dr	Costa Mesa	CA	92626	**800-722-6279***	714-556-3610	163
*Admissions						
Vanished Children's Alliance (VCA) 991 W Hedding St Suite 101	San Jose	CA	95126	**800-826-4743**	408-296-1113	48-6
Vanity Fair Magazine 4 Times Sq	New York	NY	10036	**800-690-6115**	212-286-2860	449-11
Vanner Inc 4282 Reynolds Dr	Hilliard	OH	43026	**800-227-6937**	614-771-2718	252
Vans Inc 15700 Shoemaker Ave	Santa Fe Springs	CA	90670	**800-826-7800**	562-565-8267	296
Vantage Data Solutions 5889 S Greenwood Plaza Blvd Suite 201	Englewood	CO	80111	**800-568-5665**		621
Vantage Mobility International (VMI) 5202 S 28th Pl	Phoenix	AZ	85040	**800-348-8267**	602-243-2700	62-7
Vantage Press Inc 419 Park Ave S 18th Fl	New York	NY	10016	**800-882-3273**	212-736-1767	623-2
Vantage Products Corp 960 Almon Rd	Covington	GA	30014	**800-481-3303**	770-788-0136	690
Vantage Trailers Inc 29335 Hwy 90	Katy	TX	77494	**800-826-8245**	281-391-2664	768
VantageMed Corp 3017 Kilgore Rd Suite 180	Rancho Cordova	CA	95670	**877-879-8633**	916-638-4744	176-10
VantagePoint Funds 777 N Capitol St NW	Washington	DC	20002	**800-669-7400**	202-962-4600	517
VanTran Industries Inc PO Box 20128	Waco	TX	76702	**800-433-3346***	254-772-9740	756
*Sales						
Vapor Bus International 1010 Johnson Dr	Buffalo Grove	IL	60089	**800-631-9200**	847-777-6400	636
Varel International 1434 Patton Pl Suite 106	Carrollton	TX	75007	**800-827-3526**	972-242-1160	189
Variable Annuity Life Insurance Co (VALIC) 2929 Allen Pkwy	Houston	TX	77019	**800-633-8960**	713-522-1111	384-2
Variable Star Observers. American Assn of 25 Birch St	Cambridge	MA	02138	**800-223-0138**	617-354-0484	49-19
Varian Inc 25200 Commercentre Dr	Lake Forest	CA	92630	**800-854-0277**	949-770-9381	229
Varian Semiconductor Equipment Assoc Inc 35 Dory Rd	Gloucester	MA	01930	**800-447-1762**	978-282-2000	685
NASDAQ: VSEA						
Varian Vacuum Technologies 121 Hartwell Ave	Lexington	MA	02421	**800-882-7426***	781-861-7200	170
*Cust Svc						
Variety 5700 Wilshire Blvd Suite 120	Los Angeles	CA	90036	**800-552-3632**	323-857-6600	449-9
Variety Distributors Inc 7th & Spring Sts PO Box 728	Harlan	IA	51537	**800-274-1095**	712-755-2184	323
Variety Wholesalers Inc 3401 Gresham Lake Rd	Raleigh	NC	27615	**800-366-9144**	919-876-6000	778
Variflex Inc 5152 N Commerce Ave	Moorpark	CA	93021	**800-327-0821**	805-523-0322	701
NASDAQ: VFLX						
Variform Inc 303 W Major St PO Box 559	Kearney	MO	64060	**800-800-2244**	816-903-6400	190-4
Varig Brasil Airlines 71 S Central Ave 2nd Fl	Valley Stream	NY	11580	**800-468-2744**	516-612-0339	26
Varig Brasil Airlines Smiles Program 71 S Central Ave 2nd FL	Valley Stream	NY	11580	**800-468-2744**	516-612-0339	27
Varitronic Systems Inc 6835 Winnetka Cir	Brooklyn Park	MN	55428	**800-328-0585**	763-536-6400	112
Varscona Hotel 8208 106th St	Edmonton	AB	T6E6R9	**888-515-3355**	780-434-6111	372
Varsity Brands Inc DBA Varsity Spirit Fashions 6745 Lenox Center Ct Suite 300	Memphis	TN	38115	**800-533-8022**	901-387-4370	153-19
Varsity Clubs of America-South Bend Chapter 3800 N Main St	Mishawaka	IN	46545	**800-946-4822**	574-277-0500	373
Varsity Clubs of America-Tucson Chapter 3855 E Speedway Blvd	Tucson	AZ	85716	**800-521-3131**	520-318-3777	373
Varsity Group Inc 1850 M St NW Suite 1150	Washington	DC	20036	**877-827-2665**	202-667-3400	96
NASDAQ: VSTY						
Varsity Spirit Corp 6745 Lenox Ctr Ct Suite 300	Memphis	TN	38115	**800-533-8022**	901-387-4370	153-19
Varsity Spirit Fashions 6745 Lenox Center Ct Suite 300	Memphis	TN	38115	**800-533-8022**	901-387-4370	153-19
VarTec Telecom Inc 1600 Viceroy Dr	Dallas	TX	75235	**800-583-8832**	214-424-1000	721
Vascular Access Networks. National Assn of 11441 S State St Suite A113	Draper	UT	84020	**888-576-2826**	801-576-1824	49-8
Vasomedical Inc 180 Linden Ave	Westbury	NY	11590	**800-455-3327**	516-997-4600	249
NASDAQ: VASO						
Vassar College 124 Raymond Ave	Poughkeepsie	NY	12604	**800-827-7270**	845-437-7000	163
Vatra Mountain Valley Health Resort Rt 214 Box F	Hunter	NY	12442	**800-232-2772**	518-263-4919	697
Vatterott College Kansas City 8955 E 38th Terr	Kansas City	MO	64129	**800-466-3997**	816-861-1000	787
Vaughan & Bushnell Mfg Co 11414 Maple Ave	Hebron	IL	60034	**800-435-6000**	815-648-2446	746
Vaughan Co Inc 364 Monte-Elma Rd	Montesano	WA	98563	**888-249-2467**	360-249-4042	627
Vaughan Regional Medical Center 1015 Medical Center Pkwy	Selma	AL	36701	**800-498-8461**	334-418-4100	366-2
Vaughn College of Aeronautics & Technology 86-01 23rd Ave	East Elmhurst	NY	11369	**800-776-2376**	718-429-6600	163
Vaughn Mfg Corp 26 Old Elm St	Salisbury	MA	01952	**800-282-8446**	978-462-6683	36
Vaultus Inc 632 Broadway 10th Fl	New York	NY	10012	**800-787-9170**	212-624-4040	222
Vaupell Industrial Plastics Inc 1144 NW 53rd St	Seattle	WA	98107	**800-426-7738**	206-784-9050	593

Listing	City	State	ZIP	Toll-Free	Phone	Class
VBT Bicycle Vacations 614 Monkton Rd	Bristol	VT	05443	**800-245-3868**	802-453-4811	748
VCA (Vanished Children's Alliance) 991 W Hedding St Suite 101	San Jose	CA	95126	**800-826-4743**	408-296-1113	48-6
VCA (Vision Council of America) 1700 Diagonal Rd Suite 500	Alexandria	VA	22314	**800-424-8422**	703-548-4560	49-4
VCA Antech Inc 12401 W Olympic Blvd	Los Angeles	CA	90064	**800-966-1822**	310-571-6500	781
NASDAQ: WOOF						
VCampus Corp 1850 Centennial Pk Dr Suite 200	Reston	VA	20191	**800-915-9298**	703-893-7800	176-3
NASDAQ: VCMP						
VCF Films Inc 1100 Sutton Ave	Howell	MI	48843	**888-823-4141**	517-546-2300	589
Vcommerce Corp 9977 N 90th St Suite 200	Scottsdale	AZ	85258	**800-821-6034***	480-922-9922	39
*Cust Svc						
Vcon Inc 10535 Boyer Blvd Suite 300	Austin	TX	78758	**800-418-5328***	512-583-7700	720
*Tech Supp						
VE Holdings Inc DBA Vacation Express Inc 301 Perimeter Center N NE Suite 500	Atlanta	GA	30346	**800-309-4717**	404-315-4848	760
Vecellio & Grogan Inc 2251 Robert C Byrd Dr	Beckley	WV	25802	**800-255-6575**	304-252-6575	187-4
Veco Corp 3601 C St Suite 1000	Anchorage	AK	99503	**800-284-2812**	907-264-8100	528
Vector Marketing Co 1116 E State St	Olean	NY	14760	**800-828-0448**		561
Vector Strategic Resources Inc 555 Theodore Fremd Ave Suite B-102	Rye	NY	10580	**866-832-8676**	914-921-1900	193
Vectren Communications Services 421 John St	Evansville	IN	47713	**888-326-6782**	812-437-6700	195
Vectren Corp 20 NW 4th St	Evansville	IN	47708	**800-227-1376**	812-491-4000	355-5
NYSE: VVC						
Vectron International 166 Glover Ave	Norwalk	CT	06850	**888-328-7661**	203-853-4433	252
Vedior North America 60 Harvard Mill Sq	Wakefield	MA	01880	**800-648-2469**	781-213-1500	707
Vee Bar Guest Ranch 2091 State Hwy 130	Laramie	WY	82070	**800-483-3227**	307-745-7036	238
Vee Neal Aviation Inc 200 Pleasant Unity Rd Suite 109	Latrobe	PA	15650	**800-278-2710**	724-539-4533	63
Veeder-Root 125 Powder Forest Dr	Simsbury	CT	06070	**800-879-0301**	860-651-2700	200
Veeder-Root Red Jacket Div 125 Powder Forest Dr	Simsbury	CT	06070	**800-873-3313**	860-651-2700	627
Veetronix Inc 1311 W Pacific	Lexington	NE	68850	**800-445-0007**	308-324-6661	803
Vega Group 7220 Washington Ave	New Orleans	LA	70125	**800-771-2979**	504-488-5222	183
Vega Holdings Inc 4065 Hollis St	Emeryville	CA	94608	**800-877-1771**	510-496-6666	52
Vegas Valley Book Festival Nevada Humanities Committee PO Box 8029	Reno	NV	89507	**800-382-5023**	775-784-6587	277
Vegetable Juices Inc 7400 S Narragansett Ave	Bedford Park	IL	60638	**888-776-9752**	708-924-9500	291-20
Vegetarian Times Magazine PO Box 1327	Elmhurst	IL	60126	**800-829-3340***	630-516-4008	449-13
*Orders						
Vehicle Institute of America. Specialty 2 Jenner St Suite 150	Irvine	CA	92618	**800-887-2887**	949-727-3727	49-21
Vehicle Safety Mfg LLC 408 Central Ave	Newark	NJ	07107	**800-832-7233**	973-643-3000	430
Vehicular Technology Society. IEEE IEEE Operations Ctr 445 Hoes Ln	Piscataway	NJ	08854	**800-678-4333**	732-981-0060	49-19
Velcro USA Inc 406 Brown Ave	Manchester	NH	03108	**800-225-0180**	603-669-4880	583
Velda Farms LLC 402 S Kentucky Ave Suite 500	Lakeland	FL	33801	**800-795-4649***	863-686-4441	291-27
*Cust Svc						
Veldkamp's Flowers 9501 W Colfax Ave	Lakewood	CO	80215	**800-247-3730**	303-232-2673	287
Vellano Brothers Inc 7 Hemlock St	Latham	NY	12110	**800-342-9855**	518-785-5537	378
Vellumoid Inc 54 Rockdale St	Worcester	MA	01606	**800-609-5558**	508-853-2500	321
Velocity Express Corp 512 Sharptown Rd	Bridgeport	NJ	08014	**877-990-0199**	856-294-0111	536
NASDAQ: VEXP						
Velsicol Chemical Corp 10400 W Higgins Rd Suite 600	Rosemont	IL	60018	**800-843-7759***	847-298-9000	142
*Cust Svc						
Velux-Greenwood Inc 450 Old Brickyard Rd	Greenwood	SC	29648	**800-688-3589**	864-941-4700	482
Velvet Cloak Inn 1505 Hillsborough St	Raleigh	NC	27605	**800-334-4372**	919-828-0333	373
Venable LLP 1800 Mercantile Bank & Trust Bldg 2 Hopkins Plaza	Baltimore	MD	21201	**800-966-9877**	410-244-7400	419
Vendome Copper & Brass Works Inc 729 Franklin St	Louisville	KY	40202	**800-247-6245**	502-587-1930	293
Venetian Resort Hotel & Casino 3355 Las Vegas Blvd S	Las Vegas	NV	89109	**877-283-6423**	702-414-1000	655
Vengroff Williams & Assoc Inc PO Box 19715	Irvine	CA	92623	**888-374-2600**	949-263-1300	157
Venice Gondolier 200 E Venice Ave	Venice	FL	34285	**800-799-7861**	941-207-1000	522-4
Vennard College 2300 8th Ave E PO Box 29	University Park	IA	52595	**800-686-8391**	641-673-8391	163
Vent Products Co Inc 1901 S Kilbourn Ave	Chicago	IL	60623	**800-368-8368**	773-521-1900	688
Ventana Canyon - A Wyndham Luxury Resort. Lodge at 6200 N Clubhouse Ln	Tucson	AZ	85750	**800-828-5701**	520-577-1400	655
Ventana Canyon Resort. Loews 7000 N Resort Dr	Tucson	AZ	85750	**800-234-5117**	520-299-2020	655
Ventana Inn 48123 Hwy 1	Big Sur	CA	93920	**800-628-6500**	831-667-2331	655
Ventana Medical Systems Inc 1910 Innovation Pk Dr	Tucson	AZ	85737	**800-227-2155**	520-887-2155	468
NASDAQ: VMSI						
Ventas Inc 10350 Ormsby Pk Pl Suite 300	Louisville	KY	40223	**800-877-4836**	502-357-9000	641
NYSE: VTR						
Ventiv Health Inc 200 Cottontail Ln	Somerset	NJ	08873	**800-416-0555**		194
NASDAQ: VTIV						
Ventura County Star 5250 Ralston St	Ventura	CA	93003	**800-221-7827**	805-650-2900	522-2
Ventura Educational Systems PO Box 425	Grover Beach	CA	93483	**800-336-1022**	805-473-7387	176-3

Name / Address	City	State	Zip	Toll-Free	Phone	Class
Ventura Foods LLC 40 Point Dr	Brea	CA	92821	**800-327-3906**	714-257-3700	291-30
Ventura Foods LLC Sunnyland Div 3900 Vanderbilt Rd	Birmingham	AL	35217	**800-338-8682**	205-808-3514	291-30
Ventura Visitors & Convention Bureau 89 S California St Suite C	Ventura	CA	93001	**800-333-2989**	805-648-2075	205
VenturCom Inc 29 Sawyer Rd	Waltham	MA	02543	**800-334-8649**	781-647-3000	176-12
Venture Marine Inc 1525 53rd St	West Palm Beach	FL	33407	**800-960-3434**	561-845-8557	91
Venture Tape Corp 30 Commerce Rd	Rockland	MA	02370	**800-343-1076**	781-331-5900	717
Venture Travel & Tours Inc 965 Bethel Rd	Columbus	OH	43214	**800-859-8687**	614-442-8687	748
VentureOut 575 Pierce St Suite 604	San Francisco	CA	94117	**888-431-6789**	415-626-5678	748
VentureWire 800 Plaza 2 Harborside Finanacial Ctr	Jersey City	NJ	07311	**800-326-3613**	866-291-1800	521-1
Venturi Inc PO Box 6348 *Cust Svc	Traverse City	MI	49696	**800-968-0104***	231-929-7732	596
Venus Book Club Bookspan 1225 S Market St	Mechanicsburg	PA	17055	**800-688-4442**		94
Venus Industries 41-50 24th St	Long Island City	NY	11101	**800-221-6097**	718-729-4300	730-5
Venus Laboratories Inc 855 Lively Blvd	Wood Dale	IL	60191	**800-592-1900**	630-595-1902	149
Venus Swimwear 11711 Marco Beach Dr 1 Venus Plaza	Jacksonville	FL	32224	**800-366-7946**	904-645-6000	153-17
Venus Wafers Inc 70 Research Rd	Hingham	MA	02043	**800-545-4538**	781-740-1002	291-9
Vera Bradley Designs 2208 Production Rd	Fort Wayne	IN	46808	**800-975-8372**	260-482-4673	343
Vera Wang 225 W 39th St 9th Fl	New York	NY	10018	**800-839-8372**	212-575-6400	273
Verbatim Corp 1200 West WT Harris Blvd	Charlotte	NC	28262	**800-538-8589**	704-547-6500	644
Verdelli Farms Inc 7505 Grayson Rd	Harrisburg	PA	17111	**800-422-8344**	717-561-2900	12-1
Verdigris Valley Electric Co-op PO Box 219	Collinsville	OK	74021	**800-870-5948**	918-371-2584	244
Verdin Co 444 Reading Rd	Cincinnati	OH	45202	**800-543-0488**	513-241-4010	151
Verendrye Electric Co-op Inc 615 Hwy 52 W	Velva	ND	58790	**800-472-2141**	701-338-2855	244
VERIBANC Inc 1 Social St	Woonsocket	RI	02895	**800-442-2657**	401-766-5300	212
Vericon Resources Inc 2358 Perimeter Park Dr Suite 370	Atlanta	GA	30341	**800-795-3784**	770-457-9922	621
Veridicom Inc 999 3rd Ave	Seattle	WA	98104	**800-363-1418**	206-224-6206	85
Verified Credentials Inc 20890 Kenbridge Ct	Lakeville	MN	55044	**800-473-4934**	952-985-7200	621
Verifine Dairy Products Co Inc 1606 Erie Ave	Sheboygan	WI	53081	**800-236-6455**	920-457-7733	291-27
Veriflo Div Parker Hannifin Corp 250 Canal Blvd	Richmond	CA	94804	**800-962-4074**	510-235-9590	200
VeriFone Inc 2455 Augustine Dr *NYSE: PAY*	Santa Clara	CA	95054	**800-837-4366**	408-232-7800	603
Verilink Corp 127 Jetplex Cir *NASDAQ: VRLK*	Madison	AL	35758	**800-926-0085**	256-327-2001	496
Verint Systems Inc 330 S Service Rd *NASDAQ: VRNT*	Melville	NY	11747	**800-967-1028**	631-962-9600	720
Verint Video Solutions 9105 Guilford Rd	Columbia	MD	21046	**800-638-5969**	301-483-8930	681
Verio Inc 8005 S Chester St Suite 200	Centennial	CO	80112	**888-558-3746**	303-645-1900	390
VeriSign Inc 487 E Middlefield Rd *NASDAQ: VRSN* ■ *Sales	Mountain View	CA	94043	**866-893-6565***	650-961-7500	389
Veritas DGC Inc 10300 Townpark Dr *NYSE: VTS*	Houston	TX	77072	**800-344-4266**	832-351-8300	527
VERITAS Software Corp 350 Ellis St *NASDAQ: VRTSE*	Mountain View	CA	94043	**800-327-2232**	650-527-8000	176-12
Veritech Corp 37 Prospect St	East Longmeadow	MA	01028	**800-525-5912**	413-525-3368	502
Verity Inc 892 Ross Dr *NASDAQ: VRTY*	Sunnyvale	CA	94089	**800-935-6246**	408-541-1500	176-7
Verizon Airfone 2809 Butterfield Rd *Cust Svc	Oak Brook	IL	60522	**800-247-3663***	630-572-1800	721
Verizon Communications 1095 Ave of the Americas *NYSE: VZ*	New York	NY	10036	**800-621-9900**	212-395-2121	721
Verizon Credit Inc 201 N Franklin St Suite 3300	Tampa	FL	33602	**800-483-7988**	813-229-6000	214
Verizon Directories 2200 W Airfield Dr *Orders	DFW Airport	TX	75261	**800-888-8448***	972-453-7000	623-6
Verizon Information Services 2200 W Airfield Dr	DFW Airport	TX	75261	**877-814-6854**	972-453-7000	623-6
Verizon Logistics 5615 High Point Dr	Irving	TX	75038	**800-433-4837**	972-751-4100	455
Verizon Online 4055 Corporate Dr Suite 400	Grapevine	TX	76051	**877-483-3648**		390
Verizon Wireless 180 Washington Valley Rd	Bedminster	NJ	07921	**800-214-3555**	908-306-7000	721
Vermilion Community College 1900 E Camp St	Ely	MN	55731	**800-657-3608**	218-365-7200	160
Vermilion Energy Trust 2800 400 4th Ave SW *TSE: VET.un*	Calgary	AB	T2P0J4	**866-895-8101**	403-269-4884	529
Vermont						
Child Support Office 103 S Main St	Waterbury	VT	05671	**800-786-3214**	802-241-2319	335
Crime Victim Services Center 58 S Main St	Waterbury	VT	05676	**800-750-1213**	802-241-1255	335
Emergency Management Office 103 S Main St	Waterbury	VT	05671	**800-347-0488**	802-244-8721	335
Historic Preservation Div National Life Bldg Drawer 20	Montpelier	VT	05620	**800-341-2211**	802-828-3211	335
Housing & Community Affairs Dept National Life Bldg Drawer 20	Montpelier	VT	05620	**800-622-4553**	802-828-3211	335
Parks Div 103 S Main St Bldg 10S *Campground Resv	Waterbury	VT	05671	**888-409-7579***	802-241-3655	335
Student Assistance Corp PO Box 2000	Winooski	VT	05404	**800-642-3177**	802-655-9602	711
Tourism & Marketing Dept 134 State St	Montpelier	VT	05602	**800-837-6668**	802-828-3236	335
Vital Records Section PO Box 70	Burlington	VT	05402	**800-439-5008**	802-863-7275	335
Vermont Academy PO Box 500	Saxtons River	VT	05154	**800-560-1876**	802-869-6229	611
Vermont American Corp 101 S 5th St Suite 2300	Louisville	KY	40202	**800-626-2834**	502-625-2000	746
Vermont Assn of Realtors 148 State St	Montpelier	VT	05602	**866-248-6182**	802-229-0513	642
Vermont Castings Inc PO Box 501 *Prod Info	Bethel	VT	05032	**800-227-8683***	802-234-2300	352
Vermont Electric Co-op Inc 182 School St	Johnson	VT	05656	**800-832-2667**	802-635-2331	244
Vermont Law School PO Box 96	South Royalton	VT	05068	**800-227-1395**	802-831-1001	164-1
Vermont Life Magazine 6 Baldwin St	Montpelier	VT	05602	**800-284-3243**	802-828-3241	449-22
Vermont Medical Society 134 Main St	Montpelier	VT	05601	**800-640-8767**	802-223-7898	466
Vermont Mutual Insurance Co PO Box 188	Montpelier	VT	05601	**800-451-5000**	802-223-2341	384-4
Vermont Public Television (VPT) 204 Ethan Allen Ave	Colchester	VT	05446	**800-639-7811**	802-655-4800	620
Vermont Pure Holdings Ltd 2281 Vermont Rt 66 *AMEX: VPS* ■ *Cust Svc	Randolph	VT	05060	**800-939-9119***	802-728-3600	792
Vermont Structural Slate Co Inc 3 Prospect St PO Box 98	Fair Haven	VT	05743	**800-343-1900**	802-265-4933	710
Vermont Symphony Orchestra 2 Church St Suite 19	Burlington	VT	05401	**800-876-9293**	802-864-5741	563-3
Vermont Technical College PO Box 500	Randolph Center	VT	05061	**800-442-8821**	802-728-1000	787
Vermont Teddy Bear Co Inc 6655 Shelburne Rd *NASDAQ: BEAR*	Shelburne	VT	05482	**800-988-8277**	802-985-3001	750
Vermont Transit Co Inc 345 Pine St	Burlington	VT	05401	**800-552-8737**	802-862-9671	108
Vermont Tubbs 1 Tubbs Ave	Brandon	VT	05733	**800-327-7026**	802-247-3414	314-2
Vermont's North Country Chamber of Commerce 246 The Causeway	Newport	VT	05855	**800-635-4643**	802-334-7782	137
Vernay Laboratories Inc 120 E South College St	Yellow Springs	OH	45387	**800-837-6291**	937-767-7261	664
Vernon Daily Record 3214 Wilbarger St	Vernon	TX	76384	**800-234-9014**	940-552-5454	522-2
Vernon Downs 14 Ruth St	Vernon	NY	13476	**877-777-8559**	315-829-2201	628
Vernon Electric Co-op 110 N Main St	Westby	WI	54667	**800-447-5051**	608-634-3121	244
Vernon Manor Hotel 400 Oak St	Cincinnati	OH	45219	**800-543-3999**	513-281-3300	373
Vernon Parish Library 1401 Nolan Trace	Leesville	LA	71446	**800-737-2231**	337-239-2027	426
Vernon Tool Co Ltd 503 Jones Rd	Oceanside	CA	92054	**800-452-1542**	760-433-5860	447
Vero Beach Press-Journal PO Box 1268	Vero Beach	FL	32961	**888-988-8376**	772-562-2315	522-2
Versa Press Inc 1465 Springbay Rd	East Peoria	IL	61611	**800-447-7829**	309-822-8272	614
VersaForm Systems Corp 591 W Hamilton Ave Suite 201 *Sales	Campbell	CA	95008	**800-678-1111***	408-370-2662	176-10
Versant Corp 6539 Dumbarton Cir *NASDAQ: VSNT*	Fremont	CA	94555	**800-837-7268**	510-789-1500	176-1
Versar Inc 6850 Versar Ctr *AMEX: VSR* ■ *Cust Svc	Springfield	VA	22151	**800-283-7727***	703-750-3000	258
Versata Inc 300 Lakeside Dr Suite 1300 *NASDAQ: VATA*	Oakland	CA	94612	**800-984-7638**	510-628-1000	176-1
Verso Books 180 Varick St 10th Fl *Sales	New York	NY	10014	**800-233-4830***	212-807-9680	623-2
Vertex Engineering Services Inc 400 Libbey Pkwy	Weymouth	MA	02189	**888-298-5162**	781-952-6000	191
Vertex Inc 1041 Old Cassatt Rd	Berwyn	PA	19312	**800-355-3500**	610-640-4200	176-1
Vertex Pharmaceuticals Inc 130 Waverly St *NASDAQ: VRTX*	Cambridge	MA	02139	**800-294-2465**	617-444-6100	86
Vertical Communications Inc 5 Cambridge Ctr *Sales	Cambridge	MA	02142	**800-914-9985***	617-354-0600	176-7
Vertis Inc 250 W Pratt St 18th Fl	Baltimore	MD	21201	**800-577-3569**	410-528-9800	615
Vescio Threading Co 14002 Anson Ave	Santa Fe Springs	CA	90670	**800-361-4218**	562-802-1868	446
Vesco Oil Corp 16055 W 12-Mile Rd	Southfield	MI	48076	**800-527-5358**	248-557-1600	569
Vest HD Financial Services 6333 N State Hwy 161 4th Fl	Irving	TX	75038	**800-821-8254**	972-870-6000	393
Vesta Insurance Group Inc 3760 River Run Dr *NYSE: VTA*	Birmingham	AL	35243	**800-444-2955**	205-970-7000	355-4
Vestcom International Inc 5 Henderson Dr	West Caldwell	NJ	07006	**800-865-1821**	973-287-1000	9
Vestin Group Inc 2901 El Camino Ave Suite 206 *NASDAQ: VSTN*	Las Vegas	NV	89102	**800-232-7613**	702-227-0965	498
Veterans Affairs Lakeside Medical Center 333 E Huron St	Chicago	IL	60611	**800-644-1243**	312-569-8387	366-6
Veterans Affairs Medical Center 3701 Loop Rd E	Tuscaloosa	AL	35404	**888-269-3045**	205-554-2000	366-6
Veterans Affairs Medical Center 2400 Hospital Rd	Tuskegee	AL	36083	**800-214-8387**	334-727-0550	366-6
Veterans Affairs Medical Center 500 Hwy 89 N	Prescott	AZ	86313	**800-949-1005**	928-445-4860	366-6
Veterans Affairs Medical Center 1100 N College Ave	Fayetteville	AR	72703	**800-691-8387**	479-443-4301	366-6
Veterans Affairs Medical Center 5901 E 7th St	Long Beach	CA	90822	**888-769-8387**	562-826-8000	366-6
Veterans Affairs Medical Center 3350 La Jolla Village Dr	San Diego	CA	92101	**800-331-8387**	858-552-8585	366-6
Veterans Affairs Medical Center 1055 Clermont St	Denver	CO	80220	**888-336-8262**	303-399-8020	366-6
Veterans Affairs Medical Center 1601 Kirkwood Hwy	Wilmington	DE	19805	**800-450-8262**	302-994-2511	366-6

Name / Address	City	State	ZIP	Toll-Free	Phone	Class
Veterans Affairs Medical Center 1201 NW 16th St	Miami	FL	33125	**888-276-1785**	305-324-4455	366-6
Veterans Affairs Medical Center 7305 N Military Trail	West Palm Beach	FL	33410	**800-972-8262**	561-882-8262	366-6
Veterans Affairs Medical Center 1670 Clairmont Rd	Decatur	GA	30033	**800-944-9726**	404-321-6111	366-6
Veterans Affairs Medical Center 3001 Green Bay Rd	North Chicago	IL	60064	**800-393-0865**	847-688-1900	366-6
Veterans Affairs Medical Center 2121 Lake Ave	Fort Wayne	IN	46805	**800-360-8387**	260-426-5431	366-6
Veterans Affairs Medical Center 1700 E 38th St	Marion	IN	46953	**800-498-8792**	765-674-3321	366-6
Veterans Affairs Medical Center 3600 30th St	Des Moines	IA	50310	**800-294-8387**	515-699-5999	366-6
Veterans Affairs Medical Center 1515 W Pleasant St	Knoxville	IA	50138	**800-816-8878**	641-842-3101	366-6
Veterans Affairs Medical Center 5500 E Kellogg St	Wichita	KS	67218	**888-878-6881**	316-685-2221	366-6
Veterans Affairs Medical Center 1601 Perdido St	New Orleans	LA	70112	**800-935-8387**	504-568-0811	366-6
Veterans Affairs Medical Center 10 N Greene St	Baltimore	MD	21201	**800-463-6295**	410-605-7000	366-6
Veterans Affairs Medical Center 325 E 'H' St	Iron Mountain	MI	49801	**800-215-8262**	906-774-3300	366-6
Veterans Affairs Medical Center 1500 Weiss St	Saginaw	MI	48602	**800-406-5143**	989-497-2500	366-6
Veterans Affairs Medical Center 1 Veterans Dr	Minneapolis	MN	55417	**866-414-5058**	612-725-2000	366-6
Veterans Affairs Medical Center 400 Veterans Ave	Biloxi	MS	39531	**800-296-8872**	228-523-5000	366-6
Veterans Affairs Medical Center 4801 E Linwood Blvd	Kansas City	MO	64128	**800-525-1483**	816-861-4700	366-6
Veterans Affairs Medical Center 915 N Grand Blvd	Saint Louis	MO	63106	**800-228-5459**	314-487-0400	366-6
Veterans Affairs Medical Center 600 S 70th St	Lincoln	NE	68510	**800-451-5796**	402-489-3802	366-6
Veterans Affairs Medical Center 4101 Woolworth Ave	Omaha	NE	68105	**800-608-8806**	402-346-8800	366-6
Veterans Affairs Medical Center 718 Smyth Rd	Manchester	NH	03104	**800-892-8384**	603-624-4366	366-6
Veterans Affairs Medical Center 151 Knollcroft Rd	Lyons	NJ	07939	**800-927-1000**	908-647-0180	366-6
Veterans Affairs Medical Center 1501 San Pedro Dr SE	Albuquerque	NM	87108	**800-465-8262**	505-265-1711	366-6
Veterans Affairs Medical Center 76 Veterans Ave	Bath	NY	14810	**877-845-3247**	607-664-4000	366-6
Veterans Affairs Medical Center 3495 Bailey Ave	Buffalo	NY	14215	**800-532-8387**	716-834-9200	366-6
Veterans Affairs Medical Center 79 Middleville Rd	Northport	NY	11768	**800-827-1000**	631-261-4400	366-6
Veterans Affairs Medical Center 800 Irving Ave	Syracuse	NY	13210	**800-221-2883**	315-425-4400	366-6
Veterans Affairs Medical Center 2300 Ramsey St	Fayetteville	NC	28301	**800-771-6106**	910-488-2120	366-6
Veterans Affairs Medical Center 2101 Elm St N	Fargo	ND	58102	**800-410-9723**	701-232-3241	366-6
Veterans Affairs Medical Center 3200 Vine St	Cincinnati	OH	45220	**888-267-7873**	513-861-3100	366-6
Veterans Affairs Medical Center 10701 East Blvd	Cleveland	OH	44106	**888-350-3100**	216-791-3800	366-6
Veterans Affairs Medical Center 921 NE 13th St	Oklahoma City	OK	73104	**866-835-5273**	405-270-0501	366-6
Veterans Affairs Medical Center 3710 US Veterans Hospital Rd	Portland	OR	97239	**888-233-8305**	503-220-8262	366-6
Veterans Affairs Medical Center 325 New Castle Rd	Butler	PA	16001	**800-362-8262**	724-287-4781	366-6
Veterans Affairs Medical Center 1400 Black Horse Hill Rd	Coatesville	PA	19320	**800-290-6172**	610-384-7711	366-6
Veterans Affairs Medical Center 135 E 38th St	Erie	PA	16504	**800-274-8387**	814-868-8661	366-6
Veterans Affairs Medical Center 1700 S Lincoln Ave	Lebanon	PA	17042	**800-409-8771**	717-272-6621	366-6
Veterans Affairs Medical Center 3900 Woodland Ave	Philadelphia	PA	19104	**800-949-1001**	215-823-5800	366-6
Veterans Affairs Medical Center University Dr C	Pittsburgh	PA	15240	**800-309-8398**	412-688-6000	366-6
Veterans Affairs Medical Center 113 Comanche Rd	Fort Meade	SD	57741	**800-743-1070**	605-347-2511	366-6
Veterans Affairs Medical Center 500 N 5th St	Hot Springs	SD	57747	**800-764-5370**	605-745-2000	366-6
Veterans Affairs Medical Center 6010 Amarillo Blvd W	Amarillo	TX	79106	**800-687-8262**	806-355-9703	366-6
Veterans Affairs Medical Center 215 N Main St	White River Junction	VT	05009	**866-687-8387**	802-295-9363	366-6
Veterans Affairs Medical Center 1540 Spring Valley Dr	Huntington	WV	25704	**800-827-8244**	304-429-6741	366-6
Veterans Affairs Medical Center 510 Butler Ave	Martinsburg	WV	25401	**800-817-3807**	304-263-0811	366-6
Veterans Affairs Medical Center 5000 W National Ave	Milwaukee	WI	53295	**888-469-6614**	414-384-2000	366-6
Veterans Affairs Medical Center 500 E Veterans St	Tomah	WI	54660	**800-872-8662**	608-372-3971	366-6
Veterans Affairs Medical Center 1898 Fort Rd	Sheridan	WY	82801	**800-370-0250**	307-672-3473	366-6
Veterans Affairs Puget Sound Medical Center Marrow Transplant Unit 1660 S Columbian Way	Seattle	WA	98108	**800-329-8387**	206-764-2189	758
Veterans Affairs US Dept of 810 Vermont Ave NW	Washington	DC	20420	**800-827-1000**	202-273-6000	336-15
Veterans of America. Paralyzed 801 18th St NW	Washington	DC	20006	**800-424-8200**	202-872-1300	48-19
Veterans of America. Vietnam 8605 Cameron St Suite 400	Silver Spring	MD	20910	**800-882-1316**	301-585-4000	48-19
Veterans Benefits Administration Education Service 1800 G St NW	Washington	DC	20006	**800-442-4551**	202-273-7132	711
Veterans. Disabled American 3725 Alexandria Pike	Cold Spring	KY	41076	**877-426-2838**	859-441-7300	48-19
Veterans Home of California-Barstow 100 E Veterans Pkwy	Barstow	CA	92311	**800-746-0606**	760-252-6200	780
Veterans Home of California-Chula Vista 700 E Naples Ct	Chula Vista	CA	91911	**888-857-2146**	619-482-6010	780
Veterans Home of California-Yountville PO Box 1200	Yountville	CA	94599	**800-404-8387**	707-944-4541	780
Veterans Memorial Civic & Convention Center 7 Town Sq	Lima	OH	45801	**877-377-0674**	419-224-5222	204
Veterinary Economics Magazine 8033 Flint St	Lenexa	KS	66214	**800-255-6864**	913-492-4300	449-16
Veterinary Medical Assn. Colorado 789 Sherman St Suite 550	Denver	CO	80203	**800-228-5429**	303-318-0447	782
Veterinary Medical Assn. Florida 7131 Lake Ellenor Dr	Orlando	FL	32809	**800-992-3862**	407-851-3862	782
Veterinary Medical Assn. Georgia 2814 Spring Rd Suite 217	Atlanta	GA	30339	**800-853-1625**	678-309-9800	782
Veterinary Medical Assn. Louisiana 8550 United Plaza Blvd Suite 1001	Baton Rouge	LA	70809	**800-524-2996**	225-928-5862	782
Veterinary Medical Assn. Maryland 8015 Corporate Dr Suite A	Baltimore	MD	21236	**888-884-6862**	410-931-3332	782
Veterinary Medical Assn. North Carolina 1611 Jones Franklin Rd Suite 108	Raleigh	NC	27606	**800-446-2862**	919-851-5850	782
Veterinary Medical Assn. North Dakota 921 S 9th St Suite 120	Bismarck	ND	58504	**877-637-6386**	701-221-7740	782
Veterinary Medical Assn. Ohio 3168 Riverside Dr	Columbus	OH	43221	**800-662-6862**	614-486-7253	782
Veterinary Medical Assn. Oregon 1880 Lancaster Dr NE Suite 118	Salem	OR	97305	**800-235-3502**	503-399-0311	782
Veterinary Medical Assn. Pennsylvania 905 W Governor Rd Suite 320	Hershey	PA	17033	**888-550-7862**	717-533-7934	782
Veterinary Medical Assn. Rhode Island 11 S Angell St Suite 347	Providence	RI	02906	**877-521-0103**		782
Veterinary Medical Assn. Tennessee 618 Church St Suite 220	Nashville	TN	37219	**800-697-3587**	615-254-3687	782
Veterinary Medical Assn. Virginia 2314-C Commerce Ctr Dr	Rockville	VA	23146	**800-937-8862**	804-749-8058	782
Veterinary Medical Assn. Washington State PO Box 962	Bellevue	WA	98009	**800-399-7862**	425-454-8381	782
Veterinary Medical Assn. Wisconsin 301 N Broom St	Madison	WI	53703	**888-254-5202**	608-257-3665	782
Veterinary Medical Society. New York State 9 Highland Ave	Albany	NY	12205	**800-876-9867**	518-437-0787	782
Veterinary Medicine Magazine 8033 Flint St	Lenexa	KS	66214	**800-255-6864**	913-492-4300	449-16
Veterinary Pet Insurance Inc 3060 Saturn St	Brea	CA	92821	**800-872-7387**		384-1
Veterinary Pharmacies of America 2854 Antoine Dr	Houston	TX	77092	**877-838-7979**	713-688-3321	574
VetLife 1001 Office Pk Rd Suite 201	West Des Moines	IA	50265	**888-462-3493**	515-224-0788	574
Vetoquinol Canada Inc 2000 ch Georges	Lavaltrie	QC	J0K1H0	**800-363-1700**	450-586-2252	574
Vetoquinol EVSCO Pharmaceuticals 101 Lincoln Ave	Buena	NJ	08310	**800-387-2607**		574
VetriCare 590 Main St Suite B	Templeton	CA	93465	**800-238-5999**	805-434-5999	574
VF Activewear 4408 W Linebaugh Ave	Tampa	FL	33624	**800-444-5574**	813-963-6153	153-3
VF Imageware 3375 Joseph Martin Hwy	Martinsville	VA	24112	**800-832-6469**	276-632-5601	153-3
VF Intimates 3025 Windward Plaza Suite 600	Alpharetta	GA	30005	**800-366-8339**	770-753-0900	153-18
VF Jeanswear LP 335 Church Ct PO Box 21488 *Orders	Greensboro	NC	27420	**800-888-8010***	336-332-3400	153-11
VFA Inc 266 Summer St	Boston	MA	02210	**800-693-3132**	617-772-8277	176-1
VFL Technology Corp 16 Hagerty Blvd	West Chester	PA	19382	**800-882-8358**	610-918-1100	791
VHA Inc 220 E Las Colinas Blvd	Irving	TX	75039	**800-842-5146**	972-830-0000	455
Vi-Chem Corp 55 Cottage Grove St SW	Grand Rapids	MI	49507	**800-477-8501**	616-247-8501	594-2
Vi-Jon Labs Inc 8515 Page Ave	Saint Louis	MO	63114	**800-325-8167**	314-427-1000	211
Via Christi Rehabilitation Center 1151 N Rock Rd	Wichita	KS	67206	**800-667-4241**	316-634-3400	366-4
VIA Metropolitan Transit 800 W Myrtle St	San Antonio	TX	78212	**866-362-4200**	210-362-2000	460
VIA NET.WORKS Inc 3575 Piedmont Rd Suite 710 *NASDAQ: VNWI*	Atlanta	GA	30305	**800-749-1706**	404-926-3611	390
VIA Rail Canada Inc 3 Place Ville-Marie Suite 500	Montreal	QC	H3B2C9	**800-681-2561**	514-871-6000	635
ViaCell Inc 245 1st St 15th Fl *NASDAQ: VIAC*	Cambridge	MA	02142	**866-874-2235**	617-577-7744	86
ViaCirq 400 South Point Blvd Bldg 501 Suite 230 *Cust Svc	Canonsburg	PA	15317	**877-952-6100***	724-745-2362	468
Viacom Outdoor Inc 2502 N Black Canyon Hwy	Phoenix	AZ	85009	**800-966-9569**	602-246-9569	8
viaLink Co 13155 Noel Rd Suite 700	Dallas	TX	75240	**888-842-5465**	972-934-5500	176-7
ViaSource Funding Group LLC 81 E Water St	Toms River	NJ	08753	**888-828-4404**	732-280-8500	783
ViaTech Publishing Solutions 1440 5th Ave	Bay Shore	NY	11706	**800-645-8558**	631-968-8500	87
Viatical Benefactors LLC 100 Galleria Pkwy Suite 440	Atlanta	GA	30339	**888-404-4484**	770-951-4760	783
Viatical & Life Settlement Assn of America (VLSAA) 800 Mayfair Cir	Orlando	FL	32803	**800-842-9811**	407-894-3797	49-9
Viatical Settlements Inc 10801 NE Reinking Rd	Kansas City	MO	64156	**800-650-3333**	816-792-3663	783
Viatran Corp 300 Industrial Dr	Grand Island	NY	14073	**800-688-0030**	716-773-1700	252
Vicksburg Convention & Visitors Bureau 1221 Washington St	Vicksburg	MS	39183	**800-221-3536**	601-636-9421	205
Vicksburg-Warren County Chamber of Commerce 2020 Mission 66	Vicksburg	MS	39180	**888-842-5728**	601-636-1012	137
Vicon Industries Inc 89 Arkay Dr *AMEX: VII* ■ *Cust Svc	Hauppauge	NY	11788	**800-645-9116***	631-952-2288	633
Vicor Corp 25 Frontage Rd *NASDAQ: VICR*	Andover	MA	01810	**800-869-5300**	978-470-2900	252

				Toll-Free	Phone	Class
Victaulic Co of America						
4901 Kesslersville Rd	Easton	PA	18040	**800-742-5842***	610-559-3300	584
*Sales						
Victim Assistance. National Organization for 1730 Park Rd NW	Washington	DC	20010	**800-879-6682**	202-232-6682	48-8
Victims of Crime. National Center for						
2000 M St NW Suite 480	Washington	DC	20036	**800-394-2255**	202-467-8700	48-8
Victims of Predatory Abduction. Jimmy Ryce Center for						
908 Coquina Ln	Vero Beach	FL	32963	**800-546-7923**	772-492-0200	48-6
Victor Equipment Co 2800 Airport Rd	Denton	TX	76207	**800-426-1888**	940-566-2000	798
Victor Graphics Inc 1211 Bernard Dr	Baltimore	MD	21223	**800-899-8303**	410-233-8300	614
Victor L Phillips Co						
4100 Gardner Ave	Kansas City	MO	64120	**800-878-9290**	816-241-9290	353
Victor Printing Inc 1 Victor Way	Sharon	PA	16146	**800-443-2845**	724-342-2106	111
Victor Technology Inc						
780 W Belden Ave	Addison	IL	60101	**800-628-2420**	630-268-8400	171-2
Victoria Advocate PO Box 1518	Victoria	TX	77902	**800-234-8108**	361-575-1451	522-2
Victoria Cruises Inc 57-08 39th Ave	Woodside	NY	11377	**800-348-8084**	212-818-1680	218
Victoria Inns & Suites Hwy 315	Pittston	PA	18640	**800-937-4667**	570-655-1234	373
Victoria Regent Hotel 1234 Wharf St	Victoria	BC	V8W3H9	**800-663-7472**	250-386-2211	372
Victoria Theatre 138 N Main St	Dayton	OH	45402	**888-228-3630**	937-228-3630	562
Victoria Vaudeville Theater						
1228 Market St	Wheeling	WV	26003	**800-505-7464**	304-233-7464	562
Victoria Vogue Inc 90 Southland Dr	Bethlehem	PA	18017	**800-967-7833**	610-865-1500	211
Victorian Condo-Hotel & Conference Center 6300 Seawall Blvd	Galveston	TX	77551	**800-231-6363**	409-740-3555	373
Victorian Homes 109 14th St	Middlebury	IN	46540	**800-999-5841**	574-825-5841	495
Victorian Inn 487 Foam St	Monterey	CA	93940	**800-232-4141**	831-373-8000	373
Victorian Paper Co 15600 W 99th St	Lenexa	KS	66219	**800-700-2035***	913-438-3995	322
*Cust Svc						
Victoria's Secret Direct LLC						
3425 Morse Crossing	Columbus	OH	43219	**800-888-1500**	614-337-5000	451
Victoria's Secret Stores						
4 Limited Pkwy	Reynoldsburg	OH	43068	**800-411-5116**	614-577-7000	155-6
Victory Aviation Inc						
2710 County Rd 60	Auburn	IN	46706	**800-837-5517**	260-927-4040	14
Victory Electric Co-op Assn Inc						
PO Box 1335	Dodge City	KS	67801	**800-279-7915**	620-227-2139	244
Victory Funds PO Box 182593	Columbus	OH	43218	**800-539-3863**		517
Victory Plastics International						
25 Shelley Rd	Haverhill	MA	01835	**800-541-5108***	978-373-1551	589
*Cust Svc						
Victory Refrigeration Inc						
110 Woodcrest Rd	Cherry Hill	NJ	08003	**800-523-5008**	856-428-4200	650
Victory Studios 2247 15th Ave W	Seattle	WA	98119	**888-282-1776**	206-282-1776	501
Victory Supermarkets Inc						
75 N Main St	Leominster	MA	01453	**800-536-1955**	978-840-2200	339
Victory White Metal Co						
6100 Roland Ave	Cleveland	OH	44127	**800-635-5050**	216-271-1400	476
Video Display Corp						
1868 Tucker Industrial Rd	Tucker	GA	30084	**800-241-5005***	770-938-2080	171-4
NASDAQ: VIDE ■ *Cust Svc						
Video Event Magazine						
86 Elm St	Peterborough	NH	03458	**800-677-8847**	603-924-7271	449-9
Video King Gaming Systems						
3211 Nebraska Ave	Council Bluffs	IA	51501	**800-635-9912**	712-323-1488	317
Video Products Distributors						
150 Parkshore Dr	Folsom	CA	95630	**800-366-2111**	916-605-1500	500
Video Software Dealers Assn (VSDA)						
16530 Ventura Blvd Suite 400	Encino	CA	91436	**800-955-8732**	818-385-1500	49-18
Video Store Magazine						
201 E Sandpointe Ave Suite 600	Santa Ana	CA	92707	**800-854-3112**	714-513-8400	449-21
Videoflicks.com Inc 1654 Avenue Rd	Toronto	ON	M5M3Y1	**800-690-2879**	416-782-5084	784
Videojet Technologies Inc						
1500 Mittel Blvd	Wood Dale	IL	60191	**800-843-3610***	630-860-7300	379
*Cust Svc						
Videomaker Magazine 1350 E 9th St	Chico	CA	95928	**888-884-3226**	530-891-8410	449-9
Videotek Inc 243 Shoemaker Rd	Pottstown	PA	19464	**800-800-5719***	610-327-2292	633
*Sales						
Videotex Systems Inc 10255 Miller Rd	Dallas	TX	75238	**800-888-4336**	972-231-9200	176-8
Vidmar Storage Technologies. Stanley						
11 Grammes Rd PO Box 1151	Allentown	PA	18105	**800-523-9462**	610-797-6600	281
Vie de France Bakery						
2070 Chain Bridge Rd Suite 500	Vienna	VA	22182	**800-446-4404**	703-442-9205	69
Viejas Casino 5000 Willows Rd	Alpine	CA	91901	**800-847-6537**	619-445-5400	133
Vienna Sausage Mfg Co						
2501 N Damen Ave	Chicago	IL	60647	**800-621-8183**	773-278-7800	291-26
Vietnam Veterans of America (VVA)						
8605 Cameron St Suite 400	Silver Spring	MD	20910	**800-882-1316**	301-585-4000	48-19
ViewCast Corp						
17300 N Dallas Pkwy Suite 2000	Dallas	TX	75248	**800-540-4119**	972-488-7200	174
Viewlocity Inc						
3475 Piedmont Rd Suite 1700	Atlanta	GA	30305	**877-512-8900**	404-267-6400	176-10
Viewpoint Corp 498 7th Ave 18th Fl	New York	NY	10018	**866-843-9764**	212-201-0800	176-8
NASDAQ: VWPT						
ViewSonic Corp 381 Brea Canyon Rd	Walnut	CA	91789	**800-888-8583**	909-444-8800	171-4
Viewsonics Inc						
3103 N Andrews Ave Ext	Pompano Beach	FL	33064	**800-645-7600**	954-971-8439	633
Vigil Allan Ford 6790 Mt Zion Blvd	Marrow	GA	30260	**800-222-3597**	678-364-3673	57
Vigilant Insurance Co						
15 Mountain View Rd	Warren	NJ	07059	**800-252-4670**	908-903-2000	384-4
Vignette Corp						
1301 S Mopac Expy Bldg 4	Austin	TX	78746	**888-608-9900**	512-741-4300	176-1
NASDAQ: VIGN						
Viking Acoustical Corp						
21480 Heath Ave	Lakeville	MN	55044	**800-328-8385**	952-469-3405	314-1
Viking Components Inc						
30200 Avenida de Las Banderas	Rancho Santa Margarita	CA	92688	**800-338-2361**	949-643-7255	613
Viking Corp 210 N Industrial Pk Dr	Hastings	MI	49058	**800-968-9501**	269-945-9501	681
Viking Drill & Tool Inc 355 State St	Saint Paul	MN	55107	**800-328-4655**	651-227-8911	484
Viking Electric Supply Inc						
451 Industrial Blvd W	Minneapolis	MN	55413	**800-435-3345**	612-627-1300	245
Viking Energy Royalty Trust						
330 5th Ave SW Calgary Pl Suite 400	Calgary	AB	T2P0L4	**877-292-2527**	403-268-3175	662
Viking Engineering & Development Inc						
5750 Main St NE	Fridley	MN	55432	**800-328-2403***	763-571-2400	809
*Sales						
Viking Forest Products LLC						
7615 Smetana Ln Suite 140	Eden Prairie	MN	55344	**800-733-3801**	952-941-6512	190-3
Viking Metal Cabinet Co Inc						
5321 W 65th St	Chicago	IL	60638	**800-776-7767**	708-594-1111	281
Viking Office Products Inc						
950 W 190 St	Torrance	CA	90502	**800-421-1222***	310-225-4500	451
*Cust Svc						
Viking River Cruises						
21820 Burbank Blvd	Woodland Hills	CA	91367	**877-668-4546**	818-227-1234	218
Viking Seafoods Inc 50 Crystal St	Malden	MA	02148	**800-225-3920**	781-324-1050	291-14
Viking Trailways 201 Glendale Rd	Joplin	MO	64804	**800-400-2779**	417-781-2779	109
Villa Florence Hotel						
225 Powell St	San Francisco	CA	94102	**800-553-4411**	415-397-7700	373
Villa Furniture Mfg 502 E Julianna St	Anaheim	CA	92801	**888-707-7272**	714-535-7273	678
Villa Julie College						
1525 Green Spring Valley Rd	Stevenson	MD	21153	**877-468-6852**	410-486-7000	163
Villa Lighting Supply Inc						
1218 S Vandeventer Ave	Saint Louis	MO	63110	**800-325-0963**	314-531-2600	386
Villa Roma Resort & Conference Center						
356 Villa Roma Rd	Callicoon	NY	12723	**800-727-8455**	845-887-4880	655
Villa Royale Inn						
1620 Indian Trail	Palm Springs	CA	92264	**800-245-2314**	760-327-2314	373
Village Bay Spa at Lake Arrowhead Resort						
27984 Hwy 189	Lake Arrowhead	CA	92352	**800-800-6792**	909-744-3000	698
Village at Breckenridge Resort						
535 S Park Ave	Breckenridge	CO	80424	**800-332-0424**	970-453-2000	655
Village Farms LP						
7 Christopher Way	Eatontown	NJ	07724	**877-777-7718**	732-676-3000	11-11
Village on the Green 500 Village Pl	Longwood	FL	32779	**800-432-8833***	407-788-2300	659
*Mktg						
Village Homes of Colorado Inc						
6 W Dry Creek Cir	Littleton	CO	80120	**866-752-2322**	303-795-1976	639
Village Inn 400 W 48th Ave	Denver	CO	80216	**800-800-3644**	303-296-2121	657
Village Inn Motel						
1875 Mohawk Blvd	Springfield	OR	97477	**800-327-6871**	541-747-4546	373
Village Latch Inn 101 Hill St	Southampton	NY	11968	**800-545-2824**	631-283-2160	373
Village Nurseries 1589 N Main St	Orange	CA	92867	**800-542-0209**	714-279-3100	318
Village South Inc 3180 Biscayne Blvd	Miami	FL	33137	**800-443-3784**	305-573-3784	712
Village Voice 36 Cooper Sq	New York	NY	10003	**800-875-2997***	212-475-3300	522-4
*Cust Svc						
VillageEDOCS Inc						
14471 Chambers Rd Suite 105	Tustin	CA	92780	**800-866-0883**	714-734-1030	176-7
Villager Lodge 1 Sylvan Way	Parsippany	NJ	07054	**888-821-5738**	973-428-9700	369
Villager Lodge Franchise Systems Inc						
1 Sylvan Way	Parsippany	NJ	07054	**888-821-5738**	973-428-9700	369
Hearthside by Villager						
1 Sylvan Way	Parsippany	NJ	07054	**888-821-5738**	973-428-9700	369
Villager Lodge 1 Sylvan Way	Parsippany	NJ	07054	**888-821-5738**	973-428-9700	369
Villager Premier 1 Sylvan Way	Parsippany	NJ	07054	**888-821-5738**	973-428-9700	369
Villager Premier 1 Sylvan Way	Parsippany	NJ	07054	**888-821-5738**	973-428-9700	369
Villages of Lake Sumter Inc						
1100 Main St	The Villages	FL	32159	**800-346-4556**	352-753-2270	639
Villagio Inn & Spa						
6481 Washington St	Yountville	CA	94599	**800-351-1133**	707-944-8877	373
Villamare						
27-C Coligny Plaza	Hilton Head Island	SC	29928	**800-854-6802**	843-842-6212	373
Villas of Grand Cypress						
1 N Jacaranda	Orlando	FL	32836	**800-835-7377**	407-239-4700	655
Villas de Santa Fe 400 Griffin St	Santa Fe	NM	87501	**800-869-6790**	505-988-3000	373
Villas by the Sea Resort						
1175 N Beachview Dr	Jekyll Island	GA	31527	**800-841-6262**	912-635-2521	655
Villas at Sunny Acres						
2501 E 104th Ave	Denver	CO	80233	**800-447-2092**	303-452-4181	659
Villaume Industries Inc						
2926 Lone Oak Cir	Saint Paul	MN	55121	**800-488-3610***	651-454-3610	805
*Cust Svc						
Villere's Florist 1107 Veterans Blvd	Metairie	LA	70005	**800-845-5373**	504-833-3716	287
Villeroy & Boch Tableware Ltd						
5 Vaughn Dr Suite 303	Princeton	NJ	08540	**800-845-5376**	609-734-7800	357
Vilter Mfg Corp						
5555 S Packard Ave PO Box 8904	Cudahy	WI	53110	**800-862-2677***	414-744-0111	650
*Orders						
Vim & Vigor Magazine						
1010 E Missouri Ave	Phoenix	AZ	85014	**800-282-5850**	602-395-5850	449-13
Vimco Concrete Accessories Inc						
300 Hansen Access Rd	King of Prussia	PA	19406	**888-468-4626**	610-768-0500	190-1
Vimich Traffic Logistics Inc						
12201 Tecumseh Rd E	Tecumseh	ON	N8N1M3	**800-284-1045**	519-735-6933	440
Vincennes Sun-Commercial						
PO Box 396	Vincennes	IN	47591	**800-876-9955**	812-886-9955	522-2
Vincennes University 1002 N 1st St	Vincennes	IN	47591	**800-742-9198**	812-888-4313	160
Jasper Campus 850 College Ave	Jasper	IN	47546	**800-809-8852**	812-482-3030	160
Vincent Implements Inc 8258 Hwy 45	Martin	TN	38237	**800-624-8754**	731-587-3824	270
Vincor International Inc						
441 Courtneypark Dr E	Mississauga	ON	L5T2V3	**800-265-9463**	905-564-6900	81-3
TSE: VN						
Vindicator The						
107 Vindicator Sq PO Box 780	Youngstown	OH	44501	**800-686-5199**	330-747-1471	522-2
Vineland (Greater) Chamber of Commerce 2115 S Delsea Dr	Vineland	NJ	08360	**800-309-0019**	856-691-7400	137
Vineyard National Bancorp						
9590 Foothill Blvd	Rancho Cucamonga	CA	91730	**800-442-4996**	909-987-0177	71
NASDAQ: VNBC						
Vinings Investment Properties Trust						
2839 Paces Ferry Rd NW Suite 880	Atlanta	GA	30339	**800-849-5868**	770-984-9500	641
Vinson Carl Veterans Affairs Medical Center 1826 Veterans Blvd	Dublin	GA	31021	**800-595-5229**	478-272-1210	366-6
Vintage Books 1745 Broadway	New York	NY	10019	**800-733-3000***	212-751-2600	623-2
*Orders						
Vintage Inn Napa Valley						
6541 Washington St	Yountville	CA	94599	**800-351-1133**	707-944-1112	373
Vintex Inc 1 Mount Forest Dr	Mount Forest	ON	N0G2L2	**800-846-8399**	519-323-0100	730-2
Vintners Assn. American						
1212 New York Ave NW Suite 425	Washington	DC	20005	**800-879-4637**	202-783-2756	49-6

Name / Address	City	State	ZIP	Toll-Free	Phone	Class
Vintners Inn 4350 Barnes Rd	Santa Rosa	CA	95403	**800-421-2584**	707-575-7350	373
Vinyl Siding Institute (VSI) 1667 K St NW Suite 1000	Washington	DC	20006	**888-367-8741**	202-974-5200	49-13
Vinyl Source Inc 427 Thatcher Ln	Youngstown	OH	44515	**800-824-4067**	330-792-6511	591
Vinylex Corp 2636 Byington Rd	Knoxville	TN	37931	**800-624-4435**	865-690-2211	589
Violence Hotline. National Domestic PO Box 161810	Austin	TX	78716	**800-799-7233**	512-794-1133	48-6
Violence. National Resource Center on Domestic 6400 Flank Dr Suite 1300	Harrisburg	PA	17112	**800-537-2238**	717-545-6400	48-6
VIP (Value In Pharmaceuticals) 3000 Alt Blvd	Grand Island	NY	14072	**800-724-3784**	716-773-4600	237
VIP Tickets 14515 Ventura Blvd Suite 210	Sherman Oaks	CA	91403	**800-328-4253**	818-907-1548	735
VIP Tour & Charter Bus Co 129-137 Fox St	Portland	ME	04101	**800-337-4457**	207-772-4457	748
VIPride.com 15111 N Hayden Rd Suite 300	Scottsdale	AZ	85260	**877-474-4847**	480-905-1234	433
ViPS Inc 1 W Pennsylvania Ave Suite 700	Towson	MD	21204	**888-289-8477**	410-832-8300	176-10
Vira Mfg Inc 1 Buckingham Ave	Perth Amboy	NJ	08861	**800-305-8472**	732-442-8472	281
Viracon Inc 800 Park Dr	Owatonna	MN	55060	**800-533-2080**	507-451-9555	325
Virage Logic Corp 47100 Bayside Pkwy *NASDAQ: VIRL*	Fremont	CA	94538	**877-360-6690**	510-360-8000	686
Viragen Inc 865 SW 78th Ave Suite 100 *AMEX: VRA*	Plantation	FL	33324	**888-847-2436**	954-233-8746	86
Virbac Corp 3200 Meacham Blvd	Fort Worth	TX	76137	**800-338-3659**	817-831-5030	568
Virchow Krause & Co LLP 10 Terrace Ct	Madison	WI	53718	**800-362-7301**	608-249-6622	2
Virco Mfg Corp 2027 Harpers Way *AMEX: VIR* ■ *Cust Svc	Torrance	CA	90501	**800-448-4726***	310-533-0474	314-3
Virgin Atlantic Airways Ltd 747 Belden Ave	Norwalk	CT	06850	**800-862-8621**	203-750-2000	26
Virgin Atlantic Flying Club 747 Belden Ave	Norwalk	CT	06850	**800-365-9500**		27
Virgin Megastores USA c/o SJ Communications 17012 Enadia Way	Lake Balboa	CA	91406	**877-484-7446**	818-881-3889	514
Virginia *Child Support Enforcement Div* 730 E Broad St	Richmond	VA	23219	**800-468-8894**	804-692-1501	335
College Savings Plan PO Box 607	Richmond	VA	23218	**888-567-0540**	804-786-0719	711
Criminal Injuries Compensation Fund 11513 Allecingie Pkwy	Richmond	VA	23235	**800-522-4007**	804-378-3434	335
Housing Development Authority 601 S Belvidere St	Richmond	VA	23220	**800-968-7837**	804-782-1986	335
Rehabilitative Services Dept 8004 Franklin Farms Dr	Richmond	VA	23229	**800-552-5019**	804-662-7000	335
State Parks Div 203 Governor St Suite 213 *Resv	Richmond	VA	23219	**800-933-7275***	804-786-1712	335
Tourism Corp 901 E Byrd St	Richmond	VA	23219	**800-847-4882**	804-786-2051	335
Virginia Assn of Realtors 10231 Telegraph Rd	Glen Allen	VA	23059	**800-755-8271**	804-264-5033	642
Virginia Baptist Hospital 3300 Rivermont Ave	Lynchburg	VA	24503	**800-423-5535**	434-947-4000	366-2
Virginia Beach Convention & Visitor Bureau 2101 Parks Ave Suite 500	Virginia Beach	VA	23451	**800-700-7702**	757-437-4700	205
Virginia Beach Resort Hotel & Conference Center 2800 Shore Dr	Virginia Beach	VA	23451	**800-468-2722**	757-481-9000	655
Virginia Chamber of Commerce 9 S 5th St	Richmond	VA	23219	**800-477-7682**	804-644-1607	138
Virginia Commonwealth University 821 W Franklin St	Richmond	VA	23284	**800-841-3638**	804-828-0100	163
Virginia Credit Union 7500 Boulders View Dr	Richmond	VA	23225	**800-285-5051**	804-323-6800	216
Virginia Crossings Resort 1000 Virginia Ctr Pkwy	Glen Allen	VA	23059	**888-444-6553**	804-262-1010	655
Virginia Dare Extract Co Inc 882 3rd Ave	Brooklyn	NY	11232	**800-847-4500**	718-788-1776	291-15
Virginia Financial Group Inc 102 S Main St *NASDAQ: VFGI*	Culpeper	VA	22701	**800-825-4003**	540-825-4800	355-2
Virginia Fork Produce Inc PO Box 148	Edenton	NC	27932	**800-334-7716**	252-482-2165	11-11
Virginia Gazette 216 Ironbound Rd	Williamsburg	VA	23188	**800-944-6908**	757-220-1736	522-4
Virginia Intermont College 1013 Moore St	Bristol	VA	24201	**800-451-1842**	276-669-6101	163
Virginia International Terminals Inc PO Box 1387	Norfolk	VA	23501	**800-541-2431**	757-440-7000	457
Virginia Journal of Education 116 S 3rd St	Richmond	VA	23219	**800-552-9554**	804-648-5801	449-8
Virginia KMP Corp 4100 Platinum Way	Dallas	TX	75237	**800-285-8567**	214-330-7731	15
Virginia Marti College 11724 Detroit Ave	Lakewood	OH	44107	**800-473-4350**	216-221-8584	159
Virginia Medical News 4205 Dover Rd	Richmond	VA	23221	**800-746-6768**	804-353-2721	449-16
Virginia Medical Society 4205 Dover Rd	Richmond	VA	23221	**800-746-6768**	804-353-2721	466
Virginia Military Institute 319 Letcher Ave	Lexington	VA	24450	**800-767-4207**	540-464-7207	163
Virginia Mirror Co Inc PO Box 5431	Martinsville	VA	24115	**800-826-4776**	276-632-9816	325
Virginia Natural Gas Inc 5100 E Virginia Beach Blvd *Cust Svc	Norfolk	VA	23502	**866-229-3578***	757-466-5400	774
Virginia Peninsula Chamber of Commerce 1919 Commerce Dr Suite 320	Hampton	VA	23666	**800-556-1822**	757-262-2000	137
Virginia Plastics Co Inc 3453 Aerial Way Dr	Roanoke	VA	24018	**888-905-2225**	540-981-9700	804
Virginia Press Services Inc 11529 Nuckols Rd	Glen Allen	VA	23059	**800-849-8717**	804-521-7570	612

Name / Address	City	State	ZIP	Toll-Free	Phone	Class
Virginia Railway Express (VRE) 1500 King St Suite 200	Alexandria	VA	22314	**800-743-3873**	703-684-1001	460
Virginia Risk Co 9200 Keystone Crossing Suite 300	Indianapolis	IN	46240	**800-523-6944**	317-818-2089	384-7
Virginia Satellite Educational Network (VSEN) PO Box 2120	Richmond	VA	23218	**800-246-8736**	804-692-0335	620
Virginia State University 1 Haydens Dr	Petersburg	VA	23806	**800-871-7611**	804-524-5000	163
Virginia Theatre 245 W 52nd St	New York	NY	10019	**800-432-7250**	212-239-6200	732
Virginia Transformer Corp 220 Glade View Dr	Roanoke	VA	24012	**800-882-3944**	540-345-9892	756
Virginia Veterinary Medical Assn 2314-C Commerce Ctr Dr	Rockville	VA	23146	**800-937-8862**	804-749-8058	782
Virginia Wesleyan College 1584 Wesleyan Dr	Norfolk	VA	23502	**800-737-8684**	757-455-3200	163
Virginian Lodge 750 W Broadway PO Box 1052	Jackson Hole	WY	83001	**800-262-4999**	307-733-2792	373
Virginian-Pilot 150 N Bramelton Ave	Norfolk	VA	23510	**800-446-2004**	757-446-2000	522-2
Virginian Suites 1500 Arlington Blvd	Arlington	VA	22209	**800-275-2866**	703-522-9600	373
ViroLogic Inc 345 Oyster Point Blvd *NASDAQ: VLGC* ■ *Cust Svc	South San Francisco	CA	94080	**800-777-0177***	650-635-1100	229
Virtronic/Four Seasons 4680 Parkway Dr Suite 200	Mason	OH	45040	**877-844-5032**	513-398-3695	10
Virtual Ink Inc 20 Guest St Suite 520	Boston	MA	02135	**877-696-4646**	617-987-0410	171-1
Virtual Turf 1800 Industrial Pk Dr PO Box 732	Grand Haven	MI	49417	**800-560-7795**	616-847-9121	701
VirtualBank 3801 PGA Blvd Suite 700 PO Box 109638	Palm Beach Gardens	FL	33410	**877-998-2265**	561-776-8860	71
Virtuoso 500 Main St Suite 400	Fort Worth	TX	76102	**800-401-4274**	817-870-0300	761
ViryaNet Ltd 2 Willow St *NASDAQ: VRYA*	Southborough	MA	01745	**800-661-7096**	508-490-8600	176-1
Visa International PO Box 8999	San Francisco	CA	94128	**800-847-2911**	650-432-3200	213
Visalia Chamber of Commerce 720 W Mineral King Ave	Visalia	CA	93291	**877-847-2542**	559-734-5876	137
Visalia Convention & Visitors Bureau 303 E Acequia Ave	Visalia	CA	93291	**800-524-0303**	559-713-4000	205
Visara International Inc 6833 Mt Herman Rd	Morrisville	NC	27560	**888-334-4380**	919-882-0200	174
Viscount Gort Hotel 1670 Portage Ave	Winnipeg	MB	R3J0C9	**800-665-1122**	204-775-0451	372
Viscount Suite Hotel 4855 E Broadway Blvd	Tucson	AZ	85711	**800-527-9666**	520-745-6500	373
Visible Computer Supply Inc 1750 Wallace Ave	Saint Charles	IL	60174	**800-323-0628**	630-377-2586	111
Visible Systems Corp 201 Spring St *Sales	Lexington	MA	02421	**800-684-7425***	781-778-0200	176-1
VisiNet 715 Middle Ground Blvd *Cust Svc	Newport News	VA	23606	**800-286-0674***	757-873-4500	387
Vision Care 108 Acorn Hill Ln	Apex	NC	27502	**888-657-4448**	919-303-2584	265
Vision Council of America (VCA) 1700 Diagonal Rd Suite 500	Alexandria	VA	22314	**800-424-8422**	703-548-4560	49-4
Vision-Ease Lens Inc 700 54th Ave N *Cust Svc	Saint Cloud	MN	56302	**800-328-3449***	320-251-8782	531
Vision Fitness 500 South CP Ave	Lake Mills	WI	53551	**800-335-4348**	920-648-4090	263
Vision Institute. Better Vision Council of America 1700 Diagonal Rd Suite 500	Alexandria	VA	22314	**800-424-8422**	703-548-4560	48-17
Vision-Sciences Inc 9 Strathmore Rd *NASDAQ: VSCI*	Natick	MA	01760	**800-874-9975**	508-650-9971	375
Vision Service Plan (VSP) 3333 Quality Dr *Cust Svc	Rancho Cordova	CA	95670	**800-852-7600***	916-851-5000	384-3
Vision Solutions Inc 17911 Von Karman Ave 5th Fl	Irvine	CA	92614	**800-683-4667**	949-253-6500	176-12
Visioneer Inc 5673 Gibraltar Dr Suite 150 *Cust Svc	Pleasanton	CA	94588	**888-229-4172***	925-251-6300	171-7
Visions Federal Credit Union 24 McKinley Ave	Endicott	NY	13760	**800-242-2120**	607-754-7900	216
VisionTek Inc 1610 Colonial Pkwy	Inverness	IL	60067	**800-680-4424**	224-836-3000	613
VisitBritain 551 5th Ave Suite 701	New York	NY	10176	**800-462-2748**	212-986-2266	764
Visiting Health Professionals 68 Sweeten Creek Rd	Asheville	NC	28803	**800-627-1533**	828-252-2255	358
Visiting Nurse Assns of America (VNAA) 99 Summer St Suite 1700	Boston	MA	02110	**800-426-2547**	617-737-3200	49-8
Visiting Nurse Corp of Colorado 390 Grant St	Denver	CO	80203	**888-862-9693**	303-744-6363	358
Visiting Nurse Service of New York Hospice Care 1250 Broadway 7th Fl	New York	NY	10001	**888-867-1225**	212-609-1900	365
Viskase Corp 625 Willowbrook Centre Pkwy	Willowbrook	IL	60527	**800-323-8562**	630-789-4900	538
Vista Alliance Eye Care Assoc 160 E 56th St 9th Fl	New York	NY	10022	**888-695-2745**	212-758-3838	785
Vista Bakery Inc 3000 Mt Pleasant St PO Box 888	Burlington	IA	52601	**800-553-2343**	319-754-6551	291-9
Vista Color Lab Inc 2048 Fulton Rd	Cleveland	OH	44113	**800-890-0062**	216-651-2830	338
Vista Health Plan 300 S Park Rd	Hollywood	FL	33021	**800-447-5116**	954-962-3008	384-3
Vista Host Inc 10370 Richmond Ave Suite 150	Houston	TX	77042	**800-688-4782**	713-267-5800	369
VISTA Inc 29516 Southfield Rd Suite 104	Southfield	MI	48076	**888-873-8478**	248-559-3500	392
Vista Paint Corp 2020 E Orangethorpe Ave	Fullerton	CA	92831	**800-698-4782**	714-680-3800	540
Vista RMS 950 Herndon Pkwy Suite 360	Herndon	VA	20170	**888-535-7401**	703-481-6030	707
Vista Verde Guest & Ski Ranch Box 465	Steamboat Springs	CO	80477	**800-526-7433**	970-879-3858	238
VistaCare Hospice 6431 S East St	Indianapolis	IN	46227	**800-480-9408**	317-788-0300	365
VistaCare Hospice 5201 Venice NE Suite A&B	Albuquerque	NM	87113	**888-605-1969**	505-821-5404	365
VistaCare Hospice 1515 W Calle Sur St	Hobbs	NM	88240	**800-658-6844**	505-392-2060	365

Company / Address	City	State	ZIP	Toll-Free	Phone	Class
VistaCare Hospice						
8135 Beechmont Ave	Cincinnati	OH	45255	**800-865-5980**	513-474-2550	365
Vistamax Inc 6723 Mowry Ave	Newark	CA	94560	**866-758-4782**		172
Vistar/VSA Corp						
12650 E Arapahoe Rd Bldg D	Englewood	CO	80112	**800-880-9900**	303-662-7100	292-8
Vistawall Architectural Products						
803 Airport Rd	Terrell	TX	75160	**800-869-4567**	972-563-2624	232
Visteon Corp 17000 Rotunda Dr	Dearborn	MI	48121	**800-847-8366**	313-755-2867	60
NYSE: VC						
Vistronix Inc						
8401 Greensboro Dr Suite 500	McLean	VA	22102	**800-483-2434**	703-734-2270	178
Visual Departures Ltd PO Box 1326	Passaic	NJ	07055	**800-628-2003**	973-405-6455	580
Visual Graphic Systems Inc						
500 10th Ave 7th Fl	New York	NY	10018	**800-203-0301**	212-563-5600	692
Visual Impairments. National Assn for Parents of Children with						
PO Box 317	Watertown	MA	02471	**800-562-6265**	617-972-7441	48-17
Visual Marketing Inc 154 W Erie St	Chicago	IL	60610	**800-662-8640**	312-664-9177	231
Visual Networks Inc 2092 Gaither Rd	Rockville	MD	20850	**800-240-4010**	301-296-2300	176-7
NASDAQ: VNWK						
Visual Numerics Inc						
2500 Wilcrest Dr Suite 200	Houston	TX	77042	**800-222-4675**	713-784-3131	176-1
VISX Inc 3400 Central Expy	Santa Clara	CA	95051	**800-998-2020**	408-733-2020	415
NYSE: EYE						
Vita Foam Inc 1900 Stuart St	Chattanooga	TN	37406	**800-627-3972***	423-698-3408	590
*Cust Svc						
Vita Food Products Inc						
2222 W Lake St	Chicago	IL	60612	**800-989-8482**	312-738-4500	291-13
AMEX: VSF						
Vita-Mix Corp 8615 Usher Rd	Cleveland	OH	44138	**800-848-2649**	440-235-4840	37
Vita Olympic Inc 2222 Surrett Dr	High Point	NC	27263	**800-431-1171**	336-431-1171	590
Vita Plus Corp 1508 W Badger Rd	Madison	WI	53713	**800-362-8334**	608-256-1988	438
Vitacost.com Inc						
2055 High Ridge Rd	Boynton Beach	FL	33426	**800-793-2601**	561-752-8888	236
Vital Signs Inc 20 Campus Rd	Totowa	NJ	07512	**800-932-0760**	973-790-1330	468
NASDAQ: VITL						
Vitality Food Service Inc						
400 N Tampa St Suite 1700	Tampa	FL	33602	**888-863-6726**	813-301-4600	291-20
Vitamin Shoppe Inc						
2101 91st St	North Bergen	NJ	07047	**800-223-1216**		236
Vitamin Specialties Co						
8160 Ogontz Ave	Wyncote	PA	19095	**800-365-8482**	215-885-3804	350
Vitarich Foods Inc 4365 Arnold Ave	Naples	FL	34104	**800-817-9999**	239-430-2266	291-11
VITAS Healthcare Corp						
100 S Biscayne Blvd Suite 1500	Miami	FL	33131	**800-950-9200**	305-374-4143	358
VITAS Healthcare Corp						
600 Holiday Plaza Dr Suite 200	Matteson	IL	60443	**800-938-4827**	708-748-8777	365
VITAS Healthcare Corp						
2501 Parkview Dr Suite 600	Fort Worth	TX	76102	**800-593-5855**	817-870-7000	365
VITAS Healthcare Corp						
18333 Egret Bay Suite 550	Houston	TX	77058	**800-822-8525**	281-335-3401	365
VITAS Healthcare Corp						
4828 Loop Central Dr Suite 890	Houston	TX	77081	**800-938-4827**	713-663-7777	365
VITAS Healthcare Corp						
5430 Fredericksburg Rd						
Suite 200	San Antonio	TX	78229	**800-938-4827**	210-348-4300	365
VITAS Healthcare Corp						
2675 N Mayfair Rd Suite 480	Wauwatosa	WI	53226	**800-938-4827**	414-257-2600	365
VITAS Healthcare Corp of California						
16030 Ventura Blvd Suite 600	Encino	CA	91436	**800-757-4242**	818-760-2273	365
VITAS Healthcare Corp of California						
220 Commerce Suite 100	Irvine	CA	92802	**800-486-6157**	714-921-2273	365
VITAS Healthcare Corp of California						
9655 Granite Ridge Dr Suite 300	San Diego	CA	92123	**800-966-8705**	858-499-8901	365
VITAS Healthcare Corp of California						
990 W 190th St Suite 120	Torrance	CA	90502	**800-966-7757**	310-324-2273	365
VITAS Healthcare Corp of Central Florida						
5151 Adanson St Suite 200	Orlando	FL	32804	**800-390-5370**	407-875-0028	365
VITAS Healthcare Corp of Pennsylvania						
1740 Walton Rd Suite 100	Blue Bell	PA	19422	**800-209-1080**	610-260-6020	365
VITAS Healthcare Corp of San Gabriel						
Cities 598 S Grand Ave	Covina	CA	91724	**800-966-8709**	626-918-2273	365
VITAS Hospice Care 5411 N Land Dr	Atlanta	GA	30342	**800-938-4827**	404-874-8313	365
VITAS Innovative Hospice Care						
100 S Biscayne Blvd Suite 1500	Miami	FL	33131	**800-938-4827**	305-374-4143	365
Viterbo University 900 Viterbo Dr	La Crosse	WI	54601	**800-848-3726**	608-796-3000	163
Vitesse Semiconductor Corp						
741 Calle Plano	Camarillo	CA	93012	**800-848-3773**	805-388-3700	686
NASDAQ: VTSS						
Vitner CJ & Co 4202 W 45th St	Chicago	IL	60632	**800-397-7629**	773-523-7900	291-35
Vitran Express Inc 6500 E 30th St	Indianapolis	IN	46219	**800-366-0150**	317-803-6400	769
Vitro Seating Products Inc						
201 Madison St	Saint Louis	MO	63102	**800-325-7093***	314-241-2265	314-1
*Cust Svc						
Viva International Group						
3140 Rt 22 W	Branchburg	NJ	08876	**800-345-8482**	908-595-6200	531
Vivian Beaumont Theatre						
150 W 65th St	New York	NY	10023	**800-432-7250**	212-239-6200	732
Vivian Industries Inc 680 S Pardue St	Vivian	LA	71082	**800-256-7579**	318-375-3241	91
Vivre Inc 11 E 26th St 15th Fl	New York	NY	10010	**800-411-6515**	212-739-6205	227
Vivus Inc 1172 Castro St	Mountain View	CA	94040	**888-367-6873**	650-934-5200	572
NASDAQ: VVUS						
Vivyland 350 Detroit St Suite 206	Denver	CO	80206	**888-621-5266**	303-893-8038	130
Vizcaya 2019 21st St	Sacramento	CA	95818	**800-456-2019**	916-455-5243	373
Vizzawash Inc DBA Wash Tub						
16035 University Oak	San Antonio	TX	78249	**866-493-8822**	210-493-8822	62-1
VLSAA (Viatical & Life Settlement Assn of America) 800 Mayfair Cir	Orlando	FL	32803	**800-842-9811**	407-894-3797	49-9
VMI (Vantage Mobility International)						
5202 S 28th Pl	Phoenix	AZ	85040	**800-348-8267**	602-243-2700	62-7
VML 250 Richards Rd	Kansas City	MO	64116	**800-990-2468**	816-283-0700	4
VMS Inc 203 E Cary St Suite 200	Richmond	VA	23219	**888-547-4404**	804-553-4001	267
VNA of America (VNAA)						
99 Summer St Suite 1700	Boston	MA	02110	**800-426-2547**	617-737-3200	49-8
VNA of Cleveland Hospice						
2500 E 22nd St	Cleveland	OH	44115	**800-862-5253**	216-931-1450	365
VNA Hospice Alliance						
168 Industrial Dr	Northampton	MA	01060	**800-244-1060**	413-584-1060	365
VNA Hospice Care						
9450 Manchester Rd Suite 206	Saint Louis	MO	63119	**800-392-4740**	314-918-7171	365
VNA Hospice of IRC 1110 35th Ln	Vero Beach	FL	32960	**800-749-5760**	772-567-5551	365
VNA & Hospice of Northern California						
1900 Powell St Suite 300	Emeryville	CA	94608	**888-600-7744**	510-450-8596	365
VNA & Hospice Partners in Caring						
500 S Hamilton St	Saginaw	MI	48602	**800-862-4968**	989-799-6020	365
VNA & Hospice of South Texas						
8721 Botts St	San Antonio	TX	78217	**800-773-7292**	210-804-5200	365
VNA & Hospice of Southern California						
150 W 1st St Suite 270	Claremont	CA	91711	**888-357-3574**	909-624-3574	365
VNA & Hospice of Southwest Michigan Hospice 348 N						
Burdick St	Kalamazoo	MI	49007	**800-343-1396**	269-343-1396	365
VNA Hospice Western Pennsylvania						
154 Hindman Rd	Butler	PA	16001	**800-245-3042**	724-282-6806	365
VNA of Houston Hospice						
2905 Sackett St	Houston	TX	77098	**800-375-6877**	713-520-8115	365
VNA of Manchester & Southern New Hampshire 1850 Elm St	Manchester	NH	03104	**800-624-6084**	603-622-3781	365
VNA of the Midlands Hospice						
1941 S 42nd St Suite 225	Omaha	NE	68105	**800-456-8869**	402-342-5566	365
VNS of Rhode Island Hospice Program						
6 Blackstone Valley Pl Suite 515	Lincoln	RI	02865	**800-828-4034**	401-769-5670	365
VNU Business Publications USA						
770 Broadway	New York	NY	10003	**800-451-1741**	646-654-5500	623-2
Vocational Training News Newsletter						
360 Hiatt Dr	Palm Beach Gardens	FL	33418	**800-638-8437**	800-341-7874	521-4
Vocus Inc 4296 Forbes Blvd	Lanham	MD	20706	**800-345-5572**	301-459-2590	39
Voda One Corp						
1010 S 120th St Suite 100	Omaha	NE	68154	**877-642-7750**		172
Vodavi Technology Inc						
4717 E Hilton Ave Suite 400	Phoenix	AZ	85034	**800-843-4863**	480-443-6000	720
NASDAQ: VTEK						
Vogt Tube Ice						
1000 W Ormsby Ave Suite 19	Louisville	KY	40210	**800-853-8648**	502-635-3000	650
Vogue Magazine 4 Times Sq	New York	NY	10036	**800-690-6115**	212-286-2860	449-11
Vogue Pool Products 9031 Salley	LaSalle	QC	H8R2C8	**800-363-3232**	514-363-3232	714
Vogue Tire & Rubber Co Inc						
1101 Feehanville Dr	Mount Prospect	IL	60056	**800-323-1466**	847-297-1900	739
Voice Magazine						
400 N 3rd St PO Box 1724	Harrisburg	PA	17105	**800-944-7732**	717-255-7134	449-8
Voice Power Telecommunications Inc						
PO Box 187	Austin	TX	78767	**800-613-6470**	512-419-4600	721
Voicecom						
5900 Windward Pkwy Suite 500	Alpharetta	GA	30005	**800-384-4357**	404-262-8400	721
VoiceWorld Inc						
383 Kingston Ave Suite 257	Brooklyn	NY	11213	**800-283-4759**	718-221-1400	176-7
Volckening Inc 6700 3rd Ave	Brooklyn	NY	11220	**800-221-0876**	718-836-4000	293
Volk Corp						
23936 Industrial Park Dr	Farmington Hills	MI	48335	**800-521-6799***	248-477-6700	459
*Cust Svc						
Volkert & Assoc Inc 3809 Moffett Rd	Mobile	AL	36618	**800-340-1070**	251-342-1070	258
Volkl Sport America						
19 Technology Dr	West Lebanon	NH	03784	**800-264-4579**	603-298-0314	701
Volkssport Assn. American						
1001 Pat Booker Rd						
Suite 101	Universal City	TX	78148	**800-830-9255**	210-659-2112	48-22
Volkswagen of America Inc						
3800 Hamlin Rd	Auburn Hills	MI	48326	**800-822-8987**	248-754-5000	59
Vollmer Assoc 50 W 23rd St 8th Fl	New York	NY	10010	**800-564-3434**	212-366-5600	258
Vollrath Co LLC						
1236 N 18th St PO Box 611	Sheboygan	WI	53082	**800-624-2051**	920-457-4851	295
Vollwerth & Co PO Box 239	Hancock	MI	49930	**800-562-7620**	906-482-1550	291-26
Volt Directory Systems & Services						
1 Sentry Pkwy Suite 1000	Blue Bell	PA	19422	**800-897-2508**	610-825-7720	623-6
Volt Information Sciences Inc Maintech Div 39 Paterson Ave	Wallington	NJ	07057	**800-426-8324**	973-614-1700	178
Volt Services Group						
1212 Ave of the Americas 9th Fl	New York	NY	10036	**800-367-8658**	212-719-7800	707
Volt Telecom Group Inc						
3039 Premiere Pkwy	Duluth	GA	30097	**800-521-8658**	678-957-4700	258
Volt VIEWtech Inc 5109 E La Palma	Anaheim	CA	92807	**800-998-8658**	714-695-3300	455
Voltek Div Sekisui America Corp						
100 Shepard St	Lawrence	MA	01843	**800-225-0668***	978-685-2557	590
*Cust Svc						
Volume Services America Holdings Inc DBA Centerplate 201 E						
Broad St	Spartanburg	SC	29306	**800-698-6992**	864-598-8600	294
AMEX: CVP						
Volunteer Center National Network. Points of Light Foundation &						
1400 'I' St NW Suite 800	Washington	DC	20005	**800-750-7653**	202-729-8000	48-5
Volunteer Fire Council. National						
1050 17th St NW Suite 490	Washington	DC	20036	**888-275-6832**	202-887-5700	49-4
Volunteer Program. Retired & Senior						
PO Box 70675	Washington	DC	20024	**800-424-8867**		196
Volunteer Software						
628 S 2nd Ave W	Missoula	MT	59801	**800-391-9446**	406-721-0113	176-1
Volunteer State Community College						
1480 Nashville Pike	Gallatin	TN	37066	**888-335-8722**	615-452-8600	160
Volunteer.Gov/Gov						
1600 Pennsylvania Ave NW	Washington	DC	20500	**877-872-2677**		196
Volunteers of America						
1660 Duke St	Alexandria	VA	22314	**800-899-0089**	703-341-5000	48-5
Volunteers in Overseas Cooperative Assistance. Agricultural Cooperative Development International/ 50 F St NW						
Suite 1075	Washington	DC	20001	**800-929-8622**	202-638-4661	48-5
Volvo Cars of North America						
7 Volvo Dr	Rockleigh	NJ	07647	**800-458-1552***	201-768-7300	59
*Cust Svc						
Vomela Specialty Co						
380 Saint Peter St Suite 705	Saint Paul	MN	55102	**800-645-1012**	651-228-2200	692
Von Duprin Exit Device Div Ingersoll-Rand Co						
2720 Tobey Dr	Indianapolis	IN	46219	**800-999-0408***	317-897-9944	345
*Cust Svc						

Name / Address	City	State	Zip	Toll-Free	Phone	Class
Von Hoffmann Corp 1000 Camera Ave	Saint Louis	MO	63126	800-325-2463	314-966-0909	614
Von Roll Isola USA 1 W Campbell Rd	Schenectady	NY	12306	800-654-7652	518-344-7100	490
Vontobel Asset Management Inc 450 Park Ave 7th Fl	New York	NY	10022	800-445-8872	212-415-7000	393
Voodoo Films Inc 728 E Hennepin Ave	Minneapolis	MN	55414	888-866-3666	612-617-0000	503
Voorhees College 1411 Voorhees Rd PO Box 678	Denmark	SC	29042	800-446-6250	803-793-3351	163
Voorhees Pediatric Facility 1304 Laurel Oak Rd	Voorhees	NJ	08043	888-877-3100	856-346-3300	441
Voorwood Co 2350 Barney St	Anderson	CA	96007	800-225-3879	530-365-3311	809
Vornado Air Circulation Systems Inc 415 E 13th St	Andover	KS	67002	800-297-0883	316-733-0035	18
Vornado Realty Trust 210 Rt 4 E *NYSE: VNO*	Paramus	NJ	07652	800-242-4119	201-587-1000	641
Vorwerk USA Co LP 1335 Bennette Dr Suite 111	Longwood	FL	32750	888-867-9375	407-830-9988	361
Voss Belting & Specialty Co 6965 N Hamlin Ave	Lincolnwood	IL	60712	800-323-3935	847-673-8900	364
Voss Lighting 1601 Cushman Dr	Lincoln	NE	68512	800-828-8677	402-328-2281	245
Vote. Project 6805 Oak Creek Dr	Columbus	OH	43229	800-546-8683	614-523-2560	48-7
Vote Smart. Project 1 Common Ground	Philipsburg	MT	59858	888-868-3762	406-859-8683	48-7
Voters. League of Women 1730 M St NW Suite 1000	Washington	DC	20036	800-249-8683	202-429-1965	48-7
Voto Manufacturers Sales Co 500 N 3rd St	Steubenville	OH	43952	800-848-4010	740-282-3621	378
Vox Medica Inc 210 W Washington Sq	Philadelphia	PA	19106	800-842-6482	215-238-8500	4
Voyager Emblems Inc 3707 Lockport Rd	Sanborn	NY	14132	800-268-2204	716-731-4121	256
Voyager Hotel 501 K St	Anchorage	AK	99501	800-247-9070	907-277-9501	373
Voyageur Asset Management Inc 100 S 5th St Suite 2300	Minneapolis	MN	55402	800-553-2143	612-376-7000	393
Voyageur Inn 200 Viking Dr	Reedsburg	WI	53959	800-444-4493	608-524-6431	373
Voyageur Lakewalk Inn 333 E Superior St	Duluth	MN	55802	800-258-3911	218-722-3911	373
Voyetra Turtle Beach Inc 5 Odell Plaza	Yonkers	NY	10701	800-233-9377	914-966-0600	613
VPI LLC 3123 S 9th St *Orders	Sheboygan	WI	53081	800-874-4240*	920-458-4664	589
VPOP Technologies Inc 365 E Avenida de los Arboles PMB 1014 *Sales	Thousand Oaks	CA	91360	888-811-8767*	805-529-9374	795
VPT (Vermont Public Television) 204 Ethan Allen Ave	Colchester	VT	05446	800-639-7811	802-655-4800	620
VRE (Virginia Railway Express) 1500 King St Suite 200	Alexandria	VA	22314	800-743-3873	703-684-1001	460
VRMA (Vacation Rental Managers Assn) PO Box 1202	Santa Cruz	CA	95061	800-871-8762	831-426-8762	49-17
VS & A Communications Partners 350 Park Ave 7th Fl	New York	NY	10022	800-935-4990	212-935-4990	779
VSDA (Video Software Dealers Assn) 16530 Ventura Blvd Suite 400	Encino	CA	91436	800-955-8732	818-385-1500	49-18
VSE Corp 2550 Huntington Ave *NASDAQ: VSEC*	Alexandria	VA	22303	800-455-4873	703-960-4600	258
VSEN (Virginia Satellite Educational Network) PO Box 2120	Richmond	VA	23218	800-246-8736	804-692-0335	620
VSI (Vinyl Siding Institute) 1667 K St NW Suite 1000	Washington	DC	20006	888-367-8741	202-974-5200	49-13
VSM Abrasives 1012 E Wabash St	O'Fallon	MO	63366	800-737-0176	636-272-7432	1
VSM Sewing Inc 31000 Viking Pkwy	Westlake	OH	44145	800-541-3357	440-808-6550	38
Vstore.com c/o Vcommerce Corp 9977 N 90th St Suite 200	Scottsdale	AZ	85258	800-821-6034	480-922-9922	795
VT Inc DBA Van Enterprises 8500 W Shawnee Mission Pkwy Suite 200	Shawnee Mission	KS	66202	800-747-4400	913-432-6400	57
VTA (Santa Clara Valley Transportation Authority) 3331 N 1st St	San Jose	CA	95134	800-894-9908	408-321-5555	460
VTA Management Services Inc 1901 Emmons Ave Suite 200	Brooklyn	NY	11235	800-874-3469	718-615-0049	455
VTech Electronics North America LLC 1155 W Dundee St Suite 130	Arlingtn Heights	IL	60004	800-521-2010	847-400-3600	750
VTech Innovations LP 9590 SW Gemini Dr Suite 120	Beaverton	OR	97008	800-835-8023	503-596-1200	720
VTS Investigations LLC PO Box 971	Elgin	IL	60121	800-538-4464	847-888-4464	392
VU Media Duplication 1420 Blake St	Denver	CO	80202	800-637-4336	303-534-5503	644
Vuitton Louis NA Inc 19 E 57th St *Cust Svc	New York	NY	10022	866-884-8866*	212-931-2000	155-6
Vulcan Chemicals 1200 Urban Center Dr *Cust Svc	Birmingham	AL	35242	800-633-8280*	205-298-3000	142
Vulcan Corp 30 Garfield Pl Suite 1040 *Sales	Cincinnati	OH	45202	800-447-1146*	513-621-2850	663
Vulcan-Hart Corp 2006 Northwestern Pkwy *Cust Svc	Louisville	KY	40203	800-999-9815*	502-778-2791	293
Vulcan Inc 410 E Berry Ave	Foley	AL	36535	800-633-6845	251-943-1541	151
Vulcan Industries Inc 300 Display Dr	Moody	AL	35004	888-444-4417	205-640-2400	231
Vulcan Information Packaging Div EBSCO Industries Inc PO Box 29	Vincent	AL	35178	800-633-4526	205-672-2241	87
Vulcan Life Insurance Co PO Box 1980	Carmel	IN	46032	800-544-0467		384-2
Vulcan Materials Co Western Div 3200 San Fernando Rd	Los Angeles	CA	90065	800-225-6280	323-258-2777	710
Vulcan Service PO Box 522	Birmingham	AL	35201	800-841-9600	205-991-1374	97
Vutec Corp 2741 NE 4th Ave	Pompano Beach	FL	33064	800-770-4700	954-545-9000	580
VVA (Vietnam Veterans of America) 8605 Cameron St Suite 400	Silver Spring	MD	20910	800-882-1316	301-585-4000	48-19
VVP America Inc 965 Ridge Lake Blvd Suite 300	Memphis	TN	38120	800-238-6057	901-767-7111	325
VWR Scientific Products Corp 1310 Goshen Pkwy	West Chester	PA	19380	800-932-5000	610-431-1700	467
Vycera Communications Inc 12750 High Bluff Dr Suite 200 *Cust Svc	San Diego	CA	92130	800-705-3500*	858-792-2400	721
Vyse Gelatin Co 5010 N Rose St	Schiller Park	IL	60176	800-533-2152	847-678-4780	291-22
Vystar Credit Union 4949 Blanding Blvd *Cust Svc	Jacksonville	FL	32210	800-445-6289*	904-777-6000	216
Vytech Industries Inc 5201 Old Pearman Dairy Rd	Anderson	SC	29625	800-225-8531	864-224-8771	588
Vyvx Integrated Transmission Services 1 Technology Ctr	Tulsa	OK	74103	800-364-0807	918-547-5760	669

W

Name / Address	City	State	Zip	Toll-Free	Phone	Class
W Atlee Burpee Co 300 Park Ave *Cust Svc	Warminster	PA	18974	800-333-5808*	215-674-4900	684
W & H Co-op Oil Co Inc 407 13th St N	Humboldt	IA	50548	800-392-3816	515-332-2782	319
W Hotel Atlanta at Perimeter Center 111 Perimeter Ctr W	Atlanta	GA	30346	800-683-6100	770-396-6800	373
W Hotel Honolulu Diamond Head 2885 Kalakaua Ave	Honolulu	HI	96815	888-627-7816	808-922-1700	373
W Hotel Los Angeles Westwood 930 Hilgard Ave	Los Angeles	CA	90024	800-421-2317	310-208-8765	373
W Hotel New Orleans-French Quarter 316 Chartres St	New Orleans	LA	70130	800-448-4927	504-581-1200	373
W Hotel New York 541 Lexington Ave	New York	NY	10022	877-946-8357	212-755-1200	373
W Hotel New York-The Court 130 E 39th St	New York	NY	10016	877-946-8357	212-685-1100	373
W Hotel New York Times Square 1567 Broadway *Resv	New York	NY	10036	877-946-8357*	212-930-7400	373
W Hotel San Francisco 181 3rd St	San Francisco	CA	94103	800-946-8357	415-777-5300	373
W Hotel Seattle 1112 4th Ave	Seattle	WA	98101	877-946-8357	206-264-6000	373
W Hotels 1111 Westchester Ave	White Plains	NY	10604	877-443-4585	914-640-8100	369
W Magazine 7 W 34th St 3rd Fl	New York	NY	10001	800-289-0390	212-630-4000	449-11
W Publishing Group PO Box 141000 *Cust Svc	Nashville	TN	37214	800-251-4000*	615-889-9000	623-4
W & R Funds 6300 Lamar Ave	Shawnee Mission	KS	66202	800-366-5465	913-236-2000	517
W Suites Newark 8200 Gateway Blvd	Newark	CA	94560	877-946-8357	510-494-8800	373
WA Brown & Son Inc 209 Long Meadow Dr	Salisbury	NC	28147	800-438-2316	704-636-5131	650
WA Butler Co 5600 Blazer Pkwy	Dublin	OH	43017	800-848-5983	614-761-9095	574
WA Charnstrom Co 5391 12th Ave E *Cust Svc	Shakopee	MN	55379	800-328-2962*	952-403-0303	462
WA Cleary Corp 1049 Rt 27	Somerset	NJ	08873	800-238-7813	732-247-8000	276
WA Kraft Corp 199 Wildwood Ave	Woburn	MA	01801	800-969-6121	781-938-9100	507
WA Roosevelt Co 2727 Commerce St	La Crosse	WI	54603	800-279-2726	608-781-2000	601
WA Whitney Co 650 Race St	Rockford	IL	61105	800-435-2823	815-964-6771	448
WA Whitney Corp Boyar-Schultz Div 650 Race St	Rockford	IL	61105	800-435-2823	815-964-6771	447
WA Wilde Co 201 Summer St	Holliston	MA	01746	800-933-9453	508-429-5515	5
WAAY-TV Ch 31 (ABC) 1000 Monte Sano Blvd SE	Huntsville	AL	35801	877-799-9229	256-533-3131	726
Wabash Alloys LLP PO Box 466	Wabash	IN	46992	800-348-0571	260-563-7461	476
Wabash College 301 W Wabash Ave	Crawfordsville	IN	47933	800-492-2274	765-362-1400	163
Wabash Computer Products Inc 4720 W 90th St *Cust Svc	Tulsa	OK	74132	800-323-9868*	918-447-8977	644
Wabash County Rural Electric Membership Corp 350 Wedcor Ave	Wabash	IN	46992	800-563-2146	260-563-2146	244
Wabash Electric Supply Inc 1400 S Wabash St	Wabash	IN	46992	800-552-7777	260-563-4146	245
Wabash Life Insurance Co PO Box 1917	Carmel	IN	46032	800-525-7662	317-817-6100	384-2
Wabash National Corp PO Box 6129 *NYSE: WNC* ■ *Sales	Lafayette	IN	47903	800-937-4784*	765-771-5300	768
Wabash Plain Dealer 123 W Canal St	Wabash	IN	46992	800-659-6321	260-563-2131	522-2
Wabash Valley College 2200 College Dr	Mount Carmel	IL	62863	866-982-4322	618-262-8641	160
Wabash Valley Service Co Inc 909 N Court St	Grayville	IL	62844	888-869-8127	618-375-2311	272
WABB-FM 97.5 (CHR) 1551 Springhill Ave	Mobile	AL	36604	800-678-9736	251-432-5572	631
WABX-FM 107.5 (CR) 20 NW 3rd St	Evansville	IN	47708	800-879-1372	812-424-8284	631
Wachovia Corp 301 S College St *NYSE: WB*	Charlotte	NC	28288	800-922-4684	704-374-6161	355-2
Wachovia Education Finance 11000 White Rock Rd	Rancho Cordova	CA	85670	800-347-7667		215
Wachovia Mortgage Corp 1100 Corporate Ctr Dr	Raleigh	NC	27607	800-654-9322		498
Wachs EH Co 100 Shepard St	Wheeling	IL	60090	800-323-8185	847-537-8800	447
Wachtell Lipton Rosen & Katz 51 W 52nd St	New York	NY	10019	800-848-0301	212-403-1000	419
Wachters' Organic Sea Products Corp 550 Sylvan St	Daly City	CA	94014	800-682-7100	650-757-9851	786
Wackenhut Airline Services Inc 4200 Wackenhut Dr Suite 100	Palm Beach Gardens	FL	33410	800-683-6853	561-622-5656	682
Wackenhut Corp 4200 Wackenhut Dr Suite 100	Palm Beach Gardens	FL	33410	800-922-6488	561-622-5656	682
Wackenhut Corp Nuclear Services Div 4200 Wackenhut Dr Suite 100	Palm Beach Gardens	FL	33410	800-683-6853	561-622-5656	682
Wackenhut International Inc 4200 Wackenhut Dr Suite 100	Palm Beach Gardens	FL	33410	800-683-6853	561-622-5656	682

Name / Address	City	State	ZIP	Toll-Free	Phone	Class
Wackenhut Services Inc 4200 Wackenhut Dr Suite 100	Palm Beach Gardens	FL	33410	**800-922-6488**	561-622-5656	682
Wackenhut Sports Security Inc 4200 Wackenhut Dr Suite 100	Palm Beach Gardens	FL	33410	**800-683-6853**	561-622-5656	682
Wackenhut Training Institute 4200 Wackenhut Dr Suite 100	Palm Beach Gardens	FL	33410	**800-922-6488**	561-622-5656	787
Wacker Chemical Corp DBA Wacker Silicones 3301 Sutton Rd	Adrian	MI	49221	**800-248-0063**	517-264-8500	142
Wacker Corp N 92 W 15000 Anthony Ave	Menomonee Falls	WI	53051	**800-770-0957**	262-255-0500	189
Wacker Siltronic Corp 7200 NW Front Ave	Portland	OR	97210	**800-922-5371**	503-243-2020	686
Waco Convention & Visitors Bureau 100 Washington Ave	Waco	TX	76701	**800-321-9226**	254-750-5810	205
Waco Scaffolding & Equipment Co PO Box 318028	Cleveland	OH	44131	**800-901-2282**	216-749-8900	482
Waco Tribune-Herald PO Box 2588	Waco	TX	76702	**800-678-8742**	254-757-5757	522-2
Wacoal America 1 Wacoal Plaza	Lyndhurst	NJ	07071	**800-526-6286**	201-933-8400	153-18
Wacom Technology Corp 1311 SE Cardinal Ct	Vancouver	WA	98683	**800-922-9348**	360-896-9833	171-1
WACY-TV Ch 32 (UPN) 1391 North Rd	Green Bay	WI	54313	**800-800-6619**	920-490-0320	726
Wada Farms Potatoes Inc 2058 Jennie Lee Dr	Idaho Falls	ID	83404	**800-657-5565**	208-542-2898	11-11
Waddell & Reed Advisors Funds 6300 Lamar Ave	Shawnee Mission	KS	66202	**800-366-5465**	913-236-2000	517
Waddell & Reed Financial Inc 6300 Lamar Ave *NYSE: WDR*	Shawnee Mission	KS	66202	**888-923-3355**	913-236-2000	393
Wade College 2350 Stemmons Fwy Suite M 5120	Dallas	TX	75207	**800-624-4850**	214-637-3530	158
Wade Tours Inc 797 Burdeck St	Schenectady	NY	12306	**800-955-9233**	518-355-4500	748
Wade-Trim Group Inc 25251 Northline Rd	Taylor	MI	48180	**800-482-2864**	734-947-9700	258
Wadena Timberroots PO Box 109 *Sales	Wadena	MN	56482	**800-982-4863***	218-631-2607	671
WADO-AM 1280 (Span) 485 Madison Ave 3rd Fl	New York	NY	10022	**800-999-1280**	212-310-6000	631
WAER-FM 88.3 (Jazz) 795 Ostram Ave	Syracuse	NY	13244	**888-918-3688**	315-443-4021	631
WAEZ-FM 94.9 (CHR) 901 E Valley Dr	Bristol	VA	24201	**888-937-4487**	276-669-8112	631
WAFB-TV Ch 9 (CBS) 844 Government St	Baton Rouge	LA	70802	**800-223-9232**	225-383-9999	726
Waffle House Inc 5986 Financial Dr	Norcross	GA	30071	**800-882-9235**	770-729-5700	657
Wager Robert H Co 570 Montroyal Rd	Rural Hall	NC	27045	**800-562-7024**	336-969-6909	776
Waggoners Trucking PO Box 31357	Billings	MT	59107	**800-999-9097**	406-248-1919	769
Wagner & Brown Ltd 300 N Marienfeld St Suite 1100	Midland	TX	79702	**800-777-7936**	432-682-7936	525
Wagner College 1 Campus Rd	Staten Island	NY	10301	**800-221-1010**	718-390-3411	163
Wagner ER Mfg Co Inc 4611 N 32nd St	Milwaukee	WI	53209	**800-558-5596**	414-871-5080	345
Wagner Odon Gallery 196 Davenport Rd	Toronto	ON	M5R1J2	**800-551-2465**	416-962-0438	42
Wagner Oil Co 500 Commerce St Suite 600	Fort Worth	TX	76102	**800-457-5332**	817-335-2222	525
Wagner-Smith Co PO Box 672	Dayton	OH	45401	**800-775-7799**	937-298-7481	188-4
Wagner Spray Tech Corp 1770 Fernbrook Ln	Plymouth	MN	55447	**800-328-8251**	763-553-0759	170
Wagon Wheel Village 435 N Cache St	Jackson	WY	83001	**800-323-9279**	307-733-2357	373
Wagoner Construction Co Inc PO Box 1127	Salisbury	NC	28145	**800-222-1027**	704-633-1431	186
WAGT-TV Ch 26 (NBC) PO Box 1526	Augusta	GA	30903	**800-924-8639**	706-826-0026	726
Wah Chang 1600 Old Salem Rd NE	Albany	OR	97321	**888-926-4211**	541-926-4211	476
Wahl Clipper Corp 2900 Locust St	Sterling	IL	61081	**800-767-9245**	815-625-6525	211
Wahl Refractories Inc 767 SR 19 S	Fremont	OH	43420	**800-837-9245**	419-334-2658	649
Wahpeton Visitors Bureau 118 N 6th St	Wahpeton	ND	58075	**800-892-6673**	701-642-8744	205
Waikiki Beachcomber Hotel 2300 Kalakaua Ave	Honolulu	HI	96815	**800-622-4646**	808-922-4646	373
Waikiki Gateway Hotel 2070 Kalakaua Ave	Honolulu	HI	96815	**800-247-1903**	808-955-3741	373
Waikiki Joy Hotel 320 Lewers St	Honolulu	HI	96815	**800-321-2558**	808-923-2300	373
Waikiki Parc Hotel 2233 Helumoa Rd	Honolulu	HI	96815	**800-422-0450**	808-921-7272	373
Waikiki Resort Hotel 2460 Koa Ave	Honolulu	HI	96815	**800-367-5116**	808-922-4911	373
Waikiki Resort & Spa. Hyatt Regency 2424 Kalakaua Ave	Honolulu	HI	96815	**800-233-1234**	808-923-1234	655
Waikiki Royal Suites 255 Beach Walk	Honolulu	HI	96815	**800-535-0085**	808-926-5641	373
Waikoloa Beach Marriott 69-275 Waikoloa Beach Dr	Waikoloa	HI	96738	**800-688-7444**	808-886-6789	373
Wainwright Bank & Trust Co 63 Franklin St *NASDAQ: WAIN*	Boston	MA	02110	**800-444-2265**	617-478-4000	71
Wainwright HC & Co Inc 245 Park Ave 44th Fl	New York	NY	10167	**800-727-7176**	212-856-5700	679
WAIQ-TV Ch 26 (PBS) 1255 Madison Ave	Montgomery	AL	36107	**800-239-5239**	334-264-9900	726
Waitt Media Inc 1125 S 103rd St Suite 200	Omaha	NE	68124	**888-656-0634**	402-697-8000	629
WAKA-TV Ch 8 (CBS) 3020 Eastern Blvd	Montgomery	AL	36116	**800-467-0401**	334-271-8888	726
Wake Electric Membership Corp 414 E Wait Ave	Wake Forest	NC	27587	**800-474-6300**	919-863-6300	244
Wakefield's Inc 1212 Quintard Ave	Anniston	AL	36201	**800-333-1552**	256-237-9521	155-2
Wakeman/Walworth Inc PO Box 7376	Alexandria	VA	22307	**800-876-2545**	703-768-9600	623-9
Wako Chemicals USA Inc 1600 Bellwood Rd	Richmond	VA	23237	**800-992-9256**	804-271-7677	229
Wakunaga of America Co Ltd 23501 Madero	Mission Viejo	CA	92691	**800-421-2998**	949-855-2776	786
Wal-Mart Foundation 702 SW 8th St	Bentonville	AR	72716	**800-530-9925**		299
Wal-Mart Realty 2001 SE 10th St	Bentonville	AR	72716	**800-925-6278**	479-273-4000	641
Wal-Mart Stores Inc 702 SW 8th St *NYSE: WMT* ■ *Cust Svc	Bentonville	AR	72716	**800-925-6278***	479-273-4000	227
Wal-Mart Stores Inc Supercenter Div 702 SW 8th St	Bentonville	AR	72716	**800-925-6278**	479-273-4000	227
Walbuck Crayon Co PO Box 367	Lawrence	MA	01842	**800-626-0099**	978-974-0220	43
Walch J Weston Publisher PO Box 658	Portland	ME	04104	**800-558-2846**	207-772-2846	623-2
Walco International Inc 520 S Main St	Grapevine	TX	76051	**877-289-9252**	817-601-6000	468
Walco Tool & Engineering Co 18954 Airport Rd	Lockport	IL	60441	**800-808-9365**	815-834-0225	446
Walczak Lumber Inc PO Box 340	Clifford	PA	18413	**800-445-1215**	570-222-9651	541
Wald Relocation Services Ltd 8708 W Little York Rd Suite 190	Houston	TX	77040	**800-527-1408**	713-512-4800	508
Walden Book Co Inc 100 Phoenix Dr	Ann Arbor	MI	48108	**800-566-6616**	734-477-1100	96
Walden Farms 1209 W St Georges Ave	Linden	NJ	07036	**800-229-1706**	908-925-9494	291-19
Waldinger Corp 2601 Bell Ave	Des Moines	IA	50321	**800-225-0638**	515-284-1911	188-14
Waldner's Business Environment 125 Rt 110	Farmingdale	NY	11735	**800-473-9253**	631-694-1522	315
Waldon/Laymore Inc 401 Capacity Dr	Longview	TX	75604	**800-323-0135**	903-759-0610	462
Waldorf-Astoria - A Hilton Hotel 301 Park Ave	New York	NY	10022	**800-925-3673**	212-355-3000	373
Waldorf College 106 S 6th St	Forest City	IA	50436	**800-292-1903**	641-585-2450	160
Waldorf Towers - A Conrad Hotel 100 E 50th St	New York	NY	10022	**800-445-8667**	212-355-3100	373
Waldorf Towers Hotel 860 Ocean Dr	Miami Beach	FL	33139	**800-933-2322**	305-531-7684	373
Wale Apparatus Co Inc PO Box D	Hellertown	PA	18055	**800-444-9253**	610-838-7047	329
Walgreen Co 200 Wilmot Rd *NYSE: WAG* ■ *Cust Svc	Deerfield	IL	60015	**800-289-2273***	847-940-2500	236
Walker Component Group 420 E 58th Ave	Denver	CO	80216	**800-876-8686**	303-292-5537	245
Walker County Chamber of Commerce 204 19th St E Suite 101	Jasper	AL	35501	**888-384-4571**	205-384-4571	137
Walker Georgia & Assoc Inc PO Box 584	Raymore	MO	64083	**800-385-2423**	816-331-3211	384-1
Walker Information Inc 3939 Priority Way S Dr	Indianapolis	IN	46240	**800-334-3939**	317-843-3939	458
Walker JH Trucking Co Inc 152 N Hollywood Rd	Houma	LA	70364	**800-535-5992**	985-868-8330	769
Walker Magnetics Group Inc 20 Rockdale St	Worcester	MA	01606	**800-962-4638**	508-853-3232	484
Walker MS Inc 20 3rd Ave	Somerville	MA	02143	**800-776-5808**	617-776-6700	81-1
Walker Oil Co PO Box 215	Nottingham	PA	19362	**800-468-6005**	610-932-8524	311
Walker Process Equipment 840 N Russell Ave	Aurora	IL	60506	**800-992-5537**	630-892-7921	793
Walker Stainless Equipment Co Inc 625 State St	New Lisbon	WI	53950	**800-356-5734**	608-562-3151	293
Walker Tool & Die Inc 2411 Walker Ave NW	Grand Rapids	MI	49544	**888-925-5377**	616-453-5471	745
Walker Wire & Steel Co 660 E Ten-Mile Rd	Ferndale	MI	48220	**800-521-2070**	248-399-4800	800
Walker & Zanger Inc 31 Warren Pl	Mount Vernon	NY	10550	**800-634-0866**	914-667-1600	190-1
Walking Adventures International PO Box 871000	Vancouver	WA	98687	**800-779-0353**	360-260-9393	748
Wall Colmonoy Corp 30261 Stephenson Hwy	Madison Heights	MI	48071	**800-521-2412**	248-585-6400	22
Wall Industries Inc 1615 N Lee St	Spencer	NC	28159	**888-289-9255**	704-637-7414	207
Wall Street Digest 8830 S Tamiami Trail Suite 110	Sarasota	FL	34238	**800-785-5050**	941-954-5500	521-9
Wall Street Journal PO Box 300 *Cust Svc	Princeton	NJ	08543	**800-568-7625***	609-520-4000	522-3
Walla Walla College 125 SW 4th Ave	College Place	WA	99324	**800-541-8900**	509-527-2327	163
Walla Walla Community College 500 Tausick Way	Walla Walla	WA	99362	**877-992-9922**	509-522-2500	160
Walla Walla Union-Bulletin PO Box 1358	Walla Walla	WA	99362	**800-423-5617**	509-525-3300	522-2
Walla Walla Valley Chamber of Commerce 29 E Sumach St	Walla Walla	WA	99362	**877-998-4748**	509-525-0850	137
Wallace Cleo Centers Westminster Campus 8405 Church Ranch Blvd	Westminster	CO	80021	**800-456-2536**	303-466-7391	366-1
Wallace Community College 1141 Wallace Dr	Dothan	AL	36303	**800-543-2426**	334-983-3521	160
Wallace Foundation 2 Park Ave 23rd Fl	New York	NY	10016	**800-771-9701**	212-251-9700	300
Wallace Hardware Co Inc PO Box 6004	Morristown	TN	37815	**800-776-0976**	423-586-5650	346
Wallace Metal Products 1800 Roberts Dr	Anniston	AL	36207	**888-831-9675**	256-831-4826	479
Wallach & Co Inc 107 W Federal St	Middleburg	VA	20118	**800-237-6615**	540-687-3166	384-7
Wallover Oil Co Inc 1032 Pennsylvania Ave *Sales	East Liverpool	OH	43920	**800-662-9626***	330-385-9336	530
Walls Industries Inc 1905 N Main St	Cleburne	TX	76033	**800-433-1765**	817-645-4366	153-19
Walman Optical Co Inc 801 12th Ave N	Minneapolis	MN	55411	**800-873-9256**	612-520-6000	531
Walmart.com 7000 Marina Blvd	Brisbane	CA	94005	**800-966-6546**	650-837-5000	227
Walnut Street Securities Inc 260 Madison Ave 11th Fl	New York	NY	10016	**800-873-7702**	212-354-8800	679
Walpole Woodworkers Inc 767 East St PO Box 151	Walpole	MA	02081	**800-343-6948**	508-668-2800	275
Walsh & Assoc Inc 1400 Macklind Ave	Saint Louis	MO	63110	**800-949-2574**	314-781-2520	144
Walsh Brothers Inc PO Box 1711	Phoenix	AZ	85001	**800-527-3437**	602-252-6971	315
Walsh Group Inc 929 W Adams St	Chicago	IL	60607	**800-759-2574**	312-563-5400	185
Walsh University 2020 E Maple St	North Canton	OH	44720	**800-362-9846**	330-499-7090	163
Walshire Assurance Co PO Box 3709	York	PA	17402	**800-876-3350**	717-757-0000	355-4
Walsworth Publishing Co Inc 306 N Kansas Ave	Marceline	MO	64658	**800-369-2646**	660-376-3543	623-2

Name / Address	City	State	Zip	Toll-Free	Phone	Class
Walt Disney Interactive 601 Circle 7 Dr	Glendale	CA	91201	**800-228-0988**	818-553-5000	176-6
Walt Disney World Dolphin 1500 Epcot Resorts Blvd	Lake Buena Vista	FL	32830	**800-227-1500**	407-934-4000	655
Walt Disney World Swan 1200 Epcot Resorts Blvd	Lake Buena Vista	FL	32830	**800-248-7926**	407-934-3000	655
Waltek Inc 14310 Sunfish Lake Blvd NW	Ramsey	MN	55303	**800-937-9496**	763-427-3181	301
Walter Haas & Sons Inc 123 W 23rd St	Hialeah	FL	33010	**800-552-3845**	305-883-2257	692
Walter Industries Inc 4211 W Boy Scout Blvd *NYSE: WLT*	Tampa	FL	33607	**800-888-9258**	813-871-4811	184
Walter Jim Homes Inc PO Box 31601	Tampa	FL	33631	**800-492-5837**	813-871-4811	186
Walter Kerr Theatre 219 W 48th St	New York	NY	10036	**800-432-7250**	212-239-6200	732
Walter Oil & Gas Corp 1100 Louisiana St Suite 200	Houston	TX	77002	**888-756-7880**	713-659-1221	527
Walter P Chrysler Museum 1 Chrysler Dr	Auburn Hills	MI	48326	**888-456-1924**	248-944-0001	509
Walter Waukesha Inc 1111 Sentry Dr	Waukesha	WI	53186	**800-945-5554**	262-542-4426	484
Walters State Community College 500 S Davy Crockett Pkwy	Morristown	TN	37813	**800-225-4770**	423-585-2600	160
Walters & Wolf 41450 Boscell Rd	Fremont	CA	94538	**800-969-9653**	510-490-1115	188-6
Waltham Services Inc 817 Moody St	Waltham	MA	02453	**800-562-9287**	781-893-1810	567
Walthers William K Inc 5601 W Florist Ave	Milwaukee	WI	53218	**800-877-7171**	414-527-0770	750
Walton Izaak League of America 707 Conservation Ln	Gaithersburg	MD	20878	**800-453-5463**	301-548-0150	48-13
Walton Press 402 Mayfield Dr	Monroe	GA	30655	**800-354-0235**	770-267-2596	545
Walton Rehabilitation Hospital 1355 Independence Dr	Augusta	GA	30901	**800-366-6055**	706-724-7746	366-4
Wam!net Inc 10900 Hampshire Ave S Suite 150	Bloomington	MN	55438	**800-585-3666**		39
WAMC-FM 90.3 (NPR) 318 Central Ave	Albany	NY	12206	**800-323-9262**	518-465-5233	631
WAMC/Northeast Public Radio 318 Central Ave	Albany	NY	12206	**800-323-9262**	518-465-5233	620
Wampfler Inc 8091 Production Ave	Florence	KY	41042	**800-326-2899**	859-814-2100	609
Wampole Laboratories LLC 2 Research Way *Cust Svc	Princeton	NJ	08540	**800-257-9525***	609-627-8000	229
Wanderbird Cruises DBA Rockport Schooner Cruises PO Box 987	Rockport	ME	04856	**866-732-2473**	207-230-1049	217
Wanke Cascade Co 6330 N Cutter Cir	Portland	OR	97217	**800-365-5053**	503-289-8609	356
Wannado City 12801 Sunrise Blvd Anchor D	Sunrise	FL	33323	**888-926-6236**	954-838-7100	32
Wapusk National Park PO Box 127	Churchill	MB	R0B0E0	**888-748-2928**	204-675-8863	553
War Revolution & Peace. Hoover Institution on Stanford University 434 Galvez Mall	Stanford	CA	94305	**877-466-8374**	650-723-1754	654
Warburg Pincus Funds 466 Lexington Ave	New York	NY	10017	**800-888-3697**	212-878-0600	517
Ward Aluminum Casting Co 642 Growth Ave	Fort Wayne	IN	46808	**866-427-8700**	260-426-8700	303
Ward-Kraft Inc 2401 Cooper St	Fort Scott	KS	66701	**800-821-4021**	620-223-5500	111
Ward Log Homes PO Box 72 *Cust Svc	Houlton	ME	04730	**800-341-1566***	207-532-6531	107
Ward Machinery Co 10615 Beaver Dam Rd	Hunt Valley	MD	21030	**800-847-9273**	410-584-7700	546
Ward Products LLC 633 Nassau St	New Brunswick	NJ	08902	**877-732-4095**	732-846-7500	633
Ward Transformer Sales & Service Inc PO Box 90609	Raleigh	NC	27675	**800-334-9600**	919-787-3553	756
Ward Trucking Corp PO Box 1553	Altoona	PA	16603	**800-458-3625**	814-944-0803	769
Wareforce.com Inc 19 Morgan	Irvine	CA	92618	**800-258-2622**	949-639-8934	172
Warehouse Home Furnishings Distributors Inc DBA Farmers Furniture 2005 Veterans Blvd Suite 1	Dublin	GA	31040	**800-456-0424**	478-272-4000	316
Warehouse Logistics Assn. International 2800 River Rd Suite 260	Des Plaines	IL	60018	**800-525-0165**	847-813-4699	49-21
Warfield Electric Co Inc 175 Industry Ave	Frankfort	IL	60423	**800-435-9346**	815-469-4094	507
Waring Products Inc 314 Ella T Grasso Ave	Torrington	CT	06790	**800-269-6640**	860-496-3100	37
Warm Co 954 E Union St	Seattle	WA	98122	**800-234-9276**	206-320-9276	730-1
Warm Springs Rehabilitation Hospital 5101 Medical Dr	San Antonio	TX	78229	**800-451-1350**	210-616-0100	366-4
Warmington Group 3090 Pullman St Suite A	Costa Mesa	CA	92626	**800-925-9709**	714-557-5511	639
Warnaco Swimwear Group Inc 6040 Bandini Blvd *Cust Svc	Los Angeles	CA	90040	**800-547-8770***	323-726-1262	153-17
Warner Bros Publications 15800 NW 48th Ave	Miami	FL	33014	**800-327-7643**	305-620-1500	623-7
Warner Chilcott Laboratories 100 Enterprise Dr Rockaway 80 Corporate Ctr Suite 280	Rockaway	NJ	07866	**800-521-8813**	973-442-3200	573
Warner Co 9201 W Belmont Ave	Franklin Park	IL	60131	**800-621-1143**	847-737-8000	789
Warner Electric 449 Gardner St	South Beloit	IL	61080	**800-234-3369**	815-389-3771	609
Warner Mfg Co 13435 Industrial Park Blvd	Minneapolis	MN	55441	**800-234-7708**	763-559-4740	746
Warner Pacific College 2219 SE 68th Ave	Portland	OR	97215	**800-582-7885**	503-775-4366	163
Warner Southern College 13895 Hwy 27	Lake Wales	FL	33859	**800-949-7248**	863-638-1426	163
Warner Vineyards Inc 706 S Kalamazoo St	Paw Paw	MI	49079	**800-756-5357**	269-657-3165	81-3
Warner/Chappell Music Inc 10585 Santa Monica Blvd	Los Angeles	CA	90025	**800-327-7643**	310-441-8600	623-7
Warp Bros Flex-O-Glass Inc 4647 W Augusta Blvd	Chicago	IL	60651	**800-621-3345**	773-261-5200	538
Warrantech Consumer Products Services Inc 2200 Hwy 121	Bedford	TX	76021	**800-544-9510**	817-283-7267	687
Warrantech Corp Inc 2200 Hwy 121	Bedford	TX	76021	**800-544-9510**	817-283-7267	687
Warrantech Home Service Co 2200 Hwy 121	Bedford	TX	76021	**800-544-9510**	817-283-7267	687
Warrantech International Inc 2200 Hwy 121	Beford	TX	76021	**800-544-9510**	817-283-7267	687
Warren Communications News Inc 2115 Ward Ct NW	Washington	DC	20037	**800-771-9202**	202-872-9200	623-9
Warren County Rural Electric Membership Corp 15 Midway St	Williamsport	IN	47993	**800-872-7319**	765-762-6114	244
Warren Distributing Corp 226 Glenwood Ave	Raleigh	NC	27603	**800-333-7227**	919-828-9100	38
Warren Electric Co-op Inc 320 E Main St	Youngsville	PA	16371	**800-364-8640**	814-563-7548	244
Warren Featherbone Co DBA Alexis Playsafe 999 Chestnut St SE	Gainesville	GA	30503	**800-253-9476**	770-535-3000	153-4
Warren Properties Inc PO Box 469114	Escondido	CA	92046	**877-927-7361**	760-480-6211	641
Warren Sewell Clothing Co 126 Hamilton Ave	Bremen	GA	30110	**800-876-9722**	770-537-2391	153-12
Warren Shade Co Inc 2825 E Hennepin Ave	Minneapolis	MN	55413	**800-937-0008**	612-331-5939	88
Warren Transport Inc PO Box 420	Waterloo	IA	50704	**800-553-2792**	319-233-6113	769
Warrenton-Fauquier Flight Center 5075 Airport Rd Warrenton-Fauquier Airport PO Box 239	Midland	VA	22728	**800-296-4062**	540-788-4959	63
Warrior & Gulf Navigation Co PO Box 11397	Chickasaw	AL	36671	**800-452-6100**	251-452-6000	309
Warsaw Chemical Co Inc 390 Argonne Rd	Warsaw	IN	46580	**800-548-3396**	574-267-3251	149
Wartburg College 100 Wartburg Blvd	Waverly	IA	50677	**800-772-2085**	319-352-8200	163
Wartsila North America Inc 16330 Air Center Blvd	Houston	TX	77032	**800-676-9945**	281-233-6200	259
Warwick Hotel Denver 1776 Grant St	Denver	CO	80203	**800-525-2888**	303-861-2000	373
Warwick Hotel New York 65 W 54th St	New York	NY	10019	**800-223-4099**	212-247-2700	373
Warwick Hotel Seattle 401 Lenora St	Seattle	WA	98121	**800-426-9280**	206-443-4300	373
Warwick International Hotels Inc 65 W 54th St	New York	NY	10019	**800-223-4099**	212-247-2700	369
Warwick Manor Behavioral Health 3680 Warwick Rd	East New Market	MD	21631	**800-344-6423**	410-943-8108	712
Warwick Regis Hotel San Francisco 490 Geary St	San Francisco	CA	94102	**800-827-3447**	415-928-7900	373
Warwick Valley Telephone Co DBA WVT Communications 47 Main St PO Bo 592 *NASDAQ: WWVY* ■ *Cust Svc	Warwick	NY	10990	**800-952-7642***	845-986-1101	721
Wasatch Academy 120 S 100 W	Mount Pleasant	UT	84647	**800-634-4690**	435-462-1400	611
Wasatch Electric Co Inc 1574 S West Temple	Salt Lake City	UT	84115	**800-999-4511**	801-487-4511	188-4
Wasco Products Inc 22 Pioneer Ave PO Box 351	Sanford	ME	04073	**800-388-0293**	207-324-8060	325
Wascomat of America PO Box 960338	Inwood	NY	11096	**800-645-2205**	516-371-4400	38
Wash Depot Holdings Inc 435 Eastern Ave	Malden	MA	02148	**800-339-3949**	781-324-2000	62-1
Wash Tub 16035 University Oak	San Antonio	TX	78249	**866-493-8822**	210-493-8822	62-1
Washburn University 1700 SW College Ave	Topeka	KS	66621	**800-332-0291**	785-231-1010	163
Washex Inc 5000 Central Fwy N *Sales	Wichita Falls	TX	76306	**800-433-0933***	940-855-3990	418
Washington						
Bill Status PO Box 40600	Olympia	WA	98504	**800-562-6000**	360-786-7573	425
Child Support Div PO Box 45860	Olympia	WA	98504	**800-457-6202**	360-664-5440	335
Crime Victim Compensation Program PO Box 44520	Olympia	WA	98504	**800-547-8367**	360-902-5355	335
Health Dept PO Box 47890	Olympia	WA	98504	**800-525-0127**	360-236-4501	335
Historical Society 1911 Pacific Ave	Tacoma	WA	98402	**888-238-4378**	253-272-3500	335
Housing Finance Commission 1000 2nd Ave Suite 2700	Seattle	WA	98104	**800-767-4663**	206-464-7139	335
Mental Health Div PO Box 45320	Olympia	WA	98504	**888-713-6010**	360-902-8070	335
State Parks & Recreation Commission PO Box 42650 *Campground Resv	Olympia	WA	98504	**888-226-7688***	360-902-8500	335
Veterans Affairs Dept PO Box 41150	Olympia	WA	98504	**800-562-2308**	360-753-5586	335
Vocational Rehabilitation Div PO Box 45340	Olympia	WA	98504	**800-637-5627**	360-438-8000	335
Washington Area Chamber of Commerce 323 W Main St	Washington	MO	63090	**888-792-7466**	636-239-2715	137
Washington Assn of Realtors 504 E 14th Ave Suite 200	Olympia	WA	98501	**800-562-6024**	360-943-3100	642
Washington Banking Co 321 SE Pioneer Way *NASDAQ: WBCO*	Oak Harbor	WA	98277	**800-290-6508**	360-679-3121	355-2
Washington Beef Inc PO Box 832	Toppenish	WA	98948	**800-289-2333**	509-865-2121	465
Washington Booker T Insurance Co PO Box 697	Birmingham	AL	35201	**800-228-4180**	205-328-5454	384-2
Washington Cable Supply Inc 4600-D Boston Way	Lanham	MD	20706	**800-888-0738**	301-577-1200	245
Washington Chain & Supply Inc PO Box 3645	Seattle	WA	98124	**800-851-3429**	206-623-8500	759
Washington College 300 Washington Ave	Chestertown	MD	21620	**800-410-2800**	410-778-2800	163
Washington Convention Center 801 Mt Vernon Pl NW	Washington	DC	20001	**800-368-9000**	202-249-3000	204
Washington Corp PO Box 16630	Missoula	MT	59808	**800-832-7329**	406-523-1300	258
Washington County Chamber of Commerce 314 S Austin St	Brenham	TX	77833	**888-273-6426**	979-836-3695	137
Washington County Convention & Visitors Bureau 5075 SW Griffith Dr Suite 120	Beaverton	OR	97005	**800-537-3149**	503-644-5555	205
Washington Court Hotel 525 New Jersey Ave NW	Washington	DC	20001	**800-321-3010**	202-628-2100	373
Washington DC Accommodations 2201 Wisconsin Ave NW Suite C-120	Washington	DC	20007	**800-554-2220**	202-289-2220	368
Washington Dental Service 9706 4th Ave NE	Seattle	WA	98115	**800-554-1907**	206-522-1300	384-3
Washington Document Service Inc 1023 15th St NW 12th Fl	Washington	DC	20005	**800-728-5201**	202-628-5200	621

Name / Address	City	State	Zip	Toll-Free	Phone	Class
Washington Duke Inn & Golf Club 3001 Cameron Blvd	Durham	NC	27705	**800-443-3853**	919-490-0999	373
Washington Electric Co-op Inc PO Box 664	Marietta	OH	45750	**877-594-9324**	740-373-2141	244
Washington Electric Co-op Inc PO Box 8	East Montpelier	VT	05651	**800-932-5245**	802-223-5245	244
Washington Electric Membership Corp PO Box 598	Sandersville	GA	31082	**800-552-2577**	478-552-2577	244
Washington Evening Journal PO Box 471	Washington	IA	52353	**800-369-0341**	319-653-2191	522-2
Washington Examiner 6408 Edsall Rd	Alexandria	VA	22312	**800-531-1223**	703-560-4000	522-2
Washington Express Service LLC 12240 Indian Creek Ct Suite 100	Beltsville	MD	20705	**800-939-5463**	301-210-0899	536
Washington Eye Bank 815 Park Ave	Baltimore	MD	21201	**800-756-4824**	410-752-2020	265
Washington Federal Inc 425 Pike St *NASDAQ: WFSL*	Seattle	WA	98101	**800-324-9375**	206-624-7930	355-2
Washington Federal Savings & Loan Assn 425 Pike St	Seattle	WA	98101	**800-324-9375**	206-624-7930	71
Washington Gas & Light Co 101 Constitution Ave NW	Washington	DC	20080	**800-752-7520**	703-750-4440	774
Washington Homes Inc 1802 Brightseat Rd	Landover	MD	20785	**800-342-5944**	301-772-8900	639
Washington & Jefferson College 60 S Lincoln St	Washington	PA	15301	**888-926-3529**	724-222-4400	163
Washington Missourian PO Box 336	Washington	MO	63090	**888-239-7701**	636-239-7701	522-4
Washington Mutual Bank 1201 3rd Ave	Seattle	WA	98101	**800-788-7000**	206-461-2000	71
Washington Mutual Bank FA 400 E Main St	Stockton	CA	95290	**800-788-7000**	209-460-2888	71
Washington Mutual Inc 1201 3rd Ave *NYSE: WM*	Seattle	WA	98101	**800-756-8000**	206-461-2000	71
Washington Mutual Mortgage Loan Corp 4305 Harrison Blvd Suite 10	Ogden	UT	84403	**800-756-8000**	801-626-2203	498
Washington National Cathedral 3101 Wisconsin Ave NW	Washington	DC	20016	**800-622-6304**	202-537-6200	509
Washington National Insurance Co 11815 N Pennsylvania St	Carmel	IN	46032	**800-933-9301**		384-2
Washington National Opera 2600 Virginia Ave NW Suite 104	Washington	DC	20037	**800-876-7372**	202-295-2420	563-2
Washington Ornamental Iron Works Inc 17926 S Broadway	Gardena	CA	90248	**800-332-4766**	310-327-8660	188-14
Washington Pavilion of Arts & Science 301 S Main Ave	Sioux Falls	SD	57104	**877-927-4728**	605-367-7397	509
Washington Plaza Hotel 10 Thomas Cir NW Massachusetts Ave at 14th St	Washington	DC	20005	**800-424-1140**	202-842-1300	373
Washington Post 1150 15th St NW	Washington	DC	20071	**800-627-1150**	202-334-6000	522-2
Washington Post Co 1150 15th St NW *NYSE: WPO*	Washington	DC	20071	**800-627-1150**	202-334-6000	184
Washington Post Writers Group 1150 15th St NW	Washington	DC	20071	**800-879-9794**	202-334-6375	520
Washington Publishing Co 5740 Industry Ln 2nd Fl	Frederick	MD	21704	**800-972-4334**	301-696-0050	176-11
Washington Real Estate Investment Trust 6110 Executive Blvd Suite 800 *NYSE: WRE*	Rockville	MD	20852	**800-565-9748**	301-984-9400	641
Washington Regional Hospice 34 W Colt Square Dr Suite 1	Fayetteville	AR	72703	**888-611-1094**	479-463-1161	365
Washington Savings Bank FSB 4201 Mitchellville Rd Suite 100 *AMEX: WSB*	Bowie	MD	20716	**800-843-7250**	301-352-3130	71
Washington Service Bureau Inc. CCH 1015 15th St NW 10th Fl	Washington	DC	20005	**800-955-5219**	202-312-6600	621
Washington Square Hotel 103 Waverly Pl	New York	NY	10011	**800-222-0418**	212-777-9515	373
Washington State Bar Assn 2101 4th Ave Suite 400	Seattle	WA	98121	**800-945-9722**	206-727-8200	73
Washington State Bar News 2101 4th Ave 4th Fl	Seattle	WA	98121	**800-945-9722**	206-727-8215	449-15
Washington State Employees Credit Union 400 E Union Ave	Olympia	WA	98501	**800-562-0999**	360-943-7911	216
Washington State History Museum 1911 Pacific Ave	Tacoma	WA	98402	**888-238-4373**	253-272-3500	509
Washington State Medical Assn 2033 6th Ave Suite 1100	Seattle	WA	98121	**800-552-0612**	206-441-9762	466
Washington State University	Pullman	WA	99164	**800-468-6978**	509-335-3564	163
Washington State Veterinary Medical Assn PO Box 962	Bellevue	WA	98009	**800-399-7862**	425-454-8381	782
Washington Suites 100 S Reynolds St	Alexandria	VA	22304	**877-736-2500**	703-370-9600	373
Washington Suites Georgetown 2500 Pennsylvania Ave NW	Washington	DC	20037	**877-736-2500**	202-333-8060	373
Washington Theological Union 6896 Laurel St NW	Washington	DC	20012	**800-334-9922**	202-726-8800	164-3
Washington Times-Herald PO Box 471	Washington	IN	47501	**800-235-4113**	812-254-0480	522-2
Washington Trust Bancorp Inc 23 Broad St *NASDAQ: WASH*	Westerly	RI	02891	**800-475-2265**	401-348-1200	355-2
Washington University 1 Brookings Dr	Saint Louis	MO	63130	**800-638-0700**	314-935-5000	163
Washington Wizards 601 F St NW	Washington	DC	20004	**800-551-7328**	202-661-5000	703
Washingtonian Magazine 1828 L St NW Suite 200	Washington	DC	20036	**877-532-6083**	202-296-3600	449-22
Wasserstrom Co 477 S Front St	Columbus	OH	43215	**800-999-9277**	614-228-6525	295
Wasserstrom N & Sons Inc 2300 Lockbourne Rd	Columbus	OH	43207	**800-444-4697**	614-228-5550	295
Waste Assn of North America. Solid 100 Wayne Ave Suite 700	Silver Spring	MD	20910	**800-467-9262**	301-585-2898	48-12
Waste. Citizens Against Government 1301 Connecticut Ave NW Suite 400	Washington	DC	20036	**800-232-6479**	202-467-5300	48-7
Waste Industries Inc 3301 Benson Dr Suite 601	Raleigh	NC	27609	**800-647-9946**	919-325-3000	791
Waste Management Assn. Air & 420 Fort Duquesne Blvd 1 Gateway Ctr 3rd Fl	Pittsburgh	PA	15222	**800-270-3444**	412-232-3444	48-12
Waste Management Inc 1001 Fannin St Suite 4000 *NYSE: WMI*	Houston	TX	77002	**800-633-7871**	713-512-6200	791
Waste Management & Research Center. Illinois 1 E Hazelwood Dr	Champaign	IL	61820	**800-407-0261**	217-333-8940	654
Waste Technology Corp 5400 Rio Grande Ave	Jacksonville	FL	32254	**800-231-9286**	904-355-5558	537
WatchGuard Technologies Inc 505 5th Ave S Suite 500 *NASDAQ: WGRD* ■ *Sales	Seattle	WA	98104	**800-734-9905***	206-521-8340	174
Watchmakers-Clockmakers Institute. American 701 Enterprise Dr	Harrison	OH	45030	**866-367-2924**	513-367-9800	49-4
WatchMeGrow LLC 4405 7th Ave Suite 201	Lacey	WA	98503	**800-483-5597**		145
Watcon Inc PO Box 2829	South Bend	IN	46680	**800-492-8266**	574-287-3397	143
Water Action. Clean 4455 Connecticut Ave NW Suite A-300	Washington	DC	20008	**800-709-2837**	202-895-0420	48-13
Water Assn. International Bottled 1700 Diagonal Rd Suite 650	Alexandria	VA	22314	**800-928-3711**	703-683-5213	49-6
Water Conservation Society. Soil & 945 SW Ankeny Rd	Ankeny	IA	50021	**800-843-7645**	515-289-2331	48-13
Water Environment Federation (WEF) 601 Wythe St	Alexandria	VA	22314	**800-666-0206**	703-684-2400	48-13
Water Fund. Clean 4455 Connecticut Ave NW Suite A300-16	Washington	DC	20008	**800-709-2837**	202-895-0432	48-13
Water Furnace International Inc 9000 Conservation Way	Fort Wayne	IN	46809	**800-222-5667**	260-478-5667	352
Water Mania 6073 W Hwy 192	Kissimmee	FL	34747	**800-527-3092**	407-396-2626	32
Water Saver Faucet Co 701 W Erie St 2nd Fl *Parts	Chicago	IL	60610	**800-973-7278***	312-666-5500	598
Water Ski Hall of Fame & Museum. American 1251 Holy Cow Rd	Polk City	FL	33868	**800-533-2972**	863-324-2472	511
Water Ski. USA 1251 Holy Cow Rd	Polk City	FL	33868	**800-533-2972**	863-324-4341	48-22
Water Technologies. Association of 8201 Greensboro Dr Suite 300	McLean	VA	22102	**800-858-6683**	703-610-9012	48-2
Water & Wastes Digest 380 E Northwest Hwy Suite 200	Des Plaines	IL	60016	**800-220-7851**	847-391-1000	449-21
Water Works Assn. American 6666 W Quincy Ave	Denver	CO	80235	**800-926-7337**	303-794-7711	48-12
Waterbury Farrel Technologies Inc 200 1st Gulf Blvd	Brampton	ON	L6W4T5	**800-387-3834**	905-455-0402	661
Watercolor Magic Magazine 4700 E Galbraith Rd *Cust Svc	Cincinnati	OH	45236	**800-811-9834***	513-531-2690	449-2
Waterfield Mortgage Co Inc 7500 W Jefferson Blvd	Fort Wayne	IN	46804	**800-444-9847**	260-434-8411	498
Waterford Hotel & Conference Center 11360 US Hwy 1	Palm Beach Gardens	FL	33408	**888-696-9692**	561-624-7186	370
Waterford Wedgwood USA Inc 1330 Campus Pkwy *Cust Svc	Wall	NJ	07719	**888-938-7911***	732-938-5800	357
Waterfowl Foundation. Delta 1305 E Central Ave	Bismarck	ND	58501	**888-987-3695**	701-222-8857	48-3
Waterfront Plaza Hotel 10 Washington St	Oakland	CA	94607	**800-729-3638**	510-836-3800	373
Watergate Hotel 2650 Virginia Ave NW	Washington	DC	20037	**800-289-1555**	202-965-2300	373
Watergate. Swissotel Washington - The 2650 Virginia Ave NW	Washington	DC	20037	**800-289-1555**	202-965-2300	373
Waterloo Cedar Falls Courier PO Box 540	Waterloo	IA	50704	**800-798-1730**	319-291-1400	522-2
Waterloo Convention & Visitor Bureau 313 E 5th St	Waterloo	IA	50703	**800-728-8431**	319-233-8350	205
Waterloo Industries Inc 100 E 4th St	Waterloo	IA	50703	**800-833-8851**	319-235-7131	479
Waterman Steamship Corp 1 Whitehall St 20th Fl	New York	NY	10004	**888-972-5274**	212-747-8550	307
Waterous Co 125 Hardman Ave	South Saint Paul	MN	55075	**800-488-1228**	651-450-5000	627
Waters Corp 34 Maple St *NYSE: WAT*	Milford	MA	01757	**800-252-4752**	508-478-2000	410
Waters Edge Hotel 25 Main St	Tiburon	CA	94920	**800-738-7477**	415-789-5999	373
Water's Edge Resort 1525 Boston Post Rd	Westbrook	CT	06498	**800-222-5901**	860-399-5901	655
Watersaver Co Inc 5870 E 56th Ave	Commerce City	CO	80022	**800-525-2424**	303-289-1818	589
Watertech Whirlpool Bath & Spa 2507 Plymouth Rd	Johnson City	TN	37601	**800-289-8827**	423-926-1470	367
Waterton Lakes Lodge Box 4 101 Clematis Ave	Waterton Park	AB	T0K2M0	**888-985-6343**	403-859-2150	655
Watertown Co-op Elevator Assn 810 Burlington Northern Dr	Watertown	SD	57201	**888-882-3039**	605-886-3039	272
Watertown Daily Times 260 Washington St	Watertown	NY	13601	**800-642-6222**	315-782-1000	522-2
Watertown Public Opinion PO Box 10	Watertown	SD	57201	**800-658-5401**	605-886-6901	522-2
Waterville Valley Resort 1 Ski Area Rd PO Box 540	Waterville Valley	NH	03215	**800-468-2553**	603-236-8311	655
Waterway Guide Magazine 326 1st St Suite 400	Annapolis	MD	21403	**800-233-3359**	443-482-9377	449-22
Waterwood National Resort 1 Waterwood Pkwy	Huntsville	TX	77320	**877-441-5211**	936-891-5211	655
Watkins Inc PO Box 5570	Winona	MN	55987	**800-243-9423**	507-457-3300	361
Watkins Mfg Corp 1280 Park Ctr Dr	Vista	CA	92083	**800-999-4688**	760-598-6464	367
Watkins Motor Lines Inc PO Box 95002	Lakeland	FL	33804	**800-284-4544**	863-687-4545	769
Watley AB Inc 90 Park Ave 26th Fl	New York	NY	10016	**888-229-2853**	212-500-6500	679
Watlow Winona 1241 Bundy Blvd	Winona	MN	55987	**800-833-7492**	507-454-5300	201
Watne Inc Realtors 408 N Broadway	Minot	ND	58703	**800-568-5311**	701-852-1156	638
Watonwan Farm Service 208 S Main	Delavan	MN	56023	**800-830-0447**	507-854-3204	272
Watonwan Farm Service 233 W Ciro St	Truman	MN	56088	**800-657-3282**	507-776-2831	271

Name / Address	City	State	ZIP	Toll-Free	Phone	Class
Watsco Inc 2665 S Bayshore Dr Suite 901 *NYSE: WSO*	Coconut Grove	FL	33133	**800-492-8726**	305-714-4100	15
Watson Kunda & Sons DBA Kunda Beverage 349 S Henderson Rd	King of Prussia	PA	19406	**800-262-2323**	610-265-3113	82-1
Watson Laboratories Inc 311 Bonnie Cir	Corona	CA	92880	**800-272-5525**	951-270-1400	573
Watson Pharmaceuticals Inc 311 Bonnie Cir *NYSE: WPI*	Corona	CA	92880	**800-272-5525**	951-493-5300	572
Watson Quality Food Inc PO Box 215	Blackwood	NJ	08012	**800-257-7870**	856-227-0594	608
Watson Wyatt & Co 1717 H St NW Suite 800	Washington	DC	20006	**800-675-7282**	202-715-7000	192
Watt Harvey & Co Atlanta Airport PO Box 20787	Atlanta	GA	30320	**800-241-6103**	404-767-7501	384-2
Watters & Martin Inc 3800 Village Ave	Norfolk	VA	23502	**800-446-8205**	757-857-0651	346
Watts Fluidair Inc 9 Cutts Rd	Kittery	ME	03904	**877-467-4323**	207-439-9511	777
Waukesha Cherry-Burrell Corp 611 Sugar Creek Rd	Delavan	WI	53115	**800-252-5200**	262-728-1900	627
Waukesha Electric Systems Inc 400 S Prairie Ave	Waukesha	WI	53186	**800-835-2732**	262-547-0121	756
Waukesha Memorial Hospital 725 American Ave	Waukesha	WI	53188	**800-326-2011**	262-928-1000	366-2
Wausau A Mutual Co. Employers Insurance Co of 2000 Westwood Dr	Wausau	WI	54401	**800-435-4401**	715-845-5211	384-4
Wausau Business Insurance Co 2000 Westwood Dr	Wausau	WI	54401	**800-435-4401**	715-845-5211	384-4
Wausau Central Wisconsin Convention & Visitors Bureau 10204 Park Plaza Suite B	Mosinee	WI	54455	**888-948-4748**	715-355-8788	205
Wausau Chemical Corp 2001 N River Dr	Wausau	WI	54403	**800-950-6656**	715-842-2285	142
Wausau Daily Herald PO Box 1286	Wausau	WI	54402	**800-477-4838**	715-842-2101	522-2
Wausau General Insurance Co 2000 Westwood Dr	Wausau	WI	54401	**800-435-4401**	715-845-5211	384-4
Wausau Hospital 333 Pine Ridge Blvd	Wausau	WI	54401	**800-283-2881**	715-847-2121	366-2
Wausau Papers Otis Mill Inc 1 Mill St	Jay	ME	04239	**800-876-5772**	207-897-7200	547
Wausau Service Corp 2000 Westwood Dr	Wausau	WI	54401	**800-435-4401**	715-845-5211	384-4
Wausau Underwriters Insurance Co 2000 Westwood Dr	Wausau	WI	54401	**800-435-4401**	715-845-5211	384-4
Wausau Window & Wall Systems 1415 West St	Wausau	WI	54401	**877-678-2983**	715-845-2161	232
Wauwatosa Savings Bank 11200 W Plank Ct	Wauwatosa	WI	53226	**888-686-7272**	414-918-0500	71
Wauwinet The PO Box 2580 Wauwinet Rd	Nantucket	MA	02584	**800-426-8718**	508-228-0145	373
WAV Inc 2380 Prospect Dr	Aurora	IL	60504	**800-678-2419**	630-818-1000	174
WAVA-FM 105.1 (Rel) 1901 N Moore St Suite 200	Arlington	VA	22209	**888-293-9282**	703-807-2266	631
Wave Systems Corp 480 Pleasant St *NASDAQ: WAVX*	Lee	MA	01238	**888-669-9283**	413-243-1600	176-1
Wave Three Software Inc 11696 Sorrento Valley Rd Suite J	San Diego	CA	92121	**888-408-8422**	858-720-7240	176-7
WaveLink Corp 11332 NE 122nd Way Suite 300 *Tech Supp	Kirkland	WA	98034	**888-699-9283***	425-823-0111	176-7
Waverly Mills Inc 23 3rd St *Cust Svc	Laurinburg	NC	28352	**800-496-9276***	910-276-1441	730-9
Wawa Inc 260 W Baltimore Pike	Media	PA	19063	**800-283-9292**	610-358-8000	203
Wawona Frozen Foods Inc 100 W Alluvial Ave	Clovis	CA	93611	**800-669-2966**	559-299-2901	291-21
Wax Museum at Fisherman's Wharf 145 Jefferson St Suite 500	San Francisco	CA	94133	**800-439-4305**	415-885-4834	509
Waxman Industries Inc 24460 Aurora Rd	Bedford Heights	OH	44146	**800-531-3342**	440-439-1830	601
WAXN-TV Ch 64 (ABC) 1901 N Tryon St	Charlotte	NC	28206	**800-367-9762**	704-338-9999	726
WAXQ-FM 104.3 (CR) 1180 6th Ave 6th Fl	New York	NY	10036	**888-872-1043**	212-575-1043	631
Wayest Safety Inc 3745 NW 37th Pl	Oklahoma City	OK	73112	**800-256-1003**	405-942-7101	667
WAYJ-FM 88.7 (Rel) 1860 Boyscout Dr Suite 202	Fort Myers	FL	33907	**888-936-1929**	239-936-1929	631
Wayland Academy 101 N University Ave	Beaver Dam	WI	53916	**800-860-7725**	920-885-3373	611
Wayland Baptist University 1900 W 7th St	Plainview	TX	79072	**800-588-1928**	806-291-1000	163
Wayne Combustion Systems 801 Glasgow Ave	Fort Wayne	IN	46814	**800-443-4625**	260-425-9200	352
Wayne Community College 3000 Wayne Memorial Dr Box 8002	Goldsboro	NC	27533	**866-414-5064**	919-735-5151	160
Wayne County Chamber of Commerce 303 Commercial St	Honesdale	PA	18431	**800-433-9008**	570-253-1960	137
Wayne County Community College District 801 W Fort St	Detroit	MI	48226	**800-300-2118**	313-496-2600	160
Wayne County Convention & Visitors Bureau 428 W Liberty St	Wooster	OH	44691	**800-362-6474**	330-264-1800	205
Wayne-Dalton Corp 1 Door Dr PO Box 67	Mount Hope	OH	44660	**800-827-3667**	330-674-7015	232
Wayne Div Dresser Inc 3814 Jarrett Way	Austin	TX	78728	**800-289-2963**	512-388-8311	625
Wayne Div Smith Dairy 1590 NW 11th St	Richmond	IN	47375	**800-875-9296**	765-935-7521	291-27
Wayne Farms Enterprises LLC 1020 County Rd 114	Jack	AL	36346	**800-223-2569**	334-897-3435	608
Wayne Farms LLC 4110 Continental Dr	Oakwood	GA	30566	**800-392-0844**	678-450-3100	11-8
Wayne General Hospital 950 Matthew Dr	Waynesboro	MS	39367	**877-521-9781**	601-735-5151	366-2
Wayne Homes LLC 3777 Boettler Oaks Dr	Uniontown	OH	44685	**800-686-5354**	330-896-7611	186
Wayne Hummer Investments LLC 300 S Wacker Dr Suite 1500	Chicago	IL	60606	**800-621-4477**	312-431-1700	679
Wayne Industries 1400 8th St N	Clanton	AL	35045	**800-225-3148**	205-755-5580	692
Wayne J Griffin Electric Inc 116 Hopping Brook Rd	Holliston	MA	01746	**800-421-0151**	508-429-8830	188-4
Wayne Mills Co Inc 130 W Berkley St	Philadelphia	PA	19144	**800-220-8053**	215-842-2134	730-5
Wayne State College 1111 Main St	Wayne	NE	68787	**800-228-9972**	402-375-7000	163
Wayne State University 6050 Cass Ave	Detroit	MI	48202	**877-978-4636**	313-577-2424	163
Wayne-White Counties Electric Co-op PO Drawer E	Fairfield	IL	62837	**888-871-7695**	618-842-2196	244
Wayne Wire Cloth Products Inc 200 E Dresden St	Kalkaska	MI	49646	**800-654-7688**	231-258-9187	676
Waynesboro Hospital 501 E Main St	Waynesboro	PA	17268	**888-227-3822**	717-765-4000	366-2
Waynesburg College 51 W College St	Waynesburg	PA	15370	**800-225-7393**	724-627-8191	163
Waynesville Country Club Inn 176 Country Club Dr	Waynesville	NC	28786	**800-627-6250**	828-456-3551	655
Waypoint Bank PO Box 1711	Harrisburg	PA	17105	**866-929-7646**	717-236-4041	71
WAYZ-FM 104.7 (Ctry) 10960 John Wayne Dr	Greencastle	PA	17225	**888-950-1047**	717-597-9200	631
WAZE-TV Ch 19 (WB) 1277 N St Joseph Ave	Evansville	IN	47720	**888-488-1900**	812-425-1900	726
WB Marvin Mfg Co 211 Glenn Ave	Urbana	OH	43078	**800-733-1706**	937-653-7131	37
WB McCloud & Co 2500 W Higgins Rd Suite 850 *Cust Svc	Hoffman Estates	IL	60195	**800-332-7805***	847-585-0650	567
WB McGuire Co 1 Hudson Ave	Hudson	NY	12534	**800-624-8473**	518-828-7652	462
WB Place LLC 368 W Sumner St	Hartford	WI	53027	**800-826-4433**	262-673-3130	424
WBAL-TV Ch 11 (NBC) 3800 Hooper Ave	Baltimore	MD	21211	**800-677-9225**	410-467-3000	726
WBANA (Wild Blueberry Assn of North America) 59 Cottage St po bOX 180	Bar Harbor	ME	04609	**800-233-9453**	207-288-2655	48-2
WBCT-FM 93.7 (Ctry) 77 Monroe Center St NW Suite 1000	Grand Rapids	MI	49503	**800-633-9393**	616-459-1919	631
WBDX-FM 102.7 (Rel) 5512 Ringgold Rd Suite 214	Chattanooga	TN	37412	**877-262-5103**	423-892-1200	631
WBGL-FM 91.7 (Rel) 2108 W Springfield Ave	Champaign	IL	61821	**866-917-9245**	217-359-8232	631
WBHM-FM 90.3 (NPR) 650 11th St S	Birmingham	AL	35294	**800-444-9246**	205-934-2606	631
WBHT-FM 97.1 (CHR) 600 Baltimore Dr	Wilkes-Barre	PA	18702	**800-447-5000**	570-824-9000	631
WBHY-FM 88.5 (Rel) PO Box 1328	Mobile	AL	36633	**888-473-8488**	251-473-8488	631
WBIQ-TV Ch 10 (PBS) 2112 11th Ave S Suite 400	Birmingham	AL	35205	**800-239-5233**	205-328-8756	726
WBKI-TV Ch 34 (WB) 1601 Alliant Ave	Louisville	KY	40299	**877-541-3434**	502-809-3400	726
WBNI-FM 89.1 (NPR) 3204 Clairmont Ct	Fort Wayne	IN	46808	**800-471-9264**	260-452-1189	631
WBNX-TV Ch 55 (WB) 2690 State Rd	Cuyahoga Falls	OH	44223	**800-367-8855**	330-922-5500	726
WBSC-TV Ch 40 (WB) 110 Technology Dr	Asheville	NC	28803	**800-288-8813**	864-226-9292	726
WBSN-FM 89.1 (Rel) 3939 Gentilly Blvd	New Orleans	LA	70126	**800-480-3600**	504-816-8000	631
WBUD-AM 1260 (Oldies) 109 Walters Ave	Trenton	NJ	08638	**800-678-9599**	609-771-8181	631
WBUR-FM 90.9 (NPR) 890 Commonwealth Ave	Boston	MA	02215	**800-909-9287**	617-353-2790	631
WC Bradley Char-Broil 1442 Belfast Ave *Cust Svc	Columbus	GA	31904	**800-352-4111***	706-324-0421	36
WC McQuaide Inc 153 Macridge Ave	Johnstown	PA	15904	**800-456-0292**	814-269-6000	769
WC & AN Miller Cos 4701 Sangamore Rd	Bethesda	MD	20816	**800-599-4711**	301-229-4000	186
WC & AN Miller Realtors 4910 Massachusetts Ave NW Suite 119	Washington	DC	20016	**877-362-1300**	202-362-1300	638
WCAA-FM 105.9 (Span) 485 Madison Ave 3rd Fl	New York	NY	10022	**866-927-1059**	212-310-6000	631
WCBB-TV Ch 10 (PBS) 1450 Lisbon St	Lewiston	ME	04240	**800-884-1717**	207-783-9101	726
WCBM-AM 680 (N/T) 1726 Reisterstown Rd Suite 117	Baltimore	MD	21208	**800-922-6680**	410-580-6800	631
WCBU-FM 89.9 (NPR) 1501 W Bradley Ave	Peoria	IL	61625	**888-488-9228**	309-677-3690	631
WCCO-TV Ch 4 (CBS) 90 S 11th St	Minneapolis	MN	55403	**800-444-9226**	612-339-4444	726
WCEU-TV Ch 15 (PBS) 1200 W International Speedway Blvd	Daytona Beach	FL	32114	**800-638-9238**	386-254-4415	726
WCF (Women's Campaign Fund) 734 15th St NW Suite 500	Washington	DC	20005	**800-446-8170**	202-393-8164	48-7
WCHS-TV Ch 8 (ABC) 1301 Piedmont Rd	Charleston	WV	25301	**888-696-9247**	304-346-5358	726
WCI Communities Inc 24301 Walden Ctr Dr *NYSE: WCI*	Bonita Springs	FL	34134	**800-924-2290**	239-947-2600	639
WCIC-FM 91.5 (Rel) 3902 W Baring Trace	Peoria	IL	61615	**800-353-9191**	309-282-9191	631
WCL Co PO Box 3588	City of Industry	CA	91744	**800-331-3816**	626-968-5523	346
WCLV/Seaway Productions 26501 Renaissance Pkwy	Cleveland	OH	44128	**800-491-8863**	216-464-0900	632
WCNY-FM 91.3 (NPR) 506 Old Liverpool Rd	Liverpool	NY	13088	**800-451-9269**	315-453-2424	631
WCNY-TV Ch 24 (PBS) PO Box 2400	Syracuse	NY	13220	**800-451-9269**	315-453-2424	726
WCQR-FM 88.3 (Rel) 2312 Pine St	Gray	TN	37659	**888-477-5676**	423-477-5676	631
WCQS-FM 88.1 (NPR) 73 Broadway	Asheville	NC	28801	**800-768-6698**	828-253-6875	631
WCRF-FM 103.3 (Rel) 9756 Barr Rd	Cleveland	OH	44141	**800-283-9273**	440-526-1111	631
WCSH-TV Ch 6 (NBC) 1 Congress Sq	Portland	ME	04101	**800-464-1213**	207-828-6666	726
WCTV-TV Ch 6 (CBS) 4000 County Rd 12	Tallahassee	FL	32312	**800-375-4204**	850-893-6666	726
WCVE-TV Ch 23 (PBS) 23 Sesame St	Richmond	VA	23235	**800-476-8440**	804-320-1301	726
WD-40 Co 1061 Cudahy Pl *NASDAQ: WDFC*	San Diego	CA	92110	**800-448-9340**	619-275-1400	530

Name / Address	City	State	ZIP	Toll-Free	Phone	Class
WD Tire Warehouse Inc 3805 E Livingston Ave	Columbus	OH	43227	**800-634-7883**	614-461-8944	740
WDAM-TV Ch 7 (NBC) PO Box 16269	Hattiesburg	MS	39404	**800-844-9326**	601-544-4730	726
WDAS-AM 1480 (Rel) 23 W City Line Ave	Bala Cynwyd	PA	19004	**877-894-1480**	610-617-8500	631
WDAS-FM 105.3 (Urban AC) 23 W City Line Ave	Bala Cynwyd	PA	19004	**877-894-1053**	610-617-8500	631
WDAZ-TV Ch 8 (ABC) 2220 S Washington St	Grand Forks	ND	58201	**800-732-4361**	701-775-2511	726
WDBJ-TV Ch 7 (CBS) 2807 Hershberger Rd NW	Roanoke	VA	24017	**800-777-9325**	540-344-7000	726
WDCO-FM 89.7 (NPR) 260 14th St NW	Atlanta	GA	30318	**800-222-4788**	404-685-2400	631
WDCO-TV Ch 29 (PBS) 260 14th St NW	Atlanta	GA	30318	**800-222-6006**	404-685-2400	726
WDEL-AM 1150 (N/T) 2727 Shipley Rd	Wilmington	DE	19810	**800-544-1150**	302-478-2700	631
WDIO-TV Ch 10 (ABC) 10 Observation Rd	Duluth	MN	55811	**800-477-1013**	218-727-6864	726
WDIV-TV Ch 4 (NBC) 550 W Lafayette Blvd	Detroit	MI	48226	**800-654-8221**	313-222-0500	726
WDJA-AM 1420 (N/T) 2710 W Atlantic Ave	Delray Beach	FL	33445	**888-278-0098**	561-278-1420	631
WDL Systems 220 Chatham Business Dr *Sales	Pittsboro	NC	27312	**800-548-2319***	919-545-2500	172
WDMA (Window & Door Manufacturers Assn) 1400 E Touhy Ave Suite 470	Des Plaines	IL	60018	**800-223-2301**	847-299-5200	49-3
WDNA-FM 88.9 (Jazz) 4848 SW 74th Ct	Miami	FL	33155	**866-688-9362**	305-662-8889	631
WDSD-FM 92.9 (Ctry) 1575 McKee Rd Suite 206	Dover	DE	19904	**888-929-9373**	302-674-1410	631
WDSE-TV Ch 8 (PBS) 632 Niagara Ct	Duluth	MN	55811	**888-563-9373**	218-724-8568	726
WE Aubuchon Co Inc 95 Aubuchon Dr	Westminster	MA	01473	**800-282-4393**	978-874-0521	359
WE Bassett Co 100 Trap Falls Rd Ext	Shelton	CT	06484	**800-394-8746**	203-929-8483	211
We Care Health Services Inc 151 Bloor St W Suite 602	Toronto	ON	M5S1S4	**888-429-3227**	416-922-7601	358
We Energies PO Box 2046	Milwaukee	WI	53201	**800-242-9437**	414-221-2345	774
WE Yoder Inc 41 S Maple St	Kutztown	PA	19530	**800-889-5149**	610-683-7383	187-8
WEA Mfg 1400 E Lackawanna Ave	Olyphant	PA	18448	**800-323-1263**	570-383-2471	239
WEAO-TV Ch 49 (PBS) 1750 Campus Center Dr	Kent	OH	44240	**800-544-4549**	330-677-4549	726
WEAR-TV Ch 3 (ABC) 4990 Mobile Hwy	Pensacola	FL	32506	**866-856-9327**	850-456-3333	726
WearGuard Corp 141 Longwater Dr	Norwell	MA	02061	**800-272-0308**	781-871-4100	451
Weather Shield Mfg Inc 1 Weather Shield Plaza PO Box 309 *Prod Info	Medford	WI	54451	**800-222-2995***	715-748-2100	234
Weatherby Inc 3100 El Camino Real	Atascadero	CA	93422	**800-334-4423**	805-466-1767	279
Weatherford Chamber of Commerce 401 Fort Worth St	Weatherford	TX	76086	**888-594-3801**	817-596-3801	137
Weatherford College 225 College Park Dr	Weatherford	TX	76086	**800-287-5471**	817-594-5471	160
Weatherford Completion Systems 11420 W Hwy 80 E	Midland	TX	79711	**800-777-7957**	432-563-7957	528
Weatherford-Enterra-Pearland Mfg Co 3810 Magnolia St	Pearland	TX	77581	**800-331-3387**	281-652-1300	661
Weatherford International Inc 515 Post Oak Blvd Suite 200 *NYSE: WFT*	Houston	TX	77027	**800-257-3826**	713-693-4000	526
Weathermatic 3301 W Kingsley Rd	Garland	TX	75041	**888-484-3776**	972-278-6131	420
Weatherproof Garment Co 1071 Ave of the Americas 8th Fl	New York	NY	10018	**800-645-7788**	212-695-7716	153-12
Weathervane Seafood Restaurant 31 Badgers Island W	Kittery	ME	03904	**800-654-4639**	207-439-0335	657
Weaver Brothers Inc 2230 Spar Ave	Anchorage	AK	99501	**800-478-4600**	907-278-4526	769
Weaver Daniel Co PO Box 525	Lebanon	PA	17042	**800-932-8377**	717-274-6100	291-26
Weaver Industries Inc 425 S 4th St	Denver	PA	17517	**800-292-7670**	717-336-7507	446
Weaver & Tidwell LLP 1600 W 7th St Suite 300	Fort Worth	TX	76102	**800-332-7952**	817-332-7905	2
Weavexx Corp 51 Flex Way	Youngsville	NC	27596	**800-932-8399**	919-556-7235	730-3
Web Base Inc 133 E De La Guerra St	Santa Barbara	CA	93101	**800-225-8885**	805-275-4505	176-1
Web Communications LLC 8005 S Chester St Suite 200	Englewood	CO	80112	**888-893-2266**		795
Web Content Report 316 N Michigan Ave Suite 400	Chicago	IL	60601	**800-878-5331**	312-960-4100	521-3
Web Graphics PO Box 308	Glens Falls	NY	12801	**800-833-8863**	518-792-6501	111
Web Offset Assn (WOA) 200 Deer Run Rd	Sewickley	PA	15143	**800-910-4283**	412-741-6860	49-16
Web Press Corp 22023 68th Ave S	Kent	WA	98032	**800-424-1411**	253-395-3343	617
Web Service Co Inc 3690 Redondo Beach Ave	Redondo Beach	CA	90278	**800-421-6897**	323-772-5131	38
Web Services Strategies 37 Broadway Suite 1	Arlington	MA	02474	**800-964-8702**	781-648-8700	521-3
Webb Del Corp 15111 N Pima Rd Suite 100	Scottsdale	AZ	85260	**800-808-8088**		639
Webb FW 237 Albany St	Boston	MA	02118	**800-453-1100**	617-227-2240	378
Webb Jervis B Co 34375 W 12-Mile Rd	Farmington Hills	MI	48331	**800-526-9322**	248-553-1220	206
Webb Mfg Co 1241 Carpenter St	Philadelphia	PA	19147	**800-932-2634**	215-336-5570	718
Webb Murray & Assoc Inc 2615 Beltway 8 E	Pasadena	TX	77503	**800-288-7428**	281-991-4227	691
Webb School PO Box 488	Bell Buckle	TN	37020	**888-733-9322**	931-389-9322	611
Webb Wheel Products Inc 2310 Industrial Dr SW *Cust Svc	Cullman	AL	35055	**800-633-3256***	256-739-6660	60
WebBalanced Technologies LLC 6206 Discount Dr	Fort Wayne	IN	46818	**877-366-7233**		176-7
Webber Energy Fuels 700 Main St	Bangor	ME	04401	**800-932-2371**	207-942-5501	569
Webber International University 1201 N Scenic Hwy	Babson Park	FL	33827	**800-741-1844**	863-638-1431	163
WEBC-AM 560 (N/T) 14 E Central Entrance	Duluth	MN	55811	**888-932-2560**	218-727-4500	631
Webcrafters Inc 2211 Fordem Ave	Madison	WI	53704	**800-356-8200**	608-244-3561	614
WebCT Inc 6 Kimball Ln Suite 310	Lynnfield	MA	01940	**877-932-2863**	781-309-1000	176-7
Weben-Jarco Inc 4007 Platinum Way	Dallas	TX	75237	**800-527-6449**	214-637-0530	92
Weber County Library 2464 Jefferson Ave	Ogden	UT	84401	**888-618-0564**	801-337-2617	426
Weber Marking Systems Inc 711 W Algonquin Rd *Sales	Arlington Heights	IL	60005	**800-225-0883***	847-364-8500	404
Weber Ron & Assoc Inc 185 Plains Rd Suite 302 E	Milford	CT	06460	**800-835-6584**	203-799-0000	722
Weber State University 3850 University Cir	Ogden	UT	84408	**800-848-7770**	801-626-6000	163
Weber-Stephen Products Co 200 E Daniels Rd *Cust Svc	Palatine	IL	60067	**800-446-1071***	847-934-5700	36
Weber-Valentine Co 1099 E Morse Ave *Cust Svc	Elk Grove Village	IL	60007	**800-323-9642***	847-439-7111	616
Weber's Inn 3050 Jackson Rd	Ann Arbor	MI	48103	**800-443-3050**	734-769-2500	373
WebEx Communications Inc 307 West Tasman Dr *NASDAQ: WEBX*	San Jose	CA	95134	**877-509-3239**	408-435-7000	176-7
WebFlyer.com 1930 Frequent Flyer Pt *Cust Svc	Colorado Springs	CO	80915	**800-209-2870***	719-572-2787	762
Webhire Inc 91 Hartwell Ave	Lexington	MA	02421	**877-932-4473**	781-869-5000	39
WebMD Corp 669 River Dr Center 2 *NASDAQ: HLTH*	Elmwood Park	NJ	07407	**877-469-3263**	201-703-3400	39
Webmedx Inc 564 Alpha Dr	Pittsburgh	PA	15238	**888-932-6339**	412-968-9244	755
WEBN-FM 102.7 (Rock) 8044 Montgomery Rd Suite 650	Cincinnati	OH	45236	**800-616-9236**	513-686-8300	631
Webplan One Lincoln Ctr 18 W 140 Butterfield Rd 15th Fl	Oakbrook Terrace	IL	60181	**866-236-3249**	613-592-5780	176-10
Webroot Software Inc PO Box 19816	Boulder	CO	80308	**800-772-9383**	303-442-3813	176-12
Websense Inc 10240 Sorrento Valley Rd *NASDAQ: WBSN*	San Diego	CA	92121	**800-723-1166**	858-320-8000	176-7
Websource 161 Ave of the Americas 3rd Fl	New York	NY	10013	**800-221-3213**	212-255-1600	543
Webster Bank 145 Bank St Webster Plaza	Waterbury	CT	06702	**800-325-2424**		71
Webster City Federal Bancorp 820 Des Moines St *NASDAQ: WCFB*	Webster City	IA	50595	**866-263-0293**	515-832-3071	355-2
Webster Electric Co-op PO Box 87	Marshfield	MO	65706	**800-643-4305**	417-859-2216	244
Webster Financial Corp PO Box 10305 WFD 730 *NYSE: WBS*	Waterbury	CT	06726	**800-325-2424**		355-2
Webster Industries Inc 58 Pulaski St	Peabody	MA	01960	**800-225-0796**	978-532-2000	67
Webster Industries Inc 325 Hall St	Tiffin	OH	44883	**800-243-9327**	419-447-8232	206
Webster Industries Inc PO Box 297 *Sales	Bangor	WI	54614	**800-284-2173***	608-486-2341	671
Webster Watch Co Assoc 44 E 32nd St 7th Fl *Orders	New York	NY	10016	**800-289-8963***	212-889-3560	403
WebSurveyor Corp 505 Huntmar Park Dr Suite 225	Herndon	VA	20170	**800-787-8755**	703-481-9326	176-7
Weck Closure Systems LLC 2917 Weck Dr	Research Triangle Park	NC	27709	**800-334-9751**	919-544-8000	468
WeddingChannel.com 888 S Figueroa St Suite 700	Los Angeles	CA	90017	**888-750-1550**		322
Wedgewood Hotel 845 Hornby St	Vancouver	BC	V6Z1V1	**800-663-0666**	604-689-7777	372
Wedgewood Resort Hotel 212 Wedgewood Dr	Fairbanks	AK	99701	**800-528-4916**	907-452-1442	373
Wedgworth Farms Inc 651 NW 9th St PO Box 2076	Belle Glade	FL	33430	**800-477-2077**	561-996-2076	11-9
Wednesday Magazine 20 E Gregory St	Kansas City	MO	64114	**800-274-8867**	816-361-0616	522-4
WEDR-FM 99.1 (Urban) 2741 N 29th Ave	Hollywood	FL	33020	**866-991-5269**	954-584-7117	631
Weed USA Inc 275 Old County Line Rd Suite D	Westerville	OH	43081	**800-933-3758**	614-568-0060	701
Weekender The PO Box 189	Bel Air	MD	21014	**888-879-1710**	410-838-4400	522-4
Weeki Wachee Springs 6131 Commercial Way	Spring Hill	FL	34606	**800-678-9335**	352-596-2062	32
Weekly of Business Aviation Newsletter 1200 G St NW Suite 900	Washington	DC	20005	**800-752-4959**	202-383-2350	521-13
Weekly Reader Corp 200 First Stamford Pl 2nd Fl *Cust Svc	Stamford	CT	06912	**800-446-3355***	203-705-3500	242
Weekly Standard Magazine 1150 17th St NW Suite 505 *Cust Svc	Washington	DC	20036	**800-274-7293***	202-293-4900	449-17
Weekly World News Magazine 1000 American Media Way	Boca Raton	FL	33467	**800-628-5632**	561-989-1227	449-11
Weeks-Lerman Group 58-38 Page Pl	Maspeth	NY	11378	**800-544-5959**	718-803-5000	523
Weeks Seed Co Inc 2103 Chestnut St	Greenville	NC	27834	**800-322-1234**	252-757-1234	684
Weeres Industries Corp 1045 33rd St S	Saint Cloud	MN	56301	**800-397-6686**	320-251-3551	91
Weetabix Co Inc 20 Cameron St	Clinton	MA	01510	**800-343-0590**	978-368-0991	291-4
WEF (Water Environment Federation) 601 Wythe St	Alexandria	VA	22314	**800-666-0206**	703-684-2400	48-13
Wegener Communications Inc 11350 Technology Cir	Duluth	GA	30097	**800-848-9467**	770-623-0096	633
Wegmans Food Markets Inc 1500 Brooks Ave	Rochester	NY	14624	**800-934-6267**	585-328-2550	339
Wego Chemical & Mineral Corp 239 Great Neck Rd	Great Neck	NY	11021	**877-489-6645**	516-487-3510	144
WEGW-FM 107.5 (Rock) 1015 Main St	Wheeling	WV	26003	**800-668-7426**	304-232-1170	631
Wehadkee Yarn Mills Inc 802 3rd Ave	West Point	GA	31833	**800-996-9276**	706-645-1331	730-9
WEHT-TV Ch 25 (ABC) 800 Marywood Dr	Henderson	KY	42420	**800-879-8549**	270-826-9566	726
Weibel Vineyards 1 Winemaster Way	Lodi	CA	95240	**800-932-9463**	209-365-9463	81-3

Company	City	State	ZIP	Toll-Free	Phone	Class
Weichert Realtors 1625 Rt 10 E	Morris Plains	NJ	07950	**800-872-7653**	973-267-7777	638
Weichert Relocation Resources Inc 120 Longwater Dr	Norwell	MA	02061	**800-926-8774**	781-871-4500	652
Weider Nutrition International Inc 2002 S 5070 West *NYSE: WNI*	Salt Lake City	UT	84104	**800-453-9542**	801-975-5000	786
Weider Publications Inc 21100 Erwin St	Woodland Hills	CA	91367	**800-423-5590**	818-884-6800	623-9
Weidmuller Inc 821 Southlake Blvd *Cust Svc	Richmond	VA	23236	**800-849-9343***	804-794-2877	803
Weidner Center for the Performing Arts 2420 Nicolet Dr University of Wisconsin at Green Bay	Green Bay	WI	54311	**800-328-8587**	920-465-2726	562
Weigh-Tronix Inc 1000 Armstrong Dr	Fairmont	MN	56031	**800-533-0456**	507-238-4461	672
Weight Watchers Gourmet Food Co 357 6th Ave Heinz 57 Ctr	Pittsburgh	PA	15222	**800-762-0228**	412-237-5757	291-11
Weight Watchers International Inc 175 Crossways Pk W *NYSE: WTW*	Woodbury	NY	11797	**800-651-6000**	516-390-1400	797
Weil Cliff Inc 8043 Industrial Pk Rd	Mechanicsville	VA	23116	**800-446-9345**	804-746-1321	403
Weil Joseph & Sons Inc 825 E 26th St	La Grange Park	IL	60526	**800-621-5955**	708-579-9595	549
Weiler & Co Inc 1116 E Main St *Sales	Whitewater	WI	53190	**800-558-9507***	262-473-5254	293
Weiler Corp 1 Wildwood Dr	Cresco	PA	18326	**800-835-9999**	570-595-7495	104
Weiler Welding Co Inc 324 E 2nd St	Dayton	OH	45402	**800-526-9353**	937-222-8312	585
Weimar Institute 20601 W Paoli Ln PO Box 486	Weimar	CA	95736	**800-525-9192**	530-637-4111	163
Weinbrenner Shoe Co Inc 108 S Polk St *Cust Svc	Merrill	WI	54452	**800-826-0002***	715-536-5521	296
Weingarten Realty Investors 2600 Citadel Plaza Dr Suite 300 *NYSE: WRI*	Houston	TX	77008	**800-688-8865**	713-866-6000	641
Weinschel Corp 5305 Spectrum Dr *Cust Svc	Frederick	MD	21703	**800-638-2048***	301-846-9222	252
WEIQ-TV Ch 42 (PBS) 2112 11th Ave S Suite 400	Birmingham	AL	35205	**800-239-5233**	205-328-8756	726
Weirs Furniture Village 3219 Knox St	Dallas	TX	75205	**888-889-3477**	214-528-0321	316
Weirton Medical Center 601 Colliers Way	Weirton	WV	26062	**800-243-4962**	304-797-6000	366-2
Weiser Lock A Masco Co 6700 Weiser Lock Dr	Tucson	AZ	85746	**800-677-5625**	520-741-6200	345
Weis/Robart Partitions Inc 3737 S Venoy Rd	Wayne	MI	48184	**800-223-9347**	734-467-8711	281
Weiss Homes Inc 828 E Jefferson Blvd	South Bend	IN	46617	**888-336-7373**	574-234-7373	639
Weiss Kurt Greenhouses Inc 95 Main St	Center Moriches	NY	11934	**800-858-2555**	631-878-2500	363
Weitz Funds 1125 S 103rd St Suite 600	Omaha	NE	68124	**800-304-9745**	402-391-1980	517
WEKU-FM 88.9 (Clas) 521 Lancaster Ave 102 Perkins Bldg-EKU	Richmond	KY	40475	**800-621-8890**	859-622-1660	631
Welarco Fabrications Inc 7400 W Plank Rd	Peoria	IL	61604	**800-447-6464**	309-697-9400	480
Welch Allyn Inc 4341 State Street Rd *Cust Svc	Skaneateles Falls	NY	13153	**800-535-6663***	315-685-4100	355-3
Welch Allyn Medical Products 4341 State Street Rd	Skaneateles Falls	NY	13153	**800-535-6663**	315-685-4100	249
Welch Allyn Monitoring Inc 8500 SW Creekside Pl *Cust Svc	Beaverton	OR	97008	**800-289-2500***	503-530-7500	249
Welch Packaging Group 1020 Herman St	Elkhart	IN	46516	**800-246-2475**	574-295-2460	101
Welco Technologies 200 Technicenter Dr Suite 205	Milford	OH	45150	**800-715-6006**	513-831-5335	507
Welcome Funds Inc 301 Yamato Rd	Boca Raton	FL	33431	**877-227-4484**	561-862-0244	783
Welcome Home Inc 309 Raleigh St	Wilmington	NC	28412	**800-348-4088**	910-791-4312	357
Welcome Wagon 245 Newtown Rd Suite 500 PO box 9101	Plainview	NY	11803	**800-779-3526**		652
Weld Mold Co PO Box 298	Brighton	MI	48116	**800-521-9755**	810-229-9521	798
Weld Tooling Corp 3001 W Carson St	Pittsburgh	PA	15204	**800-245-3186**	412-331-1776	798
Welded Construction LP 26933 Eckel Rd	Perrysburg	OH	43551	**800-874-3548**	419-874-3548	187-10
Welder Training & Testing Institute 1144 N Graham St	Allentown	PA	18109	**800-223-9884**	610-820-9551	787
Welding Society. American 550 NW Le Jeune Rd	Miami	FL	33126	**800-443-9353**	305-443-9353	49-3
Weldon Tool Co 200 Front St	Millersburg	PA	17061	**800-622-7742**	717-692-2113	484
Weldon Williams & Lick Inc PO Box 168	Fort Smith	AR	72902	**800-242-4995**	479-783-4113	615
Welfare Foundation Inc. Public 1200 U St NW	Washington	DC	20009	**800-275-7934**	202-965-1800	300
Welk Resort Branson 1984 State Hwy 165	Branson	MO	65616	**800-505-9355**	417-336-3575	655
Well Path Community Health Plans 6330 Quadrangle Dr Suite 500	Chapel Hill	NC	27517	**800-935-7284**	919-493-1210	384-3
Well Spa at Miramonte Resort 45-000 Indian Wells Ln	Indian Wells	CA	92210	**800-237-2926**	760-837-1652	698
Well Spouse Foundation 63 W Main St Suite H	Freehold	NJ	07728	**800-838-0879**	732-577-8899	48-6
Wella Corp 6109 DeSoto Ave	Woodland Hills	CA	91367	**800-829-4422**	818-999-5112	211
Wellborn Cabinet Inc 38669 Hwy 77	Ashland	AL	36251	**800-762-4475**	256-354-7151	116
WellCare of New York PO Box 1652	Newburgh	NY	12551	**800-288-5441**		384-3
WellChoice Inc 11 W 42 St *NYSE: WC*	New York	NY	10036	**800-261-5962**	212-476-1000	384-3
Wellco Enterprises Inc 150 Westwood Cir *AMEX: WLC*	Waynesville	NC	28786	**800-840-3155**	828-456-3545	296
Wellesley Inn & Suites 700 Rt 46 E	Fairfield	NJ	07004	**800-444-8888**	973-882-1010	369
Wellington Hotel 871 7th Ave	New York	NY	10019	**800-652-1212**	212-247-3900	373
Wellington Inc 1140 Monticello Hwy PO Box 244	Madison	GA	30650	**800-221-5054**	706-342-1916	207
Wellington West Capital Inc 200 Waterfront Dr Suite 400	Winnipeg	MB	R3B3P1	**800-461-6314**	204-925-2250	393
Wellmark Blue Cross & Blue Shield of Iowa 636 Grand Ave	Des Moines	IA	50309	**800-526-8995**	515-245-4500	384-3
Wellmark Blue Cross & Blue Shield of South Dakota 1601 W Madison St	Sioux Falls	SD	57104	**800-952-1976**	605-373-7200	384-3
Wellmark Inc 636 Grand Ave	Des Moines	IA	50309	**800-362-1697**	515-245-4500	384-3
Wellmark of South Dakota Inc DBA Wellmark Blue Cross & Blue Shield of South Da 1601 W Madison St	Sioux Falls	SD	57104	**800-952-1976**	605-373-7200	384-3
Wellness Institute. National 1300 College Ct PO Box 827	Stevens Point	WI	54481	**800-243-8694**	715-342-2969	48-17
Wellness Plan The 2888 W Grand Blvd *Cust Svc	Detroit	MI	48202	**800-680-9355***	313-875-4200	384-3
WellPath Select Inc 6 Coliseum Ctr 2815 Coliseum Ctr Dr Suite 550	Charlotte	NC	28217	**800-470-4523**	704-357-1421	384-3
Wellpoint Behavioral Health/Blue Cross 9655 Granite Ridge Dr 6th Fl	San Diego	CA	92123	**800-999-7222**	858-571-8300	454
WellPoint Inc 120 Monument Cir Suite 200 *NYSE: WLP*	Indianapolis	IN	46204	**800-331-1476**	317-488-6000	384-3
WellPoint Pharmacy Management 8407 Fallbrook Ave	West Hills	CA	91304	**800-700-2533**		575
Wells Bloomfield Industries 2 Erik Cir PO Box 280	Verdi	NV	89439	**800-777-0450**	775-345-0444	293
Wells Cargo Inc 1503 W McNaughton St	Elkhart	IN	46514	**800-348-7553**	574-264-9661	768
Wells College PO Box 500	Aurora	NY	13026	**800-952-9355**	315-364-3370	163
Wells-CTI Inc 2102 W Quail Ave Suite 2	Phoenix	AZ	85027	**800-348-2505**	623-581-5330	803
Wells' Dairy Inc 1 Blue Bunny Dr	Le Mars	IA	51031	**800-942-3800**	712-546-4000	291-25
Wells Fargo Bank Indiana NA 111 E Wayne St	Fort Wayne	IN	46802	**800-869-3557**	260-461-6401	71
Wells Fargo Bank Minnesota South NA 21 1st St SW	Rochester	MN	55902	**800-869-3557**	507-285-2800	71
Wells Fargo Bank Montana NA 175 N 27th St	Billings	MT	59101	**800-869-3557**	406-657-1903	71
Wells Fargo Bank South Dakota NA 101 N Phillips Ave	Sioux Falls	SD	57104	**800-321-4141**	605-575-6900	71
Wells Fargo Bank Texas NA 40 NE Loop 410	San Antonio	TX	78216	**800-869-3557**	210-856-5000	71
Wells Fargo Bank Wisconsin NA 735 W Wisconsin Ave	Milwaukee	WI	53233	**800-236-9000**	414-224-4429	71
Wells Fargo Business Credit 109 S 7th St Norwest Ctr	Minneapolis	MN	55402	**800-634-6224**	612-673-8500	214
Wells Fargo & Co 420 Montgomery St 12th Fl *NYSE: WFC*	San Francisco	CA	94104	**800-869-3557**		355-2
Wells Fargo Education Financial Services PO Box 5185	Sioux Falls	SD	57117	**800-658-3567**		215
Wells Fargo Equipment Finance Inc 733 Marquette Ave Investors Bldg Suite 700	Minneapolis	MN	55402	**800-322-6220**	612-667-9876	214
Wells Fargo Financial Leasing PO Box 4943	Syracuse	NY	13221	**800-451-3322**		214
Wells Fargo Foundation 550 California St 7th Fl	San Francisco	CA	94104	**888-886-1785**	415-396-3567	299
Wells Fargo Funds PO Box 8266	Boston	MA	02266	**800-222-8222**		517
Wells Fargo History Museum 420 Montgomery St	San Francisco	CA	94163	**800-411-4932**	415-396-2619	509
Wells Fargo Home Mortgage 405 SW 5th St	Des Moines	IA	50328	**800-288-3212**	515-237-6000	498
Wells Fargo Insurance Inc 600 S Hwy 169 12th Fl	Saint Louis Park	MN	55426	**800-328-2791**	612-667-5600	383
Wells Fargo Investments 420 Montgomery St 5th Fl	San Francisco	CA	94104	**800-621-7609**		679
Wells Financial Corp 53 1st St SW	Wells	MN	56097	**800-944-5869**	507-553-3151	355-2
Wells-Gardner Electronics Corp 9500 W 55th St Suite A *AMEX: WGA*	McCook	IL	60525	**800-336-6630**	708-290-2100	171-4
Wells JV Inc PO Box 520	Sharptown	MD	21861	**800-638-7697**	410-883-3196	671
Wells Lamont Corp 6640 W Touhy Ave	Niles	IL	60714	**800-323-2830**	847-647-8200	153-8
Wells Lamont Industry Group 6640 W Touhy Ave	Niles	IL	60714	**800-247-3295**		153-8
Wells Mfg Co 2100 W Lake Shore Dr	Woodstock	IL	60098	**800-227-6455**	815-338-3900	302
Wells Mfg Corp PO Box 70	Fond du Lac	WI	54936	**800-558-9770**	920-922-5900	60
Wells Pet Food Corp 617 S 'D' St	Monmouth	IL	61462	**800-447-8435**	309-734-3121	568
Wells Real Estate Investment Trust 6200 The Corners Pkwy	Norcross	GA	30092	**800-282-1581**	770-449-7800	640
Wellstone Mills 856 S Pleasantburg Dr	Greenville	SC	29607	**877-867-6455**	864-242-1293	730-3
WEMT-TV Ch 39 (Fox) 3206 Hanover Rd	Johnson City	TN	37604	**800-376-3939**	423-283-3900	726
WEMU-FM 89.1 (NPR) PO Box 980350	Ypsilanti	MI	48198	**888-299-8910**	734-487-2229	631
WEMX-FM 94.1 (Urban) 650 Wooddale Blvd	Baton Rouge	LA	70806	**800-499-9410**	225-926-1106	631
Wenaas AGS Inc 202 E Larkspur St	Victoria	TX	77904	**888-576-2668**	361-576-2668	153-19
Wenatchee Valley College 1300 5th St	Wenatchee	WA	98801	**877-982-4968**	509-682-6800	160
Wenatchee World 14 N Mission St	Wenatchee	WA	98801	**800-572-4433**	509-663-5161	522-2
Wendell August Forge Inc 620 Madison Ave	Grove City	PA	16127	**800-923-4438**	724-458-8360	322
Wendell's Inc 6601 Bunker Lake Blvd NW	Ramsey	MN	55303	**800-328-3692**	763-576-8200	459
Wendland's Farm Products Inc 405 S 2nd St	Temple	TX	76504	**800-792-3038**	254-773-5211	438
Wendt-Bristol Health Services Corp 921 Jasonway Ave	Columbus	OH	43214	**800-230-7990**	614-221-6000	376
Wenger Corp 555 Park Dr	Owatonna	MN	55060	**800-733-0393**	507-455-4100	516
Wenger Mfg Inc 714 Main St	Sabetha	KS	66534	**800-833-0174**	785-284-2133	293
Wenger North America Inc 15 Corporate Dr *Cust Svc	Orangeburg	NY	10962	**800-431-2996***	845-365-3500	219

	City	State	ZIP	Toll-Free	Phone	Class
Wenke Greenhouses Co						
2525 N 30th St	Kalamazoo	MI	49048	**800-311-7209**	269-349-7882	363
Wentworth-Douglass Hospital						
789 Central Ave	Dover	NH	03820	**877-201-7100**	603-742-5252	366-2
Wentworth Group Inc						
901 S Trooper Rd	Norristown	PA	19403	**800-222-7569**	610-650-0600	641
Wentworth Institute of Technology						
550 Huntington Ave	Boston	MA	02115	**800-556-0610**	617-989-4590	163
Wentworth Mansion						
149 Wentworth St	Charleston	SC	29401	**888-466-1886**	843-853-1886	373
WEPN-AM 1050 (Sports)						
2 Penn Plaza 17th Fl	New York	NY	10121	**800-919-3776**	212-613-3800	631
Wequassett Inn Resort & Golf Club						
2173 Rt 28	East Harwich	MA	02645	**800-225-7125**	508-432-5400	655
WERN-FM 88.7 (NPR)						
821 University Ave	Madison	WI	53706	**800-747-7444**	608-263-2121	631
Werner Co 100 National Dr	Anniston	AL	36207	**800-225-5630**	256-831-8600	476
Werner Co 93 Werner Rd	Greenville	PA	16125	**888-532-3770**	724-588-2550	412
Werner Electric Supply Co						
2341 Industrial Dr	Neenah	WI	54956	**800-236-5026**	920-729-4500	245
Werner Enterprises Inc PO Box 45308	Omaha	NE	68145	**800-228-2240**	402-895-6640	769
NASDAQ: WERN						
Werres Corp 807 E South St	Frederick	MD	21701	**800-638-6563**	301-620-4000	378
Wert Bookbinding Inc						
9975 Allentown Blvd	Grantville	PA	17028	**800-344-9378***	717-469-0626	93
*Cust Svc						
Werzalit of America Inc PO Box 373	Bradford	PA	16701	**800-999-3730**	814-362-3881	489
Wes-Garde Components Group Inc						
190 Elliott St	Hartford	CT	06114	**800-275-7089**	860-525-6907	245
WesBanco Inc 1 Bank Plaza	Wheeling	WV	26003	**800-328-3369**	304-234-9000	355-2
NASDAQ: WSBC						
Weschler Instruments Div Hughes Corp						
16900 Foltz Pkwy	Cleveland	OH	44149	**800-557-0064**	440-238-2550	247
Wesco						
52828 NW Shoe Factory Ln PO						
Box 607	Scappoose	OR	97056	**800-326-2711**	503-543-7114	296
Wesco Cedar Inc PO Box 40847	Eugene	OR	97404	**800-547-2511**	541-688-5020	190-4
Wesco Fabrics Inc 4001 Forest St	Denver	CO	80216	**800-950-9372**	303-388-4101	731
Wesco Inc 1460 Whitehall Rd	Muskegon	MI	49445	**800-968-0200**	231-719-4300	319
Wesco Industrial Products Inc						
PO Box 47	Lansdale	PA	19446	**800-445-5681**	215-699-7031	462
Wescom Credit Union						
123 S Marengo Ave	Pasadena	CA	91101	**888-493-7266**	626-535-1000	216
Wescon Products Co 2533 S West St	Wichita	KS	67217	**800-835-0160**	316-942-7266	202
WesCorp (Western Corporate Federal						
Credit Union) 924 Overland Ct	San Dimas	CA	91773	**800-442-4366**	909-394-6300	216
Weslaco Area Chamber of Commerce						
205 W Railroad	Weslaco	TX	78596	**888-968-2102**	956-968-2102	137
Wesley Biblical Seminary						
787 E Northside Dr	Jackson	MS	39206	**800-788-9571**	601-366-8880	164-3
Wesley College 120 N State St	Dover	DE	19901	**800-937-5398**	302-736-2300	163
Wesley College PO Box 1070	Florence	MS	39073	**800-748-9972**	601-845-2265	163
Wesley Medical Center 550 N Hillside	Wichita	KS	67214	**800-362-0288**	316-962-2000	366-2
Wesleyan College 4760 Forsyth Rd	Macon	GA	31210	**800-447-6610**	478-477-1110	163
Wesleyan University Press						
215 Long Ln	Middletown	CT	06459	**800-421-1561***	860-685-7711	623-5
*Orders						
West American Insurance Co						
9450 Seward Rd	Fairfield	OH	45014	**800-843-6446**	513-867-3000	384-4
West Bend Area Chamber of						
Commerce 548 S Main St	West Bend	WI	53095	**888-338-8666**	262-338-2666	137
West Bend Housewares LLC						
1100 Schmidt Rd	West Bend	WI	53090	**800-269-8805**	262-334-2311	37
West Bend Mutual Insurance Co						
1900 S 18th Ave	West Bend	WI	53095	**800-236-5010**	262-334-5571	384-4
West Boca Times						
1701 Green Rd Suite B	Deerfield Beach	FL	33064	**800-275-8820**	954-698-6397	522-4
West Branch/Ogemaw County						
Travelers & Visitors Bureau						
422 W Houghton Ave	West Branch	MI	48661	**800-755-9091**	989-345-2821	205
West Central Co-op						
406 1st St PO Box 68	Ralston	IA	51459	**800-522-1946**	712-667-3200	270
West Central Steel Inc						
2011 W Gorton Ave NW	Willmar	MN	56201	**800-992-8853**	320-235-4070	483
West Central Tribune PO Box 839	Willmar	MN	56201	**800-450-1150**	320-235-1150	522-2
West Chester Chamber Alliance						
7617 Voice of America						
Centre Dr	West Chester	OH	45069	**877-924-3783**	513-777-3600	137
West Chester University						
100 S High St	West Chester	PA	19383	**877-315-2165**	610-436-1000	163
West Coast Bancorp						
5335 Meadows Rd Suite 201	Lake Oswego	OR	97035	**800-895-3345**	503-684-0884	355-2
NASDAQ: WCBO						
West Coast Bank 506 SW Coast Hwy	Newport	OR	97365	**800-895-3345***	541-265-6666	71
*Cust Svc						
West Coast Charters Inc						
19711 Campus Dr Suite 200	Santa Ana	CA	92707	**800-352-6153**	949-852-8340	14
West Coast Connection						
318 Indian Trace Suite 336	Weston	FL	33326	**888-868-7882**	954-888-9780	748
West Coast Door Inc 3102 S Pine St	Tacoma	WA	98409	**800-445-5919**	253-272-4269	234
West Coast Industries Inc						
10 Jackson St	San Francisco	CA	94101	**800-243-3150**	415-621-6656	314-1
West Coast Life Insurance Co						
343 Sansome St	San Francisco	CA	94104	**800-366-9378**	415-591-8200	384-2
West Coast Shoe Co						
52828 NW Shoe Factory Ln PO						
Box 607	Scappoose	OR	97056	**800-326-2711**	503-543-7114	296
West Coast Tag & Label Co						
PO Box 4099	West Hills	CA	91308	**800-742-8247**	818-710-8484	404
West Coast Wire Rope & Rigging Inc						
2900 NW 29th Ave	Portland	OR	97210	**800-275-0482**	503-228-9353	802
West Corp 9910 Maple St	Omaha	NE	68134	**800-542-1000**	402-571-7700	722
NASDAQ: WSTC						
West Elizabeth Lumber Co						
1 Chicago Ave	Elizabeth	PA	15037	**800-289-9352**	412-384-3900	190-3
West Essex Graphics Inc						
305 Fairfield Ave	Fairfield	NJ	07004	**800-221-5859**	973-227-2400	770
West-Fair Electric Contractors Inc						
PO Box 298	Hawthorne	NY	10532	**800-525-0585**	914-769-8050	188-4

	City	State	ZIP	Toll-Free	Phone	Class
West Feliciana Historical						
Society Museum						
11757 Ferdinand St	Saint Francisville	LA	70775	**800-789-4221**	225-635-6330	509
West Florida Electric Co-op						
PO Box 127	Graceville	FL	32440	**800-342-7400**	850-263-3231	244
West Group PO Box 64526	Saint Paul	MN	55164	**800-328-4880***	651-687-7000	623-2
*Cust Svc						
West Harvest Inn						
17803 Stony Plain Rd	Edmonton	AB	T5S1B4	**800-661-6993**	780-484-8000	372
West Hawaii Today PO Box 789	Kailua-Kona	HI	96745	**800-355-3911**	808-329-9311	522-2
West-Herr Automotive Group Inc						
S-5025 Camp Rd	Hamburg	NY	14075	**800-933-5701**	716-649-5640	57
West Hills College 300 Cherry Ln	Coalinga	CA	93210	**800-266-1114**	559-934-2000	160
West Hollywood Convention &						
Visitors Bureau						
8687 Melrose Ave Suite M38	West Hollywood	CA	90069	**800-368-6020**	310-289-2525	205
West Houston Medical Center						
12141 Richmond Ave	Houston	TX	77082	**800-265-8624**	281-558-3444	366-2
West JS Milling Co Inc 501 9th St	Modesto	CA	95353	**800-675-9378***	209-577-3221	438
*Cust Svc						
West Kentucky Rural Electric Co-op						
Corp PO Box 589	Mayfield	KY	42066	**877-495-7322**	270-247-1321	244
West Legal Directory 610 Opperman Dr	Eagan	MN	55123	**800-328-9378**	651-687-7000	623-6
West Liberty State College						
PO Box 295	West Liberty	WV	26074	**800-732-6204**	304-336-5000	163
West Music Inc						
1212 5th St PO Box 5521	Coralville	IA	52241	**800-373-2000**	319-351-2000	515
West Nottingham Academy						
1079 Firetower Rd	Colora	MD	21917	**800-962-1744**	410-658-5556	611
West Oregon Electric Co-op Inc						
PO Box 69	Vernonia	OR	97064	**800-777-1276**	503-429-3021	244
West Penetone Corp						
700 Gotham Pkwy	Carlstadt	NJ	07072	**800-631-1652**	201-567-3000	149
West Pharmaceutical Services Inc						
101 Gordon Dr	Lionville	PA	19341	**800-345-9800**	610-594-2900	469
NYSE: WST						
West Plains Electric Co-op Inc						
PO Box 1038	Dickinson	ND	58602	**800-627-8470**	701-483-5111	244
West River Electric Assn Inc PO Box 412	Wall	SD	57790	**888-279-2135**		244
West Shore Community College						
PO Box 277	Scottville	MI	49454	**800-848-9722**	231-845-6211	160
West Star Aviation Inc						
796 Heritage Way	Grand Junction	CO	81506	**800-255-4193**	970-243-7500	25
West Tennessee Regional Blood Center						
Inc 828 North Pkwy	Jackson	TN	38305	**800-924-6572**	731-427-4431	90
West Texas A & M University						
2501 4th Ave	Canyon	TX	79016	**800-999-8268**	806-651-2000	163
West Valley Construction Co Inc						
580 McGlincey Ln	Campbell	CA	95008	**800-588-5510**	408-371-5510	187-10
West Valley Medical Center						
1717 Arlington Ave	Caldwell	ID	83605	**800-937-8860**	208-459-4641	366-2
West Vancouver Chamber of						
Commerce 1310 Marine Dr	West Vancouver	BC	V7T1B5	**888-471-9996**	604-926-6614	136
West Virginia						
Bill Status State Capitol						
Rm MB27	Charleston	WV	25305	**800-642-8650**	304-347-4831	425
Child Support Enforcement Bureau						
350 Capitol St Rm 147	Charleston	WV	25301	**800-249-3778**	304-558-3780	335
Consumer Protection Div						
812 Quarrier St 6th Fl	Charleston	WV	25301	**800-368-8808**	304-558-8986	335
Crime Victims Compensation Fund						
1900 Kanawha Blvd E						
Rm W-334	Charleston	WV	25305	**800-624-8650**	304-347-4850	335
Housing Development Fund						
814 Virginia St E	Charleston	WV	25301	**800-933-9843**	304-345-6475	335
Parks & Recreation						
1900 E Kanawha Blvd E Bldg 3						
Rm 714	Charleston	WV	25305	**800-225-5982**	304-558-2764	335
Tourism Div						
2101 Washington St E	Charleston	WV	25305	**800-225-5982**	304-558-2200	335
Veterans Affairs Div						
1321 Plaza East Suite 101	Charleston	WV	25301	**888-838-2332**	304-558-3662	335
West Virginia Correctional Industries						
617 Leon Sullivan Way	Charleston	WV	25301	**800-525-5381**	304-558-6054	618
West Virginia Electric Corp						
PO Box 1587	Fairmont	WV	26554	**800-982-3532**	304-363-6900	188-4
West Virginia Newspaper Publishing						
Co 1251 Earl L Core Rd	Morgantown	WV	26505	**800-654-4676**	304-292-6301	623-8
West Virginia Press Services Inc						
3422 Pennsylvania Ave	Charleston	WV	25302	**800-235-6881**	304-342-6908	612
West Virginia Public Theatre						
PO Box 4270	Morgantown	WV	26504	**877-999-9878**	304-598-0144	563-4
West Virginia School Journal						
1558 Quarrier St	Charleston	WV	25311	**800-642-8261**	304-346-5315	449-8
West Virginia State Medical Assn						
4301 MacCorkle Ave	Charleston	WV	25364	**800-257-4747**	304-925-0342	466
West Virginia State University						
Barron Dr PO Box 1000	Institute	WV	25112	**800-987-2112**	304-766-3000	163
West Virginia University						
PO Box 6009	Morgantown	WV	26506	**800-344-9881**	304-293-2124	163
Institute of Technology						
405 Fayette Pike	Montgomery	WV	25136	**888-554-8324**	304-442-3071	163
West Virginia Wesleyan College						
59 College Ave	Buckhannon	WV	26201	**800-722-9933**	304-473-8000	163
West-Ward Pharmaceutical Corp						
465 Industrial Way W	Eatontown	NJ	07724	**800-631-2174***	732-542-1191	573
*Cust Svc						
West Wind Inn 3345 W Gulf Dr	Sanibel	FL	33957	**800-824-0476**	239-472-1541	655
West Window Corp						
PO Drawer 3071	Martinsville	VA	24115	**800-446-4167**	276-638-2394	232
WESTA (Western Assn of Travel						
Agencies) 5933 NE Win Sivers Dr						
Suite 202	Portland	OR	97220	**800-288-8191**	503-251-8170	761
Westaff Inc 298 N Wiget Ln	Walnut Creek	CA	94598	**800-872-8367**	925-930-5300	707
NASDAQ: WSTF						
Westamerica Bancorp						
4550 Mangels Blvd	Fairfield	CA	834585	**800-848-1088**		355-2
AMEX: WABC						

Name / Address	City	State	ZIP	Toll-Free	Phone	Class
Westamerica Bank 4560 Mangels Blvd	Fairfield	CA	94534	**800-848-1088**		71
Westan Inc 360 Church St	Westfield	PA	16950	**800-352-8952**	814-367-5951	424
Westar Energy 818 S Kansas Ave *NYSE: WR*	Topeka	KS	66612	**800-794-4780**	785-575-8500	774
Westar Energy Inc 818 S Kansas Ave *NYSE: WR* ■ *Cust Svc	Topeka	KS	66612	**800-794-4780***	785-575-6300	355-3
Westat Inc 1650 Research Blvd	Rockville	MD	20850	**800-937-8281**	301-251-1500	458
Westbank & District Chamber of Commerce 2375 Pamela Rd Unit 4	Westbank	BC	V4T2H9	**866-768-3378**	250-768-3378	136
Westbend Vineyards 5394 Williams Rd	Lewisville	NC	27023	**877-901-5032**	336-945-5032	50
Westbrook College 716 Stevens Ave	Portland	ME	04103	**800-477-4863**	207-797-7261	163
Westby Co-op Creamery 401 S Main St	Westby	WI	54667	**800-492-9282**	608-634-3181	291-5
Westchester County Office of Tourism 222 Mamaroneck Ave Suite 100	White Plains	NY	10605	**800-833-9282**	914-995-8500	205
Westchester Fire Insurance Co 305 Madison Ave PO Box 1973	Morristown	NJ	07962	**800-227-3745**	973-490-6600	384-4
Westchester Lace Inc 3901 Liberty Ave	North Bergen	NJ	07047	**800-699-5223**	201-864-2150	730-4
WestCoast Hospitality Corp 201 W North River Dr Suite 100 *NYSE: WEH*	Spokane	WA	99201	**800-325-4000**	509-459-6100	369
Red Lion Hotels Inc 201 W North River Dr Suite 100	Spokane	WA	99201	**800-325-4000**	509-459-6100	369
WestCoast Hotels Inc 201 W North River Dr Suite 100	Spokane	WA	99201	**800-325-4000**	509-459-6100	369
WestCoast Hospitality Corp GuestAwards Program 201 W North River Dr Suite 100	Spokane	WA	99201	**800-325-4000**		371
WestCoast Hotels Inc 201 W North River Dr Suite 100	Spokane	WA	99201	**800-325-4000**	509-459-6100	369
Westcon Group Inc 520 White Plains Rd Suite 100	Tarrytown	NY	10591	**800-527-9516**	914-829-7000	172
Westcorp Inc 23 Pasteur *NYSE: WES*	Irvine	CA	92618	**800-289-8004**	949-727-1000	355-2
Westdale Realty Co 300 E Beltline Ave NE	Grand Rapids	MI	49506	**800-968-8770**	616-949-9400	638
Westell Technologies Inc 750 N Commons Dr *NASDAQ: WSTL*	Aurora	IL	60504	**800-323-6883**	630-898-2500	720
Westerlay Roses Inc 3504 Via Real	Carpinteria	CA	93013	**800-959-7673**	805-684-5411	363
Westerly Sun The 56 Main St	Westerly	RI	02891	**800-937-8759**	401-596-7791	522-2
Westerman Cos Alten Engineering Div 245 N Broad St	Bremen	OH	43107	**800-338-8265**	740-569-4143	700
Western Air & Refrigeration Co 15914 S Avalon Blvd	Compton	CA	90220	**800-927-1331**	310-327-4400	188-10
Western Aircraft Inc 4300 S Kennedy St	Boise	ID	83705	**800-333-3442**	208-338-1800	63
Western American Life PO Box 833879	Richardson	TX	75083	**866-629-2677**	972-699-2770	384-2
Western Assn of Travel Agencies (WESTA) 5933 NE Win Sivers Dr Suite 202	Portland	OR	97220	**800-288-8191**	503-251-8170	761
Western Badge & Trophy Co 1716 W Washington Blvd	Los Angeles	CA	90007	**800-367-4332**	323-735-1201	766
Western Baptist College 5000 Deer Pk Dr SE	Salem	OR	97301	**800-845-3005**	503-581-8600	163
Western Beverages Inc 4545 E 51st Ave	Denver	CO	80216	**877-701-2337**	303-388-5751	82-1
Western Canada Wilderness Committee (WCWC) 227 Abbott St	Vancouver	BC	V6B2K7	**800-661-9453**	604-683-8220	48-13
Western Carolina University	Cullowhee	NC	28723	**800-928-2369**	828-227-7211	163
Western Co-op Transport Assn PO Box 327	Montevideo	MN	56265	**800-992-8817**	320-269-5531	769
Western Connecticut State University 181 White St	Danbury	CT	06810	**877-837-9278**	203-837-8200	163
Western Corporate Federal Credit Union (WesCorp) 924 Overland Ct	San Dimas	CA	91773	**800-442-4366**	909-394-6300	216
Western Datacom Co Inc 959 Bassett Rd	Cleveland	OH	44145	**800-262-3311**	440-835-1510	496
Western Digital Corp 20511 Lake Forest Dr *NYSE: WDC*	Lake Forest	CA	92630	**800-832-4778**	949-672-7000	171-8
Western Discovery International 507 Casazza Dr Suite C	Reno	NV	89502	**800-843-5061**	775-329-9933	748
Western Diversified Casualty Insurance Co 2345 Waukegan Rd Suite 210	Bannockburn	IL	60015	**800-323-5771**	847-948-8988	384-4
Western Electronics LLC 1550 S Tech Ln	Meridian	ID	83642	**888-857-5775**	208-377-1557	613
Western Enterprises Inc 875 Bassett Rd	Westlake	OH	44145	**800-783-7890**		798
Western Exterminator Co 305 N Crescent Way	Anaheim	CA	92801	**800-640-0694**	714-517-9000	567
Western Extralite Co 1470 Liberty St	Kansas City	MO	64102	**800-279-8833**	816-421-8404	245
Western Financial Bank FSB 15750 Alton Pkwy	Irvine	CA	92618	**877-932-1234**	949-727-1000	71
Western Forest Products Inc 435 Trunk Rd 3rd Fl *TSE: WEF*	Duncan	BC	V9L2P9	**800-880-7471**	250-748-3711	439
Western Forge & Flange Co PO Box 327	Santa Clara	CA	95052	**800-352-6433**	408-727-7000	474
Western Fraternal Life Assn 1900 1st Ave NE	Cedar Rapids	IA	52402	**800-535-5472**	319-363-2653	384-2
Western Gas Resources Inc 1099 18th St Suite 1200 *NYSE: WGR*	Denver	CO	80202	**800-677-5603**	303-452-5603	774
Western Group 1637 N Warson Rd *Cust Svc	Saint Louis	MO	63132	**800-325-2801***	314-427-6733	188-7
Western Hoist Inc 2200 Haffly Ave	National City	CA	91950	**888-994-6478**	619-474-3361	462
Western Illinois University 1 University Cir	Macomb	IL	61455	**877-742-5948**	309-298-1414	163

Name / Address	City	State	ZIP	Toll-Free	Phone	Class
Western Industries Inc Chilton Products Div 300 E Breed St	Chilton	WI	53014	**877-671-7063**	920-849-2381	593
Western Inventory Service Ltd 192 Bridgeland Ave	Toronto	ON	M6A1Z4	**800-268-6848**	416-781-5563	391
Western Iowa Co-op PO Box 106	Hornick	IA	51026	**800-488-3201**	712-874-3211	271
Western Iowa Power Co-op PO Box 428	Denison	IA	51442	**800-253-5189**	712-263-2943	244
Western Iowa Tech Community College 4647 Stone Ave	Sioux City	IA	51106	**800-352-4649**	712-274-6400	787
Western Kentucky Gas Co Inc PO Box 650205	Dallas	TX	75265	**888-954-4321**	972-934-9227	774
Western Kentucky University 1 Big Red Way	Bowling Green	KY	42101	**800-495-8463**	270-745-0111	163
Western Lime Corp PO Box 57	West Bend	WI	53095	**800-433-0036**	262-334-3005	432
Western Looseleaf Div Cal/West United Inc 12160 Sherman Way	North Hollywood	CA	91605	**800-233-4201**	818-765-4200	87
Western Maryland Hospice Center 1500 Pennsylvania Ave	Hagerstown	MD	21742	**877-964-2262**	301-791-4400	366-5
Western Massachusetts Electric Co 1 Federal St Bldg 111-4	Springfield	MA	01105	**800-286-2000**	413-785-5871	774
Western Mattress & Furniture Co 117 E Concho Ave	San Angelo	TX	76903	**800-880-4507**	325-653-4507	463
Western Medical Center Santa Ana 1001 N Tustin Ave	Santa Ana	CA	92705	**800-777-7464**	714-835-3555	366-2
Western Mental Health Institute 11100 Hwy 64 W	Bolivar	TN	38008	**800-548-0635**	731-228-2000	366-3
Western Metal Lath & Steel Framing Systems Inc 6510 General Dr	Riverside	CA	92509	**800-365-5284**	951-360-3500	688
Western Museum of Mining & Industry 1025 N Gate Rd	Colorado Springs	CO	80921	**800-752-6588**	719-488-0880	509
Western National Mutual Insurance Co 5350 W 78th St	Edina	MN	55439	**877-862-8808**	952-835-5350	384-4
Western Nebraska Community College 1601 E 27th St	Scottsbluff	NE	69361	**800-348-4435**	308-635-3606	160
Western Nevada Community College 2201 W College Pkwy	Carson City	NV	89703	**800-748-5690**	775-445-3277	160
Western Nevada Supply Co 950 S Rock Blvd	Sparks	NV	89431	**800-648-1230**	775-359-5800	601
Western New England College 1215 Wilbraham Rd	Springfield	MA	01119	**800-325-1122**	413-782-3111	163
D'Amour Library 1215 Wilbraham Rd	Springfield	MA	01119	**800-325-1122**	413-782-1535	426
Western New Mexico University 1000 W College Ave	Silver City	NM	88061	**800-872-9668**	505-538-6011	163
Western Numerical Control 983 Golden Gate Terr	Grass Valley	CA	95945	**800-538-5108**	530-477-7575	616
Western Oilfields Supply Co PO Box 2248	Bakersfield	CA	93303	**800-742-7246**	661-399-9124	261-4
Western Ophthalmics Corp 19019 36th Ave W Suite G	Lynnwood	WA	98036	**800-426-9938**	425-672-9332	532
Western Organics Inc 420 E Southern Ave	Tempe	AZ	85202	**800-352-3245**	602-269-5756	288
Western Outdoors Magazine 185 Avenida La Plata *Cust Svc	San Clemente	CA	92673	**800-290-2929***	949-366-0030	449-22
Western Pacific Storage Systems Inc 300 E Arrow Hwy	San Dimas	CA	91773	**800-732-9777**	909-451-0303	281
Western Pennsylvania Hospital Hematology/Oncology Patient Care Unit 4800 Friendship Ave Suite 2303 NT	Pittsburgh	PA	15224	**866-680-0004**	412-578-4707	758
Western Petroleum Co 9531 W 78th St Suite 102	Eden Prairie	MN	55344	**800-972-3835**	952-941-9090	569
Western Piece Dyers & Finishers Inc 2845 W 48th Pl	Chicago	IL	60632	**866-493-7839**	773-523-7000	730-7
Western Pioneer Inc 4601 Shilshole Ave NW	Seattle	WA	98107	**800-426-6783**	206-789-1930	307
Western Plastic Products Inc 1556 W Esther St	Long Beach	CA	90813	**800-453-1881**	562-435-4881	10
Western Power & Equipment 6407-B NE 117th Ave	Vancouver	WA	98662	**800-333-2346**	360-253-2346	353
Western Psychological Services 12031 Wilshire Blvd	Los Angeles	CA	90025	**800-648-8857**	310-478-2061	623-2
Western Recreational Vehicles 3401 W Washington Ave	Yakima	WA	98903	**800-888-4133**	509-457-4133	120
Western Reflections 261 Commerce Way *Cust Svc	Gallatin	TN	37066	**800-521-2004***	615-451-9700	431
Western Regional Off-Track Betting Corp 700 Ellicott St	Batavia	NY	14020	**800-724-2000**	585-343-1423	317
Western Research Institute 365 N 9th St	Laramie	WY	82072	**888-436-6974**	307-721-2011	654
Western Reserve Academy 115 College St	Hudson	OH	44236	**800-784-3776**	330-650-9717	611
Western Reserve Group 1685 Cleveland Rd	Wooster	OH	44691	**800-362-0426**	330-262-9060	384-4
Western Reserve Life Assurance Co of Ohio 570 Carillon Pkwy	Saint Petersburg	FL	33716	**800-851-9777**	727-299-1800	384-2
Western Saddlery & Moser Leather Co 1191 Hooven Ave *Cust Svc	Hamilton	OH	45015	**800-874-1167***	513-889-0500	424
Western Security Bank 1704 Dearborn	Missoula	MT	59801	**800-453-6874**	406-721-3700	71
Western Seminary 5511 SE Hawthorne Blvd	Portland	OR	97215	**877-517-1800**	503-517-1800	164-3
Western Sizzlin Inc 1338 Plantation Rd	Roanoke	VA	24012	**800-247-8325**	540-345-3195	657
Western Slope Sales Service Inc 636 Potrero Ave	San Francisco	CA	94110	**888-777-2770**	415-282-2770	323
Western & Southern Financial Group 400 Broadway	Cincinnati	OH	45202	**800-333-5222**	513-629-1800	355-4
Western-Southern Life Assurance Co 400 Broadway	Cincinnati	OH	45202	**800-333-5222**	513-629-1800	384-2
Western & Southern Life Insurance Co 400 Broadway	Cincinnati	OH	45202	**800-333-5222**	513-629-1800	384-2
Western State College of Colorado 600 N Adams St College Heights	Gunnison	CO	81231	**800-876-5309**	970-943-0120	163

Name	Address	City	State	ZIP	Toll-Free	Phone	Class
Western States Envelope Co	4480 N 132nd St	Butler	WI	53007	**800-558-0514**	262-781-5540	260
Western States Equipment Co	500 E Overland Rd	Meridian	ID	83642	**800-852-2287**	208-888-2287	353
Western States Ticket Service	143 W McDowell Rd	Phoenix	AZ	85003	**800-326-0331**	602-254-3300	735
Western States Weeklies Inc	PO Box 600600	San Diego	CA	92160	**800-280-2985**	619-280-2985	623-8
Western Steer Family Steakhouse	129 Fast Ln PO Box 3130	Mooresville	NC	28117	**877-704-5939**	704-660-5939	657
Western Stockmens Inc	223 Rodeo Ave	Caldwell	ID	83605	**800-624-9425**	208-459-0777	438
Western Sugar Co	7555 E Hampden Ave Suite 600	Denver	CO	80231	**800-523-7497**	303-830-3939	291-38
Western Technologies Inc	3737 E Broadway Rd	Phoenix	AZ	85040	**800-580-3737**	602-437-3737	191
Western Telematic Inc	5 Sterling	Irvine	CA	92618	**800-854-7226**	949-586-9950	496
Western Texas College	6200 College Ave	Snyder	TX	79549	**888-468-6982**	325-573-8511	160
Western Tire Co	2700 E Main St	Farmington	NM	87402	**800-589-2414**	505-326-2231	62-5
Western Towboat Co Inc	617 NW 40th St	Seattle	WA	98107	**800-932-9651**	206-789-9000	457
Western Trailer Co	6700 Business Way	Boise	ID	83716	**888-344-2539**	208-344-2539	768
Western Uniform & Towel Service Inc	1707 N Mosley St	Wichita	KS	67214	**800-214-2342**	316-264-2342	434
Western Union North America	6200 S Quebec St *Cust Svc	Greenwood Village	CO	80111	**800-325-6000***	303-488-8000	70
Western United Life Assurance Co	PO Box 9000	Post Falls	ID	83877	**800-247-2045**	208-292-3900	384-2
Western Upper Peninsula Convention & Visitor Bureau	PO Box 706	Ironwood	MI	49938	**800-522-5657**	906-932-4850	205
Western Village Inn & Casino	815 Nickel Blvd	Sparks	NV	89434	**800-648-1170**	775-331-1069	133
Western Warehouse	11205 Montgomery Blvd NE	Albuquerque	NM	87111	**800-532-4888**	505-296-8344	155-5
Western Water Co	102 Washington Ave	Point Richmond	CA	94801	**877-928-9282**	510-234-7400	774
Western Wire Group	4025 NW Express Ave	Portland	OR	97210	**800-547-9192**	503-222-1644	676
Western Wireless Corp DBA Cellular One	3650 131st Ave SE Suite 600 *NASDAQ: WWCA*	Bellevue	WA	98006	**800-873-2349**	425-313-5200	721
Western Wisconsin Technical College	304 N 6th St	La Crosse	WI	54602	**800-248-9982**	608-785-9200	787
Western Wood Preserving Co	PO Box 1250	Sumner	WA	98390	**800-472-7714**	253-863-8191	806
Western World Inc	200 N Kit Ave	Caldwell	ID	83605	**800-247-2535**	208-459-0842	768
Western Wyoming Community College	2500 College Dr	Rock Springs	WY	82901	**800-226-1181**	307-382-1600	160
Westfalia Separator Inc	100 Fairway Ct	Northvale	NJ	07647	**800-722-6622**	201-767-3900	411
Westfalia Technologies Inc	3655 Sandhurst Dr	York	PA	17402	**800-673-2522**	717-764-1115	206
WestFarm Foods	635 Elliott Ave W	Seattle	WA	98119	**800-333-6455**	206-284-7220	291-27
Westfield Cos	PO Box 5001	Westfield Center	OH	44251	**800-368-3530**	330-887-0101	384-4
Westfield Court	77 3rd St	Stamford	CT	06905	**800-443-3245**	203-327-4551	659
Westfield Financial Inc	141 Elm St *AMEX: WFD*	Westfield	MA	01085	**800-995-5734**	413-568-1911	355-2
Westfield Group	1 Park Cir PO Box 5001	Westfield Center	OH	44251	**800-243-0210**	330-887-0101	384-4
Westfield National Insurance Co	PO Box 5001	Westfield Center	OH	44251	**800-368-3530**	330-887-0101	384-4
Westfields Resort & Conference Center. Marriott	14750 Conference Center Dr	Chantilly	VA	20151	**800-635-5666**	703-818-0300	370
Westford Regency Inn & Conference Center	219 Littleton Rd	Westford	MA	01886	**800-543-7801**	978-692-8200	373
Westgate Hotel	1055 2nd Ave	San Diego	CA	92101	**800-221-3802**	619-238-1818	373
Westgate Payne Fabrics Inc	1517 W North Carrier Pkwy Suite 116	Grand Prairie	TX	75050	**800-527-2517**	972-647-2323	583
Westgate Resorts	5601 Windhover Dr	Orlando	FL	32819	**800-925-9999**	407-351-3383	738
Westglow Spa	2845 Hwy 221 S	Blowing Rock	NC	28605	**800-562-0807**	828-295-4463	697
Westhampton College	The Deanery 28 Westhampton Way	University of Richmond	VA	23173	**800-700-1662**	804-289-8440	163
Westin Beach Resort Key Largo	97000 S Overseas Hwy MM 97	Key Largo	FL	33037	**800-937-8461**	305-852-5553	655
Westin La Cantera Resort	16641 La Cantera Pkwy	San Antonio	TX	78256	**800-937-8461**	210-558-6500	655
Westin Century Plaza Hotel & Spa	2025 Ave of the Stars	Los Angeles	CA	90067	**800-937-8461**	310-277-2000	373
Westin City Center Dallas	650 N Pearl St	Dallas	TX	75201	**888-625-5144**	214-979-9000	373
Westin Diplomat Resort & Spa	3555 S Ocean Dr	Hollywood	FL	33019	**888-627-9057**	954-602-6000	655
Westin Hotels & Resorts	1111 Westchester Ave	White Plains	NY	10604	**877-443-4585**	914-640-8100	369
Westin Innisbrook Golf Resort	36750 US Hwy 19 N	Palm Harbor	FL	34684	**800-456-2000**	727-942-2000	655
Westin Kierland Resort & Spa	6902 E Greenway Pkwy	Scottsdale	AZ	85254	**888-625-5144**	480-624-1000	655
Westin Mission Hills Resort	71333 Dinah Shore Dr	Rancho Mirage	CA	92270	**800-937-8461**	760-328-5955	655
Westin La Paloma Resort & Spa	3800 E Sunrise Dr	Tucson	AZ	85718	**888-627-7201**	520-742-6000	655
Westin Resort Hilton Head Island	2 Grasslawn Ave	Hilton Head Island	SC	29928	**800-937-8461**	843-681-4000	655
Westin Resort & Spa Whistler	4090 Whistler Way	Whistler	BC	V0N1B4	**888-634-5577**	604-905-5000	655
Westin Resort Tremblant	100 ch Kandahar	Mont-Tremblant	QC	J8E1E2	**800-937-8461**	819-681-8000	655
Westin Savannah Harbor Resort & Spa	1 Resort Dr	Savannah	GA	31421	**800-937-8461**	912-201-2000	655
Westin Stonebriar Resort	1549 Legacy Dr	Frisco	TX	75034	**800-937-8461**	972-668-8000	655
Westinghouse Lighting Corp	12401 McNulty Rd *Orders	Philadelphia	PA	19154	**800-999-2226***	215-671-2000	431
WestJet Airlines Ltd	5055 11th St NE *TSE: WJA*	Calgary	AB	T2E8N4	**888-293-7853**	403-444-2600	26
Westlake Plastics Co	PO Box 127	Lenni	PA	19052	**800-999-1700**	610-459-1000	593
Westland Co-op	2112 Indianapolis Rd	Crawfordsville	IN	47933	**800-878-0952**	765-362-6700	272
Westland Corp	PO Box 9268	Wichita	KS	67277	**800-247-1144**	316-721-1144	745
Westmark Anchorage	720 W 5th Ave	Anchorage	AK	99501	**800-544-0970**	907-276-7676	373
Westmark Baranof	127 N Franklin St	Juneau	AK	99801	**800-544-0970**	907-586-2660	373
Westmark Fairbanks Hotel & Conference Center	813 Noble St	Fairbanks	AK	99701	**800-544-0970**	907-456-7722	373
Westmark Hotels Inc	221 1st Ave W Suite 100	Seattle	WA	98119	**800-544-0970**	206-301-5224	369
Westminster-Canterbury Richmond	1600 Westbrook Ave	Richmond	VA	23227	**800-445-9904**	804-264-6000	659
Westminster College	501 Westminster Ave	Fulton	MO	65251	**800-475-3361**	573-642-3361	163
Westminster College	319 S Market St	New Wilmington	PA	16172	**800-942-8033**	724-946-8761	163
Westminster College of Salt Lake City	1840 S 1300 East	Salt Lake City	UT	84105	**800-748-4753**	801-484-7651	163
Westminster Place	3200 Grant St	Evanston	IL	60201	**800-896-9095**	847-492-4800	659
Westmont College	955 La Paz Rd	Santa Barbara	CA	93108	**800-777-9011**	805-565-6000	163
Westmont Hospitality Group Inc	5847 San Felipe St Suite 4650	Houston	TX	77057	**800-468-3512**	713-782-9100	369
Westmoreland County Community College	400 Armbrust Rd	Youngwood	PA	15697	**800-262-2103**	724-925-4000	160
Weston George Bakeries Inc	55 Paradise Ln	Bay Shore	NY	11706	**800-842-9595**	631-273-6000	291-1
Weston Plaza Hotel & Conference Center	2725 Cassopolis St	Elkhart	IN	46514	**800-521-8400**	574-264-7502	373
Westover Scientific Inc	18421 Bothell-Everett Hwy Suite 110	Bothell	WA	98012	**800-304-3202**	425-398-1298	410
WestPoint Stevens Inc Sales Div	1185 Ave of the Americas *Cust Svc	New York	NY	10036	**800-533-8229***	212-930-2000	356
Westport Corp	10 E 34th St	New York	NY	10016	**800-457-7782**	212-779-5900	422
Westport Inn	1595 Post Rd E	Westport	CT	06880	**800-446-8997**	203-259-5236	373
Westra Construction Inc	W7185 Hwy 49	Waupun	WI	53963	**800-388-3545**	920-324-3545	185
Westrum Development Co Inc	370 Commerce Dr Suite 100	Fort Washington	PA	19034	**800-937-8786**	215-283-2190	639
Westville 1850's Village	1 ML King Blvd	Lumpkin	GA	31815	**888-733-1850**	229-838-6310	509
Westward Look Resort	245 E Ina Rd	Tucson	AZ	85704	**800-722-2500**	520-297-1151	655
Westwood College of Technology	7350 N Broadway	Denver	CO	80221	**800-875-6050**	303-650-5050	787
Westwood Computer Corp	11 Diamond Rd	Springfield	NJ	07081	**800-800-8805**	973-376-4242	172
Westwood Lodge Hospital	45 Clapboardtree Rd	Westwood	MA	02090	**800-222-2237**	781-762-7764	366-3
Westye Group	PO Box 111400	Carrollton	TX	75011	**800-441-9260**	972-416-6677	38
Wet 'n Wild Emerald Pointe	3910 S Holden Rd	Greensboro	NC	27406	**800-555-5900**	336-852-9721	32
Wet 'n Wild Orlando	6200 International Dr	Orlando	FL	32819	**800-992-9453**	407-351-1800	32
Wet Seal Inc	26972 Burbank Ave *NASDAQ: WTSLA*	Foothill Ranch	CA	92610	**800-735-7325**	949-583-9029	155-6
WetFeet.com	609 Mission St Suite 400	San Francisco	CA	94105	**800-926-4562**	415-284-7900	257
Wetherill Assoc Inc	1101 Enterprise Dr	Royersford	PA	19468	**800-877-3340**	610-495-2200	61
WeTip Inc	PO Box 1296	Rancho Cucamonga	CA	91729	**800-782-7463**	909-987-5005	48-8
WETK-TV Ch 33 (PBS)	204 Ethan Allen Ave	Colchester	VT	05446	**800-639-7811**	802-655-4800	726
Wetlandsbank Inc	3215 NW 10th Terr Suite 209	Fort Lauderdale	FL	33309	**888-301-1707**	954-462-1707	191
WETP-TV Ch 2 (PBS)	1611 E Magnolia Ave	Knoxville	TN	37917	**800-595-0220**	865-595-0220	726
WETS-FM 89.5 (NPR)	89 Drive East Tennessee State University	Johnson City	TN	37614	**888-895-9387**	423-439-6440	631
Wetsel Inc	961 Liberty St	Harrisonburg	VA	22802	**800-572-4018**	540-434-6753	684
WEVO-FM 89.1 (N/T)	207 N Main St	Concord	NH	03301	**800-262-1816**	603-228-8910	631
Weyerhaeuser Co	PO Box 9777 *NYSE: WY*	Federal Way	WA	98063	**800-525-5440**	253-924-2345	184
WF Meyers Co	1017 14th St PO Box 426	Bedford	IN	47421	**800-457-4055**	812-275-4485	447
WF Young Inc	PO Box 1990	East Longmeadow	MA	01028	**800-628-9653**	413-526-9999	572
WFAE-FM 90.7 (NPR)	8801 JM Keynes Dr Suite 91	Charlotte	NC	28262	**800-876-9323**	704-549-9323	631
WFCA (World Floor Covering Assn)	2211 Howell Ave	Anaheim	CA	92806	**800-624-6880**	714-978-6440	49-4
WFDD-FM 88.5 (NPR)	56 Wake Forest Rd	Winston-Salem	NC	27109	**800-262-8850**	336-758-8850	631
WFFF-TV Ch 44 (Fox)	298 Mountain View Dr	Colchester	VT	05446	**888-400-4855**	802-660-9333	726
WF&FSA (Wholesale Florist & Florist Supplier Assn)	147 Old Solomons Island Rd Suite 302	Annapolis	MD	21401	**888-289-3372**	410-573-0400	49-18
WFI (Wireless Facilities Inc)	4810 Eastgate Mall *NASDAQ: WFII*	San Diego	CA	92121	**888-824-0017**	858-228-2000	195
WFIE-TV Ch 14 (NBC)	1115 Mt Auburn Rd	Evansville	IN	47720	**800-832-0014**	812-426-1414	726
WFIU-FM 103.7 (Clas)	Indiana University 1229 E 7th St	Bloomington	IN	47405	**877-285-9348**	812-855-1357	631
WFLA-TV Ch 8 (NBC)	200 S Parker St	Tampa	FL	33606	**800-348-9352**	813-228-8888	726
WFLC-FM 97.3 (AC)	2741 N 29th Ave	Hollywood	FL	33020	**866-227-9730**	954-584-7117	631
WFMF-FM 102.5 (CHR)	5555 Hilton Ave Suite 500	Baton Rouge	LA	70808	**888-235-6673**	225-231-1860	631
WFMJ-TV Ch 21 (NBC)	101 W Boardman St	Youngstown	OH	44503	**800-488-9365**	330-744-8611	726

Name / Address	City	State	ZIP	Toll-Free	Phone	Class
WFR Mutual Insurance Holding Co 1526 K St	Lincoln	NE	68508	**800-869-0355**	402-476-6500	355-4
WFRE-FM 99.9 (Ctry) 5966 Grove Hill Rd	Frederick	MD	21703	**877-999-9373**	301-663-4181	631
WFRN-AM 1270 (Rel) 25802 CR 26	Elkhart	IN	46517	**800-522-9376**	574-875-5166	631
WFS Financial Inc 23 Pasteur *NASDAQ: WFSI*	Irvine	CA	92618	**800-289-8004**	949-727-1000	215
WFSQ-FM 91.5 (Clas) 1600 Red Barber Plaza	Tallahassee	FL	32310	**800-829-8809**	850-487-3086	631
WFSU-FM 88.9 (NPR) 1600 Red Barber Plaza	Tallahassee	FL	32310	**800-829-8809**	850-487-3086	631
WFSU-TV Ch 11 (PBS) 1600 Red Barber Plaza	Tallahassee	FL	32310	**800-322-9378**	850-487-3170	726
WFTS-TV Ch 28 (ABC) 4045 N Himes Ave	Tampa	FL	33607	**800-234-9387**	813-354-2800	726
WFUM-FM 91.1 (NPR) 535 W William St Suite 110	Ann Arbor	MI	48103	**800-728-9386**	734-764-9210	631
WFWA-TV Ch 39 (PBS) 2501 E Coliseum Blvd	Fort Wayne	IN	46805	**888-484-8839**	260-484-8839	726
WFXP-TV Ch 66 (Fox) 8455 Peach St	Erie	PA	16509	**888-989-9538**	814-864-2400	726
WFYR-FM 97.3 (Ctry) 120 Eaton St	Peoria	IL	61603	**866-673-0973**	309-676-5000	631
WG Block Co 1414 Mississippi Blvd PO Box 280	Bettendorf	IA	52722	**800-397-1651**	563-823-2080	180
WG Grinders 2002 Cotter St	Lewis Center	OH	43035	**877-447-3354**	614-766-2313	657
WG Leffelman & Sons Inc 340 N Metcalf Ave	Amboy	IL	61310	**800-957-2513**	815-857-2513	270
WGAw (Writers Guild of America West) 7000 W 3rd St	Los Angeles	CA	90048	**800-548-4532**	323-951-4000	405
WGBG-FM 98.5 (CR) 20200 Dupont Blvd	Georgetown	DE	19947	**888-780-0970**	302-856-2567	631
WGCU-FM 90.1 (NPR) 10501 FGCU Blvd	Fort Myers	FL	33965	**888-824-0030**	239-590-2500	631
WGCU-TV Ch 30 (PBS) 10501 FGCU Blvd	Fort Myers	FL	33965	**888-824-0030**	239-590-2300	726
WGCX-FM 95.7 (Rel) 2070 N Palafox St	Pensacola	FL	32501	**800-441-2636**	850-434-1230	631
WGET-AM 1320 (AC) 1560 Fairfield Rd	Gettysburg	PA	17325	**800-366-9489**	717-334-3101	631
WGGS-TV Ch 16 (Ind) 3409 Rutherford Rd Ext	Taylors	SC	29687	**800-849-3683**	864-244-1616	726
WGI Heavy Minerals Inc 1875 N Lakewood Dr Suite 201 *TSE: WG*	Coeur d'Alene	ID	83814	**888-542-7638**	208-666-6000	493-3
WGL Holdings Inc 101 Constitution Ave NW *NYSE: WGL*	Washington	DC	20080	**800-752-7520**	703-750-2000	355-5
WGLO-FM 95.5 (CR) 120 Eaton St	Peoria	IL	61603	**888-676-9595**	309-676-5000	631
WGME-TV Ch 13 (CBS) 1335 Washington Ave	Portland	ME	04103	**800-766-9330**	207-797-1313	726
WGNA-FM 107.7 (Ctry) 800 New Loudon Rd Suite 4200	Latham	NY	12110	**800-476-1077**	518-782-1474	631
WGRD-FM 97.9 (Rock) 50 Monroe Ave NW Suite 500	Grand Rapids	MI	49503	**800-957-3979**	616-451-4800	631
WGRZ-TV Ch 2 (NBC) 259 Delaware Ave	Buffalo	NY	14202	**877-849-2200**	716-849-2200	726
WGST-AM 640 (N/T) 1819 Peachtree Rd NE Suite 700	Atlanta	GA	30309	**800-776-4638**	404-367-0640	631
WGTE-FM 91.3 (NPR) 1270 S Detroit Ave	Toledo	OH	43614	**800-243-9483**	419-380-4600	631
WGTE-TV Ch 30 (PBS) PO Box 30	Toledo	OH	43614	**800-243-9483**	419-380-4600	726
WGTS-FM 91.9 (Rel) 7600 Flower Ave	Takoma Park	MD	20912	**877-948-7919**	301-891-4200	631
WGTV-TV Ch 8 (PBS) 260 14th St NW	Atlanta	GA	30318	**800-222-6006**	404-685-2400	726
WGTY-FM 107.7 (Ctry) 1560 Fairfield Rd	Gettysburg	PA	17325	**800-366-9489**	717-334-3101	631
WGVU-FM 88.5 (NPR) 301 W Fulton St	Grand Rapids	MI	49504	**800-442-2771**	616-331-6666	631
WGVU-TV Ch 35 (PBS) 301 W Fulton St	Grand Rapids	MI	49504	**800-442-2771**	616-331-6666	726
WGXA-TV Ch 24 (Fox) 599 ML King Jr Blvd	Macon	GA	31201	**800-592-4240**	478-745-2424	726
WGZO-FM 103.1 (AC) 401 Mall Blvd Suite 101D	Savannah	GA	31406	**888-844-1031**	912-351-9830	631
WH Bagshaw Co Inc PO Box 766	Nashua	NH	03061	**800-343-7467**	603-883-7758	478
WH Freeman & Co 41 Madison Ave 35th Fl	New York	NY	10010	**800-903-3019**	212-576-9400	623-2
WH Salisbury & Co 7520 N Long Ave	Skokie	IL	60077	**877-406-4501**	847-679-6700	566
WHAD-FM 90.7 (NPR) 111 E Kilbourn Ave Suite 2375	Milwaukee	WI	53202	**800-486-8655**	414-227-2040	631
Whalers' Cove Sportfishing Lodge Mile 1 Killisnoo Rd PO Box 101	Angoon	AK	99820	**800-423-3123**	907-788-3123	655
Whaling Mfg Co 451 Quarry St	Fall River	MA	02723	**800-225-8554**	508-678-9061	153-5
Wham-O Inc 5903 Christie Ave	Emeryville	CA	94608	**877-469-4266**	510-596-4202	750
Wharton Center for the Performing Arts Michigan State University	East Lansing	MI	48824	**800-942-7866**	517-432-2000	562
Wharton County Electric Co-op Inc PO Box 31	El Campo	TX	77437	**800-460-6271**	979-543-6271	244
Wharton County Junior College 911 Boling Hwy	Wharton	TX	77488	**800-561-9252**	979-532-4560	160
Sugar Land Campus 550 Julie Rivers Dr	Sugar Land	TX	77478	**800-561-9252**	281-243-8410	160
Wharton Group 101 S Livingston Ave	Livingston	NJ	07039	**800-521-2725**	973-992-5775	383
Wharton-Smith Inc 750 County Rd 15 PO Box 471028	Lake Monroe	FL	32747	**888-393-0068**	407-321-8410	187-10
What Works in Teaching & Learning Newsletter 360 Hiatt Dr *Sales	Palm Beach Gardens	FL	33418	**800-621-5463***	561-622-6520	521-4
Whatcom Hospice 800 E Chestnut St Suite 1C	Bellingham	WA	98225	**800-573-5877**	360-733-5877	365
Whatman Inc 9 Bridewell Pl	Clifton	NJ	07014	**800-441-6555**	973-773-5800	410
Wheat Belt Public Power District PO Box 177	Sidney	NE	69162	**800-261-7114**	308-254-5871	244
Wheat Ridge Ministries 1 Pierce Pl Suite 250E	Itasca	IL	60143	**800-762-6748**	630-766-9066	48-20
Wheatland Electric Co-op Inc PO Box 230	Scott City	KS	67871	**800-762-0436**	620-872-5885	244
Wheatland Rural Electric Assn 2154 South Rd	Wheatland	WY	82201	**800-344-3351**	307-322-2125	244
Wheatland Tube Co 900 Haddon Ave	Collingswood	NJ	08108	**800-257-8182**	856-854-5400	481
Wheatmark Inc 610 E Delano St Suite 104	Tucson	AZ	85705	**888-934-0888**	520-798-0888	623-2
Wheaton College 501 E College Ave	Wheaton	IL	60187	**800-222-2419**	630-752-5000	163
Wheaton-Dumont Farmer Co-op 1115 Broadway	Wheaton	MN	56296	**800-258-7444**	320-563-8152	272
Wheaton River Minerals Ltd 200 Burrard St Suite 1560 *TSE: WRM*	Vancouver	BC	V6C3L6	**800-567-6223**	604-696-3000	492
Wheaton USA Inc 5176 Harding Hwy	Mays Landing	NJ	08330	**800-442-7533**	609-625-2291	329
Wheaton Van Lines Inc PO Box 50800	Indianapolis	IN	46250	**800-932-7799**	317-849-7900	508
WHEC-TV Ch 10 (NBC) 191 East Ave	Rochester	NY	14604	**800-284-9432**	585-546-5670	726
Wheel Manufacturers. Institute of Caster & 8720 Red Oak Blvd Suite 201	Charlotte	NC	28217	**800-345-1815**	704-676-1190	49-13
Wheel & Sprocket Inc 5722 S 108th St	Hales Corners	WI	53130	**800-362-4537**	414-529-6600	702
Wheelabrator Technologies Inc 4 Liberty Ln W	Hampton	NH	03842	**800-682-0026**	603-929-3000	791
Wheeled Coach Industries Inc 2737 N Forsyth Rd	Winter Park	FL	32792	**800-342-0720**	407-677-7777	505
Wheeler Industries 7261 Investment Dr *Sales	North Charleston	SC	29418	**800-343-0803***	843-552-1251	609
Wheeler Mfg 107 Main Ave PO Box 629 *Orders	Lemmon	SD	57638	**800-843-1937***	605-374-3848	401
Wheeler-Rex PO Box 688	Ashtabula	OH	44005	**800-321-7950**	440-998-2788	746
Wheeling Convention & Visitors Bureau 1401 Main St	Wheeling	WV	26003	**800-828-3097**	304-233-7709	205
Wheeling Corrugating Co 1134 Market St *Sales	Wheeling	WV	26003	**800-922-3325***	304-234-2300	709
Wheeling Jesuit University 316 Washington Ave	Wheeling	WV	26003	**800-624-6992**	304-243-2000	163
Wheeling-Pittsburgh Corp 1134 Market St *NASDAQ: WPSC*	Wheeling	WV	26003	**800-441-8190**	304-234-2400	709
Wheeling Symphony Orchestra 1025 Main St Suite 811	Wheeling	WV	26003	**800-395-9241**	304-232-6100	563-3
Wheelock College 200 The Riverway	Boston	MA	02215	**800-734-5212**	617-879-2206	163
Wheelock Inc 273 Branchport Ave *Cust Svc	Long Branch	NJ	07740	**800-631-2148***	732-222-6880	681
Wheels Etc 15186 Foothill Blvd	Fontana	CA	92335	**800-758-4737**	909-350-8200	740
Wheelwright Museum of the American Indian 704 Camino Lejo	Santa Fe	NM	87505	**800-607-4636**	505-982-4636	509
WHEMCO Inc 5 Hot Metal St	Pittsburgh	PA	15203	**800-800-7686**	412-390-2700	661
Where Baltimore Magazine 301 S 19th St Suite 1-S	Philadelphia	PA	19103	**866-368-3604**	215-893-5100	449-22
Where New York Magazine 79 Madison Ave	New York	NY	10016	**800-666-8336**	212-636-2700	449-22
Where Philadelphia Magazine 301 S 19th St Suite 1-S	Philadelphia	PA	19103	**866-368-3604**	215-893-5100	449-22
Whetstone Valley Electric Co-op PO Box 512	Milbank	SD	57252	**800-568-6631**	605-432-5331	244
Whibco Inc 87 E Commerce St	Bridgeton	NJ	08302	**800-631-8010**	856-455-9200	493-4
WHIL-FM 91.3 (NPR) PO Box 8509	Mobile	AL	36689	**800-239-9445**	251-380-4685	631
WHIQ-TV Ch 25 (PBS) 2112 11th Ave S Suite 400	Birmingham	AL	35205	**800-239-5233**	205-328-8756	726
Whirl Air Flow Corp 20055 177th St	Big Lake	MN	55309	**800-373-3461**	763-262-1200	206
Whirlpool Corp 2000 M-63 N *NYSE: WHR*	Benton Harbor	MI	49022	**800-253-1301**	269-923-5000	36
Whirlpool Corp KitchenAid Div 2000 M-63 N	Benton Harbor	MI	49022	**800-253-1301**	269-923-5000	37
Whirlpool Corp North American Region 2000 M-63 N	Benton Harbor	MI	49022	**800-253-1301**	269-923-5000	36
Whirlwind Building Systems Inc 8234 Hansen Rd	Houston	TX	77075	**800-324-9992**	713-946-7140	106
Whiskey Pete's Hotel & Casino 100 W Primm Blvd	Primm	NV	89019	**800-386-7867**	702-382-4388	133
Whistler Blackcomb Mountain Ski Resort 4545 Blackcomb Way	Whistler	BC	V0N1B4	**800-766-0449**	604-932-3434	655
Whistler Group Inc 13016 N Walton Blvd *Cust Svc	Bentonville	AR	72712	**800-531-0004***	479-273-6012	519
Whistler SB & Sons Inc PO Box 207	Akron	NY	14001	**800-828-1010**	716-542-4141	745
Whistling Acres Guest Ranch 44325 Minnesota Creek Rd PO Box 88	Paonia	CO	81428	**800-346-1420**	970-527-4560	238
Whitacre Greer Fireproofing Inc 1400 S Mahoning Ave	Alliance	OH	44601	**800-947-2837**	330-823-1610	148
Whitaker House/Anchor Distributors 30 Hunt Valley Cir *Orders	New Kensington	PA	15068	**800-444-4484***	724-334-7000	623-4
Whitaker Newsletters Inc PO Box 241	Burtonsville	MD	20866	**800-359-6049**	301-384-1573	623-9
Whitaker Oil Co Inc 1557 Marietta Rd NW	Atlanta	GA	30318	**800-221-0521**	404-355-8220	144
Whitcomb Frank W Construction Corp PO Box 1000	Walpole	NH	03608	**800-238-7283**	603-445-5555	187-4
White Bag Co Inc 8027 Hwy 161 N	North Little Rock	AR	72117	**800-527-1733**	501-835-1444	67
White Barn Candle Co 7 Limited Pkwy E	Reynoldsburg	OH	43068	**800-395-1001**	614-856-6000	122
White Brothers 24845 Corbit Pl	Yorba Linda	CA	92887	**800-854-1899**	714-692-3404	61
White Brothers Trucking Co PO Box 82	Wasco	IL	60183	**800-323-4762**	630-584-3810	769
White Cap Industries Inc 1723 S Ritchie St	Santa Ana	CA	92705	**800-922-9922**	714-258-3300	190-3
White Castle System Inc 555 W Goodale St	Columbus	OH	43215	**866-272-8372**	614-228-5781	657
White Cloud Coffee Co 199 E 52nd St	Boise	ID	83714	**800-627-0309**	208-322-1166	291-7

Name / Address	City	State	Zip	Toll-Free	Phone	Class
White Clover Dairy Inc 489 Holland Ct	Kaukauna	WI	54130	**800-878-5765**	920-766-5765	291-5
White Co 1750 S Brentwood Blvd Suite 301	Saint Louis	MO	63144	**888-221-9679**	314-961-4480	641
White Coffee Corp 1835 38th St	Long Island City	NY	11105	**800-221-0140**	718-204-7900	291-7
White County Chamber of Commerce 122 N Main St	Cleveland	GA	30528	**800-392-8279**	706-865-5356	137
White County Medical Center 3214 E Race Ave	Searcy	AR	72143	**888-562-7520**	501-268-6121	366-2
White County Rural Electric Membership Corp PO Box 599	Monticello	IN	47960	**800-844-7161**	574-583-7161	244
White Directory Publishers Inc 1945 Sheridan Dr	Buffalo	NY	14223	**800-388-8255**	716-875-9100	623-6
White Dove Ltd 3201 Harvard Ave	Cleveland	OH	44105	**888-649-6061**	216-341-0200	463
White Electrical Construction Co PO Box 19629	Atlanta	GA	30325	**888-519-4483**	404-351-5740	188-4
White Electronic Designs Corp 3601 E University Dr *NASDAQ: WEDC*	Phoenix	AZ	85034	**800-326-9556**	602-437-1520	686
White Elephant Inn & Cottages 50 Easton St	Nantucket	MA	02554	**800-475-2637**	508-228-2500	373
White Flower Farm 30 Irene St *Cust Svc	Torrington	CT	06790	**800-411-6159***	860-496-9624	318
White Inn 52 E Main St	Fredonia	NY	14063	**888-373-3664**	716-672-2103	373
White Knight Engineered Products 94 Glenn Bridge Rd	Arden	NC	28704	**800-743-4700**	828-687-0940	566
White Laboratories Inc 110 Bomar Ct Suite 122	Longwood	FL	32750	**800-327-2014**	407-869-0107	211
White LB Co Inc W 6636 LB White Rd	Onalaska	WI	54650	**800-345-7200**	608-783-5691	352
White Lily Foods Co 218 E Depot Ave	Knoxville	TN	37917	**800-264-5459**	865-546-5511	291-23
White Lion Motel 912 Capitol Landing Rd	Williamsburg	VA	23185	**800-368-1055**	757-229-3931	373
White Mountain Adventures 107 Boulder Crescent Suite 7	Canmore	AB	T1W1K9	**800-408-0005**	403-678-4099	748
White Mountain Hotel & Resort West Side Rd	North Conway	NH	03860	**800-533-6301**	603-356-7100	655
White Mountain Passenger Lines Inc 1041 E Hall St PO Box 460	Show Low	AZ	85902	**866-255-4819**	928-537-4539	109
White Mountain School 371 W Farm Rd	Bethlehem	NH	03574	**800-545-7813**	603-444-2928	611
White Mountain Traders 100 Factory St	Nashua	NH	03060	**800-648-6505**	603-889-5115	153-13
White Oak Corp 7 W Main St	Plainville	CT	06062	**800-828-6195**	860-747-1627	187-4
White Oaks Conference Resort & Spa 253 Taylor Rd	Niagara-on-the-Lake	ON	L0S1J0	**800-263-5766**	905-688-2550	370
White RH Construction Co Inc 41 Central St	Auburn	MA	01501	**800-922-8182**	508-832-3295	187-10
White River Distributors Inc PO Box 2037	Batesville	AR	72503	**800-548-7219**	870-793-2374	473
White River Paper Co 118 Rt 14	Hartford	VT	05047	**800-639-7226**	802-295-3188	549
White River State Park 801 W Washington St	Indianapolis	IN	46204	**800-665-9056**	317-233-2434	554
White River Valley Electric Co-op Inc PO Box 969	Branson	MO	65615	**800-879-4056**	417-335-9335	244
White Rock Distilleries Inc PO Box 1829	Lewiston	ME	04241	**800-628-5441**	207-783-1433	81-1
White Rock Products Corp 1616 Whitestone Expy	Whitestone	NY	11357	**800-969-7625**	718-746-3400	81-2
White Sands of La Jolla 7450 Olivetas Ave	La Jolla	CA	92037	**800-892-7817**	858-454-4201	659
White SS Medical Products Inc 151 Old New Brunswick Rd *Cust Svc	Piscataway	NJ	08854	**888-779-4483***	732-752-8300	468
White SS Technologies Inc 151 Old New Brunswick Rd	Piscataway	NJ	08854	**800-872-2673**	732-752-8300	609
White Stallion Ranch 9251 W Twin Peaks Rd	Tucson	AZ	85743	**888-977-2624**	520-297-0252	238
White Star Tours 26 E Lancaster Ave	Reading	PA	19607	**800-437-2323**	610-775-5000	748
White Sulphur Springs Resort & Spa 3100 White Sulphur Springs Rd	Saint Helena	CA	94574	**800-593-8873**	707-963-8588	697
White Systems Inc 30 Boright Ave	Kenilworth	NJ	07033	**800-275-1442**	908-272-6700	281
White Tire Distributors Inc 1513 Seibel Dr NE	Roanoke	VA	24012	**800-476-9448**	540-342-3183	740
White Way Sign 1317 N Clybourn Ave	Chicago	IL	60610	**800-621-4122**	312-642-6580	692
White Wolf Publishing Co 1554 Litton Dr *Orders	Stone Mountain	GA	30083	**800-454-9653***	404-292-1819	623-2
Whiteface Club & Resort PO Box 231 Whiteface Inn Rd	Lake Placid	NY	12946	**800-422-6757**	518-523-2551	655
Whitehall Furniture 201 E Martin St	Orleans	IN	47452	**800-467-3585**	812-865-3898	314-1
Whitehall Group Div Cadmus Communications Corp 2750 Whitehall Park Dr	Charlotte	NC	28273	**800-733-4318**	704-583-6600	615
Whitehall Hotel 105 E Delaware Pl	Chicago	IL	60611	**800-323-7500**	312-944-6300	373
Whitehall Jewellers Inc 155 N Wacker Dr Suite 500 *NYSE: JWL*	Chicago	IL	60606	**800-621-0771**	312-782-6800	402
Whitehall Printing Co 4244 Corporate Sq	Naples	FL	34104	**800-321-9290**	239-643-6464	614
Whitehill Lighting & Supplies Inc 1524 N Atherton St	State College	PA	16803	**800-326-9940**	814-238-2449	245
Whitehouse Irvin H & Sons Co 4600 Jennings Ln	Louisville	KY	40218	**800-626-5859**	502-966-4176	188-8
White's Electronics Inc 1011 Pleasant Valley Rd *Sales	Sweet Home	OR	97386	**800-547-6911***	541-367-6121	464
Whitewater. American 1424 Fenwick Ln	Silver Spring	MD	20910	**866-262-8429**	301-589-9453	48-23
Whitewater Valley Rural Electric Membership Corp PO Box 349	Liberty	IN	47353	**800-529-5557**	765-458-5171	244
Whiting Auditorium 1241 E Kearsley St	Flint	MI	48503	**888-823-6837**	810-237-7333	562
Whiting Corp 26000 Whiting Way	Monee	IL	60449	**800-255-8594**	708-587-2000	462
Whiting-Turner Contracting Co 300 E Joppa Rd	Baltimore	MD	21286	**800-638-4279**	410-821-1100	185
Whitlam Label Co Inc 24800 Sherwood Ave	Center Line	MI	48015	**800-755-2235**	586-757-5100	404
Whitlock Group 3900 Gaskins Rd	Richmond	VA	23233	**800-726-9843**	804-273-9100	245
Whitlock Packaging Corp 1701 S Lee St	Fort Gibson	OK	74434	**800-833-9382**	918-478-4300	291-20
Whitman Albert & Co 6340 Oakton St	Morton Grove	IL	60053	**800-255-7675**	847-581-0033	623-2
Whitman College 345 Boyer Ave	Walla Walla	WA	99362	**877-462-9448**	509-527-5111	163
Whitman Requardt & Assoc 801 S Caroline St	Baltimore	MD	21231	**800-787-7100**	410-235-3450	258
Whitmire Micro-Gen Research Laboratories Inc 3568 Tree Court Industrial Blvd	Saint Louis	MO	63122	**800-777-8570**	636-225-5371	276
Whitney The - A Wyndham Historic Hotel 610 Poydras St	New Orleans	LA	70130	**800-996-3426**	504-581-4222	373
Whitney Holding Corp 228 St Charles Ave *NASDAQ: WTNY*	New Orleans	LA	70130	**800-383-6538**	504-586-7272	355-2
Whitney Hotel 700 Woodrow St	Columbia	SC	29205	**800-637-4008**	803-252-0845	373
Whitney JC & Co 225 N Michigan Ave	Chicago	IL	60601	**800-529-4486**	312-431-6000	451
Whitney JH & Co LLC 177 Broad St 15th Fl	Stamford	CT	06901	**800-881-6085**	203-973-1400	779
Whitney National Bank 228 St Charles Ave	New Orleans	LA	70130	**800-347-7272**	504-586-7272	71
Whitney Tool Co Inc 906 R St	Bedford	IN	47421	**800-536-1971**	812-275-4491	447
Whitney WA Co 650 Race St	Rockford	IL	61105	**800-435-2823**	815-964-6771	448
Whitten Pumps Inc 502 County Line Rd	Delano	CA	93215	**800-287-4578**	661-725-0250	627
Whittet-Higgins Co 33 Higginson Ave PO Box 8 *Sales	Central Falls	RI	02863	**800-972-8070***	401-728-0700	609
Whittier Daily News 7612 Green Leaf Ave	Whittier	CA	90602	**800-788-1200**	562-698-0955	522-2
Whittier Law School 3333 Harbor Blvd	Costa Mesa	CA	92626	**800-808-8188**	714-444-4141	164-1
Whittier Wood Products Inc 3787 W 1st Ave	Eugene	OR	97402	**800-653-3336**	541-687-0213	314-2
Whitworth College 300 W Hawthorne Rd	Spokane	WA	99251	**800-533-4668**	509-777-1000	163
WHNN-FM 96.1 (Oldies) 1740 Champagne Dr N	Saginaw	MI	48604	**877-479-9466**	989-776-2100	631
WHNT-TV Ch 19 (CBS) PO Box 19	Huntsville	AL	35804	**800-533-8819**	256-533-1919	726
Who Needs Two? 707 Lake Cook Rd Suite 115	Deerfield	IL	60015	**888-246-8499**	847-564-8499	735
WHO-TV Ch 13 (NBC) 1801 Grand Ave	Des Moines	IA	50309	**800-835-1313**	515-242-3500	726
Wholesale Art & Hobby Distributors Inc 7207 114th Ave N Suite CF	Largo	FL	33773	**800-227-2520**	727-548-1999	44
Wholesale Electric Supply Co LP 4040 Guls Fwy PO Box 230197	Houston	TX	77223	**800-486-8563**	713-748-6100	245
Wholesale Electric Supply Inc 1400 Waterall St	Texarkana	TX	75501	**800-869-8672**	903-794-3404	245
Wholesale Florist & Florist Supplier Assn (WF&FSA) 147 Old Solomons Island Rd Suite 302	Annapolis	MD	21401	**888-289-3372**	410-573-0400	49-18
Wholesale Marketers Assn. American 2750 Prosperity Ave Suite 550	Fairfax	VA	22031	**800-482-2962**	703-208-3358	49-18
Wholesale Tire Co PO Box 1637	Victoria	TX	77902	**800-950-8119**	361-578-2945	740
Wholesale Tire Inc PO Box 1660	Clarksburg	WV	26302	**800-772-5752**	304-624-8465	740
Wholey Robert & Co Inc 1501 Penn Ave	Pittsburgh	PA	15222	**800-248-0568**	412-261-3693	292-5
WHOT-FM 101.1 (CHR) 4040 Simon Rd	Youngstown	OH	44512	**800-989-9468**	330-783-1000	631
WHQT-FM 105.1 (Urban) 2741 N 29th Ave	Hollywood	FL	33020	**888-550-9105**	954-584-7117	631
WHTZ-FM 100.3 (CHR) PO Box 7100	New York	NY	10150	**800-242-0100**	212-239-2300	631
WHUR-FM 96.3 (Urban AC) 529 Bryant St NW	Washington	DC	20059	**800-221-9487**	202-806-3500	631
WHXT-FM 103.9 (Urban) 1900 Pineview Rd	Columbia	SC	29209	**877-874-1039**	803-376-1039	631
WHY (World Hunger Year Inc) 505 8th Ave Suite 2100	New York	NY	10018	**800-548-6479**	212-629-8850	48-5
WHYN-AM 560 (N/T) 1331 Main St	Springfield	MA	01103	**800-331-9496**	413-781-1011	631
WHYN-FM 93.1 (AC) 1331 Main St	Springfield	MA	01103	**888-293-9310**	413-781-1011	631
WI (Wilderness Inquiry) 808 14th Ave SE	Minneapolis	MN	55414	**800-728-0719**	612-676-9400	48-23
Wi-LAN Inc 2891 Sunridge Way NE	Calgary	AB	T1Y7K7	**800-258-6876**	403-273-9133	496
WIBC (Women's International Bowling Congress) 5301 S 76th St	Greendale	WI	53129	**800-514-2695**	414-421-9000	48-22
Wichita Convention & Visitors Bureau 100 S Main St Suite 100	Wichita	KS	67202	**800-288-9424**	316-265-2800	205
Wichita Falls Convention & Visitors Bureau 1000 5th St PO Box 630	Wichita Falls	TX	76301	**800-799-6732**	940-716-5500	205
Wichita State University 1845 Fairmount St	Wichita	KS	67260	**800-362-2594**	316-978-3456	163
Wick Building Systems Inc 405 Walter Rd	Mazomanie	WI	53560	**800-356-9682**	608-795-4281	495
Wick Communications Inc 333 W Wilcox Dr Suite 302	Sierra Vista	AZ	85635	**800-777-9425**	520-458-0200	623-8
Wickaninnish Inn PO Box 250	Tofino	BC	V0R2Z0	**800-333-4604**	250-725-3100	372
Wickes Inc 706 N Deerpath Dr	Vernon Hills	IL	60061	**800-558-1232**	847-367-3400	190-3
Wicks 'N' Sticks PO Box 1965	Cypress	TX	77410	**800-873-3714**	713-856-7442	122
Wicks Pipe Organ Co 1100 5th St *Cust Svc	Highland	IL	62249	**800-444-9425***	618-654-2191	516
Wicomico County Convention & Visitors Bureau 8480 Ocean Hwy	Delmar	MD	21875	**800-332-8687**	410-548-4914	205
WICS (Women in Community Service Inc) 1900 N Beauregard St Suite 103	Alexandria	VA	22311	**800-442-9427**	703-671-0500	48-24
WICS-TV Ch 20 (NBC) 2680 E Cook St	Springfield	IL	62703	**800-263-9720**	217-753-5620	726
Wide-Lite Corp PO Box 606	San Marcos	TX	78667	**800-235-3214**	512-392-5821	431
Widener University School of Law Harrisburg 3800 Vartan Way	Harrisburg	PA	17110	**888-943-3637**	717-541-3900	164-1
Widener University School of Law Wilmington 4601 Concord Pike	Wilmington	DE	19803	**888-943-3637**	302-477-2100	164-1
Wider Church Ministries 700 Prospect Ave NE 7th Fl	Cleveland	OH	44115	**866-822-8224**	216-736-3200	48-20

Name / Address	City	State	Zip	Toll-Free	Phone	Class
Widmer Bros Brewing Co 929 N Russell St	Portland	OR	97227	**800-943-6371**	503-281-2437	103
Widmer's Wine Cellars Inc 1 Lake Niagra Ln	Naples	NY	14512	**800-836-5253**	585-374-6311	81-3
Widows. Society of Military 5535 Hempstead Way	Springfield	VA	22151	**800-842-3451**	703-750-1342	48-19
Wi$e Up Women Dept of Labor Women's Bureau 200 Constitution Ave NW	Washington	DC	20210	**800-827-5335**		196
Wiedemann Church Products PO Box 677	Muscatine	IA	52761	**800-553-9664**	563-263-6642	597
Wieland Furniture Inc 13737 Main St PO Box 1000	Grabill	IN	46741	**888-943-5263**	260-627-3686	314-3
Wieland John Homes & Neighborhoods Inc 1950 Sullivan Rd	Atlanta	GA	30337	**800-376-4663**	770-996-2400	639
Wiers Farm Inc PO Box 385	Willard	OH	44890	**800-825-6525**	419-935-0131	11-11
Wiese Industries Inc 1501 5th St PO Box 39	Perry	IA	50220	**800-568-4391**	515-465-9854	269
Wiesenthal Simon Center 1399 S Roxbury Dr	Los Angeles	CA	90035	**800-900-9036**	310-553-9036	48-8
Wieser & Cawley Inc 1301 Colegate Dr	Marietta	OH	45750	**800-339-0094**	740-373-1676	316
Wieser Concrete Products Inc W3716 US Hwy 10	Maiden Rock	WI	54750	**800-325-8456**	715-647-2311	181
Wig America Co 265 McCone Ave	Hayward	CA	94545	**800-338-7600**	510-887-0670	342
Wiggins Lift Co Inc PO Box 5187	Oxnard	CA	93031	**800-350-7821**	805-485-7821	462
Wigwam Mills Inc 3402 Crocker Ave	Sheboygan	WI	53082	**800-558-7760**	920-457-5551	153-10
Wigwam Resort 300 Wigwam Blvd	Litchfield Park	AZ	85340	**800-327-0396**	623-935-3811	655
WIHT-FM 99.5 (CHR) 1801 Rockville Pike 6th Fl	Rockville	MD	20852	**877-995-4681**	301-231-8231	631
Wika Instrument Corp 1000 Wiegand Blvd	Lawrenceville	GA	30043	**888-945-2872**	770-513-8200	200
WIKY-FM 104.1 (AC) 1162 Mt Auburn Rd	Evansville	IN	47736	**800-454-9459**	812-424-8284	631
WIL Research Laboratories Inc 1407 George Rd *Cust Svc	Ashland	OH	44805	**800-221-9610***	419-289-8700	728
Wilberforce University 1055 N Bickett Rd PO Box 1001	Wilberforce	OH	45384	**800-367-8568**	937-376-2911	163
Wilbert Funeral Services Inc 2913 Gardner Rd	Broadview	IL	60155	**800-323-7188**	708-865-1600	134
Wilbert Inc PO Box 147	Forest Park	IL	60130	**800-323-7188**	708-865-1600	181
Wilbur Chocolate Co Inc 48 N Broad St	Lititz	PA	17543	**800-233-0139**	717-626-1131	291-8
Wilbur Curtis Co Inc 6913 Acco St	Montebello	CA	90640	**800-421-6150**	323-837-2300	293
Wilco Farmers 200 Industrial Way	Mount Angel	OR	97362	**800-382-5339**	503-845-6122	272
Wilcom Inc 73 Daniel Webster Hwy	Belmont	NH	03220	**800-222-1898**	603-524-2622	633
Wilcox Farms Inc 40400 Harts Lake Valley Rd	Roy	WA	98580	**800-568-6456**	360-458-7774	11-8
Wilcox Frozen Foods Inc 2200 Oakdale Ave	San Francisco	CA	94124	**800-827-7858**	415-282-4116	292-6
Wild Animal Baby Magazine 8925 Leesburg Pike	Vienna	VA	22184	**800-822-9910**		449-6
Wild Animal Safari 1300 Oak Grove Rd	Pine Mountain	GA	31822	**800-367-2751**	706-663-8744	811
Wild Bird Centers of America Inc 7370 MacArthur Blvd	Glen Echo	MD	20812	**800-945-3247**	301-229-9585	518
Wild Bird Shop 123 S Hemlock	Cannon Beach	OR	97110	**800-281-9806**	503-436-9806	518
Wild Birds Unlimited 11711 N College Ave Suite 146	Carmel	IN	46032	**800-326-4928**	317-571-7100	518
Wild Blueberry Assn of North America (WBANA) 59 Cottage St po bOX 180	Bar Harbor	ME	04609	**800-233-9453**	207-288-2655	48-2
Wild Dunes Resort 5757 Palm Blvd	Isle of Palms	SC	29451	**800-845-8880**	843-886-6000	655
Wild Flavors Inc 1261 Pacific Ave	Erlanger	KY	41018	**888-945-3352**	859-342-3600	291-15
Wild Oats Markets Inc 3375 Mitchell Ln. *NASDAQ: OATS*	Boulder	CO	80301	**877-542-9453**	303-440-5220	350
Wild Palms Hotel 910 E Fremont Ave	Sunnyvale	CA	94087	**800-538-1600**	408-738-0500	373
Wild Rice Electric Co-op Inc PO Box 438	Mahnomen	MN	56557	**800-244-5709**	218-935-2517	244
Wild Rose Ranch PO Box 181	Kimberley	BC	V1A2Y6	**800-324-6188**	250-422-3403	238
Wild Turkey Federation. National 770 Augusta Rd PO Box 530 *Cust Svc	Edgefield	SC	29824	**800-843-6983***	803-637-3106	48-3
Wilde Automotive Group 1603 E Moreland Blvd	Waukesha	WI	53186	**800-236-5567**	262-542-0771	57
Wilde WA Co 201 Summer St	Holliston	MA	01746	**800-933-9453**	508-429-5515	5
Wilder Construction Co Inc 1525 E Marine View Dr	Everett	WA	98201	**800-377-0954**	425-551-3100	187-4
Wilder Laura Ingalls Museum & Home 3068 Hwy A	Mansfield	MO	65704	**877-924-7126**	417-924-3626	509
Wilderness Committee. Western Canada 227 Abbott St	Vancouver	BC	V6B2K7	**800-661-9453**	604-683-8220	48-13
Wilderness Inquiry (WI) 808 14th Ave SE	Minneapolis	MN	55414	**800-728-0719**	612-676-9400	48-23
Wilderness Society 1615 M St NW	Washington	DC	20036	**800-843-9453**	202-833-2300	48-13
Wilderness Trails Ranch 1766 County Rd 302	Durango	CO	81303	**800-527-2624**	970-247-0722	238
Wilderness Travel 1102 9th St	Berkeley	CA	94710	**800-368-2794**	510-558-2488	748
Wildlife Art Magazine 1428 E Cliff Rd	Burnsville	MN	55337	**800-221-6547**	952-736-1020	449-2
Wildlife Coalition. International 70 E Falmouth Hwy	East Falmouth	MA	02536	**800-548-8704**	508-548-8328	48-3
Wildlife Conservation Magazine 2300 Southern Blvd	Bronx	NY	10460	**800-786-8226**	718-220-6876	449-19
Wildlife Conservation Society (WCS) 2300 Southern Blvd	Bronx	NY	10460	**800-234-5128**	718-220-5100	48-3
Wildlife. Defenders of 1130 17th St NW	Washington	DC	20036	**800-989-8981**	202-682-9400	48-3
Wildlife Federation. Canadian 350 Michael Cowpland Dr	Kanata	ON	K2M2W1	**800-563-9453**	613-599-9594	48-13
Wildlife Federation. National 11100 Wildlife Center Dr *Cust Svc	Reston	VA	20190	**800-822-9919***	703-438-6000	48-3
Wildlife Foundation. African 1400 16th St NW Suite 120	Washington	DC	20036	**888-494-5354**	202-939-3333	48-3
Wildlife Fund Canada. World 245 Eglinton Ave E Suite 410	Toronto	ON	M4P3J1	**800-267-2632**	416-489-8800	48-3
Wildlife Fund. World 1250 24th St NW Suite 500	Washington	DC	20037	**800-225-5993**	202-293-4800	48-3
Wildlife Pharmaceuticals Inc 1635 Blue Spruce Dr Suite 202	Fort Collins	CO	80524	**877-883-9283**	970-484-6267	574
Wildlife Refuge Assn. National 1010 Wisconsin Ave NW Suite 200	Washington	DC	20007	**877-396-6972**	202-333-9075	48-13
Wildlife Research Education & Conservation. Jane Goodall Institute for 8700 Georgia Ave Suite 500	Silver Spring	MD	20910	**800-592-5263**	301-565-0086	48-3
Wildlife West Nature Park 87 N Frontage Rd	Edgewood	NM	87015	**877-815-9453**	505-281-7655	811
Wildman Frederick & Sons Ltd 311 E 53rd St	New York	NY	10022	**800-733-9463**	212-355-0700	82-3
WildPackets Inc 1340 Treat Blvd Suite 500	Walnut Creek	CA	94597	**800-466-2447**	925-937-3200	176-12
Wildtime Foods PO Box 10695	Eugene	OR	97440	**800-356-4458**	541-747-1654	291-4
Wildwood Express Trucking 12416 E Swanson Ave	Kingsburg	CA	93631	**800-627-3115**	559-897-1035	769
Wildwood Park for the Performing Arts 20919 Denny Rd	Little Rock	AR	72223	**888-278-7727**	501-821-7275	562
Wildwoods Convention Center 4501 Boardwalk	Wildwood	NJ	08260	**800-995-9732**	609-729-9000	204
Wiley College 711 Wiley Ave *Admissions	Marshall	TX	75670	**800-658-6889***	903-927-3311	163
Wiley John & Sons Inc 111 River St *NYSE: JWa* ■ *Sales	Hoboken	NJ	07030	**800-225-5945***	201-748-6000	623-2
Wileys Custom Water Skis 1417 S Trenton	Seattle	WA	98108	**800-962-0785**	206-762-1300	701
Wilfley AR & Sons Inc 7350 E Progress Pl Suite 200	Englewood	CO	80111	**800-525-9930**	303-779-1777	627
Wilhelm Trucking Co PO Box 10363 *Cust Svc	Portland	OR	97296	**800-275-3974***	503-227-0561	769
Wilkes-Barre (Greater) Chamber of Business & Industry 2 Public Sq PO Box 5340	Wilkes-Barre	PA	18710	**800-331-0912**	570-823-2101	137
Wilkes University 84 W South St	Wilkes-Barre	PA	18766	**800-945-5378**	570-824-4651	163
Wilkins-Rogers Inc 27 Frederick Rd *Cust Svc	Ellicott City	MD	21043	**800-735-3585***	410-465-5800	291-23
Will & Baumer Inc 100 Buckley St	Liverpool	NY	13288	**800-733-7337**	315-451-1000	122
Will Rogers Memorial Museum 1720 W Will Rogers Blvd	Claremore	OK	74017	**800-324-9455**	918-341-0719	509
Will Vision & Laser Centers 8100 NE Pkwy Dr Suite 125	Vancouver	WA	98662	**877-542-3937**	360-885-1327	785
Willamette University 900 State St	Salem	OR	97301	**877-542-2787**	503-370-6303	163
Willamette Valley Co 1075 Arrowsmith St	Eugene	OR	97402	**800-333-9826**	541-484-9621	540
Willamette Valley Hospice 1015 3rd St NW	Salem	OR	97304	**800-555-2431**	503-588-3600	365
Willamette Valley Vineyards Inc 8800 Enchanted Way SE *NASDAQ: WVVI* ■ *Sales	Turner	OR	97392	**800-344-9463***	503-588-9463	81-3
Willamette View 12705 SE River Rd	Milwaukie	OR	97222	**800-446-0670**	503-654-6581	659
Willbros Engineers Inc 2087 E 71st St	Tulsa	OK	74136	**800-434-8970**	918-496-0400	258
Willdan 2125 E Katella Ave Suite 200	Anaheim	CA	92806	**800-424-9144**	714-940-6300	258
Willert Home Products Inc 4044 Park Ave	Saint Louis	MO	63110	**800-325-9680**	314-772-2822	149
Willett Hall 3701 Willett Dr	Portsmouth	VA	23707	**800-488-6761**	757-393-5460	562
Willey RC & Son Inc 2601 S 300 W	Salt Lake City	UT	84115	**800-444-3876**	801-461-3900	316
William A Smith Construction Co Inc 6060 Armour Dr	Houston	TX	77020	**800-925-5011**	713-673-6208	187-8
William Arthur Inc 7 Alewive Park Rd PO Box 460	West Kennebunk	ME	04094	**800-985-6581**	207-985-6581	542-3
William B Eerdmans Publishing Co 255 Jefferson Ave SE	Grand Rapids	MI	49503	**800-253-7521**	616-459-4591	623-2
William B Reily & Co Inc 640 Magazine St	New Orleans	LA	70130	**800-535-1961**	504-524-6131	291-19
William Barnet & Son Inc 1300 Hayne St	Arcadia	SC	29320	**800-922-7638**	864-576-7154	594-1
William Blair Capital Partners 222 W Adams St	Chicago	IL	60606	**800-621-0687**	312-236-1600	779
William Blair & Co LLC 222 W Adams St	Chicago	IL	60606	**800-621-0687**	312-236-1600	679
William Carey College 498 Tuscan Ave	Hattiesburg	MS	39401	**800-962-5991**	601-318-6051	163
William F Renk & Sons Inc 6800 Wilburn Rd	Sun Prairie	WI	53590	**800-289-7365**	608-837-7351	11-5
William Glen Inc 2651 El Paseo Ln	Sacramento	CA	95821	**800-842-3322**	916-485-3000	357
William H Sadlier Inc 9 Pine St 2nd Fl	New York	NY	10005	**800-582-5437**	212-227-2120	623-2
William Howard Taft University 201 E Sandpointe Ave Suite 400	Santa Ana	CA	92707	**800-882-4555**	714-850-4800	163
William J Kline & Son Inc 1 Venner Rd	Amsterdam	NY	12010	**800-453-6397**	518-843-1100	623-8
William Jewell College 500 College Hill WJC Box 1002	Liberty	MO	64068	**800-753-7009**	816-781-7700	163
William K Walthers Inc 5601 W Florist Ave	Milwaukee	WI	53218	**800-877-7171**	414-527-0770	750
William L Bonnell Co 25 Bonnell St	Newnan	GA	30263	**800-846-8885**	770-253-2020	476
William Marvy Co Inc 1540 St Clair Ave	Saint Paul	MN	55105	**800-874-2651**	651-698-0726	78
William Mitchell College of Law 875 Summit Ave	Saint Paul	MN	55105	**888-962-5529**	651-227-9171	164-1
William Morrow & Co 10 E 53rd St *Cust Svc	New York	NY	10022	**800-242-7737***	212-207-7000	623-2
William Paca House & Garden 186 Prince George St	Annapolis	MD	21401	**800-603-4020**	410-263-5553	50
William Paterson University of New Jersey 300 Pompton Rd	Wayne	NJ	07470	**877-978-3923**	973-720-2000	163

Name / Address	City	State	ZIP	Toll-Free	Phone	Class
William Penn College 201 Trueblood Ave	Oskaloosa	IA	52577	**800-779-7366**	641-673-1001	163
William Penn Life Insurance Co of New York 100 Quentin Roosevelt Blvd	Garden City	NY	11530	**800-346-4773**	516-794-3700	384-2
William Powell Co 2503 Spring Grove Ave	Cincinnati	OH	45214	**800-888-2583**	513-852-2000	776
William R Peterson Oil Co 276 Main St Suite 1 PO box 31	Portland	CT	06480	**800-622-6971**	860-342-3560	311
William Rigg Co 777 Main St Suite C-50	Fort Worth	TX	76102	**800-275-4449**	817-335-4444	383
William Russell Ltd 1710 Midway Rd	Odenton	MD	21113	**800-638-9667**	410-551-3600	281
William S Hein & Co Inc 1285 Main St	Buffalo	NY	14209	**800-828-7571**	716-882-2600	623-2
William Steinen Mfg Co 29 E Halsey Rd	Parsippany	NJ	07054	**800-724-3343**	973-887-6400	598
William Tyndale College 35700 W 12 Mile Rd	Farmington Hills	MI	48331	**800-483-0707**	248-553-7200	163
William V MacGill & Co 1000 N Lombard Rd	Lombard	IL	60148	**800-323-2841**	630-889-0500	467
William Woods University 1 University Ave	Fulton	MO	65251	**800-995-3159**	573-642-2251	163
William Wright Co 85 South St	West Warren	MA	01092	**800-628-9362**	413-436-7732	730-5
Williams Advanced Materials 2978 Main St	Buffalo	NY	14214	**800-327-1355**	716-837-1000	476
Williams Baptist College 60 W Fulbright St	Walnut Ridge	AR	72476	**800-722-4434**	870-886-6741	163
Williams Bus Lines Inc PO Box 1272	Springfield	VA	22151	**888-448-7433**	703-560-5355	110
Williams Coal Seam Gas Royalty Trust 901 Main St Bank of America Plaza 17th Fl *NYSE: WTU*	Dallas	TX	75202	**800-365-6544**	214-209-2364	662
Williams Controls Inc 14100 SW 72nd Ave *Cust Svc	Portland	OR	97224	**800-547-1889***	503-684-8600	60
Williams Cos Inc 1 Williams Ctr *NYSE: WMB*	Tulsa	OK	74102	**800-945-5426**	918-573-2000	355-3
Williams Distributing Corp 880 Burnett Rd	Chicopee	MA	01020	**800-332-9634**	413-594-4900	82-1
Williams Distributing Corp 658 Richmond St NW	Grand Rapids	MI	49504	**800-748-0503**	616-456-1613	38
Williams Energy Services 1 Williams Ctr PO Box 2400	Tulsa	OK	74102	**800-945-5426**	918-573-2000	527
Williams Gas Pipelines Transco PO Box 1396	Houston	TX	77251	**888-215-8475**	713-215-2000	320
Williams Gun Sight Co Inc 7389 Lapeer Rd	Davison	MI	48423	**800-530-9028**	810-653-2131	279
Williams Industries Inc 2201 E Michigan Rd	Shelbyville	IN	46176	**800-383-4701**	317-392-4701	593
Williams Jack Tire Co Inc PO Box 3655	Scranton	PA	18505	**800-833-5051**	570-457-5000	62-5
Williams JH Oil Co Inc 1237 E Twiggs St	Tampa	FL	33602	**800-683-0536**	813-228-7776	569
Williams Mullin 1021 E Cary St 2 James Ctr 16th Fl	Richmond	VA	23219	**888-783-8181**	804-643-1991	419
Williams AT Oil Co 5446 University Pkwy	Winston-Salem	NC	27105	**800-642-0945**	336-767-6280	319
Williams Robert C American Museum of Papermaking 500 10th St NW	Atlanta	GA	30318	**800-558-6611**	404-894-7840	509
Williams Scotsman Inc 8211 Town Ctr Dr	Baltimore	MD	21236	**800-782-1500**	410-931-6000	495
Williams Service Group Inc 2076 West Park Pl	Stone Mountain	GA	30087	**800-892-0992**	770-879-4000	185
Williams-Sonoma Inc 3250 Van Ness Ave *NYSE: WSM* ■ *Cust Svc	San Francisco	CA	94109	**800-541-1262***	415-421-7900	357
Williams Supply Inc 210 7th St	Roanoke	VA	24016	**800-533-6969**	540-343-9333	245
Williams White & Co 600 River Dr	Moline	IL	61265	**877-797-7650**	309-797-7650	448
Williamsburg Area Convention & Visitors Bureau 421 N Boundary St	Williamsburg	VA	23185	**800-368-6511**	757-253-0192	205
Williamsburg Hospitality House 415 Richmond Rd	Williamsburg	VA	23185	**800-932-9192**	757-229-4020	373
Williamsburg Inn 136 E Francis St	Williamsburg	VA	23185	**800-447-8679**	757-229-1000	655
Williamsburg Lodge 310 S England St	Williamsburg	VA	23185	**800-447-8679**	757-229-1000	373
Williamsburg Millwork Corp PO Box 427	Bowling Green	VA	22427	**888-699-8900**	804-994-2151	541
Williamsburg Pottery Factory Inc Rt 60 W	Lightfoot	VA	23090	**800-768-8379**	757-564-3326	357
Williamsburg Soap & Candle Co 7521 Richmond Rd *Orders	Williamsburg	VA	23188	**800-367-9722***	757-564-3354	122
Williamsburg Technical College 601 MLK Jr Ave	Kingstree	SC	29556	**800-768-2021**	843-355-4110	160
Williamson County-Franklin Chamber of Commerce PO Box 156	Franklin	TN	37065	**800-356-3445**	615-794-1225	137
Williamson County Tourism 109 2nd Ave S Suite 137	Franklin	TN	37064	**800-356-3445**	615-794-1225	205
Williamson County Tourism Bureau 1602 Sioux Dr	Marion	IL	62959	**800-433-7399**	618-997-3690	205
Williamson-Dickie Mfg Co 509 W Vickery Blvd	Fort Worth	TX	76104	**800-336-7201**	817-336-7201	153-19
Williamson HB Co PO Box 1687 *Orders	Mount Vernon	IL	62864	**800-851-2467***	618-244-9000	304
Williamson Law Book Co 790 Canning Pkwy	Victor	NY	14564	**800-733-9522**	585-924-3400	614
Williamson Printing Corp 6700 Denton Dr	Dallas	TX	75235	**800-843-5423**	214-352-1122	615
Williamson TD Inc 5725 S Lewis St Suite 300	Tulsa	OK	74105	**888-839-6766**	918-447-5001	526
Williamsport Bureau of Transportation 1500 W 3rd St	Williamsport	PA	17701	**800-248-9287**	570-326-2500	109
Williamsport Sun-Gazette 252 W 4th St	Williamsport	PA	17701	**800-339-0289**	570-326-1551	522-2
Williard Inc 375 Highland Ave	Jenkintown	PA	19046	**800-827-5030**	215-885-5000	188-10
Willie G's 1510 W Loop South	Houston	TX	77027	**800-552-6379**	713-850-1010	657
Willingway Hospital 311 Jones Mill Rd	Statesboro	GA	30458	**800-242-9455**	912-764-6236	712
Willis Group Holdings Ltd 7 Hanover Sq *NASDAQ: WSH*	New York	NY	10004	**800-234-8596**	212-344-8888	383
Willis Shaw Express Inc 201 N Elm St	Elm Springs	AR	72728	**800-643-3540**	479-248-7261	769
Williston Basin Interstate Pipeline Co 1250 W Century Ave	Bismarck	ND	58503	**800-238-8350**	701-530-1600	320
Williston Daily Herald PO Box 1447	Williston	ND	58802	**800-950-2165**	701-572-2165	522-2
Williston State College PO Box 1326	Williston	ND	58802	**888-863-9455**	701-774-4200	160
Willits Footwear Worldwide PO Box B	Halifax	PA	17032	**800-544-3633**	717-896-3411	296
Willitts Designs International 1129 Industrial Ave	Petaluma	CA	94952	**800-358-9184**	707-778-7211	330
Willmar Poultry Co Inc PO Box 753	Willmar	MN	56201	**800-328-8842**	320-235-8850	11-8
Willmar Regional Treatment Center 1550 Hwy 71 NE	Willmar	MN	56201	**800-657-3898**	320-231-5100	366-3
Willo Products Co Inc 2115 Veterans Dr SE	Decatur	AL	35601	**800-633-3276**	256-353-7161	232
Willow Brook Foods Inc PO Box 50190	Springfield	MO	65805	**800-423-2366**	417-862-3612	11-8
Willow Creek Press Inc 9931 Hwy 70 W PO Box 147	Minocqua	WI	54548	**800-850-9453**	715-358-7010	130
Willow Grove Bancorp Inc Welsh & Norristown Rds *NASDAQ: WGBC*	Maple Glen	PA	19002	**800-647-5405**	215-646-5405	355-2
Willow Ridge 421 Landmark Dr	Wilmington	NC	28410	**800-388-2012**		451
Willow Stream Spa at the Fairmont Banff Springs 405 Spray Ave	Banff	AB	T1L1J4	**800-404-1772**	403-762-1772	698
Willow Stream Spa at the Fairmont Empress 633 Humboldt St	Victoria	BC	V8W1A6	**866-854-7444**	250-995-4650	698
Willow Stream Spa at Fairmont Scottsdale Princess 7575 E Princess Dr	Scottsdale	AZ	85255	**800-257-7544**	480-585-2732	698
Willow Stream Spa at the Turnberry Isle Resort & Club 19999 W Country Club Dr	Aventura	FL	33180	**800-327-7028**	305-933-6930	698
Willow Valley Resort & Conference Center 2416 Willow Street Pike	Lancaster	PA	17602	**800-444-1714**	717-464-2711	655
Willows The 1 Lyman St	Westborough	MA	01581	**800-464-4730**	508-366-4730	659
Willows Chamber of Commerce 118 W Sycamore	Willows	CA	95988	**888-799-4254**	530-934-8150	137
Willows Historic Palm Springs Inn 412 W Tahquitz Canyon Way	Palm Springs	CA	92262	**800-966-9597**	760-320-0771	373
Willows Hotel 555 W Surf St	Chicago	IL	60657	**800-787-3108**	773-528-8400	373
Willows Lodge 14580 NE 145th St	Woodinville	WA	98072	**877-424-3930**	425-424-3900	373
Willsie Cap & Gown Co 1220 S 13th St	Omaha	NE	68108	**800-234-4696**	402-341-6536	153-14
Wilmar Industries Inc 200 E Park Dr Suite 200	Mount Laurel	NJ	08054	**800-345-3000**	856-439-1222	601
Wilmer Service Line 220 E Monument Ave	Dayton	OH	45402	**888-494-5637**		111
Wilmes Window Mfg Co 234 W 23rd St	Ferdinand	IN	47532	**800-477-1811**	812-367-1811	233
Wilmington College 320 N DuPont Hwy	New Castle	DE	19720	**877-967-5464**	302-328-9401	163
Wilmington College of Ohio 251 Ludovic St	Wilmington	OH	45177	**800-341-9318**	937-382-6661	163
Wilmington Fibre Specialty Co 700 Washington St	New Castle	DE	19720	**800-220-5132**	302-328-7525	588
Wilmington (Greater) Convention & Visitors Bureau 100 W 10th St Suite 20	Wilmington	DE	19801	**800-422-1181**	302-652-4088	205
Wilmington Savings Fund Society FSB 838 Market St	Wilmington	DE	19801	**800-292-9594**	302-792-6000	71
Wilmington Treatment Center 2520 Troy Dr	Wilmington	NC	28401	**800-992-3671**	910-762-2727	712
Wilmington Trust Co 1100 N Market St	Wilmington	DE	19890	**800-441-7120**	302-651-1000	71
Wilmington Trust Corp 1100 N Market St 1st Fl *NYSE: WL*	Wilmington	DE	19890	**800-523-2378**	302-651-1000	355-2
Wilshire Grand Hotel & Center 930 Wilshire Blvd	Los Angeles	CA	90017	**888-773-2888**	213-688-7777	373
Wilshire Mfg Co 645 Myles Standish Blvd	Taunton	MA	02780	**800-443-4695**	508-824-1970	431
Wilshire Target Funds Inc PO Box 9807	Providence	RI	02940	**888-200-6796**		517
Wilshire Technologies 5861 Edison Pl	Carlsbad	CA	92008	**800-433-3340**	760-929-7200	566
Wilson Air Center 2930 Winchester Rd Memphis International Airport	Memphis	TN	38118	**800-464-2992**	901-345-2992	63
Wilson Bus Lines Inc PO Box 415	East Templeton	MA	01438	**800-253-5235**	978-632-3894	108
Wilson College 1015 Philadelphia Ave	Chambersburg	PA	17201	**800-421-8402**	717-264-4141	163
Wilson-Cook Medical Inc 4900 Bethania Stn Rd	Winston-Salem	NC	27105	**800-245-4717**	336-744-0157	468
Wilson Daily Times PO Box 2447	Wilson	NC	27894	**800-849-8811**	252-243-5151	522-2
Wilson Edgar H Convention Centre 200 Coliseum Dr	Macon	GA	31217	**877-532-6144**	478-751-9152	204
Wilson Foods Co LLC 1811 W 1700 South	Salt Lake City	UT	84104	**800-950-8226**	801-972-5633	291-36
Wilson H Co 555 W Taft Dr	South Holland	IL	60473	**800-245-7224**	708-339-5111	314-1
Wilson Hotel Management Co Inc 8700 Trail Lake Dr W Suite 300	Memphis	TN	38125	**800-945-7667**	901-346-8800	369
Wilson HW Co 950 University Ave	Bronx	NY	10452	**800-367-6770**	718-588-8400	623-2
Wilson Industrial Sales Co Inc PO Box 425	Brook	IN	47922	**800-633-5427**	219-275-7333	144
Wilson Learning Corp 8000 W 78th St Suite 200	Edina	MN	55439	**800-328-7937**	952-944-2880	753
Wilson Memorial Hospital 915 W Michigan St	Sidney	OH	45365	**800-589-9641**	937-498-2311	366-2
Wilson Mills DBA Catalano's Stop & Shop 5612 Wilson Mills Rd	Highland Heights	OH	44143	**800-991-5444**	440-442-8800	339

Name / Address	City	State	ZIP	Toll-Free	Phone	Class
Wilson N Jones Medical Center 500 N Highland Ave	Sherman	TX	75092	877-870-6696	903-870-4611	366-2
Wilson Quarterly Magazine 1300 Pennsylvania Ave NW 1 Woodrow Wilson Plaza *Orders	Washington	DC	20004	800-829-5108*	202-691-4000	449-11
Wilson Ranch. Freestone Inn at 31 Early Winters Dr	Mazama	WA	98833	800-639-3809	509-996-3906	655
Wilson Supply Co PO Box 1492	Houston	TX	77251	800-228-2893	713-237-3700	378
Wilson Thomas C Inc 21-11 44th Ave	Long Island City	NY	11101	800-230-2636	718-729-3360	747
Wilson Trailer Co 4400 S Lewis Blvd	Sioux City	IA	51106	800-798-2002	712-252-6500	768
Wilson Trophy Co 1724 Frienza Ave	Sacramento	CA	95815	800-325-4911	916-927-9733	766
Wilson Trucking Corp PO Box 200	Fishersville	VA	22939	800-494-5766	540-949-3200	769
Wilson Valerie Travel Inc 475 Park Ave S	New York	NY	10016	800-776-1116	212-532-3400	760
Wilson Visitors Bureau PO Box 2882	Wilson	NC	27894	800-497-7398	252-243-8440	205
Wilson WindowWare Inc 5421 California Ave SW	Seattle	WA	98136	800-762-8383	206-938-1740	176-12
Wilsonart International Inc 2400 Wilson Pl *Cust Svc	Temple	TX	76504	800-433-3222*	254-207-7000	588
WilsonMiller Inc 3200 Bailey Ln Suite 200	Naples	FL	34105	800-649-4336	239-649-4040	258
Wilsons The Leather Experts Inc 7401 Boone Ave N *NASDAQ: WLSN*	Brooklyn Park	MN	55428	800-967-6270	763-391-4000	155-5
WilTel Communications LLC 1 Technology Ctr	Tulsa	OK	74103	800-945-5426	918-547-6000	387
Wilton Armetale Co PO Box 600	Mount Joy	PA	17552	800-553-2048	717-653-4444	477
Wilton House Museum 215 S Wilton Rd	Richmond	VA	23226	877-994-5866	804-282-5936	509
Wilton Industries Inc 2240 W 75th St	Woodridge	IL	60517	800-994-5866	630-963-7100	477
Wilton Industries Inc Rowoco Div 2240 W 75th St	Woodridge	IL	60517	800-772-7100	630-963-7100	477
Wilton Tool Group 2420 Vantage Dr	Elgin	IL	60123	800-519-7381	847-851-1000	746
WILX-TV Ch 10 (NBC) 500 American Rd	Lansing	MI	48911	800-968-1024	517-393-0110	726
Wimmer Cos 4650 Shelby Air Dr	Memphis	TN	38118	800-548-2537	901-362-8900	623-2
Wimmer's Meat Products Inc PO Box 286 *Sales	West Point	NE	68788	800-358-0761*	402-372-2437	291-26
WIN Energy Rural Electric Membership Corp PO Box 577	Vincennes	IN	47591	800-882-5140	812-882-5140	244
Winbond Electronics Corp America 2727 N 1st St	San Jose	CA	95134	800-825-4473	408-943-6666	686
WinBook Computer Corp 2701 Charter St Suite A	Columbus	OH	43228	800-468-1633	614-334-1496	171-3
Winchell's Donut House 2223 Wellington Ave Suite 300	Santa Ana	CA	92701	877-541-5554	714-565-1800	69
Winchester-Auburn Mills Inc 70 Dundas St *Cust Svc	Deseronto	ON	K0K1X0	800-634-8011*	781-935-4110	207
Winchester Carton Corp PO Box 597	Eutaw	AL	35462	800-633-5967	205-372-3337	102
Winchester Div Olin Corp 427 N Shamrock St	East Alton	IL	62024	800-356-2666	618-258-2000	279
Winchester News-Gazette PO Box 429	Winchester	IN	47394	800-782-2508	765-584-4501	522-2
Winchester Star 2 N Kent St	Winchester	VA	22601	800-296-8639	540-667-3200	522-2
Winchester Systems Inc 149 Middlesex Tpke *Cust Svc	Burlington	MA	01803	800-325-3700*	781-265-0200	174
Winco Inc 5516 SW 1st Ln	Ocala	FL	34474	800-237-3377	352-854-2929	314-3
Winco Window Co Inc 6200 Maple Ave	Saint Louis	MO	63130	800-525-8089	314-725-8088	232
WinCraft Inc 1124 W 5th St	Winona	MN	55987	800-533-8006	507-454-5510	323
WinCup 7980 W Buckeye Rd	Phoenix	AZ	85043	800-292-2877	623-936-1791	590
Wind River Ranch PO Box 3410	Estes Park	CO	80517	800-523-4212	970-586-4212	238
Wind River Systems Inc 500 Wind River Way *NASDAQ: WIND*	Alameda	CA	94501	800-545-9463	510-748-4100	176-12
Wind Walker Guest Ranch PO Box 7	Spring City	UT	84662	888-606-9463	435-462-0282	238
Windemuller Electric Inc 1176 Electric Ave	Wayland	MI	49348	800-333-3641	616-877-8770	188-4
Windermere Relocation Inc 4040 Lake Washington Blvd NE Suite 201	Kirkland	WA	98033	800-735-7029	425-216-7100	652
Windfall Assoc 981 Chestnut St	Newton Upper Falls	MA	02464	877-946-3325	617-969-1790	195
Windjammer Barefoot Cruises Ltd 1759 Bay Rd	Miami Beach	FL	33139	800-327-2601	305-672-6453	217
Windmill Health Products 21 Dwight Pl	Fairfield	NJ	07004	800-822-4320	973-575-6591	786
Windmill Inn of Ashland 2525 Ashland St	Ashland	OR	97520	800-547-4747	541-482-8310	373
Windmill Inn at Saint Philip's Plaza Tucson 4250 N Campbell Ave	Tucson	AZ	85718	800-547-4747	520-577-0007	373
WinDough.com Inc 11669 Countryview Ln	Boca Raton	FL	33428	888-668-6278		443
Window & Door Manufacturers Assn (WDMA) 1400 E Touhy Ave Suite 470	Des Plaines	IL	60018	800-223-2301	847-299-5200	49-3
Windowmaster Products Inc 1111 Pioneer Way	El Cajon	CA	92020	800-862-7722	619-444-6123	232
Windquest Co Inc 3311 Windquest Dr	Holland	MI	49424	800-562-4257	616-399-3311	805
Windsor Arms Hotel 18 Saint Thomas St	Toronto	ON	M5S3E7	877-999-2767	416-971-9666	372
Windsor Corporate Suites 4212 Stearns Hills Rd	Waltham	MA	02451	800-888-7368	781-899-5100	209
Windsor Court Hotel 300 Gravier St	New Orleans	LA	70130	800-262-2662	504-523-6000	373
Windsor Factory Supply Ltd 730 N Service Rd	Windsor	ON	N8X3J3	800-387-2659	519-966-2202	378
Windsor Fashions Inc 4533 Pacific Blvd	Vernon	CA	90058	888-494-6376	323-282-9000	155-6
Windsor Group 11700 Great Oak Way	Atlanta	GA	30022	800-852-8055	678-627-6000	384-4
Windsor Hotel 125 W Lamar St	Americus	GA	31709	888-297-9567	229-924-1555	373
Windsor Industries Inc 1351 W Stanford Ave	Englewood	CO	80110	800-444-7654	303-762-1800	379
Windsor Steven Inc 6535 Arlington Blvd	Falls Church	VA	22042	800-765-3487	703-533-9784	155-3
Windsor Vineyards Po Box 368	Windsor	CA	95492	800-289-9463	707-836-5000	310-5
Windsor Windows & Doors 900 S 19th St	West Des Moines	IA	50265	800-218-6186	515-223-6660	234
Windstar Cruises 300 Elliott Ave W *Resv	Seattle	WA	98119	800-258-7245*	206-281-3535	217
Windward Seafoods 8550 NW 17 St Suite 105	Miami	FL	33126	800-780-3474	305-591-8550	292-5
Wine Club 2110 E McFadden Ave Suite E	Santa Ana	CA	92705	800-966-5432	714-835-6485	435
Wine Spectator Magazine 387 Park Ave S 8th Fl *Orders	New York	NY	10016	800-752-7799*	212-684-4224	449-14
Wine & Spirits Shippers Assn Inc (WSSA) 11800 Sunrise Valley Dr Suite 332	Reston	VA	22091	800-368-3167	703-860-2300	49-6
Wine.com Inc 114 Sansome St 6th Fl	San Francisco	CA	94104	877-289-6886		435
WineAmerica 1212 New York Ave NW Suite 425	Washington	DC	20005	800-879-4637	202-783-2756	49-6
Winebrenner Theological Seminary 950 N Main St	Findlay	OH	45840	800-992-4987	419-434-4200	164-3
Winegard Co 3000 Kirkwood St *Cust Svc	Burlington	IA	52601	800-288-8094*	319-754-0600	633
Winery at Wolf Creek 2637 S Cleveland-Massillon Rd	Norton	OH	44203	800-436-0426	330-666-9285	50
Wing Enterprises Inc PO Box 3100	Springville	UT	84663	800-453-1192	801-489-3684	412
Wingate Inns International Inc 1 Sylvan Way	Parsippany	NJ	07054	800-228-1000	973-428-9700	369
Wingate University 220 N Camden St	Wingate	NC	28174	800-755-5550	704-233-8000	163
Wingfoot Commercial Tire Systems LLC 1000 S 21st St	Fort Smith	AR	72901	800-643-7330	479-788-6400	62-5
Wingra Stone Co PO Box 44284	Madison	WI	53744	800-249-6908	608-271-5555	181
Wings Financial Credit Union 14985 Glazier Ave	Apple Valley	MN	55124	800-692-2274	952-997-8000	216
Wings Foundation 8725 W 14th Ave Suite 150	Lakewood	CO	80215	800-373-8671	303-238-8660	48-21
Wings To Go Inc 846 Ritchie Hwy Suite 1 B	Severna Park	MD	21146	800-552-9464		657
Wings Nile Cruises 11350 McCormick Rd Suite 703	Hunt Valley	MD	21031	800-869-4647	410-771-0925	218
Wings Tours Inc 11350 McCormick Rd Suite 703	Hunt Valley	MD	21031	800-869-4647	410-771-0925	748
Wink Davis Equipment Co Inc 4938 S Atlanta Rd Suite 800	Atlanta	GA	30080	800-341-5459	404-266-2290	378
Winkelman Babe Productions PO Box 407	Brainerd	MN	56401	800-333-0471	218-822-4424	727
Winkler Inc PO Box 68	Dale	IN	47523	800-621-3843	812-937-4421	292-8
Winmark Corp 4200 Dahlberg Dr Suite 100 *NASDAQ: WINA*	Minneapolis	MN	55422	800-433-2540	763-520-8500	658
Winn Devon Art Group 6015 6th Ave S	Seattle	WA	98108	800-875-4150	206-763-9544	623-10
Winn Transportation 1831 Westwood Ave	Richmond	VA	23227	800-296-9466	804-358-9466	108
Winnebago Industries Inc 605 W Crystal Lake Rd *NYSE: WGO*	Forest City	IA	50436	800-643-4892	641-585-3535	120
Winnemucca Convention & Visitors Authority 50 W Winnemucca Blvd	Winnemucca	NV	89445	800-962-2638	775-623-5071	205
Winner International LLC 32 W State St	Sharon	PA	16146	800-258-2321	724-981-1152	681
Winner Livestock Auction Co 31690 Livestock Barn Rd	Winner	SD	57580	800-201-0451	605-842-0451	437
Winona Convention & Visitors Bureau 67 Main St	Winona	MN	55987	800-657-4972	507-452-2272	205
Winona Daily News 601 Franklin St	Winona	MN	55987	800-328-2182	507-454-6500	522-2
Winona Monument Co Inc 174 W 3rd St	Winona	MN	55987	800-657-4411	507-452-4672	710
Winona State University 175 W Mark St	Winona	MN	55987	800-342-5978	507-457-5000	163
Winship Cancer Institute Bone Marrow Transplant/Hematology/Leukemia Clinic Emory Univ School of Medicine 1365 Clifton Rd NE Suite B1106	Atlanta	GA	30322	888-946-7447	404-778-4342	758
Winstar Interactive Media 100 Park Ave 6th Fl *Cust Svc	New York	NY	10017	888-961-8800*	212-896-8310	6
Winstead Sechrest & Minick PC 1201 Elm St Suite 5400	Dallas	TX	75270	800-850-8737	214-745-5400	419
Winsted Precision Ball Corp 159 Colebrook River Rd	Winsted	CT	06098	800-462-3075	860-379-2788	77
Winston Brothers Inc 160 Southampton St	Boston	MA	02118	800-457-4901	617-541-1100	287
Winston F2S Corp 1604 Cherokee Trace	White Oak	TX	75693	800-527-8465	903-757-7341	526
Winston Harry Inc 718 5th Ave	New York	NY	10019	800-988-4110	212-245-2000	401
Winston Industries LLC 2345 Carton Dr	Louisville	KY	40299	800-234-5286	502-495-5400	293
Winston Personnel Service Inc 122 E 42nd St	New York	NY	10068	800-494-6786	212-557-8181	262
Winston Rods 500 S Main St	Twin Bridges	MT	59754	800-237-8763	406-684-5674	701
Winston-Salem Convention & Visitors Bureau 200 Brookstown Ave	Winston-Salem	NC	27101	800-331-7018	336-728-4200	205
Winston-Salem Journal 418 N Marshall St	Winston-Salem	NC	27102	800-642-0925	336-727-7211	522-2
Winston-Salem Southbound Railway Co 4550 Overdale Rd	Winston-Salem	NC	27107	888-631-8223	336-788-9407	634
Winston-Salem State University 601 ML King Jr Dr	Winston-Salem	NC	27110	800-257-4052	336-750-2000	163

				Toll-Free	Phone	Class
Winston & Strawn						
35 W Wacker Dr Suite 4200	Chicago	IL	60601	**800-946-7866**	312-558-5600	419
Winter August & Sons Inc						
2323 N Roemer Rd	Appleton	WI	54911	**800-236-8882**	920-739-8881	188-13
Winter Brothers Material Co						
13098 Gravois Rd	Saint Louis	MO	63127	**800-722-5424**	314-843-1400	490
Winter CJ Machine Technologies Inc						
167 Ames St	Rochester	NY	14611	**800-288-7655**	585-429-5000	448
Winter Garden Quality Foods						
304 Commerce St	New Oxford	PA	17350	**800-242-7637**	717-624-4911	291-36
Winter Park Chamber of Commerce						
150 N New York Ave	Winter Park	FL	32789	**877-972-4262**	407-644-8281	137
Winter Park Resort						
150 Alpenglobe Way PO Box 36	Winter Park	CO	80482	**800-979-0332**	303-892-0961	655
Winter Park Resort Travel Services						
PO Box 36	Winter Park	CO	80482	**800-525-3538**	970-726-5587	368
Winter Sports Inc						
3812 Big Mountain Rd PO Box 1400	Whitefish	MT	59937	**800-858-5439**	406-862-1900	369
Wintergarden Spa & Fitness Center at Wintergreen Resort Rt 664						
PO Box 706	Wintergreen	VA	22958	**800-266-2444**	434-325-8185	698
Wintersilks Inc 14 S Carroll St	Madison	WI	53703	**800-648-7455**	608-280-9000	451
Winterthur Museum Garden & Library						
5105 Kennett Pike	Winterthur	DE	19735	**800-448-3883**	302-888-4600	509
Winthrop-Atkins Co Inc						
35 E Main St	Middleboro	MA	02346	**888-463-7888**	508-947-4600	548-1
Wintzer GA & Son Co						
5 N Blackhoof St PO Box 406	Wapakoneta	OH	45895	**800-331-1801**	419-738-3771	291-12
Winzeler Gear Inc						
7355 W Wilson Ave	Harwood Heights	IL	60706	**800-621-2397**	708-867-7971	593
Winzen Film Inc 1212 Elm St	Sulphur Springs	TX	75482	**800-779-7595**	903-885-7595	589
WIOQ-FM 102.1 (CHR)						
1 Bala Plaza Suite 243	Bala Cynwyd	PA	19004	**800-521-1021**	610-667-8100	631
Wipe-Tex International Corp						
110 E 153rd St	Bronx	NY	10451	**800-643-9607**	718-665-0013	497
Wire Belt Co of America						
154 Harvey Rd	Londonderry	NH	03053	**800-922-2637***	603-644-2500	206
*Cust Svc						
Wire Rope Corp of America Inc						
PO Box 288	Saint Joseph	MO	64502	**800-343-2808**	816-233-0287	802
Wired Magazine						
520 3rd St 3rd Fl	San Francisco	CA	94107	**800-769-4733**	415-276-5000	449-7
Wirefab Inc 919 Millbury St	Worcester	MA	01607	**800-879-4731***	508-754-5359	75
*Sales						
Wiregrass Electric Co-op Inc						
PO Box 158	Hartford	AL	36344	**800-239-4602**	334-588-2223	244
Wiregrass Hospice PO Drawer 2127	Dothan	AL	36302	**800-626-1101**	334-794-9101	365
Wireless Facilities Inc (WFI)						
4810 Eastgate Mall	San Diego	CA	92121	**888-824-0017**	858-228-2000	195
NASDAQ: WFII						
Wireless Flash News Service						
827 Washington St	San Diego	CA	92103	**800-790-2444**	619-220-7191	520
Wireless Infrastructure Assn. PCIA -						
500 Montgomery St Suite 700	Alexandria	VA	22314	**800-759-0300**	703-739-0300	49-20
Wireless Xcessories Group Inc						
1840 County Line Rd Suite 301	Huntingdon Valley	PA	19006	**800-233-0013**	215-322-4600	252
AMEX: XWG						
Wiremold Co 60 Woodlawn St	West Hartford	CT	06110	**800-621-0049***	860-233-6251	803
*Sales						
Wiremold Co Brooks Electronics Div						
13200 Townsend Rd	Philadelphia	PA	19154	**800-523-0130**	215-969-3803	803
Wirerope Works Inc						
100 Maynard St	Williamsport	PA	17701	**800-541-7673***	570-326-5146	802
*Cust Svc						
Wis-Pak Foods Inc 200 S Ember Ln	Milwaukee	WI	53233	**800-323-0639**	414-645-6500	291-26
Wisco Envelope Co PO Box 880	Tullahoma	TN	37388	**800-777-9677**	931-455-4584	260
Wisco Industries Inc 736 Janesville St	Oregon	WI	53575	**800-999-4726**	608-835-3106	36
Wisco Products Inc						
109 Commercial St	Dayton	OH	45402	**800-367-6570**	937-228-2101	688
Wisconsin						
Bill Status 1 E Main St	Madison	WI	53708	**800-362-9472**	608-266-9960	425
Education Investment Program (EdVest) PO Box 7871	Madison	WI	53707	**888-338-3789**	608-264-7899	711
Housing & Economic Development Authority PO Box 1728	Madison	WI	53701	**800-334-6873**	608-266-7884	335
Insurance Commission PO Box 7873	Madison	WI	53707	**800-236-8517**	608-266-3585	335
Tourism Dept 201 W Washington Ave 2nd Fl	Madison	WI	53707	**800-432-8747**	608-266-2161	335
Veterans Affairs Dept PO Box 7843	Madison	WI	53707	**800-947-8387**	608-266-1311	335
Vocational Rehabilitation Div PO Box 7852	Madison	WI	53707	**800-442-3477**	608-243-5600	335
Wisconsin Aviation Inc						
1741 River Dr	Watertown	WI	53094	**800-657-0761**	920-261-4567	63
Wisconsin Box Co Inc						
929 Townline Rd	Wausau	WI	54402	**800-876-6658**	715-842-2248	199
Wisconsin Brick & Block Corp						
6399 Nesbitt Rd	Madison	WI	53719	**800-601-2889**	608-845-8636	181
Wisconsin Cheeseman Inc						
301 Broadway Dr	Sun Prairie	WI	53590	**800-698-1721***	608-837-5166	291-5
*Orders						
Wisconsin Coach Lines Inc						
1520 Arcadian Ave	Waukesha	WI	53186	**800-236-2015**	262-542-8861	108
Wisconsin Dells Visitors & Convention Bureau						
701 Superior St	Wisconsin Dells	WI	53965	**800-223-3557**	608-254-8088	205
Wisconsin Dental Assn						
111 E Wisconsin Ave Suite 1300	Milwaukee	WI	53202	**800-364-7646**	414-276-4520	225
Wisconsin Dept of Public Instruction Library Services Div 125 S Webster St PO Box 7841	Madison	WI	53707	**800-441-4563**	608-266-3390	426
Wisconsin Distributors Inc						
900 Progress Way	Sun Prairie	WI	53590	**800-373-2921**	608-834-2337	82-3
Wisconsin Energy Corp						
231 W Michigan St	Milwaukee	WI	53203	**800-558-3303**	414-221-2345	355-5
NYSE: WEC						
Wisconsin Indianhead Technical College						
Ashland Campus 2100 Beaser Ave	Ashland	WI	54806	**800-243-9482**	715-682-4591	787
New Richmond Campus 1019 S Knowles Ave	New Richmond	WI	54017	**800-243-9482**	715-246-6561	787
Rice Lake Campus 1900 College Dr	Rice Lake	WI	54868	**800-243-9482**	715-234-7082	787
Superior Campus 600 N 21 St	Superior	WI	54880	**800-243-9482**	715-394-6677	787
Wisconsin Lutheran College						
8800 W Bluemound Rd	Milwaukee	WI	53226	**888-947-5884**	414-443-8800	163
Wisconsin Machine Tool Corp						
3225 Gateway Rd Suite 100	Brookfield	WI	53045	**800-243-3078**	262-317-3048	447
Wisconsin Maritime Museum						
75 Maritime Dr	Manitowoc	WI	54220	**866-724-2356**	920-684-0218	509
Wisconsin Medical Journal						
330 E Lakeside St	Madison	WI	53715	**800-362-9080**	608-257-6781	449-16
Wisconsin National Life Insurance Co 2801 Hwy 280 S	Birmingham	AL	35223	**800-955-4304**	205-879-9230	384-2
Wisconsin Paper & Products Co						
PO Box 13455	Milwaukee	WI	53213	**800-242-0790**	414-771-3771	543
Wisconsin Public Radio (WPR)						
821 University Ave	Madison	WI	53706	**800-442-7110**	608-263-3970	620
Wisconsin Public Service Corp						
PO Box 19001	Green Bay	WI	54307	**800-450-7260**		774
Wisconsin Public Television (WPT)						
821 University Ave	Madison	WI	53706	**800-422-9707**	608-263-2121	620
Wisconsin. State Bar of						
5302 Eastpark Blvd	Madison	WI	53718	**800-728-7788**	608-257-3838	73
Wisconsin State Farmer PO Box 152	Waupaca	WI	54981	**800-236-3313**	715-258-5546	522-4
Wisconsin State Journal						
1901 Fish Hatchery Rd	Madison	WI	53713	**800-362-8333**	608-252-6100	522-2
Wisconsin State Medical Society						
330 E Lakeside St	Madison	WI	53701	**866-442-3800**	608-257-6781	466
Wisconsin Trails Magazine						
1131 Mills St PO Box 317	Black Earth	WI	53515	**800-236-8088**	608-767-8000	449-22
Wisconsin Veterinary Medical Assn						
301 N Broom St	Madison	WI	53703	**888-254-5202**	608-257-3665	782
Wisconsin Vision Inc						
6310 W Blue Mound Rd	Milwaukee	WI	53213	**800-705-7011**	414-778-5360	533
Wise Business Forms Inc 150 Kriess Rd	Butler	PA	16001	**888-813-9473**	724-789-9700	111
Wise Co Inc 5535 Pleasant View Rd	Memphis	TN	38134	**800-251-2622**	901-388-0155	678
Wise El Santo Co Inc						
11000 Linpage Pl	Saint Louis	MO	63132	**800-727-8541**	314-428-3100	667
Wise Electric Co-op Inc PO Box 269	Decatur	TX	76234	**888-627-9326**	940-627-2167	244
Wise Foods Inc						
245 Town Pk Dr Suite 475	Kennesaw	GA	30144	**800-438-9473**	770-426-5821	291-35
Wise Metals Group						
857 Elkridge Landing Rd Suite 600	Linthicum	MD	21090	**800-818-9473**	410-636-6500	674
Wise Solutions Inc						
47911 Halyard Dr	Plymouth	MI	48170	**800-554-8565**	734-456-2100	176-2
Wise Tag & Label Co Inc						
7035 Central Hwy	Pennsauken	NJ	08109	**800-222-1327**	856-663-2400	404
Wiseco Piston Inc						
7201 Industrial Park Blvd	Mentor	OH	44060	**800-321-1364**	440-951-6600	128
Wish Foundation Inc. Special						
5340 E Main St Suite 208	Columbus	OH	43213	**800-486-9474**	614-575-9474	48-5
WISH List						
499 S Capitol St SW Suite 408	Washington	DC	20003	**800-756-9474**	202-479-1230	48-7
Wisp Mountain Resort Hotel & Conference Center Deep Creek Lake 290 Marsh Hill Rd	McHenry	MD	21541	**800-462-9477**	301-387-5581	655
Wispak Transport Inc						
11225 W County Line Rd	Milwaukee	WI	53224	**800-558-0560**	414-410-8282	769
Wiss Janney Elstner Assoc Inc						
330 Pfingsten Rd	Northbrook	IL	60062	**800-345-3199**	847-272-7400	258
Wissahickon Hospice						
1 Presidential Blvd Suite 125	Bala Cynwyd	PA	19004	**800-700-8807**	610-617-2400	365
Wist Office Products Co						
107 W Julie Dr	Tempe	AZ	85283	**800-999-9478**	480-921-2900	524
Wistar Institute 3601 Spruce St	Philadelphia	PA	19104	**800-724-6633**	215-898-3700	654
Witchcraft Tape Products Inc						
100 Klitchman Dr	Coloma	MI	49038	**800-521-0931**	269-468-3399	717
WITF-FM 89.5 (NPR)						
1982 Locust Ln	Harrisburg	PA	17109	**800-366-9483**	717-236-6000	631
WITF-TV Ch 33 (PBS)						
1982 Locust Ln	Harrisburg	PA	17109	**800-366-9483**	717-236-6000	726
Withers Broadcasting Co						
PO Box 1508	Mount Vernon	IL	62864	**800-333-1577**	618-242-3500	629
WITI (Women in Technology International)						
13351 Riverside Dr Suite 441	Sherman Oaks	CA	91423	**800-334-9484**	818-788-9484	49-19
WITL-FM 100.7 (Ctry)						
3200 Pine Tree Rd	Lansing	MI	48911	**800-968-7749**	517-393-1010	631
Witmer's Inc PO Box 368	Columbiana	OH	44408	**888-427-6025**	330-427-2147	270
Witness Systems Inc						
300 Colonial Ctr Pkwy Suite 600	Roswell	GA	30076	**888-394-8637**	770-754-1900	176-7
NASDAQ: WITS						
Witt Printing Co Inc						
301 Oak St	El Dorado Springs	MO	64744	**800-641-4342**	417-876-4721	111
Witte Co Inc PO Box 47	Washington	NJ	07882	**866-265-4071**	908-689-6500	293
Wittek Golf Supply Co Inc						
3650 N Avondale Ave	Chicago	IL	60618	**800-869-1800**	773-463-2636	701
Wittenberg University						
200 W Ward St PO Box 720	Springfield	OH	45501	**800-677-7558**	937-327-6231	163
Wittichen Supply Co Inc						
1600 3rd Ave S	Birmingham	AL	35233	**800-239-5294**	205-251-8203	651
Wittke Inc						
1496 Brier Park Crescent NW	Medicine Hat	AB	T1C1T8	**877-948-8531**	403-527-8806	505
Wittnauer International Co						
26-15 Brooklyn Queens Expy	Woodside	NY	11377	**800-431-1863***	718-204-3300	151
*Orders						
Witzco Trailers Inc						
6101 McIntosh Rd	Sarasota	FL	34238	**888-922-9900**	941-922-5301	768
WIWB-TV Ch 14 (WB)						
975 Parkview Rd Suite 4	Green Bay	WI	54304	**877-352-1000**	920-983-9014	726
Wizard Computer Services						
6908 Engle Rd Suite J	Middleburg Heights	OH	44130	**800-486-0060**	440-891-0060	173
Wizards of the Coast Inc						
1801 Land Ave SW	Renton	WA	98055	**800-324-6496***	425-226-6500	750
*Cust Svc						

Name / Address	City	State	ZIP	Toll-Free	Phone	Class
WizCom International Ltd 1 Campus Dr	Parsippany	NJ	07054	**877-949-2661**	973-496-3500	332
Wizcom Technologies Inc 257 Great Rd	Acton	MA	01720	**888-777-0552**	978-635-5357	171-7
WJ Byrnes & Co Inc 880 Mitten Rd Suite C	Burlingame	CA	94010	**800-733-1142**	650-692-1142	306
WJ Communications Inc 401 River Oaks Pkwy *NASDAQ: WJCI*	San Jose	CA	95134	**800-951-4401**	408-577-6200	633
WJ Savage Co Inc 100 Indel Ave PO Box 156	Rancocas	NJ	08073	**877-779-8763**	609-267-8000	447
WJAB-FM 90.9 (Jazz) Alabama A&M University Telecommunications Ctr PO Box 1687	Normal	AL	35762	**800-845-9746**	256-372-5795	631
WJBX-FM 99.3 (Alt) 20125 S Tamiami Trail	Estero	FL	33928	**800-937-7465**	239-495-2100	631
WJFK-FM 106.7 (N/T) 10800 Main St	Fairfax	VA	22030	**800-636-1067**	703-691-1900	631
WJHL-TV Ch 11 (CBS) 338 E Main St	Johnson City	TN	37601	**800-606-9545**	423-926-2151	726
WJQK-FM 99.3 (Rel) 425 Centerstone Ct Suite 1	Zeeland	MI	49464	**888-993-1260**	616-931-9930	631
WJRF-FM 89.5 (Rel) 425 W Superior St Suite 300	Duluth	MN	55802	**800-727-4487**	218-722-3017	631
WJSP-TV Ch 28 (PBS) 260 14th St NW	Atlanta	GA	30318	**800-222-4788**	404-685-2400	726
WJWL-AM 900 (Nost) 20200 Dupont Blvd	Georgetown	DE	19947	**888-780-0970**	302-856-2567	631
WJXX-TV Ch 25 (ABC) 1070 E Adams St	Jacksonville	FL	32202	**800-352-8812**	904-354-1212	726
WJZW-FM 105.9 (NAC) 4400 Jenifer St NW 4th Fl	Washington	DC	20015	**800-779-1059**	202-686-3100	631
WKAP-AM 1470 (Oldies) 1541 Alta Dr Suite 400	Whitehall	PA	18052	**800-659-1965**	610-434-1742	631
WKBW-TV Ch 7 (ABC) 7 Broadcast Plaza	Buffalo	NY	14202	**800-234-9529**	716-845-6100	726
WKCF-TV Ch 18 (WB) 31 Skyline Dr	Lake Mary	FL	32746	**877-411-2899**	407-670-3018	726
WKCQ-FM 98.1 (Ctry) 2000 Whittier St	Saginaw	MI	48601	**800-262-0098**	989-752-8161	631
WKGM-AM 940 (Rel) 13379 Great Spring Rd	Smithfield	VA	23430	**800-706-4769**	757-357-9546	631
WKIT-FM 100.3 (Rock) 861 Broadway	Bangor	ME	04401	**800-287-1003**	207-990-2800	631
WKKT-FM 96.9 (Ctry) 801 Wood Ridge Ctr Dr	Charlotte	NC	28217	**800-332-1029**	704-714-9444	631
WKLB-FM 99.5 (Ctry) 55 Morrissey Blvd	Boston	MA	02125	**888-784-0995**	617-822-9600	631
WKLE-TV Ch 46 (PBS) 600 Cooper Dr	Lexington	KY	40502	**800-432-0951**	859-258-7000	726
WKLQ-FM 94.5 (Rock) 60 Monroe Center St NW 3rd Fl	Grand Rapids	MI	49503	**800-785-1073**	616-774-8461	631
WKMG-TV Ch 6 (CBS) 4466 N John Young Pkwy	Orlando	FL	32804	**888-853-6060**	407-291-6000	726
WKMJ-TV Ch 68 (PBS) 600 Cooper Dr	Lexington	KY	40502	**800-432-0951**	859-258-7000	726
WKNN-FM 99.1 (Ctry) 286 DeBuys Rd	Biloxi	MS	39531	**800-898-9900**	228-388-2323	631
WKNO-FM 91.1 (NPR) 900 Getwell Rd PO Box 241880	Memphis	TN	38124	**800-766-9566**	901-325-6544	631
WKPC-TV Ch 15 (PBS) 600 Cooper Dr	Lexington	KY	40502	**800-432-0951**	859-258-7000	726
WKRN-TV Ch 2 (ABC) 441 Murfreesboro Rd	Nashville	TN	37210	**800-242-9576**	615-369-7222	726
WKRR-FM 92.3 (CR) 192 E Lewis St	Greensboro	NC	27406	**800-762-5923**	336-274-8042	631
WKSU-FM 89.7 (NPR) 1613 E Summit St	Kent	OH	44240	**800-672-2132**	330-672-3114	631
WKTU-FM 103.5 (CHR) 525 Washington Blvd 16th Fl	Jersey City	NJ	07310	**800-245-1035**	201-420-3700	631
WKXU-FM 101.1 (Ctry) 1109 Tower Dr	Burlington	NC	27215	**800-272-6404**	336-584-0126	631
WKXW-FM 101.5 (N/T) 109 Walters Ave	Trenton	NJ	08638	**800-678-9599**	609-771-8181	631
WKZL-FM 107.5 (CHR) 192 E Lewis St	Greensboro	NC	27406	**800-682-1075**	336-274-8042	631
WL Jenkins Co 1445 Whipple Ave SW	Canton	OH	44710	**800-426-7021**	330-477-3407	691
WLAT-AM 910 (Span) 330 Main St	Hartford	CT	06106	**866-910-6342**	860-524-0001	631
WLBW-FM 92.1 (Oldies) 351 Tilghman Rd	Salisbury	MD	21804	**800-762-0105**	410-742-1923	631
WLBZ-TV Ch 2 (NBC) 329 Mt Hope Ave	Bangor	ME	04402	**800-244-6306**	207-942-4821	726
WLCL-FM 105.7 (Oldies) 1819 Peachtree Rd NE Suite 700	Atlanta	GA	30309	**800-776-4638**	404-367-0640	631
WLDE-FM 101.7 (Oldies) 347 W Berry St Suite 417	Fort Wayne	IN	46802	**888-450-1017**	260-423-3676	631
WLEX-TV Ch 18 (NBC) PO Box 1457	Lexington	KY	40588	**800-255-4566**	859-259-1818	726
WLIB-AM 1190 (N/T) 3 Park Ave 41st Fl	New York	NY	10016	**866-303-2270**	212-447-1000	631
WLLL-AM 930 (Rel) PO Box 11375	Lynchburg	VA	24506	**888-224-9809**	434-385-9555	631
WLOS-TV Ch 13 (ABC) 110 Technology Dr	Asheville	NC	28803	**800-288-8813**	828-684-1340	726
WLPB-TV Ch 27 (PBS) 7733 Perkins Rd	Baton Rouge	LA	70810	**800-272-8161**	225-767-5660	726
WLRH-FM 89.3 (NPR) University of Alabama-Huntsville John Wright Dr	Huntsville	AL	35899	**800-239-9574**	256-895-9574	631
WLUK-TV Ch 11 (Fox) 787 Lombardi Ave	Green Bay	WI	54304	**800-242-8067**	920-494-8711	726
WLVE-FM 93.9 (NAC) 7601 Riviera Blvd	Miramar	FL	33023	**877-456-8394**	954-862-2000	631
WLYT-FM 102.9 (AC) 801 Wood Ridge Ctr Dr	Charlotte	NC	28217	**800-332-1029**	704-714-9444	631
WM Barr & Co Inc 205 Channel Ave	Memphis	TN	38113	**800-782-9928**	901-775-0100	540
WM Brode Co 100 Elizabeth St PO Box 299	Newcomerstown	OH	43832	**800-848-9217**	740-498-5121	187-2
W/M Display Group 1040-50 W 40th St	Chicago	IL	60609	**800-443-2000**	773-254-3700	281
WM Financial Services Inc PO Box 145432	Cincinnati	OH	45290	**800-331-3426**		679
WM Group of Funds PO Box 9757	Providence	RI	02940	**800-222-5852**		517
Wm Wrigley Jr Co 410 N Michigan Ave *NYSE: WWY*	Chicago	IL	60611	**888-824-9681**	312-644-2121	291-6
WMAE-FM 89.5 (NPR) 3825 Ridgewood Rd	Jackson	MS	39211	**800-922-9698**	601-432-6565	631
WMAH-FM 90.3 (NPR) 3825 Ridgewood Rd	Jackson	MS	39211	**800-922-9698**	601-432-6800	631
WMAL-AM 630 (N/T) 4400 Jenifer St NW 4th Fl	Washington	DC	20015	**888-630-9625**	202-686-3100	631
WMBD-AM 1470 (N/T) 331 Fulton St Suite 1200	Peoria	IL	61602	**800-698-1470**	309-637-3700	631
WMBM-AM 1490 (Rel) 13242 NW 7th Ave	North Miami	FL	33168	**888-599-9626**	305-769-1100	631
WMBS-AM 590 (Oldies) 44 S Mt Vernon Ave	Uniontown	PA	15401	**866-590-9627**	724-438-3900	631
WMBW-FM 88.9 (Rel) PO Box 73026	Chattanooga	TN	37407	**800-621-9629**	423-629-8900	631
WMCU-FM 89.7 (Rel) 600 SW 3rd St Suite 2290	Pompano Beach	FL	33060	**866-897-9628**	954-545-7600	631
WMEA-FM 90.1 (NPR) 309 Marginal Way	Portland	ME	04101	**800-884-1717**	207-874-6570	631
WMEH-FM 90.9 (NPR) 65 Texas Ave	Bangor	ME	04401	**800-884-1717**	207-941-1010	631
WMEZ-FM 94.1 (AC) 6085 Quinette Rd	Pace	FL	32571	**888-741-0941**	850-994-5357	631
WMF/USA 85 Price Pkwy	Farmingdale	NY	11735	**800-999-6347**	631-293-3990	356
WMGS-FM 92.9 (AC) 600 Baltimore Dr	Wilkes-Barre	PA	18702	**800-447-5000**	570-824-9000	631
WMGT-TV Ch 41 (NBC) 301 Poplar St	Macon	GA	31201	[illegible]	478-745-4141	726
WMH Tool Group Inc 2420 Vantage Dr	Elgin	IL	60123	**800-274-6848**	847-649-3010	746
WMHR-FM 102.9 (Rel) 4044 Makyes Rd	Syracuse	NY	13215	**800-677-1881**	315-469-5051	631
WMHT-TV Ch 17 (PBS) 17 Fern Ave	Schenectady	NY	12306	**800-477-9648**	518-357-1700	726
WMIT-FM 106.9 (Rel) PO Box 159	Black Mountain	NC	28711	**800-330-9648**	828-669-8477	631
WMMPA (Wood Moulding & Millwork Producers Assn) 507 First St	Woodland	CA	95695	**800-550-7889**	530-661-9591	49-3
WMPB-TV Ch 67 (PBS) 11767 Owings Mills Blvd	Owings Mills	MD	21117	**800-223-3678**	410-356-5600	726
WMPI-FM 105.3 (Ctry) 22 E McClain Ave	Scottsburg	IN	47170	**800-441-1053**	812-752-3688	631
WMPN-FM 91.3 (NPR) 3825 Ridgewood Rd	Jackson	MS	39211	**866-262-9643**	601-432-6800	631
WMPT-TV Ch 22 (PBS) 11767 Owings Mills Blvd	Owings Mills	MD	21117	**800-223-3678**	410-356-5600	726
WMT-AM 600 (N/T) 600 Old Marion Rd	Cedar Rapids	IA	52402	**800-332-5401**	319-395-0530	631
WMT-FM 96.5 (AC) 600 Old Marion Rd NE	Cedar Rapids	IA	52402	**800-332-5401**	319-395-0530	631
WMTV-Ch 15 (NBC) 615 Forward Dr	Madison	WI	53711	**800-894-4222**	608-274-1515	726
WMU (Woman's Missionary Union) 100 Missionary Ridge	Birmingham	AL	35242	**800-968-7301**	205-991-8100	48-20
WMVX-FM 106.5 (AC) 6200 Oak Tree Blvd 4th Fl	Independence	OH	44131	**800-829-1065**	216-520-2600	631
WMXJ-FM 102.7 (Oldies) 20450 NW 2nd Ave	Miami	FL	33169	**800-226-1027**	305-521-5100	631
WMZQ-FM 98.7 (Ctry) 1801 Rockville Pike 6th Fl	Rockville	MD	20852	**800-505-0098**	301-231-8231	631
WNA Comet East Inc 6 Stuart Rd	Chelmsford	MA	01824	**800-225-0939**	978-256-6551	596
WNDU-TV Ch 16 (NBC) 54516 US 31 N	South Bend	IN	46637	**800-631-6397**	574-631-1616	726
WNEM-TV Ch 5 (CBS) 107 N Franklin St	Saginaw	MI	48607	**800-522-9636**	989-755-8191	726
WNEO-TV Ch 45 (PBS) 1750 Campus Center Dr	Kent	OH	44240	**800-554-4549**	330-677-4549	726
WNEP-TV Ch 16 (ABC) 16 Montage Mountain Rd	Moosic	PA	18507	**800-982-4374**	570-346-7474	726
WNEW-FM 102.7 (AC) 888 7th Ave 9th Fl	New York	NY	10106	**877-649-1027**	212-489-1027	631
WNJN-FM 89.7 (NPR) PO Box 777	Trenton	NJ	08625	**800-792-8645**	609-777-5000	631
WNNH-FM 99.1 (Oldies) 11 Kimball Dr Unit 114	Hooksett	NH	03106	**800-228-9664**	603-225-1160	631
WNOE-FM 101.1 (Ctry) 929 Howard Ave	New Orleans	LA	70113	**800-543-9663**	504-679-7300	631
WNPB-TV Ch 24 (PBS) 191 Scott Ave	Morgantown	WV	26508	**888-596-9729**	304-284-1440	726
WNSR-AM 560 (Sports) 435 37th Ave N	Nashville	TN	37209	**888-228-6123**	615-844-1039	631
WNVY-AM 1090 (Rel) 2070 N Palafox St	Pensacola	FL	32501	**800-441-2636**	850-434-1230	631
WNYT-TV Ch 13 (NBC) 15 N Pearl St	Albany	NY	12204	**800-999-9698**	518-436-4791	726
WO Grubb Steel Erection Inc 5120 Jefferson Davis Hwy	Richmond	VA	23234	**800-344-6824**	804-271-9471	188-14
WOA (Web Offset Assn) 200 Deer Run Rd	Sewickley	PA	15143	**800-910-4283**	412-741-6860	49-16
WOCCU (World Council of Credit Unions Inc) 5710 Mineral Point Rd	Madison	WI	53705	**800-356-2644**	608-231-7130	49-2
WOCN (Wound Ostomy & Continence Nurses Society) 4700 W Lake Ave	Glenview	IL	60025	**888-224-9626**		49-8
WOCQ-FM 103.9 (CHR) 20200 Dupont Blvd	Georgetown	DE	19947	**888-780-0970**	302-856-2567	631
WOGG-FM 94.9 (Ctry) 123 Blaine Rd	Brownsville	PA	15417	**866-937-6449**	724-938-2000	631
WOI-AM 640 (NPR) Iowa State University 2022 Communications Bldg	Ames	IA	50011	**800-861-8000**	515-294-2025	631
WOIO-TV Ch 19 (CBS) 1717 E 12th St	Cleveland	OH	44114	**877-929-1943**	216-771-1943	726
WOKO-FM 98.9 (Ctry) PO Box 4489	Burlington	VT	05406	**800-354-9890**	802-658-1230	631
WOLC-FM 102.5 (Rel) 11890 Crisfield Ln PO Box 130	Princess Anne	MD	21853	**877-569-9652**	410-543-9652	631
Wolf Envelope Co 725 S Adams Rd Suite 275	Birmingham	MI	48009	**800-466-9653**	248-258-5700	260
Wolf Gordon Inc 33-00 47th Ave	Long Island City	NY	11101	**800-347-0550**	718-361-6611	540
Wolf John Florist 6228 Waters Ave	Savannah	GA	31406	**800-944-6435**	912-352-9843	287
Wolf Laurel Ski Resort 578 Valley View Cir	Mars Hill	NC	28754	**800-817-4111**	828-689-4111	655
Wolf Range Co 19600 S Alameda St	Compton	CA	90221	**888-435-9653**	310-637-3737	293
Wolf X-Ray Corp 420 Hempstead Tpke *Cust Svc	West Hempstead	NY	11552	**800-356-9729***	516-485-7000	580

Alphabetical Section

Name / Address	City	State	ZIP	Toll-Free	Phone	Class
Wolferman's Inc 14350 Santa Fe Trail Dr *Cust Svc	Lenexa	KS	66215	**800-919-1888***	913-888-4499	291-1
Wolff Bros Supply Inc 6078 Wolff Rd	Medina	OH	44256	**800-879-6533**	330-725-3451	245
Wolff Corporate Housing 9514 E Montgomery Rd Suite 20	Spokane	WA	99206	**800-528-9519**	509-444-1690	373
Wolfgang DE Candy Co 50 E 4th Ave	York	PA	17404	**800-248-4273**	717-843-5536	291-8
Wolfkill Feed & Fertilizer Corp PO Box 578	Monroe	WA	98272	**800-525-4539**	360-794-7065	438
Wolfmark 1026 W Van Buren St *Cust Svc	Chicago	IL	60607	**800-621-3435***	312-563-5510	153-13
Wolf's Head Oil Co PO Box 2967	Houston	TX	77252	**800-468-6457**	713-546-4000	530
Wolfson Casing Corp 700 S Fulton Ave	Mount Vernon	NY	10550	**800-221-8042**	914-668-9000	291-26
Wolverine Packing Co Inc 2535 Rivard St	Detroit	MI	48207	**800-521-1390**	313-259-7500	465
Wolverine Slipper Group 3290 Benchmark Dr Benchmark Bldg B	Ladson	SC	29456	**800-253-2184**		296
Wolverine Tractor & Equipment Co 25900 W Eight-Mile Rd	Southfield	MI	48034	**800-686-7482**	248-356-5200	270
Wolverine Tube Inc 200 Clinton Ave W Suite 1000 *NYSE: WLV*	Huntsville	AL	35801	**800-633-3972**	256-890-0460	481
Wolverine World Wide Inc 9345 Courtland Dr NE *NYSE: WWW*	Rockford	MI	49351	**800-626-8696**	616-866-5500	296
Woman's Day Magazine 1633 Broadway 44th Fl	New York	NY	10019	**800-234-2960**	212-767-6000	449-11
Woman's Life Insurance Society 1338 Military St PO Box 5020	Port Huron	MI	48061	**800-521-9292**	810-985-5191	384-2
Woman's Missionary Union (WMU) 100 Missionary Ridge	Birmingham	AL	35242	**800-968-7301**	205-991-8100	48-20
Woman's Society of Certified Public Accountants. American 136 S Keowee St	Dayton	OH	45402	**800-297-2721**	937-222-1872	49-1
Woman's Touch Magazine 1445 Boonville Ave	Springfield	MO	65802	**877-840-4800**	417-862-1271	449-18
Woman's World Magazine 270 Sylvan Ave	Englewood Cliffs	NJ	07632	**800-216-6981**	201-569-0006	449-11
Womeldorf Inc PO Box 829	Du Bois	PA	15801	**800-245-6339**	814-849-8347	769
Women. 9to5 National Assn of Working 152 W Wisconsin Ave Suite 408	Milwaukee	WI	53203	**800-522-0925**	414-274-0925	48-24
Women & Aging. National Center on Brandeis University Heller Graduate School MS 035	Waltham	MA	02454	**800-929-1995**	781-736-3866	48-6
Women Alive 1566 S Burnside Ave	Los Angeles	CA	90019	**800-554-4876**	323-965-1564	48-17
Women. American Assn of University 1111 16th St NW	Washington	DC	20036	**800-326-2289**	202-785-7700	49-5
Women Business Owners. National Assn of 8405 Greensboro Dr Suite 800	McLean	VA	22102	**800-556-2926**	703-506-3268	49-12
Women in Community Service Inc (WICS) 1900 N Beauregard St Suite 103	Alexandria	VA	22311	**800-442-9427**	703-671-0500	48-24
Women in Construction. National Assn of 327 S Adams St	Fort Worth	TX	76104	**800-552-3506**	817-877-5551	49-3
Women (International). National Assn of Insurance 1847 E 15th St	Tulsa	OK	74104	**800-766-6249**	918-744-5195	49-9
Women in Military Service for America Memorial Memorial Dr Arlington National Cemetery	Arlington	VA	22211	**800-222-2294**	703-533-1155	50
Women in Military Service for America Memorial Foundation Inc Dept 560	Washington	DC	20042	**800-222-2294**	703-533-1155	48-19
Women. National Council of Jewish 53 W 23rd St 6th Fl	New York	NY	10010	**800-829-6259**	212-645-4048	48-24
Women. RVing PO Box 1940	Apache Junction	AZ	85217	**888-557-8464**	480-671-6226	48-23
Women in Science Inc. Association for 1200 New York Ave NW Suite 650	Washington	DC	20005	**800-886-2947**	202-326-8940	49-19
Women in Sport. National Assn for Girls & 1900 Association Dr	Reston	VA	20191	**800-213-7193**	703-476-3400	48-22
Women in Technology International (WITI) 13351 Riverside Dr Suite 441	Sherman Oaks	CA	91423	**800-334-9484**	818-788-9484	49-19
Women United. Church 475 Riverside Dr Rm 1626	New York	NY	10115	**800-298-5551**	212-870-2347	48-20
Women Voters. League of 1730 M St NW Suite 1000	Washington	DC	20036	**800-249-8683**	202-429-1965	48-7
Women Work! National Network for Women's Employment 1625 K St NW Suite 300	Washington	DC	20006	**800-235-2732**	202-467-6346	48-24
Women's Assn. American Business 9100 Ward Pkwy	Kansas City	MO	64114	**800-228-0007**	816-361-6621	49-12
Women's Campaign Fund (WCF) 734 15th St NW Suite 500	Washington	DC	20005	**800-446-8170**	202-393-8164	48-7
Women's Golf Unlimited Inc 18 Gloria Ln	Fairfield	NJ	07004	**800-526-2250**	973-227-7783	701
Women's Growth Capital Fund 1054 31st St NW Suite 110	Washington	DC	20007	**888-640-8051**	202-342-1431	395
Women's Health Boutique Franchise System Inc 12715 Telge Rd	Cypress	TX	77429	**888-280-2053**	281-256-4100	305
Women's Health. Office on Office on Women's Health 200 Independence Ave SW Rm 730B	Washington	DC	20201	**800-994-9662**	202-690-7650	336-6
Women's International Bowling Congress (WIBC) 5301 S 76th St	Greendale	WI	53129	**800-514-2695**	414-421-9000	48-22
Women's League. Older 1750 New York Ave NW Suite 350	Washington	DC	20006	**800-825-3695**	202-783-6686	48-6
Women's Memorial Memorial Dr Arlington National Cemetery	Arlington	VA	22211	**800-222-2294**	703-533-1155	50
Women's Memorial Foundation Dept 560	Washington	DC	20042	**800-222-2294**	703-533-1155	48-19
Women's Sports Foundation Eisenhower Pk	East Meadow	NY	11554	**800-227-3988**	516-542-4700	48-22
Women's Sports Hall of Fame. International Eisenhower Pk Parking Field 6	East Meadow	NY	11554	**800-227-3988**	516-542-4700	511
Women's Wear Daily Magazine 7 W 34th St 3rd Fl	New York	NY	10001	**800-289-0273**	212-630-4000	449-11
Women's Zionist Organization of America Inc. Hadassah 50 W 58th St	New York	NY	10019	**888-303-3640**	212-355-7900	48-20
Wonder View Inn & Suites 50 Eden St PO Box 25	Bar Harbor	ME	04609	**888-439-8439**	207-288-3358	373
Wonder Wash/Wonder Lube Management Inc 1601 Caledonia St Suite 1	La Crosse	WI	54603	**800-261-9274**	608-783-5525	62-1
Wonderland Amusement Park 2601 Dumas Dr	Amarillo	TX	79107	**800-383-4712**	806-383-4712	32
Wonderlic Inc 1795 N Butterfield Rd	Libertyville	IL	60048	**800-323-3742**	847-680-4900	623-10
Wood County Electric Co-op Inc PO Box 1827	Quitman	TX	75783	**800-762-2203**	903-763-2203	244
Wood County Telephone Co 440 E Grand Ave	Wisconsin Rapids	WI	54494	**800-421-9282**	715-421-8111	721
Wood Flooring Assn. National 111 Chesterfield Industrial Blvd	Chesterfield	MO	63005	**800-422-4556**	636-519-9663	49-3
Wood-Fruitticher Grocery Co Inc 2900 Alton Rd	Birmingham	AL	35210	**800-489-4500**	205-836-9663	292-8
Wood Group Turbo Power Inc 14820 NW 60th Ave	Miami Lakes	FL	33014	**800-403-6737**	305-820-3225	25
Wood Moulding & Millwork Producers Assn (WMMPA) 507 First St	Woodland	CA	95695	**800-550-7889**	530-661-9591	49-3
Wood Preservers Inc PO Box 158	Warsaw	VA	22572	**800-368-2536**	804-333-4022	806
Wood Structures Inc 20 Pomerleau St	Biddeford	ME	04005	**800-341-9612**	207-282-7556	805
Wood & Tait Inc PO Box 6180	Kamuela	HI	96743	**800-774-8585**		392
Wood Tobe-Coburn School 8 E 40th St	New York	NY	10016	**800-394-9663**	212-686-9040	158
Woodard & Curran 41 Hutchins Dr	Portland	ME	04102	**800-426-4262**	207-774-2112	258
Woodberry Forest School 241 Woodberry Station	Woodberry Forest	VA	22989	**888-798-9371**	540-672-3900	611
Woodbridge Winery 5950 E Woodbridge Rd	Acampo	CA	95220	**888-766-6328**	209-369-5861	50
Woodbury Business Forms Inc 101 Lukken Industrial Dr E	LaGrange	GA	30241	**800-241-8116**	706-882-2977	111
Woodbury County Rural Electric Co-op Assn 1495 Humboldt Ave	Moville	IA	51039	**800-469-3125**	712-873-3125	244
Woodbury Financial Services Inc PO Box 64271	Saint Paul	MN	55164	**800-800-2000**	651-738-4000	393
Woodbury Pewterers Inc 860 Main St S	Woodbury	CT	06798	**800-648-2014**	203-263-2668	693
Woodbury University 7500 Glenoaks Blvd	Burbank	CA	91510	**800-784-9663**	818-767-0888	163
Woodcraft Supply Co 560 Airport Industrial Park *Cust Svc	Parkersburg	WV	26102	**800-535-4482***	304-428-4866	45
Woodfin Suite Hotels LLC 12730 High Bluff Dr Suite 250	San Diego	CA	92130	**800-237-8811**	858-794-2338	369
Chase Suite Hotels by Woodfin 12730 High Bluff Dr Suite 250	San Diego	CA	92130	**800-237-8811**	858-794-2338	369
Woodford Mfg Co 2121 Waynoka Rd *Sales	Colorado Springs	CO	80915	**800-621-6032***	719-574-0600	598
Woodgrain Millworks Inc PO Box 566	Fruitland	ID	83619	**800-452-3801**	208-452-3801	489
Woodhead LP 3411 Woodhead Dr *Mktg	Northbrook	IL	60062	**800-225-7724***	847-272-7990	803
Woodhill Supply Inc 4665 Beidler Rd	Willoughby	OH	44094	**800-362-6111**	440-269-1100	601
Woodland Aviation Inc 17992 County Rd 94B Watts-Woodland Airport	Woodland	CA	95695	**800-442-1333**	530-662-9631	63
Woodland Chamber of Commerce 307 1st St	Woodland	CA	95695	**888-843-2636**	530-662-7327	137
Woodland Owners Assn. National 374 Maple Ave E Suite 310	Vienna	VA	22180	**800-476-8733**	703-255-2700	48-2
Woodlands The 9700 Leavenworth Rd	Kansas City	KS	66109	**800-695-7223**	913-299-3434	628
Woodlands Resort & Conference Center 2301 N Millbend Dr	The Woodlands	TX	77380	**800-433-2624**	281-367-1100	370
Woodlands Resort & Inn 125 Parsons Rd	Summerville	SC	29483	**800-774-9999**	843-875-2600	655
Woodmark Hotel on Lake Washington 1200 Carillon Point	Kirkland	WA	98033	**800-822-3700**	425-822-3700	373
Woodmen Accident & Life Co 1526 K St	Lincoln	NE	68508	**800-869-0355**	402-476-6500	384-2
WOODMEN Magazine 1700 Farnam St	Omaha	NE	68102	**800-225-3108**	402-342-1890	449-10
Woodmen of the World/Omaha Woodmen Life Insurance Society 1700 Farnam St	Omaha	NE	68102	**800-225-3108**	402-342-1890	384-2
Woodruff Energy 73 Water St	Bridgeton	NJ	08302	**800-557-1121**	856-455-1111	311
Woodruff House 988 Bond St	Macon	GA	31201	**800-837-2911**	478-301-2715	50
Woods Equipment Co 2606 S Illinois Rt 2	Oregon	IL	61061	**800-319-6637**	815-732-2141	269
Woods Industries Canada Inc 375 Kennedy Rd	Toronto	ON	M1K2A3	**800-561-4321**	416-267-4610	803
Woods Industries Inc 510 3rd Ave SW	Carmel	IN	46032	**800-428-6168**	317-844-7261	803
Woods Resort 2201 Roark Valley Rd	Branson	MO	65616	**800-935-2345**	417-332-3550	373
Woods Resort & Conference Center Mountain Lake Rd PO Box 5	Hedgesville	WV	25427	**800-248-2222**	304-754-7977	655
Woodside Fund 350 Marine Pkwy Suite 300	Redwood Shores	CA	94065	**888-368-5545**	650-610-8050	779
Woodsmith Magazine 2200 Grand Ave	Des Moines	IA	50312	**800-333-5075**	515-282-7000	449-14
Woodson & Bozeman Inc 3870 New Getwell Rd	Memphis	TN	38118	**800-876-4243**	901-362-1500	38
Woodstock Inn & Resort 14 The Green	Woodstock	VT	05091	**800-448-7900**	802-457-1100	655

Name / Address	City	State	ZIP	Toll-Free	Phone	Class
Woodward FST 700 N Centennial St	Zeeland	MI	49464	**800-253-3295**	616-772-9171	486
Woodward Governor Co 5001 N 2nd St *NASDAQ: WGOV*	Loves Park	IL	61111	**888-273-8839**	815-877-7441	22
Woodward News PO Box 928	Woodward	OK	73802	**888-389-6960**	580-256-2200	522-2
Woodway USA W229 N591 Foster Ct	Waukesha	WI	53186	**800-966-3929**	262-548-6235	263
Woodwind & Brasswind 4004 Technology Dr	South Bend	IN	46628	**800-348-5003**	574-251-3500	515
Woody Tire Co Inc 1606 50th St	Lubbock	TX	79412	**800-530-4818**	806-747-4556	740
Woolaroc Ranch Museum & Wildlife Preserve Hwy 123 S	Bartlesville	OK	74003	**888-966-5276**	918-336-0307	509
Woolf Aircraft Products Inc 6401 Cogswell Rd	Romulus	MI	48174	**800-367-5475**	734-721-5330	584
Woolley's Petite Suites 2721 Hotel Terrace Dr	Santa Ana	CA	92705	**800-762-2597**	714-540-1111	373
Woolrich Inc 2 Mill St	Woolrich	PA	17779	**800-995-1299**	570-769-6464	153-5
Wooster Brush Co 604 Madison Ave	Wooster	OH	44691	**800-392-7246**	330-264-4440	104
Wooster Products Inc 1000 Spruce St	Wooster	OH	44691	**800-321-4936**	330-264-2844	482
Worcester County Convention & Visitors Bureau 30 Worcester Center Blvd	Worcester	MA	01608	**800-231-7557**	508-755-7400	205
Worcester Envelope Co 22 Millbury St PO Box 406	Auburn	MA	01501	**800-343-1300**	508-832-5394	200
Worcester Insurance Co 120 Front St Suite 400	Worcester	MA	01608	**800-225-7387**	508-751-8100	384-4
Worcester State College 486 Chandler St	Worcester	MA	01602	**866-972-2255**	508-793-8000	163
Worcester Telegram & Gazette Inc PO Box 15012	Worcester	MA	01615	**800-678-6680**	508-793-9100	623-8
Word Dean Co Ltd 1245 River Rd PO Box 310330	New Braunfels	TX	78131	**800-683-3926**	830-625-2365	187-4
WORD-FM 101.5 (Rel) 7 Parkway Ctr Suite 625	Pittsburgh	PA	15220	**800-320-8255**	412-937-1500	631
Worden Co Inc 199 E 17th St	Holland	MI	49423	**800-748-0561**	616-392-1848	314-3
WordMark International Corp 944 Torrey Pines Dr	Paso Robles	CA	93446	**800-835-2400**	805-237-9900	176-1
WordsWorth Books 30 Brattle St	Cambridge	MA	02138	**800-899-2202**	617-354-5201	96
Work Committee. National Right to 8001 Braddock Rd Suite 500	Springfield	VA	22160	**800-325-7892**	703-321-8510	49-12
Work Options Group Inc 1100 S McCaslin Blvd Suite 200	Superior	CO	80027	**888-610-2273**	303-604-6545	65
Workbench Magazine 2200 Grand Ave	Des Moines	IA	50312	**800-311-3991**	515-282-7000	449-14
Workbrain Inc 3440 Preston Ridge Rd Suite 100	Alpharetta	GA	30005	**866-967-5272**	678-713-6014	39
Workforce 2000 1903 Central Dr Suite 200	Bedford	TX	76021	**800-522-9778**	817-868-7277	619
Working Assets Long Distance Service 101 Market St Suite 700 *Cust Svc	San Francisco	CA	94105	**800-788-0898***	415-369-2000	721
Working Capital Co 3736 Mt Diablo Blvd Suite 310	Lafayette	CA	94549	**800-899-3836**	925-283-4433	268
Working Mother Magazine 60 E 42nd St 27th Fl	New York	NY	10165	**800-627-0690**	212-351-6400	449-11
Working Mother Media Inc 60 E 42nd St 27th	New York	NY	10165	**800-627-0690**	212-351-6400	623-9
Working Together Newsletter 360 Hiatt Dr	Palm Beach Gardens	FL	33418	**800-621-5463**	561-622-6520	521-2
Working Women. 9to5 National Assn of 152 W Wisconsin Ave Suite 408	Milwaukee	WI	53203	**800-522-0925**	414-274-0925	48-24
WorkLife Benefits Inc 25115 Ave Sanford Suite 200	Valencia	CA	91355	**800-628-5437**	661-775-2200	65
Workman Publishing 708 Broadway	New York	NY	10003	**800-722-7202**	212-254-5900	623-2
Workmen's Circle/Arbeter Ring 45 E 33rd St 4th Fl	New York	NY	10016	**800-922-2558**	212-889-6800	49-9
Workplace Integrators 30800 Telegraph Rd Suite 4700	Bingham Farms	MI	48025	**800-429-9172**	248-430-2345	315
Workplace Systems Inc 562 Mammoth Rd	Londonderry	NH	03053	**800-258-9700**	603-622-3727	314-1
Workscape Inc 500 Old Connecticut Path Bldg A	Framingham	MA	01701	**888-605-9620**	508-861-5500	39
Workspaces Inc 14311 SE 77th Ct	Newcastle	WA	98059	**800-466-4123**	425-226-4398	314-1
Workstream Inc 495 March Rd Suite 300 *NASDAQ: WSTM*	Ottawa	ON	K2K3G1	**877-327-8483**	613-270-0619	707
World Aviation Directory 1200 G St NW Suite 900	Washington	DC	20005	**800-551-2015**	609-426-5000	623-6
World Book Inc 233 N Michigan Ave 20th Fl	Chicago	IL	60601	**800-255-1750**	312-729-5800	361
World Book Publishing 233 N Michigan Ave Suite 2000 *Sales	Chicago	IL	60601	**800-967-5325***	312-729-5800	623-2
World Carpets Inc 31 S Green St *Cust Svc	Dalton	GA	30720	**800-241-4900***	800-233-4490	131
World Class Automotive Group 3333 Inwood Rd	Dallas	TX	75235	**800-898-4295**	214-358-8800	57
World Concern 19303 Fremont Ave N	Seattle	WA	98133	**800-755-5022**	206-546-7201	48-5
World Council of Credit Unions Inc (WOCCU) 5710 Mineral Point Rd	Madison	WI	53705	**800-356-2644**	608-231-7130	49-2
World Courier Inc 1313 4th Ave	New Hyde Park	NY	11040	**800-223-4461**	516-354-2600	536
World Dryer Corp 5700 McDermott Dr	Berkeley	IL	60163	**800-323-0701**	708-449-6950	37
World Floor Covering Assn (WFCA) 2211 Howell Ave	Anaheim	CA	92806	**800-624-6880**	714-978-6440	49-4
World Food Chemical News 1725 K St NW Suite 506	Washington	DC	20006	**800-272-7737**	202-887-6320	521-12
World Fuel Services Corp 9800 NW 41st St Suite 400 *NYSE: INT*	Miami	FL	33178	**800-345-3818**	305-428-8000	569
World Future Society 7910 Woodmont Ave Suite 450	Bethesda	MD	20814	**800-989-8274**	301-656-8274	49-19
World of Golf 4500 Tamiami Trail N	Naples	FL	34103	**800-505-9998**	239-263-4999	702
World Golf Village Resort. Renaissance 500 S Legacy Trail	Saint Augustine	FL	32092	**888-740-7020**	904-940-8000	655
World Gym International 3223 Washington Blvd	Marina del Rey	CA	90292	**800-544-7441**	310-827-7705	349
World Hunger Year Inc (WHY) 505 8th Ave Suite 2100	New York	NY	10018	**800-548-6479**	212-629-8850	48-5
World Inspection Network International Inc 6500 6th Ave NW	Seattle	WA	98117	**800-967-8127**	206-728-8100	360
World Minerals Inc 130 Castilian Dr	Santa Barbara	CA	93117	**800-893-4445**	805-562-0200	403
World Neighbors Inc 4127 NW 122nd St	Oklahoma City	OK	73120	**800-242-6387**	405-752-9700	48-5
World Oil Co 9302 Garfield Ave	South Gate	CA	90280	**800-266-6551**	562-928-0100	570
World Omni Financial Corp 120 NW 12th Ave *Cust Svc	Deerfield Beach	FL	33442	**866-663-9663***	954-429-2200	215
World Opportunities International/Help the Children 1875 Century Park E Suite 700	Los Angeles	CA	90067	**800-464-7187**	323-466-7187	48-5
World Paper Inc 76 Ethel Ave	Hawthorne	NJ	07506	**800-385-5911**	973-238-1750	130
World Politics. Institute of 1521 16th St NW	Washington	DC	20036	**888-566-9497**	202-462-2101	654
World Press Review 700 Broadway 3rd Fl	New York	NY	10003	**800-862-2966**	212-982-8880	449-17
World Savings Bank FSB 11601 Wilshire Blvd	Los Angeles	CA	90025	**800-468-7283**	310-477-8004	71
World Sleep Products Inc 12 Esquire Rd	North Billerica	MA	01862	**800-370-8700**	978-667-6648	463
World Society for the Protection of Animals (WSPA) 34 Deloss St	Framingham	MA	01702	**800-883-9772**	508-879-8350	48-3
World Spice Inc 223-235 Highland Pkwy	Roselle	NJ	07203	**800-234-1060**	908-245-0600	291-37
World Supply Inc 3425 W Cahuenga Blvd	Hollywood	CA	90068	**800-399-6753**	323-851-1350	45
World Trade Center Boston 164 Northern Ave	Boston	MA	02210	**800-367-9822**	617-385-5000	810
World Trade Center Cleveland Tower City Ctr 50 Public Sq Suite 824	Cleveland	OH	44113	**888-304-4769**	216-621-3300	810
World Trade Center Rio Grande Valley at McAllen 200 S 10th St Suite 401	McAllen	TX	78501	**888-874-8638**	956-686-1982	810
World Travel Bureau Inc 620 N Main St	Santa Ana	CA	92701	**800-899-3370**	714-835-8111	760
World Travel Inc 1724 W Schuylkill Rd	Douglassville	PA	19518	**800-341-2014**	610-327-9000	760
World Vision Inc PO Box 9716	Federal Way	WA	98063	**800-777-5777**	253-815-1000	48-5
World of Watches 14001 NW 4th St	Sunrise	FL	33325	**800-222-0077**	954-453-2821	151
World Wide Pet Supply Assn Inc (WWPSA) 406 S 1st Ave	Arcadia	CA	91006	**800-999-7295**	626-447-2222	49-18
World Wide Press Inc 801 River Dr S	Great Falls	MT	59405	**800-548-9888**	406-727-7812	750
World Wide Windows LLC/Gould Drapewear 840 Barry St	Bronx	NY	10474	**800-223-8990**	718-361-8120	235
World of Wigs 2305 E 17th St	Santa Ana	CA	92705	**800-794-5572**	714-547-4461	342
World Wildlife Fund (WWF) 1250 24th St NW Suite 500	Washington	DC	20037	**800-225-5993**	202-293-4800	48-3
World Wildlife Fund Canada 245 Eglinton Ave E Suite 410	Toronto	ON	M4P3J1	**800-267-2632**	416-489-8800	48-3
World Wrapps 401 2nd Ave S Suite 150	Seattle	WA	98104	**888-233-9727**	206-233-9727	657
World*Class Learning Materials 111 Kane St	Baltimore	MD	21224	**800-638-6470**	410-633-0730	242
Worldata 3000 N Military Trail	Boca Raton	FL	33431	**800-331-8102**	561-393-8200	6
WorldatWork 14040 N Northsight Blvd	Scottsdale	AZ	85260	**877-951-9191**	480-951-9191	49-12
WorldClass Travel Network 7900 Xerxes Ave S 115 Wells Fargo Plaza	Bloomington	MN	55431	**800-234-3576**	952-835-8636	761
WorldKey.net Inc 837 E Ave Suite Q-9	Palmdale	CA	93550	**888-776-2930**	661-274-4443	390
WorldMark The Club 9805 Willows Rd NE	Redmond	WA	98052	**800-722-3487**	425-498-1950	738
World's Best Rated Cigar Co 6826 NW 77th Ct	Miami	FL	33166	**877-562-4427**		741-2
World's Finest Chocolate Inc 4801 S Lawndale Ave	Chicago	IL	60632	**800-366-2462**	773-847-4600	291-8
Worldsites Inc 5915 Airport Rd Suite 300	Toronto	ON	L4V1T1	**888-678-7588**	905-678-7588	7
WorldStrides 590 Peter Jefferson Pkwy Suite 300	Charlottesville	VA	22911	**800-468-5899**	434-982-8600	748
Worldtek Travel Inc 111 Water St	New Haven	CT	06511	**800-243-1723**	203-772-0470	761
WorldTravel BTI 1055 Lenox Park Blvd Suite 420	Atlanta	GA	30319	**800-342-3234**	404-841-6600	761
Worldwide Equipment Inc Kentucky Rt 1428 E PO Box 1370	Prestonsburg	KY	41653	**800-307-4746**	606-874-2172	505
Worldwide Express 2501 Cedar Springs Rd Suite 450	Dallas	TX	75201	**800-758-7447**	214-720-2400	536
Worldwide Holidays Inc 7800 Red Rd Suite 112	South Miami	FL	33143	**800-327-9854**	305-665-0841	760
Worldwide Sign Systems 446 N Cecil St PO Box 338	Bonduel	WI	54107	**800-874-3334**	715-758-2146	692
Worldwide Sport Nutrition 851 Broken Sound Pkwy NW Suite 255	Boca Raton	FL	33487	**800-854-5019**	561-241-9400	291-11
Worldwide Travel & Cruise Assoc Inc 150 S University Dr Suite E	Plantation	FL	33324	**800-881-8484**	954-452-8800	760
Wornick Co 10825 Kenwood Rd	Cincinnati	OH	45242	**800-860-4555**	513-794-9800	291-36
Woronoco Bancorp Inc 31 Court St *AMEX: WRO*	Westfield	MA	01085	**888-972-4123**	413-568-9141	355-2
Wort Hotel 50 N Glenwood	Jackson	WY	83001	**800-322-2727**	307-733-2190	373
Worth Co PO Box 88	Stevens Point	WI	54481	**800-944-1899**	715-344-6081	701
Worth & Co Inc 6263 Kellers Church Rd	Pipersville	PA	18947	**800-220-5130**	267-362-1100	188-10

Name / Address	City	State	Zip	Toll-Free	Phone	Class
Worth Magazine 1177 Ave of the Americas 10th Fl	New York	NY	10036	**800-777-1851*** *Circ	212-223-3100	449-11
Worth Sports PO Box 88104	Tullahoma	TN	37388	**800-282-9637*** *Cust Svc	931-455-0691	701
Wortham John L & Son LLP 2727 Allen Pkwy	Houston	TX	77019	**888-896-5623**	713-526-3366	383
Worthen Industries Inc 3 E Spit Brook Rd	Nashua	NH	03060	**800-967-8436**	603-888-5443	3
Worthington Biochemical Corp 730 Vassar Ave	Lakewood	NJ	08701	**800-445-9603**	732-942-1660	229
Worthington Communities 9240 Marketplace Rd Suite 2	Fort Myers	FL	33912	**877-560-4666**	239-561-4666	639
Worthington Cylinder Corp 200 Old E Wilson Bridge Rd	Columbus	OH	43085	**800-323-6224**	614-438-3013	92
Worthington Industries Inc 200 Old Wilson Bridge Rd *NYSE: WOR*	Columbus	OH	43085	**800-944-2255**	614-438-3210	709
Worthington Steel Co 1127 Dearborn Dr	Columbus	OH	43085	**800-944-3733**	614-438-3205	709
WOS Inc 2985 S Ridge Rd Suite B	Green Bay	WI	54304	**800-888-4454**	920-336-0690	531
WOSC-FM 95.9 (Rock) 351 Tilghman Rd	Salisbury	MD	21804	**800-762-0105**	410-742-1923	631
Wound Ostomy & Continence Nurses Society (WOCN) 4700 W Lake Ave	Glenview	IL	60025	**888-224-9626**		49-8
WOW Playgrounds 2851 Polk St	Hollywood	FL	33020	**800-432-2283**	954-925-2800	340
WOWK-TV Ch 13 (CBS) 555 5th Ave	Huntington	WV	25701	**800-234-9695**	304-525-1313	726
WOWO-AM 1190 (N/T) 2915 Maples Rd	Fort Wayne	IN	46816	**800-333-1190**	260-447-5511	631
WOWT-TV Ch 6 (NBC) 3501 Farnam St	Omaha	NE	68131	**800-688-2431**	402-346-6666	726
Wozniak Industries Inc Commercial Forged Products Div 5757 W 65th St	Bedford Park	IL	60638	**800-637-2695**	708-458-1220	474
WP Carey & Co LLC 50 Rockefeller Plaza 2nd Fl *NYSE: WPC*	New York	NY	10020	**800-972-2739**	212-492-1100	641
WPBG-FM 93.3 (Oldies) 331 Fulton St Suite 1200	Peoria	IL	61602	**800-310-0930**	309-637-3700	631
WPBT-TV Ch 2 (PBS) 14901 NE 20th Ave	Miami	FL	33181	**800-222-9728**	305-949-8321	726
WPC Florida PO Box 35189	Panama City	FL	32412	**800-763-2811**	850-763-2811	181
WPCS-FM 89.5 (Rel) 250 Brent Ln	Pensacola	FL	32503	**800-726-1191**	850-479-6570	631
WPDE-TV Ch 15 (ABC) 1194 Atlantic Ave	Conway	SC	29526	**800-698-9733**	843-234-9733	726
WPEO-AM 1020 (Rel) 1708 Highview Rd	East Peoria	IL	61611	**800-728-1020**	309-698-9736	631
WPGA-TV Ch 58 (ABC) 1691 Forsyth St	Macon	GA	31201	**800-225-5222**	478-745-5858	726
WPKX-FM 97.9 (Ctry) 1331 Main St	Springfield	MA	01103	**800-345-9759**	413-781-1011	631
WPLM-FM 99.1 (AC) 17 Columbus	Plymouth	MA	02360	**877-327-9991**	508-746-1390	631
WPLN-FM 90.3 (NPR) 630 Mainstream Dr	Nashville	TN	37228	**877-760-2903**	615-760-2903	631
WPNN-AM 790 (N/T) 3801 N Pace Blvd	Pensacola	FL	32505	**888-433-1141**	850-433-1141	631
WPR (Wisconsin Public Radio) 821 University Ave	Madison	WI	53706	**800-442-7110**	608-263-3970	620
WPRO-AM 630 (N/T) 1502 Wampanoag Trail	East Providence	RI	02915	**800-321-9776**	401-433-4200	631
WPS Resources Corp 700 N Adams St *NYSE: WPS*	Green Bay	WI	54307	**800-450-7260**	920-433-4901	355-5
WPT (Wisconsin Public Television) 821 University Ave	Madison	WI	53706	**800-422-9707**	608-263-2121	620
WPTD-TV Ch 16 (PBS) 110 S Jefferson St	Dayton	OH	45402	**800-247-1614**	937-220-1600	726
WPTF-AM 680 (N/T) 3012 Highwoods Blvd Suite 200	Raleigh	NC	27604	**800-662-7979**	919-876-0674	631
WPX Delivery Solutions 3320 W Valley Hwy N Suite 110	Auburn	WA	98001	**800-562-1091**	253-796-2301	536
WPXI-TV Ch 11 (NBC) 11 Television Hill	Pittsburgh	PA	15214	**800-237-9794**	412-237-1100	726
WPXN-TV Ch 31 (PAX) 1330 Ave of the Americas 32nd Fl	New York	NY	10019	**800-646-7296**	212-757-3100	726
WPXP-TV Ch 67 (PAX) 601 Clearwater Rd	West Palm Beach	FL	33401	**800-646-7296**	561-659-4122	726
WQCD-FM 101.9 (NAC) 395 Hudson St 7th Fl	New York	NY	10014	**800-423-1019**	212-352-1019	631
WQDR-FM 94.7 (Ctry) 3012 Highwoods Blvd Suite 200	Raleigh	NC	27604	**800-233-9470**	919-876-0674	631
WQED-FM 89.3 (Clas) 4802 5th Ave	Pittsburgh	PA	15213	**800-876-1316**	412-622-1436	631
WQED-TV Ch 13 (PBS) 4802 5th Ave	Pittsburgh	PA	15213	**800-876-1316**	412-622-1300	726
WQHQ-FM 104.7 (AC) 351 Tilghman Rd	Salisbury	MD	21804	**800-762-0105**	410-742-1923	631
WQHT-FM 97.1 (Urban) 395 Hudson St 7th Fl	New York	NY	10014	**800-223-9797**	212-229-9797	631
WQKC-FM 93.7 (Ctry) PO Box 806	Seymour	IN	47274	**800-633-9370**	812-522-1390	631
WQLN-FM 91.3 (NPR) 8425 Peach St	Erie	PA	16509	**800-727-8854**	814-864-3001	631
WQLN-TV Ch 54 (PBS) 8425 Peach St	Erie	PA	16509	**800-727-8854**	814-864-3001	726
WQN Inc 14911 Quorum Dr Suite 140 *NASDAQ: WQNI*	Dallas	TX	75254	**866-661-6176**	972-361-1980	721
WQSA-FM 99.9 (N/TI) 1006 1st St	Perry	GA	31069	**800-705-8770**	478-218-7756	631
WR Case & Sons Cutlery Co Owens Way	Bradford	PA	16701	**800-523-6350**	814-368-4123	219
WR Grace & Co 7500 Grace Dr *NYSE: GRA*	Columbia	MD	21044	**888-398-4646**	410-531-4000	143
WR Hambrecht & Co 539 Bryant St Suite 100	San Francisco	CA	94107	**877-673-6476*** *Cust Svc	415-551-8600	679
WR Kelso Co Inc 10201 N Hague Rd	Indianapolis	IN	46256	**800-352-5859**	317-845-5858	188-12
WRAL-FM 101.5 (AC) 711 Hillsborough St	Raleigh	NC	27603	**800-849-6101**	919-890-6101	631
WRAL-TV Ch 5 (CBS) 2619 Western Blvd	Raleigh	NC	27606	**800-245-9725**	919-821-8555	726
Wrap-On Co Inc 5550 W 70th Pl	Bedford Park	IL	60638	**800-621-6947**	708-496-2150	800
WRAZ-TV Ch 50 (Fox) 512 S Mangum St	Durham	NC	27701	**877-369-5050**	919-595-5050	726
WRBS-FM 95.1 (Rel) 3600 Georgetown Rd	Baltimore	MD	21227	**800-899-0951**	410-247-4100	631

Name / Address	City	State	Zip	Toll-Free	Phone	Class
Wrentham Steel Products Co 30 Kendrick St	Wrentham	MA	02093	**800-251-2166**	508-384-2166	448
Wrestling Assn. New York Arm PO Box 670952	Flushing	NY	11367	**877-692-2767**	718-544-4592	48-22
Wrestling. USA 6155 Lehman Dr	Colorado Springs	CO	80918	**800-999-8531**	719-598-8181	48-22
WRFX-FM 99.7 (CR) 801 Wood Ridge Ctr Dr	Charlotte	NC	28217	**800-332-1029**	704-714-9444	631
Wricley Nut Products Co 480 Pattison Ave	Philadelphia	PA	19148	**800-523-1303**	215-467-1106	291-28
Wright Brand Foods Inc PO Box 1779	Vernon	TX	76385	**800-772-0844**	940-553-1811	291-26
Wright Business Forms Inc 2525 Braga Dr	Broadview	IL	60155	**800-487-2204**	708-865-7600	111
Wright Business Graphics 18440 NE San Rafael St	Portland	OR	97230	**800-547-8397**	503-661-2525	111
Wright Color Graphics 626 Sonora Ave	Glendale	CA	91201	**800-695-3355**	818-246-8877	614
Wright ET & Co Inc 1356 Williams St	Chippewa Falls	WI	54729	**800-934-1022**		451
Wright Express Corp 97 Darling Ave *NYSE: WXS*	South Portland	ME	04106	**800-761-7181**	207-773-8171	213
Wright GA Inc Direct Marketing Div 4105 Holly St	Denver	CO	80216	**800-824-5886**	303-333-4453	5
Wright Group/McGraw-Hill 19201 120th Ave NE Suite 100	Bothell	WA	98011	**800-523-2371*** *Sales	425-486-8011	623-2
Wright-Hennepin Co-op Electric Assn PO Box 330	Rockford	MN	55373	**800-943-2667**	763-477-3000	244
Wright Investors' Service 440 Wheelers Farms Rd	Milford	CT	06460	**800-232-0013**	203-783-4400	393
Wright-K Technology Inc 2025 E Genesee Ave	Saginaw	MI	48601	**800-752-3103**	989-752-3103	485
Wright Line LLC 160 Gold Star Blvd	Worcester	MA	01606	**800-225-7348**	508-852-4300	314-1
Wright & McGill Co DBA Eagle Claw Fishing Tackle 4245 E 46th Ave	Denver	CO	80216	**800-628-0108**	303-321-1481	701
Wright Medical Group Inc 5677 Airline Rd *NASDAQ: WMGI*	Arlington	TN	38002	**800-238-7188**	901-867-9971	469
Wright Medical Technology Inc 5677 Airline Rd	Arlington	TN	38002	**800-238-7188**	901-867-9971	469
Wright-Patt Credit Union 2455 Executive Park Blvd	Fairborn	OH	45324	**800-762-0047**	937-912-7000	216
Wright State University 3640 Colonel Glenn Hwy	Dayton	OH	45435	**800-247-1770*** *Admissions	937-775-3333	163
Wright of Thomasville Corp 5115 Prospect St	Thomasville	NC	27360	**800-678-9019**	336-472-4200	404
Wright Tool Co 1 Wright Dr	Barberton	OH	44203	**800-321-2902**	330-848-3702	746
Wright Travel Inc 2505 21st Ave S Suite 500	Nashville	TN	37212	**800-643-5992**	615-783-1111	760
Wright Tree Service Inc PO Box 1718	Des Moines	IA	50306	**800-882-1216**	515-277-6291	765
Wright William E Ltd 85 South St	West Warren	MA	01092	**800-628-9362**	413-436-7732	730-5
Wright's Knitwear Corp 10 E 34th St	New York	NY	10016	**800-952-8788**	212-779-2600	153-3
Wrigley Mansion 2501 E Telawa Trail	Phoenix	AZ	85016	**888-879-7201**	602-955-4079	50
Wrigley Wm Jr Co 410 N Michigan Ave *NYSE: WWY*	Chicago	IL	60611	**888-824-9681**	312-644-2121	291-6
Wrigley Wm Jr Co 410 N Michigan Ave *NYSE: WWY*	Chicago	IL	60611	**888-824-9681**	312-644-2121	291-6
Wrisco Industries Inc 355 Hiatt Dr Suite B	Palm Beach Gardens	FL	33418	**800-627-2646**	561-626-5700	483
Writer's Digest 4700 E Galbraith Rd	Cincinnati	OH	45236	**800-888-6880*** *Cust Svc	513-531-2690	449-21
Writer's Digest Book Club 4700 E Galbraith Rd	Cincinnati	OH	45236	**800-888-6880*** *Cust Svc	513-531-2690	94
Writers Guild of America West (WGAw) 7000 W 3rd St	Los Angeles	CA	90048	**800-548-4532**	323-951-4000	405
Writing Magazine 3001 Cindel Dr	Delran	NJ	08075	**800-446-3355**	856-786-5500	449-6
WRKF-FM 89.3 (NPR) 3050 Valley Creek Dr	Baton Rouge	LA	70808	**888-926-3050**	225-926-3050	631
WRKS-FM 98.7 (Urban) 395 Hudson St 7th Fl	New York	NY	10014	**800-288-5477**	212-242-9870	631
WRLK-TV Ch 35 (PBS) 1101 George Rogers Blvd	Columbia	SC	29201	**800-922-5437**	803-737-3200	726
WRNE-AM 980 (Urban) 312 E Nine-Mile Rd Suite 29D	Pensacola	FL	32514	**866-478-8866**	850-478-6000	631
WRNN-TV Ch 62 (Ind) 437 5th Ave	New York	NY	10016	**800-824-3302**	212-725-2666	726
WRNX-FM 100.9 (AAA) 98 Lower Westfield Rd 3rd Fl	Holyoke	MA	01040	**800-977-1009**	413-536-1105	631
WROL-AM 950 (Rel) PO Box 9121	Boston	MA	02171	**888-659-0590**	617-423-0213	631
WRQ Inc 1500 Dexter Ave N	Seattle	WA	98109	**800-872-2829*** *Sales	206-217-7500	176-1
WRR Environmental Services Co Inc 5200 SR-93	Eau Claire	WI	54701	**800-727-8760**	715-834-9624	653
WRS Motion Picture & Video Laboratory 1000 Napor Blvd	Pittsburgh	PA	15205	**800-345-6977*** *Cust Svc	412-937-7700	501
WRTI-FM 90.1 (NPR) 1509 Cecil B Moore Ave 3rd Fl	Philadelphia	PA	19122	**800-245-8776**	215-204-8405	631
WS Emerson Co Inc 15 Acme Rd	Brewer	ME	04412	**800-789-6120**	207-989-3410	154
WS Hampshire Inc 365 Keyes Ave	Hampshire	IL	60140	**800-541-0251**	847-683-4400	710
WS Packaging Group Inc 1102 Jefferson St	Algoma	WI	54201	**800-236-3424**	920-487-3424	404
WSAZ-TV Ch 3 (NBC) PO Box 2115	Huntington	WV	25721	**800-834-8515**	304-697-4780	726
WSBT-TV Ch 22 (CBS) 300 W Jefferson Blvd	South Bend	IN	46601	**800-872-3141**	574-233-3141	726
WSBY-FM 98.9 (Urban AC) 351 Tilghman Rd	Salisbury	MD	21804	**800-762-0105**	410-742-1923	631
WSCL-FM 89.5 (NPR) PO Box 2596 Salisbury University	Salisbury	MD	21801	**800-543-6895**	410-543-6895	631
WSEC-TV Ch 14 (PBS) PO Box 6248	Springfield	IL	62708	**800-232-3605**	217-206-6647	726

	City	State	Zip	Toll-Free	Phone	Class
WSFJ-TV Ch 51 (PAX) 3948 Townsfair Way Suite 220	Columbus	OH	43219	**800-517-5151**	614-416-6080	726
WSFS Bank 838 Market St	Wilmington	DE	19801	**800-292-9594**	302-792-6000	71
WSFS Financial Corp 838 N Market St *NASDAQ: WSFS*	Wilmington	DE	19801	**888-973-7226**	302-792-6000	355-2
WSHA-FM 88.9 (Jazz) 118 E South St	Raleigh	NC	27601	**800-241-0421**	919-546-8430	631
WSHU-FM 91.1 (NPR) 5151 Park Ave	Fairfield	CT	06825	**800-937-6045**	203-365-6604	631
WSKO-AM 790 (Sports) 1502 Wampanoag Trail	East Providence	RI	02915	**888-345-0790**	401-433-4200	631
WSKY-TV Ch 4 (Ind) 1417 N Battlefield Blvd Suite 160	Chesapeake	VA	23320	**800-414-0911**	757-382-0004	726
WSLS-TV Ch 10 (NBC) PO Box 10	Roanoke	VA	24022	**800-800-9757**	540-981-9110	726
WSM-AM 650 (Ctry) 2804 Opryland Dr	Nashville	TN	37214	**877-878-4650**	615-889-6595	631
WSOC-TV Ch 9 (ABC) 1901 N Tryon St	Charlotte	NC	28206	**800-367-9762**	704-338-9999	726
WSOS-FM 94.1 (AC) 2715 Stratton Blvd	Saint Augustine	FL	32084	**877-829-9767**	904-824-0833	631
WSPA (World Society for the Protection of Animals) 34 Deloss St	Framingham	MA	01702	**800-883-9772**	508-879-8350	48-3
WSPA-TV Ch 7 (CBS) PO Box 1717	Spartanburg	SC	29304	**800-207-6397**	864-576-7777	726
WSSA (Wine & Spirits Shippers Assn Inc) 11800 Sunrise Valley Dr Suite 332	Reston	VA	22091	**800-368-3167**	703-860-2300	49-6
WSTH-FM 106.1 (Ctry) 1501 13th Ave	Columbus	GA	31901	**800-445-4106**	706-576-3000	631
WSTO-FM 96.1 (CHR) 20 NW 3rd St 13th Fl	Evansville	IN	47708	**800-879-1372**	812-424-8284	631
WSTW-FM 93.7 (CHR) 2727 Shipley Rd	Wilmington	DE	19810	**800-544-9370**	302-478-2700	631
WSUA-AM 1260 (Span) 2100 Coral Way 2nd Fl	Miami	FL	33145	**800-441-1260**	305-285-1260	631
WSVH-FM 91.1 (NPR) 12 Ocean Science Cir	Savannah	GA	31411	**800-673-7332**	912-598-3300	631
WSWT-FM 106.9 (AC) 331 Fulton St Suite 1200	Peoria	IL	61602	**800-579-1069**	309-637-3700	631
WT Burnett & Co Inc 1500 Bush St	Baltimore	MD	21230	**800-638-0606**	410-837-3000	590
WTB Financial Corp PO Box 2127	Spokane	WA	99210	**800-788-4578**	509-353-4122	355-2
WTBC-AM 1230 (N/T) 2110 McFarland Blvd E Suite C	Tuscaloosa	AL	35404	**800-518-1977**	205-758-5523	631
WTIU-TV Ch 30 (PBS) 1229 E 7th St	Bloomington	IN	47405	**800-662-3311**	812-855-5900	726
WTKE-FM 98.1 (Sports) 21 Miracle Strip Pkwy	Fort Walton Beach	FL	32548	**877-981-0981**	850-244-1400	631
WTKR-TV Ch 3 (CBS) 720 Boush St	Norfolk	VA	23510	**800-375-0901**	757-446-1000	726
WTKX-FM 101.5 (Rock) 6485 Pensacola Blvd	Pensacola	FL	32505	**888-357-7625**	850-473-0400	631
WTLV-TV Ch 12 (NBC) 1070 E Adams St	Jacksonville	FL	32202	**800-352-8812**	904-354-1212	726
WTOV-TV Ch 9 (NBC) 9 Red Donley Plaza	Mingo Junction	OH	43938	**800-288-0799**	740-282-0911	726
WTRF-TV Ch 7 (CBS) 96 16th St	Wheeling	WV	26003	**800-777-9873**	304-232-7777	726
WTS Inc 1100 Olive Way Suite 1100	Seattle	WA	98101	**877-987-7253**	206-436-3300	39
WTSP-TV Ch 10 (CBS) 11450 Gandy Blvd N	Saint Petersburg	FL	33702	**800-393-6610**	727-577-1010	726
WTSU-FM 89.9 (NPR) Troy State University Wallace Hall	Troy	AL	36082	**800-800-6616**	334-670-3268	631
WTTG-TV Ch 5 (Fox) 5151 Wisconsin Ave NW	Washington	DC	20016	**800-988-4885**	202-244-5151	726
WTVD-TV Ch 11 (ABC) 411 Liberty St	Durham	NC	27701	**800-467-4440**	919-683-1111	726
WTVP-TV Ch 47 (PBS) PO Box 1347	Peoria	IL	61654	**800-837-4747**	309-677-4747	726
WTVW-TV Ch 7 (Fox) 477 Carpenter St	Evansville	IN	47708	**800-511-6009**	812-424-7777	726
WTWR-FM 98.3 (CHR) 14930 LaPlaisance Rd Suite 113	Monroe	MI	48161	**888-578-0098**	734-242-6600	631
WTXF-TV Ch 29 (Fox) 330 Market St	Philadelphia	PA	19106	**800-220-6397**	215-925-2929	726
WTZR-FM 99.3 (Alt) 901 E Valley Dr	Bristol	VA	24201	**866-770-7625**	276-669-8112	631
WUAB-TV Ch 43 (UPN) 1717 E 12th St	Cleveland	OH	44114	**800-929-0132**	216-771-1943	726
WUAL-FM 91.5 (NPR) University of Alabama Phifer Hall Suite 166	Tuscaloosa	AL	35487	**800-654-4262**	205-348-6644	631
Wuesthoff Brevard Hospice 8060 Spyglass Hill Rd	Viera	FL	32940	**800-259-2007**	321-253-2222	365
Wuesthoff Hospital 110 Longwood Ave	Rockledge	FL	32955	**800-742-9175**	321-636-2211	366-2
WUIS-FM 91.9 (NPR) University of Illinois at Springfield 1 University Plaza	Springfield	IL	62703	**866-206-9847**	217-206-6516	631
Wulfrath Refractories Inc 6th & Center Sts PO Box 28	Tarentum	PA	15084	**800-245-1801**	724-224-8800	649
WUMB-FM 91.9 (Folk) 100 Morrissey Blvd	Boston	MA	02125	**800-573-2100**	617-287-6900	631
WUNC-FM 91.5 (NPR) University of North Carolina Box 0915	Chapel Hill	NC	27599	**800-962-9862**	919-966-5454	631
WUNC-TV Ch 4 (PBS) PO Box 14900	Research Triangle Park	NC	27709	**800-906-5050**	919-549-7000	726
WUPW-TV Ch 36 (Fox) 4 Seagate Bldg	Toledo	OH	43604	**866-369-6397**	419-244-3600	726
Wurst Henry Inc 1331 Saline St	North Kansas City	MO	64116	**800-775-5851**	816-842-3113	615
Wurth Service Supply Inc 4935 W 86th St	Indianapolis	IN	46268	**800-428-4686**	317-704-1000	346
Wurzburg Inc 710 S 4th St PO Box 710	Memphis	TN	38101	**800-274-4885**	901-525-1441	549
WUSF-FM 89.7 (NPR) 4202 E Fowler Ave WRB 219	Tampa	FL	33620	**800-741-9090**	813-974-8700	631
WUSF-TV Ch 16 (PBS) 4202 E Fowler Ave	Tampa	FL	33620	**800-654-3703**	813-974-4000	726
WUWF-FM 88.1 (NPR) University of West Florida 11000 University Pkwy	Pensacola	FL	32514	**800-239-9893**	850-474-2787	631
WVAA-AM 1390 (Ctry) 272 Dorset St	South Burlington	VT	05403	**800-286-9537**	802-863-1010	631
WVAN-TV Ch 9 (PBS) 260 14th St NW	Atlanta	GA	30318	**800-222-6006**	404-685-2400	726
WVCY-TV Ch 30 (Ind) 3434 W Kilbourn Ave	Milwaukee	WI	53208	**800-729-9829**	414-935-3000	726
WVII-TV Ch 7 (ABC) 371 Target Industrial Cir	Bangor	ME	04401	**800-499-9844**	207-945-6457	726
WVIT-TV Ch 30 (NBC) 1422 New Britain Ave	West Hartford	CT	06110	**800-523-9848**	860-521-3030	726
WVKF-FM 95.7 (CHR) 1015 Main St	Wheeling	WV	26003	**800-668-7426**	304-232-1170	631
WVKS-FM 92.5 (CHR) 125 S Superior St	Toledo	OH	43602	**877-547-7366**	419-244-8321	631
WVPE-FM 88.1 (NPR) 2424 California Rd	Elkhart	IN	46514	**888-399-9873**	574-262-5660	631
WVPN-FM 88.5 (NPR) 600 Capitol St	Charleston	WV	25301	**888-596-9729**	304-556-4900	631
WVPS-FM 107.9 (NPR) 365 Troy Ave	Colchester	VT	05446	**800-639-2192**	802-655-9451	631
WVT Communications 47 Main St PO Bo 592 *NASDAQ: WWVY* ■ *Cust Svc	Warwick	NY	10990	**800-952-7642***	845-986-1101	721
WVTF-FM 89.1 (NPR) 3520 Kingsbury Ln	Roanoke	VA	24014	**800-856-8900**	540-231-8900	631
WVXU-FM 91.7 (NPR) 3800 Victory Pkwy	Cincinnati	OH	45207	**800-230-3576**	513-731-9898	631
WW Grainger Inc 100 Grainger Pkwy *NYSE: GWW*	Lake Forest	IL	60045	**888-361-8649**	847-535-1000	245
WW Norton & Co Inc 500 5th Ave	New York	NY	10110	**800-223-2584**	212-354-5500	623-2
WWAX-FM 92.1 (CHR) 501 Lake Ave S Suite 200-A	Duluth	MN	55802	**877-921-5477**	218-728-9500	631
WWDC-FM 101.1 (Rock) 1801 Rockville Pike Suite 405	Rockville	MD	20852	**800-333-2101**	301-587-7100	631
WWDL-FM 104.9 (Oldies) 1049 N Sekol Rd	Scranton	PA	18504	**888-577-4487**	570-344-1221	631
WWF (World Wildlife Fund) 1250 24th St NW Suite 500	Washington	DC	20037	**800-225-5993**	202-293-4800	48-3
WWFE-AM 670 (Span) 330 SW 27th Ave Suite 207	Miami	FL	33135	**888-541-9933**	305-541-3300	631
WWFG-FM 99.9 (Ctry) 351 Tilghman Rd	Salisbury	MD	21804	**800-762-0105**	410-742-1923	631
WWFM-FM 89.1 (Clas) 1200 Old Trenton Rd	Trenton	NJ	08650	**800-622-9936**	609-587-8989	631
WWGR-FM 101.9 (Ctry) 10915 K-Nine Dr	Bonita Springs	FL	34135	**877-787-1019**	239-495-8383	631
WWJC-AM 850 (Rel) 1120 E McCuen St	Duluth	MN	55808	**877-626-2738**	218-626-2738	631
WWMB-TV Ch 21 (UPN) 1194 Atlantic Ave	Conway	SC	29526	**800-698-9733**	843-234-9733	726
WWMT-TV Ch 3 (CBS) 590 W Maple St	Kalamazoo	MI	49008	**800-875-3333**	269-388-3333	726
WWNO-FM 89.9 (NPR) University of New Orleans Lake Front Campus	New Orleans	LA	70148	**800-286-7002**	504-280-7000	631
WWPR-FM 105.1 (Urban) 1120 6th Ave	New York	NY	10036	**800-585-1051**	212-704-1051	631
WWPSA (World Wide Pet Supply Assn Inc) 406 S 1st Ave	Arcadia	CA	91006	**800-999-7295**	626-447-2222	49-18
WWW Internet Fund PO Box 25910	Lexington	KY	40524	**888-999-8331**		517
WWZZ-FM 103.9 (AC) 1300 Idaho Ave NW Suite 200	Washington	DC	20016	**800-987-2104**	202-895-5000	631
WXBM-FM 102.7 (Ctry) 6085 Quintette Rd	Pace	FL	32571	**800-626-9926**	850-994-5357	631
WXBQ-FM 96.9 (Ctry) 901 E Valley Dr	Bristol	VA	24201	**800-332-3697**	276-669-8112	631
WXCY-FM 103.7 (Ctry) 707 Revolution St	Havre de Grace	MD	21078	**800-788-9929**	410-939-1100	631
WXEL-FM 90.7 (NPR) PO Box 6607	West Palm Beach	FL	33405	**800-915-9935**	561-737-8000	631
WXEL-TV Ch 42 (PBS) PO Box 6607	West Palm Beach	FL	33405	**800-915-9935**	561-737-8000	726
WXOK-AM 1460 (Rel) 650 Wooddale Blvd	Baton Rouge	LA	70806	**800-499-1460**	225-926-1106	631
WXTW-FM 102.3 (Alt) 2000 Lower Huntington Rd	Fort Wayne	IN	46819	**877-747-7711**	260-747-1511	631
WXXA-TV Ch 23 (Fox) 28 Corporate Cir	Albany	NY	12203	**800-999-2882**	518-862-2323	726
Wyandot Inc 135 Wyandot Ave	Marion	OH	43302	**800-992-6368**	740-383-4031	291-35
Wyandot Lake Water Park 10101 Riverside Dr	Powell	OH	43065	**800-328-9283**	614-889-9283	32
Wyandot Tractor & Implement Co PO Box 147	Upper Sandusky	OH	43351	**800-472-9554**	419-294-2349	270
Wyatt Inc 4545 Campbells Run Rd	Pittsburgh	PA	15205	**800-966-5801**	412-787-5800	188-9
Wyatt-Quarles Seed Co 730 US Hwy 70 W	Garner	NC	27529	**800-662-7591**	919-772-4243	270
WYCL-FM 107.3 (Oldies) 6485 Pensacola Blvd	Pensacola	FL	32505	**888-345-1073**	850-473-0400	631
Wycliffe Bible Translators PO Box 628200	Orlando	FL	32862	**800-992-5433**	407-852-3611	48-20
WYEP-FM 91.3 (Var) 2313 E Carson St	Pittsburgh	PA	15203	**877-381-9900**	412-381-9131	631
Wyeth BioPharm 1 Burtt Rd	Andover	MA	01810	**800-934-5556**	978-475-9214	572
Wyeth Consumer Health Care International Inc 5 Giralda Farms *Cust Svc	Madison	NJ	07940	**800-322-3129***	973-660-5000	572
Wyeth Corp 5 Giralda Farms *NYSE: WYE*	Madison	NJ	07940	**800-322-3129**	973-660-5000	355-3
Wyeth Corp Fort Dodge Animal Health Div 9225 Indian Creek Pkwy Bldg 32 Suite 400	Overland Park	KS	66210	**800-477-1365**	913-664-7000	574
Wyffels Hybrids Inc 13344 US Hwy 6	Geneseo	IL	61254	**800-369-7833**	309-944-8344	11-5
Wylie Mfg Co 101 N Main St *Sales	Petersburg	TX	79250	**800-722-4001***	806-667-3566	269
Wyman-Gordon Co 244 Worcester St	North Grafton	MA	01536	**800-343-6070**	508-839-4441	474
Wyman Jasper & Son PO Box 100	Milbridge	ME	04658	**800-341-1758**	207-546-2311	310-1
Wyndham ByRequest Program 1950 N Stemmons Fwy Suite 6001	Dallas	TX	75207	**800-347-7559**	214-863-1000	371
Wyndham Casa Marina Resort 1500 Reynolds St	Key West	FL	33040	**800-626-0777**	305-296-3535	655
Wyndham Condado Plaza Hotel & Casino 999 Ashford Ave	San Juan	PR	00907	**800-468-5228**	787-721-1000	655
Wyndham El Conquistador Resort & Country Club 1000 El Conquistador Ave	Fajardo	PR	00738	**800-996-3426**	787-863-1000	655

Name / Address	City	State	Zip	Toll-Free	Phone	Class
Wyndham El San Juan Hotel & Casino 6063 Isla Verde Ave	Carolina	PR	00979	**800-996-3426**	787-791-1000	655
Wyndham Hotels & Resorts 1950 Stemmons Fwy Suite 6001	Dallas	TX	75207	**800-996-3426**	214-863-1000	369
Wyndham International Inc 1950 Stemmons Fwy Suite 6001	Dallas	TX	75207	**800-996-3426**	214-863-1000	369
AMEX: WBR						
Summerfield Suites by Wyndham 1950 Stemmons Fwy Suite 6001	Dallas	TX	75207	**800-833-4353**	214-863-1000	369
Wyndham Hotels & Resorts 1950 Stemmons Fwy Suite 6001	Dallas	TX	75207	**800-996-3426**	214-863-1000	369
Wyndham Luxury Resorts 1950 Stemmons Fwy Suite 6001	Dallas	TX	75207	**800-996-3426**	214-863-1000	369
Wyndham Luxury Resort. Boulders Resort & Golden Door Spa - A 34631 N Tom Darlington Dr PO Box 2090	Carefree	AZ	85377	**800-553-1717**	480-488-9009	655
Wyndham Luxury Resort. Carmel Valley Ranch Resort - A 1 Old Ranch Rd	Carmel	CA	93923	**800-422-7635**	831-625-9500	655
Wyndham Luxury Resort. Lodge at Ventana Canyon - A 6200 N Clubhouse Ln	Tucson	AZ	85750	**800-828-5701**	520-577-1400	655
Wyndham Luxury Resorts 1950 Stemmons Fwy Suite 6001	Dallas	TX	75207	**800-996-3426**	214-863-1000	369
Wyndham Orlando Resort 8001 International Dr	Orlando	FL	32819	**800-421-8001**	407-351-2420	655
Wyndham Palace Resort & Spa in the Walt Disney World Resort 1900 Buena Vista Dr	Lake Buena Vista	FL	32830	**800-996-3426**	407-827-2727	655
Wyndham Peachtree Conference Center 2443 Hwy 54 W	Peachtree City	GA	30269	**800-996-3426**	770-487-2000	370
Wyndham Peaks Resort & Golden Door Spa 136 Country Club Dr	Telluride	CO	81435	**800-789-2220**	970-728-6800	655
Wyndham Reach Resort 1435 Simonton St	Key West	FL	33040	**800-996-3426**	305-296-5000	655
Wynfrey Hotel 1000 Riverchase Galleria	Birmingham	AL	35244	**800-996-3739**	205-987-1600	373
Wynn Las Vegas 3131 Las Vegas Blvd S	Las Vegas	NV	89109	**888-320-7123**	702-770-7000	373
Wynn Oil Co 1050 W 5th St	Azusa	CA	91702	**800-989-8363**	626-334-0231	143
Wynn Resorts Ltd 3131 Las Vegas Blvd S	Las Vegas	NV	89109	**866-770-7108**	702-733-4444	369
NASDAQ: WYNN						
Wynne Residential Corporate Housing 2214 Westwood Ave	Richmond	VA	23230	**800-338-8534**	804-359-8534	209
Wynne Transport Service Inc 2222 N 11th St	Omaha	NE	68108	**800-383-9330**	402-342-4001	769
Wynnwood Suites 1909 Atlantic Ave	Virginia Beach	VA	23451	**800-372-4900**	757-425-0650	373
Wyo-Ben Inc 1345 Discovery Dr	Billings	MT	59102	**800-548-7055***	406-652-6351	493-2
*Cust Svc						
Wyoming						
Bill Status State Capitol Bldg Rm 213	Cheyenne	WY	82002	**800-342-9570**	307-777-7881	425
Professional Teaching Standards Board 1920 Thomes Ave Suite 400	Cheyenne	WY	82001	**800-675-6893**	307-777-7291	335
State Parks & Historical Sites Div 122 W 25th St 1st Fl E	Cheyenne	WY	82002	**877-996-7275***	307-777-5598	335
*Campground Resv						
Tourism Div 214 W 15th St	Cheyenne	WY	82002	**800-225-5996**	307-777-2828	335
Veterans' Affairs Commission 5905 CY Ave	Casper	WY	82604	**800-832-5987**	307-265-7372	335
Wyoming Assn of Realtors PO Box 2312	Casper	WY	82602	**800-676-4085**	307-237-4085	642
Wyoming Democratic Party 254 N Center St Suite 205	Casper	WY	82601	**800-729-3367**	307-473-1457	605-1
Wyoming Medical Center 1233 E 2nd St	Casper	WY	82601	**800-822-7201**	307-577-7201	366-2
Wyoming Public Television 2660 Peck Ave	Riverton	WY	82501	**800-495-9788**	307-856-6944	620
Wyoming Seminary 201 N Sprague Ave	Kingston	PA	18704	**877-996-7364**	570-270-2160	611
Wyoming Tribune-Eagle 702 W Lincolnway	Cheyenne	WY	82001	**800-561-6268**	307-634-3361	522-2
WyoTech 4373 N 3rd St	Laramie	WY	82072	**800-521-7158**	307-742-3776	787
WYOU-TV Ch 22 (CBS) 409 Lackawanna Ave	Scranton	PA	18503	**800-422-9968**	570-961-2222	726
Wyrulec Co PO Box 359	Lingle	WY	82223	**800-628-5266**	307-837-2225	244
Wyse Technology Inc 3471 N 1st St	San Jose	CA	95134	**800-800-9973**	408-473-1200	171-3
Wysong & Miles Co Inc 4820 US 29 N	Greensboro	NC	27405	**800-299-7664**	336-621-3960	448
WYTV-TV Ch 33 (ABC) 3800 Shady Run Rd	Youngstown	OH	44502	**800-686-2930**	330-783-2930	726
WZBH-FM 93.5 (Rock) 20200 Dupont Blvd	Georgetown	DE	19947	**888-780-0970**	302-856-2567	631
WZEB-FM 101.7 (AC) 20200 Dupont Blvd	Georgetown	DE	19947	**888-780-0970**	302-856-2567	631
WZPX-TV Ch 43 (PAX) 2610 Horizon Dr Suite E	Grand Rapids	MI	49546	**877-729-8843**	616-222-4343	726
WZVN-TV Ch 26 (ABC) 3719 Central Ave	Fort Myers	FL	33901	**800-741-8820**	239-939-2020	726
WZZR-FM 94.3 (N/T) PO Box 0093	Port Saint Lucie	FL	34985	**877-927-6969**	772-335-9300	631

X

Name / Address	City	State	Zip	Toll-Free	Phone	Class
X-Cel Optical Co Inc 806 S Benton Dr	Sauk Rapids	MN	56379	**800-747-9235**	320-251-8404	531
X-Gen Pharmaceuticals Inc PO Box 445	Big Flats	NY	14814	**866-390-4411**	607-732-4411	573
X-Rite Inc 3100 44th St SW	Grandville	MI	49418	**800-248-9748**	616-534-7664	410
NASDAQ: XRIT						
Xand Corp 11 Skyline Dr	Hawthorne	NY	10532	**800-522-2823**	914-592-8282	455
Xanodyne Pharmaceuticals Inc 7300 Turfway Rd Suite 300	Florence	KY	41042	**877-926-6396**	859-371-6383	573
Xanser Corp 2435 N Central Expy Suite 700	Richardson	TX	75080	**800-488-7973**	972-699-4000	355-3
NYSE: XNR						
Xante Corp 2800 Dauphin St Suite 100	Mobile	AL	36606	**800-926-8839**	251-473-6502	171-6
Xantech Corp 13100 Telfair Ave 2nd Fl	Sylmar	CA	91342	**800-843-5465***	818-362-0353	52
*Sales						
Xanterra Parks & Resorts 14001 E Iliff Ave Suite 600	Aurora	CO	80014	**888-297-2757**	303-338-6000	267
Xaos Tools Inc 582 San Luis Rd	Berkeley	CA	94707	**800-833-9267**	510-525-5465	176-8
XATA Corp 151 E Cliff Rd Suite 10	Burnsville	MN	55337	**800-262-9282***	952-894-3680	519
NASDAQ: XATA ■ *Tech Supp						
Xavier University 3800 Victory Pkwy	Cincinnati	OH	45207	**800-344-4698**	513-745-3000	163
Xavier University of Louisiana 1 Drexel Dr	New Orleans	LA	70125	**877-928-4378***	504-486-7411	163
*Admissions						
Xcel Energy Inc PO Box 840	Denver	CO	80201	**800-772-7858**	303-571-7511	774
Xcel Energy Inc 800 Nicollet Mall	Minneapolis	MN	55401	**800-328-8226**	612-330-5500	774
NYSE: XEL						
Xechem International Inc 100 Jersey Ave Bldg B Suite 310	New Brunswick	NJ	08901	**800-858-5854**	732-247-3300	572
Xenogen Corp 860 Atlantic Ave	Alameda	CA	94501	**877-936-6436**	510-291-6100	86
NASDAQ: XGEN						
Xeroderma Pigmentosum Society Inc (XPS) 437 Snydertown Rd	Craryville	NY	12521	**877-977-2873**	518-851-2612	48-17
Xerox Canada Inc 5650 Yonge St	North York	ON	M2M4G7	**800-275-9376**	416-229-3769	578
Xerox Corp 800 Long Ridge Rd	Stamford	CT	06904	**800-842-0024**	203-968-3000	578
NYSE: XRX						
Xerox Corp Omnifax Div 9715 Burnet Rd	Austin	TX	78758	**800-221-8330**	512-719-5566	113
Xerox Global Services Inc 411 Eagleview Blvd	Exton	PA	19341	**800-884-4736**	610-458-5500	178
Xertrex International Inc 1530 W Glenlake Ave	Itasca	IL	60143	**800-822-2437**	630-773-4020	550
Xertrex International Inc Tabbies Div 1530 W Glenlake Ave	Itasca	IL	60143	**800-822-2437**	630-773-4020	550
Xerxes Corp 7901 Xerxes Ave S Suite 201	Minneapolis	MN	55431	**800-394-3490**	952-887-1890	198
XETA Technologies Inc 1814 W Tacoma St	Broken Arrow	OK	74012	**800-845-9145***	918-664-8200	720
NASDAQ: XETA ■ *Cust Svc						
XETRA-FM 91.1 (Alt) 9660 Granite Ridge Dr	San Diego	CA	92123	**866-690-1150**	619-291-9191	631
Xetron Div Neumade Products Corp 30-40 Pecks Ln	Newtown	CT	06470	**800-526-0722**	203-270-1100	580
Xilinx Inc 2100 Logic Dr	San Jose	CA	95124	**800-494-5469**	408-559-7778	686
NASDAQ: XLNX						
Xillix Technologies Corp 13775 Commerce Pkwy Suite 100	Richmond	BC	V6V2V4	**800-665-2236**	604-278-5000	375
XL Brands 237 Nance Rd NE	Calhoun	GA	30701	**800-367-4583**	706-625-0025	143
XL Specialty Insurance Co 20 N Martingale Rd Suite 200	Schaumburg	IL	60173	**800-394-3909**	847-517-2990	384-5
Xlibris Corp International Plaza 2 Suite 340	Philadelphia	PA	19113	**888-795-4274**	610-915-5214	623-2
XM Satellite Radio Holdings Inc 1500 Eckington Pl NE	Washington	DC	20002	**877-967-2346**	202-380-4000	669
NASDAQ: XMSR						
XO Communications Inc 11111 Sunset Hills Rd	Reston	VA	20190	**800-900-6398**	703-547-2000	721
Xodiax 733 Barret Ave	Louisville	KY	40204	**866-838-4722**	502-315-6000	174
XOMA Ltd 2910 7th St	Berkeley	CA	94710	**800-544-9662**	510-204-7200	86
NASDAQ: XOMA						
XP ForeSight Co 990 Benicia Ave	Sunnyvale	CA	94085	**800-276-9378**	408-732-7777	245
Xpedx Paper Store 3351 W Addison St	Chicago	IL	60618	**800-866-6332**	773-463-6423	524
Xplor International 24238 Hawthorne Blvd	Torrance	CA	90505	**800-669-7567**	310-373-3633	48-9
XPRESStrade LLC 10 S Wacker Dr Suite 2550	Chicago	IL	60606	**800-947-6228**	312-715-6228	167
XPS (Xeroderma Pigmentosum Society Inc) 437 Snydertown Rd	Craryville	NY	12521	**877-977-2873**	518-851-2612	48-17
XS Smith Inc PO Box X	Red Bank	NJ	07701	**800-631-2226**	732-222-4600	106
xSides Corp 821 2nd Ave	Seattle	WA	98104	**800-396-7877**	206-336-1600	176-12
Xspedius Communication LLC 555 Winghaven Blvd Suite 300	O Fallon	MO	63368	**877-962-9100**	636-625-7000	721
Xtek Inc 11451 Reading Rd	Cincinnati	OH	45241	**888-332-9835**	513-733-7800	446
Xtend Communications Corp 171 Madison Ave	New York	NY	10016	**800-342-5910***	212-951-7600	176-7
*Cust Svc						
XTRA Corp 1801 Park 270 Dr	Saint Louis	MO	63146	**800-325-1453**	314-579-9300	261-6
XTRA Intermodal 100 Tower Dr	Burr Ridge	IL	60527	**800-344-9872**	630-789-3200	767
Xtra Mart 221 Quinebaug Rd	North Grosvenordale	CT	06255	**800-243-6366**	860-935-5200	203
Xtria 2435 N Central Expy Suite 700	Richardson	TX	75080	**866-769-2987**	972-699-4000	178
Xybernaut Corp 12701 Fair Lakes Cir Suite 550	Fairfax	VA	22033	**888-992-3777**	703-631-6925	171-2
NASDAQ: XYBR						
Xybernet Inc 10640 Scripps Ranch Blvd	San Diego	CA	92131	**800-228-9026***	858-530-1900	176-10
*Cust Svc						
Xycom Automation Inc 750 N Maple Rd	Saline	MI	48176	**800-289-9266**	734-429-4971	171-3
XyEnterprise 30 New Crossing Rd	Reading	MA	01867	**800-925-1269**	781-756-4400	176-8
Xyvision Enterprise Solutions Inc 30 New Crossing Rd	Reading	MA	01867	**800-925-1269**	781-756-4400	176-8

Y

Name / Address	City	State	Zip	Toll-Free	Phone	Class
Y-ME National Breast Cancer Organization 212 W Van Buren St	Chicago	IL	60607	**800-221-2141**	312-986-8338	48-17

Name / Address	City	State	ZIP	Toll-Free	Phone	Class
Y-Tex Corp 1825 Big Horn Ave	Cody	WY	82414	**800-443-6401**	307-587-5515	276
Y-W Electric Assn Inc PO Box Y	Akron	CO	80720	**800-660-2291**	970-345-2291	244
Yachting Magazine 18 Marshall St Suite 114	South Norwalk	CT	06854	**800-999-0869**	203-299-5900	449-4
Yachtsman Resort Hotel 1400 N Ocean Blvd	Myrtle Beach	SC	29577	**800-868-8886**	843-448-1441	373
Yacktman Asset Management Co 1110 W Lake Cook Rd Suite 385	Buffalo Grove	IL	60089	**800-356-6356**	847-325-0707	393
Yaffa Wigs 4118 13th Ave	Brooklyn	NY	11219	**800-233-0660**	718-436-4280	342
Yaffe Iron & Metal Co Inc PO Box 916	Muskogee	OK	74402	**800-759-2333**	918-687-7543	674
Yahoo! Photos 701 1st Ave	Sunnyvale	CA	94089	**888-267-7574**	408-349-3300	577
Yahoo! Search Marketing Solutions 74 N Pasadena Ave 3rd Fl	Pasadena	CA	91103	**888-811-4686**	626-685-5600	677
Yakima Convention Center 10 N 8th St	Yakima	WA	98901	**800-221-0751**	509-575-6062	204
Yakima Federal Savings & Loan Assn 118 E Yakima Ave	Yakima	WA	98901	**800-331-3225**	509-248-2634	71
Yakima Herald-Republic PO Box 9668	Yakima	WA	98909	**800-343-2799**	509-248-1251	522-2
Yale Electric Supply Co 296 Freeport St	Dorchester	MA	02122	**800-289-9253**	617-825-9253	35
Yale Norton Inc 1902 Airport Rd	Monroe	NC	28110	**800-438-1951**	704-283-2101	345
Yale Residential Security Products Inc 2725B Northwoods Pkwy *Cust Svc	Norcross	GA	30071	**800-542-7562***	678-728-7400	345
Yale Security Group 1902 Airport Rd	Monroe	NC	28110	**800-438-1951**	704-283-2101	345
Yale University Press 302 Temple St *Sales	New Haven	CT	06511	**800-987-7323***	203-432-0960	623-5
YALSA (Young Adult Library Services Assn) 50 E Huron St	Chicago	IL	60611	**800-545-2433**	312-280-4390	49-11
Yamaha Electronics Corp 6660 Orangethorpe Ave *Cust Svc	Buena Park	CA	90620	**800-492-6242***	714-522-9105	52
Yamaha Motor Corp USA 6555 Katella Ave *Cust Svc	Cypress	CA	90630	**800-962-7926***	714-761-7300	506
Yamana Gold Inc 150 York St Suite 1902 *AMEX: AUY*	Toronto	ON	M5H3S5	**888-809-0925**	416-815-0220	492
Yamato Corp PO Box 15070	Colorado Springs	CO	80935	**800-538-1702**	719-591-1500	672
Yamato Transport USA Inc 80 Seaview Dr	Secaucus	NJ	07094	**800-492-6286**	201-583-9696	536
Yampa Valley Electric Assn Inc PO Box 771218	Steamboat Springs	CO	80477	**888-873-9832**	970-879-1160	244
Yanke Group of Cos 2815 Lorne Ave	Saskatoon	SK	S7J0S5	**800-667-7988**	306-955-4221	769
Yankee Candle Co Inc 16 Yankee Candle Way *NYSE: YCC*	South Deerfield	MA	01373	**800-839-6038**	413-665-8306	322
Yankee Energy System Inc 107 Selden St	Berlin	CT	06037	**800-286-5000**	203-639-4000	774
Yankee Inn 461 Pittsfield Rd	Lenox	MA	01240	**800-835-2364**	413-499-3700	373
Yankee Magazine 1121 Main St	Dublin	NH	03444	**800-288-4284**	603-563-8111	449-22
Yankee Peddler Inn 113 Touro St	Newport	RI	02840	**800-427-9444**	401-846-1323	373
Yankee Publishing Inc PO Box 520	Dublin	NH	03444	**800-729-9265**	603-563-8111	623-9
Yankelovich Inc 20 Glover Ave 2nd Fl N	Norwalk	CT	06850	**800-926-5356**	203-846-0100	458
Yankton Daily Press & Dakotan PO Box 56	Yankton	SD	57078	**800-743-2968**	605-665-7811	522-2
Yankton Printing Co PO Box 56	Yankton	SD	57078	**800-743-2968**	605-665-7811	623-8
Yantra Corp 1 Park W	Tewksbury	MA	01876	**888-292-6872**	978-513-6000	176-7
Yardley Products Corp PO Box 357	Yardley	PA	19067	**800-457-0154**	215-493-2700	345
Yardville National Bancorp 2465 Kuser Rd *NASDAQ: YANB*	Hamilton Square	NJ	08690	**888-443-5754**	609-585-5100	355-2
Yardville National Bank 2465 Kuser Rd	Hamilton Township	NJ	08690	**800-548-9545**	609-585-5100	71
Yarema Die & Engineering Co Inc 300 Minnesota Rd	Troy	MI	48083	**800-989-2830**	248-585-2830	745
Yarnell Ice Cream Co 205 S Spring St	Searcy	AR	72143	**800-666-2414**	501-268-2414	291-25
Yarrow Resort Hotel 1800 Park Ave	Park City	UT	84060	**800-927-7694**	435-649-7000	373
Yaskawa Electric America Inc 2121 Norman Dr	Waukegan	IL	60085	**800-927-5292**	847-887-7000	202
Yates-American Machine Co Inc 2880 Kennedy Dr	Beloit	WI	53511	**800-752-6377**	608-364-0333	809
Yavapai College 1100 E Sheldon St	Prescott	AZ	86301	**800-922-6787**	928-445-7300	160
Verde Valley Campus 601 Black Hills Dr	Clarkdale	AZ	86324	**800-922-6787**	928-634-7501	160
Yavapai Regional Medical Center 1003 Willow Creek Rd	Prescott	AZ	86301	**877-843-9762**	928-445-2700	366-2
Yaya's Flame Broiled Chicken 521 S Dort Hwy	Flint	MI	48503	**800-754-1242**	810-235-6550	657
Yazoo County Chamber of Commerce 212 E Broadway	Yazoo City	MS	39194	**800-748-8875**	662-746-1273	137
Yazoo Mills Inc PO Box 369 *Cust Svc	New Oxford	PA	17350	**800-242-5216***	717-624-8993	125
YBP Library Services 999 Maple St	Contoocook	NH	03229	**800-258-3774**	603-746-3102	97
YDA PO Box 77496	Washington	DC	20013	**877-639-8585**	202-639-8585	48-7
YDI Wireless Inc DBA Terabeam Wireless 8000 Lee Hwy	Falls Church	VA	22042	**888-297-9090**	703-205-0600	720
Yeager Skanska Inc 1995 Agua Mansa Rd	Riverside	CA	92509	**800-222-5360**	951-684-5360	187-4
Yeatts Transfer Co PO Box 687	Altavista	VA	24517	**800-446-0939**	434-369-5695	769
Yeck Brothers Co 2222 Arbor Blvd	Dayton	OH	45439	**800-417-2767**	937-294-4000	5
Yellow Book USA 193 EAB Plaza	Uniondale	NY	11556	**877-512-7710**	516-730-1900	623-6
Yellow Freight System Inc 10990 Roe Ave	Overland Park	KS	66211	**800-458-3323**	913-344-3000	769
Yellow Pages Assn (YPA) 820 Kirts Blvd Suite 100	Troy	MI	48084	**800-841-0639**	248-244-6200	49-16
Yellow Roadway Corp 10990 Roe Ave *NASDAQ: YELL*	Overland Park	KS	66211	**800-458-3323**	913-696-6100	355-3
YellowBrix Inc 44 Canal Center Plaza Suite 110	Alexandria	VA	22314	**800-945-9150**	703-548-3300	176-7
Yellowstone Coalition. Greater 13 S Willson Ave Suite 2	Bozeman	MT	59775	**800-775-1834**	406-586-1593	48-13

Name / Address	City	State	ZIP	Toll-Free	Phone	Class
Yellowstone Jetcenter 456 Gallatin Field Rd	Belgrade	MT	59714	**800-700-5381**	406-388-4152	14
Yellowstone Valley Electric Co-op PO Box 249	Huntley	MT	59037	**800-736-5323**	406-348-3411	244
Yenkin-Majestic Paint Corp 1920 Leonard Ave	Columbus	OH	43219	**800-848-1898**	614-253-8511	540
Yeo & Yeo CPA 3023 Davenport Ave	Saginaw	MI	48602	**800-968-0110**	989-793-9830	2
YesAsia.com Inc 1192 Cherry Ave	San Bruno	CA	94066	**888-716-5753**	650-517-5100	514
yesmail inc 959 Skyway Rd Suite 150	San Carlos	CA	94070	**877-937-6245**	650-620-1200	7
Yetter Mfg Co Inc 109 S McDonough St	Colchester	IL	62326	**800-447-5777**	309-776-4111	269
YFC/USA PO Box 4478	Englewood	CO	80155	**800-735-3252**	303-843-9000	48-20
Yingling Aircraft Inc 2010 Airport Rd	Wichita	KS	67277	**800-835-0083**	316-943-3246	759
YK International Co 3246 W Montrose Ave	Chicago	IL	60618	**800-621-0086**	773-583-5270	342
YMCA of the USA 101 N Wacker Dr 14th Fl	Chicago	IL	60606	**800-872-9622**	312-977-0031	48-6
YMT Vacations 8831 Aviation Blvd	Inglewood	CA	90301	**800-922-9000**	310-649-3820	760
Yoder Brothers Inc 115 3rd St SE	Barberton	OH	44203	**800-321-9573**	330-745-2143	363
Yogi Bear's Jellystone Park Camp Resorts 50 W Techne Center Dr Suite G *Sales	Milford	OH	45150	**800-626-3720***	513-831-2100	121
Yogo Inn 211 E Main St	Lewistown	MT	59457	**800-860-9646**	406-538-8721	373
Yokogawa Corp of America 2 Dart Rd	Newnan	GA	30265	**800-258-2552**	770-253-7000	247
Yokohama Tire Corp 601 S Acacia Ave	Fullerton	CA	92831	**800-423-4544**	714-870-3800	739
Yolles Group Inc 163 Queen St E Suite 200	Toronto	ON	M5A1S1	**800-572-1759**	416-363-8123	258
Yonex Corp 20140 S Western Ave	Torrance	CA	90501	**800-449-6639**	310-793-3800	701
Yoplait USA Inc PO Box 1113	Minneapolis	MN	55440	**800-967-5248**	763-764-7600	291-27
Yorba Linda Star 1771 S Lewis St	Anaheim	CA	92805	**877-469-7344**	714-634-1567	522-4
York Barbell Co Inc 3300 Board Rd *Cust Svc	York	PA	17402	**800-358-9675***	717-767-6481	263
York Building Products Co Inc PO Box 1708	York	PA	17405	**800-673-2408**	717-848-2831	181
York College 1125 E 8th St	York	NE	68467	**800-950-9675**	402-362-4441	163
York Container Co 138 Mt Scion Rd	York	PA	17402	**800-772-9675**	717-757-7611	101
York County Chamber of Commerce 1 Market Way E	York	PA	17401	**888-878-9675**	717-848-4000	137
York County Convention & Visitors Bureau 155 W Market St	York	PA	17401	**888-858-9675**	717-852-9675	205
York County Convention & Visitors Bureau 130 E Main St Suite 101	Rock Hill	SC	29731	**800-866-5200**	803-329-5200	205
York County Transportation Authority 1230 Roosevelt Ave	York	PA	17404	**800-632-9063**	717-846-5562	460
York Daily Record PO Box 15122	York	PA	17405	**800-682-1334**	717-771-2000	522-2
York Dispatch 205 N George St	York	PA	17401	**800-483-5517**	717-854-1575	522-2
York Electric Co-op Inc PO Box 150	York	SC	29745	**800-582-8810**	803-684-4247	244
York Group Inc 2 Northshore Ctr Suite 100	Pittsburgh	PA	15212	**800-223-4964**	412-995-1600	134
York Hotel 940 Sutter St	San Francisco	CA	94109	**800-808-9675**	415-885-6800	373
York International Corp Engineered Systems Group 5005 York Dr	Norman	OK	73069	**877-874-7378**	405-364-4040	15
York International Corp Unitary Products Group 5005 York Dr	Norman	OK	73069	**877-874-7378**	405-364-4040	16
YORK Label 405 Willow Springs Ln *Cust Svc	York	PA	17402	**888-800-9675***	717-266-9675	404
York News-Times PO Box 279	York	NE	68467	**800-334-4530**	402-362-4478	522-2
York Refrigeration Systems Frick 100 CV Ave	Waynesboro	PA	17268	**800-487-2653**	717-762-2121	650
York Region Tourism 17250 Young St Box 147 4th Fl	Newmarket	ON	L3Y6Z1	**888-448-0000**	905-883-3442	763
York Stamping DBA Wallace Metal Products 1800 Roberts Dr	Anniston	AL	36207	**888-831-9675**	256-831-4826	479
York Sunday News 205 N George St	York	PA	17401	**800-483-5517**	717-854-1575	522-4
York Technical College 452 S Anderson Rd	Rock Hill	SC	29730	**800-922-8324**	803-327-8000	160
York Wallcoverings Inc 750 Linden Ave PO Box 5166	York	PA	17405	**800-453-9281**	717-846-4456	789
York Water Co 130 E Market St PO Box 15089 *NASDAQ: YORW*	York	PA	17405	**800-750-5561**	717-845-3601	774
Yorkraft Inc PO Box 2386 *Cust Svc	York	PA	17405	**800-872-2044***	717-845-3666	281
Yorktowne Hotel 48 E Market St	York	PA	17401	**800-233-9324**	717-848-1111	373
Yorktowne Inc 100 Redco Ave	Red Lion	PA	17356	**800-777-0065**	717-244-4011	116
Yoshinoya Beef Bowl 1603 W Sepulveda Blvd	Torrance	CA	90501	**800-576-8017**	310-539-8319	657
Yost Superior Co PO Box 1487	Springfield	OH	45501	**800-544-4570**	937-323-7591	705
Youbet.com Inc 1950 Sawtelle Blvd Suite 180 *NASDAQ: UBET*	Los Angeles	CA	90025	**888-968-2388**	310-444-3300	443
Young AB Cos Inc 15305 Stony Creek Way	Noblesville	IN	46060	**800-886-7001**	317-565-5000	601
Young Adult Library Services Assn (YALSA) 50 E Huron St	Chicago	IL	60611	**800-545-2433**	312-280-4390	49-11
Young America Corp 717 Faxon Rd	Young America	MN	55397	**800-533-4529**	952-467-3366	722
Young America's Foundation 110 Elden St	Herndon	VA	20170	**800-292-9231**	703-318-9608	48-7
Young & Assoc Ltd 2625 Butterfield Rd Suite 216 South	Oak Brook	IL	60523	**800-553-2503**	630-573-2500	194
Young Brothers Ltd PO Box 3288	Honolulu	HI	96801	**800-572-2743**	808-543-9311	307
Young Chemical Co 6465 Eastland Rd	Brook Park	OH	44142	**800-248-3009**	440-234-3200	144
Young Contractors Inc 2001 Marlin Hwy 6	Waco	TX	76705	**800-460-2324**	254-754-2324	187-4
Young Corp 3231 Utah Ave S	Seattle	WA	98134	**800-321-9090**	206-624-1071	189
Young Democrats of America PO Box 77496	Washington	DC	20013	**877-639-8585**	202-639-8585	48-7
Young Group Ltd 1054 Central Industrial Dr	Saint Louis	MO	63110	**800-331-3080**	314-771-3080	188-12
Young Harris College PO Box 116	Young Harris	GA	30582	**800-241-3754**	706-379-3111	160
Young Innovations Inc 13705 Shoreline Ct E *NASDAQ: YDNT*	Earth City	MO	63045	**800-325-1881**	314-344-0010	469

Company / Address	City	State	Zip	Toll-Free	Phone	Class
Young Men's Christian Assn of the USA 101 N Wacker Dr 14th Fl	Chicago	IL	60606	**800-872-9622**	312-977-0031	48-6
Young Mfg Co Inc PO Box 167	Beaver Dam	KY	42320	**800-545-6595**	270-274-3306	489
Young Pecan Shelling Co PO Box 5779 *Sales	Florence	SC	29502	**800-829-6864***	843-664-2330	291-28
Young Presidents' Organization (YPO) 451 S Decker Dr Suite 200	Irving	TX	75062	**800-773-7976**	972-650-4600	49-12
Young Supply Co 888 W Baltimore St	Detroit	MI	48202	**800-872-3280**	313-875-3280	601
Young Touchstone Inc 200 Smith Ln *Sales	Jackson	TN	38301	**800-238-8230***	731-424-5045	16
Young Transportation & Tours 843 Riverside Dr	Asheville	NC	28804	**800-622-5444**	828-258-0084	108
Young WF Inc PO Box 1990	East Longmeadow	MA	01028	**800-628-9653**	413-526-9999	572
Young Women's Christian Assn 1015 18th St NW Suite 1100	Washington	DC	20036	**800-992-2871**	202-467-0801	48-6
Younger Optics 2925 California St	Torrance	CA	90503	**800-366-5367**	310-783-1533	531
Young's Commercial Transfer 44 S Lotas St	Porterville	CA	93257	**800-289-1639**	559-784-6651	769
Young's Market Co LLC 2164 N Batavia St	Orange	CA	92865	**800-317-6150**	714-283-4933	82-3
Young's Plant Farm Inc 863 Airport Rd	Auburn	AL	36830	**800-304-8609**	334-821-3500	363
Young's Richard Intelligence Report 7811 Montrose Rd	Potomac	MD	20854	**800-301-8969**	301-340-2100	521-9
Youngsoft Inc 49197 Wixom Tech Dr Suite B	Wixom	MI	48393	**888-470-4553**	248-675-1200	175
Youngstown Historical Center of Industry & Labor 151 W Wood St	Youngstown	OH	44503	**800-262-6137**	330-743-5934	509
Youngstown State University 1 University Plaza	Youngstown	OH	44555	**877-468-6978**	330-941-3000	163
Youngstown/Mahoning County Convention & Visitors Bureau 3620 Starr Centre Dr	Canfield	OH	44406	**800-447-8201**	330-286-0089	205
Younkers Inc 701 Walnut St *Acctg	Des Moines	IA	50309	**800-530-6886***	515-244-1112	227
Your Big Backyard Magazine 8925 Leesburg Pike	Vienna	VA	22184	**800-611-1599**		449-6
Your Money Magazine 520 Lake Cook Rd Suite 500	Deerfield	IL	60015	**800-777-0025**	847-607-3000	449-11
Your New Pryor Report: Managers Edge 2807 N Parham Rd Suite 200 *Cust Svc	Richmond	VA	23294	**800-722-9221***	804-762-9600	521-2
Your Northwest 31461 NE Bell Rd	Sherwood	OR	97140	**888-252-0699**	503-554-9060	333
Your True Greetings 2215 Farmersville Rd	Bethlehem	PA	18020	**800-241-2704**	610-694-8028	130
Yourga Trucking Inc 145 JH Yourga Pl	Wheatland	PA	16161	**800-245-1722**	724-981-3600	769
Youth Advocacy Coalition. National 1638 R St NW Suite 300	Washington	DC	20009	**800-541-6922**	202-319-7596	48-6
Youth. America's Promise - The Alliance for 909 N Washington St Suite 400	Alexandria	VA	22314	**800-365-0153**	703-684-4500	48-6
Youth for Christ/USA PO Box 4478	Englewood	CO	80155	**800-735-3252**	303-843-9000	48-20
Youth & Communities. Center for Brandeis University 60 Turner St 2nd Fl	Waltham	MA	02453	**800-343-4205**	781-736-3770	654
Youth Services International Inc 1819 Main St Suite 1000	Sarasota	FL	34236	**800-275-3766**	941-953-9199	210
Youth Soccer Organization. American 12501 S Isis Ave *Cust Svc	Hawthorne	CA	90250	**800-872-2976***	310-643-6455	48-22
Youth Sport Institute. North American 4985 Oak Garden Dr	Kernersville	NC	27284	**800-767-4916**	336-784-4926	48-22
Youth Sports Coaches Assn. National 2050 Vista Pkwy	West Palm Beach	FL	33411	**800-729-2057**	561-684-1141	48-22
Youth Sports. National Alliance for 2050 Vista Pkwy	West Palm Beach	FL	33411	**800-729-2057**	561-684-1141	48-22
Youth for Understanding International Exchange 6400 Goldsboro Rd Suite 100	Bethesda	MD	20817	**800-424-3691**	240-235-2100	48-11
YP Corp 4840 E Jasmine St Suite 105	Mesa	AZ	85205	**800-300-3209**	480-654-9646	623-6
YP.Com 4840 E Jasmine St Suite 105	Mesa	AZ	85205	**800-300-3209**	480-654-9646	677
YPA (Yellow Pages Assn) 820 Kirts Blvd Suite 100	Troy	MI	48084	**800-841-0639**	248-244-6200	49-16
YPO (Young Presidents' Organization) 451 S Decker Dr Suite 200	Irving	TX	75062	**800-773-7976**	972-650-4600	49-12
Ypsilanti Area Visitors & Convention Bureau 106 W Michigan Ave	Ypsilanti	MI	48197	**800-265-9045**	734-483-4444	205
Yrrid Software Inc 507 Monroe St	Chapel Hill	NC	27516	**800-443-0065**	919-968-7858	176-12
YSI Inc 1700-1725 Brannum Ln *Cust Svc	Yellow Springs	OH	45387	**800-765-4974***	937-767-7241	200
Yum! Brands Inc 1441 Gardiner Ln *NYSE: YUM*	Louisville	KY	40213	**800-225-5532**	502-874-8300	656
Yuma Convention & Visitors Bureau 377 S Main St Suite 102	Yuma	AZ	85364	**800-293-0071**	928-783-0071	205
Yuma Daily Sun 2055 Arizona Ave	Yuma	AZ	85364	**800-995-9862**	928-783-3333	522-2
Yurman David Designs Inc 729 Madison Ave	New York	NY	10021	**800-226-1400**	212-896-1550	401
YUSA Corp 151 Jamison Rd SW	Washington Court House	OH	43160	**800-395-0335**	740-335-0335	664
Yves Rocher Inc 50 Briarhollow Rd Suite 500-W	Houston	TX	77027	**800-222-6222**	713-626-2255	361
YWCA USA 1015 18th St NW Suite 1100	Washington	DC	20036	**800-992-2871**	202-467-0801	48-6

Z

Company / Address	City	State	Zip	Toll-Free	Phone	Class
Z-Axis Corp 5445 DTC Pkwy Suite 450	Greenwood Village	CO	80111	**800-827-2947**	303-713-0200	436

Company / Address	City	State	Zip	Toll-Free	Phone	Class
Z Cavaricci 5807 Smithway St	City of Commerce	CA	90040	**866-685-3267**		153-21
Z Gallerie Inc 1855 W 139th St	Gardena	CA	90249	**800-358-8288**	310-527-6811	357
Z-Tel Communications Inc 601 S Harbour Island Blvd Suite 220	Tampa	FL	33602	**800-511-4572**	813-273-6261	721
Z-World Inc 2900 Spafford St	Davis	CA	95616	**888-362-3387**	530-757-4616	613
Za Spa at Hotel Zaza 2332 Leonard St	Dallas	TX	75201	**800-597-8399**	214-550-9492	698
Zabar's & Co Inc 2245 Broadway	New York	NY	10024	**800-697-6301**	212-787-2000	333
Zachary Confections Inc 2130 W SR-28 *Cust Svc	Frankfort	IN	46041	**800-445-4222***	765-659-4751	291-8
Zachys Wine & Liquor Inc 16 East Pkwy	Scarsdale	NY	10583	**800-723-0241**	914-723-0241	435
Zack Electronics Inc 1070 Hamilton Rd	Duarte	CA	91010	**800-466-0449**	626-303-0655	245
Zacky Farms 13200 Crossroads Pkwy N Suite 250	City of Industry	CA	91746	**800-888-0235**	562-641-2020	292-10
Zaentz Saul Co 2600 10th St	Berkeley	CA	94710	**800-227-0466**	510-549-1528	501
Zagat Survey LLC 4 Columbus Cir 3rd Fl	New York	NY	10019	**800-333-3421**	212-977-6000	623-10
Zak Designs Inc 1603 S Garfield Rd	Spokane	WA	99201	**800-331-1089**	509-244-0555	356
Zale Corp 901 W Walnut Hill Ln *NYSE: ZLC* ■ *Cust Svc	Irving	TX	75038	**800-866-9700***	972-580-4000	402
Zale Corp Bailey Banks & Biddle Div 901 W Walnut Hill Ln *Cust Svc	Irving	TX	75038	**800-651-4222***	972-580-4000	402
Zale Corp Gordon's Jewelers Div 901 W Walnut Hill Ln *Cust Svc	Irving	TX	75038	**888-467-3661***	972-580-4000	402
Zale Corp Zales Jewelers Div 901 W Walnut Hill Ln *Cust Svc	Irving	TX	75038	**800-866-9700***	972-580-4000	402
Zales Jewelers Div Zale Corp 901 W Walnut Hill Ln *Cust Svc	Irving	TX	75038	**800-866-9700***	972-580-4000	402
Zambelli Internationale Fireworks Mfg 20 S Mercer St 2nd Fl	New Castle	PA	16101	**800-245-0397**	724-658-6611	264
Zane State College 1555 Newark Rd	Zanesville	OH	43701	**800-686-8324**	740-454-2501	787
Zaner-Bloser Inc PO Box 16764	Columbus	OH	43216	**800-421-3018**	614-486-0221	623-2
Zanesville-Muskingum County Convention & Visitors Bureau 205 N 5th St	Zanesville	OH	43701	**800-743-2303**	740-455-8282	205
Zantaz Inc 5671 Gibraltar Dr	Pleasanton	CA	94588	**800-636-0095**	925-598-3000	39
ZAP 501 4th St *Orders	Santa Rosa	CA	95401	**800-251-4555***	707-525-8658	759
Zappos.com 271 Omega Pkwy Suite 104	Shepherdsville	KY	40165	**888-492-7767**	502-543-7200	451
Zarlink Semiconductor Inc 400 March Rd *NYSE: ZL*	Ottawa	ON	K2K3H4	**800-325-4927**	613-592-0200	686
Zarn LLC 12700 General Dr	Charlotte	NC	28273	**800-227-5885**	704-588-9191	198
Zartic Inc 438 Lavender Dr *Cust Svc	Rome	GA	30165	**800-992-8172***	706-234-3000	291-26
Zaxby's Franchising Inc 1040 Sounder's Blvd	Athens	GA	30606	**866-892-9297**	706-353-8107	657
ZDial Inc PO Box 626	West Chester	PA	19380	**888-737-1001**	610-692-9205	390
Zebco Corp 6101 E Apache St	Tulsa	OK	74115	**800-588-9030**	918-836-5581	701
Zebra Books Kensington Publishing Corp 850 3rd Ave	New York	NY	10022	**800-221-2647**	212-407-1500	623-2
Zebra Technologies Corp 333 Corporate Woods Pkwy *NASDAQ: ZBRA*	Vernon Hills	IL	60061	**800-423-0422**	847-634-6700	171-6
Zee Medical Inc 22 Corporate Pk	Irvine	CA	92606	**800-841-8417**	949-252-9500	467
Zeeland Chemicals Inc 215 N Centennial St	Zeeland	MI	49464	**800-223-0453**	616-772-2193	470
Zeeman Mfg Co Inc 2303 John Glenn Dr	Chamblee	GA	30341	**800-732-2779**	770-451-5476	153-12
Zeigler Brothers Inc 400 Gardner Station Rd	Gardners	PA	17324	**800-841-6800**	717-677-6181	438
Zeigler MH & Sons Inc 1513 N Broad St	Lansdale	PA	19446	**800-854-6123**	215-855-5161	291-20
Zeigler RL Co Inc PO Box 1640	Tuscaloosa	AL	35403	**800-392-6328**	205-758-3621	465
Zeiss Carl Inc Industrial Measuring Technology Div 6250 Sycamore Ln N	Maple Grove	MN	55369	**800-752-6181**	763-744-2400	484
Zeiss Carl Optical Inc 13017 N Kingston Ave *Cust Svc	Chester	VA	23836	**800-338-2984***	804-530-8300	531
Zeks Compressed Air Solutions 1302 Goshen Pkwy	West Chester	PA	19380	**800-888-2323**	610-692-9100	170
Zellers Inc 8925 Torbram Rd *Cust Svc	Brampton	ON	L6T4G1	**888-226-2225***	905-792-4400	155-2
ZeniMax Media Inc 1370 Piccard Dr Suite 120	Rockville	MD	20850	**800-677-0700**	301-948-2200	176-6
Zenith Engraving Co PO Box 870	Chester	SC	29706	**800-551-7535**	803-377-1911	770
Zenith Insurance Co PO Box 9055	Van Nuys	CA	91409	**800-448-4356**	818-713-1000	384-4
Zenith National Insurance Corp 21255 Califa St *NYSE: ZNT*	Woodland Hills	CA	91367	**800-448-4356**	818-713-1000	355-4
Zenith Products Corp 400 Lukens Dr	New Castle	DE	19720	**800-892-3986**	302-326-8200	314-2
Zenithstar Insurance Co 1101 Capital of Texas Hwy S Bldg J	Austin	TX	78746	**800-841-3987**	512-306-1700	384-4
Zep Mfg Co 1310 Seaboard Industrial Blvd NW	Atlanta	GA	30318	**877-428-9937**	404-352-1680	149
Zepak Corp 26755 SW 95th Ave PO Box 789	Wilsonville	OR	97070	**800-248-7732**	503-682-1248	717
Zephyr Egg Co Inc 4622 Gall Blvd	Zephyrhills	FL	33542	**800-488-6543**	813-782-1521	11-8
Zephyr Mfg Co Inc 200 Mitchell Rd	Sedalia	MO	65301	**800-821-7197**	660-827-0352	104
Zephyrhills Natural Spring Water 777 W Putnam Ave	Greenwich	CT	06830	**800-950-9398**	203-531-4100	792
Zepto Metrix Corp 872 Main St *Cust Svc	Buffalo	NY	14202	**800-274-5487***	716-882-0920	229
Zerand Corp 15800 W Overland Dr	New Berlin	WI	53151	**800-889-9984**	262-827-3800	546
Zero Knowledge Systems Inc 375 President Kennedy	Montreal	QC	H3A2J5	**866-286-2636**	514-286-2636	176-9
Zero-Max Inc 13200 6th Ave N	Plymouth	MN	55441	**800-533-1731**	763-546-4300	609

Company / Address	City	State	Zip	Toll-Free	Phone	Class
Zero Mfg Inc 500 W 200 North	North Salt Lake	UT	84054	**800-545-1030**	801-298-5900	444
Zero's Subs 2859 Virginia Beach Blvd Suite 105	Virginia Beach	VA	23452	**800-588-0782**	757-486-8338	657
Zeta Phi Beta Sorority Inc 145 Kennedy St NW 2nd Fl	Washington	DC	20011	**800-368-5772**	202-387-3103	48-16
Zeta Psi Fraternity of North America 15 S Henry St	Pearl River	NY	10965	**800-477-1847**	845-735-1847	48-16
Zetec Inc 1370 NW Mall St	Issaquah	WA	98027	**800-643-1771**	425-392-5316	247
ZEVEX International Inc 4314 ZEVEX Pk Ln *NASDAQ: ZVXI*	Salt Lake City	UT	84123	**800-970-2337**	801-264-1001	469
Zhone Technologies Inc 7001 Oakport St *NASDAQ: ZHNE*	Oakland	CA	94621	**877-946-6320**	510-777-7000	720
Zia Natural Skincare 1337 Evans Ave	San Francisco	CA	94124	**800-334-7546**	415-642-8339	211
Zicka Walker Homes Inc 7861 E Kemper Rd	Cincinnati	OH	45249	**800-652-1745**	513-247-3500	639
Ziebart International Corp 1290 E Maple Rd	Troy	MI	48083	**800-877-1312**	248-588-4100	62-1
Zieger & Sons Inc 6215 Ardleigh St	Philadelphia	PA	19138	**800-752-2003**	215-438-7060	288
Ziff Davis Media Inc 28 E 28th St	New York	NY	10016	**800-336-2423**	212-503-3500	623-9
Ziglar Zig Ziglar Training Systems 15303 Dallas Pkwy Suite 550	Addison	TX	75001	**800-527-0306**	972-233-9191	561
ZiLOG Inc 532 Race St	San Jose	CA	95126	**800-662-6211**	408-558-8500	686
Zimmer Holdings Inc 1800 W Center St *NYSE: ZMH*	Warsaw	IN	46581	**800-613-6131**	574-267-6131	469
Zimmerman & Partners Advertising 2200 W Commercial Blvd Suite 300	Fort Lauderdale	FL	33309	**800-248-8522**	954-731-2900	4
Zimmerman Sign Co 1500 N Bolton St	Jacksonville	TX	75766	**800-888-1327**	903-589-2100	692
Zims Inc 4370 S 300 West *Orders	Salt Lake City	UT	84107	**800-453-6420***	801-268-2505	323
Zinc Corp of America 300 Frankfort Rd *Cust Svc	Monaca	PA	15061	**800-648-8897***	724-774-1020	141
Zink John Co LLC PO Box 21220	Tulsa	OK	74121	**800-421-9242**	918-234-1800	352
Zink Safety Equipment 15101 W 110th St	Lenexa	KS	66219	**800-255-1101**	913-492-9444	667
Zink & Triest Co Inc 150 Domorah Dr	Montgomeryville	PA	18936	**800-537-5070**	215-469-1950	291-15
Zionist Organization of America Inc. Hadassah Women's 50 W 58th St	New York	NY	10019	**888-303-3640**	212-355-7900	48-20
Zions Bancorp 1 S Main St Suite 1380 *NASDAQ: ZION*	Salt Lake City	UT	84111	**800-789-2265**	801-524-4787	355-2
Zippertubing Co 13000 S Broadway	Los Angeles	CA	90061	**800-321-8178**	310-527-0488	589
ZipRealty Inc 2000 Powell St Suite 1555 *NASDAQ: ZIPR*	Emeryville	CA	94608	**800-225-5947**	510-735-2600	638
Zix Corp 2711 N Haskell Rd Suite 2300 *NASDAQ: ZIXI*	Dallas	TX	75204	**888-771-4049**	214-370-2000	176-12
ZLand Inc PO Box 3469	Costa Mesa	CA	92628	**888-682-0911**		39
ZLB Behring LLC 1020 1st Ave	King of Prussia	PA	19406	**800-683-1288**	610-878-4000	572
ZNAT Insurance Co PO Box 9055	Van Nuys	CA	91409	**800-448-4356**	818-713-1000	384-4
Zodiac American Pools Inc 265 Industrial Blvd *Cust Svc	Midway	GA	31320	**800-338-1013***	912-880-7665	714
Zodiac Pool Care Inc 2028 NW 25th Ave	Pompano Beach	FL	33069	**800-937-7873**	954-935-8200	793
Zoeller Co 3649 Kane Run Rd	Louisville	KY	40211	**800-928-7867**	502-778-2731	627
Zolatone Div Surface Protection Industries Inc 3360 E Pico Blvd	Los Angeles	CA	90023	**800-372-6292**	323-269-9231	540
ZOLL Medical Corp 269 Mill Rd *NASDAQ: ZOLL*	Chelmsford	MA	01824	**800-348-9011**	978-421-9655	249
Zoltek Cos Inc 3101 McKelvey Rd *NASDAQ: ZOLT*	Bridgeton	MO	63044	**800-325-4409**	314-291-5110	127
Zondervan 5300 Patterson Ave SE *Cust Svc	Grand Rapids	MI	49530	**800-727-1309***	616-698-6900	623-4
Zones Inc 1102 15th St SW *NASDAQ: ZONS*	Auburn	WA	98001	**800-258-2088**	253-205-3000	172
Zoo Sauvage de Saint-Felicien 2230 boul du Jardin	Saint-Felicien	QC	G8K2P8	**800-667-5687**	418-679-0543	811
ZooAmerica North American Wildlife Park 100 W Hersheypark Dr	Hershey	PA	17033	**800-437-7439**	717-534-3860	811
Zoom Seating 1644 Crystal Ave	Kansas City	MO	64126	**866-839-9666**		314-1
Zoom Technologies Inc 207 South St *NASDAQ: ZOOM*	Boston	MA	02111	**800-666-6191**	617-423-1072	496
Zortec International 124 12th Ave S Suite 210	Nashville	TN	37203	**800-361-7005**	615-361-7000	176-2
Zotos International Inc 100 Tokeneke Rd	Darien	CT	06820	**800-242-9283**	203-655-8911	211
Zuckerman-Honickman Inc 191 S Gulph Rd	King of Prussia	PA	19406	**800-523-1475**	610-962-0100	378
Zuken USA 238 Littleton Rd Suite 100	Westford	MA	01886	**800-447-7332**	978-692-4900	176-5
Zumar Industries Inc PO Box 2883	Santa Fe Springs	CA	90670	**800-654-7446**	562-941-4633	692
Zumiez Inc 6300 Merrill Creek Pkwy Suite B *NASDAQ: ZUMZ*	Everett	WA	98203	**877-828-6929**	425-551-1500	155-2
Zurich North America 1400 American Ln	Schaumburg	IL	60196	**800-382-2150**		384-5
Zurn Cast Metals Operation 1301 Raspberry St	Erie	PA	16502	**877-875-1404**	814-455-0921	302
Zwaanendael Inn 142 2nd St	Lewes	DE	19958	**800-824-8754**	302-645-6466	373
Zygo Corp Laurel Brook Rd *NASDAQ: ZIGO*	Middlefield	CT	06455	**800-994-6669**	860-347-8506	534
ZyLAB North America LLC 600 17th St Suite 2800 S	Denver	CO	80202	**866-995-2262**		176-1
Zyliss USA Corp 19751 Descartes	Foothill Ranch	CA	92610	**888-794-7623**	949-699-1884	477
Zymed Laboratories Inc 561 Eccles Ave	South San Francisco	CA	94080	**800-874-4494**	650-871-4494	229
ZymeTx Inc 655 Research Pkwy Suite 554	Oklahoma City	OK	73104	**888-817-1314**	405-809-1314	86
ZymoGenetics Inc 1201 Eastlake Ave E *NASDAQ: ZGEN*	Seattle	WA	98102	**800-775-6686**	206-442-6600	86
Zyng Inc 4710 rue St Ambroise Suite 320	Montreal	QC	H4C2C7	**888-966-6353**	514-288-8800	657
ZyQuest Inc 1580 Mid-Valley Dr	De Pere	WI	54115	**800-992-0533**	920-617-7615	178
ZyXEL Communications Inc 1130 N Miller St	Anaheim	CA	92806	**800-255-4101**	714-632-0882	496
zZounds Music 65 Greenwood Ave	Midland Park	NJ	07432	**800-996-8637**		515
Zzyzx Peripherals Inc 5550 Morehouse Dr	San Diego	CA	92121	**800-876-7818**	858-558-7800	174

Classified Section

Listings in the Classified Section are organized alphabetically under subject headings denoting a business or organization type. These headings are fully outlined in the Index to Classified Headings located at the back of this book. "See" and "See Also" references are included in this section to help locate appropriate subject categories. Alphabetizing is on a word-by-word rather than letter-by-letter basis. For a detailed explanation of the scope and arrangement of listings in ***Toll-Free Phone Book USA***, please refer to "How To Use This Directory" at the beginning of this book. An explanation of individual page elements is also provided under the "Sample Entry" on the back inside cover of the book.

1 ABRASIVE PRODUCTS

Company	City	State	Zip	Toll-Free	Phone
3M Abrasive Systems Div 3M Center Bldg 223-6N-01	Saint Paul	MN	55144	**800-742-9546**	651-737-6501
3M Manufacturing & Industry Solutions 3M Ctr	Saint Paul	MN	55144	**888-364-3577**	651-733-1110
Boride Products Inc 2879 Aero Park Dr	Traverse City	MI	49686	**800-662-2131**	231-946-2100
Bullard Abrasives Inc 50 Hopkinton Rd	Westborough	MA	01581	**800-227-4469**	508-366-4465
Camel Grinding Wheels 7525 N Oak Park Ave	Niles	IL	60714	**800-760-6987**	847-647-5994
CITCO Operations 357 Washington St	Chardon	OH	44024	**800-242-7366**	440-285-9181
Comco Inc 2151 N Lincoln St	Burbank	CA	91504	**800-796-6626**	818-841-5500
Composition Materials Co Inc 125 Old Gate Ln	Milford	CT	06460	**800-262-7763**	203-874-6500
Diagrind Inc 10491 W 164th Pl	Orland Park	IL	60467	**800-790-4333**	708-460-4333
Diamond Innovations 6325 Huntley Rd *Cust Svc	Worthington	OH	43085	**800-443-1455***	614-438-2000
Ervin Industries Inc 3893 Research Pk Dr	Ann Arbor	MI	48108	**800-748-0055**	734-769-4600
Formax Mfg Corp 168 Wealthy St SW	Grand Rapids	MI	49503	**800-242-2833**	616-456-5458
Gemtex 60 Belfield Rd	Toronto	ON	M9W1G1	**800-387-5100**	416-245-5605
Glit/Microtron 809 Broad St	Wrens	GA	30833	**800-431-2976**	706-547-6555
JacksonLea PO Box 699	Conover	NC	28613	**800-438-6880**	828-464-1376
Klingspor Abrasives Inc 2555 Tate Blvd SE	Hickory	NC	28602	**800-645-5555**	828-322-3030
Marvel Abrasive Products Inc 6230 S Oak Park Ave	Chicago	IL	60638	**800-621-0673**	773-586-8700
Merit Abrasive Products Inc 7301 Orangewood Ave PO Box 3195	Garden Grove	CA	92842	**800-421-1936**	714-677-1144
Moyco Technologies Inc 200 Commerce Dr	Montgomeryville	PA	18936	**800-331-8837**	215-855-4300
National Metal Abrasive Inc PO Box 150	Wadsworth	OH	44282	**800-837-8505**	330-334-1566
Norton Co 1 New Bond St	Worcester	MA	01606	**800-543-4335**	508-795-5000
Pacific Grinding Wheel Co 13120 State Ave	Marysville	WA	98271	**800-688-9328**	360-659-6201
Radiac Abrasives Inc 1015 S College Ave	Salem	IL	62881	**800-851-1095**	618-548-4200
Raytech Industries 475 Smith St *Cust Svc	Middletown	CT	06457	**800-225-9626***	860-632-2020
Sancap Abrasives 16123 Armour St NE	Alliance	OH	44601	**800-433-6663**	330-821-3510
Sandusky-Chicago Abrasive Wheel Co 1100 W Barker Ave	Michigan City	IN	46360	**800-843-4980**	219-879-6601
Schaffner Mfg Co Inc 21 Herron Ave Schaffner Ctr	Pittsburgh	PA	15202	**800-292-9903**	412-761-9902
Spedecut Abrasives 10042 Rancho Rd	Adelanto	CA	92301	**800-423-4836**	760-246-6850
Standard Abrasives Inc 4201 Guardian St	Simi Valley	CA	93063	**800-423-5444**	805-520-5800
Universal SuperAbrasives 84 O'Leary Dr	Bensenville	IL	60106	**800-323-6676**	630-238-3300
VSM Abrasives 1012 E Wabash St	O'Fallon	MO	63366	**800-737-0176**	636-272-7432

2 ACCOUNTING FIRMS

Company	City	State	Zip	Toll-Free	Phone
Beard Miller Co LLP 2609 Keiser Blvd PO Box 311	Reading	PA	19603	**800-267-9405**	610-376-2833
Blue & Co LLC 12800 N Meridian St Suite 400	Carmel	IN	46032	**800-717-2583**	317-848-8920
Cherry Bekaert & Holland LLP 1700 Bayberry Ct Suite 300	Richmond	VA	23226	**800-849-8281**	804-673-4224
Clifton Gunderson LLC 301 SW Adams St Suite 900	Peoria	IL	61656	**800-450-4565**	309-671-4500
Cohen & Co CPA 1350 Euclid Ave Suite 800	Cleveland	OH	44115	**800-229-1099**	216-579-1040
Cohn JH LLP 75 Eisenhower Pkwy 2nd Fl	Roseland	NJ	07068	**800-879-2571**	973-228-3500
Crowe Chizek & Co LLP 330 E Jefferson Blvd PO Box 7	South Bend	IN	46624	**800-276-9301**	574-232-3992
Decosimo Joseph & Co CPA 2 Union Sq Tallan Bldg Suite 1100	Chattanooga	TN	37402	**800-782-8382**	423-756-7100
Elliott Davis & Co 200 E Broad St PO Box 6286	Greenville	SC	29606	**800-503-4721**	864-242-3370
Fiducial Inc 450 Park Ave 15th Fl	New York	NY	10022	**800-283-1040**	212-207-4700
Goodman & Co LLP 1 Commercial Pl Suite 800	Norfolk	VA	23510	**888-899-5100**	757-624-5100
Honkamp Krueger Financial Services 2355 JFK Rd	Dubuque	IA	52002	**800-791-8994**	563-582-2855
Jefferson Wells International 200 S Executive Dr Suite 440	Brookfield	WI	53005	**800-826-5099**	262-957-3400
JH Cohn LLP 75 Eisenhower Pkwy 2nd Fl	Roseland	NJ	07068	**800-879-2571**	973-228-3500
Joseph Decosimo & Co CPA 2 Union Sq Tallan Bldg Suite 1100	Chattanooga	TN	37402	**800-782-8382**	423-756-7100
Larson Allen Weishair & Co LLP 220 S 6th St Suite 300	Minneapolis	MN	55402	**888-335-6080**	612-376-4500
Marcum & Kliegman LLP 130 Crossways Park Dr	Woodbury	NY	11797	**800-921-0777**	516-921-6000
Moss Adams LLP 1001 4th Ave 31st Fl	Seattle	WA	98154	**800-243-4936**	206-223-1820
Olsen Thielen & Co Ltd 223 Little Canada Rd	Saint Paul	MN	55117	**800-866-4521**	651-483-4521
Padgett Business Services Inc 160 Hawthorne Park	Athens	GA	30606	**800-723-4388**	706-548-1040
Plante & Moran LLP 27400 Northwestern Hwy	Southfield	MI	48034	**800-827-1280**	248-352-2500
PRG-Schultz International Inc 600 Galleria Pkwy Suite 100 *NASDAQ: PRGX*	Atlanta	GA	30339	**800-752-5894**	770-779-3900
RSM McGladrey Inc 3600 American Blvd W 3rd Fl	Bloomington	MN	55431	**800-274-3978**	952-835-9930
Schenck Business Solutions 200 E Washington St	Appleton	WI	54911	**800-236-2246**	920-731-8111
Suby Von Haden & Assoc SC 1221 John Q Hammons Dr PO Box 44966	Madison	WI	53744	**800-279-2616**	608-831-8181
Tofias Fleishman Shapiro & Co PC 350 Massachusetts Ave	Cambridge	MA	02139	**888-761-8835**	617-761-0600
Virchow Krause & Co LLP 10 Terrace Ct	Madison	WI	53718	**800-362-7301**	608-249-6622
Weaver & Tidwell LLP 1600 W 7th St Suite 300	Fort Worth	TX	76102	**800-332-7952**	817-332-7905
Yeo & Yeo CPA 3023 Davenport Ave	Saginaw	MI	48602	**800-968-0110**	989-793-9830

3 ADHESIVES & SEALANTS

Company	City	State	Zip	Toll-Free	Phone
3M Automotive Aftermarket Div 3M Center Bldg 223-6N-01	Saint Paul	MN	55144	**800-364-3577**	
3M Canada Co PO Box 5757	London	ON	N6A4T1	**800-265-1840**	519-451-2500
3M Manufacturing & Industry Solutions 3M Ctr	Saint Paul	MN	55144	**888-364-3577**	651-733-1110
3M Transportation Div 3M Ctr	Saint Paul	MN	55144	**888-364-3577**	651-733-1110
Adhesives Research Inc 400 Seaks Run Rd	Glen Rock	PA	17327	**800-445-6240**	717-235-7979
Arlon Adhesives & Films 2811 S Harbor Blvd	Santa Ana	CA	92704	**800-854-0361**	714-540-2811
Atlas Minerals & Chemicals Inc 1227 Valley Rd *Cust Svc	Mertztown	PA	19539	**800-523-8269***	610-682-7171
Avery Dennison Corp 150 N Orange Grove Blvd *NYSE: AVY* ■ *Cust Svc	Pasadena	CA	91103	**800-252-8379***	626-304-2000
Bondo Corp 3700 Atlanta Industrial Pkwy NW	Atlanta	GA	30331	**800-622-8754**	404-696-2730
Bostik Inc 11320 Watertown Plank Rd	Wauwatosa	WI	53226	**800-558-4302**	414-774-2250
Brady Coated Products 6555 W Good Hope Rd	Milwaukee	WI	53223	**800-635-7557**	414-358-6600
CFC International Inc 500 State St *NASDAQ: CFCI*	Chicago Heights	IL	60411	**800-323-3399**	708-891-3456
Childers Products Co 1370 E 40th St	Houston	TX	77022	**800-231-1024**	713-691-7002
Colloid Environmental Technologies Co (CETCO) 1500 W Shure Dr	Arlington Heights	IL	60004	**800-527-9948**	847-392-5800
Custom Building Products 13001 Seal Beach Blvd	Seal Beach	CA	90740	**800-272-8786**	562-598-8808
DAP Inc 2400 Boston St Suite 200 *Cust Svc	Baltimore	MD	21224	**800-584-3840***	410-675-2100
Darex 62 Whittemore Ave	Cambridge	MA	02140	**800-232-6100**	617-498-4571
Degussa Building Systems 889 Valley Park Dr *Cust Svc	Shakopee	MN	55379	**800-433-9517***	952-496-6000
Devcon Inc 30 Endicott St	Danvers	MA	01923	**800-626-7226**	978-777-1100
Dynea USA Inc 1600 Valley River Dr Suite 390	Eugene	OR	97401	**800-862-1332**	541-687-8840
Eclectic Products Inc 1075 Arrowsmith St 2nd Fl Suite B	Eugene	OR	97402	**800-693-4667**	541-284-4667
EFTEC North America LLC 31601 Research Park Dr	Madison Heights	MI	48071	**800-633-7789**	248-585-2200
Euclid Chemical Co 19218 Redwood Rd	Cleveland	OH	44110	**800-321-7628**	216-531-9222
FiberCast Inc 25 S Main St	Sand Springs	OK	74063	**800-331-4406**	918-245-6651
Foster Products Corp 601 Campus Dr Suite C-7	Arlington Heights	IL	60004	**800-231-9541**	847-358-9500
Fox Industries Inc 3100 Falls Cliff Rd	Baltimore	MD	21211	**888-760-0369**	410-243-8856
Franklin International 2020 Bruck St	Columbus	OH	43207	**800-877-4583**	614-443-0241
Geocel Corp PO Box 398	Elkhart	IN	46515	**800-348-7615**	574-264-0645
HB Fuller Co 1200 Willow Lake Blvd PO Box 64683 *NYSE: FUL*	Saint Paul	MN	55164	**800-828-2981**	651-236-5900
Henkel Surface Technologies 32100 Stephenson Hwy	Madison Heights	MI	48071	**800-521-6895**	248-583-9300
Hercules Chemical Co Inc 111 South St	Passaic	NJ	07055	**800-221-9330**	973-778-5000
Houghton International Inc 950 Madison St PO Box 930	Valley Forge	PA	19482	**888-459-9844**	610-666-4000
Illinois Tool Works Inc TACC Div 56 Air Station Industrial Pk	Rockland	MA	02370	**800-503-6991**	781-878-7015
Industrial Adhesives Inc 4244 W 6th Ave	Eugene	OR	97402	**800-451-2580**	541-683-6677
IPS Corp 455 W Victoria St	Compton	CA	90220	**800-421-2677**	310-898-3300
ITW Insulcast Inc 565 Eagle Rock Ave	Roseland	NJ	07068	**800-631-7841**	973-403-0261
Key Polymer Corp 17 Shepherd St	Lawrence	MA	01843	**888-539-7659**	978-683-9411
Kindt-Collins Co 12651 Elmwood Ave	Cleveland	OH	44111	**800-321-3170**	216-252-4122
Laticrete International Inc 91 Amity Rd	Bethany	CT	06524	**800-243-4788**	203-393-0010
Loctite Corp 1001 Trout Brook Crossing	Rocky Hill	CT	06067	**800-842-0041**	860-571-5100
Loctite Corp North American Group 1001 Trout Brook Crossing *Cust Svc	Rocky Hill	CT	06067	**800-243-4874***	860-571-5100
Lord Corp 111 Lord Dr	Cary	NC	27511	**800-524-2885**	919-468-5979
M-D Building Products Inc 4041 N Santa Fe Ave *Cust Svc	Oklahoma City	OK	73118	**800-654-8454***	405-528-4411
MACCO Adhesives 925 Euclid Ave Suite 900	Cleveland	OH	44115	**800-634-0015**	216-344-7304

Company	City	State	Zip	Toll-Free	Phone
MACtac 4560 Darrow Rd	Stow	OH	44224	**800-762-2822**	330-688-1111
MAPEI Corp 1851 NW 22nd St	Fort Lauderdale	FL	33311	**800-426-2734**	954-485-8575
Metalcrete Industries Inc 10330 Brecksville Rd	Cleveland	OH	44141	**800-526-5602**	440-526-5600
Morgan Adhesives Co DBA MACtac 4560 Darrow Rd	Stow	OH	44224	**800-762-2822**	330-688-1111
National Starch & Chemical Co 10 Finderne Ave	Bridgewater	NJ	08807	**800-797-4992**	908-685-5000
Norton & Son Inc 148 E 5th St	Bayonne	NJ	07002	**800-631-3440**	201-437-0770
Nylok Corp 15260 Hallmark Dr	Macomb	MI	48042	**800-826-5161**	586-786-0100
Ohio Sealants Inc 7405 Production Dr	Mentor	OH	44060	**800-321-3578**	440-255-8900
Pacer Technology 9420 Santa Anita Ave	Rancho Cucamonga	CA	91730	**800-538-3091**	909-987-0550
Para-Chem Southern Inc PO Box 127	Simpsonville	SC	29681	**800-763-7272**	864-967-7691
Pecora Corp 165 Wambold Rd	Harleysville	PA	19438	**800-523-6688**	215-723-6051
Red Devil Inc 2400 Vauxhall Rd	Union	NJ	07083	**800-423-3845**	908-688-6900
Sika Corp 201 Polito Ave	Lyndhurst	NJ	07071	**800-933-7452**	201-933-8800
Sovereign Packaging Group PO Box 1092	Buffalo	NY	14240	**800-888-4910**	716-856-4910
Sovereign Specialty Chemicals 6315 Wiehe Rd	Cincinnati	OH	45237	**800-365-1301**	513-351-1300
Synkoloid Co 148 E 5th St	Bayonne	NJ	07002	**800-631-3440**	201-437-0770
TACC Div Illinois Tool Works Inc 56 Air Station Industrial Pk	Rockland	MA	02370	**800-503-6991**	781-878-7015
TEC Specialty Products Inc 315 S Hicks Rd *Cust Svc	Palatine	IL	60067	**800-832-9002***	847-358-9500
Tremco Inc Roofing Div 3735 Green Rd	Beachwood	OH	44122	**800-852-6013**	216-292-5000
Uniseal Inc PO Box 6288	Evansville	IN	47719	**800-443-6297**	812-425-1361
Worthen Industries Inc 3 E Spit Brook Rd	Nashua	NH	03060	**800-967-8436**	603-888-5443

4 ADVERTISING AGENCIES

SEE ALSO Public Relations Firms

Company	City	State	Zip	Toll-Free	Phone
4WARD Intellect Inc 550 Alden Rd Suite 107	Markham	ON	L3R6A8	**866-892-6297**	905-513-7360
AMPM Inc 1380 E Wackerly Rd	Midland	MI	48642	**800-530-9100**	989-837-8800
Arnold Worldwide 101 Huntington Ave	Boston	MA	02199	**800-782-4893**	617-587-8000
Bernard Hodes Group 220 E 42 St	New York	NY	10017	**888-438-9911**	212-999-9000
Bernstein-Rein 4600 Madison Ave Suite 1500	Kansas City	MO	64112	**800-571-6246**	816-756-0640
CoActive Marketing Group Inc 415 Northern Blvd *NASDAQ: CMKG*	Great Neck	NY	11021	**800-680-9998**	516-465-4600
Cole & Weber/Red Cell 308 Occidental Ave S	Seattle	WA	98104	**800-262-8515**	206-447-9595
Cranford Johnson Robinson Woods 303 W Capitol Ave	Little Rock	AR	72201	**888-383-2579**	501-975-6251
Creative Alliance Inc 437 W Jefferson St	Louisville	KY	40202	**800-525-0294**	502-584-8787
Davis Elen Advertising 865 S Figueroa St 12th Fl	Los Angeles	CA	90017	**800-729-4322**	213-688-7000
DDB Worldwide 437 Madison Ave	New York	NY	10022	**800-332-3336**	212-415-2000
Desktop Imagery 2733 Concession Rd 7	Bowmanville	ON	L1C3K6	**800-579-9253**	905-263-2666
Deutsch Inc 111 8th Ave 14th Fl	New York	NY	10011	**800-287-3457**	212-981-7600
DraftWorldwide 633 N Saint Clair St	Chicago	IL	60611	**800-288-8755**	312-944-3500
DVC 44 Whippany Rd	Morristown	NJ	07960	**800-526-8712**	973-775-6700
Euro RSCG Worldwide 350 Hudson St 6th Fl	New York	NY	10014	**800-263-7590**	212-886-2000
Fahlgren Inc 414 Walnut St Suite 1006	Cincinnati	OH	45202	**800-543-2663**	513-241-9200
Fallon 50 S 6th St Suite 2500	Minneapolis	MN	55402	**888-321-2345**	612-321-2345
Foth Ron Advertising 8100 N High St	Columbus	OH	43235	**888-766-3684**	614-888-7771
Greer Margolis Mitchell Burns & Assoc 1010 Wisconsin Ave NW Suite 800	Washington	DC	20007	**800-283-7606**	202-338-8700
Hal Lewis Group 1700 Market St 6th Fl	Philadelphia	PA	19103	**888-778-6115**	215-563-4461
HMS Partners 250 Civic Ctr Dr Suite 440	Columbus	OH	43215	**866-415-1010**	614-222-2548
HSR Business to Business 300 E-Business Way Suite 500	Cincinnati	OH	45241	**800-243-2648**	513-671-3811
JWT Specialized Communications 5200 W Century Blvd Suite 310	Los Angeles	CA	90045	**800-676-7080**	310-665-8700
Keller Crescent Co Inc 1100 E Louisiana St	Evansville	IN	47711	**800-457-3837**	812-464-2461
Liggett-Stashower Inc 1228 Euclid Ave 2nd Fl	Cleveland	OH	44115	**800-877-4573**	216-348-8500
Lyons Lavey Nickel & Swift Inc 220 E 42nd St 3rd Fl	New York	NY	10017	**800-599-0188**	212-771-3000
Mars Advertising Co Inc 2377 Southfield Rd	Southfield	MI	48075	**800-521-9317**	248-936-2200
Martin-Williams Advertising 60 S 6th St Suite 2800	Minneapolis	MN	55402	**800-632-1388**	612-340-0800
Moroch Partners 3625 N Hall St Suite 1100	Dallas	TX	75219	**800-916-4327**	214-520-9700
Mullen 36 Essex St	Wenham	MA	01984	**800-363-6010**	978-468-1155
NAS Recruitment Communications 1 Infinity Corporate Ctr Dr	Cleveland	OH	44125	**866-627-7327**	216-478-0300
Periscope 921 Washington Ave S	Minneapolis	MN	55415	**800-339-2103**	612-339-2100
Resource Interactive 343 N Front St	Columbus	OH	43215	**800-550-5815**	
Risdall Advertising Agency 550 Main St	New Brighton	MN	55112	**888-747-3255**	651-631-1098
Ron Foth Advertising 8100 N High St	Columbus	OH	43235	**888-766-3684**	614-888-7771
Saint John & Partners Advertising & Public Relations 5220 Belfort Rd Suite 400	Jacksonville	FL	32256	**800-642-2828**	904-281-2500
Sawtooth Group 100 Woodbridge Ctr Dr Suite 102	Woodbridge	NJ	07095	**800-636-6365**	732-636-6600
Shaker Recruitment Advertising & Communications 1100 Lake St	Oak Park	IL	60301	**800-323-5170**	708-383-5320
SpiralWest Inc 325 Pine St	Sausalito	CA	94965	**888-774-7259**	415-332-6797
TBWA Chiat/Day Inc 488 Madison Ave 7th Fl	New York	NY	10022	**877-666-2347**	212-804-1000
Ten United Pittsburgh 420 Fort Duquesne Blvd Suite 1900 1Gateway Ctr	Pittsburgh	PA	15222	**800-937-3657**	412-471-5300
Trone Advertising 4035 Piedmont Pkwy	High Point	NC	27265	**877-493-3043**	336-886-1622
UniWorld Group Inc 100 Ave of the Americas 15th Fl	New York	NY	10013	**800-900-2958**	212-219-1600
VML 250 Richards Rd	Kansas City	MO	64116	**800-990-2468**	816-283-0700
Vox Medica Inc 210 W Washington Sq	Philadelphia	PA	19106	**800-842-6482**	215-238-8500
Zimmerman & Partners Advertising 2200 W Commercial Blvd Suite 300	Fort Lauderdale	FL	33309	**800-248-8522**	954-731-2900

ADVERTISING DISPLAYS

SEE Displays - Exhibit & Trade Show; Displays - Point-of-Purchase; Signs

5 ADVERTISING SERVICES - DIRECT MAIL

Company	City	State	Zip	Toll-Free	Phone
Accurate Mailings Inc 215 O'Neill Ave	Belmont	CA	94002	**800-732-3290**	650-591-5601
Advanced Technology Marketing 6053 W Century Blvd Suite 200	Los Angeles	CA	90045	**800-624-4303**	310-642-1881
ADVO Inc 1 Targeting Ctr *NYSE: AD*	Windsor	CT	06095	**800-238-6462**	860-285-6100
American Student List LLC 330 Old Country Rd	Mineola	NY	11501	**888-462-5600**	516-248-6100
Americomm Direct Marketing 1065 Bristol Rd	Mountainside	NJ	07092	**888-737-5478**	908-232-3800
CadmusCom 1801 Bayberry Ct Suite 200	Richmond	VA	23226	**800-476-2973**	804-287-5680
Centron Data Services Co 1175 Devin Dr *Cust Svc	Norton Shores	MI	49441	**800-732-8787***	231-798-1221
ChoicePoint Precision Marketing 8600 N Industrial Rd	Peoria	IL	61615	**800-786-6880**	309-689-1000
Classic Letter Co 2850 S Jefferson Ave	Saint Louis	MO	63118	**877-551-5596**	314-664-0023
ClientLogic Corp 3102 W End Ave Suite 900	Nashville	TN	37203	**877-935-6442**	615-301-7100
Corporate Express Promotional Marketing 1400 N Price Rd	Saint Louis	MO	63132	**800-325-1965**	314-432-1800
Creative Automation Co 220 Fencl Ln	Hillside	IL	60162	**800-773-1588**	708-449-2800
DMW Worldwide 1325 Morris Dr	Wayne	PA	19087	**877-744-3699**	610-407-0407
Donnelley Marketing 5711 S 86th Cir	Omaha	NE	68127	**888-508-0866**	402-593-4500
EBSCO Industries Inc Publisher Promotion & Fulfillment Div 5724 Hwy 280 E	Birmingham	AL	35242	**800-633-4931**	205-991-1177
Focus Direct Inc 9707 Broadway	San Antonio	TX	78217	**800-299-9185**	210-805-9185
GA Wright Inc Direct Marketing Div 4105 Holly St	Denver	CO	80216	**800-824-5886**	303-333-4453
Haines & Co Inc 8050 Freedom Ave NW	North Canton	OH	44720	**800-843-8452**	330-494-9111
Harte-Hanks Inc PO Box 269 *NYSE: HHS*	San Antonio	TX	78291	**800-456-9748**	210-829-9000
Hecks Direct Mail & Printing Service Inc 202 W Florence Ave	Toledo	OH	43605	**800-997-4325**	419-661-6000
Heritage Publishing Co 2402 Wildwood Ave	Sherwood	AR	72120	**800-643-8822**	501-835-5000
Hibbert Group 21 Muirhead Ave	Trenton	NJ	08638	**888-442-2378**	609-394-7500
Johnson & Quin Inc 7460 N Lehigh Ave	Niles	IL	60714	**800-272-3770**	847-588-4800
JS & A Group Inc 3350 Palms Centre Dr	Las Vegas	NV	89103	**800-323-6400**	702-798-9000
Leifer Group 9393 W 110th St Suite 500	Overland Park	KS	66210	**877-676-9200**	913-385-9200
Lewis Systems Inc 325 E Oliver St	Baltimore	MD	21202	**800-533-5394**	410-539-5100
Lortz Direct Marketing Inc 13936 Gold Cir	Omaha	NE	68144	**800-366-7686**	402-334-9446
Market Data Retrieval 1 Forest Pkwy	Shelton	CT	06484	**800-333-8802**	203-926-4800
Money Mailer Inc 14271 Corporate Dr	Garden Grove	CA	92843	**800-234-2771**	714-265-4100
Moore Wallace Response Marketing Services 1200 S Lakeside Dr	Bannockburn	IL	60015	**800-745-0780**	847-607-6000
MWA Direct Inc 8600 109th Ave N Suite 100	Champlin	MN	55316	**800-967-9154**	763-576-4111
Newgen Results Corp 10243 Genetic Center Dr	San Diego	CA	92121	**800-763-9436**	858-346-5000
News America Marketing 1211 Ave of the Americas 5th Fl	New York	NY	10036	**800-462-0852**	212-782-8000
Odell Simms & Assoc 7704 Leesburg Pike	Falls Church	VA	22043	**800-662-7400**	703-903-9797
Priority Publications 6700 France Ave S Suite 200	Edina	MN	55435	**800-727-6397**	952-920-9928
Proven Direct W165 N5761 Ridgewood Dr	Menomonee Falls	WI	53051	**866-890-6245**	262-703-0760
RDI Marketing Services 9920 Carver Rd	Cincinnati	OH	45242	**800-388-7636**	513-984-5927
RR Donnelley Logistics 7501 S Quincy St	Willowbrook	IL	60527	**800-800-7447**	
SmartDM Inc 822 Airpark Ctr Dr	Nashville	TN	37217	**888-816-0925**	615-850-3000
Summit R & D Group 8515 Blue Jacket	Lenexa	KS	66214	**800-843-7347**	913-888-6222
Super Coups Inc 350 Revolutionary Dr	East Taunton	MA	02718	**800-626-2620**	508-977-2000
Tension Envelope Corp 819 E 19th St	Kansas City	MO	64108	**800-388-5122**	816-471-3800
United Marketing Solutions 7644 Dynatech Ct	Springfield	VA	22153	**800-368-3501**	703-644-0200
USA Direct Inc 2901 Blackbridge Rd	York	PA	17402	**800-441-1850**	717-852-1000
Val-Pak Direct Marketing System Inc 8605 Largo Lakes Dr	Largo	FL	33773	**800-237-6266**	727-393-1270
WA Wilde Co 201 Summer St	Holliston	MA	01746	**800-933-9453**	508-429-5515
Wilde WA Co 201 Summer St	Holliston	MA	01746	**800-933-9453**	508-429-5515
Wright GA Inc Direct Marketing Div 4105 Holly St	Denver	CO	80216	**800-824-5886**	303-333-4453
Yeck Brothers Co 2222 Arbor Blvd	Dayton	OH	45439	**800-417-2767**	937-294-4000

6 ADVERTISING SERVICES - MEDIA BUYERS

Company	City	State	Zip	Toll-Free	Phone
Berry Co 3170 Kettering Blvd	Dayton	OH	45401	**800-366-2379**	937-296-2121
Carat USA 2450 Colorado Ave Suite 300 E	Santa Monica	CA	90404	**800-847-6334**	310-255-1000
EBSCO Industries Inc Publisher Promotion & Fulfillment Div 5724 Hwy 280 E	Birmingham	AL	35242	**800-633-4931**	205-991-1177
Horizon Media Inc 630 3rd Ave 3rd Fl	New York	NY	10017	**800-633-4201**	212-916-8600
Media Networks Inc 1 Station Pl 5th Fl	Stamford	CT	06902	**800-225-3457**	203-967-3100
Winstar Interactive Media 100 Park Ave 6th Fl *Cust Svc	New York	NY	10017	**888-961-8800***	212-896-8310
Working Mother Media Inc 60 E 42nd St 27th	New York	NY	10165	**800-627-0690**	212-351-6400
Worldata 3000 N Military Trail	Boca Raton	FL	33431	**800-331-8102**	561-393-8200

7 ADVERTISING SERVICES - ONLINE

Company	City	State	Zip	Toll-Free	Phone
24/7 Real Media Inc 132 W 31st St 9th Fl *NASDAQ: TFSM*	New York	NY	10001	**877-247-2477**	212-231-7100

Company / Address	City	State	ZIP	Toll-Free	Phone
Active Decisions Inc 1400 Fashion Island Blvd Suite 500	San Mateo	CA	94404	**866-662-3847**	650-342-0500
Active Network 1020 Prospect St Suite 250	La Jolla	CA	92037	**888-543-7223***	858-551-9916
*Cust Svc					
Big Bad Inc 321 Summer St	Boston	MA	02210	**877-296-4287**	617-338-7770
Blattner Brunner Inc 11 Stanwix St 5th Fl	Pittsburgh	PA	15222	**800-545-5372**	412-995-9500
Blue Cat Design 4753 Mast Woods Rd	Port Hope	ON	L1A3V5	**888-258-8228**	905-753-1017
Commission Junction Inc 530 E Montecito St	Santa Barbara	CA	93103	**800-761-1072**	805-730-8000
CoolSavings Inc 360 N Michigan Ave Suite 1900	Chicago	IL	60601	**888-426-6654**	312-224-5000
E-centives Inc 6901 Rockledge Dr 6th Fl	Bethesda	MD	20817	**877-323-6848**	240-333-6100
Enhance Interactive Inc 360 West 4800 N	Provo	UT	84604	**800-840-1012**	801-705-7125
GSI Commerce Inc 935 1st Ave	King of Prussia	PA	19406	**877-708-4305**	610-265-3229
NASDAQ: GSIC					
HouseValues Inc 15 Lake Bellevue Dr Suite 100	Bellevue	WA	98005	**877-450-0088**	425-454-0088
NASDAQ: SOLD					
IconMedialab Inc 22 4th St 9th Fl	San Francisco	CA	94103	**866-426-6871**	415-278-0471
iProspect.com Inc 311 Arsenal St	Watertown	MA	02472	**800-522-1152**	617-923-7000
LinkShare Corp 215 Park Ave S 8th Fl	New York	NY	10003	**800-875-5645**	646-654-6000
LSF Network Inc 395 Oyster Pt Blvd Suite 110	South San Francisco	CA	94080	**877-616-8226**	
MyPoints.com Inc 188 The Embarcadero 5th Fl	San Francisco	CA	94105	**888-262-4528**	415-615-1100
ValueClick Inc 4353 Park Terrace Dr	Westlake Village	CA	91361	**877-825-8323**	818-575-4500
NASDAQ: VCLK					
Worldsites Inc 5915 Airport Rd Suite 300	Toronto	ON	L4V1T1	**888-678-7588**	905-678-7588
Yahoo! Search Marketing Solutions 74 N Pasadena Ave 3rd Fl	Pasadena	CA	91103	**888-811-4686**	626-685-5600
yesmail Inc 959 Skyway Rd Suite 150	San Carlos	CA	94070	**877-937-6245**	650-620-1200

8 ADVERTISING SERVICES - OUTDOOR ADVERTISING

Company / Address	City	State	ZIP	Toll-Free	Phone
Attracta Sign Co 1468 James Rd	Rogers	MN	55374	**866-339-0603**	763-428-6377
Bowlin Travel Centers Inc 150 Louisiana Blvd NE	Albuquerque	NM	87108	**800-334-2236**	505-266-5985
Kubin-Nicholson Corp 5880 N 60th St	Milwaukee	WI	53218	**800-858-9557**	414-461-8100
Lamar Advertising Co 5551 Corporate Blvd	Baton Rouge	LA	70808	**800-235-2627**	225-926-1000
NASDAQ: LAMR					
Lamar Outdoor Advertising 5953 Susquehanna Plaza Dr	York	PA	17406	**800-632-9014**	717-252-1528
May Advertising International Ltd 1200 Forum Way S	Fort Worth	TX	76140	**800-800-4629**	817-336-5671
National Print Group Inc National Posters Div 1001 Latta St	Chattanooga	TN	37406	**800-624-0408**	423-622-1106
Obie Media Corp 4211 W 11th Ave	Eugene	OR	97402	**800-233-6243**	541-686-8400
NASDAQ: OBIE					
Viacom Outdoor Inc 2502 N Black Canyon Hwy	Phoenix	AZ	85009	**800-966-9569**	602-246-9569
Waitt Media Inc 1125 S 103rd St Suite 200	Omaha	NE	68124	**888-656-0634**	402-697-8000

9 ADVERTISING SERVICES (MISC)

Company / Address	City	State	ZIP	Toll-Free	Phone
AdMasters 16901 Dallas Pkwy Suite 204	Addison	TX	75001	**877-236-2783**	972-866-9300
DG Systems 750 W John Carpenter Fwy Suite 700	Irving	TX	75039	**800-335-4347**	972-581-2000
NASDAQ: DGIT					
Digital Generation Systems Inc 750 W John Carpenter Fwy Suite 700	Irving	TX	75039	**800-335-4347**	972-581-2000
NASDAQ: DGIT					
EBSCO Professional Partnership Group PO Box 830705	Birmingham	AL	35283	**800-528-3476**	205-991-1188
Hospitality Marketing Concepts Inc 15751 Rockfield Blvd Suite 200	Irvine	CA	92618	**866-212-4462**	949-454-1800
MemberWorks Inc 680 Washington Blvd	Stamford	CT	06901	**800-374-6135**	203-324-7635
NASDAQ: MBRS					
Sperry & Hutchinson Co Inc 45 Congress St Bldg L	Salem	MA	01970	**800-435-5674**	978-740-5600
Student Advantage Inc 280 Summer St	Boston	MA	02210	**800-333-2920**	617-912-2011
Vestcom International Inc 5 Henderson Dr	West Caldwell	NJ	07006	**800-865-1821**	973-287-1000

10 ADVERTISING SPECIALTIES

SEE ALSO Signs; Smart Cards; Trophies, Plaques, Awards

Company / Address	City	State	ZIP	Toll-Free	Phone
Aakron Rule Corp 8 Indianola Ave	Akron	NY	14001	**800-828-1570**	716-542-5483
Adco Litho Line Inc 2700 W Roosevelt Rd	Broadview	IL	60155	**800-875-2326**	708-345-8200
Adimage Promotional Group 2300 Main St	Hugo	MN	55038	**800-344-8809**	651-426-0820
Adventures in Advertising 101 Commerce St	Oshkosh	WI	54901	**800-460-7836**	920-236-7272
Alexander Mfg Co 12978 Tesson Ferry Rd	Saint Louis	MO	63128	**800-467-5343**	314-842-3344
American Identity 7500 W 110th St	Overland Park	KS	66210	**800-848-8028**	913-319-3100
Americanna Co 29 Aldrin Rd	Plymouth	MA	02360	**888-747-5550***	508-747-5550
*Cust Svc					
Amsterdam Printing & Litho Corp 166 Wallins Corners Rd	Amsterdam	NY	12010	**800-833-6231**	518-842-6000
Arnold Pen Co 15 N Union St	Petersburg	VA	23803	**800-296-6612**	804-733-6612
Arthur Blank & Co Inc 225 Rivermoor St	Boston	MA	02132	**800-776-7333**	617-325-9600
Atlas Pen & Pencil Corp 3040 N 29th Ave	Hollywood	FL	33020	**800-327-3232**	954-920-4444
Barrett LW Co Inc 55 S Zuni St PO Box 19430	Denver	CO	80219	**888-312-0888**	303-934-5755
Bastian Co 122 N Genesee St	Geneva	NY	14456	**800-609-0097**	315-789-8000
Belaire Products Inc 763 S Broadway St	Akron	OH	44311	**800-886-3224**	330-253-3116
Bergamot Inc 820 Wisconsin St	Delavan	WI	53115	**800-922-6733***	262-728-5572
*Cust Svc					
Blank Arthur & Co Inc 225 Rivermoor St	Boston	MA	02132	**800-776-7333**	617-325-9600
Brown & Bigelow Inc 345 Plato Blvd E	Saint Paul	MN	55107	**800-628-1755***	651-293-7000
*Cust Svc					
Churchwell Co 3031 E Bay St	Jacksonville	FL	32202	**800-245-0075**	904-356-5721
Crown Products Inc 3107 Halls Mill Rd	Mobile	AL	36606	**800-367-2769**	251-476-7777
Dard Products Inc 912 Custer Ave	Evanston	IL	60202	**800-323-2925**	847-328-5000
Dunn Mfg Inc 1400 Goldmine Rd	Monroe	NC	28110	**800-868-7111**	704-283-2147
EBSCO Promotional Products 825 5th Ave S	Birmingham	AL	35233	**800-756-7023**	205-323-4618
Elliott Sales Corp 2502 S 12th St	Tacoma	WA	98405	**800-576-3945**	253-383-3883
Emblem & Badge Inc 747 N Main St	Providence	RI	02940	**800-875-5444**	401-331-5444
Ever-Lite Co Inc 1717 N Bayshore Dr Unit 1632	Miami	FL	33132	**800-891-4670**	305-577-0819
Exclusive Findings 29 Delaine St	Providence	RI	02909	**800-342-9560**	401-421-3661
Flair Communications Agency Inc 214 W Erie St	Chicago	IL	60610	**800-621-8317**	312-943-5959
Francis & Lusky LLC 1450 Elm Hill Pike	Nashville	TN	37210	**800-251-3711**	615-242-0501
Geiger 70 Mt Hope Ave	Lewiston	ME	04240	**888-222-4276**	207-755-2000
Geiger Brothers Promotional Marketing 2010 Oakgrove Rd	Hattiesburg	MS	39402	**800-264-9291**	601-264-1991
HALO Branded Solutions 1980 Industrial Dr	Sterling	IL	61081	**800-683-4256**	815-625-0980
Hit Promotional Products Inc 7150 Bryan Dairy Rd	Largo	FL	33777	**800-237-6305**	727-541-5561
House of Specialties 5451 Able Ct	Mobile	AL	36693	**800-348-2422**	251-438-2422
Lewtan Industries Corp 30 High St	Hartford	CT	06103	**800-539-8268**	860-278-9800
LW Barrett Co Inc 55 S Zuni St PO Box 19430	Denver	CO	80219	**888-312-0888**	303-934-5755
MARC Promotions 7172 Lakeview Pkwy W Dr	Indianapolis	IN	46268	**800-422-8851**	317-290-3516
Marco 2640 Commerce Dr	Harrisburg	PA	17110	**800-232-1121**	717-545-1060
Marietta Corp 37 Huntington St	Cortland	NY	13045	**800-431-3023**	607-753-6746
Mid-America Merchandising Inc 204 W 3rd St	Kansas City	MO	64105	**800-333-6737**	816-471-5600
MMG Works/Status Promotions 106 W 11th St Suite 500	Kansas City	MO	64105	**800-945-4044**	816-472-5988
Morco Inc 125 High St	Cochranton	PA	16314	**800-247-4093**	814-425-7476
Myron Corp 205 Maywood Ave	Maywood	NJ	07607	**800-526-9766**	201-843-6464
National Pen Corp 16885 Via Del Compo Ct Suite 100	San Diego	CA	92127	**800-854-1000**	858-675-3000
Neely Mfg Inc 2178 Hwy 2	Corydon	IA	50060	**800-247-1785**	641-872-1100
Newton Mfg Co 1123 1st Ave E	Newton	IA	50208	**800-500-7227**	641-792-4121
Norscot Group Inc 1000 W Donges Bay Rd	Mequon	WI	53092	**800-653-3313**	262-241-3313
Norwood Promotional Products Inc 318 E 7th St	Auburn	IN	46706	**800-827-5151**	260-925-1700
Norwood Souvenir 202 F Ave NW	Cedar Rapids	IA	52405	**800-413-8371**	319-366-7831
Numo Mfg Co 1072 E Hwy 175	Kaufman	TX	75142	**800-253-0434**	972-962-5400
Perrygraf Co 25 W 550 Geneva Rd Suite 1934	Carol Stream	IL	60188	**800-423-5329**	630-784-0100
Pilgrim Plastic Products Co 1200 W Chestnut St	Brockton	MA	02301	**877-343-7810**	508-436-6300
Prime Resources Corp 1100 Boston Ave	Bridgeport	CT	06610	**800-873-7746**	203-331-9100
Quikey Mfg Co 1500 Industrial Pkwy	Akron	OH	44310	**877-901-1200**	330-633-8106
Rainbow Magnetics Inc 3221 W MacArthur Blvd	Santa Ana	CA	92704	**800-248-6200***	714-540-4777
*Sales					
Sanders Mfg Co 1422 Lebanon Rd	Nashville	TN	37210	**866-254-6611**	615-254-6611
Shaw & Slavsky Inc 13821 Elmira Ave	Detroit	MI	48227	**800-521-7527**	313-834-3990
Sport It Inc 12041 World Trade Dr Suite 2	San Diego	CA	92128	**888-233-2659**	858-592-6532
Vanguard East 1172 Azalea Garden Rd	Norfolk	VA	23502	**800-221-1264**	757-857-3600
Virtronic/Four Seasons 4680 Parkway Dr Suite 200	Mason	OH	45040	**877-844-5032**	513-398-3695
Western Plastic Products Inc 1556 W Esther St	Long Beach	CA	90813	**800-453-1881**	562-435-4881

AGRICULTURAL CHEMICALS

SEE Fertilizers & Pesticides

AGRICULTURAL MACHINERY & EQUIPMENT

SEE Farm Machinery & Equipment - Mfr; Farm Machinery & Equipment - Whol

11 AGRICULTURAL PRODUCTS

SEE ALSO Fruit Growers; Horse Breeders; Horticultural Products Growers; Seed Companies

11-1 Cattle Ranches, Farms, Feedlots (Beef Cattle)

Company / Address	City	State	ZIP	Toll-Free	Phone
Agri Beef Co 1555 Shoreline Dr 3rd Fl	Boise	ID	83702	**800-657-6305**	208-338-2500
Ainsworth Feed Yards Co PO Box 267	Ainsworth	NE	69210	**800-438-3148**	402-387-2455
AzTx Cattle Co PO Box 390	Hereford	TX	79045	**800-999-5065**	806-364-8871
Coyote Lake Feedyard Inc 1287 FM 1731	Muleshoe	TX	79347	**800-299-3321**	806-946-3321
Dinklage Feed Yards Inc PO Box 274	Sidney	NE	69162	**888-343-5940**	308-254-5941
Ford County Feed Yard Inc 12466 US Hwy 400	Ford	KS	67842	**800-783-2739**	620-369-2252
Friona Feedyard PO Box 806	Friona	TX	79035	**800-658-6086**	806-265-3574
Friona Industries LP 500 S Taylor St Suite 601	Amarillo	TX	79101	**800-658-6014**	806-374-1811
Garden City Feed Yard 1805 W Annie Scheer Rd	Garden City	KS	67846	**800-272-4191**	620-275-4191
Great Bend Feeding Inc 355 NW 30 Ave	Great Bend	KS	67530	**800-792-2508**	620-792-2508
Henry C Hitch Feedyards PO Box 1559	Guymon	OK	73942	**800-951-2533**	580-338-2533
Hitch Feeders II Inc 521 50th Rd	Satanta	KS	67870	**800-951-6181**	620-275-6181
Hitch Henry C Feedyards PO Box 1559	Guymon	OK	73942	**800-951-2533**	580-338-2533
Ingalls Feed Yard 10505 US Hwy 50	Ingalls	KS	67853	**800-477-6907**	620-335-5174
JR Simplot Co 999 Main St	Boise	ID	83702	**800-635-5008**	208-336-2110
King Ranch Inc PO Box 1090	Kingsville	TX	78364	**800-375-6411**	361-592-6411
Littlefield Feedyard RR 1 Box 26	Amherst	TX	79312	**800-687-5141**	806-385-5141
Paco Feed Yard Inc PO Box 956	Friona	TX	79035	**800-725-3433**	806-265-3281

Classified Section

Cattle Ranches, Farms, Feedlots (Beef Cattle) (Cont'd)

Company	City	State	Zip	Toll-Free	Phone
Pride Feeders I Ltd RR 2 Box 67	Hooker	OK	73945	**800-872-7251**	580-253-6381
Randall County Feedyard 15000 FM 2219	Amarillo	TX	79119	**800-658-6063**	806-499-3701
Simplot JR Co 999 Main St	Boise	ID	83702	**800-635-5008**	208-336-2110
Swisher County Cattle Co PO Box 129	Tulia	TX	79088	**800-658-6064**	806-627-4231
Thomas County Feeders Inc 1762 US Hwy 83	Colby	KS	67701	**800-257-2409**	785-462-3947

11-2 Cotton Farms

Company	City	State	Zip	Toll-Free	Phone
Delta & Pine Land Co PO Box 157 *NYSE: DLP*	Scott	MS	38772	**800-321-8989**	662-742-3351
E Ritter & Co Inc 106 Frisco St	Marked Tree	AR	72365	**800-323-0355**	870-358-2200
Paymaster Technology Corp 1 Cotton Row	Scott	MS	38772	**800-321-8989**	662-742-3351

11-3 Dairy Farms

Company	City	State	Zip	Toll-Free	Phone
Hollandia Dairy Inc 622 E Mission Rd	San Marcos	CA	92069	**800-794-0978**	760-744-3222
Kreider Farms 1461 Lancaster Rd	Manheim	PA	17545	**888-665-4415**	717-665-4415
Marburger Farm Dairy Inc 1506 Mars Evans City Rd	Evans City	PA	16033	**800-331-1295**	724-538-4752
Maytag Dairy Farms Inc 2282 E 8th N	Newton	IA	50208	**800-247-2458**	641-792-1133

11-4 General Farms

Company	City	State	Zip	Toll-Free	Phone
Millhaven Co Inc 1705 Millhaven Rd	Sylvania	GA	30467	**800-421-8043**	912-829-4742
Tosh Farms 1586 Atlantic Ave	Henry	TN	38231	**888-243-4885**	731-243-4861

11-5 Grain Farms

Company	City	State	Zip	Toll-Free	Phone
AgriNorthwest 7404 W Hood Pl Suite B	Kennewick	WA	99336	**800-333-8175**	509-734-1195
Agripro Seeds Inc 2369 330th St	Slater	LA	50244	**877-247-4776**	
DuPont Agriculture & Nutrition 1007 Market St DuPont Bldg	Wilmington	DE	19898	**800-441-7515**	302-774-1000
Fred Gutwein & Sons Inc 15691 W 600 S *Cust Svc	Francesville	IN	47946	**800-457-2700***	219-567-9141
Gutwein Fred & Sons Inc 15691 W 600 S *Cust Svc	Francesville	IN	47946	**800-457-2700***	219-567-9141
Hoegemeyer Hybrids Inc 1755 Hoegemeyer Rd	Hooper	NE	68031	**800-245-4631**	402-654-3399
Moews Seed Co Inc Rt 89 S	Granville	IL	61326	**800-663-9795**	815-339-2201
Pfister Hybrid Corn Co 187 N Fayette St	El Paso	IL	61738	**888-647-3478**	309-527-6010
Pioneer Hi-Bred International Inc 400 Locust St Capital Sq Suite 800	Des Moines	IA	50309	**800-247-6803**	515-248-4800
Renk William F & Sons Inc 6800 Wilburn Rd	Sun Prairie	WI	53590	**800-289-7365**	608-837-7351
Sommer Brothers Seed Co PO Box 248	Pekin	IL	61555	**800-747-2127**	309-346-2127
William F Renk & Sons Inc 6800 Wilburn Rd	Sun Prairie	WI	53590	**800-289-7365**	608-837-7351
Wyffels Hybrids Inc 13344 US Hwy 6	Geneseo	IL	61254	**800-369-7833**	309-944-8344

11-6 Hog Farms

Company	City	State	Zip	Toll-Free	Phone
Cargill Inc 15407 McGinty Rd	Wayzata	MN	55391	**800-227-4455**	952-742-7575
Clougherty Packing Co DBA Farmer John Meats 3049 E Vernon Ave *Sales	Los Angeles	CA	90058	**800-432-7637***	323-583-4621
Farmer John Meats 3049 E Vernon Ave *Sales	Los Angeles	CA	90058	**800-432-7637***	323-583-4621
Hog Slat 206 Fayetteville St	Newton Grove	NC	28366	**800-949-4647**	910-594-0219
Murphy Brown LLC PO Box 759	Rose Hill	NC	28458	**800-311-9458**	910-289-2111
PIC USA 3033 Nashville Rd PO Box 348	Franklin	KY	42135	**800-325-3398**	270-586-9224
Smithfield Foods Inc 200 Commerce St *NYSE: SFD*	Smithfield	VA	23430	**800-276-6158**	757-365-3000
Tosh Farms 1586 Atlantic Ave	Henry	TN	38231	**888-243-4885**	731-243-4861
Tyson Foods Inc 2210 W Oaklawn Dr *NYSE: TSN*	Springdale	AR	72762	**800-643-3410**	479-290-4000

11-7 Mushroom Growers

Company	City	State	Zip	Toll-Free	Phone
Money's Mushrooms Ltd 24 Duncan St 5th Fl	Toronto	ON	M5V2B8	**800-661-8623**	416-977-1400
Monterey Mushrooms Inc 60 Westgate Dr	Watsonville	CA	95076	**800-333-6874**	831-763-5300
Ostrom Mushroom Farms 8323 Steilacoom Rd SE	Olympia	WA	98513	**800-640-7408**	360-491-1410
Phillips Mushroom Farms Inc 1011 Kaolin Rd	Kennett Square	PA	19348	**800-722-8818**	610-444-4492
Sylvan Inc PO Box 249	Saxonburg	PA	16056	**866-352-7520**	724-352-7520

11-8 Poultry & Eggs Production

Company	City	State	Zip	Toll-Free	Phone
Allen's Hatchery Inc 126 N Shipley St	Seaford	DE	19973	**800-777-8966**	302-629-9163
Amick Farms Inc PO Box 2309	Leesville	SC	29070	**800-926-4257**	803-532-1400
Aviagen Group 5015 Bradford Dr	Huntsville	AL	35805	**800-826-9685**	256-890-3800
Cargill Turkey Products 1 Kratzer Rd *Cust Svc	Harrisonburg	VA	22802	**800-233-8457***	540-568-1400
Cobb-Vantress Inc PO Box 1030	Siloam Springs	AR	72761	**800-749-9719**	479-524-3166
Cooper Farms 22348 County Rd 140	Oakwood	OH	45873	**888-594-8759**	419-594-3325
Creighton Brothers LP PO Box 220	Atwood	IN	46502	**800-847-3447**	574-267-3101
Durbin Marshall Food Corp 2830 Commerce Blvd	Irondale	AL	35210	**800-768-2456**	205-956-3505
Echo Lake Farm Produce Co PO Box 279	Burlington	WI	53105	**800-888-3447**	262-763-9551
Hickman's Egg Ranch Inc 7403 N 91st Ave	Glendale	AZ	85305	**800-224-2123**	623-872-1120
Hubbard ISA PO Box 415	Walpole	NH	03608	**800-482-2442**	603-756-3311
Jaindl Farms 3150 Coffeetown Rd	Orefield	PA	18069	**800-475-6654**	610-395-3333
Jennie-O Turkey Store 2505 Willmar Ave SW	Willmar	MN	56201	**800-328-1756**	320-235-2622
JFC Inc PO Box 1106	Saint Cloud	MN	56302	**800-328-8236**	320-251-3570
Mar-Jac Poultry Inc PO Box 1017	Gainesville	GA	30503	**800-226-0561**	770-536-0561
Marshall Durbin Food Corp 2830 Commerce Blvd	Irondale	AL	35210	**800-768-2456**	205-956-3505
Michael Foods Inc 301 Carlson Pkwy Suite 400	Minnetonka	MN	55305	**800-325-4270**	952-258-4000
Perdue Farms Inc PO Box 1537	Salisbury	MD	21802	**800-457-3738**	410-543-3000
Ross Breeders Inc 5015 Bradford Dr NW	Huntsville	AL	35805	**800-826-9685**	256-890-3800
Tampa Farm Service Inc 14425 Haynes Rd	Dover	FL	33527	**800-441-3447**	813-659-0605
Tyson Foods Inc 2210 W Oaklawn Dr *NYSE: TSN*	Springdale	AR	72762	**800-643-3410**	479-290-4000
Wayne Farms LLC 4110 Continental Dr	Oakwood	GA	30566	**800-392-0844**	678-450-3100
Wilcox Farms Inc 40400 Harts Lake Valley Rd	Roy	WA	98580	**800-568-6456**	360-458-7774
Willmar Poultry Co Inc PO Box 753	Willmar	MN	56201	**800-328-8842**	320-235-8850
Willow Brook Foods Inc PO Box 50190	Springfield	MO	65805	**800-423-2366**	417-862-3612
Zephyr Egg Co Inc 4622 Gall Blvd	Zephyrhills	FL	33542	**800-488-6543**	813-782-1521

11-9 Sugarcane & Sugarbeets Growers

Company	City	State	Zip	Toll-Free	Phone
Wedgworth Farms Inc 651 NW 9th St PO Box 2076	Belle Glade	FL	33430	**800-477-2077**	561-996-2076

11-10 Tree Nuts Growers

Company	City	State	Zip	Toll-Free	Phone
Blue Diamond Growers 1802 C St	Sacramento	CA	95814	**888-285-1351**	916-442-0771
Green Valley Pecan Co 1625 E Sahuarita Rd	Sahuarita	AZ	85629	**800-533-5269**	520-791-2852
Hammons Products Co 105 Hammons Dr PO Box 140	Stockton	MO	65785	**888-429-6887**	417-276-5181
Mauna Loa Macadamia Nut Corp HC01 Box 3 *Cust Svc	Hilo	HI	96720	**800-832-9993***	808-982-6562

11-11 Vegetable Farms

Company	City	State	Zip	Toll-Free	Phone
Accursio Sam S & Sons Farms PO Box 901767	Homestead	FL	33090	**800-233-6826**	305-246-3455
Anthony Farms Inc 290 Depot St	Scandinavia	WI	54977	**800-826-0456**	715-467-2212
Bengard Tom Ranch Inc PO Box 80090	Salinas	CA	93912	**800-546-3517**	831-422-9021
Betteravia Farms PO Box 5845	Santa Maria	CA	93456	**800-328-8816**	805-925-2417
Bo-Jac Seed Co 245 1500th Ave	Mount Pulaski	IL	62548	**800-397-2069**	217-792-5001
Borzynski Brothers Distributing Inc PO Box 133	Franksville	WI	53126	**800-248-0420**	262-886-1623
Buurma Farms Inc 3909 Kok Rd	Willard	OH	44890	**888-428-8762**	419-935-6411
Byrd Foods Inc PO Box 318	Parksley	VA	23421	**800-777-2973**	757-665-5194
Christopher Ranch 305 Bloomfield Ave	Gilroy	CA	95020	**800-321-9333**	408-847-1100
CROPP Cooperative 1 Organic Way	LaFarge	WI	54639	**888-444-6455**	608-625-2602
Dole Fresh Vegetables Co PO Box 1759 *Sales	Salinas	CA	93902	**800-333-5454***	831-754-5244
Earthbound Farm 1721 San Juan Hwy	San Juan Bautista	CA	95045	**800-690-3200**	831-623-7880
Farming Technology Corp 6950 Neuhaus St	Houston	TX	77061	**800-395-2004**	713-923-5807
Fresh Express Inc 950 E Blanco Rd *Cust Svc	Salinas	CA	93901	**800-242-5472***	831-422-5917
Greenheart Farms Inc PO Box 1510	Arroyo Grande	CA	93421	**800-549-5531**	805-481-2234
Growers Marketing Service Inc PO Box 2595	Lakeland	FL	33806	**800-476-2037**	863-644-2414
Harris Farms Inc 23300 W Oakland Ave	Coalinga	CA	93210	**800-691-1199**	559-884-2477
Hartung Brothers Inc 918 Deming Way Suite 200	Madison	WI	53717	**800-362-2522**	608-829-6000
Martori Farms 7332 E Butherus Dr	Scottsdale	AZ	85260	**800-627-8674**	480-998-1444
Nash Produce Co 6160 S North Carolina 58	Nashville	NC	27856	**800-334-3032**	252-443-6011
Offutt RD Co PO Box 7160	Fargo	ND	58106	**877-444-7363**	701-237-6062
Petrocco Farms 14110 Brighton Rd	Brighton	CO	80601	**888-876-2207**	303-659-6498
RD Offutt Co PO Box 7160	Fargo	ND	58106	**877-444-7363**	701-237-6062
Sam S Accursio & Sons Farms PO Box 901767	Homestead	FL	33090	**800-233-6826**	305-246-3455
San Miguel Produce Inc 4444 Naval Air Rd	Oxnard	CA	93033	**888-347-3367**	805-488-0981
Six L's Packing Co Inc 315 E New Market Rd	Immokalee	FL	34142	**800-554-6606**	239-657-4221
Tanimura & Antle Inc PO Box 4070	Salinas	CA	93912	**800-772-4542**	831-455-2950
Taylor & Fulton Inc 932 5th Ave W	Palmetto	FL	34221	**800-457-5577**	941-729-3883
Tom Bengard Ranch Inc PO Box 80090	Salinas	CA	93912	**800-546-3517**	831-422-9021
Tri-Campbell Farms 15111 Hwy 17	Grafton	ND	58237	**877-999-7783**	701-352-3116
Village Farms LP 7 Christopher Way	Eatontown	NJ	07724	**877-777-7718**	732-676-3000
Virginia Fork Produce Inc PO Box 148	Edenton	NC	27932	**800-334-7716**	252-482-2165
Wada Farms Potatoes Inc 2058 Jennie Lee Dr	Idaho Falls	ID	83404	**800-657-5565**	208-542-2898
Wiers Farm Inc PO Box 385	Willard	OH	44890	**800-825-6525**	419-935-0131

12 AGRICULTURAL SERVICES

12-1 Crop Preparation Services

Company	City	State	Zip	Toll-Free	Phone
Belair Packing House 1626 90th Ave	Vero Beach	FL	32966	**800-567-1154**	772-567-1151
Borg Produce Co 1601 E Olympic Blvd Bldg 100 Suite 101	Los Angeles	CA	90021	**800-808-2674**	213-688-9388
Cargill AgHorizons PO Box 9300 MS 19	Minneapolis	MN	55440	**800-227-4455**	952-742-7575
DiMare Brothers/New England Farms Packing Co 84 New England Produce Ctr	Chelsea	MA	02150	**800-510-3700**	617-889-3800
Dole Fresh Vegetables Co PO Box 1759 *Sales	Salinas	CA	93902	**800-333-5454***	831-754-5244
Dundee Citrus Growers Assn 111 1st St N	Dundee	FL	33838	**800-447-1574**	863-439-1574
Fillmore-Piru Citrus Assoc 355 N Main St PO Box 350	Piru	CA	93040	**800-524-8787**	805-524-3551
Fresh Express Inc 950 E Blanco Rd *Cust Svc	Salinas	CA	93901	**800-242-5472***	831-422-5917

Company / Address	City	State	ZIP	Toll-Free	Phone
Great Lakes Packers Inc 400 Great Lakes Pkwy PO Box 366	Bellevue	OH	44811	**800-624-8464**	419-483-2956
Haines City Citrus Growers Assn 8 Willard Ave *Sales	Haines City	FL	33845	**800-422-4245***	863-422-1174
Hazelnut Growers of Oregon 401 N 26th Ave	Cornelius	OR	97113	**800-273-4676**	503-648-4176
Index Fresh Inc 18184 Slover Ave	Bloomington	CA	92316	**800-352-6931**	909-877-1577
Lake Region Packing Assn Inc 124 S Joanna Ave PO Box 1477	Tavares	FL	32778	**800-780-3400**	352-343-3111
Mann Packing Co Inc PO Box 690	Salinas	CA	93902	**800-285-1002**	831-422-7405
Mariani Packing Co Inc 500 Crocker Dr	Vacaville	CA	95688	**800-231-1287**	707-452-2800
Northern Fruit Co Inc 220 3rd St NE	East Wenatchee	WA	98802	**800-234-6651**	509-884-6651
Pleasant Valley Potato Inc 275 E Elmore St PO Box 538	Aberdeen	ID	83210	**888-867-7783**	208-397-4194
River Ranch Fresh Foods 1156 Abbott St	Salinas	CA	93901	**800-538-5868**	831-758-1390
Verdelli Farms Inc 7505 Grayson Rd	Harrisburg	PA	17111	**800-422-8344**	717-561-2900

12-2 Livestock Improvement Services

Company / Address	City	State	ZIP	Toll-Free	Phone
ABS Global Inc 1525 River Rd *Cust Svc	DeForest	WI	53532	**800-356-5331***	608-846-3721
Accelerated Genetics E 10890 Penny Ln	Baraboo	WI	53913	**800-451-9275**	608-356-8357
Alta Genetics Inc RR 2	Balzac	AB	T0M0E0	**800-932-2855**	403-226-0666
COBA/Select Sires Inc 1224 Alton Darby Creek Rd	Columbus	OH	43228	**800-837-2621**	614-878-5333
Cobb-Vantress Inc PO Box 1030	Siloam Springs	AR	72761	**800-749-9719**	479-524-3166
Dairy One 730 Warren Rd	Ithaca	NY	14850	**800-344-2697**	607-257-1272
Genex Co-op Inc/CRI 100 MBC Dr	Shawano	WI	54166	**888-333-1783**	715-526-2141
Reproduction Enterprises Inc 908 N Prairie Rd	Stillwater	OK	74075	**866-734-2855**	405-377-8037
SEK Genetics 9305 70th Rd	Galesburg	KS	66740	**800-443-6389**	620-763-2211
Taurus Service Inc Grift Flat Rd PO Box 164	Mehoopany	PA	18629	**800-836-5123**	570-833-5123

13 AIR CARGO CARRIERS

Company / Address	City	State	ZIP	Toll-Free	Phone
Aeronet Worldwide PO Box 17239	Irvine	CA	92623	**800-552-3869**	949-474-3000
Air Canada Cargo LaGuardia International Airport Hangar 5B	Flushing	NY	11371	**800-688-2274**	718-899-9128
Air New Zealand Cargo Sales JFK International Airport Cargo Plaza Bldg 87	Jamaica	NY	11430	**800-400-0153**	718-244-1333
Air Traffic Management Inc 16550 Air Ctr Blvd *Cust Svc	Houston	TX	77032	**800-231-0221***	281-821-2002
Alaska Airlines Cargo Services 19300 International blvd	Seattle	WA	98188	**800-426-0333**	206-433-3200
Alitalia Executive Cargo Div JFK International Airport N Boundry Rd Bldg 79	Jamaica	NY	11430	**800-221-4745**	718-244-8500
America West Cargo 1329 S 27th St	Phoenix	AZ	85034	**800-292-2274**	480-693-2900
American Airlines Inc Cargo Div PO Box 619616	DFW Airport	TX	75261	**800-227-4622**	817-967-2400
Ameriflight Inc 4700 Empire Ave Hangar 1	Burbank	CA	91505	**800-800-4538**	818-980-5005
Amerijet International Inc 2800 S Andrews Ave	Fort Lauderdale	FL	33316	**800-786-6944**	954-359-0077
Antillas Air JFK International Airport Cargo Bldg 68	Jamaica	NY	11430	**800-447-0417**	718-917-6855
Arrow Air Inc 2000 NW 62nd Ave Bldg 711	Miami	FL	33122	**800-871-3370**	305-871-3116
Austrian Airlines Cargo JFK International Airport Cargo Bldg 67 Rm 3111	Jamaica	NY	11430	**800-637-2957**	718-995-2274
Capital Cargo International Airlines 6200 Hazeltine National Dr	Orlando	FL	32822	**800-593-9119**	407-855-2004
Cargo Services Inc 1601 NW 70th Ave	Miami	FL	33126	**800-597-6010**	305-599-9333
Cargolux Airlines International 238 Lawrence Ave	South San Francisco	CA	94080	**800-722-2023**	650-225-0747
Cathay Pacific Cargo 6040 Avion Dr Suite 338	Los Angeles	CA	90045	**800-628-6960**	310-417-0052
China Airlines Cargo Sales & Service 11201 Aviation Blvd	Los Angeles	CA	90045	**800-421-1289**	310-646-4293
Continental Airlines Inc Cargo Div DBA Continental Cargo 1600 Smith St	Houston	TX	77002	**800-421-2456**	
Continental Cargo 1600 Smith St	Houston	TX	77002	**800-421-2456**	
Delta Air Cargo 1600 Aviation Blvd Hartsfield-Atlanta International Airport	Atlanta	GA	30320	**800-352-2746**	
East Coast Air Charter Inc PO Box 7137	Statesville	NC	28687	**888-277-7434**	704-838-1991
Empire Airlines Inc 2115 Government Way	Coeur d'Alene	ID	83814	**800-392-9233**	208-667-5400
Evergreen International Airlines Inc 3850 Three-Mile Ln	McMinnville	OR	97128	**800-383-5338**	503-472-0011
Evergreen International Aviation Inc 3850 Three Mile Ln	McMinnville	OR	97128	**800-472-9361**	503-472-9361
Gemini Air Cargo 44965 Aviation Dr Suite 300	Dulles	VA	20166	**888-359-4221**	703-260-8100
Iberia Air Cargo 6065 NW 18th St Bldg 716D	Miami	FL	33122	**800-221-6002**	305-526-6771
Kalitta Flying Service 818 Willow Run Airport	Ypsilanti	MI	48198	**800-845-3390**	734-484-0088
Kitty Hawk Inc 1515 W 20th St PO Box 612787 *AMEX: KHK*	DFW Airport	TX	75261	**800-486-3780**	972-456-2200
LanChile Cargo Group PO Box 520846	Miami	FL	33152	**800-735-5526**	305-871-4980
Lloyd Aereo Boliviano Airlines Cargo 1651 NW 68 Ave Bldg 706 *Cust Svc	Miami	FL	33131	**800-489-4118***	305-526-5565
Lufthansa Cargo USA 3400 Peachtree Rd Lenox Towers Suite 1225	Atlanta	GA	30326	**877-542-2746**	404-814-5311
Lynden Air Cargo LLC 6441 S Airpark Pl	Anchorage	AK	99502	**888-243-7248**	907-243-6150
Martinair Holland Cargo 5550 Glades Rd Suite 600	Boca Raton	FL	33431	**800-366-3734**	561-391-1313
MartinAire Partners LP 4745 Frank Luke Dr	Addison	TX	75001	**800-282-3828**	972-349-5700
Northern Air Cargo Inc 3900 W International Airport Rd	Anchorage	AK	99502	**800-727-2141**	907-243-3331
Northwest Airlines Cargo Div 5101 Northwest Dr	Saint Paul	MN	55111	**800-692-2746**	
Polar Air Cargo 2000 Westchester Ave	Purchase	NY	10577	**800-462-2012**	
Qantas Airways Cargo 6555 W Imperial Hwy	Los Angeles	CA	90045	**800-227-0290**	310-665-2280
Ryan International Airlines Inc 266 N Main St	Wichita	KS	67202	**800-727-0457**	316-265-7400
Service by Air Inc 222 Crossways Pk Dr	Woodbury	NY	11797	**800-243-5545**	516-921-4101
South Florida Air Cargo 1801 NW 66 Ave Bldg 709 Tower 1	Miami	FL	33122	**800-327-2578**	305-871-7780
Southwest Airlines Air Cargo 8028 Aviation Pl	Dallas	TX	75235	**800-533-1222**	214-792-5534
Tampa Airlines Cargo 1650 NW 66th Ave Bldg 708 Suite 206	Miami	FL	33122	**800-327-1520**	305-526-6720
Thai Airways International Cargo 6501 W Imperial Hwy	Los Angeles	CA	90045	**800-426-8678**	310-670-8592
United Airlines Cargo Services Div PO Box 66100	Chicago	IL	60666	**800-822-2746**	847-700-5004

14 AIR CHARTER SERVICES

SEE ALSO Aviation - Fixed-Base Operations; Helicopter Transport Services

Company / Address	City	State	ZIP	Toll-Free	Phone
Active Aero Group 2068 E St *Cust Svc	Belleville	MI	48111	**800-872-5387***	734-547-7200
Aero Air LLC 2050 NE 25th Ave	Hillsboro	OR	97124	**800-448-2376**	503-640-3711
Air America Jet Charter Inc 9000 Randolph St	Houston	TX	77061	**888-423-9110**	713-640-2900
Air Charter Team 10015 NW Ambassador Dr Suite 202	Kansas City	MO	64153	**800-205-6610**	816-283-3280
Air Royale International Inc 9100 Wilshire Blvd Suite 420	Beverly Hills	CA	90212	**800-776-9253**	310-289-9800
AirFlite Inc 3250 AirFlite Way	Long Beach	CA	90807	**800-241-3548**	562-490-6200
Allegiant Air 3301 N Buffalo Dr Suite B-9 *Resv	Las Vegas	NV	89129	**800-432-3810***	702-851-7300
American Air Charter Network PO Box 569	Melville	NY	11747	**800-393-2538**	516-768-3202
American Flight Group 1974 Baltimore Annapolis Blvd	Annapolis	MD	21401	**877-234-5387**	410-757-6329
American Jet Charter 5901 Philip J Rhoads Hanger 14 Wiley Post Airport	Bethany	OK	73008	**800-495-5453**	405-495-5453
Atkin Air 1420 Flightline Dr Suite B	Lincoln	CA	95648	**800-924-2471**	916-645-6242
Aviation Charter Services 6551 Pierson Dr	Indianapolis	IN	46241	**800-522-2296**	317-244-7200
Avstar Aviation 12 N Haven Ln	East Northport	NY	11731	**800-575-2359**	631-499-0048
Berry Aviation Inc 1807 Airport Dr	San Marcos	TX	78666	**800-229-2379**	512-353-2379
Bluffton Flying Service Co 1080 Navajo Dr	Bluffton	OH	45817	**800-468-6359**	419-358-7045
Bridgeford Flying Services 2030 Airport Rd Napa County Airport	Napa	CA	94558	**800-229-6272**	707-224-0887
CAI (Chrysler Aviation Inc) 7120 Hayvenhurst Ave Suite 309	Van Nuys	CA	91406	**800-995-0825**	818-989-7900
Champion Air 8009 34th Ave S Suite 500	Bloomington	MN	55425	**800-922-2606**	952-814-8700
Charter Flight Inc 5400 Airport Dr	Charlotte	NC	28208	**800-521-3148**	704-359-9124
Charter Services Inc 8400 Airport Blvd Bldg 31	Mobile	AL	36608	**800-657-1555**	251-633-6090
Chrysler Aviation Inc (CAI) 7120 Hayvenhurst Ave Suite 309	Van Nuys	CA	91406	**800-995-0825**	818-989-7900
Clay Lacy Aviation 7435 Valjean Ave	Van Nuys	CA	91406	**800-423-2904**	818-989-2900
Colgan Air Services 2709 Fanta Reed Rd	La Crosse	WI	54603	**800-658-9498**	608-783-8359
Corporate Express Business & Charter Airline 445 Palmer Rd NE Calgary Esso Avitat	Calgary	AB	T2E7G4	**800-661-8151**	403-216-4050
Corporate Flight Inc 6150 Highland Rd	Waterford	MI	48327	**800-767-2473**	248-666-8800
East Coast Flight Services Inc 29111 Newman Rd Easton Municipal Airport *Sales	Easton	MD	21601	**800-554-0550***	410-820-6633
Elite Aviation LLC 7501 Hayvenhurst Pl	Van Nuys	CA	91406	**888-334-7777**	818-988-5387
Era Aviation Inc Louisiana Lake Charles Municipal Airport PO Box 6550	Lake Charles	LA	70606	**800-256-2372**	337-478-6131
Exec Air Montana Inc 2430 Airport Rd	Helena	MT	59601	**800-513-2190**	406-442-2190
Executive Fliteways 1 Clark Rd	Ronkonkoma	NY	11779	**800-533-3363**	631-588-5454
Executive Jet 4556 Airport Rd	Cincinnati	OH	45226	**800-451-2822**	513-979-6600
Fairwind Air Charter 2555 SE Dixie Hwy	Stuart	FL	34996	**800-989-9665**	772-288-4130
Flight Options 26180 Curtiss Wright Pkwy	Richmond Heights	OH	44143	**800-433-1285**	216-261-3500
Flightstar Corp 7 Airport Rd Willard Airport	Savoy	IL	61874	**800-747-4777**	217-351-7700
Hop-A-Jet Inc 5525 NW 15th Ave Suite 150	Fort Lauderdale	FL	33309	**800-556-6633**	954-771-5779
International Jet Aviation Services 12401 Aviator Way	Englewood	CO	80112	**800-858-5891**	303-790-0414
Jet Air Jet Charter 547 Perimeter Rd Hanger 2 PO Box 178207	Nashville	TN	37217	**888-812-6604**	615-361-1007
Jet Aviation Business Jets Inc 112 Charles A Lindbergh Dr	Teterboro	NJ	07608	**800-736-8538**	201-462-4100
Jet Resource Inc 455 Wilmer Ave Lunken Airport Hangar 27	Cincinnati	OH	45226	**800-404-5387**	513-762-6909
JetCorp 18152 Edison Ave	Chesterfield	MO	63005	**800-325-4811**	636-530-7000
KaiserAir Inc 8735 Earhart Rd	Oakland	CA	94621	**800-538-2625**	510-569-9622
Key Air Inc 3 Juliano Dr Waterbury-Oxford Airport	Oxford	CT	06478	**800-258-6975**	203-264-0605
Lacy Clay Aviation 7435 Valjean Ave	Van Nuys	CA	91406	**800-423-2904**	818-989-2900
LR Services 600 Hayden Cir	Allentown	PA	18109	**888-675-9650**	610-266-2500
Lynx Air International 3402 SW 9th Ave	Fort Lauderdale	FL	33315	**888-596-9247**	954-772-9808
Maine Aviation Corp 1001 Westbrook St	Portland	ME	04102	**888-359-7600**	207-780-1811
Mar-El Aviation Inc DBA Jet Air Jet Charter 547 Perimeter Rd Hanger 2 PO Box 178207	Nashville	TN	37217	**888-812-6604**	615-361-1007
Mayo Aviation Inc 7735 S Peoria St	Englewood	CO	80112	**800-525-0194**	303-790-9777
Midsouth Aviation Alliance Corp 2432 Winchester Rd	Memphis	TN	38116	**800-893-6222**	901-396-7318
Million Air Interlink Inc 8501 Telephone Rd	Houston	TX	77061	**888-589-9059**	713-640-4000
MissionAir 704 Southgate Rd	Saint Andrews	MB	R1A3P8	**877-231-2992**	204-231-2992
Mountainbird Inc DBA Salmon Air 29 Hamner Dr	Salmon	ID	83467	**800-448-3413**	208-756-6211
Nashville Jet 110 Tune Airport Dr	Nashville	TN	37209	**800-824-4778**	615-350-8400
North American Air Charter Inc 90 Arrival Ave Long Island MacArthur Airport	Ronkonkoma	NY	11779	**800-516-4430**	631-737-4430
Pacific Coast Jet Charter Inc PO Box 419074	Rancho Cordova	CA	95741	**800-655-3599**	916-631-6507

Toll-Free *Phone*

Paragon Air
Kahului Airport Commuter Airline Terminal
PO Box 575 Kahului HI 96733 **800-428-1231** 808-244-3356
Pentastar Aviation 7310 Highland Rd Waterford MI 48327 **800-662-9612** 248-666-3630
Personal Jet Charter Inc
5401 E Perimeter Rd Fort Lauderdale FL 33309 **800-432-1538** 954-776-4515
Petersen Aviation 7155 Valjean Ave Van Nuys CA 91406 **800-451-7270** 818-989-2300
Piedmont Hawthorne Aviation
3821 N Liberty St Winston-Salem NC 27105 **800-259-1940*** 336-776-6060
*Sales
Planemasters Ltd
32 W 611 Tower Rd DuPage Airport West Chicago IL 60185 **800-994-6400** 630-513-2100
Premier Jets
2140 NE 25th Ave Hillsboro Airport Hillsboro OR 97124 **800-635-8583** 503-640-2927
Presidential Aviation
1725 NW 51st Pl Fort Lauderdale
Executive Airport Hangar 71 Fort Lauderdale FL 33309 **888-772-8622** 954-772-8622
Priester Aviation 1061 S Wolf Rd Wheeling IL 60090 **888-323-7887** 847-537-1133
PrivatAir Inc 611 Access Rd Stratford CT 06615 **800-380-4009** 203-337-4600
Raytheon Aircraft Charter & Management
10225 E Kellogg Wichita KS 67201 **800-519-6283**
Ryan International Airlines Inc 266 N Main St Wichita KS 67202 **800-727-0457** 316-265-7400
Salmon Air 29 Hamner Dr Salmon ID 83467 **800-448-3413** 208-756-6211
San Juan Airlines Co
4000 Airport Rd Suite A Anacortes WA 98221 **800-874-4434** 360-293-4691
Sentient Jet Inc
600 Cordwainer Dr Executive Jet
Corporate Ctr Norwell MA 02061 **877-324-9538** 781-763-0200
Skyservice Airlines Inc 31 Fasken Dr Etobicoke ON M9W1K6 **800-701-9448** 416-679-5700
Southwest Jet Aviation Ltd
14988 N 78th Way Scottsdale
Municipal Airport Scottsdale AZ 85260 **800-991-7076** 480-991-7076
Spirit Aviation Inc
16233 Vanowen St Hangar 1 Van Nuys CA 91406 **800-995-1865** 818-989-4642
Sunbird Air Services Inc 1251 W Blee Rd Springfield OH 45502 **800-537-2711** 937-322-2711
Sunset Aviation 351 Airport Rd Novato CA 94945 **800-359-7861** 415-897-4522
Superior Air Charter Inc
3650 Biddle Rd Suite 16 Medford OR 97504 **800-793-1030** 541-772-5660
Tag Aviation USA Inc
111 Anza Blvd Suite 200 Burlingame CA 94010 **800-331-1930** 650-342-1717
Tas Group Inc DBA Air Charter Team
10015 NW Ambassador Dr Suite 202 Kansas City MO 64153 **800-205-6610** 816-283-3280
Tavaero Jet Charter 7930 Airport Blvd Houston TX 77061 **800-343-3771** 713-643-6043
TDM Inc DBA Colgan Air Services
2709 Fanta Reed Rd La Crosse WI 54603 **800-658-9498** 608-783-8359
Tulip City Air Service Inc
1581 S Washington Ave Holland MI 49423 **800-748-0515** 616-392-7831
Twin Cities Air Service 81 Airport Dr Auburn ME 04210 **800-564-3882** 207-782-3882
United Executive Jet Inc DBA JetCorp
18152 Edison Ave Chesterfield MO 63005 **800-325-4811** 636-530-7000
Victory Aviation Inc 2710 County Rd 60 Auburn IN 46706 **800-837-5517** 260-927-4040
West Coast Charters Inc
19711 Campus Dr Suite 200 Santa Ana CA 92707 **800-352-6153** 949-852-8340
Yellowstone Jetcenter 456 Gallatin Field Rd Belgrade MT 59714 **800-700-5381** 406-388-4152

AIR CONDITIONING EQUIPMENT - AUTOMOTIVE

SEE Air Conditioning & Heating Equipment - Residential

AIR CONDITIONING EQUIPMENT - WHOL

SEE Plumbing, Heating, Air Conditioning Equipment & Supplies - Whol

15 AIR CONDITIONING & HEATING EQUIPMENT - COMMERCIAL/INDUSTRIAL

SEE ALSO Air Conditioning & Heating Equipment - Residential; Refrigeration Equipment - Mfr

Toll-Free *Phone*

Absolut Aire Inc 5496 N Riverview Dr Kalamazoo MI 49004 **800-804-4000** 269-382-1875
AEC Inc 801 AEC Dr Wood Dale IL 60191 **800-966-1060** 630-595-1060
Airtek Inc 4087 Walden Ave Lancaster NY 14086 **800-451-6023** 716-685-4040
Aitken Products Inc PO Box 151 Geneva OH 44041 **800-569-9341** 440-466-5711
Anderson-Snow Corp 9225 Ivanhoe St Schiller Park IL 60176 **800-346-2645** 847-678-3823
Birdwell Co 3708 Greenhouse Rd Houston TX 77084 **800-237-2095** 281-492-1786
Blissfield Mfg Co 626 Depot St Blissfield MI 49228 **800-626-1772*** 517-486-2121
*Cust Svc
Bry-Air Inc 10793 SR 37 W Sunbury OH 43074 **877-427-9247** 740-965-2974
Cargocaire Div Munters Corp PO Box 640 Amesbury MA 01913 **800-843-5360*** 978-388-0600
*Sales
Carrier Corp 1 Carrier Pl Farmington CT 06034 **800-227-7437** 860-674-3000
ClimateMaster Inc 7300 SW 44th St Oklahoma City OK 73179 **800-299-9747** 405-745-6000
Colmac Coil Mfg Inc PO Box 571 Colville WA 99114 **800-845-6778** 509-684-2595
DiversiTech Inc 2530 Lantrac Ct Decatur GA 30035 **800-995-2222** 770-593-0900
Dri-Steem Humidifier Co
14949 Technology Dr Eden Prairie MN 55344 **800-328-4447** 952-949-2415
Duro Dyne Corp 81 Spence St Bay Shore NY 11706 **800-899-3876** 631-249-9000
EasyHeat Div EGS Electrical Group LLC
2 Connecticut S Dr East Granby CT 06026 **800-523-7636** 860-653-1600
EGS Electrical Group LLC EasyHeat Div
2 Connecticut S Dr East Granby CT 06026 **800-523-7636** 860-653-1600
Factory Air Conditioning Corp
330 Culebra Rd San Antonio TX 78201 **800-487-1037** 210-732-9984
Friedrich Air Conditioning Co
4200 N Pan Am Expy PO Box 1540 San Antonio TX 78295 **800-541-6645** 210-225-2000
Fritze Keyspan LLC 1 Chapin Rd Pine Brook NJ 07058 **800-626-7799*** 973-808-0411
*Cust Svc
Goettl Air Conditioning Inc 1845 W 1st St Tempe AZ 85281 **800-334-6494** 602-275-1515
Hastings HVAC Inc PO Box 669 Hastings NE 68902 **800-228-4243*** 402-463-9821
*Cust Svc
Henry Technologies 701 S Main St Chatham IL 62629 **800-327-2272** 217-483-2406
Howden Buffalo Inc 2029 W Dekalb St Camden SC 29020 **800-321-8885*** 803-713-2200
*Sales
ICE-CAP Inc 275 Grand Blvd Westbury NY 11590 **800-782-2765** 516-704-0200
IGC Polycold Systems Inc
3800 Lakeville Hwy Petaluma CA 94954 **888-476-5926** 707-769-7000
IPAC 2000 PO Box 290 Niagara Falls NY 14304 **800-388-3211** 716-283-6464
ITW Vortec 10125 Carver Rd Cincinnati OH 45242 **800-441-7475** 513-891-7474
J & D Mfg Inc 6200 Hwy 12 Eau Claire WI 54701 **800-848-7998*** 715-834-1439
*Cust Svc
Kooltronic Inc 30 Pennington-Hopewell Rd Pennington NJ 08534 **800-321-5665** 609-466-3400
Lakewood Engineering & Mfg Co
501 N Sacramento Blvd Chicago IL 60612 **800-621-4277** 773-722-4300
Layton Mfg Corp 825 Remsen Ave Brooklyn NY 11236 **800-545-8002** 718-498-6000
LE Rabjohn Inc 1833 N Daly St Los Angeles CA 90031 **800-559-3737** 323-221-9163
Lintern Corp 8685 Station St Mentor OH 44061 **800-321-3638** 440-255-9333
Lomanco Inc 2101 W Main St Jacksonville AR 72078 **800-643-5596** 501-982-6511
Mammoth Inc 101 W 82nd St Chaska MN 55318 **800-328-3321** 952-361-2711
Maradyne Corp 4540 W 160th St Cleveland OH 44135 **800-537-7444** 216-362-0755
Marc Climatic Inc 1611 Elmview Dr Houston TX 77080 **800-397-0131** 713-464-8587
Master-Bilt Products 908 Hwy 15 N New Albany MS 38652 **800-647-1284** 662-534-9061
Munters Corp PO Box 6428 Fort Myers FL 33911 **800-446-6868** 239-936-1555
Munters Corp Cargocaire Div PO Box 640 Amesbury MA 01913 **800-843-5360*** 978-388-0600
*Sales
Niagara Blower Co Inc 673 Ontario St Buffalo NY 14207 **800-426-5169** 716-875-2000
Nordyne Inc 8000 Phoenix Pkwy O'Fallon MO 63366 **888-667-4822** 636-561-7300
Oasis Corp 265 N Hamilton Rd Columbus OH 43213 **800-950-3226** 614-861-1350
Packless Industries PO Box 20668 Waco TX 76702 **800-347-4859*** 254-666-7700
*Cust Svc
Packless Metal Hose Inc DBA Packless Industries
PO Box 20668 Waco TX 76702 **800-347-4859*** 254-666-7700
*Cust Svc
Phelps Fan Mfg Co Inc 10701 I-30 Little Rock AR 72209 **800-742-6899** 501-568-5550
Phoenix Mfg Inc 3655 E Roeser Rd Phoenix AZ 85040 **800-325-6952** 602-437-1034
Rabjohn LE Inc 1833 N Daly St Los Angeles CA 90031 **800-559-3737** 323-221-9163
RAE Corp Technical Systems Div PO Box 1206 Pryor OK 74361 **888-498-8922** 918-825-7222
Rama Corp 600 W Esplanade Ave San Jacinto CA 92583 **800-472-5670** 951-654-7351
Refrigeration Research Inc 525 N 5th St Brighton MI 48116 **800-311-8469** 810-227-1151
Rheem Mfg Co 405 Lexington Ave 22nd Fl New York NY 10174 **800-432-8373*** 212-916-8100
*Cust Svc
Rink Systems Inc 1103 Hershey St Albert Lea MN 56007 **800-944-7930** 507-373-9175
Ruud Mfg Co 405 Lexington Ave 22nd Fl New York NY 10174 **800-432-8373*** 212-916-8100
*Cust Svc
Sealed Unit Parts Co Inc 2230 Landmark Pl Allenwood NJ 08720 **800-333-9125** 732-223-6644
Skuttle Mfg Co 101 Margaret St Marietta OH 45750 **800-848-9786** 740-373-9169
Slant Fin Corp 100 Forest Dr Greenvale NY 11548 **800-775-4552** 516-484-2600
ThermoElectric Cooling America Corp
4048 W Schubert Ave Chicago IL 60639 **888-832-2872** 773-342-4900
Traulsen & Co Inc 4401 Blue Mound Rd Fort Worth TX 76106 **800-825-8220** 817-625-9671
Virginia KMP Corp 4100 Platinum Way Dallas TX 75237 **800-285-8567** 214-330-7731
Watsco Inc
2665 S Bayshore Dr Suite 901 Coconut Grove FL 33133 **800-492-8726** 305-714-4100
NYSE: WSO
York International Corp Engineered Systems Group 5005 York Dr Norman OK 73069 **877-874-7378** 405-364-4040
York International Corp Unitary Products Group
5005 York Dr Norman OK 73069 **877-874-7378** 405-364-4040

16 AIR CONDITIONING & HEATING EQUIPMENT - RESIDENTIAL

SEE ALSO Air Conditioning & Heating Equipment - Commercial/Industrial

Toll-Free *Phone*

Amana Appliances Inc 2800 220th Trail Amana IA 52204 **800-843-0304*** 319-622-5511
*Cust Svc
Armstrong Air Conditioning Inc
421 Monroe St Bellevue OH 44811 **800-448-5872** 419-483-4840
Behr Climate Systems 5020 Augusta Dr Fort Worth TX 76106 **800-247-6558** 817-624-7273
Butler Vent-A-Matic Corp
100 Washington Rd Mineral Wells TX 76067 **800-433-1626** 940-325-7887
Carrier Corp Carrier Transicold Div
6304 Thompson Rd Bldg TR-20 East Syracuse NY 13057 **800-255-7382** 315-432-6000
Evans Tempcon Inc 701 Ann St NW Grand Rapids MI 49504 **800-354-7088** 616-361-2681
Friedrich Air Conditioning Co
4200 N Pan Am Expy PO Box 1540 San Antonio TX 78295 **800-541-6645** 210-225-2000
GE Consumer Products Appliance Pk Louisville KY 40225 **800-626-2000** 502-452-4311
International Comfort Products Corp
650 Heil Quaker Ave Lewisburg TN 37091 **800-458-6650** 931-359-3511
National System of Garage Ventilation Inc
714 N Church St Decatur IL 62521 **800-728-8368** 217-423-7314
Rheem Mfg Co 405 Lexington Ave 22nd Fl New York NY 10174 **800-432-8373*** 212-916-8100
*Cust Svc
Ruud Mfg Co 405 Lexington Ave 22nd Fl New York NY 10174 **800-432-8373*** 212-916-8100
*Cust Svc
Simpson Mfg Co Inc
4120 Dublin Blvd Suite 400 Dublin CA 94568 **800-925-5099** 925-560-9000
NYSE: SSD
TPI Corp PO Box 4973 Johnson City TN 37602 **800-251-0382** 423-477-4131
TransPro Inc 100 Gando Dr New Haven CT 06513 **800-755-2160** 203-401-6450
AMEX: TPR
Whirlpool Corp 2000 M-63 N Benton Harbor MI 49022 **800-253-1301** 269-923-5000
NYSE: WHR
York International Corp Unitary Products Group
5005 York Dr Norman OK 73069 **877-874-7378** 405-364-4040
Young Touchstone Inc 200 Smith Ln Jackson TN 38301 **800-238-8230*** 731-424-5045
*Sales

17 AIR FARE CONSOLIDATORS

Toll-Free *Phone*

Air by Pleasant
4025 Camino del Rio S Suite 210 San Diego CA 92108 **800-877-8111** 619-282-3455

				Toll-Free	Phone
Air-Supply Inc 350 5th Ave Empire State Bldg Suite 6724	New York	NY	10118	**800-671-9961**	212-695-1647
C & H International 4751 Wilshire Blvd Suite 201	Los Angeles	CA	90010	**800-833-8888**	323-933-2288
DER Travel Services 9501 W Devon Ave Suite 301	Rosemont	IL	60018	**800-782-2424**	847-430-0000
Global Network Tours Inc DBA Air-Supply Inc 350 5th Ave Empire State Bldg Suite 6724	New York	NY	10118	**800-671-9961**	212-695-1647
Mill Run Tours Inc 424 Madison Ave 11th Fl	New York	NY	10017	**800-645-5786**	212-486-9840
Picasso Travel 350 5th Ave Suite 1417	New York	NY	10118	**800-525-3632**	212-244-5454
Premier Gateway Inc 320 SW Stark St Suite 315	Portland	OR	97204	**800-777-8369**	503-294-6478
Solar Tours 1629 'K' St NW Suite 604	Washington	DC	20006	**800-388-7652**	202-861-5864
Trans Am Travel Inc 4300 King St Suite 130	Alexandria	VA	22302	**800-822-7600**	703-998-7676

18 AIR PURIFICATION EQUIPMENT - HOUSEHOLD

SEE ALSO Appliances - Small - Mfr

				Toll-Free	Phone
AAF International Corp 10300 Ormsby Park Pl Suite 600	Louisville	KY	40223	**888-223-2003**	502-637-0011
Air Quality Engineering Inc 7140 Northland Dr N	Brooklyn Park	MN	55428	**800-328-0787**	763-531-9823
Airguard Industries Inc 3807 Bishop Ln	Louisville	KY	40218	**800-999-3458**	502-969-2304
ALFCO Div Home Care Industries Inc 1 Lisbon St *Cust Svc	Clifton	NJ	07013	**800-240-7998***	973-365-1600
Dayton Reliable Air Filter Inc 2294 N Moraine Dr *Orders	Dayton	OH	45439	**800-699-0747***	937-293-4611
Electrocorp 595 Portal St Suite A	Cotati	CA	94931	**800-525-0711**	707-665-9616
Gaylord Industries Inc 10900 SW Avery St	Tualatin	OR	97062	**800-547-9696**	503-691-2010
Home Care Industries Inc ALFCO Div 1 Lisbon St *Cust Svc	Clifton	NJ	07013	**800-240-7998***	973-365-1600
Indoor Purification Systems Inc 887 N McCormick Way Suite 3	Layton	UT	84041	**888-812-1516**	801-444-0606
Lakewood Engineering & Mfg Co 501 N Sacramento Blvd	Chicago	IL	60612	**800-621-4277**	773-722-4300
Permatron Group 1180 Pratt Blvd	Elk Grove Village	IL	60007	**800-882-8012**	847-434-1421
PuriTec 7251 W Lake Mead Blvd Suite 300	Las Vegas	NV	89128	**888-491-4100**	702-562-8802
Purolator Products Air Filtration Co 880 Facet Rd	Henderson	NC	27536	**800-334-6659**	252-492-1141
Research Products Corp 1015 E Washington Ave	Madison	WI	53703	**800-334-6011**	608-257-8801
RPS Products Inc 281 Keyes Ave	Hampshire	IL	60140	**800-683-7030**	847-683-3400
Spencer Turbine Co 600 Day Hill Rd	Windsor	CT	06095	**800-232-4321**	860-688-8361
Sterilone 2125 Biscayne Blvd Suite 580	Miami Beach	FL	33137	**877-271-1057**	305-572-0660
Tjernlund Products Inc 1601 9th St	White Bear Lake	MN	55110	**800-255-4208**	651-426-2993
Trion Inc 101 McNeill Rd	Sanford	NC	27330	**866-829-2440**	919-775-2201
United Air Specialists Inc 4440 Creek Rd	Cincinnati	OH	45242	**800-252-4647**	513-891-0400
Vornado Air Circulation Systems Inc 415 E 13th St	Andover	KS	67002	**800-297-0883**	316-733-0035

19 AIR PURIFICATION EQUIPMENT - INDUSTRIAL

				Toll-Free	Phone
AAF International Corp 10300 Ormsby Park Pl Suite 600	Louisville	KY	40223	**888-223-2003**	502-637-0011
Advantec MFS Inc 6723 Sierra Ct Suite A	Dublin	CA	94568	**800-334-7132**	925-479-0625
Aget Mfg Co 1408 E Church St	Adrian	MI	49221	**800-832-2438**	517-263-5781
Air Quality Engineering Inc 7140 Northland Dr N	Brooklyn Park	MN	55428	**800-328-0787**	763-531-9823
Aircon Filter Mfg Co 441 Green St	Philadelphia	PA	19123	**800-833-3019**	215-922-5222
Airflow Systems Inc 11221 Pagemill Rd	Dallas	TX	75243	**800-818-6185**	214-503-8008
Airguard Industries Inc 3807 Bishop Ln	Louisville	KY	40218	**800-999-3458**	502-969-2304
Airtech Corp 4260 W Artesia Ave	Fullerton	CA	92833	**800-634-4453**	714-562-9295
Alanco Technologies Inc 15575 N 83rd Way Suite 3 *NASDAQ: ALAN*	Scottsdale	AZ	85260	**800-303-7566**	480-607-1010
ALFCO Div Home Care Industries Inc 1 Lisbon St *Cust Svc	Clifton	NJ	07013	**800-240-7998***	973-365-1600
Amerex Industries Inc 665 Molly Ln Suite 110	Woodstock	GA	30189	**800-359-2586**	770-693-2100
Andersen 2000 Inc 306 Dividend Dr	Peachtree City	GA	30269	**800-241-5424**	770-486-2000
Anguil Environmental Systems Inc 8855 N 55th St	Milwaukee	WI	53223	**800-488-0230**	414-365-6400
Baghouse & Industrial Sheet Metal Services Inc 1731 Pomona Rd	Corona	CA	92880	**866-997-3784**	951-272-6610
Barnebey & Sutcliffe Corp 835 N Cassady Ave	Columbus	OH	43219	**800-886-2272**	614-258-9501
Barron Industries Inc 105 19th St S	Irondale	AL	35210	**800-226-3267**	205-956-3441
Beckett Air Inc 37850 Taylor Industrial Pkwy	North Ridgeville	OH	44039	**800-831-7839**	440-327-9999
BHA Group Inc 8800 E 63rd St	Kansas City	MO	64133	**800-821-2222**	816-356-8400
Blocksom & Co 450 St John Rd Suite 710	Michigan City	IN	46360	**800-745-1408**	219-874-3231
Camfil Farr Co 2121 E Paulhan St	Rancho Dominguez	CA	90220	**800-333-7320**	310-668-6300
Clarcor Inc 840 Crescent Ctr Dr Suite 600 *NYSE: CLC*	Franklin	TN	37067	**800-252-7267**	615-771-3100
Cleanroom Systems 7000 Performance Dr	North Syracuse	NY	13212	**800-825-3268**	315-452-7400
Clements National Co 6650 S Narragansett Ave	Chicago	IL	60638	**800-966-0016**	708-594-5890
CMI Schneible Co 714 N Saginaw St	Holly	MI	48442	**800-627-6508**	248-634-8211
Crown Andersen Inc 306 Dividend Dr *NASDAQ: CRAN*	Peachtree City	GA	30269	**800-241-5424**	770-486-2000
CSM Worldwide Inc 269 Sheffield St Suite 305	Mountainside	NJ	07092	**800-952-5227**	908-233-2882
CUNO Inc 400 Research Pkwy *NASDAQ: CUNO*	Meriden	CT	06450	**800-243-6894**	203-237-5541
Daw Technologies Inc 1600 W 2200 S Suite 201	Salt Lake City	UT	84119	**800-596-0901**	801-977-3100
Disa Systems Inc 102 Transit Ave	Thomasville	NC	27360	**800-532-0830**	336-889-5599
Eco-Air Products Inc 9455 Cabot Dr	San Diego	CA	92126	**800-284-8111**	858-271-8111
Electrocorp 595 Portal St Suite A	Cotati	CA	94931	**800-525-0711**	707-665-9616
Environmental Elements Corp 3700 Koppers St	Baltimore	MD	21227	**800-333-4331**	410-368-7000
Epcon Industrial Systems Inc 17777 Interstate 45 S	Conroe	TX	77385	**800-447-7872**	936-273-1774
Fedder RP Corp 1237 E Main St	Rochester	NY	14609	**800-288-1660**	585-288-1600
Filtration Group Inc 912 E Washington St	Joliet	IL	60433	**800-739-4600**	815-726-4600
Flex-Kleen Div Met-Pro Corp 955 Hawthorn Dr	Itasca	IL	60143	**800-621-0734**	630-775-0707
Gardner Denver Blower Div 100 Gardner Pk	Peachtree City	GA	30269	**800-543-7736**	770-632-5000
Gaylord Industries Inc 10900 SW Avery St	Tualatin	OR	97062	**800-547-9696**	503-691-2010
Great Lakes Filter 301 Arch Ave	Hillsdale	MI	49242	**800-521-8565**	
Griffin Environmental Co Inc 7066 Interstate Island Rd	Syracuse	NY	13209	**877-293-8789**	315-451-5300
Hartzell Fan Inc 910 S Downing St	Piqua	OH	45356	**800-336-3267**	937-773-7411
Home Care Industries Inc ALFCO Div 1 Lisbon St *Cust Svc	Clifton	NJ	07013	**800-240-7998***	973-365-1600
Howden Buffalo Inc 2029 W Dekalb St *Sales	Camden	SC	29020	**800-321-8885***	803-713-2200
King Engineering Corp 3201 S State St *Cust Svc	Ann Arbor	MI	48106	**800-959-0128***	734-662-5691
La Calhene Inc 1325 Field Ave S	Rush City	MN	55069	**800-322-7604**	320-358-4713
Lakewood Engineering & Mfg Co 501 N Sacramento Blvd	Chicago	IL	60612	**800-621-4277**	773-722-4300
Lydall Inc 1 Colonial Rd *NYSE: LDL*	Manchester	CT	06045	**800-365-9325**	860-646-1233
M-D Pneumatics Div Tuthill Corp 4840 W Kearney St	Springfield	MO	65803	**800-825-6937**	417-865-8715
McIntire Co 745 Clark Ave	Bristol	CT	06010	**800-437-9247**	860-585-0050
Met-Pro Corp Flex-Kleen Div 955 Hawthorn Dr	Itasca	IL	60143	**800-621-0734**	630-775-0707
Midwesco Filter Resources Inc 385 Battaile Dr	Winchester	VA	22601	**800-336-7300**	540-667-8500
NAO Inc 1284 E Sedgley Ave *Cust Svc	Philadelphia	PA	19134	**800-523-3495***	215-743-5300
National Filter Media Corp 691 N 400 West	Salt Lake City	UT	84103	**800-777-4248**	801-363-6736
Parker Hannifin Corp Finite Filtratio & Separation Div 500 Glaspie St	Oxford	MI	48371	**800-521-4357**	248-628-6400
Paxton Products Corp 10125 Carver Rd	Cincinnati	OH	45242	**800-441-7475**	513-891-7474
Precipitator Services Group Inc 1625 Broad St	Elizabethton	TN	37643	**800-345-0484**	423-543-7331
Process Equipment Inc 2770 Welborn St	Pelham	AL	35124	**800-765-9863**	205-663-5330
Purafil Inc 2654 Weaver Way	Doraville	GA	30340	**800-222-6367**	770-662-8545
Purolator Products Air Filtration Co 880 Facet Rd	Henderson	NC	27536	**800-334-6659**	252-492-1141
Revcor Inc 251 Edwards Ave	Carpentersville	IL	60110	**800-323-8261**	847-428-4411
RP Fedder Corp 1237 E Main St	Rochester	NY	14609	**800-288-1660**	585-288-1600
RPS Products Inc 281 Keyes Ave	Hampshire	IL	60140	**800-683-7030**	847-683-3400
Sly Inc 8300 Dow Cir	Strongsville	OH	44136	**800-334-2957**	440-891-3200
Sonic Air Systems Inc 1050 Beacon St	Brea	CA	92821	**800-827-6642**	714-255-0124
Spencer Turbine Co 600 Day Hill Rd	Windsor	CT	06095	**800-232-4321**	860-688-8361
Steelcraft Corp 2700 Jackson Ave	Memphis	TN	38108	**800-238-4012**	901-452-5200
Terra Universal Inc 165 Freedom Ave	Anaheim	CA	92801	**800-767-0100**	714-526-0100
Tjernlund Products Inc 1601 9th St	White Bear Lake	MN	55110	**800-255-4208**	651-426-2993
Tri-Dim Filter Corp 93 Industrial Dr Bldg 2	Louisa	VA	23093	**800-458-9835**	540-967-2600
Tri-Mer Corp 1400 Monroe St	Owosso	MI	48867	**800-688-7838**	989-723-7838
Trion Inc 101 McNeill Rd	Sanford	NC	27330	**866-829-2440**	919-775-2201
Turbosonic Technologies Inc 239 New Rd Bldg B-205	Parsippany	NJ	07054	**800-882-9280**	973-244-9544
Tuthill Corp M-D Pneumatics Div 4840 W Kearney St	Springfield	MO	65803	**800-825-6937**	417-865-8715
United Air Specialists Inc 4440 Creek Rd	Cincinnati	OH	45242	**800-252-4647**	513-891-0400

20 AIR TRAFFIC CONTROL SERVICES

				Toll-Free	Phone
Federal Aviation Administration (FAA) 800 Independence Ave SW	Washington	DC	20591	**800-322-7873**	202-267-3484
NAV CANADA 77 Metcalfe St	Ottawa	ON	K1P5L6	**800-876-4693**	613-563-5588

21 AIRCRAFT

SEE ALSO Airships

				Toll-Free	Phone
American Eurocopter Corp 2701 Forum Dr	Grand Prairie	TX	75052	**800-873-0001**	972-641-0000
Bell Helicopter Textron Inc PO Box 482	Fort Worth	TX	76101	**800-359-2355**	817-280-2011
Bombardier Aerospace Learjet 1 Learjet Way	Wichita	KS	67209	**800-289-5327**	316-946-2000
Embraer Aircraft Corp 276 SW 34th St	Fort Lauderdale	FL	33315	**800-362-7237**	954-359-3700
Erickson Air-Crane Co 3100 Willow Springs Rd PO Box 3247	Central Point	OR	97502	**800-424-2413**	541-664-5544
Mooney Aircraft Corp Louis Schreiner Field	Kerrville	TX	78028	**800-456-3033**	830-896-6000
Sabreliner Corp 3551 Doniphan Dr	Neosho	MO	64850	**800-325-4663**	417-451-1810
Tiger Aircraft LLC 226 Pilot Way	Martinsburg	WV	25401	**877-808-4437**	304-260-0038

22 AIRCRAFT ENGINES & ENGINE PARTS

				Toll-Free	Phone
A & B Aerospace Inc 612 Ayon Ave	Azusa	CA	91702	**888-999-9397**	626-334-2976
AAR Corp 1100 N Wood Dale Rd 1 AAR Pl *NYSE: AIR*	Wood Dale	IL	60191	**800-422-2213**	630-227-2000

				Toll-Free	Phone
Aircraft Parts Corp 100 Corporate Dr.	Holtsville	NY	11742	**877-427-2634**	631-289-0077
Engine Components Inc 9503 Middlex Dr	San Antonio	TX	78217	**800-324-2359**	210-820-8100
Gros-Ite Industries 1790 New Britain Ave	Farmington	CT	06032	**800-242-1790**	860-677-2603
Lycoming Engines 652 Oliver St.	Williamsport	PA	17701	**800-258-3279**	570-323-6181
Parker Hannifin Corp 6035 Parkland Blvd	Cleveland	OH	44124	**800-272-7537***	216-896-3000
NYSE: PH ■ *Cust Svc					
Pratt & Whitney Canada Inc					
1000 Marie-Victorin Blvd	Longueuil	QC	J4G1A1	**800-268-8000**	450-677-9411
Pratt & Whitney Government Engines & Space Propulsion Div					
PO Box 109600	West Palm Beach	FL	33410	**800-327-3246**	561-796-2000
Rolls-Royce North America					
14850 Conference Ctr Dr Suite 100	Chantilly	VA	20151	**800-274-5387**	703-834-1700
Wall Colmonoy Corp					
30261 Stephenson Hwy	Madison Heights	MI	48071	**800-521-2412**	248-585-6400
Woodward Governor Co 5001 N 2nd St	Loves Park	IL	61111	**888-273-8839**	815-877-7441
NASDAQ: WGOV					

23 AIRCRAFT PARTS & AUXILIARY EQUIPMENT

SEE ALSO Precision Machined Products

				Toll-Free	Phone
AAR Cargo Systems 12633 Inkster Rd	Livonia	MI	48150	**800-247-1273**	734-522-2000
AAR Composites 14201 Myerlake Cir	Clearwater	FL	33760	**888-227-3597**	727-539-8585
AAR Corp 1100 N Wood Dale Rd 1 AAR Pl	Wood Dale	IL	60191	**800-422-2213**	630-227-2000
NYSE: AIR					
Aeronca Inc 2320 Wedekind Dr	Middletown	OH	45042	**800-991-1387**	513-422-2751
B/E Aerospace Inc 1400 Corporate Ctr Way	Wellington	FL	33414	**888-223-2376**	561-791-5000
NASDAQ: BEAV					
CEF Industries Inc 320 S Church St	Addison	IL	60101	**800-888-6419**	630-628-2299
Goodrich Corp Aircraft Interior Products Div					
3414 S 5th St	Phoenix	AZ	85040	**888-419-4344**	602-232-4000
Honeywell Aerospace 1944 E Sky Harbor Cir	Phoenix	AZ	85034	**800-601-3099**	
Honeywell Inc Aircraft Landing Systems					
3520 Westmoor St	South Bend	IN	46628	**800-707-4555**	574-231-2000
Middle River Aircraft Systems					
103 Chesapeake Pk Plaza	Baltimore	MD	21220	**800-880-9975**	410-682-1000
Sargent Fletcher Inc 9400 E Flair Dr	El Monte	CA	91731	**800-504-0101**	626-443-7171

24 AIRCRAFT RENTAL

SEE ALSO Aviation - Fixed-Base Operations

				Toll-Free	Phone
Jetscape Inc					
408 S Andrews Ave Suite 200	Fort Lauderdale	FL	33301	**800-355-5387**	954-763-4737
Jones Aviation Service Inc					
1234 Clyde Jones Rd	Sarasota	FL	34243	**800-945-6637**	941-355-8100
Pinnacle Air 802 Airport Rd	Springdale	AR	72764	**800-828-4462**	479-751-4462

25 AIRCRAFT SERVICE & REPAIR

				Toll-Free	Phone
AAR Corp 1100 N Wood Dale Rd 1 AAR Pl	Wood Dale	IL	60191	**800-422-2213**	630-227-2000
NYSE: AIR					
AeroThrust Corp PO Box 522236	Miami	FL	33152	**800-228-0665**	305-871-1790
American Avionics Inc 7023 Perimeter Rd S	Seattle	WA	98108	**800-518-5858***	206-763-8530
*Sales					
Basler Turbo Conversions Inc PO Box 2305	Oshkosh	WI	54903	**800-558-0254**	920-236-7820
Christiansen Aviation Inc PO Box 702412	Tulsa	OK	74170	**800-331-5550**	918-299-2687
Composite Technology Inc 1001 Ave R	Grand Prairie	TX	75050	**888-284-1972**	972-606-4400
Curtiss-Wright Controls Inc					
15800 John J Delaney Dr Suite 200	Charlotte	NC	28277	**877-319-8468**	704-869-4600
Cutter Aviation					
2802 E Old Tower Rd Sky Harbor International Airport	Phoenix	AZ	85034	**800-234-5382**	602-273-1237
Downtown Airpark Inc 1701-A N Cimarron Rd	Yukon	OK	73099	**800-253-1456**	405-350-1161
Duncan Aviation Inc PO Box 81887	Lincoln	NE	68501	**800-228-4277**	402-475-2611
EADS Sogerma Barfield Inc 4101 NW 29th St	Miami	FL	33142	**800-321-1039**	305-894-5400
Elliott Aviation Inc 6601 74th Ave	Milan	IL	61264	**800-447-6711**	309-799-3183
Emery Air Charter Inc 1 Airport Cir	Rockford	IL	61125	**800-435-8090**	815-968-8287
Evergreen Air Center Inc Pinal Air Pk Rd	Marana	AZ	85653	**800-624-6838**	520-682-4181
Evergreen International Aviation Inc					
3850 Three Mile Ln	McMinnville	OR	97128	**800-472-9361**	503-472-9361
Garrett Aviation 6201 W Imperial Hwy	Los Angeles	CA	90045	**800-942-7738**	310-568-3700
Honeywell Inc Aircraft Landing Systems					
3520 Westmoor St	South Bend	IN	46628	**800-707-4555**	574-231-2000
Jet Aviation 112 Charles A Lindbergh Dr	Teterboro	NJ	07608	**800-538-0832**	201-288-8400
L-3 Communications Flight International Aviation LLC 1 Lear Dr	Newport News	VA	23602	**800-358-4685**	757-886-5500
Martin Aviation 19300 Ike Jones Rd	Santa Ana	CA	92707	**800-793-9191**	714-210-2945
McKinley Air Transport Inc PO Box 2406	North Canton	OH	44720	**800-225-6446**	330-499-3316
Million Air Interlink Inc 8501 Telephone Rd	Houston	TX	77061	**888-589-9059**	713-640-4000
Northern Air Inc 5500 44th St SE	Grand Rapids	MI	49512	**800-262-4953**	616-336-4700
Priester Aviation 1061 S Wolf Rd	Wheeling	IL	60090	**888-323-7887**	847-537-1133
Rockford Motors Inc DBA Emery Air Charter Inc					
1 Airport Cir	Rockford	IL	61125	**800-435-8090**	815-968-8287
Rolls-Royce Engine Services Inc					
7200 Earhart Rd	Oakland	CA	94621	**800-622-2677**	510-613-1000
Sabreliner Corp 7733 Forsyth Blvd Suite 1500	Clayton	MO	63105	**800-325-4663**	314-863-6880
Sierra Industries Inc					
Garner Municipal Airport 122 Howard Langford Dr	Uvalde	TX	78802	**888-835-9377**	830-278-4381
Standard Aero Ltd 33 Allen Dyne Rd	Winnipeg	MB	R3H1A1	**888-836-4433**	204-775-9711
Summit Aviation Inc PO Box 258	Middletown	DE	19709	**800-441-9343**	302-834-5400
TAG Aviation Inc 6855 34th Ave S	Minneapolis	MN	55450	**800-726-1673**	612-726-1673
Telford Aviation Inc 154 Maine St	Bangor	ME	04401	**800-639-4809**	207-262-6098

				Toll-Free	Phone
Triumph Instruments & Avionics					
1425 Grand Central Ave	Glendale	CA	91201	**800-525-6696**	818-246-8431
Tulsair Beechcraft Inc PO Box 582470	Tulsa	OK	74158	**800-331-4071**	918-835-7651
West Star Aviation Inc					
796 Heritage Way	Grand Junction	CO	81506	**800-255-4193**	970-243-7500
Wood Group Turbo Power Inc					
14820 NW 60th Ave	Miami Lakes	FL	33014	**800-403-6737**	305-820-3225

26 AIRLINES - COMMERCIAL

SEE ALSO Air Cargo Carriers; Air Charter Services; Airlines - Frequent Flyer Programs

				Toll-Free	Phone
Aer Lingus 538 Broadhollow Rd Suite 3	Melville	NY	11747	**800-474-7424**	631-577-5700
Aerolineas Argentinas					
51 E 42nd St Suite 1600	New York	NY	10017	**800-333-0276**	212-542-8880
AeroMexico					
3663 N Sam Houston Pkwy E Suite 500	Houston	TX	77032	**800-237-6639**	281-372-3420
Air Canada 7373 Cote Vertu W	Saint-Laurent	QC	H4Y1H4	**888-247-2262**	514-422-5000
Air Canada Jazz 310 Goudey Dr	Enfield	NS	B2T1E4	**866-222-6688***	902-873-5000
*Cust Svc					
Air China 150 E 52 St	New York	NY	10022	**800-982-8802**	212-371-9898
Air France 125 W 55th St	New York	NY	10019	**800-237-2747***	212-830-4000
*Resv					
Air India 570 Lexington Ave 15th Fl	New York	NY	10022	**800-223-7776**	212-407-1300
Air Jamaica 95-25 Queens Blvd 7th Fl	Rego Park	NY	11374	**800-523-5585**	718-830-0622
Air Midwest Inc DBA US Airways Express					
2203 Air Cargo Rd	Wichita	KS	67209	**800-428-4322**	316-942-8137
Air New Zealand Ltd					
1960 E Grand Ave Suite 900	El Segundo	CA	90245	**800-262-1234**	310-648-7000
Air Sunshine Inc PO Box 22237	Fort Lauderdale	FL	33335	**800-327-8900**	954-434-8900
Air Tahiti Nui 1990 E Grand Ave	El Segundo	CA	90245	**877-824-4846***	310-662-1860
*Cust Svc					
AirTran Airways 9955 AirTran Blvd	Orlando	FL	32827	**800-247-8726**	407-251-5600
Alaska Airlines Inc PO Box 68900	Seattle	WA	98168	**800-252-7522***	206-433-3200
*Resv					
Alitalia Airlines 350 5th Ave 37th Fl	New York	NY	10118	**800-223-5730**	212-903-3300
All Nippon Airways Co Ltd					
1251 Ave of the Americas 8th Fl	New York	NY	10020	**800-235-9262**	
Allegiant Air 3301 N Buffalo Dr Suite B-9	Las Vegas	NV	89129	**800-432-3810***	702-851-7300
*Resv					
Aloha Airlines Inc PO Box 30028	Honolulu	HI	96820	**800-367-5250**	808-484-1111
America West Airlines Inc					
4000 E Sky Harbor Blvd	Phoenix	AZ	85034	**800-235-9292**	480-693-0800
American Airlines Inc PO Box 619616	DFW Airport	TX	75261	**800-433-7300**	817-963-1234
Asiana Airlines Inc					
3530 Wilshire Blvd Suite 1700	Los Angeles	CA	90010	**800-227-4262**	213-365-4500
ATA Airlines Inc 7337 W Washington St	Indianapolis	IN	46231	**800-435-9282***	317-247-4000
*Resv					
Austrian Airlines					
1720 Whitestone Expy Suite 500	Whitestone	NY	11357	**800-843-0002**	718-670-8600
Avianca Airlines 8125 NW 53rd St Suite 111	Miami	FL	33166	**800-284-2622**	
Bearskin Airlines PO Box 1447	Sioux Lookout	ON	P8T1C1	**800-465-2327**	807-737-3474
Big Sky Airlines 1601 Aviation Pl	Billings	MT	59105	**800-237-7788**	406-247-3910
British Airways 75-20 Astoria Blvd	Jackson Heights	NY	11370	**800-247-9297**	347-418-4000
BWIA International Airways					
5805 Blue Lagoon Dr Suite 340	Miami	FL	33126	**800-327-0204**	305-261-0393
CanJet Airlines PO Box 980	Enfield	NS	B2T1R6	**800-809-7777***	902-973-7800
*Resv					
Cape Air 660 Barnstable Rd	Hyannis	MA	02601	**800-352-0714**	508-771-6944
Cathay Pacific Airways					
300 Continental Blvd Suite 500	El Segundo	CA	90245	**800-233-2742**	310-615-1113
Cayman Airways Ltd					
8400 NW 52nd St Suite 210	Miami	FL	33166	**800-422-9626**	305-266-6760
China Airlines Ltd					
6053 W Century Blvd Suite 800	Los Angeles	CA	90045	**800-227-5118**	310-641-8888
Comair Delta Connection 77 Comair Blvd	Erlanger	KY	41018	**800-727-2550**	859-767-2550
Continental Airlines Inc 1600 Smith St	Houston	TX	77002	**800-525-0280**	713-324-5000
NYSE: CAL					
Continental Express 1600 Smith St HQSCE	Houston	TX	77002	**877-324-2639**	713-324-5000
NYSE: XJT					
Czech Airlines					
1350 Ave of the Americas Suite 601	New York	NY	10019	**800-223-2365**	212-765-6545
Delta Air Lines Inc					
PO Box 20706 Hartsfiled-Atlanta Airport	Atlanta	GA	30320	**800-221-1212**	404-715-2600
NYSE: DAL					
Delta Connection 444 S River Rd	Saint George	UT	84790	**800-221-1212**	435-634-3000
EgyptAir 720 5th Ave 11th Fl	New York	NY	10019	**800-334-6787**	212-581-5600
El Al Israel Airlines Ltd 15 E 26th St 6th Fl	New York	NY	10010	**800-223-6700**	212-852-0600
Era Aviation Inc 6160 Carl Brady Dr	Anchorage	AK	99502	**800-866-8394**	907-243-6633
Ethiopian Airlines 336 E 45th St 3rd Fl	New York	NY	10017	**800-445-2733**	212-867-0095
EVA Airways 12440 E Imperial Hwy Suite 250	Norwalk	CA	90650	**800-695-1188**	562-565-6000
ExpressJet Airlines Inc 1600 Smith St HQSCE	Houston	TX	77002	**877-324-2639**	713-324-5000
NYSE: XJT					
Finnair 228 E 45th St	New York	NY	10017	**800-950-5000**	212-499-9000
Frontier Airlines 7001 Tower Rd	Denver	CO	80249	**800-265-5505**	720-374-4200
Garuda Indonesian Airlines					
3050 Post Oak Blvd Suite 1320	Houston	TX	77056	**800-342-7832**	713-877-1942
Great Lakes Airlines 1022 Airport Pkwy	Cheyenne	WY	82001	**800-554-5111**	307-432-7000
Great Lakes Aviation Ltd DBA Great Lakes Airlines 1022 Airport Pkwy	Cheyenne	WY	82001	**800-554-5111**	307-432-7000
Grupo Taca PO Box 590628	Miami	FL	33159	**800-251-1351**	305-871-1587
Gulfstream International Airlines					
1815 Griffin Rd Suite 400	Dania Beach	FL	33004	**800-457-4853**	954-266-3000
Hawaiian Airlines Inc					
3375 Koapaka St Suite G350	Honolulu	HI	96819	**800-367-5320**	808-835-3700
AMEX: HA					
Hooters Air 1704 Oak St	Myrtle Beach	SC	29577	**888-359-4668**	843-916-4600
Horizon Air Industries Inc					
19521 International Blvd S PO Box 68977	Seattle	WA	98168	**800-523-1223**	206-241-6757
Iberia Airlines of Spain					
5835 Blue Lagoon Dr Suite 350	Miami	FL	33126	**800-772-4642**	305-267-7747
Icelandair					
5950 Symphony Woods Rd Suite 410	Columbia	MD	21044	**800-223-5500**	410-715-1600
Japan Airlines 461 5th Ave 6th Fl	New York	NY	10017	**800-525-3663**	212-838-4400
JetBlue Airways 118-29 Queens Blvd	Forest Hills	NY	11375	**800-538-2583**	718-286-7900
Kenmore Air Harbor Inc 6321 NE 175th St	Kenmore	WA	98028	**800-543-9595**	425-486-1257

Name / Address	City	State	Zip	Toll-Free	Phone
Korean Air 6101 W Imperial Hwy	Los Angeles	CA	90045	**800-438-5000**	310-417-5200
LAB Airlines 225 SE 1st St	Miami	FL	33131	**800-337-0918**	305-374-4600
LACSA 3600 Wilshire Blvd Suite 100P *Sales	Los Angeles	CA	90010	**800-225-2272***	213-385-9424
LanChile Airlines 9700 S Dixie Hwy 11th Fl	Miami	FL	33156	**800-735-5526**	305-670-1961
LanPeru Airlines 9700 S Dixie Hwy 11th Fl	Miami	FL	33156	**800-735-5526**	305-670-9999
Lauda Air 1155 Connecticut Ave NW Suite 602	Washington	DC	20036	**800-843-0002**	202-955-0023
Lloyd Aereo Boliviano DBA LAB Airlines 225 SE 1st St	Miami	FL	33131	**800-337-0918**	305-374-4600
LOT Polish Airlines 500 5th Ave Suite 408	New York	NY	10110	**800-223-0593**	212-869-1074
LTU International Airways 20803 Biscayne Blvd Suite 401	North Miami Beach	FL	33180	**866-266-5588**	305-932-1595
Lufthansa USA 1640 Hempstead Tpke *Resv	East Meadow	NY	11554	**800-581-6400***	516-296-9200
Lynx Air International 3402 SW 9th Ave	Fort Lauderdale	FL	33315	**888-596-9247**	954-772-9808
Malaysia Airlines 100 N Sepulveda Blvd Suite 400	El Segundo	CA	90245	**800-552-9264**	310-535-9288
Malev-Hungarian Airlines 90 John St Suite 312	New York	NY	10038	**800-223-6884**	212-566-9944
Martinair 5550 Glades Rd Suite 600	Boca Raton	FL	33431	**800-627-8462**	561-391-6165
Mesa Airlines 410 N 44th St Suite 700	Phoenix	AZ	85008	**800-637-2247**	602-685-4000
Mexicana Airlines 6151 W Century Blvd Suite 1124	Los Angeles	CA	90045	**800-531-7923**	310-646-0401
Midwest Airlines Inc 6744 S Howell Ave	Oak Creek	WI	53154	**800-452-2022**	414-570-4000
New England Airlines Inc 56 Airport Rd	Westerly	RI	02891	**800-243-2460**	401-596-2460
Northwest Airlines Inc (NWA) 2700 Lone Oak Pkwy	Eagan	MN	55121	**800-225-2525**	612-726-2111
Northwest/KLM 2700 Lone Oak Pkwy	Eagan	MN	55121	**800-225-2525**	612-726-2111
NWA (Northwest Airlines Inc) 2700 Lone Oak Pkwy	Eagan	MN	55121	**800-225-2525**	612-726-2111
Olympic Airways 7000 Austin St	Forest Hills	NY	11375	**800-736-5717**	718-269-2200
Pacific Wings Kahului Airport Commuter Terminal 1 Kahului Airport Rd	Kahului	HI	96732	**888-575-4547**	808-873-0877
Pakistan International Airlines Corp 505 8th Ave 14th Fl	New York	NY	10018	**800-221-2552**	212-760-8484
Peninsula Airways Inc 6100 Boeing Ave	Anchorage	AK	99502	**800-448-4226**	907-243-2485
Philippine Airlines Inc 116 McDonnell Rd *Resv	San Francisco	CA	94128	**800-435-9725***	650-877-4818
Piedmont Airlines Inc DBA US Airways Express 5443 Airport Terminal Rd	Salisbury	MD	21804	**800-354-3394**	410-742-2996
Pinnacle Airlines Inc 1689 Nonconnah Blvd Suite 111 *NASDAQ: PNCL*	Memphis	TN	38132	**800-603-4594**	901-348-4100
PSA Airlines Inc DBA US Airways Express 3400 Terminal Dr	Vandalia	OH	45377	**800-235-0986**	937-454-1116
Qantas Airways Ltd 6080 Center Dr Suite 400	Los Angeles	CA	90045	**800-227-4500**	310-726-1400
Qatar Airways 399 Thornall St	Edison	NJ	08837	**877-777-2827**	732-321-1701
Royal Air Maroc 55 E 59th St Suite 17B	New York	NY	10022	**800-344-6726**	212-750-5115
Royal Jordanian Airlines 6 E 43rd St 27th Fl	New York	NY	10017	**800-223-0470**	212-949-0060
Royal Nepal Airlines North America 16250 Ventura Blvd Suite 115	Encino	CA	91436	**800-266-3725**	
Saudi Arabian Airlines 12555 N Burrough Dr	Houston	TX	77067	**800-472-8342**	281-873-1000
Scandinavian Airlines System 9 Polito Ave	Lyndhurst	NJ	07071	**800-221-2350**	201-896-3600
Singapore Airlines Ltd 5670 Wilshire Blvd 18th Fl	Los Angeles	CA	90036	**800-742-3333**	323-934-8833
Skyservice Airlines Inc 31 Fasken Dr	Etobicoke	ON	M9W1K6	**800-701-9448**	416-679-5700
Song Airways LLC PO Box 20504	Atlanta	GA	30320	**800-359-7664**	
South African Airways 515 E Las Olas Blvd 16th Fl	Fort Lauderdale	FL	33301	**800-722-9675**	954-769-5000
Southwest Airlines Co 2702 Love Field Dr *NYSE: LUV* ■ *Resv	Dallas	TX	75235	**800-435-9792***	214-792-4000
Spirit Airlines Inc 2800 Executive Way	Miramar	FL	33025	**800-772-7117**	954-447-7965
SriLankan Airlines 1936 Wilshire Blvd	Los Angeles	CA	90057	**877-915-2652**	213-483-8808
Sun Country Airlines Inc 1300 Mendota Heights Rd	Mendota Heights	MN	55120	**800-359-6786**	651-681-3900
Surinam Airways Ltd 7270 NW 12th St Suite 255	Miami	FL	33126	**800-327-6864**	305-599-1196
Swiss International Airlines Ltd 10 E 53rd St	New York	NY	10022	**877-359-7947**	
TACA International Airlines 6824 Veterans Blvd Suite 100-A	Metairie	LA	70003	**800-535-8780**	504-887-7847
TAP Air Portugal 399 Market St *Resv	Newark	NJ	07105	**800-221-7370***	973-344-4490
Ted PO Box 66100 *Resv	Chicago	IL	60666	**800-225-5833***	877-228-1327
Thai Airways International Ltd 222 N Sepulveda Blvd Suite 1950	El Segundo	CA	90245	**800-426-5204**	310-640-0097
Turkish Airlines 437 Madison Ave	New York	NY	10022	**800-874-8875**	
Ukraine International Airlines 1643-A W Henderson	Cleburne	TX	76033	**800-876-0114**	817-641-3478
United Airlines Inc PO Box 66100	Chicago	IL	60666	**800-241-6522**	847-700-4000
United Express 1200 E Algonquin Rd	Elk Grove Township	IL	60007	**800-241-6522**	847-700-4000
US Airways Express 2203 Air Cargo Rd	Wichita	KS	67209	**800-428-4322**	316-942-8137
US Airways Express 5443 Airport Terminal Rd	Salisbury	MD	21804	**800-354-3394**	410-742-2996
US Airways Express 3400 Terminal Dr	Vandalia	OH	45377	**800-235-0986**	937-454-1116
US Airways Express 2345 Crystal Dr Crystal Pk 4	Arlington	VA	22227	**800-428-4322**	703-872-7000
US Airways Inc 2345 Crystal Dr Crystal Pk 4	Arlington	VA	22227	**800-428-4322**	703-872-7000
US Airways Shuttle Inc La Guardia Airport	Flushing	NY	11371	**800-428-4322**	718-397-6200
USA 3000 Airlines 335 Bishop Hollow Rd Suite 100	Newtown Square	PA	19073	**877-872-3000**	610-325-1280
Varig Brasil Airlines 71 S Central Ave 2nd Fl	Valley Stream	NY	11580	**800-468-2744**	516-612-0339
Virgin Atlantic Airways Ltd 747 Belden Ave	Norwalk	CT	06850	**800-862-8621**	203-750-2000
WestJet Airlines Ltd 5055 11th St NE *TSE: WJA*	Calgary	AB	T2E8N4	**888-293-7853**	403-444-2600

27 AIRLINES - FREQUENT FLYER PROGRAMS

Name / Address	City	State	Zip	Toll-Free	Phone
Aer Lingus Airlines Gold Circle Club 538 Broadhollow Rd	Melville	NY	11747	**800-474-7424**	
AeroMexico Club Premier 3663 N Sam Houston Pkwy E Suite 500	Houston	TX	77032	**800-247-3737**	
Air Canada Aeroplan PO Box 15000 Station Airport	Dorval	QC	H4Y1H5	**866-689-8080**	800-361-5373
Air China Companion Club 150 E 52nd St	New York	NY	10022	**800-982-8802**	212-371-9898
Air France Frequence Plus 235 King St E	Kitchener	ON	N2G4N5	**800-375-8723**	519-772-3570
Air Jamaica 7th Heaven 8300 NW 33rd St Suite 440	Miami	FL	33122	**800-523-5585**	305-670-3222
Air New Zealand Airpoints 1960 E Grand Ave Suite 300	El Segundo	CA	90245	**800-223-9494**	800-262-1234
AirTran Airways A-Plus Rewards 1224 Bob Harman Rd	Savannah	GA	31408	**888-327-5878**	
Alaska Airlines Mileage Plan PO Box 24948 Customer Service Ctr	Seattle	WA	98124	**800-654-5669**	
Alitalia Airlines MilleMiglia Club 350 5th Ave 36th Fl *Cust Svc	New York	NY	10118	**800-223-5730***	888-525-4825
All Nippon Airways Mileage Club (ANA) 2050 W 190th St Suite 100	Torrance	CA	90504	**800-262-4653**	310-782-3000
Aloha Airlines AlohaPass PO Box 30028	Honolulu	HI	96820	**800-367-5250**	
America West Airlines FlightFund PO Box 20050	Phoenix	AZ	85036	**800-247-5691**	
American Airlines AAdvantage Program PO Box 619620	DFW Airport	TX	75261	**800-882-8880**	
Asiana Airlines Asiana Club 3530 Wilshire Blvd Suite 1700 *Resv	Los Angeles	CA	90010	**800-227-4262***	213-365-4500
ATA Travel Awards 7337 W Washington St	Indianapolis	IN	46231	**800-435-9282**	317-247-4000
British Airways Executive Club PO Box 1757	Minneapolis	MN	55440	**800-955-2748**	
Cathay Pacific Asia Miles 300 Continental Blvd Suite 500	El Segundo	CA	90245	**866-892-2598**	
China Airlines Dynasty Flyer 6053 W Century Blvd Suite 800	Los Angeles	CA	90045	**800-227-5118**	
Club Tiare 1990 E Grand Ave	El Segundo	CA	90245	**877-824-4846**	310-662-1860
Continental Airlines OnePass 900 Grand Plaza Dr	Houston	TX	77067	**800-621-7467**	713-952-1630
Czech Airlines OK Plus 1350 Ave of the Americas Suite 601	New York	NY	10019	**800-223-2365**	212-765-6545
Delta Air Lines SkyMiles SkyMiles Service Ctr Dept 654 PO Box 20532	Atlanta	GA	30320	**800-323-2323**	
EgyptAir Plus 720 5th Ave 11th FL	New York	NY	10019	**800-334-6787**	212-581-5600
El Al Israel Airlines Matmid Frequent Flyer Club 15 E 26th St	New York	NY	10010	**800-223-6700**	212-852-0604
EVA Air Evergreen Club 12440 E Imperial Hwy Suite 250	Norwalk	CA	90650	**800-695-1188**	562-565-6000
Finnair Plus 228 E 45th St	New York	NY	10017	**800-950-3387**	
Frontier Airlines EarlyReturns PO Box 17304 *Cust Svc	Denver	CO	80217	**800-265-5505***	866-263-2759
GlobalPass 6355 NW 36th St Suite 600	Miami	FL	33166	**877-946-4537**	305-870-7500
Hawaiian Airlines HawaiianMiles PO Box 30008	Honolulu	HI	96820	**877-426-4537**	
Iberia Airlines Plus Program 5835 Blue Lagoon Dr Suite 350	Miami	FL	33126	**800-721-4122**	305-267-7747
Icelandair Customer Club 5950 Symphony Woods Rd Suite 410	Columbia	MD	21044	**800-223-5500**	800-757-7242
Independence Air iCLUB 45200 Business Ct	Dulles	VA	20166	**800-359-3594**	703-650-6000
Japan Airlines Mileage Bank 300 Continental Blvd Suite 401	El Segundo	CA	90245	**800-525-6453**	
JetBlue TrueBlue 6322 S 3000 East Fl G-1 Suite G-10	Salt Lake City	UT	84121	**800-538-2583**	801-365-2528
Korean Air Skypass 1813 Wilshire Blvd Suite 400	Los Angeles	CA	90057	**800-525-4480**	
LanPass 9700 S Dixie Hwy 11th FL	Miami	FL	33156	**866-435-9526**	305-670-9999
Mabuhay Miles 116 McDonnell Rd	San Francisco	CA	94128	**800-747-1959**	
Malev Hungarian Airlines Duna Club 90 John St Suite 312	New York	NY	10038	**800-223-6884**	212-566-9944
Mexicana Airlines Frecuenta 482 W San Ysidro Blvd Suite 754	San Ysidro	CA	92173	**800-531-7901**	
Midwest Airlines Midwest Miles 6744 S Howell Ave Dept 16	Oak Creek	WI	53154	**800-452-2022**	414-570-4000
Miles & More PO Box 946	Santa Clarita	CA	91380	**800-581-6400**	
Northwest Airlines WorldPerks 601 Oak St	Chisholm	MN	55719	**800-447-3757**	
Qantas Airways Frequent Flyer Program 6080 Center Dr	Los Angeles	CA	90045	**800-227-4220**	310-726-1400
Qatar Airways Privilege Club 399 Thornall St	Edison	NJ	08837	**877-777-2827**	732-321-1701
Saudi Arabian Airlines Alfursan Program 12555 N Burrough Dr	Houston	TX	77067	**800-472-8342**	281-873-1000
Scandinavian Airlines System EuroBonus (SAS) 9 Polito Ave	Lyndhurst	NJ	07071	**800-437-5807**	
Singapore Airlines KrisFlyer 5670 Wilshire Blvd Suite 1900	Los Angeles	CA	90036	**800-742-3333**	
South African Airways Voyager 515 E Las Olas Blvd Sun Trust Bldg 16th Fl	Fort Lauderdale	FL	33301	**800-359-7220**	954-769-5000
Southwest Airlines Rapid Rewards PO Box 36657	Dallas	TX	75235	**800-445-9267**	
SriLankan Airlines Skywards 1936 Wilshire Blvd	Los Angeles	CA	90057	**877-915-2652**	213-483-8808
Swiss TravelClub 10 E 53rd St	New York	NY	10022	**877-359-7947**	
Thai Airways Royal Orchid Plus 222 N Sepulveda Blvd Suite 1950	El Segundo	CA	90245	**800-426-5204**	
Turkish Airlines Miles & Miles 437 Madison Ave	New York	NY	10022	**800-874-8875**	
Ukraine International Airlines Panorama Club 1643-A W Henderson	Cleburne	TX	76033	**800-876-0114**	817-641-3478
United Airlines Mileage Plus PO Box 28870	Tucson	AZ	85726	**800-421-4655**	
Varig Brasil Airlines Smiles Program 71 S Central Ave 2nd FL	Valley Stream	NY	11580	**800-468-2744**	516-612-0339
Virgin Atlantic Flying Club 747 Belden Ave	Norwalk	CT	06850	**800-365-9500**	

28 AIRPORTS

SEE ALSO Ports & Port Authorities

Name / Address	City	State	Zip	Toll-Free	Phone
Akron-Canton Regional Airport (CAK)	North Canton	OH	44720	**888-434-2359**	330-896-2385

Classified Section

				Toll-Free	Phone
Baltimore-Washington International Airport (BWI)	Baltimore	MD	21240	**800-435-9294**	410-859-7111
Bismarck Municipal Airport (BIS)	Bismarck	ND	58502	**800-453-4244**	701-222-6502
Colorado Springs Municipal Airport (COS)	Colorado Springs	CO	80916	**800-462-6774**	719-550-1900
Dallas-Fort Worth International Airport (DFW)	Dallas	TX	75261	**800-762-0238**	972-574-8888
Dayton International Airport (DAY)	Vandalia	OH	45377	**877-359-3291**	937-454-8200
Denver International Airport (DEN)	Denver	CO	80249	**800-247-2336**	303-342-2000
Edmonton International Airport (YEG)	Edmonton	AB	T5J2T2	**800-268-7134**	780-890-8900
Lehigh Valley International Airport (ABE)	Allentown	PA	18103	**888-359-5842**	610-266-6000
Logan International Airport (BOS)	Boston	MA	02128	**800-235-6426**	617-561-1818
Mobile Regional Airport (MOB)	Mobile	AL	36608	**800-357-5373**	251-633-0313
Tampa International Airport (TPA)	Tampa	FL	33607	**800-767-8882**	813-870-8700
Theodore Francis Green State Airport (PVD)	Warwick	RI	02886	**888-268-7222**	401-737-4000

29 AIRSHIPS

SEE ALSO Aircraft

				Toll-Free	Phone
ILC Dover Inc 1 Moonwalker Rd	Frederica	DE	19946	**800-631-9567**	302-335-3911

30 ALL-TERRAIN VEHICLES

SEE ALSO Sporting Goods

				Toll-Free	Phone
Cycle Country Accessories Corp 2188 Hwy 86 PO Box 239 *AMEX: ATC*	Milford	IA	51351	**800-841-2222**	712-338-2701
Recreatives Industries Inc 60 Depot St	Buffalo	NY	14206	**800-255-2511**	716-855-2226
Yamaha Motor Corp USA 6555 Katella Ave *Cust Svc	Cypress	CA	90630	**800-962-7926***	714-761-7300

31 AMBULANCE SERVICES

				Toll-Free	Phone
Acadian Ambulance & Air Med Services Inc PO Box 98000	Lafayette	LA	70509	**800-259-3333**	337-291-3333
Air Response Inc 7211 S Peoria St Suite 200	Englewood	CO	80112	**800-631-6565**	303-858-9967
AirEvac Services Inc 2630 Sky Harbor Blvd	Phoenix	AZ	85034	**800-421-6111**	602-244-9327
American Medical Response 6200 S Syracuse Way Suite 200	Greenwood Village	CO	80111	**800-375-0564**	303-614-8500
CJ Systems Aviation Group Inc 57 Allegheny County Airport	West Mifflin	PA	15122	**800-245-0230**	412-466-2500
MEDjet International Inc 1000 Urban Ctr Dr	Birmingham	AL	35242	**800-356-2161**	205-592-4460
National Air Ambulance 3495 SW 9th Ave	Fort Lauderdale	FL	33315	**800-525-0166**	954-359-9400
Omniflight Helicopters Inc 4650 Airport Pkwy	Addison	TX	75001	**800-727-4644**	972-776-0130
Rural/Metro Corp 8401 E Indian School Rd *NASDAQ: RURL*	Scottsdale	AZ	85251	**800-421-5718**	480-994-3886
Skyservice Airlines Inc 31 Fasken Dr	Etobicoke	ON	M9W1K6	**800-701-9448**	416-679-5700

32 AMUSEMENT PARKS

				Toll-Free	Phone
Adventureland Park 5091 NE 56th St	Altoona	IA	50009	**800-532-1286**	515-266-2121
Busch Gardens Tampa Bay 3605 Bougainvillea Ave	Tampa	FL	33164	**888-800-5447**	813-987-5082
Busch Gardens Williamsburg 1 Busch Gardens Blvd	Williamsburg	VA	23187	**800-772-8886**	757-253-3350
Cypress Gardens Adventure Park 6000 Cypress Gardens Blvd *Tech Supp	Winter Haven	FL	33884	**800-282-2123***	863-324-2111
Dutch Wonderland Family Amusement Park 2249 Lincoln Hwy E	Lancaster	PA	17602	**866-386-2839**	717-291-1888
Grand Harbor Resort & Waterpark 350 Bell St	Dubuque	IA	52001	**866-690-4006**	563-609-4000
Hersheypark 100 W Hersheypark Dr	Hershey	PA	17033	**800-437-7439**	717-534-3900
Holiday World & Splashin' Safari 452 E Christmas Blvd	Santa Claus	IN	47579	**800-467-2682**	812-937-4401
Holy Land Experience 4655 Vineland Rd	Orlando	FL	32811	**866-872-4659**	407-872-2272
Indiana Beach 5224 E Indiana Beach Rd	Monticello	IN	47960	**800-583-4306**	574-583-4141
Islands of Adventure 1000 Universal Studios Plaza	Orlando	FL	32819	**888-837-2273**	407-363-8000
Knoebels Amusement Resort PO Box 317	Elysburg	PA	17824	**800-487-4386**	570-672-2572
Lagoon & Pioneer Village 375 N Hwy 91	Farmington	UT	84025	**800-748-5246**	801-451-8000
Lake Winnepesaukah Amusement Park 1730 Lakeview Dr	Rossville	GA	30741	**877-525-3946**	706-866-5681
LEGOLAND California 1 Legoland Dr	Carlsbad	CA	92008	**877-534-6526**	760-438-5346
Paramount's Carowinds 14523 Carowinds Blvd	Charlotte	NC	28273	**800-888-4386**	704-588-2606
Paramount's Kings Island 6300 Kings Island Dr	Kings Island	OH	45034	**800-288-0808**	513-754-5700
SeaWorld Orlando 7007 Sea World Dr	Orlando	FL	32821	**800-327-2424**	407-351-3600
SeaWorld San Antonio 10500 SeaWorld Dr	San Antonio	TX	78251	**800-722-2762**	210-523-3000
SeaWorld San Diego 500 SeaWorld Dr	San Diego	CA	92109	**800-257-4268**	619-226-3901
Silver Springs 5656 E Silver Springs Blvd	Silver Springs	FL	34488	**888-422-8727**	352-236-2121
Six Flags Fiesta Texas 17000 IH-10 W	San Antonio	TX	78257	**800-473-4378**	210-697-5000
Six Flags Kentucky Kingdom 937 Phillips Ln	Louisville	KY	40209	**800-727-3267**	502-366-2231
Six Flags New England Route 159 1623 Main St	Agawam	MA	01001	**800-370-7488**	413-786-9300
Universal Studios Florida 1000 Universal Studios Plaza	Orlando	FL	32819	**888-837-2237**	407-363-8000
Universal Studios Hollywood 100 Universal City Plaza	Universal City	CA	91608	**800-864-8377**	818-622-3801
Universal's Islands of Adventure 1000 Universal Studios Plaza	Orlando	FL	32819	**888-837-2273**	407-363-8000
Valleyfair 1 Valleyfair Dr	Shakopee	MN	55379	**800-386-7433**	952-445-7600
Wannado City 12801 Sunrise Blvd Anchor D	Sunrise	FL	33323	**888-926-6236**	954-838-7100
Water Mania 6073 W Hwy 192	Kissimmee	FL	34747	**800-527-3092**	407-396-2626
Weeki Wachee Springs 6131 Commercial Way	Spring Hill	FL	34606	**800-678-9335**	352-596-2062
Wet 'n Wild Emerald Pointe 3910 S Holden Rd	Greensboro	NC	27406	**800-555-5900**	336-852-9721
Wet 'n Wild Orlando 6200 International Dr	Orlando	FL	32819	**800-992-9453**	407-351-1800
Wonderland Amusement Park 2601 Dumas Dr	Amarillo	TX	79107	**800-383-4712**	806-383-4712
Wyandot Lake Water Park 10101 Riverside Dr	Powell	OH	43065	**800-328-9283**	614-889-9283

33 ANIMATION COMPANIES

SEE ALSO Motion Picture & Television Production; Motion Picture Production - Special Interest

				Toll-Free	Phone
Central Park Media Corp 250 W 57th St Suite 317	New York	NY	10107	**800-833-7456**	212-977-7456
Pixar Animation Studios 1200 Park Ave *NASDAQ: PIXR*	Emeryville	CA	94608	**800-888-9856**	510-752-3000

34 APPAREL FINDINGS

				Toll-Free	Phone
American Nonwovens Corp 221 Fabritek Dr	Columbus	MS	39702	**800-628-7961**	662-327-0745
Mainzer Minton Co Inc 144 Main St	Hackettstown	NJ	07840	**800-944-7632**	908-979-0800
Metric Products Inc 4671 Leahy St	Culver City	CA	90232	**800-763-8742**	310-815-9000
Mid-South Mfg Co 338 Commerce St	Jackson	TN	38301	**800-824-1622**	731-424-2525
V Western Textile Cos 3400 Treecourt Industrial Blvd	Saint Louis	MO	63122	**800-624-8731**	636-225-9400

35 APPLIANCE & HOME ELECTRONICS STORES

SEE ALSO Computer Stores; Department Stores; Furniture Stores

				Toll-Free	Phone
AAA Co Inc 6232 Bragg Blvd	Fayetteville	NC	28303	**800-850-8776**	910-867-6111
Adray Appliance Photo & Sound Center 20219 Carlysle St	Dearborn	MI	48124	**800-652-3729**	313-274-9500
At Your Service 4400 Airport Fwy	Fort Worth	TX	76117	**888-777-7115**	817-831-3113
Audio Direct 460 W Roger Rd Suite 105	Tucson	AZ	85705	**888-628-3467**	
Audio Graphic Systems Inc 2131 S Grove Ave Suite A	Ontario	CA	91761	**800-854-8547**	909-673-0070
Audio King Corp 321 W 84th Ave Suite A	Thornton	CO	80260	**800-260-2660**	303-412-2500
Auto Accents 6550 Pearl Rd	Cleveland	OH	44130	**800-567-3120**	440-888-8886
AVW - TELAV Audio Visual Solutions 4545 W Davis St	Dallas	TX	75211	**800-225-5289**	214-634-9060
Batteries Plus 925 Walnut Ridge Dr Suite 100	Hartland	WI	53029	**800-274-9155**	262-369-0690
Best Buy Co Inc 7601 Penn Ave S *NYSE: BBY*	Richfield	MN	55423	**800-369-5050**	612-291-1000
BrandsMart USA Corp 3200 SW 42nd St	Hollywood	FL	33312	**800-432-8579**	954-797-4000
Circuit City Group 9950 Mayland Dr	Richmond	VA	23233	**800-251-2665**	804-527-4000
Conn's Inc 3295 College St *NASDAQ: CONN ■ *Cust Svc*	Beaumont	TX	77701	**800-511-5750***	409-832-1696
Cook's Inc PO Box 205	Grand Haven	MI	49417	**800-499-6001**	616-842-0180
Cyberian Outpost Inc 25 N Main St	Kent	CT	06757	**877-688-7678**	860-927-2050
DeSears Appliances Inc 6430 14th St W	Bradenton	FL	34207	**800-337-3277**	941-751-7525
eCOST.com Inc 2555 W 190th St Suite 106	Torrance	CA	90504	**800-555-3613**	310-225-4044
Future Shop Ltd 6200 McKay Ave Unit 144	Burnaby	BC	V5H4L7	**800-663-2275**	604-434-3844
Good Guys Inc 1600 Harbor Bay Pkwy Suite 200	Alameda	CA	94502	**800-229-4897**	510-747-6000
Harvey Electronics Inc 205 Chubb Ave *NASDAQ: HRVE*	Lyndhurst	NJ	07071	**800-254-7836**	201-842-0078
Henshaw's Electronics Co 7622 Wornall Rd	Kansas City	MO	64114	**888-445-3434**	816-444-3434
IbuyDigital.com Inc 252 Conover St	Brooklyn	NY	11231	**866-243-4289**	646-218-2200
Interbond Corp of America 3200 SW 42nd St	Hollywood	FL	33312	**800-432-8579**	954-797-4000
Kitchen Resource LLC 3767 S 150 East	Salt Lake City	UT	84115	**800-692-6724**	801-261-3222
Let's Talk Inc 410 Townsend St Suite 100 *Orders	San Francisco	CA	94107	**866-825-5460***	415-344-0227
MCM Inc 707 N Main St	Leominster	MA	01453	**800-270-0707**	978-537-0704
NationLink Wireless 342 Cool Springs Blvd Suite 200	Franklin	TN	37067	**800-496-2355**	615-567-2224
Outpost.com 25 N Main St	Kent	CT	06757	**877-688-7678**	860-927-2050
Queen City TV & Appliance Co Inc 2430 I-85 S	Charlotte	NC	28208	**800-365-6665**	704-391-6000
RadioShack 100 Throckmorton St Suite 1800	Fort Worth	TX	76102	**800-843-7422**	817-415-3011
REX Stores Corp 2875 Needmore Rd *NYSE: RSC*	Dayton	OH	45414	**800-528-9739**	937-276-3931
Sharper Image Corp 650 Davis St *NASDAQ: SHRP*	San Francisco	CA	94111	**800-344-4444**	415-445-6000
Sound Advice Inc 2501 SW 32nd Terr *Cust Svc	Pembroke Park	FL	33023	**800-749-1897***	954-922-4434
Star Cellular 1371 S Bascom Ave	San Jose	CA	95128	**800-969-0023**	408-288-8500
Tweeter Home Entertainment Group Inc 40 Pequot Way *NASDAQ: TWTR*	Canton	MA	02021	**800-893-3837**	781-821-2900

Company / Address	City	State	ZIP	Toll-Free	Phone
Ultimate Electronics Inc 321-A W 84th Ave	Thornton	CO	80260	**800-260-2660**	303-412-2500
Yale Electric Supply Co 296 Freeport St	Dorchester	MA	02122	**800-289-9253**	617-825-9253

36 APPLIANCES - MAJOR - MFR

SEE ALSO Air Conditioning & Heating Equipment - Residential

Company / Address	City	State	ZIP	Toll-Free	Phone
AM Appliance Group 789 N Grove Rd Suite 103	Richardson	TX	75081	**800-898-1879**	972-644-8595
Anaheim Mfg Co 4240 E La Palma Ave *Cust Svc	Anaheim	CA	92807	**800-854-3229***	714-524-7770
AO Smith Corp 11270 W Park Pl Suite 170 *NYSE: AOS*	Milwaukee	WI	53224	**800-359-4065**	414-359-4000
AO Smith Water Products Co 500 Lindahl Pkwy	Ashland City	TN	37015	**800-365-8170**	615-792-4371
Bradford White Corp 725 Talamore Dr	Ambler	PA	19002	**800-523-2931**	215-641-9400
Bradley Direct 7100 Jameson Rd	Midland	GA	31820	**800-252-8248**	
Brown Stove Works Inc 1422 Carolina Ave NE	Cleveland	TN	37311	**800-251-7485**	423-476-6544
Cervitor Kitchens Inc 10775 Lower Azusa Rd	El Monte	CA	91731	**800-523-2666**	626-443-0184
Char-Broil 1442 Belfast Ave *Cust Svc	Columbus	GA	31904	**800-352-4111***	706-324-0421
CookTek Inc 810 W Washington St	Chicago	IL	60607	**888-266-5835**	312-563-9600
Crosley Corp 675 N Main St	Winston-Salem	NC	27101	**800-849-1112**	336-722-1112
Daewoo Electronics Corp of America 120 Chubb Ave	Lyndhurst	NJ	07071	**800-323-9668**	201-460-2000
Dwyer Products Corp 418 N Calumet Ave	Michigan City	IN	46360	**800-348-8508**	219-874-5236
Electric Heater Co 45 Seymour St	Stratford	CT	06615	**800-647-3165**	203-378-2659
Fisher & Paykel Appliances Inc 27 Hubble	Irvine	CA	92618	**800-863-5394**	949-790-8900
Frigidaire Home Products Co 250 Bobby Jones Expy *Sales	Augusta	GA	30907	**800-288-4924***	706-651-1751
GE Consumer Products Appliance Pk	Louisville	KY	40225	**800-626-2000**	502-452-4311
In-Sink-Erator 4700 21st St	Racine	WI	53406	**800-558-5712**	262-554-5432
Jenn-Air Co 403 W 4th St N	Newton	IA	50208	**800-688-9900**	641-792-7000
KitchenAid Div Whirlpool Corp 2000 M-63 N	Benton Harbor	MI	49022	**800-253-1301**	269-923-5000
LG Electronics USA Inc 1000 Sylvan Ave *Tech Supp	Englewood Cliffs	NJ	07632	**800-243-0000***	201-816-2000
Maytag Appliances 403 W 4th St N *Cust Svc	Newton	IA	50208	**800-688-9900***	641-792-7000
Maytag-Cleveland Cooking Products 740 King Edward Ave	Cleveland	TN	37320	**800-688-1120**	423-472-3371
Maytag Corp 403 W 4th St N *NYSE: MYG*	Newton	IA	50208	**800-688-9900**	641-792-7000
Maytag-Newton Laundry Products 403 West 4th St N	Newton	IA	50208	**800-866-9900**	641-792-7000
Miele Inc 9 Independence Way	Princeton	NJ	08540	**800-843-7231**	609-419-9898
Multi-Pak Corp 180 Atlantic St	Hackensack	NJ	07601	**800-234-7441**	201-342-7474
Northland Corp 701 Ranney Dr	Greenville	MI	48838	**800-223-3900**	616-754-5601
Peerless Premier Appliance Co 119 S 14th St	Belleville	IL	62222	**800-858-5844**	618-233-0475
Rheem Mfg Co Water Heater Div 2600 Gunter Park Dr E	Montgomery	AL	36109	**800-621-5622**	334-260-1500
Samsung Electronics America Inc 105 Challenger Rd	Ridgefield Park	NJ	07660	**800-726-7864**	201-229-4000
Sharp Electronics Corp 1 Sharp Plaza	Mahwah	NJ	07430	**800-237-4277**	201-529-8200
Siemens Home Appliances 5551 McFadden Ave	Huntington Beach	CA	92649	**888-474-3636**	
Smith AO Corp 11270 W Park Pl Suite 170 *NYSE: AOS*	Milwaukee	WI	53224	**800-359-4065**	414-359-4000
Smith AO Water Products Co 500 Lindahl Pkwy	Ashland City	TN	37015	**800-365-8170**	615-792-4371
Sub-Zero Freezer Co Inc 4717 Hammersley Rd *Prod Info	Madison	WI	53711	**800-222-7820***	608-271-2233
Tatung Co of America Inc 2850 El Presidio St	Long Beach	CA	90810	**800-827-2850**	310-637-2105
Thermador 5551 McFadden Ave	Huntington Beach	CA	92649	**800-735-4328**	714-901-6600
Vaughn Mfg Corp 26 Old Elm St	Salisbury	MA	01952	**800-282-8446**	978-462-6683
WC Bradley Char-Broil 1442 Belfast Ave *Cust Svc	Columbus	GA	31904	**800-352-4111***	706-324-0421
Weber-Stephen Products Co 200 E Daniels Rd *Cust Svc	Palatine	IL	60067	**800-446-1071***	847-934-5700
Whirlpool Corp 2000 M-63 N *NYSE: WHR*	Benton Harbor	MI	49022	**800-253-1301**	269-923-5000
Whirlpool Corp KitchenAid Div 2000 M-63 N	Benton Harbor	MI	49022	**800-253-1301**	269-923-5000
Whirlpool Corp North American Region 2000 M-63 N	Benton Harbor	MI	49022	**800-253-1301**	269-923-5000
Wisco Industries Inc 736 Janesville St	Oregon	WI	53575	**800-999-4726**	608-835-3106

37 APPLIANCES - SMALL - MFR

SEE ALSO Air Purification Equipment - Household; Vacuum Cleaners - Household

Company / Address	City	State	ZIP	Toll-Free	Phone
Abatement Technologies 2220 Northmont Pkwy Suite 100	Duluth	GA	30096	**800-634-9091**	770-689-2600
Aisin World Corp of America 24330 Garnier St	Torrance	CA	90505	**800-822-2726**	310-326-8681
Andis Co 1800 Renaissance Blvd *Cust Svc	Sturtevant	WI	53177	**800-558-9441***	262-884-2600
Applica Consumer Products Inc 3633 Flamingo Rd *Cust Svc	Miramar	FL	33027	**800-231-9786***	954-883-1000
Applica Inc 3633 Flamingo Rd *NYSE: APN*	Miramar	FL	33027	**800-557-9463**	954-883-1000
Bodum Inc 1860 Renaissance Blvd Suite 201	Sturtevant	WI	53177	**800-232-6386**	262-884-4650
Braun North America 1 Gillette Pk *Cust Svc	Boston	MA	02127	**800-272-8611***	617-463-3000
Broan-NuTone LLC 926 W State St *Cust Svc	Hartford	WI	53027	**800-558-1711***	262-673-4340
Brother International Corp 100 Somerset Corporate Blvd *Cust Svc	Bridgewater	NJ	08807	**800-276-7746***	908-704-1700
Bunn-O-Matic Corp 1400 Stevenson Dr	Springfield	IL	62703	**800-637-8606**	217-529-6601
Cadet Mfg Co Inc 2500 W 4th Plain	Vancouver	WA	98660	**800-442-2338**	360-693-2505
Casablanca Fan Co 761 Corporate Center Dr	Pomona	CA	91768	**888-227-2178**	909-629-1477
Chromalox Inc 103 Gamma Dr Ext *Cust Svc	Pittsburgh	PA	15238	**800-368-2493***	412-967-3800
Conair Corp 1 Cummings Pt Rd	Stamford	CT	06902	**800-726-6247**	203-351-9000
Craftmade International Inc 650 S Royal Ln *NASDAQ: CRFT*	Coppell	TX	75019	**800-527-2578**	972-393-3800
Cuisinart Corp 1 Cummings Pt Rd	Stamford	CT	06902	**800-726-0190**	203-975-4600
Fan-Tastic Vent Corp 2083 S Almont Ave	Imlay City	MI	48444	**800-521-0298**	810-724-3818
GE Consumer Products Appliance Pk	Louisville	KY	40225	**800-626-2000**	502-452-4311
Hamilton Beach/Proctor-Silex Inc 4421 Waterfront Dr *Cust Svc	Glen Allen	VA	23060	**800-851-8900***	804-273-9777
Hitachi Home Electronics Inc 900 Hitachi Way	Chula Vista	CA	91914	**800-981-2588**	619-591-5200
Holmes Group Inc 1 Holmes Way	Milford	MA	01757	**800-546-5637**	508-634-8050
Hunter Fan Co 2500 Frisco Ave	Memphis	TN	38114	**800-448-6837**	901-743-1360
Kaz Inc 1775 Broadway Suite 2405 *Cust Svc	New York	NY	10019	**800-241-1131***	212-586-1630
King Electrical Mfg Co 9131 10th Ave S	Seattle	WA	98108	**800-603-5464**	206-762-0400
KitchenAid Div Whirlpool Corp 2000 M-63 N	Benton Harbor	MI	49022	**800-253-1301**	269-923-5000
Krups North America 196 Boston Ave	Medford	MA	02155	**800-526-5377**	
Lasko Metal Products Inc 820 Lincoln Ave	West Chester	PA	19380	**800-394-3267**	610-692-7400
LG Electronics USA Inc 1000 Sylvan Ave *Tech Supp	Englewood Cliffs	NJ	07632	**800-243-0000***	201-816-2000
Lifetime Hoan Corp Farberware Div 1 Merrick Ave	Westbury	NY	11590	**800-252-3390**	516-683-6000
Marley Engineered Products 470 Beauty Spot Rd E	Bennettsville	SC	29512	**800-452-4179**	843-479-4006
Marvin WB Mfg Co 211 Glenn Ave	Urbana	OH	43078	**800-733-1706**	937-653-7131
Metal Ware Corp 1700 Monroe St *Cust Svc	Two Rivers	WI	54241	**800-288-4545***	920-793-1368
National Presto Industries Inc 3925 N Hastings Way *NYSE: NPK*	Eau Claire	WI	54703	**800-877-0441**	715-839-2121
Panasonic Consumer Electronics Co 1 Panasonic Way	Secaucus	NJ	07094	**888-275-2595**	201-348-7000
Rival Co 32B Spur Dr	El Paso	TX	79906	**800-557-4825**	
Rowenta Inc 196 Boston Ave	Medford	MA	02155	**800-769-3682**	781-396-0600
Salton Inc 1955 W Field Ct *NYSE: SFP*	Lake Forest	IL	60045	**800-272-5629**	847-803-4600
Sharp Electronics Corp 1 Sharp Plaza	Mahwah	NJ	07430	**800-237-4277**	201-529-8200
Singer Sewing Co PO Box 7017	La Vergne	TN	37086	**877-738-9869**	615-213-0880
Tatung Co of America Inc 2850 El Presidio St	Long Beach	CA	90810	**800-827-2850**	310-637-2105
Vita-Mix Corp 8615 Usher Rd	Cleveland	OH	44138	**800-848-2649**	440-235-4840
Waring Products Inc 314 Ella T Grasso Ave	Torrington	CT	06790	**800-269-6640**	860-496-3100
WB Marvin Mfg Co 211 Glenn Ave	Urbana	OH	43078	**800-733-1706**	937-653-7131
West Bend Housewares LLC 1100 Schmidt Rd	West Bend	WI	53090	**800-269-8805**	262-334-2311
Whirlpool Corp KitchenAid Div 2000 M-63 N	Benton Harbor	MI	49022	**800-253-1301**	269-923-5000
World Dryer Corp 5700 McDermott Dr	Berkeley	IL	60163	**800-323-0701**	708-449-6950

38 APPLIANCES - WHOL

Company / Address	City	State	ZIP	Toll-Free	Phone
Allison-Erwin Co PO Box 32308 *Sales	Charlotte	NC	28232	**800-253-0370***	704-334-8621
Almo Corp 2709 Commerce Way	Philadelphia	PA	19154	**800-345-2566**	215-698-4000
Amco McLean Corp 548 S Fulton Ave	Mount Vernon	NY	10550	**800-431-2010**	914-237-4000
Autco Distributing Inc 10900 Midwest Industrial Blvd	Saint Louis	MO	63132	**800-443-0044**	314-426-6524
Bermil Industries Corp DBA Wascomat of America PO Box 960338	Inwood	NY	11096	**800-645-2205**	516-371-4400
Blodgett Supply Co Inc PO Box 759	Williston	VT	05495	**800-223-6911**	802-864-9831
Brady Marketing Co 80 Berry Dr Suite A	Pacheco	CA	94553	**800-326-6080**	925-676-1300
Brooke Distributors Inc 16250 NW 52nd Ave	Miami	FL	33014	**800-275-8792**	305-624-9752
Collins Appliance Parts Inc 1533 Metropolitan St	Pittsburgh	PA	15233	**800-366-9969**	412-321-3700
Electrical Distributing Inc 4600 NW St Helens Rd	Portland	OR	97210	**800-932-3774**	503-226-4044
Fogel MH & Co Inc 2839 Liberty Ave	Pittsburgh	PA	15222	**800-245-2954**	412-261-3921
Fretz Corp 2001 Woodhaven Rd	Philadelphia	PA	19116	**866-987-2121**	215-671-8300
Glindmeyer Distributing Co Inc 4141 Bienville St	New Orleans	LA	70119	**800-466-1754**	504-486-6646
Goldberg Co Inc 2423-A Grenoble Rd	Richmond	VA	23294	**800-365-6533**	804-228-5700
Hamburg Brothers Inc 40 24th St	Pittsburgh	PA	15222	**800-568-4624**	412-227-6200
Helen of Troy Ltd 1 Helen of Troy Plaza *NASDAQ: HELE*	El Paso	TX	79912	**800-487-8432**	915-225-8000
Klaus Radio Inc 8400 N Allen Rd	Peoria	IL	61615	**800-545-5287**	309-691-4840
Liberty Distributors Inc PO Box 48168	Wichita	KS	67201	**800-633-9211**	316-264-7393
Luckenbach & Johnson Inc 1828 Tilghman St	Allentown	PA	18104	**800-451-7451**	610-434-6235
MH Fogel & Co Inc 2839 Liberty Ave	Pittsburgh	PA	15222	**800-245-2954**	412-261-3921
Midwest Sales & Service Inc 917 S Chapin St	South Bend	IN	46601	**800-772-7262**	574-287-3365
Nelson & Small Inc 212 Canco Rd	Portland	ME	04103	**800-341-0780**	207-775-5666
Oakton Distributors Inc 125 E Oakton St	Des Plaines	IL	60018	**800-262-5866**	847-294-5858
O'Rourke Bros Distributing Inc 3885 Elmore Ave Suite 100	Davenport	IA	52807	**800-523-4730**	563-823-1501
Peirce-Phelps Inc 2000 N 59th St	Philadelphia	PA	19131	**800-222-2742**	215-879-7000
Prudential Distributors Inc PO Box 3088	Spokane	WA	99220	**800-767-5567**	509-535-2401
Radio Distributing Co Inc 27015 Trolley Industrial Dr	Taylor	MI	48180	**800-462-1544**	313-295-4500
Roth Distributing Co 11300 W 47th St	Minnetonka	MN	55343	**800-642-3227**	952-933-4428
Rott-Keller Supply Co Inc PO Box 390	Fargo	ND	58107	**800-342-4709**	701-235-0563
Servall Co 6761 E Ten Mile Rd	Center Line	MI	48015	**800-989-7378**	586-754-1818

Classified Section

				Toll-Free	Phone
Tacony Corp 1760 Gilsinn Ln	Fenton	MO	63026	**800-482-2669**	636-349-3000
VSM Sewing Inc 31000 Viking Pkwy	Westlake	OH	44145	**800-541-3357**	440-808-6550
Warren Distributing Corp 226 Glenwood Ave.	Raleigh	NC	27603	**800-333-7227**	919-828-9100
Wascomat of America PO Box 960338	Inwood	NY	11096	**800-645-2205**	516-371-4400
Web Service Co Inc					
3690 Redondo Beach Ave	Redondo Beach	CA	90278	**800-421-6897**	323-772-5131
Westye Group PO Box 111400	Carrollton	TX	75011	**800-441-9260**	972-416-6677
Williams Distributing Corp					
658 Richmond St NW	Grand Rapids	MI	49504	**800-748-0503**	616-456-1613
Woodson & Bozeman Inc					
3870 New Getwell Rd	Memphis	TN	38118	**800-876-4243**	901-362-1500

39 APPLICATION SERVICE PROVIDERS (ASPS)

				Toll-Free	Phone
Access Data Corp 2 Chatham Ctr 11th Fl.	Pittsburgh	PA	15219	**888-799-1744**	412-201-6000
Agiliti Inc 1125 Energy Pk Dr Suite 100	Saint Paul	MN	55108	**866-244-5484***	952-918-2000
*Tech Supp					
Alliance Commerce Inc					
11950 NW 39th St Suite A	Coral Springs	FL	33065	**877-638-2777**	954-575-2300
AllMeds Inc 151 Lafayette Dr Suite 401	Oak Ridge	TN	37830	**888-343-6337**	865-482-1999
Altiris Inc 588 W 400 South	Lindon	UT	84042	**888-252-5551**	
NASDAQ: ATRS					
Appshop Inc 48089 Fremont Blvd.	Fremont	CA	94538	**800-277-7467**	510-353-2900
Ariba Inc 807 11th Ave.	Sunnyvale	CA	94089	**888-237-3131**	650-390-1000
NASDAQ: ARBA					
Avatech Solutions Inc					
10715 Red Run Blvd Suite 101	Owings Mills	MD	21117	**800-520-8000**	410-581-8080
BizLand Inc 70 Blanchard Rd	Burlington	MA	01803	**866-599-9964**	781-272-5585
Blue Martini Software Inc 2600 Campus Dr	San Mateo	CA	94403	**800-258-3627**	650-356-4000
BluePoint Data Storage Inc					
6633 NW 25th Terr	Boca Raton	FL	33496	**866-786-7390**	561-417-0324
Bowstreet Inc 200 Ames Pond Dr	Tewksbury	MA	01876	**877-663-2978**	978-863-1500
BrassRing Inc 343 Winter St.	Waltham	MA	02451	**888-265-6969**	781-530-5000
BroadVision Inc 585 Broadway	Redwood City	CA	94063	**800-269-9375**	650-542-5100
NASDAQ: BVSN					
Canopy Systems Inc 5501 Dillard Ave	Cary	NC	27511	**800-757-1354**	919-851-6177
CareScience Inc 3600 Market St 7th Fl	Philadelphia	PA	19104	**888-223-8247**	215-387-9401
Cayenta Inc 2955 Virtual Way Suite 250	Vancouver	BC	V5M4X6	**866-229-3682**	
Centric Software Inc 50 Las Colinas Ln.	San Jose	CA	95119	**800-644-1002**	408-574-7802
Chemical Safety Corp					
5901 Christie Ave Suite 502	Emeryville	CA	94608	**888-594-1100**	510-594-1000
Citadon Inc 201 Mission St Suite 2700	San Francisco	CA	94105	**800-351-5231***	415-882-1888
*Sales					
ClientSoft Inc 8323 NW 12th St Suite 216	Miami	FL	33126	**800-622-2684**	305-716-1007
CliniComp International 9655 Towne Ctr Dr	San Diego	CA	92121	**800-350-8202**	858-546-8202
Computer Programs & Systems Inc (CPSI)					
6600 Wall St	Mobile	AL	36695	**800-711-2774**	251-639-8100
NASDAQ: CPSI					
Concur Technologies Inc					
6222 185th Ave NE	Redmond	WA	98052	**800-358-0610**	425-702-8808
NASDAQ: CNQR					
Connected Corp 100 Pennsylvania Ave.	Framingham	MA	01701	**800-934-0956**	508-808-7300
Connectria Corp					
10845 Olive Blvd Suite 300	Saint Louis	MO	63141	**800-781-7820**	314-587-7000
Corio Inc 959 Skyway Rd Suite 100	San Carlos	CA	94070	**877-737-3700***	650-232-3000
*Cust Svc					
CPSI (Computer Programs & Systems Inc)					
6600 Wall St	Mobile	AL	36695	**800-711-2774**	251-639-8100
NASDAQ: CPSI					
CustomerSat Inc 1049 Terra Bella Ave	Mountain View	CA	94043	**800-372-7772**	650-234-8000
CyberData Inc 20 Max Ave	Hicksville	NY	11801	**877-942-8100**	516-942-8000
Cyveillance Inc 1555 Wilson Blvd Suite 404	Arlington	VA	22209	**888-243-0097**	703-351-1000
Dakota Imaging Inc 7130 Minstrel Way	Columbia	MD	21045	**800-833-3137**	410-381-3113
DataServ LLC					
12825 Flushing Meadows Dr Suite 100	Saint Louis	MO	63131	**877-700-3282**	314-842-1155
Digital River Inc					
9625 W 76th St Suite 150	Eden Prairie	MN	55344	**800-207-2755**	952-253-8400
NASDAQ: DRIV					
DigitalWork.com Inc 661 W Lake St Suite 2-N	Chicago	IL	60661	**877-496-7571**	312-277-4350
DocMan Technologies 31300 Bainbridge Rd	Cleveland	OH	44139	**888-636-2626**	440-542-9660
E-Builder Inc					
100 W Cypress Creek Rd Suite 845	Fort Lauderdale	FL	33309	**800-580-9322**	954-938-8032
E-Markets Inc 1606 Golden Aspen Dr Suite 110	Ames	IA	50010	**877-674-7419**	515-233-8720
eAttorney Inc					
245 Peachtree Ctr Ave Suite 2415	Atlanta	GA	30303	**800-378-6101**	
eGain Communications Corp					
345 E Middlefield Rd	Mountain View	CA	94043	**888-603-4246**	650-230-7500
NASDAQ: EGAN					
eJiva Inc 1000 Commerce Dr Suite 500	Pittsburgh	PA	15275	**877-354-8226**	412-787-2100
Electric Mail Co Inc					
3999 Henning Dr Suite 300	Burnaby	BC	V5C6P9	**800-419-7463**	604-482-1111
Employease Inc					
3295 River Exchange Dr Suite 500	Norcross	GA	30092	**888-327-3638**	770-325-7700
ePlus Inc 13595 Dulles Technology Dr.	Herndon	VA	20171	**800-827-5711**	703-984-8400
NASDAQ: PLUS					
Evant Solutions Corp					
235 Montgomery St Suite 1300	San Francisco	CA	94104	**800-316-2747**	415-283-1880
Exenet Technologies Inc					
387 Park Ave S 3rd Fl.	New York	NY	10016	**877-393-6388**	212-684-7300
FaceTime Communications Inc					
1159 Triton Dr	Foster City	CA	94404	**888-349-3223**	650-574-1600
FinancialCAD Corp					
13450 102nd Ave Suite 1753	Surrey	BC	V3T5X3	**800-304-0702**	604-957-1200
Gelco Information Network Inc					
10700 Prairie Lakes Dr	Eden Prairie	MN	55344	**800-444-6588**	952-947-1500
Glowpoint Inc 225 Long Ave.	Hillside	NJ	07205	**866-456-9764**	973-282-2000
NASDAQ: GLOW					
HealthMEDX 5100 N Towne Ctr Dr.	Ozark	MO	65721	**877-875-1200**	417-582-1816
Hire.com Inc 200 Academy Dr	Austin	TX	78704	**800-953-4473**	512-583-4400
I-Business Network LLC					
2256 Northwest Pkwy Suite E	Marietta	GA	30067	**877-336-4426**	678-627-0646
IE Discovery Inc 9101 Burnet Rd Suite 202	Austin	TX	78758	**800-656-8444**	512-833-5588
Incentivecity 7370 Bramalea Rd Suite 3	Mississauga	ON	L5S1N6	**877-387-2529**	905-362-0951
Informative Inc					
2000 Sierra Point Pkwy Suite 301	Brisbane	CA	94005	**800-829-1979***	650-534-1010
*Sales					
InsynQ Inc 1127 Broadway Plaza Suite 202	Tacoma	WA	98402	**866-796-9925**	253-284-2000
Intacct Corp 170 Knowles Dr Suite 120	Los Gatos	CA	95032	**877-704-3700**	408-884-3390
Integrity eLearning Inc					
5500 Santa Ana Canyon Rd Suite 245	Anaheim Hills	CA	92807	**888-624-6464**	714-637-9480
Internet Operations Center Inc					
200 Galleria Officentre Suite 109	Southfield	MI	48034	**800-485-4462**	248-204-8800
IntraLinks Inc 1372 Broadway 11th Fl	New York	NY	10018	**888-546-5383***	212-543-7700
*Tech Supp					
Intranets.com Inc 1 Van de Graaff Dr 6th Fl.	Burlington	MA	01803	**888-932-2600**	781-565-6000
Jamcracker Inc					
4677 Old Ironsides Dr Suite 450	Santa Clara	CA	95054	**866-559-0035**	408-496-5500
Journyx Inc 9800 N Lamar Blvd Suite 340	Austin	TX	78753	**800-755-9878**	512-834-8888
Kinzan Inc 5857 Owens Ave Suite 112	Carlsbad	CA	92008	**800-963-8424**	760-602-2900
LanVision Systems Inc					
10200 Alliance Rd Suite 200	Cincinnati	OH	45242	**800-878-5262**	513-794-7100
NASDAQ: LANV					
Learningstation.com Inc					
8008 Corporate Ctr Dr Suite 210	Charlotte	NC	28217	**888-679-7058**	704-926-5400
LiveVault Corp 201 Boston Post Rd W	Marlborough	MA	01752	**800-638-5518**	508-460-6670
Metier Ltd 3222 'N' St NW 5th Fl.	Washington	DC	20007	**877-965-9501**	202-965-9500
Mi8 Corp 601 W 26th St 11th Fl.	New York	NY	10001	**800-965-4648**	212-727-0911
Napster LLC 9044 Melrose Ave.	Los Angeles	CA	90069	**800-839-4210**	310-281-5000
NaviSite Inc 400 Minuteman Rd	Andover	MA	01810	**888-298-8222**	978-682-8300
NASDAQ: NAVI					
NetBase Corp					
4443 Brookfield Corporate Dr Suite 200	Chantilly	VA	20151	**888-456-6528***	703-814-4040
*Cust Svc					
NetSuite Inc 2955 Campus Dr Suite 100	San Mateo	CA	94403	**800-762-5524**	650-627-1000
OneMind Connect Inc					
2 Corporate Plaza Suite 100	Newport Beach	CA	92660	**877-658-5022**	949-640-0701
onProject Inc 3 Wing Dr Suite 225	Cedar Knolls	NJ	07927	**877-936-6776**	973-971-9970
OpenAir Inc 80 Lincoln St 6th Fl.	Boston	MA	02111	**888-367-1715***	617-351-0230
*Sales					
Outtask Inc 209 Madison St Suite 400	Alexandria	VA	22314	**888-662-6248**	703-837-6100
Paramount Technologies Inc					
2075 E West Maple Rd					
Suite B-203	Commerce Township	MI	48390	**800-725-4408**	248-960-0909
Passkey.com Inc 180 Old Colony Ave	Quincy	MA	02170	**800-211-4234***	617-237-8200
*Sales					
PBM Corp 20600 Chagrin Blvd Suite 450	Cleveland	OH	44122	**800-341-5809**	216-283-7999
PeopleSupport Inc					
1100 Glendon Ave Suite 1250	Los Angeles	CA	90024	**877-914-5999**	310-824-6200
NASDAQ: PSPT					
Perfect Commerce Inc					
850 NW Chipman Rd Suite 5050	Lees Summit	MO	64063	**888-726-8848**	816-448-4444
Perimeter Technology Inc					
540 N Commercial St.	Manchester	NH	03101	**800-645-1650**	603-645-1616
PhDx Systems Inc					
1001 University Blvd SE Suite 103	Albuquerque	NM	87106	**888-999-7439**	505-764-0174
Pivotal Corp 858 Beatty St Suite 700	Vancouver	BC	V6B1C1	**877-797-4595**	604-699-8000
Plumtree Software Inc 500 Sansome St	San Francisco	CA	94111	**800-810-7586**	415-263-8900
NASDAQ: PLUM					
Prodata Systems Inc					
3855 Monte Villa Pkwy Suite 105	Bothell	WA	98021	**866-487-8346**	425-487-8300
ProxyMed Inc					
2555 Davie Rd Suite 110	Fort Lauderdale	FL	33317	**800-997-7699**	954-473-1001
NASDAQ: PILL					
Punch Networks Corp 100 4th Ave N 6th Fl.	Seattle	WA	98101	**877-467-8624**	206-404-6000
PureSafety 1321 Murfreesboro Rd Suite 200	Nashville	TN	37217	**888-202-3016**	615-367-4404
PureWorks Inc DBA PureSafety					
1321 Murfreesboro Rd Suite 200	Nashville	TN	37217	**888-202-3016**	615-367-4404
QuickArrow Inc 11675 Jollyville Rd Suite 200	Austin	TX	78759	**800-914-7638**	512-381-0600
Realm Business Solutions Inc					
13727 Noel Rd Suite 800	Dallas	TX	75240	**866-697-3256**	469-791-1000
Resource Development Corp					
280 Daines St Suite 200	Birmingham	MI	48009	**800-360-7222**	248-646-2300
Responsys Inc 3 Lagwood Dr Suite 300	Redwood City	CA	94065	**800-624-5356**	650-801-7400
RightNow Technologies Inc					
40 Enterprise Blvd	Bozeman	MT	59718	**877-363-5678**	406-522-4200
NASDAQ: RNOW					
Rivio Inc 2500 Augustine Dr.	Santa Clara	CA	95054	**888-777-7077**	408-653-4400
Salesforce.com Inc					
1 Market St The Landmark Suite 300	San Francisco	CA	94105	**800-667-6389**	415-901-7000
NYSE: CRM					
Salesnet Inc 580 Harrison Ave 2nd Fl	Boston	MA	02118	**877-350-0160**	617-350-0160
SevenSpace/Nuclio Corp 20098 Ashbrook Pl	Ashburn	VA	20147	**866-977-7223**	703-726-6777
Shareholder.com					
12 Clock Tower Pl Suite 300	Maynard	MA	01754	**800-990-6397**	978-461-3111
Siebel Systems Inc 2207 Bridgepointe Pkwy	San Mateo	CA	94404	**800-647-4300**	650-295-5000
NASDAQ: SEBL					
Siemens Health Services					
51 Valley Stream Pkwy	Malvern	PA	19355	**888-767-8326**	610-219-6300
Siemens Medical Solutions Health Services Corp					
51 Valley Stream Pkwy	Malvern	PA	19355	**888-767-8326**	610-219-6300
Smart Online Inc					
PO Box 12794	Research Triangle Park	NC	27709	**800-578-9000**	919-765-5000
SourcingLink.net Inc					
16870 W Bernardo Dr Suite 400	San Diego	CA	92127	**800-717-4565**	858-385-8900
NASDAQ: SNET					
Spyre Infostructure Inc					
25 Imperial St Suite 210	Toronto	ON	M5P1B9	**888-467-7973**	416-487-7797
StorageASP Inc 515 Consumers Rd Suite 405	Toronto	ON	M2J4Z2	**877-747-0330**	416-750-4002
Syntrio 555 Howard St Suite 100	San Francisco	CA	94105	**888-858-2887**	415-951-7913
Talisma Corp 10900 NE 4th St Suite 1510	Bellevue	WA	98004	**877-934-3276**	425-688-3800
TALX Corp 1850 Borman Ct	Saint Louis	MO	63146	**800-888-8277**	314-214-7000
NASDAQ: TALX					
Toolwire Inc					
6120 Stoneridge Mall Rd Suite 110	Pleasanton	CA	94588	**866-935-8665**	925-227-8500
Totality Corp					
44 Montgomery St Suite 500	San Francisco	CA	94104	**888-486-8254**	415-402-3000
TriZetto Group Inc					
567 San Nicolas Dr Suite 360	Newport Beach	CA	92660	**800-569-1222**	949-719-2200
NASDAQ: TZIX					
UltraDNS Corp 1000 Marina Blvd Suite 600	Brisbane	CA	94005	**888-367-4812**	650-228-2300
UnicornHRO 25B Hanover Rd	Florham Park	NJ	07932	**800-343-6844**	973-360-0688
USA.NET Inc					
1155 Kelly Johnson Blvd					
Suite 400	Colorado Springs	CO	80920	**800-653-0179**	719-265-2930
USinternetworking Inc (USi Inc) 1 USi Plaza	Annapolis	MD	21401	**800-839-4874**	410-897-4400
Vcommerce Corp 9977 N 90th St Suite 200	Scottsdale	AZ	85258	**800-821-6034***	480-922-9922
*Cust Svc					
Vocus Inc 4296 Forbes Blvd	Lanham	MD	20706	**800-345-5572**	301-459-2590
Wam!net Inc					
10900 Hampshire Ave S Suite 150	Bloomington	MN	55438	**800-585-3666**	
Webhire Inc 91 Hartwell Ave.	Lexington	MA	02421	**877-932-4473**	781-869-5000

Name / Address	City	State	Zip	Toll-Free	Phone
WebMD Corp 669 River Dr Center 2 *NASDAQ: HLTH*	Elmwood Park	NJ	07407	**877-469-3263**	201-703-3400
Workbrain Inc 3440 Preston Ridge Rd Suite 100	Alpharetta	GA	30005	**866-967-5272**	678-713-6014
Workscape Inc 500 Old Connecticut Path Bldg A	Framingham	MA	01701	**888-605-9620**	508-861-5500
WTS Inc 1100 Olive Way Suite 1100	Seattle	WA	98101	**877-987-7253**	206-436-3300
Zantaz Inc 5671 Gibraltar Dr	Pleasanton	CA	94588	**800-636-0095**	925-598-3000
ZLand Inc PO Box 3469	Costa Mesa	CA	92628	**888-682-0911**	

40 AQUARIUMS - PUBLIC

SEE ALSO Botanical Gardens & Arboreta; Zoos & Wildlife Parks

Name / Address	City	State	Zip	Toll-Free	Phone
Aquarium of the Bay Pier 39	San Francisco	CA	94133	**888-732-3483**	415-623-5300
Aquarium of the Pacific 100 Aquarium Way	Long Beach	CA	90802	**888-826-7257**	562-590-3100
Audubon Aquarium of the Americas 1 Canal St	New Orleans	LA	70130	**800-774-7394**	504-565-3033
Clearwater Marine Aquarium 249 Windward Passage	Clearwater	FL	33767	**888-239-9414**	727-441-1790
Florida Aquarium 701 Channelside Dr	Tampa	FL	33602	**800-353-4741**	813-273-4000
Great Lakes Aquarium 353 Harbor Dr	Duluth	MN	55802	**877-866-3474**	218-740-3474
Key West Aquarium 1 Whitehead St	Key West	FL	33040	**800-868-7482**	305-296-2051
Marineland of Florida 9600 Ocean Shore Blvd	Marineland	FL	32080	**888-279-9194**	904-460-1275
Maui Ocean Center 192 Maalaea Rd	Wailuku	HI	96793	**800-350-5634**	808-270-7000
Monterey Bay Aquarium 886 Cannery Row	Monterey	CA	93940	**800-555-3656**	831-648-4800
Moody Gardens 1 Hope Blvd	Galveston	TX	77554	**800-582-4673**	409-744-4673
North Carolina Aquarium at Fort Fisher 900 Loggerhead Rd	Kure Beach	NC	28449	**866-301-3476**	910-458-8257
North Carolina Aquarium on Roanoke Island PO Box 967 Airport Rd	Manteo	NC	27954	**866-332-3475**	252-473-3493
Pittsburgh Zoo & PPG Aquarium 1 Wild Pl	Pittsburgh	PA	15206	**800-474-4966**	412-665-3639
Ripley's Aquarium 1110 Celebrity Cir Broadway at the Beach	Myrtle Beach	SC	29577	**800-734-8888**	843-916-0888
Sea Life Park 41-202 Kalanianaole Hwy	Waimanalo	HI	96795	**866-365-7446**	808-259-7933
SeaWorld Orlando 7007 Sea World Dr	Orlando	FL	32821	**800-327-2424**	407-351-3600
SeaWorld San Antonio 10500 SeaWorld Dr	San Antonio	TX	78251	**800-722-2762**	210-523-3000
South Carolina Aquarium PO Box 130001	Charleston	SC	29413	**800-722-6455**	843-720-1990
Tennessee Aquarium 1 Broad St	Chattanooga	TN	37401	**800-262-0695**	423-265-0695
Texas State Aquarium 2710 N Shoreline Blvd	Corpus Christi	TX	78402	**800-477-4853**	361-881-1200
Vancouver Aquarium Marine Science Center PO Box 3232	Vancouver	BC	V6B3X8	**800-931-1186**	604-659-3474

41 ARBITRATION SERVICES - LEGAL

Name / Address	City	State	Zip	Toll-Free	Phone
American Arbitration Assn Inc (AAA) 335 Madison Ave 10th Fl	New York	NY	10017	**800-778-7879**	212-716-5800
Arbitration Forums Inc 3350 Buschwood Park Dr Suite 295 *Cust Svc	Tampa	FL	33618	**800-967-8889***	813-931-4004
Council of Better Business Bureaus Inc Dispute Resolution Services & Mediation Training 4200 Wilson Blvd Suite 800	Arlington	VA	22203	**800-537-4600**	703-276-0100
Inland Valley Arbitration & Mediation Service (IVAMS) 300 S Park Ave Suite 780	Pomona	CA	91766	**800-944-8267**	909-629-6301
IVAMS (Inland Valley Arbitration & Mediation Service) 300 S Park Ave Suite 780	Pomona	CA	91766	**800-944-8267**	909-629-6301
JAMS/Endispute 500 N State College Blvd Suite 600	Orange	CA	92868	**800-352-5267**	714-939-1300
Judicate West 1851 E 1st St Suite 1450	Santa Ana	CA	92705	**800-488-8805**	714-834-1340
National Arbitration & Mediation 1010 Northern Blvd Suite 336	Great Neck	NY	11021	**877-373-8853**	516-829-4343
Resolute Systems Inc 1550 N Prospect Ave	Milwaukee	WI	53202	**800-776-6060**	414-276-4774

ARCHITECTS

SEE Engineering & Design

ART - COMMERCIAL

SEE Graphic Design

42 ART DEALERS & GALLERIES

Name / Address	City	State	Zip	Toll-Free	Phone
Heffel Gallery Ltd 2247 Granville St	Vancouver	BC	V6H3G1	**800-528-9608**	604-732-6505
Inuit Gallery of Vancouver Ltd 206 Cambie St Gastown	Vancouver	BC	V6B2M9	**888-615-8399**	604-688-7323
Loch Gallery 16 Hazelton Ave	Toronto	ON	M5R2E2	**877-227-9828**	416-964-9050
Odon Wagner Gallery 196 Davenport Rd	Toronto	ON	M5R1J2	**800-551-2465**	416-962-0438
Pace Prints 32 E 57th St 3rd Fl	New York	NY	10022	**877-440-7223**	212-421-3237
Wagner Odon Gallery 196 Davenport Rd	Toronto	ON	M5R1J2	**800-551-2465**	416-962-0438

43 ART MATERIALS & SUPPLIES - MFR

SEE ALSO Pens, Pencils, Parts

Name / Address	City	State	Zip	Toll-Free	Phone
Adco Inc 13911 Distribution Way	Dallas	TX	75234	**800-486-4583**	972-484-6177
Alvin & Co Inc 1335 Blue Hills Ave	Bloomfield	CT	06002	**800-444-2584**	860-243-8991
American Art Clay Co Inc (AMACO) 66 Guion Rd	Indianapolis	IN	46254	**800-374-1600**	317-244-6871
American Mat & Frame Co PO Box 2064	Morgan Hill	CA	95038	**800-537-0984**	408-778-1150
American Metalcraft Inc 2074 George St	Melrose Park	IL	60160	**800-333-9133**	708-345-1177
Ampersand Art Supply 1500 E 4th St	Austin	TX	78702	**800-822-1939**	512-322-0278
ART Studio Clay Co 9320 Michigan Ave	Sturtevant	WI	53177	**800-323-0212**	262-884-4278
Artist Brand Canvas 2448 Loma Ave *Orders	South El Monte	CA	91733	**888-579-2704***	626-579-2740
Badger Air Brush Co 9128 W Belmont Ave	Franklin Park	IL	60131	**800-222-7553**	847-678-3104
Binney & Smith Inc 1100 Church Ln	Easton	PA	18044	**800-272-9652**	610-253-6271
Canson Inc 21 Industrial Dr	South Hadley	MA	01075	**800-628-9283**	413-538-9250
Chartpak Inc 1 River Rd	Leeds	MA	01053	**800-628-1910**	413-584-5446
DecoArt Inc PO Box 297	Stanford	KY	40484	**800-367-3047**	606-365-3193
Duncan Enterprises 5673 E Shields Ave	Fresno	CA	93727	**800-458-7010**	559-291-4444
Duro Art Industries Inc 1832 Juneway Terr	Chicago	IL	60626	**800-621-5144**	773-743-3430
Gare Inc 165 Rosemont St	Haverhill	MA	01832	**888-511-4273**	978-373-9131
Georgie's Ceramic & Clay Co Inc 756 NE Lombard St	Portland	OR	97211	**800-999-2529**	503-283-1353
Golden Artists Colors Inc 188 Bell Rd	New Berlin	NY	13411	**800-959-6543**	607-847-6154
Houston Art 10770 Moss Ridge Rd *Cust Svc	Houston	TX	77043	**800-272-3804***	713-462-1086
Jack Richeson & Co Inc 557 Marcella Dr	Kimberly	WI	54136	**800-233-2404**	920-738-0744
National Artcraft Supply Co 7996 Darrow Rd *Orders	Twinsburg	OH	44087	**800-526-7419***	330-963-6011
Paasche Airbrush Co 4311 N Normandy *Sales	Chicago	IL	60634	**800-621-1907***	773-867-9191
Plaid Enterprises Inc 3225 Westech Dr	Norcross	GA	30092	**800-842-4197**	678-291-8100
Richeson Jack & Co Inc 557 Marcella Dr	Kimberly	WI	54136	**800-233-2404**	920-738-0744
Royal Brush Mfg Inc 6707 Broadway	Merrillville	IN	46410	**800-247-2211**	219-660-4170
Sanford Corp 2707 Butterfield Rd *Cust Svc	Oak Brook	IL	60523	**800-438-3703***	800-323-0749
Sargent Art Inc 100 E Diamond Ave	Hazleton	PA	18201	**800-424-3596**	570-454-3596
Smooth-On Inc 2000 Saint John St	Easton	PA	18042	**800-766-6841**	610-252-5800
Staedtler Inc 21900 Plummer St	Chatsworth	CA	91311	**800-800-3691**	818-882-6000
Super Brush Co 165 Front St Suite 4	Chicopee	MA	01013	**800-272-0591**	413-592-4195
Tara Materials Inc PO Box 646	Lawrenceville	GA	30046	**800-241-8129**	770-963-5256
Testor Corp 440 Blackhawk Park Ave	Rockford	IL	61104	**800-962-3741**	815-962-6654
Utrecht 6 Corporate Dr	Cranbury	NJ	08512	**800-223-9132**	609-409-8001
Walbuck Crayon Co PO Box 367	Lawrence	MA	01842	**800-626-0099**	978-974-0220

44 ART MATERIALS & SUPPLIES - WHOL

Name / Address	City	State	Zip	Toll-Free	Phone
A & B Smith Co 1383 Frey Industrial Pk	Pittsburgh	PA	15235	**800-288-1776**	412-242-5400
Charrette Corp 31 Olympia Ave	Woburn	MA	01801	**800-747-3776**	781-935-6000
Craft Wholesalers Inc 77 Cypress St SW	Reynoldsburg	OH	43068	**800-666-5858**	740-964-6210
Crafts Etc Ltd 7717 SW 44th St	Oklahoma City	OK	73179	**800-888-0321**	405-745-1200
Creative Hobbies Inc 900 Creek Rd	Bellmawr	NJ	08031	**800-843-5456**	856-933-2540
D & L Stained Glass Supply Inc 4939 N Broadway	Boulder	CO	80304	**800-525-0940**	303-449-8737
Darice Inc 13000 Darice Pkwy	Strongsville	OH	44149	**800-321-1494**	440-238-9150
Decorator & Craft Corp (DC & C) 428 S Zelta St	Wichita	KS	67207	**800-835-3013**	316-685-6265
Howells-Craftland 6030 NE 112th Ave	Portland	OR	97220	**800-547-0368**	503-255-2002
King Art & Craft Supply Co Inc 142 N Main St PO Box 671	Herkimer	NY	13350	**800-777-1975**	315-866-5500
MacPherson's-Artcraft 1351 Ocean Ave	Emeryville	CA	94608	**800-289-9800**	510-428-9011
Pioneer Wholesale Co 500 W Bagley Rd	Berea	OH	44017	**888-234-5400**	440-234-5400
Sax Arts & Crafts Inc 2725 S Moorland Rd *Cust Svc	New Berlin	WI	53151	**800-558-6696***	262-784-6880
Sbar's Inc 14 Sbar Blvd	Moorestown	NJ	08057	**800-989-7227**	856-234-8220
Sepp Leaf Products Inc 381 Park Ave S Suite 1301	New York	NY	10016	**800-971-7377**	212-683-2840
Wholesale Art & Hobby Distributors Inc 7207 114th Ave N Suite CF	Largo	FL	33773	**800-227-2520**	727-548-1999

ART SCHOOLS

SEE Colleges - Fine Arts

45 ART SUPPLY STORES

Name / Address	City	State	Zip	Toll-Free	Phone
Aaron Brothers Inc 1221 S Beltline Rd	Coppell	TX	75019	**888-372-6464**	972-409-1300
Al Friedman Co Inc 44 W 18th St	New York	NY	10011	**800-204-6352**	212-243-9000
Alabama Art Supply Inc 1006 23rd St S *Cust Svc	Birmingham	AL	35205	**800-749-4741***	205-322-4741
Art Essentials 32 E Victoria St	Santa Barbara	CA	93101	**877-965-5456**	805-965-5456
Art Hardware 402 S Nevada Ave	Colorado Springs	CO	80903	**800-355-4229**	719-635-2348
Art Supply Warehouse 6672 Westminster Blvd	Westminster	CA	92683	**800-854-6467**	714-891-3626
Art & Woodcrafters Supply 671 Hwy 165 *Orders	Branson	MO	65616	**800-786-4818***	417-335-8382
Artists Alternative 10 Sims Rd	West Hartford	CT	06117	**800-927-8258**	860-236-3803
Asel Art Supply 2701 Cedar Springs Rd	Dallas	TX	75201	**888-273-5278**	214-871-2425
Ben Franklin Stores 7601 Durand Ave	Racine	WI	53408	**800-992-9307**	262-681-7000
Blick Dick Co PO Box 1267 *Orders	Galesburg	IL	61402	**800-447-8192***	309-343-6181
Charrette Corp 31 Olympia Ave	Woburn	MA	01801	**800-747-3776**	781-935-6000

Name / Address	City	State	Zip	Toll-Free	Phone
Commercial Art Supply 935 Erie Blvd E	Syracuse	NY	13210	**800-669-2787**	315-474-1000
Continental Art Supplies 7041 Reseda Blvd	Reseda	CA	91335	**800-499-5146**	818-345-1044
Deck The Walls Inc 101 S Hanley Rd Suite 1280	Saint Louis	MO	63105	**866-719-8200**	314-719-8200
Dick Blick Co PO Box 1267 *Orders	Galesburg	IL	61402	**800-447-8192***	309-343-6181
Douglas & Sturgess Inc 730 Bryant St	San Francisco	CA	94107	**888-278-7883**	415-896-6283
Evergreen Art Works 2388 Cumberland Sq Dr	Bettendorf	IA	52722	**800-468-7280**	563-359-8324
Fastframe USA Inc 1200 Lawrence Dr Suite 300	Newbury Park	CA	91320	**888-863-7263**	805-498-4463
Flax Art & Design 240 Valley Dr	Brisbane	CA	94005	**800-343-3529**	
Friedman Al Co Inc 44 W 18th St	New York	NY	10011	**800-204-6352**	212-243-9000
Georgie's Ceramic & Clay Co Inc 756 NE Lombard St	Portland	OR	97211	**800-999-2529**	503-283-1353
Great Frame Up Systems Inc 101 S Hanley Rd Suite 1280	Saint Louis	MO	63105	**866-719-8200**	314-719-8200
Herweck's Art & Drafting Supplies 300 Broadway St	San Antonio	TX	78205	**800-725-1349**	210-227-1349
HR Meininger Co 499 Broadway	Denver	CO	80203	**800-950-2787**	303-698-3838
Jerry's Artarama 248-12 Union Tpke	Bellerose	NY	11426	**800-221-2323**	718-343-0777
Jo-Ann Fabrics & Crafts 5555 Darrow Rd	Hudson	OH	44236	**888-739-4120**	330-656-2600
Meininger HR Co 499 Broadway	Denver	CO	80203	**800-950-2787**	303-698-3838
Miami Clay Co 270 NE 183rd St	Miami	FL	33179	**800-651-4695**	305-651-4695
Michaels Stores Inc 8000 Bent Branch Dr *NYSE: MIK* ■ *Cust Svc	Irving	TX	75063	**800-642-4235***	972-409-1300
New York Central Art Supply 62 3rd Ave	New York	NY	10003	**800-950-6111**	212-473-7705
Pat Catan's Craft Centers 13000 Darice Pkwy	Strongsville	OH	44149	**800-321-1494**	440-238-9150
Pearl Paint Co Inc 308 Canal St	New York	NY	10013	**800-221-6845**	212-431-7932
Pierce Art Center 9801 Nicollet Ave	Bloomington	MN	55420	**800-338-9801**	952-884-1991
Plaza Artists Materials 173 Madison Ave	New York	NY	10016	**800-327-3200**	212-689-2870
Promotions Unlimited Corp DBA Ben Franklin Stores 7601 Durand Ave	Racine	WI	53408	**800-992-9307**	262-681-7000
Rex Artist Supplies 2263 SW 37th Ave	Miami	FL	33145	**800-739-2782**	305-445-1413
Riverside Art Shop 1600 Grand Army Hwy	Somerset	MA	02726	**800-354-9899**	508-672-6735
Seattle Art Supply Inc 2108 Western Ave	Seattle	WA	98121	**800-223-2787**	206-223-2787
Spokane Art Supply Inc N 1303 Monroe St	Spokane	WA	99201	**800-556-5568**	509-327-6622
Starvin' Artist Supplies 757 W Golf Rd	Schaumburg	IL	60194	**800-427-8478**	847-843-3600
Sterling Art Supply 18871 Teller Ave	Irvine	CA	92612	**800-953-2953**	949-553-0101
Tandy Leather Co 3847 E Loop 820 S	Fort Worth	TX	70119	**888-890-1611**	817-451-1480
Texas Art Supply 2001 Montrose Blvd	Houston	TX	77006	**800-888-9278**	713-526-5221
Thomson's Art Store 184 Mamaroneck Ave	White Plains	NY	10601	**800-287-4885**	914-949-4885
Woodcraft Supply Co 560 Airport Industrial Park *Cust Svc	Parkersburg	WV	26102	**800-535-4482***	304-428-4866
World Supply Inc 3425 W Cahuenga Blvd	Hollywood	CA	90068	**800-399-6753**	323-851-1350

46 ASPHALT PAVING & ROOFING MATERIALS

Name / Address	City	State	Zip	Toll-Free	Phone
American Asphalt Paving Co 500 Chase Rd	Shavertown	PA	18708	**800-326-9362**	570-696-1181
APAC Inc 900 Ashwood Pkwy Suite 700	Atlanta	GA	30338	**800-241-7074**	770-392-5300
Brewer Co 1354 US Hwy 50	Milford	OH	45150	**800-394-0017**	513-576-6300
Capitol Aggregates Ltd 11551 Nacogdoches Rd	San Antonio	TX	78217	**800-292-5315**	210-655-3010
CertainTeed Corp 750 E Swedesford Rd *Prod Info	Valley Forge	PA	19482	**800-782-8777***	610-341-7000
Community Asphalt Corp 14005 NW 186th St	Hialeah	FL	33018	**800-741-0806**	305-829-0700
Crafco Inc 420 N Roosevelt Ave	Chandler	AZ	85226	**800-528-8242**	602-276-0406
Dalton Enterprises Inc 131 Willow St	Cheshire	CT	06410	**800-851-5606**	203-272-3221
Dewitt Products Co 5860 Plumer Ave *Cust Svc	Detroit	MI	48209	**800-962-8599***	313-554-0575
Fields Corp 2240 Taylor Way	Tacoma	WA	98421	**800-627-4098**	253-627-4098
Gardner Asphalt Corp 4161 E 7th Ave	Tampa	FL	33605	**800-237-1155**	813-248-2101
Garland Co Inc 3800 E 91st St	Cleveland	OH	44105	**800-321-9336**	216-641-7500
Glenn O Hawbaker Inc 1952 Waddle Rd	State College	PA	16803	**800-221-1355**	814-237-1444
Gulf States Asphalt Co Inc PO Box 508	South Houston	TX	77587	**800-662-0987**	713-941-4410
Henry Co 2911 E Slauson Ave	Huntington Park	CA	90255	**800-486-1278**	323-583-5000
Highway Materials Inc 1750 Walton Rd	Blue Bell	PA	19422	**800-822-3779**	610-832-8000
JPS Elastomerics Corp 9 Sullivan Rd	Holyoke	MA	01040	**800-621-7663**	413-533-8100
Karnak Chemical Corp 330 Central Ave	Clark	NJ	07066	**800-526-4236**	732-388-0300
Kool Seal Inc 1499 Enterprise Pkwy	Twinsburg	OH	44087	**888-321-5665**	330-425-4717
Malarkey Roofing Co 3131 N Columbia Blvd	Portland	OR	97217	**800-545-1191**	503-283-1191
Midland Asphalt Corp 640 Young St	Tonawanda	NY	14150	**800-573-0400**	716-692-0730
Neyra Industries 10700 Evendale Dr	Cincinnati	OH	45241	**800-543-7077**	513-733-1000
Pace Products Inc 8950 Bond St	Overland Park	KS	66214	**888-389-8203**	913-469-5588
Package Pavement Co Inc PO Box 408	Stormville	NY	12582	**800-724-8193**	845-221-2224
Palmer Asphalt Co Inc PO Box 58	Bayonne	NJ	07002	**800-352-9898**	201-339-0855
Perma Glas-Mesh Inc 345 3rd St Suite 615	Niagara Falls	NY	14303	**800-762-6694**	716-285-0731
Pike Industries Inc 3 Eastgate Park Rd	Belmont	NH	03220	**800-283-7453**	603-527-5100
RMC Pacific Materials Inc 6601 Koll Center Pkwy PO box 5252	Pleasanton	CA	94566	**800-227-5186**	925-462-7181
Russell Standard Corp PO Box 479	Bridgeville	PA	15017	**800-323-3053**	412-221-7300
Sarnafil Inc 100 Dan Rd	Canton	MA	02021	**800-451-2504**	781-828-5400
Seaboard Asphalt Products Co 3601 Fairfield Rd	Baltimore	MD	21226	**800-536-0332**	410-355-0330
Suit-Kote Corp 1911 Lorings Crossing Rd	Cortland	NY	13045	**800-622-5636**	607-753-1100
Tamko Roofing Products Inc PO Box 1404	Joplin	MO	64802	**800-641-4691**	417-624-6644
US Intec Inc PO Box 2845 *Tech Supp	Port Arthur	TX	77643	**800-624-6832***	409-724-7024
Vance Bros Inc PO Box 300107	Kansas City	MO	64130	**800-821-8549**	816-923-4325
Vulcan Materials Co Western Div 3200 San Fernando Rd	Los Angeles	CA	90065	**800-225-6280**	323-258-2777

47 ASSOCIATION MANAGEMENT COMPANIES

Name / Address	City	State	Zip	Toll-Free	Phone
Allen Marketing & Management 810 E 10th St PO Box 1897	Lawrence	KS	66044	**800-627-0932**	785-843-1235
Association Management Consultants Inc 409 Granville St Suite 218	Vancouver	BC	V6C1T2	**866-668-5344**	604-669-5344
Association Managers Inc 9001 Braddock Rd Suite 380	Springfield	VA	22151	**800-403-3374**	703-426-8100
BLF Management Ltd 1152 Goodale Blvd	Columbus	OH	43216	**866-298-3576**	614-221-9580
Cantrall & Assoc 2517 Eastlake Ave E Suite 200	Seattle	WA	98102	**800-837-6186**	206-322-6990
Center for Association Growth 1926 Waukegan Rd Suite 1	Glenview	IL	60025	**800-492-6462**	847-657-6700
Center for Association Resources Inc 1901 N Roselle Rd	Schaumburg	IL	60195	**888-705-1434**	847-885-5680
CM Services Inc 800 Roosevelt Rd Bldg C Suite 312	Glen Ellyn	IL	60137	**800-613-6672**	630-858-7337
eGroupManager 1819 Clarkson Rd Suite 301	Chesterfield	MO	63017	**800-992-8044**	636-530-7700
FSA Group LLC 304 W Liberty St Suite 201	Louisville	KY	40202	**800-620-6422**	502-583-3783
Interactive Management Inc 11166 Huron St Suite 27	Denver	CO	80234	**800-243-1233**	303-433-4446
J Edgar Eubanks & Assoc 1 Windsor Cove Suite 305	Columbia	SC	29223	**800-445-8629**	803-252-5646
National Administration Co DBA eGroupManager 1819 Clarkson Rd Suite 301	Chesterfield	MO	63017	**800-992-8044**	636-530-7700
Pathfinder Group 6009 Quinpool Rd Suite 700	Halifax	NS	B3K5J7	**800-200-7284**	902-425-2445
Raybourn Group International Inc 7150 Winton Dr Suite 300	Indianapolis	IN	46268	**800-362-2546**	317-328-4636
Resource Management Plus Inc 1211 Locust St	Philadelphia	PA	19107	**800-408-8951**	215-545-7222
Synergy Resource Group Inc 3131 Fernbrook Ln Suite 111	Plymouth	MN	55447	**888-990-9959**	763-566-5999
Talley Management Group Inc 19 Mantua Rd	Mount Royal	NJ	08061	**888-423-4233**	856-423-7222

48 ASSOCIATIONS & ORGANIZATIONS - GENERAL

SEE ALSO Performing Arts Organizations; Political Action Committees; Political Parties (Major)

48-1 Accreditation & Certification Organizations

Name / Address	City	State	Zip	Toll-Free	Phone
Accreditation Council for Accountancy & Taxation (ACAT) 1010 N Fairfax St	Alexandria	VA	22314	**888-289-7763**	703-549-2228
American Osteopathic Assn (AOA) 142 E Ontario St	Chicago	IL	60611	**800-621-1773**	312-202-8000
Certified Financial Planner Board of Standards Inc 1670 Broadway Suite 600	Denver	CO	80202	**888-237-6275**	303-830-7500
Commission on Accreditation for Law Enforcement Agencies (CALEA) 10302 Eaton Pl Suite 100	Fairfax	VA	22030	**800-368-3757**	703-352-4225
Commission on Accreditation of Rehabilitation Facilities (CARF) 4891 E Grant Rd	Tucson	AZ	85712	**888-281-6531**	520-325-1044
Commission on Office Laboratory Accreditation (COLA) 9881 Broken Land Pkwy Suite 200	Columbia	MD	21046	**800-981-9883**	410-381-6581
Community Health Accreditation Program Inc (CHAP) 39 Broadway Suite 710	New York	NY	10006	**800-656-9656**	212-480-8828
Continuing Care Accreditation Commission (CCAC) 1730 Rhode Island Ave NW Suite 209	Washington	DC	20036	**866-888-1122**	202-587-5001
Council on Accreditation (COA) 120 Wall St 11th Fl	New York	NY	10005	**866-262-8088**	212-797-3000
Council on Occupational Education 41 Perimeter Ctr East NE Suite 640	Atlanta	GA	30346	**800-917-2081**	770-396-3898
Middle States Assn of Colleges & Schools 3624 Market St	Philadelphia	PA	19104	**800-355-1258**	215-662-5600
National Assn for the Education of Young Children (NAEYC) 1509 16th St NW	Washington	DC	20036	**800-424-2460**	202-232-8777
National League for Nursing Accrediting Commission Inc (NLNAC) 61 Broadway 33rd Fl	New York	NY	10006	**800-669-1656**	212-363-5555
North Central Assn Higher Learning Commission 30 N La Salle St Suite 2400	Chicago	IL	60602	**800-621-7440**	312-263-0456
Southern Assn of Colleges & Schools 1866 Southern Ln	Decatur	GA	30033	**800-248-7701**	404-679-4500

48-2 Agricultural Organizations

Name / Address	City	State	Zip	Toll-Free	Phone
Agriculture Council of America (ACA) 11020 King St Suite 205	Overland Park	KS	66210	**888-982-4329**	913-491-1895
American Angus Assn (AAA) 3201 Frederick Ave	Saint Joseph	MO	64506	**800-821-5478**	816-383-5100
American Assn of Bovine Practitioners (AABP) PO Box 1755	Rome	GA	30162	**800-269-2227**	706-232-2220
American Farmland Trust (AFT) 1200 18th St NW Suite 800	Washington	DC	20036	**800-431-1499**	202-331-7300
American Forage & Grassland Council (AFGC) PO Box 94	Georgetown	TX	78627	**800-944-2342**	
American Forest Foundation (AFF) 1111 19th St NW Suite 780	Washington	DC	20036	**888-889-4466**	202-463-2462
American Forest & Paper Assn (AF&PA) 1111 19th St NW Suite 800	Washington	DC	20036	**800-878-8878**	202-463-2700
American Royal Assn 1701 American Royal Ct	Kansas City	MO	64102	**800-821-5857**	816-221-9800
American Seed Trade Assn (ASTA) 225 Reinekers Ln Suite 650	Alexandria	VA	22314	**888-890-7333**	703-837-8140
American Society of Agricultural Engineers (ASAE) 2950 Niles Rd *Orders	Saint Joseph	MI	49085	**800-695-2723***	269-429-0300
American Society of Landscape Architects (ASLA) 636 'I' St NW	Washington	DC	20001	**800-787-2752**	202-898-2444
American Soybean Assn (ASA) 12125 Woodcrest Executive Dr Suite 100	Saint Louis	MO	63141	**800-688-7692**	314-576-1770
ASAE (American Society of Agricultural Engineers) 2950 Niles Rd *Orders	Saint Joseph	MI	49085	**800-695-2723***	269-429-0300

Organization	City	State	ZIP	Toll-Free	Phone
Association of Consulting Foresters of America (ACF) 312 Montgomery St Suite 208	Alexandria	VA	22314	**888-540-8733**	703-548-0990
Association of Water Technologies (AWT) 8201 Greensboro Dr Suite 300	McLean	VA	22102	**800-858-6683**	703-610-9012
California Redwood Assn (CRA) 405 Enfrente Dr Suite 200	Novato	CA	94949	**888-225-7339**	415-382-0662
Cotton Inc 6399 Weston Pkwy	Cary	NC	27513	**800-334-5868**	919-678-2220
Farm Aid 11 Ward St Suite 200	Somerville	MA	02143	**800-327-6243**	617-354-2922
Farmers Educational & Cooperative Union of America 11900 E Cornell Ave	Aurora	CO	80014	**800-347-1961**	303-337-5500
Forest Products Society 2801 Marshall Ct.	Madison	WI	53705	**800-354-7164**	608-231-1361
Golf Course Superintendents Assn of America (GCSAA) 1421 Research Park Dr	Lawrence	KS	66049	**800-472-7878**	785-841-2240
Holstein Assn USA Inc 1 Holstein Pl *Orders	Brattleboro	VT	05302	**800-952-5200***	802-254-4551
Hoo-Hoo International PO Box 118	Gurdon	AR	71743	**800-979-9950**	870-353-4997
International Society of Arboriculture (ISA) 1400 W Anthony Dr PO Box 3129	Champaign	IL	61826	**888-472-8733**	217-355-9411
Livestock Marketing Assn (LMA) 10510 NW Ambassador Dr	Kansas City	MO	64153	**800-821-2048**	816-891-0502
Mohair Council of America 233 W Twohig Rd PO Box 5337	San Angelo	TX	76902	**800-583-3161**	325-655-3161
National Agri-Marketing Assn (NAMA) 11020 King St Suite 205	Overland Park	KS	66210	**800-530-5646**	913-491-6500
National Cotton Council of America 1918 North Pkwy	Memphis	TN	38112	**800-377-9030**	901-274-9030
National Crop Insurance Services (NCIS) 7201 W 129th St Suite 200	Overland Park	KS	66213	**800-951-6247**	913-685-2767
National Family Farm Coalition (NFFC) 110 Maryland Ave NE Suite 307	Washington	DC	20002	**800-639-3276**	202-543-5675
National Farmers Organization (NFO) 528 Billy Sunday Rd Suite 100	Ames	IA	50010	**800-247-2110**	515-292-2000
National Farmers Union 11900 E Cornell Ave	Aurora	CO	80014	**800-347-1961**	303-337-5500
National FFA Organization 6060 FFA Dr.	Indianapolis	IN	46268	**800-772-0939**	317-802-6060
National Grain & Feed Assn (NGFA) 1250 I St NW Suite 1003	Washington	DC	20005	**800-680-9223**	202-289-0873
National Grange 1616 H St NW	Washington	DC	20006	**888-447-2643**	202-628-3507
National Woodland Owners Assn (NWOA) 374 Maple Ave E Suite 310	Vienna	VA	22180	**800-476-8733**	703-255-2700
NCIS (National Crop Insurance Services) 7201 W 129th St Suite 200	Overland Park	KS	66213	**800-951-6247**	913-685-2767
Professional Landcare Network (PLANET) 950 Herndon Pkwy Suite 450	Herndon	VA	20170	**800-395-2522**	703-736-9666
Smokeless Tobacco Council 1627 K St NW Suite 700	Washington	DC	20006	**800-272-7144**	202-452-1252
United Producers Inc 5909 Cleveland Ave	Columbus	OH	43231	**800-456-3276**	614-890-6666
United Soybean Board (USB) 16640 Chesterfield Grove Rd Suite 130	Chesterfield	MO	63005	**800-989-8721**	636-530-1777
US Apple Assn 8233 Old Courthouse Rd Suite 200	Vienna	VA	22182	**800-781-4443**	703-442-8850
Wild Blueberry Assn of North America (WBANA) 59 Cottage St po bOX 180	Bar Harbor	ME	04609	**800-233-9453**	207-288-2655

48-3 Animals & Animal Welfare Organizations

Organization	City	State	ZIP	Toll-Free	Phone
African Wildlife Foundation (AWF) 1400 16th St NW Suite 120	Washington	DC	20036	**888-494-5354**	202-939-3333
American Animal Hospital Assn (AAHA) PO Box 150899	Denver	CO	80215	**800-252-2242**	303-986-2800
American Assn of Equine Practitioners (AAEP) 4075 Iron Works Pkwy	Lexington	KY	40511	**800-443-0177**	859-233-0147
American Boarding Kennels Assn (ABKA) 1702 E Pikes Peak Ave	Colorado Springs	CO	80909	**877-570-7788**	719-667-1600
American Humane Assn (AHA) 63 Inverness Dr E	Englewood	CO	80112	**800-227-4645**	303-792-9900
American Quarter Horse Assn (AQHA) PO Box 200	Amarillo	TX	79168	**800-414-7433**	806-376-4811
Animal Protection Institute (API) 1122 'S' St	Sacramento	CA	95814	**800-348-7387**	916-447-3085
ASPCA Animal Poison Control Center 1717 S Philo Rd Suite 36	Urbana	IL	61802	**888-426-4435**	217-337-5030
Atlantic Salmon Federation (ASF) PO Box 5200	Saint Andrews	NB	E5B3S8	**800-565-5666**	506-529-1033
Bat Conservation International (BCI) PO Box 162603	Austin	TX	78716	**800-538-2287**	512-327-9721
Bird Studies Canada PO Box 160	Port Rowan	ON	N0E1M0	**888-448-2473**	519-586-3531
Canadian Federation of Humane Societies (CFHS) 30 Concourse Gate Suite 102	Ottawa	ON	K2E7V7	**888-678-2347**	613-224-8072
Canadian Kennel Club (CKC) 89 Skyway Ave Suite 100	Etobicoke	ON	M9W6R4	**800-250-8040**	416-675-5511
Canadian Peregrine Foundation 250 Merton St Suite 104	Toronto	ON	M4S1B1	**888-709-3944**	416-481-1233
Certified Horsemanship Assn (CHA) 5318 Old Bullard Rd	Tyler	TX	75703	**800-399-0138**	903-509-2473
Defenders of Wildlife 1130 17th St NW	Washington	DC	20036	**800-989-8981**	202-682-9400
Delta Waterfowl Foundation 1305 E Central Ave	Bismarck	ND	58501	**888-987-3695**	701-222-8857
Dian Fossey Gorilla Fund International 800 Cherokee Ave SE	Atlanta	GA	30315	**800-851-0203**	404-624-5881
Ducks Unlimited Inc 1 Waterfowl Way	Memphis	TN	38120	**800-453-8257**	901-758-3825
Friends of Animals Inc (FoA) 777 Post Rd Suite 205	Darien	CT	06820	**800-321-7387**	203-656-1522
International Fund for Animal Welfare (IFAW) 411 Main St PO Box 193	Yarmouth Port	MA	02675	**800-932-4329**	508-744-2000
International Society for Animal Rights (ISAR) 965 Griffin Pond Rd	Clarks Summit	PA	18411	**800-543-4727**	570-586-2200
International Wildlife Coalition (IWC) 70 E Falmouth Hwy	East Falmouth	MA	02536	**800-548-8704**	508-548-8328
Jane Goodall Institute for Wildlife Research Education & Conservation (JGI) 8700 Georgia Ave Suite 500	Silver Spring	MD	20910	**800-592-5263**	301-565-0086
National Anti-Vivisection Society (NAVS) 53 W Jackson Blvd Suite 1552	Chicago	IL	60604	**800-888-6287**	312-427-6065
National Dog Registry (NDR) PO Box 116	Woodstock	NY	12498	**800-637-3647**	845-679-2355
National Wild Turkey Federation (NWTF) 770 Augusta Rd PO Box 530 *Cust Svc	Edgefield	SC	29824	**800-843-6983***	803-637-3106
National Wildlife Federation (NWF) 11100 Wildlife Center Dr *Cust Svc	Reston	VA	20190	**800-822-9919***	703-438-6000
People for the Ethical Treatment of Animals (PETA) 501 Front St *Orders	Norfolk	VA	23510	**800-483-4366***	757-622-7382
Ruffed Grouse Society (RGS) 451 McCormick Rd	Coraopolis	PA	15108	**888-564-6747**	412-262-4044
Save the Manatee Club (SMC) 500 N Maitland Ave	Maitland	FL	32751	**800-432-5646**	407-539-0990
Tennessee Walking Horse Breeders' & Exhibitors' Assn (TWHBEA) PO Box 286	Lewisburg	TN	37091	**800-359-1574**	931-359-1574
Thoroughbred Owners & Breeders Assn (TOBA) PO Box 4367	Lexington	KY	40544	**888-606-8622**	859-276-2291
Trout Unlimited (TU) 1300 N 17th St Suite 500	Arlington	VA	22209	**800-834-2419**	703-522-0200
Wildlife Conservation Society (WCS) 2300 Southern Blvd	Bronx	NY	10460	**800-234-5128**	718-220-5100
World Society for the Protection of Animals (WSPA) 34 Deloss St	Framingham	MA	01702	**800-883-9772**	508-879-8350
World Wildlife Fund (WWF) 1250 24th St NW Suite 500	Washington	DC	20037	**800-225-5993**	202-293-4800
World Wildlife Fund Canada 245 Eglinton Ave E Suite 410	Toronto	ON	M4P3J1	**800-267-2632**	416-489-8800

48-4 Arts & Artists Organizations

Organization	City	State	ZIP	Toll-Free	Phone
American Assn of Community Theatre (AACT) 8402 BriarWood Cir	Lago Vista	TX	78645	**866-687-2228**	512-267-0711
American Craft Council 72 Spring St 6th Fl	New York	NY	10012	**800-836-3470**	212-274-0630
American Federation of Arts (AFA) 41 E 65th St	New York	NY	10021	**800-232-0270**	212-988-7700
American Federation of Musicians of the US & Canada (AFM) 1501 Broadway Suite 600	New York	NY	10036	**800-762-3444**	212-869-1330
American Guild of Musical Artists (AGMA) 1430 Broadway 14th Fl	New York	NY	10018	**800-543-2462**	212-265-3687
American Guild of Organists (AGO) 475 Riverside Dr Suite 1260	New York	NY	10115	**800-246-5115**	212-870-2310
American Institute of Architects (AIA) 1735 New York Ave NW *Orders	Washington	DC	20006	**800-365-2724***	202-626-7300
American Institute of Graphic Arts (AIGA) 164 5th Ave	New York	NY	10010	**800-548-1634**	212-807-1990
American Society of Cinematographers (ASC) 1782 N Orange Dr	Hollywood	CA	90028	**800-448-0145**	323-969-4333
American Society of Composers Authors & Publishers (ASCAP) 1 Lincoln Plaza	New York	NY	10023	**800-952-7227**	212-621-6000
Bix Beiderbecke Memorial Society PO Box 3688	Davenport	IA	52808	**888-249-5487**	563-324-7170
Clowns of America International (COAI) PO Box C	Richeyville	PA	15358	**888-522-5696**	
Country Music Assn (CMA) 1 Music Cir S	Nashville	TN	37203	**800-998-4636**	615-244-2840
Drum Corps International (DCI) 470 S Irmen Dr *Orders	Addison	IL	60101	**800-495-7469***	630-628-7888
International Interior Design Assn (IIDA) 13-500 Merchandise Mart	Chicago	IL	60654	**888-799-4432**	312-467-1950
Metropolitan Opera Guild 70 Lincoln Ctr Plaza 6th Fl	New York	NY	10023	**800-829-2525**	212-769-7000
Motion Picture Assn (MPA) 15503 Ventura Blvd.	Encino	CA	91436	**800-662-6797**	818-995-6600
Motion Picture Assn of America (MPAA) 15503 Ventura Blvd	Encino	CA	91436	**800-662-6797**	818-995-6600
National Academy of Recording Arts & Sciences 3402 Pico Blvd.	Santa Monica	CA	90405	**800-423-2017**	310-392-3777
Professional Photographers of America Inc (PPA) 229 Peachtree St NE Suite 2200	Atlanta	GA	30303	**800-786-6277**	404-522-8600
Recording Academy 3402 Pico Blvd.	Santa Monica	CA	90405	**800-423-2017**	310-392-3777
Recording Industry Assn of America Inc (RIAA) 1330 Connecticut Ave NW Suite 300	Washington	DC	20036	**800-223-2328**	202-775-0101
SESAC Inc 55 Music Sq E	Nashville	TN	37203	**800-826-9996**	615-320-0055
Writers Guild of America West (WGAw) 7000 W 3rd St	Los Angeles	CA	90048	**800-548-4532**	323-951-4000

48-5 Charitable & Humanitarian Organizations

Organization	City	State	ZIP	Toll-Free	Phone
ACDI/VOCA (ACDI/VOCA) 50 F St NW Suite 1075	Washington	DC	20001	**800-929-8622**	202-638-4661
Action Against Hunger 247 W 37th St Suite 1201	New York	NY	10018	**877-777-1420**	212-967-7800
Adventist Community Services 12501 Old Columbia Pike	Silver Spring	MD	20904	**877-227-2702**	301-680-6438
Adventist Development & Relief Agency International (ADRA) 12501 Old Columbia Pike	Silver Spring	MD	20904	**800-424-2372**	301-680-6380
American Anti-Slavery Group Inc 198 Tremont St Suite 421	Boston	MA	02116	**800-884-0719**	617-426-8161
American Assn of Fund-Raising Counsel (AAFRC) 4700 W Lake Ave	Glenview	IL	60025	**800-462-2372**	847-375-4709
American Jewish World Service (AJWS) 45 W 36th St 10th Fl	New York	NY	10018	**800-889-7146**	212-736-2597
American Lebanese Syrian Associated Charities (ALSAC) 501 St Jude Pl	Memphis	TN	38105	**800-822-6344**	901-578-2000
American Leprosy Missions (ALM) 1 ALM Way	Greenville	SC	29601	**800-543-3135**	864-271-7040
American ORT 817 Broadway 10th Fl	New York	NY	10003	**800-364-9678**	212-353-5800
American Refugee Committee (ARC) 430 Oak Grove St Suite 204	Minneapolis	MN	55403	**800-875-7060**	612-872-7060
AmeriCares Foundation 88 Hamilton Ave	Stamford	CT	06902	**800-486-4357**	203-658-9500
America's Second Harvest 35 E Wacker Dr Suite 2000	Chicago	IL	60601	**800-771-2303**	312-263-2303
Amigos de las Americas 5618 Star Ln.	Houston	TX	77057	**800-231-7796**	713-782-5290
Amnesty International USA (AIUSA) 5 Penn Plaza 14th Fl	New York	NY	10001	**800-266-3789**	212-807-8400
ANGELCARE PO Box 600370	San Diego	CA	92160	**888-264-5227**	619-795-6234
Association of Fundraising Professionals (AFP) 1101 King St Suite 700	Alexandria	VA	22314	**800-666-3863**	703-684-0410
Association of Gospel Rescue Missions (AGRM) 1045 Swift Ave	Kansas City	MO	64116	**800-624-5156**	816-471-8020
Bread for the World 50 F St NW Suite 500 *Cust Svc	Washington	DC	20001	**800-822-7323***	202-639-9400

Classified Section

Charitable & Humanitarian Organizations (Cont'd)

Organization	City	State	Zip	Toll-Free	Phone
Brother's Brother Foundation 1200 Galveston Ave	Pittsburgh	PA	15233	**888-323-1916**	412-321-3160
CARE USA 151 Ellis St NE	Atlanta	GA	30303	**800-422-7385**	404-681-2552
Catholic Medical Mission Board (CMMB) 10 W 17th St	New York	NY	10011	**800-678-5659**	212-242-7757
Catholic Relief Services (CRS) 209 W Fayette St	Baltimore	MD	21201	**800-235-2772**	410-625-2220
Children Inc PO Box 5381	Richmond	VA	23220	**800-538-5381**	804-359-4562
Children International 2000 E Red Bridge Rd	Kansas City	MO	64131	**800-888-3089**	816-942-2000
Children's Survival Fund Inc 4211 Surfside Cir	Missouri City	TX	77459	**800-426-9885**	281-403-3808
Christian Appalachian Project 322 Crab Orchard St	Lancaster	KY	40446	**866-270-4227**	859-792-3051
Christian Blind Mission International (CBMI) 450 E Park Ave	Greenville	SC	29601	**800-937-2264**	864-239-0065
Christian Disaster Response International 922 Magnolia Ave	Auburndale	FL	33823	**800-430-1235**	863-967-4357
Christian Reformed World Relief Committee (CRWRC) 2850 Kalamazoo Ave SE	Grand Rapids	MI	49560	**800-552-7972**	616-224-0740
Christian Relief Services 2550 Huntington Ave Suite 200	Alexandria	VA	22303	**800-337-3543**	703-317-9086
Church World Service 475 Riverside Dr 7th Fl	New York	NY	10115	**800-456-1310**	212-870-2061
Church World Service Emergency Response Program 475 Riverside Dr 7th Fl	New York	NY	10115	**800-297-1516**	212-870-3151
Citizens Network for Foreign Affairs (CNFA) 1111 19th St NW Suite 900	Washington	DC	20036	**888-872-2632**	202-296-3920
Community Health Charities 200 N Glebe Rd Suite 801	Arlington	VA	22203	**800-654-0845**	703-528-1007
Compassion International PO Box 65000	Colorado Springs	CO	80962	**800-336-7539**	719-487-7000
Concern America PO Box 1790	Santa Ana	CA	92702	**800-266-2376**	714-953-8575
Council on Foundations 1828 L St NW Suite 300	Washington	DC	20036	**800-673-9036**	202-466-6512
CRISTA Ministries 19303 Fremont Ave N	Seattle	WA	98133	**800-442-4003**	206-546-7200
Direct Relief International 27 S La Patera Ln	Santa Barbara	CA	93117	**800-676-1638**	805-964-4767
Doctors Without Borders USA Inc 333 7th Ave 2nd Fl	New York	NY	10001	**888-392-0392**	212-679-6800
Enterprise Foundation 10227 Wincopin Cir Suite 500	Columbia	MD	21044	**800-624-4298**	410-964-1230
Episcopal Migration Ministries (EMM) 815 2nd Ave	New York	NY	10017	**800-334-7626**	212-716-6252
Episcopal Relief & Development 815 2nd Ave	New York	NY	10017	**800-334-7626**	
Evangelical Council for Financial Accountability (ECFA) 440 W Jubal Early Dr Suite 130	Winchester	VA	22601	**800-323-9473**	540-535-0103
Farm Aid 11 Ward St Suite 200	Somerville	MA	02143	**800-327-6243**	617-354-2922
Feed the Children PO Box 36	Oklahoma City	OK	73101	**800-627-4556**	405-942-0228
Food for All 201 Park Washington Ct	Falls Church	VA	22046	**800-896-5101**	703-237-3677
Food for the Hungry Inc 1224 E Washington St Phoenix	Scottsdale	AZ	85034	**800-248-6437**	480-998-3100
Freedom from Hunger 1644 DaVinci Ct	Davis	CA	95616	**800-708-2555**	530-758-6200
Goodwill Industries International Inc 15810 Industrial Dr	Rockville	MD	20855	**800-741-0197**	301-530-6500
Habitat for Humanity International Inc 121 Habitat St	Americus	GA	31709	**800-422-4828**	229-924-6935
Healing the Children (HTC) PO Box 9065	Spokane	WA	99209	**877-432-5543**	509-327-4281
Heart to Heart International 401 S Clairborne Rd Suite 302	Olathe	KS	66062	**800-764-5220**	913-764-5200
Hebrew Immigrant Aid Society (HIAS) 333 7th Ave 17th Fl	New York	NY	10001	**800-442-7714**	212-967-4100
Heifer Project International (HPI) PO Box 1692	Merrifield	VA	22116	**800-422-0474**	501-907-2900
Helen Keller International 352 Park Ave S 12th Fl	New York	NY	10010	**877-535-5374**	212-532-0544
Housing Assistance Council (HAC) 1025 Vermont Ave NW Suite 606	Washington	DC	20005	**800-989-4422**	202-842-8600
Hunger Project The 15 E 26th St Suite 1401	New York	NY	10010	**800-228-6691**	212-251-9100
Independent Charities of America 21 Tamal Vista Blvd Suite 209	Corte Madera	CA	94925	**800-477-0733**	
Independent Order of Foresters (IOF) 789 Don Mills Rd	Toronto	ON	M3C1T9	**800-828-1540**	416-429-3000
Independent Sector 1200 18th St NW Suite 200 *Orders	Washington	DC	20036	**888-860-8118***	202-467-6100
INMED Partnerships for Children 45449 Severn Way Suite 161	Sterling	VA	20166	**800-521-1175**	703-444-4477
International Aid Inc 17011 W Hickory St	Spring Lake	MI	49456	**800-968-7490**	616-846-7490
International Medical Corps (IMC) 1919 Santa Monica Blvd Suite 300	Santa Monica	CA	90404	**800-481-4462**	310-826-7800
International Orthodox Christian Charities (IOCC) 110 West Rd Suite 360	Baltimore	MD	21204	**877-803-4622**	410-243-9820
Lutheran Disaster Response 8765 W Higgins Rd	Chicago	IL	60631	**800-638-3522**	773-380-2822
Lutheran World Relief (LWR) 700 Light St	Baltimore	MD	21230	**800-597-5972**	410-230-2700
Make-A-Wish Foundation of America 3550 N Central Ave Suite 300	Phoenix	AZ	85012	**800-722-9474**	602-279-9474
MAP International PO Box 215000	Brunswick	GA	31521	**800-225-8550**	912-265-6010
Medecins Sans Frontieres 333 7th Ave 2nd Fl	New York	NY	10001	**888-392-0392**	212-679-6800
Mennonite Central Committee (MCC) 21 S 12th St PO Box 500	Akron	PA	17501	**888-563-4676**	717-859-1151
Mercy Corps 3015 SW 1st Ave	Portland	OR	97201	**800-292-3355**	503-796-6800
Mercy-USA for Aid & Development Inc (M-USA) 44450 Pinetree Dr Suite 201	Plymouth	MI	48170	**800-556-3729**	734-454-0011
National Assn for the Exchange of Industrial Resources (NAEIR) 560 McClure St	Galesburg	IL	61401	**800-562-0955**	309-343-0704
National Hunger Clearinghouse 505 8th Ave Suite 2100	New York	NY	10018	**800-453-2648**	212-629-8850
National Peace Corps Assn (NPCA) 1900 L St NW Suite 205	Washington	DC	20036	**800-424-8580**	202-293-7728
National Peace Foundation (NPF) 666 11th St NW Suite 202	Washington	DC	20001	**800-237-3223**	202-783-7030
National Student Campaign Against Hunger & Homelessness (NSCAHH) 233 N Pleasant St Suite 32	Amherst	MA	01002	**800-664-8647**	413-253-6417
Northwest Medical Teams International (NWMTI) PO Box 10	Portland	OR	97207	**800-959-4325**	503-624-1000
OIC International 240 W Tulpehocken St	Philadelphia	PA	19144	**800-653-6424**	215-842-0860
Operation USA 8320 Melrose Ave Suite 200	Los Angeles	CA	90069	**800-678-7255**	323-658-8876
ORBIS International Inc 520 8th Ave 11th Fl	New York	NY	10018	**800-672-4787**	646-674-5500
Outreach International PO Box 210	Independence	MO	64051	**888-833-1235**	816-833-0883
Oxfam America 26 West St	Boston	MA	02111	**800-776-9326**	617-482-1211
Partners of the Americas 1424 K St NW Suite 700	Washington	DC	20005	**800-322-7844**	202-628-3300
People-to-People Health Foundation 255 Carter Hall Ln	Millwood	VA	22646	**800-544-4673**	540-837-2100
Points of Light Foundation & Volunteer Center National Network 1400 'I' St NW Suite 800	Washington	DC	20005	**800-750-7653**	202-729-8000
Population Connection 1400 16th St NW Suite 320	Washington	DC	20036	**800-767-1956**	202-332-2200
Presbyterian Disaster Assistance (PDA) 100 Witherspoon St	Louisville	KY	40202	**888-728-7228**	502-569-5839
Project HOPE 255 Carter Hall Ln	Millwood	VA	22646	**800-544-4673**	540-837-2100
ProLiteracy Worldwide 1320 Jamesville Ave	Syracuse	NY	13210	**800-448-8878**	315-422-9121
Random Acts of Kindness Foundation 1727 Tremont Pl	Denver	CO	80202	**800-660-2811**	303-297-1964
Rebuilding Together 1536 16th St NW	Washington	DC	20036	**800-473-4229**	202-483-9083
Refugees International (RI) 1705 'N' St NW	Washington	DC	20036	**800-733-8433**	202-828-0110
Research!America 1101 King St Suite 520	Alexandria	VA	22314	**800-366-2873**	703-739-2577
Salvation Army PO Box 269	Alexandria	VA	22313	**800-725-2769**	703-684-5500
Save the Children Federation Inc 54 Wilton Rd	Westport	CT	06880	**800-728-3843**	203-221-4000
Senior Gleaners Inc 1951 Bell Ave	Sacramento	CA	95838	**800-585-1530**	916-925-3240
Sertoma International 1912 E Meyer Blvd	Kansas City	MO	64132	**800-593-5646**	816-333-8300
Share Our Strength 1730 'M' St NW Suite 700	Washington	DC	20036	**800-969-4767**	202-393-2925
Smile Train Inc 245 5th Ave Suite 2201	New York	NY	10016	**877-543-7645**	212-689-9199
Society of Saint Andrew 3383 Sweet Hollow Rd	Big Island	VA	24526	**800-333-4597**	434-299-5956
Southeast Asia Resource Action Center (SEARAC) 1628 16th St NW 3rd Fl	Washington	DC	20009	**800-600-9188**	202-667-4690
Special Wish Foundation Inc 5340 E Main St Suite 208	Columbus	OH	43213	**800-486-9474**	614-575-9474
TechnoServe 49 Day St	Norwalk	CT	06854	**800-999-6757**	203-852-0377
Trickle Up Program Inc 104 W 27th St 12th Fl	New York	NY	10001	**866-246-9980**	212-255-9980
UNICEF (United Nations Children's Fund) 3 UN Plaza *Orders	New York	NY	10017	**800-553-1200***	212-326-7000
Unitarian Universalist Service Committee (UUSC) 130 Prospect St	Cambridge	MA	02139	**800-388-3920**	617-868-6600
United Methodist Committee on Relief (UMCOR) 475 Riverside Dr Suite 330	New York	NY	10115	**800-554-8583**	212-870-3814
United Nations Children's Fund (UNICEF) 3 UN Plaza *Orders	New York	NY	10017	**800-553-1200***	212-326-7000
United Way of America 701 N Fairfax St	Alexandria	VA	22314	**800-892-2757**	703-836-7100
USA for UNHCR 1775 K St NW Suite 290	Washington	DC	20006	**800-770-1100**	202-296-1115
Volunteers of America 1660 Duke St	Alexandria	VA	22314	**800-899-0089**	703-341-5000
World Concern 19303 Fremont Ave N	Seattle	WA	98133	**800-755-5022**	206-546-7201
World Hunger Year Inc (WHY) 505 8th Ave Suite 2100	New York	NY	10018	**800-548-6479**	212-629-8850
World Neighbors Inc 4127 NW 122nd St	Oklahoma City	OK	73120	**800-242-6387**	405-752-9700
World Opportunities International/Help the Children 1875 Century Park E Suite 700	Los Angeles	CA	90067	**800-464-7187**	323-466-7187
World Vision Inc PO Box 9716	Federal Way	WA	98063	**800-777-5777**	253-815-1000

48-6 Children & Family Advocacy Organizations

Organization	City	State	Zip	Toll-Free	Phone
AARP 601 'E' St NW	Washington	DC	20049	**888-687-2277**	202-434-2277
Adopt America Network 1025 N Reynolds Rd	Toledo	OH	43615	**800-246-1731**	419-534-3350
Adoption ARC Inc 4701 Pine St Suite J-7	Philadelphia	PA	19143	**800-884-4004**	215-748-1441
Alliance for Aging Research 2021 K St NW Suite 305	Washington	DC	20006	**800-639-2421**	202-293-2856
Alliance for Retired Americans 888 16th St NW Ste 520	Washington	DC	20006	**888-373-6497**	202-974-8222
American Academy of Pediatrics (AAP) 141 Northwest Point Blvd	Elk Grove Village	IL	60007	**800-433-9016**	847-434-4000
American Assn of Homes & Services for the Aging (AAHSA) 2519 Connecticut Ave NW	Washington	DC	20008	**800-508-9442**	202-783-2242
American Assn of Retired Persons 601 'E' St NW	Washington	DC	20049	**888-687-2277**	202-434-2277
American Coalition for Fathers & Children (ACFC) 1420 Spring Hill Rd	McLean	VA	22102	**800-978-3237**	
American Culinary Federation Chef & Child Foundation 180 Center Place Way	Saint Augustine	FL	32095	**800-624-9458**	904-824-4468
American Humane Assn (AHA) 63 Inverness Dr E	Englewood	CO	80112	**800-227-4645**	303-792-9900
American Professional Society on the Abuse of Children (APSAC) 107 Amberside Dr	Goose Creek	SC	29445	**877-402-7722**	843-764-2905
American Senior Fitness Assn (SFA) PO Box 2575	New Smyrna Beach	FL	32170	**800-243-1478**	386-423-6634
American SIDS Institute 509 Augusta Dr	Marietta	GA	30067	**800-232-7437**	770-426-8746
American Society on Aging (ASA) 833 Market St Suite 511	San Francisco	CA	94103	**800-537-9728**	415-974-9600
America's Promise - The Alliance for Youth 909 N Washington St Suite 400	Alexandria	VA	22314	**800-365-0153**	703-684-4500
Association for Children for Enforcement of Support (ACES) PO Box 7842	Fredericksburg	VA	22404	**800-738-2237**	
Association for Couples in Marriage Enrichment (ACME) PO Box 10596	Winston-Salem	NC	27108	**800-634-8325**	336-724-1526
Believe In Tomorrow National Children's Foundation 6601 Frederick Rd	Baltimore	MD	21228	**800-933-5470**	410-744-1032
Cal Farley's Boys Ranch 600 W 11th St	Amarillo	TX	79174	**800-687-3722**	806-372-2341
Canadian Assn of Retired Persons (CARP) 1304-27 Queen St E	Toronto	ON	M5C2M6	**800-363-9736**	416-363-8748
Child Find of America Inc 7 Cummings Ln	Highland	NY	12528	**800-426-5678**	845-691-4666
Child Find Canada 212-2211 McPhillips St	Winnipeg	MB	R3G0N4	**800-387-7962**	204-339-5584

Organization	City	State	ZIP	Toll-Free	Phone
Child Quest International 307 Orchard City Dr Suite 108	Campbell	CA	95008	**888-818-4673**	408-287-4673
Child Welfare League of America (CWLA) 440 1st St NW 3rd Fl	Washington	DC	20001	**800-407-6273**	202-638-2952
Childhelp USA 15757 N 78th St	Scottsdale	AZ	85260	**800-422-4453**	480-922-8212
Children of Aging Parents 1609 Woodbourne Rd Suite 302A	Levittown	PA	19057	**800-227-7294**	215-945-6900
Children Awaiting Parents Inc (CAP) 595 Blossom Rd Suite 306	Rochester	NY	14610	**888-835-8802**	585-232-5110
Children Inc PO Box 5381	Richmond	VA	23220	**800-538-5381**	804-359-4562
Children of the Night 14530 Sylvan St	Van Nuys	CA	91411	**800-551-1300**	818-908-4474
Children's Defense Fund (CDF) 25 'E' St NW	Washington	DC	20001	**800-233-1200**	202-628-8787
Children's Rights Council (CRC) 6200 Editors Park Dr Suite 103	Hyattsville	MD	20782	**800-787-5437**	301-559-3120
Christian Children's Fund Inc (CCF) 2821 Emerywood Pkwy	Richmond	VA	23294	**800-776-6767**	804-756-2700
Christian Foundation for Children & Aging (CFCA) 1 Elmwood Ave	Kansas City	KS	66103	**800-875-6564**	913-384-6500
Common Sense About Kids & Guns 1225 'I' St NW Suite 1100	Washington	DC	20005	**877-955-5437**	202-546-0200
Communities in Schools Inc (CIS) 277 S Washington St Suite 210	Alexandria	VA	22314	**800-247-4543**	703-519-8999
Connect For Kids 1625 K St NW Suite 1100	Washington	DC	20006	**877-236-8666**	202-638-5770
Covenant House 346 W 17th St	New York	NY	10011	**800-999-9999**	212-727-4000
Dream Factory Inc 1218 S 3rd St	Louisville	KY	40203	**800-456-7556**	502-637-8700
Experience Works Inc 2200 Clarendon Blvd Suite 1000	Arlington	VA	22201	**866-397-9757**	703-522-7272
FaithTrust Institute 2400 N 45th St Suite 10	Seattle	WA	98103	**877-860-2255**	206-634-1903
Family Research Council (FRC) 801 G St NW	Washington	DC	20001	**800-225-4008**	202-393-2100
Find the Children 2656 29th St Suite 203	Santa Monica	CA	90405	**888-477-6721**	310-314-3213
First Candle/SIDS Alliance 1314 Bedford Ave Suite 210	Baltimore	MD	21208	**800-221-7437**	410-653-8226
Focus on the Family 8605 Explorer Dr	Colorado Springs	CO	80920	**800-232-6459***	719-531-3400
*Sales					
Girls & Boys Town 14100 Crawford St	Boys Town	NE	68010	**800-448-3000**	402-498-1300
Girls Inc 120 Wall St 3rd Fl	New York	NY	10005	**800-374-4475**	212-509-2000
Gray Panthers 733 15th St NW Suite 437	Washington	DC	20005	**800-280-5362**	202-737-6637
Human Life International (HLI) 4 Family Life Ln	Front Royal	VA	22630	**800-549-5433***	540-635-7884
*Orders					
Jewish Board of Family & Children Services (JBFCS) 120 W 57th St	New York	NY	10019	**888-523-2769**	212-582-9100
Jimmy Ryce Center for Victims of Predatory Abduction (JRC) 908 Coquina Ln	Vero Beach	FL	32963	**800-546-7923**	772-492-0200
MOPS International 2370 S Trenton Way	Denver	CO	80231	**800-929-1287**	303-733-5353
Mothers Against Drunk Driving (MADD) 511 E John Carpenter Fwy Suite 700	Irving	TX	75062	**800-438-6233**	214-744-6233
National Adoption Center 1500 Walnut St Suite 701	Philadelphia	PA	19102	**800-862-3678**	215-735-9988
National Adult Day Services Assn (NADSA) 8201 Greensboro Dr Suite 300	McLean	VA	22102	**800-424-9046**	703-610-9000
National Assn of Child Care Professionals (NACCP) 7610 Hwy 71 W Suite E	Austin	TX	78735	**800-537-1118**	512-301-5557
National Assn of Child Care Resource & Referral Agencies (NACCRRA) 1319 F St NW Suite 500	Washington	DC	20004	**800-424-2246**	202-393-5501
National Assn for Family Child Care (NAFCC) 5202 Pinemont Dr	Salt Lake City	UT	84123	**800-359-3817**	801-269-9338
National Assn of Service & Conservation Corps (NASCC) 666 11th St NW Suite 1000	Washington	DC	20001	**800-666-2722**	202-737-6272
National Caregiving Foundation 801 N Pitt St Suite 116	Alexandria	VA	22314	**800-930-1357**	703-299-9300
National Center for Family Literacy (NCFL) 325 W Main St Suite 300	Louisville	KY	40202	**877-326-5481**	502-584-1133
National Center for Missing & Exploited Children (NCMEC) 699 Prince St	Alexandria	VA	22314	**800-843-5678**	703-274-3900
National Center on Women & Aging Brandeis University Heller Graduate School MS 035	Waltham	MA	02454	**800-929-1995**	781-736-3866
National Child Abuse Hotline 15757 N 78th St	Scottsdale	AZ	85260	**800-422-4453**	480-922-8212
National Child Care Assn (NCCA) 1016 Rosser St	Conyers	GA	30012	**800-543-7161**	770-922-8198
National Child Safety Council (NCSC) 4065 Page Ave	Jackson	MI	49204	**800-327-5107**	517-764-6070
National Council for Adoption (NCFA) 225 N Washington St	Alexandria	VA	22314	**866-212-3678**	703-299-6633
National Council on the Aging (NCOA) 300 D St SW Suite 801	Washington	DC	20024	**800-424-9046**	202-479-1200
National Council on Family Relations (NCFR) 3989 Central Ave NE Suite 550	Minneapolis	MN	55421	**888-781-9331**	763-781-9331
National Court Appointed Special Advocate Assn (CASA) 100 W Harrison St North Tower Suite 500	Seattle	WA	98119	**800-628-3233**	206-270-0072
National Dissemination Center for Children with Disabilities 1825 Connecticut Ave	Washington	DC	20009	**800-695-0285**	202-884-8200
National Domestic Violence Hotline (NDVH) PO Box 161810	Austin	TX	78716	**800-799-7233**	512-794-1133
National Family Caregivers Assn (NFCA) 10400 Connecticut Ave Suite 500	Kensington	MD	20895	**800-896-3650**	301-942-6430
National Foster Parent Assn (NFPA) 7512 Stanich Ave Suite 6	Gig Harbor	WA	98335	**800-557-5238**	253-853-4000
National Inhalant Prevention Coalition (NIPC) 2904 Kerbey Ln	Austin	TX	78703	**800-269-4237**	512-480-8953
National Interfaith Coalition on Aging (NICA) 300 D St SW	Washington	DC	20024	**800-424-9046**	202-479-1200
National Organization of Mothers of Twins Clubs Inc (NOMOTC) PO Box 438	Thompsons Station	TN	37179	**877-540-2200**	615-595-0936
National Resource Center on Domestic Violence (NRCDV) 6400 Flank Dr Suite 1300	Harrisburg	PA	17112	**800-537-2238**	717-545-6400
National Resource Center on Native American Aging (NRCNAA) 501 N Columbia Rd Rm 4531	Grand Forks	ND	58202	**800-896-7628**	701-777-3437
National Resource Center for Special Needs Adoptions 16250 Northland Dr Suite 120	Southfield	MI	48075	**877-767-5437**	248-443-7080
National Runaway Switchboard (NRS) 3080 N Lincoln Ave	Chicago	IL	60657	**800-621-4000**	773-880-9860
National Urban Technology Center 55 John St Suite 300	New York	NY	10038	**800-998-3212**	212-528-7350
National Youth Advocacy Coalition (NYAC) 1638 R St NW Suite 300	Washington	DC	20009	**800-541-6922**	202-319-7596
North America Missing Children Assn Inc 136 Rt 420 Hwy	South Esk	NB	E1V4N8	**800-260-0753**	506-627-1209
Older Women's League (OWL) 1750 New York Ave NW Suite 350	Washington	DC	20006	**800-825-3695**	202-783-6686
Orphan Foundation of America (OFA) 12020-D N Shore Dr	Reston	VA	20190	**800-950-4673**	571-203-0270
Parents of Murdered Children (POMC) 100 E 8th St Suite B-41	Cincinnati	OH	45202	**888-818-7662**	513-721-5683
Parents Without Partners (PWP) 1650 S Dixie Hwy Suite 510	Boca Raton	FL	33432	**800-637-7974**	561-391-8833
Plan USA 155 Plan Way	Warwick	RI	02886	**800-556-7918**	401-738-5600
Planned Parenthood Federation of America 434 W 33rd St	New York	NY	10001	**800-829-7732**	212-541-7800
Prevent Child Abuse America 200 S Michigan Ave 17th Fl	Chicago	IL	60604	**800-244-5373**	312-663-3520
Promise Keepers 4045 Pecos St PO Box 11798	Denver	CO	80211	**800-888-7595**	303-964-7600
Rainbows 2100 Golf Rd Suite 370	Rolling Meadows	IL	60008	**800-266-3206**	847-952-1770
RAINN (Rape Abuse & Incest National Network) 635-B Pennsylvania Ave SE	Washington	DC	20003	**800-656-4673**	202-544-1034
Rape Abuse & Incest National Network (RAINN) 635-B Pennsylvania Ave SE	Washington	DC	20003	**800-656-4673**	202-544-1034
Seniors Coalition 4401 Fair Lakes Ct Suite 210	Fairfax	VA	22033	**800-325-9891**	703-631-4211
SER - Jobs for Progress National Inc 5215 N O'Connor Blvd Suite 2550	Irving	TX	75039	**800-427-2306**	972-506-7815
SOS Children's Villages-USA 1317 F St NW Suite 550	Washington	DC	20004	**800-886-5767**	202-347-7920
Spaulding for Children 16250 Northland Dr Suite 120	Southfield	MI	48075	**877-767-5437**	248-443-7080
Stand For Children 516 SE Morrison St Suite 206	Portland	OR	97214	**800-663-4032**	503-235-2305
Stars of David International Inc 3175 Commercial Ave Suite 100	Northbrook	IL	60062	**800-782-7349**	847-509-9929
Stepfamily Assn of America (SAA) 650 J St Suite 205	Lincoln	NE	68508	**800-735-0329**	402-477-7837
Stepfamily Foundation 333 West End Ave Suite 11C	New York	NY	10023	**800-759-7837**	212-877-3244
Students Against Destructive Decisions (SADD) 255 Main St	Marlborough	MA	01752	**877-723-3462**	508-481-3568
TOUGHLOVE International 100 Mechanics St	Doylestown	PA	18901	**800-333-1069**	215-348-7090
Vanished Children's Alliance (VCA) 991 W Hedding St Suite 101	San Jose	CA	95126	**800-826-4743**	408-296-1113
Well Spouse Foundation 63 W Main St Suite H	Freehold	NJ	07728	**800-838-0879**	732-577-8899
YMCA of the USA 101 N Wacker Dr 14th Fl	Chicago	IL	60606	**800-872-9622**	312-977-0031
Young Men's Christian Assn of the USA 101 N Wacker Dr 14th Fl	Chicago	IL	60606	**800-872-9622**	312-977-0031
YWCA USA 1015 18th St NW Suite 1100	Washington	DC	20036	**800-992-2871**	202-467-0801

48-7 Civic & Political Organizations

Organization	City	State	ZIP	Toll-Free	Phone
ACU (American Conservative Union) 1007 Cameron St	Alexandria	VA	22314	**800-228-7345**	703-836-8602
Alliance for Better Campaigns 1990 M St NW Suite 200	Washington	DC	20036	**888-637-3389**	202-659-1300
American Conservative Union (ACU) 1007 Cameron St	Alexandria	VA	22314	**800-228-7345**	703-836-8602
Americans for Democratic Action (ADA) 1625 K St NW Suite 210	Washington	DC	20006	**800-787-2734**	202-785-5980
Americans for Fair Taxation PO Box 27487	Houston	TX	77227	**800-324-7829**	713-963-9023
Americans United for Separation of Church & State 518 C St NE	Washington	DC	20002	**800-875-3707**	202-466-3234
Association of Community Organizations for Reform Now (ACORN) 739 8th St SE	Washington	DC	20003	**877-552-2676**	202-547-2500
CapitolWatch PO Box 71	Great Falls	VA	22066	**888-468-9282**	202-544-2600
Christian Coalition of America PO Box 37030	Washington	DC	20013	**888-440-2262**	202-479-6900
Citizens Against Government Waste (CAGW) 1301 Connecticut Ave NW Suite 400	Washington	DC	20036	**800-232-6479**	202-467-5300
Citizens Committee for the Right to Keep & Bear Arms (CCRKBA) 12500 NE 10th Pl	Bellevue	WA	98005	**800-426-4302**	425-454-4911
Close Up Foundation Inc 44 Canal Ctr Plaza	Alexandria	VA	22314	**800-256-7387**	703-706-3300
Common Cause 1250 Connecticut Ave NW Suite 600	Washington	DC	20036	**800-926-1064**	202-833-1200
Concord Coalition 1011 Arlington Blvd Suite 300	Arlington	VA	22209	**888-333-4248**	703-894-6222
Congress Watch 215 Pennsylvania Ave SE 3rd Fl	Washington	DC	20003	**800-289-3787**	202-546-4996
Constitutional Rights Foundation 601 S Kingsley Dr	Los Angeles	CA	90005	**800-488-4273**	213-487-5590
Council of the Americas 680 Park Ave	New York	NY	10021	**800-733-2342**	212-628-3200
Council of Canadians 170 Laurier Ave W Suite 700	Ottawa	ON	K1P5V5	**800-387-7177**	613-233-2773
EMILY's List 1120 Connecticut Ave NW Suite 1100	Washington	DC	20036	**800-683-6459**	202-326-1400
Evangelicals for Social Action (ESA) 10 E Lancaster Ave	Wynnewood	PA	19096	**800-650-6600**	610-645-9390
Families USA 1334 G St NW Suite 300	Washington	DC	20005	**800-593-5041**	202-628-3030
Federation for American Immigration Reform (FAIR) 1666 Connecticut Ave NW Suite 400	Washington	DC	20009	**877-627-3247**	202-328-7004
Foreign Policy Assn (FPA) 470 Park Ave S 2nd Fl	New York	NY	10016	**800-628-5754**	212-481-8100
Foundation for Moral Law Inc PO Box 231264	Montgomery	AL	36123	**866-317-0800**	334-262-1245
FreedomWorks 1775 Pennsylvania Ave NW 11th Fl	Washington	DC	20006	**888-564-6273**	202-783-3870
Global Exchange 2017 Mission St Suite 303	San Francisco	CA	94110	**800-497-1994**	415-255-7296
HALT - An Organization of Americans for Legal Reform 1612 K St NW Suite 510	Washington	DC	20006	**888-367-4258**	202-887-8255
Judicial Watch Inc PO Box 44444	Washington	DC	20026	**888-593-8442**	202-646-5172
Junior Chamber International (JCI) 15645 Olive Blvd	Chesterfield	MO	63017	**800-905-5499**	636-449-3100

Civic & Political Organizations (Cont'd)

Organization	City	State	Zip	Toll-Free	Phone
League of Women Voters (LWV) 1730 M St NW Suite 1000	Washington	DC	20036	**800-249-8683**	202-429-1965
National Assn of Town Watch (NATW) 1 E Wynnewood Rd Suite 102	Wynnewood	PA	19096	**800-648-3688**	610-649-7055
National Committee to Preserve Social Security & Medicare (NCPSSM) 10 G St NE Suite 600	Washington	DC	20002	**800-966-1935**	202-216-0420
National Taxpayers Union (NTU) 108 N Alfred St	Alexandria	VA	22314	**800-829-4258**	703-683-5700
People for the American Way (PFAW) 2000 M St NW Suite 400	Washington	DC	20036	**800-326-7329**	202-467-4999
Population-Environment Balance Inc 2000 P St NW Suite 600	Washington	DC	20036	**800-866-6269**	202-955-5700
Population Reference Bureau (PRB) 1875 Connecticut Ave NW Suite 520	Washington	DC	20009	**800-877-9881**	202-483-1100
Project Vote 6805 Oak Creek Dr	Columbus	OH	43229	**800-546-8683**	614-523-2560
Project Vote Smart 1 Common Ground	Philipsburg	MT	59858	**888-868-3762**	406-859-8683
US Junior Chamber of Commerce PO Box 7	Tulsa	OK	74102	**800-529-2337**	918-584-2481
US Term Limits (USTL) 240 Waukegan Rd Suite 200	Glenview	IL	60025	**800-733-6440**	202-379-3000
WISH List 499 S Capitol St SW Suite 408	Washington	DC	20003	**800-756-9474**	202-479-1230
Women's Campaign Fund (WCF) 734 15th St NW Suite 500	Washington	DC	20005	**800-446-8170**	202-393-8164
Young America's Foundation 110 Elden St	Herndon	VA	20170	**800-292-9231**	703-318-9608
Young Democrats of America PO Box 77496	Washington	DC	20013	**877-639-8585**	202-639-8585

48-8 Civil & Human Rights Organizations

Organization	City	State	Zip	Toll-Free	Phone
Americans for Effective Law Enforcement (AELE) 841 W Touhy Ave	Park Ridge	IL	60068	**800-763-2802**	847-685-0700
Amnesty International USA (AIUSA) 5 Penn Plaza 14th Fl	New York	NY	10001	**800-266-3789**	212-807-8400
Asian American Legal Defense & Education Fund (AALDEF) 99 Hudson St 12th Fl	New York	NY	10013	**800-966-5946**	212-966-5932
Becket Fund for Religious Liberty 1350 Connecticut Ave NW Suite 605	Washington	DC	20036	**800-232-5385**	202-955-0095
Center for Individual Rights (CIR) 1233 20th St NW Suite 300	Washington	DC	20036	**877-426-2665**	202-833-8400
Center for Reproductive Rights 120 Wall St 14th Fl	New York	NY	10005	**800-786-9711**	917-637-3600
Children's Rights Council (CRC) 6200 Editors Park Dr Suite 103	Hyattsville	MD	20782	**800-787-5437**	301-559-3120
Corporate Accountability International 46 Plympton St	Boston	MA	02118	**800-688-8797**	617-695-2525
Crime Stoppers International PO Box 614	Arlington	TX	76004	**800-245-0009**	817-451-9229
Disability Rights Center Inc 18 Low Ave	Concord	NH	03301	**800-834-1721**	603-228-0432
End-of-Life Choices PO Box 101810	Denver	CO	80250	**800-247-7421**	303-639-1202
Facing History & Ourselves National Foundation Inc 16 Hurd Rd	Brookline	MA	02445	**800-856-9039**	617-232-1595
Human Rights Campaign 1640 Rhode Island Ave NW	Washington	DC	20036	**800-777-4723**	202-628-4160
Institute for Health Freedom 1825 'I' St NW Suite 400	Washington	DC	20006	**888-616-1976**	202-429-6610
International Task Force on Euthanasia & Assisted Suicide PO Box 760	Steubenville	OH	43952	**800-958-5678**	740-282-3810
Media Watch PO Box 618	Santa Cruz	CA	95061	**800-631-6355**	831-423-6355
Medicare Rights Center (MRC) 1460 Broadway 17th Fl *hotline	New York	NY	10036	**800-333-4114***	212-869-3850
NAACP (National Assn for the Advancement of Colored People) 4805 Mount Hope Dr	Baltimore	MD	21215	**877-622-2798**	410-358-8900
National Abortion Federation (NAF) 1755 Massachusetts Ave NW Suite 600	Washington	DC	20036	**800-772-9100**	202-667-5881
National Assn for the Advancement of Colored People (NAACP) 4805 Mount Hope Dr	Baltimore	MD	21215	**877-622-2798**	410-358-8900
National Center for Juvenile Justice (NCJJ) 3700 S Water St Suite 200	Pittsburgh	PA	15203	**800-577-6903**	412-227-6950
National Center for Victims of Crime (NCVC) 2000 M St NW Suite 480	Washington	DC	20036	**800-394-2255**	202-467-8700
National Coalition to Abolish the Death Penalty (NCADP) 920 Pennsylvania Ave SE	Washington	DC	20003	**888-286-2237**	202-543-9577
National Conference for Community & Justice (NCCJ) 475 Park Ave S 19th Fl	New York	NY	10016	**800-352-6225**	212-545-1300
National Court Appointed Special Advocate Assn (CASA) 100 W Harrison St North Tower Suite 500	Seattle	WA	98119	**800-628-3233**	206-270-0072
National Organization for the Reform of Marijuana Laws (NORML) 1600 K St NW Suite 501	Washington	DC	20006	**888-676-6765**	202-483-5500
National Organization for Victim Assistance (NOVA) 1730 Park Rd NW	Washington	DC	20010	**800-879-6682**	202-232-6682
NORML (National Organization for the Reform of Marijuana Laws) 1600 K St NW Suite 501	Washington	DC	20006	**888-676-6765**	202-483-5500
Prison Fellowship Ministries (PF) PO Box 1550	Merrifield	VA	22116	**877-498-0100**	703-478-0100
Rutherford Institute PO Box 7482	Charlottesville	VA	22906	**800-225-1791**	434-978-3888
Second Amendment Foundation 12500 NE 10th Pl	Bellevue	WA	98005	**800-426-4302**	425-454-7012
Simon Wiesenthal Center 1399 S Roxbury Dr	Los Angeles	CA	90035	**800-900-9036**	310-553-9036
Urban Land Institute (ULI) 1025 Thomas Jefferson St NW Suite 500W *Orders	Washington	DC	20007	**800-321-5011***	202-624-7000
WeTip Inc PO Box 1296	Rancho Cucamonga	CA	91729	**800-782-7463**	909-987-5005
Wiesenthal Simon Center 1399 S Roxbury Dr	Los Angeles	CA	90035	**800-900-9036**	310-553-9036

48-9 Computer & Internet Organizations

Organization	City	State	Zip	Toll-Free	Phone
ACM (Association for Computing Machinery) 1515 Broadway 17th Fl	New York	NY	10036	**800-342-6626**	212-869-7440
Association for Computing Machinery (ACM) 1515 Broadway 17th Fl	New York	NY	10036	**800-342-6626**	212-869-7440
Association for Interactive Marketing (AIM) 1430 Broadway 8th Fl	New York	NY	10018	**888-337-0008**	212-790-1406
Black Data Processing Associates (BDPA) 6301 Ivy Ln Suite 700	Greenbelt	MD	20770	**800-727-2372**	301-220-2180
Business Software Alliance (BSA) 1150 18th St Suite 700	Washington	DC	20036	**888-667-4722**	202-872-5500
CommerceNet 510 Logue Ave	Mountain View	CA	94043	**888-255-1900**	650-962-2600
Computer Measurement Group (CMG) 151 Fries Mill Rd Suite 104	Turnersville	NJ	08012	**800-436-7264**	856-401-1700
Consortium for School Networking (CoSN) 1710 Rhode Island Ave NW Suite 900	Washington	DC	20036	**866-267-8747**	202-861-2676
Document Management Industries Assn (DMIA) 433 E Monroe Ave	Alexandria	VA	22301	**800-336-4641**	703-836-6232
Encompass 401 N Michigan Ave 22nd Fl	Chicago	IL	60611	**877-354-9887**	312-321-5151
Independent Computer Consultants Assn (ICCA) 11131 S Towne Sq Suite F	Saint Louis	MO	63123	**800-774-4222**	314-892-1675
Institute for Certification of Computing Professionals (ICCP) 2350 E Devon Ave Suite 115	Des Plaines	IL	60018	**800-843-8227**	847-299-4227
Institute for Computer Capacity Management 1020 8th Ave S Suite 6	Naples	FL	34102	**800-531-6143**	239-261-8945
Interex PO Box 3439	Sunnyvale	CA	94088	**800-468-3739**	408-747-0227
International Tandem Users' Group (ITUG) 401 N Michigan	Chicago	IL	60611	**800-845-4884**	312-321-6851
Mozilla Foundation 1350 Villa St Suite C *Tech Supp	Mountain View	CA	94041	**888-586-4539***	650-903-0888
National Urban Technology Center 55 John St Suite 300	New York	NY	10038	**800-998-3212**	212-528-7350
UniForum Assn PO Box 3177	Annapolis	MD	21043	**800-333-8649**	410-715-9500
Xplor International 24238 Hawthorne Blvd	Torrance	CA	90505	**800-669-7567**	310-373-3633

48-10 Consumer Interest Organizations

Organization	City	State	Zip	Toll-Free	Phone
Accuracy in Media Inc (AIM) 4455 Connecticut Ave NW Suite 330	Washington	DC	20008	**800-787-4567**	202-364-4401
American Homeowners Assn (AHA) 1100 Summer St 1st Fl *Cust Svc	Stamford	CT	06905	**800-470-2242***	203-323-7715
Auriton Solutions 1700 W Hwy 36 Suite 301	Roseville	MN	55113	**877-332-8700**	651-631-8000
Call for Action 5272 River Rd Suite 300	Bethesda	MD	20816	**800-647-1756**	301-657-8260
Carpet & Rug Institute (CRI) 310 S Holiday Ave	Dalton	GA	30720	**800-882-8846**	706-278-3176
Funeral Consumers Alliance 33 Patchen Rd	South Burlington	VT	05403	**800-765-0107**	802-865-8300
Funeral Service Consumer Assistance Program PO Box 486	Elm Grove	WI	53122	**800-662-7666**	
Insurance Information Institute (III) 110 William St 24th Fl	New York	NY	10038	**800-331-9146**	212-346-5500
International Fabricare Institute (IFI) 12251 Tech Rd	Silver Spring	MD	20904	**800-638-2627**	301-622-1900
Internet Fraud Watch c/o National Fraud Information Ctr 1701 K St NW Suite 1200	Washington	DC	20006	**800-876-7060**	202-835-3323
Myvesta.org Inc 6 Taft Ct Suite 200	Rockville	MD	20850	**800-698-3782**	301-762-5270
National Assn of Child Care Resource & Referral Agencies (NACCRRA) 1319 F St NW Suite 500	Washington	DC	20004	**800-424-2246**	202-393-5501
National Committee for Quality Assurance (NCQA) 2000 L St NW Suite 500	Washington	DC	20036	**800-236-5903**	202-955-3500
National Consumers League (NCL) 1701 K St NW Suite 1200	Washington	DC	20006	**800-876-7060**	202-835-3323
National Foundation for Credit Counseling (NFCC) 801 Roeder Rd Suite 900	Silver Spring	MD	20910	**800-388-2227**	301-589-5600
National Fraud Information Center (NFIC) 1701 K St NW Suite 1200	Washington	DC	20006	**800-876-7060**	202-835-3323
Philanthropic Research Inc 427 Scotland St	Williamsburg	VA	23185	**800-784-9378**	757-229-4631
Private Citizen Inc PO Box 233	Naperville	IL	60566	**800-288-5865**	630-393-2370

48-11 Educational Associations & Organizations

Organization	City	State	Zip	Toll-Free	Phone
A Better Chance 240 W 35th St 9th Fl	New York	NY	10001	**800-543-7181**	646-346-1310
American Indian College Fund 8333 Greenwood Blvd	Denver	CO	80221	**800-776-3863**	303-426-8900
American Institute for Foreign Study (AIFS) 9 W Broad St	Stamford	CT	06902	**800-727-2437**	203-399-5000
Association of Boarding Schools (TABS) 4455 Connecticut Ave NW Suite A-200	Washington	DC	20008	**800-541-5908**	202-966-8705
Bands of America Inc (BOA) 39 W Jackson Pl	Indianapolis	IN	46225	**800-848-2263**	317-636-2263
Center for Education Reform 1001 Connecticut Ave NW Suite 204	Washington	DC	20036	**800-521-2118**	202-822-9000
Challenger Center for Space Science Education 1250 N Pitt St	Alexandria	VA	22314	**800-987-8277**	703-683-9740
College Board 45 Columbus Ave	New York	NY	10023	**800-927-4302**	212-713-8000
College Parents of America (CPA) 8300 Boone Blvd Suite 500	Vienna	VA	22182	**888-256-4627**	703-761-6702
Communities in Schools Inc (CIS) 277 S Washington St Suite 210	Alexandria	VA	22314	**800-247-4543**	703-519-8999
Facing History & Ourselves National Foundation Inc 16 Hurd Rd	Brookline	MA	02445	**800-856-9039**	617-232-1595
Family Career & Community Leaders of America (FCCLA) 1910 Association Dr	Reston	VA	20191	**800-234-4425**	703-476-4900
FBLA (Future Business Leaders of America - Phi Beta Lambda Inc) 1912 Association Dr	Reston	VA	20191	**800-325-2946**	703-860-3334
FIRST 200 Bedford St	Manchester	NH	03101	**800-871-8326**	603-666-3906
Foundation Center 79 5th Ave 2nd Fl	New York	NY	10003	**800-424-9836**	212-620-4230
Future Business Leaders of America - Phi Beta Lambda Inc (FBLA-PBL) 1912 Association Dr	Reston	VA	20191	**800-325-2946**	703-860-3334
Great Books Foundation 35 E Wacker Dr Suite 2300	Chicago	IL	60601	**800-222-5870**	312-332-5870
Health Occupations Students of America (HOSA) 6021 Morriss Rd Suite 111	Flower Mound	TX	75028	**800-321-4672**	972-874-0062
Intercollegiate Studies Institute (ISI) 3901 Centerville Rd	Wilmington	DE	19807	**800-526-7022**	302-652-4600

Organization	City	State	ZIP	Toll-Free	Phone
JACAN (Junior Achievement of Canada) 2275 Lakeshore Blvd W Suite 306	Toronto	ON	M8V3Y3	**800-265-0699**	416-622-4602
Junior Achievement of Canada (JACAN) 2275 Lakeshore Blvd W Suite 306	Toronto	ON	M8V3Y3	**800-265-0699**	416-622-4602
Junior State of America (JSA) 400 S El Camino Real Suite 300	San Mateo	CA	94402	**800-334-5353**	650-347-1600
National Alliance of Blind Students Inc 1155 15th St NW Suite 1004	Washington	DC	20005	**800-424-8666**	202-467-5081
National Center for Family Literacy (NCFL) 325 W Main St Suite 300	Louisville	KY	40202	**877-326-5481**	502-584-1133
National Congress of Parents & Teachers 541 N Fairbanks Ct Suite 1300	Chicago	IL	60611	**800-307-4782**	312-670-6782
National Honor Society (NHS) 1904 Association Dr	Reston	VA	20191	**800-253-7746**	703-860-0200
National Society for Experiential Education (NSEE) 515 King St Suite 240	Alexandria	VA	22314	**800-803-4170**	703-706-9552
Reading Is Fundamental Inc (RIF) 1825 Connecticut Ave NW Suite 400	Washington	DC	20009	**877-743-7323**	202-673-0020
Scholarship America 1 Scholarship Way	Saint Peter	MN	56082	**800-537-4180**	507-931-1682
SkillsUSA-VICA Inc PO Box 3000	Leesburg	VA	20177	**800-321-8422***	703-777-8810
*Orders					
TABS (Association of Boarding Schools) 4455 Connecticut Ave NW Suite A-200	Washington	DC	20008	**800-541-5908**	202-966-8705
United Negro College Fund Inc (UNCF) 8260 Willow Oaks Corporate Dr Suite 400	Fairfax	VA	22031	**800-331-2244**	703-205-3400
US Student Assn (USSA) 1413 K St NW 9th Fl	Washington	DC	20005	**877-877-2669**	202-347-8772
Youth for Understanding International Exchange 6400 Goldsboro Rd Suite 100	Bethesda	MD	20817	**800-424-3691**	240-235-2100

48-12 Energy & Natural Resources Organizations

Organization	City	State	ZIP	Toll-Free	Phone
Air & Waste Management Assn (A&WMA) 420 Fort Duquesne Blvd 1 Gateway Ctr 3rd Fl	Pittsburgh	PA	15222	**800-270-3444**	412-232-3444
American Assn of Petroleum Geologists (AAPG) 1444 S Boulder Ave	Tulsa	OK	74119	**800-364-2274**	918-584-2555
American Assn of Professional Landmen (AAPL) 4100 Fossil Creek Blvd	Fort Worth	TX	76137	**888-566-2275**	817-847-7700
American Oil Chemists Society (AOCS) 2211 W Bradley Ave	Champaign	IL	61821	**800-336-2627**	217-359-2344
American Public Gas Assn (APGA) 201 Massachusetts Ave NE Suite C-4	Washington	DC	20002	**800-927-4204**	202-464-2742
American Water Works Assn (AWWA) 6666 W Quincy Ave	Denver	CO	80235	**800-926-7337**	303-794-7711
Association of Energy Service Companies (AESC) 10200 Richmond Ave Suite 275	Houston	TX	77042	**800-692-0771**	713-781-0758
Edison Electric Institute (EEI) 701 Pennsylvania Ave NW	Washington	DC	20004	**800-334-4688**	202-508-5000
Environmental Industry Assns 4301 Connecticut Ave NW Suite 300	Washington	DC	20008	**800-927-5007**	202-244-4700
Independent Petroleum Assn of America (IPAA) 1201 15th St NW Suite 300	Washington	DC	20005	**800-433-2851**	202-857-4722
Interstate Oil & Gas Compact Commission (IOGCC) 900 NE 23rd St PO Box 53127	Oklahoma City	OK	73152	**800-822-4015**	405-525-3556
Methanol Institute (MI) 4100 N Fairfax Dr Suite 740	Arlington	VA	22203	**888-275-0768**	703-248-3636
National Ground Water Assn (NGWA) 601 Dempsey Rd	Westerville	OH	43081	**800-551-7379**	614-898-7791
National Rural Electric Cooperative Assn (NRECA) 4301 Wilson Blvd	Arlington	VA	22203	**866-673-2299**	703-907-5500
NGWA (National Ground Water Assn) 601 Dempsey Rd	Westerville	OH	43081	**800-551-7379**	614-898-7791
Petroleum Technology Transfer Council (PTTC) 16010 Barkers Point Ln Suite 220	Houston	TX	77079	**888-843-7882**	281-921-1720
Society of Petroleum Engineers (SPE) 222 Palisades Creek Dr	Richardson	TX	75080	**800-456-6863**	972-952-9393
Solid Waste Assn of North America (SWANA) 100 Wayne Ave Suite 700	Silver Spring	MD	20910	**800-467-9262**	301-585-2898
SWANA (Solid Waste Assn of North America) 100 Wayne Ave Suite 700	Silver Spring	MD	20910	**800-467-9262**	301-585-2898

48-13 Environmental Organizations

Organization	City	State	ZIP	Toll-Free	Phone
Adirondack Council 103 Hand Ave Suite 3	Elizabethtown	NY	12932	**877-873-2240**	518-873-2240
America the Beautiful Fund 725 15th St NW Suite 605	Washington	DC	20005	**800-522-3557**	202-638-1649
American Farmland Trust (AFT) 1200 18th St NW Suite 800	Washington	DC	20036	**800-431-1499**	202-331-7300
American Forests 734 15th St NW Suite 800 PO Box 2000	Washington	DC	20013	**800-368-5748**	202-955-4500
American PIE 316 Oak St PO Box 676	Northfield	MN	55057	**800-320-2743**	507-645-5613
American Public Information on the Environment 316 Oak St PO Box 676	Northfield	MN	55057	**800-320-2743**	507-645-5613
American Rivers 1025 Vermont Ave NW Suite 720	Washington	DC	20005	**800-296-6900**	202-347-7550
Appalachian Mountain Club (AMC) 5 Joy St	Boston	MA	02108	**800-262-4455***	617-523-0636
*Orders					
Canadian Wildlife Federation (CWF) 350 Michael Cowpland Dr	Kanata	ON	K2M2W1	**800-563-9453**	613-599-9594
Civil War Preservation Trust (CWPT) 1331 H St NW Suite 1001	Washington	DC	20005	**888-606-1400**	202-367-1861
Clean Water Action 4455 Connecticut Ave NW Suite A-300	Washington	DC	20008	**800-709-2837**	202-895-0420
Clean Water Fund (CWF) 4455 Connecticut Ave NW Suite A300-16	Washington	DC	20008	**800-709-2837**	202-895-0432
Co-op America 1612 K St NW Suite 600	Washington	DC	20006	**800-584-7336**	202-872-5307
Coastal Conservation Assn (CCA) 6919 Portwest Dr Suite 100	Houston	TX	77024	**800-201-3474**	713-626-4234
Conservation International (CI) 1919 M St NW Suite 600	Washington	DC	20036	**800-406-2306**	202-912-1000
Conservation Treaty Support Fund (CTSF) 3705 Cardiff Rd	Chevy Chase	MD	20815	**800-654-3150**	301-654-3150
Cousteau Society 710 Settlers Landing Rd	Hampton	VA	23669	**800-441-4395**	757-722-9300
Earth Share 7735 Old Georgetown Rd Suite 900	Bethesda	MD	20814	**800-875-3863**	240-333-0300
Earthwatch Institute 3 Clock Tower Pl Suite 100	Maynard	MA	01754	**800-776-0188**	978-461-0081
Environmental Defense 257 Park Ave S 17th Fl	New York	NY	10010	**800-505-0703**	212-505-2100
Environmental Information Assn (EIA) 6935 Wisconsin Ave Suite 306	Chevy Chase	MD	20815	**888-343-4342**	301-961-4999
Environmental Law Institute (ELI) 2000 L St NW Suite 620	Washington	DC	20036	**800-433-5120**	202-939-3800
Forest Landowners Assn (FLA) 3776 La Vista Rd Suite 250	Tucker	GA	30084	**800-325-2954**	404-325-2954
Freshwater Society 2500 Shadywood Rd	Excelsior	MN	55331	**888-471-9773**	952-471-9773
Friends of the Earth 1717 Massachusetts Ave NW Suite 600	Washington	DC	20036	**877-843-8687**	202-783-7400
Friends of the Earth Canada 260 Saint Patrick St Suite 300	Ottawa	ON	K1N5K5	**888-385-4444**	613-241-0085
Friends of the River 915 20th St	Sacramento	CA	95814	**888-464-2477**	916-442-3155
Grand Canyon Trust 2601 N Fort Valley Rd	Flagstaff	AZ	86001	**888-428-5550**	928-774-7488
Great Lakes United (GLU) Buffalo State College Cassety Hall 1300 Elmwood Ave	Buffalo	NY	14222	**800-846-0142**	716-886-0142
Greater Yellowstone Coalition (GYC) 13 S Willson Ave Suite 2	Bozeman	MT	59775	**800-775-1834**	406-586-1593
Greenpeace Canada 250 Dundas St W Suite 605	Toronto	ON	M5T2Z5	**800-320-7183**	416-597-8408
Greenpeace USA 702 H St NW Suite 300	Washington	DC	20001	**800-326-0959**	202-462-1177
Izaak Walton League of America (IWLA) 707 Conservation Ln	Gaithersburg	MD	20878	**800-453-5463**	301-548-0150
National Arbor Day Foundation 211 N 12th St	Lincoln	NE	68508	**888-448-7337**	402-474-5655
National Assn for Olmsted Parks 733 15th St NW Suite 700	Washington	DC	20005	**866-666-6905**	202-783-6606
National Forest Foundation Fort Missoula Rd Bldg 27 Suite 3	Missoula	MT	59804	**866-733-4633**	406-542-2805
National Parks Conservation Assn (NPCA) 1300 19th St NW Suite 300	Washington	DC	20036	**800-628-7275**	202-223-6722
National Trust for Historic Preservation 1785 Massachusetts Ave NW	Washington	DC	20036	**800-944-6847**	202-588-6000
National Wildlife Refuge Assn (NWRA) 1010 Wisconsin Ave NW Suite 200	Washington	DC	20007	**877-396-6972**	202-333-9075
Nature Canada 1 Nicholas St Suite 606	Ottawa	ON	K1N7B7	**800-267-4088**	613-562-3447
Nature Conservancy 4245 N Fairfax Dr Suite 100	Arlington	VA	22203	**800-628-6860***	703-841-5300
*Cust Svc					
Nature Conservancy of Canada 110 Eglinton Ave W Suite 400	Toronto	ON	M4R1A3	**800-465-0029**	416-932-3202
Ocean Conservancy 1725 DeSales St NW Suite 600	Washington	DC	20036	**800-519-1541**	202-429-5609
Rails-to-Trails Conservancy (RTC) 1100 17th St NW 10th Fl	Washington	DC	20036	**800-888-7747***	202-331-9696
*Orders					
Rainforest Action Network (RAN) 221 Pine St Suite 500	San Francisco	CA	94104	**800-989-7246**	415-398-4404
Royal Oak Foundation 26 Broadway Suite 950	New York	NY	10004	**800-913-6565**	212-480-2889
Save-the-Redwoods League 114 Sansome St Rm 1200	San Francisco	CA	94104	**888-836-0005**	415-362-2352
Sierra Club of Canada 1 Nicholas St Suite 412	Ottawa	ON	K1N7B7	**888-810-4204**	613-241-4611
Sierra Club Foundation 85 2nd St Suite 750	San Francisco	CA	94105	**800-216-2110**	415-995-1780
Sierra Legal Defense Fund 131 Water St Suite 214	Vancouver	BC	V6B4M3	**800-926-7744**	604-685-5618
Soil & Water Conservation Society (SWCS) 945 SW Ankeny Rd	Ankeny	IA	50021	**800-843-7645**	515-289-2331
Student Conservation Assn (SCA) 689 River Rd PO Box 550	Charlestown	NH	03603	**888-722-9675**	603-543-1700
Tree Care Industry Assn (TCIA) 3 Perimeter Rd Unit 1	Manchester	NH	03103	**800-733-2622**	603-314-5380
Trust for Public Land (TPL) 116 New Montgomery St 4th Fl	San Francisco	CA	94105	**800-729-6428**	415-495-4014
Union of Concerned Scientists (UCS) 2 Brattle Sq	Cambridge	MA	02238	**800-664-8276**	617-547-5552
Water Environment Federation (WEF) 601 Wythe St	Alexandria	VA	22314	**800-666-0206**	703-684-2400
Western Canada Wilderness Committee (WCWC) 227 Abbott St	Vancouver	BC	V6B2K7	**800-661-9453**	604-683-8220
Wilderness Society 1615 M St NW	Washington	DC	20036	**800-843-9453**	202-833-2300

48-14 Ethnic & Nationality Organizations

Organization	City	State	ZIP	Toll-Free	Phone
Africa-America Institute (AAI) 420 Lexington Ave Suite 1706	New York	NY	10170	**800-745-3899**	212-949-5666
First Nations Development Institute 2300 Fallhill Ave Suite 412	Fredericksburg	VA	22401	**800-682-5384**	540-371-5615
National Council of La Raza (NCLR) 1111 19th St NW Suite 1000	Washington	DC	20036	**800-311-6257**	202-785-1670
National Slovak Society of the USA (NSS) 351 Valley Brook Rd	McMurray	PA	15317	**800-488-1890**	724-731-0094
Order of the Sons of Italy in America (OSIA) 219 'E' St NE	Washington	DC	20002	**800-547-6742**	202-547-2900
Sons of Norway 1455 W Lake St	Minneapolis	MN	55408	**800-945-8851**	612-827-3611
Ukrainian National Assn PO Box 280	Parsippany	NJ	07054	**800-253-9862**	973-292-9800
US Hispanic Chamber of Commerce 2175 K St NW Suite 100	Washington	DC	20037	**800-874-2286**	202-842-1212

48-15 Fraternal & Social Organizations

Organization	City	State	ZIP	Toll-Free	Phone
American Mensa Ltd 1229 Corporate Dr W	Arlington	TX	76006	**800-666-3672**	817-607-0060
Association of Junior Leagues International Inc (AJLI) 90 William St Suite 200	New York	NY	10038	**800-955-3248**	212-683-1515
Boys & Girls Clubs of America 1230 W Peachtree St NW	Atlanta	GA	30309	**800-854-2582**	404-487-5700
Camp Fire USA 4601 Madison Ave	Kansas City	MO	64112	**800-669-6884**	816-756-1950
Civitan International 1 Civitan Pl PO Box 130744	Birmingham	AL	35213	**800-248-4826**	205-591-8910
Cosmopolitan International 7341 W 80th St	Overland Park	KS	66204	**800-648-4331**	913-648-4330

Fraternal & Social Organizations (Cont'd)

Organization / Address	City	State	ZIP	Toll-Free	Phone
DeMolay International 10200 N Ambassabor Dr	Kansas City	MO	64153	**800-336-6529***	816-891-8333
*Orders					
FOP (Fraternal Order of Police) 1410 Donelson Pike Suite A-17	Nashville	TN	37217	**800-451-2711**	615-399-0900
Fraternal Order of Police (FOP) 1410 Donelson Pike Suite A-17	Nashville	TN	37217	**800-451-2711**	615-399-0900
General Grand Chapter Order of the Eastern Star 1618 New Hampshire Ave NW	Washington	DC	20009	**800-648-1182**	202-667-4737
Girl Scouts of the USA 420 5th Ave	New York	NY	10018	**800-223-0624**	212-852-8000
Independent Order of Odd Fellows 422 Trade St	Winston-Salem	NC	27101	**800-235-8358**	336-725-5955
Knights of Columbus 1 Columbus Plaza	New Haven	CT	06510	**800-524-3611**	203-752-4000
National Exchange Club 3050 W Central Ave	Toledo	OH	43606	**800-924-2643**	419-535-3232
National Grange 1616 H St NW	Washington	DC	20006	**888-447-2643**	202-628-3507
Optimist International 4494 Lindell Blvd	Saint Louis	MO	63108	**800-500-8130**	314-371-6000
Ruritan National PO Box 487	Dublin	VA	24084	**877-787-8727***	540-674-5431
*Orders					
Up With People 1675 Broadway Suite 1460	Denver	CO	80202	**877-264-8856**	303-460-7100

48-16 Greek Letter Societies

Organization / Address	City	State	ZIP	Toll-Free	Phone
Alpha Chi National College Honor Scholarship Society Harding University PO Box 12249	Searcy	AR	72149	**800-477-4225**	501-279-4443
Alpha Epsilon Pi Fraternity Inc 8815 Wesleyan Rd	Indianapolis	IN	46268	**800-223-2374**	317-876-1913
Alpha Omega International Dental Fraternity 500 Commonwealth Dr	Warrendale	PA	15086	**800-677-8468**	724-778-3419
Alpha Sigma Phi National Fraternity 710 Adams St	Carmel	IN	46032	**800-800-1845**	317-843-1911
Beta Theta Pi 5134 Bonham Rd	Oxford	OH	45056	**800-800-2382**	513-523-7591
Chi Omega Fraternity 3395 Players Club Pkwy	Memphis	TN	38125	**800-488-4664**	901-748-8600
Delta Theta Phi 38640 Butternut Ridge Rd	Elyria	OH	44035	**800-783-2600**	440-458-4381
Eta Sigma Gamma 2000 University Ave	Muncie	IN	47306	**800-715-2559**	765-285-2258
Gamma Beta Phi Society 78-A Mitchell Rd Suite 204	Oak Ridge	TN	37830	**800-628-9920**	865-483-6212
Kappa Alpha Theta Fraternity 8740 Founders Rd	Indianapolis	IN	46268	**800-526-1870**	317-876-1870
Kappa Delta Pi 3707 Woodview Trace	Indianapolis	IN	46268	**800-284-3167**	317-871-4900
Kappa Delta Sorority 3205 Players Ln	Memphis	TN	38125	**800-536-1897**	901-748-1897
Kappa Kappa Gamma 530 E Town St PO Box 38	Columbus	OH	43216	**866-554-1870**	614-228-6515
Kappa Kappa Iota 1875 E 15th St	Tulsa	OK	74104	**800-678-0389**	918-744-0389
Kappa Kappa Psi National Honorary Band Fraternity PO Box 849	Stillwater	OK	74076	**800-543-6505**	405-372-2333
Lambda Chi Alpha International Fraternity 8741 Founders Rd	Indianapolis	IN	46268	**800-209-6837**	317-872-8000
Mu Phi Epsilon International Music Fraternity 4705 N Sonora Ave Suite 114	Fresno	CA	93722	**888-259-1471**	559-227-1898
National Fraternity of Kappa Delta Rho 331 S Main St	Greensburg	PA	15601	**800-536-5371**	724-838-7100
Omicron Delta Epsilon PO Box 1486	Hattiesburg	MS	39403	**800-584-5514**	601-264-3115
Phi Alpha Theta Univ of South Florida 4202 E Fowler Ave SOC 107	Tampa	FL	33620	**800-394-8195**	813-974-8212
Phi Delta Kappa International (PDK) 408 N Union St PO Box 789	Bloomington	IN	47402	**800-766-1156**	812-339-1156
Phi Delta Phi International Legal Fraternity 1426 21st St NW	Washington	DC	20036	**800-368-5606**	202-223-6801
Phi Kappa Psi 510 Lockerbie St	Indianapolis	IN	46202	**800-486-1852**	317-632-1852
Phi Kappa Tau 5221 Morning Sun Rd	Oxford	OH	45056	**800-758-1906**	513-523-4193
Phi Mu Fraternity 3558 Habersham at Northlake	Tucker	GA	30084	**888-744-6836**	770-496-5582
Pi Lambda Phi Fraternity Inc 304 Federal Rd Suite 113	Brookfield	CT	06804	**800-394-7573**	203-740-1044
Pi Lambda Theta PO Box 6626	Bloomington	IN	47407	**800-487-3411**	
Pi Sigma Epsilon (PSE) 3747 Howell Ave	Milwaukee	WI	53207	**800-761-9350**	414-328-1952
Psi Upsilon Fraternity 3003 E 96th St	Indianapolis	IN	46240	**800-394-1833**	317-571-1833
Sigma Alpha Epsilon Fraternity (SAE) 1856 Sheridan Rd	Evanston	IL	60201	**800-233-1856**	847-475-1856
Sigma Alpha Mu Fraternity 9245 N Meridian St Suite 105	Indianapolis	IN	46260	**888-369-9361**	317-846-0600
Sigma Phi Epsilon Fraternity 310 S Boulevard	Richmond	VA	23220	**800-313-1901**	804-353-1901
Sigma Pi Fraternity PO Box 1897	Brentwood	TN	37024	**888-744-6274**	
Sigma Theta Tau International 550 W North St	Indianapolis	IN	46202	**888-634-7575**	317-634-8171
Sigma Xi Scientific Research Society PO Box 13975	Research Triangle Park	NC	27709	**800-243-6534**	919-549-4691
Tau Beta Pi Assn PO Box 2697	Knoxville	TN	37901	**800-828-2382**	865-546-4578
Tau Beta Sigma National Honorary Band Sorority PO Box 849	Stillwater	OK	74076	**800-543-6505**	405-372-2333
Theta Delta Chi Inc 214 Lewis Wharf	Boston	MA	02110	**800-999-1847**	617-742-8886
Theta Phi Alpha Fraternity Inc 27025 Knickerbocker Rd	Bay Village	OH	44140	**877-843-8274**	440-899-9282
Theta Tau Professional Engineering Fraternity 815 Brazos St Suite 710	Austin	TX	78701	**800-264-1904**	512-472-1904
Theta Xi Fraternity PO Box 411134	Saint Louis	MO	63141	**800-783-6294**	314-993-6294
Zeta Phi Beta Sorority Inc 145 Kennedy St NW 2nd Fl	Washington	DC	20011	**800-368-5772**	202-387-3103
Zeta Psi Fraternity of North America 15 S Henry St	Pearl River	NY	10965	**800-477-1847**	845-735-1847

48-17 Health & Health-Related Organizations

Organization / Address	City	State	ZIP	Toll-Free	Phone
Alliance for Aging Research 2021 K St NW Suite 305	Washington	DC	20006	**800-639-2421**	202-293-2856
ALS Assn 27001 Agoura Rd Suite 150	Calabasas Hills	CA	91301	**800-782-4747**	818-880-9007
Alzheimer's Assn 225 N Michigan Ave Suite 1700	Chicago	IL	60601	**800-272-3900**	312-335-8700
American Assn of Drugless Practitioners (AADP) 2705 61st St	Galveston	TX	77551	**888-764-2237**	409-741-9000
American Assn on Mental Retardation (AAMR) 444 N Capitol St NW Suite 846	Washington	DC	20001	**800-424-3688**	202-387-1968
American Assn of Naturopathic Physicians (AANP) 3201 New Mexico Ave NW Suite 350	Washington	DC	20016	**866-538-2267**	202-895-1392
American Assn of Oriental Medicine (AAOM) PO Box 162340	Sacramento	CA	95816	**866-455-7999**	916-443-4770
American Autoimmune Related Disease Assn (AARDA) 22100 Gratiot Ave	Eastpointe	MI	48021	**800-598-4668**	586-776-3900
American Bone Marrow Donor Registry 2733 North St	Mandeville	LA	70448	**800-745-2452**	985-626-1749
American Botanical Council 6200 Manor Rd	Austin	TX	78723	**800-373-7105**	512-926-4900
American Brain Tumor Assn (ABTA) 2720 River Rd	Des Plaines	IL	60018	**800-886-2282**	847-827-9910
American Cancer Society (ACS) 1599 Clifton Rd NE	Atlanta	GA	30329	**800-227-2345**	404-320-3333
American Chronic Pain Assn (ACPA) PO Box 850	Rocklin	CA	95677	**800-533-3231**	916-632-0922
American Council of the Blind (ACB) 1155 15th St NW Suite 1004	Washington	DC	20005	**800-424-8666**	202-467-5081
American Council for Drug Education (ACDE) c/o Phoenix House 164 W 74th St	New York	NY	10023	**800-378-4435**	212-595-5810
American Council on Exercise (ACE) 4851 Paramount Dr	San Diego	CA	92123	**800-825-3636**	858-279-8227
American Council for Headache Education (ACHE) 19 Mantua Rd	Mount Royal	NJ	08061	**800-255-2243**	856-423-0258
American Diabetes Assn (ADA) 1701 N Beauregard St	Alexandria	VA	22311	**800-232-3472**	703-549-1500
American Dietetic Assn (ADA) 120 S Riverside Plaza Suite 2000	Chicago	IL	60606	**800-877-1000**	312-899-0040
American Foundation for AIDS Research (amfAR) 120 Wall St 13th Fl	New York	NY	10005	**800-392-6327**	212-806-1600
American Foundation for the Blind (AFB) 11 Penn Plaza Suite 300	New York	NY	10001	**800-232-5463**	212-502-7600
American Foundation for Suicide Prevention (AFSP) 120 Wall St 22nd Fl	New York	NY	10005	**888-333-2377**	212-363-3500
American Foundation for Urologic Disease (AFUD) 1000 Corporate Blvd Suite 410	Linthicum	MD	21090	**800-828-7866**	410-689-3990
American Heart Assn (AHA) 7272 Greenville Ave	Dallas	TX	75231	**800-242-8721**	214-373-6300
American Holistic Nurses' Assn (AHNA) 2733 E Lakin Dr Suite 2	Flagstaff	AZ	86004	**800-278-2462**	928-526-2196
American Kidney Fund (AKF) 6110 Executive Blvd Suite 1010	Rockville	MD	20852	**800-638-8299**	301-881-3052
American Leprosy Missions (ALM) 1 ALM Way	Greenville	SC	29601	**800-543-3135**	864-271-7040
American Liver Foundation (ALF) 75 Maiden Ln Suite 603	New York	NY	10038	**800-465-4837**	212-668-1000
American Lung Assn (ALA) 61 Broadway 6th Fl	New York	NY	10006	**800-586-4872**	212-315-8700
American Lyme Disease Foundation Inc (ALDF) 293 Rt 100	Somers	NY	10589	**800-876-5963**	914-277-6970
American Obesity Assn (AOA) 1250 24th St NW Suite 300	Washington	DC	20037	**800-986-2373**	202-776-7711
American Parkinson Disease Assn (APDA) 1250 Hyland Blvd Suite 4B	Staten Island	NY	10305	**800-223-2732**	718-981-8001
American Polarity Therapy Assn (APTA) PO Box 19858	Boulder	CO	80308	**800-359-5620**	303-545-2080
American Prostate Society 7188 Ridge Rd PO Box 870	Hanover	MD	21076	**800-308-1106**	410-859-3735
American SIDS Institute 509 Augusta Dr	Marietta	GA	30067	**800-232-7437**	770-426-8746
American Social Health Assn (ASHA) PO Box 13827	Research Triangle Park	NC	27709	**800-277-8922**	919-361-8400
American Tinnitus Assn (ATA) 65 SW Yamhill	Portland	OR	97205	**800-634-8978**	503-248-9985
Arc of the US 1010 Wayne Ave Suite 650	Silver Spring	MD	20910	**800-433-5255**	301-565-3842
Arthritis Foundation 1330 W Peachtree St Suite 100	Atlanta	GA	30309	**800-283-7800**	404-872-7100
Associated Bodywork & Massage Professionals (ABMP) 1271 Sugarbush Dr	Evergreen	CO	80439	**800-458-2267**	303-674-8478
Association for Research & Enlightenment (ARE) 215 67th St	Virginia Beach	VA	23451	**800-333-4499**	757-428-3588
Asthma & Allergy Foundation of America (AAFA) 1233 20th St NW Suite 402	Washington	DC	20036	**800-727-8462**	202-466-7643
Autism Society of America (ASA) 7910 Woodmont Ave Suite 300	Bethesda	MD	20814	**800-328-8476**	301-657-0881
AVSC International Inc 440 9th Ave 3rd Fl	New York	NY	10001	**800-564-2872**	212-561-8000
BEGINNINGS for Parents of Children Who Are Deaf or Hard of Hearing Inc 3714 A Benson Dr	Raleigh	NC	27619	**800-541-4327**	919-850-2746
Better Hearing Institute (BHI) 515 King St Suite 420	Alexandria	VA	22314	**888-432-7435**	703-684-3391
Better Vision Institute (BVI) Vision Council of America 1700 Diagonal Rd Suite 500	Alexandria	VA	22314	**800-424-8422**	703-548-4560
Bloch RA Cancer Foundation 4400 Main St	Kansas City	MO	64111	**800-433-0464**	816-932-8453
Brain Injury Assn of America 8201 Greensboro Dr Suite 611	McLean	VA	22102	**800-444-6443**	703-761-0750
Campaign for Tobacco-Free Kids 1400 'I' St NW Suite 1200	Washington	DC	20005	**800-284-5437**	202-296-5469
Cancer Care Inc 275 7th Ave 22nd Fl	New York	NY	10001	**800-813-4673**	212-712-8080
Cancer Research & Prevention Foundation 1600 Duke St Suite 500	Alexandria	VA	22314	**800-227-2732**	703-836-4412
Candlelighters Childhood Cancer Foundation PO Box 498	Kensington	MD	20895	**800-366-2223**	301-962-3520
Canine Companions for Independence (CCI) 2965 Dutton Ave	Santa Rosa	CA	95407	**800-572-2275**	707-577-1700
Center on Human Policy 805 S Crouse Ave	Syracuse	NY	13244	**800-894-0826**	315-443-3851
Center for Practical Bioethics 1100 Walnut St Suite 2900	Kansas City	MO	64106	**800-344-3829**	816-221-1100
Children & Adults with Attention-Deficit/Hyperactivity Disorder (CHADD) 8181 Professional Pl Suite 201	Landover	MD	20785	**800-233-4050**	301-306-7070
Children's Organ Transplant Assn (COTA) 2501 Cota Dr	Bloomington	IN	47403	**800-366-2682**	812-336-8872
Children's Wish Foundation International 8615 Roswell Rd	Atlanta	GA	30350	**800-323-9474**	770-393-9474
Christopher Reeve Paralysis Foundation 500 Morris Ave	Springfield	NJ	07081	**800-225-0292**	973-379-2690
Cleft Palate Foundation (CPF) 1504 E Franklin St Suite 102	Chapel Hill	NC	27514	**800-242-5338**	919-933-9044
Cornelia de Lange Syndrome Foundation Inc (CdLS) 302 W Main St Suite 100	Avon	CT	06001	**800-753-2357**	860-676-8166
Creutzfeldt-Jakob Disease Foundation Inc PO Box 5312	Akron	OH	44334	**800-659-1991**	330-665-5590
Crohn's & Colitis Foundation of America (CCFA) 386 Park Ave S 17th Fl	New York	NY	10016	**800-932-2423**	212-685-3440

	City	State	Zip	Toll-Free	Phone
Cystic Fibrosis Foundation 6931 Arlington Rd Suite 200	Bethesda	MD	20814	**800-344-4823**	301-951-4422
DBSA (Depression & Bipolar Support Alliance) 730 N Franklin St Suite 501	Chicago	IL	60610	**800-826-3632**	312-642-0049
Depression & Bipolar Support Alliance (DBSA) 730 N Franklin St Suite 501	Chicago	IL	60610	**800-826-3632**	312-642-0049
Diabetes Exercise & Sports Assn (DESA) 8001 Montcastle Dr	Nashville	TN	37221	**800-898-4322**	
Disability Rights Center Inc 18 Low Ave	Concord	NH	03301	**800-834-1721**	603-228-0432
Disabled & Alone/Life Services for the Handicapped 352 Park Ave S 11th Fl	New York	NY	10010	**800-995-0066**	212-532-6740
Dystonia Medical Research Foundation 1 E Wacker Dr Suite 2430	Chicago	IL	60601	**800-377-3978**	312-755-0198
Easter Seals 230 W Monroe St Suite 1800	Chicago	IL	60606	**800-221-6827**	312-726-6200
Elizabeth Glaser Pediatric AIDS Foundation 2950 31st St Suite 125	Santa Monica	CA	90405	**888-499-4673**	310-314-1459
Endometriosis Assn 8585 N 76th Pl	Milwaukee	WI	53223	**800-992-3636**	414-355-2200
EngenderHealth 440 9th Ave 3rd Fl	New York	NY	10001	**800-564-2872**	212-561-8000
Epilepsy Foundation 4351 Garden City Dr	Landover	MD	20785	**800-332-1000**	301-459-3700
FaithTrust Institute 2400 N 45th St Suite 10	Seattle	WA	98103	**877-860-2255**	206-634-1903
Families of Spinal Muscular Atrophy PO Box 196	Libertyville	IL	60048	**800-886-1762**	847-367-7620
Family of the Americas Foundation PO Box 1170	Dunkirk	MD	20754	**800-443-3395**	301-627-3346
Family Caregiver Alliance (FCA) 180 Montgomery St Suite 1100	San Francisco	CA	94104	**800-445-8106**	415-434-3388
Feingold Assn of the US 540 E Main St Suite N	Riverhead	NY	11901	**800-321-3287**	631-369-9340
First Candle/SIDS Alliance 1314 Bedford Ave Suite 210	Baltimore	MD	21208	**800-221-7437**	410-653-8226
Food Allergy & Anaphylaxis Network (FAAN) 11781 Lee Jackson Hwy Suite 160	Fairfax	VA	22033	**800-929-4040**	703-691-3179
Foundation Fighting Blindness 11435 Cron Hill Dr	Owings Mills	MD	21117	**800-683-5555**	410-568-0150
Freedom From Fear (FFF) 308 Seaview Ave	Staten Island	NY	10305	**888-442-2022**	718-351-1717
Gay Men's Health Crisis (GMHC) 119 W 24th St	New York	NY	10011	**800-243-7692**	212-367-1000
Genetic Alliance Inc 4301 Connecticut Ave NW Suite 404	Washington	DC	20008	**800-336-4363**	202-966-5557
Gift of Life Bone Marrow Foundation 7700 Congress Ave Suite 2201	Boca Raton	FL	33487	**800-962-7769**	561-988-0100
Gilda Radner Familial Ovarian Cancer Registry Roswell Park Cancer Institute Elm & Carlton Sts	Buffalo	NY	14263	**800-682-7426**	716-845-4503
Glaucoma Research Foundation 490 Post St Suite 1427	San Francisco	CA	94102	**800-826-6693**	415-986-3162
Guide Dog Foundation for the Blind Inc 371 E Jericho Tkpe	Smithtown	NY	11787	**800-548-4337**	631-265-2121
Guide Dogs of America 13445 Glenoaks Blvd	Sylmar	CA	91342	**800-459-4843**	818-362-5834
Guide Dogs for the Blind 350 Los Ranchitos Rd	San Rafael	CA	94903	**800-295-4050**	415-499-4000
HEATH Resource Center George Washington Univ 2121 K St NW Suite 220	Washington	DC	20037	**800-544-3284**	202-973-0904
Hepatitis Foundation International (HFI) 504 Blick Dr	Silver Spring	MD	20904	**800-891-0707**	301-622-4200
Herb Research Foundation (HRF) 4140 15th St	Boulder	CO	80304	**800-748-2617**	303-449-2265
Hospice Education Institute 3 Unity Sq PO Box 98	Machiasport	ME	04655	**800-331-1620**	207-255-8800
Human Growth Foundation 997 Glen Cove Ave Suite 5	Glen Head	NY	11545	**800-451-6434**	516-671-4041
Humor Project Inc 480 Broadway Suite 210	Saratoga Springs	NY	12866	**800-225-0330***	518-587-8770
*Orders					
Huntington's Disease Society of America (HDSA) 158 W 29th St 7th Fl	New York	NY	10001	**800-345-4372**	212-242-1968
Hysterectomy Educational Resources & Services Foundation (HERS) 422 Bryn Mawr Ave	Bala Cynwyd	PA	19004	**888-750-4377**	610-667-7757
Immune Deficiency Foundation (IDF) 40 W Chesapeake Ave Suite 308	Towson	MD	21204	**800-296-4433**	410-321-6647
International Cesarean Awareness Network Inc (ICAN) 1304 Kingsdale Ave	Redondo Beach	CA	90278	**800-686-4226**	310-542-6400
International Childbirth Education Assn (ICEA) 8060 26th Ave SE	Minneapolis	MN	55425	**800-624-4934***	952-854-8660
*Sales					
International Dyslexia Assn (IDA) 8600 LaSalle Rd Chester Bldg Suite 382	Baltimore	MD	21286	**800-222-3123**	410-296-0232
International Hearing Society (IHS) 16880 Middlebelt Rd Suite 4	Livonia	MI	48154	**800-521-5247**	734-522-7200
Juvenile Diabetes Research Foundation International (JDRF) 120 Wall St	New York	NY	10005	**800-533-2873**	212-785-9500
Kristin Brooks Hope Center (KBHC) 2001 N Beauregard St 12th Fl	Alexandria	VA	22311	**800-784-2433**	703-684-7722
La Leche League International Inc (LLL) 1400 N Meacham Rd	Schaumburg	IL	60173	**800-525-3243**	847-519-7730
Lamaze International 2025 M St NW Suite 800	Washington	DC	20036	**800-368-4404**	202-367-1128
Learning Disabilities Assn of America (LDA) 4156 Library Rd	Pittsburgh	PA	15234	**888-300-6710**	412-341-1515
Leukemia & Lymphoma Society 475 Park Ave S 8th Fl	New York	NY	10016	**800-955-4572**	212-448-9206
Lighthouse International 111 E 59th St	New York	NY	10022	**800-829-0500**	212-821-9200
Little People of America (LPA) 5289 NE Elam Young Pkwy Suite F-700	Hillsboro	OR	97124	**888-572-2001**	503-846-1562
Living Bank PO Box 6725	Houston	TX	77625	**800-528-2971**	713-961-9431
Lupus Foundation of America Inc (LFA) 2000 L St Suite 710	Washington	DC	20036	**800-558-0121**	202-349-1155
Lyme Disease Foundation Inc (LDF) Box 332	Tolland	CT	06084	**800-886-5963**	860-525-2000
Lymphoma Research Foundation 8800 Venice Blvd Suite 207	Los Angeles	CA	90034	**800-500-9976**	310-204-7040
Make Today Count 1235 E Cherokee St	Springfield	MO	65804	**800-432-2273**	417-885-3324
Male Survivor 5505 Connecticut Ave NW PMB 103	Washington	DC	20015	**800-738-4181**	
MedicAlert Foundation International 2323 Colorado Ave	Turlock	CA	95382	**800-432-5378***	209-668-3333
*Cust Svc					
Medicare Rights Center (MRC) 1460 Broadway 17th Fl	New York	NY	10036	**800-333-4114***	212-869-3850
*hotline					
Mended Hearts 7272 Greenville Ave	Dallas	TX	75231	**888-432-1899**	214-706-1442

	City	State	Zip	Toll-Free	Phone
Multiple Sclerosis Foundation (MSF) 6350 N Andrews Ave	Fort Lauderdale	FL	33309	**800-225-6495**	954-776-6805
Muscular Dystrophy Assn (MDA) 3300 E Sunrise Dr	Tucson	AZ	85718	**800-572-1717**	520-529-2000
Myasthenia Gravis Foundation of America (MGFA) 1821 University Ave W Suite S256	Saint Paul	MN	55104	**800-541-5454**	651-917-6256
NARIC (National Rehabilitation Information Center) 4200 Forbes Blvd Suite 202	Lanham	MD	20706	**800-346-2742**	301-459-5900
National Alliance for the Mentally Ill (NAMI) 2107 Wilson Blvd Suite 300	Arlington	VA	22201	**800-950-6264**	703-524-7600
National Assn of Certified Natural Health Professionals 714 E Winona Ave	Warsaw	IN	46580	**800-321-1005**	
National Assn for Continence (NAFC) 62 Columbus St	Charleston	SC	29403	**800-252-3337**	843-377-0900
National Assn for Holistic Aromatherapy (NAHA) 3327 W Indian Trail Rd	Spokane	WA	99208	**888-275-6242**	509-325-3419
National Assn for Parents of Children with Visual Impairments (NAPVI) PO Box 317	Watertown	MA	02471	**800-562-6265**	617-972-7441
National Breast Cancer Coalition (NBCC) 1101 17th St NW Suite 1300	Washington	DC	20036	**800-622-2838**	202-296-7477
National Center for Assault Prevention (NCAP) 606 Delsea Dr	Sewell	NJ	08080	**800-258-3189**	856-582-7000
National Center for Homeopathy (NCH) 801 N Fairfax St Suite 306	Alexandria	VA	22314	**877-624-0613**	703-548-7790
National Center for Stuttering (NCS) 200 E 33rd St	New York	NY	10016	**800-221-2483**	212-532-1460
National Children's Cancer Society (NCCS) 1015 Locust St Suite 600	Saint Louis	MO	63101	**800-532-6459**	314-241-1600
National Committee for Quality Assurance (NCQA) 2000 L St NW Suite 500	Washington	DC	20036	**800-236-5903**	202-955-3500
National Council on Alcoholism & Drug Dependence (NCADD) 20 Exchange Pl Suite 2902	New York	NY	10005	**800-622-2255**	212-269-7797
National Dissemination Center for Children with Disabilities 1825 Connecticut Ave	Washington	DC	20009	**800-695-0285**	202-884-8200
National Down Syndrome Congress (NDSC) 1370 Center Dr Suite 102	Atlanta	GA	30338	**800-232-6372**	770-604-9500
National Down Syndrome Society (NDSS) 666 Broadway 8th Fl	New York	NY	10012	**800-221-4602**	212-460-9330
National Eating Disorders Assn 603 Stewart St Suite 803	Seattle	WA	98101	**800-931-2237**	206-382-3587
National Fibromyalgia Partnership Inc (NFP) 140 Zinn Way PO Box 160	Linden	VA	22642	**866-725-4404**	
National Fire Protection Assn (NFPA) 1 Batterymarch Pk	Quincy	MA	02169	**800-344-3555**	617-770-3000
National Foundation of Dentistry for the Handicapped (NFDH) 1800 15th St Unit 100	Denver	CO	80202	**888-471-6334**	303-534-5360
National Gaucher Foundation (NGF) 5410 Edson Ln Suite 260	Rockville	MD	20852	**800-428-2437**	301-816-1515
National Headache Foundation (NHF) 820 N Orleans St Suite 217	Chicago	IL	60610	**888-643-5552**	
National Health Council (NHC) 1730 M St NW Suite 500	Washington	DC	20036	**800-684-6814**	202-785-3910
National Hemophilia Foundation (NHF) 116 W 32nd St 11th Fl	New York	NY	10001	**800-424-2634**	212-328-3700
National Herpes Resource Center (HRC) PO Box 13827	Research Triangle Park	NC	27709	**800-227-8922**	919-361-8488
National Hopeline Network 2001 N Beauregard St 12th Fl	Alexandria	VA	22311	**800-784-2433**	703-684-7722
National HPV & Cervical Cancer Prevention Resource Center PO Box 13827	Research Triangle Park	NC	27709	**800-277-8922**	919-361-8400
National Industries for the Blind (NIB) 1901 N Beauregard St Suite 200	Alexandria	VA	22311	**800-433-2304***	703-998-0770
*Cust Svc					
National Inhalant Prevention Coalition (NIPC) 2904 Kerbey Ln	Austin	TX	78703	**800-269-4237**	512-480-8953
National Institute for Rehabilitation Engineering (NIRE) PO Box T	Hewitt	NJ	07421	**800-736-2216**	973-853-6585
National Kidney Foundation (NKF) 30 E 33rd St Suite 1100	New York	NY	10016	**800-622-9010**	212-889-2210
National Marfan Foundation (NMF) 22 Manhasset Ave	Port Washington	NY	11050	**800-862-7326**	516-883-8712
National Marrow Donor Program (NMDP) 3001 Broadway St NE Suite 500	Minneapolis	MN	55413	**800-526-7809**	612-627-5800
National Mental Health Assn (NMHA) 2001 N Beauregard St 12th Fl	Alexandria	VA	22311	**800-969-6642***	703-684-7722
*Help Line					
National Multiple Sclerosis Society 733 3rd Ave	New York	NY	10017	**800-344-4867**	212-986-3240
National Native American AIDS Prevention Center (NNAAPC) 436 14th St Suite 1020	Oakland	CA	94612	**800-283-6880**	510-444-2051
National Neurofibromatosis Foundation 95 Pine St 16th Fl	New York	NY	10005	**800-323-7938**	212-344-6633
National Niemann-Pick Disease Foundation (NNPDF) 415 Madison Ave	Fort Atkinson	WI	53538	**877-287-3672**	920-563-0930
National Organization for Albinism & Hypopigmentation (NOAH) PO Box 959	East Hampstead	NH	03826	**800-473-2310**	603-887-2310
National Organization for Rare Disorders (NORD) 55 Kenosia Ave PO Box 1968	Danbury	CT	06813	**800-999-6673**	203-744-0100
National Osteoporosis Foundation (NOF) 1232 22nd St NW	Washington	DC	20037	**800-223-9994**	202-223-2226
National Ovarian Cancer Coalition (NOCC) 500 NE Spanish River Blvd Suite 8	Boca Raton	FL	33431	**888-682-7426**	561-393-0005
National Parkinson Foundation (NPF) 1501 NW 9th Ave	Miami	FL	33136	**800-327-4545**	305-547-6666
National Pesticide Information Center (NPIC) 333 Weniger Hall	Corvallis	OR	97331	**800-858-7378**	
National Psoriasis Foundation (NPF) 6600 SW 92nd Ave Suite 300	Portland	OR	97223	**800-723-9166**	503-244-7404
National Rehabilitation Assn (NRA) 633 S Washington St	Alexandria	VA	22314	**888-258-4295**	703-836-0850
National Rehabilitation Information Center (NARIC) 4200 Forbes Blvd Suite 202	Lanham	MD	20706	**800-346-2742**	301-459-5900
National Reye's Syndrome Foundation (NRSF) 426 N Lewis St	Bryan	OH	43506	**800-233-7393**	419-636-2679
National Rosacea Society 800 S Northwest Hwy Suite 200	Barrington	IL	60010	**888-662-5874**	847-382-8971
National Safety Council (NSC) 1121 Spring Lake Dr	Itasca	IL	60143	**800-621-7619**	630-285-1121
National Spinal Cord Injury Assn (NSCIA) 6701 Democracy Blvd Suite 300-9	Bethesda	MD	20817	**800-962-9629**	

Health & Health-Related Organizations (Cont'd)

Organization	City	State	Zip	Toll-Free	Phone
National Stroke Assn (NSA) 9707 E Easter Ln	Englewood	CO	80112	**800-787-6537**	303-649-9299
National Stuttering Assn (NSA) 119 W 40th St 14th Fl	New York	NY	10018	**800-364-1677**	212-944-4050
National Tay-Sachs & Allied Diseases Assn (NTSAD) 2001 Beacon St Suite 204	Brighton	MA	02135	**800-906-8723**	617-277-4463
National Vaccine Information Center (NVIC) 421-E Church St	Vienna	VA	22180	**800-909-7468**	703-938-3783
National Wellness Institute (NWI) 1300 College Ct PO Box 827	Stevens Point	WI	54481	**800-243-8694**	715-342-2969
North American Menopause Society (NAMS) 5900 Landerbrook Dr Suite 195	Mayfield Heights	OH	44124	**800-774-5342**	440-442-7550
Oley Foundation Albany Medical Ctr 214 Hun Memorial MC A-28	Albany	NY	12208	**800-776-6539**	518-262-5079
Oral Health America 410 N Michigan Ave Suite 352	Chicago	IL	60611	**800-523-3438**	312-836-9900
Paget Foundation for Paget's Disease of Bone & Related Disorders 120 Wall St Suite 1602	New York	NY	10005	**800-237-2438**	212-509-5335
Parkinson's Disease Foundation (PDF) 710 W 168th St	New York	NY	10032	**800-457-6676**	212-923-4700
Partnership for a Drug-Free America 405 Lexington Ave Suite 1601	New York	NY	10174	**888-575-3115**	212-922-1560
Pedorthic Footwear Assn (PFA) 7150 Columbia Gateway Dr Suite G	Columbia	MD	21046	**800-673-8447**	410-381-7278
Phoenix Society for Burn Survivors 2153 Wealthy St SE Suite 215	East Grand Rapids	MI	49506	**800-888-2876**	616-458-2773
Physicians' Committee for Responsible Medicine (PCRM) 5100 Wisconsin Ave NW Suite 400	Washington	DC	20016	**866-416-7276**	202-686-2210
Practical Allergy Research Foundation 1421 Colvin Blvd	Buffalo	NY	14223	**800-787-8780**	716-875-5578
Prader-Willi Syndrome Assn (USA) 5700 Midnight Pass Rd Suite 6	Sarasota	FL	34242	**800-926-4797**	941-312-0400
Prevent Blindness America 211 W Wacker Dr Suite 1700	Chicago	IL	60606	**800-331-2020**	312-363-6001
RA Bloch Cancer Foundation 4400 Main St	Kansas City	MO	64111	**800-433-0464**	816-932-8453
Radner Gilda Familial Ovarian Cancer Registry Roswell Park Cancer Institute Elm & Carlton Sts	Buffalo	NY	14263	**800-682-7426**	716-845-4503
Recording for the Blind & Dyslexic (RFB&D) 20 Roszel Rd	Princeton	NJ	08540	**800-221-4792**	609-452-0606
Research to Prevent Blindness Inc (RPB) 645 Madison Ave 21st Fl	New York	NY	10022	**800-621-0026**	212-752-4333
Restless Legs Syndrome Foundation Inc 819 2nd St SW	Rochester	MN	55902	**877-463-6757**	507-287-6465
Rolf Institute of Structural Integration 5055 Chaparral Ct Suite 103	Boulder	CO	80301	**800-530-8875**	303-449-5903
Safe Tables Our Priority (STOP) PO Box 4352	Burlington	VT	05406	**800-350-7867**	802-863-0555
SAVE - Suicide Awareness Voices of Education 9001 Bloomington Fwy Suite 150	Bloomington	MN	55420	**888-511-7283**	952-946-7998
Scleroderma Foundation 12 Kent Way Suite 101	Byfield	MA	01922	**800-722-4673**	978-463-5843
Scoliosis Assn Inc 2500 N Military Trail	Boca Raton	FL	33431	**800-800-0669**	561-994-4435
Sickle Cell Disease Assn of America (SCDAA) 16 S Calvert St Suite 600	Baltimore	MD	21202	**800-421-8453**	410-528-1555
Simon Foundation for Incontinence PO Box 815	Wilmette	IL	60091	**800-237-4666**	847-864-3913
Skin Cancer Foundation 245 5th Ave Suite 1403	New York	NY	10016	**800-754-6490**	212-725-5176
Spina Bifida Assn of America (SBAA) 4590 MacArthur Blvd NW Suite 250	Washington	DC	20007	**800-621-3141**	202-944-3285
Starlight Starbright Children's Foundation 5900 Wilshire Blvd Suite 2530	Los Angeles	CA	90036	**800-274-7827**	323-634-0080
Stuttering Foundation of America 3100 Walnut Grove Rd Suite 603	Memphis	TN	38111	**800-992-9392**	901-452-7343
Susan G Komen Breast Cancer Foundation 5005 LBJ Fwy Suite 250	Dallas	TX	75244	**800-462-9273**	972-855-1600
Thyroid Foundation of America Inc (TFA) 1 Longfellow Pl Suite 1518	Boston	MA	02114	**800-832-8321**	617-534-1500
TOPS Club Inc 4575 S 5th St	Milwaukee	WI	53207	**800-932-8677**	414-482-4620
Touch for Health Kinesiology Assn PO Box 392	New Carlisle	OH	45344	**800-466-8342**	937-845-3404
Tourette Syndrome Assn Inc 42-40 Bell Blvd Suite 205	Bayside	NY	11361	**888-486-8738**	718-224-2999
Turner Syndrome Society of the US 14450 TC Jester Suite 260	Houston	TX	77014	**800-365-9944**	832-249-9988
UCP National 1660 L St NW Suite 700	Washington	DC	20036	**800-872-5827**	202-776-0406
United Cerebral Palsy 1660 L St NW Suite 700	Washington	DC	20036	**800-872-5827**	202-776-0406
United Network for Organ Sharing (UNOS) 700 N 4th St	Richmond	VA	23219	**888-894-6361**	804-330-8500
United Ostomy Assn (UOA) 19772 MacArthur Blvd Suite 200	Irvine	CA	92612	**800-826-0826**	949-660-8624
Well Spouse Foundation 63 W Main St Suite H	Freehold	NJ	07728	**800-838-0879**	732-577-8899
Women Alive 1566 S Burnside Ave	Los Angeles	CA	90019	**800-554-4876**	323-965-1564
Xeroderma Pigmentosum Society Inc (XPS) 437 Snydertown Rd	Craryville	NY	12521	**877-977-2873**	518-851-2612
Y-ME National Breast Cancer Organization 212 W Van Buren St	Chicago	IL	60607	**800-221-2141**	312-986-8338

48-18 Hobby Organizations

Organization	City	State	Zip	Toll-Free	Phone
Academy of Model Aeronautics (AMA) 5161 E Memorial Dr	Muncie	IN	47302	**800-435-9262**	765-287-1256
American Contract Bridge League (ACBL) 2990 Airways Blvd *Sales	Memphis	TN	38116	**800-264-2743***	901-332-5586
American Craft Council 72 Spring St 6th Fl	New York	NY	10012	**800-836-3470**	212-274-0630
American Federation of Astrologers (AFA) 6535 S Rural Rd	Tempe	AZ	85283	**888-301-7630**	480-838-1751
American Horticultural Society (AHS) 7931 E Boulevard Dr	Alexandria	VA	22308	**800-777-7931**	703-768-5700
American Numismatic Assn (ANA) 818 N Cascade Ave	Colorado Springs	CO	80903	**800-367-9723**	719-632-2646
American Rose Society (ARS) 8877 Jefferson Paige Rd	Shreveport	LA	71119	**800-637-6534**	318-938-5402
Craft & Hobby Assn (CHA) 319 E 54th St	Elmwood Park	NJ	07407	**800-822-0494**	201-794-1133
Experimental Aircraft Assn (EAA) 3000 Poberezny Rd	Oshkosh	WI	54902	**800-236-4800**	920-426-4800
Knitting Guild of America (TKGA) 1100-H Brandywine Blvd PO Box 3388	Zanesville	OH	43702	**800-969-6069**	740-452-4541
National Craft Assn (NCA) 2012 Ridge Rd E Suite 120	Rochester	NY	14622	**800-715-9594**	585-266-5472
National Garden Clubs Inc (NGC) 4401 Magnolia Ave Suite 1600	Saint Louis	MO	63110	**800-550-6007**	314-776-7574
National Gardening Assn (NGA) 1100 Dorset St	South Burlington	VT	05403	**800-538-7476**	802-863-5251
National Genealogical Society (NGS) 3108 Columbia Pike Suite 300	Arlington	VA	22204	**800-473-0060**	703-525-0050
National Needlework Assn (TNNA) 1100-H Brandywine Blvd PO Box 3388	Zanesville	OH	43702	**800-889-8662**	740-455-6773
Society for the Preservation & Encouragement of Barber Shop Quartet Singing in America 7930 Sheridan Rd	Kenosha	WI	53143	**800-876-7464**	262-653-8440
Sports Car Club of America (SCCA) PO Box 19400	Topeka	KS	66610	**800-770-2055**	785-357-7222
Sweet Adelines International 9110 S Toledo Ave	Tulsa	OK	74137	**800-992-7464**	918-622-1444
US Chess Federation 3068 US Rt 9 W Suite 100 *Sales	New Windsor	NY	12553	**800-388-5464***	845-562-8350

48-19 Military, Veterans, Patriotic Organizations

Organization	City	State	Zip	Toll-Free	Phone
Air Force Assn (AFA) 1501 Lee Hwy	Arlington	VA	22209	**800-727-3337**	703-247-5800
Air Force Sergeants Assn (AFSA) 5211 Auth Rd	Suitland	MD	20746	**800-638-0594**	301-899-3500
American Legion 700 N Pennsylvania St *Cust Svc	Indianapolis	IN	46204	**800-433-3318***	317-630-1200
American Society of Military Comptrollers (ASMC) 415 N Alfred	Alexandria	VA	22314	**800-462-5637**	703-549-0360
AMVETS 4647 Forbes Blvd	Lanham	MD	20706	**877-726-8387**	301-459-9600
Armed Forces Communications & Electronics Assn (AFCEA) 4400 Fair Lakes Ct	Fairfax	VA	22033	**800-336-4583**	703-631-6100
Armed Services Mutual Benefit Assn (ASMBA) PO Box 160384	Nashville	TN	37216	**800-251-8434**	615-851-0800
Army Distaff Foundation 6200 Oregon Ave NW	Washington	DC	20015	**800-541-4255**	202-541-0105
Association of Old Crows (AOC) 1000 N Payne St Suite 300	Alexandria	VA	22314	**888-653-2769**	703-549-1600
Association of the US Army (AUSA) 2425 Wilson Blvd	Arlington	VA	22201	**800-336-4570**	703-841-4300
Disabled American Veterans (DAV) 3725 Alexandria Pike	Cold Spring	KY	41076	**877-426-2838**	859-441-7300
Enlisted Assn of the National Guard of the US (EANGUS) 3133 Mt Vernon Ave	Alexandria	VA	22305	**800-234-3264**	703-519-3846
Fleet Reserve Assn (FRA) 125 N West St	Alexandria	VA	22314	**800-372-1924**	703-683-1400
Marine Corps Assn (MCA) PO Box 1775	Quantico	VA	22134	**800-336-0291**	703-640-6161
Marine Corps League (MCL) PO Box 3070	Merrifield	VA	22116	**800-625-1775**	703-207-9588
Marine Corps Reserve Assn (MCRA) 337 Potomac Ave	Quantico	VA	22134	**800-927-6270**	703-630-3772
Military Benefit Assn (MBA) PO Box 221110	Chantilly	VA	20153	**800-336-0100**	703-968-6200
Military Officers Assn of America (MOAA) 201 N Washington St	Alexandria	VA	22314	**800-234-6622**	703-549-2311
MOAA (Military Officers Assn of America) 201 N Washington St	Alexandria	VA	22314	**800-234-6622**	703-549-2311
National Assn for Uniformed Services (NAUS) 5535 Hempstead Way	Springfield	VA	22151	**800-842-3451**	703-750-1342
National Committee for Employer Support of the Guard & Reserve (ESGR) 1555 Wilson Blvd Suite 200	Arlington	VA	22209	**800-336-4590**	703-696-1386
National Guard Assn of the US (NGAUS) 1 Massachusetts Ave NW Suite 200	Washington	DC	20001	**888-226-4287**	202-789-0031
Naval Enlisted Reserve Assn (NERA) 6703 Farragut Ave	Falls Church	VA	22042	**800-776-9020**	703-534-1329
Naval Reserve Assn (NRA) 1619 King St	Alexandria	VA	22314	**866-672-4968**	703-548-5800
Navy League of the US 2300 Wilson Blvd	Arlington	VA	22201	**800-356-5760**	703-528-1775
Navy-Marine Corps Relief Society (NMCRS) 4015 Wilson Blvd 10th Fl	Arlington	VA	22203	**800-654-8364**	703-696-4904
Non-Commissioned Officers Assn (NCOA) 10635 IH-35 N *Cust Svc	San Antonio	TX	78233	**800-662-2620***	210-653-6161
Paralyzed Veterans of America (PVA) 801 18th St NW	Washington	DC	20006	**800-424-8200**	202-872-1300
Reserve Officers Assn of the US (ROA) 1 Constitution Ave NE	Washington	DC	20002	**800-809-9448**	202-479-2200
Society of American Military Engineers (SAME) 607 Prince St	Alexandria	VA	22314	**800-336-3097**	703-549-3800
Society of Military Widows (SMW) 5535 Hempstead Way	Springfield	VA	22151	**800-842-3451**	703-750-1342
Tailhook Assn 9696 Businesspark Ave	San Diego	CA	92131	**800-322-4665**	858-689-9223
US Naval Institute 291 Wood Rd	Annapolis	MD	21402	**800-233-8764**	410-268-6110
Vietnam Veterans of America (VVA) 8605 Cameron St Suite 400	Silver Spring	MD	20910	**800-882-1316**	301-585-4000
Women in Military Service for America Memorial Foundation Inc Dept 560	Washington	DC	20042	**800-222-2294**	703-533-1155

48-20 Religious Organizations

Organization	City	State	Zip	Toll-Free	Phone
American Baptist Assn (ABA) 4605 N State Line Ave	Texarkana	TX	75503	**800-264-2482**	903-792-2783
American Baptist Churches USA PO Box 851	Valley Forge	PA	19482	**800-222-3872**	610-768-2000
American Bible Society 1865 Broadway	New York	NY	10023	**800-322-4253**	212-408-1200
American Theological Library Assn (ATLA) 250 S Wacker Dr Suite 1600	Chicago	IL	60606	**888-665-2852**	312-454-5100
American Tract Society (ATS) 1624 N 1st St	Garland	TX	75040	**800-548-7228**	972-276-9408

Classified Section

Organization	City	State	ZIP	Toll-Free	Phone
Assemblies of God (A/G) 1445 N Boonville Ave	Springfield	MO	65802	**800-641-4310**	417-862-2781
Association of Gospel Rescue Missions (AGRM) 1045 Swift Ave	Kansas City	MO	64116	**800-624-5156**	816-471-8020
Avant Ministries 10000 N Oak Trafficway	Kansas City	MO	64155	**800-468-1892**	816-734-8500
Baptist General Conference (BGC) 2002 S Arlington Heights Rd	Arlington Heights	IL	60005	**800-323-4215**	847-228-0200
Bible League PO Box 28000	Chicago	IL	60628	**866-825-4636**	708-367-8500
Billy Graham Evangelistic Assn 1 Billy Graham Pkwy PO Box 1270	Charlotte	NC	28201	**877-247-2426**	704-401-2432
B'nai B'rith International 2020 K St NW 7th Fl	Washington	DC	20006	**888-388-4224**	202-857-6600
Campus Crusade for Christ International 100 Lake Hart Dr	Orlando	FL	32832	**877-924-7478**	407-826-2000
Catholic Church Extension Society of the USA 150 S Wacker Dr 20th Fl	Chicago	IL	60606	**800-842-7804**	312-236-7240
CBInternational (CBI) 1501 W Mineral Ave	Littleton	CO	80120	**800-487-4224**	720-283-2000
Central Conference of American Rabbis (CCAR) 355 Lexington Ave 18th Fl	New York	NY	10017	**800-935-2227**	212-972-3636
Christian Endeavor International 309 S Main St	Mount Vernon	OH	43050	**800-260-3234**	740-397-2622
Christian Reformed Church in North America (CRC) 2850 Kalamazoo Ave SE	Grand Rapids	MI	49560	**800-272-5125**	616-241-1691
Christophers The 12 E 48th St	New York	NY	10017	**888-298-4050**	212-759-4050
Church of the Brethren 1451 Dundee Ave	Elgin	IL	60120	**800-323-8039**	847-742-5100
Church of God Ministries 1201 E 5th St	Anderson	IN	46012	**800-848-2464**	765-642-0256
Church of God World Missions PO Box 8016	Cleveland	TN	37320	**800-345-7492**	423-478-7190
Church Women United (CWU) 475 Riverside Dr Rm 1626	New York	NY	10115	**800-298-5551**	212-870-2347
Community of Christ 1001 W Walnut St	Independence	MO	64050	**800-825-2806**	816-833-1000
Connecting Businessmen to Christ (CBMC) 5746 Marlin Rd Suite 602 Osborne Center	Chattanooga	TN	37411	**800-575-2262**	423-698-4444
Episcopal Church USA 815 2nd Ave	New York	NY	10017	**800-334-7626**	212-716-6000
Evangelical Lutheran Church in America (ELCA) 8765 W Higgins Rd	Chicago	IL	60631	**800-638-3522**	773-380-2700
Evangelical Training Assn (ETA) 1620 Penny Ln	Schaumburg	IL	60173	**800-369-8291**	630-540-7840
Fellowship of Christian Athletes (FCA) 8701 Leeds Rd	Kansas City	MO	64129	**800-289-0909**	816-921-0909
First Church of Christ Scientist 175 Huntington Ave	Boston	MA	02115	**800-288-7090**	617-450-2000
Graham Billy Evangelistic Assn 1 Billy Graham Pkwy PO Box 1270	Charlotte	NC	28201	**877-247-2426**	704-401-2432
Hadassah Women's Zionist Organization of America Inc 50 W 58th St	New York	NY	10019	**888-303-3640**	212-355-7900
IFCA International PO Box 810	Grandville	MI	49468	**800-347-1840**	616-531-1840
International Bible Society (IBS) 1820 Jet Stream Dr *Cust Svc	Colorado Springs	CO	80921	**800-524-1588***	719-488-9200
International Church of the Foursquare Gospel (ICFG) 1910 W Sunset Blvd Suite 200	Los Angeles	CA	90026	**888-635-4234**	213-989-4200
International Lutheran Laymen's League 660 Mason Ridge Ctr Dr	Saint Louis	MO	63141	**800-944-3450**	314-317-4100
Jewish National Fund (JNF) 42 E 69th St	New York	NY	10021	**888-563-0099**	212-879-9300
Jimmy Swaggart Ministries (JSM) 8919 World Ministry Blvd *Orders	Baton Rouge	LA	70810	**800-288-8350***	225-768-8300
Lutheran Church Missouri Synod (LCMS) 1333 S Kirkwood Rd	Saint Louis	MO	63122	**888-843-5267**	314-965-9000
Mission Aviation Fellowship (MAF) 1849 N Wabash Ave	Redlands	CA	92374	**800-359-7623**	909-794-1151
National Assn of Congregational Christian Churches (NACCC) 8473 S Howell Ave	Oak Creek	WI	53154	**800-262-1620**	414-764-1620
National Assn of Free Will Baptists (NAFWB) 5233 Mt View Rd	Antioch	TN	37013	**877-767-7659**	615-731-6812
National Baptist Convention USA Inc 1700 Baptist World Ctr Dr	Nashville	TN	37207	**866-531-3054**	615-228-6292
New Tribes Mission (NTM) 1000 E 1st St	Sanford	FL	32771	**866-547-2460**	407-323-3430
Presbyterian Church (USA) 100 Witherspoon St	Louisville	KY	40202	**888-728-7228**	502-569-5000
Progressive National Baptist Convention Inc (PNBC) 601 50th St NE	Washington	DC	20019	**800-876-7622**	202-396-0558
Promise Keepers 4045 Pecos St PO Box 11798	Denver	CO	80211	**800-888-7595**	303-964-7600
Reformed Church in America 475 Riverside Dr 18th Fl	New York	NY	10115	**800-722-9977**	212-870-3071
Religious Science International (RSI) 901 E 2nd Ave Suite 301	Spokane	WA	99202	**800-662-1348**	509-624-7000
Salvation Army PO Box 269	Alexandria	VA	22313	**800-725-2769**	703-684-5500
Seat of the Soul Foundation 1257 Siskiyou Blvd Suite 57	Ashland	OR	97520	**888-440-7685**	541-482-8999
Swaggart Jimmy Ministries 8919 World Ministry Blvd *Orders	Baton Rouge	LA	70810	**800-288-8350***	225-768-8300
United Church of Christ (UCC) 700 Prospect Ave	Cleveland	OH	44115	**866-822-8224**	216-736-2100
Urban Alternative PO Box 4000	Dallas	TX	75208	**800-800-3222**	214-943-3868
Wheat Ridge Ministries 1 Pierce Pl Suite 250E	Itasca	IL	60143	**800-762-6748**	630-766-9066
Wider Church Ministries 700 Prospect Ave NE 7th Fl	Cleveland	OH	44115	**866-822-8224**	216-736-3200
Woman's Missionary Union (WMU) 100 Missionary Ridge	Birmingham	AL	35242	**800-968-7301**	205-991-8100
Wycliffe Bible Translators PO Box 628200	Orlando	FL	32862	**800-992-5433**	407-852-3611
Youth for Christ/USA PO Box 4478	Englewood	CO	80155	**800-735-3252**	303-843-9000

48-21 Self-Help Organizations

Organization	City	State	ZIP	Toll-Free	Phone
Al-Anon Family Group Headquarters Inc 1600 Corporate Landing Pkwy	Virginia Beach	VA	23454	**888-425-2666**	757-563-1600
Alateen 1600 Corporate Landing Pkwy	Virginia Beach	VA	23454	**888-425-2666**	757-563-1600
Calix Society 2555 Hazelwood Ave	Saint Paul	MN	55109	**800-398-0524**	651-773-3117
Candlelighters Childhood Cancer Foundation PO Box 498	Kensington	MD	20895	**800-366-2223**	301-962-3520
Chemically Dependent Anonymous (CDA) PO Box 4425	Annapolis	MD	21403	**800-232-4673**	410-369-6556
Co-Anon Family Groups PO Box 12722	Tucson	AZ	85732	**800-898-9985**	520-513-5028
Cocaine Anonymous World Services Inc (CA) 3740 Overland Ave Suite C	Los Angeles	CA	90034	**800-347-8998**	310-559-5833
Compassionate Friends PO Box 3696	Oak Brook	IL	60522	**877-969-0010**	630-990-0010
Concerned United Birthparents Inc (CUB) PO Box 230457	Encinitas	CA	92023	**800-822-2777**	
DignityUSA Inc 1500 Massachusetts Ave NW	Washington	DC	20005	**800-877-8797**	202-861-0017
Families Anonymous (FA) PO Box 3475	Culver City	CA	90231	**800-736-9805**	310-815-8010
Marijuana Anonymous World Services (MA) PO Box 2912	Van Nuys	CA	91404	**800-766-6779**	
Overcomers Outreach PO Box 2208	Oakhurst	CA	93644	**800-310-3001**	559-692-2630
Pathways to Peace Inc PO Box 259	Cassadaga	NY	14718	**800-775-4212**	716-595-3884
Rational Recovery PO Box 800	Lotus	CA	95651	**800-303-2873**	530-621-2667
Rest Ministries Inc PO Box 502928	San Diego	CA	92150	**888-751-7378**	858-486-4685
Sex Addicts Anonymous (SAA) PO Box 70949	Houston	TX	77270	**800-477-8191**	713-869-4902
SHARE Pregnancy & Infant Loss Support Inc St Joseph's Health Ctr 300 1st Capitol Dr	Saint Charles	MO	63301	**800-821-6819**	636-947-6164
Survivors Network of Those Abused by Priests (SNAP) PO Box 6416	Chicago	IL	60680	**877-409-2720**	312-409-2720
Take Root PO Box 930	Kalama	WA	98625	**888-766-8674**	360-673-3720
TOPS Club Inc 4575 S 5th St	Milwaukee	WI	53207	**800-932-8677**	414-482-4620
Twinless Twins Support Group International (TTSG) PO Box 980481	Ypsilanti	MI	48198	**888-205-8962**	
Wings Foundation 8725 W 14th Ave Suite 150	Lakewood	CO	80215	**800-373-8671**	303-238-8660

48-22 Sports Organizations

Organization	City	State	ZIP	Toll-Free	Phone
Adventure Cycling Assn 150 E Pine St PO Box 8308	Missoula	MT	59802	**800-755-2453**	406-721-1776
Aerobics & Fitness Assn of America (AFAA) 15250 Ventura Blvd Suite 200	Sherman Oaks	CA	91403	**877-968-7263**	818-905-0040
Amateur Softball Assn of America Inc (ASA) 2801 NE 50th St	Oklahoma City	OK	73111	**800-654-8337**	405-424-5266
American Alliance for Health Physical Education Recreation & Dance (AAHPERD) 1900 Association Dr	Reston	VA	20191	**800-213-7193**	703-476-3400
American Bicycle Assn (ABA) 1645 W Sunrise Blvd	Gilbert	AZ	85233	**800-886-1269**	480-961-1903
American Bowling Congress (ABC) 5301 S 76th St	Greendale	WI	53129	**800-514-2695**	414-421-6400
American Canoe Assn (ACA) 7432 Alban Station Blvd Suite B-232	Springfield	VA	22150	**800-929-5162**	703-451-0141
American Council on Exercise (ACE) 4851 Paramount Dr	San Diego	CA	92123	**800-825-3636**	858-279-8227
American Grandprix Assn (AGA) 1301 6th Ave W Suite 406	Bradenton	FL	34205	**800-237-8924**	941-744-5465
American Motorcyclist Assn (AMA) 13515 Yarmouth Dr	Pickerington	OH	43147	**800-262-5646**	614-856-1900
American Poolplayers Assn (APA) 1000 Lake St Louis Blvd Suite 325	Lake Saint Louis	MO	63367	**800-372-2536**	636-625-8611
American Running Assn 4405 East-West Hwy Suite 405	Bethesda	MD	20814	**800-776-2732**	301-913-9517
American Senior Fitness Assn (SFA) PO Box 2575	New Smyrna Beach	FL	32170	**800-243-1478**	386-423-6634
American Volkssport Assn (AVA) 1001 Pat Booker Rd Suite 101	Universal City	TX	78148	**800-830-9255**	210-659-2112
American Watercraft Assn PO Box 1993	Ashburn	VA	20147	**800-913-2921**	
American Youth Soccer Organization (AYSO) 12501 S Isis Ave *Cust Svc	Hawthorne	CA	90250	**800-872-2976***	310-643-6455
Aquatic Exercise Assn (AEA) PO Box 1609	Nokomis	FL	34274	**888-232-9283**	941-486-8600
ATP Tour Inc 201 ATP Tour Blvd	Ponte Vedra Beach	FL	32082	**800-527-4811**	904-285-8000
Cross Country Ski Areas Assn 259 Bolton Rd	Winchester	NH	03470	**877-779-2754**	603-239-4341
Fellowship of Christian Athletes (FCA) 8701 Leeds Rd	Kansas City	MO	64129	**800-289-0909**	816-921-0909
Hockey North America (HNA) PO Box 78	Sterling	VA	20167	**800-446-2539**	703-430-8100
IDEA Inc 10455 Pacific Ctr Ct	San Diego	CA	92121	**800-999-4332**	858-535-8979
International Collegiate Licensing Assn (ICLA) 24651 Detroit Rd	Westlake	OH	44145	**800-996-2232**	440-892-4000
International Health Racquet & Sportsclub Assn (IHRSA) 263 Summer St 8th Fl	Boston	MA	02210	**800-228-4772**	617-951-0055
International Sports Sciences Assn (ISSA) 400 E Gutierrez St	Santa Barbara	CA	93101	**800-892-4772**	805-884-8111
Jockeys' Guild Inc PO Box 150	Monrovia	CA	91017	**866-465-6257**	626-305-5605
Major Indoor Soccer League (MISL) 1175 Post Rd E	Westport	CT	06880	**866-647-5638**	203-222-4900
National Aeronautic Assn (NAA) 1815 N Fort Myer Dr Suite 500	Arlington	VA	22209	**800-644-9777**	703-527-0226
National Alliance for Youth Sports 2050 Vista Pkwy	West Palm Beach	FL	33411	**800-729-2057**	561-684-1141
National Assn of Collegiate Directors of Athletics (NACDA) 24651 Detroit Rd	Westlake	OH	44145	**800-996-2232**	440-892-4000
National Assn for Girls & Women in Sport (NAGWS) 1900 Association Dr	Reston	VA	20191	**800-213-7193**	703-476-3400
National Assn of Police Athletic Leagues (PAL) 618 US Hwy 1 Suite 201	North Palm Beach	FL	33408	**800-725-7743**	561-844-1823
National Assn of Sports Officials (NASO) 2017 Lathrop Ave	Racine	WI	53405	**800-733-6100**	262-632-5448
National Assn of Underwater Instructors (NAUI) 1232 Tech Blvd	Tampa	FL	33619	**800-553-6284**	813-628-6284
National Athletic Trainers Assn (NATA) 2952 Stemmons Fwy Suite 200	Dallas	TX	75247	**800-879-6282**	214-637-6282
National Dart Assn (NDA) 5613 W 74th St	Indianapolis	IN	46278	**800-808-9884**	317-387-1299
National Federation of State High School Assns (NFHS) PO Box 690 *Cust Svc	Indianapolis	IN	46206	**800-776-3462***	317-972-6900
National Football League Players Assn (NFLPA) 2021 L St NW Suite 600	Washington	DC	20036	**800-372-2000**	202-463-2200
National Golf Foundation (NGF) 1150 S US Hwy 1 Suite 401	Jupiter	FL	33477	**800-733-6006**	561-744-6006
National Health Club Assn 640 Plaza Dr Suite 300	Highlands Ranch	CO	80129	**800-765-6422**	303-753-6422
National Hockey League Players Assn (NHLPA) 777 Bay St Suite 2400	Toronto	ON	M5G2C8	**800-363-4625**	416-408-4040
National Little Britches Rodeo Assn (NLBRA) 1045 W Rio Grande St	Colorado Springs	CO	80906	**800-763-3694**	719-389-0333
National Rifle Assn of America (NRA) 11250 Waples Mill Rd *Membership	Fairfax	VA	22030	**800-672-3888***	703-267-1000

Sports Organizations (Cont'd)

Organization	City	State	Zip	Toll-Free	Phone
National Senior Golf Assn (NSGA) 3672 Nottingham Way	Hamilton Square	NJ	08690	**800-282-6772**	609-631-8145
National Soccer Coaches Assn of America (NSCAA) 6700 Squibb Rd Suite 215	Mission	KS	66202	**800-458-0678**	913-362-1747
National Strength & Conditioning Assn (NSCA) 1885 Bob Johnson Dr	Colorado Springs	CO	80906	**800-815-6826**	719-632-6722
National Thoroughbred Racing Assn (NTRA) 2525 Harrodsburg Rd	Lexington	KY	40504	**800-722-3287**	859-223-5444
National Youth Sports Coaches Assn (NYSCA) 2050 Vista Pkwy	West Palm Beach	FL	33411	**800-729-2057**	561-684-1141
New York Arm Wrestling Assn (NYAWA) PO Box 670952	Flushing	NY	11367	**877-692-2767**	718-544-4592
North American Youth Sport Institute (NAYSI) 4985 Oak Garden Dr	Kernersville	NC	27284	**800-767-4916**	336-784-4926
PGA of America 100 Ave of the Champions	Palm Beach Gardens	FL	33418	**800-477-6465**	561-624-8400
Professional Assn of Diving Instructors International (PADI) 30151 Tomas St *Sales	Rancho Santa Margarita	CA	92688	**800-729-7234***	949-858-7234
Professional Golfer's Assn 100 Ave of the Champions	Palm Beach Gardens	FL	33418	**800-477-6465**	561-624-8400
Professional Tennis Registry PO Box 4739	Hilton Head Island	SC	29930	**800-421-6200**	843-785-7244
Special Olympics Inc 1133 19th St NW 11th Fl.	Washington	DC	20036	**800-700-8585**	202-628-3630
Sports Turf Managers Assn 805 New Hampshire St Suite E	Lawrence	KS	66044	**800-323-3875**	785-843-2549
US Biathlon Assn 29 Ethan Allen Ave	Colchester	VT	05446	**800-242-8456**	802-654-7833
US Bobsled & Skeleton Federation (USBSF) 196 Old Military Rd	Lake Placid	NY	12946	**800-262-7533**	518-523-1842
US Curling Assn PO Box 866	Stevens Point	WI	54481	**888-287-5377**	715-344-1199
US Golf Assn (USGA) PO Box 708 *Orders	Far Hills	NJ	07931	**800-336-4446***	908-234-2300
US Parachute Assn (USPA) 1440 Duke St	Alexandria	VA	22314	**800-371-8772**	703-836-3495
US Power Squadrons (USPS) PO Box 30423	Raleigh	NC	27622	**888-367-8777**	919-821-0281
US Professional Tennis Assn (USPTA) 3535 Briarpark Dr Suite 1	Houston	TX	77042	**800-877-8248**	713-978-7782
US Racquet Stringers Assn (USRSA) 330 Main St	Vista	CA	92084	**888-900-3545**	760-536-1177
US Racquetball Assn (USRA) 1685 W Uintah St	Colorado Springs	CO	80904	**800-234-5396**	719-635-5396
US Rowing Assn 201 S Capitol Ave Suite 400	Indianapolis	IN	46225	**800-314-4769**	317-237-5656
US Sailing Assn 15 Maritime Dr PO Box 1260	Portsmouth	RI	02871	**800-877-2451**	401-683-0800
US Soccer Federation 1801 S Prairie Ave	Chicago	IL	60616	**800-759-9636**	312-808-1300
US Speedskating PO Box 450639	Westlake	OH	44145	**800-634-4766**	440-899-0128
US Tennis Assn (USTA) 70 W Red Oak Ln	White Plains	NY	10604	**800-990-8782**	914-696-7000
US Trotting Assn (USTA) 750 Michigan Ave	Columbus	OH	43215	**800-887-8782**	614-224-2291
USA Water Ski 1251 Holy Cow Rd	Polk City	FL	33868	**800-533-2972**	863-324-4341
USA Wrestling 6155 Lehman Dr	Colorado Springs	CO	80918	**800-999-8531**	719-598-8181
USPS (US Power Squadrons) PO Box 30423	Raleigh	NC	27622	**888-367-8777**	919-821-0281
Women's International Bowling Congress (WIBC) 5301 S 76th St	Greendale	WI	53129	**800-514-2695**	414-421-9000
Women's Sports Foundation Eisenhower Pk	East Meadow	NY	11554	**800-227-3988**	516-542-4700
YMCA of the USA 101 N Wacker Dr 14th Fl.	Chicago	IL	60606	**800-872-9622**	312-977-0031
Young Men's Christian Assn of the USA 101 N Wacker Dr 14th Fl.	Chicago	IL	60606	**800-872-9622**	312-977-0031

48-23 Travel & Recreation Organizations

Organization	City	State	Zip	Toll-Free	Phone
Adirondack Mountain Club 814 Goggins Rd. *Orders	Lake George	NY	12845	**800-395-8080***	518-668-4447
America Outdoors 5816 Kingston Pike	Knoxville	TN	37919	**800-524-4814**	865-558-3595
American Assn for Leisure & Recreation (AALR) 1900 Association Dr.	Reston	VA	20191	**800-213-7193**	703-476-3400
American Camp Assn (ACA) 5000 SR-67 N	Martinsville	IN	46151	**800-428-2267**	765-342-8456
American Hiking Society (AHS) 1422 Fenwick Ln	Silver Spring	MD	20910	**800-972-8608**	301-565-6704
American Park & Recreation Society (APRS) c/o National Recreation & Park Assn 22377 Belmont Ridge Rd	Ashburn	VA	20148	**800-626-6772**	703-858-4741
American Society of Travel Agents (ASTA) 1101 King St Suite 200	Alexandria	VA	22314	**800-440-2782**	703-739-2782
American Whitewater (AW) 1424 Fenwick Ln	Silver Spring	MD	20910	**866-262-8429**	301-589-9453
Amusement & Music Operators Assn (AMOA) 33 W Higgins Rd Suite 830	South Barrington	IL	60010	**800-937-2662**	847-428-7699
Appalachian Mountain Club (AMC) 5 Joy St *Orders	Boston	MA	02108	**800-262-4455***	617-523-0636
Association of Corporate Travel Executives (ACTE) 515 King St Suite 340	Alexandria	VA	22314	**800-228-3669**	703-683-5322
Back Country Horsemen of America (BCHA) PO Box 1367	Graham	WA	98338	**888-893-5161**	360-832-2461
Boat Owners Assn of the US 880 S Pickett St.	Alexandria	VA	22304	**800-937-9307**	703-823-9550
BoatUS 880 S Pickett St	Alexandria	VA	22304	**800-937-9307**	703-823-9550
Bowling Proprietors Assn of America Inc (BPAA) 615 Six Flags Dr PO Box 5802	Arlington	TX	76005	**800-343-1329**	817-649-5105
CrossSphere 546 E Main St	Lexington	KY	40508	**800-682-8886**	859-226-4444
Elderhostel Inc 11 Ave de Lafayette	Boston	MA	02111	**877-426-8056**	617-426-7788
Escapees RV Club 100 Rainbow Dr	Livingston	TX	77351	**888-757-2582**	936-327-8873
Family Campers & RVers (FCRV) 4804 Transit Rd Bldg 2	Depew	NY	14043	**800-245-9755**	716-668-6242
Family Motor Coach Assn (FMCA) 8291 Clough Pike	Cincinnati	OH	45244	**800-543-3622**	513-474-3622
Go RVing Coalition 1896 Preston White Dr	Reston	VA	20191	**888-467-8464**	703-620-6003
Good Sam Recreational Vehicle Club PO Box 6888	Englewood	CO	80155	**800-234-3450**	
Ice Age Park & Trail Foundation 207 E Buffalo St Suite 515	Milwaukee	WI	53202	**800-227-0046**	414-278-8518
International Airline Passengers Assn (IAPA) 5204 Tennyson Pkwy	Plano	TX	75024	**800-821-4272**	972-404-9980
International Assn of Fairs & Expositions (IAFE) 3043 E Cairo	Springfield	MO	65802	**800-516-0313**	417-862-5771
International Council of Cruise Lines (ICCL) 2111 Wilson Blvd 8th Fl	Arlington	VA	22201	**800-595-9338**	703-522-8463
International Gay & Lesbian Travel Assn (IGLTA) 4331 N Federal Hwy Suite 304	Fort Lauderdale	FL	33308	**800-448-8550**	954-776-2626
International Mountain Bicycling Assn (IMBA) 207 Canyon Blvd Suite 301 PO Box 7578	Boulder	CO	80306	**888-442-4622**	303-545-9011
Leave No Trace Center for Outdoor Ethics Inc PO Box 997	Boulder	CO	80306	**800-332-4100**	303-442-8222
Lewis & Clark Trail Heritage Foundation PO Box 3434	Great Falls	MT	59404	**888-701-3434**	406-454-1234
Loners on Wheels (LoW) PO Box 1060-WB	Cape Girardeau	MO	63702	**888-569-4478**	
National Caves Assn PO Box 280	Park City	KY	42160	**866-552-2837**	270-749-2228
National Club Assn (NCA) 1201 15th St NW Suite 450	Washington	DC	20005	**800-625-6221**	202-822-9822
National Golf Course Owners Assn (NGCOA) 291 Seven Farms Dr 2nd Fl.	Charleston	SC	29492	**800-933-4262**	843-881-9956
National Indian Gaming Assn (NIGA) 224 2nd St SE	Washington	DC	20003	**800-286-6442**	202-546-7711
National Recreation & Park Assn (NRPA) 22377 Belmont Ridge Rd.	Ashburn	VA	20148	**800-626-6772**	703-858-0784
National Recreational Vehicle Owners Club PO Box 520	Gonzalez	FL	32560	**800-281-9186**	850-937-8354
National Society for Park Resources (NSPR) c/o National Recreation & Park Assn 22377 Belmont Ridge Rd	Ashburn	VA	20148	**800-626-6772**	703-858-0784
North Country Trail Assn (NCTA) 229 E Main St	Lowell	MI	49331	**866-445-3628**	616-897-5987
Oregon-California Trails Assn PO Box 1019	Independence	MO	64051	**888-811-6282**	816-252-2276
Pacific Crest Trail Assn (PCTA) 5325 Elkhorn Blvd PMB 256	Sacramento	CA	95842	**888-728-7245**	916-349-2109
Relais & Chateaux Assn 148 E 63 St.	New York	NY	10012	**800-735-2478**	212-319-4880
RVing Women PO Box 1940	Apache Junction	AZ	85217	**888-557-8464**	480-671-6226
Society of Park & Recreation Educators (SPRE) c/o National Recreation & Park Assn 22377 Belmont Ridge Rd	Ashburn	VA	20148	**800-626-6772**	703-858-0784
Special Military Active Retired Travel Club (SMART) 600 University Office Blvd Suite 1A	Pensacola	FL	32504	**800-354-7681**	
Travel Institute 148 Linden St Suite 305	Wellesley	MA	02482	**800-542-4282**	781-237-0280
Wilderness Inquiry (WI) 808 14th Ave SE	Minneapolis	MN	55414	**800-728-0719**	612-676-9400

48-24 Women's Organizations

Organization	City	State	Zip	Toll-Free	Phone
9to5 National Assn of Working Women 152 W Wisconsin Ave Suite 408	Milwaukee	WI	53203	**800-522-0925**	414-274-0925
Girls Inc 120 Wall St 3rd Fl	New York	NY	10005	**800-374-4475**	212-509-2000
National Assn for Female Executives (NAFE) 60 E 42nd St 27th Fl	New York	NY	10165	**800-927-6233**	212-351-6400
National Center on Women & Aging Brandeis University Heller Graduate School MS 035	Waltham	MA	02454	**800-929-1995**	781-736-3866
National Council of Jewish Women (NCJW) 53 W 23rd St 6th Fl.	New York	NY	10010	**800-829-6259**	212-645-4048
Ninety-Nines Inc 4300 Amelia Earhart Rd.	Oklahoma City	OK	73159	**800-944-1929**	405-685-7969
Women in Community Service Inc (WICS) 1900 N Beauregard St Suite 103	Alexandria	VA	22311	**800-442-9427**	703-671-0500
Women Work! National Network for Women's Employment 1625 K St NW Suite 300	Washington	DC	20006	**800-235-2732**	202-467-6346
Women's Sports Foundation Eisenhower Pk	East Meadow	NY	11554	**800-227-3988**	516-542-4700
YWCA USA 1015 18th St NW Suite 1100	Washington	DC	20036	**800-992-2871**	202-467-0801

49 ASSOCIATIONS & ORGANIZATIONS - PROFESSIONAL & TRADE

SEE ALSO Bar Associations - State; Dental Associations - State; Labor Unions; Library Associations - State & Province; Medical Associations - State; Pharmacy Associations - State; Realtor Associations - State; Veterinary Medical Associations - State

49-1 Accountants Associations

Organization	City	State	Zip	Toll-Free	Phone
AACE International - Assn for the Advancement of Cost Engineering (AACE) 209 Prairie Ave Suite 100	Morgantown	WV	26501	**800-858-2678**	304-296-8444
Accountants Global Network 2851 S Parker Rd Suite 850	Aurora	CO	80014	**800-782-2272**	303-743-7880
AGN International-North America (AGN) 2851 S Parker Rd Suite 850	Aurora	CO	80014	**800-782-2272**	303-743-7880
American Institute of Certified Public Accountants (AICPA) 1211 Ave of the Americas	New York	NY	10036	**888-777-7077**	212-596-6200
American Institute of Professional Bookkeepers (AIPB) 6001 Montrose Rd Suite 500	Rockville	MD	20852	**800-622-0121**	301-770-7300
American Woman's Society of Certified Public Accountants (AWSCPA) 136 S Keowee St	Dayton	OH	45402	**800-297-2721**	937-222-1872
Association of Certified Fraud Examiners (ACFE) 716 West Ave.	Austin	TX	78701	**800-245-3321**	512-478-9070
Association of Government Accountants (AGA) 2208 Mt Vernon Ave	Alexandria	VA	22301	**800-242-7211**	703-684-6931
Association of Healthcare Internal Auditors (AHIA) PO Box 449	Onsted	MI	49265	**888-275-2442**	517-467-7729
BKR International 19 Fulton St Suite 306	New York	NY	10038	**800-257-4685**	212-964-2115
CPA Auto Dealer Consultants Assn (CADCA) 10831 Old Mill Rd Suite 400	Omaha	NE	68154	**888-475-4476**	402-778-7922
CPA Manufacturing Services Assn 10831 Old Mill Rd Suite 400	Omaha	NE	68154	**888-475-4476**	402-778-7922
Foundation for Accounting Education 3 Park Ave 18th Fl	New York	NY	10016	**800-537-3635**	212-719-8300

				Toll-Free	Phone
Hospitality Financial & Technology Professionals (HFTP) 11709 Boulder Ln Suite 110	Austin	TX	78726	**800-856-4242**	512-249-5333
IGAF Worldwide 2250 Satellite Blvd Suite 115	Duluth	GA	30097	**800-272-4423**	678-417-7730
Institute of Management Accountants Inc (IMA) 10 Paragon Dr	Montvale	NJ	07645	**800-638-4427**	201-573-9000
National Assn of State Boards of Accountancy (NASBA) 150 4th Ave N Suite 700	Nashville	TN	37219	**800-272-3926**	615-880-4200
National Assn of Tax Professionals (NATP) 720 Association Dr	Appleton	WI	54914	**800-558-3402**	920-749-1040
National CPA Health Care Advisors Assn (HCAA) 10831 Old Mill Rd Suite 400	Omaha	NE	68154	**888-475-4476**	402-778-7922
National Society of Accountants (NSA) 1010 N Fairfax St	Alexandria	VA	22314	**800-966-6679**	703-549-6400
Not-for-Profit Services Assn (NSA) 10831 Old Mill Rd Suite 400	Omaha	NE	68154	**888-475-4476**	402-778-7922

49-2 Banking & Finance Professionals Associations

				Toll-Free	Phone
ABA (American Bankers Assn) 1120 Connecticut Ave NW *Cust Svc	Washington	DC	20036	**800-226-5377***	202-663-5000
ABA Marketing Network 1120 Connecticut Ave NW	Washington	DC	20036	**800-226-5377**	202-663-5268
American Assn of Individual Investors (AAII) 625 N Michigan Ave	Chicago	IL	60611	**800-428-2244**	312-280-0170
American Bankers Assn (ABA) 1120 Connecticut Ave NW *Cust Svc	Washington	DC	20036	**800-226-5377***	202-663-5000
Bank Administration Institute (BAI) 1 N Franklin St Suite 1000 *Cust Svc	Chicago	IL	60606	**800-224-9889***	312-553-4600
Certified Financial Planner Board of Standards Inc 1670 Broadway Suite 600	Denver	CO	80202	**888-237-6275**	303-830-7500
CFA Institute 560 Ray C Hunt Dr PO Box 3668	Charlottesville	VA	22903	**800-247-8132**	434-951-5499
Community Banking Advisory Network (CBAN) 10831 Old Mill Rd Suite 400	Omaha	NE	68154	**888-475-4476**	402-778-7922
Credit Union Executives Society (CUES) 5510 Research Park Dr	Madison	WI	53711	**800-252-2664**	608-271-2664
Credit Union National Assn (CUNA) 5710 Mineral Point Rd	Madison	WI	53705	**800-356-9655**	608-231-4000
Financial Managers Society (FMS) 100 W Monroe St Suite 810 *Cust Svc	Chicago	IL	60603	**800-275-4367***	312-578-1300
Financial Planning Assn (FPA) 5775 Glenridge Dr NE Suite B300	Atlanta	GA	30328	**800-945-4237**	404-845-0011
Independent Community Bankers of America (ICBA) 1 Thomas Cir NW Suite 400	Washington	DC	20005	**800-422-8439**	202-659-8111
Mortgage Bankers Assn (MBA) 1919 Pennsylvania Ave NW	Washington	DC	20006	**800-793-6222**	202-557-2700
NACHA - Electronic Payments Assn (NACHA) 13665 Dulles Technology Dr Suite 300	Herndon	VA	20171	**800-487-9180**	703-561-1100
NASD (National Assn of Securities Dealers Inc) 1735 K St NW	Washington	DC	20006	**800-289-9999**	202-728-8000
National Assn of Credit Management (NACM) 8840 Columbia 100 Pkwy	Columbia	MD	21045	**800-955-8815**	410-740-5560
National Assn of Federal Credit Unions (NAFCU) 3138 10th St N	Arlington	VA	22201	**800-336-4644**	703-522-4770
National Assn of Investors Corp (NAIC) PO Box 220	Royal Oak	MI	48068	**877-275-6242**	248-583-6242
National Assn of Personal Financial Advisors (NAPFA) 3250 N Arlington Suite 109	Arlington Heights	IL	60004	**800-366-2732**	847-537-7722
National Assn of Securities Dealers Inc (NASD) 1735 K St NW	Washington	DC	20006	**800-289-9999**	202-728-8000
National Automated Clearing House Assn 13665 Dulles Technology Dr Suite 300	Herndon	VA	20171	**800-487-9180**	703-561-1100
National Federation of Community Development Credit Unions (NFCDCU) 120 Wall St 10th Fl	New York	NY	10005	**800-437-8711**	212-809-1850
National Futures Assn (NFA) 200 W Madison St	Chicago	IL	60606	**800-366-6321**	312-781-1300
National Home Equity Mortgage Assn (NHEMA) 1301 Pennsylvania Ave NW Suite 500	Washington	DC	20004	**800-342-1121**	202-347-1210
North American Securities Administrators Assn (NASAA) 10 G St NE Suite 710	Washington	DC	20002	**888-846-2722**	202-737-0900
RMA - Risk Management Assn 1650 Market St 1 Liberty Pl Suite 2300 *Cust Svc	Philadelphia	PA	19103	**800-677-7621***	215-446-4000
Smart Card Alliance Inc 191 Clarkville Rd	Princeton Junction	NJ	08550	**800-556-6828**	609-799-5654
Viatical & Life Settlement Assn of America (VLSAA) 800 Mayfair Cir	Orlando	FL	32803	**800-842-9811**	407-894-3797
World Council of Credit Unions Inc (WOCCU) 5710 Minerial Point Rd	Madison	WI	53705	**800-356-2644**	608-231-7130

49-3 Construction Industry Associations

				Toll-Free	Phone
AGC (Associated General Contractors of America) 333 John Carlyle St Suite 200	Alexandria	VA	22314	**800-242-1766**	703-548-3118
AMD (Association of Millwork Distributors) 10047 Robert Trent Jones Pkwy	New Port Richey	FL	34655	**800-786-7274**	727-372-3665
American Fence Assn (AFA) 800 Roosevelt Rd Bldg C-20	Glen Ellyn	IL	60137	**800-822-4342**	630-942-6598
American Society of Heating Refrigerating & Air-Conditioning Engineers Inc (ASHRAE) 1791 Tullie Cir NE *Cust Svc	Atlanta	GA	30329	**800-527-4723***	404-636-8400
American Society of Home Inspectors (ASHI) 932 Lee St Suite 101	Des Plaines	IL	60016	**800-743-2744**	847-759-2820
American Society of Professional Estimators (ASPE) 2525 Perimeter Place Dr Suite 102	Nashville	TN	37214	**888-378-6283**	615-316-9200
American Welding Society (AWS) 550 NW Le Jeune Rd	Miami	FL	33126	**800-443-9353**	305-443-9353
Associated General Contractors of America (AGC) 333 John Carlyle St Suite 200	Alexandria	VA	22314	**800-242-1766**	703-548-3118
Associated Locksmiths of America (ALOA) 3003 Live Oak St	Dallas	TX	75204	**800-532-2562**	214-827-1701
Association of Millwork Distributors (AMD) 10047 Robert Trent Jones Pkwy	New Port Richey	FL	34655	**800-786-7274**	727-372-3665
Building Material Dealers Assn (BMDA) 12540 SW Main St Suite 200	Tigard	OR	97223	**800-666-2632**	503-624-0561
Cedar Shake & Shingle Bureau 7101 Horne St Suite 2	Mission	BC	V2V7A2	**800-843-3578**	604-820-7700
Construction Specifications Institute (CSI) 99 Canal Ctr Plaza Suite 300	Alexandria	VA	22314	**800-689-2900**	703-684-0300
Interlocking Concrete Pavement Institute (ICPI) 1444 'I' St NW Suite 700	Washington	DC	20005	**800-241-3652**	202-712-9036
International Assn of Electrical Inspectors (IAEI) 901 Waterfall Way Suite 602	Richardson	TX	75080	**800-786-4234**	972-235-1455
International Council of Employers of Bricklayers & Allied Craftworkers 1730 Rhode Island Ave NW Suite 419	Washington	DC	20036	**888-880-8222**	202-457-9040
International Masonry Institute (IMI) James Brice House 42 East St	Annapolis	MD	21401	**800-803-0295**	410-280-1305
Manufactured Housing Institute (MHI) 2101 Wilson Blvd Suite 610	Arlington	VA	22201	**800-505-5500**	703-558-0400
Mason Contractors Assn of America (MCAA) 33 S Roselle Rd	Schaumburg	IL	60193	**800-536-2225**	847-301-0001
Mechanical Contractors Assn of America (MCAA) 1385 Piccard Dr	Rockville	MD	20850	**800-556-3653**	301-869-5800
MHI (Manufactured Housing Institute) 2101 Wilson Blvd Suite 610	Arlington	VA	22201	**800-505-5500**	703-558-0400
Monument Builders of North America (MBNA) 401 N Michigan Ave Suite 2200	Chicago	IL	60611	**800-233-4472**	312-321-5143
National Assn of Home Builders (NAHB) 1201 15th St NW	Washington	DC	20005	**800-368-5242**	202-266-8200
National Assn of Home Inspectors Inc (NAHI) 4248 Park Glen Rd	Minneapolis	MN	55416	**800-448-3942**	952-928-4641
National Assn of Minority Contractors 666 11th St NW Suite 520	Washington	DC	20001	**866-688-6262**	202-347-8259
National Assn of the Remodeling Industry (NARI) 780 Lee St Suite 200	Des Plaines	IL	60016	**800-611-6274**	847-298-9200
National Assn of Tower Erectors (NATE) 8 2nd St SE	Watertown	SD	57201	**888-882-5865**	605-882-5865
National Assn of Women in Construction (NAWIC) 327 S Adams St	Fort Worth	TX	76104	**800-552-3506**	817-877-5551
National Conference of States on Building Codes & Standards (NCSBCS) 505 Huntmar Park Dr Suite 210	Herndon	VA	20170	**800-362-2633**	703-437-0100
National Council of Examiners for Engineering & Surveying (NCEES) 280 Seneca Creek Rd	Clemson	SC	29631	**800-250-3196**	864-654-6824
National Frame Builders Assn (NFBA) 4840 Bob Billings Pkwy Suite 1000	Lawrence	KS	66049	**800-557-6957**	785-843-2444
National Hardwood Lumber Assn (NHLA) 6830 Raleigh-LaGrange Rd	Memphis	TN	38134	**800-933-0318**	901-377-1818
National Insulation Assn (NIA) 99 Canal Center Plaza Suite 222	Alexandria	VA	22314	**877-968-7642**	703-683-6422
National Kitchen & Bath Assn (NKBA) 687 Willow Grove St	Hackettstown	NJ	07840	**800-843-6522**	908-852-0033
National Parking Assn (NPA) 1112 16th St NW Suite 300	Washington	DC	20036	**800-647-7275**	202-296-4336
National Precast Concrete Assn (NPCA) 10333 N Meridian St Suite 272	Indianapolis	IN	46290	**800-366-7731**	317-571-9500
National Roofing Contractors Assn (NRCA) 10255 W Higgins Rd Suite 600 *Cust Svc	Rosemont	IL	60018	**800-323-9545***	847-299-9070
National Stone Sand & Gravel Assn (NSSGA) 1605 King St	Alexandria	VA	22314	**800-342-1415**	703-525-8788
National Utility Contractors Assn (NUCA) 4301 N Fairfax Dr Suite 360	Arlington	VA	22203	**800-662-6822**	703-358-9300
National Wood Flooring Assn (NWFA) 111 Chesterfield Industrial Blvd	Chesterfield	MO	63005	**800-422-4556**	636-519-9663
North American Building Material Distribution Assn (NBMDA) 401 N Michigan Ave Suite 2400	Chicago	IL	60611	**888-747-7862**	312-644-6610
North American Wholesale Lumber Assn (NAWLA) 3601 Algonquin Rd Suite 400	Rolling Meadows	IL	60008	**800-527-8258**	847-870-7470
Painting & Decorating Contractors of America (PDCA) 11960 Westline Industrial Dr Suite 201	Saint Louis	MO	63146	**800-332-7322**	314-514-7322
Plumbing-Heating-Cooling Contractors National Assn (PHCC) 180 S Washington St	Falls Church	VA	22040	**800-533-7694**	703-237-8100
Refrigeration Service Engineers Society (RSES) 1666 Rand Rd	Des Plaines	IL	60016	**800-297-5660**	847-297-6464
Sheet Metal Workers International Assn (SMWIA) 1750 New York Ave NW 6th Fl	Washington	DC	20006	**800-457-7694**	202-783-5880
Window & Door Manufacturers Assn (WDMA) 1400 E Touhy Ave Suite 470	Des Plaines	IL	60018	**800-223-2301**	847-299-5200
Wood Moulding & Millwork Producers Assn (WMMPA) 507 First St	Woodland	CA	95695	**800-550-7889**	530-661-9591

49-4 Consumer Sales & Service Professionals Associations

				Toll-Free	Phone
AeA: Advancing the Business of Technology 5201 Great America Pkwy Suite 520	Santa Clara	CA	95054	**800-284-4232**	408-987-4200
American Apparel & Footwear Assn (AAFA) 1601 N Kent St Suite 1200	Arlington	VA	22209	**800-520-2262**	703-524-1864
American Bio-Recovery Assn (ABRA) 2020 Pennsylvania Ave NW Suite 456	Washington	DC	20006	**888-979-2217**	888-979-2272
American Gem Trade Assn (AGTA) 3030 LBJ Fwy Suite 840	Dallas	TX	75234	**800-972-1162**	214-742-4367
American Lighting Assn (ALA) 2050 Stemmons Fwy Suite 10046	Dallas	TX	75342	**800-605-4448**	214-698-9898
American Pet Products Manufacturers Assn (APPMA) 255 Glenville Rd	Greenwich	CT	06831	**800-452-1225**	203-532-0000
American Rental Assn (ARA) 1900 19th St	Moline	IL	61265	**800-334-2177**	309-764-2475
American Watchmakers-Clockmakers Institute (AWI) 701 Enterprise Dr	Harrison	OH	45030	**866-367-2924**	513-367-9800
Aspirin Foundation of America 1555 Connecticut Ave NW Suite 200	Washington	DC	20036	**800-432-3247**	
Association of Pool & Spa Professionals (APSP) 2111 Eisenhower Ave	Alexandria	VA	22314	**800-323-3996**	703-838-0083

Consumer Sales & Service Professionals Associations (Cont'd)

Organization / Address	City	State	ZIP	Toll-Free	Phone
Association of Specialists in Cleaning & Restoration (ASCR) 8229 Cloverleaf Dr Suite 460	Millersville	MD	21108	**800-272-7012**	410-729-9900
Awards & Recognition Assn (ARA) 4700 W Lake Ave	Glenview	IL	60025	**800-344-2148**	847-375-4800
Carpet & Rug Institute (CRI) 310 S Holiday Ave	Dalton	GA	30720	**800-882-8846**	706-278-3176
Coin Laundry Assn (CLA) 1315 Butterfield Rd Suite 212	Downers Grove	IL	60515	**800-570-5629**	630-963-5547
Contact Lens Manufacturers Assn PO Box 29398	Lincoln	NE	68529	**800-344-9060**	402-465-4122
Diamond Council of America (DCA) 3212 West End Ave Suite 202	Nashville	TN	37203	**877-283-5669**	615-385-5301
Diving Equipment & Marketing Assn (DEMA) 3750 Convoy St Suite 310	San Diego	CA	92111	**800-862-3483**	858-616-6408
Extra Touch Florist Assn (ETF) 137 N Larchmont Blvd Suite 529	Los Angeles	CA	90019	**888-419-1515**	323-735-7272
Gemological Institute of America (GIA) 5345 Armada Dr	Carlsbad	CA	92008	**800-421-7250**	760-603-4000
Home Furnishings International Assn (HFIA) 2050 Stemmons World Trade Center Suite 170 PO Box 420807	Dallas	TX	75342	**800-942-4663**	214-741-7632
Independent Jewelers Organization (IJO) 25 Seir Hill Rd	Norwalk	CT	06850	**800-624-9252**	203-846-4215
International Cemetery & Funeral Assn (ICFA) 1895 Preston White Dr Suite 220	Reston	VA	20191	**800-645-7700**	703-391-8400
International Engraved Graphics Assn 305 Plus Park Blvd *x209	Nashville	TN	37217	**800-821-3138***	615-366-1094
International Executive Housekeepers Assn (IEHA) 1001 Eastwind Dr Suite 301	Westerville	OH	43081	**800-200-6342**	614-895-7166
International Fabricare Institute (IFI) 12251 Tech Rd	Silver Spring	MD	20904	**800-638-2627**	301-622-1900
International Order of the Golden Rule (OGR) 13523 Lakefront Dr	Bridgeton	MO	63045	**800-637-8030**	314-209-7142
International Precious Metals Institute (IPMI) 4400 Bayou Blvd Suite 18	Pensacola	FL	32503	**866-289-8484**	850-476-1156
International Sign Assn (ISA) 707 N Saint Asaph St	Alexandria	VA	22314	**888-472-7446**	703-836-4012
Jewelers of America (JA) 52 Vanderbilt Ave 19th Fl	New York	NY	10017	**800-223-0673**	646-658-0246
Manufacturing Jewelers & Suppliers of America (MJSA) 45 Royal Little Dr	Providence	RI	02904	**800-444-6572**	401-274-3840
National Assn of Institutional Linen Management (NAILM) 2130 Lexington Rd Suite H	Richmond	KY	40475	**800-669-0863**	859-624-0177
National Funeral Directors Assn (NFDA) 13625 Bishop's Dr	Brookfield	WI	53005	**800-228-6332**	262-789-1880
National Funeral Directors & Morticians Assn (NFDMA) 3951 Snapfinger Pkwy Suite 570	Decatur	GA	30035	**800-434-0958**	404-286-6680
National Home Furnishings Assn (NHFA) 3010 Tinsley Dr Suite 101	High Point	NC	27265	**800-888-9590**	336-886-6100
National Shoe Retailers Assn (NSRA) 7150 Columbia Gateway Dr Suite G	Columbia	MD	21046	**800-673-8446**	410-381-8282
National Sporting Goods Assn (NSGA) 1601 Feehanville Dr Suite 300	Mount Prospect	IL	60056	**800-815-5422**	847-296-6742
National Volunteer Fire Council (NVFC) 1050 17th St NW Suite 490	Washington	DC	20036	**888-275-6832**	202-887-5700
Paint & Decorating Retailers Assn (PDRA) 403 Axminister Dr	Fenton	MO	63026	**800-737-0107**	636-326-2636
Pedorthic Footwear Assn (PFA) 7150 Columbia Gateway Dr Suite G	Columbia	MD	21046	**800-673-8447**	410-381-7278
Pet Industry Joint Advisory Council (PIJAC) 1220 19th St NW Suite 400	Washington	DC	20036	**800-553-7387**	202-452-1525
Recreation Vehicle Industry Assn (RVIA) 1896 Preston White Dr	Reston	VA	20191	**800-336-0154**	703-620-6003
Salon Assn (TSA) 15825 N 71st St Suite 100	Scottsdale	AZ	85254	**800-211-4872**	480-281-0429
School Home & Office Products Assn (SHOPA) 3131 Elbee Rd	Dayton	OH	45439	**800-854-7467**	937-297-2250
Selected Independent Funeral Homes 500 Lake Cook Rd Suite 205	Deerfield	IL	60015	**800-323-4219**	847-236-9401
Society of American Florists (SAF) 1601 Duke St	Alexandria	VA	22314	**800-336-4743**	703-836-8700
Textile Rental Services Assn (TRSA) 1800 Diagonal Rd Suite 200	Alexandria	VA	22314	**800-868-8772**	703-519-0029
Tire Industry Assn (TIA) 1532 Pointer Ridge Pl Suite E	Bowie	MD	20716	**800-876-8372**	301-430-7280
Uniform & Textile Service Assn (UTSA) 1300 N 17th St Suite 750	Arlington	VA	22209	**800-486-6745**	703-247-2600
Vision Council of America (VCA) 1700 Diagonal Rd Suite 500	Alexandria	VA	22314	**800-424-8422**	703-548-4560
World Floor Covering Assn (WFCA) 2211 Howell Ave	Anaheim	CA	92806	**800-624-6880**	714-978-6440

49-5 Education Professionals Associations

Organization / Address	City	State	ZIP	Toll-Free	Phone
American Assn of Family & Consumer Sciences (AAFCS) 400 N Columbus St Suite 202	Alexandria	VA	22314	**800-424-8080**	703-706-4600
American Assn of School Administrators (AASA) 801 N Quincy St Suite 700	Arlington	VA	22203	**800-771-1162**	703-528-0700
American Assn of University Professors (AAUP) 1012 14th St NW Suite 500	Washington	DC	20005	**800-424-2973**	202-737-5900
American Assn of University Women (AAUW) 1111 16th St NW	Washington	DC	20036	**800-326-2289**	202-785-7700
American Dental Education Assn (ADEA) 1400 K St NW Suite 1100	Washington	DC	20005	**800-353-2237**	202-289-7201
American Federation of School Administrators (AFSA) 1729 21st St NW	Washington	DC	20009	**800-354-2372**	202-986-4209
American Library Assn (ALA) 50 E Huron St	Chicago	IL	60611	**800-545-2433**	312-944-6780
American Medical Student Assn (AMSA) 1902 Association Dr	Reston	VA	20191	**800-767-2266**	703-620-6600
American School Counselor Assn (ASCA) 1101 King St Suite 625	Alexandria	VA	22314	**800-306-4722**	703-683-2722
American School Health Assn (ASHA) 7263 State Rt 43 PO Box 708	Kent	OH	44240	**800-445-2742**	330-678-1601
American Society for Training & Development (ASTD) 1640 King St Box 1443	Alexandria	VA	22313	**800-628-2783**	703-683-8100
Association for Advanced Training in the Behavioral Sciences (AATBS) 5126 Ralston St	Ventura	CA	93003	**800-472-1931**	805-676-3030
Association for Career & Technical Education (ACTE) 1410 King St	Alexandria	VA	22314	**800-826-9972**	703-683-3111
Association for Childhood Education International (ACEI) 17904 Georgia Ave Suite 215	Olney	MD	20832	**800-423-3563**	301-570-2111
Association of Christian Schools International (ACSI) 731 Chapel Hills Dr *Cust Svc	Colorado Springs	CO	80920	**800-367-0798***	719-528-6906
Association for Continuing Higher Education (ACHE) 2001 Mabelene Rd	Charleston	SC	29406	**800-807-2243**	843-574-6658
Association for Educational Communications & Technology (AECT) 1800 N Stonelake Dr Suite 2	Bloomington	IN	47404	**877-677-2328**	812-335-7675
Association of Governing Boards of Universities & Colleges (AGB) 1 Dupont Cir NW Suite 400	Washington	DC	20036	**800-356-6317**	202-296-8400
Association of Program Directors in Internal Medicine (APDIM) 2501 M St NW Suite 550	Washington	DC	20037	**800-622-4558**	202-887-9450
Association for Supervision & Curriculum Development (ASCD) 1703 N Beauregard St	Alexandria	VA	22311	**800-933-2723**	703-578-9600
Association of Test Publishers 1201 Pennsylvania Ave Suite 300	Washington	DC	20004	**866-240-7909**	
Broadcast Education Assn (BEA) 1771 'N' St NW	Washington	DC	20036	**888-380-7222**	202-429-5354
Business Professionals of America 5454 Cleveland Ave	Columbus	OH	43231	**800-334-2007**	614-895-7277
Christian Schools International (CSI) 3350 E Paris Ave SE	Grand Rapids	MI	49512	**800-635-8288**	616-957-1070
Conference on College Composition & Communication (CCCC) 1111 W Kenyon Rd	Urbana	IL	61801	**800-369-6283**	217-328-3870
Council for Advancement & Support of Education (CASE) 1307 New York Ave NW Suite 1000 *Orders	Washington	DC	20005	**800-554-8536***	202-328-5900
Council for Exceptional Children (CEC) 1110 N Glebe Rd Suite 300	Arlington	VA	22201	**888-232-7733**	703-620-3660
Council on International Educational Exchange (CIEE) 7 Custom House St 3rd Fl *Cust Svc	Portland	ME	04101	**888-268-6245***	207-553-7600
Council for Professional Recognition 2460 16th St NW	Washington	DC	20009	**800-424-4310**	202-265-9090
Hispanic Assn of Colleges & Universities (HACU) 8415 Datapoint Dr Suite 400	San Antonio	TX	78229	**800-780-4228**	210-692-3805
Independent Educational Consultants Assn (IECA) 3251 Old Lee Hwy Suite 510	Fairfax	VA	22030	**800-808-4322**	703-591-4850
International Society for Technology in Education (ISTE) 480 Charnelton St	Eugene	OR	97401	**800-336-5191**	541-302-3777
MENC: National Assn for Music Education 1806 Robert Fulton Dr	Reston	VA	20191	**800-336-3768**	703-860-4000
Middle States Assn of Colleges & Schools 3624 Market St	Philadelphia	PA	19104	**800-355-1258**	215-662-5600
Music Teachers National Assn (MTNA) 441 Vine St Suite 505	Cincinnati	OH	45202	**888-512-5278**	513-421-1420
National Assn of Biology Teachers (NABT) 12030 Sunrise Valley Dr Suite 110	Reston	VA	20191	**800-406-0775**	703-264-9696
National Assn for Campus Activities (NACA) 13 Harbison Way	Columbia	SC	29212	**800-845-2338**	803-732-6222
National Assn of Catholic School Teachers (NACST) 1700 Sansom St Suite 903	Philadelphia	PA	19103	**800-996-2278**	215-665-0993
National Assn for College Admission Counseling (NACAC) 1631 Prince St	Alexandria	VA	22314	**800-822-6285**	703-836-2222
National Assn of Colleges & Employers (NACE) 62 Highland Ave	Bethlehem	PA	18017	**800-544-5272**	610-868-1421
National Assn for the Education of Young Children (NAEYC) 1509 16th St NW	Washington	DC	20036	**800-424-2460**	202-232-8777
National Assn of Elementary School Principals (NAESP) 1615 Duke St	Alexandria	VA	22314	**800-386-2377**	703-684-3345
National Assn of State Boards of Education (NASBE) 277 S Washington St Suite 100	Alexandria	VA	22314	**800-368-5023**	703-684-4000
National Council on Economic Education (NCEE) 1140 6th Ave 2nd Fl	New York	NY	10036	**800-338-1192**	212-730-7007
National Council for the Social Studies (NCSS) 8555 16th St Suite 500	Silver Spring	MD	20910	**800-296-7840**	301-588-1800
National Council of Teachers of English (NCTE) 1111 W Kenyon Rd	Urbana	IL	61801	**800-369-6283**	217-328-3870
National Council of Teachers of Mathematics (NCTM) 1906 Association Dr *Orders	Reston	VA	20191	**800-235-7566***	703-620-9840
National Middle School Assn (NMSA) 4151 Executive Pkwy Suite 300	Westerville	OH	43081	**800-528-6672**	614-895-4730
National Science Teachers Assn (NSTA) 1840 Wilson Blvd *Sales	Arlington	VA	22201	**800-722-6782***	703-243-7100
National Staff Development Council (NSDC) 5995 Fairfield Rd Suite 4	Oxford	OH	45056	**800-727-7288**	513-523-6029
North Central Assn Higher Learning Commission 30 N La Salle St Suite 2400	Chicago	IL	60602	**800-621-7440**	312-263-0456
Research Libraries Group Inc (RLG) 2029 Stierlin Ct Suite 100	Mountain View	CA	94043	**800-537-7546**	650-962-9951
Society of Park & Recreation Educators (SPRE) c/o National Recreation & Park Assn 22377 Belmont Ridge Rd	Ashburn	VA	20148	**800-626-6772**	703-858-0784
Southern Assn of Colleges & Schools 1866 Southern Ln	Decatur	GA	30033	**800-248-7701**	404-679-4500
Trees for Tomorrow (TFT) 519 Sheridan St E PO Box 609	Eagle River	WI	54521	**800-838-9472**	715-479-6456

49-6 Food & Beverage Industries Professional Associations

Organization / Address	City	State	ZIP	Toll-Free	Phone
American Beverage Licensees (ABL) 5101 River Rd Suite 108	Bethesda	MD	20816	**800-311-8999**	301-656-1494
American Culinary Federation Inc (ACF) 180 Sector Place Way	Saint Augustine	FL	32095	**800-624-9458**	904-824-4468
Beer Institute 122 C St NW Suite 750	Washington	DC	20001	**800-379-2739**	202-737-2337
Chocolate Manufacturers Assn (CMA) 8320 Old Courthouse Rd Suite 300	Vienna	VA	22182	**800-433-1200**	703-790-5011

Organization / Address	City	State	Zip	Toll-Free	Phone
Distilled Spirits Council of the US Inc (DISCUS) 1250 'I' St NW Suite 400	Washington	DC	20005	**888-862-7597**	202-628-3544
Food Products Assn (FPA) 1350 'I' St NW Suite 300	Washington	DC	20005	**800-355-0983**	202-639-5900
Institute of Food Technologists (IFT) 525 W Van Buren St Suite 1000	Chicago	IL	60607	**800-438-3663**	312-782-8424
International Assn for Food Protection (IAFP) 6200 Aurora Ave Suite 200W	Des Moines	IA	50322	**800-369-6337**	515-276-3344
International Bottled Water Assn (IBWA) 1700 Diagonal Rd Suite 650	Alexandria	VA	22314	**800-928-3711**	703-683-5213
International Food Service Executives Assn (IFSEA) 836 San Bruno Ave	Henderson	NV	89015	**888-234-3732**	702-564-0997
Meat Industry Suppliers Assn (MISA) Food Processing Machinery Assn 200 Dangerfield Rd 1st Fl	Alexandria	VA	22314	**800-331-8816**	703-684-1080
National Assn of Pizzeria Operators 908 S 8th St Suite 200	Louisville	KY	40203	**800-489-8324**	502-736-9500
National Assn for the Specialty Food Trade Inc (NASFT) 120 Wall St 27th Fl	New York	NY	10005	**800-627-3869**	212-482-6440
National Beer Wholesalers Assn (NBWA) 1101 King St Suite 600	Alexandria	VA	22314	**800-300-6417**	703-683-4300
National Confectioners Assn (NCA) 8320 Old Courthouse Rd Suite 300	Vienna	VA	22182	**800-433-1200**	703-790-5750
National Milk Producers Federation (NMPF) 2101 Wilson Blvd Suite 400	Arlington	VA	22201	**888-549-7600**	703-243-6111
National Nutritional Foods Assn (NNFA) 3931 MacArthur Blvd Suite 101	Newport Beach	CA	92660	**800-966-6632**	949-622-6272
National Restaurant Assn (NRA) 1200 17th St NW	Washington	DC	20036	**800-424-5156**	202-331-5900
RBA - Retailer's Bakery Assn 14239 Park Center Dr	Laurel	MD	20707	**800-638-0924**	301-725-2149
Retail Confectioners International (RCI) 1807 Glenview Rd Suite 204	Glenview	IL	60025	**800-545-5381**	847-724-6120
Snack Food Assn 1711 King St Suite 1	Alexandria	VA	22314	**800-628-1334**	703-836-4500
Wine & Spirits Shippers Assn Inc (WSSA) 11800 Sunrise Valley Dr Suite 332	Reston	VA	22091	**800-368-3167**	703-860-2300
WineAmerica 1212 New York Ave NW Suite 425	Washington	DC	20005	**800-879-4637**	202-783-2756

49-7 Government & Public Administration Professional Associations

Organization / Address	City	State	Zip	Toll-Free	Phone
American Assn of Motor Vehicle Administrators (AAMVA) 4301 Wilson Blvd Suite 400	Arlington	VA	22203	**800-515-8881**	703-522-4200
American Correctional Assn (ACA) 4380 Forbes Blvd	Lanham	MD	20706	**800-222-5646**	301-918-1800
American Foreign Service Assn 2101 'E' St NW	Washington	DC	20037	**800-704-2372**	202-338-4045
Association of Public-Safety Communications Officials International Inc 351 N Williamson Blvd	Daytona Beach	FL	32114	**888-272-6911**	386-322-2500
Association of Social Work Boards (ASWB) 400 Southridge Pkwy Suite B	Culpeper	VA	22701	**800-225-6880**	540-829-6880
Association of State & Provincial Psychology Boards (ASPPB) 7177 Halcyon Summit Dr	Montgomery	AL	36117	**800-448-4069**	334-832-4580
Commission on Accreditation for Law Enforcement Agencies (CALEA) 10302 Eaton Pl Suite 100	Fairfax	VA	22030	**800-368-3757**	703-352-4225
Conference of State Bank Supervisors (CSBS) 1155 Connecticut Ave NW 5th Fl	Washington	DC	20036	**800-886-2727**	202-296-2840
Council of State Governments (CSG) 2760 Research Park Dr PO Box 11910 *Sales	Lexington	KY	40578	**800-800-1910***	859-244-8000
CSBS (Conference of State Bank Supervisors) 1155 Connecticut Ave NW 5th Fl	Washington	DC	20036	**800-886-2727**	202-296-2840
Federation of State Medical Boards of the US Inc (FSMB) 400 Fuller Wiser Rd Suite 300	Euless	TX	76039	**800-876-5396**	817-868-4000
International Assn of Chiefs of Police (IACP) 515 N Washington St	Alexandria	VA	22314	**800-843-4227**	703-836-6767
International Assn of Plumbing & Mechanical Officials (IAPMO) 5001 E Philadelphia St	Ontario	CA	91761	**800-854-2766**	909-472-4100
International Institute of Municipal Clerks (IIMC) 8331 Utica Ave Suite 200	Rancho Cucamonga	CA	91730	**800-251-1639**	909-944-4162
International Municipal Signal Assn (IMSA) 165 E Union St PO Box 539	Newark	NY	14513	**800-723-4672**	315-331-2182
International Society of Fire Service Instructors (ISFSI) 2425 Hwy 49 E	Pleasant View	TN	37146	**800-435-0005**	
National Academy of Public Administration 1100 New York Ave NW Suite 1090 E	Washington	DC	20005	**800-883-3190**	202-347-3190
National American Indian Housing Council (NAIHC) 900 2nd St NE Suite 305	Washington	DC	20002	**800-284-9165**	202-789-1754
National Assn of Attorneys General (NAAG) 750 1st St NE Suite 1100	Washington	DC	20002	**888-245-6224**	202-326-6000
National Assn of Housing & Redevelopment Officials (NAHRO) 630 'I' St NW	Washington	DC	20001	**877-866-2476**	202-289-3500
National Assn of Social Workers (NASW) 750 1st St NE Suite 700	Washington	DC	20002	**800-638-8799**	202-408-8600
National Assn of State Fire Marshals (NASFM) PO Box 4137	Clifton Park	NY	12065	**877-996-2736**	518-371-0018
National Center for State Courts (NCSC) 300 Newport Ave	Williamsburg	VA	23185	**800-616-6164**	757-253-2000
National Conference of States on Building Codes & Standards (NCSBCS) 505 Huntmar Park Dr Suite 210	Herndon	VA	20170	**800-362-2633**	703-437-0100
National Fire Protection Assn (NFPA) 1 Batterymarch Pk	Quincy	MA	02169	**800-344-3555**	617-770-3000
National Institute of Governmental Purchasing (NIGP) 151 Spring St Suite 300	Herndon	VA	20170	**800-367-6447**	703-736-8900
National Sheriffs' Assn (NSA) 1450 Duke St	Alexandria	VA	22314	**800-424-7827**	703-836-7827
National Volunteer Fire Council (NVFC) 1050 17th St NW Suite 490	Washington	DC	20036	**888-275-6832**	202-887-5700
Northwestern University Center for Public Safety (NUCPS) 600 Foster	Evanston	IL	60204	**800-323-4011**	847-491-5476
Police Executive Research Forum (PERF) 1120 Connecticut Ave NW Suite 930	Washington	DC	20036	**888-202-4563**	202-466-7820
Public Technology Inc 1301 Pennsylvania Ave NW Suite 800	Washington	DC	20004	**800-852-4934**	202-626-2400

49-8 Health & Medical Professionals Associations

Organization / Address	City	State	Zip	Toll-Free	Phone
Academy of General Dentistry (AGD) 211 E Chicago Ave Suite 900	Chicago	IL	60611	**888-243-3368**	312-440-4300
Academy of Managed Care Pharmacy (AMCP) 100 N Pitt St Suite 400	Alexandria	VA	22314	**800-827-2627**	703-683-8416
Academy of Osseointegration 85 W Algonquin Rd Suite 550	Arlington Heights	IL	60005	**800-656-7736**	847-439-1919
Academy of Students of Pharmacy American Pharmacists Assn 2215 Constitution Ave NW	Washington	DC	20037	**800-237-2742**	202-628-4410
AHA (American Hospital Assn) 1 N Franklin St	Chicago	IL	60606	**800-424-4301**	312-422-3000
AMA (American Medical Assn) 515 N State St	Chicago	IL	60610	**800-621-8335**	312-464-5000
American Academy of Allergy Asthma & Immunology (AAAAI) 611 E Wells St 4th Fl	Milwaukee	WI	53202	**800-822-2762**	414-272-6071
American Academy of Ambulatory Care Nursing (AAACN) 200 E Holly Ave Box 56	Pitman	NJ	08080	**800-262-6877**	856-256-2350
American Academy of Audiology (AAA) 11730 Plaza America Dr Suite 300	Reston	VA	22190	**800-222-2336**	703-790-8466
American Academy of Cosmetic Dentistry (AACD) 5401 World Dairy Dr	Madison	WI	53718	**800-543-9220**	608-222-8583
American Academy of Disability Evaluating Physicians (AADEP) 150 N Wacker Dr Suite 1420	Chicago	IL	60606	**800-456-6095**	312-658-1171
American Academy of Facial Plastic & Reconstructive Surgery (AAFPRS) 310 S Henry St	Alexandria	VA	22314	**800-332-3223**	703-299-9291
American Academy of Family Physicians (AAFP) 11400 Tomahawk Creek Pkwy	Leawood	KS	66211	**800-274-2237**	913-906-6000
American Academy of Neurology (AAN) 1080 Montreal Ave	Saint Paul	MN	55116	**800-879-1960**	651-695-2717
American Academy of Ophthalmology 655 Beach St	San Francisco	CA	94109	**800-222-3937**	415-561-8500
American Academy of Pediatrics (AAP) 141 Northwest Point Blvd	Elk Grove Village	IL	60007	**800-433-9016**	847-434-4000
American Academy of Periodontology (AAP) 737 N Michigan Ave Suite 800	Chicago	IL	60611	**800-282-4867**	312-787-5518
American Assn of Colleges of Podiatric Medicine (AACPM) 1350 Piccard Dr Suite 322	Rockville	MD	20850	**800-922-9266**	301-990-7400
American Assn of Critical-Care Nurses (AACN) 101 Columbia	Aliso Viejo	CA	92656	**800-809-2273**	949-362-2000
American Assn of Diabetes Educators (AADE) 100 W Monroe St Suite 400	Chicago	IL	60603	**800-338-3633**	312-424-2426
American Assn of Endodontists (AAE) 211 E Chicago Ave Suite 1100	Chicago	IL	60611	**800-872-3636**	312-266-7255
American Assn of Gynecological Laparoscopists (AAGL) 13021 E Florence Ave	Santa Fe Springs	CA	90670	**800-554-2245**	562-946-8774
American Assn of Healthcare Consultants (AAHC) 5938 N Drake Ave	Chicago	IL	60659	**888-350-2242**	
American Assn of Medical Assistants (AAMA) 20 N Wacker Dr Suite 1575	Chicago	IL	60606	**800-228-2262**	312-899-1500
American Assn of Medical Review Officers (AAMRO) PO Box 12873	Research Triangle Park	NC	27709	**800-489-1839**	919-489-5407
American Assn for Medical Transcription (AAMT) 100 Sycamore Ave	Modesto	CA	95354	**800-982-2182**	209-527-9620
American Assn of Neurological Surgeons (AANS) 5550 Meadowbrook Dr	Rolling Meadows	IL	60068	**888-566-2267**	847-378-0500
American Assn of Neuroscience Nurses (AANN) 4700 W Lake Ave	Glenview	IL	60025	**888-557-2266**	847-375-4733
American Assn of Nutritional Consultants (AANC) 401 Kings Hwy	Winona Lake	IN	46590	**888-828-2262**	574-269-6165
American Assn of Occupational Health Nurses (AAOHN) 2920 Brandywine Rd Suite 100	Atlanta	GA	30341	**888-646-4631**	770-455-7757
American Assn of Oral & Maxillofacial Surgeons (AAOMS) 9700 W Bryn Mawr Ave	Rosemont	IL	60018	**800-822-6637**	847-678-6200
American Assn of Oriental Medicine (AAOM) PO Box 162340	Sacramento	CA	95816	**866-455-7999**	916-443-4770
American Assn of Orthodontists (AAO) 401 N Lindbergh Blvd	Saint Louis	MO	63141	**800-424-2841**	314-993-1700
American Assn of Physician Specialists Inc (AAPS) 2296 Henderson Mill Rd Suite 206	Atlanta	GA	30345	**800-447-9397**	770-939-8555
American Assn of Poison Control Centers (AAPCC) 3201 New Mexico Ave Suite 330	Washington	DC	20016	**800-222-1222**	202-362-7217
American Autoimmune Related Disease Assn (AARDA) 22100 Gratiot Ave	Eastpointe	MI	48021	**800-598-4668**	586-776-3900
American Burn Assn (ABA) 625 N Michigan Ave Suite 1530	Chicago	IL	60611	**800-548-2876**	312-642-9260
American Cancer Society (ACS) 1599 Clifton Rd NE	Atlanta	GA	30329	**800-227-2345**	404-320-3333
American Chiropractic Assn (ACA) 1701 Clarendon Blvd 2nd Fl	Arlington	VA	22209	**800-986-4636**	703-276-8800
American Cleft Palate-Craniofacial Assn 104 S Estes Dr Suite 204	Chapel Hill	NC	27514	**800-242-5338**	919-933-9044
American College for Advancement in Medicine (ACAM) 23121 Verdugo Dr Suite 204	Laguna Hills	CA	92653	**800-532-3688**	949-583-7666
American College of Allergy Asthma & Immunology (ACAAI) 85 W Algonquin Rd Suite 550	Arlington Heights	IL	60005	**800-842-7777**	847-427-1200
American College of Cardiology (ACC) 9111 Old Georgetown Rd *Cust Svc	Bethesda	MD	20814	**800-253-4636***	301-897-5400
American College of Chest Physicians (ACCP) 3300 Dundee Rd	Northbrook	IL	60062	**800-343-2227**	847-498-1400
American College of Dentists (ACD) 839 Quince Orchard Blvd Suite J	Gaithersburg	MD	20878	**888-223-1920**	301-977-3223
American College of Emergency Physicians (ACEP) PO Box 619911	Dallas	TX	75261	**800-798-1822**	972-550-0911
American College of Eye Surgeons (ACES) 334 E Lake Rd Suite 135	Palm Lake Harbor	FL	34685	**888-335-0077**	727-480-8542
American College of Foot & Ankle Surgeons (ACFAS) 8725 W Higgins Rd Suite 555	Chicago	IL	60631	**800-421-2237**	773-693-9300
American College of Health Care Administrators (ACHCA) 300 N Lee St Suite 301	Alexandria	VA	22314	**888-882-2422**	703-739-7900

Health & Medical Professionals Associations (Cont'd)

Organization	City	State	Zip	Toll-Free	Phone
American College of Osteopathic Family Physicians (ACOFP) 330 E Algonquin Rd Suite 1	Arlington Heights	IL	60005	**800-323-0794**	847-228-6090
American College of Physician Executives (ACPE) 4890 W Kennedy Blvd Suite 200	Tampa	FL	33609	**800-562-8088**	813-287-2000
American College of Physicians (ACP) 190 N Independence Mall W	Philadelphia	PA	19106	**800-523-1546**	215-351-2400
American College of Radiology (ACR) 1891 Preston White Dr	Reston	VA	20191	**800-227-5463**	703-648-8900
American College of Surgeons (ACS) 633 N Saint Clair St	Chicago	IL	60611	**800-621-4111**	312-202-5000
American Dental Hygienists' Assn (ADHA) 444 N Michigan Ave Suite 3400	Chicago	IL	60611	**800-243-2342**	312-440-8900
American Diabetes Assn (ADA) 1701 N Beauregard St	Alexandria	VA	22311	**800-232-3472**	703-549-1500
American Dietetic Assn (ADA) 120 S Riverside Plaza Suite 2000	Chicago	IL	60606	**800-877-1600**	312-899-0040
American Federation for Aging Research (AFAR) 70 W 40th St 11th Fl	New York	NY	10018	**888-582-2327**	212-703-9977
American Health Care Assn (AHCA) 1201 L St NW	Washington	DC	20005	**800-321-0343**	202-842-4444
American Health Information Management Assn (AHIMA) 233 N Michigan Ave Suite 2150	Chicago	IL	60601	**800-335-5535**	312-233-1100
American Healthcare Radiology Administrators (AHRA) 490-B Boston Post Rd Suite 101	Sudbury	MA	01776	**800-334-2472**	978-443-7591
American Heart Assn (AHA) 7272 Greenville Ave	Dallas	TX	75231	**800-242-8721**	214-373-6300
American Hospital Assn (AHA) 1 N Franklin St	Chicago	IL	60606	**800-424-4301**	312-422-3000
American Institute of Ultrasound in Medicine (AIUM) 14750 Sweitzer Ln Suite 100	Laurel	MD	20707	**800-638-5352**	301-498-4100
American Lung Assn (ALA) 61 Broadway 6th Fl	New York	NY	10006	**800-586-4872**	212-315-8700
American Medical Assn (AMA) 515 N State St	Chicago	IL	60610	**800-621-8335**	312-464-5000
American Medical Directors Assn (AMDA) 10480 Little Patuxent Pkwy Suite 760	Columbia	MD	21044	**800-876-2632**	410-740-9743
American Medical Rehabilitation Providers Assn (AMRPA) 1710 'N' St NW	Washington	DC	20036	**888-346-4624**	202-223-1920
American Medical Technologists (AMT) 710 Higgins Rd	Park Ridge	IL	60068	**800-275-1268**	847-823-5169
American Nephrology Nurses' Assn (ANNA) 200 E Holly Ave	Pitman	NJ	08080	**888-600-2662**	856-256-2320
American Nurses Assn (ANA) 8515 Georgia Ave Suite 400	Silver Spring	MD	20910	**800-274-4262**	301-628-5000
American Orthopaedic Society for Sports Medicine (AOSSM) 6300 N River Rd Suite 500	Rosemont	IL	60018	**877-321-3500**	847-292-4900
American Osteopathic Assn (AOA) 142 E Ontario St	Chicago	IL	60611	**800-621-1773**	312-202-8000
American Pharmacists Assn (APhA) 2215 Constitution Ave NW	Washington	DC	20037	**800-237-2742**	202-628-4410
American Physical Therapy Assn (APTA) 1111 N Fairfax St	Alexandria	VA	22314	**800-999-2782**	703-684-2782
American Podiatric Medical Assn (APMA) 9312 Old Georgetown Rd	Bethesda	MD	20814	**800-275-2762**	301-571-9200
American Professional Practice Assn (APPA) 350 Fairway Dr Suite 200	Deerfield Beach	FL	33441	**800-221-2168**	954-571-1877
American Prosthodontic Society (APS) 426 Hudson St	Hackensack	NJ	07601	**877-499-3500**	201-440-7699
American Registry of Diagnostic Medical Sonographers (ARDMS) 51 Monroe St Plaza East 1	Rockville	MD	20850	**800-541-9754**	301-738-8401
American Roentgen Ray Society (ARRS) 44211 Slatestone Ct	Leesburg	VA	20176	**800-438-2777**	703-729-3353
American Society for Aesthetic Plastic Surgery (ASAPS) 11081 Winners Cir	Los Alamitos	CA	90720	**800-364-2147**	562-799-2356
American Society of Cataract & Refractive Surgery (ASCRS) 4000 Legato Rd Suite 850	Fairfax	VA	22033	**800-451-1339**	703-591-2220
American Society for Clinical Investigation (ASCI) 35 Research Dr Suite 300	Ann Arbor	MI	48103	**866-660-2724**	734-222-6050
American Society of Clinical Oncology (ASCO) 1900 Duke St Suite 200	Alexandria	VA	22314	**888-282-2552**	703-299-0150
American Society for Clinical Pathology (ASCP) 2100 W Harrison St *Cust Svc	Chicago	IL	60612	**800-621-4142***	312-738-1336
American Society for Colposcopy & Cervical Pathology (ASCCP) 20 W Washington St Suite 1	Hagerstown	MD	21740	**800-787-7227**	301-733-3640
American Society of Consultant Pharmacists (ASCP) 1321 Duke St	Alexandria	VA	22314	**800-355-2727**	703-739-1300
American Society of Contemporary Medicine Surgery & Ophthalmology 820 N Orleans St Suite 208	Chicago	IL	60610	**800-621-4002**	312-440-0699
American Society for Parenteral & Enteral Nutrition (ASPEN) 8630 Fenton St Suite 412	Silver Spring	MD	20910	**800-727-4567**	301-587-6315
American Society of PeriAnesthesia Nurses (ASPAN) 10 Melrose Ave Suite 110	Cherry Hill	NJ	08003	**877-737-9696**	856-616-9600
American Society of Plastic Surgeons (ASPS) 444 E Algonquin Rd	Arlington Heights	IL	60005	**888-475-2784**	847-228-9900
American Society of Radiologic Technologists (ASRT) 15000 Central Ave SE	Albuquerque	NM	87123	**800-444-2778**	505-298-4500
American Society for Surgery of the Hand (ASSH) 6300 N River Rd Suite 600	Rosemont	IL	60018	**888-576-2774**	847-384-8300
American Society for Therapeutic Radiology & Oncology (ASTRO) 12500 Fair Lakes Cir Suite 375	Fairfax	VA	22033	**800-962-7876**	703-502-1550
American Speech-Language-Hearing Assn (ASHA) 10801 Rockville Pike	Rockville	MD	20852	**800-498-2071**	301-897-5700
American Trauma Society 8903 Presidential Pkwy Suite 512	Upper Marlboro	MD	20772	**800-556-7890**	301-420-4189
American Urological Assn (AUA) 1000 Corporate Blvd	Linthicum	MD	21090	**866-746-4282**	410-689-3700
America's Blood Centers (ABC) 725 15th St NW Suite 700	Washington	DC	20005	**888-872-5663**	202-393-5725
AORN Inc 2170 S Parker Rd Suite 300	Denver	CO	80231	**800-755-2676**	303-755-6300
Association for the Advancement of Medical Instrumentation (AAMI) 1110 N Glebe Rd Suite 220	Arlington	VA	22201	**800-332-2264**	703-525-4890
Association for Applied Psychophysiology & Biofeedback (AAPB) 10200 W 44th Ave Suite 304	Wheat Ridge	CO	80033	**800-477-8892**	303-422-8436

Organization	City	State	Zip	Toll-Free	Phone
Association of Emergency Physicians (AEP) 911 Whitewater Dr	Mars	PA	16046	**866-772-1818**	724-772-1818
Association of Military Surgeons of the US (AMSUS) 9320 Old Georgetown Rd	Bethesda	MD	20814	**800-761-9320**	301-897-8800
Association of Nurses in AIDS Care (ANAC) 3538 Ridgewood Rd	Akron	OH	44333	**800-260-6780**	330-670-0101
Association for Professionals in Infection Control & Epidemiology Inc (APIC) 1275 K St NW Suite 1000	Washington	DC	20005	**888-278-2742**	202-789-1890
Association of Program Directors in Internal Medicine (APDIM) 2501 M St NW Suite 550	Washington	DC	20037	**800-622-4558**	202-887-9450
Association of Schools of Allied Health Professions (ASAHP) 1730 M St NW Suite 500	Washington	DC	20036	**800-497-8080**	202-293-4848
Association of Staff Physician Recruiters (ASPR) 1711 W County Rd B Suite 300N	Roseville	MN	55113	**800-830-2777**	651-635-0359
Association of Women's Health Obstetric & Neonatal Nurses (AWHONN) 2000 L St NW Suite 740	Washington	DC	20036	**800-673-8499**	202-261-2400
Asthma & Allergy Foundation of America (AAFA) 1233 20th St NW Suite 402	Washington	DC	20036	**800-727-8462**	202-466-7643
Canadian Academy of Sport Medicine 1010 Polytek St Unit 14 Suite 100	Ottawa	ON	K1J9H9	**877-585-2394**	613-748-5851
Canadian Assn of Emergency Physicians (CAEP) 1785 Alta Vista Dr Suite 104	Ottawa	ON	K1G3Y6	**800-463-1158**	613-523-3343
Children's Hospice International (CHI) 901 N Pitt St Suite 230	Alexandria	VA	22314	**800-242-4453**	703-684-0330
College of American Pathologists (CAP) 325 Waukegan Rd	Northfield	IL	60093	**800-323-4040**	847-832-7000
Commission on Office Laboratory Accreditation (COLA) 9881 Broken Land Pkwy Suite 200	Columbia	MD	21046	**800-981-9883**	410-381-6581
Emergency Nurses Assn 915 Lee St	Des Plaines	IL	60016	**800-900-9659**	847-460-4000
Federation of State Medical Boards of the US Inc (FSMB) 400 Fuller Wiser Rd Suite 300	Euless	TX	76039	**800-876-5396**	817-868-4000
Gynecologic Oncology Group (GOG) 1600 JFK Blvd Suite 1020	Philadelphia	PA	19103	**800-225-3053**	215-854-0770
Healthcare Financial Management Assn (HFMA) 2 Westbrook Corporate Ctr Suite 700	Westchester	IL	60154	**800-252-4362**	708-531-9600
Hospice Foundation of America (HFA) 1621 Connecticut Ave NW Suite 300	Washington	DC	20009	**800-854-3402**	202-638-5419
Institute for the Advancement of Human Behavior (IAHB) 4370 Alpine Rd Suite 209	Portola Valley	CA	94028	**800-258-8411**	650-851-8411
International Academy of Compounding Pharmacists (IACP) PO Box 1365	Sugar Land	TX	77487	**800-927-4227**	281-933-8400
International Assn of Ocular Surgeons 820 N Orleans St Suite 208	Chicago	IL	60610	**800-621-4002**	312-440-0699
International Chiropractors Assn (ICA) 1110 N Glebe Rd Suite 1000	Arlington	VA	22201	**800-423-4690**	703-528-5000
International Congress of Oral Implantologists (ICOI) 248 Lorraine Ave 3rd Fl	Upper Montclair	NJ	07043	**800-442-0525**	973-783-6300
International Society for Peritoneal Dialysis (ISPD) 66 Martin St	Milton	ON	L9T2R2	**888-834-1001**	905-875-2456
Lamaze International 2025 M St NW Suite 800	Washington	DC	20036	**800-368-4404**	202-367-1128
Medical Group Management Assn (MGMA) 104 Inverness Terr E	Englewood	CO	80112	**877-275-6462**	303-799-1111
National Abortion Federation (NAF) 1755 Massachusetts Ave NW Suite 600	Washington	DC	20036	**800-772-9100**	202-667-5881
National Assn of Dental Laboratories (NADL) 325 John Knox Rd Suite L-103	Tallahassee	FL	32303	**800-950-1150**	850-205-5626
National Assn of Directors of Nursing Administration in Long Term Care (NADONA/LTC) 10101 Alliance Rd Suite 140	Cincinnati	OH	45242	**800-222-0539**	513-791-3679
National Assn for Healthcare Quality (NAHQ) 4700 W Lake Ave	Glenview	IL	60025	**800-966-9392**	847-375-4720
National Assn of Managed Care Physicians (NAMCP) 4435 Waterfront Dr Suite 101 PO Box 4765	Glen Allen	VA	23058	**800-722-0376**	804-527-1905
National Assn of Neonatal Nurses (NANN) 4700 W Lake Ave	Glenview	IL	60025	**800-451-3795**	847-375-3660
National Assn of Orthopaedic Nurses (NAON) 401 N Michigan Ave Suite 2200	Chicago	IL	60611	**800-289-6266**	
National Assn of Physician Recruiters (NAPR) PO Box 150127	Altamonte Springs	FL	32715	**800-726-5613**	407-774-7880
National Assn of School Nurses (NASN) PO Box 1300	Scarborough	ME	04070	**877-627-6476**	207-883-2117
National Assn of Vascular Access Networks (NAVAN) 11441 S State St Suite A113	Draper	UT	84020	**888-576-2826**	801-576-1824
National Community Pharmacists Assn (NCPA) 100 Daingerfield Rd	Alexandria	VA	22314	**800-544-7447**	703-683-8200
National Council on Problem Gambling Inc 208 G St NE 1st Fl	Washington	DC	20002	**800-522-4700**	202-547-9204
National Home Infusion Assn (NHIA) 205 Daingerfield Rd	Alexandria	VA	22314	**800-544-7447**	703-549-3740
National Hospice & Palliative Care Organization (NHPCO) 1700 Diagonal Rd Suite 625 *Help Line	Alexandria	VA	22314	**800-658-8898***	703-837-1500
National Kidney Foundation (NKF) 30 E 33rd St Suite 1100	New York	NY	10016	**800-622-9010**	212-889-2210
National League for Nursing (NLN) 61 Broadway	New York	NY	10006	**800-669-1656**	212-363-5555
National Medical Assn (NMA) 1012 10th St NW	Washington	DC	20001	**800-662-0554**	202-347-1895
National Nursing Staff Development Organization (NNSDO) 7794 Grow Dr	Pensacola	FL	32514	**800-489-1995**	850-474-0995
National Organization for Rare Disorders (NORD) 55 Kenosia Ave PO Box 1968	Danbury	CT	06813	**800-999-6673**	203-744-0100
National Pharmacy Technicians Assn (NPTA) 3920 FM 1960 W Suite 380	Houston	TX	77068	**888-247-8700**	281-866-7900
North American Menopause Society (NAMS) 5900 Landerbrook Dr Suite 195	Mayfield Heights	OH	44124	**800-774-5342**	440-442-7550
North American Spine Society (NASS) 22 Calendar Ct 2nd Fl	La Grange	IL	60525	**877-774-6337**	708-588-8080
Oncology Nursing Society (ONS) 125 Enterprise Dr	Pittsburgh	PA	15275	**866-257-4667**	412-859-6100
Optical Laboratories Assn (OLA) 11096-A Lee Hwy Suite 101	Fairfax	VA	22030	**800-477-5652**	703-359-2830

Classified Section

				Toll-Free	Phone
Optical Society of America (OSA) 2010 Massachusetts Ave NW	Washington	DC	20036	800-762-6960	202-223-8130
Opticians Assn of America (OAA) 12100 Sunset Hills Rd Suite 130	Reston	VA	20190	800-443-8997	703-437-4377
Physicians' Committee for Responsible Medicine (PCRM) 5100 Wisconsin Ave NW Suite 400	Washington	DC	20016	866-416-7276	202-686-2210
Radiology Business Management Assn (RBMA) 8001 Irvine Center Dr Suite 1060	Irvine	CA	92618	888-224-7262	949-340-5000
Society of Diagnostic Medical Sonography (SDMS) 2745 N Dallas Pkwy Suite 350	Plano	TX	75093	800-229-9506	214-473-8057
Society of Gastroenterology Nurses & Associates Inc (SGNA) 401 N Michigan Ave	Chicago	IL	60611	800-245-7462	312-321-5165
Society for Healthcare Strategy & Market Development American Hospital Assn 1 N Franklin St 28th Fl	Chicago	IL	60606	800-242-2626	312-422-3888
Society of Interventional Radiology (SIR) 10201 Lee Hwy Suite 500	Fairfax	VA	22030	800-488-7284	703-691-1805
Society of Laparoendoscopic Surgeons (SLS) 7330 SW 62nd Pl Suite 410	South Miami	FL	33143	800-446-2659	305-665-9959
Southern Medical Assn (SMA) 35 Lakeshore Dr	Birmingham	AL	35209	800-423-4992	205-945-1840
US Pharmacopeia (USP) 12601 Twinbrook Pkwy	Rockville	MD	20852	800-877-6209	301-881-0666
Visiting Nurse Assns of America (VNAA) 99 Summer St Suite 1700	Boston	MA	02110	800-426-2547	617-737-3200
Wound Ostomy & Continence Nurses Society (WOCN) 4700 W Lake Ave	Glenview	IL	60025	888-224-9626	

49-9 Insurance Industry Associations

				Toll-Free	Phone
ACORD PO Box 1529	Pearl River	NY	10965	800-444-3341	845-620-1700
American Assn of Insurance Services (AAIS) 1745 S Naperville Rd	Wheaton	IL	60187	800-564-2247	630-681-8347
American Institute for CPCU & Insurance Institute of America (AICPCU/IIA) 720 Providence Rd PO Box 3016	Malvern	PA	19355	800-644-2101	610-644-2100
American Nuclear Insurers (ANI) 95 Glastonbury Blvd	Glastonbury	CT	06033	888-561-3433	860-682-1301
America's Health Insurance Plans (AHIP) 601 Pennsylvania Ave NW Suite 500	Washington	DC	20004	877-291-2247*	202-778-3200
*Cust Svc					
Association for Advanced Life Underwriting (AALU) 2901 Telestar Ct	Falls Church	VA	22042	888-275-0092	703-641-9400
CPCU Society 720 Providence Rd Kahler Hall PO Box 3009	Malvern	PA	19355	800-932-2728	
GAMA International 2901 Telestar Ct	Falls Church	VA	22042	800-345-2687*	703-770-8184
*Cust Svc					
Independent Insurance Agents & Brokers of America Inc (IIABA) 127 S Peyton St	Alexandria	VA	22314	800-221-7917	703-683-4422
Institute for Business & Home Safety (IBHS) 4775 E Fowler Ave	Tampa	FL	33617	866-675-4247	813-286-3400
Insurance Information Institute (III) 110 William St 24th Fl	New York	NY	10038	800-331-9146	212-346-5500
Insurance Research Council (IRC) 718 Providence Rd PO Box 3025	Malvern	PA	19355	800-644-2101	610-644-2212
LIMRA International Inc 300 Day Hill Rd	Windsor	CT	06095	800-285-7792*	860-688-3358
*Cust Svc					
LOMA 2300 Windy Ridge Pkwy Suite 600	Atlanta	GA	30339	800-275-5662	770-951-1770
Million Dollar Round Table (MDRT) 325 W Touhy Ave	Park Ridge	IL	60068	800-879-6378	847-692-6378
National Assn of Insurance & Financial Advisors (NAIFA) 2901 Telestar Ct	Falls Church	VA	22042	877-866-2432*	703-770-8100
*Sales					
National Assn of Insurance Women (International) 1847 E 15th St	Tulsa	OK	74104	800-766-6249	918-744-5195
National Assn of Mutual Insurance Companies (NAMIC) 3601 Vincennes Rd PO Box 875525	Indianapolis	IN	46268	800-336-2642	317-875-5250
National Assn of Professional Insurance Agents (PIA) 400 N Washington St	Alexandria	VA	22314	800-742-6900	703-836-9340
National Crop Insurance Services (NCIS) 7201 W 129th St Suite 200	Overland Park	KS	66213	800-951-6247	913-685-2767
National Insurance Crime Bureau (NICB) 10330 S Roberts Rd	Palos Hills	IL	60465	800-447-6282	708-430-2430
NCIS (National Crop Insurance Services) 7201 W 129th St Suite 200	Overland Park	KS	66213	800-951-6247	913-685-2767
Professional Liability Underwriting Society 5353 Wayzata Blvd Suite 600	Minneapolis	MN	55416	800-845-0778	952-746-2580
Reinsurance Assn of America (RAA) 1301 Pennsylvania Ave NW Suite 900	Washington	DC	20004	800-638-3651	202-638-3690
Risk & Insurance Management Society Inc (RIMS) 655 3rd Ave 2nd Fl	New York	NY	10017	800-711-0317	212-286-9292
Self-Insurance Institute of America Inc (SIIA) PO Box 1237	Simpsonville	SC	29681	800-851-7789	864-962-2208
Society of Certified Insurance Counselors PO Box 27027	Austin	TX	78755	800-633-2165	512-345-7932
Society of Financial Service Professionals (SFSP) 270 S Bryn Mawr Ave	Bryn Mawr	PA	19010	800-392-6900	610-526-2500
Viatical & Life Settlement Assn of America (VLSAA) 800 Mayfair Cir	Orlando	FL	32803	800-842-9811	407-894-3797
Workmen's Circle/Arbeter Ring 45 E 33rd St 4th Fl	New York	NY	10016	800-922-2558	212-889-6800

49-10 Legal Professionals Associations

				Toll-Free	Phone
ABA (American Bar Assn) 750 N Lake Shore Dr	Chicago	IL	60611	800-285-2221	312-988-5000
ABA Commission on Domestic Violence 740 15th St NW 9th Fl	Washington	DC	20005	800-799-7233	202-662-1737
American Academy of Psychiatry & the Law (AAPL) 1 Regency Dr PO Box 30	Bloomfield	CT	06002	800-331-1389	860-242-5450
American Arbitration Assn Inc (AAA) 335 Madison Ave 10th Fl	New York	NY	10017	800-778-7879	212-716-5800
American Bar Assn (ABA) 750 N Lake Shore Dr	Chicago	IL	60611	800-285-2221	312-988-5000
American Land Title Assn (ALTA) 1828 L St NW Suite 705	Washington	DC	20036	800-787-2582	202-296-3671
American Law Institute (ALI) 4025 Chestnut St	Philadelphia	PA	19104	800-253-6397	215-243-1600
Association of Trial Lawyers of America (ATLA) 1050 31st St NW	Washington	DC	20007	800-424-2725	202-965-3500
Battered Women's Justice Project 2104 4th Ave S Suite B	Minneapolis	MN	55404	800-903-0111	612-824-8768
Commercial Law League of America (CLLA) 150 N Michigan Ave Suite 600	Chicago	IL	60601	800-978-2552	312-781-2000
Defense Research Institute (DRI) 150 N Michigan Ave Suite 300	Chicago	IL	60601	800-667-8108	312-795-1101
Environmental Law Institute (ELI) 2000 L St NW Suite 620	Washington	DC	20036	800-433-5120	202-939-3800
False Claims Act Legal Center 1220 19th St NW Suite 501	Washington	DC	20036	800-873-2573	202-296-4826
Food & Drug Law Institute (FDLI) 1000 Vermont Ave NW Suite 200	Washington	DC	20005	800-956-6293	202-371-1420
Hispanic National Bar Assn (HNBA) 815 Connecticut Ave NW Suite 500	Washington	DC	20006	877-221-6569	202-223-4777
Law Firm Services Assn (LFSA) 10831 Old Mill Rd Suite 400	Omaha	NE	68154	800-475-4476	402-778-7922
National Assn for Court Management (NACM) National Ctr for State Courts 300 Newport Ave	Williamsburg	VA	23185	800-616-6165	757-259-1841
National Assn of Enrolled Agents (NAEA) 1120 Connecticut Ave NW Suite 460	Washington	DC	20036	800-424-4339	202-822-6232
National Assn of Estate Planners & Councils (NAEPC) 1120 Chester Ave Suite 470	Cleveland	OH	44114	866-226-2224	
National Assn of Professional Process Servers (NAPPS) PO Box 4547	Portland	OR	97208	800-477-8211	503-222-4180
National Bar Assn (NBA) 1225 11th St NW	Washington	DC	20001	800-621-2988	202-842-3900
National Center for Juvenile Justice (NCJJ) 3700 S Water St Suite 200	Pittsburgh	PA	15203	800-577-6903	412-227-6950
National Court Reporters Assn (NCRA) 8224 Old Courthouse Rd	Vienna	VA	22182	800-272-6272	703-556-6272
National Network of Estate Planning Attorneys Inc (NNEPA) 1 Valmont Plaza 4th Fl	Omaha	NE	68154	888-837-4090	402-964-3700
Practising Law Institute (PLI) 810 7th Ave 26th Fl	New York	NY	10019	800-260-4754	212-824-5700
Taxpayers Against Fraud Education Fund (TAF) 1220 19th St NW Suite 501	Washington	DC	20036	800-873-2573	202-296-4826

49-11 Library & Information Science Associations

				Toll-Free	Phone
American Assn of School Librarians (AASL) 50 E Huron St	Chicago	IL	60611	800-545-2433	312-280-4386
American Library Assn (ALA) 50 E Huron St	Chicago	IL	60611	800-545-2433	312-944-6780
American Theological Library Assn (ATLA) 250 S Wacker Dr Suite 1600	Chicago	IL	60606	888-665-2852	312-454-5100
Association of College & Research Libraries (ACRL) 50 E Huron St	Chicago	IL	60611	800-545-2433	312-280-2519
Association for Library Collections & Technical Services (ALCTS) 50 E Huron St	Chicago	IL	60611	800-545-2433	312-280-5038
Association for Library Service to Children (ALSC) 50 E Huron St	Chicago	IL	60611	800-545-2433	312-280-2163
Association for Library Trustees & Advocates (ALTA) 50 E Huron St	Chicago	IL	60611	800-545-2433	312-280-2161
Association of Specialized & Cooperative Library Agencies (ASCLA) 50 E Huron St	Chicago	IL	60611	800-545-2433	312-280-4395
Friends of Libraries USA (FOLUSA) 1420 Walnut St Suite 450	Philadelphia	PA	19102	800-936-5872	215-790-1674
Library Administration & Management Assn (LAMA) 50 E Huron St	Chicago	IL	60611	800-545-2433	312-280-5036
Library & Information Technology Assn (LITA) 50 E Huron St	Chicago	IL	60611	800-545-2433	312-280-4270
Online Computer Library Center Inc (OCLC) 6565 Frantz Rd	Dublin	OH	43017	800-848-5878	614-764-6000
Public Library Assn (PLA) 50 E Huron St	Chicago	IL	60611	800-545-2433	312-280-5752
Reference & User Services Assn (RUSA) 50 E Huron St	Chicago	IL	60611	800-545-2433	312-280-4398
Young Adult Library Services Assn (YALSA) 50 E Huron St	Chicago	IL	60611	800-545-2433	312-280-4390

49-12 Management & Business Professional Associations

				Toll-Free	Phone
American Business Women's Assn (ABWA) 9100 Ward Pkwy	Kansas City	MO	64114	800-228-0007	816-361-6621
American Businesspersons Assn (ABA) 350 Fairway Dr Suite 200	Deerfield Beach	FL	33441	800-221-2168	954-571-1877
American Cash Flow Assn (ACFA) 255 S Orange Ave Suite 600	Orlando	FL	32801	800-253-1294	407-206-6523
American Chamber of Commerce Executives (ACCE) 4875 Eisenhower Ave Suite 250	Alexandria	VA	22304	800-394-2223	703-998-0072
American Management Assn (AMA) 1601 Broadway	New York	NY	10019	800-262-9699	212-586-8100
American Seminar Leaders Assn (ASLA) 2405 E Washington Blvd	Pasadena	CA	91104	800-735-0511	626-791-1211
American Small Businesses Assn (ASBA) 206 E College St Suite 201B	Grapevine	TX	76051	800-942-2722	817-488-8770
American Society of Association Executives (ASAE) 1575 'I' St NW	Washington	DC	20005	888-950-2723	202-626-2723
APQC 123 Post Oak Ln 3rd Fl	Houston	TX	77024	800-776-9676	713-681-4020
ARMA International 13725 W 109th St Suite 101	Lenexa	KS	66215	800-422-2762	913-341-3808
Association for Corporate Growth (ACG) 1926 Waukegan Rd Suite 1	Glenview	IL	60025	800-699-1331	847-657-6730
Association of Executive Search Consultants (AESC) 12 E 41st St 17th Fl	New York	NY	10017	877-843-2372	212-398-9556
Association of Fundraising Professionals (AFP) 1101 King St Suite 700	Alexandria	VA	22314	800-666-3863	703-684-0410
Association for Manufacturing Technology (AMT) 7901 Westpark Dr	McLean	VA	22102	800-524-0475	703-893-2900
Association for Services Management International (AFSMI) 1342 Colonial Blvd Suite 25	Fort Myers	FL	33907	800-333-9786	239-275-7887

Management & Business Professional Associations (Cont'd)

Organization	City	State	Zip	Toll-Free	Phone
Business Executives for National Security (BENS) 1717 Pennsylvania Ave NW Suite 350	Washington	DC	20006	**800-296-2125**	202-296-2125
Chief Executives Organization 7920 Norfolk Ave Suite 400	Bethesda	MD	20814	**800-634-2655**	301-656-9220
Christian Management Assn 635 Camino De Los Mares Suite 205	San Clemente	CA	92673	**800-727-4262**	949-487-0900
Employee Relocation Council (ERC) 1717 Pennsylvania Ave NW Suite 800	Washington	DC	20006	**888-372-2255**	202-857-0857
ESOP Assn 1726 M St NW Suite 501	Washington	DC	20036	**866-366-3832**	202-293-2971
Institute of Business Appraisers (IBA) 6950 Cypress Rd Suite 209	Plantation	FL	33317	**800-299-4130**	954-584-1144
Institute of Certified Professional Managers (ICPM) James Madison University MSC 5504	Harrisonburg	VA	22807	**800-568-4120**	540-568-3247
Institute of Management Consultants USA Inc (IMC USA) 2025 M St NW Suite 800	Washington	DC	20036	**800-221-2557**	202-367-1134
Institute for Supply Management (ISM) 2055 Centennial Cir *Cust Svc	Tempe	AZ	85284	**800-888-6276***	480-752-6275
International Assn of Assembly Managers (IAAM) 635 Fritz Dr	Coppell	TX	75019	**800-935-4226**	972-906-7441
International Assn of Business Communicators (IABC) 1 Hallidie Plaza Suite 600	San Francisco	CA	94102	**800-766-4222**	415-544-4700
International Assn for Human Resource Information Management (IHRIM) PO Box 1086	Burlington	MA	01803	**800-946-6363**	781-273-3697
International Assn of Workforce Professionals (IAPES) 1801 Louisville Rd	Frankfort	KY	40601	**888-898-9960**	502-223-4459
International Customer Service Assn (ICSA) 401 N Michigan Ave 22nd Fl	Chicago	IL	60611	**800-360-4272**	312-321-6800
International Foundation of Employee Benefit Plans (IFEBP) 18700 W Bluemond Rd PO Box 69	Brookfield	WI	53008	**888-334-3327**	262-786-6700
International Public Management Assn for Human Resources (IPMA-HR) 1617 Duke St	Alexandria	VA	22314	**800-220-4762**	703-549-7100
International Society of Certified Employee Benefit Specialists (ISCEBS) 18700 W Bluemond Rd PO Box 209	Brookfield	WI	53008	**888-334-3327**	262-786-8771
National Assn of Certified Valuation Analysts (NACVA) 1111 E Brickyard Rd Suite 200	Salt Lake City	UT	84106	**800-677-2009**	801-486-0600
National Assn for Female Executives (NAFE) 60 E 42nd St 27th Fl	New York	NY	10165	**800-927-6233**	212-351-6400
National Assn of Manufacturers (NAM) 1331 Pennsylvania Ave NW Suite 600	Washington	DC	20004	**800-814-8468**	202-637-3000
National Assn of Parliamentarians (NAP) 213 S Main St	Independence	MO	64050	**888-627-2929**	816-833-3892
National Assn for the Self-Employed (NASE) PO Box 612067 DFW Airport	Dallas	TX	75261	**800-232-6273**	
National Assn of Women Business Owners (NAWBO) 8405 Greensboro Dr Suite 800	McLean	VA	22102	**800-556-2926**	703-506-3268
National Business Assn (NBA) 5151 Beltline Rd Suite 1150	Dallas	TX	75254	**800-456-0440**	972-458-0900
National Contract Management Assn (NCMA) 8260 Greensboro Dr Suite 200	McLean	VA	22102	**800-344-8096**	571-382-0082
National Federation of Independent Business (NFIB) 1201 F St NW Suite 200	Washington	DC	20004	**800-552-6342**	202-554-9000
National Notary Assn (NNA) 9350 DeSoto Ave	Chatsworth	CA	91313	**800-876-6827**	818-739-4000
National Right to Work Committee (NRTWC) 8001 Braddock Rd Suite 500	Springfield	VA	22160	**800-325-7892**	703-321-8510
National Small Business Assn (NSBA) 1156 15th St NW Suite 1100	Washington	DC	20005	**800-345-6728**	202-393-8830
PRISM International 605 Benson Rd Suite B	Garner	NC	27529	**800-336-9793**	919-771-0657
Professional Convention Management Assn (PCMA) 2301 S Lake Shore Dr Suite 1001	Chicago	IL	60616	**877-827-7262**	312-423-7262
Professional Records & Information Services Management International 605 Benson Rd Suite B	Garner	NC	27529	**800-336-9793**	919-771-0657
Project Management Institute (PMI) 4 Campus Blvd	Newtown Square	PA	19073	**866-276-4764**	610-356-4600
SCORE Assn 409 3rd St SW 6th Fl	Washington	DC	20024	**800-634-0245**	202-205-6762
Society for Advancement of Management (SAM) Texas A&M Univ Corpus Christi College of Business 6300 Ocean Dr FC111	Corpus Christi	TX	78412	**888-827-6077**	361-825-6045
Society for Human Resource Management (SHRM) 1800 Duke St	Alexandria	VA	22314	**800-283-7476**	703-548-3440
TEC International Inc 11452 El Camino Real Suite 400	San Diego	CA	92130	**800-274-2367**	858-627-4050
WorldatWork 14040 N Northsight Blvd	Scottsdale	AZ	85260	**877-951-9191**	480-951-9191
Young Presidents' Organization (YPO) 451 S Decker Dr Suite 200	Irving	TX	75062	**800-773-7976**	972-650-4600

49-13 Manufacturing Industry Professional & Trade Associations

Organization	City	State	Zip	Toll-Free	Phone
American Foundry Society (AFS) 1695 N Penny Ln	Schaumburg	IL	60173	**800-537-4237**	847-824-0181
American Galvanizers Assn (AGA) 6881 S Holly Cir Suite 108	Centennial	CO	80112	**800-468-7732**	720-554-0900
American Society for Quality (ASQ) 600 N Plankinton Ave	Milwaukee	WI	53201	**800-248-1946**	414-272-8575
APICS - Assn for Operations Management 5301 Shawnee Rd	Alexandria	VA	22312	**800-444-2742**	703-354-8851
ASM International 9639 Kinsman Rd	Materials Park	OH	44073	**800-336-5152**	440-338-5151
Building Service Contractors Assn International (BSCAI) 10201 Lee Hwy Suite 225	Fairfax	VA	22030	**800-368-3414**	703-359-7090
Copper Development Assn Inc 260 Madison Ave 16th Fl	New York	NY	10016	**800-232-3282**	212-251-7200
Crane Manufacturers Assn of America (CMAA) 8720 Red Oak Blvd Suite 201	Charlotte	NC	28217	**800-345-1815**	704-676-1190
Embalming Chemical Manufacturers Assn 1370 Honeyspot Rd Ext	Stratford	CT	06615	**800-243-6104**	203-375-2984
Fabricators & Manufacturers Assn International (FMA) 833 Featherstone Rd	Rockford	IL	61107	**800-432-2832**	815-399-8700
Food Processing Machinery Assn (FPMA) 200 Daingerfield Rd	Alexandria	VA	22314	**800-833-4337**	703-684-1080
Independent Battery Manufacturers Assn (IBMA) 401 N Michigan Ave 24th Fl	Chicago	IL	60611	**800-237-6126**	312-245-1074
Industrial Fabrics Assn International (IFAI) 1801 County Rd 'B' W	Roseville	MN	55113	**800-225-4324**	651-222-2508
Institute of Caster & Wheel Manufacturers (ICWM) 8720 Red Oak Blvd Suite 201	Charlotte	NC	28217	**800-345-1815**	704-676-1190
Institute of Industrial Engineers (IIE) 3577 Parkway Ln Suite 200 *Cust Svc	Norcross	GA	30092	**800-494-0460***	770-449-0460
Institute of Packaging Professionals (IoPP) 1601 N Bond St Suite 101	Naperville	IL	60563	**800-432-4085**	630-544-5050
Institute of Paper Science & Technology (IPST) 500 10th St NW	Atlanta	GA	30332	**800-558-6611**	404-894-5700
International Ground Source Heat Pump Assn (IGSHPA) Oklahoma State University 374 Cordell S	Stillwater	OK	74078	**800-626-4747**	405-744-5175
Material Handling Industry of America (MHIA) 8720 Red Oak Blvd Suite 201	Charlotte	NC	28217	**800-345-1815**	704-676-1190
National Glass Assn (NGA) 8200 Greensboro Dr Suite 302	McLean	VA	22102	**866-342-5642**	703-442-4890
National Tooling & Machining Assn (NTMA) 9300 Livingston Rd	Fort Washington	MD	20744	**800-248-6862**	301-248-6200
Packaging Machinery Manufacturers Institute (PMMI) 4350 N Fairfax Dr Suite 600	Arlington	VA	22203	**800-275-7664**	703-243-8555
Reusable Industrial Packaging Assn (RIPA) 8401 Corporate Dr Suite 450	Landover	MD	20785	**800-533-3786**	301-577-3786
Sewn Products Equipment Suppliers Assn (SPESA) 5107 Falls of the Neuse Suite B15	Raleigh	NC	27609	**888-447-7372**	919-872-8909
Society of Manufacturing Engineers (SME) 1 SME Dr	Dearborn	MI	48121	**800-733-4763**	313-271-1500
Society for Mining Metallurgy & Exploration Inc (SME) 8307 Shaffer Pkwy	Littleton	CO	80127	**800-763-3132**	303-973-9550
Steel Tank Institute (STI) 570 Oakwood Rd	Lake Zurich	IL	60047	**800-275-1300**	847-438-8265
Technical Assn of the Pulp & Paper Industry (TAPPI) 15 Technology Pkwy S *Sales	Norcross	GA	30092	**800-332-8686***	770-446-1400
Vinyl Siding Institute (VSI) 1667 K St NW Suite 1000	Washington	DC	20006	**888-367-8741**	202-974-5200

49-14 Media Professionals Associations

Organization	City	State	Zip	Toll-Free	Phone
Accuracy in Media Inc (AIM) 4455 Connecticut Ave NW Suite 330	Washington	DC	20008	**800-787-4567**	202-364-4401
Association of Independents in Radio (AIR) 328 Flatbush Ave Suite 322	Brooklyn	NY	11238	**888-937-2477**	
Inter American Press Assn (IAPA) 1801 SW 3rd Ave 7th Fl	Miami	FL	33129	**877-747-4272**	305-634-2465
National Assn of Hispanic Journalists (NAHJ) 529 14th St NW National Press Bldg Suite 1000	Washington	DC	20045	**888-346-6245**	202-662-7145
National Cable Television Cooperative Inc (NCTC) 11200 Corporate Ave	Lenexa	KS	66219	**800-825-0357**	913-599-5900
National Federation of Community Broadcasters (NFCB) 970 Broadway Suite 1000	Oakland	CA	94612	**888-280-6322**	510-451-8200
National Newspaper Assn (NNA) Univ of Missouri 127 Neff Annex PO Box 7540	Columbia	MO	65205	**800-829-4662**	573-882-5800
Newsletter & Electronic Publishers Assn (NEPA) 1501 Wilson Blvd Suite 509	Arlington	VA	22209	**800-356-9302**	703-527-2333
Radio-Television News Directors Assn (RTNDA) 1600 K St NW Suite 700	Washington	DC	20006	**800-807-8632**	202-659-6510
Satellite Broadcasting & Communications Assn (SBCA) 1730 M St NW Suite 600	Washington	DC	20036	**800-541-5981**	202-349-3620

49-15 Mental Health Professionals Associations

Organization	City	State	Zip	Toll-Free	Phone
American Academy of Child & Adolescent Psychiatry (AACAP) 3615 Wisconsin Ave NW	Washington	DC	20016	**800-333-7636**	202-966-7300
American Academy of Psychiatry & the Law (AAPL) 1 Regency Dr PO Box 30	Bloomfield	CT	06002	**800-331-1389**	860-242-5450
American Council of Hypnotist Examiners 700 S Central Ave	Glendale	CA	91204	**800-894-9766**	818-242-1159
American Counseling Assn (ACA) 5999 Stevenson Ave	Alexandria	VA	22304	**800-347-6647**	703-823-9800
American Group Psychotherapy Assn (AGPA) 25 E 21st St 6th Fl	New York	NY	10010	**877-668-2472**	212-477-2677
American Mental Health Counselors Assn (AMHCA) 801 N Fairfax St Suite 304	Alexandria	VA	22314	**800-326-2642**	703-548-6002
American Psychiatric Assn (APA) 1000 Wilson Blvd Suite 1825	Arlington	VA	22209	**888-357-7924**	703-907-7300
American Psychological Assn (APA) 750 1st St NE	Washington	DC	20002	**800-374-2721**	202-336-5500
Association for Advancement of Behavior Therapy (AABT) 305 7th Ave 16th Fl	New York	NY	10001	**800-685-2228**	212-647-1890
International Assn of Marriage & Family Counselors (IAMFC) c/o American Counseling Assn 5999 Stevenson Ave	Alexandria	VA	22304	**800-545-2223**	703-823-9800
NAADAC - Assn for Addiction Professionals 901 N Washington St Suite 600	Alexandria	VA	22314	**800-548-0497**	703-741-7686
National Resource Center on Homelessness & Mental Illness (NRC) 345 Delaware Ave	Delmar	NY	12054	**800-444-7415**	518-439-7415
SAVE - Suicide Awareness Voices of Education 9001 Bloomington Fwy Suite 150	Bloomington	MN	55420	**888-511-7283**	952-946-7998
Society for Social Work Leadership in Health Care 1211 Locust St	Philadelphia	PA	19107	**866-237-9542**	215-599-6134

49-16 Publishing & Printing Professional Associations

Name / Address	City	State	Zip	Toll-Free	Phone
American Book Producers Assn (ABPA) 160 5th Ave	New York	NY	10010	**800-209-4575**	212-645-2368
Association of Directory Publishers (ADP) 116 Cass St	Traverse City	MI	49684	**800-267-9002**	
Children's Book Council (CBC) 12 W 37th St 2nd Fl *Orders	New York	NY	10018	**800-999-2160***	212-966-1990
Digital Printing & Imaging Assn (DPI) 10015 Main St	Fairfax	VA	22031	**888-385-3588**	703-385-1339
Editorial Freelancers Assn (EFA) 71 W 23rd St Suite 1910	New York	NY	10010	**866-929-5400**	212-929-5400
Independent Press Assn (IPA) 2729 Mission St Suite 201	San Francisco	CA	94110	**877-463-9624**	415-643-4401
International Assn of Printing House Craftsmen (IAPHC) 7042 Brooklyn Blvd	Minneapolis	MN	55429	**800-466-4274**	763-560-1620
International Reprographic Assn (IRgA) 401 N Michigan Ave	Chicago	IL	60611	**800-833-4742**	312-245-1026
Magazine Publishers of America (MPA) 810 7th Ave 24th Fl	New York	NY	10019	**888-567-3228**	212-872-3700
National Assn for Printing Leadership (NAPL) 75 W Century Rd *Cust Svc	Paramus	NJ	07652	**800-642-6275***	201-634-9600
PrintImage International 70 E Lake St Suite 333	Chicago	IL	60601	**800-234-0040**	312-726-8015
Printing Industries of America/Graphic Arts Technical Foundation (PIA/GATF) 200 Deer Run Rd	Sewickley	PA	15143	**800-910-4283**	412-741-6860
Specialty Graphic Imaging Assn (SGIA) 10015 Main St	Fairfax	VA	22031	**888-385-3588**	703-385-1335
Web Offset Assn (WOA) 200 Deer Run Rd	Sewickley	PA	15143	**800-910-4283**	412-741-6860
Yellow Pages Assn (YPA) 820 Kirts Blvd Suite 100	Troy	MI	48084	**800-841-0639**	248-244-6200

49-17 Real Estate Professionals Associations

Name / Address	City	State	Zip	Toll-Free	Phone
American Homeowners Foundation (AHF) 6776 Little Falls Rd	Arlington	VA	22213	**800-489-7776**	703-536-7776
American Society of Appraisers (ASA) 555 Herndon Pkwy Suite 125	Herndon	VA	20170	**800-272-8258**	703-478-2228
Building Owners & Managers Assn International (BOMA) 1201 New York Ave NW Suite 300	Washington	DC	20005	**800-426-6292**	202-408-2662
Building Owners & Managers Institute 1521 Ritchie Hwy	Arnold	MD	21012	**800-235-2664**	410-974-1410
CoreNet Global Inc 260 Peachtree St NW Suite 1500	Atlanta	GA	30303	**800-726-8111**	404-589-3200
Council of Real Estate Brokerage Managers (CRB) 430 N Michigan Ave Suite 300	Chicago	IL	60611	**800-621-8738**	312-321-4400
Council of Residential Specialists 430 N Michigan Ave Suite 300	Chicago	IL	60611	**800-462-8841**	312-321-4400
Institute of Business Appraisers (IBA) 6950 Cypress Rd Suite 209	Plantation	FL	33317	**800-299-4130**	954-584-1144
Institute of Real Estate Management (IREM) 430 N Michigan Ave	Chicago	IL	60611	**800-837-0706**	312-329-6000
National Assn of Industrial & Office Properties (NAIOP) 2201 Cooperative Way 3rd Fl	Herndon	VA	20171	**800-666-6780**	703-904-7100
National Assn of Master Appraisers 303 W Cypress St	San Antonio	TX	78212	**800-229-6262**	210-271-0781
National Assn of Real Estate Investment Trusts (NAREIT) 1875 'I' St NW Suite 600	Washington	DC	20006	**800-362-7348**	202-739-9400
National Assn of REALTORS 430 N Michigan Ave	Chicago	IL	60611	**800-874-6500**	312-329-8200
National Assn of Residential Property Managers (NARPM) 8317 Cross Pk Dr Suite 150	Austin	TX	78754	**800-782-3452**	512-381-6091
National Assn of Royalty Owners (NARO) PO Box 5779	Norman	OK	73070	**800-558-0557**	405-573-2972
National Council of Exchangors (NCE) 630 Quintana Rd Suite 150	Morro Bay	CA	93442	**800-324-1031**	
Real Estate Buyer's Agent Council (REBAC) 430 N Michigan Ave	Chicago	IL	60611	**800-648-6224**	312-329-8656
Realtors Land Institute 430 N Michigan Ave	Chicago	IL	60611	**800-441-5263**	312-329-8440
Vacation Rental Managers Assn (VRMA) PO Box 1202	Santa Cruz	CA	95061	**800-871-8762**	831-426-8762

49-18 Sales & Marketing Professional Associations

Name / Address	City	State	Zip	Toll-Free	Phone
ABA (American Booksellers Assn) 828 S Broadway	Tarrytown	NY	10591	**800-637-0037**	914-591-2665
American Advertising Federation (AAF) 1101 Vermont Ave NW Suite 500	Washington	DC	20005	**800-999-2231**	202-898-0089
American Assn of Franchisees & Dealers (AAFD) 3500 5th Ave Suite 103	San Diego	CA	92103	**800-733-9858**	619-209-3775
American Booksellers Assn (ABA) 828 S Broadway	Tarrytown	NY	10591	**800-637-0037**	914-591-2665
American International Automobile Dealers Assn (AIADA) 211 N Union St Suite 300	Alexandria	VA	22314	**800-462-4232**	703-519-7800
American Machine Tool Distributors' Assn (AMTDA) 1445 Research Blvd Suite 450	Rockville	MD	20850	**800-878-2683**	301-738-1200
American Marketing Assn (AMA) 311 S Wacker Dr Suite 5800	Chicago	IL	60606	**800-262-1150**	312-542-9000
American Wholesale Marketers Assn (AWMA) 2750 Prosperity Ave Suite 550	Fairfax	VA	22031	**800-482-2962**	703-208-3358
Associated Equipment Distributors (AED) 615 W 22nd St	Oak Brook	IL	60523	**800-388-0650**	630-574-0650
Association of Progressive Rental Organizations (APRO) 1504 Robin Hood Trail	Austin	TX	78703	**800-204-2776**	512-794-0095
Association of Retail Marketing Services 10 Drs James Parker Blvd Suite 103	Red Bank	NJ	07701	**866-231-6310**	732-842-5070
Automotive Distribution Network DBA Parts Plus 5050 Poplar Ave Suite 2020	Memphis	TN	38157	**800-727-8112**	901-682-9090
Beauty & Barber Supply Institute (BBSI) 15825 N 71st St Suite 100	Scottsdale	AZ	85254	**800-468-2274**	480-281-0424
Business Marketing Assn (BMA) 400 N Michigan Ave 15th Fl	Chicago	IL	60611	**800-664-4262**	312-822-0005
Business Technology Assn (BTA) 12411 Wornall Rd	Kansas City	MO	64145	**800-316-9721**	816-941-3100
CBA International 9240 Explorer Dr PO Box 62000	Colorado Springs	CO	80962	**800-252-1950**	719-265-9895
Chain Drug Marketing Assn (CDMA) 43157 W Nine-Mile Rd PO Box 995	Novi	MI	48376	**800-935-2362**	248-449-9300
Christian Booksellers Assn 9240 Explorer Dr PO Box 62000	Colorado Springs	CO	80962	**800-252-1950**	719-265-9895
Clio Awards Inc 770 Broadway 6th Fl	New York	NY	10003	**800-946-2546**	212-683-4300
Electronic Retailing Assn (ERA) 2000 N 14th St Suite 300	Arlington	VA	22201	**800-987-6462**	703-841-1751
Electronics Representatives Assn (ERA) 444 N Michigan Ave Suite 1960	Chicago	IL	60611	**800-776-7377**	312-527-3050
Health Industry Distributors Assn (HIDA) 310 Montgomery St Suite 520	Alexandria	VA	22314	**800-549-4432**	703-549-4432
Heating Airconditioning & Refrigeration Distributors International (HARDI) 1389 Dublin Rd	Columbus	OH	43215	**888-253-2128**	614-488-1835
International Franchise Assn (IFA) 1350 New York Ave NW Suite 900	Washington	DC	20005	**800-543-1038**	202-628-8000
International Home Furnishings Representatives Assn (IHFRA) 209 S Main St	High Point	NC	27260	**800-889-3920**	336-889-3920
International Sanitary Supply Assn (ISSA) 7373 N Lincoln Ave	Lincolnwood	IL	60712	**800-225-4772**	847-982-0800
Machinery Dealers National Assn (MDNA) 315 S Patrick St	Alexandria	VA	22314	**800-872-7807**	703-836-9300
Mailing & Fulfillment Service Assn (MFSA) 1421 Prince St Suite 410	Alexandria	VA	22314	**800-333-6272**	703-836-9200
Manufacturers' Agents National Assn (MANA) 1 Spectrum Pointe Dr Suite 150	Lake Forest	CA	92630	**877-626-2776**	949-859-4040
Medical Marketing Assn (MMA) 74 New Montgomery St Suite 230	San Francisco	CA	94105	**800-551-2173**	415-764-4807
NAMM - International Music Products Assn 5790 Armada Dr	Carlsbad	CA	92008	**800-767-6266**	760-438-8001
National Agri-Marketing Assn (NAMA) 11020 King St Suite 205	Overland Park	KS	66210	**800-530-5646**	913-491-6500
National Assn of Chain Drug Stores (NACDS) 413 N Lee St	Alexandria	VA	22314	**800-678-6223**	703-549-3001
National Assn of College Stores (NACS) 500 E Lorain St	Oberlin	OH	44074	**800-622-7498**	440-775-7777
National Assn of Convenience Stores (NACS) 1600 Duke St *Cust Svc	Alexandria	VA	22314	**800-966-6227***	703-684-3600
National Assn of Electrical Distributors Inc (NAED) 1100 Corporate Sq Dr Suite 100	Saint Louis	MO	63132	**888-791-2512**	314-991-9000
National Assn for Retail Marketing Services (NARMS) PO Box 906	Plover	WI	54467	**888-526-2767**	715-342-0948
National Auctioneers Assn (NAA) 8880 Ballentine St	Overland Park	KS	66214	**888-541-8084**	913-541-8084
National Automobile Dealers Assn (NADA) 8400 Westpark Dr	McLean	VA	22102	**800-252-6232**	703-821-7000
National Cotton Council of America 1918 North Pkwy	Memphis	TN	38112	**800-377-9030**	901-274-9030
National Electronic Distributors Assn (NEDA) 1111 Alderman Dr Suite 400	Alpharetta	GA	30005	**800-347-6332**	678-393-9990
National Electronics Service Dealers Assn (NESDA) 3608 Pershing Ave	Fort Worth	TX	76107	**800-946-0201**	817-921-9061
National Independent Automobile Dealers Assn (NIADA) 2521 Brown Blvd	Arlington	TX	76006	**800-682-3837**	817-640-3838
National Independent Flag Dealers Assn (NIFDA) 214 N Hale St	Wheaton	IL	60187	**877-544-3524**	630-510-4500
National Luggage Dealers Assn (NLDA) 1817 Elmdale Ave	Glenview	IL	60026	**866-998-6869**	847-998-6869
National Lumber & Building Material Dealers Assn (NLBMDA) 40 Ivy St SE	Washington	DC	20003	**800-634-8645**	202-547-2230
National Minority Supplier Development Council (NMSDC) 1040 Ave of the Americas 2nd Fl	New York	NY	10018	**888-396-1110**	212-944-2430
National Retail Federation (NRF) 325 7th St NW Suite 1100	Washington	DC	20004	**800-673-4692**	202-783-7971
National Retail Hardware Assn (NRHA) 5822 W 74th St *Cust Svc	Indianapolis	IN	46278	**800-772-4424***	317-290-0338
National School Supply & Equipment Assn (NSSEA) 8380 Colesville Rd Suite 250	Silver Spring	MD	20910	**800-395-5550**	301-495-0240
National Shoe Retailers Assn (NSRA) 7150 Columbia Gateway Dr Suite G	Columbia	MD	21046	**800-673-8446**	410-381-8282
North American Building Material Distribution Assn (NBMDA) 401 N Michigan Ave Suite 2400	Chicago	IL	60611	**888-747-7862**	312-644-6610
North American Retail Dealers Assn (NARDA) 10 E 22nd St Suite 310	Lombard	IL	60148	**800-621-0298**	630-953-8950
North American Wholesale Lumber Assn (NAWLA) 3601 Algonquin Rd Suite 400	Rolling Meadows	IL	60008	**800-527-8258**	847-870-7470
NPTA Alliance 500 Bi-County Blvd Suite 200E	Farmingdale	NY	11735	**800-355-6782**	631-777-2223
Paint & Decorating Retailers Assn (PDRA) 403 Axminister Dr	Fenton	MO	63026	**800-737-0107**	636-326-2636
Parts Plus 5050 Poplar Ave Suite 2020	Memphis	TN	38157	**800-727-8112**	901-682-9090
Petroleum Marketers Assn of America (PMAA) 1901 N Fort Myer Dr Suite 500	Arlington	VA	22209	**800-300-7622**	703-351-8000
Photo Marketing Assn International (PMA) 3000 Picture Pl	Jackson	MI	49201	**800-762-9287**	517-788-8100
Point-of-Purchase Advertising International (POPAI) 1660 L St NW 10th Fl	Washington	DC	20036	**888-407-6724**	202-530-3000
Promotional Products Assn International (PPAI) 3125 Skyway Cir N	Irving	TX	75038	**888-492-6891**	972-252-0404
Public Relations Society of America (PRSA) 33 Maiden Ln 11th Fl	New York	NY	10038	**800-937-7772**	212-995-2230
Qualitative Research Consultants Assn Inc (QRCA) PO Box 967	Camden	TN	38320	**888-674-7722**	731-584-8080
Radio Advertising Bureau (RAB) 261 Madison Ave 23rd Fl	New York	NY	10016	**800-252-7234**	212-681-7200
Retail Advertising & Marketing Assn (RAMA) 325 7th St NW Suite 1100	Washington	DC	20004	**800-673-4692**	202-661-3052
Society for Marketing Professional Services (SMPS) 99 Canal Center Plaza Suite 330	Alexandria	VA	22314	**800-292-7677**	703-549-6117
Souvenirs Gifts & Novelties Trade Assn 10 E Athens Ave Suite 208	Ardmore	PA	19003	**800-284-5451**	610-645-6940
Specialty Tools & Fasteners Distributors Assn (STAFDA) 500 Elm Grove Rd	Elm Grove	WI	53122	**800-352-2981**	262-784-4774

Sales & Marketing Professional Associations (Cont'd)

Name / Address	City	State	ZIP	Toll-Free	Phone
Video Software Dealers Assn (VSDA) 16530 Ventura Blvd Suite 400	Encino	CA	91436	**800-955-8732**	818-385-1500
Wholesale Florist & Florist Supplier Assn (WF&FSA) 147 Old Solomons Island Rd Suite 302	Annapolis	MD	21401	**888-289-3372**	410-573-0400
World Wide Pet Supply Assn Inc (WWPSA) 406 S 1st Ave	Arcadia	CA	91006	**800-999-7295**	626-447-2222

49-19 Technology, Science, Engineering Professionals Associations

Name / Address	City	State	ZIP	Toll-Free	Phone
AIIM - Enterprise Content Management Assn 1100 Wayne Ave Suite 1100	Silver Spring	MD	20910	**800-477-2446**	301-587-8202
AIM Global - Assn for Automatic Identification & Mobility (AIM) 125 Warrendale-Bayne Rd	Warrendale	PA	15086	**800-338-0206**	724-934-4470
American Assn for the Advancement of Science (AAAS) 1200 New York Ave NW	Washington	DC	20005	**800-731-4939**	202-326-6400
American Assn for Clinical Chemistry Inc (AACC) 2101 L St NW Suite 202 *Cust Svc	Washington	DC	20037	**800-892-1400***	202-857-0717
American Assn of Engineering Societies (AAES) 1828 L St NW Suite 906 *Orders	Washington	DC	20036	**888-400-2237***	202-296-2237
American Assn of Pharmaceutical Scientists (AAPS) 2107 Wilson Blvd Suite 700	Arlington	VA	22201	**877-998-2277**	703-243-2800
American Assn of Variable Star Observers (AAVSO) 25 Birch St	Cambridge	MA	02138	**800-223-0138**	617-354-0484
American Chemical Society (ACS) 1155 16th St NW	Washington	DC	20036	**800-227-5558**	202-872-4600
American Geophysical Union (AGU) 2000 Florida Ave NW	Washington	DC	20009	**800-966-2481**	202-462-6900
American Institute of Aeronautics & Astronautics (AIAA) 1801 Alexander Bell Dr Suite 500	Reston	VA	20191	**800-639-2422**	703-264-7500
American Institute of Biological Sciences (AIBS) 1444 'I' St NW Suite 200	Washington	DC	20005	**800-992-2427**	202-628-1500
American Institute of Chemical Engineers (AIChE) 3 Park Ave *Cust Svc	New York	NY	10016	**800-242-4363***	212-591-7338
American Mathematical Society (AMS) 201 Charles St PO Box 6248 *Cust Svc	Providence	RI	02940	**800-321-4267***	401-455-4000
American Nuclear Society (ANS) 555 N Kensington Ave	La Grange Park	IL	60526	**800-323-3044**	708-352-6611
American Society of Human Genetics (ASHG) 9650 Rockville Pike	Bethesda	MD	20814	**866-486-4363**	301-571-1825
American Society of Limnology & Oceanography (ASLO) 5400 Bosque Blvd Suite 680	Waco	TX	76710	**800-929-2756**	254-399-9635
American Society of Mechanical Engineers (ASME) 3 Park Ave. *Cust Svc	New York	NY	10016	**800-843-2763***	212-591-7722
American Society for Nondestructive Testing Inc (ASNT) 1711 Arlingate Ln *Orders	Columbus	OH	43228	**800-222-2768***	614-274-6003
American Society for Photobiology (ASP) 810 E 10th St	Lawrence	KS	66044	**800-627-0629**	785-843-1235
American Statistical Assn (ASA) 1429 Duke St	Alexandria	VA	22314	**888-231-3473**	703-684-1221
AOAC International 481 N Frederick Ave Suite 500	Gaithersburg	MD	20877	**800-379-2622**	301-924-7077
Association for Women in Science Inc (AWIS) 1200 New York Ave NW Suite 650	Washington	DC	20005	**800-886-2947**	202-326-8940
Audio Engineering Society 60 E 42nd St Rm 2520	New York	NY	10165	**800-541-7299**	212-661-8528
Custom Electronic Design & Installation Assn (CEDIA) 7150 Winton Dr Suite 300	Indianapolis	IN	46268	**800-669-5329**	317-328-4336
Drug Chemical & Associated Technologies Assn (DCAT) 1 Washington Blvd Suite 7	Robbinsville	NJ	08691	**800-640-3228**	609-448-1000
Electronics Technicians Assn International (ETA) 5 Depot St	Greencastle	IN	46135	**800-288-3824**	765-653-8262
Electrophoresis Society 1202 Ann St	Madison	WI	53713	**800-462-3417**	608-258-1565
Engineering Contractors' Assn (ECA) 8310 Florence Ave	Downey	CA	90240	**800-293-2240**	562-861-0929
Federation of American Societies for Experimental Biology (FASEB) 9650 Rockville Pike	Bethesda	MD	20814	**800-433-2732**	301-530-7000
Genetics Society of America (GSA) 9650 Rockville Pike	Bethesda	MD	20814	**866-486-4363**	301-634-7300
Geological Society of America (GSA) 3300 Penrose Pl PO Box 9140	Boulder	CO	80301	**800-472-1988**	303-447-2020
IEEE Aerospace & Electronics Systems Society IEEE Operations Ctr 445 Hoes Ln	Piscataway	NJ	08854	**800-678-4333**	732-981-0060
IEEE Antennas & Propagation Society (APS) IEEE Operations Ctr 445 Hoes Ln	Piscataway	NJ	08854	**800-678-4333**	732-981-0060
IEEE Broadcast Technology Society (BTS) IEEE Operations Ctr 445 Hoes Ln	Piscataway	NJ	08854	**800-678-4333**	732-981-0060
IEEE Circuits & Systems Society (CAS) IEEE Operations Ctr 445 Hoes Ln	Piscataway	NJ	08854	**800-678-4333**	732-981-0060
IEEE Communications Society (COMSOC) IEEE Operations Ctr 445 Hoes Ln	Piscataway	NJ	08854	**800-678-4333**	732-981-0060
IEEE Components Packaging & Manufacturing Technology Society 445 Hoes Ln PO Box 1331	Piscataway	NJ	08855	**800-678-4333**	732-562-5529
IEEE Consumer Electronics Society (CES) IEEE Operations Ctr 445 Hoes Ln	Piscataway	NJ	08854	**800-678-4333**	732-981-0060
IEEE Control Systems Society (CSS) IEEE Operations Ctr 445 Hoes Ln	Piscataway	NJ	08854	**800-678-4333**	732-981-0060
IEEE Dielectrics & Electrical Insulation Society IEEE Operations Ctr 445 Hoes Ln	Piscataway	NJ	08854	**800-678-4333**	732-981-0060
IEEE Education Society (ES) IEEE Operations Ctr 445 Hoes Ln	Piscataway	NJ	08854	**800-678-4333**	732-981-0060
IEEE Electromagnetic Compatibility Society (EMC) IEEE Operations Ctr 445 Hoes Ln	Piscataway	NJ	08854	**800-678-4333**	732-981-0060
IEEE Electron Devices Society (EDS) IEEE Operations Ctr 445 Hoes Ln	Piscataway	NJ	08854	**800-678-4333**	732-981-0060
IEEE Engineering Management Society (EMS) IEEE Operations Ctr 445 Hoes Ln	Piscataway	NJ	08854	**800-678-4333**	732-981-0060
IEEE Engineering in Medicine & Biology Society (EMB) IEEE Operations Ctr 445 Hoes Ln	Piscataway	NJ	08854	**800-678-4333**	732-981-0060
IEEE Geoscience & Remote Sensing Society (GRSS) IEEE Operations Ctr 445 Hoes Ln	Piscataway	NJ	08854	**800-678-4333**	732-981-0060
IEEE Industrial Electronics Society (IES) IEEE Operations Ctr 445 Hoes Ln	Piscataway	NJ	08854	**800-678-4333**	732-981-0060
IEEE Industry Applications Society IEEE Operations Ctr 445 Hoes Ln	Piscataway	NJ	08854	**800-678-4333**	732-981-0060
IEEE Information Theory Society (IT) IEEE Operations Ctr 445 Hoes Ln	Piscataway	NJ	08854	**800-678-4333**	732-981-0060
IEEE Instrumentation & Measurement Society (IM) IEEE Operations Ctr 445 Hoes Ln	Piscataway	NJ	08854	**800-678-4333**	732-981-0060
IEEE Lasers & Electro-Optics Society (LEOS) IEEE Operations Ctr 445 Hoes Ln	Piscataway	NJ	08854	**800-678-4333**	732-981-0060
IEEE Magnetics Society IEEE Operations Ctr 445 Hoes Ln	Piscataway	NJ	08854	**800-678-4333**	732-981-0060
IEEE Microwave Theory & Techniques Society (MTT-S) IEEE Operations Ctr 445 Hoes Ln	Piscataway	NJ	08854	**800-678-4333**	732-981-0060
IEEE Neural Networks Society (NNS) IEEE Operations Ctr 445 Hoes Ln	Piscataway	NJ	08854	**800-678-4333**	732-981-0060
IEEE Nuclear & Plasma Sciences Society (NPSS) IEEE Operations Ctr 445 Hoes Ln	Piscataway	NJ	08854	**800-678-4333**	732-981-0060
IEEE Oceanic Engineering Society (OES) IEEE Operations Ctr 445 Hoes Ln	Piscataway	NJ	08854	**800-678-4333**	732-981-0060
IEEE Power Electronics Society (PELS) IEEE Operations Ctr 445 Hoes Ln	Piscataway	NJ	08854	**800-678-4333**	732-981-0060
IEEE Power Engineering Society (PES) IEEE Operations Ctr 445 Hoes Ln	Piscataway	NJ	08854	**800-678-4333**	732-981-0060
IEEE Product Safety Engineering Society IEEE Operations Ctr 445 Hoes Ln	Piscataway	NJ	08854	**800-678-4333**	732-981-0060
IEEE Professional Communication Society (PCS) IEEE Operations Ctr 445 Hoes Ln	Piscataway	NJ	08854	**800-678-4333**	732-981-0060
IEEE Reliability Society (RS) IEEE Operations Ctr 445 Hoes Ln	Piscataway	NJ	08854	**800-678-4333**	732-981-0060
IEEE Robotics & Automation Society (RAS) IEEE Operations Ctr 445 Hoes Ln	Piscataway	NJ	08854	**800-678-4333**	732-981-0060
IEEE Signal Processing Society IEEE Operations Ctr 445 Hoes Ln	Piscataway	NJ	08854	**800-678-4333**	732-981-0060
IEEE Society on Social Implications of Technology (SSIT) IEEE Operations Ctr 445 Hoes Ln	Piscataway	NJ	08854	**800-678-4333**	732-981-0060
IEEE Solid State Circuits Society (SSCS) IEEE Operations Ctr 445 Hoes Ln	Piscataway	NJ	08854	**800-678-4333**	732-981-0060
IEEE Systems Man & Cybernetics Society (SMC) IEEE Operations Ctr 445 Hoes Ln	Piscataway	NJ	08854	**800-678-4333**	732-981-0060
IEEE Ultrasonics Ferroelectrics & Frequency Control Society IEEE Operations Ctr 445 Hoes Ln	Piscataway	NJ	08854	**800-678-4333**	732-981-0060
IEEE Vehicular Technology Society (VTS) IEEE Operations Ctr 445 Hoes Ln	Piscataway	NJ	08854	**800-678-4333**	732-981-0060
Institute of Electrical & Electronics Engineers (IEEE) 3 Park Ave 17th Fl	New York	NY	10016	**800-678-4333**	212-419-7900
Institute for Operations Research & the Management Sciences (INFORMS) 7240 Parkway Dr Suite 310	Hanover	MD	21076	**800-446-3676**	443-757-3500
International Center for Technology Assessment (ICTA) 660 Pennsylvania Ave SE Suite 302	Washington	DC	20003	**800-600-6664**	202-547-9359
International Society of Certified Electronics Technicians (ISCET) 3608 Pershing Ave	Fort Worth	TX	76107	**800-946-0201**	817-921-9101
Laser Institute of America (LIA) 13501 Ingenuity Dr Suite 128	Orlando	FL	32826	**800-345-2737**	407-380-1553
Mathematical Assn of America (MAA) 1529 18th St NW	Washington	DC	20036	**800-741-9415**	202-387-5200
Microscopy Society of America (MSA) 230 E Ohio St Suite 400	Chicago	IL	60611	**800-538-3672**	312-644-1527
Nail Manufacturers Council (NMC) 401 N Michigan Ave	Chicago	IL	60611	**800-868-4265**	312-245-1575
National Academy of Sciences (NAS) 500 5th St NW	Washington	DC	20001	**800-624-6242**	202-334-2138
National Assn of Radio & Telecommunications Engineers (NARTE) 167 Village St	Medway	MA	02053	**800-896-2783**	508-533-8333
National Council on Radiation Protection & Measurements (NCRP) 7910 Woodmont Ave Suite 400	Bethesda	MD	20814	**800-229-2652**	301-657-2652
National Geographic Society 1145 17th St NW *Orders	Washington	DC	20036	**800-647-5463***	202-857-7000
National Society of Professional Engineers (NSPE) 1420 King St	Alexandria	VA	22314	**800-285-6773**	703-684-2800
New York Academy of Sciences 2 E 63rd St	New York	NY	10021	**800-843-6927**	212-838-0230
Semiconductor Equipment & Materials International (SEMI) 3081 Zenker Rd	San Jose	CA	95134	**800-974-7364**	408-943-6900
Society for the Advancement of Material & Process Engineering (SAMPE) 1161 Park View Dr	Covina	CA	91724	**800-562-7360**	626-331-0616
Society of Cable Telecommunications Engineers (SCTE) 140 Philips Rd	Exton	PA	19341	**800-542-5040**	610-363-6888
Society of Environmental Toxicology & Chemistry (SETAC) 1010 N 12th Ave	Pensacola	FL	32501	**888-899-2088**	850-469-1500
Society for Industrial & Applied Mathematics (SIAM) 3600 Market St 6th Fl	Philadelphia	PA	19104	**800-447-7426**	215-382-9800
Society for Sedimentary Geology (SEPM) 6128 E 38th St Suite 308	Tulsa	OK	74135	**800-865-9765**	918-610-3361
Synthetic Organic Chemical Manufacturers Assn (SOCMA) 1850 M St NW Suite 700	Washington	DC	20036	**888-377-0778**	202-721-4100
Women in Technology International (WITI) 13351 Riverside Dr Suite 441	Sherman Oaks	CA	91423	**800-334-9484**	818-788-9484
World Future Society 7910 Woodmont Ave Suite 450	Bethesda	MD	20814	**800-989-8274**	301-656-8274

49-20 Telecommunications Professionals Associations

Name / Address	City	State	ZIP	Toll-Free	Phone
American Public Communications Council Inc (APCC) 625 Slaters Ln Suite 104	Alexandria	VA	22314	**800-868-2722**	703-739-1322

Name / Address	City	State	ZIP	Toll-Free	Phone
Communications Supply Service Assn (CSSA) 5700 Murray St	Little Rock	AR	72209	**800-252-2772**	501-562-7666
Industrial Telecommunications Assn Inc (ITA) 1110 N Glebe Rd Suite 500	Arlington	VA	22201	**800-482-8282**	703-528-5115
International Communications Industries Assn (ICIA) 11242 Waples Mill Rd Suite 200	Fairfax	VA	22030	**800-659-7469**	703-273-7200
National Systems Contractors Assn (NSCA) 625 1st St SE Suite 420	Cedar Rapids	IA	52401	**800-446-6722**	319-366-6722
PCIA - Wireless Infrastructure Assn 500 Montgomery St Suite 700	Alexandria	VA	22314	**800-759-0300**	703-739-0300
Society of Telecommunications Consultants (STC) PO Box 416	Fall River Mills	CA	96028	**800-782-7670**	530-336-7070
Telecommunications Industry Assn (TIA) 2500 Wilson Blvd Suite 300	Arlington	VA	22201	**800-799-6682**	703-907-7700

49-21 Transportation Industry Associations

Name / Address	City	State	ZIP	Toll-Free	Phone
Air Transport Assn of America (ATA) 1301 Pennsylvania Ave NW Suite 1100	Washington	DC	20004	**800-319-2463**	202-626-4000
Aircraft Owners & Pilots Assn (AOPA) 421 Aviation Way	Frederick	MD	21701	**800-872-2672**	301-695-2000
American Ambulance Assn (AAA) 8201 Greensboro Dr Suite 300	McLean	VA	22102	**800-523-4447**	703-610-9018
American International Automobile Dealers Assn (AIADA) 211 N Union St Suite 300	Alexandria	VA	22314	**800-462-4232**	703-519-7800
American Pilots Assn 499 S Capitol St SW Suite 409	Washington	DC	20003	**800-527-4568**	202-484-0700
American Traffic Safety Services Assn (ATSSA) 15 Riverside Pkwy Suite 100	Fredericksburg	VA	22406	**800-272-8772**	540-368-1701
American Trucking Assns (ATA) 2200 Mill Rd	Alexandria	VA	22314	**800-282-5463**	703-838-1700
Association of American Railroads (AAR) 50 F St NW *Cust Svc	Washington	DC	20001	**800-544-7245***	202-639-2100
Association of Retail Travel Agents (ARTA) 73 White Bridge Rd Box 238	Nashville	TN	37205	**800-969-6069**	
Automotive Engine Rebuilders Assn (AERA) 330 Lexington Dr	Buffalo Grove	IL	60089	**888-326-2372**	847-541-6550
Automotive Oil Change Assn (AOCA) 12810 Hillcrest Rd Suite 221	Dallas	TX	75230	**800-331-0329**	972-458-9468
Automotive Service Assn (ASA) 1901 Airport Fwy *Cust Svc	Bedford	TX	76021	**800-272-7467***	817-283-6205
Coalition Against Bigger Trucks (CABT) 901 N Pitt St Suite 310	Alexandria	VA	22314	**888-222-8123**	703-535-3131
Coalition for Auto Repair Equality (CARE) 119 Oronoco St Suite 300	Alexandria	VA	22314	**800-229-5380**	703-519-7555
Community Transportation Assn of America (CTAA) 1341 G St NW Suite 1000	Washington	DC	20005	**800-527-8279**	202-628-1480
Dangerous Goods Advisory Council (DGAC) 1100 H St NW Suite 740	Washington	DC	20005	**800-634-1598**	202-289-4550
Helicopter Assn International (HAI) 1635 Prince St	Alexandria	VA	22314	**800-435-4976**	703-683-4646
I-CAR Inter-Industry Conference on Auto Collision Repair (I-CAR) 3701 Algonquin Rd Suite 400	Rolling Meadows	IL	60008	**800-422-7872**	847-590-1191
Intelligent Transportation Society of America 1100 17th St NW Suite 1200	Washington	DC	20036	**800-374-8472**	202-484-4847
International Airlines Travel Agent Network (IATAN) 300 Garden City Plaza Suite 342	Garden City	NY	11530	**800-294-2826**	516-663-6000
International Motor Coach Group Inc (IMG) 8645 College Blvd Suite 220	Overland Park	KS	66210	**888-447-3466**	913-906-0111
International Safe Transit Assn (ISTA) 1400 Abbott Rd Suite 160	East Lansing	MI	48823	**888-367-4782**	517-333-3437
International Warehouse Logistics Assn (IWLA) 2800 River Rd Suite 260	Des Plaines	IL	60018	**800-525-0165**	847-813-4699
IWLA (International Warehouse Logistics Assn) 2800 River Rd Suite 260	Des Plaines	IL	60018	**800-525-0165**	847-813-4699
Jewelers Shipping Assn (JSA) 125 Carlsbad St	Cranston	RI	02920	**800-688-4572**	401-943-6490
National Air Traffic Controllers Assn (NATCA) 1325 Massachusetts Ave NW	Washington	DC	20005	**800-266-0895**	202-628-5451
National Air Transportation Assn (NATA) 4226 King St	Alexandria	VA	22302	**800-808-6282**	703-845-9000
National Assn of Marine Surveyors Inc (NAMS) PO Box 9306	Chesapeake	VA	23321	**800-822-6267**	757-638-9638
National Automobile Dealers Assn (NADA) 8400 Westpark Dr	McLean	VA	22102	**800-252-6232**	703-821-7000
National Automotive Radiator Service Assn (NARSA) 15000 Commerce Pkwy Suite C	Mount Laurel	NJ	08054	**800-551-3232**	856-439-1575
National Motorists Assn (NMA) 402 W 2nd St	Waunakee	WI	53597	**800-882-2785**	608-849-6000
National Truck Equipment Assn (NTEA) 37400 Hills Tech Dr	Farmington Hills	MI	48331	**800-441-6832**	248-489-7090
NATSO Inc 1737 King St Suite 200	Alexandria	VA	22314	**888-275-2876**	703-549-2100
Owner-Operator Independent Drivers Assn (OOIDA) 1 NW OOIDA Dr	Grain Valley	MO	64029	**800-444-5791**	816-229-5791
Passenger Vessel Assn (PVA) 801 N Quincy St Suite 200	Arlington	VA	22203	**800-807-8360**	703-807-0100
Professional Aviation Maintenance Assn (PAMA) 717 Princess St	Alexandria	VA	22314	**866-865-7262**	703-683-3171
Recreation Vehicle Industry Assn (RVIA) 1896 Preston White Dr	Reston	VA	20191	**800-336-0154**	703-620-6003
Self Storage Assn (SSA) 6506 Louisdale Rd Suite 315	Springfield	VA	22150	**888-735-3784**	703-921-9123
Shipowners Claims Bureau (SCB) 60 Broad St 37th Fl	New York	NY	10004	**800-730-2535**	212-847-4500
Society of Automotive Engineers Inc (SAE) 400 Commonwealth Dr	Warrendale	PA	15096	**877-606-7323**	724-776-4841
Specialty Vehicle Institute of America (SVIA) 2 Jenner St Suite 150	Irvine	CA	92618	**800-887-2887**	949-727-3727
Towing & Recovery Assn of America (TRAA) 2121 Eisenhower Ave Suite 200	Alexandria	VA	22314	**800-728-0136**	703-684-7734
Transportation Research Board (TRB) 500 5th St NW	Washington	DC	20001	**800-424-9818**	202-334-2934
United Motorcoach Assn (UMA) 113 S West St 4th Fl	Alexandria	VA	22314	**800-424-8262**	703-838-2929

50 ATTRACTIONS

SEE ALSO Amusement Parks; Aquariums - Public; Art Dealers & Galleries; Botanical Gardens & Arboreta; Museums; Museums & Halls of Fame - Sports; Museums - Children's; Parks - National - Canada; Parks - National & State - US; Performing Arts Facilities; Planetariums; Zoos & Wildlife Parks

Name / Address	City	State	ZIP	Toll-Free	Phone
Arkansas Arts Center 501 E 9th St	Little Rock	AR	72202	**800-264-2787**	501-372-4000
Art Concepts on Broadway 924 Broadway Plaza	Tacoma	WA	98402	**800-758-7459**	253-272-2202
Barefoot Landing 4898 Hwy 17 S	North Myrtle Beach	SC	29582	**800-272-2320**	843-272-8349
Beauvoir-Jefferson Davis Home 2244 Beach Blvd	Biloxi	MS	39531	**800-570-3818**	228-388-9074
Biltmore Estate 1 Approach Rd *Resv	Asheville	NC	28803	**800-858-4130***	828-225-1333
Black Hills Caverns 2600 Cavern Rd	Rapid City	SD	57702	**800-837-9358**	605-343-0542
Blount Mansion 200 W Hill Ave	Knoxville	TN	37901	**888-654-0016**	865-525-2375
Brielmaier House 710 Beach Blvd	Biloxi	MS	39530	**800-245-6943**	228-374-3105
Carson Hot Springs 1500 Hot Springs Rd	Carson City	NV	89706	**888-917-3711**	775-885-8844
Chateau Elan Winery 100 Tour de France	Braselton	GA	30517	**800-233-9463**	678-425-0900
Chateau Julien Wine Estate 8940 Carmel Valley Rd	Carmel	CA	93923	**800-966-2601**	831-624-2600
Chateau Ste Michelle Winery 14111 NE 145th St	Woodinville	WA	98072	**800-267-6793**	425-415-3300
Columbia Winery 14030 NE 145th St	Woodinville	WA	98072	**800-488-2347**	425-488-2776
Corn Palace 604 N Main St	Mitchell	SD	57301	**800-257-2676**	605-996-5031
Cosanti Historic Site 6433 Doubletree Ranch Rd	Paradise Valley	AZ	85253	**800-752-3187**	480-948-6145
Crystal Cathedral 12141 Lewis St	Garden Grove	CA	92840	**877-456-7900**	714-971-4000
Destrehan Plantation 13034 River Rd	Destrehan	LA	70047	**877-453-2095**	985-764-9315
Eckhart House 810 Main St Old Town	Wheeling	WV	26003	**888-700-0118**	304-232-5439
Eola Hills Wine Cellars 501 S Pacific Hwy 99 West	Rickreall	OR	97371	**800-291-6730**	503-623-2405
Everglades Holiday Park 21940 Griffin Rd	Fort Lauderdale	FL	33332	**800-226-2244**	954-434-8111
Flint Cultural Center 1178 Robert T Longway Blvd	Flint	MI	48503	**888-823-6837**	810-237-7333
Foretich House 710 Beach Blvd	Biloxi	MS	39530	**800-245-6943**	228-374-3105
Forks of Cheat Winery Stewart Town Rd	Morgantown	WV	26508	**877-989-4637**	304-598-2019
Fort Meigs State Memorial 29100 W River Rd	Perrysburg	OH	43551	**800-283-8916**	419-874-4121
Fortifications of Quebec National Historic Site 100 Saint-Louis St PO Box 2474	Quebec	QC	G1R3Z7	**800-463-6769**	418-648-7016
Fourth Avenue 4th Ave-betw University Blvd & 9th St	Tucson	AZ	85705	**800-933-2477**	520-624-5004
Frank Lloyd Wright's Darwin D Martin House 125 Jewett Pkwy	Buffalo	NY	14214	**877-377-3858**	716-856-3858
Gerald R Ford Conservation Center 1326 S 32nd St	Omaha	NE	68105	**800-833-6747**	402-595-1180
Glensheen Mansion 3300 London Rd	Duluth	MN	55804	**888-454-4536**	218-726-8980
Greenwood Plantation 6838 Highland Rd	Saint Francisville	LA	70775	**800-259-4475**	225-655-4475
Gruet Winery 8400 Pan American Fwy NE	Albuquerque	NM	87113	**888-857-9463**	505-821-0055
Guenther House 205 E Guenther St	San Antonio	TX	78204	**800-235-8186**	210-227-1061
Harborplace & The Gallery 200 E Pratt St	Baltimore	MD	21202	**800-427-2671**	410-332-4191
Historic Roswell District 617 Atlanta St	Roswell	GA	30075	**800-776-7935**	770-640-3253
Honeywood Winery 1350 Hines St SE	Salem	OR	97302	**800-726-4101**	503-362-4111
Hoover Dam Hwy 93	Boulder City	NV	89006	**866-291-8687**	702-294-3517
Huber's Orchard & Winery 19816 Huber Rd	Starlight	IN	47106	**800-345-9463**	812-923-3463
Isaac Carter Cabin 1701 Old Richton Rd	Petal	MS	39465	**800-638-6877**	601-268-3220
James J Hill House 240 Summit Ave	Saint Paul	MN	55102	**888-727-8386**	651-297-2555
Jefferson Barracks National Cemetery 2900 Sheridan Rd	Saint Louis	MO	63125	**800-535-1117**	314-260-8691
John's Pass Village & Boardwalk 150 John's Pass Boardwalk Pl	Madeira Beach	FL	33708	**800-755-0677**	727-398-6577
King Estate Winery 80854 Territorial Rd	Eugene	OR	97405	**800-884-4441**	541-942-9874
Latah Creek Winery 13030 E Indiana Ave	Spokane	WA	99216	**800-528-2427**	509-926-0164
Lava Hot Springs 430 E Main St PO Box 669	Lava Hot Springs	ID	83246	**800-423-8597**	208-776-5221
LaVelle Vineyards 89697 Sheffler Rd	Elmira	OR	97437	**800-645-8463**	541-935-9406
Lewis & Clark Monument Frontier Park	Saint Charles	MO	63303	**800-366-2427**	
Lewis & Clark National Historic Trail c/o National Park Service 601 Riverfront Dr	Omaha	NE	68102	**888-237-3252**	402-661-1804
Linville Caverns US 221 N	Marion	NC	28752	**800-419-0540**	828-756-4171
Llano Estacado Winery FM 1585 3.2 miles E of US 87 S	Lubbock	TX	79404	**800-634-3854**	806-745-2258
Loudoun House 209 Castlewood Dr	Lexington	KY	40505	**800-914-7990**	859-254-7024
Mathias Ham House Historic Site 2241 Lincoln Ave	Dubuque	IA	52001	**800-226-3369**	563-557-9545
Mazza Vineyards & Winery 11815 E Lake Rd	North East	PA	16428	**800-796-9463**	814-725-8695
McKelligon Canyon 3 McKelligon Rd	El Paso	TX	79930	**800-915-8482**	915-581-0700
Michael-David Vineyards 4580 W Hwy 12	Lodi	CA	95242	**888-707-9463**	209-368-7384
Miss Laura's Visitor Center 2 N 'B' St	Fort Smith	AR	72901	**800-637-1477**	479-783-8888
Morris-Butler House 1204 N Park Ave	Indianapolis	IN	46202	**800-450-4534**	317-636-5409
National Shrine of Saint John Neumann 1019 N 5th St	Philadelphia	PA	19123	**888-315-1860**	215-627-3080
Ocean Walk Shoppes at the Village 250 N Atlantic Ave	Daytona Beach	FL	32118	**877-845-9255**	
OK Corral 308 E Allen St	Tombstone	AZ	85638	**800-518-1566**	520-457-3456
Oklahoma City National Memorial PO Box 323	Oklahoma City	OK	73101	**888-542-4673**	405-235-3313
Oklahoma Heritage Center 201 NW 14th St	Oklahoma City	OK	73103	**888-501-2059**	405-235-4458
Old Alabama Town 301 Columbus St	Montgomery	AL	36104	**888-240-1850**	334-240-4500
Old German Free School Building 507 E 10th St	Austin	TX	78701	**866-482-4847**	512-482-0927
Oldest Wooden School House 14 Saint George St	Saint Augustine	FL	32084	**888-653-7245**	904-824-0192
Oliver Winery 8024 N SR-37	Bloomington	IN	47404	**800-258-2783**	812-876-5800
Orfila Vineyards & Winery 13455 San Pasqual Rd	Escondido	CA	92025	**800-868-9463**	760-738-6500
Parliament Building (Hotel du Parlement) 1045 rue des Parlementaires	Quebec	QC	G1A1A3	**866-337-8837**	418-641-2638
Paul Laurence Dunbar House 219 N Paul Laurence Dunbar St	Dayton	OH	45407	**800-860-0148**	937-224-7061
Pier 39 Beach & Embarcadero Sts	San Francisco	CA	94133	**800-325-7437**	415-981-7437
Ponce de Leon's Fountain of Youth 11 Magnolia Ave	Saint Augustine	FL	32084	**800-356-8222**	904-829-3168

Listing	City	State	ZIP	Toll-Free	Phone
Raccoon Mountain Caverns					
319 W Hills Dr	Chattanooga	TN	37419	**800-823-2267**	423-821-9403
Riveredge Nature Center					
4458 W Hawthorne Dr Box 26	Newburg	WI	53060	**800-287-8098**	262-375-2715
Rock City Gardens 1400 Patten Rd	Lookout Mountain	GA	30750	**800-854-0675**	706-820-2531
Rosedown Plantation & Gardens					
12501 Hwy 10	Saint Francisville	LA	70775	**888-376-1867**	225-635-3332
Ruby Falls 1720 S Scenic Hwy	Chattanooga	TN	37409	**800-755-7105**	423-821-2544
Saint Marks Historic Railroad State Trail					
W of 363 S of 319 (Capital Circle)	Tallahassee	FL	32301	**877-822-5208**	850-245-2052
Sakonnet Vineyards 162 W Main Rd	Little Compton	RI	02837	**800-919-4637**	401-635-8486
San Sebastian Winery 157 King St	Saint Augustine	FL	32084	**888-352-9463**	904-826-1594
Santa Fe Southern Railway					
410 S Guadalupe St	Santa Fe	NM	87501	**888-989-8600**	505-989-8600
Sears Tower 233 S Wacker Dr	Chicago	IL	60606	**877-759-3325**	312-875-9449
Shirley Plantation					
501 Shirley Plantation Rd	Charles City	VA	23030	**800-232-1613**	804-829-5121
Space Needle 400 Broad St	Seattle	WA	98109	**800-937-9582***	206-905-2200
*Resv					
Stepping Stone Falls 5161 Branch Rd	Flint	MI	48506	**800-648-4242**	810-736-7100
Stone Hill Winery 601 State Hwy 165	Branson	MO	65616	**888-926-9463**	417-334-1897
Stone Mountain Park					
Hwy 78 PO Box 689	Stone Mountain	GA	30086	**800-317-2006**	770-498-5690
Temple Square 50 W North Temple St	Salt Lake City	UT	84150	**800-453-3860**	801-240-1245
Travellers Rest Plantation & Museum					
636 Farrell Pkwy	Nashville	TN	37220	**866-832-8197**	615-832-8197
US Navy Memorial & Naval Heritage Center					
701 Pennsylvania Ave NW Suite 123	Washington	DC	20004	**800-821-8892**	202-737-2300
USS Alabama Battleship Memorial Park					
2703 Battleship Pkwy	Mobile	AL	36602	**800-426-4929**	251-433-2703
USS Missouri Memorial					
1 Arizona Memorial Pl USS Bowfin Submarine Museum	Honolulu	HI	96818	**888-877-6477**	808-423-2263
Westbend Vineyards 5394 Williams Rd	Lewisville	NC	27023	**877-901-5032**	336-945-5032
William Paca House & Garden					
186 Prince George St	Annapolis	MD	21401	**800-603-4020**	410-263-5553
Winery at Wolf Creek					
2637 S Cleveland-Massillon Rd	Norton	OH	44203	**800-436-0426**	330-666-9285
Women in Military Service for America Memorial Memorial Dr Arlington National Cemetery	Arlington	VA	22211	**800-222-2294**	703-533-1155
Women's Memorial					
Memorial Dr Arlington National Cemetery	Arlington	VA	22211	**800-222-2294**	703-533-1155
Woodbridge Winery 5950 E Woodbridge Rd	Acampo	CA	95220	**888-766-6328**	209-369-5861
Woodruff House 988 Bond St	Macon	GA	31201	**800-837-2911**	478-301-2715
Wrigley Mansion 2501 E Telawa Trail	Phoenix	AZ	85016	**888-879-7201**	602-955-4079

51 AUCTIONS

Listing	City	State	ZIP	Toll-Free	Phone
Ableauctions.com Inc 1963 Lougheed Hwy	Coquitlam	BC	V3K3T8	**888-599-2253**	604-521-2253
AMEX: AAC					
ADESA Inc 13085 Hamilton Crossing Blvd	Carmel	IN	46032	**800-862-7882**	317-815-1100
NYSE: KAR					
Auction Block 1502 S I-35 Suite 200	Lancaster	TX	75146	**866-890-0400**	972-230-0400
Auction Systems Auctioneers & Appraisers Inc					
3030 E Washington St	Phoenix	AZ	85034	**800-801-8880**	602-252-4842
BidWay.com Inc 401 N Brand Blvd Suite 540	Glendale	CA	91203	**877-424-3229**	818-956-2040
Butterfields 220 San Bruno Ave	San Francisco	CA	94103	**800-223-2854**	415-861-7500
Dalton Auction Co Inc PO Box 1462	Dalton	GA	30722	**888-249-5831**	706-278-7441
Davis Harry & Co 1725 Blvd of Allies	Pittsburgh	PA	15219	**800-775-2289**	412-765-1170
DoveBid Inc 1241 E Hillsdale Blvd	Foster City	CA	94404	**800-665-1042**	650-571-7400
Doyle New York 175 E 87th St	New York	NY	10128	**800-808-0902**	212-427-2730
eBay Inc 2145 Hamilton Ave	San Jose	CA	95125	**800-322-9266**	408-558-7400
NASDAQ: EBAY					
Gallery of History Inc					
3601 W Sahara Ave Suite 207	Las Vegas	NV	89102	**800-425-5379**	702-364-1000
NASDAQ: HIST					
Gordon Brothers Corp 40 Broad St Suite 800	Boston	MA	02109	**800-487-4882**	617-422-6542
Greg Manning Auctions Inc					
775 Passaic Ave	West Caldwell	NJ	07006	**800-221-0243**	973-882-0004
NASDAQ: GMAI					
Harry Davis & Co 1725 Blvd of Allies	Pittsburgh	PA	15219	**800-775-2289**	412-765-1170
Henderson Auctions Co					
13340 Florida Blvd PO Box 336	Livingston	LA	70754	**800-850-2252**	225-686-2252
icollector.com 1963 Lougheed Hwy	Coquitlam	BC	V3K3T8	**866-313-0123**	604-521-3369
Insurance Auto Auctions Inc					
850 E Algonquin Rd Suite 100	Schaumburg	IL	60173	**800-872-1501**	847-839-3939
Kennedy-Wilson Inc					
9601 Wilshire Blvd Suite 220	Beverly Hills	CA	90210	**800-522-6664**	310-887-6400
NASDAQ: KWIC					
Kruse International 5540 County Rd 11A	Auburn	IN	46706	**800-968-4444**	219-925-5600
Manning Greg Auctions Inc					
775 Passaic Ave	West Caldwell	NJ	07006	**800-221-0243**	973-882-0004
NASDAQ: GMAI					
Max Rouse & Sons Inc					
361 S Robertson Blvd	Beverly Hills	CA	90211	**800-421-0816**	310-360-9200
Priceline.com Inc 800 Connecticut Ave	Norwalk	CT	06854	**800-774-2354**	203-299-8000
NASDAQ: PCLN					
Ritchie Bros Auctioneers Inc 6500 River Rd	Richmond	BC	V6X4G5	**800-663-1739**	604-273-7564
NYSE: RBA					
Rouse Max & Sons Inc					
361 S Robertson Blvd	Beverly Hills	CA	90211	**800-421-0816**	310-360-9200
Theriault's PO Box 151	Annapolis	MD	21404	**800-966-3655**	410-224-3655
uBid Inc 8550 W Bryn Mawr Ave Suite 200	Chicago	IL	60631	**888-900-8243**	773-272-5000

52 AUDIO & VIDEO EQUIPMENT

Listing	City	State	ZIP	Toll-Free	Phone
Alpine Electronics of America					
19145 Gramercy Pl	Torrance	CA	90501	**800-257-4631**	310-326-8000
Altec Lansing Technologies Inc					
PO Box 277 Rt 6	Milford	PA	18337	**800-258-3288**	570-296-6444
Amplivox Inc 3149 MacArthur Blvd	Northbrook	IL	60062	**800-267-5486**	847-498-9000
Andrea Electronics Corp					
65 Orville Dr Suite 110	Bohemia	NY	11716	**800-442-7787**	631-719-1800
AMEX: AND					
Atlas Sound 1601 Jack McKay Blvd	Ennis	TX	75119	**800-876-3333**	972-875-8413
Audio Command Systems 694 Main St	Westbury	NY	11590	**800-382-2939**	516-997-5800
Audiosears Corp 2 South St	Stamford	NY	12167	**800-533-7863**	607-652-7305
Audiovox Corp 150 Marcus Blvd	Hauppauge	NY	11788	**800-645-4994**	631-231-7750
NASDAQ: VOXX					
Automated Voice Systems Inc (AVSI)					
17059 El Cajon Ave	Yorba Linda	CA	92886	**888-505-2026**	714-524-4488
AVSI (Automated Voice Systems Inc)					
17059 El Cajon Ave	Yorba Linda	CA	92886	**888-505-2026**	714-524-4488
Biamp Systems Inc 10074 SW Arctic Dr	Beaverton	OR	97005	**800-826-1457**	503-641-7287
Blaupunkt Div Robert Bosch Corp					
2800 S 25th Ave	Broadview	IL	60155	**800-323-1943***	708-865-5200
*Sales					
Bogen Communications International Inc					
50 Spring St	Ramsey	NJ	07446	**800-999-2809**	201-934-8500
Bose Corp The Mountain	Framingham	MA	01701	**800-444-2673***	508-879-7330
*Sales					
Boston Acoustics Inc 300 Jubilee Dr	Peabody	MA	01960	**800-288-6148**	978-538-5000
NASDAQ: BOSA					
Cambridge Soundworks Inc					
100 Brickstone Sq 5th Fl	Andover	MA	01810	**800-945-4434**	978-623-4400
Citizen Systems America Corp					
363 Van Ness Way Suite 404	Torrance	CA	90501	**800-421-6516**	310-781-1460
Clarion Corp of America					
661 W Redondo Beach Blvd	Gardena	CA	90247	**800-462-5274**	310-327-9100
Community Light & Sound Inc 333 E 5th St	Chester	PA	19013	**800-523-4934**	610-876-3400
Creative Labs Inc 1901 McCarthy Blvd	Milpitas	CA	95035	**800-998-1000***	408-428-6600
*Cust Svc					
Daewoo Electronics Corp of America					
120 Chubb Ave	Lyndhurst	NJ	07071	**800-323-9668**	201-460-2000
Digidesign Inc 2001 Junipero Serra Blvd	Daly City	CA	94014	**800-333-2137**	650-731-6300
Digit Professional Inc 3926 Varsity Dr	Ann Arbor	MI	48108	**877-767-8862**	734-677-0840
Digital Innovations					
3436 N Kennicott Suite 200	Arlington Heights	IL	60004	**888-762-7858**	847-463-9000
Directed Electronics Inc 1 Viper Way	Vista	CA	92081	**800-876-0800**	760-598-6200
Dolby Laboratories Inc 100 Potrero Ave	San Francisco	CA	94103	**800-983-6529**	415-558-0200
NYSE: DLB					
Dynamic Instruments Inc					
3860 Calle Fortunada	San Diego	CA	92123	**800-793-3358**	858-278-4900
e.Digital Corp 13114 Evening Creek Dr S	San Diego	CA	92128	**877-278-1574**	858-679-1504
Educational Technology Inc 2224 Hewlett Ave	Merrick	NY	11566	**800-942-2136***	516-623-3200
*Cust Svc					
Euphonix Inc 220 Portage Ave	Palo Alto	CA	94306	**800-579-7836**	650-855-0400
Extron Electronics USA 1230 S Lewis St	Anaheim	CA	92805	**800-633-9876***	714-491-1500
*Tech Supp					
Fujitsu Ten Corp of America					
19600 S Vermont Ave	Torrance	CA	90502	**800-233-2216**	310-327-2151
Harman International Industries Inc					
1101 Pennsylvania Ave NW Suite 1010	Washington	DC	20004	**800-336-4525***	202-393-1101
NYSE: HAR ■ *Cust Svc					
Harman Kardon Inc 250 Crossways Pk Dr	Woodbury	NY	11797	**800-336-4525**	516-496-3400
Hitachi Home Electronics Inc					
900 Hitachi Way	Chula Vista	CA	91914	**800-981-2588**	619-591-5200
International Video-Conferencing Inc					
180 Adams Ave	Hauppauge	NY	11788	**800-224-7083**	631-273-5800
JBL Professional 8400 Balboa Blvd	Northridge	CA	91329	**800-852-5776**	818-894-8850
JVC Co of America 1700 Valley Rd	Wayne	NJ	07470	**800-526-5308**	973-317-5000
Kenwood USA Corp PO Box 22745	Long Beach	CA	90801	**800-536-9663**	310-639-9000
KLH Audio Systems 11131 Dora St	Sun Valley	CA	91352	**800-854-4441**	818-767-2843
Klipsch LLC 137 County Rd 278	Hope	AR	71801	**800-554-7724**	870-777-6751
Koss Corp 4129 N Port Washington Ave	Milwaukee	WI	53212	**800-872-5677**	414-964-5000
NASDAQ: KOSS					
Law Enforcement Associates Corp					
100 Hunter Pl	Youngsville	NC	27596	**800-354-9669**	919-554-4700
Lenoxx Electronics Corp 2 Germak Dr	Carteret	NJ	07008	**800-315-5885**	718-633-4480
LKG Industries Inc 3660 Publisher's Dr	Rockford	IL	61109	**800-645-2262**	815-874-2301
Logitech Inc 6505 Kaiser Dr	Fremont	CA	94555	**800-231-7717***	510-795-8500
*Sales					
LOUD Technologies Inc					
16220 Wood Red Rd NE	Woodinville	WA	98072	**800-258-6883**	425-487-4333
Lowell Mfg Co 100 Integram Dr	Pacific	MO	63069	**800-325-9660**	636-257-3400
Matsushita Avionics Systems					
22333 29th Dr SE	Bothell	WA	98021	**800-755-2684**	425-415-9000
Matsushita Electric Corp of America					
1 Panasonic Way	Secaucus	NJ	07094	**888-275-2595**	201-348-7000
McIntosh Laboratory Inc 2 Chambers St	Binghamton	NY	13903	**800-538-6576**	607-723-3512
Metra Electronics Corp 460 Walker St	Holly Hill	FL	32117	**800-221-0932***	386-257-1186
*Sales					
Mitsubishi Digital Electronics America Inc					
9351 Jeronimo Rd	Irvine	CA	92618	**800-332-2119**	949-465-6000
Mitsubishi Electric & Electronics USA Inc					
5665 Plaza Dr	Cypress	CA	90630	**800-843-2515**	714-220-2500
MTX Corp 4545 E Baseline Rd	Phoenix	AZ	85042	**800-225-5689**	602-438-4545
Omnitronics LLC 341 Harbor St PO Box 120	Conneaut	OH	44030	**888-872-3104**	440-593-1111
Otari Corp 9420 Lurline Ave Unit C	Chatsworth	CA	91311	**800-735-1786**	818-734-1785
Panasonic Consumer Electronics Co					
1 Panasonic Way	Secaucus	NJ	07094	**888-275-2595**	201-348-7000
Philips Consumer Electronics PO Box 467300	Atlanta	GA	31146	**800-531-0039***	770-821-2400
*Cust Svc					
Phoenix Gold International Inc					
9300 N Decatur St	Portland	OR	97203	**800-950-1449**	503-286-9300
Pictorvision 7701 Haskel Ave Suite B	Van Nuys	CA	91406	**800-876-5583**	818-785-9881
Pioneer Electronics (USA) Inc					
2265 E 220th St	Long Beach	CA	90810	**800-421-1404***	310-952-2000
*Cust Svc					
Polk Audio Inc 5601 Metro Dr	Baltimore	MD	21215	**800-377-7655**	410-358-3600
Primo Microphones Inc 1805 Couch Dr	McKinney	TX	75069	**800-767-7466**	972-548-9807
QSC Audio Products Inc					
1675 MacArthur Blvd	Costa Mesa	CA	92626	**800-854-4079**	714-754-6175
ReQuest Inc					
100 Saratoga Village Blvd Suite 44	Ballston Spa	NY	12020	**800-236-2812***	518-899-1254
*Cust Svc					
Roanwell Corp 2564 Park Ave	Bronx	NY	10451	**866-292-3301**	718-401-0288
Robert Bosch Corp Blaupunkt Div					
2800 S 25th Ave	Broadview	IL	60155	**800-323-1943***	708-865-5200
*Sales					
Rockford Corp 600 S Rockford Dr	Tempe	AZ	85281	**800-669-9899**	480-967-3565
NASDAQ: ROFO					
Samsung Electronics America Inc					
105 Challenger Rd	Ridgefield Park	NJ	07660	**800-726-7864**	201-229-4000
Sanyo Mfg Corp 3333 Sanyo Rd	Forrest City	AR	72335	**800-877-5032**	870-633-5030

Company	City	State	Zip	Toll-Free	Phone
SDI Technologies Inc 1299 Main St *Cust Svc	Rahway	NJ	07065	**800-888-4491***	732-574-9000
Sharp Electronics Corp 1 Sharp Plaza	Mahwah	NJ	07430	**800-237-4277**	201-529-8200
Sherwood America 13101 Moore St	Cerritos	CA	90703	**800-777-8755**	562-741-0960
Shure Inc 5800 W Touhy Ave	Niles	IL	60714	**800-257-4873**	847-866-2200
Sima Products Corp 140 Pennsylvania Ave Bldg 5	Oakmont	PA	15139	**800-345-7462**	412-828-3700
Sony Corp of America 550 Madison Ave	New York	NY	10022	**800-282-2848**	212-833-6800
Sony Electronics Inc 1 Sony Dr *Cust Svc	Park Ridge	NJ	07656	**800-222-7669***	201-930-1000
Southern Audio Services 15049 Florida Blvd	Baton Rouge	LA	70819	**800-843-8823**	225-272-7135
Stancil Corp 2644 S Croddy Way	Santa Ana	CA	92704	**800-782-6245**	714-546-2002
TDK USA Corp 901 Franklin Ave	Garden City	NY	11530	**800-835-8273**	516-535-2600
Telex Communications Inc 12000 Portland Ave S *Sales	Burnsville	MN	55337	**800-828-6107***	952-884-4051
Toshiba America Inc 1251 Ave of the Americas 41st Fl	New York	NY	10020	**800-457-7777**	212-596-0600
Vega Holdings Inc 4065 Hollis St	Emeryville	CA	94608	**800-877-1771**	510-496-6666
Xantech Corp 13100 Telfair Ave 2nd Fl *Sales	Sylmar	CA	91342	**800-843-5465***	818-362-0353
Yamaha Electronics Corp 6660 Orangethorpe Ave *Cust Svc	Buena Park	CA	90620	**800-492-6242***	714-522-9105

53 AUTO CLUBS

Company	City	State	Zip	Toll-Free	Phone
AAA Alabama 2400 Acton Rd	Birmingham	AL	35243	**800-521-8124**	205-978-7000
AAA Allied Group Inc 15 W Central Pkwy	Cincinnati	OH	45202	**800-543-2345**	513-762-3100
AAA Arizona 3144 N 7th Ave	Phoenix	AZ	85013	**800-352-5382**	602-274-1116
AAA Ashland County 502 Claremont Ave	Ashland	OH	44805	**800-222-4357**	419-289-8133
AAA Blue Grass/Kentucky 155 N MLK Blvd	Lexington	KY	40507	**800-568-5222**	859-233-1111
AAA Carolinas 6600 AAA Dr	Charlotte	NC	28212	**800-477-4222**	704-569-3600
AAA Central Penn 2023 Market St	Harrisburg	PA	17103	**877-848-9990**	717-236-4021
AAA Chicago Motor Club 975 Meridian Lake Dr	Aurora	IL	60504	**866-968-7222**	630-328-7000
AAA Colorado 4100 E Arkansas Ave	Denver	CO	80222	**877-244-9790**	303-753-8800
AAA Columbiana County 516 Broadway St	East Liverpool	OH	43920	**800-222-4357**	330-385-2020
AAA East Penn 1020 Hamilton St	Allentown	PA	18105	**800-552-6679**	610-434-5141
AAA East Tennessee 100 W 5th Ave	Knoxville	TN	37917	**800-234-1222**	865-637-1910
AAA Hawaii 1130 N Nimitz Hwy Suite A-170	Honolulu	HI	96817	**800-736-2886**	808-593-2221
AAA Hoosier Motor Club 3750 Guion Rd	Indianapolis	IN	46222	**800-624-9820**	317-923-3311
AAA Kentucky 435 E Broadway	Louisville	KY	40202	**800-727-2552**	502-582-3311
AAA Massillon Auto Club 1972 Wales Rd NE	Massillon	OH	44646	**800-222-4357**	330-833-1084
AAA Miami Valley 825 S Ludlow St	Dayton	OH	45402	**800-624-2321**	937-224-2801
AAA Michigan 1 Auto Club Dr	Dearborn	MI	48126	**800-222-6424**	313-336-1234
AAA Mid-Atlantic 2040 Market St	Philadelphia	PA	19103	**888-859-5161**	215-864-5000
AAA Minnesota/Iowa 600 W Travelers Trail	Burnsville	MN	55337	**800-222-1333**	952-707-4500
AAA Missouri 12901 N Forty Dr	Saint Louis	MO	63141	**800-222-4357**	314-523-7350
AAA MountainWest 2100 11th Ave	Helena	MT	59601	**800-332-6119**	406-447-8100
AAA Nebraska 910 N 96th St	Omaha	NE	68114	**800-222-6327**	402-390-1000
AAA New Mexico Inc 10501 Montgomery Blvd NE	Albuquerque	NM	87111	**800-846-0377**	505-291-6611
AAA North Dakota 1801 38th St SW	Fargo	ND	58103	**800-342-4254**	701-282-6222
AAA North Jersey 418 Hamburg Tpke	Wayne	NJ	07470	**800-222-4357**	973-956-2200
AAA of Northern California Nevada & Utah 150 Van Ness Ave *Cust Svc	San Francisco	CA	94102	**800-922-8228***	415-565-2012
AAA Northern New England 68 Marginal Way	Portland	ME	04104	**800-222-4357**	207-780-6800
AAA Northwest Ohio 7150 W Central Ave	Toledo	OH	43617	**800-428-0060**	419-843-1200
AAA Ohio Auto Club 90 E Wilson Bridge Rd	Worthington	OH	43085	**800-282-0585**	614-431-7800
AAA Oklahoma 2121 E 15th St	Tulsa	OK	74104	**800-222-2582**	918-748-1000
AAA Oregon/Idaho 600 SW Market St *Cust Svc	Portland	OR	97201	**800-452-1643***	503-222-6734
AAA South Dakota 1300 Industrial Ave	Sioux Falls	SD	57104	**800-222-4545**	605-336-3690
AAA Southern New England 110 Royal Little Dr	Providence	RI	02904	**800-222-7448**	401-868-2000
AAA Southern Pennsylvania 2840 Eastern Blvd	York	PA	17402	**800-222-1469**	717-600-8700
AAA Washington-Inland 1745 114th Ave SE	Bellevue	WA	98004	**800-562-2582**	425-462-2222
AAA Western & Central New York 100 International Dr	Buffalo	NY	14221	**800-836-2582**	716-633-9860
AAA Wisconsin 8401 Excelsior Dr	Madison	WI	53717	**800-236-1300**	608-836-6555
AARP Motoring Plan 200 N Martingale Rd	Schaumburg	IL	60173	**800-555-1121**	
ACA (Auto Club of America Corp) 9411 N Georgia St	Oklahoma City	OK	73120	**800-411-2007**	405-751-4430
Allstate Motor Club 51 W Higgins Rd	South Barrington	IL	60010	**800-255-2582**	847-551-2300
Auto Club of America Corp (ACA) 9411 N Georgia St	Oklahoma City	OK	73120	**800-411-2007**	405-751-4430
Auto Club Ltd 106 E 6th St Suite 900	Austin	TX	78701	**866-247-3728**	512-343-4588
Automobile Club of Southern California 2601 S Figueroa St	Los Angeles	CA	90007	**800-400-4222**	213-741-3686
AutoVantage 100 Connecticut Ave	Norwalk	CT	06850	**800-876-7787**	
BCAA (British Columbia Automobile Assn) 4567 Canada Way	Burnaby	BC	V5G4T1	**800-222-4357**	604-268-5000
BP MotorClub 200 N Martingale Rd	Schaumburg	IL	60196	**800-334-3300**	
Brickell Financial Services Motor Club Inc DBA Road America Motor Club 7300 Corporate Ctr Dr Suite 601	Miami	FL	33126	**800-262-7262**	305-392-4300
British Columbia Automobile Assn (BCAA) 4567 Canada Way	Burnaby	BC	V5G4T1	**800-222-4357**	604-268-5000
CAA Alberta Motor Assn 10310 39A Ave NW	Edmonton	AB	T6J6R7	**800-642-3810**	780-430-5555
CAA Central Ontario 60 Commerce Valley Dr E	Thornhill	ON	L3T7P9	**800-268-3750**	905-771-3000
CAA Manitoba 870 Empress St	Winnipeg	MB	R3C2Z3	**800-222-4357**	204-262-6166
CAA Maritimes 378 Westmorland Rd	Saint John	NB	E2J2G4	**800-561-8807**	506-634-1400
CAA Mid-Western Ontario 148 Manitou Dr	Kitchener	ON	N2G4W8	**800-265-8975**	519-894-2582
CAA Niagara 3271 Schmon Pkwy	Thorold	ON	L2V4Y6	**800-263-7272**	905-984-8585
CAA North & East Ontario 2525 Carling Ave	Ottawa	ON	K2B7Z2	**800-267-8713**	613-820-1890
CAA Quebec 444 Bouvier St	Quebec	QC	G2J1E3	**800-686-9243**	418-624-2424
CAA Saskatchewan 200 Albert St N	Regina	SK	S4R5E2	**800-564-6222**	306-791-4321
California State Automobile Assn 150 Van Ness Ave *Cust Svc	San Francisco	CA	94102	**800-922-8228***	415-565-2012
Chevron Travel Club Inc PO Box P	Concord	CA	94524	**800-222-0585**	
Cross Country Automotive Services 4040 Mystic Valley Pkwy	Medford	MA	02155	**800-833-5500**	
Exxon Travel Club PO Box 660460	Dallas	TX	75266	**800-833-9966**	
Ford Auto Club Inc PO Box 660460	Dallas	TX	75226	**800-348-5220**	
GE Motor Club Inc 200 N Martingale Rd *Cust Svc	Schaumburg	IL	60173	**800-616-9286***	800-417-6368
GM Motor Club PO Box 3580	Southfield	MI	48037	**800-705-0055**	
Gulf Motor Club 929 N Plum Grove Rd	Schaumburg	IL	60173	**800-633-3224**	
Motor Club of America Enterprises Inc 3200 Wilshire Blvd	Oklahoma City	OK	73156	**800-288-2889**	
National Motor Club of America Inc 6500 Beltline Rd Suite 200	Irving	TX	75063	**800-523-4582**	972-999-4400
Ohio Motorists Assn 5700 Brecksville Rd	Independence	OH	44131	**800-711-5370**	216-606-6100
Pinnacle Motor Club 3801 William D Tate St Suite 800	Grapevine	TX	76051	**800-446-1289**	
Road America Motor Club 7300 Corporate Ctr Dr Suite 601	Miami	FL	33126	**800-262-7262**	305-392-4300
Roadgard Motor Club 11222 Quail Roost Dr	Miami	FL	33157	**800-432-8603**	
Travelers Motor Club 720 NW 50th St	Oklahoma City	OK	73154	**800-654-9208**	405-848-1711
Trilegiant Corp DBA AutoVantage 100 Connecticut Ave	Norwalk	CT	06850	**800-876-7787**	
US Auto Club Motoring Div Inc PO Box 660460	Dallas	TX	75226	**800-348-2761**	

54 AUTO SUPPLY STORES

Company	City	State	Zip	Toll-Free	Phone
Am-Pac Tire Pros Inc 917 6th Ave N	Birmingham	AL	35203	**800-875-4655**	205-322-4651
Bennett Auto Supply Inc 3141 SW 10th St	Pompano Beach	FL	33069	**800-723-6638**	954-335-8700
Champion Auto Stores Inc 2565 Kasota Ave	Saint Paul	MN	55108	**800-899-6528**	651-644-6448
Discount Tire Co 20225 N Scottsdale Rd	Scottsdale	AZ	85255	**800-347-4348**	480-606-6000
Hedahls Inc 100 E Broadway	Bismarck	ND	58502	**800-433-2457**	701-223-8393
Murray's Discount Auto Stores 8080 Hagerty Rd	Belleville	MI	48111	**800-946-8772**	734-957-8080
Original Parts Group Inc 5252 Bolsa Ave	Huntington Beach	CA	92649	**800-243-8355**	714-230-6000
Peerless Tyre Co 5000 Kingston St	Denver	CO	80239	**800-999-7810**	303-371-4300
Pep Boys - Manny Moe & Jack 3111 W Allegheny Ave *NYSE: PBY*	Philadelphia	PA	19132	**800-737-2697**	215-227-9000
Town Fair Tire Co Inc 460 Coe Ave	East Haven	CT	06512	**800-972-2245**	203-467-8600

55 AUTOMATIC MERCHANDISING EQUIPMENT & SYSTEMS

SEE ALSO Food Service

Company	City	State	Zip	Toll-Free	Phone
AIR-serv Group LLC 1370 Mendota Heights Rd	Mendota Heights	MN	55120	**800-227-5336**	651-454-0518
American Vending Sales Inc 750 Morse Ave	Elk Grove Village	IL	60007	**800-441-0009**	847-439-9400
Automatic Products International Ltd 75 Plato Blvd W	Saint Paul	MN	55107	**800-523-8363**	651-224-4391
Betson Enterprises Inc 303 Patterson Plank Rd	Carlstadt	NJ	07072	**800-524-2343**	201-438-1300
Birmingham Vending Co 540 2nd Ave N	Birmingham	AL	35204	**800-288-7635**	205-324-7526
Coin Acceptors Inc 300 Hunter Ave	Saint Louis	MO	63124	**800-325-2646**	314-725-0100
Coinstar Inc 1800 114th Ave SE *NASDAQ: CSTR*	Bellevue	WA	98004	**800-928-2274**	425-943-8000
Crane Merchandising Systems 12955 Enterprise Way	Bridgeton	MO	63044	**800-325-8811**	314-298-3500
Dixie-Narco Inc PO Drawer 719	Williston	SC	29853	**800-688-9090**	803-266-5000
Fawn Vendors Inc 8040 University Blvd	Des Moines	IA	50325	**800-247-2801**	515-274-3641
Federal Machine Corp 8040 University Blvd	Des Moines	IA	50325	**800-247-2446**	515-274-1555
Harcourt Outlines Inc 7765 S 175 West PO Box 128	Milroy	IN	46156	**800-428-6584**	765-629-2625
LM Becker & Co Inc PO Box 1459	Appleton	WI	54912	**888-869-6569**	920-739-5269
Mars Electronics International (MEI) 1301 Wilson Dr *Cust Svc	West Chester	PA	19380	**800-345-8215***	610-430-2500
Melo-Tone Vending Inc 130 Broadway	Somerville	MA	02145	**800-322-7741**	617-666-4900
Money Control Inc 34099 Melinz Pkwy	Eastlake	OH	44095	**800-321-0765**	440-946-3000
Northwestern Corp PO Box 490	Morris	IL	60450	**800-942-1316**	815-942-1300
Rowe International Inc 1500 Union Ave SE	Grand Rapids	MI	49507	**800-636-2787**	616-243-3633

56 AUTOMATIC TELLER MACHINES (ATMS)

Company	City	State	Zip	Toll-Free	Phone
Cardtronics Inc 3110 Hayes Rd Suite 300	Houston	TX	77082	**800-786-9666**	281-596-9988
Cash Systems Inc 3201 W County Rd 42 Suite 106 *AMEX: CKN* ■ *Sales	Burnsville	MN	55306	**877-600-8399***	952-895-8399
Diebold Inc 5995 Mayfair Rd *NYSE: DBD*	North Canton	OH	44720	**800-999-3600**	330-490-4000
Electronic Cash Systems Inc 22512 Avenida Empresa	Rancho Santa Margarita	CA	92688	**888-327-2864**	949-888-9955
Frisco Bay Industries Ltd 160 Graveline St	Saint-Laurent	QC	H4T1R7	**800-463-7472**	514-738-7300
NCR Corp 1700 S Patterson Blvd *NYSE: NCR* ■ *Cust Svc	Dayton	OH	45479	**800-531-2222***	937-445-5000
Tidel Engineering Inc 2310 McDaniel Dr	Carrollton	TX	75006	**800-678-7577**	972-484-3358
Tranax Technologies Inc 44320 Nobel Dr	Fremont	CA	94538	**888-340-2484**	510-770-2227
Triton Systems Inc 522 E Railroad St	Long Beach	MS	39560	**800-259-6672**	228-868-1317

57 AUTOMOBILE DEALERS & GROUPS

SEE ALSO Automobile Sales & Related Services - Online

Name / Address	City	State	Zip	Toll-Free	Phone
#1 Cochran of Monroeville 4520 William Penn Hwy	Monroeville	PA	15146	**877-262-4726**	412-373-3333
Allan Vigil Ford 6790 Mt Zion Blvd	Marrow	GA	30260	**800-222-3597**	678-364-3673
Allen Samuels Auto Group 301 Owen Ln	Waco	TX	76710	**800-762-8850**	254-761-6800
America's Car-Mart Inc 1501 SE Walton Blvd Suite 213 *NASDAQ: CRMT*	Bentonville	AR	72712	**800-264-2535**	479-464-9944
Ancira Enterprises Inc 6111 Bandera Rd	San Antonio	TX	78238	**800-299-5286**	210-681-4900
AutoNation Inc 110 SE 6th St *NYSE: AN*	Fort Lauderdale	FL	33301	**800-899-4911**	954-769-7000
Barrett Holdings Inc 15423 I-10 W	San Antonio	TX	78249	**800-234-3466**	210-341-2800
Bella Automotive Group 5895 NW 167th St	Hialeah	FL	33015	**800-779-8696**	305-364-9800
Bill Heard Enterprises 200 Brookstone Ctr Pkwy Suite 205	Columbus	GA	31904	**800-833-0479**	706-323-1111
Bob Rohrman Auto Group 701 Sagamore Pkwy S	Lafayette	IN	47905	**800-488-3534**	765-448-1000
Boyland Auto Group Inc 710 W Marine Dr	Astoria	OR	97103	**888-760-9303**	503-325-6411
Buchanan Automotive Group 707 S Washington Blvd	Sarasota	FL	34236	**800-282-5633**	941-366-5230
Burt Automotive Network 5200 S Broadway	Englewood	CO	80113	**800-535-2878**	303-761-0333
Capital Ford Inc 4900 Capital Blvd	Raleigh	NC	27616	**800-849-3166**	919-790-4600
Collins Auto Group 4220 Bardstown Rd	Lousiville	KY	40218	**800-258-2455**	502-459-9550
Courtesy Chevrolet 1233 E Camelback Rd	Phoenix	AZ	85014	**800-555-9322**	602-279-3232
Dothan Chrysler-Dodge Inc 4074 Ross Clark Cir NW	Dothan	AL	36303	**800-792-3007**	334-794-0606
DriveTime Corp 4020 E Indian School Rd	Phoenix	AZ	85018	**800-863-7483**	602-852-6600
Earnhardt Auto Centers 1301 N Arizona Ave	Gilbert	AZ	85233	**800-497-8740**	480-926-4000
Ed Morse Automotive Group Inc 6363 NW 6th Way Suite 400	Fort Lauderdale	FL	33309	**800-336-6773**	954-351-0055
Elder Automotive Group 777 John R	Troy	MI	48083	**800-585-4005**	248-585-4000
Folsom Lake Ford Inc 12755 Folsom Blvd	Folsom	CA	95630	**800-655-0555**	916-353-2000
Freehold Chevrolet 3712 Rt 9 S PO Box 6697	Freehold	NJ	07728	**800-648-8656**	732-462-1324
Galpin Motors Inc 15505 Roscoe Blvd	North Hills	CA	91343	**800-464-2574**	818-787-3800
Germain Motor Co 4130 Morse Crossing	Columbus	OH	43219	**866-771-2178**	614-478-2002
Gettel Automotive Group 3480 Bee Ridge Rd	Sarasota	FL	34239	**888-468-8696**	941-921-2655
Gillman Cos 10595 W Sam Houston Pkwy S	Houston	TX	77099	**800-933-7809**	713-776-7000
Gonzales Automotive Group 5800 Firestone Blvd	South Gate	CA	90280	**888-318-5337**	562-776-2330
Hall Automotive 441 Viking Dr	Virginia Beach	VA	23452	**800-242-4255**	757-431-9944
Huffines Auto Group 4500 W Plano Pkwy	Plano	TX	75093	**866-522-5138**	972-867-6000
Kelley Automotive Group 633 Ave of Autos	Fort Wayne	IN	46804	**800-434-4750**	260-434-4700
Ken Garff Automotive Group 195 E University Pkwy	Orem	UT	84058	**888-323-5869**	801-374-1751
Keyes Automotive Group 5855 Van Nuys Blvd	Van Nuys	CA	91401	**800-974-7709**	818-782-0122
Lou Fusz Automotive Network Inc 925 N Lindbergh Blvd	Saint Louis	MO	63141	**800-371-7819**	314-994-1500
Love Chrysler Plymouth Inc 4331 S Staples St	Corpus Christi	TX	78411	**866-460-5683**	361-991-5683
Lupient Automotive Group 750 Pennsylvania Ave S	Minneapolis	MN	55426	**800-328-0608**	763-544-6666
McCombs Enterprises 755 E Mulberry Ave Suite 600	San Antonio	TX	78212	**800-460-4883**	210-821-6523
Mike Shaw Chevrolet Buick Saab 1080 S Colorado Blvd	Denver	CO	80246	**800-223-1615**	303-757-6161
Penske Automotive Group 3534 N Peck Rd	El Monte	CA	91731	**800-355-6646**	626-580-6000
Phil Long Dealerships 1212 Motor City Dr	Colorado Springs	CO	80906	**800-685-5664**	719-575-7100
Popular Ford Sales Inc 2505 Coney Island Ave	Brooklyn	NY	11223	**888-622-9122**	718-376-5600
Ron Tonkin Dealerships 122 NE 122nd Ave	Portland	OR	97230	**800-460-5328**	503-255-4100
Russ Darrow Group W133 N8569 Executive Pkwy	Menomonee Falls	WI	53051	**800-732-7769**	262-250-9600
Sam Swope Auto Group LLC 10 Swope Auto Ctr	Louisville	KY	40299	**800-228-9086**	502-499-5000
Silver Star Automotive Group 3905 Auto Mall Dr	Thousand Oaks	CA	91362	**800-995-5175**	805-371-5400
Tamiami Automotive Group 8250 SW 8th St	Miami	FL	33144	**800-845-2886**	305-266-5500
Tuttle-Click Automotive Group 41 Auto Center Dr	Irvine	CA	92618	**800-926-8253**	949-598-4800
Van Enterprises 8500 W Shawnee Mission Pkwy Suite 200	Shawnee Mission	KS	66202	**800-747-4400**	913-432-6400
VT Inc DBA Van Enterprises 8500 W Shawnee Mission Pkwy Suite 200	Shawnee Mission	KS	66202	**800-747-4400**	913-432-6400
West-Herr Automotive Group Inc S-5025 Camp Rd	Hamburg	NY	14075	**800-933-5701**	716-649-5640
Wilde Automotive Group 1603 E Moreland Blvd	Waukesha	WI	53186	**800-236-5567**	262-542-0771
World Class Automotive Group 3333 Inwood Rd	Dallas	TX	75235	**800-898-4295**	214-358-8800

AUTOMOBILE LEASING

SEE Credit & Financing - Commercial; Credit & Financing - Consumer; Fleet Leasing & Management

58 AUTOMOBILE SALES & RELATED SERVICES - ONLINE

SEE ALSO Automobile Dealers & Groups

Name / Address	City	State	Zip	Toll-Free	Phone
Autobytel Inc 18872 MacArthur Blvd *NASDAQ: ABTL*	Irvine	CA	92612	**888-422-8999**	949-225-4500
Automobile Consumer Services Inc 6249 Stewart Rd	Cincinnati	OH	45227	**800-223-4882**	513-527-7700
Automotive Information Center 18872 MacArthur Blvd	Irvine	CA	92612	**888-422-8999**	949-862-1335
AutoTrader.com LLC 5775 Peachtree Dunwoody Rd Suite A-200	Atlanta	GA	30342	**800-353-9350**	404-269-8000
AutoVIN Inc 50 Mansell Ct Suite 200	Roswell	GA	30076	**877-428-8684**	678-585-8000
Autoweb.com Inc 18872 MacArthur Blvd	Irvine	CA	92612	**888-422-8999**	949-225-4500
Carfax Inc 10304 Eaton Pl Suite 500	Fairfax	VA	22030	**800-274-2277**	703-934-2664
CarPrices.com c/o AutoFusion Corp 9605 Scranton Rd Suite 450	San Diego	CA	92121	**800-410-7354**	
CarsDirect.com Inc 909 N Sepulveda Blvd *Cust Svc	El Segundo	CA	90245	**800-431-2500***	310-280-4000
CarSmart 18872 MacArthur Blvd	Irvine	CA	92612	**888-422-8999**	949-862-1335
DealerNet c/o Cobalt Group Inc 2200 1st Ave S Suite 400	Seattle	WA	98134	**800-909-8244**	206-269-6363
Kelley Blue Book Co Inc 5 Oldfield	Irvine	CA	92618	**800-258-3266**	949-770-7704

59 AUTOMOBILES - MFR

SEE ALSO All Terrain Vehicles; Motor Vehicles - Commercial & Special Purpose; Motorcycles & Motorcycle Parts & Accessories; Snowmobiles

Name / Address	City	State	Zip	Toll-Free	Phone
Acura Div American Honda Motor Co Inc 1919 Torrance Blvd	Torrance	CA	90501	**800-382-2238**	310-783-2000
American Honda Motor Co Inc Acura Div 1919 Torrance Blvd	Torrance	CA	90501	**800-382-2238**	310-783-2000
American Isuzu Motors Inc 13340 183rd St *Cust Svc	Cerritos	CA	90702	**800-255-6727***	562-229-5000
Audi of America 3800 Hamlin Rd	Auburn Hills	MI	48326	**800-367-2834**	248-340-5000
BMW of North America Inc PO Box 1227	Westwood	NJ	07675	**800-526-0818**	201-307-4000
Buick Motor Div General Motors Corp 300 Renaissance Ctr *Cust Svc	Detroit	MI	48265	**800-521-7300***	313-556-5000
Cadillac Motor Car Div General Motors Corp 300 Renaissance Ctr *Cust Svc	Detroit	MI	48265	**800-458-8006***	313-556-5000
Chevrolet Motor Div General Motors Corp 300 Renaissance Ctr *Cust Svc	Detroit	MI	48265	**800-222-1020***	313-556-5000
DaimlerChrysler Canada Inc PO Box 1621 Stn A	Windsor	ON	N9A4H6	**800-265-6904**	519-973-2000
DaimlerChrysler Corp 1000 Chrysler Dr *NYSE: DCX*	Auburn Hills	MI	48326	**800-992-1997**	248-576-5741
DaimlerChrysler Corp Dodge Div 1000 Chrysler Dr *Cust Svc	Auburn Hills	MI	48326	**800-992-1997***	248-576-5741
DaimlerChrysler Corp Eagle Div 800 Chrysler Dr E *Cust Svc	Auburn Hills	MI	48326	**800-992-1997***	248-576-5741
DaimlerChrysler Corp Jeep Div 800 Chrysler Dr E *Cust Svc	Auburn Hills	MI	48326	**800-992-1997***	248-576-5741
DaimlerChrysler Corp Plymouth Div 800 Chrysler Dr E *Cust Svc	Auburn Hills	MI	48326	**800-992-1997***	248-576-5741
Dodge Div DaimlerChrysler Corp 1000 Chrysler Dr *Cust Svc	Auburn Hills	MI	48326	**800-992-1997***	248-576-5741
Eagle Div DaimlerChrysler Corp 800 Chrysler Dr E *Cust Svc	Auburn Hills	MI	48326	**800-992-1997***	248-576-5741
Ford Motor Co PO Box 6248 *NYSE: F*	Dearborn	MI	48126	**800-392-3673**	313-322-3000
General Motors of Canada Ltd 1908 Colonel Sam Dr	Oshawa	ON	L1H8P7	**800-263-3777**	905-644-5000
General Motors Corp Buick Motor Div 300 Renaissance Ctr *Cust Svc	Detroit	MI	48265	**800-521-7300***	313-556-5000
General Motors Corp Cadillac Motor Car Div 300 Renaissance Ctr *Cust Svc	Detroit	MI	48265	**800-458-8006***	313-556-5000
General Motors Corp Chevrolet Motor Div 300 Renaissance Ctr *Cust Svc	Detroit	MI	48265	**800-222-1020***	313-556-5000
General Motors Corp Pontiac Div 300 Renaissance Ctr *Cust Svc	Detroit	MI	48265	**800-762-2737***	313-556-5000
General Motors Corp Pontiac-GMC Div 300 Renaissance Ctr *Cust Svc	Detroit	MI	48265	**800-762-2737***	313-556-5000
General Motors Corp Saturn Corp Div 100 Saturn Pkwy MD 371-999-S24 *Cust Svc	Spring Hill	TN	37174	**800-553-6000***	931-486-5000
Hyundai Motor America 10550 Talbert Ave *Cust Svc	Fountain Valley	CA	92728	**800-633-5151***	714-965-3000
Infiniti Div Nissan Motor Corp USA PO Box 191	Gardena	CA	90248	**800-647-7263**	310-532-3111
Jaguar Cars North America 555 MacArthur Blvd *Cust Svc	Mahwah	NJ	07430	**800-452-4827***	201-818-8500
Jeep Div DaimlerChrysler Corp 800 Chrysler Dr E *Cust Svc	Auburn Hills	MI	48326	**800-992-1997***	248-576-5741
Land Rover North America Inc 555 MacArthur Rd	Mahwah	NJ	07430	**800-637-6837**	201-818-8500
Lexus Div Toyota Motor Sales USA Inc 19001 S Western Ave *Cust Svc	Torrance	CA	90509	**800-331-4331***	310-468-4000
Lincoln-Mercury Co 16800 Executive Plaza Dr PO Box 6248	Dearborn	MI	48121	**800-521-4140**	
Lotus Cars USA Inc 2236 Northmont Pkwy	Duluth	GA	30096	**800-245-6887**	770-476-6540
Mazda North American Operations 7755 Irvine Ctr Dr *Cust Svc	Irvine	CA	92618	**800-222-5500***	949-727-1990

				Toll-Free	Phone
Mercedes-Benz USA 1 Mercedes Dr	Montvale	NJ	07645	**800-222-0100***	201-573-0600
*Cust Svc					
Mitsubishi Canada Ltd					
200 Granville St Suite 2800	Vancouver	BC	V6C1G6	**877-348-9988**	604-654-8000
Nissan Canada Inc 5290 Orbitor Dr	Mississauga	ON	L4W4Z5	**800-387-0122**	905-629-2888
Nissan Motor Corp USA Infiniti Div					
PO Box 191	Gardena	CA	90248	**800-647-7263**	310-532-3111
Peugeot Motors of America Inc					
150 Clove Rd Overlook at Great Notch	Little Falls	NJ	07424	**800-223-0587**	973-812-4444
Plymouth Div DaimlerChrysler Corp					
800 Chrysler Dr E	Auburn Hills	MI	48326	**800-992-1997***	248-576-5741
*Cust Svc					
Pontiac Div General Motors Corp					
300 Renaissance Ctr	Detroit	MI	48265	**800-762-2737***	313-556-5000
*Cust Svc					
Pontiac-GMC Div General Motors Corp					
300 Renaissance Ctr	Detroit	MI	48265	**800-762-2737***	313-556-5000
*Cust Svc					
Porsche Cars North America Inc					
980 Hammond Dr Suite 1000	Atlanta	GA	30328	**800-545-8039**	770-290-3500
Saab Cars USA Inc 300 Renaissance Ctr	Detroit	MI	48265	**800-722-2872**	313-556-5000
Saturn Corp Div General Motors Corp					
100 Saturn Pkwy MD 371-999-S24	Spring Hill	TN	37174	**800-553-6000***	931-486-5000
*Cust Svc					
Subaru of America Inc PO Box 6000	Cherry Hill	NJ	08034	**800-782-2783***	856-488-8500
*Cust Svc					
Toyota Canada Inc 1 Toyota Pl	Scarborough	ON	M1H1H9	**888-869-6828***	416-438-6320
*Cust Svc					
Toyota Motor Sales USA Inc					
19001 S Western Ave	Torrance	CA	90509	**800-331-4331***	310-468-4000
*Cust Svc					
Toyota Motor Sales USA Inc Lexus Div					
19001 S Western Ave	Torrance	CA	90509	**800-331-4331***	310-468-4000
*Cust Svc					
Volkswagen of America Inc					
3800 Hamlin Rd	Auburn Hills	MI	48326	**800-822-8987**	248-754-5000
Volvo Cars of North America 7 Volvo Dr	Rockleigh	NJ	07647	**800-458-1552***	201-768-7300
*Cust Svc					

60 AUTOMOTIVE PARTS & SUPPLIES - MFR

SEE ALSO Carburetors, Pistons, Piston Rings, Valves; Electrical Equipment for Internal Combustion Engines; Engines & Turbines; Gaskets, Packing, Sealing Devices; Hose & Belting - Rubber or Plastics; Motors (Electric) & Generators

				Toll-Free	Phone
Aamp of America Inc					
13160 56th Ct Suite 508	Clearwater	FL	33760	**800-477-2267**	727-572-9255
Acadia Polymers Inc					
Park at Valley Pointe 5251 Concourse Dr					
Suite 3	Roanoke	VA	24019	**800-444-6165**	540-265-2700
Accuride Corp 7140 Office Cir	Evansville	IN	47715	**800-626-7096***	812-962-5000
NYSE: ACW ■ *Cust Svc					
Airtex Products 407 W Main St	Fairfield	IL	62837	**800-880-3056**	618-842-2111
Aisin World Corp of America					
24330 Garnier St	Torrance	CA	90505	**800-822-2726**	310-326-8681
Alma Products Co 2000 Michigan Ave	Alma	MI	48801	**877-427-2625**	989-463-1151
AMBAC International Inc					
594 Spears Creek Church Rd	Pontiac	SC	29045	**800-628-6894**	803-735-1400
American Axle & Mfg Holdings Inc					
1840 Holbrook Ave	Detroit	MI	48212	**800-299-2953**	313-758-3600
NYSE: AXL					
American Racing Equipment Inc					
19067 S Reyes Ave	Rancho Dominguez	CA	90221	**800-421-5800**	310-635-7806
American Rubber Products Corp					
315 Brighton St	La Porte	IN	46350	**800-348-8842**	219-326-1315
ASC Inc 1 ASC Ctr	Southgate	MI	48195	**800-640-0191**	734-285-4911
Autocam Corp 4070 E Paris Ave	Kentwood	MI	49512	**800-747-6978**	616-698-0707
Baldwin Filters Inc 4400 E Hwy 30	Kearney	NE	68848	**800-822-5394**	308-234-1951
Bean John Co 309 Exchange Ave	Conway	AR	72032	**800-362-8326**	501-450-1500
Capsonic Automotive Inc 460 S 2nd St	Elgin	IL	60123	**888-981-1500**	847-888-7300
Cardone Industries Inc 5501 Whitaker Ave	Philadelphia	PA	19124	**800-777-4780***	215-912-3000
*Cust Svc					
Carlisle Industrial Brake					
1031 E Hillside Dr	Bloomington	IN	47401	**800-873-6361**	812-336-3811
Clarcor Inc 840 Crescent Ctr Dr Suite 600	Franklin	TN	37067	**800-252-7267**	615-771-3100
NYSE: CLC					
Clevite Engine Parts 1350 Eisenhower Pl	Ann Arbor	MI	48108	**800-338-8786**	734-975-4777
Consolidated Metco Inc					
13940 N Rivergate Blvd	Portland	OR	97203	**800-547-9473***	503-286-5741
*Sales					
Cummins Inc PO Box 3005	Columbus	IN	47201	**800-343-7357**	812-377-5000
NYSE: CMI					
Dacco Inc PO Box 2789	Cookeville	TN	38502	**800-443-2226**	931-528-7581
Dayton Parts Inc					
3500 Industrial Rd PO Box 5795	Harrisburg	PA	17110	**800-225-2159**	717-255-8500
Delco Remy International Inc					
2902 Enterprise Dr	Anderson	IN	46013	**800-372-5131**	765-778-6499
Dura Automotive Systems Inc					
2791 Research Dr	Rochester Hills	MI	48309	**800-362-3872**	248-299-7500
NASDAQ: DRRA					
Durakon Industries Inc 2101 N Lapeer Rd	Lapeer	MI	48446	**800-955-3993***	810-664-0850
*Cust Svc					
Edelbrock Corp 2700 California St	Torrance	CA	90503	**800-739-3737**	310-781-2222
NASDAQ: EDEL					
EnPro Industries Inc					
5605 Carnegie Blvd Suite 500	Charlotte	NC	28209	**866-663-6776**	704-731-1500
NYSE: NPO					
Federal-Mogul Corp					
26555 Northwestern Hwy	Southfield	MI	48034	**800-560-1400***	248-354-7700
*Cust Svc					
Firestone Industrial Products Co					
12650 Hamilton Crossing Blvd	Carmel	IN	46032	**800-888-0650**	317-818-8600
Fleetguard Inc 2931 Elm Hill Pike	Nashville	TN	37214	**800-777-7064**	615-367-0040
Fleetline Products					
784 Bill Jones Industrial Dr	Springfield	TN	37172	**800-332-6653**	615-384-4338
Fontaine Truck Equipment Co					
2490 Pinson Valley Pkwy	Birmingham	AL	35217	**800-824-3033**	205-841-8582
Freudenberg-NOK General Partnership					
47690 E Anchor Ct	Plymouth	MI	48170	**800-533-5656**	734-451-0020
Glacier Garlock Bearings					
700 Mid Atlantic Pkwy PO Box 189	Thorofare	NJ	08086	**800-222-0147**	856-848-3200
Global Technovations Inc					
7108 Fairway Dr Suite 130	Palm Beach Gardens	FL	33418	**800-285-7708**	561-775-5756
Go/Dan Industries 100 Gando Dr	New Haven	CT	06513	**800-755-2160**	203-562-5121
Grote Industries Inc 2600 Lanier Dr	Madison	IN	47250	**800-457-9540**	812-273-2121
Gunite Corp 302 Peoples Ave	Rockford	IL	61104	**800-677-3786**	815-490-6364
Hastings Mfg Co 325 N Hanover St	Hastings	MI	49058	**800-776-1012**	269-945-2491
Hayden Automotive PO Box 77550	Corona	CA	92877	**800-621-3233**	951-736-2665
Hayes Lemmerz International Inc					
15300 Centennial Dr	Northville	MI	48167	**800-521-0515**	734-737-5000
NASDAQ: HAYZ					
Hennessy Industries Inc					
1601 JP Hennesey Dr	La Vergne	TN	37086	**800-688-6359**	615-641-5122
Holland USA 1950 Industrial Blvd	Muskegon	MI	49442	**800-237-8932**	231-773-3271
Holley Performance Products Inc					
1801 Russellville Rd	Bowling Green	KY	42101	**800-638-0032***	270-782-2900
*Sales					
Hopkins Mfg Corp 428 Peyton St	Emporia	KS	66801	**800-524-1458**	620-342-7320
Hutchens Industries Inc					
215 N Patterson Ave	Springfield	MO	65802	**800-654-8824**	417-862-5012
Indian Head Industries Inc					
8530 Cliff Cameron Dr	Charlotte	NC	28269	**800-527-1534**	704-547-7411
Indian Head Industries Inc MGM Brakes Div					
8530 Cliff Cameron Dr	Charlotte	NC	28269	**800-527-1534**	704-547-7411
ITW Fibre Glass-Evercoat 6600 Cornell Rd	Cincinnati	OH	45242	**800-729-7600**	513-489-7600
Jasper Engine & Transmission Exchange Inc					
815 Wernsing Rd PO Box 650	Jasper	IN	47547	**800-827-7455**	812-482-1041
John Bean Co 309 Exchange Ave	Conway	AR	72032	**800-362-8326**	501-450-1500
Johnson Controls Inc					
5757 N Green Bay Ave	Milwaukee	WI	53209	**800-972-8040**	414-524-1200
NYSE: JCI					
JSJ Corp 700 Robbins Rd	Grand Haven	MI	49417	**800-867-3208**	616-842-6350
Kuss Corp 2150 Industrial Dr	Findlay	OH	45840	**800-252-5877***	419-423-9040
*Sales					
Lund International Holdings Inc					
911 Lund Blvd Suite 100	Anoka	MN	55303	**800-377-5863**	763-576-4200
MacLean-Fogg Co 1000 Allanson Rd	Mundelein	IL	60060	**800-323-4536**	847-566-0010
Marmon-Herrington Co 13001 Magisterial Dr	Louisville	KY	40223	**800-227-0727**	502-253-0277
Masterack-Crown Inc 4171 B Lincolnway E	Wooster	OH	44691	**800-321-4934***	330-262-6010
*Cust Svc					
Melling Tool Co PO Box 1188	Jackson	MI	49204	**800-777-8172**	517-787-8172
MGM Brakes Div Indian Head Industries Inc					
8530 Cliff Cameron Dr	Charlotte	NC	28269	**800-527-1534**	704-547-7411
Neapco Inc PO Box 399	Pottstown	PA	19464	**800-821-2374**	610-323-6000
OSRAM Sylvania Electronic Components &					
Materials 100 Endicott St	Danvers	MA	01923	**800-544-4828**	978-777-1900
Penda Corp 2344 W Wisconsin St	Portage	WI	53901	**800-356-7704**	608-742-5301
Perfection Clutch Co 100 Perfection Way	Timmonsville	SC	29161	**800-258-8312**	843-326-5544
Peterson Mfg Co 4200 E 135th St	Grandview	MO	64030	**800-821-3490**	816-765-2000
Pretty Products Inc 437 Cambridge Rd	Coshocton	OH	43812	**800-837-9160**	740-622-3522
R & B Inc 3400 E Walnut St	Colmar	PA	18915	**800-523-2492**	215-997-1800
NASDAQ: RBIN					
Raybestos Products Co					
1204 Darlington Ave	Crawfordsville	IN	47933	**800-428-0825**	765-362-3500
SmarTire Systems Inc					
13151 Vanier Pl Suite 150	Richmond	BC	V5V2J1	**888-982-3001**	604-276-9884
NASDAQ: SMTR					
Stanadyne Corp 92 Deerfield Rd	Windsor	CT	06095	**800-929-0919**	860-525-0821
Stemco LP 300 Industrial Blvd PO Box 1989	Longview	TX	75606	**800-527-8492**	903-758-9981
Strattec Security Corp					
3333 W Good Hope Rd	Milwaukee	WI	53209	**888-710-5770**	414-247-3333
NASDAQ: STRT					
Superior Industries International Inc					
7800 Woodley Ave	Van Nuys	CA	91406	**800-545-9882**	818-781-4973
NYSE: SUP					
TeleflexGFI Control Systems LP					
100 Hollinger Crescent	Kitchener	ON	N2K2Z3	**800-667-4275**	519-576-4270
Tenneco Automotive Inc 500 N Field Dr	Lake Forest	IL	60045	**800-777-9564**	847-482-5000
NYSE: TEN					
TI Automotive 12345 E Nine-Mile Rd	Warren	MI	48090	**800-521-2500**	586-758-6500
Titan International Inc 2701 Spruce St	Quincy	IL	62301	**800-872-2327**	217-228-6011
NYSE: TWI					
Titan Wheel Corp 2701 Spruce St	Quincy	IL	62301	**800-518-4826**	217-228-6011
Tractech Inc 11445 Stephens Dr	Warren	MI	48090	**800-328-3850**	586-759-3850
Triangle Suspension Systems Inc Maloney Rd	Du Bois	PA	15801	**800-458-6077**	814-375-7211
Trico Products Corp					
3255 W Hamlin Rd	Rochester Hills	MI	48309	**888-565-9632**	248-371-1700
Tuthill Transport Technologies					
1205 Industrial Pk Dr	Mount Vernon	MO	65712	**800-753-0050***	417-466-2178
*Cust Svc					
Universal Automotive Industries Inc					
11859 S Central Ave	Alsip	IL	60803	**800-301-2725**	708-293-4050
NASDAQ: UVSL					
Universal Mfg Co 405 Diagonal St PO Box 190	Algona	IA	50511	**800-545-9350**	515-295-3557
US Chemical & Plastics PO Box 709	Massillon	OH	44648	**800-321-0672**	330-830-6000
Visteon Corp 17000 Rotunda Dr	Dearborn	MI	48121	**800-847-8366**	313-755-2867
NYSE: VC					
Webb Wheel Products Inc					
2310 Industrial Dr SW	Cullman	AL	35055	**800-633-3256***	256-739-6660
*Cust Svc					
Wells Mfg Corp PO Box 70	Fond du Lac	WI	54936	**800-558-9770**	920-922-5900
Williams Controls Inc 14100 SW 72nd Ave	Portland	OR	97224	**800-547-1889***	503-684-8600
*Cust Svc					

61 AUTOMOTIVE PARTS & SUPPLIES - WHOL

				Toll-Free	Phone
Ace Tool Co 7337 Bryan Dairy Rd	Largo	FL	33777	**800-777-5910**	727-544-4331
Arrow Speed Warehouse 686 S Adams St	Kansas City	KS	66105	**800-255-4606**	913-321-1200
Atlantic Mobile Home & RV Supplier Corp					
4828 High Point Rd	Greensboro	NC	27407	**800-334-6976**	336-299-4691
Automotive Parts Headquarters					
125 29th Ave S	Saint Cloud	MN	56301	**800-247-0339**	320-252-5411
AW Imported Auto Parts Inc 52 Hwy 35	Eatontown	NJ	07724	**800-631-5589**	732-542-5600

				Toll-Free	Phone
Bell Industries Inc					
1960 E Grand Ave Suite 560	El Segundo	CA	90245	**800-782-2355**	310-563-2355
AMEX: BI					
Bell Industries Inc Recreational Products Group					
580 Yankee Doodle Rd Suite 1200	Eagan	MN	55121	**800-388-2355**	651-450-9020
Bendix Commercial Vehicle Systems LLC					
901 Cleveland St	Elyria	OH	44035	**800-247-2725**	440-329-9000
Birmingham Electric Battery Co					
2230 2nd Ave S	Birmingham	AL	35233	**800-446-0919**	205-458-0581
Brake & Wheel Parts Industries Inc					
2415 W 21st St	Chicago	IL	60608	**800-621-8836**	773-847-7000
CAP Warehouse 3108 Losee Rd	North Las Vegas	NV	89030	**800-879-7901**	702-642-7801
Carolina Rim & Wheel Co					
1308 Upper Asbury Dr	Charlotte	NC	28206	**800-532-6219**	704-334-7276
Carolinas Auto Supply House Inc					
2135 Tipton Dr	Charlotte	NC	28206	**800-438-4070**	704-334-4646
Charleston Auto Parts Inc DBA CAP Warehouse 3108 Losee Rd	North Las Vegas	NV	89030	**800-879-7901**	702-642-7801
Coast Distribution System					
350 Woodview Ave	Morgan Hill	CA	95037	**800-495-5858**	408-782-6686
AMEX: CRV					
Custom Chrome Inc 16100 Jacqueline Ct	Morgan Hill	CA	95037	**800-729-3332**	408-778-0500
Distributors Warehouse Inc 1900 N 10th St	Paducah	KY	42001	**800-892-9966**	270-442-8201
Drive Train Industries Inc 3301 Brighton Blvd	Denver	CO	80216	**800-525-6177**	303-292-5176
Edwards Frank Co 3626 Parkway Blvd	West Valley City	UT	84120	**800-366-8851**	801-736-8000
Flowers Auto Parts Co 935 Hwy 70 Se	Hickory	NC	28601	**800-395-6272***	828-322-5414
*Cust Svc					
Frank Edwards Co 3626 Parkway Blvd	West Valley City	UT	84120	**800-366-8851**	801-736-8000
General Truck Parts & Equipment Co					
3835 W 42nd St	Chicago	IL	60632	**800-621-3914**	773-247-6900
Global Motorsport Group					
16100 Jacqueline Ct	Morgan Hill	CA	95037	**800-359-5700**	408-778-0500
Globe Motorists Supply Co Inc					
560 S 3rd Ave	Mount Vernon	NY	10550	**888-884-7278**	914-668-6430
Gooch Brake & Equipment Co					
506 Grand Blvd	Kansas City	MO	64106	**800-444-3216**	816-421-3085
Hahn Automotive Warehouse Inc					
415 W Main St	Rochester	NY	14608	**800-456-0365**	585-235-1595
Hedahls Inc 100 E Broadway	Bismarck	ND	58502	**800-433-2457**	701-223-8393
Henderson Wheel & Warehouse Supply					
1825 S 300 West	Salt Lake City	UT	84115	**800-748-5111**	801-486-2073
InterAmerican Motor Corp					
8901 Canoga Ave	Canoga Park	CA	91304	**800-874-8925**	818-678-1200
International Brake Industries Inc					
1840 McCullough St	Lima	OH	45801	**800-537-2838**	419-227-4421
Interstate Battery System of America Inc					
12770 Merit Dr Suite 400	Dallas	TX	75251	**800-541-8419**	972-991-1444
Intraco Corp 530 Stephenson Hwy	Troy	MI	48083	**800-595-6900**	248-585-6900
Jarvis Supply Co Inc 114 W 8th St	Winfield	KS	67156	**800-522-8058**	620-221-3113
Johnson Industries 5944 Peachtree Corners E	Norcross	GA	33071	**800-922-8111***	770-441-1128
*Orders					
Keystone Automotive Industries Inc					
700 E Bonita Ave	Pomona	CA	91767	**800-772-5557**	909-624-8041
NASDAQ: KEYS					
LKQ Corp 120 N LaSalle St Suite 3300	Chicago	IL	60602	**877-557-2677**	312-621-1950
NASDAQ: LKQX					
Midwest Truck & Auto Parts					
4200 S Morgan St	Chicago	IL	60609	**800-934-2727**	312-225-1550
Mighty Distributing System of America Inc					
650 Engineering Dr	Norcross	GA	30092	**800-829-3900**	770-448-3900
PACCAR Parts 750 Houser Way N	Renton	WA	98055	**800-477-0251**	425-254-4400
Pam Cos 200 S Petro Ave	Sioux Falls	SD	57107	**800-456-2660**	605-336-1788
Parts Central Inc 3243 Whitfield St	Macon	GA	31204	**800-226-9396**	478-745-0878
Pioneer Inc 5184 Pioneer Rd	Meridian	MS	39301	**800-647-6272**	601-483-5211
Plaza Fleet Parts Inc 1520 S Broadway	Saint Louis	MO	63104	**800-325-7618**	314-231-5047
Quaker City Motor Parts Co					
680 N Broad St	Middletown	DE	19709	**800-538-6272**	302-378-9862
Reliable Automotive 10600 Mastin St	Overland Park	KS	66212	**800-521-9901***	913-894-9090
*Cust Svc					
Replacement Parts Inc					
1901 E Roosevelt Rd	Little Rock	AR	72206	**877-282-6591**	501-375-1215
Ridge Co Inc 1535 S Main St	South Bend	IN	46613	**800-348-2409**	574-234-3143
Rim & Wheel Service Inc 1014 Gest St	Cincinnati	OH	45203	**800-783-6940**	513-721-6940
Six Robblees' Inc					
11010 Tukwila International Blvd	Tukwila	WA	98168	**800-275-7499**	206-767-7970
Six States Distributors Inc					
247 W 1700 South	Salt Lake City	UT	84115	**800-453-5703**	801-488-4666
Tucker Rocky Distributing Inc					
4900 Alliance Gateway Fwy	Fort Worth	TX	76177	**800-283-8787**	817-258-9000
Twinco Romax 4635 Willow Dr	Medina	MN	55340	**800-682-3800**	763-478-2360
Universal Automotive Industries Inc					
11859 S Central Ave	Alsip	IL	60803	**800-301-2725**	708-293-4050
NASDAQ: UVSL					
Wetherill Assoc Inc 1101 Enterprise Dr	Royersford	PA	19468	**800-877-3340**	610-495-2200
White Brothers 24845 Corbit Pl	Yorba Linda	CA	92887	**800-854-1899**	714-692-3404

62 AUTOMOTIVE SERVICES

SEE ALSO Gas Stations

62-1 Appearance Care - Automotive

				Toll-Free	Phone
Autobell Car Wash Inc 1521 E 3rd St	Charlotte	NC	28204	**800-582-8096**	
Color-Glo International 7111 Ohms Ln	Minneapolis	MN	55439	**800-333-8523**	952-835-1338
Dr Vinyl & Assoc Ltd					
821 NW Commerce Dr	Lee's Summit	MO	64086	**800-531-6600**	816-525-6060
Fleetwash Inc 273 Passaic Ave	Fairfield	NJ	07004	**800-847-3735**	973-882-8314
Jax Car Wash Inc 28845 Telegraph Rd	Southfield	MI	48034	**866-529-5273**	248-353-4700
Precision Auto Care Inc 748 Miller Dr SE	Leesburg	VA	20175	**800-438-8863**	703-777-9095
Spot-Not Car Washes Inc PO Box 1269	Joplin	MO	64802	**800-682-7629**	417-781-6233
Vizzawash Inc DBA Wash Tub					
16035 University Oak	San Antonio	TX	78249	**866-493-8822**	210-493-8822
Wash Depot Holdings Inc 435 Eastern Ave	Malden	MA	02148	**800-339-3949**	781-324-2000
Wash Tub 16035 University Oak	San Antonio	TX	78249	**866-493-8822**	210-493-8822
Wonder Wash/Wonder Lube Management Inc					
1601 Caledonia St Suite 1	La Crosse	WI	54603	**800-261-9274**	608-783-5525

				Toll-Free	Phone
Ziebart International Corp 1290 E Maple Rd	Troy	MI	48083	**800-877-1312**	248-588-4100

62-2 Glass Replacement - Automotive

				Toll-Free	Phone
All Star Glass Co Inc 1845 Morena Blvd	San Diego	CA	92110	**800-225-4185**	619-275-3343
Auto Glass National 1537 W Alameda	Denver	CO	80223	**800-388-0104**	303-722-9600
Auto Glass Specialists Inc					
1200 John Q Hammons Dr Suite 300	Madison	WI	53717	**800-558-1000**	608-271-5484
Cindy Rowe Auto Glass 4750 Lindle Rd	Harrisburg	PA	17111	**800-882-4639**	717-939-7551
Diamond/Triumph Auto Glass Inc					
220 Division St	Kingston	PA	18704	**800-452-7143**	570-287-9915
Glass Doctor 1020 N University Parks Dr	Waco	TX	76707	**800-280-9959**	254-745-2480
Glass Specialty System Inc PO Box 737	Bloomington	IL	61702	**800-500-0500**	309-664-1087
Guardian Glass Co					
24150 Haggerty Rd	Farmington Hills	MI	48335	**800-621-8682**	248-471-0180
Harmon Autoglass					
4000 Olson Memorial Hwy Suite 600	Minneapolis	MN	55422	**800-352-0777**	763-521-5100
Martin Glass Co Inc 25 Center Plaza	Belleville	IL	62220	**800-325-1946**	618-277-1946
NOVUS Auto Glass Repair & Replacement					
12800 Hwy 13 S	Minneapolis	MN	55378	**800-328-1137**	952-944-8000
Rowe Cindy Auto Glass 4750 Lindle Rd	Harrisburg	PA	17111	**800-882-4639**	717-939-7551
Royal Glass Co					
9241 Hampton Overlook	Capital Heights	MD	20743	**800-509-4495**	301-808-2855
Safelite Glass Corp 2400 Farmers Dr 5th Fl	Columbus	OH	43235	**800-835-2257**	614-210-9465
Speedy Auto & Glass Inc					
9675 SE 36th St	Mercer Island	WA	98040	**800-533-6545**	206-232-9500
SuperGlass Windshield Repair					
6101 Chancellor Dr Suite 200	Orlando	FL	32809	**888-771-2700**	407-240-1920
Synergistic International Inc DBA Glass Doctor					
1020 N University Parks Dr	Waco	TX	76707	**800-280-9959**	254-745-2480

62-3 Mufflers & Exhaust Systems Repair - Automotive

				Toll-Free	Phone
Car-X Assoc Corp					
1375 E Woodfield Rd Suite 500	Schaumburg	IL	60173	**800-359-2359**	847-273-8920
Meineke Car Care Centers					
128 S Tryon St Suite 900	Charlotte	NC	28202	**800-275-5200**	704-377-8855
Midas International Corp					
1300 Arlington Heights Rd	Itasca	IL	60143	**800-621-0144**	630-438-3000
Monro Muffler Brake Inc 200 Holleder Pkwy	Rochester	NY	14615	**800-876-6676**	585-647-6400
NASDAQ: MNRO					

62-4 Paint & Body Work - Automotive

				Toll-Free	Phone
1-Day Paint & Body Centers Inc					
21801 S Western Ave	Torrance	CA	90501	**800-448-1908**	310-328-0390
Caliber Collision Centers					
17771 Cowan Ave Suite 100	Irvine	CA	92614	**888-225-3237**	949-224-0300
CARSTAR Quality Collision Service					
8400 W 110th St Suite 200	Overland Park	KS	66210	**800-227-7827**	913-451-1294
Collex Collision Experts					
44700 Enterprise Dr	Clinton Township	MI	48038	**888-426-5539**	586-954-3850
Colors on Parade 642 Century Cir	Conway	SC	29526	**800-929-3363**	843-347-8818
Dent Clinic Canada Inc					
711 48th Ave SE Suite 6	Calgary	AB	T2G4X2	**888-722-3368**	403-255-3111
Dent Doctor Inc 11301 W Markham St	Little Rock	AR	72211	**800-946-3368**	501-224-0500
Dent Wizard International					
4710 Earth City Expway	Bridgeton	MO	63044	**800-336-8949**	314-592-1800
Earl Scheib Inc					
15206 Ventura Blvd Suite 200	Sherman Oaks	CA	91403	**800-639-3275**	818-981-9992
Gerber Auto Collision & Glass Centers Inc					
8250 Skokie Blvd	Skokie	IL	60077	**800-479-1230**	847-679-0510
M2 Collision Centers Inc					
1100 Colorado Ave 2nd Fl	Santa Monica	CA	90401	**877-623-6796**	310-399-3887
Maaco Auto Painting & Body Works					
381 Brooks Rd	King of Prussia	PA	19406	**800-523-1180**	610-265-6606
True2Form Collision Repair Centers					
4853 Galaxy Pkwy Suite E	Cleveland	OH	44128	**888-223-8783**	216-591-0730

62-5 Repair Service (General) - Automotive

				Toll-Free	Phone
All Tune & Lube Brakes & More Inc					
8334 Veteran's Hwy	Millersville	MD	21108	**800-935-8863**	410-987-1011
ATL International Inc 8334 Veterans Hwy	Millersville	MD	21108	**800-935-8863**	410-987-1011
Belle Tire Inc 3500 Enterprise Dr	Allen Park	MI	48101	**800-352-3553**	313-271-9400
Big O Tires Inc					
12650 E Briarwood Ave Suite 2D	Englewood	CO	80112	**800-321-2446**	303-728-5500
Bob Sumerel Tires & Service Inc					
3646 E Broad St	Columbus	OH	43213	**800-858-0421**	614-237-6325
Bridgestone Americas Holding Inc					
535 Marriott Dr	Nashville	TN	37214	**800-543-7522***	615-937-5000
*Cust Svc					
Clark Tire & Auto Supply Co Inc					
220 S Center St	Hickory	NC	28602	**800-968-3092**	828-322-2303
Craven Tire & Auto Inc 2728 Dorr Ave	Fairfax	VA	22031	**800-284-6211**	703-698-8505
Econo Lube N' Tune Inc PO Box 2470	Newport Beach	CA	92658	**800-478-3795**	949-851-2259
Express Oil Change 190 W Valley Ave	Birmingham	AL	35209	**888-945-1771**	205-945-1771
Fyda Freightliner Youngstown Inc					
5260 76th Dr	Youngstown	OH	44515	**800-837-3932**	330-797-0224
Grease Monkey International Inc					
633 17th St Suite 400	Denver	CO	80202	**800-822-7706**	303-308-1660
Heartland Automotive Services Inc					
11308 Davenport St	Omaha	NE	68154	**800-417-7308**	402-333-0990
Jack Williams Tire Co Inc PO Box 3655	Scranton	PA	18505	**800-833-5051**	570-457-5000
Jiffy Lube International Inc 700 Milam St	Houston	TX	77002	**800-327-9532**	713-546-4000
Jubitz Corp 33 NE Middlefield Rd	Portland	OR	97211	**800-399-5480**	503-283-1111
Lucor Inc 790 Pershing Rd	Raleigh	NC	27608	**800-216-2553**	919-828-9511
Merchant's Inc 9073 Euclid Ave	Manassas	VA	20110	**800-368-3130**	703-368-3171
Morgan Tire & Auto Inc					
2021 Sunnydale Blvd	Clearwater	FL	33765	**800-269-4424**	727-442-8388
NESC Williams Inc 18 Harrison St	Zanesville	OH	43701	**800-453-4644**	740-453-0375
Parrish Tire Co Inc 5130 Indiana Ave	Winston-Salem	NC	27106	**800-849-8473**	336-767-0202

Name / Address	City	State	Zip	Toll-Free	Phone
Precision Auto Care Inc 748 Miller Dr SE	Leesburg	VA	20175	**800-438-8863**	703-777-9095
Precision Tune Auto Care Inc PO Box 5000	Leesburg	VA	20177	**800-438-8863**	703-777-9095
Somerset Tire Services Inc 400 W Main St	Bound Brook	NJ	08805	**800-445-1434**	732-356-8500
Speedee Oil Change & Tune-Up Inc PO Box 1350	Madisonville	LA	70447	**800-451-7461**	985-845-1919
Sullivan Tire Co Inc 41 Accord Park Dr	Norwell	MA	02061	**800-892-1955**	781-982-1550
Sumerel Bob Tires & Service Inc 3646 E Broad St	Columbus	OH	43213	**800-858-0421**	614-237-6325
Tire Distribution Systems Inc 11900 W 44th Ave	Wheat Ridge	CO	80033	**800-541-8473**	303-422-2300
Tire Kingdom Inc 823 Donald Ross Rd	Juno Beach	FL	33408	**800-383-3040**	561-842-4290
Tire-Rama Inc PO Box 23509	Billings	MT	59104	**800-828-1642**	406-245-4006
Tires Plus 2021 Sunnydale Blvd	Clearwater	FL	33765	**800-269-4424**	727-441-3727
Tires Plus Total Car Care 2021 Sunnydale Blvd	Clearwater	FL	33765	**800-269-4424**	727-441-3727
Transtek Inc PO Box 4174	Harrisburg	PA	17111	**800-871-1935**	717-564-6151
Tuffy Auto Service Centers 1414 Baronial Plaza Dr	Toledo	OH	43615	**800-228-8339**	419-865-6900
Western Tire Co 2700 E Main St	Farmington	NM	87402	**800-589-2414**	505-326-2231
Williams Jack Tire Co Inc PO Box 3655	Scranton	PA	18505	**800-833-5051**	570-457-5000
Wingfoot Commercial Tire Systems LLC 1000 S 21st St	Fort Smith	AR	72901	**800-643-7330**	479-788-6400

62-6 Transmission Repair - Automotive

Name / Address	City	State	Zip	Toll-Free	Phone
AAMCO Transmissions Inc 1 Presidential Blvd *Cust Svc	Bala Cynwyd	PA	19004	**800-523-0401***	610-668-2900
All Tune Transmissions 8334 Veteran's Hwy	Millersville	MD	21108	**800-935-8863**	410-987-1011
Certified Transmission Rebuilders Inc 1801 S 54th St	Omaha	NE	68106	**800-554-7520**	402-558-2117
Cottman Transmission Systems Inc 240 New York Dr	Fort Washington	PA	19034	**800-394-6116**	215-643-5885
Lee Myles Transmissions 140 Rt 17 N	Paramus	NJ	07652	**800-426-5114**	201-262-0555
Mr Transmission 9675 Yonge St 2nd Fl	Richmond Hill	ON	L4C1V7	**800-373-8432**	905-884-1511
Transmission USA 4444 W 147th St	Midlothian	IL	60445	**800-377-9247**	708-389-5922

62-7 Van Conversions

Name / Address	City	State	Zip	Toll-Free	Phone
Associated Rollx Vans 6591 Hwy 13 W	Savage	MN	55378	**800-956-6668**	952-890-7851
Clock Conversions 6700 Clay Ave	Grand Rapids	MI	49548	**800-732-5625**	616-698-9400
Elk Automotive Inc 3012 Mobile Dr	Elkhart	IN	46514	**800-289-3551**	574-264-0768
Monaco Coach Corp 91320 Coburg Industrial Way *NYSE: MNC*	Coburg	OR	97408	**800-634-0855**	541-686-8011
Royale Coach 1330 Wade Dr	Elkhart	IN	46514	**877-466-6226**	
Sherrod Vans Inc 6464 Greenland Rd	Jacksonville	FL	32258	**800-824-6333**	904-268-3321
Sidewinder Conversions 45681Yale Rd W	Chilliwack	BC	V2P2N1	**888-266-2299**	604-792-2082
Starcraft Corp 2703 College Ave	Goshen	IN	46528	**800-348-7440**	574-533-1105
Vantage Mobility International (VMI) 5202 S 28th Pl	Phoenix	AZ	85040	**800-348-8267**	602-243-2700
VMI (Vantage Mobility International) 5202 S 28th Pl	Phoenix	AZ	85040	**800-348-8267**	602-243-2700

63 AVIATION - FIXED-BASE OPERATIONS

SEE ALSO Air Cargo Carriers; Air Charter Services; Aircraft Rental; Aircraft Service & Repair

Name / Address	City	State	Zip	Toll-Free	Phone
ACM Aviation Inc 1475 Airport Blvd	San Jose	CA	95110	**800-359-7538**	408-286-3832
Aero Industries Inc 5690 Clarkson Rd Richmond International Airport	Richmond	VA	23250	**800-845-1308**	804-222-7211
Aero-Smith Inc 214 Aviation Way	Martinsburg	WV	25401	**800-550-2507**	304-262-2507
Aerodynamics Inc 6544 Highland Rd	Waterford	MI	48327	**800-235-9234**	248-666-3500
Aircraft Specialists Inc 6005 Propeller Ln	Sellersburg	IN	47172	**800-356-3723**	812-246-4696
Arlins Aircraft Service Inc 36 Gallatin Field	Belgrade	MT	59714	**800-953-2471**	406-388-1351
Avion Flight Centre Inc 2506 N Pliska Dr	Midland	TX	79711	**800-759-3359**	432-563-2033
Banyan Air Service Inc 1575 W Commercial Blvd	Fort Lauderdale	FL	33309	**800-200-2031**	954-491-3170
Basler Turbo Conversions Inc Basler Flight Service Div PO Box 2464	Oshkosh	WI	54903	**800-558-0254**	920-236-7827
BMG Aviation Inc 984 S Kirby Rd	Bloomington	IN	47403	**888-457-3787**	812-825-7979
Business Aviation Services 3501 Aviation Ave	Sioux Falls	SD	57104	**800-888-1646**	605-336-7791
Cav-Air LLC 2011 S Perimeter Rd Suite L	Fort Lauderdale	FL	33309	**800-537-4454**	954-491-4454
Central Flying Service Inc 1501 Bond St	Little Rock	AR	72202	**800-888-5387**	501-375-3245
Columbia Air Services LLC 112 Caruso Dr	Trenton	ME	04605	**888-756-8648**	207-667-5534
Cook Aviation Inc 970 S Kirby Rd	Bloomington	IN	47403	**800-880-3499**	812-825-2392
Crow Executive Air Inc 28331 Lemoyne Rd Toledo Metcalf Airport	Millbury	OH	43447	**800-972-2769**	419-838-6921
Crystal Shamrock Inc 6000 Douglas Dr N	Minneapolis	MN	55429	**800-533-2214**	763-533-2214
Dassault Falcon 191 N DuPont Hwy New Castle County Airport	New Castle	DE	19720	**800-441-9390**	302-322-7000
DB Aviation Inc 3550 N McAree Rd	Waukegan	IL	60087	**800-638-4990**	847-263-5600
Deer Horn Aviation Ltd Co DBA Avion Flight Centre Inc 2506 N Pliska Dr	Midland	TX	79711	**800-759-3359**	432-563-2033
Dulles Aviation Inc 10501 Observation Rd Manassas Regional Airport	Manassas	VA	20110	**888-835-8934**	703-361-2171
Eagle Aviation 2861 Aviation Way Columbia Metropolitan Airport	West Columbia	SC	29170	**800-848-6359**	803-822-5577
Edwards Jet Center 1691 Aviation Pl	Billings	MT	59105	**800-755-9624**	406-252-0508
Epps Aviation Inc 1 Aviation Way DeKalb Peachtree Airport	Atlanta	GA	30341	**800-462-0104**	770-458-9851
Fairchild Dornier Inc 10823 NE Entrance Rd	San Antonio	TX	78216	**800-327-2313**	210-824-2313
Felts Field Aviation Inc 5829 E Rutter Ave	Spokane	WA	99212	**800-676-5538**	509-535-9011
Fletcher Aviation Inc 9000 Randolph St	Houston	TX	77061	**800-329-4647**	713-649-8700
Fletcher Group DBA Fletcher Aviation Inc 9000 Randolph St	Houston	TX	77061	**800-329-4647**	713-649-8700
Flightcraft Inc 90454 Boeing Dr	Eugene	OR	97402	**800-776-6312**	541-688-9291
Fort Lauderdale Jet Center 1100 Lee Wagner Blvd	Fort Lauderdale	FL	33315	**800-394-5388**	954-359-3200
Frederick Aviation 330 Aviation Way	Frederick	MD	21701	**800-545-9393**	301-662-8156
Galvin Flying Service 7149 Perimeter Rd	Seattle	WA	98108	**800-341-4102**	206-763-0350
Grand Aire Express Inc 11777 W Airport Service Rd	Swanton	OH	43558	**800-704-7263**	419-865-1780
Grand Strand Aviation DBA Ramp 66 2800 Terminal St	North Myrtle Beach	SC	29582	**800-433-8918**	843-272-5337
Hagerstown Aviation Services Inc 18627 Jarkey Dr	Hagerstown	MD	21742	**800-889-6094**	301-733-5200
Holman Aviation Co 1940 Airport Ct	Great Falls	MT	59404	**800-843-7613**	406-453-7613
Hunt Pan Am Aviation Inc 505 S Minnesota Ave Brownsville/South Padre International Airport	Brownsville	TX	78521	**800-888-7524**	956-542-9111
Jet Aviation International Inc 1515 Perimeter Rd	West Palm Beach	FL	33406	**800-758-5387**	561-233-7233
Kansas City Aviation Center Inc 15325 Pflumm Rd Johnson County Executive Airport *Sales	Olathe	KS	66062	**800-720-5222***	913-782-0530
Lane Aviation Corp 4389 International Gateway	Columbus	OH	43219	**800-848-6263**	614-237-3747
Loyd's Aviation Services Inc 2813 Hangar Way	Bakersfield	CA	93308	**800-284-1334**	661-393-1334
Maine Instrument Flight Augusta State Airport PO Box 2	Augusta	ME	04332	**888-643-3597**	207-622-1211
Malloy Air East Inc Francis S Gabreski Airport	Westhampton Beach	NY	11978	**888-673-9888**	631-288-5410
McCall Aviation PO Box 771	McCall	ID	83638	**800-992-6559**	208-634-7137
Miami Executive Aviation Inc 15001 NW 42 Ave	Miami	FL	33054	**800-861-1343**	305-687-8410
Mid-Ohio Aviation 6020 N Honeytown Rd	Smithville	OH	44677	**800-669-4243**	330-669-2671
Midwest Corporate Aviation 3512 N Webb Rd	Wichita	KS	67226	**800-435-9622**	316-636-9700
Millenium Aviation 2365 Bernville Rd Reading Regional Airport	Reading	PA	19605	**800-366-9419**	610-374-0100
Million Air 4300 Westgrove Dr	Addison	TX	75001	**800-248-1602**	972-248-1600
Montgomery Aviation Corp 4525 Selma Hwy	Montgomery	AL	36108	**800-392-8044**	334-288-7334
National Jets Air Center 3495 SW 9th Ave	Fort Lauderdale	FL	33315	**800-525-0166**	954-359-9400
Newport Jet Center 19711 Campus Dr Suite 100	Santa Ana	CA	92707	**800-500-5061**	949-851-5061
Northside Aviation Inc McCollum Airport PO Box 490	Kennesaw	GA	30156	**800-754-4300**	770-422-4300
Panorama Flight Service Inc 67 Tower Rd	White Plains	NY	10604	**888-359-7266**	914-328-9800
Pensacola Aviation Center Inc 4145 Jerry L Maygarden Rd	Pensacola	FL	32504	**800-874-6580**	850-434-0636
Personal Jet Charter Inc 5401 E Perimeter Rd	Fort Lauderdale	FL	33309	**800-432-1538**	954-776-4515
Piedmont Hawthorne Aerocentre 4360 Agar Dr	Richmond	BC	V7B1A3	**888-298-7326**	604-279-9922
Piedmont Hawthorne Aviation 3821 N Liberty St *Sales	Winston-Salem	NC	27105	**800-259-1940***	336-776-6060
Ramp 66 2800 Terminal St	North Myrtle Beach	SC	29582	**800-433-8918**	843-272-5337
Regional Jet Center 12344 Tower Dr	Bentonville	AR	72712	**866-962-3835**	479-205-1100
Richmor Aviation Inc 1142 Rt 94 Columbia County Airport	Hudson	NY	12534	**800-331-6101**	518-828-9461
Saint Paul Flight Center 270 Airport Rd	Saint Paul	MN	55107	**800-368-0107**	651-227-8108
Santa Fe Jet Center Inc 121 Aviation Dr Bldg 3005	Santa Fe	NM	87507	**800-263-7695**	505-471-2525
Showalter Flying Services Orlando Executive Airport PO Box 140753	Orlando	FL	32814	**800-894-7331**	407-894-7331
Signature Flight Support 201 S Orange Ave Suite 1100	Orlando	FL	32801	**800-428-5597**	407-648-7200
Silverhawk Aviation Inc 1751 W Kearney Ave	Lincoln	NE	68524	**800-479-5851**	402-475-8600
Sky Bright Inc 65 Aviation Dr	Gilford	NH	03246	**800-639-6012**	603-528-6818
Skyservice Airlines Inc 31 Fasken Dr	Etobicoke	ON	M9W1K6	**800-701-9448**	416-679-5700
SkyTech Inc 550 Airport Rd	Rock Hill	SC	29732	**888-386-3596**	803-366-5108
Southwest Airport Services Inc 11811 N Brantly St Ellington Field Bldg 500	Houston	TX	77034	**800-426-5237**	281-484-6551
Stevens Aviation Inc 600 Delaware St Donaldson Industrial Pk	Greenville	SC	29605	**800-359-7838**	864-879-6000
TAC Air Inc 701 S Robison Rd	Texarkana	TX	75504	**800-772-0077**	903-794-3835
Telford Aviation Inc 154 Maine St	Bangor	ME	04401	**800-639-4809**	207-262-6098
Trajen Inc 10510 Superfortress Ave	Mather	CA	95655	**800-565-2647**	916-368-1455
Vee Neal Aviation Inc 200 Pleasant Unity Rd Suite 109	Latrobe	PA	15650	**800-278-2710**	724-539-4533
Warrenton-Fauquier Flight Center 5075 Airport Rd Warrenton-Fauquier Airport PO Box 239	Midland	VA	22728	**800-296-4062**	540-788-4959
Western Aircraft Inc 4300 S Kennedy St	Boise	ID	83705	**800-333-3442**	208-338-1800
Wilson Air Center 2930 Winchester Rd Memphis International Airport	Memphis	TN	38118	**800-464-2992**	901-345-2992
Wisconsin Aviation Inc 1741 River Dr	Watertown	WI	53094	**800-657-0761**	920-261-4567
Woodland Aviation Inc 17992 County Rd 94B Watts-Woodland Airport	Woodland	CA	95695	**800-442-1333**	530-662-9631

64 BABY PRODUCTS

SEE ALSO Clothing & Accessories - Mfr - Children's & Infants' Clothing; Furniture - Mfr - Household Furniture; Paper Products - Mfr - Sanitary Paper Products; Toys, Games, Hobbies

Name / Address	City	State	Zip	Toll-Free	Phone
Basic Comfort Inc 5151 Franklin St	Denver	CO	80216	**800-456-8687**	303-778-7535
Britax Child Safety Inc 13501 S Ridge Dr	Charlotte	NC	28273	**888-427-4829**	704-409-1700
Car Seat Specialty PO Box 3194	Rock Hill	SC	29732	**877-912-1313**	

Company	City	State	ZIP	Toll-Free	Phone
Central Specialties Ltd 220-D Exchange Dr	Crystal Lake	IL	60014	**800-873-4370**	815-459-6000
Crown Crafts Infant Products Inc 711 W Walnut St	Compton	CA	90220	**800-421-0526**	310-763-8100
Dorel Industries Inc 12345 Albert Hudson St Suite 100 *NASDAQ: DIIB* ■ *Cust Svc	Montreal	QC	H1G3L1	**800-544-1108***	514-323-5701
Evenflo Co Inc 1801 Commerce Dr	Piqua	OH	45356	**800-233-5921**	937-415-3300
First Years Inc 1 Kiddie Dr	Avon	MA	02322	**800-533-6708**	508-588-1220
GRACO Children's Products Inc 150 Oaklands Blvd	Exton	PA	19341	**800-345-4109**	610-884-8000
Kolcraft Enterprises Inc 10832 NC Hwy 211 E *Cust Svc	Aberdeen	NC	28315	**800-453-7673***	910-944-9345
Peg-Perego USA Inc 3625 Independence Dr *Cust Svc	Fort Wayne	IN	46808	**800-728-2108***	260-482-8191
Playtex Products Inc 300 Nyala Farms Rd *NYSE: PYX*	Westport	CT	06880	**800-999-9700**	203-341-4000
Rubbermaid Home Products 1147 Akron Rd	Wooster	OH	44691	**888-895-2110**	330-264-6464
Safety 1st Inc 45 Dan Rd	Canton	MA	02021	**800-962-7233**	781-364-3100
Triboro Quilt Mfg Inc 172 S Broadway	White Plains	NY	10605	**800-227-2077**	914-428-7551

65 BACKUP CARE SERVICES

Company	City	State	ZIP	Toll-Free	Phone
Caregivers on Call 50 Broadway	Lynbrook	NY	11563	**800-225-1200**	516-887-1200
Lifecare Inc 400 Nyala Farms Rd	Westport	CT	06880	**800-873-4636**	203-226-2680
Work Options Group Inc 1100 S McCaslin Blvd Suite 200	Superior	CO	80027	**888-610-2273**	303-604-6545
WorkLife Benefits Inc 25115 Ave Sanford Suite 200	Valencia	CA	91355	**800-628-5437**	661-775-2200

66 BAGS - PAPER

Company	City	State	ZIP	Toll-Free	Phone
Bagcraft Packaging LLC 3900 W 43rd St	Chicago	IL	60632	**800-621-8468**	773-254-8000
Bancroft Bag Inc 425 Bancroft Blvd	West Monroe	LA	71292	**800-551-4950**	318-387-2550
Bemis Pet Products PO Box 9066	Omaha	NE	68109	**800-541-4303**	402-734-6262
Bonita Pioneer Packaging Products Inc 7333 SW Bonita Rd	Portland	OR	97224	**800-677-7725**	503-684-6542
Chase Packaging Inc 1300 Marshall Ave *Cust Svc	Newport News	VA	23607	**800-532-3345***	757-247-6676
Colonial Bag Co PO Box 929	Lake Park	GA	31636	**800-392-4875**	229-559-8484
Duro Bag Mfg Co 7600 Empire Dr	Florence	KY	41042	**800-879-3876**	859-581-8200
Hood Packaging Corp 25 Woodgreen Pl	Madison	MS	39110	**800-321-8115**	601-853-7260
Mid-America Packaging LLC 3501 Jefferson Pkwy	Pine Bluff	AR	71602	**800-469-5120**	870-541-5120
Pacific Bag Inc 2045 120th Ave NE Suite 100	Bellevue	WA	98005	**800-562-2247**	425-455-1128
Portco Corp 3601 SE Columbia Way Suite 260	Vancouver	WA	98661	**800-676-8666**	360-696-1641
Stewart Sutherland Inc 5411 E 'V' Ave	Vicksburg	MI	49097	**800-253-1034**	269-649-0530
Uniflex Inc 383 W John St	Hicksville	NY	11802	**800-223-0564**	516-932-2000
White Bag Co Inc 8027 Hwy 161 N	North Little Rock	AR	72117	**800-527-1733**	501-835-1444

67 BAGS - PLASTICS

Company	City	State	ZIP	Toll-Free	Phone
American Transparent Plastics Corp 180 National Rd *Orders	Edison	NJ	08817	**800-942-8725***	732-287-3000
Ampac Packaging LLC 12025 Tricon Rd	Cincinnati	OH	45246	**800-543-7030**	513-671-1777
Armand Mfg Inc 2399 Silver Wolf Dr	Henderson	NV	89015	**800-343-7982**	702-565-7500
Associated Bag Co 400 W Boden St	Milwaukee	WI	53207	**800-926-6100**	414-769-1000
Bema Film Systems Inc 744 N Oaklawn Ave	Elmhurst	IL	60126	**800-833-6657**	630-279-7800
Clear View Bag Co 7137 Prospect Church Rd	Thomasville	NC	27361	**800-670-6483**	336-885-8131
CPI Plastics Group Ltd 979 Gana Ct	Mississauga	ON	L5S1N9	**800-251-9566**	416-798-9333
Duro Bag Mfg Co 7600 Empire Dr	Florence	KY	41042	**800-879-3876**	859-581-8200
FlexSol Packaging Corp 560 Ferry St	Newark	NJ	07105	**800-496-1998**	973-465-0266
Fortune Plastics Inc Williams Ln PO Box 637	Old Saybrook	CT	06475	**800-243-0306**	860-388-3426
Heritage Bags 1648 Diplomat Dr	Carrollton	TX	75006	**800-527-2247**	972-241-5525
Home Care Industries Inc 1 Lisbon St	Clifton	NJ	07013	**888-772-2100**	973-365-1600
Hood Packaging Corp 25 Woodgreen Pl	Madison	MS	39110	**800-321-8115**	601-853-7260
International Poly Bag Inc 990 Park Ctr Dr Suite G	Vista	CA	92083	**800-976-5922**	760-598-2468
Mercury Plastics Inc 14825 Salt Lake Ave	City of Industry	CA	91746	**800-831-2517**	626-961-0165
Mercury Plastics Inc 123 Willamette Ln	Bowling Green	KY	42101	**800-347-0338**	270-782-8026
Pacific Bag Inc 2045 120th Ave NE Suite 100	Bellevue	WA	98005	**800-562-2247**	425-455-1128
Pactiv Corp 1900 W Field Ct *NYSE: PTV*	Lake Forest	IL	60045	**888-828-2850**	847-482-2000
Papercon Inc 2700 Apple Valley Rd NE	Atlanta	GA	30319	**800-241-0619**	404-261-7205
Pitt Plastics Inc 1400 Atkinson Ave	Pittsburg	KS	66762	**800-835-0366**	620-231-4030
Poly-America Inc 2000 W Marshall Dr	Grand Prairie	TX	75051	**800-527-3322**	972-647-4374
Poly-Pak Industries Inc 125 Spagnoli Rd	Melville	NY	11747	**800-969-1995**	631-293-6767
Portco Corp 3601 SE Columbia Way Suite 260	Vancouver	WA	98661	**800-676-8666**	360-696-1641
Presto Products Co 670 N Perkins St	Appleton	WI	54912	**800-558-3525**	920-739-9471
Putnam Plastics Inc 255 S Alex Rd	West Carrollton	OH	45449	**800-457-3099**	937-866-6261
Ronpak Inc 4301 New Brunswick Ave *Cust Svc	South Plainfield	NJ	07080	**888-766-7251***	732-968-8000
Shields Bag & Printing Co 1009 Rock Ave	Yakima	WA	98902	**800-541-8630**	509-248-7500
Southeastern Plastics Corp 15 Home News Row	New Brunswick	NJ	08901	**800-966-2247**	732-846-8500
Star Packaging Corp 453 85th Cir	College Park	GA	30349	**800-252-5414**	404-763-2800
Tyco Plastics Inc 1401 W 94th St	Bloomington	MN	55431	**800-873-3941**	952-884-7281
Uniflex Inc 383 W John St	Hicksville	NY	11802	**800-223-0564**	516-932-2000
Union Industries Inc 10 Admiral St	Providence	RI	02908	**800-556-6454**	401-274-7000
Webster Industries Inc 58 Pulaski St	Peabody	MA	01960	**800-225-0796**	978-532-2000
White Bag Co Inc 8027 Hwy 161 N	North Little Rock	AR	72117	**800-527-1733**	501-835-1444

68 BAGS - TEXTILE

SEE ALSO Handbags, Totes, Backpacks; Luggage, Bags, Cases

Company	City	State	ZIP	Toll-Free	Phone
A Rifkin Co 1400 Sans Souci Pkwy *Cust Svc	Wilkes-Barre	PA	18706	**800-458-7300***	570-825-9551
Aceco Industrial Packaging 166 Frelinghuysen Ave	Newark	NJ	07114	**800-832-2247**	973-242-2200
Bulk Lift International Inc 1013 Tamarac Dr	Carpentersville	IL	60110	**800-879-2247**	847-428-6059
Fox Packaging Co 2200 Fox Dr	McAllen	TX	78504	**800-336-6369**	956-682-6176
Fulton-Denver Co 3500 Wynkoop St	Denver	CO	80216	**800-776-6715**	303-294-9292
GEM Group 9 International Way	Lawrence	MA	01843	**800-800-3200**	978-691-2000
Halsted Corp 78 Halladay St	Jersey City	NJ	07304	**800-843-5184**	201-433-3323
Harry Miller Co Inc 850 Albany St	Boston	MA	02119	**800-225-5598**	617-427-2300
HBD Inc 3901 Riverdale Rd	Greensboro	NC	27406	**800-403-2247**	336-275-4800
Indian Valley Industries Inc 60-100 Corliss Ave	Johnson City	NY	13790	**800-659-5111**	607-729-5111
J & M Industries 300 Ponchatoula Pkwy	Ponchatoula	LA	70454	**800-989-1002**	985-386-6000
Langston Cos Inc 1760 S 3rd St *Cust Svc	Memphis	TN	38101	**800-627-5224***	901-774-4440
LBU Inc 217 Brook Ave	Passaic	NJ	07055	**800-678-4528**	973-773-4800
Max Katz Inc 235 S LaSalle St	Indianapolis	IN	46201	**800-225-3729**	317-635-9561
Menardi 1 Maxwell Dr	Trenton	SC	29847	**800-321-3218**	803-663-6551
Mid-America Packaging LLC 3501 Jefferson Pkwy	Pine Bluff	AR	71602	**800-469-5120**	870-541-5120
Miller Harry Canvas Co Inc 850 Albany St	Boston	MA	02119	**800-225-5598**	617-427-2300
Morgan Brothers Bag Co Inc PO Box 25577	Richmond	VA	23260	**800-368-2247**	804-355-9107
NYP Corp 805 E Grand St	Elizabeth	NJ	07201	**800-524-1052**	908-351-6550
Sacramento Bag Mfg Co 530 Q St	Sacramento	CA	95814	**800-287-2247**	916-441-6121
Scholle Custom Packaging Inc 201 W Glocheski Dr	Manistee	MI	49660	**800-968-5211**	231-723-5211
Super Sack Mfg Corp 11510 Data Dr	Dallas	TX	75218	**800-331-9200**	214-340-7060

69 BAKERIES

Company	City	State	ZIP	Toll-Free	Phone
Atlanta Bread Co International Inc 1955 Lake Park Dr Suite 400	Smyrna	GA	30080	**800-398-3728**	770-432-0933
Au Bon Pain 19 Fid Kennedy Ave	Boston	MA	02210	**800-825-5227**	617-423-2100
Awrey Bakeries Inc 12301 Farmington Rd	Livonia	MI	48150	**800-950-2253**	734-522-1100
Big Apple Bagels 500 Lake Cook Rd Suite 475	Deerfield	IL	60015	**800-251-6101**	847-948-7520
C-Street Bakery 2930 W Maple St	Sioux Falls	SD	57107	**800-336-1320**	605-336-6961
Cheryl & Co Inc 646 McCorkle Blvd	Westerville	OH	43082	**800-443-8124**	614-891-8822
Cinnabon World Famous Cinnamon Rolls 6 Concourse Pkwy Suite 1700	Atlanta	GA	30328	**866-232-4401**	770-391-9500
Collin Street Bakery Inc 401 W 7th Ave *Sales	Corsicana	TX	75110	**800-504-1896***	903-872-8111
Cookie Bouquet 6757 Arapaho Rd Suite 707	Dallas	TX	75248	**800-752-8412**	972-386-7334
Cookies in Bloom Inc 12700 Hillcrest Rd Suite 251	Dallas	TX	75230	**800-222-3104**	972-490-8644
Damascus Bakery Inc 56 Gold St	Brooklyn	NY	11201	**800-367-7482**	718-855-1457
Daylight Corp 11707 E 11th St	Tulsa	OK	74128	**800-331-2245**	918-438-0800
Dunkin' Donuts Inc 14 Pacella Park Dr *Cust Svc	Randolph	MA	02368	**800-859-5339***	781-961-4000
Einstein/Noah Bagel Corp 1687 Cole Blvd *Cust Svc	Golden	CO	80401	**800-660-3200***	303-568-8000
Gold Medal Bakery Inc 21 Penn St	Fall River	MA	02724	**800-642-7568**	508-674-5766
Gonnella Baking Co 2002 W Erie St	Chicago	IL	60612	**800-262-3442**	312-733-2020
Great American Bagel 519 N Cass Ave	Westmont	IL	60559	**888-224-3563**	630-963-3393
Great American Cookie Co Inc 4685 Frederick Dr SW	Atlanta	GA	30336	**800-332-4856**	404-696-1700
Great Harvest Bread Co 28 S Montana St	Dillon	MT	59725	**800-442-0424**	406-683-6842
Haas Baking Co 9769 Reavis Park Dr	Saint Louis	MO	63123	**800-325-3171**	314-631-6100
Honey Dew Assoc Inc 35 Braintree Hill Office Park Suite 205	Braintree	MA	02184	**800-946-6393**	781-849-3000
J & J Restaurant Group LLC 505 W Roseville Rd	Lancaster	PA	17601	**800-233-0128**	717-299-0968
Just Desserts Inc 550 85th Ave	Oakland	CA	94621	**800-253-4438**	510-567-2910
Krispy Kreme Doughnuts Inc 370 Knollwood St Suite 500 *NYSE: KKD*	Winston-Salem	NC	27103	**800-334-1243**	336-725-2981
La Madeleine Inc 6688 N Central Expy Suite 700	Dallas	TX	75206	**800-400-5840**	214-696-6962
Manhattan Bagel Co Inc 100 Horizon Ctr Blvd	Hamilton	NJ	08691	**800-308-2457**	609-631-7000
Maple Donuts Inc 3455 E Market St	York	PA	17402	**800-627-5348**	717-757-7826
Mrs Fields Original Cookies Inc 2855 E Cottonwood Pkwy Suite 400	Salt Lake City	UT	84121	**800-348-6311**	801-736-5600
Noah's New York Bagels Inc 255 Ygnacio Valley Rd Suite 200	Walnut Creek	CA	90601	**800-936-6247**	925-979-6000
Panera Bread Co 6710 Clayton Rd *NASDAQ: PNRA*	Richmond Heights	MO	63117	**800-301-5566**	314-633-7100
Rotella's Italian Bakery Inc 6949 S 108th St	La Vista	NE	68128	**800-759-0360**	402-592-6600
Saint Louis Bread Co 6710 Clayton Rd	Richmond Heights	MO	63117	**800-301-5566**	314-633-7100
Southern Maid Donut Flour Co 3615 Cavalier Dr	Garland	TX	75042	**800-936-6887**	972-272-6425
Tim Hortons 4150 Tuller Rd Suite 236	Dublin	OH	43017	**888-376-4835**	614-791-4200
Vie de France Bakery 2070 Chain Bridge Rd Suite 500	Vienna	VA	22182	**800-446-4404**	703-442-9205
Winchell's Donut House 2223 Wellington Ave Suite 300	Santa Ana	CA	92701	**877-541-5554**	714-565-1800

70 BANKING-RELATED SERVICES

				Toll-Free	Phone
Automatic Funds Transfer Services 151 S Landers St Suite C	Seattle	WA	98134	**800-275-2033**	206-254-0975
Bankserv 222 Kearny St Suite 400	San Francisco	CA	94108	**888-354-3535**	415-217-4581
Cecorp 8 Chrysler	Irvine	CA	92618	**800-854-6861**	949-583-0792
Comdata Corp 5301 Maryland Way	Brentwood	TN	37027	**800-266-3282**	615-370-7000
Credit Union 24 Inc 2473 Care Dr Suite 1	Tallahassee	FL	32308	**877-570-2824**	850-701-2824
CU24 19 British American Blvd	Latham	NY	12110	**800-453-1466**	518-437-8100
First Data Integrated Payment Systems Financial Services Div 6200 S Quebec St	Greenwood Village	CO	80111	**800-208-3131**	303-488-8000
Game Financial Corp 1550 Utica Ave S Suite 100	Saint Louis Park	MN	55416	**800-363-3372**	952-591-3000
InteliData Technologies Corp 11600 Sunrise Valley Dr Suite 100 *NASDAQ: INTD*	Reston	VA	20191	**800-878-1053**	703-259-3000
Lydian Trust Co 3801 PGA Blvd	Palm Beach Gardens	FL	33410	**866-659-5055**	561-776-8860
Mastercard/Cirrus ATM Network 2200 Mastercard Blvd	O'Fallon	MO	63366	**800-300-3069**	636-722-6100
Midwest Payment Systems 38 Fountain Sq Plaza	Cincinnati	OH	45263	**800-972-3030**	513-579-5300
MoneyGram International Inc 1550 Utica Ave S Suite 100 *NYSE: MGI*	Saint Louis Park	MN	55416	**800-328-5678**	952-591-3000
NetBank Payment Systems Inc 200 Briarwood W Dr	Jackson	MS	39206	**800-523-2104**	601-956-1222
Star Systems Inc 495 N Keller Rd Suite 500	Maitland	FL	32751	**888-233-7337**	321-263-3000
Travelers Express Co Inc 1550 Utica Ave S Suite 100	Minneapolis	MN	55416	**800-542-3590**	952-591-3000
Travelex Worldwide Money 29 Broadway	New York	NY	10006	**800-815-1795**	212-363-6206
Universal Money Centers Inc 6800 Squibb Rd	Shawnee Mission	KS	66202	**800-234-6860**	913-831-2055
Western Union North America 6200 S Quebec St *Cust Svc	Greenwood Village	CO	80111	**800-325-6000***	303-488-8000

71 BANKS - COMMERCIAL & SAVINGS

SEE ALSO Credit & Financing - Commercial; Credit & Financing - Consumer; Credit Unions; Holding Companies - Bank Holding Companies

				Toll-Free	Phone
1st Community Bank 2911 N Westwood Blvd	Poplar Bluff	MO	63901	**888-831-3620**	573-778-0101
Acacia Federal Savings Bank 7600 Leesburg Pike East Bldg Suite 200	Falls Church	VA	22043	**800-950-0270**	703-506-8100
Advanta National Bank PO Box 15555	Wilmington	DE	19850	**800-441-7306**	
Alliance Bank 541 Lawrence Rd *NASDAQ: ALLB*	Broomall	PA	19008	**800-550-4387**	610-353-2900
Amarillo National Bank 410 S Taylor St Plaza One	Amarillo	TX	79101	**800-262-3733**	806-378-8000
Amboy National Bank 3590 US Hwy 9 S	Old Bridge	NJ	08857	**800-942-6269**	732-591-8700
AMCORE Bank NA 501 7th St	Rockford	IL	61104	**888-426-2673**	815-968-1259
Amegy Bank of Texas 4400 Post Oak Pkwy	Houston	TX	77027	**800-287-0301**	713-235-8800
American Bank 4029 W Tilghman St	Allentown	PA	18104	**888-366-6622**	610-366-1800
American Express Centurion Bank 4315 S 2700 W	Salt Lake City	UT	84130	**888-356-1006**	801-945-3000
American Savings Bank FSB 915 Fort St	Honolulu	HI	96804	**800-272-2566**	808-531-6262
Ameriserv Financial 216 Franklin St	Johnstown	PA	15901	**800-837-2265**	814-533-5300
AmSouth Bank 1900 5th Ave N	Birmingham	AL	35203	**800-284-4100**	205-326-5164
AnchorBank PO Box 7933	Madison	WI	53707	**800-252-6246**	608-252-8700
Apple Bank for Savings 122 E 42nd St 9th Fl	New York	NY	10168	**800-722-6888**	212-224-6400
Ascenia Bank PO Box 436029	Louisville	KY	40253	**877-369-2265**	502-499-4800
Associated Bank Green Bay NA 200 N Adams St	Green Bay	WI	54301	**800-236-3479**	920-433-3200
Associated Bank Illinois NA 612 N Main St *Cust Svc	Rockford	IL	61103	**800-358-6064***	815-987-3500
Associated Bank Milwaukee 401 E Kilbourn Ave	Milwaukee	WI	53202	**800-236-8866**	414-271-1786
Associated Bank North 303 S 1st Ave	Wausau	WI	54402	**800-236-7160**	715-845-4301
Atlantic Bank of New York 960 Ave of the Americas	New York	NY	10001	**800-535-2269**	212-967-7425
Banco Comercial Portugues 2 Wall St	New York	NY	10005	**800-746-7828**	212-306-7800
Banco Popular de Puerto Rico PO Box 36-2708	San Juan	PR	00936	**888-724-3650**	787-765-9800
Banco Santander Puerto Rico PO Box 362589 GPO	San Juan	PR	00936	**800-726-8263**	787-759-7070
Bancorp Bank 405 Silverside Rd *NASDAQ: TBBK* ■ *Cust Svc	Wilmington	DE	19809	**800-545-0289***	302-385-5000
BancorpSouth 2910 W Jackson St	Tupelo	MS	38801	**888-797-7711**	662-680-2000
Bangor Savings Bank PO Box 930	Bangor	ME	04402	**877-226-4671**	207-942-5211
Bank of America NA 699 S Mill Ave Suite 101	Tempe	AZ	85281	**800-299-2265**	480-804-9481
Bank of America NA 101 S Tryon St	Charlotte	NC	28255	**800-432-1000**	704-386-5478
Bank Financial 21110 S Western Ave	Olympia Fields	IL	60461	**800-244-2265**	708-747-2000
Bank of Hawaii 111 S King St	Honolulu	HI	96813	**888-643-3888**	808-538-4171
Bank Leumi USA 420 Lexington Ave	New York	NY	10170	**800-892-5430**	917-542-2343
Bank of Marin 50 Madera Blvd *NASDAQ: BMRC*	Corte Madera	CA	94925	**800-654-5111**	415-927-2265
Bank of Montreal 3 Times Sq	New York	NY	10036	**800-363-9992**	212-758-6300
Bank of Montreal 119 Saint Jacques St *NYSE: BMO*	Montreal	QC	H2Y1L6	**800-363-9992**	514-877-7373
Bank of New Hampshire NA PO Box 487 *Cust Svc	Farmington	NH	03835	**800-224-5563***	603-755-2255
Bank of New York 1 Wall St	New York	NY	10286	**800-225-5269**	212-635-6748
Bank of Newport PO Box 450	Newport	RI	02840	**800-234-8586**	401-846-3400
Bank of North Dakota 700 E Main Ave	Bismarck	ND	58501	**800-472-2166**	701-328-5600
Bank of Oklahoma NA PO Box 2300 *Cust Svc	Tulsa	OK	74192	**800-234-6181***	918-588-6000
Bank One 1 Bank One Plaza	Chicago	IL	60670	**877-226-5663**	312-732-4000
Bank of the West 180 Montgomery St	San Francisco	CA	94104	**800-575-6677**	925-942-8300
BankAtlantic 1750 E Sunrise Blvd	Fort Lauderdale	FL	33304	**800-741-1700**	954-760-5000
Banknorth Massachusetts 295 Park Ave *Cust Svc	Worcester	MA	01610	**800-390-6443***	508-752-2584
BankUnited FSB 255 Alhambra Cir Suite 100	Coral Gables	FL	33134	**800-440-9646**	305-569-2000
Banner Bank PO Box 907	Walla Walla	WA	99362	**800-272-9933**	509-526-8734
BB & T Bank 3233 Thomasville Rd	Tallahassee	FL	32308	**888-385-3301**	850-385-3300
Beal Bank SSB 6000 Legacy Dr	Plano	TX	75024	**800-404-4494**	469-467-5000
Beneficial Mutual Savings Bank 530 Walnut St	Philadelphia	PA	19106	**800-784-8490**	215-864-6000
Berkshire Bank PO Box 1308	Pittsfield	MA	01202	**800-773-5601**	413-443-5601
Bluebonnet Savings Bank FSB 8150 N Central Expy Suite 1900	Dallas	TX	75206	**800-878-3111**	214-365-1300
Boston Federal Savings Bank 17 New England Executive Park	Burlington	MA	01803	**800-688-2372**	781-272-0230
Branch Banking & Trust Co of South Carolina PO Box 408	Greenville	SC	29602	**800-226-5228**	864-242-8000
Branch Banking & Trust Co of Virginia 109 E Main St	Norfolk	VA	23510	**800-226-5228**	757-823-7800
Brookline Savings Bank 160 Washington St	Brookline	MA	02445	**888-730-3554**	617-730-3500
Busey Bank 201 W Main St	Urbana	IL	61801	**888-384-1010**	217-384-4500
California Bank & Trust 11622 El Camino Real Suite 200	San Diego	CA	92130	**800-400-6080**	858-793-7400
California Commerce Bank 2029 Century Pk E 42nd Fl	Los Angeles	CA	90067	**800-222-1234**	
Canadian Imperial Bank of Commerce 199 Bay St Commerce Court W *NYSE: BCM*	Toronto	ON	M5L1A2	**800-465-2422**	416-980-2211
Cape Cod Five Cents Savings Bank 19 West Rd	Orleans	MA	02653	**888-333-0555**	508-240-0555
Capital Crossing Bank 101 Summer St *NASDAQ: CAPX*	Boston	MA	02110	**888-880-3880**	617-880-1000
Capitol Federal Savings Bank 700 S Kansas Ave	Topeka	KS	66603	**800-432-2926**	785-235-1341
Carolina First Bank 102 S Main St	Greenville	SC	29601	**800-476-6400**	864-255-7900
Cathay Bank 777 N Broadway	Los Angeles	CA	90012	**800-922-8429**	213-625-4700
Central Pacific Bank 220 S King St PO Box 3590	Honolulu	HI	96811	**800-342-8422**	808-544-0500
Centura Bank DBA RBC Centura 1417 Centura Hwy	Rocky Mount	NC	27804	**800-236-8872**	252-454-4400
Charter One Bank 1215 Superior Ave	Cleveland	OH	44114	**800-553-8981**	216-566-5300
CharterBank 600 3rd Ave	West Point	GA	31833	**800-763-4444**	706-645-1391
Chase Bank 1 Chase Manhattan Plaza	New York	NY	10081	**800-935-9935**	212-270-6000
Chevy Chase Bank FSB 7501 Wisconsin Ave	Bethesda	MD	20814	**800-987-2265**	240-497-4102
Chinatrust Bank USA 22939 Hawthorne Blvd	Torrance	CA	90505	**888-839-9000**	310-791-2828
Chittenden Bank 2 Burlington Sq	Burlington	VT	05402	**800-752-0006**	802-658-4000
Citibank (Delaware) 1 Penns Way	New Castle	DE	19720	**800-341-4727**	302-323-3801
Citibank FSB 245 Market St	San Francisco	CA	94105	**866-248-4937**	
Citibank NA 399 Park Ave	New York	NY	10022	**800-627-3999**	
Citibank (Nevada) NA 8701 W Sahara Ave	Las Vegas	NV	89117	**866-248-4937**	
Citibank (New York State) 3330 Monroe Ave	Pittsford	NY	14618	**800-934-1609**	
Citibank (South Dakota) NA 701 E 60th St N	Sioux Falls	SD	57117	**800-843-0777**	605-331-2626
Citibank (West) FSB 950 Market St	San Francisco	CA	94104	**866-248-4937**	
Citizens Bank 919 Market St	Wilmington	DE	19801	**888-910-4100**	302-421-2228
Citizens Bank 328 S Saginaw St 1 Citizens Banking Ctr	Flint	MI	48502	**800-825-7200**	810-766-7500
Citizens Bank of Massachusetts 28 State St	Boston	MA	02109	**800-922-9999**	617-725-5900
Citizens Bank New Hampshire 875 Elm St	Manchester	NH	03101	**800-922-9999**	603-634-6000
Citizens Bank of Rhode Island 1 Citizens Plaza *Cust Svc	Providence	RI	02903	**800-922-9999***	401-456-7000
Citizens Business Bank 701 N Haven Ave Suite 350	Ontario	CA	91764	**888-222-5432**	909-980-4030
Citizens Financial Services 707 Ridge Rd	Munster	IN	46321	**800-334-5869**	219-836-5500
Citizens First Savings Bank 525 Water St	Port Huron	MI	48060	**800-922-5308**	810-987-8300
Citizens Trust Bank PO Box 4485	Atlanta	GA	30303	**800-547-1344**	404-659-5959
City Bank PO Box 97007 *NASDAQ: CTBK*	Lynnwood	WA	98046	**800-569-0006**	425-745-5933
City National Bank 400 N Roxbury Dr *Cust Svc	Beverly Hills	CA	90210	**800-773-7100***	310-888-6000
City National Bank of Florida 450 E Las Olas Blvd	Fort Lauderdale	FL	33301	**800-762-2489**	954-467-6667
City National Bank of West Virginia 3601 McCorckle Ave	Charleston	WV	25304	**877-203-8700**	304-926-3300
Coastal Federal Bank 2619 Oak St	Myrtle Beach	SC	29577	**800-613-8179**	843-205-2000
Cole Taylor Bank 1965 N Milwaukee Ave	Chicago	IL	60647	**800-727-2265**	773-927-7000
College Savings Bank 5 Vaughn Dr	Princeton	NJ	08540	**800-888-2723**	609-987-3700
Colonial Bank 1 Commerce St	Montgomery	AL	36104	**888-285-5886**	334-240-5000
Columbia Bank 7168 Columbia Gateway Dr	Columbia	MD	21046	**800-314-7714**	410-730-5000
Columbia Savings Bank 19-01 Rt 208 *Cust Svc	Fair Lawn	NJ	07410	**800-522-4167***	201-796-3600
Columbia State Bank PO Box 2156	Tacoma	WA	98401	**800-305-1905**	253-305-1900
Columbus Bank & Trust Co 1148 Broadway	Columbus	GA	31901	**800-334-9007**	706-649-2012
Comerica Bank 500 Woodward Ave	Detroit	MI	48226	**800-643-4418**	248-371-5000
Comerica Bank-California 333 W Santa Clara St	San Jose	CA	95113	**800-888-3595**	408-556-5000
Comerica Bank-Texas 753 W Illinois Ave	Dallas	TX	75224	**800-925-2160**	214-630-3030
Commerce Bank NA 1000 Walnut St *Cust Svc	Kansas City	MO	64106	**800-453-2265***	816-234-2000
Commercebank NA 220 Alhambra Cir	Coral Gables	FL	33134	**888-629-4810**	305-460-8701
Commercial Capital Bancorp Inc 8105 Irvine Ctr Dr 15th Fl *NASDAQ: CCBI*	Irvine	CA	92618	**877-387-5574**	949-585-7500
Commercial Federal Bank FSB 13220 California St	Omaha	NE	68154	**800-228-5023**	402-514-5306
Community Bank NA PO Box 509	Canton	NY	13617	**800-835-2993**	315-386-4553
Community Bank of Northern Virginia 107 Free Ct	Sterling	VA	20164	**800-430-5305**	703-430-5600
Community First National Bank 520 Main Ave	Fargo	ND	58124	**800-232-2318**	701-293-2200
Community Trust Bank NA 346 N Mayo Trail	Pikeville	KY	41501	**800-422-1090**	606-432-1414
Compass Bank 15 S 20th St *Cust Svc	Birmingham	AL	35233	**800-239-4357***	205-933-3000
Corus Bank NA 2401 N Halsted St	Chicago	IL	60614	**800-555-5710**	773-935-6000
Country Bank for Savings 75 Main St	Ware	MA	01082	**800-322-8233**	413-967-6221
Cross Country Bank 800 Delaware Ave	Wilmington	DE	19801	**800-334-3180**	302-326-4200
Cupertino National Bank & Trust 20230 Stevens Creek Blvd	Cupertino	CA	95014	**888-650-8008**	408-996-1144
Discover Bank 12 Read's Way	New Castle	DE	19720	**800-347-7000**	302-323-7110
Dollar Bank FSB 3 Gateway Ctr	Pittsburgh	PA	15222	**800-828-5527**	412-261-4900
E*Trade Bank 671 N Glebe Rd	Arlington	VA	22203	**800-382-2651**	703-247-3700
East-West Bank 415 Huntington Dr	San Marino	CA	91108	**888-888-3932**	626-799-8998
Eastern Bank 195 Market St	Lynn	MA	01903	**800-327-8376**	781-599-2100
Encore Bank 1220 Augusta Dr	Houston	TX	77057	**800-727-3193**	713-787-3100
ESB Bank 600 Lawrence Ave	Ellwood City	PA	16117	**800-533-4193**	724-758-5584

Bank / Address	City	State	ZIP	Toll-Free	Phone
Evergreen Bank NA 237 Glen St	Glens Falls	NY	12801	**888-792-1151**	518-792-1151
F & M Bank Wisconsin 205 E 4th St	Kaukauna	WI	54130	**800-806-1692**	920-766-8160
Farmers First Bank 24 N Cedar St	Lititz	PA	17543	**800-311-3182**	717-626-4735
Farmers & Mechanics Bank 110 Thomas Johnson Dr	Frederick	MD	21702	**800-445-3626**	301-694-4000
Farmers & Mechanics Bank 3 Sunset Rd	Burlington	NJ	08016	**800-523-4175**	609-386-2400
Fidelity Bank 100 E English St	Wichita	KS	67202	**800-658-1637**	316-265-2261
Fidelity Federal Bank & Trust 205 Datura St	West Palm Beach	FL	33401	**800-422-3675**	561-659-9900
Fifth Third Bank 38 Fountain Sq Plaza	Cincinnati	OH	45263	**800-972-3030**	513-579-5300
Fifth Third Bank Central Ohio 21 E State St	Columbus	OH	43215	**800-972-3030**	614-341-2595
Fifth Third Bank Inc 100 Brighton Park Blvd	Frankfort	KY	40601	**800-972-3030**	502-695-0882
Fifth Third Bank Northeastern Ohio 1404 E 9th St *Cust Svc	Cleveland	OH	44114	**800-972-3030***	216-696-5300
Fifth Third Bank Northwestern Ohio 606 Madison Ave	Toledo	OH	43604	**800-972-3030**	419-259-7890
Fifth Third Bank Western Michigan 830 Pleasant St	Saint Joseph	MI	49085	**800-972-3030**	269-983-6311
Fifth Third Bank Western Ohio 110 N Main St	Dayton	OH	45402	**800-972-3030**	937-227-6500
Fireside Bank 5050 Hopyard Rd Suite 200	Pleasanton	CA	94588	**800-825-1862**	925-460-9020
First American Bank SSB 2800 S Texas Ave Suite 200	Bryan	TX	77802	**800-299-0062**	979-361-6200
First Bank 11901 Olive Blvd	Creve Coeur	MO	63141	**800-279-3600**	314-995-8700
First Calgary Savings 510 16th Ave NE Suite 200	Calgary	AB	T2E1K4	**866-923-4778**	403-230-2783
First Charter Bank 10200 David Taylor Dr	Charlotte	NC	28262	**800-601-8471**	704-786-3300
First Citizens Bank & Trust Co 3128 Smoketree Ct *Cust Svc	Raleigh	NC	27604	**888-323-4732***	919-716-7000
First Federal Bank 329 Pierce St	Sioux City	IA	51101	**800-352-4620**	712-277-0200
First Federal Bank of Arkansas FA 1401 Hwy 62 65 N	Harrison	AR	72601	**800-345-2539**	870-741-7641
First Federal Bank of California FSB 401 Wilshire Blvd	Santa Monica	CA	90401	**800-637-5540**	310-319-6000
First Federal Bank of the Midwest 601 Clinton St PO Box 248	Defiance	OH	43512	**800-472-6292**	419-782-5015
First Federal Capital Bank 605 State St *Cust Svc	La Crosse	WI	54601	**800-657-4636***	608-784-8000
First Federal Savings & Loan Assn of Charleston 34 Broad St	Charleston	SC	29401	**800-768-3248**	843-724-0800
First Federal Savings & Loan Assn of Lakewood 14806 Detroit Ave	Lakewood	OH	44107	**800-529-2780**	216-221-7300
First Financial Bank 300 High St *Cust Svc	Hamilton	OH	45011	**800-543-2265***	513-867-4700
First Hawaiian Bank 999 Bishop St	Honolulu	HI	96813	**800-843-8411**	808-525-7153
First Indiana Bank 135 N Pennsylvania St First Indiana Plaza	Indianapolis	IN	46204	**800-888-8586**	317-269-1200
First Internet Bank of Indiana 7820 Innovation Blvd Suite 210	Indianapolis	IN	46278	**888-873-3424**	
First Interstate Bank 401 N 31st St	Billings	MT	59101	**888-752-3336**	406-255-5000
First Midwest Bank NA 300 Park Blvd Suite 405 PO Box 459	Itasca	IL	60143	**800-322-3623**	630-875-7200
First National Bank Alaska 101 W 36 Ave	Anchorage	AK	99503	**800-856-4362**	907-276-6300
First National Bank of Florida PO Box 413043	Naples	FL	34101	**800-262-7600**	239-262-7600
First National Bank of Nevada 2510 S Maryland Pkwy Suite A	Las Vegas	NV	89109	**888-216-6888**	702-792-2200
First National Bank of Omaha 1620 Dodge St	Omaha	NE	68197	**800-228-4411**	402-341-0500
First Niagara Bank 6950 S Transit Rd	Lockport	NY	14094	**800-421-0004**	716-625-7500
First Place Bank 185 E Market St	Warren	OH	44481	**800-995-2646**	330-373-1221
First Republic Bank 111 Pine St 3rd Fl *NYSE: FRC*	San Francisco	CA	94111	**800-392-1400**	415-392-1400
First Tennessee Bank 165 Madison Ave	Memphis	TN	38103	**800-999-0110**	901-523-4444
FirstFed - A Division of Webster Bank 1 First FedPark	Swansea	MA	02777	**877-679-8181**	508-991-2601
Firstrust Savings Bank 1931 Cottman Ave	Philadelphia	PA	19111	**800-220-2265**	215-836-5200
Flagstar Bank FSB 5151 Corporate Dr	Troy	MI	48098	**800-945-7700**	248-312-2000
Fleet Bank 100 Federal St	Boston	MA	02110	**866-826-8989**	617-434-2200
Franklin Bank NA 24725 W 12-Mile Rd	Southfield	MI	48034	**800-527-4447**	248-358-5170
Fremont Investment & Loan 2727 E Imperial Hwy	Brea	CA	92821	**800-373-6668**	714-961-5000
Frost National Bank 100 W Houston	San Antonio	TX	78205	**800-562-6732**	210-220-4011
Fulton Bank 1 Penn Sq	Lancaster	PA	17602	**800-752-9580**	717-291-2411
Giantbank.com 6300 NE 1st Ave Suite 300	Fort Lauderdale	FL	33308	**877-446-4200**	954-958-0001
Great Southern Bank FSB 1451 E Battlefield Rd	Springfield	MO	65804	**800-749-7113**	417-887-4400
Guaranty Bank 8333 Douglas Ave	Dallas	TX	75225	**800-999-1726**	214-360-3360
Guaranty Bank SSB 4000 W Brown Deer Rd	Brown Deer	WI	53209	**800-585-5264**	414-362-4000
Hancock Bank 2510 14th St	Gulfport	MS	39501	**800-522-6542**	228-868-4000
Harbor Federal Savings Bank 100 S 2nd St	Fort Pierce	FL	34950	**888-613-2262**	772-461-2414
Harleysville National Bank & Trust Co 483 Main St	Harleysville	PA	19438	**800-423-3955**	215-256-8851
Harris Trust & Savings Bank 111 W Monroe St	Chicago	IL	60603	**888-340-2265**	312-461-2121
Hibernia National Bank 313 Carondelet St	New Orleans	LA	70130	**800-562-9007**	504-533-3333
Hickory Point Bank & Trust FSB PO Box 2548 *Cust Svc	Decatur	IL	62525	**888-424-1976***	217-875-3131
Home Federal Bank 225 S Main Ave PO Box 5000	Sioux Falls	SD	57117	**800-244-2149**	605-333-7500
Home Savings & Loan Co of Youngstown 275 Federal Plaza W	Youngstown	OH	44503	**888-999-4707**	330-742-0500
HomeFederal 218 W 2nd St	Seymour	IN	47274	**877-626-7000**	812-522-1592
HomeStreet Bank 601 Union St 2 Union Sq Suite 2000	Seattle	WA	98101	**800-654-1075**	206-623-3050
Horizon Bank 1500 Cornwall Ave	Bellingham	WA	98225	**800-955-9194**	360-733-3050
HSBC Bank Canada 885 W Georgia St Suite 200	Vancouver	BC	V6C3E9	**800-291-3888**	604-685-1000
HSBC Bank USA 1 HSBC Ctr	Buffalo	NY	14203	**800-975-4722**	716-841-2424
Hudson River Bank & Trust 1 Hudson City Ctr PO Box 76	Hudson	NY	12534	**800-352-7776**	518-828-4600
Hudson River Bank & Trust 1 Hudson City Ctr PO Box 76	Hudson	NY	12534	**800-352-7776**	518-828-4331
Hudson United Bank 1000 MacArthur Blvd	Mahwah	NJ	07430	**800-482-5465**	201-236-2600
Huntington National Bank 41 S High St	Columbus	OH	43287	**800-480-2265**	614-480-8300
IBERIABANK 1101 E Admiral Doyle Dr	New Iberia	LA	70560	**888-447-0770**	337-365-2361
Independence Community Bank 195 Montague St	Brooklyn	NY	11201	**800-732-3434**	718-722-5700
Independence Federal Savings Bank 1229 Connecticut Ave NW *NASDAQ: IFSB*	Washington	DC	20036	**888-922-6537**	202-628-5500
InsurBanc 10 Executive Dr	Farmington	CT	06032	**866-467-2262**	860-677-9701
Integra Bank NA 21 SE 3rd St	Evansville	IN	47708	**800-467-1928**	812-464-9800

Bank / Address	City	State	ZIP	Toll-Free	Phone
INTRUST Bank NA 105 N Main St	Wichita	KS	67202	**800-895-2265**	316-383-1111
Investors Savings Bank 101 JFK Pkwy	Shorthills	NJ	07078	**800-252-8119**	973-376-5100
Irwin Union Bank & Trust Co 500 Washington St	Columbus	IN	47201	**888-879-5900**	812-372-0111
Johnson Bank 4001 N Main St	Racine	WI	53402	**800-236-8586**	262-639-6010
Kearny Federal Savings Bank 614 Kearny Ave	Kearny	NJ	07032	**800-273-3406**	201-991-4100
Key Bank USA NA 22 Corporate Woods	Albany	NY	12211	**800-872-5553**	
KeyBank NA 127 Public Sq	Cleveland	OH	44114	**800-539-2968**	216-689-3000
Laredo National Bank 700 San Bernardo Ave	Laredo	TX	78040	**888-723-1151**	956-723-1151
LaSalle Bank NA 135 S LaSalle St	Chicago	IL	60603	**800-643-9600**	312-443-2000
Laurentian Bank of Canada 1981 ave McGill College *TSE: LB*	Montreal	QC	H3A3K3	**800-522-1846**	514-284-4500
Lehman Brothers Bank FSB 1000 West St Suite 200	Wilmington	DE	19801	**800-372-8464**	302-654-6179
Liberty Bank 315 Main St	Middletown	CT	06457	**800-622-6732**	860-344-7200
M & I Bank Northeast 310 W Walnut St	Green Bay	WI	54303	**888-464-5463**	920-436-1800
M & I Marshall & Ilsley Bank 770 N Water St	Milwaukee	WI	53202	**800-342-2265**	414-765-7700
M & T Bank Corp 67 Jackson St	Fishkill	NY	12524	**800-433-2265**	845-896-7644
Manufacturers & Traders Trust Co 1 M & T Plaza	Buffalo	NY	14203	**800-724-2440**	716-842-4470
MASSBANK 123 Haven St	Reading	MA	01867	**800-447-1052**	781-662-0100
Matrix Capital Bank 277 E Amador Ave	Las Cruces	NM	88001	**800-511-5081**	505-524-7748
Mayflower Co-operative Bank 30 S Main St *NASDAQ: MFLR*	Middleboro	MA	02346	**800-552-4344**	508-947-4343
MBNA America Bank NA	Wilmington	DE	19884	**800-441-7048**	
Mellon Bank NA 500 Grant St 1 Mellon Bank Ctr	Pittsburgh	PA	15258	**800-635-5662**	412-234-5000
Mercantile-Safe Deposit & Trust Co 2 Hopkins Plaza	Baltimore	MD	21201	**888-212-0100**	410-237-5569
Mid-State Bank 1026 Grand Ave PO Box 6002	Arroyo Grande	CA	93421	**800-473-7788**	805-489-4293
Middlesex Savings Bank 6 Main St	Natick	MA	01760	**800-438-6797**	508-653-0300
MidFirst Bank PO Box 76149	Oklahoma City	OK	73147	**888-643-3477**	405-943-8002
Mutual Savings Bank 4949 W Brown Deer Rd *Cust Svc	Milwaukee	WI	53223	**800-261-6888***	414-354-1500
National Bank of South Carolina 1 Broad St	Sumter	SC	29150	**800-708-5687**	803-778-8259
National City Bank 1900 E 9th St	Cleveland	OH	44114	**888-622-4932**	216-575-2000
National City Bank of Kentucky 101 S 5th St	Louisville	KY	40202	**800-727-8686**	502-581-4200
National City Bank of Michigan/Illinois 2595 Waukegan Rd *Cust Svc	Bannockburn	IL	60015	**800-925-9259***	847-317-2350
National InterBank PO Box 1245	Indianapolis	IN	46206	**877-468-7265**	
National Penn Bank PO Box 547	Boyertown	PA	19512	**800-822-3321**	610-367-6001
NBT Bank NA 52 S Broad St	Norwich	NY	13815	**800-628-2265**	
NetBank Inc 11475 Great Oaks Way Royal Ctr Three Suite 100 *NASDAQ: NTBK*	Alpharetta	GA	30022	**888-256-6932**	770-343-6006
Nevada State Bank PO Box 990	Las Vegas	NV	89125	**800-727-4743**	702-383-0009
New South Federal Savings Bank 1900 Crestwood Blvd	Irondale	AL	35210	**800-366-3030**	205-951-4000
Nexity Bank 3500 Blue Lake Dr Suite 330	Birmingham	AL	35243	**877-738-6391**	205-298-6391
North American Savings Bank FSB 12498 S 71 Hwy	Grandview	MO	64030	**800-677-6272**	816-765-2200
North Shore Bank FSB 15700 W Bluemound Rd	Brookfield	WI	53005	**800-236-4672**	262-785-1600
Northern Trust Bank of Florida NA 700 Brickell Ave	Miami	FL	33131	**800-468-2352**	305-372-1000
Northern Trust Co 50 S LaSalle St	Chicago	IL	60675	**888-289-6542**	312-630-6000
Northrim BanCorp Inc 3111 C St *NASDAQ: NRIM*	Anchorage	AK	99503	**800-478-3311**	907-562-0062
Northwest Savings Bank 301 2nd Ave	Warren	PA	16365	**800-822-2009**	814-726-2140
NOVA Savings Bank 1535 Locust St	Philadelphia	PA	19102	**877-322-6511**	215-545-6500
Oak Brook Bank 1400 16th St	Oak Brook	IL	60523	**800-536-3000**	630-571-1050
OceanFirst Bank 975 Hooper Ave	Toms River	NJ	08753	**888-623-2633**	732-240-4500
Ohio Legacy Corp 305 W Liberty St *NASDAQ: OLCB*	Wooster	OH	44691	**866-674-5301**	330-263-1955
Ohio Savings Bank FSB 1801 E 9th St	Cleveland	OH	44114	**800-860-2025**	216-622-4100
Old National Bank 420 Main St	Evansville	IN	47708	**800-731-2265**	812-464-1200
OneUnited Bank 133 Federal St	Boston	MA	02110	**877-663-8648**	617-457-4400
Pacific Capital Bank 30343 Canwood St Suite 100	Agoura Hills	CA	91301	**800-272-7200**	818-865-3300
Pacific Northwest Bank 275 SE Pioneer Way	Oak Harbor	WA	98277	**800-869-7114**	360-679-4181
Partners Trust Bank 233 Genesee St	Utica	NY	13501	**800-765-4968**	315-768-3000
Penn Federal Savings Bank 36 Ferry St	Newark	NJ	07105	**800-722-0351**	973-589-8616
People's Bank 850 Main St Bridgeport Ctr *NASDAQ: PBCT*	Bridgeport	CT	06604	**800-894-0300**	203-338-7171
Peoples First Community Bank 2305 Hwy 77	Panama City	FL	32405	**800-624-9699**	850-769-5261
Peoples Heritage Bank 1 Portland Sq PO Box 9540 *Cust Svc	Portland	ME	04112	**800-462-3666***	207-761-8500
PFF Bank & Trust 350 S Garey Ave	Pomona	CA	91767	**888-733-5465**	
Plymouth Savings Bank 226 Main St	Wareham	MA	02571	**800-426-7937**	508-295-3800
PNC Bank Advisors NA 99 High St 27th Fl	Boston	MA	02110	**800-762-3374**	
PNC Bank Delaware 300 Delaware Ave	Wilmington	DE	19899	**800-722-1172**	302-429-1011
PNC Bank NA 249 5th Ave 1 PNC Plaza	Pittsburgh	PA	15222	**888-762-2265**	412-762-2000
Presidential Online Bank 4520 East-West Hwy	Bethesda	MD	20814	**800-383-6266**	301-652-0700
Progress Bank 4 Sentry Pkwy Suite 200 *Cust Svc	Blue Bell	PA	19422	**800-945-9905***	610-825-8800
Provident Bank 830 Bergen Ave	Jersey City	NJ	07306	**800-448-7768**	201-333-1000
Provident Savings Bank FSB 3756 Central Ave	Riverside	CA	92506	**800-686-3756**	951-686-6060
Providian National Bank 295 Main St *Cust Svc	Tilton	NH	03276	**800-537-4332***	603-286-4346
RBC Centura 1417 Centura Hwy	Rocky Mount	NC	27804	**800-236-8872**	252-454-4400
Regency Savings Bank 24 N Washington St	Naperville	IL	60540	**800-933-0298**	630-357-4500
Regions Bank 417 20th St N	Birmingham	AL	35202	**800-765-6530**	205-326-7100
Republic Bank 2425 E Grand River Ave	Lansing	MI	48912	**888-722-7377**	517-483-6700
Riggs Bank 800 17th St NW	Washington	DC	20006	**800-368-5800**	202-835-5240
Rockland Trust Co 288 Union St	Rockland	MA	02370	**800-826-6100**	781-878-6100
Royal Bank of Pennsylvania 732 Montgomery Ave	Narberth	PA	19072	**800-417-5198**	610-668-4700
Royal Bank of Scotland 101 Park Ave 10th Fl	New York	NY	10178	**800-741-9607**	212-401-3200
S & T Bank 800 Philadelphia St *Cust Svc	Indiana	PA	15701	**800-325-2265***	724-349-1800

Name / Address	City	State	Zip	Toll-Free	Phone
Salem Five & Savings Bank 210 Essex St	Salem	MA	01970	**888-666-5500**	
San Diego National Bank 1420 Kettner Blvd	San Diego	CA	92101	**888-724-7362**	619-231-4989
Santa Barbara Bank & Trust 20 E Carrillo St	Santa Barbara	CA	93102	**800-320-5353**	805-564-6300
Signature Bank 565 5th Ave	New York	NY	10017	**866-744-5463**	646-822-1500
NYSE: SBNY					
Societe Generale USA 1221 Ave of the Americas	New York	NY	10020	**800-942-7575**	212-278-6000
SouthTrust Bank 420 20th St N	Birmingham	AL	35203	**800-239-2300**	205-254-5000
Sovereign Bank FSB PO Box 12646	Reading	PA	19612	**800-683-4663***	610-320-8400
*Cust Svc					
Standard Chartered Bank 1 Madison Ave	New York	NY	10010	**800-269-3101**	212-667-0700
Standard Federal Bank 2600 W Big Beaver Rd	Troy	MI	48084	**800-643-9600**	248-643-9600
State Farm Financial Services FSB PO Box 2316	Bloomington	IL	61702	**877-734-2265**	
Sterling Bank 15000 North-West Fwy	Houston	TX	77040	**888-777-8735**	713-466-8300
Sterling Savings Bank 111 N Wall St	Spokane	WA	99201	**800-772-7791**	509-624-4114
Stonebridge Bank PO Box 2425	West Chester	PA	19380	**800-807-1666**	610-280-4700
Sun National Bank 226 Landis Ave	Vineland	NJ	08360	**800-293-7701**	856-691-7700
Susquehanna Bank 100 West Rd	Baltimore	MD	21204	**800-619-0334**	410-938-8610
TCF National Bank 801 Marquette Ave	Minneapolis	MN	55402	**800-328-0728**	612-661-6500
TD Waterhouse Bank NA 1 Harborside Financial Plaza 4A 8th Fl	Jersey City	NJ	07310	**888-327-9962**	
Terre Haute First National Bank 1 First Financial Plaza	Terre Haute	IN	47807	**800-511-0045**	812-238-6000
Third Federal Savings Bank 3 Penns Trail	Newtown	PA	18940	**800-844-7345**	215-579-4600
Third Federal Savings & Loan Assn of Cleveland 7007 Broadway Ave	Cleveland	OH	44105	**800-944-7828**	216-441-6000
Tompkins Trustco Inc 110 N Tioga St Ithaca Commons	Ithaca	NY	14850	**800-273-3210**	607-273-3210
AMEX: TMP					
Trustmark National Bank 248 E Capitol St	Jackson	MS	39201	**800-844-2000**	601-208-5111
UMB Bank NA 1010 Grand Blvd	Kansas City	MO	64106	**800-821-2171**	816-860-7000
Union Federal Bank of Indianapolis 45 N Pennsylvania St	Indianapolis	IN	46204	**800-284-8585**	317-269-4700
United Bank 11185 Main St	Fairfax	VA	22030	**800-730-6169**	703-219-4850
Unizan Bank NA 422 Main St	Zanesville	OH	43701	**800-346-2011***	740-452-8444
*Cust Svc					
US Bank NA 800 Nicollet Mall	Minneapolis	MN	55402	**800-872-2657**	651-466-3000
USAA FSB 9800 Fredericksburg Rd	San Antonio	TX	78288	**800-531-8022**	210-498-1289
Vineyard National Bancorp 9590 Foothill Blvd	Rancho Cucamonga	CA	91730	**800-442-4996**	909-987-0177
NASDAQ: VNBC					
VirtualBank 3801 PGA Blvd Suite 700 PO Box 109638	Palm Beach Gardens	FL	33410	**877-998-2265**	561-776-8860
Wainwright Bank & Trust Co 63 Franklin St	Boston	MA	02110	**800-444-2265**	617-478-4000
NASDAQ: WAIN					
Washington Federal Savings & Loan Assn 425 Pike St	Seattle	WA	98101	**800-324-9375**	206-624-7930
Washington Mutual Bank 1201 3rd Ave	Seattle	WA	98101	**800-788-7000**	206-461-2000
Washington Mutual Bank FA 400 E Main St	Stockton	CA	95290	**800-788-7000**	209-460-2888
Washington Mutual Inc 1201 3rd Ave	Seattle	WA	98101	**800-756-8000**	206-461-2000
NYSE: WM					
Washington Savings Bank FSB 4201 Mitchellville Rd Suite 100	Bowie	MD	20716	**800-843-7250**	301-352-3130
AMEX: WSB					
Wauwatosa Savings Bank 11200 W Plank Ct	Wauwatosa	WI	53226	**888-686-7272**	414-918-0500
Waypoint Bank PO Box 1711	Harrisburg	PA	17105	**866-929-7646**	717-236-4041
Webster Bank 145 Bank St Webster Plaza	Waterbury	CT	06702	**800-325-2424**	
Wells Fargo Bank Indiana NA 111 E Wayne St	Fort Wayne	IN	46802	**800-869-3557**	260-461-6401
Wells Fargo Bank Minnesota South NA 21 1st St SW	Rochester	MN	55902	**800-869-3557**	507-285-2800
Wells Fargo Bank Montana NA 175 N 27th St	Billings	MT	59101	**800-869-3557**	406-657-1903
Wells Fargo Bank South Dakota NA 101 N Phillips Ave	Sioux Falls	SD	57104	**800-321-4141**	605-575-6900
Wells Fargo Bank Texas NA 40 NE Loop 410	San Antonio	TX	78216	**800-869-3557**	210-856-5000
Wells Fargo Bank Wisconsin NA 735 W Wisconsin Ave	Milwaukee	WI	53233	**800-236-9000**	414-224-4429
West Coast Bank 506 SW Coast Hwy	Newport	OR	97365	**800-895-3345***	541-265-6666
*Cust Svc					
Westamerica Bank 4560 Mangels Blvd	Fairfield	CA	94534	**800-848-1088**	
Western Financial Bank FSB 15750 Alton Pkwy	Irvine	CA	92618	**877-932-1234**	949-727-1000
Western Security Bank 1704 Dearborn	Missoula	MT	59801	**800-453-6874**	406-721-3700
Whitney National Bank 228 St Charles Ave	New Orleans	LA	70130	**800-347-7272**	504-586-7272
Wilmington Savings Fund Society FSB 838 Market St	Wilmington	DE	19801	**800-292-9594**	302-792-6000
Wilmington Trust Co 1100 N Market St	Wilmington	DE	19890	**800-441-7120**	302-651-1000
World Savings Bank FSB 11601 Wilshire Blvd	Los Angeles	CA	90025	**800-468-7283**	310-477-8004
WSFS Bank 838 Market St	Wilmington	DE	19801	**800-292-9594**	302-792-6000
Yakima Federal Savings & Loan Assn 118 E Yakima Ave	Yakima	WA	98901	**800-331-3225**	509-248-2634
Yardville National Bank 2465 Kuser Rd	Hamilton Township	NJ	08690	**800-548-9545**	609-585-5100

72 BANKS - FEDERAL RESERVE

Name / Address	City	State	Zip	Toll-Free	Phone
Federal Reserve Bank of Atlanta New Orleans Branch 525 St Charles Ave PO Box 61630	New Orleans	LA	70161	**800-562-9023**	504-593-3200
Federal Reserve Bank of Cleveland 1455 E 6th St PO Box 6387	Cleveland	OH	44101	**888-333-2538**	216-579-2000
Cincinnati Branch 150 E 4th St PO Box 45201	Cincinnati	OH	43229	**800-432-1343**	513-721-4787
Columbus Branch 965 Kingsmill Pkwy PO Box 16541	Columbus	OH	43216	**800-333-2439**	614-846-7055
Pittsburgh Branch 717 Grant St PO Box 867	Pittsburgh	PA	15230	**888-333-7488**	412-261-7800
Federal Reserve Bank of Dallas 2200 N Pearl St PO Box 655906	Dallas	TX	75265	**800-333-4460**	214-922-6000
Federal Reserve Bank of Kansas City 925 Grand Blvd	Kansas City	MO	64198	**800-333-1010**	816-881-2000
Denver Branch 1020 16th St	Denver	CO	80202	**800-333-1020**	303-572-2300
Oklahoma City Branch 226 Dean A McGee Ave PO Box 25129	Oklahoma City	OK	73125	**800-333-1030**	405-270-8400
Omaha Branch 2201 Farnam St PO Box 3958	Omaha	NE	68103	**800-333-1040**	402-221-5500
Federal Reserve Bank of Minneapolis 90 Hennepin Ave PO Box 291	Minneapolis	MN	55480	**800-553-9656**	612-204-5000
Federal Reserve Bank of New York Buffalo Branch 160 Delaware Ave	Buffalo	NY	14202	**800-234-2931**	716-849-5000
Federal Reserve Bank of Richmond Charleston Branch 1200 Airport Rd PO Box 2309	Charleston	WV	25328	**800-642-8587**	304-353-6100
Federal Reserve Bank of Saint Louis 411 Locust St PO Box 442	Saint Louis	MO	63166	**800-333-0810**	314-444-8444
Federal Reserve Bank of San Francisco 101 Market St PO Box 7702	San Francisco	CA	94120	**800-227-4133**	415-974-2000
Los Angeles Branch 950 S Grand Ave PO Box 2077	Los Angeles	CA	90051	**800-843-8123**	213-683-2300
Seattle Branch 1015 2nd Ave PO Box 3567	Seattle	WA	98124	**800-552-7244**	206-343-3600

73 BAR ASSOCIATIONS - STATE

SEE ALSO Associations & Organizations - Professional & Trade - Legal Professionals Associations

Name / Address	City	State	Zip	Toll-Free	Phone
Arizona 4201 N 24th St Suite 200	Phoenix	AZ	85016	**866-482-9227**	602-252-4804
District of Columbia 1250 H St NW 6th Fl	Washington	DC	20005	**877-333-2227**	202-737-4700
Florida 651 E Jefferson St	Tallahassee	FL	32399	**800-342-8060**	850-561-5600
Georgia 104 Marietta St NW Suite 100	Atlanta	GA	30303	**800-334-6865**	404-527-8700
Indiana 1 Indiana Sq Suite 530	Indianapolis	IN	46204	**800-266-2581**	317-639-5465
Louisiana 601 St Charles Ave	New Orleans	LA	70130	**800-421-5722**	504-566-1600
Maryland 520 W Fayette St	Baltimore	MD	21201	**800-492-1964**	410-685-7878
Massachusetts 20 West St	Boston	MA	02111	**866-627-7577**	617-338-0500
Michigan 306 Townsend St	Lansing	MI	48933	**800-968-1442**	517-372-9030
Minnesota 600 Nicollet Mall Suite 380	Minneapolis	MN	55402	**800-882-6722**	612-333-1183
Nebraska 635 S 14th St	Lincoln	NE	68501	**800-927-0117**	402-475-7091
Nevada 600 E Charleston Blvd	Las Vegas	NV	89104	**800-254-2797**	702-382-2200
New Mexico 5121 Masthead St NE	Albuquerque	NM	87109	**800-876-6227**	505-797-6000
New York 1 Elk St	Albany	NY	12207	**800-342-3661**	518-463-3200
North Carolina 208 Fayetteville St Mall	Raleigh	NC	27601	**800-662-7407**	919-828-4620
Ohio 1700 Lake Shore Dr	Columbus	OH	43204	**800-282-6556**	614-487-2050
Oklahoma PO Box 53036	Oklahoma City	OK	73152	**800-522-8065**	405-416-7000
Pennsylvania 100 South St	Harrisburg	PA	17101	**800-932-0311**	717-238-6715
Tennessee 221 4th Ave N Suite 400	Nashville	TN	37219	**800-899-6993**	615-383-7421
Texas 1414 Colorado St	Austin	TX	78701	**800-204-2222**	512-463-1463
Washington 2101 4th Ave Suite 400	Seattle	WA	98121	**800-945-9722**	206-727-8200
Wisconsin 5302 Eastpark Blvd	Madison	WI	53718	**800-728-7788**	608-257-3838

74 BASKETS - WOVEN

Name / Address	City	State	Zip	Toll-Free	Phone
Basketville Inc PO Box 710	Putney	VT	05346	**800-258-4553**	802-387-5509
Burlington Basket Co PO Box 808	Burlington	IA	52601	**800-553-2300**	319-754-6508

75 BASKETS, CAGES, RACKS, ETC - WIRE

SEE ALSO Pet Products

Name / Address	City	State	Zip	Toll-Free	Phone
Abbott Industries Inc 95-25 149th St	Jamaica	NY	11435	**800-232-5676**	718-291-0800
Apco Products Inc PO Box 236	Essex	CT	06426	**800-640-2726**	860-767-2108
Artcraft Wire Works Inc 7026 Camden Ave	Pennsauken	NJ	08110	**800-356-2830**	856-663-9334
Bright Coop Inc 803 W Seale St	Nacogdoches	TX	75964	**800-562-0730**	936-564-8378
Eastern Wire Products Co 498 Kinsley Ave	Providence	RI	02909	**800-486-3181**	401-861-1350
Glamos Wire Products Co Inc 5561 N 152nd St	Hugo	MN	55038	**800-428-6353**	651-429-5386
Harford Systems Inc 2225 Pulaski Hwy PO Box 700	Aberdeen	MD	21001	**800-664-7620**	410-272-3400
HEB Mfg Co Inc PO Box 188	Chelsea	VT	05038	**800-639-4187**	802-685-4821
InterMetro Industries Corp 651 N Washington St	Wilkes-Barre	PA	18705	**800-992-1776***	570-825-2741
*Cust Svc					
Kaspar Wire Works Inc PO Box 667	Shiner	TX	77984	**800-337-0610**	361-594-3327
Lab Products Inc 742 Sussex Ave	Seaford	DE	19973	**800-526-0469**	302-628-4300
Midwest Wire Products Inc 800 Woodward Heights	Ferndale	MI	48220	**800-989-9881**	248-399-5100
Nashville Wire Products Mfg Co 199 Polk Ave	Nashville	TN	37210	**888-743-2595**	615-743-2500
Technibilt Corp PO Box 310	Newton	NC	28658	**800-351-2278***	828-464-7388
*Cust Svc					
Tote Cart Co Inc 1802 Preston St	Rockford	IL	61102	**800-435-5709**	815-963-3414
United Steel & Wire Co 4909 Wayne Rd	Battle Creek	MI	49015	**800-227-7887**	269-962-5571
Universal Display & Fixtures Co 726 E Hwy 121	Lewisville	TX	75057	**800-235-0701**	972-221-5022
Wirefab Inc 919 Millbury St	Worcester	MA	01607	**800-879-4731***	508-754-5359
*Sales					

76 BATTERIES

Name / Address	City	State	Zip	Toll-Free	Phone
Arotech Corp 250 W 57th St Suite 310	New York	NY	10017	**888-996-4440**	212-258-3222
NASDAQ: ARTX					
Atlantic Battery Co Inc 80 Elm St	Watertown	MA	02472	**800-924-2450**	617-924-2868

Classified Section

				Toll-Free	Phone
C & D Technologies Inc 1400 Union Meeting Rd PO Box 3053	Blue Bell	PA	19422	**800-543-8630**	215-619-2700
NYSE: CHP					
Continental Battery Corp 4919 Woodall St	Dallas	TX	75247	**800-442-0081**	214-631-5701
Crown Battery Mfg Co 1445 Majestic Dr	Fremont	OH	43420	**800-487-2879**	419-334-7181
DayStarter North America 2286 Capp Rd	Saint Paul	MN	55114	**800-328-6537**	651-646-2707
Douglas Battery Mfg Co 500 Battery Dr	Winston-Salem	NC	27107	**800-368-4527**	336-650-7000
Duracell 14 Research Dr Berkshire Corporate Pk	Bethel	CT	06801	**800-551-2355**	203-796-4000
Energizer Holdings Inc 533 Maryville University Dr	Saint Louis	MO	63141	**800-383-7323**	314-985-2000
NYSE: ENR					
EnerSys 2366 Bernville Rd	Reading	PA	19605	**800-538-3627**	610-208-1991
NYSE: ENS					
Exide Technologies 210 Carnegie Ctr Suite 500	Princeton	NJ	08540	**866-289-0645**	609-627-7200
NASDAQ: XIDE					
Johnson Controls Inc 5757 N Green Bay Ave	Milwaukee	WI	53209	**800-972-8040**	414-524-1200
NYSE: JCI					
Medtronic Energy & Component Center (MECC) 6700 Shingle Creek Pkwy	Brooklyn Center	MN	55430	**800-328-2518**	763-514-1000
Moltech Power Systems 12801 NW Hwy 441	Alachua	FL	32615	**800-677-6937**	386-462-3911
Power Battery Co Inc 25 McLean Blvd	Paterson	NJ	07514	**800-783-7697**	973-523-8630
Rayovac Corp 601 Rayovac Dr	Madison	WI	53711	**800-237-7000**	608-275-3340
NYSE: ROV					
Rosco Battery Service Corp 17217 Rt 37	Johnston City	IL	62951	**800-957-3226**	618-983-5441
Tadiran US Battery Div 2 Seaview Blvd Suite 102	Port Washington	NY	11050	**800-537-1368**	516-621-4980
TNR Technical Inc 301 Central Park Dr	Sanford	FL	32771	**800-346-0601**	407-321-3011
Trojan Battery Co 12380 Clark St	Santa Fe Springs	CA	90670	**800-423-6569***	562-946-8381
*Cust Svc					
Ultralife Batteries Inc 2000 Technology Pkwy	Newark	NY	14513	**800-332-5000**	315-332-7100
NASDAQ: ULBI					
US Battery Mfg Corp 1675 Sampson Ave	Corona	CA	92879	**800-695-0945**	951-371-8090
Valence Technology Inc 301 Conestoga Way	Henderson	NV	89015	**888-825-3623**	702-558-1000
NASDAQ: VLNC					

77 BEARINGS - BALL & ROLLER

				Toll-Free	Phone
Accurate Bushing Co Inc 443 North Ave	Garwood	NJ	07027	**800-932-0076***	908-789-1121
*Sales					
Alinabal Inc 28 Woodmont Rd	Milford	CT	06460	**800-254-6763**	203-877-3241
AST Bearings 115 Main Rd	Montville	NJ	07045	**800-526-1250**	973-335-2230
Barnes Engineering Co 2715 Delta Pl	Colorado Springs	CO	80910	**800-995-6050**	719-390-6500
Bearing Inspection Inc 4422 Corporate Ctr Dr	Los Alamitos	CA	90720	**800-416-8881**	714-484-2400
Bearing Service Co of Pennsylvania 630 Alpha Dr CIDC Industrial Pk	Pittsburgh	PA	15238	**800-783-2327**	412-963-7710
Brenco Inc PO Box 389	Petersburg	VA	23804	**800-238-4712**	804-732-0202
FAG Bearings Corp 200 Park Ave	Danbury	CT	06810	**800-243-7512**	203-790-5474
General Bearing Corp 44 High St	West Nyack	NY	10994	**800-431-1766***	845-358-6000
NASDAQ: GNRL ■ *Sales					
Green Bearing Co 9801 Harvard Ave	Cleveland	OH	44105	**800-367-9014**	216-883-7800
Hartford Technologies 1022 Elm St	Rocky Hill	CT	06067	**888-840-9565**	860-571-3601
Industrial Tectonics Bearings Corp 18301 S Santa Fe Ave	Rancho Dominguez	CA	90221	**800-654-2597**	310-537-3750
Koyo Corp of USA 29570 Clemens Rd	Westlake	OH	44145	**800-321-3102**	440-835-1000
Lutco Inc 677 Cambridge St	Worcester	MA	01610	**888-588-0099**	508-756-6296
Messinger Bearings Corp 10385 Drummond Rd	Philadelphia	PA	19154	**800-203-2729**	215-739-6880
MRC Bearings Inc 402 Chandler St	Jamestown	NY	14701	**800-672-7000***	716-661-2600
*Cust Svc					
Nachi America Inc 5022 W 79th St	Indianapolis	IN	46268	**888-340-2747**	317-334-9993
Nice Ball Bearings Inc 2060 Detwiler Rd	Kulpsville	PA	19443	**800-321-6423**	215-256-6681
NSK Corp 4200 Goss Rd	Ann Arbor	MI	48105	**800-521-0605**	734-761-9500
NTN Bearing Corp of America 1600 E Bishop Ct Suite 100	Mount Prospect	IL	60056	**800-468-6528**	847-298-7500
Oiles America Corp 44099 Plymouth Oaks Blvd Suite 109	Plymouth	MI	48170	**888-645-3726**	734-414-7400
Peer Bearing Co 2200 Norman Dr S	Waukegan	IL	60085	**800-433-7337**	847-578-1000
Rotek Inc 1400 S Chillicothe Rd	Aurora	OH	44202	**800-221-8043**	330-562-4000
Schatz Bearing Corp 10 Fairview Ave	Poughkeepsie	NY	12601	**800-554-1406**	845-452-6000
SKF USA Inc 1111 Adams Ave	Norristown	PA	19403	**800-440-4753**	610-630-2800
Timken Co 1835 Dueber Ave SW	Canton	OH	44706	**800-223-1954**	330-438-3000
NYSE: TKR					
Tuthill Corp 8500 S Madison St	Burr Ridge	IL	60527	**800-888-4455**	630-382-4900
Winsted Precision Ball Corp 159 Colebrook River Rd	Winsted	CT	06098	**800-462-3075**	860-379-2788

78 BEAUTY SALON EQUIPMENT & SUPPLIES

				Toll-Free	Phone
Aerial Co Inc 2300 Aerial Dr	Marinette	WI	54143	**800-950-9565**	715-735-9323
B & S Distributing 1911 Rice St	Roseville	MN	55113	**800-328-9653**	651-488-7261
Beaute Craft Supply Co 600 W Maple Rd	Troy	MI	48084	**800-331-8277**	248-362-0400
Belvedere USA Corp 1 Belvedere Blvd	Belvidere	IL	61008	**800-435-5491**	815-544-3131
Burmax Co 28 Barretts Ave	Holtsville	NY	11742	**800-645-5118**	631-447-8700
Collins Mfg Co 2000 Bowser Rd	Cookeville	TN	38506	**800-292-6450**	931-528-5151
Dr Kern USA Inc 221 S Franklin Rd	Indianapolis	IN	46221	**800-908-9885**	317-472-0867
European Touch Ltd II 8301 W Parkland Ct	Milwaukee	WI	53223	**800-626-6912**	414-357-7016
Kaemark 1338 County Rd 28	Giddings	TX	78942	**800-766-3651**	979-542-3651
Living Earth Crafts 3210 Executive Ridge Dr	Vista	CA	92081	**800-358-8292**	760-597-2155
Marvy William Co Inc 1540 St Clair Ave	Saint Paul	MN	55105	**800-874-2651**	651-698-0726
National Salon Resources Inc 3109 Louisiana Ave N	Minneapolis	MN	55427	**800-622-0003**	763-546-9500
Pibbs Industries 133-15 32nd Ave	Flushing	NY	11354	**800-551-5020**	718-445-8046
Sally Beauty Co Inc 3001 Colorado Blvd	Denton	TX	76210	**800-275-7255**	940-898-7500
TouchAmerica PO Box 1304	Hillsborough	NC	27278	**800-678-6824**	919-732-6968
Valley Barber & Beauty Supply 413 W Harrison St	Harlingen	TX	78550	**800-292-7548**	956-423-0727
William Marvy Co Inc 1540 St Clair Ave	Saint Paul	MN	55105	**800-874-2651**	651-698-0726

79 BEAUTY SALONS

				Toll-Free	Phone
Bumble & Bumble LLC 146 E 56th St	New York	NY	10022	**800-728-6253**	212-521-6500
Cost Cutters Family Hair Care Div Regis Corp 7201 Metro Blvd	Minneapolis	MN	55439	**888-888-7778**	952-947-7777
Elizabeth Arden Red Door Spas 3822 E University Dr Suite 5	Phoenix	AZ	85034	**800-592-7336**	602-864-8191
Fiesta Salons Inc 6363 Fiesta Dr	Columbus	OH	43235	**800-825-6363**	614-766-6363
First Choice Haircutters 6465 Millcreek Dr Suite 210	Mississauga	ON	L5N5R6	**800-361-2887**	905-821-8555
Georgette Klinger Inc 501 Madison Ave	New York	NY	10022	**800-554-6437**	212-838-3200
Great Clips Inc 7700 France Ave S Suite 425	Minneapolis	MN	55435	**800-999-5959**	952-893-9088
Hair Cuttery 2815 Hartland Rd	Falls Church	VA	22043	**800-874-6288**	703-698-7090
Haircrafters/Great Expectations 7201 Metro Blvd	Minneapolis	MN	55439	**888-888-7778**	952-947-7777
John Frieda Professional Hair Care Inc 333 Ludlow St	Stanford	CT	06902	**800-521-3189***	203-762-1233
*Cust Svc					
Klinger Georgette Inc 501 Madison Ave	New York	NY	10022	**800-554-6437**	212-838-3200
Lemon Tree Inc 1 Division Ave	Levittown	NY	11756	**800-345-9156**	516-735-2828
MasterCuts Div Regis Corp 7201 Metro Blvd	Minneapolis	MN	55439	**888-888-7778**	952-947-7777
Perfect Look Salons DBA Beauty Management Inc 270 Beavercreek Rd Suite 100	Oregon City	OR	97405	**888-268-7577**	503-723-3200
Ratner Cos 1577 Spring Hill Rd Suite 500	Vienna	VA	22182	**800-874-6288**	703-698-7090
Regis Corp 7201 Metro Blvd	Minneapolis	MN	55439	**888-888-7778**	952-947-7777
NYSE: RGS					
Regis Corp Cost Cutters Family Hair Care Div 7201 Metro Blvd	Minneapolis	MN	55439	**888-888-7778**	952-947-7777
Regis Corp MasterCuts Div 7201 Metro Blvd	Minneapolis	MN	55439	**888-888-7778**	952-947-7777
Regis Corp Regis Hairstylists Div 7201 Metro Blvd	Minneapolis	MN	55439	**888-888-7778**	952-947-7777
Regis Corp SmartStyle Div 7201 Metro Blvd	Minneapolis	MN	55439	**888-888-7778**	952-947-7777
Regis Corp Supercuts Div 7201 Metro Blvd	Minneapolis	MN	55439	**888-888-7778**	952-947-7777
Regis Corp Trade Secret Div 7201 Metro Blvd	Minneapolis	MN	55439	**888-888-7778**	952-947-7777
Regis Hairstylists Div Regis Corp 7201 Metro Blvd	Minneapolis	MN	55439	**888-888-7778**	952-947-7777
SmartStyle Div Regis Corp 7201 Metro Blvd	Minneapolis	MN	55439	**888-888-7778**	952-947-7777
Stewart's Inc 604 N West Ave	Sioux Falls	SD	57104	**800-537-2625**	605-336-2775
Supercuts Div Regis Corp 7201 Metro Blvd	Minneapolis	MN	55439	**888-888-7778**	952-947-7777
TGF Precision Haircutters 8280 Westpark Dr	Houston	TX	77063	**800-622-1330**	713-952-8080
Toni & Guy USA Inc 2311 Midway Rd	Carrollton	TX	75006	**800-256-9391**	972-931-1567
Trade Secret Div Regis Corp 7201 Metro Blvd	Minneapolis	MN	55439	**888-888-7778**	952-947-7777

80 BETTER BUSINESS BUREAUS

SEE ALSO Associations & Organizations - General - Consumer Interest Organizations

				Toll-Free	Phone
Alabama (Central) & the Wiregrass Area Montgomery Branch 1210 S 20th St	Birmingham	AL	35205	**800-824-5274**	205-558-2222
Alabama (Southern) 3361 Cottage Hill Rd Suite E	Mobile	AL	36606	**800-544-4714**	251-433-5494
Arizona (Central Northeast Northwest & Southwest) 4428 N 12th St	Phoenix	AZ	85014	**877-291-6222**	602-264-1721
Ark-La-Tex 401 Edwards St Suite 125	Shreveport	LA	71101	**800-372-4222**	318-222-7575
Blountville PO Box 1178 Tri-City Airport	Blountville	TN	37617	**888-437-4222**	423-325-6616
Carolinas (Southern Piedmont) 5200 Park Rd Suite 202	Charlotte	NC	28209	**877-317-7236**	704-527-0012
Florida (Northeast) 4417 Beach Blvd Suite 202	Jacksonville	FL	32207	**800-940-1315**	904-721-2288
Florida (West) PO Box 7950	Clearwater	FL	33758	**800-525-1447**	727-535-5522
Georgia (Southeast) & South Carolina (Southeast) 6606 Abercorn St Suite 108C	Savannah	GA	31405	**800-353-1192**	912-354-7522
Georgia (Southwest) PO Box 808	Albany	GA	31702	**800-868-4222**	229-883-0744
Kansas (Except the Northeast) 328 Laura St	Wichita	KS	67211	**800-856-2417**	316-263-3146
Kentucky (Central & Eastern) 1460 Newton Pike	Lexington	KY	40511	**800-866-6668**	859-259-1008
Louisiana (Central) 5220-C Rue Verdun	Alexandria	LA	71303	**800-256-2225**	318-473-4494
Louisiana (Southwest) 2309 E Crown Lake Rd	Lake Charles	LA	70606	**800-542-7085**	337-478-6253
Missouri (Eastern) & Illinois (Southern) 12 Sunnen Dr Suite 121	Saint Louis	MO	63143	**866-996-3887**	314-645-3300
Mountain States 1730 S College Ave Suite 303	Fort Collins	CO	80525	**800-564-0371**	970-484-1348
Ohio (Central) 1335 Dublin Rd Suite 30-A	Columbus	OH	43215	**800-759-2400**	614-486-6336
Oklahoma (Eastern) 1722 S Carson Ave Suite 3200	Tulsa	OK	74119	**800-928-4222**	918-492-1266
Ontario (Eastern) & the Outaouais 130 Albert St Suite 603	Ottawa	ON	K1P5G4	**877-889-8566**	613-237-4856
Ontario (Mid-Western) 354 Charles St E	Kitchener	ON	N2G4L5	**800-459-8875**	519-579-3080
Pennsylvania (Northeastern & Central) 4099 Birney Ave	Moosic	PA	18507	**888-229-3222**	570-342-9129
Pike's Peak Region 25 N Wahsatch Ave	Colorado Springs	CO	80903	**866-206-1800**	719-636-1155
Sioux City Area 600 4th St Suite 904	Sioux City	IA	51101	**888-845-4222**	712-252-4501
Texas (Central East) 3600 Old Bullard Rd Bldg 1	Tyler	TX	75701	**800-443-0131**	903-581-5704

Classified Section

81 BEVERAGES - MFR

SEE ALSO Breweries & Microbreweries; Water - Bottled

81-1 Liquor - Mfr

	City	St	Zip	Toll-Free	Phone
Bacardi USA Inc 2100 Biscayne Blvd	Miami	FL	33137	**800-222-2734**	305-573-8511
Consolidated Distilled Products 2600 W 35th St	Chicago	IL	60632	**800-944-9450**	773-254-9000
Diageo North America 801 Main Ave	Norwalk	CT	06851	**800-847-4109**	203-359-7100
Jacquin Charles et Cie 2633 Trenton Ave	Philadelphia	PA	19125	**800-523-3811**	215-425-9300
Paramount Distillers Inc 3116 Berea Rd	Cleveland	OH	44111	**800-821-2989**	216-671-6300
Pernod Ricard USA 777 Westchester Ave	White Plains	NY	10604	**800-488-7539**	914-539-4500
Skyy Spirits Inc 1 Beach St Suite 300	San Francisco	CA	94133	**800-367-7599**	415-315-8000
Walker MS Inc 20 3rd Ave	Somerville	MA	02143	**800-776-5808**	617-776-6700
White Rock Distilleries Inc PO Box 1829	Lewiston	ME	04241	**800-628-5441**	207-783-1433

81-2 Soft Drinks - Mfr

	City	St	Zip	Toll-Free	Phone
AriZona Beverage Co 5 Dakota Dr Suite 205	Lake Success	NY	11024	**800-832-3775**	516-812-0300
Beverage Corp International 3505 NW 107th St	Miami	FL	33167	**800-226-5061**	305-714-7000
Big Red/Seven Up Bottling of South Texas 4518 Seguin Rd	San Antonio	TX	78219	**800-580-7333**	210-661-4271
Coca-Cola Co 1 Coca-Cola Plaza *NYSE: KO*	Atlanta	GA	30313	**800-438-2653**	404-676-2121
Cott Corp 207 Queen's Quay W Suite 340 *NYSE: COT*	Toronto	ON	M5J1A7	**800-994-2688**	416-203-3898
Davis Beverage Group 1530-A Bobali Dr	Harrisburg	PA	17104	**800-360-7056**	717-914-1295
Double Cola Co USA 537 Market St Suite 100	Chattanooga	TN	37402	**877-325-2659**	423-267-5691
Dr Pepper/Seven-Up Inc 5301 Legacy Dr PO Box 869077	Plano	TX	75024	**800-527-7096**	972-673-7000
Everfresh/Lacroix Beverages Inc 6600 E 9-Mile Rd	Warren	MI	48091	**800-323-3416**	586-755-9500
Faygo Beverages Inc 3579 Gratiot Ave	Detroit	MI	48207	**800-347-6591**	313-925-1600
Ferolito Vultaggio & Sons 5 Dakota Dr Suite 205	Lake Success	NY	11024	**800-832-3775**	516-812-0300
Gatorade Worldwide PO Box 049003	Chicago	IL	60604	**800-884-2867**	312-821-1000
Hansen Natural Corp 1010 Railroad St *NASDAQ: HANS*	Corona	CA	92882	**800-426-7367**	951-739-6200
Monarch Beverage Co 3424 Peachtree Rd Suite 1450	Atlanta	GA	30326	**800-241-3732**	404-262-4040
National Beverage Corp 1 N University Dr *AMEX: FIZ*	Plantation	FL	33324	**888-462-2349**	954-581-0922
Pepsi Bottling Group Inc 1 Pepsi Way *NYSE: PBG* ■ *PR	Somers	NY	10589	**800-433-2652***	914-767-6000
Polar Beverages Inc 1001 Southbridge St *Cust Svc	Worcester	MA	01610	**800-225-7410***	508-753-4300
Shasta Beverages Inc 26901 Industrial Blvd	Hayward	CA	94545	**800-326-8640**	510-783-3200
Snapple Beverage Corp 709 Westchester Ave	White Plains	NY	10604	**800-964-7842**	
South Beach Beverage Co 40 Richards Ave *Cust Svc	Norwalk	CT	06854	**800-588-0548***	203-899-7111
White Rock Products Corp 1616 Whitestone Expy	Whitestone	NY	11357	**800-969-7625**	718-746-3400

81-3 Wines - Mfr

	City	St	Zip	Toll-Free	Phone
Banfi Vintners USA 1111 Cedar Swamp Rd	Old Brookville	NY	11545	**800-645-6511**	516-626-9200
Beaulieu Vineyard 1960 St Helena Hwy	Rutherford	CA	94573	**800-264-6918**	707-967-5200
Benziger Family Winery 1883 London Ranch Rd	Glen Ellen	CA	95442	**888-490-2739**	707-935-3000
Bronco Wine Co 6342 Bystrum Rd	Ceres	CA	95307	**800-692-5780**	209-538-3131
Canandaigua Wine Co Inc 116 Buffalo St	Canandaigua	NY	14424	**888-659-7900**	585-396-7600
Clos du Bois Wines 19410 Geyserville Ave *Sales	Geyserville	CA	95441	**800-222-3189***	707-857-1651
Delicato Vineyards 12001 S Hwy 99	Manteca	CA	95336	**888-599-4637**	209-824-3600
Distillerie Stock USA Ltd 58-58 Laurel Hill Blvd	Woodside	NY	11377	**800-323-1884**	718-651-9800
Domaine Chandon Inc 1 California Dr	Yountville	CA	94599	**800-736-2892**	707-944-8844
E & J Gallo Winery 600 Yosemite Blvd	Modesto	CA	95354	**800-322-2389**	209-341-3111
Fetzer Vineyards 13601 Old River Rd	Hopland	CA	95449	**800-846-8637**	707-744-1250
Franciscan Estates 1178 Galleron Rd	Saint Helena	CA	94574	**800-529-9463**	707-963-7111
Gallo E & J Winery 600 Yosemite Blvd	Modesto	CA	95354	**800-322-2389**	209-341-3111
Heineman Beverages Inc 407 Short St	Port Clinton	OH	43452	**800-734-9115**	419-734-9100
Hogue Cellars 2800 Lee Rd	Prosser	WA	99350	**800-565-9779**	509-786-4557
Kendall-Jackson Wine Estates Ltd 425 Aviation Blvd	Santa Rosa	CA	95403	**800-544-4413**	707-544-4000
Louis M Martini Winery 254 S St Helena Hwy PO Box 112	Saint Helena	CA	94574	**800-321-9463**	707-963-2736
Malibu Hills Vineyards 29000 Newton Canyon Rd	Malibu	CA	90265	**800-814-0733**	310-463-9532
Meier's Wine Cellars Inc 6955 Plainfield Rd	Silverton	OH	45236	**800-346-2941**	513-891-2900
Mendocino Wine Co 501 Parducci Rd	Ukiah	CA	95482	**888-362-9463**	707-463-5350
Mirassou Vineyards 3000 Aborn Rd	San Jose	CA	95135	**800-775-1936**	408-274-4000
Raymond Vineyard & Cellar Inc 849 Zinfandel Ln	Saint Helena	CA	94574	**800-525-2659**	707-963-3141
Robert Mondavi Co 7801 St Helena Hwy PO Box 106	Oakville	CA	94562	**888-766-6328**	707-259-9463
Rodney Strong Vineyards 1145 Old Redwood Hwy	Healdsburg	CA	95448	**800-474-9463**	707-433-6511
Round Hill Vineyards & Cellars 1680 Silverado Trail	Saint Helena	CA	94574	**800-778-0424**	707-963-5251
Royal Wine Corp 63 Le Fante Ln	Bayonne	NJ	07002	**800-382-8299**	718-384-2400
Sebastiani Vineyards Inc 389 4th St E	Sonoma	CA	95476	**800-888-5532**	707-938-5532
Simi Winery 16275 Healdsburg Ave	Healdsburg	CA	95448	**800-746-4880**	707-433-6981
Strong Rodney Vineyards 1145 Old Redwood Hwy	Healdsburg	CA	95448	**800-474-9463**	707-433-6511
Vincor International Inc 441 Courtneypark Dr E *TSE: VN*	Mississauga	ON	L5T2V3	**800-265-9463**	905-564-6900
Warner Vineyards Inc 706 S Kalamazoo St	Paw Paw	MI	49079	**800-756-5357**	269-657-3165
Weibel Vineyards 1 Winemaster Way	Lodi	CA	95240	**800-932-9463**	209-365-9463
Widmer's Wine Cellars Inc 1 Lake Niagra Ln	Naples	NY	14512	**800-836-5253**	585-374-6311
Willamette Valley Vineyards Inc 8800 Enchanted Way SE *NASDAQ: WVVI* ■ *Sales	Turner	OR	97392	**800-344-9463***	503-588-9463
Windsor Vineyards Po Box 368	Windsor	CA	95492	**800-289-9463**	707-836-5000

82 BEVERAGES - WHOL

82-1 Beer & Ale - Whol

	City	St	Zip	Toll-Free	Phone
Allentown Beverage Co Inc 1249 N Quebec St *Cust Svc	Allentown	PA	18109	**800-852-2337***	610-432-4581
Arkansas Distributing Co LLC 800 E Barton	West Memphis	AR	72301	**877-735-3506**	870-735-3506
Atlas Distributing Corp 44 Southbridge St	Auburn	MA	01501	**800-649-6221**	508-791-6221
Banko Beverage Co 2124 Hanover Ave	Allentown	PA	18109	**800-322-9295**	610-434-0147
Barringer RH Distributing Inc 1620 Fairfax Rd	Greensboro	NC	27407	**800-273-0555**	336-854-0555
Beauchamp Distributing Co 1911 S Santa Fe Ave	Compton	CA	90221	**800-734-5102**	310-639-5320
Beer Solutions 138313 W Laurel Dr	Lake Forest	IL	60045	**800-842-4050**	847-247-0121
Beloit Beverage Co Inc 4059 W Bradley Rd	Milwaukee	WI	53209	**800-345-0005**	414-362-5000
Better Brands of Atlanta Inc 755 Jefferson St NW	Atlanta	GA	30318	**800-273-4926**	404-872-4731
Big Sky Distributors Inc 14220 Wyandotte St	Kansas City	MO	64145	**800-926-4233**	816-941-3300
Bissman Co Inc 30 W 5th St *Cust Svc	Mansfield	OH	44901	**800-321-2337***	419-524-2337
Blach Distributing Co 131 Main St	Elko	NV	89801	**888-812-5224**	775-738-7111
Block Distributing Co Inc 6511 Tri County Pkwy	Schertz	TX	78154	**800-749-7532**	210-224-7531
Blue Ridge Beverage Co Inc PO Box 700 *Cust Svc	Salem	VA	24153	**800-868-0354***	540-380-2000
Bonanza Beverage Co 6333 Ensworth St *Cust Svc	Las Vegas	NV	89119	**800-677-4166***	702-361-4166
Brewery Products Co Inc 1017 N Sherman St *Cust Svc	York	PA	17402	**800-233-9433***	717-757-3515
Buck Distributing Co Inc 15827 Commerce Ct *Cust Svc	Upper Marlboro	MD	20774	**800-750-2825***	301-952-0400
Calumet Breweries Inc 6535 Osborn Ave *Cust Svc	Hammond	IN	46320	**800-882-2739***	219-845-2242
Capital Beverage Co 2424 Del Monte St *Cust Svc	West Sacramento	CA	95691	**800-954-2667***	916-371-8164
Central Distributors Inc 15 Foss Rd *Cust Svc	Lewiston	ME	04241	**800-427-5757***	207-784-4026
City Beverage LLC 1105 E Lafayette St	Bloomington	IL	61701	**800-272-2635**	309-662-1373
City Beverages of Orlando 10928 Florida Crown Dr	Orlando	FL	32824	**800-717-7267**	407-851-7100
Clare Rose Inc 72 Clare Rose Blvd	Patchogue	NY	11772	**800-427-2833**	631-475-1840
Classic City Beverages Inc 530 Calhoun Dr	Athens	GA	30601	**800-300-0218**	706-353-1650
Coastal Beverage Co Inc 301 Harley Rd PO Box 10159	Wilmington	NC	28404	**800-229-3884**	910-799-3011
Commercial Distributing Co Inc 46 S Broad St *Cust Svc	Westfield	MA	01086	**800-332-8999***	413-562-9691
Consolidated Beverages Inc 12 Saint Mark St	Auburn	MA	01501	**800-922-8128**	508-832-5311
Couch Distributing Co Inc 104 Lee Rd	Watsonville	CA	95076	**800-542-5555**	831-724-0649
Dearing Beverage Co Inc 331 Victory Rd *Cust Svc	Winchester	VA	22602	**800-552-9550***	540-662-0561
Delaware Importers Inc 615 Lambson Ln	New Castle	DE	19720	**800-292-7890**	302-656-4487
Dutchess Beer Distributors Inc 5 Laurel St *Cust Svc	Poughkeepsie	NY	12603	**800-427-6308***	845-452-0940
Eastown Distributors 14400 Oakland Ave	Highland Park	MI	48203	**800-417-0080**	313-867-6900
Erwin Distributing Co 530 Monocacy Blvd	Frederick	MD	21701	**800-352-9165**	301-662-0372
Fox Henry A Sales Co 4494 36th St SE	Kentwood	MI	49512	**800-762-8730**	616-949-1210
Frank B Fuhrer Wholesale Co 3100 E Carson St	Pittsburgh	PA	15203	**800-837-2212**	412-488-8844
Fuhrer Frank B Wholesale Co 3100 E Carson St	Pittsburgh	PA	15203	**800-837-2212**	412-488-8844
Gate City Beverage Distributors 2505 Steele St	San Bernardino	CA	92408	**800-500-4283**	909-799-1600
General Beverage & Beer PO Box 44326	Madison	WI	53744	**800-362-3636**	608-271-1234
General Wholesale Co 1271 Tacoma Dr NW	Atlanta	GA	30318	**800-801-0772**	404-351-3626
Georgia Crown Distributing 7 Crown Cir	Columbus	GA	31907	**800-332-4830**	706-568-4580
Giglio Distributing Co Inc 155 MLK Pkwy	Beaumont	TX	77701	**800-725-2337**	409-838-1654
Girardi Distributors LLC 5 Railroad Pl	Athol	MA	01331	**800-322-1229**	978-249-3581
Gold Coast Beverage Distributors Inc 3325 NW 70th Ave	Miami	FL	33122	**800-432-0463**	305-591-9800
Golden Eagle Distributors Inc 705 E Ajo Way	Tucson	AZ	85726	**800-274-4283**	520-884-5999
Grantham Distributing Co Inc 2685 Hansrob Rd	Orlando	FL	32804	**800-226-4010**	407-299-6446
Great Bay Distributors 2310 Starkey Rd	Largo	FL	33771	**800-231-4283**	727-584-8626
Gretz Beer Co 710 E Main St	Norristown	PA	19401	**866-473-8926**	610-275-0285
Grosslein Beverages Inc 13554 Tungsten St NW *Cust Svc	Anoka	MN	55303	**800-421-5804***	763-421-5804
Gusto Brands Inc 707 Douglas St	LaGrange	GA	30240	**800-241-3232**	706-882-2573
H Dennert Distributing Corp 351 Wilmer Ave *Cust Svc	Cincinnati	OH	45226	**800-837-5659***	513-871-7272
Halo Distributing Co 200 Lombrano St	San Antonio	TX	78207	**800-749-4256**	210-735-1111
Hartford Distributors Inc PO Box 8400	Manchester	CT	06040	**800-832-7211**	860-643-2337
Heidelberg Distributing Co 1518 Dalton St *Cust Svc	Cincinnati	OH	45214	**800-486-1518***	513-421-5000
Heineken USA 360 Hamilton Ave Suite 1103	White Plains	NY	10601	**800-811-4951**	914-681-4100
High Grade Beverage Inc 891 Old Georges Rd	South Brunswick	NJ	08852	**800-221-1194**	732-821-7600
House of La Rose 4223 E 49th St	Cuyahoga Heights	OH	44125	**800-642-4379**	216-271-5500
Hub City Distributing Co 6 Princess Rd	Lawrenceville	NJ	08648	**800-551-0668**	609-844-9600
InBev USA 101 Merritt 7 PO Box 5075 *Cust Svc	Norwalk	CT	06856	**800-268-2337***	203-750-6600

Classified Section

Beer & Ale - Whol (Cont'd)

Company	City	State	Zip	Toll-Free	Phone
Iron City Distributing Co 2670 Commercial Ave *Cust Svc	Mingo Junction	OH	43938	**800-759-2671***	740-598-4171
Joe G Maloof & Co Inc 701 Comanche Rd NE	Albuquerque	NM	87107	**800-760-2293**	505-243-2293
Koerner Distributors Inc 1305 W Wabash St	Effingham	IL	62401	**800-475-5162**	217-347-7113
Kramer Beverage Co Inc 161 S 2nd Rd *Cust Svc	Hammonton	NJ	08037	**800-321-4522***	609-704-7000
Kunda Beverage 349 S Henderson Rd	King of Prussia	PA	19406	**800-262-2323**	610-265-3113
Labatt Breweries of Canada 207 Queen's Quay W Suite 299	Toronto	ON	M5J1A7	**800-268-2337**	416-361-5050
Lake Beverage Corp 900 John St	West Henrietta	NY	14586	**800-476-4049**	585-427-0090
Leon Farmer & Co PO Box 1352	Athens	GA	30603	**800-282-7009**	706-353-1166
Lion Brewery Inc 700 N Pennsylvania Ave	Wilkes-Barre	PA	18705	**800-233-8327**	570-823-8801
Luce & Son Inc 2399 Valley Rd	Reno	NV	89512	**888-296-7570**	775-785-7810
Magnolia Marketing 809 Jefferson Hwy	Jefferson	LA	70121	**800-899-6056**	504-837-1500
Maloof Joe G & Co Inc 701 Comanche Rd NE	Albuquerque	NM	87107	**800-760-2293**	505-243-2293
Maple City Ice Co Inc 371 Cleveland Rd *Cust Svc	Norwalk	OH	44857	**800-736-6091***	419-668-2531
Mautino Distributing Co 500 N Richards St *Cust Svc	Spring Valley	IL	61362	**800-851-2756***	815-664-4311
McLaughlin & Moran Inc 40 Slater Rd	Cranston	RI	02920	**800-423-0156**	401-463-5454
Merrimack Valley Distributing Co 50 Prince St	Danvers	MA	01923	**800-698-0250**	978-777-2213
Mesa Distributing Co Inc 8870 Liquid Ct	San Diego	CA	92121	**800-275-1071**	858-452-2300
Metz Beverage Co Inc 302 N Custer St	Sheridan	WY	82801	**800-821-4010**	307-672-5848
Mt Hood Beverage Co 3601 NW Yeon Ave	Portland	OR	97210	**800-788-9992**	503-274-9990
Nackard Beverage Inc 5660 E Pensdock Ave	Flagstaff	AZ	86004	**800-622-5273**	928-526-2229
New Hampshire Distributors Inc 65 Regional Dr	Concord	NH	03301	**800-852-3781**	603-224-9991
NKS Distributors Inc 399 New Churchmans Rd	New Castle	DE	19720	**800-292-9509**	302-322-1811
Northern Distributing Co Inc 319 Corinth Rd	Glens Falls	NY	12804	**800-342-9565**	518-792-3112
Odom Corp 20415 72 Ave S Suite 210	Kent	WA	98032	**800-767-6366**	253-437-3000
Pacific Beverage Co 5305 Ekwill St *Cust Svc	Santa Barbara	CA	93111	**800-325-2278***	805-964-0611
Pine State Trading Co 8 Ellis Ave	Augusta	ME	04330	**800-873-3825**	207-622-3741
Powers Distributing Co Inc 3700 Giddings Rd	Orion	MI	48359	**800-498-4008**	248-393-3700
Premier Beverage Co of Florida 9801 Premier Pkwy	Miramar	FL	33025	**800-432-2002**	954-436-9200
RH Barringer Distributing Co Inc 1620 Fairfax Rd	Greensboro	NC	27407	**800-273-0555**	336-854-0555
Ritchie & Page Distributing Co Inc 292 3rd St	Trenton	NJ	08611	**800-257-9360**	609-392-1146
Sapporo USA Inc 11 E 44 St Suite 708	New York	NY	10017	**800-827-8234**	212-922-9165
Savannah Distributing Co PO Box 1388	Savannah	GA	31402	**800-551-0777**	912-233-1167
Seneca Beverage Corp 388 Upper Oakwood Ave	Elmira	NY	14903	**800-724-0350**	607-734-6111
Silver State Liquor & Wine Inc 325 E Nugget Ave	Sparks	NV	89431	**800-543-3867**	775-331-3400
Southern Wine & Spirits Co PO Box 5603	Denver	CO	80217	**800-332-9956**	303-292-1711
Standard Beverage Corp 2416 E 37th St N	Wichita	KS	67219	**800-999-7707**	316-838-7707
Star Distributors Inc 10 Eder Rd	West Haven	CT	06516	**800-922-3501**	203-932-3636
Supreme Beverage 2100-A Jackson Ave	Huntsville	AL	35804	**800-281-1482**	256-534-1482
United Beverage Co 624 N 44th Ave	Phoenix	AZ	85043	**888-340-4962**	602-233-1900
United Distributors Inc PO Box 1077	Macon	GA	31202	**800-749-7694**	478-746-7694
Watson Kunda & Sons DBA Kunda Beverage 349 S Henderson Rd	King of Prussia	PA	19406	**800-262-2323**	610-265-3113
Western Beverages Inc 4545 E 51st Ave	Denver	CO	80216	**877-701-2337**	303-388-5751
Williams Distributing Corp 880 Burnett Rd	Chicopee	MA	01020	**800-332-9634**	413-594-4900

82-2 Soft Drinks - Whol

Company	City	State	Zip	Toll-Free	Phone
Atlas Distributing Corp 44 Southbridge St	Auburn	MA	01501	**800-649-6221**	508-791-6221
Bissman Co Inc 30 W 5th St *Cust Svc	Mansfield	OH	44901	**800-321-2337***	419-524-2337
Buffalo Rock Co PO Box 10048 *Sales	Birmingham	AL	35202	**800-822-9799***	205-942-3435
Coca-Cola Bottling Co Consolidated 4100 Coca-Cola Plaza *NASDAQ: COKE*	Charlotte	NC	28211	**800-777-2653**	704-551-4400
Dr Pepper Bottling Co of Texas 2304 Century Ctr Blvd	Irving	TX	75062	**800-696-5891**	972-579-1024
Farrell Louis E Co Inc 20 Karen Dr	South Burlington	VT	05403	**800-473-7741**	802-864-6000
Flavia Beverage Systems 1301 Wilson Dr	West Chester	PA	19380	**800-882-6629**	610-430-2500
General Beverage & Beer PO Box 44326	Madison	WI	53744	**800-362-3636**	608-271-1234
Gusto Brands Inc 707 Douglas St	LaGrange	GA	30240	**800-241-3232**	706-882-2573
High Grade Beverage Inc 891 Old Georges Rd	South Brunswick	NJ	08852	**800-221-1194**	732-821-7600
Leading Brands Inc 1500 W Georgia St Suite 1800 *NASDAQ: LBIX*	Vancouver	BC	V6G2Z6	**866-685-5200**	604-685-5200
Louis E Farrell Co Inc 20 Karen Dr	South Burlington	VT	05403	**800-473-7741**	802-864-6000
Metz Beverage Co Inc 302 N Custer St	Sheridan	WY	82801	**800-821-4010**	307-672-5848
Nehi Royal Crown Bottling & Distributing Co Inc PO Box 1687	Bowling Green	KY	42102	**800-626-5255**	270-842-8106
Seven Up Bottling Group of Kansas 2900 S Hydraulic St	Wichita	KS	67216	**800-540-0001**	316-529-3777
Southeast-Atlantic Corp 6001 Bowdendale Ave	Jacksonville	FL	32216	**800-329-2067**	904-739-1000
Southwest Canners Inc PO Box 809	Portales	NM	88130	**800-658-2085**	505-356-6623

82-3 Wine & Liquor - Whol

Company	City	State	Zip	Toll-Free	Phone
Alabama Crown Distributing 421 Industrial Ln	Birmingham	AL	35211	**800-548-1869**	205-941-1155
Badger West Wine & Spirits LLC PO Box 869	Eau Claire	WI	54701	**800-472-6674**	715-836-8600
Barton Inc 55 E Monroe St 26th Fl	Chicago	IL	60603	**800-949-7837**	312-346-9200
Ben Arnold Sunbelt Beverage Co PO Box 480	Ridgeway	SC	29130	**888-262-9787**	803-337-3500
Block Distributing Co Inc 6511 Tri County Pkwy	Schertz	TX	78154	**800-749-7532**	210-224-7531
Blue Ridge Beverage Co Inc PO Box 700 *Cust Svc	Salem	VA	24153	**800-868-0354***	540-380-2000
Central Distributors Inc 15 Foss Rd *Cust Svc	Lewiston	ME	04241	**800-427-5757***	207-784-4026
Charmer Industries Inc 19-50 48th St	Astoria	NY	11105	**800-834-3546**	718-726-2500
Commonwealth Wine & Spirits Corp PO Box 37100	Louisville	KY	40233	**800-292-3597**	502-254-8600
Consolidated Distilled Products 2600 W 35th St	Chicago	IL	60632	**800-944-9450**	773-254-9000
Constellation Brands Inc 370 Woodcliff Dr Suite 300 *NYSE: STZ*	Fairport	NY	14450	**888-724-2169**	585-218-3600
Delaware Importers Inc 615 Lambson Ln	New Castle	DE	19720	**800-292-7890**	302-656-4487
Eber Brothers Wine & Liquor Corp 155 Paragon Dr	Rochester	NY	14624	**800-776-3237**	585-349-7700
Fedway Assoc Inc 56 Hackensack Ave	South Kearny	NJ	07032	**800-433-3929**	973-624-6444
Fox Henry A Sales Co 4494 36th St SE	Kentwood	MI	49512	**800-762-8730**	616-949-1210
Frank Liquor Co Inc PO Box 620710	Middleton	WI	53562	**800-362-9550**	608-836-6000
Frederick Wildman & Sons Ltd 311 E 53rd St	New York	NY	10022	**800-733-9463**	212-355-0700
Gallo Wine Distributors Inc 345 Underhill Blvd	Syosset	NY	11791	**800-272-4255**	516-921-9005
General Beverage & Beer PO Box 44326	Madison	WI	53744	**800-362-3636**	608-271-1234
General Wholesale Co 1271 Tacoma Dr NW	Atlanta	GA	30318	**800-801-0772**	404-351-3626
Georgia Crown Distributing 7 Crown Cir	Columbus	GA	31907	**800-332-4830**	706-568-4580
Grantham Distributing Co Inc 2685 Hansrob Rd	Orlando	FL	32804	**800-226-4010**	407-299-6446
Hammer Co Inc 9450 Rosemont Dr	Streetsboro	OH	44241	**800-258-9463**	330-422-9463
Heidelberg Distributing Co 1518 Dalton St *Cust Svc	Cincinnati	OH	45214	**800-486-1518***	513-421-5000
Koerner Distributors Inc 1305 W Wabash St	Effingham	IL	62401	**800-475-5162**	217-347-7113
Lovotti Bros Distributing Co PO Box 15840	Sacramento	CA	95852	**800-473-3911**	916-441-3911
Magnolia Marketing 809 Jefferson Hwy	Jefferson	LA	70121	**800-899-6056**	504-837-1500
Major Brands 550 E 13th Ave	North Kansas City	MO	64116	**800-467-1070**	816-221-1070
Major Brands-Columbia 1502 Business 70 W	Columbia	MO	65202	**800-264-9988**	573-443-3169
Merrimack Valley Distributing Co 50 Prince St	Danvers	MA	01923	**800-698-0250**	978-777-2213
Mt Hood Beverage Co 3601 NW Yeon Ave	Portland	OR	97210	**800-788-9992**	503-274-9990
Nackard Beverage Inc 5660 E Pensdock Ave	Flagstaff	AZ	86004	**800-622-5273**	928-526-2229
National Distributing Co Inc 1 National Dr SW	Atlanta	GA	30336	**800-282-3548**	404-696-9440
National Wine & Spirits Inc PO Box 1602	Indianapolis	IN	46206	**800-562-7359**	317-636-6092
NKS Distributors Inc 399 New Churchmans Rd	New Castle	DE	19720	**800-292-9509**	302-322-1811
Odom Corp 20415 72 Ave S Suite 210	Kent	WA	98032	**800-767-6366**	253-437-3000
Olinger Distributing Co 5337 W 78th St	Indianapolis	IN	46268	**800-366-1090**	317-876-1188
Paterno Wines International 900 Armour Dr	Lake Bluff	IL	60044	**800-950-7676**	847-604-8900
Peerless Importers Inc 16 Bridgewater St	Brooklyn	NY	11222	**800-338-3880**	718-383-5500
Pernod Ricard USA 777 Westchester Ave	White Plains	NY	10604	**800-488-7539**	914-539-4500
Phillips Distributing Corp 3010 Nob Hill Rd	Madison	WI	53713	**800-236-7269**	608-222-9177
Premier Beverage Co of Florida 9801 Premier Pkwy	Miramar	FL	33025	**800-432-2002**	954-436-9200
Premier Wine & Spirits DBA Gallo Wine Distributors Inc 345 Underhill Blvd	Syosset	NY	11791	**800-272-4255**	516-921-9005
R & R Marketing LLC 10 Patton Dr	West Caldwell	NJ	07006	**800-772-2096**	973-228-5100
Remy Amerique Inc 1350 6th Ave 7th Fl	New York	NY	10019	**800-858-9898**	212-399-4200
Republic Beverage 8045 Northcourt Rd	Houston	TX	77040	**800-292-3303**	832-782-1000
Romano Bros Beverage Co 300 E Crossroads Pkwy Bolingbrook Corp Ctr	Bolingbrook	IL	60440	**800-776-0180**	630-685-3000
Savannah Distributing Co Inc PO Box 1388	Savannah	GA	31402	**800-551-0777**	912-233-1167
Silver State Liquor & Wine Inc 325 E Nugget Ave	Sparks	NV	89431	**800-543-3867**	775-331-3400
Southern Wine & Spirits Co PO Box 5603	Denver	CO	80217	**800-332-9956**	303-292-1711
Southern Wine & Spirits Inc 1600 NW 163rd St	Miami	FL	33169	**800-432-6431**	305-625-4171
Standard Beverage Corp 2416 E 37th St N	Wichita	KS	67219	**800-999-7707**	316-838-7707
Terlato Wine Group 900 Armour Dr	Lake Bluff	IL	60044	**800-950-7676**	847-604-8900
Union Beverage Co 2600 W 35th St	Chicago	IL	60632	**800-685-6868**	773-254-9000
United Beverage Co 624 N 44th Ave	Phoenix	AZ	85043	**888-340-4962**	602-233-1900
United Distillers Products Co 4320 S 94th St	Omaha	NE	68127	**800-572-3664**	402-339-9100
United Distributors Inc PO Box 1077	Macon	GA	31202	**800-749-7694**	478-746-7694
United Liquors Ltd 175 Campanelli Dr	Braintree	MA	02185	**800-323-9666**	781-348-8000
Wildman Frederick & Sons Ltd 311 E 53rd St	New York	NY	10022	**800-733-9463**	212-355-0700
Wisconsin Distributors Inc 900 Progress Way	Sun Prairie	WI	53590	**800-373-2921**	608-834-2337
Young's Market Co LLC 2164 N Batavia St	Orange	CA	92865	**800-317-6150**	714-283-4933

83 BICYCLES & BICYCLE PARTS & ACCESSORIES

SEE ALSO Sporting Goods; Toys, Games, Hobbies

Company	City	State	Zip	Toll-Free	Phone
Aero-Fast Bicycle Co PO Box 3812	Jacksonville	FL	32206	**800-656-2376**	904-354-3339
Answer Products Inc 28209 Ave Stanford *Cust Svc	Valencia	CA	91355	**800-423-0273***	661-257-4411
Burley Design Co-op Inc 4020 Steward Rd	Eugene	OR	97402	**800-423-8445**	541-687-1644
Cane Creek Cycling Components 355 Cane Creek Rd	Fletcher	NC	28732	**800-234-2725**	828-684-3551
Diamondback Div Raleigh America Inc 6004 S 190th St Suite 101	Kent	WA	98032	**800-222-5527**	253-395-1100
EV Global Motors Co 4826 4th St	Irwindale	CA	91706	**800-871-4545**	626-813-9505
Giant Bicycle Inc 3587 Old Conejo Rd	Newbury Park	CA	91320	**800-874-4268**	805-267-4600
Huffy Bicycle Co 901 Pleasant Valley Dr	Springboro	OH	45066	**800-872-2453**	937-743-5011
K2 Bike 19215 Vashon Hwy SW	Vashon	WA	98070	**800-426-1617**	206-463-3631
Raleigh America Inc Diamondback Div 6004 S 190th St Suite 101	Kent	WA	98032	**800-222-5527**	253-395-1100
Raleigh USA 6004 S 190th St Suite 101	Kent	WA	98032	**800-222-5527**	253-395-1100
Smith Mfg Co DBA Aero-Fast Bicycle Co PO Box 3812	Jacksonville	FL	32206	**800-656-2376**	904-354-3339
Specialized Bicycle Components 15130 Concord Cir	Morgan Hill	CA	95037	**877-808-8154**	408-779-6229
Sun Wheels & Ramps 2156 N Detroit St	Warsaw	IN	46580	**888-478-6746**	574-267-3281
Terry Precision Bicycles for Women Inc 1657 E Park Dr *Orders	Macedon	NY	14502	**800-289-8379***	315-986-2103

84 BIO-RECOVERY SERVICES

Company	City	State	ZIP	Toll-Free	Phone
Advanced Ozone Engineering Inc 6038 Oakwood Ave	Cincinnati	OH	45224	**800-588-3871**	513-681-3871
Bio Cleaning Specialists Inc PO Box 18622	Minneapolis	MN	55418	**888-283-8898**	651-765-2429
Bio-Recovery Corp 51-49 47th St	Woodside	NY	11377	**877-246-2532**	718-729-2600
Bio-Recovery Services of America LLC 552 Danberry St	Toledo	OH	43609	**800-699-6522**	419-381-8255
Bio-Scene Recovery Inc 13191 Meadow St NE Suite A	Alliance	OH	44601	**877-380-5500**	330-823-5500
Biocare Inc PO Box 817	Easley	SC	29641	**800-875-9396**	864-855-3400
BioClean Inc PO Box 3062	Arlington	WA	98223	**888-412-6300**	360-435-8170
Crime & Death Scene Cleaning PO Box 828	Ipswich	MA	01938	**877-366-8348**	978-356-7007
Grangeville Environmental Services 585 McAllister St	Hanover	PA	17331	**866-437-5151**	717-637-6152
Loss Recovery Systems Inc 10 Dwight Pk Dr	Syracuse	NY	13209	**800-724-3473**	315-451-9111
Metro Restoration Inc PO Box 115	Thornton	IL	60476	**877-570-1315**	708-339-6300
Midwest Crisis Cleaning Inc 1011 Burgess Ave	Crystal City	MO	63019	**877-937-4862**	636-937-4862
Peerless Cleaners Inc 519 N Monroe St	Decatur	IL	62522	**800-879-7056**	217-423-7703
Red Alert Bio-Response Service Inc PO Box 941629	Houston	TX	77094	**800-570-1833**	281-993-0016
Trade-Winds Environmental Restoration Inc 100 Sweeneydale Ave	Bay Shore	NY	11706	**800-282-8701**	631-435-8900

85 BIOMETRIC IDENTIFICATION EQUIPMENT & SOFTWARE

Company	City	State	ZIP	Toll-Free	Phone
AcSys Biometrics Corp 399 Pearl St	Burlington	ON	L7R2M8	**877-842-7687**	905-634-4111
Aspect Business Solutions 7550 IH-10 W 14th Fl	San Antonio	TX	78229	**800-609-8113**	210-256-8300
Bio Medic Data Systems Inc 1 Silas Rd	Seaford	DE	19973	**800-526-2637**	302-628-4100
BioLink Technologies International Inc 599 Lexington Ave 38th Fl	New York	NY	10022	**866-994-3843**	212-572-6344
Biometric Access Corp 2555 IH-35 Suite 200	Round Rock	TX	78664	**800-873-4133**	512-246-3760
Bioscrypt Inc 5450 Explorer Dr Suite 500 *TSE: BYT*	Mississauga	ON	L4W5M1	**800-845-0096**	905-624-7700
BNX Systems Corp 1953 Gallows Rd Suite 500	Vienna	VA	22182	**800-397-7561**	703-734-9200
Communication Intelligence Corp 275 Shoreline Dr Suite 500 *Sales	Redwood Shores	CA	94065	**800-888-8242***	650-802-7888
Count Me In LLC 601 W Golf Rd Suite 108	Mount Prospect	IL	60056	**800-958-8779**	847-981-8779
Datastrip Inc 211 Welsh Pool Rd Suite 100	Exton	PA	19341	**800-548-2517**	610-594-6130
Digital Persona Inc 720 Bay Rd Suite 100	Redwood City	CA	94063	**877-378-2738**	650-474-4000
Honeywell Aerospace 1944 E Sky Harbor Cir	Phoenix	AZ	85034	**800-601-3099**	
International Biometric Group LLC 1 Battery Park Plaza	New York	NY	10004	**888-424-8424**	212-809-9491
Iridian Technologies Inc 1245 N Church St Suite 3	Moorestown	NJ	08057	**866-474-3426**	856-222-9090
NEC Solutions (America) Inc 1250 N Arlington Heights Rd Suite 400	Itasca	IL	60143	**800-632-4636**	630-467-5000
SAFLINK Corp 777 108th Ave NE Suite 2100	Bellevue	WA	98004	**800-762-9595**	425-278-1100
Sagem Morpho Inc 1145 Broadway Suite 200	Tacoma	WA	98402	**800-346-2674**	253-383-3617
SecuGen Corp 2356 Walsh Ave	Santa Clara	CA	95051	**866-942-8800**	408-727-7787
SIRCHIE Finger Print Laboratories Inc 100 Hunter Pl	Youngsville	NC	27596	**800-356-7311**	919-554-2244
Veridicom Inc 999 3rd Ave	Seattle	WA	98104	**800-363-1418**	206-224-6206

86 BIOTECHNOLOGY COMPANIES

SEE ALSO Diagnostic Products; Medicinal Chemicals & Botanical Products; Pharmaceutical Companies; Pharmaceutical Companies - Generic Drugs

Company	City	State	ZIP	Toll-Free	Phone
Allos Therapeutics Inc 11080 Circle Point Rd Suite 200 *NASDAQ: ALTH*	Westminster	CO	80020	**888-255-6702**	303-426-6262
Altana Pharma Inc 435 N Service Rd W 1st Fl	Oakville	ON	L6M4X8	**888-367-3331**	905-469-9333
Amgen Canada Inc 6755 Mississauga Rd Suite 400	Mississauga	ON	L5N7Y2	**800-665-4273**	905-542-7277
Amgen Inc 1 Amgen Ctr Dr *NASDAQ: AMGN*	Thousand Oaks	CA	91320	**800-926-4369**	805-447-1000
Antibodies Inc PO Box 1560	Davis	CA	95617	**800-824-8540**	530-758-4400
Aphton Corp 80 SW 8th St *NASDAQ: APHT*	Miami	FL	33130	**877-274-8660**	305-374-7338
Applera Corp 301 Merritt 7	Norwalk	CT	06856	**800-761-5381**	203-840-2000
ArQule Inc 19 Presidential Way *NASDAQ: ARQL*	Woburn	MA	01801	**800-644-5000**	781-994-0300
Array BioPharma Inc 1885 33rd St *NASDAQ: ARRY*	Boulder	CO	80301	**877-633-2436**	303-381-6600
Aventis Pasteur Inc Discovery Dr *Orders	Swiftwater	PA	18370	**800-822-2463***	570-839-7187
Aventis Pharmaceuticals Inc 300 Somerset Corp Blvd *NYSE: AVE*	Bridgewater	NJ	08807	**800-981-2491**	908-231-4000
Aviron 297 N Bernardo Ave	Mountain View	CA	94043	**877-633-4411**	650-691-9214
Bayer CropScience 2 Alexander Dr	Research Triangle Park	NC	27709	**800-523-0258**	919-549-2000
Biocine Div Chiron Corp 4560 Horton St	Emeryville	CA	94608	**800-524-4766**	510-655-8730
Biogen Idec Inc 14 Cambridge Ctr *NASDAQ: BIIB*	Cambridge	MA	02142	**800-262-4363**	617-679-2000
Biomira Inc 2011 94th St *NASDAQ: BIOM*	Edmonton	AB	T6N1H1	**877-234-0444**	780-450-3761
Bioniche Life Sciences Inc PO Box 1570 *TSE: BNC*	Belleville	ON	N8N5J2	**800-265-5464**	613-966-8058
Bionutrics Inc 2415 E Cambelback Rd Suite 700	Phoenix	AZ	85016	**800-508-7432**	602-508-0112
Biopure Corp 11 Hurley St *NASDAQ: BPUR ■ *Cust Svc*	Cambridge	MA	02141	**888-337-0929***	617-234-6500
BioReliance Corp 14920 Broschart Rd	Rockville	MD	20850	**800-553-5372**	301-738-1000
BioSphere Medical Inc 1050 Hingham St *NASDAQ: BSMD*	Rockland	MA	02370	**800-394-0295**	781-681-7900
Bone Care International Inc 1600 Aspen Commons *NASDAQ: BCII*	Middleton	WI	53562	**888-389-3300**	608-662-7800
Cambrex Bioscience 97 South St	Hopkinton	MA	01748	**877-676-5888**	508-497-0700
Cardiome Pharma Corp 6196 Agronomy Rd 6th Fl *NASDAQ: CRME*	Vancouver	BC	V6T1Z3	**800-330-9928**	604-677-6905
Celera Genomics Group 45 W Gude Dr *NYSE: CRA*	Rockville	MD	20850	**877-235-3721**	240-453-3000
Celgene Corp 7 Powder Horn Dr *NASDAQ: CELG*	Warren	NJ	07059	**888-423-5436**	732-271-1001
Cell Genesys Inc 500 Forbes Blvd *NASDAQ: CEGE*	South San Francisco	CA	94080	**800-648-6747**	650-266-3000
Cell Therapeutics Inc 201 Elliott Ave W Suite 400 *NASDAQ: CTIC*	Seattle	WA	98119	**800-215-2355**	206-282-7100
Centocor Inc 200 Great Valley Pkwy	Malvern	PA	19355	**888-874-3083**	610-651-6000
Cephalon Inc 145 Brandywine Pkwy *NASDAQ: CEPH*	West Chester	PA	19380	**800-675-8415**	610-344-0200
Chesapeake Biological Laboratories Inc 1111 S Paca St	Baltimore	MD	21230	**800-441-4225**	410-843-5000
Chiron Corp 4560 Horton St *NASDAQ: CHIR*	Emeryville	CA	94608	**800-524-4766**	510-655-8730
Chiron Corp Biocine Div 4560 Horton St	Emeryville	CA	94608	**800-524-4766**	510-655-8730
Chiron Therapeutics 4560 Horton St	Emeryville	CA	94608	**800-524-4766**	510-655-8729
Chiron Vaccines 4560 Horton St	Emeryville	CA	94608	**800-524-4766**	510-655-8729
Ciphergen Biosystems Inc 6611 Dumbarton Cir *NASDAQ: CIPH*	Fremont	CA	94555	**888-864-3770**	510-505-2100
Cohesion Technologies Inc 2500 Faber Pl	Palo Alto	CA	94303	**877-264-3746**	650-320-5500
CollaGenx Pharmaceuticals Inc 41 University Dr Suite 200 *NASDAQ: CGPI*	Newtown	PA	18940	**800-613-7847**	215-579-7388
Colorado Serum Co 4950 York St *Orders	Denver	CO	80216	**800-525-2065***	303-295-7527
CombiMatrix Corp 6500 Harbour Heights Pkwy Suite 301 *NASDAQ: CBMX*	Mukilteo	WA	98275	**800-985-2269**	425-493-2000
Connetics Corp 3290 W Bayshore Rd *NASDAQ: CNCT*	Palo Alto	CA	94303	**888-969-2628**	650-843-2800
Cook Biotech Inc 1425 Innovation Pl	West Lafayette	IN	47906	**888-299-4224**	765-497-3355
Corixa Corp 1900 9th Ave Suite 1100 *NASDAQ: CRXA*	Seattle	WA	98101	**888-426-7492**	206-366-3700
Covance Inc 210 Carnegie Ctr *NYSE: CVD*	Princeton	NJ	08540	**888-268-2623**	609-452-8550
Cryolife Inc 1655 Roberts Blvd NW *NYSE: CRY*	Kennesaw	GA	30144	**800-438-8285**	770-419-3355
Cubist Pharmaceuticals Inc 65 Hayden Ave *NASDAQ: CBST*	Lexington	MA	02421	**877-528-2478**	781-860-8660
CuraGen Corp 555 Long Wharf Dr 11th Fl *NASDAQ: CRGN*	New Haven	CT	06511	**888-436-6643**	203-401-3330
CV Therapeutics Inc 3172 Porter Dr *NASDAQ: CVTX*	Palo Alto	CA	94304	**877-475-2790**	650-384-8500
Cypress Bioscience Inc 4350 Executive Dr Suite 325 *NASDAQ: CYPB*	San Diego	CA	92121	**800-452-7646**	858-452-2323
Cytogen Corp 650 College Rd E *NASDAQ: CYTO*	Princeton	NJ	08540	**800-833-3533**	609-750-8200
Cytokinetics Inc 280 E Grand Ave *NASDAQ: CYTK*	South San Francisco	CA	94080	**877-394-2986**	650-624-3000
Dendreon Corp 3005 1st Ave *NASDAQ: DNDN*	Seattle	WA	98121	**877-256-4545**	206-256-4545
Dimethaid Research Inc 1405 Denison St *TSE: DMX*	Markham	ON	L3R5V2	**888-398-3463**	905-415-1446
Diversa Corp 4955 Directors Pl *NASDAQ: DVSA*	San Diego	CA	92121	**800-523-2990**	858-526-5000
Dow AgroSciences LLC 9330 Zionsville Rd	Indianapolis	IN	46268	**800-258-1470**	317-337-3000
Draxis Health Inc 6870 Goreway Dr 2nd Fl *NASDAQ: DRAX*	Mississauga	ON	L4V1P1	**877-550-4515**	905-677-5500
EntreMed Inc 9640 Medical Ctr Dr *NASDAQ: ENMD*	Rockville	MD	20850	**888-368-7363**	240-864-2600
Enzo Biochem Inc 60 Executive Blvd *NYSE: ENZ*	Farmingdale	NY	11735	**800-522-5052**	631-755-5500
Epoch Biosciences Inc 21720 23rd Dr SE Suite 150 *NASDAQ: EBIO*	Bothell	WA	98021	**800-562-5544**	425-482-5555
Genaera Corp 5110 Campus Dr *NASDAQ: GENR*	Plymouth Meeting	PA	19462	**800-522-8973**	610-941-4020
Genaissance Pharmaceuticals Inc 5 Science Pk *NASDAQ: GNSC*	New Haven	CT	06511	**877-476-4363**	203-773-1450
Genencor International Inc 925 Page Mill Rd	Palo Alto	CA	94304	**800-847-5311**	650-846-7500
Genentech Inc 1 DNA Way *NYSE: DNA*	South San Francisco	CA	94080	**800-551-2231**	650-225-1000
Generex Biotechnology Corp 33 Harbour Sq Suite 202 *NASDAQ: GNBT*	Toronto	ON	M5J2G2	**800-391-6755**	416-364-2551
Genitope Corp 525 Penobscot Dr *NASDAQ: GTOP*	Redwood City	CA	94063	**866-436-4867**	650-482-2000
Genomic Solutions Inc 4355 Varsity Dr Suite E	Ann Arbor	MI	48108	**877-436-6642**	734-975-4800
Genta Inc 2 Connell Dr *NASDAQ: GNTA*	Berkeley Heights	NJ	07922	**888-322-2264**	908-286-9800
GenVec Inc 65 W Watkins Mill Rd *NASDAQ: GNVC*	Gaithersburg	MD	20878	**877-943-6832**	240-632-0740
Genzyme Corp 500 Kendall St *NASDAQ: GENZ*	Cambridge	MA	02142	**800-326-7002**	617-252-7500
Gilead Sciences Inc 333 Lakeside Dr *NASDAQ: GILD*	Foster City	CA	94404	**800-445-3235**	650-574-3000
Grifols USA Inc 2410 Lillyvale Ave	Los Angeles	CA	90032	**800-421-0008**	323-225-2221
GTC Biotherapeutics Inc 175 Crossing Blvd Suite 410 *NASDAQ: GTCB*	Framingham	MA	01702	**800-326-7002**	508-620-9700
Guilford Pharmaceuticals Inc 6611 Tributary St *NASDAQ: GLFD*	Baltimore	MD	21224	**800-453-3746**	410-631-6300

Company	City	State	Zip	Toll-Free	Phone
Incara Pharmaceuticals Corp 79 TW Alexander Dr Bldg 4401 Suite 200	Research Triangle Park	NC	27709	**888-290-0528**	919-558-8688
Incyte Corp Rt 141 & Henry Clay Rd Bldg E-336 *NASDAQ: INCY* ■ *Sales	Wilmington	DE	19880	**877-746-2983***	302-498-6700
Inflazyme Pharamceuticals Ltd 5600 Parkwood Way Suite 425	Richmond	BC	V6V2M2	**800-315-3660**	604-279-8511
Inhibitex Inc 1165 Sanctuary Pkwy Suite 400 *NASDAQ: INHX*	Alpharetta	GA	30004	**866-784-3510**	678-746-1100
InKine Pharmaceutical Co 1787 Sentry Pkwy W Bldg 18 Suite 440 *NASDAQ: INKP*	Blue Bell	PA	19422	**800-759-9350**	215-283-6850
Inspire Pharmaceuticals Inc 4222 Emperor Blvd Suite 200 *NASDAQ: ISPH*	Durham	NC	27703	**877-800-4536**	919-941-9777
Integra LifeSciences Holdings Corp 311 Enterprise Dr *NASDAQ: IART*	Plainsboro	NJ	08536	**800-654-2873**	609-275-0500
Introgen Therapeutics Inc 301 Congress Ave Suite 1850 *NASDAQ: INGN*	Austin	TX	78701	**800-320-5010**	512-708-9310
Inveresk Research Group Inc 11000 Weston Pkwy	Cary	NC	27709	**800-421-1952**	919-460-9005
Invitrogen Corp 1600 Faraday Ave *NASDAQ: IVGN* ■ *Sales	Carlsbad	CA	92008	**800-955-6288***	760-603-7200
IOMED Inc 2441 S 3850 West Suite A *AMEX: IOX*	Salt Lake City	UT	84120	**800-621-3347**	801-975-1191
ISTA Pharmaceuticals Inc 15279 Alton Pkwy Suite 100 *NASDAQ: ISTA*	Irvine	CA	92618	**866-264-8568**	949-788-6000
JRH Biosciences Inc 13804 W 107th St	Lenexa	KS	66215	**800-255-6032**	913-469-5580
Leo Pharma Inc 123 Commerce Valley Dr E Suite 400	Thornhill	ON	L3T7W8	**800-668-7234**	905-886-9822
Lescarden Inc 420 Lexington Ave Suite 212	New York	NY	10170	**888-581-2076**	212-687-1050
Lexicon Genetics Inc 8800 Technology Forest Pl *NASDAQ: LEXG*	The Woodlands	TX	77381	**800-578-1972**	281-863-3000
LifeCore Biomedical Inc 3515 Lyman Blvd *NASDAQ: LCBM* ■ *Cust Svc	Chaska	MN	55318	**800-752-2663***	952-368-4300
Ligand Pharmaceuticals Inc 10275 Science Ctr Dr *NASDAQ: LGND*	San Diego	CA	92121	**800-964-5793**	858-550-7500
LiphaTech Inc 3600 W Elm St	Milwaukee	WI	53209	**888-331-7900**	
Lundbeck Canada Inc 413 St-Jacques St W Suite FB-230	Montreal	QC	H2Y1N9	**800-586-2325**	514-844-8515
Martek Biosciences Corp 6480 Dobbin Rd *NASDAQ: MATK*	Columbia	MD	21045	**888-652-7246**	410-740-0081
Maxygen Inc 515 Galveston Dr *NASDAQ: MAXY*	Redwood City	CA	94063	**888-629-9436**	650-298-5300
Medicines Co 200 5th Ave *NASDAQ: MDCO*	Waltham	MA	02451	**800-656-4662**	781-464-1500
MedImmune Inc 1 MedImmune Way *NASDAQ: MEDI*	Gaithersburg	MD	20878	**877-633-4411**	301-398-0000
Microbix Biosystems Inc 341 Bering Ave	Toronto	ON	M8Z3A8	**800-794-6694**	416-234-1624
Miravant Medical Technologies 336 Bollay Dr	Santa Barbara	CA	93117	**800-685-2959**	805-685-9880
Myogen Inc 7575 W 103rd Ave Suite 102 *NASDAQ: MYOG*	Westminster	CO	80021	**877-696-4361**	303-410-6666
Myriad Genetics Inc 320 Wakara Way *NASDAQ: MYGN*	Salt Lake City	UT	84108	**800-469-7423**	801-582-3400
Nabi Biopharmaceuticals 5800 Pk of Commerce Blvd NW *NASDAQ: NABI*	Boca Raton	FL	33487	**800-635-1766**	561-989-5800
Nastech Pharmaceutical Co Inc 3450 Monte Villa Pkwy *NASDAQ: NSTK*	Bothell	WA	98021	**888-627-2579**	425-908-3600
Nektar Therapeutics 150 Industrial Rd *NASDAQ: NKTR*	San Carlos	CA	94070	**800-438-1985**	650-631-3100
NeoRx Corp 300 Elliott Ave W Suite 500 *NASDAQ: NERX*	Seattle	WA	98119	**800-736-3679**	206-281-7001
Neurochem Inc 275 Armand Frappier *NASDAQ: NRMX*	Laval	QC	H7V4A7	**877-680-4500**	450-680-4500
Neurocrine Biosciences Inc 12790 El Camino Real *NASDAQ: NBIX*	San Diego	CA	92130	**800-876-3522**	858-617-7600
Novavax Inc 508 Lapp Rd *NASDAQ: NVAX*	Malvern	PA	19355	**888-669-9111**	484-913-1200
Novogen Inc 1 Landmark Sq Suite 240 *NASDAQ: NVGN*	Stamford	CT	06901	**888-480-8529**	203-327-1188
Nymox Pharmaceutical Corp 9900 Cavendish Blvd Suite 306 *NASDAQ: NYMX*	Saint-Laurent	QC	H4M2V2	**800-936-9669**	514-332-3222
Oakwood Laboratories LLC 7670 1st Pl Suite A	Oakwood	OH	44146	**888-625-9352**	440-359-0000
OraPharma Inc 732 Louis Dr	Warminster	PA	18974	**888-553-6010**	215-956-2200
Orchid Cellmark Inc 4390 Rt 1 *NASDAQ: ORCH*	Princeton	NJ	08540	**888-398-9352**	609-750-2200
Orphan Medical Inc 13911 Ridgedale Dr Suite 250 *NASDAQ: ORPH*	Minnetonka	MN	55305	**888-867-7426**	952-513-6900
Ortho BioTech Products LP PO Box 6914 *Cust Svc	Bridgewater	NJ	08807	**800-325-7504***	908-541-4000
OSG Ivers-Lee Ltd 31 Hansen Rd S	Brampton	ON	L6W3H7	**800-387-1188**	905-451-5535
Osteotech Inc 51 James Way *NASDAQ: OSTE*	Eatontown	NJ	07724	**800-537-9842**	732-542-2800
Oxis International Inc 6040 N Cutter Cir Suite 317	Portland	OR	97217	**800-547-3686**	503-283-3911
Penwest Pharmaceuticals Co 2981 Rt 22 *NASDAQ: PPCO*	Patterson	NY	12563	**800-431-2457**	845-878-8400
Peregrine Pharmaceuticals Inc 14272 Franklin Ave Suite 100 *NASDAQ: PPHM*	Tustin	CA	92780	**800-694-5334**	714-508-6000
Pharmacyclics Inc 995 E Arques Ave *NASDAQ: PCYC*	Sunnyvale	CA	94085	**800-458-0330**	408-774-0330
PharMingen Inc 10975 Torreyana Rd	San Diego	CA	92121	**800-848-6227**	858-812-8800
Pozen Inc 1414 Raleigh Rd Suite 400 *NASDAQ: POZN*	Chapel Hill	NC	27517	**888-264-1828**	919-913-1030
Pressure BioSciences Inc 375 West St *NASDAQ: PBIO*	West Bridgewater	MA	02379	**800-676-1881**	508-580-1900
Procyon BioPharma Inc 1650 Transcanada Hwy Suite 200	Dorval	QC	H9P1H7	**877-776-2966**	514-685-9283
QLT Inc 887 Great Northern Way *TSE: QLT*	Vancouver	BC	V5T4T5	**800-663-5486**	604-707-7000
Questcor Pharmaceuticals Inc 3260 Whipple Rd *AMEX: QSC*	Union City	CA	94587	**800-411-3065**	510-400-0700
Raven Biological Laboratories Inc 8607 Park Dr	Omaha	NE	68127	**800-728-5702**	402-593-0781
Regeneration Technologies Inc 11621 Research Cir *NASDAQ: RTIX*	Alachua	FL	32615	**877-343-6832**	386-418-8888
Regeneron Pharmaceuticals Inc 777 Old Saw Mill River Rd *NASDAQ: REGN*	Tarrytown	NY	10591	**800-637-8322**	914-347-7000
Repligen Corp 41 Seyon St *NASDAQ: RGEN* ■ *Sales	Waltham	MA	02453	**800-622-2259***	781-449-9560
Roche Bioscience 3431 Hillview Ave	Palo Alto	CA	94304	**800-796-8395**	650-855-5050
Sanofi-Synthelabo Canada Inc 15 Allstate Pkwy	Markham	ON	L3R5B4	**800-668-7401**	905-513-4444
Scios Inc 6500 Paseo Padre Pkwy	Fremont	CA	94555	**800-972-4670**	510-248-2500
Sequenom Inc 3595 John Hopkins Ct *NASDAQ: SQNM*	San Diego	CA	92121	**877-443-6663**	858-202-9000
Serologicals Corp 5655 Spalding Dr *NASDAQ: SERO*	Norcross	GA	30092	**800-842-9099**	678-728-2000
Serono Inc 1 Technology Pl	Rockland	MA	02370	**800-283-8088**	781-982-9000
StressGen Biotechnologies Corp 4243 Glanford Ave Suite 360	Victoria	BC	V8Z4B9	**800-661-4970**	250-744-2011
SuperGen Inc 4140 Dublin Blvd Suite 200 *NASDAQ: SUPG*	Dublin	CA	94568	**800-353-1075**	925-560-0100
SYN-X Pharma Inc 1 Marmac Dr	Toronto	ON	M9W1E7	**877-246-7593**	416-798-3445
Targeted Genetics Corp 1100 Olive Way Suite 100 *NASDAQ: TGEN*	Seattle	WA	98101	**800-828-6022**	206-623-7612
Therics Inc 115 Campus Dr	Princeton	NJ	08540	**888-784-3742**	609-514-7200
Third Wave Technologies Inc 502 S Rosa Rd *NASDAQ: TWTI*	Madison	WI	53719	**888-898-2357**	608-273-8933
Titan Pharmaceuticals Inc 400 Oyster Point Blvd Suite 505 *AMEX: TTP*	South San Francisco	CA	94080	**800-500-6608**	650-244-4990
Vertex Pharmaceuticals Inc 130 Waverly St *NASDAQ: VRTX*	Cambridge	MA	02139	**800-294-2465**	617-444-6100
ViaCell Inc 245 1st St 15th Fl *NASDAQ: VIAC*	Cambridge	MA	02142	**866-874-2235**	617-577-7744
Viragen Inc 865 SW 78th Ave Suite 100 *AMEX: VRA*	Plantation	FL	33324	**888-847-2436**	954-233-8746
Xenogen Corp 860 Atlantic Ave *NASDAQ: XGEN*	Alameda	CA	94501	**877-936-6436**	510-291-6100
XOMA Ltd 2910 7th St *NASDAQ: XOMA*	Berkeley	CA	94710	**800-544-9662**	510-204-7200
ZymeTx Inc 655 Research Pkwy Suite 554	Oklahoma City	OK	73104	**888-817-1314**	405-809-1314
ZymoGenetics Inc 1201 Eastlake Ave E *NASDAQ: ZGEN*	Seattle	WA	98102	**800-775-6686**	206-442-6600

87 BLANKBOOKS & BINDERS

SEE ALSO Checks - Personal & Business

Company	City	State	Zip	Toll-Free	Phone
Abco Inc 1621 Wall St	Dallas	TX	75215	**800-969-2226**	214-565-1191
ACCO Brands Inc 300 Tower Pkwy	Lincolnshire	IL	60069	**800-222-6462**	847-541-9500
ACCO Canada Inc 5 Precido Ct	Brampton	ON	L6S6B7	**800-268-3447**	905-595-3100
AD Industries Inc 12160 Sherman Way	North Hollywood	CA	91605	**800-233-4201**	818-765-4200
Advanced Looseleaf Technologies Inc 1424 Somerset Ave	Dighton	MA	02715	**800-339-6354**	508-669-6354
Allison Payment Systems LLC 2200 Production Dr	Indianapolis	IN	46241	**800-755-2440**	317-808-2400
American Thermoplastic Co 106 Gamma Dr	Pittsburgh	PA	15238	**800-245-6600**	412-967-0900
Antioch Publishing Co 888 Dayton St	Yellow Springs	OH	45387	**800-543-2397**	937-767-7379
Art Leather Mfg Co Inc 45-10 94th St	Elmhurst	NY	11373	**888-252-5286**	718-699-6300
Artistic Direct Inc 1316 College Ave *Cust Svc	Elmira	NY	14901	**800-845-3720***	607-733-5541
Avery Dennison Corp 150 N Orange Grove Blvd *NYSE: AVY* ■ *Cust Svc	Pasadena	CA	91103	**800-252-8379***	626-304-2000
Blackbourn Media Packaging Div Fey Industries 200 4th Ave N	Edgerton	MN	56128	**800-842-7550**	
Blair Industries Inc 116 E Missouri St	Scott City	MO	63780	**800-624-3150**	573-264-2146
Bobley Harmann Publishing Co 311 Crossways Park Dr *Cust Svc	Woodbury	NY	11797	**800-323-1692***	516-364-1800
Cardinal Brands 643 Massachusetts Suite 200	Lawrence	KS	66044	**800-444-3508**	785-344-1400
Chilcote Co 2140-60 Superior Ave *Sales	Cleveland	OH	44114	**800-827-5679***	216-781-6000
Colad Group 801 Exchange St	Buffalo	NY	14210	**800-950-1755**	716-961-1776
Consolidated Looseleaf Inc 649 Alden St	Fall River	MA	02722	**800-289-3523**	508-676-8580
Continental Binder & Specialty Corp 407 W Compton Blvd	Gardena	CA	90248	**800-872-2897**	310-324-8227
CR Gibson Inc 404 BNA Dr Bldg 200 Suite 600	Nashville	TN	37217	**800-243-6004**	615-724-2900
Customcraft Binder Corp 21 Addison Ln	Greenvale	NY	11548	**800-428-0934**	516-484-4020
D Davis Kenny Co Inc 4810 Greatland	San Antonio	TX	78218	**800-594-2045**	210-662-9882
Data Management Inc 537 New Britain Ave *Orders	Farmington	CT	06034	**800-243-1969***	860-677-8586
Day Runner Inc 101 O'Neil Rd	Sydney	NY	13838	**800-323-0500**	607-563-9411
Day-Timers Inc 1 Willow Ln	East Texas	PA	18046	**800-457-5702**	610-398-1151
Dayton Legal Blank Inc 875 Congress Pk Dr	Dayton	OH	45459	**800-262-8480**	937-435-4405
Dilley Mfg Co 215 E 3rd St	Des Moines	IA	50309	**800-247-5087**	515-288-7289
EBSCO Industries Inc Vulcan Information Packaging Div PO Box 29	Vincent	AL	35178	**800-633-4526**	205-672-2241
Eckhart & Co Inc 4011 W 54th St	Indianapolis	IN	46254	**800-443-3791**	317-347-2665
Eskco Inc 700 Liberty Ln	Dayton	OH	45449	**800-783-7526**	937-865-0498
Esselte Corp 48 S Service Rd Suite 400 *Cust Svc	Melville	NY	11747	**800-645-6051***	631-675-5700
Esselte Pendaflex Corp 1625 E Duane Blvd	Kankakee	IL	60901	**800-888-2115**	815-933-3351

	City	State	Zip	Toll-Free	Phone
Executive Greetings Inc 120 Greenwoods Industrial Pk. *Cust Svc	New Hartford	CT	06057	**800-562-5468***	860-379-9911
Fey Industries Blackbourn Media Packaging Div 200 4th Ave N	Edgerton	MN	56128	**800-842-7550**	
Fey Industries Inc 200 4th Ave N.	Edgerton	MN	56128	**800-533-5340**	507-442-4311
Forbes Products Corp 45 High Tech Dr	Rush	NY	14543	**800-836-7237**	585-334-4800
Formflex Inc PO Box 218	Bloomingdale	IN	47832	**800-255-7659**	765-498-8900
General Binding Corp 1 GBC Plaza *NASDAQ: GBND* ■ *Orders	Northbrook	IL	60062	**800-723-4000***	847-272-3700
General Loose Leaf Bindery Co 3811 Hawthorn Ct	Waukegan	IL	60087	**800-621-0493**	847-244-9700
General Products 4045 N Rockwell St	Chicago	IL	60618	**800-888-1934**	773-463-2424
HC Miller Co 3030 Lowell Dr	Green Bay	WI	54311	**800-829-6555**	
Holum & Sons Co Inc 740 N Burr Oak Dr	Westmont	IL	60559	**800-447-4479**	630-654-8222
Kenny D Davis Co Inc 4810 Greatland	San Antonio	TX	78218	**800-594-2045**	210-662-9882
Kunz Business Products Co 1600 Penn St	Huntingdon	PA	16652	**800-458-3442**	814-643-4320
Kurtz Brothers Co Inc PO Box 392	Clearfield	PA	16830	**800-252-3811**	814-765-6561
M & F Case International Inc 717 School St *Cust Svc	Pawtucket	RI	02860	**800-343-8820***	401-722-4830
MeadWestvaco Consumer & Office Products 10 W 2nd St	Dayton	OH	45402	**800-648-6323**	937-495-6323
Michael Lewis Simon Products Co Inc 201 Mittel Dr	Wood Dale	IL	60191	**800-323-8808**	630-350-1060
Miller HC Co 3030 Lowell Dr	Green Bay	WI	54311	**800-829-6555**	
NAPCO Inc 535 Napco Rd	Sparta	NC	28675	**800-854-8621**	336-372-5228
Pioneer Photo Albums Inc 9801 Deering Ave	Chatsworth	CA	91311	**800-366-3686**	818-882-2161
Roaring Spring Blank Book Co 740 Spang St *Cust Svc	Roaring Spring	PA	16673	**800-441-1653***	814-224-5141
Samsill Corp 5740 Hartman Rd	Fort Worth	TX	76119	**800-255-1100**	817-536-1906
Southwest Plastic Binding Co Inc 109 Millwell Ct	Maryland Heights	MO	63043	**800-325-3628**	314-739-4400
Spiral Binding Co Inc 1 Maltese Dr	Totowa	NJ	07511	**800-631-3572**	973-256-0666
Superior Press Inc 11930 Hamden Pl	Santa Fe Springs	CA	90670	**888-590-7998**	562-948-1866
Trendex Inc 240 E Maryland Ave Suite 100	Saint Paul	MN	55117	**800-328-9200**	651-489-4655
Twentieth Century Plastics Inc 205 S Puente St	Brea	CA	92821	**800-767-0777**	714-441-4500
Union Group 649 Alden St	Fall River	MA	02722	**800-289-3523**	508-676-8580
ViaTech Publishing Solutions 1440 5th Ave	Bay Shore	NY	11706	**800-645-8558**	631-968-8500
Vulcan Information Packaging Div EBSCO Industries Inc PO Box 29	Vincent	AL	35178	**800-633-4526**	205-672-2241
Western Looseleaf Div Cal/West United Inc 12160 Sherman Way	North Hollywood	CA	91605	**800-233-4201**	818-765-4200

88 BLINDS & SHADES

	City	State	Zip	Toll-Free	Phone
Aeroshade Inc 433 Oakland Ave	Waukesha	WI	53186	**800-331-7179**	262-547-2101
Beauti-Vue Products Inc 8555 194th Ave Bristol Industrial Pk	Bristol	WI	53104	**800-558-9431**	262-857-2306
Blind Maker 2013 Centimeter Cir	Austin	TX	78758	**800-999-5444**	512-835-5333
Budget Blinds Inc 1927 N Glassell St	Orange	CA	92865	**800-420-5374**	714-637-2108
C-Mor Co 7 Jewell St	Garfield	NJ	07026	**800-631-3830**	973-478-3900
Comfortex Window Fashions Inc 21 Elm St *Cust Svc	Maplewood	NY	12189	**800-843-4151***	518-273-3333
Fashion Tech Inc 2010 SE 8th Ave	Portland	OR	97214	**800-444-8822**	503-238-0666
Friedland Ralph & Brothers Inc 17 Industrial Dr	Cliffwood Beach	NJ	07735	**800-631-2162**	732-290-9800
Hunter Douglas 2 Parkway & Rt 17 S	Upper Saddle River	NJ	07458	**800-436-7366**	201-327-8200
Kenney Mfg Co 1000 Jefferson Blvd *Cust Svc	Warwick	RI	02886	**800-753-6639***	401-739-2200
Kirsch Div Newell Rubbermaid Inc 916 S Arcade Ave	Freeport	IL	61032	**800-328-7290**	815-235-4171
Levolor Div Newell Rubbermaid Inc 4110 Premier Dr	High Point	NC	27265	**800-232-2028**	336-812-8181
Mark Window Products Inc 2900 S Fairview St	Santa Ana	CA	92704	**800-427-4127**	714-641-1411
Mill Supply Div 264 Morse St	Hamden	CT	06517	**800-243-6648**	203-777-7668
Newell Rubbermaid Inc Kirsch Div 916 S Arcade Ave	Freeport	IL	61032	**800-328-7290**	815-235-4171
Newell Rubbermaid Inc Levolor Div 4110 Premier Dr	High Point	NC	27265	**800-232-2028**	336-812-8181
Northern Cross Industries Inc 92 Hardwood Way	Brattleboro	VT	05301	**800-257-4501**	802-257-4501
Ralph Friedland & Brothers Inc 17 Industrial Dr	Cliffwood Beach	NJ	07735	**800-631-2162**	732-290-9800
Source Northwest Inc 8329 216th St SE *Cust Svc	Woodinville	WA	98072	**800-426-1321***	360-512-3535
Southland Window Fashions 408 Arlington St	Houston	TX	77007	**800-299-9030**	713-863-7761
Springs Industries Inc 205 N White St	Fort Mill	SC	29715	**800-438-6709**	803-547-1500
Sun Control Products Inc 11 E Veterans Memorial Hwy	Kasson	MN	55944	**800-533-0010**	507-634-2081
Superior Shade & Blind Co Inc 1541 N Powerline Rd	Pompano Beach	FL	33069	**800-325-9018**	954-975-8122
Warren Shade Co Inc 2825 E Hennepin Ave	Minneapolis	MN	55413	**800-937-0008**	612-331-5939

89 BLISTER PACKAGING

	City	State	Zip	Toll-Free	Phone
Andex Industries Inc 1911 4th Ave N	Escanaba	MI	49829	**800-338-9882**	906-786-6070
Card Pak Inc 29601 Solon Rd	Solon	OH	44139	**800-824-3342**	440-542-3100
Dot Packaging Group Inc 1500 Paramount Pkwy	Batavia	IL	60510	**800-323-6160**	630-879-0121
Placon Corp 6096 McKee Rd	Madison	WI	53719	**800-541-1535**	608-271-5634
Sharp Corp 23 Carland Rd	Conshohocken	PA	19428	**800-892-6197**	610-279-3550

90 BLOOD CENTERS

SEE ALSO Laboratories - Drug-Testing; Laboratories - Genetic Testing; Laboratories - Medical

	City	State	Zip	Toll-Free	Phone
Belle Bonfils Memorial Blood Center 717 Yosemite St	Denver	CO	80230	**800-365-0006**	303-341-4000
Blood Assurance Inc 700 E 3rd St	Chattanooga	TN	37403	**800-962-0628**	423-756-0966
Blood Center of Central Iowa 431 E Locust St	Des Moines	IA	50309	**800-287-4903**	515-288-0276
Blood Center of Southeastern Wisconsin PO Box 2178	Milwaukee	WI	53201	**800-257-3840**	414-933-5000
Blood Centers of the Pacific 270 Masonic Ave	San Francisco	CA	94118	**888-393-4483**	415-567-6400
Carter BloodCare 2205 Hwy 121	Bedford	TX	76021	**800-366-2834**	817-412-5000
Central California Blood Center 3445 N 1st St	Fresno	CA	93726	**800-404-2500**	559-224-2900
Central Kentucky Blood Center 330 Waller Ave	Lexington	KY	40504	**800-775-2522**	859-276-2534
Coastal Bend Blood Center 5025 Deepwood Cir	Corpus Christi	TX	78415	**800-299-4943**	361-855-4943
Community Blood Center of Greater Kansas City-Saint Joseph 3122 Frederick Ave	Saint Joseph	MO	64506	**800-725-6791**	816-232-6791
Community Blood Center of the Ozarks 2230 S Glenstone	Springfield	MO	65804	**800-280-5337**	417-227-5000
Community Blood Services of Illinois 1408 W University Ave	Urbana	IL	61801	**800-217-4483**	217-367-2202
Delta Blood Bank 65 N Commerce St	Stockton	CA	95201	**800-244-6794**	209-943-3831
Florida Georgia Blood Alliance 536 W 10th St	Jacksonville	FL	32206	**800-447-1479**	904-353-8263
Florida's Blood Centers 345 W Michigan St Suite 106	Orlando	FL	32806	**888-936-6283**	407-999-8400
Gulf Coast Regional Blood Center 1400 La Concha Ln	Houston	TX	77054	**888-482-5663**	713-790-1200
Heartland Blood Centers 1200 N Highland Ave	Aurora	IL	60506	**800-786-4483**	630-892-7055
Hemacare Corp 4954 Van Nuys Blvd	Sherman Oaks	CA	91403	**888-481-1538**	818-986-3883
Hoxworth Blood Center University of Cincinnati Medical Center 3130 Highland Ave ML0055	Cincinnati	OH	45267	**800-265-1515**	513-558-1200
Inland Northwest Blood Center 210 W Cataldo Ave	Spokane	WA	99201	**800-423-0151**	509-624-0151
Lifeblood/Mid-South Regional Blood Center 1040 Madison Ave	Memphis	TN	38104	**888-543-3256**	901-522-8585
LIFELINE Blood Services 828 North Pkwy	Jackson	TN	38305	**800-924-6572**	731-427-4431
LifeSource Blood Services 1205 N Milwaukee Ave	Glenview	IL	60025	**800-486-0680**	847-298-9660
Michigan Community Blood Centers 1036 Fuller Ave NE	Grand Rapids	MI	49503	**866-642-5663**	616-774-2300
Michigan Community Blood Centers Northwest 2575 Aero Pk Dr	Traverse City	MI	49686	**800-935-5311**	231-935-3030
Mississippi Valley Regional Blood Center 5500 Lakeview Pkwy	Davenport	IA	52807	**800-747-5401**	563-359-5401
Puget Sound Blood Center 921 Terry Ave	Seattle	WA	98104	**800-366-2831**	206-292-6500
Rhode Island Blood Center 405 Promenade St	Providence	RI	02908	**800-283-8385**	401-453-8360
Rock River Valley Blood Center 419 N 6th St	Rockford	IL	61107	**866-889-9073**	815-965-8751
Sacramento Medical Foundation Blood Center 1625 Stockton Blvd	Sacramento	CA	95816	**800-995-4420**	916-456-1500
San Diego Blood Bank 440 Upas St	San Diego	CA	92103	**800-479-3902**	619-296-6393
Siouxland Community Blood Bank 1019 Jones St	Sioux City	IA	51102	**800-798-4208**	712-252-4208
South Texas Blood & Tissue Center 6211 IH-10 W	San Antonio	TX	78201	**800-292-5534**	210-731-5555
Southeast Iowa Blood Center 1007 Pennsylvania Ave	Ottumwa	IA	52501	**800-452-1097**	641-682-8149
Southeastern Community Blood Center 1731 Riggins Rd	Tallahassee	FL	32308	**800-722-2218**	850-877-7181
Stewart Regional Blood Center 815 S Baxter Ave	Tyler	TX	75701	**800-252-5584**	903-535-5400
United Blood Services of Arkansas					
Fort Smith 5300 S 'U' St	Fort Smith	AR	72903	**800-934-9415**	479-452-5880
Hot Springs 1635 Higdon Ferry Rd	Hot Springs	AR	71913	**800-286-2116**	501-624-0667
United Blood Services of Mississippi					
Meridian 1115 25th Ave	Meridian	MS	39301	**877-582-2482**	601-482-2482
Tupelo 4326 S Eason Blvd	Tupelo	MS	38803	**800-844-8870**	662-842-8870
United Blood Services of Montana Billings 1444 Grand Ave	Billings	MT	59102	**800-365-4450**	406-248-9168
United Blood Services of Nevada Reno 1125 Terminal Way	Reno	NV	89502	**800-627-4928**	775-329-6451
United Blood Services of New Mexico Albuquerque 1515 University Blvd NE	Albuquerque	NM	87102	**800-333-8037**	505-843-6227
United Blood Services of North Dakota					
Bismarck 517 S 7th St	Bismarck	ND	58502	**800-456-6159**	701-258-4512
Fargo 1320 1st Ave N	Fargo	ND	58102	**800-293-8203**	701-293-9453
United Blood Services of Texas					
El Paso 2325 Pershing Dr	El Paso	TX	79903	**800-333-7128**	915-544-5422
McAllen 1312 Pecan Blvd	McAllen	TX	78501	**888-827-4376**	956-682-1314
San Angelo 2020 W Beauregard St	San Angelo	TX	76901	**800-756-0024**	325-223-7500
West Tennessee Regional Blood Center Inc 828 North Pkwy	Jackson	TN	38305	**800-924-6572**	731-427-4431

91 BOATS - RECREATIONAL

	City	State	Zip	Toll-Free	Phone
Aquasport Marine Corp 1651 Whitfield Ave	Sarasota	FL	34243	**800-755-1099**	941-755-5800
Arima Marine International Inc 47 37th St NE	Auburn	WA	98002	**800-811-6440**	253-939-7980
Blue Wave Boats Hwy 69 S	Checotah	OK	74426	**800-432-6768**	918-473-6768
Bluewater Inc 811 E Maple Ave	Mora	MN	55051	**800-733-7127**	320-679-3811
Caribiana Sea Skiffs 8920 County Rd 65	Foley	AL	36535	**888-203-4883**	251-981-4442
Carolina Skiff Inc 3231 Fulford Rd	Waycross	GA	31503	**800-422-7543**	912-287-0547
Cigarette Racing Team Inc 4355 NW 128th St	Opa Locka	FL	33054	**800-347-4327**	305-931-4564
Cobalt Boats 1715 N 8th St	Neodesha	KS	66757	**800-835-0256**	620-325-2653
Concept Boats Corp 2410 NW 147th St	Opalocka	FL	33054	**888-635-8712**	305-635-8712
Correct Craft Inc 6100 S Orange Ave	Orlando	FL	32809	**800-346-2092**	407-855-4141
Donzi Marine PO Box 987	Tallevast	FL	34270	**800-624-3304**	941-727-0622

Company	City	State	Zip	Toll-Free	Phone
Famous Craft Inc 7921 15th St E	Sarasota	FL	34243	**888-244-3244**	941-358-3121
Fiberglass Engineering Inc DBA Cobalt Boats 1715 N 8th St	Neodesha	KS	66757	**800-835-0256**	620-325-2653
Genmar Industries Inc 80 S 8th St 2900 IDS Ctr	Minneapolis	MN	55402	**800-328-5557**	612-339-7600
Grand Banks Yachts Ltd 2 Marina Plaza	Newport	RI	02840	**800-809-0909**	401-848-7550
Hobie Cat Co 4925 Oceanside Blvd	Oceanside	CA	92056	**800-462-4349**	760-758-9100
Hunter Marine Corp PO Box 1030	Alachua	FL	32616	**800-771-5556**	386-462-3077
Johnson Outdoors Inc 555 Main St *NASDAQ: JOUT*	Racine	WI	53403	**800-299-2592**	262-631-6600
Johnson Outdoors Watercraft Sport & Leisure Group 4855 Broadmoor Ave SE	Grand Rapids	MI	49512	**800-552-6287**	616-698-3000
Larson Boats 700 Paul Larson Memorial Dr	Little Falls	MN	56345	**800-255-3622**	320-632-5481
Livingston Boats PO Box 819	Elma	WA	98541	**866-482-5580**	360-482-5580
Luhrs Corp 255 Diesel Rd	Saint Augustine	FL	32084	**800-829-5847**	904-829-0500
Mainship Corp 255 Diesel Rd	Saint Augustine	FL	32084	**800-829-5847**	904-829-0500
MasterCraft Boat Co 100 Cherokee Cove Dr	Vonore	TN	37885	**800-443-8774**	423-884-2221
Maverick Boat Co Inc 3207 Industrial 29th St	Fort Pierce	FL	34946	**888-742-5569**	772-465-0631
Playbuoy Pontoon Mfg Inc 903 Michigan Ave PO Box 698	Alma	MI	48801	**800-334-2913**	989-463-2112
Pro-Line Boats Inc PO Box 1348	Crystal River	FL	34423	**800-344-1281**	352-795-4111
Pursuit Boats 3901 St Lucie Blvd	Fort Pierce	FL	34946	**800-947-8778**	772-465-6006
Regal Marine Industries Inc 2300 Jetport Dr	Orlando	FL	32809	**800-877-3425**	407-851-4360
Rinalli Boats Ltd 1600 N King St	Seguin	TX	78155	**866-746-2554**	830-372-3300
Skeeter Products Inc 1 Skeeter Rd	Kilgore	TX	75662	**800-753-3837**	903-984-0541
Stamas Yacht Inc 300 Pampas Ave *Sales	Tarpon Springs	FL	34689	**800-782-6271***	727-937-4118
Starcraft Marine LLC 201 Starcraft Dr PO Box 517	Topeka	IN	46571	**800-535-5722**	260-593-2500
Tartan Yachts 1920 Fairport Nursery Rd	Fairport Harbor	OH	44077	**888-330-3484**	440-354-3111
Thunderbird Products Inc 2200 W Monroe St	Decatur	IN	46733	**800-736-7685**	
Triumph Boats 100 Golden Dr	Durham	NC	27705	**800-564-4225**	919-382-3149
Venture Marine Inc 1525 53rd St	West Palm Beach	FL	33407	**800-960-3434**	561-845-8557
Vivian Industries Inc 680 S Pardue St	Vivian	LA	71082	**800-256-7579**	318-375-3241
Weeres Industries Corp 1045 33rd St S	Saint Cloud	MN	56301	**800-397-6686**	320-251-3551

92 BOILER SHOPS

Company	City	State	Zip	Toll-Free	Phone
Ace Tank & Equipment Co PO Box 9039	Seattle	WA	98109	**877-223-8265**	206-281-5000
Adamson Global Technology Corp 13200 Ramblewood Dr	Chester	VA	23836	**800-525-7703**	804-748-6453
Aerofin Corp 4621 Murray Pl PO Box 10819	Lynchburg	VA	24506	**800-237-6346**	434-845-7081
Alpine Engineered Products Inc PO Box 2225	Pompano Beach	FL	33061	**800-735-8055**	954-781-3333
American Welding & Tank Co PO Box 8870	Camp Hill	PA	17001	**800-445-6709**	717-763-5080
API Heat Transfer 2777 Walden Ave	Buffalo	NY	14225	**877-274-4328**	716-684-9700
Ardco Corp 8250 E 40th Ave	Denver	CO	80207	**800-544-9013**	303-399-2934
Arrow Tank & Engineering Co 650 N Emerson St	Cambridge	MN	55008	**888-892-7769**	763-689-3360
AstroCosmos Metallurgical Div 4047 E Lincoln Way	Wooster	OH	44691	**800-231-6601**	330-264-8639
Autoclave Engineers Div Snap-Tite 8325 Hessinger Dr	Erie	PA	16509	**800-458-0409**	814-838-5700
Babcock & Wilcox Co 20 S Van Buren Ave	Barberton	OH	44203	**800-222-2625**	330-753-4511
CB & I Trusco Tank 4388 Santa Fe Rd	San Luis Obispo	CA	93401	**800-487-8265**	805-544-9155
CB Mills Div Chicago Boiler Co 1300 Northwestern Ave	Gurnee	IL	60031	**800-969-7343**	847-662-4000
Chicago Boiler Co 1300 Northwestern Ave	Gurnee	IL	60031	**800-969-7343**	847-662-4000
Chicago Boiler Co CB Mills Div 1300 Northwestern Ave	Gurnee	IL	60031	**800-969-7343**	847-662-4000
Clawson Tank Co Inc 4545 Clawson Tank Dr	Clarkston	MI	48346	**800-272-1367**	248-625-8700
Columbian Tectank 2101 S 21st St PO Box 996	Parsons	KS	67357	**800-421-2788**	620-421-0200
Connell LP 1 International Pl 31st Fl	Boston	MA	02110	**800-276-4746**	617-737-2700
Ecodyne MRM Inc 607 1st St SW	Massillon	OH	44646	**888-891-1201**	330-832-5091
Enerfab Inc 4955 Spring Grove Ave	Cincinnati	OH	45232	**800-966-7322**	513-641-0500
Erdle Perforating Co 100 Pixley Industrial Pkwy	Rochester	NY	14624	**800-627-4700**	585-247-4700
GE Nuclear Energy 175 Curtner Ave	San Jose	CA	95150	**800-626-2004**	408-925-1000
Harrington & King Perforating Co Inc 5655 W Fillmore St	Chicago	IL	60644	**800-621-3869**	773-626-1800
Harsco Corp Gas Technologies Group PO Box 8316 *Cust Svc	Camp Hill	PA	17001	**800-821-2975***	717-763-5060
Holman Boiler Works Inc 1956 Singleton Blvd *Sales	Dallas	TX	75212	**800-331-1956***	214-637-0020
ITT Standard 175 Standard Pkwy	Cheektowaga	NY	14227	**800-447-7700**	716-897-2800
James Machine Works Inc 1521 Adams St	Monroe	LA	71201	**800-259-6104**	318-322-6104
Marley Cooling Technologies 7401 W 129th St	Overland Park	KS	66213	**800-462-7539**	913-664-7400
MiTek Industries Inc 14515 N Outer 40 Rd Suite 300	Chesterfield	MO	63017	**800-325-8075**	314-434-1200
Modern Welding Co Inc 2880 New Hartford Rd	Owensboro	KY	42303	**800-922-1932**	270-685-4404
Mohawk Mfg Inc 2175 Beechgrove Pl	Utica	NY	13501	**800-765-3110**	315-793-3000
New Centennial Inc 420 10th Ave PO Box 708	Columbus	GA	31902	**800-241-7541**	706-323-6446
Ohmstede Ltd 895 N Main St	Beaumont	TX	77701	**800-568-2328**	409-833-6375
Park International Corp 1401 Freeman Ave PO Box 4189	Long Beach	CA	90804	**800-624-9118**	562-494-7002
Plant Maintenance Service Corp 3000 Fite Rd	Memphis	TN	38127	**800-514-9701**	901-353-9880
PVI Industries Inc 3209 Galvez Ave PO Box 7124	Fort Worth	TX	76111	**800-784-8326**	817-335-9531
Q3 JMC Inc 605 Miami St	Urbana	OH	43078	**800-767-1422**	937-652-2181
Ross Technology Corp 104 N Maple Ave	Leola	PA	17540	**800-345-8170**	717-656-2095
Roy E Hanson Jr Mfg 1924 Compton Ave	Los Angeles	CA	90011	**800-421-9395**	213-747-7514
Snap-Tite Autoclave Engineers Div 8325 Hessinger Dr	Erie	PA	16509	**800-458-0409**	814-838-5700
Standard Perforating & Mfg 3636 S Kedzie Ave	Chicago	IL	60632	**800-621-0273**	773-254-3232
Superior Boiler Works Inc 3524 E 4th St PO Box 1527	Hutchinson	KS	67504	**800-444-6693**	620-662-6693
Superior Die Set Corp 900 W Drexel Ave	Oak Creek	WI	53154	**800-558-6040**	414-764-4900
Superior Fabricators Inc PO Box 0539	Baldwin	LA	70514	**800-960-7271**	337-923-7271
Sussman Automatic Corp 43-20 34th St	Long Island City	NY	11101	**800-238-3535**	718-937-4500
Thermasys Heat Transfer 2760 Gunter Park Dr W	Montgomery	AL	36109	**800-233-3201**	334-277-1810
Tranter Inc 1900 Old Burk Hwy	Wichita Falls	TX	76307	**800-414-6908**	940-723-7125
Tranter Inc Texas Div 1900 Old Burk Hwy	Wichita Falls	TX	76306	**800-414-6908**	940-723-7125
Trinity Industries Inc LPG Containers Div 2525 N Stemmons Fwy	Dallas	TX	75207	**888-558-8265**	214-589-8213
Weben-Jarco Inc 4007 Platinum Way	Dallas	TX	75237	**800-527-6449**	214-637-0530
Worthington Cylinder Corp 200 Old E Wilson Bridge Rd	Columbus	OH	43085	**800-323-6224**	614-438-3013

93 BOOK BINDING & RELATED WORK

SEE ALSO Printing Companies - Book Printers

Company	City	State	Zip	Toll-Free	Phone
Bindagraphics Inc 2701 Wilmarco Ave	Baltimore	MD	21223	**800-326-0300**	410-362-7200
Booksource Inc 1230 Macklind Ave	Saint Louis	MO	63110	**800-444-0435**	314-647-0600
Bound to Stay Bound Books Inc 1880 W Morton Ave	Jacksonville	IL	62650	**800-637-6586**	217-245-5191
Chilcote Co 2140-60 Superior Ave *Sales	Cleveland	OH	44114	**800-827-5679***	216-781-6000
Heckman Bindery Inc 1010 N Sycamore St	North Manchester	IN	46962	**800-334-3628**	260-982-2107
Library Binding Service 1801 Thompson Ave	Des Moines	IA	50316	**800-247-5323**	515-262-3191
McCain Bindery Systems Inc 3802 W 128th St *Cust Svc	Alsip	IL	60803	**800-225-9363***	708-824-9600
National Library Bindery Co 100 Hembree Park Dr	Roswell	GA	30076	**800-422-7908**	770-442-5490
Perma-Bound 617 E Vandalia Rd	Jacksonville	IL	62650	**800-637-6581**	217-243-5451
Precision Technology Inc 39 Sheep Davis Rd	Pembroke	NH	03275	**800-362-7717**	603-224-9989
Reindl Bindery Co Inc 111 E Reindl Way	Glendale	WI	53212	**800-878-1121**	414-906-1111
Sagebrush Education Resources 2101 N Topeka Blvd	Topeka	KS	66608	**800-255-3502**	785-233-4252
Wert Bookbinding Inc 9975 Allentown Blvd *Cust Svc	Grantville	PA	17028	**800-344-9378***	717-469-0626

94 BOOK, MUSIC, VIDEO CLUBS

Company	City	State	Zip	Toll-Free	Phone
Adventure Library 141 Tompkins Ave *Cust Svc	Pleasantville	NY	10570	**800-823-7323***	914-747-0777
African American Literature Book Club (AALBC) 55 W 116th St Suite 195	Harlem	NY	10026	**866-603-8394**	
Architects & Designers Book Service Doubleday Select Inc 101 Park Ave 23rd Fl	New York	NY	10178	**800-321-7323**	
Audio Book Club Inc 2 Ridgedale Ave	Cedar Knolls	NJ	07927	**800-688-4442**	973-539-9528
Behavioral Science Book Service Doubleday Select Inc 101 Park Ave 23rd Fl	New York	NY	10178	**800-321-7323**	
Black Expressions Doubleday Direct Inc 1225 S Market St	Mechanicsburg	PA	17055	**800-688-4442**	
Computer Books Direct Doubleday Select Inc 101 Park Ave 2nd Fl	New York	NY	10178	**800-321-7323**	
Conservative Book Club PO Box 97197	Washington	DC	20090	**877-222-1964**	202-216-0600
Discovery Channel Book Club Doubleday Select Inc 101 Park Ave 2nd Fl	New York	NY	10178	**800-321-7323**	
Doubleday Book Club Doubleday Direct Inc 1225 S Market St	Mechanicsburg	PA	17055	**800-688-4442**	
Doubleday Direct Inc 1225 S Market St	Mechanicsburg	PA	17055	**800-688-4442**	
Doubleday Large Print Home Library Doubleday Direct Inc 1225 S Market St	Mechanicsburg	PA	17055	**800-688-4442**	
DVD Avenue PO Box 820	Clinton	MD	20735	**800-990-4159**	301-856-4159
DVD Overnight Inc PO Box 4681	Philadelphia	PA	19127	**877-383-1099**	215-483-0733
Early Childhood Teachers' Club Doubleday Select Inc 101 Park Ave 2nd Fl	New York	NY	10178	**800-321-7323**	
GameFly Inc PO Box 6019	Inglewood	CA	90312	**888-986-6400**	
Gameznflix Inc 6960 Eastgate Blvd	Lebanon	TN	37088	**800-613-1543**	
Garden & Landscape Design Book Club Doubleday Select Inc 101 Park Ave 23rd Fl	New York	NY	10178	**800-321-7323**	
Good Cook Book-of-the-Month Club Inc 1271 Ave of the Americas 3rd Fl	New York	NY	10020	**800-233-1066**	212-522-4200
HomeStyle Books Book-of-the-Month Club Inc 1271 Ave of the Americas 3rd Fl	New York	NY	10020	**800-233-1066**	212-522-4200
Library of Science Book Club Doubleday Select Inc 101 Park Ave 2nd Fl	New York	NY	10178	**800-321-7323**	
Library of Speech-Language Pathology Doubleday Select Inc 101 Park Ave 2nd Fl	New York	NY	10178	**800-321-7323**	
Literary Guild Doubleday Direct Inc 1225 S Market St	Mechanicsburg	PA	17055	**800-688-4442**	
Military Book Club Doubleday Direct Inc 1225 S Market St	Mechanicsburg	PA	17055	**800-688-4442**	
Musical Heritage Society 1710 Hwy 35 *Cust Svc	Oakhurst	NJ	07755	**800-333-4647***	732-531-7000
Mystery Guild Doubleday Direct Inc 1225 S Market St	Mechanicsburg	PA	17055	**800-688-4442**	
NetFlix Inc 970 University Ave *NASDAQ: NFLX* ■ *Cust Svc	Los Gatos	CA	95032	**888-638-3549***	408-399-3700
Nurse's Book Society Doubleday Select Inc 101 Park Ave 2nd Fl	New York	NY	10178	**800-321-7323**	

Name / Address	City	State	ZIP	Toll-Free	Phone
Outdoorsman's Edge Doubleday Direct Inc 1225 S Market St	Mechanicsburg	PA	17055	**800-688-4442**	
Prevention Book Club 33 E Minor St	Emmaus	PA	18098	**800-914-9363***	610-967-5171
*Cust Svc					
Primary Teachers' Book Club Doubleday Select Inc 101 Park Ave 2nd Fl	New York	NY	10178	**800-321-7323**	
Reader's Subscription Doubleday Select Inc 101 Park Ave 2nd Fl	New York	NY	10178	**800-321-7323**	
Scholastic Arrow Book Club Scholastic Inc 557 Broadway	New York	NY	10012	**800-724-6527***	212-343-6100
*Orders					
Scholastic Firefly Book Club Scholastic Inc 557 Broadway	New York	NY	10012	**800-724-6527***	212-343-6100
*Orders					
Scholastic Lucky Book Club Scholastic Inc 557 Broadway	New York	NY	10012	**800-724-6527***	212-343-6100
*Orders					
Scholastic Seesaw Book Club PO Box 7503	Jefferson City	MO	65102	**800-724-2424**	
Scholastic TAB Book Club Scholastic Inc 557 Broadway	New York	NY	10012	**800-724-6527***	212-343-6100
*Orders					
Science Fiction Book Club Doubleday Direct Inc 1225 S Market St	Mechanicsburg	PA	17055	**800-688-4442**	
Stage & Screen BOOKSPAN 1225 S Market St	Mechanicsburg	PA	17055	**800-688-4442**	
TrollCarnival Book Club PO Box 7504	Jefferson City	MO	65102	**800-654-3037**	
Venus Book Club Bookspan 1225 S Market St	Mechanicsburg	PA	17055	**800-688-4442**	
Writer's Digest Book Club 4700 E Galbraith Rd	Cincinnati	OH	45236	**800-888-6880***	513-531-2690
*Cust Svc					

95 BOOK PRODUCERS

Name / Address	City	State	ZIP	Toll-Free	Phone
Evanston Publishing Inc 4824 Brownsboro Ctr	Louisville	KY	40207	**800-594-5190**	502-899-1919
Scientific American Inc 415 Madison Ave	New York	NY	10017	**800-333-1199***	212-451-8550
*Cust Svc					

96 BOOK STORES

Name / Address	City	State	ZIP	Toll-Free	Phone
A1Books.com 35 Love Ln	Netcong	NJ	07857	**877-212-6657***	973-426-9995
*Cust Svc					
Amazon.com Inc PO Box 81226	Seattle	WA	98108	**800-201-7575***	206-622-2335
NASDAQ: AMZN ■ *Cust Svc					
Archambault Group Inc 500 rue Sainte-Catherine E	Montreal	QC	H2L2C6	**877-849-8589**	514-849-6206
Atlantic Book Warehouse 979 Bethlehem Pike	Montgomeryville	PA	18936	**800-237-7323**	215-661-0450
Book Passage 51 Tamal Vista Blvd	Corte Madera	CA	94925	**800-999-7909**	415-835-1020
Book Soup 8818 Sunset Blvd	West Hollywood	CA	90069	**800-764-2665**	310-659-3110
BookPeople 603 N Lamar	Austin	TX	78703	**800-853-9757**	512-472-5050
Books & Books 265 Aragon Ave	Coral Gables	FL	33134	**888-626-6576**	305-442-4408
Books on the Square 471 Angell St	Providence	RI	02906	**888-669-9660**	401-331-9097
BookSense.com 828 S Broadway	Tarrytown	NY	10591	**800-637-0037**	914-591-2665
Borders Group Inc 100 Phoenix Dr	Ann Arbor	MI	48108	**800-566-6616***	734-477-1100
NYSE: BGP ■ *Cust Svc					
Borders Inc 100 Phoenix Dr	Ann Arbor	MI	48108	**800-566-6616***	734-477-1100
*Cust Svc					
Boulder Book Store 1107 Pearl St	Boulder	CO	80302	**800-244-4651**	303-447-2074
Cody's Books Inc 2454 Telegraph Ave	Berkeley	CA	94704	**800-995-1180**	510-845-7852
Deseret Book Co PO Box 30178	Salt Lake City	UT	84130	**800-453-4532***	801-534-1515
*Sales					
EBSCO Book Services PO Box 1943	Birmingham	AL	35201	**800-815-9627***	205-991-6600
*Cust Svc					
eFollett.com 1818 Swift Dr	Oak Brook	IL	60522	**800-381-5151**	
Elliott Bay Book Company 101 S Main St	Seattle	WA	98104	**800-962-5311**	206-624-6600
Follett Corp 2233 West St	River Grove	IL	60171	**800-621-4345**	708-583-2000
Follett Higher Education Group 1818 Swift Dr	Oak Brook	IL	60523	**800-323-4506**	630-279-2330
Full Circle Bookstore 50 Penn Pl	Oklahoma City	OK	73118	**800-683-7323**	405-842-2900
Grason PO Box 669007	Charlotte	NC	28254	**800-487-0433**	
Half.com Inc 500 S Gravers Rd	Plymouth Meeting	PA	19462	**800-545-9857***	610-567-1090
*Cust Svc					
Harvard Coop Society 1400 Massachusetts Ave	Cambridge	MA	02138	**800-242-1882**	617-499-2000
Hastings Entertainment Inc 3601 Plains Blvd	Amarillo	TX	79102	**877-427-8464***	806-351-2300
NASDAQ: HAST ■ *Cust Svc					
LibertyTree 100 Swan Way	Oakland	CA	94621	**800-927-8733**	510-568-6047
Little Professor Book Centers Inc PO Box 3160	Ann Arbor	MI	48106	**800-899-6232**	734-663-8733
Matthews Book Co Inc 11559 Rock Island Ct	Maryland Heights	MO	63043	**800-633-2665**	314-432-1400
Matthews Medical & Scientific Book Inc 11559 Rock Island Ct	Maryland Heights	MO	63043	**800-633-2665**	314-432-1400
Media Play 10400 Yellow Circle Dr	Minnetonka	MN	55343	**800-371-4425***	952-932-7700
*Cust Svc					
Northshire Bookstore 4869 Main St	Manchester Center	VT	05255	**800-437-3700**	802-362-2200
Olsson's Books & Records 106 S Union St	Alexandria	VA	22314	**800-989-8084**	703-684-0032
Page One Bookstore 11018 Montgomery Blvd NE	Albuquerque	NM	87111	**800-521-4122**	505-294-2026
Parable Christian Stores 3563 Empleo St	San Luis Obispo	CA	93401	**888-644-0500**	805-543-2644
Poisoned Pen Bookstore 4014 N Goldwater Blvd	Scottsdale	AZ	85251	**888-560-9919**	480-947-2974
Politics & Prose Bookstore 5015 Connecticut Ave	Washington	DC	20008	**800-722-0790**	202-364-1919
Powell's Books Inc 7 NW 9th Ave	Portland	OR	97209	**800-878-7323**	503-228-0540
Powell's City of Books 1005 W Burnside St	Portland	OR	97209	**800-878-7323**	503-228-4651
Prairie Lights Bookstore 15 S Dubuque St	Iowa City	IA	52240	**800-295-2665**	319-337-2681
ReadMe.Doc Discount Computer Books Inc PO Box 21450	Lehigh Valley	PA	18002	**800-678-1473**	610-317-8800
Shaman Drum Bookshop 311-315 S State St	Ann Arbor	MI	48104	**800-490-7023**	734-662-7407
Social Studies School Service 10200 Jefferson Blvd Box 802	Culver City	CA	90232	**800-421-4246**	310-839-2436
Square Books 160 Courthouse Sq	Oxford	MS	38655	**800-648-4001**	662-236-2262
Stacey's 581 Market St	San Francisco	CA	94105	**800-233-8467**	415-421-4687
Steve's Books & Magazines 2612 S Harvard	Tulsa	OK	74114	**888-743-0989**	918-743-3544
Tatnuck Bookseller & Sons 335 Chandler St	Worcester	MA	01602	**800-642-6657**	508-756-7644
Tattered Cover Book Store Inc 1628 16th St	Denver	CO	80202	**800-833-9327**	303-436-1070
University Press Books 2430 Bancroft Way	Berkeley	CA	94704	**800-676-8722**	510-548-0585
Varsity Group Inc 1850 M St NW Suite 1150	Washington	DC	20036	**877-827-2665**	202-667-3400
NASDAQ: VSTY					
Walden Book Co Inc 100 Phoenix Dr	Ann Arbor	MI	48108	**800-566-6616**	734-477-1100
WordsWorth Books 30 Brattle St	Cambridge	MA	02138	**800-899-2202**	617-354-5201
YesAsia.com Inc 1192 Cherry Ave	San Bruno	CA	94066	**888-716-5753**	650-517-5100

97 BOOKS, PERIODICALS, NEWSPAPERS - WHOL

Name / Address	City	State	ZIP	Toll-Free	Phone
Advanced Marketing Services Inc 5880 Oberlin Dr Suite 400	San Diego	CA	92121	**800-695-3580**	858-457-2500
NYSE: MKT					
Austin News Agency Inc 4414 E Saint Elmo Rd	Austin	TX	78744	**800-542-0060**	512-447-6026
Baker & Taylor Books 2709 Water Ridge Pkwy Suite 500	Charlotte	NC	28217	**800-775-1800**	704-357-3500
Baker & Taylor Inc 2550 W Tyvola Rd Suite 300	Charlotte	NC	28217	**800-775-1800**	704-998-3100
BellSouth Directory Sales Center 2200 Riverchase Ctr Suite 600	Birmingham	AL	35244	**800-241-4558**	
Blackwell North America Inc 6024 SW Jean Rd Bldg G	Lake Oswego	OR	97035	**800-547-6426**	503-684-1140
Blackwell's Information Services 160 9th Ave	Runnemede	NJ	08078	**800-221-3306**	856-312-2690
BMI Educational Services PO Box 800	Dayton	NJ	08810	**800-222-8100**	732-329-6991
Book Wholesalers Inc DBA BWI 1847 Mercer Rd Suite D	Lexington	KY	40511	**800-888-4478**	859-231-9789
Bookazine Co Inc 75 Hook Rd	Bayonne	NJ	07002	**800-221-8112**	201-339-7777
Booksource Inc 1230 Macklind Ave	Saint Louis	MO	63110	**800-444-0435**	314-647-0600
Brodart Co Book Services Div 500 Arch St	Williamsport	PA	17701	**800-233-8467**	570-326-2461
BWI 1847 Mercer Rd Suite D	Lexington	KY	40511	**800-888-4478**	859-231-9789
Chas Levy Circulating Co 1930 George St Unit 1	Melrose Park	IL	60160	**800-549-5389**	
Directory Distributing Assoc 172 Distribution Dr	Birmingham	AL	35209	**800-682-4000**	
Directory Distributing Assoc 160 Corporate Woods Ct	Bridgeton	MO	63044	**800-325-1964**	314-592-8600
EBSCO Reception Room Subscription Services PO Box 830460	Birmingham	AL	35283	**800-527-5901**	
Educational Development Corp 10302 E 55th Pl	Tulsa	OK	74146	**800-475-4522**	918-622-4522
NASDAQ: EDUC					
Empire State News Corp 2800 Walden Ave	Cheektowaga	NY	14225	**800-414-6247**	716-681-1100
Follett Corp 2233 West St	River Grove	IL	60171	**800-621-4345**	708-583-2000
Follett Educational Services 1433 International Pkwy	Woodridge	IL	60517	**800-621-4272**	630-972-5600
Follett Library Resources 1340 Ridgeview Dr	McHenry	IL	60050	**888-511-5114**	815-759-1700
Harlequin Enterprises Ltd Distribution Center 3010 Walden Ave	Depew	NY	14043	**800-873-8635**	716-684-1800
Independent Publishers Group 814 N Franklin St	Chicago	IL	60610	**800-888-4741***	312-337-0747
*Orders					
Ingram Book Group 1 Ingram Blvd	La Vergne	TN	37086	**800-937-8000**	615-793-5000
JA Majors Co 1401 Lakeway Dr	Lewisville	TX	75057	**800-633-1851**	972-353-1100
MBS Textbook Exchange Inc 2711 W Ash St	Columbia	MO	65203	**800-325-0530**	573-445-2243
Midwest Library Service Inc 11443 St Charles Rock Rd	Bridgeton	MO	63044	**800-325-8833**	314-739-3100
MindBranch Inc 160 Water St	Williamstown	MA	01267	**800-774-4410**	413-458-7600
Nebraska Book Co Inc 4700 S 19th St	Lincoln	NE	68512	**800-869-0366**	402-421-7300
NetLibrary Inc 4888 Pearl East Cir Suite 103	Boulder	CO	80301	**800-413-4557**	303-415-2548
Publishers Group Inc 1400 65th St Suite 250	Emeryville	CA	94608	**800-788-3123**	510-595-3664
Publishers Group West 1400 65th St Suite250	Emeryville	CA	94608	**800-788-3123**	510-595-3664
Quality Books Inc 1003 West Pines Rd	Oregon	IL	61061	**800-323-4241***	815-732-4450
*Cust Svc					
Rittenhouse Book Distributors Inc 511 Feheley Dr	King of Prussia	PA	19406	**800-345-6425***	610-277-1414
*Cust Svc					
Riverside Distributors 636 S Oak St	Iowa Falls	IA	50126	**800-247-5111**	641-648-4271
Saint Marie's Gopher News Co 9000 10th Ave N	Minneapolis	MN	55427	**800-279-2665**	763-546-5300
Scholastic Book Fairs Inc 1080 Greenwood Blvd	Lake Mary	FL	32746	**800-874-4809**	407-829-7300
Southwestern/Great American 2451 Atrium Way	Nashville	TN	37214	**800-251-1542***	615-391-2500
*Cust Svc					
Spring Arbor Distributors 1 Ingram Blvd	La Vergne	TN	37086	**800-395-4340**	
Texas Book Co 8501 Technology Cir	Greenville	TX	75403	**800-527-1016**	903-455-6937
Turtleback Books 5701 Manufacturers Dr	Madison	WI	53704	**800-448-8939**	
Vulcan Service PO Box 522	Birmingham	AL	35201	**800-841-9600**	205-991-1374
YBP Library Services 999 Maple St	Contoocook	NH	03229	**800-258-3774**	603-746-3102

98 BOTANICAL GARDENS & ARBORETA

SEE ALSO Zoos & Wildlife Parks

Name / Address	City	State	ZIP	Toll-Free	Phone
Bellingrath Gardens & Home 12401 Bellingrath Garden Rd	Theodore	AL	36582	**800-247-8420**	251-973-2217
Brookgreen Gardens 1931 Brookgreen Dr	Murrells Inlet	SC	29576	**800-849-1931**	843-235-6000
Butchart Gardens 800 Benvenuto Ave	Brentwood Bay	BC	V8M1J8	**866-652-4422**	250-652-4422

Classified Section

Name / Address	City	State	ZIP	Toll-Free	Phone
Callaway Gardens Resort PO Box 2000	Pine Mountain	GA	31822	**800-225-5292**	706-663-2281
Cedar Crest College 100 College Dr	Allentown	PA	18104	**800-360-1222**	610-437-4471
Chimney Rock Park Hwy 64/74A PO Box 39	Chimney Rock	NC	28720	**800-277-9611**	828-625-9611
Cincinnati Zoo & Botanical Garden 3400 Vine St	Cincinnati	OH	45220	**800-944-4776**	513-281-4701
Dawes Arboretum 7770 Jacksontown Rd SE	Newark	OH	43056	**800-443-2937**	740-323-2355
Dow Gardens 1018 W Main St	Midland	MI	48640	**800-362-4874**	989-631-2677
Fetzer Vineyards 13601 Old River Rd	Hopland	CA	95449	**800-846-8637**	707-744-1250
Franklin Park Conservatory & Botanical Garden 1777 E Broad St	Columbus	OH	43203	**800-241-7275**	614-645-8733
Frederik Meijer Gardens & Sculpture Park 1000 East Beltline Ave NE	Grand Rapids	MI	49525	**888-974-1580**	616-957-1580
Gardens of the American Rose Center 8877 Jefferson-Paige Rd	West Shreveport	LA	71119	**800-637-6534**	318-938-5402
Garvan Woodland Gardens 550 Arkridge Rd PO Box 22240	Hot Springs	AR	71903	**800-366-4664**	501-262-9300
Georgia Golf Hall of Fame Botanical Gardens 1 Eleventh St	Augusta	GA	30901	**888-874-4443**	706-724-4443
Green Bay Botanical Garden PO Box 12644	Green Bay	WI	54307	**877-355-4224**	920-490-9457
Hillwood Museum & Gardens 4155 Linnean Ave NW	Washington	DC	20008	**877-445-5966**	202-686-8500
Huntsville Botanical Garden 4747 Bob Wallace Ave	Huntsville	AL	35805	**877-930-4447**	256-830-4447
Hywet Stan Hall & Gardens 714 N Portage Path	Akron	OH	44403	**888-836-5533**	330-836-5533
Idaho Botanical Garden 2355 N Penitentiary Rd	Boise	ID	83712	**877-527-8233**	208-343-8649
International Peace Garden PO Box 419	Boissevain	MB	R0K0E0	**800-432-6733**	204-534-2510
International Peace Garden Rt 1 Box 116	Dunseith	ND	58329	**888-432-6733**	701-263-4390
Lady Bird Johnson Wildflower Center 4801 LaCrosse Ave	Austin	TX	78739	**877-945-3357**	512-292-4200
Lakewold Gardens 12317 Gravelly Lake Dr SW	Lakewood	WA	98499	**888-858-4106**	253-584-4106
Longwood Gardens 1001 Conservatory Rd	Kennett Square	PA	19348	**800-737-5500**	610-388-1000
Magnolia Plantation & Gardens 3550 Ashley River Rd	Charleston	SC	29414	**800-367-3517**	843-571-1266
Meijer Frederik Gardens & Sculpture Park 1000 East Beltline Ave NE	Grand Rapids	MI	49525	**888-974-1580**	616-957-1580
Niagara Parks Botanical Gardens 2565 Niagara Pkwy N PO box 150	Niagara Falls	ON	L2E6T2	**877-642-7275**	905-356-8554
Oregon Garden 879 W Main St PO Box 155	Iverton	OR	97381	**877-674-2733**	503-874-8100
Philbrook Museum of Art & Gardens 2727 S Rockford Rd	Tulsa	OK	74114	**800-324-7941**	918-749-7941
Pierre Native Plant Arboretum Izaak Walton Rd	Pierre	SD	57501	**800-228-5254**	605-773-3594
Polynesian Cultural Center 55-370 Kamehameha Hwy	Laie	HI	96762	**800-367-7060**	808-293-3000
Schreiner's Iris Gardens 3625 Quinaby Rd NE	Salem	OR	97303	**800-525-2367**	503-393-3232
Shambhala Mountain Center 4921 County Rd 68C	Red Feather Lakes	CO	80545	**888-788-7221**	970-881-2184
Stan Hywet Hall & Gardens 714 N Portage Path	Akron	OH	44403	**888-836-5533**	330-836-5533
Tryon Palace Historic Sites & Gardens 610 Pollock St	New Bern	NC	28562	**800-767-1560**	252-514-4900
Vanderbilt University 2201 W End Ave	Nashville	TN	37235	**800-288-0432**	615-322-7311
Washington National Cathedral 3101 Wisconsin Ave NW	Washington	DC	20016	**800-622-6304**	202-537-6200
Winterthur Museum Garden & Library 5105 Kennett Pike	Winterthur	DE	19735	**800-448-3883**	302-888-4600

BOTTLES - GLASS

SEE Glass Jars & Bottles

99 BOTTLES - PLASTICS

Name / Address	City	State	ZIP	Toll-Free	Phone
Alpha Plastics Inc 1555 Page Industrial Blvd	Saint Louis	MO	63132	**800-421-4772**	314-427-4300
American Quality Products 9115-1 Dice Rd	Santa Fe Springs	CA	90670	**800-245-3737**	562-946-1616
Colt's Plastics Co PO Box 429	Dayville	CT	06241	**800-222-2658**	860-774-2277
Lerman Container Co 10 Great Hill Rd	Naugatuck	CT	06770	**800-453-7626**	203-723-6681
NEW Plastics Corp 112 4th St	Luxemburg	WI	54217	**800-666-5207**	920-845-2326
Novapak Corp 370 Stevers Crossing Rd	Philmont	NY	12565	**800-672-7721**	518-672-7721
Premier Plastics 635 E 15th St	Tacoma	WA	98421	**800-422-6864**	253-627-2151
Progressive Plastics Inc 14801 Emery Ave	Cleveland	OH	44135	**800-252-0053**	216-252-5595
PVC Container Corp 2 Industrial Way W	Eatontown	NJ	07724	**800-975-2784**	732-542-0060
Quality Containers of New England 247 Portland St Suite 300	Yarmouth	ME	04096	**800-639-1550**	207-846-5420
Silgan Plastics Corp 14515 N Outer Forty Suite 210	Chesterfield	MO	63017	**800-274-5426**	314-542-9223

100 BOWLING CENTERS

Name / Address	City	State	ZIP	Toll-Free	Phone
AMF Bowling Worldwide Inc 8100 AMF Dr	Mechanicsville	VA	23111	**800-342-5263**	804-730-4000
Bowl New England Inc 215 Lower Mountain View Dr	Colchester	VT	05446	**800-633-3535**	802-655-3468

101 BOXES - CORRUGATED & SOLID FIBER

Name / Address	City	State	ZIP	Toll-Free	Phone
Advanced Design & Packaging Inc 5090 McDougall Dr SW	Atlanta	GA	30336	**800-333-2487**	404-699-1952
Akers Packaging Service Inc 2820 Lefferson Rd	Middletown	OH	45044	**800-327-7308**	513-422-6312
Aldelano Packaging Corp 3525 Walnut Ave Suite A	Chino	CA	91710	**800-509-9212**	909-861-3970
Artistic Carton Co 1975 Big Timber Rd	Elgin	IL	60123	**877-784-7842**	847-741-0247
Arvco Container Corp 845 Gibson St	Kalamazoo	MI	49001	**800-968-9128**	269-381-0900
Atlas Container Corp 8140 Telegraph Rd	Severn	MD	21144	**800-394-4894**	410-551-6300
Bates Container Inc 6433 Davis Blvd	North Richland Hills	TX	76180	**800-792-8736**	817-498-3200
Beacon Container Corp 700 W 1st St	Birdsboro	PA	19508	**888-211-5530**	610-582-2222
Buckeye Container Inc 3350 Long Rd	Wooster	OH	44691	**800-686-8692**	330-264-6336
Cameo Container Corp 1415 W 44th St	Chicago	IL	60609	**800-621-1030**	773-254-1030
Carolina Container Co 909 Prospect St	High Point	NC	27260	**800-627-0825**	336-883-7146
Carton Service Inc First Quality Dr	Shelby	OH	44875	**800-533-7744**	419-342-5010
Cornell Paper & Box Inc 162 Van Dyke St	Brooklyn	NY	11231	**888-251-1297**	718-875-3202
Corrugated Supplies Corp 5101 W 65th St	Bedford Park	IL	60638	**888-826-2738**	708-458-5525
Delta Corrugated Paper Products Corp W Ruby & Railroad Ave	Palisades Park	NJ	07650	**800-932-6937**	201-941-1910
Franks Industries Inc 924 S Meridian PO Box 127	Sunman	IN	47041	**800-446-4844**	812-623-1140
Gibraltar Packaging Group Inc DBA Great Plains Packaging Co 2000 Summit Ave	Hastings	NE	68902	**800-456-1366**	402-463-1366
Great Lakes Packaging Corp W 190 N 11393 Carnegie Dr	Germantown	WI	53022	**800-261-4572**	262-255-2100
Great Northern Corp 395 Stroebe Rd	Appleton	WI	54914	**800-236-3671**	920-739-3671
Green Bay Packaging Inc 1700 N Webster Ct	Green Bay	WI	54302	**800-558-4008**	920-433-5111
HP Neun Co Inc 75 N Main St	Fairport	NY	14450	**800-724-2641**	585-388-1360
Key Container Corp 21 Campbell St	Pawtucket	RI	02861	**800-343-8811**	401-723-2000
Lawrence Paper Co 2801 Lakeview Rd	Lawrence	KS	66049	**800-535-4553**	785-843-8111
Liberty Carton Co 870 Louisiana Ave S	Minneapolis	MN	55426	**800-328-1784**	763-540-9600
Lone Star Corrugated Container Corp 700 N Wildwood	Irving	TX	75061	**800-552-6937**	972-579-1551
Longview Fibre Co Central & Eastern Container Div 3832 N 3rd St	Milwaukee	WI	53212	**800-929-8111**	414-264-8100
Love Box Co Inc PO Box 546	Wichita	KS	67201	**800-937-5229**	316-838-0851
Menasha Corp 1645 Bergstrom Rd	Neenah	WI	54956	**800-558-5073**	920-751-1000
Menasha Packaging Co 1645 Bergstrom Rd	Neenah	WI	54956	**800-558-5073**	920-751-1000
Multi-Wall Corp Div Real Reel Corp 50 Taylor Dr *Cust Svc	East Providence	RI	02916	**800-992-4166***	401-434-1070
National Packaging Cos Display Group 105 Ave L	Newark	NJ	07105	**800-589-5808**	973-589-2155
Neun HP Co Inc 75 N Main St	Fairport	NY	14450	**800-724-2641**	585-388-1360
North American Container Corp 5851 Riverview Rd	Mableton	GA	30126	**800-929-3468**	404-691-0611
Packaging Corp of America 1900 W Field Ct *NYSE: PKG*	Lake Forest	IL	60045	**888-828-2850**	847-482-2000
Pactiv Corp 1900 W Field Ct *NYSE: PTV*	Lake Forest	IL	60045	**888-828-2850**	847-482-2000
Rand-Whitney Container Corp 1 Agrand St	Worcester	MA	01607	**800-370-9111**	508-791-2301
Real Reel Corp Multi-Wall Corp Div 50 Taylor Dr *Cust Svc	East Providence	RI	02916	**800-992-4166***	401-434-1070
Rock-Tenn Co 504 Thrasher St *NYSE: RKT*	Norcross	GA	30071	**800-762-5836**	770-448-2193
Rock-Tenn Co Corrugated Packaging & Display Div 504 Thrasher St	Norcross	GA	30071	**800-762-5836**	770-448-2193
RTS Packaging LLC 504 Thrasher St	Norcross	GA	30071	**800-822-1914**	770-448-2244
Smurfit-Stone Container Corp 150 N Michigan Ave 17th Fl *NASDAQ: SSCC*	Chicago	IL	60601	**877-772-2999**	312-346-6600
Stronghaven Inc 5090 MacDougall Dr SW	Atlanta	GA	30336	**800-233-2487**	404-699-9680
Tecumseh Corrugated Box Co 707 S Evans	Tecumseh	MI	49286	**800-837-8374**	517-423-2126
Temple-Inland Forest Products Corp 303 S Temple Dr	Diboll	TX	75941	**800-262-5512**	936-829-5511
Tharco Inc 2222 Grant Ave	San Lorenzo	CA	94580	**800-772-2332**	510-276-8600
TimBar Packaging & Display 148 N Penn St PO Box 449	Hanover	PA	17331	**800-572-6061**	717-632-4727
Unicorr Connecticut Container Corp 455 Sackett Point Rd	North Haven	CT	06473	**800-229-4269**	203-248-2161
Welch Packaging Group 1020 Herman St	Elkhart	IN	46516	**800-246-2475**	574-295-2460
York Container Co 138 Mt Scion Rc	York	PA	17402	**800-772-9675**	717-757-7611

102 BOXES - PAPERBOARD

Name / Address	City	State	ZIP	Toll-Free	Phone
AGI Inc 1950 N Ruby St	Melrose Park	IL	60160	**800-677-9110**	708-344-9100
Aldelano Packaging Corp 3525 Walnut Ave Suite A	Chino	CA	91710	**800-509-9212**	909-861-3970
Apex Paper Box Co 5601 Walworth Ave *Cust Svc	Cleveland	OH	44102	**800-438-2269***	216-631-4000
Astronics Corp 1801 Elmwood Ave *NASDAQ: ATRO*	Buffalo	NY	14207	**800-666-3722**	716-447-9013
Burd & Fletcher Co Inc 5151 E Geospace Dr	Independence	MO	64056	**800-821-2776**	816-257-0291
Cadmus Communications Corp Whitehall Group Div 2750 Whitehall Park Dr	Charlotte	NC	28273	**800-733-4318**	704-583-6600
Carton Service Inc First Quality Dr	Shelby	OH	44875	**800-533-7744**	419-342-5010
Complemar Partners 175 Humboldt St	Rochester	NY	14610	**800-388-5126**	585-647-5800
Cornell Paper & Box Inc 162 Van Dyke St	Brooklyn	NY	11231	**888-251-1297**	718-875-3202
Dee Paper Co Inc 100 Broomall St	Chester	PA	19013	**800-359-0041**	610-876-9285
Diamond Packaging Co Inc PO Box 23620	Rochester	NY	14692	**800-333-4079**	585-334-8030
Field Container Co LP 1500 Nicholas Blvd	Elk Grove Village	IL	60007	**888-343-5334**	847-437-1700
Flashfold Carton Inc 1140 Hayden St	Fort Wayne	IN	46803	**800-589-9060**	260-423-9431
Franks Industries Inc 924 S Meridian PO Box 127	Sunman	IN	47041	**800-446-4844**	812-623-1140
Gibraltar Packaging Group Inc DBA Great Plains Packaging Co 2000 Summit Ave	Hastings	NE	68902	**800-456-1366**	402-463-1366
Gift Box Corp of America 225 5th Ave Rm 1223	New York	NY	10010	**800-443-8269**	212-684-5113
Graphic Packaging International 4455 Table Mountain Dr *NYSE: GPK*	Golden	CO	80403	**800-677-2886**	303-215-4600
Great Plains Packaging Co 2000 Summit Ave	Hastings	NE	68902	**800-456-1366**	402-463-1366
Harvard Folding Box Co Inc 71 Linden St	Lynn	MA	01905	**800-876-1246**	781-598-1600
HP Neun Co Inc 75 N Main St	Fairport	NY	14450	**800-724-2641**	585-388-1360
Hub Folding Box Co Inc 774 Norfolk St	Mansfield	MA	02048	**800-334-1113**	508-339-0005

Classified Section

Company	City	State	Zip	Toll-Free	Phone
Huhtamaki Americas 9201 Packaging Dr	DeSoto	KS	66018	**800-255-4243**	913-583-3025
Love Box Co Inc PO Box 546	Wichita	KS	67201	**800-937-5229**	316-838-0851
Mafcote Industries Inc 108 Main St *Cust Svc	Norwalk	CT	06851	**800-526-4280***	203-847-8500
Malnove Inc 13434 F St	Omaha	NE	68137	**800-228-9877**	402-330-1100
Menasha Corp 1645 Bergstrom Rd	Neenah	WI	54956	**800-558-5073**	920-751-1000
MOD-PAC Corp 1801 Elmwood Ave *NASDAQ: MPAC* ■ *Cust Svc	Buffalo	NY	14207	**800-666-3722***	716-873-0640
Neun HP Co Inc 75 N Main St	Fairport	NY	14450	**800-724-2641**	585-388-1360
Pactiv Corp 1900 W Field Ct *NYSE: PTV*	Lake Forest	IL	60045	**888-828-2850**	847-482-2000
Panoramic Inc 1500 N Parker Dr	Janesville	WI	53545	**800-333-1394**	608-754-8850
Paragon Packaging Inc 49-B Sherwood Terr	Lake Bluff	IL	60044	**888-615-0065**	847-615-0065
Resolution Packaging Inc 3 Borinski Dr Suite E	Lincoln Park	NJ	07035	**800-556-1321**	973-633-7795
Rex Packaging 136 Eastport Rd	Jacksonville	FL	32218	**800-821-0798**	904-757-5210
Rice Packaging Inc 356 Somers Rd	Ellington	CT	06029	**800-367-6725**	860-872-8341
Rock-Tenn Co 504 Thrasher St *NYSE: RKT*	Norcross	GA	30071	**800-762-5836**	770-448-2193
Rock-Tenn Co Folding Carton Div PO Box 4098	Norcross	GA	30091	**800-762-5836**	770-448-2193
Saint Joseph Packaging Inc 4515 Easton Rd	Saint Joseph	MO	64503	**800-383-3000**	816-233-3181
Seaboard Folding Box Corp 35 Daniels St	Fitchburg	MA	01420	**800-225-6313**	978-342-8921
Smurfit-Stone Container Corp 150 N Michigan Ave 17th Fl *NASDAQ: SSCC*	Chicago	IL	60601	**877-772-2999**	312-346-6600
Sonoco Products Co 1 N 2nd St *NYSE: SON*	Hartsville	SC	29550	**800-377-2692**	843-383-7000
Sterling Paper Co 2155 E Castor Ave	Philadelphia	PA	19134	**800-745-5350**	215-744-5350
Tetra Pak Inc 101 Corporate Woods Pkwy	Vernon Hills	IL	60061	**800-358-3872**	847-955-6000
Whitehall Group Div Cadmus Communications Corp 2750 Whitehall Park Dr	Charlotte	NC	28273	**800-733-4318**	704-583-6600
Winchester Carton Corp PO Box 597	Eutaw	AL	35462	**800-633-5967**	205-372-3337

103 BREWERIES & MICROBREWERIES

SEE ALSO Malting Products

Company	City	State	Zip	Toll-Free	Phone
Abita Brewing Co 21084 Hwy 36	Covington	LA	70433	**800-737-2311**	985-893-3143
Anheuser-Busch Inc 1 Busch Pl *Cust Svc	Saint Louis	MO	63118	**800-342-5283***	314-577-2000
Boston Beer Co 75 Arlington St *NYSE: SAM*	Boston	MA	02116	**800-372-1131**	617-368-5000
BridgePort Brewing Co 1318 NW Northrup St	Portland	OR	97209	**888-834-7546**	503-241-7179
Full Sail Brewing Co 506 Columbia St	Hood River	OR	97031	**888-244-2337**	541-386-2281
Harpoon Brewery 306 Northern Ave	Boston	MA	02210	**888-427-7666**	617-574-9551
Heineken USA 360 Hamilton Ave Suite 1103	White Plains	NY	10601	**800-811-4951**	914-681-4100
InBev USA 101 Merritt 7 PO Box 5075 *Cust Svc	Norwalk	CT	06856	**800-268-2337***	203-750-6600
Jacob Leinenkugel Brewing Co Hwy 124 N PO Box 368	Chippewa Falls	WI	54729	**888-534-6437**	715-723-5557
Labatt Breweries of Canada 207 Queen's Quay W Suite 299	Toronto	ON	M5J1A7	**800-268-2337**	416-361-5050
Latrobe Brewing Co 119 Jefferson St	Latrobe	PA	15650	**800-245-7892**	724-537-5545
Lion Brewery Inc 700 N Pennsylvania Ave	Wilkes-Barre	PA	18705	**800-233-8327**	570-823-8801
Malt Products Corp 88 Market St	Saddle Brook	NJ	07663	**800-526-0180**	201-845-4420
Molson Coors Brewing Co 1225 17th St Suite 1875 *NYSE: TAP*	Denver	CO	80202	**800-642-6116**	303-277-6661
New Belgium Brewing Co 500 Linden St	Fort Collins	CO	80524	**888-622-4044**	970-221-0524
Odell Brewing Co 800 E Lincoln Ave	Fort Collins	CO	80524	**888-887-2797**	970-498-9070
Pabst Brewing Co 121 Interpark Blvd Suite 300	San Antonio	TX	78216	**800-935-2337**	210-226-0231
Pyramid Breweries Inc 91 S Royal Brougham Way *NASDAQ: PMID*	Seattle	WA	98134	**800-603-3336**	206-682-8322
Rogue Ales Co 2320 OSU Dr	Newport	OR	97365	**800-850-1115**	541-867-3660
Samuel Adams Boston Beer Co 30 Germania St	Boston	MA	02130	**800-372-1131**	617-522-9080
Widmer Bros Brewing Co 929 N Russell St	Portland	OR	97227	**800-943-6371**	503-281-2437

BROKERS

SEE Commodity Contracts Brokers & Dealers; Electronic Communications Networks (ECNs); Insurance Agents, Brokers, Services; Mortgage Lenders & Loan Brokers; Real Estate Agents & Brokers; Securities Brokers & Dealers

104 BRUSHES & BROOMS

SEE ALSO Art Materials & Supplies - Mfr

Company	City	State	Zip	Toll-Free	Phone
Advanced Products Co 1021 Spring Garden St	Philadelphia	PA	19123	**800-755-9852**	215-232-5926
American Brush Co Inc 112 Industrial Blvd	Claremont	NH	03743	**800-225-0392**	603-542-9951
Anderson Products Inc 1040 Southbridge St	Worcester	MA	01610	**800-755-6101**	508-755-6100
Arnold SM Inc 7901 Michigan Ave *Cust Svc	Saint Louis	MO	63111	**800-325-7865***	314-544-4103
Bestt Liebco Corp 1201 Jackson St	Philadelphia	PA	19148	**800-523-9095**	215-336-3400
Brushes Corp 5400 Smith Rd	Brook Park	OH	44142	**800-967-9697**	216-267-8084
Brushtech Inc PO Box 1130 *Cust Svc	Plattsburgh	NY	12901	**800-346-0818***	518-563-8420
Butler Home Products Inc 311 Hopping Brook Rd PO Box 8000	Holliston	MA	01746	**800-343-3368**	508-429-8100
Carlisle Sanitary Maintenance Products 402 S Black River St	Sparta	WI	54656	**800-356-8366**	608-269-2151
Cleveland Wood Products 3871 W 150th St	Cleveland	OH	44111	**800-969-9695**	216-252-1190
Cosgrove Enterprises 16000 NW 49th Ave	Miami	FL	33014	**800-888-3396**	305-623-6700
Crystal Lake Mfg Inc 2225 Hwy 14 W PO Box 159	Autaugaville	AL	36003	**800-633-8720**	334-365-3342
Danline Inc 1 Silver Ct	Springfield	NJ	07081	**800-552-7874**	973-376-1000
Detroit Quality Brush Mfg 32165 Schoolcraft Rd	Livonia	MI	48150	**800-722-3037**	734-525-5660
Felton Brush Inc 7 Burton Dr	Londonderry	NH	03053	**800-258-9702**	603-425-0200
Fuller Brush Co 1 Fuller Way *Cust Svc	Great Bend	KS	67530	**800-438-5537***	620-792-1711
Gordon Brush Mfg Co Inc 6247 Randolph St	Commerce	CA	90040	**800-950-7950**	323-724-7777
Greenwood Mop & Broom Inc PO Drawer 1426	Greenwood	SC	29648	**800-635-6849**	864-227-8411
Harper Brush Works Inc 400 N 2nd	Fairfield	IA	52556	**800-223-7894**	641-472-5186
Industrial Brush Co Inc PO Box 869	Fairfield	NJ	07007	**800-241-9860**	973-575-0455
Industrial Brush Corp PO Box 2608	Pomona	CA	91769	**800-228-6146**	909-591-9341
Industries for the Blind 3220 W Vliet St	Milwaukee	WI	53208	**800-642-8778**	414-933-4319
Keystone Plastics Inc 3451 S Clinton Ave	South Plainfield	NJ	07080	**800-635-5238**	908-561-1300
Laitner Brush Co 1561 Laitner Dr *Cust Svc	Traverse City	MI	49686	**800-423-6805***	231-929-3300
Libman Co 220 N Sheldon St	Arcola	IL	61910	**800-646-6262**	217-268-4200
Linzer Products Corp 248 Wyandanch Ave	Wyandanch	NY	11798	**800-221-0787**	631-253-3333
Magnolia Brush Mfg Inc 1001 N Cedar PO Box 932	Clarksville	TX	75426	**800-248-2261**	903-427-2261
Mill-Rose Co 7995 Tyler Blvd	Mentor	OH	44060	**800-321-3533**	440-255-9171
Milwaukee Dustless Brush Co 10930 W Lapham St	Milwaukee	WI	53214	**800-632-3220**	414-476-1147
Newell Rubbermaid Inc Shur-Line Div 4051 S Iowa Ave	Saint Francis	WI	53235	**800-558-3958**	414-481-4500
O-Cedar Brands Inc 505 N Railroad Ave	North Lake	IL	60164	**800-332-8690**	
Ohio Brush Co 2680 Lisbon Rd	Cleveland	OH	44104	**888-411-3265**	216-791-3265
Osborn International 5401 Hamilton Ave *Cust Svc	Cleveland	OH	44114	**800-720-3358***	216-361-1900
Padco Inc 2220 Elm St SE	Minneapolis	MN	55414	**800-328-5513**	612-378-7270
PFERD Milwaukee Brush Co Inc 30 Jytek Dr	Leominster	MA	01453	**800-336-3444**	978-840-6420
Prager Brush Co Inc 730 Echo St NW	Atlanta	GA	30318	**800-241-5696**	404-875-9292
Richards Brush Co 5200 4th Ave S *Cust Svc	Seattle	WA	98108	**800-732-1110***	206-623-3720
Rutland Products 86 Center St PO Box 340	Rutland	VT	05702	**800-544-1307**	802-775-5519
Sanderson-MacLeod Inc 1199 S Main St	Palmer	MA	01069	**866-522-3481**	413-283-3481
Shur-Line Div Newell Rubbermaid Inc 4051 S Iowa Ave	Saint Francis	WI	53235	**800-558-3958**	414-481-4500
Signature Works Inc 1 Signature Dr	Hazlehurst	MS	39083	**800-647-2468**	601-894-1771
SM Arnold Inc 7901 Michigan Ave *Cust Svc	Saint Louis	MO	63111	**800-325-7865***	314-544-4103
Super Brush Co 165 Front St Suite 4	Chicopee	MA	01013	**800-272-0591**	413-592-4195
Sweepster Inc 2800 N Zeeb Rd	Dexter	MI	48130	**800-456-7100**	734-996-9116
Universal Brush Mfg Co 16200 Dixie Hwy	Markham	IL	60428	**800-323-3474**	708-331-1700
Weiler Corp 1 Wildwood Dr	Cresco	PA	18326	**800-835-9999**	570-595-7495
Wooster Brush Co 604 Madison Ave	Wooster	OH	44691	**800-392-7246**	330-264-4440
Zephyr Mfg Co Inc 200 Mitchell Rd	Sedalia	MO	65301	**800-821-7197**	660-827-0352

105 BUILDING MAINTENANCE SERVICES

SEE ALSO Cleaning Services

Company	City	State	Zip	Toll-Free	Phone
Colin Service Systems Inc 170 Hamilton Ave	White Plains	NY	10601	**800-873-2654**	914-289-2000
Denali Ventures Inc 5613 DTC Pkwy Suite 200	Greenwood Village	CO	80111	**877-290-5590**	
FBG Service Corp 407 S 27th Ave	Omaha	NE	68131	**800-777-8326**	402-346-4422
OneSource 1600 Parkwood Cir Suite 400	Atlanta	GA	30339	**800-424-4477**	770-436-9900

106 BUILDINGS - PREFABRICATED - METAL

Company	City	State	Zip	Toll-Free	Phone
Aluma Shield Industries Inc 725 Summer Hill Dr	Deland	FL	32724	**888-882-5862**	386-626-6789
American Steel Building Co Inc 12218 Robin Blvd	Houston	TX	77045	**800-877-8335**	713-433-5661
Arrow Group Industries Inc 1680 Rt 23 N	Wayne	NJ	07474	**800-851-1085**	973-696-6900
Behlen Mfg Co 4025 E 23rd St	Columbus	NE	68601	**800-553-5520**	402-564-3111
Conley's Mfg & Sales Inc 4344 E Mission Blvd	Montclair	CA	91763	**800-377-8441**	909-627-0981
Dura-Bilt Products Inc PO Box 188	Wellsburg	NY	14894	**800-233-4251**	570-596-2000
Erect-A-Tube Inc 701 W Park St	Harvard	IL	60033	**800-624-9219**	815-943-4091
Four Seasons Sunrooms 5005 Veterans Memorial Hwy	Holbrook	NY	11741	**800-368-7732**	631-563-4000
Garco Building Systems 2714 S Garfield Rd	Airway Heights	WA	99001	**800-941-2291**	509-244-5611
Gulf States Manufacturers 101 Airport Rd PO Box 1128	Starkville	MS	39760	**800-844-4853**	662-323-8021
Imperial Industries Inc 505 Industrial Park Ave	Mosinee	WI	54455	**800-558-2945**	715-359-0200
Kay Home Products 26210 Emery Rd Suite 101	Cleveland	OH	44128	**800-600-7009**	216-896-6900
Mesco Metal Buildings 400 N Kimball Ave PO Box 93629	Southlake	TX	76092	**800-556-3726**	817-488-8511
Metal Building Components Inc 10943 Sam Houston Pkwy W	Houston	TX	77064	**877-713-6224**	281-445-8555
Metal Sales Mfg Corp 7800 State Rd 60	Sellersburg	IN	47172	**800-406-7387**	812-246-1935
Mid-West Metallic Building Co 7301 Fairview St	Houston	TX	77041	**800-777-9378**	713-466-7788
Miracle Steel Corp 600 Oakwood Rd PO Box 1266	Watertown	SD	57201	**888-508-4545**	605-886-7885
Mobile Mini Inc 7420 S Kyrene Rd Suite 101 *NASDAQ: MINI*	Tempe	AZ	85283	**800-288-5669**	480-894-6311
Morton Buildings Inc 252 W Adams St	Morton	IL	61550	**800-426-6686**	309-263-7474
National Greenhouse Co 6 Industrial Dr	Pana	IL	62557	**800-826-9314**	217-562-9333

Classified Section

				Toll-Free	Phone
NCI Building Systems Inc 7301 Fairview St	Houston	TX	77041	**800-777-9378**	713-466-7788
NYSE: NCS					
Pacific Building Systems					
2100 N Pacific Hwy	Woodburn	OR	97071	**800-727-7844**	503-981-9581
Package Industries Inc 15 Harback Rd	Sutton	MA	01590	**800-225-7242**	508-865-5871
Parkline Inc PO Box 65	Winfield	WV	25213	**800-786-4855**	304-586-2113
Porta-Fab Corp					
18080 Chesterfield Airport Rd	Chesterfield	MO	63005	**800-325-3781**	636-537-5555
PorterCorp 4240 N 136th Ave	Holland	MI	49424	**800-354-7721**	616-399-1963
Red Dot Corp 1209 W Corsicana St	Athens	TX	75751	**800-657-2234***	903-675-9181
*Cust Svc					
Rigid Building Systems Ltd					
18933 Aldine Westfield Rd	Houston	TX	77073	**888-467-4443**	281-443-9065
Ruffin Building Systems Inc 6914 Hwy 2	Oak Grove	LA	71263	**800-421-4232***	318-428-2305
*Sales					
Smith XS Inc PO Box X	Red Bank	NJ	07701	**800-631-2226**	732-222-4600
Southern Structures Inc					
918 Young St PO Box 52005	Lafayette	LA	70505	**800-264-5981**	337-856-5981
Star Building Systems 8600 S I-35	Oklahoma City	OK	73149	**800-879-7827**	405-636-2010
Stuppy Greenhouse Mfg Inc					
120 E 12th Ave	North Kansas City	MO	64116	**800-877-5025**	816-842-3071
Super Secur Mfg Co					
15125 Proctor Ave	City of Industry	CA	91746	**800-591-9880**	626-333-2543
Temo Sunrooms Inc 20400 Hall Rd	Clinton Township	MI	48038	**800-344-8366**	586-286-0410
Trachte Building Systems Inc					
314 Wilburn Rd	Sun Prairie	WI	53590	**800-356-5824**	608-837-7899
Truss-T Structures Inc DBA Pacific Building					
Systems 2100 N Pacific Hwy	Woodburn	OR	97071	**800-727-7844**	503-981-9581
Tyler Building Systems LP 3535 Shiloh Rd	Tyler	TX	75707	**800-442-8979**	903-561-3000
Whirlwind Building Systems Inc					
8234 Hansen Rd	Houston	TX	77075	**800-324-9992**	713-946-7140
XS Smith Inc PO Box X	Red Bank	NJ	07701	**800-631-2226**	732-222-4600

107 BUILDINGS - PREFABRICATED - WOOD

				Toll-Free	Phone
Adrian Home Builders Inc PO Box 266	Adrian	GA	31002	**800-642-7380**	478-668-3231
All American Homes of Kansas LLC DBA All					
American KanBuild PO Box 259	Osage City	KS	66523	**800-343-2783**	785-528-4163
American Standard Building Systems Inc					
PO Box 4908	Martinsville	VA	24115	**800-888-4908**	276-638-3991
AmerLink Log Homes Ltd 7991 Beasley Rd	Whitakers	NC	27891	**800-872-4254**	252-977-2545
Atlantic Meeco Inc 1501 E Gene Stipe Blvd	McAlester	OK	74501	**800-627-4621**	918-423-6833
Aurora Modular Industries					
17300 Perris Blvd	Moreno Valley	CA	92551	**800-670-4515**	951-571-2200
Barden & Robeson Corp 103 Kelly Ave	Middleport	NY	14105	**800-724-0141**	716-735-3732
Benchmark Industries Inc 630 Hay Ave	Brookville	OH	45309	**800-833-4096**	937-833-4091
Butler Mfg Co Lester Building Systems Div					
1111 2nd Ave S	Lester Prairie	MN	55354	**800-826-4439**	320-395-2531
Deck House Inc 930 Main St	Acton	MA	01720	**800-727-3325**	978-263-7000
Design Homes Inc					
600 N Marquette Rd	Prairie du Chien	WI	53821	**800-627-9443**	608-326-6041
Dickinson Homes Inc					
404 S Stephenson Ave	Iron Mountain	MI	49801	**800-343-8179**	906-774-5800
Dynamic Homes Inc 525 Roosevelt Ave	Detroit Lakes	MN	56501	**800-492-4833**	218-847-2611
Farwest Homes PO Box 480	Chehalis	WA	98532	**800-752-0500**	360-748-3351
Fleetwood Homes of California Inc					
7007 Jurupa Ave	Riverside	CA	92504	**800-999-9265**	951-688-5353
Foremost Industries Inc					
2375 Buchanan Trail W	Greencastle	PA	17225	**877-284-5334**	717-597-7166
Heritage Log Homes Inc PO Box 8080	Sevierville	TN	37864	**800-456-4663**	865-453-0140
Homes by Keystone Inc					
13338 Midvale Rd PO Box 69	Waynesboro	PA	17268	**800-890-7926**	717-762-1104
International Homes of Cedar Inc					
PO Box 886	Woodinville	WA	98072	**800-767-7674**	360-668-8511
Lester Building Systems Div Butler Mfg Co					
1111 2nd Ave S	Lester Prairie	MN	55354	**800-826-4439**	320-395-2531
Lincoln Logs Ltd 5 Riverside Dr	Chestertown	NY	12817	**800-833-2461**	518-494-5500
Lindal Cedar Homes Inc PO Box 24426	Seattle	WA	98124	**800-426-0536***	206-725-0900
*Prod Info					
Manufactured Structures Corp					
3089 E Fort Wayne Rd PO Box 350	Rochester	IN	46975	**800-662-5344**	574-223-4794
Miller Building Systems Inc 58120 CR 3 S	Elkhart	IN	46517	**800-423-2559**	574-295-1214
Morgan Building Systems Inc					
2800 McCree Rd	Garland	TX	75041	**800-935-0321**	972-864-7300
Muncy Homes Inc 1567 Rt 442	Muncy	PA	17756	**800-788-1555**	570-546-2261
Nationwide Custom Homes 1100 Rives Rd	Martinsville	VA	24115	**800-216-7001**	276-632-7101
New England Homes Inc 270 Ocean Rd	Greenland	NH	03840	**800-800-8831**	603-436-8830
Northeastern Log Homes Inc 492 Scott Hwy	Groton	VT	05046	**800-992-6526**	802-584-3336
Northern Log Homes Inc 300 Bomarc Rd	Bangor	ME	04401	**800-553-7311**	207-942-6869
Original Lincoln Logs Ltd 5 Riverside Dr	Chestertown	NY	12817	**800-833-2461**	518-494-5500
Pacific Modern Homes Inc 9723 Railroad St	Elk Grove	CA	95624	**800-395-1011***	916-685-9514
*Sales					
Pan Abode Cedar Homes Inc					
4350 Lake Washington Blvd N	Renton	WA	98056	**800-782-2633**	425-255-8260
Pittsville Homes Inc PO Box C	Pittsville	WI	54466	**888-248-8371**	715-884-2511
Rycenga Homes Inc 17127 Hickory St	Spring Lake	MI	49456	**800-424-8040***	616-842-8040
*Sales					
Simplex Industries Inc 1 Simplex Dr	Scranton	PA	18504	**800-233-4233**	570-346-5113
Stratford Homes LP 402 S Weber Ave	Stratford	WI	54484	**800-448-1524**	715-687-3133
Sun Building Systems 9 Stauffer Industrial Pk	Taylor	PA	18517	**888-740-8218**	570-562-0110
Timberland Homes Inc 1201 37th St NW	Auburn	WA	98001	**800-488-5036**	253-735-3435
Town & Country Cedar Homes Co					
4772 US Hwy 131 S	Petoskey	MI	49770	**800-968-3178**	231-347-4360
Unibilt Industries Inc PO Box 373	Vandalia	OH	45377	**800-777-9942**	937-890-7570
Ward Log Homes PO Box 72	Houlton	ME	04730	**800-341-1566***	207-532-6531
*Cust Svc					
Wick Building Systems Inc 405 Walter Rd	Mazomanie	WI	53560	**800-356-9682**	608-795-4281

108 BUS SERVICES - CHARTER

				Toll-Free	Phone
A Yankee Line 370 W 1st St	Boston	MA	02127	**800-942-8890**	617-268-8890
Agape Tours Inc 1210 US Hwy 281	Wichita Falls	TX	76310	**800-460-2641**	940-767-4935
All West Coachlines Inc 7701 Wilbur Way	Sacramento	CA	95828	**800-843-2121**	916-423-4000
Alpha Omega Tours & Charters					
PO Box 97	Medical Lake	WA	99022	**800-351-1060**	509-624-4116
Anderson Coach & Tour Co					
1 Anderson Plaza	Greenville	PA	16125	**800-345-3435**	724-588-8310
Arrow Line Inc 19 George St	East Hartford	CT	06108	**800-243-9560**	860-289-1531
Arrow Stage Lines 720 E Norfolk Ave	Norfolk	NE	68701	**800-672-8302**	402-371-3850
Atlantic Coach 600 S Military Hwy	Virginia Beach	VA	23464	**800-258-9061**	757-420-3135
Atlantic Express Transportation Group Inc					
7 North St	Staten Island	NY	10302	**800-336-3886**	718-442-7000
Audubon Trails Coach Lines Inc					
1807 Moll Ln	Evansville	IN	47725	**800-255-5234**	812-867-2098
B & C Bus Lines 427 Continental Dr	Maryville	TN	37804	**877-812-2287**	865-983-4653
Bieber Carl R Tourways Inc 320 Fair St	Kutztown	PA	19530	**800-243-2374**	610-683-7333
Blue Lakes Charters & Tours					
12154 N Saginaw Rd	Clio	MI	48420	**800-282-4287**	810-686-4287
Boise-Winnemucca Stage Lines Inc					
1105 La Pointe St	Boise	ID	83706	**800-448-5692**	208-336-3300
Butler Motor Transit Co Inc PO Box 1602	Butler	PA	16003	**800-222-8750**	724-282-1000
Carl R Bieber Tourways Inc 320 Fair St	Kutztown	PA	19530	**800-243-2374**	610-683-7333
Central West of Texas Inc					
3426 W Gilbert Rd	Grand Prairie	TX	75050	**800-533-1939**	972-399-1059
Chenango Valley Bus Lines Inc					
105 Chenango St	Binghamton	NY	13901	**800-647-6471**	607-723-9408
Chippewa Trails 510 E South Ave	Chippewa Falls	WI	54729	**800-657-4469**	715-726-2440
Classic Transportation Group					
1600 Locust Ave	Bohemia	NY	11716	**800-666-4949**	631-567-5100
Colorado Charter Lines & Tours					
4960 Locust St	Commerce City	CO	80022	**800-821-7491**	303-287-0239
Croswell Bus Lines Inc 975 W Main St	Williamsburg	OH	45176	**800-782-8747**	513-724-2206
Cyr Bus Lines 153 Gilman Falls Ave	Old Town	ME	04468	**800-244-2335**	207-827-2335
DATTCO Inc 583 South St	New Britain	CT	06051	**800-229-4879**	860-229-4878
Elite Coach 1685 W Main St	Ephrata	PA	17522	**800-722-6206**	717-733-7710
Excellent Adventures Inc					
6215 Commodity Ct	Fort Wayne	IN	46818	**800-552-3893**	260-489-3556
Eyre Bus Service Inc 13600 Triadelphia Rd	Glenelg	MD	21737	**800-321-3973**	410-442-1330
Flack Tours PO Box 725	Waddington	NY	13694	**800-842-9747**	315-393-7160
Free Enterprise System Inc					
1254 S West St	Indianapolis	IN	46225	**800-255-1337**	317-634-7433
Great American Coach Co					
4220 Howard Ave	New Orleans	LA	70125	**866-596-2698**	504-212-5925
Great Southern Coaches Inc 900 Burke Ave	Jonesboro	AR	72401	**800-251-5569**	870-935-5569
Greyhound Canada Transportation Corp					
180 Dundas St W Suite 300	Toronto	ON	M5G1Z8	**800-661-8747**	416-594-0343
Hawkeye Stages Inc 703 Dudley St	Decorah	IA	52101	**800-323-3368**	563-382-3639
Indian Trails Inc 109 E Comstock St	Owosso	MI	48867	**800-292-3831**	989-725-5105
Jack Rabbit Lines Inc 301 N Dakota Ave	Sioux Falls	SD	57104	**800-678-6543**	605-336-3339
Jackson Tour & Travel Inc					
4500 55 Highland Village Suite 258	Jackson	MS	39216	**800-873-8572**	601-981-8415
James River Bus Lines 915 N Allen Ave	Richmond	VA	23220	**877-342-7300**	804-342-7300
King Ward Coach Lines 110 N Bridge St	Holyoke	MA	01040	**800-639-4805**	413-539-5858
Lamers Bus Lines Inc 2407 S Point Rd	Green Bay	WI	54313	**800-236-1240**	920-496-3600
Leprechaun Lines PO Box 2628	Newburgh	NY	12550	**800-624-4217**	845-565-7900
Maverick Coach Lines Ltd 7984 Webster Rd	Delta	BC	V4G1G6	**888-842-2448**	604-940-2332
Mid-America Charter Lines					
2513 E Higgins Rd	Elk Grove Village	IL	60007	**800-323-0312**	847-437-3779
Mid-American Coaches Inc PO Box 1609	Washington	MO	63090	**800-365-8687**	636-239-4700
Northern Tours 2740 Bauer St	Eau Claire	WI	54701	**800-735-8687**	715-834-1463
Northfield Lines Inc 32611 Northfield Blvd	Northfield	MN	55057	**888-670-8068**	507-645-5267
Northwest Iowa Transportation Inc					
2755 200th St	Fort Dodge	IA	50501	**877-776-1700**	515-576-5519
Onondaga Coach Corp PO Box 277	Auburn	NY	13021	**800-451-1570**	315-255-2216
Painter Bus Lines Inc 1 N Main St	Del Rio	TX	78840	**800-256-2757**	830-775-7515
Peoria Charter Coach Co 2600 NE Adams St	Peoria	IL	61603	**800-448-0572**	309-688-9523
Peter Pan Bus Lines Inc 1776 Main St	Springfield	MA	01102	**800-237-8747**	413-781-2900
Premier Coach Co Inc 67 Champlain Dr	Colchester	VT	05446	**800-532-1811**	802-655-4456
Red Carpet Charters PO Box 94626	Oklahoma City	OK	73143	**888-878-5100**	405-672-5100
Rimrock Stages Inc PO Box 988	Billings	MT	59103	**800-255-7655**	406-245-5392
Riteway Bus Service Inc Motorcoach Div					
W201 N13900 Fond du Lac Ave	Richfield	WI	53076	**800-776-7026**	414-677-3282
Rohrer Bus Service 190 Pic Rite Ln	Lewisburg	PA	17837	**800-487-8687**	570-524-5800
Royal American Charter Lines Inc					
17725 Volbrecht Rd	Lansing	IL	60438	**800-323-5281**	708-474-7474
S & O Coach Lines Inc 6630 Fly Rd	East Syracuse	NY	13057	**800-242-4244**	315-431-4462
Salter Bus Lines Inc 212 Hudson Ave	Jonesboro	LA	71251	**800-223-8056**	318-259-2522
SBS Transit Inc 3747 Colorado Ave	Sheffield Village	OH	44054	**800-548-5304**	440-949-8121
Shafer's Bus Lines Div Southern Bus Stages					
Inc 750 Harry L Dr	Johnson City	NY	13790	**800-287-8986**	607-797-2006
Sierra Nevada Stage Lines 2050 Glendale Ave	Sparks	NV	89431	**800-822-6009**	775-331-2877
Southern Bus Stages Inc Shafer's Bus Lines					
Div 750 Harry L Dr	Johnson City	NY	13790	**800-287-8986**	607-797-2006
Southern Coach Co 1300 E Pettigrew St	Durham	NC	27701	**800-222-4793**	919-688-1230
Star of Indiana Charter Services Inc					
8111 N SR 37	Bloomington	IN	47404	**800-933-0097**	812-876-7851
Starr Tours 2531 E State St	Trenton	NJ	08619	**800-782-7703**	609-587-0626
Storer Coachways 3519 McDonald Ave	Modesto	CA	95358	**800-621-3383**	209-521-8250
Sun Valley Stages Inc PO Box 936	Twin Falls	ID	83303	**800-574-8661**	208-733-3921
Swarthout Coaches Inc 115 Graham Rd	Ithaca	NY	14850	**800-772-7267**	607-257-2277
Terrian Transportation Inc DBA King Ward Coach					
Lines 110 N Bridge St	Holyoke	MA	01040	**800-639-4805**	413-539-5858
Van Galder Bus Co 715 S Pearl St	Janesville	WI	53548	**800-747-7407**	608-752-5407
Vermont Transit Co Inc 345 Pine St	Burlington	VT	05401	**800-552-8737**	802-862-9671
Wilson Bus Lines Inc PO Box 415	East Templeton	MA	01438	**800-253-5235**	978-632-3894
Winn Transportation 1831 Westwood Ave	Richmond	VA	23227	**800-296-9466**	804-358-9466
Wisconsin Coach Lines Inc					
1520 Arcadian Ave	Waukesha	WI	53186	**800-236-2015**	262-542-8861
Young Transportation & Tours					
843 Riverside Dr	Asheville	NC	28804	**800-622-5444**	828-258-0084

109 BUS SERVICES - INTERCITY & RURAL

SEE ALSO Bus Services - School; Mass Transportation (Local & Suburban)

				Toll-Free	Phone
Adirondack Trailways 499 Hurley Ave	Hurley	NY	12443	**800-858-8555**	845-339-4230
Bonanza Bus Lines Inc 1 Bonanza Way	Providence	RI	02904	**888-331-7500**	401-331-7500
Capitol Trailways Inc PO Box 3353	Harrisburg	PA	17105	**800-333-8444**	717-233-7673
City Bus 1500 W 3rd St	Williamsport	PA	17701	**800-248-9287**	570-326-2500
Colorado Valley Transit Inc					
108 Cardinal Ln PO Box 940	Columbus	TX	78934	**800-548-1068**	979-732-6281

Classified Section

	City	State	ZIP	Toll-Free	Phone
Geauga County Transit 12555 Merritt Rd.	Chardon	OH	44024	**888-287-7190**	440-285-2222
Greater Laconia Transit Agency 50 Airport Rd	Gilford	NH	03249	**800-294-2496**	603-528-2496
Greyhound Canada Transportation Corp 180 Dundas St W Suite 300	Toronto	ON	M5G1Z8	**800-661-8747**	416-594-0343
Jefferson Lines 2100 E 26th St	Minneapolis	MN	55404	**800-767-5333***	612-332-8745
*Cust Svc					
Jefferson Partners LP 2100 E 26th St	Minneapolis	MN	55404	**800-767-5333***	612-332-8745
*Cust Svc					
Laidlaw Transit Services Inc 5360 College Blvd Suite 200	Overland Park	KS	66211	**800-821-3451**	913-345-1986
Lamers Bus Lines Inc 2407 S Point Rd	Green Bay	WI	54313	**800-236-1240**	920-496-3600
Ozark Regional Transit 2423 E Robinson Ave	Springdale	AR	72764	**800-865-5901**	479-756-5901
Parker County Transportation Service Inc PO Box 1055	Mineral Wells	TX	76068	**866-521-1391**	
Pelivan Transit 333 S Oak St PO Drawer B	Big Cabin	OK	74332	**800-482-4594**	918-783-5793
Peter Pan Bus Lines Inc 1776 Main St	Springfield	MA	01102	**800-237-8747**	413-781-2900
Powder River Transportation 1700 E Hwy 14-16 PO Box 218	Gillette	WY	82717	**800-442-3682**	307-682-0960
Rides Mass Transit District (RMTD) PO Box 190	Rosiclare	IL	62982	**877-667-6122**	618-285-3342
Rimrock Stages Inc PO Box 988	Billings	MT	59103	**800-255-7655**	406-245-5392
Rural Transit Enterprises Coordinated Inc (RTEC) 100 Main St PO Box 746	Mount Vernon	KY	40456	**800-321-7832**	606-256-9835
Suburban Transit Corp 750 Somerset St	New Brunswick	NJ	08901	**800-222-0492**	732-249-1100
Thunderbird Rural Public Transportation System 4860 Knickerbocker St PO Box 60050	San Angelo	TX	76906	**800-728-2592**	325-944-9666
Trans-Bridge Lines Inc 2012 Industrial Dr	Bethlehem	PA	18017	**800-962-9135**	610-868-6001
Tri-State Coach Lines Inc 2101 W 37th Ave	Gary	IN	46408	**800-248-8747**	219-884-0054
Valley Transit Co Inc 215 N 'A' St	Harlingen	TX	78550	**800-580-4710**	956-423-4710
Viking Trailways 201 Glendale Rd	Joplin	MO	64804	**800-400-2779**	417-781-2779
White Mountain Passenger Lines Inc 1041 E Hall St PO Box 460	Show Low	AZ	85902	**866-255-4819**	928-537-4539
Williamsport Bureau of Transportation 1500 W 3rd St	Williamsport	PA	17701	**800-248-9287**	570-326-2500
Wisconsin Coach Lines Inc 1520 Arcadian Ave	Waukesha	WI	53186	**800-236-2015**	262-542-8861

110 BUS SERVICES - SCHOOL

	City	State	ZIP	Toll-Free	Phone
A & E Transport Services Inc 101 W Utica St Suite 2	Oswego	NY	13126	**800-724-0614**	315-343-2804
Atlantic Express Transportation Group Inc 7 North St	Staten Island	NY	10302	**800-336-3886**	718-442-7000
Cyr John T & Sons Inc 153 Gilman Falls Ave	Old Town	ME	04468	**800-244-2335**	207-827-2335
DATTCO Inc School Bus Div 583 South St	New Britain	CT	06051	**800-229-4879**	860-229-4878
Davidsmeyer Bus Service 2513 E Higgins Rd	Elk Grove Village	IL	60007	**800-323-0312**	847-437-3767
Dean Transportation Inc 4812 Aurelius Rd	Lansing	MI	48910	**800-282-3326**	517-319-8300
Durham School Services Inc 9011 Mountain Ridge Dr Suite 200	Austin	TX	78759	**800-950-0485**	512-343-6292
H & L Bloom Inc School Bus Div 28 Grovenor St	Taunton	MA	02780	**800-323-3009**	508-822-1442
Hastings Bus Co 425 31st St E	Hastings	MN	55033	**888-290-2429**	651-437-1888
John T Cyr & Sons Inc 153 Gilman Falls Ave	Old Town	ME	04468	**800-244-2335**	207-827-2335
Kobussen Buses Ltd W914 County Rd CE	Kaukauna	WI	54130	**800-447-0116**	920-766-0606
Krise Bus Service Inc 119 Bus Ln	Punxsutawney	PA	15767	**800-782-9769**	814-938-5250
Laidlaw International Inc School Bus Div 3221 N Service Rd	Burlington	ON	L7R3Y8	**800-563-6072**	905-336-1800
Michael's Transportation Service Inc 140 Yolano Dr	Vallejo	CA	94589	**800-295-2448**	707-643-2099
Mid-Columbia Bus Co 73458 Bus Barn Ln	Pendleton	OR	97801	**888-291-7513**	541-276-5621
Ridge Road Express Inc 5355 Junction Rd	Lockport	NY	14094	**800-847-4887**	716-625-9211
Riteway Bus Service Inc Motorcoach Div W201 N13900 Fond du Lac Ave	Richfield	WI	53076	**800-776-7026**	414-677-3282
Romano's School Bus Service 1065 Belvoir Rd	Plymouth Meeting	PA	19462	**800-877-2871**	610-272-7671
Safety Bus Service 7200 Park Ave	Pennsauken	NJ	08109	**800-367-7233**	856-665-2662
SBS Transit Inc 3747 Colorado Ave	Sheffield Village	OH	44054	**800-548-5304**	440-949-8121
Student Transportation of America Inc 3349 Hwy 138 Bldg B Suite D	Wall	NJ	07719	**888-942-2250**	732-280-4200
Williams Bus Lines Inc PO Box 1272	Springfield	VA	22151	**888-448-7433**	703-560-5355

111 BUSINESS FORMS

SEE ALSO Printing Companies - Commercial Printers

	City	State	ZIP	Toll-Free	Phone
Ace Forms of Kansas Inc 2900 N Rotary Terr	Pittsburg	KS	66762	**800-223-9287**	620-232-9290
Adams Business Forms Inc 200 Jackson St	Topeka	KS	66603	**800-444-0038**	785-233-4101
Allied Business Documents 333 Bucklin St	Providence	RI	02907	**800-556-6310**	401-461-1700
Allison Payment Systems LLC 2200 Production Dr	Indianapolis	IN	46241	**800-755-2440**	317-808-2400
Amsterdam Printing & Litho Corp 166 Wallins Corners Rd	Amsterdam	NY	12010	**800-833-6231**	518-842-6000
Apex Color 200 N Lee St	Jacksonville	FL	32204	**800-367-6790**	904-358-2928
Apperson Print Management Services 6855 E Gage Ave	Los Angeles	CA	90040	**800-877-2341**	562-927-4718
Arrow Business Forms & Labels PO Box 297	Medfield	MA	02052	**800-468-3676**	508-359-2344
B & D Litho Inc 3820 N 38th Ave	Phoenix	AZ	85019	**800-735-0375***	602-269-2526
*Cust Svc					
Bankers Systems Inc 6815 Saukview Dr	Saint Cloud	MN	56303	**800-397-2341**	320-251-3060
Belknap Business Forms Inc 215 W Lake Rd	Mayville	NY	14757	**800-828-8350***	716-753-5300
*Cust Svc					
Bernadette Business Forms Inc 8950 Pershall Rd	Saint Louis	MO	63042	**800-862-7288**	314-522-1700
Bestforms Inc 1135 Avenida Acaso	Camarillo	CA	93012	**800-350-0618**	805-388-0503
Business Forms Inc 3498 Grand Ave	Pittsburgh	PA	15225	**800-451-8086**	412-331-3300
Calibrated Forms Co Inc 537 N East Ave	Columbus	KS	66725	**800-237-7576**	
Central States Business Forms Inc 2500 Industrial Pkwy	Dewey	OK	74029	**800-331-0920**	918-534-1280
Champion Industries Inc 2450-90 1st Ave	Huntington	WV	25703	**800-624-3431**	304-528-2791
NASDAQ: CHMP					
Colwell Systems Inc 201 Kenyon Rd	Champaign	IL	61821	**800-637-1140***	217-351-5400
*Cust Svc					
Computer Stock Forms Inc 324 S Washington St	Greenfield	OH	45123	**800-543-5565**	937-981-7751
Corporate Express Document & Print Management 4205 S 96th St	Omaha	NE	68127	**800-228-9277**	402-339-0900
Curtis 1000 Inc 1725 Breckinridge Pkwy Suite 500	Duluth	GA	30096	**800-683-8162**	678-380-9095
Custom Business Forms Inc 210 Edge Pl.	Minneapolis	MN	55418	**800-234-1221**	612-789-0002
Data Papers Inc 95 Line Bluff Rd	Muncy	PA	17756	**800-233-3032**	570-546-2201
Data Source Inc 1400 Universal Ave	Kansas City	MO	64120	**800-829-3369**	816-483-3282
Datatel Resources Corp 1729 Pennsylvania Ave	Monaca	PA	15061	**800-245-2688**	724-775-5300
DFS Group 12 South St	Townsend	MA	01469	**800-225-9528**	
DSFI 450 S Lombard Rd	Addison	IL	60101	**800-828-1411***	630-627-7777
*Cust Svc					
Dupli-Systems Inc 8260 Dow Cir	Strongsville	OH	44136	**800-321-1610**	440-234-9415
Executive Greetings Inc 120 Greenwoods Industrial Pk.	New Hartford	CT	06057	**800-562-5468***	860-379-9911
*Cust Svc					
Falcon Business Forms Inc PO Box 326	Corsicana	TX	75151	**800-442-6262**	903-874-6583
Flesh Co 2118 59th St	Saint Louis	MO	63110	**800-869-3330**	314-781-4400
Forms Manufacturers Inc 312 E Forest Ave	Girard	KS	66743	**800-835-0614**	620-724-8225
Freedom Graphic Services Inc 1101 S Janesville St	Milton	WI	53563	**800-334-3540**	608-868-7007
GBF Graphics Inc 7300 Niles Ctr Rd	Skokie	IL	60077	**800-423-8326**	847-677-1700
Genoa Business Forms Inc 445 Park Ave	Sycamore	IL	60178	**800-383-2801**	815-895-2800
Global DocuGraphix 2329 Circadian Way	Santa Rosa	CA	95407	**800-325-3120**	707-527-6022
Gulf Business Forms Inc 2460 S IH-35	San Marcos	TX	78667	**800-433-4853**	512-353-8313
Haven Business Forms Inc 6 Greek Ln	Edison	NJ	08817	**800-341-2245**	732-287-1750
Highland Computer Forms Inc 1025 W Main St	Hillsboro	OH	45133	**800-669-5213**	937-393-4215
Holden Graphic Services 607 Washington Ave N	Minneapolis	MN	55401	**800-423-1099**	612-339-0241
Hospital Forms & Systems Corp 8900 Ambassador Row	Dallas	TX	75247	**800-527-5081**	214-634-8900
Howard Press Inc 450 W 1st Ave	Roselle	NJ	07203	**800-223-0648**	908-245-4400
Hygrade Business Group Inc 232 Entin Rd	Clifton	NJ	07014	**800-836-7714**	973-249-6700
Imperial Graphics Inc 3100 Walkent Dr NW	Grand Rapids	MI	49544	**800-777-2591**	616-784-0100
Interform Solutions 1901 Mayview Rd	Bridgeville	PA	15017	**800-945-7746**	412-221-3300
International Business Systems Inc 431 Yerkes Rd	King of Prussia	PA	19406	**800-220-1255**	610-265-7997
Kaye-Smith 720 Lind Ave SW	Renton	WA	98055	**800-822-9987**	425-228-8600
Maggio Data Forms Printing Ltd 1735 Expy Dr N	Hauppauge	NY	11788	**800-783-6313**	631-348-0343
Miami Systems Corp 10001 Alliance Rd	Cincinnati	OH	45242	**800-543-4540**	513-793-0110
Moore North America 1200 S Lakeside Dr	Bannockburn	IL	60015	**800-745-0780**	847-607-6000
National Business Forms Inc 100 Pennsylvania Ave	Greeneville	TN	37743	**800-722-8544***	423-638-7691
*Cust Svc					
New England Business Service Inc (NEBS) 500 Main St	Groton	MA	01471	**800-225-6380***	978-448-6111
*Sales					
New Jersey Business Forms Mfg Co 55 W Sheffield Ave	Englewood	NJ	07631	**800-466-6523**	201-569-4500
Newport Printing Systems 4120 Birch St Suite 108	Newport Beach	CA	92660	**800-660-1988**	949-261-8248
Northstar Computer Forms Inc 7130 Northland Cir N	Brooklyn Park	MN	55428	**800-765-6787**	763-531-7340
Paris Business Products 122 Kissel Rd	Burlington	NJ	08016	**800-523-6454***	609-387-7300
*Cust Svc					
Performance Office Papers 21673 Cedar Ave	Lakeville	MN	55044	**800-458-7189**	952-469-1400
PrintEdd Products of North America 2641 Forum Dr	Grand Prairie	TX	75052	**800-367-6728**	972-988-3133
Printegra Inc 403 Westpark Ct Suite A	Peachtree City	GA	30269	**800-422-6070**	770-631-6070
Printgraphics Inc 1170 Industrial Park Dr	Vandalia	OH	45377	**800-543-7510**	937-898-3008
Pummill Business Forms Inc 903 Chicago Dr	Grand Rapids	MI	49509	**888-786-6455**	616-475-9000
Rapidforms Inc 301 Grove Rd	Thorofare	NJ	08086	**800-257-8354***	856-384-1144
*Cust Svc					
Relizon Co 220 E Monument Ave	Dayton	OH	45402	**866-789-8999**	937-228-5000
Rotary Forms Press Inc 835 S High St	Hillsboro	OH	45133	**800-654-2876**	937-393-3426
Royal Business Forms Inc 3301 Ave 'E' East	Arlington	TX	76011	**800-255-9303**	817-640-5248
Safeguard Business Systems Inc 8585 N Stemmons Fwy Suite 600 N	Dallas	TX	75247	**800-338-0636**	214-905-3935
SFI Inc 225 W Olney Rd	Norfolk	VA	23510	**800-899-8713**	757-622-8001
Socrates Media LLC DBA Made E-Z Products LLC 227 W Monroe St Suite 500	Chicago	IL	60606	**800-822-4566**	312-762-5600
Specialized Printed Forms Inc 352 Center St	Caledonia	NY	14423	**800-688-2381**	585-538-2381
Standard Register Co PO Box 1167	Dayton	OH	45401	**800-755-6405**	937-221-1000
NYSE: SR					
Sterling Business Forms 5300 Crater Lake Ave	Central Point	OR	97502	**800-759-3676***	541-779-3173
*Cust Svc					
Stry-Lenkoff Co Inc 1100 W Broadway St	Louisville	KY	40232	**800-626-8247**	502-587-6804
TOPS 2275 Cabot Dr	Lisle	IL	60532	**800-444-4660**	630-588-6000
United Business Forms Inc 8482 W Allens Bridge Rd	Greeneville	TN	37743	**800-547-5351**	423-639-5551
Unz & Co 8 Easy St	Bound Brook	NJ	08805	**800-631-3098**	732-868-0706
Vallis Form Service Inc 1966 Quincy Ct	Glendale Heights	IL	60139	**800-323-0246**	630-893-2940
Victor Printing Inc 1 Victor Way	Sharon	PA	16146	**800-443-2845**	724-342-2106
Visible Computer Supply Inc 1750 Wallace Ave	Saint Charles	IL	60174	**800-323-0628**	630-377-2586
Ward-Kraft Inc 2401 Cooper St	Fort Scott	KS	66701	**800-821-4021**	620-223-5500
Web Graphics PO Box 308	Glens Falls	NY	12801	**800-833-8863**	518-792-6501
Wilmer Service Line 220 E Monument Ave	Dayton	OH	45402	**888-494-5637**	
Wise Business Forms Inc 150 Kriess Rd	Butler	PA	16001	**888-813-9473**	724-789-9700
Witt Printing Co Inc 301 Oak St	El Dorado Springs	MO	64744	**800-641-4342**	417-876-4721
Woodbury Business Forms Inc 101 Lukken Industrial Dr E	LaGrange	GA	30241	**800-241-8116**	706-882-2977
Wright Business Forms Inc 2525 Braga Dr	Broadview	IL	60155	**800-487-2204**	708-865-7600
Wright Business Graphics 18440 NE San Rafael St	Portland	OR	97230	**800-547-8397**	503-661-2525

112 BUSINESS MACHINES - MFR

SEE ALSO Business Machines - Whol; Computer Equipment; Photocopying Equipment

Company / Address	City	State	Zip	Toll-Free	Phone
Agissar Corp 526 Benton St	Stratford	CT	06615	**800-627-8256**	203-375-8662
Allegheny Paper Shredders Corp PO Box 80	Delmont	PA	15626	**800-245-2497**	724-468-4300
Amano Cincinnati Inc 140 Harrison Ave	Roseland	NJ	07068	**800-526-2559**	973-403-1900
Better Packages Inc 255 Canal St	Shelton	CT	06484	**800-237-9151**	203-926-3700
Bidwell Industrial Group Inc 2055 S Main St	Middletown	CT	06457	**800-235-0999**	860-346-9283
Bind-It Corp 150 Commerce Dr	Hauppauge	NY	11788	**800-645-5110**	631-234-2500
BOWE Bell & Howell Mail & Messaging Technologies 3791 S Alston Ave	Durham	NC	27713	**800-220-3030**	919-767-7595
Brother International Corp 100 Somerset Corporate Blvd *Cust Svc	Bridgewater	NJ	08807	**800-276-7746***	908-704-1700
Burn James International 211 Cottage St	Poughkeepsie	NY	12601	**800-431-4610**	845-454-8200
Canon Consumer Imaging & Information Systems Group 15955 Alton Pkwy *Sales	Irvine	CA	92618	**800-848-4123***	949-753-4000
Canon USA Inc 1 Canon Plaza *NYSE: CAJ*	Lake Success	NY	11042	**800-828-4040**	516-488-6700
Cummins-Allison Corp 891 Feehanville Dr	Mount Prospect	IL	60056	**800-786-5528**	847-299-9550
Diagraph Corp 1 Missouri Research Pk Dr	Saint Charles	MO	63304	**800-526-2531**	
Dictaphone Corp 3191 Broadbridge Ave	Stratford	CT	06614	**800-942-6374**	203-381-7000
Dynetics Engineering Corp 515 Bond St	Lincolnshire	IL	60069	**800-888-8110**	847-541-7300
Ecco Business Systems Inc 60 W 38th St 4th Fl	New York	NY	10018	**800-682-3226**	212-921-4545
Fellowes Inc 1789 Norwood Ave	Itasca	IL	60143	**800-945-4545**	630-893-1600
Frisco Bay Industries Ltd 160 Graveline St	Saint-Laurent	QC	H4T1R7	**800-463-7472**	514-738-7300
General Binding Corp 1 GBC Plaza *NASDAQ: GBND* ■ *Orders	Northbrook	IL	60062	**800-723-4000***	847-272-3700
Global Payment Technologies Inc 425 B Oser Ave *NASDAQ: GPTX*	Hauppauge	NY	11788	**800-472-2506**	631-231-1177
Imagistics International Inc 100 Oakview Dr *NYSE: IGI*	Trumbull	CT	06611	**800-945-9708**	203-365-7000
Industrial Paper Shredders Inc 707 Ellsworth Ave PO Box 180	Salem	OH	44460	**888-637-4733**	330-332-0024
International Business Machines Corp (IBM) New Orchard Rd *NYSE: IBM*	Armonk	NY	10504	**800-426-4968**	914-766-1900
James Burn International 211 Cottage St	Poughkeepsie	NY	12601	**800-431-4610**	845-454-8200
Lathem Time Corp 200 Selig Dr SW	Atlanta	GA	30336	**800-241-4990**	404-691-0400
Lexmark International Inc 740 W New Circle Rd *NYSE: LXK* ■ *Cust Svc	Lexington	KY	40550	**800-539-6275***	859-232-2000
Lynde-Ordway Co Inc 3308 W Warner Ave	Santa Ana	CA	92704	**800-762-7057**	714-957-1311
Michael Business Machines Corp 3134 Industry Dr *Cust Svc	North Charleston	SC	29418	**800-223-2508***	843-552-2700
Neopost Inc 30955 Huntwood Ave *Cust Svc	Hayward	CA	94544	**800-827-4543***	510-489-6800
Neopost Inc Canada 150 Steelcase Rd W	Markham	ON	L3R3J9	**800-636-7678**	905-475-3722
Olivetti Office USA Inc 379 Campus Dr 2nd Fl	Somerset	NJ	08875	**888-261-4555**	732-627-9977
Paymaster Technologies Inc 900 Pratt Blvd	Elk Grove Village	IL	60007	**800-462-4477**	847-758-1234
Pitney Bowes Inc 1 Elmcroft Rd *NYSE: PBI*	Stamford	CT	06926	**800-672-6937**	203-356-5000
Royal Consumer Information Products Inc 379 Campus Dr *Sales	Somerset	NJ	08875	**888-261-4555***	732-627-9977
Security Check PO Box 1211	Oxford	MS	38655	**800-634-4484**	662-234-0440
Security Engineered Machinery Co Inc PO Box 1045 *Sales	Westborough	MA	01581	**800-225-9293***	508-366-1488
Sharp Electronics Corp 1 Sharp Plaza	Mahwah	NJ	07430	**800-237-4277**	201-529-8200
Staplex Co 777 5th Ave *Cust Svc	Brooklyn	NY	11232	**800-221-0822***	718-768-3333
Swintec Corp 320 W Commercial Ave	Moonachie	NJ	07074	**800-225-0867**	201-935-0115
Varitronic Systems Inc 6835 Winnetka Cir	Brooklyn Park	MN	55428	**800-328-0585**	763-536-6400
Global Imaging Systems Inc 3820 Northdale Blvd Suite 200A *NASDAQ: GISX*	Tampa	FL	33624	**888-628-7834**	813-960-5508
IKON Office Solutions Inc 70 Valley Stream Pkwy *NYSE: IKN*	Malvern	PA	19355	**800-983-2898**	610-296-8600
Konica Minolta Business Solutions 500 Day Hill Rd	Windsor	CT	06095	**800-456-6422**	860-683-2222
Lewan & Assoc Inc 1400 S Colorado Blvd	Denver	CO	80222	**800-553-9265**	303-759-5440
Merchants Solutions Co 4422 Roosevelt Rd	Hillside	IL	60162	**800-244-1160**	708-449-6650
New Age Electronics Inc 21950 Arnold Ctr Rd	Carson	CA	90810	**800-234-0300**	310-549-0000
Numeridex Inc 632 Wheeling Rd	Wheeling	IL	60090	**800-323-7737**	847-541-8840
OPENFIELD Solutions 5800 Ambler Dr Suite 215 *TSE: SYS*	Mississauga	ON	L4W4J4	**800-387-3262**	905-507-4333
Pitney Bowes Inc 1 Elmcroft Rd *NYSE: PBI*	Stamford	CT	06926	**800-672-6937**	203-356-5000
Secap USA Inc 10 Clipper Rd	West Conshohocken	PA	19428	**800-523-0320**	610-825-6205
Standard Duplicating Machines Corp 10 Connector Rd	Andover	MA	01810	**800-526-4774**	978-470-1920
Stewart Engineering Supply Inc 3221 E Pioneer Pkwy	Arlington	TX	76010	**800-533-1265**	817-640-1767
Systech Retail Systems Inc DBA OPENFIELD Solutions 5800 Ambler Dr Suite 215 *TSE: SYS*	Mississauga	ON	L4W4J4	**800-387-3262**	905-507-4333
Xerox Corp Omnifax Div 9715 Burnet Rd	Austin	TX	78758	**800-221-8330**	512-719-5566

BUSINESS ORGANIZATIONS

SEE Associations & Organizations - Professional & Trade - Management & Business Professional Associations; Chambers of Commerce - Canadian; Chambers of Commerce - US - Local; Chambers of Commerce - US - State

113 BUSINESS MACHINES - WHOL

SEE ALSO Business Machines - Mfr; Computer Equipment & Software - Whol; Photocopying Equipment

Company / Address	City	State	Zip	Toll-Free	Phone
3M Canada Co PO Box 5757	London	ON	N6A4T1	**800-265-1840**	519-451-2500
Canon Business Solutions-Northeast Inc 125 Park Ave 7th Fl	New York	NY	10017	**800-627-2679**	212-850-1000
Canon Business Solutions-Southeast Inc 300 Commerce Sq Blvd	Burlington	NJ	08016	**800-220-4000**	609-387-8700
Cash Register Sales Inc 2909 Anthony Ln NE	Minneapolis	MN	55418	**800-333-4949**	612-781-3474
Danka Office Imaging Co Inc 7940 Marshall Dr	Lenexa	KS	66214	**800-336-4323**	913-495-5000
Datamax Office Systems Inc 6717 Waldemar Ave	Saint Louis	MO	63139	**800-325-9299**	314-647-2500
Dieterich-Post Co 616 Monterey Pass Rd	Monterey Park	CA	91754	**800-955-3729**	626-289-5021
Dresco Reproduction Inc 12603 Allard St	Santa Fe Springs	CA	90670	**800-423-5834**	562-863-6677
El Dorado Trading Group Inc 760 San Antonio Rd	Palo Alto	CA	94303	**800-227-8292**	650-494-6600
FDC Corp 360 Bonnie Ln	Elk Grove Village	IL	60007	**800-848-5622**	847-437-3990
FP Mailing Solutions 140 N Mitchell Ct	Addison	IL	60101	**800-341-6052**	

114 BUSINESS SERVICE CENTERS

Company / Address	City	State	Zip	Toll-Free	Phone
Advanced Business Fulfillment Inc (ABF Inc) 3183 Rider Trail S	Earth City	MO	63045	**800-804-7430**	314-770-2986
AIM Mail Centers 15550-D Rockfield Blvd	Irvine	CA	92618	**800-669-4246**	949-837-4151
Allegra Network LLC 21680 Haggerty Rd	Northville	MI	48167	**800-726-9050**	248-596-8600
AlphaGraphics Inc 268 S State St Suite 300	Salt Lake City	UT	84111	**800-955-6246**	801-595-7270
Duncan-Parnell Inc 900 S McDowell St	Charlotte	NC	28204	**800-849-7708**	704-372-7766
FedEx Kinko's Office & Print Services Inc 13155 Noel Rd Suite 1600 *Cust Svc	Dallas	TX	75240	**800-254-6567***	214-550-7000
Group O Inc 4905 77th Ave	Milan	IL	61264	**800-752-0730**	309-736-8300
Handle With Care Packaging Store 5675 DTC Blvd Suite 280	Greenwood Village	CO	80111	**800-525-6309**	303-741-6626
Kinko's (now FedEx Kinko's Office & Print Services Inc) 13155 Noel Rd Suite 1600 *Cust Svc	Dallas	TX	75240	**800-254-6567***	214-550-7000
Mail Boxes Etc 6060 Cornerstone Ct W	San Diego	CA	92121	**800-456-0414**	858-455-8800
Navis Logistics Network 5675 DTC Blvd Suite 280	Greenwood Village	CO	80111	**800-525-6309**	303-741-6626
Navis Pack & Ship Centers 5675 DTC Blvd Suite 280	Greenwood Village	CO	80111	**800-525-6309**	303-741-6626
Office Depot Inc 2200 Old Germantown Rd *NYSE: ODP*	Delray Beach	FL	33445	**800-937-3600**	561-278-4800
Packaging & Shipping Specialists 5211 85th St Suite 104	Lubbock	TX	79424	**800-877-8884**	
Packaging Store The 5675 DTC Blvd Suite 280	Greenwood Village	CO	80111	**800-525-6309**	303-741-6626
Pak Mail Centers of America Inc 7173 S Havana St Suite 600	Englewood	CO	80112	**800-778-6665**	303-957-1000
Parcel Plus Inc 12715 Telge Rd	Cypress	TX	77429	**800-662-5553**	281-256-4100
PostalAnnex+ Inc 7580 Metropolitan Dr Suite 200	San Diego	CA	92108	**800-456-1525**	619-563-4800
PostNet Postal & Business Centers 181 N Arroyo Grande Blvd Suite 100-A	Henderson	NV	89074	**800-841-7171**	702-792-7100
Sir Speedy Inc 26722 Plaza Dr	Mission Viejo	CA	92691	**800-854-8297**	949-348-5000
Staples Inc 500 Staples Dr *NASDAQ: SPLS*	Framingham	MA	01702	**877-235-9088**	508-253-5000
TRM Corp 5208 NE 122nd Ave *NASDAQ: TRMM*	Portland	OR	97230	**800-877-8762**	503-257-8766

115 BUYER'S GUIDES - ONLINE

SEE ALSO Investment Guides - Online

Company / Address	City	State	Zip	Toll-Free	Phone
Bankrate.com 11811 US Hwy 1 Suite 101	North Palm Beach	FL	33408	**800-243-7720**	561-630-2400
CardWeb.com Inc 10 N Jefferson St	Frederick	MD	21701	**800-260-7448**	301-631-9100
Dr Toy 268 Bush St	San Francisco	CA	94104	**800-551-8697**	

116 CABINETS - WOOD

SEE ALSO Construction - Special Trade Contractors - Carpentry & Flooring Contractors; Furniture - Mfr - Household Furniture

Company / Address	City	State	Zip	Toll-Free	Phone
American Woodmark Corp 3102 Shawnee Dr *NASDAQ: AMWD*	Winchester	VA	22601	**800-677-8182**	540-665-9100

Classified Section

Company	City	State	Zip	Toll-Free	Phone
Bloch Industries 140 Commerce Dr	Rochester	NY	14623	**800-992-5624**	585-334-9600
Brandom Cabinets Co 211 Campus Dr *Cust Svc	Keene	TX	76059	**800-366-8001***	817-645-8841
Cal Door 5755 Rossi Ln Suite A	Gilroy	CA	95020	**888-225-3667**	408-846-9805
California Kitchen Cabinet Door Corp 5755 Rossi Ln Suite A	Gilroy	CA	95020	**888-225-3667**	408-846-9805
Canac A Kohler Co 360 John St	Thornhill	ON	L3T3M9	**800-226-2248**	905-881-2153
Canyon Creek Cabinet Co 16726 Tye St SE	Monroe	WA	98272	**800-228-1830**	425-481-6860
Chandlers Plywood Products Inc PO Box 9009	Huntington	WV	25704	**800-624-3502**	304-429-1311
Conestoga Wood Specialties Inc 245 Reading Rd	East Earl	PA	17519	**800-964-3667**	717-445-6701
Continental Cabinet Inc 2841 Pierce St	Dallas	TX	75233	**800-786-6421**	214-467-4444
Crystal Cabinet Works Inc 1100 Crystal Dr	Princeton	MN	55371	**800-347-5045**	763-389-4187
Decore-ative Specialties Inc 2772 S Peck Rd	Monrovia	CA	91016	**800-729-7277**	626-254-9191
Haas Cabinet Co Inc 625 W Utica St	Sellersburg	IN	47172	**800-457-6458**	812-246-4431
Huntwood Industries 3808 N Sullivan Rd Bldg 26	Spokane	WA	99216	**800-873-7350**	509-924-5858
Kitchen Craft of Canada Ltd 1180 Springfield Rd	Winnipeg	MB	R2C2Z2	**800-463-9707**	204-224-3211
Legacy Cabinets LLC PO Box 730	Eastaboga	AL	36260	**800-813-1112**	256-831-4888
Marsh Furniture Co Inc 1001 S Centennial St	High Point	NC	27260	**800-756-2774**	336-884-7363
McConnell Cabinets Inc 13110 Louden Ln	City of Industry	CA	91746	**800-794-7895**	626-937-2200
Merillat Industries Inc PO Box 1946	Adrian	MI	49221	**800-575-8763**	517-263-0771
Mouser Custom Cabinetry PO Box 2527	Elizabethtown	KY	42702	**800-345-7537**	270-737-7477
Norcraft Cos LLC 3020 Denmark Ave Suite 100	Eagan	MN	55121	**800-297-0661**	651-234-3300
Patrick Industries Inc 1800 S 14th St *NASDAQ: PATK*	Elkhart	IN	46516	**800-331-2151**	574-294-7511
Plato Woodwork Inc PO Box 98	Plato	MN	55370	**800-328-5924**	320-238-2193
Prestige Inc 101 S 8th St	Neodesha	KS	66757	**800-328-4006**	620-325-8500
Quality Cabinets 515 Big Stone Gap Rd	Duncanville	TX	75137	**800-284-3888**	972-298-6103
Regal Kitchens Inc 8600 NW South River Dr	Miami	FL	33166	**800-432-0731**	305-885-0111
Rich Maid Kabinetry Inc 633 W Lincoln Ave	Myerstown	PA	17067	**800-295-2912**	717-866-2112
RSI Home Products Inc 400 E Orangethorpe Ave	Anaheim	CA	92801	**888-774-8062**	714-449-2200
Rutt HandCrafted Cabinetry 215 Diller Ave *Cust Svc	New Holland	PA	17557	**800-220-7888***	717-351-1700
Ultracraft Co 6163 Old 421 Rd	Liberty	NC	27298	**800-262-4046**	336-622-4281
Valley Cabinet Inc 845 Prosper Rd	De Pere	WI	54115	**800-236-8981**	920-336-3174
Wellborn Cabinet Inc 38669 Hwy 77	Ashland	AL	36251	**800-762-4475**	256-354-7151
Yorktowne Inc 100 Redco Ave	Red Lion	PA	17356	**800-777-0065**	717-244-4011

117 CABLE & OTHER PAY TELEVISION SERVICES

Company	City	State	Zip	Toll-Free	Phone
Adelphia Communications Corp 5619 DTC Pkwy	Greenwood Village	CO	80111	**800-892-7300**	303-268-6300
Bresnan Communications Co 1 Manhattanville Rd	Purchase	NY	10577	**888-909-4357**	914-641-3300
CableAmerica Corp 4120 E Valley Auto Dr	Mesa	AZ	85206	**800-327-4375**	480-558-7260
Cebridge Connections PO Box 139400	Tyler	TX	75713	**877-423-2743**	800-999-8876
Cebridge Connections PO Box 139400	Tyler	TX	75713	**800-999-8876**	
Cogeco Cable Inc 5 Pl Ville-Marie Suite 915	Montreal	QC	H3B2G2	**866-384-4837**	514-874-2600
Comcast Cable Communications Inc 200 Cresson Blvd *Cust Svc	Oaks	PA	19456	**800-266-2278***	610-650-3000
Direct Satellite Services 315 Quail Ridge Dr	Westmont	IL	60559	**888-475-3474**	630-887-0277
DIRECTV Inc PO Box 956 *Cust Svc	El Segundo	CA	90245	**800-347-3288***	310-535-5000
DISH Network 9601 S Meridian Blvd	Englewood	CO	80112	**800-333-3474**	303-723-1000
Galaxy Cablevision PO Box 1007 *Cust Svc	Sikeston	MO	63801	**800-365-6988***	573-472-8200
James Cable Partners 38710 N Woodward Ave Suite 180	Bloomfield Hills	MI	48304	**877-834-9487**	248-647-1080
LodgeNet Entertainment Corp 3900 W Innovation St *NASDAQ: LNET*	Sioux Falls	SD	57107	**888-563-4363**	605-988-1330
Mediacom Communications Corp 100 Crystal Run Rd *NASDAQ: MCCC*	Middletown	NY	10941	**888-692-9090**	845-695-2600
Midcontinent Communications PO Box 5010	Sioux Falls	SD	57117	**800-888-1300**	605-229-1775
Northland Communications Corp 101 Stewart St Suite 700	Seattle	WA	98101	**800-448-0273**	206-674-3900
Omega Communications Inc 29 E Maryland SE	Indianapolis	IN	46204	**800-622-6728**	317-264-4010
On Command Corp 4610 S Ulster St 6th Fl	Denver	CO	80237	**800-797-7654**	720-873-3200
Pencor Services Inc 613 3rd St	Palmerton	PA	18071	**800-634-6572**	610-826-2552
Persona Inc 17 Duffy Pl PO Box 12155 Station A	Saint John's	NL	A1B4L1	**866-737-7662**	709-754-3775
RCN Corp 105 Carnegie Ctr *NASDAQ: RCNI*	Princeton	NJ	08540	**800-746-4726**	609-734-3700
Rogers Communications Inc 333 Bloor St E *NYSE: RG*	Toronto	ON	M4W1G9	**888-620-7777**	416-935-7777
Seren Innovations Inc 15 S 5th St Suite 500	Minneapolis	MN	55402	**800-427-8686**	612-395-3500
Service Electric Cable TV & Communications 2260 Ave A	Bethlehem	PA	18017	**800-232-9100**	610-865-9100
Shaw Communications Inc 630 3rd Ave SW Suite 900 *NYSE: SJR*	Calgary	AB	T2P4L4	**888-750-7429**	403-750-4500
Superstar Dept 1142	Tulsa	OK	74182	**800-642-8080**	
Superstar Satellite Entertainment 7140 S Lewis Ave	Tulsa	OK	74136	**800-225-5772**	918-488-4100
Time Warner Cable 290 Harbor Dr	Stamford	CT	06902	**800-950-2266**	203-328-0600
Time Warner Communications Inc 1266 Dublin Rd	Columbus	OH	43215	**800-492-9324**	614-481-5050
TiVo Inc 2160 Gold St *NASDAQ: TIVO*	Alviso	CA	95002	**877-367-8486**	408-519-9100
Vyvx Integrated Transmission Services 1 Technology Ctr	Tulsa	OK	74103	**800-364-0807**	918-547-5760

118 CABLE REELS

Company	City	State	Zip	Toll-Free	Phone
American Reeling Devices Inc 15 Airpark Vista Blvd *Sales	Dayton	NV	89403	**800-354-7335***	775-246-1000
Coxreels 6720 S Clementine Ct *Cust Svc	Tempe	AZ	85283	**800-269-7335***	480-820-6396
Cumberland Wood Products Inc PO Box 68	Helenwood	TN	37755	**800-635-7335**	423-569-6363
Gleason Reel Corp PO Box 26	Mayville	WI	53050	**800-571-0166**	920-387-4120
Hannay Reels Inc 553 SR 143	Westerlo	NY	12193	**877-467-3357**	518-797-3791
Insul-8 Corp 10102 F St	Omaha	NE	68127	**800-521-4888**	402-339-9300
Reelcraft Industries Inc 1 Reelcraft Ctr PO Box 248	Columbia City	IN	46725	**800-444-3134**	260-248-8188
Tayloreel Corp PO Box 476	Oakwood	GA	30566	**877-503-1612**	770-503-1612

119 CAMERAS & RELATED SUPPLIES - RETAIL

Company	City	State	Zip	Toll-Free	Phone
Abe's of Maine Cameras & Electronics 1957 Coney Island Ave	Brooklyn	NY	11223	**800-227-0400**	718-645-0900
Adorama Camera Inc 42 W 18th St	New York	NY	10011	**800-223-2500**	212-741-0052
B & H Photo-Video-Pro Audio Corp 420 9th Ave	New York	NY	10001	**800-947-9954**	212-444-6600
Black Photo Corp 371 Gough Rd	Markham	ON	L3R4B6	**800-668-3826**	905-475-2777
Calumet Photographic Inc 890 Supreme Dr *Cust Svc	Bensenville	IL	60106	**800-453-2550***	630-860-7447
Camasco Group 5000 Armand-Frappier St	Saint-Hubert	QC	J3Z1G5	**877-361-4472**	514-856-7750
Cambridge Camera 34 Franklin Ave	Brooklyn	NY	11205	**800-221-2253**	718-858-5002
Camera Corner Inc PO Box 1899	Burlington	NC	27216	**800-868-2462**	336-228-0251
Camera Expert 5000 Armand-Frappier St	Saint-Hubert	QC	J3Z1G5	**877-361-4472**	514-856-7750
CameraWorld.com 2010 Main St Suite 400	Irvine	CA	92614	**800-226-3721**	949-442-0202
Canoga Camera Corp 22065 Sherman Way	Canoga Park	CA	91303	**800-201-4201**	818-346-5506
Central Camera Co 230 S Wabash Ave	Chicago	IL	60606	**800-421-1899**	312-427-5580
Cress Photo PO Box 4262	Wayne	NJ	07474	**888-480-3456**	973-694-1280
Dodd Co DBA Dodd Camera & Video 2077 E 30th St	Cleveland	OH	44115	**800-507-1676**	216-361-6817
Dury's 701 Ewing Ave	Nashville	TN	37203	**800-824-2379**	615-255-3456
F-11 Photographic Supplies 16 E Main St *Sales	Bozeman	MT	59715	**800-548-0203***	406-587-1300
Focus Camera Inc 905 McDonald Ave	Brooklyn	NY	11219	**800-221-0828**	718-436-6262
Get Smart Products 578 Nepperham Ave	Yonkers	NY	10701	**800-827-0673**	914-709-0600
Helix Ltd 310 S Racine Ave	Chicago	IL	60607	**800-334-3549**	312-421-6000
Kenmore Camera Inc 18031 67th Ave NE	Kenmore	WA	98028	**888-485-7447**	425-485-7447
Light Impressions Inc PO Box 787	Brea	CA	92822	**800-828-6216**	714-441-4539
Porter's Camera Store PO Box 628	Cedar Falls	IA	50613	**800-553-2001**	319-268-0104
Projector Solution 181 Avenida La Pata Suite 100	San Clemente	CA	92673	**800-701-9869**	949-940-2400
Ritz Camera Centers Inc 6711 Ritz Way *Orders	Beltsville	MD	20705	**877-690-0099***	301-419-0000
Samy's Camera Inc 431 S Fairfax Ave	Los Angeles	CA	90036	**800-321-4726**	323-938-2420
Unique Photo Inc 11 Vreeland Rd	Florham Park	NJ	07932	**800-631-0300**	973-377-5555

120 CAMPERS, TRAVEL TRAILERS, MOTOR HOMES

Company	City	State	Zip	Toll-Free	Phone
Alfa Leisure Inc 13501 5th St	Chino	CA	91710	**800-373-3372**	909-628-5574
Beaver Coaches Inc PO Box 5639 *Sales	Bend	OR	97708	**800-423-2837***	541-389-1144
Coach House Motorhomes Inc 3480 Technology Dr	Nokomis	FL	34275	**800-235-0984**	941-485-0984
Coachmen Recreational Vehicles Corp 423 N Main St	Middlebury	IN	46540	**800-353-7383**	574-825-8500
Cool Amphibious Manufacturers International LLC 31 Hawkes Rd	Bluffton	SC	29910	**888-926-6553**	843-757-4133
Custom Fiberglass Mfg Corp 1711 Harbor Ave	Long Beach	CA	90813	**800-768-4867**	562-432-5454
Foretravel Inc 1221 NW Stallings Dr	Nacogdoches	TX	75964	**800-955-6226**	936-564-8367
Four Wheel Campers 1460 Churchill Downs Ave	Woodland	CA	95776	**800-242-1442**	530-666-1442
Georgie Boy Mfg Inc 69950 Hwy M 62	Edwardsburg	MI	49112	**877-876-9024**	269-663-3415
Gulf Stream Coach Inc 503 S Oakland Ave PO Box 1005	Nappanee	IN	46550	**800-289-8787**	574-773-7761
Holiday Rambler Div Monaco Coach Corp 606 Nelson's Pkwy	Wakarusa	IN	46573	**800-650-7337**	574-862-7211
Horizons Inc 2618 Mid America Dr	Junction City	KS	66441	**800-235-3140**	785-238-7575
Jayco Inc 903 S Main St *Cust Svc	Middlebury	IN	46540	**877-825-4782***	574-825-5861
Lance Camper Corp 43120 Venture St	Lancaster	CA	93535	**800-423-7996**	661-949-3322
Leland Engineering Inc 501 S Miller Dr	White Pigeon	MI	49099	**800-669-7681**	269-483-7681
Monaco Coach Corp 91320 Coburg Industrial Way *NYSE: MNC*	Coburg	OR	97408	**800-634-0855**	541-686-8011
Monaco Coach Corp Holiday Rambler Div 606 Nelson's Pkwy	Wakarusa	IN	46573	**800-650-7337**	574-862-7211
National RV Holdings Inc 3411 N Perris Blvd *NYSE: NVH*	Perris	CA	92571	**800-322-6007**	951-943-6007
Newell Coach Corp PO Box 511	Miami	OK	74354	**888-363-9355**	918-542-3344
Nu-Wa Industries Inc 3701 Johnson Rd	Chanute	KS	66720	**800-835-0676**	620-431-2088
Peterson Industries Inc 616 E Hwy 36	Smith Center	KS	66967	**800-368-3759**	785-282-6825
Rexhall Industries Inc 46147 7th St W	Lancaster	CA	93534	**800-929-5280**	661-726-0565
Shasta Industries PO Box 30 *Cust Svc	Middlebury	IN	46540	**800-233-5571***	574-825-8555
Skyline Corp 2520 By-Pass Rd *NYSE: SKY*	Elkhart	IN	46514	**800-348-7469**	574-294-6521
Sunline Coach Co Inc 245 S Muddy Creek Rd	Denver	PA	17517	**800-827-6406**	717-336-2858
Western Recreational Vehicles 3401 W Washington Ave	Yakima	WA	98903	**800-888-4133**	509-457-4133
Winnebago Industries Inc 605 W Crystal Lake Rd *NYSE: WGO*	Forest City	IA	50436	**800-643-4892**	641-585-3535

121 CAMPGROUND OPERATORS

Company / Address	City	State	Zip	Toll-Free	Phone
Leisure Systems Inc DBA Yogi Bear's Jellystone Park Camp Resorts 50 W Techne Center Dr Suite G *Sales	Milford	OH	45150	**800-626-3720***	513-831-2100
Outdoor Resorts of America Inc 79-687 Country Club Rd Suite 201	Bermuda Dunes	CA	92201	**800-541-2582**	760-345-2046
Thousand Trails Inc 3801 Parkwood Blvd Suite 100	Frisco	TX	75034	**800-328-6226**	214-618-7200

122 CANDLES

SEE ALSO Gift Shops

Company / Address	City	State	Zip	Toll-Free	Phone
Candle-Lite Div Lancaster Colony Corp PO Box 42364	Cincinnati	OH	45242	**800-718-7018**	513-563-1113
Candleman Corp 1120 Industrial Pk Rd PO Box 731	Brainerd	MN	56401	**800-328-3453**	218-829-0592
Continental Candle Co Inc 1420 W Walnut St	Compton	CA	90220	**800-421-1035**	310-537-9300
Dadant & Sons Inc 51 S 2nd St	Hamilton	IL	62341	**800-637-7468**	217-847-3324
General Wax & Candle Co 6858 Beck Ave PO Box 9398	North Hollywood	CA	91609	**800-543-0642**	818-765-5808
Home Fragrance Holdings 8323 Fairbanks White Oak Rd *Cust Svc	Houston	TX	77040	**800-256-5689***	713-466-4600
Knorr Beeswax Products Inc 1965 Kellogg Ave	Carlsbad	CA	92008	**800-807-2337**	760-431-2007
Lancaster Colony Corp Candle-Lite Div PO Box 42364	Cincinnati	OH	45242	**800-718-7018**	513-563-1113
Lumi-Lite Candle Co Inc 102 Sundale Rd PO Box 97	Norwich	OH	43767	**800-288-2340**	740-872-3248
Mack-Miller Candle Co Inc 202 SHeridan Rd	Liverpool	NY	13090	**800-522-6353**	315-453-9665
Mason Candlelight Co 8729 Aviation Blvd	Inglewood	CA	90301	**800-556-2766**	
Muench-Kreuzer Candle Co 617 E Hiawatha Blvd	Syracuse	NY	13208	**800-448-7884**	315-471-4515
Root Candles Co 623 W Liberty St	Medina	OH	44256	**800-289-7668**	330-725-6677
White Barn Candle Co 7 Limited Pkwy E	Reynoldsburg	OH	43068	**800-395-1001**	614-856-6000
Wicks 'N' Sticks PO Box 1965	Cypress	TX	77410	**800-873-3714**	713-856-7442
Will & Baumer Inc 100 Buckley St	Liverpool	NY	13288	**800-733-7337**	315-451-1000
Williamsburg Soap & Candle Co 7521 Richmond Rd *Orders	Williamsburg	VA	23188	**800-367-9722***	757-564-3354
Yankee Candle Co Inc 16 Yankee Candle Way *NYSE: YCC*	South Deerfield	MA	01373	**800-839-6038**	413-665-8306

123 CANDY STORES

Company / Address	City	State	Zip	Toll-Free	Phone
Candy Bouquet International Inc 423 E 3rd St	Little Rock	AR	72201	**877-226-3901**	501-375-9990
Gardners Candies Inc 2600 Adams Ave	Tyrone	PA	16686	**800-242-2639**	814-684-3925
Gertrude Hawk Chocolates Inc 9 Keystone Pk	Dunmore	PA	18512	**800-822-2032**	570-342-7556
Gorant Candies Inc 8301 Market St	Youngstown	OH	44512	**800-572-4139**	330-726-8821
Hebert Candy Mansion 575 Hartford Tpke	Shrewsbury	MA	01545	**800-642-7702**	508-845-8051
Lammes Candies Since 1885 Inc 200 B Parker Dr Suite 500	Austin	TX	78728	**800-252-1885**	512-310-1885
Quality Candy Shoppes Inc PO Box 070581	Milwaukee	WI	53207	**800-972-2658**	414-483-4500
See's Candies Inc 210 El Camino Real *Cust Svc	South San Francisco	CA	94080	**800-951-7337***	650-761-2490

124 CANS - METAL

SEE ALSO Containers - Metal (Barrels, Drums, Kegs)

Company / Address	City	State	Zip	Toll-Free	Phone
Bertels Can Co 485 Stuart Rd *Cust Svc	Wilkes-Barre	PA	18706	**800-829-0578***	570-829-0524
BWAY Corp 8607 Roberts Dr Suite 250	Atlanta	GA	30350	**800-527-2267**	770-587-0888
BWAY Corp 8607 Roberts Dr Suite 250	Atlanta	GA	30350	**800-527-2267**	770-645-4800
Can Corp of America Inc PO Box 170	Blandon	PA	19510	**800-441-0876**	610-926-3044
Crown Cork & Seal Co 1 Crown Way *NYSE: CCK*	Philadelphia	PA	19154	**800-523-3644**	215-698-5100
Crown Holdings Inc DBA Crown Cork & Seal Co 1 Crown Way *NYSE: CCK*	Philadelphia	PA	19154	**800-523-3644**	215-698-5100
JL Clark Mfg Co 923 23rd Ave	Rockford	IL	61104	**800-252-7267**	815-962-8861
Protectoseal Co 225 W Foster Ave	Bensenville	IL	60106	**800-323-2268**	630-595-0800
Rexam Inc 4201 Congress St Suite 340	Charlotte	NC	28209	**800-289-2800**	704-551-1500
Ring Container Technology 1 Industrial Pk Dr	Oakland	TN	38060	**800-280-7464**	901-465-3607
Sexton Can Co Inc 23 E St	Cambridge	MA	02141	**888-739-8662**	617-577-8999
South Texas Can Co Inc 103 E Benge Rd	Fort Gibson	OK	74434	**800-776-2107**	918-478-2117
Spartanburg Steel Products Inc PO Box 6428	Spartanburg	SC	29304	**800-334-6318**	864-585-5216

125 CANS, TUBES, DRUMS - PAPER (FIBER)

Company / Address	City	State	Zip	Toll-Free	Phone
Acme Spirally Wound Paper Products Inc 4810 W 139th St PO Box 35320	Cleveland	OH	44135	**800-274-2797**	216-267-2950
Custom Paper Tubes Inc PO Box 35140	Cleveland	OH	44135	**800-766-2527**	216-362-2964
Greif Inc 425 Winter Rd *NYSE: GEF*	Delaware	OH	43015	**800-354-7343**	740-549-6000
Hayes Mfg Group Inc Core Div PO Box 595	Neenah	WI	54957	**800-236-8001**	920-725-7056
Industrial Paper Tube Inc 1335 E Bay Ave	Bronx	NY	10474	**800-345-0960**	718-893-5000
Laminations 3010 E Venture Dr	Appleton	WI	54911	**800-925-2626**	920-831-0596
Michael's Cooperage Co Inc 363 W Pershing Rd	Chicago	IL	60609	**800-262-6281**	773-268-6281
Midwest Paper Tube & Can Corp PO Box 510006 *Cust Svc	New Berlin	WI	53151	**800-577-1400***	262-782-7300
Multi-Wall Corp Div Real Reel Corp 50 Taylor Dr *Cust Svc	East Providence	RI	02916	**800-992-4166***	401-434-1070
NYSCO Products Inc 2350 Lafayette Ave	Bronx	NY	10473	**800-227-8685**	718-792-9000
Ox Paper Tube & Core Inc 331 Maple Ave	Hanover	PA	17331	**800-414-2476**	717-630-0230
Pacific Paper Tube Inc 1025 98th Ave	Oakland	CA	94603	**888-377-8823**	510-562-8823
Real Reel Corp Multi-Wall Corp Div 50 Taylor Dr *Cust Svc	East Providence	RI	02916	**800-992-4166***	401-434-1070
Self-Seal Container Corp 401 E 4th St	Bridgeport	PA	19405	**800-334-1428**	610-275-2300
Sonoco Products Co 1 N 2nd St *NYSE: SON*	Hartsville	SC	29550	**800-377-2692**	843-383-7000
Stonington Corp 111 Mosher St *Cust Svc	Holyoke	MA	01040	**800-370-2673***	413-493-1500
TEKPAK Inc 1410 S Washington St	Marion	AL	36756	**800-876-8841**	334-683-6121
Yazoo Mills Inc PO Box 369 *Cust Svc	New Oxford	PA	17350	**800-242-5216***	717-624-8993

126 CAR RENTAL AGENCIES

SEE ALSO Fleet Leasing & Management; Truck Rental & Leasing

Company / Address	City	State	Zip	Toll-Free	Phone
Ace Rent-A-Car 5806 W Washington St	Indianapolis	IN	46241	**800-242-7368**	317-243-6336
Advantage Rent-A-Car 1343 Hallmark Dr *Cust Svc	San Antonio	TX	78216	**800-777-5500***	210-344-4712
Affiliated Car Rental LC DBA Sensible Car Rental Inc 96 Freneau Ave Suite 2	Matawan	NJ	07747	**800-367-5159**	732-583-8500
Affordable Car Rental System Inc 96 Freneau Ave Suite 2	Matawan	NJ	07747	**800-631-2290**	732-290-8300
Alamo Rent A Car Inc 6929 N Lakewood Ave Suite 100	Tulsa	OK	74117	**800-327-9633**	918-401-6000
Auto Europe 39 Commercial St	Portland	ME	04101	**800-223-5555**	207-842-2000
Avis Rent A Car System Inc 6 Sylvan Way	Parsippany	NJ	07054	**800-331-1212**	973-496-3500
Budget Rent A Car System Inc 6 Sylvan Way	Parsippany	NJ	07054	**800-527-0700**	973-496-3500
Car Rental Express 3337 W 4th Ave	Vancouver	BC	V6R1N6	**888-557-8188**	604-714-5911
Discount Car & Truck Rentals Ltd 720 Arrow Rd	North York	ON	M9M2M1	**866-742-5968**	416-744-0123
Dollar Rent A Car Inc 5330 E 31st St	Tulsa	OK	74135	**800-800-4000**	918-669-3000
Enterprise Rent-A-Car 600 Corporate Pk Dr	Saint Louis	MO	63105	**800-325-8007**	314-512-5000
Europe by Car Inc 62 William St 7th Fl	New York	NY	10005	**800-223-1516**	212-581-3040
Hertz Corp 225 Brae Blvd	Park Ridge	NJ	07656	**800-654-3131**	201-307-2000
Kemwel Inc 39 Commercial St	Portland	ME	04112	**800-678-0678**	207-842-2285
National Car Rental 6929 N Lakewood Ave Suite 100	Tulsa	OK	74117	**800-227-7368**	918-401-6000
Payless Car Rental System Inc 2350 N 34th St N	Saint Petersburg	FL	33713	**800-729-5377**	727-321-6352
Rent-A-Wreck of America LLC 10324 S Dolfield Rd	Owings Mills	MD	21117	**800-535-1391**	410-581-5755
Sensible Car Rental Inc 96 Freneau Ave Suite 2	Matawan	NJ	07747	**800-367-5159**	732-583-8500
Thrifty Car Rental 5310 E 31st St	Tulsa	OK	74135	**800-367-2277**	918-665-3930
Triangle Rent A Car Co 4226A South Blvd	Charlotte	NC	28209	**800-643-7368**	704-527-1900
U-Save Auto Rental of America Inc 4780 I-55 N Suite 300	Jackson	MS	39211	**800-438-2300**	601-713-4333
Vanguard Car Rental USA 6929 N Lakewood Ave Suite 100	Tulsa	OK	74117	**800-837-0032**	918-401-6000

127 CARBON & GRAPHITE PRODUCTS

Company / Address	City	State	Zip	Toll-Free	Phone
Advance Carbon Products Inc 2036 National Ave	Hayward	CA	94545	**800-283-1249**	510-293-5930
Calcarb Inc 110 Indel Ave	Rancocas	NJ	08073	**800-732-5432**	609-261-4325
Carbone of America 400 Myrtle Ave *Cust Svc	Boonton	NJ	07005	**800-526-0877***	973-334-0700
Helwig Carbon Products Inc 8900 W Tower Ave	Milwaukee	WI	53224	**800-365-3113**	414-354-2411
National Electrical Carbon Products Inc 251 Forrester Dr	Greenville	SC	29607	**800-543-6322**	864-458-7700
Pyrotek Inc 9503 E Montgomery Ave	Spokane	WA	99206	**800-797-6835**	509-926-6212
Saturn Industries Inc 157 Union Tpke	Hudson	NY	12534	**800-775-1651**	518-828-9956
SGL Carbon Corp 307 Jamestown Rd	Morganton	NC	28655	**800-828-6601**	828-437-3221
Superior Graphite Co 10 S Riverside Plaza Suite 1470 *Orders	Chicago	IL	60606	**800-325-0337***	312-559-2999
Zoltek Cos Inc 3101 McKelvey Rd *NASDAQ: ZOLT*	Bridgeton	MO	63044	**800-325-4409**	314-291-5110

128 CARBURETORS, PISTONS, PISTON RINGS, VALVES

SEE ALSO Aircraft Engines & Engine Parts; Automotive Parts & Supplies - Mfr

Company / Address	City	State	Zip	Toll-Free	Phone
America's Double Seal Ring Co 2065 Montgomery St	Fort Worth	TX	76107	**800-397-7777**	817-738-6581
C Lee Cook Co 916 S 8th St	Louisville	KY	40203	**877-266-5226**	502-587-6783

Classified Section

Company / Address	City	State	Zip	Toll-Free	Phone
France Compressor Products 4410 Greenbriar Dr	Stafford	TX	77477	**800-675-6646**	281-207-4600
Grant Piston Rings 1360 N Jefferson St	Anaheim	CA	92807	**800-854-3540**	714-996-0050
Grover Corp PO Box 340080	Milwaukee	WI	53234	**800-776-3602**	414-384-9472
Hastings Mfg Co 325 N Hanover St	Hastings	MI	49058	**800-776-1012**	269-945-2491
Holley Performance Products Inc 1801 Russellville Rd *Sales	Bowling Green	KY	42101	**800-638-0032***	270-782-2900
Intercoastal Mfg Co 10975 SW 11 St Bldg A Suite 150	Beaverton	OR	97005	**800-547-6644**	503-574-2200
Jones LE Co 1200 34th Ave	Menominee	MI	49858	**800-535-6637**	906-863-4411
LE Jones Co 1200 34th Ave	Menominee	MI	49858	**800-535-6637**	906-863-4411
Martin Wells Industries PO Box 01406	Los Angeles	CA	90001	**800-421-6000**	323-581-6266
Safety Seal Piston Ring Co 4000 Airport Rd *Sales	Marshall	TX	75672	**800-962-3631***	903-938-9241
Tomco Auto Products Co Inc 4330 E 26th St	Los Angeles	CA	90023	**800-858-3458**	323-268-4830
United Engine & Machine Co Inc 4909 Goni Rd	Carson City	NV	89706	**800-648-7970**	775-882-7790
Wiseco Piston Inc 7201 Industrial Park Blvd	Mentor	OH	44060	**800-321-1364**	440-951-6600

129 CARD SHOPS

SEE ALSO Gift Shops

Company / Address	City	State	Zip	Toll-Free	Phone
American Greetings Corp Carlton Cards Div 1 American Rd *Sales	Cleveland	OH	44144	**800-321-3040***	216-252-7300
AmericanGreetings.com Inc 1 American Rd	Cleveland	OH	44144	**888-749-5884**	216-889-5000
Card & Gift Gallery Inc 4200 S East St	Indianapolis	IN	46227	**800-893-3115**	317-783-1555
CardStore.com 1195 Park Ave Suite 211	Emeryville	CA	94608	**877-822-2737**	510-595-6775
Carlton Cards Div American Greetings Corp 1 American Rd *Sales	Cleveland	OH	44144	**800-321-3040***	216-252-7300
Hallmark Cards Inc 2501 McGee St	Kansas City	MO	64108	**800-425-5627**	816-274-5111
Papyrus Franchise Corp 500 Chadbourne Rd	Fairfield	CA	94533	**800-333-6724**	707-425-8006
Recycled Paper Greetings Inc 3636 N Broadway *Cust Svc	Chicago	IL	60613	**800-777-9494***	773-348-6410
Scribbles & Giggles 1 American Rd *Cust Svc	Cleveland	OH	44144	**800-527-9560***	216-252-8800
Snow's Cards & Gifts 1609 1st Ave S	Birmingham	AL	35233	**800-937-6697**	205-322-1397
Stork News of America Inc 1305 Hope Mills Rd Suite A	Fayetteville	NC	28304	**800-633-6395**	910-426-1357

130 CARDS - GREETING - MFR

Company / Address	City	State	Zip	Toll-Free	Phone
Alef Judaica 8440 Warner Dr	Culver City	CA	90232	**800-262-2533**	310-202-0024
Alfred Mainzer Inc 27-08 40th Ave	Long Island City	NY	11101	**800-222-2737**	718-392-4200
Allen & John Inc 2505 N Shirk Rd	Visalia	CA	93278	**800-803-7527**	
Amber Lotus Publishing 1250 Addison St Studio 214	Berkeley	CA	94702	**800-326-2375**	510-225-0149
Amberley Greeting Card Co 11510 Goldcoast Dr	Cincinnati	OH	45249	**800-262-3759**	513-489-2775
American Greetings Corp 1 American Rd *NYSE: AM* ■ *Sales	Cleveland	OH	44144	**800-321-3040***	216-252-7300
Ancient Images Greeting Cards 44 N 100 West	Moab	UT	84532	**800-891-6635**	435-259-4087
Anna Griffin Inc 733 Lambert Dr	Atlanta	GA	30324	**888-817-8170**	404-817-8170
Avanti Press Inc 155 W Congress St Suite 200	Detroit	MI	48226	**800-228-2684**	313-961-0022
B Designs Inc 23 Noel St Suite 2	Amesbury	MA	01913	**800-978-3575**	978-388-1052
B Shackman Co Inc 9964 W Miller Dr	Galesburg	MI	49053	**800-221-7656**	269-484-1000
Backyard Oaks 401 E 8th St Suite 310	Sioux Falls	SD	57103	**800-456-8208**	605-338-1968
Barton Cotton Inc 1405 Parker Rd	Baltimore	MD	21227	**800-638-4652**	410-247-4800
Bayview Press 30 Knox St PO Box 153	Thomaston	ME	04861	**800-903-2346**	207-354-9919
Birchcraft Studios Inc 10 Railroad St	Abington	MA	02351	**800-333-0405**	781-878-5152
Birchcraft Studios Inc PO Box 328	Rockland	MA	02370	**800-333-0405**	781-878-5151
Blue Mountain Arts Inc PO Box 4549 *Sales	Boulder	CO	80306	**800-545-8573***	303-449-0536
Bonair Daydreams PO Box 3741	Farmington	NM	87499	**888-226-6247**	505-326-1684
Candy Care Inc W 58th St	New York	NY	10019	**888-423-8823**	212-421-1234
Caravan International & EthnoGraphics PO Box 768	Colleyville	TX	76034	**800-442-0036**	817-577-2988
CardInTheBox 350 S Rohlwing Rd Suite 200	Addison	IL	60101	**877-212-1121**	630-953-8882
Carole Joy Creations Inc 6 Production Dr Unit 1 *Sales	Brookfield	CT	06804	**800-223-6945***	203-740-4490
Caspari Inc 116 E 27th St 11th Fl *Sales	New York	NY	10016	**800-227-7274***	212-685-9798
ClaudiaM Publications PO Box 925	Huntington	NY	11743	**800-241-0776**	631-424-7074
Closerie Publishing 1952 S La Cienega Blvd	Los Angeles	CA	90034	**800-295-9909**	310-559-9704
Colors By Design 7723 Densmore Ave	Van Nuys	CA	91406	**800-832-8436**	818-376-1226
Copperplate Publishing Inc 1901 Lexington Ave N	Roseville	MN	55113	**888-772-6001**	651-487-8575
Creative Card Co Inc 7700 W 79th St *Cust Svc	Bridgeview	IL	60455	**800-621-3684***	708-563-9780
Curiosities Greeting Cards 64 Heather Rd	Buffalo	NY	14225	**877-424-4401**	716-837-7256
Current USA Inc 1005 E Woodmen Rd *Cust Svc	Colorado Springs	CO	80920	**800-525-7170***	719-594-4100
DaySpring Cards Inc PO Box 1010	Siloam Springs	AR	72761	**800-944-8000**	479-524-9301
Design Design Inc 19 La Grave SE	Grand Rapids	MI	49503	**800-334-3348**	616-774-2448
Designer Greetings Inc 250 Arlington Ave PO Box 140729	Staten Island	NY	10314	**800-654-6960**	718-981-7700
Different Drumbeats 400 Murrasy Hollow Rd	Shushan	NY	12873	**800-957-6548**	518-854-7446
Egreetings Network Inc 1 American Rd	Cleveland	OH	44144	**800-321-3040**	216-252-7300
Executive Greetings Inc 120 Greenwoods Industrial Pk *Cust Svc	New Hartford	CT	06057	**800-562-5468***	860-379-9911
Family Cards USA 892 Riverside St	Portland	ME	04103	**877-765-3422**	207-797-9738
Fantus Paper Products DBA PS Greetings Inc 5730 N Tripp Ave *Sales	Chicago	IL	60646	**800-621-8823***	773-267-6069
Fotofolio Inc 561 Broadway *Sales	New York	NY	10012	**800-955-3686***	212-226-0923
Freedom Greeting Card Co Inc 774 American Dr *Sales	Bensalem	PA	19020	**800-359-3301***	215-604-0300
FSG Crest LLC 354 W Armory Dr	South Holland	IL	60473	**877-747-1225**	708-210-0800
Gallant Greetings Corp 4300 United Pkwy	Schiller Park	IL	60176	**800-621-4279**	847-671-6500
Gina B Designs Inc 12700 Industrial Pk Blvd Suite 40	Plymouth	MN	55441	**800-228-4856**	763-559-7595
Glenrock International Inc 985 E Linden Ave	Linden	NJ	07036	**800-442-6374**	908-862-3433
Graphique De France 9 State St *Sales	Woburn	MA	01801	**800-444-1464***	781-935-3405
Great Arrow Graphics 2495 Main St Suite 457	Buffalo	NY	14214	**800-835-0490**	716-836-0408
Griffin Anna Inc 733 Lambert Dr	Atlanta	GA	30324	**888-817-8170**	404-817-8170
Hallmark Cards Inc 2501 McGee St	Kansas City	MO	64108	**800-425-5627**	816-274-5111
Hallmark International 2501 McGee St	Kansas City	MO	64108	**800-425-5627**	816-274-5111
Heart-Felt Greetings II Inc 1367 Fairview Blvd	Fairview	TN	37062	**800-818-9099**	615-799-8562
Idesign Greetings Inc 12020 W Ripley Ave	Milwaukee	WI	53226	**800-432-3301**	414-475-7176
InterArt Distribution DBA Sunrise Greetings 1145 Sunrise Greetings Ct *Sales	Bloomington	IN	47404	**800-457-4045***	812-336-9900
ITB Solutions DBA CardInTheBox 350 S Rohlwing Rd Suite 200	Addison	IL	60101	**877-212-1121**	630-953-8882
Kinka Cards 1 Orchard Park Rd	Madison	CT	06443	**800-635-4652**	
Krause Design Inc PO Box 240-319	Dorchester	MA	02124	**877-572-8730**	617-436-2661
Laughing Elephant 3645 Interlake Ave N	Seattle	WA	98103	**800-354-0400**	206-447-9229
Laura & Co Inc PO Box 1238	Yelm	WA	98597	**866-439-1715**	360-894-1418
Laurel Ink 911 N 145th St	Seattle	WA	98133	**800-850-0081**	206-767-4300
Leanin' Tree Inc 6055 Longbow Dr	Boulder	CO	80301	**800-777-8716**	303-530-1442
Marian Heath Greeting Cards Inc 9 Kendrick Rd *Sales	Wareham	MA	02571	**800-338-3740***	508-291-0766
Masterpiece Studios 2080 Lookout Dr Box 8240	North Mankato	MN	56002	**800-447-0219**	507-388-8788
Max & Lucy 5444 E Washington St Suite 3	Phoenix	AZ	85034	**877-975-5050**	602-275-5050
Meri Meri 525 Harbor Blvd	Bwlmont	CA	94002	**800-733-4770**	650-508-2300
Museum Facsimilies 117 4th St	Pittsfield	MA	01201	**800-499-0020**	413-499-0020
NCPL Inc DBA Northern Cards 5694 Ambler Dr	Mississauga	ON	L4W2K9	**877-627-7444**	905-625-4944
New England Art Publisher Inc DBA Birchcraft Studios Inc PO Box 328	Rockland	MA	02370	**800-333-0405**	781-878-5151
NobleWorks Inc 123 Grand St *Sales	Hoboken	NJ	07030	**800-346-6253***	201-420-0095
Northern Cards 5694 Ambler Dr	Mississauga	ON	L4W2K9	**877-627-7444**	905-625-4944
Northern Cards 5694 Ambler Dr	Mississauga	ON	L4W2K9	**877-627-7444**	905-625-4944
Northern Exposure Greeting Cards 461 Sebastopol Ave	Santa Rosa	CA	95401	**800-237-3524**	707-546-2153
Nouvelles Images Inc 22 Eagle Rd	Danbury	CT	06810	**800-345-1383**	203-730-1004
NRN Designs 5142 Argosy Ave	Huntington Beach	CA	92649	**800-421-6958**	714-898-6363
Nu-Art Publishers Inc 6247 W 74th St	Bedford Park	IL	60638	**800-323-0398**	708-496-4900
Oatmeal Studios Inc 35 Town Rd *Cust Svc	Rochester	VT	05767	**800-628-6325***	802-767-3171
Ooh La Lu! 1377 N Trail Creek Way	Eagle	ID	83616	**866-664-5258**	208-939-8940
Palm Press Inc 1442A Walnut St PMB 120	Berkeley	CA	94709	**800-322-7256**	510-486-0502
Paper Magic Group Inc 401 Adams Ave Suite 501 *Cust Svc	Scranton	PA	18510	**800-258-1044***	570-961-3863
Paper Prince 2001 Kennedy St NE	Minneapolis	MN	55413	**800-717-1574**	612-378-4691
Paperdoll Co 4944 Encino Ave	Encino	CA	91316	**866-223-1145**	818-906-8411
PaperTroupe Ltd 2975 W Soffel Ave	Melrose Park	IL	60160	**888-338-9244**	708-338-3838
Paramount Cards Inc 400 Pine St	Pawtucket	RI	02860	**800-554-5017**	401-726-0800
Parker Publications Inc PO Box 483	North Salem	NY	10560	**866-968-7872**	914-763-6933
Peaceable Kingdom Press 950 Gilman St	Berkeley	CA	94710	**800-444-7778**	510-558-2051
Penny Laine Papers 2211 Century Ctr Blvd Suite 110	Irving	TX	75062	**800-456-6484**	972-812-3000
Persimmon Press PO Box 297	Belmont	CA	94002	**800-910-5080**	
Portal Publications Ltd PO Box 6172	Novato	CA	94948	**800-227-1720**	415-884-6200
Postcards from the Moon 1525 Summit Ave	Seattle	WA	98122	**800-872-1410**	206-861-1971
PostMark Press Inc 16 Spruce St	Watertown	MA	02472	**888-924-3520**	617-924-3520
Posty Cards Inc 1600 Olive St *Sales	Kansas City	MO	64127	**800-554-5018***	816-231-2323
Potluck Press 1229 21st Ave E	Seattle	WA	98112	**877-818-5500**	206-323-8310
PS Greetings Inc 5730 N Tripp Ave *Sales	Chicago	IL	60646	**800-621-8823***	773-267-6069
Pulp Couture 230 W Huron St Suite 2E	Chicago	IL	60610	**800-404-6968**	312-420-2139
Queen of Cards 10008 S 67th E Pl	Tulsa	OK	74133	**888-899-2508**	918-299-1850
Recycled Paper Greetings Inc 3636 N Broadway *Cust Svc	Chicago	IL	60613	**800-777-9494***	773-348-6410
Red Farm Studio Co Inc 1135 Roosevelt Ave	Pawtucket	RI	02862	**800-556-7090**	401-728-9300
Renaissance Greeting Cards Inc 10 Renaissance Way	Sanford	ME	04073	**800-688-9998**	207-324-4153
Saltbox Illustrations 75 Green St Box 299	Clinton	MA	01510	**800-322-3866**	978-368-8711
Schurman Fine Papers 500 Chadbourne Rd Box 6030 *Sales	Fairfield	CA	94533	**800-333-6724***	707-428-0200
Sillies Greeting Card Co 14551 Judicial Rd Suite 130	Burnsville	MN	55306	**800-355-9148**	952-892-5666
Sole Source Inc 63820 Clausen Dr	Bend	OR	97701	**800-285-1657**	541-389-0360
Spirit Inspired PO Box 7904	Atlanta	GA	30357	**877-474-8460**	404-792-3664
StellArt 2012 Waltzer Rd	Santa Rosa	CA	95403	**866-621-1987**	707-569-1378
Sunrise Greetings 1145 Sunrise Greetings Ct *Sales	Bloomington	IN	47404	**800-457-4045***	812-336-9900
Sunshine Art Studios Inc 270 Main St	Agawam	MA	01001	**800-873-7681**	413-821-8700
Sunshine Girl Creations Inc 11115 Excelsior Blvd	Hopkins	MN	55343	**866-899-3632**	952-931-2464
Suzy's Zoo Corp 2355 Northside Dr Suite 202 *Cust Svc	San Diego	CA	92108	**800-780-9066***	619-282-9401
Tagline Greetings 1100 Irvine Blvd Suite 123	Tustin	CA	92780	**800-782-4546**	714-662-5807
Up With Paper 3255 Fairfield Ave PO Box 3962	Bridgeport	CT	06605	**800-852-7677**	203-337-4540
US Allegiance Inc 63004 Layton Ave	Bend	OR	97701	**800-327-1402**	541-330-6282
Vivyland 350 Detroit St Suite 206	Denver	CO	80206	**888-621-5266**	303-893-8038
William Arthur Inc 7 Alewive Park Rd PO Box 460	West Kennebunk	ME	04094	**800-985-6581**	207-985-6581
Willow Creek Press Inc 9931 Hwy 70 W PO Box 147	Minocqua	WI	54548	**800-850-9453**	715-358-7010
World Paper Inc 76 Ethel Ave	Hawthorne	NJ	07506	**800-385-5911**	973-238-1750
Your True Greetings 2215 Farmersville Rd	Bethlehem	PA	18020	**800-241-2704**	610-694-8028

131 CARPETS & RUGS

SEE ALSO Flooring - Resilient; Tile - Ceramic (Wall & Floor)

	City	State	ZIP	Toll-Free	Phone
Aladdin Mills Inc 2001 Antioch Rd	Dalton	GA	30720	**800-241-4072**	706-277-1100
Artisans Inc 716 River St	Calhoun	GA	30701	**800-311-8756**	706-629-9265
Atlas Carpet Mills Inc					
2200 Saybrook Ave	City of Commerce	CA	90040	**800-272-8527**	323-724-9000
Barrett Carpet Mills Inc 2216 Abutment Rd	Dalton	GA	30721	**800-241-4064**	706-277-2114
Beaulieu of America Inc 1414 Cleveland Hwy	Dalton	GA	30721	**800-633-2328**	706-370-4000
Bentley Mills Inc					
14641 E Don Julian Rd	City of Industry	CA	91746	**800-423-4709**	626-333-4585
Bigelow Commercial Div Mohawk Industries Inc					
160 S Industrial Blvd	Calhoun	GA	30703	**800-233-4490***	706-629-7721
*Cust Svc					
Blue Ridge Carpet Mills 1546 Progress Rd	Ellijay	GA	30540	**800-241-5945**	706-276-2001
Burlington Industries LLC					
804 Green Valley Rd Suite 300	Greensboro	NC	27408	**800-523-7888**	336-379-6220
Camelot Carpet Mills Inc 17111 Red Hill Ave	Irvine	CA	92614	**800-854-3258**	949-477-2299
Capel Inc 831 N Main St	Troy	NC	27371	**800-334-3711**	910-572-7000
Capitol Adhesives USA Dixie Mfg Co Div					
300 Cross Plains Blvd	Dalton	GA	30720	**800-831-8381**	706-277-6241
Carousel Carpet Mills Inc 1 Carousel Ln	Ukiah	CA	95482	**866-227-6873**	707-485-0333
Collins & Aikman Corp Floorcoverings Div					
PO Box 1447	Dalton	GA	30722	**800-241-4902**	706-259-9711
Couristan Inc 2 Executive Dr	Fort Lee	NJ	07024	**800-223-6186**	201-585-8500
Dixie Group Inc 345-B Nowlin Ln	Chattanooga	TN	37421	**800-241-4211**	706-876-5800
NASDAQ: DXYN					
Dixie Mfg Co Div Capitol Adhesives USA					
300 Cross Plains Blvd	Dalton	GA	30720	**800-831-8381**	706-277-6241
Dorsett Industries Inc 1304 May St	Dalton	GA	30721	**800-241-4035**	706-278-1961
Durkan Patterned Carpet Inc 405 Virgil Dr	Dalton	GA	30721	**800-241-4580**	706-278-7037
F Schumacher & Co 79 Madison Ave	New York	NY	10016	**800-556-0040**	212-213-7900
Galaxy Carpet Mills Inc 235 Industrial Blvd	Chatsworth	GA	30705	**800-835-6070**	706-695-9611
Georgia Tufters LLC 416 S River St	Calhoun	GA	30701	**800-232-2607**	706-629-4516
Glenoit LLC 3002 Anaconda Rd	Tarboro	NC	27886	**800-829-0984**	252-823-2124
Gulistan Carpet Inc 3140 Hwy 5	Aberdeen	NC	28315	**800-869-2727**	910-944-2371
Interface Flooring Systems Inc					
1503 Orchard Hill Rd	LaGrange	GA	30240	**800-336-0225**	706-882-1891
J & J Industries Inc 818 J & J Dr	Dalton	GA	30721	**800-241-4585**	706-278-4454
Karastan Div Mohawk Industries Inc					
335 Summit Rd	Eden	NC	27288	**800-845-8877***	336-627-7200
*Cust Svc					
Lees Carpets Div Mohawk Industries Inc					
706 Green Valley Rd	Greensboro	NC	27408	**800-523-5647**	336-378-9162
Len-Dal Carpets Inc PO Box 39	Chatsworth	GA	30705	**800-241-4030**	706-695-4533
Mannington Carpets Inc PO Box 12281	Calhoun	GA	30701	**800-241-2262**	706-629-7301
Maples Industries Inc					
2210 Moody Ridge Rd	Scottsboro	AL	35768	**800-537-3304**	256-259-1327
Marglen Industries Inc					
1748 Ward Mountain Rd NE	Rome	GA	30161	**800-627-4536**	706-295-5621
Masland Carpets Inc 716 Bill Myles Dr	Saraland	AL	36571	**800-633-0468**	251-675-9080
Milliken & Co KEX Div					
201 Lukken Industrial Dr W MS 801	LaGrange	GA	30240	**800-342-5539**	
Mohawk Carpet Corp 160 S Industrial Blvd	Calhoun	GA	30703	**800-241-4494**	706-629-7721
Mohawk Commercial Business					
443 Nathaniel Dr	East Dublin	GA	31027	**800-554-6637**	478-272-7711
Mohawk Home 3090 Sugar Valley Rd NW	Sugar Valley	GA	30746	**800-843-4473**	706-629-7916
Mohawk Industries Inc 160 S Industrial Blvd	Calhoun	GA	30703	**800-241-4494**	706-629-7721
NYSE: MHK					
Mohawk Industries Inc Bigelow Commercial Div					
160 S Industrial Blvd	Calhoun	GA	30703	**800-233-4490***	706-629-7721
*Cust Svc					
Mohawk Industries Inc Karastan Div					
335 Summit Rd	Eden	NC	27288	**800-845-8877***	336-627-7200
*Cust Svc					
Mohawk Industries Inc Lees Carpets Div					
706 Green Valley Rd	Greensboro	NC	27408	**800-523-5647**	336-378-9162
Oriental Weavers Group Sphinx Div					
3252 Lower Dug Gap Rd SW	Dalton	GA	30720	**800-832-8020**	706-277-9666
Patcraft Commercial Div Queen Carpet Co					
616 Duvall Rd	Chatsworth	GA	30705	**800-241-4014**	706-279-4000
Prince Street Technologies Ltd					
14641 E Don Jillian Rd	City of Industry	CA	91746	**800-221-3684**	626-333-4585
Queen Carpet Co Patcraft Commercial Div					
616 Duvall Rd	Chatsworth	GA	30705	**800-241-4014**	706-279-4000
Royalty Carpet Mills Inc 17111 Red Hill Ave	Irvine	CA	92614	**800-854-8331**	949-474-4000
Rug Barn Inc					
234 Industrial Park Rd PO Box 1187	Abbeville	SC	29620	**800-784-2276**	800-626-7033
S & S Mills Inc 205 Boring Dr	Dalton	GA	30721	**800-392-6890**	706-277-3677
Shaw Industries Inc 616 E Walnut Ave	Dalton	GA	30721	**800-742-9872**	706-278-3812
Stainmaster 175 Townmark Dr	Kennesaw	GA	30144	**800-438-7668**	877-446-8478
Synthetic Industries Inc					
309 LaFayette Rd	Chickamauga	GA	30707	**800-258-3121**	706-375-3121
Tuftex Carpet Mills					
15305 Valley View Ave	Santa Fe Springs	CA	90670	**877-224-7429**	562-921-0951
Unique Carpets Ltd 7360 Jurupa Ave	Riverside	CA	92504	**800-547-8266**	951-352-8125
World Carpets Inc 31 S Green St	Dalton	GA	30720	**800-241-4900***	800-233-4490
*Cust Svc					

132 CASINO COMPANIES

SEE ALSO Games & Gaming

	City	State	ZIP	Toll-Free	Phone
Alliance Gaming Corp 6601 S Bermuda Rd	Las Vegas	NV	89119	**877-462-2559**	702-896-7700
NYSE: AGI					
Ameristar Casinos Inc					
3773 Howard Hughes Pkwy Suite 490-S	Las Vegas	NV	89109	**866-921-9229**	702-567-7000
NASDAQ: ASCA					
Argosy Gaming Co 219 Piasa St	Alton	IL	62002	**800-336-7568**	618-474-7500
NYSE: AGY					
Boomtown Inc PO Box 399	Verdi	NV	89439	**800-648-3790**	775-345-6000
Boyd Gaming Corp 2950 Industrial Rd	Las Vegas	NV	89109	**800-695-2455**	702-792-7200
NYSE: BYD					
Casino Magic Corp					
711 Casino Magic Dr	Bay Saint Louis	MS	39520	**800-562-4425**	228-467-9257
Century Casinos Inc					
200-220 E Bennett Ave	Cripple Creek	CO	80813	**888-966-2257**	719-689-0333
NASDAQ: CNTY					
Coast Casinos Inc 4500 W Tropicana Ave	Las Vegas	NV	89103	**888-365-7111**	702-365-7111
Delaware North Cos Gaming & Entertainment					
40 Fountain Plaza	Buffalo	NY	14202	**800-828-7240**	716-858-5000
Exber Inc 600 E Freemont St	Las Vegas	NV	89101	**800-634-6703**	702-385-5200
Fond du Lac Band of Lake Superior Chippewa					
1720 Big Lake Rd	Cloquet	MN	55720	**800-365-1613**	218-879-4593
Harrah's Entertainment Inc 1 Harrah's Ct	Las Vegas	NV	89119	**800-442-6443**	702-407-6000
NYSE: HET					
Ho-Chunk Nation PO Box 667	Black River Falls	WI	54615	**800-294-9343**	715-284-9343
Imperial Palace Inc 3535 Las Vegas Blvd S	Las Vegas	NV	89109	**800-634-6441**	702-731-3311
Isle of Capri Casinos Inc					
1641 Popps Ferry Rd Suite B-1	Biloxi	MS	39532	**800-843-4753**	228-396-7000
NASDAQ: ISLE					
Kerzner International Ltd					
1000 S Pine Island Rd	Plantation	FL	33324	**800-321-3000**	954-809-2000
NYSE: KZL					
Lakes Entertainment Inc					
130 Cheshire Ln Suite 101	Minnetonka	MN	55305	**800-946-9464**	952-449-9092
NASDAQ: LACO					
Majestic Investor Holdings LLC					
1 Buffington Harbor Dr	Gary	IN	46406	**888-225-8258**	219-977-7777
Mashantucket Pequot Gaming Enterprise					
Inc PO Box 3777	Mashantucket	CT	06338	**800-752-9244**	860-312-3000
Mille Lacs Band of Ojibwe 43408 Oodena Dr	Onamia	MN	56359	**800-709-6445**	320-532-4181
MTR Gaming Group Inc PO Box 358	Chester	WV	26034	**800-804-0468**	304-387-8300
NASDAQ: MNTG					
President Casinos Inc 800 N 1st St	Saint Louis	MO	63102	**800-772-3647**	314-622-3000
Primm Valley Resorts 31900 S Las Vegas Blvd	Primm	NV	89019	**800-386-7867**	702-382-1212
Red Lake Gaming Enterprises Inc					
PO Box 543	Red Lake	MN	56671	**800-568-6649**	218-679-2111
Saint Croix Chippewa Tribe of Wisconsin					
24663 Angeline Ave	Webster	WI	54893	**800-236-2195**	715-349-2195
Station Casinos Inc 2411 W Sahara Ave	Las Vegas	NV	89102	**800-544-2411**	702-367-2411
NYSE: STN					

133 CASINOS

SEE ALSO Games & Gaming

	City	State	ZIP	Toll-Free	Phone
Casino Arizona at Salt River 524 N 92nd St	Scottsdale	AZ	85256	**877-724-4687**	480-850-7777
Fort McDowell Casino					
Fort McDowell Rd Hwy 87	Scottsdale	AZ	85264	**800-843-3678**	480-837-1424
Harrah's Ak-Chin Casino Resort					
15406 Maricopa Rd	Maricopa	AZ	85239	**888-302-3293**	480-802-3091
Harrah's Phoenix Ak-Chin Casino Resort					
15406 Maricopa Rd	Maricopa	AZ	85239	**800-427-7247**	480-802-5000
Augustine Casino 84-001 Ave 54	Coachella	CA	92236	**888-752-9294**	760-391-9500
Barona Valley Ranch Resort & Casino					
1932 Wildcat Canyon Rd	Lakeside	CA	92040	**888-722-7662**	619-443-2300
Bicycle Casino 7301 Eastern Ave	Bell Gardens	CA	90201	**800-292-0015**	562-806-4646
Chumash Casino 3400 E Hwy 246	Santa Ynez	CA	93460	**800-728-9997**	805-686-0855
Eagle Mountain Casino 681 S Tule Rd	Porterville	CA	93257	**800-903-3353**	559-788-6220
Fantasy Springs Resort Casino					
84-245 Indio Springs Pkwy	Indio	CA	92203	**800-827-2946**	760-342-5000
Harrah's Rincon Casino & Resort					
777 Harrah's Rincon Way	Valley Center	CA	92082	**877-777-2457**	760-751-3100
Morongo Casino Resort & Spa					
49500 Seminole Dr PO Box 366	Cabazon	CA	92230	**800-252-4499**	951-849-3080
Pala Casino Resort & Spa					
11154 Hwy 76 PO Box 40	Pala	CA	92059	**877-946-7252**	760-510-5100
Pechanga Resort & Casino					
45000 Pechanga Pkwy	Temecula	CA	92592	**877-711-2946**	951-693-1819
San Manuel Indian Bingo & Casino					
777 San Manuel Blvd	Highland	CA	92346	**800-359-2464**	909-864-5050
Spa Hotel & Casino					
100 N Indian Canyon Dr	Palm Springs	CA	92262	**800-854-1279**	760-325-1461
Spa Resort Casino 401 E Amado Rd	Palm Springs	CA	92262	**800-854-1279**	760-883-1000
Spotlight 29 Casino 46-200 Harrison Pl	Coachella	CA	92236	**866-878-6729**	760-775-5566
Sycuan Casino & Resort 5469 Casino Way	El Cajon	CA	92019	**800-279-2826**	619-445-6002
Viejas Casino 5000 Willows Rd	Alpine	CA	91901	**800-847-6537**	619-445-5400
Bronco Billy's Casino 233 E Bennett Ave	Cripple Creek	CO	80813	**877-989-2142**	719-689-2142
Bullwhackers Casino 101 Gregory St	Black Hawk	CO	80422	**800-426-2855**	
Isle of Capri Casino 401 Main St	Black Hawk	CO	80422	**800-843-4753**	
Midnight Rose Hotel & Casino					
256 E Bennett Ave	Cripple Creek	CO	80813	**888-461-7529**	719-689-2446
Sky Ute Casino 14826 Hwy 172 N	Ignacio	CO	81137	**888-842-4180**	970-563-3000
Ute Mountain Casino 3 Weeminuche Dr	Towaoc	CO	81334	**800-258-8007**	970-565-8800
Foxwoods Resort Casino					
39 Norwich Westerly Rd	Ledyard	CT	06339	**800-752-9244**	860-312-3000
Mohegan Sun Resort & Casino					
1 Mohegan Sun Blvd	Uncasville	CT	06382	**888-226-7711**	860-862-8000
Palm Beach Casino Line					
1 E 11th St Suite 500	Riviera Beach	FL	33404	**800-841-7447**	561-845-2101
SeaEscape Entertainment Inc					
3045 N Federal Hwy	Fort Lauderdale	FL	33306	**877-732-3722**	954-453-2200
Seminole Casino Hollywood					
4150 N State Rd 7	Hollywood	FL	33021	**866-222-7466**	954-961-3220
Seminole Casino Immokalee 506 S 1st St	Immokalee	FL	34143	**800-218-0007**	
Seminole Coconut Creek Casino					
5550 NW 40th St	Coconut Creek	FL	33073	**866-222-2466**	954-977-6700
Seminole Hard Rock Hotel & Casino					
Hollywood 1 Seminole Way	Hollywood	FL	33314	**800-937-0010**	954-327-7625
Seminole Hard Rock Hotel & Casino Tampa					
5223 N Orient Rd	Tampa	FL	33610	**800-282-7016**	813-621-1302
SunCruz Casino 647 E Dania Beach Blvd	Dania Beach	FL	33004	**800-474-3423**	954-929-3880
SunCruz Casino - Port Canaveral					
610 Glen Cheek Dr	Cape Canaveral	FL	32920	**800-474-3423**	321-783-2770
Argosy's Alton Belle Casino 219 Piasa St	Alton	IL	62002	**800-336-7568**	
Casino Queen 200 S Front St	East Saint Louis	IL	62201	**800-777-0777**	618-874-5000
Empress Casino 2300 Empress Dr	Joliet	IL	60436	**888-436-7737**	815-744-9400
Harrah's Joliet 151 N Joliet St	Joliet	IL	60432	**800-427-7247**	815-740-7800
Harrah's Metropolis Casino 100 E Front St	Metropolis	IL	62960	**800-929-5905**	618-524-2628

Classified Section

Name / Address	City	State	ZIP	Toll-Free	Phone
Par-A-Dice Riverboat Casino 21 Blackjack Blvd	East Peoria	IL	61611	800-727-2342	309-698-7711
Argosy Casino Cincinnati 777 Argosy Pkwy	Lawrenceburg	IN	47025	888-274-6797*	812-539-8000
*Resv					
Belterra Casino Resort 777 Belterra Dr	Belterra	IN	47020	888-235-8377*	812-427-7777
*Resv					
Blue Chip Casino Inc 2 Easy St	Michigan City	IN	46350	888-879-7711	219-879-7711
Casino Aztar 421 NW Riverside Dr	Evansville	IN	47708	800-342-5386	812-433-4000
Grand Victoria Casino & Resort by Hyatt 600 Grand Victoria Dr	Rising Sun	IN	47040	800-472-6311	812-438-1234
Resorts East Chicago 777 Harrah's Blvd	East Chicago	IN	46312	877-496-1777	219-378-3000
Trump Casino Hotel 1 Buffington Harbor Dr	Gary	IN	46406	888-218-7867	219-977-7000
Ameristar Casino Hotel Council Bluffs 2200 River Rd	Council Bluffs	IA	51501	877-462-7827	712-328-8888
Bluffs Run Casino 2701 23rd Ave	Council Bluffs	IA	51501	800-238-2946	712-323-2500
Harrah's Council Bluffs 1 Harrah's Blvd	Council Bluffs	IA	51501	888-598-8451	712-329-6000
Meskwaki Bingo Hotel Casino 1504 305th St	Tama	IA	52339	800-728-4263	641-484-2108
Rhythm City Casino 101 W River Dr	Davenport	IA	52801	800-262-8711	563-322-2628
Harrah's Prairie Band Casino & Hotel 12305 150th Rd	Mayetta	KS	66509	800-427-7247	785-966-7777
Bally's Casino New Orleans 1 Stars & Stripes Blvd	New Orleans	LA	70126	800-572-2559	504-248-3200
Boomtown Casino New Orleans 4132 Peters Rd	Harvey	LA	70058	800-366-7711	504-366-7711
Boomtown Hotel Casino 300 Riverside Dr	Bossier City	LA	71111	877-862-4428	318-746-0711
Coushatta Casino Resort 777 Coushatta Dr PO Box 1510	Kinder	LA	70648	800-584-7263	337-738-7300
Harrah's Lake Charles Casino & Hotel 505 N Lakeshore Dr	Lake Charles	LA	70601	800-427-7247	337-437-1500
Harrah's New Orleans 512 S Peter St	New Orleans	LA	70130	800-847-5299	504-533-6000
Isle of Capri Casino & Hotel 711 Isle of Capri Blvd	Bossier City	LA	71111	800-843-4753	318-678-7777
Isle of Capri Lake Charles 100 W Lake Ave	West Lake	LA	70669	800-843-4753	337-430-0711
Paragon Casino Resort 711 Paragon Pl	Marksville	LA	71351	800-946-1946	318-253-1946
Sam's Town Hotel & Casino Shreveport 315 Clyde Fant Pkwy	Shreveport	LA	71101	877-429-0711	318-424-7777
Treasure Chest Casino 5050 Williams Blvd	Kenner	LA	70065	800-298-0711	504-443-8000
Kewadin Casinos 3039 Mackinac Tr	Saint Ignace	MI	49781	800-539-2346	906-643-7071
Leelanau Sands Casino 2521 NW Bayshore Dr	Suttons Bay	MI	49682	800-922-2946	231-271-4104
MGM Grand Detroit Casino 1300 John C Lodge	Detroit	MI	48226	877-888-2121	313-393-7777
MotorCity Casino 2901 Grand River Ave	Detroit	MI	48201	877-777-0711	313-237-7711
Soaring Eagle Casino & Resort 6800 E Soaring Eagle Blvd	Mount Pleasant	MI	48858	877-232-4532	989-775-5777
Black Bear Casino 1785 Hwy 210 PO Box 777	Carlton	MN	55718	888-771-0777	218-878-2327
Grand Casino Hinckley 777 Lady Luck Dr	Hinckley	MN	55037	800-472-6321	320-384-7777
Grand Casino Mille Lacs 777 Grand Ave PO Box 343	Onamia	MN	56359	800-626-5825	320-532-7777
Jackpot Junction Casino Hotel 39375 County Hwy 24 PO Box 420	Morton	MN	56270	800-946-2274	507-644-3000
Mystic Lake Casino 2400 Mystic Lake Blvd	Prior Lake	MN	55372	800-262-7799	952-445-9000
Treasure Island Resort & Casino 5734 Sturgeon Lake Rd	Welch	MN	55089	800-222-7077	651-388-6300
Ameristar Casino Hotel Vicksburg 4116 Washington St	Vicksburg	MS	39180	800-700-7770	601-638-1000
Bally's Casino Tunica 1450 Bally's Blvd Casino Ctr	Robinsonville	MS	38664	800-382-2559	662-357-1500
Boomtown Casino Biloxi 676 Bayview Ave	Biloxi	MS	39530	800-627-0777	228-435-7000
Casino Magic Bay Saint Louis 711 Casino Magic Dr	Bay Saint Louis	MS	39520	800-562-4425	228-467-9257
Casino Magic Biloxi 195 Beach Blvd	Biloxi	MS	39530	800-562-4425	228-386-4600
Fitzgeralds Casino & Hotel Tunica 711 Lucky Ln	Robinsonville	MS	38664	888-766-5825	662-363-5825
Gold Strike Casino Resort 1010 Casino Ctr Dr	Robinsonville	MS	38664	888-245-7829*	662-357-1111
*Resv					
Grand Casino Biloxi 265 Beach Blvd	Biloxi	MS	39530	800-946-2946	228-436-2946
Grand Casino Gulfport 3215 W Beach Blvd	Gulfport	MS	39501	800-946-7777	228-870-7777
Grand Casino Tunica 13615 Old Hwy 61 N	Robinsonville	MS	38664	800-946-4946	662-363-2788
Harrah's Vicksburg 1310 Mulberry St	Vicksburg	MS	39180	800-843-2343	601-636-3423
Hollywood Casino & Hotel 1150 Casino Strip Blvd PO Box 218	Robinsonville	MS	38664	800-871-0711	662-357-7700
Horseshoe Casino & Hotel 1021 Casino Ctr Dr	Robinsonville	MS	38664	800-303-7463	662-357-5500
Imperial Palace Mississippi 850 Bayview Ave	Biloxi	MS	39530	800-436-3000	228-436-3000
Isle of Capri Casino 777 Isle of Capri Pkwy	Lula	MS	38644	800-789-5825	662-363-4600
Isle of Capri Casino Resort 151 Beach Blvd	Biloxi	MS	39530	800-843-4753	228-435-5400
Pearl River Resort 13541 Hwy 16 W	Choctaw	MS	39350	800-557-0711	601-650-1234
President Casino Broadwater Resort 2110 Beach Blvd	Biloxi	MS	39531	800-843-7737	228-388-2211
Resorts Tunica 1100 Casino Strip Blvd PO Box 750	Robinsonville	MS	38664	866-797-7111*	662-363-7777
*Resv					
Sam's Town Hotel & Gambling Hall 1477 Casino Strip Blvd	Robinsonville	MS	38664	800-456-0711	662-363-0700
Sheraton Casino & Hotel 1107 Casino Center Dr	Robinsonville	MS	38664	800-391-3777	662-363-4900
Treasure Bay Casino Resort 1980 Beach Blvd	Biloxi	MS	39531	800-747-2839	228-388-6610
Ameristar Casino Saint Charles 1260 S Main St PO Box 720	Saint Charles	MO	63301	800-325-7777	636-940-4300
Argosy Casino Kansas City 777 NW Argosy Pkwy	Riverside	MO	64150	800-900-3423	816-746-3100
Harrah's Saint Louis Casino & Hotel 777 Casino Center Dr	Maryland Heights	MO	63043	800-427-7247	314-770-8100
Isle of Capri Casino 1800 E Front St	Kansas City	MO	64120	800-843-4753	816-855-7777
President Casino on the Admiral 802 N 1st St	Saint Louis	MO	63102	800-772-3647	314-622-1111
Aladdin Resort & Casino 3667 Las Vegas Blvd S	Las Vegas	NV	89109	877-333-9474	702-785-5555
Arizona Charlie's Hotel & Casino 740 S Decatur Blvd	Las Vegas	NV	89107	800-342-2695	702-258-5111
Atlantis Casino Resort 3800 S Virginia St	Reno	NV	89502	800-723-6500	775-825-4700
Bally's Las Vegas 3645 Las Vegas Blvd S	Las Vegas	NV	89109	800-225-5977*	702-739-4111
*Resv					
Binion's Horseshoe Hotel & Casino 128 E Fremont St	Las Vegas	NV	89101	800-237-6537	702-382-1600
Boardwalk Hotel & Casino 3750 Las Vegas Blvd S	Las Vegas	NV	89109	800-635-4581	702-735-2400
Boomtown Casino & Hotel Reno 2100 Garson Rd	Verdi	NV	89439	800-648-3790	775-345-6000
Boulder Station Hotel & Casino 4111 Boulder Hwy	Las Vegas	NV	89121	800-683-7777	702-432-7777
Buffalo Bill's Resort & Casino 31700 S Las Vegas Blvd	Primm	NV	89019	800-386-7867	702-382-1111
Cactus Pete's Resort Casino 1385 Hwy 93 PO Box 508	Jackpot	NV	89825	800-821-1103	775-755-2321
Caesars Palace Las Vegas 3570 Las Vegas Blvd S	Las Vegas	NV	89109	800-634-6661	702-731-7110
Caesars Tahoe 55 Hwy 50 PO Box 5800	Stateline	NV	89449	800-648-3353	775-588-3515
California Hotel & Casino 12 Ogden Ave	Las Vegas	NV	89101	800-634-6255	702-385-1222
Carson Nugget Casino 507 N Carson St	Carson City	NV	89702	800-426-5239	775-882-1626
Circus Circus Hotel & Casino Las Vegas 2880 Las Vegas Blvd S	Las Vegas	NV	89109	800-634-3450*	702-734-0410
*Resv					
Circus Circus Hotel & Casino Reno 500 N Sierra St	Reno	NV	89503	800-648-5010	775-329-0711
Colorado Belle Hotel & Casino 2100 S Casino Dr	Laughlin	NV	89029	800-477-4837*	702-298-4000
*Resv					
Don Laughlin's Riverside Resort & Casino 1650 Casino Dr	Laughlin	NV	89029	800-227-3849	702-298-2535
Edgewater Hotel & Casino 2020 Casino Dr	Laughlin	NV	89029	800-677-4837	702-298-2453
El Cortez Hotel & Casino 600 E Fremont St	Las Vegas	NV	89101	800-634-6703	702-385-5200
Eldorado Hotel Casino 345 N Virginia St	Reno	NV	89501	800-648-5966*	775-786-5700
*Resv					
Excalibur Hotel & Casino 3850 Las Vegas Blvd S	Las Vegas	NV	89109	800-937-7777*	702-597-7777
*Resv					
Fiesta Casino Hotel 2400 N Rancho Dr	Las Vegas	NV	89130	800-731-7333	702-631-7000
Fitzgeralds Casino & Hotel Reno 255 N Virginia St PO Box 40130	Reno	NV	89504	800-535-5825	775-785-3300
Flamingo Las Vegas 3555 Las Vegas Blvd S	Las Vegas	NV	89109	800-732-2111*	702-733-3111
*Resv					
Flamingo Laughlin 1900 S Casino Dr	Laughlin	NV	89029	800-352-6464*	702-298-5111
*Resv					
Fremont Hotel & Casino 200 E Fremont St	Las Vegas	NV	89101	800-634-6182	702-385-3232
Gold Coast Hotel & Casino 4000 W Flamingo Rd	Las Vegas	NV	89103	888-402-6278	702-367-7111
Gold Strike Hotel & Gambling Hall 1 Main St PO Box 19278	Jean	NV	89019	800-634-1359	702-477-5000
Golden Nugget Hotel 129 E Fremont St	Las Vegas	NV	89101	800-634-3454	702-385-7111
Golden Nugget Laughlin 2300 S Casino Dr	Laughlin	NV	89029	800-237-1739	702-298-7111
Harrah's Lake Tahoe PO Box 8	Stateline	NV	89449	800-427-7247	775-588-6611
Harrah's Las Vegas 3475 Las Vegas Blvd S	Las Vegas	NV	89109	800-427-7247	702-369-5000
Harrah's Laughlin 2900 S Casino Dr PO Box 33000	Laughlin	NV	89029	800-427-7247	702-298-4600
Harrah's Reno 219 N Center St	Reno	NV	89501	800-427-7247	775-786-3232
Harveys Resort Hotel & Casino Hwy 50 PO Box 128	Stateline	NV	89449	800-427-8397	775-588-2411
Hilton Reno Resort & Casino 2500 E 2nd St	Reno	NV	89595	800-501-2651	775-789-2000
Hyatt Regency Lake Tahoe Resort & Casino 111 Country Club Dr	Incline Village	NV	89451	800-233-1234	775-832-1234
Imperial Palace Hotel & Casino 3535 Las Vegas Blvd S	Las Vegas	NV	89109	800-634-6441	702-731-3311
John Ascuaga's Nugget Hotel Casino 1100 Nugget Ave	Sparks	NV	89431	800-648-1177	775-356-3300
Las Vegas Club 18 E Fremont St	Las Vegas	NV	89101	800-634-6532	702-385-1664
Las Vegas Hilton 3000 Paradise Rd	Las Vegas	NV	89109	800-732-7117	702-732-5111
Luxor Hotel & Casino 3900 Las Vegas Blvd S	Las Vegas	NV	89119	800-288-1000*	702-262-4000
*Resv					
Mandalay Bay Resort & Casino 3950 Las Vegas Blvd S	Las Vegas	NV	89119	877-632-7800	702-632-7777
MGM Grand Hotel & Casino 3799 Las Vegas Blvd S	Las Vegas	NV	89109	800-929-1111	702-891-1111
Monte Carlo Resort & Casino 3770 Las Vegas Blvd S	Las Vegas	NV	89109	800-311-8999	702-730-7777
Nevada Landing Hotel & Casino 2 Goodsprings Rd	Jean	NV	89019	800-628-6682	702-387-5000
New Frontier The 3120 Las Vegas Blvd S	Las Vegas	NV	89109	800-634-6966	702-794-8200
New York New York Hotel & Casino 3790 Las Vegas Blvd S	Las Vegas	NV	89109	800-693-6763	702-740-6969
Orleans Las Vegas Hotel & Casino 4500 W Tropicana Ave	Las Vegas	NV	89103	888-365-7111	702-365-7111
Palace Station Hotel & Casino 2411 W Sahara Ave	Las Vegas	NV	89102	800-634-3101	702-367-2411
Paris Las Vegas 3655 Las Vegas Blvd S	Las Vegas	NV	89109	888-266-5687	702-946-7000
Peppermill Hotel & Casino 2707 S Virginia St	Reno	NV	89502	800-282-2444	775-826-2121
Railroad Pass Hotel & Casino 2800 S Boulder Hwy	Henderson	NV	89015	800-654-0877	702-294-5000
Rio All-Suite Hotel & Casino 3700 W Flamingo Rd	Las Vegas	NV	89103	888-746-7482	702-777-7777
River Palms Resort & Casino 2700 S Casino Dr	Laughlin	NV	89029	800-835-7904	702-298-2242
Riviera Hotel & Casino 2901 Las Vegas Blvd S	Las Vegas	NV	89109	800-634-6753*	702-734-5110
*Resv					
Sahara Hotel & Casino 2535 Las Vegas Blvd S	Las Vegas	NV	89109	888-696-2121	702-737-2111
Sam's Town Hotel & Gambling Hall 5111 Boulder Hwy	Las Vegas	NV	89122	800-634-6371	702-456-7777
Sands Regency Hotel & Casino 345 N Arlington Ave	Reno	NV	89501	800-648-3553*	775-348-2200
*Resv					
Santa Fe Station 4949 N Rancho Dr	Las Vegas	NV	89130	866-767-7771	702-658-4900
Silver Legacy Resort & Casino 407 N Virginia St	Reno	NV	89501	800-687-8733	775-329-4777
Silverton Hotel & Casino 3333 Blue Diamond Rd	Las Vegas	NV	89139	800-588-7711	702-263-7777
Stardust Resort & Casino 3000 Las Vegas Blvd S	Las Vegas	NV	89109	800-634-6757	702-732-6111
Stratosphere Tower Hotel & Casino 2000 S Las Vegas Blvd	Las Vegas	NV	89104	800-998-6937	702-380-7777
Texas Station Gambling Hall & Hotel 2101 Texas Star Ln	North Las Vegas	NV	89032	800-654-8888*	702-631-1000
*Resv					
Treasure Island Hotel & Casino 3300 Las Vegas Blvd S	Las Vegas	NV	89109	800-944-7444	702-894-7111
Tropicana Resort & Casino 3801 Las Vegas Blvd S	Las Vegas	NV	89109	888-826-8767*	702-739-2222
*Resv					
Western Village Inn & Casino 815 Nickel Blvd	Sparks	NV	89434	800-648-1170	775-331-1069
Whiskey Pete's Hotel & Casino 100 W Primm Blvd	Primm	NV	89019	800-386-7867	702-382-4388
Wynn Las Vegas 3131 Las Vegas Blvd S	Las Vegas	NV	89109	888-320-7123	702-770-7000
Atlantic City Hilton Boston & Pacific Ave	Atlantic City	NJ	08401	877-432-7139	609-347-7111

				Toll-Free	Phone
Bally's Atlantic City 1900 Boardwalk & Park Pl	Atlantic City	NJ	08401	**800-772-7777**	609-340-2000
Caesars Atlantic City 2100 Pacific Ave	Atlantic City	NJ	08401	**800-443-0104**	609-348-4411
Harrah's Atlantic City 777 Harrah's Blvd	Atlantic City	NJ	08401	**800-427-7247**	609-441-5000
Resorts Atlantic City 1133 Boardwalk	Atlantic City	NJ	08401	**800-336-6378**	609-344-6000
Sands Hotel & Casino 136 S Kentucky Ave	Atlantic City	NJ	08401	**800-227-2637**	609-441-4000
Showboat Atlantic City 801 Boardwalk	Atlantic City	NJ	08401	**800-427-7247**	609-343-4000
Tropicana Casino & Resort 2831 Boardwalk	Atlantic City	NJ	08401	**800-843-8767**	609-340-4000
Trump Marina Hotel & Casino Huron Ave & Brigantine Blvd *Resv	Atlantic City	NJ	08401	**800-777-8477***	609-441-2000
Trump Plaza Hotel & Casino 2225 Mississippi Ave	Atlantic City	NJ	08401	**800-677-7378**	609-441-6000
Trump Taj Mahal Casino Resort 1000 Boardwalk & Virginia Ave *Resv	Atlantic City	NJ	08401	**800-825-8786***	609-449-1000
Cities of Gold Casino 10-B Cities of Gold Rd	Santa Fe	NM	87506	**800-455-3313**	505-455-3313
Sandia Casino 30 Rainbow Rd NE	Albuquerque	NM	87113	**800-526-9366**	505-796-7500
Turning Stone Casino Resort 5218 Patrick Rd	Verona	NY	13478	**800-771-7711**	315-361-7711
Harrah's Cherokee Casino & Hotel 777 Casino Dr	Cherokee	NC	28719	**800-427-7247**	828-497-7777
Casino Niagara 5705 Falls Ave	Niagara Falls	ON	L2G7M9	**888-946-3255**	905-374-3598
Casino Windsor 377 Riverside Dr E	Windsor	ON	N9A7H7	**800-991-7777**	519-258-7878
Speaking Rock Casino & Entertainment Centre 122 S Old Pueblo Rd	El Paso	TX	79907	**800-772-2646**	915-860-7777
Emerald Queen Casino 2102 Alexander Ave	Tacoma	WA	98421	**888-831-7655**	253-594-7777
Muckleshoot Indian Casino 2402 Auburn Way S	Auburn	WA	98002	**800-804-4944**	253-804-4444
Skagit Valley Casino Resort 5984 N Darrk Ln	Bow	WA	98232	**877-275-2448**	360-724-7777
Tulalip Casino 10200 Quil Ceda Blvd	Tulalip	WA	98271	**888-272-1111**	360-651-1111
Ho-Chunk Casino S 3214 Hwy 12	Baraboo	WI	53913	**800-746-2486**	608-356-6210
Lake of the Torches Resort Casino 510 Old Abe Rd	Lac du Flambeau	WI	54538	**800-258-6724**	715-588-7070
Oneida Bingo & Casino 2020 Airport Dr	Oneida	WI	54155	**800-238-4263**	920-497-8118
Saint Croix Casino & Hotel 777 US Hwys 8 & 63	Turtle Lake	WI	54889	**800-846-8946**	715-986-4777

134 CASKETS & VAULTS

SEE ALSO Mortuary, Crematory, Cemetery Companies

				Toll-Free	Phone
Astral Industries Inc 7375 US 27 S PO Box 638 *Sales	Lynn	IN	47355	**800-874-1070***	765-874-2525
Aurora Casket Co Inc 10944 Marsh Rd PO Box 29 *Cust Svc	Aurora	IN	47001	**800-457-1111***	812-926-1111
Balanced Line Casket Co 15 S Boundary St	Cambridge City	IN	47327	**800-382-6934**	765-478-3501
Casket Royale 137 Lafayette Rd	Hampton Falls	NH	03844	**800-791-4169**	603-929-1515
Clark Grave Vault Co 375 E 5th Ave	Columbus	OH	43201	**800-848-3570**	614-294-3761
Delta Casket Co 821 Lone Oak Dr	West Point	MS	39773	**800-647-6310**	662-494-4151
Loretto Casket Co 110 W Commerce St	Loretto	TN	38469	**800-225-9105**	931-853-6921
Matthews International Corp 2 Northshore Ctr Suite 200 *NASDAQ: MATW*	Pittsburgh	PA	15212	**800-223-4964**	412-442-8200
Norwalk-Wilbert Vault Co 425 Harral Ave	Bridgeport	CT	06604	**800-826-9406**	203-366-5678
Paul Casket Co 505 S Green St	Cambridge City	IN	47327	**800-521-8202**	765-478-3991
Providence Casket Co 1 Industrial Cir	Lincoln	RI	02865	**800-848-2999**	401-726-1700
Sound Casket Inc 20350 71st Ave NE Suite F	Arlington	WA	98223	**800-735-7274**	425-259-6012
Wilbert Funeral Services Inc 2913 Gardner Rd	Broadview	IL	60155	**800-323-7188**	708-865-1600
Wilbert Inc PO Box 147	Forest Park	IL	60130	**800-323-7188**	708-865-1600
York Group Inc 2 Northshore Ctr Suite 100	Pittsburgh	PA	15212	**800-223-4964**	412-995-1600

135 CEMENT

				Toll-Free	Phone
Ash Grove Cement Co PO Box 25900	Overland Park	KS	66225	**800-545-1886**	913-451-8900
California Portland Cement Co 2025 E Financial Way Suite 200	Glendora	CA	91741	**800-272-1891**	626-852-6200
Capitol Aggregates Ltd 11551 Nacogdoches Rd	San Antonio	TX	78217	**800-292-5315**	210-655-3010
Carter-Waters Corp 2440 W Pennway St	Kansas City	MO	64108	**800-444-2570**	816-471-2570
Centex Corp 2728 N Harwood St *NYSE: CTX*	Dallas	TX	75201	**888-847-5130**	214-981-5000
CGM Inc 1445 Ford Rd	Bensalem	PA	19020	**800-523-6570**	215-638-4400
Coastal Cement Corp 36 Drydock Ave	Boston	MA	02210	**800-828-8352**	617-350-0183
Continental Cement Co LLC 14755 N Outer 40 Suite 514	Chesterfield	MO	63017	**800-625-1144**	636-532-7440
Dragon Products Co 38 Preble St	Portland	ME	04104	**800-828-8352**	207-774-6355
Eastern Cement Corp 13250 Eastern Ave	Palmetto	FL	34221	**800-282-7798**	941-729-7311
ESSROC Materials Inc 3251 Bath Pike	Nazareth	PA	18064	**800-523-9238**	610-837-6725
Federal White Cement Ltd PO Box 548 *Sales	Woodstock	ON	N4S7Y5	**800-265-1806***	519-485-5410
GCC Dacotah 501 N Saint Onge St	Rapid City	SD	57702	**800-843-8324**	605-721-7100
Giant Cement Holding Inc 320-D Midland Pkwy	Summerville	SC	29485	**800-845-1174**	843-851-9898
Glens Falls Lehigh Cement Co 313 Warren St	Glens Falls	NY	12801	**800-833-4157**	518-792-1137
Holcim (US) Inc 1100 Victors Way Suite 50	Ann Arbor	MI	48108	**800-831-9507**	734-821-7000
Inland Cement Ltd PO Box 3961	Edmonton	AB	T5L4P8	**800-252-9304**	780-420-2500
Keystone Cement Co PO Box A	Bath	PA	18014	**800-523-5442**	610-837-1881
Knife River Corp 1915 N Kavaney Dr	Bismarck	ND	58501	**800-982-5339**	701-223-1771
Lehigh Cement Co North America 7660 Imperial Way	Allentown	PA	18195	**800-523-5488**	610-366-4600
Lehigh Southwest Cement Co 2300 Clayton Rd Suite 300	Concord	CA	94520	**888-554-5010**	925-609-6920
Monarch Cement Co 449 1200 St PO Box 1000	Humboldt	KS	66748	**800-362-0570**	620-473-2223
Prairie Group Inc 7601 W 79th St *Sales	Bridgeview	IL	60455	**800-649-3690***	708-458-0400
Rinker Materials Corp 1501 Belvedere Rd	West Palm Beach	FL	33406	**800-226-5521**	561-833-5555
Rio Grande Portland Cement Co 4253 Montgomery Blvd NE Suite 210	Albuquerque	NM	87109	**800-234-2266**	505-881-5303
RMC Carolina Materials Inc PO Box 19178	Greensboro	NC	27419	**800-849-6894**	336-294-1124
RMC Pacific Materials Inc 6601 Koll Center Pkwy PO box 5252	Pleasanton	CA	94566	**800-227-5186**	925-462-7181
Texas-Lehigh Cement Co PO Box 610	Buda	TX	78610	**800-388-5408**	512-295-6111
Titan America Inc 1151 Azalea Garden Rd	Norfolk	VA	23502	**800-468-7622**	757-858-6500

136 CHAMBERS OF COMMERCE - CANADIAN

				Toll-Free	Phone
Belleville & District Chamber of Commerce 5 Moira St E	Belleville	ON	K8N5B3	**888-852-9992**	613-962-4597
Cambridge Chamber of Commerce 750 Hespeler Rd	Cambridge	ON	N3H5L8	**800-749-7560**	519-622-2221
Chamber of Commerce of Kitchener & Waterloo 80 Queen St N PO Box 2367	Kitchener	ON	N2H6L4	**888-672-4282**	519-576-5000
Chambre de Commerce du Quebec 576 E Saint Catherine St Suite 200	Montreal	QC	H2L2E1	**888-595-8110**	514-522-1885
Comox Valley Chamber of Commerce 2040 Cliffe Ave	Courtenay	BC	V9N2L3	**888-357-4471**	250-334-3234
Dryden District Chamber of Commerce 284 Government St	Dryden	ON	P8N2P3	**800-667-0935**	807-223-2622
Enterprise Fredericton 570 Queen St	Fredericton	NB	E3B6Z6	**800-200-1180**	506-444-4686
Kelowna Chamber of Commerce 544 Harvey Ave	Kelowna	BC	V1Y6C9	**800-663-4345**	250-861-1515
Leamington District Chamber of Commerce PO Box 321	Leamington	ON	N8H3W3	**800-250-3336**	519-326-2721
North Bay & District Chamber of Commerce 1375 Seymour St PO Box 747	North Bay	ON	P1B8J8	**888-249-8998**	705-472-8480
North Vancouver Chamber of Commerce 124 W 1st St Suite 102	North Vancouver	BC	V7M3N3	**877-880-4699**	604-987-4488
Penticton & Wine Country Chamber of Commerce 888 Westminster Ave W	Penticton	BC	V2A8S2	**800-663-5052**	250-492-4103
West Vancouver Chamber of Commerce 1310 Marine Dr	West Vancouver	BC	V7T1B5	**888-471-9996**	604-926-6614
Westbank & District Chamber of Commerce 2375 Pamela Rd Unit 4	Westbank	BC	V4T2H9	**866-768-3378**	250-768-3378

137 CHAMBERS OF COMMERCE - US - LOCAL

SEE ALSO Associations & Organizations - General - Civic & Political Organizations

Alabama

				Toll-Free	Phone
Calhoun County Chamber of Commerce 1330 Quintard Ave	Anniston	AL	36201	**800-489-1087**	256-237-3536
Bessemer Area Chamber of Commerce 321 N 18th St	Bessemer	AL	35020	**888-423-7736**	205-425-3253
Chilton County Chamber of Commerce 500 5th Ave N	Clanton	AL	35045	**800-553-0493**	205-755-2400
Cullman Area Chamber of Commerce 301 2nd Ave SW	Cullman	AL	35055	**800-313-5114**	256-734-0454
Decatur-Morgan County Chamber of Commerce 515 6th Ave NE	Decatur	AL	35602	**800-353-0005**	256-353-5312
Dothan Area Chamber of Commerce 102 Jamestown Blvd	Dothan	AL	36301	**800-221-1027**	334-792-5138
Eufaula/Barbour County Chamber of Commerce 333 E Broad St	Eufaula	AL	36027	**800-524-7529**	334-687-6664
Shoals Chamber of Commerce 612 S Court St	Florence	AL	35630	**877-764-4661**	256-764-4661
Chamber - Gadsden & Etowah County PO Box 185	Gadsden	AL	35902	**800-238-6924**	256-543-3472
Greenville Area Chamber of Commerce 1 Depot Sq	Greenville	AL	36037	**800-959-0717**	334-382-3251
Walker County Chamber of Commerce 204 19th St E Suite 101	Jasper	AL	35501	**888-384-4571**	205-384-4571
Mobile Area Chamber of Commerce 451 Government St	Mobile	AL	36602	**800-422-6951**	251-433-6951
Ozark Area Chamber of Commerce 294 Painter Ave	Ozark	AL	36360	**800-582-8497**	334-774-9321
Phenix City-Russell County Chamber of Commerce 1107 Broad St	Phenix City	AL	36867	**800-892-2248**	334-298-3639
Greater Jackson County Chamber of Commerce PO Box 973	Scottsboro	AL	35768	**800-259-5508**	256-259-5500
Selma-Dallas County Chamber of Commerce 912 Selma Ave	Selma	AL	36701	**800-457-3562**	334-875-7241

Arizona

				Toll-Free	Phone
Apache Junction Chamber of Commerce 567 W Apache Trail	Apache Junction	AZ	85220	**800-252-3141**	480-982-3141
Bullhead Area Chamber of Commerce 1251 Hwy 95	Bullhead City	AZ	86429	**800-987-7457**	928-754-4121
Chandler Chamber of Commerce 25 S Arizona Pl Suite 201	Chandler	AZ	85225	**800-963-4571**	480-963-4571
Glendale Chamber of Commerce 7105 N 59th Ave	Glendale	AZ	85301	**800-437-8669**	623-937-4754
Rim Country Regional Chamber of Commerce 100 W Main St	Payson	AZ	85547	**800-672-9766**	928-474-4515
Peoria Chamber of Commerce 10601 N 83rd Dr	Peoria	AZ	85385	**800-580-2645**	623-979-3601
Prescott Chamber of Commerce 117 W Goodwin St	Prescott	AZ	86303	**800-266-7534**	928-445-2000
Graham County Chamber of Commerce 1111 Thatcher Blvd	Safford	AZ	85546	**888-837-1841**	928-428-2511

Arkansas

Organization / Address	City	State	Zip	Toll-Free	Phone
Greater Hot Springs Chamber of Commerce 659 Ouachita Ave	Hot Springs	AR	71901	**800-467-4636**	501-321-1700
Magnolia-Columbia County Chamber of Commerce 202 N Pine St	Magnolia	AR	71753	**800-482-3330**	870-234-4352
Mountain Home Area Chamber of Commerce 1023 Hwy 62 E	Mountain Home	AR	72653	**800-822-3536**	870-425-5111
Rogers-Lowell Area Chamber of Commerce 317 W Walnut St	Rogers	AR	72756	**800-364-1240**	479-636-1240
Springdale Chamber of Commerce 202 W Emma	Springdale	AR	72765	**800-972-7261**	479-872-2222

California

Organization / Address	City	State	Zip	Toll-Free	Phone
Kern County Board of Trade PO Bin 1312	Bakersfield	CA	93302	**800-500-5376**	661-861-2367
Beverly Hills Chamber of Commerce 239 S Beverly Dr	Beverly Hills	CA	90212	**800-345-2210**	310-248-1000
Chico Chamber of Commerce 300 Salem St	Chico	CA	95928	**800-852-8570**	530-891-5556
Dana Point Chamber of Commerce 24681 La Plaza Suite 115	Dana Point	CA	92629	**800-290-4262**	949-496-1555
Encinitas Chamber of Commerce 138 Encinitas Blvd	Encinitas	CA	92024	**800-953-6041**	760-753-6041
Greater Eureka Chamber of Commerce 2112 Broadway	Eureka	CA	95501	**800-356-6381**	707-442-3738
Mendocino Coast Chamber of Commerce 332 N Main St PO Box 1141	Fort Bragg	CA	95437	**800-726-2780**	707-961-6300
Garden Grove Chamber of Commerce 12866 Main St Suite 102	Garden Grove	CA	92840	**800-959-5560**	714-638-7950
Goleta Valley Chamber of Commerce PO Box 781 5582 Calle Real Suite A	Goleta	CA	93116	**800-646-5382**	805-967-4618
Hemet Jacinto Valley Chamber of Commerce 615 N San Jacinto St	Hemet	CA	92543	**800-334-9344**	951-658-3211
Indio Chamber of Commerce 82921 Indio Blvd	Indio	CA	92201	**800-444-6346**	760-347-0676
Irvine Chamber of Commerce 2485 McCabe Way Suite 150	Irvine	CA	92614	**800-558-4262**	949-660-9112
Amador County Chamber of Commerce PO Box 596	Jackson	CA	95642	**800-649-4988**	209-223-0350
Greater Lakeport Chamber of Commerce 875 Lakeport Blvd PO Box 295	Lakeport	CA	95453	**866-525-3767**	707-263-5092
Lompoc Valley Chamber of Commerce & Visitors Bureau PO Box 626	Lompoc	CA	93438	**800-240-0999**	805-736-4567
National City Chamber of Commerce 901 National City Blvd	National City	CA	91950	**800-292-4624**	619-477-9339
Novato Chamber of Commerce 807 DeLong Ave	Novato	CA	94945	**800-897-1164**	415-897-1164
Orange Chamber of Commerce 439 E Chapman Ave	Orange	CA	92866	**800-938-0073**	714-538-3581
Oroville Area Chamber of Commerce 1789 Montgomery St	Oroville	CA	95965	**800-655-4653**	530-538-2542
Paradise Chamber of Commerce 5550 Sky Way Suite 1	Paradise	CA	95969	**888-845-2769**	530-877-9356
El Dorado County Chamber of Commerce 542 Main St	Placerville	CA	95667	**800-457-6279**	530-621-5885
San Pedro Peninsula Chamber of Commerce 390 W 7th St	San Pedro	CA	90731	**888-447-3376**	310-832-7272
San Rafael Chamber of Commerce 817 Mission Ave	San Rafael	CA	94901	**800-454-4163**	415-454-4163
Santa Clara Chamber of Commerce 1850 Warburton Ave	Santa Clara	CA	95050	**800-272-6822**	408-244-8244
Santa Maria Valley Chamber of Commerce 614 S Broadway	Santa Maria	CA	93454	**800-331-3779**	805-925-2403
Sebastopol Area Chamber of Commerce 265 S Main St	Sebastopol	CA	95472	**877-828-4748**	707-823-3032
Greater Tehachapi Chamber of Commerce PO Box 401	Tehachapi	CA	93581	**866-822-4180**	661-822-4180
Visalia Chamber of Commerce 720 W Mineral King Ave	Visalia	CA	93291	**877-847-2542**	559-734-5876
Willows Chamber of Commerce 118 W Sycamore	Willows	CA	95988	**888-799-4254**	530-934-8150
Woodland Chamber of Commerce 307 1st St	Woodland	CA	95695	**888-843-2636**	530-662-7327

Colorado

Organization / Address	City	State	Zip	Toll-Free	Phone
Cañon City Chamber of Commerce 403 Royal Gorge Blvd	Canon City	CO	81212	**800-876-7922**	719-275-2331
Durango Area Chamber of Commerce 111 S Camino del Rio	Durango	CO	81303	**888-414-0835**	970-247-0312
Fort Morgan Area Chamber of Commerce 300 Main St	Fort Morgan	CO	80701	**800-354-8660**	970-867-6702
Grand Junction Area Chamber of Commerce 360 Grand Ave	Grand Junction	CO	81501	**800-352-5286**	970-242-3214
La Veta/Cuchara Chamber of Commerce PO Box 32	La Veta	CO	81055	**866-615-3676**	719-742-3676
Montrose Chamber of Commerce 1519 E Main St	Montrose	CO	81401	**800-923-5515**	970-249-5000
Greater Pueblo Chamber of Commerce 302 N Santa Fe Ave	Pueblo	CO	81003	**800-233-3446**	719-542-1704
Vail Valley Chamber of Commerce 100 E Meadow Dr Suite 34	Vail	CO	81657	**800-525-3875**	970-476-1000

Connecticut

Organization / Address	City	State	Zip	Toll-Free	Phone
Mystic Chamber of Commerce 14 Holmes St	Mystic	CT	06355	**866-572-9578**	860-572-9578

Delaware

Organization / Address	City	State	Zip	Toll-Free	Phone
Central Delaware Economic Development Council 435 N Dupont Hwy	Dover	DE	19903	**800-624-2522**	302-678-3028
Rehoboth Beach-Dewey Beach Chamber of Commerce 501 Rehoboth Ave	Rehoboth Beach	DE	19971	**800-441-1329**	302-227-2233

Florida

Organization / Address	City	State	Zip	Toll-Free	Phone
Amelia Island-Fernandina Beach-Yulee Chamber of Commerce 961687 Gateway Blvd Suite 101-G	Amelia Island	FL	32034	**800-226-3542**	904-261-3248
Lower Keys Chamber of Commerce 31020 Overseas Hwy	Big Pine Key	FL	33043	**800-872-3722**	305-872-2411
Bonita Springs Area Chamber of Commerce 25071 Chamber of Commerce Dr	Bonita Springs	FL	34135	**800-226-2943**	239-992-2943
Flagler County Chamber of Commerce 20 Airport Rd	Bunnell	FL	32110	**800-881-1022**	386-437-0106
Cape Coral Chamber of Commerce 2051 Cape Coral Pkwy E	Cape Coral	FL	33904	**800-226-9609**	239-549-6900
Dunnellon Area Chamber of Commerce PO Box 868	Dunnellon	FL	34430	**800-830-2087**	352-489-2320
Englewood/Cape Haze Chamber of Commerce 601 S Indiana Ave	Englewood	FL	34223	**800-603-7198**	941-474-5511
Greater Fort Myers Chamber of Commerce PO Box 9289	Fort Myers	FL	33902	**800-366-3622**	239-332-3624
Fort Myers Beach Chamber of Commerce 17200 San Carlos Blvd	Fort Myers Beach	FL	33931	**800-782-9283**	239-454-7500
Greater Hollywood Chamber of Commerce 330 N Federal Hwy	Hollywood	FL	33020	**800-231-5562**	954-923-4000
Greater Homestead/Florida City Chamber of Commerce 43 N Krome Ave	Homestead	FL	33030	**888-352-4891**	305-247-2332
Islamorada Chamber of Commerce PO Box 915	Islamorada	FL	33036	**800-322-5397**	305-664-4503
Jupiter Tequesta Juno Beach Chamber of Commerce 800 N US Hwy 1	Jupiter	FL	33477	**800-616-7402**	561-746-7111
Key West Chamber of Commerce 402 Wall St	Key West	FL	33040	**800-527-8539**	305-294-2587
Palms West Chamber of Commerce PO Box 1062	Loxahatchee	FL	33470	**800-790-2364**	561-790-6200
Greater Marathon Chamber of Commerce 12222 Overseas Hwy	Marathon	FL	33050	**800-262-7284**	305-743-5417
Marco Island Chamber of Commerce 1102 N Collier Blvd	Marco Island	FL	34145	**800-788-6272**	239-394-7549
Melbourne-Palm Bay Area Chamber of Commerce 1005 E Strawbridge Ave	Melbourne	FL	32901	**800-771-9922**	321-724-5400
Cocoa Beach Area Chamber of Commerce 400 Fortenberry Rd	Merritt Island	FL	32952	**877-321-8474**	321-459-2200
Greater Miami Chamber of Commerce 1601 Biscayne Blvd	Miami	FL	33132	**888-660-5955**	305-350-7700
Southeast Volusia Chamber of Commerce 115 Canal St	New Smyrna Beach	FL	32168	**877-460-8410**	386-428-2449
Ocala-Marion County Chamber of Commerce 110 E Silver Springs Blvd	Ocala	FL	34470	**888-629-8051**	352-629-8051
Greater Plant City Chamber of Commerce 106 N Evers St	Plant City	FL	33563	**800-760-2315**	813-754-3707
Gadsden County Chamber of Commerce 208 N Adams St	Quincy	FL	32351	**800-627-9231**	850-627-9231
Greater Sebring Chamber of Commerce 309 Circle Park Dr	Sebring	FL	33870	**877-844-6007**	863-385-8448
Greater Tampa Chamber of Commerce 615 Channelside Dr Suite 108	Tampa	FL	33602	**800-298-2672**	813-228-7777
Greater Winter Haven Area Chamber of Commerce 401 Ave 'B' NW	Winter Haven	FL	33881	**800-871-7027**	863-293-2138
Winter Park Chamber of Commerce 150 N New York Ave	Winter Park	FL	32789	**877-972-4262**	407-644-8281

Georgia

Organization / Address	City	State	Zip	Toll-Free	Phone
Albany Area Chamber of Commerce 225 W Broad Ave	Albany	GA	31701	**800-475-8700**	229-434-8700
Bainbridge-Decatur County Chamber of Commerce PO Box 755	Bainbridge	GA	39818	**800-243-4774**	229-246-4774
Gordon County Chamber of Commerce 300 S Wall St	Calhoun	GA	30701	**800-887-3811**	706-625-3200
Chatsworth-Murray County Chamber of Commerce 126 N 3rd Ave	Chatsworth	GA	30705	**800-969-9490**	706-695-6060
White County Chamber of Commerce 122 N Main St	Cleveland	GA	30528	**800-392-8279**	706-865-5356
Greater Columbus Chamber of Commerce 1200 6th Ave	Columbus	GA	31902	**800-360-8552**	706-327-1566
Habersham County Chamber of Commerce PO Box 366	Cornelia	GA	30531	**800-835-2559**	706-778-4654
Douglas-Coffee County Chamber of Commerce 211 S Gaskin Ave	Douglas	GA	31533	**888-426-3334**	912-384-1873
Henry County Chamber of Commerce 1709 Hwy 20 W West Ridge Business Ctr	McDonough	GA	30253	**800-436-7926**	770-957-5786
Moultrie-Colquitt County Chamber of Commerce 116 1st Ave SE	Moultrie	GA	31768	**888-408-4748**	229-985-2131
Catoosa County Area Chamber of Commerce 264 Catoosa Cir	Ringgold	GA	30736	**877-965-5201**	706-965-5201
Polk County Chamber of Commerce/Development Authority 604 Goodyear St	Rockmart	GA	30153	**800-226-2517**	770-684-8760
Greater Rome Chamber of Commerce 1 Riverside Pkwy	Rome	GA	30161	**800-234-3154**	706-291-7663
Savannah Area Chamber of Commerce 101 E Bay St	Savannah	GA	31401	**877-728-2662**	912-644-6400
Effingham County Chamber of Commerce 520 W 3rd St PO Box 1078	Springfield	GA	31329	**866-754-3301**	912-754-3301
Tifton-Tift County Chamber of Commerce 100 Central Ave	Tifton	GA	31794	**800-550-8438**	229-382-6200

Hawaii

Organization / Address	City	State	Zip	Toll-Free	Phone
Kaua'i Chamber of Commerce PO Box 1969	Lihue	HI	96766	**800-262-1400**	808-245-7363

Idaho

Organization / Address	City	State	Zip	Toll-Free	Phone
Coeur d'Alene Area Chamber of Commerce 1621 N 3rd St Suite 100	Coeur d'Alene	ID	83814	**877-782-9232**	208-664-3194

Idaho (Cont'd)

Name / Address	City	State	Zip	Toll-Free	Phone
Greater Idaho Falls Chamber of Commerce 630 W Broadway	Idaho Falls	ID	83402	**866-365-6943**	208-523-1010
Lewiston Chamber of Commerce 111 Main St Suite 120	Lewiston	ID	83501	**800-473-3543**	208-743-3531
Moscow Chamber of Commerce 411 S Main St	Moscow	ID	83843	**800-380-1801**	208-882-1800
Sun Valley/Ketchum Chamber & Visitors Bureau PO Box 2420	Sun Valley	ID	83353	**800-634-3347**	208-726-3423
Twin Falls Area Chamber of Commerce 858 Blue Lakes Blvd N	Twin Falls	ID	83301	**866-894-6325**	208-733-3974

Illinois

Name / Address	City	State	Zip	Toll-Free	Phone
Danville Area Chamber of Commerce 28 W North St	Danville	IL	61832	**800-373-6201**	217-442-1887
Greater Marion Area Chamber of Commerce 2305 W Main St	Marion	IL	62959	**800-699-1760**	618-997-6311

Indiana

Name / Address	City	State	Zip	Toll-Free	Phone
Goshen Chamber of Commerce 232 S Main St	Goshen	IN	46526	**800-307-4204**	574-533-2102
Dearborn County Chamber of Commerce 555 Eads Pkwy E Suite 175	Greendale	IN	47025	**800-322-8198**	812-537-0814
Logansport/Cass County Chamber of Commerce 300 E Broadway Suite 103	Logansport	IN	46947	**800-425-2071**	574-753-6388
Muncie-Delaware County Chamber of Commerce 401 S High St	Muncie	IN	47305	**800-336-1373**	765-288-6681
Shelby County Chamber of Commerce 501 N Harrison St	Shelbyville	IN	46176	**800-318-4083**	317-398-6647

Iowa

Name / Address	City	State	Zip	Toll-Free	Phone
Burlington/West Burlington Area Chamber of Commerce 610 N 4th St Suite 200	Burlington	IA	52601	**800-827-4837**	319-752-6365
Clinton Area Chamber of Commerce 333 4th Ave S	Clinton	IA	52733	**800-828-5702**	563-242-5702
Council Bluffs Area Chamber of Commerce 7 N 6th St	Council Bluffs	IA	51503	**800-228-6878**	712-325-1000
Greater Des Moines Partnership 700 Locust St Suite 100	Des Moines	IA	50309	**800-376-9059**	515-286-4950
Dubuque Area Chamber of Commerce 300 Main St	Dubuque	IA	52004	**800-798-4748**	563-557-9200
Ottumwa Area Chamber of Commerce 217 E Mian St	Ottumwa	IA	52501	**800-564-5274**	641-682-3465

Kansas

Name / Address	City	State	Zip	Toll-Free	Phone
Hutchinson/Reno County Chamber of Commerce 117 N Walnut St	Hutchinson	KS	67501	**800-691-4262**	620-662-3391
Manhattan Area Chamber of Commerce 501 Poyntz Ave	Manhattan	KS	66502	**800-759-0134**	785-776-8829
Olathe Chamber of Commerce 142 N Cherry St	Olathe	KS	66061	**800-921-5678**	913-764-1050
Pittsburg Area Chamber of Commerce 117 W 4th St	Pittsburg	KS	66762	**800-879-1112**	620-231-1000
Shawnee Area Chamber of Commerce 15100 W 67th St Suite 202	Shawnee	KS	66217	**888-550-7282**	913-631-6545

Kentucky

Name / Address	City	State	Zip	Toll-Free	Phone
Ashland Alliance Chamber of Commerce PO Box 830	Ashland	KY	41105	**888-524-6860**	606-324-5111
Bardstown-Nelson County Chamber of Commerce 1 Court Sq	Bardstown	KY	40004	**866-894-9545**	502-348-9545
Glasgow-Barren County Chamber of Commerce 118 E Public Sq	Glasgow	KY	42141	**800-264-3161**	270-651-3161
Hopkinsville-Christian County Chamber of Commerce 2800 Port Campbell Blvd	Hopkinsville	KY	42240	**800-842-9959**	270-885-9096
Oldham County Chamber of Commerce 412 E Main ST	LaGrange	KY	40031	**800-813-9953**	502-222-1635
Greater Louisville Inc 614 W Main St	Louisville	KY	40202	**800-500-1066**	502-625-0000
Murray-Calloway County Chamber of Commerce 805 N 12th St	Murray	KY	42071	**800-900-5171**	270-753-5171

Louisiana

Name / Address	City	State	Zip	Toll-Free	Phone
Monroe Chamber of Commerce 212 Walnut St Suite 100	Monroe	LA	71201	**888-531-9535**	318-323-3461
Iberville Parish Chamber of Commerce 23675 Church St	Plaquemine	LA	70764	**888-687-3560**	225-687-3560
Ruston/Lincoln Chamber of Commerce 104 E Mississippi Ave	Ruston	LA	71270	**800-392-9032**	318-255-2031
Greater Shreveport Chamber of Commerce 400 Edwards St	Shreveport	LA	71101	**800-448-5432**	318-677-2500
Greater Slidell Area Chamber of Commerce 118 W Hall Ave	Slidell	LA	70460	**800-471-3758**	985-643-5678

Maine

Name / Address	City	State	Zip	Toll-Free	Phone
Bar Harbor Chamber of Commerce 93 Cottage St PO Box 158	Bar Harbor	ME	04609	**888-540-9990**	207-288-5103
Southern Midcoast Maine Chamber 59 Pleasant St	Brunswick	ME	04011	**800-725-8797**	207-725-8797
Calais Regional Chamber of Commerce 39 Union St	Calais	ME	04619	**888-422-3112**	207-454-2308
Greater Lincoln Lakes Region Chamber of Commerce 256 W Broadway	Lincoln	ME	04457	**888-794-8065**	207-794-8065

Maryland

Name / Address	City	State	Zip	Toll-Free	Phone
Harford County Chamber of Commerce 108 S Bond St	Bel Air	MD	21014	**800-682-8536**	410-838-2020
Garrett County Chamber of Commerce 15 Visitors Ctr Dr	McHenry	MD	21541	**800-387-5237**	301-387-4386
Ocean City Chamber of Commerce 12320 Ocean Gateway	Ocean City	MD	21842	**888-626-3386**	410-213-0144

Massachusetts

Name / Address	City	State	Zip	Toll-Free	Phone
Falmouth Chamber of Commerce 20 Academy Ln	Falmouth	MA	02540	**800-526-8532**	508-548-8500
Cape Ann Chamber of Commerce 33 Commercial St	Gloucester	MA	01930	**800-321-0133**	978-283-1601
Cape Cod Chamber of Commerce Rt 6 & 132	Hyannis	MA	02601	**888-332-2732**	508-362-3225
Hyannis Area Chamber of Commerce 1481 Rt 132 PO Box 100	Hyannis	MA	02601	**800-449-6647**	508-362-5230
Tri-Community Area Chamber of Commerce 380 Main St	Sturbridge	MA	01566	**888-788-7274**	508-347-2761
Blackstone Valley Chamber of Commerce 110 Church St	Whitinsville	MA	01588	**800-841-0919**	508-234-9090

Michigan

Name / Address	City	State	Zip	Toll-Free	Phone
Alpena Area Chamber of Commerce 235 W Chisholm St PO Box 65	Alpena	MI	49707	**800-425-7362**	989-354-4181
Delta County Area Chamber of Commerce 230 Ludington St	Escanaba	MI	49829	**888-335-8264**	906-786-2192
Chamber of Commerce - Grand Haven-Spring Lake-Ferrysburg 1 S Harbor Dr	Grand Haven	MI	49417	**800-303-4096**	616-842-4910
Keweenaw Peninsula Chamber of Commerce 902 College Ave	Houghton	MI	49931	**866-304-5722**	906-482-5240
Dickinson Area Partnership 600 S Stephenson Ave	Iron Mountain	MI	49801	**800-236-2447**	906-774-2002
Four Flags Area Chamber of Commerce 321 E Main St	Niles	MI	49120	**888-683-8361**	269-683-3720
Greater Port Huron Area Chamber of Commerce 920 Pine Grove Ave	Port Huron	MI	48060	**800-361-0526**	810-985-7101

Minnesota

Name / Address	City	State	Zip	Toll-Free	Phone
Alexandria Lakes Area Chamber of Commerce 206 Broadway	Alexandria	MN	56308	**800-235-9441**	320-763-3161
Apple Valley Chamber of Commerce 7300 W 147th St Suite 101	Apple Valley	MN	55124	**800-301-9435**	952-432-8422
Bemidji Area Chamber of Commerce 300 Bemidji Ave	Bemidji	MN	56601	**800-458-2223**	218-444-3541
Brainerd Lakes Area Chamber of Commerce PO Box 356	Brainerd	MN	56401	**800-450-2838**	218-829-2838
Cloquet Area Chamber of Commerce 225 Sunnyside Dr	Cloquet	MN	55720	**800-554-4350**	218-879-1551
Detroit Lakes Regional Chamber of Commerce 700 Washington Ave	Detroit Lakes	MN	56501	**800-542-3992**	218-847-9202
Grand Rapids Area Chamber of Commerce 1 NW 3rd St	Grand Rapids	MN	55744	**800-472-6366**	218-326-6619
Hastings Area Chamber of Commerce & Tourism Bureau 111 E 3rd St	Hastings	MN	55033	**888-612-6122**	651-437-6775
Lakeville Area Chamber of Commerce & Convention & Visitors Bureau PO Box 12	Lakeville	MN	55044	**888-525-3845**	952-469-2020
Owatonna Area Chamber of Commerce & Tourism 320 Hoffman Dr	Owatonna	MN	55060	**800-423-6466**	507-451-7970
Saint Cloud Area Chamber of Commerce 110 6th Ave S	Saint Cloud	MN	56301	**800-264-2040**	320-251-2940
Minnesota Chamber of Commerce 400 Robert St N Suite 1500	Saint Paul	MN	55101	**800-821-2230**	651-292-4650
Leech Lake Area Chamber of Commerce PO Box 1089	Walker	MN	56484	**800-833-1118**	218-547-1313

Mississippi

Name / Address	City	State	Zip	Toll-Free	Phone
Panola Partnership Inc 150-A Public Sq	Batesville	MS	38606	**888-872-6652**	662-563-3126
Brookhaven-Lincoln County Chamber of Commerce 230 S Whitworth Ave	Brookhaven	MS	39601	**800-613-4667**	601-833-1411
Clarksdale-Coahoma County Chamber of Commerce & Industrial Foundation 1540 DeSoto Ave	Clarksdale	MS	38614	**800-626-3760**	662-627-7337
Cleveland-Bolivar County Chamber of Commerce 600 3rd St	Cleveland	MS	38732	**800-295-7473**	662-843-2712
Alliance The PO Box 1089	Corinth	MS	38835	**877-347-0545**	662-287-5269
Area Development Partnership 1 Convention Center Plaza	Hattiesburg	MS	39401	**800-238-4288**	601-296-7500
Jones County Chamber of Commerce PO Box 527	Laurel	MS	39441	**800-392-9629**	601-428-0574
Pike County Chamber of Commerce & Economic Development District 112 N Railroad Blvd	McComb	MS	39648	**800-399-4404**	601-684-2291
Oxford-Lafayette County Chamber of Commerce 299 W Jackson Ave	Oxford	MS	38655	**800-880-6967**	662-234-4651
Philadelphia-Neshoba County Chamber of Commerce 410 Poplar Ave PO Box 330	Philadelphia	MS	39350	**877-752-2643**	601-656-1000

				Toll-Free	Phone
Southaven Chamber of Commerce 8700 Northwest Dr Suite 100	Southaven	MS	38671	**800-272-6551**	662-342-6114
Starkville Area Chamber of Commerce 1 Research Blvd Suite 204	Starkville	MS	39759	**800-649-8687**	662-323-3322
Vicksburg-Warren County Chamber of Commerce 2020 Mission 66	Vicksburg	MS	39180	**888-842-5728**	601-636-1012
Yazoo County Chamber of Commerce 212 E Broadway	Yazoo City	MS	39194	**800-748-8875**	662-746-1273

Missouri

				Toll-Free	Phone
Branson/Lakes Area Chamber of Commerce PO Box 1897	Branson	MO	65615	**800-214-3661**	417-334-4136
Cassville Area Chamber of Commerce 504 Main St	Cassville	MO	65625	**866-847-2814**	417-847-2814
Chesterfield Chamber of Commerce 101 Chesterfield Business Pkwy	Chesterfield	MO	63005	**888-242-4262**	636-532-3399
Kingdom of Callaway Chamber of Commerce 409 Court St	Fulton	MO	65251	**800-257-3554**	573-642-3055
Lebanon Area Chamber of Commerce 186 N Adams St	Lebanon	MO	65536	**888-588-5710**	417-588-3256
Lee's Summit Chamber of Commerce 220 SE Main St	Lee's Summit	MO	64063	**888-816-5757**	816-524-2424
Rolla Area Chamber of Commerce 1301 Kingshighway St	Rolla	MO	65401	**888-809-3817**	573-364-3577
Saint Joseph Area Chamber of Commerce 3003 Frederick Ave	Saint Joseph	MO	64506	**800-748-7856**	816-232-4461
Saint Louis Regional Commerce & Growth Assn 1 Metropolitan Sq Suite 1300	Saint Louis	MO	63102	**877-785-7242**	314-231-5555
Sedalia Area Chamber of Commerce 600 E 3rd St	Sedalia	MO	65301	**800-827-5295**	660-826-2222
Springfield Area Chamber of Commerce 202 S John Q Hammons Pkwy	Springfield	MO	65806	**800-879-7504**	417-862-5567
Washington Area Chamber of Commerce 323 W Main St	Washington	MO	63090	**888-792-7466**	636-239-2715

Montana

				Toll-Free	Phone
Billings Area Chamber of Commerce 815 S 27th St	Billings	MT	59101	**800-735-2635**	406-245-4111
Butte-Silver Bow Chamber of Commerce 1000 George St	Butte	MT	59701	**800-735-6814**	406-723-3177
Great Falls Area Chamber of Commerce 710 1st Ave N	Great Falls	MT	59401	**800-735-8535**	406-761-4434
Helena Area Chamber of Commerce 225 Cruse Ave	Helena	MT	59601	**800-743-5362**	406-442-4120

Nebraska

				Toll-Free	Phone
Kearney Area Chamber of Commerce 1007 2nd Ave	Kearney	NE	68847	**800-652-9435**	308-237-3101

Nevada

				Toll-Free	Phone
Elko Area Chamber of Commerce 1405 Idaho St	Elko	NV	89801	**800-428-7143**	775-738-7135
Carson Valley Chamber of Commerce & Visitors Authority 1513 Hwy 395 N	Gardnerville	NV	89410	**800-727-7677**	775-782-8144

New Jersey

				Toll-Free	Phone
Southern Ocean County Chamber of Commerce 265 W 9th St	Ship Bottom	NJ	08008	**800-292-6372**	609-494-7211
Greater Vineland Chamber of Commerce 2115 S Delsea Dr	Vineland	NJ	08360	**800-309-0019**	856-691-7400

New Mexico

				Toll-Free	Phone
Alamogordo Chamber of Commerce 1301 N White Sands Blvd	Alamogordo	NM	88310	**800-826-0294**	505-437-6120
Carlsbad Chamber of Commerce 302 S Canal St	Carlsbad	NM	88220	**800-221-1224**	505-887-6516
Clovis/Curry County Chamber of Commerce 215 N Main St	Clovis	NM	88101	**800-261-7656**	505-763-3435
Farmington Chamber of Commerce 105 N Orchard Ave	Farmington	NM	87401	**888-325-0279**	505-325-0279
Grants/Cibola County Chamber of Commerce 100 N Iron St	Grants	NM	87020	**800-748-2142**	505-287-4802
Hobbs Chamber of Commerce 400 N Marland Blvd	Hobbs	NM	88240	**800-658-6291**	505-397-3202
Las Vegas-San Miguel Chamber of Commerce PO Box 128	Las Vegas	NM	87701	**800-832-5947**	505-425-8631
Roswell Chamber of Commerce 131 W 2nd St	Roswell	NM	88202	**877-849-7679**	505-623-5695
Silver City-Grant County Chamber of Commerce 201 N Hudson St	Silver City	NM	88061	**800-548-9378**	505-538-3785

New York

				Toll-Free	Phone
Montgomery County Chamber of Commerce 366 W Main St PO Box 309	Amsterdam	NY	12010	**800-743-7337**	518-842-8200
Genesee County Chamber of Commerce 210 E Main St	Batavia	NY	14020	**800-622-2686**	585-343-7440
Greater Binghamton Chamber of Commerce 49 Court St	Binghamton	NY	13902	**800-836-6740**	607-772-8860
Buffalo Niagara Partnership 665 Main St Suite 200	Buffalo	NY	14203	**800-241-0474**	716-852-7100
Saint Lawrence County Chamber of Commerce 101 Main St	Canton	NY	13617	**877-228-7810**	315-386-4000
Corning Area Chamber of Commerce 1 W Market St Suite 302	Corning	NY	14830	**866-463-6264**	607-936-4686
Delaware County Chamber of Commerce 114 Main St	Delhi	NY	13753	**800-642-4443**	607-746-2281
Greater East Aurora Chamber of Commerce 431 Main St	East Aurora	NY	14052	**800-441-2881**	716-652-8444
Chemung County Chamber of Commerce 400 E Church St	Elmira	NY	14901	**800-627-5892**	607-734-5137
Livingston County Chamber of Commerce 4635 Millennium Dr	Geneseo	NY	14454	**800-538-7365**	585-243-2222
Adirondack Regional Chambers of Commerce 5 Warren St	Glens Falls	NY	12801	**888-516-7247**	518-798-1761
Fulton County Regional Chamber of Commerce 2 N Main St	Gloversville	NY	12078	**800-676-3858**	518-725-0641
Hamburg Chamber of Commerce 8 S Buffalo St	Hamburg	NY	14075	**877-322-6890**	716-649-7917
Huntington Township Chamber of Commerce 164 Main St	Huntington	NY	11743	**888-361-5710**	631-423-6100
Kenmore-Town of Tonawanda Chamber of Commerce 3411 Delaware Ave	Kenmore	NY	14217	**888-281-1680**	716-874-1202
Lake Placid/Essex County Visitors Bureau 2610 Main St Suite 2 Olympic Ctr	Lake Placid	NY	12946	**800-447-5224**	518-523-2445
Long Beach Chamber of Commerce 350 National Blvd	Long Beach	NY	11561	**866-563-3275**	516-432-6000
Lewis County Chamber of Commerce 7383-C Utica Blvd	Lowville	NY	13367	**800-724-0242**	315-376-2213
Herkimer County Chamber of Commerce 28 W Main St	Mohawk	NY	13407	**877-984-4636**	315-866-7820
Chenango County Chamber of Commerce 19 Eaton Ave	Norwich	NY	13815	**800-556-8596**	607-334-1400
Otsego County Chamber 12 Carbon St	Oneonta	NY	13820	**877-568-7346**	607-432-4500
Saratoga County Chamber of Commerce 28 Clinton St	Saratoga Springs	NY	12866	**800-526-8970**	518-584-3255
Chamber of Schenectady County 306 State St	Schenectady	NY	12305	**800-962-8007**	518-372-5656
Schoharie County Chamber of Commerce 315 Main St PO Box 400	Schoharie	NY	12157	**800-418-4748**	518-295-7033

North Carolina

				Toll-Free	Phone
Asheville Area Chamber of Commerce 151 Haywood St	Asheville	NC	28801	**800-257-1300**	828-258-6101
Black Mountain-Swannanoa Chamber of Commerce 201 E State St	Black Mountain	NC	28711	**800-669-2301**	828-669-2300
Brevard-Transylvania Chamber of Commerce 35 W Main St	Brevard	NC	28712	**800-648-4523**	828-883-3700
Cary Chamber of Commerce 307 N Academy St	Cary	NC	27513	**800-919-2279**	919-467-1016
Lake Norman Chamber of Commerce 20916 Torrence Chapel Rd PO Box 760	Cornelius	NC	28031	**800-305-2508**	704-892-1922
Elizabeth City Area Chamber of Commerce 502 E Ehringhaus St	Elizabeth City	NC	27909	**888-258-4832**	252-335-4365
Gaston Chamber of Commerce 601 W Franklin Blvd	Gastonia	NC	28052	**800-348-8461**	704-864-2621
Cabarrus Regional Chamber of Commerce 3003 Dale Earnhardt Blvd	Kannapolis	NC	28083	**800-848-3702**	704-782-4000
Carteret County Chamber of Commerce 801 Arendell St Suite 1	Morehead City	NC	28557	**800-622-6278**	252-726-6350
Greater Mount Airy Chamber of Commerce 200 N Main St	Mount Airy	NC	27030	**800-948-0949**	336-786-6116
Richmond County Chamber of Commerce 505 Rockingham Rd	Rockingham	NC	28380	**800-858-1688**	910-895-9058
Brunswick County Chamber of Commerce PO Box 1185	Shallotte	NC	28459	**800-426-6644**	910-754-6644
Jackson County Chamber of Commerce 773 W Main St	Sylva	NC	28779	**800-962-1911**	828-586-2155
Haywood County Chamber of Commerce PO Box 600	Waynesville	NC	28786	**877-456-3073**	828-456-3021

Ohio

				Toll-Free	Phone
Greater Akron Chamber 1 Cascade Plaza 17th Fl	Akron	OH	44308	**800-621-8001**	330-376-5550
Canton Regional Chamber of Commerce 222 Market Ave N	Canton	OH	44702	**800-533-4302**	330-456-7253
Carroll County Chamber of Commerce & Economic Development 61 N Lisbon St	Carrollton	OH	44615	**800-956-4684**	330-627-4811
Pickaway County Chamber of Commerce 135 W Main	Circleville	OH	43113	**800-897-9420**	740-474-4923
Greater Cleveland Partnership 50 Public Sq Suite 200	Cleveland	OH	44113	**800-562-7121**	216-621-3300
Greater Columbus Chamber of Commerce 37 N High St	Columbus	OH	43215	**800-950-1321**	614-221-1321
Coshocton County Chamber of Commerce 101 N Whitewoman St	Coshocton	OH	43812	**800-589-2430**	740-622-5411
Findlay-Hancock County Chamber of Commerce 123 E Main Cross St	Findlay	OH	45840	**800-424-3326**	419-422-3313
Brown County Chamber of Commerce 110 E State St	Georgetown	OH	45121	**888-276-9664**	937-378-4784
Logan-Hocking Chamber of Commerce PO Box 838	Logan	OH	43138	**800-414-6731**	740-385-6836
Union County Chamber of Commerce 227 E 5th St	Marysville	OH	43040	**800-642-0087**	937-642-6279
Newark & Licking County Chamber of Commerce 50 W Locust St	Newark	OH	43055	**800-589-8224**	740-345-9757
Portsmouth Area Chamber of Commerce 324 Chillicothe St PO Box 509	Portsmouth	OH	45662	**800-648-2574**	740-353-7647
Shelby Chamber of Commerce 142 N Gamble St Suite A	Shelby	OH	44875	**888-245-2426**	419-342-2426
Greater Lawrence County Area Chamber of Commerce PO Box 488	South Point	OH	45680	**800-408-1334**	740-377-4550
Springfield-Clark County Chamber of Commerce 333 N Limestone St Suite 201	Springfield	OH	45503	**800-803-1553**	937-325-7621
Tiffin Area Chamber of Commerce 62 S Washington St	Tiffin	OH	44883	**800-253-3314**	419-447-4141

Ohio (Cont'd)

Organization / Address	City	State	Zip	Toll-Free	Phone
Champaign County Chamber of Commerce 113 Miami St	Urbana	OH	43078	**877-873-5764**	937-653-5764
West Chester Chamber Alliance 7617 Voice of America Centre Dr	West Chester	OH	45069	**877-924-3783**	513-777-3600
Adams County Chamber of Commerce PO Box 398	West Union	OH	45693	**888-223-5454**	937-544-5454

Oklahoma

Organization / Address	City	State	Zip	Toll-Free	Phone
Greater Enid Chamber of Commerce PO Box 907	Enid	OK	73702	**888-229-2443**	580-237-2494
Lawton Chamber of Commerce & Industry 629 SW 'C' Ave Suite A	Lawton	OK	73501	**800-872-4540**	580-355-3541
Greater Oklahoma City Chamber of Commerce 123 Park Ave	Oklahoma City	OK	73102	**800-616-1114**	405-297-8900
Stillwater Chamber of Commerce 409 S Main St	Stillwater	OK	74076	**800-593-5573**	405-372-5573

Oregon

Organization / Address	City	State	Zip	Toll-Free	Phone
Bend Chamber of Commerce 777 NW Wall St Suite 200	Bend	OR	97701	**800-905-2363**	541-382-3221
Bay Area Chamber of Commerce 50 Central Ave	Coos Bay	OR	97420	**800-824-8486**	541-269-0215
Florence Area Chamber of Commerce 290 Hwy 101	Florence	OR	97439	**800-524-4864**	541-997-3128
Grants Pass Chamber of Commerce 1995 NW Vine St PO Box 970	Grants Pass	OR	97528	**800-547-5927**	541-476-7717
Klamath County Chamber of Commerce 706 Main St	Klamath Falls	OR	97601	**877-552-6284**	541-884-5193
Greater Newport Chamber of Commerce 555 SW Coast Hwy	Newport	OR	97365	**800-262-7844**	541-265-8801
Springfield Chamber of Commerce 101 S 'A' St PO Box 155	Springfield	OR	97477	**866-346-1651**	541-746-1651

Pennsylvania

Organization / Address	City	State	Zip	Toll-Free	Phone
Beaver County Chamber of Commerce 300 S Walnut Ln 202300	Beaver	PA	15009	**888-832-7591**	724-775-3944
Erie Regional Chamber & Growth Partnership 208 E Bayfront Pkwy	Erie	PA	16507	**800-524-3743**	814-454-7191
Franklin Area Chamber of Commerce 1259 Liberty St	Franklin	PA	16323	**888-547-2377**	814-432-5823
Wayne County Chamber of Commerce 303 Commercial St	Honesdale	PA	18431	**800-433-9008**	570-253-1960
Greater Johnstown/Cambria County Chamber of Commerce 111 Market St	Johnstown	PA	15901	**800-790-4522**	814-536-5107
Armstrong County Chamber of Commerce 124 Market St	Kittanning	PA	16201	**800-979-3348**	724-543-1305
Juniata Valley Area Chamber of Commerce 1 W Market St Suite 119	Lewistown	PA	17044	**877-568-9739**	717-248-6713
Clinton County Economic Partnership 212 N Jay St	Lock Haven	PA	17745	**888-388-6991**	570-748-5782
Monroeville Area Chamber of Commerce 4268 Northern Pike	Monroeville	PA	15146	**888-753-5522**	412-856-0622
Laurel Highlands Chamber of Commerce 537 W Main St	Mount Pleasant	PA	15666	**888-547-7521**	724-547-7521
Greater Pittsburgh Chamber of Commerce 425 6th Ave 11th Fl	Pittsburgh	PA	15219	**800-843-8772**	412-392-4500
Schuylkill Chamber of Commerce 91 S Progress Ave	Pottsville	PA	17901	**800-755-1942**	570-622-1942
Greater Susquehanna Valley Chamber of Commerce 104 S Susquehanna Trail PO Box 10	Shamokin Dam	PA	17876	**800-410-2880**	570-743-4100
Fayette Chamber of Commerce 65 W Main St	Uniontown	PA	15401	**800-916-9365**	724-437-4571
Greater Wilkes-Barre Chamber of Business & Industry 2 Public Sq PO Box 5340	Wilkes-Barre	PA	18710	**800-331-0912**	570-823-2101
York County Chamber of Commerce 1 Market Way E	York	PA	17401	**888-878-9675**	717-848-4000

Rhode Island

Organization / Address	City	State	Zip	Toll-Free	Phone
East Bay Chamber of Commerce 16 Cutler St Suite 102	Warren	RI	02885	**888-278-9948**	401-245-0750

South Carolina

Organization / Address	City	State	Zip	Toll-Free	Phone
Greater Aiken Chamber of Commerce PO Box 892	Aiken	SC	29802	**800-542-4536**	803-641-1111
Kershaw County Chamber of Commerce 607 S Broad St	Camden	SC	29020	**800-968-4037**	803-432-2525
Dillon County Chamber of Commerce 100 N MacArthur Ave	Dillon	SC	29536	**800-444-6838**	843-774-8551
Georgetown County Chamber of Commerce 1001 Front St	Georgetown	SC	29442	**800-777-7705**	843-546-8436
Greater Hartsville Chamber of Commerce 214 N 5th St PO Box 578	Hartsville	SC	29550	**888-427-8720**	843-332-6401
Hilton Head Island - Bluffton Chamber of Commerce 1 Chamber Dr	Hilton Head Island	SC	29928	**800-523-3373**	843-785-3673
Clarendon County Chamber of Commerce 19 N Brooks St	Manning	SC	29102	**800-731-5253**	803-435-4405
Berkeley County Chamber of Commerce PO Box 968	Moncks Corner	SC	29461	**800-882-0337**	843-761-8238
Myrtle Beach Area Chamber of Commerce 1200 N Oak St	Myrtle Beach	SC	29577	**800-356-3016**	843-626-7444
Orangeburg County Chamber of Commerce 155 Riverside Dr	Orangeburg	SC	29116	**800-545-6153**	803-534-6821
Union County Chamber of Commerce 135 W Main St	Union	SC	29379	**877-202-8755**	864-427-9039

South Dakota

Organization / Address	City	State	Zip	Toll-Free	Phone
Aberdeen Area Chamber of Commerce 516 S Main St	Aberdeen	SD	57401	**800-874-9038**	605-225-2860
Brookings Area Chamber of Commerce 2308 6th St E	Brookings	SD	57006	**800-699-6125**	605-692-6125
Pierre Area Chamber of Commerce 800 W Dakota Ave	Pierre	SD	57501	**800-962-2034**	605-224-7361

Tennessee

Organization / Address	City	State	Zip	Toll-Free	Phone
Clarksville Area Chamber of Commerce 312 Madison St	Clarksville	TN	37041	**800-530-2487**	931-647-2331
Cleveland/Bradley Chamber of Commerce 225 Keith St	Cleveland	TN	37320	**800-472-6588**	423-472-6587
Cookeville Area-Putnam County Chamber of Commerce 1 W 1st St	Cookeville	TN	38501	**800-264-5541**	931-526-2211
Crossville Cumberland County Chamber of Commerce 34 S Main St	Crossville	TN	38555	**877-465-3861**	931-484-8444
Jefferson County Chamber of Commerce PO Box 890	Dandridge	TN	37725	**877-237-3847**	865-397-9642
Dickson County Chamber of Commerce 119 Hwy 70 E	Dickson	TN	37055	**877-718-4967**	615-446-2349
Fayetteville-Lincoln County Chamber of Commerce 208 S Elk Ave	Fayetteville	TN	37334	**888-433-1238**	931-433-1234
Williamson County-Franklin Chamber of Commerce PO Box 156	Franklin	TN	37065	**800-356-3445**	615-794-1225
Jackson Area Chamber of Commerce 197 Auditorium St	Jackson	TN	38301	**800-858-5596**	731-423-2200
Johnson City/Jonesborough/Washington County Chamber of Commerce 603 E Market St	Johnson City	TN	37601	**800-852-3392**	423-461-8000
Lawrence County Chamber of Commerce 1609 N Locust Ave PO Box 86	Lawrenceburg	TN	38464	**877-388-4911**	931-762-4911
Rutherford County Chamber of Commerce 501 Memorial Blvd	Murfreesboro	TN	37129	**800-716-7560**	615-893-6565
Nashville Chamber of Commerce 211 Commerce St Suite 100	Nashville	TN	37201	**800-657-6910**	615-743-3000
Paris-Henry County Chamber of Commerce 2508 Eastwood St	Paris	TN	38242	**800-345-1103**	731-642-3431
Shelbyville-Bedford County Chamber of Commerce 100 N Cannon Blvd	Shelbyville	TN	37160	**888-662-2525**	931-684-3482
Claiborne County Chamber of Commerce 3222 Hwy 25 E Suite 1	Tazewell	TN	37879	**800-332-8164**	423-626-4149

Texas

Organization / Address	City	State	Zip	Toll-Free	Phone
Alice Chamber of Commerce 612 E Main St	Alice	TX	78332	**877-992-5423**	361-664-3454
Alvin-Manvel Area Chamber of Commerce 105 W Willis St	Alvin	TX	77511	**800-331-4063**	281-331-3944
Arlington Chamber of Commerce 505 E Border St	Arlington	TX	76010	**800-834-3928**	817-275-2613
Greater Austin Chamber of Commerce 210 Barton Springs Rd Suite 400	Austin	TX	78704	**800-856-5602**	512-478-9383
Washington County Chamber of Commerce 314 S Austin St	Brenham	TX	77833	**888-273-6426**	979-836-3695
Bryan-College Station Chamber of Commerce 4001 E 29th St Suite 175	Bryan	TX	77802	**800-777-8292**	979-260-5200
Canyon Chamber of Commerce 1518 5th Ave	Canyon	TX	79015	**800-999-9481**	806-655-1183
Brazosport Area Chamber of Commerce 420 W Hwy 332	Clute	TX	77531	**888-477-2505**	979-265-2505
Greater Conroe-Lake Conroe Area Chamber of Commerce 505 W Davis St	Conroe	TX	77301	**800-283-6645**	936-756-6644
Greater Conroe/Lake Conroe Area Chamber of Commerce PO Box 2347	Conroe	TX	77305	**800-283-6645**	936-756-6644
Corsicana Area Chamber of Commerce 120 N 12th St	Corsicana	TX	75110	**877-376-7477**	903-874-4731
Del Rio Chamber of Commerce 1915 Veterans Blvd	Del Rio	TX	78840	**800-889-8149**	830-775-3551
Denton Chamber of Commerce 414 Parkway St	Denton	TX	76202	**888-381-1818**	940-382-9693
Eagle Pass Chamber of Commerce 1511 W Henderson St	Eagle Pass	TX	78853	**888-355-3224**	830-773-3224
Edinburg Chamber of Commerce 602 W University	Edinburg	TX	78540	**800-800-7214**	956-383-4974
Greater El Paso Chamber of Commerce 10 Civic Ctr Plaza	El Paso	TX	79901	**800-651-8065**	915-534-0500
Gainesville Area Chamber of Commerce 101 S Culberson St	Gainesville	TX	76241	**888-585-4468**	940-665-2831
Greater Cedar Creek Lake Area Chamber of Commerce 1907 W Main St	Gun Barrel City	TX	75156	**877-222-5253**	903-887-3152
Harlingen Area Chamber of Commerce 311 E Tyler St	Harlingen	TX	78550	**800-531-7346**	956-423-5440
Huntsville-Walker County Chamber of Commerce 1327 11th St	Huntsville	TX	77340	**800-289-0389**	936-295-8113
Greater Killeen Chamber of Commerce 1 Santa Fe Plaza	Killeen	TX	76540	**800-869-8265**	254-526-9551
Lewisville Chamber of Commerce 551 N Valley Pkwy	Lewisville	TX	75067	**800-657-9571**	972-436-9571
Lubbock Chamber of Commerce 1301 Broadway Suite 101	Lubbock	TX	79401	**800-321-5822**	806-761-7000
Lufkin/Angelina County Chamber of Commerce 1615 S Chestnut st	Lufkin	TX	75901	**800-409-5659**	936-634-6644
Greater Marshall Chamber of Commerce 213 W Austin St	Marshall	TX	75670	**800-953-7868**	903-935-7868
McAllen Chamber of Commerce 120 Ash Ave	McAllen	TX	78505	**877-622-5536**	956-682-2871
Mesquite Chamber of Commerce 617 N Ebrite St	Mesquite	TX	75149	**800-541-2355**	972-285-0211
Midland Chamber of Commerce 109 N Main St	Midland	TX	79701	**800-624-6435**	432-683-3381

Classified Section

				Toll-Free	Phone
Mineral Wells Area Chamber of Commerce 511 E Hubbard St	Mineral Wells	TX	76067	**800-252-6989**	940-325-2557
Mission Chamber of Commerce 220 E 9th St	Mission	TX	78572	**800-580-2700**	956-585-2727
New Braunfels Chamber of Commerce 390 S Seguin St	New Braunfels	TX	78130	**800-572-2626**	830-625-2385
Odessa Chamber of Commerce 700 N Grant Suite 200	Odessa	TX	79761	**800-780-4678**	432-332-9111
Lamar County Chamber of Commerce 1125 Bonham St	Paris	TX	75460	**800-727-4789**	903-784-2501
Plainview Chamber of Commerce 710 W 5th St	Plainview	TX	79072	**800-658-2685**	806-296-7431
Richardson Chamber of Commerce 411 Belle Grove Dr	Richardson	TX	75080	**800-777-8001**	972-234-4141
Round Rock Chamber of Commerce 212 E Main St	Round Rock	TX	78664	**800-747-3479**	512-255-5805
Rowlett Chamber of Commerce 3910 Main St	Rowlett	TX	75088	**800-796-8644**	972-475-3200
San Angelo Chamber of Commerce 418 W Avenue B	San Angelo	TX	76903	**800-375-1206**	325-655-4136
San Marcos Area Chamber of Commerce 202 N CM Allen Pkwy	San Marcos	TX	78667	**888-200-5620**	512-393-5900
Sherman Area Chamber of Commerce 307 W Washington St Suite 100	Sherman	TX	75090	**888-893-1188**	903-893-1184
Hopkins County Chamber of Commerce 1200 Houston St	Sulphur Springs	TX	75482	**888-300-6623**	903-885-6515
Temple Chamber of Commerce 2 N 5th St	Temple	TX	76501	**800-374-9123**	254-773-2105
Texarkana Chamber of Commerce 819 State Line Ave	Texarkana	TX	75501	**877-275-5289**	903-792-7191
Tyler Area Chamber of Commerce 315 N Broadway Ave	Tyler	TX	75702	**800-235-5712**	903-592-1661
Weatherford Chamber of Commerce 401 Fort Worth St	Weatherford	TX	76086	**888-594-3801**	817-596-3801
Weslaco Area Chamber of Commerce 205 W Railroad	Weslaco	TX	78596	**888-968-2102**	956-968-2102

Utah

				Toll-Free	Phone
Chamber Ogden/Weber 2484 Washington Blvd Suite 400	Ogden	UT	84401	**888-621-8306**	801-621-8300
Tooele County Chamber of Commerce 201 N Main PO Box 460	Tooele	UT	84074	**800-378-0690**	435-882-0690

Vermont

				Toll-Free	Phone
Central Vermont Chamber of Commerce 33 Stewart Rd	Barre	VT	05641	**877-887-3678**	802-229-5711
Bennington Area Chamber of Commerce 100 Veterans Memorial Dr	Bennington	VT	05201	**800-229-0252**	802-447-3311
Brattleboro Area Chamber of Commerce 180 Main St	Brattleboro	VT	05301	**877-254-4565**	802-254-4565
Lake Champlain Regional Chamber of Commerce 60 Main St Suite 100	Burlington	VT	05401	**877-686-5253**	802-863-3489
Addison County Chamber of Commerce 2 Court St	Middlebury	VT	05753	**800-733-8376**	802-388-7951
Vermont's North Country Chamber of Commerce 246 The Causeway	Newport	VT	05855	**800-635-4643**	802-334-7782
Northeast Kingdom Chamber of Commerce 51 Depot Sq Suite 3	Saint Johnsbury	VT	05819	**800-639-6379**	802-748-3678

Virginia

				Toll-Free	Phone
Bedford Area Chamber of Commerce 305 E Main St	Bedford	VA	24523	**800-933-9535**	540-586-9401
Culpeper County Chamber of Commerce & Visitors Center 109 S Commerce St	Culpeper	VA	22701	**888-285-7373**	540-825-8628
Virginia Peninsula Chamber of Commerce 1919 Commerce Dr Suite 320	Hampton	VA	23666	**800-556-1822**	757-262-2000
Loudoun County Chamber of Commerce 101 Blue Seal Dr Suite 100	Leesburg	VA	20177	**800-578-5222**	703-777-2176
Martinsville-Henry County Chamber of Commerce 115 Broad St	Martinsville	VA	24112	**866-632-3378**	276-632-6401

Washington

				Toll-Free	Phone
Grays Harbor Chamber of Commerce 506 Duffy St	Aberdeen	WA	98520	**800-321-1924**	360-532-1924
Moses Lake Area Chamber of Commerce 324 S Pioneer Way	Moses Lake	WA	98837	**800-992-6234**	509-765-7888
Port Orchard Chamber of Commerce 1014 Bay St Suite 8	Port Orchard	WA	98366	**800-982-8139**	360-876-3505
Pullman Chamber of Commerce 415 N Grand Ave	Pullman	WA	99163	**800-365-6948**	509-334-3565
Richland Chamber of Commerce 710-A George Washington Way	Richland	WA	99352	**877-218-7729**	509-946-1651
Shelton-Mason County Chamber of Commerce 221 W Railroad Ave	Shelton	WA	98584	**800-576-2021**	360-426-2021
Southwest King County Chamber of Commerce 14220 Interurban Ave S	Tukwila	WA	98168	**800-638-8613**	206-575-1633
Walla Walla Valley Chamber of Commerce 29 E Sumach St	Walla Walla	WA	99362	**877-998-4748**	509-525-0850

West Virginia

				Toll-Free	Phone
Beckley-Raleigh County Chamber of Commerce 245 N Kanawha St	Beckley	WV	25801	**800-718-1474**	304-252-7328
Jefferson County Chamber of Commerce PO Box 426	Charles Town	WV	25414	**800-624-0577**	304-725-2055
Elkins-Randolph County Chamber of Commerce 315 Railroad Ave Suite 1	Elkins	WV	26241	**800-422-3304**	304-636-2717
Marion County Chamber of Commerce 110 Adams St	Fairmont	WV	26554	**800-296-3379**	304-363-0442
Greater Greenbrier Chamber of Commerce 540 N Jefferson St Box 17 Suite N	Lewisburg	WV	24901	**800-833-2068**	304-645-1000
Martinsburg-Berkeley County Chamber of Commerce 198 Viking Way	Martinsburg	WV	25401	**800-332-9007**	304-267-4841
Morgantown Area Chamber of Commerce 1009 University Ave	Morgantown	WV	26507	**800-618-2525**	304-292-3311
Fayette County Chamber of Commerce 310 Oyler Ave	Oak Hill	WV	25901	**800-927-0263**	304-465-5617

Wisconsin

				Toll-Free	Phone
Greater Beloit Chamber of Commerce 520 E Grand Ave	Beloit	WI	53511	**800-683-2774**	608-365-8835
Greater La Crosse Area Chamber of Commerce 712 Main St	La Crosse	WI	54601	**800-889-0539**	608-784-4880
Manitowoc-Two Rivers Area Chamber of Commerce 1515 Memorial Dr PO Box 903	Manitowoc	WI	54221	**800-262-7892**	920-684-5575
Greater Menomonie Area Chamber of Commerce 342 E Main St	Menomonie	WI	54751	**800-283-1862**	715-235-9087
Merrill Area Chamber of Commerce 120 S Mill St	Merrill	WI	54452	**877-907-2757**	715-536-9474
Shawano Country Chamber of Commerce 213 E Green Bay St	Shawano	WI	54166	**800-235-8528**	715-524-2139
Sheboygan County Chamber of Commerce 712 Riverfront Dr Suite 101	Sheboygan	WI	53081	**800-457-9497**	920-457-9491
West Bend Area Chamber of Commerce 548 S Main St	West Bend	WI	53095	**888-338-8666**	262-338-2666

Wyoming

				Toll-Free	Phone
Casper Area Chamber of Commerce 500 N Center St	Casper	WY	82602	**866-234-5311**	307-234-5311
Laramie Area Chamber of Commerce 800 S 3rd St	Laramie	WY	82070	**866-876-1012**	307-745-7339
Rock Springs Chamber of Commerce 1897 Dewar Dr	Rock Springs	WY	82901	**800-463-8637**	307-362-3771
Sheridan County Chamber of Commerce PO Box 707	Sheridan	WY	82801	**800-453-3650**	307-672-2485

138 CHAMBERS OF COMMERCE - US - STATE

				Toll-Free	Phone
US Chamber of Commerce 1615 H St NW	Washington	DC	20062	**800-638-6582**	202-659-6000
Alabama Business Council PO Box 76	Montgomery	AL	36101	**800-665-9647**	334-834-6000
Arizona Chamber of Commerce 1221 E Osborne Rd Suite 100	Phoenix	AZ	85014	**800-498-6973**	602-248-9172
California Chamber of Commerce PO Box 1736	Sacramento	CA	95812	**800-772-2399**	916-444-6670
Delaware State Chamber of Commerce PO Box 671	Wilmington	DE	19899	**800-292-9507**	302-655-7221
Florida Chamber of Commerce 136 S Bruno St	Tallahassee	FL	32301	**877-521-1200**	850-521-1200
Georgia Chamber of Commerce 235 Peachtree St NE Suite 900	Atlanta	GA	30303	**800-241-2286**	404-223-2264
Hawaii Chamber of Commerce 1132 Bishop St Suite 402	Honolulu	HI	96813	**800-464-2924**	808-545-4300
Illinois State Chamber of Commerce 311 S Wacker Dr Suite 1500	Chicago	IL	60606	**800-322-4722**	312-983-7100
Indiana State Chamber of Commerce 115 W Washington St Suite 850-S PO Box 44926	Indianapolis	IN	46204	**800-824-6885**	317-264-3110
Iowa Assn of Business & Industry 904 Walnut St Suite 100	Des Moines	IA	50309	**800-383-4224**	515-280-8000
Louisiana Assn of Business & Industry 3113 Valley Creek Dr	Baton Rouge	LA	70808	**888-816-5224**	225-928-5388
Michigan Chamber of Commerce 600 S Walnut St	Lansing	MI	48933	**800-748-0266**	517-371-2100
Minnesota Chamber of Commerce 400 Robert St N Suite 1500	Saint Paul	MN	55101	**800-821-2230**	651-292-4650
Mississippi Economic Council PO Box 23276	Jackson	MS	39225	**800-748-7626**	601-969-0022
New Hampshire Business & Industry Assn 122 N Main St 3rd Fl	Concord	NH	03301	**800-540-5388**	603-224-5388
[New York] Business Council of New York State Inc 152 Washington Ave	Albany	NY	12210	**800-358-1202**	518-465-7511
North Dakota (Greater) Assn PO Box 2639	Bismarck	ND	58502	**800-382-1405**	701-222-0929
Ohio Chamber of Commerce 230 E Town St	Columbus	OH	43215	**800-622-1893**	614-228-4201
Oklahoma State Chamber 330 NE 10th St	Oklahoma City	OK	73104	**800-364-6465**	405-235-3669
Pennsylvania Chamber of Business & Industry 417 Walnut St	Harrisburg	PA	17101	**800-225-7224**	717-255-3252
South Carolina Chamber of Commerce 1201 Main St Suite 1700	Columbia	SC	29201	**800-799-4601**	803-799-4601
Texas Assn of Business & Chamber of Commerce 1209 Nueces St	Austin	TX	78701	**800-856-6721**	512-477-6721
Virginia Chamber of Commerce 9 S 5th St	Richmond	VA	23219	**800-477-7682**	804-644-1607
[Washington] Association of Washington Business PO Box 658	Olympia	WA	98507	**800-521-9325**	360-943-1600

139 CHECK CASHING SERVICES

				Toll-Free	Phone
ACE Cash Express Inc 1231 Greenway Dr Suite 800 *NASDAQ: AACE* ■ *Sales	Irving	TX	75038	**800-713-3338***	972-550-5000

Company / Address	City	State	ZIP	Toll-Free	Phone
Advance America Cash Advance Centers Inc					
135 N Church St	Spartanburg	SC	29306	**866-640-4227**	864-342-5600
NYSE: AEA					
America's Cash Express					
1231 Greenway Dr Suite 800	Irving	TX	75038	**800-713-3338***	972-550-5000
NASDAQ: AACE ■ *Sales					
Cash Plus Inc 3002 Dow Ave Suite 120	Tustin	CA	92780	**888-707-2274**	714-731-2274
Mister Money USA 2057 Vermont Dr	Fort Collins	CO	80525	**800-827-7296**	970-493-0574
Pay-O-Matic Corp 160 Oak Dr	Syosset	NY	11791	**888-729-3773**	516-496-4900
TeleCheck International Inc					
5251 Westheimer Rd	Houston	TX	77056	**800-835-3243**	713-331-7600

140 CHECKS - PERSONAL & BUSINESS

Company / Address	City	State	ZIP	Toll-Free	Phone
Artistic Checks Inc PO Box 1000	Mabelvale	AR	72103	**800-243-2577**	
Check Printers Inc 1530 Antioch Pike	Antioch	TN	37013	**800-766-1217**	615-277-7100
CheckCrafters Inc PO Box 100	Edgewood	MD	21040	**888-404-5245**	
Checks In The Mail Inc					
2435 Goodwin Ln	New Braunfels	TX	78135	**800-639-2432**	830-609-5500
Checks Unlimited PO Box 35630	Colorado Springs	CO	80935	**800-565-8332**	
Clarke American Checks Inc					
10931 Laureate Dr	San Antonio	TX	78249	**800-382-0818**	210-697-8888
Classic Checks Inc PO Box 2	Edgewood	MD	21040	**800-354-3588**	
Custom Direct 1802 Fashion Ct	Joppa	MD	21085	**800-354-3540**	410-679-3300
Deluxe Business Forms 3680 Victoria St N	Shoreview	MN	55126	**800-328-7205***	651-483-7111
*Cust Svc					
Image Checks Inc PO Box 548	Little Rock	AR	72203	**800-562-8768**	
Printegra Inc 403 Westpark Ct Suite A	Peachtree City	GA	30269	**800-422-6070**	770-631-6070
Safeguard Business Systems Inc					
8585 N Stemmons Fwy Suite 600 N	Dallas	TX	75247	**800-338-0636**	214-905-3935
Wilmer Service Line 220 E Monument Ave	Dayton	OH	45402	**888-494-5637**	

CHEMICALS - AGRICULTURAL

SEE Fertilizers & Pesticides

141 CHEMICALS - INDUSTRIAL (INORGANIC)

Company / Address	City	State	ZIP	Toll-Free	Phone
Air Liquide America LP					
2700 Post Oak Blvd Suite 1800	Houston	TX	77056	**877-855-9533**	713-624-8000
Air Products & Chemicals Inc					
7201 Hamilton Blvd	Allentown	PA	18195	**800-345-3148***	610-481-4911
NYSE: APD ■ *Prod Info					
Akzo Nobel Inc 525 W Van Buren St	Chicago	IL	60607	**800-227-7070***	312-544-7000
*Cust Svc					
Alcoa World Chemicals 501 W Park Rd	Leetsdale	PA	15056	**800-643-8771**	412-630-2800
Americhem Inc 225 Broadway St E	Cuyahoga Falls	OH	44221	**800-228-3476**	330-929-4213
Ampacet Corp 660 White Plains Rd	Tarrytown	NY	10591	**800-888-4267***	914-631-6600
*Cust Svc					
Ashta Chemicals Inc 3509 Middle Rd	Ashtabula	OH	44004	**800-492-5082***	440-997-5221
*Cust Svc					
ATOFINA Chemicals Inc 2000 Market St	Philadelphia	PA	19103	**800-533-5552**	215-419-7000
BASF Canada 345 Carlingview Dr	Toronto	ON	M9W6N9	**800-267-2955***	416-675-3611
*Cust Svc					
BASF Corp 3000 Continental Dr N	Mount Olive	NJ	07828	**800-526-1072**	973-426-2600
NYSE: BF					
Bio-Lab Inc 1735 N Brown Rd	Lawrenceville	GA	30043	**800-859-7946**	404-378-1753
BOC Gases America 575 Mountain Ave	Murray Hill	NJ	07974	**800-262-4273***	908-464-8100
*Cust Svc					
BOC Group 575 Mountain Ave	Murray Hill	NJ	07974	**800-932-0803**	908-665-2400
Cabot Corp 2 Seaport Ln Suite 1300	Boston	MA	02210	**800-853-5407**	617-345-0100
NYSE: CBT					
Calgon Carbon Corp 500 Calgon Carbon Rd	Pittsburgh	PA	15205	**800-422-7266***	412-787-6700
NYSE: CCC ■ *Cust Svc					
Carus Corp 315 5th St	Peru	IL	61354	**800-435-6856**	815-223-1500
CDR Pigments & Dispersions					
305 Ring Rd	Elizabethtown	KY	42701	**800-898-3421**	270-737-1700
Criterion Catalysts & Technologies					
16825 Northchase Dr Suite 1000	Houston	TX	77060	**800-777-2650**	281-874-2600
Dow Chemical Co 2030 Dow Ctr	Midland	MI	48674	**800-331-6451***	989-636-1000
NYSE: DOW ■ *Cust Svc					
DuPont EI de Nemours & Co Inc					
1007 Market St	Wilmington	DE	19898	**800-441-7515**	302-774-1000
NYSE: DD					
DuPont Titanium Technologies					
1007 Market St PO Box 80036	Wilmington	DE	19898	**800-441-7515**	302-774-1000
EI DuPont de Nemours & Co Inc					
1007 Market St	Wilmington	DE	19898	**800-441-7515**	302-774-1000
NYSE: DD					
Elementis Chromium					
3800 Buddy Lawrence Dr PO Box 9912	Corpus Christi	TX	78469	**800-531-3188***	361-883-6421
*Cust Svc					
Elementis Pigments Inc					
2051 Lynch Ave	East Saint Louis	IL	62204	**800-323-7796***	618-646-2110
*Cust Svc					
EMD Chemicals Inc 480 S Democrat Rd	Gibbstown	NJ	08027	**800-222-0342***	856-423-6300
*Cust Svc					
Engelhard Corp 101 Wood Ave	Iselin	NJ	08830	**800-631-9505**	732-205-5000
NYSE: EC					
Erachem Comilog Inc 610 Pittman Rd	Baltimore	MD	21226	**800-789-2686**	410-789-8800
FMC Corp Industrial Chemicals Group					
1735 Market St	Philadelphia	PA	19103	**800-621-4500**	215-299-6000
General Chemical Group Inc					
90 E Halsey Rd	Parsippany	NJ	07054	**800-631-8050***	973-515-0900
*Cust Svc					
Hawkins Inc 3100 E Hennepin Ave	Minneapolis	MN	55413	**800-328-5460**	612-331-6910
NASDAQ: HWKN					
Henkel Corp					
2200 Renaissance Blvd Suite 200	Gulph Mills	PA	19406	**800-521-5317**	610-270-8100
Heucotech Ltd 99 Newbold Rd	Fairless Hills	PA	19030	**800-438-2224**	215-736-0712
INEOS Silicas Americas 111 Ingalls Ave	Joliet	IL	60435	**800-775-3651**	815-727-3651
Interstate Chemical Co Inc					
2797 Freedland Rd	Hermitage	PA	16148	**800-422-2436**	724-981-3771
JCI Jones Chemicals Inc					
100 Sunny Sol Blvd	Caledonia	NY	14423	**800-255-3789**	585-538-2314
Johnson Matthey Inc Catalysts & Chemicals Div 2001 Nolte Dr	West Deptford	NJ	08066	**800-444-1411**	856-853-8000
Jones Hamilton Co 8400 Enterprise Dr	Newark	CA	94560	**877-797-5426**	510-797-2471
Kemira Chemicals Inc					
245 TownPark Dr Suite 200	Kennesaw	GA	30144	**800-347-1542**	770-436-1542
Martin Marietta Magnesia Specialties Inc					
195 Chesapeake Pk Plaza Suite 200	Baltimore	MD	21220	**800-648-7400**	410-780-5500
Mississippi Chemical Corp					
3622 Hwy 49 E PO Box 388	Yazoo City	MS	39194	**800-433-1351**	662-746-4131
National Welders Supply Co Inc					
810 Gesco St	Charlotte	NC	28208	**800-866-4422**	704-333-5475
Norit Americas Inc					
3200 W University Ave PO Box 790	Marshall	TX	75671	**800-641-9245**	903-923-1000
Noveon Hilton-Davis Inc					
2235 Langdon Farm Rd	Cincinnati	OH	45237	**800-477-1022***	513-841-4000
*Cust Svc					
Occidental Chemical Corp 5005 LBJ Fwy	Dallas	TX	75244	**800-570-8880**	972-404-3300
OMYA Inc 100 North Point Ctr E Suite 310	Alpharetta	GA	30022	**800-749-6692**	770-751-7030
Phibro Animal Health Corp					
400 Kelby St 1 Parker Plaza	Fort Lee	NJ	07024	**800-223-0434**	201-944-6020
Pioneer Cos Inc 700 Louisiana St Suite 4300	Houston	TX	77002	**800-423-4117**	713-570-3200
NASDAQ: PONR					
Potash Corp 1101 Skokie Blvd	Northbrook	IL	60062	**800-645-2183**	847-849-4200
Potash Corp of Saskatchewan Inc					
122 1st Ave S Suite 500	Saskatoon	SK	S7K7G3	**800-667-3930**	306-933-8500
NYSE: POT					
PQ Corp 1200 W Swedes Ford Rd	Berwyn	PA	19312	**800-944-7411***	610-651-4200
*Cust Svc					
Praxair Inc 39 Old Ridgebury Rd	Danbury	CT	06810	**800-772-9247**	203-837-2000
NYSE: PX					
Reilly Industries Inc 300 N Meridian St	Indianapolis	IN	46204	**800-888-3536***	317-247-8141
*Admitting					
Rutgers Organics Corp 201 Struble Rd	State College	PA	16801	**800-458-3434**	814-238-2424
Sensient Colors Inc 2526 Baldwin St	Saint Louis	MO	63106	**800-325-8110**	314-889-7600
Silberline Mfg Co Inc					
130 Lincoln Dr PO Box B	Tamaqua	PA	18252	**800-348-4824**	570-668-6050
Solvay America Inc 3333 Richmond Ave	Houston	TX	77098	**800-231-6313**	713-525-6000
Solvay Interox Inc 3333 Richmond Ave	Houston	TX	77098	**800-468-3769**	713-525-6500
Sud-Chemie Inc 1600 W Hill St	Louisville	KY	40210	**800-626-5355**	502-634-7200
Synalloy Corp 2155 W Croft Cir	Spartanburg	SC	29302	**800-763-1001***	864-585-3605
NASDAQ: SYNL ■ *Orders					
TETRA Technologies Inc 25025 I-45 N	The Woodlands	TX	77380	**800-327-7817**	281-367-1983
NYSE: TTI					
Texas United Corp 4800 San Felipe	Houston	TX	77056	**800-554-8658**	713-877-1793
TOR Minerals International Inc					
722 Burleson St	Corpus Christi	TX	78302	**888-464-0147**	361-882-5175
NASDAQ: TORM					
UOP LLC 25 E Algonquin Rd	Des Plaines	IL	60017	**800-877-6184**	847-391-2000
US Borax Inc 26877 Tourney Rd	Valencia	CA	91355	**800-533-4872**	661-287-5400
USEC Inc 6903 Rockledge Dr 4th Fl	Bethesda	MD	20817	**800-273-7754**	301-564-3200
NYSE: USU					
Vulcan Chemicals 1200 Urban Center Dr	Birmingham	AL	35242	**800-633-8280***	205-298-3000
*Cust Svc					
Zinc Corp of America 300 Frankfort Rd	Monaca	PA	15061	**800-648-8897***	724-774-1020
*Cust Svc					

142 CHEMICALS - INDUSTRIAL (ORGANIC)

Company / Address	City	State	ZIP	Toll-Free	Phone
Ampacet Corp 660 White Plains Rd	Tarrytown	NY	10591	**800-888-4267***	914-631-6600
*Cust Svc					
ATOFINA Chemicals Inc 2000 Market St	Philadelphia	PA	19103	**800-533-5552**	215-419-7000
BASF Canada 345 Carlingview Dr	Toronto	ON	M9W6N9	**800-267-2955***	416-675-3611
*Cust Svc					
BASF Corp 3000 Continental Dr N	Mount Olive	NJ	07828	**800-526-1072**	973-426-2600
NYSE: BF					
BASF Corp Chemical Div					
333 Mount Hope Ave	Rockaway	NJ	07866	**800-669-2273***	973-895-8000
*Cust Svc					
Bayer Corp 100 Bayer Rd	Pittsburgh	PA	15205	**800-662-2927**	412-777-2000
NYSE: BAY					
Bayer Corp Chemicals Div 100 Bayer Rd	Pittsburgh	PA	15205	**800-662-2927**	412-777-2000
Bayer Inc 77 Belfield Rd	Toronto	ON	M9W1G6	**800-622-2937**	416-248-0771
Blackman Uhler LLC 2155 W Croft Cir	Spartanburg	SC	29302	**800-832-8985**	864-585-3661
BP Chemicals 150 W Warrenville Rd	Naperville	IL	60563	**877-701-2726**	630-420-5111
CasChem Inc 40 Ave A	Bayonne	NJ	07002	**800-227-2436**	201-858-7900
Chemstar Products Co 3915 Hiawatha Ave	Minneapolis	MN	55406	**800-328-5037**	612-722-0079
Chevron Phillips Chemical Co LP					
10001 Six Pines Dr	The Woodlands	TX	77380	**800-231-1212**	832-813-4100
Clariant Corp 4000 Monroe Rd	Charlotte	NC	28205	**800-631-8077***	704-331-7000
*Cust Svc					
Cognis Corp 5051 Estecreek Dr	Cincinnati	OH	45232	**800-543-7370***	513-482-3000
*Cust Svc					
Corsicana Technologies Inc 2733 E Hwy 31	Corsicana	TX	75110	**800-477-5353**	903-874-9500
CP Hall Co 311 S Wacker Dr Suite 4700	Chicago	IL	60606	**800-762-6198**	312-554-7400
Dow Chemical Canada Inc					
250 6th Ave SW Suite 2200	Calgary	AB	T2P3H7	**800-433-4398**	403-267-3500
Dow Chemical Co 2030 Dow Ctr	Midland	MI	48674	**800-331-6451***	989-636-1000
NYSE: DOW ■ *Cust Svc					
DSM Chemicals North America Inc					
1 Columbia Nitrogen Rd	Augusta	GA	30901	**800-825-4376**	706-849-6600
Eastman Chemical Co PO Box 431	Kingsport	TN	37662	**800-327-8626***	423-229-2000
NYSE: EMN ■ *Cust Svc					
EMD Chemicals Inc 480 S Democrat Rd	Gibbstown	NJ	08027	**800-222-0342***	856-423-6300
*Cust Svc					
Ferro Corp Grant Chemical Div					
111 W Irene Rd	Zachary	LA	70791	**800-325-3578**	225-654-6801
Ferro Corp Polymer Additives Div					
7050 Krick Rd	Walton Hills	OH	44146	**800-321-9946**	216-641-8580
Gantrade Corp 210 Summit Ave Bldg B	Montvale	NJ	07645	**800-426-8723**	201-573-1955
GE Petrochemicals Inc SR 892	Washington	WV	26181	**800-643-4346***	304-863-7778
*Cust Svc					

Company	City	State	Zip	Toll-Free	Phone
GE Silicones 260 Hudson River Rd	Waterford	NY	12188	**800-332-3390***	518-237-3330
*Cust Svc					
Grant Chemical Div Ferro Corp					
111 W Irene Rd	Zachary	LA	70791	**800-325-3578**	225-654-6801
Hall CP Co 311 S Wacker Dr Suite 4700	Chicago	IL	60606	**800-762-6198**	312-554-7400
Hercules Inc					
1313 N Market St Hercules Plaza	Wilmington	DE	19894	**800-441-7600**	302-594-5000
NYSE: HPC					
Heucotech Ltd 99 Newbold Rd	Fairless Hills	PA	19030	**800-438-2224**	215-736-0712
Huntsman Corp 500 Huntsman Way	Salt Lake City	UT	84108	**800-421-2411**	801-584-5700
NYSE: HUN					
ICC Industries Inc 460 Park Ave	New York	NY	10022	**800-422-1720**	212-521-1700
Inolex Chemical Co					
Jackson & Swanson Sts	Philadelphia	PA	19148	**800-521-9891***	215-271-0800
*Cust Svc					
International Specialty Products Inc					
1361 Alps Rd	Wayne	NJ	07470	**800-365-7353**	973-628-4000
JLM Industries Inc 8675 Hidden River Pkwy	Tampa	FL	33637	**800-457-3743**	813-632-3300
Magruder Color Co Inc 1029 Newark Ave	Elizabeth	NJ	07208	**800-631-4461**	973-242-1300
Methanex Corp 200 Burrard St Suite 1800	Vancouver	BC	V6C3M1	**800-900-6384**	604-661-2600
NASDAQ: MEOH					
Millennium Chemicals Inc					
20 Wight Ave Suite 100	Hunt Valley	MD	21030	**866-225-5642**	410-229-4400
Mitsui Chemicals America Inc					
2500 Westchester Ave Suite 110	Purchase	NY	10577	**800-682-2377**	914-253-0777
Niacet Corp 400 47th St	Niagara Falls	NY	14304	**800-828-1207**	716-285-1474
Perstorp Polyols Inc 600 Matzinger Rd	Toledo	OH	43612	**800-537-0280***	419-729-5448
*Cust Svc					
PMC Specialties Group Inc 501 Murray Rd	Cincinnati	OH	45217	**800-543-2466**	513-242-3300
Reilly Industries Inc 300 N Meridian St	Indianapolis	IN	46204	**800-888-3536***	317-247-8141
*Admitting					
Rhodia Inc 259 Prospect Plains Rd CN 7500	Cranbury	NJ	08512	**888-776-7337***	609-860-4000
*Cust Svc					
RT Vanderbilt Co Inc 30 Winfield St	Norwalk	CT	06855	**800-243-6064***	203-853-1400
*Cust Svc					
Sensient Colors Inc 2526 Baldwin St	Saint Louis	MO	63106	**800-325-8110**	314-889-7600
Shell Chemicals Canada Ltd 400 4th Ave	Calgary	AB	T2P0J4	**888-791-4314**	
Shin-Etsu Silicones of America 1150 Damar Dr	Akron	OH	44305	**800-544-1745**	330-630-9860
Sigma-Aldrich Chemical Co					
3050 Spruce St	Saint Louis	MO	63103	**800-325-3010***	314-771-5765
*Sales					
Sunoco Chemicals					
1801 Market St 10 Penn Ctr	Philadelphia	PA	19103	**800-786-6261**	215-977-3321
Sunoco Inc 1801 Market St	Philadelphia	PA	19103	**800-786-6261**	215-977-3000
NYSE: SUN					
Synalloy Corp 2155 W Croft Cir	Spartanburg	SC	29302	**800-763-1001***	864-585-3605
NASDAQ: SYNL ■ *Orders					
Texas Petrochemicals LP					
3 Riverway Suite 1500	Houston	TX	77056	**877-584-3256**	713-627-7474
Vanderbilt Chemical Corp 30 Winfield St	Norwalk	CT	06855	**800-243-6064**	203-853-1400
Vanderbilt RT Co Inc 30 Winfield St	Norwalk	CT	06855	**800-243-6064***	203-853-1400
*Cust Svc					
Velsicol Chemical Corp					
10400 W Higgins Rd Suite 600	Rosemont	IL	60018	**800-843-7759***	847-298-9000
*Cust Svc					
Vulcan Chemicals 1200 Urban Center Dr	Birmingham	AL	35242	**800-633-8280***	205-298-3000
*Cust Svc					
Wacker Chemical Corp DBA Wacker Silicones					
3301 Sutton Rd	Adrian	MI	49221	**800-248-0063**	517-264-8500
Wausau Chemical Corp 2001 N River Dr	Wausau	WI	54403	**800-950-6656**	715-842-2285

CHEMICALS - MEDICINAL

SEE Medicinal Chemicals & Botanical Products

143 CHEMICALS - SPECIALTY

Company	City	State	Zip	Toll-Free	Phone
Airosol Co Inc 1101 Illinois PO Box 120	Neodesha	KS	66757	**800-633-9576**	620-325-2666
Alex C Fergusson Inc					
5000 Letterkenny Rd Suite 220	Chambersburg	PA	17201	**800-345-1329**	717-264-9147
Alfa Aesar Co 26 Parkridge Rd 2nd Fl	Ward Hill	MA	01835	**800-343-0660**	978-521-6300
Allied Diagnostic Imaging Resources Inc					
5440-A Oakbrook Pkwy	Norcross	GA	30093	**800-262-9333**	770-448-0250
AM Todd Co 1717 Douglas Ave	Kalamazoo	MI	49005	**800-968-2603**	269-343-2603
Ameron International Performance Coatings & Finishes Group 13010 Morris Road					
Suite 400	Alpharetta	GA	30004	**800-926-3766**	678-393-0653
AMREP Inc 990 Industrial Park Dr	Marietta	GA	30062	**800-241-7766***	770-422-2071
*Cust Svc					
Anderson Chemical Co PO Box 1041	Litchfield	MN	55355	**800-366-2477**	320-693-2477
Angstrom Technologies Inc					
1895 Airport Exchange Blvd Suite 110	Erlanger	KY	41018	**800-543-7358***	859-282-0020
*Cust Svc					
Apollo Chemical Corp 1105 Southerland St	Graham NC	NC	27253	**800-374-3827**	336-226-1161
Athea Laboratories Inc					
7855 N Faulkner Rd PO Box 240014	Milwaukee	WI	53224	**800-743-6417**	414-354-6417
Baker Hughes Inc Baker Petrolite Div					
12645 W Airport Blvd	Sugar Land	TX	77478	**800-231-3606**	281-276-5400
Baker Petrolite Div Baker Hughes Inc					
12645 W Airport Blvd	Sugar Land	TX	77478	**800-231-3606**	281-276-5400
Benchmark Inc 4660 13th St	Wyandotte	MI	48192	**800-521-9107**	734-285-0900
Bercen Inc 1381 Cranston St	Cranston	RI	02920	**800-525-0595**	401-943-7400
BG Products Inc					
740 S Wichita St PO Box 1282	Wichita	KS	67201	**800-961-6228**	316-265-2686
Birchwood Laboratories Inc					
7900 Fuller Rd	Eden Prairie	MN	55344	**800-328-6156**	952-937-7900
BP Chemicals 150 W Warrenville Rd	Naperville	IL	60563	**877-701-2726**	630-420-5111
Brulin & Co Inc 2920 Dr AJ Brown Ave	Indianapolis	IN	46205	**800-776-7149**	317-923-3211
Buckman Laboratories Inc					
1256 N McLean Blvd	Memphis	TN	38108	**800-282-5626**	901-278-0330
Cabot Corp 2 Seaport Ln Suite 1300	Boston	MA	02210	**800-853-5407**	617-345-0100
NYSE: CBT					
Cabot Corp Inkjet Colorants Div					
157 Concord Rd	Billerica	MA	01821	**800-526-7591***	978-663-3455
*Cust Svc					
Cabot Microelectronics Corp					
870 N Commons Dr	Aurora	IL	60504	**800-811-2756**	630-375-6631
NASDAQ: CCMP					
Cabot Specialty Fluids					
10001 Woodlock Forest Dr					
Suite 275	The Woodlands	TX	77380	**888-273-7455**	281-298-9955
Chem Lab Products Inc 5160 E Airport Dr	Ontario	CA	91761	**800-745-4536**	909-390-9912
Chemetall Oakite 50 Valley Rd	Berkeley Heights	NJ	07922	**800-526-4473**	908-464-6900
Chemical Packaging Corp					
2700 SW 14th St	Pompano Beach	FL	33069	**800-327-1835***	954-974-5440
*Cust Svc					
CHT R Beitlich Corp 5046 Old Pineville Rd	Charlotte	NC	28217	**800-277-4941**	704-523-4242
Ciba Specialty Chemicals					
540 White Plains Rd	Tarrytown	NY	10591	**800-431-1900**	914-785-2000
Claire Mfg Co 500 Vista Ave	Addison	IL	60101	**800-252-4731***	630-543-7600
*Sales					
Clariant Corp 4000 Monroe Rd	Charlotte	NC	28205	**800-631-8077***	704-331-7000
*Cust Svc					
Cognis Corp 5051 Estecreek Dr	Cincinnati	OH	45232	**800-543-7370***	513-482-3000
*Cust Svc					
Columbian Chemicals Co					
1800 W Oak Commons Ct	Marietta	GA	30062	**800-235-4003**	770-792-9400
Contact Industries Inc 641 Dowd Ave	Elizabeth	NJ	07201	**800-536-3170**	908-351-5900
Coral Chemical Co 135 Le Baron St	Waukegan	IL	60085	**800-228-4646**	847-336-8100
Cortec Corp 4119 White Bear Pkwy	Saint Paul	MN	55110	**800-426-7832**	651-429-1100
CPAC Inc 2364 Leicester Rd	Leicester	NY	14481	**800-828-6011***	585-382-3223
NASDAQ: CPAK ■ *Cust Svc					
CRC Industries Inc 885 Louis Dr	Warminster	PA	18974	**800-272-4620***	215-674-4300
*Cust Svc					
Croda Inc 300-A Columbus Cir	Edison	NJ	08837	**888-252-7632**	732-417-0800
Crystal Inc 601 W 8th St	Lansdale	PA	19446	**800-525-3842**	215-368-1661
Degussa Admixtures Inc					
23700 Chagrin Blvd	Beachwood	OH	44122	**800-628-9990**	216-839-7500
Degussa Corp 379 Interpace Pkwy Bldg 3	Parsippany	NJ	07054	**800-334-8772**	973-541-8000
Degussa Wall Systems Inc					
3550 St Johns Bluff Rd S	Jacksonville	FL	32224	**800-322-7825**	904-996-6000
Delta Chemical Corp 2601 Cannery Ave	Baltimore	MD	21226	**800-282-5322**	410-354-0100
Dexter Chemical LLC 845 Edgewater Rd	Bronx	NY	10474	**800-339-9111**	718-542-7700
Diversified Chemical Technologies Inc					
15477 Woodrow Wilson St	Detroit	MI	48238	**800-243-1424**	313-867-5444
Dober Chemical Group					
14461 S Waverly Ave	Midlothian	IL	60445	**800-323-4983**	708-388-7700
DSM Desotech Inc 1122 Saint Charles St	Elgin	IL	60120	**800-223-7191**	847-697-0400
Eltech Systems Corp 100 7th Ave Suite 300	Chardon	OH	44024	**800-795-6832**	440-285-0300
Enthone-OMI Inc 350 Frontage Rd	West Haven	CT	06516	**800-496-8326**	203-934-8611
Eureka Chemical Co					
234 Lawrence Ave	South San Francisco	CA	94080	**888-387-3522**	650-761-3536
Fergusson Alex C Inc					
5000 Letterkenny Rd Suite 220	Chambersburg	PA	17201	**800-345-1329**	717-264-9147
Foseco Metallurgical Inc 20200 Sheldon Rd	Cleveland	OH	44142	**800-321-3132**	440-826-4548
Frank Miller & Sons Inc					
13831 S Emerald Ave	Riverdale	IL	60827	**800-423-6358**	708-201-7200
Fremont Industries Inc					
4400 Valley Industrial Blvd N PO Box 67	Shakopee	MN	55379	**800-436-1238**	952-445-4121
Genleco Inc 200 N Laflin St	Chicago	IL	60607	**800-223-8217**	312-421-2383
Gold Eagle Co 4400 S Kildare Ave	Chicago	IL	60632	**800-621-1251**	773-376-4400
Grace WR & Co 7500 Grace Dr	Columbia	MD	21044	**888-398-4646**	410-531-4000
NYSE: GRA					
H Krevit & Co Inc 73 Welton St	New Haven	CT	06511	**800-922-6626**	203-772-3350
Harcros Chemicals Inc 5200 Speaker Rd	Kansas City	KS	66106	**800-765-4748**	913-321-3131
Henkel Surface Technologies					
32100 Stephenson Hwy	Madison Heights	MI	48071	**800-521-6895**	248-583-9300
Hercules Inc					
1313 N Market St Hercules Plaza	Wilmington	DE	19894	**800-441-7600**	302-594-5000
NYSE: HPC					
Hickman Williams & Co					
550 Forest Ave Suite 16	Plymouth	MI	48170	**800-862-1890**	734-414-9575
Honeywell Specialty Chemicals					
101 Columbia Rd	Morristown	NJ	07962	**800-222-0094**	973-455-2145
Houghton Chemical Corp 52 Cambridge St	Boston	MA	02134	**800-777-2466**	617-254-1010
Hydrite Chemical Co 300 N Patrick Blvd	Brookfield	WI	53045	**800-558-9566**	262-792-1450
ICI American Holdings Inc					
10 Finderne Ave	Bridgewater	NJ	08807	**800-998-9986**	908-203-2800
Intercontinental Chemical Corp					
4660 Spring Grove Ave	Cincinnati	OH	45232	**800-543-2075**	513-541-7100
International Chemical Co					
2628 N Mascher St	Philadelphia	PA	19133	**800-541-2504**	215-739-2313
ITW Chemtronics Inc 8125 Cobb Centre Dr	Kennesaw	GA	30152	**800-645-5244**	770-424-4888
ITW Texwipe 3000 E Rt 17 S	Mahwah	NJ	07430	**800-839-9473**	201-327-9100
Kao Specialties Americas LLC					
243 Woodline St PO Box 2316	High Point	NC	27261	**800-727-2214**	336-884-2214
Kester Solder Co 515 E Touhy Ave	Des Plaines	IL	60018	**800-253-7837**	847-297-1600
King Industries Inc Science Rd	Norwalk	CT	06852	**800-431-7900**	203-866-5551
Kolene Corp 12890 Westwood Ave	Detroit	MI	48223	**800-521-4182**	313-273-9220
Lawter International Inc 8601 95th St	Pleasant Prairie	WI	53158	**800-775-2983**	262-947-7300
LPS Laboratories 4647 Hugh Howell Rd	Tucker	GA	30084	**800-241-8334**	770-934-7800
Lubrizol Corp 29400 Lakeland Blvd	Wickliffe	OH	44092	**800-522-4125**	440-943-4200
NYSE: LZ					
Lucas-Milhaupt Inc 5656 S Pennsylvania Ave	Cudahy	WI	53110	**800-558-3856**	414-769-6000
MacDermid Inc 245 Freight St	Waterbury	CT	06702	**800-325-4158**	203-575-5700
NYSE: MRD					
Master Builders 23700 Chagrin Blvd	Beachwood	OH	44122	**800-628-9990**	216-839-7500
McGean 2910 Harvard Ave	Cleveland	OH	44105	**800-932-7006***	216-441-4900
*Orders					
McGean-Rohco Inc DBA McGean					
2910 Harvard Ave	Cleveland	OH	44105	**800-932-7006***	216-441-4900
*Orders					
Met-Pro Corp Stiles-Kem Div					
1570 S Lakeside Dr	Waukegan	IL	60085	**800-562-1537**	847-689-1100
Michelman Inc 9080 Shell Rd	Cincinnati	OH	45236	**800-477-0498**	513-793-7766
Millennium Specialty Chemicals					
601 Crestwood St	Jacksonville	FL	32208	**800-231-6728**	904-768-5800
Miller Frank & Sons Inc					
13831 S Emerald Ave	Riverdale	IL	60827	**800-423-6358**	708-201-7200
Miller-Stephenson Chemical Co					
55 Backus Ave	Danbury	CT	06810	**800-992-2424***	203-743-4447
*Tech Supp					
Monroe Fluid Technology Inc					
36 Draffin Rd Box 810	Hilton	NY	14468	**800-828-6351**	585-392-3434
Montello Inc 6106 E 32nd Pl Suite 100	Tulsa	OK	74135	**800-331-4628**	918-665-1170
Mount Pulaski Products Inc					
908 N Vine St	Mount Pulaski	IL	62548	**800-577-2627**	217-792-3211

Company / Address	City	State	Zip	Toll-Free	Phone
Multisorb Technologies Inc 325 Harlem Rd	West Seneca	NY	14224	**800-445-9890***	716-824-8900
*Cust Svc					
Nalco Co 1601 W Diehl Rd	Naperville	IL	60563	**877-813-3523**	630-305-1000
NYSE: NLC					
National Starch & Chemical Co 10 Finderne Ave	Bridgewater	NJ	08807	**800-797-4992**	908-685-5000
Northern Technologies International Corp (NTIC) 6680 N Hwy 49	Lino Lakes	MN	55014	**800-328-2433**	651-784-1250
AMEX: NTI					
Noveon Inc 9911 Brecksville Rd	Cleveland	OH	44141	**800-380-5397**	216-447-5000
Nox-Crete Inc 1444 S 20th St	Omaha	NE	68108	**800-369-9800**	402-341-2080
NTIC (Northern Technologies International Corp) 6680 N Hwy 49	Lino Lakes	MN	55014	**800-328-2433**	651-784-1250
AMEX: NTI					
OM Group Inc 811 Sharon Dr	Westlake	OH	44145	**800-321-9696**	440-899-2950
NYSE: OMG					
OMNOVA Solutions Inc Performance Chemicals Div 165 S Cleveland Ave	Mogadore	OH	44260	**888-353-4173***	330-628-9925
*Cust Svc					
Pavco Inc 4450 Cranwood Pkwy	Warrensville Heights	OH	44128	**800-321-7735***	216-332-1000
*Orders					
Peach State Labs Inc 180 Burlington Rd PO Box 5424	Rome	GA	30162	**800-634-1653**	706-291-8743
Penford Corp 7094 S Revere Pkwy	Englewood	CO	80112	**800-204-7369**	303-649-1900
NASDAQ: PENX					
Penray Cos Inc 440 Denniston Ct	Wheeling	IL	60090	**800-373-6729**	847-459-5000
Phelps Dodge Corp 1 N Central Ave	Phoenix	AZ	85004	**800-528-1182**	602-366-8100
NYSE: PD					
Pilot Chemical Co 11756 Burke St	Santa Fe Springs	CA	90670	**800-707-4568**	562-698-6778
PMC Global Inc 12243 Branford St	Sun Valley	CA	91352	**800-423-5632**	818-896-1101
Prime Leather Finishes Co Inc 205 S 2nd St	Milwaukee	WI	53204	**800-558-7285**	414-276-1668
PVS Chemicals Inc 10900 Harper Ave	Detroit	MI	48213	**800-787-6659**	313-921-1200
Quaker Chemical Corp 901 Hector St	Conshohocken	PA	19428	**800-523-7010**	610-832-4000
NYSE: KWR					
Radiator Specialty Co 1900 Wilkinson Blvd	Charlotte	NC	28208	**800-438-4532**	704-377-6555
Resolution Specialty Materials 200 Railroad St	Roebuck	SC	29376	**800-476-4476**	864-253-8400
Rhein Chemie Corp 1014 Whitehead Rd Ext	Trenton	NJ	08638	**800-289-2436***	609-771-9100
*Cust Svc					
Rochester Midland Corp 333 Hollenbeck St PO Box 31515	Rochester	NY	14603	**800-836-1627**	585-336-2200
Rohm & Haas Electronic Materials 455 Forest St	Marlborough	MA	01752	**800-832-6200**	508-481-7950
Ronson Corp Campus Dr Corporate Pk 3	Somerset	NJ	08875	**800-526-4281**	732-469-8300
NASDAQ: RONC					
Rycoline Products Inc 5540 N Northwest Hwy	Chicago	IL	60630	**800-621-1003**	773-775-6755
Scholler Inc 95 James Way Suite 100	Southampton	PA	18966	**800-220-1504**	215-942-0200
Sigma-Aldrich Corp 3050 Spruce St	Saint Louis	MO	63103	**800-325-3010**	314-771-5765
NASDAQ: SIAL					
Sika Corp 201 Polito Ave	Lyndhurst	NJ	07071	**800-933-7452**	201-933-8800
Solutek Corp 94 Shirley St	Boston	MA	02119	**800-403-0770**	617-445-5335
Spartan Chemical Co Inc 1110 Spartan Dr	Maumee	OH	43537	**800-537-8990**	419-531-5551
Specco Industries Inc 13087 Main St	Lemont	IL	60439	**800-441-6646**	630-257-5060
Sprayway Inc 500 S Vista Ave	Addison	IL	60101	**800-332-9000**	630-628-3000
Standard Tar Products Co 2456 W Cornell St	Milwaukee	WI	53209	**800-825-7650**	414-873-7650
Stapleton Technologies Inc 1350 W 12th St	Long Beach	CA	90813	**800-266-0541**	562-437-0541
Stepan Co 22 W Frontage Rd	Northfield	IL	60093	**800-745-7837***	847-446-7500
NYSE: SCL ■ *Tech Supp					
Stiles-Kem Div Met-Pro Corp 1570 S Lakeside Dr	Waukegan	IL	60085	**800-562-1537**	847-689-1100
Stoner Inc 1070 Robert Fulton Hwy	Quarryville	PA	17566	**800-227-5538**	717-786-7355
Sweetwater Technologies PO Box 1473	Temecula	CA	92593	**888-711-7575**	951-303-0999
Sybron Chemicals Inc PO Box 66	Birmingham	NJ	08011	**800-678-0020**	609-893-1100
Symons Corp 200 E Touhy Ave	Des Plaines	IL	60018	**800-800-7601**	847-298-3200
Symrise Inc 300 North St	Teterboro	NJ	07608	**800-422-1559**	201-288-3200
Technical Chemical Co 3327 Pipeline Rd	Cleburne	TX	76033	**800-527-0885**	817-645-6088
Texas Refinery Corp 840 N Main St	Fort Worth	TX	76106	**800-827-0711**	817-332-1161
Thatcher Co PO Box 27407	Salt Lake City	UT	84127	**800-348-0034**	801-972-4587
Todd AM Co 1717 Douglas Ave	Kalamazoo	MI	49005	**800-968-2603**	269-343-2603
United Laboratories Inc 320 37th Ave	Saint Charles	IL	60174	**800-323-2594**	630-377-0900
United Salt Corp 4800 San Felipe St	Houston	TX	77056	**800-554-8658**	713-877-2600
Watcon Inc PO Box 2829	South Bend	IN	46680	**800-492-8266**	574-287-3397
WR Grace & Co 7500 Grace Dr	Columbia	MD	21044	**888-398-4646**	410-531-4000
NYSE: GRA					
Wynn Oil Co 1050 W 5th St	Azusa	CA	91702	**800-989-8363**	626-334-0231
XL Brands 237 Nance Rd NE	Calhoun	GA	30701	**800-367-4583**	706-625-0025

144 CHEMICALS & RELATED PRODUCTS - WHOL

Company / Address	City	State	Zip	Toll-Free	Phone
AEP Colloids Div SARCOM Inc 393 Church St PO Box 3425	Saratoga Springs	NY	12866	**800-848-0658**	518-584-4105
Airgas Inc 259 N Radnor-Chester Rd Suite 100	Radnor	PA	19087	**800-255-2165**	610-687-5253
NYSE: ARG					
Astro Chemicals Inc 64-94 Shaw's Ln	Springfield	MA	01104	**800-223-0776**	413-781-7240
Barton Solvents Inc 1920 NE Broadway Ave	Des Moines	IA	50313	**800-383-6488**	515-265-7998
Basic Chemicals Solutions LLC (BCS) 525 Seaport Blvd	Redwood City	CA	94063	**888-810-4787**	650-363-1661
Becker DB Co Inc 54 Old Hwy 22	Clinton	NJ	08809	**800-394-3991**	908-730-6010
Brenntag Great Lakes LLC PO Box 444	Butler	WI	53007	**800-558-8501**	262-252-3550
Brenntag Mid-South Inc 1405 Hwy 136 W	Henderson	KY	42419	**800-950-7267**	270-830-1200
Brenntag Southwest Inc 610 Fisher Rd	Longview	TX	75604	**800-945-1858**	903-759-7151
Cachat MF Co 14600 Detroit Ave Suite 600	Lakewood	OH	44107	**800-729-8900**	216-228-8900
Canada Colors & Chemicals Ltd 80 Scarsdale Rd	Don Mills	ON	M3B2R7	**800-387-8006**	416-449-7750
Chemcentral Corp 7050 W 71st St	Bedford Park	IL	60499	**800-331-6174**	708-594-7000
Chemroy Canada Inc 106 Summerlea Rd	Brampton	ON	L6T4X3	**888-243-6769**	905-789-0701
Chemsolv Inc 1140 Industry Ave SE	Roanoke	VA	24103	**800-523-3099**	540-427-4000
Coastal Chemical Co Inc 3520 Veterans Memorial	Abbeville	LA	70510	**800-535-3862***	337-893-3862
*Cust Svc					
Coyne George S Chemical Co 3015 State Rd	Croydon	PA	19021	**800-523-1230**	215-785-3000
Dar-tech Inc 16485 Rockside Rd	Cleveland	OH	44137	**800-228-7347**	216-663-7600
DB Becker Co Inc 54 Old Hwy 22	Clinton	NJ	08809	**800-394-3991**	908-730-6010
Durr Marketing Assoc Inc 1300 Lower Rodi Rd	Turtle Creek	PA	15145	**800-937-3877**	412-829-2300
EMCO Chemical Distributors Inc 2100 Commonwealth Ave	North Chicago	IL	60064	**800-267-3626**	847-689-2200
ET Horn Co 16141 Heron Ave	La Mirada	CA	90638	**800-442-4676**	714-523-8050
Gallade Chemical Inc 1230 E St Gertrude Pl	Santa Ana	CA	92707	**800-325-8431**	714-546-9901
Gallard-Schlesinger Industries Inc 245 Newtown Rd Suite 305	Plainview	NY	11803	**800-645-3044**	516-683-6900
George S Coyne Chemical Co 3015 State Rd	Croydon	PA	19021	**800-523-1230**	215-785-3000
GS Robins & Co 126 Chouteau Ave	Saint Louis	MO	63102	**800-777-5155**	314-621-5165
Harcros Chemicals Inc 5200 Speaker Rd	Kansas City	KS	66106	**800-765-4748**	913-321-3131
Haviland Enterprises Inc 421 Ann St NW	Grand Rapids	MI	49504	**800-456-1134**	616-361-6691
Hess John R & Co Inc 400 Station St PO Box 3615	Cranston	RI	02910	**800-828-4377**	401-785-9300
Hill Brothers Chemical Co 1675 N Main St	Orange	CA	92867	**800-994-8801**	714-998-8800
HM Royal Inc 689 Pennington Ave	Trenton	NJ	08618	**800-257-9452**	609-396-9176
Horn ET Co 16141 Heron Ave	La Mirada	CA	90638	**800-442-4676**	714-523-8050
Hydrite Chemical Co 300 N Patrick Blvd	Brookfield	WI	53045	**800-558-9566**	262-792-1450
ICC Chemical Corp 460 Park Ave	New York	NY	10022	**800-422-1720**	212-521-1700
Ideal Chemical & Supply Co 4025 Air Park St	Memphis	TN	38118	**800-232-6776**	901-363-7720
Independent Chemical Corp 79-51 Cooper Ave	Glendale	NY	11385	**800-892-2578**	718-894-0700
Industrial Chemicals Inc 2042 Montreat Dr	Birmingham	AL	35216	**800-476-2042**	205-823-7330
JLM Industries Inc 8675 Hidden River Pkwy	Tampa	FL	33637	**800-457-3743**	813-632-3300
JLM Marketing Inc 8675 Hidden River Pkwy	Tampa	FL	33637	**800-457-3743**	813-632-3300
John R Hess & Co Inc 400 Station St PO Box 3615	Cranston	RI	02910	**800-828-4377**	401-785-9300
KA Steel Chemicals Inc 15185 Main St PO Box 729	Lemont	IL	60439	**800-677-8335**	630-257-3900
Kraft Chemical Co 1975 N Hawthorne Ave	Melrose Park	IL	60160	**800-345-5200**	708-345-5200
LCI Ltd 415 Pablo Ave N	Jacksonville Beach	FL	32240	**800-578-7891**	904-241-1200
Mays Chemical Co Inc 5611 E 71st St	Indianapolis	IN	46220	**800-525-4803**	317-842-8722
McCullough & Assoc PO Box 29803	Atlanta	GA	30359	**800-969-1606**	404-325-1606
MF Cachat Co 14600 Detroit Ave Suite 600	Lakewood	OH	44107	**800-729-8900**	216-228-8900
Mozel Inc 1900 W Gate Dr	Columbia	IL	62236	**800-260-5348**	618-281-3040
Palmer Holland Inc 25000 Country Club Blvd Suite 400	North Olmsted	OH	44070	**800-635-4822**	440-686-2300
Plaza Group Inc 10375 Richmond Ave Suite 1620	Houston	TX	77042	**800-876-3738**	713-266-0707
Ribelin Sales Inc 3857 Miller Pk Dr	Garland	TX	75042	**800-374-1594**	972-272-1594
Robins GS & Co 126 Chouteau Ave	Saint Louis	MO	63102	**800-777-5155**	314-621-5165
Rosen's Inc 1120 Lake Ave	Fairmont	MN	56031	**800-798-2000**	507-238-4201
Royal HM Inc 689 Pennington Ave	Trenton	NJ	08618	**800-257-9452**	609-396-9176
SARCOM Inc AEP Colloids Div 393 Church St PO Box 3425	Saratoga Springs	NY	12866	**800-848-0658**	518-584-4105
Sasol Wax Americas Inc 2 Corporate Dr Suite 434	Shelton	CT	06484	**800-423-7071**	203-925-4300
Solvents & Chemicals Inc 4704 Shank Rd PO Box 490	Pearland	TX	77581	**800-622-3990**	281-485-5377
Superior Solvents & Chemicals 400 W Regent St	Indianapolis	IN	46225	**800-553-5480**	317-781-4400
Tanner Industries Inc 735 Davisville Rd 3rd Fl	Southampton	PA	18966	**800-643-6226**	215-322-1238
Tarr LLC 2429 N Borthwick	Portland	OR	97227	**800-422-5069**	503-288-5294
Tilley Chemical Co Inc 501 Chesapeake Pk Plaza	Baltimore	MD	21220	**800-638-6968**	410-574-4500
TransChemical Inc 419 E DeSoto Ave	Saint Louis	MO	63147	**888-873-6481**	314-231-6905
Ulrich Chemical Inc 3111 N Post Rd	Indianapolis	IN	46226	**800-844-8632**	317-898-8632
United Mineral & Chemical Corp 1100 Valley Brook Ave	Lyndhurst	NJ	07071	**800-777-0505**	201-507-3300
Univar USA Inc PO Box 34325	Seattle	WA	98124	**800-234-4588**	425-889-3400
Van Horn Metz & Co 201 E Elm St	Conshohocken	PA	19428	**800-523-0424**	610-828-4500
Walsh & Assoc Inc 1400 Macklind Ave	Saint Louis	MO	63110	**800-949-2574**	314-781-2520
Wego Chemical & Mineral Corp 239 Great Neck Rd	Great Neck	NY	11021	**877-489-6645**	516-487-3510
Whitaker Oil Co Inc 1557 Marietta Rd NW	Atlanta	GA	30318	**800-221-0521**	404-355-8220
Wilson Industrial Sales Co Inc PO Box 425	Brook	IN	47922	**800-633-5427**	219-275-7333
Young Chemical Co 6465 Eastland Rd	Brook Park	OH	44142	**800-248-3009**	440-234-3200

145 CHILD CARE MONITORING SYSTEMS - INTERNET

Company / Address	City	State	Zip	Toll-Free	Phone
Kids-World.net c/o SecurityBase.com PO Box 52282	Irvine	CA	92619	**877-801-0354**	
KinderCam Inc 5500 Peachtree Pkwy	Norcross	GA	30092	**888-522-6123**	678-966-3000
ParentWatch Inc 49 W 37th St 14th Fl	New York	NY	10018	**800-696-2664**	212-869-8282
WatchMeGrow LLC 4405 7th Ave Suite 201	Lacey	WA	98503	**800-483-5597**	

146 CHILDREN'S LEARNING CENTERS

Company / Address	City	State	Zip	Toll-Free	Phone
Bright Horizons Family Solutions Inc 200 Talcott Ave S	Watertown	MA	02472	**800-324-4386**	617-673-8000
NASDAQ: BFAM					
COMPUTER EXPLORERS Inc 12715 Telge Rd	Cypress	TX	77429	**800-531-5053**	281-256-4100
Educate Inc 1001 Fleet St	Baltimore	MD	21202	**888-338-2283**	410-843-8000
Futurekids Inc 1000 N Studebaker Rd Suite 1	Long Beach	CA	90815	**800-765-8000**	562-296-1111
Gymboree Corp Play & Music Program 700 Airport Blvd Suite 200	Burlingame	CA	94010	**800-222-7758**	650-579-0600
Huntington Learning Centers Inc 954 Kinderkamack Rd	River Edge	NJ	07661	**800-226-5327**	201-261-8600
Kiddie Academy International Inc 108 Wheel Rd Suite 200	Bel Air	MD	21015	**800-554-3343**	410-515-0788
KinderCare Learning Centers Inc 650 NE Holladay St Suite 1400	Portland	OR	97232	**800-633-1488**	503-872-1300
Kumon North America Inc 300 Frank W Burr Blvd Glenpointe Ctr E 5th Fl	Teaneck	NJ	07666	**800-222-6284**	201-928-0444
La Petite Academy Inc 130 S Jefferson	Chicago	IL	60661	**800-527-3848**	312-789-1200

				Toll-Free	Phone
Learning Care Group Inc 38345 W Ten-Mile Rd Suite 100 *NASDAQ: LCGI*	Farmington Hills	MI	48335	**800-425-1212**	248-476-3200
Mad Science Group 8360 Bougainville St Suite 201	Montreal	QC	H4P2G1	**800-586-5231**	514-344-4181
New Horizon Kids Quest Inc 16355 36th Ave N Suite 700	Plymouth	MN	55446	**800-941-1007**	763-557-1111
Primrose School Franchising Co 3660 Cedarcrest Rd	Acworth	GA	30101	**800-745-0677**	770-529-4100
SCORE! Educational Centers 66 Franklin St Suite 300	Oakland	CA	94607	**800-497-2673**	510-817-3700
Tutor Time Learning Systems Inc 621 NW 53rd St Suite 115	Boca Raton	FL	33487	**800-275-1235**	561-237-2200

147 CIRCUS, CARNIVAL, FESTIVAL OPERATORS

				Toll-Free	Phone
Big Apple Circus 505 8th Ave 19th Fl	New York	NY	10018	**800-922-3772**	212-268-2500
Cirque du Soleil Inc 8400 2nd Ave	Montreal	QC	H1Z4M6	**800-678-2119**	514-722-2324
Feld Entertainment Inc 8607 Westwood Center Dr	Vienna	VA	22182	**800-298-3858**	703-448-4000
International Renaissance Festivals Ltd PO Box 315	Crownsville	MD	21032	**800-296-7304**	410-266-7304

148 CLAY PRODUCTS - STRUCTURAL

SEE ALSO Construction Materials - Brick, Stone, Related Materials

				Toll-Free	Phone
Acme Brick Co 2821 W 7th St	Fort Worth	TX	76107	**800-433-5650**	817-332-4101
Boral Bricks Inc 1630 Arthern Rd	Augusta	GA	30903	**800-580-3842**	706-823-8802
Brick & Tile Corp of Lawrenceville 16024 Governor Harrison Pkwy	Lawrenceville	VA	23868	**877-274-2582**	434-848-3151
Castaic Brick Inc 32201 Castaic Lake Dr	Castaic	CA	91384	**800-227-8242**	661-259-3066
Cherokee Brick & Tile Co Inc 3250 Waterville Rd	Macon	GA	31206	**800-277-2745**	478-781-6800
Colloid Environmental Technologies Co (CETCO) 1500 W Shure Dr	Arlington Heights	IL	60004	**800-527-9948**	847-392-5800
Cunningham Brick Co Inc 701 N Main St	Lexington	NC	27292	**800-672-6181**	336-248-8541
Denver Brick Co 401 Prairie Hawk Dr	Castle Rock	CO	80109	**800-332-7724**	303-688-6952
Endicott Clay Products Co 57120 707 Rd	Endicott	NE	68350	**800-927-9179**	402-729-3315
Endicott Tile LLC 57120 707 Rd	Endicott	NE	68350	**800-927-9179**	402-729-3315
General Shale Products LLC 3211 N Roan St *Cust Svc	Johnson City	TN	37601	**800-414-4661***	423-282-4661
Hanson Brick & Tile 15720 John J Delany Dr	Charlotte	NC	28277	**877-426-7668**	704-341-8750
Henry Brick Co Inc 3409 Water Ave	Selma	AL	36703	**800-548-7576**	334-875-2600
International Chimney Corp 55 S Long St	Williamsville	NY	14221	**800-828-1446**	716-634-3967
Interstate Brick Co 9780 S 5200 West	West Jordan	UT	84088	**800-233-8654**	801-280-5200
Irvins Interstate Brick & Block Co Inc 2301 N Hawthorne Ln	Indianapolis	IN	46218	**800-837-3384**	317-547-9511
Jenkins Brick Co Inc 201 N 6th St PO Box 91	Montgomery	AL	36104	**888-215-5700**	334-834-2210
Kansas Brick & Tile Inc PO Box 450 *Cust Svc	Hoisington	KS	67544	**800-999-0480***	620-653-2157
Kinney Brick Co 100 Prosperity Rd	Albuquerque	NM	87105	**800-464-4605**	505-877-4550
Lee Brick & Tile Co 3704 Hawkins Ave	Sanford	NC	27330	**800-672-7559**	919-774-4800
Logan Clay Products Co 201 S Walnut St	Logan	OH	43138	**800-848-2141**	740-385-2184
Ludowici Roof Tile Inc 4757 Tile Plant Rd PO Box 69 *Cust Svc	New Lexington	OH	43764	**800-945-8453***	740-342-1995
Marion Ceramics Inc Hwy 301 N	Marion	SC	29571	**800-845-4010**	843-423-1311
McNear Brick & Block 1 McNear Brickyard Rd	San Rafael	CA	94901	**888-442-6811**	415-454-6811
MCP Industries Inc Mission Clay Products Div 1655 E 6th St	Corona	CA	92879	**800-795-6067**	951-736-1881
Mission Clay Products Div MCP Industries Inc 1655 E 6th St	Corona	CA	92879	**800-795-6067**	951-736-1881
Mutual Materials Co 605 119th Ave NE	Bellevue	WA	98005	**800-477-3008**	425-452-2300
Old Virginia Brick Co 2500 W Main St	Salem	VA	24153	**800-879-8227**	540-389-2357
Palmetto Brick Co 3501 Brickyard Rd	Wallace	SC	29596	**800-922-4423**	843-537-7861
Pine Hall Brick Co 2701 Shorefair Dr	Winston-Salem	NC	27105	**800-952-7425**	336-721-7536
Redland Brick Inc 15718 Clear Spring Rd	Williamsport	MD	21795	**800-366-2742**	301-223-7700
Riverside Brick & Supply Co 12th & Maury St	Richmond	VA	23224	**800-666-0444**	804-232-6786
Robinson Brick Co 1845 W Dartmouth Ave	Denver	CO	80110	**800-477-9002**	303-783-3000
Stark Ceramics Inc 600 W Church St	East Canton	OH	44730	**800-321-0662**	330-488-1211
Statesville Brick Co 391 Brickyard Rd	Statesville	NC	28677	**800-522-4716**	704-872-4123
Superior Clay Corp 6566 Superior Rd SE	Uhrichsville	OH	44683	**800-848-6166**	740-922-4122
Tri-State Brick & Tile Co Inc 2050 Forest Ave	Jackson	MS	39286	**800-962-2101**	601-981-1410
Triangle Brick Co 6523 Hwy 55	Durham	NC	27713	**800-672-8547**	919-544-1796
US Tile Co Inc 909 W Railroad St	Corona	CA	92882	**800-252-9548**	951-737-0200
Whitacre Greer Fireproofing Inc 1400 S Mahoning Ave	Alliance	OH	44601	**800-947-2837**	330-823-1610

149 CLEANING PRODUCTS

SEE ALSO Mops, Sponges, Wiping Cloths

				Toll-Free	Phone
3M Automotive Aftermarket Div 3M Center Bldg 223-6N-01	Saint Paul	MN	55144	**800-364-3577**	
3M Commercial Care Div 3M Center Bldg 223-4N-14	Saint Paul	MN	55144	**800-847-3021**	800-626-8578
3M Consumer & Office Div 3M Ctr *NYSE: MMM*	Saint Paul	MN	55144	**800-364-3577**	651-733-1110
3M Safety Security & Protection Services Div 3M Ctr	Saint Paul	MN	55144	**800-364-3577**	651-733-1110
3M Transportation Div 3M Ctr	Saint Paul	MN	55144	**888-364-3577**	651-733-1110
ABC Compounding Co Inc 6970 Jonesboro Rd	Morrow	GA	30260	**800-795-9222**	770-968-9222
Abso-Clean Industries Inc 199 Wales Ave	Tonawanda	NY	14150	**800-837-5000**	716-693-2111
Adco Inc 900 W Main St	Sedalia	MO	65301	**800-821-7556**	660-826-3300
Advanced Sterilization Products 33 Technology Dr	Irvine	CA	92618	**800-595-0200**	949-581-5799
AJ Funk & Co Inc 1471 Timber Dr	Elgin	IL	60123	**877-225-3865**	847-741-6760
American Cleaning Co 39-30 Review Ave	Long Island City	NY	11101	**888-929-7587**	718-392-8080
Angelus Shoe Polish Co 8640 National Blvd PO Box 883	Culver City	CA	90232	**800-722-4848**	310-836-3314
Armor All Products Corp PO Box 24305	Oakland	CA	94623	**800-222-7784**	510-271-7000
Arrow-Magnolia International 2646 Rodney Ln *NASDAQ: ARWM*	Dallas	TX	75229	**800-527-2101**	972-247-7111
Austin James Co 115 Downieville Rd PO Box 827	Mars	PA	16046	**800-245-1942**	724-625-1535
Aztex Wax Products 5225 Middlebrook Pike	Knoxville	TN	37921	**800-369-5357**	865-588-5357
BAF Industries Inc 1910 S Yale St	Santa Ana	CA	92704	**800-437-9893**	714-540-3850
Brulin & Co Inc 2920 Dr AJ Brown Ave	Indianapolis	IN	46205	**800-776-7149**	317-923-3211
Buckeye International Inc 2700 Wagner Pl	Maryland Heights	MO	63043	**800-321-2583**	314-291-1900
Bullen Chemical Co PO Box 37	Folcroft	PA	19032	**800-444-8900**	610-534-8900
Butcher Co 8310 16th St	Sturtevant	WI	53177	**800-795-9550**	
C & H Chemical Inc 222 Starkey St	Saint Paul	MN	55107	**800-966-2909**	651-227-4343
Camco Chemical Co 8150 Holton Dr *Cust Svc	Florence	KY	41042	**800-354-1001***	859-727-3200
Car Brite Inc 1910 S State Ave	Indianapolis	IN	46203	**800-347-2439**	317-788-9925
Car-Freshner Corp 21205 Little Tree Dr	Watertown	NY	13601	**800-545-5454**	315-788-6250
Carroll Co 2900 W Kingsley Rd	Garland	TX	75041	**800-527-5722**	972-278-1304
Champion Chemical Co 8319 S Greenleaf Ave	Whittier	CA	90602	**800-621-7868**	562-945-1456
Chemetall Oakite 50 Valley Rd	Berkeley Heights	NJ	07922	**800-526-4473**	908-464-6900
Chemical Specialties Mfg Corp (Chemspec) 901 N Newkirk St *Sales	Baltimore	MD	21205	**800-638-7370***	410-675-4800
ChemPro Inc 141 Venture Blvd PO Box 2708	Spartanburg	SC	29304	**800-835-3712**	864-587-9308
Chemspec (Chemical Specialties Mfg Corp) 901 N Newkirk St *Sales	Baltimore	MD	21205	**800-638-7370***	410-675-4800
Concord Chemical Co 1700 Federal St	Camden	NJ	08105	**800-282-2436**	856-966-1526
Correlated Products Inc PO Box 42387	Indianapolis	IN	46242	**800-428-3266**	317-243-3248
Damon Industries Inc PO Box 2120	Alliance	OH	44601	**800-362-9850**	330-821-5310
Delta Carbona Products Co 376 Hollywood Ave Suite 208	Fairfield	NJ	07004	**888-746-5599**	973-808-6260
Dial Corp 15501 N Dial Blvd *Cust Svc	Scottsdale	AZ	85260	**800-258-3425***	480-754-3425
Diamond Chemical Co Inc PO Box 7428	East Rutherford	NJ	07073	**800-654-7627**	201-935-4300
Dubois Chemicals Inc 200 Crowne Point Place	Sharonville	OH	45241	**800-543-4906**	513-326-8800
Dura Wax Co 4101 W Albany St	McHenry	IL	60050	**800-435-5705**	815-385-5000
Ecolab Inc 370 N Wabasha St *NYSE: ECL*	Saint Paul	MN	55102	**800-392-3392**	651-293-2233
Emulso Corp 301 Ellicott St	Buffalo	NY	14203	**800-724-7667**	716-854-2889
Faultless Starch/Bon Ami Co 1025 W 8th St *Cust Svc	Kansas City	MO	64101	**800-821-5565***	816-842-1230
Fine Organics Corp 420 Kuller Rd PO Box 2277	Clifton	NJ	07015	**800-526-7480**	973-478-1000
Frank Miller & Sons Inc 13831 S Emerald Ave	Riverdale	IL	60827	**800-423-6358**	708-201-7200
Funk AJ & Co Inc 1471 Timber Dr	Elgin	IL	60123	**877-225-3865**	847-741-6760
Glissen Chemical Co Inc 1321 58th St	Brooklyn	NY	11219	**800-356-9922**	718-436-4200
Granitize Products Inc 11022 Vulcan St	South Gate	CA	90280	**800-553-6866**	562-923-5438
Guardian Chemical Co PO Box 93667	Atlanta	GA	30377	**800-241-6742**	404-873-1692
Hill Mfg Co Inc 1500 Jonesboro Rd SE	Atlanta	GA	30315	**800-445-5123**	404-522-8364
Hillyard Chemical Co Inc 302 N 4th St	Saint Joseph	MO	64501	**800-365-1555**	816-233-1321
ITW Dymon 805 E Old 56 Hwy	Olathe	KS	66061	**800-289-3966**	913-397-9889
James Austin Co 115 Downieville Rd PO Box 827	Mars	PA	16046	**800-245-1942**	724-625-1535
Johnson SC & Son Inc 1525 Howe St	Racine	WI	53403	**800-494-4855**	262-260-2000
Kay Chemical Co 8300 Capital Dr	Greensboro	NC	27409	**800-333-4300**	336-668-7290
KozaK Auto DryWash Inc PO Box 910	Batavia	NY	14021	**800-237-9927**	585-343-8111
Loren Products 250 Canal St	Lawrence	MA	01840	**800-274-6068**	978-685-0911
LPS Laboratories 4647 Hugh Howell Rd	Tucker	GA	30084	**800-241-8334**	770-934-7800
M-Chem Industries Corp 1607 Derwent Way	Delta	BC	V3M6K8	**800-663-9925**	
Madison Chemical Co Inc 3141 Clifty Dr	Madison	IN	47250	**800-345-1915**	812-273-6000
Magic American Corp 23700 Mercantile Rd *Cust Svc	Cleveland	OH	44122	**800-321-6330***	216-464-2353
Malco Products Inc PO Box 892	Barberton	OH	44203	**800-253-2526**	330-753-0361
Meguiar's Inc 17991 Mitchell S *Cust Svc	Irvine	CA	92614	**800-347-5700***	949-752-8000
Micro Care Corp 595 John Downey Dr	New Britain	CT	06051	**800-638-0125**	860-827-0626
Miller Frank & Sons Inc 13831 S Emerald Ave	Riverdale	IL	60827	**800-423-6358**	708-201-7200
Mission Kleensweep Products Inc 2433 Birkdale St	Los Angeles	CA	90031	**888-201-8866**	323-223-1405
Mother's Polishes Waxes & Cleaners 5456 Industrial Dr	Huntington Beach	CA	92649	**800-221-8257**	714-891-3364
National Chemicals Inc PO Box 32 *Cust Svc	Winona	MN	55987	**800-533-0027***	507-454-5640
Navico Inc DBA Navy Brand Mfg Co 3670 Scarlet Oak Blvd	Saint Louis	MO	63122	**800-325-3312**	636-861-5500
Navy Brand Mfg Co 3670 Scarlet Oak Blvd	Saint Louis	MO	63122	**800-325-3312**	636-861-5500
NCH Corp 2727 Chemsearch Blvd	Irving	TX	75062	**800-243-6835**	972-438-0226
New Pig Corp 1 Pork Ave	Tipton	PA	16684	**800-468-4647**	814-684-0101
Nord-Viscount Corp 50 Lawrence Ave	Brooklyn	NY	11230	**866-278-7674**	718-854-5586
Northern Labs Inc PO Box 850	Manitowoc	WI	54221	**800-558-7621**	920-684-7137
Nuvite Chemical Compounds Corp 213 Freeman St	Brooklyn	NY	11222	**800-394-8351**	718-383-8351
Ocean Bio-Chem Inc 4041 SW 47th Ave *NASDAQ: OBCI*	Fort Lauderdale	FL	33314	**800-327-8583**	954-587-6280
Orange Glo International 8200 E Maplewood Ave Suite 703	Greenwood Village	CO	80111	**800-781-7529**	303-740-1909
Panther Industries Inc 600 N Beach St	Fort Worth	TX	76111	**800-433-7664**	817-834-7164
Peck's Products Co 1220 Switzer Ave	Saint Louis	MO	63147	**800-325-8891**	314-385-5454
Reckitt Benckiser Inc PO Box 225 *Cust Svc	Parsippany	NJ	07054	**800-888-0192***	973-633-3600
Safeguard Chemical Corp 411 Wales Ave	Bronx	NY	10454	**800-536-3170**	718-585-3170
SC Johnson & Son Inc 1525 Howe St	Racine	WI	53403	**800-494-4855**	262-260-2000
Scot Laboratories Div Scott Fetzer Co 16841 Park Circle Dr	Chagrin Falls	OH	44023	**800-486-7268**	440-543-3033
Scott Fetzer Co Scot Laboratories Div 16841 Park Circle Dr	Chagrin Falls	OH	44023	**800-486-7268**	440-543-3033
Scott's Liquid Gold Inc 4880 Havana St	Denver	CO	80239	**800-447-1919**	303-373-4860

Company	City	State	Zip	Toll-Free	Phone
Selig Chemical Industries Inc 115 Kendall Park Ln	Atlanta	GA	30336	**800-447-3544**	
Seventh Generation Inc 212 Battery St Suite A	Burlington	VT	05401	**800-456-1191**	802-658-3773
Share Corp 7821 N Faulkner Rd	Milwaukee	WI	53224	**800-776-7192**	414-355-4000
Simoniz USA 201 Boston Tpke	Bolton	CT	06043	**800-227-5536**	860-646-0172
State Industrial Products 3100 Hamilton Ave	Cleveland	OH	44114	**800-782-2436**	216-861-7114
Stearns Packaging Corp 4200 Sycamore Ave	Madison	WI	53714	**800-655-5008**	608-246-5150
Summit Industries Inc 839 Pickens Industrial Dr	Marietta	GA	30062	**800-241-6996**	770-590-0600
Sunshine Makers Inc 15922 Pacific Coast Hwy	Huntington Harbour	CA	92649	**800-228-0709**	714-840-1319
Turtle Wax Inc 5655 W 73rd St	Chicago	IL	60638	**800-323-9883**	708-563-3600
Unit Chemical Corp 4161 Redwood Ave	Los Angeles	CA	90066	**800-879-8648**	323-870-1923
Venus Laboratories Inc 855 Lively Blvd	Wood Dale	IL	60191	**800-592-1900**	630-595-1902
Warsaw Chemical Co Inc 390 Argonne Rd	Warsaw	IN	46580	**800-548-3396**	574-267-3251
WD-40 Co 1061 Cudahy Pl *NASDAQ: WDFC*	San Diego	CA	92110	**800-448-9340**	619-275-1400
West Penetone Corp 700 Gotham Pkwy	Carlstadt	NJ	07072	**800-631-1652**	201-567-3000
Willert Home Products Inc 4044 Park Ave	Saint Louis	MO	63110	**800-325-9680**	314-772-2822
Zep Mfg Co 1310 Seaboard Industrial Blvd NW	Atlanta	GA	30318	**877-428-9937**	404-352-1680

150 CLEANING SERVICES

SEE ALSO Bio-Recovery Services; Building Maintenance Services

Company	City	State	Zip	Toll-Free	Phone
Amtech Lighting Services 2390 E Orangewood Ave Suite 100	Anaheim	CA	92806	**800-423-4481**	714-940-4000
BearCom Building Services 7022 South 400 W	Midvale	UT	84047	**888-569-9533**	801-569-9500
Bonus Building Care Inc PO Box 300	Indianola	OK	74442	**800-931-1102**	918-823-4990
Boston's Best Chimney Sweep 80 Rear Bacon St	Waltham	MA	02451	**800-660-6708**	781-893-6611
Braco Window Cleaning Service Inc 1 Braco International Blvd	Wilder	KY	41076	**877-878-7091**	859-442-6000
Chem-Dry Carpet Drapery & Upholstery Cleaning 1530 N 1000 W	Logan	UT	84321	**800-841-6583**	435-755-0099
Clean-Tech Co 2815 Olive St	Saint Louis	MO	63103	**800-852-2388**	314-652-2388
CleanNet USA Inc 9861 Brokenland Pkwy Suite 208	Columbia	MD	21046	**800-735-8838**	410-720-6444
Cleanol Services Inc 60 Norelco Dr	Toronto	ON	M9L2X6	**800-263-9430**	416-745-5221
Clola Enterprises LP 2324 Ridgepoint Dr Suite A	Austin	TX	78754	**800-833-2923**	512-615-3400
Coverall North America Inc 500 W Cypress Creek Rd Suite 580	Fort Lauderdale	FL	33309	**800-537-3371**	954-351-1110
Davis Paul Restoration Inc 1 Independence Dr Suite 2300	Jacksonville	FL	32202	**800-722-1818**	904-737-2779
Deluxe Carpet Cleaning Co Inc 5907 High Grove Rd	Grandview	MO	64030	**800-733-0078**	816-763-3331
Duraclean International Inc 220 Campus Dr *Cust Svc	Arlington Heights	IL	60004	**800-251-7070***	847-704-7100
GCA Services Group 100 Four Falls Corporate Ctr	West Conshohocken	PA	19428	**800-422-8760**	610-834-7555
Healthcare Services Group Inc 3220 Tillman Dr Suite 300 *NASDAQ: HCSG*	Bensalem	PA	19020	**800-523-2248**	215-639-4274
Heaven's Best Carpet & Upholstery Cleaning PO Box 607	Rexburg	ID	83440	**800-359-2095**	208-359-1106
Hospital Housekeeping Systems 322 Congress Ave 2nd Fl	Austin	TX	78701	**800-229-2028**	512-478-1888
HydroChem Industrial Services Inc 900 Georgia Ave	Deer Park	TX	77536	**800-934-9376**	713-393-5600
International Master Care Janitorial Franchising Inc 555 6th St Suite 327	New Westminster	BC	V3L5H1	**800-889-2799**	604-525-8221
Jan-Pro Franchising Systems International Inc 383 Strand Industrial Dr	Little River	SC	29566	**800-668-1001**	843-399-9895
Jani-King International Inc 16885 Dallas Pkwy	Addison	TX	75001	**800-552-5264**	972-991-0900
Jantize America Inc 15449 Middlebelt Rd	Livonia	MI	48154	**800-968-9182**	734-421-4733
Langenwalter Carpet Dyeing 1111 S Richfield Rd	Placentia	CA	92870	**800-422-4370**	714-528-7610
Magikist Monarch Drapery & Carpet Cleaners Inc 16619 S Kilbourn St	Oak Forest	IL	60452	**800-244-4336**	773-378-8600
Maid Brigade USA/Minimaid Canada 4 Concourse Pkwy Suite 200	Atlanta	GA	30328	**800-722-6243**	770-551-9630
Maids International The 4820 Dodge St	Omaha	NE	68132	**800-843-6243**	402-558-5555
Merry Maids 3839 Forrest Hill-Irene Rd	Memphis	TN	38125	**800-798-8000**	901-597-8100
Mini Maid Services 2727 Canton Rd Suite 550	Marietta	GA	30066	**800-627-6464**	770-422-3565
Molly Maid Inc 3948 Ranchero Dr	Ann Arbor	MI	48108	**800-665-5962**	734-822-6800
MPW Industrial Services Group Inc 9711 Lancaster Rd SE *NASDAQ: MPWG*	Hebron	OH	43025	**800-827-8790**	740-927-8790
OpenWorks 4742 N 24th St Suite 300	Phoenix	AZ	85016	**800-777-6736**	602-224-0440
Paul Davis Restoration Inc 1 Independence Dr Suite 2300	Jacksonville	FL	32202	**800-722-1818**	904-737-2779
Professional Carpet Systems Inc 4211 Atlantic Ave	Raleigh	NC	27604	**800-925-5055**	919-875-8871
Rainbow International 1010 N University Park Dr	Waco	TX	76707	**800-583-9100**	254-745-2444
Service One Cleaning Consultants & Management 5104 N Orange Blossom Trail Suite 220	Orlando	FL	32810	**800-522-7111**	
ServiceMaster Clean 3839 Forrest Hill Irene Rd	Memphis	TN	38125	**800-242-0442**	901-597-7500
Servpro Industries Inc 575 Airport Rd	Gallatin	TN	37066	**800-826-9586**	615-451-0600
Sparkle International Inc 26851 Richmond Rd	Cleveland	OH	44146	**800-321-0770**	216-464-4212
Stanley Steemer International Inc 5500 Stanley Steemer Pkwy	Dublin	OH	43016	**800-848-7496**	614-764-2007
Steam Brothers Inc 2124 E Sweet Ave	Bismarck	ND	58504	**800-767-5064**	701-222-1263
Steamatic Inc 303 Arthur St	Fort Worth	TX	76107	**800-544-1303**	817-332-1575
Swisher Hygiene Co 6849 Fairview Rd	Charlotte	NC	28210	**800-444-4138**	704-364-7707
Swisher International Inc 6849 Fairview Rd	Charlotte	NC	28210	**800-444-4138**	704-364-7707
Vanguard Cleaning Systems Inc 655 Mariners Island Blvd Suite 303	San Mateo	CA	94404	**800-564-6422**	650-594-1500

151 CLOCKS, WATCHES, RELATED DEVICES, PARTS

Company	City	State	Zip	Toll-Free	Phone
Baume & Mercier Inc 645 5th Ave	New York	NY	10022	**800-683-2286**	212-593-0444
Benrus Watch Co Inc 33-00 Northern Blvd	Long Island City	NY	11101	**800-221-0131**	
Berger MZ & Co Inc 33-00 Northern Blvd	Long Island City	NY	11101	**800-221-0131**	
Casio Inc 570 Mt Pleasant Ave *Cust Svc	Dover	NJ	07801	**800-634-1895***	973-361-5400
Citizen Watch Co of America Inc 1200 Wall St W	Lyndhurst	NJ	07071	**800-321-1023**	201-438-8150
Colibri/Park Lane Assoc Inc Linden Div 100 Niantic Ave *Sales	Providence	RI	02907	**800-556-7354***	401-943-2100
Elgin Watch Co 33-00 Northern Blvd	Long Island City	NY	11101	**800-221-0131**	
Emperor Clock LLC 328 S Greeno Rd *Orders	Fairhope	AL	36532	**800-642-0011***	251-928-2316
Fossil Inc 2280 N Greenville Ave *NASDAQ: FOSL*	Richardson	TX	75082	**800-969-0900**	972-234-2525
Hamilton Watch Co Inc 1200 Harbor Blvd *Cust Svc	Weehawken	NJ	07086	**800-456-5354***	201-271-1400
Jules Jurgensen Helbros International 101 W City Ave	Bala Cynwyd	PA	19004	**800-220-1233**	610-667-3500
MZ Berger & Co Inc 33-00 Northern Blvd	Long Island City	NY	11101	**800-221-0131**	
Pyramid Technologies Inc 48 Elm St	Meriden	CT	06450	**888-479-7264**	203-238-0550
RADO USA 1200 Harbor Blvd	Weehawken	NJ	07086	**877-839-5223**	201-271-1400
Ridgeway Clock Co 1131 Mica Rd PO Box 407 *Cust Svc	Ridgeway	VA	24148	**800-828-4441***	276-956-3111
Seiko Instruments USA Inc 2990 W Lomita Blvd	Torrance	CA	90505	**800-358-0880**	310-517-7050
Skagen Designs Inc 640 Maestro Dr Suite 100	Reno	NV	89511	**800-937-3576**	775-850-5500
Speidel Corp 25 Fairmount Ave	East Providence	RI	02914	**800-441-2200**	401-519-2000
Swatch Group 1200 Harbor Blvd 7th Fl	Weehawken	NJ	07087	**800-456-5354**	201-271-1400
Tag Heuer USA 966 S Springfield Ave	Springfield	NJ	07081	**800-321-4832**	973-467-1890
Timex Corp 555 Christian Rd	Middlebury	CT	06762	**800-367-8463**	203-346-5000
Verdin Co 444 Reading Rd	Cincinnati	OH	45202	**800-543-0488**	513-241-4010
Vulcan Inc 410 E Berry Ave	Foley	AL	36535	**800-633-6845**	251-943-1541
Wittnauer International Co 26-15 Brooklyn Queens Expy *Orders	Woodside	NY	11377	**800-431-1863***	718-204-3300
World of Watches 14001 NW 4th St	Sunrise	FL	33325	**800-222-0077**	954-453-2821

152 CLOSURES - METAL OR PLASTICS

Company	City	State	Zip	Toll-Free	Phone
Alliance Plastics Inc 3123 Station Rd	Erie	PA	16510	**877-728-9227**	814-899-7671
Carpin Mfg Inc 411 Austin Rd	Waterbury	CT	06705	**800-227-7461**	203-574-2556
Carplugs LLC 2150 Elmwood Ave	Buffalo	NY	14207	**888-227-5847**	716-876-9855
Crest Mfg Co 5 Hood Dr PO Box 368	Lincoln	RI	02865	**800-652-7378**	401-333-1350
Lerman Container Co 10 Great Hill Rd	Naugatuck	CT	06770	**800-453-7626**	203-723-6681
Magenta Corp 3800 N Milwaukee Ave	Chicago	IL	60641	**800-387-4378**	773-777-5050
Niagara Plastics Co 7090 Edinboro Rd *Sales	Erie	PA	16509	**800-458-0465***	814-868-3671
Penn-Wheeling Metal Closure & Caps 1701 Wheeling Ave	Glen Dale	WV	26038	**800-999-2567**	304-845-3402
Portola Packaging Inc 898 Faulstich Ct	San Jose	CA	95112	**800-767-8652**	408-573-2000
Portola Tech International Inc 85 Fairmount St	Woonsocket	RI	02895	**800-556-7630**	401-765-0600
Saint-Gobain Calmar Inc 333 S Turnbull Canyon Rd	City of Industry	CA	91745	**800-841-4112**	626-937-2600
StockCap 123 Manufacturers Dr	Arnold	MO	63010	**800-827-2277**	636-282-6800
Tipper Tie Inc 2000 Lufkin Rd	Apex	NC	27502	**800-331-2905**	919-362-8811
Top-Seal Corp 2236 E University Dr	Phoenix	AZ	85034	**800-452-8677**	602-629-9000

153 CLOTHING & ACCESSORIES - MFR

SEE ALSO Baby Products; Clothing & Accessories - Whol; Fashion Design Houses; Footwear; Leather Goods - Personal; Personal Protective Equipment & Clothing

153-1 Athletic Apparel

Company	City	State	Zip	Toll-Free	Phone
Ashworth Inc 2765 Loker Ave W *NASDAQ: ASHW*	Carlsbad	CA	92008	**800-800-8443**	760-438-6610
Betlin Inc 4411 Marketing Pl	Groveport	OH	43125	**800-923-8546**	614-443-0248
Bike Athletic Co 3303 Cumberland Blvd	Atlanta	GA	30339	**800-251-9230**	678-742-8255
Bristol Products Corp 700 Shelby St *Orders	Bristol	TN	37620	**800-336-8775***	423-968-4140
Capezio/Ballet Makers Inc 1 Campus Rd	Totowa	NJ	07512	**800-595-9002**	973-595-9000
Choi Brothers Inc 3401 W Division St	Chicago	IL	60651	**800-524-2464**	773-489-2800
CranBarry Inc 330 C Lynnway	Lynn	MA	01901	**800-992-2021**	781-586-0111
Cutter & Buck Inc 701 N 34th St Suite 400 *NASDAQ: CBUK*	Seattle	WA	98103	**800-929-9299**	206-622-4191
DeLong Sportswear Inc 821 5th Ave	Grinnell	IA	50112	**800-733-5664**	641-236-3106
Dodger Industries 1702 21st St	Eldora	IA	50627	**800-247-7879**	641-939-5464
Elite Sportswear LP 2136 N 13th St *Cust Svc	Reading	PA	19604	**800-345-4087***	610-921-1469
Fila USA Inc 1 Fila Way	Sparks	MD	21152	**800-787-3452**	410-773-3000
Gear for Sports Inc 9700 Commerce Pkwy	Lenexa	KS	66219	**800-423-5044**	913-693-3200
Hilton Apparel Group 1859 Bowles Ave	Fenton	MO	63026	**800-323-5590**	
Jantzen Inc 424 NE 18th Ave	Portland	OR	97232	**800-626-0215**	503-238-5000
King Louie International Inc 13500 15th St	Grandview	MO	64030	**800-521-5212**	816-765-5212
Marker International 1070 W 2300 S	Salt Lake City	UT	84119	**800-453-3862**	801-972-2100
MJ Soffe Co 1 Soffe Dr	Fayetteville	NC	28312	**800-723-4223**	910-483-2500
Moving Comfort Inc 4500 Southgate Pl Suite 800	Chantilly	VA	20151	**800-763-6000**	703-631-1000

Company	City	State	Zip	Toll-Free	Phone
No Fear 2251 Faraday Ave	Carlsbad	CA	92008	**800-266-3327**	760-931-9550
Onfield Apparel Group LLC					
8677 LogoAthletic Ct	Indianapolis	IN	46219	**800-955-6467**	317-895-7000
Pacific Trail Inc					
1700 Westlake Ave N Suite 200	Seattle	WA	98109	**800-877-8878**	206-270-5300
Race Face Components Inc					
100 Braid St Unit 100	New Westminster	BC	V3L3P4	**800-527-9244**	604-527-9996
Royal Textile Mills Inc 929 Firetower Rd	Yanceyville	NC	27379	**800-334-9361**	336-694-4121
Russell Corp 755 Lee St	Alexander City	AL	35010	**800-729-2905**	256-500-4000
NYSE: RML					
Russell Corp Russell Athletic Div					
755 Lee St	Alexander City	AL	35010	**800-729-2905**	256-500-4000
Salomon North America 5055 N Greeley Ave	Portland	OR	97217	**877-272-5666**	971-234-2300
Sara Lee Branded Apparel					
1000 E Hanes Mill Rd	Winston-Salem	NC	27105	**800-685-7557**	336-519-4400
Shaffer Sportswear Mfg Inc					
224 N Washington St	Neosho	MO	64850	**800-643-3300***	417-451-9444
*Orders					
Southland Athletic Mfg Co 714 E Grove	Terrell	TX	75160	**800-527-7637**	972-563-3321
Sports Belle Inc 6723 Pleasant Ridge Rd	Knoxville	TN	37921	**800-888-2063***	865-938-2063
*Sales					
Stone International LLC					
317 Neely Ferry Rd Suite 3	Mauldin	SC	29662	**800-762-2637***	864-288-4822
*Cust Svc					
Tighe Industries Inc 333 E 7th Ave	York	PA	17404	**800-839-1039**	717-252-1578

153-2 Belts (Leather, Plastics, Fabric)

Company	City	State	Zip	Toll-Free	Phone
Chambers Belt Co Inc					
3230 E Broadway Rd Suite A-200	Phoenix	AZ	85040	**800-528-1388**	602-276-0016
French Craft Leather Goods Co Inc					
234 W 24th St	Los Angeles	CA	90007	**800-541-0088**	213-746-6771
Gem Dandy Inc 200 W Academy St	Madison	NC	27025	**800-334-5101**	336-548-9624
Humphreys Inc 2009 W Hastings St	Chicago	IL	60608	**800-621-8541***	312-997-2358
*Cust Svc					
Leegin Creative Leather Co					
14022 Nelson Ave	City of Industry	CA	91746	**800-235-8748**	626-961-9381
M Aron Corp 350 5th Ave Suite 3005	New York	NY	10118	**800-899-2766**	212-643-8883
Tandy Brands Accessories Inc					
690 E Lamar Blvd Suite 200	Arlington	TX	76011	**800-570-7443**	817-548-0090
NASDAQ: TBAC					
TGL 300 Wilson Ave	Norwalk	CT	06854	**800-587-1584**	203-853-4747
Trafalgar Ghurka Ltd 300 Wilson Ave	Norwalk	CT	06854	**800-587-1584**	203-853-4747

153-3 Casual Wear (Men's & Women's)

Company	City	State	Zip	Toll-Free	Phone
Alps Sportswear Mfg Co 15 Union St	Lawrence	MA	01840	**800-262-7010**	978-683-2438
Attraction Inc 672 rue du Parc	Lac-Drolet	QC	G0Y1C0	**800-567-6095**	819-549-2477
Badger Sportswear Inc 850 Meacham Rd	Statesville	NC	28677	**800-868-0105**	704-876-4648
Big Dog Holdings Inc 121 Gray Ave	Santa Barbara	CA	93101	**800-244-3647***	805-963-8727
NASDAQ: BDOG ■ *Sales					
Big Dog Sportswear 121 Gray Ave	Santa Barbara	CA	93101	**800-642-3647***	805-963-8727
*Orders					
Bobby Jones Retail Corp					
1155 N Clinton Ave	Rochester	NY	14621	**888-603-8968***	800-295-2000
*Cust Svc					
Champion Products Inc					
1000 E Hanes Mill Rd	Winston-Salem	NC	27105	**800-999-2249**	336-519-6500
Crazy Shirts Inc 99-969 Iwaena St	Aiea	HI	96701	**800-771-2720**	808-487-9919
Cross Creek Apparel LLC					
3330 Cumberland Blvd Suite 1000	Atlanta	GA	30339	**800-321-1138**	678-742-8000
Deckers Outdoor Corp 495-A S Fairview Ave	Goleta	CA	93117	**800-858-5342**	805-967-7611
NASDAQ: DECK					
Delta Apparel Inc					
2750 Premier Pkwy Suite 100	Duluth	GA	30097	**800-285-4456**	678-775-6900
AMEX: DLA					
Dickie Walker Marine Inc					
1405 S Coast Hwy	Oceanside	CA	92054	**800-548-2234**	760-450-0360
NASDAQ: DWMA					
Duck Head Apparel Co Inc 4902 W Waters Ave	Tampa	FL	33634	**888-385-8825**	813-249-4900
Eddie Bauer Inc 15010 NE 36th St	Redmond	WA	98052	**800-426-8020***	425-755-6100
*Orders					
Fortune Dogs Inc DBA Big Dog Sportswear					
121 Gray Ave	Santa Barbara	CA	93101	**800-642-3647***	805-963-8727
*Orders					
Fortune Fashions Industries LLC					
4700 S Boyle Ave	Vernon	CA	90058	**800-788-6550**	323-277-7740
Garan Inc 350 5th Ave 19th Fl	New York	NY	10118	**800-326-0225**	212-563-2000
Gildan Activewear Inc 725 Montee de Liesse	Montreal	QC	H4T1P5	**800-668-8337**	514-735-2023
NYSE: GSE					
Hamrick Industries 742 Peachoid Rd	Gaffney	SC	29341	**800-487-5411**	864-489-6095
Hilfiger Tommy Sportswear Inc					
25 W 39th St	New York	NY	10018	**800-888-8802**	212-840-8888
IC Isaacs & Co Inc 3840 Bank St	Baltimore	MD	21224	**800-537-5995**	410-342-8200
JanSport Inc N 850 County Hwy CB	Appleton	WI	54914	**800-558-8404***	920-734-5708
*Cust Svc					
Kellwood New England 300 Manley St	Brockton	MA	02303	**800-225-6987***	508-588-7200
*Cust Svc					
North Face Inc 2013 Farallon Dr	San Leandro	CA	94577	**800-535-3331**	510-618-3500
Ocean Pacific Apparel Corp 3 Studebaker	Irvine	CA	92618	**800-562-3269**	949-580-1888
Pomare Ltd 700 N Nimitz Hwy	Honolulu	HI	96817	**800-272-5282**	808-524-3966
Quiksilver Inc 15202 Graham St	Huntington Beach	CA	92649	**800-576-4004**	714-889-2200
NYSE: ZQK					
Russell Corp Jerzees Div 755 Lee St	Alexander City	AL	35010	**800-729-2905**	256-500-4000
Seattle Pacific Industries 21216 72nd Ave S	Kent	WA	98032	**800-777-1145**	206-282-8889
Sherry Mfg Co Inc 3287 NW 65th St	Miami	FL	33147	**800-741-4750**	305-693-7000
Sport-Haley Inc 4600 E 48th Ave	Denver	CO	80216	**800-627-9211**	303-320-8800
NASDAQ: SPOR					
Tommy Hilfiger USA Inc 25 W 39th St	New York	NY	10018	**800-888-8802**	212-840-8888
VF Activewear 4408 W Linebaugh Ave	Tampa	FL	33624	**800-444-5574**	813-963-6153
VF Imageware 3375 Joseph Martin Hwy	Martinsville	VA	24112	**800-832-6469**	276-632-5601
Wright's Knitwear Corp 10 E 34th St	New York	NY	10016	**800-952-8788**	212-779-2600

153-4 Children's & Infants' Clothing

Company	City	State	Zip	Toll-Free	Phone
Alexis Playsafe 999 Chestnut St SE	Gainesville	GA	30503	**800-253-9476**	770-535-3000
Bentex Group Inc 100 W 33rd St Suite 1030	New York	NY	10001	**800-451-0285**	212-594-4250
Byer California 66 Potrero Ave	San Francisco	CA	94103	**800-998-2937**	415-626-7844
Garan Inc 350 5th Ave 19th Fl	New York	NY	10118	**800-326-0225**	212-563-2000
Gerber Childrenswear Inc					
7005 Pelham Rd Suite D	Greenville	SC	29602	**800-642-4452**	864-987-5200
IFG Corp 34 W 33rd St	New York	NY	10001	**800-930-9601**	212-629-9600
Isfel Co Inc 900 Hart St	Rahway	NJ	07065	**800-927-8760**	732-382-3100
Lollytogs Ltd 100 W 33rd St Suite 1012	New York	NY	10001	**800-262-5437**	212-594-4740
Mini Togs Inc 3030 Aurora Ave	Monroe	LA	71211	**800-588-6227**	318-388-4916
OshKosh B'Gosh Inc 112 Otter Ave	Oshkosh	WI	54901	**800-282-4674**	920-231-8800
NASDAQ: GOSHA					
S Schwab Co Inc					
12101 Upper Potomac Industrial Pk	Cumberland	MD	21502	**800-533-5437**	301-729-4488
Spencers Inc 238 Willow St	Mount Airy	NC	27030	**800-633-9111**	336-789-9111
Warren Featherbone Co DBA Alexis Playsafe					
999 Chestnut St SE	Gainesville	GA	30503	**800-253-9476**	770-535-3000

153-5 Coats (Overcoats, Jackets, Raincoats, etc)

Company	City	State	Zip	Toll-Free	Phone
Essex Mfg Inc 350 5th Ave Suite 501	New York	NY	10118	**800-648-6010**	212-239-0080
Forecaster of Boston 1 Ace St	Fall River	MA	02720	**800-760-7000**	508-676-6200
Helly Hansen US Inc					
3326 160th Ave SE Kenyon Ctr Suite 200	Bellevue	WA	98008	**800-435-5901**	425-378-8700
High Sierra Sport Co					
880 Corporate Woods Pkwy	Vernon Hills	IL	60061	**800-323-9590**	847-913-1100
Holloway Sportswear Inc 2633 Campbell Rd	Sidney	OH	45365	**800-331-5156**	937-596-6193
La Cross/Rainfair Inc					
18550 NE Riverside Pkwy	Portland	OR	97230	**800-558-5990**	503-766-1005
Levy Group Inc 512 7th Ave 3rd Fl	New York	NY	10018	**800-223-2073**	212-398-0707
London Fog Industries					
1700 Westlake Ave N Suite 200	Seattle	WA	98109	**800-877-8878**	206-270-5300
MECA Sportswear Inc					
4225 White Bear Suite 400	Vadnais Heights	MN	55110	**800-729-6322**	651-638-3800
Pacific Trail Inc					
1700 Westlake Ave N Suite 200	Seattle	WA	98109	**800-877-8878**	206-270-5300
Pendleton Woolen Mills Inc					
2516 SE Mailwell Dr	Portland	OR	97222	**800-760-4844**	503-226-4801
RefrigiWear Inc 54 Breakstone Dr	Dahlonega	GA	30533	**800-645-3744***	706-864-5757
*Cust Svc					
Rennoc Corp 3501 Southeast Blvd	Vineland	NJ	08360	**800-372-7100***	856-327-5400
*Cust Svc					
Sport-Haley Inc 4600 E 48th Ave	Denver	CO	80216	**800-627-9211**	303-320-8800
NASDAQ: SPOR					
Sport Obermeyer Ltd USA Inc 115 AABC	Aspen	CO	81611	**800-525-4203**	970-925-5060
Standard Mfg Co Inc 750 2nd Ave	Troy	NY	12182	**800-227-1056***	518-235-2200
*Cust Svc					
Whaling Mfg Co 451 Quarry St	Fall River	MA	02723	**800-225-8554**	508-678-9061
Woolrich Inc 2 Mill St	Woolrich	PA	17779	**800-995-1299**	570-769-6464

153-6 Costumes

Company	City	State	Zip	Toll-Free	Phone
Art Stone Enterprises 1795 Express Dr N	Smithtown	NY	11787	**800-522-8897**	631-582-9500
Bevan Mfg Co 4451 Rt 130	Burlington	NJ	08016	**800-222-8125**	609-386-6501
Costume Specialists Inc 211 N 5th St	Columbus	OH	43215	**800-596-9357**	614-464-2115
Curtain Call Costumes 333 E 7th Ave	York	PA	17404	**888-808-0801**	717-852-6910
Disguise 11906 Tech Ctr Ct	Poway	CA	92064	**800-786-4864**	858-391-3600

153-7 Fur Goods

Company	City	State	Zip	Toll-Free	Phone
Bloch Berman Brothers Inc					
345 7th Ave 19th Fl	New York	NY	10001	**800-382-3877***	212-255-0940
*Cust Svc					

153-8 Gloves & Mittens

Company	City	State	Zip	Toll-Free	Phone
Ansell Occupational Healthcare					
1300 Walnut St	Coshocton	OH	43812	**800-800-0444***	740-622-4311
*Cust Svc					
Berlin Glove Co Inc 150 W Franklin St	Berlin	WI	54923	**800-236-3367**	920-361-5050
Boss Mfg Co 221 W 1st St	Kewanee	IL	61443	**800-447-4581***	309-852-2131
*Cust Svc					
Brookville Glove Mfg Co Inc					
5-15 Western Ave	Brookville	PA	15825	**800-322-7324**	814-849-7324
Carolina Glove Co Inc PO Drawer 820	Newton	NC	28658	**800-438-6888**	828-464-1132
Fairfield Line Inc 605 W Stone PO Box 500	Fairfield	IA	52556	**800-247-3383**	641-472-3191
Fownes Brothers & Co Inc 16 E 34th St	New York	NY	10016	**800-345-6837**	212-683-0150
Gloves Inc 50 Suffolk Rd	Mansfield	MA	02048	**800-225-6076**	508-339-2590
Grandoe Corp PO Box 713	Gloversville	NY	12078	**800-472-6363**	518-725-8641
Guard-Line Inc 215 S Louise St PO Box 1030	Atlanta	TX	75551	**800-527-8822**	903-796-4111
Illinois Glove Co 3701 Commercial Ave	Northbrook	IL	60062	**800-342-5458**	847-291-1700
Kinco International 4286 NE 185th Ave	Portland	OR	97230	**800-547-8410**	503-674-9002
Magid Glove & Safety Mfg Co					
2060 N Kolmar Ave	Chicago	IL	60639	**800-444-8010**	773-384-2070
Manzella Productions 80 Sonwil Dr	Buffalo	NY	14225	**800-645-6837**	716-681-8880
MCR Safety 5321 E Shelby Dr	Memphis	TN	38118	**800-955-6887**	901-795-5810
Midwest Quality Gloves Inc					
835 Industrial Rd	Chillicothe	MO	64601	**800-821-3028**	660-646-2165
Montpelier Glove & Safety Co Inc					
129 N Main St PO Box 7	Montpelier	IN	47359	**800-645-3931**	765-728-2481
North Star Glove Co 2916 S Steele St	Tacoma	WA	98409	**800-423-1616**	253-627-7107
Perfect Fit Glove Co Inc 85 Innsbruck Dr	Buffalo	NY	14227	**800-245-6837**	716-668-2000
Saranac Glove Co 999 LOmbardi Ave	Green Bay	WI	54304	**800-727-2622**	920-435-3737
Seal Glove Mfg Inc 525 North St	Millersburg	PA	17061	**800-992-5444**	717-692-4747
Southern Glove Mfg Co Inc 749 AC Little Dr	Newton	NC	28658	**800-222-1113***	828-464-4884
*Cust Svc					
Swany America Corp 109 Balzano Dr	Johnstown	NY	12095	**800-237-9269**	518-725-2000
Totes Isotoner Corp 9655 International Blvd	Cincinnati	OH	45246	**800-762-8712**	513-682-8200
Wells Lamont Corp 6640 W Touhy Ave	Niles	IL	60714	**800-323-2830**	847-647-8200
Wells Lamont Industry Group 6640 W Touhy Ave	Niles	IL	60714	**800-247-3295**	

153-9 Hats & Caps

Company	City	State	Zip	Toll-Free	Phone
180s Inc 720 S Montford Ave	Baltimore	MD	21224	**877-725-4386**	410-534-6320
Ahead 270 Samuel Barnet Blvd	New Bedford	MA	02745	**800-282-2246**	508-999-4466
American Needle Inc 1275 Bush Pkwy	Buffalo Grove	IL	60089	**800-356-7589**	847-215-0011
Ashworth Inc 2765 Loker Ave W	Carlsbad	CA	92008	**800-800-8443**	760-438-6610
NASDAQ: ASHW					
Bancroft Cap Co Inc 1122 S 2nd St	Cabot	AR	72023	**800-345-8784**	501-843-6561
Bayly Inc 4151 N 29th Ave	Hollywood	FL	33020	**800-882-0255**	954-923-0255
Bollman Hat Co 110 E Main St	Adamstown	PA	19501	**800-451-4287**	717-484-4361
Drew Pearson Marketing Inc 15006 Beltway Dr	Addison	TX	75001	**800-879-0880**	972-702-8055
F & M Hat Co Inc 103 Walnut St PO Box 40	Denver	PA	17517	**800-953-4287**	717-336-5505
Hatco Inc 601 Marion Dr	Garland	TX	75042	**800-288-6579**	972-494-0511
Imperial Headwear Inc 5200 E Evans Ave	Denver	CO	80222	**800-933-9444***	303-757-1166
*Cust Svc					
Julie Hat Co Inc 5948 Industrial Blvd PO Box 518	Patterson	GA	31557	**800-841-2592**	912-647-2031
Korber Hats Inc 394 Kilburn St	Fall River	MA	02724	**800-428-9911***	508-672-7033
*Cust Svc					
MPC Promotions Inc 2026 Shepherdsville Rd	Louisville	KY	40218	**800-331-0989**	502-451-4900
New Era Cap Co Inc 8061 Erie Rd	Derby	NY	14047	**800-989-0445**	716-549-0445
Onfield Apparel Group LLC 8677 LogoAthletic Ct	Indianapolis	IN	46219	**800-955-6467**	317-895-7000
Paramount Apparel International Inc 1 Paramount Dr PO Box 98	Bourbon	MO	65441	**800-255-4287**	573-732-4411
Pearson Drew Marketing Inc 15006 Beltway Dr	Addison	TX	75001	**800-879-0880**	972-702-8055
Pro-Line Cap Co 1332 N Main St	Fort Worth	TX	76106	**800-227-2456**	817-246-1978
Texace Corp 402 W Nueva St PO Box 7429	San Antonio	TX	78207	**800-835-8973**	210-227-7551
Town Talk Inc 6310 Cane Run Rd PO Box 58157	Louisville	KY	40268	**800-626-2220**	502-933-7575

153-10 Hosiery & Socks

Company	City	State	Zip	Toll-Free	Phone
Americal Corp 389 Americal Rd PO Box 1419	Henderson	NC	27536	**800-633-9707**	252-762-2000
Bossong Hosiery Mills Inc 840 W Salisbury St	Asheboro	NC	27203	**800-833-8895**	336-625-2175
Crescent Inc 527 Willson St PO Box 669	Niota	TN	37826	**877-807-7625**	423-568-2101
DeSoto Mills Inc 3850 Sand Valley Rd PO Box 680228	Fort Payne	AL	35968	**800-551-7625**	256-845-6700
Emby Hosiery Corp 3905 2nd Ave	Brooklyn	NY	11232	**800-287-6916**	718-499-6300
Fox River Mills Inc 227 Poplar Stq PO Box 298	Osage	IA	50461	**800-247-1815**	641-732-3798
Gold Toe Brands Inc 661 Plaid St	Burlington	NC	27215	**800-523-8265***	336-229-3700
*Cust Svc					
Hampshire Group Ltd PO Box 2667	Anderson	SC	29622	**800-275-3520**	864-225-6232
NASDAQ: HAMP					
HCI Direct Inc 3050 Tillman Dr	Bensalem	PA	19020	**800-989-3695**	215-244-9600
Jefferies Socks LLC 1176 N Church St	Burlington	NC	27217	**800-334-6831***	336-226-7315
*Cust Svc					
Jockey International Inc 2300 60th St PO Box 1417	Kenosha	WI	53140	**800-562-5391**	262-658-8111
Johnson Hosiery Mills Inc 2808 Main Ave NW	Hickory	NC	28601	**800-438-1511**	828-322-6185
Keepers International Inc 20720 Marilla St	Chatsworth	CA	91311	**800-797-6257**	818-882-5000
Lavitt Paul Mills Inc 1517 'F' Ave SE	Hickory	NC	28602	**800-825-7285**	828-328-2463
Mayer Berkshire Corp 25 Edison Dr	Wayne	NJ	07470	**800-245-6789**	973-696-6200
Moretz Inc 514 W 21st St	Newton	NC	28658	**800-438-9127**	828-464-0751
Mountain High Hosiery Ltd 675 Gateway Center Dr	San Diego	CA	92102	**800-528-5355**	619-262-9202
Neuville Industries Inc 9451 Neuville Ave PO Box 286	Hildebran	NC	28637	**800-334-2587**	828-397-5566
Paul Lavitt Mills Inc 1517 'F' Ave SE	Hickory	NC	28602	**800-825-7285**	828-328-2463
Premiere Direct/Legwear Express 227 Avery Ave	Morganton	NC	28655	**800-280-1222***	828-439-8724
*Orders					
Renfro Corp 661 Linville Rd	Mount Airy	NC	27030	**800-334-9091**	336-719-8000
Sara Lee Branded Apparel 1000 E Hanes Mill Rd	Winston-Salem	NC	27105	**800-685-7557**	336-519-4400
Shogren Hosiery Mfg Co 225 Wilshire Ave SW	Concord	NC	28025	**888-206-0002**	704-786-5617
Tefron USA Inc 201 St Germain Ave SW	Valdese	NC	28690	**800-554-5541**	828-879-6500
Thor-Lo Inc 2210 Newton Dr	Statesville	NC	28677	**888-846-7567**	704-872-6522
Trimfit Inc 1900 Frost Rd Suite 111	Bristol	PA	19007	**800-347-7697**	215-781-0600
Twin City Knitting Co Inc 104 Rock Barn Rd NE PO Box 1179	Conover	NC	28613	**800-438-6884***	828-464-4830
*Cust Svc					
Wigwam Mills Inc 3402 Crocker Ave	Sheboygan	WI	53082	**800-558-7760**	920-457-5551

153-11 Jeans

Company	City	State	Zip	Toll-Free	Phone
Aalfs Mfg Co 1005 4th St	Sioux City	IA	51101	**888-412-2537**	712-252-1877
Guess? Inc 1444 S Alameda St	Los Angeles	CA	90021	**800-394-8377**	213-765-3100
NYSE: GES					
Innovo Group Inc 2633 Kingston Pike Suite 100	Knoxville	TN	37919	**800-627-2621**	865-546-1110
NASDAQ: INNO					
Jordache Ltd 1400 Broadway 15th Fl	New York	NY	10018	**888-295-3267**	212-643-8400
Kayo of California Inc 161 W 39th St	Los Angeles	CA	90037	**800-233-6140**	323-233-6107
Lee Jeans 1 Lee Dr	Merriam	KS	66202	**800-453-3348**	913-384-4000
Levi Strauss & Co 1155 Battery St	San Francisco	CA	94111	**800-872-5384**	415-501-6000
Reed Mfg Co Inc 1321 S Veterans Blvd	Tupelo	MS	38801	**800-647-1280**	662-842-4472
Strauss Levi & Co 1155 Battery St	San Francisco	CA	94111	**800-872-5384**	415-501-6000
VF Jeanswear LP 335 Church Ct PO Box 21488	Greensboro	NC	27420	**800-888-8010***	336-332-3400
*Orders					

153-12 Men's Clothing

Company	City	State	Zip	Toll-Free	Phone
After Six Inc 240 Collins Industrial Dr	Athens	GA	30601	**800-554-8212***	706-543-5286
*Cust Svc					
Antigua Sportswear Inc 16651 N 84 Ave	Peoria	AZ	85382	**800-528-3133**	623-523-6000
Asher Winer Co 208 Lurgan Ave	Shippensburg	PA	17257	**800-556-8001**	717-532-4146
Barrow Mfg Co Inc 83 Horton St	Winder	GA	30680	**800-476-0047**	770-867-2121
Berle Mfg Co 1411 Folly Rd	Charleston	SC	29412	**800-845-4503**	843-762-7150
Boss Hugo Fashions Inc 601 W 26th St Suite 845	New York	NY	10001	**800-484-6207**	212-940-0600
Bowdon Mfg Co 127 N Carrol St	Bowdon	GA	30108	**800-937-7242**	770-258-7201
Carabella Corp 17662 Armstrong Ave	Irvine	CA	92614	**800-227-2235***	949-263-2300
*Cust Svc					
Chesterfield Mfg Corp 2359 Perimeter Pointe Pkwy	Charlotte	NC	28208	**800-322-1746**	704-283-0001
Christian Dior 712 5th Ave 37th Fl	New York	NY	10019	**800-929-3467**	212-582-0500
Corbin Ltd 208 Lurgan Ave	Shippensburg	PA	17257	**800-950-3330**	717-532-4146
Crown Clothing Corp 340 Vanderbilt Ave	Norwood	MA	02062	**800-225-8950**	781-769-0001
David Peyser Sportswear Inc 8890 Spence St	Bay Shore	NY	11706	**800-367-7900**	631-231-7788
Dior Christian 712 5th Ave 37th Fl	New York	NY	10019	**800-929-3467**	212-582-0500
Fishman & Tobin Inc 625 Ridge Pike Bldg E Suite 320	Conshohocken	PA	19428	**800-367-2772**	610-828-8400
Freeman H & Son Inc 411 N Cranberry Rd	Westminster	MD	21157	**800-468-0689**	410-857-5774
Gitman Brothers Shirt Co Inc 1350 Ave of the Americas Suite 1115	New York	NY	10019	**800-526-3929***	212-581-6968
*Cust Svc					
Gitman & Co 2309 Chestnut St	Ashland	PA	17921	**800-526-3929**	570-875-3100
Gordon Kenneth IAG 1209 Distributors Row	New Orleans	LA	70123	**800-234-1433***	504-734-1433
*Cust Svc					
Granite Knitwear Inc 805 S Salberry Ave Hwy 52S	Granite Quarry	NC	28072	**800-476-9944**	704-279-5526
H Freeman & Son Inc 411 N Cranberry Rd	Westminster	MD	21157	**800-468-0689**	410-857-5774
Haggar Clothing Co 11511 Luna Rd Two Colinas Crossing	Dallas	TX	75234	**800-942-4427**	214-352-8481
NASDAQ: HGGR					
Hardwick Clothes Inc 3800 Old Tasso Rd NE	Cleveland	TN	37312	**800-251-6392**	423-476-6534
Hartmarx Inc 101 N Wacker Dr	Chicago	IL	60606	**800-327-4466**	312-372-6300
Hartz & Co 1341 Hughes Ford Rd	Frederick	MD	21701	**800-638-8170**	301-662-7500
Hickey-Freeman Co Inc 1155 N Clinton Ave	Rochester	NY	14621	**800-295-2000***	585-467-7240
*Cust Svc					
HMXTailored Co 2020 Elmwood Ave	Buffalo	NY	14207	**800-874-5000**	716-874-5000
Hubbard Co Inc 208 Lurgan Ave	Shippensburg	PA	17257	**800-241-1226**	717-532-4146
Hugo Boss Fashions Inc 601 W 26th St Suite 845	New York	NY	10001	**800-484-6207**	212-940-0600
Individualized Shirts Co 581 Cortland St	Perth Amboy	NJ	08861	**888-474-4787**	732-826-8400
James Tom Co 424 S Lynn Riggs Blvd	Claremore	OK	74017	**800-237-2140**	918-341-3773
Jos A Bank Clothiers 500 Hanover Pike	Hampstead	MD	21074	**800-999-7472***	410-239-2700
NASDAQ: JOSB ■ *Cust Svc					
Kenneth Gordon IAG Inc 1209 Distributors Row	New Orleans	LA	70123	**800-234-1433***	504-734-1433
*Cust Svc					
Merrill-Sharpe Ltd 250 Clearbrook Rd	Elmsford	NY	10523	**800-832-0159**	914-347-8686
Northern Isles 300 Manley St	Brockton	MA	02303	**800-666-5105**	508-513-3013
Nu-Look Fashions Inc 5080 Sinclair Rd Suite 200	Columbus	OH	43229	**800-800-4500**	614-885-4936
Oxxford Clothes Inc 1220 W Van Buren St	Chicago	IL	60607	**888-469-9367**	312-829-3600
Palm Beach Co 2020 Elmwood Ave	Buffalo	NY	14207	**800-543-1919**	716-874-5000
Perry Ellis International Inc 3000 NW 107th Ave	Miami	FL	33172	**800-327-7587**	305-592-2830
NASDAQ: PERY					
Peyser David Sportswear Inc 8890 Spence St	Bay Shore	NY	11706	**800-367-7900**	631-231-7788
Phillips-Van Heusen Corp 200 Madison Ave	New York	NY	10016	**800-777-1726**	212-381-3500
NYSE: PVH					
PremiumWear Inc 5500 Feltl Rd	Minnetonka	MN	55343	**800-347-6098***	952-979-1700
*Cust Svc					
Savane International Div 4902 W Waters Ave	Tampa	FL	33634	**800-327-2464**	813-249-4900
Seitchik Industries Inc 1843 W Allegheny Ave	Philadelphia	PA	19132	**800-523-0814**	215-226-0200
Sewell Clothing Co Inc 115 Pacific Ave	Bremen	GA	30110	**800-241-1221**	770-537-3862
Sewell Warren Clothing Co 126 Hamilton Ave	Bremen	GA	30110	**800-876-9722**	770-537-2391
State-O-Maine 1372 Broadway Suite 1800	New York	NY	10018	**866-456-6843**	212-302-1070
Tom James Co 424 S Lynn Riggs Blvd	Claremore	OK	74017	**800-237-2140**	918-341-3773
Warren Sewell Clothing Co 126 Hamilton Ave	Bremen	GA	30110	**800-876-9722**	770-537-2391
Weatherproof Garment Co 1071 Ave of the Americas 8th Fl	New York	NY	10018	**800-645-7788**	212-695-7716
Zeeman Mfg Co Inc 2303 John Glenn Dr	Chamblee	GA	30341	**800-732-2779**	770-451-5476

153-13 Neckwear

Company	City	State	Zip	Toll-Free	Phone
Bost Neckwear Co Inc 503 Industrial Pk PO Box 1065	Asheboro	NC	27204	**800-334-8441**	336-625-6650
Burma Bibas Inc 597 5th Ave 10th Fl	New York	NY	10017	**800-362-0037**	212-750-2500
Carter & Holmes 3645 W Irving Park Rd	Chicago	IL	60618	**800-621-4646**	773-588-2626
Echo Design Group 10 E 40th St 16th Fl	New York	NY	10016	**800-331-3246**	212-686-8771
Fendrich Industries Inc 7025 Augusta Rd	Greenville	SC	29605	**800-845-2744**	864-299-0600
Mallory & Church LLC 676 S Industrial Way	Seattle	WA	98108	**800-255-8437**	206-587-2100
Marlin Ralph & Co 1814 Dolphin Dr Suite A	Waukesha	WI	53186	**800-922-8437**	262-549-5100
MMG Corp 1717 Olive St	Saint Louis	MO	63103	**800-264-8437**	314-421-2182
New York Accessories Group Inc 411 5th Ave 4th Fl	New York	NY	10016	**800-366-7254**	212-532-7911
Paris Accessories Inc 350 5th Ave 70th Fl	New York	NY	10118	**800-223-7557**	212-868-0500
Ralph Marlin & Co 1814 Dolphin Dr Suite A	Waukesha	WI	53186	**800-922-8437**	262-549-5100
Randa Corp 120 W 45th St 38th Fl	New York	NY	10036	**800-632-5843**	212-768-8800
Tie King Inc 243 44th St	Brooklyn	NY	11232	**800-852-9261**	718-768-8484
White Mountain Traders 100 Factory St	Nashua	NH	03060	**800-648-6505**	603-889-5115
Wolfmark 1026 W Van Buren St	Chicago	IL	60607	**800-621-3435***	312-563-5510
*Cust Svc					

153-14 Robes (Ceremonial)

Company	City	State	Zip	Toll-Free	Phone
Academic Choir Apparel 20644 Superior St	Chatsworth	CA	91311	**800-626-5000**	818-886-8697
CM Almy Inc 1 Ruth Rd	Pittsfield	ME	04967	**800-225-2569**	207-487-3232
Herff Jones Inc Cap & Gown Div 1000 N Market St	Champaign	IL	61820	**800-637-1124**	217-351-9500
Jostens Inc 5501 American Blvd W	Minneapolis	MN	55437	**800-235-4774**	952-830-3300
Oak Hall Industries 840 Union St	Salem	VA	24153	**800-456-7623**	540-387-0000
Robert Gaspard Co Inc 200 N Janacek Rd	Brookfield	WI	53045	**800-784-6868**	262-784-6800
Thomas Creative Apparel 1 Harmony Pl	New London	OH	44851	**800-537-2575**	419-929-1506
Willsie Cap & Gown Co 1220 S 13th St	Omaha	NE	68108	**800-234-4696**	402-341-6536

153-15 Sleepwear

Company / Address	City	State	Zip	Toll-Free	Phone
Eileen West 525 Brannan St Suite 410	San Francisco	CA	94107	**800-421-0731**	415-957-9378
Faris Brothers of California Inc 12801 Arroyo St	Sylmar	CA	91342	**800-433-2747**	818-898-2377
LSC LLC DBA Eileen West 525 Brannan St Suite 410	San Francisco	CA	94107	**800-421-0731**	415-957-9378
Milco Industries Inc 550 E 5th St	Bloomsburg	PA	17815	**800-867-0288**	570-784-0400
Miss Elaine Inc 8430 Valcour Ave	Saint Louis	MO	63123	**800-458-1422**	314-631-1900
O'Bryan Brothers Inc 4220 W Belmont Ave	Chicago	IL	60641	**800-627-9262**	773-283-3000
Universal Mfg Corp 318 Gidney St	Shelby	NC	28150	**800-553-8648**	704-487-4359
VF Intimates 3025 Windward Plaza Suite 600	Alpharetta	GA	30005	**800-366-8339**	770-753-0900

153-16 Sweaters (Knit)

Company / Address	City	State	Zip	Toll-Free	Phone
Hampshire Group Ltd PO Box 2667 *NASDAQ: HAMP*	Anderson	SC	29622	**800-275-3520**	864-225-6232
Pine State Knitwear Co Inc 630 Independence Blvd	Mount Airy	NC	27030	**800-542-1533**	336-789-9121
Schuessler Knitting Mills 1523 N Fremont St	Chicago	IL	60622	**800-227-5648**	312-642-1490

153-17 Swimwear

Company / Address	City	State	Zip	Toll-Free	Phone
AH Schreiber Co 460 W 34th St 10th Fl	New York	NY	10001	**800-724-1612**	212-564-2700
Apparel Ventures Inc 13809 S Figueroa St	Los Angeles	CA	90061	**800-289-7946**	310-538-4980
Baltex Swimsuits 1350 Mazurette St	Montreal	QC	H4N1H2	**888-225-8391**	514-383-1850
Beach Patrol Inc 1165 E 230th St	Carson	CA	90745	**800-446-1101**	310-522-2700
Blue Sky Swimwear 729 E International Speedway Blvd *Orders	Daytona Beach	FL	32118	**800-799-6445***	386-255-9009
Carabella Corp 17662 Armstrong Ave *Cust Svc	Irvine	CA	92614	**800-227-2235***	949-263-2300
Christina America Inc 9880 Rue Clark *Cust Svc	Montreal	QC	H3L2R3	**800-463-7946***	514-381-2365
Jantzen Inc 424 NE 18th Ave	Portland	OR	97232	**800-626-0215**	503-238-5000
Manhattan Beachwear Inc 6560 Bandini Blvd	Los Angeles	CA	90040	**800-279-2987**	323-887-7448
Ocean Pacific Apparel Corp 3 Studebaker	Irvine	CA	92618	**800-562-3269**	949-580-1888
Quiksilver Inc 15202 Graham St *NYSE: ZQK*	Huntington Beach	CA	92649	**800-576-4004**	714-889-2200
Schreiber AH Co 460 W 34th St 10th Fl	New York	NY	10001	**800-724-1612**	212-564-2700
TYR Sport 15391 Springdale St	Huntington Beach	CA	92649	**800-252-7878**	714-897-0799
Venus Swimwear 11711 Marco Beach Dr 1 Venus Plaza	Jacksonville	FL	32224	**800-366-7946**	904-645-6000
Warnaco Swimwear Group Inc 6040 Bandini Blvd *Cust Svc	Los Angeles	CA	90040	**800-547-8770***	323-726-1262

153-18 Undergarments

Company / Address	City	State	Zip	Toll-Free	Phone
Bali Co 5660 University Pkwy *Cust Svc	Winston-Salem	NC	27105	**800-225-4872***	336-519-6053
Delta Galil USA 150 Meadowlawn Pkwy	Secaucus	NJ	07094	**800-645-4461**	201-902-0055
Eveden Ltd 65 Sprague St	Hyde Park	MA	02136	**800-733-8964**	617-361-7559
Gelmart Industries Inc 136 Madison Ave 4th Fl	New York	NY	10016	**800-746-0014**	212-743-6900
Indera Mills Co 350 W Maple St PO Box 309	Yadkinville	NC	27055	**800-334-8605**	336-679-4440
JE Morgan Knitting Mills Inc 143 Mahanoy Ave PO Box 390	Tamaqua	PA	18252	**800-448-8240**	570-668-3330
Jockey International Inc 2300 60th St PO Box 1417	Kenosha	WI	53140	**800-562-5391**	262-658-8111
Lady Ester Lingerie Corp 33 E 33rd St	New York	NY	10016	**800-937-2413**	212-684-4446
Leading Lady Cos 24050 Commerce Pk *Cust Svc	Beachwood	OH	44122	**800-321-4804***	216-464-5490
Reliable of Milwaukee Inc 233 E Chicago St PO Box 563	Milwaukee	WI	53201	**800-336-6876**	414-272-5084
Robinson Mfg Co Inc 798 Market St PO Box 338	Dayton	TN	37321	**800-251-7286**	423-775-2212
Sara Lee Branded Apparel 1000 E Hanes Mill Rd	Winston-Salem	NC	27105	**800-685-7557**	336-519-4400
Spencers Inc 238 Willow St	Mount Airy	NC	27030	**800-633-9111**	336-789-9111
Spirite Industries Inc 150 S Dean St	Englewood	NJ	07631	**800-272-6897**	201-871-4910
Tefron USA Inc 201 St Germain Ave SW	Valdese	NC	28690	**800-554-5541**	828-879-6500
Under Armour Performance Apparel 1020 Hull St	Baltimore	MD	21230	**888-427-6687**	410-468-2512
VF Intimates 3025 Windward Plaza Suite 600	Alpharetta	GA	30005	**800-366-8339**	770-753-0900
Wacoal America 1 Wacoal Plaza	Lyndhurst	NJ	07071	**800-526-6286**	201-933-8400

153-19 Uniforms & Work Clothes

Company / Address	City	State	Zip	Toll-Free	Phone
Action Sports Systems Inc 617 Carbon City Rd	Morganton	NC	28655	**800-631-1091**	828-584-8000
Algy Costume & Uniform Co 440 NE 1st Ave	Hallandale	FL	33009	**800-458-2549**	954-457-8100
All-Bilt Uniform Fashion 30-00 47th Ave	Long Island City	NY	11101	**800-221-2980**	718-706-1414
Barco of California 350 W Rosecrans Ave	Gardena	CA	90248	**800-421-1874**	310-323-7315
Berne Apparel Co 2100 Summit St	New Haven	IN	46774	**800-843-7657**	260-469-3136
Best Mfg Inc 10 Exchange Pl 22nd Fl	Jersey City	NJ	07302	**800-843-3233**	201-356-3800
Blauer Mfg Co Inc 20 Aberdeen St	Boston	MA	02215	**800-225-6715**	617-536-6606
Carhartt Inc 5750 Mercury Dr	Dearborn	MI	48126	**800-358-3825**	313-271-8460
Choi Brothers Inc 3401 W Division St	Chicago	IL	60651	**800-524-2464**	773-489-2800
Cintas Corp 6800 Cintas Blvd *NASDAQ: CTAS*	Mason	OH	45262	**800-786-4367**	513-459-1200
DeMoulin Brothers & Co Inc 1025 S 4th St	Greenville	IL	62246	**800-228-8134**	618-664-2000
Dennis Uniform Mfg Co Inc 135 SE Hawthorne Blvd *Orders	Portland	OR	97214	**800-544-7123***	503-238-7123
Earl's Apparel Inc 908 S 4th St PO Box 939	Crockett	TX	75835	**800-527-3148**	936-544-5521
Elbeco Inc 4203 Pottsville Pike	Reading	PA	19605	**800-468-4654**	610-921-0651
Elder Mfg Co Inc 999 Executive Pkwy Suite 300	Saint Louis	MO	63141	**800-829-8880**	314-469-1120
Encompass Group LLC 615 Macon Rd	McDonough	GA	30253	**800-284-4540**	770-957-3981
Fechheimer Brothers Co Inc 4545 Malsbary Rd	Cincinnati	OH	45242	**800-543-1939**	513-793-5400
Flight Suits Ltd 1675 Pioneer Way	El Cajon	CA	92020	**800-748-6693**	619-440-6976
French Toast 100 W 33rd St Suite 1012	New York	NY	10001	**800-262-5437**	212-594-4740
Garment Corp of America 801 W 41st St 3rd Fl *Cust Svc	Miami Beach	FL	33140	**800-944-4500***	305-531-4040
Howard Uniform Co Inc 313 W Baltimore St	Baltimore	MD	21201	**800-628-8299**	410-727-3086
I Spiewak & Sons Inc 469 7th Ave 10th Fl *Cust Svc	New York	NY	10018	**800-223-6850***	212-695-1620
Key Industries Inc 400 Marble Rd	Fort Scott	KS	66701	**800-835-0365**	620-223-2000
King LC Mfg Co Inc 24 7th St PO Box 367	Bristol	TN	37620	**800-826-2510**	423-764-5188
Landau Uniforms Inc 8410 W Sandidge Rd	Olive Branch	MS	38654	**800-238-7513**	662-895-7200
LC King Mfg Co Inc 24 7th St PO Box 367	Bristol	TN	37620	**800-826-2510**	423-764-5188
Leventhal Ltd 1295 Northern Blvd	Manhasset	NY	11030	**800-847-4095**	516-365-9540
Lion Apparel Inc 6450 Poe Ave	Dayton	OH	45414	**800-548-6614**	937-898-1949
National Spirit Group Ltd 2010 Merritt Dr	Garland	TX	75041	**800-527-4366**	972-840-1233
OshKosh B'Gosh Inc 112 Otter Ave *NASDAQ: GOSHA*	Oshkosh	WI	54901	**800-282-4674**	920-231-8800
Polkton Mfg Co Inc 6713 E Marshville Blvd PO Box 220	Marshville	NC	28103	**800-445-0044**	704-624-3200
Protexall Inc 77 S Henderson St PO Box 1287	Galesburg	IL	61402	**800-334-8939**	309-342-3106
Red Kap Industries Inc 545 Marriott Dr Suite 200	Nashville	TN	37214	**800-733-5271**	615-565-5000
Riverside Mfg Co 301 Riverside Dr	Moultrie	GA	31768	**800-841-8677**	229-985-5210
Rubin Brothers Inc 2241 S Halsted St	Chicago	IL	60608	**800-632-2308**	312-942-1111
School Apparel Inc 1099 Sneath Ln	San Bruno	CA	94066	**800-227-3215**	650-827-7400
SCORE American Soccer Co Inc 726 E Anaheim St	Wilmington	CA	90744	**800-626-7774**	310-830-6161
Spiewak I & Sons Inc 469 7th Ave 10th Fl *Cust Svc	New York	NY	10018	**800-223-6850***	212-695-1620
Stanbury Uniforms Inc 108 Stanbury Industrial Dr PO Box 100	Brookfield	MO	64628	**800-826-2246**	660-258-2246
Standard Textile Co Inc 1 Knollcrest	Cincinnati	OH	45237	**800-888-5000**	513-761-9255
Superior Uniform Group Inc 10055Seminole Blvd *AMEX: SGC ■ *Cust Svc*	Seminole	FL	33772	**800-727-8643***	727-397-9611
Topps Safety Apparel Inc 2516 E State Rd 14	Rochester	IN	46975	**800-348-2990**	574-223-4311
Union Line Inc 2241 S Halsted St	Chicago	IL	60608	**800-632-2308**	312-942-1111
Universal Overall Co 1060 W Van Buren St *Cust Svc	Chicago	IL	60607	**800-621-3344***	312-226-3336
Varsity Brands Inc DBA Varsity Spirit Fashions 6745 Lenox Center Ct Suite 300	Memphis	TN	38115	**800-533-8022**	901-387-4370
Varsity Spirit Corp 6745 Lenox Ctr Ct Suite 300	Memphis	TN	38115	**800-533-8022**	901-387-4370
Varsity Spirit Fashions 6745 Lenox Center Ct Suite 300	Memphis	TN	38115	**800-533-8022**	901-387-4370
Walls Industries Inc 1905 N Main St	Cleburne	TX	76033	**800-433-1765**	817-645-4366
Wenaas AGS Inc 202 E Larkspur St	Victoria	TX	77904	**888-576-2668**	361-576-2668
Williamson-Dickie Mfg Co 509 W Vickery Blvd	Fort Worth	TX	76104	**800-336-7201**	817-336-7201

153-20 Western Wear (Except Hats & Boots)

Company / Address	City	State	Zip	Toll-Free	Phone
Karman Inc 14707 E 2nd Ave 3rd Fl	Aurora	CO	80011	**800-825-6555**	303-893-2320
Miller International Inc Rocky Mountain Clothing Co Div 8500 Zuni St	Denver	CO	80260	**800-688-4449**	303-428-5696
Niver Western Wear Inc PO Box 10122	Fort Worth	TX	76185	**800-433-5752**	817-924-4299
Rockmount Ranch Wear Mfg Co 1626 Wazee St	Denver	CO	80202	**800-776-2566**	303-629-7777
Rocky Mountain Clothing Co Div Miller International Inc 8500 Zuni St	Denver	CO	80260	**800-688-4449**	303-428-5696
Sidran Inc 14280 Gillis Rd *Cust Svc	Farmers Branch	TX	75244	**800-969-5015***	214-352-7979

153-21 Women's Clothing

Company / Address	City	State	Zip	Toll-Free	Phone
Alfred Angelo Inc 1301 Virginia Dr Suite 110	Fort Washington	PA	19034	**800-504-7263**	215-659-5300
bebe stores Inc 400 Valley Dr *NASDAQ: BEBE*	Brisbane	CA	94005	**877-232-3777**	415-715-3900
Bleyle Inc 14 St John Cir *Cust Svc	Newnan	GA	30265	**800-241-3437***	770-253-2792
Bowdon Mfg Co 127 N Carrol St	Bowdon	GA	30108	**800-937-7242**	770-258-7201
Bridal Originals 1700 Saint Louis Rd	Collinsville	IL	62234	**800-876-4696**	618-345-4499
Byer California 66 Potrero Ave	San Francisco	CA	94103	**800-998-2937**	415-626-7844
Carabella Corp 17662 Armstrong Ave *Cust Svc	Irvine	CA	92614	**800-227-2235***	949-263-2300
Christian Dior 712 5th Ave 37th Fl	New York	NY	10019	**800-929-3467**	212-582-0500
Crown Clothing Corp 340 Vanderbilt Ave	Norwood	MA	02062	**800-225-8950**	781-769-0001
Crystal Springs Apparel 206 W Railroad Ave	Crystal Springs	MS	39059	**800-633-4635**	601-892-4551
Darue of California Inc 14102 S Broadway	Los Angeles	CA	90059	**800-733-3375**	310-323-1350
Dior Christian 712 5th Ave 37th Fl	New York	NY	10019	**800-929-3467**	212-582-0500
Donna Karan International Inc 550 7th Ave 15th Fl	New York	NY	10018	**800-231-0884**	212-789-1500
Graff Californiawear 1515 E 15th St	Los Angeles	CA	90021	**800-421-8692**	213-749-0171
Halmode Apparel Inc 1400 Broadway 11th Fl	New York	NY	10018	**800-388-0938**	212-564-7800
Jessica McClintock Inc 1400 16th St	San Francisco	CA	94103	**800-333-5301**	415-553-8200
JLM Couture Inc 225 W 37th St 5th Fl *NASDAQ: JLMC*	New York	NY	10018	**800-924-6475**	212-921-7058
Karan Donna International Inc 550 7th Ave 15th Fl	New York	NY	10018	**800-231-0884**	212-789-1500
Leon Levin Inc 250 W 39th St 5th Fl	New York	NY	10018	**800-822-3363**	212-575-1900
Leon Max Inc 3100 New York Dr	Pasadena	CA	91107	**800-345-3813**	626-797-6886
McClintock Jessica Inc 1400 16th St	San Francisco	CA	94103	**800-333-5301**	415-553-8200
MHSS Enterprises 4200 N 29th Ave	Hollywood	FL	33020	**800-990-6696**	954-894-9494
Northern Isles 300 Manley St	Brockton	MA	02303	**800-666-5105**	508-513-3013

Women's Clothing (Cont'd)

Company / Address	City	State	ZIP	Toll-Free	Phone
Outer Banks Sportswear 1000 E Hanes Mill Rd PO Box 15901	Winston-Salem	NC	27105	**800-438-2029**	
Perry Mfg Co 100 Woltz St	Mount Airy	NC	27030	**800-922-8384**	336-786-6171
Polo Ralph Lauren Corp 650 Madison Ave *NYSE: RL*	New York	NY	10022	**888-475-7674**	212-318-7000
Saint John Knits Inc 17522 Armstrong Ave	Irvine	CA	92614	**877-755-8463**	949-863-1171
Sally Lou Fashions Corp 1400 Broadway 6th Fl	New York	NY	10018	**800-258-1540**	212-354-9670
Tanner Cos LLC 581Rock Rd	Rutherfordton	NC	28139	**800-669-3662**	828-287-4205
Tarrant Apparel Group 3151 E Washington Blvd *NASDAQ: TAGS*	Los Angeles	CA	90023	**800-780-8250**	323-780-8250
Ursula of Switzerland Inc 31 Mohawk Ave	Waterford	NY	12188	**800-826-4041**	518-237-2580
Z Cavaricci 5807 Smithway St	City of Commerce	CA	90040	**866-685-3267**	

154 CLOTHING & ACCESSORIES - WHOL

Company / Address	City	State	ZIP	Toll-Free	Phone
Ben Elias Industries Corp 1400 Broadway 29th Fl	New York	NY	10018	**800-354-2769**	212-354-8300
Bounty Trading Corp 1370 Broadway 14th Fl	New York	NY	10018	**800-526-8689**	212-279-5900
Broder Bros Co 45555 Port St	Plymouth	MI	48170	**800-521-0850**	734-454-4800
Continental Sportswear 135 W 27th St	New York	NY	10001	**800-543-5007**	212-966-3404
Crew Outfitters 579 W High St	Aurora	MO	65605	**888-567-2739**	
Elias Ben Industries Corp 1400 Broadway 29th Fl	New York	NY	10018	**800-354-2769**	212-354-8300
Herman's Inc 2820 Blackhawk Rd *Cust Svc	Rock Island	IL	61201	**800-447-1295***	309-788-9568
International Women's Apparel 610 Uhler Rd *Cust Svc	Easton	PA	18040	**800-735-7848***	610-258-9143
Jacob Ash Co Inc 301 Munson Ave	McKees Rocks	PA	15136	**800-245-6111**	412-331-6660
RGA Accessories Inc 350 5th Ave Suite 2101	New York	NY	10118	**800-221-8828**	212-273-9200
Romerovski Corp 450 W Westfield Ave	Roselle Park	NJ	07204	**800-852-9944**	908-241-3000
South Carolina Tees Inc PO Box 66	Columbia	SC	29202	**800-829-5000**	803-256-1393
Sussex Co Inc PO Box 749	Milford	DE	19963	**800-537-5995**	302-422-8037
TSC Apparel LLC 12080 Mosteller Rd	Cincinnati	OH	45241	**800-543-7230**	513-771-1138
Tucker Rocky Distributing Inc 4900 Alliance Gateway Fwy	Fort Worth	TX	76177	**800-283-8787**	817-258-9000
WS Emerson Co Inc 15 Acme Rd	Brewer	ME	04412	**800-789-6120**	207-989-3410

155 CLOTHING STORES

SEE ALSO Department Stores

155-1 Children's Clothing Stores

Company / Address	City	State	ZIP	Toll-Free	Phone
Babies 'R' Us 545 Rt 17 S	Paramus	NJ	07652	**800-869-7787**	201-251-3191
Children's Orchard Inc 900 Victors Way Suite 200	Ann Arbor	MI	48108	**800-999-5437**	734-994-9199
Children's Place Retail Stores Inc 915 Secaucus Rd *NASDAQ: PLCE*	Secaucus	NJ	07094	**800-527-5355**	201-558-2400
GapKids 1 Harrison St	San Francisco	CA	94105	**800-333-7899**	650-952-4400
Gymboree Corp 500 Howard St *NASDAQ: GYMB*	San Francisco	CA	94105	**800-222-7758**	415-278-7000
Limited Too 8323 Walton Pkwy	New Albany	OH	43054	**800-934-4496**	614-775-3500
Mia Bambini Inc 360 Merrimack St Riverwalk Building 9	Lawrence	MA	01843	**800-766-1254**	978-682-3600
Once Upon A Child 4200 Dahlberg Dr Suite 100	Minneapolis	MN	55422	**800-433-2540**	763-520-8500

155-2 Family Clothing Stores

Company / Address	City	State	ZIP	Toll-Free	Phone
Bob's Stores Inc 160 Corporate Ct	Meriden	CT	06450	**866-333-2627**	203-235-5775
Dawahares Inc 1845 Alexandria Dr	Lexington	KY	40504	**800-677-9108**	859-278-0422
Eblens Casual Clothing 299 Industrial Ln	Torrington	CT	06790	**800-464-2898**	860-489-3073
Factory 2-U Stores Inc 4000 Ruffin Rd	San Diego	CA	92123	**877-443-2286**	858-627-1800
Foursome Inc 841 Lake St E	Wayzata	MN	55391	**888-368-7766**	952-473-4667
Goody's Family Clothing Inc PO Box 22000 *NASDAQ: GDYS*	Knoxville	TN	37933	**800-224-3114**	865-966-2000
Hamrick Industries 742 Peachoid Rd	Gaffney	SC	29341	**800-487-5411**	864-489-6095
Kittery Trading Post 301 US Rt 1	Kittery	ME	03904	**888-587-6246**	207-439-2700
Old Navy Clothing Co 1 Harrison St *Cust Svc	San Francisco	CA	94105	**800-653-6289***	650-952-4400
Palais Royal 10201 S Main St	Houston	TX	77025	**800-324-3244**	713-667-5601
Peter Harris Clothes 952 Troy-Schenectady Rd	Latham	NY	12110	**800-444-1650**	518-785-1650
Puritan of Cape Cod 408 Main St	Hyannis	MA	02601	**800-924-0606**	508-775-2400
Rogers Department Store Inc 1001 28th St SW	Grand Rapids	MI	49509	**800-727-7643**	616-538-6000
Ross Stores Inc 8333 Central Ave *NASDAQ: ROST*	Newark	CA	94560	**800-289-7677**	510-505-4400
Sharpe Dry Goods Co Inc 200 N Broadway St	Checotah	OK	74426	**800-238-6491**	918-473-2233
Syms Corp 1 Syms Way *NYSE: SYM*	Secaucus	NJ	07094	**800-322-7967**	201-902-9600
TJ Maxx 770 Cochituate Rd *Cust Svc	Framingham	MA	01701	**800-926-6299***	508-390-1000
Wakefield's Inc 1212 Quintard Ave	Anniston	AL	36201	**800-333-1552**	256-237-9521
Zellers Inc 8925 Torbram Rd *Cust Svc	Brampton	ON	L6T4G1	**888-226-2225***	905-792-4400
Zumiez Inc 6300 Merrill Creek Pkwy Suite B *NASDAQ: ZUMZ*	Everett	WA	98203	**877-828-6929**	425-551-1500

155-3 Men's Clothing Stores

Company / Address	City	State	ZIP	Toll-Free	Phone
Alfred Dunhill North America Ltd 645 5th Ave	New York	NY	10022	**800-776-4053**	212-888-4000
Bachrach Clothing Inc 1 Bachrach Ct	Decatur	IL	62526	**800-222-4722**	217-875-1020
Brooks Brothers Inc 346 Madison Ave	New York	NY	10017	**800-444-1613**	212-682-8800
C & R Clothiers Inc 5803 Glenmont Dr	Houston	TX	77081	**800-447-8487**	713-295-7200
Carroll & Co 425 N Canon Dr	Beverly Hills	CA	90210	**800-238-9400**	310-273-9060
Casual Male Inc 555 Turnpike St	Canton	MA	02021	**800-767-0319**	781-828-9300
Dunhill Alfred North America Ltd 645 5th Ave	New York	NY	10022	**800-776-4053**	212-888-4000
Express 2 Limited Pkwy *Cust Svc	Columbus	OH	43230	**800-477-8844***	614-415-4000
Frederick Paul Inc 223 W Poplar St	Fleetwood	PA	19522	**800-247-1417**	610-944-0909
Hugestore.com 427 S Illinois St	Indianapolis	IN	46225	**800-259-7283**	317-321-9999
International Male 741 F St	San Diego	CA	92101	**800-293-9333**	619-544-9900
Jos A Bank Clothiers 500 Hanover Pike *NASDAQ: JOSB* ■ *Cust Svc	Hampstead	MD	21074	**800-999-7472***	410-239-2700
K & G Men's Center Inc 1225 Chattahoochee Ave NW	Atlanta	GA	30318	**800-351-7987**	404-351-7987
Louis Boston 234 Berkeley St	Boston	MA	02116	**800-225-5135**	617-262-6100
Men's Wearhouse Inc 40650 Encyclopedia Cir *NYSE: MW*	Fremont	CA	94538	**800-777-8580**	510-723-8200
Miltons Inc 250 Granite St	Braintree	MA	02184	**800-645-8667**	781-848-1880
Patrick James Inc 3457 W Shaw Ave	Fresno	CA	93711	**888-427-6003**	559-275-4300
Paul Frederick Inc 223 W Poplar St	Fleetwood	PA	19522	**800-247-1417**	610-944-0909
Repp Ltd Big & Tall Stores 555 Turnpike St	Canton	MA	02021	**800-690-7377**	781-828-9300
Rochester Big & Tall 700 Mission St	San Francisco	CA	94103	**800-282-8200**	415-982-6455
Rubenstein Brothers Inc 102 St Charles Ave	New Orleans	LA	70130	**800-725-7823**	504-581-6666
Steven Windsor Inc 6535 Arlington Blvd	Falls Church	VA	22042	**800-765-3487**	703-533-9784

155-4 Men's & Women's Clothing Stores

Company / Address	City	State	ZIP	Toll-Free	Phone
Abercrombie & Fitch Co 6301 Fitch Pass *NYSE: ANF*	New Albany	OH	43054	**800-666-2595**	614-283-6500
American Eagle Outfitters 150 Thorn Hill Dr *NASDAQ: AEOS* ■ *Cust Svc	Warrendale	PA	15086	**888-232-4535***	724-776-4857
Banana Republic 1 Harrison St	San Francisco	CA	94105	**800-333-7899**	650-952-4400
Bergdorf Goodman Inc 754 5th Ave *Cust Svc	New York	NY	10019	**800-218-4918***	212-753-7300
Buckle Inc 2407 W 24th St *NYSE: BKE*	Kearney	NE	68845	**800-626-1255**	308-236-8491
Cohoes Fashions Inc 43 Mohawk St	Cohoes	NY	12047	**800-736-8765**	518-237-0524
Duck Head Apparel Co Inc 4902 W Waters Ave	Tampa	FL	33634	**888-385-8825**	813-249-4900
Eddie Bauer Inc 15010 NE 36th St *Orders	Redmond	WA	98052	**800-426-8020***	425-755-6100
Gap Inc 2 Folsom St *NYSE: GPS*	San Francisco	CA	94105	**800-333-7899**	650-952-4400
Harold's Stores Inc 5919 Maple Ave *AMEX: HLD*	Dallas	TX	75235	**800-949-3533**	214-366-0600
Hirshleifer J & Son Inc 2080 Northern Blvd	Manhasset	NY	11030	**800-401-9313**	516-627-3566
J Crew Group Inc 770 Broadway	New York	NY	10003	**800-932-0043**	212-209-2500
J Hirshleifer & Son Inc 2080 Northern Blvd	Manhasset	NY	11030	**800-401-9313**	516-627-3566
Korshak Stanley 500 Crescent Ct Suite 100	Dallas	TX	75201	**800-972-5959**	214-871-3600
Mark Fore & Strike Inc 6500 Park of Commerce Blvd *Orders	Boca Raton	FL	33487	**800-327-3627***	561-241-1700
Mark Shale 10441 Beaudin Blvd Suite 100	Woodridge	IL	60517	**800-488-2686**	630-427-1100
Pacific Sunwear of California Inc 3450 E Miraloma Ave *NASDAQ: PSUN*	Anaheim	CA	92806	**800-444-6770**	714-414-4000
Patagonia Inc 259 W Santa Clara Dr PO Box 150 *Cust Svc	Ventura	CA	93001	**800-638-6464***	805-643-8616
Paul Stuart Inc Madison Ave & 45th St *Orders	New York	NY	10017	**800-678-8278***	212-682-0320
Rodes Apparel 4938 Brownsboro Rd	Louisville	KY	40222	**800-950-7633**	502-584-3112
Shale Mark Co 10441 Beaudin Blvd Suite 100	Woodridge	IL	60517	**800-488-2686**	630-427-1100
Stanley Korshak 500 Crescent Ct Suite 100	Dallas	TX	75201	**800-972-5959**	214-871-3600

155-5 Specialty Clothing Stores

Company / Address	City	State	ZIP	Toll-Free	Phone
Hilo Hattie 700 N Nimitz Hwy	Honolulu	HI	96817	**800-233-8912**	808-524-3966
Life Uniform Co 2132 Kratky Rd	Saint Louis	MO	63114	**800-325-8033**	314-824-2900
Luskey's/Ryon's Western Stores Inc 2601 N Main St	Fort Worth	TX	76106	**800-725-7966**	817-625-2391
Mark's Work Warehouse 30-1035 64th Ave SE	Calgary	AB	T2H2J7	**800-663-6275**	403-692-7793
Modell's Sporting Goods 498 7th Ave 20th Fl	New York	NY	10018	**800-250-7405**	212-822-1000
Pro Image Franchise LLC 233 N 1250 West Suite 200	Centerville	UT	84014	**888-477-6326**	801-296-9999
Warnaco Swimwear Group Inc 6040 Bandini Blvd *Cust Svc	Los Angeles	CA	90040	**800-547-8770***	323-726-1262
Western Warehouse 11205 Montgomery Blvd NE	Albuquerque	NM	87111	**800-532-4888**	505-296-8344
Wilsons The Leather Experts Inc 7401 Boone Ave N *NASDAQ: WLSN*	Brooklyn Park	MN	55428	**800-967-6270**	763-391-4000

155-6 Women's Clothing Stores

Company / Address	City	State	ZIP	Toll-Free	Phone
5-7-9 Shops 1000 Pennsylvania Ave	Brooklyn	NY	11207	**800-435-5556**	718-485-3000
A Nose For Clothes 13100 SW 128th St	Miami	FL	33186	**877-870-6673**	305-253-8631
AnnTaylor Inc 142 W 57th St	New York	NY	10019	**800-677-6788**	212-541-3300
AnnTaylor Stores Corp 142 W 57th St *NYSE: ANN*	New York	NY	10019	**800-677-6788**	212-541-3300
Anthony's Inc 5000 Georgia Ave	West Palm Beach	FL	33405	**800-324-1380**	561-588-7336
August Max 100 Phoenix Ave	Enfield	CT	06082	**800-662-8042**	860-741-0771
Avenue Stores Inc 365 W Passaic St	Rochelle Park	NJ	07662	**877-708-8740**	201-845-0880
Balliet's Inc 1900 NW Expy	Oklahoma City	OK	73118	**877-841-8078**	405-848-7811

	City	State	Zip	Toll-Free	Phone
Bluefly Inc 42 W 39th St 9th Fl	New York	NY	10018	**877-258-3359**	212-944-8000
NASDAQ: BFLY					
Cache Inc 1440 Broadway 5th Fl	New York	NY	10018	**800-788-2224**	212-575-3200
NASDAQ: CACH					
Casual Corner Group Inc 100 Phoenix Ave	Enfield	CT	06082	**800-789-5348**	860-741-0771
Catherines Stores Corp 3742 Lamar Ave	Memphis	TN	38118	**800-289-6372**	901-363-3900
Cato Corp 8100 Denmark Rd	Charlotte	NC	28273	**800-488-0619**	704-554-8510
NYSE: CTR					
Charlotte Russe 4645 Morena Blvd	San Diego	CA	92117	**877-266-9327**	858-587-9900
Chico's FAS Inc 11215 Metro Pkwy	Fort Myers	FL	33912	**888-855-4986**	239-277-6200
NYSE: CHS					
Claire's Accessories					
2400 W Central Rd	Hoffman Estates	IL	60195	**800-252-4737**	847-765-1100
Daffodil 163 Pearl St	Essex Junction	VT	05452	**800-795-1305**	802-879-0212
David's Bridal Inc 1001 Washington St	Conshohocken	PA	19428	**800-823-2403**	610-943-5000
Deb Shops Inc 9401 Blue Grass Rd	Philadelphia	PA	19114	**800-676-6700**	215-676-6000
NASDAQ: DEBS					
Drapers & Damons 9 Pasteur	Irvine	CA	92618	**800-843-1174**	949-784-3000
Embry's & Co					
3363 Tates Creek Rd Suite 212	Lexington	KY	40502	**800-236-2797**	859-266-9785
Fendi NA Inc 720 5th Ave 5th Fl	New York	NY	10019	**800-336-3469**	212-767-0100
Frederick's of Hollywood Inc					
6608 Hollywood Blvd	Hollywood	CA	90028	**800-323-9525**	323-466-5151
Girlshop Inc 154 W 14th St 9th Fl	New York	NY	10011	**888-450-7467**	212-645-6240
Henig Inc 4135 Carmichael Rd	Montgomery	AL	36106	**800-521-2037**	334-277-7610
Henri Bendel Inc 712 5th Ave	New York	NY	10019	**800-423-6335**	212-247-1100
Irresistibles 7 Hawkes St	Marblehead	MA	01945	**800-555-9865**	781-631-1248
Johnny Appleseed's Inc 30 Tozer Rd	Beverly	MA	01915	**800-767-6666***	978-922-2040
*Cust Svc					
Joyce Leslie Inc 135 W Commercial Ave	Moonachie	NJ	07074	**800-526-6216**	201-804-7800
Lady Grace Stores Inc 61 Exchange St	Malden	MA	02148	**800-922-0504**	781-322-1721
Lane Bryant Inc 8655 E Broad St	Reynoldsburg	OH	43068	**800-876-8728**	614-577-4000
Limited The 3 Limited Pkwy	Columbus	OH	43230	**800-945-9000**	614-415-2000
Limited Brands Inc 3 Limited Pkwy	Columbus	OH	43230	**800-945-9000**	614-415-7000
NYSE: LTD					
Louis Vuitton NA Inc 19 E 57th St	New York	NY	10022	**866-884-8866***	212-931-2000
*Cust Svc					
Mandee Shop 12 Vreeland Ave	Totowa	NJ	07512	**800-969-2446**	973-890-0021
Motherhood Maternity 456 N 5th St	Philadelphia	PA	19123	**800-291-7800**	215-873-2200
Mothers Work Inc 456 N 5th St	Philadelphia	PA	19123	**800-291-7800**	215-873-2200
NASDAQ: MWRK					
New York & Co 450 W 33rd St 5th Fl	New York	NY	10001	**800-723-5333**	212-736-1222
NYSE: NWY					
Petite Sophisticate 100 Phoenix Ave	Enfield	CT	06082	**800-662-8042**	860-741-0771
Styles for Less					
12728 S Shoemaker Ave	Santa Fe Springs	CA	90670	**800-929-3466**	562-229-3400
Swim 'n Sport Retail Inc 2396 NW 96th Ave	Miami	FL	33172	**800-497-2111**	305-593-5071
Talbots Inc 1 Talbots Dr	Hingham	MA	02043	**800-225-8200**	781-749-7600
NYSE: TLB					
Tootsies 4045 Westheimer Rd	Houston	TX	77027	**800-580-2220**	713-629-9990
Victoria's Secret Stores 4 Limited Pkwy	Reynoldsburg	OH	43068	**800-411-5116**	614-577-7000
Vuitton Louis NA Inc 19 E 57th St	New York	NY	10022	**866-884-8866***	212-931-2000
*Cust Svc					
Wet Seal Inc 26972 Burbank Ave	Foothill Ranch	CA	92610	**800-735-7325**	949-583-9029
NASDAQ: WTSLA					
Windsor Fashions Inc 4533 Pacific Blvd	Vernon	CA	90058	**888-494-6376**	323-282-9000

156 COFFEE & TEA STORES

	City	State	Zip	Toll-Free	Phone
Barnie's Coffee & Tea Co Inc					
2126 Landstreet Rd Suite 300	Orlando	FL	32809	**800-456-1416**	407-854-6600
Brewster's Coffee Co Inc					
500 Lake Cook Rd Suite 475	Deerfield	IL	60015	**800-251-6101**	847-948-7520
Bucks County Coffee Co					
2250 W Cabot Blvd	Langhorne	PA	19047	**800-844-8790***	215-741-1855
*Sales					
Caribou Coffee Co Inc					
3900 Lakebreeze Ave N	Brooklyn Center	MN	55429	**888-227-4268***	763-533-2525
*Cust Svc					
Coffee Bean & Tea Leaf					
1945 S La Cienega Blvd	Los Angeles	CA	90034	**800-832-5323**	310-237-2326
Coffee Beanery Ltd 3429 Pierson Pl	Flushing	MI	48433	**800-728-2326**	810-733-1020
Coffee People Inc 28 Executive Park Suite 200	Irvine	CA	92614	**800-354-5282**	949-260-1600
Diedrich Coffee Inc 28 Executive Pk Suite 200	Irvine	CA	92614	**800-354-5282**	949-260-1600
NASDAQ: DDRX					
Gloria Jean's Gourmet Coffees					
28 Executive Pk Suite 200	Irvine	CA	92614	**800-354-5282**	949-260-1600
International Coffee & Tea Inc					
1945 S La Cienega Blvd	Los Angeles	CA	90034	**800-854-6252**	310-237-2326
McNulty's Tea & Coffee Co Inc					
109 Christopher St	New York	NY	10014	**800-356-5200**	212-242-5351
Moxie Java International LLC					
199 E 52nd St Suite 100	Boise	ID	83714	**800-659-6963**	208-322-7773
New World Coffee 100 Horizon Ctr Blvd	Hamilton	NJ	08691	**800-308-2457**	609-631-7000
Pannikin Coffee & Tea 675 G St	San Diego	CA	92101	**800-232-6482**	619-239-7891
Peet's Coffee & Tea Inc 1400 Park Ave	Emeryville	CA	94608	**800-999-2132***	510-594-2100
NASDAQ: PEET ■ *Orders					
PJ's Coffee Franchises LLC					
2800 Hessmer Ave Suite C	Metairie	LA	70002	**800-749-5547**	504-454-9459
Seattle's Best Coffee Co 2401 Utah Ave S	Seattle	WA	98134	**800-611-7793**	
Second Cup Ltd 6303 Airport Rd	Mississauga	ON	L4V1R8	**800-338-2610**	905-405-6700
Starbucks Corp 2401 Utah Ave S	Seattle	WA	98134	**800-782-7282**	206-447-1575
NASDAQ: SBUX					
Treats International Franchise Corp					
418 Preston St	Ottawa	ON	K1S4N2	**800-461-4003**	613-563-4073
Tully's Coffee Corp 3100 Airport Way S	Seattle	WA	98134	**800-968-8559**	206-233-2070

157 COLLECTION AGENCIES

	City	State	Zip	Toll-Free	Phone
Alden Curtis & Michaels Ltd					
1170 Broadway Suite 316	New York	NY	10001	**800-569-3877**	212-532-7996
Alexander & Hamilton Inc 2618 Edenborn Ave	Metairie	LA	70002	**800-627-2539**	504-887-9153
Allen Daniel Assoc Inc					
411 Waverly Oaks Rd Suite 113	Waltham	MA	02454	**800-882-2100**	781-647-7722
Allied International Credit Corp					
16635 Young St Suite 26	Newmarket	ON	L3X1V6	**888-478-8181**	905-470-8181
Associated Creditors Exchange Inc					
3443 N Central Ave Suite 1100	Phoenix	AZ	85012	**800-280-3800**	602-954-6554
Barry Jon & Associates Inc PO Box 127	Concord	NC	28026	**800-264-0384**	704-723-4200
Bonneville Billing & Collection Inc					
PO Box 150621	Ogden	UT	84415	**800-660-6138**	801-621-7880
Capital Asset Research Corp Ltd					
3960 RCA Blvd Suite 6002	Palm Beach Gardens	FL	33410	**800-888-8293**	561-776-5000
CMI Group Inc 4200 International Pkwy	Carrollton	TX	75007	**800-377-7713**	972-862-4200
Collectcorp Corp					
300 International Dr Amherst Ctr					
Suite 100	Williamsville	NY	14221	**888-935-1104**	416-961-9622
Collection Co of America 700 Longwater Dr	Norwell	MA	02061	**800-886-9177**	781-681-4300
Collecto Inc DBA Collection Co of America					
700 Longwater Dr	Norwell	MA	02061	**800-886-9177**	781-681-4300
Computer Credit Inc 640 W 4th St	Winston-Salem	NC	27101	**800-942-2995**	336-761-1524
Credit Collections Inc					
2915 N Classen Blvd Suite 100	Oklahoma City	OK	73106	**866-723-2455**	405-290-2000
Credit Control Services Inc					
2 Wells Ave Suite 1	Newton	MA	02459	**800-998-5000**	617-965-2000
Diversified Account Systems of Georgia Inc					
1331 Citizens Pkwy Suite 110	Morrow	GA	30260	**800-226-1464**	770-961-5400
Diversified Adjustment Service Inc					
600 Coon Rapids Blvd	Coon Rapids	MN	55433	**800-279-3733**	763-780-1042
Diversified Collection Services Inc					
333 N Canyons Pkwy Suite 100	Livermore	CA	94551	**800-327-9467**	925-960-4800
Dun & Bradstreet Receivable Management					
Services 899 Eaton Ave	Bethlehem	PA	18025	**800-999-3867**	610-882-7000
Dynamic Recovery Services Inc					
2775 Villa Creek Dr Suite 290	Dallas	TX	75234	**800-886-8088**	972-241-5611
Encore Capital Group Inc 5775 Roscoe Ct	San Diego	CA	92123	**888-327-7774**	
GC Services LP 6330 Gulfton St	Houston	TX	77081	**800-756-6524**	713-777-4441
General Revenue Corp 11501 Northlake Dr	Cincinnati	OH	45249	**800-234-1472**	513-469-1472
Gulf Coast Collection Bureau Inc					
3621 Webber St	Sarasota	FL	34232	**888-839-6999**	941-927-6999
Hospital Billing & Collection Service Ltd					
118 Lukens Dr	New Castle	DE	19720	**877-254-9580**	302-552-8000
JJ MacIntyre Co 1801 California Ave	Corona	CA	92881	**800-621-9859**	951-898-4300
Jon Barry & Associates Inc PO Box 127	Concord	NC	28026	**800-264-0384**	704-723-4200
LC Financial Inc 16119 Vanowen St	Van Nuys	CA	91406	**800-800-4523**	818-780-9300
Leland Scott & Assoc Inc					
4275 Little Rd Suite 101	Arlington	TX	76016	**800-808-5061**	817-478-1888
LTD Financial Services LP					
7322 Southwest Fwy Suite 1600	Houston	TX	77074	**800-414-2101**	713-414-2100
MacIntyre JJ Co 1801 California Ave	Corona	CA	92881	**800-621-9859**	951-898-4300
National Action Financial Services Inc					
3587 Parkway Ln	Norcross	GA	30092	**800-452-2411**	770-248-9909
National Revenue Corp 4000 E 5th Ave	Columbus	OH	43219	**800-789-7862**	614-864-3377
Nationwide Credit Inc					
2015 Vaughn Rd Bldg 300	Kennesaw	GA	30144	**800-456-4729**	770-644-7400
Nationwide Recovery Systems Inc					
2304 Tarpley Rd Suite 134	Carrollton	TX	75006	**800-458-6357**	972-798-1000
NCO Financial Systems Inc					
507 Prudential Rd	Horsham	PA	19044	**800-220-2274**	215-441-3000
NCO Group Inc 507 Prudential Rd	Horsham	PA	19044	**800-220-2274**	215-441-3000
NASDAQ: NCOG					
NCO Group Inc Commercial Services Div					
3850 N Causeway Blvd 2nd Fl	Metairie	LA	70002	**800-745-6007**	504-834-8800
NCO Portfolio Management Inc					
507 Prudential Rd	Horsham	PA	19044	**800-220-2274**	215-441-3000
Outsourcing Solutions Inc					
390 S Woods Mill Rd Suite 350	Chesterfield	MO	63017	**800-962-5191**	314-576-0022
Portfolio Recovery Assoc LLC					
120 Corporate Blvd	Norfolk	VA	23502	**888-772-7326**	757-519-9300
NASDAQ: PRAA					
Recovery's Unlimited Inc PO Box 1349	Melville	NY	11747	**800-507-4275**	516-222-1200
Risk Management Alternatives Inc					
2675 Breckinridge Blvd	Duluth	GA	30096	**800-275-7075**	770-925-5000
Second Millennium Equity Services Inc					
796 Deer Park Ave	Babylon	NY	11703	**877-227-4466**	
Sterling Phillips & Assoc Inc					
4739 Utica St Suite 212	Metairie	LA	70006	**800-375-5773**	504-887-0202
Surpas Resource Corp					
3120 Hayes Rd Suite 200	Houston	TX	77082	**800-934-1240**	281-529-3140
Transworld Systems Inc					
5880 Commerce Blvd	Rohnert Park	CA	94928	**800-435-1526**	707-584-4225
United Recovery Systems Inc					
5800 N Course Dr	Houston	TX	77072	**800-568-0399**	713-977-1234
United Resource Systems Inc					
10075 W Colfax Ave	Lakewood	CO	80215	**800-441-7364**	303-205-0152
Van Ru Credit Corp					
1350 E Touhy Ave Suite 300E	Des Plaines	IL	60018	**800-468-2678**	847-824-2414
Vengroff Williams & Assoc Inc PO Box 19715	Irvine	CA	92623	**888-374-2600**	949-263-1300

158 COLLEGES - BUSINESS

SEE ALSO Colleges & Universities - Four-Year; Colleges - Junior; Vocational & Technical Schools

	City	State	Zip	Toll-Free	Phone
AEC Southern Ohio College					
309 Buttermilk Pike	Fort Mitchell	KY	41017	**800-888-1445**	859-341-5627
AEC Southern Ohio College					
1011 Glendale Milford Rd	Cincinnati	OH	45215	**800-888-1445**	513-771-2424
AIB College of Business 2500 Fleur Dr	Des Moines	IA	50321	**800-444-1921**	515-244-4221
Allentown Business School					
2809 E Saucon Valley Rd	Center Valley	PA	18034	**800-227-9109**	610-791-5100
Andover College 901 Washington Ave	Portland	ME	04103	**800-639-3110**	207-774-6126
Baker College Auburn Hills Campus					
1500 University Dr	Auburn Hills	MI	48326	**888-429-0410**	248-340-0600
Bay State College 122 Commonwealth Ave	Boston	MA	02116	**800-815-3276**	617-236-8000
Beal College 99 Farm Rd	Bangor	ME	04401	**800-660-7351**	207-947-4591
Berkeley College New York City Campus					
3 E 43rd St	New York	NY	10017	**800-446-5400**	212-986-4343
Blair College 1815 Jet Wing Dr	Colorado Springs	CO	80916	**888-741-4271**	719-574-1082

	City	State	ZIP	Toll-Free	Phone
Bradford School 2469 Stelzer Rd	Columbus	OH	43219	**800-678-7981**	614-416-6200
Brown College 1440 Northland Dr	Mendota Heights	MN	55120	**800-627-6966**	651-905-3400
Brown Mackie College 2106 S 9th St	Salina	KS	67401	**800-365-0433**	785-825-5422
Lenexa Campus 9705 Lenexa Dr	Lenexa	KS	66215	**800-635-9101**	913-768-1900
Bryant & Stratton College Richmond					
8141 Hull St Rd	Richmond	VA	23235	**800-735-2420**	804-745-2444
Career Colleges of Chicago					
11 E Adams St 2nd Fl	Chicago	IL	60603	**877-859-6300**	312-895-6300
Central Carolina Technical College					
506 N Guignard Dr	Sumter	SC	29150	**800-221-8711**	803-778-1961
Central Pennsylvania College					
College Hill Rd	Summerdale	PA	17093	**800-759-2727**	717-732-0702
College of Westchester 325 Central Ave	White Plains	NY	10606	**800-333-4924**	914-948-4442
Commonwealth Business College					
Merrillville 1000 E 80th Pl Suite 101N	Merrillville	IN	46410	**800-258-3321**	219-769-3321
Michigan City 325 E US Hwy 20	Michigan City	IN	46360	**800-519-2416**	219-877-3100
Davis College 4747 Monroe St	Toledo	OH	43623	**800-477-7021**	419-473-2700
Daymar College 3361 Buckland Sq	Owensboro	KY	42301	**800-960-4090**	270-926-4040
DuBois Business College 1 Beaver Dr	Du Bois	PA	15801	**800-692-6213**	814-371-6920
Duff's Business Institute					
100 Forbes Ave Suite 1200	Pittsburgh	PA	15222	**888-279-3314**	412-261-4520
Duluth Business University					
4724 Mike Colalilo Dr	Duluth	MN	55807	**800-777-8406**	218-722-4000
Erie Business Center					
Main 246 W 9th St	Erie	PA	16501	**800-352-3743**	814-456-7504
South 170 Cascade Galleria	New Castle	PA	16101	**800-722-6227**	724-658-0066
Florida Metropolitan University					
3319 W Hillsborough Ave	Tampa	FL	33614	**877-225-0009**	813-879-6000
George Meany Center for Labor Studies;					
Meany George Center for Labor					
Studies 10000 New Hampshire Ave	Silver Spring	MD	20903	**800-462-4237**	301-431-6400
Gibbs College of Boston 126 Newbury St	Boston	MA	02116	**800-675-4557**	617-578-7100
Gibbs College of Norwalk 10 Norden Pl	Norwalk	CT	06855	**800-845-5333**	203-838-4173
Golden Gate University 536 Mission St	San Francisco	CA	94105	**800-448-4968**	415-442-7000
Hagerstown Business College					
18618 Crestwood Dr	Hagerstown	MD	21742	**800-422-2670**	301-739-2670
Hamilton College - Lincoln 1821 K St	Lincoln	NE	68508	**800-742-7738**	402-474-5315
Hamilton College - Omaha 3350 N 90th St	Omaha	NE	68134	**800-642-1456**	402-572-8500
Heald College					
Concord 5130 Commercial Cir	Concord	CA	94520	**800-755-3550**	925-288-5800
Fresno 255 W Bullard Ave	Fresno	CA	93704	**800-284-0844**	559-438-4222
Hayward 25500 Industrial Blvd	Hayward	CA	94545	**800-755-3550**	510-783-2100
Honolulu 1500 Kapiolani Blvd	Honolulu	HI	96814	**800-755-3550**	808-955-1500
Portland 625 SW Broadway 2nd Fl	Portland	OR	97205	**800-432-5344**	503-229-0492
Salinas 1450 N Main St	Salinas	CA	93906	**800-755-3550**	831-443-1700
San Francisco 350 Mission St	San Francisco	CA	94105	**800-432-5398**	415-808-3000
Herzing College 3355 Lenox Rd Suite 100	Atlanta	GA	30326	**800-473-4533**	404-816-4533
Huntington Junior College 900 5th Ave	Huntington	WV	25701	**800-344-4522**	304-697-7550
ICM School of Business 10 Wood St	Pittsburgh	PA	15222	**800-441-5222**	412-261-2647
Indiana Business College					
550 E Washington St	Indianapolis	IN	46204	**800-999-9229**	317-264-5656
International Business College					
5699 Coventry Ln	Fort Wayne	IN	46804	**800-589-6363**	260-432-8702
Jefferson Community College					
4000 Sunset Blvd	Steubenville	OH	43952	**800-682-6553**	740-264-5591
JF Drake State Technical College					
3421 Meridian St N	Huntsville	AL	35811	**888-413-7253**	256-539-8161
Jones International Ltd 9697 E Mineral Ave	Englewood	CO	80112	**800-525-7002**	303-792-3111
Jones International University Ltd					
9697 E Mineral Ave	Englewood	CO	80112	**800-811-5663**	303-784-8045
Katharine Gibbs School New York					
50 W 40th St 1st Fl	New York	NY	10018	**800-843-0738**	212-867-9300
Lamson College 1126 N Scottsdale Rd Suite 17	Tempe	AZ	85281	**800-898-7017**	480-898-7000
Latter Day Saints Business College					
411 E South Temple St	Salt Lake City	UT	84111	**800-999-5767**	801-524-8100
McIntosh College 23 Cataract Ave	Dover	NH	03820	**800-624-6867**	603-742-1234
Michiana College 1030 E Jefferson Blvd	South Bend	IN	46617	**800-743-2447**	574-237-0774
Monroe College 2501 Jerome Ave	Bronx	NY	10468	**800-556-6676**	718-933-6700
National College of Business & Technology					
1813 E Main St	Salem	VA	24153	**800-664-1886**	540-986-1800
Bluefield 100 Logan St	Bluefield	VA	24605	**800-664-1886**	276-326-3621
Pikeville 288 S Mayo Trail Suite 2	Pikeville	KY	41501	**800-664-1886**	606-432-5477
Roanoke Valley 1813 E Main St	Salem	VA	24153	**800-664-1886**	540-986-1800
National Labor College					
10000 New Hampshire Ave	Silver Spring	MD	20903	**800-462-4237**	301-431-6400
New England College of Finance					
89 South St 1 Lincoln Plaza	Boston	MA	02111	**888-696-6323**	617-951-2350
Newport Business Institute					
945 Greensburg Rd	Lower Burrell	PA	15068	**800-752-7695**	724-339-7542
Newport Business Institute 941 W 3rd St	Williamsport	PA	17701	**800-962-6971**	570-326-2869
Northwestern Business College					
4829 N Lipps Ave	Chicago	IL	60630	**800-396-5613**	773-777-4220
Owensboro Community & Technical College					
4800 New Hartford Rd	Owensboro	KY	42303	**866-755-6282**	270-686-4400
Penn Commercial Inc 242 Oak Spring Rd	Washington	PA	15301	**888-309-7484**	724-222-5330
South University Montgomery Campus					
5355 Vaughn Rd	Montgomery	AL	36116	**866-629-2901**	334-395-8800
Springfield College 1010 W Sunshine St	Springfield	MO	65807	**800-475-2669**	417-864-7220
Taylor Business Institute					
23 W 17th St 7th Fl	New York	NY	10011	**800-959-9999**	212-229-1963
TCI College of Technology 320 W 31st St	New York	NY	10001	**800-878-8246**	212-594-4000
Thompson Institute 5650 Derry St	Harrisburg	PA	17111	**800-272-4632**	717-564-4112
Utica School of Commerce 201 Bleecker St	Utica	NY	13501	**800-321-4872**	315-733-2307
Wade College					
2350 Stemmons Fwy Suite M 5120	Dallas	TX	75207	**800-624-4850**	214-637-3530
Wood Tobe-Coburn School 8 E 40th St	New York	NY	10016	**800-394-9663**	212-686-9040

COLLEGES - CANADIAN

SEE Universities - Canadian

159 COLLEGES - FINE ARTS

SEE ALSO Colleges & Universities - Four-Year; Vocational & Technical Schools

	City	State	ZIP	Toll-Free	Phone
Ai Miami International University of Art & Design					
1501 Biscayne Blvd	Miami	FL	33132	**800-225-9023**	305-428-5700
American Academy of Art					
332 S Michigan Ave Suite 300	Chicago	IL	60604	**888-461-0600**	312-461-0600
American Academy of Dramatic Arts					
1336 N La Brea Ave	Hollywood	CA	90028	**800-222-2867**	323-464-2777
American Academy of Dramatic Arts					
120 Madison Ave	New York	NY	10016	**800-463-8990**	212-686-9244
Antonelli Institute 300 Montgomery Ave	Erdenheim	PA	19038	**800-722-7871**	215-836-2222
Art Institute of Atlanta					
6600 Peachtree Dunwoody Rd 100					
Embassy Row	Atlanta	GA	30328	**800-275-4242**	770-394-8300
Art Institute of California-San Diego					
7650 Mission Valley Rd	San Diego	CA	92108	**800-591-2422**	858-598-1200
Art Institute of Colorado 1200 Lincoln St	Denver	CO	80203	**800-275-2420**	303-837-0825
Art Institute of Dallas 8080 Park Ln Suite 100	Dallas	TX	75231	**800-275-4243**	214-692-8080
Art Institute of Fort Lauderdale					
1799 SE 17th St	Fort Lauderdale	FL	33316	**800-275-7603**	954-463-3000
Art Institute of Houston 1900 Yorktown St	Houston	TX	77056	**800-275-4244**	713-623-2040
Art Institute of Minnesota 15 S 9th St	Minneapolis	MN	55402	**800-777-3643**	612-332-3361
Art Institute of Philadelphia					
1622 Chestnut St	Philadelphia	PA	19103	**800-275-2474**	215-567-7080
Art Institute of Pittsburgh					
420 Blvd of the Allies	Pittsburgh	PA	15219	**800-275-2470**	412-263-6600
Art Institute of Seattle 2323 Elliott Ave	Seattle	WA	98121	**800-275-2471**	206-448-0900
Art Institute of Tampa					
4401 N Himes Ave Suite 150	Tampa	FL	33614	**866-703-3277**	813-873-2112
Bradley Academy for Visual Arts					
1409 Williams Rd	York	PA	17402	**800-864-7725**	717-755-2300
Brooks College 4825 E Pacific Coast Hwy	Long Beach	CA	90804	**800-421-3775**	562-498-2441
Fashion Institute of Design &					
Merchandising 919 S Grand Ave	Los Angeles	CA	90015	**800-421-0127***	213-624-1200
*Admissions					
San Francisco 55 Stockton St	San Francisco	CA	94108	**800-422-3436**	415-675-5200
Institute of American Indian Arts					
83 Avan Nu Po	Santa Fe	NM	87508	**800-804-6422***	505-424-2300
*Admissions					
International Fine Arts College					
1501 Biscayne Blvd	Miami	FL	33132	**800-225-9023**	305-373-4684
Virginia Marti College 11724 Detroit Ave	Lakewood	OH	44107	**800-473-4350**	216-221-8584

160 COLLEGES - JUNIOR

SEE ALSO Colleges & Universities - Four-Year; Colleges - Business; Colleges - Fine Arts; Colleges - Tribal; Vocational & Technical Schools

Alabama

	City	State	ZIP	Toll-Free	Phone
Calhoun Community College PO Box 2216	Decatur	AL	35609	**800-626-3628**	256-306-2500
Central Alabama Community College					
1675 Cherokee Rd	Alexander City	AL	35010	**800-643-2657**	256-215-4255
Faulkner State Community College					
Bay Minette 1900 US Hwy 31 S	Bay Minette	AL	36507	**800-231-3752**	251-580-2100
Fairhope 440 Fairhope Ave	Fairhope	AL	36532	**800-231-3752**	251-990-0420
Gulf Shores 3301 Gulf Shores Pkwy	Gulf Shores	AL	36542	**800-231-3752**	251-968-3101
Gadsden State Community College					
PO Box 227	Gadsden	AL	35902	**800-226-5563**	256-549-8200
Jefferson State Community College					
2601 Carson Rd	Birmingham	AL	35215	**800-239-5900**	205-853-1200
Marion Military Institute 1101 Washington St	Marion	AL	36756	**800-664-1842**	334-683-2306
Wallace Community College 1141 Wallace Dr	Dothan	AL	36303	**800-543-2426**	334-983-3521

Alaska

	City	State	ZIP	Toll-Free	Phone
Kodiak College 117 Benny Benson Dr	Kodiak	AK	99615	**800-486-7660**	907-486-4161
University of Alaska Anchorage Kodiak College					
117 Benny Benson Dr	Kodiak	AK	99615	**800-486-7660**	907-486-4161
University of Alaska Southeast Sitka Campus					
1332 Seward Ave	Sitka	AK	99835	**800-478-6653**	907-747-6653

Arizona

	City	State	ZIP	Toll-Free	Phone
Arizona Western College PO Box 929	Yuma	AZ	85366	**888-293-0392**	928-317-6000
Central Arizona College 8470 N Overfield Rd	Coolidge	AZ	85228	**800-237-9814**	520-426-4444
Cochise College 4190 W Hwy 80	Douglas	AZ	85607	**800-966-7943**	520-364-7943
Sierra Vista Campus					
901 N Colombo Ave	Sierra Vista	AZ	85635	**800-966-7943**	520-515-0500
Coconino Community College					
2800 S Lone Tree Rd	Flagstaff	AZ	86001	**800-350-7122**	928-527-1222
Eastern Arizona College 615 N Stadium Ave	Thatcher	AZ	85552	**800-678-3808**	928-428-8472
Mesa Community College 1833 W Southern Ave	Mesa	AZ	85202	**866-532-4983**	480-461-7000
Mohave Community College					
1971 Jagerson Ave	Kingman	AZ	86401	**800-678-3695**	928-757-0879
Lake Havasu Campus					
1977 W Acoma Blvd	Lake Havasu City	AZ	86403	**888-203-4394**	928-855-7812
Mohave Valley Campus 3400 Hwy 95	Bullhead City	AZ	86442	**888-203-4395**	928-758-3926
North Mohave Campus PO Box 980	Colorado City	AZ	86021	**800-678-3992**	928-875-2799
Northland Pioneer College PO Box 610	Holbrook	AZ	86025	**800-266-7845**	928-532-6111
Pima Community College					
4905 E Broadway Blvd	Tucson	AZ	85709	**800-860-7462**	520-206-4500
West Campus 2202 W Anklam Rd	Tucson	AZ	85709	**800-860-7462**	520-206-6600
Rio Salado College 2323 W 14th St	Tempe	AZ	85281	**800-729-1197**	480-517-8540
Yavapai College 1100 E Sheldon St	Prescott	AZ	86301	**800-922-6787**	928-445-7300
Verde Valley Campus 601 Black Hills Dr	Clarkdale	AZ	86324	**800-922-6787**	928-634-7501

Arkansas

	City	St	ZIP	Toll-Free	Phone
Arkansas State University					
Beebe 1000 Iowa St	Beebe	AR	72012	**800-632-9985**	501-882-6452
Newport 7648 Victory Blvd	Newport	AR	72112	**800-976-1676**	870-512-7800
Crowley's Ridge College 100 College Dr	Paragould	AR	72450	**800-264-1096**	870-236-6901
East Arkansas Community College					
1700 Newcastle Rd	Forrest City	AR	72335	**877-797-3222**	870-633-4480
National Park Community College					
101 College Dr	Hot Springs	AR	71913	**800-760-1825**	501-760-4222
North Arkansas College 1515 Pioneer Dr	Harrison	AR	72601	**800-679-6622**	870-743-3000
NorthWest Arkansas Community College					
1 College Dr	Bentonville	AR	72712	**800-995-6922**	479-636-9222
South Arkansas Community College					
PO Box 7010	El Dorado	AR	71731	**800-955-2289**	870-862-8131
University of Arkansas at Fort Smith					
PO Box 3649	Fort Smith	AR	72913	**888-512-5466**	479-788-7000

California

	City	St	ZIP	Toll-Free	Phone
Allan Hancock College 800 S College Dr	Santa Maria	CA	93454	**800-338-8731**	805-922-6966
Barstow College 2700 Barstow Rd	Barstow	CA	92311	**877-336-6868**	760-252-2411
Butte College 3536 Butte Campus Dr	Oroville	CA	95965	**800-933-8322***	530-895-2511
*Hum Res					
Cerro Coso Community College					
Mammoth Campus PO Box 1865	Mammoth Lakes	CA	93546	**888-537-6932**	760-934-2875
College of the Redwoods					
7351 Tompkins Hill Rd	Eureka	CA	95501	**800-641-0400**	707-476-4100
Del Norte Campus					
883 W Washington Blvd	Crescent City	CA	95531	**800-641-0400**	707-465-2300
Mendocino Coast Campus					
1211 Del Mar Dr	Fort Bragg	CA	95437	**800-641-0400**	707-961-1001
College of the Siskiyous 800 College Ave	Weed	CA	96094	**888-397-4339**	530-938-4461
Copper Mountain Community College					
6162 Rotary Way PO Box 1398	Joshua Tree	CA	92252	**866-366-3791**	760-366-3791
D-Q University PO Box 409	Davis	CA	95617	**866-468-6378**	530-758-0470
Feather River College 570 Golden Eagle Ave	Quincy	CA	95971	**800-442-9799**	530-283-0202
Grossmont College					
8800 Grossmont College Dr	El Cajon	CA	92020	**866-476-7766**	619-644-7000
Grossmont-Cuyamaca Community College					
District 8800 Grossmont College Dr	El Cajon	CA	92020	**866-476-7766**	619-644-7010
Lassen Community College PO Box 3000	Susanville	CA	96130	**800-461-9389**	530-257-6181
MiraCosta College 1 Barnard Dr	Oceanside	CA	92056	**888-201-8480**	760-757-2121
Mount Saint Mary's College Doheny Campus					
10 Chester Pl	Los Angeles	CA	90007	**800-999-9893***	213-477-2561
*Admissions					
Napa Valley College 2277 Napa-Vallejo Hwy	Napa	CA	94558	**800-826-1077**	707-253-3005
Santa Rosa Junior College					
1501 Mendocino Ave	Santa Rosa	CA	95401	**800-564-7752**	707-527-4011
Taft College 29 Emmons Park Dr	Taft	CA	93268	**800-379-6784**	661-763-4282
West Hills College 300 Cherry Ln	Coalinga	CA	93210	**800-266-1114**	559-934-2000

Colorado

	City	St	ZIP	Toll-Free	Phone
Aims Community College 5401 20th St	Greeley	CO	80634	**800-301-5388**	970-330-8008
Colorado Mountain College					
Alpine Campus					
1330 Bob Adams Dr	Steamboat Springs	CO	80487	**800-621-8559**	970-870-4444
Roaring Fork Campus					
3000 County Rd 114	Glenwood Springs	CO	81601	**800-621-8559**	970-945-7481
Colorado Northwestern Community College					
500 Kennedy Dr	Rangely	CO	81648	**800-562-1105**	970-675-2261
Craig Campus 50 College Dr	Craig	CO	81625	**800-562-1105**	970-824-7071
Front Range Community College Larimer					
Campus 4616 S Shields St	Fort Collins	CO	80526	**800-289-3722**	970-226-2500
Lamar Community College 2401 S Main St	Lamar	CO	81052	**800-968-6920**	719-336-2248
Northeastern Junior College 100 College Ave	Sterling	CO	80751	**800-626-4637**	970-521-6600
Pikes Peak Community College					
5675 S Academy Blvd	Colorado Springs	CO	80906	**800-456-6847**	719-576-7711
Pueblo Community College 900 W Orman Ave	Pueblo	CO	81004	**888-642-6017**	719-549-3200
Trinidad State Junior College 600 Prospect St	Trinidad	CO	81082	**800-621-8752**	719-846-5011

Connecticut

	City	St	ZIP	Toll-Free	Phone
Asnuntuck Community College 170 Elm St	Enfield	CT	06082	**800-501-3967**	860-253-3000
Briarwood College 2279 Mount Vernon Rd	Southington	CT	06489	**800-952-2444**	860-628-4751
Capital Community College 950 Main St	Hartford	CT	06103	**800-894-6126**	860-906-5000
Hartford College for Women					
1265 Asylum Ave	Hartford	CT	06105	**866-468-6429***	860-768-5600
*Admissions					
Mitchell College 437 Pequot Ave	New London	CT	06320	**800-443-2811**	860-701-5000

Florida

	City	St	ZIP	Toll-Free	Phone
Brevard Community College					
Cocoa 1519 Clearlake Rd	Cocoa	FL	32922	**888-747-2802**	321-632-1111
Melbourne 3865 N Wickham Rd	Melbourne	FL	32935	**888-747-2802**	321-632-1111
Palm Bay 250 Community College Pkwy	Palm Bay	FL	32909	**888-747-2802**	321-632-1111
Titusville 1311 N US 1	Titusville	FL	32796	**888-747-2802**	321-632-1111
Edison Community College					
Charlotte Campus 26300 Airport Rd	Punta Gorda	FL	33950	**800-749-2322**	941-637-5629
Collier County Campus					
7007 Lely Cultural Pkwy	Naples	FL	34113	**800-749-2322**	239-732-3701
Lee County Campus					
8099 College Pkwy SW	Fort Myers	FL	33919	**800-749-2322**	239-489-9054
Florida College 119 N Glen Arven Ave	Temple Terrace	FL	33617	**800-326-7655**	813-988-5131
Florida Community College at Jacksonville					
Downtown Campus 101 W State St	Jacksonville	FL	32202	**877-633-5950**	904-633-8100
Gulf Coast Community College					
5230 W Hwy 98	Panama City	FL	32401	**800-311-3685**	850-769-1551
Indian River Community College					
3209 Virginia Ave	Fort Pierce	FL	34981	**866-866-4722**	772-462-4700
Palm Beach Community College					
Central Campus 4200 Congress Ave	Lake Worth	FL	33461	**866-576-7222**	561-868-3350
Palm Beach Gardens Campus					
3160 PGA Blvd	Palm Beach Gardens	FL	33410	**866-576-7222**	561-207-5300
Pasco-Hernando Community College					
10230 Ridge Rd	New Port Richey	FL	34654	**877-879-7422**	727-847-2727
Pensacola Junior College 1000 College Blvd	Pensacola	FL	32504	**888-897-3605**	850-484-1000
South University West Palm Beach					
Campus 1760 N Congress Ave	West Palm Beach	FL	33409	**866-629-2902**	561-697-9200

Georgia

	City	St	ZIP	Toll-Free	Phone
Abraham Baldwin Agricultural College					
2802 Moore Hwy ABAC 3	Tifton	GA	31793	**800-733-3653**	229-386-3236
Andrew College 413 College St	Cuthbert	GA	39840	**800-664-9250**	229-732-2171
Coastal Georgia Community College					
3700 Altama Ave	Brunswick	GA	31520	**800-675-7235**	912-264-7235
Dalton State College 213 N College Dr	Dalton	GA	30720	**800-829-4436**	706-272-4436
Darton College 2400 Gillionville Rd	Albany	GA	31707	**866-775-1214**	229-430-6742
Emmanuel College PO Box 129	Franklin Springs	GA	30639	**800-860-8800**	706-245-7226
Emory University Oxford College PO Box 1418	Oxford	GA	30054	**800-723-8328**	770-784-8328
Floyd College PO Box 1864	Rome	GA	30162	**800-332-2406**	706-802-5000
Georgia Military College 201 E Green St	Milledgeville	GA	31061	**800-342-0413**	478-445-2700
Macon State College 100 College Station Dr	Macon	GA	31206	**800-272-7619**	478-471-2700
Oxford College PO Box 1418	Oxford	GA	30054	**800-723-8328**	770-784-8328
South Georgia College 100 W College Pk Dr	Douglas	GA	31533	**800-342-6364**	912-389-4510
Truett-McConnell College 100 Alumni Dr	Cleveland	GA	30528	**800-226-8621**	706-865-2134
Young Harris College PO Box 116	Young Harris	GA	30582	**800-241-3754**	706-379-3111

Hawaii

	City	St	ZIP	Toll-Free	Phone
Maui Community College					
310 W Kaahumanu Ave	Kahului	HI	96732	**800-479-6692**	808-984-3267

Idaho

	City	St	ZIP	Toll-Free	Phone
North Idaho College					
1000 W Garden Ave	Coeur d'Alene	ID	83814	**877-404-4536**	208-769-3300

Illinois

	City	St	ZIP	Toll-Free	Phone
Black Hawk College					
East Campus 1501 Illinois Hwy 78	Kewanee	IL	61443	**800-233-5671**	309-852-5671
Quad Cities Campus 6600 34th Ave	Moline	IL	61265	**800-334-1311**	309-796-5000
Carl Sandburg College					
2400 Tom L Wilson Blvd	Galesburg	IL	61401	**877-236-1862**	309-344-2518
Danville Area Community College					
2000 E Main St	Danville	IL	61832	**888-455-3222**	217-443-3222
Frontier Community College 2 Frontier Dr	Fairfield	IL	62837	**877-464-3687**	618-842-3711
Joliet Junior College 1215 Houbolt Rd	Joliet	IL	60431	**800-636-9886**	815-729-9020
Lincoln Land Community College					
5250 Shepherd Rd PO Box 19256	Springfield	IL	62794	**800-727-4161**	217-786-2200
Lincoln Trail College 11220 State Hwy 1	Robinson	IL	62454	**866-582-4322**	618-544-8657
Olney Central College 305 N West St	Olney	IL	62450	**866-622-4322**	618-395-4351
Robert Morris College DuPage Campus					
905 Meridian Lake Dr	Aurora	IL	60504	**800-762-5960**	
Rock Valley College 3301 N Mulford Rd	Rockford	IL	61114	**800-973-7821**	815-921-7821
Southeastern Illinois College					
3575 College Rd	Harrisburg	IL	62946	**866-338-2742**	618-252-6376
Springfield College in Illinois					
1500 N 5th St	Springfield	IL	62702	**800-635-7289**	217-525-1420
Triton College 2000 N 5th Ave	River Grove	IL	60171	**800-942-7404**	708-456-0300
Wabash Valley College 2200 College Dr	Mount Carmel	IL	62863	**866-982-4322**	618-262-8641

Indiana

	City	St	ZIP	Toll-Free	Phone
Vincennes University 1002 N 1st St	Vincennes	IN	47591	**800-742-9198**	812-888-4313
Jasper Campus 850 College Ave	Jasper	IN	47546	**800-809-8852**	812-482-3030

Iowa

	City	St	ZIP	Toll-Free	Phone
Des Moines Area Community College					
2006 S Ankeny Blvd	Ankeny	IA	50021	**800-362-2127**	515-964-6200
Des Moines Area Community College					
1125 Hancock Dr	Boone	IA	50036	**800-362-2127**	515-432-7203
Ellsworth Community College					
1100 College Ave	Iowa Falls	IA	50126	**800-322-9235**	641-648-4611
Hawkeye Community College					
1501 E Orange Rd	Waterloo	IA	50704	**800-670-4769**	319-296-2320
Indian Hills Community College					
525 Grandview Ave	Ottumwa	IA	52501	**800-726-2585**	641-683-5111
Iowa Central Community College					
330 Ave M	Fort Dodge	IA	50501	**800-362-2793**	515-576-7201
Iowa Lakes Community College					
300 S 18th St	Estherville	IA	51334	**800-242-5106**	712-362-2604
Iowa Western Community College					
Clarinda Campus 923 E Washington St	Clarinda	IA	51632	**800-521-2073**	712-542-5117
Council Bluffs Campus					
2700 College Rd Box 4-C	Council Bluffs	IA	51502	**800-432-5852**	712-325-3200
Kirkwood Community College					
6301 Kirkwood Blvd SW	Cedar Rapids	IA	52404	**800-332-2055**	319-398-5411
Muscatine Community College					
152 Colorado St	Muscatine	IA	52761	**888-336-3907**	563-288-6001
North Iowa Area Community College					
500 College Dr	Mason City	IA	50401	**888-466-4222**	641-423-1264

Iowa (Cont'd)

				Toll-Free	Phone
Northeast Iowa Community College					
Calmar Campus PO Box 400	Calmar	IA	52132	**800-728-2256**	563-562-3263
Dubuque Campus 700 Main St	Dubuque	IA	52001	**800-728-7367**	563-557-8271
Peosta Campus 10250 Sundown Rd	Peosta	IA	52068	**800-728-7367**	563-556-5110
Northwest Iowa Community College 603 W Park St	Sheldon	IA	51201	**800-352-4907**	712-324-5061
Scott Community College 500 Belmont Rd	Bettendorf	IA	52722	**888-336-3907**	563-441-4001
Southwestern Community College 1501 W Townline St	Creston	IA	50801	**800-247-4023**	641-782-7081
Waldorf College 106 S 6th St	Forest City	IA	50436	**800-292-1903**	641-585-2450

Kansas

				Toll-Free	Phone
Barton County Community College 245 NE 30th Rd	Great Bend	KS	67530	**800-722-6842**	620-792-2701
Central Christian College PO Box 1403	McPherson	KS	67460	**800-835-0078**	620-241-0723
Cloud County Community College 2221 Campus Dr	Concordia	KS	66901	**800-729-5101**	785-243-1435
Coffeyville Community College 400 W 11th St	Coffeyville	KS	67337	**800-782-4732**	620-251-7700
Colby Community College 1255 S Range Ave	Colby	KS	67701	**888-634-9350**	785-462-3984
Cowley County Community College PO Box 1147	Arkansas City	KS	67005	**800-593-2222**	620-442-0430
Dodge City Community College 2501 N 14th Ave	Dodge City	KS	67801	**800-367-3222**	620-225-1321
Fort Scott Community College 2108 S Horton St	Fort Scott	KS	66701	**800-874-3722**	620-223-2700
Garden City Community College 801 Campus Dr	Garden City	KS	67846	**800-658-1696**	620-276-7611
Hesston College PO Box 3000	Hesston	KS	67062	**800-995-2757**	620-327-4221
Hutchinson Community College 1300 N Plum St	Hutchinson	KS	67501	**800-289-3501**	620-665-3500
Independence Community College PO Box 708	Independence	KS	67301	**800-842-6063**	620-331-4100
Johnson County Community College 12345 College Blvd	Overland Park	KS	66210	**866-896-5893**	913-469-8500
Labette Community College 200 S 14th St	Parsons	KS	67357	**888-522-3883**	620-421-6700
Seward County Community College PO Box 1137	Liberal	KS	67905	**800-373-9951**	620-624-1951

Kentucky

				Toll-Free	Phone
Ashland Community College 1400 College Dr	Ashland	KY	41101	**800-370-7191**	606-329-2999
Big Sandy Community & Technical College 1 Bert T Combs Dr	Prestonsburg	KY	41653	**888-641-4132**	606-886-3863
Elizabethtown Community College 600 College Street Rd	Elizabethtown	KY	42701	**877-246-2322**	270-769-2371
Hazard Community & Technical College 1 Community College Dr	Hazard	KY	41701	**800-246-7521**	606-436-5721
Lexington Community College Cooper Dr 203 Oswald Bldg	Lexington	KY	40506	**866-774-4872**	859-257-4872
Madisonville Community College 2000 College Dr	Madisonville	KY	42431	**866-227-4812**	270-821-2250
Somerset Community College 808 Monticello St	Somerset	KY	42501	**877-629-9722**	606-679-8501
Southeast Community College 700 College Rd	Cumberland	KY	40823	**888-274-7322**	606-589-2145
Middlesboro Campus 1300 Chichester Ave	Middlesboro	KY	40965	**888-274-7322**	606-242-2145
Whitesburg Campus 2 Long Ave	Whitesburg	KY	41858	**888-274-7322**	606-633-0279

Louisiana

				Toll-Free	Phone
Louisiana State University Alexandria Campus 8100 US Hwy 71 S *Admissions	Alexandria	LA	71302	**888-473-6417***	318-445-3672
Southern University Shreveport 3050 ML King Jr Dr	Shreveport	LA	71107	**800-458-1472**	318-674-3300

Maine

				Toll-Free	Phone
Kennebec Valley Community College 92 Western Ave	Fairfield	ME	04937	**800-528-5882**	207-453-5000

Maryland

				Toll-Free	Phone
Baltimore City Community College 2901 Liberty Heights Ave	Baltimore	MD	21215	**888-203-1261**	410-462-8000
College of Southern Maryland PO Box 910	La Plata	MD	20646	**800-933-9177**	301-934-2251
Prince Frederick Campus 3205 Brooms Island Rd	Port Republic	MD	20676	**800-933-9177**	410-586-3056
Saint Mary's Campus 22950 Hollywood Rd	Leonardtown	MD	20650	**800-933-9177**	240-725-5300
Essex Community College 7201 Rossville Blvd	Baltimore	MD	21237	**800-832-0262**	410-682-6000
Hagerstown Community College 11400 Robinwood Dr	Hagerstown	MD	21742	**866-422-2468**	301-790-2800
Howard Community College 10901 Little Patuxent Pkwy	Columbia	MD	21044	**800-234-9981**	410-772-4800

Massachusetts

				Toll-Free	Phone
Bay Path College 588 Longmeadow St	Longmeadow	MA	01106	**800-782-7284**	413-567-0621
Becker College 61 Sever St	Worcester	MA	01609	**877-523-2537**	508-791-9241
Cape Cod Community College 2240 Iyanough Rd	West Barnstable	MA	02668	**877-846-3672**	508-362-2131
Dean College 99 Main St	Franklin	MA	02038	**877-879-3326**	508-541-1508
Fisher College 118 Beacon St	Boston	MA	02116	**800-446-1226**	617-236-8800
Marian Court College 35 Littles Pt Rd	Swampscott	MA	01907	**800-418-9868**	781-595-6768
Quincy College 34 Coddington St	Quincy	MA	02169	**800-698-1700**	617-984-1600

Michigan

				Toll-Free	Phone
Alpena Community College 666 Johnson St	Alpena	MI	49707	**888-468-6222**	989-356-9021
Bay Mills Community College 12214 W Lakeshore Dr	Brimley	MI	49715	**800-844-2622**	906-248-3354
Bay de Noc Community College 2001 N Lincoln Rd	Escanaba	MI	49829	**800-221-2001**	906-786-5802
Finlandia University 601 Quincy St	Hancock	MI	49930	**800-682-7604**	906-482-5300
Glen Oaks Community College 62249 Shimmel Rd	Centreville	MI	49032	**888-994-7818**	269-467-9945
Gogebic Community College E 4946 Jackson Rd	Ironwood	MI	49938	**800-682-5910**	906-932-4231
Henry Ford Community College 5101 Evergreen Rd	Dearborn	MI	48128	**800-585-4322**	313-845-9600
Jackson Community College 2111 Emmons Rd	Jackson	MI	49201	**888-522-7344**	517-787-0800
Lansing Community College 520 N Washington Sq	Lansing	MI	48901	**800-644-4522**	517-483-1957
Macomb Community College South Campus 14500 E 12-Mile Rd	Warren	MI	48088	**866-622-6624**	586-445-7000
Monroe County Community College 1555 S Raisinville Rd	Monroe	MI	48161	**877-937-6222**	734-242-7300
Muskegon Community College 221 S Quarterline Rd	Muskegon	MI	49442	**866-711-4622**	231-773-9131
North Central Michigan College 1515 Howard St	Petoskey	MI	49770	**888-298-6605**	231-348-6605
Northwestern Michigan College 1701 E Front St	Traverse City	MI	49686	**800-748-0566**	231-995-1000
Southwestern Michigan College 58900 Cherry Grove Rd	Dowagiac	MI	49047	**800-456-8675**	269-782-1000
Niles Area Campus 2229 US 12 E	Niles	MI	49120	**800-456-8675**	269-687-1600
Wayne County Community College District 801 W Fort St	Detroit	MI	48226	**800-300-2118**	313-496-2600
West Shore Community College PO Box 277	Scottville	MI	49454	**800-848-9722**	231-845-6211

Minnesota

				Toll-Free	Phone
Alexandria Technical College 1601 Jefferson St	Alexandria	MN	56308	**888-234-1222**	320-762-0221
Bethany Lutheran College 700 Luther Dr	Mankato	MN	56001	**800-944-3066**	507-344-7000
Central Lakes College					
Brainerd Campus 501 W College Dr	Brainerd	MN	56401	**800-933-0346**	218-855-8000
Staples Campus 1830 Airport Rd	Staples	MN	56479	**800-247-6836**	218-894-5100
Century College 3300 Century Ave N	White Bear Lake	MN	55110	**800-228-1978**	651-779-3200
College of Saint Catherine Minneapolis 601 25th Ave S	Minneapolis	MN	55454	**800-945-4599**	651-690-7700
Fond du Lac Tribal & Community College 2101 14th St	Cloquet	MN	55720	**800-657-3712**	218-879-0800
Hibbing Community College 1515 E 25th St	Hibbing	MN	55746	**800-224-4422**	218-262-6700
Itasca Community College 1851 E Hwy 169	Grand Rapids	MN	55744	**800-996-6422**	218-327-4460
Lake Superior College 2101 Trinity Rd	Duluth	MN	55811	**800-432-2884**	218-733-7600
Leech Lake Tribal College PO Box 180	Cass Lake	MN	56633	**888-829-4240**	218-335-4200
Mesabi Range Community & Technical College 1100 Industrial Pk Dr PO Box 648	Eveleth	MN	55734	**800-657-3860**	218-741-3095
Minneapolis Community & Technical College 1501 Hennepin Ave	Minneapolis	MN	55403	**800-247-0911**	612-659-6200
Minnesota State Community & Technical College Fergus Falls 1414 College Way	Fergus Falls	MN	56537	**877-450-3322**	218-739-7500
Minnesota West Community & Technical College 1450 Collegeway	Worthington	MN	56187	**800-657-3966**	507-372-3400
Normandale Community College 9700 France Ave S	Bloomington	MN	55431	**866-880-8740**	952-487-8200
North Hennepin Community College 7411 85th Ave N	Brooklyn Park	MN	55445	**800-818-0395**	763-424-0702
Northland Community & Technical College 1101 US Hwy 1 E	Thief River Falls	MN	56701	**800-959-6282**	218-681-0701
Rainy River Community College 1501 Hwy 71	International Falls	MN	56649	**800-456-3996**	218-285-7722
Ridgewater College					
Hutchinson Campus 2 Century Ave SE PO Box 1097	Hutchinson	MN	55350	**800-222-4424**	320-587-3636
Willmar Campus 2101 15th Ave NW	Willmar	MN	56201	**800-722-1151**	320-235-5114
Riverland Community College 1900 8th Ave NW	Austin	MN	55912	**800-247-5039**	507-433-0600
Rochester Community & Technical College 851 30th Ave SE	Rochester	MN	55904	**800-247-1296**	507-285-7210
Vermilion Community College 1900 E Camp St	Ely	MN	55731	**800-657-3608**	218-365-7200

Mississippi

				Toll-Free	Phone
Coahoma Community College 3240 Friars Point Rd	Clarksdale	MS	38614	**800-844-1222**	662-621-4205
East Central Community College PO Box 129	Decatur	MS	39327	**877-462-3222**	601-635-2126
Hinds Community College Utica Campus Hwy 18 W	Utica	MS	39175	**800-446-3722**	601-354-2327
Holmes Community College PO Box 369	Goodman	MS	39079	**800-465-6374**	662-472-2312
Meridian Community College 910 Hwy 19 N	Meridian	MS	39307	**800-622-8431**	601-483-8241
Mississippi Gulf Coast Community College PO Box 548	Perkinston	MS	39573	**866-735-1122**	601-928-5211
Northeast Mississippi Community College 101 Cunningham Blvd	Booneville	MS	38829	**800-555-2154**	662-728-7751

Missouri

				Toll-Free	Phone
Cottey College 1000 W Austin Blvd	Nevada	MO	64772	**888-526-8839**	417-667-8181

Classified Section

				Toll-Free	Phone
Crowder College 601 Laclede Ave	Neosho	MO	64850	**866-238-7788**	417-451-3223
Moberly Area Community College 101 College Ave	Moberly	MO	65270	**800-622-2070**	660-263-4110
North Central Missouri College 1301 Main St	Trenton	MO	64683	**800-880-6180**	660-359-3948
Three Rivers Community College 2080 Three Rivers Blvd	Poplar Bluff	MO	63901	**877-879-8722**	573-840-9600

Montana

				Toll-Free	Phone
Blackfeet Community College PO Box 819	Browning	MT	59417	**800-549-7457**	406-338-5421
Dawson Community College PO Box 421	Glendive	MT	59330	**800-821-8320**	406-377-3396
Flathead Valley Community College 777 Grandview Dr	Kalispell	MT	59901	**800-313-3822**	406-756-3822
Miles Community College 2715 Dickinson St	Miles City	MT	59301	**800-541-9281**	406-874-6100
Salish Kootenai Community College PO Box 70	Pablo	MT	59855	**877-752-6553**	406-275-4800

Nebraska

				Toll-Free	Phone
McCook Community College 1205 E 3rd St	McCook	NE	69001	**800-658-4348**	308-345-8100
Metropolitan Community College PO Box 3777	Omaha	NE	68103	**800-228-9553**	402-457-2400
Mid-Plains Community College					
McDonald-Belton Campus 601 W State Farm Rd	North Platte	NE	69101	**800-658-4308**	308-535-3700
Southeast Community College-Beatrice 4771 W Scott St	Beatrice	NE	68310	**800-233-5027**	402-228-3468
Southeast Community College-Lincoln 8800 'O' St	Lincoln	NE	68520	**800-642-4075**	402-471-3333
Western Nebraska Community College 1601 E 27th St	Scottsbluff	NE	69361	**800-348-4435**	308-635-3606

Nevada

				Toll-Free	Phone
Community College of Southern Nevada					
Cheyenne Campus 3200 E Cheyenne Ave	North Las Vegas	NV	89030	**800-492-5728**	702-651-4000
Western Nevada Community College 2201 W College Pkwy	Carson City	NV	89703	**800-748-5690**	775-445-3277

New Hampshire

				Toll-Free	Phone
Chester College of New England 40 Chester St	Chester	NH	03036	**800-974-6372**	603-887-4401
Hesser College 3 Sundial Ave	Manchester	NH	03103	**800-526-9231**	603-668-6660

New Jersey

				Toll-Free	Phone
Camden County College PO Box 200 College Dr	Blackwood	NJ	08012	**888-228-2466**	856-227-7200
County College of Morris 214 Center Grove Rd	Randolph	NJ	07869	**888-226-8001**	973-328-5000
Fairleigh Dickinson University Metropolitan Campus 1000 River Rd	Teaneck	NJ	07666	**800-338-8803**	201-692-2000
Mercer County Community College PO Box B	Trenton	NJ	08690	**800-392-6222**	609-586-4800
James Kerney Campus N Broad & Academy St	Trenton	NJ	08608	**800-392-6222**	609-586-4800
West Windsor Campus 1200 Old Trenton Rd	West Windsor	NJ	08550	**800-392-6222**	609-586-4800
Ocean County College PO Box 2001	Toms River	NJ	08753	**877-622-3477**	732-255-0400

New Mexico

				Toll-Free	Phone
Doña Ana Branch Community College Box 30001 Dept 3DA	Las Cruces	NM	88003	**800-903-7503**	505-527-7500
Eastern New Mexico University Roswell Campus PO Box 6000	Roswell	NM	88202	**800-243-6687**	505-624-7000
New Mexico Junior College 5317 Lovington Hwy	Hobbs	NM	88240	**800-657-6260**	505-392-4510
New Mexico Military Institute 101 W College Blvd *Admitting	Roswell	NM	88201	**800-421-5376***	505-624-8050
New Mexico State University Carlsbad Campus 1500 University Dr	Carlsbad	NM	88220	**888-888-2199**	505-234-9200
San Juan College 4601 College Blvd	Farmington	NM	87402	**800-864-4871**	505-326-3311

New York

				Toll-Free	Phone
Alfred State College 10 Upper College Dr	Alfred	NY	14802	**800-425-3733**	607-587-4215
Borough of Manhattan Community College 199 Chambers St Rm S-300	New York	NY	10007	**877-669-2622**	212-220-1265
Broome Community College 901 Front St	Binghamton	NY	13902	**800-836-0689**	607-778-5000
Clinton Community College 136 Clinton Point Dr	Plattsburgh	NY	12901	**800-552-1160**	518-562-4200
Dutchess Community College 53 Pendell Rd	Poughkeepsie	NY	12601	**800-763-3933**	845-431-8010
Erie Community College 121 Ellicott St	Buffalo	NY	14203	**800-836-0981**	716-842-2770
South Campus 4041 Southwestern Blvd	Orchard Park	NY	14127	**800-836-0983**	716-851-1003
Farmingdale State University 2350 Broad Hollow Rd	Farmingdale	NY	11735	**877-432-7646**	631-420-2000
Hudson Valley Community College 80 Vandenburgh Ave	Troy	NY	12180	**877-325-4822**	518-629-4822
Jamestown Community College 525 Faulkner St	Jamestown	NY	14702	**800-388-8557**	716-665-5220
Jefferson Community College 1220 Coffeen St	Watertown	NY	13601	**888-435-6522**	315-786-2200
Morrisville State College PO Box 901	Morrisville	NY	13408	**800-258-0111**	315-684-6000
North Country Community College 23 Santanoni Ave	Saranac Lake	NY	12983	**888-879-6222**	518-891-2915
Paul Smith's College of Arts & Sciences Rt 30 & 86 PO box 265	Paul Smiths	NY	12970	**800-421-2605**	518-327-6227
Rockland Community College 145 College Rd	Suffern	NY	10901	**800-722-7666**	845-574-4000
Sage College of Albany 140 New Scotland Ave	Albany	NY	12208	**888-837-9724**	518-292-1730
State University of New York College of Technology at Alfred 10 Upper College Dr	Alfred	NY	14802	**800-425-3733**	607-587-4215
State University of New York College of Technology at Canton 34 Cornell Dr	Canton	NY	13617	**800-388-7123**	315-386-7011
State University of New York College of Technology at Delhi 2 Main St	Delhi	NY	13753	**800-963-3544**	607-746-4000
SUNY Canton 34 Cornell Dr	Canton	NY	13617	**800-388-7123**	315-386-7011
SUNY Delhi 2 Main St	Delhi	NY	13753	**800-963-3544**	607-746-4000
SUNY Rockland 145 College Rd	Suffern	NY	10901	**800-722-7666**	845-574-4000
SUNY Ulster Cottekill Rd	Stone Ridge	NY	12484	**800-724-0833**	845-687-5000
Tompkins Cortland Community College 170 North St	Dryden	NY	13053	**888-567-8211**	607-844-8211
Ulster County Community College Cottekill Rd	Stone Ridge	NY	12484	**800-724-0833**	845-687-5000

North Carolina

				Toll-Free	Phone
Brevard College 400 N Broad St	Brevard	NC	28712	**800-527-9090**	828-883-8292
Brunswick Community College PO Box 30	Supply	NC	28462	**800-754-1050**	910-754-6900
Lenoir Community College PO Box 188	Kinston	NC	28502	**800-848-5497**	252-527-6223
Louisburg College 501 N Main St	Louisburg	NC	27549	**800-775-0208**	919-496-2521
Mayland Community College PO Box 547	Spruce Pine	NC	28777	**800-462-9526**	828-765-7351
Montgomery Community College 1011 Page St	Troy	NC	27371	**800-839-6222**	910-576-6222
Peace College 15 E Peace St	Raleigh	NC	27604	**800-732-2347**	919-508-2000
Sandhills Community College 3395 Airport Rd	Pinehurst	NC	28374	**800-338-3944**	910-692-6185
South Piedmont Community College PO Box 126	Polkton	NC	28135	**800-766-0319**	704-272-7635
Southwestern Community College 447 College Dr	Sylva	NC	28779	**800-447-4091**	828-586-4091
Wayne Community College 3000 Wayne Memorial Dr Box 8002	Goldsboro	NC	27533	**866-414-5064**	919-735-5151

North Dakota

				Toll-Free	Phone
Bismarck State College 1500 Edwards Ave	Bismarck	ND	58501	**800-445-5073**	701-224-5400
Cankdeska Cikana Community College PO Box 269	Fort Totten	ND	58335	**888-783-1463**	701-766-4415
Lake Region State College 1801 College Dr N	Devils Lake	ND	58301	**800-443-1313**	701-662-1514
Minot State University Bottineau 105 Simrall Blvd	Bottineau	ND	58318	**800-542-6866**	701-228-5451
North Dakota State College of Science 800 6th St N	Wahpeton	ND	58076	**800-342-4325**	701-671-2401
Williston State College PO Box 1326	Williston	ND	58802	**888-863-9455**	701-774-4200

Ohio

				Toll-Free	Phone
Cincinnati State Technical & Community College 3520 Central Pkwy	Cincinnati	OH	45223	**877-569-0115**	513-569-1500
Clermont College 4200 Clermont College Dr	Batavia	OH	45103	**866-446-2822**	513-732-5200
Columbus State Community College 550 E Spring St	Columbus	OH	43215	**800-621-6407**	614-287-2400
Cuyahoga Community College					
Eastern Campus 4250 Richmond Rd	Highland Hills	OH	44122	**800-954-8742**	216-987-2024
Metropolitan Campus 2900 Community College Ave	Cleveland	OH	44115	**800-954-8742**	216-987-4200
Western Campus 11000 Pleasant Valley Rd	Parma	OH	44130	**800-954-8742**	216-987-5000
Edison State Community College 1973 Edison Dr	Piqua	OH	45356	**800-922-3722**	937-778-8600
Kettering College of Medical Arts 3737 Southern Blvd	Kettering	OH	45429	**800-433-5262**	937-395-8601
Lakeland Community College 7700 Clocktower Dr	Kirtland	OH	44094	**800-589-8520**	440-953-7000
Lorain County Community College 1005 N Abbe Rd	Elyria	OH	44035	**800-995-5222**	440-365-5222
Miami University Middletown Campus 4200 E University Blvd	Middletown	OH	45042	**800-662-2262**	513-727-3200
Ohio University Southern Campus 1804 Liberty Ave	Ironton	OH	45638	**800-626-0513**	740-533-4600
Owens Community College					
Findlay 300 Davis St	Findlay	OH	45840	**800-346-3529**	419-429-3500
Toledo 30335 Oregon Rd	Perrysburg	OH	43551	**800-466-9367**	419-661-7000
Terra Community College 2830 Napoleon Rd	Fremont	OH	43420	**800-334-3886**	419-334-8400
University of Akron Wayne College 1901 Smucker Rd	Orrville	OH	44667	**800-221-8308**	330-683-2010
Wayne College 1901 Smucker Rd	Orrville	OH	44667	**800-221-8308**	330-683-2010

Oklahoma

				Toll-Free	Phone
Bacone College 2299 Old Bacone Rd	Muskogee	OK	74403	**888-682-5514**	918-683-4581
Northern Oklahoma College 1220 E Grand St PO Box 310	Tonkawa	OK	74653	**888-429-5715**	580-628-6200
Oklahoma State University Oklahoma City 900 N Portland Ave	Oklahoma City	OK	73107	**800-560-4099**	405-947-4421
Redlands Community College 1300 S Country Club Rd	El Reno	OK	73036	**866-415-6367**	405-262-2552
Rogers State University Bartlesville Campus 4001 E Adams Rd	Bartlesville	OK	74006	**800-256-7511**	918-335-3500

Oregon

				Toll-Free	Phone
Clatsop Community College 1653 Jerome Ave	Astoria	OR	97103	**866-252-8767**	503-325-0910
Rogue Community College					
3345 Redwood Hwy	Grants Pass	OR	97527	**800-411-6508**	541-956-7500
Southwestern Oregon Community College					
1988 Newmark Ave	Coos Bay	OR	97420	**800-962-2838**	541-888-2525

Pennsylvania

				Toll-Free	Phone
Butler County Community College PO Box 1203	Butler	PA	16003	**888-826-2829**	724-287-8711
Community College of Beaver County					
1 Campus Dr	Monaca	PA	15061	**800-335-0222**	724-775-8561
Delaware County Community College					
901 S Media Line Rd	Media	PA	19063	**800-543-0146**	610-359-5000
Harcum College 750 Montgomery Ave	Bryn Mawr	PA	19010	**800-345-2600**	610-525-4100
Keystone College 1 College Green	La Plume	PA	18440	**877-426-5534**	570-945-6953
Lackawanna College 501 Vine St	Scranton	PA	18509	**877-346-3552**	570-961-7810
Lehigh Carbon Community College					
4525 Education Pk Dr	Schnecksville	PA	18078	**800-414-3975**	610-799-2121
Luzerne County Community College					
1333 S Prospect St	Nanticoke	PA	18634	**800-377-5222**	570-740-0200
Northampton Community College					
3835 Green Pond Rd	Bethlehem	PA	18020	**877-543-0998**	610-861-5300
Penn State DuBois 1 College Pl	Du Bois	PA	15801	**800-346-7627**	814-375-4700
Penn State Fayette Rt 119 N	Uniontown	PA	15401	**877-568-4130**	724-430-4100
Penn State Mont Alto 1 Campus Dr	Mont Alto	PA	17237	**800-392-6173**	717-749-6000
Penn State York 1031 Edgecomb Ave	York	PA	17403	**800-778-6227**	717-771-4000
Pennsylvania State University					
Altoona College 3000 Ivyside Pk	Altoona	PA	16601	**800-848-9843**	814-949-5466
Beaver Campus of the Commonwealth College					
100 University Dr	Monaca	PA	15061	**877-564-6778**	724-773-3500
DuBois Campus of Commonwealth College					
1 College Pl	Du Bois	PA	15801	**800-346-7627**	814-375-4700
Fayette Campus of Commonwealth College					
Rt 119 N	Uniontown	PA	15401	**877-568-4130**	724-430-4100
Mont Alto Campus of Commonwealth College					
1 Campus Dr	Mont Alto	PA	17237	**800-392-6173**	717-749-6000
York Campus 1031 Edgecomb Ave	York	PA	17403	**800-778-6227**	717-771-4000
Reading Area Community College					
10 S 2nd St PO Box 1706	Reading	PA	19603	**800-626-1665**	610-372-4721
University of Pittsburgh at Titusville					
504 E Main St	Titusville	PA	16354	**888-878-0462**	814-827-5668
Valley Forge Military Academy & College					
1001 Eagle Rd	Wayne	PA	19087	**800-234-8362**	610-989-1300
Westmoreland County Community College					
400 Armbrust Rd	Youngwood	PA	15697	**800-262-2103**	724-925-4000

South Carolina

				Toll-Free	Phone
Greenville Technical College					
506 S Pleasantburg Dr	Greenville	SC	29606	**800-723-0673**	864-250-8000
Brashier Campus PO Box 5616	Greenville	SC	29606	**800-723-0673**	864-228-5000
Greer Campus PO Box 5616	Greenville	SC	29606	**800-723-0673**	864-848-2000
Midlands Technical College PO Box 2408	Columbia	SC	29202	**800-922-8038**	803-738-1400
North Greenville College PO Box 1892	Tigerville	SC	29688	**800-468-6642**	864-977-7000
University of South Carolina Salkehatchie					
PO Box 617	Allendale	SC	29810	**800-922-5500**	803-584-3446
University of South Carolina Union PO Box 729	Union	SC	29379	**800-768-5566**	864-429-8728
Williamsburg Technical College					
601 MLK Jr Ave	Kingstree	SC	29556	**800-768-2021**	843-355-4110
York Technical College 452 S Anderson Rd	Rock Hill	SC	29730	**800-922-8324**	803-327-8000

South Dakota

				Toll-Free	Phone
Kilian Community College 300 E 6th St	Sioux Falls	SD	57103	**800-888-1147**	605-221-3100
Presentation College 1500 N Main St	Aberdeen	SD	57401	**800-437-6060**	605-225-1634

Tennessee

				Toll-Free	Phone
Hiwassee College					
225 Hiwassee College Dr	Madisonville	TN	37354	**800-356-2187**	423-442-2001
Martin Methodist College 433 W Madison St	Pulaski	TN	38478	**800-467-1273**	931-363-9804
Motlow State Community College					
PO Box 8500	Lynchburg	TN	37352	**800-654-4877**	931-393-1500
Roane State Community College					
276 Patton Ln	Harriman	TN	37748	**800-343-9104**	865-354-3000
Southwest Tennessee Community College					
PO Box 780	Memphis	TN	38101	**877-717-7822**	901-333-5000
Volunteer State Community College					
1480 Nashville Pike	Gallatin	TN	37066	**888-335-8722**	615-452-8600
Walters State Community College					
500 S Davy Crockett Pkwy	Morristown	TN	37813	**800-225-4770**	423-585-2600

Texas

				Toll-Free	Phone
Central Texas College					
6200 W Central Texas Expy	Killeen	TX	76549	**800-792-3348**	254-526-1595
Clarendon College PO Box 968	Clarendon	TX	79226	**800-687-9737**	806-874-3571
Coastal Bend College 3800 Charco Rd	Beeville	TX	78102	**866-722-2838**	361-358-2838
Del Mar College					
East Campus 101 Baldwin Blvd	Corpus Christi	TX	78404	**800-652-3357**	361-698-1200
West Campus 101 Baldwin Blvd	Corpus Christi	TX	78404	**800-652-3357**	361-698-1737
Frank Phillips College PO Box 5118	Borger	TX	79008	**800-687-2056**	806-457-4200
Jacksonville College 105 BJ Albritton Dr	Jacksonville	TX	75766	**800-256-8522**	903-586-2518
Kingwood College 20000 Kingwood Dr	Kingwood	TX	77339	**800-883-7939**	281-312-1600
Lamar State College					
Orange 410 Front St	Orange	TX	77630	**800-884-7750**	409-883-7750
Port Arthur PO Box 310	Port Arthur	TX	77641	**800-477-5872**	409-983-4921
Lon Morris College					
800 College Ave Administrative Bldg	Jacksonville	TX	75766	**800-259-5753**	903-589-4000
Navarro College 3200 W 7th Ave	Corsicana	TX	75110	**800-628-2776**	903-874-6501
Northeast Texas Community College					
1735 Chapel Hill Rd	Mount Pleasant	TX	75455	**800-870-0142**	903-572-1911
Paris Junior College 2400 Clarksville St	Paris	TX	75460	**800-232-5804**	903-785-7661
Saint Philip's College 1801 ML King Dr	San Antonio	TX	78203	**866-493-3940**	210-531-3200
Temple College 2600 S 1st St	Temple	TX	76504	**800-460-4636**	254-298-8300
Texas Southmost College					
80 Fort Brown St	Brownsville	TX	78520	**800-850-0160**	956-544-8200
Texas State Technical College Harlingen					
Campus 1902 N Loop 499	Harlingen	TX	78550	**800-852-8784**	956-364-4000
Trinity Valley Community College Athens					
100 Cardinal Dr	Athens	TX	75751	**866-882-2937**	903-675-6200
Tyler Junior College PO Box 9020	Tyler	TX	75711	**800-687-5680**	903-510-2523
Weatherford College 225 College Park Dr	Weatherford	TX	76086	**800-287-5471**	817-594-5471
Western Texas College 6200 College Ave	Snyder	TX	79549	**888-468-6982**	325-573-8511
Wharton County Junior College					
911 Boling Hwy	Wharton	TX	77488	**800-561-9252**	979-532-4560
Sugar Land Campus 550 Julie Rivers Dr	Sugar Land	TX	77478	**800-561-9252**	281-243-8410

Utah

				Toll-Free	Phone
College of Eastern Utah 451 E 400 North	Price	UT	84501	**800-336-2381**	435-637-2120
San Juan Campus 639 W 100 S	Blanding	UT	84511	**800-395-2969**	435-678-2201
Dixie State College 225 S 700 East	Saint George	UT	84770	**888-324-2998**	435-652-7500
Snow College 150 E College Ave	Ephraim	UT	84627	**800-848-3399***	435-283-7000

*PR

Vermont

				Toll-Free	Phone
Champlain College PO Box 670	Burlington	VT	05402	**800-570-5858**	802-658-0800

Virginia

				Toll-Free	Phone
Lord Fairfax Community College Middletown					
Campus 173 Skirmisher Ln	Middletown	VA	22645	**800-906-5322**	540-868-7000
New River Community College PO Box 1127	Dublin	VA	24084	**866-462-6722**	540-674-3600
Southside Virginia Community College					
109 Campus Dr	Alberta	VA	23821	**888-220-7822**	434-949-1000
Tidewater Community College					
Chesapeake Campus 1428 Cedar Rd	Chesapeake	VA	23322	**800-371-0898**	757-822-5100
Portsmouth Campus 7000 College Dr	Portsmouth	VA	23703	**800-371-0898**	757-822-2124
Virginia Beach Campus					
1700 College Crescent	Virginia Beach	VA	23453	**800-371-0898**	757-822-7100

Washington

				Toll-Free	Phone
Northwest Indian College 2522 Kwina Rd	Bellingham	WA	98226	**866-676-2772**	360-676-2772
Olympic College 1600 Chester Ave	Bremerton	WA	98337	**800-259-6718**	360-792-6050
Shelton 937 W Alpine Way	Shelton	WA	98584	**800-259-6718**	360-427-2119
Skagit Valley College					
2405 E College Way	Mount Vernon	WA	98273	**877-385-5360**	360-416-7600
Spokane Community College					
1810 N Greene St	Spokane	WA	99217	**800-248-5644**	509-533-7000
Spokane Falls Community College					
3410 W Fort George Wright Dr	Spokane	WA	99224	**888-509-7944**	509-533-3500
Walla Walla Community College					
500 Tausick Way	Walla Walla	WA	99362	**877-992-9922**	509-522-2500
Wenatchee Valley College 1300 5th St	Wenatchee	WA	98801	**877-982-4968**	509-682-6800

West Virginia

				Toll-Free	Phone
Potomac State College 101 Fort Ave	Keyser	WV	26726	**800-262-7332**	304-788-6800

Wisconsin

				Toll-Free	Phone
College of the Menominee Nation					
PO Box 1179	Keshena	WI	54135	**800-567-2344**	715-799-5600
Lac Courte Oreilles Ojibwa Community College					
13466 W Trepania Rd	Hayward	WI	54843	**888-526-6221**	715-634-4790
Nicolet Area Technical College					
PO Box 518	Rhinelander	WI	54501	**800-544-3039**	715-365-4410
University of Wisconsin Colleges					
780 Regent St	Madison	WI	53715	**888-463-6892**	608-262-1783
Marathon County 518 S 7th Ave	Wausau	WI	54401	**888-367-8962**	715-261-6100

Wyoming

				Toll-Free	Phone
Casper College 125 College Dr	Casper	WY	82601	**800-442-2963**	307-268-2110
Central Wyoming College 2660 Peck Ave	Riverton	WY	82501	**800-735-8418**	307-855-2000
Eastern Wyoming College 3200 W 'C' St	Torrington	WY	82240	**800-658-3195**	307-532-8200
Laramie County Community College					
1400 E College Dr	Cheyenne	WY	82007	**800-522-2993**	307-778-5222
Northwest College 231 W 6th St	Powell	WY	82435	**800-560-4692**	307-754-6000
Sheridan College PO Box 1500	Sheridan	WY	82801	**800-913-9139**	307-674-6446
Western Wyoming Community College					
2500 College Dr	Rock Springs	WY	82901	**800-226-1181**	307-382-1600

161 COLLEGES - TRIBAL

SEE ALSO Colleges - Junior

Name / Address	City	State	ZIP	Toll-Free	Phone
Bay Mills Community College 12214 W Lakeshore Dr	Brimley	MI	49715	**800-844-2622**	906-248-3354
Blackfeet Community College PO Box 819	Browning	MT	59417	**800-549-7457**	406-338-5421
Cankdeska Cikana Community College PO Box 269	Fort Totten	ND	58335	**888-783-1463**	701-766-4415
College of the Menominee Nation PO Box 1179	Keshena	WI	54135	**800-567-2344**	715-799-5600
D-Q University PO Box 409	Davis	CA	95617	**866-468-6378**	530-758-0470
Fond du Lac Tribal & Community College 2101 14th St	Cloquet	MN	55720	**800-657-3712**	218-879-0800
Institute of American Indian Arts 83 Avan Nu Po	Santa Fe	NM	87508	**800-804-6422***	505-424-2300
*Admissions					
Lac Courte Oreilles Ojibwa Community College 13466 W Trepania Rd	Hayward	WI	54843	**888-526-6221**	715-634-4790
Leech Lake Tribal College PO Box 180	Cass Lake	MN	56633	**888-829-4240**	218-335-4200
Northwest Indian College 2522 Kwina Rd	Bellingham	WA	98226	**866-676-2772**	360-676-2772
Salish Kootenai Community College PO Box 70	Pablo	MT	59855	**877-752-6553**	406-275-4800
Si Tanka University					
Eagle Butte 435 N Elm St	Eagle Butte	SD	57625	**800-710-7159**	605-964-8011
Huron 333 9th St SW	Huron	SD	57350	**800-710-7159**	605-352-8721
Southwestern Indian Polytechnic Institute 9169 Coors Rd	Albuquerque	NM	87184	**800-586-7474**	505-346-2346

162 COLLEGES & UNIVERSITIES - CHRISTIAN

SEE ALSO Colleges & Universities - Jesuit

Name / Address	City	State	ZIP	Toll-Free	Phone
Abilene Christian University ACU Box 29000	Abilene	TX	79699	**800-460-6228***	325-674-2000
*Admissions					
Anderson University 1100 E 5th St	Anderson	IN	46012	**800-428-6414***	765-649-9071
*Admissions					
Asbury College 1 Macklem Dr	Wilmore	KY	40390	**800-888-1818**	859-858-3511
Ave Maria University 1025 Commons Cir	Naples	FL	34119	**877-283-8648**	239-280-2511
Belhaven College 1500 Peachtree St	Jackson	MS	39202	**800-960-5940**	601-968-5928
Bethel College 1001 W McKinley Ave	Mishawaka	IN	46545	**800-422-4101**	574-257-3339
Bethel University 3900 Bethel Dr	Saint Paul	MN	55112	**800-255-8706**	651-638-6400
Biola University 13800 Biola Ave	La Mirada	CA	90639	**800-652-4652***	562-903-6000
*Admissions					
Bluffton University 1 University Dr	Bluffton	OH	45817	**800-488-3257**	419-358-3257
Bryan College PO Box 7000	Dayton	TN	37321	**800-277-9522**	423-775-2041
California Baptist University 8432 Magnolia Ave	Riverside	CA	92504	**877-228-8866**	951-689-5771
Calvin College 3201 Burton St SE	Grand Rapids	MI	49546	**800-688-0122**	616-957-6000
Campbellsville University 1 University Dr	Campbellsville	KY	42718	**800-264-6014**	270-789-5000
Carson-Newman College 1646 Russell Ave	Jefferson City	TN	37760	**800-678-9061**	865-475-9061
Cedarville University 251 N Main St	Cedarville	OH	45314	**800-233-2784**	937-766-2211
College of the Ozarks PO Box 17	Point Lookout	MO	65726	**800-222-0525**	417-334-6411
Colorado Christian University 8787 W Alameda Ave	Lakewood	CO	80226	**800-443-2484**	303-963-3200
Cornerstone University 1001 E Beltline Ave NE	Grand Rapids	MI	49525	**800-787-9778***	616-222-1426
*Admissions					
Crichton College 255 N Highland Ave	Memphis	TN	38111	**800-960-9777**	901-320-9700
Crown College 8700 College View Dr	Saint Bonifacius	MN	55375	**800-682-7696**	952-446-4100
Dallas Baptist University 3000 Mountain Creek Pkwy	Dallas	TX	75211	**800-460-1328**	214-333-7100
Dordt College 498 4th Ave NE	Sioux Center	IA	51250	**800-343-6738**	712-722-6000
Eastern Mennonite University 1200 Park Rd	Harrisonburg	VA	22802	**800-368-2665***	540-432-4118
*Admissions					
Eastern Nazarene College 23 E Elm Ave	Quincy	MA	02170	**800-883-6288**	617-745-3000
Erskine College PO Box 338	Due West	SC	29639	**800-241-8721**	864-379-2131
Evangel University 1111 N Glenstone Ave	Springfield	MO	65802	**800-382-6435**	417-865-2811
Fresno Pacific University 1717 S Chestnut Ave	Fresno	CA	93702	**800-660-6089**	559-453-2039
Geneva College 3200 College Ave	Beaver Falls	PA	15010	**800-847-8255**	724-846-5100
George Fox University 414 N Meridian St	Newberg	OR	97132	**800-765-4369**	503-538-8383
Gordon College 255 Grapevine Rd	Wenham	MA	01984	**800-343-1379**	978-927-2300
Goshen College 1700 S Main St	Goshen	IN	46526	**800-348-7422**	574-535-7000
Grace College 200 Seminary Dr	Winona Lake	IN	46590	**800-544-7223**	574-372-5100
Greenville College 315 E College Ave	Greenville	IL	62246	**800-345-4440**	618-664-7100
Hardin-Simmons University 2200 Hickory St	Abilene	TX	79698	**800-568-2692**	325-670-1000
Hope International University 2500 E Nutwood Ave	Fullerton	CA	92831	**800-762-1294**	714-879-3901
Houghton College 1 Willard Ave	Houghton	NY	14744	**800-777-2556**	585-567-9200
Houston Baptist University 7502 Fondren Rd	Houston	TX	77074	**800-969-3210**	281-649-3000
Howard Payne University 1000 Fisk Ave	Brownwood	TX	76801	**800-950-8465**	325-646-2502
Huntington College 2303 College Ave	Huntington	IN	46750	**800-642-6493**	260-356-6000
Indiana Wesleyan University 4201 S Washington St	Marion	IN	46953	**800-332-6901**	765-677-2138
Judson College 302 Bibb St	Marion	AL	36756	**800-447-9472**	334-683-6161
Kentucky Christian University 100 Academic Pkwy	Grayson	KY	41143	**800-522-3181***	606-474-3000
*Admissions					
King College 1350 King College Rd	Bristol	TN	37620	**800-362-0014***	423-968-1187
*Admissions					
Lee University 1120 N Ocoee St	Cleveland	TN	37311	**800-533-9930**	423-614-8000
LeTourneau University 2100 S Mobberly	Longview	TX	75602	**800-759-8811**	903-753-0231
Lipscomb University 3901 Granny White Pike	Nashville	TN	37204	**800-333-4358**	615-269-1000
Malone College 515 25th St NW	Canton	OH	44709	**800-521-1146**	330-471-8100
Master's College 21726 Placerita Canyon Rd	Santa Clarita	CA	91321	**800-568-6248**	661-259-3540
Messiah College 1 College Ave	Grantham	PA	17027	**800-233-4220**	717-766-2511
MidAmerica Nazarene University 2030 E College Way	Olathe	KS	66062	**800-800-8887**	913-782-3750
Mississippi College 200 S Capitol St	Clinton	MS	39058	**800-738-1236**	601-925-3000
Montreat College 310 Gaither Cir	Montreat	NC	28757	**800-622-6968**	828-669-8011
Mount Vernon Nazarene University 800 Martinsburg Rd	Mount Vernon	OH	43050	**800-782-2435**	740-397-1244
North Greenville College PO Box 1892	Tigerville	SC	29688	**800-468-6642**	864-977-7000
North Park University 3225 W Foster Ave	Chicago	IL	60625	**800-888-6728**	773-244-5500
Northwest Christian College 828 E 11th Ave	Eugene	OR	97401	**877-463-6622**	541-343-1641
Northwest Nazarene University 623 Holly St	Nampa	ID	83686	**877-668-4968***	208-467-8011
*Admissions					
Northwest University 5520 108th Ave NE	Kirkland	WA	98033	**800-669-3781***	425-822-8266
*Admissions					
Northwestern College 101 7th St SW	Orange City	IA	51041	**800-747-4757**	712-707-7000
Northwestern College 3003 Snelling Ave N	Saint Paul	MN	55113	**800-827-6827***	651-631-5100
*Admissions					
Nyack College 1 South Blvd	Nyack	NY	10960	**800-336-9225***	845-358-1710
*Admissions					
Oklahoma Christian University PO Box 11000	Oklahoma City	OK	73136	**800-877-5010**	405-425-5000
Olivet Nazarene University 1 University Ave	Bourbonnais	IL	60914	**800-648-1463**	815-939-5011
Oral Roberts University 7777 S Lewis Ave	Tulsa	OK	74171	**800-678-8876**	918-495-6161
Palm Beach Atlantic University PO Box 24708	West Palm Beach	FL	33416	**888-468-6722**	561-803-2000
Redeemer University College 777 Garner Rd E	Ancaster	ON	L9K1J4	**877-779-0913**	905-648-2131
Roberts Wesleyan College 2301 Westside Dr	Rochester	NY	14624	**800-777-4792***	585-594-6000
*Admissions					
Seattle Pacific University 3307 3rd Ave W	Seattle	WA	98119	**800-366-3344**	206-281-2000
Simpson University 2211 College View Dr	Redding	CA	96003	**800-598-2493**	530-226-4606
Southeastern University 1000 Longfellow Blvd	Lakeland	FL	33801	**800-500-8760**	863-667-5000
Southern Nazarene University 6729 NW 39th Expy	Bethany	OK	73008	**800-648-9899**	405-789-6400
Southern Wesleyan University 907 Wesleyan Dr	Central	SC	29630	**800-282-8798**	864-644-5000
Southwest Baptist University 1600 University Ave	Bolivar	MO	65613	**800-526-5859**	417-326-5281
Spring Arbor University 106 E Main St	Spring Arbor	MI	49283	**800-968-0011**	517-750-1200
Sterling College 125 W Cooper	Sterling	KS	67579	**800-346-1017**	620-278-2173
Tabor College 400 S Jefferson St	Hillsboro	KS	67063	**800-822-6799**	620-947-3121
Taylor University 236 W Reade Ave	Upland	IN	46989	**800-882-3456**	765-998-2751
Trevecca Nazarene University 333 Murfreesboro Rd	Nashville	TN	37210	**888-210-4868**	615-248-1200
Trinity Christian College 6601 W College Dr	Palos Heights	IL	60463	**800-748-0085**	708-597-3000
Trinity International University 2065 Half Day Rd	Deerfield	IL	60015	**800-822-3225**	847-317-7000
Trinity Western University 7600 Glover Rd	Langley	BC	V2Y1Y1	**888-468-6898**	604-888-7511
Union University 1050 Union University Dr	Jackson	TN	38305	**800-338-6466**	731-661-5210
University of Sioux Falls 1101 W 22nd St	Sioux Falls	SD	57105	**800-888-1047**	605-331-5000
Vanguard University of Southern California 55 Fair Dr	Costa Mesa	CA	92626	**800-722-6279***	714-556-3610
*Admissions					
Warner Pacific College 2219 SE 68th Ave	Portland	OR	97215	**800-582-7885**	503-775-4366
Warner Southern College 13895 Hwy 27	Lake Wales	FL	33859	**800-949-7248**	863-638-1426
Wayland Baptist University 1900 W 7th St	Plainview	TX	79072	**800-588-1928**	806-291-1000
Waynesburg College 51 W College St	Waynesburg	PA	15370	**800-225-7393**	724-627-8191
Western Baptist College 5000 Deer Pk Dr SE	Salem	OR	97301	**800-845-3005**	503-581-8600
Westmont College 955 La Paz Rd	Santa Barbara	CA	93108	**800-777-9011**	805-565-6000
Wheaton College 501 E College Ave	Wheaton	IL	60187	**800-222-2419**	630-752-5000
Whitworth College 300 W Hawthorne Rd	Spokane	WA	99251	**800-533-4668**	509-777-1000
William Tyndale College 35700 W 12 Mile Rd	Farmington Hills	MI	48331	**800-483-0707**	248-553-7200
Williams Baptist College 60 W Fulbright St	Walnut Ridge	AR	72476	**800-722-4434**	870-886-6741

163 COLLEGES & UNIVERSITIES - FOUR-YEAR

SEE ALSO Colleges & Universities - Christian; Colleges & Universities - Graduate & Professional Schools; Colleges & Universities - Historically Black; Colleges & Universities - Jesuit; Colleges - Business; Colleges - Fine Arts; Colleges - Junior; Military Service Academies; Universities - Canadian; Vocational & Technical Schools

Alabama

Name / Address	City	State	ZIP	Toll-Free	Phone
Alabama State University 915 S Jackson St	Montgomery	AL	36104	**800-253-5037**	334-229-4100
Athens State University 300 N Beaty St	Athens	AL	35611	**800-522-0272**	256-233-8100
Auburn University 202 Mary Martin Hall	Auburn University	AL	36849	**800-282-8769**	334-844-6425
Montgomery PO Box 244023	Montgomery	AL	36124	**800-227-2649**	334-244-3000
Birmingham-Southern College 900 Arkadelphia Rd	Birmingham	AL	35254	**800-523-5793**	205-226-4600
Faulkner University 5345 Atlanta Hwy	Montgomery	AL	36109	**800-879-9816**	334-272-5820
Heritage Christian University 3625 Helton Dr PO Box HCU	Florence	AL	35630	**800-367-3565**	256-766-6610
Huntingdon College 1500 E Fairview Ave	Montgomery	AL	36106	**800-763-0313**	334-833-4497
Jacksonville State University 700 Pelham Rd N	Jacksonville	AL	36265	**800-231-5291**	256-782-5781
Judson College 302 Bibb St	Marion	AL	36756	**800-447-9472**	334-683-6161
Miles College 5500 Myron Massey Blvd	Fairfield	AL	35064	**800-445-0708**	205-929-1000
Oakwood College 7000 Adventist Blvd	Huntsville	AL	35896	**800-824-5312**	256-726-7356
Samford University 800 Lakeshore Dr	Birmingham	AL	35229	**800-888-7218**	205-726-3673
Southern Christian University 1200 Taylor Rd	Montgomery	AL	36117	**800-351-4040**	334-387-3877
Spring Hill College 4000 Dauphin St	Mobile	AL	36608	**800-742-6704**	251-380-4000
Stillman College PO Box 1430	Tuscaloosa	AL	35403	**800-841-5722***	205-349-4240
*Admissions					
Troy State University 600 University Ave	Troy	AL	36082	**800-551-9716**	334-670-3100
Montgomery PO Drawer 4419	Montgomery	AL	36103	**800-355-8786**	334-834-1400
Phenix City Campus 1 University Pl	Phenix City	AL	36869	**888-876-9787**	334-297-1007
Tuskegee University	Tuskegee	AL	36088	**800-622-6531***	334-727-8011
*Admissions					
University of Alabama Box 870132	Tuscaloosa	AL	35487	**800-933-2262**	205-348-6010

Alabama (Cont'd)

				Toll-Free	Phone
University of Alabama at Birmingham 1530 3rd Ave S HUC260	Birmingham	AL	35294	**800-421-8743**	205-934-4011
University of Alabama in Huntsville 301 Sparkman Dr.	Huntsville	AL	35899	**800-824-2255**	256-824-6070
University of Mobile 5735 College Pkwy	Mobile	AL	36613	**800-946-7267**	251-675-5990
University of Montevallo Station 6030	Montevallo	AL	35115	**800-292-4349**	205-665-6030
University of North Alabama 1 Harrison Plaza	Florence	AL	35632	**800-825-5862**	256-765-4100
University of South Alabama 307 University Blvd	Mobile	AL	36688	**800-872-5247**	251-460-6101
University of West Alabama Station 4 UWA	Livingston	AL	35470	**800-621-8044**	205-652-3400

Alaska

				Toll-Free	Phone
Alaska Bible College PO Box 289	Glennallen	AK	99588	**800-478-7884**	907-822-3201
Alaska Pacific University 4101 University Dr.	Anchorage	AK	99508	**800-252-7528**	907-564-8248
Sheldon Jackson College 801 Lincoln St.	Sitka	AK	99835	**800-478-4556**	907-747-5221
University of Alaska Fairbanks PO Box 757480	Fairbanks	AK	99775	**800-478-1823**	907-474-7500
Northwest Campus 400 E Front St Pouch 400	Nome	AK	99702	**800-478-2202**	907-443-2201
University of Alaska Southeast Juneau Campus 11120 Glacier Hwy.	Juneau	AK	99801	**877-465-4827**	907-465-6457

Arizona

				Toll-Free	Phone
American Indian College of the Assemblies of God 10020 N 15th Ave	Phoenix	AZ	85021	**800-933-3828**	602-944-3335
Embry-Riddle Aeronautical University Prescott Campus 3700 Willow Creek Rd.	Prescott	AZ	86301	**800-888-3728**	928-777-3728
Grand Canyon University 3300 W Camelback Rd	Phoenix	AZ	85017	**800-800-9776**	602-249-3300
International Baptist College 2150 E Southern Ave.	Tempe	AZ	85282	**800-422-4858**	480-838-7070
Northern Arizona University PO Box 4084	Flagstaff	AZ	86011	**888-667-3628**	928-523-5511
Ottawa University 10020 N 25th Ave	Phoenix	AZ	85021	**800-235-9586**	602-371-1188
Ottawa University 10020 N 25th Ave	Phoenix	AZ	85021	**800-235-9586**	602-371-1188
Ottawa University 13402 N Scottsdale Rd Suite B170	Scottsdale	AZ	85254	**800-235-9586**	602-749-5184
Prescott College 220 Grove Ave	Prescott	AZ	86301	**877-350-2100**	928-778-2090
Southwestern College 2625 E Cactus Rd.	Phoenix	AZ	85032	**800-247-2697**	602-992-6101
University of Phoenix 4605 E Elwood St	Phoenix	AZ	85040	**800-776-4867**	480-966-7400

Arkansas

				Toll-Free	Phone
Arkansas State University PO Box 1630	State University	AR	72467	**800-643-0080**	870-972-3024
Arkansas Tech University 1605 Coliseum Dr	Russellville	AR	72801	**800-582-6953**	479-968-0389
Harding University 900 E Center Ave	Searcy	AR	72149	**800-477-4407**	501-279-4000
Henderson State University 1100 Henderson St	Arkadelphia	AR	71999	**800-228-7333**	870-230-5000
Hendrix College 1600 Washington Ave.	Conway	AR	72032	**800-277-9017**	501-329-6811
Lyon College PO Box 2317	Batesville	AR	72503	**800-423-2542**	870-793-9813
Ouachita Baptist University 410 Ouachita St	Arkadelphia	AR	71998	**800-342-5628**	870-245-5000
Philander Smith College 1 Trudie Kibbe Reed Dr	Little Rock	AR	72202	**800-446-6772**	501-375-9845
Southern Arkansas University 100 E University St	Magnolia	AR	71753	**800-332-7286**	870-235-4000
University of Arkansas 232 Hunt Hall	Fayetteville	AR	72701	**800-377-8632**	479-575-5346
University of Arkansas - Monticello PO Box 3600	Monticello	AR	71656	**800-844-1826**	870-367-6811
University of Arkansas Pine Bluff 1200 N University Dr *Admissions	Pine Bluff	AR	71601	**800-264-6585***	870-575-8000
University of the Ozarks 415 N College Ave	Clarksville	AR	72830	**800-264-8636**	479-754-3839
Williams Baptist College 60 W Fulbright St	Walnut Ridge	AR	72476	**800-722-4434**	870-886-6741

California

				Toll-Free	Phone
Academy of Art University 79 New Montgomery St.	San Francisco	CA	94105	**800-544-2787**	415-274-2200
Alliant International University 10455 Pomerado Rd	San Diego	CA	92131	**866-825-5426**	858-271-4300
American InterContinental University Los Angeles 12655 W Jefferson Blvd	Los Angeles	CA	90066	**800-333-2652**	310-302-2000
Art Institute of California-San Francisco 1170 Market St	San Francisco	CA	94102	**888-493-3261**	415-865-0198
Azusa Pacific University 1915 W Orangewood Ave	Orange	CA	92868	**800-272-0111**	714-935-0260
Bethany College of the Assemblies of God 800 Bethany Dr	Scotts Valley	CA	95066	**800-843-9410**	831-438-3800
Biola University 13800 Biola Ave *Admissions	La Mirada	CA	90639	**800-652-4652***	562-903-6000
Brooks Institute of Photography 801 Alston Rd	Santa Barbara	CA	93108	**888-304-3456**	805-966-3888
California Baptist University 8432 Magnolia Ave	Riverside	CA	92504	**877-228-8866**	951-689-5771
California College of Arts & Crafts 1111 8th St	San Francisco	CA	94107	**800-447-1278**	415-703-9500
California Institute of the Arts 24700 McBean Pkwy	Valencia	CA	91355	**800-545-2787**	661-255-1050
California Institute of Technology 1200 E California Blvd	Pasadena	CA	91125	**800-568-8324**	626-395-6811
California Lutheran University 60 W Olsen Rd	Thousand Oaks	CA	91360	**877-258-3678**	805-493-3135
California Maritime Academy 200 Maritime Academy Dr	Vallejo	CA	94590	**800-561-1945**	707-654-1000
California Pacific University 1017 E Grand Ave	Escondido	CA	92025	**800-458-9667**	760-739-7730
California State University Bakersfield 9001 Stockdale Hwy	Bakersfield	CA	93311	**800-788-2782**	661-664-2011
California State University Chico	Chico	CA	959290722	**800-542-4426**	530-898-6321
Christian Heritage College 2100 Greenfield Dr	El Cajon	CA	92019	**800-676-2242**	619-441-2200
City University Los Angeles PO Box 4277	Inglewood	CA	90309	**800-262-8388**	310-671-0783
Cogswell Polytechnical College 1175 Bordeaux Dr	Sunnyvale	CA	94089	**800-264-7955**	408-541-0100
Coleman College 7380 Parkway Dr	La Mesa	CA	91942	**800-430-2030**	619-465-3990
Concordia University 1530 Concordia W	Irvine	CA	92612	**800-229-1200**	949-854-8002
Fresno Pacific University 1717 S Chestnut Ave.	Fresno	CA	93702	**800-660-6089**	559-453-2039
Hebrew Union College Los Angeles 3077 University Ave	Los Angeles	CA	90007	**800-899-0925**	213-749-3424
Hope International University 2500 E Nutwood Ave	Fullerton	CA	92831	**800-762-1294**	714-879-3901
Humboldt State University 1 Harpst St	Arcata	CA	95521	**866-850-9556**	707-826-3011
John F Kennedy University 100 Ellinwood Way	Pleasant Hill	CA	94523	**800-696-5358**	925-969-3300
Kennedy-Western University 30301 Agoura Rd	Agoura Hills	CA	91301	**800-635-2900**	818-707-4300
La Sierra University 4500 Riverwalk Pkwy	Riverside	CA	92515	**800-874-5587**	951-785-2000
Laguna College of Art & Design 2222 Laguna Canyon Rd	Laguna Beach	CA	92651	**800-255-0762**	949-376-6000
Loyola Marymount University 1 LMU Dr	Los Angeles	CA	90045	**800-568-4636**	310-338-2700
Master's College 21726 Placerita Canyon Rd	Santa Clarita	CA	91321	**800-568-6248**	661-259-3540
Menlo College 1000 El Camino Real	Atherton	CA	94027	**800-556-3656**	650-543-3753
Mills College 5000 MacArthur Blvd	Oakland	CA	94613	**800-876-4557**	510-430-2135
Monterey Institute of International Studies 460 Pierce St	Monterey	CA	93940	**800-824-7235**	831-647-4123
Mount Saint Mary's College 12001 Chalon Rd	Los Angeles	CA	90049	**800-999-9893**	310-954-4250
National University 11255 N Torrey Pines Rd	La Jolla	CA	92037	**800-628-8648**	858-642-8000
New College of California 50 Fell St	San Francisco	CA	94102	**800-335-6262**	415-241-1300
Notre Dame de Namur University 1500 Ralston Ave.	Belmont	CA	94002	**800-263-0545**	650-508-3600
Occidental College 1600 Campus Rd.	Los Angeles	CA	90041	**800-825-5262**	323-259-2700
Otis College of Art & Design 9045 Lincoln Blvd	Los Angeles	CA	90045	**800-527-6847**	310-665-6820
Pacific Union College 1 Angwin Ave	Angwin	CA	94508	**800-862-7080**	707-965-6311
Pacific Western University 1650 Westwood Blvd Suite 205	Los Angeles	CA	90024	**800-423-3244**	310-446-5503
Patten University 2433 Coolidge Ave	Oakland	CA	94601	**877-472-8836**	510-261-8500
Pitzer College 1050 N Mills Ave	Claremont	CA	91711	**800-748-9371**	909-621-8129
Rudolf Steiner College 9200 Fair Oaks Blvd	Fair Oaks	CA	95628	**800-515-8203**	916-961-8727
Saint Mary's College of California 1928 St Mary's Rd	Moraga	CA	94575	**800-800-4762**	925-631-4000
Samuel Merritt College 370 Hawthorne Ave	Oakland	CA	94609	**800-607-6377**	510-869-6576
San Francisco Art Institute 800 Chestnut St	San Francisco	CA	94133	**800-345-7324**	415-771-7020
Scripps College 1030 Columbia Ave	Claremont	CA	91711	**800-770-1333**	909-621-8000
Simpson University 2211 College View Dr	Redding	CA	96003	**800-598-2493**	530-226-4606
South Baylo University 1126 N Brookhurst St	Anaheim	CA	92801	**888-642-2956**	714-533-1495
Thomas Aquinas College 10000 N Ojai Rd	Santa Paula	CA	93060	**800-634-9797**	805-525-4417
University of Judaism 15600 Mulholland Dr	Los Angeles	CA	90077	**888-853-6763**	310-476-9777
University of the Pacific 3601 Pacific Ave	Stockton	CA	95211	**800-959-2867**	209-946-2011
University of Redlands 1200 E Colton Ave PO Box 3080	Redlands	CA	92374	**800-455-5064**	909-335-4074
University of San Diego 5998 Alcala Pk	San Diego	CA	92110	**800-248-4873**	619-260-4600
University of San Francisco 2130 Fulton St *Admissions	San Francisco	CA	94117	**800-225-5873***	415-422-5555
University of La Verne 1950 3rd St	La Verne	CA	91750	**800-876-4858**	909-593-3511
Vanguard University of Southern California 55 Fair Dr *Admissions	Costa Mesa	CA	92626	**800-722-6279***	714-556-3610
Weimar Institute 20601 W Paoli Ln PO Box 486	Weimar	CA	95736	**800-525-9192**	530-637-4111
Westmont College 955 La Paz Rd	Santa Barbara	CA	93108	**800-777-9011**	805-565-6000
William Howard Taft University 201 E Sandpointe Ave Suite 400	Santa Ana	CA	92707	**800-882-4555**	714-850-4800
Woodbury University 7500 Glenoaks Blvd	Burbank	CA	91510	**800-784-9663**	818-767-0888

Colorado

				Toll-Free	Phone
Adams State College 208 Edgemont Blvd	Alamosa	CO	81102	**800-824-6494**	719-587-7712
Beth-El College of Nursing & Health Sciences 1420 Austin Bluffs Pkwy	Colorado Springs	CO	80933	**800-990-8227**	719-262-4422
Colorado Christian University 3800 Automation Way Suite 101	Fort Collins	CO	80525	**800-443-2484**	970-223-8505
Colorado Christian University 8787 W Alameda Ave	Lakewood	CO	80226	**800-443-2484**	303-963-3200
Colorado College 14 E Cache La Poudre St	Colorado Springs	CO	80903	**800-542-7214**	719-389-6344
Colorado School of Mines 1500 Illinois St	Golden	CO	80401	**800-446-9488**	303-273-3000
Mesa State College 1100 North Ave	Grand Junction	CO	81501	**800-982-6372**	970-248-1020
Regis University 3333 Regis Blvd	Denver	CO	80221	**800-568-8932**	303-458-4100
Regis University 1501 Academy Ct	Fort Collins	CO	80524	**800-390-0891**	970-472-2200
Colorado Springs 7450 Campus Dr	Colorado Springs	CO	80920	**800-568-8932**	
University of Colorado at Colorado Springs PO Box 7150	Colorado Springs	CO	80933	**800-990-8227**	719-262-3000
University of Denver 2199 S University Blvd	Denver	CO	80208	**800-525-9495**	303-871-2036
University of Northern Colorado 501 20th St	Greeley	CO	80639	**888-700-4862**	970-351-2881
US Air Force Academy Dept of the Air Force Headquarters USAFA	USAF Academy	CO	80840	**800-379-1455**	719-333-1110
Western State College of Colorado 600 N Adams St College Heights	Gunnison	CO	81231	**800-876-5309**	970-943-0120

Connecticut

				Toll-Free	Phone
Albertus Magnus College 700 Prospect St	New Haven	CT	06511	**800-578-9160**	203-773-8550
Connecticut College 270 Mohegan Ave	New London	CT	06320	**888-553-8760**	860-439-2000
Eastern Connecticut State University 83 Windham St	Willimantic	CT	06226	**877-353-3278**	860-465-5000

				Toll-Free	Phone
Quinnipiac University 275 Mt Carmel Ave	Hamden	CT	06518	**800-462-1944**	203-582-8200
Teikyo Post University 800 Country Club Rd	Waterbury	CT	06723	**800-345-2562**	203-596-4500
University of Bridgeport 126 Park Ave	Bridgeport	CT	06604	**800-392-3582**	203-576-4000
University of Hartford					
200 Bloomfield Ave	West Hartford	CT	06117	**800-947-4303**	860-768-4296
University of New Haven					
300 Boston Post Rd	West Haven	CT	06516	**800-342-5864**	203-932-7000
US Coast Guard Academy					
15 Mohegan Ave	New London	CT	06320	**800-883-8724**	860-444-8444
Western Connecticut State University					
181 White St	Danbury	CT	06810	**877-837-9278**	203-837-8200

Delaware

				Toll-Free	Phone
Goldey Beacom College					
4701 Limestone Rd	Wilmington	DE	19808	**800-833-4877**	302-998-8814
Wesley College 120 N State St	Dover	DE	19901	**800-937-5398**	302-736-2300
Wilmington College 320 N DuPont Hwy	New Castle	DE	19720	**877-967-5464**	302-328-9401

District of Columbia

				Toll-Free	Phone
Catholic University of America					
620 Michigan Ave NE	Washington	DC	20064	**800-673-2772**	202-319-5000
Corcoran College of Art & Design					
500 17th St NW	Washington	DC	20006	**888-267-2672**	202-639-1800
George Washington University					
2121 'I' St NW	Washington	DC	20052	**800-447-3765**	202-994-1000
Mount Vernon College					
2100 Foxhall Rd NW	Washington	DC	20007	**800-447-3765**	202-242-6672
Howard University 2400 6th St NW	Washington	DC	20059	**800-822-6363**	202-806-6100
Mount Vernon College					
2100 Foxhall Rd NW	Washington	DC	20007	**800-447-3765**	202-242-6672
Strayer University 1133 15th St NW	Washington	DC	20005	**888-360-1588**	202-408-2400
Takoma Park Campus					
6830 Laurel St NW	Washington	DC	20012	**877-722-8100**	202-722-8100

Florida

				Toll-Free	Phone
Baptist College of Florida 5400 College Dr	Graceville	FL	32440	**800-328-2660**	850-263-3261
Barry University 11300 NE 2nd Ave	Miami Shores	FL	33161	**800-756-6000**	305-899-3000
Bethune-Cookman College					
640 Mary McLeod Bethune Blvd	Daytona Beach	FL	32114	**800-448-0228**	386-255-1401
Clearwater Christian College					
3400 Gulf to Bay Blvd	Clearwater	FL	33759	**800-348-4463**	727-726-1153
Eckerd College 4200 54th Ave S	Saint Petersburg	FL	33711	**800-456-9009**	727-867-1166
Edward Waters College 1658 Kings Rd	Jacksonville	FL	32209	**888-898-3191***	904-366-2715
*Admissions					
Embry-Riddle Aeronautical University					
Daytona Beach Campus 600 S Clyde					
Morris Blvd	Daytona Beach	FL	32114	**800-862-2416**	386-226-6000
Flagler College 74 King St	Saint Augustine	FL	32084	**800-304-4208**	904-829-6481
Florida Atlantic University 777 Glades Rd	Boca Raton	FL	33431	**800-299-4328**	561-297-3000
Davie Campus 2912 College Ave	Davie	FL	33314	**800-764-2222**	954-236-1000
Fort Lauderdale Campus					
111 E Las Olas Blvd	Fort Lauderdale	FL	33301	**800-764-2222**	954-762-5200
Florida Christian College					
1011 Bill Beck Blvd	Kissimmee	FL	34744	**888-468-6322**	407-847-8966
Florida Gulf Coast University					
10501 FGCU Blvd S	Fort Myers	FL	33965	**888-889-1095**	239-590-1000
Florida Institute of Technology					
150 W University Blvd	Melbourne	FL	32901	**800-888-4348**	321-674-8000
Florida Metropolitan University					
Orlando North 5421 Diplomat Cir	Orlando	FL	32810	**800-628-5870**	407-628-5870
Pinellas					
2471 McMullen Booth Rd Suite 200	Clearwater	FL	33759	**800-353-3687**	727-725-2688
Pompano Beach					
225 N Federal Hwy	Pompano Beach	FL	33062	**800-468-0168**	954-783-7339
Florida Southern College					
111 Lake Hollingsworth Dr	Lakeland	FL	33801	**800-274-4131**	863-680-4131
Florida State University Panama City					
Campus 4750 Collegiate Dr	Panama City	FL	32405	**866-539-7588**	850-872-4750
Hobe Sound Bible College PO Box 1065	Hobe Sound	FL	33475	**800-881-5534**	772-546-5534
International Academy of Design					
5225 Memorial Hwy	Tampa	FL	33634	**800-222-3369**	813-881-0007
International College Fort Myers Campus					
8695 College Pkwy Suite 217	Fort Myers	FL	33919	**800-466-0019**	239-482-0019
Jacksonville University					
2800 University Blvd N	Jacksonville	FL	32211	**800-225-2027**	904-256-8000
Jones College 5353 Arlington Expy	Jacksonville	FL	32211	**800-331-0176**	904-743-1122
Logos Christian College					
8159 Arlington Expy Suite 29	Jacksonville	FL	32211	**800-252-4253**	904-745-3311
Lynn University 3601 N Military Trail	Boca Raton	FL	33431	**800-544-8035**	561-237-7900
Northwood University Florida Campus					
2600 N Military Trail	West Palm Beach	FL	33409	**800-458-8325**	561-478-5500
Nova Southeastern University					
3301 College Ave	Fort Lauderdale	FL	33314	**800-541-6682**	954-262-8000
Palm Beach Atlantic University					
PO Box 24708	West Palm Beach	FL	33416	**888-468-6722**	561-803-2000
Pensacola Christian College 250 Brent Ln	Pensacola	FL	32503	**800-722-4636**	850-478-8496
Ringling School of Art & Design					
2700 N Tamiami Trail	Sarasota	FL	34234	**800-255-7695**	941-351-5100
Saint Thomas University 16401 NW 37th Ave	Miami	FL	33054	**800-367-9010**	305-628-6546
Southeastern University					
1000 Longfellow Blvd	Lakeland	FL	33801	**800-500-8760**	863-667-5000
Stetson University 421 N Woodland Blvd	DeLand	FL	32723	**800-688-0101**	386-822-7000
Tampa Technical Institute 2410 E Bush Blvd	Tampa	FL	33612	**800-992-4850**	813-935-5700
Trinity International University South Florida					
Campus 111 NW 183rd St Suite 500	Miami	FL	33169	**877-392-3586**	305-770-5100
University of Saint Augustine					
1 University Blvd	Saint Augustine	FL	32086	**800-241-1027**	904-826-0084
University of South Florida					
Lakeland Campus 3433 Winter Lake Rd	Lakeland	FL	33803	**800-873-5636**	863-667-7000
Tampa Campus 4202 E Fowler Ave	Tampa	FL	33620	**877-873-2855**	813-974-2011
University of Tampa 401 W Kennedy Blvd	Tampa	FL	33606	**800-733-4773**	813-253-6228
University of West Florida					
11000 University Pkwy	Pensacola	FL	32514	**800-263-1074**	850-474-2000
Warner Southern College 13895 Hwy 27	Lake Wales	FL	33859	**800-949-7248**	863-638-1426
Webber International University					
1201 N Scenic Hwy	Babson Park	FL	33827	**800-741-1844**	863-638-1431

Georgia

				Toll-Free	Phone
Agnes Scott College 141 E College Ave	Decatur	GA	30030	**800-868-8602**	404-471-6000
Albany State University 504 College Dr	Albany	GA	31705	**800-822-7267**	229-430-4600
American InterContinental University Atlanta					
3330 Peachtree Rd NE	Atlanta	GA	30326	**800-255-6839**	404-965-5700
Armstrong Atlantic State University					
11935 Abercorn St	Savannah	GA	31419	**800-633-2349**	912-927-5275
Atlanta Christian College 2605 Ben Hill Rd	East Point	GA	30344	**800-776-1222**	404-761-8861
Atlanta College of Art 1280 Peachtree St NE	Atlanta	GA	30309	**800-832-2104**	404-733-5001
Augusta State University 2500 Walton Way	Augusta	GA	30904	**800-341-4373**	706-737-1632
Berry College 2277 Martha Berry Hwy	Mount Berry	GA	30149	**800-237-7942**	706-232-5374
Brenau University 1 Centennial Cir	Gainesville	GA	30501	**800-252-5119**	770-534-6299
Brewton-Parker College Hwy 280	Mount Vernon	GA	30445	**800-342-1087**	912-583-2241
Clark Atlanta University					
223 James P Brawley Dr SW	Atlanta	GA	30314	**800-688-3228***	404-880-8000
*Admissions					
Columbus State University					
4225 University Ave	Columbus	GA	31907	**866-264-2035**	706-568-2001
Emory University 200 Jones Ctr	Atlanta	GA	30322	**800-727-6036**	404-727-6036
Georgia College & State University					
231 W Hancock St CB 23	Milledgeville	GA	31061	**800-342-0471**	478-445-5004
Georgia Southwestern State University					
800 Wheatley St	Americus	GA	31709	**800-338-0082**	229-928-1273
LaGrange College 601 Broad St	LaGrange	GA	30240	**800-593-2885**	706-880-8000
Medical College of Georgia 1120 15th St	Augusta	GA	30912	**800-736-2273**	706-721-0211
Mercer University 1400 Coleman Ave	Macon	GA	31207	**800-637-2378**	478-301-2700
Morehouse College 830 Westview Dr SW	Atlanta	GA	30314	**800-851-1254***	404-681-2800
*Admissions					
North Georgia College & State University	Dahlonega	GA	30597	**800-498-9581**	706-864-1800
Oglethorpe University 4484 Peachtree Rd NE	Atlanta	GA	30319	**800-428-4484**	404-261-1441
Paine College 1235 15th St	Augusta	GA	30901	**800-476-7703**	706-821-8200
Piedmont College 165 Central Ave	Demorest	GA	30535	**800-277-7020**	706-778-8033
Reinhardt College 7300 Reinhardt College Cir	Waleska	GA	30183	**877-346-4273**	770-720-5600
Savannah College of Art & Design					
PO Box 2072	Savannah	GA	31402	**800-869-7223**	912-525-5100
Shorter College 315 Shorter Ave	Rome	GA	30165	**800-868-6980**	706-233-7319
Southern Polytechnic State University					
1100 S Marietta Pkwy	Marietta	GA	30060	**800-635-3204**	678-915-4188
Spelman College 350 Spelman Ln SW	Atlanta	GA	30314	**800-982-2411***	404-681-3643
*Admissions					
Toccoa Falls College 328 Chappel Dr	Toccoa Falls	GA	30598	**800-868-3257**	706-886-6831
Valdosta State University					
1500 N Patterson St	Valdosta	GA	31698	**800-618-1878**	229-333-5800
Wesleyan College 4760 Forsyth Rd	Macon	GA	31210	**800-447-6610**	478-477-1110

Hawaii

				Toll-Free	Phone
Chaminade University 3140 Waialae Ave	Honolulu	HI	96816	**800-735-3733**	808-735-4711
Hawaii Pacific University					
1164 Bishop St Suite 200	Honolulu	HI	96813	**866-225-5478**	808-544-0237
Windward Hawaii Loa Campus					
45-045 Kamehameha Hwy	Kaneohe	HI	96744	**866-225-5478**	808-236-3500
University of Hawaii					
Hilo 200 W Kawili St	Hilo	HI	96720	**800-897-4456**	808-974-7414
Manoa 2600 Campus Rd Rm 001	Honolulu	HI	96822	**800-823-9771**	808-956-8975
West Oahu 96-129 Ala Ike	Pearl City	HI	96782	**866-299-8656**	808-454-4742

Idaho

				Toll-Free	Phone
Albertson College of Idaho					
2112 Cleveland Blvd	Caldwell	ID	83605	**800-224-3246**	208-459-5011
Boise Bible College 8695 W Marigold St	Boise	ID	83714	**800-893-7755**	208-376-7731
Boise State University 1910 University Dr	Boise	ID	83725	**800-824-7017**	208-426-1156
Lewis-Clark State College 500 8th Ave	Lewiston	ID	83501	**800-933-5272**	208-792-2210
Northwest Nazarene University 623 Holly St	Nampa	ID	83686	**877-668-4968***	208-467-8011
*Admissions					
University of Idaho PO Box 444264	Moscow	ID	83844	**888-884-3246**	208-885-6111
Boise 322 E Front St	Boise	ID	83702	**866-264-7384**	208-334-2999

Illinois

				Toll-Free	Phone
Augustana College 639 38th St	Rock Island	IL	61201	**800-798-8100**	309-794-7000
Aurora University 347 S Gladstone Ave	Aurora	IL	60506	**800-742-5281**	630-844-5533
Benedictine University 5700 College Rd	Lisle	IL	60532	**888-829-6363**	630-829-6000
Blackburn College 700 College Ave	Carlinville	IL	62626	**800-233-3550**	217-854-3231
Bradley University 1501 W Bradley Ave	Peoria	IL	61625	**800-447-6460**	309-676-7611
Concordia University 7400 Augusta St	River Forest	IL	60305	**800-285-2668**	708-771-8300
DePaul University 1 E Jackson Blvd 9th Fl	Chicago	IL	60604	**800-433-7285**	312-362-8300
Eastern Illinois University 600 Lincoln Ave	Charleston	IL	61920	**800-252-5711**	217-581-5000
Elmhurst College 190 Prospect Ave	Elmhurst	IL	60126	**800-697-1871**	630-617-3400
Eureka College 300 E College Ave	Eureka	IL	61530	**888-438-7352**	309-467-6350
Governors State University					
1 University Pkwy	University Park	IL	60466	**800-478-8478**	708-534-5000
Greenville College 315 E College Ave	Greenville	IL	62246	**800-345-4440**	618-664-7100
Harrington College of Design					
200 W Madison St Suite 200	Chicago	IL	60606	**877-939-4975**	312-939-4975
Illinois College 1101 W College Ave	Jacksonville	IL	62650	**866-464-5265**	217-245-3000
Illinois Institute of Art					
350 N Orleans St Suite 136-L	Chicago	IL	60654	**800-351-3450**	312-280-3500
Illinois Institute of Technology 10 W 33rd St	Chicago	IL	60616	**800-448-2329**	312-567-3025
Illinois State University	Normal	IL	61790	**800-366-2478**	309-438-2111

Illinois (Cont'd)

Name / Address	City	State	Zip	Toll-Free	Phone
Illinois Wesleyan University PO Box 2900	Bloomington	IL	61702	**800-332-2498**	309-556-3031
International Academy of Design & Technology					
1 N State St Suite 400	Chicago	IL	60602	**877-222-3369**	312-980-9200
Kendall College 2408 Orrington Ave	Evanston	IL	60201	**877-588-8860**	847-866-1300
Knox College 2 E South St	Galesburg	IL	61401	**800-678-5669**	309-341-7100
Lake Forest College 555 N Sheridan Rd	Lake Forest	IL	60045	**800-828-4751**	847-234-3100
Lewis University					
1 University Pkwy Box 295	Romeoville	IL	60446	**800-897-9000**	815-838-0500
Loyola University Chicago					
820 N Michigan Ave	Chicago	IL	60611	**800-262-2373**	312-915-6000
Lake Shore Campus 6525 N Sheridan Rd	Chicago	IL	60626	**800-262-2373**	773-274-3000
School of Professional Studies					
6525 N Sheridan Rd	Chicago	IL	60626	**800-756-9652**	773-262-8100
MacMurray College 447 E College Ave	Jacksonville	IL	62650	**800-252-7485**	217-479-7000
McKendree College 701 College Rd	Lebanon	IL	62254	**800-232-7228**	618-537-4481
Millikin University 1184 W Main St	Decatur	IL	62522	**800-373-7733**	217-424-6211
Moody Bible Institute 820 N La Salle St	Chicago	IL	60610	**800-356-6639**	312-329-4400
National-Louis University 2840 Sheridan Rd	Evanston	IL	60201	**800-443-5522**	847-475-1100
Chicago Campus 122 S Michigan Ave	Chicago	IL	60603	**800-443-5522**	312-621-9650
Wheaton Campus 200 S Naperville Rd	Wheaton	IL	60187	**800-443-5522**	630-668-3838
National University of Health Sciences					
200 E Roosevelt Rd	Lombard	IL	60148	**800-826-6285**	630-629-2000
North Central College 30 N Brainard St	Naperville	IL	60540	**800-411-1861**	630-637-5800
North Park University 3225 W Foster Ave	Chicago	IL	60625	**800-888-6728**	773-244-5500
Northern Illinois University PO Box 3001	DeKalb	IL	60115	**800-892-3050**	815-753-1000
Olivet Nazarene University					
1 University Ave	Bourbonnais	IL	60914	**800-648-1463**	815-939-5011
Principia College 1 Maybeck Pl	Elsah	IL	62028	**800-277-4648**	618-374-2131
Quincy University 1800 College Ave	Quincy	IL	62301	**800-688-4295**	217-228-5210
Robert Morris College					
Chicago Campus 401 S State St	Chicago	IL	60605	**800-225-1520**	312-935-6800
Orland Park Campus 43 Orland Sq Dr	Orland Park	IL	60462	**800-225-1520**	708-460-8000
Springfield Campus 3101 Montvale Dr	Springfield	IL	62704	**800-868-9300**	217-793-2500
Rockford College 5050 E State St	Rockford	IL	61108	**800-892-2984**	815-226-4000
Roosevelt University 430 S Michigan Ave	Chicago	IL	60605	**877-277-5978**	312-341-3500
Saint Xavier University 3700 W 103rd St	Chicago	IL	60655	**800-462-9288**	773-298-3000
School of the Art Institute of Chicago					
37 S Wabash Ave	Chicago	IL	60603	**800-232-7242**	312-899-5219
Shimer College PO Box 500	Waukegan	IL	60079	**800-215-7173**	847-623-8400
Trinity Christian College					
6601 W College Dr	Palos Heights	IL	60463	**800-748-0085**	708-597-3000
Trinity International University					
2065 Half Day Rd	Deerfield	IL	60015	**800-822-3225**	847-317-7000
University of Illinois Springfield					
1 University Plaza	Springfield	IL	62703	**800-252-8533**	217-206-6174
VanderCook College of Music					
3140 S Federal St	Chicago	IL	60616	**800-448-2655**	312-225-6288
Western Illinois University 1 University Cir	Macomb	IL	61455	**877-742-5948**	309-298-1414
Wheaton College 501 E College Ave	Wheaton	IL	60187	**800-222-2419**	630-752-5000

Indiana

Name / Address	City	State	Zip	Toll-Free	Phone
Anderson University 1100 E 5th St	Anderson	IN	46012	**800-428-6414***	765-649-9071
*Admissions					
Ball State University	Muncie	IN	47306	**800-482-4278**	765-285-8300
Bethel College 1001 W McKinley Ave	Mishawaka	IN	46545	**800-422-4101**	574-257-3339
Butler University 4600 Sunset Ave	Indianapolis	IN	46208	**800-368-6852**	317-940-8000
Calumet College of Saint Joseph					
2400 New York Ave	Whiting	IN	46394	**877-700-9100**	219-473-4215
DePauw University 313 S Locust St	Greencastle	IN	46135	**800-447-2495**	765-658-4800
Earlham College 801 National Rd W	Richmond	IN	47374	**800-327-5426**	765-983-1200
Franklin College 101 Branigin Blvd	Franklin	IN	46131	**800-852-0232**	317-738-8000
Goshen College 1700 S Main St	Goshen	IN	46526	**800-348-7422**	574-535-7000
Grace College 200 Seminary Dr	Winona Lake	IN	46590	**800-544-7223**	574-372-5100
Hanover College PO Box 108	Hanover	IN	47243	**800-213-2178**	812-866-7000
Huntington College 2303 College Ave	Huntington	IN	46750	**800-642-6493**	260-356-6000
Indiana Institute of Technology					
1600 E Washington Blvd	Fort Wayne	IN	46803	**888-666-8324**	260-422-5561
Indiana State University 210 N 7th St	Terre Haute	IN	47809	**800-742-0891**	812-237-2121
Indiana University					
East Campus 2325 Chester Blvd	Richmond	IN	47374	**800-959-3278**	765-973-8200
Kokomo Campus PO Box 9003	Kokomo	IN	46904	**888-875-4485**	765-455-9217
Northwest Campus 3400 Broadway	Gary	IN	46408	**888-968-7486**	219-980-6500
South Bend Campus					
1700 Mishawaka Ave Box 7111	South Bend	IN	46634	**877-462-4872**	574-237-4111
Indiana University-Purdue University Fort					
Wayne 2101 E Coliseum Blvd	Fort Wayne	IN	46805	**800-324-4739**	260-481-6100
Indiana Wesleyan University					
4201 S Washington St	Marion	IN	46953	**800-332-6901**	765-677-2138
Manchester College					
604 E College Ave	North Manchester	IN	46962	**800-852-3648**	260-982-5000
Marian College 3200 Cold Spring Rd	Indianapolis	IN	46222	**800-772-7264**	317-955-6000
Martin University 2171 Avondale Pl	Indianapolis	IN	46218	**866-344-3114**	317-543-3235
Oakland City University 138 N Lucretia St	Oakland City	IN	47660	**800-737-5125**	812-749-4781
Rose-Hulman Institute of Technology					
5500 Wabash Ave	Terre Haute	IN	47803	**800-248-7448**	812-877-1511
Saint Mary-of-the-Woods					
College 3301 St Mary Rd	Saint Mary-of-the-Woods	IN	47876	**800-926-7692**	812-535-5106
Saint Mary's College	Notre Dame	IN	46556	**800-551-7621**	574-284-4587
Taylor University 236 W Reade Ave	Upland	IN	46989	**800-882-3456**	765-998-2751
Fort Wayne Campus					
1025 W Rudisill Blvd	Fort Wayne	IN	46807	**800-233-3922**	260-456-2111
Tri-State University 1 University Blvd	Angola	IN	46703	**800-347-4878**	260-665-4100
University of Evansville 1800 Lincoln Ave	Evansville	IN	47722	**800-423-8633**	812-479-2000
University of Indianapolis					
1400 E Hanna Ave	Indianapolis	IN	46227	**800-232-8634**	317-788-3368
University of Saint Francis 2701 Spring St	Fort Wayne	IN	46808	**800-729-4732**	260-434-3100
University of Southern Indiana					
8600 University Blvd	Evansville	IN	47712	**800-467-1965**	812-464-8600
Valparaiso University 1700 Chapel Dr	Valparaiso	IN	46383	**888-468-2576**	219-464-5000
Wabash College 301 W Wabash Ave	Crawfordsville	IN	47933	**800-492-2274**	765-362-1400

Iowa

Name / Address	City	State	Zip	Toll-Free	Phone
Briar Cliff University 3303 Rebecca St	Sioux City	IA	51104	**800-662-3303**	712-279-5321
Buena Vista University 610 W 4th St	Storm Lake	IA	50588	**800-383-2821**	712-749-2351
Central College 812 University St	Pella	IA	50219	**877-462-3687**	641-628-5285
Coe College 1220 1st Ave NE	Cedar Rapids	IA	52402	**877-225-5263**	319-399-8500
Cornell College 600 1st St W	Mount Vernon	IA	52314	**800-747-1112**	319-895-4215
Dordt College 498 4th Ave NE	Sioux Center	IA	51250	**800-343-6738**	712-722-6000
Drake University 2507 University Ave	Des Moines	IA	50311	**800-443-7253**	515-271-3181
Emmaus Bible College 2570 Asbury Rd	Dubuque	IA	52001	**800-397-2425**	563-588-8000
Franciscan University 400 N Bluff Blvd	Clinton	IA	52732	**800-242-4153**	563-242-4023
Graceland University 1 University Pl	Lamoni	IA	50140	**800-346-9208**	641-784-5000
Grand View College 1200 Grandview Ave	Des Moines	IA	50316	**800-444-6083**	515-263-2800
Grinnell College 1103 Park St	Grinnell	IA	50112	**800-247-0113**	641-269-3600
Iowa State University 100 Alumni Hall	Ames	IA	50011	**800-262-3810**	515-294-4111
Iowa Wesleyan College 601 N Main St	Mount Pleasant	IA	52641	**800-582-2383**	319-385-8021
Loras College 1450 Alta Vista St	Dubuque	IA	52001	**800-245-6727**	563-588-7100
Luther College 700 College Dr	Decorah	IA	52101	**800-458-8437**	563-387-2000
Maharishi University of Management					
1000 N 4th St	Fairfield	IA	52557	**800-369-6480**	641-472-7000
Mount Mercy College					
1330 Elmhurst Dr NE	Cedar Rapids	IA	52402	**800-248-4504**	319-368-6460
Northwestern College 101 7th St SW	Orange City	IA	51041	**800-747-4757**	712-707-7000
Saint Ambrose University 518 W Locust St	Davenport	IA	52803	**800-383-2627**	563-333-6000
Simpson College 701 N 'C' St	Indianola	IA	50125	**800-362-2454**	515-961-6251
University of Dubuque 2000 University Ave	Dubuque	IA	52001	**800-722-5583**	563-589-3000
University of Northern Iowa					
1222 W 27th St	Cedar Falls	IA	50614	**800-772-2037**	319-273-2281
Upper Iowa University PO Box 1859	Fayette	IA	52142	**800-553-4150**	563-425-5200
Vennard College					
2300 8th Ave E PO Box 29	University Park	IA	52595	**800-686-8391**	641-673-8391
Wartburg College 100 Wartburg Blvd	Waverly	IA	50677	**800-772-2085**	319-352-8200
William Penn College 201 Trueblood Ave	Oskaloosa	IA	52577	**800-779-7366**	641-673-1001

Kansas

Name / Address	City	State	Zip	Toll-Free	Phone
Baker University 618 8th St	Baldwin City	KS	66006	**800-873-4282**	785-594-6451
Barclay College 607 N Kingman St	Haviland	KS	67059	**800-862-0226**	620-862-5252
Benedictine College 1020 N 2nd St	Atchison	KS	66002	**800-467-5340**	913-367-5340
Bethany College 421 N 1st St	Lindsborg	KS	67456	**800-826-2281**	785-227-3311
Bethel College 300 E 27th St	North Newton	KS	67117	**800-522-1887**	316-283-2500
Emporia State University					
1200 Commercial PO Box 34	Emporia	KS	66801	**877-468-6378**	620-341-1200
Fort Hays State University 600 Park St	Hays	KS	67601	**800-628-3478**	785-628-4000
Friends University 2100 University St	Wichita	KS	67213	**800-794-6945**	316-295-5000
Kansas State University Anderson Hall	Manhattan	KS	66506	**800-232-0133**	785-532-6250
Kansas Wesleyan University 100 E Claflin Ave	Salina	KS	67401	**800-874-1154**	785-827-5541
McPherson College PO Box 1402	McPherson	KS	67460	**800-365-7402**	620-241-0731
MidAmerica Nazarene University					
2030 E College Way	Olathe	KS	66062	**800-800-8887**	913-782-3750
Newman University 3100 McCormick Ave	Wichita	KS	67213	**877-639-6268**	316-942-4291
Ottawa University 1001 S Cedar St	Ottawa	KS	66067	**800-755-5200**	785-242-5200
Pittsburg State University					
1701 S Broadway St	Pittsburg	KS	66762	**800-854-7488**	620-231-7000
Southwestern College 100 College St	Winfield	KS	67156	**800-846-1543**	620-221-4150
Sterling College 125 W Cooper	Sterling	KS	67579	**800-346-1017**	620-278-2173
Tabor College 400 S Jefferson St	Hillsboro	KS	67063	**800-822-6799**	620-947-3121
University of Saint Mary					
4100 S 4th St Trafficway	Leavenworth	KS	66048	**800-752-7043**	913-682-5151
Washburn University 1700 SW College Ave	Topeka	KS	66621	**800-332-0291**	785-231-1010
Wichita State University 1845 Fairmount St	Wichita	KS	67260	**800-362-2594**	316-978-3456

Kentucky

Name / Address	City	State	Zip	Toll-Free	Phone
Alice Lloyd College 100 Purpose Rd	Pippa Passes	KY	41844	**888-280-4252***	606-368-2101
*Admissions					
Asbury College 1 Macklem Dr	Wilmore	KY	40390	**800-888-1818**	859-858-3511
Bellarmine University 2001 Newburg Rd	Louisville	KY	40205	**800-274-4723**	502-452-8000
Berea College 101 Chestnut St	Berea	KY	40403	**800-326-5948**	859-985-3000
Brescia University 717 Frederica St	Owensboro	KY	42301	**877-273-7242**	270-685-3131
Campbellsville University					
1 University Dr	Campbellsville	KY	42718	**800-264-6014**	270-789-5000
Centre College of Kentucky 600 W Walnut St	Danville	KY	40422	**800-423-6236**	859-238-5350
Cumberland College 816 Walnut St	Williamsburg	KY	40769	**800-343-1609**	606-549-2200
Eastern Kentucky University					
521 Lancaster Ave	Richmond	KY	40475	**800-465-9191**	859-622-1000
Georgetown College 400 E College St	Georgetown	KY	40324	**800-788-9985**	502-863-8000
Kentucky Christian University					
100 Academic Pkwy	Grayson	KY	41143	**800-522-3181***	606-474-3000
*Admissions					
Kentucky Wesleyan College PO Box 1039	Owensboro	KY	42302	**800-999-0592**	270-852-3120
Lindsey Wilson College					
210 Lindsey Wilson St	Columbia	KY	42728	**800-264-0138**	270-384-2126
Midway College 512 E Stephens St	Midway	KY	40347	**800-755-0031**	859-846-4421
Morehead State University					
150 University Blvd	Morehead	KY	40351	**800-585-6781**	606-783-2221
Murray State University PO Box 9	Murray	KY	42071	**800-272-4678**	270-762-3741
Northern Kentucky University					
Nunn Dr	Highland Heights	KY	41099	**800-637-9948**	859-572-5100
Pikeville College 147 Sycamore St	Pikeville	KY	41501	**866-232-7700**	606-218-5250
Spalding University 851 S 4th St	Louisville	KY	40203	**800-896-8941**	502-585-9911
Sullivan University 3101 Bardstown Rd	Louisville	KY	40205	**800-844-1354**	502-456-6504
Thomas More College					
333 Thomas More Pkwy	Crestview Hills	KY	41017	**800-825-4557**	859-344-3332
Transylvania University 300 N Broadway	Lexington	KY	40508	**800-872-6798**	859-233-8300
Union College 310 College St	Barbourville	KY	40906	**800-489-8646**	606-546-4151
University of Kentucky 100 Funkhouser Bldg	Lexington	KY	40536	**866-900-4685**	859-257-9000
University of Louisville 2301 S 3rd St	Louisville	KY	40292	**800-334-8635**	502-852-5555
Western Kentucky University					
1 Big Red Way	Bowling Green	KY	42101	**800-495-8463**	270-745-0111

Louisiana

Name / Address	City	State	Zip	Toll-Free	Phone
Centenary College 2911 Centenary Blvd	Shreveport	LA	71104	**800-234-4448**	318-869-5011
Dillard University 2601 Gentilly Blvd	New Orleans	LA	70122	**800-216-6637**	504-816-4670
Louisiana Tech University 305 Wisteria St	Ruston	LA	71272	**800-528-3241**	318-257-0211
Loyola University 6363 St Charles Ave	New Orleans	LA	70118	**800-456-9652**	504-865-2011
McNeese State University 4205 Ryan St	Lake Charles	LA	70609	**800-622-3352**	337-475-5000

				Toll-Free	Phone
Newcomb College 108 Newcomb Hall	New Orleans	LA	70118	**800-873-9283**	504-865-5422
Nicholls State University 906 E 1st St	Thibodaux	LA	70310	**877-642-4655**	985-446-8111
Our Lady of Holy Cross College					
4123 Woodland Dr	New Orleans	LA	70131	**800-259-7744**	504-394-7744
Southeastern Louisiana University					
752 University Stn	Hammond	LA	70402	**800-222-7358**	985-549-2000
Southern University & A & M College					
Branch Post Office	Baton Rouge	LA	70813	**800-256-1531**	225-771-4500
Tulane University 6823 St Charles Ave	New Orleans	LA	70118	**800-873-9283**	504-865-5000
University of Louisiana at Lafayette					
104 University Cir	Lafayette	LA	70503	**800-752-6553**	337-482-1000
University of Louisiana at Monroe					
700 University Ave	Monroe	LA	71209	**800-372-5127**	318-342-5430
University of New Orleans					
Administrative Bldg Rm 103 Lakefront	New Orleans	LA	70148	**800-256-5866**	504-280-6000
Xavier University of Louisiana					
1 Drexel Dr	New Orleans	LA	70125	**877-928-4378***	504-486-7411
*Admissions					

Maine

				Toll-Free	Phone
Colby College 4000 Mayflower Hill	Waterville	ME	04901	**800-723-3032**	207-872-3000
College of the Atlantic 105 Eden St	Bar Harbor	ME	04609	**800-528-0025**	207-288-5015
Husson College 1 College Cir	Bangor	ME	04401	**800-448-7766**	207-941-7000
Maine College of Art 97 Spring St	Portland	ME	04101	**800-639-4808**	207-775-3052
Maine Maritime Academy	Castine	ME	04420	**800-227-8465**	207-326-4311
New England Bible College					
879 Sawyer St	South Portland	ME	04116	**800-286-1859**	207-799-5979
Saint Joseph's College 278 Whites Bridge Rd	Standish	ME	04084	**800-338-7057**	207-893-7746
Thomas College 180 W River Rd	Waterville	ME	04901	**800-339-7001**	207-859-1111
University of Maine 5713 Chadbourne Hall	Orono	ME	04469	**877-486-2364**	207-581-1110
Fort Kent 23 University Dr	Fort Kent	ME	04743	**888-879-8635**	207-834-7500
Machias 9 O'Brien Ave	Machias	ME	04654	**888-468-6866**	207-255-1200
University of New England					
11 Hills Beach Rd	Biddeford	ME	04005	**800-477-4863**	207-283-0171
Westbrook College 716 Stevens Ave	Portland	ME	04103	**800-477-4863**	207-797-7261
University of Southern Maine PO Box 9300	Portland	ME	04104	**800-800-4876**	207-780-4141
Westbrook College 716 Stevens Ave	Portland	ME	04103	**800-477-4863**	207-797-7261

Maryland

				Toll-Free	Phone
Baltimore Hebrew University					
5800 Park Heights Ave	Baltimore	MD	21215	**888-248-7420**	410-578-6900
Bowie State University 14000 Jericho Park Rd	Bowie	MD	20715	**877-772-6943**	301-860-4000
Capitol College 11301 Springfield Rd	Laurel	MD	20708	**800-950-1992**	301-369-2800
College of Notre Dame of Maryland					
4701 N Charles St	Baltimore	MD	21210	**800-435-0300**	410-435-0100
Columbia Union College 7600 Flower Ave	Takoma Park	MD	20912	**800-835-4212**	301-891-4000
Coppin State University 2500 W North Ave	Baltimore	MD	21216	**800-635-3674**	410-951-3600
Goucher College 1021 Dulaney Valley Rd	Baltimore	MD	21204	**800-468-2437**	410-337-6000
Hood College 401 Rosemont Ave	Frederick	MD	21701	**800-922-1599**	301-696-3400
Loyola College 4501 N Charles St	Baltimore	MD	21210	**800-221-9107**	410-617-2000
McDaniel College 2 College Hill	Westminster	MD	21157	**800-638-5005**	410-848-7000
Mount Saint Mary's University					
16300 Old Emmitsburg Rd	Emmitsburg	MD	21727	**800-448-4347**	301-447-5214
Peabody Conservatory of Music					
1 E Mt Vernon Pl	Baltimore	MD	21202	**800-368-2521**	410-659-8110
Peabody Institute of the Johns Hopkins University Peabody Conservatory of Music 1 E Mt Vernon Pl	Baltimore	MD	21202	**800-368-2521**	410-659-8110
Saint Mary's College of Maryland					
18952 E Fisher Rd	Saint Mary's City	MD	20686	**800-492-7181**	240-895-5000
Salisbury University 1101 Camden Ave	Salisbury	MD	21801	**888-543-0148**	410-543-6000
Sojourner-Douglass College					
500 N Caroline St	Baltimore	MD	21205	**800-732-2630**	410-276-0306
Towson University 8000 York Rd	Towson	MD	21252	**800-225-5878**	410-704-2000
University of Baltimore 1420 N Charles St	Baltimore	MD	21201	**877-277-5982**	410-837-4200
University of Maryland Baltimore County					
1000 Hilltop Cir	Baltimore	MD	21250	**800-862-2482**	410-455-2902
University of Maryland University College					
3501 University Blvd E	Adelphi	MD	20783	**800-888-8682**	301-985-7000
US Naval Academy 117 Decatur Rd	Annapolis	MD	21402	**888-249-7707**	410-293-1000
Villa Julie College					
1525 Green Spring Valley Rd	Stevenson	MD	21153	**877-468-6852**	410-486-7000
Washington College 300 Washington Ave	Chestertown	MD	21620	**800-410-2800**	410-778-2800

Massachusetts

				Toll-Free	Phone
American International College					
1000 State St	Springfield	MA	01109	**800-242-3142***	413-737-7000
*Admissions					
Anna Maria College 50 Sunset Ln	Paxton	MA	01612	**800-344-4586**	508-849-3300
Assumption College 500 Salisbury St	Worcester	MA	01609	**888-882-7786**	508-767-7000
Atlantic Union College 338 Main St	South Lancaster	MA	01561	**800-282-2030**	978-368-2239
Babson College 231 Forest St	Babson Park	MA	02457	**800-488-3696**	781-235-1200
Bay Path College 588 Longmeadow St	Longmeadow	MA	01106	**800-782-7284**	413-567-0621
Bentley College 175 Forest St	Waltham	MA	02452	**800-523-2354**	781-891-2244
Berklee College of Music 1140 Boylston St	Boston	MA	02215	**800-421-0084**	617-747-2221
Boston College 140 Commonwealth Ave	Chestnut Hill	MA	02467	**800-360-2522**	617-552-8000
Brandeis University 415 South St	Waltham	MA	02454	**800-622-0622**	781-736-2000
Clark University 950 Main St	Worcester	MA	01610	**800-462-5275**	508-793-7711
College of the Holy Cross 1 College St	Worcester	MA	01610	**800-442-2421**	508-793-2011
Curry College 1071 Blue Hill Ave	Milton	MA	02186	**800-669-0686**	617-333-2210
Eastern Nazarene College 23 E Elm Ave	Quincy	MA	02170	**800-883-6288**	617-745-3000
Elms College 291 Springfield St	Chicopee	MA	01013	**800-255-3567**	413-592-3189
Endicott College 376 Hale St	Beverly	MA	01915	**800-325-1114**	978-927-0585
Gordon College 255 Grapevine Rd	Wenham	MA	01984	**800-343-1379**	978-927-2300
Hampshire College 89 West St	Amherst	MA	01002	**877-937-4267**	413-549-4600
Hebrew College 160 Herrick Rd	Newton Center	MA	02459	**800-866-4814**	617-559-8600
Lasell College 1844 Commonwealth Ave	Newton	MA	02466	**888-527-3554**	617-243-2000
Lesley University 29 Everett St	Cambridge	MA	02138	**800-999-1959**	617-868-9600
Massachusetts College of Pharmacy & Health Sciences 179 Longwood Ave	Boston	MA	02115	**800-225-5506**	617-732-2800
Massachusetts Maritime Academy					
101 Academy Dr	Buzzards Bay	MA	02532	**800-544-3411**	508-830-5000
Montserrat College of Art 23 Essex St	Beverly	MA	01915	**800-836-0487**	978-922-8222
Newbury College 129 Fisher Ave	Brookline	MA	02445	**800-639-2879**	617-730-7000
Nichols College PO Box 5000	Dudley	MA	01571	**800-470-3379**	508-943-1560
Pine Manor College 400 Heath St	Chestnut Hill	MA	02467	**800-762-1357**	617-731-7000
Regis College 235 Wellesley St	Weston	MA	02493	**866-438-7344**	781-768-7000
School of the Museum of Fine Arts					
230 The Fenway	Boston	MA	02115	**800-643-6078**	617-267-6100
Simmons College 300 The Fenway	Boston	MA	02115	**800-345-8468**	617-521-2000
Springfield College 263 Alden St	Springfield	MA	01109	**800-343-1257**	413-748-3000
Suffolk University 8 Ashburton Pl	Boston	MA	02108	**800-678-3365**	617-573-8000
Wentworth Institute of Technology					
550 Huntington Ave	Boston	MA	02115	**800-556-0610**	617-989-4590
Western New England College					
1215 Wilbraham Rd	Springfield	MA	01119	**800-325-1122**	413-782-3111
Wheelock College 200 The Riverway	Boston	MA	02215	**800-734-5212**	617-879-2206
Worcester State College 486 Chandler St	Worcester	MA	01602	**866-972-2255**	508-793-8000

Michigan

				Toll-Free	Phone
Adrian College 110 S Madison St	Adrian	MI	49221	**800-877-2246**	517-265-5161
Albion College 611 E Porter St	Albion	MI	49224	**800-858-6770**	517-629-1000
Alma College 614 W Superior St	Alma	MI	48801	**800-321-2562**	989-463-7111
Andrews University 100 US 31	Berrien Springs	MI	49104	**800-253-2874**	269-471-7771
Aquinas College 1607 Robinson Rd SE	Grand Rapids	MI	49506	**800-678-9593**	616-459-8281
Baker College					
Cadillac Campus 9600 E 13th St	Cadillac	MI	49601	**888-313-3463**	231-876-3100
Clinton Township Campus					
34950 Little Mack Ave	Clinton Township	MI	48035	**888-272-2842**	586-791-6610
Flint Campus 1050 W Bristol Rd	Flint	MI	48507	**800-964-4299**	810-767-7600
Jackson Campus 2800 Springport Rd	Jackson	MI	49202	**888-343-3683**	517-788-7800
Muskegon Campus 1903 Marquette Ave	Muskegon	MI	49442	**800-937-0337**	231-777-8800
Owosso Campus 1020 S Washington St	Owosso	MI	48867	**800-879-3797**	989-729-3300
Port Huron Campus 3403 Lapeer Rd	Port Huron	MI	48060	**888-262-2442**	810-985-7000
Calvin College 3201 Burton St SE	Grand Rapids	MI	49546	**800-688-0122**	616-957-6000
Central Michigan University					
102 Warriner Hall	Mount Pleasant	MI	48859	**888-292-5366**	989-774-4000
Cleary University 3601 Plymouth Rd	Ann Arbor	MI	48105	**800-589-1979**	734-332-4477
College for Creative Studies 201 E Kirby St	Detroit	MI	48202	**800-952-2787**	313-872-3118
Concordia University 4090 Geddes Rd	Ann Arbor	MI	48105	**800-253-0680**	734-995-7300
Cornerstone University					
1001 E Beltline Ave NE	Grand Rapids	MI	49525	**800-787-9778***	616-222-1426
*Admissions					
Davenport University					
Grand Rapids Campus					
415 E Fulton St	Grand Rapids	MI	49503	**800-632-9569**	616-451-3511
Lansing Campus 220 E Kalamazoo St	Lansing	MI	48933	**800-686-1600**	517-484-2600
Warren Campus 27650 Dequindre Rd	Warren	MI	48092	**800-724-7708**	586-558-8700
Eastern Michigan University	Ypsilanti	MI	48197	**800-468-6368**	734-487-1849
Ferris State University 420 Oak St	Big Rapids	MI	49307	**800-433-7747**	231-591-2000
Grace Bible College 1011 Aldon St SW	Wyoming	MI	49509	**800-968-1887**	616-538-2330
Grand Valley State University 1 Campus Dr	Allendale	MI	49401	**800-748-0246**	616-331-2025
Great Lakes Christian College					
6211 W Willow Hwy	Lansing	MI	48917	**800-937-4522***	517-321-0242
*Admissions					
Hope College 141 E 12th St DeWitt Ctr	Holland	MI	49423	**800-968-7850**	616-395-7850
Kalamazoo College 1200 Academy St	Kalamazoo	MI	49006	**800-253-3602**	269-337-7166
Kendall College of Art & Design of Ferris State University 17 Fountain St NW	Grand Rapids	MI	49503	**800-676-2787**	616-451-2787
Kettering University 1700 W 3rd Ave	Flint	MI	48504	**800-955-4464**	810-762-9500
Lake Superior State University					
650 W Easterday Ave	Sault Sainte Marie	MI	49783	**888-800-5778**	906-632-6841
Lawrence Technological University					
21000 W 10-Mile Rd	Southfield	MI	48075	**800-225-5588**	248-204-3160
Madonna University 36600 Schoolcraft Rd	Livonia	MI	48150	**800-852-4951**	734-432-5339
Marygrove College 8425 W McNichols Rd	Detroit	MI	48221	**866-313-1927**	313-927-1200
Michigan Technological University					
1400 Townsend Dr	Houghton	MI	49931	**888-688-1885**	906-487-2335
Northern Michigan University					
1401 Presque Isle Ave	Marquette	MI	49855	**800-682-9797**	906-227-2650
Northwood University Michigan Campus					
4000 Whiting Dr	Midland	MI	48640	**800-457-7878**	989-837-4200
Oakland University					
Walton Blvd & Squirrel Rd	Rochester	MI	48309	**800-625-8648**	248-370-2100
Olivet College 320 S Main St	Olivet	MI	49076	**800-456-7189**	269-749-7000
Reformed Bible College					
3333 East Beltline Ave NE	Grand Rapids	MI	49525	**800-511-3749**	616-222-3000
Rochester College 800 W Avon Rd	Rochester Hills	MI	48307	**800-521-6010**	248-218-2011
Saginaw Valley State University					
7400 Bay Rd	University Center	MI	48710	**800-968-9500**	989-964-4000
Siena Heights University					
1247 E Siena Heights Dr	Adrian	MI	49221	**800-521-0009**	517-263-0731
Spring Arbor University 106 E Main St	Spring Arbor	MI	49283	**800-968-0011**	517-750-1200
University of Detroit Mercy					
4001 W McNichols Rd	Detroit	MI	48219	**800-635-5020***	313-993-1000
*Admissions					
Wayne State University 6050 Cass Ave	Detroit	MI	48202	**877-978-4636**	313-577-2424
William Tyndale College					
35700 W 12 Mile Rd	Farmington Hills	MI	48331	**800-483-0707**	248-553-7200

Minnesota

				Toll-Free	Phone
Augsburg College					
2211 Riverside Ave S CB 143	Minneapolis	MN	55454	**800-788-5678**	612-330-1000
Bemidji State University					
1500 Birchmont Dr NE	Bemidji	MN	56601	**888-345-1721**	218-755-2001
Bethel University 3900 Bethel Dr	Saint Paul	MN	55112	**800-255-8706**	651-638-6400
Carleton College 1 N College St	Northfield	MN	55057	**800-995-2275**	507-646-4000
College of Saint Benedict					
37 S College Ave	Saint Joseph	MN	56374	**800-249-9840**	320-363-5011
College of Saint Catherine					
2004 Randolph Ave	Saint Paul	MN	55105	**800-945-4599**	651-690-6000
College of Saint Scholastica					
1200 Kenwood Ave	Duluth	MN	55811	**800-447-5444**	218-723-6000
Concordia College Moorhead 901 S 8th St	Moorhead	MN	56562	**800-699-9897**	218-299-4000
Concordia University 275 Syndicate St N	Saint Paul	MN	55104	**800-333-4705**	651-641-8278
Crossroads College 920 Mayowood Rd SW	Rochester	MN	55902	**800-456-7651**	507-288-4563
Crown College 8700 College View Dr	Saint Bonifacius	MN	55375	**800-682-7696**	952-446-4100

Minnesota (Cont'd)

				Toll-Free	Phone
Gustavus Adolphus College 800 W College Ave	Saint Peter	MN	56082	**800-487-8288**	507-933-8000
Hamline University 1536 Hewitt Ave	Saint Paul	MN	55104	**800-753-9753**	651-523-2207
Macalester College 1600 Grand Ave	Saint Paul	MN	55105	**800-231-7974**	651-696-6357
Mankato State University 122 Taylor Ctr	Mankato	MN	56001	**800-722-0544**	507-389-1822
Minneapolis College of Art & Design 2501 Stevens Ave S	Minneapolis	MN	55404	**800-874-6223**	612-874-3760
Minnesota State University Moorhead 1104 7th Ave S	Moorhead	MN	56563	**800-593-7246**	218-477-2161
National American University Roseville Campus 1550 W Hwy 36	Roseville	MN	55113	**800-843-8892**	651-644-1265
National Technological University 155 5th Ave S Suite 600	Minneapolis	MN	55401	**800-582-9976**	866-688-6797
North Central University 910 Elliot Ave S	Minneapolis	MN	55404	**800-289-6222**	612-343-4480
Northwestern College 3003 Snelling Ave N *Admissions	Saint Paul	MN	55113	**800-827-6827***	651-631-5100
Oak Hills Christian College 1600 Oak Hills Rd SW	Bemidji	MN	56601	**888-751-8670**	218-751-8670
Pillsbury Baptist Bible College 315 S Grove Ave	Owatonna	MN	55060	**800-747-4557**	507-451-2710
Saint Cloud State University 720 4th Ave S	Saint Cloud	MN	56301	**800-369-4260**	320-255-3822
Saint John's University	Collegeville	MN	56321	**800-245-6467**	320-363-2196
Saint Mary's University of Minnesota 700 Terrace Heights	Winona	MN	55987	**800-635-5987**	507-452-4430
Saint Olaf College 1520 St Olaf Ave	Northfield	MN	55057	**800-800-3025**	507-646-2222
Southwest Minnesota State University 1501 State St	Marshall	MN	56258	**800-642-0684**	507-537-7021
University of Minnesota Crookston 2900 University Ave Selvig Hall	Crookston	MN	56716	**800-232-6466**	218-281-6510
University of Minnesota Duluth 10 University Dr	Duluth	MN	55812	**800-232-1339**	218-726-8000
University of Minnesota Morris 600 E 4th St	Morris	MN	56267	**800-992-8863**	320-589-6035
University of Minnesota Rochester 855 30th Ave SE	Rochester	MN	55904	**800-947-0117**	507-280-2838
University of Minnesota Twin Cities 231 Pillsbury Dr SE Williamson Hall	Minneapolis	MN	55455	**800-752-1000**	612-625-5000
University of Saint Thomas 2115 Summit Ave	Saint Paul	MN	55105	**800-328-6819**	651-962-5000
Winona State University 175 W Mark St	Winona	MN	55987	**800-342-5978**	507-457-5000

Mississippi

				Toll-Free	Phone
Belhaven College 1500 Peachtree St	Jackson	MS	39202	**800-960-5940**	601-968-5928
Blue Mountain College PO Box 160	Blue Mountain	MS	38610	**800-235-0136**	662-685-4771
Delta State University 1003 W Sunflower Rd	Cleveland	MS	38732	**800-468-6378**	662-846-3000
Jackson State University 1400 John R Lynch St	Jackson	MS	39217	**800-848-6817**	601-979-2121
Magnolia Bible College 822 S Huntington St	Kosciusko	MS	39090	**800-748-8655**	662-289-2896
Millsaps College 1701 N State St	Jackson	MS	39210	**800-352-1050**	601-974-1000
Mississippi College 200 S Capitol St	Clinton	MS	39058	**800-738-1236**	601-925-3000
Mississippi University for Women 1100 College St W-Box 1613	Columbus	MS	39701	**877-462-8439**	662-329-4750
Rust College 150 E Rust Ave	Holly Springs	MS	38635	**888-886-8492**	662-252-8000
Tougaloo College 500 W County Line Rd *Admissions	Tougaloo	MS	39174	**888-424-2566***	601-977-7700
Wesley College PO Box 1070	Florence	MS	39073	**800-748-9972**	601-845-2265
William Carey College 498 Tuscan Ave	Hattiesburg	MS	39401	**800-962-5991**	601-318-6051

Missouri

				Toll-Free	Phone
Avila University 11901 Wornall Rd	Kansas City	MO	64145	**800-462-8452**	816-942-8400
Baptist Bible College 628 E Kearney St	Springfield	MO	65803	**800-228-5754**	417-268-6060
Calvary Bible College & Seminary 15800 Calvary Rd	Kansas City	MO	64147	**800-326-3960**	816-322-0110
Central Bible College 3000 N Grant Ave	Springfield	MO	65803	**800-831-4222**	417-833-2551
Central Christian College of the Bible 911 E Urbandale Dr	Moberly	MO	65270	**888-263-3900**	660-263-3900
Central Methodist College 411 Central Methodist Sq	Fayette	MO	65248	**888-262-1854**	660-248-3391
Central Missouri State University	Warrensburg	MO	64093	**800-729-2678**	660-543-4111
College of the Ozarks PO Box 17	Point Lookout	MO	65726	**800-222-0525**	417-334-6411
Columbia College 1001 Rogers St	Columbia	MO	65216	**800-231-2391**	573-875-8700
Columbia College-Jefferson City 3314 Emerald Ln	Jefferson City	MO	65109	**800-231-2391**	573-634-3250
Culver-Stockton College 1 College Hill	Canton	MO	63435	**800-537-1883**	573-288-6000
Deaconess College of Nursing 6150 Oakland Ave	Saint Louis	MO	63139	**800-942-4310**	314-768-3044
Drury University 900 N Benton Ave	Springfield	MO	65802	**800-922-2274**	417-873-7879
Evangel University 1111 N Glenstone Ave	Springfield	MO	65802	**800-382-6435**	417-865-2811
Fontbonne University 6800 Wydown Blvd	Saint Louis	MO	63105	**800-205-5862**	314-862-3456
Graceland University 1401 W Truman Rd	Independence	MO	64050	**800-833-0524**	816-833-0524
Hannibal-LaGrange College 2800 Palmyra Rd	Hannibal	MO	63401	**800-454-1119**	573-221-3675
Kansas City Art Institute 4415 Warwick Blvd	Kansas City	MO	64111	**800-522-5224**	816-474-5224
Lincoln University 820 Chestnut St *Admissions	Jefferson City	MO	65102	**800-521-5052***	573-681-5000
Maryville University of Saint Louis 13550 Conway Rd	Saint Louis	MO	63141	**800-627-9855**	314-529-9300
Missouri Southern State University 3950 E Newman Rd	Joplin	MO	64801	**800-606-6772**	417-625-9300
Missouri Western State College 4525 Downs Dr	Saint Joseph	MO	64507	**800-662-7041**	816-271-4266
Northwest Missouri State University 800 University Dr	Maryville	MO	64468	**800-633-1175**	660-562-1212
Ozark Christian College 1111 N Main St	Joplin	MO	64801	**800-299-4622**	417-624-2518
Park University 8700 NW River Pk Dr	Parkville	MO	64152	**800-745-7275**	816-741-2000
Rockhurst University 1100 Rockhurst Rd	Kansas City	MO	64110	**800-842-6776**	816-501-4000
Saint Louis Christian College 1360 Grandview Dr	Florissant	MO	63033	**800-887-7522**	314-837-6777
Saint Louis College of Pharmacy 4588 Parkview Pl	Saint Louis	MO	63110	**800-278-5267**	314-367-8700
Saint Louis University 221 N Grand Blvd	Saint Louis	MO	63103	**800-758-3678**	314-977-2222
Southwest Baptist University 1600 University Ave	Bolivar	MO	65613	**800-526-5859**	417-326-5281
Southwest Missouri State University 901 S National Ave	Springfield	MO	65804	**800-492-7900**	417-836-5000
Stephens College 1200 E Broadway	Columbia	MO	65215	**800-876-7207**	573-442-2211
Truman State University 100 E Normal St	Kirksville	MO	63501	**800-892-7792**	660-785-4000
University of Missouri Kansas City 5100 Rockhill Rd	Kansas City	MO	64110	**800-775-8652**	816-235-1000
University of Missouri Rolla 1870 Miner Cir G2 Parker Hall	Rolla	MO	65409	**800-522-0938**	573-341-4111
University of Missouri Saint Louis 1 University Blvd	Saint Louis	MO	63121	**888-462-8675**	314-516-5000
Washington University 1 Brookings Dr	Saint Louis	MO	63130	**800-638-0700**	314-935-5000
Westminster College 501 Westminster Ave	Fulton	MO	65251	**800-475-3361**	573-642-3361
William Jewell College 500 College Hill WJC Box 1002	Liberty	MO	64068	**800-753-7009**	816-781-7700
William Woods University 1 University Ave	Fulton	MO	65251	**800-995-3159**	573-642-2251

Montana

				Toll-Free	Phone
Carroll College 1601 N Benton Ave	Helena	MT	59625	**800-992-3648**	406-447-4300
Montana State University					
Bozeman PO Box 172190	Bozeman	MT	59717	**888-678-2287**	406-994-2452
Northern PO Box 7751	Havre	MT	59501	**800-662-6132**	406-265-3700
Montana Tech of the University of Montana 1300 W Park St	Butte	MT	59701	**800-445-8324**	406-496-4101
Rocky Mountain College 1511 Poly Dr	Billings	MT	59102	**800-877-6259**	406-657-1000
University of Great Falls 1301 20th St S	Great Falls	MT	59405	**800-856-9544**	406-761-8210
University of Montana 32 Campus Dr	Missoula	MT	59812	**800-462-8636**	406-243-6266

Nebraska

				Toll-Free	Phone
Bellevue University 1000 Galvin Rd S	Bellevue	NE	68005	**800-756-7920**	402-291-8100
Chadron State College 1000 Main St	Chadron	NE	69337	**800-242-3766**	308-432-6263
Clarkson College 101 S 42nd St	Omaha	NE	68131	**800-647-5500**	402-552-3100
College of Saint Mary 1901 S 72nd St	Omaha	NE	68124	**800-926-5534**	402-399-2400
Concordia University 800 N Columbia Ave	Seward	NE	68434	**800-535-5494**	402-643-3651
Creighton University 2500 California Plaza	Omaha	NE	68178	**800-282-5835**	402-280-2700
Dana College 2848 College Dr	Blair	NE	68008	**800-444-3262**	402-426-9000
Doane College 1014 Boswell Ave	Crete	NE	68333	**800-333-6263**	402-826-2161
Lincoln Campus 303 N 52nd St New Century Bldg	Lincoln	NE	68504	**800-333-6263**	402-466-4774
Grace University 1311 S 9th St	Omaha	NE	68108	**800-383-1422**	402-449-2800
Hastings College 710 N Turner Ave	Hastings	NE	68901	**800-532-7642**	402-463-2402
Midland Lutheran College 900 N Clarkson St	Fremont	NE	68025	**800-642-8382**	402-721-5480
Nebraska Wesleyan University 5000 St Paul Ave	Lincoln	NE	68504	**800-541-3818**	402-466-2371
Peru State College 600 Hoyt St	Peru	NE	68421	**800-742-4412**	402-872-3815
Platte Valley Bible College PO Box 1227	Scottsbluff	NE	69363	**888-305-8083**	308-632-6933
Union College 3800 S 48th St	Lincoln	NE	68506	**800-228-4600**	402-488-2331
University of Nebraska					
Kearney 905 W 25th St	Kearney	NE	68849	**800-532-7639**	308-865-8441
Lincoln 501 N 14th St	Lincoln	NE	68588	**800-742-8800**	402-472-7211
Wayne State College 1111 Main St	Wayne	NE	68787	**800-228-9972**	402-375-7000
York College 1125 E 8th St	York	NE	68467	**800-950-9675**	402-362-4441

New Hampshire

				Toll-Free	Phone
Colby-Sawyer College 541 Main St	New London	NH	03257	**800-272-1015**	603-526-2010
Daniel Webster College 20 University Dr	Nashua	NH	03063	**800-325-6876**	603-577-6000
Franklin Pierce College					
Concord Campus 5 Chenell Dr	Concord	NH	03301	**800-325-1090**	603-228-1155
Keene Campus 17 Bradco St	Keene	NH	03431	**800-325-1090**	603-357-0079
Lebanon Campus 24 Airport Rd Suite 19	West Lebanon	NH	03784	**800-325-1090**	603-298-5549
Nashua Campus 20 Cotton Rd	Nashua	NH	03063	**800-325-1090**	603-889-4143
Portsmouth Campus 73 Corporate Dr	Portsmouth	NH	03801	**800-325-1090**	603-433-2000
Rindge Campus 20 College Rd Box 60	Rindge	NH	03461	**800-437-0048**	603-899-4000
Salem Campus 12 Industrial Way	Salem	NH	03079	**800-325-1090**	603-898-1263
Keene State College 229 Main St	Keene	NH	03435	**800-572-1909**	603-352-1909
Magdalen College 511 Kearsarge Mountain Rd	Warner	NH	03278	**877-498-1723**	603-456-2656
New England College 26 Bridge St	Henniker	NH	03242	**800-521-7642**	603-428-2211
Plymouth State University 17 High St	Plymouth	NH	03264	**800-842-6900**	603-535-2237
Rivier College 420 Main St	Nashua	NH	03060	**800-447-4843**	603-888-1311
Saint Anselm College 100 St Anselm Dr	Manchester	NH	03102	**888-426-7356**	603-641-7500
Southern New Hampshire University 2500 N River Rd	Manchester	NH	03106	**800-642-4968**	603-668-2211

New Jersey

				Toll-Free	Phone
Bloomfield College 467 Franklin St	Bloomfield	NJ	07003	**800-848-4555**	973-748-9000
Caldwell College 9 Ryerson Ave	Caldwell	NJ	07006	**888-864-9516**	973-228-4424
Centenary College 400 Jefferson St	Hackettstown	NJ	07840	**800-236-8679**	908-852-1400
College of Saint Elizabeth 2 Convent Rd	Morristown	NJ	07960	**800-210-7900**	973-290-4000
Fairleigh Dickinson University 285 Madison Ave	Madison	NJ	07940	**800-338-8803**	973-593-8500
Georgian Court University 900 Lakewood Ave	Lakewood	NJ	08701	**800-458-8422**	732-364-2200
Monmouth University 400 Cedar Ave	West Long Branch	NJ	07764	**800-543-9671**	732-571-3456
Montclair State University 1 Normal Ave	Upper Montclair	NJ	07043	**800-331-9205**	973-655-4000
New Jersey City University 2039 JFK Blvd	Jersey City	NJ	07305	**888-441-6528**	201-200-2000
New Jersey Institute of Technology 323 ML King Jr Blvd	Newark	NJ	07102	**800-926-6548**	973-596-3000
Rider University 2083 Lawrenceville Rd	Lawrenceville	NJ	08648	**800-257-9026**	609-896-5000
Rowan University 201 Mullica Hill Rd	Glassboro	NJ	08028	**800-447-1165**	856-256-4000
Saint Peter's College 2641 JFK Blvd	Jersey City	NJ	07306	**888-772-9933**	201-915-9000
Seton Hall University 400 S Orange Ave	South Orange	NJ	07079	**800-738-6648**	973-761-9332
Stevens Institute of Technology Castle Point on the Hudson	Hoboken	NJ	07030	**800-458-5323**	201-216-5194
Thomas Edison State College 101 W State St	Trenton	NJ	08608	**888-442-8372**	609-984-1102

	City	State	ZIP	Toll-Free	Phone
William Paterson University of New Jersey 300 Pompton Rd	Wayne	NJ	07470	**877-978-3923**	973-720-2000

New Mexico

	City	State	ZIP	Toll-Free	Phone
College of Santa Fe 1600 St Michaels Dr	Santa Fe	NM	87505	**800-456-2673**	505-473-6011
Albuquerque Campus 4501 Indian School Rd	Albuquerque	NM	87110	**800-456-2673**	505-884-2732
College of the Southwest 6610 N Lovington Hwy	Hobbs	NM	88240	**800-530-4400**	505-392-6561
Eastern New Mexico University Station 7	Portales	NM	88130	**800-367-3668**	505-562-2178
National American University Albuquerque Campus 4775 Indian School Rd NE Suite 200	Albuquerque	NM	87110	**800-843-8892**	505-265-7517
New Mexico Highlands University 1005 University St	Las Vegas	NM	87701	**877-850-9064**	505-425-7511
New Mexico Institute of Mining & Technology Campus Stn	Socorro	NM	87801	**800-428-8324**	505-835-5614
New Mexico State University PO Box 30001 MSC-3A	Las Cruces	NM	88003	**800-662-6678**	505-646-3121
Saint John's College Santa Fe Campus 1160 Camino Cruz Blanca	Santa Fe	NM	87505	**800-331-5232**	505-984-6060
University of New Mexico University Hill NE	Albuquerque	NM	87131	**800-225-5866**	505-277-0111
Gallup 200 College Rd	Gallup	NM	87301	**800-225-5866**	505-863-7500
Western New Mexico University 1000 W College Ave	Silver City	NM	88061	**800-872-9668**	505-538-6011

New York

	City	State	ZIP	Toll-Free	Phone
Adelphi University 1 South Ave	Garden City	NY	11530	**800-233-5744**	516-877-3000
Alfred University Saxon Dr	Alfred	NY	14802	**800-541-9229**	607-871-2115
Canisius College 2001 Main St	Buffalo	NY	14208	**800-843-1517**	716-883-7000
Cazenovia College 22 Sullivan St	Cazenovia	NY	13035	**800-654-3210**	315-655-7000
City College of New York 138th St & Convent Ave	New York	NY	10031	**800-286-9937**	212-650-7000
Clarkson University 10 Clarkson Ave	Potsdam	NY	13699	**800-527-6577**	315-268-6400
College of New Rochelle 29 Castle Pl	New Rochelle	NY	10805	**800-933-5923**	914-654-5452
College of Saint Rose 432 Western Ave	Albany	NY	12203	**800-637-8556**	518-454-5150
Concordia College 171 White Plains Rd	Bronxville	NY	10708	**800-937-2655**	914-337-9300
Daemen College 4380 Main St	Amherst	NY	14226	**800-462-7652**	716-839-3600
Dominican College 470 Western Hwy	Orangeburg	NY	10962	**866-432-4636**	845-359-7800
Dowling College 150 Idle Hour Blvd	Oakdale	NY	11769	**800-369-5464**	631-244-3000
D'Youville College 320 Porter Ave	Buffalo	NY	14201	**800-777-3921**	716-881-3200
Elmira College 1 Park Place	Elmira	NY	14901	**800-935-6472**	607-735-1724
Empire State College 1 Union Ave	Saratoga Springs	NY	12866	**800-847-3000**	518-587-2100
Excelsior College 7 Columbia Cir	Albany	NY	12203	**888-647-2388**	518-464-8500
Fashion Institute of Technology 227 W 27th St	New York	NY	10001	**800-468-6348**	212-217-7650
Fordham University 441 E Fordham Rd	Bronx	NY	10458	**800-367-3426**	718-817-1000
College at Lincoln Center 113 W 60th St	New York	NY	10023	**800-367-3426**	212-636-6710
Hamilton College 198 College Hill Rd	Clinton	NY	13323	**800-843-2655**	315-859-4421
Hilbert College 5200 S Park Ave	Hamburg	NY	14075	**800-649-8003**	716-649-7900
Hobart & William Smith Colleges 300 Pulteney St	Geneva	NY	14456	**800-852-2256**	315-781-3000
Hofstra University 100 Hofstra University	Hempstead	NY	11549	**800-463-7872**	516-463-6700
Houghton College 1 Willard Ave	Houghton	NY	14744	**800-777-2556**	585-567-9200
W Seneca Campus 810 Union Rd	West Seneca	NY	14224	**800-247-6448**	716-674-6363
Iona College 715 North Ave	New Rochelle	NY	10801	**800-231-4662**	914-633-2502
Ithaca College 953 Danby Rd	Ithaca	NY	14850	**800-429-4274**	607-274-3011
Keuka College 141Central Ave	Keuka Park	NY	14478	**800-355-3852**	315-279-5000
Laboratory Institute of Merchandising 12 E 53rd St	New York	NY	10022	**800-677-1323**	212-752-1530
Le Moyne College 1419 Salt Springs Rd	Syracuse	NY	13214	**800-333-4733**	315-445-4100
Long Island University *Brooklyn Campus* 1 University Plaza	Brooklyn	NY	11201	**800-548-7526**	718-488-1011
CW Post Campus 720 Northern Blvd	Greenvale	NY	11548	**800-548-7526**	516-299-2000
Southampton College 239 Montauk Hwy	Southampton	NY	11968	**800-548-7526**	631-287-8010
Manhattan College 4513 Manhattan College Pkwy	Bronx	NY	10471	**800-622-9235**	718-862-8000
Manhattanville College 2900 Purchase St	Purchase	NY	10577	**800-328-4553**	914-323-5464
Mannes College of Music 150 W 85th St	New York	NY	10024	**800-292-3040**	212-580-0210
Marymount College 100 Marymount Ave	Tarrytown	NY	10591	**800-724-4312**	914-332-8295
Marymount Manhattan College 221 E 71st St	New York	NY	10021	**800-627-9668**	212-517-0400
Medaille College 18 Agassiz Cir	Buffalo	NY	14214	**800-292-1582**	716-884-3281
Mercy College 555 Broadway	Dobbs Ferry	NY	10522	**800-637-2969**	914-693-4500
Bronx Campus 1200 Water Pl	Bronx	NY	10461	**800-637-2969**	718-518-7710
White Plains Campus 277 Martine Ave	White Plains	NY	10601	**800-637-2969**	914-948-3666
Yorktown Heights Campus 2651 Strang Blvd	Yorktown Heights	NY	10598	**800-637-2969**	914-245-6100
Metropolitan College of New York 75 Varick St	New York	NY	10013	**800-338-4465**	212-343-1234
Molloy College 1000 Hempstead Ave PO Box 5002	Rockville Centre	NY	11571	**888-466-5569**	516-678-5000
Mount Saint Mary College 330 Powell Ave	Newburgh	NY	12550	**888-937-6762**	845-569-3248
Nazareth College of Rochester 4245 East Ave	Rochester	NY	14618	**800-462-3944**	585-586-2525
New York Institute of Technology New York Institute of Technology Northern Blvd	Old Westbury	NY	11568	**800-345-6948**	516-686-1015
Islip Campus Carlton Ave	Central Islip	NY	11722	**800-873-6948**	631-348-3200
Manhattan Campus 1855 Broadway	New York	NY	10023	**800-345-6948**	212-261-1500
New York School of Interior Design 170 E 70th St	New York	NY	10021	**800-336-9743**	212-472-1500
Niagara University	Niagara University	NY	14109	**800-462-2111**	716-286-8700
Nyack College 1 South Blvd *Admissions	Nyack	NY	10960	**800-336-9225***	845-358-1710
Pace University 1 Pace Plaza	New York	NY	10038	**866-722-3338**	212-346-1200
Parsons School of Design 2 W 13th St	New York	NY	10011	**800-252-0852**	212-229-8900
Plattsburgh State 101 Broad St	Plattsburgh	NY	12901	**888-673-0012**	518-564-2040
Polytechnic University 6 Metrotech Ctr	Brooklyn	NY	11201	**800-765-9832**	718-260-3600
Pratt Institute 200 Willoughby Ave	Brooklyn	NY	11205	**800-331-0834**	718-636-3600
Rensselaer Polytechnic Institute 110 8th St	Troy	NY	12180	**800-448-6562**	518-276-6216
Roberts Wesleyan College 2301 Westside Dr *Admissions	Rochester	NY	14624	**800-777-4792***	585-594-6000
Russell Sage College 45 Ferry St	Troy	NY	12180	**888-837-9724**	518-244-2217
Saint Bonaventure University Rt 417 PO Box D	Saint Bonaventure	NY	14778	**800-462-5050**	716-375-2400
Saint John Fisher College 3690 East Ave	Rochester	NY	14618	**800-444-4640**	585-385-8000
Saint Lawrence University 23 Romoda Dr	Canton	NY	13617	**800-285-1856**	315-229-5261
Saint Thomas Aquinas College 125 Rt 340	Sparkill	NY	10976	**800-999-7822**	845-398-4000
Sarah Lawrence College 1 Meadway	Bronxville	NY	10708	**800-888-2858**	914-337-0700
School of Visual Arts 209 E 23rd St	New York	NY	10010	**800-436-4204**	212-592-2000
Siena College 515 Loudon Rd	Loudonville	NY	12211	**800-457-4362**	518-783-2423
State University of New York College of Agriculture & Technology at Cobleskill Rt 7	Cobleskill	NY	12043	**800-295-8988**	518-255-5525
State University of New York College of Environmental Science & Forestry 1 Forestry Dr	Syracuse	NY	13210	**800-777-7373**	315-470-6500
State University of New York College at Fredonia 178 Central Ave	Fredonia	NY	14063	**800-252-1212**	716-673-3251
State University of New York College at Geneseo 1 College Cir	Geneseo	NY	14454	**866-245-5211**	585-245-5211
State University of New York College at Oneonta Ravine Pkwy	Oneonta	NY	13820	**800-786-9123**	607-436-3500
State University of New York Institute of Technology (SUNYIT) PO Box 3050	Utica	NY	13504	**800-786-9832**	315-792-7500
State University of New York at New Paltz 75 S Manheim Blvd	New Paltz	NY	12561	**888-639-7589**	845-257-2121
State University of New York at Plattsburgh 101 Broad St	Plattsburgh	NY	12901	**888-673-0012**	518-564-2040
State University of New York at Potsdam 44 Pierrpont Ave	Potsdam	NY	13676	**877-768-7326**	315-267-2000
SUNY Cobleskill Rt 7	Cobleskill	NY	12043	**800-295-8988**	518-255-5525
SUNY Fredonia 178 Central Ave	Fredonia	NY	14063	**800-252-1212**	716-673-3251
SUNY Genesco 1 College Cir	Geneseo	NY	14454	**866-245-5211**	585-245-5211
SUNY Institute of Technology PO Box 3050	Utica	NY	13504	**800-786-9832**	315-792-7500
SUNY New Paltz 75 S Manheim Blvd	New Paltz	NY	12561	**888-639-7589**	845-257-2121
SUNY Oneonta Ravine Pkwy	Oneonta	NY	13820	**800-786-9123**	607-436-3500
SUNY Potsdam 44 Pierrpont Ave	Potsdam	NY	13676	**877-768-7326**	315-267-2000
Union College 807 Union St	Schenectady	NY	12308	**888-843-6688**	518-388-6000
University at Albany 1400 Washington Ave	Albany	NY	12222	**800-293-7869**	518-442-3300
University at Albany 1400 Washington Ave	Albany	NY	12222	**800-293-7869**	518-443-5555
University at Buffalo 15 Capen Hall	Buffalo	NY	14260	**888-822-3648**	716-645-2450
US Merchant Marine Academy 300 Steamboat Rd	Kings Point	NY	11024	**866-546-4778**	516-773-5000
US Military Academy Admissions Bldg 606	West Point	NY	10996	**800-822-8762**	845-938-5746
Utica College of Syracuse University 1600 Burrstone Rd	Utica	NY	13502	**800-782-8884**	315-792-3111
Vassar College 124 Raymond Ave	Poughkeepsie	NY	12604	**800-827-7270**	845-437-7000
Vaughn College of Aeronautics & Technology 86-01 23rd Ave	East Elmhurst	NY	11369	**800-776-2376**	718-429-6600
Wagner College 1 Campus Rd	Staten Island	NY	10301	**800-221-1010**	718-390-3411
Wells College PO Box 500	Aurora	NY	13026	**800-952-9355**	315-364-3370

North Carolina

	City	State	ZIP	Toll-Free	Phone
Barber-Scotia College 145 Cabarrus Ave W *Admissions	Concord	NC	28025	**800-267-3910***	704-789-2902
Barton College PO Box 5000	Wilson	NC	27893	**800-345-4973**	252-399-6300
Belmont Abbey College 100 Belmont-Mt Holly Rd	Belmont	NC	28012	**888-222-0110**	704-825-6700
Bennett College 900 E Washington St *Admissions	Greensboro	NC	27401	**800-413-5323***	336-273-4431
Campbell University PO Box 546	Buies Creek	NC	27506	**800-334-4111**	910-893-1290
Catawba College 2300 W Innes St	Salisbury	NC	28144	**800-228-2922**	704-637-4111
Chowan College 200 Jones Dr	Murfreesboro	NC	27855	**800-488-4101**	252-398-6500
Davidson College Box 7156	Davidson	NC	28035	**800-768-0380**	704-894-2000
Elizabeth City State University 1704 Weeksville Rd CB 901 *Admissions	Elizabeth City	NC	27909	**800-347-3278***	252-335-3305
Elon University PO Box 398	Elon	NC	27244	**800-334-8448**	336-278-2000
Fayetteville State University 1200 Murchison Rd *Admissions	Fayetteville	NC	28301	**800-222-2594***	910-672-1111
Gardner-Webb University PO Box 817	Boiling Springs	NC	28017	**800-253-6472**	704-406-4498
Greensboro College 815 W Market St	Greensboro	NC	27401	**800-346-8226**	336-272-7102
Guilford College 5800 W Friendly Ave	Greensboro	NC	27410	**800-992-7759**	336-316-2100
Heritage Bible College PO Box 1628	Dunn	NC	28335	**800-297-6351**	910-892-4268
High Point University 833 Montlieu Ave	High Point	NC	27262	**800-345-6993**	336-841-9216
Johnson C Smith University 100 Beatties Ford Rd *Admissions	Charlotte	NC	28216	**800-782-7303***	704-378-1000
Lees-McRae College PO Box 128	Banner Elk	NC	28604	**800-280-4562**	828-898-5241
Lenoir-Rhyne College 510 7th Ave NE PO Box 7227	Hickory	NC	28603	**800-277-5721**	828-328-1741
Livingstone College 701 W Monroe St	Salisbury	NC	28144	**800-835-3435**	704-216-6000
Mars Hill College 100 Athletics St	Mars Hill	NC	28754	**866-642-4968**	828-689-1201
Meredith College 3800 Hillsborough St	Raleigh	NC	27607	**800-637-3348**	919-760-8581
Methodist College 5400 Ramsey St	Fayetteville	NC	28311	**800-488-7110**	910-630-7000
Montreat College 310 Gaither Cir	Montreat	NC	28757	**800-622-6968**	828-669-8011
Mount Olive College 634 Henderson St	Mount Olive	NC	28365	**800-653-0854**	919-658-2502
North Carolina A & T State University 1601 E Market St *Admissions	Greensboro	NC	27411	**800-443-8964***	336-334-7500
North Carolina Wesleyan College 3400 N Wesleyan Blvd	Rocky Mount	NC	27804	**800-488-6292**	252-985-5100
Pfeiffer University 48380 Hwy 52 N	Misenheimer	NC	28109	**800-338-2060**	704-463-1360
Queens University of Charlotte 1900 Selwyn Ave	Charlotte	NC	28274	**800-849-0202**	704-337-2212
Roanoke Bible College 715 N Poindexter St	Elizabeth City	NC	27909	**800-722-8980**	252-334-2070
Saint Andrews Presbyterian College 1700 Dogwood Mile	Laurinburg	NC	28352	**800-763-0198**	910-277-5000
Saint Augustine's College 1315 Oakwood Ave *Admissions	Raleigh	NC	27610	**800-948-1126***	919-516-4016
Salem College 601 S Church St	Winston-Salem	NC	27101	**800-327-2536**	336-721-2600
Shaw University 118 E South St *Admissions	Raleigh	NC	27601	**800-214-6683***	919-546-8275
University of North Carolina Asheville 1 University Heights	Asheville	NC	28804	**800-531-9842**	828-251-6600
University of North Carolina Pembroke PO Box 1510	Pembroke	NC	28372	**800-949-8627**	910-521-6000
University of North Carolina Wilmington 601 S College Rd	Wilmington	NC	28403	**800-228-5571**	910-962-3000

North Carolina (Cont'd)

Name	City	State	ZIP	Toll-Free	Phone
Western Carolina University	Cullowhee	NC	28723	**800-928-2369**	828-227-7211
Wingate University 220 N Camden St	Wingate	NC	28174	**800-755-5550**	704-233-8000
Winston-Salem State University 601 ML King Jr Dr	Winston-Salem	NC	27110	**800-257-4052**	336-750-2000

North Dakota

Name	City	State	ZIP	Toll-Free	Phone
Dickinson State University 291 Campus Dr	Dickinson	ND	58601	**800-279-4295**	701-483-2090
Jamestown College 6081 College Ln	Jamestown	ND	58405	**800-336-2554**	701-252-3467
Mayville State University 330 3rd St NE	Mayville	ND	58257	**800-437-4104**	701-788-2301
Minot State University 500 University Ave W	Minot	ND	58707	**800-777-0750**	701-858-3000
North Dakota State University 1301 12th Ave N	Fargo	ND	58105	**800-488-6378**	701-231-8011
Trinity Bible College 50 S 6th Ave	Ellendale	ND	58436	**800-523-1603**	701-349-3621
University of North Dakota PO Box 8357	Grand Forks	ND	58202	**800-225-5863**	701-777-2011
Valley City State University 101 College St SW	Valley City	ND	58072	**800-532-8641**	701-845-7990

Ohio

Name	City	State	ZIP	Toll-Free	Phone
Allegheny Wesleyan College 2161 Woodsdale Rd	Salem	OH	44460	**800-292-3153**	330-337-6403
Antioch College 795 Livermore St	Yellow Springs	OH	45387	**800-543-9436**	937-767-7331
Art Academy of Cincinnati 1125 Saint Gregory St	Cincinnati	OH	45202	**800-323-5692**	513-721-5205
Ashland University 401 College Ave	Ashland	OH	44805	**800-882-1548**	419-289-4142
Baldwin-Wallace College 275 Eastland Rd	Berea	OH	44017	**877-292-7759**	440-826-2900
Bluffton University 1 University Dr	Bluffton	OH	45817	**800-488-3257**	419-358-3257
Capital University 1 E Main St	Columbus	OH	43209	**800-289-6289**	614-236-6011
Case Western Reserve University 10900 Euclid Ave	Cleveland	OH	44106	**800-967-8898**	216-368-4450
Cedarville University 251 N Main St	Cedarville	OH	45314	**800-233-2784**	937-766-2211
Central State University 1400 Brush Row Rd PO Box 1004	Wilberforce	OH	45384	**800-388-2781**	937-376-6011
Cincinnati Bible College & Seminary 2700 Glenway Ave	Cincinnati	OH	45204	**800-949-4222**	513-244-8100
Circleville Bible College PO Box 458	Circleville	OH	43113	**800-701-0222**	740-474-8896
Cleveland Institute of Art 11141 East Blvd	Cleveland	OH	44106	**800-223-4700**	216-421-7400
Cleveland State University 2121 Euclid Ave	Cleveland	OH	44115	**888-278-6446**	216-687-2000
College of Mount Saint Joseph 5701 Delhi Rd	Cincinnati	OH	45233	**800-654-9314**	513-244-4200
College of Wooster 1189 Beall Ave	Wooster	OH	44691	**800-877-9905**	330-263-2000
Defiance College 701 N Clinton St	Defiance	OH	43512	**800-520-4632**	419-784-4010
Denison University 100 Main St	Granville	OH	43023	**800-336-4766**	740-587-0810
Franklin University 201 S Grant Ave	Columbus	OH	43215	**877-341-6300**	614-797-4700
Heidelberg College 310 E Market St	Tiffin	OH	44883	**800-434-3352**	419-448-2000
Hiram College PO Box 67	Hiram	OH	44234	**800-362-5280**	330-569-5169
Kent State University 500 E Main St	Kent	OH	44242	**800-988-5368**	330-672-2121
Kenyon College 8854 Ranson Hall	Gambier	OH	43022	**800-848-2468**	740-427-5000
Lake Erie College 391 W Washington St	Painesville	OH	44077	**800-533-4996**	440-375-7000
Lourdes College 6832 Convent Blvd	Sylvania	OH	43560	**800-878-3210**	419-885-3211
Malone College 515 25th St NW	Canton	OH	44709	**800-521-1146**	330-471-8100
Marietta College 215 5th St	Marietta	OH	45750	**800-331-7896**	740-376-4643
Miami University Middletown Campus 4200 E University Blvd	Middletown	OH	45042	**800-662-2262**	513-727-3200
Mount Union College 1972 Clark Ave	Alliance	OH	44601	**800-334-6682**	330-823-2590
Mount Vernon Nazarene University 800 Martinsburg Rd	Mount Vernon	OH	43050	**800-782-2435**	740-397-1244
Muskingum College 163 Stormont St	New Concord	OH	43762	**800-752-6082**	740-826-8211
Myers University 112 Prospect Ave E	Cleveland	OH	44115	**877-366-9377**	216-696-9000
Notre Dame College of Ohio 4545 College Rd	South Euclid	OH	44121	**877-632-6446**	216-381-1680
Ohio Dominican University 1216 Sunbury Rd	Columbus	OH	43219	**800-955-6446**	614-253-2741
Ohio Northern University 525 S Main St	Ada	OH	45810	**888-408-4668**	419-772-2000
Ohio University					
Chillicothe Campus 101 University Dr	Chillicothe	OH	45601	**877-462-6824**	740-774-7200
Eastern Campus 45425 National Rd	Saint Clairsville	OH	43950	**800-648-3331**	740-695-1720
Southern Campus 1804 Liberty Ave	Ironton	OH	45638	**800-626-0513**	740-533-4600
Ohio Wesleyan University 61 S Sandusky St University Hall	Delaware	OH	43015	**800-862-0612**	740-369-4431
Otterbein College 1 Otterbein College	Westerville	OH	43081	**800-488-8144**	614-823-1500
Shawnee State University 940 2nd St	Portsmouth	OH	45662	**800-959-2778**	740-351-3221
Tiffin University 155 Miami St	Tiffin	OH	44883	**800-968-6446**	419-447-6442
Union Institute & University 440 E McMillan St	Cincinnati	OH	45206	**800-486-3116**	513-861-6400
University of Akron 381 Buchtel Mall	Akron	OH	44325	**800-655-4884***	330-972-7077
*Admissions					
University of Dayton 300 College Pk	Dayton	OH	45469	**800-837-7433**	937-229-1000
University of Findlay 1000 N Main St	Findlay	OH	45840	**800-548-0932**	419-422-8313
University of Toledo 2801 W Bancroft St	Toledo	OH	43606	**800-586-5336**	419-530-4636
Urbana University 579 College Way	Urbana	OH	43078	**800-787-2262**	937-484-1301
Ursuline College 2550 Lander Rd	Pepper Pike	OH	44124	**888-877-8546**	440-449-4200
Walsh University 2020 E Maple St	North Canton	OH	44720	**800-362-9846**	330-499-7090
Wilberforce University 1055 N Bickett Rd PO Box 1001	Wilberforce	OH	45384	**800-367-8568**	937-376-2911
Wilmington College of Ohio 251 Ludovic St	Wilmington	OH	45177	**800-341-9318**	937-382-6661
Wittenberg University 200 W Ward St PO Box 720	Springfield	OH	45501	**800-677-7558**	937-327-6231
Wright State University 3640 Colonel Glenn Hwy	Dayton	OH	45435	**800-247-1770***	937-775-3333
*Admissions					
Xavier University 3800 Victory Pkwy	Cincinnati	OH	45207	**800-344-4698**	513-745-3000
Youngstown State University 1 University Plaza	Youngstown	OH	44555	**877-468-6978**	330-941-3000

Oklahoma

Name	City	State	ZIP	Toll-Free	Phone
Cameron University 2800 W Gore Blvd	Lawton	OK	73505	**888-454-7600**	580-581-2200
Heartland Baptist Bible College 4700 NW 10th St Bldg D	Oklahoma City	OK	73127	**877-943-9330**	405-943-9330
Northeastern State University 601 N Grand Ave	Tahlequah	OK	74464	**800-722-9614**	918-456-5511
Tahlequah 600 N Grand Ave	Tahlequah	OK	74464	**800-722-9614**	918-456-5511
Oklahoma Christian University PO Box 11000	Oklahoma City	OK	73136	**800-877-5010**	405-425-5000
Oklahoma City University 2501 N Blackwelder Ave	Oklahoma City	OK	73106	**800-633-7242**	405-521-5000
Oklahoma Panhandle State University 323 Eagle Blvd	Goodwell	OK	73939	**800-664-6778**	580-349-2611
Oklahoma State University Tulsa 700 N Greenwood Ave	Tulsa	OK	74106	**800-364-0710**	918-594-8000
Oral Roberts University 7777 S Lewis Ave	Tulsa	OK	74171	**800-678-8876**	918-495-6161
Rogers State University 1701 W Will Rogers Blvd	Claremore	OK	74017	**800-256-7511**	918-343-7546
Saint Gregory's University 1900 W MacArthur Dr	Shawnee	OK	74873	**888-784-7347**	405-878-5100
Southeastern Oklahoma State University 1405 N 4th St	Durant	OK	74701	**800-435-1327**	580-745-2000
Southern Nazarene University 6729 NW 39th Expy	Bethany	OK	73008	**800-648-9899**	405-789-6400
University of Oklahoma 1000 Asp Ave	Norman	OK	73019	**877-488-1674**	405-325-0311
University of Sciences & Arts of Oklahoma 1727 W Alabama Ave	Chickasha	OK	73018	**800-933-8726**	405-224-3140
University of Tulsa 600 S College Ave	Tulsa	OK	74104	**800-331-3050**	918-631-2307

Oregon

Name	City	State	ZIP	Toll-Free	Phone
Art Institute of Portland 1122 NW Davis St	Portland	OR	97209	**888-228-6528**	503-228-6528
Cascade College 9101 E Burnside St	Portland	OR	97216	**800-550-7678**	503-255-7060
Concordia University 2811 NE Holman St	Portland	OR	97211	**800-321-9371**	503-288-9371
Eastern Oregon University 1 University Blvd	La Grande	OR	97850	**800-452-8639**	541-962-3393
Eugene Bible College 2155 Bailey Hill Rd	Eugene	OR	97405	**800-322-2638**	541-485-1780
George Fox University 414 N Meridian St	Newberg	OR	97132	**800-765-4369**	503-538-8383
Lewis & Clark College 0615 SW Palatine Hill Rd	Portland	OR	97219	**800-444-4111**	503-768-7040
Linfield College 900 SE Baker St	McMinnville	OR	97128	**800-640-2287**	503-883-2200
Marylhurst University 17600 Pacific Hwy PO Box 261	Marylhurst	OR	97036	**800-634-9982**	503-636-8141
Northwest Christian College 828 E 11th Ave	Eugene	OR	97401	**877-463-6622**	541-343-1641
Oregon Institute of Technology 3201 Campus Dr	Klamath Falls	OR	97601	**800-422-2017**	541-885-1155
Oregon State University	Corvallis	OR	97331	**800-291-4192**	541-737-0123
Pacific University 2043 College Way	Forest Grove	OR	97116	**877-722-8648**	503-357-6151
Portland State University 724 SW Harrison St	Portland	OR	97201	**800-547-8887**	503-725-3000
Reed College 3203 SE Woodstock Blvd	Portland	OR	97202	**800-547-4750**	503-771-1112
University of Portland 5000 N Willamette Blvd	Portland	OR	97203	**800-227-4568**	503-943-7911
Warner Pacific College 2219 SE 68th Ave	Portland	OR	97215	**800-582-7885**	503-775-4366
Western Baptist College 5000 Deer Pk Dr SE	Salem	OR	97301	**800-845-3005**	503-581-8600
Willamette University 900 State St	Salem	OR	97301	**877-542-2787**	503-370-6303

Pennsylvania

Name	City	State	ZIP	Toll-Free	Phone
Albright College PO Box 15234	Reading	PA	19612	**800-252-1856**	610-921-2381
Allegheny College 520 N Main St	Meadville	PA	16335	**800-521-5293**	814-332-3100
Alvernia College 400 Saint Bernadine St	Reading	PA	19607	**888-258-3764**	610-796-8200
Arcadia University 450 S Easton Rd	Glenside	PA	19038	**888-232-8373**	215-572-2900
Bryn Mawr College 101 N Merion Ave	Bryn Mawr	PA	19010	**800-262-1885**	610-526-5000
Cabrini College 610 King of Prussia Rd	Radnor	PA	19087	**800-848-1003**	610-902-8100
California University of Pennsylvania 250 University Ave	California	PA	15419	**888-412-0479**	724-938-4000
Carlow College 3333 5th Ave	Pittsburgh	PA	15213	**800-333-2275**	412-578-6000
Cedar Crest College 100 College Dr	Allentown	PA	18104	**800-360-1222**	610-437-4471
Chatham College Woodland Rd	Pittsburgh	PA	15232	**800-837-1290**	412-365-1100
Chestnut Hill College 9601 Germantown Ave	Philadelphia	PA	19118	**800-248-0052**	215-248-7000
Cheyney University of Pennsylvania 1837 University Cir PO Box 200	Cheyney	PA	19319	**800-243-9639**	610-399-2275
Clarion University of Pennsylvania 840 Wood St	Clarion	PA	16214	**800-672-7171**	814-393-2000
Venango Campus 1801 W 1st St	Oil City	PA	16301	**800-672-7171**	814-676-6591
College Misericordia 301 Lake St	Dallas	PA	18612	**866-262-6363**	570-674-6400
Delaware Valley College of Science & Agriculture 700 E Butler Ave	Doylestown	PA	18901	**800-233-5825**	215-489-2211
DeSales University 2755 Station Ave	Center Valley	PA	18034	**800-228-5114**	610-282-1100
Dickinson College PO Box 1773	Carlisle	PA	17013	**800-644-1773**	717-245-1231
Drexel University 3141 Chestnut St	Philadelphia	PA	19104	**800-237-3935**	215-895-2000
Duquesne University 600 Forbes Ave	Pittsburgh	PA	15282	**800-456-0590**	412-396-6000
East Stroudsburg University 200 Prospect St	East Stroudsburg	PA	18301	**877-230-5547**	570-422-3600
Edinboro University of Pennsylvania	Edinboro	PA	16444	**800-626-2203**	814-732-2761
Franklin & Marshall College PO Box 3003	Lancaster	PA	17604	**877-678-9111**	717-291-3911
Gannon University 109 University Sq	Erie	PA	16541	**800-426-6668**	814-871-7000
Geneva College 3200 College Ave	Beaver Falls	PA	15010	**800-847-8255**	724-846-5100
Gettysburg College 300 N Washington St	Gettysburg	PA	17325	**800-431-0803**	717-337-6000
Gratz College 7605 Old York Rd	Melrose Park	PA	19027	**800-475-4635**	215-635-7300
Gwynedd-Mercy College PO Box 901	Gwynedd Valley	PA	19437	**800-342-5462**	215-646-7300
Immaculata University 1145 King Rd	Immaculata	PA	19345	**888-428-6329**	610-647-4400
Indiana University of Pennsylvania Sutton Hall 1011 South Dr Suite 117	Indiana	PA	15705	**800-442-6830**	724-357-2230
Juniata College 1700 Moore St	Huntingdon	PA	16652	**877-586-4282**	814-643-4310
King's College 133 N River St	Wilkes-Barre	PA	18711	**800-955-5777**	570-208-5900
Kutztown University PO Box 730	Kutztown	PA	19530	**877-628-1915**	610-683-4000
Lancaster Bible College 901 Eden Rd PO Box 83403	Lancaster	PA	17608	**800-544-7335**	717-569-7071
Lebanon Valley College 101 N College Ave	Annville	PA	17003	**800-445-6181**	717-867-6100
Lincoln University 1570 Old Baltimore Pike PO Box 179	Lincoln University	PA	19352	**800-790-0191***	610-932-8300
*Admissions					
Lock Haven University	Lock Haven	PA	17745	**800-233-8978**	570-893-2011
Lycoming College 700 College Pl	Williamsport	PA	17701	**800-345-3920**	570-321-4000
Mansfield University Alumni Hall	Mansfield	PA	16933	**800-577-6826**	570-662-4000
Marywood University 2300 Adams Ave	Scranton	PA	18509	**866-279-9663**	570-348-6234
Mercyhurst College 501 E 38th St	Erie	PA	16546	**800-825-1926**	814-824-2202
Messiah College 1 College Ave	Grantham	PA	17027	**800-233-4220**	717-766-2511
Moore College of Art & Design 20th & The Pkwy	Philadelphia	PA	19103	**800-523-2025**	215-965-4014

				Toll-Free	Phone
Mount Aloysius College 7373 Admiral Perry Hwy	Cresson	PA	16630	888-823-2220	814-886-6383
Neumann College 1 Neumann Dr	Aston	PA	19014	800-963-8626	610-459-0905
Peirce College 1420 Pine St	Philadelphia	PA	19102	888-467-3472	215-545-6400
Penn State Harrisburg 777 W Harrisburg Pike	Middletown	PA	17057	800-222-2056	717-948-6000
Pennsylvania State University Harrisburg Campus of Capital College 777 W Harrisburg Pike	Middletown	PA	17057	800-222-2056	717-948-6000
Philadelphia Biblical University 200 Manor Ave	Langhorne	PA	19047	800-366-0049	215-752-5800
Philadelphia University 4201 Henry Ave	Philadelphia	PA	19144	800-951-7287	215-951-2800
Point Park University 201 Wood St	Pittsburgh	PA	15222	800-321-0129	412-391-4100
Robert Morris University 6001 University Blvd	Moon Township	PA	15108	800-762-0097	412-262-8200
Rosemont College 1400 Montgomery Ave	Rosemont	PA	19010	800-331-0708	610-527-0200
Saint Francis University 169 Lakeview Dr	Loretto	PA	15940	866-342-5738	814-472-3000
Saint Vincent College 300 Fraser Purchase Rd	Latrobe	PA	15650	800-782-5549	724-532-6600
Seton Hill University 1 Seton Hill Dr	Greensburg	PA	15601	800-826-6234	724-838-4255
Slippery Rock University	Slippery Rock	PA	16057	800-929-4778	724-738-9000
Susquehanna University 514 University Ave	Selinsgrove	PA	17870	800-326-9672	570-374-0101
Swarthmore College 500 College Ave	Swarthmore	PA	19081	800-667-3110	610-328-8300
Thiel College 75 College Ave	Greenville	PA	16125	800-248-4435	724-589-2000
University of the Arts 320 S Broad St	Philadelphia	PA	19102	800-616-2787	215-717-6000
University of Pittsburgh					
Bradford 300 Campus Dr	Bradford	PA	16701	800-872-1787	814-362-7500
Johnstown 157 Blackington Hall	Johnstown	PA	15904	800-765-4875	814-269-7050
University of the Sciences 600 S 43rd St	Philadelphia	PA	19104	866-304-8747	215-596-8800
University of Scranton 800 Linden St St Thomas Hall	Scranton	PA	18510	888-727-2686	570-941-7400
Valley Forge Christian College 1401 Charlestown Rd	Phoenixville	PA	19460	800-432-8322	610-935-0450
Washington & Jefferson College 60 S Lincoln St	Washington	PA	15301	888-926-3529	724-222-4400
Waynesburg College 51 W College St	Waynesburg	PA	15370	800-225-7393	724-627-8191
West Chester University 100 S High St	West Chester	PA	19383	877-315-2165	610-436-1000
Westminster College 319 S Market St	New Wilmington	PA	16172	800-942-8033	724-946-8761
Wilkes University 84 W South St	Wilkes-Barre	PA	18766	800-945-5378	570-824-4651
Wilson College 1015 Philadelphia Ave	Chambersburg	PA	17201	800-421-8402	717-264-4141

Rhode Island

				Toll-Free	Phone
Bryant College 1150 Douglas Pike	Smithfield	RI	02917	800-622-7001	401-232-6000
Johnson & Wales University 8 Abbott Park Pl	Providence	RI	02903	800-342-5598	401-598-1000
Providence College 549 River Ave	Providence	RI	02918	800-721-6444	401-865-1000
Rhode Island School of Design 2 College St	Providence	RI	02903	800-364-7473	401-454-6100
Roger Williams University 1 Old Ferry Rd	Bristol	RI	02809	800-458-7144	401-253-1040
Salve Regina University 100 Ochre Point Ave	Newport	RI	02840	888-467-2583	401-847-6650

South Carolina

				Toll-Free	Phone
Allen University 1530 Harden St	Columbia	SC	29204	877-625-5368	803-376-5700
Anderson College 316 Blvd	Anderson	SC	29621	800-542-3594	864-231-2030
Benedict College 1600 Harden St	Columbia	SC	29204	800-868-6598	803-256-4220
Bob Jones University 1700 Wade Hampton Blvd	Greenville	SC	29614	800-252-6363*	864-242-5100
*Admissions					
Charleston Southern University 9200 University Blvd	Charleston	SC	29406	800-947-7474	843-863-7000
Citadel The 171 Moultrie St	Charleston	SC	29409	800-868-1842	843-953-5230
Claflin University 400 Magnolia St	Orangeburg	SC	29115	800-922-1276	803-535-5339
Coastal Carolina University PO Box 261954	Conway	SC	29528	800-277-7000	843-349-2026
Coker College 300 E College Ave	Hartsville	SC	29550	800-950-1908	843-383-8000
Columbia International University 7435 Monticello Rd	Columbia	SC	29203	800-777-2227	803-754-4100
Converse College 580 E Main St	Spartanburg	SC	29302	800-766-1125	864-596-9000
Erskine College PO Box 338	Due West	SC	29639	800-241-8721	864-379-2131
Francis Marion University PO Box 100547	Florence	SC	29501	800-368-7551	843-661-1362
Johnson & Wales University Charleston 701 E Bay St	Charleston	SC	29403	800-868-1522	843-727-3000
Lander University 320 Stanley Ave	Greenwood	SC	29649	888-452-6337	864-388-8307
Limestone College 1115 College Dr	Gaffney	SC	29340	800-795-7151	864-489-7151
Medical University of South Carolina 171 Ashley Ave	Charleston	SC	29425	800-424-6872	843-792-9241
Newberry College 2100 College St	Newberry	SC	29108	800-845-4955	803-276-5010
Presbyterian College 503 S Broad St	Clinton	SC	29325	800-476-7272	864-833-2820
South Carolina State University 300 College St NE	Orangeburg	SC	29117	800-260-5956*	803-536-7000
*Admissions					
Southern Wesleyan University 907 Wesleyan Dr	Central	SC	29630	800-282-8798	864-644-5000
University of South Carolina	Columbia	SC	29208	800-922-9755	803-777-7000
Aiken 471 University Pkwy	Aiken	SC	29801	888-969-8722	803-648-6851
Sumter 200 Miller Rd	Sumter	SC	29150	888-872-7868	803-775-8727
Upstate 800 University Way	Spartanburg	SC	29303	800-277-8727	864-503-5246
Voorhees College 1411 Voorhees Rd PO Box 678	Denmark	SC	29042	800-446-6250	803-793-3351

South Dakota

				Toll-Free	Phone
Augustana College 2001 S Summit Ave	Sioux Falls	SD	57197	800-727-5516	605-274-0770
Black Hills State University 1200 University St	Spearfish	SD	57799	800-255-2478	605-642-6011
Dakota State University 820 N Washington Ave	Madison	SD	57042	888-378-9988	605-256-5139
Dakota Wesleyan University 1200 W University Ave	Mitchell	SD	57301	800-333-8506	605-995-2600
Mount Marty College 1105 W 8th St	Yankton	SD	57078	800-658-4552	605-668-1011
National American University 321 Kansas City St	Rapid City	SD	57701	800-843-8892	605-394-4800
Sioux Falls Campus 2801 S Kiwanis Ave Suite 100	Sioux Falls	SD	57105	800-388-5430	605-334-5430
Northern State University 1200 S Jay St	Aberdeen	SD	57401	800-678-5330	605-626-3011
Si Tanka University					
Eagle Butte 435 N Elm St	Eagle Butte	SD	57625	800-710-7159	605-964-8011
Huron 333 9th St SW	Huron	SD	57350	800-710-7159	605-352-8721
South Dakota School of Mines & Technology 501 E Saint Joseph St	Rapid City	SD	57701	800-544-8162	605-394-2414
South Dakota State University PO Box 2201	Brookings	SD	57007	800-952-3541	605-688-4121
University of Sioux Falls 1101 W 22nd St	Sioux Falls	SD	57105	800-888-1047	605-331-5000
University of South Dakota 414 E Clark St	Vermillion	SD	57069	877-269-6837	605-677-5341

Tennessee

				Toll-Free	Phone
Austin Peay State University 601 College St	Clarksville	TN	37044	800-844-2778	931-221-7661
Belmont University 1900 Belmont Blvd	Nashville	TN	37212	800-563-6765	615-460-6000
Bryan College PO Box 7000	Dayton	TN	37321	800-277-9522	423-775-2041
Carson-Newman College 1646 Russell Ave	Jefferson City	TN	37760	800-678-9061	865-475-9061
Christian Brothers University 650 East Pkwy S	Memphis	TN	38104	800-288-7576	901-321-3000
Crichton College 255 N Highland Ave	Memphis	TN	38111	800-960-9777	901-320-9700
Cumberland University 1 Cumberland Sq	Lebanon	TN	37087	800-467-0562	615-444-2562
East Tennessee State University PO Box 70731	Johnson City	TN	37614	800-462-3878	423-439-4213
Fisk University 1000 17th Ave N	Nashville	TN	37208	800-443-3475	615-329-8500
Free Will Baptist Bible College 3606 West End Ave	Nashville	TN	37205	800-763-9222	615-383-1340
Freed-Hardeman University 158 E Main St	Henderson	TN	38340	800-630-3480	731-989-6000
Johnson Bible College 7900 Johnson Dr	Knoxville	TN	37998	800-827-2122	865-573-4517
King College 1350 King College Rd	Bristol	TN	37620	800-362-0014*	423-968-1187
*Admissions					
Lambuth University 705 Lambuth Blvd	Jackson	TN	38301	800-526-2884	731-425-2500
Lane College 545 Lane Ave	Jackson	TN	38301	800-960-7533*	731-426-7500
*Admissions					
Lee University 1120 N Ocoee St	Cleveland	TN	37311	800-533-9930	423-614-8000
LeMoyne-Owen College 807 Walker Ave	Memphis	TN	38126	800-737-7778*	901-774-9090
*Admissions					
Lincoln Memorial University 6965 Cumberland Gap Pkwy	Harrogate	TN	37752	800-325-0900	423-869-3611
Lipscomb University 3901 Granny White Pike	Nashville	TN	37204	800-333-4358	615-269-1000
Maryville College 502 E Lamar Alexander Pkwy	Maryville	TN	37804	800-597-2687	865-981-8000
Memphis College of Art Overton Park 1930 Poplar Ave	Memphis	TN	38104	800-727-1088	901-272-5151
Middle Tennessee State University 1301 E Main St	Murfreesboro	TN	37132	800-433-6878	615-898-2300
Rhodes College 2000 North Pkwy	Memphis	TN	38112	800-844-5969	901-843-3000
Southern Adventist University 4881 Taylor Cir	Collegedale	TN	37315	800-768-8437	423-238-2111
Tennessee State University 3500 John A Merritt Blvd PO Box 9609	Nashville	TN	37209	888-463-6878*	615-963-5000
*Admissions					
Tennessee Technological University PO Box 5006	Cookeville	TN	38505	800-255-8881	931-372-3101
Tennessee Temple University 1815 Union Ave	Chattanooga	TN	37404	800-553-4050	423-493-4100
Tennessee Wesleyan College PO Box 40	Athens	TN	37371	800-742-5892	423-745-7504
Trevecca Nazarene University 333 Murfreesboro Rd	Nashville	TN	37210	888-210-4868	615-248-1200
Tusculum College 60 Shiloh Rd Hwy 107	Greeneville	TN	37743	800-729-0256	423-636-7300
Union University 1050 Union University Dr	Jackson	TN	38305	800-338-6466	731-661-5210
University of Memphis	Memphis	TN	38152	800-669-2678	901-678-2040
University of the South 735 University Ave	Sewanee	TN	37383	800-522-2234	931-598-1238
University of Tennessee	Knoxville	TN	37996	800-221-8657	865-974-1000
University of Tennessee Chattanooga 615 McCallie Ave	Chattanooga	TN	37403	800-882-6627	423-425-4662
University of Tennessee Martin 554 University St	Martin	TN	38238	800-829-8861	731-881-7020
Vanderbilt University 2201 W End Ave	Nashville	TN	37235	800-288-0432	615-322-7311

Texas

				Toll-Free	Phone
Abilene Christian University ACU Box 29000	Abilene	TX	79699	800-460-6228*	325-674-2000
*Admissions					
Angelo State University 2601 West Ave N Box 11014	San Angelo	TX	76909	800-946-8627	325-942-2041
Austin College 900 N Grand Ave	Sherman	TX	75090	800-442-5363	903-813-3000
Austin Graduate School of Theology 1909 University Ave	Austin	TX	78705	866-287-4723	512-476-2772
Baylor University 1311 S 5th St	Waco	TX	76798	800-229-5678	254-710-1011
Concordia University at Austin 3400 IH-35 N	Austin	TX	78705	800-865-4282	512-486-2000
Criswell College 4010 Gaston Ave	Dallas	TX	75246	800-899-0012	214-821-5433
Dallas Baptist University 3000 Mountain Creek Pkwy	Dallas	TX	75211	800-460-1328	214-333-7100
Dallas Christian College 2700 Christian Pkwy	Dallas	TX	75234	800-688-1029	972-241-3371
Hardin-Simmons University 2200 Hickory St	Abilene	TX	79698	800-568-2692	325-670-1000
Houston Baptist University 7502 Fondren Rd	Houston	TX	77074	800-969-3210	281-649-3000
Howard Payne University 1000 Fisk Ave	Brownwood	TX	76801	800-950-8465	325-646-2502
LeTourneau University 2100 S Mobberly	Longview	TX	75602	800-759-8811	903-753-0231
Lubbock Christian University 5601 19th St	Lubbock	TX	79407	800-933-7601	806-796-8800
McMurry University S 14 St & Sayles Blvd	Abilene	TX	79697	800-460-2392	325-793-3800
Midwestern State University 3410 Taft Blvd	Wichita Falls	TX	76308	800-842-1922	940-397-4000
Northwood University Texas Campus 1114 W FM 1382	Cedar Hill	TX	75104	800-927-9663	972-291-1541
Our Lady of the Lake University 411 SW 24th St	San Antonio	TX	78207	800-436-6558	210-434-6711
Paul Quinn College 3837 Simpson Stuart Rd	Dallas	TX	75241	800-237-2648	214-376-1000
Prairie View A & M University PO Box 3089	Prairie View	TX	77446	800-787-7826	936-857-2626
Rice University 6100 Main St	Houston	TX	77005	800-527-6957	713-348-0000
Saint Edward's University 3001 S Congress Ave	Austin	TX	78704	800-555-0164	512-448-8500
Saint Mary's University 1 Camino Santa Maria	San Antonio	TX	78228	800-367-7868	210-436-3126
Sam Houston State University 1903 University Ave	Huntsville	TX	77340	866-232-7528	936-294-1111
Schreiner University 2100 Memorial Blvd	Kerrville	TX	78028	800-343-4919	830-792-7217
Southern Methodist University 6425 Boaz Ln	Dallas	TX	75205	800-323-0672	214-768-2000

Texas (Cont'd)

Name / Address	City	State	Zip	Toll-Free	Phone
Southwestern Adventist University 100 W Hillcrest Dr	Keene	TX	76059	**800-433-2240**	817-645-3921
Southwestern Assemblies of God University 1200 Sycamore St	Waxahachie	TX	75165	**888-937-7248**	972-937-4010
Southwestern Christian College PO Box 10	Terrell	TX	75160	**800-925-9357**	972-524-3341
Southwestern University PO Box 770	Georgetown	TX	78627	**800-252-3166**	512-863-1200
Sul Ross State University E Hwy 90	Alpine	TX	79832	**888-722-7778**	432-837-8011
Tarleton State University PO Box T-0030	Stephenville	TX	76402	**800-687-8236**	254-968-9125
Texas A & M University - Commerce PO Box 3011	Commerce	TX	75428	**888-868-2682**	903-886-5081
Texas A & M University - Corpus Christi 6300 Ocean Dr	Corpus Christi	TX	78412	**800-482-6822**	361-825-2624
Texas A & M University at Galveston 200 Seawolf Pkwy Bldg 3026	Galveston	TX	77553	**877-322-4443**	409-740-4428
Texas Christian University TCU Box 297013	Fort Worth	TX	76129	**800-828-3764**	817-257-7490
Texas Lutheran University 1000 W Court St	Seguin	TX	78155	**800-771-8521**	830-372-8000
Texas State University-San Marcos 601 University Dr	San Marcos	TX	78666	**866-798-2287**	512-245-2111
Texas Tech University PO Box 45005	Lubbock	TX	79409	**888-270-3369**	806-742-1480
Texas Wesleyan University 1201 Wesleyan St	Fort Worth	TX	76105	**800-580-8980**	817-531-4444
Texas Woman's University PO Box 425589	Denton	TX	76204	**888-948-9984**	940-898-2000
Trinity University 1 Trinity Pl	San Antonio	TX	78212	**800-874-6489**	210-999-7207
University of Dallas 1845 E Northgate Dr	Irving	TX	75062	**800-628-6999**	972-721-5000
University of Houston Victoria 3007 N Ben Wilson St	Victoria	TX	77901	**877-970-4848**	361-570-4848
University of the Incarnate Word 4301 Broadway St	San Antonio	TX	78209	**800-749-9673**	210-829-6000
University of Mary Hardin-Baylor 900 College St UMHB Box 8004	Belton	TX	76513	**800-727-8642**	254-295-8642
University of North Texas PO Box 311277	Denton	TX	76203	**800-868-8211**	940-565-2681
University of Saint Thomas 3800 Montrose Blvd	Houston	TX	77006	**800-856-8565**	713-522-7911
University of Texas Arlington 701 S Nedderman Dr	Arlington	TX	76019	**800-687-2882**	817-272-6287
University of Texas Brownsville 80 Fort Brown St	Brownsville	TX	78520	**800-850-0160**	956-544-8200
University of Texas Permian Basin 4901 E University Blvd	Odessa	TX	79762	**866-552-8872**	432-552-2605
University of Texas San Antonio 6900 North Loop 1604 W	San Antonio	TX	78249	**800-669-0919**	210-458-4011
University of Texas Tyler 3900 University Blvd	Tyler	TX	75799	**800-888-9537**	903-566-7000
Wayland Baptist University 1900 W 7th St	Plainview	TX	79072	**800-588-1928**	806-291-1000
West Texas A & M University 2501 4th Ave	Canyon	TX	79016	**800-999-8268**	806-651-2000
Wiley College 711 Wiley Ave	Marshall	TX	75670	**800-658-6889***	903-927-3311

*Admissions

Utah

Name / Address	City	State	Zip	Toll-Free	Phone
University of Utah 201 S 1460 East	Salt Lake City	UT	84112	**800-868-5618**	801-581-7200
Weber State University 3850 University Cir	Ogden	UT	84408	**800-848-7770**	801-626-6000
Westminster College of Salt Lake City 1840 S 1300 East	Salt Lake City	UT	84105	**800-748-4753**	801-484-7651

Vermont

Name / Address	City	State	Zip	Toll-Free	Phone
Bennington College 1 College Dr	Bennington	VT	05201	**800-833-6845**	802-442-5401
Burlington College 95 North Ave	Burlington	VT	05401	**800-862-9616**	802-862-9616
Castleton State College 86 Seminary St	Castleton	VT	05735	**800-639-8521**	802-468-5611
College of Saint Joseph in Vermont 71 Clement Rd	Rutland	VT	05701	**877-270-9998**	802-773-5900
Goddard College 123 Pitkin Rd	Plainfield	VT	05667	**800-468-4888**	802-454-8311
Green Mountain College 1 College Cir	Poultney	VT	05764	**800-776-6675**	802-287-8000
Johnson State College 337 College Hill	Johnson	VT	05656	**800-635-2356**	802-635-2356
Lyndon State College 1001 College Rd PO Box 919	Lyndonville	VT	05851	**800-225-1998**	802-626-6413
Marlboro College 2582 South Rd PO Box A	Marlboro	VT	05344	**800-343-0049**	802-257-4333
Norwich University 158 Harmon Dr	Northfield	VT	05663	**800-468-6679**	802-485-2000
Saint Michael's College 1 Winooski Pk	Colchester	VT	05439	**800-762-8000**	802-654-2000
Southern Vermont College 982 Manison Dr	Bennington	VT	05201	**800-378-2782**	802-442-5427
Union Institute & University Vermont College 36 College St	Montpelier	VT	05602	**800-336-6794**	802-828-8500

Virginia

Name / Address	City	State	Zip	Toll-Free	Phone
Averett University 420 W Main St	Danville	VA	24541	**800-283-7388**	434-791-4996
Bluefield College 3000 College Dr	Bluefield	VA	24605	**800-872-0175**	276-326-3682
Bridgewater College 402 E College St	Bridgewater	VA	22812	**800-759-8328**	540-828-5375
Christendom College 134 Christendom Dr	Front Royal	VA	22630	**800-877-5456**	540-636-2900
Christopher Newport University 1 University Pl	Newport News	VA	23606	**800-333-4268**	757-594-7000
Eastern Mennonite University 1200 Park Rd	Harrisonburg	VA	22802	**800-368-2665***	540-432-4118
*Admissions					
Emory & Henry College PO Box 10	Emory	VA	24327	**800-848-5493**	276-944-4121
Ferrum College PO Box 1000	Ferrum	VA	24088	**800-868-9797**	540-365-2121
George Mason University 4400 University Dr MS N3A4	Fairfax	VA	22030	**888-627-6612**	703-993-1000
Hampden-Sydney College PO Box 667	Hampden-Sydney	VA	23943	**800-755-0733**	434-223-6120
Hampton University 100 E Queen St	Hampton	VA	23668	**800-624-3328***	757-727-5000
*Admissions					
Hollins University 7916 Williamson Rd	Roanoke	VA	24020	**800-456-9595**	540-362-6401
Liberty University 1971 University Blvd	Lynchburg	VA	24502	**800-543-5317**	434-582-2000
Longwood University 201 High St	Farmville	VA	23909	**800-281-4677**	434-395-2060
Lynchburg College 1501 Lakeside Dr	Lynchburg	VA	24501	**800-426-8101**	434-544-8100
Mary Baldwin College PO Box 1500	Staunton	VA	24402	**800-468-2262**	540-887-7019
Marymount University 2807 N Glebe Rd	Arlington	VA	22207	**800-548-7638**	703-522-5600
Old Dominion University	Norfolk	VA	23529	**800-348-7926**	757-683-3000
Radford University Norwood St & Rt 11	Radford	VA	24142	**800-890-4265**	540-831-5000
Randolph-Macon College PO Box 5005	Ashland	VA	23005	**800-888-1762**	804-798-8372
Randolph-Macon Woman's College 2500 Rivermont Ave	Lynchburg	VA	24503	**800-745-7692**	434-947-8000
Roanoke College 221 College Ln	Salem	VA	24153	**800-388-2276**	540-375-2500
Saint Paul's College 115 College Dr	Lawrenceville	VA	23868	**800-678-7071**	434-848-3111
Shenandoah University 1460 University Dr	Winchester	VA	22601	**800-432-2266**	540-665-4581
Southern Virginia University 1 University Hill Dr	Buena Vista	VA	24416	**800-229-8420**	540-261-8400
Strayer University					
Alexandria Campus 2730 Eisenhower Ave	Alexandria	VA	22314	**888-478-7293**	703-329-9100
Arlington Campus 2121 15th St N	Arlington	VA	22201	**888-478-7293**	703-892-5100
Fredericksburg Campus 4500 Plank Rd	Fredericksburg	VA	22407	**800-765-8680**	540-785-8800
Sweet Briar College 134 Chappel Rd	Sweet Briar	VA	24595	**800-381-6142**	434-381-6100
University of Mary Washington 1301 College Ave	Fredericksburg	VA	22401	**800-468-5614**	540-654-1000
University of Richmond	Richmond	VA	23173	**800-700-1662**	804-289-8000
University of Virginia's College at Wise 1 College Ave	Wise	VA	24293	**888-282-9324**	276-328-0102
Virginia Commonwealth University 821 W Franklin St	Richmond	VA	23284	**800-841-3638**	804-828-0100
Virginia Intermont College 1013 Moore St	Bristol	VA	24201	**800-451-1842**	276-669-6101
Virginia Military Institute 319 Letcher Ave	Lexington	VA	24450	**800-767-4207**	540-464-7207
Virginia State University 1 Haydens Dr	Petersburg	VA	23806	**800-871-7611**	804-524-5000
Virginia Wesleyan College 1584 Wesleyan Dr	Norfolk	VA	23502	**800-737-8684**	757-455-3200
Westhampton College The Deanery 28 Westhampton Way	University of Richmond	VA	23173	**800-700-1662**	804-289-8440

Washington

Name / Address	City	State	Zip	Toll-Free	Phone
Antioch University 2326 6th Ave	Seattle	WA	98121	**888-268-4477**	206-441-5352
Central Washington University 400 E University Way	Ellensburg	WA	98926	**866-298-4968**	509-963-1111
City University of Bellevue 11900 NE 1st St	Bellevue	WA	98005	**800-426-5596**	425-637-1010
Cornish College of the Arts 1000 Lenora St	Seattle	WA	98121	**800-726-2787**	206-323-1400
Eastern Washington University 101 Sutton Hall	Cheney	WA	99004	**888-740-1914**	509-359-6200
Gonzaga University 502 E Boone Ave	Spokane	WA	99258	**800-986-9585**	509-328-4220
Henry Cogswell College 3002 Colby Ave	Everett	WA	98201	**866-411-4221**	425-258-3351
Heritage College 3240 Fort Rd	Toppenish	WA	98948	**888-272-6190**	509-865-8500
Northwest University 5520 108th Ave NE	Kirkland	WA	98033	**800-669-3781***	425-822-8266
*Admissions					
Pacific Lutheran University 1010 122nd St S	Tacoma	WA	98447	**800-274-6758**	253-531-6900
Puget Sound Christian College 1618 Hewitt Ave	Everett	WA	98201	**888-775-8699**	425-257-3090
Saint Martin's College 5300 Pacific Ave SE	Lacey	WA	98503	**800-368-8803**	360-438-4311
Seattle Bible College 2363 NW 80th St	Seattle	WA	98117	**877-722-9673**	206-784-1888
Seattle Pacific University 3307 3rd Ave W	Seattle	WA	98119	**800-366-3344**	206-281-2000
Seattle University 901 12th Ave	Seattle	WA	98122	**800-542-0833**	206-296-6000
University of Puget Sound 1500 N Warner St	Tacoma	WA	98416	**800-396-7191**	253-879-3611
University of Washington Tacoma 1900 Commerce St	Tacoma	WA	98402	**800-736-7750**	253-692-4400
Walla Walla College 125 SW 4th Ave	College Place	WA	99324	**800-541-8900**	509-527-2327
Washington State University	Pullman	WA	99164	**800-468-6978**	509-335-3564
Whitman College 345 Boyer Ave	Walla Walla	WA	99362	**877-462-9448**	509-527-5111
Whitworth College 300 W Hawthorne Rd	Spokane	WA	99251	**800-533-4668**	509-777-1000

West Virginia

Name / Address	City	State	Zip	Toll-Free	Phone
Alderson-Broaddus College College Hill Rd	Philippi	WV	26416	**800-263-1549***	304-457-1700
*Admissions					
Appalachian Bible College PO Box ABC	Bradley	WV	25818	**800-678-9222**	304-877-6428
Bethany College Main St	Bethany	WV	26032	**800-922-7611**	304-829-7000
Bluefield State College 219 Rock St	Bluefield	WV	24701	**800-654-7798**	304-327-4000
Concord University PO Box 1000	Athens	WV	24712	**800-344-6679**	304-384-3115
Davis & Elkins College 100 Campus Dr	Elkins	WV	26241	**800-624-3157**	304-637-1900
Fairmont State College 1201 Locust Ave	Fairmont	WV	26554	**800-641-5678**	304-367-4000
Glenville State College 200 High St	Glenville	WV	26351	**800-924-2010**	304-462-7361
Mountain State University 609 S Kanawha St	Beckley	WV	25801	**800-766-6067**	304-253-7351
Ohio Valley College 1 Campus View Dr	Vienna	WV	26105	**877-446-8668**	304-865-6000
Salem International University 223 W Main St	Salem	WV	26426	**800-283-4562**	304-782-5011
Shepherd University 301 King St	Shepherdstown	WV	25443	**800-344-5231**	304-876-5000
University of Charleston 2300 MacCorkle Ave SE	Charleston	WV	25304	**800-995-4682**	304-357-4800
West Liberty State College PO Box 295	West Liberty	WV	26074	**800-732-6204**	304-336-5000
West Virginia State University Barron Dr PO Box 1000	Institute	WV	25112	**800-987-2112**	304-766-3000
West Virginia University PO Box 6009	Morgantown	WV	26506	**800-344-9881**	304-293-2124
Institute of Technology 405 Fayette Pike	Montgomery	WV	25136	**888-554-8324**	304-442-3071
West Virginia Wesleyan College 59 College Ave	Buckhannon	WV	26201	**800-722-9933**	304-473-8000
Wheeling Jesuit University 316 Washington Ave	Wheeling	WV	26003	**800-624-6992**	304-243-2000

Wisconsin

Name / Address	City	State	Zip	Toll-Free	Phone
Alverno College PO Box 343922	Milwaukee	WI	53234	**800-933-3401**	414-382-6100
Beloit College 700 College St	Beloit	WI	53511	**800-356-0751**	608-363-2500
Cardinal Stritch University 6801 N Yates Rd	Milwaukee	WI	53217	**800-347-8822**	414-410-4000
Carroll College 100 N East Ave	Waukesha	WI	53186	**800-227-7655**	262-547-1211
Carthage College 2001 Alford Pk Dr	Kenosha	WI	53140	**800-351-4058**	262-551-8500
Concordia University Wisconsin 12800 N Lake Shore Dr	Mequon	WI	53097	**888-628-9472**	262-243-5700
Edgewood College 1000 Edgewood College Dr	Madison	WI	53711	**800-444-4861**	608-663-4861
Lakeland College W 3718 South Dr	Plymouth	WI	53073	**800-569-2166**	920-565-2111
Lawrence University PO Box 599	Appleton	WI	54912	**888-201-6017**	920-832-7000
Maranatha Baptist Bible College Inc 745 W Main St	Watertown	WI	53094	**800-622-2947**	920-261-9300
Marian College of Fond du Lac 45 S National Ave	Fond du Lac	WI	54935	**800-262-7426**	920-923-7650
Marquette University 1442 W Wisconsin Ave	Milwaukee	WI	53233	**800-222-6544**	414-288-7700
Milwaukee Institute of Art & Design 273 E Erie St	Milwaukee	WI	53202	**888-749-6423**	414-276-7889

				Toll-Free	Phone
Milwaukee School of Engineering 1025 N Broadway St	Milwaukee	WI	53202	**800-332-6763**	414-277-6763
Mount Mary College 2900 N Menomonee River Pkwy	Milwaukee	WI	53222	**800-321-6265**	414-256-1219
Northland Baptist Bible College W10085 Pike Plains Rd	Dunbar	WI	54119	**888-466-7845**	715-324-5245
Northland College 1411 Ellis Ave	Ashland	WI	54806	**800-753-1840**	715-682-1699
Ripon College 300 Seward St	Ripon	WI	54971	**800-947-4766**	920-748-8337
Saint Norbert College 100 Grant St	De Pere	WI	54115	**800-236-4878**	920-403-3005
Silver Lake College 2406 S Alverno Rd	Manitowoc	WI	54220	**800-236-4752**	920-686-6175
University of Wisconsin Eau Claire 105 Garfield Ave PO Box 4004	Eau Claire	WI	54701	**888-463-6893**	715-836-2637
University of Wisconsin Platteville 1 University Plaza	Platteville	WI	53818	**800-362-5515**	608-342-1125
University of Wisconsin Stout 802 S Broadway	Menomonie	WI	54751	**800-447-8688**	715-232-1232
Viterbo University 900 Viterbo Dr	La Crosse	WI	54601	**800-848-3726**	608-796-3000
Wisconsin Lutheran College 8800 W Bluemound Rd	Milwaukee	WI	53226	**888-947-5884**	414-443-8800

Wyoming

				Toll-Free	Phone
University of Wyoming 1000 E University Ave Dept 3435	Laramie	WY	82071	**800-342-5996**	307-766-5160

164 COLLEGES & UNIVERSITIES - GRADUATE & PROFESSIONAL SCHOOLS

164-1 Law Schools

				Toll-Free	Phone
Appalachian School of Law PO Box 2825	Grundy	VA	24614	**800-895-7411**	276-935-4349
California Western School of Law 225 Cedar St	San Diego	CA	92101	**800-255-4252**	
Drake University School of Law 2507 University Ave	Des Moines	IA	50311	**800-443-7253**	515-271-2824
Gonzaga University School of Law 721 N Cincinnati St	Spokane	WA	99258	**800-793-1710***	509-328-4220
*Admissions					
Hamline University School of Law 1536 Hewitt Ave	Saint Paul	MN	55104	**800-388-3688**	651-523-2461
Mercer University Walter F George School of Law 1021 Georgia Ave	Macon	GA	31207	**800-637-2378**	478-301-2605
Michigan State University DCL College of Law 368 Law College Bldg	East Lansing	MI	48824	**800-844-9352**	517-432-6810
Northern Illinois University College of Law 1425 W Lincoln Hwy	DeKalb	IL	60115	**800-892-3050**	815-753-8559
Nova Southeastern University Shepard Broad Law Center 3305 College Ave	Fort Lauderdale	FL	33314	**800-986-6529**	954-262-6100
Penn State Dickinson School of Law 150 S College St	Carlisle	PA	17013	**800-840-1122**	717-240-5000
Pennsylvania State University Dickinson School of Law 150 S College St	Carlisle	PA	17013	**800-840-1122**	717-240-5000
Saint John's University School of Law 8000 Utopia Pkwy	Jamaica	NY	11439	**888-978-5647**	718-990-6611
Saint Mary's University School of Law 1 Camino Santa Maria	San Antonio	TX	78228	**800-367-7868**	210-436-3523
Seton Hall University School of Law 1 Newark Ctr	Newark	NJ	07102	**888-415-7271**	973-642-8747
Southern University Law Center PO Box 9294	Baton Rouge	LA	70813	**800-537-1135**	225-771-6297
Texas Wesleyan University School of Law 1515 Commerce St	Fort Worth	TX	76102	**800-733-9529**	817-212-4000
University of Detroit Mercy School of Law 651 E Jefferson Ave	Detroit	MI	48226	**866-428-1610**	313-596-0264
University of Idaho College of Law University of Idaho College of Law PO Box 442321	Moscow	ID	83844	**888-884-3246**	208-885-4977
University of South Dakota School of Law 414 E Clark St	Vermillion	SD	57069	**877-269-6837**	605-677-5443
Valparaiso University School of Law 656 S Greenwich St	Valparaiso	IN	46383	**888-825-7652**	219-465-7829
Vermont Law School PO Box 96	South Royalton	VT	05068	**800-227-1395**	802-831-1001
Whittier Law School 3333 Harbor Blvd	Costa Mesa	CA	92626	**800-808-8188**	714-444-4141
Widener University School of Law Harrisburg 3800 Vartan Way	Harrisburg	PA	17110	**888-943-3637**	717-541-3900
Widener University School of Law Wilmington 4601 Concord Pike	Wilmington	DE	19803	**888-943-3637**	302-477-2100
William Mitchell College of Law 875 Summit Ave	Saint Paul	MN	55105	**888-962-5529**	651-227-9171

164-2 Medical Schools

				Toll-Free	Phone
Cincinnati Children's Hospital Medical Center 3333 Burnet Ave	Cincinnati	OH	45229	**800-344-2462**	513-636-4200
Dartmouth Medical School 1 Rope Ferry Rd	Dartmouth	NH	03755	**877-367-1797**	603-650-1200
Loma Linda University School of Medicine	Loma Linda	CA	92350	**800-422-4558**	909-558-4467
Oregon Health & Science University School of Medicine 3181 SW Sam Jackson Park Rd L-109	Portland	OR	97239	**800-775-5460**	503-494-7800
State University of New York Upstate Medical University 766 Irving Ave	Syracuse	NY	13210	**800-736-2171**	315-464-4570
SUNY Upstate Medical University 766 Irving Ave	Syracuse	NY	13210	**800-736-2171**	315-464-4570
Uniformed Services University of the Health Sciences 4301 Jones Bridge Rd	Bethesda	MD	20814	**800-772-1743**	
University of California Irvine College of Medicine Medical Education Bldg 802	Irvine	CA	92697	**800-824-5388**	949-824-5388
University of Ottawa Faculty of Medicine 75 Laurier Ave E Tabaret Hall	Ottawa	ON	K1N6N5	**877-868-8292**	613-562-5700
University of Texas Medical Branch at Galveston 301 University Blvd	Galveston	TX	77555	**800-228-1841**	409-772-2618

164-3 Theological Schools

				Toll-Free	Phone
Abilene Christian University ACU Box 29000	Abilene	TX	79699	**800-460-6228***	325-674-2000
*Admissions					
Anderson University 1100 E 5th St	Anderson	IN	46012	**800-428-6414***	765-649-9071
*Admissions					
Andover Newton Theological School 210 Herrick Rd	Newton Centre	MA	02459	**800-964-2687**	617-964-1100
Aquinas Institute of Theology 3642 Lindell Blvd	St. Louis	MO	63108	**800-977-3869**	314-977-3882
Assemblies of God Theological Seminary 1435 N Glenstone Ave	Springfield	MO	65802	**800-467-2487**	417-268-1000
Bangor Theological Seminary 300 Union St	Bangor	ME	04401	**800-287-6781**	207-942-6781
Barry University 11300 NE 2nd Ave	Miami Shores	FL	33161	**800-756-6000**	305-899-3000
Bethany Theological Seminary 615 National Rd W	Richmond	IN	47374	**800-287-8822**	765-983-1800
Biblical Theological Seminary 200 N Main St	Hatfield	PA	19440	**800-235-4021**	215-368-5000
Biola University 13800 Biola Ave	La Mirada	CA	90639	**800-652-4652***	562-903-6000
*Admissions					
Briercrest Seminary 510 College Dr	Caronport	SK	S0H0S0	**888-232-0531**	306-756-3200
Calvin Theological Seminary 3233 Burton St SE	Grand Rapids	MI	49546	**800-388-6034**	616-957-6036
Campbell University PO Box 546	Buies Creek	NC	27506	**800-334-4111**	910-893-1290
Canadian Southern Baptist Seminary 200 Seminary View	Cochrane	AB	T4C2G1	**877-922-2727**	403-932-6622
Catholic University of America 620 Michigan Ave NE	Washington	DC	20064	**800-673-2772**	202-319-5000
Central Baptist Theological Seminary 741 N 31st St	Kansas City	KS	66102	**800-677-2287**	913-371-5313
Christian Theological Seminary 1000 W 42nd St	Indianapolis	IN	46208	**800-585-0108**	317-924-1331
Church Divinity School of the Pacific 2451 Ridge Rd	Berkeley	CA	94709	**800-353-2377**	510-204-0700
Cincinnati Bible College & Seminary 2700 Glenway Ave	Cincinnati	OH	45204	**800-949-4222**	513-244-8100
Columbia International University 7435 Monticello Rd	Columbia	SC	29203	**800-777-2227**	803-754-4100
Cornerstone University 1001 E Beltline Ave NE	Grand Rapids	MI	49525	**800-787-9778***	616-222-1426
*Admissions					
Covenant Theological Seminary 12330 Conway Rd	Saint Louis	MO	63141	**800-264-8064**	314-434-4044
Earlham School of Religion 228 College Ave	Richmond	IN	47374	**800-432-1377**	765-983-1423
Eastern Baptist Theological Seminary 6 Lancaster Ave	Wynnewood	PA	19096	**800-220-3287**	610-896-5000
Eastern Mennonite University 1200 Park Rd	Harrisonburg	VA	22802	**800-368-2665***	540-432-4118
*Admissions					
Eden Theological Seminary 475 E Lockwood Ave	Saint Louis	MO	63119	**800-969-3627**	314-961-3627
Evangelical School of Theology 121 S College St	Myerstown	PA	17067	**800-532-5775**	717-866-5775
Gardner-Webb University M Christopher White School of Divinity 110 S Main St Noel Hall	Boiling Springs	NC	28017	**800-619-3761**	704-406-4400
Garrett-Evangelical Theological Seminary 2121 Sheridan Rd	Evanston	IL	60201	**800-736-4627**	847-866-3900
Jesuit School of Theology at Berkeley 1735 LeRoy Ave	Berkeley	CA	94709	**800-824-0122**	510-549-5000
La Sierra University 4500 Riverwalk Pkwy	Riverside	CA	92515	**800-874-5587**	951-785-2000
Lancaster Theological Seminary 555 W James St	Lancaster	PA	17603	**800-393-0654**	717-393-0654
Lincoln Christian Seminary 100 Campus View Dr	Lincoln	IL	62656	**888-522-5228**	217-732-3168
Lipscomb University 3901 Granny White Pike	Nashville	TN	37204	**800-333-4358**	615-269-1000
Louisville Presbyterian Theological Seminary 1044 Alta Vista Rd	Louisville	KY	40205	**800-264-1839**	502-895-3411
Lutheran School of Theology at Chicago 1100 E 55th St	Chicago	IL	60615	**800-635-1116**	773-256-0700
Lutheran Theological Seminary at Gettysburg 61 Seminary Ridge	Gettysburg	PA	17325	**800-658-8437**	717-334-6286
Lutheran Theological Seminary at Philadelphia 7301 Germantown Ave	Philadelphia	PA	19119	**800-286-4616**	215-248-4616
Mennonite Brethren Biblical Seminary 4824 E Butler Ave	Fresno	CA	93727	**800-251-6227**	559-251-8628
Michigan Theological Seminary 41550 E Ann Arbor Trail	Plymouth	MI	48170	**888-687-2737**	734-207-9581
Mount Saint Mary's University 16300 Old Emmitsburg Rd	Emmitsburg	MD	21727	**800-448-4347**	301-447-5214
Nazarene Theological Seminary 1700 E Meyer Blvd	Kansas City	MO	64131	**800-831-3011**	816-333-6254
New Brunswick Theological Seminary 17 Seminary Pl	New Brunswick	NJ	08901	**800-445-6287**	732-247-5241
Newman Theological College 15611 St Albert Trail	Edmonton	AB	T6V1H3	**800-386-7231**	780-447-2993
Oakland City University 138 N Lucretia St	Oakland City	IN	47660	**800-737-5125**	812-749-4781
Oral Roberts University 7777 S Lewis Ave	Tulsa	OK	74171	**800-678-8876**	918-495-6161
Pacific Lutheran Theological Seminary 2770 Marin Ave	Berkeley	CA	94708	**800-235-7587**	510-524-5264
Reformed Theological Seminary 5422 Clinton Blvd	Jackson	MS	39209	**800-543-2703**	601-923-1600
Regent College 5800 University Blvd	Vancouver	BC	V6T2E4	**800-663-8664**	604-224-3245
Roberts Wesleyan College 2301 Westside Dr	Rochester	NY	14624	**800-777-4792***	585-594-6000
*Admissions					
Saint Andrew's College 1121 College Dr	Saskatoon	SK	S7N0W3	**877-664-8970**	306-966-8970
Saint John's University	Collegeville	MN	56321	**800-245-6467**	320-363-2196
Samford University 800 Lakeshore Dr	Birmingham	AL	35229	**800-888-7218**	205-726-3673
Shaw University 118 E South St	Raleigh	NC	27601	**800-214-6683***	919-546-8275
*Admissions					
Southern Baptist Theological Seminary 2825 Lexington Rd	Louisville	KY	40280	**800-626-5525**	502-897-4011
Taylor University College & Seminary 11525 23rd Ave	Edmonton	AB	T6J4T3	**800-567-4988**	780-431-5200
Trinity Episcopal School for Ministry 311 11th St	Ambridge	PA	15003	**800-874-8754**	724-266-3838
Trinity International University 2065 Half Day Rd	Deerfield	IL	60015	**800-822-3225**	847-317-7000

Theological Schools (Cont'd)

	City	State	ZIP	Toll-Free	Phone
Trinity Western University 7600 Glover Rd	Langley	BC	V2Y1Y1	**888-468-6898**	604-888-7511
Tyndale University College & Seminary 25 Ballyconnor Ct	Toronto	ON	M2M4B3	**877-896-3253**	416-226-6380
Union Theological Seminary & Presbyterian School of Christian Education 3401 Brook Rd	Richmond	VA	23227	**800-229-2990**	804-355-0671
University of Saint Thomas 2115 Summit Ave	Saint Paul	MN	55105	**800-328-6819**	651-962-5000
University of the South 735 University Ave	Sewanee	TN	37383	**800-522-2234**	931-598-1238
Washington Theological Union 6896 Laurel St NW	Washington	DC	20012	**800-334-9922**	202-726-8800
Wesley Biblical Seminary 787 E Northside Dr	Jackson	MS	39206	**800-788-9571**	601-366-8880
Western Seminary 5511 SE Hawthorne Blvd	Portland	OR	97215	**877-517-1800**	503-517-1800
Winebrenner Theological Seminary 950 N Main St	Findlay	OH	45840	**800-992-4987**	419-434-4200

165 COLLEGES & UNIVERSITIES - HISTORICALLY BLACK

	City	State	ZIP	Toll-Free	Phone
Alabama State University 915 S Jackson St	Montgomery	AL	36104	**800-253-5037**	334-229-4100
Albany State University 504 College Dr	Albany	GA	31705	**800-822-7267**	229-430-4600
Allen University 1530 Harden St	Columbia	SC	29204	**877-625-5368**	803-376-5700
Barber-Scotia College 145 Cabarrus Ave W *Admissions	Concord	NC	28025	**800-267-3910***	704-789-2902
Benedict College 1600 Harden St	Columbia	SC	29204	**800-868-6598**	803-256-4220
Bennett College 900 E Washington St *Admissions	Greensboro	NC	27401	**800-413-5323***	336-273-4431
Bethune-Cookman College 640 Mary McLeod Bethune Blvd	Daytona Beach	FL	32114	**800-448-0228**	386-255-1401
Bluefield State College 219 Rock St	Bluefield	WV	24701	**800-654-7798**	304-327-4000
Bowie State University 14000 Jericho Park Rd	Bowie	MD	20715	**877-772-6943**	301-860-4000
Central State University 1400 Brush Row Rd PO Box 1004	Wilberforce	OH	45384	**800-388-2781**	937-376-6011
Cheyney University of Pennsylvania 1837 University Cir PO Box 200	Cheyney	PA	19319	**800-243-9639**	610-399-2275
Claflin University 400 Magnolia St	Orangeburg	SC	29115	**800-922-1276**	803-535-5339
Clark Atlanta University 223 James P Brawley Dr SW *Admissions	Atlanta	GA	30314	**800-688-3228***	404-880-8000
Coahoma Community College 3240 Friars Point Rd	Clarksdale	MS	38614	**800-844-1222**	662-621-4205
Coppin State University 2500 W North Ave	Baltimore	MD	21216	**800-635-3674**	410-951-3600
Dillard University 2601 Gentilly Blvd	New Orleans	LA	70122	**800-216-6637**	504-816-4670
Edward Waters College 1658 Kings Rd *Admissions	Jacksonville	FL	32209	**888-898-3191***	904-366-2715
Elizabeth City State University 1704 Weeksville Rd CB 901 *Admissions	Elizabeth City	NC	27909	**800-347-3278***	252-335-3305
Fayetteville State University 1200 Murchison Rd *Admissions	Fayetteville	NC	28301	**800-222-2594***	910-672-1111
Fisk University 1000 17th Ave N	Nashville	TN	37208	**800-443-3475**	615-329-8500
Hampton University 100 E Queen St *Admissions	Hampton	VA	23668	**800-624-3328***	757-727-5000
Howard University 2400 6th St NW	Washington	DC	20059	**800-822-6363**	202-806-6100
Jackson State University 1400 John R Lynch St	Jackson	MS	39217	**800-848-6817**	601-979-2121
JF Drake State Technical College 3421 Meridian St N	Huntsville	AL	35811	**888-413-7253**	256-539-8161
Johnson C Smith University 100 Beatties Ford Rd *Admissions	Charlotte	NC	28216	**800-782-7303***	704-378-1000
Lane College 545 Lane Ave *Admissions	Jackson	TN	38301	**800-960-7533***	731-426-7500
LeMoyne-Owen College 807 Walker Ave *Admissions	Memphis	TN	38126	**800-737-7778***	901-774-9090
Lincoln University 820 Chestnut St *Admissions	Jefferson City	MO	65102	**800-521-5052***	573-681-5000
Lincoln University 1570 Old Baltimore Pike PO Box 179 *Admissions	Lincoln University	PA	19352	**800-790-0191***	610-932-8300
Livingstone College 701 W Monroe St	Salisbury	NC	28144	**800-835-3435**	704-216-6000
Miles College 5500 Myron Massey Blvd	Fairfield	AL	35064	**800-445-0708**	205-929-1000
Morehouse College 830 Westview Dr SW *Admissions	Atlanta	GA	30314	**800-851-1254***	404-681-2800
North Carolina A & T State University 1601 E Market St *Admissions	Greensboro	NC	27411	**800-443-8964***	336-334-7500
Oakwood College 7000 Adventist Blvd	Huntsville	AL	35896	**800-824-5312**	256-726-7356
Paine College 1235 15th St	Augusta	GA	30901	**800-476-7703**	706-821-8200
Paul Quinn College 3837 Simpson Stuart Rd	Dallas	TX	75241	**800-237-2648**	214-376-1000
Philander Smith College 1 Trudie Kibbe Reed Dr	Little Rock	AR	72202	**800-446-6772**	501-375-9845
Prairie View A & M University PO Box 3089	Prairie View	TX	77446	**800-787-7826**	936-857-2626
Rust College 150 E Rust Ave	Holly Springs	MS	38635	**888-886-8492**	662-252-8000
Saint Augustine's College 1315 Oakwood Ave *Admissions	Raleigh	NC	27610	**800-948-1126***	919-516-4016
Saint Paul's College 115 College Dr	Lawrenceville	VA	23868	**800-678-7071**	434-848-3111
Shaw University 118 E South St *Admissions	Raleigh	NC	27601	**800-214-6683***	919-546-8275
South Carolina State University 300 College St NE *Admissions	Orangeburg	SC	29117	**800-260-5956***	803-536-7000
Southern University Shreveport 3050 ML King Jr Dr	Shreveport	LA	71107	**800-458-1472**	318-674-3300
Southern University & A & M College Branch Post Office	Baton Rouge	LA	70813	**800-256-1531**	225-771-4500
Southwestern Christian College PO Box 10	Terrell	TX	75160	**800-925-9357**	972-524-3341
Spelman College 350 Spelman Ln SW *Admissions	Atlanta	GA	30314	**800-982-2411***	404-681-3643
Stillman College PO Box 1430 *Admissions	Tuscaloosa	AL	35403	**800-841-5722***	205-349-4240
Tennessee State University 3500 John A Merritt Blvd PO Box 9609 *Admissions	Nashville	TN	37209	**888-463-6878***	615-963-5000
Tougaloo College 500 W County Line Rd *Admissions	Tougaloo	MS	39174	**888-424-2566***	601-977-7700
Tuskegee University *Admissions	Tuskegee	AL	36088	**800-622-6531***	334-727-8011
University of Arkansas Pine Bluff 1200 N University Dr *Admissions	Pine Bluff	AR	71601	**800-264-6585***	870-575-8000
Virginia State University 1 Haydens Dr	Petersburg	VA	23806	**800-871-7611**	804-524-5000
Voorhees College 1411 Voorhees Rd PO Box 678	Denmark	SC	29042	**800-446-6250**	803-793-3351
Wilberforce University 1055 N Bickett Rd PO Box 1001	Wilberforce	OH	45384	**800-367-8568**	937-376-2911
Wiley College 711 Wiley Ave *Admissions	Marshall	TX	75670	**800-658-6889***	903-927-3311
Winston-Salem State University 601 ML King Jr Dr	Winston-Salem	NC	27110	**800-257-4052**	336-750-2000
Xavier University of Louisiana 1 Drexel Dr *Admissions	New Orleans	LA	70125	**877-928-4378***	504-486-7411

166 COLLEGES & UNIVERSITIES - JESUIT

	City	State	ZIP	Toll-Free	Phone
Boston College 140 Commonwealth Ave	Chestnut Hill	MA	02467	**800-360-2522**	617-552-8000
Canisius College 2001 Main St	Buffalo	NY	14208	**800-843-1517**	716-883-7000
College of the Holy Cross 1 College St	Worcester	MA	01610	**800-442-2421**	508-793-2011
Creighton University 2500 California Plaza	Omaha	NE	68178	**800-282-5835**	402-280-2700
Fordham University 441 E Fordham Rd	Bronx	NY	10458	**800-367-3426**	718-817-1000
College at Lincoln Center 113 W 60th St	New York	NY	10023	**800-367-3426**	212-636-6710
Gonzaga University 502 E Boone Ave	Spokane	WA	99258	**800-986-9585**	509-328-4220
Le Moyne College 1419 Salt Springs Rd	Syracuse	NY	13214	**800-333-4733**	315-445-4100
Loyola College 4501 N Charles St	Baltimore	MD	21210	**800-221-9107**	410-617-2000
Loyola Marymount University 1 LMU Dr	Los Angeles	CA	90045	**800-568-4636**	310-338-2700
Loyola University 6363 St Charles Ave	New Orleans	LA	70118	**800-456-9652**	504-865-2011
Loyola University Chicago 820 N Michigan Ave	Chicago	IL	60611	**800-262-2373**	312-915-6000
Lake Shore Campus 6525 N Sheridan Rd	Chicago	IL	60626	**800-262-2373**	773-274-3000
Marquette University 1442 W Wisconsin Ave	Milwaukee	WI	53233	**800-222-6544**	414-288-7700
Regis University 3333 Regis Blvd	Denver	CO	80221	**800-568-8932**	303-458-4100
Rockhurst University 1100 Rockhurst Rd	Kansas City	MO	64110	**800-842-6776**	816-501-4000
Saint Louis University 221 N Grand Blvd	Saint Louis	MO	63103	**800-758-3678**	314-977-2222
Saint Peter's College 2641 JFK Blvd	Jersey City	NJ	07306	**888-772-9933**	201-915-9000
Seattle University 901 12th Ave	Seattle	WA	98122	**800-542-0833**	206-296-6000
Spring Hill College 4000 Dauphin St	Mobile	AL	36608	**800-742-6704**	251-380-4000
University of Detroit Mercy 4001 W McNichols Rd *Admissions	Detroit	MI	48219	**800-635-5020***	313-993-1000
University of San Francisco 2130 Fulton St *Admissions	San Francisco	CA	94117	**800-225-5873***	415-422-5555
University of Scranton 800 Linden St St Thomas Hall	Scranton	PA	18510	**888-727-2686**	570-941-7400
Wheeling Jesuit University 316 Washington Ave	Wheeling	WV	26003	**800-624-6992**	304-243-2000
Xavier University 3800 Victory Pkwy	Cincinnati	OH	45207	**800-344-4698**	513-745-3000

167 COMMODITY CONTRACTS BROKERS & DEALERS

SEE ALSO Investment Advice & Management; Securities Brokers & Dealers

	City	State	ZIP	Toll-Free	Phone
ADM Investor Services Inc 141 W Jackson Blvd 1610A Board of Trade Bldg	Chicago	IL	60604	**800-243-2649**	312-435-7000
Basic Commodities Inc 863 S Orlando Ave	Winter Park	FL	32789	**800-338-7006**	407-629-2000
Cargill Investor Services Inc 233 S Wacker Dr Suite 2300	Chicago	IL	60606	**800-621-4475**	312-460-4000
Country Hedging Inc PO Box 64089	Saint Paul	MN	55164	**800-328-6530**	651-355-5151
Goldman Sachs & Co 85 Broad St	New York	NY	10004	**800-323-5678**	212-902-1000
Keeley Investment Corp 401 S La Salle St Suite 1201	Chicago	IL	60605	**800-533-5344**	312-786-5000
Koch Supply & Trading LP 4111 E 37th St N	Wichita	KS	67220	**800-245-2243**	316-828-5500
Morgan Stanley 1585 Broadway *NYSE: MWD*	New York	NY	10036	**800-223-2440**	212-761-4000
NetFutures 150 S Wacker Dr Suite 2350	Chicago	IL	60606	**888-449-6784**	312-277-0051
optionsXpress Inc 39 S LaSalle St Suite 220 *NASDAQ: OXPS*	Chicago	IL	60603	**888-280-8020**	312-630-3300
Orion Futures 1905 W Busch Blvd	Tampa	FL	33612	**888-769-9399**	813-876-9662
Paragon Investments 9941 NW Hwy 24 Suite 3	Silver Lake	KS	66539	**888-452-8751**	
Rand Financial Services Inc 141 W Jackson Blvd Suite 1950	Chicago	IL	60604	**800-842-7263**	312-559-8800
Refco Inc 550 W Jackson Blvd Suite 1300	Chicago	IL	60661	**800-365-9310**	312-788-2000
RJ O'Brien & Assoc 222 S Riverside Plaza Suite 900	Chicago	IL	60606	**800-621-0757**	312-373-5000
XPRESStrade LLC 10 S Wacker Dr Suite 2550	Chicago	IL	60606	**800-947-6228**	312-715-6228

168 COMMUNICATIONS TOWER OPERATORS

SEE ALSO Construction - Heavy Construction Contractors - Communications Lines & Towers Construction

	City	State	ZIP	Toll-Free	Phone
Alternative Networking Inc DBA ANI Site Development 1300 Riverland Rd	Fort Lauderdale	FL	33312	**800-733-9929**	954-581-9929

Classified Section

Company	City	State	Zip	Toll-Free	Phone
American Tower Corp 116 Huntington Ave 11th Fl *NYSE: AMT*	Boston	MA	02116	**877-282-7483**	617-375-7500
ANI Site Development 1300 Riverland Rd	Fort Lauderdale	FL	33312	**800-733-9929**	954-581-9929
Atlantic Tower Corp 10197 Maple Leaf Ct	Ashland	VA	23005	**800-826-8616**	804-550-7490
Centerpointe Communications 2106 W Pioneer Pkwy Suite 131	Arlington	TX	76013	**877-277-6811**	817-277-6811
Central Tower Inc 2855 Hwy 261	Newburgh	IN	47630	**800-664-8222**	812-853-0595
CLS Group 1015 Waterwood Pkwy Suite D	Edmond	OK	73034	**800-580-5460**	405-348-5460
DukeNet Communications Inc 400 S Tryon St	Charlotte	NC	28202	**800-873-3853**	704-382-7111
Global Signal Inc 301 N Cattleman Rd Suite 300 *NYSE: GSE*	Sarasota	FL	34232	**888-748-3482**	941-364-8886
LTS Wireless Inc 311 S LHS Dr	Lumberton	TX	77657	**800-255-5471**	409-755-4038
Millennium Telecom LLC 310 60th St NW	Sauk Rapids	MN	56379	**877-720-6249**	320-253-5489
SBA Communications Corp 5900 Broken Sound Pkwy NW *NASDAQ: SBAC*	Boca Raton	FL	33487	**800-487-7483**	561-995-7670
SCANA Communications Inc 1426 Main St MC 107 *Cust Svc	Columbia	SC	29201	**800-679-5463***	803-217-7383
Shaffer Communications Group Inc 8584 Katy Fwy Suite 300	Houston	TX	77024	**800-243-7525**	713-463-0022
SpectraSite Inc 100 Regency Forest Dr Suite 400 *NYSE: SSI*	Cary	NC	27511	**888-468-0112**	919-468-0112
Spectrum Resources Tower LP 6400 Arlington Blvd Suite 1000	Falls Church	VA	22042	**888-508-6937**	703-533-1312
Spectrum Site Management Corp 6060 N Central Expy Suite 642	Dallas	TX	75206	**800-966-8885**	214-540-0359

169 COMMUNITIES - ONLINE

SEE ALSO Internet Service Providers (ISPs)

Company	City	State	Zip	Toll-Free	Phone
Alloy Inc 151 W 26th St 11th Fl *NASDAQ: ALOYE ■ *Cust Svc*	New York	NY	10001	**888-452-5569***	212-244-4307
America Online Inc (AOL) 22000 AOL Way *Orders	Dulles	VA	20166	**888-265-8002***	703-265-1000
AOL (America Online Inc) 22000 AOL Way *Orders	Dulles	VA	20166	**888-265-8002***	703-265-1000
Blackvoices.com Inc 435 N Michigan Ave Suite L2	Chicago	IL	60611	**877-765-1350**	312-222-4326
iVillage Inc 500 7th Ave 14th Fl *NASDAQ: IVIL*	New York	NY	10018	**800-977-1436**	212-600-6000
lawyers.com Martindale-Hubbell 121 Chanlon Rd	New Providence	NJ	07974	**800-526-4902**	908-464-6800
SeniorNet 121 2nd St 7th Fl	San Francisco	CA	94105	**800-747-6848**	415-495-4990
SHRM Global Forum 1800 Duke St	Alexandria	VA	22314	**800-283-7476**	703-548-3440

COMPRESSORS - AIR CONDITIONING & REFRIGERATION

SEE Air Conditioning & Heating Equipment - Commercial/Industrial

170 COMPRESSORS - AIR & GAS

Company	City	State	Zip	Toll-Free	Phone
Beach-Russ Co 544 Union Ave	Brooklyn	NY	11211	**800-543-3903**	718-388-4090
Briggs & Stratton Power Products Group LLC PO Box 239	Jefferson	WI	53549	**800-270-1408**	920-674-3750
Compressor Engineering Corp (CECO) 5440 Alder Dr	Houston	TX	77081	**800-879-2326**	713-664-7333
Cooper Energy Services 11800 Charles St	Houston	TX	77041	**888-423-7463**	713-856-1500
Cooper Turbocompressor 3101 Broadway	Buffalo	NY	14225	**877-805-7911**	716-896-6600
Corken Inc 3805 NW 36th St	Oklahoma City	OK	73112	**800-631-4929**	405-946-5576
CSI Compressor Systems Inc 3809 S FM 1788 PO Box 60760	Midland	TX	79711	**800-365-1170**	432-563-1170
Curtis Dyna-Fog Ltd 17335 US Hwy 31 N	Westfield	IN	46074	**800-544-8990**	317-896-2561
Curtis-Toledo Inc 1905 Kienlen Ave	Saint Louis	MO	63133	**800-925-5431**	314-383-1300
Delavan Spray Technologies Div Goodrich Corp PO Box 969	Bamberg	SC	29003	**800-621-9357**	803-245-4347
Elliott Turbomachinery Co 901 N 4th St	Jeannette	PA	15644	**800-635-2208**	724-527-2811
Fountainhead Group Inc 23 Garden St	New York Mills	NY	13417	**800-311-9903**	315-736-0037
Gardner Denver Inc 1800 Gardner Expy *NYSE: GDI*	Quincy	IL	62305	**800-682-9868**	217-222-5400
Gardner Denver Water Jetting Systems Inc 12300 N Houston Rosslyn Rd	Houston	TX	77086	**800-231-3628**	281-448-5800
Gast Mfg Inc PO Box 97	Benton Harbor	MI	49023	**800-952-4278**	269-926-6171
Goodrich Corp Delavan Spray Technologies Div PO Box 969	Bamberg	SC	29003	**800-621-9357**	803-245-4347
Grimmer Industries Inc DBA GrimmerSchmidt Compressors 1015 N Hurricane Rd	Franklin	IN	46131	**800-428-9703**	317-736-8416
GrimmerSchmidt Compressors 1015 N Hurricane Rd	Franklin	IN	46131	**800-428-9703**	317-736-8416
Gusmer Corp 1 Gusmer Dr	Lakewood	NJ	08701	**800-367-4767**	732-370-9000
ITW Automotive Refinishing 1724 Indian Wood Cir	Maumee	OH	43537	**800-445-3988**	419-891-8100
ITW Industrial Finishing 195 International Blvd	Glendale Heights	IL	60139	**800-992-4657**	630-237-5000
ITW Ransburg 320 Phillips Ave *Cust Svc	Toledo	OH	43612	**800-726-8097***	419-470-2000
Mattson Spray Equipment 230 W Coleman St	Rice Lake	WI	54868	**800-877-4857**	715-234-1617
Nash Elmo Industries 9 Trefoil Dr	Trumbull	CT	06611	**800-553-6274**	203-459-3900
NEAC Compressor Service USA Inc 191 Howard St	Franklin	PA	16323	**800-458-0453**	814-437-3711
Norwalk Co Inc 20 N Water St	Norwalk	CT	06854	**800-556-5001**	203-838-4766
Saylor Beall Mfg Co Inc 400 N Kibbee St	Saint Johns	MI	48879	**800-248-9001**	989-224-2371
Scales Air Compressor Corp 110 Voice Rd	Carle Place	NY	11514	**800-777-9096**	516-248-9096
Sharpe Mfg Co 8750 Pioneer Blvd	Santa Fe Springs	CA	90670	**800-742-7731**	562-908-6800
Smith Air Compressors 1761 Genesis Dr	La Porte	IN	46350	**800-635-6587**	219-324-7776
Spencer Turbine Co 600 Day Hill Rd	Windsor	CT	06095	**800-232-4321**	860-688-8361
Squire Cogswell/Aeros Instruments Inc 1111 Lakeside Dr	Gurnee	IL	60031	**800-448-0770**	847-855-0500
Sullair Corp 3700 E Michigan Blvd	Michigan City	IN	46360	**800-785-5247**	219-879-5451
Sullivan-Palatek Inc River Rd	Claremont	NH	03743	**800-334-5022**	603-543-3131
Sulzer Metco US Inc 1101 Prospect Ave	Westbury	NY	11590	**800-638-2699**	516-334-1300
Thomas Industries Inc 4360 Brownsboro Rd Suite 300 *NYSE: TII*	Louisville	KY	40207	**800-626-2847**	502-893-4600
Tuthill Vacuum Systems 4840 W Kearney St	Springfield	MO	65803	**800-225-3810**	417-865-8115
Varian Vacuum Technologies 121 Hartwell Ave *Cust Svc	Lexington	MA	02421	**800-882-7426***	781-861-7200
Wagner Spray Tech Corp 1770 Fernbrook Ln	Plymouth	MN	55447	**800-328-8251**	763-553-0759
Zeks Compressed Air Solutions 1302 Goshen Pkwy	West Chester	PA	19380	**800-888-2323**	610-692-9100

171 COMPUTER EQUIPMENT

SEE ALSO Automatic Teller Machines (ATMs); Business Machines - Mfr; Computer Networking Products & Systems; Flash Memory Devices; Modems; Point-of-Sale (POS) & Point-of-Information (POI) Systems

171-1 Computer Input Devices

Company	City	State	Zip	Toll-Free	Phone
3M Touch Systems 300 Griffin Brook Dr	Methuen	MA	01844	**866-407-6666**	978-659-9000
Advanced Input Devices Inc 600 W Wilbur Ave	Coeur d'Alene	ID	83815	**800-444-5923**	208-765-8000
Andrea Electronics Corp 65 Orville Dr Suite 110 *AMEX: AND*	Bohemia	NY	11716	**800-442-7787**	631-719-1800
BenQ America Corp 53 Discovery	Irvine	CA	92618	**866-600-2367**	949-255-9500
Cirque Corp 2463 S 3850 West Suite A	Salt Lake City	UT	84120	**800-454-3375**	801-467-1100
Digit Professional Inc 3926 Varsity Dr	Ann Arbor	MI	48108	**877-767-8862**	734-677-0840
Electronics for Imaging Inc 303 Velocity Way *NASDAQ: EFII*	Foster City	CA	94404	**800-568-1917**	650-357-3500
Elo TouchSystems Inc 301 Constitution Dr	Menlo Park	CA	94025	**800-557-1458**	510-739-4600
Fellowes Inc 1789 Norwood Ave	Itasca	IL	60143	**800-945-4545**	630-893-1600
GTCO CalComp Inc 7125 Riverwood Dr	Columbia	MD	21046	**800-344-4723**	410-381-6688
Guillemot North America 5500 rue Saint-Laurent Suite 5000	Montreal	QC	H2T1S6	**877-484-5536**	514-279-9960
Immersion Corp 801 Fox Ln *NASDAQ: IMMR*	San Jose	CA	95131	**888-467-1900**	408-467-1900
Interlink Electronics Inc 546 Flynn Rd *NASDAQ: LINK*	Camarillo	CA	93012	**800-340-1331**	805-484-8855
iScribe 101 Redwood Shores Pkwy Suite 101	Redwood City	CA	94065	**877-483-1324**	650-620-0061
Kensington Technology Group 333 Twin Dolphin Dr 6th Fl	Redwood Shores	CA	94065	**800-243-2972**	650-572-2700
Kinesis Corp 22121 17th Ave SE Suite 112	Bothell	WA	98021	**800-454-6374**	425-402-8100
Logitech Inc 6505 Kaiser Dr *Sales	Fremont	CA	94555	**800-231-7717***	510-795-8500
Mace Group Inc 15861 Tapia St	Irwindale	CA	91706	**800-644-1132**	626-338-8787
Mad Catz Interactive Inc 7480 Mission Valley Rd Suite 101 *AMEX: MCZ*	San Diego	CA	92108	**800-831-1442**	619-683-9830
Memtron Technologies Inc 530 N Franklin St *Cust Svc	Frankenmuth	MI	48734	**800-234-7525***	989-652-2656
NaturalPoint Inc 33872 Eastgate Cir SE	Corvallis	OR	97333	**888-865-5535**	541-753-6645
Numonics Corp 101 Commerce Dr	Montgomeryville	PA	18936	**800-523-6716**	215-362-2766
PolyVision Corp 3970 Johns Creek Ct Suite 325	Suwanee	GA	30024	**800-620-7659**	678-542-3100
Seiko Instruments USA Inc Business & Home Office Products Div 2990 W Lomita Blvd	Torrance	CA	90505	**800-358-0880**	310-517-7050
SMART Technologies Inc 1207 11th Ave SW Suite 300	Calgary	AB	T3C0M5	**888-427-6278**	403-245-0333
TouchSystems Corp 220 Tradesmen Dr	Hutto	TX	78634	**800-320-5944**	512-846-2424
Virtual Ink Inc 20 Guest St Suite 520	Boston	MA	02135	**877-696-4646**	617-987-0410
Wacom Technology Corp 1311 SE Cardinal Ct	Vancouver	WA	98683	**800-922-9348**	360-896-9833

171-2 Computers - Handheld

Company	City	State	Zip	Toll-Free	Phone
Calculated Industries Inc 4840 Hytech Dr	Carson City	NV	89706	**800-854-8075**	775-885-4900
Casio Inc 570 Mt Pleasant Ave *Cust Svc	Dover	NJ	07801	**800-634-1895***	973-361-5400
DAP Technologies Corp 5525 W Cypress St Suite 205	Tampa	FL	33607	**800-229-2822**	813-969-3271
Ectaco Inc 31-21 31st St	Long Island City	NY	11106	**800-710-7920**	718-728-6110
Franklin Electronic Publishers Inc 1 Franklin Plaza *AMEX: FEP*	Burlington	NJ	08016	**800-266-5626**	609-386-2500
Hand Held Products Inc 700 Vision Dr	Skaneateles Falls	NY	13153	**800-782-4263**	315-685-4100
Hewlett-Packard Co 3000 Hanover St *NYSE: HPQ ■ *Sales*	Palo Alto	CA	94304	**800-322-4772***	650-857-1501
International Business Machines Corp (IBM) New Orchard Rd *NYSE: IBM*	Armonk	NY	10504	**800-426-4968**	914-766-1900
Itronix Corp 801 S Stevens St	Spokane	WA	99204	**800-441-1309**	509-624-6600
Kontron Mobile Computing Inc 7631 Anagram Dr	Eden Prairie	MN	55344	**888-343-5396**	952-974-7000
LXE Inc 125 Technology Pkwy	Norcross	GA	30092	**800-664-4593**	770-447-4224
palmOne Inc 400 N McCarthy Blvd *NASDAQ: PLMO*	Milpitas	CA	95035	**800-881-7256**	408-503-7000

Computers - Handheld (Cont'd)

Company / Address	City	State	ZIP	Toll-Free	Phone
Radix International Corp					
4855 Wiley Post Way	Salt Lake City	UT	84116	**800-367-9256**	801-537-1717
Royal Consumer Information Products Inc					
379 Campus Dr	Somerset	NJ	08875	**888-261-4555***	732-627-9977
*Sales					
Seiko Instruments USA Inc					
2990 W Lomita Blvd	Torrance	CA	90505	**800-358-0880**	310-517-7050
Sharp Electronics Corp 1 Sharp Plaza	Mahwah	NJ	07430	**800-237-4277**	201-529-8200
Symbol Technologies Inc 1 Symbol Plaza	Holtsville	NY	11742	**800-722-6234**	631-738-2400
NYSE: SBL					
Ultradata Systems Inc					
1240 Dielman Industrial Dr	Saint Louis	MO	63132	**800-274-0971**	314-997-2250
Victor Technology Inc 780 W Belden Ave	Addison	IL	60101	**800-628-2420**	630-268-8400
Xybernaut Corp 12701 Fair Lakes Cir Suite 550	Fairfax	VA	22033	**888-992-3777**	703-631-6925
NASDAQ: XYBR					

171-3 Computers - Other Than Handheld

Company / Address	City	State	ZIP	Toll-Free	Phone
ABS Computer Technologies Inc					
9997 E Rosehills Rd	Whittier	CA	90601	**800-876-8088***	562-695-8823
*Sales					
Acer America Corp					
2641 Orchard Pkwy Bldg 1	San Jose	CA	95134	**800-733-2237**	408-432-6200
ACMA Computers Inc 1505 Reliance Way	Fremont	CA	94539	**800-786-6888***	510-623-1212
*Sales					
Advanced Processing Laboratories Inc					
16868 Via del Campo Ct	San Diego	CA	92127	**800-822-7522**	858-674-2850
Amax Engineering Corp 1565 Reliance Way	Fremont	CA	94539	**800-889-2629***	510-651-8886
*Cust Svc					
Apple Computer Inc 1 Infinite Loop	Cupertino	CA	95014	**800-275-2273***	408-996-1010
NASDAQ: AAPL ■ *Cust Svc					
Aries Research Inc 46791 Fremont Blvd	Fremont	CA	94538	**800-282-7437**	510-413-0288
Boundless Corp 100 Marcus Blvd	Hauppauge	NY	11788	**800-342-7400**	631-342-7400
Chem USA Corp 8445 Central Ave	Newark	CA	94560	**800-866-2436**	510-608-8818
Cognex Corp 1 Vision Dr	Natick	MA	01760	**877-926-4639**	508-650-3000
NASDAQ: CGNX					
Comark Corp 93 West St	Medfield	MA	02052	**800-280-8522**	508-359-8161
CSP Inc 43 Manning Rd	Billerica	MA	01821	**800-325-3110**	978-663-7598
NASDAQ: CSPI					
CSS Laboratories Inc 1641 McGaw Ave	Irvine	CA	92614	**800-852-2680**	949-852-8161
CTC Parker Automation 50 W TechneCenter Dr	Milford	OH	45150	**800-233-3329***	513-831-2340
*Cust Svc					
Cytec Corp 10385 Brockwood Rd	Dallas	TX	75238	**888-349-8881**	214-349-8881
Datalux Corp 155 Aviation Dr	Winchester	VA	22602	**800-328-2589**	540-662-1500
Dedicated Computing					
N26 W23880 Commerce Cir	Waukesha	WI	53188	**877-523-3301**	262-951-7200
Dell Inc 1 Dell Way	Round Rock	TX	78682	**800-854-6214**	512-338-4400
NASDAQ: DELL					
Diamond Flower Electric Instrument Co USA					
Inc (DFI) 732-C Striker Ave	Sacramento	CA	95834	**800-909-4334**	916-568-1234
Diversified Technology Inc					
476 Highland Colony Pkwy	Ridgeland	MS	39157	**800-443-2667**	601-856-4121
Dolch Computer Systems 3178 Laurelview Ct	Fremont	CA	94538	**877-347-4938**	510-661-2220
EliteGroup Computer Systems Inc					
45401 Research Ave	Fremont	CA	94539	**800-829-8890**	510-226-7333
eMachines Inc 14350 Myford Rd Bldg 100	Irvine	CA	92606	**877-566-3463**	714-481-2828
Encore Real Time Computing Inc					
305 East Dr Suite A	Melbourne	FL	33204	**800-936-2673***	321-473-1008
*Cust Svc					
ENGlobal Corp					
600 Century Plaza Dr Suite 140	Houston	TX	77073	**800-411-6040**	281-821-3200
AMEX: ENG					
Gateway Inc 7565 Irvine Center Dr	Irvine	CA	92618	**800-846-2000**	949-471-7000
NYSE: GTW					
Hewlett-Packard Co 3000 Hanover St	Palo Alto	CA	94304	**800-322-4772***	650-857-1501
NYSE: HPQ ■ *Sales					
HyperData Technology USA Corp					
817 S Lemon Ave	Walnut	CA	91789	**800-786-3343**	909-468-2955
Integrix Inc 2001 Corporate Ctr Dr	Newbury Park	CA	91230	**800-300-8288**	805-376-1000
International Business Machines Corp (IBM)					
New Orchard Rd	Armonk	NY	10504	**800-426-4968**	914-766-1900
NYSE: IBM					
Itronix Corp 801 S Stevens St	Spokane	WA	99204	**800-441-1309**	509-624-6600
Keydata International Inc					
201 Circle Dr N Suite 101	Piscataway	NJ	08854	**800-486-4800**	732-868-0588
MaxVision Corp 495 Production Ave	Madison	AL	35758	**800-533-5805**	256-772-3058
Mercury Computer Systems Inc					
199 Riverneck Rd	Chelmsford	MA	01824	**800-229-2006**	978-256-1300
NASDAQ: MRCY					
Micro Electronics Inc 4119 Leap Rd	Hilliard	OH	43026	**800-634-3478**	614-850-3000
Micro Express Inc 8 Hammond Dr Suite 105	Irvine	CA	92618	**800-989-9900**	
MicronPC LLC 906 E Karcher Rd	Nampa	ID	83687	**888-464-2766**	208-893-3434
Microtech Computers Inc 4921 Legends Dr	Lawrence	KS	66049	**800-828-9533***	785-841-9513
*Tech Supp					
Miltope Corp 500 Richardson Rd S	Hope Hull	AL	36043	**800-645-8673**	334-284-8665
NEC Computers International					
10850 Gold Center Dr Suite 200	Rancho Cordova	CA	95670	**800-632-4525**	916-763-7000
Neoware Systems Inc 400 Feheley Dr	King of Prussia	PA	19406	**800-437-1551**	610-277-8300
NASDAQ: NWRE					
Network Computing Devices Inc					
10795 SW Cascade Blvd	Portland	OR	97223	**800-800-9599**	503-431-8600
Panasonic Computer Solutions Co					
1 Panasonic Way	Secaucus	NJ	07094	**800-662-3537**	201-348-7000
Pinnacle Data Systems Inc					
6600 Port Rd Suite 100	Groveport	OH	43125	**800-882-8282**	614-748-1150
AMEX: PNS					
Recortec Inc 1620 Berryessa Rd Suite A	San Jose	CA	95133	**888-732-6783**	408-928-1480
SBS Technologies Inc					
2400 Louisiana Blvd NE AFC Bldg 5					
Suite 600	Albuquerque	NM	87110	**800-727-1553**	505-875-0600
NASDAQ: SBSE					
Sharp Electronics Corp 1 Sharp Plaza	Mahwah	NJ	07430	**800-237-4277**	201-529-8200
Stealth Computer Corp					
530 Rowntree Dairy Rd Unit 5	Woodbridge	ON	L4L8H2	**888-783-2584**	905-264-9000
Sys Technology Inc 17358 Railroad St	City of Industry	CA	91748	**866-834-9155**	626-810-2345
Systemax Inc 11 Harbor Pk Dr	Port Washington	NY	11050	**800-845-6225**	516-625-1555
NYSE: SYX					

Company / Address	City	State	ZIP	Toll-Free	Phone
Tadpole Computer Inc					
20450 Stevens Creek Blvd 3rd Fl	Cupertino	CA	95014	**800-734-5483**	408-973-9944
Tangent Computer Inc 197 Airport Blvd	Burlingame	CA	94010	**800-342-9388**	650-342-9388
Toshiba America Inc					
1251 Ave of the Americas 41st Fl	New York	NY	10020	**800-457-7777**	212-596-0600
Toshiba America Information Systems Inc					
9740 Irvine Blvd	Irvine	CA	92618	**800-457-7777***	949-583-3000
*Cust Svc					
Total Control Products Inc					
2500 Austin Dr	Charlottesville	VA	22911	**800-263-6041**	434-978-5000
Transource Computers Corp					
10850 N 24th Ave Suite 102	Phoenix	AZ	85029	**800-486-3715**	602-997-8101
Twinhead Corp 48303 Fremont Blvd	Fremont	CA	94538	**800-995-8946***	510-492-0828
*Sales					
WinBook Computer Corp					
2701 Charter St Suite A	Columbus	OH	43228	**800-468-1633**	614-334-1496
Wyse Technology Inc 3471 N 1st St	San Jose	CA	95134	**800-800-9973**	408-473-1200
Xycom Automation Inc 750 N Maple Rd	Saline	MI	48176	**800-289-9266**	734-429-4971

171-4 Monitors & Displays

Company / Address	City	State	ZIP	Toll-Free	Phone
3M Display & Graphics Div 3M Ctr	Saint Paul	MN	55144	**800-384-3577**	651-733-1110
Barco Folsom LLC					
11101 Trade Center Dr	Rancho Cordova	CA	95670	**888-414-7226**	916-859-2500
Barco Media LLC 1651 N 10 West	Logan	UT	84321	**800-543-7904**	435-753-2224
BenQ America Corp 53 Discovery	Irvine	CA	92618	**866-600-2367**	949-255-9500
CTX Technology Corp					
16728 E Gale Ave	City of Industry	CA	91745	**877-688-3288***	626-363-9328
*Cust Svc					
Daktronics Inc 331 32nd Ave	Brookings	SD	57006	**800-843-9878**	605-697-4300
NASDAQ: DAKT					
Dotronix Inc 160 1st St SE	New Brighton	MN	55112	**800-720-7218**	651-633-1742
Eizo Nanao Technologies Inc					
5710 Warland Dr	Cypress	CA	90630	**800-800-5202**	562-431-5011
Envision Peripherals Inc 47490 Seabridge Dr	Fremont	CA	94538	**888-838-6388***	510-770-9988
*Tech Supp					
General Digital Corp 8 Nutmeg Rd S	South Windsor	CT	06074	**800-952-2535**	860-282-2900
Hitachi America Ltd Monitor Div					
2000 Sierra Point Pkwy	Brisbane	CA	94005	**800-562-2552**	650-589-8300
Iiyama North America Inc					
65 West St Rd Suite 101-B	Warminster	PA	18974	**800-394-4335**	215-682-9050
KDS USA 7373 Hunt Ave	Garden Grove	CA	92841	**800-237-9988**	714-379-5599
LG Electronics USA Inc					
1000 Sylvan Ave	Englewood Cliffs	NJ	07632	**800-243-0000***	201-816-2000
*Tech Supp					
NEC-Mitsubishi Electronics Display of America Inc					
500 Park Blvd Suite 1100	Itasca	IL	60143	**888-632-6487***	630-467-3000
*Sales					
NEC Solutions (America) Inc					
1250 N Arlington Heights Rd Suite 400	Itasca	IL	60143	**800-632-4636**	630-467-5000
Pioneer Electronics (USA) Inc					
2265 E 220th St	Long Beach	CA	90810	**800-421-1404***	310-952-2000
*Cust Svc					
Planar Systems Inc 1195 NW Compton Dr	Beaverton	OR	97006	**866-475-2627**	503-748-1100
NASDAQ: PLNR					
Princeton Graphics Systems Inc					
3300 Irvine Ave Suite 120	Newport Beach	CA	92660	**800-747-6249***	949-777-3379
*Cust Svc					
Proview Technology 7372 Doig Dr	Garden Grove	CA	92841	**800-776-8439**	714-799-3899
Samsung Electronics America Inc					
105 Challenger Rd	Ridgefield Park	NJ	07660	**800-726-7864**	201-229-4000
Sharp Electronics Corp 1 Sharp Plaza	Mahwah	NJ	07430	**800-237-4277**	201-529-8200
Tatung Co of America Inc					
2850 El Presidio St	Long Beach	CA	90810	**800-827-2850**	310-637-2105
Trans-Lux Corp 110 Richards Ave	Norwalk	CT	06854	**800-243-5544**	203-853-4321
AMEX: TLX					
Trans-Lux Fair-Play Inc					
1700 Delaware Ave	Des Moines	IA	50317	**800-247-0265**	515-265-5305
Video Display Corp 1868 Tucker Industrial Rd	Tucker	GA	30084	**800-241-5005***	770-938-2080
NASDAQ: VIDE ■ *Cust Svc					
ViewSonic Corp 381 Brea Canyon Rd	Walnut	CA	91789	**800-888-8583**	909-444-8800
Wells-Gardner Electronics Corp					
9500 W 55th St Suite A	McCook	IL	60525	**800-336-6630**	708-290-2100
AMEX: WGA					
Xycom Automation Inc 750 N Maple Rd	Saline	MI	48176	**800-289-9266**	734-429-4971

171-5 Multimedia Equipment & Supplies

Company / Address	City	State	ZIP	Toll-Free	Phone
Altec Lansing Technologies Inc					
PO Box 277 Rt 6	Milford	PA	18337	**800-258-3288**	570-296-6444
Boston Acoustics Inc 300 Jubilee Dr	Peabody	MA	01960	**800-288-6148**	978-538-5000
NASDAQ: BOSA					
Cambridge Soundworks Inc					
100 Brickstone Sq 5th Fl	Andover	MA	01810	**800-945-4434**	978-623-4400
Creative Labs Inc 1901 McCarthy Blvd	Milpitas	CA	95035	**800-998-1000***	408-428-6600
*Cust Svc					
FOCUS Enhancements Inc 1370 Dell Ave	Campbell	CA	95008	**800-338-3348**	408-866-8300
NASDAQ: FCSE					
Guillemot North America					
5500 rue Saint-Laurent Suite 5000	Montreal	QC	H2T1S6	**877-484-5536**	514-279-9960
Kinyo Co Inc 14235 Lomitas Ave	La Puente	CA	91746	**800-735-4696**	626-333-3711
Pinnacle Systems Inc					
280 N Bernardo Ave	Mountain View	CA	94043	**800-522-8783***	650-526-1600
NASDAQ: PCLE ■ *Sales					

171-6 Printers

Company / Address	City	State	ZIP	Toll-Free	Phone
AMT Datasouth Corp 4765 Calle Quetzal	Camarillo	CA	93012	**800-215-9192**	805-388-5799
Astro-Med Inc 600 E Greenwich Ave	West Warwick	RI	02893	**800-343-4039**	401-828-4000
NASDAQ: ALOT					
Avery Dennison Printer Systems Div					
7722 Dungan Rd	Philadelphia	PA	19111	**800-395-2282**	215-725-4700
Brother International Corp					
100 Somerset Corporate Blvd	Bridgewater	NJ	08807	**800-276-7746***	908-704-1700
*Cust Svc					

Company	City	State	Zip	Toll-Free	Phone
Canon Consumer Imaging & Information Systems Group 15955 Alton Pkwy *Sales	Irvine	CA	92618	**800-848-4123***	949-753-4000
Canon USA Inc 1 Canon Plaza *NYSE: CAJ*	Lake Success	NY	11042	**800-828-4040**	516-488-6700
Casio Inc 570 Mt Pleasant Ave *Cust Svc	Dover	NJ	07801	**800-634-1895***	973-361-5400
Citizen Systems America Corp 363 Van Ness Way Suite 404	Torrance	CA	90501	**800-421-6516**	310-781-1460
Datamax Corp 4501 Parkway Commerce Blvd	Orlando	FL	32808	**800-321-2233**	407-578-8007
Digital Design Inc 67 Sand Park Rd	Cedar Grove	NJ	07009	**800-967-7746**	973-857-0900
Eastman Kodak Co 343 State St *NYSE: EK*	Rochester	NY	14650	**800-242-2424**	585-724-4000
Encad Inc A Kodak Co 6059 Cornerstone Ct W	San Diego	CA	92121	**877-362-2387**	858-452-0882
Epson America Inc 3840 Kilroy Airport Way *Cust Svc	Long Beach	CA	90806	**800-533-3731***	562-981-3840
Fargo Electronics Inc 6533 Flying Cloud Dr *NASDAQ: FRGO*	Eden Prairie	MN	55344	**800-327-4622**	952-941-9470
Fuji Photo Film USA Inc 200 Summit Lake Dr	Valhalla	NY	10595	**800-755-3854**	914-789-8100
GCC Printers USA 209 Burlington Rd *Sales	Bedford	MA	01730	**800-422-7777***	781-275-5800
Hewlett-Packard Co 3000 Hanover St *NYSE: HPQ* ■ *Sales	Palo Alto	CA	94304	**800-322-4772***	650-857-1501
Imaje Co 1650 Airport Rd Suite 101	Kennesaw	GA	30144	**800-462-5302**	770-421-7700
International Business Machines Corp (IBM) New Orchard Rd *NYSE: IBM*	Armonk	NY	10504	**800-426-4968**	914-766-1900
Kodak Co 343 State St *NYSE: EK*	Rochester	NY	14650	**800-242-2424**	585-724-4000
Konica Minolta Printing Solutions USA Inc 1 Magnum Pass	Mobile	AL	36618	**800-523-2696**	251-633-4300
Kroy LLC 3830 Kelley Ave	Cleveland	OH	44114	**888-888-5769**	216-426-5600
Lexmark International Inc 740 W New Circle Rd *NYSE: LXK* ■ *Cust Svc	Lexington	KY	40550	**800-539-6275***	859-232-2000
NEC Solutions (America) Inc 1250 N Arlington Heights Rd Suite 400	Itasca	IL	60143	**800-632-4636**	630-467-5000
Oki America Inc 785 N Mary Ave	Sunnyvale	CA	94085	**800-654-3282**	408-720-1900
Oki Data Americas Inc 2000 Bishops Gate Blvd. *Cust Svc	Mount Laurel	NJ	08054	**800-654-3282***	856-235-2600
Paxar Corp 105 Corporate Park Dr *NYSE: PXR*	White Plains	NY	10604	**888-447-2927**	914-697-6800
Pentax Imaging Co 600 12th St Suite 300	Golden	CO	80401	**800-543-6144**	303-799-8000
Plastic Card Systems Inc 31 Pierce St PO Box 1070	Northborough	MA	01532	**800-742-2273**	508-351-6210
Primera Technology Inc 2 Carlson Pkwy Suite 375	Plymouth	MN	55447	**800-797-2772**	763-475-6676
Printek Inc 1517 Townline Rd	Benton Harbor	MI	49022	**800-368-4636**	269-925-3200
Printronix Inc 14600 Myford Rd *NASDAQ: PTNX*	Irvine	CA	92606	**800-665-6210**	714-368-2300
Ricoh Corp 5 Dedrick Pl	West Caldwell	NJ	07006	**800-637-4264**	973-882-2000
Ricoh Printing Systems America Inc 2635-A Park Center Dr *Cust Svc	Simi Valley	CA	93065	**800-887-8848***	805-578-4000
RISO Inc 300 Rosewood Dr Suite 210	Danvers	MA	01923	**800-876-7476**	978-777-7377
Roland DGA Corp 15363 Barranca Pkwy	Irvine	CA	92618	**800-542-2307**	949-727-2100
Samsung Electronics America Inc 105 Challenger Rd	Ridgefield Park	NJ	07660	**800-726-7864**	201-229-4000
Seiko Instruments USA Inc 2990 W Lomita Blvd	Torrance	CA	90505	**800-358-0880**	310-517-7050
Seiko Instruments USA Inc Business & Home Office Products Div 2990 W Lomita Blvd	Torrance	CA	90505	**800-358-0880**	310-517-7050
Seiko Instruments USA Inc Micro Printer Div 2990 W Lomita Blvd	Torrance	CA	90505	**800-553-6570**	310-517-7778
Sharp Electronics Corp 1 Sharp Plaza	Mahwah	NJ	07430	**800-237-4277**	201-529-8200
Star Micronics America Inc 1150 King George's Post Rd	Edison	NJ	08837	**800-782-7636**	732-623-5500
Stratix Corp 4920 Avalon Ridge Pkwy Suite 600	Norcross	GA	30071	**800-343-0343**	770-326-7580
TallyGenicom 4500 Daly Dr Suite 100	Chantilly	VA	20151	**800-436-4266**	703-633-8700
Telpar Inc 1550 Lakeway Dr Suite 500	Lewisville	TX	75057	**800-872-4886**	972-420-4700
TransAct Technologies Inc 7 Laser Ln *NASDAQ: TACT*	Wallingford	CT	06492	**800-243-8941**	203-269-1198
TROY Group Inc 2331 S Pullman St	Santa Ana	CA	92705	**877-324-3254**	949-250-3280
Unimark Inc 9910 Widmer Rd *Cust Svc	Lenexa	KS	66215	**800-255-6356***	913-649-2424
Xante Corp 2800 Dauphin St Suite 100	Mobile	AL	36606	**800-926-8839**	251-473-6502
Xerox Corp 800 Long Ridge Rd *NYSE: XRX*	Stamford	CT	06904	**800-842-0024**	203-968-3000
Zebra Technologies Corp 333 Corporate Woods Pkwy *NASDAQ: ZBRA*	Vernon Hills	IL	60061	**800-423-0422**	847-634-6700

171-7 Scanning Equipment

Company	City	State	Zip	Toll-Free	Phone
Accu-Sort Systems Inc 511 School House Rd	Telford	PA	18969	**800-227-2633**	215-723-0981
Agfa Corp 100 Challenger Rd	Ridgefield Park	NJ	07660	**800-581-2432**	201-440-2500
BenQ America Corp 53 Discovery	Irvine	CA	92618	**866-600-2367**	949-255-9500
BOWE Bell + Howell Co 760 S Wolf Rd	Wheeling	IL	60090	**800-327-4608**	847-675-7600
Canon Consumer Imaging & Information Systems Group 15955 Alton Pkwy *Sales	Irvine	CA	92618	**800-848-4123***	949-753-4000
Canon USA Inc 1 Canon Plaza *NYSE: CAJ*	Lake Success	NY	11042	**800-828-4040**	516-488-6700
CardScan Inc 810 Memorial Dr 3rd Fl	Cambridge	MA	02139	**800-942-6739**	617-492-4200
Computerwise Inc 302 N Winchester Ln	Olathe	KS	66062	**800-255-3739**	913-829-0600
Eastman Kodak Co 343 State St *NYSE: EK*	Rochester	NY	14650	**800-242-2424**	585-724-4000
Eastman Kodak Co Digital & Applied Imaging Div 343 State St	Rochester	NY	14650	**800-242-2424**	800-698-3324
Epson America Inc 3840 Kilroy Airport Way *Cust Svc	Long Beach	CA	90806	**800-533-3731***	562-981-3840
Fujitsu Computer Products of America Inc 2904 Orchard Pkwy	San Jose	CA	95134	**800-626-4686**	408-432-6333
GTCO CalComp Inc 7125 Riverwood Dr	Columbia	MD	21046	**800-344-4723**	410-381-6688
Hand Held Products Inc 700 Vision Dr	Skaneateles Falls	NY	13153	**800-782-4263**	315-685-4100
Hewlett-Packard Co 3000 Hanover St *NYSE: HPQ* ■ *Sales	Palo Alto	CA	94304	**800-322-4772***	650-857-1501
Hitachi Canada Ltd 2495 Meadowpine Blvd	Mississauga	ON	L5N6C3	**800-906-4482**	905-821-4545
iCAD Inc 4 Townsend W Suite 17 *NASDAQ: ICAD*	Nashua	NH	03063	**800-444-6983**	603-882-5200
Indala 6850-B Santa Teresa Blvd *Sales	San Jose	CA	95119	**800-779-8663***	408-361-4700
InPath Devices 3610 Dodge St Suite 200	Omaha	NE	68131	**800-988-1914**	402-345-9200
Intelli-Check Inc 246 Crossways Park W *AMEX: IDN*	Woodbury	NY	11797	**800-444-9542**	516-992-1900
Kodak Co 343 State St *NYSE: EK*	Rochester	NY	14650	**800-242-2424**	585-724-4000
Metrologic Instruments Inc 90 Coles Rd *NASDAQ: MTLG* ■ *Sales	Blackwood	NJ	08012	**800-436-3876***	856-228-8100
NCR Corp 1700 S Patterson Blvd *NYSE: NCR* ■ *Cust Svc	Dayton	OH	45479	**800-531-2222***	937-445-5000
Peripheral Dynamics Inc 5150 Campus Dr Whitemarsh Industrial Pk	Plymouth Meeting	PA	19462	**800-523-0253**	610-825-7090
PSC Inc 959 Terry St	Eugene	OR	97402	**800-695-5700**	541-683-5700
Ricoh Corp 5 Dedrick Pl	West Caldwell	NJ	07006	**800-637-4264**	973-882-2000
Roland DGA Corp 15363 Barranca Pkwy	Irvine	CA	92618	**800-542-2307**	949-727-2100
Scan-Optics Inc 169 Progress Dr	Manchester	CT	06040	**800-543-8681**	860-645-7878
Scantron Corp 34 Parker	Irvine	CA	92618	**800-722-6876**	949-639-7500
Siemens Logistics & Assembly Systems Inc Postal Automation Div 1401 Nolan Ryan Expy	Arlington	TX	76011	**800-433-5175**	817-436-7000
Socket Communications Inc 37400 Central Ct *NASDAQ: SCKT*	Newark	CA	94560	**800-552-3300**	510-744-2700
SPYRUS Inc 2355 Oakland Rd Suite 1	San Jose	CA	95131	**800-277-9787**	408-953-0700
Stratix Corp 4920 Avalon Ridge Pkwy Suite 600	Norcross	GA	30071	**800-343-0343**	770-326-7580
Symbol Technologies Inc 1 Symbol Plaza *NYSE: SBL*	Holtsville	NY	11742	**800-722-6234**	631-738-2400
Visioneer Inc 5673 Gibraltar Dr Suite 150 *Cust Svc	Pleasanton	CA	94588	**888-229-4172***	925-251-6300
Wizcom Technologies Inc 257 Great Rd	Acton	MA	01720	**888-777-0552**	978-635-5357

171-8 Storage Devices

Company	City	State	Zip	Toll-Free	Phone
Apricorn Inc 12191 Kirkham Rd	Poway	CA	92064	**800-458-5448**	858-513-2000
BenQ America Corp 53 Discovery	Irvine	CA	92618	**866-600-2367**	949-255-9500
CMS Peripherals Inc 3095 Redhill Ave *Sales	Costa Mesa	CA	92626	**800-327-5773***	714-424-5520
Creative Labs Inc 1901 McCarthy Blvd *Cust Svc	Milpitas	CA	95035	**800-998-1000***	408-428-6600
DataDirect Networks 9320 Lurline Ave	Chatsworth	CA	91311	**888-438-6768**	818-700-7600
Datalink Corp 8170 Upland Cir *NASDAQ: DTLK*	Chanhassen	MN	55317	**800-448-6314**	952-944-3462
Digital Peripheral Solutions Inc 8015 E Crystal Dr	Anaheim	CA	92807	**800-559-4777**	714-692-5573
Engenio Information Technologies Inc 1621 Barber Ln *Tech Supp	Milpitas	CA	95035	**866-625-3993***	408-433-8000
Exabyte Corp 2108 55th St *NASDAQ: EXBT* ■ *Cust Svc	Boulder	CO	80301	**800-445-7736***	303-442-4333
EXP Computer Inc 920 S Oyster Bay Rd Unit B *Sales	Hicksville	NY	11801	**800-397-6922***	516-942-0507
Fujitsu Computer Products of America Inc 2904 Orchard Pkwy	San Jose	CA	95134	**800-626-4686**	408-432-6333
Hewlett-Packard Co 3000 Hanover St *NYSE: HPQ* ■ *Sales	Palo Alto	CA	94304	**800-322-4772***	650-857-1501
Hitachi America Ltd Computer Div 2000 Sierra Pt Pkwy	Brisbane	CA	94005	**800-225-1741**	650-589-8300
Hitachi Data Systems Corp 750 Central Expy	Santa Clara	CA	95050	**800-227-1930**	408-970-1000
Imation Corp 1 Imation Pl *NYSE: IMN*	Oakdale	MN	55128	**888-466-3456**	651-704-4000
Interactive Media Corp DBA Kanguru Solutions 1360 Main St *Sales	Millis	MA	02054	**888-526-4878***	508-376-4245
International Business Machines Corp (IBM) New Orchard Rd *NYSE: IBM*	Armonk	NY	10504	**800-426-4968**	914-766-1900
LG Electronics USA Inc 1000 Sylvan Ave *Tech Supp	Englewood Cliffs	NJ	07632	**800-243-0000***	201-816-2000
Luminex Software Inc 6840 Indiana Ave Suite 130	Riverside	CA	92506	**888-586-4639**	951-781-4100
Mace Group Inc 15861 Tapia St	Irwindale	CA	91706	**800-644-1132**	626-338-8787
Maxtor Corp 500 McCarthy Blvd *NYSE: MXO*	Milpitas	CA	95035	**800-262-9867**	408-894-5000
Micro Solutions Inc 132 W Lincoln Hwy	DeKalb	IL	60115	**800-890-7227**	815-756-3411
Microboards Technology LLC 8150 Mallory Ct PO Box 846	Chanhassen	MN	55317	**800-646-8881**	952-556-1600
Mitsumi Electronics Corp 5808 W Campus Circle Dr *Tech Supp	Irving	TX	75063	**800-648-7864***	972-550-7300
NEC Solutions (America) Inc 1250 N Arlington Heights Rd Suite 400	Itasca	IL	60143	**800-632-4636**	630-467-5000
Phoenix International 812 W Southern Ave	Orange	CA	92865	**800-203-4800**	714-283-4800
Pioneer Electronics (USA) Inc 2265 E 220th St *Cust Svc	Long Beach	CA	90810	**800-421-1404***	310-952-2000
Plasmon Plc 400 Inverness Pkwy Suite 310	Englewood	CO	80112	**800-451-6845**	720-873-2500
Plextor Corp 48383 Fremont Blvd Suite 120	Fremont	CA	94538	**800-886-3935**	510-440-2000
Procom Technology Inc 58 Discovery	Irvine	CA	92618	**800-800-8600**	949-852-1000
Qualstar Corp 3990-B Heritage Oak Ct *NASDAQ: QBAK*	Simi Valley	CA	93063	**800-468-0680**	805-583-7744
Quantum Corp 501 Sycamore Dr *NYSE: DSS* ■ *Tech Supp	Milpitas	CA	95035	**800-826-8022***	408-944-4000
Quantum/ATL PO Box 57100	Irvine	CA	92619	**800-677-6268**	949-856-7800
Rimage Corp 7725 Washington Ave S *NASDAQ: RIMG*	Minneapolis	MN	55439	**800-445-8288**	952-944-8144
Samsung Electronics America Inc 105 Challenger Rd	Ridgefield Park	NJ	07660	**800-726-7864**	201-229-4000
Shaffstall Corp 8531 Bash St	Indianapolis	IN	46250	**800-923-8439**	317-842-2077

Storage Devices (Cont'd)

Company	City	State	ZIP	Toll-Free	Phone
Storage Technology Corp 1 StorageTek Dr *NYSE: STK*	Louisville	CO	80028	**800-877-9220**	303-673-5151
TDK USA Corp 901 Franklin Ave	Garden City	NY	11530	**800-835-8273**	516-535-2600
Western Digital Corp 20511 Lake Forest Dr *NYSE: WDC*	Lake Forest	CA	92630	**800-832-4778**	949-672-7000

172 COMPUTER EQUIPMENT & SOFTWARE - WHOL

SEE ALSO Business Machines - Whol; Electrical & Electronic Equipment & Parts - Whol

Company	City	State	ZIP	Toll-Free	Phone
Agilysys Inc 6065 Parkland Blvd *NASDAQ: AGYS*	Cleveland	OH	44124	**800-362-9127**	440-720-8500
Ahearn & Soper Inc 100 Woodbine Downs Blvd	Rexdale	ON	M9W5S6	**800-263-4258**	416-675-3999
Analytical Computer Services 11500 Northwest Fwy Suite 320	Houston	TX	77092	**888-744-9451**	713-681-0039
Arrow Electronics Inc 25 Hub Dr *NYSE: ARW* ■ *Sales	Melville	NY	11747	**800-777-2776***	516-391-1300
Arrow Electronics Inc SBM Div 11455 Lakefield Dr	Duluth	GA	30097	**888-228-2101**	770-623-3430
Arrow Enterprise Computing Solutions MOCA Div 5230 Pacific Concourse Dr Bldg 2 4th Fl *Sales	Los Angeles	CA	90045	**800-786-3425***	310-643-1400
Arrow Enterprise Storage Solutions 18750 Lake Dr E	Chanhassen	MN	55317	**800-229-3475**	952-949-0053
ASI Corp 48289 Fremont Blvd	Fremont	CA	94538	**800-210-0274**	510-226-8000
Atlantix Global Systems 1 Sun Ct	Norcross	GA	30092	**888-786-2727**	770-248-7700
Avnet Inc 2211 S 47th St *NYSE: AVT*	Phoenix	AZ	85034	**888-822-8638**	480-643-2000
Avnet Technology Solutions 8700 S Price Rd	Tempe	AZ	85284	**800-409-1483**	480-794-6900
Azerty Inc 13 Centre Dr	Orchard Park	NY	14127	**800-888-8080**	716-662-0200
Bell Microproducts Inc 1941 Ringwood Ave *NASDAQ: BELM*	San Jose	CA	95131	**800-800-1513**	408-451-9400
Best Computer Supplies 895 E Patriot Blvd Suite 110	Reno	NV	89511	**800-544-3472**	775-850-2600
Caliber Computer Corp 45531 Northport Loop W	Fremont	CA	94538	**800-748-9834**	510-353-1220
Champion Solutions Group 791 Park of Commerce Blvd	Boca Raton	FL	33487	**800-771-7000**	561-997-2900
Computer Parts Unlimited Inc 3949 Heritage Oak Ct	Simi Valley	CA	93063	**800-644-4494**	805-306-2500
Comstor Inc 14850 Conference Ctr Dr Suite 200	Chantilly	VA	20151	**800-955-9590**	703-345-5100
D & H Distributing Co Inc 2525 N 7th St	Harrisburg	PA	17110	**800-877-1200**	717-236-8001
Data Impressions Inc 13180 Paramount Blvd	South Gate	CA	90280	**800-677-3031**	562-630-8788
Data Sales Co Inc 3450 W Burnsville Pkwy	Burnsville	MN	55337	**800-328-2730**	952-890-8838
Digital Storage Inc 7611 Green Meadows Dr	Lewis Center	OH	43035	**800-232-3475**	740-548-7179
En Pointe Technologies Inc 100 N Sepulveda Blvd 19th Fl *NASDAQ: ENPT*	El Segundo	CA	90245	**800-800-4214**	310-725-5200
GE Access 11300 Westmoor Cir *Sales	Westminster	CO	80031	**800-733-9333***	303-545-1000
GE Information Technology Solutions Inc 1101 Pacific Ave	Erlanger	KY	41018	**877-505-5557**	859-815-7000
General Data Co Inc 4354 Ferguson Dr	Cincinnati	OH	45245	**800-733-5252**	513-752-7978
Global Computer Supplies 11 Harbor Pk Dr *Sales	Port Washington	NY	11050	**800-845-6225***	516-625-6200
GST/E-Systems 2929 E Imperial Hwy Suite 170	Brea	CA	92821	**800-833-0128**	714-572-8020
GTSI Corp 3901 Stonecroft Blvd *NASDAQ: GTSI*	Chantilly	VA	20151	**800-999-4874**	703-502-2000
Infotel Distributing 6990 SR 36	Fletcher	OH	45326	**800-682-0422**	937-368-2650
Ingram Micro Inc 1600 E St Andrew Pl *NYSE: IM* ■ *Sales	Santa Ana	CA	92705	**800-456-8000***	714-566-1000
KeyLink Systems Group 6675 Parkland Blvd	Solon	OH	44139	**800-539-5465**	440-498-6900
LA Computer Center 450 N Oak St	Inglewood	CA	90302	**800-689-3933**	310-671-4444
Manchester Technologies Inc 160 Oser Ave *NASDAQ: MANC*	Hauppauge	NY	11788	**800-378-1231**	631-435-1199
Max Group Corp 17011 Green Dr	City of Industry	CA	91745	**800-256-9040**	626-935-0050
Media Sciences International Inc 40 Boroline Rd *AMEX: GFX*	Allendale	NJ	07401	**888-376-8378**	201-236-4311
Merisel Inc 200 Continental Blvd *NASDAQ: MSEL* ■ *Sales	El Segundo	CA	90245	**800-637-4735***	310-615-3080
MOCA Div Arrow Enterprise Computing Solutions 5230 Pacific Concourse Dr Bldg 2 4th Fl *Sales	Los Angeles	CA	90045	**800-786-3425***	310-643-1400
Navarre Corp 7400 49th Ave N *NASDAQ: NAVR*	New Hope	MN	55428	**800-728-4000**	763-535-8333
Optical Laser Inc 5702 Bolsa Ave Suite 100	Huntington Beach	CA	92649	**800-776-9215**	714-379-4400
Pacific Magtron International Corp 1600 California Cir	Milpitas	CA	95035	**800-998-2822**	408-956-8888
PC Wholesale 444 Scott Dr	Bloomingdale	IL	60108	**800-525-4727**	630-307-1700
Peak Technologies Inc 9200 Berger Rd	Columbia	MD	21046	**800-950-6372**	410-312-6000
Phoenix Computer Assoc Inc 10 Sasco Hill Rd	Fairfield	CT	06824	**800-432-1815**	203-319-3060
Programmer's Paradise Inc 1157 Shrewsbury Ave Suite C *NASDAQ: PROG*	Shrewsbury	NJ	07702	**800-445-7899**	732-389-8950
Provantage Corp 7249 Whipple Ave NW	North Canton	OH	44720	**800-336-1166**	330-494-3781
SBM Div Arrow Electronics 11455 Lakefield Dr	Duluth	GA	30097	**888-228-2101**	770-623-3430
ScanSource Inc 6 Logue Ct *NASDAQ: SCSC*	Greenville	SC	29615	**800-944-2432**	864-288-2432
SED International Inc 4916 N Royal Atlanta Dr *Sales	Tucker	GA	30084	**800-444-8962***	770-491-8962
Softmart Inc 450 Acorn Ln *Cust Svc	Downingtown	PA	19335	**800-328-1319***	610-518-4000
Software Spectrum Inc 2140 Merritt Dr	Garland	TX	75041	**800-624-0503**	972-840-6600
Solarcom Holdings Inc 1 Sun Ct	Norcross	GA	30092	**888-786-3282**	770-449-6116
Support Net Inc 4400 W 96th St	Indianapolis	IN	46268	**800-255-3390**	317-735-0200
SYNNEX Corp 839 Pellham Ridge Dr *NYSE: SNX*	Greenville	SC	29615	**800-756-9888**	
Tech Data Corp 5350 Tech Data Dr *NASDAQ: TECD*	Clearwater	FL	33760	**800-237-8931**	727-539-7429
Vistamax Inc 6723 Mowry Ave	Newark	CA	94560	**866-758-4782**	
Voda One Corp 1010 S 120th St Suite 100	Omaha	NE	68154	**877-642-7750**	
Wareforce.com Inc 19 Morgan	Irvine	CA	92618	**800-258-2622**	949-639-8934
WDL Systems 220 Chatham Business Dr *Sales	Pittsboro	NC	27312	**800-548-2319***	919-545-2500
Westcon Group Inc 520 White Plains Rd Suite 100	Tarrytown	NY	10591	**800-527-9516**	914-829-7000
Westwood Computer Corp 11 Diamond Rd	Springfield	NJ	07081	**800-800-8805**	973-376-4242
Zones Inc 1102 15th St SW *NASDAQ: ZONS*	Auburn	WA	98001	**800-258-2088**	253-205-3000

COMPUTER & INTERNET TRAINING PROGRAMS

SEE Training & Certification Programs - Computer & Internet

173 COMPUTER MAINTENANCE & REPAIR

Company	City	State	ZIP	Toll-Free	Phone
Advanced Microelectronics Inc 6001 E Old Hwy 50	Vincennes	IN	47591	**800-264-8851**	812-726-4500
Cera Services 10960 E Crystal Falls Pkwy Suite 500	Leander	TX	78641	**800-966-3070**	512-259-5151
Computer Specialists Inc 904 Wind River Ln Suite 100	Gaithersburg	MD	20878	**800-505-4365**	301-921-8860
Comtek Computer Systems 2751 Mercantile Dr Suite 100	Rancho Cordova	CA	95742	**800-823-4450**	916-859-7000
Data Exchange Corp 3600 Via Pescador	Camarillo	CA	93012	**800-237-7911**	805-388-1711
Datatech Depot 1371 N Miller St	Anaheim	CA	92806	**800-888-8181**	714-996-7500
DBK Concepts Inc 12905 SW 129 Ave	Miami	FL	33186	**800-725-7226**	305-596-7226
DecisionOne Corp 50 E Swedesford Rd	Frazer	PA	19355	**800-767-2876**	610-296-6000
Everprint International Inc 18021 Cortney Ct	City of Industry	CA	91748	**800-984-5777**	626-913-2888
Expetic Technology Service 12 2nd Ave SW	Aberdeen	SD	57401	**888-297-2292**	605-225-4122
Geek Squad Inc 1213 Washington Ave N	Minneapolis	MN	55401	**888-237-8289**	612-343-4335
Genesis Computer Repair & Sales 121 F Grafton Station Ln	Yorktown	VA	23692	**866-289-4277**	757-833-6262
ICM Corp 4025 Steve Reynolds Blvd Suite 120 *Cust Svc	Norcross	GA	30093	**800-654-8013***	770-381-2947
Interactive Services Group Inc 600 Delran Pkwy Suite C	Delran	NJ	08075	**800-566-3310**	
Jaguar Computer Systems Inc 4135 Indus Way	Riverside	CA	92503	**800-540-0548**	951-273-7950
Matthijssen Inc 14 Rt 10	East Hanover	NJ	07936	**800-845-2200**	973-887-1100
Media Sciences International Inc 40 Boroline Rd *AMEX: GFX*	Allendale	NJ	07401	**888-376-8378**	201-236-4311
NCE Computer Group 1973 Friendship Dr Suite B *Cust Svc	El Cajon	CA	92020	**800-767-2587***	619-212-3000
Scantron Service Group 2020 S 156th Cir	Omaha	NE	68130	**800-228-3628**	402-697-3000
Sierra Inc 2635 Golf Ave	Racine	WI	53404	**800-722-7263**	262-638-1851
Sun Valley Technical Repair Inc 15555 Concord Cir	Morgan Hill	CA	95037	**800-250-5858**	408-779-4115
Technology Innovations Inc 555 E Easy St	Simi Valley	CA	93065	**800-286-0651**	805-426-1000
Telemechanics Inc 6791-A Whitfield Industrial Ave	Sarasota	FL	34243	**800-227-7485**	941-751-3452
Wizard Computer Services 6908 Engle Rd Suite J	Middleburg Heights	OH	44130	**800-486-0060**	440-891-0060

174 COMPUTER NETWORKING PRODUCTS & SYSTEMS

SEE ALSO Computer Software - Systems & Utilities Software; Modems; Telecommunications Equipment & Systems

Company	City	State	ZIP	Toll-Free	Phone
3Com Corp 5403 Betsy Ross Dr *NASDAQ: COMS* ■ *Cust Svc	Santa Clara	CA	95054	**800-638-3266***	408-326-5000
Acceris Communications Solutions 1001 Brinton Rd	Pittsburgh	PA	15221	**800-447-2111**	412-244-6600
Advanced Digital Information Corp 11431 Willows Rd NE *NASDAQ: ADIC*	Redmond	WA	98052	**800-336-1233**	425-881-8004
Allied Telesyn International Corp 19800 North Creek Pkwy Suite 200	Bothell	WA	98011	**800-424-4284**	425-487-8880
AM Communications Inc 1900 AM Dr	Quakertown	PA	18951	**800-248-9004**	215-538-8700
American Megatrends Inc 6145-F Northbelt Pkwy	Norcross	GA	30071	**800-828-9264**	770-263-8181
American Research Corp 602 Monterey Pass Rd	Monterey Park	CA	91754	**888-462-3899**	626-284-1904
Applied Innovation Inc 5800 Innovation Dr *NASDAQ: AINN*	Dublin	OH	43016	**800-247-9482**	614-798-2000
Arcom Control Systems 7500 W 161st St	Overland Park	KS	66085	**888-941-2224**	913-549-1000
ASA Computers Inc 2354 Calle del Mundo	Santa Clara	CA	95054	**800-732-5727**	408-654-2901
Asante Technologies Inc 2223 Oakland Rd	San Jose	CA	95131	**800-303-9121**	408-435-8388

Classified Section

Company / Address	City	State	ZIP	Toll-Free	Phone
Avici Systems Inc 101 Billerica Ave	North Billerica	MA	01862	**877-292-8424**	978-964-2000
NASDAQ: AVCI					
Axis Communications Inc 100 Apollo Dr	Chelmsford	MA	01824	**800-444-2947**	978-614-2000
Belkin Corp 501 W Walnut St	Compton	CA	90220	**800-223-5546**	310-898-1100
Black Box Corp 1000 Park Dr	Lawrence	PA	15055	**877-877-2269**	724-746-5500
NASDAQ: BBOX					
Blue Coat Systems Inc 650 Almanor Ave	Sunnyvale	CA	94085	**888-462-3569**	408-220-2200
NASDAQ: BCSI					
Brocade Communications Systems Inc					
1745 Technology Dr	San Jose	CA	95110	**877-501-2723**	408-333-8000
NASDAQ: BRCD					
Bytex Corp					
113 Cedar St 495 Commerce Pk Suite S2	Milford	MA	01757	**800-227-1145**	508-422-9422
CalAmp Corp 12670 High Bluff Dr	San Diego	CA	92130	**888-554-2024**	858-554-1400
Cambex Corp 115 Flanders Rd	Westborough	MA	01581	**800-325-5565**	508-983-1200
Chatsworth Products Inc					
31425 Agoura Rd	Westlake Village	CA	91361	**800-834-4969**	818-735-6100
Ciprico Inc 17400 Medina Rd Suite 800	Plymouth	MN	55447	**800-727-4669**	763-551-4000
NASDAQ: CPCI					
Cisco Systems Inc 170 W Tasman Dr	San Jose	CA	95134	**800-553-6387**	408-526-4000
NASDAQ: CSCO					
CNet Technology Inc 1455 McCandless Dr	Milpitas	CA	95035	**800-486-2638**	408-934-0800
CNT (Computer Network Technology Corp)					
6000 Nathan Ln N	Minneapolis	MN	55442	**800-638-8324**	763-268-6000
NASDAQ: CMNT					
Communication Devices Inc 1 Forstmann Ct	Clifton	NJ	07011	**800-359-8561**	973-772-6997
Compex Inc 840 Columbia St Suite B	Brea	CA	92821	**800-279-8891**	714-482-0333
Compsee Inc 400 N Main St	Mount Gilead	NC	27306	**800-768-5248**	910-439-6141
CompuCom Systems Inc 7171 Forest Ln	Dallas	TX	75230	**800-597-0555***	972-856-3600
*Cust Svc					
Computer Network Technology Corp (CNT)					
6000 Nathan Ln N	Minneapolis	MN	55442	**800-638-8324**	763-268-6000
NASDAQ: CMNT					
Comtrol Corp					
6655 Wedgewood Rd Suite 120	Maple Grove	MN	55311	**800-926-6876**	763-494-4100
Continental Resources Inc					
175 Middlesex Tpke	Bedford	MA	01730	**800-937-4688**	781-275-0850
Converged Access Inc 31 Dunham Rd	Billerica	MA	08121	**888-748-2720**	978-436-9111
Crossroads Systems Inc 8300 N MoPac Expy	Austin	TX	78759	**800-643-7148**	512-349-0300
NASDAQ: CRDS					
Crystal Group Inc 850 Kacena Rd	Hiawatha	IA	52233	**800-378-1636**	319-378-1636
Cubix Corp 2800 Lockheed Way	Carson City	NV	89706	**800-829-0554***	775-883-7611
*Sales					
Cyberdata Corp 2555 Garden Rd	Monterey	CA	93940	**800-292-3723**	831-373-2601
CyberGuard Corp 350 SW 12th Ave	Deerfield Beach	FL	33442	**800-666-4273**	954-958-3900
NASDAQ: CGFW					
D-Link Systems Inc					
17595 Mt Herrmann St	Fountain Valley	CA	92708	**800-326-1688**	949-788-0805
Daly Computers Inc					
22521 Gateway Center Dr	Clarksburg	MD	20871	**800-955-3259**	301-670-0381
Dell Inc 1 Dell Way	Round Rock	TX	78682	**800-854-6214**	512-338-4400
NASDAQ: DELL					
Digi International Inc 11001 Bren Rd E	Minnetonka	MN	55343	**800-344-4273**	952-912-3444
NASDAQ: DGII					
Digilog Inc 2360 Maryland Rd	Willow Grove	PA	19090	**800-344-4564***	215-830-9400
*Cust Svc					
Dot Hill Systems Corp 6305 El Camino Real	Carlsbad	CA	92009	**800-872-2783**	760-931-5500
NASDAQ: HILL					
Echelon Corp 550 Meridian Ave	San Jose	CA	95126	**800-324-3566**	408-938-5200
NASDAQ: ELON					
Egenera Inc 165 Forest St	Marlborough	MA	01752	**800-316-3976**	508-858-2600
Electronics for Imaging Inc					
303 Velocity Way	Foster City	CA	94404	**800-568-1917**	650-357-3500
NASDAQ: EFII					
Eltek Energy LLC 115 Erick St	Crystal Lake	IL	60014	**800-447-3484**	815-459-9090
Emulex Corp 3333 Susan St	Costa Mesa	CA	92626	**800-854-7112**	714-662-5600
NYSE: ELX					
Equant 400 Galleria Pkwy Tower 400	Atlanta	GA	30339	**888-731-3100**	678-346-3000
eSoft Inc 295 Interlocken Blvd Suite 500	Broomfield	CO	80021	**888-903-7638**	303-444-1600
Extreme Networks Inc 3585 Monroe St	Santa Clara	CA	95051	**888-257-3000**	408-579-2800
NASDAQ: EXTR					
Ezenia! Inc 154 Middlesex Tpke	Burlington	MA	01803	**800-966-2301**	781-505-2100
NASDAQ: EZEN					
F5 Networks Inc 401 Elliott Ave W	Seattle	WA	98119	**888-882-4447**	206-272-5555
NASDAQ: FFIV					
Forsythe Technology Inc 7770 Frontage Rd	Skokie	IL	60077	**800-843-4488**	847-675-8000
Foundry Networks Inc 2100 Gold St	Alviso	CA	95002	**888-887-2652**	408-586-1700
NASDAQ: FDRY					
Fujitsu Computer Systems Corp					
1250 E Arques Ave	Sunnyvale	CA	94085	**877-213-6674**	408-746-6000
Futurex Inc 864 Old Boerne Rd	Bulverde	TX	78163	**800-251-5112**	830-980-9782
GlassHouse Technologies Inc					
200 Crossing Blvd	Framingham	MA	01702	**800-767-4535**	508-879-5729
Hitachi Internetworking					
2000 Sierra Point Pkwy	Brisbane	CA	94005	**800-927-9070**	650-244-7759
iLinc Communications Inc					
2999 N 44th St Suite 650	Phoenix	AZ	85018	**877-736-8347**	602-952-1200
AMEX: ILC					
IMC Networks Corp 19772 Pauling	Foothill Ranch	CA	92610	**800-624-1070**	949-465-3000
Informer Computer Systems Inc					
12711 Western Ave	Garden Grove	CA	92841	**800-650-4636**	714-891-1112
Integrix Inc 2001 Corporate Ctr Dr	Newbury Park	CA	91230	**800-300-8288**	805-376-1000
Interphase Corp 2901 N Dallas Pkwy Suite 200	Plano	TX	75093	**800-327-8638**	214-654-5000
NASDAQ: INPH					
Juniper Networks Inc 1194 N Mathilda Ave	Sunnyvale	CA	94089	**888-586-4737**	408-745-2000
NASDAQ: JNPR					
LGC Wireless Inc 2540 Junction Ave	San Jose	CA	95134	**800-530-9960**	408-952-2400
Linksys 18582 Teller Ave	Irvine	CA	92612	**800-326-7114**	949-823-3000
Mace Group Inc 15861 Tapia St	Irwindale	CA	91706	**800-644-1132**	626-338-8787
Marathon Technologies Corp 295 Foster St	Littleton	MA	01460	**800-884-6425**	978-489-1100
Marvell Semiconductor Inc 700 1st Ave	Sunnyvale	CA	94089	**800-752-3334**	408-222-2500
McDATA Corp					
380 Interlocken Crescent Suite 600	Broomfield	CO	80021	**800-545-5773**	720-558-8000
NASDAQ: MCDTA					
Medea Corp 5525 Oakdale Ave	Woodland Hills	CA	91364	**888-296-3332**	818-880-0303
Micro Design International Inc					
45 Skyline Dr Suite 1017	Lake Mary	FL	32746	**800-228-0891**	407-472-6000
MiLAN Technology 1329 Moffett Pk Dr	Sunnyvale	CA	94089	**800-466-4526**	408-744-2775
MTI Technology Corp 14661 Franklin Ave	Tustin	CA	92780	**800-999-9684**	714-481-7800
NASDAQ: MTIC					
MTM Technologies Inc 850 Canal St 3rd Fl	Stamford	CT	06902	**800-468-6782**	203-975-3700
NASDAQ: MTMC					
NETGEAR Inc 4500 Great America Pkwy	Santa Clara	CA	95054	**888-638-4327***	408-907-8000
NASDAQ: NTGR ■ *Cust Svc					
Network Appliance Inc 495 E Java Dr	Sunnyvale	CA	94089	**800-443-4537***	408-822-6000
NASDAQ: NTAP ■ *Sales					
Network Equipment Technologies Inc					
6900 Paseo Padre Pkwy	Fremont	CA	94555	**888-828-8080**	510-713-7300
NYSE: NWK					
NLynx Technologies Inc 8313 Hwy 71 W	Austin	TX	78735	**888-659-6967***	512-301-8000
*Tech Supp					
Nortel Networks Corp					
8200 Dixie Rd Suite 100	Brampton	ON	L6T5P6	**800-666-7835**	905-863-0000
NYSE: NT					
Overland Storage Inc 4820 Overland Ave	San Diego	CA	92123	**800-729-8725**	858-571-5555
NASDAQ: OVRL					
OvisLink Technologies Corp					
1301 John Reed Ct	City of Industry	CA	91745	**888-605-6847**	626-854-1805
Packeteer Inc 10201 N De Anza Blvd	Cupertino	CA	95014	**800-697-2253**	408-873-4400
NASDAQ: PKTR					
Plaintree Systems Inc 110 Decosta St	Arnprior	ON	K7S3X1	**800-461-0062**	613-623-3434
Polycom Inc 4750 Willow Rd	Pleasanton	CA	94588	**866-476-5926**	925-924-6000
NASDAQ: PLCM					
PrimeArray Systems Inc 127 Riverneck Rd	Chelmsford	MA	01824	**800-433-5133**	978-654-6250
Racore Technology Corp					
4125 S 6000 West	West Valley City	UT	84128	**877-252-9779**	801-973-9779
RedSiren Inc 650 Smithfield St Suite 910	Pittsburgh	PA	15222	**877-360-7602**	412-281-4427
Safari Technologies Inc 411 Washington St	Otsego	MI	49078	**888-694-7230**	269-694-9471
SafeNet Inc 4690 Millennium Dr	Belcamp	MD	21017	**800-533-3958***	410-931-7500
NASDAQ: SFNT ■ *Sales					
SARCOM Inc					
8337 Green Meadows Dr N Suite A	Lewis Center	OH	43035	**800-326-3962**	614-854-1300
segNET Technologies Inc					
9 Landing Rd PO Box 369	Enfield	NH	03748	**800-763-5556**	603-643-5883
Server Technology Inc 1040 Sandhill Dr	Reno	NV	89521	**800-835-1515**	775-284-2000
SIGCOM 4230 Beechwood Dr	Greensboro	NC	27410	**877-474-4266**	336-547-9700
SMC Networks Inc 38 Tesla	Irvine	CA	92618	**800-762-4968**	949-679-8000
SOHOware Inc 3050 Coronado Dr	Santa Clara	CA	95054	**800-632-1118**	408-565-9888
Solectek Corp					
6370 Nancy Ridge Dr Suite 109	San Diego	CA	92121	**800-437-1518**	858-450-1220
SonicWALL Inc 1143 Borregas Ave	Sunnyvale	CA	94089	**888-222-6563**	408-745-9600
NASDAQ: SNWL					
Spectrum Communications Cabling Services Inc					
226 N Lincoln Ave	Corona	CA	92882	**800-319-8711**	951-371-0549
Stampede Technologies Inc 80 Rhoades Ctr Dr	Dayton	OH	45458	**800-763-3423**	937-291-5035
SteelCloud Co 1306 Squire Ct	Dulles	VA	20166	**800-296-3866**	703-450-0400
NASDAQ: SCLD					
Storage Engine Inc 1 Sheila Dr Bldg 6A	Tinton Falls	NJ	07724	**866-734-8899**	732-747-6995
Sun Microsystems Inc 4150 Network Cir	Santa Clara	CA	95054	**800-786-0404**	650-960-1300
NASDAQ: SUNW					
Sycamore Networks Inc 220 Mill Rd	Chelmsford	MA	01824	**877-792-2667**	978-250-2900
NASDAQ: SCMR					
Symon Communications Inc					
500 N Central Expy Suite 175	Plano	TX	75074	**800-827-9666**	972-578-8484
Sys Technology Inc 17358 Railroad St	City of Industry	CA	91748	**866-834-9155**	626-810-2345
Systech Corp 16510 Via Esprillo	San Diego	CA	92127	**800-800-8970**	858-674-6500
Systemax Inc 11 Harbor Pk Dr	Port Washington	NY	11050	**800-845-6225**	516-625-1555
NYSE: SYX					
Telebyte Inc 270 Pulaski Rd	Greenlawn	NY	11740	**800-835-3298**	631-423-3232
Telkonet Inc					
20374 Seneca Meadows Pkwy	Germantown	MD	20876	**866-375-8446**	240-912-1800
AMEX: TKO					
TransNet Corp 45 Columbia Rd	Somerville	NJ	08876	**800-526-4965**	908-253-0500
Transource Computers Corp					
10850 N 24th Ave Suite 102	Phoenix	AZ	85029	**800-486-3715**	602-997-8101
Trendware International Inc 3135 Kashiwa St	Torrance	CA	90505	**888-326-6061**	310-891-1100
UNICOM Electric Inc 907 S Canada Ct	City of Industry	CA	91748	**800-346-6668**	626-964-7873
Unimark Inc 9910 Widmer Rd	Lenexa	KS	66215	**800-255-6356***	913-649-2424
*Cust Svc					
US Robotics Corp 935 National Pkwy	Schaumburg	IL	60173	**877-710-0884**	847-874-2000
ViewCast Corp 17300 N Dallas Pkwy Suite 2000	Dallas	TX	75248	**800-540-4119**	972-488-7200
Visara International Inc					
6833 Mt Herman Rd	Morrisville	NC	27560	**888-334-4380**	919-882-0200
WatchGuard Technologies Inc					
505 5th Ave S Suite 500	Seattle	WA	98104	**800-734-9905***	206-521-8340
NASDAQ: WGRD ■ *Sales					
WAV Inc 2380 Prospect Dr	Aurora	IL	60504	**800-678-2419**	630-818-1000
Winchester Systems Inc					
149 Middlesex Tpke	Burlington	MA	01803	**800-325-3700***	781-265-0200
*Cust Svc					
Xodiax 733 Barret Ave	Louisville	KY	40204	**866-838-4722**	502-315-6000
Zzyzx Peripherals Inc 5550 Morehouse Dr	San Diego	CA	92121	**800-876-7818**	858-558-7800

175 COMPUTER PROGRAMMING SERVICES - CUSTOM

SEE ALSO Computer Software; Computer Systems Design Services

Company / Address	City	State	ZIP	Toll-Free	Phone
Access Innovations Inc 131 Adams St NE	Albuquerque	NM	87108	**800-926-8328**	505-265-3591
Alliance Consulting					
2005 Market St 32nd Fl	Philadelphia	PA	19103	**800-706-3339**	215-569-8722
Construx Software					
11820 Northup Way Suite E-200	Bellevue	WA	98005	**866-296-6300**	425-636-0100
Edge Systems LLC					
1805 High Point Dr Suite 103	Naperville	IL	60563	**800-352-3343***	630-810-9669
*Tech Supp					
GDI Infotech Inc 3775 Varsity Dr	Ann Arbor	MI	48108	**800-608-7682**	734-477-6900
Paladin Data Systems Corp					
19362 Powder Hill Pl NE	Poulsbo	WA	98370	**800-532-8448**	360-779-2400
SEI Information Technology					
1420 Kensington Rd Suite 102	Oak Brook	IL	60523	**888-734-7343**	630-413-5050
Susquehanna Technologies DBA SusQtech					
600 Pegasus Ct Suite 100	Winchester	VA	22602	**888-603-0304**	540-723-8700
Tallan Inc					
628 Hebron Ave Bldg 2 Suite 502	Glastonbury	CT	06033	**800-677-3693**	860-633-3693
Youngsoft Inc 49197 Wixom Tech Dr Suite B	Wixom	MI	48393	**888-470-4553**	248-675-1200

COMPUTER RESELLERS

SEE Computer Equipment & Software - Whol

176 COMPUTER SOFTWARE

SEE ALSO Application Service Providers (ASPs); Computer Equipment & Software - Whol; Computer Networking Products & Systems; Computer Programming Services - Custom; Computer Stores; Computer Systems Design Services; Educational Materials & Supplies

176-1 Business Software (General)

Company	City	State	Zip	Toll-Free	Phone
4D Inc 3031 Tisch Way Suite 902	San Jose	CA	95128	**800-785-3303**	408-557-4600
ACOM Solutions Inc 2850 E 29th St	Long Beach	CA	90806	**800-347-3638**	562-424-7899
Action Technologies Inc					
10970 International Blvd 2nd Fl	Oakland	CA	94603	**800-967-5356**	510-638-8300
Actuate Corp					
701 Gateway Blvd 6th Fl	South San Francisco	CA	94080	**800-914-2259***	650-837-2000
NASDAQ: ACTU ■ *Sales					
Adobe Systems Inc 345 Park Ave	San Jose	CA	95110	**800-833-6687**	408-536-6000
NASDAQ: ADBE					
AdStar Inc 4553 Glencoe Ave Suite 325	Marina del Rey	CA	90292	**800-752-5187**	310-577-8255
NASDAQ: ADST					
AdWare Systems Inc					
5111 Commerce Crossings Dr Suite 200	Louisville	KY	40229	**800-626-2027**	502-810-5000
Agile Software Corp 6373 San Ignacio Ave	San Jose	CA	95119	**888-594-5736**	408-284-4000
NASDAQ: AGIL					
AgilQuest Corp 9407 Hull St	Richmond	VA	23236	**888-745-7455**	804-745-0467
Agresso Americas					
8150 Corporate Park Dr Suite 130	Cincinnati	OH	45242	**888-848-3776**	513-564-0400
American Business Systems Inc					
315 Littleton Rd	Chelmsford	MA	01824	**800-356-4034**	978-250-9600
American Software Inc 470 E Paces Ferry Rd	Atlanta	GA	30305	**800-726-2946**	404-261-4381
NASDAQ: AMSWA					
Applix Inc 289 Turnpike Rd	Westborough	MA	01581	**800-827-7549**	508-870-0300
NASDAQ: APLX					
APPX Software Inc					
11363 San Jose Blvd Suite 301	Jacksonville	FL	32223	**800-879-2779**	904-880-5560
AskSam Systems Inc 121 S Jefferson St	Perry	FL	32347	**800-800-1997**	850-584-6590
Astea International Inc 240 Gibraltar Rd	Horsham	PA	19044	**800-878-4657**	215-682-2500
NASDAQ: ATEA					
Atos Origin 5599 San Felipe Suite 300	Houston	TX	77056	**866-875-8902**	713-513-3000
Avexus 10182 Telesis Ct Suite 600	San Diego	CA	92121	**800-413-2797***	858-352-3300
*Sales					
Avolent Inc 444 De Haro St Suite 100	San Francisco	CA	94107	**800-553-5505**	415-553-6400
AXS-One Inc 301 Rt 17 N	Rutherford	NJ	07070	**800-828-7660***	201-935-3400
AMEX: AXO ■ *Sales					
Baudville Inc 5380 52nd St SE	Grand Rapids	MI	49512	**800-728-0888***	616-698-0888
*Orders					
Best Software Inc 56 Technology Dr	Irvine	CA	92618	**866-308-2378**	949-753-1222
Best Software Inc CRM Div					
8800 N Gainey Ctr Dr Suite 200	Scottsdale	AZ	85258	**800-643-6400**	480-368-3700
Best Software Inc Nonprofit & Government Div					
12301 Research Blvd Bldg 4 Suite 350	Austin	TX	78759	**800-647-3863**	512-454-5004
Best Software Inc Small Business Div					
1505 Pavilion Pl	Norcross	GA	30093	**800-285-0999***	770-492-6414
*Sales					
Best Software Inc Specialty Products Div					
2325 Dulles Corner Blvd Suite 800	Herndon	VA	20171	**800-424-9392**	703-793-2700
Blackbaud Inc 2000 Daniel Island Dr	Charleston	SC	29492	**800-468-8996***	843-216-6200
NASDAQ: BLKB ■ *Cust Svc					
Blue Pumpkin Software Inc					
884 Hermosa Ct Suite 100	Sunnyvale	CA	94086	**877-257-6756**	408-830-5400
BMC Software Inc 2101 City West Blvd	Houston	TX	77042	**800-841-2031**	713-918-8800
NYSE: BMC					
Bottomline Technologies Inc					
325 Corporate Dr	Portsmouth	NH	03801	**800-243-2528**	603-436-0700
NASDAQ: EPAY					
Bradmark Technologies Inc					
4265 San Felipe Suite 800	Houston	TX	77027	**800-621-2808**	713-621-2808
Brady Identification Solutions					
6555 W Good Hope Rd	Milwaukee	WI	53223	**800-537-8791***	414-358-6600
*Cust Svc					
Business Objects SA 3030 Orchard Pkwy	San Jose	CA	95134	**800-527-0580**	408-953-6000
NASDAQ: BOBJ					
Champs Software Inc					
1255 N Vantage Pt Dr	Crystal River	FL	34429	**800-322-6647**	352-795-2362
Cincom Systems Inc 55 Merchant St	Cincinnati	OH	45246	**800-888-0115**	513-612-2300
Claritas Inc 1525 Wilson Blvd Suite 1200	Arlington	VA	22209	**800-234-5973**	703-812-2700
Clarity Systems Ltd					
2 Sheppard Ave E Suite 800	Toronto	ON	M2N5Y7	**877-410-5070**	416-250-5500
ClearStory Systems					
2 Westborough Business Pk					
Suite 2000	Westborough	MA	01581	**800-546-6600**	508-870-4000
Cognos Corp 15 Wayside Rd	Burlington	MA	01803	**800-426-4667***	781-229-6600
*Orders					
Cognos Inc					
3755 Riverside Dr PO Box 9707 Stn T	Ottawa	ON	K1V1B7	**800-637-7447**	613-738-1440
NASDAQ: COGN					
Commence Corp 200 Tornillo Way	Tinton Falls	NJ	07712	**877-266-6362**	732-380-9100
Computer Assoc International Inc					
1 Computer Assoc Plaza	Islandia	NY	11749	**800-225-5224**	631-342-6000
NYSE: CA					
Computer Science Innovations Inc					
1235 Evans Rd	Melbourne	FL	32904	**800-289-2923**	321-676-2923
Compuware Corp 1 Campus Martius	Detroit	MI	48226	**800-292-7432**	313-227-7300
NASDAQ: CPWR					
Comsquared Systems Inc					
5125 Peachtree Industrial Blvd	Norcross	GA	30092	**800-592-3766**	770-734-5300
Concur Technologies Inc					
6222 185th Ave NE	Redmond	WA	98052	**800-358-0610**	425-702-8808
NASDAQ: CNQR					
CorVu Corp 3400 W 66th St Suite 445	Edina	MN	55435	**800-610-0769**	952-944-7777
Cyma Systems Inc					
2330 W University Dr Suite 7	Tempe	AZ	85281	**800-292-2962**	480-303-2962
D & B Sales & Marketing Solutions					
460 Totten Pond Rd 7th Fl	Waltham	MA	02451	**800-590-0065***	781-672-9200
*Prod Info					
Data Pro Accounting Software Inc					
150 2nd Ave N 16th Fl	Saint Petersburg	FL	33701	**800-237-6377**	727-803-1500
Datamatics Management Services Inc					
330 New Brunswick Ave	Fords	NJ	08863	**800-673-0366**	732-738-9600
Datanautics Inc					
2953 Bunker Hill Ln Suite 100	Santa Clara	CA	95054	**888-422-2783**	408-350-1300
Dazel An HP Software Co 14231 Tandem Blvd	Austin	TX	78728	**800-357-8357**	512-494-7300
Decisioneering Inc					
1515 Arapahoe St Suite 1311	Denver	CO	80202	**800-289-2550**	303-534-1515
Deltek Systems Inc 13880 Dulles Corner Ln	Herndon	VA	20171	**800-456-2009**	703-734-8606
Demantra Inc 230 3rd Ave	Waltham	MA	02451	**866-336-2687**	781-810-1700
Deploy Solutions Inc					
100 Lowder Brook Dr Suite 1100	Westwood	MA	02090	**877-463-3756**	781-461-9024
diCarta Inc 1 Circle Star Way	San Carlos	CA	94070	**888-342-2782**	650-474-3800
Document Sciences Corp					
6339 Paseo del Lago	Carlsbad	CA	92009	**800-420-2620**	760-602-1400
NASDAQ: DOCX					
DST Systems Inc 333 W 11th St	Kansas City	MO	64105	**888-378-4636**	816-435-8600
NYSE: DST					
Dynalogic Inc 2021 Eastlake Ave E	Seattle	WA	98102	**800-735-0433**	206-323-9050
e-talk Corp 4040 W Royal Ln Suite 100	Irving	TX	75063	**800-835-6357**	972-819-3100
E*Trade Financial Corp Corporate Services					
4500 Bohannon Dr	Menlo Park	CA	94025	**800-786-2575**	650-331-6000
E.piphany Inc 475 Concar Dr	San Mateo	CA	94402	**877-764-4163**	650-578-7200
NASDAQ: EPNY					
eCredit.com Inc 20 CareMatrix Dr	Dedham	MA	02026	**800-276-2321**	781-752-1200
Edge Technologies Inc					
3702 Pender Dr Suite 420	Fairfax	VA	22030	**888-771-3343**	703-691-7900
edocs Inc 1 Apple Hill Dr Suite 301	Natick	MA	01760	**877-336-3362**	508-652-8600
Elcom International Inc 10 Oceana Way	Norwood	MA	02062	**800-713-3993**	781-440-3333
Emerging Technology Solutions Inc					
10698 Deerfield Rd Suite 100 PO					
Box 1024	Franktown	CO	80116	**800-558-4269**	303-688-1987
Enterworks Inc 19886 Ashburn Rd	Ashburn	VA	20147	**888-242-8356**	703-723-6740
ePartners Inc 1304 W Walnut Hill Ln Suite 300	Irving	TX	75038	**888-883-9797**	972-751-0078
Epicor Software Corp					
18200 Von Karman Suite 1000	Irvine	CA	92612	**800-999-1809**	949-585-4000
NASDAQ: EPIC					
Epsilon Inc 601 Edgewater Dr	Wakefield	MA	01880	**800-225-3333**	781-685-6000
eSignal 3955 Point Eden Way	Hayward	CA	94545	**800-367-4670***	510-266-6000
*Sales					
eTEK International Inc					
5445 DTC Pkwy PH-4	Greenwood Village	CO	80111	**800-888-6894**	303-488-3499
ETS Inc 1115 E Brigadoon Ct	Salt Lake City	UT	84117	**800-387-7003**	801-265-2497
Evoke Software Inc					
12357 Riata Trace Pkwy Suite C-200	Austin	TX	78727	**877-333-3427**	512-372-9370
Evolutionary Technologies International Inc					
816 Congress Ave Suite 1450	Austin	TX	78701	**800-856-8800**	512-383-3000
Exact Software North America					
8800 Lyra Dr Suite 350	Columbus	OH	43240	**800-468-0834**	614-410-2600
FileMaker Inc 5201 Patrick Henry Dr	Santa Clara	CA	95054	**800-325-2747***	408-987-7000
*Cust Svc					
FirePond Inc 8009 S 34th Ave Suite 1050	Minneapolis	MN	55425	**888-662-7722**	952-229-2300
Fischer International Systems Corp					
3584 Mercantile Ave	Naples	FL	34104	**800-776-7258**	239-643-1500
FlexiInternational Software Inc					
2 Enterprise Dr	Shelton	CT	06484	**800-353-9492**	203-925-3040
FrontRange Solutions Inc					
1125 Kelly Johnson Blvd	Colorado Springs	CO	80920	**800-776-7889**	719-531-5007
FRx Software Corp					
4700 S Syracuse Pkwy Suite 150	Denver	CO	80237	**800-379-8733**	303-741-8000
GBA Systems					
1501 Highwoods Blvd Suite 201	Greensboro	NC	27410	**800-422-3267**	336-668-4555
Geac AEC Business Solutions					
3707 W Cherry St	Tampa	FL	33607	**888-284-4232***	813-874-3344
*Tech Supp					
Global Shop Solutions Inc					
975 Evergreen Cir	The Woodlands	TX	77380	**800-364-5958***	281-681-1959
*Sales					
Global Software Inc					
3200 Atlantic Ave Suite 200	Raleigh	NC	27604	**800-326-3444***	919-872-7800
*Mktg					
Glovia International LLC					
1940 E Mariposa Ave	El Segundo	CA	90245	**888-245-6842**	310-563-7000
Group 1 Software Inc					
4200 Parliament Pl Suite 600	Lanham	MD	20706	**800-368-5806**	301-731-2300
GSE Systems Inc 9189 Red Branch Rd	Columbia	MD	21045	**800-638-7912***	410-772-3500
AMEX: GVP ■ *Cust Svc					
Halogen Software Inc 17 Auriga Dr	Ottawa	ON	K2E7Y9	**866-566-7778**	613-744-2254
HarrisData 611 N Barker Rd Suite 200	Brookfield	WI	53045	**800-225-0585**	262-784-9099
HighJump Software 6455 City West Pkwy	Eden Prairie	MN	55344	**800-328-3271**	952-947-4088
HK Systems Inc 2855 S James Dr	New Berlin	WI	53151	**800-424-7365**	262-860-7000
Hyperion Solutions Corp					
1344 Crossman Ave	Sunnyvale	CA	94089	**800-858-1666**	408-744-9500
NASDAQ: HYSL					
i2 Technologies Inc One i2 Pl 11701 Luna Rd	Dallas	TX	75234	**800-800-3288**	469-357-1000
iCIMS Inc 1301 Concord Ctr Suite 2 Hwy 36	Hazlet	NJ	07730	**800-889-4422**	732-847-1941
iEmployee 699 Fall River Ave	Seekonk	MA	02771	**800-884-6504**	508-336-4441
Indus International Inc					
3301 Windy Ridge Pkwy	Atlanta	GA	30339	**800-554-6387**	770-952-8444
NASDAQ: IINT					
Info Directions Inc 833 Phillips Rd	Victor	NY	14564	**888-924-4110**	585-924-4110
Infodata Systems Inc					
12150 Monument Dr Suite 400	Fairfax	VA	22033	**800-336-4939***	703-934-5205
*Sales					
Infoglide Software Corp					
6300 Bridge Point Pkwy Bldg 3 Suite 200	Austin	TX	78730	**800-338-2441**	512-532-3500
Informatica Corp 2100 Seaport Blvd	Redwood City	CA	94063	**800-653-3871**	650-385-5000
NASDAQ: INFA					
Infosys Technologies Ltd					
1 Spectrum Pointe Suite 350	Lake Forest	CA	92630	**800-485-4636**	949-455-9161
Innovative Systems Inc					
790 Holiday Dr Bldg 11	Pittsburgh	PA	15220	**800-622-6390**	412-937-9300
Insevo Inc 2600 Campus Dr	San Mateo	CA	94403	**888-243-8762***	650-571-9798
*Sales					
Inspiration Software Inc					
7412 SW Beaverton Hillsdale Hwy					
Suite 102	Portland	OR	97225	**800-877-4292**	503-297-3004

Classified Section

Company	City	State	ZIP	Toll-Free	Phone
Intelogistics Corp					
8411 W Oakland Pk Blvd Suite 300	Fort Lauderdale	FL	33351	**877-453-5700**	954-343-5588
InterAmerica Technologies Inc					
8150 Leesburg Pike Suite 1400	Vienna	VA	22182	**800-945-8329**	703-893-3514
International Business Machines Corp (IBM)					
New Orchard Rd	Armonk	NY	10504	**800-426-4968**	914-766-1900
NYSE: IBM					
InterraTech Corp 11 Federal St	Camden	NJ	08103	**888-589-4889**	856-614-5400
Intraware Inc 25 Orinda Way Suite 101	Orinda	CA	94563	**888-446-8729**	925-253-4500
NASDAQ: ITRA					
Intuit Inc PO Box 7850	Mountain View	CA	94039	**800-446-8848***	650-944-6000
NASDAQ: INTU ■ *Cust Svc					
Intuitive Mfg Systems Inc					
12131 113th Ave NE Suite 200	Kirkland	WA	98034	**877-549-2149**	425-821-0740
IPNet Solutions Inc					
4100 Newport Pl Suite 800	Newport Beach	CA	92660	**888-882-6600**	949-476-4451
K-Systems Inc 5060 Ritter Rd Suite 2-A	Mechanicsburg	PA	17055	**800-221-0204**	717-795-7711
Lawson Software Inc 380 Saint Peter St	Saint Paul	MN	55102	**800-477-1357**	651-767-7000
NASDAQ: LWSN					
Level 8 Systems Inc 8000 Regency Pkwy	Cary	NC	27511	**866-538-3588**	919-380-5000
Lotus Development Corp					
55 Cambridge Pkwy	Cambridge	MA	02142	**800-343-5414***	617-577-8500
*Sales					
Macro 4 Inc 35 Waterview Blvd	Parsippany	NJ	07054	**800-866-6224***	973-402-8000
*Cust Svc					
Made2Manage Systems Inc					
450 E 96th St Suite 300	Indianapolis	IN	46240	**800-626-0220**	317-249-1200
Magna Solutions					
1220 Lebourgneuf Blvd Suite 250	Quebec	QC	G2K2G4	**800-361-0528**	418-622-8003
MainControl Inc 7900 Westpark Dr Suite T500	McLean	VA	22102	**800-981-3328**	703-749-2308
Malvern Systems Inc					
81 Lancaster Ave Suite 216	Malvern	PA	19355	**800-296-9642**	610-296-9642
ManageSoft Corp 10 Post Office Sq Suite 600N	Boston	MA	02109	**800-441-4330**	617-532-1600
Marimba Inc 440 Clyde Ave	Mountain View	CA	94043	**888-930-5282**	650-930-5282
Meridian Project Systems					
1180 Iron Point Rd Suite 300	Folsom	CA	95630	**800-850-2660**	916-294-2000
MetaEdge Corp 1257 Tasman Dr Suite C	Sunnyvale	CA	94089	**888-755-9100**	408-752-9977
Micro Planning International Inc					
2225 Buchtel Blvd Suite 505	Denver	CO	80210	**800-852-7526**	
MicroBiz Corp 1 Park Way	Upper Saddle River	NJ	07458	**800-385-0072**	201-785-1311
Microsoft Corp 1 Microsoft Way	Redmond	WA	98052	**800-426-9400***	425-882-8080
NASDAQ: MSFT ■ *Sales					
Microsoft Great Plains Business Solutions					
1 Lone Tree Rd	Fargo	ND	58104	**888-477-7877**	701-281-6500
Modern Mind Software Inc					
801 1st Ave S Suite 200	Seattle	WA	98134	**888-784-2929**	
MRO Software Inc 100 Crosby Dr	Bedford	MA	01730	**800-243-7734***	781-280-2000
NASDAQ: MROI ■ *Cust Svc					
Multi-Ad Services Inc 1720 W Detweiller Dr	Peoria	IL	61615	**800-348-6485**	309-692-1530
MYOB US Inc 300 Roundhill Dr	Rockaway	NJ	07866	**800-322-6962***	973-586-2200
*Cust Svc					
Nakoma Group					
16795 Von Karman Ave Suite 240	Irvine	CA	92606	**877-891-2811**	949-222-0244
Neon Systems Inc					
14100 SW Fwy Suite 500	Sugar Land	TX	77478	**800-505-6366**	281-491-4200
NASDAQ: NEON					
Newport Wave Inc 15 McLean	Irvine	CA	92620	**800-999-2611**	949-651-1099
NovaSoft Information Technology Corp					
3705 Quakerbridge Rd Suite 112	Mercerville	NJ	08619	**888-668-2763**	609-588-5500
Novell Inc 1800 S Novell Pl	Provo	UT	84606	**800-453-1267**	801-861-7000
NASDAQ: NOVL					
NuView Systems Inc					
155 West Street Suite 7	Wilmington	MA	01887	**800-244-7654**	978-988-7884
OAO Technology Solutions Inc					
7500 Greenway Ctr Dr 16th Fl	Greenbelt	MD	20770	**800-720-9030**	301-486-0400
Object/FX Corp 10 2nd St NE Suite 400	Minneapolis	MN	55413	**800-762-7748**	612-312-2002
Objectivity Inc					
640 W California Ave Suite 210	Sunnyvale	CA	94086	**800-767-6259**	408-992-7100
Onyx Software Corp					
1100 112th Ave NE Suite 100	Bellevue	WA	98004	**888-275-6699**	425-451-8060
NASDAQ: ONXS					
Open Systems Inc					
1157 Valley Park Dr Suite 105	Shakopee	MN	55379	**800-328-2276***	952-496-2465
*Sales					
Oracle Corp 500 Oracle Pkwy	Redwood Shores	CA	94065	**800-672-2531***	650-506-7000
NASDAQ: ORCL ■ *Sales					
Palisade Corp 31 Decker Rd	Newfield	NY	14867	**800-432-7475**	607-277-8000
Paperclip Software Inc					
611 US Rte 46	Hasbrouck Heights	NJ	07604	**800-929-3503**	201-329-6300
Passport Corp					
140 E Ridgewood Ave Mack Ctr III	Paramus	NJ	07652	**800-926-6736**	201-634-1100
PeopleClick.com Inc 2 Hannover Sq 7th Fl	Raleigh	NC	27601	**877-820-4400**	919-645-2800
PeopleSoft Inc 4460 Hacienda Dr	Pleasanton	CA	94588	**800-380-7638**	925-225-3000
Percussion Software Inc					
92 Montvale Ave Suite 2100	Stoneham	MA	02180	**800-283-0800**	781-438-9900
Peregrine Systems Inc					
3611 Valley Center Dr	San Diego	CA	92130	**800-638-5231**	858-481-5000
Personnel Data Systems Inc (PDS)					
650 Sentry Pkwy Suite 200	Blue Bell	PA	19422	**800-243-8737**	610-828-4294
Pilot Software Inc 1 Canal Pk	Cambridge	MA	02141	**800-944-0094**	617-374-9400
Platform Computing Corp 3760 14th Ave	Markham	ON	L3R3T7	**877-528-3676**	905-948-8448
Portal Software Inc 10200 S De Anza Blvd	Cupertino	CA	95014	**888-767-8259**	408-572-2000
NASDAQ: PRSF					
Powerway Inc 6919 Hillsdale Ct	Indianapolis	IN	46250	**800-964-9004**	317-598-1760
Primavera Systems Inc					
3 Bala Plaza W Suite 700	Bala Cynwyd	PA	19004	**800-423-0245***	610-667-8600
*Sales					
Primus Knowledge Solutions Inc					
1601 5th Ave Suite 1900	Seattle	WA	98101	**800-277-4427**	206-292-1000
NASDAQ: PKSI					
Princeton Softech Inc 111 Campus Dr	Princeton	NJ	08540	**800-457-7060**	609-627-5500
Progress Software Corp 14 Oak Pk	Bedford	MA	01730	**800-477-6473**	781-280-4000
NASDAQ: PRGS					
Provia Software Inc					
5460 Corporate Grove Blvd SE	Grand Rapids	MI	49512	**877-776-8421**	616-285-3311
Provue Development Corp					
18411 Gothard St Unit A	Huntington Beach	CA	92648	**800-966-7878**	714-841-7779
QAD Inc 6450 Via Real	Carpinteria	CA	93013	**800-373-1144***	805-684-6614
NASDAQ: QADI ■ *Sales					
QNX Software Sytems Ltd					
175 Terence Matthews Crescent	Kanata	ON	K2M1W8	**800-363-9001**	613-591-0931
Quadstone Inc 286 Congress St 6th Fl	Boston	MA	02210	**800-821-8031**	617-457-5200
Quest Software Inc					
8001 Irvine Center Dr Suite 600	Irvine	CA	92618	**800-306-9329**	949-754-8000
NASDAQ: QSFT					
Quicken PO Box 7850	Mountain View	CA	94039	**800-446-8848***	650-944-6000
NASDAQ: INTU ■ *Cust Svc					
Realtime Software Corp					
950 Lee St Suite 200	Des Plaines	IL	60016	**800-323-1143**	847-803-1100
Red Wing Software Inc 491 Hwy 19	Red Wing	MN	55066	**800-732-9464**	651-388-1106
RedPrairie Corp					
20700 Swenson Dr Suite 200	Waukesha	WI	53186	**800-990-2632**	262-317-2000
Rentrak Corp					
7700 NE Ambassador Pl 1 Airport Ctr	Portland	OR	97220	**800-929-5656**	503-284-7581
NASDAQ: RENT					
Ross Systems Inc 2 Concourse Pkwy Suite 800	Atlanta	GA	30328	**877-767-7462**	770-351-9600
S2 Systems Inc 4965 Preston Pk Blvd Suite 100	Plano	TX	75093	**800-527-4131**	972-599-5600
SAP America Inc					
3999 W Chester Pike	Newtown Square	PA	19073	**800-727-5872**	610-661-1000
Satori Software Inc 2815 2nd Ave Suite 500	Seattle	WA	98121	**800-553-6477**	206-443-0765
Scala North America Inc					
300 International Pkwy Suite 230	Heathrow	FL	32746	**888-722-5241**	407-333-8829
Sciforma Corp 985 University Ave	Los Gatos	CA	95032	**800-533-9876***	408-354-0144
*Sales					
SCO Group Inc 355 S 520 West Suite 100	Lindon	UT	84042	**888-553-3305**	801-765-4999
NASDAQ: SCOX					
SeeBeyond Technology Corp					
181 W Huntington Dr	Monrovia	CA	91016	**800-425-0541**	626-471-6000
NASDAQ: SBYN					
SEEC Inc					
Park West 1 Suite 200 Cliff Mine Rd	Pittsburgh	PA	15275	**800-682-7332**	412-893-0300
Segue Software Inc 201 Spring St	Lexington	MA	02421	**800-287-1329**	781-402-1000
NASDAQ: SEGU					
Select Business Solutions 6260 Lookout Rd	Boulder	CO	80301	**888-472-7347**	303-305-4115
Selectica Inc 3 W Plumeria Dr	San Jose	CA	95134	**877-712-9560**	408-570-9700
NASDAQ: SLTC					
ServiceWare Technologies Inc					
333 Allegheny Ave Suite 301	Oakmont	PA	15139	**800-572-5748**	412-826-1158
Silvon Software Inc					
900 Oakmont Lane Suite 400	Westmont	IL	60559	**800-874-5866**	630-655-3313
SMARTS (System Management ARTS Inc)					
44 S Broadway	White Plains	NY	10601	**877-276-2787**	914-948-6200
Software AG USA 11190 Sunrise Valley Dr	Reston	VA	20191	**800-525-7859**	703-860-5050
Solution 6 North America					
3525 Piedmont Rd Bldg 8 Suite 500	Atlanta	GA	30305	**877-608-4369**	404-720-3600
Sooner Micro Systems Inc PO Box 470666	Tulsa	OK	74147	**800-324-9393**	918-664-8383
Source Technologies Inc					
2910 Whitehall Pk Dr	Charlotte	NC	28273	**800-922-8501**	704-969-7500
Speedware Corp					
9999 Cavendish Blvd Suite 100	Saint-Laurent	QC	H4M2X5	**800-361-6782**	514-747-7007
Spescom Software Inc					
10052 Mesa Ridge Ct Suite 100	San Diego	CA	92121	**800-992-6784**	858-625-3000
SPSS Inc 233 S Wacker Dr 11th Fl	Chicago	IL	60606	**800-543-2185**	312-651-3000
NASDAQ: SPSS					
SRC Software Inc 13190 SW 68th Pkwy	Portland	OR	97223	**800-544-3477**	503-608-3300
Stamps.com Inc					
3420 Ocean Park Blvd Suite 1040	Santa Monica	CA	90405	**888-434-0055**	310-581-7200
NASDAQ: STMP					
Sterling Commerce Inc 4600 Lakehurst Ct	Dublin	OH	43016	**800-876-9772**	614-793-7000
Sybase Inc 1 Sybase Dr	Dublin	CA	94568	**800-879-2273**	925-236-5000
NYSE: SY					
SYSPRO 959 S Coast Dr Suite 100	Costa Mesa	CA	92626	**800-369-8649**	714-437-1000
System Management ARTS Inc (SMARTS)					
44 S Broadway	White Plains	NY	10601	**877-276-2787**	914-948-6200
Taleo Corp 575 Market St 8th Fl	San Francisco	CA	94105	**888-836-3669**	415-538-9068
NASDAQ: TLEO					
Tangram Enterprise Solutions Inc					
11000 Regency Pkwy Suite 301	Cary	NC	27511	**800-482-6472**	919-653-6000
TECSYS Inc 87 Prince St 5th Fl	Montreal	QC	H3C2M7	**800-922-8649**	514-866-0001
Telelogic North America Inc 9401 Jeronimo Rd	Irvine	CA	92618	**877-275-4777***	949-830-8022
*Sales					
TenFold Corp 698 W 10000 S Suite 200	South Jordan	UT	84095	**800-836-3653**	801-495-1010
Tivoli Systems Inc					
9442 Capital of Texas Hwy N Plaza 1					
Suite 100	Austin	TX	78759	**877-848-6541**	512-436-8000
Tomax Corp 224 S 200 West	Salt Lake City	UT	84101	**800-255-8120**	801-990-0909
Trados Inc 1292 Hammerwood Ave	Sunnyvale	CA	94089	**888-487-2367**	408-743-3500
Transcentive Inc 2 Enterprise Dr	Shelton	CT	06484	**888-340-4267**	203-944-7300
TreeAge Software Inc 1075 Main St	Williamstown	MA	01267	**800-254-1911**	413-458-0104
TREEV Inc 13454 Sunrise Valley Dr Suite 400	Herndon	VA	20171	**800-254-0994**	703-478-2260
Trilogy Software Inc 5001 Plaza on the Lake	Austin	TX	78746	**877-292-3266**	512-874-3100
Triversity Inc 3550 Victoria Pk Ave Suite 400	Toronto	ON	M2H2N5	**888-287-4629**	416-791-7100
Ultimate Software Group Inc					
2000 Ultimate Way	Weston	FL	33326	**800-432-1729**	954-331-7000
NASDAQ: ULTI					
UniLink Software Inc 7322 Newman Blvd	Dexter	MI	48130	**800-968-0600***	734-426-5860
*Cust Svc					
Unz & Co 8 Easy St	Bound Brook	NJ	08805	**800-631-3098**	732-868-0706
Valiant 110 Crossways Park Dr	Woodbury	NY	11797	**800-521-4555**	516-390-1100
Versant Corp 6539 Dumbarton Cir	Fremont	CA	94555	**800-837-7268**	510-789-1500
NASDAQ: VSNT					
Versata Inc 300 Lakeside Dr Suite 1300	Oakland	CA	94612	**800-984-7638**	510-628-1000
NASDAQ: VATA					
Vertex Inc 1041 Old Cassatt Rd	Berwyn	PA	19312	**800-355-3500**	610-640-4200
VFA Inc 266 Summer St	Boston	MA	02210	**800-693-3132**	617-772-8277
Vignette Corp 1301 S Mopac Expy Bldg 4	Austin	TX	78746	**888-608-9900**	512-741-4300
NASDAQ: VIGN					
ViryaNet Ltd 2 Willow St	Southborough	MA	01745	**800-661-7096**	508-490-8600
NASDAQ: VRYA					
Visible Systems Corp 201 Spring St	Lexington	MA	02421	**800-684-7425***	781-778-0200
*Sales					
Visual Numerics Inc					
2500 Wilcrest Dr Suite 200	Houston	TX	77042	**800-222-4675**	713-784-3131
Volunteer Software 628 S 2nd Ave W	Missoula	MT	59801	**800-391-9446**	406-721-0113
Wave Systems Corp 480 Pleasant St	Lee	MA	01238	**888-669-9283**	413-243-1600
NASDAQ: WAVX					
Web Base Inc 133 E De La Guerra St	Santa Barbara	CA	93101	**800-225-8885**	805-275-4505
WordMark International Corp					
944 Torrey Pines Dr	Paso Robles	CA	93446	**800-835-2400**	805-237-9900
WRQ Inc 1500 Dexter Ave N	Seattle	WA	98109	**800-872-2829***	206-217-7500
*Sales					
ZyLAB North America LLC					
600 17th St Suite 2800 S	Denver	CO	80202	**866-995-2262**	

176-2 Computer Languages & Development Tools

Company	City	State	Zip	Toll-Free	Phone
Accelerated Technology Inc 734 N University Blvd	Mobile	AL	36608	**800-468-6853**	251-208-3400
ARC International 2025 Gateway Pl Suite 140	San Jose	CA	95110	**866-272-3344**	408-437-3400
Borland Software Corp 100 Enterprise Way *NASDAQ: BORL* ■ *Cust Svc	Scotts Valley	CA	95066	**800-331-0877***	831-431-1000
BSQUARE Corp 110 110th Ave NE Suite 200 *NASDAQ: BSQR*	Bellevue	WA	98004	**888-820-4500**	425-519-5900
BulletProof Corp 2400 E Las Olas Blvd Suite 332	Fort Lauderdale	FL	33301	**800-505-0105**	954-828-9400
California Software Corp 1241 Puerta del Sol	San Clemente	CA	92673	**800-841-1532**	949-498-9300
Data Access Corp 14000 SW 119th Ave	Miami	FL	33186	**800-451-3539**	305-238-0012
DDC-I Inc 400 N 5th St Suite 1050	Phoenix	AZ	85004	**800-221-8643**	602-275-7172
FMS Inc 8100 Boone Blvd Suite 310	Vienna	VA	22182	**888-367-7801**	703-356-4700
Forth Inc 5155 W Rosecrans Ave Suite 1018	Hawthorne	CA	90250	**800-553-6784**	310-491-3356
Green Hills Software Inc 30 W Sola St	Santa Barbara	CA	93101	**800-765-4733**	805-965-6044
ILOG Inc 1080 Linda Vista Ave	Mountain View	CA	94043	**800-367-4564**	650-567-8000
Integrated Computer Solutions Inc 201 Broadway	Cambridge	MA	02139	**800-800-4271**	617-621-0060
LANSA Inc 3010 Highland Pkwy Suite 950	Downers Grove	IL	60515	**800-457-4083**	630-874-7000
Lattice Inc 1751 S Naperville Rd Suite 100 *Sales	Wheaton	IL	60187	**800-444-4309***	630-949-3250
MDBS Inc 1305 Cumberland Ave	West Lafayette	IN	47906	**800-445-6327**	765-463-7200
Mix Software Inc 1203 Berkeley Dr	Richardson	TX	75081	**800-333-0330**	972-238-8554
MKS Inc 410 Albert St *Sales	Waterloo	ON	N2L3V3	**800-265-2797***	519-884-2251
Object/FX Corp 10 2nd St NE Suite 400	Minneapolis	MN	55413	**800-762-7748**	612-312-2002
Prolifics 116 John St 20th Fl	New York	NY	10038	**800-458-3313**	212-267-7722
Recital Corp 100 Cummings Ctr Suite 318J	Beverly	MA	01915	**800-873-7443**	978-921-5594
Revelation Software 99 Kinderkamack Rd	Westwood	NJ	07675	**800-262-4747**	201-594-1422
Rogue Wave Software Inc 5500 Flatiron Pkwy	Boulder	CO	80301	**800-487-3217**	303-473-9118
SemWare Corp 730 Elk Cove Ct	Kennesaw	GA	30152	**800-467-3692**	678-355-9810
SlickEdit Inc 3000 Aerial Center Pkwy Suite 120	Morrisville	NC	27560	**800-934-3348**	919-473-0070
Sunbelt Computer Systems Inc 13090 Swan Lake Rd CR 468 *Sales	Tyler	TX	75704	**800-359-5907***	903-881-0400
Thoroughbred Software International Inc 285 Davidson Ave Suite 302	Somerset	NJ	08873	**800-524-0430**	732-560-1377
UniPress Software Inc 2025 Lincoln Hwy	Edison	NJ	08817	**800-222-0550**	732-287-2100
Wise Solutions Inc 47911 Halyard Dr	Plymouth	MI	48170	**800-554-8565**	734-456-2100
Zortec International 124 12th Ave S Suite 210	Nashville	TN	37203	**800-361-7005**	615-361-7000

176-3 Educational & Reference Software

Company	City	State	Zip	Toll-Free	Phone
American Education Corp 7506 N Broadway Ext Suite 505 *Sales	Oklahoma City	OK	73116	**800-222-2811***	405-840-6031
Atari Inc 417 5th Ave 8th Fl *NASDAQ: ATAR*	New York	NY	10016	**800-898-1438**	212-726-6500
Authoria Inc 300 5th Ave	Waltham	MA	02451	**877-628-8467**	781-530-2000
Automated Training Systems Corp 4545 E Industrial St Suite 5B	Simi Valley	CA	93063	**800-426-8737**	805-520-1509
Blackboard Inc 1899 L St NW 5th Fl *NASDAQ: BBBB*	Washington	DC	20036	**800-424-9299**	202-463-4860
Broderbund LLC 500 Redwood Blvd	Novato	CA	94947	**800-395-0277**	415-382-4400
CompassLearning Inc 9920 Pacific Heights Blvd Suite 500 *Cust Svc	San Diego	CA	92121	**800-247-1380***	858-587-0087
Corporate Solutions 303 Riding Trail Ct	Leesburg	VA	20176	**800-622-4686**	
Electronic Courseware Systems Inc 1713 S State St *Orders	Champaign	IL	61820	**800-832-4965***	217-359-7099
Gamco Industries Inc 325 N Kirkwood Dr Suite 200	Saint Louis	MO	63122	**888-726-8100**	314-909-1670
Grolier Electronic Publishing Inc 90 Old Sherman Tpke	Danbury	CT	06816	**800-955-9877**	203-797-3500
Individual Software Inc 4255 Hopyard Rd Suite 2	Pleasanton	CA	94588	**800-822-3522**	925-734-6767
Insightful Corp 1700 Westlake Ave N Suite 500 *NASDAQ: IFUL*	Seattle	WA	98109	**800-569-0123**	206-283-8802
Inspiration Software Inc 7412 SW Beaverton Hillsdale Hwy Suite 102	Portland	OR	97225	**800-877-4292**	503-297-3004
Lightspan Inc 10140 Campus Pt Dr	San Diego	CA	92121	**888-425-5543**	858-824-8000
LJ Technical Systems Inc 85 Corporate Dr	Holtsville	NY	11742	**800-237-3482**	631-758-1616
MedTech USA 6310 San Vicente Blvd Suite 404	Los Angeles	CA	90048	**800-640-8000**	323-964-1000
Milliken Publishing Co Inc 11643 Lilburn Park Dr	Saint Louis	MO	63146	**800-325-4136**	314-991-4220
MindPlay Educational Software 440 S Williams Blvd Suite 206	Tucson	AZ	85711	**800-221-7911**	520-888-1800
NCS Pearson Inc 5601 Green Valley Dr Suite 220	Bloomington	MN	55437	**800-431-1421**	952-681-3000
Nordic Software Inc PO Box 83499	Lincoln	NE	68501	**800-306-6502**	402-489-1557
Optimum Resource Inc 18 Hunter Rd	Hilton Head Island	SC	29926	**888-784-2592**	843-689-8000
PLATO Learning Inc 10801 Nesbitt Ave S *NASDAQ: TUTR*	Bloomington	MN	55437	**800-869-2000**	952-832-1000
Queue Inc 1450 Barnum Ave Suite 207	Bridgeport	CT	06610	**800-232-2224**	203-335-0906
Renaissance Learning Inc 2911 Peach St *NASDAQ: RLRN*	Wisconsin Rapids	WI	54494	**800-338-4204**	715-424-3636
Riverdeep Inc 500 Redwood Blvd	Novato	CA	94947	**800-825-4420**	415-763-4700
Saba Software Inc 2400 Bridge Pkwy *NASDAQ: SABA*	Redwood Shores	CA	94065	**877-803-1900**	650-696-3840
Scientific Learning Corp 300 Frank H Ogawa Plaza Suite 500 *NASDAQ: SCIL*	Oakland	CA	94612	**888-665-9707**	510-444-3500
Siboney Corp PO Box 221029	Saint Louis	MO	63122	**888-726-8100**	314-822-3163
Simon & Schuster Interactive 1230 Ave of the Americas	New York	NY	10020	**800-223-2348**	212-698-7000
SmartCertify Direct 25400 US Hwy 19N Suite 285 *Orders	Clearwater	FL	33763	**800-653-4933***	727-724-8994
Snyder Tom Productions Inc 80 Coolidge Hill Rd	Watertown	MA	02472	**800-342-0236**	617-926-6000
SumTotal Systems Inc 2444 Charleston Rd *NASDAQ: SUMT*	Mountain View	CA	94043	**866-768-6825**	650-934-9500
Sunburst Technology 101 Castleton St	Pleasantville	NY	10570	**800-321-7511**	914-747-3310
Thompson ISI ResearchSoft 2141 Palomar Airport Rd Suite 350	Carlsbad	CA	92009	**800-722-1227**	760-438-5526
Tom Snyder Productions Inc 80 Coolidge Hill Rd	Watertown	MA	02472	**800-342-0236**	617-926-6000
Transparent Language Inc 9 Executive Park Dr	Merrimack	NH	03054	**800-730-2230**	603-262-6300
True BASIC Inc 1523 Maple St	Hartford	VT	05047	**800-436-2111**	802-296-2711
VCampus Corp 1850 Centennial Pk Dr Suite 200 *NASDAQ: VCMP*	Reston	VA	20191	**800-915-9298**	703-893-7800
Ventura Educational Systems PO Box 425	Grover Beach	CA	93483	**800-336-1022**	805-473-7387
Wright Group/McGraw-Hill 19201 120th Ave NE Suite 100 *Sales	Bothell	WA	98011	**800-523-2371***	425-486-8011

176-4 Electronic Purchasing & Procurement Software

Company	City	State	Zip	Toll-Free	Phone
Apptis Inc 14155 Newbrook Dr	Chantilly	VA	20151	**800-338-8866**	703-279-3000
Ariba Inc 807 11th Ave *NASDAQ: ARBA*	Sunnyvale	CA	94089	**888-237-3131**	650-390-1000
BroadVision Inc 585 Broadway *NASDAQ: BVSN*	Redwood City	CA	94063	**800-269-9375**	650-542-5100
Commerce One Inc One Market St Steuart Tower Suite 1300	San Francisco	CA	94105	**800-628-2761**	415-644-8700
Computer Assoc International Inc 1 Computer Assoc Plaza *NYSE: CA*	Islandia	NY	11749	**800-225-5224**	631-342-6000
Covisint One Campus Martius	Detroit	MI	48226	**888-222-1700**	248-827-6000
eB2B Commerce Inc 665 Broadway	New York	NY	10012	**877-853-3222**	212-477-1700
Epylon Corp 1340 Treat Blvd Suite 210	Walnut Creek	CA	94597	**888-211-7438**	925-407-1020
Global eXchange Services Inc 100 Edison Park Dr	Gaithersburg	MD	20878	**800-560-4347**	301-340-4000
i2 Technologies Inc One i2 Pl 11701 Luna Rd	Dallas	TX	75234	**800-800-3288**	469-357-1000
International Business Machines Corp (IBM) New Orchard Rd *NYSE: IBM*	Armonk	NY	10504	**800-426-4968**	914-766-1900
MarketAxess Holdings Inc 140 Broadway 42nd Fl *NASDAQ: MKTX*	New York	NY	10005	**877-638-0037**	212-813-6000
NOVA Information Systems 1 Concourse Pkwy Suite 300	Atlanta	GA	30328	**800-725-1243**	770-396-1456
Open Solutions RDS Technologies 7820 Innovation Blvd Suite 100	Indianapolis	IN	46278	**800-888-2112**	317-610-3500
PayNet Merchant Services Inc 2000 Town Center Suite 2260	Southfield	MI	48075	**888-855-8644**	248-354-1111
PeopleSoft Inc 4460 Hacienda Dr	Pleasanton	CA	94588	**800-380-7638**	925-225-3000
SciQuest Inc 5151 McCrimmon Pkwy Suite 216	Morrisville	NC	27560	**800-233-1121**	919-659-2100
Siebel Systems Inc 2207 Bridgepointe Pkwy *NASDAQ: SEBL*	San Mateo	CA	94404	**800-647-4300**	650-295-5000
Transora 10 S Riverside Plaza Suite 2000	Chicago	IL	60606	**877-872-5984**	312-463-4000

176-5 Engineering Software

Company	City	State	Zip	Toll-Free	Phone
Accelrys Inc 9685 Scranton Rd *NASDAQ: ACCL*	San Diego	CA	92121	**800-756-4674**	858-799-5000
Advanced Visual Systems Inc 300 5th Ave *Sales	Waltham	MA	02451	**800-728-1600***	781-890-4300
Algor Inc 150 Beta Dr	Pittsburgh	PA	15238	**800-482-5467**	412-967-2700
Altium Inc 17140 Bernardo Center Dr Suite 100	San Diego	CA	92128	**800-488-0680**	858-485-4600
ANSYS Inc 275 Technology Dr *NASDAQ: ANSS*	Canonsburg	PA	15317	**800-937-3321**	724-746-3304
Ashlar Inc 12731 Research Blvd Bldg A	Austin	TX	78759	**800-877-2745**	512-250-2186
Autodesk Inc 111 McInnis Pkwy *NASDAQ: ADSK* ■ *Prod Info	San Rafael	CA	94903	**800-964-6432***	415-507-5000
Bentley Systems Inc 685 Stockton Dr	Exton	PA	19341	**800-236-8539**	610-458-5000
Bionetics Corp Ketron Div 44425 Pecan Ct Suite 200	California	MD	20619	**800-922-3278**	301-862-3092
Bohannan Huston Inc 7500 Jefferson St NE Courtyard 1	Albuquerque	NM	87109	**800-877-5332**	505-823-1000
Cadence Design Systems Inc 2655 Seely Ave *NYSE: CDN* ■ *Cust Svc	San Jose	CA	95134	**800-746-6223***	408-943-1234
CambridgeSoft Corp 100 CambridgePark Dr	Cambridge	MA	02140	**800-315-7300**	617-588-9100
Citect Inc 30000 Mill Creek Ave Suite 300	Alpharetta	GA	30022	**888-248-3281**	770-521-7511
Data Description Inc 840 Hanshaw Rd 2nd Fl	Ithaca	NY	14850	**800-573-5121**	607-257-1000
Disk Software Inc 109 S Murphy Rd	Plano	TX	75094	**800-635-7760**	972-423-7288
Evolution Computing 7000 N 16th St Suite 120 #514	Phoenix	AZ	85020	**800-874-4028**	602-749-9476
Geocomp Corp 1145 Massachusetts Ave *Cust Svc	Boxborough	MA	01719	**800-822-2669***	978-635-0012
Gibbs & Assoc 323 Science Dr	Moorpark	CA	93021	**800-654-9399**	805-523-0004
Intergraph Corp 288 Dunlop Blvd *NASDAQ: INGR*	Huntsville	AL	35824	**800-345-4856**	256-730-2000
Kubotek USA 100 Locke Rd	Marlborough	MA	01752	**800-372-3872**	508-229-2020
LINDO Systems Inc 1415 N Dayton St *Sales	Chicago	IL	60622	**800-441-2378***	312-988-7422
Manufacturing & Consulting Services Inc 7633 E Acoma Dr Suite 104	Scottsdale	AZ	85260	**800-932-9329**	480-991-8700
MAPICS Inc 1000 Windward Concourse Pkwy Suite 100 *NASDAQ: MAPX*	Alpharetta	GA	30005	**888-362-7427**	678-319-8000
Mentor Graphics Corp 8005 SW Boeckman Rd *NASDAQ: MENT*	Wilsonville	OR	97070	**800-592-2210**	503-685-7000

Company / Address	City	State	ZIP	Toll-Free	Phone
Moldflow Corp 430 Boston Post Rd NASDAQ: MFLO	Wayland	MA	01778	**800-284-6653**	508-358-5848
MSC.Software Corp 2 MacArthur Pl	Santa Ana	CA	92707	**800-345-2078**	714-444-5112
National Instruments Corp 11500 N Mopac Expy NASDAQ: NATI ■ *Cust Svc	Austin	TX	78759	**800-433-3488***	512-794-0100
Planit Solutions Inc 3800 Palisades Dr	Tuscaloosa	AL	35405	**800-280-6932**	205-556-9199
Simulation Sciences Inc 26561 Rancho Pkwy S	Lake Forest	CA	92630	**800-746-7241**	949-455-8150
SofTech Inc 2 Highwood Dr Suite 200	Tewksbury	MA	01876	**800-800-3702**	978-640-6222
Tecnomatix Technologies Inc 21500 Haggerty Rd Suite 300	Northville	MI	48167	**800-304-8326**	248-699-2500
Tripos Inc 1699 S Hanley Rd NASDAQ: TRPS	Saint Louis	MO	63144	**800-323-2960**	314-647-1099
Zuken USA 238 Littleton Rd Suite 100	Westford	MA	01886	**800-447-7332**	978-692-4900

176-6 Games & Entertainment Software

Company / Address	City	State	ZIP	Toll-Free	Phone
Abacus Software Inc 5130 Patterson St SE *Sales	Grand Rapids	MI	49512	**800-451-4319***	616-698-0330
Alienware Corp 12400 SW 134 Ct Bay 8	Miami	FL	33186	**866-287-6727**	305-251-9797
Apogee Software Inc 1999 S Bascom Ave Suite 325	Campbell	CA	95008	**800-337-3256**	408-369-9001
Atari Inc 417 5th Ave 8th Fl NASDAQ: ATAR	New York	NY	10016	**800-898-1438**	212-726-6500
Buena Vista Games 500 S Buena Vista St	Burbank	CA	91521	**800-228-0988**	
Cyan Inc 14617 N Newport Hwy	Mead	WA	99021	**800-219-4119**	509-468-0807
Disney Consumer Products 500 S Buena Vista St *PR	Burbank	CA	91521	**800-723-4763***	818-560-1000
Electronic Arts Inc 209 Redwood Shores Pkwy NASDAQ: ERTS ■ *Sales	Redwood City	CA	94065	**877-324-2637***	650-628-1500
Her Interactive Inc 1150 114th Ave SE Suite 200 *Orders	Bellevue	WA	98004	**800-561-0908***	425-889-2900
iEntertainment Network Inc 124 Quade Dr	Cary	NC	27513	**800-438-4263**	919-678-8301
Konami of America Inc 1400 Bridge Pkwy Suite 101	Redwood City	CA	94065	**888-212-0573**	
MakeMusic! Inc 6210 Bury Dr NASDAQ: MMUS	Eden Prairie	MN	55346	**800-843-2066**	952-937-9611
Maxis Inc 2121 N California Blvd Suite 600	Walnut Creek	CA	94596	**800-245-4525**	925-933-5630
Nintendo of America Inc 4822 150th Ave NE *Cust Svc	Redmond	WA	98052	**800-255-3700***	425-882-2040
Simon & Schuster Interactive 1230 Ave of the Americas	New York	NY	10020	**800-223-2348**	212-698-7000
Walt Disney Interactive 601 Circle 7 Dr	Glendale	CA	91201	**800-228-0988**	818-553-5000
ZeniMax Media Inc 1370 Piccard Dr Suite 120	Rockville	MD	20850	**800-677-0700**	301-948-2200

176-7 Internet & Communications Software

Company / Address	City	State	ZIP	Toll-Free	Phone
ACE*COMM Corp 704 Quince Orchard Rd Suite 100 NASDAQ: ACEC	Gaithersburg	MD	20878	**800-989-5566**	301-721-3000
Active Voice LLC 2033 6th Ave Suite 500 *Sales	Seattle	WA	98121	**877-864-8948***	206-441-4700
Adaptive Micro Systems Inc 7840 N 86th St	Milwaukee	WI	53224	**800-558-7022**	414-357-2020
ADB Systems International Inc 302 East Mall Suite 300	Etobicoke	ON	M9B6C7	**888-287-7467**	416-640-0400
Aether Systems Inc 11460 Cronridge Dr NASDAQ: AETH	Owings Mills	MD	21117	**888-812-6767**	410-654-6400
Akamai Technologies Inc 8 Cambridge Ctr NASDAQ: AKAM	Cambridge	MA	02142	**877-425-2624**	617-444-3000
Alexa Internet PO Box 29141	San Francisco	CA	94129	**888-882-5392**	415-561-6900
Amcom Software Inc 5555 W 78th St	Minneapolis	MN	55439	**800-852-8935**	952-829-7445
Anonymizer Inc 5694 Mission Ctr Rd Box 426	San Diego	CA	92108	**888-270-0141**	619-725-3180
AnyDoc Software Inc 401 E Jackson St Suite 1200	Tampa	FL	33602	**800-775-3222**	813-222-0414
Apex Voice Communications Inc 15250 Ventura Blvd 3rd Fl	Sherman Oaks	CA	91403	**800-727-3970**	818-379-8400
Apropos Technology Inc 1 Tower Ln 28th Fl NASDAQ: APRS	Oakbrook Terrace	IL	60181	**877-277-6767**	630-472-9600
Ariba Inc 807 11th Ave NASDAQ: ARBA	Sunnyvale	CA	94089	**888-237-3131**	650-390-1000
Attachmate Corp 3617 131st Ave SE	Bellevue	WA	98006	**800-426-6283**	425-644-4010
Authorize.Net Corp 915 S 500 East Suite 200 *Tech Supp	American Fork	UT	84003	**877-447-3938***	801-492-6450
Automation Technology Inc 2001 Gateway Pl Suite 100 *Sales	San Jose	CA	95110	**888-805-6322***	408-350-7020
Axeda Systems Inc 277 Great Valley Pkwy NASDAQ: XEDA	Malvern	PA	19355	**800-700-0362**	610-407-7300
BackWeb Technologies Inc 2077 Gateway Pl Suite 500 NASDAQ: BWEB	San Jose	CA	95110	**800-863-0100**	408-933-1700
Big Sky Technologies 9325 Sky Park Ct Suite 120	San Diego	CA	92123	**800-736-2751**	858-715-5000
Blast Inc 220 Chatham Business Dr	Pittsboro	NC	27312	**800-242-5278**	919-542-3007
C-ME.com 4349 Baldwin Ave Suite A	El Monte	CA	91731	**888-564-6263**	626-636-2530
Callware Technologies Inc 2755 E Cottonwood Pkwy 4th Fl	Salt Lake City	UT	84121	**800-888-4226**	801-937-6800
Captaris Inc 10885 NE 4th St Suite 400 NASDAQ: CAPA	Bellevue	WA	98004	**800-443-0806**	425-455-6000
Century Software 5284 S Commerce Dr Suite C-134	Salt Lake City	UT	84107	**800-877-3088**	801-268-3088
CertifiedMail.com Inc 35 Airport Rd Suite 120	Morristown	NJ	07960	**800-672-7233**	973-455-1245
ClearCommerce Corp 11921 N Mopac Expy Suite 400	Austin	TX	78759	**888-725-9345**	512-832-0132
ClickSoftware Inc 35 Corporate Dr Suite 140 NASDAQ: CKSW	Burlington	MA	01803	**888-438-3308**	781-272-5903
CommTouch Software Ltd 1300 Crittenden Ln Suite 103 NASDAQ: CTCH	Mountain View	CA	94043	**800-638-6824**	650-864-2000
Comspec Digital Products Inc PO Box 178	Jacksonville	TX	75766	**800-490-6893**	832-443-4487
Concerto Software 6 Technology Pk Dr	Westford	MA	01886	**800-999-4458**	978-952-0200
Conquest Systems Inc 1023 15th St NW Suite 500	Washington	DC	20005	**800-719-8817**	202-289-4240
Corillian Corp 3400 NW John Olsen Pl NASDAQ: CORI	Hillsboro	OR	97124	**800-863-6445**	503-629-3500
Cothern Computer Systems Inc 1640 Lelia Dr Suite 200	Jackson	MS	39216	**800-844-1155**	601-969-1155
Cyber Merchants Exchange Inc 4349 Baldwin Ave Suite A	El Monte	CA	91731	**888-564-6263**	626-636-2530
CyberSource Corp 1295 Charleston Rd NASDAQ: CYBS	Mountain View	CA	94043	**888-802-9237**	650-965-6000
Deerfield.com 4241 Old US 27 S	Gaylord	MI	49735	**800-599-8856**	989-732-8856
Digital Insight Corp 26025 Mureau Rd NASDAQ: DGIN	Calabasas	CA	91302	**888-344-4674**	818-871-0000
Dynamic Instruments Inc 3860 Calle Fortunada	San Diego	CA	92123	**800-793-3358**	858-278-4900
Dynarand LLC 55 Francisco St Suite 780	San Francisco	CA	94133	**888-794-4877**	415-293-1340
e-SIM Ltd 225 S Lake Ave Suite 300	Pasadena	CA	91101	**800-368-5835**	626-584-7810
Edify Corp 2840 San Thomas Expy	Santa Clara	CA	95051	**800-944-0056**	408-982-2000
eGain Communications Corp 345 E Middlefield Rd NASDAQ: EGAN	Mountain View	CA	94043	**888-603-4246**	650-230-7500
Enterprise Messaging Services 10 Mystic Ln	Malvern	PA	19355	**877-367-5050**	610-701-7002
Extended Systems Inc 5777 N Meeker Ave NASDAQ: XTND	Boise	ID	83713	**800-235-7576**	208-322-7575
EXTOL International Inc 474 N Centre St PO Box 1010	Pottsville	PA	17901	**888-334-3986**	570-628-5500
FAR Voice Inc 16645 W Greenfield Ave	New Berlin	WI	53154	**888-661-8885**	262-797-4550
Fast Search & Transfer Inc 93 Worcester St	Wellesley Hills	MA	02481	**888-871-3839**	781-304-2400
FileNet Corp 3565 Harbor Blvd NASDAQ: FILE	Costa Mesa	CA	92626	**800-345-3638**	714-327-3400
FirstLogic Inc 100 Harborview Plaza	La Crosse	WI	54601	**888-215-6442**	608-782-5000
Forgent Networks Inc 108 Wild Basin Rd NASDAQ: FORG	Austin	TX	78746	**888-323-8835**	512-437-2700
Funk Software Inc 222 3rd St	Cambridge	MA	02142	**800-828-4146**	617-497-6339
FutureSoft Inc 12012 Wickchester Ln Suite 600	Houston	TX	77079	**800-989-8908**	281-496-9400
GeoTrust Inc 40 Washington St Suite 20	Wellesley Hills	MA	02481	**800-944-0492**	781-235-4677
Hilgraeve Inc 111 Conant Avenue Suite A *Sales	Monroe	MI	48161	**800-826-2760***	734-243-0576
HTI Voice & Internet Solutions Inc 2 Mt Royal Ave	Marlborough	MA	01752	**800-255-4241**	508-485-8400
Imecom Group 8 Governor Wentworth Hwy	Wolfeboro	NH	03894	**800-329-9099**	603-569-0600
Information Builders Inc 2 Penn Plaza	New York	NY	10121	**800-969-4636**	212-736-4433
Infowave Software Inc 4664 Lougheed Hwy Suite 200	Burnaby	BC	V5C5T5	**800-463-6928**	604-473-3600
Inktomi 4100 E 3rd Ave	Foster City	CA	94404	**888-465-8664**	650-653-2800
Integra Telecom 1201 NE Lloyd Blvd Suite 500	Portland	OR	97232	**800-727-8484**	503-453-8000
IntelliNet Technologies Inc 1990 W New Haven Ave Suite 307	Melbourne	FL	32904	**888-726-0686**	321-726-0686
IntelliReach Corp 20 CareMatrix Dr	Dedham	MA	02026	**800-219-9838**	781-410-3000
Intellisync Corp 2550 N 1st St Suite 500 NASDAQ: SYNC	San Jose	CA	95131	**800-248-2795**	408-321-7650
Interact Inc 1225 L St Suite 600	Lincoln	NE	68508	**800-242-8649**	402-476-8786
Interactive Intelligence Inc 7601 Interactive Way NASDAQ: ININ	Indianapolis	IN	46278	**800-267-1364**	317-872-3000
Intershop Communications Inc 410 Townsend St Suite 125	San Francisco	CA	94107	**800-736-5197**	415-844-1500
Ion Networks Inc 120 Corporate Blvd	Sout Plainfield	NJ	07080	**800-722-8986**	908-546-3900
IONA Technologies Inc 200 West St 4th Fl NASDAQ: IONA	Waltham	MA	02451	**800-672-4948**	781-902-8000
Jones Cyber Solutions Ltd 9697 E Mineral Ave	Englewood	CO	80112	**800-944-2923**	303-784-3600
Jones International Ltd 9697 E Mineral Ave	Englewood	CO	80112	**800-525-7002**	303-792-3111
Keynote Systems Inc 777 Mariners Island Blvd NASDAQ: KEYN	San Mateo	CA	94404	**888-539-7978**	650-522-1000
Koko Interactive PO Box 55	Caldwell	NJ	07006	**877-468-5656**	212-333-5387
Lan Supervision Inc (LSVi) 3000 Executive Pkwy Suite 200 *Tech Supp	San Ramon	CA	94583	**800-820-8188***	925-355-0234
Language Automation Inc 1670 S Amphlett Blvd Suite 214	San Mateo	CA	94402	**800-571-4685**	650-571-7877
LINK2GOV Corp 1 Burton Hills Blvd Suite 300	Nashville	TN	37215	**800-483-7072**	615-297-2770
Macromedia Inc 600 Townsend St Suite 500-W NASDAQ: MACR ■ *Cust Svc	San Francisco	CA	94103	**800-470-7211***	415-252-2000
Market Central Inc 1650 Gum Branch Rd Suite A	Jacksonville	NC	28540	**888-773-3501**	910-937-0725
Mark/Space Softworks 654 N Santa Cruz Ave Suite 300	Los Gatos	CA	95030	**800-799-1718**	408-293-7299
Micromuse Inc 139 Townsend St 5th Fl NASDAQ: MUSE	San Francisco	CA	94107	**800-638-2665**	415-538-9090
Mindmaker Inc 100 Century Center Ct Suite 800	San Jose	CA	95112	**877-277-4786**	408-467-9200
Mirror Image Internet Inc 49 Dragon Ct	Woburn	MA	01801	**866-374-4113**	781-376-1100
Moai Technologies Inc 100 1st Ave Suite 900	Pittsburgh	PA	15222	**800-814-1548**	412-454-5550
MODCOMP Inc 1650 W McNab Rd	Fort Lauderdale	FL	33309	**800-327-3287**	954-974-1380
Momentum Systems Ltd 41 Twosome Dr Suite 9	Moorestown	NJ	08057	**800-279-1384**	856-727-0777
Muze Inc 304 Hudson St 8th Fl	New York	NY	10013	**800-935-4848**	212-824-0300
Netscape Communications Corp 466 Ellis St *Tech Supp	Mountain View	CA	94043	**800-411-0707***	650-254-1900
NetScout Systems Inc 310 Littleton Rd NASDAQ: NTCT	Westford	MA	01886	**800-999-5946**	978-614-4000
netViz Corp 12 S Summit Ave Suite 300	Gaithersburg	MD	20877	**800-827-1856**	301-258-5087
Nexgenix Inc 320 Commerce	Irvine	CA	92602	**800-663-9436**	714-665-6200
NICE Systems Inc 301 Rt 17 N 10th Fl	Rutherford	NJ	07070	**888-577-6423**	201-964-2600
OmTool Ltd 8A Industrial Way NASDAQ: OMTL	Salem	NH	03079	**800-886-7845**	603-898-8900

Internet & Communications Software (Cont'd)

Company / Address	City	State	Zip	Toll-Free	Phone
One Touch Systems Inc 40 Airport Pkwy	San Jose	CA	95110	**888-777-9677**	408-436-4600
Open Text Corp 185 Columbia St W *NASDAQ: OTEX* ■ *Sales	Waterloo	ON	N2L5Z5	**888-450-2547***	519-888-7111
Open Text Corp (USA) 100 Tri-State International Pkwy 3rd Fl *Sales	Lincolnshire	IL	60069	**800-507-5777***	847-267-9330
OpenConnect Systems Inc 2711 LBJ Fwy Suite 700	Dallas	TX	75234	**800-551-5881**	972-484-5200
Path 1 Network Technologies Inc 6215 Ferris Sq Suite 140 *AMEX: PNO*	San Diego	CA	92121	**877-663-7284**	858-450-4220
Phoenix Technologies Ltd 915 Murphy Ranch Rd *NASDAQ: PTEC*	Milpitas	CA	95035	**800-677-7305**	408-570-1000
PlaceWare Inc 295 N Bernardo Ave *Sales	Mountain View	CA	94043	**888-526-6170***	650-526-6100
Pragmatech Software Inc 15 Trafalgar Sq	Nashua	NH	03063	**800-401-9580**	603-249-1400
ProtoNet PO Box 8781	Calabasas	CA	91372	**800-551-0636**	818-876-0636
PureEdge Solutions 4396 W Saanich Rd	Victoria	BC	V8Z3E9	**888-517-2675**	250-708-8000
QSA ToolWorks LLC 64 W 48th St 9th Fl	New York	NY	10036	**800-784-7018**	516-935-9151
Quigo Technologies Inc 377 5th Ave 6th Fl	New York	NY	10016	**866-333-7932**	212-213-2363
Raindance Communications Inc 1157 Century Dr *NASDAQ: RNDC*	Louisville	CO	80027	**800-878-7326**	303-928-2400
RAINfinity 2740 Zanker Rd Suite 200	San Jose	CA	95134	**877-724-6333**	408-382-5000
Red Bridge Interactive Inc 2 Richmond Sq Suite 113K	Providence	RI	02906	**877-367-4676**	401-223-1141
Resonate Inc 385 Moffett Park Dr	Sunnyvale	CA	94089	**877-737-6628**	408-548-5600
RuleSpace Inc 111 SW 5th Ave Suite 2100	Portland	OR	97204	**800-387-8373**	503-290-5100
Sane Solutions LLC 35 Belver Ave Suite 230	North Kingstown	RI	02852	**800-407-3570**	401-295-4809
Security Software Systems Inc 1998 Bucktail Ln	Sugar Grove	IL	60554	**888-835-7278**	630-466-1038
Selectica Inc 3 W Plumeria Dr *NASDAQ: SLTC*	San Jose	CA	95134	**877-712-9560**	408-570-9700
Sendmail Inc 6425 Christie Ave 4th Fl	Emeryville	CA	94608	**888-594-3150**	510-594-5400
SER Solutions Inc 21680 Ridgetop Cir *Sales	Sterling	VA	20166	**800-274-5676***	703-948-5500
Smith Micro Software Inc 51 Columbia Suite 200 *NASDAQ: SMSI*	Aliso Viejo	CA	92656	**800-964-7674**	949-362-5800
Software 602 Inc 8833 Perimeter Pk Blvd Suite 702	Jacksonville	FL	32216	**888-468-6602**	904-642-5400
Software Labs Inc PO Box 6064	Bellevue	WA	98008	**800-569-7900**	425-653-2432
Soliton Inc 99 Wall St 17th Fl	New York	NY	10005	**800-201-0569**	212-344-3988
Stellent Inc 7777 Golden Triangle Dr *NASDAQ: STEL*	Eden Prairie	MN	55344	**800-989-8774**	952-903-2000
SupportSoft Inc 575 Broadway *NASDAQ: SPRT*	Redwood City	CA	94063	**877-493-2778**	650-556-9440
Surety LLC 12950 Worldgate Dr Suite 150	Herndon	VA	20170	**800-298-3115**	703-707-9901
SurfControl USA 5550 Scotts Valley Dr	Scotts Valley	CA	95066	**800-368-3366**	831-440-2500
Sybase Inc 1 Sybase Dr *NYSE: SY*	Dublin	CA	94568	**800-879-2273**	925-236-5000
Symantec Corp 20330 Stevens Creek Blvd *NASDAQ: SYMC* ■ *Cust Svc	Cupertino	CA	95014	**800-441-7234***	408-517-8000
SyVox 1850 I-30	Rockwall	TX	75087	**866-436-3782**	972-938-1653
Tally Systems Corp PO Box 70	Hanover	NH	03755	**800-262-3877**	603-643-1300
Teknowledge Corp 1800 Embarcadero Rd *NASDAQ: TEKC*	Palo Alto	CA	94303	**800-285-0500**	650-424-0500
Tenebril Inc 75 Federal St 6th Fl	Boston	MA	02110	**800-790-9060**	617-912-6600
Timecruiser Computing Corp 9 Law Dr 3rd Fl	Fairfield	NJ	07004	**877-450-9482**	973-244-7856
Tumbleweed Communications Corp 700 Saginaw Dr *NASDAQ: TMWD*	Redwood City	CA	94063	**800-696-1978**	650-216-2000
Unify Corp 2101 Arena Blvd Suite 100	Sacramento	CA	95834	**800-248-6439**	916-928-6400
Verity Inc 892 Ross Dr *NASDAQ: VRTY*	Sunnyvale	CA	94089	**800-935-6246**	408-541-1500
Vertical Communications Inc 5 Cambridge Ctr *Sales	Cambridge	MA	02142	**800-914-9985***	617-354-0600
viaLink Co 13155 Noel Rd Suite 700	Dallas	TX	75240	**888-842-5465**	972-934-5500
VillageEDOCS Inc 14471 Chambers Rd Suite 105	Tustin	CA	92780	**800-866-0883**	714-734-1030
Visual Networks Inc 2092 Gaither Rd *NASDAQ: VNWK*	Rockville	MD	20850	**800-240-4010**	301-296-2300
VoiceWorld Inc 383 Kingston Ave Suite 257	Brooklyn	NY	11213	**800-283-4759**	718-221-1400
Wave Three Software Inc 11696 Sorrento Valley Rd Suite J	San Diego	CA	92121	**888-408-8422**	858-720-7240
WaveLink Corp 11332 NE 122nd Way Suite 300 *Tech Supp	Kirkland	WA	98034	**888-699-9283***	425-823-0111
WebBalanced Technologies LLC 6206 Discount Dr	Fort Wayne	IN	46818	**877-366-7233**	
WebCT Inc 6 Kimball Ln Suite 310	Lynnfield	MA	01940	**877-932-2863**	781-309-1000
WebEx Communications Inc 307 West Tasman Dr *NASDAQ: WEBX*	San Jose	CA	95134	**877-509-3239**	408-435-7000
Websense Inc 10240 Sorrento Valley Rd *NASDAQ: WBSN*	San Diego	CA	92121	**800-723-1166**	858-320-8000
WebSurveyor Corp 505 Huntmar Park Dr Suite 225	Herndon	VA	20170	**800-787-8755**	703-481-9326
Wind River Systems Inc 500 Wind River Way *NASDAQ: WIND*	Alameda	CA	94501	**800-545-9463**	510-748-4100
Witness Systems Inc 300 Colonial Ctr Pkwy Suite 600 *NASDAQ: WITS*	Roswell	GA	30076	**888-394-8637**	770-754-1900
Xtend Communications Corp 171 Madison Ave *Cust Svc	New York	NY	10016	**800-342-5910***	212-951-7600
Yantra Corp 1 Park W	Tewksbury	MA	01876	**888-292-6872**	978-513-6000
YellowBrix Inc 44 Canal Center Plaza Suite 110	Alexandria	VA	22314	**800-945-9150**	703-548-3300

176-8 Multimedia & Design Software

Company / Address	City	State	Zip	Toll-Free	Phone
3D Systems Inc 26081 Ave Hall *NASDAQ: TDSC*	Valencia	CA	91355	**800-653-1993**	661-295-5600
ACD Systems International Inc PO Box 36 *TSE: ASA*	Saanichton	BC	V8M2C3	**800-579-5309**	250-544-6700
Adobe Systems Inc 345 Park Ave *NASDAQ: ADBE*	San Jose	CA	95110	**800-833-6687**	408-536-6000
Alias Systems Corp 210 King St E	Toronto	ON	M5A1J7	**800-447-2542**	416-362-9181
Animation Factory Inc 2000 W 42nd St Suite C	Sioux Falls	SD	57105	**800-525-2475**	605-339-4722
Apple Computer Inc 1 Infinite Loop *NASDAQ: AAPL* ■ *Cust Svc	Cupertino	CA	95014	**800-275-2273***	408-996-1010
Arts & Letters Corp 4306 Sunbelt Dr	Addison	TX	75001	**888-853-9292**	972-661-8960
ATI Inc 361 Sinclair-Frontage Rd	Milpitas	CA	95035	**800-536-2212**	408-942-1780
Auto FX Software 141 Village St Suite 2	Birmingham	AL	35242	**800-839-2008**	205-980-0056
Avid Technology Inc 1 Park W Metropolitan Technology Pk *NASDAQ: AVID*	Tewksbury	MA	01876	**800-949-2843**	978-640-6789
Bitstream Inc 245 1st St *NASDAQ: BITS*	Cambridge	MA	02142	**800-522-3668**	617-497-6222
Caligari Corp 1959 Landings Dr	Mountain View	CA	94043	**800-351-7620**	650-390-9600
Concurrent Computer Corp 4375 River Green Pkwy Suite 100 *NASDAQ: CCUR*	Duluth	GA	30096	**877-978-7363**	678-258-4000
Corel Corp 1600 Carling Ave *Orders	Ottawa	ON	K1Z8R7	**800-772-6735***	613-728-8200
cVideo Inc 10967 Via Frontera *Tech Supp	San Diego	CA	92127	**800-724-8562***	858-385-2000
DeLorme 2 DeLorme Dr *Sales	Yarmouth	ME	04096	**800-452-5931***	207-846-7000
DocuCorp International Inc 5910 N Central Expy Suite 800 *NASDAQ: DOCC*	Dallas	TX	75206	**800-928-6000**	214-891-6500
HydroCAD Software Solutions LLC 216 Chocorua Mountain Hwy	Chocorua	NH	03817	**800-927-7246**	603-323-8666
Image Labs International 151 Evergreen Dr	Bozeman	MT	59715	**800-785-5995**	406-585-7225
Infowave Software Inc 4664 Lougheed Hwy Suite 200	Burnaby	BC	V5C5T5	**800-463-6928**	604-473-3600
Inmagic Inc 200 Unicorn Pk Dr 4th Fl *Sales	Woburn	MA	01801	**800-229-8398***	781-938-4442
International Microcomputer Software Inc 100 Rowland Way Suite 300	Novato	CA	94945	**800-833-8082**	415-878-4000
IPIX Corp 1009 Commerce Park Dr Suite 400 *NASDAQ: IPIX*	Oak Ridge	TN	37830	**888-909-4749**	865-220-6500
Jasc Software Inc 7905 Fuller Rd *Orders	Eden Prairie	MN	55344	**800-622-2793***	952-930-9800
Liquid Digital Media Inc 999 Main St	Redwood City	CA	94063	**866-443-6386**	650-549-2000
Macromedia Inc 600 Townsend St Suite 500-W *NASDAQ: MACR* ■ *Cust Svc	San Francisco	CA	94103	**800-470-7211***	415-252-2000
MapInfo Corp 1 Global View *NASDAQ: MAPS*	Troy	NY	12180	**800-552-2511**	518-285-6000
Media 100 Inc 450 Donald Lynch Blvd	Marlborough	MA	01752	**800-773-1770**	508-460-1600
MicroVision Development Inc 5541 Fermi Ct Suite 120	Carlsbad	CA	92008	**800-998-4555**	760-438-7781
Nemetschek North America 7150 Riverwood Dr	Columbia	MD	21046	**888-646-4223**	410-290-5114
NewTek Inc 5131 Beckwith Blvd *Cust Svc	San Antonio	TX	78249	**800-862-7837***	210-370-8000
Paragon Imaging Inc 400 W Cummings Pk Suite 2050	Woburn	MA	01801	**800-937-6881**	781-937-9800
Patton & Patton Software Corp 3815 N Oracle Rd	Tucson	AZ	85705	**800-525-0082**	520-888-6500
PC/Nametag 124 Horizon Dr	Verona	WI	53593	**800-233-9767**	877-626-3824
Peerless Systems Corp 2381 Rosecrans Ave *NASDAQ: PRLS*	El Segundo	CA	90245	**800-362-5738**	310-536-0908
Pegasus Imaging Corp 4522 Spruce St Suite 200 *Sales	Tampa	FL	33607	**800-875-7009***	813-875-7575
Quark Inc 1800 Grant St *Cust Svc	Denver	CO	80203	**800-676-4575***	303-894-8888
RealNetworks Inc 2601 Elliott Ave Suite 1000 *NASDAQ: RNWK* ■ *Cust Svc	Seattle	WA	98121	**888-768-3248***	206-674-2700
Roxio Inc 455 El Camino Real *NASDAQ: ROXI* ■ *Cust Svc	Santa Clara	CA	95050	**866-279-7694***	408-367-3100
Scan-Optics Inc 169 Progress Dr	Manchester	CT	06040	**800-543-8681**	860-645-7878
Sigma Design 5521 Jackson St *Sales	Alexandria	LA	71303	**888-990-0900***	318-449-9900
SoftPress Systems Ltd 3020 Bridgeway Suite 310	Sausalito	CA	94965	**800-853-6454**	415-331-4820
Sonic Solutions 101 Rowland Way *NASDAQ: SNIC*	Novato	CA	94945	**888-766-4248**	415-893-8000
Strata Inc 567 S Valley View Suite 1 *Sales	Saint George	UT	84770	**800-678-7282***	435-628-5218
Superscape Inc 131 Calle Iglesia Suite 200	San Clemente	CA	92672	**800-965-7411**	
TechSmith Corp 2405 Woodlake Dr	Okemos	MI	48864	**800-517-3001**	517-381-2300
think3 Inc 312 Walnut St Suite 2470	Cincinnati	OH	45202	**800-323-6770**	513-263-6770
Three D Graphics Inc 11340 W Olympic Blvd Suite 352	Los Angeles	CA	90064	**800-913-0008**	310-231-3330
Ulead Systems Inc 20000 Mariner Ave Suite 200	Torrance	CA	90503	**800-858-5323**	310-896-6388
URW America Inc 93 Canaan Back Rd	Barrington	NH	03825	**800-229-8791**	603-664-2130
Videotex Systems Inc 10255 Miller Rd	Dallas	TX	75238	**800-888-4336**	972-231-9200
Viewpoint Corp 498 7th Ave 18th Fl *NASDAQ: VWPT*	New York	NY	10018	**866-843-9764**	212-201-0800
Xaos Tools Inc 582 San Luis Rd	Berkeley	CA	94707	**800-833-9267**	510-525-5465
XyEnterprise 30 New Crossing Rd	Reading	MA	01867	**800-925-1269**	781-756-4400
Xyvision Enterprise Solutions Inc 30 New Crossing Rd	Reading	MA	01867	**800-925-1269**	781-756-4400

176-9 Personal Software

Company / Address	City	State	Zip	Toll-Free	Phone
Avery Dennison Corp 150 N Orange Grove Blvd *NYSE: AVY* ■ *Cust Svc	Pasadena	CA	91103	**800-252-8379***	626-304-2000
Corel Corp 1600 Carling Ave *Orders	Ottawa	ON	K1Z8R7	**800-772-6735***	613-728-8200
Equis International 90 S 400 W Suite 620 *Sales	Salt Lake City	UT	84101	**800-882-3040***	801-265-9996

Company	City	State	ZIP	Toll-Free	Phone
Intuit Inc PO Box 7850 *NASDAQ: INTU* ■ *Cust Svc	Mountain View	CA	94039	**800-446-8848***	650-944-6000
Microsoft Corp 1 Microsoft Way *NASDAQ: MSFT* ■ *Sales	Redmond	WA	98052	**800-426-9400***	425-882-8080
Nolo.com 950 Parker St *Cust Svc	Berkeley	CA	94710	**800-728-3555***	510-549-1976
PhotoSpin Inc 4030 Palos Verdes Dr N Suite 200	Rolling Hills Estates	CA	90274	**888-246-1313**	310-265-1313
Quicken PO Box 7850 *NASDAQ: INTU* ■ *Cust Svc	Mountain View	CA	94039	**800-446-8848***	650-944-6000
Smyth Systems Inc 7100 Whipple Ave NW	North Canton	OH	44720	**800-767-6984**	330-499-6392
Sonic Foundry Inc 1617 Sherman Ave *NASDAQ: SOFO*	Madison	WI	53704	**800-577-6642**	608-256-3133
Stevens Creek Software LLC PO Box 2126	Cupertino	CA	95015	**800-823-4279**	408-725-0424
Symantec Corp 20330 Stevens Creek Blvd *NASDAQ: SYMC* ■ *Cust Svc	Cupertino	CA	95014	**800-441-7234***	408-517-8000
Zero Knowledge Systems Inc 375 President Kennedy	Montreal	QC	H3A2J5	**866-286-2636**	514-286-2636

176-10 Professional Software (Industry-Specific)

Company	City	State	ZIP	Toll-Free	Phone
3M Manufacturing & Industry Solutions 3M Ctr	Saint Paul	MN	55144	**888-364-3577**	651-733-1110
ACE*COMM Corp 704 Quince Orchard Rd Suite 100 *NASDAQ: ACEC*	Gaithersburg	MD	20878	**800-989-5566**	301-721-3000
Activant Solutions Inc 804 Las Cimas Pkwy	Austin	TX	78746	**800-678-5266**	512-328-2300
Advantage Credit International 15 W Strong St Suite 20A	Pensacola	FL	32501	**800-600-2510**	850-470-9336
Advent Software Inc 301 Brannan St 6th Fl *NASDAQ: ADVS*	San Francisco	CA	94107	**800-727-0605**	415-543-7696
AGRIS Corp 1600 N Lorraine St	Hutchinson	KS	67501	**800-795-7995**	620-669-9811
Allscripts Healthcare Solutions 2401 Commerce Ave *NASDAQ: MDRX*	Libertyville	IL	60048	**800-654-0889**	847-680-3515
Alogent Corp 4005 Windward Plaza 2nd Fl	Alpharetta	GA	30005	**888-333-6030**	770-752-6400
AMICAS Inc 239 Ethan Allen Hwy *NASDAQ: AMCS*	Ridgefield	CT	06877	**800-278-0037**	203-438-3654
AMS Services Inc 3 Waterside Crossing *Sales	Windsor	CT	06095	**800-444-4813***	860-602-6000
Anchor Computer Inc 1900 New Hwy	Farmingdale	NY	11735	**800-728-6262**	631-293-6100
Applied Information Management Sciences Inc PO Box 2970	Monroe	LA	71207	**800-729-2467**	318-323-2467
ARI Network Services Inc 11425 W Lake Pk Dr Suite 900	Milwaukee	WI	53224	**800-233-6997**	414-278-7676
ASI DataMyte Inc 2800 Campus Dr Suite 60	Plymouth	MN	55441	**800-207-5631**	763-553-1040
Atex Media Command Inc 24 Crosby Dr	Bedford	MA	01730	**800-872-2839**	781-275-2323
Avicis Inc 21670 Ridgetop Cir	Sterling	VA	20166	**888-591-9985**	703-480-3000
BancTec Inc 4435 Spring Valley Rd	Dallas	TX	75244	**800-226-2832**	972-960-1666
BNA Software Div Tax Management Inc 1250 23rd St NW	Washington	DC	20037	**800-424-2938**	202-728-7962
BNS Co 200 Frenchtown Rd Precision Pk	North Kingstown	RI	02852	**800-283-3600**	401-886-2000
Brodart Co 500 Arch St	Williamsport	PA	17701	**800-233-8467**	570-326-2461
C & S Marketing 10360 Old Placerville Rd Suite 100	Sacramento	CA	95827	**888-288-2009**	916-362-9609
CAM Commerce Solutions Inc 17075 Newhope St Suite A *NASDAQ: CADA*	Fountain Valley	CA	92708	**800-726-3282**	714-241-9241
CareCentric Inc 2625 Cumberland Pkwy Suite 310 *Sales	Atlanta	GA	30339	**800-254-9872***	678-264-4400
Castek Software Factory Inc 438 University Ave Suite 700	Toronto	ON	M5G2K8	**866-922-7835**	416-777-2550
Catalyst International Inc 8989 N Deerwood Dr	Milwaukee	WI	53223	**800-236-4600**	414-362-6800
Cedara Software Corp 6509 Airport Rd	Mississauga	ON	L4V1S7	**800-724-5970**	905-672-2100
Cerner DHT Inc 2800 Rockcreek Pkwy	Kansas City	MO	64119	**866-221-8877**	816-221-1024
Circa Information Technologies Inc 12001 Woodruff Ave Suite H	Downey	CA	90241	**877-992-4722**	562-803-1594
CliniComp International 9655 Towne Ctr Dr	San Diego	CA	92121	**800-350-8202**	858-546-8202
Cobalt Group Inc 2200 1st Ave S Suite 400	Seattle	WA	98134	**800-909-8244**	206-269-6363
CodeCorrect Inc 1200 Chesterly Dr Suite 260	Yakima	WA	98902	**877-937-3600**	509-453-0400
Command Alkon Inc 1800 International Park Dr Suite 400	Birmingham	AL	35243	**800-624-1872**	205-879-3282
Compumedics USA Ltd 7850 Paseo del Norte Suite 101	El Paso	TX	79912	**877-717-3975**	915-845-5600
Construction Systems Software Inc 494 Covered Bridge	Schertz	TX	78154	**800-979-6494**	210-979-6494
Continental Computer Corp 2200 East Matthews Ave	Jonesboro	AR	72401	**800-874-1413**	870-932-0081
CPASoftware 125 W Romana St Suite 500	Pensacola	FL	32501	**800-272-7123**	850-434-2685
Creative Computer Applications Inc 26115-A Mureau Rd *AMEX: CAP*	Calabasas	CA	91302	**800-437-9000**	818-880-6700
CSG Systems International Inc 7887 E Belleview Ave Suite 1000 *NASDAQ: CSGS*	Englewood	CO	80111	**800-366-2744**	303-804-4000
DataCert Inc 3100 Timmons Suite 310	Houston	TX	77027	**800-770-5121**	713-572-3282
Datastream Systems Inc 50 Datastream Plaza *NASDAQ: DSTM*	Greenville	SC	29605	**800-955-6775**	864-422-5001
Datatel Inc 4375 Fair Lakes Ct	Fairfax	VA	22033	**800-328-2835**	703-968-9000
De La Rue Retail Payment Solutions 25 Rockwood Pl	Englewood	NJ	07631	**800-526-0494**	201-894-1700
Dentrix Dental Systems Inc 727 E Utah Valley Dr Suite 500	American Fork	UT	84003	**800-336-8749**	801-763-9300
Destination Direct PO Box 65119	Port Ludlow	WA	98365	**888-227-5225**	
Digital Insight Corp 26025 Mureau Rd *NASDAQ: DGIN*	Calabasas	CA	91302	**888-344-4674**	818-871-0000
DIS Corp 1315 Cornwall Ave *Cust Svc	Bellingham	WA	98225	**800-426-8870***	360-733-7610
Dynix Corp 400 W Dynix Dr	Provo	UT	84604	**800-288-8020**	801-223-5200
Eagle Point Software Corp 4131 Westmark Dr	Dubuque	IA	52002	**800-678-6565**	563-556-8392
eBenX Inc 605 N Hwy 169 Suite LL	Minneapolis	MN	55441	**800-810-2352**	763-614-2000
Eclipsys Corp 1750 Clint Moore Rd *NASDAQ: ECLP*	Boca Raton	FL	33487	**888-325-4779**	561-322-4321
Electronics for Imaging Inc 303 Velocity Way *NASDAQ: EFII*	Foster City	CA	94404	**800-568-1917**	650-357-3500
eMed Technologies Corp 76 Blanchard Rd	Burlington	MA	01803	**800-883-8989**	781-862-0000
eMerge Interactive Inc 10305 102nd Terr *NASDAQ: EMRG*	Sebastian	FL	32958	**800-945-5310**	772-581-9700
Emerging Information Systems Inc 500 - 330 Saint Mary Ave	Winnipeg	MB	R3C3Z5	**888-692-3474**	204-943-3474
Environmental Systems Research Institute Inc 380 New York St *Sales	Redlands	CA	92373	**800-447-9778***	909-793-2853
Equis International 90 S 400 W Suite 620 *Sales	Salt Lake City	UT	84101	**800-882-3040***	801-265-9996
eResearch Technology Inc 30 S 17th St 8th Fl *NASDAQ: ERES*	Philadelphia	PA	19103	**800-704-9698**	215-972-0420
Fidelity Information Services Inc 601 Riverside Avenue	Jacksonville	FL	32204	**800-874-7359**	
Final Draft Inc 26707 W Agoura Rd Suite 205	Calabasas	CA	91302	**800-231-4055**	818-995-8995
Financial Engines Inc 1804 Embarcadero Rd	Palo Alto	CA	94303	**888-443-8577**	650-565-4900
Financial Fusion Inc 561 Virginia Rd Bldg 5	Concord	MA	01742	**800-842-0885**	978-287-1975
First DataBank Inc 1111 Bayhill Dr Suite 350	San Bruno	CA	94066	**800-633-3453**	650-588-5454
Follett Software Co 1391 Corporate Dr	McHenry	IL	60050	**800-323-3397**	815-344-8700
Gannett Media Technologies International 151 W 4th St Suite 201 *Sales	Cincinnati	OH	45202	**800-801-3771***	513-665-3777
General Dynamics C4 Systems 400 John Quincy Adams Rd Bldg 80	Taunton	MA	02780	**888-483-2472**	508-880-4000
Genomic Solutions Inc 4355 Varsity Dr Suite E	Ann Arbor	MI	48108	**877-436-6642**	734-975-4800
GeoGraphix 1805 Shea Ctr Dr Suite 400	Highlands Ranch	CO	80129	**800-296-0596**	303-779-8080
Global Turnkey Systems Inc 2001 Rt 46 Suite 203 *Help Line	Parsippany	NJ	07054	**800-221-1746***	973-331-1010
gomembers Inc 11720 Sunrise Valley Dr Suite 300	Reston	VA	20191	**888-288-4634**	703-620-9600
Heartlab Inc 1 Crosswind Rd	Westerly	RI	02891	**800-959-3205**	401-596-0592
Hyphen Solutions Inc 5055 Keller Springs Rd Suite 200 *Cust Svc	Addison	TX	75001	**877-508-2547***	972-728-8100
IHS Energy Group 15 Inverness Way E	Englewood	CO	80112	**800-645-3282**	303-736-3000
ImageWare Systems Inc 10883 Thornmint Rd *AMEX: IW*	San Diego	CA	92127	**800-842-4199**	858-673-8600
IMPAC Medical Systems Inc 100 W Evelyn Ave	Mountain View	CA	94041	**888-464-6722**	650-623-8800
Incyte Corp Rt 141 & Henry Clay Rd Bldg E-336 *NASDAQ: INCY* ■ *Sales	Wilmington	DE	19880	**877-746-2983***	302-498-6700
Inmagic Inc 200 Unicorn Pk Dr 4th Fl *Sales	Woburn	MA	01801	**800-229-8398***	781-938-4442
Innovative Technologies Corp 1020 Woodman Dr Suite 100	Dayton	OH	45432	**800-745-8050**	937-252-2145
InterAct Public Safety Systems Inc 45 Patton Ave	Asheville	NC	28801	**800-768-3911**	828-254-9876
Interactive Market Systems Inc 770 Broadway	New York	NY	10003	**800-223-7942**	646-654-5900
Intercim Corp 501 E Hwy 13	Burnsville	MN	55337	**800-343-3734**	952-894-9010
Island Pacific Inc 19800 MacArthur Blvd Suite 1200 *AMEX: IPI*	Irvine	CA	92612	**800-944-3847**	949-476-2212
Jenzabar Inc 5 Cambridge Ctr 11th Fl	Cambridge	MA	02142	**877-536-0222**	617-492-9099
JPMorgan Chase Vastera 45025 Aviation Dr Suite 200	Dulles	VA	20166	**800-275-1374**	703-661-9006
Kewill Systems PLC 100 Nickerson Rd	Marlborough	MA	01752	**877-872-2379**	508-229-4400
Lacerte Software Corp 5601 Headquarters Dr	Plano	TX	75024	**800-765-4065**	
Land & Legal Solutions Inc 300 S Hamilton Ave	Greensburg	PA	15601	**800-245-7900**	724-853-8992
Landmark Graphics Corp 2101 CityWest Blvd	Houston	TX	77242	**800-207-3098**	713-839-2000
Library Corp The 3801 E Florida Ave Suite 300	Denver	CO	80210	**888-439-2275**	303-758-3030
Management Information Control Systems Inc (MICS) 2025 9th St	Los Osos	CA	93402	**800-838-6427**	805-543-7000
Market Scan Information Systems Inc 31416 Agoura Rd Suite 110	Westlake Village	CA	91361	**800-658-7226**	818-575-2000
Marshall & Swift 911 Wilshire Blvd Suite 1600	Los Angeles	CA	90017	**800-544-2678**	213-683-9000
McKesson Information Solutions 5995 Windward Pkwy	Alpharetta	GA	30005	**800-981-8601**	404-338-6000
Med Diversified Inc 100 Brickstone Sq 5th Fl	Andover	MA	01810	**888-656-9903**	978-323-2500
Media Cybernetics LP 8484 Georgia Ave Suite 200 *Sales	Silver Spring	MD	20910	**800-992-4256***	301-495-3305
Medical Manager Health Systems 3001 N Rocky Point Dr E Suite 400	Tampa	FL	33607	**800-330-3612**	813-287-2990
MedPlus Inc 4690 Parkway Dr	Mason	OH	45040	**800-444-6235**	513-229-5500
Merrick Systems Inc 4801 Woodway Suite 100E	Houston	TX	77056	**800-842-8389**	713-355-6800
MetaSolv Inc 5556 Tennyson Pkwy *NASDAQ: MSLV*	Plano	TX	75024	**800-925-2940**	972-403-8300
MicroBilt Corp 1640 Airport Rd Suite 115	Kennesaw	GA	30144	**800-884-4747**	
MICS (Management Information Control Systems Inc) 2025 9th St	Los Osos	CA	93402	**800-838-6427**	805-543-7000
NaviSys Inc 499 Thornall St	Edison	NJ	08837	**800-775-3592**	732-549-3663
net-linx Publishing Solutions Inc 1740 N Market Blvd	Sacramento	CA	95834	**800-445-4744**	916-830-2400
New England Computer Services Inc 168 Boston Post Rd Suites 6 & 7 *Sales	Madison	CT	06443	**800-766-6327***	203-245-3999
NIC Inc 10540 S Ridgeview Rd *NASDAQ: EGOV*	Olathe	KS	66061	**877-234-3468**	913-498-3468
nPassage Inc 2505 2nd Ave Suite 405	Seattle	WA	98121	**888-486-7447**	206-441-8782
OpenTable Inc 799 Market St 4th Fl	San Francisco	CA	94103	**800-673-6822**	415-344-4200
Patient Infosystems Inc 46 Prince St 1st Fl	Rochester	NY	14607	**800-276-2575**	585-242-7200
PCi Services Inc 30 Winter St 12th Fl	Boston	MA	02108	**800-261-3111**	617-535-3000
Peace Software Inc 6205 Blue Lagoon Dr Suite 500	Miami	FL	33126	**866-407-3223**	305-341-2400
Peopleware Inc 110 110th Ave NE Suite 590	Bellevue	WA	98004	**800-869-7166**	425-454-6444
Phase Forward Inc 880 Winter St *NASDAQ: PFWD*	Waltham	MA	02451	**888-703-1122**	781-890-7878

Classified Section

Professional Software (Industry-Specific) (Cont'd)

Company / Address	City	State	ZIP	Toll-Free	Phone
ProCard Inc 1819 Denver W Dr Bldg 26 Suite 265	Golden	CO	80401	**800-469-6578**	303-279-2255
ProSight Inc 9600 SW Barnes Rd Suite 300	POrtland	OR	97255	**877-531-9121**	503-889-4800
QS/1 Data Systems PO Box 6052	Spartanburg	SC	29304	**800-845-7558**	864-503-9455
QuadraMed Corp 22 Pelican Way *AMEX: QD*	San Rafael	CA	94901	**800-473-7633**	415-482-2100
Quality Systems Inc 18191 Von Karman Ave Suite 450 *NASDAQ: QSII* ■ *Cust Svc	Irvine	CA	92612	**800-888-7955***	949-255-2600
Quovadx Inc 6400 S Fiddler's Green Cir Suite 1000 *NASDAQ: QVDX*	Englewood	CO	80111	**800-723-3033**	303-488-2019
RainMaker Software Inc 475 Sentry Pkwy Suite 4000 *Cust Svc	Blue Bell	PA	19422	**800-341-4012***	610-567-3400
Ramesys Hospitality Inc 1 Cragwood Rd Suite 202	South Plainfield	NJ	07080	**800-888-8819**	908-941-1300
Realigent Inc 2800 Saturn Ave Suite 200	Brea	CA	92821	**800-704-9302**	714-993-4295
RealLegal.com 3025 S Parker Rd 12th Fl	Aurora	CO	80014	**888-584-9988**	303-584-9988
Red Wing Software Inc 491 Hwy 19	Red Wing	MN	55066	**800-732-9464**	651-388-1106
RESUMate Inc 135 E Bennett St Suite 5 *Cust Svc	Saline	MI	48176	**800-530-9310***	734-429-8510
Retek Inc 950 Nicollet Mall	Minneapolis	MN	55403	**877-517-3835**	612-587-5000
RiskWatch Inc 2568A Riva Rd Suite 300	Annapolis	MD	21401	**800-448-4666**	410-224-4773
S1 Corp 3500 Lenox Rd Suite 200 *NASDAQ: SONE*	Atlanta	GA	30326	**888-457-2237**	404-923-3500
SalesLink Corp 425 Medford St	Charlestown	MA	02129	**888-231-2568**	617-886-4800
Scantron Corp 34 Parker	Irvine	CA	92618	**800-722-6876**	949-639-7500
Scott Studios Corp 13375 Stemmons Fwy	Dallas	TX	75234	**888-438-7268**	972-620-2211
Severn Trent Systems 20405 State Hwy 249 Suite 600	Houston	TX	77070	**800-231-4611**	281-320-7100
Siemens Logistics & Assembly Systems 507 Plymouth Ave	Grand Rapids	MI	49505	**877-725-7500**	616-913-6200
Sirsi Corp 101 Washington St SE *Sales	Huntsville	AL	35801	**800-917-4774***	256-704-7000
SISCOM 100 Arapahoe Ave Suite 2	Boulder	CO	80302	**800-325-6307**	303-449-0442
SocialPlus.com Inc 356 W 40th St 3rd Fl	New York	NY	10018	**888-701-2004**	212-244-7723
Softrax Corp 45 Shawmut Rd	Canton	MA	02021	**888-476-3872**	781-830-9200
SolidWorks Corp 300 Baker Ave	Concord	MA	01742	**800-693-9000**	978-371-5011
Solucient 1007 Church St Suite 700	Evanston	IL	60201	**800-366-7526**	847-424-4400
SQN Signature Systems 65 Indel Ave 2nd Fl	Rancocas	NJ	08073	**888-744-7226**	609-261-5500
Stok Software Inc 373 Nesconset Hwy Suite 287	Hauppauge	NY	11788	**888-448-8668**	631-232-2228
SunGard Collegis Inc 2300 Maitland Center Pkwy Suite 340	Maitland	FL	32751	**800-800-1874**	407-660-1199
SunGard Energy Systems 825 3rd Ave 28th Fl	New York	NY	10022	**877-230-6551**	212-888-3600
SunGard HTE Inc 1000 Business Center Dr	Lake Mary	FL	32746	**800-727-8088**	407-304-3235
SunGard SCT Inc 4 Country View Rd	Malvern	PA	19355	**800-223-7036**	610-647-5930
Synopsys Inc 700 E Middlefield Rd *NASDAQ: SNPS*	Mountain View	CA	94043	**800-541-7737**	650-584-5000
System Innovators Inc 10550 Deerwood Park Blvd Suite 700	Jacksonville	FL	32256	**800-963-5000**	904-281-9090
T2 Systems Inc 7835 Woodland Dr Suite 250	Indianapolis	IN	46278	**800-434-1502**	317-524-5500
Tax Management Inc BNA Software Div 1250 23rd St NW	Washington	DC	20037	**800-424-2938**	202-728-7962
Telcordia Technologies Inc 1 Telcordia Dr *Sales	Piscataway	NJ	08854	**800-521-2673***	732-699-2000
Telum International Corp 175 Commerce Valley Dr W Suite 230	Woodbridge	ON	L3T3A2	**888-278-9211**	905-882-4784
Thomson Elite 5100 W Goldleaf Cir Suite 100 *Cust Svc	Los Angeles	CA	90056	**800-274-9287***	323-642-5200
Track Data Corp 56 Pine St *NASDAQ: TRAC*	New York	NY	10005	**800-223-0113**	212-943-4555
TradeStation Group Inc 8050 SW 10th St Suite 2000 *NASDAQ: TRAD*	Plantation	FL	33324	**800-871-3577**	954-652-7000
TransWorks 9910 Dupont Circle Dr E Suite 200	Fort Wayne	IN	46825	**800-435-4691**	260-487-4400
Ulticom Inc 1020 Briggs Rd *NASDAQ: ULCM* ■ *Sales	Mount Laurel	NJ	08054	**888-295-6664***	856-787-2700
Universal Tax Systems 6 Mathis Dr *Sales	Rome	GA	30165	**800-755-9473***	706-232-7757
Urchin Software Corp 2165 India St *Sales	San Diego	CA	92101	**888-887-2446***	619-233-1400
US Digital Corp 11100 NE 34th Cir	Vancouver	WA	98682	**800-736-0194**	360-260-2468
VantageMed Corp 3017 Kilgore Rd Suite 180	Rancho Cordova	CA	95670	**877-879-8633**	916-638-4744
VersaForm Systems Corp 591 W Hamilton Ave Suite 201 *Sales	Campbell	CA	95008	**800-678-1111***	408-370-2662
Viewlocity Inc 3475 Piedmont Rd Suite 1700	Atlanta	GA	30305	**877-512-8900**	404-267-6400
VIPS Inc 1 W Pennsylvania Ave Suite 700	Towson	MD	21204	**888-289-8477**	410-832-8300
WebMD Corp 669 River Dr Center 2 *NASDAQ: HLTH*	Elmwood Park	NJ	07407	**877-469-3263**	201-703-3400
Webplan One Lincoln Ctr 18 W 140 Butterfield Rd 15th Fl	Oakbrook Terrace	IL	60181	**866-236-3249**	613-592-5780
Xybernet Inc 10640 Scripps Ranch Blvd *Cust Svc	San Diego	CA	92131	**800-228-9026***	858-530-1900

176-11 Service Software

Company / Address	City	State	ZIP	Toll-Free	Phone
360Commerce 11400 Burnet Rd Suite 5200	Austin	TX	78758	**800-897-8663**	512-491-2600
American HealthNet 2110 S 169th Plaza	Omaha	NE	68130	**800-745-4712**	402-733-2700
Applied Systems Inc 200 Applied Pkwy	University Park	IL	60466	**800-999-5368**	708-534-5575
Aptech Computer Systems Inc 135 Delta Dr	Pittsburgh	PA	15238	**800-245-0720**	412-963-7440
ARINC Inc 2551 Riva Rd	Annapolis	MD	21401	**800-492-2182**	410-266-4000
Aristotle Publishing Inc 205 Pennsylvania Ave SE	Washington	DC	20003	**800-243-4401**	202-543-8345
Bankers Systems Inc 6815 Saukview Dr	Saint Cloud	MN	56303	**800-397-2341**	320-251-3060
CACTUS Software 7301 Mission Rd Suite 300	Prairie Village	KS	66208	**800-776-2305**	913-677-0092
Camstar Systems Inc 900 E Hamilton Ave Suite 400	Campbell	CA	95008	**800-237-2841**	408-559-5700
Cerner Corp 2800 Rockcreek Pkwy *NASDAQ: CERN* ■ *Hum Res	Kansas City	MO	64117	**800-255-1024***	816-221-1024
CGI Information Systems 600 Federal St	Andover	MA	01810	**800-637-3799**	978-946-3000
Computer Technology Corp DBA CACTUS Software 7301 Mission Rd Suite 300	Prairie Village	KS	66208	**800-776-2305**	913-677-0092
Convera Corp 1921 Gallows Rd Suite 200 *NASDAQ: CNVR*	Vienna	VA	22182	**800-755-7005**	703-761-3700
Datamann Inc 1994 Hartford Ave	Wilder	VT	05088	**800-451-4263**	802-295-6600
Digital Solutions Inc 4200 Industrial Park Dr *Cust Svc	Altoona	PA	16602	**888-222-3081***	814-944-0405
DPSI Inc 4905 Koger Blvd Suite 101	Greensboro	NC	27409	**800-897-7233**	336-854-7700
eMeta Corp 81 Franklin St Suite 500	New York	NY	10013	**800-804-0103**	
EOS International 2382 Faraday Ave Suite 350 *Tech Supp	Carlsbad	CA	92008	**888-728-8746***	760-431-8400
Firstwave Technologies Inc 2859 Paces Ferry Rd Suite 1000 *NASDAQ: FSTW*	Atlanta	GA	30339	**800-540-6061**	770-431-1200
Fiserv Insurance Solutions 2110 Wiley Blvd SW	Cedar Rapids	IA	52404	**800-943-2851**	319-398-1800
Gallagher Financial Systems 1500 San Remo Ave Suite 251	Coral Gables	FL	33146	**800-989-9998**	305-665-5099
Geac Restaurant Systems 175 Ledge St	Nashua	NH	03060	**888-432-2773**	603-889-5152
H & M Systems Software Inc 600 E Crescent Ave Suite 203 *Cust Svc	Upper Saddle River	NJ	07458	**800-367-3366***	201-934-3414
I Levy & Assoc Inc 1630 Des Peres Rd Suite 300	Saint Louis	MO	63131	**800-297-6717**	314-822-0810
IHS Group 15 Inverness Way E	Englewood	CO	80112	**800-320-4555**	303-790-0600
Infor Global Solutions 11720 Amber Park Dr Suite 400	Alpharetta	GA	30004	**866-244-5479**	678-393-5000
Information Handling Services Group Inc 15 Inverness Way E	Englewood	CO	80112	**800-320-4555**	303-790-0600
Inforum Inc 801 Crescent Ctr Dr Suite 400	Franklin	TN	37067	**800-829-0600**	615-778-6300
Insurance Data Processing Inc 1 Washington Sq	Wyncote	PA	19095	**800-523-6745**	215-885-2150
Intelligent Health Systems 4275 Executive Sq Suite 550	La Jolla	CA	92037	**800-487-5772**	858-453-3600
Jobscope Corp PO Box 6767	Greenville	SC	29606	**800-443-5794**	864-458-3100
Kirchman Corp PO Box 2269 *Cust Svc	Orlando	FL	32802	**800-327-1892***	407-831-3001
Liberty FITECH Systems 3098 Piedmont Rd NE Suite 200	Atlanta	GA	30305	**800-275-4374**	404-262-2298
Liquent Inc 1300 Virginia Dr Suite 125	Fort Washington	PA	19034	**800-515-3777**	215-619-6000
Management Technology America Ltd 8233 Via Paseo del Norte Bldg C Suite 100	Scottsdale	AZ	85258	**800-366-6633**	480-998-0200
Manatron Inc 510 E Milham Ave *NASDAQ: MANA* ■ *Cust Svc	Portage	MI	49002	**800-666-5300***	269-567-2900
McKesson Pharmacy Systems 30881 Schoolcraft Rd	Livonia	MI	48150	**800-521-1758**	734-427-2000
MDL Information Systems Inc 14600 Catalina St *Cust Svc	San Leandro	CA	94577	**800-326-3002***	510-895-1313
Medical Manager MacHealth 210 Gateway Mall Suite 102	Lincoln	NE	68505	**800-888-4344**	402-466-8100
Mediware Information Systems Inc 11711 W 79th St *NASDAQ: MEDW*	Lenexa	KS	66214	**800-255-0026**	913-307-1000
Meta Health Technology Inc 330 7th Ave 14th Fl	New York	NY	10001	**800-334-6840**	212-695-5870
Metafile Information Systems Inc 2900 43rd St NW *Sales	Rochester	MN	55901	**800-638-2445***	507-286-9232
MicroStrategy Inc 1861 International Dr *NASDAQ: MSTR*	McLean	VA	22102	**800-927-1868**	703-848-8600
Misys Healthcare Systems LLC 8529 Six Forks Rd	Raleigh	NC	27615	**800-334-8534**	919-847-8102
Mortgage Computer Applications Inc 2650 Washington Blvd Suite 203 *Cust Svc	Ogden	UT	84401	**800-421-3277***	801-621-3900
MPSI Systems Inc 4343 S 118th East Ave *Cust Svc	Tulsa	OK	74146	**800-727-6774***	918-877-6774
Private Business Inc 9020 Overlook Blvd PO Box 1603 *NASDAQ: PBIZ*	Brentwood	TN	37024	**800-235-5584**	
Proscape Technologies Inc 1155 Business Ctr Dr	Horsham	PA	19044	**800-459-9300**	215-441-0300
Sandata Technologies Inc 26 Harbor Park Dr *Sales	Port Washington	NY	11050	**800-544-7263***	516-484-4400
Settlement Services Corp 1004 W Taft Ave *Sales	Orange	CA	92865	**800-767-7832***	714-998-1111
SunGard Insurance Systems 2000 S Dixie Hwy	Miami	FL	33133	**800-669-3372**	305-858-8200
SunGard Pentamation Inc 3 W Broad St Suite 1 *Cust Svc	Bethlehem	PA	18018	**800-333-3619***	610-691-3616
TCI Solutions Inc 17752 Skypark Cir Suite 160	Irvine	CA	92614	**800-621-7452**	949-476-1122
Technical Services Assoc Inc (TSA) 2 Kacey Ct	Mechanicsburg	PA	17055	**800-388-1415**	717-691-5691
Timberline Software Corp 15195 NW Greenbriar Pkwy	Beaverton	OR	97006	**800-628-6583**	503-690-6775
TimeValue Software 4 Jenner St Suite 100 *Sales	Irvine	CA	92618	**800-426-4741***	949-727-1800
TruStar Solutions Inc 10029 E 126th St Suite D	Fishers	IN	46038	**888-547-4472**	317-813-0500
TSA (Technical Services Assoc Inc) 2 Kacey Ct	Mechanicsburg	PA	17055	**800-388-1415**	717-691-5691
Unicru Inc 9525 SW Gemini Dr	Beaverton	OR	97008	**800-933-6321**	503-596-3100
United Data Systems 959 Broad St *Sales	Augusta	GA	30901	**800-241-2404***	706-823-9723
Washington Publishing Co 5740 Industry Ln 2nd Fl	Frederick	MD	21704	**800-972-4334**	301-696-0050

176-12 Systems & Utilities Software

Company / Address	City	State	ZIP	Toll-Free	Phone
Accelr8 Technology Corp 7000 Broadway Bldg 3-307 *AMEX: AXK*	Denver	CO	80221	**800-582-8898**	303-863-8088

Company / Address	City	State	ZIP	Toll-Free	Phone
ActivCard Inc 6623 Dumbarton Cir; *NASDAQ: ACTI*	Fremont	CA	94555	**800-529-9499**	510-574-0100
activePDF Inc 27405 Puerta Real Suite 100	Mission Viejo	CA	92691	**866-468-6733**	949-582-9002
Adaptive Solutions Inc 1301 Azalea Rd Suite 101	Mobile	AL	36693	**800-299-3045**	251-666-3045
Aladdin Knowledge Systems Ltd 2920 N Arlington Heights Rd; *NASDAQ: ALDN*	Arlington Heights	IL	60004	**800-562-2543**	847-818-3800
Allen Systems Group Inc (ASG) 1333 3rd Ave S	Naples	FL	34102	**800-932-5536**	239-435-2200
Allume Systems Inc 245 Westridge Dr	Watsonville	CA	95076	**800-732-8881**	831-761-6200
Altiris Inc 588 W 400 South; *NASDAQ: ATRS*	Lindon	UT	84042	**888-252-5551**	
Aonix North America Inc 5040 Shoreham Pl Suite 100	San Diego	CA	92122	**800-972-6649**	858-457-2700
Apex CoVantage LLC 198 Van Buren St Suite 120	Herndon	VA	20170	**800-628-2739**	703-709-3000
ASG (Allen Systems Group Inc) 1333 3rd Ave S	Naples	FL	34102	**800-932-5536**	239-435-2200
Aspect Business Solutions 7550 IH-10 W 14th Fl	San Antonio	TX	78229	**800-609-8113**	210-256-8300
Atos Origin 5599 San Felipe Suite 300	Houston	TX	77056	**866-875-8902**	713-513-3000
Authentium Inc 7121 Fairway Dr Suite 102	Palm Beach Gardens	FL	33418	**800-423-9147**	561-575-3200
Auto-trol Technology Corp 12500 N Washington St	Denver	CO	80241	**800-233-2882**	303-452-4919
Avatier Corp 12647 Alcosta Blvd Suite 400	San Ramon	CA	94583	**800-609-8610**	925-831-4746
Aventail Corp 808 Howell St 2nd Fl	Seattle	WA	98101	**877-283-6824**	206-215-1111
Avista Advantage 1313 N Atlantic St 5th Fl	Spokane	WA	99201	**800-767-4197**	
Award Software International Div Phoenix Technologies Ltd 411 E Plumeria Dr	San Jose	CA	95134	**800-677-7305**	408-570-1000
BakBone Software Inc 10145 Pacific Heights Blvd Suite 500	San Diego	CA	92121	**877-939-2663**	858-450-9009
Basis International Ltd 5901 Jefferson St NE; *Orders	Albuquerque	NM	87109	**800-423-1394***	505-345-5232
BEA Systems Inc 2315 N 1st St; *NASDAQ: BEAS*	San Jose	CA	95131	**800-817-4232**	408-570-8000
BenchmarkQA Inc 3800 American Blvd W Suite 1580	Minneapolis	MN	55431	**877-425-2581**	952-392-2381
Beta Systems Software Inc 6411 Ivy Ln Suite 610	Greenbelt	MD	20770	**800-475-1168**	301-486-4600
BindView Development Corp 5151 San Felipe 22nd Fl; *NASDAQ: BVEW*	Houston	TX	77056	**800-813-5869**	713-561-4000
Blue Lance Inc 1700 W Loop S Suite 1100	Houston	TX	77027	**800-856-2583**	713-680-1187
Certicom Corp 5520 Explorer Dr 4th Fl	Mississauga	ON	L4W5L1	**800-561-6100**	905-507-4220
Check Point Software Technologies Ltd 800 Bridge Pkwy; *NASDAQ: CHKP*	Redwood City	CA	94065	**800-429-4391**	650-628-2000
Cincom Systems Inc 55 Merchant St	Cincinnati	OH	45246	**800-888-0115**	513-612-2300
Citadel Security Software Inc 8750 N Central Expy	Dallas	TX	75231	**800-962-0701**	214-520-9292
Citrix Systems Inc 851 W Cypress Creek Rd; *NASDAQ: CTXS*	Fort Lauderdale	FL	33309	**800-393-1888**	954-267-3000
Cognetics Corp PO Box 386	Princeton Junction	NJ	08550	**800-229-8437**	609-799-5005
Columbia Data Products Inc 925 Sunshine Ln Suite 1080; *Sales	Altamonte Springs	FL	32714	**800-613-6288***	407-869-6700
Communication Intelligence Corp 275 Shoreline Dr Suite 500; *Sales	Redwood Shores	CA	94065	**800-888-8242***	650-802-7888
ComponentOne LLC 4516 Henry St Suite 500	Pittsburgh	PA	15213	**800-858-2739**	412-681-4343
Computer Assoc International Inc 1 Computer Assoc Plaza; *NYSE: CA*	Islandia	NY	11749	**800-225-5224**	631-342-6000
Computer Conversions Inc 13230 Evening Creek Dr Suite 202	San Diego	CA	92128	**800-328-2911**	858-746-3007
Comtech Publishing Ltd 2835 Juliann Way; *Orders	Reno	NV	89509	**800-456-7005***	775-825-9000
Concord Communications Inc 400-600 Nickerson Rd; *NASDAQ: CCRD*	Marlborough	MA	01752	**800-851-8725**	508-460-4646
CSI International Inc 8120 State Rt 138	Williamsport	OH	43164	**800-795-4914**	740-420-5400
CSP Inc 43 Manning Rd; *NASDAQ: CSPI*	Billerica	MA	01821	**800-325-3110**	978-663-7598
CyberTeams Inc 5714-B Industry Ln; *Sales	Frederick	MD	21704	**888-832-5575***	301-682-8885
Cyrano Inc 26 Parker St	Newburyport	MA	01950	**800-714-4900**	978-462-0737
DataDirect Technologies 3202 Tower Oaks Blvd Suite 300	Rockville	MD	20852	**800-876-3101**	301-468-8501
DataMirror Corp 3100 Steeles Ave E Suite 1100; *NASDAQ: DMCX*	Markham	ON	L3R8T3	**800-362-5955**	905-415-0310
DataViz Inc 612 Wheelers Farms Rd	Milford	CT	06460	**800-733-0030**	203-874-0085
Datawatch Corp 175 Cabot St Suite 503; *NASDAQ: DWCH*	Lowell	MA	01854	**800-445-3311**	978-441-2200
Descartes Systems Group Inc 120 Randall Dr; *NASDAQ: DSGX*	Waterloo	ON	N2V1C6	**800-419-8495**	519-746-8110
Digicomp Research Corp 930 Danby Rd; *Cust Svc	Ithaca	NY	14850	**800-457-6000***	607-273-5900
Digimarc Corp 9405 SW Gemini Dr; *NASDAQ: DMRC*	Everton	OR	97008	**800-344-4627**	503-469-4800
Digital Persona Inc 720 Bay Rd Suite 100	Redwood City	CA	94063	**877-378-2738**	650-474-4000
Direct Insite Corp 80 Orville Dr Suite 100; *NASDAQ: DIRI*	Bohemia	NY	11716	**800-619-0757**	631-244-1500
Diversified Software Systems Inc 18635 Sutter Blvd	Morgan Hill	CA	95037	**800-273-3774**	408-778-9914
Diversinet Corp 2225 Sheppard Ave E Suite 1801	Toronto	ON	M2J5C2	**800-357-7050**	416-756-2324
EasyLink Services Corp 33 Knightbridge Rd; *NASDAQ: EASY*	Piscataway	NJ	08854	**800-624-5266**	732-652-3500
EMC Legato 2350 W El Camino Real; *Tech Supp	Mountain View	CA	94040	**877-534-2867***	650-210-7000
Entrust Inc 16633 Dallas Pkwy Suite 800; *NASDAQ: ENTU* ■ *Sales	Addison	TX	75001	**888-690-2424***	972-713-5800
Esker Inc 100 E 7th Ave	Stillwater	OK	74074	**800-343-7070**	405-533-5500
Executive Software International Inc 7590 N Glenoaks Blvd; *Sales	Burbank	CA	91504	**800-829-6468***	818-771-1600
Expert Choice Inc 1501 Lee Hwy Suite 302	Arlington	VA	22209	**888-259-6400**	703-243-5595
FileStream Inc 333 Glen Head Rd	Old Brookville	NY	11545	**800-732-3002**	516-759-4100
Finjan Software Inc 2025 Gateway Pl Suite 180	San Jose	CA	95110	**888-346-5268**	408-452-9700
Forvus Research Inc 742-200 McKnight Dr	Knightdale	NC	27545	**888-323-4887**	919-954-0063
Fujitsu Computer Systems Corp 1250 E Arques Ave	Sunnyvale	CA	94085	**877-213-6674**	408-746-6000
Greenwald Industries 212 Middlesex Ave	Chester	CT	06412	**800-221-0982**	860-526-0800
GroupSystems.com 520 Zang St Suite 211	Broomfield	CO	80021	**800-368-6338**	303-468-8680
Heroix Corp 57 Wells Ave	Newton	MA	02459	**800-229-6500**	617-527-1550
Hitachi Data Systems Corp 750 Central Expy	Santa Clara	CA	95050	**800-227-1930**	408-970-1000
Hummingbird Ltd 1 Sparks Ave; *NASDAQ: HUMC*	Toronto	ON	M2H2W1	**877-359-4866**	416-496-2200
Information Security Corp 1141 Lake Cook Rd Suite D	Deerfield	IL	60015	**800-203-5563**	847-405-0500
Innodata Isogen Inc 3 University Plaza Dr Suite 506; *NASDAQ: INOD*	Hackensack	NJ	07601	**800-567-4784**	201-488-1200
Integic Corp 14585 Avion Pkwy	Chantilly	VA	20151	**800-874-2344**	703-222-2840
Integralis US 111 Founders Plaza 13th Fl	East Hartford	CT	06108	**877-557-1475**	860-291-0851
International Business Machines Corp (IBM) New Orchard Rd; *NYSE: IBM*	Armonk	NY	10504	**800-426-4968**	914-766-1900
Internet Security Systems Inc 6303 Barfield Rd; *NASDAQ: ISSX*	Atlanta	GA	30328	**888-901-7477**	404-236-2600
Intrusion Inc 1101 E Arapaho Rd; *NASDAQ: INTZ*	Richardson	TX	75081	**800-862-6637**	972-234-6400
Ipswitch Inc 10 Maguire Rd Suite 220	Lexington	MA	02421	**800-793-4825**	781-676-5700
Kroll Ontrack Inc 9023 Columbine Rd; *Sales	Eden Prairie	MN	55347	**800-872-2599***	952-937-1107
LapLink Software Inc 10210 NE Points Dr Suite 400	Kirkland	WA	98033	**800-343-8080**	425-952-6000
Lattice Inc 1751 S Naperville Rd Suite 100; *Sales	Wheaton	IL	60187	**800-444-4309***	630-949-3250
Livermore Software Laboratories Inc 1830 S Kirkwood Rd Suite 205	Houston	TX	77077	**800-240-5754**	281-759-3274
Luminex Software Inc 6840 Indiana Ave Suite 130	Riverside	CA	92506	**888-586-4639**	951-781-4100
Macrovision Corp 2830 De La Cruz Blvd; *NASDAQ: MVSN*	Santa Clara	CA	95050	**800-622-7686**	408-743-8600
Magic Software Enterprises Inc 17310 Red Hill Ave Suite 270; *NASDAQ: MGIC*	Irvine	CA	92614	**800-345-6244**	949-250-1718
Mainsoft Corp 224 Airport Pkwy Suite 300	San Jose	CA	95110	**800-624-6946**	408-200-4000
Mainstay 1320 Flynn Rd Suite 401; *Orders	Camarillo	CA	93012	**800-362-2605***	805-484-9400
Management Science Assoc Inc 6565 Penn Ave	Pittsburgh	PA	15206	**800-672-4636**	412-362-2000
Mandarin Library Automation Inc 1060 Holland Dr Suite 36	Boca Raton	FL	33487	**800-426-7477**	561-995-4010
Mangosoft Inc 12 Pine St Ext	Nashua	NH	03060	**888-886-2646**	603-324-0400
MARX International Inc 2900 Chamblee-Tucker Rd Bldg 9 Suite 100	Atlanta	GA	30341	**800-627-9468**	770-986-8887
Maxum Development Corp PO Box 315	Crystal Lake	IL	60039	**800-813-3410**	815-444-0100
McAfee Inc 3965 Freedom Cir; *NYSE: MFE*	Santa Clara	CA	95054	**888-847-8766**	408-988-3832
McCabe & Assoc Inc 9700 Patuxent Dr Suite 103	Columbia	MD	21045	**800-638-6316**	410-381-3710
Mercury Interactive Corp 379 N Whisman Rd; *NASDAQ: MERQ*	Mountain View	CA	94043	**800-837-8911**	650-603-5200
Metrowerks 7700 W Parmer Ln	Austin	TX	78729	**800-377-5416**	512-996-5300
Micro 2000 Inc 1100 E Broadway Suite 301	Glendale	CA	91205	**800-864-8008**	818-547-0125
Microsoft Corp 1 Microsoft Way; *NASDAQ: MSFT* ■ *Sales	Redmond	WA	98052	**800-426-9400***	425-882-8080
Mitem Corp 640 Menlo Ave; *Sales	Menlo Park	CA	94025	**800-826-4836***	650-323-1500
Neon Software Inc 244 Lafayette Cir; *Sales	Lafayette	CA	94549	**800-334-6366***	925-283-9771
Netegrity Inc 201 Jones Rd; *NASDAQ: NETE*	Waltham	MA	02451	**800-325-9870**	781-890-1700
NetIQ Corp 3553 N 1st St; *NASDAQ: NTIQ* ■ *Sales	San Jose	CA	95134	**888-323-6768***	408-856-3000
NetManage Inc 20883 Stevens Creek Blvd; *NASDAQ: NETM*	Cupertino	CA	95014	**800-558-7656**	408-973-7171
NetPro Computing Inc 4747 N 22 St Suite 400	Phoenix	AZ	85016	**800-998-5090**	602-346-3600
Network Appliance Inc 495 E Java Dr; *NASDAQ: NTAP* ■ *Sales	Sunnyvale	CA	94089	**800-443-4537***	408-822-6000
Network Computing Devices Inc 10795 SW Cascade Blvd	Portland	OR	97223	**800-800-9599**	503-431-8600
Norman Data Defense Systems Inc 9302 Lee Hwy Suite 950A	Fairfax	VA	22031	**888-466-6762**	703-267-6109
NovaStor Corp 80-B W Cochran St	Simi Valley	CA	93065	**800-668-2786**	805-579-6700
NSI Software 2 Hudson Pl Suite 700	Hoboken	NJ	07030	**800-775-4674**	201-656-2121
NTP Software 427-3 Amherst St Suite 381	Nashua	NH	03063	**800-226-2755**	603-622-4400
Open Systems Management Inc 1511 3rd Ave Suite 905	Seattle	WA	98101	**866-601-8011**	206-583-8373
OpenNetwork Technologies Inc 13577 Feather Sound Dr	Clearwater	FL	33762	**877-561-9500**	727-561-9500
Oracle Corp 500 Oracle Pkwy; *NASDAQ: ORCL* ■ *Sales	Redwood Shores	CA	94065	**800-672-2531***	650-506-7000
Peoplesmith Software Inc 50 Cole Pkwy Suite 34; *Sales	Scituate	MA	02066	**800-777-2460***	781-545-7300
Perceptics Corp 9737 Cogdill Rd Suite 200	Knoxville	TN	37932	**800-448-8544**	865-966-9200
Persistence Software Inc 1720 S Amphlett Blvd 3rd Fl; *Sales	San Mateo	CA	94402	**800-803-8491***	650-372-3600
Pervasive Software Inc 12365 Riata Trace Pkwy Bldg B; *NASDAQ: PVSW*	Austin	TX	78727	**800-287-4383**	512-231-6000
Phoenix Technologies Ltd 915 Murphy Ranch Rd; *NASDAQ: PTEC*	Milpitas	CA	95035	**800-677-7305**	408-570-1000
Phoenix Technologies Ltd Award Software International Div 411 E Plumeria Dr	San Jose	CA	95134	**800-677-7305**	408-570-1000
Pragma Systems Inc 3700 W Parmer Ln Suite 100; *Sales	Austin	TX	78727	**800-224-1675***	512-219-7270
Process Software Corp 959 Concord St	Framingham	MA	01701	**800-722-7770**	508-879-6994
Quick Eagle Networks Inc 217 Humboldt Ct	Sunnyvale	CA	94089	**888-280-5465**	408-745-6200
RadView Software Inc 7 New England Executive Pk; *NASDAQ: RDVW*	Burlington	MA	01803	**888-723-8439**	781-238-1111

Systems & Utilities Software (Cont'd)

Company	City	State	ZIP	Toll-Free	Phone
Raining Data Corp 17500 Cartwright Rd	Irvine	CA	92614	**800-367-7425**	949-442-4400
NASDAQ: RDTA					
Raxco Software Inc					
6 Montgomery Village Ave Suite 500	Gaithersburg	MD	20879	**800-546-9728***	301-527-0803
*Tech Supp					
Red Hat Inc 1801 Varsity Dr	Raleigh	NC	27606	**888-733-4281**	919-754-3700
NASDAQ: RHAT					
Relais International					
1690 Woodward Dr Suite 215	Ottawa	ON	K2C3R8	**888-294-5244**	613-226-5571
RSA Security Inc 174 Middlesex Tpke	Bedford	MA	01730	**800-301-5000**	781-515-5000
NASDAQ: RSAS					
SAFLINK Corp 777 108th Ave NE Suite 2100	Bellevue	WA	98004	**800-762-9595**	425-278-1100
Saztec International 900 Middlesex Tpke	Billerica	MA	01821	**800-888-4664**	978-901-9614
ScanSoft Inc 9 Centennial Dr	Peabody	MA	01960	**800-248-6550***	978-977-2000
NASDAQ: SSFT ■ *Cust Svc					
Secure Computing Corp 4810 Hardwood Rd	San Jose	CA	95124	**800-692-5625**	408-979-6100
NASDAQ: SCUR					
Serengeti Systems Inc 812 W 11th St 3rd Fl	Austin	TX	78701	**800-634-3122**	512-345-2211
ShowCase Div SPSS Inc					
233 S Wacker Dr 11th Fl	Chicago	IL	60606	**800-259-1028**	
Simtrol Inc 2200 Norcross Pkwy Suite 255	Norcross	GA	30071	**800-423-0769**	770-242-7566
Smart Card Solutions LLC 229 E Capitol Dr	Hartland	WI	53029	**888-225-6442**	262-369-3400
Software Engineering of America Inc					
1230 Hempstead Tpke	Franklin Square	NY	11010	**800-272-7322**	516 328-7000
Software Pursuits Inc					
1500 Fashion Island Blvd Suite 205	San Mateo	CA	94404	**800-367-4823**	650-372-0900
Soliton Inc 99 Wall St 17th Fl	New York	NY	10005	**800-201-0569**	212-344-3988
Sophos Inc 6 Kimball Ln Suite 400	Lynnfield	MA	01940	**888-767-4679**	781-973-0110
SPSS Inc ShowCase Div					
233 S Wacker Dr 11th Fl	Chicago	IL	60606	**800-259-1028**	
SPYRUS Inc 2355 Oakland Rd Suite 1	San Jose	CA	95131	**800-277-9787**	408-953-0700
SSP Litronic 17861 Cartwright Rd	Irvine	CA	92614	**800-454-8766**	949-851-1085
Stalker Software Inc					
655 Redwood Hwy Suite 275	Mill Valley	CA	94941	**800-262-4722**	415-383-7164
Stratus Technologies 111 Powdermill Rd	Maynard	MA	01754	**800-787-2887**	978-461-7000
Sun Microsystems Inc 4150 Network Cir	Santa Clara	CA	95054	**800-786-0404**	650-960-1300
NASDAQ: SUNW					
Sunbelt Software USA 101 N Garden Ave	Clearwater	FL	33755	**888-688-8457**	727-562-0101
Symantec Corp 20330 Stevens Creek Blvd	Cupertino	CA	95014	**800-441-7234***	408-517-8000
NASDAQ: SYMC ■ *Cust Svc					
Symark Software					
30401 Agoura Rd Suite 200	Agoura Hills	CA	91301	**800-234-9072**	818-575-4000
SystemSoft Corp 275 Grove St Suite I-300	Newton	MA	02466	**800-796-0088**	617-614-4315
Tally Systems Corp PO Box 70	Hanover	NH	03755	**800-262-3877**	603-643-1300
Tarantella Inc 425 Encinal St	Santa Cruz	CA	95060	**800-995-9806***	831-427-7222
NASDAQ: TTLA ■ *Sales					
TeamQuest Corp 1 TeamQuest Way	Clear Lake	IA	50428	**800-551-8326**	641-357-2700
TechSmith Corp 2405 Woodlake Dr	Okemos	MI	48864	**800-517-3001**	517-381-2300
Telesensory Inc 520 Almanor Ave	Sunnyvale	CA	94085	**800-804-8004***	408-616-8700
*Cust Svc					
Tenebril Inc 75 Federal St 6th Fl	Boston	MA	02110	**800-790-9060**	617-912-6600
Thales e-Security Inc					
2200 N Commerce Pkwy Suite 200	Weston	FL	33326	**888-744-4976**	954-888-6200
Thermo CRS 5344 John Lucas Dr	Burlington	ON	L7L6A6	**800-365-7587**	905-332-2000
TrendMicro Inc					
10101 N De Anza Blvd Suite 200	Cupertino	CA	95014	**800-228-5651**	408-257-1500
Tripwire Inc 326 SW Broadway 3rd Fl	Portland	OR	97205	**800-874-7947**	503-276-7500
TruSecure Corp					
13650 Dulles Technology Dr Suite 500	Herndon	VA	20171	**888-627-2281**	703-480-8200
Trust Digital Inc 7900 W Park Dr Suite A50	McLean	VA	22102	**888-760-9401**	703-760-9400
UniPress Software Inc 2025 Lincoln Hwy	Edison	NJ	08817	**800-222-0550**	732-287-2100
V Communications Inc					
2290 N 1st St Suite 101	San Jose	CA	95131	**800-648-8266**	408-965-4000
V-ONE Corp 20300 Century Blvd Suite 200	Germantown	MD	20874	**800-495-8663**	301-515-5200
VenturCom Inc 29 Sawyer Rd	Waltham	MA	02543	**800-334-8649**	781-647-3000
VERITAS Software Corp 350 Ellis St	Mountain View	CA	94043	**800-327-2232**	650-527-8000
NASDAQ: VRTSE					
Vision Solutions Inc					
17911 Von Karman Ave 5th Fl	Irvine	CA	92614	**800-683-4667**	949-253-6500
WatchGuard Technologies Inc					
505 5th Ave S Suite 500	Seattle	WA	98104	**800-734-9905***	206-521-8340
NASDAQ: WGRD ■ *Sales					
Webroot Software Inc PO Box 19816	Boulder	CO	80308	**800-772-9383**	303-442-3813
WildPackets Inc					
1340 Treat Blvd Suite 500	Walnut Creek	CA	94597	**800-466-2447**	925-937-3200
Wilson WindowWare Inc					
5421 California Ave SW	Seattle	WA	98136	**800-762-8383**	206-938-1740
Wind River Systems Inc 500 Wind River Way	Alameda	CA	94501	**800-545-9463**	510-748-4100
NASDAQ: WIND					
xSides Corp 821 2nd Ave	Seattle	WA	98104	**800-396-7877**	206-336-1600
Yrrid Software Inc 507 Monroe St	Chapel Hill	NC	27516	**800-443-0065**	919-968-7858
Zix Corp 2711 N Haskell Rd Suite 2300	Dallas	TX	75204	**888-771-4049**	214-370-2000
NASDAQ: ZIXI					

177 COMPUTER STORES

SEE ALSO Appliance & Home Electronics Stores

Company	City	State	ZIP	Toll-Free	Phone
A Matter of Fax 105 Harrison Ave	Harrison	NJ	07029	**800-433-3329**	973-482-3700
CDW Corp 200 N Milwaukee Ave	Vernon Hills	IL	60061	**800-828-4239**	847-465-6000
NASDAQ: CDWC					
ClubMac Inc 19 Morgan St	Irvine	CA	92618	**800-258-2622**	949-768-8130
CompUSA Inc 14951 N Dallas Pkwy	Dallas	TX	75254	**800-278-4685**	972-982-4000
Computers4SURE.com Inc 6 Cambridge Dr	Trumbull	CT	06611	**800-585-4080***	203-615-7000
*Cust Svc					
Cyberian Outpost Inc 25 N Main St	Kent	CT	06757	**877-688-7678**	860-927-2050
Dartek Computer Supply Corp					
175 Ambassador Dr	Naperville	IL	60540	**800-553-8223**	630-355-3000
Dell Inc 1 Dell Way	Round Rock	TX	78682	**800-854-6214**	512-338-4400
NASDAQ: DELL					
GameStop Corp 2250 William D Tate Ave	Grapevine	TX	76051	**800-288-9020**	817-424-2000
NYSE: GME					
Gateway Inc 7565 Irvine Center Dr	Irvine	CA	92618	**800-846-2000**	949-471-7000
NYSE: GTW					
Insight Enterprises Inc 6820 S Harl Ave	Tempe	AZ	85283	**800-467-4448**	480-333-3000
NASDAQ: NSIT					
MacConnection 730 Milford Rd Rt 101A	Merrimack	NH	03054	**800-800-0014**	603-683-2000
Outpost.com 25 N Main St	Kent	CT	06757	**877-688-7678**	860-927-2050
PC Connection Inc 730 Milford Rd Rt 101A	Merrimack	NH	03054	**800-800-1111**	603-683-2000
NASDAQ: PCCC					
PC Connection Inc MacConnection Div DBA					
MacConnection 730 Milford Rd Rt 101A	Merrimack	NH	03054	**800-800-0014**	603-683-2000
PC Mall Inc 2555 W 190th St	Torrance	CA	90504	**800-413-3833**	310-354-5600
NASDAQ: MALL					
Software Etc Stores Inc					
2250 William D Tate Ave	Grapevine	TX	76051	**800-288-9020**	817-424-2000
TigerDirect Inc 7795 W Flagler St Suite 35	Miami	FL	33144	**800-955-1888**	305-415-2200

178 COMPUTER SYSTEMS DESIGN SERVICES

SEE ALSO Web Site Design Services

Company	City	State	ZIP	Toll-Free	Phone
Abacus Technology Corp					
5454 Wisconsin Ave Suite 1100	Chevy Chase	MD	20815	**800-225-2135**	301-907-8500
Advanced Information Systems Group Inc					
2180 W SR 434 Suite 6150	Longwood	FL	32779	**800-780-2598**	407-774-7181
Advanced Resource Technologies Inc					
2800 Eisenhower Ave 4th Fl E	Alexandria	VA	22314	**800-796-9936**	703-836-8811
AETEA Information Technology Inc					
1445 Research Blvd Suite 300	Rockville	MD	20850	**888-772-3832**	301-721-4200
AGSI 3390 Peachtree Rd NE Suite 350	Atlanta	GA	30326	**800-768-2474**	404-816-7577
American Systems Corp 13990 Parkeast Cir	Chantilly	VA	20151	**800-733-2721**	703-968-6300
Analysts International Corp					
3601 W 76th St	Minneapolis	MN	55435	**800-800-5044**	952-835-5900
NASDAQ: ANLY					
Anteon International Corp					
3211 Jermantown Rd Suite 700	Fairfax	VA	22030	**800-242-0230**	703-246-0200
NYSE: ANT					
Arlington Computer Products Inc					
851 Commerce Ct	Buffalo Grove	IL	60089	**800-548-5105***	847-541-6333
*Orders					
Atos Origin 5599 San Felipe Suite 300	Houston	TX	77056	**866-875-8902**	713-513-3000
Bay State Computers Inc					
4601 Presidents Dr Suite 130	Lanham	MD	20706	**800-266-3783**	301-306-0008
BearingPoint Inc 1676 International Dr	McLean	VA	22102	**866-276-4768**	703-747-3000
NYSE: BE					
Bell Industries Inc					
1960 E Grand Ave Suite 560	El Segundo	CA	90245	**800-782-2355**	310-563-2355
AMEX: BI					
Bell Industries Inc Tech.logix Group					
3502 Woodview Trace Suite 100	Indianapolis	IN	46268	**800-722-1599**	317-227-6700
Berbee Information Networks Corp					
5520 Research Pk Dr	Madison	WI	53711	**888-888-8835**	608-288-3000
BORN Information Services Group					
301 Carlson Pkwy Suite 500	Minnetonka	MN	55305	**800-469-2676**	952-258-6000
Calence Inc					
1620 W Fountainhead Pkwy Suite 400	Tempe	AZ	85282	**877-225-3623**	480-889-9500
Camber Corp 635 Discovery Dr NW	Huntsville	AL	35806	**800-998-7988**	256-922-0200
Carreker Corp 4055 Valley View Ln Suite 1000	Dallas	TX	75244	**800-486-1981**	972-458-1981
NASDAQ: CANI					
CIBER Inc					
5251 DTC Pkwy Suite 1400	Greenwood Village	CO	80111	**800-242-3799**	303-220-0100
NYSE: CBR					
Clarkston Consulting					
1007 Slater Rd Suite 400	Durham	NC	27703	**800-652-4274**	919-484-4400
Cognizant Technology Solutions Corp					
500 Glenpointe Ctr W 7th Fl	Teaneck	NJ	07666	**888-937-3277**	201-801-0233
NASDAQ: CTSH					
CompuCom Systems Inc Excell Data Div					
1756 114th Ave SE Suite 220	Bellevue	WA	98004	**800-539-2355**	425-974-2000
Computech Resources Inc 1375 W Main Ave	De Pere	WI	54115	**877-500-3330**	920-336-1387
Computer Analytical Systems Inc (CASI)					
1418 S 3rd St	Louisville	KY	40208	**800-977-3475**	502-635-2019
Computer & Hi-tech Management Inc					
596 Lynnhaven Pkwy	Virginia Beach	VA	23452	**800-768-4111**	757-486-8838
Computer Horizons Corp					
49 Old Bloomfield Ave	Mountain Lakes	NJ	07046	**800-321-2421**	973-299-4000
NASDAQ: CHRZ					
Computer Methods Corp					
525 Rt 73 S Suite 300	Marlton	NJ	08053	**800-969-4360**	856-596-4360
Computer Sciences Corp					
2100 E Grand Ave	El Segundo	CA	90245	**800-342-5272**	310-615-0311
NYSE: CSC					
Computer Task Group Inc (CTG)					
800 Delaware Ave	Buffalo	NY	14209	**800-992-5350**	716-882-8000
NYSE: CTG					
Computer Technology Assoc (CTA)					
12530 Parklawn Dr Suite 300	Rockville	MD	20852	**800-753-9201**	301-581-3200
Cotelligent Inc					
655 Montgomery St Suite 1000	San Francisco	CA	94111	**888-683-6400**	415-477-9900
Covansys Corp					
32605 W 12 Mile Rd Suite 250	Farmington Hills	MI	48334	**877-642-2274**	248-488-2088
NASDAQ: CVNSE					
Cybertech Systems Inc					
1250 E Diehl Rd Suite 403	Naperville	IL	60563	**800-874-1985**	630-472-3200
Daou Systems Inc 412 Creamery Way Suite 300	Exton	PA	19341	**800-578-3268**	610-594-2700
Data Return LLC					
222 W Las Colinas Blvd Suite 350E	Irving	TX	75039	**800-767-1514**	972-869-0770
Datashare Corp 9485 Priority Way W Dr	Indianapolis	IN	46240	**800-228-5465**	317-569-7485
Datatec Systems Inc 1275 Alderman Dr	Alpharetta	GA	30005	**800-631-2524**	770-667-8488
NASDAQ: DATC					
DCC Services LLC					
1100 Poydras St Suite 1350	New Orleans	LA	70163	**800-309-1213**	504-585-7346
Delta CompuTec Inc 900 Huyler St	Teterboro	NJ	07608	**800-477-8586**	201-440-8585
Delta Corporate Services Inc					
129 Littleton Rd	Parsippany	NJ	07054	**800-335-8220**	973-334-6260
Design Strategy Corp 600 3rd Ave 25th Fl	New York	NY	10016	**800-331-8726**	212-370-0000
DigitalNet Holdings Inc 2525 Network Pl	Herndon	VA	20171	**800-999-3732**	703-563-7500
NASDAQ: DNET					
DPE Systems Inc 425 Pontius Ave N Suite 430	Seattle	WA	98109	**800-541-6566**	206-223-3737
Dynamic Decisions Inc 31 Suttons Ln	Piscataway	NJ	08854	**800-689-9908**	732-819-3946

	City	State	ZIP	Toll-Free	Phone
Dynamics Research Corp 60 Frontage Rd *NASDAQ: DRCO*	Andover	MA	01810	**800-522-4321**	978-475-9090
ea inc 1130 Iron Point Rd Suite 288	Folsom	CA	95630	**800-399-2828**	916-608-1868
Edgewater Technology Inc 20 Harvard Mill Sq *NASDAQ: EDGW*	Wakefield	MA	01880	**800-233-7924**	781-246-3343
EDS Canada 33 Yonge St Suite 500	Toronto	ON	M5E1G4	**800-814-9038**	416-814-4500
Electronic Warfare Assoc Inc (EWA Inc) 13873 Park Center Rd Suite 500	Herndon	VA	20171	**888-392-0002**	703-904-5700
Everdream Corp 6591 Dumbarton Cir	Fremont	CA	94555	**877-437-3264**	510-818-5500
EWA Inc (Electronic Warfare Assoc Inc) 13873 Park Center Rd Suite 500	Herndon	VA	20171	**888-392-0002**	703-904-5700
Excell Data Div CompuCom Systems Inc 1756 114th Ave SE Suite 220	Bellevue	WA	98004	**800-539-2355**	425-974-2000
Force 3 Inc 2147 Priest Bridge Dr Suite 1	Crofton	MD	21114	**800-391-0204**	301-261-0204
GE Capital IT Management Services 2480 Meadowvale Blvd	Mississauga	ON	L5N7Y1	**800-268-2106**	905-816-3000
Getronics 290 Concord Rd	Billerica	MA	01821	**800-225-0654**	978-625-5000
Global Consultants Inc 25 Airport Rd	Morristown	NJ	07960	**877-264-6424**	973-889-5200
Government Micro Resources Inc 7403 Gateway Ct *Cust Svc	Manassas	VA	20109	**800-220-4672***	703-330-1199
GramTel USA PO Box 720	South Bend	IN	46624	**866-481-7622**	574-472-4726
Hartford Computer Group Inc 1610 Colonial Pkwy	Inverness	IL	60067	**800-680-4424**	224-836-3000
Healthlink Inc 13620 Reese Blvd E Suite 100	Huntersville	NC	28078	**800-382-7094**	704-947-8848
Howard Systems International 281 Tresser Blvd	Stamford	CT	06901	**800-326-4860**	203-324-4600
Iconixx Corp 5301 Hollister Suite 400	Houston	TX	77040	**877-426-6499**	713-934-0200
Immedient 4582 S Ulster St Pkwy Suite 200	Denver	CO	80237	**800-324-3469**	303-770-7200
Impact Innovations Group 8850 Stanford Blvd Suite 4000	Columbia	MD	21045	**877-239-2333**	410-872-5400
Indotronix International Corp 331 Main St	Poughkeepsie	NY	12601	**800-800-8442**	845-473-1137
Information Analysis Inc 11240 Waples Mill Rd Suite 400	Fairfax	VA	22030	**800-829-7614**	703-383-3000
Information Systems Support Inc 13 Firstfield Rd Suite 100	Gaithersburg	MD	20878	**800-288-2095**	301-896-0500
InfoTech USA Inc 7 Kingsbridge Rd	Fairfield	NJ	07004	**800-305-8201**	973-227-8772
INNOLOG (Innovative Logistics Techniques Inc) 2010 Corporate Ridge 9th Fl	McLean	VA	22102	**800-466-6564**	703-506-1555
Innovative Logistics Techniques Inc (INNOLOG) 2010 Corporate Ridge 9th Fl	McLean	VA	22102	**800-466-6564**	703-506-1555
Integrated Information Systems Inc 2250 W 14th St	Tempe	AZ	85281	**877-447-7755**	480-752-5000
Integrated Systems Analysts Inc 2800 Shirlington Rd Suite 1100	Arlington	VA	22206	**800-929-3436**	703-824-0700
Integro Inc 1350 17th St Suite 300	Denver	CO	80202	**888-575-9300**	303-575-9300
Interlink Group LLC 98 Inverness Dr E Suite 150	Englewood	CO	80112	**888-533-1307**	303-542-7100
James River Technical Inc 4439 Cox Rd	Glen Allen	VA	23060	**800-296-0027**	804-935-0150
Keane Inc 100 City Sq *NYSE: KEA*	Boston	MA	02129	**800-365-3263**	617-241-9200
Levanta Inc 650 Townsend St Suite 225	San Francisco	CA	94103	**888-546-4878**	415-354-4878
Lighthouse Computer Services Inc 6 Blackstone Valley Pl Suite 205	Lincoln	RI	02865	**888-542-8030**	401-334-0799
Maden Technologies 2110 Washington Blvd Suite 200	Arlington	VA	22204	**800-601-5112**	703-769-4440
Mainline Information Systems Inc 1700 Summit Lake Dr	Tallahassee	FL	32317	**800-811-4429**	850-219-5000
Maintech Div Volt Information Sciences Inc 39 Paterson Ave	Wallington	NJ	07057	**800-426-8324**	973-614-1700
MANDEX Inc 12500 Fair Lakes Cir Suite 125	Fairfax	VA	22033	**888-662-6339**	703-227-0900
Meridian Group 9 Parkway N Suite 500	Deerfield	IL	60015	**800-811-2674**	847-940-1200
META Group Inc 208 Harbor Dr 4th Fl	Stamford	CT	06912	**800-756-6382**	203-973-6700
Metters Industries Inc 8200 Greensboro Dr Suite 500	McLean	VA	22102	**800-638-8377**	703-821-3300
Multimax Inc 1441 McCormick Dr	Largo	MD	20774	**800-339-8828**	301-925-8222
NCI Information Systems Inc 11730 Plaza America Dr	Reston	VA	20190	**888-409-5457**	703-707-6900
NetSolve Inc 9500 Amberglen Blvd *NASDAQ: NTSL*	Austin	TX	78729	**800-638-7658**	512-340-3000
NewAgeSys Inc 5 Vaughn Dr Suite 310	Princeton	NJ	08540	**888-863-9243**	609-919-9800
Nextira One Federal 510 Spring St Suite 200 *Cust Svc	Herndon	VA	20170	**800-822-8374***	703-885-7900
Niteo Partners Inc 379 Thornall St 5th Fl	Edison	NJ	08837	**888-406-5033**	732-767-0400
NuWare Technology Corp Inc 100 Wood Ave S Suite 306	Iselin	NJ	08830	**800-688-9273**	732-494-0550
OAO Technology Solutions Inc 7500 Greenway Ctr Dr 16th Fl	Greenbelt	MD	20770	**800-720-9030**	301-486-0400
Open Systems Solutions Inc 710 Floral Vale Blvd	Yardley	PA	19067	**800-898-6774**	215-579-8111
Paragon Computer Professionals Inc 25 Commerce Dr 2nd Fl	Cranford	NJ	07016	**800-462-5582**	908-709-6767
Perot Systems Corp 2300 W Plano Pkwy *NYSE: PER*	Plano	TX	75075	**888-407-3768**	972-577-0000
Pointe Technology Group Inc 8201 Corporate Dr Suite 700	Landover	MD	20785	**800-730-6171**	301-306-4400
Pomeroy IT Solutions Inc 1020 Petersburg Rd *NASDAQ: PMRY*	Hebron	KY	41048	**800-846-8727**	859-586-1515
Presearch Inc 8500 Executive Park Ave Suite 400	Fairfax	VA	22031	**800-922-9259**	703-876-6400
Presidio Corp 7601 Ora Glen Dr Suite 100	Greenbelt	MD	20770	**800-452-6926**	301-313-2000
RCG Information Technology Inc 379 Thornall St 14th Fl	Edison	NJ	08837	**800-333-7816**	732-744-3500
Resource One Computer Systems Inc 1159 Dublin Rd	Columbus	OH	43215	**800-393-7627**	614-485-4800
RiverPoint Group LLC 9450 W Bryn Mawr Ave Suite 700	Rosemont	IL	60018	**800-297-5601**	847-233-9600
RWD Technologies Inc 5521 Research Park Dr	Baltimore	MD	21228	**877-952-8301**	410-869-1000
Satyam Computer Services Ltd 1 Gatehall Dr Suite 301	Parsippany	NJ	07054	**800-450-7605**	973-656-0650
Sayers Group LLC 1150 Feehanville Dr	Mount Prospect	IL	60056	**800-323-5357**	847-391-4040
SecureInfo Corp 211 North Loop 1604 E Suite 200	San Antonio	TX	78232	**888-677-9351**	210-403-5600
SETA Corp 6862 Elm St Suite 600	McLean	VA	22101	**888-753-6240**	703-821-8178
Siemens Logistics & Assembly Systems 507 Plymouth Ave	Grand Rapids	MI	49505	**877-725-7500**	616-913-6200
SM Consulting Inc 1306 Concourse Dr Suite 200	Linthicum	MD	21090	**888-476-2937**	410-691-5200
SMS Data Products Group Inc 1501 Farm Credit Dr	McLean	VA	22102	**800-331-1767**	703-709-9898
Software Technology Group 2455 Parleys Way Suite 150	Salt Lake City	UT	84109	**888-595-1001**	801-595-1000
Stanley Assoc Inc 300 N Washington St Suite 400	Alexandria	VA	22314	**866-774-0577**	703-684-1125
Stopka & Assoc 975 Weiland Rd Suite 100	Buffalo Grove	IL	60089	**800-984-7031**	847-215-3900
Sumaria Systems Inc 99 Rosewood Dr Suite 140	Danvers	MA	01923	**888-245-9810**	978-739-4200
Sykes Enterprises Inc 400 N Ashley Dr Suite 2800 *NASDAQ: SYKE*	Tampa	FL	33602	**800-867-9537**	813-274-1000
Syntegra USA 4201 Lexington Ave N	Arden Hills	MN	55126	**800-257-6736**	651-415-2999
Sytel Inc 6430 Rockledge Dr Suite 400	Bethesda	MD	20817	**888-866-0881**	301-530-1000
TAMSCO (Technical & Management Services Corp) 4041 Powder Mill Rd Suite 700	Calverton	MD	20705	**800-282-6727**	301-595-0710
Tech.logix Group of Bell Industries Inc 3502 Woodview Trace Suite 100	Indianapolis	IN	46268	**800-722-1599**	317-227-6700
Technical & Management Services Corp (TAMSCO) 4041 Powder Mill Rd Suite 700	Calverton	MD	20705	**800-282-6727**	301-595-0710
Technical Resource Connection Inc 12320 Racetrack Rd	Tampa	FL	33626	**800-872-2992**	813-891-6084
Technology Solutions Co (TSC) 205 N Michigan Ave Suite 1500 *NASDAQ: TSCC*	Chicago	IL	60601	**800-819-2250**	312-228-4500
TechTeam Global Inc 27335 W Eleven-Mile Rd *NASDAQ: TEAM*	Southfield	MI	48034	**800-522-4451**	248-357-2866
Tier Technologies Inc 10780 Parkridge Blvd Suite 400 *NASDAQ: TIER*	Reston	VA	20191	**800-789-8437**	571-382-1000
TRI-COR Industries Inc 4600 Forbes Blvd Suite 205	Lanham	MD	20706	**800-764-7275**	301-731-6140
Vistronix Inc 8401 Greensboro Dr Suite 500	McLean	VA	22102	**800-483-2434**	703-734-2270
Volt Information Sciences Inc Maintech Div 39 Paterson Ave	Wallington	NJ	07057	**800-426-8324**	973-614-1700
Xerox Global Services Inc 411 Eagleview Blvd	Exton	PA	19341	**800-884-4736**	610-458-5500
Xtria 2435 N Central Expy Suite 700	Richardson	TX	75080	**866-769-2987**	972-699-4000
ZyQuest Inc 1580 Mid-Valley Dr	De Pere	WI	54115	**800-992-0533**	920-617-7615

179 CONCERT, SPORTS, OTHER LIVE EVENT PRODUCERS & PROMOTERS

	City	State	ZIP	Toll-Free	Phone
AMS Entertainment 1213 State St Suite J	Santa Barbara	CA	93101	**800-267-3548**	805-899-4000
Complete Music Inc 7877 L St	Omaha	NE	68127	**800-843-3866**	402-339-0001
Gilmore Entertainment Group PO Box 7576	Myrtle Beach	SC	29572	**800-843-6779**	843-449-4444
Harlem Globetrotters International Inc 400 E Van Buren St Suite 300	Phoenix	AZ	85004	**800-641-4667**	602-258-0000
House of Blues Entertainment Inc 6255 Sunset Blvd 16th Fl	Hollywood	CA	90028	**800-843-2583**	323-769-4600
Miss America Organization 2 Miss America Way Suite 1000	Atlantic City	NJ	08401	**800-282-6477**	609-345-7571

180 CONCRETE - READY-MIXED

	City	State	ZIP	Toll-Free	Phone
Aggregate Industries Inc 888 Dunbarton Rd	Manchester	NH	03102	**800-322-7665**	603-627-7666
American Materials LLC PO Box 1246	Eau Claire	WI	54702	**866-421-7625**	715-835-2251
AVR Inc AME Ready Mix PO Box 307 *Cust Svc	Elk River	MN	55330	**800-374-8544***	763-441-2800
Berks Products Corp 726 Spring St	Reading	PA	19604	**800-282-2375**	610-374-5131
Binkley & Ober Inc PO Box 7	East Petersburg	PA	17520	**800-860-0441**	717-569-0441
Block WG Co 1414 Mississippi Blvd PO Box 280	Bettendorf	IA	52722	**800-397-1651**	563-823-2080
Blue Rock Industries 58 Main St	Westbrook	ME	04092	**800-439-2561**	207-854-2561
Bonded Concrete Inc 303 Rt 155	Watervliet	NY	12189	**800-252-8589**	518-273-5800
Bornhoft Concrete Products Inc 150 County Rd 8	Tyler	MN	56178	**800-257-5576**	507-247-5575
Boston Sand & Gravel Co Inc 169 Portland St PO Box 9187	Boston	MA	02114	**800-624-2724**	617-227-9000
Brown Joe Co Inc PO Box 1669	Ardmore	OK	73402	**800-444-4293**	580-223-4555
Building Products Corp 950 Freeburg Ave	Belleville	IL	62220	**800-233-1996**	618-233-4427
Cadman Inc PO Box 97038	Redmond	WA	98073	**888-322-6847**	425-868-1234
Campbell Concrete & Materials PO Box 1147	Cleveland	TX	77328	**800-749-1843**	281-592-5201
Capitol Aggregates Ltd 11551 Nacogdoches Rd	San Antonio	TX	78217	**800-292-5315**	210-655-3010
Cemstone Products Co 2025 Centre Pointe Blvd Suite 300	Mendota Heights	MN	55120	**800-642-3887**	651-688-9292
Central Builders Supply Co Inc PO Box 152	Sunbury	PA	17801	**800-326-9361**	570-286-6461
Central Ready-Mix Concrete Inc 5013 W State St	Milwaukee	WI	53208	**800-258-0010**	414-258-7000
Century Ready-Mix Corp 3250 Armand St PO Box 4420	Monroe	LA	71211	**800-732-3969**	318-322-4444
Chaney Enterprises PO Box 548	Waldorf	MD	20604	**800-492-3495**	301-932-5000
Concrete Materials Corp 106 Industry Rd	Richmond	KY	40475	**877-623-4238**	859-623-4238
Dolese Brothers Co 20 NW 13th St	Oklahoma City	OK	73103	**800-375-2311**	405-235-2311
Dragon Products Co 38 Preble St	Portland	ME	04104	**800-828-8352**	207-774-6355
Eastern Concrete Materials Inc 475 Market St	Elmwood Park	NJ	07407	**800-822-7242**	201-797-7979
Elkins Builders Supply Co 5 11th St	Elkins	WV	26241	**800-339-2640**	304-636-2640
Florida Rock Industries Inc 155 E 21st St *NYSE: FRK*	Jacksonville	FL	32206	**800-874-8382**	904-355-1781
Foley Products Co PO Box 7877	Columbus	GA	31908	**800-762-6773**	706-563-7882
Gallup Sand & Gravel Co PO Box 1119	Gallup	NM	87305	**800-257-3818**	505-863-3818
Geneva Rock Products Inc PO Box 538	Orem	UT	84059	**800-464-2003**	801-765-7800
Glacier Northwest Inc PO Box 1730	Seattle	WA	98111	**800-750-0123**	206-764-3000
Griswold ST & Co Inc PO Box 849	Williston	VT	05495	**800-339-4565**	802-658-0201
Hilltop Basic Resources Inc 1 W 4th St Suite 1100	Cincinnati	OH	45202	**800-701-7973**	513-651-5000

	City	State	Zip	Toll-Free	Phone
Janesville Sand & Lycon Co 1110 Harding St	Janesville	WI	53547	**800-955-7702**	608-754-7701
Joe Brown Co Inc PO Box 1669	Ardmore	OK	73402	**800-444-4293**	580-223-4555
Joe's Ready Mix Inc PO Box 168	Sioux Center	IA	51250	**800-888-2649**	712-722-1646
Kienstra Inc 201 W Ferguson Ave	Wood River	IL	62095	**888-543-6787**	618-254-4366
King's Material Inc PO Box 368	Cedar Rapids	IA	52406	**800-332-5298**	319-363-0233
Kirkpatrick Concrete Co 2909 3rd Ave N	Birmingham	AL	35203	**800-489-0205**	205-323-8327
Krehling Industries Inc 1425 E Wiggins Pass Rd	Naples	FL	34108	**800-226-3162**	239-597-3162
Kuert Concrete Inc 3402 Lincoln Way W	South Bend	IN	46628	**866-465-8378**	574-232-9911
Kuhlman Corp 650 Beaver Creek Cir	Maumee	OH	43537	**800-669-3309**	419-897-6000
L Suzio Concrete Co Inc PO Box 748	Meriden	CT	06450	**888-789-4626**	203-237-8421
Lycon Inc PO Box 427	Janesville	WI	53547	**800-955-8758**	608-754-7701
Marshall Concrete Products Inc 1088 Industrial Ave	Danville	VA	24541	**800-537-5884**	434-792-1233
Moraine Materials Co Inc 1400 Commerce Center Dr	Franklin	OH	45005	**888-667-2463**	937-743-0650
New Holland Concrete 828 E Earl Rd PO Box 218	New Holland	PA	17557	**800-543-3860**	717-354-1200
Paramount Ready Mix Concrete Inc 13949 E Stage Rd PO Box 2823	Santa Fe Springs	CA	90670	**888-404-4125**	562-404-4125
Prairie Group Inc 7601 W 79th St	Bridgeview	IL	60455	**800-649-3690***	708-458-0400
*Sales					
Ready Mix Concrete Co PO Box 27326	Raleigh	NC	27611	**800-849-0668**	919-790-1520
Rinker Materials Corp 1501 Belvedere Rd	West Palm Beach	FL	33406	**800-226-5521**	561-833-5555
RMC Carolina Materials Inc PO Box 19178	Greensboro	NC	27419	**800-849-6894**	336-294-1124
RMC Florida Materials 801 McCue Rd	Lakeland	FL	33815	**800-282-4657**	863-688-5787
RMC Pacific Materials Inc 6601 Koll Center Pkwy PO box 5252	Pleasanton	CA	94566	**800-227-5186**	925-462-7181
Sequatchie Concrete Service Inc 406 Cedar Ave	South Pittsburg	TN	37380	**800-824-0824**	423-837-7913
Shelby Materials Inc PO Box 280	Shelbyville	IN	46176	**800-548-9516**	317-398-4485
Silvi Concrete Inc 355 Newbold Rd	Fairless Hills	PA	19030	**800-426-6273**	215-295-0777
Southern Concrete Materials Inc 35 Meadow Rd	Asheville	NC	28803	**800-288-6421**	828-253-6421
ST Griswold & Co Inc PO Box 849	Williston	VT	05495	**800-339-4565**	802-658-0201
Suzio L Concrete Co Inc PO Box 748	Meriden	CT	06450	**888-789-4626**	203-237-8421
Thomas Concrete Inc 2500 Cumberland Pkwy Suite 200	Atlanta	GA	30339	**800-633-4661**	770-431-3300
Titan America Inc 1151 Azalea Garden Rd	Norfolk	VA	23502	**800-468-7622**	757-858-6500
Transit Mix Concrete & Materials Co PO Box 5187	Beaumont	TX	77726	**800-835-4933**	409-835-4933
Vulcan Materials Co Western Div 3200 San Fernando Rd	Los Angeles	CA	90065	**800-225-6280**	323-258-2777
WG Block Co 1414 Mississippi Blvd PO Box 280	Bettendorf	IA	52722	**800-397-1651**	563-823-2080
Wingra Stone Co PO Box 44284	Madison	WI	53744	**800-249-6908**	608-271-5555

181 CONCRETE PRODUCTS - MFR

	City	State	Zip	Toll-Free	Phone
A Duchini Inc 2550 McKinley Ave	Erie	PA	16503	**800-937-7317**	814-456-7027
AC Miller Concrete Products Inc PO Box 199	Spring City	PA	19475	**800-229-2922**	610-948-4600
Accord Industries 4001 Forsyth Rd	Winter Park	FL	32792	**800-477-7675**	407-671-5200
Adams Products Co PO Box 189	Morrisville	NC	27560	**800-672-3131**	919-467-2218
Amcor Precast 801 W 12th St	Ogden	UT	84404	**800-776-8760**	801-399-1171
Americast Div Valley Blox Inc 11352 Virginia Precast Rd	Ashland	VA	23005	**800-999-2279**	804-798-6068
Beavertown Block Co Inc PO Box 337	Middleburg	PA	17842	**800-597-2565***	570-837-1744
*Cust Svc					
Bend Industries Inc 2200 S Main St	West Bend	WI	53095	**800-686-2363**	262-338-5700
Best Block Co PO Box 13707	Milwaukee	WI	53213	**800-782-7708**	262-781-7200
Betco Block & Products Inc 5400 Butler Rd	Bethesda	MD	20816	**800-486-2312**	301-654-2312
Binkley & Ober Inc PO Box 7	East Petersburg	PA	17520	**800-860-0441**	717-569-0441
Blakeslee Construction 200 N Branford Rd	Branford	CT	06405	**800-922-6203**	203-488-2500
Block USA 1572 Chelsea Ave	Memphis	TN	38108	**888-942-5625**	901-754-5115
Blocklite Corp PO Box 540	Selma	CA	93662	**800-896-0753**	559-896-0753
BNZ Materials Inc 6901 S Pierce St Suite 260	Littleton	CO	80128	**800-999-0890**	303-978-1199
Bonsal American 8201 Arrowridge Blvd PO Box 241148	Charlotte	NC	28224	**800-738-1621**	704-525-1621
Buehner Block Co 2800 SW Temple	Salt Lake City	UT	84115	**800-999-2565**	801-467-5456
Building Products Corp 950 Freeburg Ave	Belleville	IL	62220	**800-233-1996**	618-233-4427
Burtco Inc PO Box 40	Westminster Station	VT	05159	**800-451-4401**	802-722-3358
Carder Concrete Products Co 8311 W Carder Ct	Littleton	CO	80125	**800-285-2902**	303-791-1600
Cement Industries Inc 2709 Jeffcott St	Fort Myers	FL	33901	**800-332-1440**	239-332-1440
Century Group Inc PO Box 228	Sulphur	LA	70664	**800-527-5232**	337-527-5266
Chaney Enterprises PO Box 548	Waldorf	MD	20604	**800-492-3495**	301-932-5000
Christy Concrete Products Inc 5236 Arboga Rd	Marysville	CA	95901	**800-486-7070**	530-742-8368
Clayton Block Co 515 Lakewood New Egypt Rd	Lakewood	NJ	08701	**800-662-3044***	732-905-3131
*Orders					
Con Forms PO Box 308	Port Washington	WI	53074	**800-223-3676**	262-268-6800
Continental Florida Materials 13450 W Sunrise Blvd Suite 430	Sunrise	FL	33323	**888-969-9100**	954-858-0780
Crom Corp 250 SW 36th Terr	Gainesville	FL	32607	**800-289-2766**	352-372-3436
Dillon E & Co PO Box 160	Swords Creek	VA	24649	**800-234-8970**	276-873-6816
Dolese Brothers Co 20 NW 13th St	Oklahoma City	OK	73103	**800-375-2311**	405-235-2311
Domine Builders Supply Corp 100 E Highland Dr	Rochester	NY	14610	**800-836-2565**	585-271-6330
Duchini A Inc 2550 McKinley Ave	Erie	PA	16503	**800-937-7317**	814-456-7027
Dura-Stress Inc PO Box 490779	Leesburg	FL	34749	**800-342-9239**	352-787-1422
DYK Inc 351 Cypress Ln	El Cajon	CA	92020	**800-227-8181**	619-440-8181
E Dillon & Co PO Box 160	Swords Creek	VA	24649	**800-234-8970**	276-873-6816
Elk River Concrete Products Co 6550 Wedgwood Rd	Maple Grove	MN	55311	**800-557-7473**	763-545-7473
EP Henry Corp 201 Park Ave	Woodbury	NJ	08096	**800-444-3679**	856-845-6200
Fabcon Inc 6111 Hwy 13 W	Savage	MN	55378	**800-727-4444**	952-890-4444
Federal Block Corp 247 Walsh Ave	New Windsor	NY	12553	**800-724-1999**	845-561-4108
Fendt Builders Supply Inc 22005 Gill Rd	Farmington Hills	MI	48335	**888-706-9974**	248-474-3211
Florida Rock Industries Inc 155 E 21st St	Jacksonville	FL	32206	**800-874-8382**	904-355-1781
NYSE: FRK					
Foley Products Co PO Box 7877	Columbus	GA	31908	**800-762-6773**	706-563-7882
Fritz Industries Inc PO Box 170040	Dallas	TX	75217	**800-955-1323**	972-285-5471
General Shale Products LLC 3211 N Roan St	Johnson City	TN	37601	**800-414-4661***	423-282-4661
*Cust Svc					
Glacier Northwest Inc PO Box 1730	Seattle	WA	98111	**800-750-0123**	206-764-3000
Goria Enterprises PO Box 14489	Greensboro	NC	27415	**800-828-5879**	336-375-5821
Grand Blanc Cement Products 10709 S Center Rd	Grand Blanc	MI	48439	**800-875-7500**	810-694-7500
Grand River Infrastructure Inc 2701 Chicago Dr SW	Grand Rapids	MI	49519	**800-968-2662**	616-534-9645
Griswold ST & Co Inc PO Box 849	Williston	VT	05495	**800-339-4565**	802-658-0201
Hancock Concrete Products Inc 17 Atlantic Ave	Hancock	MN	56244	**800-992-8982**	320-392-5207
Hanson Building Products North America 3500 Maple Ave	Dallas	TX	75219	**800-527-2362**	214-525-5500
Hanson Pipe & Products PO Box 368	Green Cove Springs	FL	32043	**800-432-0030**	904-284-3213
Hastings Pavement Co LLC PO Box 178	Islip	NY	11751	**800-669-9294**	631-669-4900
Henry EP Corp 201 Park Ave	Woodbury	NJ	08096	**800-444-3679**	856-845-6200
High Concrete Structures Inc 125 Denver Rd	Denver	PA	17517	**800-773-2278**	717-336-9300
Iowa Prestressed Concrete Inc 601 SW 9th St Suite B	Des Moines	IA	50309	**800-826-0464**	515-243-5118
Jensen Precast 625 Bergin Way	Sparks	NV	89431	**800-648-1134**	775-359-6200
JW Peters 500 W Market St	Burlington	WI	53105	**800-877-9040**	262-763-2401
Kerr Concrete Pipe Co Inc PO Box 312	Hammonton	NJ	08037	**800-842-3755**	609-561-3400
Kienstra Inc 201 W Ferguson Ave	Wood River	IL	62095	**888-543-6787**	618-254-4366
King's Material Inc PO Box 368	Cedar Rapids	IA	52406	**800-332-5298**	319-363-0233
Kistner Concrete Products Inc 8713 Read Rd	East Pembroke	NY	14056	**800-809-2801**	585-762-8216
Krehling Industries Inc 1425 E Wiggins Pass Rd	Naples	FL	34108	**800-226-3162**	239-597-3162
Lampus RI Co 816 RI Lampus Ave	Springdale	PA	15144	**800-872-7310**	724-274-5035
Louisiana Industries PO Box 5396	Bossier City	LA	71171	**800-894-5422**	318-742-3111
Marietta Structures Corp PO Box 653	Marietta	OH	45750	**800-633-9969**	740-373-3211
Marshall Concrete Products Inc 1088 Industrial Ave	Danville	VA	24541	**800-537-5884**	434-792-1233
Martin Fireproofing Corp PO Box 27 Kenmore Stn	Buffalo	NY	14217	**800-766-3969**	716-692-3680
Mathis-Akins Concrete Block Co Inc 130 Lower Elm St	Macon	GA	31202	**888-469-0680**	478-746-5154
Metromont Prestress PO Box 2486	Greenville	SC	29602	**888-295-0383**	864-295-0295
Midwest Tile & Concrete Products Inc 4309 Webster Rd	Woodburn	IN	46797	**800-359-4701**	260-749-5173
Miller AC Concrete Products Inc PO Box 199	Spring City	PA	19475	**800-229-2922**	610-948-4600
Modern Building Materials Inc 8011 Green Bay Rd	Kenosha	WI	53142	**800-622-3166***	262-694-3166
*Cust Svc					
Molin Concrete Products Co 415 Lilac St	Lino Lakes	MN	55014	**800-336-6546**	651-786-7722
MonierLifetile Inc 7575 Irvine Ctr Dr Suite 100	Irvine	CA	92618	**800-224-2024**	949-756-1605
Montfort Bros Inc 44 Elm St	Fishkill	NY	12524	**800-724-1777**	845-896-6225
Montfort Group The 44 Elm St	Fishkill	NY	12524	**800-724-1777**	845-896-6225
Mutual Materials Co 605 119th Ave NE	Bellevue	WA	98005	**800-477-3008**	425-452-2300
NC Products Corp PO Box 27077	Raleigh	NC	27611	**800-662-1983**	919-772-6301
New Holland Concrete 828 E Earl Rd PO Box 218	New Holland	PA	17557	**800-543-3860**	717-354-1200
Oldcastle Inc 375 N Ridge Rd Suite 350	Atlanta	GA	30350	**800-899-8455**	770-804-3363
Orco Block Co Inc 8042 Katella Ave	Stanton	CA	90680	**800-473-6726**	714-527-2239
Pavestone Plus Inc RR 1 1081 Rife Rd	Cambridge	ON	N1R5S3	**800-265-6496**	519-740-6000
Pontchartrain Materials Corp 3819 France Rd	New Orleans	LA	70126	**800-255-9848**	504-949-7571
Price Brothers Co PO Box 825	Dayton	OH	45401	**800-543-5147**	937-226-8700
QUIKRETE Cos 3490 Piedmont Rd Suite 1300	Atlanta	GA	30305	**800-282-5828**	404-634-9100
RCP Block & Brick Inc 8240 Broadway	Lemon Grove	CA	91945	**800-732-7425**	619-460-7250
Reading Rock Inc 4600 Devitt Dr	Cincinnati	OH	45246	**800-482-6466**	513-874-2345
RI Lampus Co 816 RI Lampus Ave	Springdale	PA	15144	**800-872-7310**	724-274-5035
Rinker Materials Corp 1501 Belvedere Rd	West Palm Beach	FL	33406	**800-226-5521**	561-833-5555
Rinker Materials Corp Hydro Conduit Div 6560 Langfield Rd Bldg 3	Houston	TX	77092	**800-909-7763**	832-590-5300
RMC Carolina Materials Inc PO Box 19178	Greensboro	NC	27419	**800-849-6894**	336-294-1124
RMC Florida Materials 801 McCue Rd	Lakeland	FL	33815	**800-282-4657**	863-688-5787
Rockwood Retaining Walls Inc 7200 Hwy 63 N	Rochester	MN	55906	**800-535-2375**	507-288-8850
Schuster's Building Products Inc 901 E Troy Ave	Indianapolis	IN	46203	**800-424-0190**	317-787-3201
Schuylkill Products Inc 121 River St	Cressona	PA	17929	**800-631-1591**	570-385-2352
Sequatchie Concrete Service Inc 406 Cedar Ave	South Pittsburg	TN	37380	**800-824-0824**	423-837-7913
Sherman Industries PO Box 646	Madison	AL	35758	**800-239-7490**	256-772-7490
Sherman International Corp 1400 Urban Ctr Dr Suite 200	Birmingham	AL	35242	**800-277-6920**	205-970-7500
Southern Concrete Construction Co Inc PO Box 711	Albany	GA	31702	**800-768-6888**	229-435-0786
ST Griswold & Co Inc PO Box 849	Williston	VT	05495	**800-339-4565**	802-658-0201
Stanley Hardware 480 Myrtle St	New Britain	CT	06053	**800-337-4393***	860-225-5111
*Cust Svc					
Superlite Block Co Inc 4150 W Turney Ave	Phoenix	AZ	85019	**800-366-7877**	602-269-3561
Texas Concrete Co 4702 N Vine St	Victoria	TX	77904	**800-242-3511**	361-573-9145
Thomas Concrete Inc 2500 Cumberland Pkwy Suite 200	Atlanta	GA	30339	**800-633-4661**	770-431-3300
Tindall Corp PO Box 1778	Spartanburg	SC	29304	**800-849-4521**	864-576-3230
Trenwyth Industries Inc PO Box 438	Emigsville	PA	17318	**800-233-1924***	717-767-6868
*Cust Svc					
TXI Operations LP DBA Louisiana Industries PO Box 5396	Bossier City	LA	71171	**800-894-5422**	318-742-3111
United Building Centers Masonry Products Div PO Box 599	Garden City	KS	67846	**800-545-7411**	620-276-8294
Valley Blox Inc 210 Stone Spring Rd	Harrisonburg	VA	22801	**800-648-6725**	540-434-6725
Valley Blox Inc Americast Div 11352 Virginia Precast Rd	Ashland	VA	23005	**800-999-2279**	804-798-6068
Wieser Concrete Products Inc W3716 US Hwy 10	Maiden Rock	WI	54750	**800-325-8456**	715-647-2311
Wilbert Inc PO Box 147	Forest Park	IL	60130	**800-323-7188**	708-865-1600
Wingra Stone Co PO Box 44284	Madison	WI	53744	**800-249-6908**	608-271-5555
Wisconsin Brick & Block Corp 6399 Nesbitt Rd	Madison	WI	53719	**800-601-2889**	608-845-8636
WPC Florida PO Box 35189	Panama City	FL	32412	**800-763-2811**	850-763-2811
York Building Products Co Inc PO Box 1708	York	PA	17405	**800-673-2408**	717-848-2831

182 CONCRETE REINFORCING MESH

Company	City	State	ZIP	Toll-Free	Phone
CCX Inc 500 E Middle St	Hanover	PA	17331	**800-323-5585**	717-637-3795
Hohmann & Barnard Inc 30 Rasons Ct	Hauppauge	NY	11788	**800-323-7170**	631-234-0600
Insteel Industries Inc 1373 Boggs Dr	Mount Airy	NC	27030	**800-334-9504**	336-786-2141

183 CONFERENCE & EVENTS COORDINATORS

Company	City	State	ZIP	Toll-Free	Phone
Advanstar Communications Inc 7500 Old Oak Blvd	Cleveland	OH	44130	**800-225-4569**	440-243-8100
ASD/AMD Merchandise Group 2950 31st St Suite 100	Santa Monica	CA	90405	**800-421-4511**	310-396-6006
Brede Exposition Services Div Casey & Hayes Exhibits Inc 100 Industrial Pk Rd	Hingham	MA	02043	**800-835-0167**	781-741-5900
Casey & Hayes Exhibits Inc Brede Exposition Services Div 100 Industrial Pk Rd	Hingham	MA	02043	**800-835-0167**	781-741-5900
CLT Meetings/Publicis Events 340 N Primrose Dr	Orlando	FL	32803	**800-944-9797**	407-628-9700
CMP Inc 3641 Pebble Beach	Northbrook	IL	60062	**888-848-6700**	847-564-8160
Conference Management Services PO Box 2506	Monterey	CA	93942	**800-882-1891**	831-646-3377
Conference & Travel Services Inc 5701 Coventry Ln	Fort Wayne	IN	46804	**800-393-0060**	260-434-6600
Convention Consultants Historic Savannah Foundation Special Tours & Meeting Services 117 W Perry St	Savannah	GA	31401	**800-627-5030**	912-234-4088
Convention Planning Services Inc 2453 Orlando Central Pkwy	Orlando	FL	32809	**800-777-5333**	407-851-5122
Creative Concepts International 3 Waters Park Dr Suite 213	San Mateo	CA	94403	**800-222-8882**	650-357-7800
Creative Convention Services 1008 7th Ave Suite 209	Beaver Falls	PA	15010	**800-365-8501**	724-843-7501
Creative Impact Group 155 Revere Dr Suite 1	Northbrook	IL	60062	**800-445-2171**	847-945-7401
Crescent City Consultants 210 Baronne St Suite 1108	New Orleans	LA	70112	**800-899-1191**	504-561-1191
Destination Services of Colorado Inc 0150 E Beaver Creek Blvd	Avon	CO	81620	**800-372-7686**	970-476-6565
Diversified Conference Management Inc 1878 Cypress Point Ct	Ann Arbor	MI	48108	**800-458-2535**	734-665-2535
Event Planning International Corp 7731 Little Ave Suite A	Charlotte	NC	28226	**800-940-2164**	704-943-1003
Expo Group 1740 Hurd Dr	Irving	TX	75038	**800-736-7775**	972-580-9000
Gavel International Corp 2275 Half Day Rd Suite 190	Bannockburn	IL	60015	**800-544-2835**	847-945-8150
Geneva Cos 5 Park Plaza 18th Fl *Cust Svc	Irvine	CA	92614	**800-854-4643***	949-756-2200
GES Exposition Services 950 Grier Dr	Las Vegas	NV	89119	**800-443-9767**	702-263-1500
GT Consultants 3050 Eagle Watch Dr	Woodstock	GA	30189	**800-659-0345**	770-591-1343
Hansen Harry Management Inc 151 Herricks Rd Suite 1	Garden City Park	NY	11040	**800-284-6228**	516-739-2510
Harry Hansen Management Inc 151 Herricks Rd Suite 1	Garden City Park	NY	11040	**800-284-6228**	516-739-2510
Host Communications Inc 546 E Main St	Lexington	KY	40508	**888-484-4678**	859-226-4678
International Destinations Inc 2025 M St NW Suite 500	Washington	DC	20036	**800-833-5254**	202-797-1222
International Meeting Managers Inc 4550 Post Oak Pl Suite 342	Houston	TX	77027	**800-423-7175**	713-965-0566
Maritz Travel Co 1395 N Highway Dr	Fenton	MO	63099	**800-253-7562**	636-827-4000
Mayer Motivations Inc 2434 E Las Olas Blvd	Fort Lauderdale	FL	33301	**888-611-4376**	954-523-0074
MC2 10601 Baur Blvd	Saint Louis	MO	63132	**800-826-3977**	314-569-0333
Meetings & Incentives Group 21760 Stevens Creek Blvd	Cupertino	CA	95014	**800-752-9202**	408-973-1915
National Trade Productions Inc 313 S Patrick St	Alexandria	VA	22314	**800-687-7469**	703-683-8500
On the Scene 54 W Illinois St Suite 550	Chicago	IL	60610	**800-621-5327**	312-661-1440
PGI Inc 44 Canal Ctr Plaza 2nd Fl	Alexandria	VA	22314	**888-744-8326**	703-528-8484
Premier Meetings & Incentives 2150 S Washburn St	Oshkosh	WI	54903	**800-236-5095**	920-236-8030
Professional Information Management 600 Meadowland Pkwy Suite 131	Secaucus	NJ	07094	**800-237-5241**	201-866-2625
R/A Performance Group 135 Main St Suite 1120	San Francisco	CA	94105	**800-235-1446**	415-869-6500
Reed Exhibitions 275 Washington St	Newton	MA	02458	**800-732-2914**	617-630-2260
Resource Connection Inc 161 S Main St	Middleton	MA	01949	**800-649-5228**	978-777-9333
Robustelli Event Services 30 Spring St	Stamford	CT	06902	**888-258-9398**	
Rx Worldwide Meetings Inc 3060 Communications Pkwy Suite 200	Plano	TX	75093	**800-562-1713**	214-291-2920
Schneider Group 5400 Bosque Blvd Suite 680	Waco	TX	76710	**800-375-7363**	254-776-3550
Star Meetings & Events 301 N Morton St	Bloomington	IN	47404	**866-546-1687**	812-331-8800
Total Meeting Resources Inc 1435A McLendon Dr	Decatur	GA	30033	**800-783-5881**	770-496-8580
Vega Group 7220 Washington Ave	New Orleans	LA	70125	**800-771-2979**	504-488-5222

184 CONGLOMERATES

SEE ALSO Holding Companies

Company	City	State	ZIP	Toll-Free	Phone
3M Co 3M Ctr *NYSE: MMM*	Saint Paul	MN	55144	**800-364-3577**	651-733-1110
Alberto-Culver Co 2525 W Armitage Ave *NYSE: ACV*	Melrose Park	IL	60160	**800-333-0005**	708-450-3000
Andersons Inc 480 W Dussel Dr *NASDAQ: ANDE*	Maumee	OH	43537	**800-537-3370**	419-893-5050
Anheuser-Busch Cos Inc 1 Busch Pl *NYSE: BUD*	Saint Louis	MO	63118	**800-342-5283**	314-577-2000
ARAMARK Corp 1101 Market St Aramark Tower *NYSE: RMK*	Philadelphia	PA	19107	**800-999-8989**	215-238-3000
Archer Daniels Midland Co (ADM) 4666 E Faries Pkwy *NYSE: ADM*	Decatur	IL	62526	**800-637-5824**	217-424-5200
Block H & R Inc 4400 Main St *NYSE: HRB*	Kansas City	MO	64111	**800-829-7733**	816-753-6900
Brink's Co PO Box 18100 *NYSE: BCO*	Richmond	VA	23226	**877-877-9119**	804-289-9600
Canadian Tire Corp Ltd PO Box 770 Stn K *TSE: CTR*	Toronto	ON	M4P2V8	**800-387-8803**	416-480-3000
Cendant Corp 9 W 57th St 37th Fl *NYSE: CD*	New York	NY	10019	**877-446-3623**	212-413-1800
Ceridian Corp 3311 E Old Shakopee Rd *NYSE: CEN*	Minneapolis	MN	55425	**800-767-4969**	952-853-8100
Chemed Corp 255 E 5th St Chemed Ctr Suite 2600 *NYSE: CHE*	Cincinnati	OH	45202	**800-224-3633**	513-762-6900
Clear Channel Communications Inc 200 E Basse Rd *NYSE: CCU*	San Antonio	TX	78209	**888-937-6131**	210-822-2828
Clorox Co 1221 Broadway *NYSE: CLX* ■ *Cust Svc	Oakland	CA	94612	**800-292-2808***	510-271-7000
Connell Co 1 Connell Dr	Berkeley Heights	NJ	07922	**800-233-3240**	908-673-3700
Cook Group Inc PO Box 1608	Bloomington	IN	47402	**800-457-4500**	812-331-1025
Delaware North Cos Inc 40 Fountain Plaza	Buffalo	NY	14202	**800-828-7240**	716-858-5000
EBSCO Industries Inc 5724 Hwy 280 E	Birmingham	AL	35242	**800-527-5901**	205-991-6600
Ergon Inc 2829 Lakeland Dr	Jackson	MS	39232	**800-824-2626**	601-933-3000
Fortune Brands Inc 300 Tower Pkwy *NYSE: FO*	Lincolnshire	IL	60069	**800-225-2719**	847-484-4400
GE (General Electric Co) 3135 Easton Tpke *NYSE: GE* ■ *Cust Svc	Fairfield	CT	06828	**800-626-2000***	203-373-2211
General Electric Co (GE) 3135 Easton Tpke *NYSE: GE* ■ *Cust Svc	Fairfield	CT	06828	**800-626-2000***	203-373-2211
H & R Block Inc 4400 Main St *NYSE: HRB*	Kansas City	MO	64111	**800-829-7733**	816-753-6900
Hackney HT Co 502 S Gay St	Knoxville	TN	37902	**800-406-1291**	865-546-1291
Hallwood Group Inc 3710 Rawlins St Suite 1500 *AMEX: HWG*	Dallas	TX	75219	**800-225-0135**	214-528-5588
Hitachi America Ltd 50 Prospect Ave	Tarrytown	NY	10591	**800-448-2244**	914-332-5800
HNI Corp PO Box 1109 *NYSE: HNI*	Muscatine	IA	52761	**800-336-8398**	563-264-7400
Holiday Cos 4567 American Blvd W	Bloomington	MN	55437	**800-745-7411**	952-830-8700
Honeywell International Inc 101 Columbia Rd *NYSE: HON* ■ *Cust Svc	Morristown	NJ	07962	**800-707-4555***	973-455-2000
HT Hackney Co 502 S Gay St	Knoxville	TN	37902	**800-406-1291**	865-546-1291
Ilitch Holdings Inc 2211 Woodward Ave	Detroit	MI	48201	**800-722-3727**	313-983-6000
Ingram Industries Inc PO Box 23049	Nashville	TN	37202	**800-876-2047**	615-298-8200
Jefferson-Pilot Corp 100 N Greene St *NYSE: JP*	Greensboro	NC	27401	**800-487-1485**	336-691-3000
Johnson & Johnson 1 Johnson & Johnson Plaza *NYSE: JNJ*	New Brunswick	NJ	08933	**800-635-6789**	732-524-0400
Kimball International Inc 1600 Royal St *NASDAQ: KBALB*	Jasper	IN	47549	**800-482-1616**	812-482-1600
Kohler Co Inc 444 Highland Dr	Kohler	WI	53044	**800-456-4537**	920-457-4441
Loews Corp 667 Madison Ave *NYSE: LTR*	New York	NY	10021	**800-235-6397**	212-521-2000
Marmon Group Inc 225 W Washington St 19th Fl	Chicago	IL	60606	**800-621-0386**	312-372-9500
McRae Industries Inc PO Box 1239 *AMEX: MRI/A*	Mount Gilead	NC	27306	**800-768-5248**	910-439-6147
NACCO Industries Inc 5875 Landerbrook Dr Suite 300 *NYSE: NC*	Cleveland	OH	44124	**800-531-3964**	440-449-9600
Norfolk Southern Corp 3 Commercial Pl *NYSE: NSC* ■ *Cust Svc	Norfolk	VA	23510	**800-635-5768***	757-629-2600
PepsiCo Inc 700 Anderson Hill Rd *NYSE: PEP* ■ *PR	Purchase	NY	10577	**800-433-2652***	914-253-2000
Power Corp of Canada 751 Victoria Sq *TSE: POW*	Montreal	QC	H2Y2J3	**800-890-7440**	514-286-7400
Seaboard Corp 9000 W 67th St *AMEX: SEB*	Shawnee Mission	KS	66202	**800-388-4647**	913-676-8800
ServiceMaster Co 3250 Lacey Rd Suite 600 *NYSE: SVM*	Downers Grove	IL	60515	**866-782-6787**	630-663-2000
Siemens Corp 153 E 53rd St 56th Fl	New York	NY	10022	**800-743-6367**	212-258-4000
SPX Corp 13515 Ballantyne Corporate Pl *NYSE: SPW*	Charlotte	NC	28277	**800-446-2617**	704-752-4400
Steiner Corp 505 E South Temple	Salt Lake City	UT	84102	**800-408-0208**	801-328-8831
Susquehanna Pfaltzgraff Co 140 E Market St	York	PA	17401	**800-999-2811**	717-848-5500
Temple-Inland Inc 1300 S Mopac Expy *NYSE: TIN*	Austin	TX	78746	**800-826-8807**	512-434-8000
Trinity Industries Inc 2525 Stemmons Fwy *NYSE: TRN*	Dallas	TX	75207	**800-631-4420**	214-631-4420
Tyco International Ltd 9 Roszel Rd *NYSE: TYC*	Princeton	NJ	08540	**800-320-2350**	609-720-4200
United Services Automobile Assn (USAA) 9800 Fredericksburg Rd	San Antonio	TX	78288	**800-531-8222**	210-498-2211
UNOVA Inc 6001 36th Ave W *NYSE: UNA*	Everett	WA	98203	**800-829-8959**	425-265-2400
Walter Industries Inc 4211 W Boy Scout Blvd *NYSE: WLT*	Tampa	FL	33607	**800-888-9258**	813-871-4811
Washington Post Co 1150 15th St NW *NYSE: WPO*	Washington	DC	20071	**800-627-1150**	202-334-6000
Weyerhaeuser Co PO Box 9777 *NYSE: WY*	Federal Way	WA	98063	**800-525-5440**	253-924-2345

185 CONSTRUCTION - BUILDING CONTRACTORS - NON-RESIDENTIAL

Company	City	State	ZIP	Toll-Free	Phone
Abrams Construction Inc 1945 The Exchange Suite 350	Atlanta	GA	30339	**800-935-9350**	770-952-3555
Anderson Roy Corp 11400 Reichold Rd	Gulfport	MS	39503	**800-688-4003**	228-896-4000
Armada/Hoffler Construction Co 222 Central Pk Ave Suite 2100	Virginia Beach	VA	23462	**800-766-0543**	757-366-4000
Barlovento LLC 165 Hostdale Dr Suite 1	Dothan	AL	36303	**877-498-6039**	334-983-9979
Bayley Construction Co PO Box 9004	Mercer Island	WA	98040	**800-598-8884**	206-621-8884

				Toll-Free	Phone
Big-D Construction Corp 404 W 400 South Suite 550	Salt Lake City	UT	84101	**877-415-6009**	801-415-6000
Blaine Construction Corp PO Box 10147	Knoxville	TN	37939	**800-424-0426**	865-693-8900
Brasfield & Gorrie LLC 729 S 30th St	Birmingham	AL	35233	**800-239-8017**	205-328-4000
BSI Constructors Inc 6767 Southwest Ave	Saint Louis	MO	63143	**800-769-8090**	314-781-7820
BT Mancini Co Inc 876 S Milpitas Blvd	Milpitas	CA	95036	**800-488-4286**	408-942-7900
BT Mancini Co Inc Brookman Div 876 S Milpitas Blvd Suite 81	Milpitas	CA	95035	**800-488-4286**	408-942-7900
CG Schmidt Inc 11777 W Lake Pk Dr	Milwaukee	WI	53224	**800-248-1254**	414-577-1177
Clark Construction Group LLC 7500 Old Georgetown Rd	Bethesda	MD	20814	**800-827-4422**	301-272-8100
Clayco Construction Co 2199 Innerbelt Business Ctr Dr	Saint Louis	MO	63114	**888-429-3330**	314-429-5100
Daw Inc 12552 S 125 West *Sales	Draper	UT	84020	**800-748-4778***	801-553-9111
Dick Corp 1900 SR 51	Largo	PA	15025	**800-245-6577**	412-384-1000
Diffenbaugh Inc 6865 Airport Dr	Riverside	CA	92504	**800-394-5334**	951-351-6865
Donohoe Cos Inc 2101 Wisconsin Ave NW	Washington	DC	20007	**877-366-6463**	202-333-0880
Drees Co 211 Grandview Dr	Fort Mitchell	KY	41017	**800-647-1711**	859-578-4200
Facility Group Inc 2233 Lake Pk Dr Suite 100	Smyrna	GA	30080	**800-525-2463**	770-437-2700
Fisher Development Inc 1485 Bayshore Blvd Suite 152	San Francisco	CA	94124	**800-227-4392**	415-468-1717
Flintco Inc 1624 W 21st St	Tulsa	OK	74107	**800-947-2828**	918-587-8451
Fru-Con Construction Corp 15933 Clayton Rd	Ballwin	MO	63011	**800-937-8266**	636-391-6700
Gilbane Building Co Mid-Atlantic Regional Office 7901 Sandy Spring Rd Suite 500	Laurel	MD	20707	**800-445-2263**	301-317-6100
Gilbane Building Co Southwest Regional Office 1331 Lamar St Suite 1170	Houston	TX	77010	**800-445-2263**	713-209-1873
Gray James N Construction Co Inc 10 Quality St	Lexington	KY	40507	**800-950-4729**	859-281-5000
Harkins Builders Inc 2201 Warwick Way	Marriottsville	MD	21104	**888-224-5697**	410-750-2600
Haskell Co 111 Riverside Ave	Jacksonville	FL	32202	**800-733-4275**	904-791-4500
Hensel Phelps Construction Co 420 6th Ave PO Box 0	Greeley	CO	80631	**800-826-6309**	970-352-6565
Hunt Construction Group 2450 S Tibbs Ave	Indianapolis	IN	46241	**800-223-6301**	317-227-7800
James N Gray Co 10 Quality St	Lexington	KY	40507	**800-950-4729**	859-281-5000
Jaynes Corp 2906 Broadway NE	Albuquerque	NM	87107	**800-432-5204**	505-345-8591
JR Roberts Corp 7745 Greenback Ln Suite 300	Citrus Heights	CA	95610	**800-551-1534**	916-729-5600
Kinsley Construction Inc 2700 Water St	York	PA	17403	**800-546-7539**	717-741-3841
Lewis Cos 28777 Northwestern Hwy Suite 100	Southfield	MI	48034	**800-968-6808**	248-354-9005
Lyda Builders Inc 12400 Hwy 281 N Suite 200	San Antonio	TX	78216	**800-846-7026**	210-684-1770
Mancini BT Co Inc 876 S Milpitas Blvd	Milpitas	CA	95036	**800-488-4286**	408-942-7900
Mancini BT Co Inc Brookman Div 876 S Milpitas Blvd Suite 81	Milpitas	CA	95035	**800-488-4286**	408-942-7900
MGM Mirage Design Group Inc 3260 Industrial Rd	Las Vegas	NV	89109	**800-477-5110**	702-792-4600
Osborne Construction Co Inc PO Box 97010	Kirkland	WA	98083	**888-270-8221**	425-827-4221
Performance Contracting Inc 6621 E Mission Ave	Spokane	WA	99212	**800-541-4323**	509-535-4814
Perley-Halladay Assoc Inc 1442 Phoenixville Pike	West Chester	PA	19380	**800-248-5800**	610-296-5800
Pizzagalli Construction Co 50 Joy Dr	South Burlington	VT	05403	**800-760-7607**	802-658-4100
Power Construction Co LLC 2360 N Palmer Dr	Schaumburg	IL	60173	**800-307-4048**	847-925-1300
Roberts JR Corp 7745 Greenback Ln Suite 300	Citrus Heights	CA	95610	**800-551-1534**	916-729-5600
Roel Construction Co Inc 3366 Kurtz St	San Diego	CA	92110	**800-662-7635**	619-297-4156
Roy Anderson Corp 11400 Reichold Rd	Gulfport	MS	39503	**800-688-4003**	228-896-4000
Schmidt CG Inc 11777 W Lake Pk Dr	Milwaukee	WI	53224	**800-248-1254**	414-577-1177
Stellar Group 2900 Hartley Rd	Jacksonville	FL	32257	**800-488-2900**	904-260-2900
Suitt Construction Co Inc 201 E McBee Ave Suite 300	Greenville	SC	29601	**800-388-2724**	864-250-5000
Sundt Construction Inc 4101 E Irvington Rd	Tucson	AZ	85714	**800-467-5544**	520-748-7555
Tarlton Corp 5500 W Park Ave	Saint Louis	MO	63110	**888-827-5866**	314-633-3300
Taylor Ball Inc 6100 Thornton Ave Suite 200	Des Moines	IA	50321	**800-373-0330**	515-471-4700
Tishman Realty & Construction Co Inc 666 5th Ave	New York	NY	10103	**800-609-8474**	212-399-3600
Walsh Group Inc 929 W Adams St	Chicago	IL	60607	**800-759-2574**	312-563-5400
Westra Construction Inc W7185 Hwy 49	Waupun	WI	53963	**800-388-3545**	920-324-3545
Whiting-Turner Contracting Co 300 E Joppa Rd	Baltimore	MD	21286	**800-638-4279**	410-821-1100
Williams Service Group Inc 2076 West Park Pl	Stone Mountain	GA	30087	**800-892-0992**	770-879-4000

186 CONSTRUCTION - BUILDING CONTRACTORS - RESIDENTIAL

				Toll-Free	Phone
Arthur Rutenberg Homes Inc 13922 58th St N	Clearwater	FL	33760	**800-274-6637**	727-536-5900
Ball Homes LLC 3609 Walden Dr	Lexington	KY	40517	**888-268-1101**	859-268-1191
Bozzuto Group 7850 Walker Dr Suite 400	Greenbelt	MD	20770	**800-718-0200**	301-220-0100
Breeden Homes Inc 366 E 40th Ave *Sales	Eugene	OR	97405	**800-322-3198***	541-686-9431
Centex Corp 2728 N Harwood St *NYSE: CTX*	Dallas	TX	75201	**888-847-5130**	214-981-5000
Drees Co 211 Grandview Dr	Fort Mitchell	KY	41017	**800-647-1711**	859-578-4200
Eyde Construction Co PO Box 4218	East Lansing	MI	48826	**800-442-3933**	517-351-2480
Harkins Builders Inc 2201 Warwick Way	Marriottsville	MD	21104	**888-224-5697**	410-750-2600
House Doctors 575 Chamber Dr	Milford	OH	45150	**800-319-3359**	513-831-0100
JB Sandlin Cos 5137 Davis Blvd	Fort Worth	TX	76180	**800-821-4663**	817-281-3509
Jim Walter Homes Inc PO Box 31601	Tampa	FL	33631	**800-492-5837**	813-871-4811
Jones Co 16640 Chesterfield Grove Rd Suite 200	Chesterfield	MO	63005	**866-675-6637**	636-537-7000
Kopf Builders Inc 420 Avon Belden Rd	Avon Lake	OH	44012	**800-242-8913**	440-933-6908
LAS Enterprises Inc 2413 L & A Rd	Metairie	LA	70001	**800-264-1527**	504-887-1515
Levitt & Sons Corp 7777 Glades Rd Suite 410	Boca Raton	FL	33434	**800-741-5110**	561-482-5100
Miller WC & AN Cos 4701 Sangamore Rd	Bethesda	MD	20816	**800-599-4711**	301-229-4000
Nordaas American Homes Co Inc 10091 State Hwy 22 PO Box 116	Minnesota Lake	MN	56068	**800-658-7076**	507-462-3331
Purcell Construction Co 1550 Starkey Rd	Largo	FL	33771	**888-568-1555**	
Realen Homes LP 1040 Stoney Hill Rd Suite 100	Yardley	PA	19067	**800-732-5368**	215-497-0600
Rio Verde Development Inc 18815 E Four Peaks Blvd	Rio Verde	AZ	85263	**800-233-7103**	480-471-3350
Rutenberg Arthur Homes Inc 13922 58th St N	Clearwater	FL	33760	**800-274-6637**	727-536-5900
Shreve Land Co Inc 666 Travis St Suite 100	Shreveport	LA	71101	**800-259-0056**	318-226-0056
Stabile Cos Inc 21 Manchester St	Merrimack	NH	03054	**800-432-4892**	603-889-0318
Stanmar Inc 130 Boston Post Rd	Sudbury	MA	01776	**800-617-3607**	978-443-9922
TH Properties 345 Main St *Sales	Harleysville	PA	19438	**800-225-5847***	215-513-4270
Tishman Realty & Construction Co Inc 666 5th Ave	New York	NY	10103	**800-609-8474**	212-399-3600
United-Bilt Homes Inc PO Box 4346	Shreveport	LA	71134	**800-551-8955**	318-861-4572
Wagoner Construction Co Inc PO Box 1127	Salisbury	NC	28145	**800-222-1027**	704-633-1431
Walsh Group Inc 929 W Adams St	Chicago	IL	60607	**800-759-2574**	312-563-5400
Walter Jim Homes Inc PO Box 31601	Tampa	FL	33631	**800-492-5837**	813-871-4811
Wayne Homes LLC 3777 Boettler Oaks Dr	Uniontown	OH	44685	**800-686-5354**	330-896-7611
WC & AN Miller Cos 4701 Sangamore Rd	Bethesda	MD	20816	**800-599-4711**	301-229-4000

187 CONSTRUCTION - HEAVY CONSTRUCTION CONTRACTORS

187-1 Communications Lines & Towers Construction

				Toll-Free	Phone
Allied Tower Co 4646 Mandale Rd	Alvin	TX	77511	**800-207-4623**	281-331-9627
Barlovento LLC 165 Hostdale Dr Suite 1	Dothan	AL	36303	**877-498-6039**	334-983-9979
CLS Group 1015 Waterwood Pkwy Suite D	Edmond	OK	73034	**800-580-5460**	405-348-5460
Commonwealth Communications Inc 105 Carnegie Ctr	Princeton	NJ	08540	**800-746-4726**	609-734-3700
General Fiber Communications Inc 100 W Elm St Suite 300	Conshohocken	PA	19428	**866-285-3048**	610-772-2100
NAT-COM Inc 2622 Audubon Rd	Audubon	PA	19403	**800-486-7947**	610-666-7947
Radian Communications Services Corp 2700 Matheson Blvd E West Tower Suite 800	Mississauga	ON	L4W4V9	**866-472-3126**	905-212-8200
Seacomm Erectors Inc 32527 SR 2	Sultan	WA	98294	**800-497-8320**	360-793-6564
Swager Communications Inc 501 E Swager Dr	Fremont	IN	46737	**800-968-5601**	260-495-5165
Tower 2000 Inc 310 60th St NW	Sauk Rapids	MN	56379	**877-720-6249**	320-253-5489

187-2 Foundation Drilling & Pile Driving

				Toll-Free	Phone
Barcus LG & Sons Inc 1430 State Ave	Kansas City	KS	66102	**800-255-0180**	913-621-1100
Brode WM Co 100 Elizabeth St PO Box 299	Newcomerstown	OH	43832	**800-848-9217**	740-498-5121
Coastal Caisson Corp 12290 US Hwy 19 N	Clearwater	FL	33764	**800-723-0015**	727-536-4748
LG Barcus & Sons Inc 1430 State Ave	Kansas City	KS	66102	**800-255-0180**	913-621-1100
Misener Marine Construction Inc 5600 W Commerce St	Tampa	FL	33616	**866-211-9742**	813-839-8441
WM Brode Co 100 Elizabeth St PO Box 299	Newcomerstown	OH	43832	**800-848-9217**	740-498-5121

187-3 Golf Course Construction

				Toll-Free	Phone
DBI Golf 408 6th St	Prinsburg	MN	56281	**800-328-8949**	320-978-6011
Formost Construction Co 41220 Guava St	Murrieta	CA	92562	**800-247-7532**	951-698-7270
Harris Miniature Golf 141 W Burk Ave	Wildwood	NJ	08260	**888-294-6530**	609-522-4200
MacCurrach Golf Construction Inc 3501 Faye Rd	Jacksonville	FL	32226	**800-646-1581**	904-646-1581

187-4 Highway, Street, Bridge, Tunnel Construction

				Toll-Free	Phone
Adams Construction Co 523 Rutherford Ave NE	Roanoke	VA	24016	**800-523-4417**	540-982-2366
Allen Co Inc PO Box 537	Winchester	KY	40392	**888-744-3361**	859-744-3361
APAC Atlantic Inc PO Box 399	Kinston	NC	28502	**800-849-1400**	252-527-8021
APAC Inc 900 Ashwood Pkwy Suite 700	Atlanta	GA	30338	**800-241-7074**	770-392-5300
Ashmore Brothers Inc PO Box 529	Greer	SC	29652	**800-601-5884**	864-879-7311
Baker Michael Corp 100 Airside Dr Airsite Business Pk *AMEX: BKR*	Moon Township	PA	15108	**800-553-1153**	412-269-6300
Baldwin Contracting Co Inc 4509 Skyway Dr	Marysville	CA	95901	**800-682-5726**	530-742-5141
Bizzack Inc 2265 Executive Dr	Lexington	KY	40505	**800-599-0424**	859-299-8001
Blattner DH & Sons Inc 400 CR 50	Avon	MN	56310	**800-877-2866**	320-356-7351
Blue Rock Industries 58 Main St	Westbrook	ME	04092	**800-439-2561**	207-854-2561
Boh Brothers Construction Co LLC 730 S Tonti St	New Orleans	LA	70119	**800-284-3377**	504-821-2400
CA Rasmussen Inc 2360 Shasta Way	Simi Valley	CA	93065	**800-479-2888**	805-527-9330
Carlo John Inc 45000 River Ridge Dr	Clinton Township	MI	48038	**800-465-6234**	586-416-4500
Central Allied Enterprises Inc 1243 Raff Rd SW	Canton	OH	44710	**800-862-6011**	330-477-6751
Cherry Hill Construction Inc 8211 Washington Blvd	Jessup	MD	20794	**800-262-2606**	410-799-3577
Clark Construction Group LLC 7500 Old Georgetown Rd	Bethesda	MD	20814	**800-827-4422**	301-272-8100
Crowder Construction Co Inc PO Box 30007	Charlotte	NC	28230	**800-849-2966**	704-372-3541
Dean Word Co Ltd 1245 River Rd PO Box 310330	New Braunfels	TX	78131	**800-683-3926**	830-625-2365
DH Blattner & Sons Inc 400 CR 50	Avon	MN	56310	**800-877-2866**	320-356-7351
Dick Corp 1900 SR 51	Largo	PA	15025	**800-245-6577**	412-384-1000
Dickerson Florida Inc PO Drawer 719	Stuart	FL	34995	**800-772-6246**	772-287-6820
Drew James H Corp 8701 Zionsville Rd	Indianapolis	IN	46268	**800-772-7342**	317-876-3739
Duininck Brothers Inc PO Box 208	Prinsburg	MN	56281	**800-328-8949**	320-978-6011
Flatiron Structures Co Inc PO Box 2239	Longmont	CO	80502	**800-333-1760**	303-485-4050
FNF Construction Inc 115 S 48th St	Tempe	AZ	85281	**800-542-9490**	480-784-2910
Frank W Whitcomb Construction Corp PO Box 1000	Walpole	NH	03608	**800-238-7283**	603-445-5555

Classified Section

Company / Address	City	State	ZIP	Toll-Free	Phone
Fred Weber Inc 2320 Creve Coeur Mill Rd	Maryland Heights	MO	63043	**800-808-0980**	314-344-0070
Gallagher Asphalt Corp 18100 S Indiana Ave.	Thornton	IL	60476	**800-536-7160**	708-877-7160
Glasgow Inc PO Box 1089	Glenside	PA	19038	**888-222-7570**	215-884-8800
Gray & Sons Inc PO Box 8	Butler	MD	21023	**800-254-0752**	410-771-4311
Gulf Asphalt Corp 4116 US Hwy 231	Panama City	FL	32404	**800-300-0177**	850-785-4675
Herzog Contracting Corp PO Box 1089	Saint Joseph	MO	64502	**800-950-1969**	816-233-9001
Hubbard Construction Co 1936 Lee Rd 3rd Fl	Winter Park	FL	32789	**800-476-1228**	407-645-5500
Jack B Parson Cos 2350 S 1900 West	Ogden	UT	84401	**888-672-7766**	801-731-1111
James H Drew Corp 8701 Zionsville Rd	Indianapolis	IN	46268	**800-772-7342**	317-876-3739
JF Shea Co Inc 655 Brea Canyon Rd	Walnut	CA	91789	**800-755-7432**	909-594-9500
John Carlo Inc 45000 River Ridge Dr.	Clinton Township	MI	48038	**800-465-6234**	586-416-4500
John R Jurgensen Co 11641 Mosteller Rd	Cincinnati	OH	45241	**800-686-9725**	513-771-0820
Jurgensen John R Co 11641 Mosteller Rd	Cincinnati	OH	45241	**800-686-9725**	513-771-0820
Kamminga & Roodvoets Inc 3435 Broadmoor Ave SE	Grand Rapids	MI	49512	**800-632-9755**	616-949-0800
Keating PJ Co Inc 998 Reservoir Rd	Lunenburg	MA	01462	**800-441-4119**	978-582-9931
Kokosing Construction Co Inc 17531 Waterford Rd	Fredericktown	OH	43019	**800-800-6315**	740-694-6315
Lee Construction Co PO Box 7667	Charlotte	NC	28241	**800-849-5272**	704-588-5272
LeGrand Johnson Construction Co Inc PO Box 248	Logan	UT	84323	**800-286-6820**	435-752-2000
Lionmark Construction Cos 1620 Woodson Rd	Saint Louis	MO	63114	**800-392-4295**	314-991-2180
Manatt's Inc 1775 Old Six Rd	Brooklyn	IA	52211	**800-877-1258**	641-522-9206
MCC Inc PO Box 1137	Appleton	WI	54912	**800-236-8132**	920-749-3360
McCarthy Improvement Co Inc 5401 Victoria Ave	Davenport	IA	52807	**800-728-0322**	563-359-0321
Michael Baker Corp 100 Airsite Dr Airsite Business Pk. *AMEX: BKR*	Moon Township	PA	15108	**800-553-1153**	412-269-6300
Milestone Contractors LP 3410 S-650 E	Columbus	IN	47203	**800-559-7910**	812-579-5248
Modern Continental Construction Co 600 Memorial Dr	Cambridge	MA	02139	**800-833-6307**	617-864-6300
Nesbitt Contracting Co Inc 100 S Price Rd	Tempe	AZ	85281	**800-966-4188**	480-894-2831
Overstreet Paving Co 17728 US Hwy 41	Spring Hill	FL	34610	**800-741-1631**	352-796-1631
Parson Jack B Cos 2350 S 1900 West	Ogden	UT	84401	**888-672-7766**	801-731-1111
Parsons Corp 100 W Walnut St	Pasadena	CA	91124	**800-883-7300**	626-440-2000
Perry Engineering Co Inc 1945 Millwood Pike	Winchester	VA	22602	**800-272-4310**	540-667-4310
Pike Industries Inc 3 Eastgate Park Rd	Belmont	NH	03220	**800-283-7453**	603-527-5100
PJ Keating Co 998 Reservoir Rd	Lunenburg	MA	01462	**800-441-4119**	978-582-9931
Professional Construction Services Inc 8001 Downman Rd	New Orleans	LA	70126	**800-562-4318**	504-241-8001
Ranger Construction Industries Inc 101 Sansbury's Way	West Palm Beach	FL	33411	**800-969-9402**	561-793-9400
Rasmussen CA Inc 2360 Shasta Way	Simi Valley	CA	93065	**800-479-2888**	805-527-9330
Ryan Inc Eastern 786 S Military Trail	Deerfield Beach	FL	33442	**800-433-1476**	954-427-5599
Scott Construction Inc PO Box 340	Lake Delton	WI	53940	**800-843-1556**	608-254-2555
Scruggs Co Inc PO Box 2065	Valdosta	GA	31604	**800-230-7263**	229-242-2388
Shepherd Construction Co Inc 1800 Briarcliff Rd NE	Atlanta	GA	30329	**800-282-0806**	404-325-9350
Sherwood Construction Co Inc 3219 W May St	Wichita	KS	67213	**800-852-6038**	316-943-0211
Sioux Falls Construction Co Inc PO Drawer F	Sioux Falls	SD	57101	**800-888-1640**	605-336-1640
Staker & Parson Cos 2350 S 1900 W	Ogden	UT	84401	**800-748-4100**	801-731-1111
Sundt Construction Inc 4101 E Irvington Rd	Tucson	AZ	85714	**800-467-5544**	520-748-7555
Utility Contractors Inc PO Box 2079	Wichita	KS	67201	**888-766-2576**	316-265-9506
Valley Asphalt Corp 11641 Mosteller Rd	Cincinnati	OH	45241	**800-686-9725**	513-771-0820
Vecellio & Grogan Inc 2251 Robert C Byrd Dr	Beckley	WV	25802	**800-255-6575**	304-252-6575
Walsh Group Inc 929 W Adams St	Chicago	IL	60607	**800-759-2574**	312-563-5400
Washington Corp PO Box 16630	Missoula	MT	59808	**800-832-7329**	406-523-1300
Whitcomb Frank W Construction Corp PO Box 1000	Walpole	NH	03608	**800-238-7283**	603-445-5555
White Oak Corp 7 W Main St	Plainville	CT	06062	**800-828-6195**	860-747-1627
Wilder Construction Co Inc 1525 E Marine View Dr	Everett	WA	98201	**800-377-0954**	425-551-3100
Word Dean Co Ltd 1245 River Rd PO Box 310330	New Braunfels	TX	78131	**800-683-3926**	830-625-2365
Yeager Skanska Inc 1995 Agua Mansa Rd	Riverside	CA	92509	**800-222-5360**	951-684-5360
Young Contractors Inc 2001 Marlin Hwy 6	Waco	TX	76705	**800-460-2324**	254-754-2324

187-5 Marine Construction

Company / Address	City	State	ZIP	Toll-Free	Phone
Bellingham Marine Industries Inc 1001 C St	Bellingham	WA	98225	**800-733-5679**	360-676-2800
Corey Delta Inc 610 Industrial Way	Benicia	CA	94510	**800-707-2260**	707-747-7500
Great Lakes Dredge & Dock Co 2122 York Rd	Oak Brook	IL	60523	**800-323-7100**	630-574-3000
Horizon Offshore Inc 2500 Citywest Blvd Suite 2200	Houston	TX	77042	**877-361-2600**	713-361-2600
JR Filanc Construction Co Inc 4616 North Ave	Oceanside	CA	92056	**877-225-5428**	760-941-7130
King Fisher Marine Services Inc 159 Hwy 316	Port Lavaca	TX	77979	**888-553-6751**	361-552-6751
Manson Construction Co 5209 E Marginal Way S	Seattle	WA	98134	**800-262-6766**	206-762-0850
Misener Marine Construction Inc 5600 W Commerce St	Tampa	FL	33616	**866-211-9742**	813-839-8441
Modern Continental Construction Co 600 Memorial Dr	Cambridge	MA	02139	**800-833-6307**	617-864-6300
RCI Environmental Inc PO Box 1668	Sumner	WA	98390	**800-848-3777**	253-863-5300
Torch Offshore Inc 401 Whitney Ave Suite 400	Gretna	LA	70056	**800-878-6724**	504-367-7030
Washington Corp PO Box 16630	Missoula	MT	59808	**800-832-7329**	406-523-1300

187-6 Mining Construction

Company / Address	City	State	ZIP	Toll-Free	Phone
AME Inc PO Box 909	Fort Mill	SC	29716	**800-849-7766**	803-548-7766
Gunther-Nash Mining Construction Co 2 City Place Dr Suite 380	Saint Louis	MO	63141	**800-261-2611**	314-692-2611
Kokosing Construction Co Inc 17531 Waterford Rd	Fredericktown	OH	43019	**800-800-6315**	740-694-6315
Sundt Construction Inc 4101 E Irvington Rd	Tucson	AZ	85714	**800-467-5544**	520-748-7555

187-7 Plant Construction

Company / Address	City	State	ZIP	Toll-Free	Phone
Big-D Construction Corp 404 W 400 South Suite 550	Salt Lake City	UT	84101	**877-415-6009**	801-415-6000
Brasfield & Gorrie LLC 729 S 30th St	Birmingham	AL	35233	**800-239-8017**	205-328-4000
CCC Group Inc 5797 Dietrich Rd	San Antonio	TX	78219	**888-661-4251**	210-661-4251
Clark Construction Group LLC 7500 Old Georgetown Rd	Bethesda	MD	20814	**800-827-4422**	301-272-8100
Clayco Construction Co 2199 Innerbelt Business Ctr Dr	Saint Louis	MO	63114	**888-429-3330**	314-429-5100
Day & Zimmermann Group Inc 1818 Market St	Philadelphia	PA	19103	**800-523-0786**	215-299-8000
Dick Corp 1900 SR 51	Largo	PA	15025	**800-245-6577**	412-384-1000
Duke/Fluor Daniel 2300 Yorkmont Rd	Charlotte	NC	28217	**800-486-4518**	704-426-2000
Fru-Con Construction Corp 15933 Clayton Rd	Ballwin	MO	63011	**800-937-8266**	636-391-6700
Gray James N Construction Co Inc 10 Quality St	Lexington	KY	40507	**800-950-4729**	859-281-5000
Haskell Co 111 Riverside Ave	Jacksonville	FL	32202	**800-733-4275**	904-791-4500
Hunt Construction Group 2450 S Tibbs Ave	Indianapolis	IN	46241	**800-223-6301**	317-227-7800
James N Gray Co 10 Quality St	Lexington	KY	40507	**800-950-4729**	859-281-5000
JR Roberts Corp 7745 Greenback Ln Suite 300	Citrus Heights	CA	95610	**800-551-1534**	916-729-5600
Koch Specialty Plant Services 12221 E Sam Houston Pkwy N	Houston	TX	77044	**800-497-1789**	713-427-7700
Kokosing Construction Co Inc 17531 Waterford Rd	Fredericktown	OH	43019	**800-800-6315**	740-694-6315
Modern Continental Construction Co 600 Memorial Dr	Cambridge	MA	02139	**800-833-6307**	617-864-6300
Monsanto Enviro-Chem Systems Inc 14522 S Outer 40 Rd	Chesterfield	MO	63017	**800-567-8858**	314-275-5700
Parsons Corp 100 W Walnut St	Pasadena	CA	91124	**800-883-7300**	626-440-2000
Pizzagalli Construction Co 50 Joy Dr	South Burlington	VT	05403	**800-760-7607**	802-658-4100
RCI Environmental Inc PO Box 1668	Sumner	WA	98390	**800-848-3777**	253-863-5300
Roberts JR Corp 7745 Greenback Ln Suite 300	Citrus Heights	CA	95610	**800-551-1534**	916-729-5600
Shook National Corp 4977 Northcutt Pl	Dayton	OH	45414	**800-664-1844**	937-276-6666
Suitt Construction Co Inc 201 E McBee Ave Suite 300	Greenville	SC	29601	**800-388-2724**	864-250-5000
Turner Industries Ltd 8687 United Plaza Blvd Suite 500	Baton Rouge	LA	70809	**800-288-6503**	225-922-5050
US Contractors Inc 622 Commerce St	Clute	TX	77531	**800-897-9882**	979-265-7451
Walsh Group Inc 929 W Adams St	Chicago	IL	60607	**800-759-2574**	312-563-5400
Whiting-Turner Contracting Co 300 E Joppa Rd	Baltimore	MD	21286	**800-638-4279**	410-821-1100

187-8 Railroad Construction

Company / Address	City	State	ZIP	Toll-Free	Phone
Acme Construction Co Inc 7695 Bond St	Cleveland	OH	44139	**800-938-2263**	440-232-7474
Atlas Railroad Construction Co 1253 SR 519 PO Box 8	Eighty Four	PA	15330	**800-245-4980**	724-228-4500
Marta Track Constructors Inc 4390 Imeson Rd	Jacksonville	FL	32219	**888-250-5746**	
Nielsons Skanska Inc 22419 County Rd G	Cortez	CO	81321	**800-638-5545**	970-565-8000
Parsons Corp 100 W Walnut St	Pasadena	CA	91124	**800-883-7300**	626-440-2000
Smith William A Construction Co Inc 6060 Armour Dr	Houston	TX	77020	**800-925-5011**	713-673-6208
Snelson Co Inc 601 W State St	Sedro Woolley	WA	98284	**800-624-6536**	360-856-6511
Swanson Contracting Co 11701 S Mayfield Ave	Alsip	IL	60803	**800-622-6850**	708-388-0623
WE Yoder Inc 41 S Maple St	Kutztown	PA	19530	**800-889-5149**	610-683-7383
William A Smith Construction Co Inc 6060 Armour Dr	Houston	TX	77020	**800-925-5011**	713-673-6208

187-9 Refinery (Petroleum or Oil) Construction

Company / Address	City	State	ZIP	Toll-Free	Phone
ARB Inc 26000 Commercentre Dr	Lake Forest	CA	92630	**800-622-2699**	949-598-9242
Austin Industrial Inc 8031 Airport Blvd	Houston	TX	77061	**800-460-3402**	713-641-3400
Parsons Corp 100 W Walnut St	Pasadena	CA	91124	**800-883-7300**	626-440-2000
Snelson Co Inc 601 W State St	Sedro Woolley	WA	98284	**800-624-6536**	360-856-6511
Turner Industries Ltd 8687 United Plaza Blvd Suite 500	Baton Rouge	LA	70809	**800-288-6503**	225-922-5050
Underground Construction Co Inc PO Box 2000	Benicia	CA	94510	**800-227-2314**	707-746-8800

187-10 Water & Sewer Lines, Pipelines, Power Lines Construction

Company / Address	City	State	ZIP	Toll-Free	Phone
Affholder Inc 17988 Edison Ave	Chesterfield	MO	63005	**800-325-1159**	636-532-2622
APAC Inc 900 Ashwood Pkwy Suite 700	Atlanta	GA	30338	**800-241-7074**	770-392-5300
ARB Inc 26000 Commercentre Dr	Lake Forest	CA	92630	**800-622-2699**	949-598-9242
Aubrey Silvey Enterprises Inc 371 Hamp Jones Rd	Carrollton	GA	30117	**800-206-3815**	770-834-0738
B Frank Joy LLC 5335 Kilmer Pl	Hyattsville	MD	20781	**800-992-3569**	301-779-9400
Filanc JR Construction Co Inc 4616 North Ave	Oceanside	CA	92056	**877-225-5428**	760-941-7130
Fishel Co 1810 Arlingate Ln	Columbus	OH	43228	**800-347-4351**	614-274-8100
Global Industries Ltd PO Box 442 *NASDAQ: GLBL*	Sulphur	LA	70664	**800-525-3483**	337-583-5000
Hall Contracting Corp 6415 Lakeview Rd	Charlotte	NC	28269	**800-741-2117**	704-598-0818
Henkels & McCoy Inc 985 Jolly Rd	Blue Bell	PA	19422	**800-523-2568**	215-283-7600
Hubbard Construction Co 1936 Lee Rd 3rd Fl	Winter Park	FL	32789	**800-476-1228**	407-645-5500
Inco Inc PO Box 2705	Rocky Mount	NC	27802	**800-672-4626**	252-446-1174
Insituform Technologies Inc 702 Spirit 40 Park Dr *NASDAQ: INSU* ■ *Cust Svc	Chesterfield	MO	63005	**800-234-2992***	636-530-8000
Irby Construction Co Inc 815 S State St	Jackson	MS	39215	**866-687-4729**	601-960-7304
JF Shea Co Inc 655 Brea Canyon Rd	Walnut	CA	91789	**800-755-7432**	909-594-9500
Joy B Frank LLC 5335 Kilmer Pl	Hyattsville	MD	20781	**800-992-3569**	301-779-9400
JR Filanc Construction Co Inc 4616 North Ave	Oceanside	CA	92056	**877-225-5428**	760-941-7130
Koch Specialty Plant Services 12221 E Sam Houston Pkwy N	Houston	TX	77044	**800-497-1789**	713-427-7700

Water & Sewer Lines, Pipelines, Power Lines Construction (Cont'd)

Company	City	State	Zip	Toll-Free	Phone
MasTec Energy Services Inc 209 Art Bryan Dr PO Box 1	Asheboro	NC	27204	**800-672-5853**	336-672-1244
Miller Pipeline Corp 8850 Crawfordsville Rd	Indianapolis	IN	46234	**800-428-3742**	317-293-0278
Northeast Construction Inc 100 Hwy 70	Lakewood	NJ	08701	**800-879-8204**	732-364-8200
Penn Line Service Inc PO Box 462	Scottdale	PA	15683	**800-448-9110**	724-887-9110
RCI Environmental Inc PO Box 1668	Sumner	WA	98390	**800-848-3777**	253-863-5300
RH White Construction Co Inc 41 Central St	Auburn	MA	01501	**800-922-8182**	508-832-3295
Snelson Co Inc 601 W State St	Sedro Woolley	WA	98284	**800-624-6536**	360-856-6511
Spiniello Cos 12 E Daniel Rd	Fairfield	NJ	07004	**800-227-8384**	973-808-8383
Sumter Utilities Inc PO Box 579	Sumter	SC	29151	**800-678-8665**	803-469-8585
Underground Construction Co Inc PO Box 2000	Benicia	CA	94510	**800-227-2314**	707-746-8800
Utility Contractors Inc PO Box 2079	Wichita	KS	67201	**888-766-2576**	316-265-9506
Welded Construction LP 26933 Eckel Rd	Perrysburg	OH	43551	**800-874-3548**	419-874-3548
West Valley Construction Co Inc 580 McGlincey Ln	Campbell	CA	95008	**800-588-5510**	408-371-5510
Wharton-Smith Inc 750 County Rd 15 PO Box 471028	Lake Monroe	FL	32747	**888-393-0068**	407-321-8410
White RH Construction Co Inc 41 Central St	Auburn	MA	01501	**800-922-8182**	508-832-3295
Willbros Engineers Inc 2087 E 71st St	Tulsa	OK	74136	**800-434-8970**	918-496-0400

188 CONSTRUCTION - SPECIAL TRADE CONTRACTORS

188-1 Building Equipment Installation or Erection

Company	City	State	Zip	Toll-Free	Phone
AWC Commercial Window Coverings Inc 825 W Williamson Way	Fullerton	CA	92832	**800-252-2280**	714-879-3880
Baltimore Rigging Co Inc 7475 Lake Dr	Baltimore	MD	21237	**800-626-2150**	410-574-7300
Bigge Crane & Rigging Co Inc 10700 Bigge St PO Box 1657	San Leandro	CA	94577	**888-337-2444**	510-638-8100
Columbia Elevator Products Co Inc 175 N Main St	Port Chester	NY	10573	**877-265-3538**	914-937-7100
Commercial Contracting Corp 4260 N Atlantic Blvd	Auburn Hills	MI	48326	**800-521-4386**	248-209-0500
Delta/Beckwith Elevator Co 274 Southampton St	Boston	MA	02118	**800-648-8767**	617-427-5525
KONE Inc 1 Kone Ct	Moline	IL	61265	**800-334-9556**	309-764-6771
Mainco Elevator Services Inc 5-25 51st Ave	Long Island City	NY	11101	**800-464-6487**	718-786-3301
R & O Elevator Co Inc 8310 Pillsbury Ave S	Bloomington	MN	55420	**800-735-3046**	952-888-9255
San Francisco Elevator Co Inc 1940 Oakdale Ave	San Francisco	CA	94124	**800-310-1397**	415-821-1402
Schindler Elevator Corp 20 Whippany Rd	Morristown	NJ	07960	**800-225-3123**	973-397-6500
Southern Elevator Co Inc 130 O'Connor St	Greensboro	NC	27416	**800-373-0058**	336-274-2401
Taft Contracting Co Inc 9000 W 67th St	Hodgkins	IL	60525	**800-942-9385**	708-656-7500
Thyssen Elevator Co 15141 E Whittier Blvd Suite 505	Whittier	CA	90603	**800-288-3538**	562-693-9491

188-2 Carpentry & Flooring Contractors

Company	City	State	Zip	Toll-Free	Phone
Archadeck 2112 W Laburnum Ave Suite 100	Richmond	VA	23227	**800-722-4668**	804-353-6999
Bonitz Contracting Co Inc 645 Rosewood Dr	Columbia	SC	29201	**800-452-7281**	803-799-0181
Carpenter Contractors of America 941 SW 12th Ave	Pompano Beach	FL	33069	**800-959-8805**	954-781-2660
Cincinnati Floor Co Inc 5162 Broerman Ave	Cincinnati	OH	45217	**800-886-4501**	513-641-4500
Covington Flooring Co Inc 288-A Oxmore Ct	Birmingham	AL	35209	**800-824-1229**	205-328-2330
DuPont Flooring Systems 3445 Millennium Ct	Columbus	OH	43219	**800-572-7823**	614-476-1043
Hampshire John H Inc 320 W 24th St	Baltimore	MD	21211	**800-638-0076**	410-366-8900
John H Hampshire Inc 320 W 24th St	Baltimore	MD	21211	**800-638-0076**	410-366-8900
Overhead Door Co of Sacramento Inc 6756 Franklin Blvd	Sacramento	CA	95823	**800-929-3667**	916-421-3747
Partition Specialties Inc 714 C St Suite 3	San Rafael	CA	94901	**800-982-9255**	415-721-1040
Rock-Tred Corp 3415 W Howard St	Skokie	IL	60076	**800-762-8733**	847-673-8200
Schuck Component Systems Inc 8205 N 67th Ave	Glendale	AZ	85302	**800-666-3661**	623-931-3661
Turner-Brooks Inc 28811 John R Rd	Madison Heights	MI	48071	**800-560-7003**	248-548-3400

188-3 Concrete Contractors

Company	City	State	Zip	Toll-Free	Phone
Allied Erecting & Dismantling Co Inc 2100 Poland Ave	Youngstown	OH	44502	**800-624-2867**	330-744-0808
Ballard SB Construction Co 2828 Shipps Corner Rd	Virginia Beach	VA	23453	**800-296-0209**	757-440-5555
Barcus LG & Sons Inc 1430 State Ave	Kansas City	KS	66102	**800-255-0180**	913-621-1100
Blue Rock Industries 58 Main St	Westbrook	ME	04092	**800-439-2561**	207-854-2561
Goettle Construction Inc 12071 Hamilton Ave	Cincinnati	OH	45231	**800-248-8661**	513-825-8100
Hubbard Construction Co 1936 Lee Rd 3rd Fl	Winter Park	FL	32789	**800-476-1228**	407-645-5500
Inco Inc PO Box 2705	Rocky Mount	NC	27802	**800-672-4626**	252-446-1174
John Rohrer Contracting Co Inc 2820 Roe Lane Bldg S	Kansas City	KS	66103	**800-255-6119**	913-236-5005
Kent Cos Inc 130 60th St SW	Grand Rapids	MI	49548	**800-968-2345**	616-534-4909
LG Barcus & Sons Inc 1430 State Ave	Kansas City	KS	66102	**800-255-0180**	913-621-1100
Marietta Structures Corp PO Box 653	Marietta	OH	45750	**800-633-9969**	740-373-3211
Oldcastle Precast Building Systems Div 1014 Cromwell Bridge Rd	Towson	MD	21286	**800-523-9144**	410-296-1200
Pressure Concrete Inc PO Box 1303	Florence	AL	35631	**800-633-3141**	256-764-5941
RCI Environmental Inc PO Box 1668	Sumner	WA	98390	**800-848-3777**	253-863-5300
Ross Brothers Construction Co Inc PO Box 767	Ashland	KY	41105	**800-910-7222**	606-739-5139
SB Ballard Construction Co 2828 Shipps Corner Rd	Virginia Beach	VA	23453	**800-296-0209**	757-440-5555
Smock Fansler Corp 2910 W Minnesota St	Indianapolis	IN	46241	**800-281-6605**	317-248-8371
TAS Construction Inc 20105 Krahn Rd	Spring	TX	77388	**800-652-2227**	281-350-0832
Western Group 1637 N Warson Rd *Cust Svc	Saint Louis	MO	63132	**800-325-2801***	314-427-6733

188-4 Electrical Contractors

Company	City	State	Zip	Toll-Free	Phone
Althoff Industries Inc 8001 S Rt 31	Crystal Lake	IL	60014	**800-225-2443**	815-455-7000
Amelco Corp 19208 S Vermont Ave	Gardena	CA	90248	**800-788-8838**	310-327-3070
Anixter Inc 2301 Patriot Blvd	Glenview	IL	60025	**800-323-8166**	847-677-2600
APi Electric 4631 Mike Colaillo Dr	Duluth	MN	55807	**866-624-0064**	218-624-0064
Arc Electric Inc PO Box 1667	Chesapeake	VA	23327	**800-989-1053**	757-424-5164
Aschinger Electric Co PO Box 26322	Fenton	MO	63026	**800-280-4061**	636-343-1211
Baker Electric Inc 111 SW Jackson Ave	Des Moines	IA	50315	**800-779-6774**	515-288-6774
Barlovento LLC 165 Hostdale Dr Suite 1	Dothan	AL	36303	**877-498-6039**	334-983-9979
Bell Electrical Contractors Inc 128 Millwell Dr	Maryland Heights	MO	63043	**800-717-2355**	314-739-7744
Berwick Electric Co 3450 N Nevada Ave Suite 100	Colorado Springs	CO	80907	**800-442-0854**	719-632-7683
Blumenthal-Kahn Electric LP 10233 S Dolfield Rd	Owings Mills	MD	21117	**800-238-8012**	410-363-1200
Bodine Electric of Decatur Inc PO Box 976	Decatur	IL	62525	**800-252-3369**	217-423-2593
Bolton Corp 919 W Morgan St	Raleigh	NC	27603	**800-438-1098**	919 828 9021
Broadway Electrical Service Co Inc PO Box 3250	Knoxville	TN	37927	**800-516-6992**	865-524-1851
Bruce & Merrilees Electric Co 930 Cass St	New Castle	PA	16106	**800-652-5560**	724-652-5566
Casey Electric Inc 245 Preston St	Jackson	TN	38301	**800-424-0428**	731-424-7741
Coastal Mechanical Services Ltd 191 N Travis St	San Benito	TX	78586	**800-568-2612**	956-399-5157
Collins Electric Co Inc 53 2nd Ave	Chicopee	MA	01020	**800-321-4459**	413-592-9221
Compel Corp 10410 Pioneer Blvd Suite 7	Santa Fe Springs	CA	90670	**800-553-1162**	562-946-8321
Dashiell Corp PO Box 1300	Deer Park	TX	77536	**800-736-6400**	281-479-7407
Davis Electrical Constructors Inc PO Box 1907	Greenville	SC	29602	**800-849-3284**	864-250-2500
Dycom Industries Inc 4440 PGA Blvd Suite 500 *NYSE: DY*	Palm Beach Gardens	FL	33410	**877-210-0347**	561-627-7171
Dynalectric Corp 4462 Corporate Ctr Dr	Los Alamitos	CA	90720	**800-729-0444**	714-828-7000
EC Co PO Box 10286	Portland	OR	97296	**800-462-3370**	503-224-3511
EC Ernst Inc 1420 Ritchie Marlboro Rd	Capitol Heights	MD	20743	**800-683-7770**	301-350-7770
Edwin L Heim Co 1918 Greenwood St	Harrisburg	PA	17104	**800-692-7317**	717-233-8711
Electric Machinery Enterprises Inc 2515 E Hanna Ave	Tampa	FL	33610	**800-824-2557**	813-238-5010
Electrical Corp of America 7320 Arlington Ave	Raytown	MO	64133	**800-426-9453**	816-737-3206
Ernst EC Inc 1420 Ritchie Marlboro Rd	Capitol Heights	MD	20743	**800-683-7770**	301-350-7770
Flowers Construction Co Inc PO Box 1207	Hillsboro	TX	76645	**800-792-3295**	254-582-2501
G & M Electrical Contractors Co 1746 N Richmond St	Chicago	IL	60647	**800-546-8050**	773-278-8200
Gaylor Electric 11711 N College Ave Suite 150	Carmel	IN	46032	**800-878-0577**	317-843-0577
GEM Industrial Inc 6842 Commodore Dr	Walbridge	OH	43465	**800-837-5909**	419-666-6554
GR Sponaugle & Sons Inc 4391 Chambers Hill Rd	Harrisburg	PA	17111	**800-866-7036**	717-564-1515
Griffin Wayne J Electric Inc 116 Hopping Brook Rd	Holliston	MA	01746	**800-421-0151**	508-429-8830
GSL Electric Inc 8540 S Sandy Pkwy	Sandy	UT	84070	**800-221-4135**	801-565-0088
Guarantee Electrical Co 3405 Bent Ave	Saint Louis	MO	63116	**800-854-4326**	314-772-5400
Gulf States Inc 6711 E Hwy 332	Freeport	TX	77541	**800-231-9849**	979-233-5555
Heim Edwin L Co 1918 Greenwood St	Harrisburg	PA	17104	**800-692-7317**	717-233-8711
Helix Electric Inc 8260 Camino Santa Fe Suite A	San Diego	CA	92121	**800-554-3549**	858-535-0505
Highlines Construction Co Inc 701 Bridge City Ave PO Box 408	Westwego	LA	70096	**800-762-8860**	504-436-3961
Hooper Corp 2030 Pennsylvania Ave	Madison	WI	53704	**800-999-0451**	608-249-0451
Industrial Power & Lighting Corp 701 Seneca St	Buffalo	NY	14210	**800-639-3702**	716-854-1811
Interstates Electric & Engineering Co Inc PO Box 260	Sioux Center	IA	51250	**800-827-1662**	712-722-1662
JWP/Hyre Electric Co of Indiana Inc 2655 Garfield Ave	Highland	IN	46322	**800-272-9659**	219-923-6100
Koontz-Wagner Electric Co Inc 3801 Voorde Dr	South Bend	IN	46628	**800-345-2051**	574-232-2051
Long Electric Co Inc 1310 S Franklin Rd	Indianapolis	IN	46239	**800-356-2450**	317-356-2455
Mass Electric Construction Co 180 Guest St	Boston	MA	02135	**800-933-6322**	617-254-1015
Merit Electric Co Inc 6520 125th Ave N	Largo	FL	33773	**800-539-3900**	727-536-5945
Miller Electric Co 2251 Rosselle St *Sales	Jacksonville	FL	32204	**800-554-4761***	904-388-8000
Mona Electrical Co 7915 Malcolm Rd Suite 102	Clinton	MD	20735	**800-438-6662**	301-868-8400
Motor City Electric Co Inc 9446 Grinnell St	Detroit	MI	48213	**800-860-8020**	248-585-8200
Newtron Group Inc 8183 W El Cajon Dr	Baton Rouge	LA	70815	**800-644-2752**	225-927-8921
Peoples Electrical Contractors Inc 277 E Fillmore Ave	Saint Paul	MN	55107	**888-777-3409**	651-227-7711
Perreca Electric Co 520 Broadway	Newburgh	NY	12550	**800-973-7732**	845-562-4080
Petrocelli Electric Co Inc 2209 Queens Plaza N	Long Island City	NY	11101	**800-253-2721**	718-752-2200
Pike Electric Inc 100 Pike Way	Mount Airy	NC	27030	**800-343-7453**	336-789-2171
Power City Electric Inc 3327 E Olive Ave	Spokane	WA	99202	**800-877-8549**	509-535-8500
Pritchard Electric Co Inc PO Box 2503	Huntington	WV	25725	**877-457-8904**	304-529-2566
Professional Construction Services Inc 8001 Downman Rd	New Orleans	LA	70126	**800-562-4318**	504-241-8001
Ready Electric Co Inc 2030 Frankfort Ave	Louisville	KY	40206	**800-536-2512**	502-893-2511
Red Simpson Inc PO Box 12120	Alexandria	LA	71315	**800-737-4733**	318-487-1074
Regency Electric 4348 Southpoint Blvd Suite 400	Jacksonville	FL	32216	**877-309-0204**	904-281-0600
Rex Moore Electrical Contractors & Engineers 3601 Parkway Pl	West Sacramento	CA	95691	**800-266-1922**	916-372-1300
Romanoff Electric Corp 5055 Enterprise Blvd	Toledo	OH	43612	**800-866-2627**	419-726-2627
Ronco Communications & Electronics Inc 595 Sheridan Dr	Tonawanda	NY	14150	**888-879-8011**	716-873-0760
Rosendin Electric Inc 880 N Mabury Rd	San Jose	CA	95133	**800-540-4734**	408-286-2800
SASCO Electric 12900 Alondra Blvd	Cerritos	CA	90703	**800-477-4422**	562-926-0900
Shambaugh & Son LP 7614 Opportunity Dr	Fort Wayne	IN	46825	**800-234-9988**	260-487-7777
Shawver & Son Inc 144 NE 44th St	Oklahoma City	OK	73105	**800-320-5121**	405-525-9451
Southern Air Inc PO Box 4205	Lynchburg	VA	24502	**800-743-1214**	434-385-6200
Sponaugle GR & Sons Inc 4391 Chambers Hill Rd	Harrisburg	PA	17111	**800-866-7036**	717-564-1515
Starr Electric Co Inc PO Box 9298	Greensboro	NC	27429	**800-732-0241**	336-275-0241
Steiny & Co Inc 221 N Ardmore Ave PO Box 74901	Los Angeles	CA	90004	**800-350-2331**	213-382-2331

Company / Address	City	State	ZIP	Toll-Free	Phone
Sturgeon Electric Co Inc 12150 E 112th Ave	Henderson	CO	80640	**800-288-5155**	303-286-8000
Super Electric Construction Co 4300 W Chicago Ave	Chicago	IL	60651	**800-344-1936**	773-489-4400
TEC Corp PO Box 207	Sioux City	IA	51102	**800-832-2936**	712-252-4275
Totem Electric of Tacoma 2332 S Jefferson Ave	Tacoma	WA	98402	**800-562-8478**	253-383-5022
Town & Country Electric 2662 American Dr	Appleton	WI	54915	**800-274-2345**	920-738-1500
Wagner-Smith Co PO Box 672	Dayton	OH	45401	**800-775-7799**	937-298-7481
Wasatch Electric Co Inc 1574 S West Temple	Salt Lake City	UT	84115	**800-999-4511**	801-487-4511
Wayne J Griffin Electric Inc 116 Hopping Brook Rd	Holliston	MA	01746	**800-421-0151**	508-429-8830
West-Fair Electric Contractors Inc PO Box 298	Hawthorne	NY	10532	**800-525-0585**	914-769-8050
West Virginia Electric Corp PO Box 1587	Fairmont	WV	26554	**800-982-3532**	304-363-6900
White Electrical Construction Co PO Box 19629	Atlanta	GA	30325	**888-519-4483**	404-351-5740
Williard Inc 375 Highland Ave	Jenkintown	PA	19046	**800-827-5030**	215-885-5000
Windemuller Electric Inc 1176 Electric Ave	Wayland	MI	49348	**800-333-3641**	616-877-8770

188-5 Excavation Contractors

Company / Address	City	State	ZIP	Toll-Free	Phone
Allied Erecting & Dismantling Co Inc 2100 Poland Ave	Youngstown	OH	44502	**800-624-2867**	330-744-0808
APAC Inc 900 Ashwood Pkwy Suite 700	Atlanta	GA	30338	**800-241-7074**	770-392-5300
Beaver Excavating Co Inc 4650 Southway St SW	Canton	OH	44706	**800-255-3767**	330-478-2151
Bolander Carl & Sons Co Inc 251 Starkey St	Saint Paul	MN	55107	**800-676-6504**	651-224-6299
BR Kreider & Son Inc 63 Kreider Ln	Manheim	PA	17545	**800-689-7651**	717-898-7651
CA Rasmussen Inc 2360 Shasta Way	Simi Valley	CA	93065	**800-479-2888**	805-527-9330
Carl Bolander & Sons Co Inc 251 Starkey St	Saint Paul	MN	55107	**800-676-6504**	651-224-6299
Creamer J Fletcher & Son Inc 101 E Broadway	Hackensack	NJ	07601	**800-835-9801**	201-488-9800
Feutz Contractors Inc 1120 N Main St PO Box 130	Paris	IL	61944	**800-252-0273**	217-465-8402
Foundation Constructors Inc 81 Big Break Rd PO Box 97	Oakley	CA	94561	**800-841-8740**	925-625-4455
George J Igel & Co Inc 2040 Alum Creek Dr	Columbus	OH	43207	**800-345-4435**	614-445-8421
Goettle Construction Inc 12071 Hamilton Ave	Cincinnati	OH	45231	**800-248-8661**	513-825-8100
Hayward Baker Inc 1130 Annapolis Rd Suite 202	Odenton	MD	21113	**800-456-6548**	410-551-8200
Igel George J & Co Inc 2040 Alum Creek Dr	Columbus	OH	43207	**800-345-4435**	614-445-8421
Inco Inc PO Box 2705	Rocky Mount	NC	27802	**800-672-4626**	252-446-1174
Independence Excavating Inc 5720 Schaaf Rd	Independence	OH	44131	**800-524-3478**	216-524-1700
J Fletcher Creamer & Son Inc 101 E Broadway	Hackensack	NJ	07601	**800-835-9801**	201-488-9800
Kamminga & Roodvoets Inc 3435 Broadmoor Ave SE	Grand Rapids	MI	49512	**800-632-9755**	616-949-0800
Kreider BR & Son Inc 63 Kreider Ln	Manheim	PA	17545	**800-689-7651**	717-898-7651
Larry's Inc 2020 Schoonover St	Gillette	WY	82718	**800-967-1473**	307-682-5394
McAninch Corp 6800 Lake Dr Suite 125	West Des Moines	IA	50266	**800-383-3201**	515-267-2500
Moretrench American Corp 100 Stickle Ave PO Box 316	Rockaway	NJ	07866	**800-394-6673**	973-627-2100
Nelson & Belding Contractors Corp 17626 S Broadway	Gardena	CA	90248	**800-464-9969**	310-527-6200
Nicholson Construction Co 12 McClane St	Cuddy	PA	15031	**800-388-2340**	412-221-4500
Park Construction Co Inc 500 73rd St NE Suite 123	Minneapolis	MN	55432	**800-328-2556**	763-786-9800
Perry Engineering Co Inc 1945 Millwood Pike	Winchester	VA	22602	**800-272-4310**	540-667-4310
Phillips & Jordan Inc 6621 Wilbanks Rd	Knoxville	TN	37912	**800-955-0876**	865-688-8342
Pleasant Excavating Co Inc 24024 Frederick Rd Suite 200	Clarksburg	MD	20871	**800-842-1180**	301-428-0800
Professional Construction Services Inc 8001 Downman Rd	New Orleans	LA	70126	**800-562-4318**	504-241-8001
Rasmussen CA Inc 2360 Shasta Way	Simi Valley	CA	93065	**800-479-2888**	805-527-9330
Raymond Excavating Co Inc 800 Gratiot Blvd	Marysville	MI	48040	**888-837-6770**	810-364-6881

188-6 Glass & Glazing Contractors

Company / Address	City	State	ZIP	Toll-Free	Phone
Benson Industries Inc 1650 NW Naito Pkwy Suite 250	Portland	OR	97209	**800-999-5113**	503-226-7611
Cartner Glass Systems Inc PO Box 7744	Charlotte	NC	28241	**800-968-2818**	704-588-1976
Elward Construction Co 680 Harlan St	Lakewood	CO	80214	**800-933-5339**	303-239-6303
Enclos Corp 2770 Blue Water Rd	Eagan	MN	55121	**800-831-1108**	651-796-6100
Giroux Glass Inc 850 W Washington Blvd	Los Angeles	CA	90015	**800-684-5277**	213-747-7406
Karas & Karas Glass Co Inc 455 Dorchester Ave	Boston	MA	02127	**800-888-1235**	617-268-8800
Lafayette Glass Co Inc 2841 Teal Rd *Cust Svc	Lafayette	IN	47905	**800-382-7862***	765-474-1402
Lee & Cates Glass Inc 142 Madison St	Jacksonville	FL	32203	**800-433-4188**	904-354-4643
MTH Industries 1 MTH Plaza	Hillside	IL	60162	**800-231-9711**	708-498-1100
Reliant Glass & Door Systems LLC 3208 Washington Ave	Sheboygan	WI	53081	**800-234-7432**	920-458-4611
Sashco Inc 720 S Rochester Ave Suite D	Ontario	CA	91761	**800-600-3232**	909-937-8222
Walters & Wolf 41450 Boscell Rd	Fremont	CA	94538	**800-969-9653**	510-490-1115
Young Group Ltd 1054 Central Industrial Dr	Saint Louis	MO	63110	**800-331-3080**	314-771-3080

188-7 Masonry & Stone Contractors

Company / Address	City	State	ZIP	Toll-Free	Phone
Boettcher Edgar Mason Contractors Inc 1616 S Airport Rd	Traverse City	MI	49686	**800-562-3827**	231-941-5802
Brisk Waterproofing Co Inc 720 Grand Ave	Ridgefield	NJ	07657	**800-942-9228**	201-945-0210
Edgar Boettcher Mason Contractors Inc 1616 S Airport Rd	Traverse City	MI	49686	**800-562-3827**	231-941-5802
International Chimney Corp 55 S Long St	Williamsville	NY	14221	**800-828-1446**	716-634-3967
Mid-Continental Restoration Co Inc PO Box 429	Fort Scott	KS	66701	**800-835-3700**	620-223-3700
Pompano Masonry Corp 880 S Andrews Ave	Pompano Beach	FL	33069	**800-762-7425**	954-946-3033
Pyramid Masonry Contractors Inc 2330 Mellon Ct	Decatur	GA	30035	**800-345-4750**	770-987-4750
Rock & Waterscape Systems Inc 11 Whatney	Irvine	CA	92618	**800-328-9762**	949-770-1936
Western Group 1637 N Warson Rd *Cust Svc	Saint Louis	MO	63132	**800-325-2801***	314-427-6733

188-8 Painting & Paperhanging Contractors

Company / Address	City	State	ZIP	Toll-Free	Phone
Borbon Inc 7312 Walnut Ave	Buena Park	CA	90620	**800-929-1467**	714-994-0170
Cannon Sline Industrial Inc 10 Industrial Hwy MS 38	Lester	PA	19113	**800-729-4600**	610-521-2100
Certa ProPainters Ltd 150 Green Tree Rd Suite 1003	Oaks	PA	19456	**800-462-3782**	610-983-9411
Certified Coatings of California 1045 Detroit Ave	Concord	CA	94518	**888-686-5551**	925-686-1550
College Pro Painters Ltd 200 Dexter Ave 2nd Fl	Watertown	MA	02472	**800-327-2468**	617-924-1300
Hartman-Walsh Painting Co 7144 N Market St	Saint Louis	MO	63133	**800-899-3535**	314-863-1800
Hess Sweitzer Inc 2805 160th St	New Berlin	WI	53151	**800-491-4377**	262-641-9100
Irvin H Whitehouse & Sons Co 4600 Jennings Ln	Louisville	KY	40218	**800-626-5859**	502-966-4176
JP Carroll Co Inc 310 N Madison Ave	Los Angeles	CA	90004	**800-660-0162**	323-660-9230
Long Painting Co 21414 68th Ave S	Kent	WA	98032	**800-678-5664**	253-234-8050
ML McDonald Co PO Box 315	Watertown	MA	02471	**800-733-6243**	617-923-0900
NLP Enterprises Inc PO Box 349	Owings Mills	MD	21117	**800-962-9380**	410-356-7500
Partition Specialties Inc 714 C St Suite 3	San Rafael	CA	94901	**800-982-9255**	415-721-1040
Redwood Painting Co Inc 620 W 10th St	Pittsburg	CA	94565	**800-227-0622**	925-432-4500
Swanson & Youngdale Inc 6565 W 23rd St	Saint Louis Park	MN	55426	**800-486-7824**	952-545-2541
TMI Coatings Inc 2805 Dodd Rd	Saint Paul	MN	55121	**800-328-0229**	651-452-6100

188-9 Plastering, Drywall, Acoustical, Insulation Contractors

Company / Address	City	State	ZIP	Toll-Free	Phone
AC & S Inc 120 N Lime St	Lancaster	PA	17602	**800-487-7255**	717-397-3631
Allied Construction Services & Color Inc PO Box 937	Des Moines	IA	50304	**800-365-4855**	515-288-4855
APi Construction Co 2366 Rose Pl	Saint Paul	MN	55113	**800-223-4922**	651-636-4320
Baker Drywall Co Inc PO Box 38299	Dallas	TX	75238	**800-458-3480**	972-289-5534
BHN Corp 435 Madison Ave	Memphis	TN	38103	**800-238-9046**	901-521-9500
Bouma Corp 4101 Roger B Chaffee Memorial Blvd	Grand Rapids	MI	49548	**800-813-9208**	616-538-3600
CE Thurston & Sons Inc 3335 Croft St *Cust Svc	Norfolk	VA	23513	**800-444-7713***	757-855-7700
Chempower Inc 1501 Raff Rd SW	Canton	OH	44710	**800-442-4299**	330-479-4202
Circle B Co Inc 5636 S Meridian St	Indianapolis	IN	46217	**800-775-5640**	317-787-5746
Crane FL & Sons Inc PO Box 428	Fulton	MS	38843	**800-748-9523**	662-862-2172
Davenport Insulation Inc 7400 Gateway Ct	Manassas	VA	20109	**800-328-9485**	703-631-7744
Daw Technologies Inc 1600 W 2200 S Suite 201	Salt Lake City	UT	84119	**800-596-0901**	801-977-3100
Eliason & Knuth Cos Inc 13324 Chandler Rd	Omaha	NE	68138	**800-365-5760**	402-896-1614
FL Crane & Sons Inc PO Box 428	Fulton	MS	38843	**800-748-9523**	662-862-2172
Hoge-Warren-Zimmermann Co 40 W Cresentville Rd	Cincinnati	OH	45246	**800-322-3521**	513-671-3300
Irex Contracting Group 120 N Lime St	Lancaster	PA	17602	**800-487-7255**	717-397-3633
Jacobson & Co Inc PO Box 511	Elizabeth	NJ	07207	**800-352-2627**	908-355-5200
Land Coast Insulation Inc 4017 2nd St	New Iberia	LA	70560	**800-333-9424**	337-367-7741
Midwest Drywall Co Inc 1351 S Reca Ct	Wichita	KS	67209	**888-722-9559**	316-722-9559
ML McDonald Co PO Box 315	Watertown	MA	02471	**800-733-6243**	617-923-0900
Nastasi & Assoc Inc 147 Herricks Rd	Garden City Park	NY	11040	**800-353-0990**	516-746-1800
Partition Specialties Inc 714 C St Suite 3	San Rafael	CA	94901	**800-982-9255**	415-721-1040
Performance Contracting Inc 6621 E Mission Ave	Spokane	WA	99212	**800-541-4323**	509-535-4814
Precision Walls Inc 4501 Beryl Rd	Raleigh	NC	27606	**800-849-9255**	919-832-0380
Professional Construction Services Inc 8001 Downman Rd	New Orleans	LA	70126	**800-562-4318**	504-241-8001
Spectrum Interiors Inc 2652 Crescent Springs Pike	Crescent Springs	KY	41017	**888-353-2696**	859-331-2696
Thurston CE & Sons Inc 3335 Croft St *Cust Svc	Norfolk	VA	23513	**800-444-7713***	757-855-7700
Turner-Brooks Inc 28811 John R Rd	Madison Heights	MI	48071	**800-560-7003**	248-548-3400
United/Anco Industries Inc 15981 Airline Hwy	Baton Rouge	LA	70817	**800-999-8479**	225-752-2000
Wyatt Inc 4545 Campbells Run Rd	Pittsburgh	PA	15205	**800-966-5801**	412-787-5800

188-10 Plumbing, Heating, Air Conditioning Contractors

Company / Address	City	State	ZIP	Toll-Free	Phone
ACCO Engineered Systems 6265 San Fernando Rd *Cust Svc	Glendale	CA	91201	**800-998-2226***	818-244-6571
Air Comfort Corp 2550 Braga Dr	Broadview	IL	60155	**800-466-3779**	708-345-1900
Alaka'i Mechanical Corp 2655 Waiwai Loop	Honolulu	HI	96819	**800-600-1085**	808-834-1085
Aldag Honold Mechanical Inc 3509 S Business Dr	Sheboygan	WI	53082	**800-967-1712**	920-458-8777
Allied Mechanical Services Inc 2211 Miller Rd	Kalamazoo	MI	49001	**888-237-3017**	269-344-0191
Althoff Industries Inc 8001 S Rt 31	Crystal Lake	IL	60014	**800-225-2443**	815-455-7000
American Leak Detection Inc 888 Research Dr Suite 100	Palm Springs	CA	92262	**800-755-6697**	760-320-9991
Anron Heating & Air Conditioning Inc 440 Wyandanch Ave	North Babylon	NY	11704	**800-924-3336**	631-643-3433
Atlas Air Conditioning Co 4133 Southerland Rd	Houston	TX	77092	**800-460-9973**	713-460-7300
Atlas Welding & Boiler Repair 2960 Webster Ave	Bronx	NY	10458	**800-476-0556**	718-365-6600
B-G Mechanical Service Inc 32 North Rd	East Windsor	CT	06088	**800-992-7386**	860-623-7911
Baker Group 4224 Hubbell Ave	Des Moines	IA	50317	**800-789-8933**	515-262-4000
Ballard SB Construction Co 2828 Shipps Corner Rd	Virginia Beach	VA	23453	**800-296-0209**	757-440-5555
Bernhard Mechanical Contractors Inc 10321 Airline Hwy	Baton Rouge	LA	70816	**888-773-2791**	225-293-2791
Beutler Corp 4700 Lang Ave	McClellan	CA	95652	**800-238-8537**	916-646-2222

Plumbing, Heating, Air Conditioning Contractors (Cont'd)

Company	City	State	Zip	Toll-Free	Phone
Bolton Corp 919 W Morgan St	Raleigh	NC	27603	**800-438-1098**	919-828-9021
Bouchard John & Sons Co 1024 Harrison St	Nashville	TN	37203	**800-842-9156**	615-256-0112
C & R Mechanical 12825 Pennridge Dr	Bridgeton	MO	63044	**800-233-3828**	314-739-1800
Cal-Air Inc 12393 Slauson Ave	Whittier	CA	90606	**800-222-5247**	562-698-8301
CCI Mechanical Inc 758 S Redwood Rd	Salt Lake City	UT	84104	**800-521-7600**	801-973-9000
Coastal Mechanical Services LLC 394 East Dr	Melbourne	FL	32904	**800-391-5757**	321-725-3061
Coastal Mechanical Services Ltd 191 N Travis St	San Benito	TX	78586	**800-568-2612**	956-399-5157
Cobb Mechanical Contractors Inc PO Box 6729	Colorado Springs	CO	80934	**800-808-2622**	719-471-8958
Colonial Mechanical Corp 2820 Ackley Ave	Richmond	VA	23228	**800-849-5504**	804-916-1400
Comfort Systems USA Inc 777 Post Oak Blvd Suite 500 *NYSE: FIX*	Houston	TX	77056	**800-723-8431**	713-830-9600
Cox Engineering Co 35 Industrial Dr	Canton	MA	02021	**800-538-0027**	781-302-3300
Danforth John W Co 2100 Colvin Blvd	Tonawanda	NY	14150	**800-888-6119**	716-832-1940
DeBra-Kuempel 3976 Southern Ave	Cincinnati	OH	45227	**800-395-5741**	513-271-6500
Dunbar Mechanical Inc 2806 N Reynolds Rd	Toledo	OH	43615	**800-719-2201**	419-537-1900
Egan Mechanical Contractors Inc 7625 Boone Ave N	Brooklyn Park	MN	55428	**800-275-3426**	763-544-4131
Engineering & Refrigeration Inc 56 Baldwin Ave	Jersey City	NJ	07306	**800-631-3000**	201-333-4200
Fagan Co 3125 Brinkerhoff Rd	Kansas City	KS	66115	**800-966-1178**	913-621-4444
Flaherty MJ Co 1 Gateway Ctr Suite 450	Newton	MA	02458	**800-370-2280**	617-969-1492
Frank Lill & Son Inc 656 Basket Rd	Webster	NY	14580	**800-756-0490**	585-265-0490
Frank M Booth Inc 222 3rd St	Marysville	CA	95901	**800-540-9369**	530-742-7134
GEM Industrial Inc 6842 Commodore Dr	Walbridge	OH	43465	**800-837-5909**	419-666-6554
Gibb Robert & Sons Inc 205 SW 40th St	Fargo	ND	58103	**800-842-7366**	701-282-5900
Gowan Inc 5550 Airline Dr	Houston	TX	77076	**888-724-6926**	713-696-5400
GR Sponaugle & Sons Inc 4391 Chambers Hill Rd	Harrisburg	PA	17111	**800-866-7036**	717-564-1515
Gross Mechanical Contractors Inc 3622 Greenwood Blvd	Saint Louis	MO	63143	**800-641-0071**	314-645-0077
Grunau Co Inc 1100 W Anderson Ct	Oak Creek	WI	53154	**800-365-1920**	414-216-6900
Gulf States Inc 6711 E Hwy 332	Freeport	TX	77541	**800-231-9849**	979-233-5555
Har-Con Corp 551 N Shepherd Dr Suite 270	Houston	TX	77007	**800-438-0536**	713-869-8451
Harder Mechanical Contractors Inc PO Box 5118	Portland	OR	97208	**800-392-3729**	503-281-1112
Hardy Corp 430 12th St S	Birmingham	AL	35233	**800-289-4822**	205-252-7191
Heating & Plumbing Engineers Inc 407 W Fillmore Pl	Colorado Springs	CO	80907	**800-530-8592**	719-633-5414
Hill York Corp 2125 S Andrews Ave	Fort Lauderdale	FL	33316	**800-777-2971**	954-525-2971
HiMEC Inc 1400 7th St NW	Rochester	MN	55901	**888-454-4632**	507-281-4000
Hooper Corp 2030 Pennsylvania Ave	Madison	WI	53704	**800-999-0451**	608-249-0451
IMCOR-Interstate Mechanical Corp 1841 E Washington St	Phoenix	AZ	85034	**800-628-0211**	602-257-1319
Industrial Piping Inc 800 Culp Rd	Pineville	NC	28134	**800-951-0988**	704-588-1100
Interstate Mechanical Contractors Inc 3200 Henson Rd	Knoxville	TN	37921	**800-556-7072**	865-588-0180
Jackson & Blanc Inc 7929 Arjons Dr	San Diego	CA	92126	**800-236-1121**	858-831-7900
Janazzo Services Corp 140 Norton St	Milldale	CT	06467	**800-297-3931**	860-621-7381
John Bouchard & Sons Co 1024 Harrison St	Nashville	TN	37203	**800-842-9156**	615-256-0112
John W Danforth Co 2100 Colvin Blvd	Tonawanda	NY	14150	**800-888-6119**	716-832-1940
Kinetics Systems Inc 26055 SW Canyon Creek Rd	Wilsonville	OR	97070	**800-888-7597**	503-224-5200
Kuhlman Inc N 56 W 16865 Ridgewood Dr Suite 100	Menomonee Falls	WI	53051	**800-781-9229**	262-252-9400
Lawson Mechanical Contractors 6090 S Watt Ave	Sacramento	CA	95829	**800-491-8808**	916-381-5000
Lee Co Inc 331 Mallory Station Rd	Franklin	TN	37067	**888-567-7747**	615-567-1000
MacDonald-Miller Co Inc 7717 Detroit Ave SE	Seattle	WA	98106	**800-962-5979**	206-763-9400
Martin Petersen Co Inc 9800 55th St	Kenosha	WI	53144	**800-677-1326**	262-658-1326
Masters Inc 7891 Beechcraft Ave	Gaithersburg	MD	20879	**800-257-2871**	301-948-8950
McCarl's Inc 1413 9th Ave	Beaver Falls	PA	15010	**800-643-5660**	724-843-5660
McCartin McAuliffe Mechanical Contractors Inc 4508 Columbia Ave	Hammond	IN	46327	**866-998-6600**	219-931-6600
McClure Co 4101 N 6th St	Harrisburg	PA	17110	**800-382-1319**	717-232-9743
McCrea Equipment Co Inc 4463 Beech Rd	Temple Hills	MD	20748	**800-597-0091**	301-423-4585
McKenney's Inc 1056 Moreland Industrial Blvd SE	Atlanta	GA	30316	**800-489-5000**	404-622-5000
McKinstry Co 5005 3rd Ave S	Seattle	WA	98134	**800-669-6223**	206-762-3311
Mechanical Inc 2279 Rt 20 E	Freeport	IL	61032	**800-747-1955**	815-962-8050
Midwest Mechanical Group 540 Executive Dr *Svc	Willowbrook	IL	60527	**800-600-4047***	630-655-4200
MJ Flaherty Co 1 Gateway Ctr Suite 450	Newton	MA	02458	**800-370-2280**	617-969-1492
Mollenberg-Betz Inc 300 Scott St	Buffalo	NY	14204	**800-368-4998**	716-614-7473
Mr Rooter Corp 1010 N University Pk Dr	Waco	TX	76707	**800-583-8003**	254-745-2444
Murphy Co Mechanical Contractors & Engineers 1233 N Price Rd	Saint Louis	MO	63132	**800-992-6601**	314-997-6600
Nagelbush Mechanical Inc 5385 Nob Hill Rd	Sunrise	FL	33351	**800-354-3111**	954-748-7893
New England Insulation Co 55 North St	Canton	MA	02021	**800-346-6307**	781-828-6600
NewMech Cos Inc 1633 Eustis St	Saint Paul	MN	55108	**800-942-4444**	651-645-0451
Performance Contracting Group Inc 16047 W 110th St	Lenexa	KS	66219	**800-255-6866**	913-888-8600
Petersen Martin Co Inc 9800 55th St	Kenosha	WI	53144	**800-677-1326**	262-658-1326
Piedmont Mechanical Inc 116 John Dodd Rd	Spartanburg	SC	29303	**800-849-5724**	864-578-9114
Postler & Jaeckle Corp 615 South Ave	Rochester	NY	14620	**800-724-4252**	585-546-7450
Process Construction Inc 1421 Queen City Ave	Cincinnati	OH	45214	**888-251-2211**	513-251-2211
PSF Industries Inc 65 S Horton St	Seattle	WA	98134	**800-426-1204**	206-622-1252
RK Mechanical Inc 9300 E Smith Rd	Denver	CO	80207	**800-783-0075**	303-355-9696
Robert Gibb & Sons Inc 205 SW 40th St	Fargo	ND	58103	**800-842-7366**	701-282-5900
Ross Brothers Construction Co Inc PO Box 767	Ashland	KY	41105	**800-910-7222**	606-739-5139
Sanders Brothers Inc 1709 Old Georgia Hwy	Gaffney	SC	29342	**800-527-1684**	864-489-1144
SB Ballard Construction Co 2828 Shipps Corner Rd	Virginia Beach	VA	23453	**800-296-0209**	757-440-5555
Service Experts Inc 2140 Lake Pk Blvd Fl 4T	Richardson	TX	75080	**877-536-8580**	972-497-5000
Shambaugh & Son LP 7614 Opportunity Dr	Fort Wayne	IN	46825	**800-234-9988**	260-487-7777
Southern Air Inc PO Box 4205	Lynchburg	VA	24502	**800-743-1214**	434-385-6200
Southern Industrial Constructors Inc 6101 Triangle Dr	Raleigh	NC	27617	**800-851-0868**	919-782-4600
Speer Mechanical Inc 600 Oakland Park Ave	Columbus	OH	43214	**800-282-6017**	614-261-6331
Stromberg Sheet Metal Works Inc 6701 Distribution Dr	Beltsville	MD	20705	**800-348-5778**	301-931-1000
Tougher Industries Inc 175 Broadway	Albany	NY	12204	**800-836-0752**	518-465-3426
United Industrial Piping Inc 9740 Near Dr	Cincinnati	OH	45246	**800-633-9690**	513-874-2004
Western Air & Refrigeration Co 15914 S Avalon Blvd	Compton	CA	90220	**800-927-1331**	310-327-4400
Williard Inc 375 Highland Ave	Jenkintown	PA	19046	**800-827-5030**	215-885-5000
Worth & Co Inc 6263 Kellers Church Rd	Pipersville	PA	18947	**800-220-5130**	267-362-1100

188-11 Remodeling, Refinishing, Resurfacing Contractors

Company	City	State	Zip	Toll-Free	Phone
Bathcrest Inc 5195 W 4700 S	Salt Lake City	UT	84118	**800-826-6790**	801-972-1110
California Closet Co 1000 4th St Suite 800	San Rafael	CA	94901	**800-873-4264**	415-256-8500
Closet Factory 12800 S Broadway	Los Angeles	CA	90061	**800-692-5673**	310-516-7000
Coustic-Glo International 7111 Ohms Ln	Minneapolis	MN	55439	**800-333-8523**	952-835-1338
Dreammaker Bath & Kitchen by Worldwide PO Box 3146	Waco	TX	76707	**800-583-9099**	254-745-2477
Handyman Connection Inc 9403 Kenwood Rd Suite D-207	Cincinnati	OH	45242	**800-466-5530**	513-771-1122
Kitchen Solvers Inc 401 Jay St	La Crosse	WI	54601	**800-845-6779**	608-791-5516
Kitchen Tune-Up Inc 813 Circle Dr	Aberdeen	SD	57401	**800-333-6385**	605-225-4049
Kott Koatings Inc 27161 Burbank St	Foothill Ranch	CA	92610	**800-452-6161**	949-770-5055
Miracle Method US Corp 4239 N Nevada Ave Suite 115	Colorado Springs	CO	80907	**800-444-8827**	719-594-9091
Perma-Glaze Inc 1638 Research Loop Rd Suite 160	Tucson	AZ	85710	**800-332-7397**	520-722-9718
Re-Bath Corp 1055 S Country Club Dr Bldg 2	Mesa	AZ	85210	**800-426-4573**	480-844-1575

188-12 Roofing, Siding, Sheet Metal Contractors

Company	City	State	Zip	Toll-Free	Phone
ABC Seamless Siding 3001 Fiechtner Dr	Fargo	ND	58103	**800-732-6577**	701-293-5952
AC Dellovade Inc 108 Cavasina Dr	Canonsburg	PA	15317	**800-245-1556**	724-873-8190
Baker Roofing Co 517 Mercury St	Raleigh	NC	27603	**800-849-4096**	919-828-2975
Birdair Inc 65 Lawrence Bell Dr	Amherst	NY	14221	**800-622-2246**	716-633-9500
Bonland Industries Inc 50 Newark-Pompton Tpke	Wayne	NJ	07474	**800-289-7482**	973-694-3211
BT Mancini Co Inc 876 S Milpitas Blvd	Milpitas	CA	95036	**800-488-4286**	408-942-7900
Campbell John J Co Inc 6012 Resources Dr	Memphis	TN	38134	**800-274-7663**	901-372-8400
Centimark Corp 12 Grandview Cir	Canonsburg	PA	15317	**800-558-4100**	724-743-7777
Cramer Dee Inc 4221 E Baldwin Rd	Holly	MI	48442	**888-342-6995**	810-238-2664
DC Taylor Co 312 29th St NE	Cedar Rapids	IA	52402	**800-333-7763**	319-363-2073
Dee Cramer Inc 4221 E Baldwin Rd	Holly	MI	48442	**888-342-6995**	810-238-2664
Dix Corp 4024 S Grove Rd	Spokane	WA	99224	**800-827-8548**	509-838-4455
Flynn Canada Ltd 1500 Valley Rd	Winnipeg	MB	R3H1B3	**800-304-8751**	204-786-6951
Fort Roofing & Sheet Metal Works Inc 4230 Domino Ave	North Charleston	SC	29405	**800-356-6716**	843-554-9711
Gowan Inc 5550 Airline Dr	Houston	TX	77076	**888-724-6926**	713-696-5400
John J Campbell Co Inc 6012 Resources Dr	Memphis	TN	38134	**800-274-7663**	901-372-8400
Kelso WR Co Inc 10201 N Hague Rd	Indianapolis	IN	46256	**800-352-5859**	317-845-5858
Kirk & Blum Mfg Co Inc 3120 Forrer St	Cincinnati	OH	45209	**800-333-5475**	513-458-2600
National International Roofing Corp 11317 Smith Dr	Huntley	IL	60142	**800-221-7663**	847-669-3444
North American Roofing Services Inc 6151 W 80th St	Indianapolis	IN	46278	**800-876-5602**	317-875-5434
Olsson Roofing Co Inc 740 S Lake St	Aurora	IL	60506	**800-445-9655**	630-892-0449
Owen Pacific Inc 1236 S Compton Ave	Los Angeles	CA	90021	**877-693-6722**	213-747-7125
Sanders Brothers Inc 1709 Old Georgia Hwy	Gaffney	SC	29342	**800-527-1684**	864-489-1144
Schreiber Corp 2239 Fenkell St	Detroit	MI	48238	**800-275-3024**	313-864-4900
Seyforth Roofing Co Inc 2601 Wood Dr	Garland	TX	75041	**866-870-2800**	972-864-8591
SingleSource Roofing Corp 1200 McKee Ave	McKees Rocks	PA	15136	**800-777-6610**	412-771-8866
Standard Roofing Co 516 N McDonough St PO Box 1309	Montgomery	AL	36102	**800-239-5705**	334-834-3000
Taylor DC Co 312 29th St NE	Cedar Rapids	IA	52402	**800-333-7763**	319-363-2073
Top Concepts Co 13436 McGrath Rd	Houston	TX	77047	**800-856-0696**	713-434-0696
US Industries Inc 1701 1st Ave	Evansville	IN	47710	**800-264-1501**	812-425-2428
US Seamless Inc 2001 1st Ave N	Fargo	ND	58102	**888-743-3632**	701-241-8888
WR Kelso Co Inc 10201 N Hague Rd	Indianapolis	IN	46256	**800-352-5859**	317-845-5858
Young Group Ltd 1054 Central Industrial Dr	Saint Louis	MO	63110	**800-331-3080**	314-771-3080

188-13 Sprinkler System Installation (Fire Sprinklers)

Company	City	State	Zip	Toll-Free	Phone
AC & S Inc 120 N Lime St	Lancaster	PA	17602	**800-487-7255**	717-397-3631
APi Group Inc Fire Protection Group 2366 Rose Pl	Saint Paul	MN	55113	**800-223-4941**	651-636-4320
August Winter & Sons Inc 2323 N Roemer Rd	Appleton	WI	54911	**800-236-8882**	920-739-8881
Brendle Sprinkler Co Inc PO Box 210609	Montgomery	AL	36121	**800-392-8021**	334-270-8571
Comunale SA Co Inc 2900 Newpark Dr	Barberton	OH	44203	**800-776-7181**	330-706-3040
Cosco Fire Protection Inc 321 E Gardena Blvd	Gardena	CA	90248	**800-827-5612**	323-321-5155
Daly MJ & Sons Inc 110 Mattatuck Heights	Waterbury	CT	06705	**800-992-3603**	203-753-5131
Geo M Robinson & Co 852 85th Ave	Oakland	CA	94621	**800-894-8942**	510-632-7017
Martin Fireproofing Corp PO Box 27 Kenmore Stn	Buffalo	NY	14217	**800-766-3969**	716-692-3680
McDaniel Fire Systems 1055 W Joliet Rd	Valparaiso	IN	46385	**800-348-2632**	219-462-0571
MJ Daly & Sons Inc 110 Mattatuck Heights	Waterbury	CT	06705	**800-992-3603**	203-753-5131
National Automatic Sprinkler Industries 8000 Corporate Dr	Landover	MD	20785	**800-638-2603**	301-577-1700
SA Comunale Co Inc 2900 Newpark Dr	Barberton	OH	44203	**800-776-7181**	330-706-3040

188-14 Structural Steel Erection

Company	City	State	Zip	Toll-Free	Phone
Albany Steel Inc 566 Broadway	Albany	NY	12204	**800-342-9317**	518-436-4851
Allstate Steel Co Inc 130 S Jackson Ave	Jacksonville	FL	32220	**888-781-6040**	904-781-6040
Caldwell Tanks Alliance LLC 57 E Broad St	Newnan	GA	30263	**800-241-1650**	770-253-2600
CBI Services Inc 24 Read's Way	New Castle	DE	19720	**800-642-8675**	302-325-8400
CE Toland & Son 5300 Industrial Way	Benicia	CA	94510	**800-675-1166**	707-747-1000
Central Maintenance & Welding Inc 2620 Keysville Rd PO Drawer 777	Lithia	FL	33547	**877-704-7411**	813-737-1402
Century Steel Erectors Co 210 Washington Ave PO Box 490	Dravosburg	PA	15034	**888-601-8801**	412-469-8800

				Toll-Free	Phone
Dix Corp 4024 S Grove Rd	Spokane	WA	99224	**800-827-8548**	509-838-4455
Fontana Steel Inc 12451 Arron Rt	Rancho Cucamonga	CA	91739	**800-877-8758**	909-899-9993
Keller-Hall Inc 1247 Eastwood Ave	Tallmadge	OH	44278	**800-831-6147**	330-633-6160
Midwest Steel Inc 2525 E Grand Blvd	Detroit	MI	48211	**800-578-7880**	313-873-2220
Patent Construction Systems 1 Mack Centre Dr	Paramus	NJ	07652	**800-969-5600**	201-261-5600
Paxton & Vierling Steel Co 501 Ave H	Carter Lake	IA	51510	**800-831-9252**	712-347-5500
Pittsburg Tank & Tower Co Inc 1 Watertank Pl	Henderson	KY	42420	**800-499-8265**	270-826-9000
Rebar Engineering Inc 10706 Painter Ave	Santa Fe Springs	CA	90670	**800-555-9807**	562-946-2461
Schuff Steel Co 420 S 19th Ave	Phoenix	AZ	85009	**800-528-0513**	602-252-7787
Southeastern Construction & Maintenance Co Inc 1150 Pebbledale Rd PO Box 1055	Mulberry	FL	33860	**800-511-1600**	863-428-1511
Sowles Co 3045 Hwy 13 Suite 100	Eagan	MN	55121	**888-376-9537**	651-287-9700
Steel City Inc 3441 Parkwood Rd SE	Bessemer	AL	35022	**800-264-5075**	205-426-3807
Toland CE & Son 5300 Industrial Way	Benicia	CA	94510	**800-675-1166**	707-747-1000
Universal Steel Buildings Inc 2472 Sunset Dr	Grenada	MS	38902	**800-748-9967**	662-226-4512
Waldinger Corp 2601 Bell Ave	Des Moines	IA	50321	**800-225-0638**	515-284-1911
Washington Ornamental Iron Works Inc 17926 S Broadway	Gardena	CA	90248	**800-332-4766**	310-327-8660
WO Grubb Steel Erection Inc 5120 Jefferson Davis Hwy	Richmond	VA	23234	**800-344-6824**	804-271-9471

188-15 Terrazzo, Tile, Marble, Mosaic Contractors

				Toll-Free	Phone
DMI Tile & Marble Inc 3012 5th Ave S	Birmingham	AL	35233	**800-322-8449**	205-322-8473
Marblelife Inc 805 W North Carrier Pkwy Suite 220	Grand Prairie	TX	75050	**800-627-4569**	972-623-0500

188-16 Water Well Drilling

				Toll-Free	Phone
Grosch Irrigation Co Inc 3110 33rd Rd	Silver Creek	NE	68663	**800-509-2261**	308-773-2261
Ohio Drilling Co 2405 Bostic Blvd SW	Massillon	OH	44647	**800-860-2285**	330-832-1521
RE Chapman Co 30 N Main St	West Boylston	MA	01583	**800-727-6231**	508-835-6231
Rosencrantz-Bemis Enterprises Inc 1105 281 Bypass	Great Bend	KS	67530	**800-466-2467**	620-793-5512
Tri-State Drilling Inc 16940 Hwy 55 W	Plymouth	MN	55446	**800-383-1033**	763-553-1234

188-17 Wrecking & Demolition Contractors

				Toll-Free	Phone
Allied Erecting & Dismantling Co Inc 2100 Poland Ave	Youngstown	OH	44502	**800-624-2867**	330-744-0808
Bierlein Cos Inc 2000 Bay City Rd	Midland	MI	48642	**800-336-6626**	989-496-0066
Bolander Carl & Sons Co Inc 251 Starkey St	Saint Paul	MN	55107	**800-676-6504**	651-224-6299
Carl Bolander & Sons Co Inc 251 Starkey St	Saint Paul	MN	55107	**800-676-6504**	651-224-6299
Cherry Demolition 6131 Selinsky Rd	Houston	TX	77048	**800-444-1123**	713-987-0000
Invirex Demolition Co PO Box 481	Huntington	NY	11743	**800-783-2336**	631-368-4485
Nuprecon Inc 35131 SE Center St	Snoqualmie	WA	98065	**800-442-2072**	425-881-0623
O'Rourke Wrecking Co 660 Lunken Park Dr	Cincinnati	OH	45226	**800-354-9850**	513-871-1400
Penhall International Inc 1801 Penhall Way	Anaheim	CA	92803	**800-736-4255**	714-778-6677
Plant Reclamation 912 Harbour Way S	Richmond	CA	94804	**800-637-0339**	510-233-6552
RCI Environmental Inc PO Box 1668	Sumner	WA	98390	**800-848-3777**	253-863-5300
US Dismantlement LLC 2600 S Throop St	Chicago	IL	60608	**800-648-3801**	312-328-1400

189 CONSTRUCTION MACHINERY & EQUIPMENT

SEE ALSO Industrial Machinery & Equipment (Misc) - Mfr; Material Handling Equipment

				Toll-Free	Phone
Allied Construction Products LLC 3900 Kelley Ave *Cust Svc	Cleveland	OH	44114	**800-321-1046***	216-431-2600
Astec Industries Inc 4101 Jerome Ave *NASDAQ: ASTE*	Chattanooga	TN	37407	**800-468-5938**	423-867-4210
Bandit Industries Inc 6750 Millbrook Rd	Remus	MI	49340	**800-952-0178**	989-561-2270
Besser Appco 442 North WW White Rd	San Antonio	TX	78219	**800-330-5590**	210-333-1111
Bid-Well Corp PO Box 97	Canton	SD	57013	**800-843-9824**	605-987-2603
Boart Longyear Co 2640 W 1700 South *Cust Svc	Salt Lake City	UT	84104	**800-457-5778***	801-972-6430
Bomag Americas Inc 2000 Kentville Rd	Kewanee	IL	61443	**800-782-6624**	309-853-3571
Bucyrus Blades Inc 260 E Beal Ave	Bucyrus	OH	44820	**800-532-5233**	419-562-6015
Cedarapids Inc 909 17th St NE *Cust Svc	Cedar Rapids	IA	52402	**800-821-5600***	319-363-3511
Central Mine Equipment Co Inc 4215 Rider Trail N	Earth City	MO	63045	**800-325-8827**	314-291-7700
Charles Machine Works Inc PO Box 66	Perry	OK	73077	**800-654-6481**	580-336-4402
CRC Evans Pipeline International Inc 10700 E Independence St	Tulsa	OK	74116	**800-395-5192**	918-438-2100
Demag Cranes & Components 29201 Aurora Rd	Cleveland	OH	44139	**800-321-6560**	440-248-2400
ED Etnyre & Co 1333 S Daysville Rd	Oregon	IL	61061	**800-995-2116**	815-732-2116
Esco Corp 2141 NW 25th Ave	Portland	OR	97210	**800-523-3795**	503-228-2141
Franklin Equipment Co 33551 Carver Rd	Franklin	VA	23851	**800-835-7503**	757-562-6111
Gencor Industries Inc 5201 N Orange Blossom Trail	Orlando	FL	32810	**800-234-3626**	407-290-6000
Group Canam Inc 11505 1st Ave Bureau 500 *TSE: CAM*	Saint-Georges	QC	G5Y7X3	**877-499-6049**	418-228-8031
Hensley Industries Inc 2108 Joe Field Rd PO Box 29779	Dallas	TX	75229	**888-406-6262**	972-241-2321
Kennametal Inc Mining & Construction Div 1600 Technology Way	Latrobe	PA	15650	**800-446-7738**	724-539-5000
McLellan Equipment Inc 251 Shaw Rd	South San Francisco	CA	94080	**800-848-8449**	650-873-8100
Metso Dynapac Inc PO Box 615	Schertz	TX	78154	**800-867-6060**	210-474-5770
Midwestern Industries Inc 915 Oberlin Rd SW	Massillon	OH	44647	**877-474-9464**	330-837-4203
Pengo Corp 500 E Hwy 10 *Cust Svc	Laurens	IA	50554	**800-599-0211***	712-845-2540
Philadelphia Mixers Corp 1221 E Main St *Cust Svc	Palmyra	PA	17078	**800-733-1341***	717-832-2800
Pierce Pacific Mfg Inc PO Box 30509	Portland	OR	97294	**800-760-3270**	503-808-9110
Putzmeister America 1733 90th St	Sturtevant	WI	53177	**800-884-7210**	262-886-3200
Ramsey Winch Co Inc 1600 N Garnett Rd	Tulsa	OK	74116	**800-777-2760**	918-438-2760
Stone Construction Equipment Inc 8662 Main St	Honeoye	NY	14471	**800-888-9926**	585-229-5141
Swenson Spreader Co 127 Walnut St	Lindenwood	IL	61049	**888-825-7323**	815-393-4455
Symons Corp 200 E Touhy Ave	Des Plaines	IL	60018	**800-800-7601**	847-298-3200
Telsmith Inc 10910 N Industrial Dr	Mequon	WI	53092	**800-765-6601**	262-242-6600
Terex Corp Crane Div 202 Raleigh St	Wilmington	NC	28412	**800-250-2726**	910-395-8500
Trencor Inc 9600 Corporate Pk Dr	Loudon	TN	37774	**800-527-6020**	865-408-2100
Varel International 1434 Patton Pl Suite 106	Carrollton	TX	75007	**800-827-3526**	972-242-1160
Wacker Corp N 92 W 15000 Anthony Ave	Menomonee Falls	WI	53051	**800-770-0957**	262-255-0500
Young Corp 3231 Utah Ave S	Seattle	WA	98134	**800-321-9090**	206-624-1071

190 CONSTRUCTION MATERIALS

SEE ALSO Home Improvement Centers

190-1 Brick, Stone, Related Materials

				Toll-Free	Phone
Arizona Portland Cement Co 2400 N Central Ave	Phoenix	AZ	85004	**800-462-2475**	602-271-0069
Block USA 1572 Chelsea Ave	Memphis	TN	38108	**888-942-5625**	901-754-5115
Dayton/Richmond Concrete Accessories 721 Richard St	Miamisburg	OH	45342	**800-745-3700**	937-866-0711
E Stewart Mitchell Inc PO Box 2799	Baltimore	MD	21225	**800-870-6365**	410-354-0600
Franklin Industries Inc 612 10th Ave N	Nashville	TN	37203	**800-626-8147**	615-259-4222
Graniterock Co PO Box 50001	Watsonville	CA	95077	**800-327-1711**	831-768-2000
Hanson Building Products North America 3500 Maple Ave	Dallas	TX	75219	**800-527-2362**	214-525-5500
Hudson Liquid Asphalts Inc 89 Ship St	Providence	RI	02903	**800-556-3406**	401-274-2200
Ingram Materials Co 1030 Visco Dr	Nashville	TN	37210	**800-421-6998**	615-256-5111
Jack B Parson Cos 2350 S 1900 West	Ogden	UT	84401	**888-672-7766**	801-731-1111
Jaeckle Wholesale Inc 4101 Owl Creek Dr	Madison	WI	53718	**800-236-7225**	608-838-5400
Jenkins Brick Co Inc 201 N 6th St PO Box 91	Montgomery	AL	36104	**888-215-5700**	334-834-2210
Kuhlman Corp 650 Beaver Creek Cir	Maumee	OH	43537	**800-669-3309**	419-897-6000
L Thorn Co Inc PO Box 198	New Albany	IN	47151	**800-662-4594**	812-246-4461
Lyman-Richey Corp 4315 Cuming St	Omaha	NE	68131	**800-727-8432**	402-558-2727
Rio Grande Co 201 Santa Fe Dr	Denver	CO	80223	**800-864-4280**	303-825-2211
Ross Island Sand & Gravel Co PO Box 82249	Portland	OR	97282	**800-543-0230**	503-239-5504
Vimco Concrete Accessories Inc 300 Hansen Access Rd	King of Prussia	PA	19406	**888-468-4626**	610-768-0500
Walker & Zanger Inc 31 Warren Pl	Mount Vernon	NY	10550	**800-634-0866**	914-667-1600

190-2 Construction Materials (Misc)

				Toll-Free	Phone
Acoustical Material Services Inc 1620 S Maple Ave	Montebello	CA	90640	**800-486-3517**	323-721-9011
American Fence Co 2502 N 27th Ave	Phoenix	AZ	85009	**888-691-4565**	602-734-0500
APi Group Inc Materials Distribution Group 2366 Rose Pl	Saint Paul	MN	55113	**800-223-4922**	651-636-4320
Atlantic Service & Supply 130 Selig Dr	Atlanta	GA	30336	**800-859-1474**	404-699-8740
Brown DS Co 300 E Cherry St	North Baltimore	OH	45872	**800-848-1730**	419-257-3561
CR Laurence Co Inc PO Box 58923	Los Angeles	CA	90058	**800-421-6144**	323-588-1281
DS Brown Co 300 E Cherry St	North Baltimore	OH	45872	**800-848-1730**	419-257-3561
Fargo Glass & Paint Co Inc 1801 7th Ave N	Fargo	ND	58102	**800-437-4612**	701-235-4441
L & W Supply Corp 125 S Franklin St	Chicago	IL	60606	**800-621-9622**	312-606-4000
Laurence CR Co Inc PO Box 58923	Los Angeles	CA	90058	**800-421-6144**	323-588-1281
Oldcastle Glass Group 2425 Olympic Blvd Suite 525E	Santa Monica	CA	90404	**866-653-2278**	310-264-4700

190-3 Lumber & Building Supplies

				Toll-Free	Phone
84 Lumber Co 1019 Rte 519	Eighty Four	PA	15330	**800-664-1984**	724-228-8820
Allied Building Products Corp 15 E Union Ave	East Rutherford	NJ	07073	**800-541-2198**	201-507-8400
Alpine Lumber Co 1120 W 122nd Ave Suite 301	Westminster	CO	80234	**800-275-2365**	303-451-8001
American International Forest Products LLC 5560 SW 107th St	Beaverton	OR	97005	**800-366-1611**	503-641-1611
Arnold Lumber Co 251 Fairgrounds Rd	West Kingston	RI	02892	**800-339-0116**	401-783-2266
Berks Products Corp 726 Spring St	Reading	PA	19604	**800-282-2375**	610-374-5131
Birmingham International Forest Products LLC 1800 International Park Dr Suite 200	Birmingham	AL	35243	**800-767-2437**	205-972-1500
BlueLinx Holdings Inc 4300 Wildwood Pkwy *NYSE: BXC*	Atlanta	GA	30339	**888-502-2583**	770-953-7000
Buckeye Pacific LLC 4386 SW Macadam Ave Suite 200	Portland	OR	97207	**800-767-9191**	503-228-3330
Builders General Supply Co 15 Sycamore Ave	Little Silver	NJ	07739	**800-570-7227**	732-747-0808
Carolina Holdings Inc 4403 Bland Rd	Raleigh	NC	27609	**877-734-6365**	919-431-1000
Causeway Lumber Co 2601 S Andrews Ave	Fort Lauderdale	FL	33316	**800-375-5050**	954-763-1224
Chicago Lumber Co of Omaha 1324 Pierce St	Omaha	NE	68103	**800-642-8210**	402-342-0840
Edward Hines Lumber Co 1000 Corporate Grove Dr	Buffalo Grove	IL	60089	**888-334-4637**	847-353-7700
Forest City Trading Group Inc PO Box 4209	Portland	OR	97208	**800-767-3284**	503-246-8500
Foxworth-Galbraith Lumber Co 17111 Waterview Pkwy	Dallas	TX	75252	**800-688-8082**	972-437-6100
Frank Paxton Lumber Co 23925 Commerce Park Rd	Beachwood	OH	44122	**800-325-9800**	513-984-8200

Lumber & Building Supplies (Cont'd)

				Toll-Free	Phone
Higgins JE Lumber Co 6999 S Front Rd	Livermore	CA	94550	**800-241-1883**	925-245-4300
Hines Edward Lumber Co 1000 Corporate Grove Dr	Buffalo Grove	IL	60089	**888-334-4637**	847-353-7700
Huttig Building Products Inc 555 Maryville University Dr *NYSE: HBP*	Saint Louis	MO	63141	**800-325-4466**	314-216-2600
Idaho Pacific Lumber Co (IdaPac) 370 N Benjamin Ln Suite 120	Boise	ID	83704	**800-231-2310**	208-375-8052
IdaPac (Idaho Pacific Lumber Co) 370 N Benjamin Ln Suite 120	Boise	ID	83704	**800-231-2310**	208-375-8052
JE Higgins Lumber Co 6999 S Front Rd	Livermore	CA	94550	**800-241-1883**	925-245-4300
Jewett-Cameron Trading Co Ltd 32275 NW Hillcrest PO Box 1010 *NASDAQ: JCTCF*	North Plains	OR	97133	**800-547-5877**	503-647-0110
Louis & Co 895 Columbia St	Brea	CA	92821	**800-422-4389**	714-529-1771
McQuesten Co 600 Iron Horse Pk	North Billerica	MA	01862	**800-752-0129**	978-663-3435
Mill Creek Lumber & Supply 6201 S 129th East Ave PO Box 4770	Tulsa	OK	74159	**800-364-6455**	918-747-2000
Modern Builders Supply Inc 302 McClurg Rd	Youngstown	OH	44512	**800-783-4117**	330-729-2690
National Lumber Co 24595 Groesbeck Hwy	Warren	MI	48089	**800-462-9712**	586-775-8200
North Pacific 2419 Science Pkwy	Okemos	MI	48864	**800-942-8220**	517-349-8220
North Pacific Group Inc (NOR PAC) 815 NE Davis St	Portland	OR	97232	**800-547-8440**	503-231-1166
Palmer-Donavin Mfg Co 1200 Steelwood Rd	Columbus	OH	43212	**800-589-4412**	614-486-9657
Parr Lumber 5630 NW 5 Oaks Dr	Hillsboro	OR	97124	**877-849-7277**	503-614-2500
PrimeSource Building Products Inc 2115 E Beltline	Carrollton	TX	75006	**800-745-3341**	972-416-1976
Raymond Building Supply Corp 7751 Bayshore Rd	North Fort Myers	FL	33917	**877-731-7272**	239-731-8300
Richmond International Forest Products Inc 4050 Innslake Dr Suite 100	Glen Allen	VA	23060	**800-767-0111**	804-747-0111
Riverhead Building Supply Corp 1093 Pulaski St	Riverhead	NY	11901	**800-378-3650**	631-727-3650
Saxonville USA 96 Springfield Rd	Charlestown	NH	03603	**800-882-2106**	603-826-4024
Seaboard International Forest Products LLC 22 Cotton Rd Suite F PO Box 6059	Nashua	NH	03063	**800-669-6800**	603-881-3700
Stevenson Lumber 1585 Monroe Tpke PO Box 123	Stevenson	CT	06491	**800-972-4260**	203-261-2555
Stock Building Supply 4403 Bland Rd	Raleigh	NC	27609	**877-734-6365**	919-431-1000
Temple-Inland Forest Products Corp 303 S Temple Dr	Diboll	TX	75941	**800-262-5512**	936-829-5511
Timber Products Co 305 S 4th St	Springfield	OR	97477	**800-547-9520**	541-747-4577
Viking Forest Products LLC 7615 Smetana Ln Suite 140	Eden Prairie	MN	55344	**800-733-3801**	952-941-6512
West Elizabeth Lumber Co 1 Chicago Ave	Elizabeth	PA	15037	**800-289-9352**	412-384-3900
White Cap Industries Inc 1723 S Ritchie St	Santa Ana	CA	92705	**800-922-9922**	714-258-3300
Wickes Inc 706 N Deerpath Dr	Vernon Hills	IL	60061	**800-558-1232**	847-367-3400

190-4 Roofing, Siding, Insulation Materials

				Toll-Free	Phone
ABC Supply Co Inc 1 ABC Pkwy	Beloit	WI	53511	**800-366-2227**	608-362-7777
Alcoa Home Exteriors 1590 Omega Dr	Pittsburgh	PA	15205	**866-496-0370**	412-249-6000
Bartells EJ Co PO Box 4160	Renton	WA	98057	**800-468-9528**	425-228-4111
Beacon Roofing Supply Inc 1 Lakeland Park Dr	Peabody	MA	01960	**877-645-7663**	978-535-7668
Branton Industries Inc 1101 Edwards Ave	Harahan	LA	70123	**800-548-5783**	504-733-7770
Carlisle SynTec Inc PO Box 7000	Carlisle	PA	17013	**800-479-6832**	717-245-7000
Co-op Reserve Supply Inc 1100 Iron Horse Pk *Cust Svc	North Billerica	MA	01862	**800-769-2667***	978-528-5320
Collins Cos 1618 SW 1st Ave Suite 500	Portland	OR	97201	**800-329-1219**	503-227-1219
Crane Performance Siding 1441 Universal Rd	Columbus	OH	43207	**800-366-8472**	614-443-4841
EJ Bartells Co PO Box 4160	Renton	WA	98057	**800-468-9528**	425-228-4111
Gulfeagle Supply 1451 Channelside Dr *NASDAQ: EEGL*	Tampa	FL	33605	**800-986-3001**	813-636-9808
Hardie James Building Products 26300 La Alameda Ave Suite 250	Mission Viejo	CA	92691	**888-542-7343**	949-348-1800
Harvey Industries Inc 1400 Main St	Waltham	MA	02451	**800-225-5724**	781-899-3500
James Hardie Building Products 26300 La Alameda Ave Suite 250	Mission Viejo	CA	92691	**888-542-7343**	949-348-1800
Kemlite Co 23525 W Eames St	Channahon	IL	60410	**800-435-0080**	815-467-8600
MacArthur Co 2400 Wycliff St	Saint Paul	MN	55114	**800-777-7507**	651-646-2773
McClure-Johnston Co 201 Corey Ave	Braddock	PA	15104	**800-232-0018**	412-351-4300
North Carolina Foam Industries Inc 1515 Carter St	Mount Airy	NC	27030	**800-346-8229**	336-789-9161
Philadelphia Reserve Supply Co 400 Mack Dr	Croydon	PA	19021	**800-347-7726**	215-785-3141
Roofing Wholesale Co Inc 1918 W Grant St	Phoenix	AZ	85009	**800-782-2116**	602-258-3794
Saint-Gobain Corp 750 E Swedesford Rd	Valley Forge	PA	19482	**800-274-8530**	610-341-7000
SG Wholesale Roofing Supplies Inc 1000 E 6th St	Santa Ana	CA	92701	**888-747-8500**	714-568-1906
Spec Building Materials Inc 4300 West Ave	San Antonio	TX	78213	**800-588-3892**	210-342-2727
Specialty Products & Insulation Co 1097 Commercial Ave	East Petersburg	PA	17520	**800-788-7764**	717-519-4000
Standard Roofings Inc 100 Park Rd	Tinton Falls	NJ	07724	**800-624-0036**	732-542-3300
Sunniland Corp PO Box 8001	Sanford	FL	32772	**800-432-1130**	407-322-2421
Tallant Industries Inc 4900 Ondura Dr	Fredericksburg	VA	22407	**800-777-7663**	540-898-7000
Variform Inc 303 W Major St PO Box 559	Kearney	MO	64060	**800-800-2244**	816-903-6400
Wesco Cedar Inc PO Box 40847	Eugene	OR	97404	**800-547-2511**	541-688-5020

191 CONSULTING SERVICES - ENVIRONMENTAL

SEE ALSO Recyclable Materials Recovery; Remediation Services; Waste Management

				Toll-Free	Phone
ATC Assoc Inc 104 E 25th St 10th Fl	New York	NY	10010	**800-725-3282**	212-353-8280
Beck RW Inc 1001 4th Ave Suite 2500	Seattle	WA	98154	**800-285-2325**	206-695-4700
EnSafe 5724 Summer Trees Dr	Memphis	TN	38134	**800-588-7962**	901-372-7962
Environmental Compliance Services Inc (ECS) 7 Island Dock Rd	Haddam	CT	06438	**800-524-9256**	860-345-4578
Environmental & Safety Designs Inc DBA EnSafe 5724 Summer Trees Dr	Memphis	TN	38134	**800-588-7962**	901-372-7962
ERM Group Inc 350 Eagle View Blvd	Exton	PA	19341	**800-662-1124**	610-524-3500
Evans Environmental Corp 14505 Commerce Way Suite 400	Miami Lakes	FL	33016	**800-486-7458**	305-374-8300
First Environment Inc 91 Fulton St	Boonton	NJ	07005	**800-486-5869**	973-334-0003
Heath Consultants Inc 9030 Monroe Rd	Houston	TX	77061	**800-432-8487**	713-844-1300
Kemron Environmental Services Inc 8150 Leesburg Pike Suite 1410	Vienna	VA	22182	**800-777-1042**	703-893-4106
MPS Group Inc 2920 Scotten St	Detroit	MI	48210	**800-741-8779**	313-841-7588
Parsons Infrastructure & Technology 100 W Walnut St	Pasadena	CA	91124	**800-883-7300**	626-440-4000
Perma-Fix Environmental Services Inc 1940 NW 67th Pl *NASDAQ: PESI*	Gainesville	FL	32653	**800-365-6066**	352-373-4200
Retec Group 300 Baker Ave Suite 302	Concord	MA	01742	**877-222-2260**	978-371-3200
RJN Group Inc 200 W Front St	Wheaton	IL	60187	**800-227-7838**	630-682-4700
RW Beck Inc 1001 4th Ave Suite 2500	Seattle	WA	98154	**800-285-2325**	206-695-4700
S & ME Inc 3109 Spring Forest Rd *Cust Svc	Raleigh	NC	27616	**800-849-2517***	919-872-2660
Select Energy Services Inc 24 Prime Pkwy	Natick	MA	01760	**800-325-4432**	508-653-0456
Shaw Environmental & Infrastructure Inc 4171 Essen Ln	Baton Rouge	LA	70809	**800-444-9586**	225-932-2500
Spherix Inc 12051 Indian Creek Ct *NASDAQ: SPEX* ■ *Mktg	Beltsville	MD	20705	**800-727-0602***	301-419-3900
Sullivan International Group Inc 409 Camino Real Rio S Suite 204	San Diego	CA	92108	**888-744-1432**	619-260-1432
SWCA Inc 2120 N Central Ave Suite 130	Phoenix	AZ	85004	**800-828-8517**	602-274-3831
Team Inc DBA Team Industrial Services Inc 200 Hermann Dr *AMEX: TMI*	Alvin	TX	77511	**800-662-8326**	281-331-6154
Team Industrial Services Inc 200 Hermann Dr *AMEX: TMI*	Alvin	TX	77511	**800-662-8326**	281-331-6154
Tetra Tech FW Inc 1000 The American Rd	Morris Plains	NJ	07950	**800-580-3765**	973-630-8000
TRC Cos Inc 5 Waterside Crossing *NYSE: TRR*	Windsor	CT	06095	**800-365-8254**	860-289-8631
US Biosystems Inc 3231 NW 7th Ave	Boca Raton	FL	33431	**888-862-5227**	561-447-7373
Vertex Engineering Services Inc 400 Libbey Pkwy	Weymouth	MA	02189	**888-298-5162**	781-952-6000
Western Technologies Inc 3737 E Broadway Rd	Phoenix	AZ	85040	**800-580-3737**	602-437-3737
Wetlandsbank Inc 3215 NW 10th Terr Suite 209	Fort Lauderdale	FL	33309	**888-301-1707**	954-462-1707

192 CONSULTING SERVICES - HUMAN RESOURCES

SEE ALSO Professional Employer Organizations (PEOs)

				Toll-Free	Phone
CA Short Co Inc 7221 Pineville Matthews Rd Suite 600	Charlotte	NC	28277	**800-535-5690**	704-752-0119
Casco International Inc DBA CA Short Co Inc 7221 Pineville Matthews Rd Suite 600	Charlotte	NC	28277	**800-535-5690**	704-752-0119
Clark Consulting 102 S Wynstone Park Dr Suite 200 *NYSE: CLK*	North Barrington	IL	60010	**800-597-7976**	847-304-5800
Development Dimensions International 1225 Washington Pike *Mktg	Bridgeville	PA	15017	**800-933-4463***	412-257-0600
Hay Group Inc 100 Penn Sq E Wanamaker Bldg	Philadelphia	PA	19107	**800-776-1774**	215-861-2000
Lee Hecht Harrison LLC 50 Tice Blvd	Woodcliff Lake	NJ	07677	**800-611-4544**	201-782-3704
Mercer Human Resource Consulting 777 S Figueroa St	Los Angeles	CA	90017	**866-879-3384**	213-346-2200
Modern Management Inc 253 Commerce Dr Suite 105	Grayslake	IL	60030	**800-323-1331**	847-945-7400
National Center for Retirement Benefits Inc 666 Dundee Rd Suite 1200	Northbrook	IL	60062	**800-666-1000**	847-564-1111
Novations Group Inc 745 Boylston St Suite 300	Boston	MA	02116	**888-652-9975**	617-247-0214
Ricklin-Echikson Assoc 374 Millburn Ave	Millburn	NJ	07041	**800-544-2317**	973-376-2020
Right Management Consultants Inc 1818 Market St 33rd Fl	Philadelphia	PA	19103	**800-237-4448**	215-988-1588
Runzheimer International Runzheimer Pk	Rochester	WI	53167	**800-558-1702**	262-971-2200
Sibson Consulting 600 Alexander Pk Suite 208	Princeton	NJ	08540	**800-257-0486**	609-520-2700
Stanton Group 3405 Annapolis Ln N Suite 100	Plymouth	MN	55447	**800-754-9867**	763-278-4000
Systema Corp 633 Skokie Blvd Suite 240	Northbrook	IL	60062	**800-270-9530**	847-498-9530
Watson Wyatt & Co 1717 H St NW Suite 800	Washington	DC	20006	**800-675-7282**	202-715-7000

193 CONSULTING SERVICES - MANAGEMENT

SEE ALSO Association Management Companies; Management Services

				Toll-Free	Phone
Advisory Board Co 2445 M St NW *NASDAQ: ABCO*	Washington	DC	20037	**800-672-6620**	202-672-5600
AGENCY.COM Ltd 20 Exchange Pl 9th Fl	New York	NY	10005	**800-736-4644**	212-358-2600
Altman Weil Inc PO Box 625	Newtown Square	PA	19073	**800-947-2875**	610-359-9900
Answerthink Inc 1001 Brickell Bay Dr Suite 3000 *NASDAQ: ANSR*	Miami	FL	33131	**888-844-6504**	305-375-8005
Bain & Co 2 Copley Pl	Boston	MA	02116	**800-800-8338**	617-572-2000
Barnett International 1400 N Providence Rd Rose Tree Corporate Ctr Suite 2000	Media	PA	19063	**800-856-2556**	610-565-9400
Boston Consulting Group Inc 53 State St 31st Fl	Boston	MA	02109	**800-367-1989**	617-973-1200

Company	City	State	ZIP	Toll-Free	Phone
Bowne Global Solutions 6500 Wilshire Blvd Suite 700	Los Angeles	CA	90048	**800-336-9898**	323-866-1000
Byrne MRG 22 Isle of Pines Dr	Hilton Head Island	SC	29928	**888-816-8080**	
Carmody & Bloom Inc 947 Linwood Ave	Ridgewood	NJ	07450	**800-242-9000**	201-670-1700
Chang Richard Assoc 15265 Alton Pkwy Suite 300	Irvine	CA	92618	**800-756-8096**	949-727-7477
Circadian Technologies Inc 24 Hartwell Ave	Lexington	MA	02421	**800-284-5001**	781-676-6900
Corporate Dynamics Inc 200 E 5th Ave Suite 118	Naperville	IL	60563	**888-267-7396**	630-778-9991
Corporate Executive Board Co 2000 Pennsylvania Ave NW *NASDAQ: EXBD*	Washington	DC	20006	**888-777-9561**	202-777-5000
Crosby Philip Assoc II Inc PO Box 2687	Winter Park	FL	32790	**800-223-3932**	407-679-7796
Davies Consulting Inc 6935 Wisconsin Ave Suite 600	Chevy Chase	MD	20815	**800-535-6470**	301-652-4535
Dechert-Hampe & Co 27101 Puerta Real Suite 400	Mission Viejo	CA	92691	**888-790-6626**	949-282-0035
DiamondCluster International Inc 875 N Michigan Ave Suite 3000 *NASDAQ: DTPI*	Chicago	IL	60611	**800-455-5875**	312-255-5000
ECG Management Consultants Inc 1111 3rd Ave Suite 2700	Seattle	WA	98101	**800-729-7635**	206-689-2200
EnerVision Inc 2100 E Exchange Pl	Tucker	GA	30084	**888-999-8840**	770-270-7764
Excel Partnership Inc 75 Glen Rd	Sandy Hook	CT	06482	**800-374-3818**	203-426-3281
First Consulting Group Inc PO Box 22676 *NASDAQ: FCGI*	Long Beach	CA	90801	**800-251-8005**	562-624-5200
Fluor Global Services Inc 1 Enterprise Dr	Aliso Viejo	CA	92656	**800-405-6637**	949-349-2000
FMI Corp 5151 Glenwood Ave Suite 100	Raleigh	NC	27612	**800-669-1364**	919-787-8400
George S May International Co 303 S Northwest Hwy	Park Ridge	IL	60068	**800-999-3020**	847-825-8806
Gordon Rj & Co 8730 W Sunset Blvd Suite 290	West Hollywood	CA	90069	**800-746-7366**	310-734-3500
GP Deltapoint 6095 Marshalee Dr	Elkridge	MD	21075	**888-843-4784**	410-379-3600
Hay Group Inc 100 Penn Sq E Wanamaker Bldg	Philadelphia	PA	19107	**800-776-1774**	215-861-2000
HB Maynard & Co Inc 8 Parkway Ctr	Pittsburgh	PA	15220	**888-629-6273**	412-921-2400
Hildebrandt International 200 Cottontail Ln	Somerset	NJ	08873	**800-223-0937**	732-560-8888
HSB Reliability Technologies 1701 N Beauregard St Suite 400	Alexandria	VA	22311	**800-368-3371**	703-671-3800
Innovative Resources Consultant Group Inc 1 Park Plaza Suite 600	Irvine	CA	92614	**800-945-4724**	949-252-0590
International Profit Assoc Inc 1250 Barclay Blvd	Buffalo Grove	IL	60089	**800-531-7100**	847-808-5590
Julie Morgenstern's Professional Organizers 350 5th Ave Suite 828	New York	NY	10118	**866-742-6473**	212-544-8722
KEMA Consulting 3 Burlington Woods	Burlington	MA	01803	**800-892-2006**	781-273-5700
KnowledgePlanet.com 5095 Ritter Rd Suite 400	Mechanicsburg	PA	17055	**800-869-5763**	717-790-0400
KW Tunnell Co Inc 900 E 8th Ave Suite 106	King of Prussia	PA	19406	**800-532-2483**	610-337-0820
LEK Consulting 28 State St 16th Fl	Boston	MA	02109	**800-929-4535**	617-951-9500
Marakon Assoc 245 Park Ave 44th Fl	New York	NY	10167	**800-264-3000**	212-377-5000
Marasco Newton Group Ltd 2801 Clarendon Blvd	Arlington	VA	22201	**800-486-0220**	703-516-9100
May George S International Co 303 S Northwest Hwy	Park Ridge	IL	60068	**800-999-3020**	847-825-8806
Maynard HB & Co Inc 8 Parkway Ctr	Pittsburgh	PA	15220	**888-629-6273**	412-921-2400
McKinsey & Co Inc 55 E 52nd St	New York	NY	10022	**800-221-1026**	212-446-7000
Medical Doctor Assoc Inc 145 Technology Pkwy NW	Norcross	GA	30092	**800-780-3500**	770-246-9191
Mercer Management Consulting 1166 Ave of the Americas 32 Fl	New York	NY	10036	**800-532-6888**	212-345-8000
Meritus Consulting Services LLC 1899 Powers Ferry Rd Suite 205	Atlanta	GA	30339	**800-637-4887**	770-988-2600
Navigant Consulting Inc 615 N Wabash Ave *NYSE: NCI*	Chicago	IL	60611	**800-621-8390**	312-573-5600
Nolan Robert E Co Inc 90 Hopmeadow St	Simsbury	CT	06070	**800-653-1941**	860-658-1941
Organizational Dynamics Inc 790 Boston Rd Suite 201	Billerica	MA	01821	**800-634-4636**	978-671-5454
Ortloff Engineers Ltd 415 W Wall Ave Suite 2000	Midland	TX	79701	**888-367-0020**	432-685-0277
Parson Group 333 W Wacker Dr Suite 1620	Chicago	IL	60606	**800-389-8686**	312-578-1170
Perot Systems Corp Government Services Group 8550 Arlington Blvd Suite 300	Fairfax	VA	22031	**888-560-9477**	703-560-9477
Philip Crosby Assoc II Inc PO Box 2687	Winter Park	FL	32790	**800-223-3932**	407-679-7796
Pinnacle Consulting Group Inc 71 Moore Rd	Wayland	MA	01778	**800-693-7466**	508-358-8070
Power Technologies Inc 1482 Erie Blvd	Schenectady	NY	12305	**800-395-4784**	518-374-1220
Pritchett LLC 5800 Granite Pkwy Suite 455	Plano	TX	75024	**800-992-5922**	972-731-1500
Professional Bank Services Inc 6200 Dutchmans Ln Suite 305	Louisville	KY	40205	**800-523-4778**	502-451-6633
Progeny Marketing Innovations 801 Crescent Ctr Dr Suite 200	Franklin	TN	37067	**800-251-2148**	
Program Planning Professionals 3923 Ranchero Dr	Ann Arbor	MI	48108	**888-364-1182**	734-741-7770
Rapidigm Inc 4400 Campbells Run Rd	Pittsburgh	PA	15205	**800-944-6055**	412-494-9898
Rath & Strong Inc 45 Hayden Ave	Lexington	MA	02421	**800-622-2025**	781-861-1700
Resource Dynamics International Inc 3350 Boca Raton Blvd Suite A38	Boca Raton	FL	33431	**888-999-1623**	
Revere Group 1285 Baxter Pkwy Suite 15	Deerfield	IL	60015	**888-473-8373**	847-790-9800
RHR International Co 220 Gerry Dr	Wood Dale	IL	60191	**800-892-4496**	630-766-7007
Richard Chang Assoc 15265 Alton Pkwy Suite 300	Irvine	CA	92618	**800-756-8096**	949-727-7477
Rj Gordon & Co 8730 W Sunset Blvd Suite 290	West Hollywood	CA	90069	**800-746-7366**	310-734-3500
Robert E Nolan Co Inc 90 Hopmeadow St	Simsbury	CT	06070	**800-653-1941**	860-658-1941
Robert Half Management Resources (RHIMR) 2884 Sand Hill Rd Suite 200	Menlo Park	CA	94025	**888-400-7474**	650-234-6000
RSM McGladrey Inc 3600 American Blvd W 3rd Fl	Bloomington	MN	55431	**800-274-3978**	952-835-9930
Sandy Corp 1500 W Big Beaver Rd	Troy	MI	48084	**800-733-4739**	248-649-0800
Scott Madden & Assoc Inc 2626 Glenwood Ave Suite 480	Raleigh	NC	27608	**800-321-9774**	919-781-4191
Sirius Solution LLC 3700 Buffalo Speedway Suite 1100	Houston	TX	77098	**800-585-1085**	713-888-0488
Strategic Management Group Inc 3624 Market St	Philadelphia	PA	19104	**866-874-4899**	215-387-4000
Stromberg Consulting 711 3rd Ave	New York	NY	10017	**800-662-5889**	646-935-4300
Superior Consultant Holdings Corp 17570 W 12-Mile Rd	Southfield	MI	48076	**800-781-0960**	248-386-8300
Technology & Business Integrators 50 Tice Blvd	Woodcliff Lake	NJ	07677	**800-676-9470**	201-573-0400
Tenera Inc 100 Bush St Suite 850	San Francisco	CA	94104	**800-447-9388**	415-445-3200
Thomas Group Inc 5221 N O'Connor Blvd Suite 500	Irving	TX	75039	**800-826-2057**	972-869-3400
Tompkins Assoc 8970 Southall Rd	Raleigh	NC	27616	**800-789-1257**	919-876-3667
Tunnell KW Co Inc 900 E 8th Ave Suite 106	King of Prussia	PA	19406	**800-532-2483**	610-337-0820
Vector Strategic Resources Inc 555 Theodore Fremd Ave Suite B-102	Rye	NY	10580	**866-832-8676**	914-921-1900

194 CONSULTING SERVICES - MARKETING

Company	City	State	ZIP	Toll-Free	Phone
Acosta Sales & Marketing Co 500 Waters Edge Oak Creek Ctr	Lombard	IL	60148	**800-843-2750**	630-620-7600
Alexander Group Inc 14635 N Kierland Blvd Suite 200	Scottsdale	AZ	85254	**800-327-8525**	480-998-9644
ANALYTICI 150 E 42nd St 25th Fl	New York	NY	10017	**877-568-8032**	
Beverage Marketing Corp 850 3rd Ave	New York	NY	10022	**800-275-4630**	212-688-7640
Cargill AgHorizons PO Box 9300 MS 19	Minneapolis	MN	55440	**800-227-4455**	952-742-7575
Corporate Branding 470 West Ave	Stamford	CT	06902	**888-969-2726**	203-327-6333
DCI Marketing Inc 2727 W Good Hope Rd	Milwaukee	WI	53209	**800-778-4805**	414-228-7000
Faith Popcorn's BrainReserve 59 E 64th St	New York	NY	10021	**800-873-6337**	212-772-7778
Frost & Sullivan Inc 7550 W I-10 Suite 400	San Antonio	TX	78229	**877-463-7678**	210-348-1000
Fulcrum Analytics 304 Hudson St 5th Fl	New York	NY	10013	**888-421-6655**	212-651-7000
Harte-Hanks Market Intelligence 9980 Huennekens St	San Diego	CA	92121	**800-854-8409**	858-450-1667
Innotrac Corp 6655 Sugarloaf Pkwy *NASDAQ: INOC*	Duluth	GA	30097	**800-827-4666**	678-584-4000
Lexicon Branding Inc 30 Liberty Ship Way Suite 3360	Sausalito	CA	94965	**800-783-9713**	415-332-1811
PDI Inc 10 Mountainview Rd *NASDAQ: PDII*	Upper Saddle River	NJ	07458	**800-242-7494**	201-258-8450
Rainmaker Systems Inc 1800 Green Hills Rd *NASDAQ: RMKR*	Scotts Valley	CA	95066	**800-631-1545**	831-430-3800
Ronin Corp 2 Research Way 2nd Fl	Princeton	NJ	08540	**800-352-2926**	609-452-0060
Suss Consulting 801 Old York Rd Noble Plaza Suite 305	Jenkintown	PA	19046	**888-984-5900**	215-884-5900
Ventiv Health Inc 200 Cottontail Ln *NASDAQ: VTIV*	Somerset	NJ	08873	**800-416-0555**	
Young & Assoc Ltd 2625 Butterfield Rd Suite 216 South	Oak Brook	IL	60523	**800-553-2503**	630-573-2500

195 CONSULTING SERVICES - TELECOMMUNICATIONS

Company	City	State	ZIP	Toll-Free	Phone
ACRS (Associated Communications & Research Services Inc) 817 NE 63rd St	Oklahoma City	OK	73105	**800-442-3341**	405-843-9966
Ajilon Communications 3039 Premiere Pkwy Suite 900	Duluth	GA	30097	**800-843-6910**	678-584-2511
Associated Communications & Research Services Inc (ACRS) 817 NE 63rd St	Oklahoma City	OK	73105	**800-442-3341**	405-843-9966
Atcom Business Telecom Solutions PO Box 13476	Research Triangle Park	NC	27709	**800-849-8266**	919-314-1001
Behr Lawrence Assoc Inc PO Box 8026	Greenville	NC	27835	**800-522-4464**	252-757-0279
First Communications Inc 3340 W Market St	Akron	OH	44333	**800-860-1261**	330-835-2323
GLA Integrated Network Solutions LLC 5555 Winghaven Blvd	O'Fallon	MO	63366	**800-896-3355**	636-625-5700
Lawrence Behr Assoc Inc PO Box 8026	Greenville	NC	27835	**800-522-4464**	252-757-0279
Management Network Group Inc 7300 College Blvd Suite 302 *NASDAQ: TMNG*	Overland Park	KS	66210	**888-480-8664**	913-345-9315
Sonex Enterprises Inc 9990 Lee Hwy Suite 500	Fairfax	VA	22030	**888-766-3972**	703-691-8122
Technology Futures Inc 13740 N Research Blvd Bldg C	Austin	TX	78750	**800-835-3887**	512-258-8898
Telcordia Technologies Inc 1 Telcordia Dr *Sales	Piscataway	NJ	08854	**800-521-2673***	732-699-2000
Telwares Inc 4471 Legendary Dr Suite 100	Destin	FL	32541	**888-835-9273**	850-650-9800
Vectren Communications Services 421 John St	Evansville	IN	47713	**888-326-6782**	812-437-6700
WFI (Wireless Facilities Inc) 4810 Eastgate Mall *NASDAQ: WFII*	San Diego	CA	92121	**888-824-0017**	858-228-2000
Windfall Assoc 981 Chestnut St	Newton Upper Falls	MA	02464	**877-946-3325**	617-969-1790
Wireless Facilities Inc (WFI) 4810 Eastgate Mall *NASDAQ: WFII*	San Diego	CA	92121	**888-824-0017**	858-228-2000

196 CONSUMER INFORMATION RESOURCES - GOVERNMENT

Company	City	State	ZIP	Toll-Free	Phone
ADEAR Center PO Box 8250	Silver Spring	MD	20907	**800-438-4380**	301-495-3311
AIDSinfo PO Box 6303	Rockville	MD	20849	**800-448-0440**	301-519-0459
Alzheimer's Disease Education & Referral Center PO Box 8250	Silver Spring	MD	20907	**800-438-4380**	301-495-3311
Americans with Disabilities Act Information 950 Pennsylvania Ave NW	Washington	DC	20530	**800-514-0301**	
AmeriCorps USA 1201 New York Ave NW 8th Fl	Washington	DC	20525	**800-942-2677**	202-606-5000
Ask USGS 12201 Sunrise Valley Dr	Reston	VA	20192	**888-275-8747**	
Cancer Information Service (CIS) National Cancer Institute 9000 Rockville Pike Bldg 31	Bethesda	MD	20892	**800-422-6237**	301-496-4000
Consumer Product Safety Commission	Washington	DC	20207	**800-638-2772**	301-504-7908
Consumer.gov 600 Pennsylvania Ave NW	Washington	DC	20580	**877-382-4357**	202-326-2222
Education Resource Information Center (ERIC) 4483-A Forbes Blvd	Lanham	MD	20706	**800-538-3742**	
Eldercare Locator 927 15th St NW 6th Fl	Washington	DC	20005	**800-677-1116**	202-296-8130
Energy Efficiency & Renewable Energy Information Center PO Box 43165	Olympia	WA	98504	**877-337-3463**	
ERIC (Education Resource Information Center) 4483-A Forbes Blvd	Lanham	MD	20706	**800-538-3742**	

Classified Section

Name / Address	City	State	Zip	Toll-Free	Phone
Federal Citizen Information Center 201 W 8th St	Pueblo	CO	81003	**888-878-3256**	719-948-3334
Federal Student Aid Information Center PO Box 84	Washington	DC	20044	**800-433-3243**	
FedWorld.gov US Dept of Commerce 5285 Port Royal Rd	Springfield	VA	22161	**800-553-6847**	703-605-6000
FirstGov 1800 F St NW	Washington	DC	20405	**800-333-4636**	
FirstGov en Espanol 1800 F St NW	Washington	DC	20405	**800-333-4636**	
FoodSafety.gov 5600 Fishers Ln	Rockville	MD	20857	**888-723-3366**	
Girl Power! Substance Abuse & Mental Health Services Administration 5600 Fishersn Ln	Rockville	MD	20857	**800-729-6686**	
GovBenefits.gov	Washington	DC	20407	**800-333-4636**	
GovLoans.gov	Washington	DC	20405	**800-333-4636**	
Grants.gov Dept of Health & Human Services 200 Independence Ave SW	Washington	DC	20201	**800-518-4726**	
Gulf War Illness Information Helpline	Washington	DC	20420	**800-749-8387**	
Insure Kids Now! Health Resources & Services Administration 5600 Fishers Ln	Rockville	MD	20857	**877-543-7669**	
Medicare Hotline	Baltimore	MD	21207	**800-633-4227**	
MedlinePlus National Library of Medicine 8600 Rockville Pike	Bethesda	MD	20894	**888-346-3656**	301-594-5983
MedWatch 5600 Fishers Ln HFD 410	Rockville	MD	20857	**888-463-6332**	301-827-7240
National Adoption Information Clearinghouse (NAIC) 330 C St SW	Washington	DC	20447	**888-251-0075**	703-352-3488
National AIDS Hotline	Washington	DC	20201	**800-342-2437**	
National Atlas of America 508 National Ctr 12201 Sunrise Valley Dr	Reston	VA	20192	**888-275-8747**	
National Cancer Institute (NCI) 6116 Executive Blvd MSC 8322	Bethesda	MD	20892	**800-422-6237**	301-435-3848
National Center for Infectious Diseases Travelers' Health Centers for Disease Control & Prevention 1600 Clifton Rd NE	Atlanta	GA	30333	**877-394-8747**	
National Child Care Information Center (NCCIC) 243 Church St NW 2nd Fl	Vienna	VA	22180	**800-616-2242**	
National Clearinghouse for Alcohol & Drug Information PO Box 2345	Rockville	MD	20847	**800-729-6686**	301-468-2600
National Clearinghouse on Child Abuse & Neglect Information 330 C St SW	Washington	DC	20447	**800-394-3366**	703-385-7565
National Contact Center	Pueblo	CO	81009	**800-333-4636**	
National Do Not Call Registry	Washington	DC	20580	**888-382-1222**	
National Health Information Center (NHIC) PO Box 1133	Washington	DC	20013	**800-336-4797**	301-565-4167
National Immunization Program 1600 Clifton Rd NE MS E05	Atlanta	GA	30333	**800-232-2522**	404-639-8200
National Lead Information Center 422 S Clinton Ave	Rochester	NY	14620	**800-424-5323**	
National Mental Health Information Center PO Box 42557	Washington	DC	20015	**800-789-2647**	301-443-1805
National Passport Information Center	Washington	DC	20520	**877-487-2778**	
National Prevention Information Network (NPIN) PO Box 6003	Rockville	MD	20849	**800-458-5231**	301-562-1098
National Taxpayer Advocate 1111 Constitution Ave NW	Washington	DC	20224	**877-777-4778**	202-622-6100
National Women's Health Information Center 8550 Arlington Blvd Suite 300	Fairfax	VA	22031	**800-994-9662**	
Osteoporosis & Related Bone Diseases - National Resource Center 1232 22nd St NW	Washington	DC	20037	**800-624-2663**	202-223-0344
Project Safe Neighborhoods Office of Justice Programs 810 7th St NW	Washington	DC	20531	**800-458-0786**	
Ready.gov Naval Security Stn	Washington	DC	20528	**800-237-3239**	
Regulations.gov Government Printing Office	Washington	DC	20401	**888-293-6498**	
Retired & Senior Volunteer Program (RSVP) PO Box 70675	Washington	DC	20024	**800-424-8867**	
Senior Corps 1201 New York Ave NW	Washington	DC	20525	**800-424-8867**	202-606-5000
Tobacco Information & Prevention Source (TIPS) National Ctr for Chronic Disease Prevention & Health Promotion 2900 Woodcock Blvd	Atlanta	GA	30341	**800-311-3435**	
US Geological Survey (USGS) Ask USGS 12201 Sunrise Valley Dr	Reston	VA	20192	**888-275-8747**	
USA Freedom Corps 1600 Pennsylvania Ave NW West Wing	Washington	DC	20500	**877-872-2677**	
Volunteer.Gov/Gov 1600 Pennsylvania Ave NW	Washington	DC	20500	**877-872-2677**	
Wi$e Up Women Dept of Labor Women's Bureau 200 Constitution Ave NW	Washington	DC	20210	**800-827-5335**	

197 CONTAINERS - METAL (BARRELS, DRUMS, KEGS)

Name / Address	City	State	Zip	Toll-Free	Phone
Champion Co 400 Harrison St	Springfield	OH	45505	**800-328-0115***	937-324-5681
*Sales					
CSI Fabricated Metal Bins Inc 6910 W Ridge Rd	Fairview	PA	16415	**800-937-9033**	814-474-9353
Evans Industries Inc 1255 Peters Rd	Harvey	LA	70058	**800-749-6012**	504-374-6000
Greif Inc 425 Winter Rd	Delaware	OH	43015	**800-354-7343**	740-549-6000
NYSE: GEF					
Hoover Materials Handling Group Inc 2001 Westside Pkwy Suite 155	Alpharetta	GA	30004	**800-391-3561**	770-664-4047
Imperial Industries Inc 505 Industrial Park Ave	Mosinee	WI	54455	**800-558-2945**	715-359-0200
Industrial Container Services 7152 1st Ave S	Seattle	WA	98108	**800-451-3471**	206-763-2345
Innovative Fluid Handling Systems Inc 200 E 3rd St	Rock Falls	IL	61071	**800-435-7003**	815-626-1018
Justrite Mfg Co 2454 Dempster St Suite 300	Des Plaines	IL	60016	**800-469-5382**	847-298-9250
Myers Container Corp 5801 Christie Ave Suite 255	Emeryville	CA	94608	**800-228-7269**	510-652-6847
New England Container Co Inc 455 George Washington Hwy	Smithfield	RI	02917	**800-333-3109**	401-231-2100
Rayfo Inc 15629 Clayton Ave	Rosemount	MN	55068	**800-624-4764**	651-437-4441
Spartanburg Steel Products Inc PO Box 6428	Spartanburg	SC	29304	**800-334-6318**	864-585-5216
Stackbin Corp 29 Powderhill Rd	Lincoln	RI	02865	**800-333-1603***	401-333-1600
*Sales					
Trilla-Nesco Corp 2391 Cassens Dr	Fenton	MO	63026	**800-966-3786**	636-343-7333

198 CONTAINERS - PLASTICS (DRUMS, CANS, CRATES, BOXES)

Name / Address	City	State	Zip	Toll-Free	Phone
Amherst-Merritt International 5565 Red Bird Ctr Dr Suite 150	Dallas	TX	75237	**800-627-7752**	214-339-0753
Bedenbaugh Products Corp 105 Lisbon Rd	Laurens	SC	29360	**800-679-9419**	864-682-3136
Belco Mfg Co 2303 Taylors Valley Rd	Belton	TX	76513	**800-251-8265**	254-933-9000
Berry Plastics Corp 101 Oakley St	Evansville	IN	47710	**800-234-1930**	812-429-9522
Buckhorn Inc 55 W TechneCenter Dr	Milford	OH	45150	**800-543-4454**	513-831-4402
Case Design Corp 333 School Ln	Telford	PA	18969	**800-847-4176**	215-703-0130
Chem-Tainer Industries Inc 361 Neptune Ave	North Babylon	NY	11704	**800-275-2436**	631-661-8300
Contico International LLC 305 Rock Industrial Pk Dr	Saint Louis	MO	63044	**800-831-7077**	314-656-4349
Continental Mfg Co 305 Rock Industrial Pk Dr	Bridgeton	MO	63044	**800-325-1051**	314-656-4301
Fort Recovery Industries Inc 2440 SR-49	Fort Recovery	OH	45846	**800-445-5695***	419-375-4121
*Sales					
Handley Industries Inc 2101 Brooklyn Rd	Jackson	MI	49203	**800-870-5088**	517-787-8821
Hardigg Industries Inc 147 N Main St	South Deerfield	MA	01373	**800-542-7344**	413-665-2163
Hedwin Corp 1600 Roland Heights Ave	Baltimore	MD	21211	**800-638-1012**	410-467-8209
HGI Skydyne 100 River Rd	Port Jervis	NY	12771	**800-428-2273**	845-856-6655
Iroquois Products of Chicago 2220 W 56th St	Chicago	IL	60636	**800-453-3355**	773-436-3900
Jewel Case Corp 300 Niantic Ave	Providence	RI	02907	**800-441-4447**	401-943-1400
Meese Orbitron Dunne Co 535 N Midland Ave	Saddle Brook	NJ	07663	**800-829-3230**	201-796-4667
Menasha Corp 1645 Bergstrom Rd	Neenah	WI	54956	**800-558-5073**	920-751-1000
Molded Fiber Glass Tray Co 6175 US Hwy 6	Linesville	PA	16424	**800-458-6050***	814-683-4500
*Sales					
ORBIS Corp 1055 Corporate Ctr Dr	Oconomowoc	WI	53066	**800-999-8683**	262-560-5000
Plano Molding Co 431 E South St	Plano	IL	60545	**800-451-2122**	630-552-3111
Plastic Forming Co Inc 20 S Bradley Rd	Woodbridge	CT	06525	**800-732-2060**	203-397-1338
Plastic Packaging Corp 1227 Union St	West Springfield	MA	01090	**800-342-2011***	413-785-1553
*Cust Svc					
PNE Inc 7482 Presidents Dr	Orlando	FL	32809	**800-998-2525**	407-857-3888
Rehrig Pacific Co 4010 E 26th St	Los Angeles	CA	90023	**800-421-6244**	323-262-5145
River Bend Industries 2421 16th Ave S	Moorhead	MN	56560	**800-365-3070**	218-236-1818
Rocket Box Inc 125 E 144th St	Bronx	NY	10451	**800-762-5521**	718-292-5370
Ropak Corp 660 S State College Blvd	Fullerton	CA	92831	**800-367-3779**	714-870-9757
Schaefer Systems International Inc 10021 Westlake Dr	Charlotte	NC	28273	**800-876-6000**	704-944-4500
Shaw-Clayton Corp 123 Carlos Dr	San Rafael	CA	94903	**800-537-6712***	415-472-1522
*Cust Svc					
Specialty Plastic Fabricators Inc 9658 W 196th St	Mokena	IL	60448	**800-747-9509**	708-479-5501
Stack-On Products Co PO Box 489	Wauconda	IL	60084	**800-323-9601**	847-526-1611
Toter Inc PO Box 5338	Statesville	NC	28677	**800-424-0422**	704-872-8171
US Plastic Corp 1390 Newbrecht Rd	Lima	OH	45801	**800-537-9724**	419-228-2242
Xerxes Corp 7901 Xerxes Ave S Suite 201	Minneapolis	MN	55431	**800-394-3490**	952-887-1890
Zarn LLC 12700 General Dr	Charlotte	NC	28273	**800-227-5885**	704-588-9191

199 CONTAINERS - WOOD

SEE ALSO Pallets & Skids

Name / Address	City	State	Zip	Toll-Free	Phone
Abbot & Abbot Box Corp 37-11 10th St	Long Island City	NY	11101	**800-377-0037**	718-392-2600
Bluegrass Cooperage Co Inc PO Box 37210	Louisville	KY	40233	**800-364-6004**	502-368-1626
Chick Packaging Inc PO Box 80	Silver Lake	NH	03875	**800-258-4692**	603-367-8857
Corbett Package Co PO Box 210	Wilmington	NC	28402	**800-334-0684**	910-763-9991
Flight Form Cases Inc 5950 192nd St NE	Arlington	WA	98223	**800-657-1199***	360-435-6688
*Cust Svc					
Georgia Crate & Basket Co Inc 1200 Parnell St	Thomasville	GA	31792	**800-841-0001**	229-226-2541
Greif Inc 425 Winter Rd	Delaware	OH	43015	**800-354-7343**	740-549-6000
NYSE: GEF					
Martin Brothers Container & Timber Products Corp 747 Lindell St PO Box 87	Martin	TN	38237	**800-426-6984**	731-587-3171
Mautner Enterprises 155 E 76 St	New York	NY	10021	**800-628-8637**	212-452-1871
Mele Enterprises Inc 2007 Beechgrove Pl	Utica	NY	13501	**800-635-6353**	315-733-4600
Monte Package Co Inc 3752 Riverside Rd	Riverside	MI	49084	**800-653-2807**	269-849-1722
Peacock Crate Factory 225 Cash St	Jacksonville	TX	75766	**800-666-5647***	903-586-5321
*Orders					
Stearnswood Inc PO Box 50	Hutchinson	MN	55350	**800-657-0144**	320-587-2137
Texas Basket Co 100 Myrtle Dr	Jacksonville	TX	75766	**800-657-2200**	903-586-8014
Wisconsin Box Co Inc 929 Townline Rd	Wausau	WI	54402	**800-876-6658**	715-842-2248

200 CONTROLS - INDUSTRIAL PROCESS

Name / Address	City	State	Zip	Toll-Free	Phone
ADS Corp 5030 Bradford Dr NW Bldg 1 Suite 210	Huntsville	AL	35805	**800-633-7246**	256-430-3366
Alpha Technologies Services LLC 2689 Wingate Ave	Akron	OH	44314	**800-356-9886**	330-745-1641
AMETEK Power Instruments Panalarm Div 1725 Western Dr	West Chicago	IL	60185	**800-213-9568**	630-231-5900
AMETEK Sensor Technology Automation & Process Technologies Div 1080 N Crooks Rd	Clawson	MI	48017	**800-635-0289**	248-435-0700

Classified Section

Company	City	State	Zip	Toll-Free	Phone
Anarad Inc 3405 Wiley Post Rd	Carrollton	TX	75006	**888-626-3763**	972-458-6100
Anderson Instrument Co 156 Auriesville Rd	Fultonville	NY	12072	**800-833-0081**	518-922-5315
Athena Controls Inc 5145 Campus Dr	Plymouth Meeting	PA	19462	**800-782-6776**	610-828-2490
Azonix Corp 900 Middlesex Tpke Bldg 6	Billerica	MA	01821	**800-967-5558**	978-670-6300
Bacharach Inc 621 Hunt Valley Cir	New Kensington	PA	15068	**800-736-4666**	724-334-5000
Barksdale Inc 3211 Fruitland Ave	Los Angeles	CA	90058	**800-835-1060**	323-589-6181
Bristol Babcock Inc 1100 Buckingham St	Watertown	CT	06795	**800-395-5497**	860-945-2200
Brookfield Engineering Lab Inc 11 Commerce Blvd	Middleboro	MA	02346	**800-628-8139**	508-946-6200
Conax Buffalo Technologies LLC 2300 Walden Ave	Buffalo	NY	14225	**800-223-2389**	716-684-4500
Cooper Atkins Corp 33 Reeds Gap Rd	Middlefield	CT	06455	**800-835-5011***	860-349-3473
*Sales					
Crane Co Dynalco Controls Div 3690 NW 53rd St	Fort Lauderdale	FL	33309	**800-368-6666**	954-739-4300
Davis Inotek Instruments LLC 4701 Mt Hope Dr Suite J	Baltimore	MD	21215	**800-368-2516**	410-358-3900
DICKEY-john Corp 5200 Dickey-john Rd	Auburn	IL	62615	**800-637-2952**	217-438-3371
Dickson Co 930 S Westwood Ave	Addison	IL	60101	**800-323-2448**	630-543-3747
Dynalco Controls Div Crane Co 3690 NW 53rd St	Fort Lauderdale	FL	33309	**800-368-6666**	954-739-4300
Encoder Products Co 464276 Hwy 95 S PO box 249	Sagle	ID	83860	**800-366-5412**	208-263-8541
Endress+Hauser Inc 2350 Endress Pl	Greenwood	IN	46143	**800-428-4344**	317-535-7138
Environmental Systems Products Inc 11 Kripes Rd	East Granby	CT	06026	**800-446-4708**	860-653-0081
Fairchild Industrial Products Co 3920 West Point Blvd	Winston-Salem	NC	27103	**800-423-1093**	336-659-3400
Fast Heat Inc 776 Oaklawn Ave	Elmhurst	IL	60126	**800-982-4328**	630-833-5400
Fluid Components International 1755 La Costa Meadows Dr	San Marcos	CA	92078	**800-863-8703**	760-744-6950
Forney Corp 3405 Wiley Post Rd	Carrollton	TX	75006	**800-356-7740***	972-458-6100
*Cust Svc					
GE Fanuc Automation Corp 2500 Austin Dr	Charlottesville	VA	22911	**800-432-7521***	434-978-5000
*Cust Svc					
Gems Sensors Inc 1 Cowles Rd	Plainville	CT	06062	**800-378-1600**	860-747-3000
General Monitors Inc 26776 Simpatica Cir	Lake Forest	CA	92630	**866-686-0741**	949-581-4464
Hart Scientific Inc 799 E Utah Valley Dr	American Fork	UT	84003	**800-438-4278**	801-763-1600
Heraeus Electro-Nite Co 1 Summit Sq Suite 100	Langhorne	PA	19047	**800-220-1646**	215-464-4200
HO Trerice Co 12950 W Eight-Mile Rd	Oak Park	MI	48237	**888-873-7423**	248-399-8000
Honeywell ACS 11 W Spring St	Freeport	IL	61032	**800-328-5111**	
Honeywell Automation & Control Solutions 11 W Spring St	Freeport	IL	61032	**800-328-5111**	
HSQ Technology 26227 Research Rd	Hayward	CA	94545	**800-486-6684**	510-259-1334
Industrial Scientific Corp 1001 Oakdale Rd	Oakdale	PA	15071	**800-338-3287**	412-788-4353
Isco Inc 4700 Superior St PO Box 82531	Lincoln	NE	68501	**800-228-4250**	402-464-0231
K-Tron International Inc Rts 55 & 553	Pitman	NJ	08071	**800-355-8766**	856-589-0500
NASDAQ: KTII					
Kistler-Morse Corp 150 Venture Blvd	Spartanburg	SC	29306	**800-426-9010**	864-574-2763
LaMotte Co 802 Washington Ave	Chestertown	MD	21620	**800-344-3100**	410-778-3100
Magnetrol International Inc 5300 Belmont Rd	Downers Grove	IL	60515	**800-624-8765**	630-969-4000
Mahr Federal Inc 1144 Eddy St	Providence	RI	02905	**800-343-2050***	401-784-3100
*Orders					
Marsh Bellofram Corp SR 2 PO Box 305	Newell	WV	26050	**800-727-5646**	304-387-1200
McCrometer Inc 3255 W Stetson Ave	Hemet	CA	92545	**800-220-2279**	951-652-6811
Mercury Instruments Inc 3940 Virginia Ave	Cincinnati	OH	45227	**800-642-4629**	513-272-1111
Metrosonics 1060 Corporate Center Dr	Oconomowoc	WI	53066	**800-245-0779**	262-567-9157
Mikron Infrared Inc 16 Thornton Rd	Oakland	NJ	07436	**800-631-0176**	201-405-0900
NASDAQ: MIKR					
MKS Instruments Inc 90 Industrial Way	Wilmington	MA	01887	**800-227-8766**	978-284-4000
NASDAQ: MKSI					
Moore Industries International Inc 16650 Schoenborn St	North Hills	CA	91343	**800-999-2900**	818-894-7111
NRD LLC 2937 Alt Blvd PO Box 310	Grand Island	NY	14072	**800-525-8076**	716-773-7634
Omega Engineering Inc 1 Omega Dr PO Box 4047	Stamford	CT	06907	**800-826-6342**	203-359-1660
Panalarm Div AMETEK Power Instruments 1725 Western Dr	West Chicago	IL	60185	**800-213-9568**	630-231-5900
Parker Hannifin Corp Veriflo Div 250 Canal Blvd	Richmond	CA	94804	**800-962-4074**	510-235-9590
Portage Electric Products Inc 7700 Freedom Ave NW	North Canton	OH	44720	**888-464-7374**	330-499-2727
Porter Instrument Co Inc 245 Township Line Rd PO Box 907	Hatfield	PA	19440	**800-457-2001**	215-723-4000
Precision Energy Services 500 Winscott Rd	Fort Worth	TX	76126	**800-669-9326**	817-249-7200
Pressure Systems Inc 34 Research Dr	Hampton	VA	23666	**800-678-7226**	757-865-1243
Pyromation Inc 5211 Industrial Rd	Fort Wayne	IN	46825	**800-837-6805**	260-484-2580
Quest Technologies Inc 1060 Corporate Center Dr	Oconomowoc	WI	53066	**800-245-0779**	262-567-9101
RAE Systems Inc 3775 N 1st St	San Jose	CA	95134	**877-723-2878**	408-952-8200
AMEX: RAE					
Raven Industries Inc 205 E 6th St	Sioux Falls	SD	57104	**800-227-2836**	605-336-2750
NASDAQ: RAVN					
Raytheon Commercial Infrared 13532 N Central Expy MS 37	Dallas	TX	75243	**800-990-3275**	972-344-4000
Renco Encoders Inc 26 Coromar Dr	Goleta	CA	93117	**800-248-6044**	805-968-1525
Robertshaw Industrial Products 1602 Mustang Dr	Maryville	TN	37801	**800-228-7429**	865-981-3100
Rochester Gauges Inc of Texas 11616 Harry Hines Blvd	Dallas	TX	75229	**800-821-1829**	972-241-2161
Ronan Engineering Co 21200 Oxnard St	Woodland Hills	CA	91367	**800-327-6626**	818-883-5211
Rosemount Analytical Inc Process Analytical Div 6565 P Davis Industrial Pkwy	Solon	OH	44139	**800-433-6076**	330-682-9010
Rosemount Analytical Inc Uniloc Div 2400 Barranca Pkwy	Irvine	CA	92606	**800-854-8257**	949-863-1181
Rosemount Inc 8200 Market Blvd	Chanhassen	MN	55317	**800-999-9307***	952-941-5560
*Cust Svc					
Schneider Automation Inc 1 High St	North Andover	MA	01845	**800-468-5342**	978-794-0800
Scully Signal Co 70 Industrial Way	Wilmington	MA	01887	**800-272-8559**	617-692-8600
Sensidyne Inc 16333 Bay Vista Dr	Clearwater	FL	33760	**800-451-9444**	727-530-3602
Sierra Instruments Inc 5 Harris Ct Bldg L	Monterey	CA	93940	**800-866-0200**	831-373-0200
SJE-Rhombus 22650 County Hwy 6 PO Box 1708	Detroit Lakes	MN	56502	**800-746-6287**	218-847-1317
SOR Inc 14685 W 105th St	Lenexa	KS	66215	**800-676-6794**	913-888-2630
Sparton Electronics 8500 Bluewater Rd NW	Albuquerque	NM	87121	**800-772-7866**	505-892-5300
Spectronics Corp 956 Brush Hollow Rd	Westbury	NY	11590	**800-274-8888**	
Spirax Sarco Inc 1150 Northpoint Blvd	Blythewood	SC	29016	**800-883-4411**	803-714-2000
Sterling Inc 5200 W Clinton Ave	Milwaukee	WI	53223	**800-783-7835***	414-354-0970
*Cust Svc					
STI Automation Sensors 1025 W 1700 N	Logan	UT	84321	**888-525-7300**	435-753-7300
Teledyne Advanced Pollution Instrumentation 6565 Nancy Ridge Dr	San Diego	CA	92121	**800-324-5190**	858-657-9800
Teledyne Monitor Labs 35 Inverness Dr E	Englewood	CO	80112	**800-422-1499**	303-792-3300
Tescom Corp 12616 Industrial Blvd	Elk River	MN	55330	**800-447-1204**	763-241-3349
Test Automation & Controls 1036 Destrehan Ave	Harvey	LA	70058	**800-861-6792**	504-371-3000
Thermo Electric Co Inc 109 N 5th St	Saddle Brook	NJ	07663	**800-766-4020***	201-843-5800
*Sales					
Thermo Electron Corp 81 Wyman St PO Box 9056	Waltham	MA	02454	**800-678-5599**	781-622-1000
NYSE: TMO					
Thermo Environmental Instruments Inc 27 Forge Pkwy	Franklin	MA	02038	**866-282-0430**	508-520-0430
Thermo Flow Automation 9303 W Sam Houston Pkwy S	Houston	TX	77099	**800-437-7979**	713-272-0404
Thermo MeasureTech Inc 2555 N I-35	Round Rock	TX	78664	**800-736-0801**	512-388-9100
Thermometrics Inc 808 US Hwy 1	Edison	NJ	08817	**800-246-7019**	732-287-2870
Transcat Inc 35 Vantage Point Dr	Rochester	NY	14624	**800-828-1470**	585-352-7777
NASDAQ: TRNS					
Trerice HO Co 12950 W Eight-Mile Rd	Oak Park	MI	48237	**888-873-7423**	248-399-8000
Troxler Electronic Laboratories Inc 3008 Cornwallis Rd PO Box 12057	Research Triangle Park	NC	27709	**877-876-9537**	919-549-8661
TSI Inc 500 Cardigan Rd	Shoreview	MN	55126	**800-234-8822**	651-483-0900
Uniloc Div Rosemount Analytical Inc 2400 Barranca Pkwy	Irvine	CA	92606	**800-854-8257**	949-863-1181
United Electric Controls Co 180 Dexter Ave	Watertown	MA	02472	**800-545-1416**	617-926-1000
Veeder-Root 125 Powder Forest Dr	Simsbury	CT	06070	**800-879-0301**	860-651-2700
Veriflo Div Parker Hannifin Corp 250 Canal Blvd	Richmond	CA	94804	**800-962-4074**	510-235-9590
Wika Instrument Corp 1000 Wiegand Blvd	Lawrenceville	GA	30043	**888-945-2872**	770-513-8200
Yokogawa Corp of America 2 Dart Rd	Newnan	GA	30265	**800-258-2552**	770-253-7000
YSI Inc 1700-1725 Brannum Ln	Yellow Springs	OH	45387	**800-765-4974***	937-767-7241
*Cust Svc					

201 CONTROLS - TEMPERATURE - RESIDENTIAL & COMMERCIAL

Company	City	State	Zip	Toll-Free	Phone
APCOM Inc 125 Southeast Pkwy	Franklin	TN	37064	**800-251-3535**	615-794-5574
Azonix Corp 900 Middlesex Tpke Bldg 6	Billerica	MA	01821	**800-967-5558**	978-670-6300
Capp Inc 201 Marple Ave	Clifton Heights	PA	19018	**800-356-8000**	610-394-1100
Columbus Electric Mfg Co PO Box 4973	Johnson City	TN	37602	**800-251-7828**	423-477-4131
Computer Process Controls Inc 1640 Airport Rd NW Suite 104	Kennesaw	GA	30144	**800-829-2724**	770-425-2724
Cooper Atkins Corp 33 Reeds Gap Rd	Middlefield	CT	06455	**800-835-5011***	860-349-3473
*Sales					
DeltaTRAK Inc PO Box 398	Pleasanton	CA	94566	**800-962-6776**	925-467-5940
Electronic Systems USA Inc 9410 Bunsen Pkwy Suite 100	Louisville	KY	40220	**800-765-7773**	502-495-6700
FAST (Food Automation-Service Techniques Inc) 905 Honeyspot Rd	Stratford	CT	06615	**800-327-8766**	203-377-4414
Food Automation-Service Techniques Inc (FAST) 905 Honeyspot Rd	Stratford	CT	06615	**800-327-8766**	203-377-4414
Hallcrest Inc 1820 Pickwick Ln	Glenview	IL	60025	**800-527-1419**	847-998-8580
HSQ Technology 26227 Research Rd	Hayward	CA	94545	**800-486-6684**	510-259-1334
Invensys 33 Commercial St	Foxboro	MA	02035	**866-746-6477**	508-543-8750
Ircon Inc 7300 N Natchez Ave	Niles	IL	60714	**800-323-7660**	847-967-5151
Johnson Controls Inc 5757 N Green Bay Ave	Milwaukee	WI	53209	**800-972-8040**	414-524-1200
NYSE: JCI					
Johnson Controls Inc Controls Group 507 E Michigan St	Milwaukee	WI	53202	**800-275-5676**	414-274-4000
Kidde-Fenwal Inc 400 Main St	Ashland	MA	01721	**800-872-6527**	508-881-2000
Liebert Corp 1050 Dearborn Dr	Columbus	OH	43085	**800-543-2778***	614-888-0246
*Tech Supp					
Novar Controls Corp 3333 Copley Rd	Copley	OH	44321	**800-348-1235**	330-670-1010
Portage Electric Products Inc 7700 Freedom Ave NW	North Canton	OH	44720	**888-464-7374**	330-499-2727
Powers Process Controls 3400 Oakton St	Skokie	IL	60076	**800-669-4217**	847-673-6700
Robinair Div SPX Corp 655 Eisenhower Dr	Owatonna	MN	55060	**800-628-6496**	507-455-7000
SPX Corp Robinair Div 655 Eisenhower Dr	Owatonna	MN	55060	**800-628-6496**	507-455-7000
TAC Americas 1650 W Crosby Rd	Carrollton	TX	75006	**800-274-5551**	972-323-1111
Watlow Winona 1241 Bundy Blvd	Winona	MN	55987	**800-833-7492**	507-454-5300

202 CONTROLS & RELAYS - ELECTRICAL

Company	City	State	Zip	Toll-Free	Phone
ABB SSAC Inc 8220 Loop Rd	Baldwinsville	NY	13027	**800-377-7722***	315-638-1300
*Tech Supp					
Alcoa Fujikura Ltd 830 Crescent Ctr Dr Suite 600	Franklin	TN	37067	**800-627-7854**	615-778-6000
Allied Controls Inc 150 E Aurora St	Waterbury	CT	06708	**800-648-8871**	203-757-4200
AMETEK National Controls Corp 1725 Western Dr	West Chicago	IL	60185	**800-323-2593**	630-231-5900
AMX Corp 3000 Research Dr	Richardson	TX	75082	**800-222-0193**	469-624-8000
Anaheim Automation 910 E Orangefair Ln	Anaheim	CA	92801	**800-345-9401***	714-992-6990
*Sales					
Aromat Corp 629 Central Ave	New Providence	NJ	07974	**800-276-6289**	908-464-3550
ATC Diversified Electronics Inc 1827 Freedom Rd	Lancaster	PA	17601	**800-874-0619***	717-295-0500
*Cust Svc					
Bright Image Corp 4900 Harrison St	Hillside	IL	60162	**800-733-5656**	708-449-5656
Cleveland Motion Controls Inc 7550 Hub Pkwy	Cleveland	OH	44125	**800-321-8072**	216-524-8800
DST Controls 651 Stone Rd	Benicia	CA	94510	**800-251-0773**	707-745-5117
Ducommun Technologies Inc 23301 Wilmington Ave	Carson	CA	90745	**800-421-5032**	310-513-7200
Duct-O-Wire Co PO Box 519	Corona	CA	92878	**800-752-6001**	951-735-8220
Electric Regulator Corp 6189 El Camino Real	Carlsbad	CA	92009	**800-458-6566**	760-438-7873

	City	State	Zip	Toll-Free	Phone
Electroid Co 45 Fadem Rd	Springfield	NJ	07081	**800-242-7184**	973-467-8100
Electronic Theatre Controls Inc 3031 Pleasantview Rd	Middleton	WI	53562	**800-688-4116**	608-831-4116
Enercon Engineering Inc 1 Altorfer Ln	East Peoria	IL	61611	**800-218-8831**	309-694-1418
Fife Corp 222 W Memorial Rd	Oklahoma City	OK	73114	**800-333-3433**	405-755-1600
Fincor Automation Inc 3750 E Market St. *Sales	York	PA	17402	**800-334-3040***	717-751-4200
FSI/Fork Standards Inc 668 E Western Ave	Lombard	IL	60148	**800-468-6009**	630-932-9380
GE Multilin 215 Anderson Ave	Markham	ON	L6E1B3	**800-547-8629**	905-294-6222
Gerhardts Inc 819 Central Ave	Jefferson	LA	70121	**800-722-6566**	504-733-2500
Glendinning Marine Products 740 Century Cir	Conway	SC	29526	**800-500-2380**	843-399-6146
Globe Electronic Hardware Inc 34-24 56th St.	Woodside	NY	11377	**800-221-1505**	718-457-0303
Guardian Electric Mfg Co Inc 1425 Lake Ave	Woodstock	IL	60098	**800-762-0369**	815-337-0050
Honeywell ACS 11 W Spring St	Freeport	IL	61032	**800-328-5111**	
Honeywell Automation & Control Solutions 11 W Spring St	Freeport	IL	61032	**800-328-5111**	
Honeywell Sensing & Control 11 W Spring St. *Cust Svc	Freeport	IL	61032	**800-537-6945***	815-235-5500
Hubbell Industrial Controls 4301 Cheyenne Dr	Archdale	NC	27263	**800-828-4032**	336-434-2800
IDEC Corp 1175 Elko Dr	Sunnyvale	CA	94089	**800-262-4332**	408-747-0550
Johnson Controls Inc 5757 N Green Bay Ave. *NYSE: JCI*	Milwaukee	WI	53209	**800-972-8040**	414-524-1200
Johnson Controls Inc Controls Group 507 E Michigan St	Milwaukee	WI	53202	**800-275-5676**	414-274-4000
Jordan Controls Inc 5607 W Douglas Ave *Prod Info	Milwaukee	WI	53218	**800-637-5547***	414-461-9200
Joslyn Clark Controls Inc 2013 W Meeting St	Lancaster	SC	29720	**800-476-6952**	803-286-8491
Kaiser Electroprecision Corp 17000 S Red Hill Ave	Irvine	CA	92614	**800-866-5775**	949-250-1015
KB Electronics Inc 12095 NW 39th St.	Coral Springs	FL	33065	**800-221-6570**	954-346-4900
Lutron Electronics Co Inc 7200 Suter Rd. *Tech Supp	Coopersburg	PA	18036	**800-523-9466***	610-282-3800
Magnet Schultz of America Inc 401 Plaza Dr *Cust Svc	Westmont	IL	60559	**800-635-3778***	630-789-0600
Moeller Electric Corp USA 15311 Vantage Pkwy Suite 190	Houston	TX	77032	**800-451-5110**	713-933-0999
Moog Inc Seneca & Jamison Rd. *NYSE: MOG/A*	East Aurora	NY	14052	**800-664-6664**	716-652-2000
Omron Electronics Inc 1 Commerce Dr	Schaumburg	IL	60173	**800-556-6766**	847-843-7900
Ormec Systems Corp 19 Linden Pk	Rochester	NY	14625	**800-656-7632**	585-385-3520
Parker Hannifin Corp Electromechanical Automation Div 5500 Business Park Dr	Rohnert Park	CA	94928	**800-358-9068**	707-584-7558
Parker McCrory Mfg Co 2000 Forest Ave.	Kansas City	MO	64108	**800-662-1038**	816-221-2000
Payne Engineering Co Rt 29 Rocky Step Rd. *Orders	Scott Depot	WV	25560	**800-331-1345***	304-757-7353
Polytron Corp 4400 Wyland Dr.	Elkhart	IN	46516	**888-228-0246**	574-522-0246
Rockford Systems Inc 4620 Hydraulic Rd *Cust Svc	Rockford	IL	61109	**800-922-7533***	815-874-7891
SAIA-Burgess Inc PO Box 427	Vandalia	OH	45377	**800-888-9765**	937-898-3621
SBE Inc 2305 Camino Ramon Suite 200. *NASDAQ: SBEI*	San Ramon	CA	94583	**800-925-2666**	925-355-2000
Scientific Technologies Inc 6550 Dumbarton Cir *NASDAQ: STIZ*	Fremont	CA	94555	**800-221-7060**	510-608-3400
Sheffield Measurement Inc 660 S Military Rd PO Box 1658 *Cust Svc	Fond du Lac	WI	54936	**800-535-1236***	920-921-7100
SOR Inc 14685 W 105th St.	Lenexa	KS	66215	**800-676-6794**	913-888-2630
SRC Devices Inc 888 Prospect St Suite 201	San Diego	CA	92037	**866-772-8668**	858-292-8770
Sturdy Corp 1822 Carolina Beach Rd	Wilmington	NC	28401	**800-721-3282**	910-763-8261
Time Mark Corp 11440 E Pine St.	Tulsa	OK	74116	**800-862-2875**	918-438-1220
Time-O-Matic Inc 1015 Maple St	Danville	IL	61832	**800-637-2645**	217-442-0611
Unico Inc 3725 Nicholson Rd.	Franksville	WI	53126	**800-245-1859**	262-886-5678
Wescon Products Co 2533 S West St	Wichita	KS	67217	**800-835-0160**	316-942-7266
Yaskawa Electric America Inc 2121 Norman Dr	Waukegan	IL	60085	**800-927-5292**	847-887-7000

203 CONVENIENCE STORES

SEE ALSO Gas Stations; Grocery Stores

	City	State	Zip	Toll-Free	Phone
7-Eleven Inc PO Box 711 *NYSE: SE*	Dallas	TX	75221	**800-255-0711**	214-828-7011
Alimentation Couche-Tard Inc 1600 boul St Martin E Suite 200 Tower B *TSE: ATD*	Laval	QC	H7G4S7	**800-361-2612**	450-662-3272
Brower CW Inc 413 S Riverside Dr.	Modesto	CA	95354	**800-400-0477**	209-523-1828
Calfee Co of Dalton DBA Favorite Market 1503 N Tibbs Rd	Dalton	GA	30720	**800-634-2944**	706-226-4834
Convenient Food Mart Inc 467 N State St.	Painesville	OH	44077	**800-860-4844**	
Cumberland Farms Inc 777 Dedham St	Canton	MA	02021	**800-225-9702**	781-828-4900
CW Brower Inc 413 S Riverside Dr.	Modesto	CA	95354	**800-400-0477**	209-523-1828
E-Z Mart Stores Inc 602 W Falvey St.	Texarkana	TX	75501	**800-234-6502**	903-832-6502
Erickson Petroleum Corp 4567 American Blvd W	Bloomington	MN	55437	**800-745-7411**	952-830-8700
Farm Stores 5800 NW 74th Ave.	Miami	FL	33166	**800-726-3276**	305-471-5141
Favorite Market 1503 N Tibbs Rd	Dalton	GA	30720	**800-634-2944**	706-226-4834
Gibbs Oil Co LP PO Box 9151	Chelsea	MA	02150	**800-352-3558**	617-889-9000
Handy Dandy Food Stores Inc 1800 Magnavox Way	Fort Wayne	IN	46804	**800-686-2836**	260-436-1415
Jackpot Convenience Stores Inc 2737 W Commodore Way	Seattle	WA	98199	**800-552-0748**	206-286-6436
Jet Food Stores of Georgia 1106 S Harris St	Sandersville	GA	31082	**800-277-1168**	478-552-2588
Junior Food Stores of West Florida Inc DBA Tom Thumb 619 8th Ave	Crestview	FL	32536	**800-682-8486**	850-682-5171
Kwik Pantry 2801 Glenda Ave.	Fort Worth	TX	76117	**800-695-3282**	817-838-4700
Love's Travel Stops & Country Stores Inc 10601 N Pennsylvania	Oklahoma City	OK	73120	**800-388-0983**	405-751-9000
Mac's Convenience Stores Inc 10 Commander Blvd	Scarborough	ON	M1S3T2	**800-268-5574**	416-291-4441
Norkus Enterprises Inc 505 Richmond Ave	Point Pleasant Beach	NJ	08742	**800-281-4047**	732-899-4040
Ohio Valley AFM Inc 3955 Alexandria Pike	Cold Spring	KY	41076	**800-359-3971**	859-781-3800
Okay Food Co Inc 500 Abney Ave	Lufkin	TX	75902	**800-256-6455**	936-634-4648
Pantry Inc 1801 Douglas Dr *NASDAQ: PTRY*	Sanford	NC	27330	**800-476-7574**	919-774-6700
Plaid Pantries Inc 10025 SW Allen Blvd	Beaverton	OR	97005	**800-677-5243**	503-646-4246
Presto Food Stores Inc 2009 N Airport Rd	Plant City	FL	33563	**800-881-3511**	813-754-3511
QuikTrip Corp 4705 S 129th East Ave	Tulsa	OK	74134	**800-544-5749**	918-615-7700
Rosenberger's Dairies Inc 847 Forty Foot Rd PO Box 901	Hatfield	PA	19440	**800-355-9074**	215-855-9074
Sheetz Inc 5700 6th Ave.	Altoona	PA	16602	**800-487-5444**	814-946-3611
Speedway SuperAmerica LLC 500 Speedway Dr *Cust Svc	Enon	OH	45323	**800-643-1948***	937-864-3000
Stop-N-Go Inc 1 Valero Way	San Antonio	TX	78249	**800-333-3377**	210-592-2000
Tom Thumb 619 8th Ave.	Crestview	FL	32536	**800-682-8486**	850-682-5171
Uni-Marts LLC 477 E Beaver Ave *AMEX: UNI*	State College	PA	16801	**800-494-1500**	814-234-6000
Wawa Inc 260 W Baltimore Pike	Media	PA	19063	**800-283-9292**	610-358-8000
Xtra Mart 221 Quinebaug Rd	North Grosvenordale	CT	06255	**800-243-6366**	860-935-5200

204 CONVENTION CENTERS

SEE ALSO Performing Arts Facilities; Stadiums & Arenas

	City	State	Zip	Toll-Free	Phone
Albuquerque Convention Center 401 2nd St NW *Mktg	Albuquerque	NM	87102	**800-733-9918***	505-768-4575
AmericasMart 240 Peachtree St NW Suite 2200	Atlanta	GA	30303	**800-285-6278**	404-220-2659
Arthur R. Outlaw Mobile Convention Center 1 S Water St	Mobile	AL	36602	**800-566-2453**	251-208-2100
Beaumont Civic Center Complex 701 Main St.	Beaumont	TX	77701	**800-782-3081**	409-838-3435
Bell Harbor International Conference Center 2211 Alaskan Way Pier 66	Seattle	WA	98121	**888-772-4422**	206-441-6666
Benton Convention Center 301 W 5th St.	Winston-Salem	NC	27101	**800-289-5670**	336-727-2976
Birmingham-Jefferson Convention Complex 2100 Richard Arrington Jr Blvd.	Birmingham	AL	35203	**877-843-2522**	205-458-8400
Bossier Civic Center 620 Benton Rd	Bossier City	LA	71111	**800-522-4842**	318-741-8900
Buffalo Convention Center 153 Franklin St Convention Center Plaza	Buffalo	NY	14202	**800-995-7570**	716-855-5555
Casper Events Center 1 Events Dr.	Casper	WY	82601	**800-442-2256**	307-235-8441
Chattanooga Convention Center 1 Carter Plaza	Chattanooga	TN	37402	**800-962-5213**	423-756-0001
Cleveland Convention Center 500 Lakeside Ave	Cleveland	OH	44114	**800-543-2489**	216-348-2200
Concourse Exhibition Center 8th & Brannan Sts	San Francisco	CA	94103	**800-877-8522**	415-864-1500
Dallas Convention Center 650 S Griffin St.	Dallas	TX	75202	**877-850-2100**	214-939-2700
Dallas Market Center 2100 Stemmons Fwy Suite MS 150	Dallas	TX	75207	**800-325-6587**	
David L Lawrence Convention Center 1000 Fort Duquesne Blvd	Pittsburgh	PA	15222	**800-222-5200**	412-565-6000
Dayton Convention Center 22 E 5th St	Dayton	OH	45402	**800-822-3498**	937-333-4700
Duluth Entertainment Convention Center 350 Harbor Dr	Duluth	MN	55802	**800-628-8385**	218-722-5573
Earle Brown Heritage Center 6155 Earle Brown Dr	Minneapolis	MN	55430	**800-524-0239**	763-569-6300
Edgar H Wilson Convention Centre 200 Coliseum Dr	Macon	GA	31217	**877-532-6144**	478-751-9152
El Paso Convention & Performing Arts Center 1 Civic Center Plaza	El Paso	TX	79901	**800-351-6024**	915-534-0600
Elko Civic Auditorium & Convention Center 700 Moren Way	Elko	NV	89801	**800-248-3556**	775-738-4091
Florence Events Center 715 Quince St	Florence	OR	97439	**888-968-4086**	541-997-1994
Frank W Mayborn Civic & Convention Center 3303 N 3rd St	Temple	TX	76501	**800-478-0338**	254-298-5720
Frankfort Convention Center 405 Mero St.	Frankfort	KY	40601	**800-960-7200**	502-564-5335
Gateway Center 1 Gateway Dr	Collinsville	IL	62234	**800-289-2388**	618-345-8998
Gatlinburg Convention Center 303 Reagan Dr.	Gatlinburg	TN	37738	**800-343-1475**	865-436-2392
George R Brown Convention Center 1001 Avenida de Las Americas	Houston	TX	77010	**800-427-4697**	713-853-8000
Golden Spike Event Center 1000 N 1200 West	Ogden	UT	84404	**800-442-7362**	801-399-8544
Greater Columbus Convention Center 400 N High St	Columbus	OH	43215	**800-626-0241**	614-827-2500
Greater Richmond Convention Center 403 N 3rd St	Richmond	VA	23219	**800-370-9004**	804-783-7300
Greater Tacoma Convention & Trade Center 1500 Broadway Plaza	Tacoma	WA	98402	**888-227-3705**	253-830-6601
Gwinnett Center 6400 Sugarloaf Pkwy Bldg 100	Duluth	GA	30097	**800-224-6422**	770-813-7500
Harborside Event Center 1375 Monroe St	Fort Myers	FL	33901	**800-294-9516**	239-332-7600
Hawaii Convention Center 1801 Kalakaua Ave.	Honolulu	HI	96815	**800-295-6603**	808-943-3500
Henry B Gonzalez Convention Center 200 E Market St.	San Antonio	TX	78205	**877-504-8895**	210-207-8500
Horizon Convention Center 401 S High St.	Muncie	IN	47305	**888-288-8860**	765-288-8860
Hot Springs Convention Center 134 Convention Blvd	Hot Springs	AR	71901	**800-543-2284**	501-321-1705
Jekyll Island Convention Center 1 Beachview Dr	Jekyll Island	GA	31527	**877-453-5955**	912-635-3400
John B Hynes Veterans Memorial Convention Center 900 Boylston St.	Boston	MA	02115	**800-845-8800**	617-954-2000
John S Knight Convention Center 77 E Mill St	Akron	OH	44308	**800-245-4254**	330-374-8900
Kansas City Convention & Entertainment Centers 301 W 13th St.	Kansas City	MO	64105	**800-821-7060**	816-513-5000
Kentucky International Convention Center 221 4th St	Louisville	KY	40202	**800-701-5831**	502-595-4381
Lakeland Center 701 W Lime St	Lakeland	FL	33815	**800-200-4870**	863-834-8100
Las Vegas Convention Center 3150 Paradise Rd	Las Vegas	NV	89109	**800-332-5333**	702-892-0711
LifeWay Glorieta Conference Center PO Box 8 *Resv	Glorieta	NM	87535	**800-797-4222***	505-757-6161
Los Angeles Convention Center 1201 S Figueroa St	Los Angeles	CA	90015	**800-448-7775**	213-741-1151
Mayo Civic Center 30 Civic Center Dr SE	Rochester	MN	55904	**800-422-2199**	507-281-6184
McCormick Place 2301 S Lake Shore Dr.	Chicago	IL	60616	**800-263-9170**	312-791-7000

Name / Address	City	State	ZIP	Toll-Free	Phone
Meadowlands Exposition Center 355 Plaza Dr	Secaucus	NJ	07094	**888-400-3976**	201-330-7773
Memphis Cook Convention Center 255 N Main St	Memphis	TN	38103	**800-726-0915**	901-576-1200
Merchandise Mart 470 Merchandise Mart	Chicago	IL	60654	**800-677-6278**	312-527-7902
MetraPark 308 6th Ave N PO Box 2514	Billings	MT	59103	**800-366-8538**	406-256-2422
Mississippi Coast Coliseum & Convention Center 2350 Beach Blvd	Biloxi	MS	39531	**800-726-2781**	228-594-3700
Monterey Conference Center 1 Portola Plaza	Monterey	CA	93940	**800-742-8091**	831-646-3770
Moody Gardens Convention Center 1 Hope Blvd	Galveston	TX	77554	**800-582-4673**	409-744-4673
MPEC (Multi-Purpose Events Center) 1000 5th St	Wichita Falls	TX	76301	**800-799-6732**	940-716-5500
Myrtle Beach Convention Center 2101 N Oak St	Myrtle Beach	SC	29577	**800-537-1690**	843-918-1225
Natchez Convention Center 211 Main St	Natchez	MS	39120	**888-475-9744**	601-442-5881
Northwest Georgia Trade & Convention Center 2211 Dug Gap Battle Rd	Dalton	GA	30720	**800-824-7469**	706-272-7676
Oakland Convention Center 1001 Broadway	Oakland	CA	94607	**800-262-5526**	510-451-4000
Oakley-Lindsay Center 300 Civic Center Plaza Suite 237	Quincy	IL	62301	**800-978-4748**	217-223-1000
Ocean Center 101 N Atlantic Ave	Daytona Beach	FL	32118	**800-858-6444**	386-254-4500
Ocean Shores Convention Center 120 Chance ala Mer	Ocean Shores	WA	98569	**800-874-6737**	360-289-4411
Ogden Eccles Conference Center 2415 Washington Blvd.	Ogden	UT	84401	**800-337-2690**	801-395-3200
Ontario Convention Center 2000 Convention Center Way	Ontario	CA	91764	**800-455-5755**	909-937-3000
Orange County Convention Center 9800 International Dr.	Orlando	FL	32819	**800-345-9845**	407-685-9800
Oregon Convention Center 777 NE ML King Jr Blvd	Portland	OR	97232	**800-791-2250**	503-235-7575
Palais des Congres de Montreal-Convention Centre 159 rue Saint-Antoine O 9e étage	Montreal	QC	H2Z1H2	**800-268-8122**	514-871-8122
Palm Beach County Convention Center 650 Okeechobee Blvd.	West Palm Beach	FL	33401	**800-833-5733**	561-366-3019
Palm Springs Convention Center 277 N Avenida Caballeros	Palm Springs	CA	92262	**800-333-7535**	760-325-6611
Pendleton Convention Center 1601 Westgate Ave	Pendleton	OR	97801	**800-863-9358**	541-276-6569
Pennsylvania Convention Center 1101 Arch St	Philadelphia	PA	19107	**800-428-9000**	215-418-4700
Phoenix Civic Plaza Convention Center 111 N 3rd St	Phoenix	AZ	85004	**800-282-4842**	602-262-6225
Pine Bluff Convention Center 1 Convention Ctr Plaza	Pine Bluff	AR	71601	**800-536-7660**	870-536-7600
Plano Centre 2000 E Springcreek Pkwy	Plano	TX	75074	**800-817-5266**	972-422-0296
Roland E Powell Convention Center 4001 Coastal Hwy	Ocean City	MD	21842	**800-626-2326**	410-289-8311
Saint Cloud Civic Center 10 4th Ave S	Saint Cloud	MN	56301	**800-450-7272**	320-255-7272
Salem Conference Center 200 Commercial St SE *Sales	Salem	OR	97301	**877-589-1700***	503-589-1700
Salt Palace Convention Center 100 S West Temple	Salt Lake City	UT	84101	**877-547-4656**	801-534-4777
San Diego Convention Center 111 W Harbor Dr	San Diego	CA	92101	**800-525-7322**	619-525-5000
San Jose Convention & Cultural Facilities 408 Almaden Blvd	San Jose	CA	95110	**800-533-2345**	408-277-5277
San Jose McEnery Convention Center 150 W San Carlos St	San Jose	CA	95113	**800-533-2345**	408-277-3900
San Mateo County Expo Center 2495 S Delaware St	San Mateo	CA	94403	**800-338-3976**	650-574-3247
SeaGate Convention Centre 401 Jefferson Ave	Toledo	OH	43604	**800-243-4667**	419-255-3300
Seaside Civic & Convention Center 415 1st Ave	Seaside	OR	97138	**800-394-3303**	503-738-8585
Sioux City Convention Center 801 4th St	Sioux City	IA	51101	**800-593-2228**	712-279-4800
South Padre Island Convention Centre 7355 Padre Blvd	South Padre Island	TX	78597	**800-657-2373**	956-761-3000
Statehouse Convention Center Markham & Main #1 1 Statehouse Plaza	Little Rock	AR	72201	**800-844-4781**	501-376-4781
Sweeney Convention Center 201 W Marcy St	Santa Fe	NM	87504	**800-777-2489**	505-955-6200
Tallahassee-Leon County Civic Center 505 W Pensacola St	Tallahassee	FL	32301	**800-322-3602**	850-487-1691
Tampa Convention Center 333 S Franklin St	Tampa	FL	33602	**800-426-5630**	813-274-8511
Tulsa Convention Center 100 Civic Ctr	Tulsa	OK	74103	**800-678-7177**	918-596-7177
Tyson Events Center 401 Gordon Dr	Sioux City	IA	51101	**800-593-2228**	712-279-4850
Valley Forge Convention Center 1160 1st Ave	King of Prussia	PA	19406	**888-267-1500**	610-337-4000
Veterans Memorial Civic & Convention Center 7 Town Sq	Lima	OH	45801	**877-377-0674**	419-224-5222
Washington Convention Center 801 Mt Vernon Pl NW	Washington	DC	20001	**800-368-9000**	202-249-3000
Wildwoods Convention Center 4501 Boardwalk	Wildwood	NJ	08260	**800-995-9732**	609-729-9000
Yakima Convention Center 10 N 8th St	Yakima	WA	98901	**800-221-0751**	509-575-6062

205 CONVENTION & VISITORS BUREAUS

SEE ALSO Travel & Tourism Information - Canadian; Travel & Tourism Information - Foreign Travel

Listings are alphabetized by city names.

Name / Address	City	State	ZIP	Toll-Free	Phone
Aberdeen Convention & Visitors Bureau PO Box 78	Aberdeen	SD	57402	**800-645-3851**	605-225-2414
Abilene Convention & Visitors Bureau 201 NW 2nd St PO Box 146	Abilene	KS	67410	**800-569-5915**	785-263-2231
Abilene Convention & Visitors Bureau 1101 N 1st St	Abilene	TX	79601	**800-727-7704**	325-676-2556
Abingdon Convention & Visitors Bureau 335 Cummings St	Abingdon	VA	24210	**800-435-3440**	276-676-2282
Akron/Summit County Convention & Visitors Bureau 77 E Mill St	Akron	OH	44308	**800-245-4254**	330-374-7560
Albany County Convention & Visitors Bureau 25 Quackenbush Sq	Albany	NY	12207	**800-258-3582**	518-434-1217
Albany Visitors Assn 250 Broadalbin St SW Suite 110	Albany	OR	97321	**800-526-2256**	541-928-0911
Albuquerque Convention & Visitors Bureau 20 First Plaza Suite 601	Albuquerque	NM	87102	**800-733-9918**	505-842-9918
Alexandria/Pineville Area Convention & Visitors Bureau 707 Main St	Alexandria	LA	71301	**800-551-9546**	318-442-9546
Alexandria Convention & Visitors Assn 221 King St	Alexandria	VA	22314	**800-388-9119**	703-838-4200
Allegan County Tourist & Recreational Council 3255 122nd Ave Suite 102	Allegan	MI	49010	**888-425-5342**	269-686-9088
Alpena Area Convention & Visitors Bureau 235 W Chisholm St	Alpena	MI	49707	**800-425-7362**	989-354-4181
Greater Alton/Twin Rivers Convention & Visitors Bureau 200 Piasa St	Alton	IL	62002	**800-258-6645**	618-465-6676
Alvin Convention & Visitors Bureau 105 W Willis St	Alvin	TX	77511	**800-331-4063**	281-585-3359
Amana Colonies Convention & Visitors Bureau 622 46th Ave	Amana	IA	52203	**800-245-5465**	319-622-7622
Amarillo Convention & Visitor Council PO Box 9480	Amarillo	TX	79105	**800-692-1338**	806-374-1497
Lorain County Visitors Bureau 8025 Leavitt Rd	Amherst	OH	44001	**800-334-1673**	440-984-5282
Anaheim/Orange County Visitor & Convention Bureau 800 W Katella Ave	Anaheim	CA	92802	**888-598-3200**	714-765-8888
Anchorage Convention & Visitors Bureau 524 W 4th Ave	Anchorage	AK	99501	**800-478-1255**	907-276-4118
Anderson/Madison County Visitors & Convention Bureau 6335 S Scatterfield Rd	Anderson	IN	46013	**800-533-6569**	765-643-5633
Steuben County Tourism Bureau 207 S Wayne St	Angola	IN	46703	**800-525-3101**	260-665-5386
Ann Arbor Area Convention & Visitors Bureau 120 W Huron St	Ann Arbor	MI	48104	**800-888-9487**	734-995-7281
Southernmost Illinois Tourism Bureau PO Box 378	Anna	IL	62906	**800-248-4373**	618-833-9928
Fox Cities Convention & Visitors Bureau 3433 W College Ave	Appleton	WI	54914	**800-236-6673**	920-734-3358
Arlington Convention & Visitors Bureau 1905 E Randol Mill Rd	Arlington	TX	76011	**800-433-5374**	817-265-7721
Arlington Convention & Visitors Service 1100 N Glebe Rd Suite 1500	Arlington	VA	22201	**800-296-7996**	703-228-0888
Asheville Area Convention & Visitors Bureau PO Box 1010	Asheville	NC	28802	**800-257-5583**	828-258-6102
Athens Convention & Visitors Bureau 300 N Thomas St.	Athens	GA	30601	**800-653-0603**	706-357-4430
Athens County Convention & Visitors Bureau 667 E State St	Athens	OH	45701	**800-878-9767**	740-592-1819
Atlanta Convention & Visitors Bureau 233 Peachtree St NE Suite 100	Atlanta	GA	30303	**800-285-2682**	404-521-6600
Cobb County Convention & Visitors Bureau 1 Galleria Pkwy	Atlanta	GA	30339	**800-451-3480**	678-303-2622
Atlantic City Convention & Visitors Authority 2314 Pacific Ave	Atlantic City	NJ	08401	**888-228-4748**	609-449-7130
Auburn/Opelika Convention & Visitors Bureau 714 E Glenn Ave	Auburn	AL	36830	**800-321-8880**	334-887-8747
Augusta Metropolitan Convention & Visitors Bureau 1450 Greene St Suite 110	Augusta	GA	30901	**800-726-0243**	706-823-6600
Aurora Area Convention & Visitors Bureau 43 W Galena Blvd	Aurora	IL	60506	**800-477-4369**	630-897-5581
Austin Convention & Visitors Bureau 301 Congress Suite 200	Austin	TX	78701	**800-926-2282**	512-474-5171
Baker County Visitors & Convention Bureau 490 Campbell St	Baker City	OR	97814	**800-523-1235**	541-523-3356
Greater Bakersfield Convention & Visitors Bureau 515 Truxtun Ave	Bakersfield	CA	93301	**866-425-7353**	661-325-5051
Baltimore Area Convention & Visitors Assn 100 Light St 12th Fl.	Baltimore	MD	21202	**800-343-3468**	410-659-7300
Bandera County Convention & Visitors Bureau PO Box 171	Bandera	TX	78003	**800-364-3833**	830-796-3045
Greater Bangor Convention & Visitors Bureau 1 Cumberland Pl Suite 300	Bangor	ME	04401	**800-916-6673**	207-947-5205
Bardstown-Nelson County Tourist & Convention Commission PO Box 867	Bardstown	KY	40004	**800-638-4877**	502-348-4877
Clermont County Convention & Visitors Bureau 410 E Main St PO Box 100	Batavia	OH	45103	**800-796-4282**	513-732-3600
Baton Rouge Convention & Visitors Bureau 730 North Blvd.	Baton Rouge	LA	70802	**800-527-6843**	225-383-1825
Battle Creek/Calhoun County Visitors & Convention Bureau 77 E Michigan Ave Suite 100	Battle Creek	MI	49017	**800-397-2240**	269-962-2240
Gateway Tourism Council PO Box 2011	Bayonne	NJ	07002	**877-428-3930**	201-436-6009
Beaumont Convention & Visitors Bureau 801 Main St Suite 100	Beaumont	TX	77701	**800-392-4401**	409-880-3749
Greene County Convention & Visitors Bureau 1221 Meadowbridge Dr	Beavercreek	OH	45434	**800-733-9109**	937-429-9100
Washington County Convention & Visitors Bureau 5075 SW Griffith Dr Suite 120	Beaverton	OR	97005	**800-537-3149**	503-644-5555
Southern West Virginia Convention & Visitors Bureau 200 Main St	Beckley	WV	25801	**800-847-4898**	304-252-2244
Bedford County Visitors Bureau 131 S Juliana St	Bedford	PA	15522	**800-765-3331**	814-623-1771
Bellevue Area Tourism & Visitors Bureau PO Box 63	Bellevue	OH	44811	**800-562-6978**	419-483-5359
Gaston County Travel & Tourism 620 N Main St	Belmont	NC	28012	**800-849-9994**	704-825-4044
Beloit Convention & Visitors Bureau 1003 Pleasant St	Beloit	WI	53511	**800-423-5648**	608-365-4838
Bucks County Conference & Visitors Bureau 3207 Street Rd	Bensalem	PA	19020	**800-836-2825**	215-639-0300
Franklin County Tourism Bureau PO Box 1641	Benton	IL	62812	**800-661-9998**	618-439-0608
Berkeley Convention & Visitors Bureau 2015 Center St 1st Fl	Berkeley	CA	94704	**800-847-4823**	510-549-7040
Lehigh Valley Convention & Visitors Bureau 2200 Ave A	Bethlehem	PA	18017	**800-747-0561**	610-882-9200
Beverly Hills Conference & Visitors Bureau 239 S Beverly Dr	Beverly Hills	CA	90212	**800-345-2210**	310-248-1000
Greater Big Rapids Convention & Visitors Bureau 246 N State St	Big Rapids	MI	49307	**888-229-4386**	231-796-7640
Big Spring Convention & Visitor Bureau PO Box 1391	Big Spring	TX	79721	**800-734-7641**	432-263-7641
Billings Convention & Visitors Bureau PO Box 31177	Billings	MT	59107	**800-735-2635**	406-245-4111
Broome County Convention & Visitors Bureau PO Box 995	Binghamton	NY	13902	**800-836-6740**	607-772-8860

Organization / Address	City	State	ZIP	*Toll-Free*	*Phone*
Greater Birmingham Convention & Visitors Bureau 2200 9th Ave N	Birmingham	AL	35203	**800-458-8085**	205-458-8000
Bismarck-Mandan Convention & Visitors Bureau 1600 Burnt Boat Dr	Bismarck	ND	58503	**800-767-3555**	701-222-4308
Bloomington-Normal Area Convention & Visitors Bureau 3201 CIRA Dr Suite 201	Bloomington	IL	61704	**800-433-8226**	309-665-0033
Bloomington/Monroe County Convention & Visitors Bureau 2855 N Walnut St	Bloomington	IN	47404	**800-800-0037**	812-334-8900
Bloomington Convention & Visitors Bureau 7900 International Dr Suite 990	Bloomington	MN	55425	**800-346-4289**	952-858-8500
Columbia-Montour Visitors Bureau 121 Papermill Rd	Bloomsburg	PA	17815	**800-847-4810**	570-784-8279
Mercer County Convention & Visitors Bureau 500 Bland St PO Box 4088	Bluefield	WV	24701	**800-221-3206**	304-325-8438
Boise Convention & Visitors Bureau 312 S 9th St Suite 100	Boise	ID	83702	**800-635-5240**	208-344-7777
Boone Convention & Visitors Bureau 208 Howard St	Boone	NC	28607	**800-852-9506**	828-262-3516
North Carolina High Country Host 1700 Blowing Rock Rd	Boone	NC	28607	**800-438-7500**	828-264-1299
Greater Boston Convention & Visitors Bureau 2 Copley Pl Suite 105	Boston	MA	02116	**888-733-2678**	617-536-4100
Bottineau Convention & Visitor Bureau 519 Main St	Bottineau	ND	58318	**800-735-6932**	701-228-3849
Boulder Convention & Visitors Bureau 2440 Pearl St	Boulder	CO	80302	**800-444-0447**	303-442-2911
Bradenton Area Convention & Visitors Bureau PO Box 1000	Bradenton	FL	34206	**800-822-2017**	941-729-9177
Brainerd Lakes Area Convention & Visitors Bureau 124 N 6th St	Brainerd	MN	56401	**800-450-2838**	218-829-2838
Branson/Lakes Area Convention & Visitors Bureau PO Box 1897	Branson	MO	65615	**800-214-3661**	417-334-4136
Brenham/Washington County Convention & Visitor Bureau 314 S Austin St	Brenham	TX	77833	**800-225-3695**	979-836-3695
Greater Bridgeport Conference & Vistors Center 164 W Main St	Bridgeport	WV	26330	**800-368-4324**	304-842-7272
Minneapolis Metro North Convention & Visitors Bureau 6200 Shingle Creek Pkwy Suite 248	Brooklyn Center	MN	55430	**800-541-4364**	763-566-7722
Northwest Pennsylvania's Great Outdoors Visitors Bureau 175 Main St	Brookville	PA	15825	**800-348-9393**	814-849-5197
Brownsville Convention & Visitors Bureau PO Box 4697	Brownsville	TX	78523	**800-626-2639**	956-546-3721
Buena Park Convention & Visitors Office 6601 Beach Blvd Suite 200	Buena Park	CA	90621	**800-541-3953**	714-562-3560
Greater Buffalo Convention & Visitors Bureau 617 Main St Suite 200	Buffalo	NY	14203	**800-283-3256**	716-852-2356
San Mateo County Convention & Visitors Bureau 111 Anza Blvd Suite 410	Burlingame	CA	94010	**800-288-4748**	650-348-7600
Burlington/Alamance County Convention & Visitors Bureau PO Box 519	Burlington	NC	27216	**800-637-3804**	336-570-1444
Burlington Convention & Visitors Bureau 60 Main St Suite 100	Burlington	VT	05401	**877-264-3503**	802-863-3489
Cadillac Area Visitors Bureau 222 Lake St	Cadillac	MI	49601	**800-225-2537**	231-775-0657
Tourism Calgary 238 11th Ave SE Suite 200	Calgary	AB	T2G0X8	**800-661-1678**	403-263-8510
Finger Lakes Visitors Connection 25 Gorham St Box 179	Canandaigua	NY	14424	**877-386-4669**	585-394-3915
Youngstown/Mahoning County Convention & Visitors Bureau 3620 Starr Centre Dr	Canfield	OH	44406	**800-447-8201**	330-286-0089
Canton/Stark County Convention & Visitors Bureau 222 Market Ave N	Canton	OH	44702	**800-533-4302**	330-454-1439
Carbondale Convention & Tourism Bureau 1185 E Main St Suite 1046	Carbondale	IL	62901	**800-526-1500**	618-529-4451
Carlsbad Convention & Visitors Bureau 400 Carlsbad Village Dr	Carlsbad	CA	92008	**800-227-5722**	760-434-6093
Carlsbad Convention & Visitors Bureau 302 S Canal St	Carlsbad	NM	88220	**800-221-1224**	505-887-6516
Carrington Convention & Visitors Bureau PO Box 439	Carrington	ND	58421	**800-641-9668**	701-652-2524
Carson City Convention & Visitors Bureau 1900 S Carson St Suite 100	Carson City	NV	89701	**800-638-2321**	775-687-7410
Cartersville Bartow County Convention & Visitors Bureau PO Box 200397	Cartersville	GA	30120	**800-733-2280**	770-387-1357
Casper Area Convention & Visitors Bureau 330 S Center St Suite 420	Casper	WY	82601	**800-852-1889**	307-234-5362
Iron County Tourism & Convention Bureau 581 N Main	Cedar City	UT	84720	**800-354-4849**	435-586-5124
Cedar Rapids Area Convention & Visitors Bureau PO Box 5339	Cedar Rapids	IA	52406	**800-735-5557**	319-398-5009
River Country Tourism Bureau 316 E Charlotte PO Box 579	Centreville	MI	49032	**800-447-2821**	269-467-4452
Brandywine Conference & Visitors Bureau 1 Beaver Valley Rd	Chadford	PA	19317	**800-343-3983**	610-565-3679
Champaign County Convention & Visitors Bureau 1817 S Neil St Suite 201	Champaign	IL	61820	**800-369-6151**	217-351-4133
Chapel Hill/Orange County Visitors Bureau 501 W Franklin St	Chapel Hill	NC	27516	**888-968-2060**	919-968-2060
Charleston Area Convention & Visitors Bureau 423 King St	Charleston	SC	29403	**800-868-8118**	843-853-8000
Charleston Convention & Visitors Bureau 200 Civic Center Dr	Charleston	WV	25301	**800-733-5469**	304-344-5075
Charlotte Convention & Visitors Bureau 500 S College St Suite 300	Charlotte	NC	28202	**800-722-1994**	704-334-2282
Chattanooga Area Convention & Visitors Bureau 2 Broad St	Chattanooga	TN	37402	**800-322-3344**	423-756-8687
Chautauqua County Visitors Bureau PO Box 1441	Chautauqua	NY	14722	**800-242-4569**	716-357-4569
Tourism Lewis County 500 NW Chamber of Commerce Way	Chehalis	WA	98532	**800-525-3323**	360-748-8885
Cherokee Tribal Travel & Promotions 498 Tsali Blvd	Cherokee	NC	28719	**800-438-1601**	828-497-9195
Indiana Dunes - The Casual Coast 1120 S Calumet Suite 1	Chesterton	IN	46304	**800-283-8687**	219-926-2255
Cheyenne Area Convention & Visitors Bureau 121 W 15th St Suite 202	Cheyenne	WY	82001	**800-426-5009**	307-778-3133
Chicago Convention & Tourism Bureau 2301 S Lake Shore Dr McCormick Complex Lakeside Ctr	Chicago	IL	60616	**800-244-2246**	312-567-8500
Chicago Office of Tourism 78 E Washington St	Chicago	IL	60602	**877-244-2246**	312-744-2400
Greater Cincinnati Convention & Visitors Bureau 300 W 6th St	Cincinnati	OH	45202	**800-246-2987**	513-621-2142

Organization / Address	City	State	ZIP	*Toll-Free*	*Phone*
Pickaway County Visitors Bureau 135 W Main St	Circleville	OH	43113	**888-770-7425**	740-474-4923
Clarksville/Montgomery County Tourist Commission PO Box 883	Clarksville	TN	37041	**800-530-2487**	931-648-0001
Clear Lake Convention & Visitors Bureau PO Box 188	Clear Lake	IA	50428	**800-285-5338**	641-357-2159
Saint Petersburg/Clearwater Area Convention & Visitors Bureau 14450 46th St N Suite 108	Clearwater	FL	33762	**800-345-6710**	727-464-7200
Convention & Visitors Bureau of Greater Cleveland 50 Public Sq Terminal Tower Suite 3100	Cleveland	OH	44113	**800-321-1001**	216-621-4110
Cleveland/Bradley Convention & Visitors Bureau PO Box 2275	Cleveland	TN	37320	**800-472-6588**	423-472-6587
Clinton Convention & Visitors Bureau 333 4th Ave S	Clinton	IA	52732	**800-828-5702**	563-242-5702
Park County Travel Council 836 Sheridan Ave	Cody	WY	82414	**800-393-2639**	307-587-2297
Coffeyville Convention & Visitors Bureau PO Box 457	Coffeyville	KS	67337	**800-626-3357**	620-251-1194
Colby Convention & Visitors Bureau 350 S Range Ave Suite 10	Colby	KS	67701	**800-611-8835**	785-460-7643
Bryan/College Station Convention & Visitors Bureau 715 University Dr E	College Station	TX	77840	**800-777-8292**	979-260-9898
Colorado Springs Convention & Visitors Bureau 515 S Cascade Ave	Colorado Springs	CO	80903	**800-368-4748**	719-635-7506
Columbia Convention & Visitors Bureau 300 S Providence Rd	Columbia	MO	65203	**800-652-0987**	573-875-1231
Columbia Metropolitan Convention & Visitors Bureau PO Box 15	Columbia	SC	29202	**800-264-4884**	803-545-0000
Columbus Convention & Visitors Bureau 900 Front Ave	Columbus	GA	31901	**800-999-1613**	706-322-1613
Columbus Area Visitors Center 506 5th St	Columbus	IN	47201	**800-468-6564**	812-378-2622
Columbus Convention & Visitors Bureau PO Box 789	Columbus	MS	39703	**800-327-2686**	662-329-1191
Greater Columbus Convention & Visitors Bureau 90 N High St	Columbus	OH	43215	**800-354-2657**	614-221-6623
New Hampshire Office of Travel & Tourism 172 Pembroke Rd PO Box 1856	Concord	NH	03302	**800-386-4664**	603-271-2666
Bay Area Chamber of Commerce/Visitor Bureau 145 Central Ave	Coos Bay	OR	97420	**800-824-8486**	541-266-0868
Iowa City/Coralville Convention & Visitors Bureau 900 1st Ave	Coralville	IA	52241	**800-283-6592**	319-337-6592
Corinth Area Tourism Promotion Council PO Box 2158	Corinth	MS	38835	**800-748-9048**	662-287-8300
Corpus Christi Convention & Visitors Bureau 1201 N Shoreline Blvd	Corpus Christi	TX	78401	**800-678-6232**	361-881-1888
Corvallis Convention & Visitors Bureau 553 NW Harrison Blvd	Corvallis	OR	97330	**800-334-8118**	541-757-1544
Council Grove/Morris County Convention & Visitors Bureau 212 W Main St	Council Grove	KS	66846	**800-732-9211**	620-767-5882
Northern Kentucky Convention & Visitors Bureau 50 E RiverCenter Blvd Suite 100	Covington	KY	41011	**800-447-8489**	859-261-4677
Montgomery County Visitors & Convention Bureau 218 E Pike St	Crawfordsville	IN	47933	**800-866-3973**	765-362-5200
Crescent City-Del Norte County Chamber of Commerce 1001 Front St	Crescent City	CA	95531	**800-343-8300**	707-464-3174
Dallas Convention & Visitors Bureau 325 N Saint Paul St Suite 700	Dallas	TX	75201	**800-232-5527**	214-571-1000
Tucker County Convention & Visitors Bureau William Ave & 4th St PO Box 565	Davis	WV	26260	**800-782-2775**	304-259-5315
Dayton/Montgomery County Convention & Visitors Bureau 1 Chamber Plaza Suite A	Dayton	OH	45402	**800-221-8235**	937-226-8211
Daytona Beach Area Convention & Visitors Bureau 126 E Orange Ave	Daytona Beach	FL	32114	**800-544-0415**	386-255-0415
Decatur/Morgan County Convention & Visitors Bureau 719 6th Ave SE PO Box 2349	Decatur	AL	35601	**800-524-6181**	256-350-2028
Decatur Area Convention & Visitors Bureau 202 E North St	Decatur	IL	62523	**800-331-4479**	217-423-7000
Wicomico County Convention & Visitors Bureau 8480 Ocean Hwy	Delmar	MD	21875	**800-332-8687**	410-548-4914
Greater Des Moines Convention & Visitors Bureau 405 6th Ave Suite 201	Des Moines	IA	50309	**800-451-2625**	515-286-4960
Detroit Metropolitan Convention & Visitors Bureau 211 W Fort St Suite 1000	Detroit	MI	48226	**800-225-5389**	313-202-1800
Dickinson Convention & Visitors Bureau 72 E Museum Dr	Dickinson	ND	58601	**800-279-7391**	701-483-4988
Dothan Area Convention & Visitors Bureau 3311 Ross Clark Cir NW PO Box 8765	Dothan	AL	36305	**888-449-0212**	334-794-6622
Kent County Tourism Corp 435 N DuPont Hwy	Dover	DE	19901	**800-233-5368**	302-734-1736
Downers Grove Tourism & Events 801 Burlington Ave	Downers Grove	IL	60515	**800-934-0615**	630-434-5921
Drummond Island Tourism Assn PO Box 200	Drummond Island	MI	49726	**800-737-8666**	906-493-5245
Dublin Convention & Visitors Bureau 9 S High St	Dublin	OH	43017	**800-245-8387**	614-792-7666
Dubuque Convention & Visitors Bureau 300 Main St Suite 200	Dubuque	IA	52001	**800-798-4748**	563-557-9200
Atlanta's Gwinnett Convention & Visitors Bureau 6500 Sugarloaf Pkwy Suite 200	Duluth	GA	30097	**888-494-6638**	770-623-3600
Duluth Convention & Visitors Bureau 21 W Superior St Suite 100	Duluth	MN	55802	**800-438-5884**	218-722-4011
DuQuoin Tourism Commission PO Box 1037	DuQuoin	IL	62832	**800-455-9570**	618-542-8338
Durham Convention & Visitors Bureau 101 E Morgan St	Durham	NC	27701	**800-446-8604**	919-687-0288
Eagan Convention & Visitors Bureau 1501 Central Pkwy	Eagan	MN	55121	**800-324-2620**	651-675-5546
Chippewa Valley Convention & Visitors Bureau 3625 Gateway Dr Suite F	Eau Claire	WI	54701	**888-523-3866**	715-831-2345
Edmonton Tourism 9990 Jasper Ave NW 3rd Fl	Edmonton	AB	T5J1P7	**800-463-4667**	780-426-4715
Effingham Convention & Visitors Bureau 201 E Jefferson Ave	Effingham	IL	62401	**800-772-0750**	217-342-5305
El Paso Convention & Visitors Bureau 1 Civic Center Plaza	El Paso	TX	79901	**800-351-6024**	915-534-0600
Elgin Area Convention & Visitors Bureau 77 Riverside Dr	Elgin	IL	60120	**800-217-5362**	847-695-7540
Elkhart County Convention & Visitors Bureau 219 Caravan Dr	Elkhart	IN	46514	**800-262-8161**	574-262-8161
Howard County Tourism Council 8267 Main St	Ellicott City	MD	21043	**800-288-8747**	410-313-1900
Tourism Grays Harbor PO Box 1229	Elma	WA	98541	**800-621-9625**	360-482-2651
Erie Area Convention & Visitors Bureau 208 E Bayfront Pkwy Suite 103	Erie	PA	16507	**800-524-3743**	814-454-7191

Classified Section

Name / Address	City	State	ZIP	*Toll-Free*	*Phone*
Convention & Visitors Assn of Lane County Oregon PO Box 10286	Eugene	OR	97440	**800-547-5445**	541-484-5307
Eureka/Humboldt County Convention & Visitors Bureau 1034 2nd St	Eureka	CA	95501	**800-346-3482**	707-443-5097
Evansville Convention & Visitors Bureau 401 SE Riverside Dr	Evansville	IN	47713	**800-433-3025**	812-425-5402
Chester County Tourist Bureau 400 Exton Square Pkwy	Exton	PA	19341	**800-228-9933**	610-280-6145
Fairbanks Convention & Visitors Bureau 550 1st Ave	Fairbanks	AK	99701	**800-327-5774**	907-456-5774
Fairmont Convention & Visitors Bureau PO Box 976	Fairmont	MN	56031	**800-657-3280**	507-235-8585
Convention & Visitors Bureau of Marion County 110 Adams St	Fairmont	WV	26554	**800-834-7365**	304-368-1123
Tourism Bureau Southwestern Illinois 10950 Lincoln Trail	Fairview Heights	IL	62208	**800-442-1488**	618-397-1488
Fargo-Moorhead Convention & Visitors Bureau 2001 44th St SW	Fargo	ND	58103	**800-235-7654**	701-282-3653
Farmington Convention & Visitors Bureau 3041 E Main St	Farmington	NM	87402	**800-448-1240**	505-326-7602
Fayetteville Area Convention & Visitors Bureau 245 Person St	Fayetteville	NC	28301	**800-255-8217**	910-483-5311
Hamilton County Convention & Visitors Bureau 11601 Municipal Dr	Fishers	IN	46038	**800-776-8687**	317-598-4444
Flagstaff Convention & Visitors Bureau 323 W Aspen Ave	Flagstaff	AZ	86001	**800-217-2367**	928-779-7611
Flint Area Convention & Visitors Bureau 316 Water St	Flint	MI	48502	**800-253-5468***	810-232-8900
*Sales					
Florence Convention & Visitors Bureau 3290 W Radio Dr	Florence	SC	29501	**800-325-9005**	843-664-0330
Tropical Everglades Visitor Assn 160 US 1	Florida City	FL	33034	**800-388-9669**	305-245-9180
Fond du Lac Convention & Visitors Bureau 171 S Pioneer Rd	Fond du Lac	WI	54935	**800-937-9123**	920-923-3010
Fort Collins Convention & Visitors Bureau 3745 E Prospect Rd Suite 200	Fort Collins	CO	80525	**800-274-3678**	970-491-3388
Greater Fort Lauderdale Convention & Visitors Bureau 100 E Broward Blvd Suite 200	Fort Lauderdale	FL	33301	**800-356-1662**	954-765-4466
Fort Madison Convention & Visitors Bureau PO Box 425	Fort Madison	IA	52627	**800-210-8687**	319-372-5472
Lee County Visitors & Convention Bureau 12800 University Dr Suite 550	Fort Myers	FL	33907	**800-237-6444**	239-338-3500
Saint Lucie County Tourist Development Council 2300 Virginia Ave	Fort Pierce	FL	34982	**800-344-8443**	772-462-1535
Fort Smith Convention & Visitors Bureau 2 N 'B' St	Fort Smith	AR	72901	**800-637-1477**	479-783-8888
Fort Worth Convention & Visitors Bureau 415 Throckmorton St	Fort Worth	TX	76102	**800-433-5747**	817-336-8791
Frankenmuth Convention & Visitors Bureau 635 S Main St	Frankenmuth	MI	48734	**800-386-8696**	989-652-6106
Frankfort/Franklin County Tourist & Convention Commission 100 Capital Ave	Frankfort	KY	40601	**800-960-7200**	502-875-8687
Williamson County Tourism 109 2nd Ave S Suite 137	Franklin	TN	37064	**800-356-3445**	615-794-1225
Fredericksburg Convention & Visitors Bureau 302 E Austin St	Fredericksburg	TX	78624	**888-997-3600**	830-997-6523
Dodge County Convention & Visitors Bureau 605 N Broad St	Fremont	NE	68025	**800-727-8323**	402-721-2641
Fremont/Sandusky County Convention & Visitors Bureau 712 North St Suite 102	Fremont	OH	43420	**800-255-8070**	419-332-4470
Fresno Convention & Visitors Bureau 848 M St 3rd Fl	Fresno	CA	93721	**800-788-0836**	559-233-0836
Galena/Jo Daviess County Convention & Visitors Bureau 720 Park Ave	Galena	IL	61036	**800-747-9377**	815-777-3557
Galesburg Area Convention & Visitors Bureau 2163 East Main St	Galesburg	IL	61402	**800-916-3330**	309-343-2485
Gallup Convention & Visitors Bureau PO Box 600	Gallup	NM	87305	**800-242-4282**	505-863-3841
Gatlinburg Dept of Tourism & Convention Ctr 234 Historic Nature Trail	Gatlinburg	TN	37738	**800-343-1475**	865-436-2392
Georgetown Convention & Visitors Bureau PO Box 409	Georgetown	TX	78627	**800-436-8696**	512-930-3545
Gettysburg Convention & Visitors Bureau PO Box 4117	Gettysburg	PA	17325	**800-337-5015**	717-334-6274
Greater Grand Forks Convention & Visitors Bureau 4251 Gateway Dr	Grand Forks	ND	58203	**800-866-4566**	701-746-0444
Grand Junction Visitors & Convention Bureau 740 Horizon Dr	Grand Junction	CO	81506	**800-962-2547**	970-244-1480
Grand Rapids/Kent County Convention & Visitors Bureau 171 Monroe Ave NW Suite 700	Grand Rapids	MI	49503	**800-678-9859**	616-459-8287
Grand Rapids Area Convention & Visitors Bureau 1 NW 3rd St	Grand Rapids	MN	55744	**800-355-9740**	218-326-9607
Grants Pass Visitors & Convention Bureau 1995 NW Vine St	Grants Pass	OR	97526	**800-547-5927**	541-476-5510
Grapevine Convention & Visitors Bureau 1 Liberty Pk Plaza	Grapevine	TX	76051	**800-457-6338**	817-410-3185
Houma-Terrebonne Tourist Commission 114 Tourist Dr	Gray	LA	70359	**800-688-2732**	985-868-2732
Greyling Area Visitor's Council 213 N James St	Grayling	MI	49738	**800-937-8837**	989-348-2921
Greeley Convention & Visitors Bureau 902 7th Ave	Greeley	CO	80631	**800-449-3866**	970-352-3567
Packer Country Regional Tourism Office 1901 S Oneida St	Green Bay	WI	54304	**888-867-3342**	920-494-9507
Putnam County Convention & Visitors Bureau 12 W Washington St	Greencastle	IN	46135	**800-829-4639**	765-653-8743
Greensboro Area Convention & Visitors Bureau 317 S Greene St	Greensboro	NC	27401	**800-344-2282**	336-274-2282
Greenville-Pitt County Convention & Visitors Bureau 303 SW Greenville Blvd	Greenville	NC	27834	**800-537-5564**	252-329-4200
Greater Greenville Convention & Visitors Bureau 631 S Main St Suite 301	Greenville	SC	29601	**800-351-7180**	864-421-0000
Greenwood Convention & Visitors Bureau 1902 Leflore Ave	Greenwood	MS	38930	**800-748-9064**	662-453-9197
Alabama Gulf Coast Convention & Visitors Bureau PO Drawer 457	Gulf Shores	AL	36547	**800-745-7263**	251-968-7511
Mississippi Gulf Coast Convention & Visitors Bureau 942 Beach Dr	Gulfport	MS	39507	**888-467-4853**	228-896-6699
Hagerstown/Washington County Convention & Visitors Bureau 16 Public Sq Ellizabeth Hager Ctr	Hagerstown	MD	21740	**800-228-7829**	301-791-3246
Haines Visitors Bureau PO Box 530	Haines	AK	99827	**800-458-3579**	907-766-2234
Lake County Convention & Visitors Bureau 7770 Corinne Dr	Hammond	IN	46323	**800-255-5253**	219-989-7770
Hampton Conventions & Visitors Bureau 1919 Commerce Dr Suite 290	Hampton	VA	23666	**800-487-8778**	757-722-1222
Hannibal Convention & Visitors Bureau 505 N 3rd St	Hannibal	MO	63401	**866-263-4825**	573-221-2477
Jefferson County Convention & Visitors Bureau PO Box A	Harpers Ferry	WV	25425	**800-848-8687**	304-535-2627
Hershey-Capital Region Visitors Bureau 4th & Chestnut Sts Suite 208 Harrisburg Transportation Ctr	Harrisburg	PA	17101	**800-995-0969**	717-231-7788
Long Island Convention & Visitors Bureau 330 Motor Pkwy Suite 203	Hauppauge	NY	11788	**800-441-4601**	631-951-3440
Hays Convention & Visitors Bureau 1301 Pine St Suite B	Hays	KS	67601	**800-569-4505**	785-628-8202
Alpine Helen/White County Convention & Visitors Bureau PO Box 730	Helen	GA	30545	**800-858-8027**	706-878-2181
Henderson County Tourist Commission 101 N Water St Suite B	Henderson	KY	42420	**800-648-3128**	270-826-3128
Henderson County Travel & Tourism 201 S Main St	Hendersonville	NC	28792	**800-828-4244**	828-693-9708
Huntingdon County Visitors Bureau 7 Points Rd RD 1 Box 222A	Hesston	PA	16647	**888-729-7869**	814-658-0060
Hickory Metro Convention & Visitors Bureau 1960A 13th Ave Dr SE	Hickory	NC	28602	**800-509-2444**	828-322-1335
High Point Convention & Visitors Bureau 300 S Main St	High Point	NC	27260	**800-720-5255**	336-884-5255
Hilton Head Island Visitors & Convention Bureau PO Box 5647	Hilton Head Island	SC	29938	**800-523-3373**	843-785-3673
Holland Area Convention & Visitors Bureau 76 E 8th St	Holland	MI	49423	**800-506-1299**	616-394-0000
Hawaii Visitors & Convention Bureau 2270 Kalakaua Ave Suite 801	Honolulu	HI	96815	**800-464-2924**	808-923-1811
Hot Springs Convention & Visitors Bureau 134 Convention Blvd	Hot Springs	AR	71901	**800-543-2284**	501-321-2277
Houghton Lake Area Tourism & Convention Bureau 4482 W Houghton Lake Dr	Houghton Lake	MI	48629	**800-676-5330**	989-366-8474
Greater Houston Convention & Visitors Bureau 901 Bagby St Suite 100	Houston	TX	77002	**800-446-8786**	713-437-5200
Huntington County Visitors & Convention Bureau 407 N Jefferson St	Huntington	IN	46750	**800-848-4282**	260-359-8687
Cabell-Huntington Convention & Visitors Bureau PO Box 347	Huntington	WV	25708	**800-635-6329**	304-525-7333
Huntsville/Madison County Convention & Visitor's Bureau 500 Church St	Huntsville	AL	35801	**800-772-2348**	256-551-2230
Huron Chamber & Visitors Bureau 15 4th St SW	Huron	SD	57350	**800-487-6673**	605-352-0000
Greater Hutchinson Convention & Visitors Bureau 117 N Walnut St	Hutchinson	KS	67501	**800-691-4282**	620-662-3391
Incline Village/Crystal Bay Convention & Visitors Bureau 969 Tahoe Blvd	Incline Village	NV	89451	**800-468-2463**	775-832-1606
Indiana County Tourist Bureau 2334 Oakland Ave Suite 7	Indiana	PA	15701	**877-746-3426**	724-463-7505
Indianapolis Convention & Visitors Assn 200 S Capitol Ave 1 RCA Dome Suite 100	Indianapolis	IN	46225	**800-323-4639**	317-639-4282
Tourism Assn of the Dickinson County Area 600 S Stephenson Ave	Iron Mountain	MI	49801	**800-236-2447**	906-774-2945
Western Upper Peninsula Convention & Visitor Bureau PO Box 706	Ironwood	MI	49938	**800-522-5657**	906-932-4850
Irving Convention & Visitors Bureau 222 W Las Colinas Blvd Suite 1550	Irving	TX	75039	**800-247-8464**	972-252-7476
Ithaca/Tompkins County Convention & Visitors Bureau 904 E Shore Dr	Ithaca	NY	14850	**800-284-8422**	607-272-1313
Jackson County Convention & Visitors Bureau 6007 Ann Arbor Rd	Jackson	MI	49201	**800-245-5282**	517-764-4440
Metro Jackson Convention & Visitors Bureau 921 N President St	Jackson	MS	39202	**800-354-7695**	601-960-1891
Jacksonville Convention & Visitors Bureau 550 Water St Suite 1000	Jacksonville	FL	32202	**800-733-2668**	904-798-9111
Jacksonville Convention & Visitors Bureau 155 W Morton Ave	Jacksonville	IL	62650	**800-593-5678**	217-243-5678
Onslow County Tourism 1099 Gum Branch Rd	Jacksonville	NC	28541	**800-932-2144**	910-455-1113
Jamestown Promotions & Tourism Center PO Box 917	Jamestown	ND	58401	**800-222-4766**	701-251-9145
Jefferson City Convention & Visitors Bureau 213 Adams St	Jefferson City	MO	65101	**800-769-4183**	573-632-2820
Southern Indiana Convention & Tourism Bureau 315 Southern Indiana Ave	Jeffersonville	IN	47130	**800-552-3842**	812-282-6654
Johnson City Convention & Visitors Bureau 603 E Market St	Johnson City	TN	37601	**800-852-3392**	423-461-8000
Greater Johnstown/Cambria County Convention & Visitors Bureau 416 Main St Suite 100	Johnstown	PA	15901	**800-237-8590**	814-536-7993
Heritage Corridor Convention & Visitors Bureau 81 N Chicago St	Joliet	IL	60432	**800-926-2262**	815-727-2323
Joplin Convention & Visitors Bureau 602 S Main St	Joplin	MO	64801	**800-657-2534**	417-625-4789
Juneau Convention & Visitors Bureau 101 Egan Dr	Juneau	AK	99801	**888-581-2201**	907-586-2201
Kalamazoo County Convention & Visitors Bureau 346 W Michigan Ave	Kalamazoo	MI	49007	**800-530-9192**	269-381-4003
Flathead Convention & Visitors Bureau 15 Depot Pk	Kalispell	MT	59901	**800-543-3105**	406-756-9091
Cabarrus County Convention & Visitors Bureau 3003 Dale Earnhardt Blvd	Kannapolis	NC	28083	**800-848-3740**	704-782-4340
Kansas City Kansas/Wyandotte County Convention & Visitors Bureau 727 Minnesota Ave PO Box 171517	Kansas City	KS	66117	**800-264-1563**	913-321-5800
Convention & Visitors Bureau of Greater Kansas City 1100 Main St Suite 2200	Kansas City	MO	64105	**800-767-7700**	816-221-5242
Tri-Cities Convention & Visitors Bureau 6951 W Grandridge Blvd	Kennewick	WA	99336	**800-254-5824**	509-735-8486
Kenosha Area Convention & Visitors Bureau 812 56th St	Kenosha	WI	53140	**800-654-7309**	262-654-7307
Kerrville Convention & Visitors Bureau 2108 Sidney Baker St	Kerrville	TX	78028	**800-221-7958**	830-792-3535
Ketchikan Visitors Bureau 131 Front St	Ketchikan	AK	99901	**800-770-2200**	907-225-6166
Key West Visitors Center 402 Wall St	Key West	FL	33040	**800-648-6269**	305-294-2587
Monroe County Tourist Development Council 1201 White St Suite 102	Key West	FL	33040	**800-352-5397**	305-296-1552

Organization / Address	City	State	ZIP	Toll-Free	Phone
Kingsport Convention & Visitors Bureau PO Box 1403	Kingsport	TN	37662	**800-743-5282**	423-392-8820
Preston County Convention & Visitors Bureau 200 1/2 W Main St	Kingwood	WV	26537	**800-571-0912**	304-329-4660
Kinston Convention & Visitors Bureau PO Box 157	Kinston	NC	28502	**800-869-0032**	252-523-2500
Kissimmee-Saint Cloud Convention & Visitors Bureau 1925 E Irlo Bronson Memorial Hwy	Kissimmee	FL	34744	**800-327-9159**	407-847-5000
Armstrong County Tourist Bureau 125 Market St Suite 2	Kittanning	PA	16201	**888-265-9954**	724-548-3226
Great Basin Visitor Assn 507 Main St	Klamath Falls	OR	97601	**800-445-6728**	541-884-0666
Knoxville Tourism & Sports Corp 301 S Gay St	Knoxville	TN	37902	**866-790-5373**	865-523-7263
Lyon County Joint Tourism Commission 82 Days Inn Dr	Kuttawa	KY	42055	**800-355-3885**	270-388-5300
La Crosse Area Convention & Visitors Bureau 410 Veterans Memorial Dr	La Crosse	WI	54601	**800-658-9424**	608-782-2366
Greater Lafayette Convention & Visitors Bureau 301 Frontage Rd	Lafayette	IN	47905	**800-872-6648**	765-447-9999
Lafayette Convention & Visitors Commission 1400 NW Evageline Thwy	Lafayette	LA	70501	**800-346-1958**	337-232-3737
Laguna Beach Visitors & Conference Bureau 252 Broadway	Laguna Beach	CA	92651	**800-877-1115**	949-497-9229
Southwest Louisiana Convention & Visitors Bureau 1205 N Lakeshore Dr	Lake Charles	LA	70601	**800-456-7952**	337-436-9588
Lake Placid Convention & Visitors Bureau 216 Main St Olympic Ctr	Lake Placid	NY	12946	**800-447-5224**	518-523-2445
Pennsylvania Dutch Convention & Visitors Bureau 501 Greenfield Rd	Lancaster	PA	17601	**800-723-8824**	717-299-8901
Chicago Southland Convention & Visitors Bureau 2304 173rd St	Lansing	IL	60438	**888-895-8233**	708-895-8200
Greater Lansing Convention & Visitors Bureau 1223 Turner St Suite 200	Lansing	MI	48906	**800-648-6630**	517-487-0077
Prince George's County Conference & Visitors Bureau 9200 Basil Ct Suite 101	Largo	MD	20774	**888-925-8300**	301-925-8300
Marin County Visitors Bureau 1013 Larkspur Landing Cir	Larkspur	CA	94939	**866-925-2060**	415-925-2060
Las Cruces Convention & Visitors Bureau 211 N Water St	Las Cruces	NM	88001	**800-343-7827**	505-541-2444
Las Vegas Convention & Visitors Authority 3150 S Paradise Rd	Las Vegas	NV	89109	**800-332-5333**	702-892-0711
Lawrence Visitor Information Ctr 402 N 2nd St	Lawrence	KS	66044	**888-529-5267**	785-865-4499
Leavenworth Convention & Visitors Bureau 518 Shawnee St PO Box 44	Leavenworth	KS	66048	**800-844-4114**	913-682-4113
Lenexa Convention & Visitors Bureau 11180 Lackman Rd	Lenexa	KS	66219	**800-950-7867**	913-888-1414
Greenbrier County Convention & Visitors Bureau 540 N Jefferson St Suite N	Lewisburg	WV	24901	**800-833-2068**	304-645-1000
Juniata River Valley Visitors Bureau Historic Court House 1 W Market St Suite 103	Lewistown	PA	17044	**877-568-9739**	717-248-6713
Lexington Convention & Visitors Bureau 301 E Vine St	Lexington	KY	40507	**800-845-3959**	859-233-7299
Laurel Highlands Visitors Bureau 120 E Main St	Ligonier	PA	15658	**800-333-5661**	724-238-5661
Lima/Allen County Convention & Visitors Bureau 147 N Main St	Lima	OH	45801	**888-222-6075**	419-222-6075
Lincoln Convention & Visitors Bureau 1135 M St 3rd Fl	Lincoln	NE	68508	**800-423-8212**	402-434-5335
Lincoln City Visitor & Convention Bureau 801 SW Hwy 101 Suite 1	Lincoln City	OR	97367	**800-452-2151**	541-994-8378
Lisle Convention & Visitors Bureau 4746 Main St	Lisle	IL	60532	**800-733-9811**	630-769-1000
Little Rock Convention & Visitors Bureau PO Box 3232	Little Rock	AR	72203	**800-844-4781**	501-376-4781
Lodi Conference & Visitors Bureau 2545 W Turner Rd	Lodi	CA	95242	**800-798-1810**	209-365-1195
London/Laurel County Tourist Commission 140 W Daniel Boone Pkwy	London	KY	40741	**800-348-0095**	606-878-6900
Long Beach Convention & Visitors Bureau 1 World Trade Ctr Suite 300	Long Beach	CA	90831	**800-452-7829**	562-436-3645
Seminole County Convention & Visitors Bureau 1230 Douglas Ave Suite 116	Longwood	FL	32779	**800-800-7832**	407-665-2900
Los Angeles Convention & Visitors Bureau 333 S Hope St 18th Fl	Los Angeles	CA	90071	**800-228-2452**	213-624-7300
Louisville & Jefferson County Convention & Visitors Bureau 401 W Main St Suite 2300	Louisville	KY	40202	**800-792-5595**	502-584-2121
Greater Merrimack Valley Convention & Visitors Bureau 9 Central St Suite 201	Lowell	MA	01852	**800-443-3332**	978-459-6150
Lubbock Convention & Visitors Bureau 1301 Broadway St Suite 200	Lubbock	TX	79401	**800-692-4035**	806-747-5232
Lufkin Visitor & Convention Bureau 1615 S Chestnut	Lufkin	TX	75901	**800-409-5659**	936-634-6305
Lumberton Area Visitors Bureau 3431 Lackey St	Lumberton	NC	28360	**800-359-6971**	910-739-9999
Baltimore County Conference & Visitors Bureau PO Box 5426	Lutherville	MD	21094	**877-782-9630**	410-296-4886
Mackinaw Area Visitors Bureau 10300 US 23 PO Box 160	Mackinaw City	MI	49701	**800-666-0160**	231-436-5664
Macon-Bibb County Convention/Visitors Bureau 200 Cherry St	Macon	GA	31201	**800-768-3401**	478-743-3401
Madison Convention & Visitors Bureau 115 E Jefferson St	Madison	GA	30650	**800-709-7406**	706-342-4454
Greater Madison Convention & Visitors Bureau 615 E Washington Ave	Madison	WI	53703	**800-373-6376**	608-255-2537
Maggie Valley Area Convention & Visitors Bureau 2487 Soco Rd PO Box 87	Maggie Valley	NC	28751	**800-785-8259**	828-926-1686
Saint Tammany Parish Tourist & Convention Commission 68099 Hwy 59	Mandeville	LA	70471	**800-634-9443**	985-892-0520
Manhattan Convention & Visitors Bureau 501 Poyntz Ave	Manhattan	KS	66502	**800-759-0134**	785-776-8829
Manitowoc Visitor & Convention Bureau 4221 Calumet Ave PO Box 966	Manitowoc	WI	54221	**800-627-4896**	920-683-4388
Greater Mankato Chamber & Convention Bureau 112 S Riverfront Dr	Mankato	MN	56002	**800-657-4733**	507-345-4519
Mansfield/Richland County Convention & Visitors Bureau 124 N Main St	Mansfield	OH	44902	**800-642-8282**	419-525-1300
Outer Banks Visitors Bureau 1 Visitor Center Cir	Manteo	NC	27954	**800-446-6262**	252-473-2138
Williamson County Tourism Bureau 1602 Sioux Dr	Marion	IL	62959	**800-433-7399**	618-997-3690
Marion-Grant County Convention & Visitors Bureau 217 S Adams St	Marion	IN	46952	**800-662-9474**	765-668-5435
McDowell County Tourism Development Authority 1170 W Tate St	Marion	NC	28752	**888-233-6111**	828-652-1103
Marquette Country Convention & Visitors Bureau 2552 US Hwy 41 W Suite 300	Marquette	MI	49855	**800-544-4321**	906-228-7749
Marshfield Convention & Visitors Bureau 700 S Central Ave	Marshfield	WI	54449	**800-422-4541**	715-384-3454
Mason City Convention & Visitors Bureau PO Box 1128	Mason City	IA	50402	**800-423-5724**	641-422-1663
McAllen Convention & Visitors Bureau 1200 Ash St	McAllen	TX	78501	**877-622-5536**	956-682-2871
Melbourne/Palm Bay Area Convention & Visitor Bureau 1005 E Strawbridge Ave	Melbourne	FL	32901	**800-771-9922**	321-724-5400
Memphis Convention & Visitors Bureau 47 Union Ave	Memphis	TN	38103	**800-873-6282**	901-543-5300
Merced Conference & Visitors Bureau 690 W 16th St	Merced	CA	95340	**800-446-5353**	209-384-7092
Meridian/Lauderdale County Tourism Bureau 212 21st Ave PO Box 5313	Meridian	MS	39301	**888-868-7720**	601-482-8001
Mesa Convention & Visitors Bureau 120 N Center St	Mesa	AZ	85201	**800-283-6372**	480-827-4700
Greater Miami Convention & Visitors Bureau 701 Brickell Ave Suite 2700	Miami	FL	33131	**800-933-8448**	305-539-3000
LaPorte County Convention & Visitors Bureau 1503 S Meer Rd	Michigan City	IN	46360	**800-634-2650**	219-872-5055
Midland County Convention & Visitors Bureau 300 Rodd St Suite 101	Midland	MI	48640	**888-464-3526**	989-839-9901
Milledgeville-Baldwin County Convention & Visitors Bureau 200 W Hancock St	Milledgeville	GA	31061	**800-653-1804**	478-452-4687
Greater Milwaukee Convention & Visitors Bureau 101 W Wisconsin Ave Suite 425	Milwaukee	WI	53203	**800-231-0903**	414-273-3950
Greater Minneapolis Convention & Visitors Assn 250 Marquette Ave Suite 1300	Minneapolis	MN	55401	**800-445-7412**	612-767-8000
Minot Convention & Visitors Bureau 1020 S Broadway	Minot	ND	58701	**800-264-2626**	701-857-8206
Missoula Convention & Visitors Bureau 1121 E Broadway Suite 103	Missoula	MT	59802	**800-526-3465**	406-543-6623
Mobile Bay Convention & Visitors Bureau 1 S Water St	Mobile	AL	36602	**800-566-2453**	251-208-2000
Modesto Convention & Visitors Bureau 1150 9th St Suite C	Modesto	CA	95354	**888-640-8467**	209-526-5588
Quad Cities Convention & Visitors Bureau 2021 River Dr	Moline	IL	61265	**800-747-7800**	563-322-3911
Monterey County Convention & Visitors Bureau PO Box 1770	Monterey	CA	93942	**888-221-1010**	831-649-1770
Montgomery Area Chamber of Commerce Convention & Visitor Bureau 300 Water St Union Stn	Montgomery	AL	36104	**800-240-9452**	334-261-1100
Greater Montreal Convention & Tourism Bureau 1555 rue Peel Bureau 600	Montreal	QC	H3A3L8	**800-363-7777**	514-844-5400
Montrose Visitor & Convention Bureau 1519 E Main St	Montrose	CO	81401	**800-873-0244**	970-240-1414
Greater Morgantown Convention & Visitors Bureau 201 High St Suite 3	Morgantown	WV	26505	**800-458-7373**	304-292-5081
Wausau Central Wisconsin Convention & Visitors Bureau 10204 Park Plaza Suite B	Mosinee	WI	54455	**888-948-4748**	715-355-8788
Mount Vernon Convention & Visitors Bureau 200 Potomac Blvd	Mount Vernon	IL	62864	**800-252-5464**	618-242-3151
Knox County Convention & Visitors Bureau 107 S Main St	Mount Vernon	OH	43050	**800-837-5282**	740-392-6102
Muncie Visitors Bureau 425 N High St	Muncie	IN	47305	**800-568-6862**	765-284-2700
Muskegon County Convention & Visitors Bureau 610 W Western Ave	Muskegon	MI	49440	**800-250-9283**	231-724-3100
Myrtle Beach Area Convention Bureau 1200 N Oak St	Myrtle Beach	SC	29577	**800-356-3016**	843-626-7444
Nacogdoches Convention & Visitors Bureau 200 E Main St	Nacogdoches	TX	75961	**888-653-3788**	936-564-7351
Greater Naples Marco Island Everglades Convention & Visitors Bureau 3050 N Horseshoe Dr Suite 218	Naples	FL	34104	**800-688-3600**	239-403-2425
Brown County Convention & Visitors Bureau PO Box 840	Nashville	IN	47448	**800-753-3255**	812-988-7303
Nashville Convention & Visitors Bureau 211 Commerce St Suite 100	Nashville	TN	37201	**800-657-6910**	615-259-4700
Natchez Convention & Visitors Bureau 640 S Canal St Box C	Natchez	MS	39120	**800-647-6724**	601-446-6345
Craven County Convention & Visitors Bureau 203 S Front St	New Bern	NC	28560	**800-437-5767**	252-637-9400
Greater New Braunfels Chamber of Commerce PO Box 311417	New Braunfels	TX	78131	**800-572-2626**	830-625-2385
Convention & Visitors Bureau of Henry County 2020 S Memorial Dr Suite I	New Castle	IN	47362	**800-676-4302**	765-593-0764
Lawrence County Tourist Promotion Agency 229 S Jefferson St	New Castle	PA	16101	**888-284-7599**	724-654-8408
Greater New Haven Convention & Visitors Bureau 59 Elm St	New Haven	CT	06510	**800-332-7829**	203-777-8550
Connecticut's Mystic & More! PO Box 89	New London	CT	06320	**800-863-6569**	860-444-2206
New Orleans Metropolitan Convention & Visitors Bureau 2020 St Charles Ave	New Orleans	LA	70130	**800-672-6124**	504-566-5011
NYC & Co 810 7th Ave 3rd Fl	New York	NY	10019	**800-692-8474**	212-484-1200
Newberry Area Tourism Assn 4947 E County Rd 460	Newberry	MI	49868	**800-831-7292**	906-293-5739
Newport County Convention & Visitors Bureau 23 America's Cup Ave	Newport	RI	02840	**800-326-6030**	401-849-8048
Newport Beach Conference & Visitors Bureau 110 Newport Ctr Dr Suite 120	Newport Beach	CA	92660	**800-942-6278**	949-719-6100
Newport News Tourism Development Office 700 Town Ctr Dr Suite 320	Newport News	VA	23606	**888-493-7386**	757-926-1400
Newton Convention & Visitor Bureau 113 1st Ave W	Newton	IA	50208	**800-798-0299**	641-792-5545
Niagara Tourism & Convention Corp 345 3rd St Suite 605	Niagara Falls	NY	14303	**800-338-7890**	716-282-8992
Trumbull County Convention & Visitors Bureau 650 Youngstown-Warren Rd	Niles	OH	44446	**800-672-9555**	330-544-3468
Madison County Convention & Visitors Bureau 405 Madison Ave	Norfolk	NE	68701	**888-371-2932**	402-371-2932
Norfolk Convention & Visitors Bureau 232 E Main St	Norfolk	VA	23510	**800-368-3097**	757-664-6620
Norman Convention & Visitors Bureau 224 W Gray St Suite 104	Norman	OK	73069	**800-767-7260**	405-366-8095
North Platte/Lincoln County Convention & Visitors Bureau 219 S Dewey St	North Platte	NE	69103	**800-955-4528**	308-532-4729

Classified Section

Name / Address	City	State	ZIP	*Toll-Free*	*Phone*
DuPage Convention & Visitors Bureau 915 Harger Rd Suite 240	Oak Brook	IL	60523	**800-232-0502**	630-575-8070
Oak Park Area Convention and Visitors Bureau 158 N Forest Ave	Oak Park	IL	60301	**888-625-7275**	708-524-7800
Oak Ridge Convention & Visitors Bureau 302 S Tulane Ave	Oak Ridge	TN	37830	**800-887-3429**	865-482-7821
Ocean City Convention & Visitors Bureau 4001 Coastal Hwy	Ocean City	MD	21842	**800-626-2326**	410-289-8181
Oconomowoc Convention & Visitors Bureau 174 E Wisconsin Ave	Oconomowoc	WI	53066	**800-524-3744**	262-569-2185
Odessa Convention & Visitors Bureau 700 N Grant Ave Suite 200	Odessa	TX	79761	**800-780-4678**	432-333-7871
Ogden/Weber Convention & Visitors Bureau 2501 Wall Ave Union Stn Suite 201	Ogden	UT	84401	**800-255-8824**	801-627-8288
Oklahoma City Convention & Visitors Bureau 189 W Sheridan St	Oklahoma City	OK	73102	**800-225-5652**	405-297-8912
Olympia/Thurston County Visitor & Convention Bureau PO Box 7338	Olympia	WA	98507	**877-704-7500**	360-704-7544
Greater Omaha Convention & Visitors Bureau 1001 Farnam St Suite 200	Omaha	NE	68102	**800-332-1819**	402-444-4660
Onalaska Center for Commerce & Tourism 800 Oak Forest Dr	Onalaska	WI	54650	**800-873-1901**	608-781-9570
Ontario Convention & Visitors Bureau 2000 Convention Ctr Way	Ontario	CA	91764	**800-455-5755**	909-937-3000
Ontario Convention & Visitors Bureau 676 SW 5th Ave	Ontario	OR	97914	**888-889-8012**	541-889-8012
Orange Convention & Visitors Bureau 803 W Green Ave	Orange	TX	77630	**800-528-4906**	409-883-1010
Orlando/Orange County Convention & Visitors Bureau 6700 Forum Dr Suite 100	Orlando	FL	32821	**800-551-0181**	407-363-5800
Lake of the Ozarks Convention & Visitors Bureau 5815 Hwy 54	Osage Beach	MO	65065	**800-386-5253**	573-348-1599
Ottawa Visitors Center 100 W Lafayette St	Ottawa	IL	61350	**888-688-2924**	815-434-2737
Ottawa Tourism & Convention Authority 130 Albert St Suite 1800	Ottawa	ON	K1P5G4	**800-363-4465**	613-237-5150
Overland Park Convention & Visitors Bureau 9001 W 110th St Suite 100	Overland Park	KS	66210	**800-262-7275**	913-491-0123
Owatonna Area Chamber of Commerce & Tourism 320 Hoffman Dr	Owatonna	MN	55060	**800-423-6466**	507-451-7970
Owensboro-Davies County Tourist Commission 215 E 2nd St	Owensboro	KY	42303	**800-489-1131**	270-926-1100
Oxford Tourism Council 107 Courthouse Sq Suite 1	Oxford	MS	38655	**800-758-9177**	662-234-4680
Oxnard Convention & Visitors Bureau 200 W 7th St	Oxnard	CA	93030	**800-269-6273**	805-385-7545
Panama City Beach Convention & Visitors Bureau 17001 Panama City Beach Pkwy	Panama City Beach	FL	32413	**800-722-3224**	850-233-5070
Paris Convention & Visitors Bureau 1125 Bonham St	Paris	TX	75460	**800-727-4789**	903-784-2501
Park City Chamber of Commerce/Convention & Visitors Bureau 1910 Prospector Ave Suite 103	Park City	UT	84060	**800-453-1360**	435-649-6100
Parkersburg/Wood County Convention & Visitors Bureau 350 7th St	Parkersburg	WV	26101	**800-752-4982**	304-428-1130
Pasadena Convention & Visitors Bureau 171 S Los Robles Ave	Pasadena	CA	91101	**800-307-7977**	626-795-9311
North of Boston Convention & Visitors Bureau 17 Peabody Sq	Peabody	MA	01960	**877-662-9299**	978-977-7760
Pensacola Convention & Visitors Bureau 1401 E Gregory St	Pensacola	FL	32502	**800-874-1234**	850-434-1234
Peoria Area Convention & Visitors Bureau 456 Fulton St Suite 300	Peoria	IL	61602	**800-747-0302**	309-676-0303
Petoskey/Harbor Springs/Boyne Country Visitors Bureau 401 E Mitchell St	Petoskey	MI	49770	**800-845-2828**	231-348-2755
Philadelphia Convention & Visitors Bureau 1700 Market St Suite 3000	Philadelphia	PA	19103	**800-225-5745**	215-636-3300
Greater Phoenix Convention & Visitors Bureau 400 E Van Buren St 1 Arizona Ctr Suite 600	Phoenix	AZ	85004	**877-225-5749**	602-254-6500
Pierre Convention & Visitors Bureau 800 W Dakota Ave PO Box 548	Pierre	SD	57501	**800-962-2034**	605-224-7361
Pigeon Forge Dept of Tourism 2450 Parkway	Pigeon Forge	TN	37863	**800-251-9100**	865-453-8574
Pine Bluff Convention & Visitors Bureau 1 Convention Ctr Plaza	Pine Bluff	AR	71601	**800-536-7660**	870-536-7600
Greater Pittsburgh Convention & Visitors Bureau 425 6th Ave 30th Fl	Pittsburgh	PA	15219	**800-359-0758**	412-281-7711
Plano Convention & Visitors Bureau 2000 E Spring Creek Pkwy	Plano	TX	75074	**800-817-5266**	972-422-0296
Valley Forge Convention & Visitors Bureau 600 W Germantown Pike Suite 130	Plymouth Meeting	PA	19462	**800-441-3549**	610-834-1550
Ponca City Tourism 516 E Grand Ave	Ponca City	OK	74601	**866-763-8092**	
North Olympic Peninsula Visitor & Convention Bureau 338 W 1st St Suite 104	Port Angeles	WA	98362	**800-942-4042**	360-452-8552
Port Arthur Convention & Visitors Bureau 3401 Cultural Ctr Dr	Port Arthur	TX	77642	**800-235-7822**	409-985-7822
Ottawa County Visitors Bureau 770 SE Catawba Rd	Port Clinton	OH	43452	**800-441-1271**	419-734-4386
Blue Water Area Convention & Visitors Bureau 520 Thomas Edison Pkwy	Port Huron	MI	48060	**800-852-4242**	810-987-8687
Portland Oregon Visitors Assn 1000 SW Broadway Suite 2300	Portland	OR	97204	**800-962-3700**	503-275-9750
Portsmouth Convention & Visitors Bureau 505 Crawford St Suite 2	Portsmouth	VA	23704	**800-767-8782**	757-393-5327
Providence Warwick Convention & Visitors Bureau 1 W Exchange St	Providence	RI	02903	**800-233-1636**	401-274-1636
Utah Valley Convention & Visitors Bureau 111 S University Ave	Provo	UT	84601	**800-222-8824**	801-851-2100
Greater Pueblo Chamber of Commerce & Visitors Council 210 N Santa Fe	Pueblo	CO	81003	**800-233-3446**	719-542-1704
Plumas County Visitors Bureau 550 Crescent St	Quincy	CA	95971	**800-326-2247**	530-283-6345
Quincy Convention & Visitors Bureau 300 Civic Ctr Plaza Suite 237	Quincy	IL	62301	**800-978-4748**	217-223-1000
Greater Raleigh Convention & Visitors Bureau 421 Fayetteville St Mall Suite 1505	Raleigh	NC	27602	**800-849-8499**	919-834-5900
Palm Springs Desert Resorts Convention & Visitors Authority 70-100 Hwy 111	Rancho Mirage	CA	92270	**800-967-3767**	760-770-9000
Rapid City Convention & Visitors Bureau 444 Mt Rushmore Rd N	Rapid City	SD	57701	**800-487-3223**	605-343-1744
Reading & Berks County Visitors Bureau 352 Penn St	Reading	PA	19602	**800-443-6610**	610-375-4085
Redding Convention & Visitors Bureau 777 Auditorium Dr	Redding	CA	96001	**800-874-7562**	530-225-4100
Reno-Sparks Convention & Visitors Authority PO Box 837	Reno	NV	89504	**800-443-1482**	775-827-7600
Richardson Convention & Visitors Services 411 W Arapaho Rd Suite 105	Richardson	TX	75080	**888-690-7287**	972-744-4034
Richmond/Wayne County Convention & Tourism Bureau 5701 National Rd E	Richmond	IN	47374	**800-828-8414**	765-935-8687
Richmond Metropolitan Convention & Visitors Bureau 401 N 3rd St	Richmond	VA	23219	**800-370-9004**	804-782-2777
Ridgecrest Area Convention & Visitors Bureau 139 Balsam St	Ridgecrest	CA	93555	**800-847-4830**	760-375-8202
Rising Sun/Ohio County Convention & Tourism Bureau 120 N Walnut St	Rising Sun	IN	47040	**888-776-4786**	812-438-4933
Riverside Convention & Visitors Bureau 3750 University Ave Suite 175	Riverside	CA	92501	**888-913-4636**	951-222-4700
Riverside Visitors Center 3750 University Ave Suite 175	Riverside	CA	92501	**888-913-4636**	951-684-4636
Roanoke Valley Convention & Visitors Bureau 101 Shenandoah Ave NE	Roanoke	VA	24016	**800-635-5535**	540-342-6025
Tunica County Convention & Visitors Bureau 13625 Hwy 61 N	Robinsonville	MS	38664	**888-488-6422**	662-363-3800
Rochester Convention & Visitors Bureau 111 S Broadway Suite 301	Rochester	MN	55904	**800-634-8277**	507-288-4331
Greater Rochester Visitors Assn 45 East Ave Suite 400	Rochester	NY	14604	**800-677-7282**	585-546-3070
York County Convention & Visitors Bureau 130 E Main St Suite 101	Rock Hill	SC	29731	**800-866-5200**	803-329-5200
Rockford Area Convention & Visitors Bureau 102 N Main St	Rockford	IL	61101	**800-521-0849**	815-963-8111
Conference & Visitors Bureau of Montgomery County 11820 Parklawn Dr Suite 380	Rockville	MD	20852	**800-925-0880**	301-428-9702
Nash County Visitors Bureau PO Box 392	Rocky Mount	NC	27802	**800-849-6825**	252-972-5080
Greater Rome Convention & Visitors Bureau PO Box 5823	Rome	GA	30162	**800-444-1834**	706-295-5576
Roswell Convention & Visitors Bureau 617 Atlanta St	Roswell	GA	30075	**800-776-7935**	770-640-3253
Sacramento Convention & Visitors Bureau 1608 'I' St	Sacramento	CA	95814	**800-292-2334**	916-808-7777
Saginaw County Convention & Visitors Bureau 515 N Washington Ave 3rd Fl	Saginaw	MI	48607	**800-444-9979**	989-752-7164
Saint Johns County Convention & Visitors Bureau 88 Riberia St Suite 400	Saint Augustine	FL	32084	**800-653-2489**	904-829-1711
Greater Saint Charles Convention & Visitors Bureau 230 S Main St	Saint Charles	MO	63301	**800-366-2427**	636-946-7776
Saint Cloud Area Convention & Visitors Bureau 525 Hwy 10 S Suite 1	Saint Cloud	MN	56304	**800-264-2940**	320-251-4170
Saint Joseph Convention & Visitors Bureau 109 S 4th St	Saint Joseph	MO	64501	**800-785-0360**	816-233-6688
Saint Louis Convention & Visitors Commission 1 Metropolitan Sq Suite 1100	Saint Louis	MO	63102	**800-325-7962**	314-421-1023
Auglaize & Mercer Counties Convention & Visitors Bureau 900 Edgewater Dr	Saint Marys	OH	45885	**800-860-4726**	419-394-1294
Saint Paul Convention & Visitors Bureau 175 W Kellogg Blvd Suite 502	Saint Paul	MN	55102	**800-627-6101**	651-265-4900
Salem Convention & Visitors Assn 1313 Mill St SE	Salem	OR	97301	**800-874-7012**	503-581-4325
Rowan County Convention & Visitors Bureau 204 E Innes St Suite 120	Salisbury	NC	28144	**800-332-2343**	704-638-3100
Salt Lake Convention & Visitors Bureau 90 S West Temple	Salt Lake City	UT	84101	**800-541-4955**	801-521-2822
San Angelo Convention & Visitors Bureau 418 West Ave B	San Angelo	TX	76903	**800-375-1206**	325-653-1206
San Antonio Convention & Visitors Bureau 203 S Saint Marys St 2nd Fl	San Antonio	TX	78205	**800-447-3372**	210-207-6700
San Bernardino Convention & Visitors Bureau 201 N 'E' St Suite 103	San Bernardino	CA	92401	**800-867-8366**	909-889-3980
San Jose Convention & Visitors Bureau 408 Almaden Blvd	San Jose	CA	95110	**800-726-5673**	408-295-9600
Santa Barbara Visitors Bureau & Film Commission 1601 Anacapa St	Santa Barbara	CA	93101	**800-927-4688**	805-966-9222
Santa Clara Convention/Visitors Bureau 1850 Warburton Ave	Santa Clara	CA	95050	**800-272-6822**	408-244-9660
Santa Cruz County Conference & Visitors Council 1211 Ocean St	Santa Cruz	CA	95060	**800-833-3494**	831-425-1234
Santa Fe Convention & Visitors Bureau 201 W Marcy St	Santa Fe	NM	87504	**800-777-2489**	505-955-6200
Santa Maria Valley Convention & Visitors Bureau 614 S Broadway	Santa Maria	CA	93454	**800-331-3779**	805-925-2403
Santa Monica Convention & Visitors Bureau 520 Broadway Suite 250	Santa Monica	CA	90401	**800-544-5319**	310-319-6263
Beaches of South Walton Tourist Development Council PO Box 1248	Santa Rosa Beach	FL	32459	**800-822-6877**	850-267-1216
Sarasota Convention & Visitors Bureau 655 N Tamiami Trail	Sarasota	FL	34236	**800-522-9799**	941-957-1877
Sault Convention & Visitors Bureau 536 Ashman St	Sault Sainte Marie	MI	49783	**800-647-2858**	906-632-3366
Savannah Area Convention & Visitors Bureau 101 E Bay St	Savannah	GA	31401	**877-728-2662**	912-644-6401
Hardin County Convention & Visitors Bureau 495 Main St	Savannah	TN	38372	**800-552-3866**	731-925-2364
Greater Woodfield Convention & Visitors Bureau 1430 N Meacham Rd Suite 1400	Schaumburg	IL	60173	**800-847-4849**	847-490-1010
Scottsdale Convention & Visitors Bureau 4343 N Scottsdale Rd Suite 170	Scottsdale	AZ	85251	**800-782-1117**	480-421-1004
Northeast Pennsylvania Convention & Visitors Bureau 99 Glenmaura National Blvd	Scranton	PA	18507	**800-229-3526**	570-963-6363
Mercer County Convention & Visitors Bureau 50 N Water Ave	Sharon	PA	16146	**800-637-2370**	724-346-3771
Shelby County Office of Tourism 315 E Main St	Shelbyville	IL	62565	**800-874-3529**	217-774-2244
Shepherdsville-Bullitt County Tourism Commission 395 Paraquet Springs Dr	Shepherdsville	KY	40165	**800-526-2068**	502-543-8687
Sherman Convention & Visitors Council 307 W Washington St Suite 100	Sherman	TX	75090	**888-893-1188**	903-893-1184
LaGrange County Convention & Visitor Bureau 440 1/2 S Van Buren St	Shipshewana	IN	46565	**800-254-8090**	260-768-4008

Name / Address	City	State	ZIP	Toll-Free	Phone
Shreveport-Bossier Convention & Tourist Bureau 629 Spring St	Shreveport	LA	71101	**800-551-8682**	318-222-9391
Sioux City Convention Center/Auditorium/Tourism Bureau 801 4th St	Sioux City	IA	51101	**800-593-2228**	712-279-4800
Sioux Falls Convention & Visitors Bureau 200 N Phillips Ave Suite 102	Sioux Falls	SD	57104	**800-333-2072**	605-336-1620
Sitka Convention & Visitors Bureau 303 Lincoln St Suite 4	Sitka	AK	99835	**800-557-4852**	907-747-5940
Skagway Convention & Visitors Bureau 245 Broadway PO Box 1025	Skagway	AK	99840	**888-762-1898**	907-983-2854
Johnston County Visitors Bureau 1115 Industrial Pk Dr.	Smithfield	NC	27577	**800-441-7829**	919-989-8687
Snowmass Resort Assn & Convention Center 38 Snowmass Village Upper Mall PO Box 5566	Snowmass Village	CO	81615	**800-598-2006**	970-923-2000
South Bend/Mishawaka Convention & Visitors Bureau 401 E Colfax Ave Suite 310	South Bend	IN	46617	**800-828-7881**	574-234-0051
Rutherford County Tourism Development Authority 1990 US Hwy 221 S	South Forest City	NC	28043	**800-849-5998**	828-245-1492
Lake Tahoe Visitors Authority 1156 Ski Run Blvd	South Lake Tahoe	CA	96150	**800-288-2463**	530-544-5050
South Padre Island Convention & Visitors Bureau 600 Padre Blvd	South Padre Island	TX	78597	**800-767-2373**	956-761-6433
South Sioux City Convention & Visitors Bureau 3900 Dakota Ave Suite 11	South Sioux City	NE	68776	**800-793-6327**	402-494-1307
Convention & Visitors Bureau-Village of Pinehurst Southern Pines Aberdeen Area PO Box 2270	Southern Pines	NC	28388	**800-346-5362**	910-692-3330
Spokane Convention & Visitors Bureau 201 W Main Suite 301	Spokane	WA	99201	**888-776-5263**	509-747-3230
Springfield Convention & Visitors Bureau 109 N 7th St	Springfield	IL	62701	**800-545-7300**	217-789-2360
Greater Springfield Convention & Visitors Bureau 1441 Main St Suite 136	Springfield	MA	01103	**800-723-1548**	413-787-1548
Springfield Missouri Convention & Visitors Bureau 3315 E Battlefield Rd	Springfield	MO	65804	**800-678-8767**	417-881-5300
Springfield Area Convention & Visitors Bureau 333 N Limestone St Suite 201	Springfield	OH	45503	**800-803-1553**	937-325-7621
Centre County Convention & Visitors Bureau 800 E Park Ave	State College	PA	16803	**800-358-5466**	814-231-1400
Pocono Mountains Vacation Bureau 1004 Main St	Stroudsburg	PA	18360	**800-722-9199**	570-421-5791
Racine County Convention & Visitors Bureau 14015 Washington Ave	Sturtevant	WI	53177	**800-272-2463**	262-884-6400
Superior/Douglas County Convention & Visitors Bureau 205 Belknap St	Superior	WI	54880	**800-942-5313**	715-394-7716
Syracuse Convention & Visitors Bureau 572 S Salina St	Syracuse	NY	13202	**800-234-4797**	315-470-1910
Tacoma Regional Convention & Visitor Bureau 1119 Pacific Ave 5th Fl	Tacoma	WA	98402	**800-272-2662**	253-627-2836
North Lake Tahoe Resort Assn 3000 N Lake Blvd Suite 10	Tahoe City	CA	96145	**800-824-6348**	530-583-3494
Tallahassee Area Convention & Visitors Bureau 106 E Jefferson St	Tallahassee	FL	32301	**800-628-2866**	850-413-9200
Tampa Bay Convention & Visitors Bureau 400 N Tampa St Suite 2800	Tampa	FL	33602	**800-826-8358**	813-223-1111
Tawas Area Tourism & Convention Bureau PO Box 10	Tawas City	MI	48764	**877-868-2927**	
Tempe Convention & Visitors Bureau 51 W 3rd St Suite 105	Tempe	AZ	85281	**800-283-6734**	480-894-8158
Terre Haute Convention & Visitors Bureau 643 Wabash Ave	Terre Haute	IN	47807	**800-366-3043**	812-234-5555
Thief River Falls Convention & Visitors Bureau 2017 Hwy 59 SE	Thief River Falls	MN	56701	**800-827-1629**	218-681-3720
City of Thomasville Tourism Authority 401 S Broad St	Thomasville	GA	31792	**800-704-2350**	229-227-7099
Three Lakes Information Bureau 1704 Superior St PO Box 262	Three Lakes	WI	54562	**800-972-6103**	715-546-3344
Seneca County Convention & Visitors Bureau 114 S Washington St	Tiffin	OH	44883	**888-736-3221**	419-447-5866
Greater Toledo Convention & Visitors Bureau 401 Jefferson Ave	Toledo	OH	43604	**800-243-4667**	419-321-6404
Tomah Convention & Visitors Bureau 805 Superior Ave PO Box 625	Tomah	WI	54660	**800-948-6624**	608-372-2166
Topeka Convention & Visitors Bureau 1275 SW Topeka Blvd	Topeka	KS	66612	**800-235-1030**	785-234-1030
Toronto Convention & Visitors Assn 207 Queen's Quay W Suite 590	Toronto	ON	M5J1A7	**800-363-1990**	416-203-2600
Smoky Mountain Visitors Bureau 7906 E Lamar Alexander Pkwy	Townsend	TN	37882	**800-525-6834**	865-448-6134
Traverse City Convention & Visitors Bureau 101 W Grandview Pkwy	Traverse City	MI	49684	**800-940-1120**	231-947-1120
Polk County Travel & Tourism 317 N Trade St	Tryon	NC	28782	**800-440-7848**	828-859-8300
Atlanta's DeKalb Convention & Visitors Bureau 1957 Lakeside Pkwy Suite 510	Tucker	GA	30084	**800-999-6055**	770-492-5000
Metropolitan Tucson Convention & Visitors Bureau 100 S Church Ave	Tucson	AZ	85701	**800-638-8350**	520-624-1817
Tulsa Convention & Visitors Bureau 2 W 2nd St Suite 150 Williams Ctr Tower II	Tulsa	OK	74103	**800-558-3311**	918-585-1201
Tupelo Convention & Visitors Bureau 399 E Main St	Tupelo	MS	38804	**800-533-0611**	662-841-6521
Tuscaloosa Convention & Visitors Bureau 1305 Greensboro Ave	Tuscaloosa	AL	35401	**800-538-8696**	205-391-9200
Colbert County Tourism & Convention Bureau PO Box 740425	Tuscumbia	AL	35674	**800-344-0783**	256-383-0783
Tyler Convention & Visitors Bureau 315 N Broadway	Tyler	TX	75702	**800-235-5712**	903-592-1661
Oneida County Convention & Visitors Bureau PO Box 551	Utica	NY	13503	**800-426-3132**	315-724-7221
Vail Valley Tourism Bureau 100 E Meadow Dr Suite 34	Vail	CO	81657	**800-525-3875**	970-476-1000
Vallejo Convention & Visitors Bureau 495 Mare Island Way	Vallejo	CA	94590	**800-482-5535**	707-642-3653
Greater Vancouver Convention & Visitors Bureau 200 Burrard St	Vancouver	BC	V6C3L6	**800-663-6000**	604-683-2000
Ventura Visitors & Convention Bureau 89 S California St Suite C	Ventura	CA	93001	**800-333-2989**	805-648-2075
Vicksburg Convention & Visitors Bureau 1221 Washington St	Vicksburg	MS	39183	**800-221-3536**	601-636-9421
Florida's Space Coast Office of Tourism 2725 Judge Fran Jamieson Way Suite B-105	Viera	FL	32940	**877-572-3224**	321-637-5483
Iron Trail Convention & Visitors Bureau 403 1st St N	Virginia	MN	55792	**800-777-8497**	218-749-8161
Virginia Beach Convention & Visitor Bureau 2101 Parks Ave Suite 500	Virginia Beach	VA	23451	**800-700-7702**	757-437-4700
Visalia Convention & Visitors Bureau 303 E Acequia Ave	Visalia	CA	93291	**800-524-0303**	559-713-4000
Waco Convention & Visitors Bureau 100 Washington Ave	Waco	TX	76701	**800-321-9226**	254-750-5810
Wahpeton Visitors Bureau 118 N 6th St	Wahpeton	ND	58075	**800-892-6673**	701-642-8744
Northern Alleghenies Vacation Region 2883 Pennsylvania Ave W Ext	Warren	PA	16365	**800-624-7802**	814-726-1222
Kosciusko County Convention & Visitors Bureau 111 Capital Dr	Warsaw	IN	46582	**800-800-6090**	574-269-6090
Puerto Rico Convention Bureau 1730 Rhode Island Ave NW Suite 601	Washington	DC	20036	**800-875-4765**	202-457-9262
Northwest Connecticut Convention & Visitors Bureau 21 Church St	Waterbury	CT	06702	**888-588-7880**	203-597-9527
Waterloo Convention & Visitor Bureau 313 E 5th St	Waterloo	IA	50703	**800-728-8431**	319-233-8350
Tioga County Visitors Bureau 114 Main St	Wellsboro	PA	16901	**888-846-4228**	570-724-0635
West Branch/Ogemaw County Travelers & Visitors Bureau 422 W Houghton Ave	West Branch	MI	48661	**800-755-9091**	989-345-2821
West Hollywood Convention & Visitors Bureau 8687 Melrose Ave Suite M38	West Hollywood	CA	90069	**800-368-6020**	310-289-2525
Monroe-West Monroe Convention & Visitors Bureau 601 Constitution Dr	West Monroe	LA	71292	**800-843-1872**	318-387-5691
Palm Beach County Convention & Visitors Bureau 1555 Palm Beach Lakes Blvd Suite 800	West Palm Beach	FL	33401	**800-833-5733**	561-471-3995
Wheeling Convention & Visitors Bureau 1401 Main St	Wheeling	WV	26003	**800-828-3097**	304-233-7709
Westchester County Office of Tourism 222 Mamaroneck Ave Suite 100	White Plains	NY	10605	**800-833-9282**	914-995-8500
Wichita Convention & Visitors Bureau 100 S Main St Suite 100	Wichita	KS	67202	**800-288-9424**	316-265-2800
Wichita Falls Convention & Visitors Bureau 1000 5th St PO Box 630	Wichita Falls	TX	76301	**800-799-6732**	940-716-5500
Williamsburg Area Convention & Visitors Bureau 421 N Boundary St	Williamsburg	VA	23185	**800-368-6511**	757-253-0192
Martin County Travel & Tourism Authority 100 E Church St	Williamston	NC	27892	**800-776-8566**	252-792-6605
Greater Wilmington Convention & Visitors Bureau 100 W 10th St Suite 20	Wilmington	DE	19801	**800-422-1181**	302-652-4088
Cape Fear Coast Convention & Visitors Bureau 24 N 3rd St	Wilmington	NC	28401	**800-222-4757**	910-341-4030
Wilson Visitors Bureau PO Box 2882	Wilson	NC	27894	**800-497-7398**	252-243-8440
Winnemucca Convention & Visitors Authority 50 W Winnemucca Blvd	Winnemucca	NV	89445	**800-962-2638**	775-623-5071
Destination Winnipeg 259 Portage Ave	Winnipeg	MB	R3B2B4	**800-665-0204**	204-943-1970
Winona Convention & Visitors Bureau 67 Main St	Winona	MN	55987	**800-657-4972**	507-452-2272
Winston-Salem Convention & Visitors Bureau 200 Brookstown Ave	Winston-Salem	NC	27101	**800-331-7018**	336-728-4200
Central Florida Visitors & Convention Bureau 1339 Helena Rd	Winter Haven	FL	33884	**800-828-7655**	863-298-7565
Wisconsin Dells Visitors & Convention Bureau 701 Superior St	Wisconsin Dells	WI	53965	**800-223-3557**	608-254-8088
Wayne County Convention & Visitors Bureau 428 W Liberty St	Wooster	OH	44691	**800-362-6474**	330-264-1800
Worcester County Convention & Visitors Bureau 30 Worcester Center Blvd	Worcester	MA	01608	**800-231-7557**	508-755-7400
York County Convention & Visitors Bureau 155 W Market St	York	PA	17401	**888-858-9675**	717-852-9675
Ypsilanti Area Visitors & Convention Bureau 106 W Michigan Ave	Ypsilanti	MI	48197	**800-265-9045**	734-483-4444
Yuma Convention & Visitors Bureau 377 S Main St Suite 102	Yuma	AZ	85364	**800-293-0071**	928-783-0071
Zanesville-Muskingum County Convention & Visitors Bureau 205 N 5th St	Zanesville	OH	43701	**800-743-2303**	740-455-8282

Classified Section

206 CONVEYORS & CONVEYING EQUIPMENT

SEE ALSO Material Handling Equipment

Name / Address	City	State	ZIP	Toll-Free	Phone
Acco Systems Inc 12755 E Nine-Mile Rd	Warren	MI	48089	**800-521-3423**	586-755-7500
Airfloat Systems Inc 2230 Brush College Rd	Decatur	IL	62526	**800-888-0018**	217-423-6001
Allor Mfg Inc 12534 Emerson Dr	Brighton	MI	48116	**888-244-4028**	248-486-4500
Alloy Wire Belt Co 2318 Tenaya Dr	Modesto	CA	95354	**800-538-7933**	209-575-4900
Alvey Systems Inc 9301 Olive Blvd	Saint Louis	MO	63132	**800-325-1596**	314-993-4700
Ambec Inc 1320 Wards Ferry Rd	Lynchburg	VA	24502	**800-899-4406**	434-582-1200
AMF Bakery Systems 2115 W Laburnum Ave	Richmond	VA	23227	**800-225-3771**	804-355-7961
Automatic Systems Inc 9230 E 47th St	Kansas City	MO	64133	**800-366-3488**	816-356-0660
Automation Service Equipment Inc 23850 Pinewood St	Warren	MI	48091	**800-735-5940**	586-754-7480
Beltservice Corp 4143 Rider Trail N	Earth City	MO	63045	**800-727-2358**	314-344-8500
Brake Roller Co 730 E Michigan Ave	Battle Creek	MI	49016	**800-537-9940**	269-968-9311
Cambridge Inc 105 Goodwill Rd	Cambridge	MD	21613	**800-638-9560**	410-228-3000
Carman Industries Inc 1005 W Riverside Dr PO box 579	Jeffersonville	IN	47131	**800-456-7560**	812-288-4700
Christianson Systems Inc 20421 15th St SE	Blomkest	MN	56216	**800-328-8896**	320-995-6141
Conveyor Components Co 130 Seltzer Rd *Cust Svc	Croswell	MI	48422	**800-233-3233***	810-679-4211
Conveyor & Material Handling Systems 4598 SR 37	Mitchell	IN	47446	**800-551-3195**	812-849-5647
Daifuku America Corp 6700 Tussing Rd	Reynoldsburg	OH	43068	**800-531-1888**	614-863-1888
Engineered Products Inc 355 Woodruff Rd Suite 204	Greenville	SC	29607	**800-868-0145**	864-234-4888
Essmueller Co 334 Ave A PO Box 1966	Laurel	MS	39440	**800-325-7175**	601-649-2400
Feeco International Inc 3913 Algoma Rd *Mktg	Green Bay	WI	54311	**800-373-9347***	920-469-5100
FKI Logistex 1500 Lebanon Rd	Danville	KY	40422	**877-935-4564**	
Fleetwood Inc 1305 Lakeview Dr	Romeoville	IL	60446	**800-824-6609**	630-759-6800
Frost Inc 2020 Bristol Ave NW *Cust Svc	Grand Rapids	MI	49504	**800-783-6633***	616-453-7781
Garvey Corp 208 S Rt 73	Blue Anchor	NJ	08037	**800-257-8581**	609-561-2450
Grasan Equipment 440 S Illinois Ave	Mansfield	OH	44907	**800-526-4602**	419-526-4440

	Toll-Free	Phone
Hapman Conveyors 6002 E Kilgore Rd, Kalamazoo MI 49048	**800-427-6260**	269-382-8200
Interlake Material Handling Inc 1230 E Diehl Rd Suite 400, Naperville IL 60563	**800-282-8032***	630-245-8800
*Sales		
Interroll Corp 3000 Corporate Dr, Wilmington NC 28405	**800-830-9680***	910-799-1100
*Sales		
Jeffrey Chain Corp 2307 Maden Dr, Morristown TN 37813	**800-251-9012**	423-586-1951
Jervis B Webb Co 34375 W 12-Mile Rd, Farmington Hills MI 48331	**800-526-9322**	248-553-1220
Jorgensen Conveyors Inc 10303 N Baehr Rd, Mequon WI 53092	**800-325-7705**	262-242-3089
K-Tron International Inc Rts 55 & 553, Pitman NJ 08071	**800-355-8766**	856-589-0500
NASDAQ: KTII		
Krasny-Kaplan Corp 4899 Commerce Pkwy, Cleveland OH 44128	**800-631-0520**	216-292-6300
KWS Mfg Co 3041 Conveyor Dr, Burleson TX 76028	**800-543-6558**	817-295-2247
Laitram Corp 220 Laitram Ln, Harahan LA 70123	**800-533-8253**	504-733-6000
Lipe Automation Equipment 7650 Edgecomb Dr, Liverpool NY 13088	**800-448-7822**	315-457-1052
Mac Equipment Inc 7901 NW 107 Terr, Kansas City MO 64153	**800-821-2476**	816-891-9300
Martin Engineering 1 Martin Pl, Neponset IL 61345	**800-544-2947**	309-594-2384
Mayfran International 6650 Beta Dr, Mayfield Village OH 44143	**800-321-6988**	440-461-4100
Metal Equipment Co 875 Crocker Rd, Westlake OH 44145	**800-700-6326**	440-835-3100
Montague Industrial Inc PO Box 6016, Florence SC 29502	**800-922-7820**	803-775-1102
Nim-Cor Inc 575 Amherst St, Nashua NH 03061	**888-464-6267**	603-889-2153
NKC of America Inc 1584 E Brooks Rd, Memphis TN 38116	**800-532-6727**	901-396-5353
Overhead Conveyor Co 1330 Hilton Rd, Ferndale MI 48220	**800-396-2554**	248-547-3800
Prab Inc 5944 E Kilgore Rd, Kalamazoo MI 49048	**800-968-7722**	269-382-8200
Railex Corp 89-02 Atlantic Ave, Ozone Park NY 11416	**800-352-3244**	718-845-5454
Railglide Systems 12995 Hillview St, Detroit MI 48227	**800-451-5262**	313-834-0100
Ransohoff Inc 4933 Provident Dr, Cincinnati OH 45246	**800-248-9274**	513-870-0100
Rapid Industries Inc 4003 Oaklawn Dr, Louisville KY 40219	**800-727-4381**	502-968-3645
Richards-Wilcox Inc 600 S Lake St, Aurora IL 60506	**800-253-5668**	630-897-6951
Sandvik Sorting Systems Inc 500 E Burnett Ave, Louisville KY 40217	**800-926-6839**	502-636-1414
Schroeder Industries 580 W Park Rd, Leetsdale PA 15056	**800-722-4810**	724-318-1100
Shuttleworth Inc 10 Commercial Rd, Huntington IN 46750	**800-444-7412**	260-356-8500
Siemens Dematic Material Handling Automation Div 507 Plymouth Ave NE, Grand Rapids MI 49505	**800-530-9153***	616-913-6200
*Cust Svc		
Stewart Systems 808 Stewart Ave, Plano TX 75074	**800-966-5808**	972-422-5808
Sweet Mfg Co Inc 200 E Leffel Ln, Springfield OH 45505	**800-334-7254***	937-325-1511
*Cust Svc		
Swisslog Translogic 10825 E 47th Ave, Denver CO 80239	**800-525-1841**	303-371-7770
Thomas Conveyor Co 555 Burleson Blvd, Burleson TX 76028	**800-433-2217**	817-295-7151
Transco Industries Inc 5534 NE 122nd Ave, Portland OR 97230	**800-545-9991**	503-256-1955
Unex Conveying Systems Inc 50 Progress Pl, Jackson NJ 08527	**800-695-7726***	732-928-2800
*Cust Svc		
Universal Industries Inc 5800 Nordic Dr, Cedar Falls IA 50613	**800-553-4446**	319-277-7501
Webb Jervis B Co 34375 W 12-Mile Rd, Farmington Hills MI 48331	**800-526-9322**	248-553-1220
Webster Industries Inc 325 Hall St, Tiffin OH 44883	**800-243-9327**	419-447-8232
Westfalia Technologies Inc 3655 Sandhurst Dr, York PA 17402	**800-673-2522**	717-764-1115
Whirl Air Flow Corp 20055 177th St, Big Lake MN 55309	**800-373-3461**	763-262-1200
Wire Belt Co of America 154 Harvey Rd, Londonderry NH 03053	**800-922-2637***	603-644-2500
*Cust Svc		

207 CORD & TWINE

	Toll-Free	Phone
Ashaway Line & Twine Mfg Co PO Box 549, Ashaway RI 02804	**800-556-7260**	401-377-2221
Atkins & Pearce Inc 1 Braid Way, Covington KY 41017	**800-837-7477**	859-356-2001
Bridon Cordage LLC 909 16th St, Albert Lea MN 56007	**800-563-2170**	507-377-1601
Brownell & Co Inc 423 E Haddam-Moodus Rd, Moodus CT 06469	**800-222-4007**	860-873-8625
Carron Net Co Inc PO Box 177, Two Rivers WI 54241	**800-558-7768**	920-793-2217
Columbian Rope Co 145 Towery St, Guntown MS 38849	**800-692-0151**	662-348-2241
Cortland Line Co Inc 3736 Kellogg Rd, Cortland NY 13045	**800-847-6787**	607-756-2851
FNT Industries Inc 927 1st St, Menominee MI 49858	**800-338-9860***	906-863-5531
*Cust Svc		
Forten Corp 7815 Silverton Ave Suite 2-A, San Diego CA 92126	**800-722-5588**	858-693-9888
Hooven Allison Co 677 Cincinnati Ave, Xenia OH 45385	**800-543-0736**	937-372-4421
Lehigh Group 2834 Shoeneck Rd, Macungie PA 18062	**800-523-9382**	610-966-9702
New England Ropes Inc 848 Airport Rd, Fall River MA 02720	**800-333-6679**	508-678-8200
Pacific Fibre & Rope Co Inc 903 Flint Ave Suite 27, Wilmington CA 90748	**800-825-7673**	310-834-4567
Pelican Rope Works Inc 4001 W Carriage Dr, Santa Ana CA 92704	**800-464-7673**	714-545-0116
Puget Sound Rope Corp 1012 2nd St, Anacortes WA 98221	**800-366-8488**	360-293-8488
Rocky Mount Cord Co 381 N Grace St, Rocky Mount NC 27804	**800-342-9130***	252-977-9130
*Orders		
Ryan Rope Works 953 Benton Ave, Winslow ME 04901	**800-848-4495**	207-872-0031
Samson Rope Technologies Inc 2090 Thornton Rd, Ferndale WA 98248	**800-227-7673***	360-384-4669
*Cust Svc		
Sinco Inc 701 Middle St, Middletown CT 06457	**800-243-6753***	860-632-0500
*Cust Svc		
US Line Co 16 Union Ave, Westfield MA 01085	**800-456-4665**	413-562-3629
Wall Industries Inc 1615 N Lee St, Spencer NC 28159	**888-289-9255**	704-637-7414
Wellington Inc 1140 Monticello Hwy PO Box 244, Madison GA 30650	**800-221-5054**	706-342-1916
Winchester-Auburn Mills Inc 70 Dundas St, Deseronto ON K0K1X0	**800-634-8011***	781-935-4110
*Cust Svc		

208 CORK & CORK PRODUCTS

SEE ALSO Office Supplies

	Toll-Free	Phone
American Star Cork Co 33-53 62nd St, Woodside NY 11377	**800-338-3581**	718-335-3000
Amorim Industrial Solutions 26112 110th St PO Box 25, Trevor WI 53179	**800-558-3206**	262-862-2311
Expanko Cork Co Inc 3135 Lower Valley Rd, Parkesburg PA 19365	**800-345-6202***	610-593-3000
*Cust Svc		
Manton Industrial Cork Products Inc 415 Oser Ave Unit U, Hauppauge NY 11788	**800-663-1921**	631-273-0700
Maryland Cork Co Inc PO Box 126, Elkton MD 21922	**800-662-2675**	410-398-2955

209 CORPORATE HOUSING

	Toll-Free	Phone
BridgeStreet Accommodations Inc 2242 Pinnacle Pkwy, Twinsburg OH 44087	**800-278-7338**	330-405-6060
Cabernet Corporate Housing PO Box 18281, Oklahoma City OK 73154	**888-413-3463**	405-236-0066
Charles E Smith Corporate Living 400 15th St S, Arlington VA 22202	**888-234-7829**	703-920-9550
Churchill Corporate Services 56 Utter Ave, Hawthorne NJ 07506	**800-941-7458**	973-636-9400
Coast to Coast Corporate Housing PO Box 1597, Cypress CA 90630	**800-451-9466**	714-229-1881
ExecSuites 702 3rd Ave SW, Calgary AB T2P3B4	**800-667-4980**	403-294-5800
ExecuStay Corp 7595 Rickenbacker Dr, Gaithersburg MD 20879	**888-840-7829**	301-212-9660
K & M Corporate Housing Inc 16060 Caputo Dr Suite 120, Morgan Hill CA 95037	**800-646-0907**	408-782-1212
Klein & Co Corporate Housing Services Inc 6312 S Fiddlers Green Cir Suite 230E, Englewood CO 80111	**800-208-9826**	303-796-2100
Marriott International Inc ExecuStay Corp 7595 Rickenbacker Dr, Gaithersburg MD 20879	**888-840-7829**	301-212-9660
Oakwood Worldwide 2222 Corinth Ave, Los Angeles CA 90064	**800-888-0808**	310-478-1021
Preferred Living 88 Upham St, Malden MA 02148	**800-343-2177**	781-321-5793
Smith Charles E Corporate Living 400 15th St S, Arlington VA 22202	**888-234-7829**	703-920-9550
SuiteAmerica 4970 Windplay Dr Suite C-1, El Dorado Hills CA 95762	**800-363-9779**	916-367-9501
Temporary VIP Suites 43000 W Nine-Mile Rd Suite 305, Novi MI 48375	**888-847-7848**	248-347-1551
Windsor Corporate Suites 4212 Stearns Hills Rd, Waltham MA 02451	**800-888-7368**	781-899-5100
Wynne Residential Corporate Housing 2214 Westwood Ave, Richmond VA 23230	**800-338-8534**	804-359-8534

210 CORRECTIONAL FACILITIES OPERATORS

	Toll-Free	Phone
Avalon Correctional Services Inc PO Box 57012, Oklahoma City OK 73157	**800-919-9113**	405-752-8802
NASDAQ: CITY		
Cornell Cos Inc 1700 West Loop S Suite 1500, Houston TX 77027	**888-624-0816**	713-623-0790
NYSE: CRN		
Correctional Services Corp 1819 Main St Suite 1000, Sarasota FL 34236	**800-275-3766**	941-953-9199
NASDAQ: CSCQ		
Corrections Corp of America 10 Burton Hills Blvd, Nashville TN 37215	**800-624-2931**	615-263-3000
NYSE: CXW		
GEO Group Inc 621 NW 53rd St Suite 700, Boca Raton FL 33487	**800-666-5640**	561-893-0101
NYSE: GGI		
Youth Services International Inc 1819 Main St Suite 1000, Sarasota FL 34236	**800-275-3766**	941-953-9199

211 COSMETICS, SKIN CARE, AND OTHER PERSONAL CARE PRODUCTS

SEE ALSO Perfumes

	Toll-Free	Phone
ABRA Therapeutics Inc 10365 Hwy 116, Forestville CA 95436	**800-745-0761**	707-869-0761
Access Business Group LLC 7575 Fulton St E, Ada MI 49355	**800-253-6500***	616-787-5358
*Cust Svc		
Advanced Research Laboratories 1063 McGaw Ave Suite 100, Irvine CA 92614	**800-966-6960**	949-221-8238
Alchemy International Inc 14909 Community St, Panorama City CA 91402	**800-798-4801***	818-830-3374
*Orders		
Alleghany Pharmacal Corp 277 Northern Blvd, Great Neck NY 11022	**800-645-6190**	516-466-0660
Almay Inc 237 Park Ave, New York NY 10017	**800-473-8566**	212-527-4700
Aloette Cosmetics Inc 4900 Highlands Pkwy, Smyrna GA 30082	**800-256-3883**	678-444-2563
American Safety Razor Co 1 Razor Blade Ln, Verona VA 24482	**800-445-9284**	540-248-8000
At Last Naturals Inc 401 Columbus Ave, Valhalla NY 10595	**800-527-8123**	914-747-3599
Avalon Natural Cosmetics Inc 1105 Industrial Ave Suite 200, Petaluma CA 94952	**800-227-5120**	707-769-5120
Aveda Corp 4000 Pheasant Ridge Dr, Blaine MN 55449	**800-283-3224**	763-783-4000
Avon Products Inc 1251 Ave of the Americas, New York NY 10020	**800-367-2866***	212-282-5000
NYSE: AVP ■ *Cust Svc		
Bassett WE Co 100 Trap Falls Rd Ext, Shelton CT 06484	**800-394-8746**	203-929-8483
Bath & Body Works 7 Limited Pkwy E, Reynoldsburg OH 43068	**888-856-1616**	614-856-6000
Bath-and-Body.com 1021 Bay Blvd Suite S, Chula Vista CA 91911	**888-935-2639**	619-425-0829
BeautiControl Cosmetics Inc 2121 Midway Rd, Carrollton TX 75006	**800-232-8841**	972-458-0601
Beehive Botanicals Inc 16297 W Nursery Rd, Hayward WI 54843	**800-233-4483**	715-634-4274
Beiersdorf North America 187 Danbury Rd, Wilton CT 06897	**800-233-2340**	203-563-5800
Belcam Inc Delagar Div 27 Montgomery St, Rouses Point NY 12979	**800-848-9281**	
BeneFit Cosmetics 685 Market St 7th Fl, San Francisco CA 94105	**800-781-2336***	415-781-8153
*Cust Svc		
Blissworld LLC 50 Washington St 7th Fl, Brooklyn NY 11201	**888-243-8825**	212-219-8970
Bobbi Brown Professional Cosmetics Inc 767 5th Ave, New York NY 10153	**877-310-9222**	
Body Shop The 5036 One World Way, Wake Forest NC 27587	**800-747-4827***	919-554-4900
*Cust Svc		
Bonne Bell Inc 18519 Detroit Ave, Lakewood OH 44107	**800-321-1006**	216-221-0800
Bronner Brothers Inc 2141 Powers Ferry Rd, Marietta GA 30067	**800-241-6151**	770-988-0015

Company	City	State	ZIP	Toll-Free	Phone
Carter-Horner Inc 6600 Kitimat Rd	Mississauga	ON	L5N1L9	**800-387-2130**	905-826-6200
Caswell-Massey Co Ltd 121 Fieldcrest Ave	Edison	NJ	08837	**800-326-0500**	732-225-2181
CBI Laboratories 4201 Diplomacy Rd	Fort Worth	TX	76155	**800-822-7546**	972-241-7546
CCA Industries Inc 200 Murray Hill Pkwy *AMEX: CAW* ■ *Cust Svc	East Rutherford	NJ	07073	**800-524-2720***	201-330-1400
Chattem Inc 1715 W 38th St *NASDAQ: CHTT*	Chattanooga	TN	37409	**800-366-6077**	423-821-4571
Clairol Div Procter & Gamble Co 1 Blachley Rd	Stamford	CT	06922	**800-223-5800**	203-357-5000
Combe Inc 1101 Westchester Ave	White Plains	NY	10604	**800-873-7400**	914-694-5454
Cosmolab Inc 1100 Garrett Pkwy	Lewisburg	TN	37091	**800-359-6254**	931-359-6253
Cosrich Group Inc 51 LaFrance Ave	Bloomfield	NJ	07003	**888-898-9176**	973-566-6240
Crabtree & Evelyn Ltd 102 Peake Brook Rd	Woodstock	CT	06281	**800-624-5211**	860-928-2761
Del Laboratories Inc 178 EAB Plaza West Tower	Uniondale	NY	11556	**800-952-5080**	516-844-2020
Delagar Div Belcam Inc 27 Montgomery St	Rouses Point	NY	12979	**800-848-9281**	
Dial Corp 15501 N Dial Blvd *Cust Svc	Scottsdale	AZ	85260	**800-258-3425***	480-754-3425
Dudley Products Inc 1080 Old Greensboro Rd	Kernersville	NC	27284	**800-334-4150**	336-993-8800
Elizabeth Arden Inc 14100 NW 60th Ave *NASDAQ: RDEN*	Miami Lakes	FL	33014	**800-227-2445**	305-818-8000
Flents Products Co 5401 S Graham Rd	Saint Charles	MI	48655	**800-262-8221**	989-865-8221
Flowery Beauty Products Inc 107 Mill Plain Rd Suite 303	Danbury	CT	06811	**800-545-5247**	203-205-0686
Forever Living Products International Inc 7501 E McCormick Pkwy	Scottsdale	AZ	85258	**888-440-2563**	480-998-8888
Framesi USA Inc 400 Chess St	Coraopolis	PA	15108	**800-321-9648**	412-269-2950
Fuller Brush Co 1 Fuller Way *Cust Svc	Great Bend	KS	67530	**800-438-5537***	620-792-1711
Gillette Co Prudential Tower Bldg *NYSE: G* ■ *Cust Svc	Boston	MA	02199	**800-445-5388***	617-421-7000
Gloss.com Inc 767 5th Ave *Orders	New York	NY	10153	**888-550-4567***	212-572-4200
GOJO Industries Inc PO Box 991	Akron	OH	44309	**800-321-9647**	330-255-6000
Goody Products Inc 400 Galleria Pkwy Suite 1100	Atlanta	GA	30339	**800-241-4324**	770-615-4700
Guest Supply Inc PO Box 902 *Cust Svc	Monmouth Junction	NJ	08852	**800-448-3787***	609-514-9696
H2O Plus Inc 845 W Madison St *Cust Svc	Chicago	IL	60607	**800-690-2284***	312-850-9283
Hawaiian Tropic 1190 US Hwy 1 N	Ormond Beach	FL	32174	**800-874-4844**	386-677-9559
Helene Curtis Industries Inc 205 N Michigan Ave Suite 3200	Chicago	IL	60601	**800-621-2013**	312-661-0222
Henkel Corp Schwartzkopf & Henkel Div 1063 McGraw Ave Suite 100	Irvine	CA	92614	**800-326-2855**	949-794-5500
Hewitt Soap Co Inc 333 Linden Ave	Dayton	OH	45403	**800-543-2245**	937-253-1151
Hydron Technologies Inc 2201 W Sample Rd Bldg 9 Suite 7B	Pompano Beach	FL	33073	**800-449-3766**	954-861-6400
Jafra Cosmetics International 2451 Townsgate Rd	Westlake Village	CA	91361	**800-551-2345**	805-449-3000
Jason Natural Cosmetics Inc 5500 W 83rd St	Los Angeles	CA	90045	**800-527-6605**	310-838-7543
John Frieda Professional Hair Care Inc 333 Ludlow St *Cust Svc	Stanford	CT	06902	**800-521-3189***	203-762-1233
John Paul Mitchell Systems 9701 Wilshire Blvd Suite 1205 *Cust Svc	Beverly Hills	CA	90212	**800-793-8790***	310-248-3888
Johnson & Johnson Consumer Products Co 199 Grandview Rd	Skillman	NJ	08558	**800-526-3967**	908-874-1000
Kao Brands Co 2535 Spring Grove Ave	Cincinnati	OH	45214	**800-742-8798**	513-421-1400
Key West Fragrance & Cosmetics Factory Inc 540 Greene St *Orders	Key West	FL	33040	**800-445-2563***	305-293-1885
Korex Corp 50000 W Pontiac Trail PO Box 930339	Wixom	MI	48393	**800-678-7627**	248-624-0000
Lander Co Inc 200 Lenox Dr Suite 202 *Orders	Lawrenceville	NJ	08648	**800-452-6337***	609-219-0930
Lee Pharmaceuticals Inc 1434 Santa Anita Ave	South El Monte	CA	91733	**800-950-5337**	626-442-3141
L'Oreal USA Inc Soft Sheen/Carson Products Div 8522 S LaFayette	Chicago	IL	60620	**800-342-7661**	800-621-6143
Luster Products Inc 1104 W 43rd St	Chicago	IL	60609	**800-621-4255**	773-579-1800
Luzier Personalized Cosmetics Inc 7910-12 Troost Ave	Kansas City	MO	64131	**800-821-6632**	816-531-8338
MakeUpMania! of New York 154 Orchard St	New York	NY	10002	**800-711-7182**	212-533-5900
Mana Products Inc 32-02 Queens Blvd *Cust Svc	Long Island City	NY	11101	**800-221-3071***	718-361-2550
Mary Kay Inc 16251 Dallas Pkwy *Cust Svc	Addison	TX	75001	**800-627-9529***	972-687-6300
Mary Kay Inc Mfg Group 1330 Regal Row *Cust Svc	Dallas	TX	75247	**800-627-9529***	972-687-6300
Matrix Essentials Inc 30601 Carter St	Solon	OH	44139	**800-282-2822**	440-248-3700
Max Factor 1 Procter & Gamble Plaza	Cincinnati	OH	45202	**800-526-8787**	513-983-1100
Maybelline New York 575 5th Ave	New York	NY	10017	**800-944-0730**	212-818-1500
Merle Norman Cosmetics Inc 9130 Bellanca Ave	Los Angeles	CA	90045	**800-421-2060**	310-641-3000
Neutrogena Corp 5760 W 96th St *Cust Svc	Los Angeles	CA	90045	**800-217-1136***	310-642-1150
Newell Rubbermaid Inc Home & Family Group 10B Glenlake Pkwy Suite 600	Atlanta	GA	30328	**800-434-4314**	770-407-3800
Nexxus Products Co 82 Coromar Dr	Goleta	CA	93117	**800-444-6399**	805-968-6900
Norelco Consumer Products Co 1010 Washington Blvd	Stamford	CT	06912	**800-243-7884**	203-973-0200
Obagi Medical Products Inc 310 Golden Shore	Long Beach	CA	90802	**800-636-7546**	562-628-1007
Origins Natural Resources Inc 767 5th Ave *Cust Svc	New York	NY	10153	**800-723-7310***	212-572-4200
Para Laboratories Inc 100 Rose Ave	Hempstead	NY	11550	**800-645-3752**	516-538-4600
Paramount Cosmetics Inc 93 Entin Rd Suite 4	Clifton	NJ	07014	**800-522-9880**	973-472-2323
Person & Covey Inc 616 Allen Ave	Glendale	CA	91201	**800-423-2341**	818-240-1030
Pfizer Inc 235 E 42nd St *NYSE: PFE* ■ *Prod Info	New York	NY	10017	**800-733-4717***	212-573-2323
Philips Oral Healthcare Inc 35301 SE Center St	Snoqualmie	WA	98065	**800-957-9310**	425-396-2000
philosophy inc 4602 E Hammond Ln	Phoenix	AZ	85034	**800-568-3151**	480-736-8200
Playtex Products Inc 300 Nyala Farms Rd *NYSE: PYX*	Westport	CT	06880	**800-999-9700**	203-341-4000
Prestige Cosmetics Corp 1441 W Newport Center Dr	Deerfield Beach	FL	33442	**800-722-7488**	954-480-9202
Pro-Line International Inc 2121 Panoramic Cir	Dallas	TX	75212	**800-527-5879**	214-631-4247
Procter & Gamble Co Clairol Div 1 Blachley Rd	Stamford	CT	06922	**800-223-5800**	203-357-5000
Procter & Gamble Cosmetics 11050 York Rd *Cust Svc	Hunt Valley	MD	21030	**800-638-6204***	800-851-8262
Queen Helene 100 Rose Ave	Hempstead	NY	11550	**800-645-3752**	516-538-4600
Reckitt Benckiser Inc PO Box 225 *Cust Svc	Parsippany	NJ	07054	**800-888-0192***	973-633-3600
Redken Laboratories Inc 575 5th Ave *Cust Svc	New York	NY	10017	**800-423-5280***	212-818-1500
Remington Products Co LLC 601 Rayovac Dr *Cust Svc	Madison	WI	53711	**800-736-4648***	608-275-3340
Revlon Consumer Products Corp 237 Park Ave	New York	NY	10017	**800-473-8566**	212-527-4000
Rozelle Cosmetics PO Box 70	Westfield	VT	05874	**800-451-4216**	802-744-2270
Saint Ives Laboratories Inc 2525 Armitage Ave	Melrose Park	IL	60160	**800-333-6666**	708-450-3000
Sara Lee Household Products 707 Eagle View Blvd	Exton	PA	19341	**800-879-5494**	610-321-1220
Schering-Plough Corp 2000 Galloping Hill Rd *NYSE: SGP* ■ *Mktg	Kenilworth	NJ	07033	**888-793-7253***	908-298-4000
Schering-Plough HealthCare Products Corp PO Box 377 *Cust Svc	Memphis	TN	38151	**800-842-4090***	901-320-2011
Schwarzkopf & Henkel Div Henkel Corp 1063 McGraw Ave Suite 100	Irvine	CA	92614	**800-326-2855**	949-794-5500
Scolding Locks Corp 1520 W Rogers Ave	Appleton	WI	54914	**800-537-9707**	920-733-5561
Sebastian International Inc 6109 DeSoto Ave *Cust Svc	Woodland Hills	CA	91367	**800-347-4424***	818-999-5112
sephora.com Inc 525 Market St First Market Tower 3rd Fl *Cust Svc	San Francisco	CA	94105	**877-737-4672***	415-977-4300
Sheffield Laboratories 170 Broad St	New London	CT	06320	**800-222-1087**	860-442-4451
Soft Sheen/Carson Products Div L'Oreal USA Inc 8522 S LaFayette	Chicago	IL	60620	**800-342-7661**	800-621-6143
Stahl Soap Corp 1 Branca Rd	East Rutherford	NJ	07073	**800-527-5115**	201-507-5770
Star Nail Products Inc 29120 Ave Paine	Valencia	CA	91355	**800-762-6245**	661-257-7827
Stephan Co 1850 W McNab Rd *AMEX: TSC*	Fort Lauderdale	FL	33309	**800-327-4963**	954-971-0600
Stila Cosmetics 551 Madison Ave 12th Fl	New York	NY	10022	**877-565-1299**	646-282-1000
Tanning Research Labs Inc DBA Hawaiian Tropic 1190 US Hwy 1 N	Ormond Beach	FL	32174	**800-874-4844**	386-677-9559
Tom's of Maine Inc PO Box 710	Kennebunk	ME	04043	**800-367-8667**	207-985-2944
Ulta3 Inc 1135 Arbor Dr	Romeoville	IL	60446	**866-858-2266**	630-226-0020
Unilever Home & Personal Care North America 800 Sylvan Ave 1st Fl	Englewood Cliffs	NJ	07632	**800-745-9595**	201-862-2000
Unilever of Puerto Rico Inc PO Box 599	Bayamon	PR	00960	**800-981-3405**	787-740-3400
Urban Decay 729 Farad St	Costa Mesa	CA	92627	**800-784-8722**	949-631-4504
Vi-Jon Labs Inc 8515 Page Ave	Saint Louis	MO	63114	**800-325-8167**	314-427-1000
Victoria Vogue Inc 90 Southland Dr	Bethlehem	PA	18017	**800-967-7833**	610-865-1500
Wahl Clipper Corp 2900 Locust St	Sterling	IL	61081	**800-767-9245**	815-625-6525
WE Bassett Co 100 Trap Falls Rd Ext	Shelton	CT	06484	**800-394-8746**	203-929-8483
Wella Corp 6109 DeSoto Ave	Woodland Hills	CA	91367	**800-829-4422**	818-999-5112
White Laboratories Inc 110 Bomar Ct Suite 122	Longwood	FL	32750	**800-327-2014**	407-869-0107
Zia Natural Skincare 1337 Evans Ave	San Francisco	CA	94124	**800-334-7546**	415-642-8339
Zotos International Inc 100 Tokeneke Rd	Darien	CT	06820	**800-242-9283**	203-655-8911

212 CREDIT BUREAUS

Company	City	State	ZIP	Toll-Free	Phone
CBA Information Services 4 Executive Campus	Cherry Hill	NJ	08002	**800-248-0470**	856-532-6500
Coface Services North America Inc 121 Whitney Ave	New Haven	CT	06510	**800-929-8374**	203-781-3800
Equifax Inc 1550 Peachtree St NW *NYSE: EFX* ■ *Sales	Atlanta	GA	30309	**888-202-4025***	404-885-8000
Experian Inc 475 Anton Blvd	Costa Mesa	CA	92626	**888-397-3742**	714-830-7000
Fair Isaac Corp 200 Smith Ranch Rd *NYSE: FIC*	San Rafael	CA	94903	**800-444-5850**	415-472-2211
Kroll Factual Data Inc 5200 Hahns Peak Dr	Loveland	CO	80538	**800-929-3400**	970-663-5700
Merchants Credit Bureau PO Box 458	Augusta	GA	30903	**800-426-5265**	706-823-6246
Tele-Track 155 Technology Pkwy Suite 800	Norcross	GA	30092	**800-729-6981**	770-449-8809
TransUnion LLC 555 W Adams St	Chicago	IL	60661	**800-916-8800**	312-258-1717
VERIBANC Inc 1 Social St	Woonsocket	RI	02895	**800-442-2657**	401-766-5300

213 CREDIT CARD PROVIDERS & RELATED SERVICES

Company	City	State	ZIP	Toll-Free	Phone
American Express Co Inc World Financial Ctr 200 Vesey St *NYSE: AXP*	New York	NY	10285	**800-666-1775**	212-640-2000
AT & T Universal Card Services PO Box 44167	Jacksonville	FL	32231	**800-235-3549**	904-954-7500
Bank of America Card Services 1 Commercial Plaza	Norfolk	VA	23510	**800-732-9194**	757-441-4770
Bloomingdale's Credit Services 9111 Duke Blvd	Mason	OH	45040	**800-456-9529**	513-398-5221
BP Amoco Credit Card 4300 Westown Pkwy	West Des Moines	IA	50266	**800-850-6266**	800-462-6626
Capital One Financial Corp 1680 Capital One Dr *NYSE: COF*	McLean	VA	22102	**800-801-1164**	703-720-1000
ChevronTexaco Credit Card Center 2001 Diamond Blvd	Concord	CA	94520	**800-243-8766**	925-842-1000
Credit Card Sentinel Inc PO Box 4401 *Cust Svc	Carol Stream	IL	60197	**800-423-5166***	847-605-7485
Dillard's Credit Services Inc PO Box 4599	Carol Stream	IL	60197	**800-643-8278**	
Diners Club Carte Blanche 7958 S Chester St Waterview IV	Englewood	CO	80112	**800-234-6377**	303-799-9000

Name / Address	City	State	ZIP	Toll-Free	Phone
Diners Club International 8430 W Bryn Mawr Ave	Chicago	IL	60631	**800-234-6377**	773-380-5100
Discover Financial Services Inc 2500 Lake Cook Rd *Cust Svc	Riverwoods	IL	60015	**800-347-2683***	224-405-0900
ExxonMobil Credit Card Services PO Box 4598	Carol Stream	IL	60197	**800-344-4355**	
GE Capital Card Services PO Box 276	Dayton	OH	45401	**800-844-6543**	800-333-1071
Household Retail Services USA Churman's Corporate Ctr 90 Christiana Rd	New Castle	DE	19720	**800-695-6950**	302-327-2400
Intersections Inc 14901 Bogle Dr *NASDAQ: INTX*	Chantilly	VA	20151	**800-695-7536**	703-488-6100
iPayment Inc 40 Burton Hills Blvd Suite 415 *NASDAQ: IPMT* ■ *Cust Svc	Nashville	TN	37215	**800-324-9825***	615-665-1858
Macy's Credit Services 5300 Kings Island Dr *Cust Svc	Mason	OH	45040	**800-743-6229***	513-459-1500
MasterCard International Inc 2000 Purchase St	Purchase	NY	10577	**800-247-4623**	914-249-2000
Rewards Network 2 N Riverside Plaza Suite 950 *AMEX: IRN*	Chicago	IL	60606	**800-841-7102**	312-521-6767
Saks Inc 3455 Hwy 80 W	Jackson	MS	39209	**800-443-6856**	601-968-4400
Shell Credit Card 4300 Westown Pkwy	West Des Moines	IA	50266	**877-236-5153**	
TNS Merchant & Credit Card Services 1939 Roland Clarke Pl	Reston	VA	20191	**800-240-2824**	703-453-8338
Visa International PO Box 8999	San Francisco	CA	94128	**800-847-2911**	650-432-3200
Wright Express Corp 97 Darling Ave *NYSE: WXS*	South Portland	ME	04106	**800-761-7181**	207-773-8171

214 CREDIT & FINANCING - COMMERCIAL

SEE ALSO Banks - Commercial & Savings; Credit & Financing - Consumer

Name / Address	City	State	ZIP	Toll-Free	Phone
Advanta Corp PO Box 844 *NASDAQ: ADVNA*	Spring House	PA	19477	**800-327-5998**	215-657-4000
Advanta Leasing Services 40 E Clementon Rd	Gibbsboro	NJ	08026	**800-255-0022**	
AFCO Credit Corp 110 William St 29th Fl	New York	NY	10038	**800-288-2313**	212-401-4400
Agricredit Acceptance LLC PO Box 2000	Johnston	IA	50131	**800-873-2474**	515-251-2800
American Express Business Finance 390 N Sepulveda Blvd Suite 1000	El Segundo	CA	90245	**800-234-8975**	800-774-5855
American Express Credit Corp 301 N Walnut St 1 Christina Centre Suite 1002	Wilmington	DE	19801	**800-525-5450**	302-594-3350
Arkansas Capital Corp Group 200 S Commerce St Suite 400	Little Rock	AR	72201	**800-216-7237**	501-374-9247
Automotive Finance Corp (AFC) 13085 Hamilton Crossing Blvd	Carmel	IN	46032	**888-335-6675**	317-815-9645
Bank of America Leasing Corp 2059 Northlake Pkwy 4th Fl	Tucker	GA	30084	**800-299-2265**	770-270-8400
Bombardier Capital Group 261 Mountain View Dr	Colchester	VT	05446	**800-525-5871**	802-654-8100
Business Loan Express LLC 645 Madison Ave	New York	NY	10022	**888-722-5626**	212-751-5626
Church Loans & Investment Trust PO Box 8203	Amarillo	TX	79114	**800-692-1111**	806-358-3666
Comfort Financial Services PO Box 1140	Evansville	IN	47706	**866-866-1331**	
Congress Financial Corp 1133 Ave of the Americas	New York	NY	10036	**800-223-6352**	212-840-2000
Connell Finance Co Inc 1 Connell Dr	Berkeley Heights	NJ	07922	**800-233-3240**	908-673-3700
Connell Technologies Co LLC 350 Lindbergh Ave	Livermore	CA	94550	**888-301-0300**	925-455-6790
Cooperative Finance Assn Inc 10100 N Ambassador Dr Suite 315 PO Box 901532	Kansas City	MO	64190	**877-835-5232**	816-214-4200
De Lage Landen Inc 1111 Old Eagle School Rd	Wayne	PA	19087	**800-735-3273**	610-386-5000
Deere Credit Services Inc 6400 NW 86th St PO Box 6600	Johnston	IA	50131	**800-362-8580**	515-224-2800
Deere John Credit Co PO Box 6600	Johnston	IA	50131	**800-275-5322**	515-267-3000
Edison Capital 18101 Von Karman Ave Suite 1700	Irvine	CA	92612	**800-241-8101**	949-757-2400
Falcon Financial Investment Trust 15 Commerce Rd	Stamford	CT	06902	**800-771-5400**	203-967-0000
Farm Credit Leasing 5500 Wayzata Blvd Colonnade Bldg Suite 1600	Minneapolis	MN	55416	**800-328-8863**	763-797-7400
Financial Federal Corp 733 3rd Ave 24th Fl *AMEX: FIF*	New York	NY	10017	**800-480-1003**	212-599-8000
First Community Financial Corp 4000 N Central Ave Suite 100	Phoenix	AZ	85012	**800-242-3232**	602-265-7714
First South Production Credit Assn 713 S Pear Orchard Rd Suite 300	Ridgeland	MS	39157	**888-297-1722**	601-977-8394
Foothill Group Inc 2450 Colorado Ave Suite 3000W	Santa Monica	CA	90404	**800-535-1811**	310-453-7300
Ford Motor Credit Co 1 American Rd PO Box 1732	Dearborn	MI	48121	**800-727-7000**	313-322-3000
GATX Capital Corp 4 Embarcadero Ctr Suite 2200	San Francisco	CA	94111	**800-227-4289**	415-955-3200
GATX Corp 500 W Monroe St *NYSE: GMT*	Chicago	IL	60661	**800-525-4289**	312-621-6200
GE Capital Auto Financial Services 540 W Northwest Hwy *Cust Svc	Barrington	IL	60010	**800-488-5208***	847-277-4000
GE Capital Public Finance 8400 Normandale Lake Blvd Suite 470	Minneapolis	MN	55437	**800-346-3164**	952-897-5649
GE Capital Small Business Finance 635 Maryville Ctr Dr Suite 120	Saint Louis	MO	63141	**800-447-2025**	314-205-3500
GE Commercial Equipment Financing 44 Old Ridgebury Rd	Danbury	CT	06810	**800-937-4322**	203-796-1000
GE Vendor Financial Services 10 Riverview Dr	Danbury	CT	06810	**800-876-2033**	203-749-6000
Green Tree Servicing LLC 345 Saint Peter St Suite 600	Saint Paul	MN	55102	**800-423-9527**	651-293-3400
HPSC Inc 1 Beacon St 2nd Fl	Boston	MA	02109	**800-225-2488**	617-720-7200
John Deere Credit Co PO Box 6600	Johnston	IA	50131	**800-275-5322**	515-267-3000
KLC Inc DBA Unicapital Leasing 433 New Park Ave	West Hartford	CT	06110	**800-444-8333**	860-233-3663
Koch Financial Corp 17767 N Perimeter Dr Suite 101	Scottsdale	AZ	85255	**866-545-2327**	480-419-3600
Kraus-Anderson Capital Inc 523 S 8th St Suite 523	Minneapolis	MN	55404	**888-547-3983**	612-305-2934
M & I First National Leasing Corp 250 E Wisconsin Ave Suite 1400	Milwaukee	WI	53202	**800-558-9840**	414-272-2374
MarCap Corp 20 N Wacker Dr Suite 2150	Chicago	IL	60606	**800-621-1677**	312-641-0233
Medallion Financial Corp 437 Madison Ave 38th Fl *NASDAQ: TAXI*	New York	NY	10022	**877-633-2554**	212-328-2100
Metro Financial Services PO Box 970817	Dallas	TX	75397	**800-327-2274**	214-363-4557
MicroFinancial Inc 10-M Commerce Way *NYSE: MFI*	Woburn	MA	01801	**800-843-5327**	781-994-4800
NAFCO 3907 Aero Pl Suite 1	Lakeland	FL	33811	**800-999-3712**	863-644-8463
National Rural Utilities Cooperative Finance Corp 2201 Cooperative Way Woodland Pk	Herndon	VA	20171	**800-424-2954**	703-709-6700
Navistar Financial Corp 2850 W Golf Rd	Rolling Meadows	IL	60008	**800-233-9121**	847-734-4000
New York Business Development Corp 50 Beaver St 6th Fl	Albany	NY	12207	**800-923-2504**	518-463-2268
Orix Financial Services Inc 600 Town Park Ln	Kennesaw	GA	30144	**866-674-9112**	770-970-6000
PDS Gaming Corp 6171 McLeod Dr Suite L *NASDAQ: PDSG*	Las Vegas	NV	89120	**800-479-3612**	702-736-0700
Phoenix American Inc 2401 Kerner Blvd	San Rafael	CA	94901	**800-266-2344**	415-485-4500
Phoenix Growth Capital Corp 2401 Kerner Blvd	San Rafael	CA	94901	**800-227-2626**	415-485-4500
Phoenix Leasing Inc 2401 Kerner Blvd	San Rafael	CA	94901	**800-266-2344**	415-485-4500
Pitney Bowes Credit Corp 27 Waterview Dr	Shelton	CT	06484	**800-243-9506**	203-922-4000
PMC Capital Inc 17950 Preston Rd Suite 600	Dallas	TX	75252	**800-486-3223**	972-349-3200
PMC Commercial Trust 17950 Preston Rd Suite 600 *AMEX: PCC*	Dallas	TX	75252	**800-486-3223**	972-349-3200
PNC Equipment Leasing Corp 620 Liberty Ave 2 PNC Plaza 13th Fl	Pittsburgh	PA	15222	**800-762-6260**	412-762-4848
Presidential Realty Corp 180 S Broadway *AMEX: PDL/A*	White Plains	NY	10605	**800-948-2977**	914-948-1300
Rabo AG Services PO Box 668	Cedar Falls	IA	50613	**800-395-8505**	319-277-0261
SBC Capital Services 2000 W SBC Center Dr	Hoffman Estates	IL	60196	**800-346-8082**	847-290-5000
Siemens Financial Services Inc 170 Wood Ave S	Iselin	NJ	08830	**800-327-4443**	732-590-6500
Snap-on Credit Corp 1125 Tri-State Pkwy Suite 700	Gurnee	IL	60031	**877-777-8455**	847-782-7700
Systran Financial Services Corp 4949 SW Meadows Rd Suite 500	Oswego	OR	97035	**800-824-2075**	503-675-5700
Transamerica Commercial Finance Corp 11121 Carmel Commons Blvd Suite 350	Charlotte	NC	28226	**800-932-0999**	704-542-5134
Unicapital Leasing 433 New Park Ave	West Hartford	CT	06110	**800-444-8333**	860-233-3663
Universal Premium Acceptance Corp 8245 Nieman Rd Suite 100	Lenexa	KS	66214	**800-877-7848**	913-894-6150
US Bancorp Leasing & Financial Inc 13010 SW 68th Pkwy	Portland	OR	97223	**800-253-3468**	503-797-0200
Verizon Credit Inc 201 N Franklin St Suite 3300	Tampa	FL	33602	**800-483-7988**	813-229-6000
Wells Fargo Business Credit 109 S 7th St Norwest Ctr	Minneapolis	MN	55402	**800-634-6224**	612-673-8500
Wells Fargo Equipment Finance Inc 733 Marquette Ave Investors Bldg Suite 700	Minneapolis	MN	55402	**800-322-6220**	612-667-9876
Wells Fargo Financial Leasing PO Box 4943	Syracuse	NY	13221	**800-451-3322**	

215 CREDIT & FINANCING - CONSUMER

SEE ALSO Banks - Commercial & Savings; Credit & Financing - Commercial; Credit Unions

Name / Address	City	State	ZIP	Toll-Free	Phone
American General Financial Services 601 NW 2nd St	Evansville	IN	47701	**800-457-3741**	812-424-8031
AmeriCredit Corp 801 Cherry St Suite 3900 *NYSE: ACF*	Fort Worth	TX	76102	**800-937-3635**	817-302-7000
Ameristar Financial 1795 N Butterfield Rd	Libertyville	IL	60048	**800-784-1535**	847-855-2000
Arcadia Financial Ltd PO Box 1437	Eden Prairie	MN	55440	**800-486-1750**	952-944-4520
AutoNation Financial Services 110 SE 6th St *Cust Svc	Fort Lauderdale	FL	33301	**888-825-8929***	954-769-7000
BB & T Sales Finance 6402 Arlington Blvd	Falls Church	VA	22042	**800-348-6189**	703-241-3500
Central Financial Acceptance Corp 1900 S Main St	Los Angeles	CA	90007	**800-273-3486**	
Chrysler Financial Co LLC 27777 Franklin Rd *Cust Svc	Southfield	MI	48034	**800-556-8172***	248-427-6424
CitiFinancial 300 St Paul Pl *Cust Svc	Baltimore	MD	21202	**800-922-6235***	410-332-3000
Collegiate Funding Services Inc 100 Riverside Pkwy Suite 125 *NASDAQ: CFSI*	Fredericksburg	VA	22406	**800-762-6441**	540-374-1600
Comfort Financial Services PO Box 1140	Evansville	IN	47706	**866-866-1331**	
Credit Acceptance Corp 25505 W 12 Mile Rd *NASDAQ: CACC*	Southfield	MI	48034	**800-634-1506**	248-353-2700
Deere John Credit Co PO Box 6600	Johnston	IA	50131	**800-275-5322**	515-267-3000
EduCap Inc 1676 International Dr Suite 501 *Cust Svc	McLean	VA	22102	**800-865-3276***	703-442-3000
Educational Lending Group Inc 12760 High Bluff Dr Suite 210 *NASDAQ: EDLG* ■ *Cust Svc	San Diego	CA	92130	**866-311-8060***	858-793-4151
Finance Co The 16355 Laguna Canyon Rd	Irvine	CA	92618	**800-966-5100**	
First Investors Financial Services Group Inc 675 Bering Dr Suite 710 *NASDAQ: FIFS*	Houston	TX	77057	**800-722-9112**	713-977-2600
First Marblehead Corp 800 Boylston St 34th Fl *NYSE: FMD*	Boston	MA	02199	**800-895-4238**	781-639-2000
Ford Motor Credit Co 1 American Rd PO Box 1732	Dearborn	MI	48121	**800-727-7000**	313-322-3000

Company / Address	City	State	ZIP	Toll-Free	Phone
GE Capital Auto Financial Services 540 W Northwest Hwy	Barrington	IL	60010	**800-488-5208***	847-277-4000
*Cust Svc					
General Motors Acceptance Corp (GMAC) 200 Renaissance Ctr	Detroit	MI	48265	**800-200-4622**	313-556-5000
General Motors Acceptance Corp Canada (GMAC Canada) 3300 Bloor St W Suite 2800	Toronto	ON	M8X2X5	**800-616-4622**	416-234-6600
GMAC Canada (General Motors Acceptance Corp Canada) 3300 Bloor St W Suite 2800	Toronto	ON	M8X2X5	**800-616-4622**	416-234-6600
Green Tree Servicing LLC 345 Saint Peter St Suite 600	Saint Paul	MN	55102	**800-423-9527**	651-293-3400
Harley-Davison Financial Services 150 S Wacker Dr Suite 3100	Chicago	IL	60606	**800-538-3150**	312-368-9501
John Deere Credit Co PO Box 6600	Johnston	IA	50131	**800-275-5322**	515-267-3000
Key Corporate Banking & Finance 601 Oakmont Ln Suite 110	Westmont	IL	60559	**800-877-2860**	630-655-7100
MBNA Corp 1100 N King St	Wilmington	DE	19884	**800-441-7048**	302-456-8588
NYSE: KRB					
Mercedes-Benz Credit Corp PO Box 685	Roanoke	TX	76262	**800-654-6222**	
Nellie Mae Corp 50 Braintree Hill Park Suite 300	Braintree	MA	02184	**800-367-8848***	781-849-1325
*Cust Svc					
Nelnet Inc 121 S 13th St Suite 201	Lincoln	NE	68508	**888-486-4722**	402-458-2370
NYSE: NNI					
Nicholas Financial Inc 2454 McMullen-Booth Rd Bldg C	Clearwater	FL	33759	**800-237-2721**	727-726-0763
NASDAQ: NICK					
Prestige Financial 1420 S 500 West	Salt Lake City	UT	84115	**866-737-2733**	801-844-2100
Prime Rate Premium Finance Corp 2141 Enterprise Dr PO Box 100507	Florence	SC	29501	**800-777-7458***	843-669-0937
*Cust Svc					
Providian Financial Corp 201 Mission St	San Francisco	CA	94105	**800-525-7557**	415-543-0404
NYSE: PVN					
Sallie Mae Inc 12061 Bluemont Way	Reston	VA	20190	**888-272-5543***	703-810-3000
*Cust Svc					
Sears Roebuck Acceptance Corp 3711 Kennett Pike	Greenville	DE	19807	**800-729-7722**	302-434-3100
Select Portfolio Servicing Inc PO Box 65250	Salt Lake City	UT	84165	**800-258-8602**	801-293-1883
SLM Corp 12061 Bluemont Way	Reston	VA	20190	**888-272-5543**	703-810-3000
NYSE: SLM					
Student Loan Corp PO Box 6191	Sioux Falls	SD	57117	**800-967-2400**	605-331-0821
NYSE: STU					
Toyota Motor Credit Corp 19001 S Western Ave	Torrance	CA	90509	**800-392-2968***	310-787-1310
*Cust Svc					
Union Acceptance Corp 250 N Shadeland Ave	Indianapolis	IN	46219	**800-221-6809**	317-231-6400
United Student Aid Funds Inc DBA USA Funds 11100 USA Pkwy	Fishers	IN	46038	**800-824-7044**	317-849-6510
USA Funds 11100 USA Pkwy	Fishers	IN	46038	**800-824-7044**	317-849-6510
Wachovia Education Finance 11000 White Rock Rd	Rancho Cordova	CA	85670	**800-347-7667**	
Wells Fargo Education Financial Services PO Box 5185	Sioux Falls	SD	57117	**800-658-3567**	
WFS Financial Inc 23 Pasteur	Irvine	CA	92618	**800-289-8004**	949-727-1000
NASDAQ: WFSI					
World Omni Financial Corp 120 NW 12th Ave	Deerfield Beach	FL	33442	**866-663-9663***	954-429-2200
*Cust Svc					

216 CREDIT UNIONS

Credit Union / Address	City	State	ZIP	Toll-Free	Phone
Addison Avenue Federal Credit Union 1501 Pagemill Rd	Palo Alto	CA	94303	**877-233-4766**	
AEDC Federal Credit Union 550 William Northern Blvd PO Box 1210	Tullahoma	TN	37388	**800-342-3086**	931-455-5441
Affinity Federal Credit Union 73 Mountain View Blvd Bldg 200	Basking Ridge	NJ	07920	**800-325-0808**	908-860-7300
Alaska USA Federal Credit Union 4000 Credit Union Dr	Anchorage	AK	99503	**800-525-9094**	907-563-4567
Allegacy Federal Credit Union 700 Highland Oaks Dr	Winston-Salem	NC	27103	**800-782-4670**	336-774-3400
America First Credit Union 1344 W 4675 South	Riverdale	UT	84405	**800-999-3961**	801-627-0900
American Airlines Employees Federal Credit Union PO Box 155489	Fort Worth	TX	76155	**800-533-0035**	817-963-6000
American Eagle Federal Credit Union 417 Main St	East Hartford	CT	06118	**800-842-0145**	860-568-2020
Andrews Federal Credit Union PO Box 4000	Clinton	MD	20735	**800-487-5500**	301-702-5500
APCO Employees Credit Union 1608 7th Ave N	Birmingham	AL	35203	**800-249-2726**	205-257-3601
Arizona Federal Credit Union PO Box 60070	Phoenix	AZ	85082	**800-523-4603**	602-683-1000
Atlanta Postal Credit Union 3900 Crown Rd	Atlanta	GA	30380	**800-849-8431**	404-768-4126
Bank-Fund Staff Federal Credit Union PO Box 27755	Washington	DC	20038	**800-923-7328**	202-458-4300
BECU (Boeing Employees' Credit Union) PO Box 97050	Seattle	WA	98124	**800-233-2328**	206-439-5700
Bellco First Federal Credit Union PO Box 6611	Greenwood Village	CO	80155	**800-235-5261**	303-689-7800
Bethpage Federal Credit Union 899 S Oyster Bay Rd	Bethpage	NY	11714	**800-628-7070**	516-349-6700
Boeing Employees' Credit Union (BECU) PO Box 97050	Seattle	WA	98124	**800-233-2328**	206-439-5700
California Credit Union The 3330 Cahuenga Blvd W Suite 115	Los Angeles	CA	90068	**800-334-8788**	818-291-6700
Chartway Federal Credit Union 160 Newtown Rd	Virginia Beach	VA	23462	**800-678-8765**	757-552-1000
Citizens Equity First Credit Union 5401 W Dirksen Pkwy	Peoria	IL	61607	**800-633-7077**	309-633-7000
Coastal Federal Credit Union 333 St Albans Dr	Raleigh	NC	27609	**800-868-4262**	919-420-8000
Community America Credit Union 9777 Ridge Dr	Lenexa	KS	66219	**800-892-7957**	913-905-7000
Community Credit Union PO Box 830742	Richardson	TX	75083	**800-578-9009**	972-578-5000
Credit Union of Texas PO Box 517028	Dallas	TX	75251	**800-314-3828**	972-263-9497
Dearborn Federal Credit Union 400 Town Center Dr	Dearborn	MI	48126	**888-336-2700**	313-336-2700

Credit Union / Address	City	State	ZIP	Toll-Free	Phone
Delta Employees Credit Union PO Box 20541	Atlanta	GA	30320	**800-544-3328**	404-715-4725
Desert Schools Federal Credit Union PO Box 2945	Phoenix	AZ	85062	**800-456-9171***	602-433-7000
*Mktg					
Digital Employees' Federal Credit Union 220 Donald Lynch Blvd	Marlborough	MA	01752	**800-328-8797**	508-263-6700
Dow Chemical Employees' Credit Union 600 E Lyon Rd	Midland	MI	48640	**800-835-7794**	989-835-7794
Eastern Financial Florida Credit Union 3700 Lakeside Dr	Miramar	FL	33027	**800-882-5007**	954-704-5000
Eastman Credit Union PO Box 1989	Kingsport	TN	37662	**800-999-2328**	423-229-8200
Educational Employees Credit Union PO Box 5242	Fresno	CA	93755	**800-538-3328**	559-437-7700
Eglin Federal Credit Union 838 NE Eglin Pkwy	Fort Walton Beach	FL	32547	**800-367-6159**	850-862-0111
Ent Federal Credit Union 7250 Campus Dr	Colorado Springs	CO	80920	**800-525-9623**	719-574-1100
ESL Federal Credit Union 100 Kings Hwy S Suite 1200	Rochester	NY	14617	**800-848-2265**	585-336-1000
Fairwinds Federal Credit Union 3075 N Alafaya Trail	Orlando	FL	32826	**800-443-6887**	407-277-5045
Founders Federal Credit Union 607 N Main St	Lancaster	SC	29720	**800-845-1614**	803-283-5900
Georgia Telco Credit Union 1155 Peachtree St NE Suite 400	Atlanta	GA	30309	**800-533-2062**	404-874-1166
Golden One Credit Union 6507 4th Ave	Sacramento	CA	95817	**800-521-0137**	916-732-2900
Government Employees Credit Union of El Paso 7227 Viscount Blvd	El Paso	TX	79925	**800-772-4328**	915-778-9221
GTE Federal Credit Union PO Box 172599	Tampa	FL	33672	**800-241-4120**	813-871-2690
HarborOne Credit Union 68 Legion Pkwy	Brockton	MA	02301	**800-244-7592**	508-895-1000
Hudson Valley Federal Credit Union 159 Barnegat Rd	Poughkeepsie	NY	12601	**800-468-3011**	845-463-3011
Kern Schools Federal Credit Union PO Box 9506	Bakersfield	CA	93389	**800-221-3311**	661-833-7900
KeyPoint Credit Union 505 N Mathilda Ave	Sunnyvale	CA	94085	**888-844-3279**	408-731-4100
Kinecta Federal Credit Union 1440 Rosecrans Ave	Manhattan Beach	CA	90266	**800-854-9846**	310-643-5400
Langley Federal Credit Union 1055 W Mercury Blvd	Hampton	VA	23666	**800-826-7490**	757-827-7200
Lockheed Federal Credit Union 2340 Hollywood Way	Burbank	CA	91505	**800-328-5328**	818-565-2020
MacDill Federal Credit Union 6701 S Dale Mabry Hwy	Tampa	FL	33611	**800-839-6328**	813-837-2451
Mission Federal Credit Union 5785 Oberlin Dr Suite 333	San Diego	CA	92121	**800-640-5463**	858-524-2850
Mountain America Credit Union PO Box 9001	West Jordan	UT	84084	**800-748-4302**	801-325-6228
Municipal Credit Union PO Box 3205	New York	NY	10007	**800-843-1867**	212-693-4900
Navy Federal Credit Union PO Box 3000	Merrifield	VA	22119	**800-914-9494**	703-255-8500
Newport News Shipbuilding Employees Credit Union 3711 Huntington Ave	Newport News	VA	23607	**800-928-8801**	757-928-8850
North Island Financial Credit Union 2300 Boswell Rd	Chula Vista	CA	91914	**800-752-4419***	619-656-1600
*Cust Svc					
Northwest Federal Credit Union 200 Spring St	Herndon	VA	20170	**800-336-3384**	703-709-8900
Omni American Federal Credit Union PO Box 150098	Fort Worth	TX	76108	**800-695-2328**	817-246-0111
Orange County Teachers Federal Credit Union 2115 N Broadway	Santa Ana	CA	92706	**800-462-8328**	714-258-4000
Pacific Service Federal Credit Union 2850 Shadelands Dr	Walnut Creek	CA	94598	**888-858-6878**	925-296-6200
Patelco Credit Union 156 2nd St	San Francisco	CA	94105	**800-358-8228**	415-442-6200
Pennsylvania State Employees Credit Union 1 Credit Union Pl	Harrisburg	PA	17110	**800-237-7328**	717-234-8484
Pentagon Federal Credit Union 1001 N Fairfax St	Alexandria	VA	22314	**800-247-5626**	
Police & Fire Federal Credit Union 901 Arch St	Philadelphia	PA	19107	**800-228-8801**	215-931-0300
Polish & Slavic Federal Credit Union 140 Greenpoint Ave	Brooklyn	NY	11222	**800-297-2181**	718-383-6268
Portland Teachers Credit Union PO Box 3750	Portland	OR	97208	**800-527-3932**	503-228-7077
Provident Central Credit Union 303 Twin Dolphin Dr	Redwood Shores	CA	94065	**800-632-4600**	650-508-0300
Randolph-Brooks Federal Credit Union PO Box 2097	Universal City	TX	78148	**800-580-3300**	210-945-3300
Redstone Federal Credit Union 220 Wynn Dr NW	Huntsville	AL	35893	**800-234-1234**	256-837-6110
SAFE Credit Union 3720 Madison Ave	North Highlands	CA	95660	**800-733-7233**	916-979-7233
San Antonio Federal Credit Union 6061 IH 10W	San Antonio	TX	78201	**800-234-7228**	210-258-1414
San Diego County Credit Union 6545 Sequence Dr	San Diego	CA	92121	**877-732-2848**	
Schools Federal Credit Union 5210 Madison Ave	Sacramento	CA	95841	**800-962-0990**	916-569-5400
Security Service Federal Credit Union 16211 La Cantera Pkwy	San Antonio	TX	78256	**800-527-7328**	210-476-4000
South Carolina Federal Credit Union PO Box 190012	North Charleston	SC	29419	**800-845-0432**	843-797-8300
Space Coast Credit Union PO Box 419001	Melbourne	FL	32941	**800-447-7228**	321-752-2222
Star One Federal Credit Union 166 8th Ave Bldg 166	Sunnyvale	CA	94089	**800-552-1455**	408-742-2801
State Employees Credit Union 501 S Capitol Ave	Lansing	MI	48933	**800-937-7328**	517-267-7328
State Employees' Credit Union 1000 Wade Ave	Raleigh	NC	27605	**888-732-8562**	919-839-5000
State Employees Credit Union of Maryland Inc 971 Corporate Blvd	Linthicum	MD	21090	**800-879-7328**	410-487-7328
State Employees Federal Credit Union 1239 Washington Ave	Albany	NY	12206	**800-727-3328**	518-452-8234
Suncoast Schools Federal Credit Union 6804 E Hillsborough Ave	Tampa	FL	33610	**800-999-5887**	813-621-7511
Teachers Credit Union 110 S Main St	South Bend	IN	46601	**800-333-3828**	574-232-8011
Teachers Federal Credit Union 2410 N Ocean Ave	Farmingville	NY	11738	**800-341-4333**	631-698-7000
Texans Credit Union 777 E Campbell Rd	Richardson	TX	75081	**800-843-5295**	972-348-2000
Texas Dow Employees Credit Union 1001 FM 2004	Lake Jackson	TX	77566	**800-839-1154**	979-297-1154
Think Federal Credit Union 5200 Members Pkwy NW	Rochester	MN	55901	**800-288-3425**	507-288-3425
Tinker Federal Credit Union PO Box 45750	Tinker AFB	OK	73145	**800-456-4828**	405-732-0324
Tower Federal Credit Union 7901 Sandy Spring Rd	Laurel	MD	20707	**800-787-8328**	301-497-7000
Travis Federal Credit Union 1 Travis Way	Vacaville	CA	95687	**800-877-8328**	707-449-4000

Name / Address	City	State	Zip	Toll-Free	Phone
Truliant Federal Credit Union 3200 Truliant Way	Winston-Salem	NC	27103	**800-822-0382**	336-659-1955
United Nations Federal Credit Union 820 2nd Ave 12th Fl	New York	NY	10017	**800-891-2471**	212-338-8100
US Alliance Federal Credit Union 600 Midland Ave	Rye	NY	10580	**800-431-2754***	914-921-0500
*Cust Svc					
US Central Credit Union 9701 Renner Blvd	Lenexa	KS	66219	**888-872-0440**	913-227-6000
Virginia Credit Union 7500 Boulders View Dr	Richmond	VA	23225	**800-285-5051**	804-323-6800
Visions Federal Credit Union 24 McKinley Ave	Endicott	NY	13760	**800-242-2120**	607-754-7900
Vystar Credit Union 4949 Blanding Blvd	Jacksonville	FL	32210	**800-445-6289***	904-777-6000
*Cust Svc					
Washington State Employees Credit Union 400 E Union Ave	Olympia	WA	98501	**800-562-0999**	360-943-7911
Wescom Credit Union 123 S Marengo Ave	Pasadena	CA	91101	**888-493-7266**	626-535-1000
WesCorp (Western Corporate Federal Credit Union) 924 Overland Ct	San Dimas	CA	91773	**800-442-4366**	909-394-6300
Western Corporate Federal Credit Union (WesCorp) 924 Overland Ct	San Dimas	CA	91773	**800-442-4366**	909-394-6300
Wings Financial Credit Union 14985 Glazier Ave	Apple Valley	MN	55124	**800-692-2274**	952-997-8000
Wright-Patt Credit Union 2455 Executive Park Blvd	Fairborn	OH	45324	**800-762-0047**	937-912-7000

217 CRUISE LINES

SEE ALSO Casinos; Cruises - Riverboat; Ports & Port Authorities; Travel Agencies

Name / Address	City	State	Zip	Toll-Free	Phone
American Canadian Caribbean Line Inc 461 Water St	Warren	RI	02885	**800-556-7450**	401-247-0955
American Safari Cruises Inc 19221 36th Ave W Suite 208	Lynnwood	WA	98036	**888-862-8881**	425-776-4700
Aquanaut Cruise Line Ltd 241 E Commercial Blvd	Fort Lauderdale	FL	33334	**800-327-8223**	954-491-0333
Atlantic Coast Schooner Co 391 Hatchet Mountain Rd	Hope	ME	04847	**800-500-6077**	207-763-4255
Baja Expeditions Inc 2625 Garnet Ave	San Diego	CA	92109	**800-843-6967**	858-581-3311
Blackbeard Cruises PO Box 661091	Miami	FL	33266	**800-327-9600**	305-888-1226
Bluewater Adventures Ltd 252 E 1st St Suite 3	North Vancouver	BC	V7L1B3	**888-877-1770**	604-980-3800
Carnival Cruise Lines Inc 3655 NW 87th Ave	Miami	FL	33178	**888-227-6482**	305-599-2600
Celebrity Cruises 1050 Caribbean Way	Miami	FL	33132	**800-722-5941**	305-539-6000
Clipper Cruise Line Inc 11969 Westline Industrial Dr	Saint Louis	MO	63146	**800-325-0010**	314-655-6700
Costa Cruise Lines 200 S Park Rd Suite 200	Hollywood	FL	33021	**800-462-6782**	954-266-5600
Cruise West 2301 5th Ave Suite 401	Seattle	WA	98121	**888-851-8133**	206-441-8687
Crystal Cruises Inc 2049 Century Pk E Suite 1400	Los Angeles	CA	90067	**866-446-6625**	310-785-9300
Cunard Line Ltd 24303 Town Ctr Dr Suite 200	Valencia	CA	91355	**800-528-6273**	800-223-0764
Discovery Cruises Inc 1775 NW 70th Ave	Miami	FL	33126	**800-866-8687**	305-597-0336
Disney Cruise Line 210 Celebration Pl	Celebration	FL	34747	**800-511-1333**	407-566-3500
Glacier Bay Cruiseline 2101 4th Ave Suite 2200	Seattle	WA	98121	**800-451-5952***	206-623-7110
*Resv					
GlobalQuest Journeys Ltd 185 Willis Ave 2nd Fl	Mineola	NY	11501	**800-221-3254**	516-739-3690
Great Lakes Cruise Co 3270 Washtenaw Ave	Ann Arbor	MI	48104	**888-891-0203**	734-677-0900
Holland America Line 300 Elliott Ave W	Seattle	WA	98119	**800-426-0327**	206-281-3535
Imperial Majesty Cruise Line 2950 Gateway Dr	Pompano Beach	FL	33069	**800-394-3865**	954-956-9505
Lindblad Expeditions 96 Morton St 9th Fl	New York	NY	10014	**800-397-3348**	212-765-7740
Maine Windjammer Cruises PO Box 617	Camden	ME	04843	**800-736-7981**	207-236-2938
Maui-Molokai Sea Cruises 831 Eha St Suite 101	Wailuku	HI	96793	**800-468-1287**	808-242-8777
Mediterranean Shipping Co Cruises 6700 N Andrews Ave Suite 605	Fort Lauderdale	FL	33309	**800-666-9333**	954-772-6262
MSC Cruises USA Inc 6700 N Andrews Ave Suite 605	Fort Lauderdale	FL	33309	**800-666-9333**	954-772-6262
Nekton Diving Cruises 520 SE 32nd St	Fort Lauderdale	FL	33316	**800-899-6753**	954-463-9324
Norwegian Coastal Voyage Inc 405 Park Ave	New York	NY	10022	**800-323-7436**	212-319-1300
Norwegian Cruise Line Ltd 7665 Corporate Ctr Dr	Miami	FL	33126	**800-327-7030**	305-436-4000
Oceania Cruises Inc 8120 NW 53rd St Suite 100	Miami	FL	33166	**800-531-5619**	305-514-2300
Orient Lines Inc 7665 Corporate Ctr Dr	Miami	FL	33126	**800-333-7300**	305-468-2000
Party Line Cruise Co 301 Broadway Suite 142	Riviera Beach	FL	33404	**866-463-3779**	561-472-9860
Peter Deilmann Cruises 1800 Diagonal Rd Suite 170	Alexandria	VA	22314	**800-348-8287**	703-549-1741
Princess Cruise Line Ltd 24200 Town Ctr Dr	Santa Clarita	CA	91355	**800-421-0522**	661-753-0000
Quark Expeditions Inc 1019 Post Rd	Darien	CT	06820	**800-356-5699**	203-656-0499
Radisson Seven Seas Cruises 600 Corporate Dr Suite 410	Fort Lauderdale	FL	33334	**800-477-7500**	954-776-6123
ResidenSea 5200 Blue Lagoon Dr Suite 790	Miami	FL	33139	**800-970-6601**	305-264-9090
Rockport Schooner Cruises PO Box 987	Rockport	ME	04856	**866-732-2473**	207-230-1049
Royal Caribbean Cruises Ltd 1050 Caribbean Way	Miami	FL	33132	**800-398-9819**	305-539-6000
NYSE: RCL					
Royal Caribbean International 1050 Caribbean Way	Miami	FL	33132	**800-327-6700**	305-539-6000
Scotia Prince Cruises Ltd 468 Commercial St	Portland	ME	04101	**800-341-7540**	207-775-5611
Sea Cloud Cruises Inc 32-40 N Dean St	Englewood	NJ	07631	**888-732-2568**	201-227-9404
Seabourn Cruise Line 6100 Blue Lagoon Dr Suite 400	Miami	FL	33126	**800-929-9595**	305-463-3000
SeaDream Yacht Club 2601 S Bayshore Dr PH 1B	Coconut Grove	FL	33133	**800-707-4911**	305-631-6100
Silversea Cruises 110 E Broward Blvd	Fort Lauderdale	FL	33301	**800-722-9955**	954-522-4477
Star Clippers Inc 4101 Salzedo St	Coral Gables	FL	33146	**800-442-0551**	305-442-0550
Star Cruises 7665 Corporate Ctr Dr	Miami	FL	33126	**800-327-9020**	305-436-4000
Swan Hellenic Cruises 631 Commack Rd Suite 1A	Commack	NY	11725	**877-800-7926**	631-858-1263
Travel Dynamics International 132 E 70th St	New York	NY	10021	**800-257-5767**	212-517-7555
Wanderbird Cruises DBA Rockport Schooner Cruises PO Box 987	Rockport	ME	04856	**866-732-2473**	207-230-1049
Windjammer Barefoot Cruises Ltd 1759 Bay Rd	Miami Beach	FL	33139	**800-327-2601**	305-672-6453
Windstar Cruises 300 Elliott Ave W	Seattle	WA	98119	**800-258-7245***	206-281-3535
*Resv					

218 CRUISES - RIVERBOAT

SEE ALSO Casinos; Cruise Lines

Name / Address	City	State	Zip	Toll-Free	Phone
American Cruise Lines 741 Boston Post Rd Suite 200	Guilford	CT	06437	**800-814-6880**	203-453-6800
American Rivers Cruise Lines 2101 4th Ave Suite 2200	Seattle	WA	98121	**800-901-9152**	206-388-0444
American West Steamboat Co 2101 4th Ave Suite 1150	Seattle	WA	98121	**800-434-1232**	206-292-9606
Delta Queen Steamboat Co Inc 1380 Port of New Orleans Pl Robin St Wharf	New Orleans	LA	70130	**800-543-1949**	504-586-0631
French Country Waterways Ltd PO Box 2195	Duxbury	MA	02331	**800-222-1236**	781-934-2454
Gateway Riverboat Cruises 707 N 1st St	Saint Louis	MO	63102	**877-982-1410**	314-621-4040
Les Etoiles Barges 3355 Lenox Rd Suite 750	Atlanta	GA	30326	**800-280-1492**	
Peter Deilmann Cruises 1800 Diagonal Rd Suite 170	Alexandria	VA	22314	**800-348-8287**	703-549-1741
RiverBarge Excursion Lines Inc 201 Opelousas Ave	New Orleans	LA	70114	**888-462-2743**	504-365-0022
Spirit of Dubuque 400 3rd St Ice Harbor	Dubuque	IA	52001	**800-747-8093**	563-583-8093
Uniworld 17323 Ventura Blvd	Encino	CA	91316	**800-733-7820**	818-382-7820
Victoria Cruises Inc 57-08 39th Ave	Woodside	NY	11377	**800-348-8084**	212-818-1680
Viking River Cruises 21820 Burbank Blvd	Woodland Hills	CA	91367	**877-668-4546**	818-227-1234
Wings Nile Cruises 11350 McCormick Rd Suite 703	Hunt Valley	MD	21031	**800-869-4647**	410-771-0925

219 CUTLERY

SEE ALSO Silverware

Name / Address	City	State	Zip	Toll-Free	Phone
Alcas Corp 1116 E State St	Olean	NY	14760	**800-828-0448**	716-373-6141
American Safety Razor Co 1 Razor Blade Ln	Verona	VA	24482	**800-445-9284**	540-248-8000
Atlanta Cutlery Corp 2147 Gees Mill Rd	Conyers	GA	30012	**800-883-0300**	770-922-3700
Buck Knives Inc 660 S Lochsa St	Post Falls	ID	83854	**800-326-2825**	208-262-0500
Camillus Cutlery Co 54 Main St	Camillus	NY	13031	**800-344-0456***	315-672-8111
*Sales					
Case WR & Sons Cutlery Co Owens Way	Bradford	PA	16701	**800-523-6350**	814-368-4123
Clauss Cutlery Co 223 N Prospect St	Fremont	OH	43420	**800-225-2877***	419-332-7344
*Cust Svc					
Crescent Mfg Co 1310 Majestic Dr	Fremont	OH	43420	**800-537-1330**	419-332-6484
Douglas/Quikut Co 118 E Douglas Rd	Walnut Ridge	AR	72476	**800-982-5233**	870-886-6774
Excel Group 1 Merrick Ave	Westbury	NY	11590	**800-252-3390**	516-794-3355
Fiskars Brands Inc 2537 Daniels St	Madison	WI	53718	**800-500-4849**	608-259-1649
Gerber Legendary Blades Inc 14200 SW 72nd Ave	Portland	OR	97224	**800-950-6161**	503-639-6161
Goodell Inc 9440 Science Ctr Dr	Minneapolis	MN	55428	**800-542-3906***	763-531-0053
*Cust Svc					
KA-BAR Knives Inc 200 Homer St	Olean	NY	14760	**800-282-0130**	716-372-5952
Lamson & Goodnow Mfg Co 45 Conway St	Shelburne Falls	MA	01370	**800-872-6564**	413-625-6331
Midwest Tool & Cutlery Co Inc 1210 Progress St PO Box 160	Sturgis	MI	49091	**800-782-4659**	269-651-2476
Millers Forge Inc 1411 Capital Ave	Plano	TX	75074	**800-527-3474**	972-422-2145
Ontario Knife Co 26 Empire St	Franklinville	NY	14737	**800-222-5233**	716-676-5527
Pacific Handy Cutter Inc 2968 Randolph Ave	Costa Mesa	CA	92626	**800-229-2233***	714-662-1033
*Cust Svc					
Queen Cutlery Co 507 Chestnut St	Titusville	PA	16354	**800-222-5233***	814-827-3673
*Sales					
Rada Mfg Co 905 Industrial St	Waverly	IA	50677	**800-311-9691**	319-352-5454
Taylor Cutlery 1736 N Eastman Rd	Kingsport	TN	37664	**800-251-0254**	423-247-2406
Utica Cutlery Co 820 Noyes St	Utica	NY	13502	**800-888-4223**	315-733-4663
Wenger North America Inc 15 Corporate Dr	Orangeburg	NY	10962	**800-431-2996***	845-365-3500
*Cust Svc					
WR Case & Sons Cutlery Co Owens Way	Bradford	PA	16701	**800-523-6350**	814-368-4123

220 CYLINDERS & ACTUATORS - FLUID POWER

SEE ALSO Automotive Parts & Supplies - Mfr

Name / Address	City	State	Zip	Toll-Free	Phone
ARO Fluid Products Div Ingersoll-Rand Co 1 Aro Ctr PO Box 151	Bryan	OH	43506	**800-495-0276***	419-636-4242
*Cust Svc					
Bimba Mfg Co PO Box 68	Monee	IL	60449	**800-442-4622**	708-534-8544
Bosch Rexroth Corp 5150 Prairie Stone Pkwy	Hoffman Estates	IL	60192	**800-860-1055**	847-645-3600
Clippard Instrument Lab 7390 Colerain Ave	Cincinnati	OH	45239	**877-245-6247**	513-521-4261
Cross Mfg Inc 11011 King St Suite 210	Overland Park	KS	66210	**800-542-7677**	913-451-1233
Eckel Mfg Co Inc PO Box 1375	Odessa	TX	79760	**800-654-4779**	432-362-4336
Engineered Valves Div ITT Industries Inc 33 Centerville Rd	Lancaster	PA	17603	**800-366-1111**	717-291-1901
Hader/Seitz Inc PO Box 510260	New Berlin	WI	53151	**877-388-2101**	262-641-6000
Hannon Hydraulics Inc 625 N Loop 12	Irving	TX	75061	**800-333-4266**	972-438-2870

				Toll-Free	Phone
Hol-Mac Corp PO Box 349	Bay Springs	MS	39422	**800-844-3019**	601-764-4121
Humphrey Products Co 5070 East N Ave	Kalamazoo	MI	49048	**800-477-8707**	269-381-5500
Ingersoll-Rand Co ARO Fluid Products Div 1 Aro Ctr PO Box 151 *Cust Svc	Bryan	OH	43506	**800-495-0276***	419-636-4242
ITT Industries Inc Engineered Valves Div 33 Centerville Rd	Lancaster	PA	17603	**800-366-1111**	717-291-1901
Jordan Controls Inc 5607 W Douglas Ave *Prod Info	Milwaukee	WI	53218	**800-637-5547***	414-461-9200
Miller Fluid Power Corp 800 N York Rd	Bensenville	IL	60106	**800-323-8207**	630-766-3400
Norris Cylinder Co 1535 FM 1845	Longview	TX	75603	**800-527-8418**	903-757-7633
Parker Hannifin Corp 6035 Parkland Blvd *NYSE: PH* ■ *Cust Svc	Cleveland	OH	44124	**800-272-7537***	216-896-3000
Parker Instrumentation Group 6035 Parkland Blvd	Cleveland	OH	44124	**800-272-7537**	216-896-3000
PHD Inc 9009 Clubridge Dr	Fort Wayne	IN	46809	**800-624-8511**	260-747-6151
Roper Pump Co PO Box 269 *Sales	Commerce	GA	30529	**800-944-6769***	706-335-5551
Sargent Controls & Aerospace 5675 W Burlingame Rd	Tucson	AZ	85743	**800-932-5273**	520-744-1000
Shafer Valve Co 2500 Park Ave W	Mansfield	OH	44906	**800-876-4311**	419-529-4311
Sheffer Corp 6990 Cornell Rd *Sales	Cincinnati	OH	45242	**800-387-2191***	513-489-9770
SMC Pneumatics Inc 3011 N Franklin Rd	Indianapolis	IN	46226	**800-762-7621**	317-899-4440
Standex International Corp Custom Hoists Div PO Box 98	Hayesville	OH	44838	**800-837-4668**	419-368-4721
Tol-O-Matic Inc 3800 County Rd 116	Hamel	MN	55340	**800-328-2174**	763-478-8000

221 DAIRY PRODUCT STORES

				Toll-Free	Phone
Baskin-Robbins 130 Royall St	Canton	MA	02021	**800-859-5339**	781-737-3000
Brigham's Inc 30 Mill St	Arlington	MA	02476	**800-274-4426**	781-648-9000
Carvel Corp 175 Capital Blvd Suite 400	Rocky Hill	CT	06067	**800-322-4848**	860-257-4448
Carvel Franchising 200 Glenridge Point Pkwy Suite 200	Atlanta	GA	30342	**800-227-8353**	404-255-3250
CF Burger Creamery Co 8101 Greenfield Rd	Detroit	MI	48228	**800-229-2322**	313-584-4040
Cloverland Green Spring Dairy Inc 2701 Loch Raven Rd *Orders	Baltimore	MD	21218	**800-876-6455***	410-235-4477
Crystal Cream & Butter Co 1013 D St	Sacramento	CA	95814	**800-272-7326**	916-444-7200
Cumberland Farms Inc 777 Dedham St	Canton	MA	02021	**800-225-9702**	781-828-4900
Farm Stores 5800 NW 74th Ave	Miami	FL	33166	**800-726-3276**	305-471-5141
Freshens Quality Brands 1750 The Exchange	Atlanta	GA	30339	**800-633-4519**	678-627-5400
Rita's Water Ice Franchise Corp 1525 Ford Rd	Bensalem	PA	19020	**800-677-7482**	215-633-9899
Rosenberger's Dairies Inc 847 Forty Foot Rd PO Box 901	Hatfield	PA	19440	**800-355-9074**	215-855-9074
Swensen's Ice Cream Co 4175 Veterans Memorial Hwy	Ronkonkoma	NY	11779	**800-423-2763**	631-737-9898
TCBY Enterprises Inc 2855 E Cottonwood Pkwy Suite 400	Salt Lake City	UT	84121	**888-900-8229**	801-736-5600

222 DATA COMMUNICATIONS SERVICES FOR WIRELESS DEVICES

				Toll-Free	Phone
@Road Inc 47200 Bayside Pkwy *NASDAQ: ARDI*	Fremont	CA	94538	**877-428-7623**	510-668-1638
724 Solutions Inc 4101 Yonge St Suite 702 *NASDAQ: SVNX*	Toronto	ON	M2P1N6	**877-241-7378**	416-226-2900
Aether Systems Inc 11460 Cronridge Dr *NASDAQ: AETH*	Owings Mills	MD	21117	**888-812-6767**	410-654-6400
Air2Web Inc 1230 Peachtree St NE 12th Fl	Atlanta	GA	30309	**877-238-3637**	404-815-7707
BlackBerry 295 Phillip St	Waterloo	ON	N2L3W8	**877-255-2377**	519-888-7465
Cell-Loc Inc 3015 5th Ave NE Franklin Atrium Suite 220	Calgary	AB	T2A6T8	**877-569-5700**	403-569-5700
Dynamic Mobile Data Systems Inc 285 Davidson Ave Suite 501 *Tech Supp	Somerset	NJ	08873	**866-662-4363***	732-302-1700
Everypath Inc 2211 N 1st St Suite 200 *Sales	San Jose	CA	95131	**800-355-1068***	408-562-8000
GoAmerica Inc 401 Hackensack Ave *NASDAQ: GOAM*	Hackensack	NJ	07601	**888-462-4600**	201-996-1717
Intermec Technologies Corp 6001 36th Ave W *Sales	Everett	WA	98203	**800-934-3163***	425-348-2600
Linx Communications Inc 175 Crossing Blvd Suite 300	Framingham	MA	01702	**888-367-5469**	617-747-4200
Metro One Telecommunications Inc 11200 Murray Scholls Pl *NASDAQ: INFO*	Beaverton	OR	97007	**800-933-4034**	503-643-9500
Motricity 2800 Meridian Pkwy Suite 150	Durham	NC	27713	**800-746-7646**	919-287-7400
NAVTEQ Corp 222 Merchandise Mart Suite 900 *NYSE: NVT*	Chicago	IL	60654	**888-628-6277**	312-894-7000
PacketVideo Corp 10350 Science Center Dr Suite 210	San Diego	CA	92121	**877-308-2500**	858-731-5300
Remote Dynamics Inc 1155 Kas Dr Suite 100 *NASDAQ: REDI*	Richardson	TX	75081	**800-828-4696**	972-301-2000
Semotus Solutions Inc 16400 Lark Ave Suite 230 *AMEX: DLK*	Los Gatos	CA	95032	**800-775-1377**	408-358-7100
TeleCommunication Systems Inc 275 West St Suite 400 *NASDAQ: TSYS*	Annapolis	MD	21401	**800-810-0827**	410-263-7616
Vaultus Inc 632 Broadway 10th Fl	New York	NY	10012	**800-787-9170**	212-624-4040

223 DATA PROCESSING & RELATED SERVICES

SEE ALSO Electronic Transaction Processing; Payroll Services

				Toll-Free	Phone
Automatic Data Processing Inc (ADP) 1 ADP Blvd *NYSE: ADP*	Roseland	NJ	07068	**800-225-5237**	973-994-5000
CCC Information Services Group Inc 444 Merchandise Mart Plaza *NASDAQ: CCCG*	Chicago	IL	60654	**800-621-8070**	312-222-4636
ChoicePoint Inc 1000 Alderman Dr *NYSE: CPS*	Alpharetta	GA	30005	**877-317-5000**	770-752-6000
Claimsnet.com Inc 14860 Montfort Dr Suite 250	Dallas	TX	75254	**800-356-1511**	972-458-1701
Communication Data Services 1901 Bell Ave	Des Moines	IA	50315	**800-378-9982**	515-247-7500
Computer Services Inc 3901 Technology Dr	Paducah	KY	42001	**800-545-4274**	270-442-7361
Continental DataGraphics 222 N Sepulveda Blvd Suite 300	El Segundo	CA	90245	**800-862-5691**	310-662-2300
Continental Graphics Corp DBA Continental DataGraphics 222 N Sepulveda Blvd Suite 300	El Segundo	CA	90245	**800-862-5691**	310-662-2300
DPF Data Services Group Inc 1990 Swarthmore Ave	Lakewood	NJ	08701	**800-431-4416**	732-370-8840
ENVOY Corp 26 Century Blvd Suite 601	Nashville	TN	37214	**800-366-5716**	615-885-3700
Equifax Inc 1550 Peachtree St NW *NYSE: EFX* ■ *Sales	Atlanta	GA	30309	**888-202-4025***	404-885-8000
Fair Isaac Corp 200 Smith Ranch Rd *NYSE: FIC*	San Rafael	CA	94903	**800-444-5850**	415-472-2211
First Health Services Corp 4300 Cox Rd	Glen Allen	VA	23060	**800-884-2822**	804-965-7400
Fiserv Inc 255 Fiserv Dr *NASDAQ: FISV*	Brookfield	WI	53045	**800-558-8413**	262-879-5000
Hartley Data Service Inc 1807 Glenview Rd	Glenview	IL	60025	**800-433-2796**	847-724-9280
ImageMax Inc 455 Pennsylvania Ave Suite 200	Fort Washington	PA	19034	**800-873-9426**	215-628-3600
NDCHealth Corp 1 National Data Plaza *NYSE: NDC*	Atlanta	GA	30329	**800-225-5632**	404-728-2000
QRS Corp 1400 Marina Way S	Richmond	CA	94804	**800-872-8255**	510-215-5000
Scicom Data Services Ltd 10101 Bren Rd E	Minnetonka	MN	55343	**800-488-9087**	952-933-4200
SunGard Data Systems Inc 680 E Swedesford Rd *NYSE: SDS*	Wayne	PA	19087	**800-523-4970**	650-377-3897
SuperComm Inc 5001 LBJ Fwy Suite 550	Dallas	TX	75244	**800-252-9556**	972-726-2000
TDEC Inc 7735 Old Georgetown Rd Suite 1010	Bethesda	MD	20814	**800-424-8332**	301-718-0703
Users Inc 1250 Drummers Ln	Valley Forge	PA	19482	**800-523-7282**	610-687-9400

224 DATING SERVICES

				Toll-Free	Phone
Friendfinder Network Inc 445 Sherman Ave Suite C	Palo Alto	CA	94306	**800-388-0760**	650-847-3100
iMatchup.com Inc 1 Blue Hill Plaza 5th Fl	Pearl River	NY	10965	**800-222-4963**	845-620-1212
Match.com Inc 3001 George Bush Hwy Suite 100	Richardson	TX	75082	**800-926-2824**	214-827-2262
My EMatch.com LLC PO Box 66535	Saint Pete Beach	FL	33736	**800-215-7560**	727-866-1583

225 DENTAL ASSOCIATIONS - STATE

SEE ALSO Associations & Organizations - Professional & Trade - Health & Medical Professionals Associations

				Toll-Free	Phone
Arizona 4131 N 36th St	Phoenix	AZ	85018	**800-866-2732**	602-957-4777
Arkansas 2501 Crestwood Dr Suite 205	North Little Rock	AR	72116	**800-501-2732**	501-771-7650
California PO Box 13749	Sacramento	CA	95853	**800-736-7071**	916-443-0505
Florida 1111 E Tennessee St	Tallahassee	FL	32308	**800-877-9922**	850-681-3629
Georgia 7000 Peachtree Dunwoody Rd NE Bldg 17 Suite 200	Atlanta	GA	30328	**800-432-4357**	404-636-7553
Hawaii 1345 S Beretania St Suite 301	Honolulu	HI	96814	**800-359-6725**	808-593-7956
Indiana 401 W Michigan St	Indianapolis	IN	46202	**800-562-5646**	317-634-2610
Iowa 505 5th Ave Suite 333	Des Moines	IA	50309	**800-828-2181**	515-282-7250
Louisiana 7833 Office Pk Blvd	Baton Rouge	LA	70809	**800-388-6642**	225-926-1986
Massachusetts 2 Willow St Suite 200	Southborough	MA	01745	**800-943-9200**	508-480-9797
Minnesota 2236 Marshall Ave	Saint Paul	MN	55104	**800-950-3368**	651-646-7454
Montana 17 1/2 S Last Chance Gulch St	Helena	MT	59601	**800-257-4988**	406-443-2061
Nevada 8863 W Flamingo Rd Suite 102	Las Vegas	NV	89147	**800-962-6710**	702-255-4211
Oklahoma 629 NW Grand Blvd	Oklahoma City	OK	73118	**800-876-8890**	405-848-8873
Wisconsin 111 E Wisconsin Ave Suite 1300	Milwaukee	WI	53202	**800-364-7646**	414-276-4520

226 DENTAL EQUIPMENT & SUPPLIES - MFR

				Toll-Free	Phone
3M ESPE Dental Products Div 3M Ctr Bldg 275-2SE-03	Saint Paul	MN	55144	**888-364-3577**	
3M Health Care Solutions 3M Ctr Health Care Service Ctr *Prod Info	Saint Paul	MN	55144	**800-364-3577***	651-733-1110
3M Unitek 2724 South Peck Rd	Monrovia	CA	91016	**800-634-5300**	626-445-7960
A-dec Inc 2601 Crestview Dr *Cust Svc	Newberg	OR	97132	**800-547-1883***	503-538-9471
Align Technology Inc 881 Martin Ave *NASDAQ: ALGN*	Santa Clara	CA	95050	**888-822-5446**	408-470-1000

Company	City	State	ZIP	Toll-Free	Phone
American Medical Technologies Inc 5555 Bear Ln; *NASDAQ: ADLI*	Corpus Christi	TX	78405	**800-440-0310**	361-289-1145
American Orthodontics Corp 1714 Cambridge Ave	Sheboygan	WI	53081	**800-558-7687**	920-457-5051
Brasseler USA 1 Brasseler Blvd	Savannah	GA	31419	**800-841-4522**	912-925-8525
Ceramco Div Dentsply International Inc 6 Terri Ln Suite 100	Burlington	NJ	08016	**800-487-0100**	609-386-8900
Colgate Oral Pharmaceuticals One Colgate Way	Canton	MA	02021	**800-225-3756**	781-821-2880
Coltene/Whaledent Inc 235 Ascot Pkwy	Cuyahoga Falls	OH	44223	**800-221-3046**	330-916-8800
Darby Group Cos Inc 300 Jericho Quad	Jericho	NY	11753	**800-468-1001**	516-683-1800
Den-Mat Corp 2727 Skyway Dr	Santa Maria	CA	93455	**800-433-6628**	805-922-8491
Dentsply-Ceramco 6 Terri Ln	Burlington	NJ	08016	**800-487-0100**	609-386-8900
Dentsply International Inc 221 W Philadelphia St PO Box 872; *NASDAQ: XRAY*	York	PA	17405	**800-877-0020**	717-845-7511
Dentsply International Inc Ceramco Div 6 Terri Ln Suite 100	Burlington	NJ	08016	**800-487-0100**	609-386-8900
Dentsply International Inc LD Caulk Div 38 W Clarke Ave	Milford	DE	19963	**800-532-2855**	302-422-4511
Dentsply International Inc Professional Care Div 1301 Smile Way	York	PA	17404	**800-989-8825**	717-767-8500
Dentsply International Inc Rinn Div 1212 Abbott Dr	Elgin	IL	60123	**800-323-0970**	847-742-1115
Dentsply International Inc Trubyte Div 221 W Philadelphia St PO Box 872	York	PA	17405	**800-877-0020**	717-845-7511
Dentsply International Inc Tulsa Dental Div 5100 E Skelly Dr Suite 300	Tulsa	OK	74135	**800-662-1202**	918-493-6598
GC America Inc 3737 W 127th St	Alsip	IL	60803	**800-323-3386**	708-597-0900
Heraeus Kulzer Inc Dental Products Div 99 Business Pk Dr	Armonk	NY	10504	**800-343-5336**	914-273-8600
Hygenic Corp 1245 Home Ave	Akron	OH	44310	**800-321-2135**	330-633-8460
Jelenko International 99 Business Pk Dr	Armonk	NY	10504	**800-431-1785**	914-273-8600
John O Butler Co 4635 W Foster Ave	Chicago	IL	60630	**800-528-8537**	773-777-4000
Keystone Tube Co 13527 S Halsted St; *Cust Svc	Riverdale	IL	60827	**800-323-9493***	708-841-2450
Lancer Orthodontics Inc 253 Pawnee St; *Cust Svc	San Marcos	CA	92069	**800-854-2896***	760-744-5585
LifeCore Biomedical Inc 3515 Lyman Blvd; *NASDAQ: LCBM* ■ *Cust Svc	Chaska	MN	55318	**800-752-2663***	952-368-4300
MDS Matrx 145 Mid County Dr	Orchard Park	NY	14127	**800-847-1000**	716-662-6650
Midwest Dental Products Corp 901 W Oakton St; *Cust Svc	Des Plaines	IL	60018	**800-800-2888***	847-640-4800
Nobel Biocare USA Inc 22715 Savi Ranch Pkwy	Yorba Linda	CA	92887	**800-993-8100**	714-282-4800
ORMCO Corp 1717 W Collins Ave	Orange	CA	92867	**800-854-1741**	714-516-7400
Pelton & Crane A DCI Co 11727 Fruehauf Dr; *Cust Svc	Charlotte	NC	28273	**800-659-6560***	704-588-2126
Premier Dental Products Co Inc 1710 Romano Dr Box 4500	Plymouth Meeting	PA	19462	**888-773-6872**	610-239-6000
Professional Dental Technologies 267 E Main St	Batesville	AR	72501	**800-228-5595**	870-698-2300
Rinn Div Dentsply International Inc 1212 Abbott Dr	Elgin	IL	60123	**800-323-0970**	847-742-1115
Rocky Mountain Orthodontics Inc (RMO Inc) 650 W Colfax Ave	Denver	CO	80204	**800-525-6044**	303-592-8200
TP Orthodontics Inc 100 Center Plaza	La Porte	IN	46350	**800-348-8856**	219-785-2591
Tulsa Dental Div Dentsply International Inc 5100 E Skelly Dr Suite 300	Tulsa	OK	74135	**800-662-1202**	918-493-6598

227 DEPARTMENT STORES

Company	City	State	ZIP	Toll-Free	Phone
Bloomingdale's 1000 3rd Ave	New York	NY	10022	**800-950-0047**	212-705-2000
Bob's Merchandise Inc 1111 Hudson St	Longview	WA	98632	**800-292-5551**	360-425-3870
Bracker's Department Store 68 N Morley Ave	Nogales	AZ	85621	**800-635-5431**	520-287-3631
Dunlap Co 200 Bailey Ave	Fort Worth	TX	76107	**866-274-0163**	817-336-4985
Fred's Inc 4300 New Getwell Rd PO Box 18356; *NASDAQ: FRED*	Memphis	TN	38118	**800-374-7417**	901-365-8880
Gordman Inc 12100 W Center Rd	Omaha	NE	68144	**800-456-7463**	402-691-4000
GR Herberger's Inc 600 W Saint Germain St	Saint Cloud	MN	56301	**800-398-7896**	320-251-5351
Halls Merchandising Inc 200 E 25th St	Kansas City	MO	64108	**888-545-2121**	816-274-8111
Herberger's GR Inc 600 W Saint Germain St	Saint Cloud	MN	56301	**800-398-7896**	320-251-5351
JC Penney Co Inc PO Box 10001; *NYSE: JCP* ■ *Orders	Dallas	TX	75301	**800-222-6161***	972-431-1000
Kmart Corp 3100 W Big Beaver Rd; *NASDAQ: KMRT* ■ *Cust Svc	Troy	MI	48084	**866-562-7848***	248-643-1000
Kohl's Corp N 56 West 17000 Ridgewood Dr; *NYSE: KSS*	Menomonee Falls	WI	53051	**800-837-6644**	262-703-7000
Langstons Co 2224 Exchange Ave	Oklahoma City	OK	73108	**800-658-2831**	405-235-9536
Lord & Taylor 424 5th Ave	New York	NY	10018	**800-223-7440**	212-391-3344
Macy's 151 W 34th St; *Cust Svc	New York	NY	10001	**800-526-1202***	212-695-4400
Mansours Department Store Inc 26 W Lafayette Sq	LaGrange	GA	30240	**888-311-2289**	706-884-7305
Nordstrom Inc 1617 6th Ave Suite 500; *NYSE: JWN*	Seattle	WA	98101	**800-285-5800**	206-628-2111
OW Houts & Sons Inc 120 N Buckhout St; *Cust Svc	State College	PA	16801	**800-252-3583***	814-238-6701
Peebles Inc 1 Peebles St	South Hill	VA	23970	**800-723-4548**	434-447-5200
Penney JC Co Inc PO Box 10001; *NYSE: JCP* ■ *Orders	Dallas	TX	75301	**800-222-6161***	972-431-1000
Reed's 129-131 W Main St	Tupelo	MS	38804	**800-627-3337**	662-842-6453
RH Macy & Co Inc DBA Macy's 151 W 34th St; *Cust Svc	New York	NY	10001	**800-526-1202***	212-695-4400
Rogers 519 W Avalon Ave Suite 7	Muscle Shoals	AL	35661	**800-219-8245**	256-383-1828
RW Reed Co DBA Reed's 129-131 W Main St	Tupelo	MS	38804	**800-627-3337**	662-842-6453
Spiegel Inc 3500 Lacey Rd; *Orders	Downers Grove	IL	60515	**800-345-4500***	630-986-8800
Takashimaya Inc 693 5th Ave	New York	NY	10022	**800-753-2038**	212-350-0100
Target Stores 1000 Nicollet Mall	Minneapolis	MN	55403	**800-440-0680**	612-304-6073
Tongass Trading Co 201 Dock St	Ketchikan	AK	99901	**800-235-5102**	907-225-5101
Vivre Inc 11 E 26th St 15th Fl	New York	NY	10010	**800-411-6515**	212-739-6205
Wal-Mart Stores Inc 702 SW 8th St; *NYSE: WMT* ■ *Cust Svc	Bentonville	AR	72716	**800-925-6278***	479-273-4000
Wal-Mart Stores Inc Supercenter Div 702 SW 8th St	Bentonville	AR	72716	**800-925-6278**	479-273-4000
Walmart.com 7000 Marina Blvd	Brisbane	CA	94005	**800-966-6546**	650-837-5000
Younkers Inc 701 Walnut St; *Acctg	Des Moines	IA	50309	**800-530-6886***	515-244-1112

228 DEVELOPMENTAL CENTERS

Company	City	State	ZIP	Toll-Free	Phone
Altoona Center 1515 4th St	Altoona	PA	16601	**800-398-3202**	814-946-6900
Central Virginia Training Center PO Box 1098	Lynchburg	VA	24505	**866-897-6095**	434-947-6000
Devereux Foundation 2012 Renaissance Blvd	King of Prussia	PA	19406	**800-345-1292**	610-520-3000
Productive Alternatives Inc 1205 N Tower Rd	Fergus Falls	MN	56537	**800-477-7246**	218-736-5668

229 DIAGNOSTIC PRODUCTS

SEE ALSO Biotechnology Companies; Medicinal Chemicals & Botanical Products; Pharmaceutical Companies; Pharmaceutical Companies - Generic Drugs

Company	City	State	ZIP	Toll-Free	Phone
Abaxis Inc 3240 Whipple Rd; *NASDAQ: ABAX*	Union City	CA	94587	**800-822-2947**	510-675-6500
Abbott Laboratories 100 Abbott Pk Rd; *NYSE: ABT*	Abbott Park	IL	60064	**800-323-9100**	847-937-6100
Abbott Laboratories Abbott Diagnostics Div 100 Abbott Pk Rd	Abbott Park	IL	60064	**800-323-9100**	847-937-6100
Accurate Chemical & Scientific Corp 300 Shames Dr	Westbury	NY	11590	**800-645-6264**	516-333-2221
Adeza Biomedical Corp 1240 Elko Dr; *NASDAQ: ADZA* ■ *Cust Svc	Sunnyvale	CA	94089	**877-945-0208***	408-745-0975
Advanced Biotechnologies Inc 9108 Guilford Rd Rivers Pk II	Columbia	MD	21046	**800-426-0764**	301-470-3220
Aero Pharmaceuticals Inc 3848 FAU Blvd Suite 100	Boca Raton	FL	33431	**800-223-6837**	561-208-2200
Affinity Bioreagents Inc 4620 Technology Dr Suite 600	Golden	CO	80403	**800-527-4535**	303-278-4535
Akorn Inc 2500 Millbrook Dr	Buffalo Grove	IL	60089	**800-932-5676**	847-279-6100
ALerCHEK Inc 203 Anderson St	Portland	ME	04101	**877-282-9542**	207-775-2574
Allermed Laboratories Inc 7203 Convoy Ct	San Diego	CA	92111	**800-221-2748**	858-292-1060
Ambion Inc 2130 Woodward St Suite 200	Austin	TX	78744	**800-888-8804**	512-651-0200
American Diagnostica Inc 500 West Ave	Stamford	CT	06902	**888-234-4435**	203-602-7777
American Qualex International Inc 920-A Calle Negocio	San Clemente	CA	92673	**800-772-1776**	949-492-8298
Amresco Inc 30175 Solon Industrial Pkwy	Solon	OH	44139	**800-366-1313**	440-349-1313
Anachemia Chemicals Inc 3 Lincoln Blvd	Rouses Point	NY	12979	**800-323-1414**	518-297-4444
AnaSpec Inc 2149 O'Toole Ave Suite L	San Jose	CA	95131	**800-452-5530**	408-452-5055
Angus Buffers & Biochemicals 2236 Liberty Dr	Niagara Falls	NY	14304	**800-648-6689**	716-283-1434
AntiCancer Inc 7917 Ostrow St	San Diego	CA	92111	**800-511-2555**	858-654-2555
Apothecus Pharmaceutical Corp 220 Townsend Sq	Oyster Bay	NY	11771	**800-227-2393**	516-624-8200
Applera Corp 301 Merritt 7	Norwalk	CT	06856	**800-761-5381**	203-840-2000
Argonaut Technologies Inc 220 Saginaw Dr; *NASDAQ: AGNT*	Redwood City	CA	94063	**877-655-4200**	650-716-1600
Armor Forensics 13386 International Pkwy	Jacksonville	FL	32218	**800-852-0300**	904-485-1836
Athena Diagnostics Inc 377 Plantation St 4 Biotech Pk	Worcester	MA	01605	**800-394-4493**	508-756-2886
Bachem-Peninsula Laboratories Inc 305 Old Country Rd	San Carlos	CA	94070	**800-650-4442**	650-592-5392
Bayer Healthcare Diagnostics Div 511 Benedict Ave	Tarrytown	NY	10591	**800-431-1970**	914-631-8000
BD Diagnostics 7 Loveton Cir	Sparks	MD	21152	**800-666-6433**	410-316-4000
Becton Dickinson & Co 1 Becton Dr; *NYSE: BDX* ■ *Cust Svc	Franklin Lakes	NJ	07417	**888-237-2762***	201-847-6800
Berlex Laboratories Inc 6 W Belt	Wayne	NJ	07470	**888-237-2394**	973-694-4100
Binax Inc 217 Read St	Portland	ME	04103	**800-323-3199**	207-772-3988
Biodesign International 60 Industrial Pk Rd	Saco	ME	04072	**888-530-0140**	207-283-6500
BioGenex Laboratories Inc 4600 Norris Canyon Rd	San Ramon	CA	94583	**800-421-4149**	925-275-0550
Biomeda Corp 1851 Vanderbilt Rd	Texarkana	AR	71854	**800-341-8787**	870-779-8787
Biomerica Inc 1533 Monrovia Ave; *Cust Svc	Newport Beach	CA	92663	**800-854-3002***	949-645-2111
BioMerieux Inc 595 Anglum Rd	Hazelwood	MO	63042	**800-638-4835**	314-731-8500
Biosite Inc 11030 Roselle St; *NASDAQ: BSTE* ■ *Cust Svc	San Diego	CA	92121	**888-246-7483***	858-455-4808
BioSource International Inc 542 Flynn Rd; *NASDAQ: BIOI*	Camarillo	CA	93012	**800-242-0607**	805-987-0086
BiosPacific Inc 5980 Horton St Suite 225	Emeryville	CA	94608	**800-344-6686**	510-652-6155
Biotest Diagnostics Corp 66 Ford Rd Suite 220	Denville	NJ	07834	**800-522-0090**	973-625-1300
Caltag Laboratories Inc 1849 Bayshore Hwy	Burlingame	CA	94010	**800-874-4007**	650-652-0468
Calypte Biomedical Corp 5000 Hopyard Rd Suite 480; *AMEX: HIV*	Pleasanton	CA	94588	**877-225-9783**	925-730-7200
CEDARLANE Laboratories Inc 5516 8th Line RR 2	Hornby	ON	L0P1E0	**800-268-5058**	905-878-8891
Chematics Inc Hwy 13 S PO Box 293	North Webster	IN	46555	**800-348-5174**	574-834-2406
Chemicon International Inc 28820 Single Oak Dr	Temecula	CA	92590	**800-437-7500**	951-676-8080
Chiron Corp 4560 Horton St; *NASDAQ: CHIR*	Emeryville	CA	94608	**800-524-4766**	510-655-8730
Cholestech Corp 3347 Investment Blvd; *NASDAQ: CTEC*	Hayward	CA	94545	**800-733-0404**	510-732-7200
Chromaprobe Inc 378 Fee Fee Rd	Maryland Heights	MO	63043	**888-964-1400**	314-738-0001

Company / Address	City	State	ZIP	Toll-Free	Phone
Cliniqa Corp 1432 S Mission Rd	Fallbrook	CA	92028	**800-728-5205**	760-728-5205
Clontech Laboratories Inc 1290 Terra Bella Ave	Mountain View	CA	94043	**877-232-8995**	800-662-2566
Cortex Biochem Inc 1933 Davis St Suite 321	San Leandro	CA	94577	**800-888-7713**	510-568-2228
CST Technologies Inc 55 Northern Blvd Suite 200	Great Neck	NY	11021	**800-448-4407**	516-482-9001
Cytyc Corp 250 Campus Dr. *NASDAQ: CYTC*	Marlborough	MA	01752	**800-442-9892**	508-263-2900
Dade Behring Holdings Inc 1717 Deerfield Rd. *NASDAQ: DADE*	Deerfield	IL	60015	**800-948-3233**	847-267-5300
DakoCytomation 6392 Via Real *Cust Svc	Carpinteria	CA	93013	**800-400-3256***	805-566-6655
Diagnostic Chemicals Ltd 16 McCarville St.	Charlottetown	PE	C1E2A6	**800-565-0265**	902-566-1396
Diagnostic Products Corp 5700 W 96th St *NYSE: DP*	Los Angeles	CA	90045	**800-678-6699**	310-645-8200
Diagnostic Systems Laboratories Inc 445 Medical Ctr Blvd	Webster	TX	77598	**800-231-7970**	281-332-9678
Diametrics Medical Inc 2658 Patton Rd *NASDAQ: DMED*	Saint Paul	MN	55113	**800-949-4762**	651-639-8035
DiaSorin Inc 1951 Northwestern Ave	Stillwater	MN	55082	**800-328-1482**	651-439-9710
Digene Corp 1201 Clopper Rd *NASDAQ: DIGE*	Gaithersburg	MD	20878	**800-344-3631**	301-944-7000
DuPont Agriculture & Nutrition 1007 Market St DuPont Bldg	Wilmington	DE	19898	**800-441-7515**	302-774-1000
DuPont Qualicon Rt 141 Henry Clay Rd Bldg 400	Wilmington	DE	19880	**800-863-6842**	302-695-5300
E-Z-EM Inc 717 Main St *AMEX: EZM*	Westbury	NY	11590	**800-544-4624**	516-333-8230
EMD Biosciences Inc 10394 Pacific Ctr Ct. *Cust Svc	San Diego	CA	92121	**800-854-3417***	858-450-5500
Enzo Biochem Inc 60 Executive Blvd *NYSE: ENZ*	Farmingdale	NY	11735	**800-522-5052**	631-755-5500
Exalpha Biologicals Inc 5 Clock Tower Pl Suite 255	Maynard	MA	01754	**800-395-1137**	978-461-0435
Fisher Diagnostics 8365 Valley Pike PO Box 307	Middletown	VA	22645	**800-528-0494**	540-869-3200
Fisher Scientific International Inc HealthCare Div 9999 Veterans Memorial Dr	Houston	TX	77038	**800-766-7000**	281-405-4000
Gen-Probe Inc 10210 Genetic Ctr Dr *NASDAQ: GPRO*	San Diego	CA	92121	**800-523-5001**	858-410-8000
GenBio 15222 Ave of Science Suite A *Tech Supp	San Diego	CA	92128	**800-288-4368***	858-592-9300
Genzyme Corp 500 Kendall St. *NASDAQ: GENZ*	Cambridge	MA	02142	**800-326-7002**	617-252-7500
Genzyme Diagnostics 1 Kendall Sq Bldg 1400	Cambridge	MA	02139	**800-326-7002**	617-252-7500
Gibson Laboratories Inc 1040 Manchester St	Lexington	KY	40508	**800-477-4763**	859-254-9500
Goodwin Biotechnology Inc 1850 NW 69th Ave	Plantation	FL	33313	**800-814-8600**	954-321-5300
Harlan Bioproducts for Science Inc PO Box 29176	Indianapolis	IN	46229	**800-972-4362**	317-353-8810
Harlan Sprague Dawley Inc 298 S Carroll Rd	Indianapolis	IN	46229	**800-793-7287**	317-894-7521
Helena Laboratories Inc 1530 Lindbergh Dr	Beaumont	TX	77704	**800-231-5663**	409-842-3714
Hemagen Diagnostics Inc 9033 Red Branch Rd	Columbia	MD	21045	**800-495-2180**	443-367-5500
Hitachi Chemical Diagnostics 630 Clyde Ct	Mountain View	CA	94043	**800-233-6278**	650-961-5501
Home Diagnostics Inc 2400 NW 55th Ct.	Fort Lauderdale	FL	33309	**800-342-7226**	954-677-9201
Hycor Biomedical Inc 7272 Chapman Ave *Cust Svc	Garden Grove	CA	92841	**800-382-2527***	714-933-3000
IDEXX Laboratories Inc 1 IDEXX Dr *NASDAQ: IDXX*	Westbrook	ME	04092	**800-932-4399**	207-856-0300
ImmucorGamma Inc 3130 Gateway Dr PO Box 5625 *NASDAQ: BLUD* ■ *Cust Svc	Norcross	GA	30091	**800-829-2553***	770-441-2051
Immuno-Mycologics Inc 1236 E Redbud Rd	Goldsby	OK	73093	**800-654-3639**	405-288-2383
ImmunoDiagnostics Inc 21 F Olympia Ave	Woburn	MA	01801	**800-573-1700**	781-938-6300
Immunovision Inc 1820 Ford Ave	Springdale	AR	72764	**800-541-0960**	479-751-7005
InSite Vision Inc 965 Atlantic Ave *AMEX: ISV*	Alameda	CA	94501	**800-726-7483**	510-865-8800
International Immunology Corp 25549 Adams Ave	Murrieta	CA	92562	**800-843-2853**	951-677-5629
International Isotopes Inc 4137 Commerce Circle	Idaho Falls	ID	83401	**800-699-3108**	208-524-5300
Intracel Resources LLC 93 Monocacy Blvd Unit A 8	Frederick	MD	21701	**877-289-5476**	301-668-8400
Inverness Medical Innovations Inc 51 Sawyer Rd Suite 200 *AMEX: IMA*	Waltham	MA	02453	**877-696-2525**	781-647-3900
InVitro International 17751 Sky Park E Suite G	Irvine	CA	92614	**800-246-8487**	949-851-8356
Iso-Tex Diagnostics Inc PO Box 909	Friendswood	TX	77549	**800-477-4839**	281-482-1231
IVAX Diagnostics Inc 2140 N Miami Ave *AMEX: IVD*	Miami	FL	33127	**800-327-4565**	305-324-2300
Jackson ImmunoResearch Laboratories Inc 872 W Baltimore Pike	West Grove	PA	19390	**800-367-5296**	610-869-4024
Kirkegaard & Perry Laboratories Inc 2 Cessna Ct	Gaithersburg	MD	20879	**800-638-3167**	301-948-7755
KMI Diagnostics Inc 8201 Central Ave NE Suite P	Minneapolis	MN	55432	**888-523-1246**	763-780-2955
Life Sciences Inc 2900 72nd St N	Saint Petersburg	FL	33710	**800-237-4323**	727-345-9371
LifeScan Inc 1000 Gibraltar Dr	Milpitas	CA	95035	**800-227-8862**	408-263-9789
LipoScience Inc 2500 Sumner Blvd	Raleigh	NC	27616	**877-547-6837**	919-212-1999
Maine Biotechnology Services Inc 1037 R Forest Ave	Portland	ME	04103	**800-925-9476**	207-797-5454
Mallinckrodt Inc 675 McDonnell Blvd	Hazelwood	MO	63042	**888-744-1414**	314-654-2000
Medical Analysis Systems Inc 46360 Fremont Blvd.	Fremont	CA	94538	**800-582-3095**	800-232-3342
MEDTOX Diagnostics Inc 1238 Anthony Rd	Burlington	NC	27215	**800-334-1116**	336-226-6311
Meridian Bioscience Inc 3471 River Hills Dr. *NASDAQ: VIVO* ■ *Cust Svc	Cincinnati	OH	45244	**800-543-1980***	513-271-3700
Monobind Inc 100 N Point Dr.	Lake Forest	CA	92630	**800-854-6265**	949-951-2665
Moss Inc 2605 Cab Over Dr Suite 11	Hanover	MD	21076	**800-932-6677**	410-768-3442
Nabi Biopharmaceuticals 5800 Pk of Commerce Blvd NW *NASDAQ: NABI*	Boca Raton	FL	33487	**800-635-1766**	561-989-5800
National Diagnostics Inc 305 Patton Dr.	Atlanta	GA	30336	**800-526-3867**	404-699-2121
Neogen Corp 620 Lesher Pl *NASDAQ: NEOG*	Lansing	MI	48912	**800-234-5333**	517-372-9200
New Horizons Diagnostics Corp 9110 Red Branch Rd	Columbia	MD	21045	**800-888-5015**	410-992-9357
North American Scientific Inc 20200 Sunburst St. *NASDAQ: NASI*	Chatsworth	CA	91311	**800-992-6274**	818-734-8600
Oncogene Science 80 Rogers St *Sales	Cambridge	MA	02142	**888-674-3424***	617-492-7289
OraSure Technologies Inc 220 1st St *NASDAQ: OSUR*	Bethlehem	PA	18015	**800-869-3538**	610-882-1820
Ortho-Clinical Diagnostics Inc 1001 US Rt 202 N PO Box 350	Raritan	NJ	08869	**800-828-6316**	908-218-1300
Oxford Biomedical Research Inc 2165 Avon Industrial Dr.	Rochester Hills	MI	48309	**800-692-4633**	248-852-8815
Pacific Biometrics Inc 220 W Harrison St.	Seattle	WA	98119	**800-767-9151**	206-298-0068
Panbio Inc 9075 Guilford Rd	Columbia	MD	21046	**800-962-6790**	410-381-8550
Peptides International Inc 11621 Electron Dr	Louisville	KY	40299	**800-777-4779**	502-266-8787
PerkinElmer Life & Analytical Sciences Inc 549 Albany St	Boston	MA	02118	**800-446-0035**	617-482-9595
Pierce Biotechnology Inc 3747 N Meridian Rd	Rockford	IL	61101	**800-874-3723**	815-968-0747
PML Microbiologicals Inc 27120 SW 95th Ave. *Cust Svc	Wilsonville	OR	97070	**800-628-7014***	503-570-2500
Pointe Scientific Inc 5449 Research Dr.	Canton	MI	48188	**800-445-9853**	734-487-8300
Polymedco Inc 510 Furnace Dock Rd.	Cortlandt Manor	NY	10567	**800-431-2123**	914-739-5400
Polysciences Inc 400 Valley Rd *Cust Svc	Warrington	PA	18976	**800-523-2575***	215-343-6484
Promega Corp 2800 Woods Hollow Rd	Madison	WI	53711	**800-356-9526**	608-274-4330
Protide Pharmaceuticals Inc 1311 Helmo Ave	Saint Paul	MN	55128	**800-552-3569**	651-730-1500
Prozyme Inc 1933 Davis St Suite 207	San Leandro	CA	94577	**800-457-9444**	510-638-6900
Quality Biological Inc 7581 Lindbergh Dr	Gaithersburg	MD	20879	**800-443-9331**	301-840-9331
Quantimetrix Corp 2005 Manhattan Beach Blvd	Redondo Beach	CA	90278	**800-624-8380**	310-536-0006
Quidel Corp 10165 McKellar Ct. *NASDAQ: QDEL*	San Diego	CA	92121	**800-874-1517**	858-552-1100
R & D Systems Inc 614 McKinley Pl NE	Minneapolis	MN	55413	**800-343-7475**	612-379-2956
Remel Inc 12076 Santa Fe Dr	Lenexa	KS	66215	**800-255-6730**	913-888-0939
Research & Diagnostic Antibodies 4872 E 2nd St	Benicia	CA	94510	**800-858-7322**	707-746-6800
Research Organics Inc 4353 E 49th St	Cleveland	OH	44125	**800-321-0570**	216-883-8025
Roche Diagnostics Corp 9115 Hague Rd PO Box 50457 *Cust Svc	Indianapolis	IN	46256	**800-428-5076***	317-521-2000
Roche Diagnostics North America 9115 Hague Rd PO Box 50457 *Cust Svc	Indianapolis	IN	46256	**800-428-5076***	317-521-2000
Rockland Inc 650 Englesville Rd	Boyertown	PA	19512	**800-656-7625**	610-369-1008
SCIMEDX Corp 100 Ford Rd	Denville	NJ	07834	**800-221-5598**	973-625-8822
Seradyn Inc 7998 Georgetown Rd Suite 1000	Indianapolis	IN	46268	**800-428-4072**	317-610-3800
Sigma-Aldrich Corp 3050 Spruce St. *NASDAQ: SIAL*	Saint Louis	MO	63103	**800-325-3010**	314-771-5765
Southern Biotechnology Assoc Inc 160A Oxmoor Blvd.	Birmingham	AL	35209	**800-722-2255**	205-945-1774
Stratagene Inc 11011 N Torrey Pines Rd. *NASDAQ: STGN*	La Jolla	CA	92037	**800-894-1304**	858-535-5400
Strategic Diagnostics Inc 111 Pencader Dr. *NASDAQ: SDIX*	Newark	DE	19702	**800-544-8881**	302-456-6789
Synergent Biochem Inc 12038 Centralia Rd Suite C	Hawaiian Gardens	CA	90716	**800-585-8580**	562-809-3389
Techne Corp 614 McKinley Pl NE *NASDAQ: TECH*	Minneapolis	MN	55413	**800-328-2400**	612-379-8854
Teco Diagnostics 1268 N Lakeview Ave.	Anaheim	CA	92807	**800-222-9880**	714-693-7788
Theragenics Corp 5203 Bristol Industrial Way *NYSE: TGX*	Buford	GA	30518	**800-458-4372**	770-271-0233
Trinity Biotech PLC 5919 Farnsworth Ct	Carlsbad	CA	92008	**800-331-2291**	760-929-0500
Utak Laboratories Inc 25020 Ave Tibbitts	Valencia	CA	91355	**800-235-3442**	661-294-3935
Varian Inc 25200 Commercentre Dr.	Lake Forest	CA	92630	**800-854-0277**	949-770-9381
ViroLogic Inc 345 Oyster Point Blvd *NASDAQ: VLGC* ■ *Cust Svc	South San Francisco	CA	94080	**800-777-0177***	650-635-1100
Wako Chemicals USA Inc 1600 Bellwood Rd	Richmond	VA	23237	**800-992-9256**	804-271-7677
Wampole Laboratories LLC 2 Research Way *Cust Svc	Princeton	NJ	08540	**800-257-9525***	609-627-8000
Worthington Biochemical Corp 730 Vassar Ave	Lakewood	NJ	08701	**800-445-9603**	732-942-1660
Zepto Metrix Corp 872 Main St *Cust Svc	Buffalo	NY	14202	**800-274-5487***	716-882-0920
Zymed Laboratories Inc 561 Eccles Ave.	South San Francisco	CA	94080	**800-874-4494**	650-871-4494

230 DISPLAYS - EXHIBIT & TRADE SHOW

Company / Address	City	State	ZIP	Toll-Free	Phone
3D Exhibits Inc 2800 Lively Blvd	Elk Grove Village	IL	60007	**800-471-9617**	847-250-9000
Derse Exhibits Inc 1234 N 62nd St	Milwaukee	WI	53213	**800-562-2300**	414-257-2000
Downing Displays Inc 550 TechneCenter Dr.	Milford	OH	45150	**800-883-1800**	513-248-9800
Exhibitgroup/Giltspur 200 N Gary Ave	Roselle	IL	60172	**800-843-3944**	630-307-2400
Expon Exhibits 1902 Channel Dr.	West Sacramento	CA	95691	**800-783-9766**	916-371-1600
HB Stubbs Co 27027 Mound Rd	Warren	MI	48092	**800-968-2132**	586-574-9700
Heritage Exhibits 798 Albion Ave	Schaumburg	IL	60193	**800-966-9722**	847-301-4646
ICON Exhibits 8333 Clinton Pk Dr.	Fort Wayne	IN	46825	**800-320-4266**	260-483-6441
Lynch Exhibits 7 Campus Dr Burlington Business Campus	Burlington	NJ	08016	**800-343-1666**	609-387-1600
MG Design Assoc Corp 8778 100th St	Pleasant Prairie	WI	53158	**800-643-9442**	262-947-8890
Siegel Display Products 300 6th Ave N	Minneapolis	MN	55401	**800-626-0322**	612-340-1493
Skyline Displays Inc DBA Skyline Exhibits 3355 Discovery Rd	Eagan	MN	55121	**800-328-2725**	651-234-6000
Sparks Exhibits & Environments 10232 Palm Dr.	Santa Fe Springs	CA	90670	**800-925-7727**	562-941-0101

Classified Section

231 DISPLAYS - POINT-OF-PURCHASE

SEE ALSO Signs

Company	City	State	Zip	Toll-Free	Phone
Acrylic Design Assoc 6050 Nathan Ln N	Plymouth	MN	55442	**800-445-2167**	763-559-8395
AMD Industries Inc 4620 W 19th St	Cicero	IL	60804	**800-367-9999**	708-863-8900
Archbold Container Corp 800 W Barre Rd PO Box 10	Archbold	OH	43502	**800-446-2520**	419-445-8865
Array Marketing 555 W 5th St 30th Fl	Los Angeles	CA	90013	**866-452-1200**	213-533-4189
Art-Phyl Creations 16250 NW 48th Ave	Hialeah	FL	33014	**800-327-8318**	305-624-2333
Chicago Display Marketing Corp 1999 N Ruby St	Melrose Park	IL	60160	**800-681-4340**	708-681-4340
Display Smart LLC 801 W 27th Terr	Lawrence	KS	66046	**888-843-1870**	785-843-1869
Display Technology Inc 111-01 14th Ave 3rd Fl	College Point	NY	11356	**800-424-4220**	718-321-3100
Elkader Wire & Display Co 1802 Preston St	Rockford	IL	61102	**800-435-5709**	815-963-3414
Felbro Inc 3666 E Olympic Blvd	Los Angeles	CA	90023	**800-733-5276**	323-263-8686
Frank Mayer & Assoc Inc 1975 Wisconsin Ave	Grafton	WI	53024	**800-225-3987**	262-377-4700
Harbor Industries Inc 14130 172nd Ave	Grand Haven	MI	49417	**800-968-6993**	616-842-5330
Hunter Display 14 Hewlett Ave	East Patchogue	NY	11772	**800-767-2110**	631-475-5900
Lingo Mfg Co 7400 Industrial Rd *Cust Svc	Florence	KY	41042	**800-354-9771***	859-371-2662
Mayer Frank & Assoc Inc 1975 Wisconsin Ave	Grafton	WI	53024	**800-225-3987**	262-377-4700
Miller Multiplex Inc 512 Stockton St	Richmond	VA	23224	**800-757-1112**	804-232-4551
New Dimensions Research Corp 260 Spagnoli Rd	Melville	NY	11747	**800-637-8870**	631-694-1356
Rapid Displays Inc 4300 W 47th St	Chicago	IL	60632	**800-356-5775**	773-927-5000
Rock-Tenn Co 504 Thrasher St *NYSE: RKT*	Norcross	GA	30071	**800-762-5836**	770-448-2193
Sonoco Corrflex Display 701 Rickert St	Statesville	NC	28677	**800-334-8384**	704-872-7777
Thorco Industries Inc 1300 E 12th St	Lamar	MO	64759	**800-445-3375**	417-682-3375
Visual Marketing Inc 154 W Erie St	Chicago	IL	60610	**800-662-8640**	312-664-9177
Vulcan Industries Inc 300 Display Dr	Moody	AL	35004	**888-444-4417**	205-640-2400

DOORS & WINDOWS - GLASS

SEE Glass - Flat, Plate, Tempered

232 DOORS & WINDOWS - METAL

SEE ALSO Shutters - Window (All Types)

Company	City	State	Zip	Toll-Free	Phone
Aluma-Glass Industries Inc 16265 Star Rd	Nampa	ID	83687	**800-321-8273**	208-467-4491
Aluma Shield Industries Inc Butcher Boy Doors Div 725 Summerhill Dr	Deland	FL	32724	**888-882-5862**	386-626-6789
Amsco Windows Inc 1880 S 1045 West	Salt Lake City	UT	84104	**800-748-4661**	801-978-5000
Anemostat 1220 Watsoncenter Rd	Carson	CA	90745	**800-982-9000**	310-835-7500
Armaclad Inc 6806 Anthony Hwy	Waynesboro	PA	17268	**800-541-6666**	717-749-3141
ASSA ABLOY Door Security Solutions 110 Sargent Dr	New Haven	CT	06511	**800-377-3948**	203-624-5225
Atrium Cos Inc 3890 W Northwest Hwy Suite 500	Dallas	TX	75220	**800-421-6292**	214-630-5757
Babcock-Davis 9300 73rd Ave N	Brooklyn Park	MN	55428	**888-412-3726**	763-488-9200
Butcher Boy Doors Div Aluma Shield Industries Inc 725 Summerhill Dr	Deland	FL	32724	**888-882-5862**	386-626-6789
Clopay Building Products Inc PO Box 440	Baldwin	WI	54002	**800-621-3667**	715-684-3223
Columbia Mfg Corp 14400 S San Pedro St	Gardena	CA	90248	**800-729-3667**	310-327-9300
Comprehensive Mfg Services LLC DBA Courion 3044 Lambdin Ave	Saint Louis	MO	63115	**800-533-5760**	314-533-5700
Cookson Co Inc 2417 S 50th Ave	Phoenix	AZ	85043	**800-294-4358**	602-272-4244
Cornell Iron Works Inc 100 Elmwood Ave Crestwood Industrial Pk *Cust Svc	Mountain Top	PA	18707	**800-233-8366***	570-474-6773
Courion 3044 Lambdin Ave	Saint Louis	MO	63115	**800-533-5760**	314-533-5700
Creation Group Inc 53032 County Rd 13 PO Box 1025	Elkhart	IN	46515	**800-862-3131**	574-264-3131
Dunbarton Corp 868 Murray Rd	Dothan	AL	36303	**800-633-7553**	334-794-0661
Eastern Garage Door 417 Canal St	Lawrence	MA	01842	**800-766-6012**	978-683-3158
EFCO Corp 1000 County Rd	Monett	MO	65708	**800-221-4169**	417-235-3193
Elixir Industries Inc 17925 S Broadway	Gardena	CA	90247	**800-421-1942**	310-767-3400
Ellison Bronze Co Inc 125 W Main St	Falconer	NY	14733	**800-665-6445**	716-665-6522
Emco Specialties Inc 2121 E Walnut St *Cust Svc	Des Moines	IA	50317	**800-933-3626***	515-265-6101
Empire Pacific Industries 10255 SW Spokane Ct PO Box 4210	Tualatin	OR	97062	**800-473-7013**	503-692-6167
Engineered Products Inc 1844 Ardmore Blvd	Pittsburgh	PA	15221	**800-245-4814**	412-242-6900
Fleming Door Products Ltd 20 Barr Rd	Ajax	ON	L1S3X9	**800-263-7515**	905-683-3667
GADCO (General American Door Co) 5050 Baseline Rd	Montgomery	IL	60538	**800-323-0813**	630-859-3000
General Aluminum Co of Texas 1001 W Crosby Rd	Carrollton	TX	75006	**800-727-0835**	972-242-5271
General American Door Co (GADCO) 5050 Baseline Rd	Montgomery	IL	60538	**800-323-0813**	630-859-3000
Graef Windows Inc 365 McClurg Rd	Youngstown	OH	44512	**800-877-2911**	330-652-9999
Homeshield PO Box 907	Chatsworth	IL	60921	**800-323-2512**	815-635-3171
Hufcor Inc 2101 Kennedy Rd	Janesville	WI	53545	**800-356-6968**	608-756-1241
Hygrade Metal Moulding Mfg Corp 1990 Highland Ave	Bethlehem	PA	18020	**800-645-9475**	610-866-2441
International Revolving Door Co 2100 N 6th Ave *Cust Svc	Evansville	IN	47710	**800-745-4726***	812-425-3311
International Window Corp 5625 E Firestone Blvd	South Gate	CA	90280	**800-477-4032**	562-928-6411
JA Nearing Co Inc 9390 Davis Ave	Laurel	MD	20723	**800-323-6933**	301-498-5700
Jamison Door Co 55 JV Jamison Dr	Hagerstown	MD	21740	**800-532-3667**	301-733-3100
Jordan Co PO Box 18377	Memphis	TN	38181	**800-888-8848**	901-363-2121
Kane Mfg Corp 515 N Fraley St	Kane	PA	16735	**800-952-6399**	814-837-6464
Kewanee Corp 1642 Burlington Ave	Kewanee	IL	61443	**800-666-4481**	309-853-4481
Kinco Ltd 5245 Old Kings Rd	Jacksonville	FL	32254	**800-342-0244**	904-355-1476
Krieger Specialty Products Co 4880 Gregg Rd	Pico Rivera	CA	90660	**866-203-5060**	562-695-0645
LaForce Inc 1060 W Mason St	Green Bay	WI	54303	**800-236-8858**	920-497-7100
Lausell Inc PO Box 938	Bayamon	PR	00960	**800-981-7724**	787-798-7610
Lockheed Window Corp Rt 100 PO Box 166	Pascoag	RI	02859	**800-537-3061**	401-568-3061
Loxcreen Co Inc 1630 Old Dunbar Rd	West Columbia	SC	29172	**800-394-8667**	803-822-8200
M-D Building Products Inc 4041 N Santa Fe Ave *Cust Svc	Oklahoma City	OK	73118	**800-654-8454***	405-528-4411
Mannix Architectural Window Products 345 Crooked Hill Rd	Brentwood	NY	11717	**800-752-6483**	631-231-0800
Masonite Holdings Inc 1 N Dale Mabry Hwy Suite 950	Tampa	FL	33609	**800-895-2723**	813-877-2726
McKeon Door Corp 95 29th St	Brooklyn	NY	11232	**800-266-9392**	718-965-0700
Mercer Industries Inc 10760 SW Denney Rd	Beaverton	OR	97008	**800-962-7860**	503-526-3650
MI Windows & Doors Inc 650 W Market St	Gratz	PA	17030	**800-949-3818**	717-365-3300
Milgard Mfg 1010 54th Ave E	Tacoma	WA	98424	**800-562-8444**	253-922-2030
MM Systems Corp 50 MM Way	Pendergrass	GA	30567	**800-241-3460**	706-824-7500
Moss Supply Co Inc PO Box 26338	Charlotte	NC	28221	**800-438-0770**	704-596-8717
MW Manufacturers Inc 433 N Main St	Rocky Mount	VA	24151	**888-999-8400**	540-483-0211
Napco Inc 125 McFann Rd	Valencia	PA	16059	**800-786-2726**	724-898-1511
Napoleon/Lynx 111 Weires Dr	Archbold	OH	43502	**800-338-5399**	419-445-1010
National Guard Products Inc 4985 E Raines Rd	Memphis	TN	38118	**800-647-7874**	901-795-6900
Nu-Air Mfg Co 8105 Anderson Rd	Tampa	FL	33634	**800-282-6627**	813-885-1654
Nystrom Inc 9300 73rd Ave N	Brooklyn Park	MN	55428	**800-547-2635**	763-488-9200
O'Keeffe's Inc 325 Newhall St	San Francisco	CA	94124	**888-653-3333**	415-822-4222
Overhead Door Corp 1900 Crown Dr	Farmers Branch	TX	75234	**800-275-3290**	972-233-6611
Overly Mfg Co 574 W Otterman St	Greensburg	PA	15601	**800-979-7300**	724-834-7300
Peachtree Doors & Windows Inc 2744 Ramsey Rd	Gainesville	GA	30501	**800-443-5692**	770-534-8070
Peelle Co 34 Central Ave	Hauppauge	NY	11788	**800-645-1056**	631-231-6000
Peerless Products Inc 2403 S Main St	Fort Scott	KS	66701	**800-279-9999**	620-223-4610
Pemko Mfg Co Inc 4226 Transport St	Ventura	CA	93003	**800-283-9988**	805-642-2600
PGT Industries Inc 1070 Technology Dr	Nokomis	FL	34275	**877-550-6006**	941-480-1600
Pipin Industries Inc 6500 W 65th St Suite 200	Chicago	IL	60638	**888-706-8646**	708-458-3440
Portal Inc 10 Tracy Dr	Avon	MA	02322	**800-966-3030**	508-588-3030
Public Supply Co Inc 1236 NW 4th St	Oklahoma City	OK	73106	**800-259-6355**	405-272-9621
Quaker Window Products Inc PO Box 128	Freeburg	MO	65035	**800-347-0438**	573-744-5211
Raynor Garage Doors 1101 E River Rd	Dixon	IL	61021	**800-472-9667**	815-288-1431
Rebco Inc 1171-1225 Madison Ave	Paterson	NJ	07509	**800-777-0787**	973-684-0200
Reese Enterprises Inc 16350 Asher Ave	Rosemount	MN	55068	**800-328-0953**	651-423-1126
Republic Windows & Doors Inc 930 W Evergreen Ave	Chicago	IL	60622	**800-248-1775**	312-932-8000
Richards-Wilcox Inc 600 S Lake St	Aurora	IL	60506	**800-253-5668**	630-897-6951
Sears Home Improvement Products 1024 Florida Central Pkwy	Longwood	FL	32750	**800-222-5030**	407-767-0990
Sellmore Industries Inc 815 Smith St	Buffalo	NY	14206	**800-783-1900**	716-854-1600
Silver Line Building Products 1 Silver Line Dr *Sales	North Brunswick	NJ	08902	**800-234-4228***	732-435-1000
Southeastern Aluminum Products Inc 6701 Suemac Pl *Sales	Jacksonville	FL	32254	**800-243-8200***	904-781-8200
Southeastern Metals Mfg Co Inc 11801 Industry Dr	Jacksonville	FL	32218	**800-874-2335**	904-757-4200
Stanley Access Technologies 65 Scott Swamp Rd	Farmington	CT	06032	**800-722-2377**	860-677-2861
Stanley Home Decor 480 Myrtle St	New Britain	CT	06053	**800-782-6539**	860-225-5111
State Wide Aluminum 23601 CR 6 E PO Box 987	Elkhart	IN	46515	**800-860-2594**	574-262-2594
Steelcraft Mfg Co 9017 Blue Ash Rd *Cust Svc	Cincinnati	OH	45242	**800-930-8585***	513-745-6400
Steves & Sons Inc 203 Humble Ave *Sales	San Antonio	TX	78225	**800-627-5111***	210-924-5111
Super Sky Products Inc 10301 N Enterprise Dr	Mequon	WI	53092	**800-558-0467**	262-242-2000
Taylor Building Products PO Box 457	West Branch	MI	48661	**800-248-3600**	989-345-5110
Therma-Tru Corp 1687 Woodlands Dr	Maumee	OH	43537	**800-537-8827**	419-891-7400
Thermo-Twin Industries Inc 1155 Allegheny Ave	Oakmont	PA	15139	**800-641-2211**	412-826-1000
TKO Dock Doors N56 W24701 N Corporate Cir	Sussex	WI	53089	**800-575-3366**	262-820-1217
TM Window & Door 601 NW 12th Ave	Pompano Beach	FL	33069	**800-511-1746**	954-781-4430
TRACO 71 Progress Ave	Cranberry Township	PA	16066	**800-468-7226**	724-776-7000
Tubelite Inc 4878 Mackinaw Trail	Reed City	MI	49677	**800-866-2227**	231-832-2211
Vistawall Architectural Products 803 Airport Rd	Terrell	TX	75160	**800-869-4567**	972-563-2624
Wausau Window & Wall Systems 1415 West St	Wausau	WI	54401	**877-678-2983**	715-845-2161
Wayne-Dalton Corp 1 Door Dr PO Box 67	Mount Hope	OH	44660	**800-827-3667**	330-674-7015
West Window Corp PO Drawer 3071	Martinsville	VA	24115	**800-446-4167**	276-638-2394
Willo Products Co Inc 2115 Veterans Dr SE	Decatur	AL	35601	**800-633-3276**	256-353-7161
Winco Window Co Inc 6200 Maple Ave	Saint Louis	MO	63130	**800-525-8089**	314-725-8088
Windowmaster Products Inc 1111 Pioneer Way	El Cajon	CA	92020	**800-862-7722**	619-444-6123

233 DOORS & WINDOWS - VINYL

Company	City	State	Zip	Toll-Free	Phone
AlbanyDoor Systems 975A Old Norcross Rd	Lawrenceville	GA	30045	**800-252-2691**	770-962-7997
Alside Div Associated Materials Inc PO Box 2010	Akron	OH	44309	**800-922-6009**	330-929-1811
Associated Materials Inc Alside Div PO Box 2010	Akron	OH	44309	**800-922-6009**	330-929-1811
Atrium Windows & Doors 9001 Ambassador Rd	Dallas	TX	75247	**800-938-2000**	
Benjamin F Rich Co PO Box 6031	Newark	DE	19714	**800-237-4241**	302-894-0498
CertainTeed Corp 750 E Swedesford Rd *Prod Info	Valley Forge	PA	19482	**800-782-8777***	610-341-7000
Dayton Technologies 351 N Garver Rd	Monroe	OH	45050	**800-432-9560**	513-539-4444
Eagle Window & Door Inc 2045 Kerper Blvd	Dubuque	IA	52001	**800-324-5354**	563-556-2270
Harry G Barr Co 6500 S Zero St	Fort Smith	AR	72903	**800-829-2277**	479-646-7891
Kensington Windows Inc 1136 Industrial Pk Rd	Vandergrift	PA	15690	**800-444-4972**	724-845-8133
Larson Mfg Co 2333 Eastbrook Dr *Cust Svc	Brookings	SD	57006	**800-352-3360***	605-692-6115
Mathews Brothers Co PO Box 345	Belfast	ME	04915	**800-639-7203**	207-338-3360

	City	St	Zip	Toll-Free	Phone
Mikron Industries Inc 1034 6th Ave N	Kent	WA	98032	**800-456-8020**	253-854-8020
Moss Supply Co Inc PO Box 26338	Charlotte	NC	28221	**800-438-0770**	704-596-8717
PGT Industries Inc 1070 Technology Dr	Nokomis	FL	34275	**877-550-6006**	941-480-1600
Rehau Inc PO Box 1706	Leesburg	VA	20177	**800-247-9445**	703-777-5255
RubbAir Door Div Eckel Industries Inc 100 Groton Shirley Rd	Ayer	MA	01432	**800-966-7822**	978-772-0480
Slocomb Industries Inc 801 Pencader Dr	Newark	DE	19702	**800-348-6233**	302-266-7101
Soft-Lite LLC 10250 Philipp Pkwy	Streetsboro	OH	44241	**800-551-1953**	330-528-3400
Stanley Works 1000 Stanley Dr *NYSE: SWK* ■ *Cust Svc	New Britain	CT	06053	**800-262-2161***	860-225-5111
Thermal Industries Inc 301 Brushton Ave	Pittsburgh	PA	15221	**800-245-1540**	412-244-6400
Weather Shield Mfg Inc 1 Weather Shield Plaza PO Box 309 *Prod Info	Medford	WI	54451	**800-222-2995***	715-748-2100
West Window Corp PO Drawer 3071	Martinsville	VA	24115	**800-446-4167**	276-638-2394
Wilmes Window Mfg Co 234 W 23rd St	Ferdinand	IN	47532	**800-477-1811**	812-367-1811
Windsor Windows & Doors 900 S 19th St	West Des Moines	IA	50265	**800-218-6186**	515-223-6660

234 DOORS & WINDOWS - WOOD

SEE ALSO Millwork; Shutters - Window (All Types)

	City	St	Zip	Toll-Free	Phone
Algoma Hardwoods Inc 1001 Perry St	Algoma	WI	54201	**800-678-8910**	920-487-5221
Andersen Corp 100 4th Ave N	Bayport	MN	55003	**877-229-2677**	651-264-5150
Buell Door Co Inc 5200 E Grand Ave	Dallas	TX	75223	**800-556-0155**	214-827-9260
Donlin Co Inc 539 E Saint Germain St	Saint Cloud	MN	56302	**800-892-7015**	320-251-3680
Eagle Window & Door Inc 2045 Kerper Blvd	Dubuque	IA	52001	**800-324-5354**	563-556-2270
Haley Brothers Inc 6291 Orangethorpe Ave	Buena Park	CA	90620	**800-848-3240**	714-670-2112
Hurd Millwork Co Inc 575 S Whelan Ave	Medford	WI	54451	**800-433-4873**	715-748-2011
Jenkins Mfg Co Inc PO Box 249	Anniston	AL	36202	**800-633-2323**	256-831-7000
Jordan Millwork Co 1820 E 54th St N *Cust Svc	Sioux Falls	SD	57104	**800-843-0076***	605-336-1910
King Sash & Door Inc PO Box 1029	Mocksville	NC	27028	**800-642-0886**	336-768-4650
Larson Mfg Co 2333 Eastbrook Dr *Cust Svc	Brookings	SD	57006	**800-352-3360***	605-692-6115
Lifetime Doors Inc 30700 Northwestern Hwy	Farmington	MI	48334	**800-521-0500**	248-851-7700
Lincoln Wood Products Inc PO Box 375	Merrill	WI	54452	**800-967-2461**	715-536-2461
Marvin Windows & Doors 104 State Ave N	Warroad	MN	56763	**800-346-5044**	218-386-1430
Masonite Holdings Inc 1 N Dale Mabry Hwy Suite 950	Tampa	FL	33609	**800-895-2723**	813-877-2726
Mathews Brothers Co PO Box 345	Belfast	ME	04915	**800-639-7203**	207-338-3360
McPhillips Mfg Co Inc PO Box 169	Mobile	AL	36601	**800-348-6274**	251-438-1681
Norco Windows Inc 811 Factory St PO Box 140	Hawkins	WI	54530	**800-826-6793**	715-585-6311
Peachtree Doors & Windows Inc 2744 Ramsey Rd	Gainesville	GA	30501	**800-443-5692**	770-534-8070
Pella Corp 102 Main St *Cust Svc	Pella	IA	50219	**800-288-7281***	641-628-1000
Quaker Window Products Inc PO Box 128	Freeburg	MO	65035	**800-347-0438**	573-744-5211
Semling-Menke Co Inc PO Box 378	Merrill	WI	54452	**800-333-2206**	715-536-9411
SNE Enterprises Inc 888 Southview Dr	Mosinee	WI	54455	**800-826-1707**	715-693-7000
Steves & Sons Inc 203 Humble Ave *Sales	San Antonio	TX	78225	**800-627-5111***	210-924-5111
Vancouver Door Co Inc PO Box 1418	Puyallup	WA	98371	**800-999-3667**	253-845-9581
Weather Shield Mfg Inc 1 Weather Shield Plaza PO Box 309 *Prod Info	Medford	WI	54451	**800-222-2995***	715-748-2100
West Coast Door Inc 3102 S Pine St	Tacoma	WA	98409	**800-445-5919**	253-272-4269
Windsor Windows & Doors 900 S 19th St	West Des Moines	IA	50265	**800-218-6186**	515-223-6660

235 DRAPERY HARDWARE

	City	St	Zip	Toll-Free	Phone
Kenney Mfg Co 1000 Jefferson Blvd *Cust Svc	Warwick	RI	02886	**800-753-6639***	401-739-2200
Newell Rubbermaid Inc Kirsch Div 916 S Arcade Ave	Freeport	IL	61032	**800-328-7290**	815-235-4171
World Wide Windows LLC/Gould Drapewear 840 Barry St	Bronx	NY	10474	**800-223-8990**	718-361-8120

236 DRUG STORES

SEE ALSO Health Food Stores

	City	St	Zip	Toll-Free	Phone
Astrup Drugs Inc 905 N Main St	Austin	MN	55912	**800-888-9069**	507-433-7447
Bartell Drug Co 4727 Denver Ave S	Seattle	WA	98134	**877-227-8355**	206-763-2626
Click Pharmacy 8790 SW 8th St *Orders	Miami	FL	33174	**800-838-9525***	305-226-8373
CVS Corp 1 CVS Dr *NYSE: CVS* ■ *Cust Svc	Woonsocket	RI	02895	**800-746-7287***	401-765-1500
drugstore.com inc 13920 SE Eastgate Way Suite 300 *NASDAQ: DSCM*	Bellevue	WA	98005	**800-378-4786**	425-372-3200
Familymeds.com Inc 312 Farmington Ave	Farmington	CT	06032	**800-203-2776**	860-676-1222
Feelbest.com 778 Bank St	Ottawa	ON	K1S3V6	**888-689-9890**	613-234-4643
Happy Harry's Inc 326 Ruthar Dr	Newark	DE	19711	**866-994-2779**	302-366-0335
Kerr Drug Stores Inc 3220 Spring Forest Rd	Raleigh	NC	27616	**800-494-3053**	919-544-3896
Kinney Drugs Inc 29 E Main St	Gouverneur	NY	13642	**800-552-8044**	315-287-1500
Medicap Pharmacies Inc 4350 Westown Pkwy Suite 400 *Cust Svc	West Des Moines	IA	50266	**800-445-2244***	515-224-8400
Medicine Shoppe International Inc 1100 N Lindbergh Blvd *Cust Svc	Saint Louis	MO	63132	**800-325-1397***	314-993-6000
Osco Drugs 250 E Park Ctr Blvd	Boise	ID	83706	**800-541-2863**	208-395-6200
Thrifty White Stores 6901 E Fish Lake Rd Suite 118	Maple Grove	MN	55369	**800-816-2887**	763-513-4300
Vitacost.com Inc 2055 High Ridge Rd	Boynton Beach	FL	33426	**800-793-2601**	561-752-8888
Vitamin Shoppe Inc 2101 91st St	North Bergen	NJ	07047	**800-223-1216**	
Walgreen Co 200 Wilmot Rd *NYSE: WAG* ■ *Cust Svc	Deerfield	IL	60015	**800-289-2273***	847-940-2500

DRUGS - MFR

SEE Biotechnology Companies; Diagnostic Products; Medicinal Chemicals & Botanical Products; Pharmaceutical Companies; Pharmaceutical Companies - Generic Drugs; Pharmaceutical & Diagnostic Products - Veterinary; Vitamins & Nutritional Supplements

237 DRUGS & PERSONAL CARE PRODUCTS - WHOL

	City	St	Zip	Toll-Free	Phone
American Herbal Products 1440 JFK Causeway Suite 400	North Bay Village	FL	33141	**888-446-6884**	305-865-2919
AmerisourceBergen Corp 1300 Morris Dr Suite 100 *NYSE: ABC*	Chesterbrook	PA	19087	**800-829-3132**	610-727-7000
Anderson Wholesale Co PO Box 69	Muskogee	OK	74402	**800-324-9656**	918-682-5568
ASD Specialty Healthcare 4006 Beltline Rd Suite 200	Addison	TX	75001	**800-746-6273**	972-490-5551
Avatex Corp 5910 N Central Expy Suite 1780	Dallas	TX	75206	**800-654-3808**	214-365-7450
Barnes Wholesale Inc PO Box 17010	Inglewood	CA	90308	**800-227-4845**	310-641-1885
Cardinal Health Distribution 7000 Cardinal Pl	Dublin	OH	43017	**800-234-8701**	614-757-5000
Cardinal Health Specialty Pharmaceutical Distribution 401 Mason Rd	La Vergne	TN	37086	**800-879-5569**	
Cosmopolitan Cosmetics 909 3rd Ave 20th Fl	New York	NY	10022	**800-589-1412**	212-980-6400
D & K Healthcare Resources Inc 8235 Forsythe Blvd *NASDAQ: DKHR*	Saint Louis	MO	63105	**888-727-3485**	314-727-3485
Dakota Drug Inc 28 Main St N	Minot	ND	58703	**800-437-2018**	701-852-2141
Dohmen F Co W 194 North 11381 McCormick Dr	Germantown	WI	53022	**877-848-4166**	262-255-0022
F Dohmen Co W 194 North 11381 McCormick Dr	Germantown	WI	53022	**877-848-4166**	262-255-0022
Family Pharmacy 300 Chesterfield Pkwy	Malvern	PA	19355	**877-892-1254**	
HD Smith Wholesale Drug Co 4650 Industrial Dr	Springfield	IL	62703	**800-252-8090**	217-529-0211
Kinray Inc 152-35 10th Ave	Whitestone	NY	11357	**800-854-6729**	718-767-1234
McKesson Specialty Pharmaceuticals 5712 Jarvis St	New Orleans	LA	70123	**888-456-7274**	504-736-7827
Medtech Products Inc PO Box 1108	Jackson	WY	83001	**800-443-4908**	307-733-1680
Millbrook Distribution Services 88 Huntoon Memorial Hwy	Leicester	MA	01524	**800-225-7398**	508-892-8171
Morris & Dickson Co Ltd PO Box 51367	Shreveport	LA	71135	**800-388-3833**	318-797-7900
North Carolina Mutual Wholesale Drug Co PO Box 411	Durham	NC	27702	**800-800-8551**	919-596-2151
Parmed Pharmaceuticals Inc 4220 Hyde Park Blvd	Niagara Falls	NY	14305	**800-727-6331**	716-284-5666
Pharmed Group Corp 3075 NW 107th Ave	Miami	FL	33172	**800-683-7342**	305-592-2324
Quality King Distributors Inc 2060 9th Ave	Ronkonkoma	NY	11779	**800-676-5554**	631-439-2000
Reese Pharmaceutical Co PO Box 1957	Cleveland	OH	44106	**800-321-7178**	216-231-6441
Respiratory Distributors Inc 110 E Azalea Ave	Foley	AL	36535	**800-872-8672**	251-943-5844
RG Shakour Inc 254 Turnpike Rd	Westborough	MA	01581	**800-262-9090**	508-366-8282
Rochester Drug Co-op Inc PO Box 24389	Rochester	NY	14624	**800-333-0538**	585-271-7220
Shakour RG Inc 254 Turnpike Rd	Westborough	MA	01581	**800-262-9090**	508-366-8282
Smith HD Wholesale Drug Co 4650 Industrial Dr	Springfield	IL	62703	**800-252-8090**	217-529-0211
Standard Drug Co 1 Westbury Sq Bldg B	Saint Charles	MO	63301	**877-482-5874**	636-946-6557
Sun Healthcare Group Inc Pharmaceutical Services 101 Sun Ave NE	Albuquerque	NM	87109	**800-729-6600**	505-468-4168
Superior Pharmaceutical Co 1385 Kemper Meadow Dr	Cincinnati	OH	45240	**800-826-5035**	513-851-3600
Syncor International Corp 6464 Canoga Ave	Woodland Hills	CA	91367	**800-999-9098**	818-737-4000
Texas Drug Co 1101 W Vickery Blvd	Fort Worth	TX	76104	**888-378-4668**	817-335-5761
Value In Pharmaceuticals (VIP) 3000 Alt Blvd	Grand Island	NY	14072	**800-724-3784**	716-773-4600

238 DUDE RANCHES

SEE ALSO Resorts

	City	St	Zip	Toll-Free	Phone
7 D Ranch PO Box 100	Cody	WY	82414	**888-587-9885**	307-587-9885
63 Ranch Box 979	Livingston	MT	59047	**888-395-5151**	406-222-0570
Alisal Guest Ranch & Resort 1054 Alisal Rd	Solvang	CA	93463	**800-425-4725**	805-688-6411
Aspen Canyon Ranch 13206 County Rd 3	Parshall	CO	80468	**800-321-1357**	970-725-3600
Bar Lazy J Guest Ranch PO Box N	Parshall	CO	80468	**800-396-6279**	970-725-3437
Bar M Dude Ranch 58840 Bar M Ln	Adams	OR	97810	**888-824-3381**	541-566-3381
Black Mountain Ranch PO Box 219	McCoy	CO	80463	**800-967-2401**	970-653-4226
Bonanza Creek Country Guest Ranch 523 Bonanza Creek Rd	Martinsdale	MT	59053	**800-476-6045**	406-572-3366
Brush Creek Ranch HC 63 Box 10	Saratoga	WY	82331	**800-726-2499**	307-327-5241
Buffalo Horn Ranch 13825 County Rd 7	Meeker	CO	81641	**877-878-5450**	970-878-5450
Cherokee Park Ranch 436 Cherokee Hills Dr	Livermore	CO	80536	**800-628-0949**	970-493-6522
Circle Bar Guest Ranch HCR 81 Box 61	Utica	MT	59452	**888-570-0227**	406-423-5454
Circle Z Ranch PO Box 194	Patagonia	AZ	85624	**888-854-2525**	520-394-2525
CM Ranch 167 Fish Hatchery Rd	Dubois	WY	82513	**800-455-0721**	307-455-2331
Coffee Creek Ranch 4940 Coffee Creek Rd	Trinity Center	CA	96091	**800-624-4480**	530-266-3343

Name / Address	City	State	Zip	Toll-Free	Phone
Colorado Trails Ranch 12161 County Rd 240	Durango	CO	81301	**800-323-3833**	970-247-5055
Coulter Lake Guest Ranch 80 County Rd 273	Rifle	CO	81650	**800-858-3046**	970-625-1473
Crossed Sabres Ranch 829 N Fork Hwy	Wapiti	WY	82450	**800-535-8944**	307-587-3750
Deer Valley Ranch 16825 County Rd 162	Nathrop	CO	81236	**800-284-1708**	719-395-2353
Diamond J Ranch PO Box 577	Ennis	MT	59729	**877-929-4867**	406-682-4867
Drowsy Water Ranch PO Box 147	Granby	CO	80446	**800-845-2292**	970-725-3456
Eatons' Ranch 270 Eatons' Ranch Rd	Wolf	WY	82844	**800-210-1049**	307-655-9285
Echo Canyon Guest Ranch 12507 Echo Canyon Creek Rd PO Box 328	La Veta	CO	81055	**800-341-6603**	719-742-5524
Echo Valley Ranch & Spa Clinton PO Box 16	Jesmond	BC	V0K1K0	**800-253-8831**	250-459-2386
Elk Mountain Ranch PO Box 910	Buena Vista	CO	81211	**800-432-8812**	719-539-4430
Flying A Ranch 771 Flying A Ranch Rd	Pinedale	WY	82941	**888-833-3348**	307-367-2385
Flying E Ranch 2801 W Wickenburg Way	Wickenburg	AZ	85390	**888-684-2650**	928-684-2690
Fort Ranch PO Box 73	Golconda	NV	89414	**800-651-4567**	480-488-2775
Grapevine Canyon Ranch Inc PO Box 302	Pearce	AZ	85625	**800-245-9202**	520-826-3185
Greenhorn Creek Guest Ranch 2116 Greenhorn Ranch Rd	Quincy	CA	95971	**800-334-6939**	530-283-0930
Heart Six Ranch 16985 Buffalo Valley Rd PO Box 70	Moran	WY	83013	**888-543-2477**	307-543-2477
Hidden Creek Ranch 11077 E Blue Lake Rd	Harrison	ID	83833	**800-446-3833**	208-689-3209
Hideout at Flitner Ranch Resort PO Box 206	Shell	WY	82441	**800-354-8637**	307-765-2080
Historic Pines Ranch PO Box 311	Westcliffe	CO	81252	**800-446-9462**	719-783-9261
Homeplace Ranch RR 1 Site 2 Box 6	Priddis	AB	T0L1W0	**877-931-3245**	403-931-3245
Horse Prairie Ranch 3300 Bachelor Mountain Rd	Dillon	MT	59725	**888-726-2454**	406-681-3155
Horseshoe Canyon Ranch 3900 Lochridge Rd	North Little Rock	AR	72116	**800-480-9635**	501-791-2679
Kay El Bar Guest Ranch PO Box 2480	Wickenburg	AZ	85358	**800-684-7583**	928-684-7593
Kedesh Guest Ranch 1940 Hwy 14	Shell	WY	82441	**800-845-3320**	307-765-2791
King Mountain Ranch PO Box 497	Granby	CO	80446	**800-476-5464**	970-887-2511
Lake Mancos Ranch 42688 County Rd 'N'	Mancos	CO	81328	**800-325-9462**	970-533-1190
Laramie River Dude Ranch 25777 County Rd 103	Jelm	WY	82063	**800-551-5731**	970-435-5716
Latigo Ranch PO Box 237	Kremmling	CO	80459	**800-227-9655**	
Laughing Water Guest Ranch PO Box 157	Fortine	MT	59918	**800-847-5095**	406-882-4680
Lazy K Bar Guest Ranch 8401 N Scenic Dr	Tucson	AZ	85743	**800-321-7018**	520-744-3050
Lazy L & B Ranch 1072 E Fork Rd	Dubois	WY	82513	**800-453-9488**	307-455-2839
Lone Mountain Ranch PO Box 160069	Big Sky	MT	59716	**800-514-4644**	406-995-4644
Long Hollow Ranch 71105 Holmes Rd	Sisters	OR	97759	**877-923-1901**	541-923-1901
Lozier's Box R Ranch PO Box 100	Cora	WY	82925	**800-822-8466**	307-367-4868
Moose Creek Ranch 219 E Moose Creek Rd	Victor	ID	83455	**800-676-0075**	208-787-2784
Mountain Sky Guest Ranch PO Box 1219	Emigrant	MT	59027	**800-548-3392**	406-333-4911
North Fork Ranch 555395 Hwy 285	Shawnee	CO	80475	**800-843-7895**	303-838-9873
Peaceful Valley Ranch 475 Peaceful Valley Rd	Lyons	CO	80540	**800-955-6343**	303-747-2881
Powderhorn Guest Ranch 1525 County Rd 27	Powderhorn	CO	81243	**800-786-1220**	970-641-0220
Price Canyon Ranch PO Box 1065	Douglas	AZ	85608	**800-727-0065**	520-558-2383
Rainbow Trout Ranch 1484 FDR 250	Antonito	CO	81120	**800-633-3397**	719-376-5659
Rancho de la Osa Guest Ranch PO Box 1	Sasabe	AZ	85633	**800-872-6240**	520-823-4257
Ranger Creek Guest Ranch PO Box 47	Shell	WY	82441	**888-817-7787**	307-272-5107
Rawah Ranch 11447 N County Rd 103	Jelm	WY	82063	**800-820-3152**	
Rich Ranch PO Box 495	Seeley Lake	MT	59868	**800-532-4350**	406-677-2317
Rock Springs Guest Ranch 64201 Tyler Rd	Bend	OR	97701	**800-225-3833**	541-382-1957
Scott Valley Resort & Guest Ranch 223 Scott Valley Trail	Mountain Home	AR	72653	**888-855-7747**	870-425-5136
Spear-O-Wigwam Guest Ranch PO Box 1081	Sheridan	WY	82801	**888-818-3833**	
Sundance Trail Guest Ranch 17931 Red Feather Lakes Rd	Red Feather Lakes	CO	80545	**800-357-4930**	970-224-1222
Sylvan Dale Guest Ranch 2939 N County Rd 31 D	Loveland	CO	80538	**877-667-3999**	970-667-3915
Tarryall River Ranch 27001.5 County Rd 77	Lake George	CO	80827	**800-408-8407**	719-748-1214
Three Bars Cattle & Guest Ranch 9500 Wycliffe Perry Creek Rd	Cranbrook	BC	V1C7C7	**877-426-5230**	250-426-5230
Triangle C Ranch 3737 Hwy 26	Dubois	WY	82513	**800-661-4928**	307-455-2225
Triangle X Ranch 2 Triangle X Ranch Rd	Moose	WY	83012	**888-860-0005**	307-733-2183
Triple R Ranch PO Box 124	Keystone	SD	57751	**888-777-2624**	605-666-4605
Tumbling River Ranch 3715 Park County Rd 62 Box 30	Grant	CO	80448	**800-654-8770**	303-838-5981
Twin Peaks Ranch PO Box 774	Salmon	ID	83467	**800-659-4899**	208-894-2290
UXU Ranch 1710 Yellowstone Hwy	Wapiti	WY	82450	**800-373-9027**	307-587-2143
Vee Bar Guest Ranch 2091 State Hwy 130	Laramie	WY	82070	**800-483-3227**	307-745-7036
Vista Verde Guest & Ski Ranch Box 465	Steamboat Springs	CO	80477	**800-526-7433**	970-879-3858
Whistling Acres Guest Ranch 44325 Minnesota Creek Rd PO Box 88	Paonia	CO	81428	**800-346-1420**	970-527-4560
White Stallion Ranch 9251 W Twin Peaks Rd	Tucson	AZ	85743	**888-977-2624**	520-297-0252
Wild Rose Ranch PO Box 181	Kimberley	BC	V1A2Y6	**800-324-6188**	250-422-3403
Wilderness Trails Ranch 1766 County Rd 302	Durango	CO	81303	**800-527-2624**	970-247-0722
Wind River Ranch PO Box 3410	Estes Park	CO	80517	**800-523-4212**	970-586-4212
Wind Walker Guest Ranch PO Box 7	Spring City	UT	84662	**888-606-9463**	435-462-0282

239 DUPLICATION & REPLICATION SERVICES

Name / Address	City	State	Zip	Toll-Free	Phone
Avery Dennison Microreplication Div 7590 Auburn Rd MS 16X	Painesville	OH	44077	**866-358-4862**	440-358-4862
Campbell Blueprint & Supply Co Inc PO Box 820344	Memphis	TN	38182	**800-238-7564**	901-327-7385
Cleveland City Blue Printing Co 1937 Prospect Ave	Cleveland	OH	44115	**800-993-2583**	216-241-7344
Corporate Disk Co 1226 Michael Dr Suite F	Wood Dale	IL	60191	**800-634-3475**	630-616-0700
Digital Video Services 4592 40th St SE	Grand Rapids	MI	49512	**800-747-8273**	616-975-9911
Eva-Tone Soundsheets Inc 4801 Ulmerton Rd *Sales	Clearwater	FL	33762	**800-382-8663***	727-572-7000
Globalware Solutions Inc 1089 Mills Way	Redwood City	CA	94063	**800-224-6326**	650-363-2200
Media Factory Inc 48873 Kato Rd	Fremont	CA	94539	**800-879-9536**	510-438-0373
MerX City 7600 Wayzata Blvd	Golden Valley	MN	55426	**800-356-6826**	763-253-6500
Metacom Inc 251 1st Ave N 2nd Fl	Minneapolis	MN	55401	**800-236-0289**	
Online Copy Corp 48815 Kato Rd	Fremont	CA	94539	**800-833-4460**	510-226-6810
Producers & Quantity Photos Inc 6660 Santa Monica Blvd *Cust Svc	Hollywood	CA	90038	**800-843-9259***	323-467-6178
Reproduction Systems Inc 1828 Walnut St Suite 900	Kansas City	MO	64108	**800-633-6125**	816-471-1414
RT Technologies 2000 L St NW Suite B-1	Washington	DC	20036	**800-231-5758**	202-331-0576
Shaffstall Corp 8531 Bash St	Indianapolis	IN	46250	**800-923-8439**	317-842-2077
Smart Document Solutions 120 Bluegrass Valley Pkwy	Alpharetta	GA	30005	**800-367-1500**	770-360-1700
Standard Digital Imaging 4426 S 108th St	Omaha	NE	68137	**800-642-8062**	402-592-1292
T-Square Miami Blueprint Co 998 W Flagler St	Miami	FL	33130	**800-432-3360**	305-324-1234
Thomas Reprographics 600 N Central Expy	Richardson	TX	75080	**800-877-3776**	972-231-7227
Triangle Blueprint Co 2721 Brunswick Pike	Lawrenceville	NJ	08648	**800-792-8800**	609-883-3600
Victory Studios 2247 15th Ave W	Seattle	WA	98119	**888-282-1776**	206-282-1776
WEA Mfg 1400 E Lackawanna Ave	Olyphant	PA	18448	**800-323-1263**	570-383-2471

240 DUTY-FREE SHOPS

SEE ALSO Gift Shops

Name / Address	City	State	Zip	Toll-Free	Phone
American Airlines Duty Free 1166 Kane Concourse Suite 301	Bay Harbor Islands	FL	33154	**888-388-9373**	305-864-5788
Baja Duty Free 4590 Border Village Rd	San Ysidro	CA	92173	**877-438-8937**	619-428-6671
Colombian Emeralds International PO Box 5868	Fort Lauderdale	FL	33310	**800-666-3889**	954-917-2547
DUTYFREE.COM PO Box 5868	Fort Lauderdale	FL	33310	**800-666-3889**	954-978-5482
Little Switzerland Inc 6800 NW Broken Sound Pkwy	Boca Raton	FL	33487	**888-257-5488**	561-206-0080
Niagara Duty Free Shop 5726 Falls Ave	Niagara Falls	ON	L2G7T5	**877-612-4337**	905-374-3700
Peace Bridge Duty Free Inc Peace Bridge Plaza PO Box 339	Fort Erie	ON	L2A5N1	**800-361-1302**	905-871-5400

241 EDUCATIONAL INSTITUTION OPERATORS & MANAGERS

Name / Address	City	State	Zip	Toll-Free	Phone
Beacon Education Management Inc 112 Turnpike Rd Suite 107	Westborough	MA	01581	**800-789-1258**	508-836-4461
Capella Education Co 222 S 9th St 20th Fl	Minneapolis	MN	55402	**888-227-3552**	612-339-7665
Career Education Corp 2895 Greenspoint Pkwy Suite 600 *NASDAQ: CECO*	Hoffman Estates	IL	60195	**888-781-3608**	847-781-3600
College for Financial Planning Inc 6161 S Syracuse Way	Greenwood Village	CO	80111	**800-237-9990**	303-220-1200
Corinthian Colleges Inc 6 Hutton Ctr Dr Suite 400 *NASDAQ: COCO*	Santa Ana	CA	92707	**800-611-2101**	714-427-3000
Corinthian Schools Inc 6 Hutton Ctr Dr Suite 400	Santa Ana	CA	92707	**888-741-4271**	714-427-3000
DeVRY Inc 1 Tower Ln Suite 1000 *NYSE: DV*	Oakbrook Terrace	IL	60181	**800-733-3879**	630-571-7700
Lincoln Educational Services 200 Executive Dr	West Orange	NJ	07052	**877-693-8887**	973-736-9340
National Heritage Academies 3850 Broadmoor Ave SE Suite 201	Grand Rapids	MI	49512	**800-699-9235**	616-222-1700
Rhodes Colleges Inc 6 Hutton Ctr Dr Suite 400	Santa Ana	CA	92707	**888-741-4271**	714-427-3000
Strayer Education Inc 2121 15th St N *NASDAQ: STRA*	Arlington	VA	22201	**877-892-5100**	703-892-5100
Sylvan Learning Centers 1001 Fleet St	Baltimore	MD	21202	**800-627-4276**	410-843-8000
UNext.com 500 Lake Cook Rd Suite 150	Deerfield	IL	60015	**877-405-4500**	847-405-5000

EDUCATIONAL INSTITUTIONS

SEE Children's Learning Centers; Colleges & Universities - Christian; Colleges & Universities - Four-Year; Colleges & Universities - Graduate & Professional Schools; Colleges & Universities - Historically Black; Colleges & Universities - Jesuit; Colleges - Business; Colleges - Fine Arts; Colleges - Junior; Colleges - Tribal; Military Service Academies; Preparatory Schools; Universities - Canadian; Vocational & Technical Schools

242 EDUCATIONAL MATERIALS & SUPPLIES

SEE ALSO Computer Software - Educational & Reference Software; School Supplies

Name / Address	City	State	Zip	Toll-Free	Phone
American Educational Products Inc 401 W Hickory St PO Box 2121	Fort Collins	CO	80522	**800-446-8767**	970-484-7445
American Educational Products LLC Hubbard Scientific Div 401 Hickory St *Cust Svc	Fort Collins	CO	80522	**800-289-9299***	970-484-7445
American Educational Products LLC National Teaching Aids Div 401 Hickory St *Cust Svc	Fort Collins	CO	80522	**800-289-9299***	970-484-7445
American Educational Products LLC Scott Resources Div 401 Hickory St *Cust Svc	Fort Collins	CO	80522	**800-289-9299***	970-484-7445
American Greetings Corp Learning Horizons Div 1 American Rd	Cleveland	OH	44144	**800-321-3040**	216-252-7300
American Guidance Service Inc DBA AGS Publishing 4201 Woodland Rd	Circle Pines	MN	55014	**800-471-8457**	651-287-7220
Carson-Dellosa Publishing Co Inc 7027 Albert Pick Rd	Greensboro	NC	27409	**800-321-0943**	336-632-0084
Center Enterprises Inc 30 Shield St *Orders	West Hartford	CT	06110	**800-542-2214***	860-953-4423
Chenille Kraft Co 65 Ambrogio Dr	Gurnee	IL	60031	**800-621-1261**	847-249-2900
Classroom Connect Inc 8000 Marina Blvd Suite 400	Brisbane	CA	94005	**800-638-1639**	650-351-5100

Company / Address	City	State	ZIP	Toll-Free	Phone
Creative Teaching Press Inc 15342 Graham St	Huntington Beach	CA	92649	**800-444-4287**	714-895-5047
Delta Education LLC 80 Northwest Blvd	Nashua	NH	03063	**800-258-1302**	603-889-8899
Didax Educational Resources Inc 395 Main St	Rowley	MA	01969	**800-458-0024**	978-948-2340
Edcon/Imperial/AV 30 Montauk Blvd	Oakdale	NY	11769	**888-553-3266**	631-567-7227
Education Center Inc 3515 W Market St Suite 200	Greensboro	NC	27403	**800-714-7991**	336-854-0309
Educational Insights Inc 18730 S Wilmington Ave	Rancho Dominguez	CA	90220	**800-933-3277**	310-884-2000
Educational Resources 1550 Executive Dr *Orders	Elgin	IL	60123	**800-624-2926***	847-888-8300
Edupress Inc W 5527 SR 106	Fort Atlinson	WI	53538	**800-835-7978**	920-563-9751
Eureka School Div Paper Magic Group Inc 401 Adams Ave *Cust Svc	Scranton	PA	18510	**800-258-1044***	570-961-3863
Evan-Moor Educational Publishers Inc 18 Lower Ragsdale Dr	Monterey	CA	93940	**800-777-4489**	831-649-5901
Excelligence Learning Corp 2 Lower Ragsdale Dr Suite 200 *NASDAQ: LRNS*	Monterey	CA	93940	**800-627-2829**	831-333-2000
Films for the Humanities & Sciences PO Box 2053	Princeton	NJ	08543	**800-257-5126**	609-275-1400
Frank Schaffer Publications PO Box 141487	Grand Rapids	MI	49514	**800-253-5469**	800-417-3261
Frog Street Press Inc 308 E Trunk St	Crandall	TX	75114	**800-884-3764**	972-472-6896
Ghent Mfg Inc 2999 Henkle Dr	Lebanon	OH	45036	**800-543-0550**	513-932-3445
Great Source Education Group 181 Ballardvale St	Wilmington	MA	01887	**800-289-4490**	978-661-1300
Guidecraft USA 66 Grand Ave Suite 207	Englewood	NJ	07631	**800-544-6526**	201-894-5401
Hayes School Publishing Co Inc 321 Pennwood Ave	Pittsburgh	PA	15221	**800-245-6234**	412-731-4693
Hubbard Scientific Div American Educational Products LLC 401 Hickory St *Cust Svc	Fort Collins	CO	80522	**800-289-9299***	970-484-7445
Incentive Publications Inc 2400 Crestmoor Dr Suite 211 *Mktg	Nashville	TN	37215	**800-421-2830***	615-385-2934
Kimbo Educational 10 N 3rd Ave	Long Branch	NJ	07740	**800-631-2187**	732-229-4949
Lauri 51 Magnetic Ave	Smethport	PA	16749	**800-451-0520**	814-887-6921
Learning Horizons Div American Greetings Corp 1 American Rd	Cleveland	OH	44144	**800-321-3040**	216-252-7300
Learning Resources 380 N Fairway Dr	Vernon Hills	IL	60061	**800-222-3909**	847-573-8400
Learning Works 15342 Graham St	Huntington Beach	CA	92649	**800-235-5767**	714-895-5047
Learning Wrap-Ups Inc 1660 W Gordon Ave Suite 4	Layton	UT	84041	**800-992-4966**	801-497-0050
Macmillan/McGraw-Hill Div McGraw-Hill Cos Inc 2 Pennsylvania Plaza	New York	NY	10121	**800-442-9685**	212-512-2000
McDonald Publishing 567 Hanley Industrial Ct	Saint Louis	MO	63144	**800-722-8080**	314-781-7400
McGraw-Hill Cos Inc Macmillan/McGraw-Hill Div 2 Pennsylvania Plaza	New York	NY	10121	**800-442-9685**	212-512-2000
McGraw-Hill Cos Inc SRA/McGraw-Hill Div 8787 Orion Pl	Columbus	OH	43240	**800-468-4850**	614-430-6600
Milliken Publishing Co Inc 11643 Lilburn Park Dr	Saint Louis	MO	63146	**800-325-4136**	314-991-4220
Monday Morning Books 150 Bayview Dr PO Box 1134	Palo Alto	CA	94301	**800-255-6049**	
National Teaching Aids Div American Educational Products LLC 401 Hickory St *Cust Svc	Fort Collins	CO	80522	**800-289-9299***	970-484-7445
Paper Magic Group Inc Eureka School Div 401 Adams Ave *Cust Svc	Scranton	PA	18510	**800-258-1044***	570-961-3863
Replogle Globes Inc 2801 S 25th Ave	Broadview	IL	60155	**800-275-4452**	708-343-0900
Rock 'N Learn Inc 105 Commercial Cir	Conroe	TX	77304	**800-348-8445**	936-539-2731
Roylco Inc 3251 Abbeville Hwy	Anderson	SC	29624	**800-362-8656**	864-296-0043
Scholastic Corp 557 Broadway *NASDAQ: SCHL* ■ *Cust Svc	New York	NY	10012	**800-724-6527***	212-343-6100
Scholastic News 557 Broadway *Orders	New York	NY	10012	**800-724-6527***	212-343-6100
School Mate Inc 77 Conalco Dr	Jackson	TN	38302	**800-264-4108**	731-935-2000
Scott Resources Div American Educational Products LLC 401 Hickory St *Cust Svc	Fort Collins	CO	80522	**800-289-9299***	970-484-7445
SRA/McGraw-Hill Div McGraw-Hill Cos Inc 8787 Orion Pl	Columbus	OH	43240	**800-468-4850**	614-430-6600
Teacher Created Resources Inc 6421 Industry Way	Westminster	CA	92683	**888-343-4335**	714-891-7895
Teaching & Learning Co 1204 Buchanan St	Carthage	IL	62321	**800-852-1234**	217-357-2591
Touchstone Applied Science Assoc Inc 4 Hardscrabble Heights PO Box 382 *Cust Svc	Brewster	NY	10509	**800-800-2598***	845-277-8100
TREND enterprises Inc 300 9th Ave SW *Cust Svc	New Brighton	MN	55112	**800-328-0818***	651-631-2850
Twin Sisters Productions LLC 2680 W Market St	Akron	OH	44333	**800-248-8946**	330-864-3000
Weekly Reader Corp 200 First Stamford Pl 2nd Fl *Cust Svc	Stamford	CT	06912	**800-446-3355***	203-705-3500
World*Class Learning Materials 111 Kane St	Baltimore	MD	21224	**800-638-6470**	410-633-0730

243 EDUCATIONAL TESTING SERVICES - ASSESSMENT & PREPARATION

Company / Address	City	State	ZIP	Toll-Free	Phone
Association for Advanced Training in the Behavioral Sciences (AATBS) 5126 Ralston St	Ventura	CA	93003	**800-472-1931**	805-676-3030
Barron's Educational Series Inc 250 Wireless Blvd	Hauppauge	NY	11788	**800-645-3476**	631-434-3311
BISYS Education Services 1100 Circle 75 Pkwy Suite 1300	Atlanta	GA	30339	**800-241-9095**	770-659-6000
Castle Worldwide Inc 900 Perimeter Park Rd Suite G	Morrisville	NC	27560	**866-422-7853**	919-572-6880
College Board 45 Columbus Ave	New York	NY	10023	**800-927-4302**	212-713-8000
CTB/McGraw-Hill Div McGraw-Hill Cos Inc 20 Ryan Ranch Rd	Monterey	CA	93940	**800-538-9547**	831-393-0700
H & H Publishing Co Inc 1231 Kapp Drive	Clearwater	FL	33765	**800-366-4079**	727-442-7760
Harcourt Assessment Inc 19500 Bulverde Rd	San Antonio	TX	78259	**800-228-0752**	210-339-5000
Kaplan Inc 888 7th Ave 21st Fl *Cust Svc	New York	NY	10106	**800-527-8378***	212-492-5800
Kaplan Inc Test Preparation & Admissions Div 888 7th Ave 21st Fl	New York	NY	10106	**888-527-5268**	212-492-5800
McGraw-Hill Cos Inc CTB/McGraw-Hill Div 20 Ryan Ranch Rd	Monterey	CA	93940	**800-538-9547**	831-393-0700
NCS Pearson Inc 5601 Green Valley Dr Suite 220	Bloomington	MN	55437	**800-431-1421**	952-681-3000
Praxis Series Online Educational Testing Service Teaching & Learning Div Rosedale Rd	Princeton	NJ	08541	**800-772-9476**	609-771-7395
Princeton Review 2315 Broadway *NASDAQ: REVU*	New York	NY	10024	**800-333-0369**	212-874-8282
Professional Assessment for Beginning Teachers Educational Testing Service Teaching & Learning Div Rosedale Rd	Princeton	NJ	08541	**800-772-9476**	609-771-7395
Promissor Inc 1007 Church St Suite 314	Evanston	IL	60201	**800-255-1312**	847-866-2001
Promissor Inc 3 Bala Plaza W Suite 300	Bala Cynwyd	PA	19004	**888-204-6231**	610-617-5093
Riverside Publishing Co 425 Spring Lake Dr	Itasca	IL	60143	**800-323-9540**	630-467-7000
Thomson Prometric 1000 Lancaster St	Baltimore	MD	21202	**866-776-6387**	443-923-8668

244 ELECTRIC COMPANIES - COOPERATIVES (RURAL)

SEE ALSO Utility Companies

Alabama

Company / Address	City	State	ZIP	Toll-Free	Phone
Baldwin County Electric Membership Corp 19600 Hwy 59	Summerdale	AL	36580	**800-837-3374**	251-989-6247
Central Alabama Electric Co-op PO Box 681570	Prattville	AL	36068	**800-545-5735**	334-365-6762
Cherokee Electric Co-op 1550 Clarence Chestnut Bypass	Centre	AL	35960	**800-952-2667**	256-927-5524
Clarke-Washington Electric Membership Corp 1307 College Ave	Jackson	AL	36545	**800-323-9081**	251-246-9081
Coosa Valley Electric Co-op 69220 Alabama Hwy 77	Talladega	AL	35160	**800-273-7210**	256-362-4180
Covington Electric Co-op Inc 18836 US Hwy 84	Andalusia	AL	36420	**800-239-4121**	334-222-4121
Cullman Electric Co-op 1749 Eva Rd NE	Cullman	AL	35055	**800-242-1806**	256-737-3200
Dixie Electric Co-op PO Box 30	Union Springs	AL	36089	**888-349-4332**	334-738-2500
Franklin Electric Co-op Inc PO Box 10	Russellville	AL	35653	**800-451-1505**	256-332-2730
Marshall DeKalb Electric Co-op PO Box 724	Boaz	AL	35957	**800-239-3692**	256-593-4262
North Alabama Electric Co-op PO Box 628	Stevenson	AL	35772	**800-572-2900**	256-437-2281
Pea River Electric Co-op 1311 W Roy Parker Rd	Ozark	AL	36360	**800-264-7732**	334-774-2545
Pioneer Electric Co-op 300 Herbert St	Greenville	AL	36037	**800-239-3092**	334-382-6636
South Alabama Electric Co-op 13192 Hwy 231 S	Troy	AL	36081	**800-556-2060**	334-566-2060
Tallapoosa River Electric Co-op PO Box 675	Lafayette	AL	36862	**800-332-8732**	334-864-9331
Tombigbee Electric Co-op Inc PO Box 610	Guin	AL	35563	**800-621-8069**	205-468-3325
Wiregrass Electric Co-op Inc PO Box 158	Hartford	AL	36344	**800-239-4602**	334-588-2223

Alaska

Company / Address	City	State	ZIP	Toll-Free	Phone
Chugach Electric Assn Inc 5601 Minnesota Dr	Anchorage	AK	99519	**800-478-7494**	907-563-7494
Golden Valley Electrical Assn Inc PO Box 71249	Fairbanks	AK	99707	**800-770-4832**	907-452-1151

Arizona

Company / Address	City	State	ZIP	Toll-Free	Phone
Duncan Valley Electric Co-op Inc PO Box 440	Duncan	AZ	85534	**800-669-2503**	928-359-2503
Graham County Electric Co-op Inc PO Drawer B	Pima	AZ	85543	**800-577-9266**	928-485-2451
Mohave Electric Co-op Inc 1999 Arena Dr	Bullhead City	AZ	86442	**800-685-4251**	928-763-4115
Navopache Electric Co-op Inc 1878 W White Mountain Blvd	Lakeside	AZ	85929	**800-543-6324**	928-368-5118
Sulphur Springs Valley Electric Co-op Inc PO Box 820	Willcox	AZ	85644	**800-422-9288**	520-384-2221

Arkansas

Company / Address	City	State	ZIP	Toll-Free	Phone
Arkansas Valley Electric Co-op Corp 1811 W Commercial St	Ozark	AR	72949	**800-468-2176**	479-667-2176
Ashley-Chicot Electric Co-op Inc 307 E Jefferson St	Hamburg	AR	71646	**800-281-5212**	870-853-5212
Carroll Electric Co-op Corp 920 Hwy 62 Spur	Berryville	AR	72616	**800-432-9720**	870-423-2161
Craighead Electric Co-op Corp 4714 Stadium Blvd	Jonesboro	AR	72403	**800-794-5012**	870-932-8301
Farmers Electric Co-op Corp PO Box 708	Newport	AR	72112	**800-834-9055**	870-523-3691
First Electric Co-op Corp PO Box 5018	Jacksonville	AR	72078	**800-489-7405**	501-982-4545
Mississippi County Electric Co-op PO Box 7	Blytheville	AR	72316	**800-439-4563**	870-763-4563
Ozarks Electric Co-op Corp PO Box 848	Fayetteville	AR	72702	**800-521-6144**	479-521-2900
Petit Jean Electric Co-op 270 Quality Dr	Clinton	AR	72031	**800-786-7618**	501-745-2493
Rich Mountain Electric Co-op Inc PO Box 897	Mena	AR	71953	**877-828-4074**	479-394-4140
South Central Arkansas Electric Co-op PO Box 476	Arkadelphia	AR	71923	**800-814-2931**	870-246-6701
Southwest Arkansas Electric Co-op Corp PO Box 1807	Texarkana	AR	75504	**800-782-2743**	870-772-2743

California

	City	State	ZIP	Toll-Free	Phone
Plumas-Sierra Rural Electric Co op 73233 Hwy 70 Suite A	Portola	CA	96122	**800-555-2207**	530-832-4261
Surprise Valley Electric Co-op PO Box 691	Alturas	CA	96101	**866-843-2667**	530-233-3511
Trinity Public Utility District PO Box 1216	Weaverville	CA	96093	**800-968-7783**	530-623-5536

Colorado

	City	State	ZIP	Toll-Free	Phone
Empire Electric Assn Inc PO Drawer K	Cortez	CO	81321	**800-709-3726**	970-565-4444
Gunnison County Electric Assn PO Box 180	Gunnison	CO	81230	**800-726-3523**	970-641-3520
Holy Cross Energy PO Box 2150	Glenwood Springs	CO	81602	**888-347-4425**	970-945-5491
Intermountain Rural Electric Assn PO Box A	Sedalia	CO	80135	**800-332-9540**	303-688-3100
KC Electric Assn PO Box 8	Hugo	CO	80821	**800-700-3123**	719-743-2431
La Plata Electric Assn Inc PO Box 2750	Durango	CO	81302	**888-839-5732**	970-247-5786
Mountain Parks Electric Inc PO Box 170	Granby	CO	80446	**877-887-3378**	970-887-3378
Mountain View Electric Assn Inc PO Box 1600	Limon	CO	80828	**800-388-9881**	719-775-2861
Poudre Valley Rural Electric Assn Inc 7649 Rea Pkwy	Fort Collins	CO	80528	**800-432-1012**	970-226-1234
San Isabel Electric Assn 893 E Enterprise Dr	Pueblo	CO	81002	**800-279-7432**	719-547-2160
San Luis Valley Rural Electric Co-op 3625 US Hwy 160 W	Monte Vista	CO	81144	**800-332-7634**	719-852-3538
San Miguel Power Assn Inc PO Box 817	Nucla	CO	81424	**800-864-7256**	970-864-7311
Sangre de Cristo Electric Assn 2978 N US Hwy 24	Buena Vista	CO	81211	**800-933-3823**	719-395-2412
Southeast Colorado Power Assn 901 W 3rd	La Junta	CO	81050	**800-332-8634**	719-384-2551
United Power Inc PO Box 929	Brighton	CO	80601	**800-468-8809**	303-659-0551
Y-W Electric Assn Inc PO Box Y	Akron	CO	80720	**800-660-2291**	970-345-2291
Yampa Valley Electric Assn Inc PO Box 771218	Steamboat Springs	CO	80477	**888-873-9832**	970-879-1160

Delaware

	City	State	ZIP	Toll-Free	Phone
Delaware Electric Co-op Inc PO Box 600	Greenwood	DE	19950	**800-282-8595**	302-349-4571

Florida

	City	State	ZIP	Toll-Free	Phone
Central Florida Electric Co-op Inc 1124 N Young Blvd	Chiefland	FL	32644	**800-227-1302**	352-493-2511
Choctawhatchee Electric Co-op Inc 1350 W Baldwin Ave	De Funiak Springs	FL	32435	**800-342-0990**	850-892-2111
Clay Electric Co-op Inc 225 W Walker Dr	Keystone Heights	FL	32656	**800-224-4917***	352-473-8000
*Cust Svc					
Escambia River Electric Co-op Inc PO Box 428	Jay	FL	32565	**800-235-3848**	850-675-4521
Florida Keys Electric Co-op Assn 91605 Overseas Hwy PO Box 377	Tavernier	FL	33070	**800-858-8845**	305-852-2431
Glades Electric Co-op Inc PO Box 519	Moore Haven	FL	33471	**800-226-4024**	863-946-0061
Gulf Coast Electric Co-op Inc PO Box 220	Wewahitchka	FL	32465	**800-333-9392**	850-639-2216
Lee County Electric Co-op Inc PO Box 3455	North Fort Myers	FL	33918	**800-282-1643**	239-995-2121
Peace River Electric Co-op Inc 1499 US Hwy 17 N PO Box 1310	Wauchula	FL	33873	**800-282-3824**	863-773-4116
Tri-County Electric Co-op Inc PO Box 208	Madison	FL	32341	**800-999-2285**	850-973-2285
West Florida Electric Co-op PO Box 127	Graceville	FL	32440	**800-342-7400**	850-263-3231

Georgia

	City	State	ZIP	Toll-Free	Phone
Altamaha Electric Membership Corp 611 W Liberty St	Lyons	GA	30436	**800-822-4563**	912-526-8181
Amicalola Electric Membership Corp 544 Hwy 515 S	Jasper	GA	30143	**800-992-6471**	706-253-5200
Blue Ridge Mountain Electric Membership Corp 1360 Main St	Young Harris	GA	30582	**800-292-6456**	706-379-3121
Canoochee Electric Membership Corp 342 E Brazell St	Reidsville	GA	30453	**800-342-0134**	912-557-4391
Central Georgia Electric Membership Corp 923 S Mulberry St	Jackson	GA	30233	**800-222-4877**	770-775-7857
Coastal Electric Co-op 1265 S Coastal Hwy PO Box 109	Midway	GA	31320	**800-421-2343**	912-884-3311
Colquitt Electric Membership Corp 15 Rowland Dr	Moultrie	GA	31768	**800-342-8694**	229-985-3620
Coweta-Fayette Electric Membership Corp 390 N Hwy 29	Newnan	GA	30264	**877-746-4362**	770-253-5626
Diverse Power Inc PO Box 160	LaGrange	GA	30241	**800-845-8362**	706-845-2000
Flint Energies PO Box 308	Reynolds	GA	31076	**800-342-3616**	478-847-3415
Habersham Electric Membership Corp PO Box 25	Clarkesville	GA	30523	**800-640-6812**	706-754-2114
Hart Electric Membership Corp PO Box 250	Hartwell	GA	30643	**800-241-4109**	706-376-4714
Irwin Electric Membership Corp 915 W 4th St	Ocilla	GA	31774	**800-237-3745**	229-468-7415
Jackson Electric Membership Corp PO Box 38	Jefferson	GA	30549	**800-462-3691**	706-367-5281
Jefferson Energy Co-op 3077 Hwy 17 PO Box 457	North Wrens	GA	30833	**800-342-0322**	706-547-2167
Lamar Electric Membership Corp 1367 Hwy 341 S PO Box 40	Barnesville	GA	30204	**877-358-1383**	770-358-1383
Middle Georgia Electric Membership Corp PO Box 190	Vienna	GA	31092	**800-342-0144**	229-268-2671
Mitchell Electric Membership Corp PO Box 409	Camilla	GA	31730	**800-479-6034**	229-336-5221
North Georgia Electric Membership Corp 1850 Cleveland Hwy	Dalton	GA	30722	**800-282-4022**	706-259-9441
Ocmulgee Electric Membership Corp 5722 Eastman St	Eastman	GA	31023	**800-342-5509**	478-374-7001
Oconee Electric Membership Corp 3453 Hwy 80 W	Dudley	GA	31022	**800-522-2930**	478-676-3191
Okefenoke Rural Electric Membership Corp 174 E Cleveland St	Nahunta	GA	31553	**800-262-5131**	912-462-5131
Pataula Electric Membership Corp 925 Barkley St PO Box 289	Cuthbert	GA	31740	**888-631-9757**	229-732-3171
Planters Electric Membership Corp 1740 Hwy 25 N	Millen	GA	30442	**800-324-4722**	478-982-4722
Satilla Rural Electric Membership Corp 101 W 17th St PO Box 906	Alma	GA	31510	**888-738-6926**	912-632-7222
Sawnee Electric Membership Corp 543 Atlantic Hwy	Cumming	GA	30028	**800-635-9131**	770-887-2363
Sumter Electric Membership Corp PO Box 1048	Americus	GA	31709	**800-342-6978**	229-924-8041
Three Notch Electric Membership Corp PO Box 367	Donalsonville	GA	39845	**800-239-5377**	229-524-5377
Tri-County Electric Membership Corp PO Box 487	Gray	GA	31032	**800-342-3812**	478-986-3134
Washington Electric Membership Corp PO Box 598	Sandersville	GA	31082	**800-552-2577**	478-552-2577

Idaho

	City	State	ZIP	Toll-Free	Phone
Clearwater Power Co 4230 Hatwai Rd PO Box 997	Lewiston	ID	83501	**888-743-1501**	208-743-1501
Fall River Rural Electric Co-op Inc 1150 N 3400 East	Ashton	ID	83420	**800-632-5726**	208-652-7431
Idaho County Light & Power Co-op PO Box 300	Grangeville	ID	83530	**877-212-0424**	208-983-1610
Northern Lights Inc 421 Cherry St	Sagle	ID	83860	**800-326-9594**	208-263-5141
Raft River Rural Electric Co-op Inc 155 N Main St PO Box 617	Malta	ID	83342	**800-342-7732**	208-645-2211
Salmon River Electric Co-op Inc 1130 Main St PO Box 384	Challis	ID	83226	**877-806-2283**	208-879-2283

Illinois

	City	State	ZIP	Toll-Free	Phone
Adams Electric Co-op 700 Eastwood St	Camp Point	IL	62320	**800-232-4797**	217-593-7701
Clinton County Electric Co-op Inc 475 N Main St	Breese	IL	62230	**800-526-7282**	618-526-7282
Coles-Moultrie Electric Co-op 104 DeWitt Ave E PO Box 709	Mattoon	IL	61938	**888-661-2632**	217-235-0341
Corn Belt Energy Corp 1 Energy Way	Bloomington	IL	61704	**800-879-0339**	309-662-5330
Eastern Illini Electric Co-op PO Box 96	Paxton	IL	60957	**800-824-5102**	217-379-2131
Egyptian Electric Co-op Assn PO Box 38	Steeleville	IL	62288	**800-606-1505**	618-965-3434
EnerStar Power Corp 11597 Illinois Hwy 1	Paris	IL	61944	**800-635-4145**	217-463-4145
Jo-Carroll Energy PO Box 390	Elizabeth	IL	61028	**800-858-5522**	815-858-2207
Menard Electric Co-op PO Box 200	Petersburg	IL	62675	**800-872-1203**	217-632-7746
MJM Electric Co-op Inc 264 N East St PO Box 80	Carlinville	IL	62626	**800-648-4729**	217-854-3137
Norris Electric Co-op PO Box 6000	Newton	IL	62448	**877-783-8765**	618-783-8765
Rural Electric Convenience Co-op Co 3973 W SR 104 PO Box 19	Auburn	IL	62615	**800-245-7322**	217-438-6197
Shelby Electric Co-op Rt 128 N 6th St PO Box 560	Shelbyville	IL	62565	**800-677-2612**	217-774-3986
SouthEastern Illinois Electric Co-op 585 Hwy 142 S	Eldorado	IL	62930	**800-833-2611**	618-273-2611
Southern Illinois Electric Co-op 7420 US Hwy 51 S	Dongola	IL	62926	**800-762-1400**	618-827-3555
Southwestern Electric Co-op Inc PO Box 549	Greenville	IL	62246	**800-637-8667**	618-664-1025
Spoon River Electric Co-op Inc PO Box 340	Canton	IL	61520	**877-404-2572**	309-647-2700
Tri-County Electric Co-op Inc PO Drawer 309	Mount Vernon	IL	62864	**800-244-5151**	618-244-5151
Wayne-White Counties Electric Co-op PO Drawer E	Fairfield	IL	62837	**888-871-7695**	618-842-2196

Indiana

	City	State	ZIP	Toll-Free	Phone
Bartholomew County Rural Electric Membership Corp 801 2nd St	Columbus	IN	47201	**800-927-5672**	812-372-2546
Boone County Rural Electric Membership Corp 1207 Indianapolis Ave	Lebanon	IN	46052	**800-897-7362**	765-482-2390
Carroll County Rural Electric Membership Corp 119 W Franklin St	Delphi	IN	46923	**800-506-7362**	765-564-2057
Central Indiana Power Corp 2243 Main St	Greenfield	IN	46140	**800-382-5544**	317-477-2200
Clark County Rural Electric Membership Corp 7810 SR 60 PO Box L	Sellersburg	IN	47172	**800-462-6988**	812-246-3316
Daviess-Martin County Rural Electric Membership Corp 12628 E 75 N PO Box 430	Loogootee	IN	47553	**800-762-7362**	812-295-4200
Decatur County Rural Electric Membership Corp 1430 W Main St	Greensburg	IN	47240	**800-844-7362**	812-663-3391
Hendricks Power Co-op PO Box 309	Danville	IN	46122	**800-876-5473**	317-745-5473
Jackson County Rural Electric Membership Corp PO Box K	Brownstown	IN	47220	**800-288-4458**	812-358-4458
Jasper County Rural Electric Membership Corp PO Box 129	Rensselaer	IN	47978	**888-866-7362**	219-866-4601
Jay County Rural Electric Membership Corp PO Box 904	Portland	IN	47371	**800-835-7362**	260-726-7121
Kankakee Valley Rural Electric Membership Corp 114 S Main St	Wanatah	IN	46390	**800-552-2622**	219-733-2511
Kosciusko County Rural Electric Membership Corp PO Box 588	Warsaw	IN	46581	**800-790-7362**	574-267-6331
LaGrange County Rural Electric Membership Corp PO Box 147	LaGrange	IN	46761	**877-463-7165**	260-463-7165
Miami-Cass County Rural Electric Membership Corp PO Box 168	Peru	IN	46970	**800-844-6668**	765-473-6668
Noble Rural Electric Membership Corp PO Box 137	Albion	IN	46701	**800-933-7362**	260-636-2113
Orange County Rural Electric Membership Corp PO Box 208	Orleans	IN	47452	**888-337-5900**	812-865-2229
Parke County Rural Electric Membership Corp 119 W High St	Rockville	IN	47872	**800-537-3913**	765-569-3133
Rush Shelby Energy Inc 1504 S Harrison St	Shelbyville	IN	46176	**800-427-0497**	317-398-6621
South Central Indiana Rural Electric Membership Corp 300 Morton Ave PO Box 3100	Martinsville	IN	46151	**800-264-7362**	765-342-3344
Southeastern Indiana Rural Electric Membership Corp 712 Buckeye St	Osgood	IN	47037	**800-737-4111**	812-689-4111

Indiana (Cont'd)

	City	State	ZIP	Toll-Free	Phone
Southern Indiana Rural Electric Co-op Inc 1776 10th St	Tell City	IN	47586	**800-323-2316**	812-547-2316
Steuben County Rural Electric Membership Corp PO Box 359	Angola	IN	46703	**888-233-9088**	260-665-3563
Tipmont Rural Electric Membership Corp PO Box 20	Linden	IN	47955	**800-726-3953**	765-339-7211
UDWI Rural Electric Membership Corp PO Box 427	Bloomfield	IN	47424	**800-489-7362**	812-384-4446
United Rural Electric Membership Corp PO Box 605	Markle	IN	46770	**800-542-6339**	260-758-3155
Wabash County Rural Electric Membership Corp 350 Wedcor Ave	Wabash	IN	46992	**800-563-2146**	260-563-2146
Warren County Rural Electric Membership Corp 15 Midway St	Williamsport	IN	47993	**800-872-7319**	765-762-6114
White County Rural Electric Membership Corp PO Box 599	Monticello	IN	47960	**800-844-7161**	574-583-7161
Whitewater Valley Rural Electric Membership Corp PO Box 349	Liberty	IN	47353	**800-529-5557**	765-458-5171
WIN Energy Rural Electric Membership Corp PO Box 577	Vincennes	IN	47591	**800-882-5140**	812-882-5140

Iowa

	City	State	ZIP	Toll-Free	Phone
Access Energy Co-op 907 E Washington St	Mount Pleasant	IA	52641	**866-242-4232**	319-385-1577
Butler County Rural Electric Co-op 521 N Main St	Allison	IA	50602	**888-267-2726**	319-267-2726
Clarke Electric Co-op Inc 1103 N Main St	Osceola	IA	50213	**800-362-2154**	641-342-2173
Consumers Energy 2075 Marshalltown Blvd PO Box 1058	Marshalltown	IA	50158	**800-696-6552**	641-752-1593
East-Central Iowa Rural Electric Co-op PO Box 248	Urbana	IA	52345	**877-850-4343**	319-443-4343
Eastern Iowa Light & Power Co-op 600 E 5th St Po Box 3003	Wilton	IA	52778	**800-728-1242**	563-732-2211
Farmers Electric Co-op Inc 1959 Yoder Ave SW	Kalona	IA	52247	**877-426-6540**	319-683-2510
Farmers Rural Electric Co-op Inc 102 SE 6th St	Greenfield	IA	50849	**800-397-4821**	641-743-6146
Franklin Rural Electric Co-op PO Box 437	Hampton	IA	50441	**800-750-3557**	641-456-2557
Glidden Rural Electric Co-op PO Box 486	Glidden	IA	51443	**800-253-6211**	712-659-3649
Grundy County Rural Electric Co-op 102 E 'G' Ave	Grundy Center	IA	50638	**800-390-7605**	319-824-5251
Guthrie County Rural Electric Co-op Assn PO Box 7	Guthrie Center	IA	50115	**888-747-2206**	641-747-2206
Hawkeye REC PO Box 90	Cresco	IA	52136	**800-658-2243**	563-547-3801
Heartland Power Co-op 216 Jackson St PO Box 65	Thompson	IA	50478	**888-584-9732**	641-584-2251
Humboldt County Rural Electric Co-op 1210 13th St N	Humboldt	IA	50548	**800-994-3532**	515-332-1616
Iowa Lakes Electric Co-op 702 S 1st St	Estherville	IA	51334	**800-225-4532**	712-362-7870
Lyon Rural Electric Co-op PO Box 629	Rock Rapids	IA	51246	**800-658-3976**	712-472-2506
Maquoketa Valley Rural Electric Co-op PO Box 370	Anamosa	IA	52205	**800-927-6068**	319-462-3542
Nishnabotna Valley Rural Electric Co-op PO Box 714	Harlan	IA	51537	**800-234-5122**	712-755-2166
North West Rural Electric Co-op 1505 Albany Pl SE	Orange City	IA	51041	**800-383-0476**	712-707-4935
Osceola Electric Co-op Inc 204 8th St	Sibley	IA	51249	**888-754-2519**	712-754-2519
Pella Co-op Electric Assn 2615 Washington St	Pella	IA	50219	**800-619-1040**	641-628-1040
Sac County Rural Electric Co-op 601 E Main St PO Box 397	Sac City	IA	50583	**866-722-6732**	712-662-4275
Southern Iowa Electric Co-op Inc 800 E Franklin St	Bloomfield	IA	52537	**800-607-2027**	641-664-2277
Southwest Iowa Rural Electric Cooperative 626 Davis Ave	Corning	IA	50841	**888-591-1261**	641-322-3165
TIP Rural Electric Co-op PO Box 534	Brooklyn	IA	52211	**800-934-7976**	641-522-9221
Western Iowa Power Co-op PO Box 428	Denison	IA	51442	**800-253-5189**	712-263-2943
Woodbury County Rural Electric Co-op Assn 1495 Humboldt Ave	Moville	IA	51039	**800-469-3125**	712-873-3125

Kansas

	City	State	ZIP	Toll-Free	Phone
Ark Valley Electric Co-op Assn 10 E 10th St	South Hutchinson	KS	67505	**888-297-9212**	620-662-6661
Bluestem Electric Co-op Inc 614 E Hwy 24	Wamego	KS	66547	**800-558-1580**	785-456-2212
Butler Rural Electric Co-op Assn Inc 216 S Vine St	El Dorado	KS	67042	**800-464-0060**	316-321-9600
Caney Valley Electric Co-op Assn 401 Lawrence St	Cedar Vale	KS	67024	**800-310-8911**	620-758-2262
CMS Electric Co-op Inc PO Box 790	Meade	KS	67864	**800-794-2353**	620-873-2184
Doniphan Electric Co-op Assn Inc PO Box 699	Troy	KS	66087	**800-699-0810**	785-985-3523
DS & O Rural Electric Co-op Assn 129 W Main St PO Box 286	Solomon	KS	67480	**800-376-3533**	785-655-2011
Heartland Rural Electric Co-op PO Box 40	Girard	KS	66743	**888-835-9585**	620-724-8251
Kaw Valley Electric Co-op Inc 1100 SW Auburn Rd	Topeka	KS	66615	**800-794-2011**	785-478-3444
Leavenworth-Jefferson Electric Co-op Inc PO Box 70	McLouth	KS	66054	**888-796-6111**	913-796-6111
Lyon-Coffey Electric Co-op Inc PO Box 229	Burlington	KS	66839	**800-748-7395**	620-364-2116
Midwest Energy Inc PO Box 898	Hays	KS	67601	**800-222-3121**	785-625-3437
Nemaha-Marshall Electric Co-op PO Box O	Axtell	KS	66403	**866-736-2347**	785-736-2345
Pioneer Electric Co-op Inc 1850 W Oklahoma St	Ulysses	KS	67880	**800-794-9302**	620-356-1211
Prairie Land Electric Co-op Inc 1101 W Hwy 36	Norton	KS	67654	**800-577-3323**	785-877-3323
Radiant Electric Co-op Inc 100 N 15th St	Fredonia	KS	66736	**800-821-0956**	620-378-2161
Rolling Hills Electric Co 122 W Main St	Mankato	KS	66956	**877-906-5903**	785-378-3151
Sedgwick County Electric Co-op 1355 S 383rd St W PO Box 220	Cheney	KS	67025	**866-542-4732**	316-542-3131
Sumner-Cowley Electric Co-op Inc PO Box 220	Wellington	KS	67152	**888-326-3356**	620-326-3356
Twin Valley Electric Co-op PO Box 385	Altamont	KS	67330	**866-784-5500**	620-784-5500
Victory Electric Co-op Assn Inc PO Box 1335	Dodge City	KS	67801	**800-279-7915**	620-227-2139
Wheatland Electric Co-op Inc PO Box 230	Scott City	KS	67871	**800-762-0436**	620-872-5885

Kentucky

	City	State	ZIP	Toll-Free	Phone
Blue Grass Energy Co-op Corp PO Box 990	Nicholasville	KY	40340	**888-546-4243**	859-885-4191
Clark Energy Co-op Inc 264 Iron Works Rd	Winchester	KY	40392	**800-992-3269**	859-744-4251
Cumberland Valley Electric Inc Cumberland Gap Pkwy PO Box 440	Gray	KY	40734	**800-513-2677**	606-528-2677
Farmers Rural Electric Co-op Corp PO Box 1298	Glasgow	KY	42141	**800-253-2191**	270-651-2191
Fleming Mason Energy Co-op PO Box 328	Flemingsburg	KY	41041	**800-464-3144**	606-845-2661
Inter-County Energy Co-op PO Box 87	Danville	KY	40423	**888-266-7322**	859-236-4561
Jackson Energy Co-op PO Box 307	McKee	KY	40447	**800-262-7480**	606-364-1000
Jackson Purchase Energy Corp 2900 Irvin Cobb Dr	Paducah	KY	42002	**800-633-4044**	270-442-7321
Owen Electric Co-op Inc 510 S Main St PO Box 400	Owenton	KY	40359	**800-372-7612**	502-484-3471
Pennyrile Rural Electric Co-op Corp PO Box 2900 *Cust Svc	Hopkinsville	KY	42241	**800-297-4710***	270-886-2555
Salt River Electric Co-op Corp 111 W Brashear Ave	Bardstown	KY	40004	**800-221-7465**	502-348-3931
Shelby Energy Co-op Inc 620 Old Finchville Rd	Shelbyville	KY	40065	**800-292-6585**	502-633-4420
South Kentucky Rural Electrical Co-op 925 N Main St PO Box 910	Somerset	KY	42502	**800-264-5112**	606-678-4121
West Kentucky Rural Electric Co-op Corp PO Box 589	Mayfield	KY	42066	**877-495-7322**	270-247-1321

Louisiana

	City	State	ZIP	Toll-Free	Phone
Beauregard Electric Co-op Inc 1010 E 1st St	DeRidder	LA	70634	**800-367-0275**	337-463-6221
Claiborne Electric Co-op Inc 12525 Hwy 9	Homer	LA	71040	**800-929-3504**	318-927-3504
Concordia Electric Co-op Inc 1865 Hwy 84 W	Jonesville	LA	71343	**800-617-6282**	318-339-7969
Dixie Electric Membership Corp (DEMCO) PO Box 15659	Baton Rouge	LA	70895	**800-262-0221**	225-261-1221
Jefferson Davis Electric Co-op 906 N Lake Arthur Ave	Jennings	LA	70546	**800-256-5332**	337-824-4330
Pointe Coupee Electric Membership Corp PO Box 160	New Roads	LA	70760	**800-738-7232**	225-638-3751
Southwest Louisiana Electric Membership Corp 3420 Hwy 167 N	Lafayette	LA	70509	**888-275-3626**	337-896-5384

Maine

	City	State	ZIP	Toll-Free	Phone
Eastern Maine Electric Co-op Inc PO Box 425	Calais	ME	04619	**800-696-7444**	207-454-7555

Maryland

	City	State	ZIP	Toll-Free	Phone
Choptank Electric Co-op Inc 24820 Meeting House Rd	Denton	MD	21629	**877-892-0001**	410-479-0380
Southern Maryland Electric Co-op PO Box 1937	Hughesville	MD	20637	**888-440-3311**	301-274-3111

Michigan

	City	State	ZIP	Toll-Free	Phone
Alger Delta Co-op Electric Assn 426 N 9th St	Gladstone	MI	49837	**800-562-0950**	906-428-4141
Cherryland Electric Co-op 5930 US Hwy 31 S	Grawn	MI	49637	**800-442-8616**	231-486-9200
Cloverland Electric Co-op 2916 W Hwy M-28	Dafter	MI	49724	**800-562-4953**	906-635-6800
Great Lakes Energy Co-op 1323 Boyne Ave	Boyne City	MI	49712	**888-485-2537**	
HomeWorks Tri-County Electric Co-op 7973 E Grand River Ave PO Box 350	Portland	MI	48875	**800-848-9333**	517-647-7554
Midwest Energy Co-op PO Box 127	Cassopolis	MI	49031	**800-492-5989**	269-445-1000
Ontonagon County Rural Electric Assn 500 James K Paul St	Ontonagon	MI	49953	**800-562-7128**	906-884-4151
Presque Isle Electric & Gas Co-op PO Box 308	Onaway	MI	49765	**800-423-6634**	989-733-8515

Minnesota

	City	State	ZIP	Toll-Free	Phone
Agralite Electric Co-op 320 E Hwy 12	Benson	MN	56215	**800-950-8375**	320-843-4150
Arrowhead Electric Co-op Inc 5401 W Hwy 61	Lutsen	MN	55612	**800-864-3744**	218-663-7239
Beltrami Electric Co-op Inc 4111 Technology Dr NW	Bemidji	MN	56601	**800-955-6083**	218-444-2540
BENCO Electric Co-op 20946 549 Ave	Mankato	MN	56001	**888-792-3626**	507-387-7963
Brown County Rural Electric Assn PO Box 529	Sleepy Eye	MN	56085	**800-658-2368**	507-794-3331
Clearwater-Polk Electric Co-op 315 N Main Ave PO Box O	Bagley	MN	56621	**888-694-3833**	218-694-6241
Connexus Energy Co-op 14601 Ramsey Blvd	Ramsey	MN	55303	**800-642-1672**	763-323-2600
Crow Wing Co-op Power & Light Co PO Box 507	Brainerd	MN	56401	**800-648-9401**	218-829-2827
Dakota Electric Assn 4300 220th St W	Farmington	MN	55024	**800-874-3409**	651-463-6212
East Central Energy PO Box 39	Braham	MN	55006	**800-254-7944**	
Federated Rural Electric Assn PO Box 69	Jackson	MN	56143	**800-321-3520**	507-847-3520
Goodhue County Co-op Electric Assn PO Box 99	Zumbrota	MN	55992	**800-927-6864**	507-732-5117
Kandiyohi Power Co-op 1311 Hwy 71 NE	Willmar	MN	56201	**800-551-4951**	320-235-4155
Lake Country Power 2810 Elida Dr	Grand Rapids	MN	55744	**800-421-9959**	
Lake Region Co-op Electrical Assn 1401 S Broadway	Pelican Rapids	MN	56572	**800-552-7658**	218-863-1171
Lyon-Lincoln Electric Co-op Inc PO Box 639	Tyler	MN	56178	**800-927-6276**	507-247-5505
McLeod Co-op Power Assn 1231 Ford Ave N	Glencoe	MN	55336	**800-494-6272**	320-864-3148
Meeker Co-op Light & Power Assn PO Box 522	Litchfield	MN	55355	**800-232-6257**	320-693-3231
Mille Lacs Electric Co-op PO Box 230	Aitkin	MN	56431	**800-450-2191**	218-927-2191

	City	State	ZIP	Toll-Free	Phone
Minnesota Valley Co-op Light & Power Assn PO Box 717	Montevideo	MN	56265	**800-247-5051**	320-269-2163
Minnesota Valley Electric Co-op 125 Minnesota Valley Electric Dr	Jordan	MN	55352	**800-282-6832**	952-492-2313
Nobles Co-op Electric PO Box 788	Worthington	MN	56187	**800-776-0517**	507-372-7331
North Itasca Electric Co-op 301 Main Ave	Bigfork	MN	56628	**800-762-4048**	218-743-3131
North Star Electric Co-op Inc 441 State Hwy 172 NW	Baudette	MN	56623	**888-634-2202**	218-634-2202
People's Co-op Services 3935 Hwy 14 PO Box 339	Rochester	MN	55903	**800-214-2694**	507-288-4004
PKM Electric Co-op Inc 406 N Minnesota St	Warren	MN	56762	**800-552-7366**	218-745-4711
Red Lake Electric Co-op Inc 412 International Dr SW PO Box 43	Red Lake Falls	MN	56750	**800-245-6068**	218-253-2168
Redwood Electric Co-op 60 Pine St	Clements	MN	56224	**888-251-5100**	507-692-2214
Renville-Sibley Co-op Power Assn 103 Oak St	Danube	MN	56230	**800-826-2593**	320-826-2593
Roseau Electric Co-op Inc 903 3rd St NE	Roseau	MN	56751	**888-847-8840**	218-463-1543
South Central Electric Assn 71176 Tiell Dr PO Box 150	Saint James	MN	56081	**888-805-7232**	507-375-3164
Stearns Co-op Electric Assn 900 E Kraft Dr	Melrose	MN	56352	**800-962-0655**	320-256-4241
Steele-Waseca Co-op Electric PO Box 485	Owatonna	MN	55060	**800-526-3514**	507-451-7340
Todd-Wadena Electric Co-op PO Box 431	Wadena	MN	56482	**800-321-8932**	218-631-3120
Traverse Electric Co-op Inc PO Box 66	Wheaton	MN	56296	**800-927-5443**	320-563-8616
Tri-County Electric Co-op PO Box 626	Rushford	MN	55971	**800-432-2285**	507-864-7783
Wild Rice Electric Co-op Inc PO Box 438	Mahnomen	MN	56557	**800-244-5709**	218-935-2517
Wright-Hennepin Co-op Electric Assn PO Box 330	Rockford	MN	55373	**800-943-2667**	763-477-3000

Mississippi

	City	State	ZIP	Toll-Free	Phone
Coast Electric Power Assn 302 Hwy 90	Bay Saint Louis	MS	39521	**800-624-3348***	228-467-6535
*Cust Svc					
North East Mississippi Electric Power Assn 10 County Rd 2050	Oxford	MS	38655	**877-234-6331**	662-234-6331
Pearl River Valley Electric Power Assn 1422 Hwy 13 N	Columbia	MS	39429	**800-320-0312**	601-736-2666
Southern Pine Electric Power Assn 110 Risher St	Taylorsville	MS	39168	**800-231-5240**	601-785-6511
Southwest Mississippi Electric Power Assn 18671 Hwy 61	Lorman	MS	39096	**800-287-8564**	601-437-3611

Missouri

	City	State	ZIP	Toll-Free	Phone
Atchison-Holt Electric Co-op 18585 Industrial Rd	Rock Port	MO	64482	**888-744-5366**	660-744-5344
Barry Electric Co-op 4015 Main St PO Box 307	Cassville	MO	65625	**866-847-2333**	417-847-2131
Barton County Electric Co-op 91 W Hwy 160	Lamar	MO	64759	**800-286-5636**	417-682-5636
Black River Electric Co-op 2600 Hwy 67	Fredericktown	MO	63645	**800-392-4711**	573-783-3381
Boone Electric Co-op 1413 Rangeline St	Columbia	MO	65205	**800-225-8143**	573-449-4181
Callaway Electric Co-op 503 Truman Rd	Fulton	MO	65251	**888-642-4840**	573-642-3326
Citizens Electric Corp 150 Merchant St	Sainte Genevieve	MO	63670	**877-876-3511**	573-883-5339
Co-Mo Electric Co-op Inc 29868 Hwy 5	Tipton	MO	65081	**800-781-0157**	660-433-5521
Crawford Electric Co-op Inc 10301 N Service Rd	Bourbon	MO	65441	**800-677-2667**	573-732-4415
Cuivre River Electric Co-op 1112 E Cherry St	Troy	MO	63379	**800-392-3709**	636-528-8261
Farmers' Electric Co-op Inc PO Box 680	Chillicothe	MO	64601	**800-279-0496**	660-646-4281
Grundy Electric Co-op Inc 4100 Oklahoma Ave	Trenton	MO	64683	**800-279-2249**	660-359-3941
Howell-Oregon Electric Co-op Inc PO Box 649	West Plains	MO	65775	**888-463-7693**	417-256-2131
Laclede Electric Co-op PO Box M	Lebanon	MO	65536	**800-299-3164**	417-532-3164
Lewis County Rural Electric Co-op Assn PO Box 68	Lewistown	MO	63452	**888-454-4485**	573-215-4000
Macon Electric Co-op PO Box 157	Macon	MO	63552	**800-553-6901**	660-385-3157
North Central Missouri Electric Co-op Inc 1098 Hwy E PO Box 220	Milan	MO	63556	**800-279-2264**	660-265-4404
Osage Valley Electric Co-op Assn 1321 N Orange	Butler	MO	64730	**800-889-6832**	660-679-3131
Ozark Border Electric Co-op 3281 S Westwood Blvd	Poplar Bluff	MO	63902	**800-392-0567**	573-785-4631
Ozark Electric Co-op N Hwy 39 PO Box 420	Mount Vernon	MO	65712	**800-947-6393**	417-466-2144
Pemiscot-Dunklin Electric Co-op PO Box 657	Hayti	MO	63851	**800-558-6641**	573-757-6641
Platte-Clay Electric Co-op Inc 1000 W Hwy 92 PO Box 100	Kearney	MO	64060	**800-431-2131**	816-628-3121
Ralls County Electric Co-op 17594 Hwy 19	New London	MO	63459	**877-985-8711**	573-985-8711
Sac Osage Electric Co-op Inc 4815 E Hwy 54	El Dorado Springs	MO	64744	**800-876-2701**	417-876-2721
Semo Electric Co-op 505 S Main St	Sikeston	MO	63801	**800-813-5230**	573-471-5821
Tri-County Electric Co-op Assn PO Box 159	Lancaster	MO	63548	**888-457-3734**	660-457-3733
United Electric Co-op Inc PO Box 319	Savannah	MO	64485	**800-748-1488**	816-324-3155
Webster Electric Co-op PO Box 87	Marshfield	MO	65706	**800-643-4305**	417-859-2216
White River Valley Electric Co-op Inc PO Box 969	Branson	MO	65615	**800-879-4056**	417-335-9335

Montana

	City	State	ZIP	Toll-Free	Phone
Beartooth Electric Co-op Inc 1306 N Broadway St	Red Lodge	MT	59068	**800-472-9821**	406-446-2310
Big Flat Electric Co-op Inc 333 S 7th St E	Malta	MT	59538	**800-242-2040**	406-654-2040
Flathead Electric Co-op Inc 2510 Hwy 2 E	Kalispell	MT	59901	**800-735-8489**	406-752-4483
Glacier Electric Co-op Inc PO Box 2090	Cut Bank	MT	59427	**800-347-6795**	406-873-5566
Hill County Electric Co-op Inc PO Box 2330	Havre	MT	59501	**877-394-7804**	406-394-7802
Lincoln Electric Co-op Inc PO Box 628	Eureka	MT	59917	**800-442-2994**	406-889-3301
McCone Electric Co-op Inc PO Box 368	Circle	MT	59215	**800-684-3605**	406-485-3430
Missoula Electric Co-op Inc 1700 W Broadway	Missoula	MT	59808	**800-352-5200**	406-541-4433
Park Electric Co-op Inc 5706 US Hwy 89 S PO Box 1119	Livingston	MT	59047	**888-298-0657**	406-222-3100
Southeast Electric Co-op Inc 110 S Main St	Ekalaka	MT	59324	**888-485-8762**	406-775-8762
Sun River Electric Co-op Inc PO Box 309	Fairfield	MT	59436	**800-452-7516**	406-467-2526
Yellowstone Valley Electric Co-op PO Box 249	Huntley	MT	59037	**800-736-5323**	406-348-3411

Nebraska

	City	State	ZIP	Toll-Free	Phone
Burt County Public Power District 613 N 13th St	Tekamah	NE	68061	**888-835-1620**	402-374-2631
Butler County Rural Public Power District 1331 N 4th St	David City	NE	68632	**800-230-0569**	402-367-3081
Chimney Rock Public Power District 805 W 8th St	Bayard	NE	69334	**877-773-6300**	308-586-1824
Cuming County Public Power District 500 S Main St	West Point	NE	68788	**877-572-2463**	402-372-2463
Custer Public Power District 625 E South 'E' St	Broken Bow	NE	68822	**888-749-2453**	308-872-2451
Dawson Public Power District PO Box 777	Lexington	NE	68850	**800-752-8305**	308-324-2386
Elkhorn Rural Public Power District PO Box 310	Battle Creek	NE	68715	**800-675-2185**	402-675-2185
Howard Greeley Rural Public Power District PO Box 105	Saint Paul	NE	68873	**800-280-4962**	308-754-4457
KBR Rural Public Power District PO Box 187	Ainsworth	NE	69210	**800-672-0009**	402-387-1120
Loup River Public Power District PO Box 988	Columbus	NE	68602	**888-564-3172**	402-564-3171
Loup Valleys Rural Public Power District 606 'S' St	Ord	NE	68862	**888-880-3633**	308-728-3633
McCook Public Power District PO Box 1147	McCook	NE	69001	**800-658-4285**	308-345-2500
Midwest Electric Co-op Corp PO Box 970	Grant	NE	69140	**800-451-3691**	308-352-4356
Norris Public Power District PO Box 399	Beatrice	NE	68310	**800-858-4707**	402-223-4038
North Central Public Power District 1409 Main St	Creighton	NE	68729	**800-578-1060**	402-358-5112
Northeast Nebraska Public Power District 303 Logan St	Wayne	NE	68787	**800-750-9277**	402-375-1360
Northwest Rural Public Power District PO Box 249	Hay Springs	NE	69347	**800-847-0492**	308-638-4445
Perennial Public Power District 2122 S Lincoln Ave	York	NE	68467	**800-289-0288**	402-362-3355
Polk County Rural Public Power District 120 W 4th St	Stromsburg	NE	68666	**888-242-5265**	402-764-4381
South Central Public Power District 275 S Main St	Nelson	NE	68961	**800-557-5254**	402-225-2351
Southern Public Power District PO Box 1687	Grand Island	NE	68802	**800-652-2013**	308-384-2350
Southwest Public Power District 221 N Main St	Palisade	NE	69040	**800-379-7977**	308-285-3295
Stanton County Public Power District PO Box 319	Stanton	NE	68779	**877-439-2300**	402-439-2228
Twin Valleys Public Power District PO Box 160	Cambridge	NE	69022	**800-658-4266**	308-697-3315
Wheat Belt Public Power District PO Box 177	Sidney	NE	69162	**800-261-7114**	308-254-5871

Nevada

	City	State	ZIP	Toll-Free	Phone
Mount Wheeler Power Inc PO Box 15000	Ely	NV	89315	**800-977-6937**	775-289-8981
Overton Power District # 5 615 N Moapa Valley Blvd PO Box 395	Overton	NV	89040	**800-393-2512**	702-397-2512
Valley Electric Assn PO Box 237	Pahrump	NV	89041	**800-742-3330**	775-727-5312

New Hampshire

	City	State	ZIP	Toll-Free	Phone
New Hampshire Electric Co-op 579 Tenney Mountain Hwy	Plymouth	NH	03264	**800-698-2007**	603-536-1800

New Jersey

	City	State	ZIP	Toll-Free	Phone
Sussex Rural Electric Co-op PO Box 346	Sussex	NJ	07461	**877-504-6463**	973-875-5101

New Mexico

	City	State	ZIP	Toll-Free	Phone
Central New Mexico Electric Co-op Inc Hwy 55 PO Box 157	Mountainair	NM	87036	**800-339-2521**	505-847-2521
Columbus Electric Co-op Inc 900 N Gold St	Deming	NM	88031	**800-950-2667**	505-546-8838
Jemez Mountains Electric Co-op PO Box 128	Espanola	NM	87532	**888-755-2105**	505-753-2105
Kit Carson Electric Co-op Inc PO Box 587	Taos	NM	87571	**800-688-6780**	505-758-2258
Lea County Electric Co-op Inc PO Drawer 1447	Lovington	NM	88260	**800-510-5232**	505-396-3631
Otero County Electric Co-op Inc 202 Burro Ave PO Box 227	Cloudcroft	NM	88317	**800-548-4660**	505-682-2521
Socorro Electric Co-op Inc 215 E Manazannez St	Socorro	NM	87801	**800-351-7575**	505-835-0560
Springer Electric Co-op Inc PO Box 698	Springer	NM	87747	**800-288-1353**	505-483-2421

New York

	City	State	ZIP	Toll-Free	Phone
1st Rochdale Co-op Group Ltd 465 Grand St 2nd Fl	New York	NY	10002	**877-624-3253**	212-673-3900
Steuben Rural Electric Co-op Inc 9 Wilson Ave	Bath	NY	14810	**800-843-3414**	607-776-4161

North Carolina

	City	State	ZIP	Toll-Free	Phone
Albemarle Electric Membership Corp 159 Creek Dr	Hertford	NC	27944	**800-215-9915**	252-426-5735

North Carolina (Cont'd)

	City	State	ZIP	Toll-Free	Phone
Blue Ridge Electric Membership Corp 1216 Blowing Rock Blvd NE	Lenoir	NC	28645	**800-451-5474**	828-758-2383
Brunswick Electric Membership Corp 795 Ocean Hwy W	Supply	NC	28462	**800-842-5871**	910-754-4391
Cape Hatteras Electric Co-op 47109 Light Plant Rd	Buxton	NC	27920	**800-454-5616**	252-995-5616
Carteret-Craven Electric Co-op 1300 Hwy 24 W	Newport	NC	28570	**800-682-2217**	252-247-3107
Central Electric Membership Corp 128 Wilson Rd	Sanford	NC	27331	**800-446-7752**	919-774-4900
Edgecombe-Martin County Electric Membership Corp PO Box 188	Tarboro	NC	27886	**800-445-6486**	252-823-2171
EnergyUnited Electric Membership Corp PO Box 1831	Statesville	NC	28687	**800-522-3793**	704-873-5241
Haywood Electric Membership Corp 1560 Asheville Rd	Waynesville	NC	28786	**800-951-6088**	828-452-2281
Jones-Onslow Electric Membership Corp 259 Western Blvd	Jacksonville	NC	28546	**800-682-1515**	910-353-1940
Lumbee River Electric Membership Corp PO Box 830	Red Springs	NC	28377	**800-683-5571**	910-843-4131
Pee Dee Electric Membership Corp PO Box 859	Wadesboro	NC	28170	**800-992-1626**	704-694-2114
Pitt & Greene Electric Membership Corp 3989 W Wilson St	Farmville	NC	27828	**800-622-1362**	252-753-3128
Randolph Electric Membership Corp 879 McDowell Rd	Asheboro	NC	27204	**800-672-8212**	336-625-5177
Roanoke Electric Co-op 401 N Main St	Rich Square	NC	27869	**800-433-2236**	252-539-2236
Rutherford Electric Membership Corp 186 Hudlow Rd PO Box 1569	Forest City	NC	28043	**800-521-0920**	828-245-1621
South River Electric Membership Corp 17494 US 421 S PO Box 931	Dunn	NC	28335	**800-338-5530**	910-892-8071
Surry-Yadkin Electric Membership Corp PO Box 305	Dobson	NC	27017	**800-682-5903**	336-386-8241
Tideland Electric Membership Corp PO Box 159	Pantego	NC	27860	**800-637-1079**	252-943-3046
Union Power Co-op PO Box 5014	Monroe	NC	28111	**800-922-6840**	704-289-3145
Wake Electric Membership Corp 414 E Wait Ave	Wake Forest	NC	27587	**800-474-6300**	919-863-6300

North Dakota

	City	State	ZIP	Toll-Free	Phone
Cass County Electric Co-op Inc 491 Elm St	Kindred	ND	58051	**800-248-3292**	701-356-4400
Dakota Valley Electric Co-op 7296 Hwy 281	Edgeley	ND	58433	**800-342-4671**	701-493-2281
KEM Electric Co-op Inc 107 S Broadway	Linton	ND	58552	**800-472-2673**	701-254-4666
McLean Electric Co-op Inc PO Box 399	Garrison	ND	58540	**800-263-4922**	701-463-2291
Mor-Gran-Sou Electric Co-op Inc PO Box 297	Flasher	ND	58535	**800-750-8212**	701-597-3301
Mountrail-Williams Electric Co-op PO Box 1346	Williston	ND	58802	**800-279-2667**	701-577-3765
Nodak Electric Co-op Inc PO Box 13000	Grand Forks	ND	58208	**800-732-4373**	701-746-4461
Northern Plains Electric Co-op 1515 W Main St	Carrington	ND	58421	**800-882-2500**	701-652-3156
Oliver-Mercer Electric Co-op Inc 800 Highway Dr	Hazen	ND	58545	**800-748-5533**	701-748-2293
Slope Electric Co-op Inc 116 E 12th St	New England	ND	58647	**800-559-4191**	701-579-4191
Verendrye Electric Co-op Inc 615 Hwy 52 W	Velva	ND	58790	**800-472-2141**	701-338-2855
West Plains Electric Co-op Inc PO Box 1038	Dickinson	ND	58602	**800-627-8470**	701-483-5111

Ohio

	City	State	ZIP	Toll-Free	Phone
Adams Rural Electric Co-op Inc 4800 SR 125	West Union	OH	45693	**800-283-1846**	937-544-2305
Buckeye Rural Electric Co-op Inc 4848 SR 325 S	Patriot	OH	45658	**800-231-2732**	740-379-2025
Butler Rural Electric Co-op Inc 3888 Still-Beckett Rd	Oxford	OH	45056	**800-255-2732**	513-867-4400
Carroll Electric Co-op Inc 350 Canton Rd NW	Carrollton	OH	44615	**800-232-7697**	330-627-2116
Consolidated Electric Co-op Inc 5255 SR 95	Mount Gilead	OH	43338	**800-421-5863**	419-947-3055
Darke Rural Electric Co-op Inc 1120 Fort Jefferson Rd	Greenville	OH	45331	**800-776-5612**	937-548-4114
Firelands Electric Co-op Inc 1 Energy Pl PO Box 32	New London	OH	44851	**800-533-8658**	419-929-1571
Frontier Power Co PO Box 280	Coshocton	OH	43812	**800-624-8050**	740-622-6755
Hancock-Wood Electric Co-op Inc PO Box 190	North Baltimore	OH	45872	**800-445-4840**	419-257-3241
Holmes-Wayne Electric Co-op Inc PO Box 112	Millersburg	OH	44654	**877-520-1055**	330-674-1055
Licking Rural Electrification Inc PO Box 4970	Newark	OH	43058	**800-255-6815**	740-892-2791
Lorain-Medina Rural Electric Co-op Inc PO Box 158	Wellington	OH	44090	**800-222-5673**	440-647-2133
Mid Ohio Energy Co-op Inc PO Box 224	Kenton	OH	43326	**888-382-6732**	419-673-7289
Midwest Electric Inc PO Box 10	Saint Marys	OH	45885	**800-962-3830**	419-394-4110
North Central Electric Co-op Inc PO Box 475	Attica	OH	44807	**800-426-3072**	419-426-3072
North Western Electric Co-op Inc 04125 SR 576	Bryan	OH	43506	**800-647-6932**	419-636-5051
Paulding-Putman Electric Co-op 910 N Williams St	Paulding	OH	45879	**800-686-2357**	419-399-5015
Pioneer Rural Electric Co-op Inc 344 W US Rt 36 PO Box 604	Piqua	OH	45356	**800-762-0997**	937-773-2523
South Central Power Co Inc 2780 Coon Path Rd	Lancaster	OH	43130	**800-282-5064**	740-653-4422
Union Rural Electric Co-op Inc 15461 US 36E	Marysville	OH	43040	**800-642-1826**	937-642-1826
Washington Electric Co-op Inc PO Box 664	Marietta	OH	45750	**877-594-9324**	740-373-2141

Oklahoma

	City	State	ZIP	Toll-Free	Phone
Alfalfa Electric Co-op Inc 121 E Main St	Cherokee	OK	73728	**888-736-3837**	580-596-3333
Central Rural Electric Co-op 3304 S Boomer Rd	Stillwater	OK	74074	**800-375-2884**	405-372-2884
Choctaw Electric Co-op Inc Hwy 93 N PO Box 758	Hugo	OK	74743	**800-780-6486**	580-326-6486
Cimarron Electric Co-op Hwy 81 N PO Box 299	Kingfisher	OK	73750	**800-375-4121**	405-375-4121
Cookson Hills Electric Co-op Inc 1002 E Main St	Stigler	OK	74462	**800-328-2368**	918-967-4614
Cotton Electric Co-op Inc 226 N Broadway	Walters	OK	73572	**800-522-3520**	580-875-3351
East Central Oklahoma Electric Co-op Inc PO Box 1178	Okmulgee	OK	74447	**800-783-9317**	918-756-0833
Harmon Electric Assn Inc PO Box 393	Hollis	OK	73550	**800-643-7769**	580-688-3342
Indian Electric Co-op Inc PO Box 49	Cleveland	OK	74020	**800-482-2750**	918-358-2514
Kay Electric Co-op PO Box 607	Blackwell	OK	74631	**800-535-1079**	580-363-1260
Kiamichi Electric Co-op Inc PO Box 340	Wilburton	OK	74578	**800-888-2731**	918-465-2338
Kiwash Electric Co-op Inc PO Box 100	Cordell	OK	73632	**888-832-3362**	580-832-3361
Northeast Oklahoma Electric Co-op Inc 443857 E Hwy 60 PO Box 948	Vinita	OK	74301	**800-256-6405**	918-256-6405
Northwestern Electric Co-op Inc 2925 William Ave	Woodward	OK	73802	**800-375-7423**	580-256-7425
People's Electric Co-op 1130 W Main St	Ada	OK	74821	**877-455-3031**	580-332-3031
Red River Valley Rural Electric Assn 1003 Memorial Dr	Marietta	OK	73448	**800-749-3364**	580-276-3364
Rural Electric Co-op Inc PO Box 609	Lindsay	OK	73052	**800-259-3504**	405-756-3104
Southwest Rural Electric Assn 700 N Broadway	Tipton	OK	73570	**800-256-7973**	580-667-5281
Tri-County Electric Co-op Inc 302 E Glaydas St PO Box 880	Hooker	OK	73945	**800-522-3315**	580-652-2418
Verdigris Valley Electric Co-op PO Box 219	Collinsville	OK	74021	**800-870-5948**	918-371-2584

Oregon

	City	State	ZIP	Toll-Free	Phone
Blachly-Lane Electric Co-op 90680 Hwy 99	Eugene	OR	97402	**800-446-8418**	541-688-8711
Consumers Power Inc 6990 W Hills Rd	Philomath	OR	97370	**800-872-9036**	541-929-3124
Douglas Electric Co-op Inc PO Box 1327	Roseburg	OR	97470	**800-233-2733**	541-673-6616
Midstate Electric Co-op Inc PO Box 127	La Pine	OR	97739	**800-722-7219**	541-536-2126
Tillamook People's Utility District PO Box 433	Tillamook	OR	97141	**800-422-2535**	503-842-2535
West Oregon Electric Co-op Inc PO Box 69	Vernonia	OR	97064	**800-777-1276**	503-429-3021

Pennsylvania

	City	State	ZIP	Toll-Free	Phone
Adams Electric Co-op Inc 1338 Biglerville Rd	Gettysburg	PA	17325	**888-232-6732**	717-334-9211
Bedford Rural Electric Co-op Inc 8846 Lincoln Hwy	Bedford	PA	15522	**800-808-2732**	814-623-5101
Claverack Rural Electric Co-op Inc RR 2 Box 17	Wysox	PA	18854	**800-326-9799**	570-265-2167
New Enterprise Rural Electric Co-op Inc PO Box 75	New Enterprise	PA	16664	**800-270-3177**	814-766-3221
Northwestern Rural Electric Co-op Assn Inc PO Box 207	Cambridge Springs	PA	16403	**800-472-7910**	
REA Energy Co-op Inc 75 Airport Rd	Indiana	PA	15701	**800-211-5667**	724-349-4800
Somerset Rural Electric Co-op Inc 223 Industrial Pk Rd PO Box 270	Somerset	PA	15501	**800-443-4255**	814-445-4106
Sullivan County Rural Electric Co-op Inc PO Box 65	Forksville	PA	18616	**800-570-5081**	570-924-3381
Tri-County Rural Electric Co-op Inc PO Box 526	Mansfield	PA	16933	**800-343-2559**	570-662-2175
United Electric Co-op Inc PO Box 688	Du Bois	PA	15801	**888-581-8969**	814-371-8570
Valley Rural Electric Co-op Inc PO Box 477	Huntingdon	PA	16652	**800-432-0680**	814-643-2650
Warren Electric Co-op Inc 320 E Main St	Youngsville	PA	16371	**800-364-8640**	814-563-7548

South Carolina

	City	State	ZIP	Toll-Free	Phone
Aiken Electric Co-op Inc 2790 Wagener Rd	Aiken	SC	29802	**800-922-1262**	803-649-6245
Blue Ridge Electric Co-op Inc 734 W Main St	Pickens	SC	29671	**800-240-3400**	864-878-6326
Broad River Electric Co-op Inc 811 Hamrick St	Gaffney	SC	29342	**866-687-2667**	864-489-5737
Coastal Electric Co-op Inc 2269 Jefferies Hwy	Walterboro	SC	29488	**877-538-5700**	843-538-5700
Edisto Electric Co-op Inc PO Box 547	Bamberg	SC	29003	**800-433-3292**	803-245-5141
Laurens Electric Co-op Inc PO Box 700	Laurens	SC	29360	**800-942-3141**	864-682-3141
Little River Electric Co-op Inc PO Box 220	Abbeville	SC	29620	**800-459-2141**	864-366-2141
Lynches River Electric Co-op Inc PO Box 308	Pageland	SC	29728	**800-922-3486**	843-672-6111
Marlboro Electric Co-op Inc PO Box 1057	Bennettsville	SC	29512	**800-922-9174**	843-479-3855
Mid-Carolina Electric Co-op Inc PO Box 669 *Cust Svc	Lexington	SC	29071	**888-813-8000***	803-749-6555
Newberry Electric Co-op Inc PO Box 477	Newberry	SC	29108	**800-479-8838**	803-276-1121
Palmetto Electric Co-op 4063 Grays Hwy PO Box 820	Ridgeland	SC	29936	**800-922-5551**	843-726-5551
Santee Electric Co-op Inc 424 Sumter Hwy	Kingstree	SC	29556	**800-922-1604**	843-355-6187
Tri-County Electric Co-op Inc PO Box 217	Saint Matthews	SC	29135	**877-874-1215**	803-874-1215
York Electric Co-op Inc PO Box 150	York	SC	29745	**800-582-8810**	803-684-4247

South Dakota

	City	State	ZIP	Toll-Free	Phone
Black Hills Electric Co-op Inc 25197 Cooperative Way	Custer	SD	57730	**800-742-0085**	605-673-4461
Butte Electric Co-op Inc 109 S Dartmouth Ave	Newell	SD	57760	**800-928-8839**	605-456-2494
Central Electric Co-op 1420 N Main St	Mitchell	SD	57301	**800-477-2892**	605-996-7516
Charles Mix Electric Assn Inc 440 Lake St	Lake Andes	SD	57356	**800-208-8587**	605-487-7321
Cherry-Todd Electric Co-op Inc Hwy 18 PO Box 169	Mission	SD	57555	**800-856-4417**	605-856-4416
Clay-Union Electric Corp 1410 E Cherry St	Vermillion	SD	57069	**800-696-2832**	605-624-2673
Codington-Clark Electric Co-op 3 8th Ave	Watertown	SD	57201	**800-463-8938**	605-886-5848
Dakota Energy Co-op Inc 40294 US Hwy 14 PO Box 830	Huron	SD	57350	**800-353-8591**	605-352-8591
Grand Electric Co-op Inc PO Box 39	Bison	SD	57620	**800-592-1803**	605-244-5211
Lacreek Electric Assn Inc PO Box 220	Martin	SD	57551	**800-655-9324**	605-685-6581
Lake Region Electric Assn Inc PO Box 341	Webster	SD	57274	**800-657-5869**	605-345-3379
McCook Electric Co-op Inc PO Box 250	Salem	SD	57058	**800-942-3113**	605-425-2661

	City	State	ZIP	Toll-Free	Phone
Northern Electric Co-op Inc 39456 133nd St	Bath	SD	57427	**800-529-0310**	605-225-0310
Oahe Electric Co-op Inc 102 S Cranford St PO Box 216	Blunt	SD	57522	**800-640-6243**	605-962-6243
Sioux Valley-Southwestern Electric Co-op Inc 47092 SD Hwy 34	Colman	SD	57017	**800-234-1960**	605-534-3535
Southeastern Electric Co-op Inc 501 S Broadway Ave	Marion	SD	57043	**800-333-2859**	605-648-3619
West River Electric Assn Inc PO Box 412	Wall	SD	57790	**888-279-2135**	
Whetstone Valley Electric Co-op PO Box 512	Milbank	SD	57252	**800-568-6631**	605-432-5331

Tennessee

	City	State	ZIP	Toll-Free	Phone
Caney Fork Electric Co-op Inc 920 Smithville Hwy	McMinnville	TN	37111	**888-505-3030**	931-473-3116
Chickasaw Electric Co-op 17970 Hwy 64 PO Box 459	Somerville	TN	38068	**866-465-3591**	901-465-3591
Fayetteville Electric System 408 W College St	Fayetteville	TN	37334	**800-379-2534**	931-433-1522
La Follette Utilities Board PO Box 1411	La Follette	TN	37766	**800-352-1340**	423-562-3316
Mountain Electric Co-op Inc PO Box 180	Mountain City	TN	37683	**888-721-9111**	423-727-1800
Pickwick Electric Co-op 530 Mulberry Ave	Selmer	TN	38375	**800-372-8258**	731-645-3411
Sequachee Valley Electric Co-op 512 Cedar Ave PO Box 31	South Pittsburg	TN	37380	**800-923-2203**	423-837-8605
Southwest Tennessee Electric Membership Corp PO Box 989	Brownsville	TN	38012	**800-772-0472**	731-772-1322
Tennessee Valley Electric Co-op 515 Florence Rd	Savannah	TN	38372	**866-925-4916**	731-925-4916
Tri-County Electric Membership Corp PO Box 40	Lafayette	TN	37083	**800-369-2111**	615-666-2111
Upper Cumberland Electric Membership Corp 138 Gordonsville Hwy	South Carthage	TN	37030	**800-261-2940**	615-735-2940

Texas

	City	State	ZIP	Toll-Free	Phone
Bailey County Electric Co-op Inc 305 East Ave B	Muleshoe	TX	79347	**800-869-7049**	806-272-4504
Bandera Electric Co-op Inc 3172 State Hwy 16 N	Bandera	TX	78003	**866-226-3372**	830-796-3741
Big Country Electric Co-op 1010 W South 1st St	Roby	TX	79543	**888-662-2232**	325-776-2244
Bluebonnet Electric Co-op Inc 426 E Austin St	Giddings	TX	78942	**800-842-7708**	979-542-3151
Bowie-Cass Electric Co-op Inc 117 North St	Douglassville	TX	75560	**800-794-2919**	903-846-2311
Central Texas Electric Co-op Inc 386 Friendship Ln	Fredericksburg	TX	78624	**800-900-2832**	830-997-2126
Coleman County Electric Co-op Inc 3300 N Hwy 84	Coleman	TX	76834	**800-560-2128**	325-625-2128
Comanche Electric Co-op Assn PO Box 729	Comanche	TX	76442	**800-915-2533**	325-356-2533
Cooke County Electric Co-op Assn 11799 W US Hwy 82 PO Box 530	Muenster	TX	76252	**800-962-0296**	940-759-2211
CoServ Electric 7701 S Stemmons Fwy	Corinth	TX	76210	**800-274-4014**	940-321-4640
Deaf Smith Electric Co-op Inc PO Box 753	Hereford	TX	79045	**800-687-8189**	806-364-1166
Deep East Texas Electric Co-op Inc PO Box 736	San Augustine	TX	75972	**800-392-5986**	936-275-2314
Fannin County Electric Co-op Inc PO Drawer 250	Bonham	TX	75418	**800-695-9020**	903-583-2117
Farmers Electric Co-op Inc PO Box 6037	Greenville	TX	75403	**800-541-2662**	903-455-1715
Fayette Electric Co-op Inc PO Box 490	La Grange	TX	78945	**800-874-8290**	979-968-3181
Grayson-Collin Electric Co-op Inc PO Box 548	Van Alstyne	TX	75495	**800-967-5235**	903-482-7100
Greenbelt Electric Co-op Inc PO Box 948	Wellington	TX	79095	**800-527-3082**	806-447-2536
Guadalupe Valley Electric Co-op Inc PO Box 118	Gonzales	TX	78629	**800-223-4832**	830-857-1200
Hamilton County Electric Co-op Assn PO Box 753	Hamilton	TX	76531	**800-595-3401**	254-386-3123
Hilco Electric Co-op Inc PO Box 127	Itasca	TX	76055	**800-338-6425**	254-687-2331
Houston County Electric Co-op Inc PO Box 52	Crockett	TX	75835	**800-657-2445**	936-544-5641
Jasper-Newton Electric Co-op Inc 812 S Margaret Ave	Kirbyville	TX	75956	**800-231-9340**	409-423-2241
Karnes Electric Co-op Inc PO Box 7	Karnes City	TX	78118	**888-807-3952**	830-780-3952
Lamar County Electric Co-op Assn 1485 N Main St	Paris	TX	75460	**800-782-9010**	903-784-4303
Lighthouse Electric Co-op Inc PO Box 600	Floydada	TX	79235	**800-657-7192**	806-983-2814
Magic Valley Electric Co-op Inc PO Box 267	Mercedes	TX	78570	**800-880-6832**	866-225-5683
McLennan County Electric Co-op PO Box 357	McGregor	TX	76657	**800-840-2957**	254-840-2871
Medina Electric Co-op Inc PO Box 370	Hondo	TX	78861	**800-381-3334**	830-741-4384
Mid-South Electric Co-op Assn PO Box 970	Navasota	TX	77868	**888-525-6677**	936-825-5100
Navarro County Electric Co-op Inc PO Drawer 616	Corsicana	TX	75151	**800-771-9095**	903-874-7411
North Plains Electric Co-op Inc 14585 Hwy 83 N	Perryton	TX	79070	**800-272-5482**	806-435-5482
Nueces Electric Co-op 709 E Main St	Robstown	TX	78380	**800-632-9288**	361-387-2581
Panola-Harrison Electric Co-op 410 E Houston St	Marshall	TX	75670	**800-972-1093**	903-935-7936
Pedernales Electric Co-op Inc 300 Haley Rd	Johnson City	TX	78636	**888-554-4732**	830-868-7155
Rio Grande Electric Co-op Inc Hwy 90 & State Hwy 131 PO Box 1509	Brackettville	TX	78832	**800-749-1509**	830-563-2444
Rita Blanca Electric Co-op Inc PO Box 1947	Dalhart	TX	79022	**800-299-4506**	806-249-4506
Sam Houston Electric Co-op Inc 150 E Church St PO Box 1121	Livingston	TX	77351	**800-458-0381**	936-327-5711
San Bernard Electric Co-op Inc 309 W Main St	Bellville	TX	77418	**800-364-3171**	979-865-3171
San Patricio Electric Co-op Inc 402 E Sinton St	Sinton	TX	78387	**888-740-2220**	361-364-2220
South Plains Electric Co-op Inc 4727 S Loop 289 Suite 200	Lubbock	TX	79408	**800-658-2655**	806-775-7732
Southwest Texas Electric Co-op Inc 101 E Gillis St	Eldorado	TX	76936	**800-643-3980**	325-853-2544
Swisher Electric Co-op Inc 401 SW 2nd St	Tulia	TX	79088	**800-530-4344**	806-995-3567
Taylor Electric Co-op Inc PO Box 250	Merkel	TX	79536	**800-992-0086**	325-928-4715
Tri-County Electric Co-op Inc 600 Northwest Pkwy	Azle	TX	76020	**800-367-8232**	817-444-3201
Trinity Valley Electric Co-op Inc PO Box 888	Kaufman	TX	75142	**800-766-9576**	972-932-2214
Wharton County Electric Co-op Inc PO Box 31	El Campo	TX	77437	**800-460-6271**	979-543-6271
Wise Electric Co-op Inc PO Box 269	Decatur	TX	76234	**888-627-9326**	940-627-2167
Wood County Electric Co-op Inc PO Box 1827	Quitman	TX	75783	**800-762-2203**	903-763-2203

Utah

	City	State	ZIP	Toll-Free	Phone
GarKane Energy Inc PO Box 465	Loa	UT	84747	**800-747-5403**	435-836-2795

Vermont

	City	State	ZIP	Toll-Free	Phone
Vermont Electric Co-op Inc 182 School St	Johnson	VT	05656	**800-832-2667**	802-635-2331
Washington Electric Co-op Inc PO Box 8	East Montpelier	VT	05651	**800-932-5245**	802-223-5245

Virginia

	City	State	ZIP	Toll-Free	Phone
BARC Electric Co-op 100 High St	Millboro	VA	24460	**800-846-2272**	540-997-9124
Central Virginia Electric Co-op 800 Cooperative Way	Lovingston	VA	22949	**800-367-2832**	434-263-8336
Craig-Botetourt Electric Co-op PO Box 265	New Castle	VA	24127	**800-760-2232**	540-864-5121
Mecklenburg Electric Co-op PO Box 2451	Chase City	VA	23924	**800-989-4161**	434-372-6100
Northern Neck Electric Co-op Inc 85 Saint Johns St PO Box 288	Warsaw	VA	22572	**800-243-2860**	804-333-3621
Northern Virginia Electric Co-op PO Box 2710	Manassas	VA	22110	**888-335-0500**	703-335-0500
Rappahannock Electric Co-op 247 Industrial Ct	Fredericksburg	VA	22408	**800-552-3904**	540-898-8500
Shenandoah Valley Electric Co-op PO Box 236	Mount Crawford	VA	22841	**800-234-7832**	540-434-2200
Southside Electric Co-op Inc 2000 W Virgina Ave	Crewe	VA	23930	**800-552-2118**	434-645-7721

Washington

	City	State	ZIP	Toll-Free	Phone
Benton Rural Electric Assn 402 7th	Prosser	WA	99350	**800-221-6987**	509-786-2913
Columbia Rural Electric Assn Inc 115 E Main St	Dayton	WA	99328	**800-642-1231**	509-382-2578
Inland Power & Light Co Inc PO Box 4429	Spokane	WA	99220	**800-747-7151**	509-747-7151
Peninsula Light Co PO Box 78	Gig Harbor	WA	98335	**888-809-8021**	253-857-5950
Tanner Electric Co PO Box 1426	North Bend	WA	98045	**800-472-0208**	425-888-0623

West Virginia

	City	State	ZIP	Toll-Free	Phone
Harrison Rural Electrification Assn Inc Rt 6 Box 502	Clarksburg	WV	26301	**800-540-4732**	304-624-6365

Wisconsin

	City	State	ZIP	Toll-Free	Phone
Adams-Columbia Electric Co-op 401 E Lake St	Friendship	WI	53934	**800-831-8629**	608-339-3346
Barron Electric Co-op 1456 E LaSalle Ave	Barron	WI	54812	**800-322-1008**	715-537-3171
Chippewa Valley Electric Co-op 317 S 8th St	Cornell	WI	54732	**800-300-6800**	715-239-6800
Clark Electric Co-op 124 N Main St PO Box 190	Greenwood	WI	54437	**800-272-6188**	715-267-6188
Dunn Energy Co-op PO Box 220	Menomonie	WI	54751	**800-924-0630**	715-232-6240
Eau Claire Electric Co-op PO Box 368	Fall Creek	WI	54742	**800-927-5090**	715-832-1603
Jackson Electric Co-op PO Box 546	Black River Falls	WI	54615	**800-370-4607**	715-284-5385
Oakdale Electric Co-op 489 N Oakwood St	Oakdale	WI	54660	**800-241-2468**	608-372-4131
Oconto Electric Co-op 7478 Rea Rd PO Box 168	Oconto Falls	WI	54154	**800-472-8410**	920-846-2816
Pierce-Pepin Electric Co-op 7725 US Hwy 10	Ellsworth	WI	54011	**800-924-2133**	715-273-4355
Polk-Burnett Electric Co-op 1001 SR 35	Centuria	WI	54824	**800-421-0283**	715-646-2191
Price Electric Co-op Inc 508 N Lake Ave	Phillips	WI	54555	**800-884-0881**	715-339-2155
Riverland Energy Co-op 625 W Main St	Arcadia	WI	54612	**800-411-9115**	608-323-3381
Rock County Electric Co-op Assn 2815 Kennedy Rd	Janesville	WI	53547	**888-236-0665**	608-752-4550
Saint Croix Electric Co-op 1925 Ridgeway St	Hammond	WI	54015	**800-924-3407**	715-796-7000
Scenic Rivers Energy Co-op 231 N Sheridan St	Lancaster	WI	53813	**800-236-2141**	608-723-2121
Vernon Electric Co-op 110 N Main St	Westby	WI	54667	**800-447-5051**	608-634-3121

Wyoming

	City	State	ZIP	Toll-Free	Phone
Big Horn Rural Electric Co-op 208 S 5th St	Basin	WY	82410	**800-564-2419**	307-568-2419
Bridger Valley Electric Assn Inc 40014 Business Loop 1-80	Mountain View	WY	82939	**800-276-3481**	307-786-2800
Carbon Power & Light Inc 110 E Spring St	Saratoga	WY	82331	**800-359-0249**	307-326-5206
High Plains Power Inc PO Box 713	Riverton	WY	82501	**800-445-0613**	307-856-9426
High West Energy Inc PO Box 519	Pine Bluffs	WY	82082	**888-834-1657**	307-245-3261
Lower Valley Energy PO Box 188	Afton	WY	83110	**800-882-5875**	307-885-3175
Niobrara Electric Assn Inc PO Box 697	Lusk	WY	82225	**800-322-0544**	307-334-3221
Powder River Energy Corp 221 Main St	Sundance	WY	82729	**800-442-3630**	307-283-3531
Wheatland Rural Electric Assn 2154 South Rd	Wheatland	WY	82201	**800-344-3351**	307-322-2125
Wyrulec Co PO Box 359	Lingle	WY	82223	**800-628-5266**	307-837-2225

245 ELECTRICAL & ELECTRONIC EQUIPMENT & PARTS - WHOL

Company	City	State	ZIP	Toll-Free	Phone
ACF Components & Fasteners Inc					
31012 Huntwood Ave	Hayward	CA	94544	**800-227-2901***	510-487-2100
*Cust Svc					
ACI Electronics Inc 125 Michael Dr Suite 105	Syosset	NY	11791	**800-645-4955**	516-730-8182
Advanced MP Technology					
1010 Calle Sombra	San Clemente	CA	92673	**800-492-3113**	949-492-3113
AE Petsche Co Inc 2112 W Division St	Arlington	TX	76012	**800-777-9280**	817-461-9473
AF Comm Supply 8238 Neiman Rd	Lenexa	KS	66214	**800-255-6222**	913-492-6212
Airtechnics Inc 3851 N Webb Rd	Wichita	KS	67226	**800-544-4070**	316-315-1200
All American Semiconductor Inc					
16115 NW 52nd Ave	Miami	FL	33014	**800-762-2095**	305-621-8282
NASDAQ: SEMI					
ALLTEL Communications Products Inc					
13560 Morris Rd 1 ALLTEL Ctr	Alpharetta	GA	30004	**800-501-1754**	678-351-4000
America II Corp Inc					
2600 118th Ave N	Saint Petersburg	FL	33716	**800-767-2637**	727-573-0900
America II Electronics Inc					
2600 118th Ave N	Saint Petersburg	FL	33716	**800-767-2637**	727-573-0900
American Electric Supply Inc					
1872 W Pomona Rd	Corona	CA	92880	**800-877-8346**	951-734-7910
American Light 4401 Westgate Blvd Suite 310	Austin	TX	78745	**800-854-6465**	512-440-7985
American Technology Corp					
13114 Evening Creek Dr S	San Diego	CA	92128	**800-417-2346**	858-679-2114
NASDAQ: ATCO					
Anixter International Inc 2301 Patriot Blvd	Glenview	IL	60025	**800-264-9837**	224-521-8000
NYSE: AXE					
Argo International Corp 140 Franklin St	New York	NY	10013	**877-274-6468**	212-431-1700
Arrow Electronics Inc 25 Hub Dr	Melville	NY	11747	**800-777-2776***	516-391-1300
NYSE: ARW ■ *Sales					
Astrex Inc 205 Express St	Plainview	NY	11803	**800-633-6360**	516-433-1700
Avnet Inc 2211 S 47th St	Phoenix	AZ	85034	**888-822-8638**	480-643-2000
NYSE: AVT					
Barnett Inc 3333 Lenox Ave	Jacksonville	FL	32254	**800-288-2000**	904-384-6530
Bearcom Inc 4009 Distribution Dr Suite 200	Garland	TX	75041	**800-527-1670***	214-340-8876
*Sales					
Becker Electric Supply Inc 1341 E 4th St	Dayton	OH	45402	**800-762-9515**	937-226-1341
Bell Microproducts Inc 1941 Ringwood Ave	San Jose	CA	95131	**800-800-1513**	408-451-9400
NASDAQ: BELM					
Blackburn Don & Co Inc 13335 Farmington Rd	Livonia	MI	48150	**800-448-0528**	734-261-9100
Boggis-Johnson Electric Co					
2900 N 112th St PO Box 26068	Milwaukee	WI	53226	**800-333-7650**	414-475-6900
Border States Electric Supply 105 25th St N	Fargo	ND	58102	**800-676-5833**	701-293-5834
Braid Electric Co Inc 299 Cowan St	Nashville	TN	37213	**800-342-1115**	615-242-6511
Brightpoint Inc 501 Airtech Pkwy	Plainfield	IN	46168	**800-952-2355**	317-707-2355
NASDAQ: CELL					
Brightstar Corp 2010 NW 84th Ave	Miami	FL	33122	**800-381-8402**	305-477-8676
Broken Arrow Electric Supply Inc					
2350 W Vancouver	Broken Arrow	OK	74012	**877-999-2237**	918-258-3581
Buckles-Smith 801 Savaker Ave	San Jose	CA	95126	**800-833-7362**	408-280-7777
Cabletel Communications Corp					
55 Valleywood Dr	Markham	ON	L3R5L9	**800-268-3231**	905-475-1030
Cain Electrical Supply Corp					
204 Johnson St PO Box 2158	Big Spring	TX	79721	**800-749-8421**	432-263-8421
Cardello Electric Supply Co 701 N Point Dr	Pittsburgh	PA	15233	**800-333-0454**	412-322-8031
Carlton Bates Co 3600 W 69th St	Little Rock	AR	72209	**800-482-9313**	501-562-9100
Cell-Tel Government Systems Inc					
8226 Phillips Hwy Suite 290	Jacksonville	FL	32256	**800-737-7545**	904-363-1111
CellStar Corp 1730 Briercroft Ct	Carrollton	TX	75006	**800-723-9070**	972-466-5000
NASDAQ: CLST					
Cellular & Wireless Wholesale Corp					
8240 NW 30th Terr	Miami	FL	33122	**888-918-4299**	305-436-8999
Central Wholesale Electrical Distributors Inc					
1183-A Quarry Ln PO Box 1210	Pleasanton	CA	94566	**800-834-8122**	925-417-6930
Century Fasteners Corp 50-20 Ireland St	Elmhurst	NY	11373	**800-221-0769**	718-446-5000
City Lighting Products Co					
4307 W Papin St	Saint Louis	MO	63109	**800-888-2572**	314-534-1090
Clifford of Vermont 1453 VT Route 107	Royalton	VT	05068	**800-451-4381**	802-234-9921
CLS Inc 270 Locust St	Hartford	CT	06114	**800-842-8078**	860-549-1230
Codale Electric Supply Inc					
3150 S 900 West	Salt Lake City	UT	84119	**800-300-6634**	801-975-7300
Coghlin Electric/Electronics					
PO Box 5100	Westborough	MA	01581	**800-343-1201**	508-870-5000
Communications Supply Corp					
200 E Lies Rd	Carol Stream	IL	60188	**800-468-2121**	630-221-6400
Computer Components Corp DBA Universal					
Battery 1702 Hayden Dr	Carrollton	TX	75006	**800-749-0222**	972-387-0850
Corporate Telephone 56 Roland St	Boston	MA	02129	**800-274-1211**	617-625-1200
Cross Automation Inc 2001 Oak Pkwy	Belmont	NC	28012	**800-866-4568**	704-523-2222
Crum Electric Supply Co 1165 English Ave	Casper	WY	82601	**800-726-2239**	307-266-1278
Dakota Supply Group 2601 3rd Ave N	Fargo	ND	58102	**800-437-4702**	701-237-9440
Dalis HL Inc 35-35 24th St	Long Island City	NY	11106	**800-453-2547**	718-361-1100
Dee Electronics Inc 2500 16th Ave SW	Cedar Rapids	IA	52404	**800-747-3331**	319-365-7551
Dependable Component Supply Corp					
1003 E Newport Ctr Dr	Deerfield Beach	FL	33442	**800-336-7100**	954-283-5800
Desco Inc 1205 Lincolnton Rd	Salisbury	NC	28145	**800-222-2140**	704-633-6331
Digi-Key Corp 701 Brooks Ave S	Thief River Falls	MN	56701	**800-344-4539**	218-681-6674
Dominion Electric Supply Co Inc					
5053 Lee Hwy	Arlington	VA	22207	**800-525-5006**	703-536-4400
Don Blackburn & Co Inc 13335 Farmington Rd	Livonia	MI	48150	**800-448-0528**	734-261-9100
Dow Electronics Inc 8603 Adamo Dr	Tampa	FL	33619	**800-627-2900**	813-626-5195
E Sam Jones Distributor Inc					
4898 S Atlanta Rd	Smyrna	GA	30080	**800-624-9849**	404-351-3250
Eagle Electric Supply Co Inc 135 Will Dr	Canton	MA	02021	**800-462-5010**	781-302-2000
EIS Inc 13200 10th Ave N Suite E	Plymouth	MN	55441	**800-328-4662**	763-513-7300
Electric Fixture & Supply Co 1006 N 20th St	Omaha	NE	68102	**800-642-9312**	402-342-3050
Electric Supply & Equipment Co					
1812 E Wendover Ave	Greensboro	NC	27405	**800-632-0268**	336-272-4123
Electric Supply of Tampa Inc					
4407 N Manhattan Ave	Tampa	FL	33614	**800-678-1894**	813-872-1894
Electro-Matic Products Inc					
23409 Industrial Park Ct	Farmington Hills	MI	48335	**888-879-1088**	248-478-1182
Elliott Electric Supply Co					
2526 N Stallings Dr	Nacogdoches	TX	75964	**877-777-0242**	936-569-1184
Englewood Electrical Supply					
716 Belvedere Dr	Kokomo	IN	46901	**800-589-8886**	765-452-4087
Eoff Electric Co Inc 1095 25th St SE Suite A	Salem	OR	97301	**877-371-3633**	503-371-3633
Equity Utility Service Co Inc 1060-D Triad Ct	Marietta	GA	30062	**800-282-9695**	770-422-1005
Eric Electronics 2220 Lundy Ave	San Jose	CA	95131	**800-406-3742**	408-432-1111
ESCO LLC 2 S Point Dr	Lake Forest	CA	92630	**800-622-3726**	949-330-3602
Essex Brownell Inc 84 Executive Ave	Edison	NJ	08817	**800-228-8026**	732-287-3355
Facility Solutions Group					
4401 Westgate Blvd Suite 310	Austin	TX	78704	**800-854-6465**	
Farmstead Telephone Group Inc					
22 Prestige Park Cir	East Hartford	CT	06108	**800-243-0234**	860-282-0010
AMEX: FTG					
FD Lawrence Electric Co Inc					
3450 Beekman St	Cincinnati	OH	45223	**800-582-4490***	513-542-1100
*Cust Svc					
Fiber Instruments Sales Inc 161 Clear Rd	Oriskany	NY	13424	**800-500-0347***	315-736-2206
*Sales					
Fidelitone Inc 1260 Karl Ct	Wauconda	IL	60084	**800-342-2112***	847-487-3300
*Cust Svc					
Fitzpatrick Electric Supply Co					
444 Irwin Ave	Muskegon	MI	49442	**800-968-6621**	231-722-6621
Friedman Electric Supply 1321 Wyoming Ave	Exeter	PA	18643	**800-545-5517**	570-654-3371
Fromm Electric Supply Corp					
2101 Centre Ave PO Box 15147	Reading	PA	19612	**800-360-4441**	610-374-4441
Future Electronics 237 Hymus Blvd	Pointe-Claire	QC	H9R5C7	**800-388-8731**	514-694-7710
Grainger WW Inc 100 Grainger Pkwy	Lake Forest	IL	60045	**888-361-8649**	847-535-1000
NYSE: GWW					
Graybar Electric Co Inc					
34 N Meramec Ave	Saint Louis	MO	63105	**800-472-9227**	314-573-9200
H Poll Electric Co 8 N Saint Clair St	Toledo	OH	43697	**800-518-0106**	419-255-1660
Hagemeyer North America					
12117 Insurance Way	Hagerstown	MD	21740	**800-638-3552**	301-733-1212
Hammond Electronics Inc					
1230 W Central Blvd	Orlando	FL	32805	**800-929-3672***	407-849-6060
*Sales					
Hardware Specialty Co Inc					
4875 36th St	Long Island City	NY	11101	**800-800-9269**	718-361-9393
Harris Electric Supply Co Inc					
656 Wedgewood Ave	Nashville	TN	37203	**800-342-1479**	615-255-4161
Hartford Electric Supply Co (HESCO)					
571 New Park Ave PO Box 331010	West Hartford	CT	06133	**800-969-5444**	860-236-6363
Heilind Electronics Inc 58 Jonspin Rd	Wilmington	MA	01887	**800-400-7041**	978-657-4870
HESCO (Hartford Electric Supply Co)					
571 New Park Ave PO Box 331010	West Hartford	CT	06133	**800-969-5444**	860-236-6363
HL Dalis Inc 35-35 24th St	Long Island City	NY	11106	**800-453-2547**	718-361-1100
Horizon Solutions Corp 4 Access Rd	Albany	NY	12205	**800-345-4621**	518-452-6904
Houston Wire & Cable Co 10201 N Loop E	Houston	TX	77029	**800-468-9473**	713-609-2100
Hutton Communications Inc 2520 Marsh Ln	Carrollton	TX	75006	**800-435-9313**	972-417-0250
IBS Electronics Inc					
3506 Lake Center Dr Unit D	Santa Ana	CA	92704	**800-527-2888**	714-751-6633
ICS Telecom Inc 125 Highpower Rd	Rochester	NY	14623	**800-836-8677**	585-427-7000
IMS Inc 340 Progress Dr	Manchester	CT	06040	**800-666-1626**	860-649-4415
Industrial Electric Wire & Cable Inc					
5001 S Towne Dr	New Berlin	WI	53151	**800-344-2323**	262-782-2323
InfoSonics Corp 5880 Pacific Center Blvd	San Diego	CA	92121	**800-519-1599**	858-373-1600
AMEX: IFO					
Integrated Electronics Corp 420 E 58th Ave	Denver	CO	80216	**800-876-8686**	303-292-5537
Interstate Electrical Supply Inc					
2300 2nd Ave	Columbus	GA	31901	**800-903-4409**	706-324-1000
Irby Stuart C Co 815 S State St PO Box 1819	Jackson	MS	39215	**800-844-1811**	601-969-1811
Jaco Electronics Inc 145 Oser Ave	Hauppauge	NY	11788	**800-966-5226**	631-273-5500
NASDAQ: JACO					
Jasco Products Inc 311 NW 122nd St	Oklahoma City	OK	73114	**800-654-8483**	405-752-0710
JH Larson Co 10200 51st Ave N	Plymouth	MN	55442	**800-292-7970**	763-545-1717
Kendall Electric Inc 131 Grand Trunk Ave	Battle Creek	MI	49015	**800-632-5422**	269-963-5585
Kendall Industrial Supplies Inc					
4560 W Dickman Rd	Battle Creek	MI	49015	**800-632-9606**	269-965-2211
King Wire Inc 2500 Commonwealth Ave	North Chicago	IL	60064	**800-453-5464**	847-688-1100
Larson JH Co 10200 51st Ave N	Plymouth	MN	55442	**800-292-7970**	763-545-1717
Lawrence FD Electric Co Inc					
3450 Beekman St	Cincinnati	OH	45223	**800-582-4490***	513-542-1100
*Cust Svc					
Leff H Electric Co Inc 1163 E 40th St	Cleveland	OH	44114	**800-686-5333**	216-432-3000
Loeb Electric Co 915 Williams Ave	Columbus	OH	43212	**800-837-2852**	614-294-6351
Loyd's Electric Supply Inc 117 E College St	Branson	MO	65616	**800-492-4030**	417-334-2171
Major Electric Supply Inc 123 High St	Pawtucket	RI	02860	**800-444-1660**	401-724-7100
Maltby Electric Supply Co Inc					
336 7th St	San Francisco	CA	94103	**800-339-0668**	415-863-5000
Marcone Appliance Parts Inc					
2300 Clark Ave	Saint Louis	MO	63103	**800-325-7588**	314-231-7141
Mars Electric Co 38868 Mentor Ave	Willoughby	OH	44094	**800-288-6277**	440-946-2250
Marsh Electronics Inc 1563 S 101st St	Milwaukee	WI	53214	**800-558-1238***	414-475-6000
*Cust Svc					
Master Distributors Inc					
1220 Olympic Blvd	Santa Monica	CA	90404	**800-421-8153**	310-452-1229
Mayer Electric Supply Co Inc 3405 4th Ave S	Birmingham	AL	35222	**800-444-8524**	205-583-3500
McNaughton-McKay Electric Co Inc					
1357 E Lincoln Ave	Madison Heights	MI	48071	**800-527-5033**	248-399-7500
Memec Inc 3721 Valley Centre Dr	San Diego	CA	92130	**888-882-2444**	858-314-8800
Mercedes Electric Supply Inc					
8550 NW South River Dr	Miami	FL	33166	**800-636-5550**	305-887-5550
Mid-Island Electrical Supply 59 Mall Dr	Commack	NY	11725	**877-324-2636**	631-864-4242
Minnesota Electric Supply Co Inc 1209 E Hwy 12	Willmar	MN	56201	**800-992-8830**	320-235-2255
Mouser Electronics Corp 1000 N Main St	Mansfield	TX	76063	**800-346-6873**	817-804-3888
Nedco Electronics 594 American Way	Payson	UT	84651	**800-605-2323**	801-465-1790
Nelson Electric Supply Co Inc 926 State St	Racine	WI	53404	**800-994-5666**	262-637-7661
Newark In One 4801 N Ravenswood Ave	Chicago	IL	60640	**800-463-9275**	
NF Smith & Assoc LP 5306 Hollister Rd	Houston	TX	77040	**800-468-7866**	713-430-3000
Noland Co 80 29th St	Newport News	VA	23607	**800-446-8960**	757-928-9000
NASDAQ: NOLD					
Northern Video Systems Inc					
4465 Granite Dr Suite 700	Rocklin	CA	95677	**800-366-4472**	916-630-4700
Northwest Controls 188 Fox Run Dr	Defiance	OH	43512	**800-888-6932**	419-782-9479
Norvell Electronics Inc PO Box 701027	Dallas	TX	75370	**800-477-0021**	972-858-3713
Nu Horizons Electronics Corp 70 Maxess Rd	Melville	NY	11747	**888-747-6846**	631-396-5000
NASDAQ: NUHC					
Nu-Lite Electrical Wholesalers					
850 Edwards Ave	Harahan	LA	70123	**800-256-1603**	504-733-3300
Omni Cable Corp 905 Airport Rd Suite C	West Chester	PA	19380	**800-292-6664**	610-701-0100
OneSource Distributors Inc 3951 Oceanic Dr	Oceanside	CA	92056	**800-521-5092**	760-966-4500
Paige Electric Corp 1160 Springfield Rd	Union	NJ	07083	**800-327-2443**	908-687-7810
Peerless Electronics Inc 19 Wilbur St	Lynbrook	NY	11563	**800-285-2121**	516-594-3500
PEI-Genesis 2180 Hornig Rd	Philadelphia	PA	19116	**800-523-0727**	215-673-0400
Petsche AE Co Inc 2112 W Division St	Arlington	TX	76012	**800-777-9280**	817-461-9473
Pill Ralph Electrical Supply Co					
307 Dorchester Ave	Boston	MA	02127	**800-879-7455**	617-269-8200
Platt Electric Supply 10605 SW Allen Blvd	Beaverton	OR	97005	**800-257-5288**	503-641-6121
PNS Inc 581 Dado St	San Jose	CA	95131	**800-537-4767**	408-944-0500

Classified Section

Company / Address	City	State	ZIP	Toll-Free	Phone
Powell Electronics Inc 4848 S Island Ave	Philadelphia	PA	19153	**800-235-7880**	215-365-1900
Power & Telephone Supply Co Inc 2673 Yale Ave *Cust Svc	Memphis	TN	38112	**800-238-7514***	901-324-6116
Priority Wire & Cable Inc 8200 E Roosevelt Rd	North Little Rock	AR	72206	**800-945-5542**	501-372-5444
Professional Electric Products Co 33210 Lakeland Blvd	Eastlake	OH	44095	**800-872-7000**	440-946-3790
Projections Unlimited Inc 14831 Myford Rd	Tustin	CA	92780	**800-551-4405**	714-544-2700
QED Inc 1661 W 3rd Ave	Denver	CO	80223	**800-700-5011**	303-825-5011
Ralph Pill Electrical Supply Co 307 Dorchester Ave	Boston	MA	02127	**800-879-7455**	617-269-8200
Rawson & Co Inc PO Box 924288	Houston	TX	77292	**800-779-1414**	713-684-1400
Regency Lighting Co 16665 Arminta St	Van Nuys	CA	91406	**800-284-2024**	818-901-0255
Reily Electric Supply Inc 3011 Lausat St	Metairie	LA	70001	**800-662-1906**	504-835-8888
Rexel Ryall Electrical Supplies 2627 W 6th Ave	Denver	CO	80204	**800-759-2728**	303-629-7721
Reynolds Co 140-B Regal Row	Dallas	TX	75247	**800-851-0304**	214-630-9000
RF Monolithics Inc 4441 Sigma Rd *NASDAQ: RFMI*	Dallas	TX	75244	**800-704-6079**	972-233-2903
Richardson Electronics Ltd 40 W 267 Keslinger Rd PO Box 393 *NASDAQ: RELL* ■ *Sales	LaFox	IL	60147	**800-348-5580***	630-208-2200
Rockingham Electrical Supply Co Inc 187 River Rd	Newington	NH	03801	**800-727-2310**	603-436-2310
Roden Electrical Supply Co 170 Mabry Hood Rd	Knoxville	TN	37922	**800-532-8742**	865-546-8755
Rohm Electronics USA LLC 10145 Pacific Heights Blvd Suite 1000	San Diego	CA	92121	**800-955-7646**	858-625-3600
RS Electronics Inc 34443 Schoolcraft Rd	Livonia	MI	48150	**800-366-7750**	734-525-1155
Rumsey Electric Co 15 Colwell Ln	Conshohocken	PA	19428	**800-462-2402**	610-832-9000
Sager Electronics Inc 97 Libbey Industrial Pkwy	Weymouth	MA	02189	**800-541-9371**	781-682-4844
Schaedler Yesco Distribution Inc 951 S 13th St	Harrisburg	PA	17104	**800-998-1621**	717-233-1621
Schuster Electronics Inc 11320 Grooms Rd	Cincinnati	OH	45242	**800-877-6875**	513-489-1400
Scott Electric 1000 S Main St PO Box S	Greensburg	PA	15601	**800-442-8045**	724-834-4321
SED International Inc 4916 N Royal Atlanta Dr *Sales	Tucker	GA	30084	**800-444-8962***	770-491-8962
Sennheiser Electronics Corp 1 Enterprise Dr	Old Lyme	CT	06371	**877-736-6434**	860-434-9190
Shepherd Electric Supply 7401 Pulaski Hwy *Sales	Baltimore	MD	21237	**800-253-1777***	410-866-6000
Smith NF & Assoc LP 5306 Hollister Rd	Houston	TX	77040	**800-468-7866**	713-430-3000
Somera Communications Inc 5383 Hollister Ave Suite 100 *NASDAQ: SMRA*	Santa Barbara	CA	93111	**800-761-1206**	805-681-3322
Sommer Electric Corp 818 3rd St NE	Canton	OH	44704	**800-766-6373**	330-455-9454
Springfield Electric Supply Co 700 N 9th St	Springfield	IL	62708	**800-757-2101**	217-788-2100
Sprint North Supply Co Inc 600 New Century Pkwy	New Century	KS	66031	**800-755-3004**	913-791-7000
Standard Electric Co 2650 Trautner Dr PO Box 5289	Saginaw	MI	48603	**800-322-0215**	989-497-2100
Stanion Wholesale Electric Co 812 S Main St PO Box F	Pratt	KS	67124	**800-880-2008**	620-672-5678
State Electric Supply Co Inc 2010 2nd Ave *Cust Svc	Huntington	WV	25703	**800-624-3417***	304-523-7491
Steiner Electric Co Inc 1250 Touhy Ave	Elk Grove Village	IL	60007	**800-783-4637**	847-228-0400
Steven Engineering Inc 230 Ryan Way	South San Francisco	CA	94080	**800-258-9200**	650-588-9200
Stokes Electric Co Inc 1701 McCalla Ave	Knoxville	TN	37915	**800-999-0351**	865-525-0351
Stoneway Electric Supply Co 402 N Perry St	Spokane	WA	99202	**800-841-1408**	509-535-2933
Stuart C Irby Co 815 S State St PO Box 1819	Jackson	MS	39215	**800-844-1811**	601-969-1811
Summit Electric Supply Co 2900 Stanford NE	Albuquerque	NM	87107	**800-824-4400**	505-884-4400
Surface Mount Distribution Inc 1 Oldfield	Irvine	CA	92618	**800-229-7634**	949-470-7700
Taitron Components Inc 28040 W Harrison Pkwy *NASDAQ: TAIT*	Valencia	CA	91355	**800-247-2232**	661-257-6060
Tecot Electric Supply Co 55 Lukens Dr	New Castle	DE	19720	**800-344-9905**	302-421-3900
Teleco Inc 430 Woodruff Rd Suite 300	Greenville	SC	29607	**800-800-6159**	864-297-4400
Terry-Durin Co 409 7th Ave SE	Cedar Rapids	IA	52401	**800-332-8114**	319-364-4106
TESSCO Technologies Inc 11126 McCormick Rd *NASDAQ: TESS*	Hunt Valley	MD	21031	**800-472-7373**	410-229-1000
Thalner Electronics Laboratory Inc 7235 Jackson Rd	Ann Arbor	MI	48103	**800-686-7235**	734-761-4506
Tri-State Utility Products Inc 1030 Atlanta Industrial Dr	Marietta	GA	30065	**800-282-7985**	770-427-3119
TTI Inc 2441 Northeast Pkwy *Sales	Fort Worth	TX	76106	**800-845-5119***	817-740-9000
United Utility Supply Co-op Inc 4515 Bishop Ln	Louisville	KY	40218	**800-357-5232**	502-459-4011
Universal Battery 1702 Hayden Dr	Carrollton	TX	75006	**800-749-0222**	972-387-0850
Van Meter Industrial Inc 240 33rd Ave SW	Cedar Rapids	IA	52404	**800-332-8468**	319-366-5301
Viking Electric Supply Inc 451 Industrial Blvd W	Minneapolis	MN	55413	**800-435-3345**	612-627-1300
Voss Lighting 1601 Cushman Dr	Lincoln	NE	68512	**800-828-8677**	402-328-2281
Wabash Electric Supply Inc 1400 S Wabash St	Wabash	IN	46992	**800-552-7777**	260-563-4146
Walker Component Group 420 E 58th Ave	Denver	CO	80216	**800-876-8686**	303-292-5537
Washington Cable Supply Inc 4600-D Boston Way	Lanham	MD	20706	**800-888-0738**	301-577-1200
Werner Electric Supply Co 2341 Industrial Dr	Neenah	WI	54956	**800-236-5026**	920-729-4500
Wes-Garde Components Group Inc 190 Elliott St	Hartford	CT	06114	**800-275-7089**	860-525-6907
Western Extralite Co 1470 Liberty St	Kansas City	MO	64102	**800-279-8833**	816-421-8404
Whitehill Lighting & Supplies Inc 1524 N Atherton St	State College	PA	16803	**800-326-9940**	814-238-2449
Whitlock Group 3900 Gaskins Rd	Richmond	VA	23233	**800-726-9843**	804-273-9100
Wholesale Electric Supply Co LP 4040 Guls Fwy PO Box 230197	Houston	TX	77223	**800-486-8563**	713-748-6100
Wholesale Electric Supply Inc 1400 Waterall St	Texarkana	TX	75501	**800-869-8672**	903-794-3404
Williams Supply Inc 210 7th St	Roanoke	VA	24016	**800-533-6969**	540-343-9333
Wolff Bros Supply Inc 6078 Wolff Rd	Medina	OH	44256	**800-879-6533**	330-725-3451
WW Grainger Inc 100 Grainger Pkwy *NYSE: GWW*	Lake Forest	IL	60045	**888-361-8649**	847-535-1000
XP ForeSight Co 990 Benicia Ave	Sunnyvale	CA	94085	**800-276-9378**	408-732-7777
Zack Electronics Inc 1070 Hamilton Rd	Duarte	CA	91010	**800-466-0449**	626-303-0655

246 ELECTRICAL EQUIPMENT FOR INTERNAL COMBUSTION ENGINES

SEE ALSO Automotive Parts & Supplies - Mfr; Motors (Electric) & Generators

Company / Address	City	State	ZIP	Toll-Free	Phone
CE Niehoff & Co 2021 Lee St *Tech Supp	Evanston	IL	60202	**800-643-4633***	847-866-6030
Delco Remy International Inc 2902 Enterprise Dr	Anderson	IN	46013	**800-372-5131**	765-778-6499
Edge Products 1080 S Depot Dr	Ogden	UT	84404	**888-360-3343**	801-476-3343
Ennis Automotive Inc 2400 N Preston St	Ennis	TX	75120	**800-624-8813**	972-878-3896
Fisher Electric Technology 2801 72nd St N	Saint Petersburg	FL	33710	**800-789-2347**	727-345-9122
Goodall Mfg Co 7558 Washington Ave S	Eden Prairie	MN	55344	**800-328-7730**	952-941-6666
KEM Mfg Co 18-35 River Rd	Fair Lawn	NJ	07410	**800-289-5362**	201-796-8000
Motor Appliance Corp 555 Spirit of St Louis Blvd	Chesterfield	MO	63005	**800-622-3406**	636-532-3406
Niehoff CE & Co 2021 Lee St *Tech Supp	Evanston	IL	60202	**800-643-4633***	847-866-6030
Precision Parts & Remanufacturing Co 4411 SW 19th St	Oklahoma City	OK	73108	**800-654-3846**	405-681-2592
Prestolite Electric Inc 2311 Green Rd Suite B *Cust Svc	Ann Arbor	MI	48105	**800-354-0560***	734-913-6600
Prestolite Wire Corp 200 Galleria Officentre Suite 212	Southfield	MI	48034	**800-498-3132**	248-355-4422
Sure Power Industries Inc 10189 SW Avery St *Tech Supp	Tualatin	OR	97062	**800-845-6269***	503-692-5360
Transpo Electronics Inc 2150 Brengle Ave	Orlando	FL	32808	**800-327-7792**	407-298-4563
Van Bergen & Greener Inc 1818 Madison St	Maywood	IL	60153	**800-621-3889**	708-343-4700

247 ELECTRICAL SIGNALS MEASURING & TESTING INSTRUMENTS

Company / Address	City	State	ZIP	Toll-Free	Phone
Acterna Corp 1 Milestone Center Dr	Germantown	MD	20876	**800-543-1550**	301-353-1550
Actron Mfg Co 15825 Industrial Pkwy	Cleveland	OH	44135	**800-228-7667**	216-898-9200
Advanced Measurement Technology 801 S Illinois Ave	Oak Ridge	TN	37831	**800-251-9750**	865-482-4411
Advanced Test Products Inc 3270 Executive Way	Miramar	FL	33025	**800-327-5060**	954-499-5400
Aetrium Inc 2350 Helen St *NASDAQ: ATRM*	North Saint Paul	MN	55109	**800-274-3500**	651-770-2000
Agilent Technologies Inc 395 Page Mill Rd *NYSE: A*	Palo Alto	CA	94306	**877-424-4536**	650-752-5000
AMETEK Inc Dixson Div 287 27 Rd	Grand Junction	CO	81503	**888-302-0639**	970-244-1241
Analog Devices Inc 1 Technology Way PO Box 9106 *NYSE: ADI*	Norwood	MA	02062	**800-262-5643**	781-329-4700
Associated Equipment Corp 5043 Farlan Ave	Saint Louis	MO	63115	**800-949-1472**	314-385-5178
Avtron Mfg Inc 7900 E Pleasant Valley Rd	Independence	OH	44131	**800-922-9751**	216-641-8310
B & K Corp 5675 Dixie Hwy	Saginaw	MI	48601	**800-977-3775**	989-777-2111
Bird Electronic Corp 30303 Aurora Rd	Solon	OH	44139	**866-695-4569**	440-248-1200
Bruel & Kjaer Instruments Inc 2815-A Colonnades Ct	Norcross	GA	30071	**800-241-9188**	770-209-6907
Cascade Microtech Inc 2430 NW 206th Ave	Beaverton	OR	97006	**800-550-3279**	503-601-1000
Chatsworth Data Corp 20710 Lassen St	Chatsworth	CA	91311	**800-423-5217**	818-341-9200
Communications Mfg Co 2234 Colby Ave	Los Angeles	CA	90064	**800-462-5532**	310-828-3200
Credence Systems Corp 1421 California Cir *NASDAQ: CMOS*	Milpitas	CA	95035	**800-328-7045**	408-635-4300
CXR Telcom Corp 894 Faulstich Ct	San Jose	CA	95112	**800-537-5762**	510-657-8810
CyberOptics Corp 5900 Golden Hills Dr *NASDAQ: CYBE* ■ *Cust Svc	Minneapolis	MN	55416	**800-746-6315***	763-542-5000
Data Control Systems 213 Perry Pkwy	Gaithersburg	MD	20877	**800-296-3333**	301-590-3300
Delta Design Inc 12367 Crosthwaite Cir	Poway	CA	92064	**800-776-0697**	858-848-8000
DIT-MCO International Corp 5612 Brighton Terr	Kansas City	MO	64130	**800-821-2168**	816-444-9700
Dixson Div AMETEK Inc 287 27 Rd	Grand Junction	CO	81503	**888-302-0639**	970-244-1241
Dranetz-BMI 1000 New Durham Rd	Edison	NJ	08818	**800-372-6832**	732-287-3680
EXFO Electro-Optical Engineering Inc 400 Godin Ave *NASDAQ: EXFO*	Vanier	QC	G1M2K2	**800-663-3936**	418-683-0211
Fluke Biomedical 2000 Arrowhead Dr	Carson City	NV	89706	**800-648-7952**	775-883-3400
Fluke Corp 6920 Seaway Blvd	Everett	WA	98203	**800-753-5853**	425-446-6100
Giga-Tronics Inc 4650 Norris Canyon Rd *NASDAQ: GIGA*	San Ramon	CA	94583	**800-726-4442**	925-328-4650
Hickok Inc 10514 Dupont Ave *NASDAQ: HICKA*	Cleveland	OH	44108	**800-342-5080**	216-541-8060
Hipotronics Inc 1650 Rt 22	Brewster	NY	10509	**800-727-4476**	845-279-8091
Hughes Corp Weschler Instruments Div 16900 Foltz Pkwy	Cleveland	OH	44149	**800-557-0064**	440-238-2550
ILX Lightwave Corp 31950 E Frontage Rd	Bozeman	MT	59715	**800-459-9459**	406-586-1244
Itron Inc 2818 N Sullivan Rd *NASDAQ: ITRI*	Spokane	WA	99216	**800-635-5461**	509-924-9900
Ixia 26601 W Agoura Rd *NASDAQ: XXIA*	Calabasas	CA	91302	**877-367-4942**	818-871-1800
Keithley Instruments Inc 28775 Aurora Rd *AMEX: KEI*	Cleveland	OH	44139	**800-552-1115**	440-248-0400
Knopp Inc 1307 66th St	Emeryville	CA	94608	**800-227-1848**	510-653-1661
LDS Test & Measurement LLC 8333 Rockside Rd *Sales	Valley View	OH	44125	**800-468-5365***	216-328-7000
LeCroy Corp 700 Chestnut Ridge Rd *NASDAQ: LCRY*	Chestnut Ridge	NY	10977	**800-553-2769**	845-425-2000
LTX Corp 50 Rosemont Rd *NASDAQ: LTXX*	Westwood	MA	02090	**800-451-2500**	781-461-1000
Mantas Inc 13650 Dulles Technology Dr	Herndon	VA	20171	**866-462-6827**	703-673-0577
Megger 4271 Bronze Way	Dallas	TX	75237	**800-723-2861**	214-333-3201
Micro Networks Corp 324 Clark St	Worcester	MA	01606	**800-544-0052**	508-852-5400
Micromanipulator Co Inc 1555 Forrest Way *Cust Svc	Carson City	NV	89706	**800-654-5659***	775-882-7377

				Toll-Free	Phone
Monroe Electronics Inc 100 Housel Ave	Lyndonville	NY	14098	**800-821-6001**	585-765-2254
National Instruments Corp 11500 N Mopac Expy	Austin	TX	78759	**800-433-3488***	512-794-0100
NASDAQ: NATI ■ *Cust Svc					
NetTest North America Inc 6 Rhoads Dr	Utica	NY	13502	**800-443-6154**	315-266-5000
Newport Electronics Inc 2229 S Yale St	Santa Ana	CA	92704	**800-639-7678***	714-540-4914
*Cust Svc					
PerkinElmer Instruments Inc 710 Bridgeport Ave	Shelton	CT	06484	**800-762-4000**	203-925-4600
Power Measurement Ltd 2195 Keating Cross Rd	Saanichton	BC	V8M2A5	**866-466-7627**	250-652-7100
Quest Technologies Inc 1060 Corporate Center Dr	Oconomowoc	WI	53066	**800-245-0779**	262-567-9101
Racal Instruments Inc 4 Goodyear	Irvine	CA	92618	**800-722-3262***	949-859-8999
*Cust Svc					
Radiodetection Corp RR 2 Box 756	Bridgton	ME	04009	**800-524-1739**	207-647-3185
Sencore Inc 3200 Sencore Dr	Sioux Falls	SD	57107	**800-736-2673***	605-339-0100
*Cust Svc					
Snap-on Diagnostics 420 Barclay Blvd	Lincolnshire	IL	60069	**800-967-8030**	847-478-0700
Spirent Communications 15200 Omega Dr	Rockville	MD	20850	**800-385-0110**	301-590-3600
TEGAM Inc 10 Tegam Way	Geneva	OH	44041	**800-666-1010**	440-466-6100
Tektronix Inc 14200 SW Karl Braun Dr PO Box 500	Beaverton	OR	97077	**800-833-9200**	503-627-7111
NYSE: TEK					
Tempo Research Corp 1390 Aspen Way	Vista	CA	92083	**888-860-8535**	760-598-8900
Texmate Inc 995 Park Ctr Dr	Vista	CA	92081	**800-839-6283**	760-598-9899
Therma-Wave Inc 1250 Reliance Way	Fremont	CA	94539	**800-238-4376**	510-668-2200
NASDAQ: TWAV					
Trek Inc 11601 Maple Ridge Rd	Medina	NY	14103	**800-367-8735**	585-798-3140
Trilithic Inc 9710 Park Davis Dr	Indianapolis	IN	46235	**800-344-2412**	317-895-3600
Triplett Corp 1 Triplett Dr	Bluffton	OH	45817	**800-874-7538**	419-358-5015
Tyco Electronics Corp Corcom Div 844 E Rockland Rd	Libertyville	IL	60048	**800-643-8391**	847-680-7400
Weschler Instruments Div Hughes Corp 16900 Foltz Pkwy	Cleveland	OH	44149	**800-557-0064**	440-238-2550
Yokogawa Corp of America 2 Dart Rd	Newnan	GA	30265	**800-258-2552**	770-253-7000
Zetec Inc 1370 NW Mall St	Issaquah	WA	98027	**800-643-1771**	425-392-5316

248 ELECTRICAL SUPPLIES - PORCELAIN

				Toll-Free	Phone
Ceramaseal Div CeramTec North America 1033 US Rt 20	New Lebanon	NY	12125	**800-752-7325**	518-794-7800
CeramTec North America PO Box 89 1 Technology Pl	Laurens	SC	29360	**800-845-9761**	864-682-3215
CeramTec North America Ceramaseal Div 1033 US Rt 20	New Lebanon	NY	12125	**800-752-7325**	518-794-7800
CeramTec North America Electronic Applications Inc 1 Technology Pl PO Box 89	Laurens	SC	29360	**800-845-9761**	864-682-3215
CoorsTek Inc 16000 Table Mountain Pkwy	Golden	CO	80403	**800-821-6110**	303-278-4000
Fair-Rite Products Corp 1 Commerical Row PO Box J	Wallkill	NY	12589	**888-324-7748**	845-895-2055
International Ceramic Engineering 235 Brooks St	Worcester	MA	01606	**800-779-3321**	508-853-4700
Kyocera Industrial Ceramics Corp 5713 E Fourth Plain Rd	Vancouver	WA	98661	**800-826-0527**	360-696-8950
Saint-Gobain Advanced Ceramics Latrobe 4702 Rt 982	Latrobe	PA	15650	**800-438-7237**	724-539-6000
Saxonburg Ceramics Inc PO Box 688	Saxonburg	PA	16056	**800-245-1270**	724-352-1561
Steward Inc 1200 E 36th St	Chattanooga	TN	37407	**800-634-2673***	423-867-4100
*Cust Svc					

249 ELECTROMEDICAL & ELECTROTHERAPEUTIC EQUIPMENT

SEE ALSO Medical Instruments & Apparatus - Mfr

				Toll-Free	Phone
ABIOMED Inc 22 Cherry Hill Dr	Danvers	MA	01923	**800-422-8666**	978-777-5410
NASDAQ: ABMD					
Advanced Neuromodulation Systems Inc 6901 Preston Rd	Plano	TX	75024	**800-727-7846**	972-309-8000
NASDAQ: ANSI					
Affymetrix Inc 3380 Central Expy	Santa Clara	CA	95051	**888-362-2447***	408-731-5503
NASDAQ: AFFX ■ *Tech Supp					
ArthroCare Corp 680 Vaqueros Ave	Sunnyvale	CA	94085	**800-348-8929**	408-736-0224
NASDAQ: ARTC					
Aspect Medical Systems Inc 141 Needham St	Newton	MA	02464	**888-247-4633**	617-559-7000
NASDAQ: ASPM					
Astro-Med Inc 600 E Greenwich Ave	West Warwick	RI	02893	**800-343-4039**	401-828-4000
NASDAQ: ALOT					
Bio-logic Systems Corp 1 Bio-logic Plaza	Mundelein	IL	60060	**800-323-8326***	847-949-5200
NASDAQ: BLSC ■ *Cust Svc					
Bovie Aaron Medical Industries 7100 30th Ave N	Saint Petersburg	FL	33710	**800-537-2790**	727-384-2323
Bovie Medical Corp 734 Walt Whitman Rd Suite 207	Melville	NY	11747	**800-888-4999**	631-421-5452
AMEX: BVX					
CardioDynamics International Corp 6175 Nancy Ridge Dr Suite 300	San Diego	CA	92121	**800-778-4825**	858-535-0202
NASDAQ: CDIC					
CAS Medical Systems Inc 44 E Industrial Rd	Branford	CT	06405	**800-227-4414**	203-488-6056
Compex Technologies Inc 1811 Old Hwy 8	New Brighton	MN	55112	**800-551-7939**	651-631-0590
NASDAQ: CMPX					
Compumedics USA Ltd 7850 Paseo del Norte Suite 101	El Paso	TX	79912	**877-717-3975**	915-845-5600
Conmed Corp 525 French Rd	Utica	NY	13502	**800-448-6506**	315-797-8375
NASDAQ: CNMD					
Cook Vascular Inc Rt 66 River Rd PO Box 529	Leechburg	PA	15656	**800-245-4715**	724-845-8621
Criticare Systems Inc 20925 Crossroads Cir Suite 100	Waukesha	WI	53186	**800-458-4615**	262-798-8282
AMEX: CMD					
Curon Medical Inc 46117 Landing Pkwy	Fremont	CA	94538	**877-734-2873**	
NASDAQ: CURN					
Datascope Corp 14 Philips Pkwy	Montvale	NJ	07645	**800-288-2121**	201-391-8100
NASDAQ: DSCP					
Del Mar Medical Systems LLC 13 Whatney	Irvine	CA	92618	**800-423-0480**	
Draeger Medical Inc 3135 Quarry Rd	Telford	PA	18969	**800-437-2437**	215-723-9824
Dynatronics Corp 7030 Park Centre Dr	Salt Lake City	UT	84121	**800-874-6251**	801-568-7000
NASDAQ: DYNT					
EBI Medical Systems LP 100 Interpace Pkwy	Parsippany	NJ	07054	**800-526-2579**	973-299-9300
EP MedSystems Inc 575 Rt 73 N	West Berlin	NJ	08091	**800-537-6285**	856-753-8533
NASDAQ: EPMD					
Fisher & Paykel Healthcare Inc 22982 Alcalde Dr Suite 101	Laguna Hills	CA	92653	**800-446-3908**	949-470-3900
Gambro Renal Products 10810 W Collins Ave	Lakewood	CO	80215	**800-525-2623**	303-232-6800
GE Healthcare PO Box 414	Milwaukee	WI	53201	**800-558-5102**	262-544-3011
GE Healthcare Information Technologies 8200 W Tower Ave	Milwaukee	WI	53223	**800-558-5102**	414-355-5000
Guidant Corp PO Box 44906	Indianapolis	IN	46244	**800-405-9611**	317-971-2000
NYSE: GDT					
HealthTronics Inc 1301 S Capital of Texas Hwy Suite B-200	Austin	TX	78746	**888-252-6575**	512-328-2892
NASDAQ: HTRN					
IVY Biomedical Systems Inc 11 Business Park Dr	Branford	CT	06405	**800-247-4614**	203-481-4183
Medical Graphics Corp 350 Oak Grove Pkwy	Saint Paul	MN	55127	**800-333-4137**	651-484-4874
Medtronic of Canada Ltd 6733 Kitimat Rd	Mississauga	ON	L5N1W3	**800-268-5346**	905-826-6020
Medtronic Emergency Response Systems 11811 Willows Rd NE	Redmond	WA	98052	**800-442-1142**	425-867-4000
Medtronic Inc 710 Medtronic Pkwy NE	Minneapolis	MN	55432	**800-328-2518***	763-574-4000
NYSE: MDT ■ *Cust Svc					
Medtronic Perfusion Systems 7611 Northland Dr	Brooklyn Park	MN	55428	**800-328-3320**	763-391-9000
Medtronic Powered Surgical Solutions 4620 N Beach St	Fort Worth	TX	76137	**800-433-7639**	817-788-6400
Mennen Medical Corp 2540 Metropolitan Dr	Trevose	PA	19053	**800-223-2201**	215-322-9997
Meridian Medical Technologies Inc 6350 Stevens Forest Rd Suite 301	Columbia	MD	21046	**800-638-8093**	443-259-7800
Mortara Instrument Inc 7865 N 86th St	Milwaukee	WI	53224	**800-231-7437**	414-354-1600
Natus Medical Inc 1501 Industrial Rd	San Carlos	CA	94070	**800-255-3901**	650-802-0400
NASDAQ: BABY					
NeuroMetrix 62 4th Ave	Waltham	MA	02451	**888-786-7287**	781-890-9989
NASDAQ: NURO					
Oscor Inc 3816 DeSoto Blvd	Palm Harbor	FL	34683	**800-726-7267**	727-937-2511
Quinton Cardiology Systems Inc 3303 Monte Villa Pkwy	Bothell	WA	98021	**800-426-0337**	425-402-2000
NASDAQ: QUIN					
R2 Technology Inc 1195 W Fremont Ave	Sunnyvale	CA	94087	**866-243-2533**	408-481-5600
Respironics Inc 1010 Murry Ridge Ln	Murrysville	PA	15668	**800-345-6443**	724-387-5200
NASDAQ: RESP					
Respironics Novametrix Medical Systems Inc 5 Technology Dr	Wallingford	CT	06492	**800-243-3444**	203-265-7701
Saint Jude Medical Inc Heart Valve Div 1 Lillehei Plaza	Saint Paul	MN	55117	**800-328-9634**	651-483-2000
SensorMedics Corp 22745 Savi Ranch Pkwy	Yorba Linda	CA	92887	**800-231-2466**	714-283-2228
Siemens Medical Solutions Inc 51 Valley Stream Pkwy	Malvern	PA	19355	**866-872-9745**	610-448-6300
Smiths Medical PM Inc N7 W22025 Johnson Rd	Waukesha	WI	53186	**800-558-2345***	262-542-3100
*Cust Svc					
Spacelabs Medical Inc 5150 220th Ave SE	Issaquah	WA	98029	**800-287-7108**	425-657-7200
Thoratec Corp 6035 Stoneridge Dr	Pleasanton	CA	94588	**800-528-2577**	925-847-8600
NASDAQ: THOR					
Valleylab 5920 Longbow Dr	Boulder	CO	80301	**800-255-8522**	303-530-2300
Vasomedical Inc 180 Linden Ave	Westbury	NY	11590	**800-455-3327**	516-997-4600
NASDAQ: VASO					
Welch Allyn Medical Products 4341 State Street Rd	Skaneateles Falls	NY	13153	**800-535-6663**	315-685-4100
Welch Allyn Monitoring Inc 8500 SW Creekside Pl	Beaverton	OR	97008	**800-289-2500***	503-530-7500
*Cust Svc					
ZOLL Medical Corp 269 Mill Rd	Chelmsford	MA	01824	**800-348-9011**	978-421-9655
NASDAQ: ZOLL					

250 ELECTRONIC BILL PRESENTMENT & PAYMENT SERVICES

SEE ALSO Application Service Providers (ASPs)

				Toll-Free	Phone
CheckFree Corp 4411 E Jones Bridge Rd	Norcross	GA	30092	**800-305-3716***	678-375-3000
NASDAQ: CKFR ■ *Cust Svc					
Heartland Payment Systems Inc 247 Hulfish St Suite 400	Princeton	NJ	08542	**888-798-3131**	609-683-3831
Internet Billing Co Ltd (iBill) 2200 SW 10th St	Deerfield Beach	FL	33442	**888-237-1764**	954-363-4400
Metavante Corp 4900 W Brown Deer Rd	Brown Deer	WI	53223	**800-236-3282**	414-357-2290
Paytrust Inc 4900 W Brown Deer Rd	Milwaukee	WI	53223	**800-729-8787**	
Princeton eCom Corp 650 College Rd E 2nd Fl	Princeton	NJ	08540	**866-606-3000**	609-606-3000
TPI Billing Solutions PO Box 472330	Tulsa	OK	74147	**800-332-0023**	918-664-0144
TROY Group Inc 2331 S Pullman St	Santa Ana	CA	92705	**877-324-3254**	949-250-3280

251 ELECTRONIC COMMUNICATIONS NETWORKS (ECNS)

SEE ALSO Securities & Commodities Exchanges; Securities Brokers & Dealers

				Toll-Free	Phone
Archipelago Holdings LLC 100 S Wacker Dr Suite 1800	Chicago	IL	60606	**888-514-7284**	312-960-1696
Instinet Group Inc 3 Times Sq	New York	NY	10036	**800-225-5008**	212-310-9500
NASDAQ: INGP					

252 ELECTRONIC COMPONENTS & ACCESSORIES - MFR

SEE ALSO Printed Circuit Boards; Semiconductors & Related Devices

Company / Address	City	State	ZIP	Toll-Free	Phone
3M Electrical Products Div 6801 River Place Blvd 3M Austin Ctr	Austin	TX	78726	**800-245-3573**	
3M Electro & Communications Div 3M Ctr	Saint Paul	MN	55144	**800-364-3577**	651-733-1110
3M Electronic Handling & Protection Div 6801 River Place Blvd	Austin	TX	78726	**800-328-1368**	
3M Interconnect Solutions Div 6801 River Place Blvd	Austin	TX	78726	**800-225-5373**	512-984-1800
3M Transportation Div 3M Ctr	Saint Paul	MN	55144	**888-364-3577**	651-733-1110
Actown-Electrocoil Inc 2414 Highview St	Spring Grove	IL	60081	**800-531-6366**	815-675-6641
Advanced Electronic Support Products Inc 1810 NE 144th St *NASDAQ: AESP*	North Miami Beach	FL	33181	**800-446-2377**	305-944-7710
AEM Inc 11525 Sorrento Valley Rd	San Diego	CA	92121	**888-323-6462**	858-481-0210
Aerovox Inc 167 John Vertente Blvd	New Bedford	MA	02745	**800-343-3348**	508-994-9661
Aim Electronics Corp 3103 N Andrews Ave	Pompano Beach	FL	33064	**800-327-8663**	954-984-3400
Alpha Technologies Inc 3767 Alpha Way	Bellingham	WA	98226	**800-322-5742**	360-647-2360
American Power Conversion Corp (APC) 132 Fairgrounds Rd *NASDAQ: APCC* ■ *Cust Svc	West Kingston	RI	02892	**800-788-2208***	401-789-5735
AMETEK Prestolite Power & Switch 2220 Corporate Dr	Troy	OH	45373	**800-367-2002**	937-440-0800
AMETEK Sensor Technology Automation & Process Technologies Div 1080 N Crooks Rd	Clawson	MI	48017	**800-635-0289**	248-435-0700
AMETEK Solidstate Controls 875 Dearborn Dr	Columbus	OH	43085	**800-635-7300**	614-846-7500
Amphenol Aerospace 40-60 Delaware Ave	Sidney	NY	13838	**800-678-0141**	607-563-5011
Amphenol RF 4 Old Newtown Rd *Sales	Danbury	CT	06810	**800-825-5577***	203-743-9272
Amphenol Sine Systems 25371 Joy Blvd	Mount Clemens	MI	48046	**800-394-7732**	586-465-3131
Amphenol Spectra-Strip 720 Sherman Ave	Hamden	CT	06514	**800-846-6400**	203-281-3200
AmRad Engineering Inc 32 Hargrove Grade	Palm Coast	FL	32137	**800-445-6033**	386-445-6000
Anaren Microwave Inc 6635 Kirkville Rd *NASDAQ: ANEN*	East Syracuse	NY	13057	**800-544-2414**	315-432-8909
Antec Inc 47900 Fremont Blvd *Cust Svc	Fremont	CA	94538	**888-542-6832***	510-770-1200
APC (American Power Conversion Corp) 132 Fairgrounds Rd *NASDAQ: APCC* ■ *Cust Svc	West Kingston	RI	02892	**800-788-2208***	401-789-5735
Apex Microtechnology Corp 5980 N Shannon Rd	Tucson	AZ	85741	**800-421-1865**	520-690-8600
Astec America Inc 5810 Van Allen Way	Carlsbad	CA	92008	**888-412-7832**	760-930-4600
AVG Automation 343 Saint Paul Blvd	Carol Stream	IL	60188	**800-527-2841**	630-668-3900
Avnet Electronics Marketing 2211 S 47th St	Phoenix	AZ	85034	**888-822-8638**	480-643-2000
Banner Engineering Corp 9714 10th Ave N	Minneapolis	MN	55441	**888-373-6767**	763-544-3164
Beacon Power Corp 234 Ballardvale St *NASDAQ: BCON*	Wilmington	MA	01887	**888-938-9112**	978-694-9121
BEI Technologies Inc Industrial Encoder Div 7230 Hollister Ave *Sales	Goleta	CA	93117	**800-350-2727***	805-968-0782
Belkin Corp 501 W Walnut St	Compton	CA	90220	**800-223-5546**	310-898-1100
Bergquist Co 18930 W 78th St	Chanhassen	MN	55317	**800-347-4572**	952-835-2322
C & D Technologies Inc 1400 Union Meeting Rd PO Box 3053 *NYSE: CHP*	Blue Bell	PA	19422	**800-543-8630**	215-619-2700
Cambridge Products Corp 299 Johnson Ave Suite 100	Waseca	MN	56093	**800-243-8814**	507-833-8822
Celestica Inc 844 Don Mills Rd *NYSE: CLS*	Toronto	ON	M3C1V7	**888-899-9998**	416-448-5800
Ceramaseal Div CeramTec North America 1033 US Rt 20	New Lebanon	NY	12125	**800-752-7325**	518-794-7800
CeramTec North America PO Box 89 1 Technology Pl	Laurens	SC	29360	**800-845-9761**	864-682-3215
CeramTec North America Ceramaseal Div 1033 US Rt 20	New Lebanon	NY	12125	**800-752-7325**	518-794-7800
CeramTec North America Electronic Applications Inc 1 Technology Pl PO Box 89	Laurens	SC	29360	**800-845-9761**	864-682-3215
Coilcraft Inc 1102 Silver Lake Rd	Cary	IL	60013	**800-325-5045**	847-639-2361
Comdel Inc 11 Kondelin Rd	Gloucester	MA	01930	**800-468-3144**	978-282-0620
Communications & Power Industries Inc EIMAC Div DBA CPI Inc EIMAC Div 301 Industrial Rd	San Carlos	CA	94070	**800-423-4622**	650-592-1221
Corning Gilbert Inc 5310 W Camelback Rd *Cust Svc	Glendale	AZ	85301	**800-528-0199***	623-245-1050
Crystek Crystals Corp 12730 Commonwealth Dr Unit 6	Fort Myers	FL	33913	**800-237-3061**	239-561-3311
Cyberex LLC 6095 Parkland Blvd Suite 310	Mayfield Heights	OH	44124	**800-292-3739**	440-995-3200
Data Device Corp 105 Wilbur Pl *Cust Svc	Bohemia	NY	11716	**800-332-5757***	631-567-5600
Datel Inc 11 Cabot Blvd	Mansfield	MA	02048	**800-233-2765**	508-339-3000
Ducommun Technologies Inc 23301 Wilmington Ave	Carson	CA	90745	**800-421-5032**	310-513-7200
Eby Co 4300 H St	Philadelphia	PA	19124	**800-329-3430**	215-537-4700
Elgar Electronics Corp 9250 Brown Deer Rd	San Diego	CA	92121	**800-733-5427**	858-450-0085
Engineered Components Co PO Box 8121	San Luis Obispo	CA	93403	**800-235-4144**	805-544-3800
EPCOS Inc 186 Wood Ave S *NYSE: EPC*	Iselin	NJ	08830	**800-689-3717**	732-906-4300
HDR Power Systems Inc 3563 Interchange Rd	Columbus	OH	43204	**888-797-2685**	614-308-5500
Heraeus Tenevo 100 Heraeus Blvd	Buford	GA	30518	**800-848-4527**	770-945-2275
Hitachi Canada Ltd 2495 Meadowpine Blvd	Mississauga	ON	L5N6C3	**800-906-4482**	905-821-4545
Illinois Capacitor Inc 3757 W Touhy Ave	Lincolnwood	IL	60712	**800-323-5420**	847-675-1760
International Resistive Co Inc (IRC) 736 Greenway Rd	Boone	NC	28607	**800-472-6467**	828-264-8861
Interpoint Corp PO Box 97005	Redmond	WA	98073	**800-822-8782**	425-882-3100
Invensys 33 Commercial St	Foxboro	MA	02035	**866-746-6477**	508-543-8750
IRC (International Resistive Co Inc) 736 Greenway Rd	Boone	NC	28607	**800-472-6467**	828-264-8861
ITW Paktron PO Box 4539	Lynchburg	VA	24502	**888-227-7845**	434-239-6941
JDS Uniphase Corp 1768 Automation Pkwy *NASDAQ: JDSU*	San Jose	CA	95131	**800-644-8674**	408-546-5000
Jewell Instruments LLC 850 Perimeter Rd	Manchester	NH	03103	**800-227-5955**	603-669-6400
K & M Electronics Inc 11 Interstate Dr W	Springfield	MA	01089	**800-442-4334**	413-781-1350
Kaman Instrumentation Corp 3450 N Nevada Ave	Colorado Springs	CO	80907	**800-552-6267**	719-635-6867
Kay Elemetrics Corp 2 Bridgewater Ln	Lincoln Park	NJ	07035	**800-289-5297**	973-628-6200
Lambda Electronics An Invensys Co 45 Fairchild Ave Suite A	Plainview	NY	11803	**800-526-2325**	516-629-3000
Lambda Novatronics Inc 2855 W McNab Rd	Pompano Beach	FL	33069	**800-952-6909**	954-984-7000
M-Tron Industries Inc PO Box 630	Yankton	SD	57078	**800-762-8800**	605-665-9321
McDonald Technologies International Inc 1920 Diplomat Dr	Farmers Branch	TX	75234	**800-678-7046**	972-243-6767
MGE UPS Systems 1660 Scenic Ave	Costa Mesa	CA	92626	**800-438-7373**	714-557-1636
Midian Electronics Inc 2302 E 22nd St *Orders	Tucson	AZ	85713	**800-643-4267***	520-884-7981
Mitsubishi Electric & Electronics USA Inc 5665 Plaza Dr	Cypress	CA	90630	**800-843-2515**	714-220-2500
MMG North America 126 Pennsylvania Ave	Paterson	NJ	07503	**800-664-7712**	973-345-8900
Molex Inc 2222 Wellington Ct *NASDAQ: MOLX* ■ *Cust Svc	Lisle	IL	60532	**800-786-6539***	630-969-4550
Motorola Inc 1301 E Algonquin Rd *NYSE: MOT*	Schaumburg	IL	60196	**800-331-6456**	847-576-5000
MPD Inc 316 E 9th St	Owensboro	KY	42303	**866-225-5673**	270-685-6200
Murata Electronics North America Inc 2200 Lake Pk Dr	Smyrna	GA	30080	**800-241-6574**	770-436-1300
Newport Corp 1791 Deere Ave *NASDAQ: NEWP* ■ *Sales	Irvine	CA	92606	**800-222-6440***	949-863-3144
Northern Technologies Corp 23123 E Mission Ave	Liberty Lake	WA	99019	**800-456-1875**	509-927-0401
Novacap Inc 25136 Anza Dr	Valencia	CA	91355	**800-227-2447**	661-295-5920
NWL Transformers Inc 312 Rising Sun Rd	Bordentown	NJ	08505	**800-742-5695**	609-298-7300
OEM Worldwide Inc 2920 Kelly Ave PO Box 430	Watertown	SD	57201	**800-258-7989**	605-886-2519
Ohmite Mfg Co 1600 Golf Rd Suite 850	Rolling Meadows	IL	60008	**866-964-6483**	847-258-0300
ONEAC Corp 27944 N Bradley Rd	Libertyville	IL	60048	**800-327-8801**	847-816-6000
Para Systems Inc 1455 LeMay Dr	Carrollton	TX	75007	**800-238-7272**	972-446-7363
PEMSTAR Inc 3535 Technology Dr NW *NASDAQ: PMTR*	Rochester	MN	55901	**888-736-7827**	507-288-6720
Piller Inc 334 CR 49	Middletown	NY	10940	**800-597-6937**	845-355-5000
Plastronics Socket Co Inc 2601 Texas Dr *Cust Svc	Irving	TX	75062	**800-582-5822***	972-258-1906
Positronic Industries Inc PO Box 8247	Springfield	MO	65801	**800-641-4054**	417-866-2322
Post Glover LifeLink Inc 4750 Olympic Blvd Bldg B	Erlanger	KY	41018	**800-287-4123**	859-283-5900
Post Glover Resistors Inc 4750 Olympic Blvd *Cust Svc	Erlanger	KY	41018	**800-537-6144***	859-283-0778
Power-One Inc 740 Calle Plano *NASDAQ: PWER*	Camarillo	CA	93012	**800-678-9445**	805-987-8741
Powerware Corp 8609 Six Forks Rd	Raleigh	NC	27615	**800-554-3448**	919-872-3020
Precision Devices Inc 8840 N Greenview Dr	Middleton	WI	53562	**800-274-9825**	608-831-4445
Quartzdyne Inc 1020 W Atherton Dr	Salt Lake City	UT	84123	**888-353-7956**	801-266-6958
Raritan Computer Inc 400 Cottontail Ln	Somerset	NJ	08873	**800-724-8090**	732-764-8886
Samtec Inc 520 Parkeast Blvd	New Albany	IN	47150	**800-726-8329**	812-944-6733
Schumacher Electric Corp 801 Business Ctr Dr	Mount Prospect	IL	60056	**800-621-5485**	847-385-1600
Seiko Instruments USA Inc 2990 W Lomita Blvd	Torrance	CA	90505	**800-358-0880**	310-517-7050
Semiconductor Circuits Inc 49 Range Rd *Cust Svc	Windham	NH	03087	**800-448-4724***	603-893-2330
Shelly Inc 17171 Murphy Ave	Irvine	CA	92614	**888-669-9850**	949-417-8070
Sigma Electronics Inc 1027 Commercial Ave	East Petersburg	PA	17520	**866-569-2681**	717-569-2681
Simplex Inc 1139 N MacArthur Blvd	Springfield	IL	62702	**800-637-8603**	217-525-6995
SNC Mfg Co Inc 101 W Waukau Ave	Oshkosh	WI	54902	**800-558-3325**	920-231-7370
Stevens Water Monitoring Systems 5465 SW Western Ave Suite F	Beaverton	OR	97005	**800-452-5272**	503-469-8000
Suntron Corp 2401 W Grandview Rd Suite 1 *NASDAQ: SUNN*	Phoenix	AZ	85023	**866-554-1223**	602-789-6600
Taiyo Yuden (USA) Inc 1930 N Thoreau Dr Suite 190	Schaumburg	IL	60173	**800-348-2496**	847-925-0888
Telonic Berkeley Inc 2825 Laguna Canyon Rd	Laguna Beach	CA	92651	**800-854-2436**	949-494-9401
Tempo Research Corp 1390 Aspen Way	Vista	CA	92083	**888-860-8535**	760-598-8900
Total Technologies Ltd 9 Studebaker	Irvine	CA	92618	**800-669-4885**	949-465-0200
Trompeter Electronics Inc 31186 La Baya Dr	Westlake Village	CA	91362	**800-982-2629**	818-707-2020
UTC Fuel Cells 195 Governors Hwy	South Windsor	CT	06074	**866-383-5235**	860-727-2200
Valberg LLD 14792 172nd Dr SE	Monroe	WA	98272	**800-487-2206**	360-794-9885
Valpey Fisher Corp 75 South St *AMEX: VPF*	Hopkinton	MA	01748	**800-982-5737**	508-435-6831
Vanner Inc 4282 Reynolds Dr	Hilliard	OH	43026	**800-227-6937**	614-771-2718
Vectron International 166 Glover Ave	Norwalk	CT	06850	**888-328-7661**	203-853-4433
Viatran Corp 300 Industrial Dr	Grand Island	NY	14073	**800-688-0030**	716-773-1700
Vicor Corp 25 Frontage Rd *NASDAQ: VICR*	Andover	MA	01810	**800-869-5300**	978-470-2900
Weinschel Corp 5305 Spectrum Dr *Cust Svc	Frederick	MD	21703	**800-638-2048***	301-846-9222
Western Electronics LLC 1550 S Tech Ln	Meridian	ID	83642	**888-857-5775**	208-377-1557
Wireless Xcessories Group Inc 1840 County Line Rd Suite 301 *AMEX: XWG*	Huntingdon Valley	PA	19006	**800-233-0013**	215-322-4600

253 ELECTRONIC ENCLOSURES

Company / Address	City	State	ZIP	Toll-Free	Phone
AMCO Engineering Co 3801 N Rose St *Mktg	Schiller Park	IL	60176	**800-833-3156***	847-671-6670
APW Electronic Solutions 14100 Danielson St	Poway	CA	92064	**800-854-7086**	858-679-4550
APW Ltd N 22 W 23685 Ridgeview Pkwy W	Waukesha	WI	53188	**800-599-5556**	262-523-7600
Buckeye ShapeForm 555 Marion Rd	Columbus	OH	43207	**800-728-0776**	614-445-8433
Equipto Electronics Corp 351 Woodlawn Ave	Aurora	IL	60506	**800-204-7225**	630-897-4691
Global MetalForm LP 733 Davis St	Scranton	PA	18505	**800-233-4818**	570-346-3871
I-Bus Corp 2391 Zanker Rd Suite 370	San Jose	CA	95131	**800-382-4229**	408-428-6100
Swanson Engineering & Mfg Co 1133 E Redondo Blvd	Inglewood	CA	90302	**800-633-1158**	310-671-6915
TRI MAP International Inc 111 Val Dervin Pkwy	Stockton	CA	95206	**888-687-4627**	209-234-0100
Zero Mfg Inc 500 W 200 North	North Salt Lake	UT	84054	**800-545-1030**	801-298-5900

254 ELECTRONIC TRANSACTION PROCESSING

Name / Address	City	State	ZIP	Toll-Free	Phone
American Payment Systems Inc 15 Sterling Dr PO Box 5044	Wallingford	CT	06492	**800-309-7668**	203-679-4400
BA Merchant Services LLC 1231 Durrett Ln	Louisville	KY	40213	**800-949-7379**	502-315-2000
Ceridian Corp 3311 E Old Shakopee Rd *NYSE: CEN*	Minneapolis	MN	55425	**800-767-4969**	952-853-8100
ECHO (Electronic Clearing House Inc) 730 Paseo Camarillo *NASDAQ: ECHO*	Camarillo	CA	93010	**800-262-3246**	
Electracash 4404 E Pacific Coast Hwy *Cust Svc	Long Beach	CA	90804	**800-444-6952***	888-310-7312
First Data Corp 6200 S Quebec St *NYSE: FDC*	Greenwood Village	CO	80111	**800-735-3362**	303-488-8000
Global Payments Inc 10 Glenlake Pkwy North Tower *NYSE: GPN*	Atlanta	GA	30328	**800-560-2960**	770-829-8000
Lynk Systems Inc 600 Morgan Falls Rd Suite 260	Atlanta	GA	30350	**800-200-5965**	770-396-1616
National Bankcard Systems 2600 Via Fortuna Suite 240	Austin	TX	78749	**800-823-6835**	512-494-9200
NOVA Information Systems 1 Concourse Pkwy Suite 300	Atlanta	GA	30328	**800-725-1243**	770-396-1456
PayNet Merchant Services Inc 2000 Town Center Suite 2260	Southfield	MI	48075	**888-855-8644**	248-354-1111
Total System Services Inc 1600 1st Ave *NYSE: TSS*	Columbus	GA	31901	**800-241-0912**	706-649-2310

255 ELEVATORS, ESCALATORS, MOVING WALKWAYS

Name / Address	City	State	ZIP	Toll-Free	Phone
Access Industries Inc 4001 E 138th St	Grandview	MO	64030	**800-669-9047**	816-763-3100
Adams Elevator Equipment Co 6310 W Howard St	Niles	IL	60714	**800-323-0796**	847-581-2900
CemcoLift Inc 2801 Township Line Rd *Sales	Hatfield	PA	19440	**800-962-3626***	215-799-2900
DA Matot Inc 2501 Van Buren St	Bellwood	IL	60104	**800-369-1070**	708-547-1888
Delta/Beckwith Elevator Co 274 Southampton St	Boston	MA	02118	**800-648-8767**	617-427-5525
Elevator Equipment Corp 4035 Goodwin Ave	Los Angeles	CA	90039	**888-577-3326**	323-245-0147
GAL Mfg Corp 50 E 153rd St	Bronx	NY	10451	**877-425-3538**	718-292-9000
Inclinator Co of America 2200 Paxton St	Harrisburg	PA	17105	**800-343-9007**	717-234-8065
KONE Inc 1 Kone Ct	Moline	IL	61265	**800-334-9556**	309-764-6771
Mitsubishi Electric & Electronics USA Inc 5665 Plaza Dr	Cypress	CA	90630	**800-843-2515**	714-220-2500
Peelle Co 34 Central Ave	Hauppauge	NY	11788	**800-645-1056**	631-231-6000
R & O Elevator Co Inc 8310 Pillsbury Ave S	Bloomington	MN	55420	**800-735-3046**	952-888-9255
Schindler Elevator Corp 20 Whippany Rd	Morristown	NJ	07960	**800-225-3123**	973-397-6500
ThyssenKrupp Elevator 6266 Hurt Rd	Horn Lake	MS	38637	**877-230-0303**	662-393-2110

256 EMBROIDERY & OTHER DECORATIVE STITCHING

Name / Address	City	State	ZIP	Toll-Free	Phone
Branded Emblem Co Inc 7920 Foster St	Overland Park	KS	66204	**800-747-7920**	913-648-7920
CR Daniels Inc 3451 Ellicott Ctr Dr	Ellicott City	MD	21043	**800-933-2638**	410-461-2100
Fabri-Quilt Inc 901 E 14th Ave PO Box 12479	North Kansas City	MO	64116	**800-279-0622**	816-421-2000
Lion Brothers Co Inc 10246 Reisterstown Rd *Cust Svc	Owings Mills	MD	21117	**800-365-6543***	410-363-1000
Luv n' care Ltd PO Box 6050	Monroe	LA	71211	**800-588-6227**	318-388-4916
Moritz Embroidery Works Inc PO Box 187	Mount Pocono	PA	18344	**800-533-4183**	570-839-9600
National Emblem Inc 17036 S Avalon Blvd	Carson	CA	90746	**800-877-6185**	310-515-5055
Penn Emblem Co 10909 Dutton Rd	Philadelphia	PA	19154	**800-793-7366**	215-632-7800
Saint Louis Embroidery 1759 Scherer Pkwy	Saint Charles	MO	63303	**800-423-0450**	636-724-2200
Schweizer Emblem Co 1022 Busse Hwy *Cust Svc	Park Ridge	IL	60068	**800-942-5215***	847-292-1022
Standard Swiss Embroidery Co 5900 S Eastern Ave Suite 166	Commerce	CA	90040	**800-443-8357**	323-582-8057
Voyager Emblems Inc 3707 Lockport Rd	Sanborn	NY	14132	**800-268-2204**	716-731-4121

257 EMPLOYMENT SERVICES - ONLINE

Name / Address	City	State	ZIP	Toll-Free	Phone
AGRIcareers Inc PO Box 140	Massena	IA	50853	**888-224-5621**	712-779-3300
BostonWorks.com c/o Boston Globe PO Box 2378	Boston	MA	02107	**888-566-4562**	617-929-2000
BrassRing Inc 343 Winter St	Waltham	MA	02451	**888-265-6969**	781-530-5000
CareerBuilder Inc 8420 W Bryn Mawr Ave Suite 900	Chicago	IL	60631	**888-622-9022**	773-527-3600
CareerPark c/o Parker Advertising Service Inc Box 5600	Lancaster	PA	17606	**800-396-3306**	717-581-1966
CareerShop Inc 12200 W Colonial Dr	Winter Garden	FL	34787	**800-639-2060**	407-877-5992
ComputerJobs.com Inc 280 Interstate North Pkwy SE Suite 300	Atlanta	GA	30339	**800-850-0045**	770-850-0045
Computerwork.com c/o Internet Assn Group 4500 Salisbury Rd	Jacksonville	FL	32216	**800-691-8413**	904-296-1993
CyberEdit Inc 2000 Lenox Dr 3rd Fl	Lawrenceville	NJ	08648	**888-438-2633**	609-896-5401
Emplawyernet.com 1940 Westwood Blvd Suite 153	Los Angeles	CA	90025	**800-270-2688**	
Employer Central c/o College Central Network Inc 141 W 28th St 9th Fl	New York	NY	10001	**800-442-3614**	212-967-0230
EmploymentGuide.com 295 Bendix Rd 4th Fl	Virginia Beach	VA	23452	**877-876-4039**	757-446-2900
Environmental Career Opportunities c/o Brubach Corp PO Box 678	Stanardsville	VA	22973	**800-315-9777**	
ExecUNet Inc 295 Westport Ave	Norwalk	CT	06851	**800-637-3126**	203-750-1030
FlipDog.com 5 Clock Tower Pl Suite 500	Maynard	MA	01754	**877-887-3547**	
HealthCareSource Inc 8 Winchester Pl Suite 304	Winchester	MA	01890	**888-289-9979**	
HotJobs.com Ltd 406 W 31st St 9th Fl	New York	NY	10001	**877-468-5627**	212-302-0060
ihispano.com 17 N State St Suite 1700	Chicago	IL	60602	**888-252-1220**	
JobWeb c/o National Assn of Colleges & Employers 62 Highland Ave	Bethlehem	PA	18017	**800-544-5272**	610-868-1421
Law.com Lawjobs 10 Union Plaza 3rd Fl	San Francisco	CA	94102	**800-628-1160**	
Lawjobs 10 Union Plaza 3rd Fl	San Francisco	CA	94102	**800-628-1160**	
MarketingJobs.com 15275 Collier Blvd Suite 201	Naples	FL	34119	**877-348-5627**	
Med-Employ.com Inc 3905 E Martin Way Suite D	Olympia	WA	98506	**800-942-2480**	
Monster.com 5 Clock Tower Pl Suite 500	Maynard	MA	01754	**800-666-7837**	978-461-8000
MonsterTRAK 1964 Westwood Blvd 3rd Fl	Los Angeles	CA	90025	**800-999-8725**	310-474-3377
National Diversity Newspaper Job Bank c/o Morris Communications PO Box 936	Augusta	GA	30903	**800-622-6358**	
NationJob Inc 601 SW 9th St Suites J & K	Des Moines	IA	50309	**800-292-7731**	515-280-3672
Non-Profit Career Network PO Box 241	Haddam	CT	06438	**888-844-4870**	860-345-3255
Outdoor JobNet c/o Outdoor Network PO Box 1928	Boulder	CO	80306	**800-688-6387**	303-444-7117
Recruiters OnLine Network Inc (RON) 947 Essex Ln	Medina	OH	44256	**888-364-4667**	
RON (Recruiters OnLine Network Inc) 947 Essex Ln	Medina	OH	44256	**888-364-4667**	
TrueCareers Inc 12061 Bluemont Way	Reston	VA	20190	**800-441-4062**	
TV Jobs c/o Broadcast Employment Services PO Box 4116	Oceanside	CA	92052	**800-374-0119**	760-754-8177
WetFeet.com 609 Mission St Suite 400	San Francisco	CA	94105	**800-926-4562**	415-284-7900

258 ENGINEERING & DESIGN

SEE ALSO Surveying, Mapping, Related Services

Name / Address	City	State	ZIP	Toll-Free	Phone
Advantis Technologies 1400 Bluegrass Lakes Pkwy	Alpharetta	GA	30004	**888-452-7678**	770-521-5999
AEP Pro Serv 1 Riverside Plaza	Columbus	OH	43215	**800-777-1131**	614-716-1000
Alfred Benesch & Co 205 N Michigan Ave Suite 2400	Chicago	IL	60601	**877-222-9995**	312-565-0450
Allen & Hoshall Inc 1661 International Dr Suite 100	Memphis	TN	38120	**888-819-5005**	901-820-0820
Ardaman & Assoc Inc 8008 S Orange Ave	Orlando	FL	32809	**800-432-3143**	407-855-3860
Baker Michael Corp 100 Airsite Dr Airsite Business Pk *AMEX: BKR*	Moon Township	PA	15108	**800-553-1153**	412-269-6300
Barr Engineering Co 4700 W 77th St	Minneapolis	MN	55435	**800-632-2277**	952-832-2600
Bartlett & West Engineers Inc 1200 SW Executive Dr	Topeka	KS	66615	**888-200-6464**	785-272-2252
Barton JF Contracting Co PO Box 73525	Houston	TX	77273	**800-222-1472**	281-443-3800
BCM Engineers 920 Germantown Pike Suite 200	Plymouth Meeting	PA	19462	**800-221-1226**	610-313-3100
Belcan Engineering Group Inc 10200 Anderson Way	Cincinnati	OH	45242	**800-423-5226**	513-891-0972
Benesch Alfred & Co 205 N Michigan Ave Suite 2400	Chicago	IL	60601	**877-222-9995**	312-565-0450
Berger Louis Group Inc 100 Halsted St	East Orange	NJ	07018	**800-323-4098**	973-678-1960
Bergmann Assoc Inc 200 First Federal Plaza	Rochester	NY	14614	**800-724-1168**	585-232-5135
Berryman & Henigar 11590 W Bernardo Ct Suite 100	San Diego	CA	92127	**800-964-4274**	858-451-6100
Bionetics Corp 11833 Cannon Blvd Suite 100	Newport News	VA	23606	**800-868-0330**	757-873-0900
Braun Intertec Corp 11001 Hampshire Ave S	Bloomington	MN	55438	**800-279-6100**	952-995-2000
Brock Solutions Inc 86 Ardelt Ave	Kitchener	ON	N2C2C9	**877-702-7625**	519-571-1434
Brown Dayton T Inc 1175 Church St	Bohemia	NY	11716	**800-232-6300**	631-589-6300
BSW International Inc 1 W 3rd St Suite 800	Tulsa	OK	74103	**800-749-8771**	918-582-8771
Buchart Horn Inc/Basco Assoc PO Box 15040	York	PA	17405	**800-274-2224**	717-852-1400
Bucher Willis & Ratliff Corp 609 W North St	Salina	KS	67401	**800-942-9807**	785-827-3603
Burgess & Niple Inc 5085 Reed Rd	Columbus	OH	43220	**800-282-1761**	614-459-2050
C & S Cos 499 Col Eileen Collins Blvd	Syracuse	NY	13212	**877-277-6583**	315-455-2000
Carollo Engineers 3033 N 44th St Suite 101	Phoenix	AZ	85018	**800-523-5822**	602-263-9500
Carter & Burgess Inc PO Box 901058	Fort Worth	TX	76101	**800-624-7959**	817-735-6000
CAS Inc PO Box 11190	Huntsville	AL	35814	**800-729-8686**	256-895-8600
CEI Engineering Assoc Inc 3317 SW 'I' St	Bentonville	AR	72712	**800-433-4173**	479-273-9472
Chemtex International Inc 1979 Eastwood Rd	Wilmington	NC	28403	**877-243-6839**	910-509-4400
Chevron Energy Solutions 345 California St 32nd Fl	San Francisco	CA	94104	**800-982-6887**	
Civil & Environmental Consultants Inc 333 Baldwin Rd	Pittsburgh	PA	15205	**800-365-2324**	412-429-2324
Clough Harbour & Assoc 3 Winners Circle	Albany	NY	12205	**800-836-0817**	518-453-4500
Continental Glass & Plastic Inc 841 W Cermak Rd	Chicago	IL	60608	**888-676-5277**	312-666-2050
Corrpro Cos Inc 1055 W Smith Rd *NYSE: CO*	Medina	OH	44256	**800-726-5082**	330-723-5082
CUH2A Inc 1000 Lenox Dr	Lawrenceville	NJ	08648	**877-992-8422**	609-844-1212
David Evans & Assoc Inc 2100 SW River Pkwy	Portland	OR	97201	**800-721-1916**	503-223-6663
Dayton T Brown Inc 1175 Church St	Bohemia	NY	11716	**800-232-6300**	631-589-6300
DLZ Corp 6121 Huntley Rd	Columbus	OH	43229	**800-336-5352**	614-888-0040
DMJM & Harris 605 3rd Ave 31st Fl	New York	NY	10158	**800-729-3656**	212-973-2900
Duke/Fluor Daniel 2300 Yorkmont Rd	Charlotte	NC	28217	**800-486-4518**	704-426-2000
Dyer Riddle Mills & Precourt Inc 1505 E Colonial Dr	Orlando	FL	32803	**800-375-3767**	407-896-0594
EA Engineering Science & Technology Inc 11019 McCormick Rd	Hunt Valley	MD	21031	**800-777-9750**	410-584-7000
ENSCO Inc 5400 Port Royal Rd	Springfield	VA	22151	**800-367-2682**	703-321-9000

Company / Address	City	State	ZIP	Toll-Free	Phone
ENSR International 2 Technology Pk Dr	Westford	MA	01886	**800-722-2440**	978-589-3000
ENTRANCO Inc 10900 NE 8th St Suite 300	Bellevue	WA	98004	**800-454-5601**	425-454-5600
Erdman Marshall & Assoc 5117 University Ave	Madison	WI	53705	**800-550-5117**	608-238-0211
ERM Group Inc 350 Eagle View Blvd	Exton	PA	19341	**800-662-1124**	610-524-3500
Essex Corp 9150 Guilford Rd	Columbia	MD	21046	**800-533-7739**	301-939-7000
NASDAQ: KEYW					
Evans David & Assoc Inc 2100 SW River Pkwy	Portland	OR	97201	**800-721-1916**	503-223-6663
Facility Group Inc 2233 Lake Pk Dr Suite 100	Smyrna	GA	30080	**800-525-2463**	770-437-2700
Fanning/Howey Assoc Inc 1200 Irmscher Blvd	Celina	OH	45822	**888-499-2292**	419-586-2292
Fata Hunter Co Inc 1040 Iowa Ave Suite 100	Riverside	CA	92507	**800-248-6837**	951-328-0200
Fay Spofford & Thorndike LLC 5 Burlington Woods	Burlington	MA	01803	**800-835-8666**	781-221-1000
Foth & Van Dyke & Assoc Inc PO Box 19012	Green Bay	WI	54307	**800-236-8690**	920-497-2500
GAI Consultants Inc 570 Beatty Rd	Monroeville	PA	15146	**800-437-2150**	412-856-6400
Gannett Fleming Inc PO Box 67100	Harrisburg	PA	17106	**800-233-1055**	717-763-7211
Geomatrix Consultants Inc 2101 Webster St 12th Fl	Oakland	CA	94612	**800-999-6879**	510-663-4100
GeoSyntec Consultants Inc 621 NW 53rd St Suite 650	Boca Raton	FL	33487	**800-765-4436**	561-995-0900
Grant Geophysical Inc PO Box 219950	Houston	TX	77218	**800-390-5530**	281-398-9503
Greeley & Hansen 100 S Wacker Dr Suite 1400	Chicago	IL	60606	**800-837-9779**	312-558-9000
Greenhorne & O'Mara Inc 9001 Edmonston Rd	Greenbelt	MD	20770	**866-322-8905**	301-982-2800
Greenman-Pedersen Inc 325 W Main St	Babylon	NY	11702	**800-347-9221**	631-587-5060
Gresham Smith & Partners 511 Union St 1400 Nashville City Ctr	Nashville	TN	37219	**800-867-3384**	615-770-8100
Halff Assoc Inc 8616 NW Plaza Dr	Dallas	TX	75225	**800-425-3387**	214-346-6200
Halliburton Co Engineering & Construction Group DBA Kellogg Brown & Root 4100 Clinton Dr	Houston	TX	77020	**800-231-8166**	713-753-2000
Hammel Green & Abrahamson Inc 701 Washington Ave N	Minneapolis	MN	55401	**888-442-8255**	612-758-4000
Hanson Engineers Inc 1525 S 6th St	Springfield	IL	62703	**800-788-2450**	217-788-2450
Harris Group Inc 1000 Denny Way Suite 800	Seattle	WA	98109	**800-488-7410**	206-494-9400
Hart Crowser Inc 1910 Fairview Ave E	Seattle	WA	98102	**800-925-9530**	206-324-9530
Hart Engineering Corp 29 Lark Industrial Pkwy	Greenville	RI	02828	**800-492-4278**	401-949-5300
Hayes Seay Mattern & Mattern Inc PO Box 13446	Roanoke	VA	24034	**800-366-4766**	540-857-3100
Hazen & Sawyer PC 498 7th Ave 11th Fl	New York	NY	10018	**800-858-9876**	212-777-8400
HDR Engineering Inc 8404 Indian Hills Dr	Omaha	NE	68114	**800-366-4411**	402-399-1000
Healy SA Co 1910 S Highland Ave Suite 300	Lombard	IL	60148	**888-724-3259**	630-678-3110
High Technology Solutions Inc 9771 Clairmont Mesa Blvd Suite A	San Diego	CA	92124	**800-411-8483**	858-495-0508
HLW International 115 5th Ave 5th Fl	New York	NY	10003	**888-353-4601**	212-353-4600
HMC Archtiect 3270 Inland Empire Blvd	Ontario	CA	91764	**800-350-9979**	909-989-9979
Howard R Green Co 8710 Earhart Ln SW PO Box 9009	Cedar Rapids	IA	52409	**800-728-7805**	319-841-4000
HPD Systems 23562 W Main St	Plainfield	IL	60544	**800-927-0319**	815-609-2000
HSB Group Inc 1 State St PO Box 5024	Hartford	CT	06102	**800-472-1866**	860-722-1866
HW Lochner Inc 20 N Wacker Dr Suite 1200	Chicago	IL	60606	**800-327-7346**	312-372-7346
Inco Inc PO Box 2705	Rocky Mount	NC	27802	**800-672-4626**	252-446-1174
Inland Waters Pollution Control Inc 2021 S Schaefer Hwy	Detroit	MI	48217	**800-992-9118**	313-841-5800
Intrinsix Corp 33 Lyman St	Westborough	MA	01581	**800-783-0330**	508-836-4100
JF Barton Contracting Co PO Box 73525	Houston	TX	77273	**800-222-1472**	281-443-3800
Jordan Jones & Goulding Inc 6801 Governors Lake Pkwy	Norcross	GA	30071	**800-545-2373**	770-455-8555
Kaplan McLaughlin Diaz 222 Vallejo St 4th Fl	San Francisco	CA	94111	**800-822-5191**	415-398-5191
KCI Technologies Inc 10 N Park Dr	Hunt Valley	MD	21030	**800-572-7496**	410-316-7800
Keith Cos Inc 19 Technology Dr	Irvine	CA	92618	**800-735-3484**	949-923-6000
NASDAQ: TKCI					
Kellogg Brown & Root 4100 Clinton Dr	Houston	TX	77020	**800-231-8166**	713-753-2000
Kinney AM Inc 150 E 4th St	Cincinnati	OH	45202	**800-265-3682**	513-421-2265
KKE Architects Inc 300 1st Ave N	Minneapolis	MN	55401	**866-224-6499**	612-339-4200
Kling 2301 Chestnut St	Philadelphia	PA	19103	**800-888-2054**	215-569-2900
Langan Engineering & Environmental Services Inc River Drive Ctr 1	Elmwood Park	NJ	07407	**800-352-6426**	201-794-6900
LBA Group Inc 3400 Tupper Dr	Greenville	NC	27834	**800-522-4464**	252-757-0279
Louis Berger Group Inc 100 Halsted St	East Orange	NJ	07018	**800-323-4098**	973-678-1960
Malcolm Pirnie Inc 104 Corporate Park Dr	White Plains	NY	10602	**800-759-5020**	914-694-2100
Mason & Hanger Group Inc 300 W Vine St Suite 1300	Lexington	KY	40507	**800-586-2766**	859-252-9980
McLaughlin Research Corp 132 Johnnycake Hill Rd	Middletown	RI	02842	**800-556-7154**	401-849-4010
Merrick & Co 2450 S Peoria St	Aurora	CO	80014	**800-544-1714**	303-751-0741
Michael Baker Corp 100 Airsite Dr Airsite Business Pk	Moon Township	PA	15108	**800-553-1153**	412-269-6300
AMEX: BKR					
Miller Architects & Builders Inc 3335 W Saint Germain St	Saint Cloud	MN	56301	**800-772-1758**	320-251-4109
Modern Engineering Inc 633 South Blvd Suite 200	Rochester Hills	MI	48307	**800-875-6423**	248-606-6100
Moody Nolan Inc 300 Spruce St Suite 300	Columbus	OH	43215	**877-530-4984**	614-461-4664
Moreland & Altobelli Assoc Inc 2211 Beaver Ruin Rd Suite 190	Norcross	GA	30071	**800-899-4689**	770-263-5945
Nolte Assoc Inc 1750 Creekside Oaks Dr Suite 200	Sacramento	CA	95833	**800-216-6583**	916-641-1500
Operational Technologies Corp 4100 NW Loop 410 Suite 230	San Antonio	TX	78229	**800-677-8072**	210-731-0000
Ortloff Engineers Ltd 415 W Wall Ave Suite 2000	Midland	TX	79701	**888-367-0020**	432-685-0277
Outokumpu Livernois Engineering Co 25315 Kean St	Dearborn	MI	48124	**800-900-0200**	313-278-0200
Pace Resources Inc 40 S Richland Ave	York	PA	17404	**800-274-2224**	717-852-1300
Paragon Engineering Services Inc 10777 Clay Rd	Houston	TX	77041	**800-324-7272**	713-570-1000
Parsons Brinckerhoff Inc 1 Penn Plaza 2nd Fl	New York	NY	10119	**800-877-7754**	212-465-5000
Parsons Corp 100 W Walnut St	Pasadena	CA	91124	**800-883-7300**	626-440-2000
Parsons Infrastructure & Technology 100 W Walnut St	Pasadena	CA	91124	**800-883-7300**	626-440-4000
Parsons PFI 150 Federal St	Boston	MA	02110	**800-555-0532**	617-946-9400
Patton Harris Rust & Assoc PC 14532 Lee Rd	Chantilly	VA	20151	**800-550-7472**	703-449-6700
Perkins & Will 330 N Wabash Ave Suite 3600	Chicago	IL	60611	**800-837-9455**	312-755-0770
Petrocon Engineering Inc PO Box 20397	Beaumont	TX	77720	**800-256-5710**	409-840-2100
Post Buckley Schuh & Jernigan 2001 NW 107th Ave	Miami	FL	33172	**800-597-7275**	305-592-7275
Power Engineering Corp PO Box 766	Wilkes-Barre	PA	18703	**800-626-0903**	570-823-8822
Product Development Technologies Inc 600 Heathrow Dr	Lincolnshire	IL	60069	**800-747-6600**	847-821-3000
Professional Service Industries Inc 1901 S Meyers Rd Suite 400	Oakbrook Terrace	IL	60181	**800-426-2897**	630-691-1490
RBF Consulting 14725 Alton Pkwy	Irvine	CA	92618	**800-479-3808**	949-472-3505
Rentenbach Engineering Co 2400 Sutherland Ave	Knoxville	TN	37919	**800-621-4941**	865-546-2440
Rettew Assoc Inc 3020 Columbia Ave	Lancaster	PA	17603	**800-738-8395**	717-394-3721
Reynolds Smith & Hills Inc PO Box 4850 Suite 400	Jacksonville	FL	32201	**800-741-2014**	904-296-2000
RG Vanderweil Engineers Inc 274 Summer St	Boston	MA	02210	**800-726-2840**	617-423-7423
RMT Inc 744 Heartland Trail	Madison	WI	53717	**800-283-3443**	608-831-4444
RTKL Assoc Inc 901 S Bond St	Baltimore	MD	21231	**800-345-7855**	410-537-6000
Rummel Klepper & Kahl LLP 81 Mosher St	Baltimore	MD	21217	**800-787-3755**	410-728-2900
SA Healy Co 1910 S Highland Ave Suite 300	Lombard	IL	60148	**888-724-3259**	630-678-3110
Schneider Corp 8901 Otis Ave	Indianapolis	IN	46216	**800-898-0332**	317-826-7100
Scientech Inc 200 S Woodruff Ave	Idaho Falls	ID	83401	**800-247-8818**	208-529-1000
SCS Engineers 3711 Long Beach Blvd 9th Fl	Long Beach	CA	90807	**800-326-9544**	562-426-9544
SE Technologies Inc 98 Vanadium Rd Bldg D 2nd Fl	Coraopolis	PA	15108	**800-685-0354**	412-221-1100
Sear-Brown Group 85 Metro Park	Rochester	NY	14623	**800-724-4131**	585-272-1814
SFA Inc 9315 Largo Dr W Suite 200	Largo	MD	20774	**800-787-2732**	301-350-0938
Shannon & Wilson Inc PO Box 300303	Seattle	WA	98103	**800-633-6800**	206-632-8020
Shive-Hattery Inc PO Box 1803	Cedar Rapids	IA	52406	**800-798-0227**	319-364-0227
Short-Elliott-Hendrickson Inc 3535 Vadnais Ctr Dr	Saint Paul	MN	55110	**800-325-2055**	651-490-2000
Sofec Inc 14741 Yorktown Plaza	Houston	TX	77070	**800-462-6003**	713-510-6600
Sonalysts Inc 215 Parkway N	Waterford	CT	06385	**800-526-8091**	860-442-4355
Spillis Candela DMJM 800 Douglas Entrance North Tower 2nd Fl	Coral Gables	FL	33134	**800-999-4727**	305-444-4691
Stratasys Inc 14950 Martin Dr	Eden Prairie	MN	55344	**888-480-3548**	952-937-3000
NASDAQ: SSYS					
STS Consultants Ltd 750 Corporate Woods Pkwy	Vernon Hills	IL	60061	**800-859-7871**	847-279-2500
Sullivan International Group Inc 409 Camino Real Rio S Suite 204	San Diego	CA	92108	**888-744-1432**	619-260-1432
Syska & Hennessy Group 11 W 42nd St	New York	NY	10036	**800-328-1600**	212-921-2300
Teledyne Brown Engineering PO Box 070007	Huntsville	AL	35807	**800-933-2091**	256-726-1000
Testwell Laboratories Inc 47 Hudson St	Ossining	NY	10562	**800-444-9013**	914-762-9000
Tetra Tech FW Inc 1000 The American Rd	Morris Plains	NJ	07950	**800-580-3765**	973-630-8000
Tolz King Duvall Anderson & Assoc Inc 444 Cedar St Suite 1500	Saint Paul	MN	55101	**800-247-1714**	651-292-4400
Trandes Corp 4601 Presidents Dr Suite 360	Lanham	MD	20706	**800-878-0201**	301-459-0200
TransCore Holdings Inc 8158 Adams Dr Bldg 200	Hummelstown	PA	17036	**800-233-2172**	717-561-2400
UEC Technologies LLC 600 Grant St Rm 1644	Pittsburgh	PA	15219	**800-245-4450**	412-433-6527
Universal Ensco Inc 1811 Bering Dr	Houston	TX	77057	**800-966-1811**	713-977-7770
Unwin Scheben Korynta Huettl Inc 2515 A St	Anchorage	AK	99503	**888-706-8754**	907-276-4245
US Laboratories Inc 7895 Convoy Ct Suite 18	San Diego	CA	92111	**800-487-0355**	858-715-5800
Vanadium Group Corp 400 Rouser Rd Bldg 2	Moon Township	PA	15108	**800-685-0354**	412-264-2030
Vanderweil RG Engineers Inc 274 Summer St	Boston	MA	02210	**800-726-2840**	617-423-7423
Versar Inc 6850 Versar Ctr	Springfield	VA	22151	**800-283-7727***	703-750-3000
AMEX: VSR ■ *Cust Svc					
Volkert & Assoc Inc 3809 Moffett Rd	Mobile	AL	36618	**800-340-1070**	251-342-1070
Vollmer Assoc 50 W 23rd St 8th Fl	New York	NY	10010	**800-564-3434**	212-366-5600
Volt Telecom Group Inc 3039 Premiere Pkwy	Duluth	GA	30097	**800-521-8658**	678-957-4700
VSE Corp 2550 Huntington Ave	Alexandria	VA	22303	**800-455-4873**	703-960-4600
NASDAQ: VSEC					
Wade-Trim Group Inc 25251 Northline Rd	Taylor	MI	48180	**800-482-2864**	734-947-9700
Washington Corp PO Box 16630	Missoula	MT	59808	**800-832-7329**	406-523-1300
Whitman Requardt & Assoc 801 S Caroline St	Baltimore	MD	21231	**800-787-7100**	410-235-3450
Willbros Engineers Inc 2087 E 71st St	Tulsa	OK	74136	**800-434-8970**	918-496-0400
Willdan 2125 E Katella Ave Suite 200	Anaheim	CA	92806	**800-424-9144**	714-940-6300
WilsonMiller Inc 3200 Bailey Ln Suite 200	Naples	FL	34105	**800-649-4336**	239-649-4040
Wiss Janney Elstner Assoc Inc 330 Pfingsten Rd	Northbrook	IL	60062	**800-345-3199**	847-272-7400
Woodard & Curran 41 Hutchins Dr	Portland	ME	04102	**800-426-4262**	207-774-2112
Yolles Group Inc 163 Queen St E Suite 200	Toronto	ON	M5A1S1	**800-572-1759**	416-363-8123

259 ENGINES & TURBINES

SEE ALSO Aircraft Engines & Engine Parts; Automotive Parts & Supplies - Mfr; Motors (Electric) & Generators

Company / Address	City	State	ZIP	Toll-Free	Phone
Alaska Diesel Electric Inc 4420 14th Ave NW	Seattle	WA	98107	**800-762-0165**	206-789-3880
Arrow Specialty Co 2301 E Independence St	Tulsa	OK	74110	**800-331-3662**	918-583-5711
Briggs & Stratton Corp PO Box 702	Milwaukee	WI	53201	**800-444-7774**	414-259-5333
NYSE: BGG					
Cascade Diesel Engine Co LLP 9800 40th Ave S	Seattle	WA	98118	**800-238-3850**	206-764-3850
Clayton Industries 4213 N Temple City Blvd	El Monte	CA	91731	**800-423-4585**	626-443-9381
Cummins Inc PO Box 3005	Columbus	IN	47201	**800-343-7357**	812-377-5000
NYSE: CMI					
DaimlerChrysler Corp 1000 Chrysler Dr	Auburn Hills	MI	48326	**800-992-1997**	248-576-5741
NYSE: DCX					
Delaware Mfg Industries Corp 3775 Commerce Ct	Wheatfield	NY	14120	**800-248-3642**	716-743-4360
Dresser-Rand Co Steam Products Div 37 Coats St PO Box 592	Wellsville	NY	14895	**800-828-2818**	585-596-3100
Electro Steam Generator Corp 7217 Lockport Pl Suite 207	Lorton	VA	22079	**800-634-8177**	703-549-0664
Elliott Turbomachinery Co 901 N 4th St	Jeannette	PA	15644	**800-635-2208**	724-527-2811
EnPro Industries Inc 5605 Carnegie Blvd Suite 500	Charlotte	NC	28209	**866-663-6776**	704-731-1500
NYSE: NPO					

Classified Section

				Toll-Free	Phone
EnPro Industries Inc Fairbanks Morse Engine 701 White Ave	Beloit	WI	53511	**800-356-6955**	608-364-4411
Fairbanks Morse Engine EnPro Industries Inc 701 White Ave	Beloit	WI	53511	**800-356-6955**	608-364-4411
Franklin Power Products Inc 400 Forsythe St *Cust Svc	Franklin	IN	46131	**800-837-7697***	317-738-2117
GE Energy 4200 Wildwood Pkwy	Atlanta	GA	30339	**800-368-1316**	
Gopher Motor Rebuilding Inc 6530 James Ave N	Minneapolis	MN	55430	**800-328-3994**	763-746-3440
Hatch & Kirk Inc 5111 Leary Ave NW	Seattle	WA	98107	**800-426-2818**	206-783-2766
Hercules Engine Components Co 2770 S Erie St	Massillon	OH	44646	**800-345-0662**	330-830-2498
Jasper Engine & Transmission Exchange Inc 815 Wernsing Rd PO Box 650	Jasper	IN	47547	**800-827-7455**	812-482-1041
Kohler Engines 444 Highland Dr	Kohler	WI	53044	**800-544-2444**	920-457-4441
Mercury Marine Ltd 2395 Meadowpine Blvd	Mississauga	ON	L5N7W6	**800-388-2166**	905-567-6372
NREC Power Systems 5222 Hwy 311	Houma	LA	70360	**800-851-6732**	985-872-5480
Penske Corp Rt 10 Green Hills PO Box 563	Reading	PA	19603	**800-222-0277**	610-775-6000
Pratt & Whitney Canada Inc 1000 Marie-Victorin Blvd	Longueuil	QC	J4G1A1	**800-268-8000**	450-677-9411
Pratt & Whitney Power Systems Inc 80 Lamberton Rd	Windsor	CT	06095	**800-525-8199**	860-565-5776
Rolls-Royce Energy System Inc 105 N Sandusky St	Mount Vernon	OH	43050	**800-284-8782**	740-393-8888
Springfield ReManufacturing Corp 650 N Broadview Pl	Springfield	MO	65802	**800-772-7700**	417-862-3501
Stewart & Stevenson Services Inc 2707 North Loop W *NYSE: SVC*	Houston	TX	77008	**800-527-3246**	713-868-7700
Tecumseh Products Co Engine & Transmission Group 900 North St *Cust Svc	Grafton	WI	53024	**800-477-1277***	262-377-2700
Wartsila North America Inc 16330 Air Center Blvd	Houston	TX	77032	**800-676-9945**	281-233-6200
Woodward Governor Co 5001 N 2nd St *NASDAQ: WGOV*	Loves Park	IL	61111	**888-273-8839**	815-877-7441

260 ENVELOPES

				Toll-Free	Phone
ADM Corp 100 Lincoln Blvd	Middlesex	NJ	08846	**800-327-0718**	732-469-0900
Alvah Bushnell Co 519 E Chelten Ave	Philadelphia	PA	19144	**800-255-7434**	215-842-9520
Ambassador Envelope Co 6705 Keaton Corp Pkwy	Saint Charles	MO	63304	**800-325-4510**	636-477-1300
American Pad & Paper Co LLC 3101 E George Bush Hwy Suite 200	Plano	TX	75082	**800-426-1368**	
AmericanChurch Div AmericanPaper Group Inc PO Box 3132	Youngstown	OH	44513	**800-250-7112**	330-758-4545
AmericanPaper Group Inc PO Box 3120	Youngstown	OH	44513	**800-431-4134**	330-758-4545
AmericanPaper Group Inc AmericanChurch Div PO Box 3132	Youngstown	OH	44513	**800-250-7112**	330-758-4545
AmericanPaper Group Inc AmericanPaper Products Co Div 8401 Southern Blvd	Youngstown	OH	44512	**800-431-4134**	330-758-4545
AmericanPaper Products Co Div AmericanPaper Group Inc 8401 Southern Blvd	Youngstown	OH	44512	**800-431-4134**	330-758-4545
Ames Safety Envelope Co 12 Tyler St	Somerville	MA	02143	**800-225-1138**	617-776-1142
Atlantic Envelope Co 1420 Peachtree St NE Suite 200	Atlanta	GA	30309	**800-225-4636**	404-853-6700
Barkley Farling Corp 5370 Hwy 42	Hattiesburg	MS	39401	**800-522-0297**	601-545-2200
Curtis 1000 Inc 1725 Breckinridge Pkwy Suite 500	Duluth	GA	30096	**800-683-8162**	678-380-9095
Heinrich Envelope Corp 925 Zane Ave N	Minneapolis	MN	55422	**800-346-7957**	763-544-3571
International Envelope Co 2 Tabas Lane *Cust Svc	Exton	PA	19341	**800-468-9835***	610-363-0900
Love Envelopes Inc 10733 E Ute St	Tulsa	OK	74116	**800-532-9747**	918-836-3535
Mackay Envelope Corp 2100 Elm St SE	Minneapolis	MN	55414	**800-622-5299**	612-331-9311
Mail-Well Envelope Co 8310 S Valley Hwy Suite 400	Englewood	CO	80112	**888-543-5439**	303-566-4500
MeadWestvaco Corp Envelope Div 2001 Roosevelt Ave	Springfield	MA	01104	**800-628-9265**	413-736-7211
Milwaukee Envelope Inc 1880 Executive Dr	Oconomowoc	WI	53006	**800-236-1980**	262-569-5555
National Envelope Corp 29-10 Hunters Pt Ave	Long Island City	NY	11101	**800-877-9551**	718-786-0300
New York Envelope Corp 29-10 Hunters Pt Ave	Long Island City	NY	11101	**800-877-9551**	718-786-0300
Old Colony Envelope Co 70 Tpke Industrial Rd *Cust Svc	Westfield	MA	01085	**800-343-1273***	413-568-2431
Oles Envelope Corp 532 E 25th St	Baltimore	MD	21218	**800-822-6537**	410-243-1520
Papercone Corp 3200 Fern Valley Rd	Louisville	KY	40213	**800-626-5308**	502-961-9493
Poly-Pak Industries Inc 125 Spagnoli Rd	Melville	NY	11747	**800-969-1995**	631-293-6767
Quality Park 2520 Como Ave	Saint Paul	MN	55108	**800-328-2990**	651-645-0251
Response Envelope Inc 1340 S Baker Ave	Ontario	CA	91761	**800-750-0046**	909-923-5855
Stora Enso North America Corp 2 Landmark Sq 3rd Fl *NYSE: SEO*	Stamford	CT	06901	**888-807-8672**	203-356-2300
Tension Envelope Corp 819 E 19th St	Kansas City	MO	64108	**800-388-5122**	816-471-3800
Top Flight Paper Products Inc 1300 Central Ave	Chattanooga	TN	37408	**800-777-3740**	423-266-8171
Tri-State Envelope Corp 20th & Market Sts 1 Orgler Pl	Ashland	PA	17921	**800-233-3102**	570-875-0433
Western States Envelope Co 4480 N 132nd St	Butler	WI	53007	**800-558-0514**	262-781-5540
Wisco Envelope Co PO Box 880	Tullahoma	TN	37388	**800-777-9677**	931-455-4584
Wolf Envelope Co 725 S Adams Rd Suite 275	Birmingham	MI	48009	**800-466-9653**	248-258-5700
Worcester Envelope Co 22 Millbury St PO Box 406	Auburn	MA	01501	**800-343-1398**	508-832-5394

261 EQUIPMENT RENTAL & LEASING

SEE ALSO Credit & Financing - Commercial; Credit & Financing - Consumer; Fleet Leasing & Management

261-1 Computer Equipment Leasing

				Toll-Free	Phone
All Service Computer Rental 600 Sylvan Ave	Englewood Cliffs	NJ	07632	**800-927-6555**	201-568-6555
Computer Sales International Inc (CSI) 9990 Old Olive St Rd	Saint Louis	MO	63141	**800-955-0960**	314-997-7010
CSI (Computer Sales International Inc) 9990 Old Olive St Rd	Saint Louis	MO	63141	**800-955-0960**	314-997-7010
Data Sales Co Inc 3450 W Burnsville Pkwy	Burnsville	MN	55337	**800-328-2730**	952-890-8838
Electro Rent Corp 6060 Sepulveda Blvd *NASDAQ: ELRC* ■ *Sales	Van Nuys	CA	91411	**800-688-1111***	818-787-2100
Forsythe MacArthur Assoc Inc 7770 Frontage Rd	Skokie	IL	60077	**800-843-4488**	847-675-8000
Halifax Corp 5250 Cherokee Ave *AMEX: HX* ■ *Cust Svc	Alexandria	VA	22312	**800-944-2543***	703-750-2202
Hitachi Credit America Ltd 800 Connecticut Ave	Norwalk	CT	06854	**800-810-0952**	203-956-3000
Meridian Technology Leasing Services 570 Lake Cook Rd Suite 300 *Cust Svc	Deerfield	IL	60015	**800-426-3090***	847-940-1200
Newport Leasing Inc 4750 Von Karman Ave *Cust Svc	Newport Beach	CA	92660	**800-678-9426***	949-476-8476
Relational Technology Services 7720 Rivers Edge Dr Suite 200	Columbus	OH	43235	**866-999-4787**	614-431-4433
Rent-A-PC Inc 265 Oser Ave	Hauppauge	NY	11788	**877-736-8272**	631-273-8888
Rush Computer Rentals 29 North Plains Rd	Wallingford	CT	06492	**800-526-7368**	203-284-8277

261-2 Heavy Equipment Rental

				Toll-Free	Phone
Allied Equipment Rentals 4969 Santa Monica Blvd	Los Angeles	CA	90029	**800-975-7368**	323-663-3251
Allied Steel Construction Co Inc PO Box 1111	Oklahoma City	OK	73101	**800-522-4658**	405-232-7531
Barnhart Crane & Rigging Inc 938 E 4th St	Richmond	VA	23224	**800-787-4767**	804-233-9221
Blanchard Machinery Inc 14301 NE 19th Ave	North Miami	FL	33181	**800-330-4242**	305-949-2581
Burke Cyril J Inc 36000 Mound Rd	Sterling Heights	MI	48310	**800-482-4952**	586-939-4400
Cloverdale Equipment Co 13133 Cloverdale St	Oak Park	MI	48237	**800-822-7999**	248-399-6600
Cyril J Burke Inc 36000 Mound Rd	Sterling Heights	MI	48310	**800-482-4952**	586-939-4400
D & D Equipment Rental Inc PO Box 2369	Santa Fe Springs	CA	90670	**866-446-1100**	562-595-4555
Equipment Corp of America PO Box 306	Coraopolis	PA	15108	**800-745-3872**	412-331-2000
Hertz Big 4 Rents Inc 5500 Commerce Blvd	Rohnert Park	CA	94928	**888-777-2700**	707-586-4444
Klochko Equipment Rental Co 2782 Corbin Ave	Melvindale	MI	48122	**800-783-7368**	313-386-7220
Marco Crane & Rigging Co 221 S 35th Ave	Phoenix	AZ	85009	**800-668-2671**	602-272-2671
Maxim Crane Works 800 Waterfront Dr	Pittsburgh	PA	15222	**866-629-4648**	412-320-4900
Medico Industries Inc 1500 Hwy 315	Wilkes-Barre	PA	18711	**800-633-0027**	570-825-7711
Morrow Equipment Co Inc 3218 Pringle Rd SE	Salem	OR	97302	**800-505-7766**	503-585-5721
National Construction Rentals Inc 15319 Chatsworth St	Mission Hills	CA	91345	**800-874-6285**	818-221-6000
NationsRent Inc 450 E Las Olas Blvd Suite 1400	Fort Lauderdale	FL	33301	**800-667-9328**	954-760-6550
Neff Corp 3750 NW 87th Ave Suite 400	Miami	FL	33178	**888-709-6333**	305-513-3350
Rental Service Corp 6929 E Greenway Pkwy Suite 200	Scottsdale	AZ	85254	**888-736-8772**	480-905-3300
Rush Enterprises Inc 555 IH 35 S Suite 500 *NASDAQ: RUSHA*	New Braunfels	TX	78130	**800-973-7874**	830-626-5200
Specialty Rental Tools & Supply Inc 1131 E FM 517	Alvin	TX	77511	**800-253-1085**	281-331-1800
Star Rentals Inc 1919 4th Ave S	Seattle	WA	98134	**800-825-7880**	206-622-7880
Sunbelt Rentals Inc 1337 Hundred Oaks Dr *Mktg	Charlotte	NC	28217	**800-452-1963***	704-348-2676
T & T Truck & Crane Service Inc 1375 N Olive St	Ventura	CA	93001	**800-655-3348**	805-488-4475
United Crane Rentals Inc 111 N Michigan Ave	Kenilworth	NJ	07033	**800-356-6260**	908-245-6260
United Rentals Inc 5 Greenwich Office Pk *NYSE: URI*	Greenwich	CT	06830	**800-877-3687**	203-622-3131
Utility Equipment Leasing Corp N4 W22610 Bluemound Rd	Waukesha	WI	53186	**800-558-0999**	262-547-1600
Waco Scaffolding & Equipment Co PO Box 318028	Cleveland	OH	44131	**800-901-2282**	216-749-8900

261-3 Home & Office Equipment Rental (General)

				Toll-Free	Phone
Aaron Rents Inc 309 E Paces Ferry Rd NE *NYSE: RNT*	Atlanta	GA	30305	**800-551-6015**	404-231-0011
Bestway Inc 7800 N Stemmons Fwy Suite 320 *NASDAQ: BSTW*	Dallas	TX	75247	**800-520-1107**	214-630-6655
Brook Furniture Rental Inc 100 Field Dr Suite 220	Lake Forest	IL	60045	**800-933-7368**	847-810-4000
Citicapital 1255 Wrights Ln	West Chester	PA	19380	**800-736-9033**	610-719-4500
ColorTyme Inc 5700 Tennyson Pkwy Suite 180	Plano	TX	75024	**800-411-8963**	972-608-5376
CORT Business Services Corp 11250 Waples Mill Rd Suite 500	Fairfax	VA	22030	**800-962-2678**	703-968-8500
CORT Furniture Rental 11250 Waples Mill Rd Suite 500	Fairfax	VA	22030	**800-962-2678**	703-968-8500
GFC Leasing Co 2101 W Beltline Hwy	Madison	WI	53713	**800-333-5905**	608-274-7877
Grand Rental Station 203 Jandus Rd	Cary	IL	60013	**800-833-3004**	847-462-5440
HSS RentX 1001 E Sunrise Blvd	Fort Lauderdale	FL	33304	**877-711-7368**	954-766-2588
Initial Tropical Plant Services 3750 W Deerfield Rd	Riverwoods	IL	60015	**800-345-0551**	847-634-4250
Lease One Systems 7305 Manchester Rd Suite C-1	Saint Louis	MO	63143	**888-645-1300**	314-645-1300
M & C Leasing Co Inc 1050 Union Rd Suite 102	West Seneca	NY	14224	**800-416-9080**	716-873-6800
Marlin Business Services Inc DBA Marlin Leasing Corp 124 Gaither Dr Suite 170 *NASDAQ: MRLN*	Mount Laurel	NJ	08054	**888-479-9123**	856-727-9526
Marlin Leasing Corp 124 Gaither Dr Suite 170 *NASDAQ: MRLN*	Mount Laurel	NJ	08054	**888-479-9123**	856-727-9526
Rent-A-Center Inc 5700 Tennyson Pkwy 3rd Fl *NASDAQ: RCII*	Plano	TX	75024	**800-275-2696**	972-801-1100
Rentway Inc 1 Rentway Pl *NYSE: RWY*	Erie	PA	16505	**800-736-8929**	814-455-5378

				Toll-Free	Phone
Rug Doctor LP 4701 Old Shepard Pl	Plano	TX	75093	**800-234-6286**	972-673-1400
Taylor Rental 203 Jandus Rd	Cary	IL	60013	**800-833-3004**	847-462-5440
Tri-Rentals Inc 3103 E Broadway Suite 400	Phoenix	AZ	85040	**800-678-3854**	602-232-9900

261-4 Industrial Equipment Rental

				Toll-Free	Phone
Able Builders Equipment Inc 7475 NW 63rd St	Miami	FL	33166	**800-864-5387**	305-592-5940
American Classic Sanitation LLC 242 E Live Oak Ave	Irwindale	CA	91706	**877-340-0004**	626-462-9110
Brockman Forklift Inc 15800 Tireman Ave	Detroit	MI	48228	**800-228-1957**	313-584-4550
Broussard Brothers Inc 25817 Louisiana Hwy 333	Abbeville	LA	70510	**800-299-5303**	337-893-5303
Chesapeake Industrial Leasing Co Inc 9512 Harford Rd	Baltimore	MD	21234	**800-782-1022**	410-661-5000
Grand Rental Station 203 Jandus Rd	Cary	IL	60013	**800-833-3004**	847-462-5440
HB Rentals LC 5813 Hwy 90 E	Broussard	LA	70518	**800-262-6790**	337-839-1641
Hertz Big 4 Rents Inc 5500 Commerce Blvd	Rohnert Park	CA	94928	**888-777-2700**	707-586-4444
Hertz Equipment Rental Corp 225 Brae Blvd	Park Ridge	NJ	07656	**800-654-3131**	201-307-2000
Horizon Fleet Services Inc 341 NW 122nd St	Oklahoma City	OK	73114	**800-357-2444**	405-755-9703
Kohler Rental Power Div of Kohler Co 4509 S Taylor Dr	Sheboygan	WI	53081	**888-769-3794**	920-459-1634
M & C Leasing Co Inc 1050 Union Rd Suite 102	West Seneca	NY	14224	**800-416-9080**	716-873-6800
M & I First National Leasing Corp 250 E Wisconsin Ave Suite 1400	Milwaukee	WI	53202	**800-558-9840**	414-272-2374
Modern Corp 4746 Model City Rd	Model City	NY	14107	**800-662-0012**	716-754-8226
Modern Equipment Sales & Rental Co 24 Brookside Dr	Wilmington	DE	19804	**800-227-2525**	302-658-5257
Quantum Analytics 363 Vintage Park Dr	Foster City	CA	94404	**800-992-4199**	650-312-0900
Safway Services Inc PO Box 1991	Milwaukee	WI	53201	**800-558-4772**	262-523-6500
Sunbelt Rentals Inc 1337 Hundred Oaks Dr *Mktg	Charlotte	NC	28217	**800-452-1963***	704-348-2676
Taylor Rental 203 Jandus Rd	Cary	IL	60013	**800-833-3004**	847-462-5440
Telogy 3200 Whipple Rd	Union City	CA	94587	**800-835-6494**	510-675-9500
Traffic Control Service Inc 1881 Betmor Ln	Anaheim	CA	92805	**800-222-8274**	714-937-0422
United Rentals Inc 5 Greenwich Office Pk *NYSE: URI*	Greenwich	CT	06830	**800-877-3687**	203-622-3131
Universal Compression Holdings Inc 4444 Brittmoore Rd *NYSE: UCO*	Houston	TX	77041	**800-234-4650**	713-335-7000
Western Oilfields Supply Co PO Box 2248	Bakersfield	CA	93303	**800-742-7246**	661-399-9124

261-5 Medical Equipment Rental

				Toll-Free	Phone
American Shared Hospital Services 4 Embarcadero Ctr Suite 3700 *AMEX: AMS*	San Francisco	CA	94111	**800-735-0641**	415-788-5300
First Lease Inc 185 Commerce Dr Unit 2	Fort Washington	PA	19034	**800-544-7607**	215-283-9727
Freedom Medical Inc 219 Welsh Pool Rd	Exton	PA	19341	**800-784-8849**	610-903-0200
M & C Leasing Co Inc 1050 Union Rd Suite 102	West Seneca	NY	14224	**800-416-9080**	716-873-6800
MEDIQ Inc 1 MEDIQ Plaza	Pennsauken	NJ	08110	**800-222-4776**	856-665-9300
Modern Medical Modalities Corp PO Box 957	Union	NJ	07083	**800-367-3926**	
Universal Hospital Services Inc 3800 W 80th St Suite 1250	Bloomington	MN	55431	**800-847-7368**	952-893-3200

261-6 Transport Equipment Rental

				Toll-Free	Phone
Andersons Inc Rail Group 480 W Dussel Dr	Maumee	OH	43537	**866-234-0505**	419-893-5050
Cronos Containers Inc 1 Front St Suite 925	San Francisco	CA	94111	**800-821-7035**	
Cronos Containers Inc 517 Rt 1 S Suite 1000	Iselin	NJ	08830	**800-221-4126**	732-602-0808
GATX Rail Canada 1600 Rene Levesque Blvd W Suite 1500	Montreal	QC	H3H1P9	**800-806-2489**	514-931-7343
GE Rail Car Services 161 N Clark St 7th Fl	Chicago	IL	60601	**888-272-5793**	312-853-5000
Greenbrier Co 1 Centerpointe Dr Suite 200 *NYSE: GBX*	Lake Oswego	OR	97035	**800-343-7188**	503-684-7000
Interpool Inc 211 College Rd E *NYSE: IPX*	Princeton	NJ	08540	**800-388-7485**	609-452-8900
Railserve Inc 1691 Phoenix Blvd Suite 110	Atlanta	GA	30349	**800-345-7245**	770-996-6838
Relco Locomotives Inc 113 Industrial Dr	Minooka	IL	60447	**800-435-6091**	815-467-3030
TTX Co 101 N Wacker Dr	Chicago	IL	60606	**800-621-5854**	312-853-3223
Union Tank Car Co 175 W Jackson Blvd Suite 2100	Chicago	IL	60604	**800-635-3770**	312-431-3111
United Rental Highway Technology 880 N Addison Rd *Cust Svc	Villa Park	IL	60181	**800-323-2462***	630-932-4600
XTRA Corp 1801 Park 270 Dr	Saint Louis	MO	63146	**800-325-1453**	314-579-9300

262 EXECUTIVE RECRUITING FIRMS

				Toll-Free	Phone
Christian & Timbers 25825 Science Pk Dr Suite 400	Cleveland	OH	44122	**800-380-9444**	216-464-8710
Cole Warren & Long Inc 2 Penn Ctr Plaza Suite 312	Philadelphia	PA	19102	**800-394-8517**	215-563-0701
Daniel & Yeager 6767 Old Madison Pike Suite 690	Huntsville	AL	35806	**800-955-1919**	256-551-1070
DHR International 10 S Riverside Plaza Suite 2220	Chicago	IL	60606	**800-782-2210**	312-782-1581
Diversified Search Cos 2005 Market St Suite 3300	Philadelphia	PA	19103	**800-423-3932**	215-732-6666
Gilbert Tweed Assoc Inc 415 Madison Ave 20th Fl	New York	NY	10017	**800-456-3932**	212-758-3000
HC Smith Ltd 20600 Chagrin Blvd Tower East Suite 200	Shaker Heights	OH	44122	**800-442-7583**	216-752-9966
Howard-Sloan Search Inc 1140 Ave of the Americas	New York	NY	10036	**800-221-1326**	212-704-0444
Klein Landau & Romm 1725 K St NW	Washington	DC	20006	**866-807-1931**	202-728-0100
Major Hagen & Africa 500 Washington St 5th Fl	San Francisco	CA	94111	**877-482-1010**	415-956-1010
Management Recruiters International Worldwide Inc 200 Public Sq 31st Fl	Cleveland	OH	44114	**800-875-4000**	216-696-1122
Medical Directions Inc 410 Saw Mill River Rd Suite 1005	Ardsley	NY	10502	**800-647-0573**	914-478-8500
Monster Worldwide Inc 622 3rd Ave 39th Fl *NASDAQ: MNST*	New York	NY	10017	**800-867-2001**	212-351-7000
MSI International Inc 245 Peachtree Ctr Ave Suite 2500	Atlanta	GA	30303	**800-801-1820**	404-659-5236
Physicians Search 5581 E Stetson Ct	Anaheim	CA	92807	**800-748-6320**	714-685-1047
Reynolds Russell Assoc Inc 200 Park Ave 23rd Fl	New York	NY	10166	**888-772-6200**	212-351-2000
Russell Reynolds Assoc Inc 200 Park Ave 23rd Fl	New York	NY	10166	**888-772-6200**	212-351-2000
Sanford Rose Assoc 3737 Embassy Pkwy Suite 200	Akron	OH	44333	**800-731-7724**	330-670-9797
Smith HC Ltd 20600 Chagrin Blvd Tower East Suite 200	Shaker Heights	OH	44122	**800-442-7583**	216-752-9966
Swan Legal Search 11500 Olympic Blvd Suite 370	Los Angeles	CA	90064	**888-860-1154**	310-445-5010
Winston Personnel Service Inc 122 E 42nd St	New York	NY	10068	**800-494-6786**	212-557-8181

263 EXERCISE & FITNESS EQUIPMENT

SEE ALSO Sporting Goods

				Toll-Free	Phone
All Pro Exercise Products Inc 2110 Harbourside Dr Suite 528	Longboat Key	FL	34228	**800-735-9287**	941-387-9432
Battle Creek Equipment Co 307 W Jackson St *Cust Svc	Battle Creek	MI	49017	**800-253-0854***	269-962-6181
Body Masters Sports Industries Inc 700 E Texas Ave	Rayne	LA	70578	**800-325-8964**	337-334-9611
Body-Solid Inc 1900 S Des Plaines Ave	Forest Park	IL	60130	**800-833-1227**	708-427-3500
Cybex International Inc 10 Trotter Dr *AMEX: CYB*	Medway	MA	02053	**888-462-9239**	508-533-4300
Fitness Quest Inc 1400 Raff Rd SW	Canton	OH	44750	**800-321-9236**	330-478-0755
Heart-Rate Inc 3190 Airport Loop Dr Bldg E	Costa Mesa	CA	92626	**800-237-2271**	714-850-9716
Heartline Fitness Products Inc 19209 Orbit Dr	Gaithersburg	MD	20879	**800-262-3348**	301-921-0661
Hoggan Health Industries Inc 8020 S 1300 West	West Jordan	UT	84088	**800-678-7888**	801-572-6500
Hoist Fitness Systems Inc 9990 Empire St Suite 130	San Diego	CA	92126	**800-548-5438**	858-578-7676
HYDRO-FIT Inc 160 Madison St *Cust Svc	Eugene	OR	97402	**800-346-7295***	541-484-4361
ICON Health & Fitness Inc 1500 S 1000 West	Logan	UT	84321	**800-999-3756**	435-750-5000
IronMaster LLC 21828 87th Ave SE Suite E	Woodinville	WA	98072	**800-533-3339**	425-408-9040
Life Fitness 5100 N River Rd	Schiller Park	IL	60176	**800-735-3867**	847-288-3300
New York Barbells 160 Home St	Elmira	NY	14904	**800-446-1833**	607-733-8038
Paramount Fitness Corp 6450 E Bandini Blvd	Los Angeles	CA	90040	**800-721-2121**	323-721-2121
Precor Inc 20031 142nd Ave NE	Woodinville	WA	98072	**800-786-8404**	425-486-9292
Pro Star Sports Inc 1133 Winchester Ave	Kansas City	MO	64126	**800-821-8482**	816-241-9737
Soloflex Inc 570 NE 53rd Ave	Hillsboro	OR	97124	**800-547-8802**	503-640-8891
Spirit Manufacturing Inc 5702 Krueger Dr	Jonesboro	AR	72401	**800-258-4555**	870-935-1107
Star Trac by Unisen Inc 14410 Myford Rd	Irvine	CA	92606	**800-228-6635**	714-669-1660
Task Industries Inc 1325 E Franklin Ave	Pomona	CA	91766	**800-961-9377**	909-629-1600
True Fitness Technology Inc 865 Hoff Rd	O'Fallon	MO	63366	**800-426-6570**	636-272-7100
Vision Fitness 500 South CP Ave	Lake Mills	WI	53551	**800-335-4348**	920-648-4090
Woodway USA W229 N591 Foster Ct	Waukesha	WI	53186	**800-966-3929**	262-548-6235
York Barbell Co Inc 3300 Board Rd *Cust Svc	York	PA	17402	**800-358-9675***	717-767-6481

264 EXPLOSIVES

				Toll-Free	Phone
Accurate Arms Co Inc 5891 Hwy 230 W	McEwen	TN	37101	**800-416-3006**	931-729-4207
Alliant Powder PO Box 6	Radford	VA	24143	**800-276-9337**	540-639-7800
Austin Powder Co 25800 Science Park Dr Suite 300	Cleveland	OH	44122	**800-321-0752**	216-464-2400
Buckley Powder Co 42 Inverness Dr E	Englewood	CO	80112	**800-333-2266**	303-790-7007
Dyno Nobel Inc 50 S Main St Crossroad Towers 11th Fl	Salt Lake City	UT	84144	**800-473-2626**	801-364-4800
Longhorn Mfg Co Inc PO Box 6060	Roswell	NM	88202	**800-248-3957**	505-347-5411
Orica USA Inc 33101 E Quincy Ave	Watkins	CO	80137	**877-336-7422**	303-268-5000
Titan Completion Products Ltd 1266 Lakeview Dr FM 661	Mansfield	TX	79088	**800-320-5110**	817-473-9321
Zambelli Internationale Fireworks Mfg 20 S Mercer St 2nd Fl	New Castle	PA	16101	**800-245-0397**	724-658-6611

265 EYE BANKS

SEE ALSO Organ & Tissue Banks; Transplant Centers - Blood Stem Cell

				Toll-Free	Phone
Alabama Eye Bank 500 Robert Jemison Rd	Birmingham	AL	35209	**800-423-7811**	205-942-2120

Name / Address	City	State	ZIP	Toll-Free	Phone
Alcon Research Ltd 6201 S Fwy	Fort Worth	TX	76134	**800-757-9195**	817-551-6929
Center for Organ Recovery & Education (CORE) 204 Sigma Dr RIDC Park	Pittsburgh	PA	15238	**800-366-6777**	412-366-6777
Central Florida Lions Eye & Tissue Bank Inc 5523 W Cypress St Suite 100	Tampa	FL	33607	**800-277-2020**	813-289-1200
Central Florida Tissue & Eye Bank Inc 8663 Commodity Cir	Orlando	FL	32819	**800-753-9109**	407-226-3888
Central Ohio Lions Eye Bank 456 W 10th Ave Suite B-0903	Columbus	OH	43210	**800-301-4960**	614-293-8114
Connecticut Eye Bank & Visual Research Foundation Inc 100 Grand St	New Britain	CT	06052	**800-355-5520**	860-224-5550
CORE (Center for Organ Recovery & Education) 204 Sigma Dr RIDC Park	Pittsburgh	PA	15238	**800-366-6777**	412-366-6777
Doheny Eye & Tissue Transplant Bank 1127 Wilshire Blvd Suite 602	Los Angeles	CA	90017	**877-348-2020**	213-482-3937
Donor Network of Arizona 201 W Coolidge	Phoenix	AZ	85013	**800-447-9477**	602-222-2200
Eye Bank of British Columbia Vancouver General Hospital 2550 Willow St Eye Care Centre 3rd Fl	Vancouver	BC	V5Z3N9	**800-667-2060**	604-875-4567
Georgia Eye Bank Inc 3060 Peachtree Rd NW Suite 130	Atlanta	GA	30305	**800-342-9812**	404-264-1900
Gift of Life Donor Program Eye Bank 2000 Hamilton St Rodin Pl Suite 201	Philadelphia	PA	19130	**800-543-6391**	215-557-8090
Idaho Lions Eye Bank 1055 N Curtis Rd	Boise	ID	83706	**800-546-6889**	208-367-2400
Indiana Lions Eye & Tissue Transplant Bank Indiana University Medical Center 702 Rotary Cir Rm 115	Indianapolis	IN	46202	**800-232-4384**	317-274-8527
International Cornea Project 9444 Balboa Ave Suite 100	San Diego	CA	92123	**888-393-2265**	858-694-0444
Laboratories at Bonfils 717 Yosemite St 2nd Fl	Denver	CO	80230	**800-321-6088**	303-365-9000
LifeShare of the Carolinas 86 Victoria Rd Bldg B	Asheville	NC	28801	**800-932-4483**	828-258-9703
LifeShare of the Carolinas 5000 D Airport Ctr Pkwy	Charlotte	NC	28208	**800-932-4483**	704-697-3303
Lions Eye Bank of Central Texas Inc 103 E Wheeler PO Box 347	Manor	TX	78653	**800-977-3937**	512-457-0638
Lions Eye Bank of Delaware Valley 2000 Hamilton St Rodin Pl Suite 301	Philadelphia	PA	19130	**800-743-6667**	215-563-1679
Lions Eye Bank of Oregon 1010 NW 22nd Ave Suite N144	Portland	OR	97210	**800-843-7793**	503-413-7523
Lions Medical Eye Bank & Research Foundation of Eastern Virginia Inc 600 Gresham Dr	Norfolk	VA	23507	**800-453-6059**	757-668-2020
Medical Eye Bank of Maryland 815 Park Ave	Baltimore	MD	21201	**800-756-4824**	410-752-2020
Michigan Eye Bank & Transplantation Center 1000 Wall St	Ann Arbor	MI	48105	**800-247-7250**	734-764-3262
Mid-America Transplant Services 1139 Olivette Executive Pkwy	Saint Louis	MO	63132	**888-376-4854**	314-991-1661
Mid-Continent Eye Bank 3306 E Central Ave	Wichita	KS	67208	**800-366-6791**	316-688-3937
Midwest Eye Banks & Transplantation Center 800 S Wells St Suite 185	Chicago	IL	60607	**800-548-4703**	312-706-9650
Minnesota Lions Eye Bank 420 Delaware St SE MMC 493	Minneapolis	MN	55455	**866-887-4448**	612-625-5159
Musculoskeletal Transplant Foundation 125 May St Suite 300	Edison	NJ	08837	**800-433-6576**	732-661-0202
National Disease Research Interchange (NDRI) 1628 John F Kennedy Blvd 8 Penn Ctr 8th Fl	Philadelphia	PA	19103	**800-222-6374**	215-557-7361
NDRI (National Disease Research Interchange) 1628 John F Kennedy Blvd 8 Penn Ctr 8th Fl	Philadelphia	PA	19103	**800-222-6374**	215-557-7361
New Mexico Lions Eye Bank 2501 Yale Blvd SE Suite 100	Albuquerque	NM	87106	**888-616-3937**	505-266-3937
North Carolina Eye Bank Inc 3622 Lyckan Pkwy	Durham	NC	27707	**800-552-9956**	
North Carolina Eye Bank Inc 3900 Westpoint Blvd Suite F	Winston-Salem	NC	27103	**800-552-9956**	336-765-0932
Northwest Lions Eye Bank 901 Boren Ave Suite 810	Seattle	WA	98104	**800-847-5786**	206-682-8500
Regional Tissue Bank QEII Health Sciences 5788 University Ave Rm 431 McKenzie Bldg Ctr	Halifax	NS	B3H1V7	**800-314-6515**	902-473-7360
Rochester Eye & Human Parts Bank DBA Rochester/Finger Lakes Eye & Tissue Bank 524 White Spruce Blvd	Rochester	NY	14623	**800-568-4321**	585-272-7890
Rochester/Finger Lakes Eye & Tissue Bank 524 White Spruce Blvd	Rochester	NY	14623	**800-568-4321**	585-272-7890
Rocky Mountain Lions Eye Bank PO Box 6026	Aurora	CO	80045	**800-444-7479**	720-848-3937
San Diego Eye Bank 9444 Balboa Ave Suite 100	San Diego	CA	92123	**800-393-2265**	858-694-0444
Sierra Eye & Tissue Donor Services 1700 Alhambra Blvd Suite 112	Sacramento	CA	95816	**800-762-8819**	916-456-1450
South Dakota Lions Eye Bank 1321 W 22nd St	Sioux Falls	SD	57105	**800-245-7846**	605-373-1008
Tissue Banks International 815 Park Ave	Baltimore	MD	21201	**800-756-4824**	410-752-2020
Transplant Services Center University of Texas 5323 Harry Hines Blvd MC 9074	Dallas	TX	75390	**800-433-6667**	214-648-2609
Upstate New York Transplant Services Inc 165 Genesee St	Buffalo	NY	14203	**800-227-4771**	716-853-6667
Vision Care 108 Acorn Hill Ln	Apex	NC	27502	**888-657-4448**	919-303-2584
Washington Eye Bank 815 Park Ave	Baltimore	MD	21201	**800-756-4824**	410-752-2020

266 FABRIC STORES

SEE ALSO Patterns - Sewing

Name / Address	City	State	ZIP	Toll-Free	Phone
Ben Franklin Stores 7601 Durand Ave	Racine	WI	53408	**800-992-9307**	262-681-7000
Calico Corners 203 Gale Ln *Cust Svc	Kennett Square	PA	19348	**800-213-6366***	610-444-9700
Everfast Inc DBA Calico Corners 203 Gale Ln *Cust Svc	Kennett Square	PA	19348	**800-213-6366***	610-444-9700
Fabric Place Inc 136 Howard St	Framingham	MA	01702	**800-556-3700**	508-872-4888
Jo-Ann Fabrics & Crafts 5555 Darrow Rd	Hudson	OH	44236	**888-739-4120**	330-656-2600
Mary Maxim Inc 2001 Holland Ave PO Box 5019	Port Huron	MI	48061	**800-962-9504**	810-987-2000

267 FACILITIES MANAGEMENT SERVICES

SEE ALSO Correctional Facilities Operators

Name / Address	City	State	ZIP	Toll-Free	Phone
American Park 'n Swap 40 Fountain Plaza	Buffalo	NY	14202	**800-828-7240**	716-858-5185
ARAMARK Food & Support Services 1101 Market St	Philadelphia	PA	19107	**800-999-8989**	215-238-3000
ARAMARK Harrison Lodging 580 White Plains Rd	Tarrytown	NY	10591	**800-422-6338**	914-631-8100
ARAMARK Uniform & Career Apparel 1101 Market St	Philadelphia	PA	19107	**800-999-8989**	215-238-3000
CA One Services 40 Fountain Plaza	Buffalo	NY	14202	**800-828-7240**	716-858-5000
Delaware North Cos Gaming & Entertainment 40 Fountain Plaza	Buffalo	NY	14202	**800-828-7240**	716-858-5000
Johnson Controls Inc 5757 N Green Bay Ave *NYSE: JCI*	Milwaukee	WI	53209	**800-972-8040**	414-524-1200
OMNIPLEX World Services Corp 14840 Conference Ctr Dr	Chantilly	VA	20151	**800-356-3406**	703-652-3100
Sodexho Inc 9801 Washingtonian Blvd	Gaithersburg	MD	20878	**800-763-3946**	301-987-4000
Sportservice Corp 40 Fountain Plaza	Buffalo	NY	14202	**800-828-7240**	716-858-5000
UNICCO Service Co 275 Grove St Suite 3-200	Auburndale	MA	02466	**800-283-9222**	617-527-5222
United Space Alliance 1150 Gemini Ave	Houston	TX	77058	**800-329-4036**	281-212-6200
VMS Inc 203 E Cary St Suite 200	Richmond	VA	23219	**888-547-4404**	804-553-4001
Xanterra Parks & Resorts 14001 E Iliff Ave Suite 600	Aurora	CO	80014	**888-297-2757**	303-338-6000

268 FACTORS

Name / Address	City	State	ZIP	Toll-Free	Phone
1st AAA Factors Inc 321 N Mall Dr	Saint George	UT	84790	**888-216-1235**	
Accelerated Business Credit Corp 101 N Westlake Blvd Suite 204	Westlake Village	CA	91362	**866-446-2888**	805-370-0234
Accord Financial Corp 77 Bloor St W *TSE: ACD*	Toronto	ON	M5S1M2	**800-967-0015**	416-961-0007
Accord Financial Inc 25 Woods Lake Rd Suite 102	Greenville	SC	29607	**800-231-2757**	864-271-4384
Account Funding Inc 16055 Ventura Blvd Suite 924	Encino	CA	91436	**800-666-3928**	
Accounts Receivable Funding Corp 317 Peoples St Suite 600	Corpus Christi	TX	78401	**800-992-1717**	361-884-7196
Action Capital Corp 230 Peachtree St Suite 910	Atlanta	GA	30303	**800-525-7767**	404-524-3181
Advantage Funding Corp 1000 Parkwood Cir Suite 300	Atlanta	GA	30339	**800-241-2274**	770-955-2274
AmeriFactors 215 Celebration Pl Suite 150	Celebration	FL	34747	**800-884-3863**	407-566-1150
Crestmark Bank 850 E Long Lake Rd	Troy	MI	48085	**888-999-6088**	248-740-0700
Diversified Funding Services Inc PO Box 873	Jonesboro	GA	30237	**888-603-0055**	770-603-0055
Goodman Factors 3010 LBJ Freeway Suite 140	Dallas	TX	75234	**877-446-6362**	972-241-3297
Hamilton Group 100 Elwood Davis Rd	North Syracuse	NY	13212	**800-351-3066**	315-413-0086
JD Factors 1611 S Pacific Coast Hwy Suite 203	Redondo Beach	CA	90277	**866-585-2274**	310-316-7170
LSQ Funding Group LC 1403 W Colonial Dr Suite B	Orlando	FL	32804	**800-474-7606**	407-206-0022
Mazon Assoc Inc 600 W Airport Fwy	Irving	TX	75062	**800-442-2740**	972-554-6967
Merchant Factors Corp 1430 Broadway 18th Fl	New York	NY	10018	**800-929-3293**	212-840-7575
Montcap Financial Corp 3500 de Maisonneuve Blvd W Suite 1510	Montreal	QC	H3Z3C1	**800-231-2977**	514-932-8223
Oxford Capital Partners LLC PO Box 61585	Potomac	MD	20859	**888-224-3035**	301-983-8000
Porter Capital Corp 2112 1st Ave N	Birmingham	AL	35203	**800-737-7344**	205-322-5442
Quantum Corporate Funding Ltd 1140 Ave of the Americas 16th Fl	New York	NY	10036	**800-352-2535**	212-768-1200
Riviera Finance 220 Ave I	Redondo Beach	CA	90277	**800-872-7484**	
Rockland Credit Finance LLC 6 Park Center Ct Suite 212	Owings Mills	MD	21117	**866-725-5263**	410-902-0393
Rosenthal & Rosenthal Inc 1370 Broadway	New York	NY	10018	**800-999-4800**	212-356-1400
RTS Financial Service 8601 Monrovia	Lenexa	KS	66215	**800-860-7926**	913-492-6351
Seven Oaks Capital 5745 Essen Ln Suite 102	Baton Rouge	LA	70810	**800-511-4588**	225-757-1919
Systran Financial Services Corp 4949 SW Meadows Rd Suite 500	Oswego	OR	97035	**800-824-2075**	503-675-5700
TCE Capital Corp 505 Consumers Rd Suite 707	Toronto	ON	M2J4V8	**800-465-0400**	416-497-7400
United California Discount Corp 2035 S Myrtle Ave	Monrovia	CA	91017	**800-228-7151**	626-303-3551
Working Capital Co 3736 Mt Diablo Blvd Suite 310	Lafayette	CA	94549	**800-899-3836**	925-283-4433

269 FARM MACHINERY & EQUIPMENT - MFR

SEE ALSO Lawn & Garden Equipment

Name / Address	City	State	ZIP	Toll-Free	Phone
ADM Alliance Nutrition Inc 1000 N 30th St	Quincy	IL	62301	**800-292-3333**	217-222-7100
Agile Mfg Inc 720 Industrial Park Rd	Anderson	MO	64831	**800-704-7356**	417-845-6065
Alamo Group Inc 1502 E Walnut St *NYSE: ALG* ■ *Cust Svc	Seguin	TX	78155	**800-356-6286***	830-379-1480
Allied Systems Co 2300 Oregon St	Sherwood	OR	97140	**800-627-0429**	503-625-2560
Amarillo Wind Machine Co 20513 Ave 256	Exeter	CA	93221	**800-311-4498**	559-592-4256
Automatic Equipment Mfg Co 1 Mill Rd Industrial Pk	Pender	NE	68047	**800-228-9289**	402-385-3051
B & H Mfg Inc 141 County Rd 34 E	Jackson	MN	56143	**800-240-3288**	507-847-2802
Behlen Mfg Co 4025 E 23rd St	Columbus	NE	68601	**800-553-5520**	402-564-3111
Berg Equipment Co 2700 W Veterans Pkwy	Marshfield	WI	54449	**800-494-1738**	715-384-2151
Bowie Industries Inc 1004 E Wise	Bowie	TX	76230	**800-433-0934**	940-872-1106
Brillion Iron Works Inc 200 Park Ave PO Box 127	Brillion	WI	54110	**800-409-9749**	920-756-2121

				Toll-Free	Phone
Brock Grain Conditioning Group 1750 W SR-28	Frankfort	IN	46041	**800-541-7900**	765-654-8517
Brown Mfg Corp 6001 E Hwy 27	Ozark	AL	36360	**800-633-8909**	334-795-6603
Broyhill Co 1 N Market Sq	Dakota City	NE	68731	**800-228-1003**	402-987-3412
Bush Hog LLC PO Box 1039 2501 Griffin Ave	Selma	AL	36701	**800-363-6096**	334-872-6261
Cal-Coast Dairy Systems Inc 424 S Tegner Rd *Cust Svc	Turlock	CA	95380	**800-732-6826***	209-634-9026
Carver Inc 1 Lummus Dr	Savannah	GA	31407	**800-458-6687**	912-748-5000
CNH LLC 600 E Peoria St	Goodfield	IL	61742	**800-432-7680**	309-965-2233
Conrad-American Inc 609 Main St	Houghton	IA	52631	**800-553-1791**	319-469-4111
Custom Products of Litchfield Inc 1715 S Sibley Ave	Litchfield	MN	55355	**800-222-5463**	320-693-3221
Cyclone Mfg Co Inc PO Box 67	Urbana	IN	46990	**800-972-6130**	260-774-3311
Dempster Industries Inc 711 S 6th St	Beatrice	NE	68310	**800-777-0212**	402-223-4026
DuraTech Industries International Inc 3780 Hwy 281 SE	Jamestown	ND	58402	**800-243-4601**	701-252-4601
Edstrom Industries Inc 819 Bakke Ave	Waterford	WI	53185	**800-558-5913**	262-534-5181
EVH Mfg LLC 4895 Red Bluff Rd	Loris	SC	29569	**888-990-2555**	843-756-4051
EZ Trail Inc Hwy 133 E Box 168	Arthur	IL	61911	**800-677-2802**	217-543-3471
Feterl Mfg Co 411 Center Ave W	Salem	SD	57058	**800-367-8660**	605-425-2206
Finn Corp 9281 Le Saint Dr	Fairfield	OH	45014	**800-543-7166**	513-874-2818
Flint Cliffs Mfg Co 1600 Bluff Rd	Burlington	IA	52601	**800-445-1867**	319-752-2781
Forsbergs Inc 1210 Pennington Ave *Cust Svc	Thief River Falls	MN	56701	**800-654-1927***	218-681-1927
Gandy Co 528 Gandrud Rd	Owatonna	MN	55060	**800-443-2476**	507-451-5430
Great Bend Mfg Co Inc 2501 Griffin Ave	Selma	AL	36701	**800-825-1701**	334-872-6261
Gregory Mfg Co Inc 506 Oak Dr	Lewiston	NC	27849	**800-233-4734**	252-348-2531
Hagie Mfg Co 721 Central Ave W	Clarion	IA	50525	**800-247-4885**	515-532-2861
Hanson Silo Co 11587 County Rd 8 SE	Lake Lillian	MN	56253	**800-450-4171**	320-664-4171
HD Hudson Mfg Co 500 N Michigan Ave Suite 2300	Chicago	IL	60611	**800-523-9284**	312-644-2830
Henderson Mfg Inc 1085 S 3rd St	Manchester	IA	52057	**800-359-4970**	563-927-2828
Herschel-Adams Inc 1301 N 14th St *Cust Svc	Indianola	IA	50125	**800-247-2167***	515-961-7481
Hiniker Co 58766 240th St	Mankato	MN	56002	**800-433-5620**	507-625-6621
Hudson HD Mfg Co 500 N Michigan Ave Suite 2300	Chicago	IL	60611	**800-523-9284**	312-644-2830
Hutchinson/Mayrath Industries 514 W Crawford St	Clay Center	KS	67432	**800-523-6993**	785-632-3133
K & M Mfg Co 308 NW 2nd St	Renville	MN	56284	**800-328-1752**	320-329-3301
Kelly Ryan Equipment Co 900 Kelly Ryan Dr	Blair	NE	68008	**800-640-6967**	402-426-2151
Krause Corp 305 S Monroe St	Hutchinson	KS	67501	**800-957-2873**	620-663-6161
Kroy Industries 701 S 17th St	Henderson	NE	68371	**800-228-2883**	402-723-5374
Lely USA Inc 1410 Vermeer Rd E PO Box 437	Pella	IA	50219	**888-245-4684**	641-621-7905
Lindsay Mfg Co 214 E 2nd St *NYSE: LNN*	Lindsay	NE	68644	**800-829-5300**	402-428-2131
Loftness Specialized Farm Equipment Inc 650 S Main St	Hector	MN	55342	**800-828-7624**	320-848-6266
LongAgribusiness LLC 111 Fairview St	Tarboro	NC	27886	**877-639-5194**	252-823-4151
LZ Truck Equipment Co Inc 1881 Rice St	Roseville	MN	55113	**800-247-1082**	651-488-2571
M & W Gear Co 1020 S Sangamon Ave	Gibson City	IL	60936	**800-221-2855**	217-784-4261
Mathews Co 500 Industrial Ave	Crystal Lake	IL	60039	**800-323-7045**	815-459-2210
Mertz Inc 1701 N Waverly	Ponca City	OK	74601	**800-654-6433**	580-762-5646
Miller Saint Nazianz Inc 511 E Main St	Saint Nazianz	WI	54232	**800-247-5557**	920-773-2121
Modern Group Ltd 1655 Louisiana St *Cust Svc	Beaumont	TX	77701	**800-231-8198***	409-833-2665
Moorfeed Corp 6996 E 32nd St	Indianapolis	IN	46226	**888-545-7171**	317-545-7171
New Holland Construction North America 245 E North Ave	Carol Stream	IL	60188	**888-290-7377**	630-260-4000
Orchard-Rite Ltd Inc PO Box 9308	Yakima	WA	98909	**800-676-4460**	509-457-9196
Orthman Mfg Inc PO Box B	Lexington	NE	68850	**800-658-3270**	308-324-4654
Osborne Industries Inc 120 N Industrial Ave	Osborne	KS	67473	**800-255-0316**	785-346-2192
P & H Mfg Co PO Box 349 *Sales	Shelbyville	IL	62565	**800-879-2123***	217-774-2123
Peerless Mfg Co US Hwy 82 E	Shellman	GA	39886	**800-225-4617**	229-679-5353
Precision Tank & Equipment Co Inc 3503 Conover Rd	Virginia	IL	62691	**800-258-4197**	217-452-7228
Rainbow Mfg Co 1 Rainbow Dr *Cust Svc	Fitzgerald	GA	31750	**800-841-0323***	229-423-4341
Reynolds International LP 5000 N 29th St	McAllen	TX	78504	**800-441-8161**	956-687-7500
Ryan Kelly Equipment Co 900 Kelly Ryan Dr	Blair	NE	68008	**800-640-6967**	402-426-2151
Shivvers Inc 614 W English St	Corydon	IA	50060	**800-245-9093**	641-872-1005
Simonsen Industries Inc 500 Hwy 31 E	Quimby	IA	51049	**800-831-4860**	712-445-2211
Sioux Steel Co 196 1/2 E 6th St	Sioux Falls	SD	57104	**800-557-4689**	605-336-1750
Stock Equipment Co 16490 Chillicothe Rd	Chagrin Falls	OH	44023	**800-289-7326**	440-543-6000
Sudenga Industries Inc 2002 Kingbird Ave	George	IA	51237	**800-314-3908**	712-475-3301
Summers Mfg Co Inc 338 Railway Ave	Maddock	ND	58348	**800-732-4347**	701-438-2855
Taylor Pittsburgh Manufacturing 7 Rocky Mount Rd	Athens	TN	37303	**800-456-7929**	423-745-3110
Toro Co Irrigation Div 5825 Jasmine St	Riverside	CA	92502	**800-664-4740**	951-688-9221
Unverferth Mfg Co Inc 18107 US 224 W	Kalida	OH	45853	**800-322-6301**	419-532-3121
Valco Inc 210 E Main St	Coldwater	OH	45828	**800-531-1064**	419-678-8731
Valmont Industries Inc 1 Valmont Plaza *NYSE: VMI*	Omaha	NE	68154	**800-825-6668**	402-963-1000
Wiese Industries Inc 1501 5th St PO Box 39	Perry	IA	50220	**800-568-4391**	515-465-9854
Woods Equipment Co 2606 S Illinois Rt 2	Oregon	IL	61061	**800-319-6637**	815-732-2141
Wylie Mfg Co 101 N Main St *Sales	Petersburg	TX	79250	**800-722-4001***	806-667-3566
Yetter Mfg Co Inc 109 S McDonough St	Colchester	IL	62326	**800-447-5777**	309-776-4111

270 FARM MACHINERY & EQUIPMENT - WHOL

				Toll-Free	Phone
A & L Distributing Co 7933 SW Cirrus Dr	Beaverton	OR	97008	**800-234-9556**	503-684-9384
Ag West Supply 9055 Rickreall Rd	Rickreall	OR	97371	**800-842-2224**	503-363-2332
Arends & Sons Inc 715 S Sangamon Ave	Gibson City	IL	60936	**800-637-6052**	217-784-4241
B & G Equipment Inc 301 E 8th St	Greeley	CO	80631	**800-382-9024**	970-352-9141
Barnett Implement Co Inc 4220 Old Hwy 99 S	Mount Vernon	WA	98273	**800-453-9274**	360-424-7995
BE Implement Co PO Box 752	Brownfield	TX	79316	**800-725-5435**	806-637-3594
Belarus Tractor International Inc 7842 N Faulkner Rd	Milwaukee	WI	53224	**800-356-2336**	414-355-2000
Bell Equipment Inc PO Box 230	Grangeville	ID	83530	**800-753-3373**	208-983-1730
Blanchard Compact Equipment 1410 Ashville Hwy	Spartanburg	SC	29303	**800-397-9075**	864-582-1245
Carco International Inc 2721 Midland Blvd	Fort Smith	AR	72904	**800-824-3215**	479-441-3270
Carroll County Equipment Co 25921 Hwy 65	Carrollton	MO	64633	**800-214-3337**	660-542-2485
Cash Hardware Co Inc 406 W Main St	Coulee City	WA	99115	**800-835-8311**	509-632-5547
Deer Trail Implement Inc 1411 S 81 Hwy Bypass PO Box 1326	McPherson	KS	67460	**800-364-4020**	620-241-3553
Dent & Co 5800 E Mabry Dr	Clovis	NM	88101	**800-748-3368**	505-763-5517
Empire Southwest Co 1725 S Country Club Dr	Mesa	AZ	85210	**800-367-4731**	480-633-4400
Farm Implement & Supply Co Inc 520 W Mill St	Plainville	KS	67663	**888-589-6029**	785-434-4824
Ferriday Farm Equipment Co Inc 503 Lake Dr Hwy 568	Ferriday	LA	71334	**800-256-4576**	318-757-4576
French Implement Co Inc 497 S Hwy 105	Charleston	MO	63834	**800-325-8622**	573-649-3021
Gardner Inc 3641 Interchange Rd	Columbus	OH	43204	**800-848-8946**	614-456-4000
German-Bliss Equipment Co Inc 624 W Spring St	Princeville	IL	61559	**800-728-4734**	309-385-4316
Giles & Ransome Inc Ransome Engine Power Div 2975 Galloway Rd	Bensalem	PA	19020	**800-753-4228**	215-639-4300
Golden Spike Equipment Co 1352 W Main St PO Box 70	Tremonton	UT	84337	**800-821-4474**	435-257-5346
Greenline Equipment 6068 S Redwood Rd	Salt Lake City	UT	84123	**888-201-5500**	801-966-4231
Grossenburg Implement Inc 31341 US Hwy 18	Winner	SD	57580	**800-658-3440**	605-842-2040
Growers Equipment Co 8674 NW 58th St	Miami	FL	33166	**800-592-7890**	305-592-7891
Hanley Co Inc 641 W Main St	Sun Prairie	WI	53590	**800-279-1422**	608-837-5111
Harcourt Equipment 313 Hwy 169 & 175 E	Harcourt	IA	50544	**800-445-5646**	515-354-5331
Hayward Distributing Co 4061 Perimeter Dr	Columbus	OH	43228	**800-282-1585**	614-272-5953
HB Duvall Inc 901 E Patrick St	Frederick	MD	21701	**800-423-4032**	301-662-1125
HC Clark Implement Co 4411 E Hwy 12	Aberdeen	SD	57401	**800-532-6747**	605-225-8170
Heath's Inc 600 W Bridge St	Monticello	IL	61856	**800-443-2847**	217-762-2534
Hector Turf & Garden Inc 1301 NW 3rd St	Deerfield Beach	FL	33442	**877-343-2867**	954-429-3200
Hillsboro Equipment Inc E18898 State Hwy 33 E PO Box 583	Hillsboro	WI	54634	**800-521-5133**	608-489-2275
Hobbs Implement Co Inc PO Box 807	Edenton	NC	27932	**800-682-6457**	252-482-7411
Hollingsworth Inc 1775 SW 30th St	Ontario	OR	97914	**800-541-1612**	541-889-7254
Holt Co of Texas 3302 South WW White Rd	San Antonio	TX	78220	**800-275-4658**	210-648-1111
Hoober Inc 3452 Old Philadelphia Pike	Intercourse	PA	17534	**800-732-0017**	717-768-8231
Hultgren Implements Inc 5698 State Hwy 175	Ida Grove	IA	51445	**800-827-1650**	712-364-3105
Hurst Farm Supply Inc 105 Ave D	Abernathy	TX	79311	**800-535-8903**	806-298-2541
Implement Sales Co LLC 1574 Stone Ridge Dr	Stone Mountain	GA	30083	**800-955-9592**	770-908-9439
Jacobi Sales Inc 425 Main St NE	Palmyra	IN	47164	**800-489-3617**	812-364-6141
James River Equipment 11047 Leadbetter Rd	Ashland	VA	23005	**800-969-6001**	804-798-6001
JD Equipment Inc 1660 US 42 NE	London	OH	43140	**800-659-5646**	614-879-6620
John Day Co 6263 Abbott Dr	Omaha	NE	68110	**800-767-2273**	402-455-8000
John Fayhee & Sons Inc 360 E Main St	Prairie City	IL	61470	**800-637-2614**	309-775-3317
Johnson Implement Co Inc 1904 Hwy 82 W	Greenwood	MS	38930	**800-898-0160**	662-453-6525
Landell-Thelen Inc 323 E Hwy 30	Shelton	NE	68876	**800-694-5674**	308-647-6811
Larchmont Engineering & Irrigation Co 11 Larchmont Ln	Lexington	MA	02420	**877-862-2550**	781-862-2550
Leoti Greentech Inc PO Drawer L	Leoti	KS	67861	**800-783-2621**	620-375-2621
Liechty Farm Equipment Inc PO Box 67	Archbold	OH	43502	**800-272-5898**	419-445-1565
McCranie Implement Co Inc PO Box 628	Hawkinsville	GA	31036	**800-245-9046**	478-892-9046
McCranie Motors & Tractors Inc PO Box 770	Unadilla	GA	31091	**800-841-4050**	478-627-3291
Meissner Tractors Inc Hwy 2 & 87 PO Box 1111	Havre	MT	59501	**800-800-3113**	406-265-5887
Miller Machinery & Supply Co 127 NE 27th St	Miami	FL	33137	**800-273-3030**	305-573-1300
Moodie Implement Inc 3701 E Hwy 14	Pierre	SD	57501	**800-742-8110**	605-224-1631
Odessa Trading Co 9 W 1st Ave	Odessa	WA	99159	**800-726-2661**	509-982-2661
Ohio Machinery Co 3993 E Royalton Rd	Broadview Heights	OH	44147	**800-837-6200**	440-526-6200
Olsen Implement Inc 2025 US Hwy 14 W	Huron	SD	57350	**800-627-5469**	605-352-7100
Peterson Tractor Co 955 Marina Blvd	San Leandro	CA	94577	**888-738-3776**	510-357-6200
Polk County Farmers Co-op DBA Ag West Supply 9055 Rickreall Rd	Rickreall	OR	97371	**800-842-2224**	503-363-2332
Puck Implement Co 402 6th St	Manning	IA	51455	**800-458-4431**	712-653-2574
R & W Supply Inc 2210 Hall Ave	Littlefield	TX	79339	**800-477-1191**	806-385-4447
Ransome Engine Power Div Giles & Ransome Inc 2975 Galloway Rd	Bensalem	PA	19020	**800-753-4228**	215-639-4300
Reliable Tractor Inc PO Box 808	Tifton	GA	31793	**800-255-4401**	229-382-4400
Revels Tractor Co Inc 2217 N Main St	Fuquay-Varina	NC	27526	**800-849-5469**	919-552-5697
Rockingham New Holland Inc 600 W Market St	Harrisonburg	VA	22802	**800-360-5313**	540-434-6791
Roeder Implement Inc 2550 Rockdale Rd	Dubuque	IA	52003	**800-557-1184**	563-557-1184
Sauder & Rippel Inc 1450 SR 251	Minonk	IL	61760	**800-825-6983**	309-432-2531
Schmidt Machine Co 7013 State Hwy 199 N	Upper Sandusky	OH	43351	**800-589-3814**	419-294-3814
Sedalia Implement Co 2205 S Limit Ave	Sedalia	MO	65301	**800-752-5476**	660-826-0466
Seedburo Equipment Co 1022 W Jackson Blvd	Chicago	IL	60607	**800-284-5779**	312-738-3700
SEMA Equipment Inc 11555 Hwy 60 Blvd	Wanamingo	MN	55983	**800-569-1377**	507-824-2256
Sloan Implement Co 120 N Business 51	Assumption	IL	62510	**800-745-4020**	217-226-4411
Spartan Distributors Inc 487 W Division St	Sparta	MI	49345	**800-822-2216**	616-887-7301
Teeter Irrigation Inc 2295 S Old Hwy 83	Garden City	KS	67846	**800-834-7481**	620-276-8257
Titan Machinery Inc PO Box 310	Wahpeton	ND	58074	**800-654-4313**	701-642-8424
Tom Hassenfritz Equipment Co 1300 W Washington St	Mount Pleasant	IA	52641	**800-634-4885**	319-385-3114
Turf Professionals Equipment Co 13899 W 101st St	Lenexa	KS	66215	**800-299-3245**	913-599-0333
Unruh-Foster Inc 501 E Texcoco St	Montezuma	KS	67867	**800-279-7283**	620-846-2215
Vincent Implements Inc 8258 Hwy 45	Martin	TN	38237	**800-624-8754**	731-587-3824
West Central Co-op 406 1st St PO Box 68	Ralston	IA	51459	**800-522-1946**	712-667-3200
WG Leffelman & Sons Inc 340 N Metcalf Ave	Amboy	IL	61310	**800-957-2513**	815-857-2513
Witmer's Inc PO Box 368	Columbiana	OH	44408	**888-427-6025**	330-427-2147
Wolverine Tractor & Equipment Co 25900 W Eight-Mile Rd	Southfield	MI	48034	**800-686-7482**	248-356-5200
Wyandot Tractor & Implement Co PO Box 147	Upper Sandusky	OH	43351	**800-472-9554**	419-294-2349
Wyatt-Quarles Seed Co 730 US Hwy 70 W	Garner	NC	27529	**800-662-7591**	919-772-4243

271 FARM PRODUCT RAW MATERIALS

				Toll-Free	Phone
ADM/GROWMARK River System Inc 4666 E Faries Pkwy	Decatur	IL	62526	**800-637-5843**	217-424-5900
Alliance Grain Co 1306 W 8th St	Gibson City	IL	60936	**800-222-2451**	217-784-4284
Andersons Inc Agriculture Group 480 W Dussel Dr	Maumee	OH	43537	**800-537-3370**	419-893-5050
Aurora Co-op Elevator Co PO Box 209	Aurora	NE	68818	**800-642-6795**	402-694-2106
Cargill Inc 15407 McGinty Rd	Wayzata	MN	55391	**800-227-4455**	952-742-7575
Central Connecticut Co-op Farmers Assn PO Box 8500	Manchester	CT	06040	**800-640-4523**	860-649-4523

Classified Section

Company	City	State	ZIP	Toll-Free	Phone
Central Iowa Co-op PO Box 190	Jewell	IA	50130	**800-728-0017**	515-827-5431
Cooperative Elevator Co PO Box 619	Pigeon	MI	48755	**800-968-0601**	989-453-4500
Dalhart Consumers Fuel Assn Inc PO Box 610	Dalhart	TX	79022	**800-249-5695**	806-249-5695
De Bruce Grain PO Box 329	Creston	IA	50801	**877-274-2676**	641-782-6411
DeBruce Grain Inc 4100 N Mulberry Dr Suite 300	Kansas City	MO	64116	**800-821-5210**	816-421-8182
Effingham Equity Inc 201 W Roadway	Effingham	IL	62401	**800-223-1337**	217-342-4101
Farmers Co-op Co 105 Garfield Ave	Farnhamville	IA	50538	**800-642-6815**	515-544-3213
Farmers Cooperative Elevator Co 208 W Depot	Dorchester	NE	68343	**800-642-6439**	402-946-2211
Frick Services Inc 3154 Depot St	Wawaka	IN	46794	**800-552-1754**	260-761-3311
Frontier Co-op Co 211 S Lincoln St	Brainard	NE	68626	**800-869-0379**	402-545-2811
Grand Prairie Co-op Inc 1 S Calhoun St	Tolono	IL	61880	**800-252-4724**	217-485-6630
Growers Co-op Inc 2500 S 13th St	Terre Haute	IN	47802	**800-283-8123**	812-235-8123
Heart of Iowa Co-op 229 E Ash St	Roland	IA	50236	**800-662-4642**	515-388-4341
Heartland Co-op 2829 Westown Pkwy Suite 350	West Des Moines	IA	50266	**800-513-3938**	515-225-1334
Interstate Commodities Inc 7 Madison St	Troy	NY	12181	**800-833-3636**	518-272-7212
MaxYield Cooperative PO Box 49	West Bend	IA	50597	**800-383-0003**	515-887-7211
Mid-Iowa Co-op PO Box 160	Conrad	IA	50621	**800-458-9753**	641-366-2040
NEW Cooperative Inc 2626 1st Ave S	Fort Dodge	IA	50501	**800-362-2233**	515-955-2040
Northwest Grain Growers Inc 850 N 4th Ave	Walla Walla	WA	99362	**800-994-4290**	509-525-6510
Pendleton Grain Growers Inc PO Box 1248	Pendleton	OR	97801	**800-422-7611**	541-276-7611
Plains Cotton Co-op Assn PO Box 2827	Lubbock	TX	79408	**800-333-8011**	806-763-8011
Pro-Pet LLC 1400 McKinley Rd	Saint Marys	OH	45885	**800-245-4125**	419-394-3374
Scoular Co 2027 Dodge St	Omaha	NE	68102	**800-488-3500**	402-342-3500
South Dakota Wheat Growers Assn 110 6th Ave SE	Aberdeen	SD	57401	**888-429-4902**	605-225-5500
Staplcotn Co-op Assn Inc 214 W Market St	Greenwood	MS	38930	**800-293-6231**	662-453-6231
Stratton Equity Co-op Co Inc PO Box 25	Stratton	CO	80836	**800-752-2068**	719-348-5347
United Farmers Co-op PO Box 310	Shelby	NE	68662	**800-742-7813**	402-527-5511
Watonwan Farm Service 233 W Ciro St	Truman	MN	56088	**800-657-3282**	507-776-2831
Western Iowa Co-op PO Box 106	Hornick	IA	51026	**800-488-3201**	712-874-3211

272 FARM SUPPLIES

Company	City	State	ZIP	Toll-Free	Phone
Ag Valley Co-op 103 S Commercial St	Maywood	NE	69038	**800-233-4551**	308-362-4244
Agri Co-op 310 Logan St	Holdrege	NE	68949	**800-658-4089**	308-995-8626
Andersons Inc Agriculture Group 480 W Dussel Dr	Maumee	OH	43537	**800-537-3370**	419-893-5050
Auglaize Farmers Co-op Inc 601 S Logan St	Wapakoneta	OH	45895	**800-472-9286**	419-739-4600
Battle Creek Farmers Co-op 400 W Front St Box 10	Battle Creek	NE	68715	**800-233-6679**	402-675-2055
Bleyhl Farm Service Inc 940 E Wine Country Rd	Grandview	WA	98930	**800-862-6806**	509-882-2248
Bradley Caldwell Inc 200 Kiwanis Blvd	Hazleton	PA	18202	**800-257-9100**	570-455-7511
Cal/West Seeds Inc 41970 E Main St	Woodland	CA	95776	**800-327-3337**	530-666-3331
Co-op Feed Dealers Inc 380 Broome Corporate Pkwy PO Box 670	Conklin	NY	13748	**800-333-0895***	607-651-9078
*Cust Svc					
CropKing.com Inc 5050 Greenwich Rd	Seville	OH	44273	**800-321-5656**	330-769-2002
Dorchester Farmers Co-op 208 W Depot	Dorchester	NE	68343	**800-642-6439**	402-946-2211
Evergreen FS Inc 402 N Hershey Rd	Bloomington	IL	61704	**877-963-2392**	309-663-2392
Farm Service Co-op 2308 Pine St	Harlan	IA	51537	**800-452-4372**	712-755-3185
Farmers Co-op Assn 105 Jackson St	Jackson	MN	56143	**800-864-3847**	507-847-4160
Farmers Co-op Oil Co 6th & Logan	Newman Grove	NE	68758	**800-898-6292**	402-447-6292
Farmers Co-op Supply & Shipping Assn 570 Commerce St	West Salem	WI	54669	**800-657-5189**	608-786-1100
Farmway Co-op Inc 204 E Court St	Beloit	KS	67420	**800-748-7038**	785-738-2241
Federation Co-op 108 N Water St	Black River Falls	WI	54615	**800-944-1784**	715-284-5354
Florida Favorite Fertilizer Inc 1607 Olive St	Lakeland	FL	33815	**800-822-4474**	863-688-2442
Frenchman Valley Farmers Co-op Exchange 143 Broadway	Imperial	NE	69033	**800-538-2667**	308-882-3200
Gold Star FS Inc 101 N East St	Cambridge	IL	61238	**800-443-8497**	309-937-3369
Hydro Agri North America Inc 100 N Tampa St Suite 3200	Tampa	FL	33602	**800-944-9376**	813-222-5700
Intermountain Farmers Assn 1147 W 2100 South	Salt Lake City	UT	84119	**800-748-4432**	801-972-2122
Jasper County Farm Bureau Co-op Assn 2530 N McKinley	Rensselaer	IN	47978	**800-828-7516**	219-866-7131
Kugler Co 209 W 3rd	McCook	NE	69001	**800-445-9116**	308-345-2280
La Salle Farmers Grain Co 317 4th St NE	Madelia	MN	56062	**800-245-5857**	507-642-3276
Land O'Lakes Inc Western Feed Div PO Box 818	Caldwell	ID	83606	**800-452-4052**	208-459-3689
Loveland Industries Inc 14520 WCR #64	Greeley	CO	80631	**800-356-8920**	970-356-8920
Martrex Inc 14525 Hwy 7	Minnetonka	MN	55345	**800-328-3627**	952-933-5000
McFarlane Mfg Co Inc 1259 Water St	Sauk City	WI	53583	**800-627-8569**	608-643-3321
Meadowland Farmers Co-op 101 1st Ave E	Lamberton	MN	56152	**800-527-5824**	507-752-7352
Meherrin Agricultural & Chemical Co Inc PO Box 200	Severn	NC	27877	**800-775-0333**	252-585-1744
Miles Farm Supplies LLC 1401 B Spring Bank Dr	Owensboro	KY	42303	**800-666-4537**	270-926-2420
NC Plus Hybrids 3820 N 56th St	Lincoln	NE	68504	**800-279-7999**	402-467-2517
NEW Cooperative Inc 2626 1st Ave S	Fort Dodge	IA	50501	**800-362-2233**	515-955-2040
Northwestern Supply Co Inc 525 Progress Rd	Waite Park	MN	56387	**800-397-6972**	320-251-0812
Panhandle Co-op Assn 401 S Beltline Hwy W	Scottsbluff	NE	69363	**800-732-4546***	308-632-5301
*Cust Svc					
Rabo AG Services PO Box 668	Cedar Falls	IA	50613	**800-395-8505**	319-277-0261
Rolling Hills Farm Service Inc 421 N 10th St	Winterset	IA	50273	**800-352-3276**	515-462-2644
Rosen's Inc 1120 Lake Ave	Fairmont	MN	56031	**800-798-2000**	507-238-4201
Royster-Clark Inc 6 Executive Dr	Collinsville	IL	62234	**800-767-2855**	618-346-7300
South Central Co-op 40 W Park Dr	Gibbon	MN	55335	**800-690-6534**	507-834-6534
Southern FS Inc 1900 E Main St	Marion	IL	62959	**800-492-7684**	618-993-2833
Stanislaus Farm Supply Co 624 E Service Rd	Modesto	CA	95358	**800-323-0725**	209-538-7070
United Suppliers Inc 30473 260th St	Eldora	IA	50627	**800-782-5123**	641-858-2341
Wabash Valley Service Co Inc 909 N Court St	Grayville	IL	62844	**888-869-8127**	618-375-2311
Watertown Co-op Elevator Assn 810 Burlington Northern Dr	Watertown	SD	57201	**888-882-3039**	605-886-3039
Watonwan Farm Service 208 S Main	Delavan	MN	56023	**800-830-0447**	507-854-3204
Westland Co-op 2112 Indianapolis Rd	Crawfordsville	IN	47933	**800-878-0952**	765-362-6700
Wheaton-Dumont Farmer Co-op 1115 Broadway	Wheaton	MN	56296	**800-258-7444**	320-563-8152

Company	City	State	ZIP	Toll-Free	Phone
Wilco Farmers 200 Industrial Way	Mount Angel	OR	97362	**800-382-5339**	503-845-6122

273 FASHION DESIGN HOUSES

SEE ALSO Clothing & Accessories - Mfr

Company	City	State	ZIP	Toll-Free	Phone
Armani Exchange 568 Broadway	New York	NY	10012	**800-717-2929**	212-431-6000
BCBG Max Azria 2761 Fruitland Ave	Vernon	CA	90058	**888-636-2224**	323-589-2224
Christian Dior 712 5th Ave 37th Fl	New York	NY	10019	**800-929-3467**	212-582-0500
Donna Karan International Inc 550 7th Ave 15th Fl	New York	NY	10018	**800-231-0884**	212-789-1500
Hugo Boss Fashions Inc 601 W 26th St Suite 845	New York	NY	10001	**800-484-6207**	212-940-0600
Jessica McClintock Inc 1400 16th St	San Francisco	CA	94103	**800-333-5301**	415-553-8200
Jhane Barnes Inc 119 W 40th St 20th Fl	New York	NY	10018	**888-465-4263**	212-575-2448
Ralph Lauren 650 Madison Ave	New York	NY	10022	**888-475-7674**	212-318-7000
Tommy Hilfiger USA Inc 25 W 39th St	New York	NY	10018	**800-888-8802**	212-840-8888
Vera Wang 225 W 39th St 9th Fl	New York	NY	10018	**800-839-8372**	212-575-6400

274 FASTENERS & FASTENING SYSTEMS

SEE ALSO Hardware - Mfr; Precision Machined Products

Company	City	State	ZIP	Toll-Free	Phone
Alcoa Fastening Systems DBA Huck Fasteners 3724 E Columbia St	Tucson	AZ	85714	**800-326-1799**	520-519-7400
Atlas Bolt & Screw Co 1628 Troy Rd	Ashland	OH	44805	**800-321-6977**	419-289-6171
B & G Mfg Co Inc 3067 Unionville Pike	Hatfield	PA	19440	**800-366-3067**	215-822-1925
Ford Fasteners Inc 110 S Newman St	Hackensack	NJ	07601	**800-272-3673**	201-487-3151
Gesipa Fasteners USA Inc 375 Phillips Blvd	Ewing	NJ	08618	**800-257-9404**	609-883-8300
Huck Fasteners 3724 E Columbia St	Tucson	AZ	85714	**800-326-1799**	520-519-7400
ITW Brands 955 National Pkwy Suite 95500	Schaumburg	IL	60173	**800-982-7178**	847-944-2260
ITW Buildex 1349 W Bryn Mawr	Itasca	IL	60143	**800-284-5339**	630-595-3500
National Rivet & Mfg Co 21 E Jefferson St	Waupun	WI	53963	**888-324-5511**	920-324-5511
Ohio Nut & Bolt Co 33 Lou Groza Blvd	Berea	OH	44017	**800-362-0291**	440-243-0200
Pan American Screw Inc 630 Reese Dr SW	Conover	NC	28613	**800-951-2222**	828-466-0060
PennEngineering & Mfg Corp 5190 Old Easton Rd	Danboro	PA	18916	**800-237-4736**	215-766-8853
Robertson Inc 97 Bronte St N	Milton	ON	L9T2N8	**800-268-5090**	905-878-2866
Scovill Fasteners Inc 1802 Scovill Dr	Clarkesville	GA	30523	**800-756-4734***	706-754-1000
*Cust Svc					
Stafast Products Inc 505 Lake Shore Blvd	Painesville	OH	44077	**800-782-3278**	440-357-5546

275 FENCES

SEE ALSO Recycled Plastics Products

Company	City	State	ZIP	Toll-Free	Phone
Acorn Wire & Iron Works Inc 4940 S Kilbourn Ave	Chicago	IL	60632	**800-552-2676**	773-585-0600
Burke-Parsons-Bowlby Corp Rt 21 S	Ripley	WV	25271	**800-745-7095**	304-372-2211
Caffall Brothers Forest Products Inc 25260 SW Pkwy PO Box 725	Wilsonville	OR	97070	**800-547-2011**	503-682-1910
Century Fence Co PO Box 466	Waukesha	WI	53187	**800-558-0507**	262-547-3331
Dare Products Inc PO Box 157	Battle Creek	MI	49016	**800-922-3273**	269-965-2307
Fi-Shock Inc 5360 N National Dr	Knoxville	TN	37914	**800-251-9288**	865-524-7380
Merchants Metals Inc 3838 N Sam Houston Pkwy E Suite 600	Houston	TX	77032	**800-254-0080**	281-372-3800
Miller Wire Works Inc 7429 Georgia Rd	Birmingham	AL	35212	**800-783-0341**	205-592-0341
Moultrie Mfg Co PO Box 2948	Moultrie	GA	31776	**800-841-8674**	229-985-1312
Tru-Link Fence Co 5440 W Touhy Ave	Skokie	IL	60077	**888-568-9300**	847-568-9300
Walpole Woodworkers Inc 767 East St PO Box 151	Walpole	MA	02081	**800-343-6948**	508-668-2800

276 FERTILIZERS & PESTICIDES

SEE ALSO Farm Supplies

Company	City	State	ZIP	Toll-Free	Phone
Agricultural Commodities Inc 2224 Oxford Rd	New Oxford	PA	17350	**800-359-8899**	717-624-8249
Agrium Inc 13131 Lake Fraser Dr SE	Calgary	AB	T2J7E8	**877-247-4861**	403-225-7000
NYSE: AGU					
Alabama Farmers Co-op Inc 121 Somerville Rd NE	Decatur	AL	35601	**800-737-6843**	256-353-6843
Amvac Chemical Corp 4100 E Washington Blvd	Los Angeles	CA	90023	**888-468-2726**	323-264-3910
Andersons DBA Erny's PO Box 452	Walton	IN	46994	**800-552-3769**	574-626-2522
Andersons Inc Processing Group 480 W Dussel Dr	Maumee	OH	43537	**800-537-3370**	419-893-5050
Atlantic FEC Fertilizer & Chemical Co 18375 SW 260 St	Homestead	FL	33031	**800-432-3413**	305-247-8800
ATOFINA Chemicals Inc 2000 Market St	Philadelphia	PA	19103	**800-533-5552**	215-419-7000
BASF Corp 3000 Continental Dr N	Mount Olive	NJ	07828	**800-526-1072**	973-426-2600
NYSE: BF					
Bayer Corp Agricultural Div 8400 Hawthorn Rd	Kansas City	MO	64120	**800-821-8556**	816-242-2000
Bayer CropScience 2 Alexander Dr	Research Triangle Park	NC	27709	**800-523-0258**	919-549-2000
Cargill Inc North America 15407 McGinty Rd	Wayzata	MN	55391	**800-227-4455**	952-742-7575
Certis USA 9145 Guilford Rd Suite 175	Columbia	MD	21046	**800-847-5620**	301-604-7340

Classified Section

Company	City	State	Zip	Toll-Free	Phone
Cleary WA Corp 1049 Rt 27	Somerset	NJ	08873	**800-238-7813**	732-247-8000
Clinton Nursery Products Inc 114 W Main St	Clinton	CT	06413	**800-289-7645**	860-669-8611
Coastal Chem Inc 8305 Otto Rd	Cheyenne	WY	82009	**800-949-6377**	307-637-2700
Dow AgroSciences LLC 9330 Zionsville Rd	Indianapolis	IN	46268	**800-258-1470**	317-337-3000
DuPont Agriculture & Nutrition 1007 Market St DuPont Bldg	Wilmington	DE	19898	**800-441-7515**	302-774-1000
DuPont Crop Protection 1007 Market St DuPont Bldg	Wilmington	DE	19898	**800-441-7515**	302-774-1000
DuPont EI de Nemours & Co Inc 1007 Market St *NYSE: DD*	Wilmington	DE	19898	**800-441-7515**	302-774-1000
EI DuPont de Nemours & Co Inc 1007 Market St *NYSE: DD*	Wilmington	DE	19898	**800-441-7515**	302-774-1000
Erny's PO Box 452	Walton	IN	46994	**800-552-3769**	574-626-2522
Farmland Industries Inc 12200 N Ambassador Dr	Kansas City	MO	64163	**800-821-8000**	816-713-7000
FMC Corp Agricultural Products Group 1735 Market St	Philadelphia	PA	19103	**800-621-4500**	215-299-6000
Frit Industries Inc PO Box 1589	Ozark	AL	36361	**800-633-7685**	334-774-2515
Growers Fertilizer Corp PO Box 1407	Lake Alfred	FL	33850	**800-343-1101**	863-956-1101
Gustafson Inc PO Box 660065	Dallas	TX	75266	**800-248-6907**	972-985-8877
Hintzsche Fertilizer Inc 2 S 181 County Line Rd PO Box 367	Maple Park	IL	60151	**800-446-3378**	630-557-2406
Hydro/Kirby Agri Service Inc PO Box 6277	Lancaster	PA	17607	**800-745-7524**	717-299-2541
Johnson SC & Son Inc 1525 Howe St	Racine	WI	53403	**800-494-4855**	262-260-2000
JR Simplot Co 999 Main St	Boise	ID	83702	**800-635-5008**	208-336-2110
JR Simplot Co AgriBusiness Group PO Box 70013	Boise	ID	83707	**800-635-9444**	208-672-2700
Kellogg Supply Inc 350 W Sepulveda Blvd **Cust Svc*	Carson	CA	90745	**800-232-2322***	310-830-2200
Kova Fertilizer Inc 1330 N Anderson St	Greensburg	IN	47240	**800-346-1569**	812-663-5081
LaRoche Industries Inc 1100 Johnson Ferry Rd	Atlanta	GA	30342	**800-226-4572**	404-851-0300
Lebanon Seaboard Corp 1600 E Cumberland St	Lebanon	PA	17042	**800-233-0628**	717-273-1685
LESCO Inc 15885 Sprague Rd *NASDAQ: LSCO*	Strongsville	OH	44136	**800-321-5325**	440-783-9250
Living Earth Technology Co 5625 Crawford Rd	Houston	TX	77041	**800-665-3826**	713-466-7360
Miller Chemical & Fertilizer Corp 120 Radio Rd	Hanover	PA	17331	**800-233-2040**	717-632-8921
Mississippi Chemical Corp 3622 Hwy 49 E PO Box 388	Yazoo City	MS	39194	**800-433-1351**	662-746-4131
Mosaic Co 12800 Whitewater Dr MS 190 *NYSE: MOS*	Minnetonka	MN	55343	**800-918-8270**	
Na-Churs/Alpine Solutions 421 Leader St	Marion	OH	43302	**800-622-4877**	740-382-5701
Nufarm America Co 1333 Burr Ridge Pkwy Suite 125A	Burr Ridge	IL	60521	**800-345-3330**	708-754-3330
Pace International LLC 1011 Western Ave Suite 807	Seattle	WA	98104	**800-247-8711**	206-264-7599
PBI/Gordon Corp PO Box 014090	Kansas City	MO	64101	**800-821-7925**	816-421-4070
Pioneer Hi-Bred International Inc 400 Locust St Capital Sq Suite 800	Des Moines	IA	50309	**800-247-6803**	515-248-4800
Potash Corp 1101 Skokie Blvd	Northbrook	IL	60062	**800-645-2183**	847-849-4200
Potash Corp of Saskatchewan Inc 122 1st Ave S Suite 500 *NYSE: POT*	Saskatoon	SK	S7K7G3	**800-667-3930**	306-933-8500
Roche Mfg Co Inc PO Box 4156	Dublin	GA	31040	**800-515-3251**	478-272-3340
Royster-Clark Inc 6 Executive Dr	Collinsville	IL	62234	**800-767-2855**	618-346-7300
Safeguard Chemical Corp 411 Wales Ave	Bronx	NY	10454	**800-536-3170**	718-585-3170
Sara Lee Household Products 707 Eagle View Blvd	Exton	PA	19341	**800-879-5494**	610-321-1220
SC Johnson & Son Inc 1525 Howe St	Racine	WI	53403	**800-494-4855**	262-260-2000
Scotts Miracle-Gro Co 14111 Scottslawn Rd *NYSE: SMG ■ *Cust Svc*	Marysville	OH	43041	**800-543-8873***	937-644-0011
Share Corp 7821 N Faulkner Rd	Milwaukee	WI	53224	**800-776-7192**	414-355-4000
Simplot JR Co 999 Main St	Boise	ID	83702	**800-635-5008**	208-336-2110
Simplot JR Co AgriBusiness Group PO Box 70013	Boise	ID	83707	**800-635-9444**	208-672-2700
Southern States Phosphate & Fertilizer Co PO Box 546	Savannah	GA	31402	**888-337-8922**	912-232-1101
Spectrum Brands 2150 Schultz Rd	Saint Louis	MO	63146	**800-341-0020**	314-427-4886
Standard Tar Products Co 2456 W Cornell St	Milwaukee	WI	53209	**800-825-7650**	414-873-7650
Stoller Enterprises Inc 4001 W Sam Houston Pkwy N Suite 100	Houston	TX	77043	**800-539-5283**	713-461-1493
Summit Chemical Co 7657 Canton Ctr Dr	Baltimore	MD	21224	**800-227-8664**	410-282-5200
Sunniland Corp PO Box 8001	Sanford	FL	32772	**800-432-1130**	407-322-2421
Syngenta Corp 2200 Concord Pike	Wilmington	DE	19803	**800-759-4500**	302-425-2000
Syngenta Crop Protection Inc PO Box 18300	Greensboro	NC	27419	**800-334-9481**	336-632-6000
Valent USA Corp 1333 N California Blvd Suite 600	Walnut Creek	CA	94596	**800-624-6094**	925-256-2700
Valley Fertilizer & Chemical Co Inc PO Box 816	Mount Jackson	VA	22842	**800-571-3121**	540-477-3121
Van Diest Supply Co PO Box 610	Webster City	IA	50595	**800-779-2424**	515-832-2366
WA Cleary Corp 1049 Rt 27	Somerset	NJ	08873	**800-238-7813**	732-247-8000
Whitmire Micro-Gen Research Laboratories Inc 3568 Tree Court Industrial Blvd	Saint Louis	MO	63122	**800-777-8570**	636-225-5371
Wolfkill Feed & Fertilizer Corp PO Box 578	Monroe	WA	98272	**800-525-4539**	360-794-7065
Y-Tex Corp 1825 Big Horn Ave	Cody	WY	82414	**800-443-6401**	307-587-5515

277 FESTIVALS - BOOK

Company	City	State	Zip	Toll-Free	Phone
Los Angeles Times Festival of Books Los Angeles Times 202 W 1st St	Los Angeles	CA	90012	**800-528-4637**	213-237-5000
National Book Festival Library of Congress 101 Independence Ave SE	Washington	DC	20540	**888-714-4696**	
Times Festival of Reading PO Box 1121	Saint Petersburg	FL	33731	**800-333-7505**	727-445-4142
Vegas Valley Book Festival Nevada Humanities Committee PO Box 8029	Reno	NV	89507	**800-382-5023**	775-784-6587

278 FESTIVALS - FILM

Company	City	State	Zip	Toll-Free	Phone
Austin Film Festival 1604 Nueces	Austin	TX	78701	**800-310-3378**	512-478-4795
Los Angeles International Film Festival American Film Institute 2021 N Western Ave	Los Angeles	CA	90027	**866-231-3378**	323-856-7600

279 FIREARMS & AMMUNITION (NON-MILITARY)

SEE ALSO Sporting Goods; Weapons & Ordnance (Military)

Company	City	State	Zip	Toll-Free	Phone
Beeman Precision Airguns 5454 Argosy Dr	Huntington Beach	CA	92649	**800-227-2744**	714-890-4800
Beretta USA Corp 17601 Beretta Dr	Accokeek	MD	20607	**800-636-3420**	301-283-2191
Colt's Mfg Co Inc PO Box 1868	Hartford	CT	06144	**800-962-2658**	860-236-6311
Crosman Corp Rts 5 & 20	East Bloomfield	NY	14443	**800-724-7486**	585-657-6161
Defense Technology / Federal Laboratories 13386 International Pkwy	Jacksonville	FL	32218	**800-773-3832**	904-741-5400
Federal Cartridge Co 900 Ehlen Dr	Anoka	MN	55303	**800-322-2342**	763-323-2300
Freedom Arms Inc 314 Hwy 239 **Orders*	Freedom	WY	83120	**800-833-4432***	307-883-2468
Hornady Mfg Co 3625 Old Potash Hwy **Cust Svc*	Grand Island	NE	68803	**800-338-3220***	308-382-1390
Lyman Products Corp 475 Smith St	Middletown	CT	06457	**800-225-9626**	860-632-2020
Marksman Products Inc 5482 Argosy Dr	Huntington Beach	CA	92649	**800-822-8005**	714-898-7535
Marlin Firearms Co 100 Kenna Dr **Cust Svc*	North Haven	CT	06473	**800-544-8892***	203-239-5621
Mossberg OF & Sons Inc 7 Grasso Ave	North Haven	CT	06473	**800-989-4867**	203-230-5300
OF Mossberg & Sons Inc 7 Grasso Ave	North Haven	CT	06473	**800-989-4867**	203-230-5300
Olin Corp Winchester Div 427 N Shamrock St	East Alton	IL	62024	**800-356-2666**	618-258-2000
Remington Arms Co Inc 870 Remington Dr PO Box 700	Madison	NC	27025	**800-243-9700**	336-548-8700
Savage Industries Inc 100 Springdale Rd	Westfield	MA	01085	**800-370-0712**	413-568-7001
SIGARMS Inc 18 Industrial Dr **Orders*	Exeter	NH	03833	**800-325-3693***	603-772-2302
Smith & Wesson Corp 2100 Roosevelt Ave **Cust Svc*	Springfield	MA	01104	**800-331-0852***	413-781-8300
Smith & Wesson Holding Corp 2100 Roosevelt Ave *AMEX: SWB*	Springfield	MA	01104	**800-331-0852**	413-781-8300
Springfield Armory 420 W Main St	Geneseo	IL	61254	**800-680-6866**	309-944-5631
US Repeating Arms Co 344 Winchester Ave	New Haven	CT	06511	**800-322-4626**	203-789-5000
Weatherby Inc 3100 El Camino Real	Atascadero	CA	93422	**800-334-4423**	805-466-1767
Williams Gun Sight Co Inc 7389 Lapeer Rd	Davison	MI	48423	**800-530-9028**	810-653-2131
Winchester Div Olin Corp 427 N Shamrock St	East Alton	IL	62024	**800-356-2666**	618-258-2000

280 FISHING - COMMERCIAL

Company	City	State	Zip	Toll-Free	Phone
American Seafoods Holdings LLC 2025 1st Ave Suite 900 *AMEX: SEA*	Seattle	WA	98121	**800-275-2019**	206-448-0300
Arctic Storm Inc 400 N 34th St Suite 306	Seattle	WA	98103	**800-929-0908**	206-547-6557
Blue North Fisheries 2930 Westlake Ave N Suite 300	Seattle	WA	98109	**877-878-3263**	206-352-9252
Bon Secour Fisheries Inc 17449 County Rd 49 S PO Box 60	Bon Secour	AL	36511	**800-633-6854**	251-949-7411
Canadian Fishing Co Foot of Gore Ave	Vancouver	BC	V6A2Y7	**888-526-2929**	604-681-0211
Canfisco Foot of Gore Ave	Vancouver	BC	V6A2Y7	**888-526-2929**	604-681-0211
Nova Fisheries 2532 Yale Ave E	Seattle	WA	98102	**888-458-6682**	206-781-2000
Ocean Beauty Seafoods Inc 1100 W Ewing St	Seattle	WA	98119	**800-877-0185**	206-285-6800
Trident Seafood Corp 5303 Shilshole Ave NW	Seattle	WA	98107	**800-367-6065**	206-783-3818

281 FIXTURES - OFFICE & STORE

SEE ALSO Furniture - Mfr - Commercial & Industrial Furniture

Company	City	State	Zip	Toll-Free	Phone
Adapto Storage Products 625 E 10th Ave	Hialeah	FL	33010	**800-923-2786**	305-499-4800
AGI Schutz Merchandising Co 376 Pine St	Forest City	NC	28043	**800-662-2150**	828-245-9871
Amco Corp 901 N Kilpatrick Ave	Chicago	IL	60651	**800-621-4023**	
Amstore Corp 540 Danforth St	Coopersville	MI	49404	**800-933-6681**	616-837-3700
Angola Wire Products Inc 803 Wohlert St	Angola	IN	46703	**800-800-7225**	260-665-9447
Architectural Bronze & Aluminum Corp 3638 W Oakton St	Skokie	IL	60076	**800-339-6581**	847-674-3638
Bassett Russ Co 8189 Byron Rd	Whittier	CA	90606	**800-350-2445**	562-945-2445
Benner-Nawman Inc 3450 Sabin Brown Rd	Wickenburg	AZ	85390	**800-992-3833**	928-684-2813
Bennett Mfg Co Inc 13315 Railroad St	Alden	NY	14004	**800-345-2142**	716-937-9161
Best-Rite Mfg PO Box D	Temple	TX	76503	**866-886-6935**	
Boden Store Fixtures Inc 5335 NE 109th Ave	Portland	OR	97220	**800-733-1923**	503-252-4728
Borroughs Corp 3002 N Burdick St	Kalamazoo	MI	49004	**800-748-0227**	269-342-0161
Boston Retail Products 400 Riverside Ave	Medford	MA	02155	**800-225-1633**	781-395-7417
Brewster Panel Inc PO Box 669	Vernon	AL	35592	**800-243-8198**	
CAH Industries Inc 1500 Midway Ct Suite W-2	Elk Grove Village	IL	60007	**800-323-0300**	847-593-0727
Cano Corp 225 Industrial Rd	Fitchburg	MA	01420	**800-237-1358**	978-342-0953
ClosetMaid PO Box 4400 **Cust Svc*	Ocala	FL	34478	**800-874-0008***	352-401-6000
Cres-Cor 5925 Heisley Rd	Mentor	OH	44060	**877-273-7267**	440-350-1100
Custom Fold Doors Inc 110 W Ash Ave	Burbank	CA	91502	**800-913-3573**	323-849-3225
Dann Dee Display Fixtures Inc 7555 N Caldwell Ave	Niles	IL	60714	**800-888-8515**	847-588-1600

				Toll-Free	Phone
Darling LA Co 1401 Hwy 49B	Paragould	AR	72450	**800-643-3499**	870-239-9564
Datum Filing Systems Inc 89 Church Rd	Emigsville	PA	17318	**800-828-8018**	717-764-6350
DeBourgh Mfg Co 27505 Otero Ave PO Box 981	La Junta	CO	81050	**800-328-8829**	719-384-8161
Dixie Store Fixtures Inc 2425 1st Ave N	Birmingham	AL	35203	**800-323-4943**	205-322-2442
Durham Mfg Co Inc PO Box 230	Durham	CT	06422	**800-243-3774**	860-349-3427
EBSCO Industries Inc Luxor Div 2245 Delany Rd	Waukegan	IL	60087	**800-323-4656**	847-244-1800
Econoco Corp 300 Karin Ln	Hicksville	NY	11801	**800-645-7032**	516-935-7700
Edwards Products Inc 11385 Sebring Dr	Cincinnati	OH	45240	**800-543-1835**	513-851-3000
Electrorack Inc 1443 S Sunkist St	Anaheim	CA	92806	**800-433-6745**	714-776-5420
Equipto Co Inc 4550 Beltway Dr *Cust Svc	Addison	TX	75001	**800-323-0801***	214-443-9800
Eugene Welding Co 2420 Wills St	Marysville	MI	48040	**800-959-0857**	810-364-7421
Ex-Cell Metal Products Inc 11240 Melrose St	Franklin Park	IL	60131	**800-392-3557**	847-451-0451
Excell Store Fixtures 80 Jutland Rd	Toronto	ON	M8Z2H1	**800-392-3551**	416-503-1234
Fixtures International Inc 501 Yale St PO Box 7774	Houston	TX	77007	**800-444-1253**	713-869-3228
Goebel Fixture Co 528 Dale St	Hutchinson	MN	55350	**800-727-4646**	320-587-2112
Hale TJ Co W 139 N 9499 Hwy 145 PO Box 250	Menomonee Falls	WI	53051	**800-236-4253**	262-255-5555
Hamilton Fixture Co 3550 Symmes Rd	Hamilton	OH	45015	**800-889-2165**	513-874-2016
Hamilton Sorter Co Inc 3158 Production Dr	Fairfield	OH	45014	**800-503-9966**	513-870-4400
Harbor Industries Inc 14130 172nd Ave	Grand Haven	MI	49417	**800-968-6993**	616-842-5330
HC Osvold Co 2828 University Ave SE	Minneapolis	MN	55414	**800-328-4827**	612-331-1581
Hirsh Industries MEG Div 502 S Green St *Cust Svc	Cambridge City	IN	47327	**800-645-3315***	765-478-3141
Hoosier Co 5421 W 86th St PO Box 681064	Indianapolis	IN	46268	**800-521-4184**	317-872-8125
Hufcor Inc 2101 Kennedy Rd	Janesville	WI	53545	**800-356-6968**	608-756-1241
Hurco Design & Mfg 200 W 33rd St	Ogden	UT	84401	**877-859-6840**	801-394-9471
InterMetro Industries Corp 651 N Washington St *Cust Svc	Wilkes-Barre	PA	18705	**800-992-1776***	570-825-2741
IVC Fixture Mfg 245 5th Ave	New York	NY	10016	**800-777-5286**	212-213-6007
Jarke Corp 750 Pinecrest Dr	Prospect Heights	IL	60070	**800-722-5255**	847-541-6500
Jesco-Wipco Industries Inc PO Box 388	Litchfield	MI	49252	**800-455-0019**	517-542-2903
JL Industries Inc 4450 W 78th Street Cir	Bloomington	MN	55435	**800-554-6077**	952-835-6850
Kardex Systems Inc PO Box 171	Marietta	OH	45750	**800-234-3654**	740-374-9300
Karges Furniture Co Inc 1501 W Maryland St	Evansville	IN	47710	**800-252-7437**	812-425-2291
Kent Corp 4446 Pinson Valley Pkwy	Birmingham	AL	35217	**800-252-5368**	205-853-3420
Killion Industries Inc 1380 Poinsettia Ave	Vista	CA	92083	**800-421-5352**	760-727-5102
Kimball International Inc Transwall Div 1220 Wilson Dr	West Chester	PA	19380	**800-441-9255**	610-429-1400
Kwik-Wall Co 1010 E Edwards St	Springfield	IL	62703	**800-280-5945**	217-522-5553
LA Darling Co 1401 Hwy 49B	Paragould	AR	72450	**800-643-3499**	870-239-9564
Lista International Corp 106 Lowland St *Cust Svc	Holliston	MA	01746	**800-722-3020***	508-429-1350
Lozier Corp 6336 Pershing Dr	Omaha	NE	68110	**800-228-9882**	402-457-8000
Lundia Div MII Inc 600 Capitol Way	Jacksonville	IL	62650	**800-726-9663**	217-243-8585
Luxor Div EBSCO Industries Inc 2245 Delany Rd	Waukegan	IL	60087	**800-323-4656**	847-244-1800
Lyon Work Space Products 420 N Main St	Montgomery	IL	60538	**800-433-8488**	630-892-8941
Madix Store Fixtures 500 Airport Rd *Cust Svc	Terrell	TX	75160	**800-776-2349***	972-563-5744
MEG Div SteelWorks Inc 502 S Green St *Cust Svc	Cambridge City	IN	47327	**800-645-3315***	765-478-3141
Metpar Corp 95 State St	Westbury	NY	11590	**888-638-7271**	516-333-2600
MII Inc Lundia Div 600 Capitol Way	Jacksonville	IL	62650	**800-726-9663**	217-243-8585
Millrock Inc 67 Federal Ave	Quincy	MA	02169	**800-645-7625**	617-890-1090
Modern Metals Industries Inc PO Box 888	El Segundo	CA	90245	**800-437-6633**	310-516-0851
Modernfold Inc 215 W New Rd	Greenfield	IN	46140	**800-869-9685**	317-468-6700
Monarch Industries Inc 99 Main St	Warren	RI	02885	**800-669-9663**	401-247-5200
National Partitions & Interiors Inc 340 W 78th Rd	Hialeah	FL	33014	**866-528-4616**	305-822-3721
October Co Inc PO Box 71	Easthampton	MA	01027	**800-628-9346**	413-527-9380
Oklahoma Fixture Co DBA Penloyd/OFC 2900 E Apache St	Tulsa	OK	74110	**800-233-3794**	918-836-3794
Osvold HC Co 2828 University Ave SE	Minneapolis	MN	55414	**800-328-4827**	612-331-1581
Pacific Fixture Co Inc 9725 Variel Ave	Chatsworth	CA	91311	**800-272-2349**	818-727-1545
Packard Industries Inc 1515 US 31 N *Orders	Niles	MI	49120	**800-253-0866***	269-684-2550
Pan-Osten Co 6944 Louisville Rd	Bowling Green	KY	42101	**800-472-6678**	270-783-3900
Penloyd/OFC 2900 E Apache St	Tulsa	OK	74110	**800-233-3794**	918-836-3794
Pentwater Wire Products Inc PO Box 947	Pentwater	MI	49449	**800-437-2871**	231-869-6911
Rapid Rack Industries Inc 14421 Bonelli St	City of Industry	CA	91746	**800-736-7225**	626-333-7225
RC Smith Co 14200 Southcross Dr W	Burnsville	MN	55306	**800-747-7648**	952-854-0711
Ready Metal Mfg Co Inc Ready Fixtures Div 4500 W 47th St	Chicago	IL	60632	**800-638-7334**	773-376-9700
Reeve Store Equipment Co 9131 Bermudez St PO Box 276	Pico Rivera	CA	90660	**800-927-3383**	562-949-2535
Republic Storage Systems Co Inc 1038 Belden Ave NE *Sales	Canton	OH	44705	**800-477-1255***	330-438-5800
RTI Shelving Systems Inc 339 Kingsland Ave	Brooklyn	NY	11222	**800-746-5846**	212-279-0435
Russ Bassett Co 8189 Byron Rd	Whittier	CA	90606	**800-350-2445**	562-945-2445
Russell William Ltd 1710 Midway Rd	Odenton	MD	21113	**800-638-9667**	410-551-3600
Sandusky Cabinets Inc PO Box 517	Arvin	CA	93203	**800-336-0674**	661-854-5551
Schulte Corp 12115 Ellington Ct	Cincinnati	OH	45249	**800-669-3225**	513-489-9300
Semasys Inc 702 Ashland St *Cust Svc	Houston	TX	77007	**800-231-1425***	713-869-8331
Smith RC Co 14200 Southcross Dr W	Burnsville	MN	55306	**800-747-7648**	952-854-0711
Southern Imperial Inc 1400 Eddy Ave *Cust Svc	Rockford	IL	61103	**800-747-4665***	815-877-7041
Southern Metal Industries Inc PO Box 219	Ringgold	GA	30736	**800-241-5246**	706-935-4486
SpaceGuard Products 711 S Commerce Dr	Seymour	IN	47274	**800-841-0680**	812-523-3044
Spacesaver Corp 1450 Janesville Ave	Fort Atkinson	WI	53538	**800-492-3434**	920-563-6362
Spectrum Industries Inc 1600 Johnson St	Chippewa Falls	WI	54729	**800-235-1262**	715-723-6750
Stanley Vidmar Storage Technologies 11 Grammes Rd PO Box 1151	Allentown	PA	18105	**800-523-9462**	610-797-6600
Streater Inc 411 S 1st Ave	Albert Lea	MN	56007	**800-527-4197**	507-373-0611
Structural Concepts Corp 888 Porter Rd	Muskegon	MI	49441	**800-433-9489**	231-798-8888
Syndicate Store Fixtures Inc 402 N Main St	Middlebury	IN	46540	**800-626-3407**	574-825-9561
Systems Mfg Corp 1037 Powers Rd *Cust Svc	Conklin	NY	13748	**800-762-7587***	607-775-1100
Tesko Welding & Mfg Co 7350 W Montrose Ave	Norridge	IL	60706	**800-621-4514**	708-452-0045
Timely Inc 10241 Norris Ave	Pacoima	CA	91331	**800-247-6242**	818-896-3094
TJ Hale Co W 139 N 9499 Hwy 145 PO Box 250	Menomonee Falls	WI	53051	**800-236-4253**	262-255-5555
Transwall Div Kimball International Inc 1220 Wilson Dr	West Chester	PA	19380	**800-441-9255**	610-429-1400
Trendway Corp PO Box 9016	Holland	MI	49422	**800-968-5344**	616-399-3900
Trion Industries Inc 297 Laird St	Wilkes-Barre	PA	18702	**800-444-4665**	570-824-1000
Unarco Material Handling Inc 701 16th Ave E	Springfield	TN	37172	**800-862-7261**	615-384-3531
United Steel & Wire Co 4909 Wayne Rd	Battle Creek	MI	49015	**800-227-7887**	269-962-5571
Universal Display & Fixtures Co 726 E Hwy 121	Lewisville	TX	75057	**800-235-0701**	972-221-5022
Viking Metal Cabinet Co Inc 5321 W 65th St	Chicago	IL	60638	**800-776-7767**	708-594-1111
Vira Mfg Inc 1 Buckingham Ave	Perth Amboy	NJ	08861	**800-305-8472**	732-442-8472
Weis/Robart Partitions Inc 3737 S Venoy Rd	Wayne	MI	48184	**800-223-9347**	734-467-8711
Western Pacific Storage Systems Inc 300 E Arrow Hwy	San Dimas	CA	91773	**800-732-9777**	909-451-0303
White Systems Inc 30 Boright Ave	Kenilworth	NJ	07033	**800-275-1442**	908-272-6700
William Russell Ltd 1710 Midway Rd	Odenton	MD	21113	**800-638-9667**	410-551-3600
W/M Display Group 1040-50 W 40th St	Chicago	IL	60609	**800-443-2000**	773-254-3700
Yorkraft Inc PO Box 2386 *Cust Svc	York	PA	17405	**800-872-2044***	717-845-3666

282 FLAGS, BANNERS, PENNANTS

				Toll-Free	Phone
Annin & Co 105 Eisenhower Pkwy	Roseland	NJ	07068	**800-526-1390**	973-228-9400
Collegiate Pacific Inc 532 Luck Ave *AMEX: BOO*	Roanoke	VA	24016	**800-336-5996**	540-981-0281
Eder Flag Mfg Co Inc 1000 W Rawson Ave	Oak Creek	WI	53154	**800-558-6044**	414-764-3522
Forest Corp 1665 Enterprise Pkwy	Twinsburg	OH	44087	**800-637-6434**	330-425-3805
Metro Flag 47 Bassett Hwy	Dover	NJ	07802	**800-666-3524**	973-366-1776
National Banner Co 11938 Harry Hines Blvd	Dallas	TX	75234	**800-527-0860**	972-241-2131
Olympus Flag & Banner 9000 W Heather Ave	Milwaukee	WI	53224	**800-558-9620**	414-355-2010
Valley Forge Flag Co Inc 1700 Conrad Weiser Pkwy *Cust Svc	Womelsdorf	PA	19567	**800-743-5247***	610-589-5888

283 FLASH MEMORY DEVICES

				Toll-Free	Phone
Advanced Micro Devices Inc PO Box 3453 *NYSE: AMD*	Sunnyvale	CA	94088	**800-538-8450**	408-732-2400
Kingston Technology Co 17600 Newhope St	Fountain Valley	CA	92708	**800-835-6575**	714-435-2600
PNY Technologies Inc 299 Webro Rd	Parsippany	NJ	07054	**800-769-7079**	973-515-9700
SimpleTech Inc 3001 Daimler St *NASDAQ: STEC*	Santa Ana	CA	92705	**800-367-7330**	949-476-1180

284 FLEET LEASING & MANAGEMENT

				Toll-Free	Phone
AMI Leasing PO Box 986	Worcester	MA	01613	**800-468-9993**	508-852-5311
Bank of America Leasing Corp 2059 Northlake Pkwy 4th Fl	Tucker	GA	30084	**800-299-2265**	770-270-8400
Donlen Corp 2315 Sanders Rd	Northbrook	IL	60062	**800-323-1483**	847-714-1400
Emkay Inc 805 W Thorndale Ave	Itasca	IL	60143	**800-621-2001**	630-250-7400
Enterprise Fleet Services 5105 Johnson Rd	Coconut Creek	FL	33073	**800-325-8007**	954-354-5400
Executive Car Leasing Inc 7807 Santa Monica Blvd	Los Angeles	CA	90046	**800-994-2277**	323-654-5000
GE Capital Fleet Services 3 Capital Dr	Eden Prairie	MN	55344	**800-469-0044**	952-828-1000
Lease Plan USA 1165 Sanctuary Pkwy	Alpharetta	GA	30004	**800-457-8721**	770-933-9090
Leasing Assoc Inc PO Box 243	Houston	TX	77001	**800-449-4807**	713-522-9771
Motorlease Corp 1506 New Britain Ave	Farmington	CT	06032	**800-243-0182**	860-677-9711
PHH Arval 940 Ridgebrook Rd	Sparks	MD	21152	**800-665-9744**	410-771-1900
Transervice Lease Corp 5 Dakota Dr Suite 209	Lake Success	NY	11042	**800-645-8018**	516-488-3400

FLOOR COVERINGS - MFR

SEE Carpets & Rugs; Flooring - Resilient; Tile - Ceramic (Wall & Floor)

285 FLOOR COVERINGS STORES

				Toll-Free	Phone
Carpet Network Inc 109 Gaither Dr Suite 302	Mount Laurel	NJ	08054	**800-428-1067**	856-273-9393
Clark-Dunbar Carpets 3232 Empire Dr	Alexandria	LA	71301	**800-256-1467**	318-445-0262
Clark & Mitchell Inc 7820 Bluffton Rd	Fort Wayne	IN	46809	**800-319-2366**	260-747-7431
Coyle Carpet One Inc 250 W Beltline Hwy	Madison	WI	53713	**800-842-6953**	608-257-0291
Ducks Carpet & Flooring 1133 Hwy 45 Bypass	Jackson	TN	38301	**800-372-1000**	731-664-2871
Harry L Murphy Inc 42 Bonaventura Dr	San Jose	CA	95134	**800-439-6777**	408-955-1100
Kensington Home Furnishings Center 200 Tilton Rd	Northfield	NJ	08225	**800-641-4844**	609-641-4800
Lumber Liquidators Inc 1455 VFW Pkwy	West Roxbury	MA	02132	**877-645-5347**	617-327-1222

Company	City	State	Zip	Toll-Free	Phone
MMM Carpets Unlimited Inc 3100 Molinaro St	Santa Clara	CA	95054	**800-355-4666**	408-988-4661
O'Krent Floor Covering Co 2075 N Loop 1604 E	San Antonio	TX	78232	**800-369-7387**	210-227-7387
Pace Stone Inc 663 Washington St	Eden	NC	27288	**800-789-0236**	336-623-2158

286 FLOORING - RESILIENT

SEE ALSO Recycled Plastics Products

Company	City	State	Zip	Toll-Free	Phone
American Floor Products Co Inc 7977 Cessna Ave	Gaithersburg	MD	20879	**800-342-0424**	301-987-0490
Amtico International Inc 6480 Roswell Rd	Atlanta	GA	30328	**800-268-4260**	404-267-1900
Armstrong World Industries Inc 2500 Columbia Ave *Cust Svc	Lancaster	PA	17603	**800-233-3823***	717-397-0611
AstroTurf Industries Inc 809 Kenner St	Dalton	GA	30721	**800-723-8873**	706-272-4200
Columbia Forest Products Inc 222 SW Columbia St Suite 1575	Portland	OR	97201	**800-547-4261**	503-224-5300
Congoleum Corp PO Box 3127 *AMEX: CGM*	Mercerville	NJ	08619	**800-274-3266**	609-584-3000
Dodge-Regupol Inc 715 Fountain Ave	Lancaster	PA	17601	**800-322-1923**	717-295-3400
Domco Tarkett Inc 1139 Lehigh Ave	Whitehall	PA	18052	**800-367-8275**	610-266-5500
Forbo Industries Inc PO Box 667 *Cust Svc	Hazleton	PA	18201	**800-842-7839***	570-459-0771
Formica Corp 10155 Reading Rd	Cincinnati	OH	45241	**800-367-6422**	513-786-3400
Hambro Forest Products Inc PO Box 129	Crescent City	CA	95531	**800-442-6276**	707-464-6131
Mannington Mills Inc 75 Mannington Mills Rd *Cust Svc	Salem	NJ	08079	**800-356-6787***	856-935-3000
Pergo Inc 3128 Highwoods Blvd Suite 100	Raleigh	NC	27604	**800-222-1827**	919-773-6000
RCA Rubber Co 1833 E Market St	Akron	OH	44305	**800-321-2340**	330-784-1291
Roppe Corp 1602 N Union St	Fostoria	OH	44830	**800-537-9527**	419-435-8546
SRI Sports Inc 701 Leander Dr	Leander	TX	78641	**800-233-5714**	512-259-0080
Stonhard Inc 1 Park Ave *Cust Svc	Maple Shade	NJ	08052	**800-854-0310***	856-779-7500
Superior Mfg Group 7171 W 65th St	Chicago	IL	60638	**800-621-2802**	708-458-4600
Tarkett Inc 1001 Yamaska St E	Farnham	QC	J2N1J7	**800-363-9276**	450-293-3173
Wilsonart International Inc 2400 Wilson Pl *Cust Svc	Temple	TX	76504	**800-433-3222***	254-207-7000

287 FLORISTS

SEE ALSO Flowers-by-Wire Services; Garden Centers

Company	City	State	Zip	Toll-Free	Phone
1-800-Flowers.com Inc 1600 Stewart Ave *NASDAQ: FLWS*	Westbury	NY	11590	**800-356-9377**	516-237-6000
Alan Preuss Florists 17680-E W Bluemound Rd	Brookfield	WI	53045	**800-839-8400**	262-786-7900
Amlings Flowerland 540 W Ogden Ave	Hinsdale	IL	60521	**888-265-4647**	630-850-5070
Anthony's Florist & Gifts Inc 701 E Hallandale Beach Blvd	Hallandale	FL	33009	**800-989-8765**	954-457-8520
Arrow Florist & Park Avenue Greenhouses Inc 757 Park Ave	Cranston	RI	02910	**800-556-7097**	401-785-1900
Bachman's Inc 6010 Lyndale Ave S	Minneapolis	MN	55419	**888-222-4626**	612-861-7600
Boesen the Florist 3422 Beaver Ave	Des Moines	IA	50310	**800-274-4761**	515-274-4761
Cactus Flower Florists 7077 E Bell Rd	Scottsdale	AZ	85254	**800-922-2887**	480-483-9200
Calyx & Corolla 185 Berry St Suite 2400	San Francisco	CA	94107	**888-882-2599**	415-626-5511
Connell's Flowers 2385 E Main St	Bexley	OH	43209	**800-790-8980**	614-237-8653
Conroy's Inc 2550 N Hollywood Way Suite 206	Burbank	CA	91505	**800-266-7697**	818-843-8280
Country Lane Flower Shops Inc 729 S Michigan Ave	Howell	MI	48843	**800-764-7673**	517-546-1111
DeLoache Flowers 2927 Millwood Ave	Columbia	SC	29205	**800-922-2707**	803-256-1681
Don Wan Florist Ltd 5644 W 63rd St	Chicago	IL	60638	**800-336-6926**	773-585-2225
Dr Delphinium Designs Inc 5806 Lovers Lane & Tollway	Dallas	TX	75225	**800-783-8790**	214-522-9911
Eastern Floral & Gift Shop 2836 Broadmoor Ave SE	Grand Rapids	MI	49512	**800-494-2202**	616-949-2200
Felly's Flowers Inc PO Box 6620	Madison	WI	53716	**800-993-7673**	608-223-3285
Field of Flowers Inc 5101 S University Dr	Davie	FL	33328	**800-963-7374**	954-680-2406
Florist 800 Network 2820 La Mirada Dr Suite J	Vista	CA	92083	**800-688-1299**	760-599-5599
Flower Pot Florists 2314 N Broadway St	Knoxville	TN	37917	**800-824-7792**	865-523-5121
Flower World 5201 Rt 38	Pennsauken	NJ	08109	**800-257-7880**	856-429-5800
FlowerClub PO Box 60910	Los Angeles	CA	90060	**800-800-7363**	405-440-6001
Flowers from Holland Ltd 835A Franklin Ct	Marietta	GA	30067	**800-647-8182**	770-380-3000
Foster City Flowers & Gifts 1185 Chess Dr Suite G	Foster City	CA	94404	**800-970-7673**	650-573-6607
Fred Allen Florist 310 E Broad St	Gadsden	AL	35903	**800-824-9181**	256-546-0437
FTD Inc 3113 Woodcreek Dr	Downers Grove	IL	60515	**800-736-3383**	630-724-6200
Higdon Florist 201 E 32nd St	Joplin	MO	64804	**800-641-4726**	417-624-7171
Howard Brothers Florists 7101 Southwestern Ave	Oklahoma City	OK	73139	**800-648-0524**	405-632-4747
IOS Brands Corp 3113 Woodcreek Dr	Downers Grove	IL	60515	**800-736-3383**	630-719-7800
John Wolf Florist 6228 Waters Ave	Savannah	GA	31406	**800-944-6435**	912-352-9843
Johnston the Florist Inc 14179 Lincoln Way	North Huntingdon	PA	15642	**800-232-4795**	412-751-2821
Joyce Florist 2729 S Hampton Rd	Dallas	TX	75224	**800-527-1520**	214-942-1776
Kato Design 3650 Austin Bluffs Suite 190	Colorado Springs	CO	80918	**800-448-3383**	719-634-8300
Ken's Flower Shop 140 W South Boundary St	Perrysburg	OH	43551	**800-253-0100**	419-874-4103
Kuhn Flowers Inc 3802 Beach Blvd	Jacksonville	FL	32207	**800-458-5846**	904-398-8601
La Rue's Flower Shop 2600 N MacArthur Blvd	Oklahoma City	OK	73127	**800-847-1462**	405-943-3314
Lehrer's Flowers Inc 3191 W 38th Ave	Denver	CO	80211	**800-537-1308**	303-455-1234
Lester's Florist Inc 2100 Bull St	Savannah	GA	31401	**800-841-1103**	912-233-6066
Long Distance Roses 8673 N Peacock Way	Hilmar	CA	95324	**800-537-6737**	
Maple Lee Flowers Inc 615 High St	Worthington	OH	43085	**800-414-0000**	614-885-5350
Martina's Flowers & Gifts 3830 Washington Rd West Town Market Sq	Martinez	GA	30907	**800-927-1204**	706-863-7172
Metropolitan Plant & Flower Exchange 459 Main St	Fort Lee	NJ	07024	**800-942-1050**	201-944-1050
Nanz & Kraft Florists Inc 141 Breckenridge Ln	Louisville	KY	40207	**800-897-6551**	502-897-6551
Norton's Flowers & Gifts 2900 Washtenaw Ave *Sales	Ypsilanti	MI	48197	**800-682-8667***	734-434-2700
Phillip's Flower Shops Inc 524 N Cass Ave	Westmont	IL	60559	**800-356-7257**	630-719-5200
Phoenix Flower Shops 5012 E Thomas Rd Suite 4	Phoenix	AZ	85018	**888-311-0404**	602-840-1200
Preuss Alan Florists 17680-E W Bluemound Rd	Brookfield	WI	53045	**800-839-8400**	262-786-7900
Proflowers.com 5005 Wateridge Vista Dr 2nd Fl	San Diego	CA	92121	**800-776-3569**	858-454-9850
Royer's Flower Shops 810 S 12th St	Lebanon	PA	17042	**888-276-9377**	717-273-2683
Russell Florist Inc 5001 Gravois Blvd	Saint Louis	MO	63116	**800-351-9003**	314-351-4676
Schroeder's Flowerland Inc 1530 S Webster Ave	Green Bay	WI	54301	**800-236-4769**	920-436-6363
Stephenson's Flower Shops 145 S Locust St	Camp Hill	PA	17011	**800-735-6937**	717-761-5990
Strange's Florist Inc 3313 Mechanicsville Pike	Richmond	VA	23223	**800-421-4070**	804-321-2200
Veldkamp's Flowers 9501 W Colfax Ave	Lakewood	CO	80215	**800-247-3730**	303-232-2673
Villere's Florist 1107 Veterans Blvd	Metairie	LA	70005	**800-845-5373**	504-833-3716
Winston Brothers Inc 160 Southampton St	Boston	MA	02118	**800-457-4901**	617-541-1100
Wolf John Florist 6228 Waters Ave	Savannah	GA	31406	**800-944-6435**	912-352-9843

288 FLOWERS & NURSERY STOCK - WHOL

SEE ALSO Horticultural Products Growers

Company	City	State	Zip	Toll-Free	Phone
Agriflora Corp 9475 NW 13th St	Miami	FL	33172	**800-851-2098**	305-477-0291
Ardinger HT & Son Co 1990 Lake Point Dr	Lewisville	TX	75057	**800-683-0498**	214-631-9830
Ball Horticultural Co 622 Town Rd	West Chicago	IL	60185	**800-879-2255**	630-231-3600
Bill Doran Co Inc 619 W Jefferson St	Rockford	IL	61103	**800-822-8815**	815-965-6042
Carlstedt Oscar G Co 577 College St	Jacksonville	FL	32204	**800-654-5739**	904-354-8474
Celebrity Inc 4520 Old Troup Hwy Suite C	Tyler	TX	75707	**800-527-8446**	903-561-3981
Claymore C Sieck Wholesale Florist 311 E Chase St	Baltimore	MD	21202	**800-624-7134**	410-685-4660
Cleveland Plant & Flower Co 12920 Corporate Dr	Parma	OH	44130	**800-688-8012**	216-898-3500
Cut Flower Wholesale Inc 2122 Faulkner Rd	Atlanta	GA	30324	**888-997-8367**	404-320-1619
Delaware Valley Wholesale Florist 520 Mantua Blvd N	Sewell	NJ	08080	**800-676-1212**	856-468-7000
Distinctive Designs International Inc 120 Sibley Dr	Russellville	AL	35653	**800-243-4787**	256-332-7390
Esprit Miami 3043 NW 107th Ave	Miami	FL	33172	**800-327-2320**	305-591-2244
Florist Distributing 2403 Bell Ave	Des Moines	IA	50321	**800-373-3741**	515-243-5228
Greenleaf Wholesale Florists Inc 13239 Weld County Rd 4	Brighton	CO	80601	**800-659-8000**	303-659-8000
Hill Floral Products Inc 2117 Peacock Rd	Richmond	IN	47374	**800-526-4733**	765-973-6660
Houff Roy Co 6200 S Oak Park Ave	Chicago	IL	60638	**800-366-1769**	773-586-8118
HT Ardinger & Son Co 1990 Lake Point Dr	Lewisville	TX	75057	**800-683-0498**	214-631-9830
Karthauser & Sons Inc W 147 N 11100 Fond du Lac Ave	Germantown	WI	53022	**800-338-8620**	262-255-7815
L & L Nursery Supply Co Inc 5350 G St	Chino	CA	91710	**800-624-2517**	909-591-0461
Lee Wholesale Floral Inc 917 N 8th St	Abilene	TX	79601	**800-677-2626**	325-673-7381
Manatee Cortez Floral Co 1320 33rd St W	Palmetto	FL	34221	**800-752-9845**	941-722-3279
Norben Import Corp 99 S Newman St	Hackensack	NJ	07601	**800-526-4652**	201-487-0855
Oscar G Carlstedt Co 577 College St	Jacksonville	FL	32204	**800-654-5739**	904-354-8474
Pennock Co 4700 Wissahickon Ave	Philadelphia	PA	19144	**800-473-1222**	215-844-6600
Pittsburgh Cut Flower Co 1901 Liberty Ave	Pittsburgh	PA	15222	**800-837-2837**	412-355-7000
Platz Flowers & Supply Inc 8501 Frontage Rd	Morton Grove	IL	60053	**888-752-8048**	847-966-3100
Reliance Trading Corp of America 2222 W 138th St	Blue Island	IL	60406	**800-782-7673**	708-597-2300
Rexius Forest By-Products Inc 1275 Bailey Hill Rd	Eugene	OR	97402	**800-285-7227**	541-342-1835
Roy Houff Co 6200 S Oak Park Ave	Chicago	IL	60638	**800-366-1769**	773-586-8118
Southern Importers Inc 3859 Battleground Ave Suite 300 *Cust Svc	Greensboro	NC	27410	**800-334-9658***	336-292-4521
Tapscott's 1403 E 18th St	Owensboro	KY	42303	**800-626-1922**	270-684-2308
Tennessee Florist Supply Inc 2713 John Deere Dr	Knoxville	TN	37917	**800-951-7451**	865-524-7451
Teters Floral Products Inc 1425 S Lillian Ave	Bolivar	MO	65613	**800-999-5996**	417-326-7654
Teufel Nursery Inc 12345 NW Barnes Rd	Portland	OR	97229	**800-483-8335**	503-646-1111
Van Bloem Gardens 500 Pirkle Ferry Rd Suite D	Cummings	GA	30130	**800-683-2852**	770-667-3344
Van Well Nursery 2821 Grant Rd	East Wenatchee	WA	98802	**800-572-1553**	509-886-8189
Van Zyverden Inc 8079 Van Zyverden Rd	Meridian	MS	39305	**800-332-2852**	601-679-8274
Western Organics Inc 420 E Southern Ave	Tempe	AZ	85202	**800-352-3245**	602-269-5756
Zieger & Sons Inc 6215 Ardleigh St	Philadelphia	PA	19138	**800-752-2003**	215-438-7060

289 FLOWERS-BY-WIRE SERVICES

Company	City	State	Zip	Toll-Free	Phone
FTD Group Inc 3113 Woodcreek Dr *NYSE: FTD*	Downers Grove	IL	60515	**800-788-9000**	630-719-7800
Teleflora Inc 11444 W Olympic Blvd 4th Fl	Los Angeles	CA	90064	**800-321-2654**	310-231-9199

290 FOIL & LEAF - METAL

Company	City	State	Zip	Toll-Free	Phone
Chemetal 39 O'Neil St	Easthampton	MA	01027	**800-807-7341**	413-529-0718
Crown Roll Leaf Inc 91 Illinois Ave	Paterson	NJ	07503	**800-631-3831**	973-742-4000
Hamilton Precision Metals Inc 1780 Rohrerstown Rd	Lancaster	PA	17601	**800-476-7065**	717-569-7061

Company	City	State	ZIP	Toll-Free	Phone
M Swift & Sons Inc 10 Love Ln	Hartford	CT	06112	**800-628-0380**	860-522-1181
October Co Inc PO Box 71	Easthampton	MA	01027	**800-628-9346**	413-527-9380
Swift M & Sons Inc 10 Love Ln	Hartford	CT	06112	**800-628-0380**	860-522-1181

291 FOOD PRODUCTS - MFR

SEE ALSO Agricultural Products; Bakeries; Beverages - Mfr; Ice - Manufactured; Livestock & Poultry Feeds - Prepared; Meat Packing Plants; Pet Products; Poultry Processing; Salt

291-1 Bakery Products - Fresh

Company	City	State	ZIP	Toll-Free	Phone
Alfred Nickles Bakery Inc 26 N Main St	Navarre	OH	44662	**800-635-1110**	330-879-5635
Amoroso's Baking Co 845 S 55th St	Lansdowne	PA	19143	**800-377-6557**	215-471-4740
Archway & Mother's Cookie Co 810 81st Ave	Oakland	CA	94621	**800-538-4842**	510-569-2323
Arnie's Inc 722 Leonard St NW	Grand Rapids	MI	49504	**800-343-4361**	616-458-1107
Bama Pie Ltd 2745 E 11th St	Tulsa	OK	74104	**800-756-2262**	918-592-0778
Brown's Bakery Inc 505 Downs St	Defiance	OH	43512	**800-468-2511**	419-784-3330
Butter Krust Baking Co Inc 249 N 11th St	Sunbury	PA	17801	**800-332-8521**	570-286-5845
Byrnes & Kiefer Co 131 Kline Ave	Callery	PA	16024	**877-444-2240**	724-538-5200
Carolina Foods Inc 1807 S Tryon St	Charlotte	NC	28203	**800-234-0441**	704-333-9812
Chattanooga Bakery Inc 900 Manufacture Rd	Chattanooga	TN	37401	**800-251-3404**	423-267-3351
Cloverhill Bakery Inc 2035 N Narragansett Ave	Chicago	IL	60639	**800-745-9822**	773-745-9800
Colchester Bakery 96 Lebanon Ave	Colchester	CT	06415	**800-554-2440**	860-537-2415
Country Hearth Breads 3355 W Memorial Blvd	Lakeland	FL	33815	**800-283-8093**	863-682-1155
Dakota Brands International 2121 13th St NE	Jamestown	ND	58401	**800-844-5073**	701-252-5073
Dinkel's Bakery 3329 N Lincoln Ave	Chicago	IL	60657	**800-822-8817**	773-281-7300
Ellison Bakery 4108 W Ferguson Rd	Fort Wayne	IN	46809	**800-711-8091**	260-747-6136
Fantini Baking Co Inc 375 Washington St	Haverhill	MA	01832	**800-223-9037**	978-373-1273
Franz Bakery 340 NE 11th Ave	Portland	OR	97232	**800-935-5679**	503-232-2191
Franz Family Bakeries Gal's Div 2006 Weller St	Seattle	WA	98144	**800-272-7323**	206-322-0931
Gal's Div Franz Family Bakeries 2006 Weller St	Seattle	WA	98144	**800-272-7323**	206-322-0931
George Weston Bakeries Inc 55 Paradise Ln	Bay Shore	NY	11706	**800-842-9595**	631-273-6000
H & S Bakery Inc 601 S Caroline St	Baltimore	MD	21231	**800-959-7655**	410-558-3096
Heiners Bakery Inc 1300 Adams Ave	Huntington	WV	25704	**800-776-8411**	304-523-8411
Horizon Snack Foods 443 W 400 North	Salt Lake City	UT	84103	**800-453-4575**	801-533-9550
HPR Bakers 290 Madsen Dr Suite 101	Bloomingdale	IL	60108	**800-366-6776**	630-671-4100
Jenny Lee Bakery Inc 620 Island Ave	McKees Rocks	PA	15136	**888-536-6933**	412-331-8900
Klosterman Baking Co Inc 4760 Paddock Rd	Cincinnati	OH	45229	**877-301-1004**	513-242-1004
Leidenheimer Baking Co 1501 Simon Bolivar Ave	New Orleans	LA	70113	**800-259-9099**	504-525-1575
Little Dutch Boy Bakery Inc 12349 S 970 East	Draper	UT	84020	**800-382-2594**	801-571-3800
Mama Kayer's Baltimore Bakery Inc 1140 Kingwood Ave	Norfolk	VA	23502	**800-627-7850**	757-855-4731
Mary of Puddin Hill Inc 201 E I-30 *Orders	Greenville	TX	75403	**800-545-8889***	903-455-2651
Maurice Lenell Cooky Co 4474 N Harlem Ave	Norridge	IL	60706	**800-323-1760**	708-456-6500
McKee Foods Corp PO Box 750 *Cust Svc	Collegedale	TN	37315	**800-522-4499***	423-238-7111
Meyer's Bakeries Inc 2700 E 3rd St	Hope	AR	71802	**800-643-1542**	870-777-9031
Montana Mills Bread Co Inc 2171 Monroe Ave Suite 205A	Rochester	NY	14618	**877-662-7323**	585-242-7540
Morabito Baking Co Inc 757 Kohn St	Norristown	PA	19401	**800-525-7747**	610-275-5419
Mrs Baird's Bakeries Inc 7301 South Fwy	Fort Worth	TX	76134	**800-366-7921**	817-293-6230
Nickles Alfred Bakery Inc 26 N Main St	Navarre	OH	44662	**800-635-1110**	330-879-5635
Old London Foods 1776 Eastchester Rd	Bronx	NY	10461	**888-266-4445**	718-409-1776
Orlando Baking Co Inc 7777 Grand Ave	Cleveland	OH	44104	**800-362-5504**	216-361-1872
Ottenberg's Bakery Inc 655 Taylor St NE	Washington	DC	20017	**800-334-7264**	202-529-5800
Pan-O-Gold Baking Co 44 E Saint Germain St	Saint Cloud	MN	56304	**800-444-7005**	320-251-9361
Parco Foods LLC 2200 W 138th St	Blue Island	IL	60406	**888-371-9200**	708-371-9200
Pechters Baking 840 Jersey St	Harrison	NJ	07029	**800-525-5779**	973-483-3374
Pepperidge Farm Inc 595 Westport Ave *PR	Norwalk	CT	06851	**888-737-7374***	203-846-7000
Philadelphia Baking Co 9400 Bluegrass Rd	Philadelphia	PA	19114	**800-775-5623**	215-464-4242
Piantedosi Baking Co Inc 240 Commercial St	Malden	MA	02148	**800-339-0080**	781-321-3400
Quinzani's Bakery 380 Harrison Ave	Boston	MA	02118	**800-999-1062**	617-426-2114
Royal Cake Co Inc 315 Cassell St	Winston-Salem	NC	27107	**800-334-5260**	336-785-8700
San Francisco French Bread Co 580 Julie Ann Way	Oakland	CA	94621	**888-661-7687**	510-729-6232
Sara Lee Bakery Group Gardner Div 3401 E Washington Ave	Madison	WI	53704	**800-676-4395**	608-244-4747
Sara Lee Food & Beverage 10151 Carver Rd	Cincinnati	OH	45242	**800-351-7111**	513-936-2000
Schafers Bakery Inc 5085 W Grand River Ave	Lansing	MI	48906	**800-347-7373**	517-886-3842
Schmidt Baking Co Inc 7801 Fitch Ln	Baltimore	MD	21236	**800-456-2253**	410-668-8200
Schwebel Baking Co 965 E Midlothian Blvd PO Box 6018	Youngstown	OH	44501	**800-860-2867**	330-783-2860
Sokol & Co 5315 Dansher Rd *Cust Svc	Countryside	IL	60525	**800-328-7656***	708-482-8250
Specialty Bakers Inc 450 S State Rd	Marysville	PA	17053	**800-233-0778**	717-957-2131
Stroehmann Bakeries Inc 255 Business Center Dr Suite 200	Horsham	PA	19044	**800-355-1260**	215-672-8010
Svenhard's Swedish Bakery Inc 335 Adeline St	Oakland	CA	94607	**800-333-7836**	510-834-5035
Tasty Baking Co 2801 W Hunting Park Ave *NYSE: TBC*	Philadelphia	PA	19129	**800-330-8677**	215-221-8500
TJ Cinnamons 1000 Corporate Dr	Fort Lauderdale	FL	33334	**800-487-2729**	954-351-5100
Turano Baking Co 6501 W Roosevelt Rd	Berwyn	IL	60402	**800-458-5662**	708-788-9220
US Bakery DBA Franz Bakery 340 NE 11th Ave	Portland	OR	97232	**800-935-5679**	503-232-2191
Vie de France Bakery 2070 Chain Bridge Rd Suite 500	Vienna	VA	22182	**800-446-4404**	703-442-9205
Weston George Bakeries Inc 55 Paradise Ln	Bay Shore	NY	11706	**800-842-9595**	631-273-6000
Wolferman's Inc 14350 Santa Fe Trail Dr *Cust Svc	Lenexa	KS	66215	**800-919-1888***	913-888-4499

291-2 Bakery Products - Frozen

Company	City	State	ZIP	Toll-Free	Phone
Athens Pastries & Frozen Foods Inc 13600 Snow Rd	Cleveland	OH	44142	**800-837-5683**	216-676-8500
Bavarian Specialty Foods 22417 S Vermont Ave	Torrance	CA	90502	**800-421-0301**	310-212-6199
Best Brands Corp 1765 Yankee Doodle Rd	Eagan	MN	55121	**800-328-2068**	651-454-5850
Bridgford Foods Corp 1308 N Patt St *NASDAQ: BRID*	Anaheim	CA	92801	**800-854-3255**	714-526-5533
Brooks Food Group Inc 940 Orange St	Bedford	VA	24523	**800-873-4934**	540-586-8284
Chef Solutions Inc 1000 Universal Dr	North Haven	CT	06473	**800-877-1157**	203-234-0115
Cookietree Bakeries PO Box 57888	Salt Lake City	UT	84157	**800-998-0111**	801-268-2253
Country Home Bakers Inc 3 Enterprise Dr Suite 404 *Cust Svc	Shelton	CT	06484	**800-243-0008***	203-225-2333
Eli's Cheesecake Co 6701 W Forest Preserve Dr	Chicago	IL	60634	**800-999-8300**	773-736-3417
Evans Frozen Baked Goods Inc PO Box 284 *Cust Svc	Cozad	NE	69130	**800-222-5641***	308-784-2409
Guttenplans Frozen Dough 100 Hwy 36	Middletown	NJ	07748	**888-422-4357**	732-495-9480
James Skinner Baking Co 4657 G St	Omaha	NE	68117	**800-358-7428**	402-734-1672
Main Street Gourmet Inc 170 Muffin Ln	Cuyahoga Falls	OH	44223	**800-678-6246**	330-929-0000
Maplehurst Inc 50 Maplehurst Dr	Brownsburg	IN	46112	**800-428-3200**	317-858-9000
Orange Bakery Inc 17751 Cowan Ave	Irvine	CA	92614	**800-576-6836**	949-863-1377
Rhino Foods Inc 79 Industrial Pkwy	Burlington	VT	05401	**800-639-3350**	802-862-0252
Sam's Cheesecake Inc 7666 Miramar Rd	San Diego	CA	92126	**800-833-8835**	858-578-3460
Sara Lee Food & Beverage 10151 Carver Rd	Cincinnati	OH	45242	**800-351-7111**	513-936-2000
Schroeder's Cosmopolitan Bakery Inc PO Box 183	Buffalo	NY	14213	**800-850-7763**	716-885-4894
Schwan's Bakery 1651 Montreal Cir	Tucker	GA	30084	**800-241-4166**	770-449-4900
Vie de France Bakery 2070 Chain Bridge Rd Suite 500	Vienna	VA	22182	**800-446-4404**	703-442-9205

291-3 Butter (Creamery)

Company	City	State	ZIP	Toll-Free	Phone
AMPI 315 N Broadway	New Ulm	MN	56073	**800-533-3580**	507-354-8295
California Dairies Inc 11709 E Artesia Blvd	Artesia	CA	90701	**800-821-5588**	562-865-1291
Challenge Dairy Products Inc 11875 Dublin Blvd Suite B230	Dublin	CA	94568	**800-733-2374**	925-828-6160
Crystal Cream & Butter Co 1013 D St	Sacramento	CA	95814	**800-272-7326**	916-444-7200
Grassland Dairy Products Co Inc PO Box 160	Greenwood	WI	54437	**800-428-8837**	715-267-6182
Land O'Lakes Inc 4001 Lexington Ave N	Arden Hills	MN	55126	**800-328-9680**	651-481-2222
Level Valley Creamery 807 Pleasant Valley Rd	West Bend	WI	53095	**800-558-1707**	262-675-6533
Milkco Inc 220 Deaverview Rd	Asheville	NC	28806	**800-842-8021**	828-254-9560
O-AT-KA Milk Products Co-op Inc PO Box 718	Batavia	NY	14021	**800-828-8152**	585-343-0536
Ramey Farmers Co-op Creamery 5139 345th Ave	Foley	MN	56329	**888-219-1768**	320-355-2313
WestFarm Foods 635 Elliott Ave W	Seattle	WA	98119	**800-333-6455**	206-284-7220

291-4 Cereals (Breakfast)

Company	City	State	ZIP	Toll-Free	Phone
Arrowhead Mills Inc PO Box 2059	Hereford	TX	79045	**800-749-0730**	806-364-0730
Beech-Nut Nutrition Corp 100 S 4th St Suite 1010	Saint Louis	MO	63102	**800-233-2468**	314-436-7667
Big G Cereals PO Box 9452	Minneapolis	MN	55440	**800-328-1144**	763-764-7600
Bob's Red Mill Natural Foods Inc 5209 SE International Way	Milwaukie	OR	97222	**800-553-2258**	503-654-3215
Breadshop Inc 16100 Foothill Blvd	Irwindale	CA	91706	**800-334-3204**	
General Mills Inc 1 General Mills Blvd *NYSE: GIS*	Minneapolis	MN	55426	**800-328-1144**	763-764-7600
General Mills Inc International Foods Div 1 General Mills Blvd	Minneapolis	MN	55426	**800-328-1144**	763-764-7600
Gilster-Mary Lee Corp 1037 State St	Chester	IL	62233	**800-851-5371**	618-826-2361
Homestead Mills PO Box 1115	Cook	MN	55723	**800-652-5233**	218-666-5233
Honeyville Grain Inc 11600 Dayton Dr	Rancho Cucamonga	CA	91730	**888-810-3212**	909-980-9500
Kellogg Co 1 Kellogg Sq *NYSE: K* ■ *Cust Svc	Battle Creek	MI	49016	**800-962-1413***	269-961-2000
Little Crow Foods PO Box 1038	Warsaw	IN	46581	**800-288-2769**	574-267-7141
Malt-O-Meal Inc 80 S 8th St Suite 2600	Minneapolis	MN	55402	**800-328-4452**	612-338-8551
Organic Milling Co 505 W Allen Ave	San Dimas	CA	91773	**800-638-8686**	909-599-0961
Pacific Grain Products International Inc PO Box 2060 *Cust Svc	Woodland	CA	95776	**800-747-0161***	530-662-5056
Quaker Oats Co 555 W Monroe St	Chicago	IL	60661	**800-555-6287**	312-821-1000
Sovex Foods PO Box 2178	Collegedale	TN	37315	**877-396-3145**	423-396-3145
US Mills Inc 200 Reservoir St Suite 202	Needham	MA	02494	**800-422-1125**	781-444-0440
Weetabix Co Inc 20 Cameron St	Clinton	MA	01510	**800-343-0590**	978-368-0991
Wildtime Foods PO Box 10695	Eugene	OR	97440	**800-356-4458**	541-747-1654

291-5 Cheeses - Natural, Processed, Imitation

Company	City	State	ZIP	Toll-Free	Phone
AMPI 315 N Broadway	New Ulm	MN	56073	**800-533-3580**	507-354-8295
Bel/Kaukauna USA 1500 E North Ave	Little Chute	WI	54140	**800-558-3500**	920-788-3524
Berner Foods Inc 2034 E Factory Rd	Dakota	IL	61018	**800-819-8199**	815-563-4222
Bongrain Cheese USA 400 S Custer Ave	New Holland	PA	17557	**800-253-6637**	717-355-8500
Brewster Dairy Inc PO Box 98	Brewster	OH	44613	**800-874-8874**	330-767-3492
Cabot Creamery Co-op Inc 1 Home Farm Way	Montpelier	VT	05602	**888-792-2268**	802-229-9361
Cacique Inc 14923 Procter Ave	La Puente	CA	91746	**800-521-6987**	626-961-3399
Calabro Cheese Corp 580 Coe Ave	East Haven	CT	06512	**800-969-1311**	203-469-1311
California Dairies Inc 11709 E Artesia Blvd	Artesia	CA	90701	**800-821-5588**	562-865-1291
ConAgra Foods Retail Products Co Dairy Foods Group 215 W Diehl Rd	Naperville	IL	60563	**800-444-7360**	630-857-5200
ConAgra Foods Retail Products Co Deli Foods Group 2001 Butterfield Rd	Downers Grove	IL	60515	**800-325-7424**	630-512-1000
Crowley Foods Inc 95 Court St	Binghamton	NY	13901	**800-637-0019**	607-779-3289
Cucina Classica Italiana Inc 2400 Main St Suite 12	Sayreville	NJ	08872	**800-524-2713**	732-727-7800
Dairy Farmers of America Inc 10220 N Ambassador Dr Northpointe Tower	Kansas City	MO	64153	**888-332-6455**	816-801-6455

				Toll-Free	Phone
F & A Cheese Corp PO Box 19127	Irvine	CA	92623	**800-634-4109**	949-221-8255
Fleur de Lait BC USA 400 S Custer Ave	New Holland	PA	17557	**800-322-2743**	717-355-8500
Galaxy Nutritional Foods Inc 2441 Viscount Row *AMEX: GXY* ■ *Cust Svc	Orlando	FL	32809	**800-808-2325***	407-855-5500
Golden Cheese Co of California 1138 W Rincon St *Cust Svc	Corona	CA	92880	**800-842-0264***	951-493-4700
Gossner Foods Inc 1051 N 1000 West	Logan	UT	84321	**800-944-0454**	435-752-9365
Great Lakes Cheese Co Inc 17825 Great Lakes Pkwy	Hiram	OH	44234	**800-677-7181**	440-834-2500
Heluva Good Cheese Inc PO Box 410	Sodus	NY	14551	**800-323-2188**	315-483-6971
Lactoprot USA Inc PO Box 7 *Cust Svc	Blue Mounds	WI	53517	**800-236-3300***	608-437-5598
Land O'Lakes Inc 4001 Lexington Ave N	Arden Hills	MN	55126	**800-328-9680**	651-481-2222
Le Sueur Cheese Co Inc 719 N Main St	Le Sueur	MN	56058	**800-247-0871**	507-665-3353
Leprino Foods Co 1830 W 38th Ave	Denver	CO	80211	**800-537-7466**	303-480-2600
Level Valley Creamery 807 Pleasant Valley Rd	West Bend	WI	53095	**800-558-1707**	262-675-6533
Lucille Farms Inc 150 River Rd *NASDAQ: LUCY*	Montville	NJ	07045	**800-654-6844**	973-334-6030
McCadam Cheese Co Inc 14 Annette St	Heuvelton	NY	13654	**800-724-3373**	315-344-2441
Miceli Dairy Products Co 2721 E 90th St	Cleveland	OH	44104	**800-551-7196**	216-791-6222
Milkco Inc 220 Deaverview Rd	Asheville	NC	28806	**800-842-8021**	828-254-9560
Pace Dairy Foods Co 2700 Valleyhigh Dr NW	Rochester	MN	55901	**800-533-1687**	507-288-6315
Sargento Foods Inc 1 Persnickety Pl	Plymouth	WI	53073	**800-558-5802**	920-893-8484
Sartori Food Corp 107 Pleasant View Rd *Cust Svc	Plymouth	WI	53073	**800-558-5888***	920-893-6061
Schreiber Foods Inc 425 Pine St	Green Bay	WI	54301	**800-344-0333**	920-437-7601
Swiss Valley Farms Co 21100 Holden Dr	Davenport	IA	52806	**800-747-6113**	563-391-3341
Westby Co-op Creamery 401 S Main St	Westby	WI	54667	**800-492-9282**	608-634-3181
WestFarm Foods 635 Elliott Ave W	Seattle	WA	98119	**800-333-6455**	206-284-7220
White Clover Dairy Inc 489 Holland Ct	Kaukauna	WI	54130	**800-878-5765**	920-766-5765
Wisconsin Cheeseman Inc 301 Broadway Dr *Orders	Sun Prairie	WI	53590	**800-698-1721***	608-837-5166

291-6 Chewing Gum

				Toll-Free	Phone
Ford Gum & Machine Co Inc 18 Newton Ave	Akron	NY	14001	**800-225-5535**	716-542-4561
Philadelphia Chewing Gum Corp N Eagle & Lawrence Rds	Havertown	PA	19083	**800-793-5548**	610-449-1700
Wm Wrigley Jr Co 410 N Michigan Ave *NYSE: WWY*	Chicago	IL	60611	**888-824-9681**	312-644-2121

291-7 Coffee - Roasted (Ground, Instant, Freeze-Dried)

				Toll-Free	Phone
Allegro Coffee Co 12799 Claude Ct *Cust Svc	Thornton	CO	80241	**800-530-3993***	303-444-4844
American Ace Inc 2500 Heiman St	Nashville	TN	37208	**800-309-0079**	615-329-0079
American Coffee Co Inc 800 Magazine St	New Orleans	LA	70130	**800-554-7234**	504-581-7234
Araban Coffee Co Inc 2 Keith Way	Hingham	MA	02043	**800-225-2474**	781-740-4441
Autocrat Coffee Inc PO Box 285	Lincoln	RI	02865	**800-288-6272**	401-333-3300
Boyd Coffee Co 19730 NE Sandy Blvd *Cust Svc	Portland	OR	97230	**800-545-4077***	503-666-4545
Cadillac Coffee Co 1801 Michael St	Madison Heights	MI	48071	**800-438-6900**	248-545-2266
Caravali Coffees Inc 717 Del Paso Rd	Sacramento	CA	95834	**800-647-5282**	916-565-5500
Coffee Holding Co Inc 4401 1st Ave *AMEX: JVA*	Brooklyn	NY	11232	**800-458-2233**	718-832-0800
Community Coffee Co PO Box 791	Baton Rouge	LA	70821	**800-688-0990**	225-291-3900
DeCoty Coffee Co Inc 1920 Austin St	San Angelo	TX	76903	**800-588-8001**	325-655-5607
deLima Paul Co Inc PO Box 4813	Syracuse	NY	13221	**800-962-8864**	315-699-5282
F Gavina & Sons Inc 2700 Fruitland Ave	Vernon	CA	90058	**800-428-4627**	323-582-0671
Farmer Brothers Co 20333 S Normandie Ave *NASDAQ: FARM*	Torrance	CA	90502	**800-735-3226**	310-787-5200
Frontier Natural Products Co-op 3021 78th St PO Box 299	Norway	IA	52318	**800-669-3275**	319-227-7996
Green Mountain Coffee Roasters Inc 33 Coffee Ln *NASDAQ: GMCR* ■ *Cust Svc	Waterbury	VT	05676	**800-432-4627***	802-244-5621
Hawaiian Isles Kona Coffee Co 2839 Mokumoa St *Orders	Honolulu	HI	96819	**800-749-9103***	808-833-2244
JFG Coffee Co 3434 Mynatt Ave	Knoxville	TN	37919	**800-627-1988**	865-546-2120
Kauai Coffee Co Inc PO Box 8	Eleele	HI	96705	**800-545-8605**	808-335-5497
McCullagh SJ Inc 245 Swan St	Buffalo	NY	14204	**800-753-3473**	716-856-3473
Melitta Canada Inc 1 Greensboro Dr Suite 202	Rexdale	ON	M9W1C8	**800-565-4882**	416-243-8979
New England Coffee Co 100 Charles St	Malden	MA	02149	**800-225-3537**	781-324-8094
Old Mansion Foods Inc 1558 W Washington St PO Box 2026	Petersburg	VA	23803	**800-476-1877**	804-862-9889
Paul deLima Co Inc PO Box 4813	Syracuse	NY	13221	**800-962-8864**	315-699-5282
Red Diamond Inc PO Box 2168	Birmingham	AL	35201	**800-292-4651**	205-254-3138
Reily William B & Co Inc 640 Magazine St	New Orleans	LA	70130	**800-535-1961**	504-524-6131
Rowland Coffee Roasters Inc 5605 NW 82 Ave	Miami	FL	33166	**800-990-9039**	305-594-9039
S & D Coffee Inc PO Box 1628 *Cust Svc	Concord	NC	28026	**800-933-2210***	704-782-3121
Sara Lee Food & Beverage 10151 Carver Rd	Cincinnati	OH	45242	**800-351-7111**	513-936-2000
SJ McCullagh Inc 245 Swan St	Buffalo	NY	14204	**800-753-3473**	716-856-3473
Stewarts Private Blend Food Inc 4110 W Wrightwood Ave	Chicago	IL	60639	**800-654-2862**	773-489-2500
Texas Coffee Co Inc PO Box 31	Beaumont	TX	77704	**800-259-3400**	409-835-3434
Torke Coffee Roasting Co Inc 3455 Paine Ave PO Box 694	Sheboygan	WI	53081	**800-242-7671**	920-458-4114
Van Rooy Coffee Co 4569 Spring Rd	Cleveland	OH	44131	**877-826-7669**	216-749-7069
White Cloud Coffee Co 199 E 52nd St	Boise	ID	83714	**800-627-0309**	208-322-1166
White Coffee Corp 1835 38th St	Long Island City	NY	11105	**800-221-0140**	718-204-7900
William B Reily & Co Inc 640 Magazine St	New Orleans	LA	70130	**800-535-1961**	504-524-6131

291-8 Confectionery Products

				Toll-Free	Phone
Adams & Brooks Inc 1915 S Hoover St PO Box 7303 *Orders	Los Angeles	CA	90007	**800-999-9808***	213-749-3226
American Licorice Co 3701 W 128th Pl	Alsip	IL	60803	**800-220-2399**	708-371-1414
Anthony-Thomas Candy Co 1777 Arlingate Ct	Columbus	OH	43228	**877-226-3921**	614-274-8405
Atkinson Candy Co 1608 W Frank Ave	Lufkin	TX	75904	**800-231-1203**	936-639-2333
Banner Candy Mfg Corp 700 Liberty Ave	Brooklyn	NY	11208	**800-221-0934**	718-647-4747
Barry Callebaut USA Inc 400 Industrial Pk Rd	Saint Albans	VT	05478	**800-556-8845**	802-524-9711
Beecher Katharine Candies 1250 Slate Hill Rd	Camp Hill	PA	17011	**800-708-3641**	717-761-5440
Ben Myerson Candy Co Inc 928 Towne Ave	Los Angeles	CA	90021	**800-421-8448**	213-623-6266
Best Sweet Inc 288 Mazeppa Rd	Mooresville	NC	28115	**888-211-5530**	704-664-4300
Blommer Chocolate Co 600 W Kinzie St	Chicago	IL	60610	**800-621-1606**	312-226-7700
Bobs Candies Inc 1315 W Oakridge Dr	Albany	GA	31707	**800-841-3602**	229-430-8300
Brach's Confections Inc 19111 N Dallas Pkwy Suite 200	Dallas	TX	75287	**800-999-0204**	972-930-3600
Brechet & Richter Co 6005 Golden Valley Rd *Sales	Minneapolis	MN	55422	**800-347-8700***	763-545-0201
Brown & Haley 1940 E 11th St	Tacoma	WA	98421	**800-426-8400**	253-620-3000
Cargill Foods 15407 McGinty Rd	Wayzata	MN	55391	**800-227-4455**	952-742-7575
Cargill Inc North America 15407 McGinty Rd	Wayzata	MN	55391	**800-227-4455**	952-742-7575
Carrie Sweet Ingredients 400 Prairie Village Dr	New Century	KS	66031	**800-255-6312**	913-780-1212
Charms Co 7401 S Cicero Ave	Chicago	IL	60629	**800-877-7655**	773-838-3400
Cherrydale Farms Inc 1035 Mill Rd	Allentown	PA	18106	**800-333-4525**	610-366-1606
Chocolates a la Carte Inc 28455 Livingston Ave *Cust Svc	Valencia	CA	91355	**800-818-2462***	661-257-3700
Dahlgren & Co Inc 1220 Sunflower St	Crookston	MN	56716	**800-346-6050**	218-281-2985
DE Wolfgang Candy Co 50 E 4th Ave	York	PA	17404	**800-248-4273**	717-843-5536
Decko Products Inc 2105 Superior St	Sandusky	OH	44870	**800-537-6143**	419-626-5757
Doumak Inc 2201 Touhy Ave	Elk Grove Village	IL	60007	**800-323-0318**	847-437-2100
Eaton Farm Confectioners Inc 30 Burbank Rd	Sutton	MA	01590	**800-343-9300**	508-865-5235
Elmer Candy Corp 401 N 5th St	Ponchatoula	LA	70454	**800-843-9537**	985-386-6166
Esther Price Candies Inc 1709 Wayne Ave	Dayton	OH	45410	**800-782-0326**	937-253-2121
Ferrara Bakery & Cafe Inc 195 Grand St 3rd Fl	New York	NY	10013	**800-871-6068**	212-226-6150
Ferrara Pan Candy Co 7301 W Harrison St	Forest Park	IL	60130	**800-323-1768**	708-366-0500
Ferrero USA Inc 600 Cottontail Ln	Somerset	NJ	08873	**800-337-7376**	732-764-9300
Fowler's Chocolate Co 100 River Rock Dr	Buffalo	NY	14207	**800-824-2263**	716-877-9983
Frankford Candy & Chocolate Co Inc 2101 Washington Ave	Philadelphia	PA	19146	**800-523-9090**	215-735-5200
Gertrude Hawk Chocolates Inc 9 Keystone Pk	Dunmore	PA	18512	**800-822-2032**	570-342-7556
Ghirardelli Chocolate Co 1111 139th Ave	San Leandro	CA	94578	**800-877-9338**	510-483-6970
Godiva Chocolatier Inc 355 Lexington Ave 16th Fl	New York	NY	10017	**800-732-7333**	212-984-5900
Goetze's Candy Co Inc 3900 E Monument St *Orders	Baltimore	MD	21205	**800-295-8058***	410-342-2010
Golden Stream Quality Foods 11899 Exit 5 Pkwy	Fishers	IN	46038	**800-837-2855**	317-845-5534
Guittard Chocolate Co 10 Guittard Rd	Burlingame	CA	94010	**800-468-2462**	650-697-4427
Harry London Candies Inc 5353 Lauby Road *Cust Svc	North Canton	OH	44720	**800-321-0444***	330-494-0833
Hawk Gertrude Chocolates Inc 9 Keystone Pk	Dunmore	PA	18512	**800-822-2032**	570-342-7556
HB Reese Candy Co 925 Reese Ave *Cust Svc	Hershey	PA	17033	**800-468-1714***	717-534-4106
Hershey Co 100 Crystal A Dr *NYSE: HSY*	Hershey	PA	17033	**800-468-1714**	
Hillside Candy Co 35 Hillside Ave	Hillside	NJ	07205	**800-524-1304**	973-926-2300
James Candy Co 1519 Boardwalk	Atlantic City	NJ	08401	**800-441-1404**	609-344-1519
Jelly Belly Candy Co 1 Jelly Belly Ln	Fairfield	CA	94533	**800-323-9380**	707-428-2800
Just Born Inc 1300 Stefko Blvd	Bethlehem	PA	18017	**800-445-5787**	610-867-7568
Kalva Corp 3940 Porett Dr	Gurnee	IL	60031	**800-525-8220**	847-336-1200
Katharine Beecher Candies 1250 Slate Hill Rd	Camp Hill	PA	17011	**800-708-3641**	717-761-5440
Koeze Co 2555 Burlingame Ave SW	Grand Rapids	MI	49509	**888-253-6887**	616-724-2601
Kopper's Chocolate Specialty Co Inc 39 Clarkson St	New York	NY	10014	**800-325-0026**	212-243-0220
Lammes Candies Since 1885 Inc 200 B Parker Dr Suite 500	Austin	TX	78728	**800-252-1885**	512-310-1885
Lindt & Sprungli USA 1 Fine Chocolate Pl	Stratham	NH	03885	**877-695-4638**	603-778-8100
London Harry Candies Inc 5353 Lauby Road *Cust Svc	North Canton	OH	44720	**800-321-0444***	330-494-0833
Lucks Co 3003 S Pine St	Tacoma	WA	98409	**800-826-7409**	206-674-7200
Madelaine Chocolate Novelties Inc 9603 Beach Channel Dr	Rockaway Beach	NY	11693	**800-322-1505**	718-945-1500
Malleys Chocolates 13400 Brookpark Rd	Cleveland	OH	44135	**800-275-6255**	216-226-8300
Marshmallow Cone Co 5141 Fischer Pl	Cincinnati	OH	45217	**800-641-8551**	513-641-2345
Masterfoods USA 800 High St	Hackettstown	NJ	07840	**800-222-0293**	908-852-1000
Masterson Co Inc 4023 W National Ave	Milwaukee	WI	53215	**800-558-0990**	414-647-1132
Maxfield Candy Co 1050 S 200 West	Salt Lake City	UT	84101	**800-288-8002**	801-355-5321
Melster Candy Co 500 E Madison St	Cambridge	WI	53523	**800-535-4401**	608-423-3221
Morley Candy Makers Inc 23770 Hall Rd	Clinton Township	MI	48036	**800-651-7263**	586-468-4300
Munson's Candy Kitchen Inc DBA Munson's Chocolates PO Box 9217	Bolton	CT	06043	**888-868-6766**	860-649-4332
Myerson Ben Candy Co Inc 928 Towne Ave	Los Angeles	CA	90021	**800-421-8448**	213-623-6266
NECCO (New England Confectionery Co) 135 American Legion Hwy	Revere	MA	02151	**800-225-5508**	781-485-4500
New England Confectionery Co (NECCO) 135 American Legion Hwy	Revere	MA	02151	**800-225-5508**	781-485-4500
Palmer Candy Co 311 Bluff St	Sioux City	IA	51103	**800-831-0828**	712-258-5543
Paradise Inc PO Drawer Y	Plant City	FL	33564	**800-330-8952**	813-752-1155
Pearson's Candy Co 2140 W 7th St *Cust Svc	Saint Paul	MN	55116	**800-328-6507***	651-698-0356
Pennsylvania Dutch Candies 1250 Slate Hill Rd	Camp Hill	PA	17011	**800-233-7082**	717-761-5440
Pez Candy Inc 35 Prindle Hill Rd	Orange	CT	06477	**800-243-6087**	203-795-0531
Price Esther Candies Inc 1709 Wayne Ave	Dayton	OH	45410	**800-782-0326**	937-253-2121
Reese HB Candy Co 925 Reese Ave *Cust Svc	Hershey	PA	17033	**800-468-1714***	717-534-4106
Russell Stover Candies Inc 4900 Oak St	Kansas City	MO	64112	**800-477-8683**	816-842-9240
See's Candies Inc 210 El Camino Real *Cust Svc	South San Francisco	CA	94080	**800-951-7337***	650-761-2490
Simon Candy Co 31 N Spruce St	Elizabethtown	PA	17022	**800-367-2441**	717-367-2441
Sorbee International Ltd 9990 Global Rd	Philadelphia	PA	19115	**800-654-3997**	215-677-5200

Confectionery Products (Cont'd)

				Toll-Free	Phone
Spangler Candy Co					
400 N Portland St PO Box 71	Bryan	OH	43506	**800-653-8638***	419-636-4221
*Sales					
Standard Candy Co Inc 715 Massman Dr	Nashville	TN	37210	**800-226-4340**	615-889-6360
Storck USA LP 325 N LaSalle St Suite 400	Chicago	IL	60610	**800-621-7772**	312-467-5700
Sweet Candy Co Inc					
3780 W Directors Row	Salt Lake City	UT	84104	**800-669-8669**	801-886-1444
Tootsie Roll Industries Inc 7401 S Cicero Ave	Chicago	IL	60629	**800-877-7655**	773-838-3400
NYSE: TR					
Wilbur Chocolate Co Inc 48 N Broad St	Lititz	PA	17543	**800-233-0139**	717-626-1131
Wolfgang DE Candy Co 50 E 4th Ave	York	PA	17404	**800-248-4273**	717-843-5536
World's Finest Chocolate Inc					
4801 S Lawndale Ave	Chicago	IL	60632	**800-366-2462**	773-847-4600
Zachary Confections Inc 2130 W SR-28	Frankfort	IN	46041	**800-445-4222***	765-659-4751
*Cust Svc					

291-9 Cookies & Crackers

				Toll-Free	Phone
Archway Cookies LLC					
67 W Michigan Ave Suite 608	Battle Creek	MI	49017	**800-444-6205**	269-962-6205
Archway & Mother's Cookie Co 810 81st Ave	Oakland	CA	94621	**800-538-4842**	510-569-2323
Bakery Resources -Ms Desserts					
2275 Rolling Run Dr	Baltimore	MD	21244	**800-876-7117***	410-281-2000
*Cust Svc					
Benzel's Pretzel Bakery Inc 5200 6th Ave	Altoona	PA	16602	**800-344-4438**	814-942-5062
Bremner Biscuit Co 4600 Joliet St	Denver	CO	80239	**800-722-1871**	303-371-8180
Bremner Inc 800 Market St PO Box 618	Saint Louis	MO	63101	**800-725-7866***	314-877-7000
*Cust Svc					
Chatham Village Foods Div T Marzetti Co					
15 Kendrick Rd	Wareham	MA	02571	**800-771-3888**	508-291-2304
Christie Cookie Co 1205 3rd Ave N	Nashville	TN	37208	**800-458-2447**	615-242-3817
Crackin Good Bakers Inc 701 N Forrest St	Valdosta	GA	31601	**800-323-7850**	229-242-7850
DF Stauffer Biscuit Co					
PO Box 1426 Belmont & 6th Ave	York	PA	17405	**800-673-2473**	717-843-9016
Ellison Bakery 4108 W Ferguson Rd	Fort Wayne	IN	46809	**800-711-8091**	260-747-6136
Ferrara Bakery & Cafe Inc					
195 Grand St 3rd Fl	New York	NY	10013	**800-871-6068**	212-226-6150
George Weston Bakeries Inc					
55 Paradise Ln	Bay Shore	NY	11706	**800-842-9595**	631-273-6000
Holland American Wafer Co					
3300 Roger B Chaffee Blvd SE	Grand Rapids	MI	49548	**800-253-8350**	616-243-0191
J & J Snack Foods Corp					
6000 Central Hwy	Pennsauken	NJ	08109	**800-486-9533**	856-665-9533
NASDAQ: JJSF					
Joy Cone Co 3435 Lamor Rd	Hermitage	PA	16148	**800-242-2663**	724-962-5747
Keystone Pretzels					
124 W Airport Rd Flyway Business Pk	Lititz	PA	17543	**888-572-4500**	717-560-1882
Lance Inc 8600 South Blvd	Charlotte	NC	28273	**800-438-1880**	704-554-1421
NASDAQ: LNCE					
Little Dutch Boy Bakery Inc 12349 S 970 East	Draper	UT	84020	**800-382-2594**	801-571-3800
Mrs Alison's Cookie Co Inc					
1600 Pk 370 Pl Suite 2	Hazelwood	MO	63042	**800-878-6772**	314-298-2595
Norse Dairy Systems PO Box 1869	Columbus	OH	43216	**800-338-7465**	614-294-4931
Pretzels Inc 123 Harvest Rd PO Box 503	Bluffton	IN	46714	**800-456-4838**	260-824-4838
Rudolph Foods Co Inc 6575 Bellefontaine Rd	Lima	OH	45804	**800-241-7675**	419-648-3611
Silver Lake Cookie Co Inc 141 Freeman Ave	Islip	NY	11751	**800-645-9048**	631-581-4000
Snyder's of Hanover 1350 York St	Hanover	PA	17331	**800-233-7125**	717-632-4477
Stauffer DF Biscuit Co					
PO Box 1426 Belmont & 6th Ave	York	PA	17405	**800-673-2473**	717-843-9016
Sturgis Tom Pretzels Inc 2267 Lancaster Pike	Reading	PA	19607	**800-817-3834**	610-775-0335
Sweet Street Desserts PO Box 15127	Reading	PA	19612	**800-793-3897***	610-921-8113
*Orders					
T Marzetti Co Chatham Village Foods Div					
15 Kendrick Rd	Wareham	MA	02571	**800-771-3888**	508-291-2304
Tom Sturgis Pretzels Inc 2267 Lancaster Pike	Reading	PA	19607	**800-817-3834**	610-775-0335
Venus Wafers Inc 70 Research Rd	Hingham	MA	02043	**800-545-4538**	781-740-1002
Vista Bakery Inc					
3000 Mt Pleasant St PO Box 888	Burlington	IA	52601	**800-553-2343**	319-754-6551
Weston George Bakeries Inc					
55 Paradise Ln	Bay Shore	NY	11706	**800-842-9595**	631-273-6000

291-10 Dairy Products - Dry, Condensed, Evaporated

				Toll-Free	Phone
Abbott Laboratories Ross Products Div					
625 Cleveland Ave	Columbus	OH	43215	**800-227-5767***	614-624-7677
*PR					
American Casein Co 109 Elbow Ln	Burlington	NJ	08016	**800-699-6455**	609-387-3130
AMPI 315 N Broadway	New Ulm	MN	56073	**800-533-3580**	507-354-8295
California Dairies Inc 11709 E Artesia Blvd	Artesia	CA	90701	**800-821-5588**	562-865-1291
Dairy Farmers of America Inc					
10220 N Ambassador Dr					
Northpointe Tower	Kansas City	MO	64153	**888-332-6455**	816-801-6455
Davisco International Inc PO Box 69	Le Sueur	MN	56058	**800-323-4503**	507-665-8811
Dietrichs Milk Products Inc 100 McKinley Ave	Reading	PA	19605	**800-526-6455**	610-929-5736
DMV USA 1285 Rudy St	Onalaska	WI	54650	**877-300-7676***	608-779-7676
*Cust Svc					
Erie Foods International Inc 401 7th Ave	Erie	IL	61250	**800-447-1887**	309-659-2233
Foremost Farms USA E10889A Penny Ln	Baraboo	WI	53913	**800-362-9196**	608-356-8316
Gehl's Guernsey Farms Inc					
N116 W15970 Main St	Germantown	WI	53022	**800-521-2873**	262-251-8570
Instantwhip Foods Inc 2200 Cardigan Ave	Columbus	OH	43215	**800-544-9447***	614-488-2536
*Cust Svc					
Jackson-Mitchell Inc PO Box 934	Turlock	CA	95381	**800-343-1185**	209-667-2019
Land O'Lakes Inc 4001 Lexington Ave N	Arden Hills	MN	55126	**800-328-9680**	651-481-2222
Maple Island Inc					
2497 7th Ave E Suite 105	North Saint Paul	MN	55109	**800-369-1022**	651-773-1000
Milnot Co 100 S 4th St Suite 1010	Saint Louis	MO	63102	**800-877-6455***	314-436-7667
*Sales					
O-AT-KA Milk Products Co-op Inc PO Box 718	Batavia	NY	14021	**800-828-8152**	585-343-0536
Penn Maid Foods Inc 10975 Dutton Rd	Philadelphia	PA	19154	**800-220-7063**	215-824-2800
Rich Products Corp 1 Robert Rich Way	Buffalo	NY	14213	**800-828-2021**	716-878-8000
Ross Products Div Abbott Laboratories					
625 Cleveland Ave	Columbus	OH	43215	**800-227-5767***	614-624-7677
*PR					
Saputo Cheese USA 325 Tompkins St	Fond du Lac	WI	54935	**800-345-9714**	920-922-0600
Sinton Dairy Foods Co LLC					
3801 N Sinton Rd	Colorado Springs	CO	80907	**800-388-4970**	719-633-3821
WestFarm Foods 635 Elliott Ave W	Seattle	WA	98119	**800-333-6455**	206-284-7220

291-11 Diet & Health Foods

				Toll-Free	Phone
AMS Health Sciences Inc					
2601 Northwest Expy Suite 1210W					
PO Box 12940	Oklahoma City	OK	73157	**800-426-4267**	405-842-0131
AMEX: AMM					
Balance Bar Co 800 W Chester Ave	Rye Brook	NY	10573	**800-678-4246***	914-335-8400
*Cust Svc					
Cascadian Farm Inc 719 Metcalf St	Sedro Woolley	WA	98284	**800-624-4123**	360-855-0100
Eden Foods Inc 701 Tecumseh Rd	Clinton	MI	49236	**800-248-0320***	517-456-7424
*Cust Svc					
Enjoy Life Foods LLC 1601 N Natchez Ave	Chicago	IL	60707	**888-503-6569**	773-889-5070
French Meadow Bakery Inc					
2610 Lyndale Ave S	Minneapolis	MN	55408	**877-669-3278**	612-870-4740
Golden Temple Inc 2545 Prairie Rd	Eugene	OR	97402	**800-285-6457**	541-461-2160
Great American Health Foods					
4075 40th Ave SW	Fargo	ND	58108	**800-437-2733**	701-356-2760
Lehman Sugarfree Confections Inc					
4512 Farragut Rd	Brooklyn	NY	11203	**800-438-3327**	718-469-3057
Medifast Inc 11445 Cronhill Dr	Owings Mills	MD	21117	**888-463-3432**	410-581-8042
AMEX: MED					
Morinda Inc PO Box 4000	Orem	UT	84059	**800-445-2969**	801-431-6000
Nutrition 21 Inc 4 Manhattanville Rd	Purchase	NY	10577	**800-699-3533**	914-701-4500
NASDAQ: NXXI					
Optimal Nutrients 1163 Chess Dr Unit F	Foster City	CA	94404	**800-966-8874**	650-525-0112
PowerBar Inc 2150 Shattuck Ave	Berkeley	CA	94704	**800-587-6937**	510-843-1330
RC Fine Foods PO Box 236	Belle Mead	NJ	08502	**800-526-3953**	908-359-5500
Seasons' Enterprises Ltd					
1790 W Cortland Ct Suite B PO Box 965	Addison	IL	60101	**800-789-0211**	630-628-0211
Sigco Sun Products Inc PO Box 331	Breckenridge	MN	56520	**800-654-4145**	218-643-8467
Slim-Fast Foods Co					
777 S Flagler Dr Suite 1400	West Palm Beach	FL	33401	**877-375-4632**	561-833-9920
Vitarich Foods Inc 4365 Arnold Ave	Naples	FL	34104	**800-817-9999**	239-430-2266
Weight Watchers Gourmet Food Co					
357 6th Ave Heinz 57 Ctr	Pittsburgh	PA	15222	**800-762-0228**	412-237-5757
Worldwide Sport Nutrition					
851 Broken Sound Pkwy NW Suite 255	Boca Raton	FL	33487	**800-854-5019**	561-241-9400

291-12 Fats & Oils - Animal or Marine

				Toll-Free	Phone
American Proteins Inc 4705 Leland Dr	Cumming	GA	30041	**800-346-7476**	770-886-2250
Baker Commodities Inc 4020 Bandini Blvd	Los Angeles	CA	90023	**800-427-0696**	323-268-2801
Carolina By-Products 1309 Industrial Dr	Fayetteville	NC	28301	**800-476-8675**	910-483-0473
Darling International Inc					
251 O'Connor Ridge Blvd Suite 300	Irving	TX	75038	**800-800-4841**	972-717-0300
AMEX: DAR					
GA Wintzer & Son Co					
5 N Blackhoof St PO Box 406	Wapakoneta	OH	45895	**800-331-1801**	419-738-3771
Griffin Industries 4221 Alexandria Pike	Cold Spring	KY	41076	**800-743-7413**	859-781-2010
Griffin Industries Inc					
4413 Tanner Church Rd	Ellenwood	GA	30294	**800-536-3935**	404-363-1320
Jacob Stern & Sons Inc					
1464 E Valley Rd	Santa Barbara	CA	93108	**800-223-7054**	805-565-1411
San Luis Tallow Co Inc PO Box 3835	San Luis Obispo	CA	93403	**800-281-8660**	805-543-8660

291-13 Fish & Seafood - Canned

				Toll-Free	Phone
Appert's Foodservice 900 S Hwy 10	Saint Cloud	MN	56304	**800-225-3883**	320-251-3200
Beaver Street Fisheries Inc					
1741 W Beaver St	Jacksonville	FL	32209	**800-874-6426**	904-354-8533
Bumble Bee Seafoods Inc PO Box 85362	San Diego	CA	92186	**800-800-8572**	858-715-4000
Cape May Foods Inc 35 Indian Trail Rd	Burleigh	NJ	08210	**800-922-1141**	609-465-4551
Chicken of the Sea International Inc					
9330 Scranton Rd Suite 500	San Diego	CA	92121	**800-456-1511**	858-558-9662
Fishking Alabama Inc PO Box 1068	Bayou La Batre	AL	36509	**800-445-0729**	251-824-2118
Florida Smoked Fish Div SeaSpecialties Inc					
1111 NW 159th Dr	Miami	FL	33169	**800-654-6682**	305-625-5112
Hegg & Hegg Elwha Fish Co					
801 Marine Dr	Port Angeles	WA	98363	**800-435-3474**	360-457-3344
Nelson Crab Inc PO Box 520	Tokeland	WA	98590	**800-262-0069**	360-267-2911
Noon Hour Food Products Inc					
215 N Des Plaines	Chicago	IL	60661	**800-621-6636***	312-382-1177
*Cust Svc					
Pacific Seafood Co PO Box 97	Clackamas	OR	97015	**800-388-1101**	503-657-1101
Rich-SeaPak Corp PO Box 20670	Saint Simons Island	GA	31522	**800-654-9731**	912-638-5000
SeaSpecialties Inc Florida Smoked Fish Div					
1111 NW 159th Dr	Miami	FL	33169	**800-654-6682**	305-625-5112
Snow's/Doxsee Inc 994 Ocean Dr	Cape May	NJ	08204	**800-459-0396**	609-884-0440
Vita Food Products Inc 2222 W Lake St	Chicago	IL	60612	**800-989-8482**	312-738-4500
AMEX: VSF					

291-14 Fish & Seafood - Fresh or Frozen

				Toll-Free	Phone
American Seafoods International					
40 Herman Melville Blvd	New Bedford	MA	02740	**800-343-8046**	508-997-0031
America's Catch Inc PO Box 584	Itta Bena	MS	38941	**800-242-0041**	662-254-7207
Blount Seafood Corp PO Box 327	Warren	RI	02885	**800-274-2526**	401-245-8800
Bon Secour Fisheries Inc					
17449 County Rd 49 S PO Box 60	Bon Secour	AL	36511	**800-633-6854**	251-949-7411
ConAgra Seafood Cos PO Box 2819	Tampa	FL	33601	**800-732-3663**	813-241-1500
ConFish Inc PO Box 271	Isola	MS	38754	**800-228-3474**	662-962-3101
Delta Pride Catfish Inc 1301 Industrial Pkwy	Indianola	MS	38751	**800-421-1045**	662-887-5401
Eastern Shore Seafood PO Box 38	Mappsville	VA	23407	**800-446-8550***	757-824-5651
*Sales					
Gorton's Inc 128 Rogers St	Gloucester	MA	01930	**800-225-0572**	978-283-3000
Gulf City Seafood Inc PO Box 1346	Pascagoula	MS	39568	**800-666-3300**	228-762-3271
King & Prince Seafood Corp					
1 King & Prince Blvd	Brunswick	GA	31520	**800-841-0205**	912-265-5155

				Toll-Free	Phone
Matlaw's Food Products Inc 135 Front Ave	West Haven	CT	06516	**800-934-8266***	203-934-5233
*Cust Svc					
Ocean Beauty Seafoods Inc 1100 W Ewing St	Seattle	WA	98119	**800-877-0185**	206-285-6800
Perona Farms Food Specialties 350 Andover Sparta Rd	Andover	NJ	07821	**800-762-8569**	973-729-7878
Sea Harvest Packing Co PO Box 818	Brunswick	GA	31521	**800-627-4300**	912-264-3212
Sea Watch International Ltd 8978 Glebe Pk Dr	Easton	MD	21601	**800-732-2526**	410-822-7500
Singleton Seafood Co 5024 Uceta Rd	Tampa	FL	33619	**800-732-3663**	813-241-1500
Stoller Fisheries Inc PO Box B	Spirit Lake	IA	51360	**800-831-5174**	712-336-1750
Tampa Bay Fisheries Inc 3060 Gallagher Rd	Dover	FL	33527	**800-234-2561**	813-752-8883
Tampa Maid Foods Inc 1600 Kathleen Rd	Lakeland	FL	33805	**800-237-7637**	863-687-4411
Trident Seafood Corp 5303 Shilshole Ave NW	Seattle	WA	98107	**800-367-6065**	206-783-3818
UniSea Inc 15400 NE 90th St PO Box 97019	Redmond	WA	98073	**800-535-8509**	425-881-8181
Viking Seafoods Inc 50 Crystal St	Malden	MA	02148	**800-225-3920**	781-324-1050

291-15 Flavoring Extracts & Syrups

				Toll-Free	Phone
American Distilling & Mfg Inc 31 E High St	East Hampton	CT	06424	**800-203-4444**	860-267-4444
BFI Innovations 420-C Airport Rd	Elgin	IL	60123	**800-323-7009**	847-214-4860
Brady Enterprises Inc 167 Moore Rd	East Weymouth	MA	02189	**800-225-5126**	781-337-5000
Danisco Cultor USA 411 E Gano PO Box 470489	Saint Louis	MO	63147	**800-851-8100**	314-436-3133
David Michael & Co Inc 10801 Decatur Rd	Philadelphia	PA	19154	**800-523-3806**	215-632-3100
Edlong Corp 225 Scott St	Elk Grove Village	IL	60007	**888-698-2783**	847-439-9230
Firmenich Inc PO Box 5880	Princeton	NJ	08543	**800-257-9591**	609-452-1000
Food Producers International 10505 Wayzata Blvd Suite 400	Minnetonka	MN	55305	**800-443-1336**	952-544-2763
Frutarom Corp 9500 Railroad Ave	North Bergen	NJ	07047	**800-526-7147**	201-861-9500
Givaudan Flavors Corp 1199 Edison Dr	Cincinnati	OH	45216	**800-892-1199**	513-948-8000
Guernsey Bel Inc 4300 S Morgan St	Chicago	IL	60609	**800-621-0271**	773-927-4000
I Rice & Co Inc 11500 Roosevelt Blvd Bldg D	Philadelphia	PA	19116	**800-232-6022**	215-673-7423
Jel Sert Co PO Box 261	West Chicago	IL	60186	**800-323-2592**	630-231-7590
Kalsec Inc PO Box 50511	Kalamazoo	MI	49005	**800-323-9320**	269-349-9711
Limpert Brothers Inc PO Box 1480	Vineland	NJ	08362	**800-691-1353**	856-691-1353
Lyons Magnus Inc 1636 S 2nd St	Fresno	CA	93702	**800-344-7130**	559-268-5966
McCormick & Co Inc Food Service Div 226 Schilling Cir	Hunt Valley	MD	21031	**800-327-6838**	410-771-7500
McCormick & Co Inc McCormick Flavor Div 226 Schilling Cir	Hunt Valley	MD	21031	**800-327-6838**	410-771-7500
McCormick & Co Inc US Consumer Products Div 211 Schilling Cir	Hunt Valley	MD	21031	**800-292-5300**	410-527-6000
Mother Murphy's Labs Inc PO Box 16846	Greensboro	NC	27416	**800-849-1277**	336-273-1737
Nielsen-Massey Vanillas Inc 1550 Shields Dr	Waukegan	IL	60085	**800-525-7873**	847-578-1550
Ottens Flavors 7800 Holstein Ave	Philadelphia	PA	19153	**800-523-0767**	215-365-7800
Quest International Flavors USA Inc 10 Painters Mill Rd	Owings Mills	MD	21117	**800-743-1399**	410-363-2550
Sea Breeze Fruit Flavors Inc 441 Rt 202	Towaco	NJ	07082	**800-732-2733**	973-334-7777
Sensient Technologies Corp 777 E Wisconsin Ave 11th Fl	Milwaukee	WI	53202	**800-558-9892**	414-271-6755
NYSE: SXT					
Sethness Products Co 3422 W Touhy Ave	Chicago	IL	60645	**888-772-1880**	847-329-2080
Slush Puppie Frozen Drink Div of Dr Pepper/Seven-Up Inc PO Box 869077	Plano	TX	75086	**800-527-7096**	
Symrise Inc 300 North St	Teterboro	NJ	07608	**800-422-1559**	201-288-3200
Technology Flavors & Fragrances Inc 10 Edison St E	Amityville	NY	11701	**800-427-3908**	631-842-7600
AMEX: TFF					
V & E Kohnstamm Inc 882 3rd Ave	Brooklyn	NY	11232	**800-847-4500**	718-788-6320
Virginia Dare Extract Co Inc 882 3rd Ave	Brooklyn	NY	11232	**800-847-4500**	718-788-1776
Wild Flavors Inc 1261 Pacific Ave	Erlanger	KY	41018	**888-945-3352**	859-342-3600
Zink & Triest Co Inc 150 Domorah Dr	Montgomeryville	PA	18936	**800-537-5070**	215-469-1950

291-16 Flour Mixes & Doughs

				Toll-Free	Phone
Abitec Corp Inc PO Box 569	Columbus	OH	43216	**800-555-1255***	614-429-6464
*Sales					
Bake'n Joy Foods Inc 351 Willow St S	North Andover	MA	01845	**800-666-4937**	978-683-1414
Best Brands Corp 1765 Yankee Doodle Rd	Eagan	MN	55121	**800-328-2068**	651-454-5850
Caravan Products Co Inc 100 Adams Dr	Totowa	NJ	07512	**800-526-5261**	973-256-8886
Cereal Food Processors Inc 2001 Shawnee Mission Pkwy	Mission Woods	KS	66205	**800-743-5687**	913-890-6300
Continental Mills Inc PO Box 88176	Seattle	WA	98138	**800-457-7744**	253-872-8400
Dawn Food Products Inc 2021 Micor Dr	Jackson	MI	49203	**800-248-1144**	517-789-4400
General Mills Inc International Foods Div 1 General Mills Blvd	Minneapolis	MN	55426	**800-328-1144**	763-764-7600
Gilster-Mary Lee Corp 1037 State St	Chester	IL	62233	**800-851-5371**	618-826-2361
Langlois Co 10810 San Sevaine Way	Mira Loma	CA	91752	**800-962-5993**	951-360-3900
Puratos Corp 1941 Old Cuthbert Rd	Cherry Hill	NJ	08034	**800-654-0036**	856-428-4300
Rhodes International Inc PO Box 25487	Salt Lake City	UT	84125	**800-876-7333**	801-972-0122
Roman Meal Co 2101 S Tacoma Way	Tacoma	WA	98409	**800-426-3600**	253-475-0964
Subco Foods Inc 4350 S Taylor Dr	Sheboygan	WI	53081	**800-473-0757**	920-457-7761

291-17 Food Emulsifiers

				Toll-Free	Phone
ADM Arkady Products 100 Paniplus Rd	Olathe	KS	66061	**800-255-6637**	913-782-8800
ADM Oil Refinery 1940 E Hull Ave	Des Moines	IA	50316	**800-637-5843**	515-263-2112
American Casein Co 109 Elbow Ln	Burlington	NJ	08016	**800-699-6455**	609-387-3130
American Ingredients Co 3947 Broadway	Kansas City	MO	64111	**800-669-4092**	816-561-9050
American Lecithin Co Inc 115 Hurley Rd Unit 2B	Oxford	CT	06478	**800-364-4416**	203-262-7100
Frutarom Corp 9500 Railroad Ave	North Bergen	NJ	07047	**800-526-7147**	201-861-9500
Honeymead Products Co PO Box 3247	Mankato	MN	56002	**800-328-3445**	507-625-7911

291-18 Fruits & Vegetables - Dried or Dehydrated

				Toll-Free	Phone
Basic American Foods 2999 Oak Rd Suite 100	Walnut Creek	CA	94597	**800-227-4050**	925-472-4000
Bernard Food Industries Inc 1125 Hartrey Ave	Evanston	IL	60204	**800-323-3663**	847-869-5222
Crystals International Inc 600 W ML King Jr Blvd	Plant City	FL	33563	**800-237-7620**	813-754-2691
Custom Food Products Inc 5145 W 123rd St	Alsip	IL	60803	**800-621-8827***	708-239-2766
*Cust Svc					
Dean Distributors Inc 1350 Bayshore Hwy Suite 400	Burlingame	CA	94010	**800-792-0816**	650-340-1738
Del Monte Foods Co 1 Market St The Landmark	San Francisco	CA	94105	**800-543-3090***	415-247-3000
NYSE: DLM ■ *Cust Svc					
Garry Packing Inc PO Box 249	Del Rey	CA	93616	**800-248-2126**	559-888-2126
Graceland Fruit Inc 1123 Main St	Frankfort	MI	49635	**800-352-7181**	231-352-7181
Idaho Fresh-Pak Inc DBA Idahoan Foods 529 N 3500 East PO Box 130	Lewisville	ID	83431	**800-635-6100**	208-754-4686
Idaho-Pacific Corp 4723 E 100 North PO Box 478	Ririe	ID	83443	**800-238-5503***	208-538-6971
*Sales					
National Raisin Co PO Box 219	Fowler	CA	93625	**800-874-3726**	559-834-5981
Nonpareil Corp 40 N 400 W	Blackfoot	ID	83221	**800-522-2223**	208-785-5880
Oregon Freeze Dry Inc PO Box 1048	Albany	OR	97321	**800-547-4060**	541-926-6001
Small Planet Foods 719 Metcalf St	Sedro Woolley	WA	98284	**800-624-4123**	360-855-0100
Stapleton-Spence Packing Co 1530 The Alameda Suite 320	San Jose	CA	95126	**800-297-8815**	408-297-8815
Sun-Maid Growers of California 13525 S Bethel Ave	Kingsburg	CA	93631	**800-272-4746***	559-896-8000
*Sales					
Sunsweet Growers Inc 901 N Walton Ave	Yuba City	CA	95993	**800-417-2253**	530-674-5010

291-19 Fruits & Vegetables - Pickled

				Toll-Free	Phone
Baumer Foods Inc 4301 Tulane Ave PO Box 19166	New Orleans	LA	70179	**800-222-0694***	504-482-5761
*Sales					
Beaverton Foods Inc PO Box 687	Beaverton	OR	97075	**800-223-8076**	503-646-8138
Cain's Foods Inc 114 E Main St PO Box 347	Ayer	MA	01432	**800-225-0601**	978-772-0300
Claussen Pickle Co 1300 Claussen Dr	Woodstock	IL	60098	**800-435-2817**	815-338-7000
Conway Import Co Inc 11051 West Addison St	Franklin Park	IL	60131	**800-323-8801**	847-455-5600
Daltons Best Maid Products Inc 1400 S Riverside Dr	Fort Worth	TX	76104	**800-447-3581**	817-335-5494
Dean Pickle & Specialty Products Co 857 School Pl	Green Bay	WI	54303	**800-558-4700**	920-497-7131
Eastern Foods Inc 1000 Naturally Fresh Blvd	Atlanta	GA	30349	**800-765-1950**	404-765-9000
Gold Pure Food Products Inc 1 Brooklyn Rd	Hempstead	NY	11550	**800-422-4681**	516-483-5600
Henri's Food Products Co Inc 8622 N 87th St	Milwaukee	WI	53224	**800-338-8831***	414-365-5720
*Cust Svc					
Ken's Foods Inc 1 D'Angelo Dr	Marlborough	MA	01752	**800-633-5800**	508-485-7540
Langlois Co 10810 San Sevaine Way	Mira Loma	CA	91752	**800-962-5993**	951-360-3900
Lawry's Foods Inc 222 E Huntington Dr	Monrovia	CA	91016	**800-952-9797**	626-930-8870
Lea & Perrins Inc 1501 Pollitt Dr	Fair Lawn	NJ	07410	**800-289-5797**	201-791-1600
Lee Kum Kee Inc 14841 don Julian Rd	City of Industry	CA	91746	**800-654-5082***	626-709-1888
*Orders					
Litehouse Inc 1109 N Ella Ave	Sandpoint	ID	83864	**800-669-3169**	208-263-7569
Maurice's Gourmet Barbeque PO Box 6847	West Columbia	SC	29171	**800-628-7423**	803-791-5887
McCormick & Co Inc McCormick Flavor Div 226 Schilling Cir	Hunt Valley	MD	21031	**800-327-6838**	410-771-7500
McIlhenny Co Hwy 329	Avery Island	LA	70513	**800-634-9599***	337-365-8173
*Orders					
Moody Dunbar Inc 3202 Hwy 107	Chuckey	TN	37641	**800-251-8202**	423-257-4712
Morehouse Foods Inc 760 Epperson Dr	City of Industry	CA	91748	**888-297-9800**	626-854-1655
Mount Olive Pickle Co PO Box 609	Mount Olive	NC	28365	**800-672-5041**	919-658-2535
Musco Olive Products Inc 17950 Via Nicolo	Tracy	CA	95376	**800-523-9828**	209-836-4600
NORPAC Foods Inc 930 W Washington St	Stayton	OR	97383	**800-733-9311***	503-769-2101
*Sales					
Olds Products Co 10700 88th Ave	Pleasant Prairie	WI	53158	**800-233-8064**	262-947-3500
Piknik Products Co Inc 3806 Day St	Montgomery	AL	36108	**800-300-8557***	334-265-1567
*Cust Svc					
Portion Pac Inc 7325 Snider Rd	Mason	OH	45040	**800-232-4829**	513-398-0400
Ralph Sechler & Son Inc 5686 State Rd 1	Saint Joe	IN	46785	**800-332-5461**	260-337-5461
Reckitt Benckiser Inc PO Box 225	Parsippany	NJ	07054	**800-888-0192***	973-633-3600
*Cust Svc					
Reily William B & Co Inc 640 Magazine St	New Orleans	LA	70130	**800-535-1961**	504-524-6131
Schwartz Pickle Co 4401 W 44th Pl	Chicago	IL	60632	**800-621-4273**	773-927-7700
Sechler Ralph & Son Inc 5686 State Rd 1	Saint Joe	IN	46785	**800-332-5461**	260-337-5461
Spectrum Organic Products Inc 5341 Old Redwood Hwy	Petaluma	CA	94952	**800-995-2705**	707-778-8900
Spring Glen Fresh Foods Inc 314 Spring Glen Dr PO Box 518	Ephrata	PA	17522	**800-641-2853**	717-733-2201
Thor-Shackel Horseradish Co 16 W 224th Shore Ct	Burr Ridge	IL	60527	**800-951-9696**	630-986-1333
TODDS Enterprises Inc 610 S 56th Ave	Phoenix	AZ	85043	**800-242-7687**	602-484-9584
Tulkoff Products Co Inc 1101 S Conkling St	Baltimore	MD	21224	**800-638-7343**	410-327-6585
Walden Farms 1209 W St Georges Ave	Linden	NJ	07036	**800-229-1706**	908-925-9494
William B Reily & Co Inc 640 Magazine St	New Orleans	LA	70130	**800-535-1961**	504-524-6131

291-20 Fruits, Vegetables, Juices - Canned or Preserved

				Toll-Free	Phone
Allen Canning Co 305 E Main St	Siloam Springs	AR	72761	**800-234-2553**	479-524-6431
AM Braswell Jr Food Co Inc 226 N Zetterower Ave	Statesboro	GA	30458	**800-673-9388**	912-764-6191
American Spoon Foods Inc 1668 Clarion Ave	Petoskey	MI	49770	**800-222-5886**	231-347-9030
Apple & Eve Inc 2 Seaview Blvd	Port Washington	NY	11050	**800-969-8018**	516-621-1122
Ardmore Farms Inc 1915 N Woodland Blvd	DeLand	FL	32720	**800-365-8423**	386-734-4634
Authentic Specialty Foods Inc 4340 Eucalyptus Ave	Chino	CA	91710	**888-236-2272**	909-631-2000
Baumer Foods Inc 4301 Tulane Ave PO Box 19166	New Orleans	LA	70179	**800-222-0694***	504-482-5761
*Sales					
Bell-Carter Foods Inc 3742 Mount Diablo Blvd	Lafayette	CA	94549	**800-252-3557**	925-284-5933
Birds Eye Foods Inc 90 Linden Oaks	Rochester	NY	14625	**800-999-5044**	585-383-1850

Fruits, Vegetables, Juices - Canned or Preserved (Cont'd)

Company	City	State	ZIP	Toll-Free	Phone
Braswell AM Jr Food Co 226 N Zetterower Ave	Statesboro	GA	30458	**800-673-9388**	912-764-6191
Bruce Foods Corp PO Box 1030	New Iberia	LA	70562	**800-299-9082**	337-365-8101
Campbell Soup Co 1 Campbell Pl *NYSE: CPB*	Camden	NJ	08103	**800-772-8467**	856-342-4800
Cargill Foods 15407 McGinty Rd	Wayzata	MN	55391	**800-227-4455**	952-742-7575
Cargill Inc North America 15407 McGinty Rd	Wayzata	MN	55391	**800-227-4455**	952-742-7575
Carriage House Cos Inc 196 Newton St	Fredonia	NY	14063	**800-828-8915**	716-673-1000
Cascadian Farm Inc 719 Metcalf St	Sedro Woolley	WA	98284	**800-624-4123**	360-855-0100
Cincinnati Preserving Co Inc 3015 E Kemper Rd	Sharonville	OH	45241	**800-222-9966**	513-771-2000
Clement Pappas & Co Inc 1045 N Parsonage Rd	Seabrook	NJ	08302	**800-257-7019**	856-455-1000
Cliffstar Corp 1 Cliffstar Ave	Dunkirk	NY	14048	**800-777-2389**	716-366-6100
ConAgra Hunt-Wesson Foodservice Co 3353 Michelson Dr	Irvine	CA	92612	**800-633-0112**	949-437-1000
Daily Juice Products 1 Daily Way	Verona	PA	15147	**800-245-2929**	412-828-9020
Del Monte Foods Co 1 Market St The Landmark *NYSE: DLM* ■ *Cust Svc	San Francisco	CA	94105	**800-543-3090***	415-247-3000
ED Smith & Sons Ltd 944 Hwy 8	Winona	ON	L8E5S3	**800-263-9246**	905-643-1211
Escalon Premier Brands 1905 McHenry Ave	Escalon	CA	95320	**800-343-9556**	209-838-7341
Friel's Inc 100 Friel Pl	Queenstown	MD	21658	**800-739-2676**	410-827-8811
Furmano Foods Inc 700 Cannery Rd PO Box 500	Northumberland	PA	17857	**877-877-6032**	570-473-3516
Giorgio Foods Inc 1161 Park Rd	Reading	PA	19605	**800-220-2139**	610-926-2139
Hanover Foods Corp 1550 York St PO Box 334	Hanover	PA	17331	**800-888-4646**	717-632-6000
Hirzel Canning Co Inc 411 Lemoyne Rd	Northwood	OH	43619	**800-837-1631**	419-693-0531
HJ Heinz Co PO Box 57 *NYSE: HNZ*	Pittsburgh	PA	15230	**800-255-5750**	412-456-5700
HR Nicholson Co 6320 Oakleaf Ave *Cust Svc	Baltimore	MD	21215	**800-638-3514***	410-764-2323
Jasper Wyman & Son PO Box 100	Milbridge	ME	04658	**800-341-1758**	207-546-2311
JM Smucker Co 1 Strawberry Ln *NYSE: SJM*	Orrville	OH	44667	**888-550-9555**	330-682-3000
Johanna Foods Inc Johanna Farm Rd	Flemington	NJ	08822	**800-727-6700**	908-788-2200
Knouse Foods Co-op Inc 800 Peach Glen-Idaville Rd	Peach Glen	PA	17375	**800-827-7537**	717-677-8181
Kuner-Empson Co PO Box 309	Brighton	CO	80601	**888-201-6440**	303-659-1710
Lawrence Foods Inc 2200 Lunt Ave	Elk Grove Village	IL	60007	**800-323-7848**	847-437-2400
Leelanau Fruit Co 2900 SW Bayshore Dr	Suttons Bay	MI	49682	**800-431-0718**	231-271-3514
LiDestri Foods Inc 815 Whitney Rd W	Fairport	NY	14450	**800-397-5222**	585-377-7700
Luigino's Inc 525 S Lake Ave	Duluth	MN	55802	**800-521-1281**	218-723-5555
Lyons Magnus Inc 1636 S 2nd St	Fresno	CA	93702	**800-344-7130**	559-268-5966
MH Zeigler & Sons Inc 1513 N Broad St	Lansdale	PA	19446	**800-854-6123**	215-855-5161
Minute Maid Co 2000 St James Pl	Houston	TX	77056	**800-888-6488**	713-888-5000
Moody Dunbar Inc 3202 Hwy 107	Chuckey	TN	37641	**800-251-8202**	423-257-4712
Morgan Foods Inc 90 W Morgan St	Austin	IN	47102	**888-430-1780**	812-794-1170
Mott's Inc 900 King St	Rye Brook	NY	10573	**800-426-4891**	914-612-4000
Mrs Clark's Foods LLC 740 SE Dalby Dr	Ankeny	IA	50021	**866-971-6500**	515-964-8100
Muir Glen Organic Tomato Products 719 Metcalf St	Sedro Woolley	WA	98284	**800-832-6345**	360-855-0100
Naked Juice Co 935 W 8th St	Azusa	CA	91702	**800-745-8423**	626-852-2500
National Fruit Product Co Inc PO Box 2040	Winchester	VA	22604	**800-551-5167**	540-662-3401
Nicholson HR Co 6320 Oakleaf Ave *Cust Svc	Baltimore	MD	21215	**800-638-3514***	410-764-2323
NORPAC Foods Inc 930 W Washington St *Sales	Stayton	OR	97383	**800-733-9311***	503-769-2101
Ocean Spray Cranberries Inc 1 Ocean Spray Dr	Lakeville-Middleboro	MA	02349	**800-662-3263**	508-946-1000
Odwalla Inc 120 Stone Pine Rd	Half Moon Bay	CA	94019	**800-639-2552**	650-726-1888
Pastorelli Food Products Inc 162 N Sangamon St	Chicago	IL	60607	**800-767-2829**	312-666-2041
Pro-Fac Co-op Inc 350 Linden Oaks *NASDAQ: PFACP*	Rochester	NY	14625	**800-999-5044**	585-218-4210
Simply Orange Juice Co 2659 Orange Ave	Apopka	FL	32703	**800-871-2653**	
Smith ED & Sons Ltd 944 Hwy 8	Winona	ON	L8E5S3	**800-263-9246**	905-643-1211
Smucker JM Co 1 Strawberry Ln *NYSE: SJM*	Orrville	OH	44667	**888-550-9555**	330-682-3000
Stanislaus Food Products Co 1202 D St	Modesto	CA	95354	**800-327-7201**	209-522-7201
Stapleton-Spence Packing Co 1530 The Alameda Suite 320	San Jose	CA	95126	**800-297-8815**	408-297-8815
Sun Orchard Inc 1198 W Fairmont Dr	Tempe	AZ	85282	**800-505-8423**	480-966-1770
Talk O'Texas Brands Inc 1610 Roosevelt St	San Angelo	TX	76905	**800-749-6572**	325-655-6077
Truitt Brothers Inc 1105 Front St NE	Salem	OR	97301	**800-547-8712**	503-362-3674
Vegetable Juices Inc 7400 S Narragansett Ave	Bedford Park	IL	60638	**888-776-9752**	708-924-9500
Vitality Food Service Inc 400 N Tampa St Suite 1700	Tampa	FL	33602	**888-863-6726**	813-301-4600
Whitlock Packaging Corp 1701 S Lee St	Fort Gibson	OK	74434	**800-833-9382**	918-478-4300
Wyman Jasper & Son PO Box 100	Milbridge	ME	04658	**800-341-1758**	207-546-2311
Zeigler MH & Sons Inc 1513 N Broad St	Lansdale	PA	19446	**800-854-6123**	215-855-5161

291-21 Fruits, Vegetables, Juices - Frozen

Company	City	State	ZIP	Toll-Free	Phone
Ardmore Farms Inc 1915 N Woodland Blvd	DeLand	FL	32720	**800-365-8423**	386-734-4634
Birds Eye Foods Inc 90 Linden Oaks	Rochester	NY	14625	**800-999-5044**	585-383-1850
Brooks Food Group Inc 940 Orange St	Bedford	VA	24523	**800-873-4934**	540-586-8284
Cascadian Farm Inc 719 Metcalf St	Sedro Woolley	WA	98284	**800-624-4123**	360-855-0100
Cherry Central Co-op Inc 1771 N US Hwy 31 S PO Box 988	Traverse City	MI	49685	**800-678-1860**	231-946-1860
Coloma Frozen Foods Inc PO Box 520	Coloma	MI	49038	**800-462-7608**	269-849-0500
Dole Food Co Inc 1 Dole Dr	Westlake Village	CA	91362	**800-232-8888**	818-879-6600
Giorgio Foods Inc 1161 Park Rd	Reading	PA	19605	**800-220-2139**	610-926-2139
Graceland Fruit Inc 1123 Main St	Frankfort	MI	49635	**800-352-7181**	231-352-7181
Heinz Frozen Food Co 357 6th Ave *Cust Svc	Pittsburgh	PA	15222	**800-892-2401***	412-237-3600
HJ Heinz Co PO Box 57 *NYSE: HNZ*	Pittsburgh	PA	15230	**800-255-5750**	412-456-5700
JR Simplot Co 999 Main St	Boise	ID	83702	**800-635-5008**	208-336-2110
JR Simplot Co Food Group 6360 S Federal Way	Boise	ID	83716	**800-635-0408**	208-384-8000
Leelanau Fruit Co 2900 SW Bayshore Dr	Suttons Bay	MI	49682	**800-431-0718**	231-271-3514
Lewis Dreyfus Citrus Inc PO Box 770399	Winter Garden	FL	34777	**800-549-4272**	407-656-1000
McCain Foods USA Inc 2905 Butterfield Rd	Oak Brook	IL	60523	**800-938-7799**	630-472-0420
McCain Snack Foods 555 N Hickory Farm Ln PO Box 2518	Appleton	WI	54913	**800-767-7377**	920-997-2828
Minute Maid Co 2000 St James Pl	Houston	TX	77056	**800-888-6488**	713-888-5000
Mrs Clark's Foods LLC 740 SE Dalby Dr	Ankeny	IA	50021	**866-971-6500**	515-964-8100
NORPAC Foods Inc 930 W Washington St *Sales	Stayton	OR	97383	**800-733-9311***	503-769-2101
Ocean Spray Cranberries Inc 1 Ocean Spray Dr	Lakeville-Middleboro	MA	02349	**800-662-3263**	508-946-1000
Patterson Frozen Foods Inc PO Box 114	Patterson	CA	95363	**800-821-1007**	209-892-2611
Pro-Fac Co-op Inc 350 Linden Oaks *NASDAQ: PFACP*	Rochester	NY	14625	**800-999-5044**	585-218-4210
Simplot JR Co 999 Main St	Boise	ID	83702	**800-635-5008**	208-336-2110
Simplot JR Co Food Group 6360 S Federal Way	Boise	ID	83716	**800-635-0408**	208-384-8000
Sun Orchard of Florida Inc PO Box 2008	Haines City	FL	33844	**877-875-8423**	863-422-5062
United Foods Inc 10 Pictsweet Dr	Bells	TN	38006	**800-367-7412**	731-422-7600
Wawona Frozen Foods Inc 100 W Alluvial Ave	Clovis	CA	93611	**800-669-2966**	559-299-2901

291-22 Gelatin

Company	City	State	ZIP	Toll-Free	Phone
ConAgra Hunt-Wesson Foodservice Co 3353 Michelson Dr	Irvine	CA	92612	**800-633-0112**	949-437-1000
Kind & Knox Gelatine Inc PO Box 927	Sioux City	IA	51102	**888-443-6183**	712-943-5516
Kraft Food Ingredients Corp 8000 Horizon Ctr Blvd	Memphis	TN	38133	**800-458-8324**	901-381-6500
Langlois Co 10810 San Sevaine Way	Mira Loma	CA	91752	**800-962-5993**	951-360-3900
Nitta Gelatin Inc 201 W Passaic St	Rochelle Park	NJ	07662	**800-278-7680**	201-368-0071
Precision Foods Inc 11457 Olde Cabin Rd	Saint Louis	MO	63141	**800-442-5242**	314-567-7400
Subco Foods Inc 4350 S Taylor Dr	Sheboygan	WI	53081	**800-473-0757**	920-457-7761
Vyse Gelatin Co 5010 N Rose St	Schiller Park	IL	60176	**800-533-2152**	847-678-4780

291-23 Grain Mill Products

Company	City	State	ZIP	Toll-Free	Phone
ACH Food Cos Inc 7171 Goodlet Farms Pkwy	Cordova	TN	38016	**800-691-1106**	901-381-3000
ADM Milling Co 8000 W 110th St Suite 300	Overland Park	KS	66210	**800-637-5843**	913-491-9400
AG Processing Inc PO Box 2047	Omaha	NE	68103	**800-247-1345**	402-496-7809
Arrowhead Mills Inc PO Box 2059	Hereford	TX	79045	**800-749-0730**	806-364-0730
Azteca Milling Co 501 W Chapin St	Edinburg	TX	78539	**800-262-7322**	956-383-4911
Bartlett & Co 4800 Main St Suite 600	Kansas City	MO	64112	**800-888-6300**	816-753-6300
Bay State Milling Co 100 Congress St	Quincy	MA	02169	**800-553-5687**	617-328-4400
Blendex Co Inc 11208 Electron Dr	Louisville	KY	40299	**800-253-6339**	502-267-1003
Cargill Foods 15407 McGinty Rd	Wayzata	MN	55391	**800-227-4455**	952-742-7575
Cargill Inc North America 15407 McGinty Rd	Wayzata	MN	55391	**800-227-4455**	952-742-7575
Cereal Food Processors Inc 2001 Shawnee Mission Pkwy	Mission Woods	KS	66205	**800-743-5687**	913-890-6300
Cereal Foods Inc 416 N Main St	McPherson	KS	67460	**800-835-2067**	620-241-2410
Farmers Rice Co-op PO Box 15223	Sacramento	CA	95851	**800-326-2799**	916-923-5100
Foxtail Foods 6075 Poplar Ave Suite 800 *Cust Svc	Memphis	TN	38119	**800-487-2253***	901-766-6400
General Mills Inc 1 General Mills Blvd *NYSE: GIS*	Minneapolis	MN	55426	**800-328-1144**	763-764-7600
Henry & Henry Inc 3765 Walden Ave	Lancaster	NY	14086	**800-828-7130**	716-685-4000
House-Autry Mills Inc 7000 US Hwy 301 S	Four Oaks	NC	27524	**800-849-0802**	919-963-6200
Illinois Cereal Mills Inc 616 S Jefferson St *Sales	Paris	IL	61944	**800-331-1716***	217-465-5331
Indian Harvest Specialtifoods Inc 1012 Paul Bunyan Dr Se *Orders	Bemidji	MN	56601	**800-346-7032***	218-751-8500
JR Short Milling Co 150 S Wacker Dr	Chicago	IL	60606	**800-544-8734**	312-559-5450
Knappen Milling Co 110 S Water St	Augusta	MI	49012	**800-562-7736**	269-731-4141
Mallet & Co Inc 51 Arch St Ext	Carnegie	PA	15106	**800-245-2757**	412-276-9000
Masterfoods USA 800 High St	Hackettstown	NJ	07840	**800-222-0293**	908-852-1000
Mennel Milling Co 128 W Crocker St	Fostoria	OH	44830	**800-688-8151**	419-435-8151
MGP Ingredients Inc 1300 Main St *NASDAQ: MGPI*	Atchison	KS	66002	**800-255-0302**	913-367-1480
Midstate Mills Inc 324 E 'A' St	Newton	NC	28658	**800-222-1032**	828-464-1611
Minnesota Corn Processors Inc 400 W Erie Rd	Marshall	MN	56258	**800-328-4150**	507-537-2676
Monahan Thomas Co Inc 202 N Oak St	Arcola	IL	61910	**800-637-7739**	217-268-4955
Morrison Milling Co 319 E Prairie St	Denton	TX	76201	**800-866-5487**	940-387-6111
North Dakota Mill PO Box 13078	Grand Forks	ND	58208	**800-538-7721**	701-795-7000
Pacific Grain Products International Inc PO Box 2060 *Cust Svc	Woodland	CA	95776	**800-747-0161***	530-662-5056
Pacific International Rice Mills Inc PO Box 652	Woodland	CA	95776	**800-747-4764**	530-666-1691
Penford Products Co PO Box 428	Cedar Rapids	IA	52406	**800-553-7294**	319-398-3700
Riviana Foods Inc PO Box 2636	Houston	TX	77252	**800-626-9522**	713-529-3251
Rocky Mountain Milling LLC 400 Platte St	Platteville	CO	80651	**888-785-7636**	970-785-2794
Roquette America Inc 1417 Exchange St	Keokuk	IA	52632	**800-553-7030**	319-524-5757
Short JR Milling Co 150 S Wacker Dr	Chicago	IL	60606	**800-544-8734**	312-559-5450
Siemer Milling Co 111 W Main St	Teutopolis	IL	62467	**800-826-1065**	217-857-3131
Stafford County Flour Mills Co PO Box 7	Hudson	KS	67545	**800-530-5640**	620-458-4121
Thomas Monahan Co Inc 202 N Oak St	Arcola	IL	61910	**800-637-7739**	217-268-4955
Uhlmann Co 1009 Central St	Kansas City	MO	64105	**800-383-8201**	816-221-8200
White Lily Foods Co 218 E Depot Ave	Knoxville	TN	37917	**800-264-5459**	865-546-5511
Wilkins-Rogers Inc 27 Frederick Rd *Cust Svc	Ellicott City	MD	21043	**800-735-3585***	410-465-5800

291-24 Honey

Company	City	State	ZIP	Toll-Free	Phone
Glorybee Foods Inc PO Box 2744	Eugene	OR	97402	**800-456-7923**	541-689-0913
Honey Acres 1557 Hwy 67 N	Ashippun	WI	53003	**800-558-7745**	920-474-4411
Honeytree Inc PO Box 310	Onsted	MI	49265	**800-968-1889**	517-467-2482
Sioux Honey Assn Co-op PO Box 388	Sioux City	IA	51102	**888-270-6956**	712-258-0638
Stoller's W Honey Inc PO Box 97	Latty	OH	45855	**888-233-6446**	419-399-5786

291-25 Ice Cream & Frozen Desserts

Company	City	State	ZIP	Toll-Free	Phone
Anderson Erickson Dairy Co 2420 E University Ave	Des Moines	IA	50317	**800-234-7257**	515-265-2521

Company	City	State	ZIP	Toll-Free	Phone
Baldwin Richardson Foods Co Inc 20201 S La Grange Rd Suite 200 *Cust Svc	Frankfort	IL	60423	**800-762-6458***	815-464-9994
Brigham's Inc 30 Mill St	Arlington	MA	02476	**800-274-4426**	781-648-9000
Broughton Foods Co 1701 Green St	Marietta	OH	45750	**800-283-2479**	740-373-4121
Cedar Crest Specialties Inc 7269 Hwy 60	Cedarburg	WI	53012	**800-877-8341**	262-377-7252
Central Dairy & Ice Cream Co 610 Madison St	Jefferson City	MO	65101	**800-422-2148**	573-635-6148
Coleman Dairy Inc 6901 I-30	Little Rock	AR	72209	**800-365-1551**	501-565-1551
Country Fresh Inc 355 Mart St SW	Grand Rapids	MI	49548	**800-748-0480**	616-243-0173
Creamland Dairies Inc 010 Indian School Rd NW	Albuquerque	NM	87102	**800-334-3865**	505-247-0721
Crossroad Farms Dairy 400 S Shortridge Rd	Indianapolis	IN	46219	**800-334-7502**	317-229-7600
Dreyer's Grand Ice Cream Holdings Inc 5929 College Ave *NASDAQ: DRYR*	Oakland	CA	94618	**800-888-3442**	510-652-8187
Edy's Grand Ice Cream 5929 College Ave	Oakland	CA	94618	**800-888-3442**	510-652-8187
Elgin Dairy Foods Inc 3707 W Harrison St	Chicago	IL	60624	**800-786-9900**	773-722-7100
Flav-O-Rich 1105 N William St	Goldsboro	NC	27530	**877-321-1158**	919-734-0728
Galliker Dairy Co Inc 143 Donald Ln	Johnstown	PA	15904	**800-477-6455**	814-266-8702
Gandy's Dairies Inc PO Box 992	San Angelo	TX	76902	**800-200-3326**	325-655-6965
Hershey Creamery Co 301 S Cameron St	Harrisburg	PA	17101	**888-240-1905**	717-238-8134
Hiland Dairy 302 S Porter St	Norman	OK	73071	**800-366-6455**	405-321-3191
Hood HP Inc 90 Everett Ave *Cust Svc	Chelsea	MA	02150	**800-662-4468***	617-887-3000
HP Hood Inc 90 Everett Ave *Cust Svc	Chelsea	MA	02150	**800-662-4468***	617-887-3000
Ice Cream Specialties 8419 Hanley Industrial Dr	Saint Louis	MO	63144	**800-662-7550**	314-962-2550
Integrated Brands 4175 Veterans Memorial Hwy	Ronkonkoma	NY	11779	**800-423-2763**	631-737-9700
J & J Snack Foods Corp 6000 Central Hwy *NASDAQ: JJSF*	Pennsauken	NJ	08109	**800-486-9533**	856-665-9533
Kemps Food Inc PO Box 7007	Lancaster	PA	17604	**800-233-2007**	717-394-5601
Kemps LLC 2929 University Ave SE	Minneapolis	MN	55414	**800-322-9566**	612-331-3775
Land O'Sun Dairies LLC 2900 Bristol Hwy	Johnson City	TN	37601	**800-683-0765**	423-283-5700
Louis Trauth Dairy Inc 16 E 11th St	Newport	KY	41071	**800-544-6455**	859-431-7553
Melody Farms/Stroh's Ice Cream Co 1000 Maple St	Detroit	MI	48207	**800-234-8871**	313-568-5100
Mid States Dairy Co 6040 N Lindbergh Blvd	Saint Louis	MO	63042	**800-473-1150**	314-731-1150
Milkco Inc 220 Deaverview Rd	Asheville	NC	28806	**800-842-8021**	828-254-9560
Perry's Ice Cream Co Inc 1 Ice Cream Plaza	Akron	NY	14001	**800-873-7797**	716-542-5492
Richman Ice Cream Co 91 18th Ave	Paterson	NJ	07513	**800-883-3332**	973-684-8935
Schwan's Sales Enterprises Inc 115 W College Dr	Marshall	MN	56258	**800-533-5290**	507-532-3274
Smith Dairy Wayne Div 1590 NW 11th St	Richmond	IN	47375	**800-875-9296**	765-935-7521
Stonyfield Farm Inc 10 Burton Dr	Londonderry	NH	03053	**800-776-2697**	603-437-4040
Sugar Creek Foods Inc 301 N El Paso St	Russellville	AR	72810	**800-445-2715**	479-968-1005
Trauth Louis Dairy Inc 16 E 11th St	Newport	KY	41071	**800-544-6455**	859-431-7553
Turkey Hill Dairy Inc 2601 River Rd	Conestoga	PA	17516	**800-688-7539**	717-872-5461
United Dairy Farmers 3955 Montgomery Rd	Cincinnati	OH	45212	**800-654-2809**	513-396-8700
Upstate Farms Co-op 25 Anderson Rd	Buffalo	NY	14225	**800-724-6455**	716-892-3156
Velda Farms LLC 402 S Kentucky Ave Suite 500 *Cust Svc	Lakeland	FL	33801	**800-795-4649***	863-686-4441
Wayne Div Smith Dairy 1590 NW 11th St	Richmond	IN	47375	**800-875-9296**	765-935-7521
Wells' Dairy Inc 1 Blue Bunny Dr	Le Mars	IA	51031	**800-942-3800**	712-546-4000
WestFarm Foods 635 Elliott Ave W	Seattle	WA	98119	**800-333-6455**	206-284-7220
Yarnell Ice Cream Co 205 S Spring St	Searcy	AR	72143	**800-666-2414**	501-268-2414

291-26 Meat Products - Prepared

Company	City	State	ZIP	Toll-Free	Phone
Alderfer Bologna Co Inc PO Box 2 *Sales	Harleysville	PA	19438	**800-341-1121***	215-256-8818
Alfery Sausage Co Inc RD 6 Box 2060	Mount Pleasant	PA	15666	**800-648-2547**	724-547-5270
American Foods Group Inc PO Box 8547	Green Bay	WI	54308	**800-345-0293**	920-437-6330
Ball Park Brands 10151 Carver Rd *Cust Svc	Cincinnati	OH	45242	**888-317-5867***	513-936-2000
Ballard's Farm Sausage Inc PO Box 699	Wayne	WV	25570	**800-346-7675**	304-272-5147
Berks Packing Co Inc PO Box 5919	Reading	PA	19610	**800-882-3757**	610-376-7291
Best Kosher Foods Corp PO Box 25111	Cincinnati	OH	45225	**888-800-0072**	513-936-2000
Best Provision Co Inc 144 Avon Ave	Newark	NJ	07108	**800-631-4466**	973-242-5000
Bison Products Co Inc PO Box 87	Buffalo	NY	14240	**800-248-2705**	716-826-2700
Blue Grass Quality Meats PO Box 17658	Crescent Springs	KY	41017	**888-236-4455**	859-331-7100
Boyle's Famous Corned Beef Co 1638 St Louis Ave	Kansas City	MO	64101	**800-821-3626**	816-221-6283
Bridgford Foods Corp 1308 N Patt St *NASDAQ: BRID*	Anaheim	CA	92801	**800-854-3255**	714-526-5533
Bryan Foods Inc PO Box 1177 *Orders	West Point	MS	39773	**800-647-6342***	662-494-3741
Buddig Carl & Co 950 W 175th St	Homewood	IL	60430	**800-621-0868**	708-798-0900
Burger's Ozark Country Cured Hams Inc 32819 Hwy 87 S	California	MO	65018	**800-203-4424**	573-796-3134
Busch Fred Foods Corp 6278 N Cicero	Chicago	IL	60646	**800-323-3981**	773-545-2650
Carando Inc 20 Carando Dr	Springfield	MA	01104	**800-628-9524**	413-781-5620
Cargill Foods 15407 McGinty Rd	Wayzata	MN	55391	**800-227-4455**	952-742-7575
Cargill Inc North America 15407 McGinty Rd	Wayzata	MN	55391	**800-227-4455**	952-742-7575
Carl Buddig & Co 950 W 175th St	Homewood	IL	60430	**800-621-0868**	708-798-0900
Carlton Food Products Inc PO Box 311385	New Braunfels	TX	78131	**800-628-9849**	830-625-7583
Carriage House Foods DBA Grand Choice Foods 1131 Dayton Ave	Ames	IA	50010	**800-250-3860**	515-232-2273
Cattaneo Brothers Inc 769 Caudill St	San Luis Obispo	CA	93401	**800-243-8537**	805-543-7188
Cher-Make Sausage Co 2915 Calumet Ave	Manitowoc	WI	54220	**800-242-7679**	920-683-5980
Chicago Meat Authority Inc 1120 W 47th Pl	Chicago	IL	60609	**800-383-3811**	773-254-3811
Chicopee Provision Co Inc 19 Sitarz St	Chicopee	MA	01014	**800-924-6328**	413-594-4765
Citterio USA Corp 5115 35th St	Long Island City	NY	11101	**800-435-8888**	718-706-7390
Clifty Farm Country Ham Co Inc PO Box 1146	Paris	TN	38242	**800-486-4267**	731-642-9740
Cloverdale Foods Co Inc 3015 34th St NW PO Box 667	Mandan	ND	58554	**800-669-9511**	701-663-9511
Coleman Natural Products Inc 5140 Race Ct Unit 4	Denver	CO	80216	**800-442-8666**	303-297-9393
ConAgra Foods International 2 Jericho Plaza Suite 304	Jericho	NY	11753	**800-275-5454**	516-949-7500
Counts Sausage Co Inc PO Box 390	Prosperity	SC	29127	**800-868-0041**	803-364-2392
Cudahy Patrick Inc 1 Sweet Apple-Wood Ln	Cudahy	WI	53110	**800-486-6900**	414-744-2000
Daniel Weaver Co PO Box 525	Lebanon	PA	17042	**800-932-8377**	717-274-6100
Dewied International Inc 5010 E IH-10	San Antonio	TX	78219	**800-992-5600**	210-661-6161
Dial Corp 15501 N Dial Blvd *Cust Svc	Scottsdale	AZ	85260	**800-258-3425***	480-754-3425
Dietz & Watson Inc 5701 Tacony St	Philadelphia	PA	19135	**800-333-1974**	215-831-9000
Emmpak Foods Inc 200 S Emmber Ln	Milwaukee	WI	53233	**800-558-4242**	414-645-6500
Essem Packing Co 14 Loon Hill Rd	Dracut	MA	01826	**800-272-0030**	978-452-2195
EW Knauss & Sons Inc 625 E Broad St	Quakertown	PA	18951	**800-648-4220**	215-536-4220
Family Brands International LLC PO Box 429	Lenoir City	TN	37771	**800-356-4455**	865-986-8005
Farm Boy Meats PO Box 996	Evansville	IN	47706	**800-852-3976**	812-425-5231
Farmland Foods Inc 7501 NW Tiffany Springs Pkey	Kansas City	MO	64153	**888-327-6526**	816-801-4300
Flint Sausage Works Inc PO Box 86	Flint	MI	48501	**800-654-7280**	810-239-3179
Fred Busch Foods Corp 6278 N Cicero	Chicago	IL	60646	**800-323-3981**	773-545-2650
Fred Usinger Inc 1030 N Old World 3rd St	Milwaukee	WI	53203	**800-558-9997**	414-276-9100
Gallo Salami 2411 Baumann Ave	San Lorenzo	CA	94580	**800-321-1097**	510-276-1300
Gold Star Sausage Co Inc PO Box 4245	Denver	CO	80204	**800-258-7229**	303-295-6400
Grand Choice Foods 1131 Dayton Ave	Ames	IA	50010	**800-250-3860**	515-232-2273
Green Bay Dressed Beef Inc PO Box 8547	Green Bay	WI	54308	**800-345-0293**	920-437-4311
Green Tree Packing Co 65 Central Ave	Passaic	NJ	07055	**800-221-5754**	973-473-1305
Gwaltney of Smithfield Ltd 601 N Church St	Smithfield	VA	23430	**800-888-7521**	757-357-3131
H & H Meat Products Inc DBA H & H Foods PO Box 358	Mercedes	TX	78570	**800-365-4632**	956-565-6363
Hansel 'n Gretel Brand Inc 79-36 Cooper Ave	Glendale	NY	11385	**800-635-3354**	718-326-0041
Hillshire Farm & Kahn's 3241 Spring Grove Ave	Cincinnati	OH	45225	**800-543-4465**	513-541-4000
Hormel Foods Corp 1 Hormel Pl *NYSE: HRL*	Austin	MN	55912	**800-523-4635**	507-437-5611
Hormel Foods International Corp 1 Hormel Pl	Austin	MN	55912	**800-523-4635**	507-437-5478
JC Potter Sausage Co 1914 Hwy 70 E	Durant	OK	74702	**800-321-8549**	580-924-2414
Jimmy Dean Foods Inc PO Box 2511	Cincinnati	OH	45225	**800-925-3326**	
Joseph McSweeney & Sons Inc PO Box 26409	Richmond	VA	23260	**800-552-6927**	804-359-6024
Karl Ehmer Inc 63-35 Fresh Pond Rd	Ridgewood	NY	11385	**800-487-5275**	718-456-8100
Kayem Foods Inc 75 Arlington St	Chelsea	MA	02150	**800-426-6100**	617-889-1600
Kessler's Inc 1201 Hummel Ave	Lemoyne	PA	17043	**800-382-1328**	717-763-7162
Klement Sausage Co Inc 207 E Lincoln Ave	Milwaukee	WI	53207	**800-553-6368**	414-744-2330
Knauss EW & Sons Inc 625 E Broad St	Quakertown	PA	18951	**800-648-4220**	215-536-4220
Kowalski Sausage Co Inc 2270 Holbrook Ave	Hamtramck	MI	48212	**800-482-2400**	313-873-8200
Kunzler & Co Inc 652 Manor St	Lancaster	PA	17604	**800-233-0203**	717-299-6301
Land O'Frost Inc 16850 Chicago Ave	Lansing	IL	60438	**800-323-3308**	708-474-7100
Levonian Brothers Inc PO Box 629 *Cust Svc	Troy	NY	12180	**800-538-6642***	518-274-3610
Maid-Rite Steak Co Inc 105 Keystone Industrial Pk	Dunmore	PA	18512	**800-233-4259**	570-343-4748
Marathon Enterprises Inc 66 E Union Ave	East Rutherford	NJ	07073	**800-722-7388**	201-935-3330
McSweeney Joseph & Sons Inc PO Box 26409	Richmond	VA	23260	**800-552-6927**	804-359-6024
Metzger Packing Co Inc 520 S 2nd St	Paducah	KY	42002	**800-347-9630**	270-442-3503
Miller Packing Co PO Box 1390	Lodi	CA	95241	**800-624-2328**	209-339-2310
Mongolia Casing Corp 4706 Grand Ave	Maspeth	NY	11378	**800-221-4887**	718-628-4500
Murry's Inc 8300 Pennsylvania Ave	Upper Marlboro	MD	20772	**800-638-5806**	301-420-6400
Neto Sausage Co Inc PO Box 578	Santa Clara	CA	95052	**888-482-6386**	408-296-0818
Oberto Sausage Co 7060 S 238th St	Kent	WA	98032	**877-234-7902**	253-437-6100
Odom's Tennessee Pride Sausage Inc 1201 Neelys Bend Rd	Madison	TN	37115	**800-327-6269**	615-868-1360
Old Wisconsin Sausage Co 2107 S 17th St	Sheboygan	WI	53081	**800-558-7840**	920-458-4304
Owens Country Sausage Inc 1403 E Lookout Dr	Richardson	TX	75082	**800-966-9367**	972-235-7181
Palmyra Bologna Co Inc DBA Seltzer's Smokehouse Meats PO Box 111	Palmyra	PA	17078	**800-282-6336**	717-838-6336
Peer Food Products Co 4631 S McDowell Ave	Chicago	IL	60609	**800-365-5644**	773-927-1440
Plumrose USA Inc 7 Lexington Ave	East Brunswick	NJ	08816	**800-526-4909**	732-257-6600
Potter JC Sausage Co 1914 Hwy 70 E	Durant	OK	74702	**800-321-8549**	580-924-2414
Premio Foods Inc 50 Utter Ave	Hawthorne	NJ	07506	**800-864-7622**	973-427-1106
Reser's Fine Foods Inc PO Box 8	Beaverton	OR	97075	**800-333-6431**	503-643-6431
Roman Corp 1810 Richard Ave	Santa Clara	CA	95050	**800-497-7462**	408-988-1222
Russer Foods Inc 665 Perry St	Buffalo	NY	14210	**800-828-1885**	716-826-6400
Saags Products Inc 1799 Factor Ave	San Leandro	CA	94577	**800-352-7224**	510-352-8000
Sabrett Food Products Corp 66 E Union Ave	East Rutherford	NJ	07073	**800-722-7388**	201-935-3330
Sara Lee Food & Beverage 10151 Carver Rd	Cincinnati	OH	45242	**800-351-7111**	513-936-2000
Schaller & Weber Inc 22-35 46th St *Orders	Astoria	NY	11105	**800-847-4115***	718-721-5480
Seltzer's Smokehouse Meats PO Box 111	Palmyra	PA	17078	**800-282-6336**	717-838-6336
Silver Star Meats Inc PO Box 393	McKees Rocks	PA	15136	**800-548-1321**	412-771-5539
Smithfield Foods Inc 200 Commerce St *NYSE: SFD*	Smithfield	VA	23430	**800-276-6158**	757-365-3000
Smithfield Ham & Products Co Inc 401 N Church St	Smithfield	VA	23430	**800-628-2242**	757-357-2121
Sparrer Sausage Co Inc 4320 W Ogden Ave	Chicago	IL	60623	**800-666-3287**	773-762-3334
Standard Casing Co Inc 60 Amity St	Jersey City	NJ	07304	**800-847-4141**	201-434-6300
Stock Yards Packing Co Inc PO Box 12450	Chicago	IL	60612	**800-621-3687**	312-733-6050
Storer Meats Co Inc 3007 Clinton Ave	Cleveland	OH	44113	**800-355-7537**	216-621-7538
Suzanna's Kitchen Inc 4025 Buford Hwy	Duluth	GA	30096	**800-241-2455**	770-476-9900
Swift & Co 1770 Promontory Cir	Greeley	CO	80634	**800-555-2588**	970-506-8000
Taylor Provision Co PO Box 5108	Trenton	NJ	08638	**800-772-7126**	609-392-1113
Texas Meat Purveyor 4241 Director Dr	San Antonio	TX	78219	**800-552-3234**	210-337-1011
Tyson Prepared Foods Inc 5701 McNutt Rd	Santa Teresa	NM	88008	**800-351-8184**	505-589-0100
Usinger Fred Inc 1030 N Old World 3rd St	Milwaukee	WI	53203	**800-558-9997**	414-276-9100
Vienna Sausage Mfg Co 2501 N Damen Ave	Chicago	IL	60647	**800-621-8183**	773-278-7800
Vollwerth & Co PO Box 239	Hancock	MI	49930	**800-562-7620**	906-482-1550
Weaver Daniel Co PO Box 525	Lebanon	PA	17042	**800-932-8377**	717-274-6100
Wimmer's Meat Products Inc PO Box 286 *Sales	West Point	NE	68788	**800-358-0761***	402-372-2437
Wis-Pak Foods Inc 200 S Ember Ln	Milwaukee	WI	53233	**800-323-0639**	414-645-6500
Wolfson Casing Corp 700 S Fulton Ave	Mount Vernon	NY	10550	**800-221-8042**	914-668-9000
Wright Brand Foods Inc PO Box 1779	Vernon	TX	76385	**800-772-0844**	940-553-1811
Zartic Inc 438 Lavender Dr *Cust Svc	Rome	GA	30165	**800-992-8172***	706-234-3000

291-27 Milk & Cream Products

Company	City	State	ZIP	Toll-Free	Phone
Agri-Mark Inc 100 Milk St	Methuen	MA	01844	**800-225-0532**	978-689-4442
Agropur Co-op Agro-alimentaire 510 rue Principale	Granby	QC	J2G7G2	**800-363-6190**	450-375-1991
Alta Dena Dairy 17637 E Valley Blvd *Orders	City of Industry	CA	91744	**800-533-2479***	626-964-6401

Milk & Cream Products (Cont'd)

Company	City	State	ZIP	Toll-Free	Phone
AMPI 315 N Broadway	New Ulm	MN	56073	**800-533-3580**	507-354-8295
Anderson Erickson Dairy Co					
2420 E University Ave	Des Moines	IA	50317	**800-234-7257**	515-265-2521
Barber Pure Milk Co 19 Green Briar Rd	Anniston	AL	36201	**800-264-4157**	256-240-9141
Brookwood Farms Dairy					
1801 Hempstead Rd PO Box 7007	Lancaster	PA	17604	**800-233-2007**	717-233-6423
Broughton Foods Co 1701 Green St	Marietta	OH	45750	**800-283-2479**	740-373-4121
California Dairies Inc 11709 E Artesia Blvd	Artesia	CA	90701	**800-821-5588**	562-865-1291
CF Burger Creamery Co 8101 Greenfield Rd	Detroit	MI	48228	**800-229-2322**	313-584-4040
Clinton Milk Co Inc 353 Morris Ave	Newark	NJ	07108	**800-223-6455**	973-642-3000
Cloverland Green Spring Dairy Inc					
2701 Loch Raven Rd	Baltimore	MD	21218	**800-876-6455***	410-235-4477
*Orders					
Coleman Dairy Inc 6901 I-30	Little Rock	AR	72209	**800-365-1551**	501-565-1551
Country Fresh Inc 355 Mart St SW	Grand Rapids	MI	49548	**800-748-0480**	616-243-0173
Crossroad Farms Dairy					
400 S Shortridge Rd	Indianapolis	IN	46219	**800-334-7502**	317-229-7600
Dairymen's Milk Co 3068 W 106th St	Cleveland	OH	44111	**800-944-2301**	216-671-2300
Dannon Co 120 White Plains Rd	Tarrytown	NY	10591	**800-321-2174**	914-366-9700
Fairmont Products Inc 15 Kishacoquillas St	Belleville	PA	17004	**800-525-9338**	717-935-2121
Farmers Co-op Dairy Inc 104 Rotary Dr	West Hazleton	PA	18202	**800-548-8787***	570-453-0203
*Cust Svc					
Farmland Dairies LLC 520 Main Ave	Wallington	NJ	07057	**800-275-4645**	973-777-2500
Flav-O-Rich 1105 N William St	Goldsboro	NC	27530	**877-321-1158**	919-734-0728
Galliker Dairy Co Inc 143 Donald Ln	Johnstown	PA	15904	**800-477-6455**	814-266-8702
Garelick Farms Inc					
124 Grove St Franklin Oaks Office Pk					
Suite 100	Franklin	MA	02038	**800-343-4982**	508-528-9000
Gillette Dairy of the Black Hills Inc					
PO Box 2553	Rapid City	SD	57709	**800-933-3247**	605-348-1500
Guida-Seibert Dairy Co 433 Park St	New Britain	CT	06051	**800-832-8929**	860-224-2404
Gustafson's Dairy Inc					
4169 County Rd 15-A	Green Cove Springs	FL	32043	**800-342-1092**	904-284-3750
H Meyer Dairy Co 415 John St	Cincinnati	OH	45215	**800-347-6455**	513-948-8811
Harrisburg Dairies Inc 2001 Herr St	Harrisburg	PA	17105	**800-692-7429**	717-233-8701
Heritage Foods LLC 4002 Westminster Ave	Santa Ana	CA	92703	**800-321-5960***	714-775-5000
*Orders					
Hiland Dairy Co PO Box 2270	Springfield	MO	65801	**800-641-4022**	417-862-9311
Hiland Dairy Foods Co 700 E Central St	Wichita	KS	67202	**800-336-0765**	316-267-4221
Hood HP Inc 90 Everett Ave	Chelsea	MA	02150	**800-662-4468***	617-887-3000
*Cust Svc					
HP Hood Inc 90 Everett Ave	Chelsea	MA	02150	**800-662-4468***	617-887-3000
*Cust Svc					
Johanna Foods Inc Johanna Farm Rd	Flemington	NJ	08822	**800-727-6700**	908-788-2200
Kemps LLC 2929 University Ave SE	Minneapolis	MN	55414	**800-322-9566**	612-331-3775
Lacto Milk Products Corp					
Johanna Farm Rd	Flemington	NJ	08822	**800-727-6700**	908-788-2200
Land O'Lakes Inc 4001 Lexington Ave N	Arden Hills	MN	55126	**800-328-9680**	651-481-2222
Lehigh Valley Dairies Inc 880 Allentown Rd	Lansdale	PA	19446	**800-937-3233**	215-855-8205
Maple Hill Farms Inc					
12 Burr Rd PO Box 767	Bloomfield	CT	06002	**800-243-0067**	860-242-9689
Marcus Dairy Inc 3 Sugar Hollow Rd	Danbury	CT	06810	**800-243-2511**	203-748-5611
Mayfield Dairy Farms Inc PO Box 310	Athens	TN	37371	**800-362-9546**	423-745-2151
McArthur Dairy Inc					
500 Sawgrass Corporate Pkwy	Sunrise	FL	33325	**877-803-6565**	954-846-1234
Meyer H Dairy Co 415 John St	Cincinnati	OH	45215	**800-347-6455**	513-948-8811
Mid States Dairy Co					
6040 N Lindbergh Blvd	Saint Louis	MO	63042	**800-473-1150**	314-731-1150
Milkco Inc 220 Deaverview Rd	Asheville	NC	28806	**800-842-8021**	828-254-9560
Oakhurst Dairy 364 Forest Ave	Portland	ME	04101	**800-482-0718**	207-772-7468
Oberlin Farms Dairy Inc DBA Dairymen's Milk					
Co 3068 W 106th St	Cleveland	OH	44111	**800-944-2301**	216-671-2300
Penn Maid Foods Inc 10975 Dutton Rd	Philadelphia	PA	19154	**800-220-7063**	215-824-2800
Prairie Farms Dairy Inc 1100 N Broadway St	Carlinville	IL	62626	**800-654-2547**	217-854-2547
Purity Dairies Inc 360 Murfreesboro Rd	Nashville	TN	37210	**800-947-6455**	615-244-1900
Readington Farms Inc 12 Mill Rd	Whitehouse	NJ	08888	**800-426-1707**	908-534-2121
Roberts Dairy					
3805 S Emanuel Cleaver II Blvd	Kansas City	MO	64128	**800-279-1692**	816-921-7370
Schneider Valley Farms Dairy					
1860 E 3rd St	Williamsport	PA	17701	**800-332-8563**	570-326-2021
Schroeder Milk Co Inc 2080 Rice St	Maplewood	MN	55113	**800-354-6775**	651-487-1471
Shamrock Foods Co Inc 2540 N 29th Ave	Phoenix	AZ	85009	**800-388-3247**	602-233-6400
Shenandoah's Pride Dairy Inc					
168 Dinkel Ave PO Box 120	Mount Crawford	VA	22841	**888-840-6001**	540-442-6000
Smith Dairy 1381 Dairy Ln	Orrville	OH	44667	**800-776-7076**	330-683-8710
Smith Dairy Wayne Div 1590 NW 11th St	Richmond	IN	47375	**800-875-9296**	765-935-7521
Southeast Milk Inc 1950 SE Hwy 484	Belleview	FL	34420	**800-598-7866**	352-245-2437
Southern Belle Dairy Co Inc PO Box 1020	Somerset	KY	42502	**800-468-4798**	606-679-1131
Stonyfield Farm Inc 10 Burton Dr	Londonderry	NH	03053	**800-776-2697**	603-437-4040
Superior Dairy Inc 4719 Navarre Rd SW	Canton	OH	44706	**800-683-2479**	330-477-4515
Tuscan Dairy Farms Inc 750 Union Ave	Union	NJ	07083	**800-672-1137**	908-686-1500
UC Milk Co Inc 234 N Scott St	Madisonville	KY	42431	**800-462-2354**	270-821-7221
United Dairy Farmers 3955 Montgomery Rd	Cincinnati	OH	45212	**800-654-2809**	513-396-8700
United Dairy Inc 300 N 5th St	Martins Ferry	OH	43935	**800-252-1542**	740-633-1451
Upstate Farms Co-op 25 Anderson Rd	Buffalo	NY	14225	**800-724-6455**	716-892-3156
Velda Farms LLC					
402 S Kentucky Ave Suite 500	Lakeland	FL	33801	**800-795-4649***	863-686-4441
*Cust Svc					
Verifine Dairy Products Co Inc					
1606 Erie Ave	Sheboygan	WI	53081	**800-236-6455**	920-457-7733
Wayne Div Smith Dairy 1590 NW 11th St	Richmond	IN	47375	**800-875-9296**	765-935-7521
WestFarm Foods 635 Elliott Ave W	Seattle	WA	98119	**800-333-6455**	206-284-7220
Wilcox Farms Inc 40400 Harts Lake Valley Rd	Roy	WA	98580	**800-568-6456**	360-458-7774
Yoplait USA Inc PO Box 1113	Minneapolis	MN	55440	**800-967-5248**	763-764-7600

291-28 Nuts - Edible

Company	City	State	ZIP	Toll-Free	Phone
AL Bazzini Co Inc 200 Food Center Dr	Bronx	NY	10474	**800-228-0172***	718-842-8644
*Cust Svc					
Azar Nut Co 1800 Northwestern Dr	El Paso	TX	79912	**800-351-8178**	915-877-4079
Bazzini AL Co Inc 200 Food Center Dr	Bronx	NY	10474	**800-228-0172***	718-842-8644
*Cust Svc					
Beer Nuts Inc 103 N Robinson St	Bloomington	IL	61701	**800-233-7688**	309-827-8580
Blue Diamond Growers 1802 C St	Sacramento	CA	95814	**888-285-1351**	916-442-0771
Dahlgren & Co Inc 1220 Sunflower St	Crookston	MN	56716	**800-346-6050**	218-281-2985
Fisher Nut Co 2299 Busse Rd	Elk Grove Village	IL	60007	**800-323-1288**	847-593-2300
Flavor House Products PO Box 8084	Dothan	AL	36304	**800-233-5979**	334-983-5643
Hines Nut Co Inc 990 S Saint Paul St	Dallas	TX	75201	**800-580-0580**	214-939-0253
John B Sanfilippo & Son Inc					
2299 Busse Rd	Elk Grove Village	IL	60007	**800-323-6887**	847-593-2300
NASDAQ: JBSS					
Kar Nut Products Co Inc 1525 Wanda Ave	Ferndale	MI	48220	**800-527-6887**	248-541-7870
King Nut Co 31900 Solon Rd	Solon	OH	44139	**800-498-5690**	440-248-8484
Koeze Co 2555 Burlingame Ave SW	Grand Rapids	MI	49509	**888-253-6887**	616-724-2601
Koinonia Partners Inc					
1324 Georgia Hwy 49 S	Americus	GA	31719	**800-569-4128**	229-924-0391
Mauna Loa Macadamia Nut Corp HC01 Box 3	Hilo	HI	96720	**800-832-9993***	808-982-6562
*Cust Svc					
Nutcracker Brands Inc PO Box 420	Billerica	MA	01821	**800-638-6887**	978-663-5400
Old Dominion Peanut Corp 208 W 24th St	Norfolk	VA	23517	**800-368-6887**	757-622-1633
Peanut Processors Inc PO Box 160	Dublin	NC	28332	**800-334-8383**	910-862-2136
Priester Pecan Co Inc PO Box 381	Fort Deposit	AL	36032	**800-277-3226**	334-227-4301
Sanfilippo John B & Son Inc					
2299 Busse Rd	Elk Grove Village	IL	60007	**800-323-6887**	847-593-2300
NASDAQ: JBSS					
South Georgia Pecan Co 309 S Lee St	Valdosta	GA	31601	**800-627-6630**	229-244-1321
Trophy Nut Co Inc 320 N 2nd St	Tipp City	OH	45371	**800-729-6887**	937-667-8478
Wricley Nut Products Co 480 Pattison Ave	Philadelphia	PA	19148	**800-523-1303**	215-467-1106
Young Pecan Shelling Co PO Box 5779	Florence	SC	29502	**800-829-6864***	843-664-2330
*Sales					

291-29 Oil Mills - Cottonseed, Soybean, Other Vegetable Oils

Company	City	State	ZIP	Toll-Free	Phone
Abitec Corp Inc PO Box 569	Columbus	OH	43216	**800-555-1255***	614-429-6464
*Sales					
ADM Oil Refinery 1940 E Hull Ave	Des Moines	IA	50316	**800-637-5843**	515-263-2112
AG Processing Inc PO Box 2047	Omaha	NE	68103	**800-247-1345**	402-496-7809
American Lecithin Co Inc					
115 Hurley Rd Unit 2B	Oxford	CT	06478	**800-364-4416**	203-262-7100
Cargill Foods 15407 McGinty Rd	Wayzata	MN	55391	**800-227-4455**	952-742-7575
Cargill Inc 15407 McGinty Rd	Wayzata	MN	55391	**800-227-4455**	952-742-7575
Cargill Inc North America 15407 McGinty Rd	Wayzata	MN	55391	**800-227-4455**	952-742-7575
Honeymead Products Co PO Box 3247	Mankato	MN	56002	**800-328-3445**	507-625-7911
Kraft Food Ingredients Corp					
8000 Horizon Ctr Blvd	Memphis	TN	38133	**800-458-8324**	901-381-6500
Owensboro Grain Co 719 E 2nd St	Owensboro	KY	42303	**800-874-0305**	270-926-2032
Southern Cotton Oil Co PO Box 1470	Decatur	IL	62525	**800-637-5824**	217-424-5526
Valley Co-op Oil Mill PO Box 533609	Harlingen	TX	78553	**800-775-3382**	956-425-4545

291-30 Oils - Edible (Margarine, Shortening, Table Oils, etc)

Company	City	State	ZIP	Toll-Free	Phone
ACH Food Cos Inc 7171 Goodlet Farms Pkwy	Cordova	TN	38016	**800-691-1106**	901-381-3000
Bertolli USA Inc 800 Sylvan Ave	Englewood Cliffs	NJ	07632	**800-908-9789**	
Central Soya 38 Colfax St	Pawtucket	RI	02860	**800-556-6777**	401-724-3800
ConAgra Hunt-Wesson Foodservice Co					
3353 Michelson Dr	Irvine	CA	92612	**800-633-0112**	949-437-1000
Creative Foods LLC PO Box 368	Osceola	AR	72370	**800-643-0006**	870-563-2601
Golden Foods/Golden Brands Inc					
PO Box 398	Louisville	KY	40201	**800-622-3055**	502-636-3712
Lou Ana Foods Inc 715 N Railroad Ave	Opelousas	LA	70570	**800-551-9080**	337-948-6561
Par-Way Tryson Co 107 Bolte Ln	Saint Clair	MO	63077	**800-844-4554**	636-629-4545
Purity Products Inc 1800 NW 70th Ave	Miami	FL	33126	**800-654-0235**	305-592-3600
Star Fine Foods 4652 E Date Ave	Fresno	CA	93725	**800-694-4872**	559-498-2900
Sunnyland Div Ventura Foods LLC					
3900 Vanderbilt Rd	Birmingham	AL	35217	**800-338-8682**	205-808-3514
Ventura Foods LLC 40 Point Dr	Brea	CA	92821	**800-327-3906**	714-257-3700
Ventura Foods LLC Sunnyland Div					
3900 Vanderbilt Rd	Birmingham	AL	35217	**800-338-8682**	205-808-3514

291-31 Pasta

Company	City	State	ZIP	Toll-Free	Phone
Everfresh Food Corp 501 Huron Blvd SE	Minneapolis	MN	55414	**800-428-9999**	612-331-6393
Gilster-Mary Lee Corp 1037 State St	Chester	IL	62233	**800-851-5371**	618-826-2361
Monterey Pasta Co 1528 Moffett St	Salinas	CA	93905	**800-588-7782**	831-753-6262
NASDAQ: PSTA					
New World Pasta Co 85 Shannon Rd	Harrisburg	PA	17112	**800-227-2782***	717-526-2200
*Sales					
Nissin Foods USA Co Inc					
2001 W Rosecrans Ave	Gardena	CA	90249	**800-664-3537***	310-327-8478
*Cust Svc					
OB Macaroni Co PO Box 53	Fort Worth	TX	76101	**800-553-4336***	817-335-4629
*Orders					
Original Italian Pasta Products Co Inc					
6 ConAgra Dr	Omaha	NE	68102	**800-563-9786**	402-595-6935
Pasta USA Inc PO Box 7399	Spokane	WA	99207	**800-456-2084**	509-489-7219
Reames Foods Inc PO Box 71159	Des Moines	IA	50325	**800-247-4194**	515-967-4254

291-32 Peanut Butter

Company	City	State	ZIP	Toll-Free	Phone
Baumer Foods Inc					
4301 Tulane Ave PO Box 19166	New Orleans	LA	70179	**800-222-0694***	504-482-5761
*Sales					
Carriage House Cos Inc 196 Newton St	Fredonia	NY	14063	**800-828-8915**	716-673-1000
ConAgra Hunt-Wesson Foodservice Co					
3353 Michelson Dr	Irvine	CA	92612	**800-633-0112**	949-437-1000
Edwards-Freeman Inc 441 E Hector St	Conshohocken	PA	19428	**877-448-6887**	610-828-7441
Fisher Nut Co 2299 Busse Rd	Elk Grove Village	IL	60007	**800-323-1288**	847-593-2300
HB Reese Candy Co 925 Reese Ave	Hershey	PA	17033	**800-468-1714***	717-534-4106
*Cust Svc					
Jimbo's Jumbos Inc PO Box 465	Edenton	NC	27932	**800-334-4771**	252-482-2193
JM Smucker Co 1 Strawberry Ln	Orrville	OH	44667	**888-550-9555**	330-682-3000
NYSE: SJM					
John B Sanfilippo & Son Inc					
2299 Busse Rd	Elk Grove Village	IL	60007	**800-323-6887**	847-593-2300
NASDAQ: JBSS					
Koeze Co 2555 Burlingame Ave SW	Grand Rapids	MI	49509	**888-253-6887**	616-724-2601
Producers Peanut Co Inc 337 Moore Ave	Suffolk	VA	23434	**800-847-5491**	757-539-7496
Sanfilippo John B & Son Inc					
2299 Busse Rd	Elk Grove Village	IL	60007	**800-323-6887**	847-593-2300
NASDAQ: JBSS					

	City	State	Zip	Toll-Free	Phone
Smucker JM Co 1 Strawberry Ln	Orrville	OH	44667	**888-550-9555**	330-682-3000
NYSE: SJM					
William B Reily & Co Inc					
640 Magazine St	New Orleans	LA	70130	**800-535-1961**	504-524-6131

291-33 Salads - Prepared

	City	State	Zip	Toll-Free	Phone
A Camacho Inc 2502 Walden Woods Dr	Plant City	FL	33566	**800-881-4534**	813-305-4534
Chef Solutions Inc 1000 Universal Dr	North Haven	CT	06473	**800-877-1157**	203-234-0115
Dole Fresh Vegetables Co PO Box 1759	Salinas	CA	93902	**800-333-5454***	831-754-5244
*Sales					
Kayem Foods Inc 75 Arlington St	Chelsea	MA	02150	**800-426-6100**	617-889-1600
Naked Juice Co 935 W 8th St	Azusa	CA	91702	**800-745-8423**	626-852-2500
Reser's Fine Foods Inc PO Box 8	Beaverton	OR	97075	**800-333-6431**	503-643-6431
Sandridge Food Corp 133 Commerce Dr	Medina	OH	44256	**800-280-7951**	330-725-2348
Star Food Products Inc PO Box 1479	Burlington	NC	27216	**800-672-5310**	336-227-4079
Suter Co Inc 258 May St	Sycamore	IL	60178	**800-435-6942**	815-895-9186

291-34 Sandwiches - Prepared

	City	State	Zip	Toll-Free	Phone
Bridgford Foods Corp 1308 N Patt St	Anaheim	CA	92801	**800-854-3255**	714-526-5533
NASDAQ: BRID					
Camino Real Foods Inc					
5785 Corporate Ave Suite 170	Cypress	CA	90630	**800-421-6201**	714-816-7900
Cloverdale Foods Co Inc					
3015 34th St NW PO Box 667	Mandan	ND	58554	**800-669-9511**	701-663-9511
Downs Food Group 400 Armstrong Blvd N	Saint James	MN	56081	**800-533-0452**	507-375-3111
Fishers Bakery & Sandwich Co					
1519 Brookside Dr	Raleigh	NC	27604	**800-849-8093**	919-832-6494
Hormel Foods Corp 1 Hormel Pl	Austin	MN	55912	**800-523-4635**	507-437-5611
NYSE: HRL					
Konop Cos 1725 Industrial Dr	Green Bay	WI	54302	**800-770-0477**	920-468-8517
Landshire Inc 9200 W Main St	Belleville	IL	62223	**800-468-3354**	618-398-8122
Sunburst Foods Inc 1002 Sunburst Dr	Goldsboro	NC	27534	**800-849-3196**	919-778-2151

291-35 Snack Foods

	City	State	Zip	Toll-Free	Phone
Bachman Co 50 N 4th St	Reading	PA	19601	**800-523-8253**	610-320-7800
Barrel O' Fun Snack Foods Co 800 4th St NW	Perham	MN	56573	**800-346-4910**	218-346-7000
Bickel's Snack Foods 1120 Zinns Quarry Rd	York	PA	17404	**800-233-1933**	717-843-0738
Cape Cod Potato Chip Co 100 Breed's Hill Rd	Hyannis	MA	02601	**888-881-2447**	508-775-3358
CJ Vitner & Co 4202 W 45th St	Chicago	IL	60632	**800-397-7629**	773-523-7900
Evans Food Products Co 4118 S Halsted St	Chicago	IL	60609	**866-254-7400**	773-254-7400
F & F Foods Inc 3501 W 48th Pl	Chicago	IL	60632	**800-621-0225**	773-927-3737
Frito-Lay Co 7701 Legacy Dr	Plano	TX	75024	**800-776-2257**	972-334-7000
General Mills Inc 1 General Mills Blvd	Minneapolis	MN	55426	**800-328-1144**	763-764-7600
NYSE: GIS					
General Mills Inc International Foods Div					
1 General Mills Blvd	Minneapolis	MN	55426	**800-328-1144**	763-764-7600
Golden Flake Snack Foods Inc					
1 Golden Flake Dr	Birmingham	AL	35205	**800-239-2447**	205-323-6161
Herr Foods Inc PO Box 300	Nottingham	PA	19362	**800-344-3777**	610-932-9330
Humpty Dumpty Snack Foods USA					
88 Pleasant Hill Rd	Scarborough	ME	04074	**800-274-2447**	207-883-8422
Husman Snack Foods Co 1621 Moore St	Cincinnati	OH	45202	**800-487-6267**	513-621-5614
Jays Foods Inc 825 E 99th St	Chicago	IL	60628	**800-621-6152**	773-731-8400
Keystone Food Products Co 3767 Hecktown Rd	Easton	PA	18045	**800-523-9426**	610-258-0888
Martin's Pastry Shop Inc					
1000 Potato Roll Ln	Chambersburg	PA	17201	**800-548-1200***	717-263-9580
*Cust Svc					
Martin's Potato Chips Inc					
5847 Lincoln Hwy W	Thomasville	PA	17364	**800-272-4477**	717-792-3565
Mike-Sell's Potato Chip Co 333 Leo St	Dayton	OH	45404	**800-257-4742**	937-228-9400
Mission Foods 2110 Santa Fe Dr	Pueblo	CO	81006	**800-821-3187**	719-543-4350
Old Dutch Foods Inc 2375 Terminal Rd	Roseville	MN	55113	**800-989-2447**	651-633-8810
Snyder of Berlin 1313 Stadium Dr	Berlin	PA	15530	**800-374-7949**	814-267-4641
Tim's Cascade Style Potato Chips					
PO Box 2302	Auburn	WA	98071	**800-533-8467**	253-833-0255
Troyer Potato Products Inc 810 Rt 97S	Waterford	PA	16441	**800-458-0485**	814-796-2611
Utz Quality Foods Co 900 High St	Hanover	PA	17331	**800-367-7629**	717-637-6644
Wise Foods Inc 245 Town Pk Dr Suite 475	Kennesaw	GA	30144	**800-438-9473**	770-426-5821
Wyandot Inc 135 Wyandot Ave	Marion	OH	43302	**800-992-6368**	740-383-4031

291-36 Specialty Foods

	City	State	Zip	Toll-Free	Phone
Alphin Brothers Inc 2302 US 301 S	Dunn	NC	28334	**800-672-4502**	910-892-8751
Amigos Canning Co Inc PO Box 37347	San Antonio	TX	78237	**800-580-3477**	210-434-0433
Armanino Foods of Distinction Inc					
30588 San Antonio St	Hayward	CA	94544	**800-255-5855**	510-441-9300
NASDAQ: ARMF					
Ateeco Inc DBA Mrs T's Pierogies					
600 E Center St PO Box 606	Shenandoah	PA	17976	**800-233-3170**	570-462-2745
Beech-Nut Nutrition Corp					
100 S 4th St Suite 1010	Saint Louis	MO	63102	**800-233-2468**	314-436-7667
Bruce Foods Corp PO Box 1030	New Iberia	LA	70562	**800-299-9082**	337-365-8101
Camino Real Foods Inc					
5785 Corporate Ave Suite 170	Cypress	CA	90630	**800-421-6201**	714-816-7900
Campbell Soup Co 1 Campbell Pl	Camden	NJ	08103	**800-772-8467**	856-342-4800
NYSE: CPB					
Castleberry's Food Co PO Box 1010	Augusta	GA	30903	**800-241-3520**	706-733-7765
Continental Mills Inc PO Box 88176	Seattle	WA	98138	**800-457-7744**	253-872-8400
Cromers Inc PO Box 163	Columbia	SC	29202	**800-322-7688**	803-779-1147
Cuisine Solutions Inc					
85 S Bragg St Suite 600	Alexandria	VA	22312	**888-285-4679**	703-270-2900
AMEX: FZN					
Culinary Foods Inc 4201 S Ashland Ave	Chicago	IL	60609	**800-621-4049**	773-650-4000
Del Monte Foods Co					
1 Market St The Landmark	San Francisco	CA	94105	**800-543-3090***	415-247-3000
NYSE: DLM ■ *Cust Svc					
Deli Express 16101 W 78th St	Eden Prairie	MN	55344	**866-787-8862**	952-937-9440
Delimex 7878 Airway Rd	San Diego	CA	92154	**800-382-6253**	619-661-5440
Eden Foods Inc 701 Tecumseh Rd	Clinton	MI	49236	**800-248-0320***	517-456-7424
*Cust Svc					
Edwards-Freeman Inc 441 E Hector St	Conshohocken	PA	19428	**877-448-6887**	610-828-7441
El Encanto Inc PO Box 293	Albuquerque	NM	87103	**800-888-7336**	505-243-2722
Ener-G Foods Inc					
5960 1st Ave S PO box 84487	Seattle	WA	98124	**800-331-5222**	206-767-6660
Fairmont Foods of Minnesota 905 E 4th St	Fairmont	MN	56031	**800-432-4411**	507-238-9001
Fernando's Foods Corp PO Box 4188	Compton	CA	90221	**800-388-5505**	310-223-1499
Gardenburger Inc					
1411 SW Morrison St Suite 400	Portland	OR	97205	**800-636-0109**	503-205-1500
Gerber Products Co 445 State St	Fremont	MI	49413	**800-443-7237**	231-928-2000
Hanover Foods Corp					
1550 York St PO Box 334	Hanover	PA	17331	**800-888-4646**	717-632-6000
Harvest States Foods 1565 1st Ave NW	New Brighton	MN	55112	**800-700-0809**	651-697-5500
Heinz Frozen Food Co 357 6th Ave	Pittsburgh	PA	15222	**800-892-2401***	412-237-3600
*Cust Svc					
HJ Heinz Co PO Box 57	Pittsburgh	PA	15230	**800-255-5750**	412-456-5700
NYSE: HNZ					
Homestead Ravioli Co Inc					
315 S Maple Ave	South San Francisco	CA	94080	**800-334-3397**	650-615-0750
Hormel Foods Corp 1 Hormel Pl	Austin	MN	55912	**800-523-4635**	507-437-5611
NYSE: HRL					
JM Smucker Co 1 Strawberry Ln	Orrville	OH	44667	**888-550-9555**	330-682-3000
NYSE: SJM					
Kedem Food Products/Royal Wine Corp					
63 Le Fante Ln	Bayonne	NJ	07002	**800-382-8299**	718-384-2400
La Choy Foodservice 3353 Michelson Dr	Irvine	CA	92612	**800-663-0112**	949-437-1000
Leon's Texas Cuisine Co 2100 Redbud Blvd	McKinney	TX	75069	**800-527-1243**	972-529-5050
Little Lady Foods Inc 2323 Pratt Blvd	Elk Grove Village	IL	60007	**800-439-1440**	847-806-1440
Luigino's Inc 525 S Lake Ave	Duluth	MN	55802	**800-521-1281**	218-723-5555
McCain Foods USA Inc 2905 Butterfield Rd	Oak Brook	IL	60523	**800-938-7799**	630-472-0420
McCain Snack Foods					
555 N Hickory Farm Ln PO Box 2518	Appleton	WI	54913	**800-767-7377**	920-997-2828
Michael Angelo's Gourmet Foods Inc					
200 Michael Angelo Way	Austin	TX	78728	**800-526-4918**	512-218-3500
Morgan Foods Inc 90 W Morgan St	Austin	IN	47102	**888-430-1780**	812-794-1170
Mott's Inc 900 King St	Rye Brook	NY	10573	**800-426-4891**	914-612-4000
Mrs Crockett's Kitchens Inc					
8821-G Forum Way	Fort Worth	TX	76140	**800-527-2523**	817-293-8164
Mrs T's Pierogies					
600 E Center St PO Box 606	Shenandoah	PA	17976	**800-233-3170**	570-462-2745
ORA Corp DBA Delimex 7878 Airway Rd	San Diego	CA	92154	**800-382-6253**	619-661-5440
Pastorelli Food Products Inc					
162 N Sangamon St	Chicago	IL	60607	**800-767-2829**	312-666-2041
Preferred Meal Systems Inc					
5240 Saint Charles Rd	Berkeley	IL	60163	**800-886-6325***	708-318-2500
*Cust Svc					
Proferas Inc 1136 Moosic St	Scranton	PA	18505	**800-360-7763**	570-342-4181
Progresso Quality Foods Co 500 W Elmer Rd	Vineland	NJ	08360	**800-200-9377**	856-691-1565
Quaker Oats Co 555 W Monroe St	Chicago	IL	60661	**800-555-6287**	312-821-1000
Readi-Bake Inc 361 Benigno Blvd	Bellmawr	NJ	08031	**800-852-2253**	440-237-3712
Reames Foods Inc PO Box 71159	Des Moines	IA	50325	**800-247-4194**	515-967-4254
Request Foods Inc PO Box 2577	Holland	MI	49422	**800-748-0378***	616-786-0900
*Sales					
Reynaldo's Mexican Food Co Inc					
4911 Mason St	South Gate	CA	90280	**800-686-4911**	
Rich Products Corp 1 Robert Rich Way	Buffalo	NY	14213	**800-828-2021**	716-878-8000
Ruiz Food Products Inc 501 S Alta Ave	Dinuba	CA	93618	**800-477-6474**	559-591-5510
Sanderson Farms Inc Foods Div					
4418 Mangum Dr	Flowood	MS	39208	**800-844-8291**	601-939-9790
Schwan's Bakery 1651 Montreal Cir	Tucker	GA	30084	**800-241-4166**	770-449-4900
Schwan's Minh Foods 1251 Scarborough Ln	Pasadena	TX	77506	**888-724-9267**	713-740-7200
Schwan's Sales Enterprises Inc					
115 W College Dr	Marshall	MN	56258	**800-533-5290**	507-532-3274
Small Planet Foods 719 Metcalf St	Sedro Woolley	WA	98284	**800-624-4123**	360-855-0100
Smucker JM Co 1 Strawberry Ln	Orrville	OH	44667	**888-550-9555**	330-682-3000
NYSE: SJM					
Specialty Brands Inc 4200 E Concours Dr	Ontario	CA	91764	**800-782-1180***	909-477-4700
*Cust Svc					
State Fair Foods 3900 Meacham Blvd	Haltom City	TX	76117	**800-641-6412**	817-427-7700
Steak-Umm Co LLC 153 Searles Rd	Pomfret Center	CT	06259	**800-394-7427**	860-928-5900
Stockpot Inc 22505 SR 9	Woodinville	WA	98072	**800-468-1611**	425-415-2000
Suter Co Inc 258 May St	Sycamore	IL	60178	**800-435-6942**	815-895-9186
TODDS Enterprises Inc 610 S 56th Ave	Phoenix	AZ	85043	**800-242-7687**	602-484-9584
Vanee Foods Co Inc 5418 McDermott Dr	Berkeley	IL	60163	**800-654-6647***	708-449-7300
*Cust Svc					
Wilson Foods Co LLC					
1811 W 1700 South	Salt Lake City	UT	84104	**800-950-8226**	801-972-5633
Winter Garden Quality Foods					
304 Commerce St	New Oxford	PA	17350	**800-242-7637**	717-624-4911
Wornick Co 10825 Kenwood Rd	Cincinnati	OH	45242	**800-860-4555**	513-794-9800

291-37 Spices, Seasonings, Herbs

	City	State	Zip	Toll-Free	Phone
Abco Laboratories Inc 2450 S Watney Way	Fairfield	CA	94533	**800-678-2226**	707-432-2200
Baltimore Spice Inc					
9740 Reisterstown Rd	Owings Mills	MD	21117	**800-365-3229**	410-363-1700
Basic American Foods					
2999 Oak Rd Suite 100	Walnut Creek	CA	94597	**800-227-4050**	925-472-4000
Benson's Gourmet Seasonings PO Box 638	Azusa	CA	91702	**800-325-5619**	626-969-4443
Blendex Co Inc 11208 Electron Dr	Louisville	KY	40299	**800-253-6339**	502-267-1003
Cargill Foods 15407 McGinty Rd	Wayzata	MN	55391	**800-227-4455**	952-742-7575
ConAgra Food Ingredients Co SpiceTec-USF					
Group 195 Alexandra Way	Carol Stream	IL	60188	**800-872-9236**	630-682-5600
Custom Food Products Inc 5145 W 123rd St	Alsip	IL	60803	**800-621-8827***	708-239-2766
*Cust Svc					
Danisco Ingredients USA Inc					
201 New Century Pkwy	New Century	KS	66031	**800-255-6837**	913-764-8100
Dirigo Spice Corp					
Thyme Square 750 Dorchester Ave	Dorchester	MA	02125	**800-345-9540**	617-436-9540
El Guapo Spice Inc 6200 E Slauson Ave	Commerce	CA	90040	**800-995-8906**	323-890-8900
Frontier Natural Products Co-op					
3021 78th St PO Box 299	Norway	IA	52318	**800-669-3275**	319-227-7996
Garden Herbs Inc 26021 Business Center Dr	Redlands	CA	92374	**800-388-9397**	909-796-2569
Griffith Laboratories USA 1 Griffith Ctr	Alsip	IL	60803	**800-346-9494***	708-371-0900
*Cust Svc					
Heller Seasonings & Ingredients Inc					
150 S Wacker Dr Suite 3200	Chicago	IL	60606	**800-323-2726**	312-456-6800
Johnny's Fine Foods Inc 319 E 25th St	Tacoma	WA	98421	**800-962-1462***	253-383-4597
*Orders					
Lawry's Foods Inc 222 E Huntington Dr	Monrovia	CA	91016	**800-952-9797**	626-930-8870

Spices, Seasonings, Herbs (Cont'd)

Company / Address	City	State	Zip	Toll-Free	Phone
McCormick & Co Inc 18 Loveton Cir *NYSE: MKC*	Sparks	MD	21152	**800-632-5847**	410-771-7301
McCormick & Co Inc Food Service Div 226 Schilling Cir	Hunt Valley	MD	21031	**800-327-6838**	410-771-7500
McCormick & Co Inc McCormick Flavor Div 226 Schilling Cir	Hunt Valley	MD	21031	**800-327-6838**	410-771-7500
McCormick & Co Inc US Consumer Products Div 211 Schilling Cir	Hunt Valley	MD	21031	**800-292-5300**	410-527-6000
McCormick Ingredients 10901 Gilroy Rd	Hunt Valley	MD	21031	**800-632-5847**	410-771-5008
Newly Weds Foods Inc 4140 W Fullerton Ave *Cust Svc	Chicago	IL	60639	**800-621-7521***	773-489-7000
Old Mansion Foods Inc 1558 W Washington St PO Box 2026	Petersburg	VA	23803	**800-476-1877**	804-862-9889
Precision Foods Inc 11457 Olde Cabin Rd	Saint Louis	MO	63141	**800-442-5242**	314-567-7400
Presco Food Seasonings Inc PO Box 152	Flemington	NJ	08822	**800-526-1713**	908-782-4919
REX Fine Foods 4100 Howard Ave	New Orleans	LA	70153	**800-344-8314**	504-822-4141
Spice Hunter Inc 184 Suburban Rd	San Luis Obispo	CA	93403	**800-444-3061**	805-544-4466
Spice World Inc 8101 Presidents Dr	Orlando	FL	32809	**800-433-4979**	407-851-9432
World Spice Inc 223-235 Highland Pkwy	Roselle	NJ	07203	**800-234-1060**	908-245-0600

291-38 Sugar & Sweeteners

Company / Address	City	State	Zip	Toll-Free	Phone
Cumberland Packing Corp 2 Cumberland St	Brooklyn	NY	11205	**800-221-1763**	718-858-4200
Imperial Sugar Co PO Box 9 *NASDAQ: IPSU*	Sugar Land	TX	77487	**800-727-8427**	281-491-9181
Monitor Sugar Co Inc 2600 S Euclid Ave	Bay City	MI	48706	**800-227-9110**	989-686-0161
NutraSweet Co 200 World Trade Ctr Merchandise Mart *Cust Svc	Chicago	IL	60654	**800-323-5321***	312-873-5000
Stadt Corp 2 Cumberland St	Brooklyn	NY	11205	**800-221-1763**	718-858-4200
Tate & Lyle North America 2200 E Eldorado St *Cust Svc	Decatur	IL	62525	**800-782-7248***	217-423-4411
Western Sugar Co 7555 E Hampden Ave Suite 600	Denver	CO	80231	**800-523-7497**	303-830-3939

291-39 Syrup - Maple

Company / Address	City	State	Zip	Toll-Free	Phone
Carriage House Cos Inc 196 Newton St	Fredonia	NY	14063	**800-828-8915**	716-673-1000
Food Producers International 10505 Wayzata Blvd Suite 400	Minnetonka	MN	55305	**800-443-1336**	952-544-2763
Foxtail Foods 6075 Poplar Ave Suite 800 *Cust Svc	Memphis	TN	38119	**800-487-2253***	901-766-6400
Kalva Corp 3940 Porett Dr	Gurnee	IL	60031	**800-525-8220**	847-336-1200
Maple Grove Farms of Vermont Inc 1052 Portland St	Saint Johnsbury	VT	05819	**800-525-2540**	802-748-5141
Richards Maple Products Inc 545 Water St	Chardon	OH	44024	**800-352-4052**	440-286-4160
Sea Breeze Fruit Flavors Inc 441 Rt 202	Towaco	NJ	07082	**800-732-2733**	973-334-7777

291-40 Tea

Company / Address	City	State	Zip	Toll-Free	Phone
American Ace Inc 2500 Heiman St	Nashville	TN	37208	**800-309-0079**	615-329-0079
Celestial Seasonings Inc 4600 Sleepytime Dr	Boulder	CO	80301	**800-351-8175**	303-581-1202
Eastern Tea Corp 1 Engelhard Dr	Monroe Township	NJ	08831	**800-221-0865**	609-860-1100
Fee Brothers Inc 453 Portland Ave	Rochester	NY	14605	**800-961-3337**	585-544-9530
JFG Coffee Co 3434 Mynatt Ave	Knoxville	TN	37919	**800-627-1988**	865-546-2120
Old Mansion Foods Inc 1558 W Washington St PO Box 2026	Petersburg	VA	23803	**800-476-1877**	804-862-9889
Oregon Chai Inc 1745 NW Marshall St	Portland	OR	97209	**888-874-2424**	
Redco Foods Inc 1 Hansen Island	Little Falls	NY	13365	**800-556-6674**	315-823-1300
S & D Coffee Inc PO Box 1628 *Cust Svc	Concord	NC	28026	**800-933-2210***	704-782-3121
Sara Lee Food & Beverage 10151 Carver Rd	Cincinnati	OH	45242	**800-351-7111**	513-936-2000
SJ McCullagh Inc 245 Swan St	Buffalo	NY	14204	**800-753-3473**	716-856-3473
Stash Tea Co Inc PO Box 910	Portland	OR	97207	**800-547-1514**	503-684-4482
Texas Coffee Co Inc PO Box 31	Beaumont	TX	77704	**800-259-3400**	409-835-3434
Van Rooy Coffee Co 4569 Spring Rd	Cleveland	OH	44131	**877-826-7669**	216-749-7069
White Coffee Corp 1835 38th St	Long Island City	NY	11105	**800-221-0140**	718-204-7900

291-41 Vinegar & Cider

Company / Address	City	State	Zip	Toll-Free	Phone
A Camacho Inc 2502 Walden Woods Dr	Plant City	FL	33566	**800-881-4534**	813-305-4534
Assouline & Ting Inc 2050 Richmond St	Philadelphia	PA	19125	**800-521-4491**	215-627-3000
Bertolli USA Inc 800 Sylvan Ave	Englewood Cliffs	NJ	07632	**800-908-9789**	
Boyajian Inc 144 Will Dr	Canton	MA	02021	**800-419-4677**	781-828-9966
Daltons Best Maid Products Inc 1400 S Riverside Dr	Fort Worth	TX	76104	**800-447-3581**	817-335-5494
Gold Pure Food Products Inc 1 Brooklyn Rd	Hempstead	NY	11550	**800-422-4681**	516-483-5600
Ken's Foods Inc 1 D'Angelo Dr	Marlborough	MA	01752	**800-633-5800**	508-485-7540
Knouse Foods Co-op Inc 800 Peach Glen-Idaville Rd	Peach Glen	PA	17375	**800-827-7537**	717-677-8181
Nakano Foods Inc 55 E Euclid Ave	Mount Prospect	IL	60056	**800-323-4358**	847-590-0059
National Fruit Product Co Inc PO Box 2040	Winchester	VA	22604	**800-551-5167**	540-662-3401
Pastorelli Food Products Inc 162 N Sangamon St	Chicago	IL	60607	**800-767-2829**	312-666-2041
Purity Products Inc 1800 NW 70th Ave	Miami	FL	33126	**800-654-0235**	305-592-3600
REX Fine Foods 4100 Howard Ave	New Orleans	LA	70153	**800-344-8314**	504-822-4141
Silver Palate PO Box 512	Cresskill	NJ	07626	**800-872-5283**	201-568-0110

291-42 Yeast

Company / Address	City	State	Zip	Toll-Free	Phone
Abco Laboratories Inc 2450 S Watney Way	Fairfield	CA	94533	**800-678-2226**	707-432-2200
ADM Arkady Products 100 Paniplus Rd	Olathe	KS	66061	**800-255-6637**	913-782-8800
Brolite Products Inc 1900 S Park Ave	Streamwood	IL	60107	**888-276-5483**	630-830-0340
DSM Food Specialties Inc 2675 Eisenhower Ave Valley Forge Corporate Ctr	Eagleville	PA	19403	**800-662-4478**	610-650-8480
Lesaffre Yeast Corp 433 E Michigan St	Milwaukee	WI	53202	**877-677-7000**	414-615-4055
Minn-Dak Yeast Co Inc 18175 Red River Rd W	Wahpeton	ND	58075	**800-348-0991**	701-642-3300
Red Star Bioproducts 5600 W Raymond St	Indianapolis	IN	46241	**800-445-0073**	317-243-3521

292 FOOD PRODUCTS - WHOL

SEE ALSO Beverages - Whol

292-1 Baked Goods - Whol

Company / Address	City	State	Zip	Toll-Free	Phone
Country Home Bakers Inc 3 Enterprise Dr Suite 404 *Cust Svc	Shelton	CT	06484	**800-243-0008***	203-225-2333
Stroehmann Bakeries Inc 255 Business Center Dr Suite 200	Horsham	PA	19044	**800-355-1260**	215-672-8010
Turano Baking Co 6501 W Roosevelt Rd	Berwyn	IL	60402	**800-458-5662**	708-788-9220

292-2 Coffee & Tea - Whol

Company / Address	City	State	Zip	Toll-Free	Phone
Becharas Brothers Coffee Co Inc 14501 Hamilton Ave	Highland Park	MI	48203	**800-944-9675**	313-869-4700
Capricorn Coffees Inc 353 10th St	San Francisco	CA	94103	**800-541-0758**	415-621-8500
Coex Coffee International Inc 2121 Ponce de Leon Blvd Suite 930	Coral Gables	FL	33134	**800-426-0343**	305-444-0568
Coffee Bean International 2181 NW Nicolai St	Portland	OR	97210	**800-877-0474**	503-227-4490
Coffee Masters Inc 7606 Industrial Ct	Spring Grove	IL	60081	**800-334-6485**	815-675-0088
Paramount Coffee Co 130 N Larch Ave	Lansing	MI	48912	**800-968-1222**	517-372-5500
Red Diamond Inc PO Box 2168	Birmingham	AL	35201	**800-292-4651**	205-254-3138
Texas Coffee Co Inc PO Box 31	Beaumont	TX	77704	**800-259-3400**	409-835-3434

292-3 Confectionery & Snack Foods - Whol

Company / Address	City	State	Zip	Toll-Free	Phone
AMCON Distributing Co 7405 Irvington Rd *AMEX: DIT*	Omaha	NE	68122	**800-369-0047**	402-331-3727
Anter Brothers Co 12501 Elmwood Ave	Cleveland	OH	44111	**800-331-5000**	216-252-4555
AW Marshall Co PO Box 16127	Salt Lake City	UT	84116	**800-273-4713**	801-328-4713
Axton Candy & Tobacco Co PO Box 32219	Louisville	KY	40232	**800-633-7816**	502-634-8000
Boyd-Bluford Inc PO Box 12240	Norfolk	VA	23541	**800-985-2828**	757-855-6036
Brown & Haley 1940 E 11th St	Tacoma	WA	98421	**800-426-8400**	253-620-3000
Bur-Bee Co PO Box 797	Walla Walla	WA	99362	**800-747-9726**	509-525-5040
Burklund Distributors Inc 2500 N Main St Suite 3	East Peoria	IL	61611	**800-322-2876**	309-694-1900
Foreign Candy Co Inc 1 Foreign Candy Dr	Hull	IA	51239	**800-767-4575**	712-439-1496
Frito-Lay Co 7701 Legacy Dr	Plano	TX	75024	**800-776-2257**	972-334-7000
Fritz Co Inc 1912 Hastings Ave	Newport	MN	55055	**800-328-1652**	651-459-9751
Hammons Products Co 105 Hammons Dr PO Box 140	Stockton	MO	65785	**888-429-6887**	417-276-5181
Hines Nut Co Inc 990 S Saint Paul St	Dallas	TX	75201	**800-580-0580**	214-939-0253
J Polep Distribution Services Inc 705 Meadow St	Chicopee	MA	01013	**800-447-6537**	413-592-4141
J Sosnick & Sons Inc 258 Littlefield Ave	South San Francisco	CA	94080	**800-443-6737**	650-952-2226
Kennedy Wholesale Inc 205 W Harvard St	Glendale	CA	91204	**877-292-2639**	818-241-9977
L & L Enterprises Inc 1307 E Maple Rd	Troy	MI	48083	**800-433-9486**	248-689-3850
L & L/Jiroch Distributing Co 1180 58th St	Wyoming	MI	49509	**800-874-5550**	616-530-6600
Marshall AW Co PO Box 16127	Salt Lake City	UT	84116	**800-273-4713**	801-328-4713
McDonald Candy Co 2350 W Broadway St	Eugene	OR	97402	**877-722-5503**	541-345-8421
Mound City Industries Inc 1315 Cherokee St	Saint Louis	MO	63118	**800-727-1548**	314-773-5200
New Britain Candy Co 24 Maple St	Wethersfield	CT	06129	**800-382-0515**	860-257-7058
Old Dutch Foods Inc 2375 Terminal Rd	Roseville	MN	55113	**800-989-2447**	651-633-8810
Peanut Processors Inc PO Box 160	Dublin	NC	28332	**800-334-8383**	910-862-2136
Pennsylvania Dutch Candies 1250 Slate Hill Rd	Camp Hill	PA	17011	**800-233-7082**	717-761-5440
Perugina Brands of America 800 N Brand Blvd 8th Fl	Glendale	CA	91203	**800-544-1672**	818-551-3530
Polep J Distribution Services Inc 705 Meadow St	Chicopee	MA	01013	**800-447-6537**	413-592-4141
Sosnick J & Sons Inc 258 Littlefield Ave	South San Francisco	CA	94080	**800-443-6737**	650-952-2226
Taste of Nature Inc 400 S Beverly Dr Suite 214 *Cust Svc	Beverly Hills	CA	90212	**800-898-2783***	310-396-4433
Trophy Nut Co Inc 320 N 2nd St	Tipp City	OH	45371	**800-729-6887**	937-667-8478
Tzetzo Brothers Inc 1100 Military Rd	Buffalo	NY	14217	**800-248-2881**	716-877-0800

292-4 Dairy Products - Whol

Company / Address	City	State	Zip	Toll-Free	Phone
Ambriola Co Inc 2 Burma Rd	Jersey City	NJ	07305	**800-962-8224**	201-434-6289
AMPI 315 N Broadway	New Ulm	MN	56073	**800-533-3580**	507-354-8295
Broughton Foods Co 1701 Green St	Marietta	OH	45750	**800-283-2479**	740-373-4121
Clofine Dairy Products Inc 1407 New Rd	Linwood	NJ	08221	**800-441-1001**	609-653-1000
Country Classic Dairies Inc DBA Darigold Farms of Montana PO Box 968	Bozeman	MT	59771	**800-321-4563**	406-586-5426
Country Fresh Inc 355 Mart St SW	Grand Rapids	MI	49548	**800-748-0480**	616-243-0173
Cream-O-Land Dairy Inc 529 Cedar Ln Box 146	Florence	NJ	08518	**800-220-6455**	609-499-3601
Crystal Farms Refrigerated Distribution Co 6465 Wayzata Blvd Suite 200	Minneapolis	MN	55426	**800-344-7382**	952-544-8101
Dairylea Co-op Inc 5001 Brittonfield Pkwy	East Syracuse	NY	13057	**800-654-8838**	315-433-0100

Classified Section

	City	State	Zip	Toll-Free	Phone
Darigold Farms of Montana PO Box 968	Bozeman	MT	59771	**800-321-4563**	406-586-5426
DMV USA 1285 Rudy St *Cust Svc	Onalaska	WI	54650	**877-300-7676***	608-779-7676
Erie Foods International Inc 401 7th Ave	Erie	IL	61250	**800-447-1887**	309-659-2233
Fleur de Lait BC USA 400 S Custer Ave	New Holland	PA	17557	**800-322-2743**	717-355-8500
Foremost Farms USA E10889A Penny Ln	Baraboo	WI	53913	**800-362-9196**	608-356-8316
Hautly Cheese Co Inc 5130 Northrup Ave	Saint Louis	MO	63110	**800-729-9339**	314-772-9339
Jack & Jill Ice Cream Co 3100 Marwin Ave	Bensalem	PA	19020	**800-220-2300**	215-639-2300
Kraft Foods International Inc 800 Westchester Ave	Rye Brook	NY	10573	**800-323-0768**	914-335-2500
Level Valley Creamery 807 Pleasant Valley Rd	West Bend	WI	53095	**800-558-1707**	262-675-6533
Maryland & Virginia Milk Producers Co-op Assn Inc 1985 Isaac Newton Sq W	Reston	VA	20190	**800-552-1976**	703-742-6800
Masters Gallery Foods Inc 328 County Hwy PP	Plymouth	WI	53073	**800-236-8431**	920-893-8431
Matanuska Maid Dairy 814 W Northern Lights Blvd	Anchorage	AK	99503	**800-478-5223**	907-561-5223
NZMP Inc 635 N 12th St Suite 101	Lemoyne	PA	17043	**800-358-9096**	717-920-4000
Pevely Dairy Co 1001 S Grand Blvd	Saint Louis	MO	63104	**800-727-4407**	314-771-4400
Plains Dairy Products 300 N Taylor St	Amarillo	TX	79107	**800-365-5608**	806-374-0385
Prairie Farms Dairy Inc 1100 N Broadway St	Carlinville	IL	62626	**800-654-2547**	217-854-2547
Purity Dairies Inc 360 Murfreesboro Rd	Nashville	TN	37210	**800-947-6455**	615-244-1900
Queensboro Farm Products Inc 156-02 Liberty Ave	Jamaica	NY	11433	**800-696-8970**	718-658-5000
Reiter Dairy Inc 1415 W Waterloo Rd	Akron	OH	44314	**800-362-0825**	330-745-1123
Roberts Dairy Co PO Box 3825	Omaha	NE	68103	**800-779-4321**	402-344-4321
Rockview Dairies Inc PO Box 668	Downey	CA	90241	**800-423-2479**	562-927-5511
Schenkel's Dairy 1019 Flax Mill Rd	Huntington	IN	46750	**800-862-6455**	260-356-4225
Simco Sales Service of Pennsylvania Inc DBA Jack & Jill Ice Cream Co 3100 Marwin Ave	Bensalem	PA	19020	**800-220-2300**	215-639-2300
Sunshine Dairy Foods Inc 801 NE 21st Ave	Portland	OR	97232	**800-544-0554**	503-234-7526
Sure Winner Foods Inc PO Box 430	Saco	ME	04072	**800-640-6447**	207-282-1258
Tuscan Dairy Farms Inc 750 Union Ave	Union	NJ	07083	**800-672-1137**	908-686-1500
Velda Farms LLC 402 S Kentucky Ave Suite 500 *Cust Svc	Lakeland	FL	33801	**800-795-4649***	863-686-4441

292-5 Fish & Seafood - Whol

	City	State	Zip	Toll-Free	Phone
Beaver Street Fisheries Inc 1741 W Beaver St	Jacksonville	FL	32209	**800-874-6426**	904-354-8533
Blount Seafood Corp PO Box 327	Warren	RI	02885	**800-274-2526**	401-245-8800
Bon Secour Fisheries Inc 17449 County Rd 49 S PO Box 60	Bon Secour	AL	36511	**800-633-6854**	251-949-7411
Empress International Ltd 10 Harbor Park Dr *Sales	Port Washington	NY	11050	**800-645-6244***	516-621-5900
Fishery Products International 18 Electronics Ave	Danvers	MA	01923	**800-374-4770**	978-777-2660
Fjord Seafoods DBA Windward Seafoods 8550 NW 17 St Suite 105	Miami	FL	33126	**800-780-3474**	305-591-8550
Gorton Slade Co Inc 4433 W 42nd Pl	Chicago	IL	60632	**800-524-8237**	773-927-2400
Handy John T Co Inc PO Box 309	Crisfield	MD	21817	**800-426-3977**	410-968-1772
Inland Seafood Corp 1222 Menlo Dr	Atlanta	GA	30318	**800-883-3474**	404-350-5850
Interamerican Trading & Products Corp PO Box 402427	Miami Beach	FL	33140	**800-999-7123**	305-885-9666
Ipswich Shellfish Co Inc 8 Hayward St	Ipswich	MA	01938	**800-477-9424**	978-356-4371
John Keeler & Co Inc 3000 NW 109th Ave	Miami	FL	33172	**888-663-2722**	305-836-6858
John T Handy Co Inc PO Box 309	Crisfield	MD	21817	**800-426-3977**	410-968-1772
Keeler John & Co Inc 3000 NW 109th Ave	Miami	FL	33172	**888-663-2722**	305-836-6858
Lobster Direct 97 Bedford Hills Rd	Bedford	NS	B4A1J8	**800-672-5297**	902-832-1680
Metropolitan Poultry & Seafood Co 1920 Stanford Ct	Landover	MD	20785	**800-522-0060**	301-772-0060
Michael's Finer Meats & Seafoods 3775 Zane Trace Dr	Columbus	OH	43228	**800-282-0518**	614-527-4900
Morley Sales Co Inc 809 W Madison St	Chicago	IL	60607	**800-828-0424**	312-829-1125
Ore-Cal Corp 634 S Crocker St	Los Angeles	CA	90021	**800-827-7474**	213-680-9540
Quirch Foods Co 7600 NW 82nd Pl	Miami	FL	33166	**800-458-5252**	305-691-3535
Robert Wholey & Co Inc 1501 Penn Ave	Pittsburgh	PA	15222	**800-248-0568**	412-261-3693
SeaSpecialties Inc 1111 NW 159th Dr	Miami	FL	33169	**800-654-6682**	305-625-5112
Slade Gorton Co Inc 4433 W 42nd Pl	Chicago	IL	60632	**800-524-8237**	773-927-2400
Southern Foods Inc 3500 Old Battleground Rd	Greensboro	NC	27410	**800-441-3663**	336-545-3800
Stavis Seafoods Inc 212 Northern Ave Suite 305	Boston	MA	02210	**800-390-5103**	617-482-6349
Sunnyvale Seafood Corp 1651 Pomona Ave	San Jose	CA	95110	**800-726-2326**	408-289-9198
Troyer Foods Inc PO Box 608	Goshen	IN	46527	**800-876-9377**	574-533-0302
Wholey Robert & Co Inc 1501 Penn Ave	Pittsburgh	PA	15222	**800-248-0568**	412-261-3693
Windward Seafoods 8550 NW 17 St Suite 105	Miami	FL	33126	**800-780-3474**	305-591-8550

292-6 Frozen Foods (Packaged) - Whol

	City	State	Zip	Toll-Free	Phone
American Frozen Foods Inc 155 Hill St	Milford	CT	06460	**800-233-5554**	203-882-6200
Cirelli Foods Inc 30 Commerce Blvd	Middleboro	MA	02346	**800-242-0939**	508-947-8778
Dot Foods Inc PO Box 192	Mount Sterling	IL	62353	**800-366-3687**	217-773-4411
Happy & Healthy Products Inc 1600 S Dixie Hwy Suite 200	Boca Raton	FL	33432	**800-378-4854**	561-367-0739
Muir-Roberts Co Inc 68 S Main St Suite 900	Salt Lake City	UT	84101	**877-268-2002**	801-363-7695
Superior Foods Inc 275 Westgate Dr	Watsonville	CA	95076	**888-373-7871**	831-728-3691
Wilcox Frozen Foods Inc 2200 Oakdale Ave	San Francisco	CA	94124	**800-827-7858**	415-282-4116

292-7 Fruits & Vegetables - Fresh - Whol

	City	State	Zip	Toll-Free	Phone
Amerifresh 4025 Delridge Way SW Suite 550	Seattle	WA	98106	**800-568-3235**	206-933-4900
Banacol Marketing Corp 2655 Le Jeune Rd Suite 1015	Coral Gables	FL	33134	**800-824-6585**	305-441-9036
Belair Produce Co Inc 7226 Parkway Dr	Hanover	MD	21076	**888-782-8008**	410-782-8000
Bell-Carter Foods Inc 3742 Mount Diablo Blvd	Lafayette	CA	94549	**800-252-3557**	925-284-5933
Besteman JA Co Inc 1060 Hall St SW	Grand Rapids	MI	49503	**800-253-4620**	616-452-2101
Bix Produce Co 1415 L'Orient St	Saint Paul	MN	55117	**800-642-9514**	651-487-8000
Calavo Growers Inc PO Box 26081 *NASDAQ: CVGW*	Santa Ana	CA	92799	**800-422-5286**	949-223-1111
Caro Foods Inc 2324 Bayou Blue Rd	Houma	LA	70364	**800-395-2276**	985-872-1483
Castellini Co PO Box 721610	Newport	KY	41072	**800-233-8560**	859-442-4600
Community Suffolk Inc 304 2nd St	Everett	MA	02149	**800-225-4470**	617-389-5200
Consumers Produce Co 1 21st St	Pittsburgh	PA	15222	**800-245-0698**	412-281-0722
Costa Fruit & Produce Inc 18 Bunker Hill Industrial Pk	Charlestown	MA	02129	**800-343-0836**	617-241-8007
Crosset Co Inc 10295 Toebben Dr	Independence	KY	41051	**800-347-4902**	859-283-5830
D'Arrigo Brothers Co of Massachusetts Inc 105 New England Produce Ctr	Chelsea	MA	02150	**800-327-7446**	617-884-0316
D'Arrigo Brothers Co of New York Inc 315 NYC Terminal Market	Bronx	NY	10474	**800-223-8080**	718-991-5900
DiMare Brothers/New England Farms Packing Co 84 New England Produce Ctr	Chelsea	MA	02150	**800-510-3700**	617-889-3800
DiMare Fresh Inc 1049 Ave H East	Arlington	TX	76011	**800-322-2184**	817-385-3000
Dixie Produce & Packaging Inc 5801 G St	Harahan	LA	70123	**800-952-5637**	504-733-7500
DNE World Fruit Sales 1900 Old Dixie Hwy	Fort Pierce	FL	34946	**800-327-6676**	772-465-1110
Dole Distribution Center 607 Ala Moana Blvd CFS-3	Honolulu	HI	96813	**800-697-9100**	808-531-5911
East Coast Fruit Co Inc 3335 Edgewood Ave N	Jacksonville	FL	32205	**800-541-4602**	904-355-7591
Federal Fruit & Produce Co 1890 E 58th Ave	Denver	CO	80216	**800-621-7166**	303-292-1303
Fresh Del Monte Produce Inc 241 Sevilla Ave *NYSE: FDP* ■ *Cust Svc	Coral Gables	FL	33134	**800-950-3683***	305-520-8400
Frieda's Inc 4465 Corporate Ctr Dr	Los Alamitos	CA	90720	**800-421-9477**	714-826-6100
General Produce Co Ltd 1330 N 'B' St	Sacramento	CA	95814	**800-366-4985**	916-441-6431
HC Schmeiding Produce Co PO Box 369	Springdale	AR	72765	**800-643-3607**	479-751-4517
Hearn Kirkwood 7251 Standard Dr	Hanover	MD	21076	**888-866-2905**	410-712-6000
Indianapolis Fruit Co Inc 4501 Massachusetts Ave	Indianapolis	IN	46218	**800-377-2425**	317-546-2425
JA Besteman Co Inc 1060 Hall St SW	Grand Rapids	MI	49503	**800-253-4620**	616-452-2101
Lee Ray-Tarantino Co Inc PO Box 2408	South San Francisco	CA	94083	**800-321-1035**	650-761-2854
Melissa's/World Variety Produce Inc 5325 S Soto St	Vernon	CA	90058	**800-468-7111**	323-588-0151
Moore Food Distributors Co 9910 Page Ave	Saint Louis	MO	63132	**800-467-7878**	314-426-1300
Movsovitz & Sons of Florida Inc 3100 Hilton St	Jacksonville	FL	32209	**800-393-3663**	904-764-7681
Muir-Roberts Co Inc 68 S Main St Suite 900	Salt Lake City	UT	84101	**877-268-2002**	801-363-7695
Oneonta Trading Corp 1 Oneonta Way	Wenatchee	WA	98804	**800-688-2191**	509-663-2631
Organic Valley Family of Farms 1 Organic Way	LaFarge	WI	54639	**888-444-6455**	608-625-2602
Paramount Export Co 175 Filbert St Suite 201	Oakland	CA	94607	**800-869-0150**	510-839-0150
Peak of the Market 1200 King Edward St	Winnipeg	MB	R3H0R5	**888-289-7325**	204-633-7325
Peirone Produce Co 524 E Trent Ave	Spokane	WA	99202	**800-552-5837**	509-838-3515
Red's Market Inc 8801 Exchange Dr	Orlando	FL	32809	**800-226-3930**	407-857-3930
Sandridge Food Corp 133 Commerce Dr	Medina	OH	44256	**800-280-7951**	330-725-2348
Schmieding HC Produce Co PO Box 369	Springdale	AR	72765	**800-643-3607**	479-751-4517
Snokist Growers Co-op PO Box 1587	Yakima	WA	98907	**800-258-0470**	509-453-5631
Superior Foods Inc 275 Westgate Dr	Watsonville	CA	95076	**888-373-7871**	831-728-3691
United Foods Inc 10 Pictsweet Dr	Bells	TN	38006	**800-367-7412**	731-422-7600

292-8 Groceries - General Line

	City	State	Zip	Toll-Free	Phone
Abbott Sysco Food Service 2400 Harrison Rd	Columbus	OH	43204	**800-686-3663**	614-272-0658
Affiliated Foods Inc 1401 Farmers Ave	Amarillo	TX	79118	**800-234-3661**	806-372-3851
AJC International 5188 Roswell Rd NW	Atlanta	GA	30342	**800-252-3663**	404-252-6750
Allen Foods Inc 8543 Page Ave	Saint Louis	MO	63114	**800-888-4855**	314-426-4100
AMCON Distributing Co 7405 Irvington Rd *AMEX: DIT*	Omaha	NE	68122	**800-369-0047**	402-331-3727
Anderson-DuBose Co 6575 Davis Industrial Pkwy	Solon	OH	44139	**800-248-1080**	440-248-8800
Associated Food Stores Inc 1850 W 2100 South *Cust Svc	Salt Lake City	UT	84119	**888-574-7100***	801-973-4400
Associated Grocers of Florida Inc 7000 NW 32nd Ave	Miami	FL	33147	**800-275-8181**	305-696-0080
Associated Grocers Inc 8600 Anselmo Ln	Baton Rouge	LA	70810	**800-637-2021**	225-769-2020
Associated Grocers Inc 3301 S Norfolk St	Seattle	WA	98118	**800-562-9729**	206-762-2100
Associated Grocers of New England Inc 725 Gold St	Manchester	NH	03108	**800-242-2248**	603-669-3250
Associated Grocers of the South 3600 Vanderbilt Rd	Birmingham	AL	35217	**800-695-6051**	205-841-6781
Associated Wholesalers Inc PO Box 67	Robesonia	PA	19551	**800-927-7771**	610-693-3161
Banta Foods Inc 1620 N Packer Rd	Springfield	MO	65803	**800-492-2682**	417-862-6644
Ben E Keith Co 7650 Will Rogers Blvd	Fort Worth	TX	76140	**877-317-6100**	817-759-6000
Brenham Wholesale Grocery Co 602 W 1st St	Brenham	TX	77833	**800-324-3232**	979-836-7925
Cash-Wa Distributing Co 401 W 4th St	Kearney	NE	68847	**800-652-0010**	308-237-3151
CB Ragland Co 2720 Eugenia Ave	Nashville	TN	37211	**800-234-4455**	615-259-4622
Core-Mark International Inc 395 Oyster Point Blvd Suite 415	South San Francisco	CA	94080	**800-622-1713**	650-589-9445
Dearborn Wholesale Grocers Inc 2801 S Western Ave	Chicago	IL	60608	**800-999-3663**	773-254-4300
DiCarlo Distributors Inc 1630 N Ocean Ave	Holtsville	NY	11742	**800-342-2756**	631-758-6000
Eby-Brown Co 280 W Shuman Blvd Suite 280	Naperville	IL	60563	**800-553-8249**	630-778-2800
Farner-Bocken Co 1751 US Hwy 30 E	Carroll	IA	51401	**800-274-8692**	712-792-3503
Feesers Inc 5561 Grayson Rd	Harrisburg	PA	17111	**800-326-2828**	717-564-4636
Food Services of America Inc 4025 Delridge Way SW Suite 400	Seattle	WA	98106	**800-372-3663**	206-933-5000
Glazier Foods Co 1520 Oliver St	Houston	TX	77007	**800-989-6411**	713-869-6411
Gordon Food Service 333 50th St SW	Grand Rapids	MI	49548	**800-968-7500**	616-530-7000
Henry Lee Div 3301 NW 125th St	Miami	FL	33167	**800-274-4533**	305-685-5851
Grocers Supply Co Inc 3131 E Holcombe Blvd	Houston	TX	77021	**800-352-8003**	713-747-5000
Grocery Supply Co 130 Hillcrest Dr	Sulphur Springs	TX	75482	**800-231-1938**	903-885-7621
Hannaford Bros Co Inc 145 Pleasant Hill Rd	Scarborough	ME	04074	**800-341-6393**	207-883-2911
IJ Co PO Box 51890	Knoxville	TN	37950	**800-251-9516**	865-970-7800
Imperial Trading Co Inc 701 Edwards Ave PO Box 23508 *Cust Svc	Elmwood	LA	70183	**800-743-1761***	504-733-1400
Institution Food House Inc 543 12th Street Dr NW	Hickory	NC	28603	**800-487-2527**	828-323-4500
Institutional Distributors Inc PO Box 520	East Bernstadt	KY	40729	**800-442-7885**	606-843-2100

Groceries - General Line (Cont'd)

Company	City	State	Zip	Toll-Free	Phone
International Multifoods Corp 110 Cheshire Ln Suite 300	Minnetonka	MN	55305	**800-866-3300**	952-594-3300
JM Swank Co 520 W Penn St	North Liberty	IA	52317	**800-593-6375**	319-626-3683
Jordano's Inc 550 S Patterson Ave	Santa Barbara	CA	93111	**800-325-2278**	805-964-0611
JT Davenport & Sons Inc PO Box 1105	Sanford	NC	27331	**800-868-7550***	919-774-9444
*Cust Svc					
Kehe Food Distributors Inc 900 N Schmidt Rd	Romeoville	IL	60446	**800-995-5343**	815-886-0700
Keith Ben E Co 7650 Will Rogers Blvd	Fort Worth	TX	76140	**877-317-6100**	817-759-6000
Kraft Foods International Inc 800 Westchester Ave	Rye Brook	NY	10573	**800-323-0768**	914-335-2500
Labatt Food Service 4500 Industry Park Dr	San Antonio	TX	78218	**800-324-8732**	210-661-4216
Laurel Grocery Co Inc PO Box 4100	London	KY	40743	**800-467-6601**	606-878-6601
Luke Soules Acosta 1920 Westridge Dr	Irving	TX	75038	**800-486-0928**	972-518-1442
Maines Paper & Food Service Co 101 Broome Corporate Pkwy	Conklin	NY	13748	**800-366-3669**	607-772-1936
McLane Co Inc 4747 McLane Pkwy	Temple	TX	76504	**800-299-1401**	254-771-7500
Millbrook Distribution Services 88 Huntoon Memorial Hwy	Leicester	MA	01524	**800-225-7398**	508-892-8171
Mountain People's Warehouse Inc 12745 Earhart Ave	Auburn	CA	95602	**800-679-8735**	530-889-9531
Nobel/Sysco Food Services Inc 1101 W 48th Ave	Denver	CO	80221	**800-366-6696**	303-458-4000
Oppenheimer Cos Inc 877 W Main St Suite 700	Boise	ID	83702	**800-727-9939**	208-343-4883
Pegler-Sysco Food Services Co 1700 Center Park Rd	Lincoln	NE	68512	**800-366-1031**	402-423-1031
PFG/AFI Foodservice 1 Center Dr	Elizabeth	NJ	07207	**800-275-0155**	908-629-1800
Piggly Wiggly Carolina Co Inc PO Box 118047	Charleston	SC	29423	**800-243-9880**	843-554-9880
Purity Wholesale Grocers Inc 5400 Broken Sound Blvd NW Suite 100	Boca Raton	FL	33487	**800-323-6838**	561-994-9360
Quality-PFG 4901 Asher Ave	Little Rock	AR	72204	**800-568-3141**	501-568-3141
Ragland CB Co 2720 Eugenia Ave	Nashville	TN	37211	**800-234-4455**	615-259-4622
Reinhart FoodService Inc 1500 Saint James St	La Crosse	WI	54603	**800-827-4010**	608-782-2660
Shamrock Foods Co Inc 2540 N 29th Ave	Phoenix	AZ	85009	**800-388-3247**	602-233-6400
Smart & Final Foodservice Distributors Inc 4343 E Fremont St	Stockton	CA	95215	**800-336-6200**	209-948-1814
Soules Luke Acosta 1920 Westridge Dr	Irving	TX	75038	**800-486-0928**	972-518-1442
Southco Distributing Co 701 Patetown Rd	Goldsboro	NC	27530	**800-969-3172**	919-735-8012
SUPERVALU Inc 11840 Valley View Rd	Eden Prairie	MN	55344	**888-256-2800***	952-828-4000
NYSE: SVU ■ *Cust Svc					
Swank JM Co 520 W Penn St	North Liberty	IA	52317	**800-593-6375**	319-626-3683
SYGMA Network Inc 2000 Westbelt Dr	Columbus	OH	43228	**800-347-7344**	614-771-3801
Thoms Proestler Co 8001 TPC Rd	Rock Island	IL	61204	**800-747-1234**	309-787-1234
Tree of Life Inc 405 Golfway W Dr	Saint Augustine	FL	32095	**800-223-2910***	904-824-1846
*Cust Svc					
Tripifoods Inc 1427 William St	Buffalo	NY	14240	**800-851-7400**	716-853-7400
Unified Western Grocers Inc 6433 S E Lake Rd	Portland	OR	97222	**800-777-3305**	503-833-1000
UniPro Foodservice Inc 2500 Cumberland Pkwy Suite 600	Atlanta	GA	30339	**800-366-7723**	770-952-0871
United Natural Foods Inc 260 Lake Rd PO Box 999	Dayville	CT	06241	**800-877-8898**	860-779-2800
NASDAQ: UNFI					
Vistar/VSA Corp 12650 E Arapahoe Rd Bldg D	Englewood	CO	80112	**800-880-9900**	303-662-7100
Winkler Inc PO Box 68	Dale	IN	47523	**800-621-3843**	812-937-4421
Wood-Fruitticher Grocery Co Inc 2900 Alton Rd	Birmingham	AL	35210	**800-489-4500**	205-836-9663

292-9 Meats & Meat Products - Whol

Company	City	State	Zip	Toll-Free	Phone
Agar Supply Co Inc 225 John Hancock Rd	Taunton	MA	02780	**800-669-6040**	508-821-2060
Auth Brothers Inc 1905 Clarkson Way	Landover	MD	20785	**800-424-2610**	301-322-8400
Bruss Co 3548 N Kostner Ave	Chicago	IL	60641	**800-621-3882**	773-282-2900
Colorado Boxed Beef Co PO Box 899	Winter Haven	FL	33882	**800-955-0636**	863-967-0636
Cusack Wholesale Meat Inc PO Box 25111	Oklahoma City	OK	73125	**800-241-6328**	405-232-2114
Deen Wholesale Meats 813 E Northside Dr	Fort Worth	TX	76102	**800-333-3953**	817-335-2257
Durham Meat Co 2026 Martin Ave	Santa Clara	CA	95050	**800-233-8742**	800-444-5687
Earp Distribution Co 6550 Kansas Ave	Kansas City	KS	66111	**800-866-3277**	913-287-3311
Empire Beef Co Inc 171 Weidner Rd	Rochester	NY	14624	**800-462-6804**	585-235-7350
Green Tree Packing Co 65 Central Ave	Passaic	NJ	07055	**800-221-5754**	973-473-1305
Harker's Distribution Inc 801 6th St SW	Le Mars	IA	51031	**800-798-9800**	712-546-8171
Holten Meat Inc 1682 Sauget Business Blvd	Sauget	IL	62206	**800-851-4684**	618-337-8400
Leidy's Inc 266 W Cherry Ln	Souderton	PA	18964	**800-222-2319**	215-723-4606
Manda Fine Meats 2445 Sorrel Ave	Baton Rouge	LA	70802	**800-343-2642**	225-344-7636
Maryland Quality Meats Inc 701 W Hamburg St	Baltimore	MD	21230	**800-368-2579**	410-539-7055
Michael's Finer Meats & Seafoods 3775 Zane Trace Dr	Columbus	OH	43228	**800-282-0518**	614-527-4900
Midamar Corp PO Box 218	Cedar Rapids	IA	52406	**800-362-3711**	319-362-3711
Middendorf Meat Co Inc 3737 N Broadway	Saint Louis	MO	63147	**800-949-6328**	314-241-4800
Nationwide Foods/Brookfield Farms 700 E 107th St	Chicago	IL	60628	**800-243-1014**	773-787-4900
Peyton Meats Inc 3 Butterfield Trail Suite 101	El Paso	TX	79906	**800-351-1024**	915-751-6632
Porky Products Corp 400 Port Carteret Dr	Carteret	NJ	07008	**800-952-0265**	732-541-0200
Quality Meats & Seafoods 700 Center St	West Fargo	ND	58078	**800-959-4250**	701-282-0202
Quirch Foods Co 7600 NW 82nd Pl	Miami	FL	33166	**800-458-5252**	305-691-3535
Randall Foods Inc 2905 E 50th St	Vernon	CA	90058	**800-372-6581**	323-587-2383
Sampco Inc 651 W Washington Blvd Suite 300	Chicago	IL	60661	**800-767-0689**	312-346-1506
Scavuzzo's Inc 2840 Gwinnot St	Kansas City	MO	64120	**800-800-4707**	816-231-1517
Schisa Brothers Inc PO Box 3350	Syracuse	NY	13220	**800-676-3287**	315-463-0213
Southern Foods Inc 3500 Old Battleground Rd	Greensboro	NC	27410	**800-441-3663**	336-545-3800
Stadler's Country Hams Inc PO Box 397	Elon	NC	27244	**800-262-1795**	336-584-1396
Troyer Foods Inc PO Box 608	Goshen	IN	46527	**800-876-9377**	574-533-0302
Wolfson Casing Corp 700 S Fulton Ave	Mount Vernon	NY	10550	**800-221-8042**	914-668-9000

292-10 Poultry, Eggs, Poultry Products - Whol

Company	City	State	Zip	Toll-Free	Phone
Acme Farms Inc PO Box 3065	Seattle	WA	98114	**800-542-8309**	206-323-4300
Agar Supply Co Inc 225 John Hancock Rd	Taunton	MA	02780	**800-669-6040**	508-821-2060
Crystal Farms Refrigerated Distribution Co 6465 Wayzata Blvd Suite 200	Minneapolis	MN	55426	**800-344-7382**	952-544-8101
Durbin Marshall Food Corp 2830 Commerce Blvd	Irondale	AL	35210	**800-768-2456**	205-956-3505
Dutt & Wagner of Virginia Inc PO Box 518	Abingdon	VA	24212	**800-688-2116**	276-628-2116
Harker's Distribution Inc 801 6th St SW	Le Mars	IA	51031	**800-798-9800**	712-546-8171
House of Raeford Farms Inc PO Box 100	Raeford	NC	28376	**800-888-7539**	910-875-5161
Lincoln Poultry & Egg Co 2005 'M' St	Lincoln	NE	68510	**800-477-4433**	402-477-3757
Marshall Durbin Food Corp 2830 Commerce Blvd	Irondale	AL	35210	**800-768-2456**	205-956-3505
Metropolitan Poultry & Seafood Co 1920 Stanford Ct	Landover	MD	20785	**800-522-0060**	301-772-0060
Norbest Inc 6875 S 900 East	Midvale	UT	84047	**800-453-5327**	801-566-5656
Nulaid Foods Inc 200 W 5th St	Ripon	CA	95366	**800-788-8871**	209-599-2121
Park Farms Inc 1925 30th St NE	Canton	OH	44705	**800-683-6511**	330-455-0241
Petaluma Poultry Processors PO Box 7368	Petaluma	CA	94955	**800-556-6789**	707-763-1904
Quirch Foods Co 7600 NW 82nd Pl	Miami	FL	33166	**800-458-5252**	305-691-3535
Randall Foods Inc 2905 E 50th St	Vernon	CA	90058	**800-372-6581**	323-587-2383
Troyer Foods Inc PO Box 608	Goshen	IN	46527	**800-876-9377**	574-533-0302
Valley Fresh Inc 680 D St	Turlock	CA	95380	**800-526-3189**	209-668-3695
Zacky Farms 13200 Crossroads Pkwy N Suite 250	City of Industry	CA	91746	**800-800-0205**	562-641-2020

292-11 Specialty Foods - Whol

Company	City	State	Zip	Toll-Free	Phone
Brechet & Richter Co 6005 Golden Valley Rd	Minneapolis	MN	55422	**800-347-8700***	763-545-0201
*Sales					
Conway Import Co Inc 11051 West Addison St	Franklin Park	IL	60131	**800-323-8801**	847-455-5600
Diaz Wholesale & Mfg Co Inc 5500 Bucknell Dr	Atlanta	GA	30336	**800-394-4639**	404-344-5421
Essex Grain Products 9 Lee Blvd	Frazer	PA	19355	**800-441-1017**	610-647-3800
Gourmet Award Foods 7225 W Marcia Rd	Milwaukee	WI	53223	**800-726-7205**	414-365-7000
I & K Distributors Inc 1600 Gressel Dr	Delphos	OH	45833	**800-472-9920**	419-695-5015
Indiana Sugars Inc 911 Virginia St	Gary	IN	46402	**800-333-9666**	219-886-9151
J Sosnick & Sons Inc 258 Littlefield Ave	South San Francisco	CA	94080	**800-443-6737**	650-952-2226
JF Braun & Sons Inc 265 Post Ave	Westbury	NY	11590	**800-997-7177**	516-997-2200
JFC International Inc 540 Forbes Blvd	South San Francisco	CA	94080	**800-633-1004**	650-873-8400
John E Koerner & Co Inc PO Box 10218	New Orleans	LA	70181	**800-333-1913**	504-734-1100
Koerner John E & Co Inc PO Box 10218	New Orleans	LA	70181	**800-333-1913**	504-734-1100
Kraft Foods International Inc 800 Westchester Ave	Rye Brook	NY	10573	**800-323-0768**	914-335-2500
Liberty Richter Inc 400 Lyster Ave	Saddle Brook	NJ	07663	**800-631-3650**	201-843-8900
Lomar Distributing 2500 Dixon St	Des Moines	IA	50316	**800-369-3663**	515-244-3105
Mitsui Foods Inc 35 Maple St	Norwood	NJ	07648	**800-777-2322**	201-750-0500
Roma Food Enterprises Inc 45 Stanford Rd	Piscataway	NJ	08854	**800-526-7662**	732-463-7662
Shonfeld's USA Inc 3100 S Susan St	Santa Ana	CA	92704	**877-447-8933**	714-429-1922
Sosnick J & Sons Inc 258 Littlefield Ave	South San Francisco	CA	94080	**800-443-6737**	650-952-2226
Sturm Foods Inc PO Box 287	Manawa	WI	54949	**800-347-8876**	920-596-2511
Sugar Foods Corp 950 3rd Ave 21st Fl	New York	NY	10022	**800-666-3285**	212-753-6900
Sunsweet Growers Inc 901 N Walton Ave	Yuba City	CA	95993	**800-417-2253**	530-674-5010

293 FOOD PRODUCTS MACHINERY

Company	City	State	Zip	Toll-Free	Phone
Acme Pizza & Bakery Equipment Inc 7039 E Slauson Ave	Commerce	CA	90040	**800-428-2263**	323-722-7900
Adamatic Corp 607 Industrial Way W	Eatontown	NJ	07724	**800-526-2807**	732-544-8400
Advance Food Service Equipment Inc 200 Heartland Blvd	Edgewood	NY	11717	**800-645-3166**	631-242-4800
Aeroglide Corp PO Box 29505	Raleigh	NC	27626	**800-722-7483**	919-851-2000
Alto-Shaam Inc PO Box 450	Menomonee Falls	WI	53052	**800-329-8744**	262-251-3800
American Permanent Ware Inc 729 3rd Ave	Dallas	TX	75226	**800-527-2100**	214-421-7366
Anderson International Corp 6200 Harvard Ave	Cleveland	OH	44105	**800-336-4730**	216-641-1112
Anetsberger Brothers Inc 180 N Anets Dr	Northbrook	IL	60062	**800-837-2638**	847-272-0770
APV Canada Inc 3280 Langstaff Rd	Concord	ON	L4K4Z8	**800-263-3958**	905-760-1852
Atlas Metal Industries 1135 NW 159th Dr	Miami	FL	33169	**800-762-7565***	305-625-2451
*Cust Svc					
Atlas Pacific Engineering Co 1 Atlas Ave	Pueblo	CO	81001	**800-227-0682**	719-948-3040
Baader-Johnson 2955 Fairfax Trafficway	Kansas City	KS	66115	**800-288-3434**	913-621-3366
Beehive Machinery Inc PO Box 5002	Sandy	UT	84091	**800-621-8438**	801-561-4211
Blakeslee Inc 1844 S Laramie Ave	Cicero	IL	60804	**800-652-5889**	708-656-0660
Brewmatic Co 20333 S Normandie Ave PO Box 2959	Torrance	CA	90509	**800-421-6860**	310-787-5444
Brogdex Co 1441 W 2nd St	Pomona	CA	91766	**800-795-5225**	909-622-1021
Brown Citrus Systems Inc 333 M Ave NW	Winter Haven	FL	33881	**800-788-8225**	863-299-2111
Brown International Corp 633 N Barranca Ave	Covina	CA	91723	**800-423-1843**	626-966-8361
C Cretors & Co 3243 N California Ave	Chicago	IL	60618	**800-228-1885**	773-588-1690
Carpigiani Corp of America 3760 Industrial Dr	Winston-Salem	NC	27105	**800-648-4389**	336-661-9893
Casa Herrerra Inc 2655 N Pine St	Pomona	CA	91767	**800-624-3916**	909-392-3930
Chester-Jensen Co Inc PO Box 908	Chester	PA	19016	**800-685-3750**	610-876-6276
Cleveland Range Co 1333 E 179th St	Cleveland	OH	44110	**800-338-2204**	216-481-4900
Colborne Corp 28495 N Ballard Dr	Lake Forest	IL	60045	**800-279-1879**	847-371-0101
Cretors C & Co 3243 N California Ave	Chicago	IL	60618	**800-228-1885**	773-588-1690
Curtis Wilbur Co Inc 6913 Acco St	Montebello	CA	90640	**800-421-6150**	323-837-2300
Delfield Co 980 S Isabella Rd	Mount Pleasant	MI	48858	**800-733-8821**	989-773-7981
Duke Mfg Co 2305 N Broadway	Saint Louis	MO	63102	**800-735-3853**	314-231-1130
Edlund Co Inc 159 Industrial Pkwy	Burlington	VT	05401	**800-772-2126**	802-862-9661
Fedco Systems Co Super Grain Div PO Box 769	Sidney	OH	45365	**800-922-6641**	937-492-4158
Food Service Supplies Inc 1020 2nd Ave	Columbia	SC	29209	**800-366-3774**	803-776-2658
Food Warming Equipment Co Inc 7900 SR 31	Crystal Lake	IL	60014	**800-222-4393***	815-459-7500
*Sales					
Garland Commercial Industries 185 E South St	Freeland	PA	18224	**800-424-2411**	570-636-1000
Globe Food Equipment Co PO Box 3209	Dayton	OH	45401	**800-347-5423**	937-299-5493
Gold Medal Products Co 10700 Medallion Dr	Cincinnati	OH	45241	**800-543-0862***	513-769-7676
*Cust Svc					

Classified Section

Company / Address	City	State	Zip	Toll-Free	Phone
Great Western Mfg Co Inc PO Box 149	Leavenworth	KS	66048	**800-682-3121**	913-682-2291
Grindmaster Crathco Systems Inc					
PO Box 35020	Louisville	KY	40232	**800-695-4500**	502-425-4776
GS Blodgett Corp 44 Lakeside Ave	Burlington	VT	05401	**800-331-5842**	802-658-6600
Hayes & Stolz Industrial Mfg Co Inc					
PO Box 11217	Fort Worth	TX	76110	**800-725-7272**	817-926-3391
Heat & Control Inc 21121 Cabot Blvd	Hayward	CA	94545	**800-227-5980**	510-259-0500
Henny Penny Corp 1219 US 35 W	Eaton	OH	45320	**800-417-8417**	937-456-4171
Hobart Corp 701 S Ridge Ave	Troy	OH	45374	**800-333-7447***	937-332-3000
*Cust Svc					
Hosokawa Micron Group 10 Chatham Rd	Summit	NJ	07901	**800-526-4491**	908-273-6360
Howes S Co Inc 25 Howard St	Silver Creek	NY	14136	**888-255-2611**	716-934-2611
Idaho Steel Products Co					
255 E Anderson St	Idaho Falls	ID	83401	**800-633-0022**	208-522-1275
Insinger Machine Co 6245 State Rd	Philadelphia	PA	19135	**800-344-4802**	215-624-4800
Invensys APV 395 Fillmore Ave	Tonawanda	NY	14150	**800-828-7667**	716-692-3000
ITW Food Equipment Group 701 S Ridge Ave	Troy	OH	45374	**800-333-7447***	937-332-3000
*Cust Svc					
Kasco Corp 1569 Tower Grove Ave	Saint Louis	MO	63110	**800-325-8940**	314-771-1550
Kwik Lok Corp PO Box 9548	Yakima	WA	98909	**800-688-5945**	509-248-4770
Load King Mfg Co PO Box 40606	Jacksonville	FL	32203	**800-531-4975**	904-354-8882
Lucks Co 3003 S Pine St	Tacoma	WA	98409	**800-826-7409**	206-674-7200
Luker Inc 514 National Ave	Augusta	GA	30901	**800-982-9534**	706-724-0244
Merco-Savory Inc 1111 N Hadley Rd	Fort Wayne	IN	46804	**800-547-2513***	260-459-8200
*Cust Svc					
Microfluidics International Corp PO Box 9101	Newton	MA	02464	**800-370-5452**	617-969-5452
Middleby Corp 1400 Toastmaster Dr	Elgin	IL	60120	**800-323-2210***	847-741-3300
NASDAQ: MIDD ■ *Cust Svc					
Miroil Div Oil Process Systems Inc					
602 N Tacoma St	Allentown	PA	18109	**800-523-9844**	610-437-4618
Nitta Casings Inc PO Box 858	Somerville	NJ	08876	**800-526-3970***	908-218-4400
*Cust Svc					
Oil Process Systems Inc Miroil Div					
602 N Tacoma St	Allentown	PA	18109	**800-523-9844**	610-437-4618
Oliver Products Co 445 6th St NW	Grand Rapids	MI	49504	**800-253-3893**	616-456-7711
Peerless Machinery Corp PO Box 769	Sidney	OH	45365	**800-999-3327**	937-492-4158
Peters Machinery Inc 500 S Vandemark Rd	Sidney	OH	45365	**800-999-3327**	937-492-4158
Piper Products Inc 300 S 84th Ave	Wausau	WI	54401	**800-558-5880**	715-842-2724
Pitco Frialator Inc PO Box 501	Concord	NH	03302	**800-258-3708**	603-225-6684
Prince Castle Inc 355 E Kehoe Blvd	Carol Stream	IL	60188	**800-722-7853**	630-462-8800
Reading Bakery Systems					
380 Old West Penn Ave	Robesonia	PA	19551	**800-693-5816**	610-693-5816
Ross Industries Inc 5321 Midland Rd	Midland	VA	22728	**800-336-6010**	540-439-3271
S Howes Co Inc 25 Howard St	Silver Creek	NY	14136	**888-255-2611**	716-934-2611
SaniServ Inc 451 E County Line Rd	Mooresville	IN	46158	**800-733-8073**	317-831-7030
Sanovo Engineering 4225 SW Kirklawn Ave	Topeka	KS	66609	**800-255-2463***	785-266-5511
*Sales					
Schlueter Co PO Box 548	Janesville	WI	53547	**800-359-1700**	608-755-5455
Server Products Inc PO Box 98	Richfield	WI	53076	**800-558-8722**	262-628-5600
Southbend Co Inc					
1100 Old Honeycutt Rd	Fuquay-Varina	NC	27526	**800-348-2558**	919-552-9161
Stork Gamco Inc PO Box 1258	Gainesville	GA	30503	**800-347-8675**	770-532-7041
Taylor Co 750 N Blackhawk Blvd	Rockton	IL	61072	**800-255-0626**	815-624-8333
Town Food Service Equipment Co					
351 Bowery	New York	NY	10003	**800-221-5032**	212-473-8355
Townsend Engineering Co PO Box 1433	Des Moines	IA	50305	**800-247-8609**	515-265-8181
Ultrafryer Systems 302 Spencer Ln	San Antonio	TX	78201	**800-545-9189**	210-731-5000
Union Standard Equipment Co 801 E 141st St	Bronx	NY	10454	**800-237-8873**	718-585-0200
Univex Corp 3 Old Rockingham Rd	Salem	NH	03079	**800-258-6358**	603-893-6191
Vendome Copper & Brass Works Inc					
729 Franklin St	Louisville	KY	40202	**800-247-6245**	502-587-1930
Volckening Inc 6700 3rd Ave	Brooklyn	NY	11220	**800-221-0876**	718-836-4000
Vulcan-Hart Corp 2006 Northwestern Pkwy	Louisville	KY	40203	**800-999-9815***	502-778-2791
*Cust Svc					
Walker Stainless Equipment Co Inc					
625 State St	New Lisbon	WI	53950	**800-356-5734**	608-562-3151
Weiler & Co Inc 1116 E Main St	Whitewater	WI	53190	**800-558-9507***	262-473-5254
*Sales					
Wells Bloomfield Industries					
2 Erik Cir PO Box 280	Verdi	NV	89439	**800-777-0450**	775-345-0444
Wenger Mfg Inc 714 Main St	Sabetha	KS	66534	**800-833-0174**	785-284-2133
Wilbur Curtis Co Inc 6913 Acco St	Montebello	CA	90640	**800-421-6150**	323-837-2300
Winston Industries LLC 2345 Carton Dr	Louisville	KY	40299	**800-234-5286**	502-495-5400
Wisco Industries Inc 736 Janesville St	Oregon	WI	53575	**800-999-4726**	608-835-3106
Witte Co Inc PO Box 47	Washington	NJ	07882	**866-265-4071**	908-689-6500
Wolf Range Co 19600 S Alameda St	Compton	CA	90221	**888-435-9653**	310-637-3737

294 FOOD SERVICE

SEE ALSO Restaurants

Company / Address	City	State	Zip	Toll-Free	Phone
Aircraft Service International Group					
201 S Orange Ave Suite 205	Orlando	FL	32801	**800-557-2744**	407-648-7373
All Seasons Services Inc					
1265 Belmont St Suite 2	Brockton	MA	02301	**888-558-2557**	508-559-9000
ARAMARK Food & Support Services					
1101 Market St	Philadelphia	PA	19107	**800-999-8989**	215-238-3000
ARAMARK Uniform & Career Apparel					
1101 Market St	Philadelphia	PA	19107	**800-999-8989**	215-238-3000
Atlas Food Systems & Services Inc					
205 Woods Lake Rd	Greenville	SC	29607	**800-476-1123**	864-232-1885
Blue Line Foodservice Distribution					
24120 Haggerty Rd	Farmington Hills	MI	48335	**866-414-2583**	248-478-6200
Canteen Correctional Services					
38 Pond St Suite 308	Franklin	MA	02030	**800-357-0012**	508-520-4334
Canteen Vending Services					
2400 Yorkmont Rd	Charlotte	NC	28217	**800-357-0012**	704-329-4000
Cara Operations Ltd 6303 Airport Rd	Mississauga	ON	L4V1R8	**800-860-4082**	905-405-6500
Cara Operations Ltd Airport Services Div					
6303 Airport Rd	Mississauga	ON	L4V1R8	**800-860-4082**	905-405-6500
Centerplate 201 E Broad St	Spartanburg	SC	29306	**800-698-6992**	864-598-8600
AMEX: CVP					
COI Foodservice 2629 Eugenia Ave	Nashville	TN	37211	**877-503-5212**	615-231-4300
Compass Group North American Div					
2400 Yorkmont Rd	Charlotte	NC	28217	**800-357-0012**	704-329-4000
Custom Food Group 2627 Midway Ave	Shreveport	LA	71108	**800-256-8828**	318-632-8000
Filterfresh Coffee Service Inc					
378 University Ave	Westwood	MA	02090	**800-461-8734**	781-461-8734
Five Star Food Service Inc 1400 17th St	Columbus	GA	31901	**800-327-0043**	706-327-0303
Forever/NPC Resorts LLC					
7500 McCormick Blvd	Scottsdale	AZ	85258	**800-455-3509**	480-998-8888
Guckenheimer Enterprises Inc					
3 Lagoon Dr Suite 325	Redwood Shores	CA	94065	**800-466-5303**	650-592-3800
Guest Services Inc 3055 Prosperity Ave	Fairfax	VA	22031	**800-345-7534**	703-849-9300
Institution Food House Inc					
543 12th Street Dr NW	Hickory	NC	28603	**800-487-2527**	828-323-4500
Institutional Distributors Inc					
PO Box 520	East Bernstadt	KY	40729	**800-442-7885**	606-843-2100
Institutional Wholesale Co					
535 Dry Valley Rd	Cookeville	TN	38503	**800-239-9588**	931-537-4000
Morrison Management Specialists Inc					
5801 Peachtree Dunwoody Rd	Atlanta	GA	30342	**800-622-1035**	404-845-3330
Open Kitchen Inc 1161 W 21st St	Chicago	IL	60608	**800-339-5334**	312-666-5334
Sanese Services Inc 6465 Busch Blvd	Columbus	OH	43229	**800-589-3410**	614-436-1234
Shamrock Food Service 3055 Prosperity Ave	Fairfax	VA	22031	**800-345-7534**	703-849-9300
Signature Services Corp 2705 Hawes Ave	Dallas	TX	75235	**800-929-5519**	214-353-2661
Sodexho Inc 9801 Washingtonian Blvd	Gaithersburg	MD	20878	**800-763-3946**	301-987-4000
Sportservice Corp 40 Fountain Plaza	Buffalo	NY	14202	**800-828-7240**	716-858-5000
Summit Food Service Distributors Inc					
580 Industrial Rd	London	ON	N5V1V1	**800-265-9267**	519-453-3410
Universal Sodexho 5749 Susitna Dr	Harahan	LA	70123	**800-535-1946**	504-733-5761
Valley Inc 4400 Mangum Dr	Flowood	MS	39232	**800-748-9985**	601-664-3100
Volume Services America Holdings Inc DBA					
Centerplate 201 E Broad St	Spartanburg	SC	29306	**800-698-6992**	864-598-8600
AMEX: CVP					

295 FOOD SERVICE EQUIPMENT & SUPPLIES

SEE ALSO Industrial Machinery & Equipment (Misc) - Mfr

Company / Address	City	State	Zip	Toll-Free	Phone
Adams-Burch Inc 1901 Stanford Ct	Landover	MD	20785	**800-347-8093***	301-341-1600
*Cust Svc					
Anderson-DuBose Co 6575 Davis Industrial Pkwy	Solon	OH	44139	**800-248-1080**	440-248-8800
Arranaga Robert & Co Inc					
216 S Alameda St	Los Angeles	CA	90012	**800-639-0059**	213-622-1261
Atlanta Fixture & Sales Co					
3185 Northeast Expy	Atlanta	GA	30341	**800-282-1977**	770-455-8844
Blue Line Foodservice Distribution					
24120 Haggerty Rd	Farmington Hills	MI	48335	**866-414-2583**	248-478-6200
Boelter Cos Inc 11100 W Silver Spring Rd	Milwaukee	WI	53225	**800-392-3278**	414-461-3400
Bolton & Hay Inc 2701 Delaware Ave	Des Moines	IA	50317	**800-362-1861**	515-265-2554
Browne-Halco Inc 2840 Morris Ave	Union	NJ	70783	**888-289-1005**	908-964-9200
Buffalo Hotel Supply Co Inc					
375 Commerce Dr PO Box 646	Amherst	NY	14226	**800-333-1678**	716-691-8080
Cambro Mfg Co 5801 Skylab Rd	Huntington Beach	CA	92647	**800-833-3003**	714-848-1555
Carlisle FoodService Products Inc					
4711 E Hefner Rd	Oklahoma City	OK	73131	**800-654-8210**	405-475-5600
Cecilware Corp 43-05 20th Ave	Long Island City	NY	11105	**800-935-2211**	718-932-1414
Curtis Restaurant Supply Co 6577 E 40th St	Tulsa	OK	74145	**800-766-2878**	918-622-7390
Don Edward & Co 2500 S Harlem Ave	North Riverside	IL	60546	**800-777-4366***	708-883-8000
*Cust Svc					
Edward Don & Co 2500 S Harlem Ave	North Riverside	IL	60546	**800-777-4366***	708-883-8000
*Cust Svc					
Gardner & Benoit Inc PO Box 7246	Charlotte	NC	28241	**800-467-6676**	704-504-1151
Golden Light Equipment Co 1010 W 6th St	Amarillo	TX	79101	**800-692-4098**	806-373-4277
Gordon Food Service 333 50th St SW	Grand Rapids	MI	49548	**800-968-7500**	616-530-7000
Henry Lee Div 3301 NW 125th St	Miami	FL	33167	**800-274-4533**	305-685-5851
Groen 1055 Mendell Davis Dr	Jackson	MS	39272	**800-676-9040**	601-372-3903
HB Hunter Co PO Box 1599	Norfolk	VA	23501	**800-446-8314**	757-664-5200
Hunter HB Co PO Box 1599	Norfolk	VA	23501	**800-446-8314**	757-664-5200
Interstate Restaurant Equipment Corp					
37 Amoskeag St	Manchester	NH	03102	**800-258-3040**	603-669-3400
King Provision Corp					
9009 Regency Square Blvd	Jacksonville	FL	32211	**888-781-5464**	904-781-9888
Kittredge Equipment Co Inc					
2155 Columbus Ave	Springfield	MA	01104	**800-423-7082**	413-788-6101
Maines Equipment & Supply Co PO Box 450	Conklin	NY	13748	**800-800-4825**	607-772-0055
Maines Paper & Food Service Co					
101 Broome Corporate Pkwy	Conklin	NY	13748	**800-366-3669**	607-772-1936
N Wasserstrom & Sons Inc					
2300 Lockbourne Rd	Columbus	OH	43207	**800-444-4697**	614-228-5550
PBI Market Equipment Inc					
2667 Gundry Ave	Signal Hill	CA	90755	**800-421-3753**	562-595-4785
RAPIDS Wholesale Equipment Co					
6201 S Gateway Dr	Marion	IA	52302	**800-899-6610**	319-364-5186
Restaurant & Stores Equipment Co					
230 W 700 South	Salt Lake City	UT	84101	**800-877-0087**	801-364-1981
Robert Arranaga & Co Inc					
216 S Alameda St	Los Angeles	CA	90012	**800-639-0059**	213-622-1261
Service Ideas Inc 2354 Ventura Dr	Woodbury	MN	55125	**800-328-4493**	651-730-8800
Singer Equipment Co Inc 3030 Kutztown Rd	Reading	PA	19605	**800-422-8126**	610-929-8000
Sofco Div US Foodservice Inc					
3366 Walden Ave	Depew	NY	14043	**800-724-2571***	716-685-6001
*Cust Svc					
Sofco Div US Foodservice Inc					
702 Potential Pkwy	Scotia	NY	12302	**800-836-7632***	518-374-7810
*Orders					
Southern Foods Inc					
3500 Old Battleground Rd	Greensboro	NC	27410	**800-441-3663**	336-545-3800
Strategic Equipment & Supply Corp					
1031 Madeira Ave	Minneapolis	MN	55405	**800-328-5133**	612-381-3100
Sunlow Inc 1071 Howell Mill Rd NW	Atlanta	GA	30318	**800-678-6569**	404-872-8135
Superior Products Catalog Co					
510 W County Rd D	Saint Paul	MN	55112	**800-328-9800***	651-636-1110
*Sales					
Traex Co 101 Traex Plaza	Dane	WI	53529	**800-356-8006**	608-849-2500
Unified Foodservice Purchasing Co-op LLC					
950 Breckenridge Ln	Louisville	KY	40207	**800-444-4144**	502-896-5900
UniPro Foodservice Inc					
2500 Cumberland Pkwy Suite 600	Atlanta	GA	30339	**800-366-7723**	770-952-0871
US Foodservice Inc Sofco Div					
3366 Walden Ave	Depew	NY	14043	**800-724-2571***	716-685-6001
*Cust Svc					
US Foodservice Inc Sofco Div					
702 Potential Pkwy	Scotia	NY	12302	**800-836-7632***	518-374-7810
*Orders					

Company	City	State	ZIP	Toll-Free	Phone
Vollrath Co LLC					
1236 N 18th St PO Box 611	Sheboygan	WI	53082	**800-624-2051**	920-457-4851
Wasserstrom Co 477 S Front St	Columbus	OH	43215	**800-999-9277**	614-228-6525
Wasserstrom N & Sons Inc					
2300 Lockbourne Rd	Columbus	OH	43207	**800-444-4697**	614-228-5550

296 FOOTWEAR

Company	City	State	ZIP	Toll-Free	Phone
Acor Orthopaedic Inc 18530 S Miles Pkwy	Cleveland	OH	44128	**800-237-2267**	216-662-4500
Acushnet Co 333 Bridge St	Fairhaven	MA	02719	**800-225-8500**	508-979-2000
adidas America 5055 N Greeley Ave	Portland	OR	97217	**888-234-3270**	971-234-2300
Aerosoles 201 Meadow Rd	Edison	NJ	08817	**800-798-9478**	732-985-6900
Airwalk International LLC					
603 Park Point Dr Suite 100	Golden	CO	80401	**800-677-1545**	303-526-2100
Aldo Shoes 2300 Emile Belanger	Saint-Laurent	QC	H4R3J4	**888-818-2536**	514-747-2536
Allen-Edmonds Shoe Corp					
201 E Seven Hills Rd	Port Washington	WI	53074	**800-235-2348***	262-235-6000
*Cust Svc					
AmAsia International Ltd 34 3rd Ave	Burlington	MA	01803	**888-877-3338**	781-229-6611
American Sporting Goods Corp 2323 Main St	Irvine	CA	92614	**800-848-0690**	949-752-6888
American West Trading Co 1751 Alpine Dr	Clarksville	TN	37040	**800-340-4466**	931-645-4466
Asics Tiger Corp 16275 Laguna Canyon Rd	Irvine	CA	92618	**800-333-8404**	949-453-8888
Athlete's Foot Group Inc 1950 Vaughn Rd	Kennesaw	GA	30144	**800-524-6444**	770-514-4500
ATP Mfg LLC 761 Great Rd	North Smithfield	RI	02896	**800-315-5246**	401-765-8600
BA Mason 1251 1st Ave	Chippewa Falls	WI	54774	**800-826-7030**	715-723-1871
Badorf Shoe Co Inc PO Box 367	Lititz	PA	17543	**800-325-1545**	717-626-8521
Barbour Welting Co Div Barbour Corp					
1001 N Montello St	Brockton	MA	02301	**800-955-9649**	508-583-8200
Bass GH & Co Inc 600 Sable Oaks Dr	South Portland	ME	04106	**800-950-2277***	207-791-4000
*Cust Svc					
Beacon Shoe Co Inc 213 Lions Estates Dr	Jonesburg	MO	63351	**800-325-7463**	636-488-5444
Birkenstock Footprint Sandals Inc					
8171 Redwood Blvd	Novato	CA	94945	**800-487-9255**	415-892-4200
Bottega Veneta Inc 635 Madison Ave	New York	NY	10022	**877-362-1715**	212-371-5511
Brooks Sports Inc					
19820 North Creek Pkwy Suite 200	Bothell	WA	98011	**800-227-6657**	425-488-3131
Brown Shoe Co Inc 8300 Maryland Ave	Saint Louis	MO	63105	**800-766-6465***	314-854-4000
NYSE: BWS ■ *Cust Svc					
Candie's Inc 400 Columbus Ave	Valhalla	NY	10595	**800-352-2634**	914-769-8600
NASDAQ: CAND					
Capezio/Ballet Makers Inc 1 Campus Rd	Totowa	NJ	07512	**800-595-9002**	973-595-9000
Carolina Shoe Co PO Box 1079	Morganton	NC	28680	**800-438-7026**	828-437-7755
Cole-Haan 1 Cole Haan Dr	Yarmouth	ME	04096	**800-488-2000**	207-846-2500
Cole Kenneth Productions Inc					
603 W 50th St	New York	NY	10019	**800-536-2653**	212-265-1500
NYSE: KCP					
Conaway-Winter Inc 718 E Park St	Willow Springs	MO	65793	**800-331-9476**	417-469-3125
Consolidated Shoe Co Inc					
22290 Timberlake Rd	Lynchburg	VA	24502	**800-368-7463**	434-239-0391
Converse Inc 1 High St	North Andover	MA	01845	**800-428-2667***	978-983-3300
*Cust Svc					
Cowtown Boot Co 11401 Gateway Blvd W	El Paso	TX	79936	**800-580-2668**	915-593-2565
D Myers & Sons Inc 4311 Erdman Ave	Baltimore	MD	21213	**800-367-7463**	410-522-7500
Danner Shoe Mfg Co					
18550 NE Riverside Pkwy	Portland	OR	97230	**800-345-0430**	503-251-1100
Deckers Outdoor Corp 495-A S Fairview Ave	Goleta	CA	93117	**800-858-5342**	805-967-7611
NASDAQ: DECK					
Drew Shoe Corp 252 Quarry Rd	Lancaster	OH	43130	**800-837-3739**	740-653-4271
DSW Shoe Warehouse 4150 E 5th Ave	Columbus	OH	43219	**800-477-8595***	614-237-7100
*Cust Svc					
E Shoe Sale Inc 60 Enterprise Ave N	Secaucus	NJ	07094	**877-474-6372**	201-319-0853
Easy Spirit Shoes 1129 Westchester Ave	White Plains	NY	10604	**800-284-9955**	914-640-6400
EJ Footwear Corp 120 Plaza Dr Suite A	Vestal	NY	13850	**800-223-5029**	607-584-5000
ES Originals Inc 450 W 33rd St 9th Fl	New York	NY	10001	**800-677-6577**	212-736-8124
Eurostar Inc 13425 S Figueroa St	Los Angeles	CA	90061	**800-276-2002***	310-354-1387
*Cust Svc					
Famous Footwear 7010 Mineral Point Rd	Madison	WI	53717	**800-888-7198***	608-829-3668
*Cust Svc					
Fancy Feet Inc 26650 Harding St	Oak Park	MI	48237	**800-858-8460**	248-398-8460
Fila USA Inc 1 Fila Way	Sparks	MD	21152	**800-787-3452**	410-773-3000
Finish Line Inc 3308 N Mitthoeffer Rd	Indianapolis	IN	46235	**800-370-6061**	317-899-1022
NASDAQ: FINL					
Foot Locker Inc 112 W 34th St	New York	NY	10120	**800-991-6682**	212-720-3700
NYSE: FL					
Foot-So-Port Shoe Corp PO Box 247	Oconomowoc	WI	53066	**800-679-7463**	262-567-4416
Footaction USA 112 W 34th St	New York	NY	10120	**800-863-8932**	212-720-3700
Georgia Boot Inc PO Box 10	Franklin	TN	37068	**800-251-3388**	615-794-1556
GH Bass & Co Inc 600 Sable Oaks Dr	South Portland	ME	04106	**800-950-2277***	207-791-4000
*Cust Svc					
Hi-Tec Sports USA Inc 4801 Stoddard Rd	Modesto	CA	95356	**800-521-1698**	209-545-1111
Hush Puppies Co 9341 Courtland Dr NE	Rockford	MI	49351	**800-626-8696**	616-866-5500
Impo International Inc PO Box 639	Santa Maria	CA	93456	**800-367-4676**	805-922-7753
In Step Promotions Inc 10821 Lakeview Ave	Lenexa	KS	66219	**800-321-1098**	913-599-5995
Iron Age Corp Robinson Plaza III Suite 400	Pittsburgh	PA	15205	**800-223-8912***	412-787-4100
*Cust Svc					
Jimlar Corp 160 Great Neck Rd	Great Neck	NY	11021	**800-883-3453**	516-829-1717
John Reyer Shoe Store					
Reyers City Ctr 40 S Water Ave	Sharon	PA	16146	**800-245-1550***	724-981-2200
*Cust Svc					
Johnston & Murphy Inc					
1415 Murfreesboro Rd	Nashville	TN	37217	**800-424-2854**	615-367-8101
Justin Boot Co Inc 610 W Daggett St	Fort Worth	TX	76104	**866-240-8853***	817-332-4385
*Cust Svc					
K-Swiss Inc 31248 Oak Crest Dr	Westlake Village	CA	91361	**800-938-8000**	818-706-5100
NASDAQ: KSWS					
Kaepa USA Inc 9050 Autobahn Dr Suite 500	Dallas	TX	75237	**800-880-9200**	972-296-7300
Keds Corp 191 Spring St	Lexington	MA	02421	**800-428-6575**	617-824-6000
Kenneth Cole Productions Inc					
603 W 50th St	New York	NY	10019	**800-536-2653**	212-265-1500
NYSE: KCP					
LA Gear Inc 844 Moraga Dr	Los Angeles	CA	90049	**800-252-4327**	310-253-7744
LaCrosse Footwear Inc					
18550 NE Riverside Pkwy	Portland	OR	97230	**800-323-2668***	503-766-1010
NASDAQ: BOOT ■ *Cust Svc					
Lady Foot Locker 112 W 34th St	New York	NY	10120	**800-877-5239**	212-720-3700
Lake Catherine Footwear PO Box 6048	Hot Springs	AR	71902	**800-826-8676**	501-262-6000
Lama Tony Boot Co Inc 1137 Tony Lama St	El Paso	TX	79915	**800-866-9526**	915-778-8311
Lehigh Safety Shoe Co 120 Plaza Dr Suite A	Vestal	NY	13850	**800-444-4086**	607-584-5000
Littonian Shoe Co PO Box 95	Littlestown	PA	17340	**888-790-3930**	717-359-5194
Lucchese Boot Co Inc 40 Walter Jones Blvd	El Paso	TX	79906	**800-637-6888**	915-778-8585
Lugz 155 6th Ave 9th Fl	New York	NY	10013	**800-648-8602**	212-691-4700
Madden Steven Ltd 52-16 Barnett Ave	Long Island City	NY	11104	**800-747-6233**	718-446-1800
NASDAQ: SHOO					
Marty's Shoes Inc 60 Enterprise Ave N	Secaucus	NJ	07094	**800-262-7897***	201-319-0500
*Cust Svc					
Meldisco 933 MacArthur Blvd	Mahwah	NJ	07430	**800-777-1330**	201-934-2000
Merrell Footwear 9341 Courtland Dr NE	Rockford	MI	49351	**888-637-7001***	616-866-5500
*Cust Svc					
Minor PW & Son Inc PO Box 678	Batavia	NY	14020	**800-524-1084**	585-343-1500
Mizuno USA 4925 Avalon Ridge Pkwy	Norcross	GA	30071	**800-333-7888**	770-441-5553
Montello Heel Mfg Inc 13 Emerson Ave	Brockton	MA	02305	**800-245-4335**	508-586-0603
Munro & Co PO Box 1157	Hot Springs	AR	71902	**800-826-8676**	501-262-6000
New Balance Athletic Shoe Inc					
20 Guest St Brighton Landing	Boston	MA	02135	**800-622-1218**	617-783-4000
Nike Inc 1 Bowerman Dr	Beaverton	OR	97005	**800-344-6453***	503-671-6453
NYSE: NKE ■ *Cust Svc					
Nina Footwear Co Inc 730 5th Ave 8th Fl	New York	NY	10019	**800-233-6462**	212-399-2323
Nine West Group Inc					
1129 Westchester Ave Nine West Plaza	White Plains	NY	10604	**800-260-2227**	914-640-6400
Nocona Boot Co 610 W Daggett St	Fort Worth	TX	76104	**800-545-8707**	817-332-4385
ONGUARD Industries 1850 Clark Rd	Havre de Grace	MD	21078	**800-365-2282**	410-272-2000
Otomix 3691 Lenawee Ave	Los Angeles	CA	90016	**800-701-7867**	310-815-4700
Payless ShoeSource Inc 3231 SE 6th St	Topeka	KS	66607	**800-444-7403***	785-233-5171
NYSE: PSS ■ *Cust Svc					
Phoenix Footwear Group Inc 107 Main St	Old Town	ME	04468	**800-341-1550**	207-827-4431
AMEX: PXG					
Priva Sport 8505 Devonshire Rd	Montreal	QC	H4P2L3	**877-568-8662**	514-341-9548
Propet USA Inc 25612 74th Ave S	Kent	WA	98032	**800-877-6738**	253-854-7600
Puma North America Inc 5 Lyberty Way	Westford	MA	01886	**800-662-7862**	978-698-1000
PW Minor & Son Inc PO Box 678	Batavia	NY	14020	**800-524-1084**	585-343-1500
Quabaug Corp 18 School St	North Brookfield	MA	01535	**800-325-5022**	508-867-7731
Red Wing Shoe Co Inc 314 Main St	Red Wing	MN	55066	**800-733-9464***	651-388-8211
*Cust Svc					
Reebok International Ltd 1895 JW Foster Blvd	Canton	MA	02021	**800-843-4444**	781-401-5000
NYSE: RBK					
Reef Brazil 9660 Chesapeake Dr	San Diego	CA	92123	**800-423-6855**	858-514-3600
RG Barry Corp 13405 Yarmouth Dr NW	Pickerington	OH	43147	**800-848-7560**	614-864-6400
Riddell Footwear 11426 Moog Dr	Saint Louis	MO	63146	**800-367-6822**	314-432-7171
Rockport Co Inc 1895 SW Foster Blvd	Canton	MA	02021	**800-762-5767**	781-401-5000
Rocky Shoes & Boots Inc 39 E Canal St	Nelsonville	OH	45764	**800-421-5151**	740-753-1951
NASDAQ: RCKY					
Salomon North America 5055 N Greeley Ave	Portland	OR	97217	**877-272-5666**	971-234-2300
Saucony Inc 13 Centennial Dr	Peabody	MA	01960	**800-365-4933**	978-532-9000
NASDAQ: SCNYA					
SBC/Sporto Corp 1100 Massachusetts Ave	Boston	MA	02125	**888-277-6786***	617-442-9778
*Cust Svc					
Sebago Inc 55 Hutcherson Dr	Gorham	ME	04038	**800-365-5505**	207-854-8474
Shoe Carnival Inc 8233 Baumgart Rd	Evansville	IN	47725	**800-430-7463***	812-867-6471
NASDAQ: SCVL ■ *Cust Svc					
Shoe Pavillion Inc 1380 Fitzgerald Dr	Pinole	CA	94564	**800-736-5523**	510-222-4405
NASDAQ: SHOE					
Shoe Show of Rocky Mountain Inc					
2201 Trinity Church Rd	Concord	NC	28027	**888-557-4637***	704-782-4143
*Cust Svc					
Shoes.com Inc					
11965 Venice Blvd Suite 404	Los Angeles	CA	90066	**888-233-6743***	310-566-7911
*Cust Svc					
Skechers USA Inc					
228 Manhattan Beach Blvd					
Suite 200	Manhattan Beach	CA	90266	**800-456-3627**	310-318-3100
NYSE: SKX					
South Cone Inc DBA Reef Brazil					
9660 Chesapeake Dr	San Diego	CA	92123	**800-423-6855**	858-514-3600
Spalding 150 Brookdale Dr	Springfield	MA	01104	**800-772-5346***	413-735-1400
*Cust Svc					
Spenco Medical Corp PO Box 2501	Waco	TX	76702	**800-877-3626**	254-772-6000
Sperry Top-Sider 191 Spring St	Lexington	MA	02421	**800-666-5689***	617-824-6000
*Cust Svc					
Steven Madden Ltd 52-16 Barnett Ave	Long Island City	NY	11104	**800-747-6233**	718-446-1800
NASDAQ: SHOO					
Stride Rite Corp 191 Spring St	Lexington	MA	02421	**800-666-5689***	617-824-6000
NYSE: SRR ■ *Cust Svc					
Super Shoe Stores Inc 601 Dual Hwy	Hagerstown	MD	21740	**888-392-2204**	301-766-7513
Taos Moccasins PO Box 708	Taos	NM	87571	**800-662-8267**	505-758-4276
Teva Sport Sandals PO Box 968	Flagstaff	AZ	86002	**800-367-8382***	928-779-5938
*Orders					
Texas Boot Co PO Box 17307	Nashville	TN	37217	**800-628-2668**	615-695-2000
Timberland Co 200 Domain Dr	Stratham	NH	03885	**800-258-0855**	603-772-9500
NYSE: TBL					
Tony Lama Boot Co Inc 1137 Tony Lama St	El Paso	TX	79915	**800-866-9526**	915-778-8311
Trimfoot Shoe Co 115 Trimfoot Terr	Farmington	MO	63640	**800-325-6116**	573-756-6616
TT Group Inc 702 Carnation Dr	Aurora	MO	65605	**800-445-0886**	417-678-2181
Vans Inc 15700 Shoemaker Ave	Santa Fe Springs	CA	90670	**800-826-7800**	562-565-8267
Weinbrenner Shoe Co Inc 108 S Polk St	Merrill	WI	54452	**800-826-0002***	715-536-5521
*Cust Svc					
Wellco Enterprises Inc 150 Westwood Cir	Waynesville	NC	28786	**800-840-3155**	828-456-3545
AMEX: WLC					
Wesco					
52828 NW Shoe Factory Ln PO Box 607	Scappoose	OR	97056	**800-326-2711**	503-543-7114
West Coast Shoe Co					
52828 NW Shoe Factory Ln PO Box 607	Scappoose	OR	97056	**800-326-2711**	503-543-7114
Willits Footwear Worldwide PO Box B	Halifax	PA	17032	**800-544-3633**	717-896-3411
Wolverine Slipper Group					
3290 Benchmark Dr Benchmark Bldg B	Ladson	SC	29456	**800-253-2184**	
Wolverine World Wide Inc					
9345 Courtland Dr NE	Rockford	MI	49351	**800-626-8696**	616-866-5500
NYSE: WWW					

297 FORESTRY SERVICES

SEE ALSO Timber Tracts

Company	City	State	ZIP	Toll-Free	Phone
Merrill & Ring Inc					
813 E 8th St PO Box 1058	Port Angeles	WA	98362	**800-827-2367**	360-452-2367
Resource Management Service Inc					
100 Corporate Ridge Suite 200	Birmingham	AL	35242	**800-995-9516**	205-991-9516

Classified Section

Name / Address	City	State	Zip	Toll-Free	Phone
Timberland Management Services Inc PO Box 819	Centreville	MS	39631	**800-306-6439**	601-645-6440
UAP Timberland LLC 140 Arkansas St	Monticello	AR	71655	**800-752-7009**	870-367-8561
Western Forest Products Inc 435 Trunk Rd 3rd Fl *TSE: WEF*	Duncan	BC	V9L2P9	**800-880-7471**	250-748-3711

298 FOUNDATIONS - COMMUNITY

SEE ALSO Associations & Organizations - General - Charitable & Humanitarian Organizations

Name / Address	City	State	Zip	Toll-Free	Phone
Arizona Community Foundation 2122 E Highland Suite 400	Phoenix	AZ	85016	**800-222-8221**	602-381-1400
California Endowment 21650 Oxnard St Suite 1200	Woodland Hills	CA	91367	**800-449-4149**	818-703-3311
Colorado Trust 1600 Sherman St	Denver	CO	80203	**888-847-9140**	303-837-1200
Dayton Foundation 2300 Kettering Tower	Dayton	OH	45423	**877-222-0410**	937-222-0410
El Pomar Foundation 10 Lake Cir	Colorado Springs	CO	80906	**800-554-7711**	719-633-7733
Foundation for the Carolinas 217 S Tryon St	Charlotte	NC	28202	**888-335-9541**	704-973-4500
Hawaii Community Foundation 1164 Bishop St Suite 800	Honolulu	HI	96813	**888-731-3863**	808-537-6333
Northwest Area Foundation 60 Plato Blvd E Suite 400	Saint Paul	MN	55107	**888-904-9821**	651-224-9635

299 FOUNDATIONS - CORPORATE

SEE ALSO Associations & Organizations - General - Charitable & Humanitarian Organizations

Name / Address	City	State	Zip	Toll-Free	Phone
AT & T Foundation 32 Ave of the Americas Rm 2417	New York	NY	10013	**800-428-8652**	212-387-4801
Bank of America Foundation 315 Montgomery St 8th Fl MS CA5-704-08-03	San Francisco	CA	94104	**888-488-9802**	415-953-3175
Cisco Systems Foundation 170 W Tasman Dr	San Jose	CA	95134	**800-553-6387**	408-527-3040
Eli Lilly & Co Foundation Lilly Corporate Ctr	Indianapolis	IN	46285	**800-545-5979**	317-276-0464
GlaxoSmithKline Foundation 5 Moore Dr	Research Triangle Park	NC	27709	**888-825-5249**	919-483-2140
Lutheran Brotherhood Foundation 625 4th Ave S Suite 1415	Minneapolis	MN	55415	**800-365-4172**	
New York Life Foundation 51 Madison Ave Suite 1600	New York	NY	10010	**800-710-7945**	212-576-7341
Sara Lee Foundation 3 First National Plaza 47th Fl	Chicago	IL	60602	**800-727-2533**	312-558-8448
SBC Foundation 130 E Travis St Suite 350	San Antonio	TX	78205	**800-591-9663**	210-351-2210
Siemens Foundation 170 Wood Ave S	Iselin	NJ	08830	**877-822-5233**	732-603-5886
Wal-Mart Foundation 702 SW 8th St	Bentonville	AR	72716	**800-530-9925**	
Wells Fargo Foundation 550 California St 7th Fl	San Francisco	CA	94104	**888-886-1785**	415-396-3567

300 FOUNDATIONS - PRIVATE

SEE ALSO Associations & Organizations - General - Charitable & Humanitarian Organizations

Name / Address	City	State	Zip	Toll-Free	Phone
Annie E Casey Foundation 701 Saint Paul St	Baltimore	MD	21202	**800-222-1099**	410-547-6600
Bill & Melinda Gates Foundation PO Box 23350	Seattle	WA	98102	**888-452-6352**	206-709-3100
Casey Annie E Foundation 701 Saint Paul St	Baltimore	MD	21202	**800-222-1099**	410-547-6600
Corporation for Public Broadcasting (CPB) 401 9th St NW	Washington	DC	20004	**800-272-2190**	202-879-9600
Dave Thomas Foundation for Adoption 4288 W Dublin Granville Rd	Dublin	OH	43017	**800-275-3832**	614-764-8454
Dow Herbert H & Grace A Foundation 1018 W Main St	Midland	MI	48640	**800-362-4849**	989-631-3699
Ewing Marion Kauffman Foundation 4801 Rockhill Rd	Kansas City	MO	64110	**800-489-4900**	816-932-1000
Gates Bill & Melinda Foundation PO Box 23350	Seattle	WA	98102	**888-452-6352**	206-709-3100
Herbert H & Grace A Dow Foundation 1018 W Main St	Midland	MI	48640	**800-362-4849**	989-631-3699
John D & Catherine T MacArthur Foundation 140 S Dearborn St Suite 1100	Chicago	IL	60603	**800-662-8004**	312-726-8000
John S & James L Knight Foundation 200 S Biscayne Blvd Suite 3300	Miami	FL	33131	**800-711-2004**	305-908-2600
Johnson Magic Foundation Inc 9100 Wilshire Blvd East Tower Suite 700	Beverly Hills	CA	90212	**888-624-4205**	310-246-4400
Knight John S & James L Foundation 200 S Biscayne Blvd Suite 3300	Miami	FL	33131	**800-711-2004**	305-908-2600
Lumina Foundation for Education 30 S Meridian St Suite 700	Indianapolis	IN	46204	**800-834-5756**	317-951-5704
MacArthur John D & Catherine T Foundation 140 S Dearborn St Suite 1100	Chicago	IL	60603	**800-662-8004**	312-726-8000
Magic Johnson Foundation Inc 9100 Wilshire Blvd East Tower Suite 700	Beverly Hills	CA	90212	**888-624-4205**	310-246-4400
Meadows Foundation Inc 3003 Swiss Ave	Dallas	TX	75204	**800-826-9431**	214-826-9431
Michael J Fox Foundation for Parkinson's Research PO Box 4777 Grand Central Stn	New York	NY	10163	**800-708-7644**	
Nellie Mae Education Foundation 1250 Hancock St Suite 205N	Quincy	MA	02169	**877-635-5436**	781-348-4200
Pew Charitable Trusts 2005 Market St 1 Commerce Sq Suite 1700	Philadelphia	PA	19103	**800-634-4850**	215-575-9050
Public Welfare Foundation Inc 1200 U St NW	Washington	DC	20009	**800-275-7934**	202-965-1800
Rockefeller Foundation 420 5th Ave	New York	NY	10018	**800-645-1133**	212-869-8500
Thomas Dave Foundation for Adoption 4288 W Dublin Granville Rd	Dublin	OH	43017	**800-275-3832**	614-764-8454
Wallace Foundation 2 Park Ave 23rd Fl	New York	NY	10016	**800-771-9701**	212-251-9700

301 FOUNDRIES - INVESTMENT

Name / Address	City	State	Zip	Toll-Free	Phone
Northern Precision Casting Co Inc PO Box 580	Lake Geneva	WI	53147	**800-934-4903**	262-248-4461
Remet Corp 210 Commons Rd	Utica	NY	13502	**800-445-2424**	315-797-8700
Waltek Inc 14310 Sunfish Lake Blvd NW	Ramsey	MN	55303	**800-937-9496**	763-427-3181
Wyman-Gordon Co 244 Worcester St	North Grafton	MA	01536	**800-343-6070**	508-839-4441

302 FOUNDRIES - IRON & STEEL

SEE ALSO Foundries - Nonferrous (Castings)

Name / Address	City	State	Zip	Toll-Free	Phone
Allegheny Technologies Inc 6 PPG Pl Suite 1000 *NYSE: ATI* ■ *Sales	Pittsburgh	PA	15222	**800-258-3586***	412-394-2800
American Cast Iron Pipe Co (ACIPCO) 2916 16th St N	Birmingham	AL	35207	**800-442-2347**	205-325-7701
American Drill Bushing Co 2000 Camfield Ave	Los Angeles	CA	90040	**800-423-4425**	323-725-1515
Atlantic States Cast Iron Pipe Co 183 Sitgreaves St	Phillipsburg	NJ	08865	**800-859-1161**	908-454-1161
Blackhawk Foundry & Machine Co 323 S Clark St	Davenport	IA	52802	**800-325-4766**	563-323-3621
Bremen Castings Inc 500 N Baltimore St	Bremen	IN	46506	**800-837-2411**	574-546-2411
Campbell Foundry Co 800 Bergen St	Harrison	NJ	07029	**800-843-4766**	973-483-5480
Castalloy Inc 1701 Industrial Ln	Waukesha	WI	53189	**800-211-0900**	262-547-0070
Columbia Steel Casting Co Inc PO Box 83095	Portland	OR	97283	**800-547-9471**	503-286-0685
Delta Centrifugal Corp PO Box 1043 *Sales	Temple	TX	76503	**800-433-3100***	254-773-9055
Duraloy Technologies Inc 120 Bridge St	Scottdale	PA	15683	**800-823-5101**	724-887-5100
East Jordan Iron Works Inc 301 Spring St	East Jordan	MI	49727	**800-874-4100**	231-536-2261
Gartland Foundry Co Inc PO Box 1564	Terre Haute	IN	47808	**800-237-0226**	812-232-0226
Goldens' Foundry & Machine Co 600 12th St	Columbus	GA	31901	**800-328-8379**	706-323-0471
Hensley Industries Inc 2108 Joe Field Rd PO Box 29779	Dallas	TX	75229	**888-406-6262**	972-241-2321
Hunt Rodney Co Inc 46 Mill St	Orange	MA	01364	**800-448-8860**	978-544-2511
Jencast 1004 W 14th	Coffeyville	KS	67337	**800-796-6630**	620-251-7802
KP Iron Foundry Inc 4731 E Vine Ave	Fresno	CA	93725	**800-655-2590**	559-233-2591
ME Global 3901 University Ave NE	Minneapolis	MN	55421	**800-328-3858**	763-788-1651
Neenah Foundry Co 2121 Brooks Ave	Neenah	WI	54956	**800-558-5075**	920-725-7000
Ohio Cast Products Inc 2408 13th St NE	Canton	OH	44705	**800-909-2278**	330-456-4784
Quaker City Castings Inc 310 Euclid St	Salem	OH	44460	**800-445-8853**	330-332-1566
Rodney Hunt Co Inc 46 Mill St	Orange	MA	01364	**800-448-8860**	978-544-2511
Russell Pipe & Foundry Co Inc Hwy 22 W	Alexander City	AL	35010	**800-824-4513**	256-234-2514
Sioux City Foundry Co 801 Division St	Sioux City	IA	51102	**800-831-0874**	712-252-4181
Sivyer Steel Corp 225 S 33rd St	Bettendorf	IA	52722	**800-474-8937**	563-355-1811
Spokane Steel Foundry Co 3808 N Sullivan Rd Bldg 1	Spokane	WA	99220	**800-541-3601**	509-924-0440
Standard Alloys & Mfg PO Box 969	Port Arthur	TX	77640	**800-231-8240**	409-983-3201
Sturgis Foundry Corp PO Box 568	Sturgis	MI	49091	**800-809-7203**	269-651-8544
Talladega Castings & Machine Co Inc 228 N Court St	Talladega	AL	35160	**800-766-6708**	256-362-5550
Talladega Machinery & Supply Co Inc PO Box 736 *Cust Svc	Talladega	AL	35161	**800-289-8672***	256-362-4124
Wells Mfg Co 2100 W Lake Shore Dr	Woodstock	IL	60098	**800-227-6455**	815-338-3900
Zurn Cast Metals Operation 1301 Raspberry St	Erie	PA	16502	**877-875-1404**	814-455-0921

303 FOUNDRIES - NONFERROUS (CASTINGS)

SEE ALSO Foundries - Iron & Steel

Name / Address	City	State	Zip	Toll-Free	Phone
Bunting Bearings Corp 1001 Holland Park Blvd	Holland	OH	43528	**888-228-9899**	419-866-7000
C & H Die Casting Inc PO Box 1170	Temple	TX	76503	**800-433-3148**	254-938-2541
Cambridge Tool & Mfg Co Inc 67 Faulkner St	North Billerica	MA	01862	**888-333-9798**	978-667-8400
Consolidated Metco Inc 13940 N Rivergate Blvd *Sales	Portland	OR	97203	**800-547-9473***	503-286-5741
Deco Products Co 506 Sanford St	Decorah	IA	52101	**800-327-9751**	
Del Mar Die Casting Co 12901 S Western Ave	Gardena	CA	90249	**800-624-7468**	323-321-0600
Delta Centrifugal Corp PO Box 1043 *Sales	Temple	TX	76503	**800-433-3100***	254-773-9055
Electric Materials Co 50 S Washington St	North East	PA	16428	**800-356-2211**	814-725-9621
Empire Die Casting Co Inc 635 Highland Rd E	Macedonia	OH	44056	**800-297-5724**	330-467-0750
Falcon Foundry Co 96 6th St	Lowellville	OH	44436	**800-253-8624**	330-536-6221
General Die Casters Inc 2150 Highland Rd	Twinsburg	OH	44087	**800-332-2278**	330-657-2300
Halex Co 23901 Aurora Rd	Bedford Heights	OH	44146	**800-749-3261**	440-439-1616
Lee Brass Co PO Box 1229	Anniston	AL	36202	**800-876-1811**	256-831-2501
Littlestown Foundry Inc 150 Charles St PO Box 69	Littlestown	PA	17340	**800-471-0844**	717-359-4141
Magnolia Metal Corp 6161 Abbott	Omaha	NE	68119	**800-228-4043**	402-455-8760

Company	City	State	Zip	Toll-Free	Phone
Matthews International Corp 2 Northshore Ctr Suite 200 *NASDAQ: MATW*	Pittsburgh	PA	15212	**800-223-4964**	412-442-8200
Matthews International Corp Bronze Div 1315 W Liberty Ave	Pittsburgh	PA	15226	**888-838-8890**	412-571-5500
NGK Metals Corp 917 US Hwy 11 S *Sales	Sweetwater	TN	37874	**800-523-8268***	423-337-5500
Piad Precision Casting Corp RD 12 Box 38	Greensburg	PA	15601	**800-441-9858**	724-838-5500
Premier Die Casting Co 1177 Rahway Ave	Avenel	NJ	07001	**800-394-3006**	732-634-3000
Premier Tool & Die Cast Corp 9886 N Tudor Rd	Berrien Springs	MI	49103	**800-417-8717**	269-471-7715
Progress Casting Group Inc 2600 Niagara Ln N	Plymouth	MN	55447	**800-866-3025**	763-557-1000
Saint Clair Die Casting LLC 225 St Clair Industrial Park Dr	Saint Clair	MO	63077	**800-367-7232**	636-629-2550
Southern Centrifugal Inc 4180 S Creek Rd	Chattanooga	TN	37406	**800-722-7277**	423-622-4131
Stroh Die Casting Co Inc 11123 W Burleigh St *Cust Svc	Milwaukee	WI	53222	**800-843-2871***	414-771-7100
Talladega Castings & Machine Co Inc 228 N Court St	Talladega	AL	35160	**800-766-6708**	256-362-5550
ThyssenKrupp Stahl Co 11 E Pacific PO Box 6	Kingsville	MO	64061	**888-395-1042**	816-597-3322
Ward Aluminum Casting Co 642 Growth Ave	Fort Wayne	IN	46808	**866-427-8700**	260-426-8700

FRAMES & MOULDINGS - METAL

SEE Doors & Windows - Metal

304 FRAMES & MOULDINGS - WOOD

Company	City	State	Zip	Toll-Free	Phone
Alexandria Moulding 95 Lochiel St E	Alexandria	ON	K0C1A0	**800-267-1773**	613-525-2784
Art-O-Rama Inc 510 5th Ave	Pelham	NY	10803	**800-421-2438**	914-738-1138
Colonial Craft 2270 Woodale Dr	Mounds View	MN	55112	**800-727-5187**	763-231-4000
Contact Lumber Co 9200 SE Sunnybrook Blvd Suite 200	Clackamas	OR	97015	**800-547-1038**	503-228-7361
Cooper Wood Products Inc 2785 Grassy Hill Rd	Rocky Mount	VA	24151	**800-262-3453**	540-483-9201
Groovfold Inc 1050 W State St	Newcomerstown	OH	43832	**800-367-1133**	740-498-8363
Harris-Tarkett Inc 2225 Eddie Williams Rd *Cust Svc	Johnson City	TN	37601	**800-842-7816***	423-928-3122
HB Williamson Co PO Box 1687 *Orders	Mount Vernon	IL	62864	**800-851-2467***	618-244-9000
Kendall-Hartcraft PO Box 11670	Huntsville	AL	35814	**800-421-7435**	256-859-5533
Kendall-Hartcraft 1480 Independence Ave PO Box 270465	Hartford	WI	53027	**800-558-7834**	262-673-3440
Larson-Juhl 3900 Steve Reynolds Blvd	Norcross	GA	30093	**800-438-5031**	770-279-5200
Marley Mouldings Ltd Hwy 11 W Bearcreek Rd	Marion	VA	24354	**800-368-3117**	276-783-8161
MillSource PO Box 170	Montevallo	AL	35115	**800-756-0199**	205-665-2546
Monarch Industries Inc 99 Main St	Warren	RI	02885	**800-669-9663**	401-247-5200
North American Enclosures Inc 65 Jetson Ln	Central Islip	NY	11722	**800-645-9209**	631-234-9500
PB & H Moulding Corp 124 Pickard Dr E	Syracuse	NY	13211	**800-746-9724**	315-455-5602
Peterson Picture Frame Co Inc 2720 W Belmont Ave	Chicago	IL	60641	**800-293-7011**	773-463-8888
Pinnacle Frames & Accents Inc 2606 Hwy 67 S PO Box 507	Pocahontas	AR	72455	**800-231-9974**	870-892-5227
Sunset Moulding Co Inc 2231 Paseo Ave	Live Oak	CA	95953	**800-824-5888**	530-695-1801
Tara Picture Frames 7615 Siempre Viva Rd	San Diego	CA	92154	**800-788-9969**	619-671-1018
Thunderbird Forest Products 8180 Industrial Pkwy	Sacramento	CA	95824	**800-824-5104**	916-381-4200
Uniek Inc 805 Uniek Dr	Waunakee	WI	53597	**800-248-6435**	608-849-9999

305 FRANCHISES

SEE ALSO Auto Supply Stores; Automotive Services; Bakeries; Beauty Salons; Business Service Centers; Candles; Car Rental Agencies; Children's Learning Centers; Cleaning Services; Construction - Special Trade Contractors - Remodeling, Refinishing, Resurfacing Contractors; Convenience Stores; Dairy Product Stores; Health Food Stores; Home Inspection Services; Hotel & Resort Operation & Management; Laundry & Drycleaning Services; Optical Goods Stores; Pest Control Services; Printing Companies - Commercial Printers; Real Estate Agents & Brokers; Restaurants; Staffing Services; Travel Agency Networks; Weight Loss Centers & Services

Company	City	State	Zip	Toll-Free	Phone
1 Hour Martinizing Dry Cleaning Stores 422 Wards Corner Rd	Loveland	OH	45140	**800-827-0207**	513-351-6211
7-Eleven Inc PO Box 711 *NYSE: SE*	Dallas	TX	75221	**800-255-0711**	214-828-7011
AAMCO Transmissions Inc 1 Presidential Blvd *Cust Svc	Bala Cynwyd	PA	19004	**800-523-0401***	610-668-2900
ABC Seamless Siding 3001 Fiechtner Dr	Fargo	ND	58103	**800-732-6577**	701-293-5952
ACE Cash Express Inc 1231 Greenway Dr Suite 800 *NASDAQ: AACE* ■ *Sales	Irving	TX	75038	**800-713-3338***	972-550-5000
Adecco Inc 175 Broad Hollow Rd *NYSE: ADO*	Melville	NY	11747	**877-632-9169**	631-844-7800
Adventures in Advertising 101 Commerce St	Oshkosh	WI	54901	**800-460-7836**	920-236-7272
Affiliated Car Rental LC DBA Sensible Car Rental Inc 96 Freneau Ave Suite 2	Matawan	NJ	07747	**800-367-5159**	732-583-8500
Affordable Car Rental System Inc 96 Freneau Ave Suite 2	Matawan	NJ	07747	**800-631-2290**	732-290-8300
Algonquin Travel Corp 130 Merton St *Cust Svc	Toronto	ON	M4S1A4	**888-599-0789***	416-485-1700
Allegra Network LLC 21680 Haggerty Rd	Northville	MI	48167	**800-726-9050**	248-596-8600
Aloette Cosmetics Inc 4900 Highlands Pkwy	Smyrna	GA	30082	**800-256-3883**	678-444-2563
AlphaGraphics Inc 268 S State St Suite 300	Salt Lake City	UT	84111	**800-955-6246**	801-595-7270
American Leak Detection Inc 888 Research Dr Suite 100	Palm Springs	CA	92262	**800-755-6697**	760-320-9991
American Poolplayers Assn (APA) 1000 Lake St Louis Blvd Suite 325	Lake Saint Louis	MO	63367	**800-372-2536**	636-625-8611
AmeriSpec Inc 889 Ridgelake Blvd	Memphis	TN	38120	**800-426-2270**	901-820-8500
Apparelmaster 123 Harrison Ave	Harrison	OH	45030	**877-543-1678**	513-202-1600
Arby's Inc 1000 Corporate Dr	Fort Lauderdale	FL	33334	**800-487-2729**	954-351-5100
Assist-2-Sell Inc 1610 Meadow Wood Ln	Reno	NV	89502	**800-528-7816**	775-688-6060
Athlete's Foot Group Inc 1950 Vaughn Rd	Kennesaw	GA	30144	**800-524-6444**	770-514-4500
ATL International Inc 8334 Veterans Hwy	Millersville	MD	21108	**800-935-8863**	410-987-1011
Atlanta Bread Co International Inc 1955 Lake Park Dr Suite 400	Smyrna	GA	30080	**800-398-3728**	770-432-0933
Au Bon Pain 19 Fid Kennedy Ave	Boston	MA	02210	**800-825-5227**	617-423-2100
Badger Daylighting Inc 6740 65th Ave	Red Deer	AB	T4P1A5	**800-465-4273**	403-343-0303
Bakers Square Restaurants Inc 400 W 48th Ave	Denver	CO	80216	**800-800-3644**	303-296-2121
Baskin-Robbins 130 Royall St	Canton	MA	02021	**800-859-5339**	781-737-3000
Bathcrest Inc 5195 W 4700 S	Salt Lake City	UT	84118	**800-826-6790**	801-972-1110
Batteries Plus 925 Walnut Ridge Dr Suite 100	Hartland	WI	53029	**800-274-9155**	262-369-0690
Bennigan's 6500 International Pkwy Suite 1000	Plano	TX	75093	**800-727-8355**	972-588-5000
Berlitz International Inc 400 Alexander Pk	Princeton	NJ	08540	**800-257-9449**	609-514-9650
Big Apple Bagels 500 Lake Cook Rd Suite 475	Deerfield	IL	60015	**800-251-6101**	847-948-7520
Big Boy Restaurants International LLC 4199 Marcy St	Warren	MI	48091	**800-837-3003**	586-759-6000
Big O Tires Inc 12650 E Briarwood Ave Suite 2D	Englewood	CO	80112	**800-321-2446**	303-728-5500
Blimpie International Inc 145 Huguenot St Suite 410	New Rochelle	NY	10801	**800-447-6258**	914-576-1006
Bojangles' Restaurants Inc 9432 Southern Pine Blvd	Charlotte	NC	28273	**800-366-9921**	704-527-2675
Bonanza Restaurants 6500 International Pkwy Suite 1000	Plano	TX	75093	**800-727-8355**	972-588-5000
Bonus Building Care Inc PO Box 300	Indianola	OK	74442	**800-931-1102**	918-823-4990
Breadeaux Pisa Inc 3308 S Leonard Rd	Saint Joseph	MO	64503	**800-835-6534**	816-364-1088
BrickKicker Inc 849 N Ellsworth St	Naperville	IL	60563	**800-821-1820**	630-420-9900
Brown's Chicken & Pasta Inc 489 W Fullerton Ave	Elmhurst	IL	60126	**888-582-7700**	630-617-8800
Budget Blinds Inc 1927 N Glassell St	Orange	CA	92865	**800-420-5374**	714-637-2108
Budget Rent A Car System Inc 6 Sylvan Way	Parsippany	NJ	07054	**800-527-0700**	973-496-3500
Burger King Restaurants of Canada Inc 401 The West Mall 7th Fl	Etobicoke	ON	M9C5J4	**888-252-8280**	416-626-6464
Butterfly Life 2404 San Ramon Valley Blvd Suite 200	San Ramon	CA	94583	**800-288-8373**	
C-Street Bakery 2930 W Maple St	Sioux Falls	SD	57107	**800-336-1320**	605-336-6961
California Closet Co 1000 4th St Suite 800	San Rafael	CA	94901	**800-873-4264**	415-256-8500
Candy Bouquet International Inc 423 E 3rd St	Little Rock	AR	72201	**877-226-3901**	501-375-9990
Captain D's LLC 1717 Elm Hill Pike Suite A-1	Nashville	TN	37210	**800-314-4819**	615-391-5461
Car-X Assoc Corp 1375 E Woodfield Rd Suite 500	Schaumburg	IL	60173	**800-359-2359**	847-273-8920
Career Blazers Inc 222 W Las Colinas Blvd Suite 1250E	Irving	TX	75039	**800-787-6750**	214-296-6700
Carl's Jr Restaurants 401 W Carl Karcher Way	Anaheim	CA	92803	**800-422-4141**	714-774-5796
Carlson Wagonlit Travel Assoc 701 Carlson Pkwy	Minnetonka	MN	55305	**800-335-8747**	763-212-4000
CARSTAR Quality Collision Service 8400 W 110th St Suite 200	Overland Park	KS	66210	**800-227-7827**	913-451-1294
Carvel Franchising 200 Glenridge Point Pkwy Suite 200	Atlanta	GA	30342	**800-227-8353**	404-255-3250
CD Warehouse Inc 900 N Broadway	Oklahoma City	OK	73102	**800-641-9394**	405-236-8742
Century 21 Real Estate Corp 1 Campus Dr	Parsippany	NJ	07054	**800-221-5737**	973-428-9700
Certa ProPainters Ltd 150 Green Tree Rd Suite 1003	Oaks	PA	19456	**800-462-3782**	610-983-9411
Champion Auto Stores Inc 2565 Kasota Ave	Saint Paul	MN	55108	**800-899-6528**	651-644-6448
Checkers Drive-In Restaurants Inc 4300 W Cypress St Suite 600 *NASDAQ: CHKR*	Tampa	FL	33607	**800-800-8072**	813-283-7000
Chem-Dry Carpet Drapery & Upholstery Cleaning 1530 N 1000 W	Logan	UT	84321	**800-841-6583**	435-755-0099
Children's Orchard Inc 900 Victors Way Suite 200	Ann Arbor	MI	48108	**800-999-5437**	734-994-9199
Church's Chicken Inc 980 Hammond Dr NE Suite 1100	Atlanta	GA	30328	**866-232-9402**	770-350-3800
CleanNet USA Inc 9861 Brokenland Pkwy Suite 208	Columbia	MD	21046	**800-735-8838**	410-720-6444
Closet Factory 12800 S Broadway	Los Angeles	CA	90061	**800-692-5673**	310-516-7000
Coffee Beanery Ltd 3429 Pierson Pl	Flushing	MI	48433	**800-728-2326**	810-733-1020
Coffee People Inc 28 Executive Park Suite 200	Irvine	CA	92614	**800-354-5282**	949-260-1600
College Pro Painters Ltd 200 Dexter Ave 2nd Fl	Watertown	MA	02472	**800-327-2468**	617-924-1300
Color-Glo International 7111 Ohms Ln	Minneapolis	MN	55439	**800-333-8523**	952-835-1338
Colors on Parade 642 Century Cir	Conway	SC	29526	**800-929-3363**	843-347-8818
ColorTyme Inc 5700 Tennyson Pkwy Suite 180	Plano	TX	75024	**800-411-8963**	972-608-5376
Complete Music Inc 7877 L St	Omaha	NE	68127	**800-843-3866**	402-339-0001
COMPUTER EXPLORERS Inc 12715 Telge Rd	Cypress	TX	77429	**800-531-5053**	281-256-4100
Contours Express Inc 156 Imperial Way	Nicholasville	KY	40356	**877-227-2282**	859-885-6441
Cookie Bouquet 6757 Arapaho Rd Suite 707	Dallas	TX	75248	**800-752-8412**	972-386-7334
Cost Cutters Family Hair Care Div Regis Corp 7201 Metro Blvd	Minneapolis	MN	55439	**888-888-7778**	952-947-7777
Cottman Transmission Systems Inc 240 New York Dr	Fort Washington	PA	19034	**800-394-6116**	215-643-5885
Country Kitchen International 801 Deming Way	Madison	WI	53717	**888-359-3235**	608-833-9633
Cousins Subs Inc N 83 W 13400 Leon Rd	Menomonee Falls	WI	53051	**800-238-9736**	262-253-7700
Coustic-Glo International 7111 Ohms Ln	Minneapolis	MN	55439	**800-333-8523**	952-835-1338
Coverall North America Inc 500 W Cypress Creek Rd Suite 580	Fort Lauderdale	FL	33309	**800-537-3371**	954-351-1110
Craig Jenny International Inc 5770 Fleet St	Carlsbad	CA	92008	**800-443-2331**	760-696-4000
Cruise Holidays International Inc 701 Carlson Pkwy	Minnetonka	MN	55305	**800-866-7245**	

Toll-Free Phone

CruiseOne Inc
1415 NW 62nd St Suite 205 .... Fort Lauderdale FL 33309 **800-832-3592** 954-958-3700
Culligan International Co 1 Culligan Pkwy....Northbrook IL 60062 **800-285-5442** 847-205-6000
Cumberland Farms Inc Gulf Div
777 Dedham St .... Canton MA 02021 **800-843-8028** 781-828-4900
Curves International Inc 100 Ritchie Rd .... Waco TX 76712 **800-848-1096** 254-399-9285
Damon's International Inc
4645 Executive Dr .... Columbus OH 43220 **800-226-7427** 614-442-7900
Davis Paul Restoration Inc
1 Independence Dr Suite 2300 .... Jacksonville FL 32202 **800-722-1818** 904-737-2779
Daylight Corp 11707 E 11th St................. Tulsa OK 74128 **800-331-2245** 918-438-0800
Deck The Walls Inc
101 S Hanley Rd Suite 1280.............Saint Louis MO 63105 **866-719-8200** 314-719-8200
Decorating Den Systems Inc
19100 Montgomery Village Ave
Suite 200 ....Montgomery Village MD 20886 **800-428-1366** 301-272-1500
Del Taco Inc
25521 Commercentre Dr Suite 200....... Lake Forest CA 92630 **800-852-7204*** 949-462-9300
*Cust Svc
Diet Center Worldwide Inc 395 Springside Dr..... Akron OH 44333 **800-656-3294** 330-665-5861
Discount Car & Truck Rentals Ltd
720 Arrow Rd .... North York ON M9M2M1 **866-742-5968** 416-744-0123
Dollar Discount Stores of America Inc
1362 Naamans Creek Rd................. Boothwyn PA 19061 **800-227-5314** 610-497-1991
Dollar Rent A Car Inc 5330 E 31st St .... Tulsa OK 74135 **800-800-4000** 918-669-3000
Domino's Pizza Inc
30 Frank Lloyd Wright Dr .... Ann Arbor MI 48106 **888-366-4667** 734-930-3030
NYSE: DPZ
Dr Vinyl & Assoc Ltd
821 NW Commerce Dr................Lee's Summit MO 64086 **800-531-6600** 816-525-6060
Dreammaker Bath & Kitchen by Worldwide
PO Box 3146 .... Waco TX 76707 **800-583-9099** 254-745-2477
Dryclean USA Inc 290 NE 68th St ....Miami FL 33138 **800-746-4583** 305-758-0066
AMEX: DCU
Dunhill Staffing Systems Inc
9190 Priority Way W Suite 204.......... Indianapolis IN 46240 **800-386-7823** 317-818-4910
Dunkin' Donuts Inc 14 Pacella Park Dr .... Randolph MA 02368 **800-859-5339*** 781-961-4000
*Cust Svc
Duraclean International Inc
220 Campus Dr ....Arlington Heights IL 60004 **800-251-7070*** 847-704-7100
*Cust Svc
Econo Lube N' Tune Inc PO Box 2470... Newport Beach CA 92658 **800-478-3795** 949-851-2259
Educate Inc 1001 Fleet St.................. Baltimore MD 21202 **888-338-2283** 410-843-8000
Einstein/Noah Bagel Corp 1687 Cole Blvd....... Golden CO 80401 **800-660-3200*** 303-568-8000
*Cust Svc
El Chico Restaurants Inc
12200 N Stemmons Fwy Suite 100............Dallas TX 75234 **800-275-1334** 972-241-5500
ERA Franchise Systems Inc 1 Campus Dr.... Parsippany NJ 07054 **800-869-1260** 973-428-9700
ET3 LLC DBA ExecuTrain Corp
2500 Northwinds Pkwy Suite 600..........Alpharetta GA 30004 **800-908-7246** 770-521-1964
Expetic Technology Service 12 2nd Ave SW... Aberdeen SD 57401 **888-297-2292** 605-225-4122
Express Oil Change 190 W Valley Ave...... Birmingham AL 35209 **888-945-1771** 205-945-1771
Express Services Inc
8516 Northwest Expy............... Oklahoma City OK 73162 **800-652-6400** 405-840-5000
Fastframe USA Inc
1200 Lawrence Dr Suite 300.......... Newbury Park CA 91320 **888-863-7263** 805-498-4463
FASTSIGNS International Inc
2550 Midway Rd Suite 150...............Carrollton TX 75006 **800-827-7446** 972-447-0777
Fiducial Franchising
10480 Little Patuxent Pkwy 3rd Fl.......... Columbia MD 21044 **800-323-9000** 410-910-5885
Figaro's Italian Pizza Inc
1500 Liberty St SE Suite 160 ....Salem OR 97302 **888-344-2767** 503-371-9318
First Action Security 18702 Crestwood Dr ... Hagerstown MD 21742 **800-342-4243** 301-797-2124
First Choice Haircutters
6465 Millcreek Dr Suite 210 .... Mississauga ON L5N5R6 **800-361-2887** 905-821-8555
Floor Coverings International
5182 Old Dixie Hwy Suite B .... Forest Park GA 30297 **800-955-4324*** 404-361-5047
*Sales
Form-You 3 International Inc 395 Springside Dr... Akron OH 44333 **800-525-6315** 330-668-1461
Four Seasons Sunrooms
5005 Veterans Memorial Hwy .... Holbrook NY 11741 **800-368-7732** 631-563-4000
Fourth R Inc 11410 NE 124th St Suite 142 ..... Kirkland WA 98034 **800-821-8653** 425-814-1001
Fox's Distribution Inc
3243 Old Frankstown Rd................ Pittsburgh PA 15239 **800-899-3697** 724-733-7888
Fred Astaire Dance Studios Inc
10 Bliss Rd .... Longmeadow MA 01106 **800-278-2473** 413-567-3200
Freshens Quality Brands 1750 The Exchange ..... Atlanta GA 30339 **800-633-4519** 678-627-5400
Friendly's Restaurants 1855 Boston Rd...... Wilbraham MA 01095 **800-966-9970** 413-543-2400
Furniture Medic Inc
3839 Forrest Hill Irene Rd................ Memphis TN 38125 **800-877-9933** 901-597-8600
Futurekids Inc
1000 N Studebaker Rd Suite 1 .... Long Beach CA 90815 **800-765-8000** 562-296-1111
Gateway Newstands Inc
9555 Yonge St Suite 400............. Richmond Hill ON L4C9M5 **800-942-5351** 905-737-7755
Glamour Shots 1300 Metropolitan Ave .... Oklahoma City OK 73108 **800-336-4550**
Gloria Jean's Gourmet Coffees
28 Executive Pk Suite 200.................... Irvine CA 92614 **800-354-5282** 949-260-1600
GNC Corp 300 6th Ave..................... Pittsburgh PA 15222 **888-462-2548*** 412-288-4600
*Cust Svc
GNC Franchising Inc 300 6th Ave........... Pittsburgh PA 15222 **800-259-5008** 412-288-4600
Godfather's Pizza Inc 9140 W Dodge Rd........ Omaha NE 68114 **800-456-8347** 402-391-1452
Golden Corral Corp 5151 Glenwood Ave ....Raleigh NC 27612 **800-284-5673** 919-781-9310
Gold's Gym International 358 Hampton Dr ...... Venice CA 90291 **800-457-5375** 310-392-3005
Golf USA
3705 W Memorial Rd Suite 801 .... Oklahoma City OK 73134 **800-488-1107** 405-751-0015
Grand Rental Station 203 Jandus Rd............. Cary IL 60013 **800-833-3004** 847-462-5440
Grease Monkey International Inc
633 17th St Suite 400...................... Denver CO 80202 **800-822-7706** 303-308-1660
Great American Bagel 519 N Cass Ave ...... Westmont IL 60559 **888-224-3563** 630-963-3393
Great American Cookie Co Inc
4685 Frederick Dr SW...................... Atlanta GA 30336 **800-332-4856** 404-696-1700
Great Clips Inc
7700 France Ave S Suite 425 .... Minneapolis MN 55435 **800-999-5959** 952-893-9088
Great Earth Vitamin Stores
1101 S Millikin Ave Suite A.................Ontario CA 91761 **800-374-7328**
Great Frame Up Systems Inc
101 S Hanley Rd Suite 1280.............Saint Louis MO 63105 **866-719-8200** 314-719-8200
Great Harvest Bread Co 28 S Montana St .... Dillon MT 59725 **800-442-0424** 406-683-6842
Guardsman FurniturePro
4999 36th St SE .... Grand Rapids MI 49512 **800-253-3957** 616-285-7877
Gymboree Corp 500 Howard St.......... San Francisco CA 94105 **800-222-7758** 415-278-7000
NASDAQ: GYMB
Gymboree Corp Play & Music Program
700 Airport Blvd Suite 200 ....Burlingame CA 94010 **800-222-7758** 650-579-0600

Haircrafters/Great Expectations
7201 Metro Blvd .... Minneapolis MN 55439 **888-888-7778** 952-947-7777
Handle With Care Packaging Store
5675 DTC Blvd Suite 280 ....Greenwood Village CO 80111 **800-525-6309** 303-741-6626
Handyman Connection Inc
9403 Kenwood Rd Suite D-207............Cincinnati OH 45242 **800-466-5530** 513-771-1122
Happy & Healthy Products Inc
1600 S Dixie Hwy Suite 200 .... Boca Raton FL 33432 **800-378-4854** 561-367-0739
Hardee's Food Systems Inc 505 N 7th St ....Saint Louis MO 63101 **800-711-4274** 314-259-6200
Health Clubs of America
500 E Broward Blvd Suite 1650 ...... Fort Lauderdale FL 33394 **800-833-5239** 954-527-5373
Heavenly Ham 5445 Triangle Pkwy Suite 400.... Norcross GA 30092 **800-989-0509** 770-752-1999
Heaven's Best Carpet & Upholstery Cleaning
PO Box 607 .... Rexburg ID 83440 **800-359-2095** 208-359-1106
Help-U-Sell Real Estate
6800 Jericho Tpke Suite 208 E............. Syosset NY 11791 **800-366-1177** 516-364-9650
Hertz Corp 225 Brae Blvd .... Park Ridge NJ 07656 **800-654-3131** 201-307-2000
Hobbytown USA 6301 S 58th St............... Lincoln NE 68516 **800-869-0424** 402-434-5385
Home Helpers Inc 10700 Montgomery Rd .....Cincinnati OH 45242 **800-216-4196** 513-563-8339
Home Instead Inc 604 N 109th Ct .... Omaha NE 68154 **888-484-5759** 402-498-4466
HomeLife Realty Services Inc
5752 176th St Unit 203.................... Surrey BC V3S4C8 **800-667-6329** 604-575-3130
Homes & Land Publishing Ltd
1830 E Park Ave .... Tallahassee FL 32301 **800-466-3546** 850-574-2111
HomeTeam Inspection Service
575 Chamber Dr .... Milford OH 45150 **800-598-5297** 513-831-1300
Hot Stuff Pizza 2930 W Maple St........... Sioux Falls SD 57107 **800-648-6227** 605-336-6961
House Doctors 575 Chamber Dr............... Milford OH 45150 **800-319-3359** 513-831-0100
HouseMaster 421 W Union Ave .... Bound Brook NJ 08805 **800-526-3939** 732-469-6565
HQ Global Workplaces Inc
15305 N Dallas Pkwy Suite 1400 .... Addison TX 75001 **800-633-4237** 972-361-8100
Huddle House Inc 2969 E Ponce de Leon Ave... Decatur GA 30030 **800-418-9555** 404-377-5700
Hungry Howie's Pizza & Subs Inc
30300 Stephenson Hwy Suite 200 ... Madison Heights MI 48071 **800-624-8122** 248-414-3300
Huntington Learning Centers Inc
954 Kinderkamack Rd .... River Edge NJ 07661 **800-226-5327** 201-261-8600
InspecTech Inc 925 N Point Pkwy Suite 400... Alpharetta GA 30005 **800-285-3001**
Interim HealthCare Inc
1601 Sawgrass Corporate Pkwy ....Sunrise FL 33323 **800-338-7786** 954-858-6000
International House of Pancakes (IHOP)
450 N Brand Blvd 7th Fl ....Glendale CA 91203 **800-241-4467** 818-240-6055
International Master Care Janitorial Franchising Inc 555 6th St
Suite 327 .... New Westminster BC V3L5H1 **800-889-2799** 604-525-8221
Jack in the Box Restaurants
9330 Balboa Ave .... San Diego CA 92123 **800-500-5225** 858-571-2121
Jackpot Convenience Stores Inc
2737 W Commodore Way.................. Seattle WA 98199 **800-552-0748** 206-286-6436
Jackson Hewitt Inc 7 Sylvan Way .... Parsippany NJ 07054 **800-234-1040** 973-496-1040
NYSE: JTX
Jamba Juice Co 1700 17th St .... San Francisco CA 94103 **800-545-9972**
Jan-Pro Franchising Systems International Inc 383 Strand Industrial Dr ....Little River SC 29566 **800-668-1001** 843-399-9895
Jani-King International Inc
16885 Dallas Pkwy .... Addison TX 75001 **800-552-5264** 972-991-0900
Jazzercise Inc 2460 Impala Dr...............Carlsbad CA 92008 **800-348-4748*** 760-476-1750
*Cust Svc
Jenny Craig International Inc 5770 Fleet St ....Carlsbad CA 92008 **800-443-2331** 760-696-4000
Jersey Mike's Franchise Systems Inc
2251 Landmark Pl................... Manasquan NJ 08736 **800-321-7676** 732-282-2323
Jiffy Lube International Inc 700 Milam St...... Houston TX 77002 **800-327-9532** 713-546-4000
KFC 1441 Gardiner Ln.................... Louisville KY 40213 **800-544-5774** 502-874-8300
Kitchen Solvers Inc 401 Jay St ....La Crosse WI 54601 **800-845-6779** 608-791-5516
Kitchen Tune-Up Inc 813 Circle Dr........... Aberdeen SD 57401 **800-333-6385** 605-225-4049
Kott Koatings Inc 27161 Burbank St ..... Foothill Ranch CA 92610 **800-452-6161** 949-770-5055
Krystal Co 1 Union Sq.................. Chattanooga TN 37402 **800-458-5841** 423-757-1550
Kumon North America Inc
300 Frank W Burr Blvd Glenpointe Ctr E
5th Fl .... Teaneck NJ 07666 **800-222-6284** 201-928-0444
LA Weight Loss Centers
747 Dresher Rd Suite 100................ Horsham PA 19044 **877-524-3571** 215-346-4300
Labor Finders International Inc
3910 RCA Blvd Suite 1001 ...... Palm Beach Gardens FL 33410 **800-864-7749** 561-627-6507
Ladies Workout Express
500 E Broward Blvd Suite 1650 ...... Fort Lauderdale FL 33394 **800-833-5239** 954-527-5373
Lady of America Franchise Corp
500 E Broward Blvd Suite 1650 ...... Fort Lauderdale FL 33394 **800-833-5239** 954-527-5373
Langenwalter Carpet Dyeing
1111 S Richfield Rd..................... Placentia CA 92870 **800-422-4370** 714-528-7610
Lawn Doctor Inc 142 SR 34................. Holmdel NJ 07733 **800-631-5660** 732-946-0029
LedgerPlus Inc 401 Saint Francis St........ Tallahassee FL 32301 **888-643-1348** 850-681-1941
Liberty Tax Service Inc
4575 Bonney Rd Suite 1040.......... Virginia Beach VA 23462 **800-790-3863** 757-493-8855
Little Caesars Inc 2211 Woodward Ave......... Detroit MI 48201 **800-722-3727** 313-983-6000
Little Gym International Inc
8970 E Raintree Dr Suite 200 .... Scottsdale AZ 85260 **888-228-2878** 480-948-2878
Little Professor Book Centers Inc
PO Box 3160 .... Ann Arbor MI 48106 **800-899-6232** 734-663-8733
Maaco Auto Painting & Body Works
381 Brooks Rd.................... King of Prussia PA 19406 **800-523-1180** 610-265-6606
MacGregor's Market 2930 W Maple St ...... Sioux Falls SD 57107 **800-648-6227** 605-336-6961
Mad Science Group
8360 Bougainville St Suite 201 ....Montreal QC H4P2G1 **800-586-5231** 514-344-4181
Maid Brigade USA/Minimaid Canada
4 Concourse Pkwy Suite 200................ Atlanta GA 30328 **800-722-6243** 770-551-9630
Maids International The 4820 Dodge St .... Omaha NE 68132 **800-843-6243** 402-558-5555
Mail Boxes Etc 6060 Cornerstone Ct W....... San Diego CA 92121 **800-456-0414** 858-455-8800
Management Recruiters International Worldwide Inc 200 Public Sq 31st Fl....... Cleveland OH 44114 **800-875-4000** 216-696-1122
Manhattan Bagel Co Inc
100 Horizon Ctr Blvd.................... Hamilton NJ 08691 **800-308-2457** 609-631-7000
Matco Tools 4403 Allen Rd ....Stow OH 44224 **800-368-6651** 330-929-4949
McDonald's Corp 1 McDonald's Plaza .... Oak Brook IL 60523 **800-234-6227** 630-623-3000
NYSE: MCD
Mean Gene's Burgers 2930 W Maple St ..... Sioux Falls SD 57107 **800-648-6227** 605-336-6961
Medicap Pharmacies Inc
4350 Westown Pkwy Suite 400..... West Des Moines IA 50266 **800-445-2244*** 515-224-8400
*Cust Svc
Medicine Shoppe International Inc
1100 N Lindbergh Blvd ....Saint Louis MO 63132 **800-325-1397*** 314-993-6000
*Cust Svc
Meineke Car Care Centers
128 S Tryon St Suite 900 .... Charlotte NC 28202 **800-275-5200** 704-377-8855

Company / Address	City	State	ZIP	Toll-Free	Phone
Merle Norman Cosmetics Inc					
9130 Bellanca Ave	Los Angeles	CA	90045	**800-421-2060**	310-641-3000
Merry Maids 3839 Forrest Hill-Irene Rd	Memphis	TN	38125	**800-798-8000**	901-597-8100
Midas International Corp					
1300 Arlington Heights Rd	Itasca	IL	60143	**800-621-0144**	630-438-3000
Mighty Distributing System of America Inc					
650 Engineering Dr	Norcross	GA	30092	**800-829-3900**	770-448-3900
Mikes Restaurants Inc					
8250 Decarie Blvd Suite 310	Montreal	QC	H4P2P5	**866-346-4537**	514-341-5544
Mini Maid Services					
2727 Canton Rd Suite 550	Marietta	GA	30066	**800-627-6464**	770-422-3565
Minuteman Press International Inc					
61 Executive Blvd	Farmingdale	NY	11735	**800-645-3006**	631-249-1370
Miracle-Ear Inc 5000 Cheshire Ln N	Plymouth	MN	55446	**800-234-7714**	763-268-4000
Miracle Method US Corp					
4239 N Nevada Ave Suite 115	Colorado Springs	CO	80907	**800-444-8827**	719-594-9091
Molly Maid Inc 3948 Ranchero Dr	Ann Arbor	MI	48108	**800-665-5962**	734-822-6800
Money Mailer Inc 14271 Corporate Dr	Garden Grove	CA	92843	**800-234-2771**	714-265-4100
Moto Photo Inc 4444 Lake Center Dr	Dayton	OH	45426	**800-733-6686**	937-854-6686
Mr Goodcents Franchise Systems Inc					
8997 Commerce Dr	DeSoto	KS	66018	**800-648-2368**	913-583-8400
Mr Hero 5755 Granger Rd Suite 200	Independence	OH	44131	**800-837-9599**	216-398-1101
Mr Rooter Corp 1010 N University Pk Dr	Waco	TX	76707	**800-583-8003**	254-745-2444
Mr Sub 4576 Yonge St	Toronto	ON	M2N6P1	**800-668-7827**	416-225-5545
Mrs Fields Original Cookies Inc					
2855 E Cottonwood Pkwy Suite 400	Salt Lake City	UT	84121	**800-348-6311**	801-736-5600
My Favorite Muffin					
500 Lake Cook Rd Suite 475	Deerfield	IL	60015	**800-251-6101**	847-948-7520
Nathan's Famous Inc					
1400 Old Country Rd Suite 400	Westbury	NY	11590	**800-628-4267**	516-338-8500
NASDAQ: NATH					
National Property Inspections Inc					
11620 Arbor St Suite 100	Omaha	NE	68144	**800-333-9807**	402-333-9807
Navis Pack & Ship Centers					
5675 DTC Blvd Suite 280	Greenwood Village	CO	80111	**800-525-6309**	303-741-6626
New Horizons Computer Learning Centers Inc					
1900 S State College Blvd Suite 100	Anaheim	CA	92806	**888-222-3380**	714-712-1000
Noah's New York Bagels Inc					
255 Ygnacio Valley Rd Suite 200	Walnut Creek	CA	90601	**800-936-6247**	925-979-6000
Norwalk Furniture Corp 100 Furniture Pkwy	Norwalk	OH	44857	**800-837-2565***	419-668-4461
*Orders					
NOVUS Auto Glass Repair & Replacement					
12800 Hwy 13 S	Minneapolis	MN	55378	**800-328-1137**	952-944-8000
Nutrilawn Inc 5397 Eglinton Ave W Suite 110	Toronto	ON	M9C5K6	**800-396-6096**	416-620-7100
Once Upon A Child					
4200 Dahlberg Dr Suite 100	Minneapolis	MN	55422	**800-433-2540**	763-520-8500
OpenWorks 4742 N 24th St Suite 300	Phoenix	AZ	85016	**800-777-6736**	602-224-0440
Orange Julius of America					
7505 Metro Blvd	Minneapolis	MN	55439	**800-679-6556**	952-830-0200
Packaging & Shipping Specialists					
5211 85th St Suite 104	Lubbock	TX	79424	**800-877-8884**	
Packaging Store The					
5675 DTC Blvd Suite 280	Greenwood Village	CO	80111	**800-525-6309**	303-741-6626
Padgett Business Services Inc					
160 Hawthorne Park	Athens	GA	30606	**800-723-4388**	706-548-1040
Pak Mail Centers of America Inc					
7173 S Havana St Suite 600	Englewood	CO	80112	**800-778-6665**	303-957-1000
Panera Bread Co 6710 Clayton Rd	Richmond Heights	MO	63117	**800-301-5566**	314-633-7100
NASDAQ: PNRA					
Papa John's International Inc					
2002 Papa John's Blvd	Louisville	KY	40299	**877-547-7272**	502-261-7272
NASDAQ: PZZA					
Parcel Plus Inc 12715 Telge Rd	Cypress	TX	77429	**800-662-5553**	281-256-4100
Party City Corp 400 Commons Way	Rockaway	NJ	07866	**800-883-2100**	973-983-0888
NASDAQ: PCTY					
Party Land Inc 5215 Militia Hill Rd	Plymouth Meeting	PA	19462	**800-778-9563**	610-941-6200
Paul Davis Restoration Inc					
1 Independence Dr Suite 2300	Jacksonville	FL	32202	**800-722-1818**	904-737-2779
Payless Car Rental System Inc					
2350 N 34th St N	Saint Petersburg	FL	33713	**800-729-5377**	727-321-6352
Pearle Vision Inc 1925 Enterprise Pkwy	Twinsburg	OH	44087	**800-282-3931**	330-486-3000
Perkins Restaurant & Bakery					
6075 Poplar Ave Suite 800	Memphis	TN	38119	**800-877-7375**	901-766-6400
Perma-Glaze Inc					
1638 Research Loop Rd Suite 160	Tucson	AZ	85710	**800-332-7397**	520-722-9718
Pet Supplies "Plus" Inc					
22670 Haggerty Rd Suite 200	Farmington Hills	MI	48335	**866-477-7747**	248-374-1900
Petland Inc 250 Riverside St	Chillicothe	OH	45601	**800-221-5935**	740-775-2464
Physicians Weight Loss Centers of America Inc					
395 Springside Dr	Akron	OH	44333	**800-205-7887**	330-666-7952
Pillar to Post Inc					
13902 N Dale Mabry Hwy Suite 300	Tampa	FL	33618	**800-294-5591**	813-962-4461
Pizza Factory Inc 49430 Rd 426	Oakhurst	CA	93644	**800-654-4840**	559-683-3377
Pizza Hut Inc 14841 N Dallas Pkwy	Dallas	TX	75254	**800-948-8488**	972-338-7700
Pizza Inn Inc 3551 Plano Pkwy	The Colony	TX	75056	**800-880-9955**	469-384-5000
NASDAQ: PZZI					
Pizza Pizza Ltd 580 Jarvis St	Toronto	ON	M4Y2H9	**800-265-9762**	416-967-1010
Play It Again Sports					
4200 Dahlberg Dr Suite 100	Minneapolis	MN	55422	**800-433-2540**	763-520-8500
Ponderosa Steakhouses					
6500 International Pkwy Suite 1000	Plano	TX	75093	**800-727-8355**	972-588-5000
Popeyes Chicken & Biscuits					
5555 Glenridge Connector NE Suite 300	Atlanta	GA	30342	**866-232-4403**	404-459-4450
PostalAnnex+ Inc					
7580 Metropolitan Dr Suite 200	San Diego	CA	92108	**800-456-1525**	619-563-4800
PostNet Postal & Business Centers					
181 N Arroyo Grande Blvd Suite 100-A	Henderson	NV	89074	**800-841-7171**	702-792-7100
Precision Auto Care Inc 748 Miller Dr SE	Leesburg	VA	20175	**800-438-8863**	703-777-9095
Precision Tune Auto Care Inc PO Box 5000	Leesburg	VA	20177	**800-438-8863**	703-777-9095
Pressed4Time Inc 8 Clock Tower Pl Suite 110	Maynard	MA	01754	**800-423-8711**	978-823-8300
Primrose School Franchising Co					
3660 Cedarcrest Rd	Acworth	GA	30101	**800-745-0677**	770-529-4100
Priority Management Systems Inc					
13251 Delf Pl Suite 420	Richmond	BC	V6V2A2	**800-221-9031**	604-214-7772
Pro Golf of America Inc					
32751 Middlebelt Rd	Farmington Hills	MI	48334	**800-521-6388**	248-737-0553
Pro Image Franchise LLC					
233 N 1250 West Suite 200	Centerville	UT	84014	**888-477-6326**	801-296-9999
Productivity Point International Inc					
2950 Gateway Center Blvd	Morrisville	NC	27560	**800-774-2727**	919-379-5611
Professional Carpet Systems Inc					
4211 Atlantic Ave	Raleigh	NC	27604	**800-925-5055**	919-875-8871
ProForma 8800 E Pleasant Valley Rd	Independence	OH	44131	**800-825-1525**	216-520-8400
Promotions Unlimited Corp DBA Ben Franklin					
Stores 7601 Durand Ave	Racine	WI	53408	**800-992-9307**	262-681-7000
Property Damage Appraisers Inc					
PO Box 9230	Fort Worth	TX	76147	**800-749-7324**	817-731-5555
Prudential Real Estate Affiliates Inc					
3333 Michelson Dr Suite 1000	Irvine	CA	92612	**800-999-1120**	949-794-7900
Putt-Putt Golf Courses of America Inc					
6350 Quadrangle Dr Suite 210	Chapel Hill	NC	27517	**888-788-8788**	910-401-9759
RadioShack					
100 Throckmorton St Suite 1800	Fort Worth	TX	76102	**800-843-7422**	817-415-3011
Rainbow International					
1010 N University Park Dr	Waco	TX	76707	**800-583-9100**	254-745-2444
Rally's Hamburgers Inc					
4300 W Cypress St Suite 600	Tampa	FL	33607	**800-800-8072**	813-283-7000
Realty Executives International					
2398 E Camelback Rd Suite 900	Phoenix	AZ	85016	**800-252-3366**	602-957-0747
Regis Corp Cost Cutters Family Hair Care					
Div 7201 Metro Blvd	Minneapolis	MN	55439	**888-888-7778**	952-947-7777
Regis Corp Supercuts Div					
7201 Metro Blvd	Minneapolis	MN	55439	**888-888-7778**	952-947-7777
Relax The Back Corp					
15901 Hawthorne Blvd Suite 401	Lawndale	CA	90260	**800-222-5728**	
RE/MAX International Inc					
8390 E Crescent Pkwy Suite 500	Greenwood Village	CO	80111	**800-525-7452***	303-770-5531
*Cust Svc					
Remedy Temp Inc 101 Enterprise Suite 100	Aliso Viejo	CA	92656	**800-828-3726**	949-425-7600
NASDAQ: REMX					
Rent-A-Wreck of America LLC					
10324 S Dolfield Rd	Owings Mills	MD	21117	**800-535-1391**	410-581-5755
Rita's Water Ice Franchise Corp					
1525 Ford Rd	Bensalem	PA	19020	**800-677-7482**	215-633-9899
Ruby Tuesday Inc 150 W Church Ave	Maryville	TN	37801	**800-325-0755**	865-379-5700
NYSE: RI					
Sandler Sales Institute					
10411 Stevenson Rd	Stevenson	MD	21153	**800-638-5686**	410-653-1993
Sbarro Inc 401 Broadhollow Rd	Melville	NY	11747	**800-766-4949***	631-715-4100
*Cust Svc					
Schlotzsky's Ltd 203 Colorado St	Austin	TX	78701	**800-846-2867***	512-236-3600
*Sales					
Sea Tow Services International Inc					
1560 Youngs Ave	Southold	NY	11971	**800-473-2869**	631-765-3660
Second Cup Ltd 6303 Airport Rd	Mississauga	ON	L4V1R8	**800-338-2610**	905-405-6700
Sensible Car Rental Inc					
96 Freneau Ave Suite 2	Matawan	NJ	07747	**800-367-5159**	732-583-8500
Service One Cleaning Consultants &					
Management 5104 N Orange Blossom Trail					
Suite 220	Orlando	FL	32810	**800-522-7111**	
ServiceMaster Clean					
3839 Forrest Hill Irene Rd	Memphis	TN	38125	**800-242-0442**	901-597-7500
Servpro Industries Inc 575 Airport Rd	Gallatin	TN	37066	**800-826-9586**	615-451-0600
Sign*A*Rama 1801 S Australian Ave	West Palm Beach	FL	33409	**800-286-8671**	561-640-5570
Signs Now Corp					
4900 Manatee Ave W Suite 201	Bradenton	FL	34209	**800-356-3373**	941-747-7747
Simple Simon's Pizza 6650 S Lewis St	Tulsa	OK	74136	**800-261-6375**	918-496-1272
Sir Speedy Inc 26722 Plaza Dr	Mission Viejo	CA	92691	**800-854-8297**	949-348-5000
Slender Lady Inc					
45 NE Loop 410 Suite 500	San Antonio	TX	78216	**888-227-8187**	210-877-1500
Smash Hit Subs 2930 W Maple St	Sioux Falls	SD	57107	**800-648-6227**	605-336-6961
Smoothie King Franchises Inc					
2400 Veterans Blvd Suite 110	Kenner	LA	70062	**800-577-4200**	504-467-4006
Snelling Personnel Services					
12801 N Central Expy Suite 700	Dallas	TX	75243	**800-766-5556**	972-239-7575
Sonic Drive-in Restaurants					
101 Park Ave Suite 1400	Oklahoma City	OK	73102	**800-569-6656**	405-280-7654
Southern Maid Donut Flour Co					
3615 Cavalier Dr	Garland	TX	75042	**800-936-6887**	972-272-6425
Sparkle International Inc					
26851 Richmond Rd	Cleveland	OH	44146	**800-321-0770**	216-464-4212
Speedee Oil Change & Tune-Up Inc					
PO Box 1350	Madisonville	LA	70447	**800-451-7461**	985-845-1919
Spherion Corp 2050 Spectrum Blvd	Fort Lauderdale	FL	33309	**866-435-7456**	954-308-7600
NYSE: SFN					
Sports Section Inc 2150 Boggs Rd Suite 200	Duluth	GA	30096	**800-321-9127**	770-622-4900
Spring Crest Window Fashions					
4375 Prado Rd Unit 104	Corona	CA	92880	**800-552-5523**	951-340-2293
Spring-Green Lawn Care Corp					
11909 Spaulding School Dr	Plainfield	IL	60544	**800-435-4051**	815-436-8777
Stained Glass Overlay Inc 1827 N Case St	Orange	CA	92865	**800-944-4746**	714-974-6124
Stanley Steemer International Inc					
5500 Stanley Steemer Pkwy	Dublin	OH	43016	**800-848-7496**	614-764-2007
Steak & Ale 6500 International Pkwy Suite 1000	Plano	TX	75093	**800-727-8355**	972-588-5000
Steamatic Inc 303 Arthur St	Fort Worth	TX	76107	**800-544-1303**	817-332-1575
Sterling Optical					
100 Quentin Roosevelt Blvd	Garden City	NY	11530	**800-332-6302**	516-390-2100
Stork News of America Inc					
1305 Hope Mills Rd Suite A	Fayetteville	NC	28304	**800-633-6395**	910-426-1357
Subway Restaurants 325 Bic Dr	Milford	CT	06460	**800-888-4848**	203-877-4281
Successories Inc 2520 Diehl Rd	Aurora	IL	60504	**800-621-1423**	630-820-7200
Super Coups Inc 350 Revolutionary Dr	East Taunton	MA	02718	**800-626-2620**	508-977-2000
Supercuts Div Regis Corp					
7201 Metro Blvd	Minneapolis	MN	55439	**888-888-7778**	952-947-7777
SuperGlass Windshield Repair					
6101 Chancellor Dr Suite 200	Orlando	FL	32809	**888-771-2700**	407-240-1920
Swensen's Ice Cream Co					
4175 Veterans Memorial Hwy	Ronkonkoma	NY	11779	**800-423-2763**	631-737-9898
Swisher Hygiene Co 6849 Fairview Rd	Charlotte	NC	28210	**800-444-4138**	704-364-7707
Swisher International Inc 6849 Fairview Rd	Charlotte	NC	28210	**800-444-4138**	704-364-7707
Taco Bueno Restaurants Inc					
3033 Kellway Dr Suite 122	Carrollton	TX	75006	**800-440-0778**	972-417-4800
Taco Cabana Inc					
8918 Tesoro Dr Suite 200	San Antonio	TX	78217	**800-357-9924**	210-804-0990
Taco John's International Inc					
808 W 20th St	Cheyenne	WY	82001	**800-854-0819**	307-635-0101
Taco Maker Inc 4605 Harrison Blvd	Ogden	UT	84403	**800-207-5804**	801-476-9780
Taco Time International Inc					
7730 E Greenway Rd Suite 104	Scottsdale	AZ	85260	**800-547-8907**	480-443-0200
Tandem Staffing Solutions Inc					
1690 S Congress Ave Suite 210	Delray Beach	FL	33445	**800-275-5000**	561-454-3500
Taylor Rental 203 Jandus Rd	Cary	IL	60013	**800-833-3004**	847-462-5440
TCBY Enterprises Inc					
2855 E Cottonwood Pkwy Suite 400	Salt Lake City	UT	84121	**888-900-8229**	801-736-5600
Terminix International Co					
860 Ridge Lake Blvd	Memphis	TN	38120	**800-654-7848**	901-766-1333
TGI Friday's Worldwide Inc 4201 Marsh Ln	Carrollton	TX	75007	**800-374-3297**	972-662-5400

	City	State	Zip	Toll-Free	Phone
Thrifty Car Rental 5310 E 31st St	Tulsa	OK	74135	**800-367-2277**	918-665-3930
Tim Hortons 4150 Tuller Rd Suite 236	Dublin	OH	43017	**888-376-4835**	614-791-4200
Tinder Box International Ltd 3 Bala Plaza E Suite 102	Bala Cynwyd	PA	19004	**800-846-3372**	610-668-4220
Togo's Eateries Inc 130 Royal St	Canton	MA	02021	**800-859-5339**	781-737-3000
Tony Roma's Famous for Ribs 9304 Forest Ln Suite 200	Dallas	TX	75243	**800-286-7662**	214-343-7800
Transmission USA 4444 W 147th St	Midlothian	IL	60445	**800-377-9247**	708-389-5922
Treats International Franchise Corp 418 Preston St	Ottawa	ON	K1S4N2	**800-461-4003**	613-563-4073
Tuffy Auto Service Centers 1414 Baronial Plaza Dr	Toledo	OH	43615	**800-228-8339**	419-865-6900
Tutor Time Learning Systems Inc 621 NW 53rd St Suite 115	Boca Raton	FL	33487	**800-275-1235**	561-237-2200
Two Men & A Truck International Inc 3400 Belle Chase Way	Lansing	MI	48911	**800-345-1070**	517-394-7210
U-Save Auto Rental of America Inc 4780 I-55 N Suite 300	Jackson	MS	39211	**800-438-2300**	601-713-4333
Unishippers Assn 746 E Winchester Suite 200	Salt Lake City	UT	84107	**800-999-8721**	801-487-0600
US Seamless Inc 2001 1st Ave N	Fargo	ND	58102	**888-743-3632**	701-241-8888
Val-Pak Direct Marketing System Inc 8605 Largo Lakes Dr	Largo	FL	33773	**800-237-6266**	727-393-1270
Vanguard Cleaning Systems Inc 655 Mariners Island Blvd Suite 303	San Mateo	CA	94404	**800-564-6422**	650-594-1500
Village Inn 400 W 48th Ave	Denver	CO	80216	**800-800-3644**	303-296-2121
Weight Watchers International Inc 175 Crossways Pk W *NYSE: WTW*	Woodbury	NY	11797	**800-651-6000**	516-390-1400
Westaff Inc 298 N Wiget Ln *NASDAQ: WSTF*	Walnut Creek	CA	94598	**800-872-8367**	925-930-5300
Western Sizzlin Inc 1338 Plantation Rd	Roanoke	VA	24012	**800-247-8325**	540-345-3195
WG Grinders 9002 Cotter St	Lewis Center	OH	43035	**877-447-3354**	614-766-2313
Wicks 'N' Sticks PO Box 1965	Cypress	TX	77410	**800-873-3714**	713-856-7442
Wild Birds Unlimited 11711 N College Ave Suite 146	Carmel	IN	46032	**800-326-4928**	317-571-7100
Women's Health Boutique Franchise System Inc 12715 Telge Rd	Cypress	TX	77429	**888-280-2053**	281-256-4100
World Gym International 3223 Washington Blvd	Marina del Rey	CA	90292	**800-544-7441**	310-827-7705
World Inspection Network International Inc 6500 6th Ave NW	Seattle	WA	98117	**800-967-8127**	206-728-8100
Worldsites Inc 5915 Airport Rd Suite 300	Toronto	ON	L4V1T1	**888-678-7588**	905-678-7588
Worldwide Express 2501 Cedar Springs Rd Suite 450	Dallas	TX	75201	**800-758-7447**	214-720-2400
Ziebart International Corp 1290 E Maple Rd	Troy	MI	48083	**800-877-1312**	248-588-4100

306 FREIGHT FORWARDERS

SEE ALSO Logistics Services (Transportation & Warehousing)

	City	State	Zip	Toll-Free	Phone
Adcom Worldwide Inc PO Box 390048	Edina	MN	55439	**800-747-7424**	952-829-7990
Air Cargo International & Domestic 180 Admiral Cochrane Dr Suite 305	Annapolis	MD	21401	**800-747-6505**	410-280-5578
Airways Freight Corp 3849 W Wedington Dr	Fayetteville	AR	72704	**800-643-3525**	479-442-6301
ALG Admiral Inc 1101 Ellis St	Bensenville	IL	60106	**800-323-0289**	630-766-3900
Allstates WorldCargo Inc 4 Lakeside Dr S	Forked River	NJ	08731	**800-575-5575**	609-693-5950
Argents Express Group 7025 Metroplex Dr	Romulus	MI	48174	**800-229-2231**	734-326-9499
Byrnes WJ & Co Inc 880 Mitten Rd Suite C	Burlingame	CA	94010	**800-733-1142**	650-692-1142
CD&L Inc 80 Wesley St *AMEX: CDV*	South Hackensack	NJ	07606	**800-899-7296**	201-487-7740
Central Global Express PO Box 698	Taylor	MI	48180	**800-982-3924**	734-955-2555
FESCO Agencies NA Inc 821 2nd Ave Suite 1100	Seattle	WA	98104	**800-275-3372**	206-583-0860
Graulich International Inc 6411 NW 35th Ave	Miami	FL	33147	**800-836-2709**	305-836-1700
Guaranteed Air Freight & Forwarding Inc 4555 McDonnell Blvd	Saint Louis	MO	63134	**800-445-0738**	314-427-7709
Hassett Air Express 877 S Rt 83	Elmhurst	IL	60126	**800-323-9422**	630-530-6515
Lynden Inc 18000 International Blvd Suite 800	Seattle	WA	98188	**800-426-3201**	206-241-8778
Phoenix International Freight Services Ltd 712 N Central Ave	Wood Dale	IL	60191	**800-959-9590**	630-766-9444
Ram International Inc 4664 World Pkwy Cir	Saint Louis	MO	63134	**800-884-4726**	314-427-3000
Senderex Cargo Inc 10425 S La Cienega Blvd	Los Angeles	CA	90045	**800-421-5846**	310-342-2900
Sho-Air International 50 Corporate Park	Irvine	CA	92606	**800-227-9111**	949-476-9111
Target Logistic Services Inc 201 W Carob St	Compton	CA	90220	**800-283-8888**	310-900-1974
Tricor America Inc 717 Airport Blvd	South San Francisco	CA	94080	**800-669-7631**	650-877-3650
WJ Byrnes & Co Inc 880 Mitten Rd Suite C	Burlingame	CA	94010	**800-733-1142**	650-692-1142

307 FREIGHT TRANSPORT - DEEP SEA (DOMESTIC PORTS)

	City	State	Zip	Toll-Free	Phone
Alaska Marine Lines Inc 5615 W Marginal Way SW	Seattle	WA	98106	**800-950-4265**	206-763-4244
Coastal Transportation Inc 4025 13th Ave W	Seattle	WA	98119	**800-544-2580**	206-282-9979
Crowley Marine Services Inc 1102 SW Massachusetts St	Seattle	WA	98134	**800-248-8632**	206-332-8000
Crowley Maritime Corp 155 Grand Ave Suite 700	Oakland	CA	94612	**800-276-9539**	510-251-7500
ENSCO Marine Co 620 Moulin Rd	Broussard	LA	70518	**800-322-8217**	337-837-9583
Farmers Co-op Shipping Assn PO Box 250	Clifton	KS	66937	**800-562-4203**	785-455-3315
Horizon Lines LLC 4064 Colony Rd Suite 200 **Cust Svc	Charlotte	NC	28211	**877-678-7447***	704-973-7000
K Line America Inc 8730 Stony Point Pkwy Suite 400	Richmond	VA	23235	**800-609-3221**	804-560-3600
Matson Navigation Co 555 12th St *Cust Svc	Oakland	CA	94607	**800-462-8766***	510-628-4000
Mormac Marine Group Inc 1 Landmark Sq Suite 710	Stamford	CT	06901	**800-669-8903**	203-977-8900
Northland Services Inc 6700 W Marginal Way SW Suite 600	Seattle	WA	98106	**800-426-3113**	206-763-3000
Overseas Shipholding Group Inc 511 5th Ave *NYSE: OSG*	New York	NY	10017	**800-223-1722**	212-953-4100
SC Loveland Co Inc PO Box 368	Pennsville	NJ	08070	**800-523-2687**	856-935-8100
Sea Star Line LLC 100 Bell Tel Way Suite 300	Jacksonville	FL	32216	**877-775-7447**	904-855-1260
Seaboard Marine Ltd 8001 NW 79th Ave	Miami	FL	33166	**800-753-0681**	305-863-4444
TECO Ocean Shipping 1300 E 8th Ave Suite F-300	Tampa	FL	33605	**800-835-4161**	813-209-4200
Totem Ocean Trailer Express Inc (TOTE) 32001 32nd Ave S Suite 200	Federal Way	WA	98001	**800-426-0074**	
Trailer Bridge Inc 10405 New Berlin Rd E *NASDAQ: TRBR*	Jacksonville	FL	32226	**800-554-1589**	904-751-7100
Waterman Steamship Corp 1 Whitehall St 20th Fl	New York	NY	10004	**888-972-5274**	212-747-8550
Western Pioneer Inc 4601 Shilshole Ave NW	Seattle	WA	98107	**800-426-6783**	206-789-1930
Young Brothers Ltd PO Box 3288	Honolulu	HI	96801	**800-572-2743**	808-543-9311

308 FREIGHT TRANSPORT - DEEP SEA (FOREIGN PORTS)

	City	State	Zip	Toll-Free	Phone
American President Lines Ltd 1111 Broadway	Oakland	CA	94607	**800-999-7733**	510-272-8000
Anderson Trucking Service Inc 203 Cooper Ave N PO Box 1377	Saint Cloud	MN	56302	**800-328-2307**	320-255-7400
APL Ltd 1111 Broadway	Oakland	CA	94607	**800-999-7733**	510-272-8000
Atlantic Container Line 194 Wood Ave S Suite 500	Iselin	NJ	08830	**800-225-1235**	732-452-5400
Brennan International Transport Inc 2665 E Del Amo Blvd	Rancho Dominguez	CA	90221	**866-427-3662**	310-637-7000
Direct Container Line Inc 857 E 230th St	Carson	CA	90745	**888-325-4325**	310-518-1773
Fednav Ltd 1000 rue de la Gauchetière O Bureau 3500	Montreal	QC	H3B4W5	**800-678-4842**	514-878-6500
Hamburg Sud North America Inc 465 South St	Morristown	NJ	07960	**800-901-7447**	973-775-5300
K Line America Inc 8730 Stony Point Pkwy Suite 400	Richmond	VA	23235	**800-609-3221**	804-560-3600
Lykes Lines Ltd LLC PO Box 31244	Tampa	FL	33631	**800-242-7447**	813-276-4600
OMI Corp 1 Station Pl Metro Ctr *NYSE: OMM*	Stamford	CT	06902	**800-344-9711**	203-602-6700
Overseas Shipholding Group Inc 511 5th Ave *NYSE: OSG*	New York	NY	10017	**800-223-1722**	212-953-4100
Seaboard Marine Ltd 8001 NW 79th Ave	Miami	FL	33166	**800-753-0681**	305-863-4444
SEACOR Marine Inc 5005 Railroad Ave	Morgan City	LA	70380	**800-989-7062**	985-385-3475
Sunmar Inc 500 108th Ave NE Suite 1710	Bellevue	WA	98004	**800-443-4127**	425-577-1870
Sunmar Shipping Inc 500 108th Ave NE Suite 1710	Bellevue	WA	98004	**800-443-4127**	425-577-1870
TECO Ocean Shipping 1300 E 8th Ave Suite F-300	Tampa	FL	33605	**800-835-4161**	813-209-4200
Tidewater Inc 601 Poydras St Suite 1900 *NYSE: TDW*	New Orleans	LA	70130	**800-678-8433**	504-568-1010
Tropical Shipping PO Box 10683	Riviera Beach	FL	33419	**800-367-6200**	561-881-3900
Waterman Steamship Corp 1 Whitehall St 20th Fl	New York	NY	10004	**888-972-5274**	212-747-8550

309 FREIGHT TRANSPORT - INLAND WATERWAYS

	City	State	Zip	Toll-Free	Phone
American Commercial Barge Lines Co 1701 E Market St	Jeffersonville	IN	47130	**800-457-6377**	812-288-0100
American Commercial Lines Inc 1701 E Market St	Jeffersonville	IN	47130	**800-457-6377**	812-288-0100
American River Transportation Co 4666 E Faries Pkwy	Decatur	IL	62526	**800-637-5824**	217-424-5200
Boston Towing & Transportation Co LP 36 New St	East Boston	MA	02128	**800-836-8847**	617-567-9100
Crowley Maritime Corp 155 Grand Ave Suite 700	Oakland	CA	94612	**800-276-9539**	510-251-7500
Fednav Ltd 1000 rue de la Gauchetière O Bureau 3500	Montreal	QC	H3B4W5	**800-678-4842**	514-878-6500
Ingram Barge Co 4400 Harding Rd 1 Belle Meade Pl	Nashville	TN	37205	**800-876-2047**	615-298-8200
L & M Bo-Truc Rental Inc 18692 W Main St	Galliano	LA	70354	**800-256-1186**	985-475-5733
Shaver Transportation Co Inc 4900 NW Front Ave	Portland	OR	97210	**888-228-8850**	503-228-8850
Warrior & Gulf Navigation Co PO Box 11397	Chickasaw	AL	36671	**800-452-6100**	251-452-6000

310 FRUIT GROWERS

SEE ALSO Agricultural Services - Crop Preparation Services; Beverages - Mfr - Wines - Mfr

310-1 Berry Growers

	City	State	Zip	Toll-Free	Phone
Driscoll Strawberry Assoc Inc PO Box 50045	Watsonville	CA	95077	**800-871-3333**	831-761-5301
Jasper Wyman & Son PO Box 100	Milbridge	ME	04658	**800-341-1758**	207-546-2311
Merrill Blueberry Farms Inc PO Box 149	Ellsworth	ME	04605	**800-711-6551**	207-667-2541

310-2 Citrus Growers

	City	State	Zip	Toll-Free	Phone
Blood's Hammock Groves 4600 Linton Blvd	Delray Beach	FL	33445	**800-255-5188**	561-498-3400

Citrus Growers (Cont'd)

Company / Address	City	State	ZIP	Toll-Free	Phone
Callery-Judge Grove 4001 Seminole-Pratt Whitney Rd	Loxahatchee	FL	33470	**800-967-2643**	561-793-1676
Egan Bernard & Co DBA DNE World Fruit Sales 1900 Old Dixie Hwy	Fort Pierce	FL	34946	**800-327-6676**	772-465-1110
Graves Brothers Co 8465 Old Dixie Hwy PO Box 700277	Wabasso	FL	32970	**877-999-8499***	772-589-4356
*Sales					
Heller Brothers Packing Corp 288 9th St	Winter Garden	FL	34787	**800-823-2124**	407-656-2124
Highland Exchange Service Co-op 5916 SR 540 E PO Box K	Waverly	FL	33877	**800-237-3989**	863-439-3661
K-Y Farms DBA Valley Fruit Inc PO Box 770	Pharr	TX	78577	**800-255-1486**	956-787-3241
Limoneira Co 1141 Cummings Rd	Santa Paula	CA	93060	**800-350-5541**	805-525-5541
Orange Cove-Sanger Citrus Assn 180 South Ave	Orange Cove	CA	93646	**800-533-8871**	559-626-4453
Seald-Sweet Growers Inc 1991 74th Ave	Vero Beach	FL	32966	**800-336-2926***	772-569-2244
*Sales					
Silver Springs Citrus Inc 25411 N Mare Ave	Howey in the Hills	FL	34737	**800-940-2277**	352-324-2101
Valley Fruit Inc PO Box 770	Pharr	TX	78577	**800-255-1486**	956-787-3241

310-3 Deciduous Tree Fruit Growers

Company / Address	City	State	ZIP	Toll-Free	Phone
Appletree Orchards Inc 12025 Four-Mile Rd NE	Lowell	MI	49331	**800-922-0635**	616-897-9216
Brewster Heights Packing Inc 908 Hwy 97	Brewster	WA	98812	**800-967-3634**	509-689-3424
Capital Agricultural Property Services Inc 801 Warrenville Rd Suite 150	Lisle	IL	60532	**800-243-2060**	630-434-9150
Cherry Central Co-op Inc 1771 N US Hwy 31 S PO Box 988	Traverse City	MI	49685	**800-678-1860**	231-946-1860
Evans Fruit Farm 200 Cowiche City Rd	Cowiche	WA	98923	**800-255-7513**	509-678-4127
Hudson Valley Farms Inc 381 Vineyard Ave	Highland	NY	12528	**800-336-2252**	845-691-2181
Lane Packing Inc Hwy 96 & 50 Ln Rd PO Box 1087	Fort Valley	GA	31030	**800-277-3224**	478-825-3592
National Fruit Product Co Inc PO Box 2040	Winchester	VA	22604	**800-551-5167**	540-662-3401
Rice Fruit Co 2760 Carlisle Rd PO Box 66	Gardners	PA	17324	**800-627-3359**	717-677-8131
Southern Orchard Supply Co DBA Lane Packing Inc Hwy 96 & 50 Ln Rd PO Box 1087	Fort Valley	GA	31030	**800-277-3224**	478-825-3592
Titan Farms 5 RW Du Bose Rd	Ridge Spring	SC	29129	**888-848-2672**	803-685-5381

310-4 Fruit Growers (Misc)

Company / Address	City	State	ZIP	Toll-Free	Phone
Brooks Tropicals Inc PO Box 900160	Homestead	FL	33090	**800-327-4833**	305-247-3544
Calavo Growers Inc PO Box 26081	Santa Ana	CA	92799	**800-422-5286**	949-223-1111
NASDAQ: CVGW					
Chiquita Brands International Inc 250 E 5th St	Cincinnati	OH	45202	**800-541-8998**	513-784-8000
NYSE: CQB					
Dole Food Co Inc 1 Dole Dr	Westlake Village	CA	91362	**800-232-8888**	818-879-6600
Fresh Del Monte Produce Inc 241 Sevilla Ave	Coral Gables	FL	33134	**800-950-3683***	305-520-8400
NYSE: FDP ■ *Cust Svc					
Martori Farms 7332 E Butherus Dr	Scottsdale	AZ	85260	**800-627-8674**	480-998-1444
Virginia Fork Produce Inc PO Box 148	Edenton	NC	27932	**800-334-7716**	252-482-2165

310-5 Grape Vineyards

Company / Address	City	State	ZIP	Toll-Free	Phone
Delicato Vineyards 12001 S Hwy 99	Manteca	CA	95336	**888-599-4637**	209-824-3600
E & J Gallo Winery 600 Yosemite Blvd	Modesto	CA	95354	**800-322-2389**	209-341-3111
Gallo E & J Winery 600 Yosemite Blvd	Modesto	CA	95354	**800-322-2389**	209-341-3111
National Raisin Co PO Box 219	Fowler	CA	93625	**800-874-3726**	559-834-5981
Scheid Vineyards Inc 305 Hilltown Rd	Salinas	CA	93908	**888-772-4343**	831-455-9990
NASDAQ: SVIN					
Stimson Lane Ltd 14111 NE 145th St	Woodinville	WA	98072	**800-267-6793**	425-488-1133
Windsor Vineyards Po Box 368	Windsor	CA	95492	**800-289-9463**	707-836-5000

311 FUEL DEALERS

Company / Address	City	State	ZIP	Toll-Free	Phone
Able Energy Inc PO Box 630	Rockaway	NJ	07866	**800-564-1012**	973-625-1012
NASDAQ: ABLE					
AC & T Co Inc 11535 Hopewell Rd	Hagerstown	MD	21740	**800-458-3835**	301-582-2700
Alvin Hollis & Co Inc 1 Hollis St	South Weymouth	MA	02190	**800-649-5090**	781-335-2100
Automotive Service Inc PO Box 2157	Reading	PA	19608	**800-383-3421**	610-678-3421
Big Stone Co-op PO Box 362	Clinton	MN	56225	**800-325-1132**	320-325-5466
Blossman Gas Inc PO Box 1110	Ocean Springs	MS	39566	**800-234-1110**	228-875-2261
Carolane Propane Gas Inc 339 S Main St	Lexington	NC	27292	**800-838-1982**	336-249-8981
Carroll Independent Fuel Co 2700 Loch Raven Rd	Baltimore	MD	21218	**800-834-8590**	410-235-1066
Cenex 5500 Cenex Dr	Inver Grove Heights	MN	55077	**800-232-3639**	651-355-6000
Cornerstone Propane Partners LP 432 Westridge Dr	Watsonville	CA	95076	**800-288-5206**	831-724-1921
Diamond/Delchester 841 Lincoln Ave	West Chester	PA	19381	**888-835-3535**	610-692-3366
Farm & Home Oil Co PO Box 389	Telford	PA	18969	**800-473-1562**	215-257-0131
Farmers Union Oil Co of Kenmare Hwy 52 S PO Box 726	Kenmare	ND	58746	**800-342-4418***	701-385-4277
*Cust Svc					
FC Haab Co Inc 2314 Market St	Philadelphia	PA	19103	**800-486-5663**	215-563-0800
Fred M Schildwachter & Sons Inc 1400 Ferris Pl	Bronx	NY	10461	**800-642-3646**	718-828-2500
Glassmere Fuel Service Inc 1967 Saxonburg Blvd	Tarentum	PA	15084	**800-235-9054**	724-224-0880
Griffith Energy Services Inc 2510 Schuster Dr	Cheverly	MD	20781	**800-633-4328**	301-322-5100
Herring Gas Co Inc 33 Main St	Meadville	MS	39653	**800-543-9049**	601-384-5833
Hollis Alvin & Co Inc 1 Hollis St	South Weymouth	MA	02190	**800-649-5090**	781-335-2100
Hometown Inc 1518 E North Ave	Milwaukee	WI	53202	**800-242-9238**	414-276-9311
Inergy LP 2 Brush Creek Blvd Suite 200	Kansas City	MO	64112	**877-446-3749**	816-842-8181
NASDAQ: NRGY					
Kingston Oil Supply Corp PO Box 760	Port Ewen	NY	12466	**800-755-6726**	845-331-0770
Kocolene Marketing LLC 1725 E Tipton St	Seymour	IN	47274	**800-457-9886**	812-522-2224
Lincoln Land Oil Co 2026 Republic St	Springfield	IL	62702	**800-238-4912**	217-523-5050
Lyon County Co-op Oil Co 1100 E Main St	Marshall	MN	56258	**888-532-9686**	507-532-9686
Martin LP Gas Inc 2606 N Longview St	Kilgore	TX	75662	**800-441-8569**	903-984-0781
Mirabito Fuel Group 44 Grand St	Sidney	NY	13838	**800-934-9480**	607-561-2700
Mitchell Supreme Fuel 532 Freeman St	Orange	NJ	07050	**800-832-7090**	973-678-1800
New London Energy 410 Bank St	New London	CT	06320	**800-944-8803**	860-271-2020
Oliver Oil Co Inc PO Box 248	Chambersburg	PA	17201	**800-634-8729**	717-264-5165
Peterson William R Oil Co 276 Main St Suite 1 PO box 31	Portland	CT	06480	**800-622-6971**	860-342-3560
Petro Heat & Power Corp 28 Southfield Ave	Stamford	CT	06902	**800-775-4645**	203-323-2121
Polsinello Fuels Inc 41 Riverside Ave	Rensselaer	NY	12144	**800-334-5823**	518-463-0084
Range Co-op Inc 102 S Hoover Rd	Virginia	MN	55792	**800-862-8628**	218-741-7393
Schildwachter Fred M & Sons Inc 1400 Ferris Pl	Bronx	NY	10461	**800-642-3646**	718-828-2500
Shipley Energy Co 550 E King St	York	PA	17405	**800-839-1849**	717-848-4100
Spencer Oil Co Inc 16410 Common Rd	Roseville	MI	48066	**800-445-7562**	586-775-5022
Star Gas Partners LP 2187 Atlantic St	Stamford	CT	06902	**800-966-9827**	203-328-7300
NYSE: SGU					
Streicher Mobile Fueling Inc 800 W Cypress Creek Rd Suite 580	Fort Lauderdale	FL	33309	**800-383-5734**	954-308-4200
NASDAQ: FUEL					
Suburban Propane Partners LP 240 Rt 10 W PO Box 206	Whippany	NJ	07981	**800-526-0620**	973-887-5300
NYSE: SPH					
Walker Oil Co PO Box 215	Nottingham	PA	19362	**800-468-6005**	610-932-8524
Webber Energy Fuels 700 Main St	Bangor	ME	04401	**800-932-2371**	207-942-5501
William R Peterson Oil Co 276 Main St Suite 1 PO box 31	Portland	CT	06480	**800-622-6971**	860-342-3560
Woodruff Energy 73 Water St	Bridgeton	NJ	08302	**800-557-1121**	856-455-1111

312 FUND-RAISING SERVICES

Company / Address	City	State	ZIP	Toll-Free	Phone
Alford Group Inc 1603 Orrington Ave 2nd Fl	Evanston	IL	60201	**800-291-8913**	847-425-9800
Bentz Whaley Flessner 7251 Ohms Ln	Minneapolis	MN	55439	**800-921-0111**	952-921-0111
Brakeley Briscoe Inc 51 Locust Ave Suite 204	New Canaan	CT	06804	**800-486-5171**	203-972-0282
Cargill Assoc Inc 4701 Altamesa Blvd	Fort Worth	TX	76133	**800-433-2233**	817-292-9374
Carlton & Co 101 Federal St Suite 1900	Boston	MA	02110	**800-622-0194**	617-342-7257
Community Counselling Service Co Inc 461 5th Ave 3rd Fl	New York	NY	10017	**800-223-6733**	212-695-1175
First Counsel Inc 428 E 4th St Suite 100	Charlotte	NC	28202	**800-313-1645**	704-342-1100
Gonser Gerber Tinker Stuhr LLP 400 E Diehl Rd Suite 380	Naperville	IL	60563	**800-446-4487**	630-505-1433
Hodge Cramer & Assoc Inc 5400 Frantz Rd Suite 120	Dublin	OH	43016	**800-978-9212**	614-761-3005
Ketchum Inc 5151 Belt Line Rd Suite 900	Dallas	TX	75254	**800-242-2161**	214-866-7600
KMA The Agency 7160 Dallas Pkwy Suite 400	Plano	TX	75024	**800-562-4161**	972-244-1900
LW Robbins Assoc 201 Summer St	Holliston	MA	01746	**800-229-5972**	508-893-0210
MacIntyre Assoc Inc 106 W State St	Kennett Square	PA	19348	**888-575-0903**	610-925-5925
PEP Direct Inc 19 Stoney Brook Dr	Wilton	NH	03086	**877-782-3782**	603-654-6141
Robbins LW Assoc 201 Summer St	Holliston	MA	01746	**800-229-5972**	508-893-0210
Ruotolo Assoc Inc 29 Broadway Suite 210	Cresskill	NJ	07626	**800-786-8656**	201-568-3898

313 FURNACES & OVENS - INDUSTRIAL PROCESS

Company / Address	City	State	ZIP	Toll-Free	Phone
Ajax Tocco Magnethermic Corp 1745 Overland Ave NE	Warren	OH	44483	**800-321-0153**	330-372-8511
Alpha 1 Induction Service Center Inc 1525 Old Alum Creek Dr	Columbus	OH	43209	**800-991-2599**	614-253-8900
AVS Inc 60 Fitchburg Rd	Ayer	MA	01432	**800-272-0710**	978-772-0710
BH Thermal Corp 1055 Gibbard Ave	Columbus	OH	43201	**800-848-7673**	614-294-3376
CCI Thermal Technologies Inc 5918 Roper Rd	Edmonton	AB	T6B3E1	**800-661-8529**	780-466-3178
Cincinnati Industrial Machinery An Armor Metal Group Co 3280 Hageman St	Cincinnati	OH	45241	**800-677-0076**	513-769-0700
Despatch Industries Inc 8860 207th St W	Lakeville	MN	55044	**800-473-7373**	952-469-5424
Detroit Radiant Product Co 21400 Hoover Rd	Warren	MI	48089	**800-222-1100**	586-756-0950
Detroit Stoker Co 1510 E 1st St	Monroe	MI	48161	**800-786-5374**	734-241-9500
Eclipse Inc 1665 Elmwood Rd	Rockford	IL	61103	**800-676-3254**	815-877-3031
Electric Heating Equipment Co 1240 Oronoque Rd	Milford	CT	06460	**800-958-9998**	203-882-0199
Fast Heat Inc 776 Oaklawn Ave	Elmhurst	IL	60126	**800-982-4328**	630-833-5400
Fostoria Industries Inc 1200 N Main St	Fostoria	OH	44830	**800-495-4025**	419-435-9201
Gas-Fired Products Inc PO Box 36485	Charlotte	NC	28236	**800-438-4936**	704-372-3485
Glenro Inc 39 McBride Ave	Paterson	NJ	07501	**800-922-0106**	973-279-5900
Glo-Quartz Electric Heater Co Inc 7084 Maple St	Mentor	OH	44060	**800-321-3574***	440-255-9701
*Sales					
Global Finishing Solutions LLC 1625 W Crosby Rd Suite 124	Carrollton	TX	75006	**800-389-5296**	
Heatrex Inc PO Box 515	Meadville	PA	16335	**800-394-6589**	814-724-1800
Inductoheat Inc 32251 N Avis Dr	Madison Heights	MI	48071	**800-642-8903**	248-585-9393
Inductotherm Corp 10 Indel Ave	Rancocas	NJ	08073	**800-257-9527**	609-267-9000
Inductotherm Industries Inc 10 Indel Ave	Rancocas	NJ	08073	**800-257-9527**	609-267-9000
Industrial Heater Corp 30 Knotter Dr	Cheshire	CT	06410	**800-822-4426**	203-250-0500
Industronics Service Co 489 Sullivan Ave PO Box 649	South Windsor	CT	06074	**800-878-1551**	860-289-1551
International Thermal Systems LLC 4697 W Greenfield Ave	Milwaukee	WI	53214	**877-683-6797**	414-672-7700
IntriCon Corp 2034 S Limekiln Pike	Dresher	PA	19025	**800-523-6500**	215-646-6600
AMEX: IIN					
Ipsen International Inc PO Box 6266	Rockford	IL	61125	**800-727-7625**	815-332-4941
John Zink Co LLC PO Box 21220	Tulsa	OK	74121	**800-421-9242**	918-234-1800
Johnson Gas Appliance Co 520 E Ave NW	Cedar Rapids	IA	52405	**800-553-5422**	319-365-5267
JT Thorpe & Son Inc 1060 Hensley St	Richmond	CA	94801	**800-577-1755**	510-233-2500
Nevo Corp 50 Haynes Ct	Ronkonkoma	NY	11779	**800-955-6836**	631-585-8787
Novatec Inc 222 E Thomas Ave	Baltimore	MD	21225	**800-237-8379**	410-789-4811

Company	City	State	ZIP	Toll-Free	Phone
Paragon Industries Inc 2011 South Town E Blvd	Mesquite	TX	75149	**800-876-4328**	972-288-7557
Pillar Industries 21905 Gateway Rd	Brookfield	WI	53045	**800-558-7733**	262-317-5300
Radyne Corp 211 W Boden St	Milwaukee	WI	53207	**800-236-8360**	414-481-8360
Ray Burner/RD Miners Co 401 Parr Blvd	Richmond	CA	94801	**800-729-2876**	510-236-4972
SECO/Warwick Corp 180 Mercer St	Meadville	PA	16335	**800-458-6071**	814-724-1400
SPX Corp Lindberg Div 304 Hart St	Watertown	WI	53094	**800-873-4468**	920-261-7000
Surface Combustion Inc 1700 Indian Wood Cir	Maumee	OH	43537	**800-537-8980**	419-891-7150
Tempco Electric Heater Mfg 607 N Central Ave	Wood Dale	IL	60191	**800-323-6859**	630-350-2252
Thermal Circuits Inc 1 Technology Way	Salem	MA	01970	**800-808-4328**	978-745-1162
Thermal Engineering Corp 2741 The Boulevard	Columbia	SC	29209	**800-331-0097**	803-783-0750
Todd Combustion Group 2 Armstrong Rd 3rd Fl	Shelton	CT	06484	**800-225-0085**	203-925-0380
Trent Inc 201 Leverington Ave	Philadelphia	PA	19127	**800-544-8736**	215-482-5000
Truheat Corp 700 Grand St	Allegan	MI	49010	**800-879-6199**	269-673-2145
Zink John Co LLC PO Box 21220	Tulsa	OK	74121	**800-421-9242**	918-234-1800

314 FURNITURE - MFR

SEE ALSO Baby Products; Cabinets - Wood; Fixtures - Office & Store; Mattresses & Adjustable Beds; Recycled Plastics Products

314-1 Commercial & Industrial Furniture

Company	City	State	ZIP	Toll-Free	Phone
Adelphia Steel Equipment Co 7372 State Rd	Philadelphia	PA	19136	**800-865-8211**	215-333-6300
Allied Plastics Co Inc 2001 Walnut St	Jacksonville	FL	32206	**800-999-0386***	904-359-0386
*Cust Svc					
Allsteel Inc 2210 2nd Ave	Muscatine	IA	52761	**888-255-7833***	563-262-4800
*Cust Svc					
Anthro Corp 10450 SW Manhasset Dr	Tualatin	OR	97062	**800-325-3841**	503-691-2556
Bestar Inc 4220 Villeneuve St	Lac-Megantic	QC	G6B2C3	**888-823-7827**	819-583-1017
TSE: BES					
Bevco Precision Mfg Co 2246A Bluemound Rd	Waukesha	WI	53186	**800-864-2991**	262-798-9200
BGD Cos Inc 275 Market St Suite 192	Minneapolis	MN	55405	**800-699-3537**	612-338-6804
Biofit Engineered Products 15500 Biofit Way	Bowling Greene	OH	43402	**800-597-0246**	419-823-1089
BK Barrit Corp 1850 E Sedgley Ave	Philadelphia	PA	19124	**888-256-2020**	215-533-3900
Borroughs Corp 3002 N Burdick St	Kalamazoo	MI	49004	**800-748-0227**	269-342-0161
Brayton International Inc 250 Swathmoore St	High Point	NC	27263	**800-627-6770**	336-434-4151
Bright Chair Co 51 Railroad Ave PO Box 269	Middletown	NY	10940	**888-524-5997**	845-343-2196
Carolina Business Furniture LLC 535 Archdale Blvd	Archdale	NC	27263	**800-763-0212**	336-431-9400
Cramer Inc 1222 Quebec St	North Kansas City	MO	64116	**800-366-6700**	816-471-4433
Dar-Ran Furniture Industries 2402 Shore St	High Point	NC	27263	**800-334-7891**	336-861-2400
Dauphin North America 300 Myrtle Ave	Boonton	NJ	07005	**800-631-1186***	973-263-1100
*Cust Svc					
Davis Furniture Industries Inc 2401 S College St	High Point	NC	27260	**877-463-2847**	336-889-2009
Design Options 5202 Eagle Trail Dr	Tampa	FL	33634	**877-800-3560***	813-885-4950
*Cust Svc					
DMI Furniture Inc 101 Bullitt Ln Suite 205	Louisville	KY	40222	**888-372-1927**	502-426-4351
Easi File Mfg Corp 6 Wrigley St	Irvine	CA	92618	**800-800-5563**	949-855-4121
Emeco Industries Inc 805 W Elm Ave PO Box 179	Hanover	PA	17331	**800-366-5951**	717-637-5951
Engineered Data Products Inc 2550 W Midway Blvd	Broomfield	CO	80020	**800-432-1337**	303-465-2800
Ergotron Inc 1181 Trapp Rd	Eagan	MN	55121	**800-888-8458***	651-681-7600
*Sales					
Executive Office Concepts Inc 1715 S Anderson Ave	Compton	CA	90220	**800-421-5927**	310-537-1657
Falcon Products Inc 9387 Dielman Industrial Dr	Saint Louis	MO	63132	**800-873-3252**	314-991-9200
Fillip Metal Cabinet Co 701 N Albany Ave	Chicago	IL	60612	**800-535-0733**	773-826-7373
Fixtures Furniture 1642 Crystal Ave	Kansas City	MO	64126	**800-821-3500***	816-241-4500
*Cust Svc					
Flex-Y-Plan Distinctive Office Furnitue PO Box CC	Fairview	PA	16415	**800-458-0552***	814-474-1565
*Cust Svc					
Flexible Furniture 323 Acorn St	Plainwell	MI	49080	**800-875-6836***	269-685-6831
*Cust Svc					
Foldcraft Co 615 Centennial Dr	Kenyon	MN	55946	**800-759-6653**	507-789-5111
Franke Foodservice Systems 305 Tech Park Dr	La Vergne	TN	37086	**888-437-2653**	615-287-8200
Geiger International Inc 6095 Fulton Industrial Blvd SW	Atlanta	GA	30336	**800-444-8812**	404-344-1100
GF Office Furniture Ltd 6655 Seville Dr	Canfield	OH	44406	**800-321-4005***	330-533-7799
*Cust Svc					
Global Industries Inc 17 W Stow Rd	Marlton	NJ	08053	**800-220-1900**	856-596-3390
Groupe Lacasse LLC 99 St-Pierre St	Sainte-Pie	QC	J0H1W0	**888-522-2773**	450-772-2495
Gunlocke Co LLC 1 Gunlocke Dr	Wayland	NY	14572	**800-828-6300***	585-728-5111
*Cust Svc					
H Wilson Co 555 W Taft Dr	South Holland	IL	60473	**800-245-7224**	708-339-5111
Harter Group Inc 11451 Harter Dr	Middlebury	IN	46540	**800-543-5449**	574-825-5871
Hausmann Industries Inc 130 Union St	Northvale	NJ	07647	**888-428-7626**	201-767-0255
Haworth Inc 1 Haworth Ctr	Holland	MI	49423	**800-344-2600**	616-393-3000
Helikon Furniture Co Inc 607 Norwich Ave	Taftville	CT	06380	**800-824-6729**	860-886-2301
Herman Miller Inc 855 E Main Ave	Zeeland	MI	49464	**888-443-4357**	616-654-3000
NASDAQ: MLHR					
HFG (Hospitality Furniture Group Mfg) 8180 NW 36th St Suite 418	Miami	FL	33166	**800-772-8826**	305-477-2882
High Point Furniture Industries Inc 1104 Bedford St PO Box 2063	High Point	NC	27261	**800-447-3462**	336-431-7101
Hirsh Industries Inc 1500 Delaware Ave	Des Moines	IA	50317	**800-872-3279**	515-265-7111
Holga Inc 7901 Woodley Ave	Van Nuys	CA	91406	**800-544-4623**	818-782-0600
HON Co 200 Oak St	Muscatine	IA	52761	**800-553-8230**	563-264-7400
Hospitality Furniture Group Mfg (HFG) 8180 NW 36th St Suite 418	Miami	FL	33166	**800-772-8826**	305-477-2882
Huot Mfg Co 550 Wheeler St N	Saint Paul	MN	55104	**800-832-3838**	651-646-1869
IAC Industries 895 Beacon St	Brea	CA	92821	**800-229-1422**	714-990-8997
Indiana Furniture Industries Inc 1224 Mill St	Jasper	IN	47546	**800-422-5727**	812-482-5727
Institutional & Office Services Inc 4 Cara Ct	Randolph	NJ	07869	**800-223-1210**	973-895-9002
Intrex LLC 40 Park St	Brooklyn	NY	11206	**877-946-8739**	718-455-5042
Invincible Office Furniture Co 842 S 26th St	Manitowoc	WI	54220	**800-558-4417**	920-682-4601
Inwood Office Environments 1108 E 15th St	Jasper	IN	47546	**800-786-6121**	812-482-6121
Izzydesign 1 Industrial Pk	Belton	TX	76513	**800-551-3227***	254-939-3517
*Cust Svc					
Jasper Desk Co 415 E 6th St	Jasper	IN	47547	**800-365-7994***	812-482-4132
*Cust Svc					
Jasper Seating Co Inc 225 Clay St	Jasper	IN	47546	**800-622-5661**	812-482-3204
Jofco International 402 E 13th St	Jasper	IN	47546	**800-235-6326**	812-482-5154
JSJ Corp 700 Robbins Rd	Grand Haven	MI	49417	**800-867-3208**	616-842-6350
KI 1330 Bellevue St	Green Bay	WI	54302	**877-231-8555**	920-468-8100
Kimball Hospitality 1205 Kimball Blvd	Jasper	IN	47549	**800-634-9510**	
Kimball Office Furniture Co 1600 Royal St	Jasper	IN	47549	**800-482-1818**	812-482-1600
Knoll Inc 1235 Water St	East Greenville	PA	18041	**800-343-5665***	215-679-7991
NYSE: KNL ■ *Cust Svc					
Lakeside Mfg Inc 4900 W Electric Ave	West Milwaukee	WI	53219	**800-558-8565**	414-902-6400
LB Furniture Industries LLC 99 S 3rd St	Hudson	NY	12534	**800-403-0833**	518-828-1501
Loewenstein Inc 206 E Frazier Ave	Liberty	NC	27298	**877-396-5356**	336-622-2201
Magna Design Inc 5804 204th St SW	Lynnwood	WA	98046	**800-233-2304**	425-776-2181
Martin Furniture 7757 St Andrews Ave	San Diego	CA	92154	**800-268-5669**	619-671-5100
Marvel Group Corp 3843 W 43rd St	Chicago	IL	60632	**800-621-8846***	773-523-4804
*Cust Svc					
Maxon Furniture Inc 21606 86th Pl S	Kent	WA	98031	**800-876-4274***	253-872-0396
*Cust Svc					
Mayline Group 619 N Commerce St	Sheboygan	WI	53081	**800-822-8037**	920-457-5537
McDowell-Craig Office Furniture 13146 Firestone Blvd	Norwalk	CA	90650	**877-921-2100**	562-921-4441
Miller Herman Inc 855 E Main Ave	Zeeland	MI	49464	**888-443-4357**	616-654-3000
NASDAQ: MLHR					
Miller Office Furniture 1212 Lincoln Dr	High Point	NC	27260	**800-438-4324**	336-819-6400
MLP Seating Corp 2125 Lively Blvd	Elk Grove Village	IL	60007	**800-723-3030**	847-956-1700
National Business Services 1601 Magoffin Ave	El Paso	TX	79901	**800-777-7807***	915-544-1271
*Sales					
National Office Furniture 1205 Kimball Blvd	Jasper	IN	47549	**800-482-1717**	
NER Data Products Inc 307 S Delsea Dr	Glassboro	NJ	08028	**800-257-5235**	856-881-5524
Neutral Posture Inc 3904 N Texas Ave	Bryan	TX	77803	**800-446-3746**	979-778-0502
Nova Solutions Inc 421 W Industrial Ave	Effingham	IL	62401	**800-730-6682**	217-342-7070
Omni International Inc 435 12th St SW PO Box 1409	Vernon	AL	35592	**800-844-6664**	205-695-9173
Open Plan Systems Inc 14140 N Washington Hwy PO Box 1810	Ashland	VA	23005	**800-849-7239**	804-228-5600
Paoli Inc 201 E Martin St	Orleans	IN	47452	**800-457-7415**	812-723-2791
Penco Products Inc 99 Brower Ave	Oaks	PA	19456	**800-562-1000**	610-666-0500
Plymold Seating 615 Centennial Dr	Kenyon	MN	55946	**800-759-6653**	507-789-5111
Pucel Enterprises Inc 1440 E 36th St	Cleveland	OH	44114	**800-336-4986**	216-881-4604
Quaker Furniture Inc 3060 Main Ave SE	Hickory	NC	28602	**800-356-5732**	828-322-1794
Reconditioned Systems Inc 444 W Fairmont Dr	Tempe	AZ	85282	**800-280-5000**	480-968-1772
Robertson Furniture Co Inc 720 Elberton St PO Box 847	Toccoa	GA	30577	**800-241-0713**	706-886-1494
Safco Products Co 9300 W Research Ctr Rd	New Hope	MN	55428	**800-328-3020**	763-536-6700
Shure Mfg Corp 1901 W Main St	Washington	MO	63090	**800-227-4873**	636-390-7100
Signore Inc 55-57 Jefferson St	Ellicottville	NY	14731	**800-828-2808**	716-699-2361
Spectrum Industries Inc 1600 Johnson St	Chippewa Falls	WI	54729	**800-235-1262**	715-723-6750
Steelcase Inc PO Box 1967	Grand Rapids	MI	49501	**888-783-3522**	616-247-2710
NYSE: SCS					
Stylex Inc Tungsten Rd PO Box 5038	Delanco	NJ	08075	**800-257-5742**	856-461-5600
Styline Industries Inc PO Box 100	Huntingburg	IN	47542	**800-521-5381**	812-683-4848
TAB Products Co 605 4th St	Mayville	WI	53050	**888-822-9777**	920-387-3131
Taylor Cos 75 Taylor St	Bedford	OH	44146	**888-758-2956**	440-232-0700
Techline USA LLC 500 S Division St	Waunakee	WI	53597	**800-356-8400**	
Tennsco Corp 201 Tennsco Dr PO Box 1888	Dickson	TN	37056	**800-251-8184***	615-446-8000
*Cust Svc					
Trendway Corp PO Box 9016	Holland	MI	49422	**800-968-5344**	616-399-3900
Tuohy Furniture Corp 42 St Albans Pl	Chatfield	MN	55923	**800-533-1696***	507-867-4280
*Cust Svc					
Ulrich Planfiling Equipment Corp 2120 4th Ave PO Box 135	Lakewood	NY	14750	**800-346-2875**	716-763-1815
United Chair Co 147 St-Pierre St	Sainte-Pie	QC	J0H1W0	**800-723-5181**	450-772-2495
Van San Corp 16735 E Johnson Dr	City of Industry	CA	91745	**800-423-1829**	626-961-7211
Viking Acoustical Corp 21480 Heath Ave	Lakeville	MN	55044	**800-328-8385**	952-469-3405
Vitro Seating Products Inc 201 Madison St	Saint Louis	MO	63102	**800-325-7093***	314-241-2265
*Cust Svc					
West Coast Industries Inc 10 Jackson St	San Francisco	CA	94101	**800-243-3150**	415-621-6656
Whitehall Furniture 201 E Martin St	Orleans	IN	47452	**800-467-3585**	812-865-3898
Wilson H Co 555 W Taft Dr	South Holland	IL	60473	**800-245-7224**	708-339-5111
Workplace Systems Inc 562 Mammoth Rd	Londonderry	NH	03053	**800-258-9700**	603-622-3727
Workspaces Inc 14311 SE 77th Ct	Newcastle	WA	98059	**800-466-4123**	425-226-4398
Wright Line LLC 160 Gold Star Blvd	Worcester	MA	01606	**800-225-7348**	508-852-4300
Zoom Seating 1644 Crystal Ave	Kansas City	MO	64126	**866-839-9666**	

314-2 Household Furniture

Company	City	State	ZIP	Toll-Free	Phone
American Moulding & Millwork Co 2801 West Ln	Stockton	CA	95204	**800-441-8231**	209-946-5800
Ameriwood Industries Inc 305 E South 1st St	Wright City	MO	63390	**800-454-0283**	636-745-3351
Ashley Furniture Industries Inc 1 Ashley Way	Arcadia	WI	54612	**800-477-2222**	608-323-3377
Baby's Dream Furniture Inc PO Box 579	Buena Vista	GA	31803	**800-835-2742**	229-649-4404
Baker Furniture 1661 Monroe Ave NW	Grand Rapids	MI	49505	**800-592-2537**	616-361-7321
Brooks Furniture Mfg Inc 110 Maples Ln	Tazewell	TN	37879	**800-427-6657**	423-626-1111
Broyhill Furniture Industries Inc 1 Broyhill Pk	Lenoir	NC	28633	**800-327-6944***	828-758-3111
*Cust Svc					
Brueton Industries Inc 145-68 228th St	Springfield Gardens	NY	11413	**800-221-6783***	718-527-3000
*Cust Svc					
Bryan Ashley International Inc 2601 Gateway Dr	Pompano Beach	FL	33069	**800-331-4225**	954-351-1199
Bush Industries Inc 1 Mason Dr	Jamestown	NY	14701	**800-228-2874**	716-665-2000
Bushline Inc 707 Industrial Park Dr	New Tazewell	TN	37825	**800-627-1682**	423-626-5246
Charles Inc 518 N 10th St	Council Bluffs	IA	51503	**800-831-5878**	712-328-2603
Charles Schneider Furniture 518 N 10th St	Council Bluffs	IA	51503	**800-831-5878**	712-328-1587
Claude Gable Co 322 Fraley Rd	High Point	NC	27263	**800-422-5331**	336-883-1351

Classified Section

Household Furniture (Cont'd)

Company	City	State	ZIP	Toll-Free	Phone
Clayton Marcus Co Inc 166 Teague Town Rd *Cust Svc	Hickory	NC	28601	**800-893-2931***	828-495-2200
Community Products LLC DBA Community Playthings 359 Gibson Hill Rd	Chester	NY	10918	**800-777-4244**	845-572-3410
DMI Furniture Inc 101 Bullitt Ln Suite 205	Louisville	KY	40222	**888-372-1927**	502-426-4351
Dorel Industries Inc 12345 Albert Hudson St Suite 100 *NASDAQ: DIIB* ■ *Cust Svc	Montreal	QC	H1G3L1	**800-544-1108***	514-323-5701
Dorel Juvenile Group 2525 State St	Columbus	IN	47201	**800-544-1108**	812-372-0141
Drexel Heritage Furnishings Inc 1925 Eastchester Dr	High Point	NC	27265	**866-450-3434**	336-888-4800
El Ran Furniture Ltd 2751 Transcanada Hwy	Pointe-Claire	QC	H9R1B4	**800-361-6546**	514-630-5656
Elegant Bebe PO Box 670235	Dallas	TX	75536	**888-886-8307**	972-239-0028
Elliott's Designs Inc 18201 Santa Fe Ave S	Rancho Dominguez	CA	90221	**800-435-5468**	310-631-4931
Evenflo Co Inc 1801 Commerce Dr	Piqua	OH	45356	**800-233-5921**	937-415-3300
Fraenkel Co Inc PO Box 15385	Baton Rouge	LA	70895	**800-847-2580**	225-275-8111
Fredman Brothers Furniture Co Inc 908 SW Washington St	Peoria	IL	61602	**800-248-5228**	309-674-2011
Gable Claude Co 322 Fraley Rd	High Point	NC	27263	**800-422-5331**	336-883-1351
Generation 2 Worldwide 113 Anderson Ct Suite 1	Dothan	AL	36301	**800-738-1140**	334-792-1144
Gold Mitchell Co 135 One Comfortable Pl	Taylorsville	NC	28681	**800-789-5401**	828-632-9200
Good Cos Inc 1118 E 223rd St	Carson	CA	90745	**800-666-8225**	310-549-2160
GuildCraft of California 18626 S Reyes Ave	Rancho Dominguez	CA	90221	**800-283-6716**	310-223-4200
Gusdorf Canada Ltd 2105 Dagenais Blvd W	Laval	QC	H7L5W9	**800-361-2304**	450-963-0808
Hekman Furniture Co 1400 Buchanan Ave SW	Grand Rapids	MI	49507	**800-253-9249**	616-452-1411
Hickory Hill Furniture Corp 501 Hoyle St	Valdese	NC	28690	**800-737-4432**	828-874-2124
Hooker Furniture Corp 440 E Commonwealth Blvd *NASDAQ: HOFT* ■ *Cust Svc	Martinsville	VA	24112	**888-462-6877***	276-632-0459
Jack-Post Corp 810 E 3rd St *Cust Svc	Buchanan	MI	49107	**800-800-4950***	269-695-7000
Jensen Industries Inc 1946 E 46th St	Los Angeles	CA	90058	**800-325-8351**	323-235-6800
Johnston Tombigbee Furniture Mfg Co 1402 Waterworks Rd	Columbus	MS	39701	**800-654-3876**	662-328-1685
Keller Mfg Co Inc 1010 Keller Dr NE	New Salisbury	IN	47161	**800-738-2240**	812-366-4001
Khoury Inc 1011 N Stephenson Ave *Cust Svc	Iron Mountain	MI	49801	**800-553-5446***	906-774-6333
KidsChairs 2201 Long Prairie Suite 107-195	Flower Mound	TX	75022	**800-993-5578**	
Kimball Home Furniture 2602 Newton St	Jasper	IN	47549	**800-482-1616**	812-482-1600
Kincaid Furniture Co Inc 240 Pleasant Hill Rd	Hudson	NC	28638	**800-438-8207**	828-728-3261
Klaussner Furniture Industries Inc 405 Lewallen Rd *Cust Svc	Asheboro	NC	27205	**800-828-9534***	336-625-6174
Leathercraft Inc 102 Section House Rd	Conover	NC	28613	**800-951-3507**	828-322-3305
Lexington Home Brands PO Box 1008	Lexington	NC	27293	**800-539-4636**	336-249-5300
Little Tikes Co 2180 Barlow Rd *Cust Svc	Hudson	OH	44236	**800-321-0183***	330-650-3000
Mantua Mfg Co 7900 Northfield Rd *Orders	Walton Hills	OH	44146	**800-333-8333***	440-232-8865
McGuire Furniture Co 1201 Bryant St	San Francisco	CA	94103	**800-662-4847**	415-626-1414
Mitchell Gold Co 135 One Comfortable Pl	Taylorsville	NC	28681	**800-789-5401**	828-632-9200
Norwalk Furniture Corp 100 Furniture Pkwy *Orders	Norwalk	OH	44857	**800-837-2565***	419-668-4461
O'Sullivan Furniture 1900 Gulf St *Cust Svc	Lamar	MO	64759	**800-327-9782***	417-682-3322
Pennsylvania House Co 137 10th St N *Cust Svc	Lewisburg	PA	17837	**800-782-9663***	570-523-1285
Robern Inc 701 N Wilson Ave	Bristol	PA	19007	**800-877-2376**	215-826-9800
Rowe Cos 1650 Tysons Blvd Suite 710 *AMEX: ROW*	McLean	VA	22102	**800-340-7693**	703-847-8670
Rowe Furniture Inc 1650 Tysons Blvd Suite 710	McLean	VA	22102	**800-334-7693**	703-847-8670
RT Mfg 1186 N Industrial Park Dr	Orem	UT	84057	**800-524-9607**	
Sauder Woodworking Co 502 Middle St PO Box 156 *Cust Svc	Archbold	OH	43502	**800-523-3987***	419-446-2711
Schnadig Corp 1111 E Touhy Ave Suite 500	Des Plaines	IL	60018	**800-468-8730**	847-803-6000
Schneider Charles Furniture 518 N 10th St	Council Bluffs	IA	51503	**800-831-5878**	712-328-1587
Shermag Inc 2171 King St W *Sales	Sherbrooke	QC	J1J2G1	**800-363-2635***	819-566-1515
Sico North America Inc 7525 Cahill Rd	Minneapolis	MN	55439	**800-328-6138**	952-941-1700
SklarPeppler Furniture Corp 617 Victoria St E	Whitby	ON	L1N5S7	**800-263-2607**	905-619-6523
Standard Furniture Mfg Co Inc 801 Hwy 31 S	Bay Minette	AL	36507	**800-827-7866**	251-937-6741
Stanley Furniture Co Inc 1641 Fairystone Pk Hwy *NASDAQ: STLY*	Stanleytown	VA	24168	**800-216-6888**	276-627-2000
Techline USA LLC 500 S Division St	Waunakee	WI	53597	**800-356-8400**	
Towne Square 2000 Inc 402 Hawkins St	Hillsboro	TX	76645	**800-356-1663**	254-582-7444
Vanguard Furniture Co Inc 109 Simpson St	Conover	NC	28613	**800-968-1702**	828-328-5631
Vermont Tubbs 1 Tubbs Ave	Brandon	VT	05733	**800-327-7026**	802-247-3414
Whittier Wood Products Inc 3787 W 1st Ave	Eugene	OR	97402	**800-653-3336**	541-687-0213
Zenith Products Corp 400 Lukens Dr	New Castle	DE	19720	**800-892-3986**	302-326-8200

314-3 Institutional & Other Public Buildings Furniture

Company	City	State	ZIP	Toll-Free	Phone
Adden Furniture Inc 26 Jackson St	Lowell	MA	01852	**800-625-3876**	978-454-7848
American Desk Mfg Co Inc PO Box 608	Temple	TX	76503	**800-433-3142**	254-778-1811
American Seating Co 401 American Seating Ctr *Cust Svc	Grand Rapids	MI	49504	**800-748-0268***	616-732-6600
Artco-Bell Corp PO Box 608	Temple	TX	76503	**800-950-5850**	254-778-1811
Bay Concepts Inc PO Box 7229	Oakland	CA	94601	**888-534-4511**	510-534-4511
Brayton International Inc 250 Swathmoore St	High Point	NC	27263	**800-627-6770**	336-434-4151
Bretford Mfg Inc 11000 Seymour Ave	Franklin Park	IL	60131	**800-521-9614**	847-678-2545
Brodart Co 500 Arch St	Williamsport	PA	17701	**800-233-8467**	570-326-2461
Brodart Co Contract Library Furniture Div 500 Arch St	Williamsport	PA	17701	**800-233-8467**	570-326-2461
Buckstaff Co PO Box 2506	Oshkosh	WI	54903	**800-755-5890**	920-235-5890
Enochs Medical Furniture Inc PO Box 50559 *Cust Svc	Indianapolis	IN	46250	**800-428-2305***	317-580-2940
Fleetwood Group Inc 11832 James St	Holland	MI	49424	**800-257-6390**	616-396-1142
Fordham Equipment Co 3308 Edson Ave	Bronx	NY	10469	**800-249-5922**	718-379-7300
Gaylord Brothers PO Box 4901 *Cust Svc	Syracuse	NY	13221	**800-634-6304***	315-457-5070
Gunlocke Co LLC 1 Gunlocke Dr *Cust Svc	Wayland	NY	14572	**800-828-6300***	585-728-5111
Hard Mfg Co Inc 230 Grider St	Buffalo	NY	14215	**800-873-4273**	716-893-1800
Herman Miller for Health Care 855 E Main Ave PO Box 302	Zeeland	MI	49464	**888-443-4357**	
Hussey Seating Co 38 Dyer St Ext	North Berwick	ME	03906	**800-341-0401**	207-676-2271
Inwood Office Environments 1108 E 15th St	Jasper	IN	47546	**800-786-6121**	812-482-6121
Irwin Seating Co Inc PO Box 2429	Grand Rapids	MI	49501	**800-759-7328**	616-784-2621
Jasper Seating Co Inc 225 Clay St	Jasper	IN	47546	**800-622-5661**	812-482-3204
KI 1330 Bellevue St	Green Bay	WI	54302	**877-231-8555**	920-468-8100
Kimball Hospitality 1205 Kimball Blvd	Jasper	IN	47549	**800-634-9510**	
KLN Steel Products Co PO Box 34690	San Antonio	TX	78265	**800-624-9101**	210-227-4747
LB Furniture Industries LLC 99 S 3rd St	Hudson	NY	12534	**800-403-0833**	518-828-1501
List Industries Inc 401 NW 12th Ave	Deerfield Beach	FL	33442	**800-776-1342**	954-429-9155
LL Sams Inc 1203 Industrial Blvd	Cameron	TX	76520	**800-537-4723**	254-697-6754
Meco Corp 1500 Industrial Rd	Greeneville	TN	37745	**800-251-7558**	423-639-1171
Midwest Folding Products Inc 1414 S Western Ave	Chicago	IL	60608	**800-621-4718**	312-666-3366
Miller Herman for Health Care 855 E Main Ave PO Box 302	Zeeland	MI	49464	**888-443-4357**	
Mitchell Furniture Systems Inc 1700 W St Paul Ave	Milwaukee	WI	53201	**800-290-5960**	414-342-3111
MITY Enterprises Inc 1301 W 400 North *NASDAQ: MITY*	Orem	UT	84057	**800-327-1692**	801-224-0589
MLP Seating Corp 2125 Lively Blvd	Elk Grove Village	IL	60007	**800-723-3030**	847-956-1700
Monroe Table Co 316 N Walnut St	Colfax	IA	50054	**800-247-2488**	515-674-3511
National Church Furnishings Co 2600 Commercial Blvd	Centralia	WA	98531	**800-225-4599**	360-736-9323
Nemschoff Chairs Inc 909 N 8th St *Cust Svc	Sheboygan	WI	53081	**800-203-8916***	920-457-7726
New Holland Church Furniture 313 Prospect St	New Holland	PA	17557	**800-648-9663**	717-354-4521
Omni International Inc 435 12th St SW PO Box 1409	Vernon	AL	35592	**800-844-6664**	205-695-9173
Overholtzer Church Furniture Inc 626 Kearney Ave *Sales	Modesto	CA	95352	**800-366-1716***	209-529-1716
Reliance Medical Products Inc 3535 Kings Mills Rd	Mason	OH	45040	**800-735-0357**	513-398-3937
Royal Seating Ltd 1110 Industrial Blvd *Cust Svc	Cameron	TX	76520	**800-460-4916***	254-697-6421
Sams LL Inc 1203 Industrial Blvd	Cameron	TX	76520	**800-537-4723**	254-697-6754
Scholarcraft Inc PO Box 170748 *Cust Svc	Birmingham	AL	35217	**888-765-5200***	205-841-1922
Sico North America Inc 7525 Cahill Rd	Minneapolis	MN	55439	**800-328-6138**	952-941-1700
Spectrum Industries Inc 1600 Johnson St	Chippewa Falls	WI	54729	**800-235-1262**	715-723-6750
Sturdisteel Co 131 Ava Dr	Hewitt	TX	76643	**800-433-3116**	254-666-5155
Sunrise Medical Continuing Care Group 5001 Joerns Dr	Stevens Point	WI	54481	**800-972-7581**	715-341-3600
Sunrise Medical Inc 2382 Faraday Ave Suite 200	Carlsbad	CA	92008	**800-278-6747**	760-930-1500
Texwood Furniture Corp 1353 W 2nd St	Taylor	TX	76574	**888-878-0000**	512-352-3000
TMI Systems Design Corp 50 S 3rd Ave West	Dickinson	ND	58601	**800-456-6716**	701-456-6716
Trinity Furniture Mfg 2885 Lorraine Ave	Temple	TX	76501	**800-256-7397**	254-778-4727
United Metal Fabricators Inc 1316 Eisenhower Blvd *Sales	Johnstown	PA	15904	**800-638-5322***	814-266-8726
Virco Mfg Corp 2027 Harpers Way *AMEX: VIR* ■ *Cust Svc	Torrance	CA	90501	**800-448-4726***	310-533-0474
Wieland Furniture Inc 13737 Main St PO Box 1000	Grabill	IN	46741	**888-943-5263**	260-627-3686
Winco Inc 5516 SW 1st Ln	Ocala	FL	34474	**800-237-3377**	352-854-2929
Worden Co Inc 199 E 17th St	Holland	MI	49423	**800-748-0561**	616-392-1848

314-4 Outdoor Furniture

Company	City	State	ZIP	Toll-Free	Phone
Basta Sole 5 Marconi *Cust Svc	Irvine	CA	92618	**800-654-7000***	949-951-2010
Belson Outdoors Inc 111 N River Rd	North Aurora	IL	60542	**800-323-5664**	630-897-8489
Bemis Mfg Co PO Box 901	Sheboygan Falls	WI	53085	**800-558-7651**	920-467-4621
Brown Jordan Co Inc 9860 Gidley St	El Monte	CA	91731	**800-743-4252**	626-443-8971
Cox Industries Inc 860 Cannon Bridge Rd	Orangeburg	SC	29115	**800-476-4401**	803-534-7467
DuMor Inc PO Box 142	Mifflintown	PA	17059	**800-494-0706**	717-436-2106
Hatteras Hammocks Inc PO Box 1602	Greenville	NC	27835	**800-643-3522**	252-758-0641
Homecrest Industries Inc PO Box 350	Wadena	MN	56482	**888-346-4852**	218-631-1000
Kay Park Recreation Corp 1301 Pine St *Cust Svc	Janesville	IA	50647	**800-553-2476***	319-987-2313
Lloyd/Flanders Industries Inc 3010 10th St	Menominee	MI	49858	**800-526-9894**	906-863-4491
Mallin Casual Furniture 1441 Peerless Way	Montebello	CA	90640	**800-251-6537**	323-513-1041
Moultrie Mfg Co PO Box 2948	Moultrie	GA	31776	**800-841-8674**	229-985-1312
RJ Thomas Mfg Co Inc PO Box 946	Cherokee	IA	51012	**800-725-5115**	712-225-5115
Syroco Inc 7528 State Fair Blvd	Baldwinsville	NY	13027	**800-853-9272**	315-635-9911
Texacraft Inc 603 SE 14th St	Ocala	FL	34471	**800-231-9790**	
Tropitone Furniture Co Inc 5 Marconi *Cust Svc	Irvine	CA	92618	**800-654-7000***	949-951-2010
Twin Oaks Hammocks 138 Twin Oaks Rd	Louisa	VA	23093	**800-688-8946**	540-894-5125
Walpole Woodworkers Inc 767 East St PO Box 151	Walpole	MA	02081	**800-343-6948**	508-668-2800

315 FURNITURE - WHOL

Company	City	State	ZIP	Toll-Free	Phone
A Pomerantz & Co 701 Market St Suite 7000	Philadelphia	PA	19106	**800-344-9135**	215-408-2100
Adirondack Chair Co Inc 31-01 Vernon Blvd	Long Island City	NY	11106	**800-477-1330**	718-932-4003
Adirondack Direct 31-01 Vernon Blvd	Long Island City	NY	11106	**800-221-2444**	718-204-4500

				Toll-Free	Phone
ATD-American Co 111-149 Greenwood Ave	Wyncote	PA	19095	**800-283-9327**	215-576-1380
Booker-Price Co 1318 McHenry St	Louisville	KY	40217	**800-928-1080**	502-637-2531
Brown & Saenger PO Box 84040	Sioux Falls	SD	57118	**800-952-3509***	605-336-1960
*Sales					
Business Furniture Corp 6102 Victory Way	Indianapolis	IN	46278	**800-774-5544**	317-216-1600
Business Interiors Inc 4141 Colorado Blvd	Denver	CO	80216	**800-373-6994**	303-321-6671
California Office Furniture Inc 1724 10th St	Sacramento	CA	95814	**877-442-6959**	916-442-6959
Carithers Wallace Courtenay Co 4343 Northeast Expy	Atlanta	GA	30340	**800-292-8220**	770-493-8200
Champion Industries Inc 2450-90 1st Ave	Huntington	WV	25703	**800-624-3431**	304-528-2791
NASDAQ: CHMP					
COECO Office Systems Co PO Box 2088	Rocky Mount	NC	27804	**800-682-6844**	252-977-1121
Dancker Sellew & Douglas 100 Broadway 5th Fl	New York	NY	10005	**800-326-2537**	212-267-2200
Decorize Inc 1938 E Phelps	Springfield	MO	65802	**877-669-3326**	417-879-3326
AMEX: DCZ					
Douron Inc 30 New Plant Ct	Owings Mills	MD	21117	**888-833-8350**	410-363-2600
Empire Office Inc 125 Maiden Ln	New York	NY	10038	**877-533-6747**	212-607-5500
Glover Equipment Inc 221 Cockeysville Rd PO Box 405	Cockeysville	MD	21030	**800-966-9016**	410-771-8000
Haldeman-Homme Inc 430 Industrial Blvd NE	Minneapolis	MN	55413	**800-795-0696**	612-331-4880
Highsmith Inc W 5527 SR 106 PO Box 800	Fort Atkinson	WI	53538	**800-558-3899**	920-563-9571
Holland House Furniture 9420 E 33rd St	Indianapolis	IN	46235	**800-634-4666**	317-895-4300
Huntington Wholesale Furniture Co Inc PO Box 1300	Huntington	WV	25715	**800-788-3858***	304-523-9415
*Orders					
KBM Office Furniture Co 320 S 1st St	San Jose	CA	95113	**800-578-4526**	408-351-7100
Kennedy Group PO Box 420136	Dallas	TX	75342	**800-527-5724**	214-748-0821
Kyle RH Furniture Co 1352 Hansford St	Charleston	WV	25301	**800-624-9170**	304-346-0671
Mastercraft Inc PO Box 326	Shipshewana	IN	46565	**800-522-5652**	260-768-4101
Missco Corp 2510 Lakeland Terr Suite 100	Jackson	MS	39216	**800-647-5333**	601-987-8600
National Business Furniture Inc PO Box 514052	Milwaukee	WI	53203	**800-558-1010***	414-276-8511
*Sales					
Office Furnishings Ltd 725 S 25th Ave	Bellwood	IL	60104	**800-728-8550**	708-547-8550
Ohio Desk Co 1122 Prospect Ave E	Cleveland	OH	44115	**800-326-0601**	216-623-0600
OneWorkplace 475 Brannan St	San Francisco	CA	94107	**800-899-4324**	415-357-2200
Pivot Interiors 2740 Zanker Rd Suite 100	San Jose	CA	95134	**800-350-7135**	408-432-5600
Pomerantz A & Co 701 Market St Suite 7000	Philadelphia	PA	19106	**800-344-9135**	215-408-2100
R & M Office Furniture Inc 9615 Oates Dr	Sacramento	CA	95827	**800-660-1756**	916-362-1756
RH Kyle Furniture Co 1352 Hansford St	Charleston	WV	25301	**800-624-9170**	304-346-0671
Ruff Thomas W & Co Inc 1114 Dublin Rd	Columbus	OH	43215	**800-828-0234**	614-487-4000
Southern Office Furniture Distributors Inc 719 N Regional Rd	Greensboro	NC	27409	**800-933-6369**	336-668-4192
Storage Equipment Co Inc 1258 Titan Dr	Dallas	TX	75247	**800-443-1791**	214-630-9221
Swindal-Powell Co 7750 Phillips Hwy	Jacksonville	FL	32256	**800-422-8903**	904-739-0100
Tangram Interiors Inc 9200 Sorensen Ave	Santa Fe Springs	CA	90670	**800-700-1377**	562-365-5000
Thomas W Ruff & Co Inc 1114 Dublin Rd	Columbus	OH	43215	**800-828-0234**	614-487-4000
Valiant Products Corp 2727 5th Ave W	Denver	CO	80204	**800-347-2727***	303-892-1234
*Cust Svc					
Waldner's Business Environment 125 Rt 110	Farmingdale	NY	11735	**800-473-9253**	631-694-1522
Walsh Brothers Inc PO Box 1711	Phoenix	AZ	85001	**800-527-3437**	602-252-6971
Wasserstrom Co 477 S Front St	Columbus	OH	43215	**800-999-9277**	614-228-6525
Workplace Integrators 30800 Telegraph Rd Suite 4700	Bingham Farms	MI	48025	**800-429-9172**	248-430-2345

316 FURNITURE STORES

SEE ALSO Department Stores

				Toll-Free	Phone
American Furniture Warehouse Co 8501 Grant St	Thornton	CO	80229	**800-992-7997**	303-289-3311
American Home Furnishings 3535 Menaul Blvd NE	Albuquerque	NM	87107	**800-876-4454**	505-883-2211
Aronson Furniture Co 3401 W 47th St	Chicago	IL	60632	**800-610-5678**	773-376-3400
Atlantic Corporate Interiors Inc 4600 Powder Mill Rd Suite 300	Beltsville	MD	20705	**800-564-3228**	301-931-3600
Babies 'R' Us 545 Rt 17 S	Paramus	NJ	07652	**800-869-7787**	201-251-3191
Badcock's Economy Furniture Store Inc 512 Clematis St	West Palm Beach	FL	33401	**800-223-2625**	561-659-1370
Baer's Furniture 1589 NW 12th Ave	Pompano Beach	FL	33069	**800-543-2092**	954-946-3792
Barn Furniture Mart Inc 6206 N Sepulveda Blvd	Van Nuys	CA	91411	**888-302-2276**	818-780-4070
Bombay Co Inc 550 Bailey Ave	Fort Worth	TX	76107	**800-829-7789**	817-347-8200
NYSE: BBA					
Breuner's 3250 Buskirk Ave	Pleasant Hill	CA	94523	**800-865-6778**	925-472-4500
Cargo Kids 2900 W Seminary Dr Suite 100	Fort Worth	TX	76133	**800-333-1402***	817-252-6861
*Cust Svc					
Darvin Furniture 15400 La Grange Rd	Orland Park	IL	60462	**800-232-7846**	708-460-4100
DeKorne Furniture Co Inc 2740 29th St SE	Grand Rapids	MI	49512	**800-968-4848**	616-949-4966
Domain Inc 51 Morgan Dr	Norwood	MA	02062	**877-436-6246**	781-769-9130
El Dorado Furniture Corp 4200 NW 167th St	Miami	FL	33054	**800-236-6256**	305-624-9700
Farmers Furniture 2005 Veterans Blvd Suite 1	Dublin	GA	31040	**800-456-0424**	478-272-4000
Franklin Interiors Inc 2740 Smallman St Suite 600	Pittsburgh	PA	15222	**800-371-5001**	412-261-2525
Fredman Brothers Furniture Co Inc 908 SW Washington St	Peoria	IL	61602	**800-248-5228**	309-674-2011
Gallery Furniture Inc 6006 I-45 N Fwy	Houston	TX	77076	**800-518-0008**	713-694-5570
Granite Furniture Co 1050 E 2100 South	Salt Lake City	UT	84106	**800-470-9077**	801-486-3333
Hansen's Furniture Inc 411 Fraine Barracks Rd	Bismarck	ND	58504	**888-221-2565**	701-223-2565
Haverty Furniture Cos Inc 780 Johnson Ferry Rd NE Suite 800	Atlanta	GA	30342	**800-241-4599**	404-443-2900
NYSE: HVT					
Haynes Furniture Co Inc 5324 Virginia Beach Blvd	Virginia Beach	VA	23462	**800-768-0348**	757-497-9681
Home Furnishings Corp DBA Breuner's 3250 Buskirk Ave	Pleasant Hill	CA	94523	**800-865-6778**	925-472-4500
Homestead House Inc PO Box 6010	Broomfield	CO	80021	**800-275-0345**	303-425-6544
Huffman Koos Inc Rt 4 & Main St	River Edge	NJ	07661	**800-648-3362***	201-343-4300
*Cust Svc					
Hurwitz-Mintz Furniture Co 227 Chartres St	New Orleans	LA	70130	**800-597-9555**	504-568-9555
IKEA 496 W Germantown Pike	Plymouth Meeting	PA	19462	**800-434-4532**	610-834-0180
Jennifer Convertibles Inc 419 Crossways Park Dr	Woodbury	NY	11797	**800-595-1422**	516-496-1900
AMEX: JEN					
Jerome's Furniture Warehouse 1401 East St	San Diego	CA	92101	**800-698-3444**	619-231-1757
Jordan's Furniture Co 100 Stockwell Dr	Avon	MA	02322	**800-846-3737**	508-580-4600
Kacey Fine Furniture 900 S Santa Fe Dr Dock 4 Unit 25	Denver	CO	80223	**800-574-1979**	303-778-6400
Kensington Home Furnishings Center 200 Tilton Rd	Northfield	NJ	08225	**800-641-4844**	609-641-4800
Kirschman Morris Co Inc 5050 Almonaster St	New Orleans	LA	70126	**800-289-9430**	504-947-6673
Lack's Stores Inc PO Box 2088	Victoria	TX	77902	**800-242-1123**	361-578-3571
Mathis Brothers Furniture Inc 3434 W Reno Ave	Oklahoma City	OK	73107	**800-329-3434**	405-943-3434
Morris Kirschman Co Inc 5050 Almonaster St	New Orleans	LA	70126	**800-289-9430**	504-947-6673
Nebraska Furniture Mart Inc 700 S 72nd St	Omaha	NE	68114	**800-359-1200**	402-397-6100
Norwalk Furniture Corp 100 Furniture Pkwy	Norwalk	OH	44857	**800-837-2565***	419-668-4461
*Orders					
Olum's of Binghamton Inc 3701 Vestal Pkwy E	Vestal	NY	13850	**800-247-0533***	607-729-5775
*Cust Svc					
Peerless Mattress & Furniture Co PO Box 7650	Flint	MI	48507	**800-253-0937**	810-230-7440
Porters of Racine 301 6th St	Racine	WI	53403	**800-558-3245**	262-633-6363
RC Willey & Son Inc 2601 S 300 W	Salt Lake City	UT	84115	**800-444-3876**	801-461-3900
RH Kuhn Co DBA Roomful Express 55th St & AVRR	Pittsburgh	PA	15201	**888-696-7378**	412-784-1250
Rhodes Furniture Co 1800 E 5th Ave	Columbus	OH	43219	**877-274-6337**	614-253-7441
Roomful Express 55th St & AVRR	Pittsburgh	PA	15201	**888-696-7378**	412-784-1250
Rooms To Go Inc 11540 US Hwy 92 E	Seffner	FL	33584	**800-766-6786***	813-623-5400
*Cust Svc					
Rotmans Furniture & Carpet 725 Southbridge St	Worcester	MA	01610	**800-768-6267**	508-755-5276
Routzahn's PO Box 663	Frederick	MD	21705	**800-132-1177**	301-662-2141
Scan International Inc 1800-I Rockville Pike	Rockville	MD	20852	**800-386-0989**	301-984-2960
Seaman Furniture Co Inc 300 Crossways Pk Dr	Woodbury	NY	11797	**800-445-2403**	516-496-9560
Sedlak Interiors Inc 34300 Solon Rd	Solon	OH	44139	**800-260-2949**	440-248-2424
See Ltd 8806 Beverly Blvd	Los Angeles	CA	90048	**800-258-8292**	310-385-1919
Selden's Home Furnishings & Interior Design 1802 62nd Ave E	Tacoma	WA	98424	**800-870-7880**	253-922-5700
Shops at Carolina Furniture 5425 Richmond Rd	Williamsburg	VA	23188	**800-582-8916**	757-565-3000
Sit 'n Sleep 3853 Overland Ave	Culver City	CA	90232	**800-675-3536**	310-842-6850
Sleepy's Inc 175 Central Ave S	Bethpage	NY	11714	**800-753-3797**	516-844-8800
Smulekoff's Fine Home Furnishings PO Box 74090	Cedar Rapids	IA	52407	**888-384-6995**	319-362-2181
Star Furniture Co Inc 16666 Barker Springs Rd	Houston	TX	77084	**800-364-6661**	281-492-6661
Steinhafels 16250 W Rogers Dr	New Berlin	WI	53151	**800-813-2358**	262-784-0500
Town & Country Furniture 6545 Airline Hwy	Baton Rouge	LA	70805	**800-375-6660**	225-355-6666
USA Baby 793 Springer Dr	Lombard	IL	60148	**800-323-4108**	630-652-0600
Value City Furniture 1800 Moler Rd	Columbus	OH	43207	**800-743-4577**	614-221-9200
Walsh Brothers Inc PO Box 1711	Phoenix	AZ	85001	**800-527-3437**	602-252-6971
Warehouse Home Furnishings Distributors Inc DBA Farmers Furniture 2005 Veterans Blvd Suite 1	Dublin	GA	31040	**800-456-0424**	478-272-4000
Weirs Furniture Village 3219 Knox St	Dallas	TX	75205	**888-889-3477**	214-528-0321
Wieser & Cawley Inc 1301 Colegate Dr	Marietta	OH	45750	**800-339-0094**	740-373-1676
Willey RC & Son Inc 2601 S 300 W	Salt Lake City	UT	84115	**800-444-3876**	801-461-3900

317 GAMES & GAMING

SEE ALSO Casino Companies; Casinos; Lotteries, Games, Sweepstakes; Toys, Games, Hobbies

				Toll-Free	Phone
Alaska Bingo Supply 3707 Woodland Dr Suite 3	Anchorage	AK	99517	**800-478-7003**	907-243-7003
Alliance Gaming Corp 6601 S Bermuda Rd	Las Vegas	NV	89119	**877-462-2559**	702-896-7700
NYSE: AGI					
American Gaming & Electronics 9500 W 55th St	McCook	IL	60525	**800-336-6630**	708-290-2100
Amtote International Inc 11200 Pepper Rd	Hunt Valley	MD	21031	**800-345-1566**	410-771-8700
Arachnid Inc 6212 Material Ave	Loves Park	IL	61111	**800-435-8319**	815-654-0212
Aristocrat Technologies 7230 Amigo St	Las Vegas	NV	89119	**800-748-4156**	702-269-5000
Bally Gaming & Systems 6601 S Bermuda Rd	Las Vegas	NV	89119	**877-462-2559**	702-896-7700
Bally-Sierra Design Group 300 Sierra Manor Dr	Reno	NV	89511	**888-404-8838**	775-850-1500
Douglas Press Inc 2810 Madison St	Bellwood	IL	60104	**800-323-0705**	708-547-8400
GameTech International Inc 900 Sandhill Rd	Reno	NV	89521	**800-487-8510**	775-850-6000
NASDAQ: GMTC					
Gaming Partners International Corp 1700 Industrial Rd	Las Vegas	NV	89102	**800-728-5766**	702-384-2425
NASDAQ: GPIC					
IGT Inc 7115 Amigo St Suite 150	Las Vegas	NV	89119	**888-254-7568**	702-263-7588
Konami Gaming Inc 7140 S Industrial Rd Suite 700	Las Vegas	NV	89118	**866-544-7568**	702-367-0573
Mikohn Gaming Corp 920 Pilot Rd	Las Vegas	NV	89119	**800-336-8449**	702-896-3890
NASDAQ: MIKN					
Poker Chips Online LLC 380 Warren Ave	Portland	ME	04103	**888-797-2200**	506-575-8827
Scientific Games Corp 750 Lexington Ave 25th Fl	New York	NY	10022	**800-367-9345**	212-754-2233
NASDAQ: SGMS					
Smart Industries Corp 1626 Delaware Ave	Des Moines	IA	50317	**800-553-2442**	515-265-9900
Sodak Gaming Inc 5301 S Hwy 16	Rapid City	SD	57701	**800-711-7322**	605-341-5400
United Tote Co 11505 Susquehanna Trail	Glen Rock	PA	17327	**800-238-8683**	717-227-4350
Valley-Dynamo 2525 Handley Ederville Rd	Richland Hills	TX	76118	**800-248-2837**	817-299-3070
Video King Gaming Systems 3211 Nebraska Ave	Council Bluffs	IA	51501	**800-635-9912**	712-323-1488
Western Regional Off-Track Betting Corp 700 Ellicott St	Batavia	NY	14020	**800-724-2000**	585-343-1423

318 GARDEN CENTERS

SEE ALSO Horticultural Products Growers; Seed Companies

Company	City	State	Zip	Toll-Free	Phone
Armstrong Garden Centers Inc 2200 E Rt 66 Suite 200	Glendora	CA	91740	**800-229-1707**	626-914-1091
Earl May Seed & Nursery 208 N Elm St	Shenandoah	IA	51603	**800-831-4193**	712-246-1020
Flowerwood Garden Center 7625 US Hwy 14	Crystal Lake	IL	60012	**800-852-3114**	815-459-6200
Gardener's Supply Co 128 Intervale Rd	Burlington	VT	05401	**800-863-1700**	802-660-3500
Greenbrier Farms Ltd 225 Sign Pine Rd	Chesapeake	VA	23322	**800-821-2141**	757-421-2141
Home Depot Inc 2455 Paces Ferry Rd *NYSE: HD* ■ *Cust Svc	Atlanta	GA	30339	**800-553-3199***	770-433-8211
Home & Garden Showplace 8600 W Bryn Mawr	Chicago	IL	60631	**888-474-9752**	
Jackson & Perkins 2500 S Pacific Hwy PO Box 1028 *Cust Svc	Medford	OR	97501	**800-872-7673***	541-776-2000
Johnson's Garden Centers 2707 W 13th St	Wichita	KS	67203	**888-542-8463**	316-942-1443
Jung JW Seed Co 335 S High St	Randolph	WI	53956	**800-297-3123**	920-326-3121
JW Jung Seed Co 335 S High St	Randolph	WI	53956	**800-297-3123**	920-326-3121
Kmart Corp 3100 W Big Beaver Rd *NASDAQ: KMRT* ■ *Cust Svc	Troy	MI	48084	**866-562-7848***	248 613 1000
Langeveld Bulb Co Inc 725 Vassar Ave	Lakewood	NJ	08701	**800-526-0467**	732-367-2000
Lowe's Cos Inc 1605 Curtis Bridge Rd *NYSE: LOW*	North Wilkesboro	NC	28697	**800-890-5932**	336-658-4000
Master Nursery Garden Centers Inc 2211 Olympic Blvd	Walnut Creek	CA	94595	**800-576-5102**	925-934-1144
McKay Nursery Co Inc 750 S Monroe St	Waterloo	WI	53594	**800-236-4242**	920-478-2121
Merrygro Farms Inc 34135 Cardinal Ln	Eustis	FL	32736	**888-637-7947**	352-589-0868
Milaeger's Inc 4838 Douglas Ave	Racine	WI	53402	**800-669-1229**	262-639-2040
North Haven Gardens Inc 7700 Northaven Rd	Dallas	TX	75230	**800-347-2342**	214-363-6715
Panhandle Co-op Assn 401 S Beltline Hwy W *Cust Svc	Scottsbluff	NE	69363	**800-732-4546***	308-632-5301
Plants of the Southwest 3095 Agua Fria Rd	Santa Fe	NM	87507	**800-788-7333**	505-438-8888
Pursley Inc 9115 58th Dr E Suite A	Bradenton	FL	34202	**800-683-7584**	941-753-7851
Rain or Shine LandscapeUSA 13126 NE Airport Way	Portland	OR	97230	**800-966-1033**	503-255-1981
Smith & Hawken Inc 4 Hamilton Landing Suite 100	Novato	CA	94949	**800-776-5558**	415-506-3700
Star Nursery Inc 125 Cassia Way	Henderson	NV	89014	**866-584-7827**	702-568-7000
Target Stores 1000 Nicollet Mall	Minneapolis	MN	55403	**800-440-0680**	612-304-6073
Van Bourgondien & Sons Inc 245 Rt 109	West Babylon	NY	11704	**800-622-9997**	631-669-3500
Village Nurseries 1589 N Main St	Orange	CA	92867	**800-542-0209**	714-279-3100
Wal-Mart Stores Inc 702 SW 8th St *NYSE: WMT* ■ *Cust Svc	Bentonville	AR	72716	**800-925-6278***	479-273-4000
White Flower Farm 30 Irene St *Cust Svc	Torrington	CT	06790	**800-411-6159***	860-496-9624

319 GAS STATIONS

SEE ALSO Convenience Stores

Company	City	State	Zip	Toll-Free	Phone
AMBEST Inc 5250 Virginia Way Suite 250	Brentwood	TN	37027	**800-910-7220**	615-371-5187
AT Williams Oil Co 5446 University Pkwy	Winston-Salem	NC	27105	**800-642-0945**	336-767-6280
Busler Enterprises Inc PO Box 23610 *Whse	Evansville	IN	47724	**800-457-3232***	812-424-7511
Chevron Corp 6001 Bollinger Canyon Rd *NYSE: CVX* ■ *Cust Svc	San Ramon	CA	94583	**800-243-8766***	925-842-1000
Crystal Flash Petroleum Corp 5221 Ivy Tech Dr	Indianapolis	IN	46268	**800-886-3835**	317-879-2849
Cumberland Farms Inc Gulf Div 777 Dedham St	Canton	MA	02021	**800-843-8028**	781-828-4900
Englefield Oil Co 447 James Pkwy	Heath	OH	43056	**800-282-1675**	740-928-8215
Erickson Oil Products Inc 1231 Industrial St	Hudson	WI	54016	**800-521-0104**	715-386-8241
ExxonMobil Corp 5959 Las Colinas Blvd *NYSE: XOM* ■ *Hum Res	Irving	TX	75039	**800-252-1800***	972-444-1000
FL Roberts & Co Inc 93 W Broad St PO Box 1964	Springfield	MA	01102	**800-628-4004**	413-781-7444
Flying J Inc 1104 Country Hill Dr	Ogden	UT	84403	**800-842-6428**	801-624-1000
Forward Corp 219 N Front St	Standish	MI	48658	**800-664-4501**	989-846-4501
Fowler MM Inc 4220 Neal Rd	Durham	NC	27705	**800-313-6635**	919-309-2925
Freedom Oil Co 814 W Chestnut St	Bloomington	IL	61701	**800-397-6147**	309-828-7750
Gibbs Oil Co LP PO Box 9151	Chelsea	MA	02150	**800-352-3558**	617-889-9000
Gillespie Oil Inc PO Box 370	Bellefontaine	OH	43311	**800-686-3835**	937-599-2085
Griffin Rip Truck Travel Center Inc PO Box 10128	Lubbock	TX	79408	**800-333-9330**	806-763-9349
Gulf Div Cumberland Farms Inc 777 Dedham St	Canton	MA	02021	**800-843-8028**	781-828-4900
Iowa 80 Group Inc PO Box 639	Walcott	IA	52773	**800-336-9889**	563-284-6965
J & H Oil Co PO Box 9464	Wyoming	MI	49509	**800-442-9110**	616-534-2181
Jubitz Corp 33 NE Middlefield Rd	Portland	OR	97211	**800-399-5480**	503-283-1111
Kent Oil Inc PO Box 908001	Midland	TX	79708	**800-375-5368**	432-699-5822
Keystops LLC PO Box 2809	Franklin	KY	42135	**800-346-6456**	270-586-8283
Lassus Brothers Oil Inc 1800 Magnavox Way	Fort Wayne	IN	46804	**800-686-2836**	260-436-1415
Midstream Fuel Service LLC 5900 Memorial Dr Suite 305	Houston	TX	77007	**800-368-5990**	713-350-6800
MM Fowler Inc 4220 Neal Rd	Durham	NC	27705	**800-313-6635**	919-309-2925
Olympian Oil Co 999 Bayhill Dr Suite 135	San Bruno	CA	94066	**800-899-4659**	650-873-8200
Petro Stopping Centers 6080 Surety Dr	El Paso	TX	79905	**800-331-8809**	915-779-4711
Pilot Travel Centers LLC PO Box 10146	Knoxville	TN	37939	**800-562-6210**	865-588-7487
RaceTrac Petroleum Inc 300 Technology Ct	Smyrna	GA	30082	**888-636-5589**	770-431-7600
Rip Griffin Truck Travel Center Inc PO Box 10128	Lubbock	TX	79408	**800-333-9330**	806-763-9349
Roberts FL & Co Inc 93 W Broad St PO Box 1964	Springfield	MA	01102	**800-628-4004**	413-781-7444
Rollette Oil Co 2104 Beloit Ave	Janesville	WI	53546	**800-362-0888**	608-754-0035
Schmitt Sales Inc 2101 St Rita's Ln	Buffalo	NY	14221	**800-873-8080**	716-639-1500
Service Oil Inc 1718 E Main Ave	West Fargo	ND	58078	**800-726-0133**	701-277-1050
Shell Oil Co PO Box 2463	Houston	TX	77252	**888-467-4355**	713-241-6161
Sinclair Oil Corp 550 E South Temple	Salt Lake City	UT	84102	**800-552-8695**	801-524-2700
Speedway SuperAmerica LLC 500 Speedway Dr *Cust Svc	Enon	OH	45323	**800-643-1948***	937-864-3000
Spencer Cos Inc 120 Woodson St NW	Huntsville	AL	35801	**800-633-2910**	256-533-1150
Swifty Oil Co Inc PO Box 1002	Seymour	IN	47274	**800-742-8497**	812-522-1640
Thornton Oil Corp 10101 Linn Station Rd Suite 200	Louisville	KY	40223	**800-928-8022**	502-425-8022
TravelCenters of America 24601 Center Ridge Rd Suite 200	Westlake	OH	44145	**800-872-7024**	440-808-9100
Triple A Oil 12342 Inwood Rd	Dallas	TX	75244	**800-657-9595**	972-503-3333
Ultramar Diamond Shamrock Corp 2200 ave McGill College	Montreal	QC	H3A3L3	**800-361-4253**	514-499-6111
W & H Co-op Oil Co Inc 407 13th St N	Humboldt	IA	50548	**800-392-3816**	515-332-2782
Walker Oil Co PO Box 215	Nottingham	PA	19362	**800-468-6005**	610-932-8524
Wesco Inc 1460 Whitehall Rd	Muskegon	MI	49445	**800-968-0200**	231-719-4300
Williams AT Oil Co 5446 University Pkwy	Winston-Salem	NC	27105	**800-642-0945**	336-767-6280

320 GAS TRANSMISSION - NATURAL GAS

Company	City	State	Zip	Toll-Free	Phone
ANR Pipeline Co PO Box 2511	Houston	TX	77011	**800-827-5267**	
ANR Storage Inc 27725 Stansbury Blvd Suite 200	Farmington Hills	MI	48334	**800-998-3847**	248-994-4100
Belden & Blake Corp 5200 Stoneham Rd	North Canton	OH	44720	**800-837-4344**	330-497-5471
CMS Panhandle Eastern Pipe Line Co 5444 Westheimer Rd	Houston	TX	77056	**800-275-7375**	713-627-4272
CMS Trunkline Gas Co 5444 Westheimer Rd	Houston	TX	77056	**800-275-7375**	713-627-4272
Columbia Gas Transmission Corp 1700 MacCorkle Ave SE	Charleston	WV	25314	**800-832-3242**	304-357-2000
Crossroads Pipeline Co 12801 Fair Lakes Pkwy	Fairfax	VA	22033	**888-499-3450**	
Dominion Transmission PO Box 2450	Clarksburg	WV	26302	**800-624-3101**	304-623-8000
Duke Energy Trading & Marketing 5400 Westheimer Ct	Houston	TX	77056	**800-873-3853**	713-260-1800
El Paso Corp 1001 Louisiana St *NYSE: EP* ■ *Cust Svc	Houston	TX	77002	**800-594-2018***	713-420-2131
Enbridge Midcoast Energy Inc 1100 Louisiana St Suite 3300	Houston	TX	77002	**888-650-8900**	713-650-8900
Enogex Inc 515 Central Park Dr Suite 600	Oklahoma City	OK	73105	**800-829-9922**	405-525-7788
Gulf South Pipeline Co LP 20 E Greenway Plaza Suite 900	Houston	TX	77046	**866-820-6000**	713-544-6000
GulfTerra Energy Partners LP 1001 Louisiana St	Houston	TX	77002	**800-594-2018**	713-420-2131
Kentucky West Virginia Gas Co LLC 748 N Lake Dr	Prestonsburg	KY	41653	**800-654-9754**	606-886-2311
Kinder Morgan Energy Partners LP 500 Dallas St Suite 1000 *NYSE: KMP*	Houston	TX	77002	**888-844-5657**	713-369-9000
Kinder Morgan Management LLC 500 Dallas St 1 Allen Ctr Suite 1000 *NYSE: KMR*	Houston	TX	77002	**800-324-2900**	713-369-9000
Kinder Morgan Texas Pipeline LP 500 Dallas St Suite 1000	Houston	TX	77002	**800-324-2900**	713-369-9000
Mid Louisiana Gas Co 1100 Louisiana St Suite 2950	Houston	TX	77002	**888-650-8900**	713-650-8900
Mississippi River Transmission Inc 9900 Clayton Rd *Cust Svc	Saint Louis	MO	63124	**800-325-4005***	314-991-9900
Penn Octane Corp 77-530 Enfield Ln Bldg D *NASDAQ: POCC*	Palm Desert	CA	92211	**877-419-6265**	760-772-9080
PG Energy Co 1 PEI Ctr *Cust Svc	Wilkes-Barre	PA	18711	**800-432-8017***	570-829-8600
Questar Gas Management Co PO Box 45601	Salt Lake City	UT	84145	**800-323-5517**	801-324-2400
Southern Natural Gas Co PO Box 2563	Birmingham	AL	35202	**800-633-8570**	205-325-7410
TC Pipelines LP 450 1st St SW *NASDAQ: TCLP*	Calgary	AB	T2P5H1	**800-361-6522**	403-920-2000
TEPPCO Partners LP 2929 Allen Pkwy *NYSE: TPP*	Houston	TX	77019	**800-877-3636**	713-759-3636
TransCanada Pipelines Ltd 450 1st St SW *NYSE: TRP*	Calgary	AB	T2P5H1	**800-661-3805**	403-920-2000
Williams Gas Pipelines Transco PO Box 1396	Houston	TX	77251	**888-215-8475**	713-215-2000
Williston Basin Interstate Pipeline Co 1250 W Century Ave	Bismarck	ND	58503	**800-238-8350**	701-530-1600

321 GASKETS, PACKING, SEALING DEVICES

SEE ALSO Automotive Parts & Supplies - Mfr

Company	City	State	Zip	Toll-Free	Phone
Akron Gasket & Packing Enterprises Inc 1244 Home Ave	Akron	OH	44310	**800-289-7318**	330-633-3742
American Casting & Mfg Corp 51 Commercial St	Plainview	NY	11803	**800-342-0333**	516-349-7010
American Packing & Gasket Co 6039 Armour Dr	Houston	TX	77020	**800-888-5223**	713-675-5271
Apple Rubber Products Inc 310 Erie St *Cust Svc	Lancaster	NY	14086	**800-828-7745***	716-684-6560
Atlantic Gasket Corp 3908 Frankford Ave	Philadelphia	PA	19124	**800-229-8881**	215-533-6400
Auburn Mfg Co 29 Stack St	Middletown	CT	06457	**800-427-5387**	860-346-6677
Bal Seal Engineering Co Inc 19650 Pauling	Foothill Ranch	CA	92610	**800-366-1006**	949-460-2100
Bar's Products 720 W Rose St	Holly	MI	48442	**800-521-7475**	248-634-8278
Beaverite Corp 128 Main St *Cust Svc	Beaver Falls	NY	13305	**800-424-6337***	315-346-6011
Bentley Mfg Co Inc 15123 Colorado Ave	Paramount	CA	90723	**800-424-2425**	562-634-4051
Brooks EJ Co 8 Microlab Rd	Livingston	NJ	07039	**800-458-7325**	973-597-2900
Burly Seal Products Co 1865 W 'D' Ave *Cust Svc	Tooele	UT	84074	**800-877-7325***	435-843-4477
California Gasket & Rubber Corp 1601 W 134th St	Gardena	CA	90249	**800-635-7084**	310-323-4250

Company	City	State	ZIP	Toll-Free	Phone
Calpico Inc 1387 San Mateo Ave	South San Francisco	CA	94080	**800-998-9115**	650-588-2241
Carbon Technology Inc 659 S County Trail	Exeter	RI	02822	**800-222-7266**	401-295-8877
CE Conover & Co Inc 4106 Blanche Rd	Bensalem	PA	19020	**800-266-6837**	215-639-6666
Chicago Gasket Co 1285 W North Ave	Chicago	IL	60622	**800-833-5666**	773-486-3060
Chicago Rawhide Industries 900 N State St *Cust Svc	Elgin	IL	60123	**800-882-0008***	847-742-7840
Chicago-Wilcox Mfg Co 16928 State St	South Holland	IL	60473	**800-323-5282**	708-339-5000
Conover CE & Co Inc 4106 Blanche Rd	Bensalem	PA	19020	**800-266-6837**	215-639-6666
Crane John Canada 423 Green Rd	Stoney Creek	ON	L8E3A1	**800-263-6860**	905-662-6191
Crane John Inc 6400 W Oakton St	Morton Grove	IL	60053	**800-732-5464**	847-967-2400
Eagle Burgmann Industries LP 10035 Brookriver Dr	Houston	TX	77040	**800-303-7735**	713-939-9515
EJ Brooks Co 8 Microlab Rd	Livingston	NJ	07039	**800-458-7325**	973-597-2900
EnPro Industries Inc 5605 Carnegie Blvd Suite 500 *NYSE: NPO*	Charlotte	NC	28209	**866-663-6776**	704-731-1500
Excelsior Inc 720 Chestnut St	Rockford	IL	61102	**800-435-4671**	815-987-2940
Flow Dry Technology Ltd 379 Albert Rd	Brookville	OH	45309	**800-533-0077**	937-833-2161
France Compressor Products 4410 Greenbriar Dr	Stafford	TX	77477	**800-675-6646**	281-207-4600
Freudenberg-NOK General Partnership 47690 E Anchor Ct	Plymouth	MI	48170	**800-533-5656**	734-451-0020
Garlock Sealing Technologies 1666 Division St	Palmyra	NY	14522	**800-448-6688**	315-597-4811
Gasket Mfg Co Inc 18001 S Main St	Gardena	CA	90248	**800-442-7538**	310-217-5600
Gaskets Inc 301 W Hwy 16 PO Box 398	Rio	WI	53960	**800-558-1833**	920-992-3137
Gunite Supply & Equipment Co 1726 S Magnolia Ave	Monrovia	CA	91016	**888-393-8635**	626-359-9361
Higbee Inc 6741 Thompson Rd N	Syracuse	NY	13221	**800-255-4800**	315-432-8021
Hoosier Gasket Corp 3333 Massachusetts Ave	Indianapolis	IN	46218	**800-442-7705**	317-545-2000
Hutchinson Seal Corp National O-Ring Div 11634 Patton Rd	Downey	CA	90241	**800-421-3837**	562-862-8163
IGS (Industrial Gasket & Shim Co Inc) 200 Country Club Rd	Meadow Lands	PA	15347	**800-229-1447**	724-222-5800
Ilene Industries Inc 301 Stanley Blvd	Shelbyville	TN	37160	**800-251-1602**	931-684-8731
Industrial Custom Products Inc 2801 37th Ave NE	Minneapolis	MN	55421	**800-654-0886**	612-781-2255
Industrial Gasket Inc 720 S Sara Rd	Mustang	OK	73064	**800-654-8433**	405-376-9393
Industrial Gasket & Shim Co Inc (IGS) 200 Country Club Rd	Meadow Lands	PA	15347	**800-229-1447**	724-222-5800
Intek Plastic Inc 800 E 10th St *Cust Svc	Hastings	MN	55033	**800-451-4544***	651-437-7700
Interface Solutions Inc 216 Wohlsen Way	Lancaster	PA	17603	**800-942-7538**	717-207-6000
ITW Southland 5700 Ward Ave	Virginia Beach	VA	23455	**800-804-4744**	757-543-5701
JM Clipper Corp 403 Industrial Dr PO Drawer 632340	Nacogdoches	TX	75964	**800-233-3900**	936-560-8900
John Crane Canada Inc 423 Green Rd	Stoney Creek	ON	L8E3A1	**800-263-6860**	905-662-6191
John Crane Inc 6400 W Oakton St	Morton Grove	IL	60053	**800-732-5464**	847-967-2400
Laird Technologies PO Box 650	Delaware Water Gap	PA	18327	**800-843-4556**	570-424-8510
Lamons Gasket Co 7300 Airport Blvd	Houston	TX	77061	**800-231-6906**	713-222-0284
Marsh Bellofram Corp SR 2 PO Box 305	Newell	WV	26050	**800-727-5646**	304-387-1200
Meirath Gasket Inc 2901 W Hunting Pk Ave	Philadelphia	PA	19129	**800-635-7284**	215-223-6000
Mesa Rubber Co 1726 S Magnolia Ave	Monrovia	CA	91016	**888-393-8635**	626-359-9361
National O-Ring Div Hutchinson Seal Corp 11634 Patton Rd	Downey	CA	90241	**800-421-3837**	562-862-8163
Netherland Rubber Co 2931 Exon Ave	Cincinnati	OH	45241	**800-582-1877**	513-733-0883
Nott-Atwater Co 1309 N Bradley Rd	Spokane	WA	99212	**800-288-7278**	509-922-4522
Ohio Gasket & Shim Co Inc 976 Evans Ave	Akron	OH	44305	**800-321-2438**	330-630-2030
Omega Shielding Products 1384 Pompton Ave	Cedar Grove	NJ	07009	**800-828-5784**	973-890-7455
Pacific States Felt & Mfg Co Inc 23850 Clawiter Rd	Hayward	CA	94545	**800-566-8866**	510-783-0277
Parker Hannifin Corp Composite Sealing Systems Div 7664 Panasonic Way	San Diego	CA	92154	**800-272-7537**	619-661-7000
Pemko Mfg Co Inc 4226 Transport St	Ventura	CA	93003	**800-283-9988**	805-642-2600
PerkinElmer Fluid Sciences Inc 11642 Old Baltimore Pike	Beltsville	MD	20705	**800-691-4666**	301-937-4010
Power Engineering & Equipment Co 20009 S Rancho Way	Rancho Dominguez	CA	90220	**800-231-6906**	310-886-1133
PPC Mechanical Seals 2769 Mission Dr	Baton Rouge	LA	70805	**800-731-7325**	225-356-4333
Press-Seal Gasket Corp 6932 Gettysburg Pike	Fort Wayne	IN	46804	**800-348-7325**	260-436-0521
Presscut Industries Inc 1540 Selene Dr Suite 100	Carrollton	TX	75006	**800-442-4924**	972-389-0615
Rotor Clip Co Inc 187 Davidson Ave *Cust Svc	Somerset	NJ	08873	**800-631-5857***	732-469-7333
Rubbercraft Corp of California 15627 S Broadway	Gardena	CA	90248	**800-782-2379**	310-328-5402
Schlegel Systems Inc 1555 Jefferson Rd	Rochester	NY	14623	**800-828-6237**	585-427-7200
Seal Methods Inc 11915 Shoemaker Ave	Santa Fe Springs	CA	90670	**800-423-4777**	562-944-0291
Sealing Devices Inc 4400 Walden Ave *Cust Svc	Lancaster	NY	14086	**800-727-3257***	716-684-7600
Sealing Equipment Products Co Inc 123 Airpark Industrial Rd *Cust Svc	Alabaster	AL	35007	**800-633-4770***	205-403-7500
Specification Rubber Products Inc 1568 1st St N	Alabaster	AL	35007	**800-633-3415**	205-663-2521
Standco Industries Inc 2701 Clinton Dr	Houston	TX	77020	**800-231-6018**	713-224-6311
Sur-Seal Gasket & Packing Inc 6156 Wesselman Rd	Cincinnati	OH	45248	**800-345-8966**	513-574-8500
T & E Industries Inc 215 Watchung Ave *Sales	Orange	NJ	07050	**800-245-7080***	973-672-5454
TRUARC Co LLC 70 E Willow St *Cust Svc	Millburn	NJ	07041	**800-228-4460***	973-926-5000
Tyden Brammall Inc 409 Hoosier Dr	Angola	IN	46703	**800-348-4777**	260-665-3176
UTEX Industries Inc 10810 Old Katy Rd	Houston	TX	77043	**800-359-9230**	713-467-1000
Vellumoid Inc 54 Rockdale St	Worcester	MA	01606	**800-609-5558**	508-853-2500

322 GIFT SHOPS

SEE ALSO Card Shops; Duty-Free Shops; Home Furnishings Stores; Nature Stores

Company	City	State	ZIP	Toll-Free	Phone
Afromart Gift Enterprises PO Box 7814	Long Beach	CA	90807	**877-215-0284**	562-426-0055
Arribas Brothers Inc PO Box 809	Windermere	FL	34786	**888-828-4840**	407-828-4840
Ashford.com 14001 NW 4th St	Sunrise	FL	33325	**888-922-9039**	954-453-2874
Barbeques Galore 10 Orchard Rd Suite 200 *NASDAQ: BBQZ*	Lake Forest	CA	92630	**800-752-3085**	949-597-2400
Brookstone Inc 1 Innovation Way *NASDAQ: BKST* ■ *Cust Svc	Merrimack	NH	03054	**800-846-3000***	603-880-9500
Candleman Corp 1120 Industrial Pk Rd PO Box 731	Brainerd	MN	56401	**800-328-3453**	218-829-0592
CM Paula Co 6049 Hi-Tek Ct	Mason	OH	45040	**800-543-4464**	513-336-3100
Disney Consumer Products 500 S Buena Vista St *PR	Burbank	CA	91521	**800-723-4763***	818-560-1000
EBSCO Industries Inc Military Service Co Div PO Box 1943	Birmingham	AL	35201	**800-255-3722**	205-991-6600
GiftCertificates.com 315 5th Ave S Suite 100	Seattle	WA	98104	**800-773-7368**	206-568-2500
Gump's 135 Post St	San Francisco	CA	94108	**800-766-7628**	415-982-1616
Hazelwood Enterprises Inc 402 N 32nd St	Phoenix	AZ	85008	**800-680-4667**	602-275-7709
Historical Research Center International Inc 2019 Corporate Dr	Boynton Beach	FL	33426	**800-940-7991**	561-732-5263
Hummel Gift Shop 1656 E Garfield Rd	New Springfield	OH	44443	**800-354-5438**	330-549-3728
Illuminations 775 Point Blvd	Petaluma	CA	94954	**800-226-3537**	707-769-2700
Limited Edition 2170 Sunrise Hwy *Orders	Merrick	NY	11566	**800-645-2864***	516-623-4400
Military Service Co Div EBSCO Industries Inc PO Box 1943	Birmingham	AL	35201	**800-255-3722**	205-991-6600
Mole Hollow Candles Ltd 3 Deerfield Ave *Cust Svc	Shelburne Falls	MA	01370	**800-445-6653***	413-625-6337
Oregon Connection 1125 S 1st St	Coos Bay	OR	97420	**800-255-5318**	541-267-7804
Paula CM Co 6049 Hi-Tek Ct	Mason	OH	45040	**800-543-4464**	513-336-3100
RedEnvelope Inc 149 New Montgomery St *NASDAQ: REDE*	San Francisco	CA	94105	**877-733-3683**	415-371-9100
San Francisco Music Box Co 3113 Woodcreek Dr	Downers Grove	IL	60515	**800-227-2190**	
Sanrio Inc 570 Eccles Ave	South San Francisco	CA	94080	**800-325-8316**	650-952-2880
Spencer Gifts Inc 6826 Black Horse Pike	Egg Harbor Township	NJ	08234	**800-762-0419**	609-645-3300
Swans Candles 8933 Gravelly Lake Dr SW	Lakewood	WA	98499	**888-848-7926**	253-584-4666
Things Remembered Inc 5500 Avion Park Dr	Highland Heights	OH	44143	**800-874-2653**	440-473-2000
Tipton & Hurst Inc 1801 N Grant St	Little Rock	AR	72207	**800-633-3036**	501-666-3333
Tuesday Morning Corp 6250 LBJ Fwy *NASDAQ: TUES*	Dallas	TX	75240	**800-457-0099**	972-387-3562
Victorian Paper Co 15600 W 99th St *Cust Svc	Lenexa	KS	66219	**800-700-2035***	913-438-3995
WeddingChannel.com 888 S Figueroa St Suite 700	Los Angeles	CA	90017	**888-750-1550**	
Wendell August Forge Inc 620 Madison Ave	Grove City	PA	16127	**800-923-4438**	724-458-8360
Wicks 'N' Sticks PO Box 1965	Cypress	TX	77410	**800-873-3714**	713-856-7442
Yankee Candle Co Inc 16 Yankee Candle Way *NYSE: YCC*	South Deerfield	MA	01373	**800-839-6038**	413-665-8306

323 GIFTS & NOVELTIES - WHOL

Company	City	State	ZIP	Toll-Free	Phone
Accoutrements PO Box 30811	Seattle	WA	98113	**800-886-2221**	425-349-3838
BalloonZone 1 American Rd *Sales	Cleveland	OH	44144	**800-321-3040***	216-252-7300
Blair Cedar & Novelty Works Inc 345 W Hwy 54	Camdenton	MO	65020	**800-325-3943**	573-346-2235
Department 56 Inc 6436 City W Pkwy 1 Village Pl *NYSE: DFS*	Eden Prairie	MN	55344	**800-348-3749**	952-944-5600
Enesco Group Inc 225 Windsor Dr *NYSE: ENC* ■ *Cust Svc	Itasca	IL	60143	**800-632-7968***	630-875-5300
Fridgedoor.com 21 Dixwell Ave	Quincy	MA	02169	**888-463-3184**	617-770-7913
Giftco Inc 700 Woodlands Pkwy	Vernon Hills	IL	60061	**800-443-8261**	847-478-8400
Hayes Specialties Corp 1761 E Genesee	Saginaw	MI	48601	**800-248-3603**	989-755-6541
Healthy Planet Products Inc 43 Moraga Way Suite 205	Orinda	CA	94563	**800-424-4422**	925-253-9595
Hornung's Golf Products Inc 815 Morris St	Fond du Lac	WI	54935	**800-323-3569**	920-922-2640
Northwestern Products Inc 721 Industrial Park Rd	Ashland	WI	54806	**800-328-7317**	715-685-9500
Novelty Advertising Co PO Box 250	Coshocton	OH	43812	**800-848-9163**	740-622-3113
Sanrio Inc 570 Eccles Ave	South San Francisco	CA	94080	**800-325-8316**	650-952-2880
Star Sales Co Inc 1803 N Central St	Knoxville	TN	37917	**800-347-9494**	865-524-0771
Unique Industries Inc 2400 S Weccacoe Ave	Philadelphia	PA	19148	**800-888-1705**	215-336-4300
Variety Distributors Inc 7th & Spring Sts PO Box 728	Harlan	IA	51537	**800-274-1095**	712-755-2184
Western Slope Sales Service Inc 636 Potrero Ave	San Francisco	CA	94110	**888-777-2770**	415-282-2770
WinCraft Inc 1124 W 5th St	Winona	MN	55987	**800-533-8006**	507-454-5510
Zims Inc 4370 S 300 West *Orders	Salt Lake City	UT	84107	**800-453-6420***	801-268-2505

324 GLASS - AUTOMOTIVE

SEE ALSO Automotive Services - Glass Replacement - Automotive

Company	City	State	ZIP	Toll-Free	Phone
Gentex Corp 600 N Centennial St *NASDAQ: GNTX*	Zeeland	MI	49464	**800-444-4689**	616-772-1800
Glasstite Inc 600 Hwy 4 N *Cust Svc	Dunnell	MN	56127	**800-533-0450***	507-695-2378
Globe Amerada Glass Co 2001 Greenleaf Ave	Elk Grove Village	IL	60007	**800-323-8776**	847-364-2900

325 GLASS - FLAT, PLATE, TEMPERED

Company / Address	City	State	ZIP	Toll-Free	Phone
ACI Distribution 965 Ridge Lake Blvd Suite 300	Memphis	TN	38120	**800-238-6057**	901-767-7111
AFG Industries Inc PO Box 929	Kingsport	TN	37662	**800-251-0441**	423-229-7200
Anthony International 12812 Arroyo St	San Fernando	CA	91342	**800-772-0900**	818-365-9451
Basco Co 7201 Snider Rd	Mason	OH	45040	**800-543-1938**	513-573-1900
Binswanger Glass 965 Ridge Lake Blvd Suite 300	Memphis	TN	38120	**800-238-6057**	901-767-7111
Binswanger Mirror PO Box 1400	Grenada	MS	38902	**800-221-8408**	662-226-5551
Cameron Glass Inc 3550 W Tacoma St	Broken Arrow	OK	74012	**800-331-3666**	918-254-6000
Cardinal Glass Co 1087 Research Pkwy	Rockford	IL	61109	**800-728-3468**	815-394-1400
Century Glass Inc 4620 Andrews St	North Las Vegas	NV	89031	**800-654-7027**	702-385-9309
D & W Inc 941 Oak St	Elkhart	IN	46514	**800-255-0829**	574-264-9674
FJ Gray & Co 217-44 98th Ave	Queens Village	NY	11429	**800-523-3320**	718-217-2943
Gray FJ & Co 217-44 98th Ave	Queens Village	NY	11429	**800-523-3320**	718-217-2943
Guardian Industries Corp 2300 Harmon Rd	Auburn Hills	MI	48326	**800-327-5888**	248-340-1800
Northwestern Industries Inc 2500 W Jameson St	Seattle	WA	98199	**800-426-2771**	206-285-3140
ODL Inc 215 E Roosevelt Ave	Zeeland	MI	49464	**800-288-1800**	616-772-9111
Oregon Glass Co 10450 SW Ridder Rd	Wilsonville	OR	97070	**800-547-0217**	503-682-3846
Rainbow Art Glass Inc 1761 Rt 34 S	Wall	NJ	07727	**800-526-2356**	732-681-6003
Saint-Gobain Corp 750 E Swedesford Rd	Valley Forge	PA	19482	**800-274-8530**	610-341-7000
Shower Rite Inc 7519 S Greenwood Ave	Chicago	IL	60619	**800-925-9131**	773-483-5400
Spectrum Glass Co PO Box 646	Woodinville	WA	98072	**800-426-3120**	425-483-6699
Stanley Home Decor 480 Myrtle St	New Britain	CT	06053	**800-782-6539**	860-225-5111
Super Sky Products Inc 10301 N Enterprise Dr	Mequon	WI	53092	**800-558-0467**	262-242-2000
Thermoseal Glass Corp 400 Water St	Gloucester	NJ	08130	**800-456-7788**	856-456-3109
Tru-Vue Glass & Artboard Co 9400 W 55th St	McCook	IL	60525	**800-621-8339***	708-485-5080
*Cust Svc					
Viracon Inc 800 Park Dr	Owatonna	MN	55060	**800-533-2080**	507-451-9555
Virginia Mirror Co Inc PO Box 5431	Martinsville	VA	24115	**800-826-4776**	276-632-9816
VVP America Inc 965 Ridge Lake Blvd Suite 300	Memphis	TN	38120	**800-238-6057**	901-767-7111
Wasco Products Inc 22 Pioneer Ave PO Box 351	Sanford	ME	04073	**800-388-0293**	207-324-8060

326 GLASS FIBERS

Company / Address	City	State	ZIP	Toll-Free	Phone
Corning Optical Fiber PO Box 7429	Endicott	NY	13760	**800-525-2524**	607-786-8125
Evanite Fiber Corp PO Box E	Corvallis	OR	97339	**800-441-5567***	541-753-1211
*Cust Svc					
Fiber Glass Industries Inc 69 Edson St	Amsterdam	NY	12010	**800-842-4413**	518-842-4000
Fiberoptics Technology Inc 1 Quassett Rd	Pomfret	CT	06258	**800-433-5248**	860-928-0443

327 GLASS JARS & BOTTLES

Company / Address	City	State	ZIP	Toll-Free	Phone
Anchor Glass Container Corp 4343 Anchor Plaza Pkwy	Tampa	FL	33634	**800-326-2467**	813-882-0000
NASDAQ: AGCC					
Glenshaw Glass Co Inc 1101 William Flynn Hwy	Glenshaw	PA	15116	**800-326-2467**	412-486-9100
New High Glass Inc 12713 SW 125th Ave	Miami	FL	33186	**800-452-7787**	305-232-0840
Saint-Gobain Containers Inc 1509 S Macedonia Ave	Muncie	IN	47302	**800-428-8642**	765-741-7000

328 GLASS PRODUCTS - INDUSTRIAL (CUSTOM)

Company / Address	City	State	ZIP	Toll-Free	Phone
Abrisa USPG PO Box 3258	Ventura	CA	93006	**800-350-5000**	805-525-4902
ACCU-GLASS Div Becton Dickinson & Co 10765 Trenton Ave	Saint Louis	MO	63132	**800-325-4796**	314-423-0300
Becton Dickinson & Co ACCU-GLASS Div 10765 Trenton Ave	Saint Louis	MO	63132	**800-325-4796**	314-423-0300
Flex-O-Lite Inc 801 Corporate Ctr Dr Suite 300	Saint Charles	MO	63304	**800-325-9525**	636-300-2700
Lancaster Glass Corp 240 W Main St	Lancaster	OH	43130	**800-264-6826**	740-653-0311
Lenoir Mirror Co Inc PO Box 1650	Lenoir	NC	28645	**800-438-8204**	828-728-3271
Naugatuck Glass Co PO Box 71	Naugatuck	CT	06770	**800-533-3513**	203-729-5227
Precision Electronic Glass Inc 1013 Hendee Rd	Vineland	NJ	08360	**800-982-4734**	856-691-2234
Richland Glass Co Inc 1640 Southwest Blvd	Vineland	NJ	08360	**800-959-0312**	
Schott Corp 3 Odell Plaza	Yonkers	NY	10701	**800-633-4505**	914-968-8900
Swift Glass Co Inc 131 W 22nd St	Elmira Heights	NY	14903	**800-537-9438**	607-733-7166

329 GLASSWARE - LABORATORY & SCIENTIFIC

Company / Address	City	State	ZIP	Toll-Free	Phone
Ace Glass Inc 1430 Northwest Blvd PO Box 688	Vineland	NJ	08360	**800-223-4524**	856-692-3333
Bellco Glass Inc 340 Edrudo Rd	Vineland	NJ	08360	**800-257-7043**	856-691-1075
Erie Scientific Co 20 Post Rd	Portsmouth	NH	03801	**800-258-0834**	603-431-8410
Kimble Glass Inc 537 Crystal Ave	Vineland	NJ	08360	**888-546-2531***	856-692-3600
*Cust Svc					
Quadrex Corp PO Box 3881	Woodbridge	CT	06525	**800-275-7033***	203-393-3112
*Sales					
Super Glass Corp 1020 E 48th St	Brooklyn	NY	11203	**800-237-2211**	718-469-9300
Wale Apparatus Co Inc PO Box D	Hellertown	PA	18055	**800-444-9253**	610-838-7047
Wheaton USA Inc 5176 Harding Hwy	Mays Landing	NJ	08330	**800-442-7533**	609-625-2291

330 GLASSWARE & POTTERY - DECORATIVE

Company / Address	City	State	ZIP	Toll-Free	Phone
Blenko Glass Co Inc Fairground Rd	Milton	WV	25541	**877-425-3656**	304-743-9081
Boehm Edward Marshall Inc 25 Princess Diana Ln	Trenton	NJ	08638	**800-257-9410**	609-392-2207
Carolina Mirror Co 600 Elkin Hwy	North Wilkesboro	NC	28659	**800-334-7245**	336-838-2151
CDP Corp 1399 Executive Dr W	Richardson	TX	75081	**800-527-4356**	972-234-8565
Ceramo Co Inc 681 Kasten Dr	Jackson	MO	63755	**800-325-8303**	573-243-3138
Crystal Clear Industries 2 Bergen Tpke	Ridgefield Park	NJ	07660	**800-841-4014***	201-440-4200
*Orders					
Culver Industries Inc 1000 Industrial Blvd Hopewell Industrial Park	Aliquippa	PA	15001	**800-862-0070**	724-857-5770
Dacra Glass Inc 1144 S State Rd 3 S	Hartford City	IN	47348	**800-359-3189**	765-348-2190
Dansk International Designs Ltd 100 Lenox Dr	Lawrenceville	NJ	08648	**800-293-2675***	609-896-2800
*Cust Svc					
Edward Marshall Boehm Inc 25 Princess Diana Ln	Trenton	NJ	08638	**800-257-9410**	609-392-2207
Enesco Corp 225 Windsor Dr	Itasca	IL	60143	**800-436-3726**	630-875-5300
Fenton Art Glass Co 700 Elizabeth St	Williamstown	WV	26187	**800-933-6766***	304-375-6122
*Cust Svc					
Fitz & Floyd Corp Inc 501 Corporate Dr	Lewisville	TX	75057	**800-243-2058**	972-874-3480
Friedman Brothers Decorative Arts Inc 9015 NW 105th Way	Medley	FL	33178	**800-327-1065**	305-887-3170
Gainey Ceramics Inc 1200 Arrow Hwy	La Verne	CA	91750	**800-451-8155***	909-593-3533
*Cust Svc					
Gardner Glass Products Inc 600 Elkin Hwy	North Wilkesboro	NC	28659	**800-334-7267**	336-651-9300
Haeger Industries Inc 7 Maiden Ln	Dundee	IL	60118	**800-288-2529**	847-426-3441
Haggerty Enterprises Inc 321 W Lake St Suite G	Elmhurst	IL	60126	**800-352-5282**	630-315-3300
LE Smith Glass Co 1900 Liberty St	Mount Pleasant	PA	15666	**800-537-6484**	724-547-3544
Lenox Inc 100 Lenox Dr	Lawrenceville	NJ	08648	**800-635-3669***	609-896-2800
*Cust Svc					
LH Selman Ltd 123 Locust St	Santa Cruz	CA	95060	**800-538-0766**	831-427-1177
Marshall Pottery 4901 Elysian Fields Rd	Marshall	TX	75670	**888-768-8721**	903-927-5400
Martin's Herend Imports Inc 21440 Pacific Blvd	Sterling	VA	20167	**800-643-7363**	703-450-1601
Media Arts Group Inc 900 Lightpost Way	Morgan Hill	CA	95037	**800-366-3733**	408-201-5000
Michel & Co PO Box 85515	San Diego	CA	92186	**800-533-7263**	
Mikasa Inc 1 Mikasa Dr	Secaucus	NJ	07096	**800-833-4681***	201-867-9210
*Cust Svc					
Royal Doulton USA Inc 200 Cottontail Ln	Somerset	NJ	08873	**800-682-4462**	732-356-7880
Stained Glass Overlay Inc 1827 N Case St	Orange	CA	92865	**800-944-4746**	714-974-6124
Steuben Glass 1 Steuben Way	Corning	NY	14830	**800-424-4240**	607-974-8584
United Design Corp PO Box 1200	Noble	OK	73068	**800-527-4883**	405-872-3468
Waterford Wedgwood USA Inc 1330 Campus Pkwy	Wall	NJ	07719	**888-938-7911***	732-938-5800
*Cust Svc					
Willitts Designs International 1129 Industrial Ave	Petaluma	CA	94952	**800-358-9184**	707-778-7211

331 GLASSWARE & POTTERY - HOUSEHOLD

SEE ALSO Table & Kitchen Supplies - China & Earthenware

Company / Address	City	State	ZIP	Toll-Free	Phone
Berney-Karp Inc 3350 E 26th St	Los Angeles	CA	90023	**800-237-6395**	323-260-7122
Dansk International Designs Ltd 100 Lenox Dr	Lawrenceville	NJ	08648	**800-293-2675***	609-896-2800
*Cust Svc					
Lenox Inc 100 Lenox Dr	Lawrenceville	NJ	08648	**800-635-3669***	609-896-2800
*Cust Svc					
Libbey Inc 300 Madison Ave	Toledo	OH	43604	**888-794-8469**	419-325-2100
NYSE: LBY					
Mikasa Inc 1 Mikasa Dr	Secaucus	NJ	07096	**800-833-4681***	201-867-9210
*Cust Svc					
Noritake Co Inc 15-22 Fair Lawn Ave	Fair Lawn	NJ	07410	**888-296-3423**	
Oneida Ltd 163-181 Kenwood Ave	Oneida	NY	13421	**800-877-6667**	315-361-3000
Pfaltzgraff Co 140 E Market St	York	PA	17401	**800-999-2811**	717-848-5500
Waterford Wedgwood USA Inc 1330 Campus Pkwy	Wall	NJ	07719	**888-938-7911***	732-938-5800
*Cust Svc					

332 GLOBAL DISTRIBUTION SYSTEMS (GDSS)

Company / Address	City	State	ZIP	Toll-Free	Phone
Amadeus North America LLC 9250 NW 36 St	Miami	FL	33178	**800-888-7971**	305-499-6000
Pegasus Solutions Inc 8350 N Central Expy Suite 1900	Dallas	TX	75206	**800-528-2422**	214-234-4000
NASDAQ: PEGS					
WizCom International Ltd 1 Campus Dr	Parsippany	NJ	07054	**877-949-2661**	973-496-3500

333 GOURMET SPECIALTY SHOPS

Company / Address	City	State	ZIP	Toll-Free	Phone
Dean & DeLuca Inc 560 Broadway	New York	NY	10012	**800-999-0306**	212-226-6800
Graber Olive House Inc 315 E 4th St	Ontario	CA	91764	**800-996-5483**	909-983-1761

Name / Address	City	State	Zip	Toll-Free	Phone
Harry & David Co 2500 S Pacific Hwy	Medford	OR	97501	**800-345-5655***	541-776-2121
*Cust Svc					
Heavenly Ham 5445 Triangle Pkwy Suite 400	Norcross	GA	30092	**800-989-0509**	770-752-1999
Hickory Farms Inc 1505 Holland Rd	Maumee	OH	43537	**800-288-7327**	419-893-7611
Honeybaked Ham Co 5445 Triangle Pkwy Suite 400	Norcross	GA	30092	**800-367-2426**	678-966-3100
Jerky Hut International PO Box 308	Hubbard	OR	97032	**800-223-5759**	503-981-7191
Logan Farms Honey Glazed Hams 10560 Westheimer Rd	Houston	TX	77042	**800-833-4267**	713-781-3773
Omaha Steaks International Inc 10909 John Galt Blvd	Omaha	NE	68137	**800-960-8400**	402-597-8370
Stew Leonard's 100 Westport Ave	Norwalk	CT	06851	**800-729-7839**	203-847-9088
Your Northwest 31461 NE Bell Rd	Sherwood	OR	97140	**888-252-0699**	503-554-9060
Zabar's & Co Inc 2245 Broadway	New York	NY	10024	**800-697-6301**	212-787-2000

334 GOVERNMENT - COUNTY

Name / Address	City	State	Zip	Toll-Free	Phone
Aleutians East Borough PO Box 349	Sand Point	AK	99661	**888-383-2699**	907-383-2699
Coconino County 219 E Cherry Ave	Flagstaff	AZ	86001	**800-559-9289**	928-774-5011
Dauphin County 2 S 2nd St	Harrisburg	PA	17101	**800-328-0058**	717-780-6300
Garfield County 55 S Main St	Panguitch	UT	84759	**800-636-8826**	435-676-8826
Hoke County PO Box 210	Raeford	NC	28376	**800-597-8751**	910-875-8751
King County 701 5th Ave Suite 3210	Seattle	WA	98104	**800-325-6165**	206-296-4040
Latah County 522 S Adams PO Box 8068	Moscow	ID	83843	**800-691-2012**	208-882-8580
Lincoln County 300 Central Ave PO Box 338	Carrizozo	NM	88301	**800-687-2705**	505-648-2394
Santa Fe County 102 Grant Ave	Santa Fe	NM	87504	**800-894-7028**	505-986-6200
Uintah County 147 E Main St	Vernal	UT	84078	**800-966-4680**	435-781-0770

335 GOVERNMENT - STATE

Name / Address	City	State	Zip	Toll-Free	Phone
Idaho State Government Information		ID		**877-443-3468**	208-334-2411
Massachusetts State Government Information		MA		**866-888-2808**	
Alabama					
Conservation & Natural Resources Dept 64 N Union St PO Box 301450	Montgomery	AL	36130	**800-262-3151**	334-242-3486
Homeland Security Dept PO Box 304115	Montgomery	AL	36130	**800-361-4454**	334-956-7250
Prepaid Affordable College Tuition (PACT) Program 100 N Union St Suite 660	Montgomery	AL	36130	**800-252-7228**	334-242-7514
Public Service Commission PO Box 304260	Montgomery	AL	36130	**800-392-8050**	334-242-5218
Rehabilitation Services Dept 2129 E South Blvd	Montgomery	AL	36116	**800-441-7607**	334-281-8780
Securities Commission 770 Washington Ave Suite 570	Montgomery	AL	36130	**800-222-1253**	334-242-2984
Senior Services Dept 770 Washington Ave Suite 470	Montgomery	AL	36130	**877-425-2243**	334-242-5743
State Parks Div 64 N Union St	Montgomery	AL	36130	**800-252-7275**	334-242-3334
Tourism & Travel Bureau 401 Adams Ave Suite 126	Montgomery	AL	36104	**800-252-2262**	334-242-4169
Alaska					
Postsecondary Education Commission 3030 Vintage Blvd	Juneau	AK	99801	**800-441-3293***	907-465-6740
*Cust Svc					
Student Aid Office 3030 Vintage Blvd	Juneau	AK	99801	**800-441-2962**	907-465-2962
Vocational Rehabilitation Div 801 W 10th St Suite 200	Juneau	AK	99801	**800-478-2815**	907-465-2814
Arizona					
Attorney General 1275 W Washington St	Phoenix	AZ	85007	**888-377-6108**	602-542-5025
Bill Status-House Capitol Complex 1700 W Washington St	Phoenix	AZ	85007	**800-352-8404**	602-542-4900
Children Youth & Families Div 1789 W Jefferson St	Phoenix	AZ	85007	**877-543-7633**	602-542-2277
Environmental Quality Dept 1110 W Washington St	Phoenix	AZ	85007	**800-234-5677**	602-207-2300
Legislature Capitol Complex 1700 W Washington St	Phoenix	AZ	85007	**800-352-8404**	602-542-4900
Rehabilitation Services Administration 1789 W Jefferson St 2nd Fl NW	Phoenix	AZ	85007	**800-563-1221**	602-542-3332
Tourism Office 1110 W Washington St Suite 155	Phoenix	AZ	85007	**888-520-3434**	602-364-3700
Arkansas					
Attorney General 323 Center St Suite 200	Little Rock	AR	72201	**800-482-8982***	501-682-2007
*Consumer Info					
Consumer Protection Div 323 Center St Tower Bldg Suite 200	Little Rock	AR	72201	**800-482-8982**	501-682-6150
Crime Victims Reparations Board 323 Center St Suite 200	Little Rock	AR	72201	**800-448-3014**	501-682-1323
Economic Development Dept 1 Capitol Mall Suite 4C-300	Little Rock	AR	72201	**800-275-2672**	501-682-1121
Financial Aid Office 114 E Capitol St	Little Rock	AR	72201	**800-547-8839**	501-371-2013
Insurance Dept 1200 W 3rd St	Little Rock	AR	72201	**800-282-9134**	501-371-2600
Parks & Tourism Dept 1 Capitol Mall	Little Rock	AR	72201	**800-628-8725**	501-682-7777
Rehabilitation Services 1616 Brookwood Dr	Little Rock	AR	72202	**800-330-0632**	501-296-1600
Vital Records Div 4815 W Markham St Slot 44	Little Rock	AR	72205	**800-637-9314**	501-661-2174
Worker's Compensation Commission PO Box 950	Little Rock	AR	72203	**800-622-4472**	501-682-3930
California					
Arts Council 1300 'I' St Suite 930	Sacramento	CA	95814	**800-201-6201**	916-322-6555
Child Support Services Dept PO Box 269112	Sacramento	CA	95826	**866-249-0773**	916-464-5000
Fair Political Practices Commission 428 J St Suite 620	Sacramento	CA	95814	**866-275-3772**	916-322-5660
Financial Institutions Dept 111 Pine St Suite 1100	San Francisco	CA	94111	**800-622-0620***	415-263-8500
*Consumer Info					
Military Dept 9800 Goethe Rd PO Box 269101	Sacramento	CA	95826	**800-321-2752**	916-854-3000
Parks & Recreation Dept PO Box 942896	Sacramento	CA	94296	**800-777-0369**	916-653-6995
Public Utilities Commission 505 Van Ness Ave	San Francisco	CA	94102	**800-848-5580**	415-703-2782
Student Aid Commission PO Box 419027	Rancho Cordova	CA	95741	**888-224-7268**	916-526-8999
Teacher Credentialing Commission 1900 Capitol Ave	Sacramento	CA	95814	**888-921-2682**	916-445-7254
Veterans Affairs Dept 1227 'O' St	Sacramento	CA	95814	**800-221-8998**	916-653-2158
Victim Compensation Program PO Box 3036	Sacramento	CA	95812	**800-777-9229**	916-324-0400
Colorado					
Arts Council 750 Pennsylvania St	Denver	CO	80203	**800-291-2787**	303-894-2617
CollegeInvest 1801 Broadway Suite 1300	Denver	CO	80202	**800-478-5651**	303-295-1981
Labor & Employment Dept 1515 Arapahoe St Tower 2 Suite 400	Denver	CO	80202	**800-390-7936**	303-318-8000
Lottery Div 201 W 8th St Suite 600	Pueblo	CO	81003	**800-999-2959**	719-546-2400
Parks & Outdoor Recreation Div 1313 Sherman St Rm 618	Denver	CO	80203	**800-678-2267***	303-866-3437
*Campground Resv					
Tourism Office 1625 Broadway Suite 1700	Denver	CO	80202	**800-265-6723**	303-892-3885
Victims Programs Office 700 Kipling St Suite 3000	Denver	CO	80215	**888-282-1080**	303-239-4442
Connecticut					
Banking Dept 260 Constitution Plaza	Hartford	CT	06103	**800-831-7225**	860-240-8299
Consumer Protection Dept 165 Capitol Ave	Hartford	CT	06106	**800-842-2649**	860-713-6020
Higher Education Dept 61 Woodland St	Hartford	CT	06105	**800-842-0229**	860-947-1800
Rehabilitation Services Bureau 25 Sigourney St 11th Fl	Hartford	CT	06106	**800-537-2549**	860-424-4844
Victim Services Office 31 Cookes St	Plainville	CT	06062	**800-822-8428**	860-747-3994
Delaware					
Higher Education Commission 820 N French St 5th Fl	Wilmington	DE	19801	**800-292-7935**	302-577-3240
Parks & Recreation Div 89 Kings Hwy	Dover	DE	19901	**877-987-2757***	302-739-4702
*Campground Resv					
Tourism Office 99 Kings Hwy	Dover	DE	19901	**866-284-7483**	302-739-4271
District of Columbia					
Convention & Tourism Corp 1212 New York Ave Suite 200	Washington	DC	20005	**800-422-8644**	202-724-5644
Employment Services Dept 609 H St NE	Washington	DC	20002	**877-319-7346**	202-698-6044
Tuition Assistance Grant Program 441 4th St NW Rm 350N	Washington	DC	20001	**877-485-6751**	202-727-2824
Florida					
Bill Status 111 W Madison St Rm 704	Tallahassee	FL	32399	**800-342-1827**	850-488-4371
Child Support Enforcement Program PO Box 8030	Tallahassee	FL	32314	**800-622-5437**	
Consumer Services Div 2005 Apalachee Pkwy	Tallahassee	FL	32399	**800-435-7352**	850-922-2966
Financial Services Dept 200 E Gaines St	Tallahassee	FL	32399	**800-342-2762**	850-413-3100
Insurance Regulation Office 200 E Gaines St	Tallahassee	FL	32399	**800-342-2762**	850-413-3132
Prepaid College Board PO Box 6567	Tallahassee	FL	32314	**800-552-4723**	850-488-8514
Recreation & Parks Div 3900 Commonwealth Blvd MS 500	Tallahassee	FL	32399	**800-326-3521***	850-245-2157
*Campground Resv					
Student Financial Assistance Office 1940 N Monroe St Suite 70	Tallahassee	FL	32303	**888-827-2004**	850-410-5200
Tourism Commission 661 E Jefferson St Suite 300	Tallahassee	FL	32301	**888-735-2872**	850-488-5607
Vocational Rehabilitation Services Div 2002 Old St Augustine Rd Bldg A	Tallahassee	FL	32301	**800-451-4327**	850-245-3399
Georgia					
Environmental Protection Div 2 ML King Jr Dr SE Suite 1152E	Atlanta	GA	30334	**888-373-5947**	404-657-5947
Parks Recreation & Historic Sites Div 2 ML King Jr Dr SE Suite 1352E	Atlanta	GA	30334	**800-862-7275**	404-656-2770
Ports Authority PO Box 2406	Savannah	GA	31402	**800-342-8012**	912-964-3811
Student Finance Commission 2082 E Exchange Pl Suite 200	Tucker	GA	30084	**800-505-4732**	770-724-9000
Tourism Div 285 Peachtree Center Ave NE Suite 1000	Atlanta	GA	30303	**800-847-4842**	404-656-2000
Hawaii Child Support Enforcement Agency 601 Kamokila Blvd Suite 251	Kapolei	HI	96707	**888-317-9081**	808-692-7000
Idaho					
Arts Commission 2410 Old Penitentiary Rd	Boise	ID	83712	**800-278-3863**	208-334-2119
Crime Victims Compensation Program PO Box 83720	Boise	ID	83720	**800-950-2110**	208-334-6000
Economic Development Div PO Box 83720	Boise	ID	83720	**800-842-5858**	208-334-2470
Tourism Div PO Box 83720	Boise	ID	83720	**800-842-5858**	208-334-2470
Illinois					
Arts Council 100 W Randolph St Suite 10-500	Chicago	IL	60601	**800-237-6994**	312-814-4831
Child Support Enforcement Div 509 S 6th St	Springfield	IL	62701	**800-447-4278**	217-524-4602
Crime Victims Services Div 100 W Randolf Rd 13th Fl	Chicago	IL	60601	**800-228-3368**	312-814-2581
Human Services Dept 100 S Grand Ave E 3rd Fl	Springfield	IL	62762	**800-843-6154**	217-557-1601
Lottery Dept 101 W Jefferson St	Springfield	IL	62702	**800-252-1775**	217-524-5155
Mental Health Div 100 W Randolf St Suite 3-400	Chicago	IL	60601	**800-252-2923**	312-814-2811
Rehabilitation Services Office 100 S Grand Ave E 3rd Fl	Springfield	IL	62762	**800-641-3929**	217-557-2507
Revenue Dept 101 W Jefferson St	Springfield	IL	62702	**800-732-8866**	217-782-3336
Student Assistance Commission 1755 Lake Cook Rd	Deerfield	IL	60015	**800-899-4722**	847-948-8500
Tourism Bureau 100 W Randolph St Suite 3-400	Chicago	IL	60601	**800-226-6632**	312-814-4732
Veterans Affairs Dept 833 S Spring St	Springfield	IL	62794	**800-437-9824**	217-782-6641
Industrial Commission 100 W Randolph St 8th Fl	Chicago	IL	60601	**866-352-3033**	312-814-6611
Indiana					
Community Development Div 1 N Capitol Ave Suite 700	Indianapolis	IN	46204	**800-824-2476**	317-232-8911
Consumer Protection Div 402 W Washington St 5th Fl	Indianapolis	IN	46204	**800-382-5516**	317-232-6330
Disability Aging & Rehabilitative Services Div 402 W Washington St Rm W451	Indianapolis	IN	46207	**800-545-7763**	317-232-1147
Family & Social Services Administration 402 W Washington St Rm W461	Indianapolis	IN	46207	**800-545-7763**	317-233-4454
Health Professions Bureau 402 W Washington St Rm W041	Indianapolis	IN	46204	**888-333-7515**	317-232-2960
Insurance Dept 311 W Washington St Suite 300	Indianapolis	IN	46204	**800-622-4461***	317-232-2385
*Cust Svc					

Agency / Address	City	State	Zip	Toll-Free	Phone
Port Commission 150 W Market St Suite 100	Indianapolis	IN	46204	**800-232-7678**	317-232-9200
State Parks & Reservoirs Div 402 W Washington Rm W-298	Indianapolis	IN	46204	**800-622-4931**	317-232-4124
Students Assistance Commission 150 W Market St Suite 500	Indianapolis	IN	46204	**888-528-4719**	317-232-2350
Tourism Div 1 N Capitol Ave Suite 700	Indianapolis	IN	46204	**888-365-6946**	317-232-8860
Victims Services Div 302 W Washington St Rm E209	Indianapolis	IN	46204	**800-353-1484**	317-232-1233
Iowa					
Child Support Recovery Unit 400 SW 8th St Suite M	Des Moines	IA	50309	**888-229-9223**	515-281-5580
College Student Aid Commission 200 10th St 4th Fl	Des Moines	IA	50309	**800-383-4222**	515-281-3501
Crime Victim Assistance Div 321 E 12th St Rm 018	Des Moines	IA	50319	**800-373-5044**	515-281-5044
Educational Examiners Board 400 E 14th St	Des Moines	IA	50319	**800-778-7856**	515-281-5849
Motor Vehicle Div 100 Euclid Ave	Des Moines	IA	50313	**800-532-1121**	515-237-3202
Tourism Office 200 E Grand Ave	Des Moines	IA	50309	**888-472-6035**	515-242-4705
Veterans Affairs Commission Camp Dodge 7700 NW Beaver Dr Bldg A6A	Johnston	IA	50131	**800-838-4692**	515-242-5331
Kansas					
Insurance Dept 420 SW 9th St	Topeka	KS	66612	**800-432-2484**	785-296-3071
Travel & Tourism Development Div 1000 SW Jackson St Suite 100	Topeka	KS	66612	**800-252-6727**	785-296-5403
Kentucky					
Consumer Protection Div 1024 Capital Center Dr Suite 200	Frankfort	KY	40601	**888-432-9257**	502-696-5389
Education Professional Standards Board 1024 Capitol Center Dr Suite 225	Frankfort	KY	40601	**888-598-7667**	502-573-4606
Fish & Wildlife Resources Dept 1 Game Farm Rd	Frankfort	KY	40601	**800-858-1549**	502-564-3400
Higher Education Assistance Authority PO Box 798	Frankfort	KY	40602	**800-928-8926**	502-696-7200
Historical Society 100 W Broadway	Frankfort	KY	40601	**877-444-7867**	502-564-1792
Housing Corp 1231 Louisville Rd	Frankfort	KY	40601	**800-633-8896**	502-564-7630
Parks Dept 500 Mero St Suite 1100	Frankfort	KY	40601	**800-255-7275**	502-564-2172
Real Estate Commission 10200 Linn Station Rd Suite 201	Louisville	KY	40223	**888-373-3300**	502-425-4273
Travel Dept 500 Mero St Suite 2200	Frankfort	KY	40601	**800-225-8747**	502-564-4930
Vocational Rehabilitation Dept 209 Saint Clair St Rm 200	Frankfort	KY	40601	**800-372-7172**	502-564-4440
Louisiana					
Bill Status State Capitol 13th Fl	Baton Rouge	LA	70804	**800-256-3793**	225-342-2456
Ethics Board 2415 Quail Dr 3rd Fl	Baton Rouge	LA	70808	**800-842-6630**	225-763-8777
Insurance Dept PO Box 94214	Baton Rouge	LA	70804	**800-259-5300**	225-342-5900
Rehabilitation Services 8225 Florida Blvd	Baton Rouge	LA	70806	**800-737-2958**	225-925-4131
State Parks Office PO Box 44426	Baton Rouge	LA	70804	**888-677-1400**	225-342-8111
Student Financial Assistance Office PO Box 91202	Baton Rouge	LA	70821	**800-259-5626**	225-922-1011
Maine					
Bill Status State House 100 State House Station	Augusta	ME	04333	**800-301-3178**	207-287-1692
Economic & Community Development Dept 59 State House Stn	Augusta	ME	04333	**800-541-5872**	207-287-2656
Emergency Management Agency 72 State House Stn	Augusta	ME	04333	**800-452-8735**	207-626-4503
Environmental Protection Dept 17 State House Stn	Augusta	ME	04333	**800-452-1942**	207-287-7688
Finance Authority of Maine (FAME) PO Box 949	Augusta	ME	04332	**800-228-3734**	207-623-3263
Parks & Land Bureau 22 State House Stn *Campground Resv	Augusta	ME	04333	**800-332-1501***	207-287-3821
Rehabilitation Services Bureau 150 State House Stn	Augusta	ME	04333	**800-760-1573**	207-624-5950
Tourism Office 59 State House Stn	Augusta	ME	04333	**888-624-6345**	207-287-5711
Maryland					
Aging Dept 301 W Preston St Rm 1007	Baltimore	MD	21201	**800-243-3425**	410-767-1100
Bill Status 90 State Cir	Annapolis	MD	21401	**800-492-7122**	410-946-5400
Chief Medical Examiner 111 Penn St	Baltimore	MD	21201	**800-833-6263**	410-333-3250
Child Support Enforcement Administration 311 W Saratoga St	Baltimore	MD	21201	**800-332-6347**	410-767-7674
Criminal Injuries Compensation Board 6776 Reisterstown Rd Suite 312	Baltimore	MD	21215	**888-679-9347**	410-585-3010
Emergency Management Agency 5401 Rue Saint Lo Dr	Reisterstown	MD	21136	**877-636-2872**	410-517-3600
Health & Mental Hygiene Dept 201 W Preston St 5th Fl	Baltimore	MD	21201	**877-463-3464**	410-767-6500
Higher Education Commision 839 Bestgate Rd Suite 400	Annapolis	MD	21401	**800-974-0203**	410-260-4500
Public Service Commission 6 Saint Paul St 16th Fl	Baltimore	MD	21202	**800-492-0474**	410-767-8000
Rehabilitation Services Div 2301 Argonne Dr	Baltimore	MD	21218	**888-554-0334**	410-554-9385
State Forest & Park Service 580 Taylor Ave Rm E-3 *Campground Resv	Annapolis	MD	21401	**888-432-2267***	410-260-8186
Student Financial Assistance Office 839 Bestgate Rd Suite 400	Annapolis	MD	21401	**800-974-1024**	410-260-4565
Tourism Development Office 217 E Redwood St 9th Fl	Baltimore	MD	21202	**800-543-1036**	410-767-3400
Treasurer 80 Calvert St Rm 109	Annapolis	MD	21401	**800-974-0468**	410-260-7533
Veterans Affairs Dept 31 Hopkins Plaza Rm 110	Baltimore	MD	21201	**800-446-4926**	410-333-4428
Vital Records Div 6550 Reisterstown Rd	Baltimore	MD	21215	**800-832-3277**	410-764-3038
Massachusetts					
Bill Status 1 Ashburton Pl Rm 1611	Boston	MA	02108	**800-392-6090**	617-727-7030
Child Support Enforcement Div 51 Sleeper St 3rd Fl	Boston	MA	02205	**800-332-2733**	617-626-4170
Educational Financing Authority 125 Summer St	Boston	MA	02110	**800-449-6332**	617-261-9760
Elder Affairs Office 1 Ashburton Pl 5th Fl	Boston	MA	02108	**800-243-4636**	617-727-7750
Travel & Tourism Office 10 Park Plaza Suite 4510	Boston	MA	02116	**800-227-6277**	617-973-8500
Michigan					
Education Trust PO Box 30198	Lansing	MI	48909	**800-638-4543**	517-335-4767
Parks & Recreation Bureau PO Box 30257 *Campground Resv	Lansing	MI	48909	**800-447-2757***	517-373-9900
Rehabilitation Services PO Box 30010	Lansing	MI	48909	**800-605-6722**	517-373-3390
Student Financial Services Bureau PO Box 30047	Lansing	MI	48909	**800-642-5626**	517-373-4897
Travel Michigan 300 N Washington Sq	Lansing	MI	48913	**888-784-7328**	517-373-0670
Minnesota					
Aging Board 444 Lafayette Rd N	Saint Paul	MN	55155	**800-657-3889**	651-296-1531
Arts Board 400 Sibley St Suite 200	Saint Paul	MN	55101	**800-866-2787**	651-215-1600
Consumer Protection Office 445 Minnesota St Suite 1400	Saint Paul	MN	55101	**800-657-3787**	651-296-3353
Crime Victims Reparations Board 445 Minnesota St Suite 2300	Saint Paul	MN	55101	**888-622-8799**	651-282-6256
Higher Education Services Office 1450 Energy Park Dr Suite 350	Saint Paul	MN	55108	**800-657-3866**	651-642-0567
Historical Society 345 Kellogg Blvd W	Saint Paul	MN	55102	**888-727-8386**	651-296-6126
Licensing Div 85 7th Pl E Suite 600	Saint Paul	MN	55101	**800-657-3978**	651-296-6319
Natural Resources Dept 500 Lafayette Rd	Saint Paul	MN	55155	**888-646-6367**	651-296-2549
Rehabilitation Services Branch 390 N Robert St 1st Fl	Saint Paul	MN	55101	**800-328-9095**	651-296-5616
Tourism Office 121 7th Pl E Suite 100	Saint Paul	MN	55101	**800-657-3700**	651-296-5029
Mississippi					
Banking & Consumer Finance Dept PO Box 23729	Jackson	MS	39225	**800-844-2499**	601-359-1031
Child Support Enforcement Div PO Box 352	Jackson	MS	39205	**800-948-4010**	601-359-4861
Consumer Protection Div PO Box 1609	Jackson	MS	39215	**800-551-1830**	601-359-1111
Contractors Board PO Box 320279	Jackson	MS	39232	**800-880-6161**	601-354-6161
Crime Victim Compensation Program PO Box 267	Jackson	MS	39205	**800-829-6766**	601-359-6766
Emergency Management Agency PO Box 4501	Jackson	MS	39296	**800-222-6362**	601-352-9100
Parks & Recreation Div PO Box 451	Jackson	MS	39205	**800-467-2757**	601-432-2266
Prepaid Affordable College Tuition Program (MPACT) PO Box 120	Jackson	MS	39205	**800-987-4450**	601-359-5255
Rehabilitation Services Dept PO Box 1698	Jackson	MS	39215	**800-443-1000**	601-853-5100
Tourism Development Div PO Box 849	Jackson	MS	39205	**866-733-6477**	601-359-3297
Missouri					
Child Support Enforcement Div PO Box 1527	Jefferson City	MO	65102	**800-859-7999**	573-751-4301
Higher Education Dept 3515 Amazonas Dr	Jefferson City	MO	65109	**800-473-6757**	573-751-2361
State Parks Div PO Box 176	Jefferson City	MO	65102	**800-334-6946**	573-751-2479
Student Assistance Resource Services (MOSTARS) 3515 Amazonas Dr	Jefferson City	MO	65109	**800-473-6757**	573-751-2361
Tourism Div PO Box 1055	Jefferson City	MO	65102	**800-877-1234**	573-526-5900
Transportation Dept PO Box 270	Jefferson City	MO	65102	**888-275-6636**	573-751-2551
Montana					
Arts Council PO Box 202201	Helena	MT	59620	**800-282-3092**	406-444-6430
Consumer Protection Office PO Box 200501	Helena	MT	59620	**800-322-2272**	406-444-4311
Historical Society 225 N Roberts St	Helena	MT	59620	**800-243-9900**	406-444-2694
Promotion Div (Travel Montana) PO Box 200533	Helena	MT	59620	**800-847-4868**	406-444-2654
Public Instruction Office PO Box 202501	Helena	MT	59620	**888-231-9393**	406-444-3095
Nebraska					
Arts Council 3838 Davenport St	Omaha	NE	68131	**800-341-4067**	402-595-2122
Bill Status 2018 State Capitol Bldg	Lincoln	NE	68509	**800-724-7456**	402-471-2877
Child Support Enforcement Div PO Box 94728	Lincoln	NE	68509	**877-631-9973**	402-471-8715
Consumer Protection Div 2115 State Capitol Bldg	Lincoln	NE	68509	**800-727-6432**	402-471-2682
Economic Development Dept PO Box 94666	Lincoln	NE	68509	**800-426-6505**	402-471-3747
Public Accountancy Board PO Box 94725	Lincoln	NE	68509	**800-564-6111**	402-471-3595
Travel & Tourism Div PO Box 98907	Lincoln	NE	68509	**877-632-7275**	402-471-3796
Vocational Rehabilitation Services Div PO Box 94987	Lincoln	NE	68509	**877-637-3422**	402-471-3644
Workers' Compensation Court PO Box 98908	Lincoln	NE	68509	**800-599-5155**	402-471-6468
Nevada					
Bill Status 401 S Carson St	Carson City	NV	89701	**800-992-6761**	775-684-6800
Child Support Enforcement Office 2527 N Carson St	Carson City	NV	89706	**800-992-0900**	775-687-4744
Consumer Affairs Div 1850 E Sahara Ave Suite 101	Las Vegas	NV	89104	**800-326-5202**	702-486-7355
Economic Development Commission 108 E Proctor St	Carson City	NV	89701	**800-336-1600**	775-687-4325
Insurance Div 788 Fairview Dr Suite 300	Carson City	NV	89701	**800-992-0900**	775-687-4270
Motor Vehicles Dept 555 Wright Way	Carson City	NV	89711	**877-368-7828**	775-684-4368
Securities Div 555 E Washington Ave Suite 5200	Las Vegas	NV	89101	**800-758-6440**	702-486-2440
Tourism Commission 401 N Carson St	Carson City	NV	89701	**800-237-0774**	775-687-4322
New Hampshire					
Housing Finance Authority PO Box 5087	Manchester	NH	03108	**800-439-7247**	603-472-8623
Travel & Tourism Development Office PO Box 1856	Concord	NH	03302	**800-386-4664**	603-271-2665
Victims' Assistance Commission 33 Capitol St	Concord	NH	03301	**800-300-4500**	603-271-1284
Worker's Compensation Div 95 Pleasant St	Concord	NH	03301	**800-272-4353**	603-271-3176
New Jersey					
Bill Status State House Annex PO Box 068	Trenton	NJ	08625	**800-792-8630**	609-292-4840
Child Support Office PO Box 716	Trenton	NJ	08625	**800-621-5437**	609-588-2385
Higher Education Student Assistance Authority 4 Quakerbridge Plaza PO Box 540	Trenton	NJ	08625	**800-792-8670**	609-588-7944
Mental Health Services Div PO Box 272	Trenton	NJ	08625	**800-382-9717**	609-777-0700
Military & Veterans' Affairs Dept 101 Eggert Crossing Rd	Lawrenceville	NJ	08648	**800-624-0508**	609-530-4600
Motor Vehicles Commission 225 E State St PO Box 160	Trenton	NJ	08666	**888-486-3339**	609-292-6500
Travel & Tourism Div PO Box 820	Trenton	NJ	08625	**800-847-4865**	609-777-0885
New Mexico					
Arts Div 228 E Palace Ave	Santa Fe	NM	87501	**800-879-4278**	505-827-6490
Children Youth & Families Dept PO Drawer 5160	Santa Fe	NM	87502	**800-610-7610**	505-827-7610
Consumer Protection Div PO Drawer 1508	Santa Fe	NM	87504	**800-300-2020**	505-827-6060
Environment Dept 1190 St Francis Dr	Santa Fe	NM	87503	**800-219-6157**	505-827-2855
Ethics Administration 325 Don Gaspar St Suite 300	Santa Fe	NM	87503	**800-477-3632**	505-827-3895
Higher Education Commission 1068 Cerrillos Rd	Santa Fe	NM	87501	**800-279-9777**	505-827-7383
Highway & Transportation Dept PO Box 1149	Santa Fe	NM	87504	**877-887-7094**	505-827-5100
Human Services Dept PO Box 2348	Santa Fe	NM	87504	**800-432-6217**	505-827-7750
Lieutenant Governor State Capitol Bldg 4th Fl	Santa Fe	NM	87503	**800-432-4406**	505-827-3050
Mortgage Finance Authority 344 4th St SW	Albuquerque	NM	87102	**800-444-6880**	505-843-6880
Secretary of State 325 Don Gaspar Ave Suite 300	Santa Fe	NM	87501	**800-477-3632**	505-827-3600
State Parks Div PO Box 1147	Santa Fe	NM	87504	**888-667-2757**	505-476-3355

	City	State	ZIP	Toll-Free	Phone
Tourism Dept 491 Old Santa Fe Trail	Santa Fe	NM	87503	**800-545-2070**	505-827-7400
Vocational Rehabilitation Div 435 St Michaels Dr Bldg D	Santa Fe	NM	87505	**800-235-5387**	505-954-8500
New York					
Agriculture & Markets Dept 10A Airline Dr	Albany	NY	12235	**800-554-4501**	518-457-3880
Athletic Commission 123 William St 20th Fl	New York	NY	10038	**866-269-3769**	212-417-5700
Bill Status 55 Elk St	Albany	NY	12210	**800-342-9860**	518-455-7545
Consumer Protection Board 5 Empire State Plaza Suite 2101	Albany	NY	12223	**800-697-1220**	518-474-3514
Empire State Development Corp 30 S Pearl St	Albany	NY	12245	**800-782-8369**	518-292-5100
Higher Education Services Corp 99 Washington Ave	Albany	NY	12255	**888-697-4372**	518-473-1574
Parks Recreation & Historic Preservation Office 1 Empire State Plaza *Campground Resv	Albany	NY	12238	**800-456-2267***	518-474-0456
Taxation & Finance Dept WA Harriman Campus Bldg 8	Albany	NY	12227	**800-225-5829**	518-457-2244
Tourism Div PO Box 2603	Albany	NY	12220	**800-225-5697**	518-474-4116
North Carolina					
Marine Fisheries Div PO Box 769	Morehead City	NC	28557	**800-682-2632**	252-726-7021
State Education Assistance Authority PO Box 14103	Research Triangle Park	NC	27709	**800-700-1775**	919-549-8614
State Ports Authority 2202 Burnett Blvd PO Box 9002	Wilmington	NC	28402	**800-334-0682**	910-763-1621
Tourism Div 301 N Wilmington St	Raleigh	NC	27601	**800-847-4862**	919-733-4171
North Dakota					
Accountancy Board 2701 S Columbia Rd	Grand Forks	ND	58201	**800-532-5904**	701-775-7100
Children & Family Services Div 600 E Boulevard Ave	Bismarck	ND	58505	**800-245-3736**	701-328-2316
Consumer Protection Div 600 E Boulevard Ave Dept 125	Bismarck	ND	58505	**800-472-2600**	701-328-3404
Human Services Dept 600 E Boulevard Ave Dept 325	Bismarck	ND	58505	**800-472-2622**	701-328-2310
Insurance Dept 600 E Boulevard Ave Dept 401	Bismarck	ND	58505	**800-247-0560**	701-328-2440
Parks & Recreation Dept 1835 E Bismarck Expy *Campground Resv	Bismarck	ND	58504	**800-807-4723***	701-328-5357
Secretary of State 600 E Boulevard Ave Dept 108	Bismarck	ND	58505	**800-352-0867**	701-328-2900
Tourism Div 604 E Boulevard Ave	Bismarck	ND	58505	**800-435-5663**	701-328-2525
Vocational Rehabilitation Div 600 S 2nd St Suite 1B	Bismarck	ND	58504	**800-755-2745**	701-328-8950
Ohio					
Agriculture Dept 8995 E Main St	Reynoldsburg	OH	43068	**800-282-1955**	614-728-6200
Child Support Office 30 E Broad St 32nd Fl	Columbus	OH	43215	**800-686-1556**	614-752-6561
Crime Victim Services 150 E Gay St 25th Fl	Columbus	OH	43215	**800-582-2877**	614-466-5610
Development Dept 77 S High St	Columbus	OH	43215	**800-848-1300**	614-466-2480
Education Dept 25 S Front St	Columbus	OH	43215	**877-644-6338**	614-466-3641
Insurance Dept 2100 Stella Ct	Columbus	OH	43215	**800-686-1526**	614-644-2658
Parks & Recreation Div 2045 Morse Rd Bldg C-3	Columbus	OH	43229	**800-282-7275**	614-265-6561
Rehabilitation Services Commission 400 E Campus View Blvd	Columbus	OH	43235	**800-282-4536**	614-438-1200
State Grants & Scholarships Office PO Box 182452	Columbus	OH	43218	**888-833-1133**	614-466-7420
Travel & Tourism Div PO Box 1001	Columbus	OH	43216	**800-282-5393**	614-466-8844
Tuition Trust Authority 580 S High St Suite 208 *Cust Svc	Columbus	OH	43215	**800-233-6734***	614-752-9400
Wildlife Div 2045 Morse Rd Bldg G	Columbus	OH	43229	**800-945-3543**	614-265-6300
Workers' Compensation Bureau 30 W Spring St	Columbus	OH	43215	**800-644-6292**	614-644-6292
Oklahoma					
Commerce Dept 900 N Stiles Ave	Oklahoma City	OK	73104	**800-879-6552**	405-815-6552
Environmental Quality Dept 707 N Robinson Ave PO Box 1677	Oklahoma City	OK	73101	**800-869-1400**	405-702-1000
Housing Finance Agency 1140 NW 63rd St Suite 200	Oklahoma City	OK	73116	**800-256-1489**	405-848-1144
Parks Div PO Box 52002	Oklahoma City	OK	73152	**800-654-8240**	405-521-3411
Rehabilitative Services Dept 3535 NW 58th St Suite 500	Oklahoma City	OK	73112	**800-845-8476**	405-951-3400
Tourism & Recreation Dept 15 N Robinson St Suite 100	Oklahoma City	OK	73105	**800-652-6552**	405-521-2406
Workers' Compensation Div 4001 N Lincoln Blvd	Oklahoma City	OK	73105	**888-269-5353**	405-528-1500
Oregon					
Fish & Wildlife Dept 3406 Cherry Ave NE	Salem	OR	97303	**800-720-6339**	503-947-6000
Parks & Recreation Dept 725 Summer St NE Suite C	Salem	OR	97301	**800-551-6949**	503-986-0667
Seniors & People with Disabilities Div 500 Summer St NE 2nd Fl	Salem	OR	97310	**800-282-2096**	503-945-5811
Student Assistance Commission 1500 Valley River Dr Suite 100	Eugene	OR	97401	**800-452-8807**	541-687-7400
Tourism Commission 670 Hawthorne Ave SE Suite 240	Salem	OR	97301	**800-547-7842**	503-378-8850
Transportation Dept 355 Capitol St NE Suite 135	Salem	OR	97301	**888-275-6368**	503-986-3200
Vocational Rehabilitation Services Office 500 Summer St NE	Salem	OR	97310	**800-452-2147**	503-945-5880
Pennsylvania					
Higher Education Assistance Agency 1200 N 7th St	Harrisburg	PA	17102	**800-692-7392**	717-720-2860
State Lottery 2850 Turnpike Industrial Dr	Middletown	PA	17057	**800-692-7481**	717-986-4699
State Parks Bureau PO Box 8551	Harrisburg	PA	17105	**888-727-2757**	717-787-6640
Tourism Office 404 North St 4th Fl	Harrisburg	PA	17120	**800-847-4872**	717-720-1301
Transportation Dept 400 North St	Harrisburg	PA	17120	**800-932-4600**	717-787-2838
Tuition Account Plan (TAP 529) PO Box 42529	Philadelphia	PA	19101	**800-440-4000**	
Vocational Rehabilitation Office 909 Green St	Harrisburg	PA	17120	**800-442-6351**	717-787-5244
Rhode Island					
Higher Education Assistance Authority 560 Jefferson Blvd	Warwick	RI	02886	**800-922-9855**	401-736-1100
Tourism Div 1 W Exchange St	Providence	RI	02903	**800-556-2484**	401-222-2601
South Carolina					
Child Support Enforcement Office PO Box 1469	Columbia	SC	29202	**800-768-5858**	803-898-9210
Consumer Affairs Dept PO Box 5757	Columbia	SC	29250	**800-922-1594**	803-734-4200
Disabilities & Special Needs Dept 3440 Harden St Ext PO Box 4706	Columbia	SC	29240	**888-376-4636**	803-898-9600
Motor Vehicles Div PO Box 1498	Blythewood	SC	29016	**800-422-1368**	803-896-5000
Securities Div PO Box 11549	Columbia	SC	29211	**877-232-5378**	803-734-9916
State Ports Authority 176 Concord St	Charleston	SC	29401	**800-845-7106**	843-723-8651
South Dakota					
Child Support Div 700 Governors Dr	Pierre	SD	57501	**800-286-9145**	605-773-3641
Crime Victims' Compensation Program 700 Governors Dr	Pierre	SD	57501	**800-696-9476**	605-773-6317
Economic Development Office 711 E Wells Ave	Pierre	SD	57501	**800-872-6190**	605-773-3301
Parks & Recreation Div 523 E Capitol Ave *Campground Resv	Pierre	SD	57501	**800-710-2267***	605-773-3391
Rehabilitation Services Div 500 E Capitol Ave	Pierre	SD	57501	**800-265-9684**	605-773-3195
Tourism Office 711 E Wells Ave	Pierre	SD	57501	**800-732-5682**	605-773-3301
Vital Records 600 E Capitol Ave	Pierre	SD	57501	**800-738-2301**	605-773-4961
Tennessee					
Baccalaureate Education System Trust (BEST) PO Box 198786	Nashville	TN	37219	**888-486-2378**	615-532-8056
Child Support Services Div 400 Deaderick St 12th Fl	Nashville	TN	37248	**800-838-6911**	615-313-4880
Mental Health & Developmental Disabilities Dept 425 5th Ave N 3rd Fl	Nashville	TN	37243	**800-669-1851**	615-532-6500
Real Estate Commission 500 James Robertson Pkwy Suite 180	Nashville	TN	37243	**800-342-4031**	615-741-2273
State Parks Div 401 Church St 7th Fl	Nashville	TN	37243	**888-867-2757**	615-532-0001
Student Assistance Corp 404 James Robertson Pkwy Suite 1950	Nashville	TN	37243	**800-257-6526**	615-741-1346
Texas					
Assistive & Rehabilitation Services Dept 4800 N Lamar Blvd 3rd Fl	Austin	TX	78756	**800-252-5204**	512-377-0500
Bill Status State Capitol 1100 Congress Ave Rm 2N-3	Austin	TX	78711	**877-824-7038**	512-463-2182
Child Support Div MC 040 PO Box 12017	Austin	TX	78711	**800-252-8014**	512-460-6000
Comptroller of Public Accounts 111 E 17th St	Austin	TX	78774	**800-531-5441**	512-463-4600
Consumer Protection Div PO Box 12548	Austin	TX	78711	**800-621-0508**	512-463-2185
Crime Victims Compensation Div PO Box 12198	Austin	TX	78711	**800-983-9933**	512-936-1200
Ethics Commission 201 E 14th St 10th Fl	Austin	TX	78701	**800-325-8506**	512-463-5800
Lottery Commission PO Box 16630	Austin	TX	78761	**800-375-6886**	512-344-5000
Parks & Wildlife Dept 4200 Smith School Rd	Austin	TX	78744	**800-792-1112**	512-389-4800
Public Utility Commission PO Box 13326	Austin	TX	78711	**888-782-8477**	512-936-7000
Tourism Div PO Box 12728	Austin	TX	78711	**800-888-8839**	512-462-9191
Vital Statistics Bureau PO Box 12040	Austin	TX	78711	**888-963-7111**	
Workers Compensation Commission 7551 Metro Center Dr	Austin	TX	78744	**800-372-7713**	512-804-4000
Utah					
Higher Education Assistance Authority 60 S 400 West	Salt Lake City	UT	84101	**877-336-7378**	801-321-7294
Parks & Recreation Div PO Box 146001 *Campground Resv	Salt Lake City	UT	84114	**800-322-3770***	801-538-7220
Rehabilitation Office 250 E 500 South	Salt Lake City	UT	84111	**800-473-7530**	801-538-7530
Travel Development Div 300 N State St	Salt Lake City	UT	84114	**800-200-1160**	801-538-1900
Vermont					
Child Support Office 103 S Main St	Waterbury	VT	05671	**800-786-3214**	802-241-2319
Crime Victim Services Center 58 S Main St	Waterbury	VT	05676	**800-750-1213**	802-241-1255
Emergency Management Office 103 S Main St	Waterbury	VT	05671	**800-347-0488**	802-244-8721
Historic Preservation Div National Life Bldg Drawer 20	Montpelier	VT	05620	**800-341-2211**	802-828-3211
Housing & Community Affairs Dept National Life Bldg Drawer 20	Montpelier	VT	05620	**800-622-4553**	802-828-3211
Parks Div 103 S Main St Bldg 10S *Campground Resv	Waterbury	VT	05671	**888-409-7579***	802-241-3655
Tourism & Marketing Dept 134 State St	Montpelier	VT	05602	**800-837-6668**	802-828-3236
Vital Records Section PO Box 70	Burlington	VT	05402	**800-439-5008**	802-863-7275
Virginia					
Child Support Enforcement Div 730 E Broad St	Richmond	VA	23219	**800-468-8894**	804-692-1501
College Savings Plan PO Box 607	Richmond	VA	23218	**888-567-0540**	804-786-0719
Criminal Injuries Compensation Fund 11513 Allecingie Pkwy	Richmond	VA	23235	**800-522-4007**	804-378-3434
Housing Development Authority 601 S Belvidere St	Richmond	VA	23220	**800-968-7837**	804-782-1986
Rehabilitative Services Dept 8004 Franklin Farms Dr	Richmond	VA	23229	**800-552-5019**	804-662-7000
State Parks Div 203 Governor St Suite 213 *Resv	Richmond	VA	23219	**800-933-7275***	804-786-1712
Tourism Corp 901 E Byrd St	Richmond	VA	23219	**800-847-4882**	804-786-2051
Washington					
Bill Status PO Box 40600	Olympia	WA	98504	**800-562-6000**	360-786-7573
Child Support Div PO Box 45860	Olympia	WA	98504	**800-457-6202**	360-664-5440
Crime Victim Compensation Program PO Box 44520	Olympia	WA	98504	**800-547-8367**	360-902-5355
Health Dept PO Box 47890	Olympia	WA	98504	**800-525-0127**	360-236-4501
Historical Society 1911 Pacific Ave	Tacoma	WA	98402	**888-238-4378**	253-272-3500
Housing Finance Commission 1000 2nd Ave Suite 2700	Seattle	WA	98104	**800-767-4663**	206-464-7139
Mental Health Div PO Box 45320	Olympia	WA	98504	**888-713-6010**	360-902-8070
State Parks & Recreation Commission PO Box 42650 *Campground Resv	Olympia	WA	98504	**888-226-7688***	360-902-8500
Veterans Affairs Dept PO Box 41150	Olympia	WA	98504	**800-562-2308**	360-753-5586
Vocational Rehabilitation Div PO Box 45340	Olympia	WA	98504	**800-637-5627**	360-438-8000
West Virginia					
Bill Status State Capitol Rm MB27	Charleston	WV	25305	**800-642-8650**	304-347-4831
Child Support Enforcement Bureau 350 Capitol St Rm 147	Charleston	WV	25301	**800-249-3778**	304-558-3780
Consumer Protection Div 812 Quarrier St 6th Fl	Charleston	WV	25301	**800-368-8808**	304-558-8986
Crime Victims Compensation Fund 1900 Kanawha Blvd E Rm W-334	Charleston	WV	25305	**800-624-8650**	304-347-4850
Housing Development Fund 814 Virginia St E	Charleston	WV	25301	**800-933-9843**	304-345-6475

	City	State	Zip	Toll-Free	Phone
Parks & Recreation 1900 E Kanawha Blvd E Bldg 3 Rm 714	Charleston	WV	25305	**800-225-5982**	304-558-2764
Tourism Div 2101 Washington St E	Charleston	WV	25305	**800-225-5982**	304-558-2200
Veterans Affairs Div 1321 Plaza East Suite 101	Charleston	WV	25301	**888-838-2332**	304-558-3662
Wisconsin					
Bill Status 1 E Main St	Madison	WI	53708	**800-362-9472**	608-266-9960
Education Investment Program (EdVest) PO Box 7871	Madison	WI	53707	**888-338-3789**	608-264-7899
Housing & Economic Development Authority PO Box 1728	Madison	WI	53701	**800-334-6873**	608-266-7884
Insurance Commission PO Box 7873	Madison	WI	53707	**800-236-8517**	608-266-3585
Tourism Dept 201 W Washington Ave 2nd Fl	Madison	WI	53707	**800-432-8747**	608-266-2161
Veterans Affairs Dept PO Box 7843	Madison	WI	53707	**800-947-8387**	608-266-1311
Vocational Rehabilitation Div PO Box 7852	Madison	WI	53707	**800-442-3477**	608-243-5600
Wyoming					
Bill Status State Capitol Bldg Rm 213	Cheyenne	WY	82002	**800-342-9570**	307-777-7881
Professional Teaching Standards Board 1920 Thomes Ave Suite 400	Cheyenne	WY	82001	**800-675-6893**	307-777-7291
State Parks & Historical Sites Div 122 W 25th St 1st Fl E *Campground Resv	Cheyenne	WY	82002	**877-996-7275***	307-777-5598
Tourism Div 214 W 15th St	Cheyenne	WY	82002	**800-225-5996**	307-777-2828
Veterans' Affairs Commission 5905 CY Ave	Casper	WY	82604	**800-832-5987**	307-266-7372

336 GOVERNMENT - US - EXECUTIVE BRANCH

	City	State	Zip	Toll-Free	Phone
Office of the US Trade Representative 600 17th St NW	Washington	DC	20508	**888-473-8787**	202-395-3230
USA Freedom Corps 1600 Pennsylvania Ave NW West Wing	Washington	DC	20500	**877-872-2677**	

336-1 US Department of Agriculture

	City	State	Zip	Toll-Free	Phone
Food & Nutrition Service Food Stamps Program 3101 Park Center Dr	Alexandria	VA	22302	**800-221-5689**	703-305-2022
Grain Inspection Packers & Stockyards Administration 1400 Independence Ave SW 10th Fl	Washington	DC	20250	**800-998-3447**	202-720-0219
National Agricultural Statistics Service (NASS) 1400 Independence Ave SW Rm 4117	Washington	DC	20250	**800-727-9540**	202-720-2707
Secretary of Agriculture Fraud Waste & Abuse Hotline	Washington	DC	20250	**800-424-9121**	
USDA Graduate School 600 Maryland Ave SW	Washington	DC	20024	**888-744-4723**	202-314-3400
USDA Meat & Poultry Hotline	Washington	DC	20250	**800-535-4555**	202-720-3333

336-2 US Department of Commerce

	City	State	Zip	Toll-Free	Phone
International Trade Administration 1401 Constitution Ave NW Hoover Bldg	Washington	DC	20230	**800-872-2723**	202-482-3809
National Technical Information Service (NTIS) 5285 Port Royal Rd *Orders	Springfield	VA	22161	**800-553-6847***	703-605-6000
FedWorld.gov US Dept of Commerce 5285 Port Royal Rd	Springfield	VA	22161	**800-553-6847**	703-605-6000
FLITE US Supreme Court Database US Dept of Commerce 5285 Port Royal Rd	Springfield	VA	22161	**800-553-6847**	703-605-6000
North American Industry Classification System (NAICS) US Census Bureau 4700 Silver Hill Rd	Washington	DC	20333	**888-756-2427**	301-763-4636
Secretary of Commerce Fraud Hotline	Washington	DC	20230	**800-424-5197**	
US Census Bureau Regional Offices					
Charlotte 901 Center Park Dr Suite 106	Charlotte	NC	28217	**800-331-7360**	704-344-6100
Dallas 8585 N Stemmons Fwy Suite 800-S	Dallas	TX	75247	**800-835-9952**	214-253-4400
Detroit 1395 Brewery Park Blvd	Detroit	MI	48207	**800-432-1495**	313-259-0056
Kansas City 1211 N 8th St	Kansas City	KS	66101	**800-728-4748**	913-551-6728
US Patent & Trademark Office	Washington	DC	20231	**800-786-9199**	703-308-4357

336-3 US Department of Defense

	City	State	Zip	Toll-Free	Phone
Defense Energy Support Center 8725 John J Kingman Rd Suite 4950	Fort Belvoir	VA	22060	**800-286-7633**	703-767-9700
Defense Information Systems Agency Network Information Center 7990 Science Applications Ct MS CV-50	Vienna	VA	22183	**800-365-3642**	703-676-1051
Defense Threat Reduction Agency 8725 John T Kingman Rd MS 6201	Fort Belvoir	VA	22060	**800-701-5096**	703-767-5870
Department of Defense (DOD) Inspector General 400 Army-Navy Dr Suite 1000	Arlington	VA	22202	**800-424-9098**	703-604-8300
Department of the Air Force Agency for National Security & Emergency Preparedness	Fort McPherson	GA	30330	**800-366-0051**	
Department of the Army					
Judge Advocate General 1777 N Kent St	Rosslyn	VA	22209	**800-208-7178**	703-697-5151
US Army Reserve Personnel Center 1 Reserve Way	Saint Louis	MO	63132	**800-318-5298**	314-592-0200
US Army War College 122 Fores Ave	Carlisle	PA	17013	**800-453-0992**	717-245-4101
Department of the Navy Military Sealift Command 914 Charles Morris Ct SE Washington Navy Yard	Washington	DC	20398	**888-732-5438**	202-685-5055
National Imagery & Mapping Agency 4600 Sangamore Rd	Bethesda	MD	20816	**800-455-0899**	301-227-3785
Network Information Center 7990 Science Applications Ct MS CV-50	Vienna	VA	22183	**800-365-3642**	703-676-1051
Secretary of Defense Defense Hotline for Fraud Waste & Abuse	Washington	DC	20301	**800-424-9098**	
Uniformed Services University of the Health Sciences (USUHS) 4301 Jones Bridge Rd *Admissions	Bethesda	MD	20814	**800-772-1743***	301-295-3103

336-4 US Department of Education

	City	State	Zip	Toll-Free	Phone
Department of Education 400 Maryland Ave SW	Washington	DC	20202	**800-872-5327**	202-401-2000
Inspector General's Fraud & Abuse Hotline	Washington	DC	20202	**800-647-8733**	
Office of Federal Student Aid 830 1st St NE Union Center Plaza	Washington	DC	20202	**800-433-3243**	
Federal Student Aid Information Center PO Box 84	Washington	DC	20044	**800-433-3243**	
National Library of Education 400 Maryland Ave SW	Washington	DC	20202	**800-424-1616**	202-205-5015

336-5 US Department of Energy

	City	State	Zip	Toll-Free	Phone
Department of Energy (DOE)					
Clean Cities Program 1000 Independence Ave SW EE-2K	Washington	DC	20585	**800-224-8437**	202-586-1573
Office of Civilian Radioactive Waste Management 1000 Independence Ave SW	Washington	DC	20585	**800-225-6972**	202-586-6842
Office of Energy Efficiency & Renewable Energy 1000 Independence Ave SW	Washington	DC	20585	**877-337-3463**	202-568-9220
Power Marketing Administrations Bonneville Power Administration 905 NE 11th Ave	Portland	OR	97232	**800-282-3713**	503-230-3000

336-6 US Department of Health & Human Services

	City	State	Zip	Toll-Free	Phone
Agency for Healthcare Research & Quality 540 Gaither Rd	Rockville	MD	20850	**800-358-9295**	301-427-1200
Agency for Toxic Substances & Disease Registry Centers for Disease Control & Prevention 1600 Clifton Rd NE Bldg 37 MS E-29	Atlanta	GA	30333	**888-422-8737**	404-498-0110
AIDSinfo PO Box 6303	Rockville	MD	20849	**800-448-0440**	301-519-0459
Alzheimer's Disease Education & Referral Center PO Box 8250	Silver Spring	MD	20907	**800-438-4380**	301-495-3311
Bureau of Health Professions Practitioner Data Banks Div 5600 Fishers Ln Parklawn Bldg *Cust Svc	Rockville	MD	20857	**800-767-6732***	301-443-2300
Cancer Information Service (CIS) National Cancer Institute 9000 Rockville Pike Bldg 31	Bethesda	MD	20892	**800-422-6237**	301-496-4000
Centers for Disease Control & Prevention (CDC)					
National Center for Environmental Health 4770 Buford Hwy Bldg 101	Chamblee	GA	30341	**888-232-6789**	770-488-7000
National Immunization Program 1600 Clifton Rd NE MS E05	Atlanta	GA	30333	**800-232-2522**	404-639-8200
National Institute for Occupational Safety & Health 200 Independence Ave SW	Washington	DC	20201	**800-356-4674**	202-401-6997
Centers for Medicare & Medicaid Services (CMS) Medicare Hotline	Baltimore	MD	21207	**800-633-4227**	
Department of Health & Human Services (HHS) Office on Women's Health 200 Independence Ave SW Rm 730B	Washington	DC	20201	**800-994-9662**	202-690-7650
Food & Drug Administration (FDA)					
Center for Devices & Radiological Health 9200 Corporate Blvd Suite 100E	Rockville	MD	20850	**800-638-2041**	
Center for Food Safety & Applied Nutrition 5100 Paint Branch Pkwy	College Park	MD	20740	**888-723-3366**	301-436-1600
FoodSafety.gov 5600 Fishers Ln	Rockville	MD	20857	**888-723-3366**	
MedWatch 5600 Fishers Ln HFD-410	Rockville	MD	20857	**888-463-6332**	301-827-7240
National Center for Toxicological Research 3900 NCTR Rd	Jefferson	AR	72079	**800-638-3321**	870-543-7000
Office of Orphan Products Development 5600 Fishers Ln	Rockville	MD	20857	**800-300-7469**	301-827-3666
Health Resources & Services Administration (HRSA) 5600 Fishers Ln	Rockville	MD	20857	**888-275-4772**	301-443-2216
HRSA (Health Resources & Services Administration) 5600 Fishers Ln	Rockville	MD	20857	**888-275-4772**	301-443-2216
National Adoption Information Clearinghouse (NAIC) 330 C St SW	Washington	DC	20447	**888-251-0075**	703-352-3488
National AIDS Hotline	Washington	DC	20201	**800-342-2437**	
National Cancer Institute (NCI) 6116 Executive Blvd MSC 8322	Bethesda	MD	20892	**800-422-6237**	301-435-3848
National Center for Complementary & Alternative Medicine (NCCAM) National Institutes of Health 31 Center Dr Bldg 31	Bethesda	MD	20892	**888-644-6226**	301-435-5042
National Center for Infectious Diseases Travelers' Health Centers for Disease Control & Prevention 1600 Clifton Rd NE	Atlanta	GA	30333	**877-394-8747**	
National Child Care Information Center (NCCIC) 243 Church St NW 2nd Fl	Vienna	VA	22180	**800-616-2242**	
National Clearinghouse for Alcohol & Drug Information PO Box 2345	Rockville	MD	20847	**800-729-6686**	301-468-2600
National Clearinghouse on Child Abuse & Neglect Information 330 C St SW	Washington	DC	20447	**800-394-3366**	703-385-7565
National Hansen's Disease Programs (NHDP) 1770 Physicians Park Dr	Baton Rouge	LA	70816	**800-642-2477**	225-756-3773
National Health Information Center (NHIC) PO Box 1133	Washington	DC	20013	**800-336-4797**	301-565-4167
National Institute of Neurological Disorders & Stroke (NINDS) 31 Center Dr Bldg 31 Rm 8A52	Bethesda	MD	20892	**800-352-9424**	301-496-9746
National Institutes of Health (NIH) Osteoporosis & Related Bone Diseases - National Resource Center 1232 22nd St NW	Washington	DC	20037	**800-624-2663**	202-223-0344

				Toll-Free	Phone
National Library of Medicine					
8600 Rockville Pike	Bethesda	MD	20894	**888-346-3656**	301-594-5983
National Mental Health Information Center					
PO Box 42557	Washington	DC	20015	**800-789-2647**	301-443-1805
National Prevention Information Network (NPIN)					
PO Box 6003	Rockville	MD	20849	**800-458-5231**	301-562-1098
National Women's Health Information Center					
8550 Arlington Blvd Suite 300	Fairfax	VA	22031	**800-994-9662**	

336-7 US Department of Homeland Security

				Toll-Free	Phone
Department of Homeland Security (DHS)					
National Disaster Medical System 500 C Street SW Suite 713	Washington	DC	20472	**800-872-6967**	
Ready.gov Naval Security Stn	Washington	DC	20528	**800-237-3239**	
Federal Emergency Management Agency (FEMA) 500 C St SW	Washington	DC	20472	**800-462-9029**	202-646-4600
National Flood Insurance Program 500 C St SW	Washington	DC	20472	**800-427-4661**	202-646-2500
FEMA (Federal Emergency Management Agency) 500 C St SW	Washington	DC	20472	**800-462-9029**	202-646-4600
Immigration & Naturalization Service (now US Citizenship & Immigration Services) 20 Massachusetts Ave NW	Washington	DC	20536	**800-870-3676**	202-514-4600
National Disaster Medical System 500 C Street SW Suite 713	Washington	DC	20472	**800-872-6967**	
National Vessel Movement Center 408 Coast Guard Dr	Kearneysville	WV	25430	**800-708-9823**	304-264-2502
US Citizenship & Immigration Services (USCIS) 20 Massachusetts Ave NW	Washington	DC	20536	**800-870-3676**	202-514-4600
US Coast Guard (USCG) National Vessel Movement Center 408 Coast Guard Dr	Kearneysville	WV	25430	**800-708-9823**	304-264-2502
US Coast Guard Academy 15 Mohegan Ave	New London	CT	06320	**800-883-8724**	860-444-8444
US Coast Guard Regional Offices Atlantic Area District 1 408 Atlantic Ave	Boston	MA	02110	**800-848-3942**	617-223-8515
US Computer Emergency Readiness Team Naval Security Stn	Washington	DC	20535	**888-282-0870**	202-401-4600
US Immigration & Customs Enforcement (ICE) 425 'I' St NW	Washington	DC	20536	**866-347-2423**	202-514-1900

336-8 US Department of Housing & Urban Development

				Toll-Free	Phone
Department of Housing & Urban Development (HUD)					
Housing Discrimination Hotline	Washington	DC	20410	**800-669-9777**	
Office of Fair Housing & Equal Opportunity 451 7th St SW MC E	Washington	DC	20410	**800-669-9777**	202-708-4252
Office of the Inspector General 451 7th St SW	Washington	DC	20410	**800-347-3735**	202-708-0430
Office of Multifamily Housing Programs 451 7th St SW	Washington	DC	20410	**800-685-8470**	202-708-2495
Department of Housing & Urban Development Regional Offices					
Pacific/Hawaii Region 450 Golden Gate Ave 8th Fl	San Francisco	CA	94102	**800-436-6446**	415-436-6550
Rocky Mountain Region 633 17th St 14th Fl	Denver	CO	80202	**800-543-9378**	303-672-5440
Federal Housing Administration (FHA) 451 7th St SW Suite 9100	Washington	DC	20410	**800-767-7460**	202-708-3600

336-9 US Department of the Interior

				Toll-Free	Phone
Bureau of Indian Affairs Regional Offices Alaska Region PO Box 25520	Juneau	AK	99802	**800-645-8397**	907-586-7177
National Wild Horse & Burro Program PO Box 3270	Sparks	NV	89432	**866-468-7826**	775-475-2222
Secretary of the Interior Fraud Hotline	Washington	DC	20240	**800-424-5081**	
US Fish & Wildlife Service (USFWS) 1849 C St NW	Washington	DC	20240	**800-344-9453**	202-208-4717
US Geological Survey (USGS) 12201 Sunrise Valley Dr	Reston	VA	20192	**888-275-8747**	703-648-4000
Ask USGS 12201 Sunrise Valley Dr	Reston	VA	20192	**888-275-8747**	
National Atlas of America 508 National Ctr 12201 Sunrise Valley Dr	Reston	VA	20192	**888-275-8747**	

336-10 US Department of Justice

				Toll-Free	Phone
Americans with Disabilities Act Information 950 Pennsylvania Ave NW	Washington	DC	20530	**800-514-0301**	
Community Oriented Policing Services Office (COPS) 1100 Vermont Ave NW 10th Fl	Washington	DC	20530	**800-421-6770**	202-616-2888
Department of Justice (DOJ)					
Office of Justice Programs 810 7th St NW Suite 6400	Washington	DC	20531	**800-421-6770**	202-307-5933
Office of Special Counsel for Immigration-Related Unfair Employment Practices 950 Pennsylvania Ave NW *Hotline	Washington	DC	20038	**800-255-7688***	202-616-5594
Department of Justice Antitrust Div 950 Pennsylvania Ave NW	Washington	DC	20530	**888-647-3258**	202-514-2421
Federal Bureau of Prisons National Institute of Corrections 1860 Industrial Cir Suite A	Longmont	CO	80501	**800-877-1461**	303-682-0213
National Criminal Justice Reference Service PO Box 6000	Rockville	MD	20849	**800-851-3420**	301-519-5500
US Marshals Service 1735 Jefferson Davis Hwy	Arlington	VA	22202	**800-336-0102**	202-307-9100

336-11 US Department of Labor

				Toll-Free	Phone
Department of Labor (DOL) 200 Constitution Ave NW	Washington	DC	20210	**866-487-2365**	202-693-4650
GovBenefits.gov	Washington	DC	20407	**800-333-4636**	
Department of Labor Women's Bureau 200 Constitution Ave NW Rm S3002	Washington	DC	20210	**800-827-5335**	202-693-6710
Department of Labor Women's Bureau Regional Offices					
Region 1 JFK Federal Bldg Rm E-270	Boston	MA	02203	**800-518-3585**	617-565-1988
Region 2 201 Varick St Rm 708	New York	NY	10014	**800-827-5335**	212-337-2389
Region 3 170 S Independence Mall W Suite 880W	Philadelphia	PA	19106	**800-379-9042**	215-861-4860
Region 4 Federal Center 61 Forsyth St SW Suite 7T95	Atlanta	GA	30303	**800-672-8356**	404-562-2336
Region 5 Federal Bldg 230 S Dearborn St Rm 1022	Chicago	IL	60604	**800-648-8183**	312-353-6985
Region 6 Federal Bldg 525 Griffin St Rm 735	Dallas	TX	75202	**888-887-6794**	214-767-6985
Region 7 1100 Main St Suite 845	Kansas City	MO	64105	**800-252-4706**	816-426-6108
Region 8 1990 Broadway Suite 1620	Denver	CO	80201	**800-299-0886**	303-844-1285
Region 9 71 Stevenson St Suite 927	San Francisco	CA	94105	**877-923-6509**	415-975-4750
Region 10 1111 3rd Ave Rm 925	Seattle	WA	98101	**888-296-7011**	206-553-1534
Mine Safety & Health Administration (MSHA) 1100 Wilson Blvd	Arlington	VA	22209	**800-746-1554**	202-693-9419
Occupational Safety & Health Administration (OSHA) 200 Constitution Ave NW	Washington	DC	20210	**800-321-6742**	202-693-1999
OSHA (Occupational Safety & Health Administration) 200 Constitution Ave NW	Washington	DC	20210	**800-321-6742**	202-693-1999

336-12 US Department of State

				Toll-Free	Phone
Bureau of Consular Affairs					
Office of Children's Issues 2201 C St NW MS SA-29	Washington	DC	20520	**888-407-4747**	202-736-9130
Overseas Citizens Services 2201 C St NW Rm 4811	Washington	DC	20520	**888-407-4747**	202-647-5225
National Passport Information Center	Washington	DC	20520	**877-487-2778**	

336-13 US Department of Transportation

				Toll-Free	Phone
Bureau of Transportation Statistics 400 7th St SW	Washington	DC	20590	**800-853-1351**	202-366-1270
Department of Transportation (DOT) Small & Disadvantaged Business Utilization Office 400 7th St SW Rm 9414	Washington	DC	20590	**800-532-1169**	202-366-1930
Federal Aviation Administration (FAA) 800 Independence Ave SW	Washington	DC	20591	**800-322-7873**	202-267-3484
Safety Hotline	Washington	DC	20591	**800-255-1111**	
Federal Highway Administration (FHWA) National Highway Institute 4600 N Fairfax Dr	Arlington	VA	22203	**877-558-6873**	703-235-0500
Federal Motor Carrier Safety Administration (FMCSA) 400 7th St SW	Washington	DC	20590	**888-832-5660**	202-366-2519
Federal Railroad Administration Regional Offices					
Region 3 61 Forsyth St SW Suite 16T20	Atlanta	GA	30303	**800-724-5993**	404-562-3800
Region 6 901 Locust St Suite 464	Kansas City	MO	64106	**800-724-5996**	816-329-3840
Maritime Administration 400 7th St SW *Hotline	Washington	DC	20590	**800-996-2723***	202-366-5812
National Highway Traffic Safety Administration (NHTSA)					
Auto Safety Hotline	Washington	DC	20590	**888-327-4236**	
National Center for Statistics & Analysis 400 7th St SW Rm 6125	Washington	DC	20590	**800-934-8517**	202-366-1503
Research & Special Programs Administration Hazardous Materials Safety Office 400 7th St SW Rm 8321	Washington	DC	20590	**800-467-4922**	202-366-0656
US Merchant Marine Academy 300 Steamboat Rd	Kings Point	NY	11024	**866-546-4778**	516-773-5000

336-14 US Department of the Treasury

				Toll-Free	Phone
Alcohol & Tobacco Tax & Trade Bureau (TTB) 650 Massachusetts Ave NW	Washington	DC	20226	**877-882-3277**	202-927-8100
National Revenue Center 550 Main St	Cincinnati	OH	45202	**800-937-8864**	513-684-3334
Bureau of the Public Debt US Savings Bonds Call Center PO Box 1328	Parkersburg	WV	26101	**800-487-2663**	304-480-6112
Comptroller of the Currency 250 'E' St SW 9th Fl	Washington	DC	20219	**800-613-6743**	202-874-4900
Department of the Treasury Office of Foreign Assets Control Pennsylvania Ave & Madison Pl NW	Washington	DC	20220	**800-306-2822**	202-622-2500
Financial Crimes Enforcement Network (FinCEN) 2070 Chain Bridge Rd PO Box 39	Vienna	VA	22183	**800-767-2825**	703-905-3520
Internal Revenue Service (IRS) 1111 Constitution Ave NW	Washington	DC	20224	**800-829-1040**	202-622-9511
National Taxpayer Advocate 1111 Constitution Ave NW	Washington	DC	20224	**877-777-4778**	202-622-6100
Tax Forms & Publications Div 1111 Constitution Ave NW	Washington	DC	20224	**800-829-3676**	202-622-5200
National Revenue Center 550 Main St	Cincinnati	OH	45202	**800-937-8864**	513-684-3334
US Mint 801 9th St NW *Cust Svc	Washington	DC	20220	**800-872-6468***	202-354-7200

336-15 US Department of Veterans Affairs

				Toll-Free	Phone
Department of Veterans Affairs (VA) 810 Vermont Ave NW	Washington	DC	20420	**800-827-1000**	202-273-6000
Small & Disadvantaged Business Utilization Office 801 'I' St NW	Washington	DC	20005	**800-949-8387**	202-565-8124
Gulf War Illness Information Helpline	Washington	DC	20420	**800-749-8387**	
Secretary of Veterans Affairs Fraud Hotline	Washington	DC	20420	**800-488-8244**	
Veterans Benefits Administration Education Service 1800 G St NW	Washington	DC	20006	**800-442-4551**	202-273-7132

336-16 US Independent Agencies & Commissions

				Toll-Free	Phone
Access Board 1331 F St NW Suite 1000	Washington	DC	20004	800-872-2253	202-272-0080
AmeriCorps USA 1201 New York Ave NW 8th Fl	Washington	DC	20525	800-942-2677	202-606-5000
Architectural & Transportation Barriers Compliance Board 1331 F St NW Suite 1000	Washington	DC	20004	800-872-2253	202-272-0080
Commodity Futures Trading Commission (CFTC) 1155 21 St NW 3 Lafayette Ctr	Washington	DC	20581	866-366-2382	202-418-5080
Consumer Product Safety Commission	Washington	DC	20207	800-638-2772	301-504-7908
Corporation for National & Community Service					
AmeriCorps USA 1201 New York Ave NW 8th Fl	Washington	DC	20525	800-942-2677	202-606-5000
Senior Corps 1201 New York Ave NW	Washington	DC	20525	800-424-8867	202-606-5000
Defense Nuclear Facilities Safety Board 625 Indiana Ave NW Suite 700	Washington	DC	20004	800-788-4016	202-694-7000
EEOC (Equal Employment Opportunity Commission) 1801 L St NW	Washington	DC	20507	800-669-4000	202-663-4900
Environmental Protection Agency (EPA) 1200 Pennsylvania Ave NW	Washington	DC	20460	888-372-8255	202-564-4700
National Lead Information Center 422 S Clinton Ave	Rochester	NY	14620	800-424-5323	
Office of Ground Water & Drinking Water 1200 Pennsylvania Ave NW	Washington	DC	20460	800-426-4791	202-564-3750
US National Response Team 1200 Pennsylvania Ave NW MC 5104A	Washington	DC	20460	800-424-8802	202-267-2675
Environmental Protection Agency Regional Offices					
Region 1 1 Congress St Suite 1100	Boston	MA	02114	888-372-7341	617-918-1111
Region 3 1650 Arch St	Philadelphia	PA	19103	800-438-2474	215-814-5000
Region 4 Federal Ctr 61 Forsyth St SW	Atlanta	GA	30303	800-241-1754	404-562-9900
Region 5 77 W Jackson Blvd	Chicago	IL	60604	800-621-8431	312-353-2000
Region 6 1445 Ross Ave Suite 1200	Dallas	TX	75202	800-887-6063	214-665-2100
Region 7 901 N 5th St	Kansas City	KS	66101	800-233-0425	913-551-7003
Region 8 999 18th St Suite 300	Denver	CO	80202	800-227-8917	303-312-6308
Region 9 75 Hawthorne St	San Francisco	CA	94105	866-372-9378	415-947-8000
Region 10 1200 6th Ave MS RA-140	Seattle	WA	98101	800-424-4372	206-553-1200
EPA (Environmental Protection Agency) 1200 Pennsylvania Ave NW	Washington	DC	20460	888-372-8255	202-564-4700
Equal Employment Opportunity Commission (EEOC) 1801 L St NW	Washington	DC	20507	800-669-4000	202-663-4900
Export-Import Bank of the US 811 Vermont Ave NW	Washington	DC	20571	800-565-3946	202-565-3946
Federal Communications Commission (FCC) 445 12th St SW	Washington	DC	20554	888-225-5322	202-418-0200
Consumer & Government Affairs Bureau 445 12th St SW	Washington	DC	20554	888-225-5322	202-418-1400
Federal Deposit Insurance Corp (FDIC) 550 17th St NW	Washington	DC	20429	877-375-3342	202-898-6947
Federal Deposit Insurance Corp Regional Offices					
Atlanta Regional Office 10 10th St NE Suite 800	Atlanta	GA	30309	800-765-3342	
Chicago Regional Office 500 W Monroe St Suite 330	Chicago	IL	60661	800-944-5343	312-382-7500
Dallas Regional Office 1910 Pacific Ave 2nd Fl	Dallas	TX	75201	800-568-9161	972-761-2092
Kansas City Regional Office 2345 Grand Blvd	Kansas City	MO	64108	800-334-9593	816-234-8000
New York Regional Office 20 Exchange Pl Rm 6014	New York	NY	10005	800-334-9593	917-320-2500
San Francisco Regional Office 25 Ecker St Suite 2300	San Francisco	CA	94105	800-756-3558	415-546-0160
Federal Election Commission 999 'E' St NW	Washington	DC	20463	800-424-9530	202-694-1100
Federal Home Loan Bank					
Atlanta 1475 Peachtree St NE	Atlanta	GA	30309	800-536-9650	404-888-8000
Cincinnati 221 E 4th St Suite 1000 PO Box 598	Cincinnati	OH	45201	888-852-6500	513-852-7500
Des Moines 907 Walnut St	Des Moines	IA	50309	800-544-0200	515-281-1000
Pittsburgh 601 Grant St	Pittsburgh	PA	15219	800-288-3400	412-288-3400
San Francisco 600 California St Suite 300 PO Box 7948	San Francisco	CA	94120	800-283-0700	415-616-1000
Seattle 1501 4th Ave 19th Fl	Seattle	WA	98101	800-283-0700	206-340-2300
Federal Trade Commission (FTC) 600 Pennsylvania Ave NW	Washington	DC	20580	877-382-4357	202-326-2222
Consumer.gov 600 Pennsylvania Ave NW	Washington	DC	20580	877-382-4357	202-326-2222
National Do Not Call Registry	Washington	DC	20580	888-382-1222	
FTC (Federal Trade Commission) 600 Pennsylvania Ave NW	Washington	DC	20580	877-382-4357	202-326-2222
General Services Administration (GSA) 1800 F St NW *Fraud Hotline	Washington	DC	20405	800-424-5210*	202-501-1231
FCIC National Contact Center	Pueblo	CO	81009	800-333-4636	
Federal Citizen Information Center 201 W 8th St	Pueblo	CO	81003	888-878-3256	719-948-3334
FirstGov 1800 F St NW	Washington	DC	20405	800-333-4636	
Merit Systems Protection Board (MSPB) 1615 M St NW	Washington	DC	20419	800-209-8960	202-653-7200
National Aeronautics & Space Administration (NASA) 300 'E' St SW	Washington	DC	20546	800-424-9183	202-358-0000
National Archives & Records Administration (NARA) 8601 Adelphi Rd	College Park	MD	20740	866-272-6272	301-837-0482
Archival Research Catalog 8601 Adelphi Rd	College Park	MD	20740	866-272-6272	
National Credit Union Administration 1775 Duke St *Fraud Hotline	Alexandria	VA	22314	800-827-9650*	703-518-6300
National Endowment for the Humanities (NEH) 1100 Pennsylvania Ave NW	Washington	DC	20506	800-634-1121	202-606-8400
National Labor Relations Board (NLRB) 1099 14th St NW	Washington	DC	20570	800-736-2983	202-273-1991
National Lead Information Center 422 S Clinton Ave	Rochester	NY	14620	800-424-5323	
National Railroad Passenger Corp DBA Amtrak 60 Massachusetts Ave NE	Washington	DC	20002	800-872-7245	202-906-3000
Neighborhood Reinvestment Corp Regional Offices North Central District 1111 W 39th St Suite 100W	Kansas City	MO	64111	800-823-1428	816-931-4176
NLRB (National Labor Relations Board) 1099 14th St NW	Washington	DC	20570	800-736-2983	202-273-1991
NRC (Nuclear Regulatory Commission)	Washington	DC	20555	800-368-5642	301-415-8200
Nuclear Regulatory Commission (NRC)	Washington	DC	20555	800-368-5642	301-415-8200
Nuclear Regulatory Commission Regional Offices					
Region 1 475 Allendale Rd	King of Prussia	PA	19406	800-432-1156	610-337-5000
Region 2 61 Forsyth St SW Suite 23T85	Atlanta	GA	30303	800-577-8510	404-562-4400
Region 3 2443 Warrenville Rd	Lisle	IL	60532	800-522-3025	630-829-9500
Region 4 611 Ryan Plaza Dr Suite 4005	Arlington	TX	76011	800-952-9677	817-860-8100
Office of Special Counsel 1730 M St NW Suite 300	Washington	DC	20036	800-872-9855	202-653-1800
Peace Corps 1111 20th St NW	Washington	DC	20526	800-424-8580	202-692-2100
Pension Benefit Guaranty Corp 1200 K St NW *Cust Svc	Washington	DC	20005	800-400-7242*	202-326-4000
Railroad Retirement Board 844 N Rush St	Chicago	IL	60611	800-808-0772	312-751-4500
SBA (Small Business Administration) 409 3rd St SW	Washington	DC	20416	800-827-5722	202-205-6600
Securities & Exchange Commission (SEC) 450 5th St NW	Washington	DC	20549	800-732-0330	202-942-0020
Office of Investor Education & Assistance 450 5th St NW	Washington	DC	20549	800-732-0330	202-942-7040
Senior Corps 1201 New York Ave NW	Washington	DC	20525	800-424-8867	202-606-5000
Small Business Administration (SBA) 409 3rd St SW	Washington	DC	20416	800-827-5722	202-205-6600
Smithsonian Institution 1000 Jefferson Dr SW	Washington	DC	20560	800-766-2149	202-357-2700
Social Security Administration (SSA) 6401 Security Blvd	Baltimore	MD	21235	800-772-1213	410-965-3120
US Chemical Safety & Hazard Investigation Board 2175 K St NW Suite 400	Washington	DC	20037	800-424-8802	202-261-7600
US Commission on Civil Rights 624 9th St NW	Washington	DC	20425	800-552-6843	202-376-7700
US National Response Team 1200 Pennsylvania Ave NW MC 5104A	Washington	DC	20460	800-424-8802	202-267-2675
US Postal Service (USPS) 475 L'Enfant Plaza West SW *Cust Svc	Washington	DC	20260	800-275-8777*	202-268-2284

337 GOVERNMENT - US - LEGISLATIVE BRANCH

SEE ALSO Legislation Hotlines

				Toll-Free	Phone
US Government Printing Office (GPO) 732 N Capitol St NW	Washington	DC	20401	866-512-1800	202-512-0000
Federal Register Online 732 N Capitol St NW	Washington	DC	20401	888-293-6498	202-512-1530

338 GRAPHIC DESIGN

SEE ALSO Typesetting & Related Services

				Toll-Free	Phone
3 Strikes Inc 1905 Elizabeth Ave	Rahway	NJ	07065	888-725-8483	732-382-3820
Ambrosi & Assoc 200 W Jackson Blvd 6th Fl	Chicago	IL	60606	888-262-7674	312-666-9200
Benchmark Imaging & Display 640 Busse Hwy	Park Ridge	IL	60068	800-626-3069	847-292-5150
BrandEquity International 2330 Washington St	Newton	MA	02462	800-969-3150	617-969-3150
Deskey Assoc Inc 120 E 8th St	Cincinnati	OH	45202	877-433-7539	513-721-6800
Dynamic Graphics Group 6000 N Forest Park Dr	Peoria	IL	61614	800-255-8800	309-688-8800
Flavia Publishing Inc 924 Anacapa St Suite B4	Santa Barbara	CA	93101	800-352-8424	805-564-6907
Kane Graphical Corp 2255 W Logan Blvd	Chicago	IL	60647	800-992-2921	773-384-1200
Metro Creative Graphics Inc 519 8th Ave	New York	NY	10018	800-223-1600	212-947-5100
Payne Printery Inc 1101 Dallas Memorial Hwy	Dallas	PA	18612	800-724-3188	570-675-1147
Prism Studios Inc 2505 Kennedy St NE	Minneapolis	MN	55413	800-659-2001	612-331-1000
Seven Worldwide Inc 225 W Superior Ave	Chicago	IL	60610	877-777-7934	312-943-0400
Signature Graphics Inc 1000 Signature Dr	Porter	IN	46304	800-356-3235	219-926-4994
Spire Inc 65 Bay St	Dorchester	MA	02125	800-653-3323	617-426-3323
Vista Color Lab Inc 2048 Fulton Rd	Cleveland	OH	44113	800-890-0062	216-651-2830

339 GROCERY STORES

SEE ALSO Bakeries; Convenience Stores; Dairy Product Stores; Gourmet Specialty Shops; Health Food Stores; Wholesale Clubs

				Toll-Free	Phone
Acme Markets Inc 75 Valley Stream Pkwy	Malvern	PA	19355	800-767-2312	610-889-4000
Alaska Commercial Co 550 W 64th Ave Suite 200	Anchorage	AK	99518	800-478-4484	907-273-4600
Albertson's Inc 250 E Parkcenter Blvd *NYSE: ABS*	Boise	ID	83706	888-746-7252	208-395-6200
ALDI Inc 1200 N Kirk Rd	Batavia	IL	60510	800-388-2534	630-879-8100
Autry Greer & Sons Inc 2850 W Main St	Prichard	AL	36612	800-477-9490	251-457-8655
Bashas' Inc PO Box 488	Chandler	AZ	85244	800-755-7292	480-895-9350
Bick's Supermarkets 1540 Vision Dr	Platteville	WI	53818	800-793-8089	608-348-2343
Big Y Foods Inc 2145 Roosevelt Ave *Cust Svc	Springfield	MA	01102	800-828-2688*	413-784-0600
Brookshire Brothers Ltd 1201 Ellen Trout Dr	Lufkin	TX	75901	800-364-6690	936-634-8155
Brown & Cole PO Box 9797	Bellingham	WA	98227	800-743-0437	360-714-9797
Catalano's Stop & Shop 5612 Wilson Mills Rd	Highland Heights	OH	44143	800-991-5444	440-442-8800
D & W Food Centers Inc 3001 Orchard Vista Dr SE	Grand Rapids	MI	49546	800-642-3728	616-940-3580
Dominick's Finer Foods Inc 711 Jorie Blvd	Oak Brook	IL	60523	877-723-3929	630-891-5000
Dorignac's Food Center Inc 710 Veterans Memorial Blvd	Metairie	LA	70005	877-712-2204	504-837-4650
Farmer Jack 18718 Borman Ave	Detroit	MI	48228	877-327-5225	313-270-1000

				Toll-Free	Phone
Felpausch Food Centers Corp 127 S Michigan Ave	Hastings	MI	49058	**800-648-6433**	269-945-3485
Fiesta Mart Inc 5235 Katy Fwy	Houston	TX	77007	**877-256-5060**	713-869-5060
Food City PO Box 488	Chandler	AZ	85244	**800-755-7292**	480-895-9350
Food Giant Supermarkets 120 Industrial Dr	Sikeston	MO	63801	**800-445-3740**	573-471-3500
Foods Inc 4343 Merle Hay Rd	Des Moines	IA	50310	**800-421-4355**	515-278-1657
Fred Meyer Inc 3800 SE 22nd Ave	Portland	OR	97202	**800-858-9202**	503-232-8844
Genuardi's Family Markets Inc 301 E Germantown Pike	Norristown	PA	19401	**877-723-3929**	610-277-6000
Giant Eagle Inc 101 Kappa Dr	Pittsburgh	PA	15238	**800-553-2324***	412-963-6200
*Cust Svc					
Giant Food Inc 6300 Sheriff Rd	Landover	MD	20785	**888-469-4426**	301-341-4100
Giant Food Stores Inc 1149 Harrisburg Pike	Carlisle	PA	17013	**800-814-4268**	717-249-4000
Hannaford Bros Co Inc 145 Pleasant Hill Rd	Scarborough	ME	04074	**800-341-6393**	207-883-2911
Harris Teeter Inc 701 Crestdale Dr	Matthews	NC	28105	**800-432-6111***	704-844-3100
*Cust Svc					
Homeland Stores Inc 28 E 33 St	Edmond	OK	73013	**800-522-5658**	405-216-2200
Houchens Industries Inc 700 Church St	Bowling Green	KY	42101	**800-846-3252**	270-843-3252
Ingles Markets Inc 2913 US Hwy 70 W	Black Mountain	NC	28711	**800-635-5066**	828-669-2941
NASDAQ: IMKTA					
K-VA-T Food Stores Inc PO Box 1158	Grundy	VA	24614	**800-253-6684**	276-623-5100
Lowes Food Stores Inc 1381 Old Mill Cir Suite 200	Winston-Salem	NC	27103	**800-669-5693**	336-659-0180
Mars Supermarkets Inc 3401 E Federal St	Baltimore	MD	21213	**888-284-7773**	410-342-0197
Mass Marketing Inc 401 Isom Bldg 100	San Antonio	TX	78216	**800-279-1149**	210-344-1960
Meijer Inc 2929 Walker Ave NW	Grand Rapids	MI	49544	**800-543-3704**	616-453-6711
Meyer Fred Inc 3800 SE 22nd Ave	Portland	OR	97202	**800-858-9202**	503-232-8844
NETGROCER.com Inc 14 Post Rd	Oakland	NJ	07436	**888-638-4762**	201-337-3900
Niemann Foods Inc 1501 N 12th St	Quincy	IL	62301	**800-800-3916**	217-221-5600
P & C Foods 1200 State Fair Blvd	Syracuse	NY	13209	**800-724-0205***	315-457-9460
*Cust Svc					
Peapod LLC 9933 Woods Dr	Skokie	IL	60077	**800-573-2763**	847-583-9400
Piggly Wiggly Carolina Co Inc PO Box 118047	Charleston	SC	29423	**800-243-9880**	843-554-9880
Piggly Wiggly Corp 2605 Sagebrush Dr Suite 200	Flower Mound	TX	75028	**800-800-8215**	972-410-2901
Publix Super Markets Inc 3300 Airport Rd	Lakeland	FL	33811	**800-342-1227***	863-688-1188
*PR					
Raley's PO Box 15618	Sacramento	CA	95852	**800-925-9989**	916-373-3333
Ralphs Grocery Co 1100 W Artesia Blvd	Compton	CA	90220	**888-437-3496***	310-884-9000
*Cust Svc					
Randalls Food Markets Inc PO Box 4506	Houston	TX	77210	**800-420-5385***	713-268-3500
*PR					
Schnuck Markets Inc 11420 Lackland Rd	Saint Louis	MO	63146	**800-264-4400**	314-994-9900
Seaway Food Town Inc 1020 Ford St	Maumee	OH	43537	**800-221-8816**	419-893-9401
Shop 'n Save Inc 10461 Manchester Rd	Kirkwood	MO	63122	**800-368-7052**	314-984-0900
Shop 'n Save Massachusetts Inc 145 Pleasant Hill Rd	Scarborough	ME	04074	**800-341-6393**	207-883-2911
Shop-Rite Supermarkets Inc PO Box 2328	Fort Oglethorpe	GA	30742	**800-742-3347**	706-861-3347
Shoppers Food Warehouse Corp 4600 Forbes Blvd	Lanham	MD	20706	**800-775-9888**	301-306-8600
ShopRite Supermarkets Inc PO Box 7812	Edison	NJ	08818	**800-746-7748**	732-417-0850
Smart & Final Inc 600 Citadel Dr	Commerce	CA	90040	**800-894-0511**	323-869-7500
NYSE: SMF					
Smith's Food & Drug Centers Inc 1550 S Redwood Rd	Salt Lake City	UT	84104	**800-444-8081**	801-974-1400
Sobeys Inc 115 King St	Stellarton	NS	B0K1S0	**888-944-0442***	902-752-8371
*Cust Svc					
SUPERVALU Inc 11840 Valley View Rd	Eden Prairie	MN	55344	**888-256-2800***	952-828-4000
NYSE: SVU ■ *Cust Svc					
Tops Markets Inc 6363 Main St	Williamsville	NY	14221	**800-522-2522**	716-635-5000
Ukrop's Super Markets Inc 600 Southlake Blvd	Richmond	VA	23236	**800-868-2270**	804-379-7300
Victory Supermarkets Inc 75 N Main St	Leominster	MA	01453	**800-536-1955**	978-840-2200
Wegmans Food Markets Inc 1500 Brooks Ave	Rochester	NY	14624	**800-934-6267**	585-328-2550
Wilson Mills DBA Catalano's Stop & Shop 5612 Wilson Mills Rd	Highland Heights	OH	44143	**800-991-5444**	440-442-8800

340 GYM & PLAYGROUND EQUIPMENT

				Toll-Free	Phone
American Athletic Inc 200 American Ave	Jefferson	IA	50129	**800-247-3978**	515-386-3125
American Playground Corp 6406 Production Dr	Anderson	IN	46013	**800-541-1602**	765-642-0288
BCI Burke Co Inc 660 Van Dyne Rd	Fond du Lac	WI	54937	**800-356-2070**	920-921-9220
Columbia Cascade Co 1975 SW 5th Ave	Portland	OR	97201	**800-547-1940**	503-223-1157
Florida Playground & Steel Co 4701 S 50th St	Tampa	FL	33619	**800-444-2655**	813-247-2812
Game-Time Inc 150 Gametime Dr	Fort Payne	AL	35968	**800-235-2440***	256-845-5610
*Sales					
Grounds For Play Inc 1401 E Dallas St	Mansfield	TX	76063	**800-552-7529**	817-477-5482
Howell Playground Equipment Inc 1714 E Fairchild	Danville	IL	61832	**800-637-5075***	217-442-0482
*Orders					
Jaypro Sports Inc 976 Hartford Tpke	Waterford	CT	06385	**800-243-0533***	860-447-3001
*Cust Svc					
Koala Corp 7881 S Wheeling Ct	Englewood	CO	80112	**888-733-3456**	303-539-8300
Landscape Structures Inc 601 7th St S	Delano	MN	55328	**800-328-0035**	763-972-3391
Miracle Recreation Equipment Co 878 Hwy 60	Monett	MO	65708	**800-523-4202**	417-235-6917
PlayCore Inc 430 Chestnut St Suite 300	Chattanooga	TN	37402	**888-404-5737**	423-756-0015
Playground Environments 82 Modular Ave	Commack	NY	11725	**800-777-6596**	631-231-1300
Playworld Systems Inc 1000 Buffalo Rd	Lewisburg	PA	17837	**800-233-8404**	570-522-9800
PW Athletic Mfg Co 140 N Gilbert Rd	Mesa	AZ	85203	**800-687-5768**	928-778-4232
Recreation Creation Inc 215 W Mechanic St	Hillsdale	MI	49242	**800-766-9458***	517-439-1591
*Cust Svc					
School-Tech Inc 745 State Cir Box 1941	Ann Arbor	MI	48106	**800-521-2832**	734-761-5072
SportsPlay Equipment Inc 5642 Natural Bridge Ave	Saint Louis	MO	63120	**800-727-8180**	314-389-4140
Swing-N-Slide Corp 1212 Barberry Dr	Janesville	WI	53545	**800-888-1232**	608-755-4777
Ultra Play Systems Inc 1675 Locust St	Red Bud	IL	62278	**800-458-5872**	618-282-8200
WOW Playgrounds 2851 Polk St	Hollywood	FL	33020	**800-432-2283**	954-925-2800

341 GYPSUM PRODUCTS

				Toll-Free	Phone
American Gypsum Co 3811 Turtlecreek Blvd Suite 1200	Dallas	TX	75219	**800-545-6302**	214-530-5500
BPB 2424 Lakeshore Rd W	Mississauga	ON	L5J1K4	**866-272-8722**	905-823-9881
BPB Gypsum 27442 Portola Pkwy Suite 100	Foothill Ranch	CA	92610	**800-426-3669**	949-282-5300
Hamilton Materials Inc 345 W Meats Ave	Orange	CA	92865	**800-331-5569**	714-637-2770
National Gypsum Co 2001 Rexford Rd	Charlotte	NC	28211	**800-628-4662**	704-365-7300
PABCO Gypsum 37849 Cherry St	Newark	CA	94560	**800-829-1577**	510-792-1577
US Gypsum Co 125 S Franklin St	Chicago	IL	60606	**800-621-9622**	312-606-4000
USG Corp 125 S Franklin St	Chicago	IL	60606	**800-621-9622**	312-606-4000
NYSE: USG					

342 HAIRPIECES, WIGS, TOUPEES

				Toll-Free	Phone
Afro World Hair Goods Inc 7276 Natural Bridge Rd	Saint Louis	MO	63121	**800-228-9424**	314-389-5194
Alfieri Charles Studio 4390 N Federal Hwy Suite 203	Fort Lauderdale	FL	33308	**800-321-2413**	954-928-1755
Alkinco 264 W 40th St	New York	NY	10018	**800-424-7118**	212-719-3070
Amekor Industries 500 Brook Rd Suite 100	Conshohocken	PA	19428	**800-345-6332**	610-825-6747
Charles Alfieri Studio 4390 N Federal Hwy Suite 203	Fort Lauderdale	FL	33308	**800-321-2413**	954-928-1755
Eva Gabor International Ltd 5900 Equitable Rd	Kansas City	MO	64120	**800-236-0326**	816-231-3700
Headstart Hair For Men Inc 3395 Cypress Gardens Rd	Winter Haven	FL	33884	**800-645-6525**	863-324-5559
Henry Margu Inc 540 Commerce Dr	Yeadon	PA	19050	**800-345-8284**	610-622-0515
HPH Corp 1529 SE 47th Terr	Cape Coral	FL	33904	**800-654-9884**	239-540-0085
Jacquelyn Wigs 15 W 37th St 4th Fl	New York	NY	10018	**800-272-2424**	212-302-2266
Jean Paree Weegs Inc 4041 S 700 East Suite 2	Salt Lake City	UT	84107	**800-422-9447***	801-328-9756
*Orders					
Jon Renau Collection 2510 Island View Way	Vista	CA	92081	**800-462-9447**	760-598-0067
Knight Peggy Solutions Inc 180 Harbor Dr Suite 221	Sausalito	CA	94965	**800-997-7753**	415-289-1777
Look of Love International 555-A N Michigan Ave	Kenilworth	NJ	07033	**800-526-7627**	908-687-9502
Louis Ferre Inc 302 5th Ave 10th Fl	New York	NY	10001	**800-695-1061**	212-239-1600
National Fiber Technology LLC 300 Canal St	Lawrence	MA	01840	**800-842-2751**	978-686-2964
Peggy Knight Solutions Inc 180 Harbor Dr Suite 221	Sausalito	CA	94965	**800-997-7753**	415-289-1777
Rene Of Paris 15551 Cabrito Rd	Van Nuys	CA	91406	**800-353-7363**	818-908-3100
TressAllure/General Wig 5800 NW 163rd St	Miami Lakes	FL	33014	**800-777-9447**	305-823-0600
Troika International Inc 1555 Los Palos St	Los Angeles	CA	90023	**800-787-6452**	323-415-0199
Wig America Co 265 McCone Ave	Hayward	CA	94545	**800-338-7600**	510-887-9579
World of Wigs 2305 E 17th St	Santa Ana	CA	92705	**800-794-5572**	714-547-4461
Yaffa Wigs 4118 13th Ave	Brooklyn	NY	11219	**800-233-0660**	718-436-4280
YK International Co 3246 W Montrose Ave	Chicago	IL	60618	**800-621-0086**	773-583-5270

343 HANDBAGS, TOTES, BACKPACKS

SEE ALSO Leather Goods - Personal; Luggage, Bags, Cases; Sporting Goods; Tarps, Tents, Covers

				Toll-Free	Phone
Accurate Flannel Bag Co 35-37 36th St 6th Fl	Long Island City	NY	11106	**800-234-9200**	718-784-7600
Allegro Mfg Inc 7250 E Oxford Way	Commerce	CA	90040	**800-833-5562**	323-724-0101
Anchor Industries Inc 1100 Burch Dr	Evansville	IN	47725	**800-544-4445**	812-867-2421
Dow Cover Co Inc 373 Lexington Ave	New Haven	CT	06513	**800-735-8877**	203-469-5394
Eastpak Corp PO Box 1817	Appleton	WI	54912	**800-222-5725**	
Etienne Aigner Group Inc 47 Brunswick Ave	Edison	NJ	08818	**800-537-7463**	732-248-9200
Fabriko Inc 318 E Confederate Blvd	Appomattox	VA	24522	**800-558-0242**	434-352-7145
GeoDesic Corp 400 Commerce Rd	Alice	TX	78332	**800-824-4153**	361-668-3766
Innovo Group Inc 2633 Kingston Pike Suite 100	Knoxville	TN	37919	**800-627-2621**	865-546-1110
NASDAQ: INNO					
JanSport Inc N 850 County Hwy CB	Appleton	WI	54914	**800-558-8404***	920-734-5708
*Cust Svc					
LBU Inc 217 Brook Ave	Passaic	NJ	07055	**800-678-4528**	973-773-4800
LeSportsac Inc 358 5th Ave 8th Fl	New York	NY	10001	**800-486-2247**	212-736-6262
North Face Inc 2013 Farallon Dr	San Leandro	CA	94577	**800-535-3331**	510-618-3500
Salomon North America 5055 N Greeley Ave	Portland	OR	97217	**877-272-5666**	971-234-2300
SeamCraft Inc 932 W Dakin St	Chicago	IL	60613	**800-322-2441**	773-281-5150
Service Mfg Corp 5414 W Roosevelt Rd	Chicago	IL	60644	**800-338-7082**	773-287-5500
Vera Bradley Designs 2208 Production Rd	Fort Wayne	IN	46808	**800-975-8372**	260-482-4673

344 HANGERS - CLOTHES

				Toll-Free	Phone
A & E Products Group Inc 1 Harmon Meadow Blvd	Secaucus	NJ	07094	**800-762-1167**	
CHC Industries 3055 Ruen Dr	Palm Harbor	FL	34685	**800-242-3665**	727-789-3000
International Innovations Inc 4107 Spicewood Springs Rd Suite 216	Austin	TX	78759	**800-708-2111**	512-502-0636
Laidlaw Corp 6625 N Scottsdale Rd	Scottsdale	AZ	85250	**800-528-8295**	480-951-0003
M & B Hangers Co 1313 Parkway Dr SE	Leeds	AL	35094	**800-227-0436**	205-699-2171
Montrose Hanger Co PO Box 1149	Wilson	NC	27894	**800-849-8038**	252-237-8038
Rochester Shoe Tree Co Inc PO Box 746	Ashland	NH	03217	**800-692-3300***	603-968-3301
*Cust Svc					

345 HARDWARE - MFR

Company / Address	City	State	ZIP	Toll-Free	Phone
Adams Rite Mfg Co 260 W Santa Fe St	Pomona	CA	91767	**800-872-3267**	909-632-2300
Amerock Corp PO Box 7018 *Cust Svc	Rockford	IL	61125	**800-435-6959***	815-963-9631
Anderson Electrical Products Inc PO Box 455	Leeds	AL	35094	**800-423-0730**	205-699-2411
Arrow Lock Co 325 Duffy Ave	Hicksville	NY	11801	**800-221-6529**	516-704-2700
ASSA Inc 110 Sargent Dr	New Haven	CT	06511	**800-235-7482**	203-603-5959
Baldwin Hardware Corp 841 E Wyomissing Blvd	Reading	PA	19611	**800-437-7448**	610-777-7811
Band-It-IDEX Inc 4799 Dahlia St	Denver	CO	80216	**800-525-0758**	303-320-4555
Baron Mfg Co 1200 Capitol Dr	Addison	IL	60101	**800-368-8585**	630-628-9110
Belwith International Ltd 3100 Broadway Ave	Grandville	MI	49418	**800-235-9484**	
Bete Fog Nozzle Inc 50 Greenfield St	Greenfield	MA	01301	**800-235-0049**	413-772-0846
Bommer Industries Inc PO Box 187	Landrum	SC	29356	**800-334-1654**	864-457-3301
Brainerd Mfg Co Inc 140 Business Pk Dr	Winston-Salem	NC	27107	**800-652-7277**	
Bronze Craft Corp 37 Will St	Nashua	NH	03060	**800-488-7747**	603-883-7747
Charles Leonard Inc 79-11 Cooper Ave	Glendale	NY	11385	**800-999-7202**	718-894-4851
Component Hardware Group Inc PO Box 2020	Lakewood	NJ	08701	**800-526-3694**	732-363-4700
Craft Inc PO Box 3049	South Attleboro	MA	02703	**800-827-2388**	508-761-7917
Daniel Edward W Co Inc 11700 Harvard Ave *Cust Svc	Cleveland	OH	44105	**800-338-2658***	216-295-2750
Dayton Superior Corp 7777 Washington Village Dr Suite 130	Dayton	OH	45459	**877-632-9866**	937-428-6360
Dixie Industries PO Box 180600	Chattanooga	TN	37406	**800-933-4943**	423-698-3323
Dor-O-Matic Inc 7350 W Wilson Ave	Harwood Heights	IL	60706	**800-543-4635**	708-867-7400
DORMA Group North America Dorma Dr	Reamstown	PA	17567	**800-523-8483**	717-336-3881
Edward W Daniel Co Inc 11700 Harvard Ave *Cust Svc	Cleveland	OH	44105	**800-338-2658***	216-295-2750
Engineered Products Co PO Box 108	Flint	MI	48501	**888-414-3726**	810-767-2050
ER Wagner Mfg Co Inc 4611 N 32nd St	Milwaukee	WI	53209	**800-558-5596**	414-871-5080
ESPE Mfg Co Inc 9220 Ivanhoe St *Cust Svc	Schiller Park	IL	60176	**800-367-3773***	847-678-8950
Faultless Caster Div FKI Industries 1421 N Garvin St *Cust Svc	Evansville	IN	47711	**800-322-9329***	812-425-1011
FKI Industries Faultless Caster Div 1421 N Garvin St *Cust Svc	Evansville	IN	47711	**800-322-9329***	812-425-1011
Folger Adam Security Inc 16300 W 103rd St	Lemont	IL	60439	**800-966-6739**	630-739-3900
Fried Brothers Inc 467 N 7th St	Philadelphia	PA	19123	**800-523-2924**	215-627-3205
Fulton Corp 303 8th Ave	Fulton	IL	61252	**800-252-0002**	815-589-3211
Guard Security Hardware 1 S Middlesex Ave *Sales	Monroe Township	NJ	08831	**800-523-1268***	609-860-9990
Guden HA Co Inc 99 Raynor Ave	Ronkonkoma	NY	11779	**800-344-6437**	631-737-2900
HA Guden Co Inc 99 Raynor Ave	Ronkonkoma	NY	11779	**800-344-6437**	631-737-2900
Hager Hinge Co 139 Victor St	Saint Louis	MO	63104	**800-325-9995**	314-772-4400
Hamilton Caster & Mfg Co 1637 Dixie Hwy	Hamilton	OH	45011	**800-733-7665**	513-863-3300
Hindley Mfg Co Inc PO Box 38	Cumberland	RI	02864	**800-323-9031**	401-722-2550
Hurd Corp PO Box 1450	Greeneville	TN	37744	**800-877-2581**	423-787-8800
Ideal Clamp 3200 Parker Dr	Saint Augustine	FL	32084	**800-221-0100**	904-829-1000
Ingersoll-Rand Co Von Duprin Exit Device Div 2720 Tobey Dr *Cust Svc	Indianapolis	IN	46219	**800-999-0408***	317-897-9944
Inwesco Inc 746 N Coney Ave	Azusa	CA	91702	**800-266-9304**	626-334-9304
Jacknob Corp 290 Oser Ave	Hauppauge	NY	11788	**888-231-9333**	631-231-9400
Jarvis Caster Group 60 Record Dr	Henderson	TN	38340	**800-995-9876**	
John Sterling Corp PO Box 469	Richmond	IL	60071	**800-367-5726**	815-678-2031
Johnson LE Products Inc 2100 Sterling Ave	Elkhart	IN	46516	**800-837-4697**	574-293-5664
Kaba Ilco Corp 400 Jeffreys Rd	Rocky Mount	NC	27804	**800-334-1381**	252-446-3321
Kason Industries Inc 57 Amlajack Blvd	Shenandoah	GA	30265	**800-935-2766**	770-251-1422
Keeler Brass Co 955 Godfrey Ave SW	Grand Rapids	MI	49503	**800-874-6522**	616-247-4000
Keystone Electronics Corp 31-07 20th Rd	Astoria	NY	11105	**800-221-5510**	718-956-8900
La Gard Inc 3330 Kashiwa St	Torrance	CA	90505	**800-523-9605**	310-325-5670
Lawrence Hardware 2 1st Ave	Sterling	IL	61081	**800-435-9568**	815-625-0360
LE Johnson Products Inc 2100 Sterling Ave	Elkhart	IN	46516	**800-837-4697**	574-293-5664
Leonard Charles Inc 79-11 Cooper Ave	Glendale	NY	11385	**800-999-7202**	718-894-4851
Liberty Hardware Mfg Corp 140 Business Park Dr	Winston-Salem	NC	27107	**800-542-3789**	336-769-4077
Master Lock Co 137 W Forest Hills Ave	Oak Creek	WI	53154	**800-308-9242**	414-571-5625
McKinney Products Inc 820 Davis St	Scranton	PA	18505	**800-346-7707**	570-346-7551
Medeco Security Locks Inc PO Box 3075	Salem	VA	24153	**800-839-3157**	540-380-5000
National Mfg Co 1 1st Ave *Cust Svc	Sterling	IL	61081	**800-346-9445***	815-625-1320
No-Sag Products Corp 2225 Production Rd	Kendallville	IN	46755	**800-345-0775**	260-347-2600
Nucor Corp Fastener Div PO Box 6100	Saint Joe	IN	46785	**800-955-6826**	260-337-1600
Parker Metal Corp 243 Stafford St	Worcester	MA	01603	**800-225-9011**	508-791-7131
Payson Casters Inc 2323 N Delaney Rd	Gurnee	IL	60031	**800-323-4552**	847-336-6200
Precision Brand Products Inc 2250 Curtiss St	Downers Grove	IL	60515	**800-535-3727**	630-969-7200
PrimeSource Building Products Inc 2115 E Beltline	Carrollton	TX	75006	**800-745-3341**	972-416-1976
Qual-Craft Industries PO Box 559	Stoughton	MA	02072	**800-231-5647**	781-344-1000
RWM Casters Co PO Box 668	Gastonia	NC	28053	**800-253-6634**	704-866-8533
S Parker Hardware Mfg Corp PO Box 9882	Englewood	NJ	07631	**800-772-7537**	201-569-1600
Sargent Mfg Co 100 Sargent Dr *Sales	New Haven	CT	06511	**800-906-6606***	203-562-2151
Securitron Magnalock Corp 550 Vista Blvd *Sales	Sparks	NV	89434	**800-624-5625***	775-355-5625
Selby Furniture Hardware Co 321 Rider Ave	Bronx	NY	10451	**800-224-0058**	718-993-3700
Simpson Strong-Tie Co Inc 4120 Dublin Blvd Suite 400	Dublin	CA	94568	**800-925-5099**	925-560-9000
Solus Industrial Innovations LLC 30152 Aventura *Cust Svc	Rancho Santa Margarita	CA	92688	**800-825-8364***	949-589-3900
Southern Tool Mfg Co Inc PO Box 12008	Winston-Salem	NC	27117	**800-334-5262**	336-788-6321
Stanley Works 1000 Stanley Dr *NYSE: SWK* ■ *Cust Svc	New Britain	CT	06053	**800-262-2161***	860-225-5111
Sterling John Corp PO Box 469	Richmond	IL	60071	**800-367-5726**	815-678-2031
Trimco/Builders Brass Works PO Box 23277	Los Angeles	CA	90023	**877-786-8387**	323-262-4191
Truth Hardware Inc 700 W Bridge St *Cust Svc	Owatonna	MN	55060	**800-866-7884***	507-451-5620
Ultra Hardware Products LLC 1777 Hylton Rd	Pennsauken	NJ	08110	**800-426-6379**	856-663-5050
Unicorp 291 Cleveland St	Orange	NJ	07050	**800-526-1389**	973-674-1700
United Fixtures Co 601 N 8th St	Niles	MI	49120	**800-468-8447**	269-683-0311
Von Duprin Exit Device Div Ingersoll-Rand Co 2720 Tobey Dr *Cust Svc	Indianapolis	IN	46219	**800-999-0408***	317-897-9944
Wagner ER Mfg Co Inc 4611 N 32nd St	Milwaukee	WI	53209	**800-558-5596**	414-871-5080
Weiser Lock A Masco Co 6700 Weiser Lock Dr	Tucson	AZ	85746	**800-677-5625**	520-741-6200
Yale Norton Inc 1902 Airport Rd	Monroe	NC	28110	**800-438-1951**	704-283-2101
Yale Residential Security Products Inc 2725B Northwoods Pkwy *Cust Svc	Norcross	GA	30071	**800-542-7562***	678-728-7400
Yale Security Group 1902 Airport Rd	Monroe	NC	28110	**800-438-1951**	704-283-2101
Yardley Products Corp PO Box 357	Yardley	PA	19067	**800-457-0154**	215-493-2700

346 HARDWARE - WHOL

Company / Address	City	State	ZIP	Toll-Free	Phone
All-Pro Fasteners Inc 1916 Peyco Dr N	Arlington	TX	76001	**800-361-6627**	817-467-5700
Allied International 13207 Bradley Ave	Sylmar	CA	91342	**800-533-8333**	818-364-2333
Amarillo Hardware Co Inc PO Box 1891	Amarillo	TX	79172	**800-949-4722**	806-376-4722
Associated Steel Corp 18200 Miles Rd	Cleveland	OH	44128	**800-441-9303**	216-475-8000
Baer Supply Co 909 Forest Edge Dr	Vernon Hills	IL	60061	**800-944-2237**	847-913-2237
Barnett Inc 3333 Lenox Ave	Jacksonville	FL	32254	**800-288-2000**	904-384-6530
Blish-Mize Co 223 S 5th St	Atchison	KS	66002	**800-995-0525**	913-367-1250
Bostwick-Braun Co PO Box 912	Toledo	OH	43697	**800-777-9640**	419-259-3600
Bradley EB Co 5080 S Alameda St	Los Angeles	CA	90058	**800-533-3030**	323-585-9201
Builders Hardware & Supply Co Inc PO Box C-79005	Seattle	WA	98119	**800-999-5158**	206-281-3700
Carlson Systems LLC PO Box 3036	Omaha	NE	68103	**800-325-8343**	402-593-5300
Cascade Wholesale Hardware Inc PO Box 1659	Hillsboro	OR	97123	**800-877-9987**	503-614-2600
Dake Div JSJ Corp 724 Robbins Rd	Grand Haven	MI	49417	**800-846-3253**	616-842-7110
Dillon Poe Supply Corp 215 Pelham Davis Cir	Greenville	SC	29615	**800-849-4300**	864-213-9000
Do it Best Corp PO Box 868	Fort Wayne	IN	46801	**800-348-1785**	260-748-5300
Earnest Machine Products Co 12502 Plaza Dr	Parma	OH	44130	**800-327-6378**	216-362-1100
EB Bradley Co 5080 S Alameda St	Los Angeles	CA	90058	**800-533-3030**	323-585-9201
Fastec Industrial Corp 23348 County Rd 6	Elkhart	IN	46514	**800-837-2505**	574-262-2505
General Fasteners Co Inc 11820 Globe Rd	Livonia	MI	48150	**800-945-2658**	734-452-2400
Grainger WW Inc 100 Grainger Pkwy *NYSE: GWW*	Lake Forest	IL	60045	**888-361-8649**	847-535-1000
Handy Hardware Wholesale Inc 8300 Tewantin Dr	Houston	TX	77061	**800-364-3835**	713-644-1495
Hans Johnsen Co Inc 8901 Chancellor Row *Sales	Dallas	TX	75247	**800-879-1515***	214-879-1550
Hardware Distribution Warehouses Inc (HDW) 6900 Woolworth Rd *Cust Svc	Shreveport	LA	71129	**800-256-8527***	318-686-8527
HDW (Hardware Distribution Warehouses Inc) 6900 Woolworth Rd *Cust Svc	Shreveport	LA	71129	**800-256-8527***	318-686-8527
Heads & Threads International LLC 200 Kennedy Dr	Sayreville	NJ	08872	**800-929-1950**	732-727-5800
Hillman Group Inc 10590 Hamilton Ave	Cincinnati	OH	45231	**800-800-4900**	513-851-4900
Home Depot Supply 10641 Scripps Summit Ct	San Diego	CA	92131	**800-233-6166**	858-831-2000
House-Hasson Hardware Inc 3125 Water Plant Rd SE	Knoxville	TN	37914	**800-333-0520**	865-525-0471
Interline Brands Inc 801 W Bay St *NYSE: IBI*	Jacksonville	FL	32204	**800-288-2000**	904-421-1400
Jensen Distribution Services 314 W Riverside Ave	Spokane	WA	99201	**800-234-1321**	509-624-1321
Johnsen Hans Co Inc 8901 Chancellor Row *Sales	Dallas	TX	75247	**800-879-1515***	214-879-1550
JSJ Corp 700 Robbins Rd	Grand Haven	MI	49417	**800-867-3208**	616-842-6350
JSJ Corp Dake Div 724 Robbins Rd	Grand Haven	MI	49417	**800-846-3253**	616-842-7110
Kentec Inc 3250 Centerville Hwy	Snellville	GA	30039	**800-241-0148**	770-985-1907
Long-Lewis Hardware Co 430 9th St N	Birmingham	AL	35203	**800-322-0492**	205-322-2561
Monroe Hardware Co PO Box 5015	Monroe	NC	28111	**800-222-1974**	704-289-3121
Moore-Handley Inc 3140 Pelham Pkwy	Birmingham	AL	35124	**800-633-3848**	205-663-8011
Parts Assoc Inc 12420 Plaza Dr	Parma	OH	44130	**800-321-1128**	216-433-7700
Porteous Fastener Co 1300 Morse Ave	Elk Grove Village	IL	60007	**800-935-2002**	847-228-6313
Ram Tool & Supply Co PO Box 320979	Birmingham	AL	35232	**800-292-6027**	205-591-2527
Reid Tool Supply Co Inc 2265 Black Creek Rd *Sales	Muskegon	MI	49444	**800-253-0421***	231-777-3951
Rock Island Corp 530 Oak Court Dr Suite 260	Memphis	TN	38117	**800-529-5701**	901-529-5700
Ryobi Technologies Inc 1428 Pearman Dairy Rd	Anderson	SC	29625	**800-525-2579**	864-226-6511
Star Stainless Screw Co 30 West End Rd	Totowa	NJ	07512	**800-631-3540**	973-256-2300
Swiss Army Brands Inc 1 Research Dr PO Box 874 *Cust Svc	Shelton	CT	06484	**800-243-4057***	203-929-6391
Techni-Tool Inc 1547 N Trooper Rd PO Box 1117 *Cust Svc	Worcester	PA	19490	**800-832-4866***	610-941-2400
Thruway Fasteners Inc 2910 Niagara Falls Blvd	North Tonawanda	NY	14120	**800-201-1619**	716-694-1434
United Hardware Distributing Co PO Box 410	Minneapolis	MN	55440	**800-835-6560**	763-559-1800
Wallace Hardware Co Inc PO Box 6004	Morristown	TN	37815	**800-776-0976**	423-586-5650
Watters & Martin Inc 3800 Village Ave	Norfolk	VA	23502	**800-446-8205**	757-857-0651
WCL Co PO Box 3588	City of Industry	CA	91744	**800-331-3816**	626-968-5523
Wurth Service Supply Inc 4935 W 86th St	Indianapolis	IN	46268	**800-428-4686**	317-704-1000
WW Grainger Inc 100 Grainger Pkwy *NYSE: GWW*	Lake Forest	IL	60045	**888-361-8649**	847-535-1000

347 HEALTH CARE PROVIDERS - ANCILLARY

SEE ALSO Home Health Services; Hospices; Vision Correction Centers

Company / Address	City	State	ZIP	Toll-Free	Phone
Amedisys Inc 11100 Mead Rd Suite 300 *NASDAQ: AMED*	Baton Rouge	LA	70816	**800-467-2662**	225-292-2031

				Toll-Free	Phone
American Healthways Inc 3841 Greenhills Village Dr Suite 300 *NASDAQ: AMHC*	Nashville	TN	37215	**800-327-3822**	615-665-1122
AmSurg Corp 20 Burton Hills Blvd 5th Fl *NASDAQ: AMSG*	Nashville	TN	37215	**800-945-2301**	615-665-1283
Apex Fitness Group 100 Camino Ruiz	Camarillo	CA	93012	**800-656-2739**	805-449-1330
BriteSmile Inc 490 N Wiget Ln *NASDAQ: BSML*	Walnut Creek	CA	94598	**800-274-8376**	925-941-6260
Curative Health Services Inc 150 Motor Pkwy 4th Fl *NASDAQ: CURE*	Hauppauge	NY	11788	**800-966-5656**	631-232-7000
DaVita Inc 601 Hawaii St *NYSE: DVA*	El Segundo	CA	90245	**800-310-4872**	310-536-2400
Dialysis Corp of America 27 Miller St Suite 2 *NASDAQ: DCAI*	Lemoyne	PA	17043	**888-730-6164**	717-730-6164
Executive Health Group 10 Rockefeller Plaza 4th Fl	New York	NY	10020	**800-362-8671**	212-332-3030
Fresenius Medical Care North America 95 Hayden Ave 2 Ledgemont Ctr *NYSE: FMS*	Lexington	MA	02420	**800-662-1237**	781-402-9000
Gambro Healthcare Inc 5200 Virginia Way	Brentwood	TN	37027	**800-467-4736**	615-320-4200
Hanger Orthopedic Group Inc 2 Bethesda Metro Ctr Suite 1200 *NYSE: HGR*	Bethesda	MD	20814	**800-765-3822**	301-986-0701
Health Fitness Corp 3600 American Blvd West Suite 560	Bloomington	MN	55431	**800-639-7913**	952-831-6830
HealthDrive Corp 25 Needham St	Newton	MA	02461	**888-964-6681**	617-964-6681
HealthSouth Corp 1 HealthSouth Pkwy	Birmingham	AL	35243	**800-765-4772**	205-967-7116
Hooper Holmes Inc 170 Mt Airy Rd *AMEX: HH*	Basking Ridge	NJ	07920	**800-782-7373**	908-766-5000
Med Tech 135 NW 100 Ave	Plantation	FL	33324	**800-786-9555**	954-434-4341
Medstone International Inc 100 Columbia Suite 100	Aliso Viejo	CA	92656	**800-633-7866**	949-448-7700
Midwest Medical Services 4280 Bluestem Rd	Charleston	IL	61920	**888-850-7377**	
Miracle-Ear Inc 5000 Cheshire Ln N	Plymouth	MN	55446	**800-234-7714**	763-268-4000
NovaCare Inc 680 American Ave	King of Prussia	PA	19406	**800-331-8840**	610-992-7200
Radiation Therapy Services Inc 2234 Colonial Blvd *NASDAQ: RTSX*	Fort Myers	FL	33907	**888-376-9729**	239-931-7275
Raytel Medical Corp 7 Waterside Crossing	Windsor	CT	06095	**800-367-1095**	860-298-6100
RehabCare Group Inc 7733 Forsyth Blvd Suite 2300 *NYSE: RHB*	Saint Louis	MO	63105	**800-677-1238**	314-863-7422
Sonus Corp 5000 Cheshire Ln N	Plymouth	MN	55446	**888-447-0443**	
SunDance Rehabilitation Corp 101 Sun Ave NE	Albuquerque	NM	87109	**800-729-6600**	505-821-3355
US Physical Therapy 1300 W Sam Houston Pkwy Suite 300 *NASDAQ: USPH*	Houston	TX	77042	**800-580-6285**	713-297-7000

348 HEALTH CARE SYSTEMS

SEE ALSO Hospitals - General Hospitals - US

				Toll-Free	Phone
Adventist Health System 111 N Orlando Ave	Winter Park	FL	32789	**800-327-9290**	407-647-4400
Advocate Health Care 2025 Windsor Dr	Oak Brook	IL	60523	**800-323-8622**	630-572-9393
Albert Einstein Healthcare Network 5501 Old York Rd	Philadelphia	PA	19141	**800-346-7834**	215-456-7010
Baptist Health Systems of South Florida 6855 Red Rd Suite 600	Coral Gables	FL	33143	**800-327-2491**	786-662-7111
Benedictine Health System 503 E 3rd St Suite 400	Duluth	MN	55805	**800-833-7208**	218-786-2370
Catholic Healthcare Partners 615 Elsinore Pl	Cincinnati	OH	45202	**800-367-9212**	513-639-2800
CHRISTUS Schumpert Health System 1 St Mary Pl	Shreveport	LA	71101	**888-336-8115**	318-681-4500
Community Health Systems Inc 155 Franklin Rd Suite 400 *NYSE: CYH*	Brentwood	TN	37027	**888-373-9600**	615-373-9600
Fairview Hospital & Healthcare Services 2450 Riverside Ave S	Minneapolis	MN	55454	**800-328-4661**	612-672-6000
Great Plains Health Alliance Inc 625 3rd St	Phillipsburg	KS	67661	**800-432-2779**	785-543-2111
HCA Inc 1 Park Plaza *NYSE: HCA*	Nashville	TN	37203	**800-828-2561**	615-344-9551
Intermountain Health Care Inc (IHC) 36 S State St 22nd Fl *Hum Res	Salt Lake City	UT	84111	**800-843-7820***	801-442-2000
Kindred Healthcare Inc 680 S 4th Ave *NASDAQ: KIND*	Louisville	KY	40202	**800-545-0749**	502-596-7300
MedStar Health 5565 Sterrett Pl 5th Fl	Columbia	MD	21044	**877-772-6505**	410-772-6500
New York-Presbyterian Healthcare System 622 W 168th St	New York	NY	10032	**877-697-9355**	212-305-2500
Oakwood Health Services Corp PO Box 2500	Dearborn	MI	48123	**800-543-9355**	313-593-7000
Palomar Pomerado Health System 15615 Pomerado Rd	Poway	CA	92064	**800-628-2880**	858-613-4000
Presbyterian Healthcare Services 1100 Central Ave SE	Albuquerque	NM	87106	**800-545-4030**	505-841-1234
Saint Mary's Good Samaritan Inc 605 N 12th St	Mount Vernon	IL	62864	**800-310-0484**	618-242-4600
Scripps Health 4275 Campus Point Ct	San Diego	CA	92121	**800-727-4777**	858-678-6111
Southern Illinois Healthcare 1239 E Main St	Carbondale	IL	62902	**866-744-2468**	618-457-5200
Sutter Health 2200 River Plaza	Sacramento	CA	95833	**800-606-7070**	916-733-8800
Triad Hospitals Inc 5800 Tennyson Pkwy *NYSE: TRI*	Plano	TX	75024	**800-238-6006**	214-473-7000
Universal Health Services Inc 367 S Gulph Rd *NYSE: UHS*	King of Prussia	PA	19406	**800-347-7750**	610-768-3300
University of Maryland Medical System 22 S Greene St	Baltimore	MD	21201	**800-492-5538**	410-328-8667
University of Pittsburgh Medical Center Health System 200 Lothrop St	Pittsburgh	PA	15213	**800-533-8762**	412-647-2345

349 HEALTH & FITNESS CENTERS

SEE ALSO Spas - Health & Fitness; Weight Loss Centers & Services

				Toll-Free	Phone
24 Hour Fitness Worldwide Inc 12647 Alcosta Blvd 5th fl	San Ramon	CA	94583	**888-256-5485**	925-543-3100
Bel Air Athletic Club 8400 E Crescent Pkwy Suite 200	Greenwood Village	CO	80111	**888-458-0489**	303-866-0800
Brick Bodies Fitness Services Inc 201 Old Padonia Mill Rd	Cockeysville	MD	21030	**877-348-3861**	410-252-8058
Butterfly Life 2404 San Ramon Valley Blvd Suite 200	San Ramon	CA	94583	**800-288-8373**	
Contours Express Inc 156 Imperial Way	Nicholasville	KY	40356	**877-227-2282**	859-885-6441
Curves International Inc 100 Ritchie Rd	Waco	TX	76712	**800-848-1096**	254-399-9285
Equinox Fitness Holdings Inc 895 Broadway	New York	NY	10003	**866-332-6549**	212-677-0180
Fitness Co 1602 Hgwy 35 South	Oakhurst	NJ	07755	**888-353-6754**	732-775-0955
Gold's Gym International 358 Hampton Dr	Venice	CA	90291	**800-457-5375**	310-392-3005
Gorilla Sports 12440 E Imperial Hwy Suite 300	Norwalk	CA	90651	**800-447-7457**	562-484-2000
Health Clubs of America 500 E Broward Blvd Suite 1650	Fort Lauderdale	FL	33394	**800-833-5239**	954-527-5373
Health Fitness Corp 3600 American Blvd West Suite 560	Bloomington	MN	55431	**800-639-7913**	952-831-6830
LA Fitness International 8105 Irvine Ctr Dr Suite 200	Irvine	CA	92618	**800-600-2540**	949-255-7400
Ladies Workout Express 500 E Broward Blvd Suite 1650	Fort Lauderdale	FL	33394	**800-833-5239**	954-527-5373
Lady of America Franchise Corp 500 E Broward Blvd Suite 1650	Fort Lauderdale	FL	33394	**800-833-5239**	954-527-5373
Life Time Fitness Inc 6442 City West Pkwy *NYSE: LTM*	Eden Prairie	MN	55344	**800-368-7543**	952-947-0000
Linda Evans Fitness Centers 2491 San Ramon Valley Blvd Suite 1 PMB 203	San Ramon	CA	94583	**800-455-4632**	925-743-3399
Little Gym International Inc 8970 E Raintree Dr Suite 200	Scottsdale	AZ	85260	**888-228-2878**	480-948-2878
New York Health & Racquet Club Inc 3 New York Plaza 18th Fl	New York	NY	10004	**800-472-2378**	212-797-1500
Pinnacle Fitness 12440 E Imperial Hwy Suite 300	Norwalk	CA	90651	**800-447-7457**	562-484-2000
Slender Lady Inc 45 NE Loop 410 Suite 500	San Antonio	TX	78216	**888-227-8187**	210-877-1500
Sports Clubs of Canada 2 Sheppard Ave E Suite 200	Willowdale	ON	M2N5Y7	**800-967-5688**	416-221-6900
World Gym International 3223 Washington Blvd	Marina del Rey	CA	90292	**800-544-7441**	310-827-7705

350 HEALTH FOOD STORES

				Toll-Free	Phone
Christopher Enterprises 155 W 250 N	Spanish Fork	UT	84660	**800-453-1406**	801-794-6800
GNC Corp 300 6th Ave *Cust Svc	Pittsburgh	PA	15222	**888-462-2548***	412-288-4600
GNC Franchising Inc 300 6th Ave	Pittsburgh	PA	15222	**800-259-5008**	412-288-4600
Great Earth Vitamin Stores 1101 S Millikin Ave Suite A	Ontario	CA	91761	**800-374-7328**	
Jamba Juice Co 1700 17th St	San Francisco	CA	94103	**800-545-9972**	
Netrition Inc 20 Petra Ln	Albany	NY	12205	**888-817-2411**	518-464-0765
Smoothie King Franchises Inc 2400 Veterans Blvd Suite 110	Kenner	LA	70062	**800-577-4200**	504-467-4006
Vitamin Specialties Co 8160 Ogontz Ave	Wyncote	PA	19095	**800-365-8482**	215-885-3804
Wild Oats Markets Inc 3375 Mitchell Ln *NASDAQ: OATS*	Boulder	CO	80301	**877-542-9453**	303-440-5220

351 HEALTH & MEDICAL INFORMATION - ONLINE

				Toll-Free	Phone
ADAM Inc 1600 RiverEdge Pkwy Suite 100 *NASDAQ: ADAM*	Atlanta	GA	30328	**800-755-2326**	770-980-0888
Alternative Medicine.com 2995 Wilderness Pl Suite 205	Boulder	CO	80301	**800-333-4325**	800-515-4325
At Health Inc 14241 NE Woodinville-Duvall Rd Suite 104	Woodinville	WA	98072	**888-284-3258**	360-668-3808
BabyCenter LLC 163 Freelon St	San Francisco	CA	94107	**866-241-2229**	415-537-0900
cancerfacts.com 1725 Westlake Ave N Suite 300 *Cust Svc	Seattle	WA	98109	**877-422-3228***	206-270-0225
eDiets.com Inc 3801 W Hillsboro Blvd *NASDAQ: DIET*	Deerfield Beach	FL	33442	**800-265-6170**	954-360-9022
eMedicine.com Inc 1004 Farnam St Suite 300	Omaha	NE	68102	**866-363-3362**	402-341-3222
eMedicineHealth.com 1004 Farnam St Suite 300	Omaha	NE	68102	**866-363-3362**	402-341-3222
Food Allergy & Anaphylaxis Network (FAAN) 11781 Lee Jackson Hwy Suite 160	Fairfax	VA	22033	**800-929-4040**	703-691-3179
HealthWeb Greater Midwest Region of the National Network Libraries of Medicine 1750 W Polk St MC 763	Chicago	IL	60612	**800-338-7657**	312-996-2464
Medicine Online Inc 18800 Delaware St Suite 650	Huntington Beach	CA	92648	**888-666-5638**	714-848-0444
MedicineNet Inc 903 Calle Amanecer Suite 300	San Clemente	CA	92673	**800-221-5698**	949-940-6500
MedlinePlus National Library of Medicine 8600 Rockville Pike	Bethesda	MD	20894	**888-346-3656**	301-594-5983
Pain.com Dannemiller Memorial Educational Foundation 5711 NW Parkway Suite 100	San Antonio	TX	78249	**800-328-2308**	210-641-8311

HEATING EQUIPMENT - ELECTRIC

SEE Air Conditioning & Heating Equipment - Residential

352 HEATING EQUIPMENT - GAS, OIL, COAL

SEE ALSO Air Conditioning & Heating Equipment - Commercial/ Industrial; Air Conditioning & Heating Equipment - Residential; Boiler Shops; Furnaces & Ovens - Industrial Process

Company / Address	City	State	Zip	Toll-Free	Phone
Aerco International Inc 159 Paris Ave	Northvale	NJ	07647	**800-526-0288**	201-768-2400
Aquatherm Industries Inc 1940 Rutgers University Blvd	Lakewood	NJ	08701	**800-535-6307**	732-905-0440
Beckett RW Corp PO Box 1289	Elyria	OH	44036	**800-645-2876**	440-327-1060
Burner Systems International Inc 3600 Cummings Rd	Chattanooga	TN	37419	**800-251-6318**	423-822-3600
Burnham Corp PO Box 3245	Lancaster	PA	17603	**877-567-4328**	717-397-4701
[illegible] Solar Corp PO Box 163	Pomona	NY	10970	**800-988-4455**	845-354-2500
DESA International 2701 Industrial Dr *Cust Svc	Bowling Green	KY	42101	**800-402-[illegible]***	270-781-9600
EFM Sales Co 302 S 4th St	Emmaus	PA	18049	**800-935-0933**	610-965-9041
Electro-Flex Heat Inc PO Box 88	Bloomfield	CT	06002	**800-585-4213**	860-242-6287
Empire Comfort Systems Inc 918 Freeburg Ave	Belleville	IL	62222	**800-851-3153**	618-233-7420
Erie Power Technologies Inc 5300 Knowledge Pkwy Suite 200	Erie	PA	16510	**800-323-3743**	814-897-7000
Gordon-Piatt Group Inc PO Box 21220	Tulsa	OK	74141	**800-638-6940**	
Hamworthy Peabody Combustion Inc 70 Shelton Technology Ctr	Shelton	CT	06484	**877-732-2639**	203-922-1199
Hearth & Home Technologies Inc 20802 Kensington Blvd	Lakeville	MN	55044	**800-669-4328**	952-985-6000
Heatilator Inc 1915 W Saunders St	Mount Pleasant	IA	52641	**800-843-2848**	319-385-9211
John Zink Co LLC PO Box 21220	Tulsa	OK	74121	**800-421-9242**	918-234-1800
Lattner Boiler Mfg Co PO Box 1527	Cedar Rapids	IA	52406	**800-345-1527**	319-366-0778
LB White Co Inc W 6636 LB White Rd	Onalaska	WI	54650	**800-345-7200**	608-783-5691
Lennox Hearth Products 1110 W Taft Ave	Orange	CA	92865	**800-854-0257**	714-921-6100
Meeder Equipment Co 12323 6th St	Rancho Cucamonga	CA	91739	**800-423-3711**	909-463-0600
New Yorker Boiler Co Inc 21 E Lincoln Ave Suite 100	Hatfield	PA	19440	**800-535-4679**	215-855-8055
North American Mfg Co Ltd 4455 E 71st St	Cleveland	OH	44105	**800-626-3477**	216-271-6000
PM Lattner Mfg Co PO Box 1527	Cedar Rapids	IA	52406	**800-345-1527**	319-366-0778
Powrmatic Inc PO Box 439	Finksburg	MD	21048	**800-966-9100**	410-833-9100
Raypak Inc 2151 Eastman Ave	Oxnard	CA	93030	**800-947-2975**	805-278-5300
Reimers Electra Steam Inc PO Box 37	Clear Brook	VA	22624	**800-872-7562**	540-662-3811
Roberts-Gordon Inc PO Box 44	Buffalo	NY	14240	**800-828-7450**	716-852-4400
RW Beckett Corp PO Box 1289	Elyria	OH	44036	**800-645-2876**	440-327-1060
Schwank Inc 2 Schwank Way at Hwy 56N	Waynesboro	GA	30830	**800-776-8459**	706-554-6191
Taco Inc 1160 Cranston St	Cranston	RI	02920	**800-822-6007**	401-942-8000
US Stove Co Inc PO Box 151	South Pittsburg	TN	37380	**800-750-2723**	423-837-2100
Utica Boilers Inc PO Box 4729	Utica	NY	13504	**800-325-5479**	315-797-1310
Vermont Castings Inc PO Box 501 *Prod Info	Bethel	VT	05032	**800-227-8683***	802-234-2300
Water Furnace International Inc 9000 Conservation Way	Fort Wayne	IN	46809	**800-222-5667**	260-478-5667
Wayne Combustion Systems 801 Glasgow Ave	Fort Wayne	IN	46814	**800-443-4625**	260-425-9200
White LB Co Inc W 6636 LB White Rd	Onalaska	WI	54650	**800-345-7200**	608-783-5691
Zink John Co LLC PO Box 21220	Tulsa	OK	74121	**800-421-9242**	918-234-1800

353 HEAVY EQUIPMENT DISTRIBUTORS

SEE ALSO Farm Machinery & Equipment - Whol; Industrial Equipment & Supplies (Misc) - Whol

Company / Address	City	State	Zip	Toll-Free	Phone
Alban Tractor Co 8531 Pulaski Hwy	Baltimore	MD	21237	**800-492-6994**	410-686-7777
Anderson Machinery Co Inc 6535 Leopard St	Corpus Christi	TX	78409	**800-308-6043**	361-289-6043
Arnold Machinery Co 2955 W 2100 South *Cust Svc	Salt Lake City	UT	84119	**800-821-0548***	801-972-4000
Balzer Pacific Equipment Co 2136 SE 8th Ave	Portland	OR	97214	**800-442-0966**	503-232-5141
Beckwith Machinery Co 4565 William Penn Hwy	Murrysville	PA	15668	**888-232-5948**	724-327-1300
Brandeis Machinery & Supply Co 1801 Watterson Trail	Louisville	KY	40299	**800-274-7253**	502-493-4380
Caspian Holdings of Delaware DBA Guyan Machinery Co PO Box 150	Chapmanville	WV	25508	**800-999-3888**	304-855-4501
Chadwick-BaRoss Inc 160 Warren Ave	Westbrook	ME	04092	**800-477-4963**	207-854-8411
Cleveland Brothers Equipment Co Inc 5300 Paxton St	Harrisburg	PA	17111	**800-482-2378**	717-564-2121
Contractors Machinery Co Inc 13200 Northend Ave	Oak Park	MI	48237	**800-572-7479**	248-543-4770
Croushorn Equipment Co Inc PO Box 796	Harlan	KY	40831	**800-861-5070**	606-573-2454
Empire Southwest Co 1725 S Country Club Dr	Mesa	AZ	85210	**800-367-4731**	480-633-4400
Feenaughty Machinery Co 4800 NE Columbia Blvd	Portland	OR	97218	**800-875-2566**	503-282-2566
General Equipment & Supplies Inc PO Box 2145	Fargo	ND	58107	**800-437-2924**	701-282-2662
Guyan Machinery Co PO Box 150	Chapmanville	WV	25508	**800-999-3888**	304-855-4501
Halton Co PO Box 3377	Portland	OR	97208	**800-452-7676**	503-288-6411
Heavy Machines Inc 3926 E Rains Rd	Memphis	TN	38118	**800-238-5591**	901-260-2200
Hoffman International Inc 300 S Randolphville Rd	Piscataway	NJ	08855	**800-446-3362**	732-752-3600
MacAllister Machinery Co Inc 7515 E 30th St PO Box 1941	Indianapolis	IN	46219	**800-227-3228**	317-545-2151
Martin Tractor Co Inc 1737 SW 42nd St	Topeka	KS	66609	**800-666-5770**	785-266-5770
Mississippi Valley Equipment Co Inc 1198 Pershall Rd	Saint Louis	MO	63137	**800-325-8001**	314-869-8600
Mustang Tractor & Equipment Co 12800 NW Fwy	Houston	TX	77040	**800-256-1001**	713-460-2000
Nortrax Equipment Co 310 Industrial Park Dr	Ashland	WI	54806	**800-472-6685**	715-682-5522
Ohio Machinery Co 3993 E Royalton Rd	Broadview Heights	OH	44147	**800-837-6200**	440-526-6200
Phillips Victor L Co 4100 Gardner Ave	Kansas City	MO	64120	**800-878-9290**	816-241-9290
Pioneer Machinery Co 3239 Sunset Blvd PO Box 3079	West Columbia	SC	29171	**888-983-9990**	803-936-9990
Power Motive Corp 5000 Vasquez Blvd	Denver	CO	80216	**800-627-0087**	303-355-5900
Roland Machinery Co 816 N Dirksen Pkwy	Springfield	IL	62702	**800-252-2926**	217-789-7711
Rudd Equipment Co 4344 Poplar Level Rd	Louisville	KY	40213	**800-283-7833**	502-456-4050
Scott Machinery Co 4055 S 500 West	Salt Lake City	UT	84123	**800-734-7441**	801-262-7441
Southeastern Equipment Co Inc 10874 E Pike Rd	Cambridge	OH	43725	**800-798-5438**	740-432-6303
Spreitzer Inc 3145 16th Ave SW	Cedar Rapids	IA	52404	**800-823-0399**	319-365-9155
Tri-State Truck & Equipment Inc 1124 Main St	Billings	MT	59103	**800-227-1132**	406-245-3188
Tyler Equipment Corp 251 Shaker Rd	East Longmeadow	MA	01028	**800-292-6351**	413-525-6351
Victor L Phillips Co 4100 Gardner Ave	Kansas City	MO	64120	**800-878-9290**	816-241-9290
Western Power & Equipment 6407-B NE 117th Ave	Vancouver	WA	98662	**800-333-2346**	360-253-2346
Western States Equipment Co 500 E Overland Rd	Meridian	ID	83642	**800-852-2287**	208-888-2287

354 HELICOPTER TRANSPORT SERVICES

SEE ALSO Air Charter Services; Ambulance Services

Company / Address	City	State	Zip	Toll-Free	Phone
Air Logistics Inc 4605 Industrial Dr	New Iberia	LA	70560	**800-365-6771**	337-365-6771
Carson Helicopters 952 Blooming Glen Rd	Perkasie	PA	18944	**800-523-2335**	215-249-3535
Coastal Helicopters Inc 8995 Yandukin Dr	Juneau	AK	99801	**800-789-5610**	907-789-5600
Corporate Helicopters of San Diego 3753 John J Montgomery Dr Suite 2	San Diego	CA	92123	**800-345-6737**	858-505-5650
Era Helicopters Inc 6160 Carl Brady Dr	Anchorage	AK	99502	**800-843-1947**	907-248-4422
Evergreen Helicopters of Alaska Inc 1936 Merrill Field Dr	Anchorage	AK	99501	**800-958-2454**	907-257-1500
Evergreen International Aviation Inc 3850 Three Mile Ln	McMinnville	OR	97128	**800-472-9361**	503-472-9361
Gateway Helicopters Ltd PO Box 21028 Aviation Ln Hangar 4	North Bay	ON	P1B9N8	**888-474-4214**	705-474-4214
Helinet Aviation Services LLC 16425 Hart St Hangar 2	Van Nuys	CA	91406	**800-221-8389**	818-902-0229
Island Express Helicopter Service 1175 Queens Hwy S	Long Beach	CA	90802	**800-228-2566**	310-510-2525
Midwest Helicopter Airways Inc 525 Executive Dr	Willowbrook	IL	60527	**800-323-7609**	630-325-7860
Petroleum Helicopters Inc 2001 SE Evangeline Thwy *NASDAQ: PHEL*	Lafayette	LA	70508	**800-235-2452**	337-235-2452
Saint Louis Helicopter LLC 18004 Edison Ave	Chesterfield	MO	63005	**800-325-4046**	636-532-1177
Skydance Helicopters 2207 Bellanca St Suite B	Minden	NV	89423	**800-882-1651**	775-782-4040
Vancouver Island Helicopters Ltd 1962 Canso Rd	North Saanich	BC	V8L5V5	**866-844-4354**	250-656-3987

355 HOLDING COMPANIES

SEE ALSO Conglomerates

355-1 Airlines Holding Companies

Company / Address	City	State	Zip	Toll-Free	Phone
America West Holdings Corp 111 W Rio Salado Pkwy *NYSE: AWA*	Tempe	AZ	85281	**800-235-9292**	480-693-0800
ATA Holdings Corp 7337 W Washington St	Indianapolis	IN	46231	**800-435-9282**	317-247-4000
Frontier Airlines Inc 7001 Tower Rd *NASDAQ: FRNT*	Denver	CO	80249	**800-265-5505**	720-374-4200
JetBlue Airways Corp 118-29 Queens Blvd *NASDAQ: JBLU*	Forest Hills	NY	11375	**800-538-2583**	718-286-7900
Mesa Air Group Inc 410 N 44th St Suite 700 *NASDAQ: MESA*	Phoenix	AZ	85008	**800-637-2247**	602-685-4000
Midwest Air Group Inc 6744 S Howell Ave *NYSE: MEH*	Oak Creek	WI	53154	**800-452-2022**	414-570-4000
Northwest Airlines Corp 2700 Lone Oak Pkwy *NASDAQ: NWAC*	Eagan	MN	55121	**800-225-2525**	612-726-2111
UAL Corp 1200 E Algonquin Rd	Elk Grove Township	IL	60007	**800-241-6522**	847-700-4000
US Airways Group Inc 2345 Crystal Dr Crystal Pk 4	Arlington	VA	22227	**800-428-4322**	703-872-7000

355-2 Bank Holding Companies

Company / Address	City	State	Zip	Toll-Free	Phone
1st Source Corp 100 N Michigan St *NASDAQ: SRCE* ■ *Cust Svc	South Bend	IN	46601	**800-513-2360***	574-235-2000
ABC Bancorp PO Box 3668 *NASDAQ: ABCB*	Moultrie	GA	31776	**888-556-2701**	229-890-1111
Abigail Adams National Bancorp Inc 1130 Connecticut Ave NW Suite 200 *NASDAQ: AANB*	Washington	DC	20036	**877-442-3267**	202-772-3600
Access Anytime Bancorp Inc 801 Pile St *NASDAQ: AABC*	Clovis	NM	88101	**888-299-4310**	505-762-4417
Advance Financial Bancorp 1015 Commerce St *NASDAQ: AFBC*	Wellsburg	WV	26070	**800-569-7650**	304-737-3531
Alabama National BanCorporation 1927 1st Ave N *NASDAQ: ALAB*	Birmingham	AL	35203	**888-583-3200**	205-583-3600

Classified Section

Company	City	State	ZIP	Toll-Free	Phone
AMCORE Financial Inc 501 7th St *NASDAQ: AMFI*	Rockford	IL	61104	**800-521-5150**	815-968-2241
Amegy Bancorp Inc 4400 Post Oak Pkwy *NASDAQ: ABNK*	Houston	TX	77027	**800-324-6705**	713-235-8800
Ameriana Bancorp 2118 Bundy Ave *NASDAQ: ASBI*	New Castle	IN	47362	**800-487-2118**	765-529-2230
American National Bankshares Inc 628 Main St *NASDAQ: AMNB*	Danville	VA	24541	**800-240-8190**	434-792-5111
AmeriServe Financial Inc 216 Franklin St *NASDAQ: ASRV* ■ *Cust Svc	Johnstown	PA	15901	**800-837-2265***	814-533-5300
AmSouth Bancorporation PO Box 11007 *NYSE: ASO*	Birmingham	AL	35288	**800-267-6884**	205-320-7151
Annapolis Bancorp Inc 1000 Bestgate Rd Suite 400 *NASDAQ: ANNB*	Annapolis	MD	21401	**800-582-2651**	410-224-4483
ASB Financial Corp 503 Chillicothe St *NASDAQ: ASBP*	Portsmouth	OH	45662	**866-866-3177**	740-354-3177
Associated Banc-Corp 1200 Hansen Rd. *NASDAQ: ASBC* ■ *PR	Green Bay	WI	54304	**800-236-2722***	920-491-7000
Auburn National Bancorporation Inc PO Box 3110 *NASDAQ: AUBN*	Auburn	AL	36831	**888-988-2162**	334-821-9200
Banc Corp 17 N 20th St *NASDAQ: TBNC*	Birmingham	AL	35203	**877-326-2365**	205-326-2265
BancorpSouth Inc 1 Mississippi Plaza *NYSE: BXS*	Tupelo	MS	38802	**888-797-7711**	662-680-2000
BancWest Corp PO Box 3200	Honolulu	HI	96847	**888-844-4444**	808-525-7000
Bank of America Corp 100 N Tryon St Suite 200 Corporate Ctr. *NYSE: BAC*	Charlotte	NC	28202	**800-299-2265**	
Bank of Hawaii Corp PO Box 2900 *NYSE: BOH*	Honolulu	HI	96846	**888-643-3888**	808-537-8272
Bank Mutual Corp 4949 W Brown Deer Rd *NASDAQ: BKMU*	Milwaukee	WI	53223	**888-358-5070**	414-354-1500
Bank of the Ozarks Inc 12615 Chenal Pkwy Suite 3100 *NASDAQ: OZRK*	Little Rock	AR	72211	**800-628-3552**	501-978-2265
BankAtlantic Bancorp Inc 1750 E Sunrise Blvd *NYSE: BBX*	Fort Lauderdale	FL	33304	**800-741-1700**	954-760-5000
BankUnited Financial Corp 255 Alhambra Cir *NASDAQ: BKUNA*	Coral Gables	FL	33134	**800-440-9646**	305-569-2000
Bar Harbor Bankshares 82 Main St PO Box 400 *AMEX: BHB*	Bar Harbor	ME	04609	**800-237-9601**	207-288-3314
Bay View Capital Corp 1840 Gateway Dr Suite 300 *NYSE: BVC*	San Mateo	CA	94404	**800-229-8439**	650-312-7300
BOE Financial Services of Virginia Inc 323 Prince St *NASDAQ: BSXT*	Tappahannock	VA	22560	**800-443-5524**	804-443-4343
Brookline Bancorp Inc 160 Washington St *NASDAQ: BRKL*	Brookline	MA	02445	**877-668-2265**	617-730-3500
Bryn Mawr Bank Corp 801 Lancaster Ave *NASDAQ: BMTC*	Bryn Mawr	PA	19010	**888-732-2080**	610-525-1700
BWC Financial Corp 1400 Civic Dr. *NASDAQ: BWCF*	Walnut Creek	CA	94596	**888-278-1079**	925-932-5353
C & F Financial Corp PO Box 391 *NASDAQ: CFFI*	West Point	VA	23181	**800-296-6246**	804-843-2360
CalFirst Bancorp 18201 Von Karman Ave Suite 700 *NASDAQ: CFNB*	Irvine	CA	92612	**800-496-4640**	949-255-0500
California First National Bancorp 18201 Von Karman Ave Suite 700 *NASDAQ: CFNB*	Irvine	CA	92612	**800-496-4640**	949-255-0500
Camden National Corp 2 Elm St. *AMEX: CAC*	Camden	ME	04843	**800-860-8821**	207-236-8821
Capital Bank Corp 4901 Glenwood Ave *NASDAQ: CBKN*	Raleigh	NC	27612	**800-308-3971**	919-645-6400
Capital City Bank Group Inc 217 N Monroe St *NASDAQ: CCBG*	Tallahassee	FL	32301	**888-671-0400**	850-671-0400
Capitol Federal Financial 700 Kansas Ave *NASDAQ: CFFN*	Topeka	KS	66603	**888-822-7333**	785-235-1341
Cardinal Financial Corp 8270 Greensboro Dr Suite 500 *NASDAQ: CFNL*	McLean	VA	22102	**800-473-3247**	703-279-5050
Carrollton Bancorp 1589 Sulphur Spring Rd *NASDAQ: CRRB*	Baltimore	MD	21227	**800-222-6566**	410-536-4600
Cascade Bancorp 1100 NW Wall St *NASDAQ: CACB*	Bend	OR	97701	**877-617-3400**	541-385-6205
Cascade Financial Corp 2828 Colby Ave *NASDAQ: CASB*	Everett	WA	98201	**800-326-8787**	425-339-5500
Center Bancorp Inc 2455 Morris Ave *NASDAQ: CNBC*	Union	NJ	07083	**800-862-3683**	908-688-9500
Central Coast Bancorp 301 Main St. *NASDAQ: CCBN*	Salinas	CA	93901	**800-660-1585**	831-422-6642
Central Federal Corp PO Box 345 *NASDAQ: GCFC*	Wellsville	OH	43968	**888-273-8255**	330-532-1517
Century Bancorp Inc 400 Mystic Ave *NASDAQ: CNBKA*	Medford	MA	02155	**800-442-1859**	781-391-4000
Charter Financial Corp 600 3rd Ave *NASDAQ: CHFN*	West Point	GA	31833	**800-763-4444**	706-645-1391
Chemical Financial Corp 333 E Main St *NASDAQ: CHFC*	Midland	MI	48640	**800-722-6050**	989-839-5350
Chester Valley Bancorp Inc 100 E Lancaster Ave *NASDAQ: CVAL*	Downingtown	PA	19335	**800-687-4529**	610-269-9700
Chittenden Corp PO Box 820 *NYSE: CHZ*	Burlington	VT	05402	**800-642-3158**	802-658-4000
Citizens Banking Corp 328 S Saginaw St. *NASDAQ: CBCF* ■ *Cust Svc	Flint	MI	48502	**800-825-7200***	810-766-7500
Citizens Financial Group Inc 1 Citizens Dr	Providence	RI	02915	**800-922-9999**	401-456-7000
Citizens First Bancorp Inc 525 Water St *NASDAQ: CTZN*	Port Huron	MI	48060	**800-922-5308**	810-987-8300
City Holding Co 25 Gatewater Rd *NASDAQ: CHCO*	Cross Lanes	WV	25313	**800-922-9236**	304-769-1100
City National Bancshares Inc 25 W Flagler St.	Miami	FL	33130	**800-435-8839**	305-577-7333
CNB Financial Corp 1 S 2nd St *NASDAQ: CCNE*	Clearfield	PA	16830	**800-492-3221**	814-765-9621
Columbia Bancorp 7168 Columbia Gateway Dr *NASDAQ: CBMD*	Columbia	MD	21044	**888-822-2265**	410-423-8000
Columbia Banking System Inc PO Box 2156 *NASDAQ: COLB*	Tacoma	WA	98401	**800-305-1905**	253-305-1900
Comerica Inc 500 Woodward Ave *NYSE: CMA*	Detroit	MI	48226	**800-521-1190**	
Commerce Bancorp Inc 1701 Rt 70 E Commerce Atrium *NYSE: CBH* ■ *Cust Svc	Cherry Hill	NJ	08034	**800-751-9000***	856-751-9000
Commerce Bancshares Inc 1000 Walnut St *NASDAQ: CBSH*	Kansas City	MO	64106	**800-892-7100**	816-234-2000
Commercial Bankshares Inc 1550 SW 57th Ave *NASDAQ: CLBK*	Miami	FL	33144	**800-752-7999**	305-267-1200
Commercial National Financial Corp 900 Ligonier St *NASDAQ: CNAF*	Latrobe	PA	15650	**800-803-2265**	724-539-3501
Commonwealth Bancshares Inc 403 Boush St *NASDAQ: CWBS*	Norfolk	VA	23510	**888-446-9862**	757-446-6900
Community Bancorp Inc 900 Canterbury Pl Suite 300 *NASDAQ: CMBC*	Escondido	CA	92025	**800-362-2252**	760-432-1100
Community Bank Shares of Indiana Inc 101 W Spring St *NASDAQ: CBIN*	New Albany	IN	47150	**866-944-2004**	812-944-2224
Community Bank System Inc 5790 Widewaters Pkwy *NYSE: CBU*	DeWitt	NY	13214	**800-724-2262**	315-445-2282
Community Banks Inc 750 E Park Dr 2nd Fl *NASDAQ: CMTY*	Harrisburg	PA	17111	**800-331-8362**	717-920-1698
Community Investors Bancorp Inc 119 S Sandusky Ave *NASDAQ: CIBI*	Bucyrus	OH	44820	**800-222-4955**	419-562-7055
Community Trust Bancorp Inc 346 N Mayo Trail *NASDAQ: CTBI*	Pikeville	KY	41501	**800-422-1090**	606-432-1414
Compass Bancshares Inc 15 S 20th St *NASDAQ: CBSS*	Birmingham	AL	35233	**800-239-2265**	205-933-3000
Cooperative Bankshares Inc 201 Market St. *NASDAQ: COOP*	Wilmington	NC	28402	**800-672-0443**	910-343-0181
Cornerstone Bancorp Inc 550 Summer St *AMEX: CBN*	Stamford	CT	06901	**800-378-6367**	203-356-0111
Corus Bankshares Inc 3959 N Lincoln Ave *NASDAQ: CORS*	Chicago	IL	60613	**800-555-5710**	773-832-3462
Cowlitz Bancorporation 927 Commerce Ave *NASDAQ: CWLZ*	Longview	WA	98632	**800-340-8865**	360-423-9800
Crazy Woman Creek Bancorp Inc PO Box 1020 *NASDAQ: CRZY*	Buffalo	WY	82834	**800-348-8971**	307-684-5591
Crescent Banking Co PO Box 668 *NASDAQ: CSNT*	Jasper	GA	30143	**800-872-7941**	678-454-2265
Cullen/Frost Bankers Inc 100 W Houston St *NYSE: CFR*	San Antonio	TX	78205	**800-562-6732**	210-220-4011
CVB Financial Corp PO Box 51000 *NASDAQ: CVBF*	Ontario	CA	91761	**888-222-5432**	909-980-4030
Dime Community Bancshares Inc 209 Havemeyer St *NASDAQ: DCOM*	Brooklyn	NY	11211	**800-321-3463**	718-782-6200
Eastern Bank Corp Inc 112 Market St	Lynn	MA	01901	**800-327-8376**	781-599-2100
Eastern Virginia Bankshares Inc 330 Hospital Rd *NASDAQ: EVBS*	Tappahannock	VA	22560	**866-443-8429**	804-443-8400
ECB Bancorp Inc 35080 US Hwy 264 *NASDAQ: ECBE*	Engelhard	NC	27824	**800-849-2265**	252-925-9411
EFC Bancorp Inc 1695 Larkin Ave *AMEX: EFC*	Elgin	IL	60123	**888-354-4632**	847-741-3900
Empire Financial Holding Co 2170 W SR 434 Suite 100 *AMEX: EFH*	Longwood	FL	32779	**800-569-3337**	407-774-1300
ESB Financial Corp 600 Lawrence Ave *NASDAQ: ESBF*	Ellwood City	PA	16117	**800-533-4193**	724-758-5584
Exchange National Bancshares Inc 132 E High St *NASDAQ: EXJF*	Jefferson City	MO	65101	**800-761-8362**	573-761-6100
FFLC Bancorp Inc PO Box 490420	Leesburg	FL	34749	**877-955-2265**	352-787-3311
FFW Corp 1205 N Cass St *NASDAQ: FFWC*	Wabash	IN	46992	**800-377-4984**	260-563-3185
Fidelity Bankshares Inc 205 Datura St *NASDAQ: FFFL*	West Palm Beach	FL	33401	**800-422-3675**	561-514-9222
Fidelity Southern Corp 3490 Piedmont Rd Suite 1550 *NASDAQ: LION*	Atlanta	GA	30305	**888-248-5466**	404-639-6500
Fifth Third Bancorp 38 Fountain Sq Plaza *NASDAQ: FITB*	Cincinnati	OH	45263	**800-972-3030**	513-579-5300
First Bancorp 341 N Main St *NASDAQ: FBNC*	Troy	NC	27371	**800-548-9377**	910-576-6171
First Banks Inc 135 N Meramec Ave	Clayton	MO	63105	**800-760-2265**	314-854-4600
First Busey Corp PO Box 17125 *NASDAQ: BUSE*	Urbana	IL	61803	**800-672-8739**	217-365-4516
First Capital Inc 220 Federal Dr NW *NASDAQ: FCAP*	Corydon	IN	47112	**800-390-1465**	812-738-2198
First Charter Corp PO Box 37937 *NASDAQ: FCTR*	Charlotte	NC	28237	**800-422-4650**	704-688-4300
First Citizens Bancorporation Inc PO box 29	Columbia	SC	29202	**888-612-4444**	803-771-8700
First Commonwealth Financial Corp 22 N 6th St Old Courthouse Sq. *NYSE: FCF*	Indiana	PA	15701	**800-711-2265**	724-349-7220
First Defiance Financial Corp 601 Clinton St *NASDAQ: FDEF*	Defiance	OH	43512	**800-472-6292**	419-782-5015
First Federal Bancorporation PO Box 458	Bemidji	MN	56619	**800-749-9606**	218-751-5120
First Federal Bancshares of Arkansas Inc 128 W Stephenson Ave *NASDAQ: FFBH*	Harrison	AR	72601	**800-345-2539**	870-741-7641
First Federal Bankshares Inc 329 Pierce St *NASDAQ: FFSX*	Sioux City	IA	51102	**800-352-4620**	712-277-0200
First Federal Capital Corp 605 State St.	La Crosse	WI	54601	**800-657-4636**	608-784-8000
First Financial Corp 1 First Financial Plaza *NASDAQ: THFF*	Terre Haute	IN	47807	**800-511-0045**	812-238-6000
First Financial Holdings Inc PO Box 118068 *NASDAQ: FFCH*	Charleston	SC	29423	**800-768-3248**	843-529-5933

Bank Holding Companies (Cont'd)

Company	City	State	Zip	Toll-Free	Phone
First Financial Service Corp 2323 Ring Rd NASDAQ: FFKY	Elizabethtown	KY	42701	**800-314-2265**	270-765-2131
First Indiana Corp 135 N Pennsylvania St First Indiana Plaza Suite 1900 NASDAQ: FINB ■ *Cust Svc	Indianapolis	IN	46204	**800-888-8586***	317-269-1200
First Keystone Financial Inc 22 W State St NASDAQ: FKFS	Media	PA	19063	**800-590-1414**	610-565-6210
First Midwest Bancorp Inc 300 Park Blvd Suite 405 NASDAQ: FMBI	Itasca	IL	60143	**800-322-3623**	630-875-7200
First Mutual Bancshares Inc 400 108th Ave NE NASDAQ: FMSB	Bellevue	WA	98004	**800-735-7303**	425-455-7300
First National Lincoln Corp PO Box 940 NASDAQ: FNLC	Damariscotta	ME	04543	**800-564-3195**	207-563-3195
First National of Nebraska Inc 1 First National Ctr	Omaha	NE	68197	**800-688-7070**	402-341-0500
First Oak Brook Bancshares Inc 1400 W 16th St NASDAQ: FOBB	Oak Brook	IL	60523	**800-536-3000**	630-571-1050
First Place Financial Corp 185 E Market St NASDAQ: FPFC	Warren	OH	44481	**800-995-2646**	330-373-1221
First South Bancorp Inc 1311 Carolina Ave NASDAQ: FSBK	Washington	NC	27889	**888-317-0097**	252-946-4178
First Southern Bancshares Inc 102 S Court St	Florence	AL	35630	**800-625-7131**	256-764-7131
First State Bancorporation 7900 Jefferson NE NASDAQ: FSNM	Albuquerque	NM	87190	**888-699-7500**	505-241-7500
First United Corp 19 S 2nd St NASDAQ: FUNC	Oakland	MD	21550	**800-296-9471**	301-334-9471
First West Virginia Bancorp Inc 1701 Warwood Ave AMEX: FWV	Wheeling	WV	26003	**866-235-1923**	304-277-1100
FirstFed Bancorp Inc 1630 4th Ave N NASDAQ: FFDB	Bessemer	AL	35020	**800-436-5112**	205-428-8472
FirstFed Financial Corp 401 Wilshire Blvd NYSE: FED	Santa Monica	CA	90401	**800-637-5540**	310-319-6000
FirstMerit Corp 3 Cascade Plaza NASDAQ: FMER	Akron	OH	44308	**888-554-4362**	330-384-8000
Flagstar Bancorp Inc 5151 Corporate Dr NYSE: FBC	Troy	MI	48098	**800-945-7700**	248-312-2000
FNB Corp 101 Sunset Ave NASDAQ: FNBN	Asheboro	NC	27203	**800-873-1172**	336-626-8300
FNB Corp 105 Arbor Dr NASDAQ: FNBP	Christiansburg	VA	24073	**800-642-7416**	540-382-4951
Frankfort First Bancorp Inc 216 W Main St NASDAQ: FKKY	Frankfort	KY	40602	**888-818-3372**	502-223-1638
Fulton Financial Corp 1 Penn Sq NASDAQ: FULT	Lancaster	PA	17602	**800-752-9580**	717-291-2411
German American Bancorp 711 Main St NASDAQ: GABC	Jasper	IN	47546	**800-482-1314**	812-482-1314
Glacier Bancorp Inc 49 Commons Loop NASDAQ: GBCI	Kalispell	MT	59901	**800-735-4371**	406-756-4200
Gold Banc Corp Inc 11301 Nall Ave NASDAQ: GLDB	Leawood	KS	66211	**866-842-4686**	913-451-8050
Great Southern Bancorp Inc PO Box 9009GS NASDAQ: GSBC ■ *Cust Svc	Springfield	MO	65808	**800-749-7113***	417-887-4400
Greater Atlantic Financial Corp 10700 Parkridge Blvd Suite P50 NASDAQ: GAFC	Reston	VA	20191	**800-296-5581**	703-391-1300
Greater Bay Bancorp 2860 W Bayshore Rd NASDAQ: GBBK	Palo Alto	CA	94301	**800-226-5262**	650-813-8200
Guaranty Bancshares Inc 100 W Arkansas St PO Box 1158 NASDAQ: GNTY	Mount Pleasant	TX	75455	**888-572-9881**	903-572-9881
Habersham Bancorp 282 Historic Hwy 441 N NASDAQ: HABC	Cornelia	GA	30531	**800-822-0316**	706-778-1000
Hancock Holding Co 2510 14th St NASDAQ: HBHC	Gulfport	MS	39501	**800-522-6542**	228-868-4000
Harbor Florida Bancshares Inc 100 S 2nd St NASDAQ: HARB	Fort Pierce	FL	34950	**800-234-1959**	772-461-2414
Harleysville National Corp 483 Main St NASDAQ: HNBC	Harleysville	PA	19438	**800-423-3955**	215-256-8851
Harleysville Savings Financial Corp 271 Main St NASDAQ: HARL	Harleysville	PA	19438	**888-256-8828**	215-256-8828
Harrington West Financial Group Inc 610 Alamo Pintado Rd NASDAQ: HWFG	Solvang	CA	93463	**800-525-4959**	805-688-6644
Harris Bankcorp Inc 111 W Monroe St 18th Fl	Chicago	IL	60603	**888-340-2265**	312-461-2121
Heritage Financial Corp 201 5th Ave SW NASDAQ: HFWA	Olympia	WA	98501	**800-455-6126**	360-943-1500
HF Financial Corp 225 S Main Ave NASDAQ: HFFC	Sioux Falls	SD	57104	**800-244-2149**	605-333-7556
HFB Financial Corp 1602 Cumberland Ave NASDAQ: HFBA	Middlesboro	KY	40965	**800-354-0182**	606-248-1095
Hibernia Corp 313 Carondelet St NYSE: HIB	New Orleans	LA	70130	**800-245-4388**	504-533-2858
High Country Bancorp Inc 7360 W Hwy 50 NASDAQ: HCBC	Salida	CO	81201	**800-201-0557**	719-539-2516
HMN Financial Inc 1016 Civic Center Dr NW NASDAQ: HMNF	Rochester	MN	55901	**888-644-4142**	507-535-1200
Home Federal Bancorp 501 Washington St NASDAQ: HOMF	Columbus	IN	47201	**800-876-4372**	812-376-3323
Home Financial Bancorp 279 E Morgan St NASDAQ: HWEN	Spencer	IN	47460	**800-690-2095**	812-829-2095
Home Street Bank Inc 601 Union St Suite 2000	Seattle	WA	98101	**800-654-1075**	206-623-3050
Horizon Financial Corp 1500 Cornwall Ave NASDAQ: HRZB	Bellingham	WA	98225	**800-955-9194**	360-733-3050
HSBC USA Inc 1 HSBC Ctr	Buffalo	NY	14203	**800-975-4722**	716-841-2424
Hudson City Bancorp Inc W 80 Century Rd NASDAQ: HCBK	Paramus	NJ	07652	**800-967-2200**	201-967-1900
Hudson United Bancorp 1000 MacArthur Blvd NYSE: HU	Mahwah	NJ	07430	**800-482-5465**	201-236-2600
Huntington Bancshares Inc 41 S High St NASDAQ: HBAN	Columbus	OH	43287	**800-480-2265**	614-480-8300
IBERIABANK Corp 1101 E Admiral Doyle Dr NASDAQ: IBKC	New Iberia	LA	70560	**800-968-0801**	337-365-2361
Independence Community Bank Corp 195 Montague St NASDAQ: ICBC	Brooklyn	NY	11201	**800-732-3434**	718-722-5300
Independent Bank Corp 288 Union St NASDAQ: INDB	Rockland	MA	02370	**800-826-6100**	781-878-6100
Independent Bank Corp 230 W Main St NASDAQ: IBCP	Ionia	MI	48846	**800-662-0102**	616-527-9450
IndyMac Bancorp Inc 155 N Lake Ave NYSE: NDE	Pasadena	CA	91101	**800-669-2300**	626-535-5901
Integra Bank Corp PO Box 868 NASDAQ: IBNK	Evansville	IN	47705	**800-467-1928**	812-464-9800
Interchange Financial Services Corp Park 80 W Plaza 2 NASDAQ: IFCJ	Saddle Brook	NJ	07663	**800-701-7718**	201-703-2265
Intervest Bancshares Corp 1 Rockefeller Plaza Suite 400 NASDAQ: IBCA	New York	NY	10020	**877-226-5462**	212-218-2800
INTRUST Financial Corp 105 N Main St	Wichita	KS	67202	**800-242-7111**	316-383-1111
Irwin Financial Corp 500 Washington St PO Box 929 NYSE: IFC	Columbus	IN	47202	**888-879-5900**	812-376-1020
ITLA Capital Corp 888 Prospect St Suite 110 NASDAQ: ITLA	La Jolla	CA	92037	**888-551-4852**	858-551-0511
Jacksonville Bancorp Inc 100 N Laura St NASDAQ: JAXB	Jacksonville	FL	32202	**888-699-5292**	904-421-3040
KeyCorp 127 Public Sq NYSE: KEY ■ *Hum Res	Cleveland	OH	44114	**888-539-2562***	216-689-3000
KNBT Bancorp Inc 90 Highland Ave NASDAQ: KNBT	Bethlehem	PA	18017	**800-996-2062**	610-861-5000
Lakeland Financial Corp 202 E Center St NASDAQ: LKFN	Warsaw	IN	46580	**800-827-4522**	574-267-6144
Landmark Bancorp Inc 800 Poyntz Ave NASDAQ: LARK	Manhattan	KS	66502	**800-322-6344**	785-565-2000
Laredo National Bancshares Inc 700 San Bernardo Ave *Mktg	Laredo	TX	78040	**888-723-1151***	956-723-1151
Leesport Financial Corp 1240 Broadcasting Rd NASDAQ: FLPB	Wyomissing	PA	19610	**888-238-3330**	610-208-0966
Lincoln Bancorp 1121 E Main St PO Box 510 NASDAQ: LNCB	Plainfield	IN	46168	**888-895-6539**	317-839-6539
LNB Bancorp Inc 457 Broadway NASDAQ: LNBB	Lorain	OH	44052	**800-860-1007**	440-244-6000
Logansport Financial Corp 723 E Broadway NASDAQ: LOGN	Logansport	IN	46947	**800-436-5151**	574-722-3855
Long Island Financial Corp 1601 Veterans Memorial Hwy Suite 120 NASDAQ: LICB	Islandia	NY	11749	**888-542-2888**	631-348-0888
LSB Corp 30 Massachusetts Ave NASDAQ: LSBX	North Andover	MA	01845	**800-730-9660**	978-725-7500
LSB Financial Corp 101 Main St NASDAQ: LSBI	Lafayette	IN	47901	**800-704-3084**	765-742-1064
M & T Bank Corp 1 M & T Plaza 5th Fl NYSE: MTB	Buffalo	NY	14203	**800-724-2440**	716-842-4200
Macatawa Bank Corp 10753 Macatawa Dr NASDAQ: MCBC	Holland	MI	49422	**877-820-2265**	616-820-1444
Madison Bancshares Group Ltd 1767 Sentry Pkwy W	Blue Bell	PA	19422	**800-848-9867**	215-641-1111
Marshall & Ilsley Corp 770 N Water St NYSE: MI	Milwaukee	WI	53202	**800-342-2265**	414-765-7801
MASSBANK Corp 123 Haven St NASDAQ: MASB	Reading	MA	01867	**800-447-1052**	781-662-0100
Matrix Bancorp Inc 700 17th St Suite 2100 NASDAQ: MTXC	Denver	CO	80202	**800-594-2079**	303-595-9898
MBNA Corp 1100 N King St NYSE: KRB	Wilmington	DE	19884	**800-441-7048**	302-456-8588
Mercantile Bank Corp 216 N Division Ave NASDAQ: MBWM	Grand Rapids	MI	49503	**888-345-6296**	616-406-3000
Merchants Bancshares Inc PO Box 1009 NASDAQ: MBVT	Burlington	VT	05402	**800-322-5222**	802-658-3400
Meta Financial Group Inc 121 E 5th PO Box 1307 NASDAQ: CASH	Storm Lake	IA	50588	**800-792-6815**	712-732-4117
MFB Corp 4100 Edison Lakes Pkwy NASDAQ: MFBC	Mishawaka	IN	46545	**800-400-0433**	574-277-4200
Mid Penn Bancorp Inc 349 Union St AMEX: MBP	Millersburg	PA	17601	**800-672-6843**	717-692-2133
Mid-State Bancshares PO Box 6002 NASDAQ: MDST	Arroyo Grande	CA	93421	**800-473-7788**	805-473-6829
Midland Financial Co 501 NW Grand Blvd	Oklahoma City	OK	73118	**800-851-5041**	405-840-7600
MidSouth Bancorp Inc 102 Versailles Blvd AMEX: MSL	Lafayette	LA	70501	**800-213-2265**	337-237-8343
MidWestOne Financial Group Inc 222 1st Ave E NASDAQ: OSKY	Oskaloosa	IA	52577	**800-303-6740**	641-673-8448
Monroe Bancorp 210 E Kirkwood Ave NASDAQ: MROE	Bloomington	IN	47408	**800-319-2664**	812-336-0201
MutualFirst Financial Inc 110 E Charles St NASDAQ: MFSF	Muncie	IN	47305	**800-382-8031**	765-747-2800
NASB Financial Inc 12498 S 71st Hwy NASDAQ: NASB	Grandview	MO	64030	**800-677-6272**	816-765-2200
National City Corp 1900 E 9th St NYSE: NCC	Cleveland	OH	44114	**800-622-8100**	216-575-2000
National Penn Bancshares Inc PO Box 547 NASDAQ: NPBC	Boyertown	PA	19512	**800-822-3321**	610-367-6001
NBC Capital Corp NBC Plaza 301 E Main St AMEX: NBY	Starkville	MS	39759	**888-622-7341**	662-323-1341
NBT Bancorp Inc 52 S Broad St NASDAQ: NBTB	Norwich	NY	13815	**800-628-2265**	607-337-2265
New Hampshire Thrift Bancshares Inc 9 Main St NASDAQ: NHTB	Newport	NH	03773	**800-281-5772**	603-863-5772
New York Community Bancorp Inc 615 Merrick Ave NYSE: NYB	Westbury	NY	11590	**888-550-9888**	516-683-4100
NewMil Bancorp Inc 19 Main St NASDAQ: NMIL	New Milford	CT	06776	**800-525-6672**	860-355-7600

Classified Section

Company	City	State	ZIP	Toll-Free	Phone
North Central Bancshares Inc 825 Central Ave *NASDAQ: FFFD*	Fort Dodge	IA	50501	**800-272-3445**	515-576-7531
North Fork Bancorp Inc 275 Broad Hollow Rd *NYSE: NFB*	Melville	NY	11747	**877-694-9111**	631-844-1000
Northeast Bancorp 158 Court St *AMEX: NBN*	Auburn	ME	04210	**800-284-5989**	207-777-6411
Northeast Indiana Bancorp Inc 648 N Jefferson St *NASDAQ: NEIB*	Huntington	IN	46750	**800-550-3372**	260-356-3311
Northeast Pennsylvania Financial Corp 12 E Broad St	Hazleton	PA	18201	**888-466-6745**	570-459-3700
Northern States Financial Corp 1601 N Lewis Ave *NASDAQ: NSFC*	Waukegan	IL	60085	**800-339-4432**	847-244-6000
Northway Financial Inc PO Box 9 *NASDAQ: NWFI*	Berlin	NH	03570	**800-442-6666**	603-752-1171
Northwest Bancorp Inc 301 2nd Ave *NASDAQ: NWSB*	Warren	PA	16365	**877-672-5678**	814-726-2140
Norwood Financial Corp 717 Main St *NASDAQ: NWFL*	Honesdale	PA	18431	**800-598-5002**	570-253-1455
OceanFirst Financial Corp 975 Hooper Ave *NASDAQ: OCFC*	Toms River	NJ	08754	**888-623-2633**	732-240-4500
Ocwen Financial Corp 1665 Palm Beach Lakes Blvd *NYSE: OCN*	West Palm Beach	FL	33401	**800-746-2936**	561-681-8000
Ohio Savings Financial Corp 1801 E 9th St Suite 200	Cleveland	OH	44114	**800-696-2222**	216-622-4100
Ohio Valley Banc Corp 420 3rd Ave *NASDAQ: OVBC*	Gallipolis	OH	45631	**800-468-6682**	740-446-2631
Old National Bancorp 1 Main St *NYSE: ONB*	Evansville	IN	47708	**800-731-2265**	812-464-1494
Old Second Bancorp Inc 37 S River St *NASDAQ: OSBC*	Aurora	IL	60506	**888-892-6565**	630-892-0202
Omega Financial Corp 366 Walker Dr *NASDAQ: OMEF*	State College	PA	16801	**800-494-1810**	814-231-7680
Oneida Financial Corp 182 Main St *NASDAQ: ONFC*	Oneida	NY	13421	**800-211-0564**	315-363-2000
PAB Bankshares Inc 3250 Valdosta Rd *AMEX: PAB*	Valdosta	GA	31602	**800-394-2321**	229-241-2775
Pacific Capital Bancorp 1 S Los Carneros Rd *NASDAQ: PCBC*	Goleta	CA	93117	**888-400-7228**	805-564-6300
Pacific Mercantile Bancorp 949 South Coast Dr *NASDAQ: PMBC*	Costa Mesa	CA	92626	**877-450-2265**	714-438-2500
Pacific Premier Bancorp Inc 1600 Sunflower Ave 2nd Fl *NASDAQ: PPBI*	Costa Mesa	CA	92626	**888-388-5433**	714-431-4000
Pamrapo Bancorp Inc 611 Ave C PO Box 98 *NASDAQ: PBCI*	Bayonne	NJ	07002	**800-680-6872**	201-339-4600
Park Bancorp Inc 5400 S Pulaski Rd *NASDAQ: PFED*	Chicago	IL	60632	**888-727-5333**	773-582-8616
Park National Corp 50 N 3rd St *AMEX: PRK*	Newark	OH	43055	**800-762-2616**	740-349-8451
Pathfinder Bancorp Inc 214 W 1st St *NASDAQ: PBHC*	Oswego	NY	13126	**800-811-5620**	315-343-0057
Patriot National Bancorp Inc 900 Bedford St *NASDAQ: PNBK*	Stamford	CT	06901	**800-762-7620**	203-324-7500
Peapack-Gladstone Financial Corp PO Box 178 *AMEX: PGC*	Gladstone	NJ	07934	**800-742-7595**	908-234-0700
Pelican Financial Inc 811 Anchor Rode Dr *AMEX: PFI*	Naples	FL	34103	**800-219-4777**	239-403-0076
PennFed Financial Service Inc 622 Eagle Rock Ave *NASDAQ: PFSB*	West Orange	NJ	07052	**800-722-0351**	973-669-7366
PennRock Financial Services Corp 1060 Main St *NASDAQ: PRFS*	Blue Ball	PA	17506	**800-346-3437**	717-354-4541
Pennsylvania Commerce Bancorp Inc 100 Senate Ave *NASDAQ: COBH*	Camp Hill	PA	17011	**800-937-2003**	717-975-5630
Peoples Bancorp Inc 138 Putnam St *NASDAQ: PEBO*	Marietta	OH	45750	**800-374-6123**	740-373-3155
Peoples Bancorp of North Carolina Inc 518 W 'C' St *NASDAQ: PEBK*	Newton	NC	28658	**800-948-7195**	828-464-5620
Peoples BancTrust Co Inc 310 Broad St *NASDAQ: PBTC*	Selma	AL	36701	**800-278-8725**	334-875-1000
Peoples Community Bancorp Inc 11 S Broadway *NASDAQ: PCBI*	Lebanon	OH	45036	**888-815-3530**	513-932-3876
People's First Properties Inc 1022 W 23rd St Suite 400	Panama City	FL	32405	**800-624-9699**	850-769-1111
People's Mutual Holdings 850 Main St	Bridgeport	CT	06604	**800-392-3009**	203-338-7171
PFF Bancorp Inc PO Box 1520 *NYSE: PFB*	Pomona	CA	91769	**888-733-5465**	909-623-2323
Plymouth Bancorp Inc 151 Campanelli Dr	Middleboro	MA	02346	**800-882-4994**	508-946-3000
PNC Financial Services Group Inc 249 5th Ave 1 PNC Plaza *NYSE: PNC*	Pittsburgh	PA	15222	**877-762-2000**	412-762-2000
Popular Inc 209 Ponce de Leon Ave *NASDAQ: BPOP*	San Juan	PR	00919	**888-724-3650**	787-765-9800
Premier Community Bankshares Inc 4095 Valley Pike *NASDAQ: PREM*	Winchester	VA	22602	**800-526-2265**	540-869-6600
Premier Financial Bancorp Inc 2883 5th Ave *NASDAQ: PFBI*	Huntington	WV	25702	**866-269-0298**	304-525-1600
Princeton National Bancorp Inc 606 S Main St *NASDAQ: PNBC*	Princeton	IL	61356	**800-293-0451**	815-875-4444
PrivateBancorp Inc 10 N Dearborn St Suite 900 *NASDAQ: PVTB*	Chicago	IL	60602	**800-662-7748**	312-683-7100
Provident Financial Holdings Inc 3756 Central Ave *NASDAQ: PROV*	Riverside	CA	92506	**800-442-5201**	951-686-6060
Providian Financial Corp 201 Mission St *NYSE: PVN*	San Francisco	CA	94105	**800-525-7557**	415-543-0404
PSB Bancorp Inc 1835 Market St 11 Penn Ctr Suite 2601 *NASDAQ: PSBI*	Philadelphia	PA	19103	**866-437-2265**	215-979-7900

Company	City	State	ZIP	Toll-Free	Phone
Pulaski Financial Corp 12300 Olive Blvd *NASDAQ: PULB*	Saint Louis	MO	63141	**800-261-0113**	314-878-2210
PVF Capital Corp 30000 Aurora Rd *NASDAQ: PVFC*	Solon	OH	44139	**800-676-2572**	440-248-7171
Rainier Pacific Financial Group Inc 1498 Pacific Ave *NASDAQ: RPFG*	Tacoma	WA	98402	**800-228-2858**	253-926-4000
RBC Centura Banks Inc 134 N Church St	Rocky Mount	NC	27804	**800-236-8872**	252-454-4400
Regions Financial Corp 417 N 20th St *NYSE: RF*	Birmingham	AL	35203	**800-734-4667**	205-326-7100
Renasant Corp 209 Troy St *AMEX: PHC*	Tupelo	MS	38802	**800-680-1601**	662-680-1001
Republic Bancorp Inc 601 W Market St *NASDAQ: RBCAA*	Louisville	KY	40202	**888-540-5363**	502-584-3600
Republic Bancorp Inc 1070 E Main St *NASDAQ: RBNC*	Owosso	MI	48867	**888-722-7377**	989-725-7337
Riggs National Corp 1503 Pennsylvania Ave NW	Washington	DC	20005	**800-368-5800**	301-887-6000
River Valley Bancorp 430 Clifty Dr *NASDAQ: RIVR*	Madison	IN	47250	**800-994-4849**	812-273-4949
Rome Bancorp Inc 100 W Dominick St *NASDAQ: ROMED*	Rome	NY	13440	**800-280-9315**	315-336-7300
Royal Bancshares of Pennsylvania Inc 732 Montgomery Ave *NASDAQ: RBPAA*	Narberth	PA	19072	**800-417-5198**	610-668-4700
S & T Bancorp Inc 43 S 9th St *NASDAQ: STBA*	Indiana	PA	15701	**800-325-2265**	724-349-1800
Sandy Spring Bancorp Inc 17801 Georgia Ave *NASDAQ: SASR*	Olney	MD	20832	**800-399-5919**	301-774-6400
SCBT Financial Corp 950 John C Calhoun Dr *NASDAQ: SCBT*	Orangeburg	SC	29115	**800-277-2175**	803-534-2175
Seacoast Banking Corp of Florida PO Box 9012 *NASDAQ: SBCF*	Stuart	FL	34995	**800-706-9991**	772-287-4000
Shore Financial Corp 25020 Shore Pkwy *NASDAQ: SHBK*	Onley	VA	23418	**800-852-8176**	757-787-1335
Simmons First National Corp 501 Main St *NASDAQ: SFNCA*	Pine Bluff	AR	71601	**800-272-2102**	870-541-1000
Slade's Ferry Bancorp 100 Slade's Ferry Ave *NASDAQ: SFBC*	Somerset	MA	02726	**800-643-7537**	508-675-2121
Sobieski Bancorp Inc 105 E Jefferson Blvd Suite 800 *NASDAQ: SOBI*	South Bend	IN	46601	**888-321-8961**	574-239-7047
South Financial Group Inc 104 S Main St *NASDAQ: TSFG* ■ *Cust Svc	Greenville	SC	29601	**800-476-6400***	864-255-7900
SouthFirst Bancshares Inc 126 N Norton Ave *AMEX: SZB*	Sylacauga	AL	35150	**800-239-1492**	256-245-4365
Southside Bancshares Inc 1201 S Beckham Ave *NASDAQ: SBSI*	Tyler	TX	75701	**800-962-4284**	903-531-7111
SouthTrust Corp PO Box 2554 *NASDAQ: SOTR*	Birmingham	AL	35290	**800-239-2300**	205-254-5000
Southwest Bancorp Inc 608 S Main St *NASDAQ: OKSB*	Stillwater	OK	74074	**800-727-2230**	405-372-2230
Southwest Georgia Financial Corp 201 1st St SE *AMEX: SGB*	Moultrie	GA	31768	**888-683-2265**	229-985-1120
Sovereign Bancorp Inc PO Box 12646 *NYSE: SOV*	Reading	PA	19612	**800-683-4663**	610-320-8400
Sterling Bancshares Inc 2550 N Loop W Suite 200 *NASDAQ: SBIB*	Houston	TX	77092	**888-777-8735**	713-466-8300
Sterling Financial Corp 111 N Wall St *NASDAQ: STSA*	Spokane	WA	99201	**800-772-7791**	509-624-4114
Summit Bank Corp 4360 Chamblee Dunwoody Rd Suite 300 *NASDAQ: SBGA*	Atlanta	GA	30341	**800-752-4343**	770-454-0400
Sun Bancorp Inc 226 Landis Ave *NASDAQ: SNBC*	Vineland	NJ	08360	**800-691-7701**	856-691-7700
SunTrust Banks Inc 303 Peachtree St NE *NYSE: STI*	Atlanta	GA	30308	**800-688-7878**	404-588-7711
Susquehanna Bancshares Inc 24 N Cedar St PO Box 1000 *NASDAQ: SUSQ*	Lititz	PA	17543	**800-311-3182**	717-626-4721
Sussex Bancorp 399 Rt 23 S *AMEX: SBB*	Franklin	NJ	07416	**800-511-9900**	973-827-2914
SY Bancorp Inc 1040 E Main St *AMEX: SYI*	Louisville	KY	40206	**800-625-9066**	502-582-2571
Taylor Capital Group Inc 9550 W Higgins Rd 5th Fl *NASDAQ: TAYC*	Rosemont	IL	60018	**800-727-2265**	847-537-0020
TCF Financial Corp 801 Marquette Ave *NYSE: TCB*	Minneapolis	MN	55402	**800-533-1723**	612-661-6500
Team Financial Inc 8 W Peoria St Suite 200 PO Box 402 *NASDAQ: TFIN*	Paola	KS	66071	**800-880-6262**	913-294-9667
Teche Holding Co 211 Willow St *AMEX: TSH*	Franklin	LA	70538	**800-256-1500**	337-828-3212
Temple-Inland Financial Services Inc 1300 S Mopac Expy	Austin	TX	78746	**800-964-9420**	512-434-8000
TF Financial Corp 3 Penns Trail *NASDAQ: THRD*	Newtown	PA	18940	**888-918-4473**	215-579-4000
TIB Financial Corp 99451 Overseas Hwy *NASDAQ: TIBB*	Key Largo	FL	33037	**800-233-6330**	305-451-4660
Timberland Bancorp Inc PO Box 697 *NASDAQ: TSBK*	Hoquiam	WA	98550	**800-562-8761**	360-533-4747
Tower Financial Corp 116 E Berry St *NASDAQ: TOFC*	Fort Wayne	IN	46802	**877-427-7220**	260-427-7000
TriCo Bancshares 63 Constitution Dr *NASDAQ: TCBK*	Chico	CA	95973	**800-922-8742**	530-898-0300
Trustmark Corp PO Box 291 *NASDAQ: TRMK*	Jackson	MS	39205	**800-844-2000**	601-208-5111
UCBH Holdings Inc 555 Montgomery St *NASDAQ: UCBH*	San Francisco	CA	94111	**800-288-3899**	415-928-0700
UMB Financial Corp 1010 Grand Blvd *NASDAQ: UMBF*	Kansas City	MO	64106	**800-821-2171**	816-860-7000
Union Bankshares Corp 212 N Main St *NASDAQ: UBSH*	Bowling Green	VA	22427	**800-546-5031**	804-633-5031
Union Financial Bancshares Inc 203 W Main St *NASDAQ: UFBS*	Union	SC	29379	**888-427-9002**	864-427-9000
United Bancorp Inc 201 S 4th St *NASDAQ: UBCP*	Martins Ferry	OH	43935	**888-275-5566**	740-633-0445
United Bancshares Inc 100 S High St *NASDAQ: UBOH*	Columbus Grove	OH	45830	**800-837-8111**	419-659-2141

Bank Holding Companies (Cont'd)

Company	City	State	ZIP	Toll-Free	Phone
United Bankshares Inc 514 Market St *NASDAQ: UBSI*	Parkersburg	WV	26101	**800-345-4862**	304-424-8800
United Community Banks Inc 63 Hwy 515 *NASDAQ: UCBI*	Blairsville	GA	30512	**866-270-7200**	706-781-2265
United Community Financial Corp 275 Federal Plaza W *NASDAQ: UCFC*	Youngstown	OH	44503	**888-822-4751**	330-742-0500
United PanAm Financial Corp 3990 Westerly Pl Suite 200 *NASDAQ: UPFC*	Newport Beach	CA	92660	**800-833-1940**	949-224-1917
Unity Bancorp Inc 64 Old Hwy 22 *NASDAQ: UNTY*	Clinton	NJ	08809	**800-540-4790**	908-730-7630
University Bancorp Inc 959 Maiden Ln *NASDAQ: UNIB*	Ann Arbor	MI	48105	**888-944-5004**	734-741-5858
Unizan Financial Corp 220 Market Ave S *NASDAQ: UNIZ*	Canton	OH	44702	**866-235-7203**	330-438-1118
US Bancorp 800 Nicollet Mall *NYSE: USB*	Minneapolis	MN	55402	**800-872-2657**	651-466-3000
US Bancorp 8534 E Kemper Rd	Cincinnati	OH	45249	**800-582-9702**	513-247-0300
USB Holding Co Inc 100 Dutch Hill Rd *AMEX: UBH*	Orangeburg	NY	10962	**800-616-3491**	845-365-4600
Valley National Bancorp 1455 Valley Rd *NYSE: VLY*	Wayne	NJ	07470	**800-522-4100**	973-305-8800
Virginia Financial Group Inc 102 S Main St *NASDAQ: VFGI*	Culpeper	VA	22701	**800-825-4003**	540-825-4800
Wachovia Corp 301 S College St *NYSE: WB*	Charlotte	NC	28288	**800-922-4684**	704-374-6161
Washington Banking Co 321 SE Pioneer Way *NASDAQ: WBCO*	Oak Harbor	WA	98277	**800-290-6508**	360-679-3121
Washington Federal Inc 425 Pike St *NASDAQ: WFSL*	Seattle	WA	98101	**800-324-9375**	206-624-7930
Washington Trust Bancorp Inc 23 Broad St *NASDAQ: WASH*	Westerly	RI	02891	**800-475-2265**	401-348-1200
Webster City Federal Bancorp 820 Des Moines St *NASDAQ: WCFB*	Webster City	IA	50595	**866-263-0293**	515-832-3071
Webster Financial Corp PO Box 10305 WFD 730 *NYSE: WBS*	Waterbury	CT	06726	**800-325-2424**	
Wells Fargo & Co 420 Montgomery St 12th Fl *NYSE: WFC*	San Francisco	CA	94104	**800-869-3557**	
Wells Financial Corp 53 1st St SW	Wells	MN	56097	**800-944-5869**	507-553-3151
WesBanco Inc 1 Bank Plaza *NASDAQ: WSBC*	Wheeling	WV	26003	**800-328-3369**	304-234-9000
West Coast Bancorp 5335 Meadows Rd Suite 201 *NASDAQ: WCBO*	Lake Oswego	OR	97035	**800-895-3345**	503-684-0884
Westamerica Bancorp 4550 Mangels Blvd *AMEX: WABC*	Fairfield	CA	834585	**800-848-1088**	
Westcorp Inc 23 Pasteur *NYSE: WES*	Irvine	CA	92618	**800-289-8004**	949-727-1000
Westfield Financial Inc 141 Elm St *AMEX: WFD*	Westfield	MA	01085	**800-995-5734**	413-568-1911
Whitney Holding Corp 228 St Charles Ave *NASDAQ: WTNY*	New Orleans	LA	70130	**800-383-6538**	504-586-7272
Willow Grove Bancorp Inc Welsh & Norristown Rds *NASDAQ: WGBC*	Maple Glen	PA	19002	**800-647-5405**	215-646-5405
Wilmington Trust Corp 1100 N Market St 1st Fl *NYSE: WL*	Wilmington	DE	19890	**800-523-2378**	302-651-1000
Woronoco Bancorp Inc 31 Court St *AMEX: WRO*	Westfield	MA	01085	**888-972-4123**	413-568-9141
WSFS Financial Corp 838 N Market St *NASDAQ: WSFS*	Wilmington	DE	19801	**888-973-7226**	302-792-6000
WTB Financial Corp PO Box 2127	Spokane	WA	99210	**800-788-4578**	509-353-4122
Yardville National Bancorp 2465 Kuser Rd *NASDAQ: YANB*	Hamilton Square	NJ	08690	**888-443-5754**	609-585-5100
Zions Bancorp 1 S Main St Suite 1380 *NASDAQ: ZION*	Salt Lake City	UT	84111	**800-789-2265**	801-524-4787

355-3 Holding Companies (General)

Company	City	State	ZIP	Toll-Free	Phone
AG Edwards Inc 1 N Jefferson Ave *NYSE: AGE*	Saint Louis	MO	63103	**877-835-7877**	314-955-3000
Alliance Capital Management Holding LP 1345 Ave of the Americas *NYSE: AC*	New York	NY	10105	**800-221-5672**	212-969-1000
American Standard Cos Inc 1 Centennial Ave *NYSE: ASD*	Piscataway	NJ	08854	**800-223-0068**	732-980-6000
Ameritrade Holding Corp PO Box 3288 *NASDAQ: AMTD*	Omaha	NE	68103	**800-237-8692**	402-331-2744
AMETEK Inc 37 N Valley Rd Bldg 4 PO Box 1764 *NYSE: AME*	Paoli	PA	19301	**800-473-1286**	610-647-2121
Armstrong Holdings Inc 2500 Columbia Ave	Lancaster	PA	17603	**800-446-8066**	717-397-0611
Atlas World Group Inc 1212 St George Rd	Evansville	IN	47711	**800-252-8885**	812-424-2222
AuthentiDate Holding Corp 2165 Technology Dr *NASDAQ: ADAT*	Schenectady	NY	12308	**800-367-5906**	518-346-7799
BCE Inc 1000 de la Gauchetiere St W Suite 3700 *NYSE: BCE*	Montreal	QC	H3B4Y7	**888-932-6666**	514-870-8777
BET Holdings II Inc 1235 'W' St NE	Washington	DC	20018	**800-626-9911**	202-608-2000
Burlington Northern Santa Fe Corp 2650 Lou Menk Dr *NYSE: BNI*	Fort Worth	TX	76131	**800-795-2673**	
Cadmus Communications Corp 1801 Bayberry Ct Suite 200 *NASDAQ: CDMS*	Richmond	VA	23226	**800-476-2973**	804-287-5680
Cardinal Health Inc 7000 Cardinal Pl *NYSE: CAH*	Dublin	OH	43017	**800-234-8701**	614-757-5000
Carnival Corp 3655 NW 87th Ave *NYSE: CCL*	Miami	FL	33178	**800-438-6744**	305-599-2600
Cavs/Gund Arena Co 1 Center Ct	Cleveland	OH	44115	**800-332-2287**	216-420-2000

Company	City	State	ZIP	Toll-Free	Phone
CBRL Group Inc 305 Hartmann Dr *NASDAQ: CBRL*	Lebanon	TN	37087	**800-333-9566**	615-444-5533
Charles Schwab Corp 101 Montgomery St *NYSE: SCH*	San Francisco	CA	94104	**800-648-5300**	415-627-7000
Circuit City Stores Inc 9950 Mayland Dr *NYSE: CC*	Richmond	VA	23233	**800-251-2665**	804-527-4000
Clark Enterprises Inc 7500 Old Georgetown Rd	Bethesda	MD	20814	**800-800-2242**	301-657-7100
Conning Corp City Place II 185 Asylum St	Hartford	CT	06103	**888-266-6464**	860-527-1131
DeBartolo Edward J Corp 7620 Marcus St	Youngstown	OH	44512	**888-965-3532**	330-965-2000
Deluxe Corp 3680 N Victoria St *NYSE: DLX*	Shoreview	MN	55126	**800-328-7205**	651-483-7111
Diamond Holding Corp 150 Marr Ave	Marietta	GA	30060	**800-556-6211**	770-590-0152
Duchossois Industries Inc 845 Larch Ave	Elmhurst	IL	60126	**800-282-6225**	630-279-3600
Dwyer Group Inc 1010 N University Parks Dr	Waco	TX	76707	**800-490-7501**	254-745-2400
Edward J DeBartolo Corp 7620 Marcus St	Youngstown	OH	44512	**888-965-3532**	330-965-2000
Edwards AG Inc 1 N Jefferson Ave *NYSE: AGE*	Saint Louis	MO	63103	**877-835-7877**	314-955-3000
Elvis Presley Enterprises Inc 3734 Elvis Presley Blvd	Memphis	TN	38186	**800-238-2000**	901-332-3322
ESCO Technologies Inc 8888 Ladue Rd Suite 200 *NYSE: ESE*	Saint Louis	MO	63124	**888-622-3726**	314-213-7200
FedEx Corp 942 S Shady Grove Road *NYSE: FDX*	Memphis	TN	38120	**800-463-3339**	901-369-3600
First Albany Cos Inc 30 S Pearl St *NASDAQ: FACT*	Albany	NY	12207	**800-833-4168**	518-447-8500
G-I Holdings Inc 1361 Alps Rd	Wayne	NJ	07470	**800-766-3411**	973-628-4032
Goodman Holding Co 2550 N Loop W Suite 400	Houston	TX	77092	**888-593-9988**	713-861-2500
Hickory Tech Corp 221 E Hickory St *NASDAQ: HTCO*	Mankato	MN	56002	**800-326-5789**	507-387-1151
Hitch Enterprises Inc PO Box 1308	Guymon	OK	73942	**800-634-8678**	580-338-8575
Home Capital Group Inc 145 King St W Suite 1910 *TSE: HCG*	Toronto	ON	M5H1J8	**800-990-7881**	416-360-4663
Huffy Corp 225 Byers Rd	Miamisburg	OH	45342	**800-872-2453**	937-866-6251
iGATE Corp 1000 Commerce Dr Parkridge 1 *NASDAQ: IGTE*	Pittsburgh	PA	15275	**800-627-8323**	412-506-1131
Impreso Inc 652 Southwestern Blvd *NASDAQ: ZCOM*	Coppell	TX	75019	**800-521-8781**	972-462-0100
Investors Capital Holdings Ltd 230 Broadway Suite 205 *AMEX: ICH*	Lynnfield	MA	01940	**800-949-1422**	781-593-8565
JB Oxford Holdings Inc 9665 Wilshire Blvd 3rd Fl *NASDAQ: JBOH*	Beverly Hills	CA	90212	**800-799-8870**	310-777-8888
Kansas City Southern 427 W 12th St *NYSE: KSU*	Kansas City	MO	64105	**800-243-8624**	816-983-1303
Kidde plc 700 Nickerson Rd	Marlborough	MA	01752	**800-309-6336**	508-481-0700
Laidlaw International Inc 55 Shuman Blvd Suite 400 *NYSE: LI*	Naperville	IL	60563	**800-524-3529**	630-848-3000
Landmark Communications Inc 150 W Brambleton Ave	Norfolk	VA	23510	**800-446-2004**	757-446-2010
Lehman Brothers Holdings Inc 745 7th Ave *NYSE: LEH*	New York	NY	10019	**800-666-2388**	212-526-7000
Liberty Diversified Industries Inc 5600 Hwy 169 N	New Hope	MN	55428	**800-421-1270**	763-536-6600
Lone Star Technologies Inc 15660 N Dallas Pkwy Suite 500 *NYSE: LSS*	Dallas	TX	75248	**800-527-4615**	972-386-3981
McKesson Corp 1 Post St *NYSE: MCK*	San Francisco	CA	94104	**800-482-3784**	415-983-8300
Morgan Keegan Inc 50 N Front St 17th Fl	Memphis	TN	38103	**800-366-7426**	901-524-4100
NewMarket Corp 330 S 4th St *NYSE: NEU*	Richmond	VA	23219	**800-625-5191**	804-788-5000
NextHealth Inc 16600 N Lago del Oro Pkwy	Tucson	AZ	85739	**888-792-5800**	
North Pittsburgh Systems Inc 4008 Gibsonia Rd *NASDAQ: NPSI*	Gibsonia	PA	15044	**800-541-9225**	724-443-9600
Oaks Group 11451 Katy Fwy Suite 505	Houston	TX	77079	**800-277-9373**	713-722-8080
Omnicom Group Inc 437 Madison Ave *NYSE: OMC*	New York	NY	10022	**800-332-3336**	212-415-3600
Otter Tail Corp 215 S Cascade St *NASDAQ: OTTR*	Fergus Falls	MN	56537	**877-688-9288**	218-739-8200
Pacer International Inc 2300 Clayton Rd Suite 1200 *NASDAQ: PACR*	Concord	CA	94520	**877-917-2237**	925-887-1400
Price T Rowe Group Inc 100 E Pratt St *NASDAQ: TROW*	Baltimore	MD	21202	**800-638-7890**	410-345-2000
Pro-Dex Inc 151 E Columbine Ave *NASDAQ: PDEX*	Santa Ana	CA	92707	**800-562-6204**	714-241-4411
Pulte Homes Inc 100 Bloomfield Hills Pkwy Suite 300 *NYSE: PHM*	Bloomfield Hills	MI	48304	**800-777-8583**	248-647-2750
Revlon Inc 237 Park Ave *NYSE: REV*	New York	NY	10017	**800-473-8566**	212-527-4000
Sanders Morris Harris Group Inc 600 Travis St Suite 3100 *NASDAQ: SMHG*	Houston	TX	77002	**800-538-0020**	713-993-4610
Sandvik Inc 1702 Nevins Rd	Fair Lawn	NJ	07410	**800-726-3845**	201-794-5000
Sara Lee Corp 70 W Madison St *NYSE: SLE*	Chicago	IL	60602	**800-621-5235**	312-726-2600
Schuff International Inc 420 S 19th Ave	Phoenix	AZ	85009	**800-528-0513**	602-252-7787
Schwab Charles Corp 101 Montgomery St *NYSE: SCH*	San Francisco	CA	94104	**800-648-5300**	415-627-7000
Siebert Financial Corp 885 3rd Ave Suite 1720 *NASDAQ: SIEB*	New York	NY	10022	**877-327-8379**	212-644-2400
T Rowe Price Group Inc 100 E Pratt St *NASDAQ: TROW*	Baltimore	MD	21202	**800-638-7890**	410-345-2000
Taylor Corp 1725 Roe Crest Dr	North Mankato	MN	56003	**800-545-6620**	507-625-2828
Thomson Corp 1 Station Pl Metro Ctr	Stamford	CT	06902	**800-354-9706**	203-539-8000
Toyota Motor North America Inc 9 W 57th St Suite 4900	New York	NY	10019	**800-331-4331**	212-223-0303
Tredegar Corp 1100 Boulders Pkwy Suite 200 *NYSE: TG*	Richmond	VA	23225	**800-411-7441**	804-330-1000
Triarc Cos Inc 280 Park Ave 41st Fl *NYSE: TRY*	New York	NY	10017	**800-787-4272**	212-451-3000

Classified Section

				Toll-Free	Phone
Union Pacific Corp 1400 Douglas St *NYSE: UNP*	Omaha	NE	68179	**888-870-8777**	402-544-5000
USF Corp 8550 W Bryn Mawr Ave Suite 700	Chicago	IL	60631	**800-873-8680**	773-824-1000
UST Inc 100 W Putnam Ave *NYSE: UST*	Greenwich	CT	06830	**800-243-8536**	203-661-1100
Welch Allyn Inc 4341 State Street Rd *Cust Svc	Skaneateles Falls	NY	13153	**800-535-6663***	315-685-4100
Westar Energy Inc 818 S Kansas Ave *NYSE: WR* ■ *Cust Svc	Topeka	KS	66612	**800-794-4780***	785-575-6300
Williams Cos Inc 1 Williams Ctr *NYSE: WMB*	Tulsa	OK	74102	**800-945-5426**	918-573-2000
Wyeth Corp 5 Giralda Farms *NYSE: WYE*	Madison	NJ	07940	**800-322-3129**	973-660-5000
Xanser Corp 2435 N Central Expy Suite 700 *NYSE: XNR*	Richardson	TX	75080	**800-488-7973**	972-699-4000
Yellow Roadway Corp 10990 Roe Ave *NASDAQ: YELL*	Overland Park	KS	66211	**800-458-3323**	913-696-6100

355-4 Insurance Holding Companies

				Toll-Free	Phone
21st Century Holding Co 4161 NW 5th St *NASDAQ: TCHC*	Plantation	FL	33317	**800-333-3477**	954-581-9993
21st Century Insurance Group 6301 Owensmouth Ave *NYSE: TW*	Woodland Hills	CA	91367	**800-443-3100**	818-704-3700
AFLAC Inc 1932 Wynnton Rd *NYSE: AFL*	Columbus	GA	31999	**800-992-3522**	706-323-3431
AIG SunAmerica Inc 1 SunAmerica Ctr 37th Fl	Los Angeles	CA	90067	**800-445-7862**	310-772-6000
Alfa Corp PO Box 11000 *NASDAQ: ALFA*	Montgomery	AL	36191	**888-964-2532**	334-288-3900
Allmerica Financial Corp 440 Lincoln St *NYSE: AFC*	Worcester	MA	01653	**800-533-7881**	508-855-1000
Allstate Corp 2775 Sanders Rd Allstate Plaza *NYSE: ALL*	Northbrook	IL	60062	**800-255-7828**	847-402-5000
AMBAC Financial Group Inc 1 State Street Plaza 15th Fl *NYSE: ABK*	New York	NY	10004	**800-221-1854**	212-668-0340
American Family Insurance Group 6000 American Pkwy	Madison	WI	53783	**800-374-0008**	608-249-2111
American Fidelity Group 2000 N Classen Blvd	Oklahoma City	OK	73106	**800-654-8489**	405-523-2000
American Medical Security Group Inc 3100 AMS Blvd *NYSE: AMZ*	Green Bay	WI	54313	**800-232-5432**	920-661-1111
American Physicians Capital Inc (APCapital) 1301 N Hagadorn Rd *NASDAQ: ACAP*	East Lansing	MI	48823	**800-748-0465**	517-351-1150
American Physicians Service Group Inc 1301 Capitol of Texas Hwy S Suite C-300 *NASDAQ: AMPH*	Austin	TX	78746	**800-252-3628**	512-328-0888
American Re Corp 555 College Rd E	Princeton	NJ	08543	**800-255-5676**	609-243-4200
Americo Life Inc 1055 Broadway	Kansas City	MO	64105	**800-982-8144**	816-391-2000
Ameritas Acacia Mutual Holding Co 5900 O St	Lincoln	NE	68510	**800-311-7871**	402-467-1122
Ameritas Holding Co 5900 O St	Lincoln	NE	68510	**800-311-7871**	402-467-1122
AmerUs Group Co 699 Walnut St *NYSE: AMH*	Des Moines	IA	50309	**800-367-3669**	515-362-3600
AmVestors Financial Corp 555 S Kansas Ave	Topeka	KS	66603	**800-255-2405**	785-232-6945
APCapital (American Physicians Capital Inc) 1301 N Hagadorn Rd *NASDAQ: ACAP*	East Lansing	MI	48823	**800-748-0465**	517-351-1150
Argonaut Group Inc 10101 Reunion Pl Suite 500 *NASDAQ: AGII*	San Antonio	TX	78216	**800-470-7958**	210-321-8400
Assurant Group 11222 Quail Roost Dr	Miami	FL	33157	**800-852-2244**	305-253-2244
Assurant Inc 1 Chase Manhattan Plaza 41st Fl *NYSE: AIZ*	New York	NY	10005	**800-859-5676**	212-859-7000
Atlantic American Corp PO Box 105480 *NASDAQ: AAME*	Atlanta	GA	30348	**800-241-1439**	404-266-5500
Benfield Blanch Inc 500 N Akard St Suite 3700	Dallas	TX	75201	**866-236-3435**	214-756-7000
Ceres Group Inc 17800 Royalton Rd *NASDAQ: CERG*	Strongsville	OH	44136	**800-321-3997**	440-572-2400
Citizens Financial Corp 12910 Shelbyville Rd Suite 300 *NASDAQ: CNFL*	Louisville	KY	40243	**800-843-7752**	502-244-2420
Citizens Inc 400 E Anderson Ln *NYSE: CIA*	Austin	TX	78752	**800-880-5044**	512-837-7100
Commerce Group Inc 211 Main St *NYSE: CGI*	Webster	MA	01570	**800-221-1605**	508-943-9000
Conseco Inc 11825 N Pennsylvania St *NYSE: CNO*	Carmel	IN	46032	**800-541-2254**	317-817-6100
Cumberland Technologies Inc 4311 W Waters Ave Suite 401	Tampa	FL	33614	**800-723-0171**	813-885-2112
CUNA Mutual Group 5910 Mineral Point Rd	Madison	WI	53705	**800-937-2644**	608-238-5851
Donegal Group Inc 1195 River Rd *NASDAQ: DGICB*	Marietta	PA	17547	**800-877-0600**	717-426-1931
EMC Insurance Group Inc 717 Mulberry St *NASDAQ: EMCI*	Des Moines	IA	50309	**800-362-2227**	515-280-2511
Erie Indemnity Co 100 Erie Insurance Pl *NASDAQ: ERIE*	Erie	PA	16530	**800-458-0811**	814-870-2000
Everest Re Group Ltd 477 Martinsville Rd *NYSE: RE*	Liberty Corner	NJ	07938	**800-551-6501**	908-604-3000
Farm Family Holdings Inc PO Box 656 *Cust Svc	Albany	NY	12201	**800-843-3276***	518-431-5000
Federated Insurance Cos PO Box 328	Owatonna	MN	55060	**800-533-0472**	507-455-5200
Fidelity National Financial Inc 601 Riverside Avenue *NYSE: FNF*	Jacksonville	FL	32204	**800-815-3969**	888-934-3354
Financial Industries Corp 6500 River Place Blvd Bldg 1	Austin	TX	78730	**800-925-6000**	512-404-5000
Financial Security Assurance Holdings Ltd 350 Park Ave 13th Fl	New York	NY	10022	**800-846-4372**	212-826-0100
Foremost Corp of America PO Box 2450	Grand Rapids	MI	49501	**877-444-6678**	616-942-3000
FPIC Insurance Group Inc 225 Water St Suite 1400 *NASDAQ: FPIC*	Jacksonville	FL	32202	**800-221-2101**	904-354-2482
GAINSCO Inc 5400 Airport Fwy Suite A	Fort Worth	TX	76117	**800-438-4246**	817-336-2500
GEICO 1 GEICO Plaza	Washington	DC	20076	**800-824-5404**	301-986-2500
General Re Corp 695 E Main St Financial Ctr	Stamford	CT	06901	**800-431-9994**	203-328-5000
GMAC Insurance Holdings Inc 1 GMAC Insurance Plaza	Saint Louis	MO	63166	**877-468-3466**	314-493-8000
Great American Financial Resources Inc 250 E 5th St *NYSE: GFR*	Cincinnati	OH	45202	**800-438-3398**	513-333-5300
Harleysville Group Inc 355 Maple Ave *NASDAQ: HGIC*	Harleysville	PA	19438	**800-222-1981**	215-256-5000
Horace Mann Educators Corp 1 Horace Mann Plaza *NYSE: HMN*	Springfield	IL	62715	**800-999-1030**	217-789-2500
Industrial Alliance Insurance & Financial Services Inc 1080 Chemin Saint-Louis *TSE: IAG*	Sillery	QC	G1K7M3	**800-463-6236**	418-684-5182
ING Americas 5780 Powers Ferry Rd NW	Atlanta	GA	30327	**800-465-3330**	770-980-3300
InterContinental Life Corp PO Box 149138	Austin	TX	78714	**800-925-6000**	512-404-5000
Interstate Insurance Group 33 W Monroe St 12th Fl	Chicago	IL	60603	**800-255-2096**	312-346-6400
Interstate National Corp 33 W Monroe St 12th Fl	Chicago	IL	60603	**800-255-2096**	312-346-6400
Investors Title Co 121 N Columbia St *NASDAQ: ITIC*	Chapel Hill	NC	27514	**800-326-4842**	919-968-2200
Kansas City Life Insurance Co PO Box 219139 *NASDAQ: KCLI*	Kansas City	MO	64121	**800-821-6164**	816-753-7000
LandAmerica Financial Group Inc 101 Gateway Center Pkwy Gateway 1 *NYSE: LFG*	Richmond	VA	23235	**800-388-8822**	804-267-8000
Legal & General America Inc 1701 Research Blvd	Rockville	MD	20850	**800-638-8428**	301-279-4800
Lifetime Healthcare Cos 165 Court St	Rochester	NY	14647	**800-847-1200**	585-454-1700
Lincoln Financial Group 1500 Market St Centre Sq West Tower Suite 3900 *NYSE: LNC*	Philadelphia	PA	19102	**800-454-6265**	215-448-1400
Lincoln National Corp DBA Lincoln Financial Group 1500 Market St Centre Sq West Tower Suite 3900 *NYSE: LNC*	Philadelphia	PA	19102	**800-454-6265**	215-448-1400
Lykes Bros Inc PO Box 2879	Tampa	FL	33601	**800-243-0494**	813-223-3981
Mann Horace Educators Corp 1 Horace Mann Plaza *NYSE: HMN*	Springfield	IL	62715	**800-999-1030**	217-789-2500
Manulife Financial Corp 200 Bloor St E *NYSE: MFC*	Toronto	ON	M4W1E5	**800-795-9767**	416-926-3000
Markel Corp 4521 Highwoods Pkwy *NYSE: MKL*	Glen Allen	VA	23060	**800-446-6671**	804-747-0136
Meadowbrook Insurance Group Inc 26600 Telegraph Rd Suite 300 *NYSE: MIG*	Southfield	MI	48034	**800-482-2726**	248-358-1100
MEEMIC Holdings Inc 691 N Squirrel Rd Suite 100	Auburn Hills	MI	48326	**888-463-3642**	248-373-5700
MGIC Investment Corp 250 E Kilbourn Ave *NYSE: MTG*	Milwaukee	WI	53202	**800-558-9900**	414-347-6480
Midland Co PO Box 1256 *NASDAQ: MLAN*	Cincinnati	OH	45201	**800-543-2644**	513-943-7100
MIIX Group Inc 2 Princess Rd	Lawrenceville	NJ	08648	**800-257-6288**	609-896-2404
Mutual of Omaha Cos Mutual of Omaha Plaza	Omaha	NE	68175	**800-775-6000**	402-342-7600
Nationwide Financial Services Inc 5100 Rings Rd *NYSE: NFS*	Dublin	OH	43017	**800-321-9332**	
Nationwide Insurance Enterprise 1 Nationwide Plaza	Columbus	OH	43215	**800-882-2822**	614-249-7111
Navigators Group Inc 1 Penn Plaza 55th Fl *NASDAQ: NAVG*	New York	NY	10119	**800-496-2901**	212-244-2333
NCRIC Group Inc 1115 30th St NW *NASDAQ: NCRI*	Washington	DC	20007	**800-613-3615**	202-969-1866
NYMAGIC Inc 919 3rd Ave 10th Fl *NYSE: NYM*	New York	NY	10022	**800-367-0224**	212-551-0600
Ohio Casualty Corp 9450 Seward Rd *NASDAQ: OCAS*	Fairfield	OH	45014	**800-843-6446**	513-603-2400
Ohio National Financial Services Inc 1 Financial Way Suite 100	Cincinnati	OH	45242	**800-366-6654**	513-794-6100
Old Republic International Corp 307 N Michigan Ave *NYSE: ORI*	Chicago	IL	60601	**800-621-0365**	312-346-8100
Pacific Mutual Holding Co 700 Newport Ctr Dr	Newport Beach	CA	92660	**800-347-7787**	
Penn Treaty American Corp 3440 Lehigh St *NYSE: PTA*	Allentown	PA	18103	**800-222-3469**	610-965-2222
Philadelphia Consolidated Holding Corp 1 Bala Plaza Suite 100 *NASDAQ: PHLY*	Bala Cynwyd	PA	19004	**877-438-7459**	610-617-7900
PICO Holdings Inc 875 Prospect St Suite 301 *NASDAQ: PICO*	La Jolla	CA	92037	**888-389-3222**	858-456-6022
PMI Group Inc 3003 Oak Rd *NYSE: PMI*	Walnut Creek	CA	94597	**800-288-1970**	925-658-7878
Power Financial Corp 751 Victoria Sq	Montreal	QC	H2Y2J3	**800-890-7440**	514-286-7400
Preserver Group Inc 95 Rt 17 S	Paramus	NJ	07653	**800-242-0332**	201-291-2000
Presidential Life Corp 69 Lydecker St *NASDAQ: PLFE*	Nyack	NY	10960	**800-926-7599**	845-358-2300
Principal Financial Group Inc 711 High St *NYSE: PFG*	Des Moines	IA	50392	**800-986-3343**	515-247-5111
ProAssurance Corp 100 Brookwood Pl *NYSE: PRA*	Birmingham	AL	35209	**800-282-6242**	205-877-4400
Progressive Corp 6300 Wilson Mills Rd *NYSE: PGR*	Mayfield Village	OH	44143	**800-321-9843**	440-461-5000
Protective Life Corp PO Box 2606 *NYSE: PL*	Birmingham	AL	35202	**800-333-3418**	205-879-9230
Reinsurance Group of America Inc 1370 Timberlake Manor Pkwy *NYSE: RGA*	Chesterfield	MO	63017	**888-736-5445**	636-736-7000
RLI Corp 9025 N Lindbergh Dr *NYSE: RLI*	Peoria	IL	61615	**800-331-4929**	309-692-1000
SAFECO Corp 4333 Brooklyn Ave NE *NASDAQ: SAFC*	Seattle	WA	98185	**800-562-1018**	206-545-5000
Saint Paul Travelers Cos Inc 385 Washington St *NYSE: STA*	Saint Paul	MN	55102	**800-328-2189**	651-310-7911
SCPIE Holdings Inc 1888 Century Park E Suite 800 *NYSE: SKP*	Los Angeles	CA	90067	**800-962-5549**	310-551-5900

Insurance Holding Companies (Cont'd)

Company	City	State	ZIP	Toll-Free	Phone
Selective Insurance Group Inc 40 Wantage Ave *NASDAQ: SIGI*	Branchville	NJ	07890	**800-777-9656**	973-948-3000
Sentry Insurance Group 1800 N Point Dr	Stevens Point	WI	54481	**800-227-0201**	715-346-6000
Skandia US Holding Corp 1 Corporate Dr Tower 1	Shelton	CT	06484	**800-628-6039**	203-926-1888
Southwestern Life Holdings Inc 8710 Freeport Pkwy Suite 150	Irving	TX	75063	**800-792-4368**	
State Auto Financial Corp 518 E Broad St *NASDAQ: STFC*	Columbus	OH	43215	**800-444-9950**	614-464-5000
Summit Holding Southeast Inc PO Box 988	Lakeland	FL	33802	**800-282-7648**	863-665-6060
Sun Life Financial Inc 150 King St W *NYSE: SLF*	Toronto	ON	M5H1J9	**800-786-5433**	416-979-9966
Swiss Re Life & Health America Inc 175 King St	Armonk	NY	10504	**877-794-7773**	914-828-8500
Symons International Group Inc 4720 Kingsway Dr	Indianapolis	IN	46205	**800-342-5243**	317-259-6300
Trenwick Group Ltd 1 Canterbury Green	Stamford	CT	06901	**866-330-6719**	203-353-5500
Triad Guaranty Inc 101 S Stratford Rd *NASDAQ: TGIC*	Winston-Salem	NC	27104	**800-451-4872**	336-723-1282
UICI 9151 Grapevine Hwy *NYSE: UCI*	North Richland Hills	TX	76180	**800-527-5504**	817-255-5200
ULLICO Inc 8403 Colesville Rd	Silver Springs	MD	20910	**800-431-5425**	202-682-0900
United Fire Group 118 2nd Ave SE	Cedar Rapids	IA	52401	**800-332-7977**	319-399-5700
United Trust Group Inc 5250 S 6th St	Springfield	IL	62703	**800-323-0050**	217-241-6300
Unitrin Inc 1 E Wacker Dr *NYSE: UTR*	Chicago	IL	60601	**800-990-0546**	312-661-4600
Universal American Financial Corp 6 International Dr Suite 190 *NASDAQ: UHCO*	Rye Brook	NY	10573	**800-332-3377**	914-934-8300
Utica Mutual Insurance Co PO Box 530	Utica	NY	13503	**800-274-1914**	315-734-2000
Vesta Insurance Group Inc 3760 River Run Dr *NYSE: VTA*	Birmingham	AL	35243	**800-444-2955**	205-970-7000
Walshire Assurance Co PO Box 3709	York	PA	17402	**800-876-3350**	717-757-0000
Western & Southern Financial Group 400 Broadway	Cincinnati	OH	45202	**800-333-5222**	513-629-1800
WFR Mutual Insurance Holding Co 1526 K St	Lincoln	NE	68508	**800-869-0355**	402-476-6500
Zenith National Insurance Corp 21255 Califa St *NYSE: ZNT*	Woodland Hills	CA	91367	**800-448-4356**	818-713-1000

355-5 Utilities Holding Companies

Company	City	State	ZIP	Toll-Free	Phone
AGL Resources Inc 10 Peachtree Pl *NYSE: ATG* ■ *Cust Svc	Atlanta	GA	30309	**800-427-5463***	404-584-4000
Allegheny Energy Inc 800 Cabin Hill Dr *NYSE: AYE* ■ *Cust Svc	Greensburg	PA	15601	**800-255-3443***	724-837-3000
Ameren Corp 1901 Chouteau Ave *NYSE: AEE*	Saint Louis	MO	63103	**800-552-7583**	314-621-3222
American Electric Power Co Inc 1 Riverside Plaza *NYSE: AEP* ■ *Cust Svc	Columbus	OH	43215	**800-277-2177***	614-716-1000
Artesian Resources Corp 664 Churchmans Rd *NASDAQ: ARTNA*	Newark	DE	19702	**800-332-5114**	302-453-6900
Black Hills Corp 625 9th St *NYSE: BKH*	Rapid City	SD	57701	**800-843-8849**	605-721-1700
CenterPoint Energy Inc 1111 Louisiana St *NYSE: CNP* ■ *Cust Svc	Houston	TX	77002	**866-735-4268***	713-207-1111
Cinergy Corp 139 E 4th St *NYSE: CIN*	Cincinnati	OH	45202	**800-544-6900**	513-421-9500
Cleco Corp 1030 Donahue Ferry Rd *NYSE: CNL* ■ *Cust Svc	Pineville	LA	71360	**800-622-6537***	318-484-7400
CMS Energy Corp 1 Energy Plaza *NYSE: CMS*	Jackson	MI	49201	**800-477-5050**	517-788-0550
Conectiv 800 King St PO Box 231	Wilmington	DE	19899	**800-266-3284**	302-429-3018
Connecticut Water Service Inc 93 W Main St *NASDAQ: CTWS*	Clinton	CT	06413	**800-286-5700**	860-669-8636
Consolidated Edison Inc 4 Irving Pl *NYSE: ED*	New York	NY	10003	**800-752-6633**	212-460-4600
Dominion Resources Inc PO Box 26532 *NYSE: D*	Richmond	VA	23261	**800-552-4034**	804-775-2500
DPL Inc 1065 Woodman Dr *NYSE: DPL*	Dayton	OH	45432	**800-322-9244**	937-224-6000
DTE Energy Co 2000 2nd Ave *NYSE: DTE*	Detroit	MI	48226	**800-477-4747**	313-235-4000
Duquesne Light Holdings Inc 411 7th Ave *NYSE: DQE*	Pittsburgh	PA	15219	**877-393-7800**	412-393-6000
Dynegy Inc 1000 Louisiana St Suite 5800 *NYSE: DYN*	Houston	TX	77002	**800-922-2104**	713-507-6400
Edison International 2244 Walnut Grove Ave *NYSE: EIX*	Rosemead	CA	91770	**800-655-4555**	626-302-1212
Emera Inc 1894 Barrington St *TSE: EMA*	Halifax	NS	B3J2W5	**800-358-1995**	902-450-0507
Energen Corp 605 Richard Arrington Blvd N *NYSE: EGN*	Birmingham	AL	35203	**800-292-4005**	205-326-2700
Entergy Corp 639 Loyola Ave *NYSE: ETR*	New Orleans	LA	70113	**800-368-3749**	504-529-5262
E'Town Corp 600 South Ave	Westfield	NJ	07090	**800-272-1325**	908-654-1234
Exelon Corp 10 S Dearborn St 37th Fl *NYSE: EXC*	Chicago	IL	60690	**800-334-7661**	312-394-7398
First Energy 76 S Main St *NYSE: FE*	Akron	OH	44308	**800-646-0400**	
FirstEnergy Corp 76 S Main St *NYSE: FE*	Akron	OH	44308	**800-646-0400**	
IPALCO Enterprises Inc PO Box 1595	Indianapolis	IN	46206	**888-261-8222**	317-261-8261
Laclede Group Inc 720 Olive St *NYSE: LG*	Saint Louis	MO	63101	**800-887-4173**	314-342-0500
LG & E Energy Corp 220 W Main St	Louisville	KY	40202	**800-331-7370**	502-627-2000
National Fuel Gas Co 6363 Main St *NYSE: NFG* ■ *Cust Svc	Williamsville	NY	14221	**800-365-3234***	716-857-7000
National Grid USA 25 Research Dr	Westborough	MA	01582	**888-424-2113**	508-389-2000
Niagara Mohawk A National Grid Co 300 Erie Blvd W	Syracuse	NY	13202	**888-424-2113**	315-474-1511
NiSource Inc 801 E 86th Ave *NYSE: NI*	Merrillville	IN	46410	**800-464-7726**	219-853-5200
Northeast Utilities 197 Selden St *NYSE: NU*	Berlin	CT	06037	**800-286-5000**	860-665-5000
NSTAR 800 Boylston St *NYSE: NST*	Boston	MA	02199	**800-592-2000**	617-424-2000
OGE Energy Corp 321 N Harvey St *NYSE: OGE*	Oklahoma City	OK	73102	**800-272-9741**	405-553-3000
Peoples Energy Corp 130 E Randolph Dr *NYSE: PGL* ■ *Cust Svc	Chicago	IL	60601	**866-556-6001***	312-240-4000
PG & E Corp 1 Market St *NYSE: PCG*	San Francisco	CA	94105	**800-743-5000**	415-267-7000
Pinnacle West Capital Corp 400 N 5th St *NYSE: PNW*	Phoenix	AZ	85004	**800-457-2983**	602-250-1000
PPL Corp 2 N 9th St *NYSE: PPL*	Allentown	PA	18101	**800-342-5775**	610-774-5151
Progress Energy Inc 411 Fayetteville St *NYSE: PGN*	Raleigh	NC	27602	**800-452-2777**	919-546-6111
Questar Corp 180 E 100 South PO Box 45360 *NYSE: STR*	Salt Lake City	UT	84145	**800-323-5517**	801-324-5000
RGS Energy Group Inc 89 East Ave	Rochester	NY	14649	**888-253-8888**	585-546-2700
SCANA Corp 1426 Main St *NYSE: SCG*	Columbia	SC	29218	**800-251-7234**	803-748-3000
Sempra Energy Corp 101 Ash St *NYSE: SRE*	San Diego	CA	92101	**800-411-7343**	619-696-2000
Sierra Pacific Resources 6226 W Sahara Ave *NYSE: SRP*	Las Vegas	NV	89146	**800-331-3134**	702 367 5000
South Jersey Industries Inc Rt 54 1 S Jersey Plaza *NYSE: SJI* ■ *Cust Svc	Folsom	NJ	08037	**888-766-9900***	609-561-9000
Sprint Corp 6200 Sprint Pkwy	Overland Park	KS	66251	**800-829-0965**	
TNP Enterprises Inc 4100 International Plaza 9th Fl Tower 2	Fort Worth	TX	76109	**800-435-2822**	817-731-0099
UIL Holdings Corp 157 Church St *NYSE: UIL*	New Haven	CT	06510	**800-722-5584**	203-499-2000
UniSource Energy Corp 1 S Church Ave *NYSE: UNS*	Tucson	AZ	85701	**800-328-8853**	520-571-4000
Vectren Corp 20 NW 4th St *NYSE: VVC*	Evansville	IN	47708	**800-227-1376**	812-491-4000
WGL Holdings Inc 101 Constitution Ave NW *NYSE: WGL*	Washington	DC	20080	**800-752-7520**	703-750-2000
Wisconsin Energy Corp 231 W Michigan St *NYSE: WEC*	Milwaukee	WI	53203	**800-558-3303**	414-221-2345
WPS Resources Corp 700 N Adams St *NYSE: WPS*	Green Bay	WI	54307	**800-450-7260**	920-433-4901

356 HOME FURNISHINGS - WHOL

Company	City	State	ZIP	Toll-Free	Phone
AA Importing Co Inc 7700 Hall St *Cust Svc	Saint Louis	MO	63147	**800-325-0602***	314-383-8800
Acme Linen Co Inc 5136 E Triggs St	City of Commerce	CA	90022	**800-255-2263**	323-266-4000
Adleta Co 1645 Diplomat Dr Suite 200	Carrollton	TX	75006	**800-423-5382**	972-620-5600
Bishop Distributing Co 5200 36th St SE *Cust Svc	Grand Rapids	MI	49512	**800-748-0363***	616-942-9734
Boston Warehouse Trading Corp 59 Davis Ave	Norwood	MA	02062	**888-923-2982**	781-769-8550
CDC Distributors 7235 Progress St PO Box 1267	Holland	OH	43528	**800-537-0154**	419-866-3567
Clarence House Imports Ltd Inc 3010 Westchester Ave	Purchase	NY	10577	**800-803-2890**	914-701-0100
Dealers Supply Co Inc 112 S Duke St	Durham	NC	27715	**800-776-6655**	919-383-7451
Decorative Crafts Inc 50 Chestnut St	Greenwich	CT	06830	**800-431-4455**	203-531-1500
Decorize Inc 1938 E Phelps *AMEX: DCZ*	Springfield	MO	65802	**877-669-3326**	417-879-3326
Dimock Gould & Co 190 22nd St	Moline	IL	61265	**800-274-4013**	309-797-0650
Fabricut Inc 9303 E 46th St	Tulsa	OK	74145	**800-999-8200**	918-622-7700
Florstar Sales Inc 1325 N Mittel Blvd	Wood Dale	IL	60191	**800-942-6285**	630-595-7500
Hoboken Floors PO Box 43205	Atlanta	GA	30336	**877-356-2687**	404-629-1425
HW Baker Linen Co Inc 500 Corporate Dr	Mahwah	NJ	07430	**800-631-0122**	201-825-2000
Interstate Supply Co 4445 Gustine Ave	Saint Louis	MO	63116	**800-324-3535**	314-481-2222
James G Hardy & Co 352 7th Ave Suite 1223	New York	NY	10001	**800-847-4076**	212-689-6680
JJ Haines & Co Inc 6950 Aviation Blvd	Glen Burnie	MD	21061	**800-922-9248**	410-760-4040
Kinder-Harris Inc 203 E 22nd St	Stuttgart	AR	72160	**800-688-8839**	870-673-1518
Koval Marketing Inc 11208 47th Ave W	Mukilteo	WA	98275	**800-972-4782**	425-347-4249
Larson Distributing Co Inc 5925 N Broadway	Denver	CO	80216	**800-736-3750**	303-296-7253
Longust Distributing Inc 2432 W Birchwood Ave	Mesa	AZ	85202	**800-352-0521**	480-820-6244
Louis Bornstein & Co 321 Washington St *Sales	Somerville	MA	02143	**800-842-1111***	617-776-3555
M Block & Sons Inc 5020 W 73rd St	Bedford Park	IL	60638	**800-621-8845**	708-728-8400
McKee Floor Covering Inc 2785 Hwy 55	Eagan	MN	55121	**800-328-2020**	651 454 1700
Milson & Louis 83 Ames St	Brockton	MA	02302	**877-835-6457**	508-559-0770
Momeni Inc 36 E 31st St 2nd Fl	New York	NY	10016	**800-536-6778**	212-532-9577
Mottahedeh & Co 225 5th Ave	New York	NY	10010	**800-242-3050**	212-685-3050
Orders Distributing Co Inc 1 Whitlee Ct *Cust Svc	Greenville	SC	29607	**888-867-3377***	864-288-4220
Peking Handicraft Inc 1388 San Mateo Ave	South San Francisco	CA	94080	**800-872-6888**	650-871-3788
Readers Wholesale Distributors Inc 1201 Naylor St	Houston	TX	77002	**800-766-0001**	713-224-8300
Revere Mills Inc 3000 S River Rd	Des Plaines	IL	60018	**800-367-8258**	847-759-6800
Sobel Westex Inc 2670 Southwestern Ave	Las Vegas	NV	89109	**800-282-3041**	702-735-4973
Sound Floor Coverings Inc 18375 Olympic Ave S *Orders	Tukwila	WA	98188	**800-288-2289***	206-575-1181
Source Northwest Inc 8329 216th St SE *Cust Svc	Woodinville	WA	98072	**800-426-1321***	360-512-3535
Stark Carpet Corp 979 3rd Ave 11th Fl	New York	NY	10022	**800-223-1224**	212-752-9000
Wanke Cascade Co 6330 N Cutter Cir	Portland	OR	97217	**800-365-5053**	503-289-8609
WestPoint Stevens Inc Sales Div 1185 Ave of the Americas *Cust Svc	New York	NY	10036	**800-533-8229***	212-930-2000
WMF/USA 85 Price Pkwy	Farmingdale	NY	11735	**800-999-6347**	631-293-3990
Zak Designs Inc 1603 S Garfield Rd	Spokane	WA	99201	**800-331-1089**	509-244-0555

357 HOME FURNISHINGS STORES

SEE ALSO Department Stores; Furniture Stores

Company	City	State	ZIP	Toll-Free	Phone
Altmeyer Home Stores Inc Rt 22 461 William Penn Hwy	Delmont	PA	15626	**800-394-6628**	724-468-3434
Bazaar Co 801 3rd Ave	Huntington	WV	25701	**877-764-0305**	304-522-0305
Bed Bath & Beyond Inc 650 Liberty Ave *NASDAQ: BBBY*	Union	NJ	07083	**800-462-3966**	908-688-0888
Besco Electric Supply Co 711 S 14th St	Leesburg	FL	34748	**800-541-6618**	352-787-4542
Bridge Kitchenware Inc 214 E 52nd St	New York	NY	10022	**800-274-3435**	212-688-4220
Bromberg & Co Inc 123 N 20th St	Birmingham	AL	35203	**800-633-4616**	205-252-0221
Calvert Retail LP PO Box 302 W Rockland Rd Suite A	Montchanin	DE	19710	**800-747-7224**	302-622-8811
Chef's Catalog 5950 Cowell Blvd *Cust Svc	Irving	TX	75039	**800-884-2433***	972-969-3100
Container Store 500 Freeport Pkwy	Coppell	TX	75019	**800-733-3532**	972-538-6000
Cooking.com 2850 Ocean Park Blvd Suite 310	Santa Monica	CA	90405	**800-663-8810**	310-450-3270
Cost Plus Inc 200 4th St *NASDAQ: CPWM*	Oakland	CA	94607	**800-777-4665**	510-893-7300
Dansk International Designs Ltd 100 Lenox Dr *Cust Svc	Lawrenceville	NJ	08648	**800-293-2675***	609-896-2800
Design Within Reach Inc 225 Bush St 20th Fl *NASDAQ: DWRI*	San Francisco	CA	94104	**800-944-2233**	415-676-6500
EBSCO Industries Inc Military Service Co Div PO Box 1943	Birmingham	AL	35201	**800-255-3722**	205-991-6600
Fina Michael C Inc 545 5th Ave	New York	NY	10017	**800-289-3462**	212-557-2500
Foreside Co 33 Hutcherson Dr *Cust Svc	Gorham	ME	04038	**800-359-8380***	207-854-4000
FurnitureFind.com Inc 311 W Jefferson Blvd	South Bend	IN	46601	**800-362-7632**	574-299-2700
Garden Ridge Corp 19411 Atrium Pl Suite 170	Houston	TX	77084	**800-216-4887**	281-579-7901
Geary's Stores Inc 351 N Beverly Dr	Beverly Hills	CA	90210	**800-243-2797**	310-273-4741
Georgia Lighting Supply Co 530 14th St NW	Atlanta	GA	30318	**800-282-0220**	404-875-4759
Granite City Electric Supply Co 19 Quincy Ave	Quincy	MA	02169	**800-850-9400**	617-472-6500
Habitat 3801 Old Seward Hwy Suite 5 University Ctr	Anchorage	AK	99503	**800-770-1856**	907-561-1856
Hammacher Schlemmer & Co 303 W Erie St	Chicago	IL	60610	**800-233-4800**	312-664-8170
International Cutlery Ltd 367 Madison Ave	New York	NY	10017	**866-487-6164**	212-924-7300
Jackalope Pottery 2820 Cerrillos Rd	Santa Fe	NM	87507	**800-753-7757**	505-471-8539
Kitchen Collection Inc 71 E Water St	Chillicothe	OH	45601	**800-292-9150**	740-773-9150
Linens 'n Things Inc 6 Brighton Rd *NYSE: LIN*	Clifton	NJ	07015	**866-568-7378**	973-778-1300
Marburn Stores Inc 225 Walker St *Cust Svc	Cliffside Park	NJ	07010	**888-627-2876***	201-943-0222
Michael C Fina Inc 545 5th Ave	New York	NY	10017	**800-289-3462**	212-557-2500
Mikasa Inc 1 Mikasa Dr *Cust Svc	Secaucus	NJ	07096	**800-833-4681***	201-867-9210
Military Service Co Div EBSCO Industries Inc PO Box 1943	Birmingham	AL	35201	**800-255-3722**	205-991-6600
Plej's Linen Supermarket 454 S Anderson Rd Suite 600	Rock Hill	SC	29730	**800-838-4599**	803-324-4284
Pratesi Linens Inc 381 Park Ave S Suite 1223	New York	NY	10016	**800-332-6925**	212-689-3150
Replacements Ltd PO Box 26029	Greensboro	NC	27420	**800-737-5223**	336-697-3000
Royal Doulton USA Inc 200 Cottontail Ln	Somerset	NJ	08873	**800-682-4462**	732-356-7880
Seattle Lighting Fixture Co 222 2nd Ave Ext S *Cust Svc	Seattle	WA	98104	**800-689-1000***	206-622-1962
Shreve Crump & Low Co Inc 330 Boylston St	Boston	MA	02116	**800-225-7088**	617-267-9100
Spring Crest Window Fashions 4375 Prado Rd Unit 104	Corona	CA	92880	**800-552-5523**	951-340-2293
Sultan & Sons 650 SW 9th Terr	Pompano Beach	FL	33069	**800-299-6601**	954-782-6600
Sur La Table 5701 6th Ave S Suite 486	Seattle	WA	98108	**800-243-0852**	206-682-7175
Villeroy & Boch Tableware Ltd 5 Vaughn Dr Suite 303	Princeton	NJ	08540	**800-845-5376**	609-734-7800
Waterford Wedgwood USA Inc 1330 Campus Pkwy *Cust Svc	Wall	NJ	07719	**888-938-7911***	732-938-5800
Welcome Home Inc 309 Raleigh St	Wilmington	NC	28412	**800-348-4088**	910-791-4312
William Glen Inc 2651 El Paseo Ln	Sacramento	CA	95821	**800-842-3322**	916-485-3000
Williams-Sonoma Inc 3250 Van Ness Ave *NYSE: WSM* ■ *Cust Svc	San Francisco	CA	94109	**800-541-1262***	415-421-7900
Williamsburg Pottery Factory Inc Rt 60 W	Lightfoot	VA	23090	**800-768-8379**	757-564-3326
Z Gallerie Inc 1855 W 139th St	Gardena	CA	90249	**800-358-8288**	310-527-6811
Zabar's & Co Inc 2245 Broadway	New York	NY	10024	**800-697-6301**	212-787-2000

358 HOME HEALTH SERVICES

SEE ALSO Hospices

Company	City	State	ZIP	Toll-Free	Phone
Alacare Home Health Services Inc 4752 Hwy 280 E	Birmingham	AL	35242	**800-852-4724**	205-981-8000
Almost Family Inc 9510 Ormsby Station Rd Suite 300 *NASDAQ: AFAM*	Louisville	KY	40223	**800-845-6987**	502-899-5355
Amedisys Inc 11100 Mead Rd Suite 300 *NASDAQ: AMED*	Baton Rouge	LA	70816	**800-467-2662**	225-292-2031
American HomePatient Inc 5200 Maryland Way Suite 400	Brentwood	TN	37027	**800-890-7271**	615-221-8884
Apria Healthcare Group Inc 26220 Enterprise Ct *NYSE: AHG*	Lake Forest	CA	92630	**800-647-5404**	949-639-2000
Arcadia Health Care 26777 Central Park Blvd Suite 200	Southfield	MI	48076	**800-733-8427**	248-352-7530
Aroostook Home Health Services 22 Birdseye Ave	Caribou	ME	04736	**877-688-9977**	207-492-8290
Bayada Nurses Home Care Specialists 290 Chester Ave	Moorestown	NJ	08057	**800-305-3000**	856-231-1000
Building Blocks Pediatric Home Health Services 18003 Sky Park Cir Suite B	Irvine	CA	92614	**800-346-9490**	949-752-9595
CareSouth Homecare Professionals 3626 Walton Way Ext Suite 2	Augusta	GA	30909	**800-241-3363**	706-855-5533
Carter Healthcare 4301 Will Rogers Pkwy Suite 100	Oklahoma City	OK	73108	**888-951-1112**	405-947-7700
Continucare Corp 80 SW 8th St Suite 2350 *AMEX: CNU*	Miami	FL	33130	**888-350-7515**	305-350-7515
Coram Healthcare Corp 1675 Broadway Suite 900	Denver	CO	80202	**800-267-2642**	303-292-4973
Gentiva Health Services Inc 3 Huntington Quadrangle Suite 200S *NASDAQ: GTIV*	Melville	NY	11747	**866-436-8487**	631-501-7000
HealthEssentials Solutions Inc 9510 Ormsby Station Rd Suite 101	Louisville	KY	40223	**877-453-5307**	502-429-7778
Help At Home Inc 17 N State St 14th Fl	Chicago	IL	60602	**800-422-1755**	312-762-9680
Home Care Supply 2155 IH-10 E	Beaumont	TX	77701	**800-871-1386**	409-835-3939
Home Health Corp of America Inc 620 Freedom Business Center Suite 105	King of Prussia	PA	19406	**800-872-5230**	610-205-2440
Home Helpers Inc 10700 Montgomery Rd	Cincinnati	OH	45242	**800-216-4196**	513-563-8339
Home Instead Inc 604 N 109th Ct	Omaha	NE	68154	**888-484-5759**	402-498-4466
Home IV Care & Nutritional Service PO Box 700	Stuarts Draft	VA	24477	**800-552-6576**	540-932-3000
HOMECALL Inc 92 Thomas Johnson Dr Suite 150	Frederick	MD	21702	**800-444-0097**	301-663-8818
Hospice Atlanta-Visiting Nurse Health System 1244 Park Vista Dr	Atlanta	GA	30319	**800-287-7849**	404-869-3000
Interim HealthCare Inc 1601 Sawgrass Corporate Pkwy	Sunrise	FL	33323	**800-338-7786**	954-858-6000
Kelly Home Care Services Inc 999 W Big Beaver Rd	Troy	MI	48084	**800-937-5355**	248-362-4444
Legum Home Health Care PO Box 700	Stuarts Draft	VA	24477	**800-552-6576**	540-932-3000
LHC Group LLC 420 W Pinhook Rd Suite A *NASDAQ: LHCG*	Lafayette	LA	70503	**800-489-1307**	337-233-1307
Lincare Holdings Inc 19387 US 19 N *NASDAQ: LNCR*	Clearwater	FL	33764	**800-284-2006**	727-530-7700
Maxim Healthcare Services 7080 Samuel Morse Dr	Columbia	MD	21046	**800-796-2946**	410-910-1500
Medical Center at Princeton Home Care 208 Bunn Dr	Princeton	NJ	08540	**800-584-4153**	609-497-4900
Medical Services of America Inc 171 Monroe Ln	Lexington	SC	29072	**800-845-5850**	803-957-0500
National Health Care Affiliates Inc 651 Delaware Ave	Buffalo	NY	14202	**800-999-6422**	716-881-4425
Option Care Inc 485 Half Day Rd Suite 300 *NASDAQ: OPTN*	Buffalo Grove	IL	60089	**800-879-6137**	847-465-2100
Pediatric Services of America Inc 310 Technology Pkwy *NASDAQ: PSAI*	Norcross	GA	30092	**800-950-1580**	770-441-1580
Personal-Touch Home Care Inc 22215 Northern Blvd	Bayside	NY	11361	**800-937-4747**	718-468-4747
RoTech Medical Corp 4506 LB McLeod Rd Suite F	Orlando	FL	32811	**800-357-3835**	407-841-2115
Sentara Home Care Services 535 Independence Pkwy Suite 200	Chesapeake	VA	23320	**888-461-5649**	757-382-4980
Sta-Home Health Agency Inc 406 Briarwood Dr Bldg 200	Jackson	MS	39206	**800-782-4663**	601-956-5100
Tender Loving Care Staff Builders 1983 Marcus Ave Suite 200	Lake Success	NY	11042	**800-444-4633**	516-358-1000
Trinity Home Care 114-02 15th Ave	College Point	NY	11356	**877-687-7369**	718-961-1634
Ultra Care Home Medical 2001 Janice Ave	Melrose Park	IL	60160	**800-222-9444**	773-804-7400
Visiting Health Professionals 68 Sweeten Creek Rd	Asheville	NC	28803	**800-627-1533**	828-252-2255
Visiting Nurse Corp of Colorado 390 Grant St	Denver	CO	80203	**888-862-9693**	303-744-6363
VITAS Healthcare Corp 100 S Biscayne Blvd Suite 1500	Miami	FL	33131	**800-950-9200**	305-374-4143
We Care Health Services Inc 151 Bloor St W Suite 602	Toronto	ON	M5S1S4	**888-429-3227**	416-922-7601

359 HOME IMPROVEMENT CENTERS

SEE ALSO Construction Materials

Company	City	State	ZIP	Toll-Free	Phone
Alaska Industrial Hardware Inc 2192 Viking Dr	Anchorage	AK	99501	**800-478-7201**	907-276-7201
Arlington Coal & Lumber Co Inc 41 Park Ave	Arlington	MA	02476	**800-649-8101**	781-643-8100
Aubuchon WE Co Inc 95 Aubuchon Dr	Westminster	MA	01473	**800-282-4393**	978-874-0521
BGE Home Products & Services Inc 7161 Columbia Gateway	Columbia	MD	21046	**888-243-4663**	410-720-6619
Carter Cos 601 Tallmadge Rd	Kent	OH	44240	**877-586-2374**	330-673-6100
Carter-Jones Lumber Co 601 Tallmadge Rd	Kent	OH	44240	**877-586-2374**	330-673-6100
Carter Lumber Co Inc 601 Tallmadge Rd	Kent	OH	44240	**877-586-2374**	330-673-6100
Contractor's Warehouse 3222 Winona Way Suite 201	North Highlands	CA	95660	**800-789-8060**	916-331-5934
Dixieline Lumber Co Inc 3250 Sports Arena Blvd	San Diego	CA	92110	**800-443-7386**	619-224-4120
EBS Building Supplies 261 State St	Ellsworth	ME	04605	**800-244-7134**	207-667-7134
EXPO Design Center 2455 Paces Ferry Rd *Cust Svc	Atlanta	GA	30339	**800-553-3199***	770-433-8211
Home Depot Inc 2455 Paces Ferry Rd *NYSE: HD* ■ *Cust Svc	Atlanta	GA	30339	**800-553-3199***	770-433-8211
Lowe's Cos Inc 1605 Curtis Bridge Rd *NYSE: LOW*	North Wilkesboro	NC	28697	**800-890-5932**	336-658-4000
Lumbermens 3773 Martin Way E Bldg A	Olympia	WA	98506	**800-842-8256**	360-456-1880
MarJam Supply Co Inc 20 Rewe St	Brooklyn	NY	11211	**800-462-7526**	718-388-6465
National Home Centers Inc 1106 N Old Missouri Rd	Springdale	AR	72765	**800-540-0529**	479-756-1700
National Lumber 71 Maple St	Mansfield	MA	02048	**800-370-9663**	508-339-8020
Northern Tool & Equipment Co 2800 Southcross Dr W	Burnsville	MN	55306	**800-221-0516**	952-894-9510
Ray Mart Inc PO Box 5548	Beaumont	TX	77726	**800-341-7788**	409-835-4744

Company / Address	City	State	ZIP	Toll-Free	Phone
Spenard Builders Supply Inc 840 K St Suite 200	Anchorage	AK	99501	**800-478-3141**	907-261-9120
Sutherland Lumber Co 4000 Main St	Kansas City	MO	64111	**800-821-2252**	816-756-3000
WE Aubuchon Co Inc 95 Aubuchon Dr	Westminster	MA	01473	**800-282-4393**	978-874-0521

360 HOME INSPECTION SERVICES

Company / Address	City	State	ZIP	Toll-Free	Phone
AmeriSpec Inc 889 Ridgelake Blvd	Memphis	TN	38120	**800-426-2270**	901-820-8500
BrickKicker Inc 849 N Ellsworth St	Naperville	IL	60563	**800-821-1820**	630-420-9900
HomeTeam Inspection Service 575 Chamber Dr	Milford	OH	45150	**800-598-5297**	513-831-1300
HouseMaster 421 W Union Ave	Bound Brook	NJ	08805	**800-526-3939**	732-469-6565
InspecTech Inc 925 N Point Pkwy Suite 400	Alpharetta	GA	30005	**800-285-3001**	
National Property Inspections Inc 11620 Arbor St Suite 100	Omaha	NE	68144	**800-333-9807**	402-333-9807
Pillar to Post Inc 13902 N Dale Mabry Hwy Suite 300	Tampa	FL	33618	**800-294-5591**	813-962-4461
World Inspection Network International Inc 6500 6th Ave NW	Seattle	WA	98117	**800-967-8127**	206-728-8100

361 HOME SALES & OTHER DIRECT SELLING

Company / Address	City	State	ZIP	Toll-Free	Phone
1-800-Mattress 31-10 48th Ave	Long Island City	NY	11101	**800-999-1000**	718-472-1200
4Life Research 9850 S 300 West *Sales	Sandy	UT	84070	**800-776-9898***	801-562-3600
Amway Corp 7575 Fulton St E	Ada	MI	49355	**800-253-6500**	616-787-6000
Avon Products Inc 1251 Ave of the Americas *NYSE: AVP* ■ *Cust Svc	New York	NY	10020	**800-367-2866***	212-282-5000
BeautiControl Cosmetics Inc 2121 Midway Rd	Carrollton	TX	75006	**800-232-8841**	972-458-0601
Color Me Beautiful Inc 14900 Conference Ctr Dr Suite 450	Chantilly	VA	20151	**800-265-6763**	703-471-6400
Colorado Prime Foods 500 Bi-County Blvd Suite 400	Farmingdale	NY	11735	**800-365-2404**	631-694-1111
Conklin Co Inc 551 Valley Park Dr	Shakopee	MN	55379	**800-888-8838**	952-445-6010
Cutco Cutlery Corp 1116 E State St	Olean	NY	14760	**800-828-0448**	
Dial-A-Mattress Operating Corp DBA 1-800-Mattress 31-10 48th Ave	Long Island City	NY	11101	**800-999-1000**	718-472-1200
Discovery Toys Inc 6400 Brisa St *Cust Svc	Livermore	CA	94550	**800-426-4777***	925-606-2600
Electrolux LLC 5956 Sherry Ln Suite 1500 *Cust Svc	Dallas	TX	75225	**800-243-9078***	214-361-4300
Floor Coverings International 5182 Old Dixie Hwy Suite B *Sales	Forest Park	GA	30297	**800-955-4324***	404-361-5047
Fuller Brush Co 1 Fuller Way *Cust Svc	Great Bend	KS	67530	**800-438-5537***	620-792-1711
Golden Neo-Life Diamite International 3500 Gateway Blvd	Fremont	CA	94538	**800-432-5848**	510-651-0405
Goldshield Elite 1501 Northpoint Pkwy Suite 100	West Palm Beach	FL	33407	**866-218-8142**	
Jafra Cosmetics International 2451 Townsgate Rd	Westlake Village	CA	91361	**800-551-2345**	805-449-3000
Mannatech Inc 600 S Royal Ln Suite 200 *NASDAQ: MTEX*	Coppell	TX	75019	**800-281-4469**	972-471-7400
Mary Kay Inc 16251 Dallas Pkwy *Cust Svc	Addison	TX	75001	**800-627-9529***	972-687-6300
Melaleuca Inc 3910 S Yellowstone Hwy *Sales	Idaho Falls	ID	83402	**800-282-3000***	208-522-0700
Midwest Marketing Inc 239 Hwy 61 PO Box 125	Bloomsdale	MO	63627	**800-662-7538**	573-483-2577
Noevir USA Inc 1095 SE Main St	Irvine	CA	92614	**800-872-8817**	949-660-1111
North American Membership Group Inc 12301 Whitewater Dr Suite 260	Minnetonka	MN	55343	**800-634-8598**	952-936-9333
Nutrition for Life International 10235 W Little York Suite 300	Houston	TX	77040	**800-800-7377**	713-460-1976
Pampered Chef Ltd 1 Pampered Chef Ln	Addison	IL	60101	**800-266-5562**	630-261-8900
Periodical Publishers Service Bureau 1 N Superior St	Sandusky	OH	44870	**800-654-9204**	419-626-0623
Pola USA Inc 251 E Victoria St	Carson	CA	90746	**800-222-6564**	310-527-9696
Princess House Inc 470 Miles Standish Blvd *Sales	Taunton	MA	02780	**800-622-0039***	508-823-0711
Reliv International Inc 136 Chesterfield Industrial Blvd *NASDAQ: RELV*	Chesterfield	MO	63005	**800-735-4887**	636-537-9715
Rocher Yves Inc 50 Briarhollow Rd Suite 500-W	Houston	TX	77027	**800-222-6222**	713-626-2255
Shaklee Corp 4747 Willow Rd	Pleasanton	CA	94588	**800-742-5533**	925-924-2000
Specialty Merchandise Corp 9447 De Soto Ave *Orders	Chatsworth	CA	91311	**800-877-7621***	818-998-3300
Stanley Home Products 1 Fuller Way *Cust Svc	Great Bend	KS	67530	**800-628-9032***	620-792-1711
Success Motivation International Inc 5000 Lakeshore Dr *Sales	Waco	TX	76710	**888-391-0050***	254-776-9966
Sunrider International 1625 Abalone Ave *Orders	Torrance	CA	90501	**888-278-6743***	310-781-3808
Tupperware Corp PO Box 2353 *NYSE: TUP* ■ *Cust Svc	Orlando	FL	32802	**800-772-4001***	407-847-3111
UndercoverWear Inc 30 Commerce Way Suite 2	Tewksbury	MA	01876	**800-733-0007**	978-851-8580
Unicity Network Inc 1201 N 800 East	Orem	UT	84097	**800-748-4334**	801-226-2224
University Subscription Service 1213 Butterfield Rd	Downers Grove	IL	60515	**800-876-1213**	630-960-3233
Vector Marketing Co 1116 E State St	Olean	NY	14760	**800-828-0448**	
Vorwerk USA Co LP 1335 Bennette Dr Suite 111	Longwood	FL	32750	**888-867-9375**	407-830-9988
Watkins Inc PO Box 5570	Winona	MN	55987	**800-243-9423**	507-457-3300
World Book Inc 233 N Michigan Ave 20th Fl	Chicago	IL	60601	**800-255-1750**	312-729-5800
Yves Rocher Inc 50 Briarhollow Rd Suite 500-W	Houston	TX	77027	**800-222-6222**	713-626-2255

362 HORSE BREEDERS

SEE ALSO Agricultural Services - Livestock Improvement Services

Company / Address	City	State	ZIP	Toll-Free	Phone
Glencrest Farm PO Box 4468	Midway	KY	40347	**800-903-0136**	859-233-7032
King Ranch Inc PO Box 1090	Kingsville	TX	78364	**800-375-6411**	361-592-6411

363 HORTICULTURAL PRODUCTS GROWERS

SEE ALSO Garden Centers; Seed Companies

Company / Address	City	State	ZIP	Toll-Free	Phone
Aldershot of New Mexico Inc 3905 Meadow Lark Ln	Mesilla Park	NM	88047	**888-768-6867**	505-523-8621
Alex R Masson Inc 12819 198th St	Linwood	KS	66052	**800-444-6210**	913-301-3281
Altman Specialty Plants Inc 3742 Bluebird Canyon Rd	Vista	CA	92084	**800-348-4881**	760-744-8191
B & H Flowers Inc 3516 Foothill Rd	Carpinteria	CA	93014	**800-682-5666**	805-684-4550
Battlefield Farms Inc 23190 Clarks Mountain Rd	Rapidan	VA	22733	**800-722-0744**	540-854-6485
Bay City Flower Co Inc PO Box 186 *Sales	Half Moon Bay	CA	94019	**800-399-5858***	650-726-5535
Blue Ridge Growers Inc 21409 Germanna Hwy	Stevensburg	VA	22741	**800-368-2030**	540-399-1636
Brand Flowers Inc 5300 Foothill Rd	Carpinteria	CA	93013	**800-549-0089**	805-684-5531
California Pajarosa PO Box 684	Watsonville	CA	95077	**800-565-6374**	831-722-6374
Color Spot Nurseries Inc 2575 Olive Hill Rd	Fallbrook	CA	92028	**800-554-4065**	760-695-1430
Costa Nursery Farms Inc 22290 SW 162nd Ave	Miami	FL	33170	**800-327-7074**	305-247-3248
Cuthbert Greenhouses Inc 4900 Hendron Rd	Groveport	OH	43125	**800-321-1939**	614-836-3866
Dallas Johnson Greenhouse Inc 2802 Twin City Dr	Council Bluffs	IA	51501	**800-445-4794**	712-366-0407
Dan Schantz Farm & Greenhouses LLC 8025 Spinnerstown Rd	Zionsville	PA	18092	**800-451-3064**	610-967-2181
DeLeon's Bromeliads Co 13745 SW 216th St	Goulds	FL	33170	**800-448-8649**	305-238-6028
Delray Plants Inc 5700 Sims Rd	Delray Beach	FL	33484	**800-854-5393**	561-498-3200
Dramm & Echter Inc 1150 Quail Gardens Dr	Encinitas	CA	92024	**800-854-7021**	760-436-0188
Ecke Paul Ranch Inc 441 Saxony Rd	Encinitas	CA	92024	**800-468-3253**	760-753-1134
El Modeno Gardens 11911 Jeffrey Rd	Irvine	CA	92602	**800-776-8111**	949-559-1234
Engelmann Hermann Greenhouses Inc 2009 Marden Rd	Apopka	FL	32703	**800-722-6435**	407-886-3434
Ever-Bloom Inc 4701 Foothill Rd	Carpinteria	CA	93013	**800-388-8112**	805-684-5566
Fernlea Nurseries Inc 294 Buck Blunt Rd	Quincy	FL	32351	**800-428-9729**	850-442-6188
Floral Plant Growers LLC 1133 Ebenezer Church Rd	Rising Sun	MD	21911	**800-637-2107**	410-658-6100
Garden State Growers 99 Locust Grove Rd	Pittstown	NJ	08867	**800-288-8484**	908-730-8888
Green Circle Growers Inc 15650 SR-511	Oberlin	OH	44074	**800-533-4266**	440-775-1411
Green Valley Floral Co 24999 Potter Rd	Salinas	CA	93908	**800-228-1255**	831-424-7691
Greenleaf Nursery Co 28406 Hwy 82	Park Hill	OK	74451	**800-331-2982**	918-457-5172
Harts Nursery of Jefferson Inc 4049 Jefferson-Scio Rd	Jefferson	OR	97352	**800-356-9335**	541-327-3366
Hermann Engelmann Greenhouses Inc 2009 Marden Rd	Apopka	FL	32703	**800-722-6435**	407-886-3434
Hines Horticulture Inc 12621 Jeffrey Rd *NASDAQ: HORT*	Irvine	CA	92620	**800-444-4499**	949-559-4444
Imperial Nurseries Inc 90 Salmon Brook St	Granby	CT	06035	**800-343-3132**	860-653-4541
Johannes Flowers Inc 4998 Foothill Rd	Carpinteria	CA	93013	**800-365-9476**	805-684-5686
Johnsen Nurseries Inc 2897 Freedom Blvd	Watsonville	CA	95076	**800-322-6529**	831-728-4205
Johnson Dallas Greenhouse Inc 2802 Twin City Dr	Council Bluffs	IA	51501	**800-445-4794**	712-366-0407
Kerry's Bromeliad Nursery Inc 21840 SW 258th St	Homestead	FL	33031	**800-331-9127**	305-247-7096
Kitayama Brothers Inc 13239 Weld County Rd 4	Brighton	CO	80601	**800-829-5323**	303-659-8005
Knox Nursery Inc 4349 N Hiawassee Rd	Orlando	FL	32818	**800-441-5669**	407-293-3721
Kocher Flower Growers 6211 Yarrow Dr Suite B	Carlsbad	CA	92009	**800-821-4421**	760-607-9100
Kurt Weiss Greenhouses Inc 95 Main St	Center Moriches	NY	11934	**800-858-2555**	631-878-2500
Mainland Nursery Inc J50 W Turner Rd	Lodi	CA	95242	**800-366-4048**	209-334-1680
Masson Alex R Inc 12819 198th St	Linwood	KS	66052	**800-444-6210**	913-301-3281
Matsui Nursery Inc 1645 Old Stage Rd	Salinas	CA	93908	**800-793-6433**	831-422-6433
Metrolina Greenhouses Inc 16400 Huntersville-Concord Rd	Huntersville	NC	28078	**800-222-2905**	704-875-1371
Mid American Growers Inc RR 1 Box 36	Granville	IL	61326	**800-892-6888**	815-339-6831
Milgro Nursery LLC 340 Rosewood Ave Suite J	Camarillo	CA	93010	**800-645-4769**	805-383-3616
Monrovia Nursery Growers 18331 E Foothill Blvd	Azusa	CA	91702	**800-999-9321**	626-334-9321
Mount Arbor Nurseries 201 E Ferguson Rd *Sales	Shenandoah	IA	51601	**800-831-4125***	712-246-4250
Mountain States Plants Corp 1421 W Gentile St	Layton	UT	84041	**800-326-4490**	801-544-8878
Neal Robinson Wholesale Greenhouses 975 Robindale Rd	Brownsville	TX	78523	**800-874-2740**	956-831-4656
Nurserymen's Exchange 475 6th St	San Francisco	CA	94103	**800-227-5630**	415-392-0078
Ocean Breeze International 3910 N Via Real	Carpinteria	CA	93013	**888-715-8888**	805-684-1747
Oglevee Ltd 152 Oglevee Ln	Connellsville	PA	15425	**800-437-4733**	724-628-8360
Pajaro Valley Greenhouses Inc 214 Lewis Rd *Cust Svc	Watsonville	CA	95077	**800-538-5922***	831-722-2773
Panzer Nursery Inc 17980 SW Baseline Rd	Beaverton	OR	97006	**888-212-5327**	503-645-1185
Parks Brothers Farm Inc 6733 Parks Rd	Van Buren	AR	72956	**800-334-5770**	479-474-1125
Paul Ecke Ranch Inc 441 Saxony Rd	Encinitas	CA	92024	**800-468-3253**	760-753-1134
Robinson Neal Wholesale Greenhouses 975 Robindale Rd	Brownsville	TX	78523	**800-874-2740**	956-831-4656
Rockwell Farms Inc 332 Rockwell Farms Rd	Rockwell	NC	28138	**800-635-6576**	704-279-5589
Rocky Mountain Growers 14095 Peyton Hwy	Peyton	CO	80831	**800-687-3001**	719-749-2510
Rod McLellan Co 159 Homer Ave	Palo Alto	CA	94301	**800-467-2443**	650-330-8990
Schantz Dan Farm & Greenhouses LLC 8025 Spinnerstown Rd	Zionsville	PA	18092	**800-451-3064**	610-967-2181
Silver Terrace Nurseries Inc 501 North St	Pescadero	CA	94060	**800-323-5977**	650-879-2110
Speedling Inc 4300 Old 41 Hwy S PO box 7238	Sun City	FL	33586	**800-771-2543**	813-645-3221

Classified Section

Name / Address	City	State	Zip	Toll-Free	Phone
Sun Valley Floral Farms Inc 3160 Upper Bay Rd	Arcata	CA	95521	**800-747-0396**	707-826-8700
Sunshine Foliage World 2060 Steve Roberts Special	Zolfo Springs	FL	33890	**800-872-0607**	863-735-0501
Ulery Greenhouse Co 2625 Old Clifton Rd *Cust Svc	Springfield	OH	45501	**800-722-5143***	937-325-5543
Van Wingerden International Inc 1856 Jeffress Rd	Fletcher	NC	28732	**800-226-3597**	828-891-4116
Weiss Kurt Greenhouses Inc 95 Main St	Center Moriches	NY	11934	**800-858-2555**	631-878-2500
Wenke Greenhouses Co 2525 N 30th St	Kalamazoo	MI	49048	**800-311-7209**	269-349-7882
Westerlay Roses Inc 3504 Via Real	Carpinteria	CA	93013	**800-959-7673**	805-684-5411
Yoder Brothers Inc 115 3rd St SE	Barberton	OH	44203	**800-321-9573**	330-745-2143
Young's Plant Farm Inc 863 Airport Rd	Auburn	AL	36830	**800-304-8609**	334-821-3500

364 HOSE & BELTING - RUBBER OR PLASTICS

SEE ALSO Automotive Parts & Supplies - Mfr

Name / Address	City	State	Zip	Toll-Free	Phone
American Hose & Industrial Rubber Inc 2545 N Broad St	Philadelphia	PA	19132	**800-533-1134**	215-223-7710
Ammeraal Beltech USA 7501 N St Louis Ave *Cust Svc	Skokie	IL	60076	**800-323-4170***	847-673-6720
Apache Hose & Belting Co Inc 4805 Bowling St SW *Cust Svc	Cedar Rapids	IA	52406	**800-553-5455***	319-365-0471
Aquapore Moisture Systems Inc 610 S 80th Ave	Tolleson	AZ	85353	**800-426-8419**	623-936-8083
Armstrong Industrial Hose Products LLC 96 Stokes Ave	Trenton	NJ	08638	**800-275-6547**	609-883-3030
Atco Rubber Products Inc 7101 Atco Dr	Fort Worth	TX	76118	**800-877-3828**	817-595-2894
Belting Industries Co Inc 20 Boright Ave	Kenilworth	NJ	07033	**800-843-2358**	908-272-8591
Carlisle Power Transmission Products Inc 1 Prestige Pl	Miamisburg	OH	45342	**866-773-2926**	937-229-8000
Chapin Watermatics Inc 740 Water St	Watertown	NY	13601	**800-242-7467**	315-782-1170
Chase-Walton Elastomers Inc 29 Apsley St	Hudson	MA	01749	**800-448-6289**	978-562-0085
Chemprene Inc 483 Fishkill Ave	Beacon	NY	12508	**800-431-9981**	845-831-2800
Coilhose Pneumatics Inc 19 Kimberly Rd	East Brunswick	NJ	08816	**800-526-2100**	732-390-8480
Colorite Plastics Co 101 Railroad Ave	Ridgefield	NJ	07657	**800-631-1577**	201-941-2900
Cooper Tire & Rubber Co 701 Lima Ave *NYSE: CTB* ■ *Cust Svc	Findlay	OH	45840	**800-854-6288***	419-423-1321
Fenner Drives 311 W Stiegel St *Sales	Manheim	PA	17545	**800-243-3374***	717-665-2421
Fenner Dunlop Conveyor Belting Americas 10125 S Tryon St *Cust Svc	Charlotte	NC	28273	**800-922-1735***	704-943-5669
Flexaust Co 1510 Armstrong Rd	Warsaw	IN	46580	**800-343-0428**	574-267-7909
Flexfab LLC 1699 W M-43 Hwy	Hastings	MI	49058	**800-331-0003**	269-945-2433
Flexon Industries Corp 1 Flexon Plaza	Newark	NJ	07114	**800-327-4673**	973-824-5527
Habasit ABT Inc 150 Industrial Park Rd	Middletown	CT	06457	**800-522-2358**	860-632-2211
Habasit Belting Inc 1400 Clinton St	Buffalo	NY	14206	**800-325-1585**	716-824-8484
HBD Industries Inc 1301 W Sandusky Ave	Bellefontaine	OH	43311	**800-543-8070**	937-593-5010
Hi-Tech Hose Inc 400 E Main St	Georgetown	MA	01833	**800-451-5985**	978-352-2077
Legg Co Inc 325 E 10th St *Sales	Halstead	KS	67056	**800-835-1003***	316-835-2256
Lockwood Products Inc 5615 SW Willow Ln	Lake Oswego	OR	97035	**800-423-1625**	503-635-8113
Mulhern Belting Inc 148 Bauer Dr	Oakland	NJ	07436	**800-253-6300**	201-337-5700
NewAge Industries Inc Plastics Technology Group 145 James Way	Southampton	PA	18966	**800-506-3924**	215-526-2300
Novaflex Hose Inc 449 Trollingwood Rd *Cust Svc	Haw River	NC	27258	**800-334-4270***	336-578-2161
Parker Fluid Connectors Group 6035 Parkland Blvd	Cleveland	OH	44124	**800-272-7537**	216-896-3000
Ro-Lab American Rubber Co Inc 8830 W Linne Rd	Tracy	CA	95304	**888-276-2993**	209-836-0965
Salem-Republic Rubber Co 475 W California Ave	Sebring	OH	44672	**800-686-4199**	330-938-9801
Snap-Tite Inc 8325 Hessinger Dr	Erie	PA	16509	**800-458-0409**	814-838-5700
Sparks Belting Co 3800 Stahl Dr SE	Grand Rapids	MI	49546	**800-451-4537**	616-949-2750
Standco Industries Inc 2701 Clinton Dr	Houston	TX	77020	**800-231-6018**	713-224-6311
Titeflex Corp 603 Hendee St	Springfield	MA	01139	**800-765-2525**	413-739-5631
Unaflex Inc 3901 NE 12th Ave	Pompano Beach	FL	33064	**800-327-1286**	954-943-5002
Voss Belting & Specialty Co 6965 N Hamlin Ave	Lincolnwood	IL	60712	**800-323-3935**	847-673-8900

365 HOSPICES

SEE ALSO Hospitals - Specialty Hospitals

Name / Address	City	State	Zip	Toll-Free	Phone
Hospice of the Valley PO Box 2745	Decatur	AL	35602	**877-260-3657**	256-350-5585
Wiregrass Hospice PO Drawer 2127	Dothan	AL	36302	**800-626-1101**	334-794-9101
Banner Home Care & Hospice 1325 N Fiesta Blvd Suite 1	Gilbert	AZ	85233	**800-293-6989**	480-497-5535
Carondelet Hospice Services 1802 W Saint Mary's Rd	Tucson	AZ	85745	**800-979-9290**	520-205-7700
Hospice Family Care 310 S Williams Blvd Suite 210	Tucson	AZ	85711	**800-839-3288**	520-790-9299
Hospice of Arizona 2222 W Northern Ave Suite A100	Phoenix	AZ	85021	**800-890-9046**	602-678-1313
RTA Hospice 511 S Mudsprings Rd	Payson	AZ	85541	**800-450-9558**	928-472-6340
Sun Health Hospice Care Services & Residence 12740 N Plaza del Rio Blvd	Peoria	AZ	85381	**800-858-9428**	623-815-2800
Tucson Medical Center Hospice 5301 E Grant Rd	Tucson	AZ	85712	**800-526-5353**	520-324-2438
Baptist Hospice 11900 Colonel Glenn Rd Suite 2000	Little Rock	AR	72210	**800-900-7474**	501-202-7474
Hospice Home Care 1501 N University Ave Suite 340	Little Rock	AR	72207	**800-479-2503**	501-666-9697
Peachtree Hospice 4300 Rogers Ave Suuite 33	Fort Smith	AR	72903	**800-752-0444**	479-494-0100
Washington Regional Hospice 34 W Colt Square Dr Suite 1	Fayetteville	AR	72703	**888-611-1094**	479-463-1161
Citrus Valley Hospice 820 N Phillips Ave	West Covina	CA	91791	**877-422-7301**	626-859-2263
Elizabeth Hospice 150 W Crest St	Escondido	CA	92025	**800-797-2050**	760-737-2050
Heartland Home Health Care & Hospice 901 Sun Valley Blvd Suite 220	Concord	CA	94520	**800-675-2273**	925-674-8610
Hinds Hospice 1616 W Shaw Ave Suite B-6	Fresno	CA	93711	**800-400-4677**	559-226-5683
Hospice of the Central Coast 2 Upper Ragsdale Bldg D Suite 210	Monterey	CA	93941	**800-492-3037**	831-649-7750
Kaiser Walnut Creek Hospice 200 Muir Rd	Martinez	CA	94553	**800-418-8300**	925-229-7800
Livingston Memorial Visiting Nurse Assn Hospice 1996 Eastman Ave Suite 101	Ventura	CA	93003	**800-540-0543**	805-642-1608
Midpeninsula Pathways Hospice 585 N Mary Ave	Sunnyvale	CA	94085	**800-900-0811**	408-773-5900
Optimal Hospice 4800 Stockdale Hwy Suite 215	Bakersfield	CA	93309	**888-597-6115**	661-387-1527
Pathways Home Health & Hospice 585 N Mary Ave	Sunnyvale	CA	94085	**888-755-7855**	408-773-5900
Ramona VNA & Hospice 890 W Stetson Ave Suite A	Hemet	CA	92543	**800-588-7862**	951-658-9288
San Diego Hospice 4311 3rd Ave	San Diego	CA	92103	**800-696-9474**	619-688-1600
TrinityCare Hospice 18331 Gridley Rd Suite F	Cerritos	CA	90703	**866-210-1055**	562-809-2150
UCD Hospice 3630 Business Dr Suite G	Sacramento	CA	95820	**800-268-9232**	916-734-2458
VITAS Healthcare Corp of California 16030 Ventura Blvd Suite 600	Encino	CA	91436	**800-757-4242**	818-760-2273
VITAS Healthcare Corp of California 220 Commerce Suite 100	Irvine	CA	92802	**800-486-6157**	714-921-2273
VITAS Healthcare Corp of California 9655 Granite Ridge Dr Suite 300	San Diego	CA	92123	**800-966-8705**	858-499-8901
VITAS Healthcare Corp of California 990 W 190th St Suite 120	Torrance	CA	90502	**800-966-7757**	310-324-2273
VITAS Healthcare Corp of San Gabriel Cities 598 S Grand Ave	Covina	CA	91724	**800-966-8709**	626-918-2273
VNA & Hospice of Northern California 1900 Powell St Suite 300	Emeryville	CA	94608	**888-600-7744**	510-450-8596
VNA & Hospice of Southern California 150 W 1st St Suite 270	Claremont	CA	91711	**888-357-3574**	909-624-3574
Hospice & Palliative Care of Western Colorado 2754 Compass Dr Suite 377	Grand Junction	CO	81506	**866-310-8900**	970-241-2212
Hospice of Northern Colorado 2726 W 11th Street Rd	Greeley	CO	80634	**800-564-5563**	970-352-8487
Connecticut Hospice 100 Double Beach Rd	Branford	CT	06405	**800-315-7654**	203-315-7500
Hospice of Southeastern Connecticut Inc PO Box 902	Uncasville	CT	06382	**877-654-4035**	860-848-5699
Compassionate Care Hospice of Delaware 5610 Kirkwood Hwy	Wilmington	DE	19808	**800-219-0092**	302-683-1000
Hospice Care of the District of Columbia 4401 Connecticut Ave Suite 700	Washington	DC	20008	**800-869-2136**	202-347-1700
Bigbend Hospice 1723 Mahan Ctr Blvd	Tallahassee	FL	32308	**800-772-5862**	850-878-5310
Good Shepherd Hospice of Mid-Florida Inc 105 Arneson Ave	Auburndale	FL	33823	**800-753-1880**	863-297-1880
Gulfside Regional Hospice Inc 6117 Trouble Creek Rd	New Port Richey	FL	34653	**800-561-4883**	727-845-5707
Hernando Pasco Hospice 12107 Majestic Blvd	Hudson	FL	34667	**800-486-8784**	727-863-7971
Hope Hospice 9470 HealthPark Cir	Fort Myers	FL	33908	**800-835-1673**	239-482-4673
Hospice by the Sea 1531 W Palmetto Park Rd	Boca Raton	FL	33486	**800-633-2577**	561-395-5031
Hospice of Lake & Sumter Inc 12300 Lane Park Rd	Tavares	FL	32778	**888-728-6234**	352-343-1341
Hospice of North Central Florida Inc 4200 NW 90th Blvd	Gainesville	FL	32606	**800-727-1889**	352-378-2121
Hospice of Palm Beach County 5300 East Ave	West Palm Beach	FL	33407	**800-287-4722**	561-848-5200
Hospice of Southwest Florida 5955 Rand Blvd	Sarasota	FL	34238	**800-959-4291**	941-923-5822
Hospice of the Treasure Coast 2500 Virginia Ave Suite 202	Fort Pierce	FL	34981	**800-375-4682**	772-465-0660
Hospice of Volusia/Flagler 3800 Woodbriar Trail	Port Orange	FL	32129	**800-272-2717**	386-322-4701
Lifepath Hospice 3010 W Azeele St	Tampa	FL	33609	**800-209-2200**	813-877-2200
VITAS Healthcare Corp of Central Florida 5151 Adanson St Suite 200	Orlando	FL	32804	**800-390-5370**	407-875-0028
VITAS Innovative Hospice Care 100 S Biscayne Blvd Suite 1500	Miami	FL	33131	**800-938-4827**	305-374-4143
VNA Hospice of IRC 1110 35th Ln	Vero Beach	FL	32960	**800-749-5760**	772-567-5551
Wuesthoff Brevard Hospice 8060 Spyglass Hill Rd	Viera	FL	32940	**800-259-2007**	321-253-2222
Heyman HospiceCare PO Box 163	Rome	GA	30162	**800-324-1078**	706-232-0807
Hospice Atlanta-Visiting Nurse Health System 1244 Park Vista Dr	Atlanta	GA	30319	**800-287-7849**	404-869-3000
Hospice of Central Georgia 3780 Eisenhower Pkwy	Macon	GA	31206	**800-211-1084**	478-633-5660
Hospice of Southwest Georgia 818 Gordon Ave	Thomasville	GA	31792	**800-290-6567**	229-227-5520
Hospice Savannah Inc PO Box 13190	Savannah	GA	31416	**888-355-4911**	912-355-2289
United Hospice-Lilburn 3945 Lawrenceville Hwy	Lilburn	GA	30047	**800-544-4798**	770-925-1143
VITAS Hospice Care 5411 N Land Dr	Atlanta	GA	30342	**800-938-4827**	404-874-8313
Advocate Hospice 1441 Branding Ave Suite 310	Downers Grove	IL	60515	**800-564-2025**	630-963-6800
Blessing Hospice PO Box 7005	Quincy	IL	62305	**800-382-8833**	217-228-5521
Carle Hospice 206-A W Anthony Dr	Champaign	IL	61822	**800-610-5547**	217-383-3151
Harbor Light Hospice 800 Roosevelt Rd Bldg C Suite 206	Glen Ellyn	IL	60137	**800-419-0542**	630-942-0100
Hospice of Northeastern Illinois 410 S Hager Ave	Barrington	IL	60010	**800-425-4444**	847-381-5599
Hospice of Southern Illinois 305 S Illinois St	Belleville	IL	62220	**800-233-1708**	618-235-1703
Joliet Area Community Hospice 250 Water Stone Cir	Joliet	IL	60431	**800-360-1817**	815-740-4104
Unity Hospice 439 E 31st St Suite 213	Chicago	IL	60616	**888-949-1188**	312-949-1188
VITAS Healthcare Corp 600 Holiday Plaza Dr Suite 200	Matteson	IL	60443	**800-938-4827**	708-748-8777
Hospice & Palliative Care of Southern Indiana 624 E Market St	New Albany	IN	47150	**800-895-5633**	812-945-4596
Hospice of South Central Indiana 2626 E 17th St	Columbus	IN	47201	**800-841-4938**	812-376-5813
Saint Vincent Hospice 8450 N Payne Rd Suite 100	Indianapolis	IN	46268	**888-780-7284**	317-338-4040
VistaCare Hospice 6431 S East St	Indianapolis	IN	46227	**800-480-9408**	317-788-0300
Cedar Valley Hospice 2101 Kimball Ave Suite 401	Waterloo	IA	50702	**800-617-1972**	319-272-2002
Hospice of Central Iowa 401 Railroad Pl	West Des Moines	IA	50265	**800-806-9934**	515-274-3400
Hospice of Siouxland 224 4th St	Sioux City	IA	51101	**800-383-4545**	712-233-4100

Classified Section

				Toll-Free	Phone
Hospice Home Health of Olathe Medical Center 20333 W 151st St TDB 2 Suite 301	Olathe	KS	66061	**800-467-4451**	913-324-8515
Hynes Harry Memorial Hospice 313 S Market St	Wichita	KS	67202	**800-767-4965**	316-265-9441
Midland Hospice Care 200 SW Frazier Cir	Topeka	KS	66606	**800-491-3691**	785-232-2044
Community Hospice 1538 Central Ave	Ashland	KY	41101	**800-926-6184**	606-329-1890
Hospice of Lake Cumberland 100 Pkwy Dr	Somerset	KY	42503	**800-937-9556**	606-679-4389
Hospice of Southern Kentucky 1027 Broadway Ave	Bowling Green	KY	42104	**800-344-9479**	270-782-3402
Hospice of the Bluegrass 2312 Alexandria Dr	Lexington	KY	40504	**800-876-6005**	859-276-5344
Jessamine County Hospice PO Box 873	Nicholasville	KY	40356	**800-279-0750**	859-887-2696
Lourdes Homecare & Hospice 2855 Jackson St	Paducah	KY	42003	**800-870-7460**	270-444-2262
Hospice of Acadiana 2600 Johnston St Suite 200	Lafayette	LA	70503	**800-738-2226**	337-232-1234
Hospice of Baton Rouge 9063 Siegen Ln	Baton Rouge	LA	70810	**800-349-8833**	225-767-4673
Hospice of Greater New Orleans 3616 S I-10 Service Rd W Suite 109	Metairie	LA	70001	**800-960-3016**	504-838-8944
Hospice of South Louisiana 7932 Park Ave	Houma	LA	70364	**800-256-1611**	985-851-4273
HealthReach Homecare & Hospice PO Box 1568	Waterville	ME	04903	**800-427-1127**	207-873-1127
Hospice of the Chesapeake 445 Defense Hwy	Annapolis	MD	21401	**800-745-6132**	410-987-2003
Seasons Hospice 7008 Security Blvd Suite 300	Baltimore	MD	21244	**888-523-6000**	410-594-9100
Baystate VNA & Hospice 50 Maple St	Springfield	MA	01102	**800-249-0290**	413-781-2317
Good Samaritan Hospice 310 Allston St	Brighton	MA	02135	**800-425-8282**	617-566-6242
Hospice Care 41 Montvale Ave	Stoneham	MA	02180	**866-279-7103**	781-279-4100
Hospice of Community Visiting Nurse Agency 141 Park St	Attleboro	MA	02703	**800-220-0110**	508-222-0118
Merrimack Valley Hospice 360 Merrimack St Bldg 9	Lawrence	MA	01843	**800-933-5593**	978-552-4000
Old Colony Hospice 14 Page Terr	Stoughton	MA	02072	**800-370-1322**	781-341-4145
VNA Hospice Alliance 168 Industrial Dr	Northampton	MA	01060	**800-244-1060**	413-584-1060
Arbor Hospice & Home Care 2366 Oak Valley Dr	Ann Arbor	MI	48103	**888-992-2273**	734-662-5999
Community Hospice & Home Care Services 32932 Warren Rd Suite 100	Westland	MI	48185	**800-444-0425**	734-522-4244
Genesys Hospice 7280 S State Rd	Goodrich	MI	48438	**888-943-9690**	810-762-4370
Good Samaritan Hospice Care 166 E Goodale Ave	Battle Creek	MI	49017	**800-254-5939**	269-660-3600
Hospice at Home PO Box 297	Stevensville	MI	49127	**800-717-3811**	269-429-7100
Hospice of Holland Inc 270 Hoover Blvd	Holland	MI	49423	**800-255-3522**	616-396-2972
Hospice of Michigan 400 Mack Ave	Detroit	MI	48201	**888-466-5656**	313-578-5000
Karmanos Cancer Institute Hospice 24601 Northwestern Hwy	Southfield	MI	48075	**800-527-6266**	248-827-1592
McLaren Hospice Service 1515 Cal Dr	Davison	MI	48423	**800-206-4806**	810-496-8855
Mid Michigan Hospice 3007 N Saginaw Rd	Midland	MI	48640	**800-852-9350**	989-633-1400
Munson Hospice 1105 6th St	Traverse City	MI	49684	**800-252-2065**	231-935-6520
Saint Joseph Mercy Home Care & Hospice 806 Airport Blvd	Ann Arbor	MI	48108	**888-884-6569**	734-327-3400
Samaritan Care Hospice 24445 Northwestern Hwy Suite 105	Southfield	MI	48075	**800-397-9360**	248-355-9900
VNA & Hospice of Southwest Michigan Hospice 348 N Burdick St	Kalamazoo	MI	49007	**800-343-1396**	269-343-1396
VNA & Hospice Partners in Caring 500 S Hamilton St	Saginaw	MI	48602	**800-862-4968**	989-799-6020
Allina Hospice & Palliative Care 2550 University Ave W Suite 180-S	Saint Paul	MN	55114	**800-261-0879**	651-635-9173
Fairview Hospice 2450 26th Ave S	Minneapolis	MN	55406	**800-285-5647**	612-728-2380
Rice Hospice 301 SW Becker Ave	Willmar	MN	56201	**800-336-7423**	320-231-4450
Delta Area Hospice Care Ltd 522 Arnold Ave	Greenville	MS	38701	**800-742-2641**	662-335-7040
Hospice Ministries PO Box 1228	Ridgeland	MS	39158	**800-273-7724**	601-898-1053
North Mississippi Medical Center Hospice 422-A E President St	Tupelo	MS	38801	**800-852-1610**	662-377-3612
Sta-Home Hospice 406 Briarwood Dr Suite 500	Jackson	MS	39206	**800-336-6557**	601-991-1933
Hands of Hope Hospice 105 N Far West Dr Suite 100	Saint Joseph	MO	64506	**800-443-1143**	816-271-7190
Saint John's Hospice Care 1378 E Republic Rd	Springfield	MO	65804	**800-330-8304**	417-820-7550
SSM Hospice 2 Harbor Bend Ct	Lake Saint Louis	MO	63367	**800-835-1212**	636-695-2050
VNA Hospice Care 9450 Manchester Rd Suite 206	Saint Louis	MO	63119	**800-392-4740**	314-918-7171
Hospice Care of Nebraska 1600 S 70th St Suite 201	Lincoln	NE	68506	**800-826-3841**	402-488-1363
VNA of the Midlands Hospice 1941 S 42nd St Suite 225	Omaha	NE	68105	**800-456-8869**	402-342-5566
Family Home Hospice 1701 W Charleston Blvd Suite 201	Las Vegas	NV	89102	**800-999-2536**	702-383-0887
Nathan Adelson Hospice 4141 S Swenson St	Las Vegas	NV	89119	**888-281-8646**	702-733-0320
Concord Regional Visiting Nurse Assoc Hospice Program PO Box 1797	Concord	NH	03302	**800-924-8620**	603-224-4093
Home Health & Hospice Care 22 Prospect St	Nashua	NH	03060	**800-887-5973**	603-882-2941
Seacoast Hospice 10 Hampton Rd	Exeter	NH	03833	**800-416-9207**	603-778-7391
VNA of Manchester & Southern New Hampshire 1850 Elm St	Manchester	NH	03104	**800-624-6084**	603-622-3781
Compassionate Care Hospice 66 Mt Prospect Ave Bldg C	Clifton	NJ	07013	**800-916-1494**	973-916-1400
Compassionate Care Hospice 600 Highland Dr Suite 624	West Hampton	NJ	08060	**800-844-4774**	609-267-1178
Home Health/Van Dyke Hospice 99 Rt 37 W	Toms River	NJ	08755	**800-338-3131**	732-818-6800
HospiceCare of South Jersey 2848 S Delsea Dr	Vineland	NJ	08360	**800-584-1515**	856-794-1515
Karen Ann Quinlan Hospice 99 Sparta Ave	Newton	NJ	07860	**800-882-1117**	973-383-0115
Lighthouse Hospice 1040 N Kings Hwy Suite 100	Cherry Hill	NJ	08034	**888-345-7742**	856-661-5600
Samaritan Hospice 5 Eves Dr Suite 300	Marlton	NJ	08053	**800-229-8183**	856-596-1600
VistaCare Hospice 5201 Venice NE Suite A&B	Albuquerque	NM	87113	**888-605-1969**	505-821-5404
VistaCare Hospice 1515 W Calle Sur St	Hobbs	NM	88240	**800-658-6844**	505-392-2060
HomeCare & Hospice 1225 W State St	Olean	NY	14760	**800-339-7011**	716-372-5735
Hospice Care in Westchester & Putnam Inc 100 S Bedford Rd	Mount Kisco	NY	10549	**800-298-6341**	914-666-4228
Hospice Care Inc 4277 Middle Settlement Rd	New Hartford	NY	13413	**800-317-5661**	315-735-6484
Visiting Nurse Service of New York Hospice Care 1250 Broadway 7th Fl	New York	NY	10001	**888-867-1225**	212-609-1900
Hospice of Alamance Caswell 914 Chapel Hill Rd	Burlington	NC	27215	**800-588-8879**	336-532-0100
Hospice of Stanly County 960 N 1st St	Albemarle	NC	28001	**800-230-4236**	704-983-4216
Hospice of Wake County Inc 1300 Saint Mary's St 4th Fl	Raleigh	NC	27605	**888-900-3959**	919-828-0890
Kitty Askins Hospice Center 2402 Wayne Memorial Dr	Goldsboro	NC	27534	**800-260-4442**	919-735-1387
Lower Cape Fear Hospice and Life Care 725-A Wellington Ave	Wilmington	NC	28401	**800-733-1476**	910-772-5444
Rowan Regional Home Health & Hospice 825A W Henderson St	Salisbury	NC	28144	**888-279-0304**	704-637-7645
Altru Hospice 1380 S Columbia Rd	Grand Forks	ND	58206	**800-545-5615**	701-780-5258
Hospice of the Red River Valley 1701 38th St SW Suite 201	Fargo	ND	58102	**800-237-4629**	701-356-1500
Bridge Home Health & Hospice 15100 Birchaven Ln	Findlay	OH	45840	**800-982-3306**	419-423-5351
Homereach Hospice 3595 Olentangy River Rd	Columbus	OH	43214	**800-300-7075**	614-566-5377
Hospice & Health Services Inc 1111 E Main St	Lancaster	OH	43130	**800-994-7077**	740-654-7077
Hospice of Central Ohio 2269 Cherry Valley Rd	Newark	OH	43055	**800-804-2505**	740-344-0311
Hospice of Cincinnati 4310 Cooper Rd	Cincinnati	OH	45242	**800-691-7255**	513-891-7700
Hospice of Dayton 324 Wilmington Ave	Dayton	OH	45420	**800-653-4490**	937-256-4490
Hospice of Medina County 797 N Court St	Medina	OH	44256	**800-700-4771**	330-722-4771
Hospice of Miami County PO Box 502	Troy	OH	45373	**800-372-0009**	937-335-5191
Hospice of North Central Ohio 1605 County Rd 1095	Ashland	OH	44805	**800-952-2207**	419-281-7107
Hospice of the Valley 5190 Market St	Youngstown	OH	44512	**800-640-5180**	330-788-1992
Hospice of Tuscarawas County 201 W 3rd St	Dover	OH	44622	**800-947-7247**	330-343-7605
Hospice of Visiting Nurse Service 3358 Ridgewood Rd	Akron	OH	44333	**800-335-1455**	330-665-1455
Hospice of Wayne County 2525 Back Orrville Rd	Wooster	OH	44691	**800-884-6547**	330-264-4899
New Life Hospice 5255 N Abbe Rd	Elyria	OH	44035	**800-770-5767**	440-934-1458
State of the Heart Home Health & Hospice 1350 N Broadway	Greenville	OH	45331	**800-417-7535**	937-548-2999
Stein Hospice Service 1200 Sycamore Line	Sandusky	OH	44870	**800-625-5269**	419-625-5269
Tricare Home Health & Hospice 205 E Palmer Ave	Bellefontaine	OH	43311	**800-886-5936**	937-593-6333
Valley Hospice 380 Summit Ave	Steubenville	OH	43952	**877-467-7423**	740-283-7487
VistaCare Hospice 8135 Beechmont Ave	Cincinnati	OH	45255	**800-865-5980**	513-474-2550
VNA of Cleveland Hospice 2500 E 22nd St	Cleveland	OH	44115	**800-862-5253**	216-931-1450
Trinity Hospice LLC 1437 S Boulder Ave Suite 1080	Tulsa	OK	74119	**800-473-4368**	918-742-7559
Legacy Visiting Nurses Assn Hospice PO Box 3426	Portland	OR	97208	**800-896-6287**	503-225-6370
Lovejoy Hospice 939 NE 8th St	Grants Pass	OR	97526	**888-758-8569**	541-474-1193
Willamette Valley Hospice 1015 3rd St NW	Salem	OR	97304	**800-555-2431**	503-588-3600
Berks VNA Hospice Program 1170 Berkshire Blvd	Wyomissing	PA	19610	**800-346-7848**	610-378-0481
Compassionate Care Hospice 3333 Street Rd Suite 235	Bensalem	PA	19020	**800-584-8165**	215-245-3525
Forbes Hospice 115 S Neville St	Pittsburgh	PA	15213	**800-381-8080**	412-325-7200
Heartland Hospice 4070 Butler Pike Suite 100	Plymouth Meeting	PA	19462	**800-807-3738**	610-941-6700
Hospice of Lancaster County 685 Good Dr PO Box 4125	Lancaster	PA	17604	**800-924-7610**	717-295-3900
Hospice Saint John 123 N Vine St	Hazleton	PA	18201	**877-438-3511**	570-459-6778
Lehigh Valley Hospice 2166 S 12th St	Allentown	PA	18103	**800-944-4354**	610-402-7400
Neighborhood Hospice 795 E Marshall St Suite 204	West Chester	PA	19380	**800-848-1155**	610-696-6511
Pinnacle Health Hospice 3705 Elmwood Dr	Harrisburg	PA	17110	**800-889-1098**	717-671-3700
Samaritan Care Hospice 653 Skippack Pike	Blue Bell	PA	19422	**800-764-6878**	215-653-7310
SUN Home Health Services & Hospice 61 Duke St	Northumberland	PA	17857	**888-478-6227**	570-473-8320
VITAS Healthcare Corp of Pennsylvania 1740 Walton Rd Suite 100	Blue Bell	PA	19422	**800-209-1080**	610-260-6020
VNA Hospice Western Pennsylvania 154 Hindman Rd	Butler	PA	16001	**800-245-3042**	724-282-6806
Wissahickon Hospice 1 Presidential Blvd Suite 125	Bala Cynwyd	PA	19004	**800-700-8807**	610-617-2400
Hospice Care of Rhode Island 169 George St	Pawtucket	RI	02860	**800-338-6555**	401-444-9070
VNS of Rhode Island Hospice Program 6 Blackstone Valley Pl Suite 515	Lincoln	RI	02865	**800-828-4034**	401-769-5670
Hospice Community Care PO Box 993	Rock Hill	SC	29731	**800-895-2273**	803-329-4663
Hospice of the Upstate 1835 Rogers Rd	Anderson	SC	29621	**800-261-8638**	864-224-3358
HospiceCare of the Piedmont 408 W Alexander Ave	Greenwood	SC	29646	**800-450-6646**	864-227-9393
McLeod Hospice 555 E Cheves St	Florence	SC	29506	**800-768-4556**	843-777-2564
Palmetto Health Home Care & Hospice 1400 Pickens St	Columbia	SC	29202	**800-238-1884**	803-296-3100
Saint Francis Hospice 414-A Pettigru St	Greenville	SC	29601	**800-277-2273**	864-233-5300
Adventa Hospice 684 Hwy 91 Suite 1	Elizabethton	TN	37643	**800-774-1404**	423-547-0852
Adventa Hospice 1423 W Morris Blvd	Morristown	TN	37814	**800-659-2633**	423-587-9484
Alive Hospice Inc 1718 Patterson St	Nashville	TN	37203	**800-327-1085**	615-327-1085
Methodist Alliance Hospice 6423 Shelby View Dr Suite 103	Memphis	TN	38134	**800-968-8326**	901-380-8169
Trinity Hospice 1049 Cresthaven Rd	Memphis	TN	38119	**800-727-6416**	901-767-6767
Ann's Haven VNA 216 W Mulberry St	Denton	TX	76201	**800-383-5435**	940-566-6550
AseraCare Hospice 1212 Palm Valley Blvd	Round Rock	TX	78664	**800-332-3982**	512-467-7423
Baptist Saint Anthony's Hospice PO Box 950	Amarillo	TX	79176	**800-315-6209**	806-212-8000
CHRISTUS Spohn Hospice 1660 S Staples St	Corpus Christi	TX	78404	**800-371-0115**	361-881-3159
Community Hospice of Texas 6100 Western Pl Suite 500	Fort Worth	TX	76107	**800-226-0373**	817-870-2795
Hendrick Hospice Care PO Box 1922	Abilene	TX	79601	**800-622-8516**	325-677-8516
Hospice at the Texas Medical Center 1905 Holcombe Blvd	Houston	TX	77030	**800-630-7894**	713-467-7423
Hospice Austin 4107 Spicewood Springs Rd Suite 100	Austin	TX	78759	**800-445-3261**	512-342-4700
Hospice Longview 1306 Pine Tree Rd	Longview	TX	75604	**800-371-1016**	903-295-1680
Hospice of Wichita Falls 4909 Johnson Rd	Wichita Falls	TX	76308	**800-378-2822**	940-691-0982
Hospice Preferred Choice 1235 N Loop W Suite 215	Houston	TX	77008	**888-646-8696**	713-864-2626
Samaritan Care Hospice 9535 Forest Ln Suite 229	Dallas	TX	75243	**800-473-2430**	972-690-6632
VITAS Healthcare Corp 2501 Parkview Dr Suite 600	Fort Worth	TX	76102	**800-593-5855**	817-870-7000
VITAS Healthcare Corp 18333 Egret Bay Suite 550	Houston	TX	77058	**800-822-8525**	281-335-3401
VITAS Healthcare Corp 4828 Loop Central Dr Suite 890	Houston	TX	77081	**800-938-4827**	713-663-7777

Name / Address	City	State	ZIP	Toll-Free	Phone
VITAS Healthcare Corp 5430 Fredericksburg Rd Suite 200	San Antonio	TX	78229	**800-938-4827**	210-348-4300
VNA & Hospice of South Texas 8721 Botts St.	San Antonio	TX	78217	**800-773-7292**	210-804-5200
VNA of Houston Hospice 2905 Sackett St	Houston	TX	77098	**800-375-6877**	713-520-8115
IHC Home Care 2250 S 1300 W Suite A	Salt Lake City	UT	84119	**800-527-1118**	801-977-9900
Hospice VNA 46 S Main St	White River Junction	VT	05001	**800-858-1696**	802-295-2604
Capital Hospice Inc 9300 Lee Hwy Suite 200	Faifax	VA	22031	**888-583-1900**	703-383-9222
Good Samaritan Hospice 3825 Electric Rd SW Suite A	Roanoke	VA	24018	**888-466-7809**	540-776-0198
Hospice of the Piedmont 2200 Old Ivy Rd Suite 2	Charlottesville	VA	22903	**800-975-5501**	434-817-6900
Hospice of the Rapidan PO Box 1715	Culpeper	VA	22701	**800-676-2012**	540-825-4840
Evergreen Community Hospice 12822 124th Ln NE	Kirkland	WA	98034	**800-442-4546**	425-899-1040
Franciscan Hospice 2901 Bridgeport Way W	University Place	WA	98466	**800-338-8305**	253-671-7000
Hospice of Spokane 121 S Arthur	Spokane	WA	99202	**888-459-0438**	509-456-0438
Providence Hospice & Home Care of Snohomish County 2731 Wetmore Ave Suite 500	Everett	WA	98201	**800-825-0045**	425-261-4800
Providence Sound Home Care & Hospice PO Box 5008	Olympia	WA	98509	**800-869-7062**	360-459-8311
Whatcom Hospice 800 E Chestnut St Suite 1C	Bellingham	WA	98225	**800-573-5877**	360-733-5877
Hospice of Huntington 1101 6th Ave	Huntington	WV	25701	**800-788-5480**	304-529-4217
Hospice of the Panhandle 122 Waverly Ct	Martinsburg	WV	25401	**800-345-6538**	304-264-0406
Kanawha Hospice Care 1143 Dunbar Ave	Dunbar	WV	25064	**800-560-8523**	304-768-8523
Beloit Regional Hospice 655 3rd St Suite 200	Beloit	WI	53511	**877-363-7421**	608-363-7200
Gundersen Lutheran at Home HomeCare & Hospice 811 Monitor St Suite 101	La Crosse	WI	54603	**800-848-5442**	608-775-8400
Hospice Alliance 10220 Prairie Ridge Blvd	Pleasant Prairie	WI	53158	**800-830-8344**	262-652-4400
HospiceCare 5395 E Cheryl Pkwy	Madison	WI	53711	**800-553-4289**	608-276-4660
Ministry Home Care Hospice Services 611 Saint Joseph Ave Saint Joseph's Hospital	Marshfield	WI	54449	**800-397-4216**	715-387-7052
Saint Agnes Home Care Hospice 239 Trowbridge Dr	Fond du Lac	WI	54936	**800-236-4156**	920-923-7950
Theda Care at Home 201 E Bell St	Neenah	WI	54956	**800-984-5554**	920-969-0919
Unity Hospice 916 Willard Dr Suite 100	Green Bay	WI	54304	**800-990-9249**	920-494-0225
VITAS Healthcare Corp 2675 N Mayfair Rd Suite 480	Wauwatosa	WI	53226	**800-938-4827**	414-257-2600

366 HOSPITALS

SEE ALSO Health Care Providers - Ancillary; Health Care Systems; Hospices; Veterans Nursing Homes - State

366-1 Children's Hospitals

Name / Address	City	State	ZIP	Toll-Free	Phone
All Children's Hospital 801 6th St S	Saint Petersburg	FL	33701	**800-456-4543**	727-898-7451
Children's Care Hospital & School 2501 W 26th St	Sioux Falls	SD	57105	**800-584-9294**	605-782-2300
Children's Healthcare of Atlanta at Egleston 1405 Clifton Rd NE	Atlanta	GA	30322	**800-250-5437**	404-325-6000
Children's Healthcare of Atlanta at Scottish Rite 1001 Johnson Ferry Rd NE	Atlanta	GA	30342	**800-250-5437**	404-256-5252
Children's Hospital 1056 E 19th Ave	Denver	CO	80218	**800-624-6553**	303-861-8888
Children's Hospital 700 Children's Dr	Columbus	OH	43205	**800-792-8401**	614-722-2000
Cincinnati Children's Hospital Medical Center 3333 Burnet Ave	Cincinnati	OH	45229	**800-344-2462**	513-636-4200
Cleo Wallace Centers Westminster Campus 8405 Church Ranch Blvd	Westminster	CO	80021	**800-456-2536**	303-466-7391
Copper Hills Youth Center 5899 W Rivendell Dr	West Jordan	UT	84088	**800-776-7116**	801-561-3377
CS Mott Children's Hospital 1500 E Medical Center Dr	Ann Arbor	MI	48109	**800-211-8181**	734-936-4000
Cumberland Hospital for Children & Adolescents 9407 Cumberland Rd	New Kent	VA	23124	**800-368-3472**	804-966-2242
Gillette Children's Specialty Healthcare 200 E University Ave	Saint Paul	MN	55101	**800-719-4040**	651-291-2848
Hospital for Sick Children 1731 Bunker Hill Rd NE	Washington	DC	20017	**800-226-4444**	202-832-4400
Inner Harbour Hospitals 4685 Dorsett Shoals Rd	Douglasville	GA	30135	**800-255-8657**	770-942-2391
Miami Children's Hospital 3100 SW 62nd Ave	Miami	FL	33155	**800-432-6837**	305-666-6511
Mott CS Children's Hospital 1500 E Medical Center Dr	Ann Arbor	MI	48109	**800-211-8181**	734-936-4000
Saint Louis Children's Hospital 1 Children's Pl	Saint Louis	MO	63110	**800-678-5437**	314-454-6000
Shriners Hospitals for Children Chicago 2211 N Oak Park Ave	Chicago	IL	60707	**800-237-5055**	773-622-5400
Shriners Hospitals for Children Cincinnati 3229 Burnet Ave	Cincinnati	OH	45229	**800-875-8580**	513-872-6000
Shriners Hospitals for Children Galveston 815 Market St	Galveston	TX	77550	**800-292-3938**	409-621-1366
Shriners Hospitals for Children Greenville 950 W Faris Rd	Greenville	SC	29605	**800-591-7564**	864-271-3444
Shriners Hospitals for Children Honolulu 1310 Punahou St	Honolulu	HI	96826	**888-888-6314**	808-941-4466
Shriners Hospitals for Children Lexington 1900 Richmond Rd	Lexington	KY	40502	**800-668-4634**	859-266-2101
Shriners Hospitals for Children Los Angeles 3160 Geneva St	Los Angeles	CA	90020	**800-237-5055**	213-388-3151
Shriners Hospitals for Children Philadelphia 3551 N Broad St	Philadelphia	PA	19140	**800-281-4050**	215-430-4000
Shriners Hospitals for Children Saint Louis 2001 S Lindbergh Blvd	Saint Louis	MO	63131	**800-237-5055**	314-432-3600
Shriners Hospitals for Children Twin Cities 2025 E River Pkwy	Minneapolis	MN	55414	**888-293-2832**	612-596-6100
Texas Children's Hospital 6621 Fannin St	Houston	TX	77030	**800-364-5437**	832-824-1000
Texas Scottish Rite Hospital for Children 2222 Welborn St	Dallas	TX	75219	**800-421-1121**	214-521-3168
Wallace Cleo Centers Westminster Campus 8405 Church Ranch Blvd	Westminster	CO	80021	**800-456-2536**	303-466-7391

366-2 General Hospitals - US

Name / Address	City	State	ZIP	Toll-Free	Phone
Aiken Regional Medical Centers 302 University Pkwy	Aiken	SC	29802	**800-245-3679**	803-641-5000
Akron General Medical Center 400 Wabash Ave	Akron	OH	44307	**800-221-4601**	330-344-6000
All Saints Health Care 3801 Spring St	Racine	WI	53405	**800-526-9309**	262-687-4011
Altoona Regional Health System Altoona Hospital 620 Howard Ave	Altoona	PA	16601	**800-946-1902**	814-946-2011
Altru Hospital 1200 S Columbia Rd	Grand Forks	ND	58201	**800-732-4277**	701-780-5000
Anderson Area Medical Center 800 N Fant St	Anderson	SC	29621	**800-825-6688**	864-261-1000
Appleton Medical Center 1818 N Meade St	Appleton	WI	54911	**800-236-4101**	920-731-4101
Arrowhead Regional Medical Center 400 N Pepper Ave	Colton	CA	92324	**877-873-2762**	909-580-1000
Audrain Medical Center 620 E Monroe St	Mexico	MO	65265	**800-748-7098**	573-582-5000
Augusta Medical Center 78 Medical Ctr Dr	Fishersville	VA	22939	**800-932-0262**	540-932-4000
Avera Saint Luke's Hospital 305 S State St	Aberdeen	SD	57401	**800-225-8537**	605-622-5000
Baptist Health of South Florida 8900 N Kendall Dr	Miami	FL	33176	**800-327-2491**	786-596-1960
Baptist Health Systems Inc 1225 N State St	Jackson	MS	39202	**800-948-6262**	601-968-1000
Baptist Medical Center 800 Prudential Dr	Jacksonville	FL	32207	**800-874-8567**	904-202-2000
Barberton Citizens Hospital 155 5th St NE	Barberton	OH	44203	**877-227-8745**	330-745-1611
Bay Area Medical Center 3100 Shore Dr	Marinette	WI	54143	**888-788-2070**	715-735-6621
Bay Regional Medical Center 1900 Columbus Ave	Bay City	MI	48708	**800-726-0666**	989-894-3000
Bayley Seton Hospital 75 Vanderbilt Ave	Staten Island	NY	10304	**800-273-1114**	718-818-6000
Beaufort Memorial Hospital 955 Ribaut Rd	Beaufort	SC	29902	**877-532-6472**	843-522-5200
Beaver Dam Community Hospital 707 S University Ave	Beaver Dam	WI	53916	**800-870-7181**	920-887-7181
Bedford Regional Medical Center 2900 W 16th St	Bedford	IN	47421	**800-755-3734**	812-275-1200
Beloit Memorial Hospital 1969 W Hart Rd	Beloit	WI	53511	**800-637-2641**	608-364-5011
Bethesda Hospital 2951 Maple Ave	Zanesville	OH	43701	**800-322-4762**	740-454-4000
Bi-County Community Hospital 13355 E Ten-Mile Rd	Warren	MI	48089	**800-423-1948**	586-759-7300
Bon Secours Cottage Hospital 468 Cadieux Rd	Grosse Pointe	MI	48230	**888-331-0954**	313-343-1000
Bon Secours Memorial Regional Medical Center 8260 Atlee Rd	Mechanicsville	VA	23116	**888-455-3766**	804-764-6000
Bon Secours Saint Mary's Hospital 5801 Bremo Rd	Richmond	VA	23226	**800-472-2011**	804-285-2011
Brooks Memorial Hospital 529 Central Ave	Dunkirk	NY	14048	**800-366-0717**	716-366-1111
Broward General Medical Center 1600 S Andrews Ave	Fort Lauderdale	FL	33316	**866-293-7866**	954-355-4400
Bryan LGH Medical Center West 2300 S 16th St	Lincoln	NE	68502	**800-742-7845**	402-475-1011
Camden-Clark Memorial Hospital 800 Garfield Ave	Parkersburg	WV	26102	**800-422-6437**	304-424-2111
Capital Medical Center 3900 Capital Mall Dr SW	Olympia	WA	98502	**888-677-9757**	360-754-5858
Catholic Medical Center 100 McGregor St	Manchester	NH	03102	**800-437-9666**	603-668-3545
Caylor-Nickel Clinic PC 1 Caylor-Nickel Sq	Bluffton	IN	46714	**800-756-2663**	260-824-3500
Cedars-Sinai Medical Center 8700 Beverly Blvd	Los Angeles	CA	90048	**800-233-2771**	310-423-3277
Centinela Freeman Regional Medical Center Memorial Campus 333 N Prairie Ave	Inglewood	CA	90301	**800-455-1933**	310-674-7050
Central Carolina Hospital 1135 Carthage St	Sanford	NC	27330	**800-292-2262**	919-774-2100
Central DuPage Hospital 25 N Winfield Rd	Winfield	IL	60190	**877-933-1600**	630-933-1600
Central Michigan Community Hospital 1221 South Dr	Mount Pleasant	MI	48858	**800-671-1453**	989-772-6700
Central Mississippi Medical Center 1850 Chadwick Dr	Jackson	MS	39204	**800-844-0919**	601-376-1000
Central Texas Medical Center 1301 Wonder World Dr	San Marcos	TX	78666	**800-508-8515**	512-353-8979
Chandler Regional Hospital 475 S Dobson Rd	Chandler	AZ	85224	**800-350-4677**	480-963-4561
Christ Hospital 2139 Auburn Ave	Cincinnati	OH	45219	**800-527-8919**	513-585-2000
City of Hope National Medical Center 1500 E Duarte Rd	Duarte	CA	91010	**866-434-4673**	626-256-4673
Civista Medical Center 701 E Charles St	La Plata	MD	20646	**800-422-8585**	301-609-4000
Clarion Hospital 1 Hospital Dr	Clarion	PA	16214	**800-522-0505**	814-226-9500
Cleveland Clinic 9500 Euclid Ave	Cleveland	OH	44195	**800-223-2273**	216-444-2200
Clinton Memorial Hospital 610 W Main St	Wilmington	OH	45177	**800-803-9648**	937-382-6611
Coffeyville Regional Medical Center 1400 W 4th St	Coffeyville	KS	67337	**800-540-2762**	620-251-1200
Colquitt Regional Medical Center 3131 S Main St	Moultrie	GA	31768	**888-262-2762**	229-985-3420
Community Health Center of Branch County 274 E Chicago St	Coldwater	MI	49036	**888-774-1471**	517-279-5400
Community Hospital of Anderson & Madison Counties 1515 N Madison Ave	Anderson	IN	46011	**800-430-4774**	765-298-4242
Community Memorial Hospital 855 Mankato Ave	Winona	MN	55987	**800-944-3960**	507-454-3650
Community Methodist Hospital 1305 N Elm St	Henderson	KY	42420	**800-467-7766**	270-827-7700
Conroe Regional Medical Center 504 Medical Ctr Blvd	Conroe	TX	77304	**888-633-2687**	936-539-1111
Corning Hospital 176 Denison Pkwy E	Corning	NY	14830	**800-295-1122**	607-937-7200
Danbury Hospital 24 Hospital Ave	Danbury	CT	06810	**800-284-3262**	203-797-7000
Deaconess Billings Clinic 2800 10th Ave N	Billings	MT	59101	**800-332-7201**	406-657-4000
Dean Medical Center 1313 Fish Hatchery Rd	Madison	WI	53715	**800-279-9966**	608-252-8000
Desert Regional Medical Center 1150 N Indian Canyon Dr	Palm Springs	CA	92262	**800-962-3765**	760-323-6511
DesPeres Hospital 2345 Dougherty Ferry Rd	Kirkwood	MO	63122	**888-457-5203**	314-821-5850
Eastern New Mexico Medical Center 405 W Country Club Rd	Roswell	NM	88201	**800-437-9275**	505-622-8170
Eastside Hospital 2700 152nd Ave NE	Redmond	WA	98052	**800-995-5658**	425-883-5151
Edinburg Regional Medical Center 1102 W Trenton Rd	Edinburg	TX	78539	**800-465-5585**	956-388-6000
Elk Regional Health Center 763 Johnsonburg Rd	Saint Marys	PA	15857	**877-391-6800**	814-781-7500
Enloe Medical Center 1531 Esplanade	Chico	CA	95926	**800-822-8102**	530-332-7300
Ephraim McDowell Regional Medical Center 217 S 3rd St	Danville	KY	40422	**800-686-4121**	859-236-4121
Erie County Medical Center 462 Grider St	Buffalo	NY	14215	**888-894-9444**	716-898-3000
Fairfield Medical Center 401 N Ewing St	Lancaster	OH	43130	**800-548-2627**	740-687-8000
Fairview General Hospital 18101 Lorain Ave	Cleveland	OH	44111	**800-323-8434**	216-476-7000
Fairview-University Medical Center University Campus 420 Delaware St SE	Minneapolis	MN	55455	**800-688-5252**	612-273-3000
Fallbrook Hospital District 624 E Elder St	Fallbrook	CA	92028	**800-647-6464**	760-728-1191
FHN Memorial Hospital 1045 W Stephenson St	Freeport	IL	61032	**800-747-4131**	815-599-6000
Finley Hospital 350 N Grandview Ave	Dubuque	IA	52001	**800-582-1891**	563-582-1881

General Hospitals - US (Cont'd)

Name / Address	City	State	ZIP	Toll-Free	Phone
Flagler Hospital 400 Health Park Blvd	Saint Augustine	FL	32086	**866-834-3278**	904-829-5155
Florida Medical Center 5000 W Oakland Park Blvd	Fort Lauderdale	FL	33313	**800-222-9355**	954-735-6000
Floyd Memorial Hospital 1850 State St	New Albany	IN	47150	**800-423-1513**	812-944-7701
Forest Park Hospital 6150 Oakland Ave	Saint Louis	MO	63139	**877-249-8557**	314-768-3000
Freeman Hospital & Health Systems 1102 W 32nd St	Joplin	MO	64804	**800-477-6610**	417-623-2801
French Hospital Medical Center 1911 Johnson Ave	San Luis Obispo	CA	93401	**800-775-5335**	805-543-5353
Gateway Regional Medical Center 2100 Madison Ave	Granite City	IL	62040	**800-559-9992**	618-798-3000
Genesys Regional Medical Center Health Park 1 Genesys Pkwy	Grand Blanc	MI	48439	**888-606-6556**	810-762-8000
Golden Valley Memorial Hospital 1600 N 2nd St	Clinton	MO	64735	**800-748-7681**	660-885-5511
Good Samaritan Hospital 10 E 31st St	Kearney	NE	68847	**800-658-4250**	308-865-7100
Good Samaritan Medical & Rehabilitation Center 800 Forest Ave	Zanesville	OH	43701	**800-322-4762**	740-454-5843
Good Samaritan Regional Medical Center 3600 NW Samaritan Dr	Corvallis	OR	97330	**888-872-0760**	541-757-5111
Grand Strand Regional Medical Ctr 809 82nd Pkwy	Myrtle Beach	SC	29572	**800-222-1859**	843-692-1000
Great Plains Regional Medical Center 601 W Leota St	North Platte	NE	69101	**800-662-0011**	308-696-8000
Great River Medical Center PO Box 108	Blytheville	AR	72316	**800-557-5591**	870-838-7300
Gulf Coast Hospital 13681 Doctors Way	Fort Myers	FL	33912	**800-440-4481**	239-768-5000
Gundersen Lutheran Medical Center 1900 South Ave	La Crosse	WI	54601	**800-362-9567**	608-785-0530
Hackley Hospital 1700 Clinton St	Muskegon	MI	49442	**800-825-4677**	231-726-3511
Hancock Memorial Hospital 801 N State St	Greenfield	IN	46140	**888-900-4677**	317-462-5544
Hanover Hospital 300 Highland Ave	Hanover	PA	17331	**800-673-2426**	717-637-3711
Harris Regional Hospital 68 Hospital Rd	Sylva	NC	28779	**800-496-2362**	828-586-7000
Hays Medical Center 2220 Canterbury Dr	Hays	KS	67601	**800-248-0073**	785-623-5000
Heartland Hospital East 5325 Faraon St	Saint Joseph	MO	64506	**800-443-1143**	816-271-6000
Highlands Regional Medical Center 5000 KY Rt 321	Prestonsburg	KY	41653	**800-533-4762**	606-886-8511
Holmes Regional Medical Center 1350 S Hickory St	Melbourne	FL	32901	**888-434-3730**	321-434-7000
Holy Redeemer Hospital & Medical Center 1648 Huntingdon Pike	Meadowbrook	PA	19046	**800-818-4747**	215-947-3000
Holy Rosary Medical Center 351 SW 9th St	Ontario	OR	97914	**877-225-4762**	541-881-7000
Hospital of Saint Raphael 1450 Chapel St	New Haven	CT	06511	**800-662-2366**	203-789-3000
Immanuel-Saint Joseph's Hospital 1025 Marsh St	Mankato	MN	56001	**800-327-3721**	507-625-4031
Indian River Memorial Hospital 1000 36th St	Vero Beach	FL	32960	**800-226-4764**	772-567-4311
Ivinson Memorial Hospital 255 N 30th St	Laramie	WY	82072	**800-854-1115**	307-742-2141
Jackson County Memorial Hospital 1200 E Pecan St	Altus	OK	73521	**800-250-9965**	580-482-4781
Jennie Stuart Medical Center 320 W 18th St PO Box 2400	Hopkinsville	KY	42241	**800-887-5762**	270-887-0100
John D Archbold Memorial Hospital PO Box 1018	Thomasville	GA	31799	**800-341-1009**	229-228-2000
Joint Township District Memorial Hospital 200 Saint Clair St	Saint Marys	OH	45885	**877-564-6897**	419-394-3335
Jones Wilson N Medical Center 500 N Highland Ave	Sherman	TX	75092	**877-870-6696**	903-870-4611
Kadlec Medical Center 888 Swift Blvd	Richland	WA	99352	**800-780-6067**	509-946-4611
Kaiser Permanente Hospital 441 N Lakeview Ave	Anaheim	CA	92807	**800-464-4000**	714-279-4000
Kaiser Permanente Hospital 99 Montecillo Rd	San Rafael	CA	94903	**800-464-4000**	415-444-2000
Kaiser Permanente Medical Center 25825 S Vermont Ave	Harbor City	CA	90710	**800-464-4000**	310-325-5111
Kaiser Permanente Medical Center 1150 Veterans Blvd	Redwood City	CA	94063	**800-464-4000**	650-299-2000
Kaiser Permanente Medical Center 1200 El Camino Real	South San Francisco	CA	94080	**800-660-1231**	650-742-2000
Kaiser Permanente Medical Center-South Sacramento 6600 Bruceville Rd	Sacramento	CA	95823	**800-464-4000**	916-688-2000
Kaiser Permanente Parma Medical Center 12301 Snow Rd	Parma	OH	44130	**800-524-7372**	216-362-2000
Kaiser Permanente Riverside Medical Center 10800 Magnolia Ave *Cust Svc	Riverside	CA	92505	**800-464-4000***	951-353-2000
Kalispell Regional Medical Ctr 310 Sunnyview Ln	Kalispell	MT	59901	**800-228-1574**	406-752-5111
Kaweah Delta Hospital 400 W Mineral King Ave	Visalia	CA	93291	**800-529-3244**	559-624-2000
King's Daughters' Hospital 1 King's Daughters' Dr	Madison	IN	47250	**800-272-5341**	812-265-5211
Kishwaukee Community Hospital 626 Bethany Rd	DeKalb	IL	60115	**800-397-1521**	815-756-1521
Labette County Medical Center 1902 S US Hwy 59	Parsons	KS	67357	**800-843-5262**	620-421-4880
Lahey Clinic 41 Mall Rd	Burlington	MA	01805	**800-524-3955**	781-744-5100
Lakewood Hospital 14519 Detroit Ave	Lakewood	OH	44107	**800-521-3955**	216-521-4200
Landmark Medical Center 115 Cass Ave	Woonsocket	RI	02895	**800-722-0175**	401-767-3211
Lanier Park Hospital 675 White Sulphur Rd	Gainesville	GA	30501	**800-388-1920**	678-343-4000
Lawrence & Memorial Hospital 365 Montauk Ave	New London	CT	06320	**888-777-9539**	860-442-0711
Lea Regional Medical Center 5419 N Lovington Hwy	Hobbs	NM	88240	**877-492-8001**	505-392-6581
Lewistown Hospital 400 Highland Ave	Lewistown	PA	17044	**800-248-0505**	717-248-5411
Lexington Memorial Hospital 250 Hospital Dr	Lexington	NC	27292	**800-442-7381**	336-248-5161
Lodi Memorial Hospital 975 S Fairmont Ave	Lodi	CA	95241	**800-876-6750**	209-334-3411
Loudoun Hospital Center 44045 Riverside Pkwy	Leesburg	VA	20176	**888-542-8477**	703-858-6000
Louise Obici Memorial Hospital 2800 Godwin Blvd	Suffolk	VA	23434	**800-237-5788**	757-934-4000
MacNeal Hospital 3249 S Oak Pk Ave	Berwyn	IL	60402	**888-622-6325**	708-795-9100
Magic Valley Regional Medical Center 650 Addison Ave W	Twin Falls	ID	83301	**800-947-4852**	208-737-2000
Marietta Memorial Hospital 401 Matthew St	Marietta	OH	45750	**800-523-3977**	740-374-1400
Marquette General Hospital 580 College Ave	Marquette	MI	49855	**800-652-9752**	906-228-9440
Mary Imogene Bassett Hospital 1 Atwell Rd	Cooperstown	NY	13326	**800-227-7388**	607-547-3456
Massillon Community Hospital 875 8th St NE	Massillon	OH	44646	**800-346-4869**	330-832-8761
Maury Regional Hospital 1224 Trotwood Ave	Columbia	TN	38401	**800-799-5053**	931-381-1111
McLaren Regional Medical Center 401 S Ballenger Hwy	Flint	MI	48532	**800-821-6517**	810-342-2000
Medical Center Enterprise 400 N Edwards St	Enterprise	AL	36330	**800-993-6837**	334-347-0584
Memorial Healthcare Center 826 W King St	Owosso	MI	48867	**800-206-8706**	989-723-5211
Memorial Hermann Memorial City Hospital 921 Gessner Rd	Houston	TX	77024	**800-392-6370**	713-932-3000
Memorial Hospital 1101 Michigan Ave	Logansport	IN	46947	**800-243-4512**	574-753-7541
Memorial Hospital 325 South Belmont St PO Box 15118	York	PA	17405	**800-436-4326**	717-843-8623
Memorial Hospital of Sweetwater County 1200 College Dr	Rock Springs	WY	82901	**800-307-3711**	307-362-3711
Memorial Medical Center of East Texas PO Box 1447	Lufkin	TX	75902	**800-348-5969**	936-634-8111
Mercy Hospital Medical Center 1111 6th Ave	Des Moines	IA	50314	**800-637-2993**	515-247-3121
Mercy Hospital of Kansas 401 Woodland Hills Blvd	Fort Scott	KS	66701	**877-336-3729**	620-223-2200
Mercy Medical Center 375 E Park Ave	Durango	CO	81301	**800-345-2516**	970-247-4311
Mercy Medical Center 301 St Paul Pl	Baltimore	MD	21202	**800-636-3729**	410-332-9000
Mercy Medical Center 1301 15th Ave W	Williston	ND	58801	**800-544-3579**	701-774-7400
Mercy Medical Center 1320 Mercy Dr	Canton	OH	44708	**800-999-8662**	330-489-1000
Mercy Medical Center North Iowa 1000 4th St SW	Mason City	IA	50401	**800-433-3883**	641-422-7000
Mercy Medical Center Redding 2175 Rosaline Ave	Redding	CA	96001	**800-521-6377**	530-225-6000
MetroHealth Medical Center 2500 MetroHealth Dr	Cleveland	OH	44109	**800-554-5251**	216-778-7800
Miami Valley Hospital 1 Wyoming St	Dayton	OH	45409	**800-544-0630**	937-223-6192
Mid Coast Hospital 123 Medical Center Dr	Brunswick	ME	04011	**877-729-0181**	207-729-0181
Middle Tennessee Medical Center 400 N Highland Ave	Murfreesboro	TN	37130	**800-596-3455**	615-849-4100
Middlesex Hospital 28 Crescent St	Middletown	CT	06457	**800-664-5031**	860-344-6110
Middletown Regional Hospital 105 McKnight Dr	Middletown	OH	45044	**800-338-4057**	513-424-2111
Midland Memorial Hospital 2200 W Illinois Ave	Midland	TX	79701	**800-833-2916**	432-685-1111
Midway Hospital Medical Center 5925 San Vincente Blvd	Los Angeles	CA	90019	**800-827-8599**	323-938-3161
Monmouth Medical Center 300 2nd Ave	Long Branch	NJ	07740	**888-661-7484**	732-222-5200
Monroe Clinic Hospital 515 22nd Ave	Monroe	WI	53566	**800-338-0568**	608-324-1000
Moore Regional Hospital 155 Memorial Dr	Pinehurst	NC	28374	**800-672-6072**	910-215-1000
Nacogdoches Medical Center 4920 Stallings Dr	Nacogdoches	TX	75961	**800-539-2772**	936-569-9481
NEA Medical Center 3024 Stadium Blvd	Jonesboro	AR	72401	**800-999-4486**	870-972-7000
New England Baptist Hospital 125 Parker Hill Ave	Boston	MA	02120	**800-340-6324**	617-754-5214
New Hanover Regional Medical Center 2131 S 17th St	Wilmington	NC	28401	**877-228-8135**	910-343-7000
Newton Medical Center 600 Medical Ctr Dr	Newton	KS	67114	**800-811-3183**	316-283-2700
NHS University Hospital 985230 Nebraska Medical Ctr	Omaha	NE	68198	**800-642-1095**	402-559-4000
Northbay Medical Center 1200 B Gale Wilson Blvd	Fairfield	CA	94533	**888-294-3600**	707-429-3600
NorthEast Medical Center 920 Church St N	Concord	NC	28025	**800-842-6868**	704-783-3000
Northern Montana Hospital 30 13th St	Havre	MT	59501	**800-352-5097**	406-265-2211
Northern Navajo Medical Center PO Box 160	Shiprock	NM	87420	**800-549-5644**	505-368-6001
Oakwood Hospital & Medical Center 18101 Oakwood Blvd	Dearborn	MI	48124	**800-543-9355**	313-593-7000
Obici Louise Memorial Hospital 2800 Godwin Blvd	Suffolk	VA	23434	**800-237-5788**	757-934-4000
Ochsner Clinic Foundation 1514 Jefferson Hwy	New Orleans	LA	70121	**800-928-6247**	504-842-3000
Ogden Regional Medical Center 5475 S 500 East	Ogden	UT	84405	**800-237-9194**	801-479-2111
Olive View Medical Center 14445 Olive View Dr	Sylmar	CA	91342	**800-970-5478**	818-364-1555
OSF Saint Francis Medical Center 530 NE Glen Oak Ave	Peoria	IL	61637	**888-627-5673**	309-655-2000
Ottumwa Regional Health Center 1001 Pennsylvania Ave	Ottumwa	IA	52501	**800-933-6742**	641-682-7511
Palmetto General Hospital 2001 W 68th St	Hialeah	FL	33016	**888-222-2020**	305-823-5000
Palms West Hospital 13001 Southern Blvd	Loxahatchee	FL	33470	**866-857-3936**	561-798-3300
Pampa Regional Medical Center 1 Medical Plaza	Pampa	TX	79065	**800-896-3684**	806-665-3721
Parkview Hospital 2200 Randallia Dr	Fort Wayne	IN	46805	**888-856-2522**	260-373-4000
Parkview Medical Center 400 W 16th St	Pueblo	CO	81003	**800-543-8984**	719-584-4000
Parkway Regional Medical Center 160 NW 170th St	North Miami Beach	FL	33169	**888-651-1100**	305-654-5050
Parma Community General Hospital 7007 Powers Blvd	Parma	OH	44129	**866-699-7244**	440-743-3000
Peace River Regional Medical Center 2500 Harbor Blvd	Port Charlotte	FL	33952	**800-226-4122**	941-766-4122
Peninsula Regional Medical Center 100 E Carroll St	Salisbury	MD	21801	**800-543-7780**	410-546-6400
Phelps County Regional Medical Center 1000 W 10th St	Rolla	MO	65401	**877-311-8899**	573-364-3100
Phoebe Putney Memorial Hospital 417 W 3rd Ave	Albany	GA	31702	**877-312-1167**	229-312-1000
Plain's Regional Medical Center 2100 ML King Blvd	Clovis	NM	88101	**800-221-3706**	505-769-2141
Portsmouth Regional Hospital 333 Borthwick Ave	Portsmouth	NH	03801	**800-685-8282**	603-436-5110
Prairie Lakes Hospital & Care Center 401 9th Ave NW	Watertown	SD	57201	**877-917-7547**	605-882-7000
Presbyterian Hospital of Greenville PO Box 1059	Greenville	TX	75403	**800-984-9223**	903-408-5000
Provena Covenant Medical Center 1400 W Park St	Urbana	IL	61801	**800-245-6697**	217-337-2000
Providence Hospital 914 S Scheuber Rd	Centralia	WA	98531	**877-736-2803**	360-736-2803
Providence Medford Medical Center 1111 Crater Lake Ave	Medford	OR	97504	**877-541-0588**	541-773-6611
Providence Saint Peter Hospital 413 Lilly Rd NE	Olympia	WA	98506	**888-492-9480**	360-491-9480
Raleigh General Hospital 1710 Harper Rd	Beckley	WV	25801	**800-368-8016**	304-256-4100
Regional Hospital of Jackson 367 Hospital Blvd	Jackson	TN	38305	**800-454-9970**	731-661-2000
Regional Medical Center 900 Hospital Dr	Madisonville	KY	42431	**800-998-5100**	270-825-5100
Regional Medical Center of Orangeburg & Calhoun Counties 3000 Saint Matthews Rd	Orangeburg	SC	29118	**800-476-3377**	803-395-2200
Regions Hospital 640 Jackson St	Saint Paul	MN	55101	**800-332-5720**	651-254-3456
Reston Hospital Center 1850 Town Ctr Pkwy	Reston	VA	20190	**800-695-9426**	703-689-9000

Name / Address	City	State	Zip	Toll-Free	Phone
Ridgeview Medical Center 500 S Maple St	Waconia	MN	55387	**800-967-4620**	952-442-2191
River Region West Campus 1111 N Frontage Rd	Vicksburg	MS	39180	**800-548-2419**	601-636-2611
Riverview Hospital 395 Westfield Rd	Noblesville	IN	46060	**800-523-6001**	317-773-0760
Robert Packer Hospital 1 Guthrie Sq	Sayre	PA	18840	**888-448-8474**	570-888-6666
Rockingham Memorial Hospital 235 Cantrell Ave	Harrisonburg	VA	22801	**800-543-2201**	540-433-4100
Rogue Valley Medical Center 2825 E Barnett Rd	Medford	OR	97504	**800-944-7073**	541-789-7000
Rutland Regional Medical Center 160 Allen St	Rutland	VT	05701	**800-649-2187**	802-775-7111
Sacred Heart Hospital 900 W Clairemont Ave	Eau Claire	WI	54701	**888-445-4554**	715-839-4121
Sacred Heart Hospital of Pensacola 5151 N 9th Ave	Pensacola	FL	32504	**800-874-1026**	850-416-7000
Sacred Heart Medical Center 1255 Hilyard St	Eugene	OR	97401	**800-288-7444**	541-686-7300
Saint Agnes HealthCare 900 Caton Ave	Baltimore	MD	21229	**800-875-8750**	410-368-6000
Saint Agnes Hospital 430 E Division St	Fond du Lac	WI	54935	**800-922-3400**	920-929-2300
Saint Alphonsus Regional Medical Center 1055 N Curtis Rd	Boise	ID	83706	**877-341-2121**	208-367-2121
Saint Anthony Hospital 1000 N Lee St	Oklahoma City	OK	73101	**800-227-6964**	405-272-7000
Saint Anthony Medical Center 5666 E State St	Rockford	IL	61108	**800-343-3185**	815-226-2000
Saint Barnabas Medical Center 94 Old Short Hills Rd	Livingston	NJ	07039	**888-724-7123**	973-533-5000
Saint Charles Mercy Hospital 2600 Navarre Ave	Oregon	OH	43616	**800-692-6363**	419-696-7200
Saint Cloud Hospital 1406 6th Ave N	Saint Cloud	MN	56303	**800-835-6652**	320-251-2700
Saint Elizabeth Hospital 1506 S Oneida St	Appleton	WI	54915	**800-223-7332**	920-738-2000
Saint Elizabeth Hospital Medical Center 1501 Hartford St	Lafayette	IN	47904	**800-371-6011**	765-423-6011
Saint Elizabeth Medical Center-North 401 E 20th St	Covington	KY	41014	**800-888-7362**	859-292-4000
Saint Francis Health Center 1700 SW 7th St	Topeka	KS	66606	**800-444-2954**	785-295-8000
Saint Francis Hospital 6161 S Yale Ave	Tulsa	OK	74136	**800-888-9599**	918-494-2200
Saint Francis Medical Center 2620 W Faidley Ave	Grand Island	NE	68803	**800-353-4896**	308-384-4600
Saint John's Medical Center 1615 Delaware St	Longview	WA	98632	**800-438-7562**	360-423-1530
Saint John's Medical Center 625 E Broadway	Jackson	WY	83001	**800-877-7078**	307-733-3636
Saint Joseph Hospital 172 Kinsley St	Nashua	NH	03060	**877-899-6345**	603-882-3000
Saint Joseph Hospital 2901 Squalicum Pkwy	Bellingham	WA	98225	**800-541-7209**	360-734-5400
Saint Joseph's Hospital & Health Center 30 7th St W	Dickinson	ND	58601	**800-446-6215**	701-456-4000
Saint Joseph's Hospital Health Center 301 Prospect Ave	Syracuse	NY	13203	**888-785-6371**	315-448-5111
Saint Joseph's Hospital of Atlanta 5665 Peachtree Dunwoody Rd NE	Atlanta	GA	30342	**800-678-5637**	404-851-7001
Saint Joseph's Medical Center 523 N 3rd St	Brainerd	MN	56401	**888-829-2861**	218-829-2861
Saint Luke Hospital East 85 N Grand Ave	Fort Thomas	KY	41075	**800-345-7151**	859-572-3100
Saint Luke Hospital West 7380 Turfway Rd	Florence	KY	41042	**800-345-7151**	859-962-5200
Saint Luke's Hospital & Regional Trauma Center 915 E 1st St	Duluth	MN	55805	**800-321-3790**	218-249-5555
Saint Luke's Hospital of New Bedford 101 Page St	New Bedford	MA	02740	**800-245-8537**	508-997-1515
Saint Luke's Regional Medical Center 2720 Stone Park Blvd	Sioux City	IA	51104	**800-352-4660**	712-279-3500
Saint Mary Medical Center 401 W Poplar St	Walla Walla	WA	99362	**800-452-3320**	509-525-3320
Saint Mary Mercy Hospital 36475 Five-Mile Rd	Livonia	MI	48154	**800-464-7492**	734-655-4800
Saint Mary's Health Care System 1230 Baxter St	Athens	GA	30606	**800-233-7864**	706-548-7581
Saint Mary's Health Center 6420 Clayton Rd	Richmond Heights	MO	63117	**800-284-2854**	314-768-8000
Saint Mary's Hospital 25500 Point Lookout Rd PO Box 527	Leonardtown	MD	20650	**800-222-1764**	301-475-8981
Saint Mary's Hospital 2251 N Shore Dr	Rhinelander	WI	54501	**800-578-0840**	715-361-2000
Saint Mary's Hospital & Medical Center 2635 N 7th St PO Box 1628	Grand Junction	CO	81502	**800-458-3888**	970-244-2273
Saint Mary's Hospital Ozaukee 13111 N Port Washington Rd	Mequon	WI	53097	**800-848-2844**	262-243-7300
Saint Mary's Medical Center 2900 1st Ave	Huntington	WV	25702	**800-978-6279**	304-526-1234
Saint Mary's Medical Center 1726 Shawano Ave	Green Bay	WI	54303	**800-666-5606**	920-498-4200
Saint Mary-Corwin Medical Center 1008 Minnequa Ave	Pueblo	CO	81004	**800-228-4039**	719-560-4000
Saint Nicholas Hospital 1601 N Taylor Dr	Sheboygan	WI	53081	**800-472-6710**	920-459-8300
Saint Vincent Charity Hospital 2351 E 22nd St	Cleveland	OH	44115	**800-451-8128**	216-861-6200
Saint Vincent Hospital 835 S Van Buren St	Green Bay	WI	54301	**800-236-3030**	920-433-0111
Salinas Valley Memorial Hospital 450 E Romie Ln	Salinas	CA	93901	**888-755-7864**	831-757-4333
Samaritan Medical Center 830 Washington St	Watertown	NY	13601	**877-888-6138**	315-785-4000
Sarasota Memorial Hospital 1700 S Tamiami Trail	Sarasota	FL	34239	**800-764-8255**	941-917-9000
Scott & White Memorial Hospital 2401 S 31st St	Temple	TX	76508	**800-792-3710**	254-724-2111
Scripps Green Hospital 10666 N Torrey Pines Rd	La Jolla	CA	92037	**800-727-4777**	858-455-9100
Scripps Memorial Hospital-La Jolla 9888 Genesee Ave	La Jolla	CA	92037	**800-727-4777**	858-457-4123
Sentara Careplex Hospital 3000 Colliseum Dr	Hampton	VA	23616	**800-736-8272**	757-736-1000
Shands Hospital at the University of Florida 1600 SW Archer Rd	Gainesville	FL	32610	**800-749-7424**	352-265-0111
Shannon Medical Center 120 E Harris Ave	San Angelo	TX	76903	**888-653-6741**	325-653-6741
Sharon Regional Health System 740 E State St	Sharon	PA	16146	**866-228-1055**	724-983-3911
Shore Memorial Hospital 9507 Hospital Ave PO Box 17	Nassawadox	VA	23413	**800-834-7035**	757-414-8000
Sinai Hospital of Baltimore 2401 W Belvedere Ave	Baltimore	MD	21215	**800-444-8233**	410-601-9000
Sinai Samaritan Medical Center 945 N 12th St	Milwaukee	WI	53201	**888-414-7762**	414-219-2000
Sonora Regional Medical Center 1000 Greenly Rd	Sonora	CA	95370	**800-235-7203**	209-532-3161
South Baldwin Regional Medical Center 1613 N McKenzie St	Foley	AL	36535	**800-580-3627**	251-949-3400
South Shore Hospital 55 Fogg Rd	South Weymouth	MA	02190	**800-472-3434**	781-340-8000
Southwestern Vermont Medical Center 100 Hospital Dr	Bennington	VT	05201	**800-543-1624**	802-442-6361
Spartanburg Regional Medical Center 101 E Wood St	Spartanburg	SC	29303	**800-868-8784**	864-560-6000
Springs Memorial Hospital 800 W Meeting St	Lancaster	SC	29720	**800-488-2567**	803-286-1481
Stormont-Vail Regional Health Center 1500 SW 10th St	Topeka	KS	66604	**800-432-2951**	785-354-6000
Sumner Regional Medical Center 555 Hartsville Pike	Gallatin	TN	37066	**800-728-4217**	615-452-4210
Sutter Davis Hospital 2000 Sutter Pl	Davis	CA	95616	**800-745-0227**	530-756-6440
Terre Haute Regional Hospital 3901 S 7th St	Terre Haute	IN	47802	**800-678-8474**	812-232-0021
Terrebonne General Medical Center 8166 Main St	Houma	LA	70360	**800-456-9121**	985-873-4141
Theda Clark Medical Center 130 2nd St	Neenah	WI	54956	**800-236-3122**	920-729-3100
Thibodaux Regional Medical Center PO Box 1118	Thibodaux	LA	70302	**800-822-8442**	985-447-5500
Thomasville Medical Center 207 Old Lexington Rd	Thomasville	NC	27360	**800-880-0110**	336-472-2000
Tift Regional Medical Center 901 E 18th St	Tifton	GA	31794	**800-648-1935**	229-382-7120
TJ Samson Community Hospital 1301 N Race St	Glasgow	KY	42141	**800-651-5635**	270-651-4444
Tucson Medical Center 5301 E Grant Rd	Tucson	AZ	85712	**800-526-5353**	520-327-5461
Tulane University Hospital & Clinic 1415 Tulane Ave	New Orleans	LA	70112	**800-588-5800**	504-588-5263
Twin County Regional Hospital 200 Hospital Dr	Galax	VA	24333	**800-295-3342**	276-236-8181
UAB Medical West PO Box 847	Bessemer	AL	35021	**877-481-7001**	205-481-7000
UCI Medical Center University of California Irvine 101 City Dr S	Orange	CA	92868	**877-824-3627**	714-456-6011
United Community Hospital 631 N Broad St Ext	Grove City	PA	16127	**877-459-5455**	724-450-7000
University Hospital SUNY Health Center at Syracuse 750 E Adams St	Syracuse	NY	13210	**877-464-5540**	315-464-5540
University Medical Center-Mesabi 750 E 34th St	Hibbing	MN	55746	**888-870-8626**	218-262-4881
University of Chicago Hospitals 5841 S Maryland Ave	Chicago	IL	60637	**800-289-6333**	773-702-1000
University of Connecticut Health Center John Dempsey Hospital 263 Farmington Ave	Farmington	CT	06030	**800-535-6232**	860-679-2000
University of Nebraska Medical Center 985230 Nebraska Medical Ctr	Omaha	NE	68198	**800-642-1095**	402-559-4000
Vanderbilt University Medical Center 1211 22nd Ave S	Nashville	TN	37232	**800-288-7777**	615-322-5000
Vaughan Regional Medical Center 1015 Medical Center Pkwy	Selma	AL	36701	**800-498-8461**	334-418-4100
Virginia Baptist Hospital 3300 Rivermont Ave	Lynchburg	VA	24503	**800-423-5535**	434-947-4000
Waukesha Memorial Hospital 725 American Ave	Waukesha	WI	53188	**800-326-2011**	262-928-1000
Wausau Hospital 333 Pine Ridge Blvd	Wausau	WI	54401	**800-283-2881**	715-847-2121
Wayne General Hospital 950 Matthew Dr	Waynesboro	MS	39367	**877-521-9781**	601-735-5151
Waynesboro Hospital 501 E Main St	Waynesboro	PA	17268	**888-227-3822**	717-765-4000
Weirton Medical Center 601 Colliers Way	Weirton	WV	26062	**800-243-4962**	304-797-6000
Wentworth-Douglass Hospital 789 Central Ave	Dover	NH	03820	**877-201-7100**	603-742-5252
Wesley Medical Center 550 N Hillside	Wichita	KS	67214	**800-362-0288**	316-962-2000
West Houston Medical Center 12141 Richmond Ave	Houston	TX	77082	**800-265-8624**	281-558-3444
West Valley Medical Center 1717 Arlington Ave	Caldwell	ID	83605	**800-937-8860**	208-459-4641
Western Medical Center Santa Ana 1001 N Tustin Ave	Santa Ana	CA	92705	**800-777-7464**	714-835-3555
White County Medical Center 3214 E Race Ave	Searcy	AR	72143	**888-562-7520**	501-268-6121
Wilson Memorial Hospital 915 W Michigan St	Sidney	OH	45365	**800-589-9641**	937-498-2311
Wilson N Jones Medical Center 500 N Highland Ave	Sherman	TX	75092	**877-870-6696**	903-870-4611
Wuesthoff Hospital 110 Longwood Ave	Rockledge	FL	32955	**800-742-9175**	321-636-2211
Wyoming Medical Center 1233 E 2nd St	Casper	WY	82601	**800-822-7201**	307-577-7201
Yavapai Regional Medical Center 1003 Willow Creek Rd	Prescott	AZ	86301	**877-843-9762**	928-445-2700

366-3 Psychiatric Hospitals

Name / Address	City	State	Zip	Toll-Free	Phone
Allentown State Hospital 1600 Hanover Ave	Allentown	PA	18109	**800-256-3571**	610-740-3200
Arbour Hospital 49 Robinwood Ave	Jamaica Plain	MA	02130	**800-828-3934**	617-522-4400
Arizona State Hospital 2500 E Van Buren St	Phoenix	AZ	85008	**877-588-5163**	602-244-1331
Brentwood A Behavioral Health Co 1006 Highland Ave	Shreveport	LA	71101	**877-678-7500**	318-678-7500
BryLin Hospitals 1263 Delaware Ave	Buffalo	NY	14209	**800-727-9546**	716-886-8200
Caritas Peace Center 2020 Newburg Rd	Louisville	KY	40205	**800-451-3637**	502-451-3330
Carrier Clinic PO Box 147	Belle Mead	NJ	08502	**800-933-3579**	908-281-1000
CenterPointe Hospital 5931 Hwy 94 S	Saint Charles	MO	63304	**800-345-5407**	636-441-7300
Central Washington Hospital PO Box 1887	Wenatchee	WA	98807	**800-365-6428**	509-662-1511
Chicago Lakeshore Hospital 4840 N Marine Dr	Chicago	IL	60640	**800-888-0560**	773-878-9700
College Hospital 10802 College Pl	Cerritos	CA	90703	**800-352-3301**	562-924-9581
Danville State Hospital 200 State Hospital Dr	Danville	PA	17821	**888-796-3476**	570-271-4500
Del Amo Hospital 23700 Camino Del Sol	Torrance	CA	90505	**800-533-5266**	310-530-1151
Dominion Hospital 2960 Sleepy Hollow Rd	Falls Church	VA	22044	**800-950-6463**	703-536-2000
Fairfax Hospital 10200 NE 132nd St	Kirkland	WA	98034	**800-435-7221**	425-821-2000
Fairmount Behavioral Health System 561 Fairthorne St	Philadelphia	PA	19128	**800-235-0200**	215-487-4000
Fergus Falls Regional Treatment Center 1400 N Union Ave	Fergus Falls	MN	56537	**800-657-3854**	218-739-7200
Focus Healthcare of Georgia 2927 Demere Rd	Saint Simons Island	GA	31522	**800-234-0420**	912-638-1999
Fort Lauderdale Hospital 1601 E Las Olas Blvd	Fort Lauderdale	FL	33301	**800-585-7527**	954-463-4321
Four Winds Hospital 800 Cross River Rd	Katonah	NY	10536	**800-528-6624**	914-763-8151
Friends Hospital 4641 Roosevelt Blvd	Philadelphia	PA	19124	**800-889-0548**	215-831-4600
Green Oaks Hospital 7808 Clodus Fields Dr	Dallas	TX	75251	**800-866-6554**	972-991-9504
Hampstead Hospital 218 East Rd	Hampstead	NH	03841	**800-600-5311**	603-329-5311
Hartgrove Hospital 520 N Ridgeway Ave	Chicago	IL	60624	**800-478-4783**	773-722-3113
Havenwyck Hospital 1525 University Dr	Auburn Hills	MI	48326	**800-401-2727**	248-373-9200
Hill Crest Behavioral Health Services 6869 5th Ave S	Birmingham	AL	35212	**800-292-8553**	205-833-9000
Holliswood Hospital 87-37 Palermo St	Holliswood	NY	11423	**800-486-3005**	718-776-8181
Holly Hill Hospital 3019 Falstaff Rd	Raleigh	NC	27610	**800-422-1840**	919-250-7000
Hudson River Psychiatric Center 10 Ross Cir	Poughkeepsie	NY	12601	**800-871-7910**	845-452-8000
Las Encinas Hospital 2900 E Del Mar Blvd	Pasadena	CA	91107	**800-792-2345**	626-795-9901
Las Vegas Medical Center 3695 Hot Springs Blvd PO Box 1388	Las Vegas	NM	87701	**800-446-5970**	505-454-2100

Psychiatric Hospitals (Cont'd)

Name / Address	City	State	Zip	Toll-Free	Phone
Meadows Psychiatric Center 132 Meadows Dr	Centre Hall	PA	16828	**800-641-7529**	814-364-2161
Menninger Clinic PO Box 809045	Houston	TX	77280	**800-351-9058**	713-275-5000
Middle Tennessee Mental Health Institute 221 Stewarts Ferry Pike	Nashville	TN	37214	**800-575-3506**	615-902-7400
Pembroke Hospital 199 Oak St. *Admissions	Pembroke	MA	02359	**800-222-2237***	781-826-8161
Peninsula Hospital 2347 Jones Bend Rd	Louisville	TN	37777	**800-526-8215**	865-970-9800
Pine Rest Christian Mental Health Services PO Box 165	Grand Rapids	MI	49508	**800-678-5500**	616-455-5000
Potomac Ridge Behavioral Health 14901 Broschart Rd	Rockville	MD	20850	**800-204-8600**	301-251-4500
Psychiatric Institute of Washington 4228 Wisconsin Ave NW	Washington	DC	20016	**800-369-2273**	202-885-5600
Retreat Healthcare PO Box 803	Brattleboro	VT	05302	**800-345-5550**	802-257-7785
Ridge Behavioral Health System 3050 Rio Dosa Dr	Lexington	KY	40509	**800-753-4673**	859-269-2325
River Park Hospital 1230 6th Ave	Huntington	WV	25701	**800-992-9101**	304-526-9111
Sheppard Pratt at Ellicott City 4100 College Ave	Ellicott City	MD	21043	**800-883-3322**	410-465-3322
Sheppard Pratt Health System 6501 N Charles St	Baltimore	MD	21204	**800-627-0330**	410-938-3000
Spring Grove Hospital Center 55 Wade Ave.	Catonsville	MD	21228	**866-734-3337**	410-402-6000
Spring Harbor Hospital 123 Andover Rd	Westbrook	ME	04092	**888-524-0080**	207-761-2200
Springfield Hospital Center 6655 Sykesville Rd	Sykesville	MD	21784	**800-333-7564**	410-795-2100
Thomas B Finan Center 10102 Country Club Rd SE PO Box 1722	Cumberland	MD	21501	**888-854-0035**	301-777-2405
Timberlawn Mental Health System 4600 Samuell Blvd	Dallas	TX	75228	**800-426-4944**	214-381-7181
Western Mental Health Institute 11100 Hwy 64 W	Bolivar	TN	38008	**800-548-0635**	731-228-2000
Westwood Lodge Hospital 45 Clapboardtree Rd	Westwood	MA	02090	**800-222-2237**	781-762-7764
Willmar Regional Treatment Center 1550 Hwy 71 NE	Willmar	MN	56201	**800-657-3898**	320-231-5100

366-4 Rehabilitation Hospitals

Name / Address	City	State	Zip	Toll-Free	Phone
Baylor Institute for Rehabilitation 3505 Gaston Ave	Dallas	TX	75246	**800-242-2334**	214-820-9300
Brooks Rehabilitation Hospital 3599 University Blvd S	Jacksonville	FL	32216	**800-487-7342**	904-858-7600
Bryn Mawr Rehabilitation Hospital 414 Paoli Pike	Malvern	PA	19355	**888-734-2241**	610-251-5400
Burke Rehabilitation Hospital 785 Mamaroneck Ave	White Plains	NY	10605	**888-992-8753**	914-597-2500
Cardinal Hill Rehabilitation Hospital 2050 Versailles Rd	Lexington	KY	40504	**800-843-1408**	859-254-5701
Charlotte Institute of Rehabilitation 1100 Blythe Blvd	Charlotte	NC	28203	**800-634-2256**	704-355-4300
Drake Center 151 W Galbraith Rd	Cincinnati	OH	45216	**800-948-0003**	513-948-2500
Gaylord Hospital Gaylord Farms Rd PO Box 400	Wallingford	CT	06492	**888-429-5673**	203-284-2800
HealthSouth Braintree Rehabilitation Hospital 250 Pond St	Braintree	MA	02184	**800-997-3422**	781-848-5353
HealthSouth Chattanooga Rehabilitation Hospital 2412 McCallie Ave	Chattanooga	TN	37404	**800-763-5189**	423-698-0221
HealthSouth Mountainview Regional Rehabilitation Hospital 1160 Van Voorhis Rd	Morgantown	WV	26505	**800-388-2451**	304-598-1100
HealthSouth Nittany Valley Rehabilitation Hospital 550 W College Ave	Pleasant Gap	PA	16823	**800-842-6026**	814-359-3421
HealthSouth North Louisiana Rehabilitation Hospital 1401 Ezell St	Ruston	LA	71270	**800-765-4772**	318-251-3126
HealthSouth Reading Rehabilitation Hospital 1623 Morgantown Rd	Reading	PA	19607	**800-755-8027**	610-796-6000
HealthSouth Rehabilitation Hospital of Altoona 2005 Valley View Blvd	Altoona	PA	16602	**800-873-4220**	814-944-3535
HealthSouth Rehabilitation Hospital of Austin 1215 Red River	Austin	TX	78701	**800-765-4772**	512-474-5700
HealthSouth Rehabilitation Hospital of Erie 143 E 2nd St	Erie	PA	16507	**800-234-4574**	814-878-1200
HealthSouth Rehabilitation Hospital of Greater Pittsburgh 2380 McGinley Rd	Monroeville	PA	15146	**800-695-4774**	412-856-2400
HealthSouth Rehabilitation Hospital of Memphis 1282 Union Ave	Memphis	TN	38104	**800-363-7342**	901-722-2000
HealthSouth Rehabilitation Hospital of North Alabama 107 Governors Dr	Huntsville	AL	35801	**800-467-3422**	256-535-2300
HealthSouth Tri-State Rehabilitation Hospital 4100 Covert Ave	Evansville	IN	47714	**800-677-3422**	812-476-9983
Helen Hayes Hospital Rt 9W	West Haverstraw	NY	10993	**888-707-3422**	845-947-3000
Institute for Rehabilitation & Research 1333 Moursund St	Houston	TX	77030	**800-447-3422**	713-799-5000
John Heinz Institute of Rehabilitation Medicine 150 Mundy St	Wilkes-Barre	PA	18702	**877-727-3422**	570-826-3800
Kessler Institute for Rehabilitation 1199 Pleasant Valley Way	West Orange	NJ	07052	**888-537-7537**	973-731-3600
Madonna Rehabilitation Hospital 5401 South St	Lincoln	NE	68506	**800-676-5448**	402-489-7102
Magee Rehabilitation Hospital 6 Franklin Plaza	Philadelphia	PA	19102	**800-966-2433**	215-587-3000
Marianjoy Rehabilitation Hospital & Clinics 26 W 171 Roosevelt Rd	Wheaton	IL	60187	**800-462-2371**	630-462-4000
Mary Free Bed Hospital & Rehabilitation Center 235 Wealthy St SE	Grand Rapids	MI	49503	**800-528-8989**	616-242-0300
Methodist Rehabilitation Center 1350 E Woodrow Wilson Dr	Jackson	MS	39216	**800-223-6672**	601-981-2611
Rancho Los Amigos National Rehabilitation Center 7601 E Imperial Hwy	Downey	CA	90242	**877-726-2461**	562-401-7111
Rehabilitation Hospital of Indiana 4141 Shore Dr	Indianapolis	IN	46254	**800-933-0123**	317-329-2000
Rehabilitation Hospital of the Pacific Inc 226 N Kuakini St	Honolulu	HI	96817	**800-973-4226**	808-531-3511
Rehabilitation Institute of Chicago 345 E Superior St *Admitting	Chicago	IL	60611	**800-354-7342***	312-238-1000
Rio Vista Rehabilitation Hospital 1740 Curie Dr	El Paso	TX	79902	**800-999-8392**	915-544-3399
Saint David's Rehabilitation Hospital 1005 E 32nd St	Austin	TX	78705	**800-533-8545**	512-867-5100
Siskin Hospital for Physical Rehabilitation 1 Siskin Plaza	Chattanooga	TN	37403	**800-474-7546**	423-634-1200
Southern Indiana Rehabilitation Hospital 3104 Blackiston Blvd	New Albany	IN	47150	**800-737-7090**	812-941-8300
Southern Kentucky Rehab 1300 Campbell Ln	Bowling Green	KY	42104	**800-989-5775**	270-782-6900
Spalding Rehabilitation Hospital 900 Potomac St	Aurora	CO	80011	**800-367-3309**	303-367-1166
SSM Rehab 6420 Clayton Rd Executive Offices	Saint Louis	MO	63117	**800-818-9494**	314-768-5300
Thoms Rehabilitation Hospital 68 Sweeten Creek Rd	Asheville	NC	28803	**800-627-1533**	828-274-2400
Via Christi Rehabilitation Center 1151 N Rock Rd	Wichita	KS	67206	**800-667-4241**	316-634-3400
Walton Rehabilitation Hospital 1355 Independence Dr	Augusta	GA	30901	**800-366-6055**	706-724-7746
Warm Springs Rehabilitation Hospital 5101 Medical Dr	San Antonio	TX	78229	**800-451-1350**	210-616-0100

366-5 Specialty Hospitals

Name / Address	City	State	Zip	Toll-Free	Phone
Arthur G James Cancer Hospital & Richard J Solove Research Institute 300 W 10th Ave	Columbus	OH	43210	**888-293-3118**	614-293-5485
Bascom Palmer Eye Institute 900 NW 17th St	Miami	FL	33136	**800-329-7000**	305-326-6000
Brigham & Women's Hospital 75 Francis St	Boston	MA	02115	**800-722-5520**	617-732-5500
City of Hope National Medical Center Beckman Research Institute 1500 E Duarte Rd	Duarte	CA	91010	**800-826-4673**	626-359-8111
Dana-Farber Cancer Institute 44 Binney St	Boston	MA	02115	**800-757-3324**	617-632-3000
Doheny Eye Institute 1450 San Pablo St	Los Angeles	CA	90033	**800-872-2273**	323-442-6300
Fox Chase Cancer Center 333 Cottman Ave	Philadelphia	PA	19111	**888-369-2427**	215-728-6900
H Lee Moffitt Cancer Center & Research Institute 12902 Magnolia Dr	Tampa	FL	33612	**800-456-3434**	813-972-4673
Hospital for Joint Diseases Orthopedic Institute 301 E 17th St	New York	NY	10003	**800-372-2887**	212-598-6000
Midwestern Regional Medical Center 2520 Elisha Ave	Zion	IL	60099	**800-322-9183**	847-872-4561
National Jewish Medical & Research Center 1400 Jackson St	Denver	CO	80206	**800-222-5864**	303-388-4461
Norris Comprehensive Cancer Center & Hospital 1441 Eastlake Ave	Los Angeles	CA	90033	**800-522-6237**	323-865-3000
Oaks Treatment Center 1407 W Stassney Ln	Austin	TX	78745	**800-843-6257**	512-464-0200
Richmond Eye & Ear Surgical Specialty Center 8700 Stony Point Pkwy	Richmond	VA	23235	**800-328-7334**	804-775-4500
Roswell Park Cancer Institute Elm & Carlton Sts	Buffalo	NY	14263	**800-685-6825**	716-845-2300
Saint Francis Health Care Center 401 N Broadway	Green Springs	OH	44836	**800-248-2552**	419-639-2626
Specialty Hospital Jacksonville 4901 Richard St	Jacksonville	FL	32207	**800-378-9497**	904-737-3120
Texas Center for Infectious Diseases 2303 SE Military Dr	San Antonio	TX	78223	**800-839-5864**	210-534-8857
Texas Orthopedic Hospital 7401 S Main St	Houston	TX	77030	**800-678-4501**	713-799-8600
UC Davis Cancer Center 4501 X St	Sacramento	CA	95817	**800-362-5566**	916-734-5800
Western Maryland Hospice Center 1500 Pennsylvania Ave	Hagerstown	MD	21742	**877-964-2262**	301-791-4400

366-6 Veterans Hospitals

Name / Address	City	State	Zip	Toll-Free	Phone
Carl T Hayden Veterans Affairs Medical Center 650 E Indian School Rd	Phoenix	AZ	85012	**800-359-8262**	602-277-5551
Carl Vinson Veterans Affairs Medical Center 1826 Veterans Blvd	Dublin	GA	31021	**800-595-5229**	478-272-1210
Central Texas Veteran's Health Care 1901 Veterans Memorial Dr	Temple	TX	76504	**800-423-2111**	254-778-4811
Dwight D Eisenhower Veterans Affairs Medical Center 4101 S 4th St	Leavenworth	KS	66048	**800-952-8387**	913-682-2000
Hunter Holmes McGuire Veterans Affairs Medical Center 1201 Broad Rock Blvd	Richmond	VA	23249	**800-784-8381**	804-675-5000
James E Van Zandt Veterans Affairs Medical Center 2907 Pleasant Valley Blvd	Altoona	PA	16602	**877-626-2500**	814-943-8164
Jerry L Pettis Memorial Veterans Affairs Medical Center 11201 Benton St *Mail Rm	Loma Linda	CA	92357	**800-741-8387***	909-825-7084
Overton Brooks Veterans Affairs Medical Center 510 E Stoner Ave	Shreveport	LA	71101	**800-863-7441**	318-221-8411
Sam Rayburn Memorial Veterans Center 1201 E 9th St	Bonham	TX	75418	**800-924-8387**	903-583-2111
Sepulveda Veterans Affairs Medical Center 16111 Plummer St	North Hills	CA	91343	**800-516-4567**	818-891-7711
Sierra NV Healthcare Systems (VA Medical Center) 1000 Locust St	Reno	NV	89502	**888-838-6256**	775-786-7200
Stratton Veterans Affairs Medical Center 113 Holland Ave	Albany	NY	12208	**800-223-4810**	518-626-5000
VA Central Alabama Veterans Health Care System 215 Perry Hill Rd	Montgomery	AL	36109	**800-214-8387**	334-272-4670
VA Hudson Valley Health Care System Franklin Delano Roosevelt Campus PO Box 100	Montrose	NY	10548	**800-269-8749**	914-737-4400
Veterans Affairs Lakeside Medical Center 333 E Huron St	Chicago	IL	60611	**800-644-1243**	312-569-8387
Veterans Affairs Medical Center 3701 Loop Rd E	Tuscaloosa	AL	35404	**888-269-3045**	205-554-2000
Veterans Affairs Medical Center 2400 Hospital Rd	Tuskegee	AL	36083	**800-214-8387**	334-727-0550
Veterans Affairs Medical Center 500 Hwy 89 N	Prescott	AZ	86313	**800-949-1005**	928-445-4860

Name / Address	City	State	Zip	Toll-Free	Phone
Veterans Affairs Medical Center 1100 N College Ave	Fayetteville	AR	72703	**800-691-8387**	479-443-4301
Veterans Affairs Medical Center 5901 E 7th St	Long Beach	CA	90822	**888-769-8387**	562-826-8000
Veterans Affairs Medical Center 3350 La Jolla Village Dr	San Diego	CA	92101	**800-331-8387**	858-552-8585
Veterans Affairs Medical Center 1055 Clermont St	Denver	CO	80220	**888-336-8262**	303-399-8020
Veterans Affairs Medical Center 1601 Kirkwood Hwy	Wilmington	DE	19805	**800-450-8262**	302-994-2511
Veterans Affairs Medical Center 1201 NW 16th St	Miami	FL	33125	**888-276-1785**	305-324-4455
Veterans Affairs Medical Center 7305 N Military Trail	West Palm Beach	FL	33410	**800-972-8262**	561-882-8262
Veterans Affairs Medical Center 1670 Clairmont Rd	Decatur	GA	30033	**800-944-9726**	404-321-6111
Veterans Affairs Medical Center 3001 Green Bay Rd	North Chicago	IL	60064	**800-393-0865**	847-688-1900
Veterans Affairs Medical Center 2121 Lake Ave	Fort Wayne	IN	46805	**800-360-8387**	260-426-5431
Veterans Affairs Medical Center 1700 E 38th St	Marion	IN	46953	**800-498-8792**	765-674-3321
Veterans Affairs Medical Center 3600 30th St	Des Moines	IA	50310	**800-294-8387**	515-699-5999
Veterans Affairs Medical Center 1515 W Pleasant St	Knoxville	IA	50138	**800-816-8878**	641-842-3101
Veterans Affairs Medical Center 5500 E Kellogg St	Wichita	KS	67218	**888-878-6881**	316-685-2221
Veterans Affairs Medical Center 1601 Perdido St	New Orleans	LA	70112	**800-935-8387**	504-568-0811
Veterans Affairs Medical Center 10 N Greene St	Baltimore	MD	21201	**800-463-6295**	410-605-7000
Veterans Affairs Medical Center 325 E 'H' St	Iron Mountain	MI	49801	**800-215-8262**	906-774-3300
Veterans Affairs Medical Center 1500 Weiss St	Saginaw	MI	48602	**800-406-5143**	989-497-2500
Veterans Affairs Medical Center 1 Veterans Dr	Minneapolis	MN	55417	**866-414-5058**	612-725-2000
Veterans Affairs Medical Center 400 Veterans Ave	Biloxi	MS	39531	**800-296-8872**	228-523-5000
Veterans Affairs Medical Center 4801 E Linwood Blvd	Kansas City	MO	64128	**800-525-1483**	816-861-4700
Veterans Affairs Medical Center 915 N Grand Blvd	Saint Louis	MO	63106	**800-228-5459**	314-487-0400
Veterans Affairs Medical Center 600 S 70th St	Lincoln	NE	68510	**800-451-5796**	402-489-3802
Veterans Affairs Medical Center 4101 Woolworth Ave	Omaha	NE	68105	**800-608-8806**	402-346-8800
Veterans Affairs Medical Center 718 Smyth Rd	Manchester	NH	03104	**800-892-8384**	603-624-4366
Veterans Affairs Medical Center 151 Knollcroft Rd	Lyons	NJ	07939	**800-927-1000**	908-647-0180
Veterans Affairs Medical Center 1501 San Pedro Dr SE	Albuquerque	NM	87108	**800-465-8262**	505-265-1711
Veterans Affairs Medical Center 76 Veterans Ave	Bath	NY	14810	**877-845-3247**	607-664-4000
Veterans Affairs Medical Center 3495 Bailey Ave	Buffalo	NY	14215	**800-532-8387**	716-834-9200
Veterans Affairs Medical Center 79 Middleville Rd	Northport	NY	11768	**800-827-1000**	631-261-4400
Veterans Affairs Medical Center 800 Irving Ave	Syracuse	NY	13210	**800-221-2883**	315-425-4400
Veterans Affairs Medical Center 2300 Ramsey St	Fayetteville	NC	28301	**800-771-6106**	910-488-2120
Veterans Affairs Medical Center 2101 Elm St N	Fargo	ND	58102	**800-410-9723**	701-232-3241
Veterans Affairs Medical Center 3200 Vine St	Cincinnati	OH	45220	**888-267-7873**	513-861-3100
Veterans Affairs Medical Center 10701 East Blvd	Cleveland	OH	44106	**888-350-3100**	216-791-3800
Veterans Affairs Medical Center 921 NE 13th St	Oklahoma City	OK	73104	**866-835-5273**	405-270-0501
Veterans Affairs Medical Center 3710 US Veterans Hospital Rd	Portland	OR	97239	**888-233-8305**	503-220-8262
Veterans Affairs Medical Center 325 New Castle Rd	Butler	PA	16001	**800-362-8262**	724-287-4781
Veterans Affairs Medical Center 1400 Black Horse Hill Rd	Coatesville	PA	19320	**800-290-6172**	610-384-7711
Veterans Affairs Medical Center 135 E 38th St	Erie	PA	16504	**800-274-8387**	814-868-8661
Veterans Affairs Medical Center 1700 S Lincoln Ave	Lebanon	PA	17042	**800-409-8771**	717-272-6621
Veterans Affairs Medical Center 3900 Woodland Ave	Philadelphia	PA	19104	**800-949-1001**	215-823-5800
Veterans Affairs Medical Center University Dr C	Pittsburgh	PA	15240	**800-309-8398**	412-688-6000
Veterans Affairs Medical Center 113 Comanche Rd	Fort Meade	SD	57741	**800-743-1070**	605-347-2511
Veterans Affairs Medical Center 500 N 5th St	Hot Springs	SD	57747	**800-764-5370**	605-745-2000
Veterans Affairs Medical Center 6010 Amarillo Blvd W	Amarillo	TX	79106	**800-687-8262**	806-355-9703
Veterans Affairs Medical Center 215 N Main St	White River Junction	VT	05009	**866-687-8387**	802-295-9363
Veterans Affairs Medical Center 1540 Spring Valley Dr	Huntington	WV	25704	**800-827-8244**	304-429-6741
Veterans Affairs Medical Center 510 Butler Ave	Martinsburg	WV	25401	**800-817-3807**	304-263-0811
Veterans Affairs Medical Center 5000 W National Ave	Milwaukee	WI	53295	**888-469-6614**	414-384-2000
Veterans Affairs Medical Center 500 E Veterans St	Tomah	WI	54660	**800-872-8662**	608-372-3971
Veterans Affairs Medical Center 1898 Fort Rd	Sheridan	WY	82801	**800-370-0250**	307-672-3473

HOSPITALS - DEVELOPMENTAL DISABILITIES

SEE Developmental Centers

367 HOT TUBS, SPAS, WHIRLPOOL BATHS

Name / Address	City	State	Zip	Toll-Free	Phone
Alaglass Pools 165 Sweet Bay Rd	Saint Matthews	SC	29135	**877-655-7179**	803-655-7179
American Whirlpool Products Corp 3050 N 29th Ct	Hollywood	FL	33020	**800-327-1394**	954-921-4400
Americh Corp 13212 Saticoy St	North Hollywood	CA	91605	**800-453-1463**	818-982-1711
Aqua Glass Corp 320 Industrial Park Dr	Adamsville	TN	38310	**800-632-0911**	731-632-0911
Aquatic Industries PO Box 889	Leander	TX	78646	**800-928-3707***	512-259-2255
*Cust Svc					
Atlantic Whirlpools Inc 8721 Glenwood Ave	Raleigh	NC	27617	**800-849-8827**	919-783-7447
Baja Products 4065 N Romero Rd	Tucson	AZ	85705	**800-845-2252**	520-887-1154
Baker Mfg Corp 7460 Chancellor Dr	Orlando	FL	32809	**800-881-2284**	407-816-9559
Bath-Tec Inc PO Box 1118	Ennis	TX	75120	**800-526-3301**	972-646-5279
Bathroom World Mfg Co 3569 NW 10th Ave	Fort Lauderdale	FL	33309	**800-566-0541**	954-566-0451
California Acrylic Industries Cal Spas 1462 E Ninth St	Pomona	CA	91766	**800-225-7727**	909-623-8781
Cameo Marble 540 Central Ct	New Albany	IN	47150	**800-447-8558**	812-944-5055
Clarke Products Inc 1170 109th St	Grand Prairie	TX	75050	**800-426-8964**	972-660-1992
Classic Spas Inc 1400 Melody Rd	Marysville	CA	95901	**800-796-7727**	530-742-7304
Dimension One Spas 2611 Business Park Dr	Vista	CA	92081	**800-345-7727**	760-727-7727
DM Industries Ltd 2320 NW 147th St	Miami	FL	33054	**800-848-2772**	305-685-5739
Fiberglass Systems Inc 4545 Enterprise St	Boise	ID	83705	**800-727-9907**	208-342-6823
Fox Pool Corp 3490 Board Rd	York	PA	17402	**800-723-1011**	717-764-8581
Gatsby Spas Inc 1003 S Alexander St Suite 7	Plant City	FL	33563	**800-393-7727**	813-754-4122
Kallista Inc 444 Highland Dr	Kohler	WI	53044	**888-452-5547**	920-457-4441
Koral Industries Inc PO Box 1270	Ennis	TX	75120	**800-627-2441**	972-875-6555
Lasco Bathware 8101 E Kaiser Blvd Suite 130	Anaheim	CA	92808	**800-877-2005**	714-993-1220
MAAX Pearl 9224 73rd Ave N	Brooklyn Park	MN	55428	**800-328-2531**	763-424-3335
Marquis Corp 596 Hoffman Rd	Independence	OR	97351	**800-275-0888**	503-838-0888
Oasis Industries Inc 1600 Mountain St	Aurora	IL	60505	**800-323-2748**	630-898-3500
Plastic Development Co Inc PO Box 4007	Williamsport	PA	17701	**800-451-1420**	570-323-3060
Royal Baths Mfg Co 14635 Chrisman Rd	Houston	TX	77039	**800-826-0074**	281-442-3400
Spurlin Industries Inc PO Box 707	Palmetto	GA	30268	**800-749-4475**	770-463-1644
Thermo Spas Inc 155 East St	Wallingford	CT	06492	**800-876-0158**	203-265-6133
Twirl Jet Spas Inc 3990 Industrial Ave	Hemet	CA	92545	**800-854-4890**	951-766-4306
Watertech Whirlpool Bath & Spa 2507 Plymouth Rd	Johnson City	TN	37601	**800-289-8827**	423-926-1470
Watkins Mfg Corp 1280 Park Ctr Dr	Vista	CA	92083	**800-999-4688**	760-598-6464

368 HOTEL RESERVATIONS SERVICES

Name / Address	City	State	Zip	Toll-Free	Phone
AAA Reservation Services 1740 Jackson Ave	New Orleans	LA	70113	**888-840-2331**	504-522-1785
Accommodations Plus 4230 Merrick Rd	Massapequa	NY	11758	**800-733-7666**	718-995-4444
Advance Reservations Inn Arizona PO Box 950	Tempe	AZ	85280	**800-456-0682**	480-990-0682
Advanced Reservation Systems Inc 1059 1st Ave	San Diego	CA	92101	**800-434-7894**	619-238-0900
Alexandria & Arlington Bed & Breakfast Network 512 S 25th St	Arlington	VA	22202	**888-549-3415**	703-549-3415
All Around the Town 270 Lafayette St Suite 804	New York	NY	10012	**800-443-3800**	212-675-5600
All Keys Reservation Service PO Box 269	Norfolk	CT	06058	**800-255-5397**	
Alliance Reservations Network 14435 N 7th St	Phoenix	AZ	85022	**800-892-2108**	602-952-2106
American Country Collection of Bed & Breakfast Homes 1353 Union St	Schenectady	NY	12308	**800-810-4948**	518-370-4948
Anchorage Alaska Bed & Breakfast Assn PO Box 242623	Anchorage	AK	99524	**888-584-5147**	907-272-5909
Annapolis Accommodations 41 Maryland Ave	Annapolis	MD	21401	**800-715-1000**	410-280-0900
Atlantic City Toll-Free Reservations PO Box 665	Northfield	NJ	08225	**800-833-7070**	609-646-7070
B & B Agency of Boston 47 Commercial Wharf #3	Boston	MA	02110	**800-248-9262**	617-720-3540
Barclay International Group 6800 Jericho Tpke	Syosset	NY	11791	**800-845-6636**	516-364-0064
Bed & Breakfast Accommodations Ltd PO Box 12011	Washington	DC	20005	**877-893-3233**	202-328-3510
Bed & Breakfast Assoc Bay Colony Ltd PO Box 57166 Babson Park Branch	Boston	MA	02457	**888-486-6018**	781-449-5302
Bed & Breakfast Atlanta Reservation Services 790 North Ave Suite 202	Atlanta	GA	30306	**800-967-3224**	404-875-0525
Bed & Breakfast & Beyond Reservation Service 3115 Napoleon Ave	New Orleans	LA	70125	**800-886-3709**	504-896-9977
Bed & Breakfast Cape Cod PO Box 1312	Orleans	MA	02653	**800-541-6226**	508-255-3824
Bed & Breakfast Directory for San Diego PO Box 3292	San Diego	CA	92163	**800-619-7666**	
Bed & Breakfast of Hawaii PO Box 449	Kapaa	HI	96746	**800-733-1632**	808-822-7771
Bed & Breakfast Inc-A Reservation Service 1021 Moss St	New Orleans	LA	70152	**800-729-4640**	504-488-4640
Bed & Breakfast of Philadelphia PO Box 21	Devon	PA	19333	**800-448-3619**	610-687-3565
Bed & Breakfast Reservations 11A Beach Rd	Gloucester	MA	01930	**800-832-2632**	617-964-1606
Bed & Breakfast Reservations 11A Beach Rd	Gloucester	MA	01930	**800-832-2632**	978-281-9505
Bed & Breakfast San Francisco PO Box 420009	San Francisco	CA	94142	**800-452-8249**	415-899-0060
Big Easy/Gulf Coast Reservation Service 233 Cottonwood Dr	Gretna	LA	70056	**800-368-4876**	504-433-2563
Branson Nights Reservations 109 N Business 65	Branson	MO	65616	**800-329-9999**	417-335-6971
Branson/Lakes Area Lodging Assn PO Box 430	Branson	MO	65615	**888-238-6782**	417-332-1400
Branson's Best Reservations 3150 Green Mountain Dr	Branson	MO	65616	**800-800-2019**	417-339-2204
Budgethotels.com Inc 1260 Hornby St Suite 104	Vancouver	BC	V6Z1W2	**800-548-4432**	
Capitol Reservations 1730 Rhode Island Ave NW Suite 1210	Washington	DC	20036	**800-847-4832**	202-452-1270

Listing	City	State	Zip	Toll-Free	Phone
Central Reservation Service 159 Lookout Pl Suite 201	Maitland	FL	32751	**800-548-3311**	407-740-6442
Central Reservation Service of New England Inc 300 Terminal C Logan International Airport	East Boston	MA	02128	**800-332-3026**	617-569-3800
Citywide Reservation Services 839 Beacon St Suite A	Boston	MA	02215	**800-468-3593**	617-267-7424
Colonial Williamsburg Reservation Center PO Box 1776	Williamsburg	VA	23187	**800-447-8679**	757-253-2277
Colorado Resort Services 2955 Village Dr	Steamboat Springs	CO	80487	**800-525-7654**	970-879-7654
Downtown Vancouver B & B Accommodations Group 515 W Pender St Suite 247	Vancouver	BC	V6B6H5	**877-454-8179**	604-454-8179
Equity Corporate Housing 913 Trinity Rd	Raleigh	NC	27607	**800-533-2370**	919-851-1511
Eugene Area Bed & Breakfast Assn 2013 Charnelton St	Eugene	OR	97405	**800-507-1354**	541-343-3553
Express Hotel Reservations 3825 Iris Ave Suite 200	Boulder	CO	80301	**800-356-1123**	303-440-8481
Florida Hotels & Discount Guide World Choice Travel 11300 US 1 Suite 300	North Palm Beach	FL	33408	**800-670-5445**	561-845-8856
Florida SunBreak 90 Alton Rd Suite 16	Miami Beach	FL	33139	**800-786-2732**	305-532-1516
Good Earth Travel Adventures Reservations PO Box 8510	Canmore	AB	T1W2V2	**888-979-9797**	403-678-9358
Grand Canyon National Park Lodges PO Box 699	Grand Canyon	AZ	86023	**888-297-2757**	928-638-2631
Greater Miami & the Beaches Hotel Assn 407 Lincoln Rd Suite 10G	Miami Beach	FL	33139	**800-531-3553**	305-531-3553
Greater Tacoma Bed & Breakfast Reservation Service 619 N 'K' St	Tacoma	WA	98403	**800-406-4088**	253-752-8175
Greek Hotel & Cruise Reservation Center 17280 Newhope St Suite 18	Fountain Valley	CA	92708	**800-736-5717**	714-641-3118
Greenville Area Central Reservations PO Box 10527	Greenville	SC	29603	**800-351-7180**	864-233-0461
Gulf Coast Hotel Reservations PO Box 116	Biloxi	MS	39533	**888-388-1006**	228-388-6117
Hawaii's Best Bed & Breakfasts PO Box 485	Laupahoehoe	HI	96764	**800-262-9912**	808-962-0100
Hilton Head Vacation Rentals 430 William Hilton Pkwy Suite 504	Hilton Head Island	SC	29926	**800-732-7671**	843-689-3010
Historic Charleston Bed & Breakfast Reservations Service 57 Broad St	Charleston	SC	29401	**800-743-3583**	843-722-6606
Hospitalite Canada 651 Notre Dame W Suite 260	Montreal	QC	H3C1H9	**800-665-1528**	514-287-9049
Hot Rooms 1 E Erie St Suite 225	Chicago	IL	60611	**800-468-3500**	773-468-7666
Hotel Locators.com 919 Garnet Ave Suite 216	San Diego	CA	92109	**800-576-0003**	
HotelNetDiscount.com 3070 Windward Plaza Suite F-302	Alpharetta	GA	30005	**800-364-1528**	770-664-1316
Hotels.com 10440 N Central Expy	Dallas	TX	75231	**800-964-6835***	214-361-7311
*Sales					
Jackson Hole Central Reservations 140 E Broadway Suite 24	Jackson	WY	83001	**800-443-6931**	307-733-4005
Jackson Hole Resort Reservations LLC PO Box 12739	Jackson	WY	83002	**800-329-9205**	307-733-6331
Key West Key 726 Passover Ln	Key West	FL	33040	**800-881-7321**	305-294-4357
Know Before You Go Reservations 4720 W Irlo Bronson Memorial Hwy	Kissimmee	FL	34746	**800-749-1993**	407-352-9813
Leading Hotels of the World 99 Park Ave	New York	NY	10016	**800-223-6800**	212-515-5600
Lexington Services 2120 Walnut Hill Ln Suite 100	Irving	TX	75038	**800-537-8483**	972-714-0585
Lodging.com 4805 N 30th St Suite 103	Colorado Springs	CO	80919	**888-563-4434**	
Luxe Worldwide Hotels 11461 Sunset Blvd	Los Angeles	CA	90049	**866-589-3411**	310-440-3090
Martha's Vineyard & Nantucket Reservations 73 Lagoon Pond Rd	Vineyard Haven	MA	02568	**800-649-5671**	508-693-7200
Myrtle Beach Reservation Service 1551 21st Ave N Suite 20	Myrtle Beach	SC	29577	**800-626-7477**	843-626-7477
National Reservation Bureau 3100 W Sahara Ave Suite 207	Las Vegas	NV	89109	**800-831-2754**	702-794-2820
New Mexico Central Reservations 800 20th St NW Suite B	Albuquerque	NM	87104	**800-466-7829**	505-766-9770
New Orleans Accommodations Bed & Breakfast Service 828 Rue Royal Suite 259	New Orleans	LA	70116	**888-240-0070**	504-561-0447
New Otani North America Reservation Center 120 S Los Angeles St	Los Angeles	CA	90012	**800-421-8795**	213-629-1114
Newport Reservations 174 Bellevue Ave Suite 203	Newport	RI	02840	**800-842-0102**	401-842-0102
Ocean City Hotel-Motel-Restaurant Assn PO Box 340	Ocean City	MD	21843	**800-626-2326**	410-289-6733
Pacific Reservation Service 2520 Westlake Ave N	Seattle	WA	98109	**800-684-2932**	206-439-7677
Preferred Hotels & Resorts Worldwide Inc 311 S Wacker Dr Suite 1900	Chicago	IL	60606	**800-323-7500**	312-913-0400
Quikbook 381 Park Ave S 3rd Fl	New York	NY	10016	**800-789-9887**	212-779-7666
Reservations USA 3171 North Pkwy	Pigeon Forge	TN	37863	**800-251-4444**	865-453-1000
Resort 2 Me 2600 Garden Rd Suite 111	Monterey	CA	93940	**800-757-5646**	831-642-6622
RSVP Martha's Vineyard PO Box 2042	Oak Bluffs	MA	02557	**866-778-7689**	508-693-9371
San Diego Concierge 4379 30th St Suite 4	San Diego	CA	92104	**800-979-9091**	619-280-4121
San Francisco Reservations 360 22nd St Suite 300	Oakland	CA	94612	**800-677-1550**	510-628-4444
Santa Fe Accommodations 320 Artist Rd	Santa Fe	NM	87501	**800-745-9910**	505-988-2800
Scottsdale Resort Accommodations 14505 N Hayden Rd Suite 341	Scottsdale	AZ	85260	**888-868-4378**	480-515-2300
Seattle Super Saver 701 Pike St Suite 800	Seattle	WA	98101	**800-535-7071**	206-461-5800
Stay Aspen Snowmass 425 Rio Grande Pl	Aspen	CO	81611	**800-670-0792**	970-925-9000
Travel Planners Inc 381 Park Ave S	New York	NY	10016	**800-221-3531**	212-532-1660
Travelweb.com 2777 Stemmons Fwy Suite 675	Dallas	TX	75207	**800-818-0033**	
Turbotrip.com 4124 S McCann Ct	Springfield	MO	65804	**800-473-7829**	
USA Hotel Guide 630 US 1 Suite 200	North Palm Beach	FL	33408	**888-729-7705**	561-845-8899
USA Hotels 860 Wyckoff Ave	Mahwah	NJ	07430	**800-343-8861**	201-847-9000
Utell International Resorts 8350 N Central Expy Suite 1900	Dallas	TX	75206	**800-223-6510**	214-234-4000
Vacation Co 42 New Orleans Rd	Hilton Head Island	SC	29928	**800-845-7018**	843-686-6100
Washington DC Accommodations 2201 Wisconsin Ave NW Suite C-120	Washington	DC	20007	**800-554-2220**	202-289-2220
Winter Park Resort Travel Services PO Box 36	Winter Park	CO	80482	**800-525-3538**	970-726-5587

369 HOTEL & RESORT OPERATION & MANAGEMENT

SEE ALSO Casino Companies; Corporate Housing; Hotel Reservations Services; Hotels & Motels (Individual) - Canada; Hotels & Motels (Individual) - US; Hotels - Conference Center; Resorts

Listing	City	State	Zip	Toll-Free	Phone
Accor Economy Lodging					
Motel 6 LP 4001 International Pkwy	Carrollton	TX	75007	**800-466-8356**	972-360-9000
Red Roof Inns Inc 4001 International Pkwy	Carrollton	TX	75007	**800-733-7663**	972-360-9000
Studio 6 4001 International Pkwy	Carrollton	TX	75007	**800-466-8356**	972-360-9000
Adam's Mark Hotels & Resorts 11330 Olive Blvd	Saint Louis	MO	63141	**800-444-2326**	314-567-9000
Admiral Benbow Inns of America Inc 2160 Kingston Ct Suite N	Marietta	GA	30067	**800-451-1986**	770-952-9145
Affinia Hospitality 500 W 37th St	New York	NY	10018	**866-246-2203***	212-465-3700
*Resv					
AFM Hospitality Corp Inc 135 Queens Plate Suite 410	Toronto	ON	M9W6V1	**800-249-3656**	416-361-1010
TSE: AFM					
AmericInn International LLC 250 Lake Dr E	Chanhassen	MN	55317	**800-634-3444**	952-294-5000
AmeriHost Franchise Systems Inc 1 Sylvan Way	Parsippany	NJ	07054	**800-889-8847**	973-428-9700
AmeriSuites 700 Rt 46 E	Fairfield	NJ	07004	**800-833-1516**	973-882-1010
Aristos International 319 S 11th St	McAllen	TX	78501	**800-527-4786**	956-631-2000
Ashford/Dromoland Castles PO Box 28966	Atlanta	GA	30358	**800-553-3719**	770-612-1701
Aspen Skiing Co LLC PO Box 1248	Aspen	CO	81612	**800-525-6200***	970-925-1220
*Sales					
Aston Hotels & Resorts 2155 Kalakaua Ave Suite 500	Honolulu	HI	96815	**800-922-7866**	808-931-1400
Atlas Hotels Inc 500 Hotel Cir N	San Diego	CA	92108	**800-772-8527**	619-291-2232
Baymont Inns & Suites Inc 100 E Wisconsin Ave Suite 1800	Milwaukee	WI	53202	**877-229-6668**	414-905-2000
Best Inns & Suites 13 Corporate Sq Suite 250	Atlanta	GA	30329	**800-237-8466**	404-321-4045
Best Western International Inc 6201 N 24th Pkwy	Phoenix	AZ	85016	**800-528-1234**	602-957-4200
Boyne USA Inc PO Box 19	Boyne Falls	MI	49713	**800-462-6963**	231-549-6000
Buckhead America Corp 50 Glen Lake Pkwy NE Suite 350	Atlanta	GA	30328	**800-432-7992**	770-393-2662
Camberley Hotel Co 4405 Northside Pkwy Suite 2124	Atlanta	GA	30327	**800-555-8000**	404-261-9600
Carlson Hospitality Worldwide PO Box 59159	Minneapolis	MN	55459	**800-333-3333**	763-212-5000
Carlson Hotels Worldwide					
Country Inns & Suites by Carlson PO Box 59159	Minneapolis	MN	55459	**800-456-4000***	763-212-1000
*Resv					
Park Inn PO Box 59159	Minneapolis	MN	55459	**800-670-7275***	763-212-1000
*Resv					
Radisson Hotels & Resorts PO Box 59159	Minneapolis	MN	55459	**800-333-3333**	763-212-5526
Castle Group Inc 500 Ala Moana Blvd Suite 555	Honolulu	HI	96813	**800-733-7753***	808-524-0900
*Sales					
Castle Resorts & Hotels 500 Ala Moana Blvd Suite 555	Honolulu	HI	96813	**800-367-5004**	808-545-3510
Cendant Corp Hospitality Div					
AmeriHost Franchise Systems Inc 1 Sylvan Way	Parsippany	NJ	07054	**800-889-8847**	973-428-9700
Days Inns Worldwide Inc 1 Sylvan Way	Parsippany	NJ	07054	**800-329-7466**	973-428-9700
Howard Johnson International Inc 1 Sylvan Way	Parsippany	NJ	07054	**800-446-4656**	973-428-9700
Ramada Franchise Systems Inc 1 Sylvan Way	Parsippany	NJ	07054	**800-932-6726**	973-428-9700
Super 8 Motels Inc 1910 8th Ave NE	Aberdeen	SD	57401	**800-800-8000**	605-225-2272
Cendant Corp Hospitality Services Div					
Travelodge Hotels Inc 1 Sylvan Way	Parsippany	NJ	07054	**800-578-7878**	973-428-9700
Villager Lodge Franchise Systems Inc 1 Sylvan Way	Parsippany	NJ	07054	**888-821-5738**	973-428-9700
Wingate Inns International Inc 1 Sylvan Way	Parsippany	NJ	07054	**800-228-1000**	973-428-9700
Chase Suite Hotels by Woodfin 12730 High Bluff Dr Suite 250	San Diego	CA	92130	**800-237-8811**	858-794-2338
Choice Hotels Canada Inc 5090 Explorer Dr Suite 500	Mississauga	ON	L4W4T9	**800-424-6423**	905-602-2222
Choice Hotels International Inc 10750 Columbia Pike	Silver Spring	MD	20901	**800-424-6423**	301-592-5000
NYSE: CHH					
Clarion Hotels 10750 Columbia Pike	Silver Spring	MD	20901	**800-424-6423**	301-592-5000
Comfort Inns 10750 Columbia Pike	Silver Spring	MD	20901	**800-424-6423**	301-592-5000
Comfort Suites 10750 Columbia Pike	Silver Spring	MD	20901	**800-424-6423**	301-592-5000
Econo Lodge 10750 Columbia Pike	Silver Spring	MD	20901	**800-424-6423**	301-592-5000
MainStay Suites 10750 Columbia Pike	Silver Spring	MD	20901	**800-424-6423**	301-592-5000
Quality Inns Hotels & Suites 10750 Columbia Pike	Silver Spring	MD	20901	**800-424-6423**	301-592-5000
Rodeway Inns 10750 Columbia Pike	Silver Spring	MD	20901	**800-424-6423**	301-592-5000
Sleep Inn & Suites 10750 Columbia Pike	Silver Spring	MD	20901	**800-424-6423**	301-592-5000
Clarion Hotels 10750 Columbia Pike	Silver Spring	MD	20901	**800-424-6423**	301-592-5000
Club Med Inc 75 Valencia Ave	Coral Gables	FL	33134	**800-258-2633**	305-925-9000
Coastal Inns Inc 515 Kennedy St Unit 5	Dieppe	NB	E1A7R9	**800-665-7829**	506-859-2486
Collection of Fine Properties PO Box 1190	Breckenridge	CO	80424	**800-627-3766**	970-453-9692
Comfort Inns 10750 Columbia Pike	Silver Spring	MD	20901	**800-424-6423**	301-592-5000
Comfort Suites 10750 Columbia Pike	Silver Spring	MD	20901	**800-424-6423**	301-592-5000
Concorde Hotels International 1 Penn Plaza Suite 2127	New York	NY	10119	**800-888-4747**	212-935-1045
Conrad Hotels 9336 Civic Ctr Dr	Beverly Hills	CA	90210	**800-445-8667**	310-278-4321
Country Inns & Suites by Carlson PO Box 59159	Minneapolis	MN	55459	**800-456-4000***	763-212-1000
*Resv					
Courtyard by Marriott 1 Marriott Dr	Washington	DC	20058	**800-321-2211**	301-380-3000
Crossland Economy Studios 100 Dunbar St	Spartanburg	SC	29306	**877-276-7752**	864-573-1600
Days Inns Worldwide Inc 1 Sylvan Way	Parsippany	NJ	07054	**800-329-7466**	973-428-9700
Delta Hotels Canadian Pacific Tower PO Box 227 TD Centre	Toronto	ON	M5K1J3	**800-268-1133***	416-874-2000
*Resv					

				Toll-Free	*Phone*
Destination Hotels & Resorts Inc					
10333 E Dry Creek Rd Suite 450	Englewood	CO	80112	**800-633-8347**	303-799-3830
Divi Resorts Inc					
6340 Quadrangle Dr Suite 300	Chapel Hill	NC	27517	**800-367-3484**	919-419-3484
Dolce International 28 W Grand Ave	Montvale	NJ	07645	**888-993-6523**	201-307-8700
Doubletree Hotels 9336 Civic Ctr Dr	Beverly Hills	CA	90210	**800-222-8733**	310-278-4321
Downtowner Inns 1726 Montreal Cir	Tucker	GA	30084	**800-251-1962**	770-270-1180
Drury Inns Inc 721 Emerson Rd Suite 400	Saint Louis	MO	63141	**800-378-7946**	314-429-2255
Econo Lodge 10750 Columbia Pike	Silver Spring	MD	20901	**800-424-6423**	301-592-5000
Embassy Suites Inc 755 Crossover Ln	Memphis	TN	38117	**800-362-2779**	901-374-5000
Exel Inns of America Inc					
4706 E Washington Ave	Madison	WI	53704	**800-367-3935**	608-241-5271
Extended Stay America Inc					
Crossland Economy Studios					
100 Dunbar St	Spartanburg	SC	29306	**877-276-7752**	864-573-1600
Extended StayAmerica Efficiency Studios					
100 Dunbar St	Spartanburg	SC	29306	**800-398-7829**	864-573-1600
StudioPLUS Deluxe Studios					
100 Dunbar St	Spartanburg	SC	29306	**888-788-3467**	864-573-1600
Fairfield Inn by Marriott 1 Marriott Dr	Washington	DC	20058	**800-228-9290**	301-380-3000
Fairmont Hotels & Resorts Inc					
100 Wellington St W TD Centre Suite 1600	Toronto	ON	M5K1B7	**800-866-5577**	416-874-2600
NYSE: FHR					
Family Inns of America Inc PO Box 10	Pigeon Forge	TN	37868	**800-251-9752**	865-453-4988
Four Points by Sheraton Hotels					
1111 Westchester Ave	White Plains	NY	10604	**877-443-4585***	914-640-8100
*Cust Svc					
Four Seasons Hotels Inc 1165 Leslie St	Toronto	ON	M3C2K8	**800-332-3442**	416-449-1750
NYSE: FS					
Golf Hosts Inc 36750 US Hwy 19 N	Palm Harbor	FL	34684	**800-456-2000**	727-942-2000
Grand Hyatt Hotels 71 S Walker Dr	Chicago	IL	60606	**800-233-1234**	312-750-1234
Grand Teton Lodge Co PO Box 240	Moran	WY	83013	**800-628-9988**	307-543-3100
Greenbrier Resort Management Co					
300 W Main St	White Sulphur Springs	WV	24986	**800-624-6070**	304-536-1110
Hampton Inn 755 Crossover Ln	Memphis	TN	38117	**800-426-7866**	901-374-5000
Hampton Inn & Suites 755 Crossover Ln	Memphis	TN	38117	**800-426-7866**	901-374-5000
Harrah's Entertainment Inc 1 Harrah's Ct	Las Vegas	NV	89119	**800-442-6443**	702-407-6000
NYSE: HET					
Harrison Conference Centers					
755 Crossover Ln	Memphis	TN	38117	**800-422-6338**	901-374-5000
Hawthorn Suites 13 Corporate Sq Suite 250	Atlanta	GA	30329	**800-527-1133**	404-321-4045
Hearthside by Villager 1 Sylvan Way	Parsippany	NJ	07054	**888-821-5738**	973-428-9700
Hershey Entertainment & Resorts Co					
PO Box 860	Hershey	PA	17033	**800-437-7439**	717-534-3131
Hilton Garden Inn 9336 Civic Ctr Dr	Beverly Hills	CA	90210	**800-445-8667**	310-278-4321
Hilton Hotels 9336 Civic Ctr Dr	Beverly Hills	CA	90210	**800-445-8667**	310-278-4321
Hilton Hotels Corp 9336 Civic Ctr Dr	Beverly Hills	CA	90210	**800-445-8667**	310-278-4321
NYSE: HLT					
Conrad Hotels 9336 Civic Ctr Dr	Beverly Hills	CA	90210	**800-445-8667**	310-278-4321
Doubletree Hotels 9336 Civic Ctr Dr	Beverly Hills	CA	90210	**800-222-8733**	310-278-4321
Embassy Suites Inc 755 Crossover Ln	Memphis	TN	38117	**800-362-2779**	901-374-5000
Hampton Inn 755 Crossover Ln	Memphis	TN	38117	**800-426-7866**	901-374-5000
Hampton Inn & Suites 755 Crossover Ln	Memphis	TN	38117	**800-426-7866**	901-374-5000
Harrison Conference Centers					
755 Crossover Ln	Memphis	TN	38117	**800-422-6338**	901-374-5000
Hilton Garden Inn 9336 Civic Ctr Dr	Beverly Hills	CA	90210	**800-445-8667**	310-278-4321
Hilton Hotels 9336 Civic Ctr Dr	Beverly Hills	CA	90210	**800-445-8667**	310-278-4321
Homewood Suites by Hilton					
755 Crossover Ln	Memphis	TN	38117	**800-225-5466**	901-374-5000
Hilton International Co 40 Wall St 41st Fl	New York	NY	10005	**800-445-8667**	212-820-1700
HLC Hotels Inc PO Box 13069	Savannah	GA	31416	**800-358-6122**	912-352-4493
Homestead Village Inc 100 Dunbar St	Spartanburg	SC	29306	**888-782-9473**	864-573-1600
Homewood Suites by Hilton					
755 Crossover Ln	Memphis	TN	38117	**800-225-5466**	901-374-5000
Hospitality International Inc 1726 Montreal Cir	Tucker	GA	30084	**800-251-1962**	770-270-1180
Downtowner Inns 1726 Montreal Cir	Tucker	GA	30084	**800-251-1962**	770-270-1180
Master Hosts Inns & Resorts					
1726 Montreal Cir	Tucker	GA	30084	**800-247-4677**	770-270-1180
Passport Inn 1726 Montreal Cir	Tucker	GA	30084	**800-251-1962**	770-270-1180
Red Carpet Inn 1726 Montreal Cir	Tucker	GA	30084	**800-251-1962**	770-270-1180
Scottish Inns 1726 Montreal Cir	Tucker	GA	30084	**800-251-1962**	770-270-1180
Howard Johnson Franchise Canada Inc					
135 Queens Plate Suite 410	Toronto	ON	M9W6V1	**800-249-4656**	416-361-1010
Howard Johnson International Inc					
1 Sylvan Way	Parsippany	NJ	07054	**800-446-4656**	973-428-9700
HTH Corp 2490 Kalakaua Ave	Honolulu	HI	96815	**800-367-6060**	808-922-1233
Hyatt Hotels Corp 71 S Walker Dr	Chicago	IL	60606	**800-233-1234**	312-750-1234
Grand Hyatt Hotels 71 S Walker Dr	Chicago	IL	60606	**800-233-1234**	312-750-1234
Hyatt Regency Hotels 71 S Walker Dr	Chicago	IL	60606	**800-233-1234**	312-750-1234
Park Hyatt Hotels 71 S Walker Dr	Chicago	IL	60606	**800-233-1234**	312-750-1234
Hyatt Regency Hotels 71 S Walker Dr	Chicago	IL	60606	**800-233-1234**	312-750-1234
Innkeeper Motels/Hotels 4829 Riverside Dr	Danville	VA	24541	**800-466-5337**	434-822-2161
Inns of America 755 Raintree Dr Suite 200	Carlsbad	CA	92009	**800-826-0778**	760-438-6661
InnSuites Hospitality Trust InnSuites Hotels Inc					
1615 E Northern Ave Suite 102	Phoenix	AZ	85020	**800-842-4242**	602-944-1500
InnSuites Hotels Inc					
1615 E Northern Ave Suite 102	Phoenix	AZ	85020	**800-842-4242**	602-944-1500
InterContinental Hotels Group Staybridge Suites					
by Holiday Inn 3 Ravinia Dr Suite 100	Atlanta	GA	30346	**800-465-4329**	770-604-2000
Jameson Inn 8 Perimeter Ctr E Suite 8050	Atlanta	GA	30346	**800-526-3766**	770-901-9020
Jameson Inns Inc 8 Perimeter Ctr E Suite 8050	Atlanta	GA	30346	**800-526-3766**	770-901-9020
NASDAQ: JAMS					
Jameson Inn 8 Perimeter Ctr E Suite 8050	Atlanta	GA	30346	**800-526-3766**	770-901-9020
Signature Inn 8 Perimeter Ctr E Suite 8050	Atlanta	GA	30346	**800-822-5252**	770-901-9020
JHM Enterprises Inc					
880 S Pleasantburg Dr Suite 3G	Greenville	SC	29607	**800-763-1100**	864-232-9944
Joie de Vivre Hospitality Inc					
567 Sutter St	San Francisco	CA	94102	**800-738-7477**	415-835-0300
Kelly Inns Ltd 3211 W Sencore Dr	Sioux Falls	SD	57107	**800-635-3559**	605-334-2371
Kimpton Hotel & Restaurant Group LLC					
222 Kearny St Suite 200	San Francisco	CA	94108	**800-546-2686**	415-397-5572
Knights Franchise Systems Inc Knights Inns					
1 Sylvan Way	Parsippany	NJ	07054	**800-418-8977**	973-428-9700
Knights Inns 1 Sylvan Way	Parsippany	NJ	07054	**800-418-8977**	973-428-9700
La Quinta Inns Inc 909 Hidden Ridge Suite 600	Irving	TX	75038	**877-204-9204**	214-492-6600
Lees Inns of America Inc 130 N State St	North Vernon	IN	47265	**800-733-5337**	812-346-5072
Leisure Hotel Group of Companies					
1600 N Lorraine St Suite 211	Hutchinson	KS	67501	**888-250-1618**	620-663-9800
Leisure Hotels LLC					
1600 N Lorraine St Suite 211	Hutchinson	KS	67501	**888-250-1618**	620-663-9800
Little America Hotels & Resorts					
500 S Main St	Salt Lake City	UT	84101	**800-453-9450**	801-363-6781
Loews Hotels 667 Madison Ave	New York	NY	10021	**800-235-6397**	212-521-2000
Luxe Worldwide Hotels					
11461 Sunset Blvd	Los Angeles	CA	90049	**866-589-3411**	310-440-3090
Luxury Collection 1111 Westchester Ave	White Plains	NY	10604	**877-443-4585***	914-640-8100
*Cust Svc					
MainStay Suites 10750 Columbia Pike	Silver Spring	MD	20901	**800-424-6423**	301-592-5000
Mandarin Oriental Hotel Group					
9841 Airport Blvd Suite 822	Los Angeles	CA	90045	**800-526-6566**	310-670-6422
Marc Resorts Hawaii					
2155 Kalakaua Ave Suite 318	Honolulu	HI	96815	**800-535-0085**	808-926-5900
Marriott Conference Centers 1 Marriott Dr	Washington	DC	20058	**800-453-0309**	301-380-3000
Marriott Hotels Resorts & Suites					
1 Marriott Dr	Washington	DC	20058	**800-228-9290**	301-380-3000
Marriott International Inc 1 Marriott Dr	Washington	DC	20058	**800-228-9290**	301-380-3000
NYSE: MAR					
Courtyard by Marriott 1 Marriott Dr	Washington	DC	20058	**800-321-2211**	301-380-3000
Fairfield Inn by Marriott 1 Marriott Dr	Washington	DC	20058	**800-228-9290**	301-380-3000
Marriott Conference Centers					
1 Marriott Dr	Washington	DC	20058	**800-453-0309**	301-380-3000
Marriott Hotels Resorts & Suites					
1 Marriott Dr	Washington	DC	20058	**800-228-9290**	301-380-3000
Renaissance Hotels 1 Marriott Dr	Washington	DC	20058	**800-638-8108**	301-380-3000
Residence Inn by Marriott 1 Marriott Dr	Washington	DC	20058	**800-638-8108**	301-380-3000
SpringHill Suites by Marriott					
1 Marriott Dr	Washington	DC	20058	**800-228-9290**	301-380-3000
TownePlace Suites by Marriott					
1 Marriott Dr	Washington	DC	20058	**800-228-9290**	301-380-3000
Master Hosts Inns & Resorts					
1726 Montreal Cir	Tucker	GA	30084	**800-247-4677**	770-270-1180
Masters Inns PO Box 13069	Savannah	GA	31416	**800-633-3434**	912-352-4493
McIntosh Inns					
440 Feheley Dr McIntosh Bldg	King of Prussia	PA	19406	**800-444-2775**	610-279-6000
Meyer Crest Ltd 2051 Hilltop Dr Suite A-26	Redding	CA	96002	**800-626-1900**	530-221-8250
Microtel Inns & Suites					
13 Corporate Sq Suite 250	Atlanta	GA	30329	**888-222-2142**	404-321-4045
Midamerica Hotels Corp					
105 S Mt Auburn Rd PO Box 1570	Cape Girardeau	MO	63702	**888-866-4326**	573-334-0546
Milner Hotels Inc 1526 Centre St	Detroit	MI	48226	**800-521-0592**	313-962-5400
Motel 6 LP 4001 International Pkwy	Carrollton	TX	75007	**800-466-8356**	972-360-9000
Nikko Hotels International					
222 Mason St	San Francisco	CA	94102	**800-645-5687**	415-394-1111
Occidental-Allegro Hotels & Resorts					
6303 Blue Lagoon Dr Suite 250	Miami	FL	33126	**800-858-2258**	305-262-5909
Oceans Resorts Inc					
2025 S Atlantic Ave	Daytona Beach Shores	FL	32118	**800-874-7420**	386-257-1950
OHANA Hotels of Hawaii 2375 Kuhio Ave	Honolulu	HI	96815	**800-462-6262**	808-921-6600
Omni Hotels 420 Decker Dr Suite 200	Irving	TX	75062	**800-843-6664**	972-730-6664
Orient Express Hotels Inc					
1155 Ave of the Americas 30th Fl	New York	NY	10036	**800-237-1236**	212-302-5055
NYSE: OEH					
Outrigger Hotels & Resorts 2375 Kuhio Ave	Honolulu	HI	96815	**800-688-7444**	808-921-6600
Pan Pacific Hotels & Resorts					
500 Post St	San Francisco	CA	94102	**800-327-8585**	415-732-7747
Park Hyatt Hotels 71 S Walker Dr	Chicago	IL	60606	**800-233-1234**	312-750-1234
Park Inn PO Box 59159	Minneapolis	MN	55459	**800-670-7275***	763-212-1000
*Resv					
Park Lane Hotels International					
55 Cyril Magnin St	San Francisco	CA	94102	**800-650-7272**	415-398-4491
Passport Inn 1726 Montreal Cir	Tucker	GA	30084	**800-251-1962**	770-270-1180
Premier Resorts & Hotels					
2600 SW 3rd Ave 6th Fl	Miami	FL	33129	**800-877-3643**	305-856-7083
Premier Resorts International PO Box 4800	Park City	UT	84060	**888-774-3533**	435-655-4800
Prime Hospitality Corp 700 Rt 46 E	Fairfield	NJ	07004	**800-444-8888**	973-882-1010
NYSE: PDQ					
AmeriSuites 700 Rt 46 E	Fairfield	NJ	07004	**800-833-1516**	973-882-1010
Prime Hotels & Resorts 700 Rt 46 E	Fairfield	NJ	07004	**866-864-3649***	973-882-1010
*Resv					
Wellesley Inn & Suites 700 Rt 46 E	Fairfield	NJ	07004	**800-444-8888**	973-882-1010
Prime Hotels & Resorts 700 Rt 46 E	Fairfield	NJ	07004	**866-864-3649***	973-882-1010
*Resv					
Prince Resorts Hawaii 100 Holomoana St	Honolulu	HI	96815	**800-774-6234**	808-956-1111
Quality Inns Hotels & Suites					
10750 Columbia Pike	Silver Spring	MD	20901	**800-424-6423**	301-592-5000
Radisson Hotels & Resorts PO Box 59159	Minneapolis	MN	55459	**800-333-3333**	763-212-5526
Ramada Franchise Systems Inc					
1 Sylvan Way	Parsippany	NJ	07054	**800-932-6726**	973-428-9700
Raphael Hotel Group 200 W 12th St	Kansas City	MO	64105	**800-821-5343**	816-421-6100
Red Carpet Inn 1726 Montreal Cir	Tucker	GA	30084	**800-251-1962**	770-270-1180
Red Lion Hotels Inc					
201 W North River Dr Suite 100	Spokane	WA	99201	**800-325-4000**	509-459-6100
Red Roof Inns Inc 4001 International Pkwy	Carrollton	TX	75007	**800-733-7663**	972-360-9000
Renaissance Hotels 1 Marriott Dr	Washington	DC	20058	**800-638-8108**	301-380-3000
Reneson Hotel Group 121 7th St	San Francisco	CA	94103	**800-444-5816**	415-626-0200
Residence Inn by Marriott 1 Marriott Dr	Washington	DC	20058	**800-638-8108**	301-380-3000
ResidenSea 5200 Blue Lagoon Dr Suite 790	Miami	FL	33139	**800-970-6601**	305-264-9090
Ritz-Carlton Hotel Co LLC					
4445 Willard Ave Suite 800	Chevy Chase	MD	20815	**800-241-3333**	301-547-4700
Riviera Holdings Corp					
2901 Las Vegas Blvd S	Las Vegas	NV	89109	**800-634-6753**	702-734-5110
AMEX: RIV					
Rodeway Inns 10750 Columbia Pike	Silver Spring	MD	20901	**800-424-6423**	301-592-5000
Rosen Hotels & Resorts Inc					
9840 International Dr	Orlando	FL	32819	**800-204-7234**	407-996-9840
Rosewood Hotels & Resorts					
500 Crescent Ct Suite 300	Dallas	TX	75201	**888-767-3966**	214-880-4200
Sandals Resorts International					
4950 SW 72nd Ave	Miami	FL	33155	**888-726-3257**	305-284-1300
Sands Regent 345 N Arlington Ave	Reno	NV	89501	**800-648-3553**	775-348-2200
NASDAQ: SNDS					
Scottish Inns 1726 Montreal Cir	Tucker	GA	30084	**800-251-1962**	770-270-1180
Shangri-La International Hotels Inc					
1501 Broadway Suite 502	New York	NY	10036	**800-942-5050**	212-768-3190
Sheraton Hotels & Resorts					
1111 Westchester Ave	White Plains	NY	10604	**800-325-3535**	914-640-8100
Shilo Inns 11600 SW Shilo Ln	Portland	OR	97225	**800-222-2244**	503-641-6565
ShoLodge Inc 130 Maple Dr N	Hendersonville	TN	37075	**800-222-2222**	615-264-8000
Shoney's Inn Inc 130 Maple Dr N	Hendersonville	TN	37075	**800-552-4667**	615-264-8000
Shoney's Inn Inc 130 Maple Dr N	Hendersonville	TN	37075	**800-552-4667**	615-264-8000
Signature Inn 8 Perimeter Ctr E Suite 8050	Atlanta	GA	30346	**800-822-5252**	770-901-9020
Sleep Inn & Suites 10750 Columbia Pike	Silver Spring	MD	20901	**800-424-6423**	301-592-5000
Snowdance LLC PO Box 699	Brownsville	VT	05037	**800-243-0011**	802-484-7000
Sonesta International Hotels Corp					
116 Huntington Ave 9th Fl	Boston	MA	02116	**800-766-3782**	617-421-5400
NASDAQ: SNSTA					
SpringHill Suites by Marriott 1 Marriott Dr	Washington	DC	20058	**800-228-9290**	301-380-3000

Name / Address	City	State	Zip	Toll-Free	Phone
Starwood Hotels & Resorts Worldwide Inc					
1111 Westchester Ave	White Plains	NY	10604	**877-443-4585***	914-640-8100
NYSE: HOT ■ *Cust Svc					
Four Points by Sheraton Hotels					
1111 Westchester Ave	White Plains	NY	10604	**877-443-4585***	914-640-8100
*Cust Svc					
Luxury Collection					
1111 Westchester Ave	White Plains	NY	10604	**877-443-4585***	914-640-8100
*Cust Svc					
Sheraton Hotels & Resorts					
1111 Westchester Ave	White Plains	NY	10604	**800-325-3535**	914-640-8100
W Hotels 1111 Westchester Ave	White Plains	NY	10604	**877-443-4585**	914-640-8100
Westin Hotels & Resorts					
1111 Westchester Ave	White Plains	NY	10604	**877-443-4585**	914-640-8100
Staybridge Suites by Holiday Inn					
3 Ravinia Dr Suite 100	Atlanta	GA	30346	**800-465-4329**	770-604-2000
Steamboat Resorts PO Box 772995	Steamboat Springs	CO	80477	**800-525-5502**	970-879-8000
Studio 6 4001 International Pkwy	Carrollton	TX	75007	**800-466-8356**	972-360-9000
StudioPLUS 100 Dunbar St	Spartanburg	SC	29306	**888-788-3467**	864-573-1600
Summerfield Suites by Wyndham					
1950 Stemmons Fwy Suite 6001	Dallas	TX	75207	**800-833-4353**	214-863-1000
Summit Hotels & Resorts					
311 S Wacker Dr Suite 1900	Chicago	IL	60606	**800-457-4000**	312-913-0400
Super 8 Motels Inc 1910 8th Ave NE	Aberdeen	SD	57401	**800-800-8000**	605-225-2272
Thriftlodge 1 Sylvan Way	Parsippany	NJ	07054	**800-578-7878**	973-428-9700
TownePlace Suites by Marriott					
1 Marriott Dr	Washington	DC	20058	**800-228-9290**	301-380-3000
Travelodge Hotels Inc 1 Sylvan Way	Parsippany	NJ	07054	**800-578-7878**	973-428-9700
Thriftlodge 1 Sylvan Way	Parsippany	NJ	07054	**800-578-7878**	973-428-9700
US Franchise Systems Inc					
13 Corporate Sq Suite 250	Atlanta	GA	30329	**888-225-5151**	404-321-4045
Best Inns & Suites					
13 Corporate Sq Suite 250	Atlanta	GA	30329	**800-237-8466**	404-321-4045
Hawthorn Suites 13 Corporate Sq Suite 250	Atlanta	GA	30329	**800-527-1133**	404-321-4045
Microtel Inns & Suites					
13 Corporate Sq Suite 250	Atlanta	GA	30329	**888-222-2142**	404-321-4045
Vagabond Inns Inc					
5933 W Century Blvd Suite 200	Los Angeles	CA	90045	**800-522-1555**	310-410-5700
Val-U Inn Motels					
16100 NW Cornell Rd Suite 100	Beaverton	OR	97006	**800-443-7777**	503-531-4000
Villager Lodge 1 Sylvan Way	Parsippany	NJ	07054	**888-821-5738**	973-428-9700
Villager Lodge Franchise Systems Inc					
1 Sylvan Way	Parsippany	NJ	07054	**888-821-5738**	973-428-9700
Hearthside by Villager 1 Sylvan Way	Parsippany	NJ	07054	**888-821-5738**	973-428-9700
Villager Lodge 1 Sylvan Way	Parsippany	NJ	07054	**888-821-5738**	973-428-9700
Villager Premier 1 Sylvan Way	Parsippany	NJ	07054	**888-821-5738**	973-428-9700
Villager Premier 1 Sylvan Way	Parsippany	NJ	07054	**888-821-5738**	973-428-9700
Vista Host Inc					
10370 Richmond Ave Suite 150	Houston	TX	77042	**800-688-4782**	713-267-5800
W Hotels 1111 Westchester Ave	White Plains	NY	10604	**877-443-4585**	914-640-8100
Warwick International Hotels Inc					
65 W 54th St	New York	NY	10019	**800-223-4099**	212-247-2700
Wellesley Inn & Suites 700 Rt 46 E	Fairfield	NJ	07004	**800-444-8888**	973-882-1010
WestCoast Hospitality Corp					
201 W North River Dr Suite 100	Spokane	WA	99201	**800-325-4000**	509-459-6100
NYSE: WEH					
Red Lion Hotels Inc					
201 W North River Dr Suite 100	Spokane	WA	99201	**800-325-4000**	509-459-6100
WestCoast Hotels Inc					
201 W North River Dr Suite 100	Spokane	WA	99201	**800-325-4000**	509-459-6100
WestCoast Hotels Inc					
201 W North River Dr Suite 100	Spokane	WA	99201	**800-325-4000**	509-459-6100
Westin Hotels & Resorts					
1111 Westchester Ave	White Plains	NY	10604	**877-443-4585**	914-640-8100
Westmark Hotels Inc 221 1st Ave W Suite 100	Seattle	WA	98119	**800-544-0970**	206-301-5224
Westmont Hospitality Group Inc					
5847 San Felipe St Suite 4650	Houston	TX	77057	**800-468-3512**	713-782-9100
Wilson Hotel Management Co Inc					
8700 Trail Lake Dr W Suite 300	Memphis	TN	38125	**800-945-7667**	901-346-8800
Wingate Inns International Inc					
1 Sylvan Way	Parsippany	NJ	07054	**800-228-1000**	973-428-9700
Winter Sports Inc					
3812 Big Mountain Rd PO Box 1400	Whitefish	MT	59937	**800-858-5439**	406-862-1900
Woodfin Suite Hotels LLC					
12730 High Bluff Dr Suite 250	San Diego	CA	92130	**800-237-8811**	858-794-2338
Chase Suite Hotels by Woodfin					
12730 High Bluff Dr Suite 250	San Diego	CA	92130	**800-237-8811**	858-794-2338
Wyndham Hotels & Resorts					
1950 Stemmons Fwy Suite 6001	Dallas	TX	75207	**800-996-3426**	214-863-1000
Wyndham International Inc					
1950 Stemmons Fwy Suite 6001	Dallas	TX	75207	**800-996-3426**	214-863-1000
AMEX: WBR					
Summerfield Suites by Wyndham					
1950 Stemmons Fwy Suite 6001	Dallas	TX	75207	**800-833-4353**	214-863-1000
Wyndham Hotels & Resorts					
1950 Stemmons Fwy Suite 6001	Dallas	TX	75207	**800-996-3426**	214-863-1000
Wyndham Luxury Resorts					
1950 Stemmons Fwy Suite 6001	Dallas	TX	75207	**800-996-3426**	214-863-1000
Wyndham Luxury Resorts					
1950 Stemmons Fwy Suite 6001	Dallas	TX	75207	**800-996-3426**	214-863-1000
Wynn Resorts Ltd 3131 Las Vegas Blvd S	Las Vegas	NV	89109	**866-770-7108**	702-733-4444
NASDAQ: WYNN					

370 HOTELS - CONFERENCE CENTER

Name / Address	City	State	Zip	Toll-Free	Phone
Aberdeen Woods Conference Center					
201 Aberdeen Pkwy	Peachtree City	GA	30269	**800-285-6338**	770-487-2666
ACE Conference Center & Country Club					
800 Ridge Pike	Lafayette Hill	PA	19444	**800-523-3000**	610-825-8000
Airlie Conference Center 6809 Airlie Rd	Warrenton	VA	20187	**800-288-9573**	540-347-1300
Ashman Court Marriott Conference Hotel					
111 W Main St	Midland	MI	48642	**877-645-3643**	989-839-0500
Auburn University Hotel & Dixon Conference					
Center 241 S College St	Auburn	AL	36830	**800-228-2876**	334-821-8200
Banff Centre 107 Tunnel Mountain Dr	Banff	AB	T1L1H5	**800-884-7574**	403-762-6100
Big EZ Lodge					
PO Box 160070 7000 Beaver Creek Rd	Big Sky	MT	59716	**877-244-3299**	406-995-7000
Biltmore Hotel & Conference Center of the					
Americas 1200 Anastasia Ave	Coral Gables	FL	33134	**800-727-1926**	305-445-1926
Burkshire Marriott Conference Hotel					
10 W Burke Ave	Towson	MD	21204	**800-435-5986**	410-324-8100
Chaminade 1 Chaminade Ln	Santa Cruz	CA	95065	**800-283-6569**	831-475-5600
Chateau Elan Resort & Conference Center					
100 rue Charlemagne	Braselton	GA	30517	**800-233-9463**	678-425-0900
Chattanoogan The 1201 S Broad St	Chattanooga	TN	37402	**877-756-1684**	423-756-3400
Cheyenne Mountain Conference Resort					
3225 Broadmoor Valley Rd	Colorado Springs	CO	80906	**800-428-8886**	719-538-4000
Clarion Hotel & Conference Center Antietam					
Creek 901 Dual Hwy	Hagerstown	MD	21740	**888-528-6738**	301-733-5100
Country Springs Hotel & Conference Center					
2810 Golf Rd	Pewaukee	WI	53072	**800-247-6640**	262-547-0201
Crystal Mountain Resort					
12500 Crystal Mountain Dr	Thompsonville	MI	49683	**800-968-7686**	231-378-2000
Del Lago Waterfront Conference Center &					
Resort 600 Del Lago Blvd	Montgomery	TX	77356	**800-863-9208**	936-582-7510
Dolce Hamilton Park 175 Park Ave	Florham Park	NJ	07932	**800-321-6000**	973-377-2424
Dolce Hayes Mansion 200 Edenvale Ave	San Jose	CA	95136	**800-420-3200**	408-226-3200
Dolce Heritage 522 Heritage Rd	Southbury	CT	06488	**800-932-3466**	203-264-8200
Dolce Skamania Lodge					
1131 SW Skamania Lodge Way	Stevenson	WA	98648	**800-221-7117**	509-427-7700
Dolce Tarrytown House 49 E Sunnyside Ln	Tarrytown	NY	10591	**800-553-8118**	914-591-8200
Donaldson Brown Hotel & Conference Center					
201 Otey St Virginia Tech Campus	Blacksburg	VA	24061	**877-200-3360**	540-231-8000
Doral Arrowwood Conference Resort					
975 Anderson Hill Rd	Rye Brook	NY	10573	**800-223-6725**	914-939-5500
Doral Forrestal Conference Center Hotel					
100 College Rd E	Princeton	NJ	08540	**800-222-1131**	609-452-7800
Doubletree Hotel & Conference Center Saint					
Louis 16625 Swingley Ridge Rd	Chesterfield	MO	63017	**800-222-8733**	636-532-5000
Doubletree Hotel & Executive Meeting Center					
Somerset 200 Atrium Dr	Somerset	NJ	08873	**800-222-8733**	732-469-2600
Doubletree Hotel Roanoke & Conference Center					
110 Shenandoah Ave	Roanoke	VA	24016	**866-594-4722**	540-985-5900
Dover Downs Hotel & Conference Center					
1131 N DuPont Hwy	Dover	DE	19901	**800-711-5882**	302-674-4600
Edith Macy Conference Center					
550 Chappaqua Rd	Briarcliff Manor	NY	10510	**800-442-6229**	914-945-8000
Emory Conference Center Hotel					
1615 Clifton Rd	Atlanta	GA	30329	**800-933-6679**	404-712-6000
Evergreen Marriott Conference Resort					
4021 Lakeview Dr	Stone Mountain	GA	30083	**800-228-9290**	770-879-9900
Founders Inn 5641 Indian River Rd	Virginia Beach	VA	23464	**800-926-4466**	757-424-5511
Georgetown University Conference Center					
3800 Reservoir Rd NW	Washington	DC	20057	**800-228-9290**	202-687-3200
Gurney's Inn Resort & Spa					
290 Old Montauk Hwy	Montauk	NY	11954	**800-848-7639**	631-668-2345
Hickory Ridge Marriott Conference Hotel					
1195 Summerhill Dr	Lisle	IL	60532	**800-334-0344**	630-971-5000
Hidden Valley Resort & Conference Center					
1 Craighead Dr	Hidden Valley	PA	15502	**800-458-0175**	814-443-8000
Hilton DFW Lakes Executive Conference					
Center 1800 Hwy 26 E	Grapevine	TX	76051	**800-445-8667**	817-481-8444
Hilton Seattle Airport & Conference Center					
17620 Pacific Hwy S	Seattle	WA	98188	**800-445-8667**	206-244-4800
Hilton University of Florida Conference Center					
1714 SW 34th St	Gainesville	FL	32607	**800-774-1500**	352-371-3600
IBM Palisades Conference Center Rt 9 W	Palisades	NY	10964	**800-426-0889**	845-732-6000
Inn at Aspen 38750 Hwy 82	Aspen	CO	81611	**800-952-1515**	970-925-1500
InterContinental Hotel & Conference Center					
Cleveland 9801 Carnegie Ave	Cleveland	OH	44106	**877-707-8999**	216-707-4100
JR's Executive Inn Riverfront					
1 Executive Blvd	Paducah	KY	42001	**800-866-3636**	270-443-8000
Kingbridge Centre 12750 Jane St	King City	ON	L7B1A3	**800-827-7221**	905-833-3086
Kingsmill Resort & Spa					
1010 Kingsmill Rd	Williamsburg	VA	23185	**800-832-5665**	757-253-1703
Lafayette Yard Marriott Conference Hotel					
1 W Lafayette St	Trenton	NJ	08608	**800-228-9290**	609-421-4000
Lakeview Scanticon Resort & Conference					
Center 1 Lakeview Dr	Morgantown	WV	26508	**800-624-8300**	304-594-1111
Lakeway Inn & Resort 101 Lakeway Dr	Austin	TX	78734	**800-525-3929**	512-261-6600
Lansdowne Resort 44050 Woodridge Pkwy	Leesburg	VA	20176	**800-541-4801**	703-729-8400
Legends at Capitol Hill 2500 Legends Cir	Prattville	AL	36066	**888-250-3767**	334-290-1235
Lodge & Spa at Breckenridge					
112 Overlook Dr	Breckenridge	CO	80424	**800-736-1607**	970-453-9300
Macy Edith Conference Center					
550 Chappaqua Rd	Briarcliff Manor	NY	10510	**800-442-6229**	914-945-8000
Marietta Conference Center & Resort					
500 Powder Springs St	Marietta	GA	30064	**888-685-2500**	770-427-2500
Marriott Kingsgate Conference Hotel at					
University of Cincinnati 151 Goodman Dr	Cincinnati	OH	45219	**800-228-9290**	513-487-3800
Marriott MeadowView Conference Resort &					
Convention Center					
1901 Meadowview Pkwy	Kingsport	TN	37660	**800-820-5055**	423-578-6600
Marriott Westfields Resort & Conference Center					
14750 Conference Center Dr	Chantilly	VA	20151	**800-635-5666**	703-818-0300
Marten House Hotel & Lilly Conference					
Center 1801 W 86th St	Indianapolis	IN	46260	**800-736-5634**	317-872-4111
Meadowood Napa Valley					
900 Meadowood Ln	Saint Helena	CA	94574	**800-458-8080**	707-963-3646
Millennium Hotel New York Broadway					
145 W 44th St	New York	NY	10036	**800-622-5569**	212-768-4400
National Center for Employee Development					
2801 E State Hwy 9	Norman	OK	73071	**866-278-4434**	405-447-9100
NAV Canada Training & Conference Center					
1950 Montreal Rd	Cornwall	ON	K6H6L2	**877-832-6416**	613-936-5000
New England Center					
15 Strafford Ave University of					
New Hampshire	Durham	NH	03824	**800-590-4334**	603-862-2712
North Maple Inn at Basking Ridge					
300 N Maple Ave	Basking Ridge	NJ	07920	**800-288-2687**	908-953-3000
Northland Inn & Executive Conference					
Center 7025 Northland Dr	Minneapolis	MN	55428	**800-441-6422**	763-536-8300
Oak Brook Hills Resort & Conference Center					
3500 Midwest Rd	Oak Brook	IL	60523	**800-445-3315**	630-850-5555
Oak Ridge Conference Center 1 Oak Ridge Dr	Chaska	MN	55318	**800-737-9588***	952-368-3100
*Sales					
Penn Stater Conference Center Hotel					
215 Innovation Blvd	State College	PA	16803	**800-233-7505**	814-863-5000
Renaissance Portsmouth Hotel & Waterfront					
Conference Center 425 Water St	Portsmouth	VA	23704	**888-839-1775**	757-673-3000
Resort at Squaw Creek					
400 Squaw Creek Rd	Olympic Valley	CA	96146	**800-327-3353**	530-583-6300

Name / Address	City	State	Zip	Toll-Free	Phone
San Luis Resort Spa & Conference Center 5222 Seawall Blvd	Galveston Island	TX	77551	**800-445-0090**	409-744-1500
San Ramon Valley Conference Center 3301 Crow Canyon Rd	San Ramon	CA	94583	**800-521-4335**	925-866-7500
Scottsdale Resort & Conference Center 7700 E McCormick Pkwy	Scottsdale	AZ	85258	**800-528-0293**	480-991-9000
Sheraton Meadowlands Hotel & Conference Center 2 Meadowlands Plaza	East Rutherford	NJ	07073	**800-325-3535**	201-896-0500
Sheraton New York Hotel & Towers 811 7th Ave	New York	NY	10019	**800-223-6550**	212-581-1000
Snowbird Ski & Summer Resort Hwy 210 PO Box 929000	Snowbird	UT	84092	**800-453-3000**	801-742-2222
Snowmass Conference Center 76 Elbert Ln	Snowmass Village	CO	81615	**800-598-2006**	970-923-2000
Spencer Conference Centre 551 Windermere Rd	London	ON	N5X2T1	**800-983-6523**	519-679-4546
Stoweflake Mountain Resort & Spa 1746 Mountain Rd PO Box 369	Stowe	VT	05672	**800-253-2232**	802-253-7355
Tempe Mission Palms Hotel & Conference Center 60 E 5th St	Tempe	AZ	85281	**800-547-8705**	480-894-1400
University Inn & Conference Center 2401 N Forest Rd	Amherst	NY	14226	**800-537-8483**	716-636-7500
University of Maryland University College Marriott Conference Center Hotel 3501 University Blvd E	Adelphi	MD	20783	**800-727-8622**	301-985-7303
University Place Conference Center & Hotel-Indianapolis 850 W Michigan St	Indianapolis	IN	46202	**800-627-2700**	317-269-9000
University Plaza Hotel & Convention Center 333 S John Q Hammons Pkwy	Springfield	MO	65806	**800-465-4329**	417-864-7333
Valley Forge Scanticon Hotel & Conference Center 1210 1st Ave	King of Prussia	PA	19406	**800-333-3333**	610-265-1500
Waterford Hotel & Conference Center 11360 US Hwy 1	Palm Beach Gardens	FL	33408	**888-696-9692**	561-624-7186
White Oaks Conference Resort & Spa 253 Taylor Rd	Niagara-on-the-Lake	ON	L0S1J0	**800-263-5766**	905-688-2550
Woodlands Resort & Conference Center 2301 N Millbend Dr	The Woodlands	TX	77380	**800-433-2624**	281-367-1100
Wyndham Peachtree Conference Center 2443 Hwy 54 W	Peachtree City	GA	30269	**800-996-3426**	770-487-2000

371 HOTELS - FREQUENT STAY PROGRAMS

Name / Address	City	State	Zip	Toll-Free	Phone
Adam's Mark Hotels Gold Mark Rewards 11330 Olive Blvd	Saint Louis	MO	63141	**800-444-2326**	314-567-9000
Baymont Guest Ovations Program 100 E Wisconsin Ave	Milwaukee	WI	53202	**866-464-2321**	414-905-2000
Best Traveler Program 13 Corporate Sq Suite 250	Atlanta	GA	30329	**800-237-8466**	404-321-4045
Best Western Gold Crown Club International 20400 N 29th Ave	Phoenix	AZ	85027	**800-237-8483**	
CHIP Hospitality Traveller's Reward Program 1600-1030 W Georgia St	Vancouver	BC	V6E2Y3	**800-431-0070**	604-646-2447
Choice Privileges Reward Program 2697 US Hwy 50 *Cust Svc	Grand Junction	CO	81503	**800-521-2121***	888-770-6800
Concorde Hotels International Prestige Card 1 Penn Plaza Suite 2127	New York	NY	10119	**800-888-4747**	212-935-1045
Country Hearth Inn Country Club 4243 Don Woody Club Dr Suite 200	Atlanta	GA	30350	**888-635-2582**	770-393-2662
Delta Hotels Privilege Program 100 Wellington St Suite 1200	Toronto	ON	M5K1J3	**888-321-3358**	416-874-2000
Drury Inns Gold Key Club PO Box 910	Cape Girardeau	MO	63702	**800-325-0581**	
Exel Inns Insider's Program 4706 E Washington Ave	Madison	WI	53704	**800-367-3935**	608-241-5271
Fairmont President's Club 650 California St 12th Fl	San Francisco	CA	94108	**800-663-7575**	415-772-7800
Gold Points Reward Network PO Box 59159	Minneapolis	MN	55459	**800-508-9000**	763-212-6900
Hilton HHonors Frequent Stay Program 2050 Chenault Dr	Carrollton	TX	75006	**800-548-8690**	972-788-0878
Hospitality International INNcentive Card Program 1726 Montreal Cir	Tucker	GA	30084	**800-247-4677**	
Hyatt Gold Passport Program PO Box 27089	Omaha	NE	68127	**800-544-9288**	
La Quinta Returns Club PO Box 2636	San Antonio	TX	78299	**800-642-4258**	
Leaders Club Services Leading Hotels of the World 99 Park Ave *Resv	New York	NY	10016	**800-223-6800***	212-515-5600
Lees Elite Club 130 N State St	North Vernon	IN	47265	**800-733-5337**	812-346-5072
Loews First Guest Recognition Program 2 2nd St Station Plaza	Rye	NY	10580	**800-563-9712**	
Marriott Hotels Rewards Program 310 Bearcat Dr *Sales	Salt Lake City	UT	84115	**800-450-4442***	800-249-0800
Masters Inn Preferred Guest Program PO Box 13069 *Resv	Savannah	GA	31416	**800-633-3434***	912-352-4493
MicroPass Rewards Program 900 Skyline Dr Suite 100	Marion	IL	62959	**888-222-2142**	800-373-0092
Omni Hotels Select Guest Program 11819 Miami St 3rd Fl *Cust Svc	Omaha	NE	68164	**877-440-6664***	800-367-6664
Prime Rewards 10 Kingsbridge Rd	Fairfield	NJ	07007	**800-982-6374**	
Prince Preferred Guest Program 100 Holomoana St	Honolulu	HI	96815	**800-774-6234**	
Priority Club Rewards PO Box 30320	Salt Lake City	UT	84130	**888-211-9874**	800-272-9273
Sandals Signature Guest Program 4950 SW 72nd Ave	Miami	FL	33155	**800-726-3257**	305-284-1300
Starwood Hotels Preferred Guest Program 111 Westchester Ave	White Plains	NY	10604	**888-625-4988**	512-834-2426
TripRewards PO Box 19807	Knoxville	TN	37939	**800-367-8747**	
WestCoast Hospitality Corp GuestAwards Program 201 W North River Dr Suite 100	Spokane	WA	99201	**800-325-4000**	
Wyndham ByRequest Program 1950 N Stemmons Fwy Suite 6001	Dallas	TX	75207	**800-347-7559**	214-863-1000

372 HOTELS & MOTELS (INDIVIDUAL) - CANADA

SEE ALSO Corporate Housing; Hotel & Resort Operation & Management; Hotel Reservations Services; Hotels & Motels (Individual) - US; Hotels - Conference Center; Hotels - Frequent Stay Programs; Resorts

Alberta

Name / Address	City	Prov	Postal Code	Toll-Free	Phone
Best Western Hospitality Inn 135 Southland Dr SE	Calgary	AB	T2J5X5	**800-528-1234**	403-278-5050
Best Western Port O'Call Hotel 1935 McKnight Blvd NE	Calgary	AB	T2E6V4	**800-661-1161**	403-291-4600
Blackfoot Inn 5940 Blackfoot Trail SE	Calgary	AB	T2H2B5	**800-661-1151**	403-252-2253
Castleton Suites 9600 Southland Cir SW	Calgary	AB	T2V5A1	**888-227-8534**	403-640-3900
Coast Plaza Hotel & Conference Center 1316 33rd St NE	Calgary	AB	T2A6B6	**800-663-1144**	403-248-8888
Delta Bow Valley 209 4th Ave SE	Calgary	AB	T2G0C6	**800-877-1133**	403-266-1980
Delta Calgary Airport 2001 Airport Rd NE	Calgary	AB	T2E6Z8	**800-268-1133**	403-291-2600
Elbow River Inn & Casino 1919 Macleod Trail SE	Calgary	AB	T2G4S1	**800-661-1463**	403-269-6771
Fairmont Palliser 133 9th Ave SW	Calgary	AB	T2P2M3	**800-441-1414**	403-262-1234
Glenmore Inn 2720 Glenmore Trail SE	Calgary	AB	T2C2E6	**800-661-3163**	403-279-8611
Greenwood Inn Calgary 3515 26th St NE	Calgary	AB	T1Y7E3	**888-233-6730**	403-250-8855
Hawthorn Hotel & Suites 618 5th Ave SW	Calgary	AB	T2P0M7	**800-661-1592**	403-263-0520
Hilton Garden Inn Calgary Airport 2335 Pegasus Rd NE	Calgary	AB	T2E8C3	**877-782-9444**	403-717-1999
Holiday Inn Calgary Downtown 119 12th Ave SW	Calgary	AB	T2R0G8	**800-661-9378**	403-266-4611
Hyatt Regency Calgary 700 Centre St SE	Calgary	AB	T2G5P6	**800-233-1234**	403-717-1234
International Hotel of Calgary 220 4th Ave SW	Calgary	AB	T2P0H5	**800-637-7200**	403-265-9600
Kensington Riverside Inn 1126 Memorial Dr NW	Calgary	AB	T2N3E3	**877-313-3733**	403-228-4442
Marriott Calgary 110 9th Ave SE	Calgary	AB	T2G5A6	**800-228-9290**	403-266-7331
Olympic Corporate Suites 400 Village Gardens SW	Calgary	AB	T3H2L1	**800-791-8788**	403-246-1040
Regency Suites Calgary 610 4th Ave SW	Calgary	AB	T2P0K1	**800-468-4044**	403-231-1000
Sandman Hotel Calgary 888 7th Ave SW	Calgary	AB	T2P3J3	**800-726-3626**	403-237-8626
Sheraton Cavalier Hotel 2620 32nd Ave NE	Calgary	AB	T1Y6B8	**800-325-3535**	403-291-0107
Westin Calgary 320 4th Ave SW	Calgary	AB	T2P2S6	**800-937-8461**	403-266-1611
Wingate Inn Calgary 400 Midpark Way SE	Calgary	AB	T2X3S4	**800-228-1000**	403-514-0099
Alberta Place Suite Hotel 10049 103rd St	Edmonton	AB	T5J2W7	**800-661-3982**	780-423-1565
Campus Tower Suite Hotel 11145 87th Ave	Edmonton	AB	T6G0Y1	**888-962-2522**	780-439-6060
Chateau Edmonton Hotel & Suites 7230 Argyll Rd	Edmonton	AB	T6C4A6	**800-465-3648**	780-465-7931
Chateau Louis Hotel & Conference Centre 11727 Kingsway	Edmonton	AB	T5G3A1	**800-661-9843**	780-452-7770
Coast Edmonton Plaza Hotel 10155 105th St	Edmonton	AB	T5J1E2	**800-663-1144**	780-423-4811
Coast Terrace Inn Edmonton South 4440 Gateway Blvd	Edmonton	AB	T6H5C2	**800-663-1144**	780-437-6010
Crowne Plaza Hotel Chateau Lacombe Edmonton 10111 Bellamy Hill	Edmonton	AB	T5J1N7	**800-661-8801**	780-428-6611
Delta Edmonton Centre Suite Hotel 10222 102nd St Eaton Ctr	Edmonton	AB	T5J4C5	**800-661-6655**	780-429-3900
Delta Edmonton South Hotel & Conference Center 4404 Gateway Blvd	Edmonton	AB	T6H5C2	**800-661-1122**	780-434-6415
Edmonton House Suite Hotel 10205 100th Ave	Edmonton	AB	T5J4B5	**888-962-2522**	780-420-4000
Executive Royal Inn West Edmonton 10010 178th St	Edmonton	AB	T5S1T3	**800-661-4879**	780-484-6000
Fairmont Hotel Macdonald 10065 100th St	Edmonton	AB	T5J0N6	**800-441-1414**	780-424-5181
Fantasyland Hotel 17700 87th Ave West Edmonton Mall	Edmonton	AB	T5T4V4	**800-737-3783**	780-444-3000
Greenwood Inn Edmonton 4485 Gateway Blvd	Edmonton	AB	T6H5C3	**888-233-6730**	780-431-1100
Hilton Garden Inn West Edmonton 17610 Stony Plain Rd	Edmonton	AB	T5S1A2	**877-782-9444**	780-443-2233
Holiday Inn Edmonton The Palace 4235 Gateway Blvd	Edmonton	AB	T6J5H2	**800-565-1222**	780-438-1222
Inn on 7th 10001 107th St	Edmonton	AB	T5J1J1	**800-661-7327**	780-429-2861
Mayfield Inn & Suites 16615 109th Ave	Edmonton	AB	T5P4K8	**800-661-9804**	780-484-0821
Ramada Hotel & Conference Center/Edmonton Inn 11834 Kingsway	Edmonton	AB	T5G3J5	**800-272-6232**	780-454-5454
Ramada Inn Edmonton 5359 Calgary Trail	Edmonton	AB	T6H4J9	**800-661-9030**	780-434-3431
Sandman Hotel West Edmonton 17635 Stony Plain Rd	Edmonton	AB	T5S1E3	**800-726-3626**	780-483-1385
Sutton Place Hotel The 10235 101st St	Edmonton	AB	T5J3E9	**800-263-9030**	780-428-7111
Tower on the Park Hotel 9715 110th St	Edmonton	AB	T5K2M1	**800-720-2179**	780-488-1626
Varscona Hotel 8208 106th St	Edmonton	AB	T6E6R9	**888-515-3355**	780-434-6111
West Harvest Inn 17803 Stony Plain Rd	Edmonton	AB	T5S1B4	**800-661-6993**	780-484-8000
Westin Edmonton 10135 100th St	Edmonton	AB	T5J0N7	**800-937-8461**	780-426-3636
Lake Louise Inn 210 Village Rd	Lake Louise	AB	T0L1E0	**800-661-9237**	403-522-3791
Post Hotel 200 Pipestone Rd PO Box 69	Lake Louise	AB	T0L1E0	**800-661-1586**	403-522-3989

British Columbia

Name / Address	City	Prov	Postal Code	Toll-Free	Phone
Accent Inns Vancouver-Burnaby 3777 Henning Dr	Burnaby	BC	V5C6N5	**800-663-0298**	604-473-5000
Executive Hotel & Conference Centre Burnaby 4201 Lougheed Hwy	Burnaby	BC	V5C3Y6	**800-590-3932**	604-298-2010
Best Western Coquitlam Inn Convention Centre 319 North Rd	Coquitlam	BC	V3K3V8	**800-668-3383**	604-931-9011
Coast Bastion Inn 11 Bastion St	Nanaimo	BC	V9R6E4	**800-663-1144**	250-753-6601
Royal Towers Hotel & Casino 140 6th St	New Westminster	BC	V3M1J4	**800-663-0202**	604-524-3777
Holiday Inn North Vancouver 700 Old Lillooet Rd	North Vancouver	BC	V7J2H5	**877-985-3111**	604-985-3111
King Pacific Lodge 255 W 1st St Suite 214	North Vancouver	BC	V7M3G8	**888-592-5464**	604-987-5452
Lonsdale Quay Hotel 123 Carrie Cates Ct	North Vancouver	BC	V7M3K7	**800-836-6111**	604-986-6111
Accent Inns Vancouver Airport 10551 St Edwards Dr	Richmond	BC	V6X3L8	**800-663-0298**	604-273-3311

British Columbia (Cont'd)

Hotel	City	Prov	Postal Code	Toll-Free	Phone
Best Western Abercorn Inn 9260 Bridgeport Rd	Richmond	BC	V6X1S1	**800-663-0085**	604-270-7576
Delta Vancouver Airport Hotel & Marina 3500 Cessna Dr	Richmond	BC	V7B1C7	**800-268-1133**	604-278-1241
Executive Airport Plaza 7311 Westminster Hwy	Richmond	BC	V6X1A3	**800-663-2878**	604-278-5555
Fairmont Vancouver Airport 3111 Grant McConachie Way Vancouver International Airport	Richmond	BC	V7B1X9	**800-441-1414**	604-207-5200
Holiday Inn Vancouver Airport 10720 Cambie Rd	Richmond	BC	V6X1K8	**800-465-4329**	604-821-1818
Marriott Vancouver Airport 7571 Westminster Hwy	Richmond	BC	V6X1A3	**800-228-9290**	604-276-2112
Radisson President Hotel & Suites Vancouver Airport 8181 Cambie Rd	Richmond	BC	V6X3X9	**866-660-1003**	604-276-8181
Ramada Plaza Vancouver Airport Conference Resort 10251 St Edwards Dr	Richmond	BC	V6X2M9	**888-298-2054**	604-278-9611
Hastings House 160 Upper Ganges Rd	Salt Spring Island	BC	V8K2S2	**800-661-9255**	250-537-2362
Aston Pacific Inn Resort & Conference Centre 1160 King George Hwy	Surrey	BC	V4A4Z2	**800-667-2248**	604-535-1432
Wickaninnish Inn PO Box 250	Tofino	BC	V0R2Z0	**800-333-4604**	250-725-3100
Atrium Inn 2889 E Hastings St	Vancouver	BC	V5K2A1	**888-428-7486**	604-254-1000
Best Western Chateau Granville 1100 Granville St	Vancouver	BC	V6Z2B6	**800-663-0575**	604-669-7070
Blue Horizon Hotel 1225 Robson St	Vancouver	BC	V6E1C3	**800-663-1333**	604-688-1411
Century Plaza Hotel & Spa 1015 Burrard St	Vancouver	BC	V6Z1Y5	**800-663-1818**	604-687-0575
Coast Plaza Hotel & Suites at Stanley Park 1763 Comox St	Vancouver	BC	V6G1P6	**800-663-1144**	604-688-7711
Coast Vancouver Airport Hotel 1041 SW Marine Dr	Vancouver	BC	V6P6L6	**800-263-1555**	604-263-1555
Crowne Plaza Hotel Georgia 801 W Georgia St	Vancouver	BC	V6C1P7	**800-663-1111**	604-682-5566
Delta Vancouver Suites 550 W Hastings St	Vancouver	BC	V6B1L6	**800-268-1133**	604-689-8188
Empire Landmark Hotel & Conference Centre 1400 Robson St	Vancouver	BC	V6G1B9	**800-830-6144**	604-687-0511
Executive Hotel Vancouver Downtown 1379 Howe St	Vancouver	BC	V6Z2R5	**888-388-3932**	604-688-7678
Fairmont Hotel Vancouver 900 W Georgia St	Vancouver	BC	V6C2W6	**800-441-1414**	604-684-3131
Fairmont Waterfront 900 Canada Place Way	Vancouver	BC	V6C3L5	**800-441-1414**	604-691-1991
Four Seasons Hotel Vancouver 791 W Georgia St	Vancouver	BC	V6C2T4	**800-332-3442**	604-689-9333
Georgian Court Hotel 773 Beatty St	Vancouver	BC	V6B2M4	**800-663-1155**	604-682-5555
Holiday Inn Hotel & Suites Vancouver Downtown 1110 Howe St	Vancouver	BC	V6Z1R2	**800-465-4329**	604-684-2151
Howard Johnson Hotel Vancouver 1176 Granville St	Vancouver	BC	V6Z1L8	**800-446-4656**	604-688-8701
Hyatt Regency Vancouver 655 Burrard St	Vancouver	BC	V6C2R7	**800-233-1234**	604-683-1234
Listel Vancouver Hotel 1300 Robson St	Vancouver	BC	V6E1C5	**800-663-5491**	604-684-8461
Lord Stanley Suites on the Park 1889 Alberni St	Vancouver	BC	V6G3G7	**888-767-7829**	604-688-9299
Metropolitan Hotel Vancouver 645 Howe St	Vancouver	BC	V6C2Y9	**800-667-2300**	604-687-1122
Pacific Palisades Hotel 1277 Robson St	Vancouver	BC	V6E1C4	**800-663-1815**	604-688-0461
Pan Pacific Hotel Vancouver 300-999 Canada Pl	Vancouver	BC	V6C3B5	**800-937-1515**	604-662-8111
Plaza 500 Hotel 500 W 12th Ave	Vancouver	BC	V5Z1M2	**800-473-1811**	604-873-1811
Quality Hotel Downtown 1335 Howe St	Vancouver	BC	V6Z1R7	**800-663-8474**	604-682-0229
Renaissance Vancouver Hotel Harbourside 1133 West Hastings St	Vancouver	BC	V6E3T2	**800-905-8582**	604-689-9211
Residence Inn Vancouver 1234 Hornby St	Vancouver	BC	V6Z1W2	**800-663-1234**	604-688-1234
Riviera Hotel 1431 Robson St	Vancouver	BC	V6G1C1	**888-699-5222**	604-685-1301
Rosedale on Robson Suite Hotel 838 Hamilton St	Vancouver	BC	V6B6A2	**800-661-8870**	604-689-8033
Rosellen Suites at Stanley Park 2030 Barclay St	Vancouver	BC	V6G1L5	**888-317-6648**	604-689-4807
Saint Regis Hotel 602 Dunsmuir St	Vancouver	BC	V6B1Y6	**800-770-7929**	604-681-1135
Sandman Hotel Vancouver 180 W Georgia St	Vancouver	BC	V6B4P4	**800-726-3626**	604-681-2211
Sheraton Suites Le Soleil 567 Hornby St	Vancouver	BC	V6C2E8	**877-632-3030**	604-632-3000
Sunset Inn Travel Apartments 1111 Burnaby St	Vancouver	BC	V6E1P4	**800-786-1997**	604-688-2474
Sutton Place Hotel Vancouver 845 Burrard St	Vancouver	BC	V6Z2K6	**800-961-7555**	604-682-5511
Vancouver Marriott Pinnacle Downtown 1128 W Hastings St	Vancouver	BC	V6E4R5	**800-228-9290**	604-684-1128
Wedgewood Hotel 845 Hornby St	Vancouver	BC	V6Z1V1	**800-663-0666**	604-689-7777
Westin Bayshore Resort & Marina 1601 Bayshore Dr	Vancouver	BC	V6G2V4	**800-228-3000**	604-682-3377
Westin Grand Vancouver 433 Robson St	Vancouver	BC	V6B6L9	**888-680-9393**	604-602-1999
Coast Harbourside Hotel & Marina 146 Kingston St	Victoria	BC	V8V1V4	**800-663-1144**	250-360-1211
Fairmont Empress 721 Government St	Victoria	BC	V8W1W5	**800-441-1414**	250-384-8111
Hotel Grand Pacific 463 Belleville St	Victoria	BC	V8V1X3	**800-663-7550**	250-386-0450
Magnolia Hotel & Spa 623 Courtney St	Victoria	BC	V8W1B8	**877-624-6654**	250-381-0999
Strathcona Hotel 919 Douglas St	Victoria	BC	V8W2C2	**800-663-7476**	250-383-7137
Victoria Regent Hotel 1234 Wharf St	Victoria	BC	V8W3H9	**800-663-7472**	250-386-2211
Coast Whistler Hotel 4005 Whistler Way	Whistler	BC	V0N1B4	**888-252-4454**	604-932-2522
Residence Inn Whistler 4899 Painted Cliff Rd	Whistler	BC	V0N1B4	**800-777-0185**	604-905-3400
Summit Lodge 4359 Main St	Whistler	BC	V0N1B4	**888-913-8811**	604-932-2778

Manitoba

Hotel	City	Prov	Postal Code	Toll-Free	Phone
Best Western Victoria Inn 1808 Wellington Ave	Winnipeg	MB	R3H0G3	**800-928-4067**	204-786-4801
Canad Inns - Club Regent Casino Hotel 1415 Regent Ave W	Winnipeg	MB	R2C3B2	**888-332-2623**	204-667-5560
Canad Inns Fort Garry 1824 Pembina Hwy	Winnipeg	MB	R3T2G2	**888-332-2623**	204-261-7450
Canad Inns Garden City 2100 McPhillips St	Winnipeg	MB	R2V3T9	**888-332-2623**	204-633-0024
Canad Inns Polo Park 1405 St Matthews Ave	Winnipeg	MB	R3G0K5	**888-332-2623**	204-775-8791
Fairmont Winnipeg 2 Lombard Pl	Winnipeg	MB	R3B0Y3	**800-441-1414**	204-957-1350
Fort Garry The 222 Broadway	Winnipeg	MB	R3C0R3	**800-665-8088**	204-942-8251
Greenwood Inn Winnipeg 1715 Wellington Ave	Winnipeg	MB	R3H0G1	**888-233-6730**	204-775-9889
Holiday Inn Winnipeg Airport West 2520 Portage Ave	Winnipeg	MB	R3J3T6	**800-665-0352**	204-885-4478
Norwood Hotel 112 Marion St	Winnipeg	MB	R2H0T1	**888-888-1878**	204-233-4475
Place Louis Riel All-Suite Hotel 190 Smith St	Winnipeg	MB	R3C1J8	**800-665-0569**	204-947-6961
Radisson Hotel Winnipeg Downtown 288 Portage Ave	Winnipeg	MB	R3C0B8	**800-333-3333**	204-956-0410
Saint Regis Hotel Winnipeg 285 Smith St	Winnipeg	MB	R3C1K9	**800-663-7344**	204-942-0171
Sheraton Winnipeg 161 Donald St	Winnipeg	MB	R3C1M3	**800-463-6400**	204-942-5300
Viscount Gort Hotel 1670 Portage Ave	Winnipeg	MB	R3J0C9	**800-665-1122**	204-775-0451

Nova Scotia

Hotel	City	Prov	Postal Code	Toll-Free	Phone
Burnside Hotel 739 Windmill Rd	Dartmouth	NS	B3B1C1	**800-830-4656**	902-468-7117
Coastal Inn Concorde 379 Windmill Rd	Dartmouth	NS	B3A1J6	**800-565-1565**	902-465-7777
Holiday Inn Harbourview 101 Wyse Rd	Dartmouth	NS	B3A1L9	**800-465-4329**	902-463-1100
Park Place Ramada Plaza Hotel 240 Brownlow Ave	Dartmouth	NS	B3B1X6	**800-561-3733**	902-468-8888
Airport Hotel Halifax 60 Bell Blvd Halifax International Airport	Enfield	NS	B2T1K3	**800-667-3333**	902-873-3000
Bluenose Inn 636 Bedford Hwy	Halifax	NS	B3M2L8	**800-565-2301**	902-443-3171
Cambridge Suites Hotel Halifax 1583 Brunswick St	Halifax	NS	B3J3P5	**800-565-1263**	902-420-0555
Casino Nova Scotia Hotel 1919 Upper Water St	Halifax	NS	B3J3J5	**866-425-4329**	902-421-1700
Citadel Halifax Hotel 1960 Brunswick St	Halifax	NS	B3J2G7	**800-565-7162**	902-422-1391
Delta Barrington 1875 Barrington St	Halifax	NS	B3J3L6	**800-268-1133**	902-429-7410
Delta Halifax 1990 Barrington St	Halifax	NS	B3J1P2	**800-268-1133**	902-425-6700
Four Points by Sheraton Halifax 1496 Hollis St	Halifax	NS	B3J3Z1	**866-444-9494**	902-423-4444
Holiday Inn Select Halifax Centre 1980 Robie St	Halifax	NS	B3H3G5	**800-465-4329**	902-423-1161
King Edward Inn 5780-88 West St	Halifax	NS	B3K1H9	**800-565-5464**	902-422-3266
Lord Nelson Hotel & Suites 1515 South Park St	Halifax	NS	B3J2L2	**800-565-0000**	902-423-6331
Prince George Hotel 1725 Market St	Halifax	NS	B3J3N9	**800-565-1567**	902-425-1986
Radisson Suite Hotel Halifax 1649 Hollis St	Halifax	NS	B3J1V8	**800-333-3333**	902-429-7233
Westin Nova Scotian 1181 Hollis St	Halifax	NS	B3H2P6	**800-937-8461**	902-421-1000

Ontario

Hotel	City	Prov	Postal Code	Toll-Free	Phone
Holiday Inn Select Brampton 30 Peel Centre Dr	Brampton	ON	L6T4G3	**800-465-4329**	905-792-9900
Langdon Hall Country House Hotel & Spa 1 Langdon Dr	Cambridge	ON	N3H4R8	**800-268-1898**	519-740-2100
Delta Toronto Airport Hotel 801 Dixon Rd	Etobicoke	ON	M9W1J5	**800-668-1444**	416-675-6100
Valhalla Inn Toronto 1 Valhalla Inn Rd	Etobicoke	ON	M9B1S9	**800-268-2500**	416-239-2391
Holiday Inn Select Ottawa West (Kanata) 101 Kanata Ave	Kanata	ON	K2T1E6	**800-465-4329**	613-271-3057
Delta London Armouries 325 Dundas St	London	ON	N6B1T9	**800-668-9999**	519-679-6111
Hilton Garden Inn Toronto/Markham 300 Commerce Valley Dr E	Markham	ON	L3T7X3	**877-782-9444**	905-709-8008
Four Points by Sheraton Toronto Airport 5444 Dixie Rd	Mississauga	ON	L4W2L2	**800-737-3211**	905-624-1144
Glenerin Inn 1695 The Collegeway	Mississauga	ON	L5L3S7	**877-991-9971**	905-828-6103
Hilton Garden Inn Toronto/Mississauga 100 Traders Blvd	Mississauga	ON	L4Z2H7	**877-782-9444**	905-890-9110
Hilton Toronto Airport 5875 Airport Rd	Mississauga	ON	L4V1N1	**800-445-8667**	905-677-9900
Holiday Inn Select Mississauga 2565 Argentia Rd	Mississauga	ON	L5N5V4	**800-465-4329**	905-542-2121
Monte Carlo Inn-Airport Suites 5 Derry Rd	Mississauga	ON	L5T2H8	**800-363-6400**	905-564-8500
Sandalwood Hotel & Suites 5050 Orbitor Dr	Mississauga	ON	L4W4X2	**800-387-3355**	905-238-9600
Marriott Niagara Falls 6740 Fallsview Blvd	Niagara Falls	ON	L2G3W6	**888-501-8916**	905-357-7300
Ramada Plaza Fallsview Niagara Falls 6732 Fallsview Blvd	Niagara Falls	ON	L2G3W6	**800-461-2492**	905-356-1501
Renaissance Fallsview Hotel 6455 Fallsview Blvd	Niagara Falls	ON	L2G3V9	**800-363-3255**	905-357-5200
Novotel Toronto North York Hotel 3 Park Home Ave	North York	ON	M2N6L3	**800-668-6835**	416-733-2929
Radisson Hotel Toronto East 55 Hallcrown Pl	North York	ON	M2J4R1	**800-333-3333**	416-493-7000
Hilton Garden Inn Toronto/Oakville 2774 S Sheridan Way	Oakville	ON	L6J7T4	**877-782-9444**	905-829-1145
Albert at Bay Suite Hotel 435 Albert St	Ottawa	ON	K1R7X4	**800-267-6644**	613-238-8858
Arosa Suites Hotel 163 McLaren St	Ottawa	ON	K2P2G4	**866-238-6783**	613-238-6783
Best Western Macies Hotel 1274 Carling Ave	Ottawa	ON	K1Z7K8	**800-528-1234**	613-728-1951
Brookstreet Hotel 525 Legget Dr	Ottawa	ON	K2K2W2	**888-826-2220**	613-271-1800
Business Inn 180 MacLaren St	Ottawa	ON	K2P0L3	**800-363-1777**	613-232-1121
Capital Hill Hotel & Suites 88 Albert St	Ottawa	ON	K1P5E9	**800-463-7705**	613-235-1413
Cartier Place Suite Hotel 180 Cooper St	Ottawa	ON	K2P2L5	**800-236-8399**	613-236-5000
Chimo Hotel 1199 Joseph Cyr St	Ottawa	ON	K1J7T4	**800-387-9779**	613-744-1060
Delta Ottawa Hotel & Suites 361 Queen St	Ottawa	ON	K1R7S9	**800-268-1133**	613-238-6000
Embassy Hotel & Suites 25 Cartier St	Ottawa	ON	K2P1J2	**800-661-5495**	613-237-2111
Embassy West Hotel 1400 Carling Ave	Ottawa	ON	K1Z7L8	**800-267-8696**	613-729-4331
Fairmont Chateau Laurier 1 Rideau St	Ottawa	ON	K1N8S7	**800-441-1414**	613-241-1414
Les Suites Hotel Ottawa 130 Besserer St	Ottawa	ON	K1N9M9	**800-267-1989**	613-232-2000
Lord Elgin Hotel 100 Elgin St	Ottawa	ON	K1P5K8	**800-267-4298**	613-235-3333
Marriott Ottawa 100 Kent St	Ottawa	ON	K1P5R7	**800-853-8463**	613-238-1122
Monterey Inn Resort 2259 Prince of Wales Dr	Ottawa	ON	K2E6Z8	**800-565-1311**	613-226-5813
Novotel Ottawa 33 Nicholas St	Ottawa	ON	K1N9M7	**800-668-6835**	613-230-3033
Residence Inn Ottawa Downtown 161 Laurier Ave W	Ottawa	ON	K1P5J2	**877-478-4838**	613-231-2020
Sheraton Ottawa Hotel 150 Albert St	Ottawa	ON	K1P5G2	**800-325-3535**	613-238-1500
Southway Inn 2431 Bank St	Ottawa	ON	K1V8R9	**877-688-4929**	613-737-0811
Westin Ottawa 11 Colonel By Dr	Ottawa	ON	K1N9H4	**800-228-3000**	613-560-7000
Best Western Primrose Hotel Downtown 111 Carlton St	Toronto	ON	M5B2G3	**800-528-1234**	416-977-8000
Best Western Roehampton Hotel & Suites 808 Mt Pleasant Rd	Toronto	ON	M4P2L2	**800-387-8899**	416-487-5101
Bond Place Hotel 65 Dundas St E	Toronto	ON	M5B2G8	**800-268-9390**	416-362-6061
Cambridge Suites Hotel Toronto 15 Richmond St E	Toronto	ON	M5C1N2	**800-463-1990**	416-368-1990
Delta Chelsea 33 Gerrard St W	Toronto	ON	M5G1Z4	**800-268-2266**	416-595-1975
Delta Toronto East 2035 Kennedy Rd	Toronto	ON	M1T3G2	**800-268-1133**	416-299-1500
Doubletree International Plaza Hotel Toronto Airport 655 Dixon Rd	Toronto	ON	M9W1J3	**800-668-3656**	416-244-1711
Fairmont Royal York 100 Front St W	Toronto	ON	M5J1E3	**800-441-1414**	416-368-2511
Four Seasons Hotel Toronto 21 Avenue Rd	Toronto	ON	M5R2G1	**800-332-3442**	416-964-0411
Glen Grove Suites 2837 Yonge St	Toronto	ON	M4N2J6	**800-565-3024**	416-489-8441
Hilton Toronto 145 Richmond St W	Toronto	ON	M5H2L2	**800-267-2281**	416-869-3456
Holiday Inn on King 370 King St W	Toronto	ON	M5V1J9	**800-263-6364**	416-599-4000

				Toll-Free	Phone
Holiday Inn Select Toronto Airport 970 Dixon Rd	Toronto	ON	M9W1J9	**800-465-4329**	416-675-7611
Holiday Inn Toronto Yorkdale 3450 Dufferin St.	Toronto	ON	M6A2V1	**800-465-4329**	416-789-5161
Hotel Victoria 56 Yonge St.	Toronto	ON	M5E1G5	**800-363-8228**	416-363-1666
InterContinental Toronto 220 Bloor St W	Toronto	ON	M5S1T8	**800-267-0010**	416-960-5200
Intercontinental Toronto Centre 225 Front St W	Toronto	ON	M5V2X3	**800-227-6963**	416-597-1400
Le Royal Meridien King Edward 37 King St E	Toronto	ON	M5C1E9	**800-543-4300**	416-863-3131
Marriott Toronto Airport 901 Dixon Road	Toronto	ON	M9W1J5	**800-228-9290**	416-674-9400
Marriott Toronto Bloor Yorkville Hotel 90 Bloor St E	Toronto	ON	M4W1A7	**800-228-9290**	416-961-8000
Marriott Toronto Eaton Centre 525 Bay St	Toronto	ON	M5G2L2	**800-228-9290**	416-597-9200
Metropolitan Hotel Toronto 108 Chestnut St.	Toronto	ON	M5G1R3	**800-668-6600**	416-977-5000
Novotel Toronto Centre 45 The Esplanade	Toronto	ON	M5E1W2	**800-668-6835**	416-367-8900
Park Hyatt Toronto 4 Avenue Rd	Toronto	ON	M5R2E8	**800-233-1234**	416-924-5471
Radisson Plaza Hotel Admiral-Toronto 249 Queen's Quay W	Toronto	ON	M5J2N5	**800-333-3333**	416-203-3333
Renaissance Toronto Hotel at Sky Dome 1 Blue Jays Way	Toronto	ON	M5V1J4	**800-237-1512**	416-341-7100
Seneca College Residence & Conference Centre 1760 Finch Ave E.	Toronto	ON	M2J5G3	**877-225-8664**	416-491-8811
Sheraton Centre Toronto Hotel 123 Queen St W	Toronto	ON	M5H2M9	**800-325-3535**	416-361-1000
Strathcona Hotel 60 York St.	Toronto	ON	M5J1S8	**800-268-8304**	416-363-3321
Sutton Place Hotel Toronto 955 Bay St.	Toronto	ON	M5S2A2	**800-268-3790**	416-924-9221
Town Inn Suites 620 Church St	Toronto	ON	M4Y2G2	**800-387-2755**	416-964-3311
Westin Prince Toronto 900 York Mills Rd	Toronto	ON	M3B3H2	**800-937-8461**	416-444-2511
Windsor Arms Hotel 18 Saint Thomas St.	Toronto	ON	M5S3E7	**877-999-2767**	416-971-9666
Wyndham Bristol Place Toronto Airport 950 Dixon Rd.	Toronto	ON	M9W5N4	**800-996-3426**	416-675-9444
Holiday Inn Select Windsor (Ambassador Bridge) 1855 Huron Church Rd	Windsor	ON	N9C2L6	**800-465-4329**	519-966-1200
Radisson Riverfront Hotel Windsor 333 Riverside Dr W	Windsor	ON	N9A5K4	**800-333-3333**	519-977-9777

Prince Edward Island

				Toll-Free	Phone
Delta Prince Edward PO Box 2170 18 Queen St.	Charlottetown	PE	C1A8B9	**800-268-1133**	902-566-2222

Quebec

				Toll-Free	Phone
Hotel Ambassadeur 321 boul Sainte-Anne	Beauport	QC	G1E3L4	**800-363-4619**	418-666-2828
Hilton Montreal Airport 12505 ch Cote-de-Liesse	Dorval	QC	H9P1B7	**800-445-8667**	514-631-2411
Hilton Lac Leamy 3 boul du Casino	Hull	QC	J8Y6X4	**866-488-7888**	819-790-6444
Holiday Inn Plaza La Chaudiere 2 rue Montcalm	Hull	QC	J8X4B4	**800-567-1962**	819-778-3880
Ramada Plaza Hotel Manoir du Casino 35 rue Laurier	Hull	QC	J8X4E9	**800-567-9607**	819-778-6111
Radisson Hotel Laval 2900 boul Le Carrefour	Laval	QC	H7T2K9	**800-333-3333**	450-682-9000
Sandman Hotel Longueuil-Montreal 999 de Serigny	Longueuil	QC	J4K2T1	**800-493-7303**	450-670-3030
Auberge du Vieux-Port 97 de la Commune E.	Montreal	QC	H2Y1J1	**888-660-7678**	514-876-0081
Best Western Europa Downtown 1240 rue Drummond	Montreal	QC	H3G1V7	**800-361-3000**	514-866-6492
Best Western Ville-Marie Hotel & Suites 3407 rue Peel	Montreal	QC	H3A1W7	**800-528-1234**	514-288-4141
Chateau Royal Hotel Suites 1420 Rue Crescent	Montreal	QC	H3G2B7	**800-363-0335**	514-848-0999
Chateau Versailles 1659 Sherbrooke St W	Montreal	QC	H3H1E3	**888-933-8111**	514-933-8111
Clarion Hotel & Suites Montreal Downtown 2100 boul de Maisonneuve O	Montreal	QC	H3H1K6	**800-361-7191**	514-931-8861
Crowne Plaza Hotel Montreal Metro Centre 505 rue Sherbrooke O	Montreal	QC	H2L4N3	**800-561-4644**	514-842-8581
Delta Centre-Ville 777 University St	Montreal	QC	H3C3Z7	**800-268-1133**	514-879-1370
Delta Montreal 475 rue President-Kennedy O	Montreal	QC	H3A1J7	**877-286-1986**	514-286-1986
Fairmont Queen Elizabeth 900 Rene Levesque Blvd W	Montreal	QC	H3B4A5	**800-441-1414**	514-861-3511
Four Points by Sheraton Montreal Centre-Ville 475 rue Sherbrooke O	Montreal	QC	H3A2L9	**800-325-3535**	514-842-3961
Gouverneur Hotel Montreal (Place-Dupuis) 1415 rue Saint-Hubert	Montreal	QC	H2L3Y9	**888-910-1111**	514-842-4881
Hilton Garden Inn Montreal/Dorval Airport 7880 Cote De Liesse	Montreal	QC	H4T1E7	**877-782-9444**	514-788-5120
Hilton Montreal Bonaventure 900 De La Gauchetiere O Suite 10750	Montreal	QC	H5A1E4	**800-267-2575**	514-878-2332
Holiday Inn Montreal Midtown 420 Sherbrooke St W	Montreal	QC	H3A1B4	**800-387-3042**	514-842-6111
Holiday Inn Select Montreal Centre-Ville 99 ave Viger O	Montreal	QC	H2Z1E9	**888-878-9888**	514-878-9888
Hotel Cantlie Suites 1110 rue Sherbrooke O	Montreal	QC	H3A1G9	**800-567-1110**	514-842-2000
Hotel du Fort 1390 Rue du Fort	Montreal	QC	H3H2R7	**800-565-6333**	514-938-8333
Hotel l'Appartement Montreal 455 rue Sherbrooke O	Montreal	QC	H3A1B7	**800-363-3010**	514-284-3634
Hotel Lord-Berri 1199 rue Berri	Montreal	QC	H2L4C6	**888-363-0363**	514-845-9236
Hotel Maritime Plaza 1155 rue Guy	Montreal	QC	H3H2P5	**800-363-6255**	514-932-1411
Hotel de la Montagne 1430 rue de la Montagne	Montreal	QC	H3G1Z5	**800-361-6262**	514-288-5656
Hotel Omni Mont-Royal 1050 rue Sherbrooke O	Montreal	QC	H3A2R6	**800-843-6664**	514-284-1110
Hotel Ruby Foo's 7655 Decarie Blvd	Montreal	QC	H4P2H2	**800-361-5419**	514-731-7701
Hotel Versailles 1808 rue Sherbrooke O	Montreal	QC	H3H1E5	**800-933-8111**	514-933-8111
Hyatt Regency Montreal 1255 rue Jeanne-Mance CP 130	Montreal	QC	H5B1E5	**800-361-8234**	514-285-1450
InterContinental Montreal 360 rue Saint-Antoine O	Montreal	QC	H2Y3X4	**800-361-3600**	514-987-9900
Le Nouvel Montreal Hotel & Spa 1740 boul Rene-Levesque W	Montreal	QC	H3H1R3	**800-363-6063**	514-931-8841
Le Saint Sulpice 414 St Sulpice	Montreal	QC	H2Y2V5	**877-785-7423**	514-282-9942
Loews Hotel Vogue 1425 rue de la Montagne	Montreal	QC	H3G1Z3	**800-465-6654**	514-285-5555
Montreal Marriott Chateau Champlain 1050 rue de la Gauchetiere	Montreal	QC	H3B4C9	**800-200-5909**	514-878-9000
Novotel Montreal Centre 1180 rue de la Montagne	Montreal	QC	H3G1Z1	**800-668-6835**	514-861-6000
Ritz-Carlton Montreal 1228 rue Sherbrooke O.	Montreal	QC	H3G1H6	**800-241-3333**	514-842-4212
Auberge Saint-Antoine 8 rue Saint-Antoine	Quebec	QC	G1K4C9	**888-692-2211**	418-692-2211
Delta Hotel Quebec 690 boul Rene-Levesque E.	Quebec	QC	G1R5A8	**888-884-7777**	418-647-1717
Fairmont Le Chateau Frontenac 1 rue des Carrieres	Quebec	QC	G1R4P5	**800-441-1414**	418-692-3861
Hilton Quebec 1100 boul Rene-Levesque E	Quebec	QC	G1K7K7	**800-447-2411**	418-647-2411
Holiday Inn Select Quebec City Downtown 395 rue de la Couronne	Quebec	QC	G1K7X4	**800-267-2002**	418-647-2611
Hotel Acadia 43 rue Sainte-Ursule	Quebec	QC	G1R4E4	**800-463-0280**	418-694-0280
Hotel Le Capitole 972 rue Saint-Jean	Quebec	QC	G1R1R5	**800-363-4040**	418-694-4040
Hotel Chateau Bellevue 16 rue de la Porte	Quebec	QC	G1R4M9	**800-463-2617**	418-692-2573
Hotel Chateau Laurier 1220 Pl George V O	Quebec	QC	G1R5B8	**800-463-4453**	418-522-8108
Hotel Clarendon 57 rue Sainte-Anne	Quebec	QC	G1R3X4	**888-554-6001**	418-692-2480
Hotel Le Clos Saint-Louis 69 rue Saint-Louis	Quebec	QC	G1R3Z2	**800-461-1311**	418-694-1311
Hotel Manoir Lafayette 661 Grande Allee E.	Quebec	QC	G1R2K4	**800-363-8203**	418-522-2652
Hotel Manoir Victoria 44 Cote du Palais	Quebec	QC	G1R4H8	**800-463-6283**	418-692-1030
Hotel Normandin 4700 boul Pierre-Bertrand	Quebec	QC	G2J1A4	**800-463-6721**	418-622-1611
Hotel le Priori 15 rue du Sault-au-Matelot	Quebec	QC	G1K3Y7	**800-351-3992**	418-692-3992
Hotel Royal Palace 775 Honore Mercier Ave	Quebec	QC	G1R6A5	**800-567-5276**	418-694-2000
L'Hotel du Vieux-Quebec 1190 rue Saint-Jean	Quebec	QC	G1R1S6	**800-361-7787**	418-692-1850
Loews Le Concorde Hotel 1225 Cours Du General De Montcalm	Quebec	QC	G1R4W6	**800-463-5256**	418-647-2222
Best Western Hotel L'Aristocrate 3100 ch Saint-Louis	Sainte-Foy	QC	G1W1R8	**800-463-4752**	418-653-2841
Chateau Bonne Entente 3400 ch Sainte-Foy	Sainte-Foy	QC	G1X1S6	**800-463-4390**	418-653-5221
Gouverneur Hotel Sainte-Foy 3030 Laurier Blvd	Sainte-Foy	QC	G1V2M5	**888-910-1111**	418-651-3030
Hotel Classique 2815 boul Laurier	Sainte-Foy	QC	G1V4H3	**800-463-1885**	418-658-2793
Hotel Germain des Pres 1200 ave Germain-des-Pres	Sainte-Foy	QC	G1V3M7	**800-463-5253**	418-658-1224
Hotel Plaza Quebec 3031 boul Laurier	Sainte-Foy	QC	G1V2M2	**800-567-5276**	418-658-2727
Hotel Quartier 2955 boul Laurier	Sainte-Foy	QC	G1V2M2	**888-818-5863**	418-650-1616
Hotel Universel 2300 ch Sainte-Foy	Sainte-Foy	QC	G1V1S5	**800-463-4495**	418-653-5250
L'Hotel Quebec 3115 ave des Hotels	Sainte-Foy	QC	G1W3Z6	**800-567-5276**	418-658-5120
Quebec Inn 7175 boul Hamel	Sainte-Foy	QC	G2G1B6	**800-567-5276**	418-872-9831
Delta Sherbrooke Hotel & Conference Centre 2685 King St W	Sherbrooke	QC	J1L1C1	**800-268-1133**	819-822-1989
Delta Trois-Rivieres Hotel & Conference Centre 1620 Notre Dame St	Trois-Rivieres	QC	G9A6E5	**800-268-1133**	819-376-1991

Saskatchewan

				Toll-Free	Phone
Delta Bessborough 601 Spadina Crescent E.	Saskatoon	SK	S7K3G8	**800-268-1133**	306-244-5521

373 HOTELS & MOTELS (INDIVIDUAL) - US

SEE ALSO Corporate Housing; Hotel & Resort Operation & Management; Hotel Reservations Services; Hotels & Motels (Individual) - Canada; Hotels - Conference Center; Hotels - Frequent Stay Programs; Resorts

Alabama

				Toll-Free	Phone
Hilton Garden Inn Auburn/Opelika 2555 Hilton Garden Dr.	Auburn	AL	36830	**877-782-9444**	334-502-3500
Alta Vista Hotel & Conference Center 260 Goodwin Crest Dr	Birmingham	AL	35209	**888-290-8099**	205-290-8000
AmeriSuites Birmingham/Inverness 4686 Hwy 280 E	Birmingham	AL	35242	**800-833-1516**	205-995-9242
AmeriSuites Birmingham/Riverchase 2980 John Hawkins Pkwy	Birmingham	AL	35244	**800-833-1516**	205-988-8444
Best Western Riverchase Inn 1800 Riverchase Dr	Birmingham	AL	35244	**800-937-8376**	205-985-7500
Crowne Plaza Hotel Birmingham-The Redmont 2101 5th Ave N	Birmingham	AL	35203	**800-227-6963**	205-324-2101
Embassy Suites Birmingham 2300 Woodcrest Pl	Birmingham	AL	35209	**800-362-2779**	205-879-7400
Holiday Inn Birmingham Airport 5000 Richard Arrington Blvd	Birmingham	AL	35212	**800-368-5533**	205-591-6900
Holiday Inn Birmingham-Homewood 260 Oxmoor Rd	Birmingham	AL	35209	**800-465-4329**	205-942-2041
Marriott Birmingham 3590 Grandview Pkwy	Birmingham	AL	35243	**800-228-9290**	205-968-3775
Pickwick Hotel 1023 20th St S	Birmingham	AL	35205	**800-255-7304**	205-933-9555
Radisson Hotel Birmingham 808 S 20th St	Birmingham	AL	35205	**800-333-3333**	205-933-9000
Residence Inn Birmingham/Inverness 3 Greenhill Pkwy	Birmingham	AL	35242	**800-331-3131**	205-991-8686
Sheraton Birmingham Hotel 2101 Richard Arrington Jr Blvd N	Birmingham	AL	35203	**800-325-3535**	205-324-5000
Tutwiler The - A Wyndham Historic Hotel 2021 Park Pl N	Birmingham	AL	35203	**800-996-3426**	205-322-2100
Wingate Inn Birmingham 800 Corporate Ridge Rd	Birmingham	AL	35242	**866-466-2426**	205-995-8586
Wynfrey Hotel 1000 Riverchase Galleria	Birmingham	AL	35244	**800-996-3739**	205-987-1600
Hilton Garden Inn Mobile East Bay/Daphne 29546 N Main St	Daphne	AL	36526	**877-782-9444**	251-625-0020
Courtyard Birmingham Homewood 500 Shades Creek Pkwy	Homewood	AL	35209	**800-321-2211**	205-879-0400
Hilton Garden Inn Birmingham/Lakeshore Drive 520 Wildwood Cir Dr N	Homewood	AL	35209	**877-782-9444**	205-314-0274
Courtyard Birmingham Hoover 1824 Montgomery Hwy S	Hoover	AL	35244	**800-321-2211**	205-988-5000
Courtyard Huntsville 4804 University Dr	Huntsville	AL	35816	**800-321-2211**	256-837-1400
Four Points by Sheraton Huntsville Airport 1000 Glenn Hearn Blvd	Huntsville	AL	35824	**800-241-7873**	256-772-9661
Hilton Huntsville 401 Williams Ave SW	Huntsville	AL	35801	**800-345-6505**	256-533-1400
Holiday Inn Huntsville Research Park 5903 University Dr NW	Huntsville	AL	35806	**800-845-7275**	256-830-0600
Marriott Huntsville 5 Tranquility Base	Huntsville	AL	35805	**800-228-9290**	256-830-2222
Radisson Suite Hotel Huntsville 6000 S Memorial Pkwy	Huntsville	AL	35802	**800-333-3333**	256-882-9400
Federal Square Suites 8781 Madison Blvd	Madison	AL	35758	**800-458-1639**	256-772-8470
Holiday Inn Huntsville-Madison 9035 Madison Blvd	Madison	AL	35758	**800-826-9563**	256-772-7170

Alabama (Cont'd)

Name / Address	City	State	Zip	Toll-Free	Phone
Radisson Inn Huntsville Airport 8721 Madison Blvd	Madison	AL	35758	**800-333-3333**	256-772-8855
Courtyard Mobile 1000 S Beltline Hwy	Mobile	AL	36609	**800-321-2211**	251-344-5200
Lafayette Plaza Hotel 301 Government St	Mobile	AL	36602	**800-692-6662**	251-694-0100
Malaga Inn 359 Church St	Mobile	AL	36602	**800-235-1586**	251-438-4701
Marriott Mobile 3101 Airport Blvd	Mobile	AL	36606	**800-228-9290**	251-380-7971
Radisson Admiral Semmes Hotel 251 Government St	Mobile	AL	36602	**800-333-3333**	251-432-8000
Residence Inn Mobile 950 W 1-165 Svc Rd S	Mobile	AL	36609	**800-331-3131**	251-304-0570
Riverview Plaza Hotel 64 S Water St	Mobile	AL	36602	**800-444-2326**	251-438-4000
Comfort Suites Montgomery 5924 Monticello Dr	Montgomery	AL	36117	**800-424-6423**	334-272-1013
Courtyard Montgomery 5555 Carmichael Rd	Montgomery	AL	36117	**800-321-2211**	334-272-5533
Embassy Suites Montgomery 300 Tallapoosa St	Montgomery	AL	36104	**800-362-2779**	334-269-5055
Fairfield Inn Montgomery 5601 Carmichael Rd	Montgomery	AL	36117	**800-228-2800**	334-270-0007
Governor's House Hotel & Conference Center 2705 E South Blvd	Montgomery	AL	36116	**866-535-5392**	334-288-2800
Hilton Garden Inn Montgomery East 1600 Interstate Pk Dr	Montgomery	AL	36109	**877-782-9444**	334-272-2225
Holiday Inn Montgomery East 1185 Eastern Bypass Blvd	Montgomery	AL	36117	**800-465-4329**	334-272-0370
Quality Inn Montgomery 5175 Carmichael Rd	Montgomery	AL	36106	**800-228-5151**	334-277-1919
Residence Inn Montgomery 1200 Hilmar Ct	Montgomery	AL	36117	**800-331-3131**	334-270-3300
Wingate Inn Montgomery 2060 Eastern Blvd	Montgomery	AL	36117	**800-228-1000**	334-244-7880
Best Western Catalina Inn 2015 McFarland Blvd	Northport	AL	35476	**800-780-7234**	205-339-5200
Hilton Garden Inn Orange Beach Beachfront 23092 Perdido Beach Blvd	Orange Beach	AL	36561	**877-782-9444**	251-974-1600
Best Western Park Plaza Motor Inn 3801 McFarland Blvd E	Tuscaloosa	AL	35405	**800-235-7282**	205-556-9690
Comfort Inn Tuscaloosa 4700 Doris Pate Dr	Tuscaloosa	AL	35405	**877-424-6423**	205-556-3232
Courtyard Tuscaloosa 4115 Courtney Dr	Tuscaloosa	AL	35401	**800-321-2211**	205-750-8384
Four Points by Sheraton Tuscaloosa Capstone 320 Paul Bryant Dr	Tuscaloosa	AL	35401	**800-477-2262**	205-752-3200
Quality Inn Tuscaloosa 4541 Old Jug Factory Rd	Tuscaloosa	AL	35405	**800-228-5151**	205-759-9878

Alaska

Name / Address	City	State	Zip	Toll-Free	Phone
Best Western Barratt Inn 4616 Spenard Rd	Anchorage	AK	99517	**800-221-7550**	907-243-3131
Black Angus Inn 1430 Gambell St	Anchorage	AK	99501	**800-770-0707**	907-272-7503
Chelsea Inn Hotel 3836 Spenard Rd	Anchorage	AK	99517	**800-770-5002**	907-276-5002
Clarion Suites Anchorage 325 W 8th Ave	Anchorage	AK	99501	**800-252-7466**	907-274-1000
Coast International Inn 3333 W International Airport Rd	Anchorage	AK	99502	**800-663-1144**	907-243-2233
Duke's 8th Avenue Hotel 630 W 8th Ave	Anchorage	AK	99501	**800-478-4837**	907-274-6213
Executive Suite Hotel 4360 Spenard Rd	Anchorage	AK	99517	**800-770-6366**	907-243-6366
Hilton Anchorage 500 W 3rd Ave	Anchorage	AK	99501	**800-245-2527**	907-272-7411
Hilton Garden Inn Anchorage 100 W Tudor Rd	Anchorage	AK	99503	**877-782-9444**	907-729-7000
Hotel Captain Cook 939 W 5th Ave	Anchorage	AK	99501	**800-843-1950**	907-276-6000
Inlet Tower Suites 1200 L St	Anchorage	AK	99501	**800-544-0786**	907-276-0110
Long House Alaskan Hotel 4335 Wisconsin St	Anchorage	AK	99517	**888-243-2133**	907-243-2133
Marriott Anchorage Downtown 820 W 7th Ave	Anchorage	AK	95501	**800-228-9290**	907-279-8000
Millennium Hotel Anchorage 4800 Spenard Rd	Anchorage	AK	99517	**800-544-0553**	907-243-2300
Puffin Inn 4400 Spenard Rd	Anchorage	AK	99517	**800-478-3346**	907-243-4044
Residence Inn Anchorage Midtown 1025 E 35th Ave	Anchorage	AK	99508	**800-331-3131**	907-563-9844
Royal Suite Lodge 3811 Minnesota Dr	Anchorage	AK	99503	**800-282-3114**	907-563-3114
Sheraton Anchorage Hotel 401 E 6th Ave	Anchorage	AK	99501	**800-325-3535**	907-276-8700
Voyager Hotel 501 K St	Anchorage	AK	99501	**800-247-9070**	907-277-9501
Westmark Anchorage 720 W 5th Ave	Anchorage	AK	99501	**800-544-0970**	907-276-7676
Bridgewater Hotel 723 1st Ave	Fairbanks	AK	99701	**800-528-4916**	907-452-6661
Captain Bartlett Inn 1411 Airport Way	Fairbanks	AK	99701	**800-544-7528**	907-452-1888
Fairbanks Hotel 517 3rd Ave	Fairbanks	AK	99701	**888-329-4685**	907-456-6411
Fairbanks Princess Riverside Lodge 4477 Pikes Landing Rd	Fairbanks	AK	99709	**800-426-0500**	907-455-4477
Golden North Motel 4888 Old Airport Rd	Fairbanks	AK	99709	**800-447-1910**	907-479-6201
Regency Fairbanks Hotel 95 10th Ave	Fairbanks	AK	99701	**800-348-1340**	907-452-3200
River's Edge Resort Cottages 4200 Boat St	Fairbanks	AK	99709	**800-770-3343**	907-474-0286
Sophie Station Hotel 1717 University Ave	Fairbanks	AK	99709	**800-528-4916**	907-479-3650
Wedgewood Resort Hotel 212 Wedgewood Dr	Fairbanks	AK	99701	**800-528-4916**	907-452-1442
Westmark Fairbanks Hotel & Conference Center 813 Noble St	Fairbanks	AK	99701	**800-544-0970**	907-456-7722
Glacier Bay Country Inn Mile 1 Tong Rd	Gustavus	AK	99826	**800-628-0912**	907-697-2288
Breakwater Inn 1711 Glacier Ave	Juneau	AK	99801	**800-544-2250**	907-586-6303
Driftwood Lodge 435 Willoughby Ave	Juneau	AK	99801	**800-544-2239**	907-586-2280
Goldbelt Hotel Juneau 51 Egan Dr	Juneau	AK	99801	**888-478-6909**	907-586-6900
Prospector Hotel 375 Whittier St	Juneau	AK	99801	**800-331-2711**	907-586-3737
Westmark Baranof 127 N Franklin St	Juneau	AK	99801	**800-544-0970**	907-586-2660
Best Western Kodiak Inn 236 W Rezanof Dr	Kodiak	AK	99615	**888-563-4254**	907-486-5712

Arizona

Name / Address	City	State	Zip	Toll-Free	Phone
Park Plaza Phoenix/Chandler 7475 W Chandler Blvd	Chandler	AZ	85226	**800-814-7000**	480-961-4444
AmeriSuites Flagstaff Interstate Crossroads 2455 S Beulah Blvd	Flagstaff	AZ	86001	**800-833-1516**	928-774-8042
Hilton Garden Inn Flagstaff 350 W Forest Meadows St	Flagstaff	AZ	86001	**877-782-9444**	928-226-8888
Hotel Monte Vista 100 N San Francisco St	Flagstaff	AZ	86001	**800-545-3068**	928-779-6971
InnSuites Hotels Flagstaff/Grand Canyon 1008 E Rt 66	Flagstaff	AZ	86001	**800-842-4242**	928-774-7356
Little America Hotel Flagstaff 2515 E Butler Ave	Flagstaff	AZ	86004	**800-352-4386**	928-779-2741
Radisson Woodlands Hotel Flagstaff 1175 W Rt 66	Flagstaff	AZ	86001	**800-333-3333**	928-773-8888
Best Western Phoenix-Glendale 5940 NW Grand Ave	Glendale	AZ	85301	**800-333-7172**	623-939-9431
Quality Inn & Suites at Talavi 5511 W Bell Rd	Glendale	AZ	85308	**800-228-5151**	602-896-8900
Best Western Grand Canyon Squire Inn Hwy 64 PO Box 130	Grand Canyon	AZ	86023	**800-622-6966**	928-638-2681
El Tovar Hotel PO Box 699	Grand Canyon	AZ	86023	**888-297-2757**	928-638-2631
Harrah's Phoenix Ak-Chin Casino Resort 15406 Maricopa Rd	Maricopa	AZ	85239	**800-427-7247**	480-802-5000
Best Western Dobson Ranch Inn & Resort 1666 S Dobson Rd	Mesa	AZ	85202	**800-528-1356**	480-831-7000
Courtyard Phoenix Mesa 1221 S Westwood St	Mesa	AZ	85210	**800-321-2211**	480-461-3000
Hilton Phoenix East/Mesa 1011 W Holmes Ave	Mesa	AZ	85210	**800-445-8667**	480-833-5555
Holiday Inn Hotel & Suites Phoenix-Mesa 1600 S Country Club Dr	Mesa	AZ	85210	**800-465-4329**	480-964-7000
Select Suites Fiesta Mall 960 W Southern Ave	Mesa	AZ	85210	**800-633-5972**	480-962-8343
Select Suites North Mesa-Sierra Madre 900 N Country Club Dr	Mesa	AZ	85201	**800-821-8005**	480-962-7940
Select Suites South Mesa-Peppertree 1318 S Vineyard St	Mesa	AZ	85210	**800-354-0893**	480-833-2959
Hermosa Inn 5532 N Palo Cristi Rd	Paradise Valley	AZ	85253	**800-241-1210**	602-955-8614
AmeriSuites Phoenix Metrocenter 10838 N 25th Ave	Phoenix	AZ	85029	**800-833-1516**	602-997-8800
Best Western Central Phoenix Inn & Suites 1100 N Central Ave	Phoenix	AZ	85004	**800-937-8376**	602-252-2100
Best Western Grace Inn at Ahwatukee 10831 S 51st St	Phoenix	AZ	85044	**800-843-6010**	480-893-3000
Crowne Plaza Hotel Phoenix Metro Center 2532 W Peoria Ave	Phoenix	AZ	85029	**800-465-4329**	602-943-2341
Doubletree Guest Suites Phoenix-Gateway Center 320 N 44th St	Phoenix	AZ	85008	**800-222-8733**	602-225-0500
Embassy Suites Phoenix-Airport at 44th St 1515 N 44th St	Phoenix	AZ	85008	**800-447-8483**	602-244-8800
Embassy Suites Phoenix-Biltmore 2630 E Camelback Rd	Phoenix	AZ	85016	**800-362-2779**	602-955-3992
Four Points by Sheraton Phoenix Metrocenter 10220 North Metro Pkwy E	Phoenix	AZ	85051	**800-325-3535**	602-997-5900
Hilton Garden Inn Phoenix Airport 3422 E Elwood St	Phoenix	AZ	85040	**877-782-9444**	602-470-0500
Hilton Garden Inn Phoenix Midtown 4000 N Central Ave	Phoenix	AZ	85012	**877-782-9444**	602-279-9811
Hilton Phoenix Airport 2435 S 47th St	Phoenix	AZ	85034	**800-445-8667**	480-894-1600
Holiday Inn Phoenix-Midtown 4321 N Central Ave	Phoenix	AZ	85012	**800-465-4329**	602-200-8888
Hotel San Carlos 202 N Central Ave	Phoenix	AZ	85004	**866-253-4121**	602-253-4121
Hyatt Regency Phoenix 122 N 2nd St	Phoenix	AZ	85004	**800-233-1234**	602-252-1234
JW Marriott Desert Ridge Resort & Spa Phoenix 5350 E Marriott Dr	Phoenix	AZ	85054	**800-898-4527**	480-293-5000
MainStay Suites at Metro Center 9455 N Black Canyon Hwy	Phoenix	AZ	85021	**800-424-6423**	602-395-0900
Marriott Phoenix Airport 1101 N 44th St	Phoenix	AZ	85008	**800-228-9290**	602-273-7373
Radisson Hotel Phoenix Airport 3333 E University Dr	Phoenix	AZ	85034	**800-333-3333**	602-437-8400
Ritz-Carlton Phoenix 2401 E Camelback Rd	Phoenix	AZ	85016	**800-241-3333**	602-468-0700
Select Suites Airport Center 4221 E McDowell Rd	Phoenix	AZ	85008	**800-845-3020**	602-267-7917
Select Suites Biltmore Center 4341 N 24th St	Phoenix	AZ	85016	**800-821-8005**	602-954-8049
Sheraton Crescent Hotel 2620 W Dunlap Ave	Phoenix	AZ	85021	**800-325-3535**	602-943-8200
Wingate Inn Phoenix 2520 N Central Ave	Phoenix	AZ	85003	**800-228-1000**	602-716-9900
Wyndham Phoenix 50 E Adams St	Phoenix	AZ	85004	**800-996-3426**	602-333-0000
Hassayampa Inn 122 E Gurley St	Prescott	AZ	86301	**800-322-1927**	928-778-9434
Courtyard North Scottsdale 17010 N Scottsdale Rd	Scottsdale	AZ	85255	**800-321-2211**	480-922-8400
Courtyard Scottsdale/Mayo Clinic 13444 E Shea Blvd	Scottsdale	AZ	85259	**800-321-2211**	480-860-4000
Hilton Garden Inn Scottsdale Old Town 7324 E Indian School Rd	Scottsdale	AZ	85251	**877-782-9444**	480-481-0400
Hilton Scottsdale Resort & Villas 6333 N Scottsdale Rd	Scottsdale	AZ	85250	**800-548-8690**	480-948-7750
Hospitality Suites Resort 409 N Scottsdale Rd	Scottsdale	AZ	85257	**800-445-5115**	480-949-5115
Marriott Scottsdale McDowell Mountains 16770 N Perimeter Dr	Scottsdale	AZ	85260	**800-228-9290**	480-502-3836
Marriott Suites Scottsdale Old Town 7325 E 3rd Ave	Scottsdale	AZ	85251	**800-228-9290**	480-945-1550
Resort Suites 7677 E Princess Blvd	Scottsdale	AZ	85255	**800-541-5203**	480-585-1234
Summerfield Suites by Wyndham Scottsdale 4245 N Drinkwater Blvd	Scottsdale	AZ	85251	**800-833-4353**	480-946-7700
L'Auberge de Sedona 301 L'Auberge Ln *Resv	Sedona	AZ	86336	**800-272-6777***	928-282-1661
AmeriSuites Tempe/Arizona Mills 1520 W Baseline Rd	Tempe	AZ	85283	**800-833-1516**	480-831-9800
AmeriSuites Tempe/Phoenix Airport 1413 W Rio Salado Pkwy	Tempe	AZ	85281	**800-833-1516**	480-804-9544
Courtyard Phoenix Tempe Downtown 601 S Ash Ave	Tempe	AZ	85281	**800-321-2211**	480-966-2800
Embassy Suites Tempe 4400 S Rural Rd	Tempe	AZ	85282	**800-362-2779**	480-897-7444
Fiesta Inn Resort 2100 S Priest Dr	Tempe	AZ	85282	**800-528-6481**	480-967-1441
Holiday Inn Phoenix-Tempe/ASU 915 E Apache Blvd	Tempe	AZ	85281	**800-553-1826**	480-968-3451
InnSuites Hotel & Suites Tempe/Phoenix Airport 1651 W Baseline Rd	Tempe	AZ	85283	**800-841-4242**	480-897-7900
Twin Palms Hotel 225 E Apache Blvd	Tempe	AZ	85281	**800-367-0835**	480-967-9431
Wyndham Buttes Resort 2000 Westcourt Way	Tempe	AZ	85282	**800-843-1986**	602-225-9000
Arizona Inn 2200 E Elm St	Tucson	AZ	85719	**800-933-1093**	520-325-1541
Best Western Inn at the Airport 7060 S Tucson Blvd	Tucson	AZ	85706	**800-772-3847**	520-746-0271
Courtyard Tucson Airport 2505 E Executive Dr	Tucson	AZ	85706	**800-321-2211**	520-573-0000
Courtyard Tucson Williams Centre 201 S Williams Blvd	Tucson	AZ	85711	**800-321-2211**	520-745-6000
Doubletree Hotel Tucson-Reid Park 445 S Alvernon Way	Tucson	AZ	85711	**800-222-8733**	520-881-4200
Embassy Suites Tucson-International Airport 7051 S Tucson Blvd	Tucson	AZ	85706	**800-362-2779**	520-573-0700
Flamingo Hotel Tucson 1300 N Stone Ave	Tucson	AZ	85705	**800-300-3533**	520-770-1910
Hilton Tucson East 7600 E Broadway Blvd	Tucson	AZ	85710	**800-445-8667**	520-721-5600
Hotel Congress 311 E Congress St	Tucson	AZ	85701	**800-722-8848**	520-622-8848
InnSuites Hotels Tucson City Center Conference Hotel & Suite Resort 475 N Granada Ave	Tucson	AZ	85701	**877-446-6589**	520-622-3000
Lodge on the Desert 306 N Alvernon Way	Tucson	AZ	85711	**800-456-5634**	520-325-3366

				Toll-Free	Phone
Marriott Tucson University Park 880 E 2nd St	Tucson	AZ	85719	**800-228-9290**	520-792-4100
Ramada Inn & Suites Palo Verde 5251 S Julian Dr	Tucson	AZ	85706	**800-272-6232**	520-294-5250
Sheraton Tucson Hotel & Suites 5151 E Grant Rd	Tucson	AZ	85712	**800-325-3535**	520-323-6262
Smuggler's Inn 6350 E Speedway Blvd	Tucson	AZ	85710	**800-525-8852**	520-296-3292
Varsity Clubs of America-Tucson Chapter 3855 E Speedway Blvd	Tucson	AZ	85716	**800-521-3131**	520-318-3777
Viscount Suite Hotel 4855 E Broadway Blvd	Tucson	AZ	85711	**800-527-9666**	520-745-6500
Windmill Inn at Saint Philip's Plaza Tucson 4250 N Campbell Ave	Tucson	AZ	85718	**800-547-4747**	520-577-0007

Arkansas

				Toll-Free	Phone
Hilton Garden Inn Bentonville 2204 SE Walton Blvd	Bentonville	AR	72712	**877-782-9444**	479-464-7300
Crescent Hotel 75 Prospect Ave	Eureka Springs	AR	72632	**877-342-9766**	479-253-9766
Aspen Hotel & Suites 2900 S 68th St	Fort Smith	AR	72903	**800-627-9417**	479-452-9000
Fifth Season Inn 2219 S Waldron Rd	Fort Smith	AR	72903	**877-452-4880**	479-452-4880
Holiday Inn Fort Smith City Center 700 Rogers Ave	Fort Smith	AR	72901	**800-465-4329**	479-783-1000
Austin Hotel & Spa 305 Malvern Ave	Hot Springs	AR	71901	**877-623-6697**	501-623-6600
Country Inn Lake Resort 1332 Airport Rd	Hot Springs	AR	71913	**800-822-7402**	501-767-3535
Downtown Hotel & Spa 135 Central Ave	Hot Springs	AR	71901	**888-624-5521**	501-624-5521
Edgewater Resort 200 Edgewater Cir	Hot Springs	AR	71913	**800-234-3687**	501-767-3311
Majestic Resort & Spa 101 Park Ave	Hot Springs	AR	71901	**800-643-1504**	501-623-5511
AmeriSuites Little Rock Financial Center 10920 Financial Center Pkwy	Little Rock	AR	72211	**800-833-1516**	501-225-1075
Capital Hotel 111 W Markham St	Little Rock	AR	72201	**800-766-7666**	501-374-7474
Courtyard Little Rock 10900 Financial Centre Pkwy	Little Rock	AR	72211	**800-321-2211**	501-227-6000
Doubletree Hotel Little Rock 424 W Markham St	Little Rock	AR	72201	**800-937-2789**	501-372-4371
Embassy Suites Little Rock 11301 Financial Centre Pkwy	Little Rock	AR	72211	**800-362-2779**	501-312-9000
Holiday Inn Presidential Conference Center 600 I-30	Little Rock	AR	72202	**866-900-7625**	501-375-2100
Peabody Little Rock 3 Statehouse Plaza	Little Rock	AR	72201	**800-527-1745**	501-906-4000
Premier Suites 11601 W Markham Rd Suite D	Little Rock	AR	72211	**800-735-2955**	501-221-7378
Cozy Acres Resort 1100 Cozy Acres Rd	Mountain Pine	AR	71956	**877-691-2699**	501-767-5023
Wyndham Riverfront Little Rock 2 Riverfront Pl	North Little Rock	AR	72114	**800-345-6565**	501-371-9000

California

				Toll-Free	Phone
Anaheim Plaza Hotel 1700 S Harbor Blvd	Anaheim	CA	92802	**800-532-4517**	714-772-5900
Carousel Inn & Suites 1530 S Harbor Blvd	Anaheim	CA	92802	**800-854-6767**	714-758-0444
Castle Inn & Suites 1734 S Harbor Blvd	Anaheim	CA	92802	**800-521-5653**	714-774-8111
Coast Anaheim Hotel 1855 S Harbor Blvd	Anaheim	CA	92802	**800-663-1144**	714-750-1811
Embassy Suites Anaheim North 3100 E Frontera St	Anaheim	CA	92806	**800-362-2779**	714-632-1221
Hilton Anaheim 777 W Convention Way	Anaheim	CA	92802	**800-222-9923**	714-750-4321
Holiday Inn Hotel & Suites Anaheim 1240 S Walnut St	Anaheim	CA	92802	**800-465-4329**	714-535-0300
Jolly Roger Inn 640 W Katella Ave	Anaheim	CA	92802	**800-854-8700**	714-772-7621
Marriott Anaheim 700 W Convention Way	Anaheim	CA	92802	**800-228-9290**	714-750-8000
Peacock Suites Resort 1745 S Anaheim Blvd	Anaheim	CA	92805	**800-522-6401**	714-535-8255
Portofino Inn & Suites 1831 South Harbor Blvd	Anaheim	CA	92802	**888-297-7143**	714-782-7600
Radisson Hotel Maingate Anaheim 1850 S Harbor Blvd	Anaheim	CA	92802	**800-333-3333**	714-750-2801
Residence Inn Anaheim/Disneyland 1700 S Clementine St	Anaheim	CA	92802	**800-331-3131**	714-533-3555
Sheraton Anaheim Hotel 900 S Disneyland Dr	Anaheim	CA	92802	**800-325-3535**	714-778-1700
Tropicana Inn & Suites 1540 S Harbor Blvd	Anaheim	CA	92802	**800-828-4898**	714-635-4082
Hilton Garden Inn Arcadia/Pasadena 199 N 2nd Ave	Arcadia	CA	91006	**877-782-9444**	626-574-6900
Residence Inn Pasadena-Arcadia 321 E Huntington Dr	Arcadia	CA	91006	**800-331-3131**	626-446-6500
Best Western Catalina Canyon Resort & Spa 888 Country Club Dr	Avalon	CA	90704	**800-253-9361**	310-510-0325
Inn on Mount Ada 398 Wrigley Rd PO Box 2560	Avalon	CA	90704	**800-608-7669**	310-510-2030
Best Western Crystal Palace Inn & Suites 2620 Buck Owens Blvd	Bakersfield	CA	93308	**800-424-4900**	661-327-9651
Best Western Hill House 700 Truxton Ave	Bakersfield	CA	93301	**800-300-4230**	661-327-4064
Clarion Hotel Bakersfield 3540 Rosedale Hwy	Bakersfield	CA	93308	**888-326-1121**	661-326-1111
Courtyard Bakersfield 3601 Marriott Dr	Bakersfield	CA	93308	**800-321-2211**	661-324-6660
Doubletree Hotel Bakersfield 3100 Camino Del Rio Ct	Bakersfield	CA	93308	**800-222-8733**	661-323-7111
Four Points by Sheraton Bakersfield 5101 California Ave	Bakersfield	CA	93309	**888-625-4988**	661-325-9700
Hilton Garden Inn Bakersfield 3625 Marriott Dr	Bakersfield	CA	93308	**800-664-4321**	661-716-1000
Holiday Inn Select Bakersfield-Convention Center 801 Truxtun Ave	Bakersfield	CA	93301	**800-465-4329**	661-323-1900
La Quinta Inn Bakersfield 3232 Riverside Dr	Bakersfield	CA	93308	**800-531-5900**	661-325-7400
Residence Inn Bakersfield 4241 Chester Ln	Bakersfield	CA	93309	**800-331-3131**	661-321-9800
Doubletree Hotel & Executive Meeting Center 200 Marina Blvd	Berkeley	CA	94710	**800-222-8733**	510-548-7920
Hotel Durant 2600 Durant Ave	Berkeley	CA	94704	**800-238-7268**	510-845-8981
Best Western Beverly Pavilion Hotel 9360 Wilshire Blvd	Beverly Hills	CA	90212	**800-441-5050**	310-273-1400
Beverly Hills Hotel 9641 Sunset Blvd	Beverly Hills	CA	90210	**800-283-8885**	310-276-2251
Beverly Hilton 9876 Wilshire Blvd	Beverly Hills	CA	90210	**800-445-8667**	310-274-7777
Crescent Hotel 403 N Crescent Dr	Beverly Hills	CA	90210	**800-451-1566**	310-247-0505
Mosaic Hotel 125 S Spalding Dr	Beverly Hills	CA	90212	**800-463-4466**	310-278-0303
Peninsula Beverly Hills 9882 S Santa Monica Blvd	Beverly Hills	CA	90212	**800-462-7899**	310-551-2888
Raffles L'Ermitage Beverly Hills 9291 Burton Way	Beverly Hills	CA	90210	**800-800-2113**	310-278-3344
Regent Beverly Wilshire - A Four Seasons Hotel 9500 Wilshire Blvd	Beverly Hills	CA	90212	**800-545-4000**	310-275-5200
Bodega Bay Lodge & Spa 103 Coast Hwy 1	Bodega Bay	CA	94923	**800-368-2468**	707-875-3525
Inn at the Tides PO Box 640 800 Hwy 1	Bodega Bay	CA	94923	**800-541-7788**	707-875-2751
Woodfin Suite Hotel Brea 3100 E Imperial Hwy	Brea	CA	92821	**888-433-9402**	714-579-3200
Marriott Rancho Santa Barbara 555 McMurray Rd	Buellton	CA	93427	**800-228-9290**	805-688-1000
Crowne Plaza San Francisco International Airport 1177 Airport Blvd	Burlingame	CA	94010	**800-411-7275**	650-342-9200
Doubletree Hotel San Francisco Airport 835 Airport Blvd	Burlingame	CA	94010	**800-222-8733**	650-344-5500
Hilton Garden Inn San Francisco Airport/Burlingame 765 Airport Blvd	Burlingame	CA	94010	**877-782-9444**	650-347-7800
Hyatt Regency San Francisco Airport 1333 Bayshore Hwy	Burlingame	CA	94010	**800-233-1234**	650-347-1234
Marriott San Francisco Airport 1800 Old Bayshore Hwy	Burlingame	CA	94010	**800-228-9290**	650-692-9100
Sheraton Gateway San Francisco Airport Hotel 600 Airport Blvd	Burlingame	CA	94010	**800-325-3535**	650-340-8500
Hilton Garden Inn Calabasas 24150 Park Sorrento	Calabasas	CA	91302	**877-782-9444**	818-591-2300
Mount View Hotel & Spa 1457 Lincoln Ave	Calistoga	CA	94515	**800-772-8838**	707-942-6877
Hilton Garden Inn Carlsbad Beach 6450 Carlsbad Blvd	Carlsbad	CA	92009	**877-782-9444**	760-476-0800
Carmel River Inn Hwy 1 at Carmel River Bridge PO Box 221609	Carmel	CA	93922	**800-882-8142**	831-624-1575
Highlands Inn - A Park Hyatt Hotel 120 Highlands Dr	Carmel	CA	93923	**800-682-4811**	831-624-3801
La Playa Hotel & Cottages-by-the-Sea PO Box 900	Carmel	CA	93921	**800-582-8900**	831-624-6476
Tickle Pink Inn at Carmel Highlands 155 Highland Dr	Carmel	CA	93923	**800-635-4774**	831-624-1244
Bernardus Lodge 415 Carmel Valley Rd	Carmel Valley	CA	93924	**888-648-9463**	831-658-3400
Best Western Chula Vista Inn 946 Broadway	Chula Vista	CA	91911	**800-528-1234**	619-691-6868
La Quinta Inn Chula Vista 150 Bonita Rd	Chula Vista	CA	91910	**800-531-5900**	619-691-1211
Claremont Inn 555 W Foothill Blvd	Claremont	CA	91711	**800-854-5733**	909-626-2411
Crowne Plaza Hotel Los Angeles-Commerce Casino 6121 E Telegraph Rd	Commerce	CA	90040	**800-227-6963**	323-728-3600
Wyndham Commerce 5757 Telegraph Rd	Commerce	CA	90040	**800-996-3426**	323-887-8100
Hilton Concord 1970 Diamond Blvd	Concord	CA	94520	**800-826-2644**	925-827-2000
Best Western Suites Hotel Coronado Island 275 Orange Ave	Coronado	CA	92118	**800-528-1234**	619-437-1666
Glorietta Bay Inn 1630 Glorietta Blvd	Coronado	CA	92118	**800-283-9383**	619-435-3101
Best Western Corte Madera Inn 56 Madera Blvd	Corte Madera	CA	94925	**800-777-9670**	415-924-1502
Marriott Suites Costa Mesa 500 Anton Blvd	Costa Mesa	CA	92626	**800-228-9290**	714-957-1100
Westin South Coast Plaza 686 Anton Blvd	Costa Mesa	CA	92626	**800-937-8461**	714-540-2500
Wyndham Garden Hotel Orange County 3350 Ave of the Arts	Costa Mesa	CA	92626	**800-996-3426**	714-751-5100
Radisson Hotel Los Angeles Westside 6161 W Centinela Ave	Culver City	CA	90230	**800-333-3333**	310-649-1776
Cypress Hotel 10050 S DeAnza Blvd	Cupertino	CA	95014	**800-499-1408**	408-253-8900
Hilton Garden Inn Cupertino 10741 N Wolfe Rd	Cupertino	CA	95014	**877-782-9444**	408-777-8787
Woodfin Suite Hotel Cypress 5905 Corporate Ave	Cypress	CA	90630	**888-433-9403**	714-828-4000
Clarion Carriage House Del Mar Inn 720 Camino Del Mar	Del Mar	CA	92014	**800-451-4515**	858-755-9765
Hilton San Diego/Del Mar 15575 Jimmy Durante Blvd	Del Mar	CA	92014	**800-833-7904**	858-792-5200
Holiday Inn Select Diamond Bar 21725 E Gateway Ctr Dr	Diamond Bar	CA	91765	**800-988-3587**	909-860-5440
Hacienda Hotel 525 N Sepulveda Blvd	El Segundo	CA	90245	**800-421-5900**	310-615-0015
Hilton Garden Inn LAX/El Segundo 2100 E Mariposa Ave	El Segundo	CA	90245	**877-782-9444**	310-726-0100
Summerfield Suites by Wyndham El Segundo/LAX 810 S Douglas St	El Segundo	CA	90245	**800-996-3426**	310-725-0100
Holiday Inn San Francisco-Oakland Bay Bridge 1800 Powell St	Emeryville	CA	94608	**800-465-4329**	510-658-9300
Woodfin Suite Hotel Emeryville 5800 Shellmound St	Emeryville	CA	94608	**888-433-9042**	510-601-5880
Hilton Garden Inn Fairfield 2200 Gateway Ct	Fairfield	CA	94533	**877-782-9444**	707-426-6900
Los Willows Inn & Spa 530 Stewart Canyon Rd	Fallbrook	CA	92028	**888-731-9400**	760-728-8121
Hilton Garden Inn Folsom 221 Iron Point Rd	Folsom	CA	95630	**877-782-9444**	916-353-1717
Hilton Garden Inn Irvine East/Lake Forest 27082 Towne Ctr Dr	Foothill Ranch	CA	92610	**877-782-9444**	949-859-4000
Crowne Plaza Hotel San Francisco/Peninsula Airport 1221 Chess Dr	Foster City	CA	94404	**800-227-6963**	650-570-5700
Best Western Garden Court Inn 5400 Mowry Ave	Fremont	CA	94538	**800-541-4909**	510-792-4300
Courtyard Fremont 47000 Lakeview Blvd	Fremont	CA	94538	**800-321-2211**	510-656-1800
Good-Nite Inn Fremont 4135 Cushing Pkwy	Fremont	CA	94538	**800-648-3466**	510-656-9307
Marriott Fremont 46100 Landing Pkwy	Fremont	CA	94538	**800-228-9290**	510-413-3700
Residence Inn Fremont Silicon Valley 5400 Farwell Pl	Fremont	CA	94536	**800-331-3131**	510-794-5900
Chateau Inn 5113 E McKinley Ave	Fresno	CA	93727	**800-445-2428**	559-456-1418
Courtyard Fresno 140 E Shaw Ave	Fresno	CA	93710	**800-321-2211**	559-221-6000
Courtyard Fresno Airport 1551 N Peach Ave	Fresno	CA	93727	**800-321-2211**	559-251-5200
Four Points by Sheraton Fresno 3737 N Blackstone Ave	Fresno	CA	93726	**800-325-3535**	559-226-2200
Piccadilly Inn Airport 5115 E McKinley Ave	Fresno	CA	93727	**800-468-3587**	559-251-6000
Piccadilly Inn Shaw 2305 W Shaw Ave	Fresno	CA	93711	**800-468-3587**	559-226-3850
Piccadilly Inn University 4961 N Cedar Ave	Fresno	CA	93726	**800-468-3587**	559-224-4200
Radisson Hotel & Conference Center Fresno 2233 Ventura St	Fresno	CA	93721	**800-333-3333**	559-268-1000
Residence Inn Fresno 5322 N Diana St	Fresno	CA	93710	**800-331-3131**	559-222-8900
San Joaquin Hotel 1309 W Shaw Ave	Fresno	CA	93711	**800-775-1309**	559-225-1309
Hilton Garden Inn Anaheim/Garden Grove 11777 Harbor Blvd	Garden Grove	CA	92840	**877-782-9444**	714-703-9100
Hyatt Regency Orange County 11999 Harbor Blvd	Garden Grove	CA	92840	**800-233-1234**	714-750-1234
Hilton Garden Inn Gilroy 6070 Monterey St	Gilroy	CA	95020	**877-782-9444**	408-840-7000
Half Moon Bay Lodge & Conference Center 2400 S Cabrillo Hwy	Half Moon Bay	CA	94019	**800-710-0778**	650-726-9000
Chateau Marmont Hotel 8221 Sunset Blvd	Hollywood	CA	90046	**800-242-8328**	323-656-1010
Hollywood Metropolitan Hotel 5825 Sunset Blvd	Hollywood	CA	90028	**800-962-5800**	323-962-5800
Hollywood Roosevelt Hotel 7000 Hollywood Blvd	Hollywood	CA	90028	**800-950-7667**	323-466-7000
Hotel Huntington Beach 7667 Center Ave	Huntington Beach	CA	92647	**877-891-0123**	714-891-0123
Hyatt Regency Huntington Beach 21100 Pacific Coast Hwy	Huntington Beach	CA	92648	**800-233-1234**	714-698-1234

California (Cont'd)

Name / Address	City	State	ZIP	Toll-Free	Phone
Atrium Hotel 18700 MacArthur Blvd	Irvine	CA	92612	**800-854-3012**	949-833-2770
Crowne Plaza Hotel Irvine-Orange County Airport 17941 Von Karman Ave	Irvine	CA	92614	**800-227-6963**	949-863-1999
Hyatt Regency Irvine 17900 Jamboree Blvd	Irvine	CA	92614	**800-233-1234**	949-975-1234
Marriott Irvine 18000 Von Karman Ave	Irvine	CA	92612	**800-228-9290**	949-553-0100
Empress Hotel 7766 Fay Ave	La Jolla	CA	92037	**888-369-9900**	858-454-3001
Hilton La Jolla Torrey Pines 10950 N Torrey Pines Rd	La Jolla	CA	92037	**800-445-8667**	858-558-1500
Hotel La Jolla 7955 La Jolla Shores Dr	La Jolla	CA	92037	**800-666-0261**	858-459-0261
Hotel Parisi 1111 Prospect	La Jolla	CA	92037	**877-472-7474**	858-454-1511
La Valencia Hotel 1132 Prospect St	La Jolla	CA	92037	**800-451-0772**	858-454-0771
San Diego Marriott La Jolla 4240 La Jolla Village Dr	La Jolla	CA	92037	**800-228-9290**	858-587-1414
Holiday Inn Select La Mirada 14299 Firestone Blvd	La Mirada	CA	90638	**800-356-6873**	714-739-8500
Residence Inn La Mirada-Buena Park 14419 Firestone Blvd	La Mirada	CA	90638	**800-331-3131**	714-523-2800
Lafayette Park Hotel 3287 Mt Diablo Blvd	Lafayette	CA	94549	**800-368-2468**	925-283-3700
Laguna Brisas Spa Hotel 1600 S Coast Hwy	Laguna Beach	CA	92651	**877-503-1461**	949-497-7272
Surf & Sand Resort 1555 South Coast Hwy	Laguna Beach	CA	92651	**888-869-7569**	949-497-4477
Vacation Village Hotel 647 S Coast Hwy	Laguna Beach	CA	92651	**800-843-6895**	949-494-8566
Heritage House Inn 5200 N Hwy 1	Little River	CA	95456	**800-235-5885**	707-937-5885
Hilton Garden Inn Livermore 2801 Constitution Dr	Livermore	CA	94551	**877-782-9444**	925-292-2000
Best Western Golden Sails Hotel 6285 E Pacific Coast Hwy	Long Beach	CA	90803	**800-762-5333**	562-596-1631
Coast Long Beach Hotel 700 Queensway Dr	Long Beach	CA	90802	**800-663-1144**	562-435-7676
Courtyard Long Beach 500 E 1st St	Long Beach	CA	90802	**800-321-2211**	562-435-8511
Holiday Inn Long Beach Airport 2640 Lakewood Blvd	Long Beach	CA	90815	**800-465-4329**	562-597-4401
Hotel Queen Mary 1126 Queens Hwy	Long Beach	CA	90802	**800-437-2934**	562-435-3511
Hyatt Regency Long Beach 200 S Pine Ave	Long Beach	CA	90802	**800-233-1234**	562-491-1234
Inn of Long Beach 185 Atlantic Ave	Long Beach	CA	90802	**800-230-7500**	562-435-3791
Marriott Long Beach 4700 Airport Plaza Dr	Long Beach	CA	90815	**800-228-9290**	562-425-5210
Renaissance Long Beach Hotel 111 E Ocean Blvd	Long Beach	CA	90802	**800-228-9898**	562-437-5900
Westin Long Beach 333 E Ocean Blvd	Long Beach	CA	90802	**800-937-8461**	562-436-3000
Residence Inn Palo Alto-Los Altos 4460 El Camino Real	Los Altos	CA	94022	**800-331-3131**	650-559-7890
Best Western Dragon Gate Inn 818 N Hill St	Los Angeles	CA	90012	**800-282-9999**	213-617-3077
Best Western Mayfair 1256 W 7th St	Los Angeles	CA	90017	**800-821-8682**	213-484-9789
Century Wilshire Hotel 10776 Wilshire Blvd	Los Angeles	CA	90024	**800-421-7223**	310-474-4506
Courtyard Los Angeles LAX/Century Boulevard 6161 W Century Blvd	Los Angeles	CA	90045	**800-529-6161**	310-649-1400
Crowne Plaza Hotel Los Angeles Airport 5985 W Century Blvd	Los Angeles	CA	90045	**888-315-3700**	310-642-7500
Doubletree Hotel Los Angeles-Westwood 10740 Wilshire Blvd	Los Angeles	CA	90024	**800-472-8556**	310-475-8711
Embassy Suites Los Angeles-International Airport North 9801 Airport Blvd	Los Angeles	CA	90045	**800-362-2779**	310-215-1000
Figueroa Hotel 939 S Figueroa St	Los Angeles	CA	90015	**800-421-9092**	213-627-8971
Four Seasons Hotel Los Angeles at Beverly Hills 300 S Doheny Dr	Los Angeles	CA	90048	**800-332-3442**	310-273-2222
Furama Hotel Los Angeles 8601 Lincoln Blvd	Los Angeles	CA	90045	**800-225-8126**	310-670-8111
Hilgard House Hotel & Suites 927 Hilgard Ave	Los Angeles	CA	90024	**800-826-3934**	310-208-3945
Hilton Los Angeles Airport 5711 W Century Blvd	Los Angeles	CA	90045	**800-445-8667**	310-410-4000
Hotel Bel-Air 701 Stone Canyon Rd	Los Angeles	CA	90077	**800-648-4097**	310-472-1211
Hotel Sofitel Los Angeles 8555 Beverly Blvd	Los Angeles	CA	90048	**800-521-7772**	310-278-5444
Howard Johnson Wilshire Royale Plaza Hotel 2619 Wilshire Blvd	Los Angeles	CA	90057	**800-421-8072**	213-387-5311
Hyatt Regency Los Angeles 711 S Hope St	Los Angeles	CA	90017	**800-233-1234**	213-683-1234
Kawada Hotel 200 S Hill St	Los Angeles	CA	90012	**800-752-9232**	213-621-4455
Le Meridien at Beverly Hills 465 S La Cienega Blvd	Los Angeles	CA	90048	**800-645-5624**	310-247-0400
Los Angeles Athletic Club 431 W 7th St	Los Angeles	CA	90014	**800-421-8777**	213-625-2211
Luxe Hotel Sunset Boulevard 11461 Sunset Blvd	Los Angeles	CA	90049	**800-468-3541**	310-476-6571
Marriott Los Angeles Airport 5855 W Century Blvd	Los Angeles	CA	90045	**800-228-9290**	310-641-5700
Marriott Los Angeles Downtown 333 S Figueroa St	Los Angeles	CA	90071	**800-228-9290**	213-617-1133
Millennium Biltmore Hotel Los Angeles 506 S Grand Ave	Los Angeles	CA	90071	**800-245-8673**	213-624-1011
Miyako Inn & Spa 328 E 1st St	Los Angeles	CA	90012	**800-228-6596**	213-617-2000
New Otani Hotel & Garden 120 S Los Angeles St	Los Angeles	CA	90012	**800-639-6826**	213-629-1200
Omni Los Angeles Hotel at California Plaza 251 S Olive St	Los Angeles	CA	90012	**800-843-6664**	213-617-3300
Orlando The 8384 W 3rd St	Los Angeles	CA	90048	**800-624-6835**	323-658-6600
Oxford Palace 745 S Oxford Ave	Los Angeles	CA	90005	**800-532-7887**	213-389-8000
Park Hyatt Los Angeles 2151 Ave of the Stars	Los Angeles	CA	90067	**800-233-1234**	310-277-1234
Radisson Hotel Midtown Los Angeles 3540 S Figueroa St	Los Angeles	CA	90007	**800-333-3333**	213-748-4141
Radisson Wilshire Plaza Hotel 3515 Wilshire Blvd	Los Angeles	CA	90010	**800-333-3333**	213-381-7411
Renaissance Los Angeles Hotel-Airport 9620 Airport Blvd	Los Angeles	CA	90045	**888-293-0523**	310-337-2800
Ritz Milner Hotel 813 S Flower St	Los Angeles	CA	90017	**800-827-0411**	213-627-6981
Saint Regis Los Angeles Hotel & Spa 2055 Ave of the Stars	Los Angeles	CA	90067	**877-787-3452**	310-277-6111
Sheraton Gateway Hotel Los Angeles Airport 6101 W Century Blvd	Los Angeles	CA	90045	**800-325-3535**	310-642-1111
Stillwell Hotel 838 S Grand Ave	Los Angeles	CA	90017	**800-553-4774**	213-627-1151
W Hotel Los Angeles Westwood 930 Hilgard Ave	Los Angeles	CA	90024	**800-421-2317**	310-208-8765
Westin Bonaventure Hotel & Suites 404 S Figueroa St	Los Angeles	CA	90071	**800-937-8461**	213-624-1000
Westin Century Plaza Hotel & Spa 2025 Ave of the Stars	Los Angeles	CA	90067	**800-937-8461**	310-277-2000
Westin Los Angeles Airport 5400 W Century Blvd	Los Angeles	CA	90045	**800-937-8461**	310-216-5858
Wilshire Grand Hotel & Center 930 Wilshire Blvd	Los Angeles	CA	90017	**888-773-2888**	213-688-7777
Hotel Los Gatos 210 E Main St	Los Gatos	CA	95030	**866-335-1700**	408-335-1700
Malibu Beach Inn 22878 Pacific Coast Hwy	Malibu	CA	90265	**800-462-5428**	310-456-6444
Marriott Manhattan Beach 1400 Parkview Ave	Manhattan Beach	CA	90266	**800-228-9290**	310-546-7511
Marina Dunes Resort 3295 Dunes Dr	Marina	CA	93933	**877-944-3863**	831-883-9478
Courtyard Los Angeles/Marina del Rey 13480 Maxella Ave	Marina del Rey	CA	90292	**800-628-0908**	310-822-8555
Marriott Marina Del Rey 4100 Admiralty Way	Marina del Rey	CA	90292	**800-228-9290**	310-301-3000
Ritz-Carlton Marina del Rey 4375 Admiralty Way	Marina del Rey	CA	90292	**800-241-3333**	310-823-1700
Mendocino Hotel & Garden Suites 45080 Main St	Mendocino	CA	95460	**800-548-0513**	707-937-0511
Acqua Hotel 555 Redwood Hwy	Mill Valley	CA	94941	**800-738-7477**	415-380-0400
Mill Valley Inn 165 Throckmorton Ave	Mill Valley	CA	94941	**800-595-2100**	415-389-6608
Clarion Hotel San Francisco Airport 401 E Millbrae Ave	Millbrae	CA	94030	**800-252-7466**	650-692-6363
Westin San Francisco Airport 1 Old Bayshore Hwy	Millbrae	CA	94030	**888-627-8404**	650-692-3500
Beverly Heritage Hotel 1820 Barber Ln	Milpitas	CA	95035	**800-443-4455**	408-943-9080
Crowne Plaza Hotel San Jose/Silicon Valley 777 Bellew Dr	Milpitas	CA	95035	**800-227-6963**	408-321-9500
Embassy Suites Milpitas-Silicon Valley 901 E Calaveras Blvd	Milpitas	CA	95035	**800-362-2779**	408-942-0400
Hilton Garden Inn San Jose/Milpitas 30 Ranch Dr	Milpitas	CA	95035	**877-782-9444**	408-719-1313
Best Western Town House Lodge 909 16th St	Modesto	CA	95354	**800-780-7234**	209-524-7261
Courtyard Modesto 1720 Sisk Rd	Modesto	CA	95350	**800-294-4040**	209-577-3825
Doubletree Hotel Modesto 1150 9th St	Modesto	CA	95354	**800-222-8733**	209-526-6000
Red Lion Hotel Modesto 1612 Sisk Rd	Modesto	CA	95350	**800-733-5466**	209-521-1612
Hilton Garden Inn Montebello 801 N Via San Clemente	Montebello	CA	90640	**877-782-9444**	323-724-5900
Bay Park Hotel 1425 Munras Ave	Monterey	CA	93940	**800-338-3564**	831-649-1020
Best Western The Beach Resort 2600 Sand Dunes Dr	Monterey	CA	93940	**800-242-8627**	831-394-3321
Casa Munras Garden Hotel 700 Munras Ave	Monterey	CA	93940	**800-222-2558**	831-375-2411
Hilton Monterey 1000 Aguajito Rd	Monterey	CA	93940	**800-234-5697**	831-373-6141
Hotel Pacific 300 Pacific St	Monterey	CA	93940	**800-554-5542**	831-373-5700
Hyatt Regency Monterey 1 Old Golf Course Rd	Monterey	CA	93940	**800-233-1234**	831-372-1234
Lone Oak Lodge 2221 N Fremont St	Monterey	CA	93940	**800-283-5663**	831-372-4924
Marriott Monterey 350 Calle Principal	Monterey	CA	93940	**800-228-9290**	831-649-4234
Monterey Bay Inn 242 Cannery Row	Monterey	CA	93940	**800-424-6242**	831-373-6242
Monterey Hotel 406 Alvarado St	Monterey	CA	93940	**800-727-0960**	831-375-3184
Monterey Plaza Hotel & Spa 400 Cannery Row	Monterey	CA	93940	**800-334-3999**	831-646-1700
Portola Plaza Hotel 2 Portola Plaza	Monterey	CA	93940	**888-222-5851**	831-649-4511
Quality Inn Monterey 1058 Munras Ave	Monterey	CA	93940	**800-361-3835**	831-372-3381
Sand Dollar Inn 755 Abrego St	Monterey	CA	93940	**800-982-1986**	831-372-7551
Spindrift Inn 652 Cannery Row	Monterey	CA	93940	**800-841-1879**	831-646-8900
Victorian Inn 487 Foam St	Monterey	CA	93940	**800-232-4141**	831-373-8000
Inn at Morro Bay 60 State Park Rd	Morro Bay	CA	93442	**800-321-9566**	805-772-5651
Hilton Garden Inn Mountain Inn 840 E El Camino Real	Mountain View	CA	94040	**877-782-9444**	650-964-1700
Hotel Avante 860 E El Camino Real	Mountain View	CA	94040	**800-538-1600**	650-940-1000
Hilton Garden Inn Napa 3585 Solano Ave	Napa	CA	94558	**877-782-9444**	707-252-0444
Marriott Napa Valley 3425 Solano Ave	Napa	CA	94558	**800-228-9290**	707-253-7433
Napa River Inn 500 Main St	Napa	CA	94559	**877-251-8500**	707-251-8500
Red Lion Inn & Suites San Diego South Bay 801 National City Blvd	National City	CA	91950	**800-733-5466**	619-336-1100
Hilton Newark/Fremont 39900 Balentine Dr	Newark	CA	94560	**800-445-8667**	510-490-8390
W Suites Newark 8200 Gateway Blvd	Newark	CA	94560	**877-946-8357**	510-494-8800
Woodfin Suite Hotel Newark 39150 Cedar Blvd	Newark	CA	94560	**888-433-9404**	510-795-1200
Four Seasons Hotel Newport Beach 690 Newport Center Dr	Newport Beach	CA	92660	**800-332-3442**	949-759-0808
Hyatt Regency Newport Beach 1107 Jamboree Rd	Newport Beach	CA	92660	**800-233-1234**	949-729-1234
Marriott Newport Beach Hotel & Tennis Club 900 Newport Center Dr	Newport Beach	CA	92660	**800-228-9290**	949-640-4000
Marriott Suites Newport Beach 500 Bayview Cir	Newport Beach	CA	92660	**800-228-9290**	949-854-4500
Radisson Hotel Newport Beach 4545 MacArthur Blvd	Newport Beach	CA	92660	**800-333-3333**	949-833-0570
Sutton Place Hotel Newport Beach 4500 MacArthur Blvd	Newport Beach	CA	92660	**800-243-4141**	949-476-2001
Beverly Garland's Holiday Inn at Universal Studios Hollywood 4222 Vineland Ave	North Hollywood	CA	91602	**800-238-3759**	818-980-8000
Marriott Norwalk 13111 Sycamore Dr	Norwalk	CA	90650	**800-228-9290**	562-863-5555
Best Western Novato Oaks Inn 215 Alameda del Prado	Novato	CA	94949	**800-625-7466**	415-883-4400
Clarion Suites Lake Merritt 1800 Madison St	Oakland	CA	94612	**800-933-4683**	510-832-2300
Hilton Oakland Airport 1 Hegenberger Rd	Oakland	CA	94621	**800-445-8667**	510-635-5000
Jack London Inn 444 Embarcadero W	Oakland	CA	94607	**800-549-8780**	510-444-2032
Marriott Oakland City Center 1001 Broadway	Oakland	CA	94607	**800-228-9290**	510-451-4000
Park Plaza Hotel Oakland 150 Hegenberger Rd	Oakland	CA	94621	**800-635-5301**	510-635-5300
Waterfront Plaza Hotel 10 Washington St	Oakland	CA	94607	**800-729-3638**	510-836-3800
Plump Jack's Squaw Valley Inn 1920 Squaw Valley Rd	Olympic Valley	CA	96146	**800-323-7666**	530-583-1576
Doubletree Hotel Ontario Airport 222 N Vineyard Ave	Ontario	CA	91764	**800-222-8733**	909-937-0900
Marriott Ontario Airport 2200 E Holt Blvd	Ontario	CA	91761	**800-228-9290**	909-975-5000
Doubletree Hotel Anaheim/Orange County 100 The City Dr	Orange	CA	92868	**800-222-8733**	714-634-4500
Casa Sirena Hotel & Marina 3605 Peninsula Rd	Oxnard	CA	93035	**800-447-3529**	805-985-6311
Channel Islands Inn & Suites 1001 E Channel Islands Blvd	Oxnard	CA	93033	**800-344-5998**	805-487-7755
Courtyard Oxnard Ventura 600 E Esplanade Dr	Oxnard	CA	93036	**800-535-4028**	805-485-9666
Embassy Suites Mandalay Beach Resort-Oxnard 2101 Mandalay Beach Rd	Oxnard	CA	93035	**800-362-2779**	805-984-2500
Deerhaven Inn & Suites 740 Crocker Ave	Pacific Grove	CA	93950	**800-525-3373**	831-373-1114
Lighthouse Lodge & Suites 1150 Lighthouse Ave	Pacific Grove	CA	93950	**800-858-1249**	831-655-2111
Mojave A Desert Resort 73721 Shadow Mountain Dr	Palm Desert	CA	92260	**866-846-8357**	760-346-6121

Classified Section

				Toll-Free	Phone
Residence Inn Palm Desert 38305 Cook St	Palm Desert	CA	92211	**800-331-3131**	760-776-0050
Ballantines Hotels in Palm Springs 1420 N Indian Canyon Dr	Palm Springs	CA	92262	**800-485-2808**	760-320-1178
Best Western Las Brisas Hotel 222 S Indian Canyon Dr	Palm Springs	CA	92262	**800-346-5714**	760-325-4372
Chase Hotel at Palm Springs 200 W Arenas Rd	Palm Springs	CA	92262	**877-532-4273**	760-320-8866
East Canyon Hotel & Spa 288 E Camino Monte Vista	Palm Springs	CA	92262	**877-324-6835**	760-320-1928
Estrella 415 S Belardo Rd	Palm Springs	CA	92262	**800-237-3687**	760-320-4117
Hyatt Regency Suites Palm Springs 285 N Palm Canyon Dr	Palm Springs	CA	92262	**800-233-1234**	760-322-9000
Ingleside Inn 200 W Ramon Rd	Palm Springs	CA	92264	**800-772-6655**	760-325-0046
Monte Vista Hotel & Spa 414 N Palm Canyon Dr	Palm Springs	CA	92262	**800-789-3188**	760-325-5641
Palm Mountain Resort & Spa 155 S Belardo Rd	Palm Springs	CA	92262	**800-622-9451**	760-325-1301
Royal Sun Inn 1700 S Palm Canyon Dr	Palm Springs	CA	92264	**800-619-4786**	760-327-1564
Villa Royale Inn 1620 Indian Trail	Palm Springs	CA	92264	**800-245-2314**	760-327-2314
Willows Historic Palm Springs Inn 412 W Tahquitz Canyon Way	Palm Springs	CA	92262	**800-966-9597**	760-320-0771
Wyndham Palm Springs 888 E Tahquitz Canyon Way	Palm Springs	CA	92262	**800-996-3426**	760-322-6000
Crowne Plaza Hotel Palo Alto 4290 El Camino Real	Palo Alto	CA	94306	**800-227-6963**	650-857-0787
Dinah's Garden Hotel 4261 El Camino Real	Palo Alto	CA	94306	**800-227-8220**	650-493-4542
Garden Court Hotel 520 Cowper St	Palo Alto	CA	94301	**800-824-9028**	650-322-9000
Rickeys - A Hyatt Hotel 4219 El Camino Real	Palo Alto	CA	94306	**800-233-1234**	650-493-8000
Westin Palo Alto 675 El Camino Real	Palo Alto	CA	94301	**800-937-8461**	650-321-4422
Hilton Pasadena 168 S Los Robles Ave	Pasadena	CA	91101	**800-445-8667**	626-577-1000
Ritz-Carlton Huntington Hotel & Spa 1401 S Oak Knoll Ave	Pasadena	CA	91106	**800-241-3333**	626-568-3900
Sheraton Pasadena Hotel 303 E Cordova St	Pasadena	CA	91101	**800-457-7940**	626-449-4000
Westin Pasadena 191 N Los Robles Ave	Pasadena	CA	91101	**800-937-8461**	626-792-2727
Paso Robles Inn 1103 Spring St	Paso Robles	CA	93446	**800-676-1713**	805-238-2660
Crowne Plaza Hotel Pleasanton 11950 Dublin Canyon Rd	Pleasanton	CA	94588	**800-227-6963**	925-847-6000
Residence Inn Pleasanton 11920 Dublin Canyon Rd	Pleasanton	CA	94588	**800-331-3131**	925-227-0500
Rose Hotel 807 Main St	Pleasanton	CA	94566	**800-843-9540**	925-846-8802
Wyndham Garden Hotel Pleasanton 5990 Stoneridge Mall Rd	Pleasanton	CA	94588	**800-996-3426**	925-463-3330
Casa Via Mar Inn & Tennis Club 377 W Channel Islands Blvd	Port Hueneme	CA	93041	**800-992-5522**	805-984-6222
Marriott Sacramento Rancho Cordova 11211 Point East Dr	Rancho Cordova	CA	95742	**800-228-9290**	916-638-1100
Hilton Garden Inn Palm Springs/Rancho Mirage 71-700 Hwy 111	Rancho Mirage	CA	92270	**877-782-9444**	760-776-9700
Hilton Garden Inn Redding 5050 Bechelli Ln	Redding	CA	96002	**877-782-9444**	530-226-5111
Crowne Plaza Hotel Redondo Beach & Marina 300 N Harbor Dr	Redondo Beach	CA	90277	**800-227-6963**	310-318-8888
Palos Verdes Inn 1700 S Pacific Coast Hwy	Redondo Beach	CA	90277	**800-421-9241**	310-316-4211
Portofino Hotel & Yacht Club 260 Portofino Way	Redondo Beach	CA	90277	**800-468-4292**	310-379-8481
Hotel Sofitel San Francisco Bay 223 Twin Dolphin Dr	Redwood City	CA	94065	**800-763-4835**	650-598-9000
Courtyard Riverside 1510 University Ave	Riverside	CA	92507	**800-321-2200**	951-276-1200
Dynasty Suites 3735 Iowa Ave	Riverside	CA	92507	**800-842-7899**	951-369-8200
Mission Inn 3649 Mission Inn Ave	Riverside	CA	92501	**800-843-7755**	951-784-0300
Rocklin Park Hotel 5450 China Garden Rd	Rocklin	CA	95677	**888-630-9400**	916-630-9400
Doubletree Hotel Sonoma Wine Country 1 Doubletree Dr	Rohnert Park	CA	94928	**800-222-8733**	707-584-5466
Hilton Garden Inn Roseville 1951 Taylor Rd	Roseville	CA	95661	**877-782-9444**	916-773-7171
Auberge du Soleil 180 Rutherford Hill Rd	Rutherford	CA	94573	**800-348-5406**	707-963-1211
Courtyard Sacramento South Natomas 2101 River Plaza Dr	Sacramento	CA	95833	**800-321-2211**	916-922-1120
Delta King Riverboat Hotel 1000 Front St	Sacramento	CA	95814	**800-825-5464**	916-444-5464
Doubletree Hotel Sacramento 2001 Point West Way	Sacramento	CA	95815	**800-222-8733**	916-929-8855
Governor's Inn 210 Richards Blvd	Sacramento	CA	95814	**800-999-6689**	916-448-7224
Heritage Hotel 1780 Tribute Rd	Sacramento	CA	95815	**800-357-9913**	916-929-7900
Hilton Garden Inn Sacramento/South Natomas 2540 Venture Oaks Way	Sacramento	CA	95833	**877-782-9444**	916-568-5400
Hilton Sacramento Arden West 2200 Harvard St	Sacramento	CA	95815	**800-445-8667**	916-922-4700
Holiday Inn Sacramento Capitol Plaza 300 J St	Sacramento	CA	95814	**800-465-4329**	916-446-0100
Holiday Inn Sacramento I-80 Northeast 5321 Date Ave	Sacramento	CA	95841	**800-465-4329**	916-338-5800
Host Airport Hotel 6945 Airport Blvd	Sacramento	CA	95837	**800-903-4678**	916-922-8071
Hyatt Regency Sacramento 1209 L St	Sacramento	CA	95814	**800-233-1234**	916-443-1234
Quality Inn Inn Sacramento 2600 Auburn Blvd	Sacramento	CA	95821	**800-424-6423**	916-487-7600
Radisson Hotel Sacramento 500 Leisure Ln	Sacramento	CA	95815	**800-333-3333**	916-922-2020
Red Lion Hotel Sacramento 1401 Arden Way	Sacramento	CA	95815	**800-733-5466**	916-922-8041
Sheraton Grand Sacramento Hotel 1230 J St	Sacramento	CA	95814	**800-325-3535**	916-447-1700
Sterling Hotel 1300 H St	Sacramento	CA	95814	**800-365-7660**	916-448-1300
Vizcaya 2019 21st St	Sacramento	CA	95818	**800-456-2019**	916-455-5243
Harvest Inn 1 Main St	Saint Helena	CA	94574	**800-950-8466**	707-963-9463
Comfort Inn San Bernardino 1909 S Business Center Dr	San Bernardino	CA	92408	**800-228-5150**	909-889-0090
Hilton San Bernardino 285 E Hospitality Ln	San Bernardino	CA	92408	**800-445-8667**	909-889-0133
La Quinta Inn San Bernardino 205 E Hospitality Ln	San Bernardino	CA	92408	**800-531-5900**	909-888-7571
Radisson Hotel San Bernardino Convention Center 295 N 'E' St	San Bernardino	CA	92401	**800-333-3333**	909-381-6181
500 West Hotel 500 W Broadway	San Diego	CA	92101	**866-500-7533**	619-234-5252
Bay Club Hotel & Marina 2131 Shelter Island Dr	San Diego	CA	92106	**800-672-0800**	619-224-8888
Best Western Bayside Inn 555 W Ash St	San Diego	CA	92101	**800-341-1818**	619-233-7500
Best Western Island Palms Hotel & Marina 2051 Shelter Island Dr	San Diego	CA	92106	**800-345-9995**	619-222-0561
Bristol Hotel 1055 1st Ave	San Diego	CA	92101	**800-662-4477**	619-232-6141
Comfort Inn & Suites Hotel Circle 2201 Hotel Circle S	San Diego	CA	92108	**800-772-6318**	619-291-2711
Courtyard San Diego Downtown 530 Broadway	San Diego	CA	92101	**800-627-7468**	619-446-3000

				Toll-Free	Phone
Courtyard San Diego Old Town 2435 Jefferson St	San Diego	CA	92110	**800-255-3544**	619-260-8500
Doubletree Club San Diego 1515 Hotel Cir S *Resv	San Diego	CA	92108	**800-489-9671***	619-881-6900
Doubletree Hotel San Diego/Mission Valley 7450 Hazard Center Dr	San Diego	CA	92108	**800-222-8733**	619-297-5466
Embassy Suites San Diego Bay-Downtown 601 Pacific Hwy	San Diego	CA	92101	**800-362-2779**	619-239-2400
Hilton San Diego Airport/Harbor Island 1960 Harbor Island Dr	San Diego	CA	92101	**800-445-8667**	619-291-6700
Hilton San Diego Mission Valley 901 Camino del Rio S	San Diego	CA	92108	**800-733-2332**	619-543-9000
Holiday Inn San Diego on the Bay 1355 N Harbor Dr	San Diego	CA	92101	**800-877-8920**	619-232-3861
Holiday Inn San Diego Bayside 4875 N Harbor Dr *Resv	San Diego	CA	92106	**800-345-9995***	619-224-3621
Holiday Inn Select San Diego North-Miramar 9335 Kearny Mesa Rd	San Diego	CA	92126	**800-262-2301**	858-695-2300
Horton Grand Hotel 311 Island Ave	San Diego	CA	92101	**800-542-1886**	619-544-1886
Hotel Solamar 435 6th Ave	San Diego	CA	92101	**877-230-0300**	619-531-8740
Humphrey's Half Moon Inn & Suites 2303 Shelter Island Dr	San Diego	CA	92106	**800-542-7400**	619-224-3411
Hyatt Regency Islandia 1441 Quivira Rd	San Diego	CA	92109	**800-233-1234**	619-224-1234
Hyatt Regency La Jolla at Aventine 3777 La Jolla Village Dr	San Diego	CA	92122	**800-233-1234**	858-552-1234
InnSuites Hotels San Diego Balboa Park Hotel & Suite Resort 2223 El Cajon Blvd	San Diego	CA	92104	**800-468-3531**	619-296-2101
La Pensione Hotel 606 W Date St	San Diego	CA	92101	**800-232-4683**	619-236-8000
Manchester Grand Hyatt San Diego 1 Market Pl	San Diego	CA	92101	**800-233-1234**	619-232-1234
Pacific Terrace Hotel 610 Diamond St	San Diego	CA	92109	**800-344-3370**	858-581-3500
Pickwick Hotel 132 W Broadway	San Diego	CA	92101	**800-826-0009**	619-234-9200
PRIME Hotel & Suites San Diego/Sorrento Mesa 5975 Lusk Blvd	San Diego	CA	92121	**800-996-3426**	858-558-1818
Radisson Hotel San Diego Harbor View 1646 Front St	San Diego	CA	92101	**800-333-3333**	619-239-6800
Ramada Inn & Suites San Diego - Gaslamp/Convention Center 830 6th St	San Diego	CA	92101	**800-272-6232**	619-531-8877
Ramada Plaza Hotel San Diego-Circle South 2151 Hotel Cir S	San Diego	CA	92108	**800-272-6232**	619-291-6500
Residence Inn San Diego Downtown 1747 Pacific Highway	San Diego	CA	92101	**800-331-3131**	619-338-8200
San Diego Marriott Hotel & Marina 333 W Harbor Dr	San Diego	CA	92101	**800-228-9290**	619-234-1500
San Diego Marriott Mission Valley 8757 Rio San Diego Dr	San Diego	CA	92108	**800-228-9290**	619-692-3800
Shelter Pointe Hotel 1551 Shelter Island Dr	San Diego	CA	92106	**800-566-2524**	619-221-8000
Sheraton San Diego Hotel & Marina 1380 Harbor Island Dr	San Diego	CA	92101	**800-325-3535**	619-291-2900
Sheraton San Diego Hotel Mission Valley 1433 Camino del Rio S	San Diego	CA	92108	**800-333-3333**	619-260-0111
US Grant Hotel - A Wyndham Historic Hotel 326 Broadway	San Diego	CA	92101	**800-237-5029**	619-232-3121
Westgate Hotel 1055 2nd Ave	San Diego	CA	92101	**800-221-3802**	619-238-1818
Westin Horton Plaza San Diego 910 Broadway Cir	San Diego	CA	92101	**800-937-8461**	619-239-2200
Woodfin Suite Hotel San Diego 10044 Pacific Mesa Blvd	San Diego	CA	92121	**888-433-2150**	858-597-0500
Wyndham San Diego at Emerald Plaza 400 W Broadway	San Diego	CA	92101	**800-996-3426**	619-239-4500
Andrews Hotel 624 Post St	San Francisco	CA	94109	**800-926-3739**	415-563-6877
Argent Hotel 50 3rd St	San Francisco	CA	94103	**877-222-6699**	415-974-6400
Argonaut Hotel 495 Jefferson St	San Francisco	CA	94109	**800-790-1415**	415-563-0800
Best Western Americania 121 7th St	San Francisco	CA	94103	**800-528-1234**	415-626-0200
Best Western Civic Center Inn 364 9th St	San Francisco	CA	94103	**800-444-5829**	415-621-2826
Best Western Tuscan Inn at Fisherman's Wharf 425 Northpoint St	San Francisco	CA	94133	**800-648-4626**	415-561-1100
Campton Place Hotel 340 Stockton St	San Francisco	CA	94108	**800-235-4300**	415-781-5555
Carlton Hotel 1075 Sutter St	San Francisco	CA	94109	**800-922-7586**	415-673-0242
Cartwright Hotel 524 Sutter St	San Francisco	CA	94102	**800-794-7661**	415-421-2865
Cathedral Hill Hotel 1101 Van Ness Ave	San Francisco	CA	94109	**800-622-0855**	415-776-8200
Chancellor Hotel on Union Square 433 Powell St	San Francisco	CA	94102	**800-428-4748**	415-362-2004
Clift The 495 Geary St	San Francisco	CA	94102	**800-652-5438**	415-775-4700
Commodore Hotel 825 Sutter St	San Francisco	CA	94109	**800-338-6848**	415-923-6800
Crowne Plaza Hotel San Francisco-Union Square 480 Sutter St	San Francisco	CA	94108	**800-243-1135**	415-398-8900
Donatello The 501 Post St	San Francisco	CA	94102	**800-227-3184**	415-441-7100
Executive Hotel Vintage Court 650 Bush St	San Francisco	CA	94108	**800-654-1100**	415-392-4666
Fairmont San Francisco 950 Mason St	San Francisco	CA	94108	**800-344-3550**	415-772-5000
Fitzgerald Hotel 620 Post St	San Francisco	CA	94109	**800-334-6835**	415-775-8100
Four Seasons Hotel San Francisco 757 Market St	San Francisco	CA	94103	**800-332-3442**	415-633-3000
Galleria Park Hotel 191 Sutter St	San Francisco	CA	94104	**866-756-3036**	415-781-3060
Grand Hyatt San Francisco 345 Stockton St	San Francisco	CA	94108	**800-233-1234**	415-398-1234
Grant Plaza Hotel 465 Grant Ave	San Francisco	CA	94108	**800-472-6899**	415-434-3883
Handlery Union Square Hotel 351 Geary St	San Francisco	CA	94102	**800-843-4343**	415-781-7800
Harbor Court Hotel 165 Steuart St	San Francisco	CA	94105	**800-346-0555**	415-882-1300
Hilton San Francisco 333 O'Farrell St	San Francisco	CA	94102	**800-445-8667**	415-771-1400
Hilton San Francisco Fisherman's Wharf 2620 Jones St	San Francisco	CA	94133	**800-228-8408**	415-885-4700
Holiday Inn San Francisco Civic Center 50 8th St	San Francisco	CA	94103	**800-243-1135**	415-626-6103
Holiday Inn San Francisco Financial District 750 Kearny St	San Francisco	CA	94108	**800-424-8292**	415-433-6600
Holiday Inn San Francisco-Fisherman's Wharf 1300 Columbus Ave	San Francisco	CA	94133	**800-465-4329**	415-771-9000
Hotel Adagio 550 Geary St	San Francisco	CA	94102	**800-228-8830**	415-775-5000
Hotel Bijou 111 Mason St	San Francisco	CA	94102	**800-771-1022**	415-771-1200
Hotel Britton 112 7th St	San Francisco	CA	94103	**800-444-5819**	415-621-7001
Hotel Cosmo 761 Post St	San Francisco	CA	94109	**800-252-7466**	415-673-6040
Hotel Del Sol 3100 Webster St	San Francisco	CA	94123	**877-433-5765**	415-921-5520
Hotel Drisco 2901 Pacific Ave	San Francisco	CA	94115	**800-634-7277**	415-346-2880
Hotel Griffon 155 Steuart St	San Francisco	CA	94105	**800-321-2201**	415-495-2100
Hotel Majestic 1500 Sutter St	San Francisco	CA	94109	**800-869-8966**	415-441-1100
Hotel Milano 55 5th St	San Francisco	CA	94103	**800-398-7555**	415-543-8555
Hotel Monaco San Francisco 501 Geary St	San Francisco	CA	94102	**866-622-5284**	415-292-0100

California (Cont'd)

Name / Address	City	State	Zip	Toll-Free	Phone
Hotel Nikko San Francisco 222 Mason St	San Francisco	CA	94102	**800-645-5687**	415-394-1111
Hotel Palomar 12 4th St	San Francisco	CA	94103	**877-294-9711**	415-348-1111
Hotel Rex 562 Sutter St	San Francisco	CA	94102	**800-433-4434**	415-433-4434
Hotel Triton 342 Grant Ave	San Francisco	CA	94108	**800-800-1299**	415-394-0500
Huntington Hotel 1075 California St	San Francisco	CA	94108	**800-227-4683**	415-474-5400
Hyatt at Fisherman's Wharf 555 N Point St	San Francisco	CA	94133	**800-233-1234**	415-563-1234
Hyatt Regency San Francisco 5 Embarcadero Ctr	San Francisco	CA	94111	**800-233-1234**	415-788-1234
Inn at the Opera 333 Fulton St	San Francisco	CA	94102	**800-325-2708**	415-863-8400
Inn at Union Square 440 Post St	San Francisco	CA	94102	**800-288-4346**	415-397-3510
InterContinental Mark Hopkins San Francisco 1 Nob Hill	San Francisco	CA	94108	**800-662-4455**	415-392-3434
Kensington Park Hotel 450 Post St	San Francisco	CA	94102	**800-553-1900**	415-788-6400
Laurel Inn 444 Presidio Ave	San Francisco	CA	94115	**800-552-8735**	415-567-8467
Mandarin Oriental San Francisco 222 Sansome St	San Francisco	CA	94104	**800-526-6566**	415-276-9888
Marriott San Francisco Downtown 55 4th St	San Francisco	CA	94103	**800-228-9290**	415-896-1600
Marriott San Francisco Fisherman's Wharf 1250 Columbus Ave	San Francisco	CA	94133	**800-525-0956**	415-775-7555
Monticello Inn 127 Ellis St	San Francisco	CA	94102	**800-669-7777**	415-392-8800
Mosser Victorian Hotel 54 4th St	San Francisco	CA	94103	**800-227-3804**	415-986-4400
Nob Hill Lambourne 725 Pine St	San Francisco	CA	94108	**800-274-8466**	415-433-2287
Omni San Francisco Hotel 500 California St	San Francisco	CA	94104	**800-843-6664**	415-677-9494
Orchard Hotel 665 Bush St	San Francisco	CA	94108	**888-717-2881**	415-362-8878
Palace Hotel 2 New Montgomery St	San Francisco	CA	94105	**800-325-3535**	415-512-1111
Pan Pacific San Francisco 500 Post St	San Francisco	CA	94102	**800-327-8585**	415-771-8600
Park Hyatt San Francisco 333 Battery St	San Francisco	CA	94111	**800-233-1234**	415-392-1234
Petite Auberge 863 Bush St	San Francisco	CA	94108	**800-365-3004**	415-928-6000
Phoenix Hotel 601 Eddy St	San Francisco	CA	94109	**800-248-9466**	415-776-1380
Pickwick Grand Heritage Hotel 85 5th St	San Francisco	CA	94103	**800-437-4824**	415-421-7500
Prescott Hotel 545 Post St	San Francisco	CA	94102	**800-271-3632**	415-563-0303
Queen Anne Hotel 1590 Sutter St	San Francisco	CA	94109	**800-227-3970**	415-441-2828
Radisson Hotel San Francisco Fisherman's Wharf 250 Beach St	San Francisco	CA	94133	**800-333-3333**	415-392-6700
Radisson Miyako Hotel San Francisco 1625 Post St	San Francisco	CA	94115	**800-333-3333**	415-922-3200
Ramada Plaza Downtown San Francisco 1231 Market St	San Francisco	CA	94103	**800-272-6232**	415-626-8000
Renaissance Parc 55 Hotel 55 Cyril Magnin St	San Francisco	CA	94102	**800-650-7272**	415-392-8000
Renaissance Stanford Court Hotel 905 California St	San Francisco	CA	94108	**800-468-3571**	415-989-3500
Ritz-Carlton San Francisco 600 Stockton St	San Francisco	CA	94108	**800-241-3333**	415-296-7465
Savoy Hotel 580 Geary St	San Francisco	CA	94102	**800-227-4223**	415-441-2700
Serrano Hotel 405 Taylor St	San Francisco	CA	94102	**877-294-9709**	415-885-2500
Sheehan Hotel 620 Sutter St	San Francisco	CA	94102	**800-848-1529**	415-775-6500
Sheraton Fisherman's Wharf Hotel 2500 Mason St	San Francisco	CA	94133	**800-325-3535**	415-362-5500
Sir Francis Drake Hotel 450 Powell St	San Francisco	CA	94102	**800-227-5480**	415-392-7755
Stratford Hotel 242 Powell St	San Francisco	CA	94102	**888-504-6835**	415-397-7080
Suites at Fisherman's Wharf 2655 Hyde St	San Francisco	CA	94109	**800-227-3608**	415-771-0200
Villa Florence Hotel 225 Powell St	San Francisco	CA	94102	**800-553-4411**	415-397-7700
W Hotel San Francisco 181 3rd St	San Francisco	CA	94103	**800-946-8357**	415-777-5300
Warwick Regis Hotel San Francisco 490 Geary St	San Francisco	CA	94102	**800-827-3447**	415-928-7900
Westin Saint Francis 335 Powell St	San Francisco	CA	94102	**800-937-8461**	415-397-7000
York Hotel 940 Sutter St	San Francisco	CA	94109	**800-808-9675**	415-885-6800
Adlon Hotel 1275 N 4th St	San Jose	CA	95112	**888-452-3566**	408-282-1000
Arena Hotel 817 The Alameda	San Jose	CA	95126	**800-954-6835**	408-294-6500
Clarion Hotel San Jose Airport 1355 N 4th St	San Jose	CA	95112	**800-453-5340**	408-453-5340
Clarion Inn San Jose 3200 Monterey Rd	San Jose	CA	95111	**800-252-7466**	408-972-2200
Courtyard San Jose Airport 1727 Technology Dr	San Jose	CA	95110	**800-321-2211**	408-441-6111
Crowne Plaza Hotel San Jose Downtown 282 Almaden Blvd	San Jose	CA	95113	**800-227-6963**	408-998-0400
Doubletree Hotel San Jose 2050 Gateway Pl	San Jose	CA	95110	**800-222-8733**	408-453-4000
Executive Inn Suites San Jose 3930 Monterey Rd	San Jose	CA	95111	**800-453-7755**	408-281-8700
Fairmont San Jose 170 S Market St	San Jose	CA	95113	**800-441-1414**	408-998-1900
Hilton San Jose & Towers 300 Almaden Blvd	San Jose	CA	95110	**800-445-8667**	408-287-2100
Hotel de Anza 233 W Santa Clara St	San Jose	CA	95113	**800-843-3700**	408-286-1000
Hyatt Sainte Claire 302 S Market St	San Jose	CA	95113	**800-233-1234**	408-298-1230
Hyatt San Jose 1740 N 1st St	San Jose	CA	95112	**800-975-1234**	408-993-1234
Marriott San Jose 301 S Market St	San Jose	CA	95113	**800-314-0928**	408-280-1300
Moorpark Hotel 4241 Moorpark Ave	San Jose	CA	95129	**877-740-6622**	408-864-0300
Radisson Plaza Hotel San Jose Airport 1471 N 4th St	San Jose	CA	95112	**800-333-3333**	408-452-0200
Staybridge Suites San Jose 1602 Crane Ct	San Jose	CA	95112	**800-833-4353**	408-436-1600
Valley Park Hotel 2404 Stevens Creek Blvd	San Jose	CA	95128	**800-954-6835**	408-293-5000
Wyndham San Jose 1350 N 1st St	San Jose	CA	95112	**800-996-3426**	408-453-6200
Hilton Garden Inn Oakland/San Leandro 510 Lewelling Blvd	San Leandro	CA	94579	**877-782-9444**	510-346-5533
Hilton Garden Inn San Mateo 2000 Bridgepointe Cir	San Mateo	CA	94404	**877-782-9444**	650-522-9000
Marriott San Mateo 1770 S Amphlett Blvd	San Mateo	CA	94402	**800-627-7468**	650-653-6000
Hilton Port of Los Angeles/San Pedro Hilton 2800 Via Cabrillo Marina	San Pedro	CA	90731	**800-445-8667**	310-514-3344
Holiday Inn San Pedro-Los Angeles Harbor 111 S Gaffey St	San Pedro	CA	90731	**800-248-3188**	310-514-1414
Sheraton Los Angeles Harbor Hotel 601 S Palos Verdes St	San Pedro	CA	90731	**800-325-3535**	310-519-8200
Doubletree Club Orange County Airport 7 Hutton Ctr Dr	Santa Ana	CA	92707	**800-644-2582**	714-751-2400
Doubletree Hotel Santa Ana/Orange County Airport 201 E MacArthur Blvd	Santa Ana	CA	92707	**800-222-8733**	714-825-3333
Embassy Suites Santa Ana-Orange County Airport 1325 E Dyer Rd	Santa Ana	CA	92705	**800-362-2779**	714-241-3800
Hampton Inn & Suites Santa Ana/Orange County Airport 2720 Hotel Terrace Dr	Santa Ana	CA	92705	**800-333-3333**	714-556-3838
Holiday Inn Santa Ana-Orange County Airport 2726 S Grand Ave	Santa Ana	CA	92705	**800-465-4329**	714-966-1955
Woolley's Petite Suites 2721 Hotel Terrace Dr	Santa Ana	CA	92705	**800-762-2597**	714-540-1111
Best Western Encina Lodge & Suites 2220 Bath St	Santa Barbara	CA	93105	**800-526-2282**	805-682-7277
Best Western Pepper Tree Inn 3850 State St	Santa Barbara	CA	93105	**800-338-0030**	805-687-5511
El Encanto Hotel & Garden Villas 1900 Lasuen Rd	Santa Barbara	CA	93103	**800-346-7039**	805-687-5000
Hotel Oceana 202 W Cabrillo Blvd	Santa Barbara	CA	93101	**800-965-9776**	805-965-4577
Hotel Santa Barbara 533 State St	Santa Barbara	CA	93101	**888-259-7700**	805-957-9300
Radisson Hotel Santa Barbara 1111 E Cabrillo Blvd	Santa Barbara	CA	93103	**800-333-3333**	805-963-0744
Santa Barbara Inn 901 E Cabrillo Blvd	Santa Barbara	CA	93103	**800-231-0431**	805-966-2285
Biltmore Hotel & Suites 2151 Laurelwood Rd	Santa Clara	CA	95054	**800-255-9925**	408-988-8411
Embassy Suites Santa Clara-Silicon Valley 2885 Lakeside Dr	Santa Clara	CA	95054	**800-362-2779**	408-496-6400
Marriott Santa Clara 2700 Mission College Blvd	Santa Clara	CA	95054	**800-228-9290**	408-988-1500
Plaza Suites Silicon Valley 3100 Lakeside Dr	Santa Clara	CA	95054	**800-345-1554**	408-748-9800
Westin Santa Clara 5101 Great America Pkwy	Santa Clara	CA	95054	**800-937-8461**	408-986-0700
Coast Santa Cruz Hotel 175 W Cliff Dr	Santa Cruz	CA	95060	**800-663-1144**	831-426-4330
Santa Maria Inn 801 S Broadway	Santa Maria	CA	93454	**800-462-4276**	805-928-7777
Fairmont Miramar Hotel Santa Monica 101 Wilshire Blvd	Santa Monica	CA	90401	**800-866-5577**	310-576-7777
Georgian Hotel 1415 Ocean Ave	Santa Monica	CA	90401	**800-538-8147**	310-395-9945
Holiday Inn Santa Monica 120 Colorado Ave	Santa Monica	CA	90401	**800-947-9175**	310-451-0676
Hotel Casa del Mar 1910 Ocean Way	Santa Monica	CA	90405	**800-898-6999**	310-581-5533
Hotel Oceana 849 Ocean Ave	Santa Monica	CA	90403	**800-777-0758**	310-393-0486
Le Merigot - A JW Marriott Beach Hotel & Spa 1740 Ocean Ave	Santa Monica	CA	90401	**888-539-7899**	310-395-9700
Loews Santa Monica Beach Hotel 1700 Ocean Ave	Santa Monica	CA	90401	**800-325-6397**	310-458-6700
Radisson Huntley Hotel 1111 2nd St	Santa Monica	CA	90403	**800-333-3333**	310-394-5454
Sheraton Delfina Santa Monica 530 W Pico Blvd	Santa Monica	CA	90405	**800-325-3535**	310-399-9344
Shutters on the Beach 1 Pico Blvd	Santa Monica	CA	90405	**800-334-9000**	310-458-0030
Hotel La Rose 308 Wilson St	Santa Rosa	CA	95401	**800-527-6738**	707-579-3200
Hyatt Vineyard Creek Hotel & Spa 170 Railroad St	Santa Rosa	CA	95401	**800-233-1234**	707-636-7100
Vintners Inn 4350 Barnes Rd	Santa Rosa	CA	95403	**800-421-2584**	707-575-7350
Casa Madrona Hotel 801 Bridgeway	Sausalito	CA	94965	**800-567-9524**	415-332-0502
Embassy Suites Monterey Bay-Seaside 1441 Canyon Del Rey	Seaside	CA	93955	**800-362-2779**	831-393-1115
Holiday Inn Swan Court 2950 Pea Soup Andersen Blvd	Selma	CA	93662	**800-462-5363**	559-891-8000
Lodge at Sonoma Renaissance Resort & Spa 1325 Broadway	Sonoma	CA	95476	**888-710-8008**	707-935-6600
MacArthur Place 29 E MacArthur St	Sonoma	CA	95476	**800-722-1866**	707-938-2929
Embassy Suites Lake Tahoe Resort 4130 Lake Tahoe Blvd	South Lake Tahoe	CA	96150	**800-988-9820**	530-544-5400
Inn by the Lake 3300 Lake Tahoe Blvd	South Lake Tahoe	CA	96150	**800-877-1466**	530-542-0330
Tahoe Seasons Resort 3901 Saddle Rd	South Lake Tahoe	CA	96150	**800-540-4874**	530-541-6700
Best Western Grosvenor Airport Hotel 380 S Airport Blvd	South San Francisco	CA	94080	**800-722-7141**	650-873-3200
Hilton Garden Inn San Francisco Airport North 670 Gateway Blvd	South San Francisco	CA	94080	**877-782-9444**	650-872-1515
Inn at Oyster Point 425 Marina Blvd	South San Francisco	CA	94080	**800-642-2720**	650-737-7633
Wingate Inn San Francisco Airport 373 S Airport Blvd	South San Francisco	CA	94080	**800-228-1000**	650-589-0600
Best Western Inn Stockton 4219 E Waterloo Rd	Stockton	CA	95215	**800-528-1234**	209-931-3131
Comfort Inn Stockton 3951 E Budweiser Ct	Stockton	CA	95215	**800-228-5150**	209-931-9341
Courtyard Stockton 3252 W March Ln	Stockton	CA	95219	**800-321-2211**	209-472-9700
La Quinta Inn Stockton 2710 W March Ln	Stockton	CA	95219	**800-531-5900**	209-952-7800
Radisson Hotel Stockton 2323 Grand Canal Blvd	Stockton	CA	95207	**800-333-3333**	209-957-9090
Residence Inn Stockton 3240 W March Ln	Stockton	CA	95219	**800-331-3131**	209-472-9800
Sheraton Sunnyvale Hotel 1100 N Mathilda Ave	Sunnyvale	CA	94089	**800-325-3535**	408-745-6000
Wild Palms Hotel 910 E Fremont Ave	Sunnyvale	CA	94087	**800-538-1600**	408-738-0500
Woodfin Suite Hotel Sunnyvale 635 E El Camino Real	Sunnyvale	CA	94087	**888-433-9405**	408-738-1700
Wyndham Sunnyvale Hotel 1300 Chesapeake Terr	Sunnyvale	CA	94089	**800-996-3426**	408-747-0999
Sea Ranch Lodge PO Box 44	The Sea Ranch	CA	95497	**800-732-7262**	707-785-2371
Thousand Oaks Inn 75 W Thousand Oaks Blvd	Thousand Oaks	CA	91360	**800-600-6878**	805-497-3701
Waters Edge Hotel 25 Main St	Tiburon	CA	94920	**800-738-7477**	415-789-5999
Marriott Torrance 3635 Fashion Way Ave	Torrance	CA	90503	**800-228-9290**	310-316-3636
Hilton Los Angeles/Universal City 555 Universal Hollywood Dr	Universal City	CA	91608	**800-445-8667**	818-506-2500
Sheraton Universal Hotel 333 Universal Hollywood Dr	Universal City	CA	91608	**800-325-3535**	818-980-1212
Hilton Garden Inn Valencia Six Flags 2771o The Old Rd	Valencia	CA	91355	**877-782-9444**	661-254-8800
Hyatt Valencia & Santa Clarita Conference Center 24500 Town Center Dr	Valencia	CA	91355	**800-233-1234**	661-799-1234
Airtel Plaza Hotel 7277 Valjean Ave	Van Nuys	CA	91406	**800-224-7835**	818-997-7676
Clocktower Inn Hotel 181 E Santa Clara St	Ventura	CA	93001	**800-727-1027**	805-652-0141
Pierpont Inn 550 Sanjon Rd	Ventura	CA	93001	**800-285-4667**	805-643-6144
Marriott Walnut Creek 2355 N Main St	Walnut Creek	CA	94596	**800-228-9290**	925-934-2000
Argyle Hotel 8358 Sunset Blvd	West Hollywood	CA	90069	**800-225-2637**	323-654-7100
Best Western Sunset Plaza Hotel 8400 Sunset Blvd	West Hollywood	CA	90069	**800-421-3652**	323-654-0750
Hyatt West Hollywood 8401 Sunset Blvd	West Hollywood	CA	90069	**800-233-1234**	323-656-1234
Le Parc Suite Hotel 733 N West Knoll Dr	West Hollywood	CA	90069	**800-578-4837**	310-855-8888
Mondrian Hotel 8440 Sunset Blvd	West Hollywood	CA	90069	**800-525-8029**	323-650-8999
Summerfield Suites by Wyndham West Hollywood 1000 Westmount Dr	West Hollywood	CA	90069	**800-833-4353**	310-657-7400
Sunset Marquis Hotel & Villas 1200 N Alta Loma Rd	West Hollywood	CA	90069	**800-858-9758**	310-657-1333
Wyndham Bel Age Hotel 1020 N San Vicente Blvd	West Hollywood	CA	90069	**800-996-3426**	310-854-1111
Hyatt Westlake Plaza in Thousand Oaks 880 S Westlake Blvd	Westlake Village	CA	91361	**800-233-1234**	805-557-1234

Name / Address	City	State	ZIP	Toll-Free	Phone
Radisson Whittier 7320 Greenleaf Ave	Whittier	CA	90602	**800-333-3333**	562-945-8511
Marriott Woodland Hills-Warner Center 21850 Oxnard St	Woodland Hills	CA	91367	**800-228-9290**	818-887-4800
Villagio Inn & Spa 6481 Washington St	Yountville	CA	94599	**800-351-1133**	707-944-8877
Vintage Inn Napa Valley 6541 Washington St	Yountville	CA	94599	**800-351-1133**	707-944-1112

Colorado

Name / Address	City	State	ZIP	Toll-Free	Phone
Hotel Jerome 330 E Main St	Aspen	CO	81611	**800-331-7213**	970-920-1000
Little Nell The 675 E Durant Ave	Aspen	CO	81611	**888-843-6355**	970-920-4600
Saint Regis Aspen 315 E Dean St	Aspen	CO	81611	**888-454-9005**	970-920-3300
Sky Hotel 709 E Durant Ave	Aspen	CO	81611	**800-882-2582**	970-925-6760
AmeriSuites Denver Airport 16250 E 40th Ave	Aurora	CO	80011	**800-833-1516**	303-371-0700
Comfort Inn Aurora 14071 E Iliff Ave	Aurora	CO	80014	**800-228-5150**	303-755-8000
Comfort Inn Denver Airport 16921 E 32nd Ave	Aurora	CO	80011	**800-228-5150**	303-367-5000
Doubletree Hotel Denver-Southeast 13696 E Iliff Pl & I-225	Aurora	CO	80014	**800-222-8733**	303-337-2800
Hilton Garden Inn Denver Airport 16475 E 40th Cir	Aurora	CO	80011	**877-782-9444**	303-371-9393
La Quinta Inn Denver Aurora 1011 S Abilene St	Aurora	CO	80012	**800-531-5900**	303-337-0206
Marriott Denver Airport at Gateway Park 16455 E 40th Cir	Aurora	CO	80011	**800-228-9290**	303-371-4333
Radisson Hotel Denver Southeast 3200 S Parker Rd	Aurora	CO	80014	**800-465-4329**	303-695-1700
Charter at Beaver Creek 120 Offerson Rd PO Box 5310	Avon	CO	81620	**800-525-6660**	970-949-6660
Pines Lodge 141 Scott Hill Rd	Avon	CO	81620	**800-859-8242**	970-845-7900
Beaver Creek Lodge 26 Avon Dale Ln	Beaver Creek	CO	81620	**800-525-7280**	970-845-9800
Saddleridge 44 Meadows Ln	Beaver Creek	CO	81620	**800-859-8242**	970-845-5450
Best Western Golden Buff Lodge 1725 28th St	Boulder	CO	80301	**800-999-2833**	303-442-7450
Boulder Mountain Lodge 91 Four-Mile Canyon Rd	Boulder	CO	80302	**800-458-0882**	303-444-0882
Bradley Boulder 2040 16th St	Boulder	CO	80302	**800-858-5811**	303-545-5200
Broker Inn 555 30th St	Boulder	CO	80303	**800-338-5407**	303-444-3330
Courtyard Boulder 4710 Pearl East Cir	Boulder	CO	80301	**800-321-2211**	303-440-4700
Foot of the Mountain Motel 200 W Arapahoe Ave	Boulder	CO	80302	**866-773-5489**	303-442-5688
Gunbarrel Guest House 6901 Lookout Rd	Boulder	CO	80301	**800-530-1513**	303-530-1513
Hotel Boulderado 2115 13th St	Boulder	CO	80302	**800-433-4344**	303-442-4344
Marriott Boulder 2660 Canyon Blvd	Boulder	CO	80302	**888-238-2178**	303-440-8877
Millennium Hotel Boulder 1345 28th St	Boulder	CO	80302	**866-866-8086**	303-443-3850
Quality Inn & Suites Boulder 2020 Arapahoe Ave	Boulder	CO	80302	**888-449-7550**	303-449-7550
Residence Inn Boulder 3030 Center Green Dr	Boulder	CO	80301	**800-331-3131**	303-449-5545
Saint Julien Hotel & Spa 900 Walnut St	Boulder	CO	80302	**877-303-0900**	720-406-9696
Sandy Point Inn 6485 Twin Lakes Rd	Boulder	CO	80301	**800-322-2939**	303-530-2939
Great Divide Lodge 550 Village Rd	Breckenridge	CO	80424	**800-321-8444**	970-453-4500
Lodge & Spa at Breckenridge 112 Overlook Dr	Breckenridge	CO	80424	**800-736-1607**	970-453-9300
Academy Hotel 8110 N Academy Blvd	Colorado Springs	CO	80920	**800-333-3333**	719-598-5770
Alikar Gardens Resort 1123 Verde Dr	Colorado Springs	CO	80910	**800-456-1123**	719-475-2564
Antlers Hilton Colorado Springs 4 S Cascade Ave	Colorado Springs	CO	80903	**800-444-2326**	719-473-5600
Apollo Park Executive Suites 805 S Circle Dr Suite 2B	Colorado Springs	CO	80910	**800-279-3620**	719-634-0286
Doubletree Hotel Colorado Springs-World Arena 1775 E Cheyenne Mountain Blvd	Colorado Springs	CO	80906	**800-222-8733**	719-576-8900
Garden of the Gods Motel 2922 W Colorado Ave	Colorado Springs	CO	80904	**800-637-0703**	719-636-5271
Hilton Garden Inn Colorado Springs 1810 Briargate Pkwy	Colorado Springs	CO	80920	**800-445-8667**	719-598-6866
Radisson Inn & Suites Colorado Springs Airport 1645 N Newport Rd	Colorado Springs	CO	80916	**800-333-3333**	719-597-7000
Satellite Hotel 411 Lakewood Cir	Colorado Springs	CO	80910	**800-423-8409**	719-596-6800
Sheraton Colorado Springs Hotel 2886 S Circle Dr	Colorado Springs	CO	80906	**800-325-3535**	719-576-5900
Wyndham Colorado Springs 5580 Tech Center Dr	Colorado Springs	CO	80919	**800-996-3426**	719-260-1800
Adam's Mark Denver 1550 Court Pl	Denver	CO	80202	**800-444-2326**	303-893-3333
Brown Palace Hotel 321 17th St	Denver	CO	80202	**800-321-2599**	303-297-3111
Burnsley Hotel 1000 Grant St	Denver	CO	80203	**800-231-3915**	303-830-1000
Courtyard Denver International Airport 6901 Tower Rd	Denver	CO	80249	**800-321-2211**	303-371-0300
Doubletree Hotel Denver 3203 Quebec St	Denver	CO	80207	**800-222-8733**	303-321-3333
Embassy Suites Denver Airport 4444 N Havana St	Denver	CO	80239	**800-362-2779**	303-375-0400
Embassy Suites Denver Downtown 1881 Curtis St	Denver	CO	80202	**800-733-3366**	303-297-8888
Embassy Suites Denver Southeast 7525 E Hampden Ave	Denver	CO	80231	**800-362-2779**	303-696-6644
Executive Tower Hotel 1405 Curtis St	Denver	CO	80202	**800-525-6651**	303-571-0300
Fairfield Inn Denver Airport 6851 Tower Rd	Denver	CO	80249	**800-228-2800**	303-576-9640
Four Points by Sheraton Denver Southeast 6363 E Hampden Ave	Denver	CO	80222	**800-228-9290**	303-758-7000
Holiday Inn Denver Downtown 1450 Glenarm Pl	Denver	CO	80202	**800-423-5128**	303-573-1450
Holiday Inn Select Denver-Cherry Creek 455 S Colorado Blvd	Denver	CO	80246	**800-465-4329**	303-388-5561
Hotel Monaco Denver 1717 Champa St	Denver	CO	80202	**800-397-5380**	303-296-1717
Hotel Teatro 1100 14th St	Denver	CO	80202	**888-727-1200**	303-228-1100
Hyatt Regency Denver 1750 Welton St	Denver	CO	80202	**800-233-1234**	303-295-1234
Hyatt Regency Tech Center 7800 E Tufts Ave	Denver	CO	80237	**800-233-1234**	303-779-1234
Loews Denver Hotel 4150 E Mississippi Ave	Denver	CO	80246	**800-235-6397**	303-782-9300
Magnolia Hotel Denver 818 17th St	Denver	CO	80202	**888-915-1110**	303-607-9000
Marriott Denver City Center 1701 California St	Denver	CO	80202	**800-228-9290**	303-297-1300
Marriott Denver Tech Center 4900 S Syracuse St	Denver	CO	80237	**800-228-9290**	303-779-1100
Oxford Hotel 1600 17th St	Denver	CO	80202	**800-228-5838**	303-628-5400
Radisson Hotel Denver Stapleton Plaza 3333 Quebec St	Denver	CO	80207	**800-333-3333**	303-321-3500
Ramada Inn Denver Downtown 1150 E Colfax Ave	Denver	CO	80218	**800-272-6232**	303-831-7700
Renaissance Denver Hotel 3801 Quebec St	Denver	CO	80207	**800-468-3571**	303-399-7500
Residence Inn Denver Downtown 2777 Zuni St	Denver	CO	80211	**800-331-3131**	303-458-5318
Warwick Hotel Denver 1776 Grant St	Denver	CO	80203	**800-525-2888**	303-861-2000
Westin Tabor Center 1672 Lawrence St	Denver	CO	80202	**800-937-8461**	303-572-9100
Wyndham Denver Tech Center 7675 E Union Ave	Denver	CO	80237	**800-996-3426**	303-770-4200
Strater Hotel 699 Main Ave	Durango	CO	81301	**800-247-4431**	970-247-4431
Lodge & Spa at Cordillera 2205 Cordillera Way	Edwards	CO	81632	**800-877-3529**	970-926-2200
Hilton Garden Inn Denver South/Meridian 9290 Meridian Blvd	Englewood	CO	80112	**877-782-9444**	303-824-1550
Summerfield Suites by Wyndham Denver South/Tech Center 9280 E Costilla Ave	Englewood	CO	80112	**800-833-4353**	303-706-1945
Holiday Inn Rocky Mountain Park 101 S St Vrain Ave	Estes Park	CO	80517	**800-803-7837**	970-586-2332
Lake Estes Inn & Suites 1650 Big Thompson Ave	Estes Park	CO	80517	**800-332-6867**	970-586-3386
Stanley Hotel 333 Wonderview Ave	Estes Park	CO	80517	**800-976-1377**	970-586-3371
Best Western University Inn 914 S College Ave	Fort Collins	CO	80524	**800-780-7234**	970-484-1984
Fort Collins Mulberry Inn 4333 E Mulberry St	Fort Collins	CO	80524	**800-234-5548**	970-493-9000
Fort Collins Plaza Inn 3709 E Mulberry St	Fort Collins	CO	80524	**800-434-5548**	970-493-7800
Holiday Inn Fort Collins-University Park 425 W Prospect Rd	Fort Collins	CO	80526	**800-465-4329**	970-482-2626
Marriott Fort Collins 350 E Horsetooth Rd	Fort Collins	CO	80525	**800-548-2635**	970-226-5200
Quality Inn & Suites Fort Collins 4001 S Mason St	Fort Collins	CO	80525	**800-228-5151**	970-282-9047
Hotel Colorado 526 Pine St	Glenwood Springs	CO	81601	**800-544-3998**	970-945-6511
Marriott Denver West 1717 Denver West Blvd	Golden	CO	80401	**800-228-9290**	303-279-9100
Adam's Mark Grand Junction 743 Horizon Dr	Grand Junction	CO	81506	**800-444-2326**	970-241-8888
Hilton Denver Tech South 7801 E Orchard Rd	Greenwood Village	CO	80111	**800-327-2242**	303-779-6161
Sheraton Denver Tech Center Hotel 7007 S Clinton St	Greenwood Village	CO	80112	**800-325-3535**	303-799-6200
Cliff House at Pikes Peak 306 Canon Ave	Manitou Springs	CO	80829	**888-212-7000**	719-685-3000
Marriott Pueblo 110 W 1st St	Pueblo	CO	81003	**800-228-9290**	719-542-3200
Redstone Inn 82 Redstone Blvd	Redstone	CO	81623	**800-748-2524**	970-963-2526
Silvertree Hotel 100 Elbert Ln	Snowmass Village	CO	81615	**800-525-9402**	970-923-3520
Stonebridge Inn 300 Carriage Way PO Box 5008	Snowmass Village	CO	81615	**800-922-7242**	970-923-2420
Ranch at Steamboat 1 Ranch Rd	Steamboat Springs	CO	80487	**800-525-2002**	970-879-3000
Radisson North Denver Graystone Castle 83 E 120th Ave	Thornton	CO	80233	**800-333-3333**	303-451-1002
Best Western Fabulous Vailglo Lodge 701 W Lionshead Cir	Vail	CO	81657	**800-541-8245**	970-476-5506
Evergreen Lodge 250 South Frontage Rd W	Vail	CO	81657	**800-284-8245**	970-476-7810
Mountain Haus 292 E Meadow Dr	Vail	CO	81657	**800-237-0922**	970-476-2434
Tivoli Lodge 386 Hanson Ranch Rd	Vail	CO	81657	**800-451-4756**	970-476-5615
Westin Westminster 10600 Westminster Blvd	Westminster	CO	80020	**800-937-8461**	303-410-5000
Iron Horse Resort 101 Iron Horse Way	Winter Park	CO	80482	**800-621-8190**	970-726-8851

Connecticut

Name / Address	City	State	ZIP	Toll-Free	Phone
Holiday Inn Bridgeport 1070 Main St	Bridgeport	CT	06604	**800-465-4329**	203-334-1234
Radisson Hotel & Conference Center Cromwell 100 Berlin Rd	Cromwell	CT	06416	**800-333-3333**	860-635-2000
Comfort Suites Danbury 89 Mill Plain Rd	Danbury	CT	06811	**800-424-6423**	203-205-0800
Inn at Ethan Allen 21 Lake Ave Ext	Danbury	CT	06811	**800-742-1776**	203-744-1776
Maron Hotel & Suites 42 Lake Ave Ext	Danbury	CT	06811	**800-333-3333**	203-791-2200
Residence Inn Danbury 22 Segar St	Danbury	CT	06810	**800-331-3131**	203-797-1256
Sheraton Danbury Hotel 18 Old Ridgebury Rd	Danbury	CT	06810	**800-325-3535**	203-794-0600
Radisson Hotel Springfield-Enfield 1 Bright Meadow Blvd	Enfield	CT	06082	**800-333-3333**	860-741-2211
Marriott Hartford-Farmington 15 Farm Springs Rd	Farmington	CT	06032	**800-228-9290**	860-678-1000
Hilton Garden Inn Hartford South/Glastonbury 85 Glastonbury Blvd	Glastonbury	CT	06033	**877-782-9444**	860-659-1025
DELAMAR Greenwich Harbor 500 Steamboat Rd	Greenwich	CT	06830	**866-335-2627**	203-661-9800
Crowne Plaza Hotel Hartford Downtown 50 Morgan St	Hartford	CT	06120	**800-227-6963**	860-549-2400
Goodwin Hotel 1 Haynes St	Hartford	CT	06103	**800-922-5006**	860-246-7500
Hilton Hartford 315 Trumbull St	Hartford	CT	06103	**800-445-8667**	860-728-5151
Inn at Mystic 3 Williams Ave PO Box 216	Mystic	CT	06355	**800-237-2415**	860-536-9604
Courtyard New Haven 30 Whalley Ave	New Haven	CT	06511	**800-321-2211**	203-777-6221
New Haven Hotel 229 George St	New Haven	CT	06510	**800-644-6835**	203-498-3100
Omni New Haven Hotel at Yale 155 Temple St	New Haven	CT	06510	**800-843-6664**	203-772-6664
Quality Inn Conference Center New Haven 100 Pond Lily Ave	New Haven	CT	06525	**800-228-5151**	203-387-6651
Residence Inn New Haven 3 Long Wharf Dr	New Haven	CT	06511	**800-331-3131**	203-777-5337
Three Chimneys Inn 1201 Chapel St	New Haven	CT	06511	**800-443-1554**	203-789-1201
Lighthouse Inn 6 Guthrie Pl	New London	CT	06320	**888-600-5681**	860-443-8411
Courtyard Norwalk 474 Main Ave	Norwalk	CT	06851	**800-321-2211**	203-849-9111
Doubletree Hotel Norwalk 789 Connecticut Ave	Norwalk	CT	06854	**888-444-2582**	203-853-3477
Hyatt Regency Greenwich 1800 E Putnam Ave	Old Greenwich	CT	06870	**800-233-1234**	203-637-1234
Marriott Hartford-Rocky Hill 100 Capital Blvd	Rocky Hill	CT	06067	**800-228-9290**	860-257-6000
Residence Inn Fairfield County-Shelton 1001 Bridgeport Ave	Shelton	CT	06484	**800-331-3131**	203-926-9000
Holiday Inn Select Stamford Downtown 700 Main St	Stamford	CT	06901	**800-408-7640**	203-358-8400
Marriott Stamford 2 Stamford Forum	Stamford	CT	06901	**800-228-9290**	203-357-9555
Sheraton Stamford Hotel 2701 Summer St	Stamford	CT	06905	**800-325-3535**	203-359-1300
Stamford Suites 720 Bedford St	Stamford	CT	06901	**866-394-4365**	203-359-7300
Westin Stamford 1 First Stamford Pl	Stamford	CT	06902	**800-937-8461**	203-967-2222
Marriott Trumbull-Merritt Parkway 180 Hawley Ln	Trumbull	CT	06611	**800-221-9855**	203-378-1400
Best Western Executive Hotel West Haven 490 Saw Mill Rd	West Haven	CT	06516	**800-528-1234**	203-933-0344
Inn at National Hall 2 Post Rd W	Westport	CT	06880	**800-628-4255**	203-221-1351
Westport Inn 1595 Post Rd E	Westport	CT	06880	**800-446-8997**	203-259-5236
Hilton Garden Inn Hartford North/Bradley International 555 Corporate Dr	Windsor	CT	06095	**877-782-9444**	860-688-6400
Marriott Hartford-Windsor Airport 28 Day Hill Rd	Windsor	CT	06095	**800-535-4028**	860-688-7500
Doubletree Hotel Bradley International Airport 16 Ella Grasso Tpke	Windsor Locks	CT	06096	**800-222-8733**	860-627-5171
Sheraton Bradley Airport Hotel 1 Bradley International Airport	Windsor Locks	CT	06096	**800-325-3535**	860-627-5311

Delaware

Name / Address	City	State	ZIP	Toll-Free	Phone
Holiday Inn Select Wilmington (Claymont) 630 Naamans Rd	Claymont	DE	19703	**800-465-4329**	302-792-2700
Adams Oceanfront Resort 4 Read St	Dewey Beach	DE	19971	**800-448-8080**	302-227-3030
Marina Suites 1117 Hwy 1	Dewey Beach	DE	19971	**888-777-3613**	302-227-1700
Comfort Inn Dover 222 S DuPont Hwy	Dover	DE	19901	**800-228-5150**	302-674-3300
Fairfield Inn & Suites Dover 655 N Dupont Hwy	Dover	DE	19901	**800-228-2800**	302-677-0900
Sheraton Dover Hotel 1570 N DuPont Hwy	Dover	DE	19901	**800-325-3535**	302-678-8500
Heritage Inn & Golf Club 2 Postal Ln	Lewes	DE	19958	**800-669-9399**	302-644-0600
Zwaanendael Inn 142 2nd St	Lewes	DE	19958	**800-824-8754**	302-645-6466
Inn at Montchanin Village Rte 100 & Kirk Rd	Montchanin	DE	19710	**800-269-2473**	302-888-2133
Courtyard Wilmington Newark/Christiana Mall 48 Geoffrey Dr	Newark	DE	19713	**800-321-2211**	302-456-3800
Hilton Wilmington/Christiana 100 Continental Dr	Newark	DE	19713	**800-348-3133**	302-454-1500
Admiral Hotel 2 Baltimore Ave	Rehoboth Beach	DE	19971	**888-882-4188**	302-227-2103
Atlantic Sands Hotel 101 N Boardwalk	Rehoboth Beach	DE	19971	**800-422-0600**	302-227-2511
Avenue Inn & Spa 33 Wilmington Ave	Rehoboth Beach	DE	19971	**800-433-5870**	302-226-2900
Bellmoor The 6 Christian St	Rehoboth Beach	DE	19971	**800-425-2355**	302-227-5800
Boardwalk Plaza Hotel 2 Olive Ave	Rehoboth Beach	DE	19971	**800-332-3224**	302-227-7169
Breakers Hotel & Suites 105 2nd St	Rehoboth Beach	DE	19971	**800-441-8009**	302-227-6688
Henlopen Hotel 511 N Boardwalk	Rehoboth Beach	DE	19971	**800-441-8450**	302-227-2551
Oceanus Motel 6 2nd St	Rehoboth Beach	DE	19971	**800-852-5011**	302-227-8200
Sandcastle Motel 123 2nd St	Rehoboth Beach	DE	19971	**800-372-2112**	302-227-0400
Sea-Esta II Motel 713 Rehoboth Ave	Rehoboth Beach	DE	19971	**800-436-6591**	302-227-8199
Best Western Brandywine Valley Inn 1807 Concord Pike	Wilmington	DE	19803	**800-537-7772**	302-656-9436
Brandywine Suites Hotel 707 N King St	Wilmington	DE	19801	**800-756-0070**	302-656-9300
Doubletree Hotel Wilmington 4727 Concord Pike	Wilmington	DE	19803	**800-222-8733**	302-478-6000
Hotel du Pont 11th & Market Sts	Wilmington	DE	19801	**800-441-9019**	302-594-3100
Sheraton Suites Wilmington 422 Delaware Ave	Wilmington	DE	19801	**800-325-3535**	302-654-8300
Spencer Hotel 700 N King St	Wilmington	DE	19801	**866-589-3411**	302-655-0400

District of Columbia

Name / Address	City	State	ZIP	Toll-Free	Phone
Best Western Downtown Capitol Hill 724 3rd St NW	Washington	DC	20001	**800-242-4831**	202-842-4466
Capital Hilton 1001 16th St NW	Washington	DC	20036	**800-445-8667**	202-393-1000
Capitol Hill Suites 200 C St SE	Washington	DC	20003	**888-627-7811**	202-543-6000
Carlyle Suites Hotel 1731 New Hampshire Ave NW	Washington	DC	20009	**800-964-5377**	202-234-3200
Channel Inn Hotel 650 Water St SW	Washington	DC	20024	**800-368-5668**	202-554-2400
Churchill Hotel 1914 Connecticut Ave NW	Washington	DC	20009	**800-424-2464**	202-797-2000
Courtyard Washington Convention Center 900 F St NW	Washington	DC	20004	**800-321-2211**	202-638-4600
Courtyard Washington Embassy Row 1600 Rhode Island Ave NW	Washington	DC	20036	**800-321-2211**	202-293-8000
Doubletree Guest Suites Washington DC 801 New Hampshire Ave NW	Washington	DC	20037	**800-222-8733**	202-785-2000
Embassy Suites Washington DC at the Chevy Chase Pavilion 4300 Military Rd NW	Washington	DC	20015	**800-760-6120**	202-362-9300
Fairmont Hotel Washington 2401 M St NW	Washington	DC	20037	**877-222-2266**	202-429-2400
Four Points by Sheraton Washington DC Downtown 1201 K St NW	Washington	DC	20005	**800-325-3535**	202-289-7600
Four Seasons Hotel Washington DC 2800 Pennsylvania Ave NW	Washington	DC	20007	**800-332-3442**	202-342-0444
George Washington University Inn 824 New Hampshire Ave NW	Washington	DC	20037	**800-426-4455**	202-337-6620
Georgetown Inn 1310 Wisconsin Ave NW	Washington	DC	20007	**800-424-2979**	202-333-8900
Governor's House Hotel 1615 Rhode Island Ave NW	Washington	DC	20036	**800-821-4367**	202-296-2100
Grand Hyatt Washington 1000 H St NW	Washington	DC	20001	**800-233-1234**	202-582-1234
Hamilton Crowne Plaza Hotel Washington DC 1001 14th St NW	Washington	DC	20005	**800-263-9802**	202-682-0111
Hay-Adams Hotel 800 16th St NW	Washington	DC	20006	**800-424-5054**	202-638-6600
Henley Park Hotel 926 Massachusetts Ave NW	Washington	DC	20001	**800-222-8474**	202-638-5200
Hilton Garden Inn Washington-Franklin Square 815 14th St NW	Washington	DC	20005	**877-782-9444**	202-783-7800
Hilton Washington Embassy Row 2015 Massachusetts Ave NW	Washington	DC	20036	**800-445-8667**	202-265-1600
Hilton Washington & Towers 1919 Connecticut Ave NW	Washington	DC	20009	**800-445-8667**	202-483-3000
Holiday Inn Washington-Capitol 550 C St SW	Washington	DC	20024	**800-465-4329**	202-479-4000
Holiday Inn Washington-Downtown 1155 14th St NW	Washington	DC	20005	**800-465-4329**	202-737-1200
Holiday Inn Washington-Georgetown 2101 Wisconsin Ave NW	Washington	DC	20007	**800-465-4329**	202-338-4600
Holiday Inn Washington on the Hill 415 New Jersey Ave NW	Washington	DC	20001	**800-465-4329**	202-638-1616
Hotel George 15 'E' St NW	Washington	DC	20001	**800-576-8831**	202-347-4200
Hotel Helix 1430 Rhode Island Ave NW	Washington	DC	20005	**866-508-0658**	202-462-9001
Hotel Lombardy 2019 Pennsylvania Ave NW	Washington	DC	20006	**800-424-5486**	202-828-2600
Hotel Monticello 1075 Thomas Jefferson St NW	Washington	DC	20007	**800-388-2410**	202-337-0900
Hotel Sofitel Lafayette Square 806 15th St NW	Washington	DC	20005	**800-763-4835**	202-730-8800
Hotel Washington 515 15th St NW	Washington	DC	20004	**800-424-9540**	202-638-5900
Hyatt Regency Washington DC on Capitol Hill 400 New Jersey Ave NW	Washington	DC	20001	**800-233-1234**	202-737-1234
Jefferson Hotel - A Loews Hotel 1200 16th St NW	Washington	DC	20036	**800-368-5966**	202-347-2200
Jurys Washington Hotel 1500 New Hampshire Ave NW	Washington	DC	20036	**800-423-6953**	202-483-6000
JW Marriott Hotel on Pennsylvania Avenue 1331 Pennsylvania Ave NW	Washington	DC	20004	**800-228-9290**	202-393-2000
Latham Hotel The 3000 M St NW	Washington	DC	20007	**800-368-5922**	202-726-5000
Lincoln Suites Downtown 1823 L St NW	Washington	DC	20036	**800-424-2970**	202-223-4320
Loews L'Enfant Plaza Hotel 480 L'Enfant Plaza SW	Washington	DC	20024	**800-635-5065**	202-484-1000
Madison The 1177 15th St NW	Washington	DC	20005	**800-424-8577**	202-862-1600
Mandarin Oriental Washington DC 1330 Maryland Ave SW	Washington	DC	20024	**888-888-1778**	202-554-8588
Marriott Wardman Park Hotel 2660 Woodley Rd NW	Washington	DC	20008	**800-228-9290**	202-328-2000
Marriott Washington 1221 22nd St NW	Washington	DC	20037	**800-228-9290**	202-872-1500
Marriott Washington at Metro Center 775 12th St NW	Washington	DC	20005	**800-228-9290**	202-737-2200
Melrose Hotel Washington DC 2430 Pennsylvania Ave NW	Washington	DC	20037	**800-635-7673**	202-955-6400
Morrison-Clark Inn 1101 11th St NW	Washington	DC	20001	**800-222-8474**	202-898-1200
Omni Shoreham Hotel 2500 Calvert St NW	Washington	DC	20008	**800-843-6664**	202-234-0700
One Washington Circle Hotel 1 Washington Cir NW	Washington	DC	20037	**800-424-9671**	202-872-1680
Park Hyatt Washington 1201 24th St NW	Washington	DC	20037	**800-233-1234**	202-789-1234
Phoenix Park Hotel 520 North Capitol St NW	Washington	DC	20001	**800-824-5419**	202-638-6900
Radisson Barcelo Hotel Washington 2121 P St NW	Washington	DC	20037	**800-333-3333**	202-293-3100
Renaissance Mayflower Hotel 1127 Connecticut Ave NW	Washington	DC	20036	**800-468-3571**	202-347-3000
Renaissance Washington DC Hotel 999 9th St NW	Washington	DC	20001	**800-228-9290**	202-898-9000
Residence Inn Washington DC Vermont Avenue 1199 Vermont Ave NW	Washington	DC	20005	**800-331-3131**	202-898-1100
Ritz-Carlton Georgetown 3100 South St NW	Washington	DC	20007	**800-241-3333**	202-912-4100
Ritz-Carlton Washington DC 1150 22nd St NW	Washington	DC	20037	**800-241-3333**	202-835-0500
River Inn 924 25th St NW	Washington	DC	20037	**800-424-2741**	202-337-7600
Saint Gregory Luxury Hotel & Suites 2033 M Street NW	Washington	DC	20036	**800-829-5034**	202-530-3600
Saint Regis Washington DC 923 16th St NW	Washington	DC	20006	**800-325-3535**	202-638-2626
Savoy Suites Georgetown 2505 Wisconsin Ave NW	Washington	DC	20007	**800-944-5377**	202-337-9700
State Plaza Hotel 2117 'E' St NW	Washington	DC	20037	**800-424-2859**	202-861-8200
Washington Court Hotel 525 New Jersey Ave NW	Washington	DC	20001	**800-321-3010**	202-628-2100
Washington Plaza Hotel 10 Thomas Cir NW Massachusetts Ave at 14th St	Washington	DC	20005	**800-424-1140**	202-842-1300
Washington Suites Georgetown 2500 Pennsylvania Ave NW	Washington	DC	20037	**877-736-2500**	202-333-8060
Watergate Hotel 2650 Virginia Ave NW	Washington	DC	20037	**800-289-1555**	202-965-2300
Westin Embassy Row 2100 Massachusetts Ave NW	Washington	DC	20008	**800-937-8461**	202-293-2100
Westin Grand Washington DC 2350 M St NW	Washington	DC	20037	**800-937-8461**	202-429-0100
Wyndham City Center 1143 New Hampshire Ave NW	Washington	DC	20037	**800-966-3426**	202-775-0800
Wyndham Washington DC 1400 M St NW	Washington	DC	20005	**800-847-8232**	202-429-1700

Florida

Name / Address	City	State	ZIP	Toll-Free	Phone
Hilton Orlando/Altamonte Springs 350 S North Lake Blvd	Altamonte Springs	FL	32715	**800-445-8667**	407-830-1985
Residence Inn Orlando-Altamonte Springs 270 Douglas Ave	Altamonte Springs	FL	32714	**800-331-3131**	407-788-7991
Sea Turtle Inn 1 Ocean Blvd	Atlantic Beach	FL	32233	**800-874-6000**	904-249-7402
Sea View Hotel 9909 Collins Ave	Bal Harbour	FL	33154	**800-447-1010**	305-866-4441
Courtyard Boca Raton 2000 NW Executive Ctr Ct	Boca Raton	FL	33431	**800-321-2211**	561-241-7070
Doubletree Guest Suites Boca Raton 701 NW 53rd St	Boca Raton	FL	33487	**800-222-8733**	561-997-9500
Marriott Boca Raton 5150 Town Center Cir	Boca Raton	FL	33486	**800-228-9290**	561-392-4600
Radisson Bridge Resort of Boca Raton 999 E Camino Real	Boca Raton	FL	33432	**800-333-3333**	561-368-9500
Radisson Suite Hotel Boca Raton 7920 Glades Rd	Boca Raton	FL	33434	**800-333-3333**	561-483-3600
Renaissance Boca Raton Hotel 2000 NW 19th St	Boca Raton	FL	33431	**800-394-7829**	561-368-5252
Celebration Hotel 700 Bloom St	Celebration	FL	34747	**888-472-6312**	407-566-6000
Adam's Mark Clearwater Beach Resort 430 S Gulfview Blvd	Clearwater Beach	FL	33767	**800-444-2326**	727-443-5714
Quality Inn Beach Resort Clearwater Beach 655 S Gulfview Blvd	Clearwater Beach	FL	33767	**800-228-5151**	727-442-7171
Shephard's Beach Resort 619 S Gulfview Blvd	Clearwater Beach	FL	33767	**800-237-8477**	727-442-5107
Doubletree Hotel Cocoa Beach Oceanfront 2080 N Atlantic Ave	Cocoa Beach	FL	32931	**800-222-8733**	321-783-9222
Grove Isle Club & Resort 4 Grove Isle Dr	Coconut Grove	FL	33133	**800-884-7683**	305-858-8300
Mayfair Hotel & Spa 3000 Florida Ave	Coconut Grove	FL	33133	**800-433-4555**	305-441-0000
Sonesta Hotel & Suites Coconut Grove 2889 McFarlane Rd	Coconut Grove	FL	33133	**800-766-3782**	305-529-2828
David William Hotel 700 Biltmore Way	Coral Gables	FL	33134	**800-757-8073**	305-445-7821
Hyatt Regency Coral Gables 50 Alhambra Plaza	Coral Gables	FL	33134	**800-233-1234**	305-441-1234
Omni Colonnade Hotel 180 Aragon Ave	Coral Gables	FL	33134	**800-843-6664**	305-441-2600
Hilton Garden Inn Fort Lauderdale/Hollywood Airport 180 SW 18th Ave	Dania Beach	FL	33004	**877-782-9444**	954-924-9204
Sheraton Fort Lauderdale Airport Hotel 1825 Griffin Rd	Dania Beach	FL	33004	**800-325-3535**	954-920-3500
Wyndham Fort Lauderdale Airport 1870 Griffin Rd	Dania Beach	FL	33004	**800-445-8667**	954-920-3300
Adam's Mark Daytona Beach Resort 100 N Atlantic Ave	Daytona Beach	FL	32118	**800-444-2326**	386-254-8200
Americano Beach Resort 1260 N Atlantic Ave	Daytona Beach	FL	32118	**800-874-1824**	386-255-7431
Beachcomer Resort 2000 N Atlantic Ave	Daytona Beach	FL	32118	**800-245-3575**	386-252-8513
Best Western La Playa Resort 2500 N Atlantic Ave	Daytona Beach	FL	32118	**800-874-6996**	386-672-0990
Daytona Beach Resort & Conference Center 2700 N Atlantic Ave	Daytona Beach	FL	32118	**800-654-6216**	386-672-3770
Daytona Inn Beach Resort 219 S Atlantic Ave	Daytona Beach	FL	32118	**800-874-1822**	386-252-3626
Desert Inn Resort 900 N Atlantic Ave	Daytona Beach	FL	32118	**800-826-1711**	386-258-6555
Double Stay Inn Oceanfront 905 S Atlantic Ave	Daytona Beach	FL	32118	**888-558-5577**	386-255-5432
Hilton Daytona Beach Oceanfront Resort 2637 S Atlantic Ave	Daytona Beach	FL	32118	**800-525-7350**	386-767-7350

Classified Section

				Toll-Free	Phone
Hilton Garden Inn Daytona Beach Airport 189 Midway Ave	Daytona Beach	FL	32114	**877-782-9444**	386-944-4000
Holiday Inn at Indigo Lakes 2620 W International Speedway Blvd	Daytona Beach	FL	32114	**800-465-4329**	386-258-6333
Inn on the Beach 1615 S Atlantic Ave	Daytona Beach	FL	32118	**800-874-0975**	386-255-0921
Radisson Resort Daytona Beach 640 N Atlantic Ave	Daytona Beach	FL	32118	**800-333-3333**	386-239-9800
Tropical Winds Oceanfront Hotel 1398 N Atlantic Ave	Daytona Beach	FL	32118	**800-245-6099**	386-258-1016
Bahama House 2001 S Atlantic Ave	Daytona Beach Shores	FL	32118	**800-571-2001**	386-248-2001
Best Western Aku Tiki Inn 2225 S Atlantic Ave	Daytona Beach Shores	FL	32118	**800-258-8454**	386-252-9631
Castaways Beach Resort 2043 S Atlantic Ave	Daytona Beach Shores	FL	32118	**866-254-2722**	386-254-8480
Hawaiian Inn 2301 S Atlantic Ave	Daytona Beach Shores	FL	32118	**800-457-0077**	386-255-5411
Holiday Inn Daytona Beach Shores 3209 S Atlantic Ave	Daytona Beach Shores	FL	32118	**800-465-4329**	386-761-2050
Palm Plaza Oceanfront Resort 3301 S Atlantic Ave	Daytona Beach Shores	FL	32118	**800-329-8662**	386-767-1711
Sun Viking Lodge 2411 S Atlantic Ave	Daytona Beach Shores	FL	32118	**800-874-4469**	386-252-6252
Treasure Island Resort 2025 S Atlantic Ave	Daytona Beach Shores	FL	32118	**800-543-5070**	386-255-8371
Embassy Suites Deerfield Beach 950 SE 20th Ave	Deerfield Beach	FL	33441	**800-362-2779**	954-426-0478
Howard Johnson Ocean Plaza Resort 2096 NE 2nd St	Deerfield Beach	FL	33441	**800-426-0084**	954-428-2850
Colony Hotel & Cabana Club 525 E Atlantic Ave	Delray Beach	FL	33483	**800-552-2363**	561-276-4123
Marriott Delray Beach 10 N Ocean Blvd	Delray Beach	FL	33483	**800-228-9290**	561-274-3200
Seagate Hotel & Beach Club 400 S Ocean Blvd	Delray Beach	FL	33483	**800-233-3581**	561-276-2421
Bahia Mar Beach Resort 801 Seabreeze Blvd	Fort Lauderdale	FL	33316	**800-333-3333**	954-764-2233
Beach Plaza Hotel 625 N Atlantic Blvd	Fort Lauderdale	FL	33304	**800-451-4711**	954-566-7631
Best Western Marina Inn & Yacht Harbor 2150 SE 17th St	Fort Lauderdale	FL	33316	**800-327-1390**	954-525-3484
Best Western Pelican Beach Resort 2000 N Atlantic Blvd	Fort Lauderdale	FL	33305	**800-525-6298**	954-568-9431
Best Western Rolling Hills Resort 3501 W Rolling Hills Cir	Fort Lauderdale	FL	33328	**800-327-7735**	954-475-0400
Courtyard Fort Lauderdale North/Cypress Creek 2440 W Cypress Creek Rd	Fort Lauderdale	FL	33309	**800-321-2211**	954-772-7770
Days Inn Bahia Cabana Beach Resort & Marina 3001 Harbor Dr	Fort Lauderdale	FL	33316	**800-323-2244**	954-524-1555
Doubletree Guest Suites Fort Lauderdale-Galleria 2670 E Sunrise Blvd	Fort Lauderdale	FL	33304	**800-222-8733**	954-565-3800
Embassy Suites Fort Lauderdale 1100 SE 17th St	Fort Lauderdale	FL	33316	**800-362-2779**	954-527-2700
Fort Lauderdale Oceanfront Hotel 440 Seabreeze Blvd	Fort Lauderdale	FL	33316	**800-222-8733**	954-524-8733
Holiday Inn Fort Lauderdale Beach 999 Fort Lauderdale Beach Blvd	Fort Lauderdale	FL	33304	**800-465-4329**	954-563-5961
Howard Johnson Ocean Edge Resort 700 N Fort Lauderdale Beach Blvd	Fort Lauderdale	FL	33304	**800-327-8578**	954-563-2451
Ireland's Inn Resort Hotel 2220 N Atlantic Blvd	Fort Lauderdale	FL	33305	**800-347-7776**	954-565-6661
Marriott Fort Lauderdale Marina 1881 SE 17th St	Fort Lauderdale	FL	33316	**800-228-9290**	954-463-4000
Marriott Fort Lauderdale North 6650 N Andrews Ave	Fort Lauderdale	FL	33309	**800-228-9290**	954-771-0440
Marriott's Beachplace Towers 21 S Fort Lauderdale Beach Blvd	Fort Lauderdale	FL	33316	**800-854-5279**	954-525-4440
Ocean Manor Resort 4040 Galt Ocean Dr	Fort Lauderdale	FL	33308	**800-955-0444**	954-566-7500
Pillars Hotel at New River Sound 111 N Birch Rd	Fort Lauderdale	FL	33304	**800-800-7666**	954-467-9639
Ramada Plaza Fort Lauderdale Beach Resort 4060 Galt Ocean Dr	Fort Lauderdale	FL	33308	**800-678-9022**	954-565-6611
Renaissance Fort Lauderdale Hotel 1617 SE 17th St	Fort Lauderdale	FL	33316	**888-503-7669**	954-626-1700
Riverside Hotel 620 E Las Olas Blvd	Fort Lauderdale	FL	33301	**800-325-3280**	954-467-0671
Sheraton Suites Cypress Creek Fort Lauderdale 555 NW 62nd St	Fort Lauderdale	FL	33309	**800-325-3535**	954-772-5400
Sheraton Yankee Clipper Hotel 1140 Seabreeze Blvd	Fort Lauderdale	FL	33316	**800-958-5551**	954-524-5551
Sheraton Yankee Trader Hotel 321 N Fort Lauderdale Beach Blvd	Fort Lauderdale	FL	33304	**800-325-3535**	954-467-1111
Westin Fort Lauderdale 400 Corporate Dr	Fort Lauderdale	FL	33334	**800-937-8461**	954-772-1331
Holiday Inn Select Fort Myers Airport 13051 Bell Tower Dr	Fort Myers	FL	33907	**800-465-4329**	239-482-2900
Holiday Inn SunSpree Resort Fort Walton Beach 573 Santa Rosa Blvd	Fort Walton Beach	FL	32548	**800-238-8686**	850-244-8686
Howard Johnson Plaza Hotel 7707 NW 103rd St	Hialeah	FL	33016	**800-446-4656**	305-825-1000
Ramada Hollywood Beach Resort Hotel 101 N Ocean Dr	Hollywood	FL	33019	**800-331-6103**	954-921-0990
Holiday Inn Hollywood Beach 2711 S Ocean Dr	Hollywood Beach	FL	33019	**800-237-4667**	954-923-8700
Adam's Mark Jacksonville 225 E Coastline Dr	Jacksonville	FL	32202	**800-444-2326**	904-633-9095
AmeriSuites Jacksonville Baymeadows 8277 Western Way Cir	Jacksonville	FL	32256	**800-833-1516**	904-737-4477
Clarion Hotel Jacksonville Airport Conference Center 2101 Dixie Clipper Rd	Jacksonville	FL	32218	**800-234-2398**	904-741-1997
Courtyard Jacksonville Airport/Northeast 14668 Duval Rd	Jacksonville	FL	32218	**800-321-2211**	904-741-1122
Courtyard Mayo Clinic Jacksonville & Beaches Area 4600 San Pablo Rd	Jacksonville	FL	32224	**800-321-2211**	904-223-1700
Embassy Suites Jacksonville-Baymeadows 9300 Baymeadows Rd	Jacksonville	FL	32256	**800-362-2779**	904-731-3555
Hilton Garden Inn Jacksonville Airport 13503 Ranch Rd	Jacksonville	FL	32218	**877-782-9444**	904-421-2700
Hilton Garden Inn Jacksonville JTB/Deerwood Park 9745 Gate Pkwy N	Jacksonville	FL	32246	**877-782-9444**	904-997-6600
Hilton Jacksonville Riverfront 1201 Riverplace Blvd	Jacksonville	FL	32207	**800-445-8667**	904-398-8800
Holiday Inn Jacksonville Airport 14670 Duval Rd	Jacksonville	FL	32218	**800-465-4329**	904-741-4404
Hyatt Regency Jacksonville Riverfront 225 Coast Line Dr	Jacksonville	FL	32202	**800-233-1234**	904-588-1234
Inn at Mayo Clinic 4400 San Pablo Rd	Jacksonville	FL	32224	**888-255-4458**	904-992-9992
Marriott Jacksonville 4670 Salisbury Rd	Jacksonville	FL	32256	**800-584-2842**	904-296-2222
Omni Jacksonville Hotel 245 Water St	Jacksonville	FL	32202	**800-843-6664**	904-355-6664
Radisson Riverwalk Hotel Jacksonville 1515 Prudential Dr	Jacksonville	FL	32207	**800-333-3333**	904-396-5100
Wingate Inn Jacksonville South 4681 Lenoir Ave	Jacksonville	FL	32216	**800-228-1000**	904-281-2600
Marriott Miami Dadeland 9090 S Dadeland Blvd	Kendall	FL	33156	**800-228-9290**	305-670-1035
Marina Del Mar Resort & Marina 527 Caribbean Dr	Key Largo	FL	33037	**800-451-3483**	305-451-4107
Alexander Palms Court 715 South St	Key West	FL	33040	**800-858-1943**	305-296-6413
Ambrosia House Tropical Lodging 615 Fleming St	Key West	FL	33040	**800-535-9838**	305-296-9838
Banyan Resort 323 Whitehead St	Key West	FL	33040	**800-853-9937**	305-296-7786
Blue Marlin Motel 1320 Simonton St	Key West	FL	33040	**800-523-1698**	305-294-2585
Blue Parrot Inn 916 Elizabeth St	Key West	FL	33040	**800-231-2473**	305-296-0033
Center Court Historic Inn & Cottages 915 Center St	Key West	FL	33040	**800-797-8787**	305-296-9292
Conch House Heritage Inn 625 Truman Ave	Key West	FL	33040	**800-207-5806**	305-293-0020
Crowne Plaza Key West La Concha Hotel 430 Duval St	Key West	FL	33040	**800-745-2191**	305-296-2991
Eden House 1015 Fleming St	Key West	FL	33040	**800-533-5397**	305-296-6868
Gardens Hotel 526 Angela St	Key West	FL	33040	**800-526-2664**	305-294-2661
Holiday Inn Key West Beachside 3841 N Roosevelt Blvd	Key West	FL	33040	**800-292-7706**	305-294-2571
Key Lime Inn 725 Truman Ave	Key West	FL	33040	**800-594-4430**	305-294-5229
Marquesa Hotel 600 Fleming St	Key West	FL	33040	**800-869-4631**	305-292-1919
Paradise Inn 819 Simonton St	Key West	FL	33040	**800-888-9648**	305-293-8007
Pegasus International Hotel 501 Southard St	Key West	FL	33040	**800-397-8148**	305-294-9323
Radisson Hotel Key West 3820 N Roosevelt Blvd	Key West	FL	33040	**800-333-3333**	305-294-5511
Sheraton Suites Key West 2001 S Roosevelt Blvd	Key West	FL	33040	**800-452-3224**	305-292-9800
Simonton Court Historic Inn & Cottages 320 Simonton St	Key West	FL	33040	**800-944-2687**	305-294-6386
Southernmost On the Beach 508 South St	Key West	FL	33040	**800-354-4455**	305-296-5611
Southernmost Motel 1319 Duval St	Key West	FL	33040	**800-354-4455**	305-296-6577
Sunrise Suites Resort 3685 Seaside Dr	Key West	FL	33040	**800-723-5200**	305-296-6661
AmeriSuites Orlando/Lake Buena Vista S 4991 Calypso Cay Way	Kissimmee	FL	34746	**800-833-1516**	407-997-1300
Celebrity Resorts Orlando 2800 N Poinciana Blvd	Kissimmee	FL	34746	**800-423-8604**	407-997-5000
Clarion Hotel Maingate 7675 W Irlo Bronson Memorial Hwy	Kissimmee	FL	34747	**800-568-3352**	407-396-4000
Doubletree Resort Orlando-Villas at Maingate 4787 W Irlo Bronson Memorial Hwy	Kissimmee	FL	34746	**800-222-8733**	407-397-0555
Hyatt Orlando 6375 W Irlo Bronson Memorial Hwy	Kissimmee	FL	34747	**800-233-1234**	407-396-1234
Star Island Resort 5000 Avenue of the Stars	Kissimmee	FL	34746	**800-513-2820**	407-997-8000
Best Western Lake Buena Vista Resort Hotel 2000 Hotel Plaza Blvd	Lake Buena Vista	FL	32830	**800-348-3765**	407-828-2424
Courtyard LBV at Walt Disney 1805 Hotel Plaza Blvd	Lake Buena Vista	FL	32830	**800-223-9930**	407-828-8888
Disney's Saratoga Springs Resort & Spa 1960 Broadway St	Lake Buena Vista	FL	32830	**800-282-9282**	407-827-1100
Doubletree Guest Suites in the Walt Disney World Resort 2305 Hotel Plaza Blvd	Lake Buena Vista	FL	32830	**800-222-8733**	407-934-1000
Grosvenor Resort at Walt Disney World Village 1850 Hotel Plaza Blvd	Lake Buena Vista	FL	32830	**800-624-4109**	407-828-4444
Hilton in the Walt Disney World Resort 1751 Hotel Plaza Blvd	Lake Buena Vista	FL	32830	**800-445-8667**	407-827-4000
Hotel Royal Plaza PO Box 22203	Lake Buena Vista	FL	32830	**800-248-7890**	407-828-2828
GulfStream Hotel 1 Lake Ave	Lake Worth	FL	33460	**888-540-0669**	561-540-6000
Little Inn by the Sea 4546 El Mar Dr	Lauderdale-by-the-Sea	FL	33308	**800-492-0311**	954-772-2450
Pier Pointe Resort 4320 El Mar Dr	Lauderdale-by-the-Sea	FL	33308	**800-331-6384**	954-776-5121
Sheraton Orlando North Hotel 600 N Lake Destiny Dr	Maitland	FL	32751	**800-325-3535**	407-660-9000
Airport Regency Hotel 1000 NW Lejeune Rd	Miami	FL	33126	**800-367-1039**	305-441-1600
AmeriSuites Miami Airport West 3655 NW 82nd Ave	Miami	FL	33166	**800-833-1516**	305-718-8292
Clarion Hotel & Suites Miami 100 SE 4th St	Miami	FL	33131	**800-424-6423**	305-374-5100
Crowne Plaza Hotel Miami International Airport 950 NW Le Jeune Rd	Miami	FL	33126	**800-227-6963**	305-446-9000
Doubletree Grand Hotel Biscayne Bay 1717 N Bayshore Dr	Miami	FL	33132	**800-222-8733**	305-372-0313
Doubletree Hotel Coconut Grove 2649 S Bayshore Dr	Miami	FL	33133	**800-222-8733**	305-858-2500
Embassy Suites Miami International Airport 3974 NW South River Dr	Miami	FL	33142	**800-362-2779**	305-634-5000
Hilton Miami Airport & Towers 5101 Blue Lagoon Dr	Miami	FL	33126	**800-445-8667**	305-262-1000
Holiday Inn Marina Park Hotel 340 Biscayne Blvd	Miami	FL	33132	**800-526-5655**	305-371-4400
Hotel Sofitel Miami 5800 Blue Lagoon Dr	Miami	FL	33126	**800-763-4835**	305-264-4888
Hyatt Regency Miami 400 SE 2nd Ave	Miami	FL	33131	**800-233-1234**	305-358-1234
InterContinental Miami 100 Chopin Plaza	Miami	FL	33131	**888-567-8725**	305-577-1000
JW Marriott Hotel Miami 1109 Brickell Ave	Miami	FL	33131	**800-228-9290**	305-374-1224
Mandarin Oriental Miami 500 Brickell Key Dr	Miami	FL	33131	**800-526-6566**	305-913-8288
Marriott Biscayne Bay 1633 N Bayshore Dr	Miami	FL	33132	**800-228-9290**	305-374-3900
Marriott Miami Airport 1201 NW Le Jeune Rd	Miami	FL	33126	**800-228-9290**	305-649-5000
Miami International Airport Hotel NW 20th St & Le Jeune Rd	Miami	FL	33122	**800-327-1276**	305-871-4100
Mutiny Hotel 2951 S Bayshore Dr	Miami	FL	33133	**888-868-8469**	305-441-2100
Radisson Hotel Miami Downtown 1601 Biscayne Blvd	Miami	FL	33132	**800-333-3333**	305-374-0000
Radisson Mart Plaza Hotel & Convention Center-Miami Airport 711 NW 72nd Ave	Miami	FL	33126	**800-333-3333**	305-261-3800
Riande Continental Miami Bayside Hotel 146 Biscayne Blvd	Miami	FL	33132	**800-742-6331**	305-358-4555
Riu Hotel Florida Beach 3101 Collins Ave	Miami	FL	33140	**888-666-8816**	305-673-5333
Sheraton Biscayne Bay Hotel 495 Brickell Ave	Miami	FL	33131	**800-325-3535**	305-373-6000
Summerfield Suites by Wyndham Miami Airport 5710 Blue Lagoon Dr	Miami	FL	33126	**800-833-4353**	305-269-1922

Florida (Cont'd)

Name / Address	City	State	ZIP	Toll-Free	Phone
Wyndham Grand Bay Hotel Coconut Grove 2669 S Bayshore Dr	Miami	FL	33133	**888-472-6229**	305-858-9600
Wyndham Miami Airport Hotel 3900 NW 21st St	Miami	FL	33142	**800-996-3426**	305-871-3800
Abbey Hotel 300 21st St	Miami Beach	FL	33139	**888-612-2239**	305-531-0031
Albion Hotel 1650 James Ave	Miami Beach	FL	33139	**888-665-0008**	305-913-1000
Alexander Hotel 5225 Collins Ave	Miami Beach	FL	33140	**800-327-6121**	305-865-6500
Avalon Majestic 700 Ocean Dr	Miami Beach	FL	33139	**800-933-3306**	305-538-0133
Barbizon Suites 530 Ocean Dr	Miami Beach	FL	33139	**800-478-6082**	305-673-1173
Beachcomber Hotel 1340 Collins Ave	Miami Beach	FL	33139	**866-859-4177**	305-531-3755
Beacon Hotel 720 Ocean Dr	Miami Beach	FL	33139	**877-674-8200**	305-674-8200
Beekman Hotel-Suites on the Ocean 9499 Collins Ave	Miami Beach	FL	33154	**800-237-9367**	305-861-4801
Bentley Beach Hotel 101 Ocean Dr	Miami Beach	FL	33139	**866-236-8539**	305-938-4600
Bentley Hotel 510 Ocean Dr	Miami Beach	FL	33139	**800-236-8510**	305-538-1700
Blue Moon Hotel 944 Collins Ave	Miami Beach	FL	33139	**800-724-1623**	305-673-2262
Capri Miami Beach Condo-Hotel 3010 Collins Ave	Miami Beach	FL	33140	**800-528-0823**	305-531-7742
Casa Grande Suite Hotel 834 Ocean Dr	Miami Beach	FL	33139	**800-688-7678**	305-672-7003
Castillo del Mar Resort 5445 Collins Ave	Miami Beach	FL	33140	**888-352-3224**	305-865-1500
Chesterfield Hotel 855 Collins Ave	Miami Beach	FL	33139	**800-244-6088**	305-531-5831
Crest Hotel & Suites 1670 James Ave	Miami Beach	FL	33139	**800-531-3880**	305-531-0321
Crystal Beach Suites & Health Club 6985 Collins Ave	Miami Beach	FL	33141	**800-435-0766**	305-865-9555
Delano The 1685 Collins Ave	Miami Beach	FL	33139	**800-555-5001**	305-538-7881
Doubletree Surfcomber Hotel Miami-South Beach 1717 Collins Ave	Miami Beach	FL	33139	**800-222-8733**	305-532-7715
Holiday Inn South Beach 2201 Collins Ave	Miami Beach	FL	33139	**800-356-6902**	305-779-3200
Hotel Astor 956 Washington Ave	Miami Beach	FL	33139	**800-270-4981**	305-531-8081
Hotel Edison 960 Ocean Dr	Miami Beach	FL	33139	**800-961-9076**	305-531-2744
Hotel Ocean 1230 Ocean Dr	Miami Beach	FL	33139	**800-783-1725**	305-672-2579
Hotel Shelley 844 Collins Ave	Miami Beach	FL	33139	**800-414-0612**	305-531-3341
Howard Johnson Plaza Hotel Dezerland Beach & Spa 8701 Collins Ave	Miami Beach	FL	33154	**800-331-9346**	305-865-6661
Indian Creek Hotel 2727 Indian Creek Dr	Miami Beach	FL	33140	**800-491-2772**	305-531-2727
Kent The 1131 Collins Ave	Miami Beach	FL	33139	**800-688-7678**	305-604-5068
La Flora Hotel 1238 Collins Ave	Miami Beach	FL	33139	**877-523-5672**	305-531-3406
Lily Guesthouse 835 Collins Ave	Miami Beach	FL	33139	**888-742-6600**	305-535-9900
Loews Miami Beach Hotel 1601 Collins Ave	Miami Beach	FL	33139	**800-235-6397**	305-604-1601
Marlin Hotel 1200 Collins Ave	Miami Beach	FL	33139	**800-688-7678**	305-604-5063
Marseilles Hotel 1741 Collins Ave	Miami Beach	FL	33139	**800-327-4739**	305-538-5711
Mercury Resort 100 Collins Ave	Miami Beach	FL	33139	**877-786-2732**	305-398-3000
National Hotel 1677 Collins Ave	Miami Beach	FL	33139	**800-327-8370**	305-532-2311
Newport Beachside Hotel & Resort 16701 Collins Ave	Miami Beach	FL	33160	**800-327-5476**	305-949-1300
Ocean Five Hotel 436 Ocean Dr	Miami Beach	FL	33139	**888-531-8122**	305-532-7093
Palms The 3025 Collins Ave	Miami Beach	FL	33140	**800-550-0505**	305-534-0505
Park Central The 640 Ocean Dr	Miami Beach	FL	33139	**800-727-5236**	305-538-1611
Penguin Hotel 1418 Ocean Dr	Miami Beach	FL	33139	**800-235-3296**	305-534-9334
President Hotel 1423 Collins Ave	Miami Beach	FL	33139	**800-235-3296**	305-538-2882
Richmond The 1757 Collins Ave	Miami Beach	FL	33139	**800-327-3163**	305-538-2331
Ritz Plaza Hotel 1701 Collins Ave	Miami Beach	FL	33139	**800-522-6400**	305-534-3500
Royal Hotel South Beach 758 Washington Ave	Miami Beach	FL	33139	**888-394-6835**	305-673-9009
Savoy on South Beach 425 Ocean Dr	Miami Beach	FL	33139	**800-237-2869**	305-532-0200
Seacoast Suites Hotel 5101 Collins Ave	Miami Beach	FL	33140	**800-969-6329**	305-865-5152
Shelborne Beach Resort 1801 Collins Ave	Miami Beach	FL	33139	**800-327-8757**	305-531-1271
South Seas Hotel 1751 Collins Ave	Miami Beach	FL	33139	**800-345-2678**	305-538-1411
Tides The 1220 Ocean Dr	Miami Beach	FL	33139	**800-688-7678**	305-604-5070
Traymore Hotel 2445 Collins Ave	Miami Beach	FL	33140	**800-445-1512**	305-534-7111
Waldorf Towers Hotel 860 Ocean Dr	Miami Beach	FL	33139	**800-933-2322**	305-531-7684
Wyndham Miami Beach Resort 4833 Collins Ave	Miami Beach	FL	33140	**800-203-8368**	305-532-3600
Courtyard Miami Lakes 15700 NW 77th Ct	Miami Lakes	FL	33016	**800-321-2211**	305-556-6665
Wellesley Inn Miami Lakes 7925 NW 154th St	Miami Lakes	FL	33016	**800-444-8888**	305-821-8274
Hilton Garden Inn Fort Lauderdale/Miramar 14501 Hotel Rd	Miramar	FL	33027	**877-782-9444**	954-438-7700
Lakeside Inn 100 N Alexander St	Mount Dora	FL	32757	**800-556-5016**	352-383-4101
Courtyard Naples 3250 Tamiami Trail N	Naples	FL	34103	**800-321-2211**	239-434-8700
Cove Inn 900 Broad Ave S	Naples	FL	34102	**800-255-4365**	239-262-7161
Doubletree Guest Suites Naples 12200 Tamiami Trail N	Naples	FL	34110	**800-222-8733**	239-593-8733
Edgewater Beach Hotel 1901 Gulf Shore Blvd N	Naples	FL	34102	**800-821-0196**	239-403-2000
Grand Inn 1100 Pine Ridge Rd	Naples	FL	34108	**877-430-3500**	239-430-3500
Inn on Fifth 699 5th Ave S	Naples	FL	34102	**888-403-8778**	239-403-8777
Inn at Pelican Bay 800 Vanderbilt Beach Rd	Naples	FL	34108	**800-597-8770**	239-597-8777
Quality Inn & Suites at Park Shore 4055 Tamiami Trail N	Naples	FL	34103	**800-895-8858**	239-649-5500
Trianon Old Naples 955 7th Ave S	Naples	FL	34102	**877-482-5228**	239-435-9600
Vanderbilt Inn on the Gulf 11000 Gulf Shore Dr N	Naples	FL	34108	**800-643-8654**	239-597-3151
Hilton Tampa Bay/North Redington Beach Resort 17120 Gulf Blvd	North Redington Beach	FL	33708	**800-445-8667**	727-391-4000
Adam's Mark Orlando 1500 Sand Lake Rd	Orlando	FL	32809	**800-444-2326**	407-859-1500
Buena Vista Suites 8203 World Center Dr	Orlando	FL	32821	**800-537-7737**	407-239-8588
Caribe Royale Resort Suites 8101 World Center Dr	Orlando	FL	32821	**800-823-8300**	407-238-8000
Courtyard Orlando Airport 7155 N Frontage Rd	Orlando	FL	32812	**800-321-2211**	407-240-7200
Courtyard Orlando International Drive 8600 Austrian Ct	Orlando	FL	32819	**800-321-2211**	407-351-2244
Doubletree Club Lake Buena Vista 12490 Apopka Vineland Rd	Orlando	FL	32836	**800-222-8733**	407-239-4646
Embassy Suites Orlando Downtown 191 E Pine St	Orlando	FL	32801	**800-362-2779**	407-841-1000
Embassy Suites Orlando/Lake Buena Vista Resort 8100 Lake Ave	Orlando	FL	32836	**800-257-8483**	407-239-1144
Enclave Suites of Orlando 6165 Carrier Dr	Orlando	FL	32819	**800-457-0077**	407-351-1155
Extended Stay Deluxe-Orlando Convention Center 8750 Universal Blvd	Orlando	FL	32819	**888-387-8420**	407-903-1500
Hard Rock Hotel at Universal Orlando - A Loews Hotel 5800 Universal Blvd	Orlando	FL	32819	**877-819-7884**	407-503-7625
Hilton Garden Inn Orlando Airport 7300 Augusta National Dr	Orlando	FL	32822	**877-782-9444**	407-240-3725
Hilton Garden Inn Orlando East/UCF 1959 N Alafaya Tr	Orlando	FL	32826	**877-782-9444**	407-992-5000
Hilton Garden Inn Orlando International Drive North 5877 American Way	Orlando	FL	32819	**877-782-9444**	407-363-9332
Holiday Inn Select Orlando International Airport 5750 TG Lee Blvd	Orlando	FL	32822	**800-465-4329**	407-851-6400
Holiday Inn Select Orlando-University Central 12125 High Tech Ave. *Resv	Orlando	FL	32817	**800-465-4329***	407-275-9000
Hyatt Regency Orlando International Airport 9300 Airport Blvd	Orlando	FL	32827	**800-233-1234**	407-825-1234
Marriott Orlando Airport 7499 Augusta National Dr	Orlando	FL	32822	**800-228-9290**	407-851-9000
Marriott Orlando Downtown 400 W Livingston St	Orlando	FL	32801	**800-574-3160**	407-843-6664
Peabody Orlando 9801 International Dr	Orlando	FL	32819	**800-732-2639**	407-352-4000
Portofino Bay Hotel at Universal Orlando - A Loews Hotel 5601 Universal Blvd	Orlando	FL	32819	**800-837-2273**	407-503-1000
Radisson Barcelo Hotel Orlando 8444 International Dr	Orlando	FL	32819	**800-333-3333**	407-345-0505
Renaissance Orlando Hotel-Airport 5445 Forbes Pl	Orlando	FL	32812	**800-228-9290**	407-240-1000
Ritz-Carlton Orlando Grande Lakes 4012 Central Florida Pkwy	Orlando	FL	32837	**800-241-3333**	407-206-2400
Rosen Centre Hotel 9840 International Dr	Orlando	FL	32819	**800-800-9840**	407-996-9840
Rosen Plaza Hotel 9700 International Dr	Orlando	FL	32819	**800-366-9700**	407-996-9700
Royal Pacific Resort - A Loews Hotel 6300 Hollywood Way	Orlando	FL	32819	**800-645-6397**	407-503-3000
Sheraton Safari Hotel Lake Buena Vista 12205 Apopka-Vineland Rd	Orlando	FL	32836	**800-325-3535**	407-239-0444
Sheraton Studio City Hotel 5905 International Dr	Orlando	FL	32819	**800-325-3535**	407-351-2100
Staybridge Suites International Drive 8480 International Dr	Orlando	FL	32819	**800-866-4549**	407-352-2400
Staybridge Suites Lake Buena Vista 8751 Suiteside Dr	Orlando	FL	32836	**800-866-4549**	407-238-0777
Westin Grand Bohemian Orlando 325 S Orange Ave	Orlando	FL	32801	**800-937-8461**	407-313-9000
Brazilian Court Hotel 301 Australian Ave	Palm Beach	FL	33480	**800-552-0335**	561-655-7740
Chesterfield Hotel 363 Cocoanut Row	Palm Beach	FL	33480	**800-243-7871**	561-659-5800
Colony Hotel 155 Hammon Ave	Palm Beach	FL	33480	**800-521-5525**	561-655-5430
Hilton Palm Beach Oceanfront Resort 2842 S Ocean Blvd	Palm Beach	FL	33480	**800-433-1718**	561-586-6542
Plaza Inn 215 Brazilian Ave. *Resv	Palm Beach	FL	33480	**800-233-2632***	561-832-8666
Doubletree Hotel Palm Beach Gardens 4431 PGA Blvd	Palm Beach Gardens	FL	33410	**800-222-8733**	561-622-2260
Marriott Palm Beach Gardens 4000 RCA Blvd	Palm Beach Gardens	FL	33410	**800-228-9290**	561-622-8888
Courtyard Pensacola 451 Creighton Rd	Pensacola	FL	32504	**800-321-2211**	850-857-7744
Dunes Hotel 333 Fort Pickens Rd	Pensacola Beach	FL	32561	**800-833-8637**	850-932-3536
Hilton Garden Inn Pensacola Beach 12 Via de Luna Dr	Pensacola Beach	FL	32561	**866-916-2999**	850-916-2999
Courtyard Fort Lauderdale/Plantation 7780 SW 6th St	Plantation	FL	33324	**800-321-2211**	954-475-1100
Holiday Inn Plantation/Sawgrass 1711 N University Dr	Plantation	FL	33322	**800-465-4329**	954-472-5600
Renaissance Fort Lauderdale-Plantation Hotel 1230 S Pine Island Rd	Plantation	FL	33324	**800-316-7708**	954-472-2252
Sheraton Suites Plantation-Fort Lauderdale 311 N University Dr	Plantation	FL	33324	**800-325-3535**	954-424-3300
Best Western Beachcomber Hotel & Villas 1200 S Ocean Blvd	Pompano Beach	FL	33062	**800-231-2423**	954-941-7830
Hilton Garden Inn Jacksonville/Pointe Vedra 45 PGA Blvd	Ponte Vedra Beach	FL	32082	**877-782-9444**	904-280-1661
Anastasia Inn 218 Anastasia Blvd	Saint Augustine	FL	32080	**888-226-6181**	904-825-2879
Bayfront Inn 138 Avenida Menendez	Saint Augustine	FL	32084	**800-558-3455**	904-824-1681
Beacher's Lodge 6970 US Hwy A1A S	Saint Augustine	FL	32080	**800-527-8849**	904-471-8849
Casa Monica Hotel 95 Cordova St	Saint Augustine	FL	32084	**888-472-6312**	904-827-1888
Conch House Marina Resort 57 Comares Ave	Saint Augustine	FL	32080	**800-940-6256**	904-829-8646
Hilton Garden Inn Saint Augustine Beach 401 A1A Beach Blvd	Saint Augustine	FL	32080	**877-782-9444**	904-471-5559
Inn at Camachee Harbor 201 Yacht Club Dr	Saint Augustine	FL	32084	**800-688-5379**	904-825-0003
Alden Beach Resort 5900 Gulf Blvd	Saint Pete Beach	FL	33706	**800-237-2530**	727-360-7081
Beach House Suites by the Don Cesar 3680 Gulf Blvd	Saint Pete Beach	FL	33706	**800-282-1116**	727-363-0001
Best Western Beachfront Resort 6200 Gulf Blvd	Saint Pete Beach	FL	33706	**800-544-4222**	727-367-1902
Coral Reef Resort 5800 Gulf Blvd	Saint Pete Beach	FL	33706	**800-352-4874**	727-363-1604
Dolphin Beach Resort 4900 Gulf Blvd	Saint Pete Beach	FL	33706	**800-237-8916**	727-360-7011
Holiday Inn Hotel & Suites Saint Petersburg Beach 5250 Gulf Blvd	Saint Pete Beach	FL	33706	**800-448-0901**	727-360-1811
Hilton Saint Petersburg Bayfront 333 1st St S	Saint Petersburg	FL	33701	**800-944-5500**	727-894-5000
Helmsley Sandcastle Hotel 1540 Ben Franklin Dr	Sarasota	FL	34236	**800-225-2181**	941-388-2181
Hyatt Sarasota 1000 Blvd of the Arts	Sarasota	FL	34236	**800-233-1234**	941-953-1234
Ritz-Carlton Sarasota 1111 Ritz-Carlton Dr	Sarasota	FL	34236	**800-241-3333**	941-309-2000
Crowne Plaza Oceanfront Singer Island 3200 N Ocean Dr	Singer Island	FL	33404	**800-327-0522**	561-842-6171
Hilton Singer Island Oceanfront 3700 N Ocean Dr	Singer Island	FL	33404	**800-941-3592**	561-848-3888
Ramada Plaza Marco Polo Beach Resort 19201 Collins Ave	Sunny Isles	FL	33160	**800-272-6232**	305-932-2233
Doubletree Ocean Point Resort & Spa 17375 Collins Ave	Sunny Isles Beach	FL	33360	**866-623-2678**	305-940-5422
Trump International Sonesta Beach Resort 18101 Collins Ave	Sunny Isles Beach	FL	33160	**800-766-3782**	305-692-5600
Crowne Plaza Hotel Sunrise-Sawgrass Mills 13400 W Sunrise Blvd	Sunrise	FL	33323	**888-633-1956**	954-851-1020
Hilton Fort Lauderdale/Sunrise 3003 N University Dr	Sunrise	FL	33322	**800-445-8667**	954-748-7000
Best Western Seminole Inn 6737 Mahan Dr	Tallahassee	FL	32308	**800-996-6537**	850-656-2938
Cabot Lodge Tallahassee North 2735 N Monroe St	Tallahassee	FL	32303	**800-223-1964**	850-386-8880
Comfort Inn Tallahassee 2727 Graves Rd	Tallahassee	FL	32303	**800-228-5150**	850-562-7200
Courtyard Tallahassee Capital 1018 Apalachee Pkwy	Tallahassee	FL	32301	**800-321-2211**	850-222-8822
Doubletree Hotel Tallahassee 101 S Adams St	Tallahassee	FL	32301	**800-222-8733**	850-224-5000
Hilton Garden Inn Tallahassee 3333 Thomasville Rd	Tallahassee	FL	32308	**877-782-9444**	850-385-3553

Classified Section

Name / Address	City	State	ZIP	Toll-Free	Phone
Holiday Inn Select Tallahassee Downtown Capitol 316 W Tennessee St	Tallahassee	FL	32301	**800-648-6135**	850-222-9555
Holiday Inn Tallahassee NW 2714 Graves Rd	Tallahassee	FL	32303	**800-465-4329**	850-562-2000
La Quinta Inn Tallahassee North 2905 N Monroe St	Tallahassee	FL	32303	**800-531-5900**	850-385-7172
Quality Inn & Suites Tallahassee 2020 Apalachee Pkwy	Tallahassee	FL	32301	**800-228-5151**	850-877-4437
Radisson Hotel Tallahassee 415 N Monroe St	Tallahassee	FL	32301	**800-333-3333**	850-224-6000
AmeriSuites Tampa Airport Westshore 4811 W Main St	Tampa	FL	33607	**800-833-1516**	813-282-1037
AmeriSuites Tampa Near Busch Gardens 11408 N 30th St	Tampa	FL	33612	**800-833-1516**	813-979-1922
Best Western Westshore Hotel 1200 N Westshore Blvd	Tampa	FL	33607	**800-528-1234**	813-282-3636
Courtyard Tampa Westshore 3805 W Cypress St	Tampa	FL	33607	**800-321-2211**	813-874-0555
Doubletree Guest Suites Tampa Bay 3050 North Rocky Point Dr W	Tampa	FL	33607	**800-222-8733**	813-888-8800
Doubletree Guest Suites Tampa Near Busch Gardens 11310 N 30th St	Tampa	FL	33612	**800-222-8733**	813-971-7690
Doubletree Hotel Tampa Westshore Airport 4500 W Cypress St	Tampa	FL	33607	**800-222-8733**	813-879-4800
Embassy Suites Tampa Airport-Westshore 555 N Westshore Blvd	Tampa	FL	33609	**800-362-2779**	813-875-1555
Grand Hyatt Tampa Bay 6200 Courtney Campbell Cswy	Tampa	FL	33607	**800-233-1234**	813-874-1234
Hilton Garden Inn Tampa East/Brandon 10309 Highland Manor Dr	Tampa	FL	33610	**877-782-9444**	813-626-6700
Hilton Tampa Airport Westshore 2225 N Lois Ave	Tampa	FL	33607	**800-345-6565**	813-877-6688
Hyatt Regency Tampa 211 N Tampa St	Tampa	FL	33602	**800-233-1234**	813-225-1234
Marriott Tampa Airport Tampa International Airport	Tampa	FL	33607	**800-228-9290**	813-879-5151
Marriott Tampa Waterside 700 S Florida Ave	Tampa	FL	33602	**800-228-9290**	813-221-4900
Marriott Tampa Westshore 1001 N Westshore Blvd	Tampa	FL	33607	**800-228-9290**	813-287-2555
Quorum Hotel Tampa-Westshore 700 N Westshore Blvd	Tampa	FL	33609	**877-478-6786**	813-289-8200
Radisson Bay Harbor Hotel 7700 W Courtney Campbell Cswy	Tampa	FL	33607	**800-333-3333**	813-281-8900
Radisson Hotel Tampa Riverwalk 200 N Ashley St	Tampa	FL	33602	**800-333-3333**	813-223-2222
Renaissance Tampa Hotel International Plaza 4200 Jim Walter Blvd	Tampa	FL	33607	**800-644-2685**	813-877-9200
Sailport Resort 2506 Rocky Point Dr	Tampa	FL	33607	**800-255-9599**	813-281-9599
Sheraton Suites Tampa Airport 4400 W Cypress St	Tampa	FL	33607	**800-325-3535**	813-873-8675
Wingate Inn Tampa 3751 E Fowler Ave	Tampa	FL	33612	**800-228-1000**	813-979-2828
Wingate Inn Tampa North 17301 Dona Michelle Dr	Tampa	FL	33647	**800-228-1000**	813-971-7676
Wyndham Harbour Island 725 S Harbour Island Blvd	Tampa	FL	33602	**800-996-3426**	813-229-5000
Wyndham Westshore 4860 W Kennedy Blvd	Tampa	FL	33609	**800-966-3426**	813-286-4400
Ocean Pointe Suites at Key Largo 500 Burton Dr	Tavernier	FL	33070	**800-882-9464**	305-853-3000
Tierra Verde Island Resort 200 Madonna Blvd	Tierra Verde	FL	33715	**800-934-0549**	727-867-8611
Courtyard West Palm Beach 600 Northpoint Pkwy	West Palm Beach	FL	33407	**800-321-2211**	561-640-9000
Crowne Plaza Hotel West Palm Beach 1601 Belvedere Rd	West Palm Beach	FL	33406	**800-227-6963**	561-689-6400
Marriott West Palm Beach 1001 Okeechobee Blvd	West Palm Beach	FL	33401	**800-376-2292**	561-833-1234
Radisson Hotel Palm Beach Airport 1808 S Australian Ave	West Palm Beach	FL	33409	**800-333-3333**	561-689-6888

Georgia

Name / Address	City	State	ZIP	Toll-Free	Phone
Hilton Garden Inn Atlanta North/Alpharetta 4025 Winward Plaza	Alpharetta	GA	30005	**877-782-9444**	770-360-7766
Hilton Garden Inn Atlanta Northpoint 10975 Georgia Ln	Alpharetta	GA	30022	**877-782-9444**	678-566-3900
Marriott Atlanta Alpharetta 5750 Windward Pkwy	Alpharetta	GA	30005	**800-228-9290**	770-754-9600
Windsor Hotel 125 W Lamar St	Americus	GA	31709	**888-297-9567**	229-924-1555
Best Western Granada Suite Hotel-Downtown 1302 W Peachtree St	Atlanta	GA	30309	**800-548-5631**	404-876-6100
Courtyard Atlanta Downtown 175 Piedmont Ave	Atlanta	GA	30303	**800-321-2211**	404-659-2727
Courtyard Atlanta Windy Hill 2045 S Park Pl	Atlanta	GA	30339	**800-321-2211**	770-955-3838
Crowne Plaza Hotel Atlanta Airport 1325 Virginia Ave	Atlanta	GA	30344	**800-227-6963**	404-768-6660
Crowne Plaza Hotel Atlanta-Perimeter NW 6345 Powers Ferry Rd NW	Atlanta	GA	30339	**800-554-0055**	770-955-1700
Crowne Plaza Hotel Atlanta-Ravinia 4355 Ashford-Dunwoody Rd	Atlanta	GA	30346	**800-554-0055**	770-395-7700
Doubletree Club Atlanta Airport 3400 Norman Berry Dr	Atlanta	GA	30344	**800-222-8733**	404-763-1600
Doubletree Guest Suites Atlanta-Galleria 2780 Windy Ridge Pkwy	Atlanta	GA	30339	**800-843-5858**	770-980-1900
Doubletree Guest Suites Atlanta-Perimeter 6120 Peachtree Dunwoody Rd	Atlanta	GA	30328	**800-222-8733**	770-668-0808
Doubletree Hotel Atlanta/Buckhead 3342 Peachtree Rd NE	Atlanta	GA	30326	**800-222-8733**	404-231-1234
Embassy Suites Atlanta Buckhead 3285 Peachtree Rd NE	Atlanta	GA	30305	**800-362-2779**	404-261-7733
Embassy Suites Atlanta at Centennial Olympic Park 267 Marietta St NW	Atlanta	GA	30313	**800-362-2779**	404-223-2300
Emory Inn 1641 Clifton Rd	Atlanta	GA	30329	**800-933-6679**	404-712-6720
Four Seasons Hotel Atlanta 75 14th St	Atlanta	GA	30309	**800-332-3442**	404-881-9898
Georgian Terrace Hotel 659 Peachtree St	Atlanta	GA	30308	**800-651-2316**	404-897-1991
Grand Hyatt Atlanta 3300 Peachtree Rd	Atlanta	GA	30305	**800-233-1234**	404-365-8100
Hilton Atlanta 255 Courtland St NE	Atlanta	GA	30303	**800-445-8667**	404-659-2000
Hilton Atlanta Airport & Towers 1031 Virginia Ave	Atlanta	GA	30354	**800-445-8667**	404-767-9000
Hilton Garden Inn Atlanta Perimeter Center 1501 Lake Hearn Dr	Atlanta	GA	30319	**877-782-9444**	404-459-0500
Holiday Inn Atlanta Downtown 101 Andrew Young International Blvd NW	Atlanta	GA	30303	**800-535-0707**	404-524-5555
Holiday Inn Select Atlanta 450 Capitol Ave SW	Atlanta	GA	30312	**800-442-6011**	404-591-2000
Howard Johnson Plaza Suites at Atlanta Underground 54 Peachtree St SW	Atlanta	GA	30303	**877-477-5549**	404-223-5555
Hyatt Regency Atlanta 265 Peachtree St NE	Atlanta	GA	30303	**800-233-1234**	404-577-1234
JW Marriott Hotel Buckhead/Lenox 3300 Lenox Rd NE	Atlanta	GA	30326	**800-228-9290**	404-262-3344
Marriott Atlanta Century Center 2000 Century Blvd NE	Atlanta	GA	30345	**800-228-9290**	404-325-0000
Marriott Atlanta Marquis 265 Peachtree Center Ave	Atlanta	GA	30303	**800-228-9290**	404-521-0000
Marriott Atlanta Northwest 200 I-North Pkwy	Atlanta	GA	30339	**800-228-9290**	770-952-7900
Marriott Atlanta Perimeter Center 246 Perimeter Center Pkwy NE	Atlanta	GA	30346	**800-228-9290**	770-394-6500
Marriott Suites Atlanta Midtown 35 14th St NE	Atlanta	GA	30309	**800-228-9290**	404-876-8888
Omni Hotel at CNN Center 100 CNN Ctr	Atlanta	GA	30335	**800-843-6664**	404-659-0000
Prime Hotel & Suites Atlanta/Perimeter 800 Hammond Dr NE	Atlanta	GA	30328	**800-982-6374**	404-252-3344
Regency Suites Hotel Midtown Atlanta 975 W Peachtree St	Atlanta	GA	30309	**800-642-3629**	404-876-5003
Renaissance Atlanta Hotel-Concourse 1 Hartsfield Centre Pkwy	Atlanta	GA	30354	**800-228-9290**	404-209-9999
Renaissance Atlanta Hotel Downtown 590 W Peachtree St NW	Atlanta	GA	30308	**800-228-9898**	404-881-6000
Renaissance Atlanta Waverly Hotel 2450 Galleria Pkwy NW	Atlanta	GA	30339	**800-468-3571**	770-953-4500
Residence Inn Atlanta-Buckhead (Lenox Park) 2220 Lake Blvd	Atlanta	GA	30319	**800-331-3131**	404-467-1660
Residence Inn Atlanta Historic Midtown 1041 W Peachtree St	Atlanta	GA	30309	**800-331-3131**	404-872-8885
Residence Inn Atlanta Midtown 17th St 1365 Peachtree St	Atlanta	GA	30309	**800-331-3131**	404-745-1000
Ritz-Carlton Atlanta 181 Peachtree St NE	Atlanta	GA	30303	**800-241-3333**	404-659-0400
Ritz-Carlton Buckhead 3434 Peachtree Rd NE	Atlanta	GA	30326	**800-241-3333**	404-237-2700
Sheraton Atlanta Hotel 165 Courtland St NE	Atlanta	GA	30303	**800-325-3535**	404-659-6500
Sheraton Buckhead Hotel Atlanta 3405 Lenox Rd NE	Atlanta	GA	30326	**800-325-3535**	404-261-9250
Sheraton Colony Square Hotel 188 14th St NE	Atlanta	GA	30361	**800-325-3535**	404-892-6000
Sheraton Suites Galleria Atlanta 2844 Cobb Pkwy SE	Atlanta	GA	30339	**800-325-3535**	770-955-3900
W Hotel Atlanta at Perimeter Center 111 Perimeter Ctr W	Atlanta	GA	30346	**800-683-6100**	770-396-6800
Westin Atlanta North at Perimeter 7 Concourse Pkwy	Atlanta	GA	30328	**800-937-8461**	770-395-3900
Westin Peachtree Plaza 210 Peachtree St NW	Atlanta	GA	30303	**800-937-8461**	404-659-1400
Wingate Inn Atlanta-Buckhead 3600 Piedmont Rd NE	Atlanta	GA	30305	**800-228-1000**	404-869-1100
Wyndham Atlanta 160 Spring St NW	Atlanta	GA	30303	**800-996-3426**	404-688-8600
Wyndham Midtown Atlanta 125 10th St NE	Atlanta	GA	30309	**800-996-3426**	404-873-4800
Wyndham Vinings 2857 Paces Ferry Rd	Atlanta	GA	30339	**800-996-3426**	770-432-5555
AmeriSuites Augusta Riverwatch Pkwy 1062 Claussen Rd	Augusta	GA	30907	**800-833-1516**	706-733-4656
Courtyard Augusta 1045 Stevens Creek Rd	Augusta	GA	30907	**800-321-2211**	706-737-3737
Fairfield Inn Augusta 201 Boy Scout Rd	Augusta	GA	30909	**800-228-2800**	706-733-8200
Holiday Inn Augusta-Gordon Hwy 2155 Gordon Hwy	Augusta	GA	30909	**800-465-4329**	706-737-2300
Partridge Inn 2110 Walton Way	Augusta	GA	30904	**800-476-6888**	706-737-8888
Radisson Riverfront Hotel Augusta 2 10th St	Augusta	GA	30901	**800-333-3333**	706-722-8900
Ramada Plaza Hotel & Convention Center Augusta 640 Broad St	Augusta	GA	30901	**800-257-5060**	706-722-5541
Sheraton Augusta Hotel 2651 Perimeter Pkwy	Augusta	GA	30909	**800-325-3535**	706-855-8100
Wingate Inn Augusta 4087 Belair Rd	Augusta	GA	30909	**800-228-1000**	706-860-8223
Wingate Inn Atlanta-Buford 1355 Mall of Georgia Blvd	Buford	GA	30519	**800-228-1000**	678-714-0248
Courtyard Atlanta Airport South/Sullivan Rd 2050 Sullivan Rd	College Park	GA	30337	**800-321-2211**	770-997-2220
Hilton Garden Inn Atlanta Airport/Millenium Center 2301 Sullivan Rd	College Park	GA	30337	**877-782-9444**	404-766-0303
Marriott Atlanta Airport 4711 Best Rd	College Park	GA	30337	**800-228-9290**	404-766-7900
Sheraton Gateway Hotel Atlanta Airport 1900 Sullivan Rd SW	College Park	GA	30337	**800-325-3535**	770-997-1100
Westin Atlanta Airport 4736 Best Rd	College Park	GA	30337	**888-627-7211**	404-762-7676
Comfort Suites Columbus 5236 Armour Rd	Columbus	GA	31904	**800-228-5150**	706-322-6666
Courtyard Columbus 3501 Courtyard Way	Columbus	GA	31909	**800-321-2211**	706-323-2323
Four Points by Sheraton Columbus Airport 5351 Sidney Simons Blvd	Columbus	GA	31904	**800-325-3535**	706-327-6868
Hilton Columbus 800 Front Ave	Columbus	GA	31901	**800-524-4020**	706-324-1800
Hilton Garden Inn Columbus 1500 Bradley Lakes Pkwy	Columbus	GA	31904	**877-782-9444**	706-660-1000
Holiday Inn Columbus-North I-85 2800 Manchester Expy	Columbus	GA	31904	**800-465-4329**	706-324-0231
Hilton Garden Inn Atlanta NE/Gwinnett Sugarloaf 2040 Sugarloaf Cir	Duluth	GA	30097	**877-782-9444**	770-495-7600
Hilton Garden Inn Atlanta North/Johns Creek 11695 Medlock Bridge Rd	Duluth	GA	30097	**877-782-9444**	770-476-1966
Marriott Atlanta Gwinnett Place 1775 Pleasant Hill Rd	Duluth	GA	30096	**800-228-9290**	770-923-1775
Residence Inn Atlanta-Gwinnett Place 1760 Pineland Rd	Duluth	GA	30096	**800-331-3131**	770-921-2202
Best Western Augusta Inn 452 Park West Dr	Grovetown	GA	30813	**800-528-1234**	706-651-9100
Best Western Riverside Inn 2400 Riverside Dr	Macon	GA	31204	**888-454-4565**	478-743-6311
Comfort Inn Macon North 2690 Riverside Dr	Macon	GA	31204	**800-847-6453**	478-746-8855
Comfort Inn Macon West 4951 Eisenhower Pkwy	Macon	GA	31206	**800-228-5150**	478-788-5500
Courtyard Macon 3990 Sheraton Dr	Macon	GA	31210	**800-321-2211**	478-477-8899
Crowne Plaza Hotel Macon 108 1st St	Macon	GA	31201	**800-227-6963**	478-746-1461
Holiday Inn Macon Conference Center 3590 Riverside Dr	Macon	GA	31298	**888-781-7666**	478-474-2610
Holiday Inn Macon West 4755 Chambers Rd	Macon	GA	31206	**877-622-6693**	478-788-0120
Quality Inn & Suites Macon 115 Riverside Pkwy	Macon	GA	31210	**800-228-5151**	478-474-4000
Residence Inn Macon 3900 Sheraton Dr	Macon	GA	31210	**800-331-3131**	478-475-4280
Wingate Inn Macon 100 Northcrest Blvd	Macon	GA	31210	**800-228-1000**	478-476-8100
Hyatt Regency Suites Perimeter Northwest 2999 Windy Hill Rd	Marietta	GA	30067	**800-233-1234**	770-956-1234
Wingate Inn Marietta 1250 Franklin Rd	Marietta	GA	30067	**800-228-1000**	770-989-0071
Wyndham Garden Hotel Atlanta Northwest 1775 Parkway Pl NW	Marietta	GA	30067	**800-996-3426**	770-428-4400
Marriott Atlanta Norcross 475 Technology Pkwy	Norcross	GA	30092	**800-228-9290**	770-263-8558
Residence Inn Atlanta Peachtree Corners 5500 Triangle Dr	Norcross	GA	30092	**800-331-3131**	770-447-1714

Georgia (Cont'd)

Hotel	City	State	ZIP	Toll-Free	Phone
Wingate Inn Norcross 5800 Peachtree Industrial Blvd	Norcross	GA	30071	**800-228-1000**	770-263-2020
Courtyard Savannah Midtown 6703 Abercorn St.	Savannah	GA	31405	**800-321-2211**	912-354-7878
Foley Inn 14 W Hull St Chippewa Sq	Savannah	GA	31401	**800-647-3708**	912-232-6622
Gastonian The 220 E Gaston St	Savannah	GA	31401	**800-322-6603**	912-232-2869
Hilton Savannah Desoto 15 E Liberty St	Savannah	GA	31401	**800-445-8667**	912-232-9000
Hyatt Regency Savannah 2 W Bay St	Savannah	GA	31401	**800-233-1234**	912-238-1234
Mansion on Forsyth Park 700 Drayton St	Savannah	GA	31401	**888-711-5114**	912-238-5158
Marriott Savannah Riverfront 100 General McIntosh Blvd	Savannah	GA	31401	**800-228-9290**	912-233-7722
Planters Inn 29 Abercorn St	Savannah	GA	31401	**800-554-1187**	912-232-5678
Quail Run Lodge 1130 Bob Harman Rd	Savannah	GA	31408	**800-627-7035**	912-964-1421
River Street Inn 115 E River St	Savannah	GA	31401	**800-253-4229**	912-234-6400
Wingate Inn Savannah 11 Gateway Blvd E.	Savannah	GA	31419	**800-228-1000**	912-925-2525
Melhana - The Grand Plantation 301 Showboat Ln.	Thomasville	GA	31792	**888-920-3030**	229-226-2290
Radisson Hotel Atlanta Northlake 4156 La Vista Rd	Tucker	GA	30084	**800-333-3333**	770-938-1026

Hawaii

Hotel	City	State	ZIP	Toll-Free	Phone
Ala Moana Hotel 410 Atkinson Dr	Honolulu	HI	96814	**800-367-6025**	808-955-4811
Aqua Bamboo 2425 Kuhio Ave	Honolulu	HI	96815	**800-367-5004**	808-922-7777
Aston Aloha Surf Hotel 444 Kanekapolei St	Honolulu	HI	96815	**800-922-7866**	808-923-0222
Aston Coconut Plaza Hotel 450 Lewers St	Honolulu	HI	96815	**877-997-6667**	808-923-8828
Aston at the Executive Centre Hotel 1088 Bishop St	Honolulu	HI	96813	**800-949-3932**	808-539-3000
Aston Pacific Monarch 2427 Kuhio Ave	Honolulu	HI	96815	**800-922-7866**	808-923-9805
Aston at the Waikiki Banyan 201 Ohua Ave	Honolulu	HI	96815	**800-922-7866**	808-922-0555
Aston Waikiki Beach Tower 2470 Kalakaua Ave.	Honolulu	HI	96815	**800-922-7866**	808-926-6400
Aston Waikiki Beachside Hotel 2452 Kalakaua Ave.	Honolulu	HI	96815	**800-922-7866**	808-931-2100
Aston Waikiki Circle Hotel 2464 Kalakaua Ave.	Honolulu	HI	96815	**877-997-6667**	808-923-1571
Aston Waikiki Sunset 229 Paoakalani Ave	Honolulu	HI	96815	**800-922-7866**	808-922-0511
Best Western Plaza Hotel 3253 N Nimitz Hwy	Honolulu	HI	96819	**800-800-4683**	808-836-3636
Coral Reef Hotel 2299 Kuhio Ave	Honolulu	HI	96815	**800-922-7866**	808-922-1262
Doubletree Alana Hotel-Waikiki 1956 Ala Moana Blvd.	Honolulu	HI	96815	**800-222-8733**	808-941-7275
Ewa Hotel Waikiki 2555 Cartwright Rd	Honolulu	HI	96815	**800-359-8639**	808-922-1677
Halekulani Hotel 2199 Kalia Rd	Honolulu	HI	96815	**800-367-2343**	808-923-2311
Honolulu Airport Hotel 3401 N Nimitz Hwy	Honolulu	HI	96819	**800-800-3477**	808-836-0661
Imperial of Waikiki 205 Lewers St.	Honolulu	HI	96815	**800-347-2582**	808-923-1827
Kahala Mandarin Oriental Hotel Hawaii Resort 5000 Kahala Ave	Honolulu	HI	96816	**800-367-2525**	808-739-8888
Marine Surf Waikiki Hotel 364 Seaside Ave	Honolulu	HI	96815	**888-456-7873**	808-923-2424
Marriott Waikiki Beach 2552 Kalakaua Ave.	Honolulu	HI	96815	**888-236-2427**	808-922-6611
Miramar Hotel at Waikiki 2345 Kuhio Ave	Honolulu	HI	96815	**800-367-2303**	808-922-2077
New Otani Kaimana Beach Hotel 2863 Kalakaua Ave.	Honolulu	HI	96815	**800-356-8264**	808-923-1555
Ocean Resort Hotel Waikiki 175 Paoakalani Ave	Honolulu	HI	96815	**800-367-2317**	808-922-3861
OHANA Islander Waikiki 270 Lewers St.	Honolulu	HI	96815	**800-688-7444**	808-923-7711
OHANA Reef Lanai 225 Saratoga Rd.	Honolulu	HI	96815	**800-462-6262**	808-923-3881
OHANA Reef Towers 227 Lewers St	Honolulu	HI	96815	**800-688-7444**	808-924-8844
OHANA Waikiki Tower 200 Lewers St	Honolulu	HI	96815	**800-462-6262**	808-922-6424
OHANA Waikiki Village 240 Lewers St.	Honolulu	HI	96815	**800-462-6262**	808-923-3881
OHANA Waikiki West 2330 Kuhio Ave	Honolulu	HI	96815	**800-462-6262**	808-922-5022
Outrigger Luana Waikiki 2045 Kalakaua Ave	Honolulu	HI	96815	**800-445-8811**	808-955-6000
Outrigger Reef on the Beach 2169 Kalia Rd	Honolulu	HI	96815	**800-688-7444**	808-923-3111
Outrigger Waikiki 2335 Kalakaua Ave.	Honolulu	HI	96815	**800-688-7444**	808-923-0711
Pacific Beach Hotel 2490 Kalakaua Ave	Honolulu	HI	96815	**800-367-6060**	808-922-1233
Pagoda Hotel 1525 Rycroft St	Honolulu	HI	96814	**800-367-6060**	808-941-6611
Park Shore Waikiki 2586 Kalakaua Ave	Honolulu	HI	96815	**800-367-2377**	808-923-0411
Queen Kapiolani Hotel 150 Kapahulu Ave	Honolulu	HI	96815	**800-367-2317**	808-922-1941
Radisson Waikiki Prince Kuhio Hotel 2500 Kuhio Ave	Honolulu	HI	96815	**888-557-4422**	808-922-0811
Renaissance Ilikai Waikiki Hotel 1777 Ala Moana Blvd.	Honolulu	HI	96815	**800-245-4524**	808-949-3811
Royal Garden at Waikiki Hotel 440 Olohana St	Honolulu	HI	96815	**800-367-5666**	808-943-0202
Sheraton Princess Kaiulani Hotel 120 Kaiulani Ave	Honolulu	HI	96815	**866-500-8313**	808-922-5811
W Hotel Honolulu Diamond Head 2885 Kalakaua Ave.	Honolulu	HI	96815	**888-627-7816**	808-922-1700
Waikiki Beachcomber Hotel 2300 Kalakaua Ave.	Honolulu	HI	96815	**800-622-4646**	808-922-4646
Waikiki Gateway Hotel 2070 Kalakaua Ave	Honolulu	HI	96815	**800-247-1903**	808-955-3741
Waikiki Joy Hotel 320 Lewers St	Honolulu	HI	96815	**800-321-2558**	808-923-2300
Waikiki Parc Hotel 2233 Helumoa Rd	Honolulu	HI	96815	**800-422-0450**	808-921-7272
Waikiki Resort Hotel 2460 Koa Ave.	Honolulu	HI	96815	**800-367-5116**	808-922-4911
Waikiki Royal Suites 255 Beach Walk	Honolulu	HI	96815	**800-535-0085**	808-926-5641
King Kamehameha's Kona Beach Hotel 75-5660 Palani Rd.	Kailua-Kona	HI	96740	**800-367-2111**	808-329-2911
Outrigger Kanaloa at Kona 78-261 Manukai St	Kailua-Kona	HI	96740	**800-688-7444**	808-322-9625
Kapalua Bay Hotel 1 Bay Dr.	Kapalua	HI	96761	**800-367-8000**	808-669-5656
Ritz-Carlton Kapalua 1 Ritz-Carlton Dr.	Kapalua	HI	96761	**800-241-3333**	808-669-6200
Maui Coast 2259 S Kihei Rd.	Kihei	HI	96753	**800-895-6284**	808-874-6284
Sheraton Maui Resort 2605 Kaanapali Pkwy	Lahaina	HI	96761	**888-782-9488**	808-661-0031
Westin Maui on Ka'anapali Beach 2365 Kaanapali Pkwy.	Lahaina	HI	96761	**800-937-8461**	808-667-2525
Molokai Lodge & Beach Village 100 Maunaloa Hwy	Maunaloa	HI	96770	**888-627-8082**	808-552-2741
Breakers at Waikiki 250 Beach Walk.	Waikiki	HI	96815	**800-426-0494**	808-923-3181
Waikoloa Beach Marriott 69-275 Waikoloa Beach Dr	Waikoloa	HI	96738	**800-688-7444**	808-886-6789
Outrigger Wailea Resort Hotel & Conference Center 3700 Wailea Alanui Dr.	Wailea	HI	96753	**800-367-2960**	808-879-1922

Idaho

Hotel	City	State	ZIP	Toll-Free	Phone
AmeriSuites Boise Towne Square Mall 925 N Milwaukee Ave	Boise	ID	83704	**800-833-1516**	208-375-1200
Ameritel Inn Boise Spectrum 7499 W Overland Rd	Boise	ID	83709	**877-800-5876**	208-323-2500
Ameritel Inn Boise Towne Square 7965 W Emerald St	Boise	ID	83704	**800-600-6001**	208-378-7000
Comfort Inn Boise Airport 2526 Airport Way	Boise	ID	83705	**800-228-5150**	208-336-0077
Courtyard Boise 222 S Broadway Ave	Boise	ID	83702	**800-321-2211**	208-331-2700
Doubletree Club Boise 475 W Park Ctr Blvd	Boise	ID	83706	**800-222-8733**	208-345-2002
Doubletree Hotel Boise-Riverside 2900 Chinden Blvd.	Boise	ID	83714	**800-222-8733**	208-343-1871
Fairfield Inn Boise 3300 S Shoshone St	Boise	ID	83705	**800-228-2800**	208-331-5656
Grove Hotel - A WestCoast Grand Hotel 245 S Capitol Blvd	Boise	ID	83702	**800-426-0670**	208-333-8000
Hilton Garden Inn Boise Spectrum 7699 W Spectrum Rd	Boise	ID	83709	**877-782-9444**	208-376-1000
Holiday Inn Boise Airport 3300 Vista Ave	Boise	ID	83705	**800-465-4329**	208-344-8365
Owyhee Plaza Hotel 1109 Main St	Boise	ID	83702	**800-233-4611**	208-343-4611
Plaza Suite Hotel 409 S Cole Rd	Boise	ID	83709	**800-376-3608**	208-375-7666
Red Lion Hotel Boise Downtowner 1800 Fairview Ave	Boise	ID	83702	**800-325-4000**	208-344-7691
Red Lion ParkCenter Suites 424 E Park Center Blvd	Boise	ID	83706	**800-733-5466**	208-342-1044
Residence Inn Boise 1401 Lusk Ave	Boise	ID	83706	**800-331-3131**	208-344-1200
Statehouse Inn 981 Grove St	Boise	ID	83702	**800-243-4622**	208-342-4622
University Inn 2360 University Dr.	Boise	ID	83706	**800-345-7170**	208-345-7170
WestCoast Grove Hotel 245 S Capitol Blvd	Boise	ID	83702	**800-426-0670**	208-333-8000
Hilton Garden Inn Boise/Eagle 145 E Riverside Dr	Eagle	ID	83616	**877-782-9444**	208-938-9600
Red Lion Idaho Falls Hotel 475 River Pkwy.	Idaho Falls	ID	83402	**800-325-4000**	208-523-8000
Knob Hill Inn 960 N Main St PO Box 800	Ketchum	ID	83340	**800-526-8010***	208-726-8010
*Resv					
Ameritel Inn Pocatello 1440 Bench Rd	Pocatello	ID	83201	**800-600-6001**	208-234-7500
Comfort Inn Pocatello 1333 Bench Rd.	Pocatello	ID	83201	**800-228-5150**	208-237-8155
Holiday Inn Pocatello 1399 Bench Rd	Pocatello	ID	83201	**800-200-8944**	208-237-1400
Red Lion Hotel Pocatello 1555 Pocatello Creek Rd	Pocatello	ID	83201	**800-733-5466**	208-233-2200

Illinois

Hotel	City	State	ZIP	Toll-Free	Phone
Sheraton Chicago Northwest 3400 W Euclid Ave	Arlington Heights	IL	60005	**800-325-3535**	847-394-2000
Chateau Hotel & Conference Center 1601 Jumer Dr.	Bloomington	IL	61704	**800-285-8637**	309-662-2020
Wyndham Garden Hotel Buffalo Grove 900 W Lake Cook Rd.	Buffalo Grove	IL	60089	**800-996-3426**	847-215-8883
Comfort Inn Champaign 305 W Market View Dr	Champaign	IL	61821	**800-228-5150**	217-352-4055
Courtyard Champaign 1811 Moreland Blvd	Champaign	IL	61820	**800-321-2211**	217-355-0411
Fairfield Inn Champaign 1807 Moreland Blvd.	Champaign	IL	61821	**800-228-2800**	217-355-0604
Hawthorn Suites LTD Champaign 101 Trade Centre Dr	Champaign	IL	61820	**800-527-1133**	217-398-3400
Best Western Hawthorne Terrace 3434 N Broadway Ave	Chicago	IL	60657	**888-675-2378**	773-244-3434
Best Western Inn of Chicago 162 E Ohio St	Chicago	IL	60611	**800-557-2378**	312-787-3100
City Suites Hotel 933 W Belmont Ave	Chicago	IL	60657	**800-248-9108**	773-404-3400
Claridge Hotel 1244 N Dearborn Pkwy.	Chicago	IL	60610	**800-245-1258**	312-787-4980
Congress Plaza Hotel & Convention Center 520 S Michigan Ave.	Chicago	IL	60605	**800-635-1666**	312-427-3800
Courtyard Chicago Downtown 30 E Hubbard St	Chicago	IL	60611	**800-321-2211**	312-329-2500
Crowne Plaza Hotel Chicago-Allerton 701 N Michigan Ave	Chicago	IL	60611	**800-227-6963**	312-440-1500
Crowne Plaza Hotel Chicago Silversmith 10 S Wabash Ave	Chicago	IL	60603	**800-227-6963**	312-372-7696
Doubletree Guest Suites Chicago-Downtown 198 E Delaware Pl	Chicago	IL	60611	**800-222-8733**	312-664-1100
Drake Hotel 140 E Walton Pl	Chicago	IL	60611	**800-553-7253**	312-787-2200
Embassy Suites Chicago Downtown 600 N State St	Chicago	IL	60610	**800-362-2779**	312-943-3800
Embassy Suites Chicago Downtown Lakefront 511 N Columbus Dr.	Chicago	IL	60611	**800-362-2779**	312-836-5900
Fairmont Chicago 200 N Columbus Dr.	Chicago	IL	60601	**800-526-2008**	312-565-8000
Fitzpatrick Chicago Hotel 166 E Superior St.	Chicago	IL	60611	**800-367-7701**	312-787-6000
Four Seasons Hotel Chicago 120 E Delaware Pl	Chicago	IL	60611	**800-332-3442**	312-280-8800
Hilton Chicago 720 S Michigan Ave.	Chicago	IL	60605	**800-445-8667**	312-922-4400
Hilton Garden Inn Chicago Downtown 10 E Grand Ave	Chicago	IL	60611	**877-782-9444**	312-595-0000
Holiday Inn Chicago City Center 300 E Ohio St	Chicago	IL	60611	**800-465-4329**	312-787-6100
Holiday Inn Chicago Mart Plaza 350 N Orleans St	Chicago	IL	60654	**800-465-4329**	312-836-5000
Hotel 71 Chicago 71 E Wacker Dr	Chicago	IL	60601	**800-621-4005**	312-346-7100
Hotel Allegro Chicago 171 W Randolph St	Chicago	IL	60601	**800-643-1500**	312-236-0123
Hotel Burnham 1 W Washington St	Chicago	IL	60602	**877-294-9712**	312-782-1111
Hotel Monaco Chicago 225 N Wabash Ave	Chicago	IL	60601	**866-610-0081**	312-960-8500
Hotel Sofitel Chicago Water Tower 20 E Chestnut St	Chicago	IL	60611	**800-763-4835**	312-324-4000
House of Blues Hotel - A Loews Hotel 333 N Dearborn St.	Chicago	IL	60610	**800-235-6397**	312-245-0333
Hyatt on Printer's Row 500 S Dearborn St	Chicago	IL	60605	**800-233-1234**	312-986-1234
Hyatt Regency Chicago 151 E Wacker Dr	Chicago	IL	60601	**800-233-1234**	312-565-1234
Hyatt Regency McCormick Place 2233 ML King Dr	Chicago	IL	60616	**800-233-1234**	312-567-1234
InterContinental Chicago 505 N Michigan Ave	Chicago	IL	60611	**800-628-2112**	312-944-4100
Le Meridien Chicago 521 N Rush St	Chicago	IL	60611	**800-543-4300**	312-645-1500
Lenox Suites Hotel 616 N Rush St.	Chicago	IL	60611	**800-445-3669**	312-337-1000
Majestic Hotel 528 W Brompton	Chicago	IL	60657	**800-727-5108**	773-404-3499
Marriott Chicago Downtown 540 N Michigan Ave	Chicago	IL	60611	**800-228-0265**	312-836-0100
Marriott Chicago O'Hare 8535 W Higgins Rd	Chicago	IL	60631	**800-228-9290**	773-693-4444
Millennium Knickerbocker Hotel Chicago 163 E Walton Pl.	Chicago	IL	60611	**800-621-8140**	312-751-8100
Omni Ambassador East 1301 N State Pkwy	Chicago	IL	60610	**800-843-6664**	312-787-7200
Omni Chicago Hotel 676 N Michigan Ave.	Chicago	IL	60611	**800-843-6664**	312-944-6664
Palmer House Hilton 17 E Monroe St	Chicago	IL	60603	**800-445-8667**	312-726-7500
Park Hyatt Chicago 800 N Michigan Ave	Chicago	IL	60611	**800-233-1234**	312-335-1234
Peninsula Chicago 108 E Superior St	Chicago	IL	60611	**866-288-8889**	312-337-2888
Radisson Hotel & Suites Downtown Chicago 160 E Huron St	Chicago	IL	60611	**800-333-3333**	312-787-2900

				Toll-Free	Phone
Ramada Inn Chicago Lake Shore 4900 S Lake Shore Dr	Chicago	IL	60615	**800-237-4933**	773-288-5800
Renaissance Chicago Hotel 1 W Wacker Dr	Chicago	IL	60601	**800-228-9290**	312-372-7200
Ritz-Carlton Chicago - A Four Seasons Hotel 160 E Pearson St	Chicago	IL	60611	**800-621-6906**	312-266-1000
Seneca Hotel 200 E Chestnut St	Chicago	IL	60611	**800-800-6261**	312-787-8900
Sheraton Chicago Hotel & Towers 301 E North Water St	Chicago	IL	60611	**800-325-3535**	312-464-1000
Sutton Place Hotel Chicago 21 E Bellevue Pl	Chicago	IL	60611	**866-378-8866**	312-266-2100
Swissotel Chicago 323 E Wacker Dr	Chicago	IL	60601	**800-654-7263**	312-565-0565
Talbott Hotel 20 E Delaware Pl	Chicago	IL	60611	**800-825-2688**	312-944-4970
Tremont Chicago 100 E Chestnut St	Chicago	IL	60611	**800-621-8133**	312-751-1900
Westin Chicago River North 320 N Dearborn Ave	Chicago	IL	60610	**800-937-8461**	312-744-1900
Westin Michigan Avenue Chicago 909 N Michigan Ave	Chicago	IL	60611	**888-627-8385**	312-943-7200
Whitehall Hotel 105 E Delaware Pl	Chicago	IL	60611	**800-323-7500**	312-944-6300
Willows Hotel 555 W Surf St	Chicago	IL	60657	**800-787-3108**	773-528-8400
Wyndham Chicago 633 N Saint Clair St	Chicago	IL	60611	**866-850-3057**	312-573-0300
Holiday Inn Select Decatur Conference Center 4191 W US Hwy 36	Decatur	IL	62522	**800-465-4329**	217-422-8800
Embassy Suites Chicago North Shore 1445 Lake Cook Rd	Deerfield	IL	60015	**800-362-2779**	847-945-4500
Hyatt Deerfield 1750 Lake Cook Rd	Deerfield	IL	60015	**800-233-1234**	847-945-3400
Marriott Suites Chicago-Deerfield 2 Parkway N	Deerfield	IL	60015	**800-228-9290**	847-405-9666
Doubletree Guest Suites Downers Grove 2111 Butterfield Rd	Downers Grove	IL	60515	**800-765-2785**	630-971-2000
Marriott Suites Chicago-Downers Grove 1500 Opus Pl	Downers Grove	IL	60515	**800-228-9290**	630-852-1500
Par-A-Dice Hotel 7 Blackjack Blvd	East Peoria	IL	61611	**800-727-2342**	309-699-7711
Stoney Creek Inn 101 Mariner's Way	East Peoria	IL	61611	**800-659-2220**	309-694-1300
Holiday Inn Hotel & Suites Elgin 495 Airport Rd	Elgin	IL	60123	**800-227-6963**	847-488-9000
Sheraton Chicago Elk Grove Village 121 Northwest Point Blvd	Elk Grove Village	IL	60007	**800-325-3535**	847-290-1600
Hotel Orrington 1710 Orrington Ave	Evanston	IL	60201	**800-843-6664**	847-866-8700
Doubletree Guest Suites Chicago North/Glenview 1400 N Milwaukee Ave	Glenview	IL	60025	**800-222-8733**	847-803-9800
Wyndham Northwest Chicago 400 Park Blvd	Itasca	IL	60143	**800-996-3426**	630-773-4000
Harrah's Joliet 151 N Joliet St	Joliet	IL	60432	**800-427-7247**	815-740-7800
Deer Path Inn 255 E Illinois Rd	Lake Forest	IL	60045	**800-788-9480**	847-234-2280
Hyatt Lisle 1400 Corporetum Dr	Lisle	IL	60532	**800-233-1234**	630-852-1234
Holiday Inn Matteson 500 Holiday Plaza Dr	Matteson	IL	60443	**800-465-4329**	708-747-3500
Holiday Inn Select Naperville 1801 N Naper Blvd	Naperville	IL	60563	**800-465-4329**	630-505-4900
Prime Hotel & Suites Chicago/Naperville 1837 Centre Point Cir	Naperville	IL	60563	**866-937-7746**	630-505-3353
Hilton Northbrook 2855 N Milwaukee Ave	Northbrook	IL	60062	**800-445-8667**	847-480-7500
Chicago Marriott Oak Brook Hotel 1401 W 22nd St	Oak Brook	IL	60523	**800-228-9290**	630-573-8555
Doubletree Hotel Chicago-Oak Brook 1909 Spring Rd	Oak Brook	IL	60523	**800-233-1234**	630-573-1234
Renaissance Oak Brook Hotel 2100 Spring Rd	Oak Brook	IL	60523	**800-468-3571**	630-573-2800
Wyndham Drake 2301 York Rd	Oak Brook	IL	60523	**800-996-3426**	630-574-5700
Hilton Oak Lawn 9333 S Cicero Ave	Oak Lawn	IL	60453	**800-445-9333**	708-425-7800
Comfort Suites Peoria 1812 W War Memorial Dr	Peoria	IL	61614	**800-517-4000**	309-688-3800
Holiday Inn Peoria City Centre 500 Hamilton Blvd	Peoria	IL	61602	**800-465-4329**	309-674-2500
Hotel Pere Marquette 501 Main St	Peoria	IL	61602	**800-447-1676**	309-637-6500
Mark Twain Hotel 225 NE Adams St	Peoria	IL	61602	**866-325-6351**	309-676-3600
Radisson Hotel Peoria 117 N Western Ave	Peoria	IL	61604	**800-285-8637**	309-673-8040
Residence Inn Peoria 2000 W War Memorial Dr	Peoria	IL	61614	**800-331-3131**	309-681-9000
Best Western Heritage Inn 420 S Murray Rd	Rantoul	IL	61866	**800-528-1234**	217-892-9292
Best Western Clock Tower Resort & Conference Center 7801 E State St	Rockford	IL	61108	**800-358-7666**	815-398-6000
Courtyard Rockford 7676 E State St	Rockford	IL	61108	**800-321-2211**	815-397-6222
Residence Inn Rockford 7542 Colosseum Dr	Rockford	IL	61107	**800-331-3131**	815-227-0013
Sweden House 4605 E State St	Rockford	IL	61108	**800-886-4138**	815-398-4130
Crowne Plaza O'Hare International Airport 5440 N River Rd	Rosemont	IL	60018	**800-227-6963**	847-671-6350
Hotel Sofitel Chicago O'Hare 5550 N River Rd	Rosemont	IL	60018	**800-763-4835**	847-678-4488
Hyatt Regency O'Hare 9300 Bryn Mawr Ave	Rosemont	IL	60018	**800-233-1234**	847-696-1234
Hyatt Rosemont 6350 N River Rd	Rosemont	IL	60018	**800-233-1234**	847-518-1234
Marriott Suites Chicago O'Hare 6155 N River Rd	Rosemont	IL	60018	**800-228-9290**	847-696-4400
Ramada Plaza Hotel O'Hare 6600 N Mannheim Rd	Rosemont	IL	60018	**800-272-6232**	847-827-5131
Sheraton Gateway Suites Chicago O'Hare 6501 N Mannheim Rd	Rosemont	IL	60018	**800-325-3535**	847-699-6300
Westin O'Hare 6100 N River Rd	Rosemont	IL	60018	**800-937-8461**	847-698-6000
AmeriSuites Chicago/Schaumburg 1851 McConnor Pkwy	Schaumburg	IL	60173	**800-833-1516**	847-330-1060
Hyatt Regency Woodfield 1800 E Golf Rd	Schaumburg	IL	60173	**800-233-1234**	847-605-1234
Marriott Chicago-Schaumburg 50 N Martingale Rd	Schaumburg	IL	60173	**800-228-9290**	847-240-0100
Staybridge Suites Schaumburg 901 E Woodfield Office Ct	Schaumburg	IL	60173	**800-238-8000**	847-619-6677
Wyndham Garden Hotel Schaumburg 800 National Pkwy	Schaumburg	IL	60173	**800-996-3426**	847-605-9222
Four Points by Sheraton Chicago O'Hare Airport 10249 W Irving Park Rd	Schiller Park	IL	60176	**800-325-3535**	847-671-6000
North Shore Skokie Hotel 9599 Skokie Blvd	Skokie	IL	60077	**800-879-4458**	847-679-7000
Comfort Inn Springfield 3442 Freedom Dr	Springfield	IL	62704	**800-228-5150**	217-787-2250
Comfort Suites Springfield 2620 S Dirksen Pkwy	Springfield	IL	62703	**800-424-6423**	217-753-4000
Courtyard Springfield 3462 Freedom Dr	Springfield	IL	62704	**800-321-2211**	217-793-5300
Crowne Plaza Hotel Springfield 3000 S Dirksen Pkwy	Springfield	IL	62703	**800-227-6963**	217-529-7777
Fairfield Inn Springfield (IL) 3446 Freedom Dr	Springfield	IL	62704	**800-228-2800**	217-793-9277
Hilton Springfield 700 E Adams St	Springfield	IL	62701	**800-445-8667**	217-789-1530
Mansion View Inn & Suites 529 S 4th St	Springfield	IL	62701	**800-252-1083**	217-544-7411
Renaissance Springfield Hotel 701 E Adams St	Springfield	IL	62701	**800-468-3571**	217-544-8800
Wingate Inn Chicago-Tinley Park 18421 N Creek Dr	Tinley Park	IL	60477	**800-228-1000**	708-532-9300
Holiday Inn Champaign/Urbana 1001 W Killarney St	Urbana	IL	61801	**800-465-4329**	217-328-7900
Sleep Inn Champaign-Urbana 1908 N Lincoln Ave	Urbana	IL	61801	**800-424-6423**	217-367-6000
Wyndham Garden Hotel Wood Dale 1200 N Mittel Blvd	Wood Dale	IL	60191	**800-996-3426**	630-860-2900

Indiana

				Toll-Free	Phone
Century Suites Hotel 300 SR-446	Bloomington	IN	47401	**800-766-5446**	812-336-7777
Courtyard Bloomington 310 S College Ave	Bloomington	IN	47403	**800-321-2211**	812-335-8000
Fairfield Inn Bloomington 120 Fairfield Dr	Bloomington	IN	47404	**800-228-2800**	812-331-1122
Indiana Memorial Union Hotel & Conference Center 900 E 7th St	Bloomington	IN	47405	**800-209-8145**	812-855-2536
Quality Inn Bloomington 1100 W Rappel Dr	Bloomington	IN	47404	**800-228-5151**	812-323-2222
Doubletree Guest Suites Indianapolis/Carmel 11355 N Meridian St	Carmel	IN	46032	**800-222-8733**	317-844-7994
Hilton Garden Inn Indianapolis/Carmel 13090 Pennsylvania St	Carmel	IN	46032	**877-782-9444**	317-581-9400
Resorts East Chicago 777 Harrah's Blvd	East Chicago	IN	46312	**877-496-1777**	219-378-3000
Caesars Indiana Casino Hotel 11999 Ave of the Emperors	Elizabeth	IN	47117	**888-766-2648**	812-969-6000
Weston Plaza Hotel & Conference Center 2725 Cassopolis St	Elkhart	IN	46514	**800-521-8400**	574-264-7502
Casino Aztar Hotel 421 NW Riverside Dr	Evansville	IN	47708	**800-544-0120**	812-433-4444
Comfort Inn Evansville East 8331 E Walnut St	Evansville	IN	47715	**800-228-5150**	812-476-3600
Executive Inn Evansville 600 Walnut St	Evansville	IN	47708	**877-424-0888**	812-424-8000
Marriott Evansville Airport 7101 Hwy 41 N	Evansville	IN	47725	**800-228-9290**	812-867-7999
Oak Meadow Lodge 11503 Browning Rd	Evansville	IN	47725	**800-933-1920**	812-867-6431
Residence Inn Evansville 8283 E Walnut St	Evansville	IN	47715	**800-331-3131**	812-471-7191
Corporate Housing Systems 6517 Constitution Dr	Fort Wayne	IN	46804	**800-430-7171**	260-436-7171
Courtyard Fort Wayne 1619 W Washington Ctr Rd	Fort Wayne	IN	46818	**800-321-2211**	260-489-1500
Don Hall's Guesthouse 1313 W Washington Center Rd	Fort Wayne	IN	46825	**800-348-1999**	260-489-2524
Hilton Fort Wayne Convention Center 1020 S Calhoun St	Fort Wayne	IN	46802	**800-445-8667**	260-420-1100
Hilton Garden Inn Fort Wayne 8615 US 24 W	Fort Wayne	IN	46804	**877-782-9444**	260-435-1777
Holiday Inn Hotel & Suites Fort Wayne Downtown 300 E Washington Blvd	Fort Wayne	IN	46802	**800-465-4329**	260-422-5511
Marriott Fort Wayne 305 E Washington Ctr Rd	Fort Wayne	IN	46825	**800-228-9290**	260-484-0411
Residence Inn Fort Wayne 4919 Lima Rd	Fort Wayne	IN	46808	**800-331-3131**	260-484-4700
Adam's Mark Indianapolis Airport 2544 Executive Dr	Indianapolis	IN	46241	**800-444-2326**	317-248-2481
Adam's Mark Indianapolis Downtown 120 W Market St	Indianapolis	IN	46204	**800-444-2326**	317-972-0600
AmeriSuites Indianapolis Keystone 9104 Keystone Crossing	Indianapolis	IN	46240	**800-833-1516**	317-843-0064
Canterbury Hotel 123 S Illinois St	Indianapolis	IN	46225	**800-538-8186**	317-634-3000
Courtyard Indianapolis at the Capitol 320 N Senate Ave	Indianapolis	IN	46204	**800-321-2211**	317-684-7733
Courtyard Indianapolis Downtown 501 W Washington St	Indianapolis	IN	46204	**800-321-2211**	317-635-4443
Crowne Plaza Hotel Indianapolis Downtown-Union Station 123 W Louisiana St	Indianapolis	IN	46225	**800-227-6963**	317-631-2221
Embassy Suites Indianapolis Downtown 110 W Washington St	Indianapolis	IN	46204	**800-362-2779**	317-236-1800
Embassy Suites Indianapolis North 3912 N Vincennes Rd	Indianapolis	IN	46268	**800-362-2779**	317-872-7700
Hilton Garden Inn Indianapolis Downtown 10 E Market St	Indianapolis	IN	46204	**877-782-9444**	317-955-9700
Holiday Inn Select Indianapolis Airport 2501 S High School Rd	Indianapolis	IN	46241	**800-465-4329**	317-244-6861
Holiday Inn Select Indianapolis-North 3850 DePauw Blvd	Indianapolis	IN	46268	**800-465-4329**	317-872-9790
Hyatt Regency Indianapolis 1 S Capitol Ave	Indianapolis	IN	46204	**800-233-1234**	317-632-1234
Marriott Indianapolis East 7202 E 21st St	Indianapolis	IN	46219	**800-228-9290**	317-352-1231
Marriott Indianapolis North 3645 River Crossing Pkwy	Indianapolis	IN	46240	**800-228-9290**	317-705-0000
Marten House Hotel & Lilly Conference Center 1801 W 86th St	Indianapolis	IN	46260	**800-736-5634**	317-872-4111
Omni Indianapolis North Hotel 8181 N Shadeland Ave	Indianapolis	IN	46250	**800-843-6664**	317-849-6668
Omni Severin Hotel 40 W Jackson Pl	Indianapolis	IN	46225	**800-843-6664**	317-634-6664
Radisson Hotel City Centre Indianapolis 31 W Ohio St	Indianapolis	IN	46204	**800-333-3333**	317-635-2000
Renaissance Tower Historic Inn 230 E 9th St	Indianapolis	IN	46204	**800-676-7786**	317-261-1652
Sheraton Indianapolis Hotel & Suites 8787 Keystone Crossing	Indianapolis	IN	46240	**800-325-3535**	317-846-2700
Westin Indianapolis 50 S Capitol Ave	Indianapolis	IN	46204	**800-937-8461**	317-262-8100
Wingate Inn Indianapolis Airport 5797 Rockville Rd	Indianapolis	IN	46224	**800-228-1000**	317-243-8310
Wingate Inn Indianapolis Northwest 6240 InTech Commons Dr	Indianapolis	IN	46278	**800-228-1000**	317-275-7000
Courtyard South Bend/Mishawaka 4825 N Main St	Mishawaka	IN	46545	**800-321-2211**	574-273-9900
Varsity Clubs of America-South Bend Chapter 3800 N Main St	Mishawaka	IN	46545	**800-946-4822**	574-277-0500
Brown County Inn 51 E State Rd 46	Nashville	IN	47448	**800-772-5249**	812-988-2291
Inn at Saint Mary's 53993 US 31-33 N	South Bend	IN	46637	**800-947-8627**	574-232-4000
Marriott South Bend 123 N Saint Joseph St	South Bend	IN	46601	**800-228-9290**	574-234-2000
Residence Inn South Bend 716 N Niles Ave	South Bend	IN	46617	**800-331-3131**	574-289-5555

Iowa

				Toll-Free	Phone
Lodge Hotel & Conference Center 900 Spruce Hills Dr	Bettendorf	IA	52722	**800-285-8637**	563-359-7141
Wingate Inn Omaha Airport 1201 Avenue H	Carter Lake	IA	51510	**800-228-1000**	712-347-6595
Best Western Longbranch Hotel & Convention Center 90 Twixt Town Rd NE	Cedar Rapids	IA	52402	**800-443-7660**	319-377-6386

Iowa (Cont'd)

Name / Address	City	State	Zip	Toll-Free	Phone
Cedar Rapids Marriott 1200 Collins Rd NE	Cedar Rapids	IA	52402	**800-541-1067**	319-393-6600
Clarion Hotel & Convention Center Cedar Rapids 525 33rd Ave SW	Cedar Rapids	IA	52404	**800-424-6423**	319-366-8671
Crowne Plaza Hotel Cedar Rapids 350 1st Ave NE	Cedar Rapids	IA	52401	**800-227-6963**	319-363-8161
Fairfield Inn Cedar Rapids 3243 Southridge Dr SW	Cedar Rapids	IA	52404	**800-228-2800**	319-364-2000
Heartland Inn Cedar Rapids 3315 Southgate Ct SW	Cedar Rapids	IA	52404	**800-334-3277**	319-362-9012
Residence Inn Cedar Rapids 1900 Dodge Road NE	Cedar Rapids	IA	52402	**800-331-3131**	319-395-0111
Courtyard Des Moines-Clive 1520 NW 114th St	Clive	IA	50325	**800-321-2211**	515-225-1222
Best Western Cantebury Inn & Suites 704 1st Ave	Coralville	IA	52241	**800-798-0400**	319-351-0400
Ameristar Casino Hotel Council Bluffs 2200 River Rd	Council Bluffs	IA	51501	**877-462-7827**	712-328-8888
Harrah's Council Bluffs 1 Harrah's Blvd.	Council Bluffs	IA	51501	**888-598-8451**	712-329-6000
Adventureland Inn I-80 & Hwy 65	Des Moines	IA	50316	**800-910-5382**	515-265-7321
Embassy Suites Des Moines on the River 101 E Locust St	Des Moines	IA	50309	**800-362-2779**	515-244-1700
Holiday Inn Des Moines Airport 6111 Flour Dr	Des Moines	IA	50321	**800-248-4013**	515-287-2400
Hotel Fort Des Moines 1000 Walnut St	Des Moines	IA	50309	**800-532-1466**	515-243-1161
Marriott Des Moines 700 Grand Ave	Des Moines	IA	50309	**800-228-9290**	515-245-5500
Quality Inn & Suites Event Center 929 3rd St	Des Moines	IA	50309	**800-903-0009**	515-282-5251
Radisson Inn Des Moines Airport 6800 Fleur Dr	Des Moines	IA	50321	**800-333-3333**	515-285-7777
Renaissance Hotel Savery 401 Locust St	Des Moines	IA	50309	**800-798-2151**	515-244-2151
Best Western Dubuque Inn 3434 Dodge St	Dubuque	IA	52003	**800-747-7760**	563-556-7760
Best Western Midway Hotel Dubuque 3100 Dodge St	Dubuque	IA	52003	**800-336-4392**	563-557-8000
Comfort Inn Dubuque 4055 McDonald Dr	Dubuque	IA	52003	**800-228-5150**	563-556-3006
Fairfield Inn Dubuque 3400 Dodge St	Dubuque	IA	52003	**800-228-2800**	563-588-2349
Heartland Inn Dubuque South 2090 Southpark Ct	Dubuque	IA	52003	**800-334-3277**	563-556-6555
Heartland Inn Dubuque West 4025 McDonald Dr	Dubuque	IA	52003	**800-334-3277**	563-582-3752
Holiday Inn Dubuque Five Flags 450 Main St	Dubuque	IA	52001	**800-465-4329**	563-556-2000
Sheraton Iowa City Hotel 210 S Dubuque St	Iowa City	IA	52240	**800-325-3535**	319-337-4058
Hotel Pattee 1112 Willis Ave	Perry	IA	50220	**888-424-4268**	515-465-3511
Hilton Garden Inn Des Moines/Urbandale 8600 Northpark Dr	Urbandale	IA	50322	**877-782-9444**	515-270-8890
Fairfield Inn West Des Moines 7225 Vista Dr	West Des Moines	IA	50266	**800-228-2800**	515-225-6100
Marriott West Des Moines 1250 Jordan Creek Pkwy	West Des Moines	IA	50266	**800-228-9290**	515-267-1500

Kansas

Name / Address	City	State	Zip	Toll-Free	Phone
Hilton Garden Inn Kansas City/Kansas 520 Minnesota Ave	Kansas City	KS	66101	**877-782-9444**	913-342-7900
Eldridge Hotel 701 Massachusetts St	Lawrence	KS	66044	**800-527-0909**	785-749-5011
Ramada Plaza Hotel Manhattan 1641 Anderson Ave	Manhattan	KS	66502	**800-962-0014**	785-539-7531
Harrah's Prairie Band Casino & Hotel 12305 150th Rd	Mayetta	KS	66509	**800-427-7247**	785-966-7777
Residence Inn Kansas City-Olathe 12215 S Strangline Rd	Olathe	KS	66062	**800-331-3131**	913-829-6700
AmeriSuites Kansas City/Overland Park-Metcalf 6801 W 112th St	Overland Park	KS	66211	**800-833-1516**	913-451-2553
Doubletree Hotel Overland Park-Corporate Woods 10100 College Blvd	Overland Park	KS	66210	**800-222-8733**	913-451-6100
Holiday Inn Hotel & Suites Overland Park 10920 Nall Ave	Overland Park	KS	66211	**800-465-4329**	913-312-0900
Holiday Inn Hotel & Suites Overland Park West 8787 Reeder Rd	Overland Park	KS	66214	**888-825-7538**	913-888-8440
Marriott Overland Park 10800 Metcalf Ave	Overland Park	KS	66210	**800-228-9290**	913-451-8000
Wyndham Garden Hotel Overland Park 7000 W 108th St	Overland Park	KS	66211	**800-996-3426**	913-383-2550
AmeriSuites Topeka Northwest 6021 SW 6th Ave	Topeka	KS	66615	**800-833-1516**	785-273-0066
Best Western Candlelight Inn 2831 SW Fairlawn Rd	Topeka	KS	66614	**800-223-8892**	785-272-9550
Capitol Plaza Hotel Topeka 1717 SW Topeka Blvd	Topeka	KS	66612	**800-579-7937**	785-431-7200
Comfort Inn Topeka 1518 SW Wanamaker Rd	Topeka	KS	66604	**800-228-5150**	785-273-5365
Fairfield Inn Topeka 1530 SW Westport Dr	Topeka	KS	66614	**800-228-2800**	785-273-6800
Holiday Inn Topeka West 605 SW Fairlawn Rd	Topeka	KS	66606	**800-822-0216**	785-272-8040
Quality Inn Topeka 1240 SW Wanamaker Rd	Topeka	KS	66604	**800-228-5151**	785-273-6969
Residence Inn Topeka 1620 SW Westport Dr	Topeka	KS	66604	**800-331-3131**	785-271-8903
Senate Luxury Suites 900 SW Tyler St	Topeka	KS	66612	**800-488-3188**	785-233-5050
Clubhouse Inn & Suites Wichita 515 S Webb Rd	Wichita	KS	67207	**800-258-2466**	316-684-1111
Hilton Garden Inn Wichita 2041 N Bradley Fair Pkwy	Wichita	KS	67206	**877-782-9444**	316-219-4444
Hilton Wichita Airport Executive Conference Center 2098 Airport Rd	Wichita	KS	67209	**800-445-8667**	316-945-5272
Holiday Inn Select Wichita 549 S Rock Rd	Wichita	KS	67207	**800-465-4329**	316-686-7131
Hotel at Old Town 830 E 1st St	Wichita	KS	67202	**877-265-3869**	316-267-4800
Hyatt Regency Wichita 400 W Waterman St	Wichita	KS	67202	**800-233-1234**	316-293-1234
Inn at the Park 3751 E Douglas Ave	Wichita	KS	67218	**800-258-1951**	316-652-0500
Inn at Tallgrass 2280 N Tara Cir	Wichita	KS	67226	**800-684-3466**	316-684-3466
Marriott Wichita 9100 Corporate Hills Dr	Wichita	KS	67207	**800-228-9290**	316-651-0333
Scotsman Inn East 465 S Webb Rd	Wichita	KS	67207	**800-477-7268**	316-684-6363
Scotsman Inn West 5922 W Kellogg St	Wichita	KS	67209	**800-950-7268**	316-943-3800

Kentucky

Name / Address	City	State	Zip	Toll-Free	Phone
Boone Tavern Hotel of Berea College 100 Main St	Berea	KY	40404	**800-366-9358**	859-985-3700
Marriott Cincinnati at RiverCenter 10 W RiverCenter Blvd	Covington	KY	41011	**800-228-9290**	859-261-2900
Hilton Greater Cincinnati Airport 7373 Turfway Rd	Florence	KY	41042	**800-445-8667**	859-371-4400
Drawbridge Inn 2477 Royal Dr	Fort Mitchell	KY	41017	**800-354-9793**	859-341-2800
Holiday Inn Frankfort Capital Plaza 405 Wilkinson Blvd	Frankfort	KY	40601	**800-465-4329**	502-227-5100
Best Western Georgetown Corporate Center Hotel 132 Darby Dr	Georgetown	KY	40324	**877-868-6555**	502-868-0055
Comfort Suites Georgetown 121 Darby Dr	Georgetown	KY	40324	**800-228-5150**	502-868-9500
Marriott Cincinnati Airport 2395 Progress Dr	Hebron	KY	41048	**800-228-9290**	859-586-0166
Campbell House Inn 1375 Harrodsburg Rd	Lexington	KY	40504	**800-354-9235**	859-255-4281
Courtyard Lexington North 775 Newtown Ct	Lexington	KY	40511	**800-321-2582**	859-253-4646
Hilton Garden Inn Lexington 1973 Plaudit Pl	Lexington	KY	40509	**877-782-9444**	859-543-8300
Hilton Suites Lexington Green 245 Lexington Green Cir	Lexington	KY	40503	**800-445-8667**	859-271-4000
Holiday Inn Lexington North 1950 Newtown Pike	Lexington	KY	40511	**800-465-4329**	859-233-0512
Hyatt Regency Lexington 401 W High St	Lexington	KY	40507	**800-233-1234**	859-253-1234
Radisson Plaza Hotel Lexington 369 W Vine St	Lexington	KY	40507	**800-333-3333**	859-231-9000
Sheraton Suites Lexington 2601 Richmond Rd	Lexington	KY	40509	**800-325-3535**	859-268-0060
Springs Inn 2020 Harrodsburg Rd	Lexington	KY	40503	**800-354-9503**	859-277-5751
AmeriSuites Louisville Bluegrass Industrial Park 701 S Hurstbourne Pkwy	Louisville	KY	40222	**800-833-1516**	502-426-0119
Camberley Brown Hotel 335 W Broadway St	Louisville	KY	40202	**800-555-8000**	502-583-1234
Courtyard Louisville East 9608 Blairwood Rd	Louisville	KY	40222	**800-321-2211**	502-429-0006
Executive Inn 970 Phillips Ln	Louisville	KY	40209	**800-626-2706**	502-367-6161
Executive West Hotel 830 Phillips Ln	Louisville	KY	40209	**800-626-2708**	502-367-2251
Galt House Hotel 140 N 4th St	Louisville	KY	40202	**800-626-1814**	502-589-5200
Hilton Garden Inn Louisville Airport 2735 Crittenden Dr	Louisville	KY	40209	**877-782-9444**	502-637-2424
Hilton Garden Inn Louisville East 1530 Alliant Ave	Louisville	KY	40299	**877-782-9444**	502-297-8066
Holiday Inn Louisville Airport East 4004 Gardiner Pt Dr	Louisville	KY	40213	**800-465-4329**	502-452-6361
Hyatt Regency Louisville 320 W Jefferson St	Louisville	KY	40202	**800-233-1234**	502-587-3434
Marriott Louisville East 1903 Embassy Square Blvd	Louisville	KY	40299	**800-228-9290**	502-499-6220
Seelbach Hilton Louisville 500 S 4th St	Louisville	KY	40202	**800-333-3399**	502-585-3200
Executive Inn Rivermont 1 Executive Blvd	Owensboro	KY	42301	**800-626-1936**	270-926-8000
JR's Executive Inn Riverfront 1 Executive Blvd	Paducah	KY	42001	**800-866-3636**	270-443-8000

Louisiana

Name / Address	City	State	Zip	Toll-Free	Phone
AmeriSuites Baton Rouge East 6080 Bluebonnet Blvd	Baton Rouge	LA	70809	**800-833-1516**	225-769-4400
Best Western Chateau Louisianne Suite Hotel 710 N Lobdell Ave	Baton Rouge	LA	70806	**800-256-6263**	225-927-6700
Best Western Richmond Suites Hotel 5668 Hilton Ave	Baton Rouge	LA	70808	**800-332-2582**	225-924-6500
Courtyard Baton Rouge Acadian Center 2421 S Acadian Thwy	Baton Rouge	LA	70808	**800-321-2211**	225-924-6400
Courtyard Baton Rouge Siegen Lane 10307 N Mall Dr	Baton Rouge	LA	70809	**800-321-2211**	225-293-7200
Embassy Suites Baton Rouge 4914 Constitution Ave	Baton Rouge	LA	70808	**800-362-2779**	225-924-6566
Hilton Garden Inn Baton Rouge Airport 3330 Harding Blvd	Baton Rouge	LA	70807	**877-782-9444**	225-357-6177
Holiday Inn Baton Rouge South 9940 Airline Hwy	Baton Rouge	LA	70816	**800-465-4329**	225-924-7021
Holiday Inn Select Executive Center Baton Rouge 4728 Constitution Ave	Baton Rouge	LA	70808	**800-465-4329**	225-925-2244
Holiday Inn Siegen 10455 Reiger Rd	Baton Rouge	LA	70809	**800-465-4329**	225-293-6880
Marriott Baton Rouge 5500 Hilton Ave	Baton Rouge	LA	70808	**800-228-9290**	225-924-5000
Sheraton Baton Rouge Convention Center Hotel 102 France St	Baton Rouge	LA	70802	**800-325-3535**	225-242-2600
Boomtown Hotel Casino 300 Riverside Dr	Bossier City	LA	71111	**877-862-4428**	318-746-0711
Isle of Capri Casino & Hotel 711 Isle of Capri Blvd	Bossier City	LA	71111	**800-843-4753**	318-678-7777
Isle of Capri Inn 3033 Hilton Dr	Bossier City	LA	71111	**800-525-5143**	318-747-2400
Ramada Inn & Conference Center Bossier 4000 Industrial Dr	Bossier City	LA	71111	**800-272-6232**	318-747-0711
Residence Inn Shreveport-Bossier City 1001 Gould Dr	Bossier City	LA	71111	**800-331-3131**	318-747-6220
Hilton Garden Inn New Orleans Airport 4535 Williams Blvd	Kenner	LA	70065	**877-782-9444**	504-712-0504
Hilton New Orleans Airport 901 Airline Dr	Kenner	LA	70062	**800-445-8667**	504-469-5000
Holiday Inn Select New Orleans Airport 2929 Williams Blvd	Kenner	LA	70062	**800-465-4329**	504-467-5611
Wingate Inn New Orleans Airport 1501 Veterans Blvd	Kenner	LA	70062	**800-228-1000**	504-305-1501
Bendel Executive Suites 213 Bendel Rd	Lafayette	LA	70503	**800-990-5708**	337-261-0604
Best Western Hotel Acadiana 1801 W Pinhook Rd	Lafayette	LA	70508	**800-826-8368**	337-233-8120
Comfort Inn Lafayette 1421 SE Evangeline Thwy	Lafayette	LA	70501	**800-800-8752**	337-232-9000
Courtyard Lafayette Airport 214 E Kaliste Saloom Rd	Lafayette	LA	70508	**800-321-2211**	337-232-5005
Hilton Lafayette 1521 W Pinhook Rd	Lafayette	LA	70503	**800-332-2586**	337-235-6111
Harrah's Lake Charles Casino & Hotel 505 N Lakeshore Dr	Lake Charles	LA	70601	**800-427-7247**	337-437-1500
Best Western Landmark Hotel 2601 Severn Ave	Metairie	LA	70002	**800-277-7575**	504-888-9500
Courtyard New Orleans-Metairie 2 Galleria Blvd	Metairie	LA	70001	**800-321-2211**	504-838-3800
Doubletree Hotel New Orleans-Lakeside 3838 N Causeway Blvd	Metairie	LA	70002	**800-222-8733**	504-836-5253
Four Points by Sheraton New Orleans Airport 6401 Veterans Memorial Blvd	Metairie	LA	70003	**800-325-3535**	504-885-5700
Holiday Inn New Orleans-Metairie 3400 S I-10 Service Rd	Metairie	LA	70001	**800-465-4329**	504-833-8201
Quality Hotel & Conference Center 2261 N Causeway Blvd	Metairie	LA	70001	**800-228-5151**	504-833-8211
Ramada Inn Natchitoches 7624 Hwy 1 Bypass	Natchitoches	LA	71457	**888-252-8281**	318-357-8281
Alexa On Royal 119 Royal St	New Orleans	LA	70130	**888-487-9643**	504-962-0600
Ambassador Hotel 535 Tchoupitoulas St	New Orleans	LA	70130	**888-527-5271**	504-527-5271
Astor Crowne Plaza-French Quarter 739 Canal St	New Orleans	LA	70130	**800-684-1127**	504-962-0500

Name / Address	City	State	Zip	Toll-Free	Phone
Avenue Plaza Hotel & Spa 2111 St Charles Ave	New Orleans	LA	70130	**800-535-9575**	504-566-1212
Baronne Plaza Hotel 201 Baronne St	New Orleans	LA	70112	**888-756-0083**	504-522-0083
Best Western French Quarter Landmark Hotel 920 N Rampart St	New Orleans	LA	70116	**800-535-7862**	504-524-3333
Best Western Parc Saint Charles 500 St Charles Ave	New Orleans	LA	70130	**800-521-7551**	504-522-9000
Bienville House Hotel 320 Decatur St	New Orleans	LA	70130	**800-535-7836**	504-529-2345
Brent House Hotel 1512 Jefferson Hwy	New Orleans	LA	70121	**800-535-3986**	504-835-5411
Chateau Dupre Hotel 131 Rue Decatur	New Orleans	LA	70130	**800-256-0135**	504-569-0600
Chateau Sonesta Hotel New Orleans 800 Iberville St	New Orleans	LA	70112	**800-766-3782**	504-586-0800
Clarion Grand Boutique Hotel New Orleans 2001 St Charles Ave	New Orleans	LA	70130	**877-427-8332**	504-558-9966
Columns The 3811 St Charles Ave	New Orleans	LA	70115	**800-445-9308**	504-899-9308
Courtyard New Orleans 124 St Charles Ave	New Orleans	LA	70130	**800-321-2211**	504-581-9005
Dauphine Orleans Hotel 415 Dauphine St	New Orleans	LA	70112	**800-521-7111**	504-586-1800
Doubletree Hotel New Orleans 300 Canal St	New Orleans	LA	70130	**800-222-8733**	504-581-1300
Embassy Suites New Orleans 315 Julia St	New Orleans	LA	70130	**800-362-2779**	504-525-1993
Fairmont New Orleans 123 Baronne St	New Orleans	LA	70112	**800-635-4440**	504-529-7111
Grenoble House 329 Dauphine St	New Orleans	LA	70112	**800-722-1834**	504-522-1331
Hilton Garden Inn New Orleans Convention Center 1001 S Peters St	New Orleans	LA	70130	**877-782-9444**	504-525-0044
Hilton Garden Inn New Orleans French Quarter/CBD 821 Gravier St	New Orleans	LA	70130	**877-782-9444**	504-324-6000
Hilton New Orleans Riverside 2 Poydras St	New Orleans	LA	70140	**800-445-8667**	504-561-0500
Historic French Market Inn 501 Rue Decatur	New Orleans	LA	70130	**888-538-5651**	504-561-5621
Holiday Inn New Orleans Chateau LeMoyne 301 Rue Dauphine	New Orleans	LA	70112	**800-747-3279**	504-581-1303
Holiday Inn New Orleans Downtown-Superdome 330 Loyola Ave	New Orleans	LA	70112	**800-535-7830**	504-581-1600
Holiday Inn New Orleans French Quarter 124 Royal St	New Orleans	LA	70130	**800-447-2830**	504-529-7211
Holiday Inn Select New Orleans Convention Center 881 Convention Center Blvd	New Orleans	LA	70130	**888-524-1881**	504-524-1881
Hotel Andrew Jackson 919 Royal St	New Orleans	LA	70116	**800-654-0224**	504-561-5881
Hotel Le Cirque 2 Lee Circle	New Orleans	LA	70130	**888-487-8782**	504-962-0900
Hotel Maison de Ville 727 Toulouse St	New Orleans	LA	70130	**800-634-1600**	504-561-5858
Hotel Monaco New Orleans 333 Saint Charles Ave	New Orleans	LA	70130	**866-685-8359**	504-561-0010
Hotel Monteleone 214 Royal St	New Orleans	LA	70130	**800-535-9595**	504-523-3341
Hotel Provincial 1024 Rue Chartres	New Orleans	LA	70116	**800-535-7922**	504-581-4995
Hotel Saint Marie 827 Toulouse St	New Orleans	LA	70112	**800-366-2743**	504-561-8951
Hotel Saint Pierre 911 Burgundy St	New Orleans	LA	70116	**800-225-4040**	504-524-4401
Hyatt Regency New Orleans 500 Poydras Plaza	New Orleans	LA	70113	**800-233-1234**	504-561-1234
InterContinental New Orleans 444 St Charles Ave	New Orleans	LA	70130	**800-327-0200**	504-525-5566
International House Hotel 221 Camp St	New Orleans	LA	70130	**800-633-5770**	504-553-9550
JW Marriott New Orleans 614 Canal St	New Orleans	LA	70130	**888-236-2427**	504-525-6500
Lamothe House Hotel 621 Esplanade Ave	New Orleans	LA	70116	**800-367-5858**	504-947-1161
Le Pavillon Hotel 833 Poydras St	New Orleans	LA	70112	**800-535-9095**	504-581-3111
Le Richelieu Hotel 1234 Chartres St	New Orleans	LA	70116	**800-535-9653**	504-529-2492
Maison Dupuy Hotel 1001 Toulouse St	New Orleans	LA	70112	**800-535-9177**	504-586-8000
Maison Orleans - A Ritz-Carlton Hotel 904 Rue Iberville	New Orleans	LA	70112	**800-241-3333**	504-670-2900
Marriott New Orleans 555 Canal St	New Orleans	LA	70130	**800-228-9290**	504-581-1000
Omni Royal Crescent Hotel 535 Gravier St	New Orleans	LA	70130	**800-843-6664**	504-527-0006
Omni Royal Orleans 621 Saint Louis St	New Orleans	LA	70140	**800-843-6664**	504-529-5333
Pelham Hotel 444 Common St	New Orleans	LA	70130	**888-211-3447**	504-522-4444
Place D'Armes Hotel 625 Saint Ann St	New Orleans	LA	70116	**800-366-2743**	504-524-4531
Plaza Suite Hotel Resort 620 S Peters St	New Orleans	LA	70130	**800-770-6721**	504-524-9500
Pontchartrain Hotel 2031 St Charles Ave	New Orleans	LA	70140	**800-777-6193**	504-524-0581
Prince Conti Hotel 830 Conti St	New Orleans	LA	70112	**800-366-2743**	504-529-4172
Queen & Crescent Hotel 344 Camp St	New Orleans	LA	70130	**800-975-6652**	504-587-9700
Radisson Hotel New Orleans 1500 Canal St	New Orleans	LA	70112	**800-333-3333**	504-522-4500
Ramada Plaza Inn on Bourbon 541 Bourbon St	New Orleans	LA	70130	**800-535-7891**	504-524-7611
Renaissance Pere Marquette Hotel 817 Common St *Resv	New Orleans	LA	70112	**800-468-3571***	504-525-1111
Ritz-Carlton New Orleans 921 Canal St	New Orleans	LA	70112	**800-241-3333**	504-524-1331
Royal Sonesta Hotel New Orleans 300 Bourbon St	New Orleans	LA	70130	**800-766-3782**	504-586-0300
Saint Ann/Marie Antoinette Hotel 717 Conti St	New Orleans	LA	70130	**888-535-3603**	504-581-1881
Saint James Hotel 330 Magazine St	New Orleans	LA	70130	**800-273-1889**	504-304-4000
Saint Louis Hotel 730 Bienville St	New Orleans	LA	70130	**800-535-9111**	504-581-7300
Sheraton New Orleans Hotel 500 Canal St	New Orleans	LA	70130	**800-325-3535**	504-525-2500
Soniat House 1133 Chartres St	New Orleans	LA	70116	**800-544-8808**	504-522-0570
W Hotel New Orleans-French Quarter 316 Chartres St	New Orleans	LA	70130	**800-448-4927**	504-581-1200
Whitney The - A Wyndham Historic Hotel 610 Poydras St	New Orleans	LA	70130	**800-996-3426**	504-581-4222
Windsor Court Hotel 300 Gravier St	New Orleans	LA	70130	**800-262-2662**	504-523-6000
Wyndham New Orleans at Canal Place 100 Rue Iberville	New Orleans	LA	70130	**800-996-3426**	504-566-7006
Wyndham Riverfront 701 Convention Center Blvd	New Orleans	LA	70130	**800-996-3426**	504-524-8200
Holiday Inn Shreveport Financial Plaza 5555 Financial Plaza	Shreveport	LA	71129	**800-465-4329**	318-688-3000
Remington Suite Hotel 220 Travis St	Shreveport	LA	71101	**800-444-6750**	318-425-5000
Sam's Town Hotel & Casino Shreveport 315 Clyde Fant Pkwy	Shreveport	LA	71101	**877-429-0711**	318-424-7777
Sheraton Shreveport Hotel 1419 E 70th St	Shreveport	LA	71105	**800-325-3535**	318-797-9900

Maine

Name / Address	City	State	Zip	Toll-Free	Phone
Best Western Senator Inn & Spa 284 Western Ave	Augusta	ME	04330	**800-528-1234**	207-622-5804
Comfort Inn Augusta Civic Center 281 Civic Center Dr	Augusta	ME	04330	**800-228-5150**	207-623-1000
Holiday Inn Augusta Civic Center 110 Community Dr	Augusta	ME	04330	**800-694-6404**	207-622-4751
Best Western White House Inn 155 Littlefield Ave	Bangor	ME	04401	**800-937-8376**	207-862-3737
Comfort Inn Bangor 750 Hogan Rd	Bangor	ME	04401	**800-228-5150**	207-942-7899
Country Inn at the Mall 936 Stillwater Ave	Bangor	ME	04401	**800-244-3961**	207-941-0200
Fairfield Inn Bangor 300 Odlin Rd	Bangor	ME	04401	**800-228-2800**	207-990-0001
Four Points by Sheraton Bangor Airport 308 Godfrey Blvd	Bangor	ME	04401	**800-325-3535**	207-947-6721
Holiday Inn Bangor-Civic Center 500 Main St	Bangor	ME	04401	**800-799-8651**	207-947-8651
Holiday Inn Bangor-Odlin Rd 404 Odlin Rd	Bangor	ME	04401	**800-914-0101**	207-947-0101
Acadia Inn 98 Eden St	Bar Harbor	ME	04609	**800-638-3636**	207-288-3500
Atlantic Eyrie Lodge 6 Norman Rd	Bar Harbor	ME	04609	**800-422-2883**	207-288-9786
Aurora Inn 51 Holland Ave	Bar Harbor	ME	04609	**800-841-8925**	207-288-3771
Balance Rock Inn 21 Albert Meadow	Bar Harbor	ME	04609	**800-753-0494**	207-288-2610
Bar Harbor Hotel-Bluenose Inn 90 Eden St	Bar Harbor	ME	04609	**800-445-4077**	207-288-3348
Bar Harbor Inn Oceanfront Resort Newport Dr Box 7	Bar Harbor	ME	04609	**800-248-3351**	207-288-3351
Bayview Hotel 111 Eden St	Bar Harbor	ME	04609	**800-356-3585**	207-288-5861
Chiltern Inn 3 Cromwell Harbor Rd	Bar Harbor	ME	04609	**800-404-0114**	207-288-0114
Cleftstone Manor 92 Eden St	Bar Harbor	ME	04609	**888-288-4951**	207-288-8086
Cromwell Harbor Motel 359 Main St *Resv	Bar Harbor	ME	04609	**800-544-3201***	207-288-3201
Edgewater Motel & Cottages Box 566	Bar Harbor	ME	04609	**888-310-9920**	207-288-3491
Harborside Hotel & Marina 55 West St	Bar Harbor	ME	04609	**800-328-5033**	207-288-5033
Ledgelawn Inn 66 Mt Desert St	Bar Harbor	ME	04609	**800-274-5334**	207-288-4596
Manor House Inn 106 West St	Bar Harbor	ME	04609	**800-437-0088**	207-288-3759
Mira Monte Inn & Suites 69 Mt Desert St	Bar Harbor	ME	04609	**800-553-5109**	207-288-4263
Park Entrance Oceanfront Motel RR2 Box 180B 15 Ocean Dr	Bar Harbor	ME	04609	**800-288-9703**	207-288-9703
Quimby House Inn 109 Cottage St	Bar Harbor	ME	04609	**800-344-5811**	207-288-5811
Snell House 21 Atlantic Ave	Bar Harbor	ME	04609	**866-763-5524**	207-288-8004
Wonder View Inn & Suites 50 Eden St PO Box 25	Bar Harbor	ME	04609	**888-439-8439**	207-288-3358
Brown's Wharf Motel 121 Atlantic Ave	Boothbay Harbor	ME	04538	**800-334-8110**	207-633-5440
Fisherman's Wharf Inn 22 Commercial St	Boothbay Harbor	ME	04538	**800-628-6872**	207-633-5090
Tugboat Inn 80 Commercial St PO Box 267	Boothbay Harbor	ME	04538	**800-248-2628**	207-633-4434
Captain Daniel Stone Inn 10 Water St	Brunswick	ME	04011	**877-573-5151**	207-725-9898
Harraseeket Inn 162 Main St	Freeport	ME	04032	**800-342-6423**	207-865-9377
Maple Hill Farm Bed & Breakfast Inn 11 Inn Rd	Hallowell	ME	04330	**800-622-2708**	207-622-2708
Ramada Inn Conference Center Lewiston/Auburn 490 Pleasant St	Lewiston	ME	04240	**800-272-6232**	207-784-2331
Bradley Inn 3063 Bristol Rd	New Harbor	ME	04554	**800-942-5560**	207-677-2105
Asticou Inn 15 Peabody Dr	Northeast Harbor	ME	04662	**800-258-3373**	207-276-3344
Kimball Terrace Inn 10 Huntington Rd	Northeast Harbor	ME	04662	**800-454-6225**	207-276-3383
Grand Beach Inn 198 E Grand Ave	Old Orchard Beach	ME	04064	**800-834-9696**	207-934-4621
Doubletree Hotel Portland 1230 Congress St	Portland	ME	04102	**800-222-8733**	207-774-5611
Eastland Park Hotel 157 High St	Portland	ME	04101	**888-671-8008**	207-775-5411
Embassy Suites Portland 1050 Westbrook St	Portland	ME	04102	**800-753-8767**	207-775-2200
Hilton Garden Inn Portland Airport 145 Jetport Blvd	Portland	ME	04102	**877-782-9444**	207-828-1117
Hilton Garden Inn Portland Downtown Waterfront 65 Commercial St	Portland	ME	04101	**877-782-9444**	207-780-0780
Holiday Inn Portland by the Bay 88 Spring St	Portland	ME	04101	**800-345-5050**	207-775-2311
Howard Johnson Plaza Hotel Portland 155 Riverside St	Portland	ME	04103	**800-446-4656**	207-774-5861
Inn at Saint John 939 Congress St	Portland	ME	04102	**800-636-9127**	207-773-6481
Portland Regency Hotel 20 Milk St	Portland	ME	04101	**800-727-3436**	207-774-4200
Coastline Inn 80 John Roberts Rd	South Portland	ME	04106	**800-470-9494**	207-772-3838
Marriott Portland Sable Oaks 200 Sable Oaks Dr	South Portland	ME	04106	**800-228-9290**	207-871-8000
Sheraton South Portland Hotel 363 Maine Mall Rd	South Portland	ME	04106	**800-325-3535**	207-775-6161

Maryland

Name / Address	City	State	Zip	Toll-Free	Phone
Courtyard Annapolis 2559 Riva Rd	Annapolis	MD	21401	**800-321-2211**	410-266-1555
Governor Calvert House 58 State Cir	Annapolis	MD	21401	**800-847-8882**	410-263-2641
Historic Inns of Annapolis 58 State Cir	Annapolis	MD	21401	**800-847-8882**	410-263-2641
Johnson Robert House 58 State Cir	Annapolis	MD	21401	**800-847-8882**	410-263-2641
Loews Annapolis Hotel 126 West St	Annapolis	MD	21401	**800-526-2593**	410-263-7777
Marriott Annapolis Waterfront 80 Compromise St	Annapolis	MD	21401	**800-336-0072**	410-268-7555
Maryland Inn 58 State Cir	Annapolis	MD	21401	**800-847-8882**	410-263-2641
Radisson Hotel Annapolis 210 Holiday Ct	Annapolis	MD	21401	**800-333-3333**	410-224-3150
Residence Inn Annapolis 170 Admiral Cochrane Dr	Annapolis	MD	21401	**800-331-3131**	410-573-0300
Sheraton Barcelo Annapolis Hotel 173 Jennifer Rd	Annapolis	MD	21401	**800-325-3535**	410-266-3131
Admiral Fell Inn 888 S Broadway	Baltimore	MD	21231	**800-292-4667**	410-522-7377
Best Western Hotel & Conference Center Baltimore 5625 O'Donnell St	Baltimore	MD	21224	**800-528-1234**	410-633-9500
Biltmore Suites 205 W Madison St	Baltimore	MD	21201	**800-868-5064**	410-728-6550
Brookshire Inner Harbor Suite Hotel 120 E Lombard St	Baltimore	MD	21202	**877-207-9046**	410-625-1300
Clarion Hotel Peabody Court 612 Cathedral St	Baltimore	MD	21201	**800-292-5500**	410-727-7101
Harbor Court Hotel 550 Light St	Baltimore	MD	21202	**800-824-0076**	410-234-0550
Hilton Garden Inn White Marsh 5015 Campbell Blvd	Baltimore	MD	21236	**877-782-9444**	410-427-0600
Holiday Inn Baltimore Inner Harbor 301 W Lombard St	Baltimore	MD	21201	**800-465-4329**	410-685-3500
Hyatt Regency Baltimore 300 Light St	Baltimore	MD	21202	**800-233-1234**	410-528-1234
Inn at the Colonnade 4 W University Pkwy	Baltimore	MD	21218	**800-222-8733**	410-235-5400
Inn at Henderson's Wharf 1000 Fell St	Baltimore	MD	21231	**800-522-2088**	410-522-7777
Marriott Baltimore-BWI Airport 1743 W Nursery Rd	Baltimore	MD	21240	**800-228-9290**	410-859-8300
Marriott Baltimore Inner Harbor 110 S Eutaw St	Baltimore	MD	21201	**800-228-9290**	410-962-0202
Marriott Baltimore Waterfront Hotel 700 Aliceanna St	Baltimore	MD	21202	**800-228-9290**	410-385-3000
Mount Vernon Hotel 24 W Franklin St	Baltimore	MD	21201	**800-245-5256**	410-727-2000
Pier 5 Hotel 711 Eastern Ave	Baltimore	MD	21202	**866-583-4162**	410-539-2000
Radisson Hotel Baltimore at Cross Keys 100 Village Sq	Baltimore	MD	21210	**800-333-3333**	410-532-6900
Radisson Plaza Lord Baltimore 20 W Baltimore St	Baltimore	MD	21201	**800-333-3333**	410-539-8400

Classified Section

Maryland (Cont'd)

				Toll-Free	Phone
Renaissance Harborplace Hotel 202 E Pratt St	Baltimore	MD	21202	**800-468-3571**	410-547-1200
Sheraton Inner Harbor Hotel 300 S Charles St	Baltimore	MD	21201	**800-325-3535**	410-962-8300
Sheraton International Hotel BWI Airport 7032 Elm Rd	Baltimore	MD	21240	**800-325-3535**	410-859-3300
Tremont Hotel Baltimore 8 E Pleasant St	Baltimore	MD	21202	**800-873-6668**	410-576-1200
Tremont Plaza Hotel Baltimore 222 Saint Paul Pl	Baltimore	MD	21202	**800-873-6668**	410-727-2222
Wyndham Baltimore Inner Harbor 101 W Fayette St	Baltimore	MD	21201	**800-996-3426**	410-752-1100
Holiday Inn Select Bethesda 8120 Wisconsin Ave	Bethesda	MD	20814	**877-888-3001**	301-652-2000
Hyatt Regency Bethesda 7400 Wisconsin Ave	Bethesda	MD	20814	**800-233-1234**	301-657-1234
Marriott Bethesda 5151 Pooks Hill Rd	Bethesda	MD	20814	**800-228-9290**	301-897-9400
Marriott Suites Bethesda 6711 Democracy Plaza	Bethesda	MD	20817	**800-228-9290**	301-897-5600
Holiday Inn Chevy Chase 5520 Wisconsin Ave	Chevy Chase	MD	20815	**800-465-4329**	301-656-1500
Colony South Hotel 7401 Surratts Rd	Clinton	MD	20735	**800-537-1147**	301-856-4500
Hilton Columbia 5485 Twin Knolls Rd	Columbia	MD	21045	**800-235-0653**	410-997-1060
Sheraton Columbia Hotel 10207 Wincopin Cir	Columbia	MD	21044	**800-325-3535**	410-730-[illegible]
Tidewater Inn & Conference Center 101 E Dover St	Easton	MD	21601	**800-237-8775**	410-822-1300
Marriott Gaithersburg Washingtonian Center 9751 Washingtonian Blvd	Gaithersburg	MD	20878	**800-393-3450**	301-590-0044
Marriott Greenbelt 6400 Ivy Ln	Greenbelt	MD	20770	**800-228-9290**	301-441-3700
Embassy Suites Baltimore-Hunt Valley 213 International Cir	Hunt Valley	MD	21030	**800-362-2779**	410-584-1400
Marriott's Hunt Valley Inn 245 Shawan Rd	Hunt Valley	MD	21031	**800-228-9290**	410-785-7000
AmeriSuites Baltimore BWI Airport 940 International Dr	Linthicum	MD	21090	**800-833-1516**	410-859-3366
Hilton Garden Inn BWI Airport 1516 Aero Dr	Linthicum	MD	21090	**877-782-9444**	410-691-0500
Holiday Inn BWI 890 Elkridge Landing Rd	Linthicum	MD	21090	**800-465-4329**	410-859-8400
Best Western Flagship Oceanfront 2600 Baltimore Ave	Ocean City	MD	21842	**800-837-3585**	410-289-3384
Breakers Hotel 3rd St & Boardwalk	Ocean City	MD	21843	**800-283-9165**	410-289-9165
Buckingham Hotel 1405 Baltimore Ave	Ocean City	MD	21842	**800-787-6246**	410-289-6246
Carousel Beachfront Hotel & Suites 11700 Coastal Hwy	Ocean City	MD	21842	**800-641-0011**	410-524-1000
Castle in the Sand Hotel 3701 Atlantic Ave	Ocean City	MD	21842	**800-552-7263**	410-289-6846
Clarion Resort Fontainebleau Hotel 10100 Coastal Hwy	Ocean City	MD	21842	**800-638-2100**	410-524-3535
Coconut Malorie 200 59th St	Ocean City	MD	21842	**800-767-6060**	410-723-6100
Commander Hotel 1401 Atlantic Ave	Ocean City	MD	21842	**888-289-6166**	410-289-6166
Dunes Manor Hotel 2800 Baltimore Ave	Ocean City	MD	21842	**800-523-2888**	410-289-1100
Fenwick Inn 13801 Coastal Hwy	Ocean City	MD	21842	**800-492-1873**	410-250-1100
Flamingo Motel 3100 Baltimore Ave	Ocean City	MD	21842	**800-394-7465**	410-289-6464
Francis Scott Key Motel 12806 Ocean Gateway PO Box 468	Ocean City	MD	21842	**800-213-0088**	410-213-0088
Holiday Inn Ocean City Oceanfront 6600 Coastal Hwy	Ocean City	MD	21842	**800-837-3588**	410-524-1600
Howard Johnson Oceanfront Plaza Hotel 1109 Atlantic Ave	Ocean City	MD	21842	**800-926-1122**	410-289-7251
Lighthouse Club Hotel 201 60th St	Ocean City	MD	21842	**888-371-5400**	410-524-5400
Phillips Beach Plaza Hotel 1301 Atlantic Ave	Ocean City	MD	21842	**800-492-5834**	410-289-9121
Plim Plaza Hotel 2nd St & Boardwalk PO Box 160	Ocean City	MD	21843	**800-837-3587**	410-289-6181
Princess Bayside Beach Hotel & Golf Center 4801 Coastal Hwy	Ocean City	MD	21842	**800-854-9785**	410-723-2900
Princess Royale Oceanfront Hotel & Conference Center 9100 Coastal Hwy	Ocean City	MD	21842	**800-476-9253**	410-524-7777
Quality Inn Ocean City Boardwalk 1601 Atlantic Ave	Ocean City	MD	21842	**800-837-3584**	410-289-4401
Quality Inn Ocean City Oceanfront 5400 Coastal Hwy	Ocean City	MD	21842	**800-837-3586**	410-524-7200
Serene Hotel & Suites 12004 Coastal Hwy	Ocean City	MD	21842	**800-542-4444**	410-250-4000
Hilton Pikesville 1726 Reisterstown Rd	Pikesville	MD	21208	**800-445-8667**	410-653-1100
Doubletree Hotel & Executive Meeting Center Rockville 1750 Rockville Pike	Rockville	MD	20852	**800-222-8733**	301-468-1100
Woodfin Suite Hotel Rockville 1380 Piccard Dr	Rockville	MD	20850	**800-966-3346**	301-590-9880
Inn at Perry Cabin 308 Watkins Ln	Saint Michaels	MD	21663	**800-722-2949**	410-745-2200
Saint Michaels Harbour Inn & Marina 101 N Harbor Rd	Saint Michaels	MD	21663	**800-955-9001**	410-745-9001
Hilton Silver Spring 8727 Colesville Rd	Silver Spring	MD	20910	**800-445-8667**	301-589-5200
Holiday Inn Select Baltimore North 2004 Greenspring Dr	Timonium	MD	21093	**800-465-4329**	410-252-7373
Sheraton Baltimore North Hotel 903 Dulaney Valley Rd	Towson	MD	21204	**800-325-3535**	410-321-7400

Massachusetts

				Toll-Free	Phone
Wyndham Andover 123 Old River Rd	Andover	MA	01810	**800-996-3426**	978-975-3600
Renaissance Bedford Hotel 44 Middlesex Tpke	Bedford	MA	01730	**800-468-3571**	781-275-5500
Wyndham Billerica Hotel 270 Concord Rd	Billerica	MA	01821	**800-996-3426**	978-670-7500
Best Western Boston - Inn at Longwood Medical 342 Longwood Ave	Boston	MA	02115	**800-937-8376**	617-731-4700
Boston Harbor Hotel 70 Rowes Wharf	Boston	MA	02110	**800-752-7077**	617-439-7000
Boston Park Plaza Hotel & Towers 64 Arlington St	Boston	MA	02116	**800-225-2008**	617-426-2000
Chandler Inn 26 Chandler St	Boston	MA	02116	**800-842-3450**	617-482-3450
Colonnade Hotel 120 Huntington Ave	Boston	MA	02116	**800-962-3030**	617-424-7000
Copley Square Hotel 47 Huntington Ave	Boston	MA	02116	**800-225-7062**	617-536-9000
Doubletree Club Boston Bayside 240 Mt Vernon St at Bayside Ctr	Boston	MA	02125	**800-222-8733**	617-822-3600
Doubletree Guest Suites Boston/Cambridge 400 Soldiers Field Rd	Boston	MA	02134	**800-222-8733**	617-783-0090
Eliot Hotel 370 Commonwealth Ave	Boston	MA	02215	**800-443-5468**	617-267-1607
Fairmont Copley Plaza Boston 138 St James Ave	Boston	MA	02116	**800-441-1414**	617-267-5300
Fifteen Beacon Hotel 15 Beacon St	Boston	MA	02108	**877-982-3226**	617-670-1500
Four Seasons Hotel Boston 200 Boylston St	Boston	MA	02116	**800-332-3442**	617-338-4400
Harborside Inn of Boston 185 State St	Boston	MA	02109	**800-437-7668**	617-723-7500
Hilton Boston Back Bay 40 Dalton St	Boston	MA	02115	**800-445-8667**	617-236-1100
Holiday Inn Boston-Logan Airport 225 McClellan Hwy	Boston	MA	02128	**800-465-4329**	617-569-5250
Holiday Inn Select Boston-Government Center 5 Blossom St	Boston	MA	02114	**800-465-4329**	617-742-7630
Hyatt Harborside 101 Harborside Dr	Boston	MA	02128	**800-233-1234**	617-568-1234
Hyatt Regency Boston 1 Ave de Lafayette	Boston	MA	02111	**800-233-1234**	617-912-1234
Langham Hotel Boston 250 Franklin St	Boston	MA	02110	**800-791-7781**	617-451-1900
Lenox Hotel 61 Exeter St	Boston	MA	02116	**800-225-7676**	617-536-5300
Marriott Boston Copley Place 110 Huntington Ave	Boston	MA	02116	**800-228-9290**	617-236-5800
Marriott Boston Long Wharf 296 State St	Boston	MA	02109	**800-228-9290**	617-227-0800
Midtown Hotel 220 Huntington Ave	Boston	MA	02115	**800-343-1177**	617-262-1000
Millennium Bostonian Hotel 26 North St Faneuil Hall Marketplace	Boston	MA	02109	**800-343-0922**	617-523-3600
Milner Hotel Boston 78 Charles St S	Boston	MA	02116	**800-453-1731**	617-426-6220
Omni Parker House 60 School St	Boston	MA	02108	**800-843-6664**	617-227-8600
Radisson Hotel Boston 200 Stuart St	Boston	MA	02116	**800-333-3333**	617-482-1800
Ritz-Carlton Boston 15 Arlington St	Boston	MA	02117	**800-241-3333**	617-536-5700
Ritz-Carlton Boston Common 10 Avery St	Boston	MA	02111	**888-698-3322**	617-574-7100
Seaport Hotel 1 Seaport Ln	Boston	MA	02210	**877-732-7678**	617-385-4000
Shawmut Inn 280 Friend St	Boston	MA	02114	**800-350-7784**	617-720-5544
Sheraton Boston Hotel 39 Dalton St	Boston	MA	02199	**800-325-3535**	617-236-2000
Tremont Boston - A Wyndham Historic Hotel 275 Tremont St	Boston	MA	02116	**888-223-7220**	617-426-1400
Westin Copley Place 10 Huntington Ave	Boston	MA	02116	**800-937-8461**	617-262-9600
Wyndham Boston Hotel 89 Broad St	Boston	MA	02110	**800-996-3426**	617-556-0006
Holiday Inn Boston-Brookline 1200 Beacon St	Brookline	MA	02440	**800-465-4329**	617-277-1200
Marriott Burlington 1 Mall Rd	Burlington	MA	01803	**800-228-9290**	781-229-6565
Charles Hotel Harvard Square 1 Bennett St	Cambridge	MA	02138	**800-882-1818**	617-864-1200
Harvard Square Hotel 110 Mt Auburn St	Cambridge	MA	02138	**800-458-5886**	617-864-5200
Hotel Marlowe Cambridge 25 Edwind H Land Blvd	Cambridge	MA	02141	**800-825-7040**	617-868-8000
Hotel@MIT - University Park 20 Sidney St	Cambridge	MA	02139	**800-222-2733**	617-577-0200
Hyatt Regency Cambridge 575 Memorial Dr	Cambridge	MA	02139	**800-233-1234**	617-492-1234
Inn at Harvard 1201 Massachusetts Ave	Cambridge	MA	02138	**800-458-5886**	617-491-2222
Marriott Cambridge 2 Cambridge Ctr	Cambridge	MA	02142	**800-228-9290**	617-494-6600
Royal Sonesta Hotel Boston 5 Cambridge Pkwy	Cambridge	MA	02142	**800-766-3782**	617-806-4200
Sheraton Commander Hotel 16 Garden St	Cambridge	MA	02138	**800-325-3535**	617-547-4800
Seafarer of Chatham 2079 Main St	Chatham	MA	02633	**800-786-2772**	508-432-1739
Radisson Hotel & Suites Chelmsford 10 Independence Dr	Chelmsford	MA	01824	**800-333-3333**	978-256-0800
Wyndham Chelsea Hotel 201 Everett Ave	Chelsea	MA	02150	**800-996-3426**	617-884-2900
Plantation Inn of New England 295 Burnett Rd	Chicopee	MA	01020	**800-248-8495**	413-592-8200
Cohasset Harbor Inn 124 Elm St	Cohasset	MA	02025	**800-252-5287**	781-383-6650
Hilton Dedham Place 25 Allied Dr	Dedham	MA	02026	**800-445-8667**	781-329-7900
Harbor View Hotel 131 N Water St PO Box 7 Martha's Vineyard	Edgartown	MA	02539	**800-225-6005**	508-627-7000
Residence Inn Boston-Foxborough 250 Foxborough Blvd	Foxborough	MA	02035	**800-331-3131**	508-698-2800
Residence Inn Boston-Franklin 4 Forge Pkwy	Franklin	MA	02038	**800-331-3131**	508-541-8188
Holiday Inn Springfield-Holyoke Holidome & Conference Center 245 Whiting Farms Rd	Holyoke	MA	01040	**800-465-4329**	413-534-3311
Radisson Hotel Hyannis 287 Iyannough Rd	Hyannis	MA	02601	**800-333-3333**	508-771-1700
Gateways Inn 51 Walker St	Lenox	MA	01240	**888-492-9466**	413-637-2532
Yankee Inn 461 Pittsfield Rd	Lenox	MA	01240	**800-835-2364**	413-499-3700
Four Points by Sheraton Leominster 99 Erdman Way	Leominster	MA	01453	**800-325-3535**	978-534-9000
Battle Green Inn 1720 Massachusetts Ave	Lexington	MA	02420	**800-343-0235**	781-862-6100
Sheraton Lexington Inn 727 Marrett Rd	Lexington	MA	02421	**800-325-3535**	781-862-8700
Best Western Royal Plaza Hotel & Trade Center 181 Boston Post Rd W	Marlborough	MA	01752	**888-543-9500**	508-460-0700
AmeriSuites Boston/Medford 116 Riverside Ave NE	Medford	MA	02155	**800-833-1516**	781-395-8500
Jared Coffin House 29 Broad St	Nantucket	MA	02554	**800-248-2405**	508-228-2400
Wauwinet The PO Box 2580 Wauwinet Rd	Nantucket	MA	02584	**800-426-8718**	508-228-0145
White Elephant Inn & Cottages 50 Easton St	Nantucket	MA	02554	**800-475-2637**	508-228-2500
Crowne Plaza Hotel Boston-Natick 1360 Worcester St	Natick	MA	01760	**800-227-6963**	508-653-8800
Sheraton Needham Hotel 100 Cabot St	Needham	MA	02494	**800-325-3535**	781-444-1110
Marriott Newton 2345 Commonwealth Ave	Newton	MA	02466	**800-228-9290**	617-969-1000
Clarion Hotel & Conference Center Northampton 1 Atwood Dr	Northampton	MA	01060	**800-582-2929**	413-586-1211
Hotel Northampton 36 King St	Northampton	MA	01060	**800-547-3529**	413-584-3100
Marriott Peabody 8-A Centennial Dr	Peabody	MA	01960	**800-228-9290**	978-977-9700
Crowne Plaza Hotel Pittsfield 1 West St	Pittsfield	MA	01201	**800-227-6963**	413-499-2000
Hawthorne Hotel 18 Washington Sq W	Salem	MA	01970	**800-729-7829**	978-744-4080
Dan'l Webster Inn 149 Main St	Sandwich	MA	02563	**800-444-3566**	508-888-3622
Hilton Garden Inn Springfield 800 W Columbus Ave	Springfield	MA	01115	**877-782-9444**	413-886-8000
Marriott Springfield 2 Boland Way	Springfield	MA	01115	**800-228-9290**	413-781-7111
Sheraton Springfield at Monarch Place 1 Monarch Pl	Springfield	MA	01144	**800-426-9004**	413-781-1010
Publick House Historic Resort 295 Main St Rt 131	Sturbridge	MA	01566	**800-782-5425**	508-347-3313
Sturbridge Host Hotel & Conference Center 366 Main St	Sturbridge	MA	01566	**800-582-3232**	508-347-7393
Stonehedge Inn 160 Pawtucket Blvd	Tyngsboro	MA	01879	**800-648-7070**	978-649-4400
Sheraton Colonial Hotel & Golf Club Boston North 1 Audubon Rd	Wakefield	MA	01880	**800-325-3535**	781-245-9300
Westin Waltham-Boston 70 3rd Ave	Waltham	MA	02451	**800-937-8461**	781-290-5600
Residence Inn Boston-Westborough 25 Connector Rd	Westborough	MA	01581	**800-331-3131**	508-366-7700
Wyndham Westborough 5400 Computer Dr	Westborough	MA	01581	**800-996-3426**	508-366-5511
Residence Inn Boston-Westford 7 Lan Dr	Westford	MA	01886	**800-331-3131**	978-392-1407
Westford Regency Inn & Conference Center 219 Littleton Rd	Westford	MA	01886	**800-543-7801**	978-692-8200
Orchards Hotel 222 Adams Rd	Williamstown	MA	01267	**800-225-1517**	413-458-9611
Crowne Plaza Hotel Boston-Woburn 2 Forbes Rd	Woburn	MA	01801	**800-227-6963**	781-932-0999
Beechwood Hotel 363 Plantation St	Worcester	MA	01605	**800-344-2589**	508-754-5789
Crowne Plaza Hotel Worcester Downtown 10 Lincoln Sq	Worcester	MA	01608	**800-628-4240**	508-791-1600

Michigan

				Toll-Free	Phone
Bell Tower Hotel 300 S Thayer St	Ann Arbor	MI	48104	**800-562-3559**	734-769-3010

				Toll-Free	Phone
Best Western Executive Plaza Ann Arbor 2900 Jackson Ave	Ann Arbor	MI	48103	**888-290-1739**	734-665-4444
Comfort Inn & Business Center Ann Arbor 2455 Carpenter Rd	Ann Arbor	MI	48108	**800-973-6101**	734-973-6100
Courtyard Ann Arbor 3205 Boardwalk	Ann Arbor	MI	48108	**800-321-2211**	734-995-5900
Dahlmann Campus Inn 615 E Huron St	Ann Arbor	MI	48104	**800-666-8693**	734-769-2200
Fairfield Inn Ann Arbor 3285 Boardwalk	Ann Arbor	MI	48108	**800-228-2800**	734-995-5200
Holiday Inn Ann Arbor North Campus 3600 Plymouth Rd	Ann Arbor	MI	48105	**800-800-5560**	734-769-9800
Residence Inn Ann Arbor 800 Victors Way	Ann Arbor	MI	48108	**800-331-3131**	734-996-5666
Sheraton Inn Ann Arbor 3200 Boardwalk	Ann Arbor	MI	48108	**800-325-3535**	734-996-0600
Weber's Inn 3050 Jackson Rd	Ann Arbor	MI	48103	**800-443-3050**	734-769-2500
Wingate Inn Auburn Hills 2200 Featherstone Rd	Auburn Hills	MI	48326	**800-228-1000**	248-334-3324
Battle Creek Inn 5050 Beckley Rd	Battle Creek	MI	49015	**800-232-3405**	269-979-1100
McCamly Plaza Hotel 50 Capital Ave SW	Battle Creek	MI	49017	**888-622-2659**	269-963-7050
Townsend Hotel 100 Townsend St	Birmingham	MI	48009	**800-548-4172**	248-642-7900
Kingsley Hotel & Suites 39475 N Woodward Ave	Bloomfield Hills	MI	48304	**800-544-6835**	248-644-1400
Dearborn Inn The - A Marriott Hotel 20301 Oakwood Blvd	Dearborn	MI	48124	**800-228-9290**	313-271-2700
Hyatt Regency Dearborn Fairlane Town Ctr	Dearborn	MI	48126	**800-233-1234**	313-593-1234
Ritz-Carlton Dearborn 300 Town Ctr Dr	Dearborn	MI	48126	**800-241-3333**	313-441-2000
Atheneum Suite Hotel & Conference Center 1000 Brush Ave	Detroit	MI	48226	**800-772-2323**	313-962-2323
Courtyard Detroit Downtown 333 E Jefferson Ave	Detroit	MI	48226	**800-321-2211**	313-222-7700
Hilton Garden Inn Detroit Downtown 351 Gratiot Ave	Detroit	MI	48226	**877-782-9444**	313-967-0900
Hotel Pontchartrain 2 Washington Blvd	Detroit	MI	48226	**800-227-6963**	313-965-0200
Hotel Saint Regis Detroit 3071 W Grand Blvd	Detroit	MI	48202	**800-848-4810**	313-873-3000
Marriott Renaissance Center Detroit Jefferson & Brush Sts	Detroit	MI	48243	**800-228-9290**	313-568-8000
Omni Detroit Hotel at River Place 1000 River Pl	Detroit	MI	48207	**800-843-6664**	313-259-9500
Ramada Inn Detroit Downtown 400 Bagley Ave	Detroit	MI	48226	**800-272-6232**	313-962-2300
Residence Inn Dearborn 5777 Southfield Service Dr	Detroit	MI	48228	**800-331-3131**	313-441-1700
Kellogg Hotel & Conference Center S Harrison Rd Michigan State University Campus	East Lansing	MI	48824	**800-875-5090**	517-432-4000
Marriott East Lansing at University Place 300 MAC Ave	East Lansing	MI	48823	**800-228-9290**	517-337-4440
Residence Inn East Lansing 1600 E Grand River Ave	East Lansing	MI	48823	**800-331-3131**	517-332-7711
Holiday Inn Flint 5353 Gateway Centre	Flint	MI	48507	**888-570-1770**	810-232-5300
Wingate Inn Grand Blanc Airport 1359 Grand Pointe Ct	Grand Blanc	MI	48439	**800-228-1000**	810-694-9900
Amway Grand Plaza Hotel 187 Monroe Ave NW	Grand Rapids	MI	49503	**800-253-3590**	616-774-2000
Best Western Midway Hotel Grand Rapids 4101 28th St	Grand Rapids	MI	49512	**800-528-1234**	616-942-2550
Comfort Inn Grand Rapids Airport 4155 28th St SE	Grand Rapids	MI	49512	**800-228-5150**	616-957-2080
Courtyard Grand Rapids Downtown 11 Monroe Ave NW	Grand Rapids	MI	49503	**800-321-2211**	616-242-6000
Crowne Plaza Hotel Grand Rapids 5700 28th St SE	Grand Rapids	MI	49546	**888-957-9575**	616-957-1770
Hilton Grand Rapids Airport 4747 28th St SE	Grand Rapids	MI	49512	**877-944-5866**	616-957-0100
Quality Inn Grand Rapids Terrace Club 4495 28th St SE	Grand Rapids	MI	49512	**800-228-5151**	616-956-8080
Radisson Hotel Grand Rapids East 3333 28th St SE	Grand Rapids	MI	49512	**800-333-3333**	616-949-9222
Residence Inn Grand Rapids-East 2701 E Beltline Ave SE	Grand Rapids	MI	49546	**800-331-3131**	616-957-8111
Sleep Inn Grand Rapids 4284 29th St SE	Grand Rapids	MI	49512	**800-753-3746**	616-975-9000
Radisson Plaza Hotel at Kalamazoo Center 100 W Michigan Ave	Kalamazoo	MI	49007	**800-333-3333**	269-343-3333
Best Western Midway Hotel Lansing 7711 W Saginaw Hwy	Lansing	MI	48917	**800-937-8597**	517-627-8471
Clarion Hotel & Conference Center Lansing 3600 Dunckel Dr	Lansing	MI	48910	**800-252-7466**	517-351-7600
Courtyard Lansing 2710 Lake Lansing Rd	Lansing	MI	48912	**800-321-2211**	517-482-0500
Holiday Inn Lansing South/Convention Center 6820 S Cedar St	Lansing	MI	48911	**800-465-4329**	517-694-8123
Quality Inn University 3121 E Grand River Ave	Lansing	MI	48912	**800-228-5151**	517-351-1440
Radisson Hotel Lansing 111 N Grand Ave	Lansing	MI	48933	**800-333-3333**	517-482-0188
Sheraton Lansing Hotel 925 S Creyts Rd	Lansing	MI	48917	**800-325-3535**	517-323-7100
Courtyard Detroit Livonia 17200 N Laurel Park Dr	Livonia	MI	48152	**800-321-2211**	734-462-2000
Marriott Livonia 17100 Laurel Park Dr N	Livonia	MI	48152	**800-228-9290**	734-462-3100
Landmark Inn 230 N Front St	Marquette	MI	49855	**800-752-6362**	906-228-2580
Wyndham Garden Hotel Novi 42100 Crescent Blvd	Novi	MI	48375	**800-996-3426**	248-344-8800
Marriott Pontiac at Centerpoint 3600 Centerpoint Pkwy	Pontiac	MI	48341	**800-228-9290**	248-253-9800
Clarion Hotel Barcelo Metro Airport 8600 Merriman Rd	Romulus	MI	48174	**800-424-6423**	734-728-7900
Courtyard Detroit Metro Airport 30653 Flynn Dr	Romulus	MI	48174	**800-321-2211**	734-721-3200
Crowne Plaza Hotel Detroit Metro Airport 8000 Merriman Rd	Romulus	MI	48174	**800-227-6963**	734-729-2600
Doubletree Hotel Detroit Metropolitan Airport 31500 Wick Rd	Romulus	MI	48174	**800-222-8733**	734-467-8000
Hilton Garden Inn Detroit Metro Airport 31800 Smith Rd	Romulus	MI	48174	**877-782-9444**	734-727-6000
Hilton Suites Detroit Metro Airport 8600 Wickham Rd	Romulus	MI	48174	**800-445-8667**	734-728-9200
Marriott Detroit Romulus at Metro Airport 30559 Flynn Dr	Romulus	MI	48174	**800-228-9290**	734-729-7555
Best Western Georgian Inn 31327 Gratiot Ave	Roseville	MI	48066	**800-477-1466**	586-294-0400
Saint Clair Inn 500 N Riverside Ave	Saint Clair	MI	48079	**800-482-8327**	810-329-2222
Marriott Southfield 27033 Northwestern Hwy	Southfield	MI	48034	**800-228-9290**	248-356-7400
Ramada Inn & Convention Center Southfield 17017 W Nine-Mile Rd	Southfield	MI	48075	**800-272-6232**	248-552-7777
Westin Southfield-Detroit 1500 Town Center Dr	Southfield	MI	48075	**800-937-8461**	248-827-4000
Best Western Sterling Inn 34911 Van Dyke Ave	Sterling Heights	MI	48312	**800-937-8376**	586-979-1400
Marriott Troy 200 W Big Beaver Rd	Troy	MI	48084	**800-228-9290**	248-680-9797
Somerset Inn 2601 W Big Beaver Rd	Troy	MI	48084	**800-228-8769**	248-643-7800
Marriott Ypsilanti at Eagle Crest 1275 S Huron St	Ypsilanti	MI	48197	**800-228-9290**	734-487-2000

Minnesota

				Toll-Free	Phone
Clarion Hotel Minneapolis Airport 5151 American Blvd W	Bloomington	MN	55437	**800-252-7466**	952-830-1300
Embassy Suites Minneapolis Airport 7901 34th Ave S	Bloomington	MN	55425	**800-362-2779**	952-854-1000
Hilton Minneapolis-Saint Paul Airport 3800 E 80th St	Bloomington	MN	55425	**800-637-7453**	952-854-2100
Holiday Inn Select Minneapolis/Saint Paul International Airport 3 Appletree Sq	Bloomington	MN	55425	**800-465-4329**	952-854-9000
Hotel Sofitel Minneapolis 5601 W 78th St	Bloomington	MN	55439	**800-876-6303**	952-835-1900
Marriott Minneapolis Airport 2020 E American Blvd	Bloomington	MN	55425	**800-228-9290**	952-854-7441
Best Western Edgewater 2400 London Rd	Duluth	MN	55812	**800-777-7925**	218-728-3601
Buena Vista Motel 1144 Mesaba Ave	Duluth	MN	55811	**800-569-8124**	218-722-7796
Canal Park Inn 250 Canal Park Dr	Duluth	MN	55802	**800-777-8560**	218-727-8821
Fitger's Inn 600 E Superior St	Duluth	MN	55802	**888-348-4377**	218-722-8826
Holiday Inn Hotel & Suites Duluth Downtown Waterfront 200 W 1st St	Duluth	MN	55802	**800-477-7089**	218-722-1202
Inn on Gitche Gumee 8517 Congdon Blvd	Duluth	MN	55804	**800-317-4979**	218-525-4979
Inn on Lake Superior 350 Canal Park Dr	Duluth	MN	55802	**888-668-4352**	218-726-1111
Mountain Villas 9525 W Skyline Pkwy	Duluth	MN	55810	**800-642-6377**	218-624-5784
Radisson Hotel Duluth-Harborview 505 W Superior St	Duluth	MN	55802	**800-333-3333**	218-727-8981
Suites at Waterfront Plaza 325 Lake Ave S	Duluth	MN	55802	**877-766-2665**	218-722-2143
Voyageur Lakewalk Inn 333 E Superior St	Duluth	MN	55802	**800-258-3911**	218-722-3911
Hilton Garden Inn Minneapolis Eagan 1975 Rahncliff Ct	Eagan	MN	55122	**877-782-9444**	651-686-4605
Hilton Garden Inn Minneapolis/Eden Prairie 6330 Point Chase	Eden Prairie	MN	55344	**877-782-9444**	952-995-9000
Hilton Garden Inn Minneapolis/Maple Grove 6350 Vinewood Ln N	Maple Grove	MN	55311	**877-782-9444**	763-509-9500
Crowne Plaza Minneapolis Northstar Hotel 618 2nd Ave S	Minneapolis	MN	55402	**800-556-7827**	612-338-2288
Doubletree Guest Suites Minneapolis 1101 LaSalle Ave	Minneapolis	MN	55403	**800-222-8733**	612-332-6800
Doubletree Hotel Minneapolis-Park Place 1500 Park Place Blvd	Minneapolis	MN	55416	**800-222-8733**	952-542-8600
Grand Hotel Minneapolis 615 2nd Ave S	Minneapolis	MN	55402	**866-843-4726**	612-339-3655
Hilton Minneapolis 1001 Marquette Ave	Minneapolis	MN	55403	**800-445-8667**	612-376-1000
Holiday Inn Minneapolis Metrodome 1500 Washington Ave S	Minneapolis	MN	55454	**800-448-3663**	612-333-4646
Hyatt Regency Minneapolis 1300 Nicollet Mall	Minneapolis	MN	55403	**800-233-1234**	612-370-1234
Marquette Hotel 710 Marquette Ave	Minneapolis	MN	55402	**800-328-4782**	612-333-4545
Marriott Minneapolis City Center 30 S 7th St	Minneapolis	MN	55402	**800-228-9290**	612-349-4000
Millennium Hotel Minneapolis 1313 Nicollet Mall	Minneapolis	MN	55403	**866-866-8086**	612-332-6000
Radisson Plaza Hotel Minneapolis 35 S 7th St	Minneapolis	MN	55402	**800-333-3333**	612-339-4900
Residence Inn Minneapolis Downtown 45 S 8th St	Minneapolis	MN	55402	**800-331-3131**	612-677-1000
Marriott Minneapolis Southwest 5801 Opus Pkwy	Minnetonka	MN	55343	**800-228-9290**	952-935-5500
Sheraton Minneapolis West Hotel 12201 Ridgedale Dr	Minnetonka	MN	55305	**800-325-3535**	952-593-0000
Wingate Inn Minneapolis 970 Helena Ave N	Oakdale	MN	55128	**866-680-3000**	651-578-8466
Saint James Hotel 406 Main St	Red Wing	MN	55066	**800-252-1875**	651-388-2846
Bell Tower Inn 1235 2nd St SW	Rochester	MN	55902	**800-448-7583**	507-289-2233
Best Western Apache 1517 16th St SW	Rochester	MN	55902	**800-552-7224**	507-289-8866
Best Western Soldier's Field Tower & Suites 401 6th St SW	Rochester	MN	55902	**800-366-2067**	507-288-2677
Blondell's Crown Square 1406 2nd St SW	Rochester	MN	55902	**800-441-5209**	507-282-9444
Fiksdal Motel 1215 2nd St SW	Rochester	MN	55902	**800-366-3451**	507-288-2671
Hilton Garden Inn Rochester Downtown 225 S Broadway	Rochester	MN	55904	**877-782-9444**	507-285-1234
Holiday Inn Rochester City Centre 220 S Broadway	Rochester	MN	55904	**800-241-1597**	507-252-8200
Kahler Grand Hotel 20 SW 2nd Ave	Rochester	MN	55902	**800-533-1655**	507-282-2581
Marriott Rochester at Mayo Clinic 101 1st Ave SW	Rochester	MN	55902	**800-228-9290**	507-280-6000
Radisson Plaza Hotel Rochester 150 S Broadway	Rochester	MN	55904	**800-333-3333**	507-281-8000
Embassy Suites Saint Paul Downtown 175 E 10th St	Saint Paul	MN	55101	**800-362-2779**	651-224-5400
Holiday Inn Saint Paul North 1201 W County Rd 'E'	Saint Paul	MN	55112	**800-777-2232**	651-636-4123
Radisson City Center Hotel Saint Paul 411 Minnesota St	Saint Paul	MN	55101	**800-333-3333**	651-291-8800
Radisson Riverfront Saint Paul 11 Kellogg Blvd E	Saint Paul	MN	55101	**800-333-3333**	651-292-1900
Saint Paul Hotel 350 Market St	Saint Paul	MN	55102	**800-292-9292**	651-292-9292
Hilton Garden Inn Minneapolis Saint Paul/Shoreview 1050 Gramsie Rd	Shoreview	MN	55126	**877-782-9444**	651-415-1956

Mississippi

				Toll-Free	Phone
Balmoral Inn 120 Balmoral Ave	Biloxi	MS	39531	**800-393-9131**	228-388-6776
Biloxi Beach Resort Inn 2736 Beach Blvd	Biloxi	MS	39531	**800-345-1570**	228-388-3310
Breakers Inn 2506 Beach Blvd	Biloxi	MS	39531	**800-624-5031**	228-388-6320
Casino Magic Biloxi 195 Beach Blvd	Biloxi	MS	39530	**800-562-4425**	228-386-4600
Isle of Capri Casino Resort 151 Beach Blvd	Biloxi	MS	39530	**800-843-4753**	228-435-5400
Royal Holiday Beach Resort 1980 Beach Blvd	Biloxi	MS	39531	**800-874-0402**	228-388-7553
Travel Inn Biloxi 2010 Beach Blvd	Biloxi	MS	39531	**800-676-4465**	228-388-5531
Wingate Inn Biloxi-D Iberville 12009 Indian River Dr	D'Iberville	MS	39540	**800-228-1000**	228-396-0036
Chateau de La Mer Resort Inn 1410 Beach Blvd	Gulfport	MS	39507	**800-257-5551**	228-896-1703
Crystal Inn Gulfport 9379 Canal Rd	Gulfport	MS	39503	**888-822-9600**	228-822-9600
Holiday Inn Gulfport Beachfront 1600 E Beach Blvd	Gulfport	MS	39501	**800-441-0887**	228-864-4310
Comfort Inn University 6541 Hwy 49	Hattiesburg	MS	39401	**800-424-6423**	601-264-1881
Best Western Metro Inn 1520 Ellis Ave	Jackson	MS	39204	**888-788-9788**	601-355-7483

Mississippi (Cont'd)

Name / Address	City	State	ZIP	Toll-Free	Phone
Clarion Hotel Jackson 400 Greymont Ave	Jackson	MS	39202	**800-252-7466**	601-969-2141
Comfort Inn Jackson Southwest 2800 Greenway Dr	Jackson	MS	39204	**800-228-5150**	601-922-5600
Courtyard Jackson 6280 Ridgewood Ct	Jackson	MS	39211	**800-321-2211**	601-956-9991
Crowne Plaza Hotel Jackson Downtown 200 E Amite St	Jackson	MS	39201	**800-227-6963**	601-969-5100
Edison Walthall Hotel 225 E Capitol St	Jackson	MS	39201	**800-932-6161**	601-948-6161
Hilton Jackson 1001 E County Line Rd	Jackson	MS	39211	**888-263-0524**	601-957-2800
Holiday Inn Hotel & Suites Jackson North 5075 I-55 N	Jackson	MS	39206	**800-465-4329**	601-366-9411
Ramada Inn Southwest Conference Center 1525 Ellis Ave	Jackson	MS	39204	**888-298-2054**	601-944-1150
Residence Inn Jackson 881 E River Pl	Jackson	MS	39202	**800-331-3131**	601-355-3599
Monmouth Plantation 36 Melrose Ave	Natchez	MS	39120	**800-828-4531**	601-442-5852
Comfort Inn Jackson Airport 235 S Pearson Rd	Pearl	MS	39208	**800-228-5150**	601-932-6009
Bally's Casino Tunica 1450 Bally's Blvd Casino Ctr	Robinsonville	MS	38664	**800-382-2559**	662-357-1500
Fitzgeralds Casino & Hotel Tunica 711 Lucky Ln	Robinsonville	MS	38664	**888-766-5825**	662-363-5825
Gold Strike Casino Resort 1010 Casino Ctr Dr *Resv	Robinsonville	MS	38664	**888-245-7829***	662-357-1111
Resorts Tunica 1100 Casino Strip Blvd PO Box 750 *Resv	Robinsonville	MS	38664	**866-797-7111***	662-363-7777
Sheraton Casino & Hotel 1107 Casino Center Dr	Robinsonville	MS	38664	**800-391-3777**	662-363-4900
Best Western Tupelo 897 Harmony Ln	Tupelo	MS	38801	**800-780-7234**	662-842-4403
Comfort Inn Tupelo 1190 N Gloster St	Tupelo	MS	38804	**800-228-5150**	662-842-5100
Courtyard Tupelo 1320 N Gloster St	Tupelo	MS	38804	**800-321-2211**	662-841-9960
Ramada Inn Tupelo 854 N Gloster St	Tupelo	MS	38801	**888-298-2054**	662-844-4111
Harrah's Vicksburg 1310 Mulberry St	Vicksburg	MS	39180	**800-843-2343**	601-636-3423

Missouri

Name / Address	City	State	ZIP	Toll-Free	Phone
Renaissance Saint Louis Hotel-Airport 9801 Natural Bridge Rd	Berkeley	MO	63134	**800-228-9290**	314-429-1100
Best Western Branson Rustic Oak 403 W Main St	Branson	MO	65616	**800-828-0404**	417-334-6464
Best Western Branson Towers 236 Shepherd of the Hills Expy	Branson	MO	65616	**800-683-1122**	417-336-4500
Best Western Center Pointe Inn 3215 W Hwy 76	Branson	MO	65616	**888-334-1894**	417-334-1894
Best Western Music Capital Inn 3257 Shepherd of the Hills Expy	Branson	MO	65616	**877-334-8378**	417-334-8378
Cascades Inn 3226 Shepherd of the Hills Expy	Branson	MO	65616	**800-588-8424**	417-335-8424
Chateau on the Lake 415 N State Hwy 265	Branson	MO	65616	**888-333-5253**	417-334-1161
Clarion Hotel at the Palace 2820 W Hwy 76 PO Box 6004	Branson	MO	65615	**800-725-2236**	417-334-7666
Grand Country Inn Grand Country Sq 1945 W Hwy 76	Branson	MO	65616	**800-828-9068**	417-335-3535
Grand Oaks Hotel 2315 Green Mountain Dr	Branson	MO	65616	**800-553-6423**	417-336-6423
Hillbilly Inn Motel 1166 W Hwy 76	Branson	MO	65616	**800-535-0739**	417-334-3946
Hotel Grand Victorian 2325 W Hwy 76	Branson	MO	65616	**800-324-8751**	417-336-2935
Lodge of the Ozarks 3431 W Hwy 76	Branson	MO	65616	**800-213-2584**	417-334-7535
Plantation Inn 3470 Keeter St	Branson	MO	65616	**800-324-8748**	417-334-3600
Radisson Hotel Branson 120 S Wildwood Dr	Branson	MO	65616	**800-333-3333**	417-335-5767
Residence Inn Branson 280 S Wildwood Dr	Branson	MO	65616	**800-331-3131**	417-336-4077
Settle Inn Resort & Conference Center 3050 Green Mountain Dr	Branson	MO	65616	**800-677-6906**	417-335-4700
Thousand Hills Golf Resort 245 S Wildwood Dr	Branson	MO	65616	**800-864-4145**	417-336-5873
Woods Resort 2201 Roark Valley Rd	Branson	MO	65616	**800-935-2345**	417-332-3550
Crowne Plaza Hotel Saint Louis 11228 Lone Eagle Dr	Bridgeton	MO	63044	**800-227-7963**	314-291-6700
Hilton Garden Inn Saint Louis/Chesterfield 16631 Chesterfield Grove Rd	Chesterfield	MO	63005	**877-782-9444**	636-532-9400
Clayton on the Park 8025 Bonhomme Ave	Clayton	MO	63105	**800-323-7500**	314-721-6543
Daniele Hotel 216 N Meramec Ave	Clayton	MO	63105	**800-325-8302**	314-721-0101
Best Western Columbia Inn 3100 I-70 Dr SE	Columbia	MO	65201	**800-362-3185**	573-474-6161
Fairfield Inn Columbia (MO) 2904 Clark Ln	Columbia	MO	65202	**800-228-2800**	573-814-2727
Holiday Inn Select Executive Center Columbia Mall 2200 I-70 Dr SW	Columbia	MO	65203	**800-465-4329**	573-445-8531
La Quinta Inn Columbia 901 Conley Rd	Columbia	MO	65201	**800-228-5150**	573-443-4141
Wingate Inn Columbia 3101 Wingate Ct	Columbia	MO	65201	**800-228-1000**	573-817-0500
Rock View Resort 1049 Parkview Dr	Hollister	MO	65672	**800-375-9530**	417-334-4678
Hilton Garden Inn Independence 19677 E Jackson Dr	Independence	MO	64057	**877-782-9444**	816-350-3000
Capitol Plaza Hotel Jefferson City 415 W McCarty St	Jefferson City	MO	65101	**800-338-8088**	573-635-1234
Hotel DeVille 319 W Miller St	Jefferson City	MO	65101	**800-392-3366**	573-636-5231
Ramada Inn & Conference Center Jefferson City 1510 Jefferson St	Jefferson City	MO	65109	**800-272-6232**	573-635-7171
Adam's Mark Kansas City 9103 E 39th St	Kansas City	MO	64133	**800-444-2326**	816-737-0200
Ameristar Casino Hotel Kansas City 3200 N Ameristar Dr	Kansas City	MO	64161	**800-499-4961**	816-414-7000
Clarion Hotel Airport 11832 NW Plaza Cir	Kansas City	MO	64153	**800-424-6423**	816-464-2345
Courtyard Kansas City Airport 7901 N Tiffany Springs Pkwy	Kansas City	MO	64153	**800-321-2211**	816-891-7500
Courtyard Kansas City South 500 E 105th St	Kansas City	MO	64131	**800-321-2211**	816-941-3333
Doubletree Hotel Kansas City 1301 Wyandotte St	Kansas City	MO	64105	**800-222-8733**	816-474-6664
Embassy Suites Kansas City Country Club Plaza 220 W 43rd St	Kansas City	MO	64111	**800-362-2779**	816-756-1720
Fairmont Kansas City at the Plaza 401 Ward Pkwy	Kansas City	MO	64112	**800-441-1414**	816-756-1500
Four Points by Sheraton Kansas City Country Club Plaza 1 E 45th St	Kansas City	MO	64111	**800-325-3535**	816-753-7400
Hilton Kansas City Airport 8801 NW 112th St	Kansas City	MO	64153	**800-445-8667**	816-891-8900
Hotel Phillips 106 W 12th St	Kansas City	MO	64105	**800-433-1426**	816-221-7000
Hyatt Regency Crown Center 2345 McGee St	Kansas City	MO	64108	**800-233-1234**	816-421-1234
Marriott Kansas City Airport 775 Brasilia Ave	Kansas City	MO	64153	**800-228-9290**	816-464-2200
Marriott Kansas City Country Club Plaza 4445 Main St	Kansas City	MO	64111	**800-228-9290**	816-531-3000
Marriott Kansas City Downtown 200 W 12th St	Kansas City	MO	64105	**800-228-9290**	816-421-6800
Quarterage Hotel 560 Westport Rd	Kansas City	MO	64111	**800-942-4233**	816-931-0001
Radisson Hotel Kansas City Airport 11828 NW Plaza Cir	Kansas City	MO	64153	**800-333-3333**	816-464-2423
Raphael Kansas City 325 Ward Pkwy	Kansas City	MO	64112	**800-821-5343**	816-756-3800
Residence Inn Downtown Union Hill 2975 Main St	Kansas City	MO	64108	**800-331-3131**	816-561-3000
Sheraton Suites Country Club Plaza 770 W 47th St	Kansas City	MO	64112	**800-325-3535**	816-931-4400
Westin Crown Center 1 E Pershing Rd	Kansas City	MO	64108	**800-228-3000**	816-474-4400
Harrah's Saint Louis Casino & Hotel 777 Casino Center Dr	Maryland Heights	MO	63043	**800-427-7247**	314-770-8100
Harrah's North Kansas City 1 Riverboat Dr	North Kansas City	MO	64116	**800-427-7247**	816-472-7777
Hilton Garden Inn Saint Louis/O'Fallon 2310 Technology Dr	O'Fallon	MO	63366	**877-782-9444**	636-625-2700
Adam's Mark Saint Louis 315 Chestnut St	Saint Louis	MO	63102	**800-444-2326**	314-241-7400
Cheshire Inn & Lodge 6300 Clayton Rd	Saint Louis	MO	63117	**800-325-7378**	314-647-7300
Courtyard Saint Louis Downtown 2340 Market St	Saint Louis	MO	63103	**800-627-7468**	314-241-9111
Doubletree Club Saint Louis Airport 9600 Natural Bridge Rd	Saint Louis	MO	63134	**800-222-8733**	314-427-7600
Drury Inn Saint Louis Union Station 201 S 20th St	Saint Louis	MO	63103	**800-378-7946**	314-231-3900
Drury Inn & Suites Saint Louis Convention Center 711 N Broadway	Saint Louis	MO	63102	**800-325-8300**	314-231-8100
Drury Plaza Hotel Saint Louis 2 S 4th St	Saint Louis	MO	63102	**800-378-7946**	314-231-3003
Embassy Suites Saint Louis Downtown 901 N 1st St	Saint Louis	MO	63102	**800-362-2779**	314-241-4200
Hilton Saint Louis Airport 10330 Natural Bridge Rd	Saint Louis	MO	63134	**800-345-5500**	314-426-5500
Hilton Saint Louis Frontenac 1335 S Lindbergh Blvd	Saint Louis	MO	63131	**800-445-8667**	314-993-1100
Holiday Inn Saint Louis-Westport 1973 Craigshire Rd	Saint Louis	MO	63146	**800-465-4329**	314-434-0100
Holiday Inn Select Saint Louis Convention Center 811 N 9th St	Saint Louis	MO	63101	**800-289-8338**	314-421-4000
Hyatt Regency Saint Louis 1 St Louis Union Stn	Saint Louis	MO	63103	**800-233-1234**	314-231-1234
Marriott Saint Louis Airport 10700 Peartree Ln	Saint Louis	MO	63134	**800-228-9290**	314-423-9700
Marriott Saint Louis Pavilion Downtown 1 S Broadway	Saint Louis	MO	63102	**800-228-9290**	314-421-1776
Marriott Saint Louis West 660 Maryville Centre Dr	Saint Louis	MO	63141	**800-352-1175**	314-878-2747
Mayfair The - A Wyndham Historic Hotel 806 Saint Charles St	Saint Louis	MO	63101	**800-996-3426**	314-421-2500
Omni Majestic Hotel 1019 Pine St	Saint Louis	MO	63101	**800-843-6664**	314-436-2355
Radisson Hotel & Suites Downtown Saint Louis 200 N 4th St	Saint Louis	MO	63102	**800-333-3333**	314-621-8200
Renaissance Grand Hotel 800 Washington Ave	Saint Louis	MO	63101	**800-468-3571**	314-621-9600
Renaissance Saint Louis Suites Hotel 827 Washington Ave	Saint Louis	MO	63101	**800-468-3571**	314-621-9700
Ritz-Carlton Saint Louis 100 Carondelet Plaza	Saint Louis	MO	63105	**800-241-3333**	314-863-6300
Seven Gables Inn 26 N Meramec Ave	Saint Louis	MO	63105	**800-433-6590**	314-863-8400
Sheraton Saint Louis City Center Hotel & Suites 400 S 14th St	Saint Louis	MO	63103	**800-325-3535**	314-231-5007
Sheraton West Port Hotel Lakeside Chalet 191 West Port Plaza Dr	Saint Louis	MO	63146	**800-325-3535**	314-878-1500
Sheraton West Port Hotel Plaza 900 West Port Plaza	Saint Louis	MO	63146	**800-325-3535**	314-434-5010
Westin Saint Louis 811 Spruce St	Saint Louis	MO	63102	**800-937-8461**	314-621-2000
Holiday Inn Select Saint Peters/Saint Charles Area 4341 Veteran's Memorial Pkwy	Saint Peters	MO	63376	**800-767-3837**	636-928-1500
Best Western State Fair Motor Inn 3120 S Limit Ave	Sedalia	MO	65301	**800-528-1234**	660-826-6100
Clarion Hotel Springfield 3333 S Glenstone Ave	Springfield	MO	65804	**800-756-7318**	417-883-6550
Holiday Inn Springfield-North I-44 2720 N Glenstone Ave	Springfield	MO	65803	**800-465-4329**	417-865-8600
Lamplighter Inn & Suites South 1772 S Glenstone Ave	Springfield	MO	65804	**800-749-7275**	417-882-1113
Residence Inn Springfield 1303 E Kingsley St	Springfield	MO	65804	**800-331-3131**	417-890-0020
Sheraton Hawthorn Park Hotel 2431 N Glenstone Ave	Springfield	MO	65803	**800-223-0092**	417-831-3131
University Plaza Hotel & Convention Center 333 S John Q Hammons Pkwy	Springfield	MO	65806	**800-465-4329**	417-864-7333

Montana

Name / Address	City	State	ZIP	Toll-Free	Phone
Best Western Ponderosa Inn 2511 1st Ave N	Billings	MT	59103	**800-628-9081**	406-259-5511
Billings Hotel & Convention Center 1223 Mullowney Ln	Billings	MT	59101	**800-537-7286**	406-248-7151
Billings Inn 880 N 29th St	Billings	MT	59101	**800-231-7782**	406-252-6800
C'mon Inn Billings 2020 Overland Ave	Billings	MT	59102	**800-655-1170**	406-655-1100
Dude Rancher Lodge 415 N 29th St	Billings	MT	59101	**800-221-3302**	406-259-5561
Fairfield Inn Billings 2026 Overland Ave	Billings	MT	59102	**800-228-2800**	406-652-5330
Holiday Inn Grand Montana 5500 Midland Rd	Billings	MT	59101	**800-465-4329**	406-248-7701
Juniper Inn 1315 N 27th St	Billings	MT	59101	**800-826-7530**	406-245-4128
Northern Hotel Billings 19 N Broadway	Billings	MT	59101	**800-542-5121**	406-245-5121
Quality Inn Billings-Homestead Park 2036 Overland Ave	Billings	MT	59102	**800-228-5151**	406-652-1320
Sheraton Billings Hotel 27 N 27th St	Billings	MT	59101	**800-325-3535**	406-252-7400
Sleep Inn Billings 4904 Southgate Dr	Billings	MT	59101	**800-228-5160**	406-254-0013
Best Western Heritage Inn Great Falls 1700 Fox Farm Rd	Great Falls	MT	59404	**800-548-8256**	406-761-1900
Comfort Inn Great Falls 1120 9th St S	Great Falls	MT	59405	**800-228-5150**	406-454-2727
Holiday Inn Great Falls 400 10th Ave S	Great Falls	MT	59405	**800-257-1998**	406-727-7200
TownHouse Inn 1411 10th Ave S	Great Falls	MT	59405	**800-442-4667**	406-761-4600
Comfort Inn Helena 750 Fee St	Helena	MT	59601	**800-228-5150**	406-443-1000
Holiday Inn Helena Downtown 22 N Last Chance Gulch	Helena	MT	59601	**800-465-4329**	406-443-2200
Jorgenson's Inn & Suites 1714 11th Ave	Helena	MT	59601	**800-272-1770**	406-442-1770
Red Lion Colonial Hotel 2301 Colonial Dr	Helena	MT	59601	**800-733-5466**	406-443-2100
Wingate Inn Helena 2007 N Oakes St	Helena	MT	59601	**866-300-7100**	406-449-3000
WestCoast Outlaw Hotel 1701 Hwy 93 S	Kalispell	MT	59901	**800-237-7445**	406-755-6100

	City	State	ZIP	Toll-Free	Phone
Yogo Inn 211 E Main St	Lewistown	MT	59457	**800-860-9646**	406-538-8721
Doubletree Hotel Missoula/Edgewater 100 Madison St	Missoula	MT	59802	**800-222-8733**	406-728-3100
Pollard The 2 N Broadway PO Box 650	Red Lodge	MT	59068	**800-765-5273**	406-446-0001

Nebraska

	City	State	ZIP	Toll-Free	Phone
New World Inn 265 33rd Ave	Columbus	NE	68601	**800-433-1492**	402-564-1492
Best Western Villager Courtyard & Gardens 5200 'O' St	Lincoln	NE	68510	**800-937-8376**	402-464-9111
Cornhusker Hotel The 333 S 13th St	Lincoln	NE	68508	**800-793-7474**	402-474-7474
Fairfield Inn Lincoln 4221 Industrial Ave	Lincoln	NE	68504	**800-228-2800**	402-476-6000
Holiday Inn Lincoln Downtown 141 N 9th St	Lincoln	NE	68508	**800-465-4329**	402-475-4011
Sleep Inn Lincoln 3400 NW 12th St	Lincoln	NE	68521	**800-753-3746**	402-475-1550
Best Western Redick Plaza Hotel 1504 Harney St	Omaha	NE	68102	**888-342-5339**	402-342-1500
Comfort Inn Omaha 8736 W Dodge Rd	Omaha	NE	68114	**800-228-5150**	402-343-1000
Comfort Inn Omaha at the Zoo 2920 S 13th Ct	Omaha	NE	68108	**800-228-5150**	402-342-8000
Courtyard Omaha Downtown 101 S 10th St	Omaha	NE	68102	**800-321-2211**	402-346-2200
Crowne Plaza Hotel Omaha Old Mill 655 N 108th Ave	Omaha	NE	68154	**800-227-6963**	402-496-0850
Doubletree Guest Suites Omaha 7270 Cedar St	Omaha	NE	68124	**800-222-8733**	402-397-5141
Doubletree Hotel Omaha-Downtown 1616 Dodge St	Omaha	NE	68102	**800-222-8733**	402-346-7600
Embassy Suites Omaha 555 S 10th St	Omaha	NE	68102	**800-362-2779**	402-346-9000
Hilton Garden Inn Omaha Downtown/Old Market Area 1005 Dodge St	Omaha	NE	68102	**877-782-9444**	402-341-4400
Holiday Inn Omaha 3321 S 72nd St	Omaha	NE	68124	**800-465-4329**	402-393-3950
Marriott Omaha 10220 Regency Cir	Omaha	NE	68114	**800-228-9290**	402-399-9000
Quality Inn Omaha 2808 S 72nd St	Omaha	NE	68124	**800-228-5151**	402-397-7137
Ramada Inn Executive Center Omaha 3650 S 72nd St	Omaha	NE	68124	**800-446-6242**	402-397-3700
Residence Inn Omaha 6990 Dodge St	Omaha	NE	68132	**800-331-3131**	402-553-8898
Sheraton Omaha Hotel 1615 Howard St	Omaha	NE	68102	**800-325-3535**	402-342-2222

Nevada

	City	State	ZIP	Toll-Free	Phone
Best Western Carson Station Hotel & Casino 900 S Carson St	Carson City	NV	89701	**800-501-2929**	775-883-0900
City Center Motel 800 N Carson St	Carson City	NV	89701	**800-338-7760**	775-882-5535
Desert Hills Motel 1010 S Carson St	Carson City	NV	89701	**800-652-7785**	775-882-1932
Railroad Pass Hotel & Casino 2800 S Boulder Hwy	Henderson	NV	89015	**800-654-0877**	702-294-5000
Ritz-Carlton Lake Las Vegas 1610 Lake Las Vegas Pkwy	Henderson	NV	89011	**800-241-3333**	702-567-4700
Alexis Park Resort 375 E Harmon Ave	Las Vegas	NV	89109	**800-582-2228**	702-796-3300
Arizona Charlie's Hotel & Casino 740 S Decatur Blvd	Las Vegas	NV	89107	**800-342-2695**	702-258-5111
Atrium Suites Hotel Las Vegas 4255 S Paradise Rd	Las Vegas	NV	89109	**800-330-7728**	702-369-4400
Barbary Coast Hotel & Casino 3595 S Las Vegas Blvd	Las Vegas	NV	89109	**888-227-2279**	702-737-7111
Best Western Mardi Gras Inn 3500 Paradise Rd	Las Vegas	NV	89109	**800-634-6501**	702-731-2020
Best Western McCarran Inn 4970 Paradise Rd	Las Vegas	NV	89119	**800-937-8376**	702-798-5530
Binion's Horseshoe Hotel & Casino 128 E Fremont St	Las Vegas	NV	89101	**800-237-6537**	702-382-1600
Boardwalk Hotel & Casino 3750 Las Vegas Blvd S	Las Vegas	NV	89109	**800-635-4581**	702-735-2400
Boulder Station Hotel & Casino 4111 Boulder Hwy	Las Vegas	NV	89121	**800-683-7777**	702-432-7777
Caesars Palace Las Vegas 3570 Las Vegas Blvd S	Las Vegas	NV	89109	**800-634-6661**	702-731-7110
California Hotel & Casino 12 Ogden Ave	Las Vegas	NV	89101	**800-634-6255**	702-385-1222
Circus Circus Hotel & Casino Las Vegas 2880 Las Vegas Blvd S *Resv	Las Vegas	NV	89109	**800-634-3450***	702-734-0410
El Cortez Hotel & Casino 600 E Fremont St	Las Vegas	NV	89101	**800-634-6703**	702-385-5200
Excalibur Hotel & Casino 3850 Las Vegas Blvd S *Resv	Las Vegas	NV	89109	**800-937-7777***	702-597-7777
Fitzgerald's Casino & Hotel Las Vegas 301 E Fremont St	Las Vegas	NV	89101	**800-274-5825**	702-388-2400
Four Queens Hotel & Casino 202 Fremont St	Las Vegas	NV	89101	**800-634-6045**	702-385-4011
Four Seasons Hotel Las Vegas 3960 Las Vegas Blvd S	Las Vegas	NV	89119	**877-632-5200**	702-632-5000
Fremont Hotel & Casino 200 E Fremont St	Las Vegas	NV	89101	**800-634-6182**	702-385-3232
Gold Coast Hotel & Casino 4000 W Flamingo Rd	Las Vegas	NV	89103	**888-402-6278**	702-367-7111
Hilton Garden Inn Las Vegas Strip South 7830 S Las Vegas Blvd	Las Vegas	NV	89123	**877-782-9444**	702-453-7830
Imperial Palace Hotel & Casino 3535 Las Vegas Blvd S	Las Vegas	NV	89109	**800-634-6441**	702-731-3311
Jackie Gaughan's Plaza Hotel & Casino 1 Main St	Las Vegas	NV	89125	**800-634-6575**	702-386-2110
Key Largo Casino & Hotel 377 E Flamingo Rd	Las Vegas	NV	89109	**800-634-6617**	702-733-7777
Las Vegas Club 18 E Fremont St	Las Vegas	NV	89101	**800-634-6532**	702-385-1664
Las Vegas Hilton 3000 Paradise Rd	Las Vegas	NV	89109	**800-732-7117**	702-732-5111
Luxor Hotel & Casino 3900 Las Vegas Blvd S *Resv	Las Vegas	NV	89119	**800-288-1000***	702-262-4000
Main Street Station Hotel & Casino 200 N Main St	Las Vegas	NV	89101	**800-713-8933**	702-387-1896
Marriott Suites Las Vegas 325 Convention Center Dr	Las Vegas	NV	89109	**800-228-9290**	702-650-2000
New York New York Hotel & Casino 3790 Las Vegas Blvd S	Las Vegas	NV	89109	**800-693-6763**	702-740-6969
Palace Station Hotel & Casino 2411 W Sahara Ave	Las Vegas	NV	89102	**800-634-3101**	702-367-2411
Paris Las Vegas 3655 Las Vegas Blvd S	Las Vegas	NV	89109	**888-266-5687**	702-946-7000
Sahara Hotel & Casino 2535 Las Vegas Blvd S	Las Vegas	NV	89109	**888-696-2121**	702-737-2111
Saint Tropez Hotel 455 E Harmon Ave	Las Vegas	NV	89109	**800-666-5400**	702-369-5400
Sam's Town Hotel & Gambling Hall 5111 Boulder Hwy	Las Vegas	NV	89122	**800-634-6371**	702-456-7777
Stardust Resort & Casino 3000 Las Vegas Blvd S	Las Vegas	NV	89109	**800-634-6757**	702-732-6111
Stratosphere Tower Hotel & Casino 2000 S Las Vegas Blvd	Las Vegas	NV	89104	**800-998-6937**	702-380-7777
Wynn Las Vegas 3131 Las Vegas Blvd S	Las Vegas	NV	89109	**888-320-7123**	702-770-7000
Colorado Belle Hotel & Casino 2100 S Casino Dr *Resv	Laughlin	NV	89029	**800-477-4837***	702-298-4000
Edgewater Hotel & Casino 2020 Casino Dr	Laughlin	NV	89029	**800-677-4837**	702-298-2453
Whiskey Pete's Hotel & Casino 100 W Primm Blvd	Primm	NV	89019	**800-386-7867**	702-382-4388
Atlantis Casino Resort 3800 S Virginia St	Reno	NV	89502	**800-723-6500**	775-825-4700
Best Western Airport Plaza Hotel & Conference Center 1981 Terminal Way	Reno	NV	89502	**800-648-3525**	775-348-6370
Circus Circus Hotel & Casino Reno 500 N Sierra St	Reno	NV	89503	**800-648-5010**	775-329-0711
Eldorado Hotel Casino 345 N Virginia St *Resv	Reno	NV	89501	**800-648-5966***	775-786-5700
Fitzgeralds Casino & Hotel Reno 255 N Virginia St PO Box 40130	Reno	NV	89504	**800-535-5825**	775-785-3300
Harrah's Reno 219 N Center St	Reno	NV	89501	**800-427-7247**	775-786-3232
Peppermill Hotel & Casino 2707 S Virginia St	Reno	NV	89502	**800-282-2444**	775-826-2121
Sands Regency Hotel & Casino 345 N Arlington Ave *Resv	Reno	NV	89501	**800-648-3553***	775-348-2200
Sundowner Hotel Casino 450 N Arlington Ave	Reno	NV	89503	**800-648-5490**	775-786-7050
Caesars Tahoe 55 Hwy 50 PO Box 5800	Stateline	NV	89449	**800-648-3353**	775-588-3515
Harrah's Lake Tahoe PO Box 8	Stateline	NV	89449	**800-427-7247**	775-588-6611
Harveys Resort Hotel & Casino Hwy 50 PO Box 128	Stateline	NV	89449	**800-427-8397**	775-588-2411

New Hampshire

	City	State	ZIP	Toll-Free	Phone
Centennial Inn 96 Pleasant St	Concord	NH	03301	**800-360-4839**	603-225-7102
Inn & Conference Center of Exeter 90 Front St	Exeter	NH	03833	**800-782-8444**	603-772-5901
Misty Harbor & Barefoot Beach Resort Rt 11B	Gilford	NH	03246	**800-336-4789**	603-293-4500
Town & Country Motor Inn Rt 2 PO Box 220	Gorham	NH	03581	**800-325-4386**	603-466-3315
Hanover Inn PO Box 151	Hanover	NH	03755	**800-443-7024**	603-643-4300
Colby Hill Inn The Oaks PO Box 779	Henniker	NH	03242	**800-531-0330**	603-428-3281
Eagle Mountain House Carter Notch Rd Box E	Jackson	NH	03846	**800-966-5779**	603-383-9111
EF Lane Hotel 30 Main St	Keene	NH	03431	**888-300-5056**	603-357-7070
Courtyard Manchester Airport 700 Huse Rd	Manchester	NH	03103	**888-844-0500**	603-641-4900
Four Points by Sheraton Manchester 55 John E Devine Dr	Manchester	NH	03103	**888-627-8142**	603-668-6110
Highlander Inn 2 Highlander Way	Manchester	NH	03103	**800-548-9248**	603-625-6426
Radisson Inn Manchester 700 Elm St	Manchester	NH	03101	**800-333-3333**	603-625-1000
Inns at Mill Falls 312 Daniel Webster Hwy	Meredith	NH	03253	**800-622-6455**	603-279-7006
Crowne Plaza Hotel Nashua 2 Somerset Pkwy	Nashua	NH	03063	**800-227-6963**	603-886-1200
Marriott Nashua 2200 Southwood Dr	Nashua	NH	03063	**800-228-9290**	603-880-9100
Sheraton Nashua Hotel 11 Tara Blvd	Nashua	NH	03062	**800-325-3535**	603-888-9970
Best Western Red Jacket Mountain View Resort 2251 White Mountain Hwy	North Conway	NH	03860	**800-752-2538**	603-356-5411
Sise Inn 40 Court St	Portsmouth	NH	03801	**877-747-3466**	603-433-1200
Snowy Owl Inn 4 Village Rd	Waterville Valley	NH	03215	**800-766-9969**	603-236-8383
Fireside Inn & Suites 25 Airport Rd	West Lebanon	NH	03784	**800-962-3198**	603-298-5906

New Jersey

	City	State	ZIP	Toll-Free	Phone
Atlantic City Hilton Boston & Pacific Ave	Atlantic City	NJ	08401	**877-432-7139**	609-347-7111
Atlantic Palace Suites Hotel 1507 Boardwalk	Atlantic City	NJ	08401	**800-527-8483**	609-344-1200
Flagship All Suites Resort 60 N Maine Ave	Atlantic City	NJ	08401	**800-647-7890**	609-343-7447
Harrah's Atlantic City 777 Harrah's Blvd	Atlantic City	NJ	08401	**800-427-7247**	609-441-5000
Holiday Inn Atlantic City Boardwalk 115 S Chelsea Ave	Atlantic City	NJ	08401	**800-548-3030**	609-348-2200
Sands Hotel & Casino 136 S Kentucky Ave	Atlantic City	NJ	08401	**800-227-2637**	609-441-4000
Showboat Atlantic City 801 Boardwalk	Atlantic City	NJ	08401	**800-427-7247**	609-343-4000
Tropicana Casino & Resort 2831 Boardwalk	Atlantic City	NJ	08401	**800-843-8767**	609-340-4000
Trump Marina Hotel & Casino Huron Ave & Brigantine Blvd *Resv	Atlantic City	NJ	08401	**800-777-8477***	609-441-2000
Trump Plaza Hotel & Casino 2225 Mississippi Ave	Atlantic City	NJ	08401	**800-677-7378**	609-441-6000
Bernards Inn 27 Mine Brook Rd	Bernardsville	NJ	07924	**888-766-0002**	908-766-0002
Hilton Philadelphia/Cherry Hill 2349 W Marlton Pike	Cherry Hill	NJ	08002	**800-445-8667**	856-665-6666
Holiday Inn Select Clinton 111 Rt 173	Clinton	NJ	08809	**800-465-4329**	908-735-5111
Hilton East Brunswick 3 Tower Ctr Blvd	East Brunswick	NJ	08816	**800-445-8667**	732-828-2000
Clarion Hotel & Towers 2055 Lincoln Hwy	Edison	NJ	08817	**800-424-6423**	732-287-3500
Hilton Newark Airport 1170 Spring St	Elizabeth	NJ	07201	**800-445-8667**	908-351-3900
Radisson Hotel & Suites Fairfield 690 Rt 46 E	Fairfield	NJ	07004	**800-333-3333**	973-227-9200
Hilton Hasbrouck Heights 650 Terrace Ave	Hasbrouck Heights	NJ	07604	**800-238-3046**	201-288-6100
Inn at Lambertville Station 11 Bridge St	Lambertville	NJ	08530	**800-524-1091**	609-397-4400
Courtyard Meadowlands 1 Polito Ave	Lyndhurst	NJ	07071	**800-321-2211**	201-896-6666
Sheraton Crossroads Hotel 1 International Blvd	Mahwah	NJ	07495	**800-325-3535**	201-529-1660
Madison Hotel 1 Convent Rd	Morristown	NJ	07960	**800-526-0729**	973-285-1800
Westin Morristown 2 Whippany Rd	Morristown	NJ	07960	**800-937-8461**	973-539-7300
Wyndham Mount Laurel 1111 Rt 73 N	Mount Laurel	NJ	08054	**800-996-3426**	856-234-7000
Wyndham Garden Hotel Mount Olive 1000 International Dr	Mount Olive	NJ	07828	**800-996-3426**	973-448-1100
Hyatt Regency New Brunswick 2 Albany St	New Brunswick	NJ	08901	**800-233-1234**	732-873-1234
Courtyard Newark Airport 600 Rts 1 & 9 S	Newark	NJ	07114	**800-321-2211**	973-643-8500
Hilton Newark Gateway Raymond Blvd 1 Gateway Ctr	Newark	NJ	07102	**800-445-8667**	973-622-5000
Marriott Newark Airport Newark International Airport	Newark	NJ	07114	**800-228-9290**	973-623-0006
Sheraton Newark Airport Hotel 128 Frontage Rd	Newark	NJ	07114	**800-325-3535**	973-690-5500
Port-O-Call Hotel 1510 Boardwalk	Ocean City	NJ	08226	**800-334-4546**	609-399-8812

New Jersey (Cont'd)

Name / Address	City	State	ZIP	Toll-Free	Phone
Marriott Park Ridge 300 Brae Blvd	Park Ridge	NJ	07656	**800-228-9290**	201-307-0800
Hilton Parsippany 1 Hilton Ct	Parsippany	NJ	07054	**800-445-8667**	973-267-7373
Regency House Hotel 140 Rt 23 N	Pompton Plains	NJ	07444	**800-696-0304**	973-696-0900
Hyatt Regency Princeton 102 Carnegie Center	Princeton	NJ	08540	**800-233-1234**	609-987-1234
Nassau Inn The 10 Palmer Square	Princeton	NJ	08542	**800-862-7728**	609-921-7500
Palmer Inn The 3499 Rt 1 S	Princeton	NJ	08540	**800-688-0500**	609-452-2500
Radisson Hotel Princeton 4355 US Hwy 1	Princeton	NJ	08540	**800-333-3333**	609-452-2400
Westin Princeton at Forrestal Village 201 Village Blvd	Princeton	NJ	08540	**800-937-8461**	609-452-7900
Oyster Point Hotel Marina & Conference Center 146 Bodman Pl	Red Bank	NJ	07701	**800-345-3484**	732-530-8200
Marriott Saddle Brook I-80 & Garden State Pkwy	Saddle Brook	NJ	07663	**800-832-6254**	201-843-9500
Crowne Plaza Hotel Meadowlands 2 Harmon Plaza	Secaucus	NJ	07094	**800-227-6963**	201-348-6900
Embassy Suites Secaucus-Meadowlands 455 Plaza Dr	Secaucus	NJ	07094	**800-362-2779**	201-864-7300
Hilton Short Hills Hotel & Spa 41 JFK Pkwy	Short Hills	NJ	07078	**800-445-8667**	973-379-0100
Marriott Somerset 110 Davidson Ave	Somerset	NJ	08873	**800-228-9290**	732-560-0500
Grand Summit Hotel 570 Springfield Ave	Summit	NJ	07901	**800-346-0773**	908-273-3000
Marriott Teaneck at Glenpointe 100 Frank W Burr Blvd	Teaneck	NJ	07666	**800-228-9290**	201-836-0600
Somerset Hills Hotel 200 Liberty Corner Rd	Warren	NJ	07059	**800-688-0700**	908-647-6700
Hanover Marriott 1401 Rt 10 E	Whippany	NJ	07981	**800-228-9290**	973-538-8811
Hilton Woodcliff Lake 200 Tice Blvd	Woodcliff Lake	NJ	07677	**800-445-8667**	201-391-3600

New Mexico

Name / Address	City	State	ZIP	Toll-Free	Phone
Amberley Suite Hotel 7620 Pan American Fwy NE	Albuquerque	NM	87109	**800-333-9806**	505-823-1300
AmeriSuites Albuquerque Airport 1400 Sunport Pl SE	Albuquerque	NM	87106	**800-833-1516**	505-242-9300
AmeriSuites Albuquerque Uptown 6901 Arvada Ave NE	Albuquerque	NM	87110	**800-833-1516**	505-872-9000
Best Western Winrock Inn 18 Winrock Ctr	Albuquerque	NM	87110	**800-866-5252**	505-883-5252
Comfort Suites Albuquerque 900 Louisiana Blvd NE	Albuquerque	NM	87110	**800-424-6423**	505-255-5566
Courtyard Albuquerque 5151 Journal Ctr Blvd	Albuquerque	NM	87109	**800-321-2211**	505-823-1919
Courtyard Albuquerque Airport 1920 Yale Blvd SE	Albuquerque	NM	87106	**800-321-2211**	505-843-6600
Doubletree Hotel Albuquerque 201 Marquette Ave NW	Albuquerque	NM	87102	**800-222-8733**	505-247-3344
Hilton Albuquerque 1901 University Blvd NE	Albuquerque	NM	87102	**800-274-6835**	505-884-2500
Hilton Garden Inn Albuquerque Airport 2601 Yale Blvd SE	Albuquerque	NM	87106	**877-782-9444**	505-765-1000
Hilton Garden Inn Albuquerque/Journal Center 5320 San Antonio Blvd	Albuquerque	NM	87109	**877-782-9444**	505-314-0800
Hyatt Regency Albuquerque 330 Tijeras Ave NW	Albuquerque	NM	87102	**800-233-1234**	505-842-1234
La Posada de Albuquerque 125 2nd St NW	Albuquerque	NM	87102	**800-777-5732**	505-242-9090
Marriott Albuquerque 2101 Louisiana Blvd NE	Albuquerque	NM	87110	**800-228-9290**	505-881-6800
Plaza Inn 900 Medical Arts NE	Albuquerque	NM	87102	**800-237-1307**	505-243-5693
Radisson Hotel & Conference Center Albuquerque 2500 Carlisle Blvd NE	Albuquerque	NM	87110	**800-333-3333**	505-888-3311
Sheraton Albuquerque Uptown Hotel 2600 Louisiana Blvd NE	Albuquerque	NM	87110	**800-252-7772**	505-881-0000
Sheraton Old Town Hotel 800 Rio Grande Blvd NW	Albuquerque	NM	87104	**800-237-2133**	505-843-6300
Wyndham Albuquerque at International Sunport 2910 Yale Blvd SE	Albuquerque	NM	87106	**800-227-1117**	505-843-7000
Best Western Mesilla Valley Inn 901 Avenida de Mesilla	Las Cruces	NM	88005	**800-327-3314**	505-524-8603
Best Western Mission Inn 1765 S Main St	Las Cruces	NM	88005	**800-390-1440**	505-524-8591
Comfort Inn Las Cruces 2585 S Valley Dr	Las Cruces	NM	88005	**800-228-5150**	505-527-2000
Fairfield Inn Las Cruces 2101 Summit Ct	Las Cruces	NM	88011	**800-228-2800**	505-522-6840
Holiday Inn de Las Cruces 201 E University Ave	Las Cruces	NM	88005	**800-465-4329**	505-526-4411
La Quinta Inn Las Cruces 790 Avenida de Mesilla	Las Cruces	NM	88005	**800-531-5900**	505-524-0331
SpringHill Suites Las Cruces 1611 Hickory Loop	Las Cruces	NM	88005	**888-772-8887**	505-541-8887
Quality Inn & Suites Los Alamos 2201 Trinity Dr	Los Alamos	NM	87544	**800-279-9279**	505-662-7211
Hilton Garden Inn Albuquerque North/Rio Rancho 1771 Rio Rancho Blvd	Rio Rancho	NM	87124	**877-782-9444**	505-896-1111
Courtyard Santa Fe 3347 Cerillos Rd	Santa Fe	NM	87507	**800-777-3347**	505-473-2800
El Rey Inn 1862 Cerillos Rd	Santa Fe	NM	87505	**800-521-1349**	505-982-1931
Eldorado Hotel 309 W San Francisco St	Santa Fe	NM	87501	**800-955-4455**	505-988-4455
Fort Marcy Hotel Suites 320 Artist Rd	Santa Fe	NM	87501	**800-745-9910**	505-988-2800
Garrett's Desert Inn 311 Old Santa Fe Trail	Santa Fe	NM	87501	**800-888-2145**	505-982-1851
Hilton Santa Fe 100 Sandoval St	Santa Fe	NM	87501	**800-336-3676**	505-988-2811
Hotel Loretto 211 Old Santa Fe Trail	Santa Fe	NM	87501	**800-727-5531**	505-988-5531
Hotel Saint Francis 210 Don Gaspar Ave	Santa Fe	NM	87501	**800-529-5700**	505-983-5700
Hotel Santa Fe 1501 Paseo de Peralta	Santa Fe	NM	87501	**800-825-9876**	505-982-1200
Inn on the Alameda 303 E Alameda St	Santa Fe	NM	87501	**800-289-2122**	505-984-2121
Inn of the Anasazi 113 Washington Ave	Santa Fe	NM	87501	**800-688-8100**	505-988-3030
Inn of the Governors 101 W Alameda St	Santa Fe	NM	87501	**800-234-4534**	505-982-4333
La Fonda 100 E San Francisco St	Santa Fe	NM	87501	**800-523-5002**	505-982-5511
Radisson Santa Fe 750 N St Francis Dr	Santa Fe	NM	87501	**800-333-3333**	505-982-5591
Villas de Santa Fe 400 Griffin St	Santa Fe	NM	87501	**800-869-6790**	505-988-3000
Best Western Kachina Lodge & Meetings Center 413 N Pueblo Rd	Taos	NM	87571	**800-937-8376**	505-758-2275

New York

Name / Address	City	State	ZIP	Toll-Free	Phone
Cocca's Inn & Suites 2 Wolf Rd	Albany	NY	12205	**888-426-2227**	518-459-2240
Courtyard Albany Airport 168 Wolf Rd	Albany	NY	12205	**800-321-2211**	518-482-8800
Courtyard Albany Thruway 1455 Washington Ave	Albany	NY	12206	**800-321-2211**	518-435-1600
Crowne Plaza Hotel Albany City Center State & Lodge Sts	Albany	NY	12207	**800-227-6963**	518-462-6611
Desmond Albany 660 Albany-Shaker Rd	Albany	NY	12211	**800-448-3500**	518-869-8100
Hilton Garden Inn Albany Airport 800 Albany Shaker Rd	Albany	NY	12211	**877-782-9444**	518-464-6666
Holiday Inn Albany-Turf on Wolf Road 205 Wolf Rd	Albany	NY	12205	**800-465-4329**	518-458-7250
Marriott Albany 189 Wolf Rd	Albany	NY	12205	**800-228-9290**	518-458-8444
Ramada Inn Albany Downtown 300 Broadway	Albany	NY	12207	**800-272-6232**	518-434-4111
Riveredge Resort Hotel 17 Holland St	Alexandria Bay	NY	13607	**800-365-6987**	315-482-9917
Marriott Buffalo Niagara 1340 Millersport Hwy	Amherst	NY	14221	**800-334-4040**	716-689-6900
Marriott Brooklyn 333 Adams St	Brooklyn	NY	11201	**800-228-9290**	718-246-7000
Adam's Mark Buffalo 120 Church St	Buffalo	NY	14202	**800-444-2326**	716-845-5100
Best Western Inn-On the Avenue 510 Delaware Ave	Buffalo	NY	14202	**800-528-1234**	716-886-8333
Courtyard Buffalo Amherst 4100 Sheridan Dr	Buffalo	NY	14221	**800-321-2211**	716-626-2300
Four Points by Sheraton Buffalo Airport 2040 Walden Ave	Buffalo	NY	14225	**800-323-3331**	716-681-2400
Hyatt Regency Buffalo 2 Fountain Plaza	Buffalo	NY	14202	**800-848-9496**	716-856-1234
Park Plaza Hotel Buffalo Airport 4243 Genesee St	Buffalo	NY	14225	**888-201-1803**	716-634-2300
Pillars Hotel 125 High St	Buffalo	NY	14203	**877-633-4667**	716-845-0112
Canandaigua Inn on the Lake 770 S Main St	Canandaigua	NY	14424	**800-228-2801**	585-394-7800
Best Western Inn Cobleskill 121 Burgin Dr	Cobleskill	NY	12043	**800-528-1234**	518-234-4321
Courtyard LaGuardia 90-10 Grand Central Pkwy	East Elmhurst	NY	11369	**800-321-2211**	718-446-4800
Crowne Plaza Hotel New York-La Guardia 104-04 Ditmars Blvd	East Elmhurst	NY	11369	**800-227-6963**	718-457-6300
Marriott LaGuardia 102-05 Ditmars Blvd	East Elmhurst	NY	11369	**800-228-9290**	718-565-8900
Courtyard Syracuse 6415 Yorktown Cir	East Syracuse	NY	13057	**800-205-6520**	315-432-0300
Embassy Suites Syracuse 6646 Old Collamer Rd	East Syracuse	NY	13057	**800-362-2779**	315-446-3200
Hilton Garden Inn Syracuse 6004 Fair Lakes Rd	East Syracuse	NY	13057	**877-782-9444**	315-431-4800
Wyndham Syracuse 6301 Rt 298	East Syracuse	NY	13057	**800-996-3426**	315-432-0200
Craftsman Inn 7300 E Genesee St	Fayetteville	NY	13066	**800-797-4464**	315-637-8000
Sheraton LaGuardia East Hotel 135-20 39th Ave	Flushing	NY	11354	**800-325-3535**	718-460-6666
White Inn 52 E Main St	Fredonia	NY	14063	**888-373-3664**	716-672-2103
Garden City Hotel 45 7th St	Garden City	NY	11530	**800-547-0400**	516-747-3000
Geneva on the Lake 1001 Lochland Rd	Geneva	NY	14456	**800-343-6382**	315-789-7190
Holiday Inn Grand Island 100 Whitehaven Rd	Grand Island	NY	14072	**800-465-4329**	716-773-1111
Hyatt Regency Wind Watch 1717 Motor Pkwy	Hauppauge	NY	11788	**800-233-1234**	631-232-9800
Marriott Islandia 3635 Express Dr N	Hauppauge	NY	11788	**800-228-9290**	631-232-3000
Clarion University Hotel & Conference Center 1 Sheraton Dr	Ithaca	NY	14850	**800-252-7466**	607-257-2000
Crowne Plaza Hotel JFK Airport 151-20 Baisley Blvd	Jamaica	NY	11434	**888-211-7996**	718-489-1000
Holiday Inn JFK Airport 144-02 135th Ave	Jamaica	NY	11436	**800-465-4329**	718-659-0200
Radisson Hotel JFK Airport 135-30 140th St	Jamaica	NY	11436	**800-333-3333**	718-322-2300
Ramada Plaza Hotel JFK International Airport Van Wyck Expy JFK International Airport Bldg 144	Jamaica	NY	11430	**800-272-6232**	718-995-9000
Georgian Resort 384 Canada St	Lake George	NY	12845	**800-525-3436**	518-668-5401
Lake Placid Lodge Whiteface Inn Rd PO Box 550	Lake Placid	NY	12946	**877-523-2700**	518-523-2700
Century House Inn 997 New Loudon Rd Rt 9	Latham	NY	12110	**888-674-6873**	518-785-0931
Clarion Inn & Suites Albany Airport 611 Troy-Schenectady Rd	Latham	NY	12110	**800-830-5205**	518-785-5891
Residence Inn Albany Airport 1 Residence Inn Dr	Latham	NY	12110	**800-331-3131**	518-783-0600
Wingate Inn Albany Airport 254 Old Wolf Rd	Latham	NY	12110	**800-228-1000**	518-869-9100
Hilton Huntington 598 Broadhollow Rd	Melville	NY	11747	**800-445-8667**	631-845-1000
Marriott Melville Long Island 1350 Old Walt Whitman Rd	Melville	NY	11747	**800-228-9290**	631-423-1600
70 Park Avenue Hotel 70 Park Ave at 38th St	New York	NY	10016	**877-707-2752**	212-973-2400
Affina Dumont Plaza 150 E 34th St	New York	NY	10016	**866-233-4642**	212-481-7600
Barclay The 111 E 48th St	New York	NY	10017	**800-327-0200**	212-755-5900
Beekman Tower Hotel 3 Mitchell Pl	New York	NY	10017	**866-233-4642**	212-355-7300
Belvedere Hotel 319 W 48th St	New York	NY	10036	**888-468-3558**	212-245-7000
Benjamin The 125 E 50th St	New York	NY	10022	**800-637-8483**	212-715-2500
Best Western Ambassador Hotel 132 W 45th St	New York	NY	10036	**800-242-8935**	212-921-7600
Best Western President Hotel 234 W 48th St	New York	NY	10036	**800-826-4667**	212-246-8800
Best Western Seaport Inn 33 Peck Slip	New York	NY	10038	**800-528-1234**	212-766-6600
Blakely Hotel 136 W 55th St	New York	NY	10019	**800-735-0710**	212-245-1800
Broadway Inn 264 W 46th St	New York	NY	10036	**800-826-6300**	212-997-9200
Carlton on Madison Ave 22 E 29th St	New York	NY	10016	**800-542-1502**	212-532-4100
Carlyle The 35 E 76th St	New York	NY	10021	**800-227-5737**	212-744-1600
Casablanca Hotel 147 W 43rd St	New York	NY	10036	**888-922-7225**	212-869-1212
Chelsea Inn 46 W 17th St	New York	NY	10011	**800-640-6469**	212-645-8989
Chelsea Savoy Hotel 204 W 23rd St	New York	NY	10011	**866-929-9353**	212-929-9353
Comfort Inn New York Central Park West 31 W 71st St	New York	NY	10023	**800-228-5150**	212-721-4770
Cosmopolitan Hotel 95 W Broadway	New York	NY	10007	**888-895-9400**	212-566-1900
Court The 130 E 39th St	New York	NY	10016	**877-946-8357**	212-685-1100
Crowne Plaza Hotel Manhattan Times Square 1605 Broadway	New York	NY	10019	**800-243-6969**	212-977-4000
Crowne Plaza Hotel New York at the United Nations 304 E 42nd St	New York	NY	10017	**800-879-8836**	212-986-8800
Days Hotel New York City Midtown 790 8th Ave	New York	NY	10019	**800-572-6232**	212-581-7000
Doubletree Guest Suites New York City 1568 Broadway	New York	NY	10036	**800-222-8733**	212-719-1600
Dream 210 W 55th St	New York	NY	10019	**866-437-3266**	212-247-2000
Dylan Hotel 52 E 41st St	New York	NY	10017	**866-553-9526**	212-338-0500
Eastgate Tower 222 E 39th St	New York	NY	10016	**800-637-8483**	212-687-8000
Essex House - A Westin Hotel 160 Central Park S	New York	NY	10019	**800-937-8461**	212-247-0300
Fitzpatrick Manhattan Hotel 687 Lexington Ave	New York	NY	10022	**800-367-7701**	212-355-0100
Flatotel International 135 W 52nd St	New York	NY	10019	**800-352-8683**	212-887-9400
Four Seasons Hotel New York 57 E 57th St	New York	NY	10022	**800-332-3442**	212-758-5700
Franklin The 164 E 87th St	New York	NY	10128	**877-847-4444**	212-369-1000
Gramercy Park Hotel 2 Lexington Ave	New York	NY	10010	**800-221-4083**	212-475-4320
Grand Hyatt New York Park Ave at Grand Central	New York	NY	10017	**800-233-1234**	212-883-1234

	City	State	ZIP	Toll-Free	Phone
Helmsley Carlton House Hotel 680 Madison Ave	New York	NY	10021	**800-221-4982**	212-838-3000
Helmsley Middletowne Hotel 148 E 48th St	New York	NY	10017	**800-221-4982**	212-755-3000
Helmsley Park Lane Hotel 36 Central Park S	New York	NY	10019	**800-221-4982**	212-371-4000
Hilton New York 1335 Ave of the Americas	New York	NY	10019	**800-445-8667**	212-586-7000
Holiday Inn Manhattan-Downtown/SoHo 138 Lafayette St	New York	NY	10013	**800-465-4329**	212-966-8898
Hotel Beacon 2130 Broadway	New York	NY	10023	**800-572-4969**	212-787-1100
Hotel Edison 228 W 47th St	New York	NY	10036	**800-637-7070**	212-840-5000
Hotel Elysee 60 E 54th St	New York	NY	10022	**800-535-9733**	212-753-1066
Hotel Giraffe 365 Park Ave S at 26th St	New York	NY	10016	**877-296-0009**	212-685-7700
Hotel Plaza Athenee 37 E 64th St	New York	NY	10021	**800-447-8800**	212-734-9100
Hotel Sofitel New York 45 W 44th St	New York	NY	10036	**877-565-9240**	212-354-8844
Hudson Hotel 356 W 58th St	New York	NY	10019	**800-444-4786**	212-554-6000
InterContinental The Barclay New York 111 E 48th St	New York	NY	10017	**800-327-0200**	212-755-5900
Iroquois New York 49 W 44th St	New York	NY	10036	**800-332-7220**	212-840-3080
Kimberly Hotel 145 E 50th St	New York	NY	10022	**800-683-0400**	212-755-0400
Kitano New York 66 Park Ave	New York	NY	10016	**800-548-2666**	212-885-7000
La Quinta Manhattan 17 W 32nd St	New York	NY	10001	**800-551-2303**	212-736-1600
Le Parker Meridien 118 W 57th St	New York	NY	10019	**800-543-4300**	212-245-5000
Library Hotel 299 Madison Ave	New York	NY	10017	**877-793-7323**	212-983-4500
Lowell The 28 E 63rd St	New York	NY	10021	**800-221-4444**	212-838-1400
Lyden Gardens 215 E 64th St	New York	NY	10021	**800-637-8483**	212-355-1230
Lyden House 320 E 53rd St	New York	NY	10022	**800-637-8483**	212-888-6070
Mark The 25 E 77th St	New York	NY	10021	**800-843-6275**	212-744-4300
Marriott Marquis New York 1535 Broadway	New York	NY	10036	**800-843-4898**	212-398-1900
Marriott New York East Side 525 Lexington Ave	New York	NY	10017	**800-228-9290**	212-755-4000
Marriott New York Financial Center 85 West St	New York	NY	10006	**800-228-9290**	212-385-4900
Melrose Hotel 140 E 63rd St	New York	NY	10021	**800-223-1020**	212-838-5700
Mercer Hotel 147 Mercer St	New York	NY	10012	**888-918-6060**	212-966-6060
Metropolitan Hotel 569 Lexington Ave	New York	NY	10022	**800-836-6471**	212-752-7000
Michelangelo Hotel 152 W 51st St	New York	NY	10019	**800-237-0990**	212-765-1900
Millennium Hotel New York Broadway 145 W 44th St	New York	NY	10036	**800-622-5569**	212-768-4400
Morgans Hotel 237 Madison Ave	New York	NY	10016	**800-334-3408**	212-686-0300
Muse The 130 W 46th St	New York	NY	10036	**877-692-6873**	212-485-2400
New York Helmsley Hotel 212 E 42nd St	New York	NY	10017	**800-221-4982**	212-490-8900
New York Palace Hotel 455 Madison Ave	New York	NY	10022	**800-697-2522**	212-888-7000
Novotel New York 226 W 52nd St	New York	NY	10019	**800-221-3185**	212-315-0100
Omni Berkshire Place 21 E 52nd St	New York	NY	10022	**800-843-6664**	212-753-5800
Park Central New York 870 7th Ave	New York	NY	10019	**800-346-1359**	212-247-8000
Park South Hotel 122 E 28th St	New York	NY	10016	**800-315-4642**	212-448-0888
Peninsula New York 700 5th Ave	New York	NY	10019	**800-262-9467**	212-956-2888
Pierre The - A Four Seasons Hotel 2 E 61st St	New York	NY	10021	**800-332-3442**	212-838-8000
Plaza Fifty 155 E 50th St	New York	NY	10022	**866-233-4642**	212-751-5710
Quality Hotel on Broadway 215 W 94th St	New York	NY	10025	**800-228-5151**	212-866-6400
Quality Hotel Times Square 157 W 47th St	New York	NY	10036	**800-424-6423**	212-768-3700
Radisson Lexington Hotel New York 511 Lexington Ave	New York	NY	10017	**800-333-3333**	212-755-4400
Ramada Plaza & Inn - New Yorker Hotel 481 8th Ave	New York	NY	10001	**800-764-4680**	212-971-0101
Regency Hotel - A Loews Hotel 540 Park Ave	New York	NY	10021	**800-235-6397**	212-759-4100
Renaissance New York Hotel 714 7th Ave	New York	NY	10036	**800-468-3571**	212-765-7676
RIHGA Royal Hotel 151 W 54th St	New York	NY	10019	**800-937-5454**	212-307-5000
Ritz-Carlton New York (Battery Park) 2 West St	New York	NY	10004	**800-704-5643**	212-344-0800
Ritz-Carlton New York (Central Park) 50 Central Park S	New York	NY	10019	**800-241-3333**	212-308-9100
Roger Smith Hotel 501 Lexington Ave	New York	NY	10017	**800-445-0277**	212-755-1400
Roger Williams The 131 Madison Ave *Resv	New York	NY	10016	**877-847-4444***	212-448-7000
Roosevelt Hotel 45 E 45th St	New York	NY	10017	**888-833-3969**	212-661-9600
Royalton Hotel 44 W 44th St	New York	NY	10036	**800-606-6090**	212-869-4400
Saint Regis New York 2 E 55th St	New York	NY	10022	**800-759-7550**	212-753-4500
Salisbury Hotel 123 W 57th St	New York	NY	10019	**888-692-5757**	212-246-1300
San Carlos Hotel 150 E 50th St	New York	NY	10022	**800-722-2012**	212-755-1800
Shelburne Murray Hill 303 Lexington Ave	New York	NY	10016	**866-233-4642**	212-689-5200
Sheraton Manhattan Hotel 790 7th Ave	New York	NY	10019	**800-325-3535**	212-581-3300
Sheraton Russell Hotel 45 Park Ave	New York	NY	10016	**800-325-3535**	212-685-7676
Sherry-Netherland Hotel 781 5th Ave	New York	NY	10022	**800-247-4377**	212-355-2800
Shoreham Hotel 33 W 55th St	New York	NY	10019	**800-553-3347**	212-247-6700
Skyline Hotel 725 10th Ave	New York	NY	10019	**800-433-1982**	212-586-3400
SoHo Grand Hotel 310 W Broadway	New York	NY	10013	**800-965-3000**	212-965-3000
Southgate Tower 371 7th Ave	New York	NY	10001	**800-637-8483**	212-563-1800
Surrey Hotel 20 E 76th St	New York	NY	10021	**800-637-8483**	212-288-3700
Swissotel New York - The Drake 440 Park Ave	New York	NY	10022	**800-372-5369**	212-421-0900
The Plaza 5th Ave & Central Park S	New York	NY	10019	**800-759-3000**	212-759-3000
Time The 224 W 49th St	New York	NY	10019	**877-846-3692**	212-246-5252
Trump International Hotel & Tower 1 Central Park W	New York	NY	10023	**888-448-7867**	212-299-1000
W Hotel New York 541 Lexington Ave	New York	NY	10022	**877-946-8357**	212-755-1200
W Hotel New York-The Court 130 E 39th St	New York	NY	10016	**877-946-8357**	212-685-1100
W Hotel New York Times Square 1567 Broadway *Resv	New York	NY	10036	**877-946-8357***	212-930-7400
Waldorf-Astoria - A Hilton Hotel 301 Park Ave	New York	NY	10022	**800-925-3673**	212-355-3000
Waldorf Towers - A Conrad Hotel 100 E 50th St	New York	NY	10022	**800-445-8667**	212-355-3100
Warwick Hotel New York 65 W 54th St	New York	NY	10019	**800-223-4099**	212-247-2700
Washington Square Hotel 103 Waverly Pl	New York	NY	10011	**800-222-0418**	212-777-9515
Wellington Hotel 871 7th Ave	New York	NY	10019	**800-652-1212**	212-247-3900
Holiday Inn Select Niagara Falls 300 3rd St	Niagara Falls	NY	14303	**800-953-2557**	716-285-3361
Doubletree Club Syracuse 6701 Buckley Rd	North Syracuse	NY	13212	**888-444-2582**	315-457-4000
Hilton Pearl River 500 Veterans Memorial Dr	Pearl River	NY	10965	**800-445-8667**	845-735-9000
Del Monte Lodge - A Renaissance Hotel 41 N Main St	Pittsford	NY	14534	**800-386-3376**	585-381-9900
Residence Inn Plainview 9 Gerhard Rd	Plainview	NY	11803	**800-331-3131**	516-433-6200
Clarion Hotel Riverside 120 E Main St	Rochester	NY	14604	**877-424-6423**	585-546-6400
Courtyard Rochester/Brighton 33 Corporate Woods	Rochester	NY	14623	**800-321-2211**	585-292-1000
Crowne Plaza Hotel Rochester 70 State St	Rochester	NY	14614	**800-227-6963**	585-546-3450
Holiday Inn Rochester Airport 911 Brooks Ave	Rochester	NY	14624	**800-465-4329**	585-328-6000
Hyatt Regency Rochester 125 E Main St	Rochester	NY	14604	**800-233-1234**	585-546-1234
Marriott Rochester Airport 1890 W Ridge Rd	Rochester	NY	14615	**800-228-9290**	585-225-6880
Park Plaza Hotel Rochester Airport 175 Jefferson Rd	Rochester	NY	14623	**800-814-7000**	585-475-1910
Strathallan Hotel 550 East Ave	Rochester	NY	14607	**800-678-7284**	585-461-5010
Roslyn Claremont Hotel 1221 Old Northern Blvd	Roslyn	NY	11576	**800-626-9005**	516-625-2700
Hilton Rye Town 699 Westchester Ave	Rye Brook	NY	10573	**800-445-8667**	914-939-6300
Hotel Saranac 100 Main St	Saranac Lake	NY	12983	**800-937-0211**	518-891-2200
Gideon Putnam Hotel & Conference Center 24 Gideon Putnam Rd	Saratoga Springs	NY	12866	**800-732-1560**	518-584-3000
Mirbeau Inn & Spa 851 W Genesee St	Skaneateles	NY	13152	**877-647-2328**	315-685-5006
Sheraton Long Island Hotel 110 Vanderbilt Motor Pkwy	Smithtown	NY	11788	**800-325-3535**	631-231-1100
Southampton Inn 91 Hill St	Southampton	NY	11968	**800-832-6500**	631-283-6500
Village Latch Inn 101 Hill St	Southampton	NY	11968	**800-545-2824**	631-283-2160
Staten Island Hotel 1415 Richmond Ave	Staten Island	NY	10314	**800-532-3532**	718-698-5000
Genesee Grande Hotel 1060 E Genesee St	Syracuse	NY	13210	**800-365-4663**	315-476-4212
Marx Hotel & Conference Center 701 E Genesee St	Syracuse	NY	13210	**877-843-6279**	315-479-7000
Sheraton University Hotel & Conference Center 801 University Ave	Syracuse	NY	13210	**800-325-3535**	315-475-3000
Castle on the Hudson 400 Benedict Ave	Tarrytown	NY	10591	**800-616-4487**	914-631-1980
Courtyard Tarrytown Greenburgh 475 White Plains Rd	Tarrytown	NY	10591	**800-321-2211**	914-631-1122
Marriott Westchester 670 White Plains Rd	Tarrytown	NY	10591	**800-228-9290**	914-631-2200
Marriott Long Island Hotel & Conference Center 101 James Doolittle Blvd	Uniondale	NY	11553	**800-228-9290**	516-794-3800
Hotel Utica 102 Lafayette St	Utica	NY	13502	**877-906-1912**	315-724-7829
Radisson Hotel Utica Centre 200 Genesee St	Utica	NY	13502	**800-333-3333**	315-797-8010
Thayer Hotel 674 Thayer Rd	West Point	NY	10996	**800-247-5047**	845-446-4731
Crowne Plaza Hotel White Plains Downtown 66 Hale Ave	White Plains	NY	10601	**800-752-4672**	914-682-0050
Esplanade Hotel 95 S Broadway	White Plains	NY	10601	**800-247-5322**	914-761-8100
Renaissance Westchester Hotel 80 W Red Oak Ln	White Plains	NY	10604	**800-468-3571**	914-694-5400
Residence Inn Westchester County 5 Barker Ave	White Plains	NY	10601	**800-331-3131**	914-761-7700
Garden Place Hotel 6615 Transit Rd	Williamsville	NY	14221	**800-427-3361**	716-635-9000
Residence Inn Buffalo-Amherst 100 Maple Rd	Williamsville	NY	14221	**800-331-3131**	716-632-6622
Royal Regency Hotel 165 Tuckahoe Rd	Yonkers	NY	10710	**800-215-3858**	914-476-6200

North Carolina

	City	State	ZIP	Toll-Free	Phone
American Court Motel 85 Merrimon Ave	Asheville	NC	28801	**800-233-3582**	828-253-4427
Applewood Manor Inn 62 Cumberland Cir	Asheville	NC	28801	**800-442-2197**	828-254-2244
Best Western Biltmore West 275 Smokey Pk Hwy	Asheville	NC	28806	**800-925-5486**	828-667-4501
Courtyard Asheville 1 Buckstone Pl	Asheville	NC	28805	**800-321-2211**	828-281-0041
Forest Manor Inn 866 Hendersonville Rd	Asheville	NC	28803	**800-866-3531**	828-274-3531
Haywood Park Hotel 1 Battery Park Ave	Asheville	NC	28801	**800-228-2522**	828-252-2522
Ramada Plaza Hotel Asheville West 435 Smoky Park Hwy	Asheville	NC	28806	**800-678-2161**	828-665-2161
Renaissance Asheville Hotel 1 Thomas Wolfe Plaza	Asheville	NC	28801	**800-468-3571**	828-252-8211
Richmond Hill Inn 87 Richmond Hill Dr	Asheville	NC	28806	**888-742-4554**	828-252-7313
Green Park Inn 9239 Valley Blvd	Blowing Rock	NC	28605	**800-852-2462**	828-295-3141
High Country Inn 1785 Hwy 105	Boone	NC	28607	**800-334-5605**	828-264-1000
Courtyard Raleigh Cary 102 Edinburgh Dr S	Cary	NC	27511	**800-321-2211**	919-481-9666
Carolina Inn 211 Pittsboro St	Chapel Hill	NC	27516	**800-962-8519**	919-933-2001
Sheraton Chapel Hill Hotel 1 Europa Dr	Chapel Hill	NC	27517	**800-325-3535**	919-968-4900
Siena Hotel 1505 E Franklin St	Chapel Hill	NC	27514	**800-223-7379**	919-929-4000
Adam's Mark Charlotte 555 S McDowell St	Charlotte	NC	28204	**800-444-2326**	704-372-4100
Ascot Inn 1025 S Tryon St	Charlotte	NC	28203	**800-333-9417**	704-377-3611
Clarion Hotel Charlotte Airport-Coliseum 321 W Woodlawn Rd	Charlotte	NC	28217	**800-424-6423**	704-523-1400
Courtyard Charlotte Airport 2700 Little Rock Rd	Charlotte	NC	28214	**800-321-2211**	704-319-9900
Courtyard Charlotte Arrowood 800 W Arrowood Rd	Charlotte	NC	28217	**800-321-2211**	704-527-5055
Courtyard Charlotte South Park 6023 Park South Dr	Charlotte	NC	28210	**800-321-2211**	704-552-7333
Courtyard Charlotte University 333 W WT Harris Blvd	Charlotte	NC	28262	**800-321-2211**	704-549-4888
Doubletree Guest Suites Charlotte/SouthPark 6300 Morrison Blvd	Charlotte	NC	28211	**800-647-8483**	704-364-2400
Doubletree Hotel Charlotte-Gateway Village 895 W Trade St	Charlotte	NC	28202	**800-222-8733**	704-347-0070
Embassy Suites Charlotte 4800 S Tryon St	Charlotte	NC	28217	**800-362-2779**	704-527-8400
Hilton Charlotte Executive Park 5624 WestPark Dr	Charlotte	NC	28217	**800-445-8667**	704-527-8000
Hilton Charlotte & Towers 222 E 3rd St	Charlotte	NC	28202	**800-445-8667**	704-377-1500
Hilton Charlotte University Place 8629 JM Keynes Dr	Charlotte	NC	28262	**800-445-8667**	704-547-7444
Hilton Garden Inn Charlotte North 9315 Statesville Rd	Charlotte	NC	28269	**877-782-9444**	704-597-7655
Hilton Garden Inn Charlotte Uptown 508 E 2nd St	Charlotte	NC	28202	**877-782-9444**	704-347-5972
Holiday Inn Woodlawn-Airport South 212 W Woodlawn Rd	Charlotte	NC	28217	**800-465-4329**	704-525-8350
Hyatt Charlotte 5501 Carnegie Blvd	Charlotte	NC	28209	**800-233-1234**	704-554-1234
Marriott Charlotte City Center 100 W Trade St	Charlotte	NC	28202	**800-228-9290**	704-333-9000
Marriott Charlotte Executive Park 5700 WestPark Dr	Charlotte	NC	28217	**800-228-9290**	704-527-9650
Morgan Hotel & Suites 315 E Woodlawn Rd	Charlotte	NC	28217	**800-522-1994**	704-522-0852
Omni Charlotte Hotel 132 E Trade St	Charlotte	NC	28202	**800-843-6664**	704-377-0400
Park Hotel 2200 Rexford Rd	Charlotte	NC	28211	**800-334-0331**	704-364-8220
Renaissance Charlotte Suites Hotel 2800 Coliseum Centre Dr	Charlotte	NC	28217	**800-468-3571**	704-357-1414
Residence Inn Charlotte Uptown 404 S Mint St	Charlotte	NC	28202	**800-331-3131**	704-340-4000
Sheraton Charlotte Airport Hotel 3315 S I-85 at Billy Graham Pkwy	Charlotte	NC	28208	**800-325-3535**	704-392-1200
Wingate Inn Charlotte-Coliseum 6057 Nations Ford Rd	Charlotte	NC	28217	**800-228-1000**	704-523-3366
Wyndham Garden Hotel Charlotte 2600 Yorkmont Rd	Charlotte	NC	28208	**800-996-3426**	704-357-9100
Harrah's Cherokee Casino & Hotel 777 Casino Dr	Cherokee	NC	28719	**800-427-7247**	828-497-7777

North Carolina (Cont'd)

				Toll-Free	Phone
Courtyard Durham-Duke University/Downtown 1815 Front St	Durham	NC	27705	**800-321-2211**	919-309-1500
Doubletree Guest Suites Raleigh/Durham 2515 Meridian Pkwy	Durham	NC	27713	**800-222-8733**	919-361-4660
Duke Towers Residential Suites 807 W Trinity Ave	Durham	NC	27701	**866-385-3869**	919-687-4444
Hilton Durham 3800 Hillsborough Rd	Durham	NC	27705	**800-445-8667**	919-383-8033
Marriott Durham at the Civic Center 201 Foster St	Durham	NC	27701	**800-228-9290**	919-768-6000
Marriott Research Triangle Park 4700 Guardian Dr	Durham	NC	27703	**800-228-9290**	919-941-6200
Millennium Hotel Durham 2800 Campus Walk Ave	Durham	NC	27705	**800-633-5379**	919-383-8575
Residence Inn Durham Research Triangle Park 201 Residence Inn Blvd	Durham	NC	27713	**800-331-3131**	919-361-1266
Sheraton Imperial Hotel & Convention Center 4700 Emperor Blvd	Durham	NC	27703	**800-325-3535**	919-941-5050
Washington Duke Inn & Golf Club 3001 Cameron Blvd	Durham	NC	27705	**800-443-3853**	919-490-0999
Wingate Inn Raleigh-Durham 5223 Page Rd	Durham	NC	27703	**800-228-1000**	919-941-2854
Wyndham Garden Hotel Durham 4620 S Miami Blvd	Durham	NC	27703	**800-972-0264**	919-941-6066
AmeriSuites Greensboro Wendover 1619 Stanley Rd	Greensboro	NC	27407	**800-833-1516**	336-852-1443
Biltmore Greensboro Hotel 111 W Washington St	Greensboro	NC	27401	**800-332-0303**	336-272-3474
Courtyard Greensboro 4400 W Wendover Ave	Greensboro	NC	27407	**800-321-2211**	336-294-3800
Embassy Suites Greensboro Airport 204 Centreport Dr	Greensboro	NC	27409	**800-362-2779**	336-668-4535
Marriott Greensboro Airport 1 Marriott Dr	Greensboro	NC	27409	**800-228-9290**	336-852-6450
Marriott Greensboro Downtown 304 N Greene St	Greensboro	NC	27401	**800-228-9290**	336-379-8000
O Henry Hotel 624 Green Valley Rd	Greensboro	NC	27408	**800-965-8259**	336-854-2000
Park Lane Hotel at Four Seasons 3005 High Point Rd	Greensboro	NC	27403	**800-942-6556**	336-294-4565
Residence Inn Greensboro 2000 Veasley St	Greensboro	NC	27407	**800-331-3131**	336-294-8600
Sheraton Greensboro at Four Seasons 3121 High Point Rd	Greensboro	NC	27407	**800-325-3535**	336-292-9161
Wingate Inn Greensboro 6007 Landmark Center Blvd	Greensboro	NC	27407	**800-228-1000**	336-854-8610
Lake Lure Inn & Conference Center PO Box 10	Lake Lure	NC	28746	**888-434-4970**	828-625-2525
Courtyard Raleigh Durham Airport 2001 Hospitality Ct	Morrisville	NC	27560	**800-321-2211**	919-467-9444
Hilton Garden Inn Raleigh-Durham Airport 1500 RDU Center Dr	Morrisville	NC	27560	**877-782-9444**	919-840-8088
Hilton Garden Inn Charlotte Pineville 425 Towne Ctr Blvd	Pineville	NC	28134	**877-782-9444**	704-889-3279
Clarion Hotel State Capitol 320 Hillsborough St	Raleigh	NC	27603	**800-424-6423**	919-832-0501
Courtyard Raleigh North 1041 Wake Towne Dr	Raleigh	NC	27609	**800-321-2211**	919-821-3400
Crabtree Summit Hotel 3908 Arrow Dr	Raleigh	NC	27612	**800-521-7521**	919-782-6868
Hilton North Raleigh 3415 Wake Forest Rd	Raleigh	NC	27609	**800-445-8667**	919-872-2323
Holiday Inn Raleigh-Brownstone 1707 Hillsborough St	Raleigh	NC	27605	**800-331-7919**	919-828-0811
Marriott Raleigh-Crabtree Valley 4500 Marriott Dr	Raleigh	NC	27612	**800-228-9290**	919-781-7000
Sheraton Raleigh Capital Center Hotel 421 S Salisbury St	Raleigh	NC	27601	**800-325-3535**	919-834-9900
Velvet Cloak Inn 1505 Hillsborough St	Raleigh	NC	27605	**800-334-4372**	919-828-0333
Wingate Inn Raleigh 2610 Westinghouse Blvd	Raleigh	NC	27604	**800-228-1000**	919-821-0888
Holiday Inn Raleigh-Durham Airport 4810 Old Page Rd	Research Triangle Park	NC	27709	**800-465-4329**	919-941-6000
Radisson Hotel Research Triangle Park 150 Park Dr PO Box 12168	Research Triangle Park	NC	27709	**800-333-3333**	919-549-8631
Snowbird Mountain Lodge 4633 Santeetlah Rd	Robbinsville	NC	28771	**800-941-9290**	828-479-3433
Pine Crest Inn 85 Pine Crest Ln	Tryon	NC	28782	**800-633-3001**	828-859-9135
Swag The 2300 Swag Rd	Waynesville	NC	28785	**800-789-7672**	828-926-0430
Adam's Mark Winston-Salem 425 N Cherry St	Winston-Salem	NC	27101	**800-444-2326**	336-725-3500
Best Western Salem Inn & Suites 127 S Cherry St	Winston-Salem	NC	27101	**800-533-8760**	336-725-8561
Brookstown Inn 200 Brookstown Ave	Winston-Salem	NC	27101	**800-845-4262**	336-725-1120
Courtyard Winston-Salem/University 3111 University Pkwy	Winston-Salem	NC	27105	**800-321-2211**	336-727-1277
Hawthorne Inn & Conference Center 420 High St	Winston-Salem	NC	27101	**800-972-3774**	336-777-3000
Holiday Inn Select Winston-Salem 5790 University Pkwy	Winston-Salem	NC	27105	**800-553-9595**	336-767-9595
Ramada Plaza Winston-Salem Coliseum 3050 University Pkwy	Winston-Salem	NC	27105	**800-272-6232**	336-723-2911
Residence Inn Winston-Salem 7835 N Point Blvd	Winston-Salem	NC	27106	**800-331-3131**	336-759-0777
Wingate Inn Winston-Salem 125 S Main St	Winston-Salem	NC	27101	**800-228-1000**	336-714-2800

North Dakota

				Toll-Free	Phone
Best Western Doublewood Inn 1400 E Interchange Ave	Bismarck	ND	58501	**800-554-7077**	701-258-7000
Best Western Ramkota 800 S 3rd St	Bismarck	ND	58504	**800-528-1234**	701-258-7700
Expressway Suites 180 E Bismarck Expy	Bismarck	ND	58504	**888-774-5566**	701-222-3311
Fairfield Inn Bismarck/North 1120 Century Ave	Bismarck	ND	58503	**800-228-2800**	701-223-9077
Fairfield Inn Bismarck/South 135 Ivy Ave	Bismarck	ND	58504	**800-228-2800**	701-223-9293
Best Western Fargo Doublewood Inn 3333 13th Ave S	Fargo	ND	58103	**800-433-3235**	701-235-3333
C'mon Inn Fargo 4338 20th Ave SW	Fargo	ND	58103	**800-334-1570**	701-277-9944
Expressway Inn 1340 S 21st Ave	Fargo	ND	58103	**800-437-0044**	701-235-3141
Holiday Inn Fargo 3803 13th Ave S	Fargo	ND	58103	**877-282-2700**	701-282-2700
Radisson Hotel Fargo 201 5th St N	Fargo	ND	58102	**800-333-3333**	701-232-7363
Ramada Plaza Suites Hotel Fargo 1635 42nd St SW	Fargo	ND	58103	**800-272-6232**	701-277-9000
Wingate Inn Fargo 4429 19th Ave SW	Fargo	ND	58103	**800-228-1000**	701-281-9133
Best Western Town House 710 1st Ave N	Grand Forks	ND	58203	**800-867-9797**	701-746-5411
C'mon Inn Grand Forks 3051 32nd Ave S	Grand Forks	ND	58201	**800-255-2323**	701-775-3320
Hilton Garden Inn Grand Forks/UND 4301 Dartmouth Dr	Grand Forks	ND	58203	**877-782-9444**	701-775-6000
Holiday Inn Grand Forks 1210 N 43rd St	Grand Forks	ND	58203	**800-465-4329**	701-772-7131
Road King Inn Columbia Mall 3300 30th Ave S	Grand Forks	ND	58201	**800-707-1391**	701-746-1391
Best Western Seven Seas Motor Inn 2611 Old Red Trail	Mandan	ND	58554	**800-597-7327**	701-663-7401

Ohio

				Toll-Free	Phone
Best Western Executive Inn Akron 2677 Gilchrist Rd	Akron	OH	44305	**800-528-1234**	330-794-1050
Comfort Inn Akron West 130 Montrose W Ave	Akron	OH	44321	**800-424-6423**	330-666-5050
Courtyard Akron Montrose 100 Springside Dr	Akron	OH	44333	**800-321-2211**	330-668-9090
Crowne Plaza Quaker Square Hotel 135 S Broadway St	Akron	OH	44308	**866-668-6689**	330-253-5970
Four Points by Sheraton Akron West 3150 W Market St	Akron	OH	44333	**800-325-3535**	330-869-9000
Hilton Akron/Fairlawn 3180 W Market St	Akron	OH	44333	**800-445-8667**	330-867-5000
Radisson Hotel Akron City Centre 20 W Mill St	Akron	OH	44308	**800-333-3333**	330-384-1500
Radisson Hotel Akron/Fairlawn 200 Montrose W Ave	Akron	OH	44321	**800-333-3333**	330-666-9300
Residence Inn Akron 120 Montrose W Ave	Akron	OH	44321	**800-331-3131**	330-666-4811
Embassy Suites Cleveland-Beachwood 3775 Park East Dr	Beachwood	OH	44122	**800-362-2779**	216-765-8066
Courtyard Cincinnati Blue Ash 4625 Lake Forest Dr	Blue Ash	OH	45242	**800-321-2211**	513-733-4334
Holiday Inn Youngstown-Boardman 7410 South Ave	Boardman	OH	44512	**800-465-4329**	330-726-1611
Four Points by Sheraton Canton 4375 Metro Cir NW	Canton	OH	44720	**877-867-7666**	330-494-6494
Residence Inn Canton 5280 Broadmoor Cir NW	Canton	OH	44709	**800-331-3131**	330-493-0004
Best Western Mariemont Inn 6880 Wooster Pike	Cincinnati	OH	45227	**800-528-1234**	513-271-2100
Cincinnatian Hotel 601 Vine St	Cincinnati	OH	45202	**800-942-9000**	513-381-3000
Crowne Plaza Hotel Cincinnati Downtown 15 W 6th St	Cincinnati	OH	45202	**888-279-8260**	513-381-4000
Doubletree Guest Suites Cincinnati/Sharonville 6300 E Kemper Rd	Cincinnati	OH	45241	**800-222-8733**	513-489-3636
Embassy Suites Cincinnati Northeast-Blue Ash 4554 Lake Forest Dr	Cincinnati	OH	45242	**800-362-2779**	513-733-8900
Garfield Suites Hotel 2 Garfield Pl	Cincinnati	OH	45202	**800-367-2155**	513-421-3355
Hampshire House Hotel & Conference Center 30 Tri-County Pkwy	Cincinnati	OH	45246	**800-543-4211**	513-772-5440
Hilton Cincinnati Netherland Plaza 35 W 5th St	Cincinnati	OH	45202	**800-843-6664**	513-421-9100
Hilton Garden Inn Cincinnati/Sharonville 11149 Dowlin Dr	Cincinnati	OH	45241	**877-782-9444**	513-772-2837
Hyatt Regency Cincinnati 151 W 5th St	Cincinnati	OH	45202	**800-233-1234**	513-579-1234
Marriott Cincinnati North 6189 Muhlhauser Rd	Cincinnati	OH	45069	**800-228-9290**	513-874-7335
Millennium Hotel Cincinnati 141 W 6th St	Cincinnati	OH	45202	**800-876-2100**	513-352-2100
Vernon Manor Hotel 400 Oak St	Cincinnati	OH	45219	**800-543-3999**	513-281-3300
Westin Cincinnati 21 E 5th St	Cincinnati	OH	45202	**800-937-8461**	513-621-7700
Wingate Inn Cincinnati-Blue Ash 4320 Glendale-Milford Rd	Cincinnati	OH	45242	**800-228-1000**	513-733-1142
Embassy Suites Cleveland Downtown 1701 E 12th St	Cleveland	OH	44114	**800-362-2779**	216-523-8000
Glidden House 1901 Ford Dr	Cleveland	OH	44106	**800-759-8358**	216-231-8900
Hilton Garden Inn Cleveland Airport 4900 Emerald Ct SW	Cleveland	OH	44135	**877-782-9444**	216-898-1898
Hilton Garden Inn Cleveland Downtown 1100 Carnegie Ave	Cleveland	OH	44115	**877-782-9444**	216-658-6400
Holiday Inn Select Cleveland City Center-Lakeshore 1111 Lakeside Ave	Cleveland	OH	44114	**800-465-4329**	216-241-5100
Hyatt Regency Cleveland at the Arcade 420 Superior Ave	Cleveland	OH	44114	**800-233-1234**	216-575-1234
InterContinental Hotel & Conference Center Cleveland 9801 Carnegie Ave	Cleveland	OH	44106	**877-707-8999**	216-707-4100
InterContinental Suites Cleveland 8800 Euclid Ave	Cleveland	OH	44106	**888-707-8999**	216-707-4300
Marriott Cleveland Airport 4277 W 150th St	Cleveland	OH	44135	**800-228-9290**	216-252-5333
Marriott Cleveland Downtown at Key Center 127 Public Sq	Cleveland	OH	44114	**800-228-9290**	216-696-9200
Radisson Hotel at Gateway-Cleveland 651 Huron Rd	Cleveland	OH	44115	**800-333-3333**	216-377-9000
Renaissance Cleveland Hotel 24 Public Sq	Cleveland	OH	44113	**800-468-3571**	216-696-5600
Ritz-Carlton Cleveland 1515 W 3rd St	Cleveland	OH	44113	**800-241-3333**	216-623-1300
Sheraton Cleveland Airport Hotel 5300 Riverside Dr	Cleveland	OH	44135	**800-325-3535**	216-267-1500
Sheraton Cleveland City Centre Hotel 777 St Clair Ave NE	Cleveland	OH	44114	**800-325-3535**	216-771-7600
Wyndham Cleveland at Playhouse Square 1260 Euclid Ave	Cleveland	OH	44115	**800-996-3426**	216-615-7500
Adam's Mark Columbus 50 N 3rd St	Columbus	OH	43215	**800-444-2326**	614-228-5050
AmeriSuites Columbus/Worthington 7490 Vantage Dr	Columbus	OH	43235	**800-833-1516**	614-846-4355
Concourse Hotel & Conference Center 4300 International Gateway	Columbus	OH	43219	**800-541-4574**	614-237-2515
Courtyard Columbus Downtown 35 W Spring St	Columbus	OH	43215	**800-321-2211**	614-228-3200
Crowne Plaza Hotel Columbus Downtown 33 Nationwide Blvd	Columbus	OH	43215	**800-227-6963**	614-461-4100
Doubletree Guest Suites Columbus 50 S Front St	Columbus	OH	43215	**800-222-8733**	614-228-4600
Embassy Suites Columbus 2700 Corporate Exchange Dr	Columbus	OH	43231	**800-362-2779**	614-890-8600
Hilton Garden Inn Columbus Airport 4265 Sawyer Rd	Columbus	OH	43219	**877-782-9444**	614-231-2869
Holiday Inn on the Lane 328 W Lane Ave	Columbus	OH	43201	**800-465-4329**	614-294-4848
Holiday Inn Worthington Hotel & Conference Center 175 Hutchinson Ave	Columbus	OH	43235	**800-465-4329**	614-885-3334
Hyatt on Capitol Square 75 E State St	Columbus	OH	43215	**800-233-1234**	614-228-1234
Hyatt Regency Columbus 350 N High St	Columbus	OH	43215	**800-233-1234**	614-463-1234
Lofts Hotel & Suites 55 E Nationwide Blvd	Columbus	OH	43215	**800-735-6387**	614-461-2663
Marriott Columbus North 6500 Doubletree Ave	Columbus	OH	43229	**800-228-9290**	614-885-1885
Ramada Plaza Hotel Columbus 4900 Sinclair Rd	Columbus	OH	43229	**800-272-6232**	614-846-0300

Name / Address	City	State	ZIP	Toll-Free	Phone
Sheraton Suites Columbus 201 Hutchinson Ave	Columbus	OH	43235	**800-325-3535**	614-436-0004
University Plaza Hotel & Conference Center 3110 Olentangy River Rd	Columbus	OH	43202	**877-677-5292**	614-267-7461
Westin Great Southern 310 S High St	Columbus	OH	43215	**800-937-8461**	614-228-3800
Wingate Inn Columbus-Polaris 8505 Pulsar Pl	Columbus	OH	43240	**800-228-1000**	614-844-5888
Sheraton Suites Akron/Cuyahoga Falls 1989 Front St	Cuyahoga Falls	OH	44221	**800-325-3535**	330-929-3000
Best Western Executive Hotel Dayton 2401 Needmore Rd	Dayton	OH	45414	**800-528-1234**	937-278-5711
Crowne Plaza Hotel Dayton 33 E 5th St	Dayton	OH	45402	**800-227-6963**	937-224-0800
Doubletree Hotel Dayton Downtown 11 S Ludlow St	Dayton	OH	45402	**800-222-8733**	937-461-4700
Marriott Dayton 1414 S Patterson Blvd	Dayton	OH	45409	**800-228-9290**	937-223-1000
Residence Inn Dayton North 7070 Poe Ave	Dayton	OH	45414	**800-331-3131**	937-898-7764
Clarion Hotel Dublin 600 Metro Pl N	Dublin	OH	43017	**800-252-7446**	614-764-2200
Hilton Garden Inn Columbus/Dublin 500 Metro Pl N	Dublin	OH	43017	**877-782-9444**	614-766-9900
Marriott Columbus Northwest 5605 Blazer Pkwy	Dublin	OH	43017	**800-228-9290**	614-791-1000
Woodfin Suite Hotel Dublin 4130 Tuller Rd	Dublin	OH	43017	**888-433-9408**	614-766-7762
Holiday Inn Fairborn Hotel & Conference Center 2800 Presidential Dr	Fairborn	OH	45324	**800-465-4329**	937-426-7800
Findlay Inn & Conference Center 200 E Main Cross St	Findlay	OH	45840	**800-825-1455**	419-422-5682
Hilton Garden Inn Columbus/Grove City 3928 Jackpot Rd	Grove City	OH	43123	**877-782-9444**	614-539-8944
Courtyard Toledo Airport 1435 E Mall Dr	Holland	OH	43528	**800-321-2211**	419-866-1001
Fairfield Inn Toledo/Holland Airport 1401 E Mall Dr	Holland	OH	43528	**800-228-2800**	419-867-1144
Hilton Cleveland South 6200 Quarry Ln	Independence	OH	44131	**800-445-8667**	216-447-1300
Hilton Garden Inn Cincinnati Northeast 6288 Tri Ridge Blvd	Loveland	OH	45140	**877-782-9444**	513-576-6999
Lafayette Hotel 101 Front St	Marietta	OH	45750	**800-331-9336**	740-373-5522
Kings Island Resort & Conference Center 5691 Kings Island Dr	Mason	OH	45040	**800-704-2439**	513-398-0115
Marriott Cincinnati Northeast 9664 Mason Montgomery Rd	Mason	OH	45040	**800-228-9290**	513-459-9800
Fairfield Inn Toledo/Maumee 521 W Dussel Dr	Maumee	OH	43537	**800-228-2800**	419-897-0865
Courtyard Dayton Mall 100 Prestige Pl	Miamisburg	OH	45342	**800-321-2211**	937-433-3131
Doubletree Guest Suites Dayton/Miamisburg 300 Prestige Pl	Miamisburg	OH	45342	**800-222-8733**	937-436-2400
Holiday Inn North Canton 4520 Everhard Rd NW	North Canton	OH	44718	**800-465-4329**	330-494-2770
Oberlin Inn 7 N Main St	Oberlin	OH	44074	**800-376-4173**	440-775-1111
Maumee Bay Resort & Conference Center 1750 Park Rd 2	Oregon	OH	43618	**800-282-7275**	419-836-1466
Holiday Inn Perrysburg-French Quarter 10630 Fremont Pike	Perrysburg	OH	43551	**888-874-2592**	419-874-3111
Fairfield Inn Youngstown 7397 Tiffany S	Poland	OH	44514	**800-228-2800**	330-726-5979
Best Western Springdale Hotel & Conference Center 11911 Sheraton Ln	Springdale	OH	45246	**800-528-1234**	513-671-6600
Holiday Inn Select Cleveland (Strongsville) 15471 Royalton Rd	Strongsville	OH	44136	**800-465-4329**	440-238-8800
Clarion Hotel Toledo Westgate 3536 Secor Rd	Toledo	OH	43606	**800-252-7466**	419-535-7070
Comfort Inn Toledo 3560 Secor Rd	Toledo	OH	43606	**800-228-5150**	419-531-2666
Hilton Toledo 3100 Glendale Ave	Toledo	OH	43614	**800-445-8667**	419-381-6800
Holiday Inn Toledo West 2340 S Reynolds Rd	Toledo	OH	43614	**800-465-4329**	419-865-1361
Radisson Hotel Toledo 101 N Summit St	Toledo	OH	43604	**800-333-3333**	419-241-3000
Wyndham Toledo 2 Seagate-Summit St	Toledo	OH	43604	**800-996-3426**	419-241-1411
Hilton Garden Inn Cleveland/Twinsburg 8971 Wilcox Dr	Twinsburg	OH	44087	**877-782-9444**	330-405-8448
Holiday Inn Westlake 1100 Crocker Rd	Westlake	OH	44145	**800-465-4329**	440-871-6000
Best Western Meander Inn 870 N Canfield-Niles Rd	Youngstown	OH	44515	**800-528-1234**	330-544-2378
Quality Inn & Suites Youngstown North 4055 Belmont Ave	Youngstown	OH	44505	**800-860-7829**	330-759-3180

Oklahoma

Name / Address	City	State	ZIP	Toll-Free	Phone
Ramada Plaza Hotel Edmond/Oklahoma City North 930 E 2nd St	Edmond	OK	73034	**800-322-4686**	405-341-3577
AmeriSuites Oklahoma City Airport 1818 S Meridian Ave	Oklahoma City	OK	73108	**800-833-1516**	405-682-3900
Biltmore Hotel Oklahoma 401 S Meridian Ave	Oklahoma City	OK	73108	**800-522-6620**	405-947-7681
Clarion Hotel Oklahoma City Airport 737 S Meridian Ave	Oklahoma City	OK	73108	**800-424-6423**	405-942-8511
Courtyard Oklahoma City Airport 4301 Highline Blvd	Oklahoma City	OK	73108	**800-321-2211**	405-946-6500
Embassy Suites Oklahoma City-Will Rogers Airport 1815 S Meridian Ave	Oklahoma City	OK	73108	**800-362-2779**	405-682-6000
Habana Inn 2200 NW 39th Expy	Oklahoma City	OK	73112	**800-988-2221**	405-528-2221
Hilton Garden Inn Oklahoma City Airport 801 S Meridian	Oklahoma City	OK	73108	**877-782-9444**	405-942-1400
Hilton Oklahoma City Northwest 2945 Northwest Expy	Oklahoma City	OK	73112	**800-445-8667**	405-848-4811
Marriott Oklahoma City 3233 Northwest Expy	Oklahoma City	OK	73112	**800-228-9290**	405-842-6633
Renaissance Oklahoma City Hotel 10 N Broadway *Resv	Oklahoma City	OK	73102	**800-468-3571***	405-228-8000
Residence Inn Oklahoma City West 4361 W Reno Ave	Oklahoma City	OK	73107	**800-331-3131**	405-942-4500
Waterford Marriott 6300 Waterford Blvd	Oklahoma City	OK	73118	**800-228-9290**	405-848-4782
Westin Oklahoma City 1 N Broadway	Oklahoma City	OK	73102	**800-937-8461**	405-235-2780
Wingate Inn Oklahoma City 2001 S Meridian Ave	Oklahoma City	OK	73108	**800-228-1000**	405-682-3600
Inn at Jarrett Farm 38009 US Hwy 75 N	Ramona	OK	74061	**877-371-1200**	918-371-1200
Adam's Mark Tulsa 100 E 2nd St	Tulsa	OK	74103	**800-444-2326**	918-582-9000
AmeriSuites Tulsa Hyde Park 7037 S Zurich Ave	Tulsa	OK	74136	**800-833-1516**	918-491-4010
Courtyard Tulsa 3340 S 79th East Ave	Tulsa	OK	74145	**800-321-2211**	918-660-0646
Doubletree Hotel Tulsa-Downtown 616 W 7th St	Tulsa	OK	74127	**800-222-8733**	918-587-8000
Doubletree Hotel Tulsa- Warren Place 6110 S Yale Ave	Tulsa	OK	74136	**800-222-8733**	918-495-1000
Embassy Suites Tulsa I-44 3332 S 79th East Ave	Tulsa	OK	74145	**800-362-2779**	918-622-4000
Hilton Garden Inn Tulsa Airport 7728 E Virgin Ct	Tulsa	OK	74115	**877-782-9444**	918-838-1444
Hilton Tulsa Southern Hills 7902 S Lewis Ave	Tulsa	OK	74136	**800-444-7263**	918-492-5000
Holiday Inn Select Tulsa 5000 E Skelly Dr	Tulsa	OK	74135	**800-836-9635**	918-622-7000
Hotel Ambassador 1324 S Main St	Tulsa	OK	74119	**888-408-8282**	918-587-8200
Marriott Tulsa Southern Hills 1902 E 71st St	Tulsa	OK	74136	**800-228-9290**	918-493-7000
Radisson Inn Tulsa Airport 2201 N 77th Ave East	Tulsa	OK	74115	**800-333-3333**	918-835-9911
Ramada Inn Tulsa Downtown 17 W 7th St	Tulsa	OK	74119	**800-585-5101**	918-585-5898
Sheraton Tulsa Hotel 10918 E 41st St	Tulsa	OK	74146	**800-325-3535**	918-627-5000

Oregon

Name / Address	City	State	ZIP	Toll-Free	Phone
Ashland Springs Hotel - A WestCoast Hotel 212 E Main St	Ashland	OR	97520	**800-325-4000**	541-488-1700
Windmill Inn of Ashland 2525 Ashland St	Ashland	OR	97520	**800-547-4747**	541-482-8310
Courtyard Portland/Beaverton 8500 SW Nimbus Dr	Beaverton	OR	97008	**800-321-2211**	503-641-3200
Greenwood Inn 10700 SW Allen Blvd	Beaverton	OR	97005	**800-289-1300**	503-643-7444
Hilton Garden Inn Portland/Beaverton 15520 NW Gateway Ct	Beaverton	OR	97006	**877-782-9444**	503-439-1717
Hallmark Resort PO Box 547	Cannon Beach	OR	97110	**800-345-5676**	503-436-1566
Surfsand Resort 148 W Gower Rd	Cannon Beach	OR	97110	**800-547-6100**	503-436-2274
Monarch Hotel & Conference Center 12566 SE 93rd Ave	Clackamas	OR	97015	**800-492-8700**	503-652-1515
Best Western Greentree Inn 1759 Franklin Blvd	Eugene	OR	97403	**800-528-1234**	541-485-2727
Campus Inn & Suites 390 E Broadway	Eugene	OR	97401	**800-888-6313**	541-343-3376
Hilton Eugene & Conference Center 66 E 6th Ave	Eugene	OR	97401	**800-937-6660**	541-342-2000
Phoenix Inn Eugene 850 Franklin Blvd	Eugene	OR	97403	**800-344-0131**	541-344-0001
Red Lion Hotel Eugene 205 Coburg Rd	Eugene	OR	97401	**800-733-5466**	541-342-5201
Valley River Inn - A WestCoast Hotel 1000 Valley River Way	Eugene	OR	97401	**800-543-8266**	541-743-1000
Driftwood Shores Resort 88416 1st Ave	Florence	OR	97439	**800-422-5091**	541-997-8263
Wingate Inn Portland-Hillsboro 5900 NE Ray Circle	Hillsboro	OR	97124	**800-228-1000**	503-844-9696
Crowne Plaza Hotel Lake Oswego 14811 Kruse Oaks Dr	Lake Oswego	OR	97035	**800-465-4329**	503-624-8400
Hilton Garden Inn Portland/Lake Oswego 14850 Kruse Oaks Dr	Lake Oswego	OR	97035	**877-782-9444**	503-684-8900
Inn at Spanish Head 4009 SW Hwy 101	Lincoln City	OR	97367	**800-452-8127**	541-996-2161
Surftides Beach Resort 2945 NW Jetty Ave	Lincoln City	OR	97367	**800-452-2159**	541-994-2191
Safari Motor Inn 345 N Hwy 99 West	McMinnville	OR	97128	**800-321-5543**	503-472-5187
Embarcadero Resort Hotel & Marina 1000 SE Bay Blvd	Newport	OR	97365	**800-547-4779**	541-265-8521
Inn at Otter Crest 301 Otter Crest Loop	Otter Rock	OR	97369	**800-452-2101**	541-765-2111
5th Avenue Suites Hotel 506 SW Washington St	Portland	OR	97204	**800-711-2971**	503-222-0001
Avalon Hotel & Spa 0455 SW Hamilton Ct	Portland	OR	97239	**888-556-4402**	503-802-5800
Benson The 309 SW Broadway	Portland	OR	97205	**800-426-0670**	503-228-2000
Courtyard Portland Airport 11550 NE Airport Way	Portland	OR	97220	**800-321-2211**	503-252-3200
Courtyard Portland North Harbour 1231 N Anchor Way	Portland	OR	97217	**800-321-2211**	503-735-1818
Doubletree Hotel Portland-Columbia River 1401 N Hayden Island Dr	Portland	OR	97217	**800-222-8733**	503-283-2111
Doubletree Hotel Portland-Lloyd Center 1000 NE Multnomah St	Portland	OR	97232	**800-222-8733**	503-281-6111
Embassy Suites Portland Downtown 319 SW Pine St	Portland	OR	97204	**800-362-2779**	503-279-9000
Four Points by Sheraton Portland East 1919 NE 181st Ave	Portland	OR	97230	**888-828-1918**	503-491-1818
Governor Hotel 611 SW 10th Ave	Portland	OR	97205	**800-554-3456**	503-224-3400
Heathman Hotel 1001 SW Broadway	Portland	OR	97205	**800-551-0011**	503-241-4100
Hilton Garden Inn Portland Airport 12048 NE Airport Way	Portland	OR	97220	**877-782-9444**	503-255-8600
Hilton Portland 921 SW 6th Ave	Portland	OR	97204	**800-445-8667**	503-226-1611
Hotel Lucia 400 SW Broadway	Portland	OR	97205	**877-225-1717**	503-225-1717
Hotel Vintage Plaza 422 SW Broadway	Portland	OR	97205	**800-263-2305**	503-228-1212
Mallory Hotel 729 SW 15th Ave	Portland	OR	97205	**800-228-8657**	503-223-6311
Mark Spencer Hotel 409 SW 11th Ave	Portland	OR	97205	**800-548-3934**	503-224-3293
Marriott Portland City Center 520 SW Broadway	Portland	OR	97205	**800-228-9290**	503-226-6300
Marriott Portland Downtown 1401 SW Naito Pkwy	Portland	OR	97201	**800-228-9290**	503-226-7600
Paramount Hotel 808 SW Taylor St	Portland	OR	97205	**800-716-6199**	503-223-9900
Residence Inn Portland Downtown Riverplace 2115 SW River Pkwy	Portland	OR	97201	**800-331-3131**	503-552-9500
RiverPlace Hotel - A WestCoast Grand Hotel 1510 SW Harbor Way	Portland	OR	97201	**800-227-1333**	503-228-3233
Sheraton Portland Airport Hotel 8235 NE Airport Way	Portland	OR	97220	**800-325-3535**	503-281-2500
Shilo Inn Hotel Portland/Beaverton 9900 SW Canyon Rd	Portland	OR	97225	**800-222-2244**	503-297-2551
Shilo Inn Suites Hotel Portland Airport 11707 NE Airport Way	Portland	OR	97220	**800-222-2244**	503-252-7500
US Suites Portland 10220 SW Nimbus St	Portland	OR	97223	**800-877-8483**	503-443-2033
WestCoast Benson Hotel 309 SW Broadway	Portland	OR	97205	**800-426-0670**	503-228-2000
WestCoast RiverPlace Hotel 1510 SW Harbor Way	Portland	OR	97201	**800-227-1333**	503-228-3233
Westin Portland 750 SW Alder St	Portland	OR	97205	**800-937-8461**	503-294-9000
Phoenix Inn Salem North 1590 Weston Ct NE	Salem	OR	97301	**888-239-9593**	503-581-7004
Phoenix Inn Salem South 4370 Commercial St SE	Salem	OR	97302	**800-445-4498**	503-588-9220
Red Lion Hotel Salem 3301 Market St NE	Salem	OR	97301	**800-248-6273**	503-370-7888
Shilo Inn Suites Salem 3304 Market St	Salem	OR	97301	**800-222-2244**	503-581-4001
Village Inn Motel 1875 Mohawk Blvd	Springfield	OR	97477	**800-327-6871**	541-747-4546
Embassy Suites Portland-Washington Square 9000 SW Washington Square Rd	Tigard	OR	97223	**800-362-2779**	503-644-4000

Pennsylvania

Name / Address	City	State	ZIP	Toll-Free	Phone
Four Points by Sheraton Hotel & Suites Lehigh Valley Airport 3400 Airport Rd	Allentown	PA	18109	**800-625-5144**	610-266-1000
Hilton Garden Inn Allentown Airport 1787-B Airport Rd	Allentown	PA	18109	**877-782-9444**	610-443-1400
Wingate Inn Allentown 4325 Hamilton Blvd	Allentown	PA	18103	**800-228-1000**	610-366-1600
Courtyard Allentown Bethlehem 2160 Motel Dr	Bethlehem	PA	18018	**800-321-2211**	610-317-6200
Radisson Hotel Bethlehem 437 Main St	Bethlehem	PA	18018	**800-333-3333**	610-625-5000
Glendorn 1000 Glendorn Dr	Bradford	PA	16701	**800-843-8568**	814-362-6511

Pennsylvania (Cont'd)

				Toll-Free	Phone
Hilton Garden Inn Allentown West 230 Sycamore Rd	Breinigsville	PA	18031	**877-782-9444**	610-398-6686
Riverside Inn 1 Fountain Ave	Cambridge Springs	PA	16403	**800-964-5173**	814-398-4645
Radisson Penn Harris Hotel & Convention Center 1150 Camp Hill Bypass	Camp Hill	PA	17011	**800-333-3333**	717-763-7117
Hilton Garden Inn Pittsburgh/Southpointe 1000 Corporate Dr	Canonsburg	PA	15317	**877-782-9444**	724-743-5000
Inn at Nichols Village 1101 Northern Blvd	Clarks Summit	PA	18411	**800-642-2215**	570-587-1135
Courtyard Pittsburgh Airport 450 Cherrington Pkwy	Coraopolis	PA	15108	**800-321-2211**	412-264-5000
Crowne Plaza Hotel Pittsburgh International Airport 1160 Thorn Run Rd Ext	Coraopolis	PA	15108	**800-627-6373**	412-262-2400
Embassy Suites Pittsburgh International Airport 550 Cherrington Pkwy	Coraopolis	PA	15108	**800-362-2779**	412-269-9070
Holiday Inn Pittsburgh Airport 8256 University Blvd	Coraopolis	PA	15108	**800-333-4835**	412-262-3600
Wyndham Pittsburgh Airport 777 Aten Rd	Coraopolis	PA	15108	**800-328-9297**	412-788-8800
Avalon Hotel 16 W 10th St	Erie	PA	16501	**800-822-5011**	814-459-2220
Bel-Air Clarion Hotel & Conference Center 2800 W 8th St	Erie	PA	16505	**800-888-8781**	814-833-1116
Comfort Inn Erie 8051 Peach St	Erie	PA	16509	**800-228-5150**	814-866-6666
Glass House Inn 3202 W 26th St	Erie	PA	16506	**800-[illegible]-7222**	814-[illegible]-7751
Lakeview-on-the-Lake Motel 8696 E Lake Rd	Erie	PA	16511	**888-558-8439**	814-899-6948
Residence Inn Erie 8061 Peach St	Erie	PA	16509	**800-331-3131**	814-864-2500
Best Western Presque Isle Country Inn 6467 Sterrettania Rd	Fairview	PA	16415	**800-528-1234**	814-838-7647
Sheraton Great Valley Hotel 707 Lancaster Pike	Frazer	PA	19355	**800-325-3535**	610-524-5500
Best Western Gettysburg Hotel 1 Lincoln Sq	Gettysburg	PA	17325	**866-378-1797**	717-337-2000
Eisenhower Inn & Conference Center 2634 Emmitsburg Rd	Gettysburg	PA	17325	**800-776-8349**	717-334-8121
Hilton Garden Inn Gettysburg 1061 York St	Gettysburg	PA	17325	**877-782-9444**	717-334-2040
James Gettys Hotel 27 Chambersburg St	Gettysburg	PA	17325	**888-900-5275**	717-337-1334
Quality Inn Larson's at General Lee's Headquarters 401 Buford Ave	Gettysburg	PA	17325	**800-228-5151**	717-334-3141
Mountain View Inn 1001 Village Dr	Greensburg	PA	15601	**800-537-8709**	724-834-5300
Crowne Plaza Hotel Harrisburg-Hershey 23 S 2nd St	Harrisburg	PA	17101	**800-227-6963**	717-234-5021
Hilton Harrisburg & Towers 1 N 2nd St	Harrisburg	PA	17101	**800-445-8667**	717-233-6000
Wingate Inn Harrisburg 1344 Eisenhower Blvd	Harrisburg	PA	17111	**800-228-1000**	717-985-1600
Wyndham Garden Hotel Harrisburg 765 Eisenhower Blvd	Harrisburg	PA	17111	**800-253-0238**	717-558-9500
Wyndham Harrisburg-Hershey 4650 Lindle Rd	Harrisburg	PA	17111	**800-996-3426**	717-564-5511
Hershey Lodge & Convention Center W Chocolate Ave & University Dr	Hershey	PA	17033	**800-533-3131**	717-533-3311
Hilton Valley Forge 251 W DeKalb Pike	King of Prussia	PA	19406	**800-445-8667**	610-337-1200
Radisson Valley Forge Hotel & Convention Center 1160 1st Ave	King of Prussia	PA	19406	**800-333-3333**	610-337-2000
Sheraton Park Ridge Hotel & Conference Center 480 N Gulph Rd	King of Prussia	PA	19406	**800-337-1801**	610-337-1800
Best Western Eden Resort Inn & Conference Center 222 Eden Rd	Lancaster	PA	17601	**800-528-1234**	717-569-6444
Sheraton Bucks County Hotel 400 Oxford Valley Rd	Langhorne	PA	19047	**800-325-3535**	215-547-4100
Leola Village Inn & Suites 38 Deborah Dr	Leola	PA	17540	**877-669-5094**	717-656-7002
Desmond Great Valley 1 Liberty Blvd	Malvern	PA	19355	**800-575-1776**	610-296-9800
Courtyard Scranton 16 Glenmaura National Blvd	Moosic	PA	18507	**800-321-2211**	570-969-2100
Lantern Lodge Motor Inn 411 N College St	Myerstown	PA	17067	**800-262-5564**	717-866-6536
Adam's Mark Philadelphia 4000 City Line Ave	Philadelphia	PA	19131	**800-444-2326**	215-581-5000
Best Western Center City Hotel 501 N 22nd St	Philadelphia	PA	19130	**800-528-1234**	215-568-8300
Best Western Independence Park Hotel 235 Chestnut St	Philadelphia	PA	19106	**800-624-2988**	215-922-4443
Chestnut Hill Hotel 8229 Germantown Ave	Philadelphia	PA	19118	**800-628-9744**	215-242-5905
Courtyard Philadelphia Airport 8900 Bartram Ave	Philadelphia	PA	19153	**800-321-2211**	215-365-2200
Crowne Plaza Hotel Philadelphia-Center City 1800 Market St	Philadelphia	PA	19103	**800-227-6963**	215-561-7500
Doubletree Hotel Philadelphia 237 S Broad St	Philadelphia	PA	19107	**800-222-8733**	215-893-1600
Embassy Suites Philadelphia-Center City 1776 Ben Franklin Pkwy	Philadelphia	PA	19103	**800-362-2779**	215-561-1776
Four Seasons Hotel Philadelphia 1 Logan Sq	Philadelphia	PA	19103	**800-332-3442**	215-963-1500
Hilton Garden Inn Philadelphia Center City 1100 Arch St	Philadelphia	PA	19107	**877-782-9444**	215-923-0100
Hilton Philadelphia Airport 4509 Island Ave	Philadelphia	PA	19153	**800-445-8667**	215-365-4150
Hilton Philadelphia City Avenue 4200 City Ave	Philadelphia	PA	19131	**800-445-8667**	215-879-4000
Holiday Inn Philadelphia City Line 4100 Presidential Blvd	Philadelphia	PA	19131	**800-465-4329**	215-477-0200
Holiday Inn Philadelphia Stadium 900 Packer Ave	Philadelphia	PA	19148	**800-424-0291**	215-755-9500
Hotel Sofitel Philadelphia 120 S 17th St	Philadelphia	PA	19103	**800-763-4835**	215-569-8300
Latham Hotel Center City 135 S 17th St	Philadelphia	PA	19103	**877-528-4261**	215-563-7474
Loews Philadelphia Hotel 1200 Market St	Philadelphia	PA	19107	**800-235-6397**	215-627-1200
Marriott Philadelphia Airport 1 Arrivals Rd	Philadelphia	PA	19153	**800-228-9290**	215-492-9000
Marriott Philadelphia Downtown 1201 Market St	Philadelphia	PA	19107	**800-228-9290**	215-625-2900
Omni Hotel at Independence Park 401 Chestnut St	Philadelphia	PA	19106	**800-843-6664**	215-925-0000
Park Hyatt Philadelphia 1415 Chancellor Ct	Philadelphia	PA	19102	**800-233-1234**	215-893-1234
Penn's View Hotel 14 N Front St	Philadelphia	PA	19106	**800-331-7634**	215-922-7600
Radisson Plaza Warwick Hotel Philadelphia 1701 Locust St	Philadelphia	PA	19103	**800-333-3333**	215-735-6000
Renaissance Philadelphia Hotel-Airport 500 Stevens Dr	Philadelphia	PA	19113	**888-887-7951**	610-521-5900
Rittenhouse Hotel 210 W Rittenhouse Sq	Philadelphia	PA	19103	**800-635-1042**	215-546-9000
Ritz-Carlton Philadelphia 10 Ave of the Arts	Philadelphia	PA	19102	**888-505-3914**	215-523-8000
Sheraton Rittenhouse Square Hotel 227 S 18th St	Philadelphia	PA	19103	**800-325-3535**	215-546-9400
Sheraton Society Hill Hotel 1 Dock St	Philadelphia	PA	19106	**800-325-3535**	215-238-6000
Sheraton Suites Philadelphia Airport 4101 Island Ave	Philadelphia	PA	19153	**800-325-3535**	215-365-6600
Sheraton University City Hotel 36th & Chestnut Sts	Philadelphia	PA	19104	**800-325-3535**	215-387-8000
Westin Philadelphia 99 S 17 St	Philadelphia	PA	19103	**800-937-8461**	215-563-1600
Wyndham Philadelphia at Franklin Plaza 17th & Race St 2 Franklin Plaza	Philadelphia	PA	19102	**800-996-3426**	215-448-2000
AmeriSuites Pittsburgh Airport 6011 Campbells Run Rd	Pittsburgh	PA	15205	**800-833-1516**	412-494-0202
Hilton Pittsburgh & Towers 600 Commonwealth Pl Gateway Ctr	Pittsburgh	PA	15222	**800-445-8667**	412-391-4600
Holiday Inn Select Pittsburgh-University Center 100 Lytton Ave	Pittsburgh	PA	15213	**800-465-4329**	412-682-6200
Marriott Pittsburgh City Center 112 Washington Pl	Pittsburgh	PA	15219	**888-456-6600**	412-471-4000
Radisson Hotel Pittsburgh Green Tree 101 Radisson Dr	Pittsburgh	PA	15205	**800-333-3333**	412-922-8400
Ramada Plaza Suites & Conference Center Pittsburgh 1 Bigelow Sq	Pittsburgh	PA	15219	**800-225-5858**	412-281-5800
Renaissance Pittsburgh Hotel 107 6th St	Pittsburgh	PA	15222	**866-454-4400**	412-562-1200
Sheraton Station Square Hotel 300 Station Square Dr W	Pittsburgh	PA	15219	**800-255-7488**	412-261-2000
Westin Convention Center Pittsburgh 1000 Penn Ave	Pittsburgh	PA	15222	**800-228-3000**	412-281-3700
Wyndham Garden Hotel Pittburgh University Place 3454 Forbes Ave	Pittsburgh	PA	15213	**800-996-3426**	412-683-2040
Victoria Inns & Suites Hwy 315	Pittston	PA	18640	**800-937-4667**	570-655-1234
Radnor Hotel 591 E Lancaster Ave	Saint Davids	PA	19087	**800-537-3000**	610-688-5800
Radisson Lackawanna Station Hotel Scranton 700 Lackawanna Ave	Scranton	PA	18503	**800-333-3333**	570-342-8300
Nittany Lion Inn 200 W Park Ave	State College	PA	16803	**800-233-7505**	814-865-8500
Cross Creek Resort 3815 SR 8	Titusville	PA	16354	**800-461-3173**	814-827-9611
Holiday Inn Select Philadelphia-Bucks County 4700 Street Rd	Trevose	PA	19053	**800-873-7263**	215-364-2000
Wyndham Valley Forge Suites 888 Chesterbrook Blvd	Wayne	PA	19087	**800-996-3426**	610-647-6700
Marriott Philadelphia West 111 Crawford Ave	West Conshohocken	PA	19428	**800-228-9290**	610-941-5600
Radisson Hotel Sharon Rt 18 & I-80	West Middlesex	PA	16159	**800-333-3333**	724-528-2501
Best Western East Mountain Inn 2400 East End Blvd	Wilkes-Barre	PA	18702	**800-528-1234**	570-822-1011
Inn at Reading 1040 Park Rd	Wyomissing	PA	19610	**800-383-9713**	610-372-7811
Sheraton Reading Hotel 1741 Papermill Rd	Wyomissing	PA	19610	**800-325-3535**	610-376-3811
Yorktowne Hotel 48 E Market St	York	PA	17401	**800-233-9324**	717-848-1111

Puerto Rico

				Toll-Free	Phone
InterContinental San Juan Resort & Casino 5961 Isla Verde Ave	Carolina	PR	00979	**800-443-2009**	787-791-6100
Ritz-Carlton San Juan Hotel Spa & Casino 6961 Ave of the Governors	Carolina	PR	00979	**800-241-3333**	787-253-1700
Radisson Ambassador Plaza Hotel & Casino 1369 Ashford Ave	Condado	PR	00907	**800-468-8512**	787-721-7300
Wyndham Old San Juan Hotel & Casino 100 Brumbaugh St	San Juan	PR	00902	**800-996-3426**	787-721-5100

Rhode Island

				Toll-Free	Phone
Courtyard Newport- Middletown 9 Commerce Dr	Middletown	RI	02842	**888-686-5067**	401-849-8000
Inn at Newport Beach 30 Wave Ave	Middletown	RI	02842	**800-786-0310**	401-846-0310
Newport Gateway Hotel 31 W Main Rd	Middletown	RI	02842	**800-427-9444**	401-847-2735
Royal Plaza Hotel 425 E Main Rd	Middletown	RI	02842	**800-825-7072**	401-846-3555
Castle Hill Inn & Resort 590 Ocean Dr	Newport	RI	02840	**888-466-1355**	401-849-3800
Harborside Inn Christie's Landing	Newport	RI	02840	**800-427-9444**	401-846-6600
Hotel Viking 1 Bellevue Ave	Newport	RI	02840	**800-556-7126**	401-847-3300
Hyatt Regency Newport 1 Goat Island	Newport	RI	02840	**800-233-1234**	401-851-1234
Jailhouse Inn 13 Marlborough St	Newport	RI	02840	**800-427-9444**	401-847-4638
Marriott Newport 25 America's Cup Ave	Newport	RI	02840	**800-458-3066**	401-849-1000
Mill Street Inn 75 Mill St	Newport	RI	02840	**800-392-1316**	401-849-9500
Newport Harbor Hotel & Marina 49 America's Cup Ave	Newport	RI	02840	**800-955-2558**	401-847-9000
SeaView Inn 240 Aquidneck Ave	Newport	RI	02842	**800-495-2046**	401-846-5000
Vanderbilt Hall Hotel 41 Mary St	Newport	RI	02840	**888-826-4255**	401-846-6200
Yankee Peddler Inn 113 Touro St	Newport	RI	02840	**800-427-9444**	401-846-1323
Holiday Inn Providence Downtown 21 Atwells Ave	Providence	RI	02903	**800-465-4329**	401-831-3900
Marriott Providence 1 Orms St	Providence	RI	02904	**800-228-9290**	401-272-2400
Providence Biltmore Hotel Kennedy Plaza 11 Dorrance St	Providence	RI	02903	**800-294-7709**	401-421-0700
Westin Providence 1 W Exchange St	Providence	RI	02903	**800-937-8461**	401-598-8000
Crowne Plaza Hotel Providence-Warwick 801 Greenwich Ave	Warwick	RI	02886	**800-227-6963**	401-732-6000
Radisson Airport Hotel Providence 2081 Post Rd	Warwick	RI	02886	**800-333-3333**	401-739-3000
Residence Inn Providence-Warwick 500 Kilvert St	Warwick	RI	02886	**800-331-3131**	401-737-7100
Sheraton Providence Airport Hotel 1850 Post Rd	Warwick	RI	02886	**800-325-3535**	401-738-4000

South Carolina

				Toll-Free	Phone
Sleep Inn Aiken 1002 Monterey Dr	Aiken	SC	29803	**800-753-3746**	803-644-9900
Rhett House Inn 1009 Craven St	Beaufort	SC	29902	**888-480-9530**	843-524-9030
Anchorage Inn 26 Vendue Range	Charleston	SC	29401	**800-421-2952**	843-723-8300
Ansonborough Inn 21 Hassell St	Charleston	SC	29401	**800-522-2073**	843-723-1655
Charleston Place 205 Meeting St	Charleston	SC	29401	**800-611-5545**	843-722-4900
Courtyard Charleston Downtown/Riverview 35 Lockwood Dr	Charleston	SC	29401	**800-321-2211**	843-722-7229
Doubletree Guest Suites Charleston-Historic District 181 Church St	Charleston	SC	29401	**800-222-8733**	843-577-2644
Embassy Suites Charleston 337 Meeting St	Charleston	SC	29403	**800-362-2779**	843-723-6900

Name / Address	City	State	Zip	Toll-Free	Phone
Holiday Inn Charleston Historic District 125 Calhoun St	Charleston	SC	29401	**877-805-7900**	843-805-7900
Holiday Inn Charleston-Riverview 301 Savannah Hwy	Charleston	SC	29407	**800-465-4329**	843-556-7100
Indigo Inn 1 Maiden Ln	Charleston	SC	29401	**800-845-7639**	843-577-5900
Lodge Alley Inn 195 E Bay St	Charleston	SC	29401	**800-456-0009**	843-722-1611
Meeting Street Inn 173 Meeting St	Charleston	SC	29401	**800-842-8022**	843-723-1882
Mills House Hotel 115 Meeting St	Charleston	SC	29401	**800-874-9600**	843-577-2400
Planters Inn 112 N Market St	Charleston	SC	29401	**800-845-7082**	843-722-2345
Town & Country Inn & Conference Center 2008 Savannah Hwy	Charleston	SC	29407	**800-334-6660**	843-571-1000
Wentworth Mansion 149 Wentworth St	Charleston	SC	29401	**888-466-1886**	843-853-1886
Adam's Mark Columbia 1200 Hampton St	Columbia	SC	29201	**800-444-2326**	803-771-7000
AmeriSuites Columbia Northeast 7525 Two Notch Rd	Columbia	SC	29223	**800-833-1516**	803-736-6666
Best Western Governor's House Hotel & Suites 1301 Main St	Columbia	SC	29201	**800-937-8376**	803-779-7790
Clarion Town House Hotel 1615 Gervais St	Columbia	SC	29201	**800-252-7466**	803-771-8711
Courtyard Columbia Northwest 347 Zimalcrest Dr	Columbia	SC	29210	**800-321-2211**	803-731-2300
Embassy Suites Columbia-Greystone 200 Stoneridge Dr	Columbia	SC	29210	**800-362-2779**	803-252-8700
Ramada Plaza Hotel Columbia NE 8105 Two Notch Rd	Columbia	SC	29223	**800-272-6232**	803-736-5600
Sheraton Columbia Hotel & Conference Center 2100 Bush River Rd	Columbia	SC	29210	**800-325-3535**	803-731-0300
Whitney Hotel 700 Woodrow St	Columbia	SC	29205	**800-637-4008**	803-252-0845
Wingate Inn Columbia Northeast 8300 Two Notch Rd	Columbia	SC	29223	**800-228-1000**	803-699-9333
AmeriSuites Greenville Haywood 40 W Orchard Park Dr	Greenville	SC	29615	**800-833-1516**	864-232-3000
Courtyard Greenville 70 Orchard Park Dr	Greenville	SC	29615	**800-321-2211**	864-234-0300
Crowne Plaza Hotel Greenville 851 Congaree Rd	Greenville	SC	29607	**800-227-6963**	864-297-6300
Embassy Suites Greenville Golf Resort & Conference Center 670 Verdae Blvd	Greenville	SC	29607	**800-362-2779**	864-676-9090
Hilton Greenville & Towers 45 W Orchard Park Dr	Greenville	SC	29615	**800-445-8667**	864-232-4747
Hyatt Regency Greenville 220 N Main St	Greenville	SC	29601	**800-233-1234**	864-235-1234
Marriott Greenville-Spartanburg Airport 1 Parkway E	Greenville	SC	29615	**800-441-1737**	864-297-0300
Westin Poinsett 120 S Main St	Greenville	SC	29601	**800-937-8461**	864-421-9700
Hilton Garden Inn Hilton Head 1575 Fording Island Rd	Hilton Head Island	SC	29926	**877-782-9444**	843-837-8111
Inn at Harbour Town 11 Lighthouse Ln	Hilton Head Island	SC	29928	**888-807-6873**	843-363-8100
Main Street Inn 2200 Main St	Hilton Head Island	SC	29926	**800-471-3001**	843-681-3001
South Beach Marina Inn & Vacation Rentals 232 South Sea Pines Dr	Hilton Head Island	SC	29928	**800-367-3909**	843-671-6498
Villamare 27-C Coligny Plaza	Hilton Head Island	SC	29928	**800-854-6802**	843-842-6212
AmeriSuites Columbia I-26 1130 Kinley Rd	Irmo	SC	29063	**800-833-1516**	803-407-1560
Boardwalk Inn 5757 Palm Blvd	Isle of Palms	SC	29451	**800-845-8880**	843-886-6000
Beverly Motel 703 N Ocean Blvd	Myrtle Beach	SC	29577	**800-843-0415**	843-448-9496
Breakers Resort & Paradise Tower 2006 N Ocean Blvd	Myrtle Beach	SC	29577	**800-845-0688**	843-626-5000
Driftwood on the Oceanfront 1600 N Ocean Blvd	Myrtle Beach	SC	29578	**800-942-3456**	843-448-1544
Embassy Suites Myrtle Beach at Kingston Plantation 9800 Queensway Blvd	Myrtle Beach	SC	29572	**800-876-0010**	843-449-0006
Holiday Inn Myrtle Beach Oceanfront/Downtown 415 S Ocean Blvd	Myrtle Beach	SC	29577	**800-845-0313**	843-448-4481
Meridian Plaza Resort 2310 N Ocean Blvd	Myrtle Beach	SC	29577	**800-323-3011**	843-626-4734
Myrtle Beach Resort 5905 S Kings Hwy	Myrtle Beach	SC	29578	**888-627-3767**	843-238-1559
Ocean Dunes Resort & Villas 201 75th Ave N	Myrtle Beach	SC	29578	**800-845-0635**	843-449-7441
Ocean Forest Villa Resort 5601 N Ocean Blvd	Myrtle Beach	SC	29577	**800-845-0347**	843-449-9661
Ocean Reef Resort 7100 N Ocean Blvd	Myrtle Beach	SC	29572	**800-542-0048**	843-449-4441
Sand Dunes Resort Hotel 201 74th Ave N	Myrtle Beach	SC	29572	**800-845-6701**	843-449-3313
Sands Beach Club All-Suite Resort Hotel 9400 Shore Dr	Myrtle Beach	SC	29572	**800-845-6999**	843-449-1531
Sands Ocean Club Resort 9550 Shore Dr	Myrtle Beach	SC	29572	**800-845-6701**	843-449-6461
Seacrest Oceanfront Resort on the South Beach 803 S Ocean Blvd	Myrtle Beach	SC	29577	**800-845-1112**	843-913-5800
Yachtsman Resort Hotel 1400 N Ocean Blvd	Myrtle Beach	SC	29577	**800-868-8886**	843-448-1441
Hilton Garden Inn Charleston Airport 5265 International Blvd	North Charleston	SC	29418	**877-782-9444**	843-308-9330
Radisson Hotel Charleston Airport 5991 Rivers Ave	North Charleston	SC	29406	**800-333-3333**	843-744-2501
Sheraton North Charleston Hotel 4770 Goer Dr	North Charleston	SC	29406	**800-325-3535**	843-747-1900
Wingate Inn Charleston Airport 5219 N Arco Ln	North Charleston	SC	29418	**800-228-1000**	843-308-9666
Litchfield Plantation Kings River Rd PO Box 290	Pawleys Island	SC	29585	**800-869-1410**	843-237-9121
Holiday Inn Columbia Airport 500 Chris Dr	West Columbia	SC	29169	**800-465-4329**	803-794-9440

South Dakota

Name / Address	City	State	Zip	Toll-Free	Phone
Brookings Inn 2500 E 6th St PO Box 557	Brookings	SD	57006	**877-831-1562**	605-692-9471
Bavarian Inn PO Box 152	Custer	SD	57730	**800-657-4312**	605-673-2802
Bullock Hotel 633 Main St	Deadwood	SD	57732	**800-336-1876**	605-578-1745
First Gold Hotel 270 Main St	Deadwood	SD	57732	**800-274-1876**	605-578-9777
Rushmore View Inn 610 Hwy 16A	Keystone	SD	57751	**800-888-2603**	605-666-4466
Best Western Ramkota Hotel 920 W Sioux Ave	Pierre	SD	57501	**800-780-7234**	605-224-6877
Comfort Inn Pierre 410 W Sioux Ave	Pierre	SD	57501	**800-228-5150**	605-224-0377
Governor's Inn 700 W Sioux Ave	Pierre	SD	57501	**888-315-2378**	605-224-4200
Foothills Inn 1625 N La Crosse St	Rapid City	SD	57701	**877-428-5666**	605-348-5640
Holiday Inn Rushmore Plaza 505 N 5th St	Rapid City	SD	57701	**800-465-4329**	605-348-4000
Hotel Alex Johnson 523 6th St	Rapid City	SD	57701	**800-888-2539**	605-342-1210
Radisson Hotel Rapid City/Mount Rushmore 445 Mt Rushmore Rd	Rapid City	SD	57701	**800-333-3333**	605-348-8300
Best Western Empire Towers 4100 W Shirley Pl	Sioux Falls	SD	57106	**888-338-3118**	605-361-3118
Best Western Ramkota Hotel 3200 W Maple St	Sioux Falls	SD	57107	**800-780-7234**	605-336-0650
Comfort Inn Sioux Falls North 5100 N Cliff Ave	Sioux Falls	SD	57104	**800-228-5150**	605-331-4490
Comfort Inn Sioux Falls South 3216 S Carolyn Ave	Sioux Falls	SD	57106	**800-228-5150**	605-361-2822
Holiday Inn Sioux Falls City Centre 100 W 8th St	Sioux Falls	SD	57104	**800-465-4329**	605-339-2000
Oaks Hotel & Convention Center 3300 W Russell St	Sioux Falls	SD	57107	**800-326-4656**	605-336-9000
Radisson Encore Hotel Sioux Falls 4300 Empire Pl	Sioux Falls	SD	57106	**800-333-3333**	605-361-6684
Residence Inn Sioux Falls 4509 W Empire Pl	Sioux Falls	SD	57106	**800-331-3131**	605-361-2202
Sheraton Sioux Falls & Convention Center 1211 West Ave N	Sioux Falls	SD	57104	**800-325-3535***	605-331-0100
*Resv					
Holiday Inn Spearfish-Northern Black Hills Hotel & Convention Center PO Box 399	Spearfish	SD	57783	**800-999-3541**	605-642-4683

Tennessee

Name / Address	City	State	Zip	Toll-Free	Phone
Hilton Knoxville Airport 2001 Alcoa Hwy	Alcoa	TN	37701	**800-445-8667**	865-970-4300
Courtyard Nashville Brentwood 103 E Park Dr	Brentwood	TN	37027	**800-321-2211**	615-371-9200
Hilton Suites Brentwood 9000 Overlook Blvd	Brentwood	TN	37027	**800-445-8667**	615-370-0111
Holiday Inn Brentwood 760 Old Hickory Blvd	Brentwood	TN	37027	**800-465-4329**	615-373-2600
Best Western Heritage Inn Chattanooga 7641 Lee Hwy	Chattanooga	TN	37421	**800-441-8034**	423-899-3311
Best Western Royal Inn 3644 Cummings Hwy	Chattanooga	TN	37419	**800-528-1234**	423-821-6840
Clarion Hotel Chattanooga 407 Chestnut St	Chattanooga	TN	37402	**800-424-6423**	423-756-5150
Comfort Suites Chattanooga 7324 Shallowford Rd	Chattanooga	TN	37421	**800-517-4000**	423-892-1500
Courtyard Chattanooga 2210 Bams Dr	Chattanooga	TN	37421	**800-321-2211**	423-499-4400
Fairfield Inn Chattanooga 2350 Shallowford Village Dr	Chattanooga	TN	37421	**800-228-2800**	423-499-3800
Hilton Garden Inn Chattanooga Downtown 311 Chestnut St	Chattanooga	TN	37402	**877-782-9444**	423-308-9000
Hilton Garden Inn Chattanooga/Hamilton Place 2343 Shallowford Village Dr	Chattanooga	TN	37421	**877-782-9444**	423-308-4400
Marriott Chattanooga Convention Center 2 Carter Plaza	Chattanooga	TN	37402	**800-841-1674**	423-756-0002
Read House Hotel & Suites 827 Broad St	Chattanooga	TN	37402	**800-691-1255**	423-266-4121
Wingate Inn Chattanooga 7312 Shallowford Rd	Chattanooga	TN	37421	**800-228-1000**	423-893-7400
Marriott Franklin Cool Springs Hotel 700 Cool Springs Blvd	Franklin	TN	37067	**800-228-9290**	615-261-6100
Brookside Resort 463 East Pkwy	Gatlinburg	TN	37738	**800-251-9597**	865-436-5611
Holiday Inn SunSpree Resort Gatlinburg 520 Historic Nature Trail	Gatlinburg	TN	37738	**800-435-9201**	865-436-9201
Park Vista Resort Hotel 705 Cherokee Orchard Rd PO Box 30	Gatlinburg	TN	37738	**800-421-7275**	865-436-9211
General Morgan Inn 111 N Main St	Greeneville	TN	37743	**800-223-2679**	423-787-1000
Doubletree Hotel Johnson City 211 Mockingbird Ln	Johnson City	TN	37604	**800-342-7336**	423-929-2000
Holiday Inn Johnson City 101 W Springbrook Dr	Johnson City	TN	37604	**800-465-4329**	423-282-4611
Clubhouse Inn & Suites Knoxville 208 Market Place Blvd	Knoxville	TN	37922	**800-258-2466**	865-531-1900
Courtyard Knoxville/Cedar Bluff 216 Langely Pl	Knoxville	TN	37922	**800-321-2211**	865-539-0600
Hilton Garden Inn West Knoxville/Cedar Bluff 216 Peregrine Way	Knoxville	TN	37922	**877-782-9444**	865-690-6511
Hilton Knoxville 501 W Church Ave	Knoxville	TN	37902	**800-445-8667**	865-523-2300
Holiday Inn Select Knoxville-Cedar Bluff 304 Cedar Bluff Rd	Knoxville	TN	37923	**800-465-4329**	865-693-1011
Holiday Inn Select Knoxville Downtown 525 Henley St	Knoxville	TN	37902	**800-465-4329**	865-522-2800
Marriott Knoxville 500 Hill Ave SE	Knoxville	TN	37915	**800-836-8031**	865-637-1234
Radisson Summit Hill Knoxville 401 W Summitt Hill Dr	Knoxville	TN	37902	**800-333-3333**	865-522-2600
AmeriSuites Memphis Primacy Parkway 1220 Primacy Pkwy	Memphis	TN	38119	**800-833-1516**	901-680-9700
Best Western Benchmark Hotel 164 Union Ave	Memphis	TN	38103	**800-380-3236**	901-527-4100
Elvis Presley's Heartbreak Hotel 3677 Elvis Presley Blvd	Memphis	TN	38116	**877-777-0606**	901-332-1000
Embassy Suites Memphis 1022 S Shady Grove Rd	Memphis	TN	38120	**800-362-2779**	901-684-1777
French Quarter Suites Hotel 2144 Madison Ave	Memphis	TN	38104	**800-843-0353**	901-728-4000
Hilton East Memphis 5069 Sanderlin Ave	Memphis	TN	38117	**800-445-8667**	901-767-6666
Holiday Inn Select Memphis Airport 2240 Democrat Rd	Memphis	TN	38132	**800-465-4329**	901-332-1130
Holiday Inn Select Memphis Downtown 160 Union Ave	Memphis	TN	38103	**888-300-5491**	901-525-5491
Madison Hotel 79 Madison Ave	Memphis	TN	38103	**888-636-7447**	901-333-1200
Marriott Memphis Downtown 250 N Main St	Memphis	TN	38103	**888-557-8740**	901-527-7300
Marriott Memphis East 2625 Thousand Oaks Blvd	Memphis	TN	38118	**800-228-9290**	901-362-6200
Park Vista Memphis 939 Ridge Lake Blvd	Memphis	TN	38120	**800-371-8065**	901-684-6664
Peabody Memphis 149 Union Ave	Memphis	TN	38103	**800-833-2548**	901-529-4000
Radisson Hotel Memphis 185 Union Ave	Memphis	TN	38103	**800-333-3333**	901-528-1800
Wingate Inn Memphis-Wolfchase 2270 N Germantown Pkwy	Memphis	TN	38016	**800-228-1000**	901-386-1110
Wyndham Garden Hotel Memphis 300 N 2nd St	Memphis	TN	38105	**800-996-3426**	901-525-1800
AmeriSuites Nashville Airport 721 Royal Pkwy	Nashville	TN	37214	**800-833-1516**	615-493-5200
AmeriSuites Nashville Opryland 220 Rudy's Cir	Nashville	TN	37214	**800-833-1516**	615-872-0422
Courtyard Nashville Airport 2508 Elm Hill Pike	Nashville	TN	37214	**800-321-2211**	615-883-9500
Courtyard Nashville Downtown 170 4th Ave N	Nashville	TN	37219	**800-687-9377**	615-256-0900
Doubletree Guest Suites Nashville Airport 2424 Atrium Way	Nashville	TN	37214	**800-222-8733**	615-889-8889
Doubletree Hotel Nashville 315 4th Ave N	Nashville	TN	37219	**800-222-8733**	615-244-8200

Tennessee (Cont'd)

Name / Address	City	State	ZIP	Toll-Free	Phone
Embassy Suites Nashville Airport 10 Century Blvd	Nashville	TN	37214	**800-362-2779**	615-871-0033
Hermitage Hotel 231 6th Ave N	Nashville	TN	37219	**888-888-9414**	615-244-3121
Hilton Garden Inn Nashville Airport 412 Royal Pkwy	Nashville	TN	37214	**877-782-9444**	615-884-0088
Holiday Inn Select Nashville-Vanderbilt (Downtown) 2613 West End Ave	Nashville	TN	37203	**800-465-4329**	615-327-4707
Holiday Inn Select Opryland/Airport 2200 Elm Hill Pike	Nashville	TN	37214	**800-633-4427**	615-883-9770
Loews Vanderbilt Hotel 2100 West End Ave	Nashville	TN	37203	**800-336-3335**	615-320-1700
Marriott Nashville 600 Marriott Dr	Nashville	TN	37214	**800-228-9290**	615-889-9300
Millennium Maxwell House Hotel Nashville 2025 Metro Center Blvd	Nashville	TN	37228	**866-866-8086**	615-259-4343
Radisson Hotel Opryland 2401 Music Valley Dr	Nashville	TN	37214	**800-333-3333**	615-889-0800
Renaissance Nashville Hotel 611 Commerce St	Nashville	TN	37203	**800-327-6618**	615-255-8400
Sheraton Music City 777 McGavok Pike	Nashville	TN	37214	**800-325-3535**	615-885-2200
Sheraton Nashville Downtown Hotel 623 Union St	Nashville	TN	37219	**800-325-3535**	615-259-2000
Union Station - A Wyndham Historic Hotel 1001 Broadway	Nashville	TN	37203	**800-996-3426**	615-726-1001
Wingate Inn Nashville Airport 000 Royal Pkwy	Nashville	TN	37214	**800-228-1000**	615-884-9777
Smoky Shadows Motel 4215 Parkway	Pigeon Forge	TN	37863	**800-282-2121**	865-453-7155

Texas

Name / Address	City	State	ZIP	Toll-Free	Phone
Ambassador Suites Abilene 4250 Ridgemont Dr	Abilene	TX	79606	**888-897-9644**	325-698-1234
Courtyard Abilene 4350 Ridgemont Dr	Abilene	TX	79606	**800-321-2211**	325-695-9600
Fairfield Inn Abilene 3902 Turner Plaza Dr	Abilene	TX	79606	**800-228-2800**	325-695-2448
La Quinta Inn Abilene 3501 Westlake Rd	Abilene	TX	79601	**800-687-6667**	325-676-1676
Quality Inn Abilene Civic Center 505 Pine St	Abilene	TX	79601	**800-588-0222**	325-676-0222
Regency Inn & Suites 3450 S Clack St	Abilene	TX	79606	**800-676-7262**	325-695-7700
Crowne Plaza Hotel North Dallas-Addison 14315 Midway Rd	Addison	TX	75001	**800-227-6963**	972-980-8877
InterContinental Dallas 15201 Dallas Pkwy	Addison	TX	75248	**800-327-0200**	972-386-6000
Wingate Inn Addison-North Dallas 4960 Arapaho Rd	Addison	TX	75001	**800-228-1000**	972-490-1212
Hilton Garden Inn Dallas/Allen 705 Central Expy S	Allen	TX	75013	**877-782-9444**	214-547-1700
Amarillo Ritz Plaza Hotel 7909 I-40 E	Amarillo	TX	79118	**800-274-5315**	806-373-3303
Ambassador Hotel 3100 I-40 W	Amarillo	TX	79102	**800-817-0521**	806-358-6161
Best Western Amarillo Inn 1610 Coulter Dr	Amarillo	TX	79106	**800-528-1234**	806-358-7861
Big Texan Motel 7701 I-40 E	Amarillo	TX	79118	**800-657-7177**	806-372-5000
Comfort Inn Amarillo Airport 1515 I-40 E	Amarillo	TX	79102	**800-228-5150**	806-376-9993
Comfort Suites Amarillo 2103 S Lakeview Dr	Amarillo	TX	79109	**888-373-8400**	806-352-8300
Fairfield Inn Amarillo 6600 I-40 W	Amarillo	TX	79106	**800-228-2800**	806-351-0172
Holiday Inn I-40 1911 I-40 E	Amarillo	TX	79102	**800-465-4329**	806-372-8741
La Quinta Amarillo West Medical Center 2108 Coulter St	Amarillo	TX	79106	**800-531-5900**	806-352-6311
Residence Inn Amarillo 6700 I-40 W	Amarillo	TX	79106	**800-331-3131**	806-354-2978
AmeriSuites Arlington 2380 E Road to Six Flags	Arlington	TX	76011	**800-833-1516**	817-649-7676
Best Western Great Southwest Inn 3501 E Division St	Arlington	TX	76011	**800-528-1234**	817-640-7722
Courtyard Dallas/Arlington by the Ballpark 1500 Nolan Ryan Expy	Arlington	TX	76011	**800-321-2211**	817-277-2774
Fairfield Inn Arlington 2500 E Lamar Blvd	Arlington	TX	76006	**800-228-2800**	817-649-5800
Hilton Arlington 2401 E Lamar Blvd	Arlington	TX	76006	**800-445-8667**	817-640-3322
Holiday Inn Arlington (Near Six Flags) 1507 N Watson Rd	Arlington	TX	76006	**877-622-5395**	817-640-7712
La Quinta Inn Dallas - Arlington Conference Center 825 N Watson Rd	Arlington	TX	76011	**800-453-7909**	817-640-4142
Residence Inn Arlington/DFW South 1050 Brookhollow Plaza Dr	Arlington	TX	76006	**800-331-3131**	817-649-7300
Wingate Inn Arlington 1024 Brookhollow Plaza Dr	Arlington	TX	76006	**800-228-1000**	817-640-8686
Wyndham Arlington-DFW Airport South 1500 Convention Center Dr	Arlington	TX	76011	**800-996-3426**	817-261-8200
Best Western Atrium North 7928 Gessner Dr	Austin	TX	78753	**800-468-3708**	512-339-7311
Clarion Inn & Suites Conference Center Austin 2200 S IH-35	Austin	TX	78704	**800-434-7378**	512-444-0561
Courtyard Austin Central 5660 N IH-35	Austin	TX	78751	**800-321-2211**	512-458-2340
Courtyard Austin Northwest/Arboretum 9409 Stonelake Blvd	Austin	TX	78759	**800-321-2211**	512-502-8100
Crowne Plaza Austin Hotel 500 N IH-35	Austin	TX	78701	**800-325-3535**	512-480-8181
Doubletree Club Austin-University Area 1617 N IH-35	Austin	TX	78702	**800-222-8733**	512-479-4000
Doubletree Guest Suites Austin 303 W 15th St	Austin	TX	78701	**800-222-8733**	512-478-7000
Doubletree Hotel Austin 6505 N IH-35	Austin	TX	78752	**800-222-8733**	512-454-3737
Driskill Hotel 604 Brazos St	Austin	TX	78701	**800-252-9367**	512-474-5911
Embassy Suites Austin Downtown-Town Lake 300 S Congress Ave	Austin	TX	78704	**800-362-2779**	512-469-9000
Embassy Suites Austin North 5901 N IH-35	Austin	TX	78723	**800-362-2779**	512-454-8004
Four Points by Sheraton Austin 7800 N IH-35	Austin	TX	78753	**800-325-3535**	512-836-8520
Four Seasons Hotel Austin 98 San Jacinto Blvd	Austin	TX	78701	**800-819-5053**	512-478-4500
Habitat Suites 500 E Highland Mall Blvd	Austin	TX	78752	**800-535-4663**	512-467-6000
Hilton Austin Airport 9515 New Airport Dr	Austin	TX	78719	**800-445-8667**	512-385-6767
Hilton Garden Inn Austin NW/Arboretum 11617 Research Blvd	Austin	TX	78759	**877-782-9444**	512-241-1600
Holiday Inn Austin-Town Lake 20 N IH-35	Austin	TX	78701	**800-465-4329**	512-472-8211
Hyatt Regency Austin 208 Barton Springs Rd	Austin	TX	78704	**800-233-1234**	512-477-1234
InterContinental Stephen F Austin 701 Congress Ave	Austin	TX	78701	**800-327-0200**	512-457-8800
Marriott Austin Airport South 4415 South IH-35	Austin	TX	78744	**800-228-9290**	512-441-7900
Marriott Austin at the Capitol 701 E 11th St	Austin	TX	78701	**800-228-9290**	512-478-1111
Omni Austin Hotel Downtown 700 San Jacinto Blvd	Austin	TX	78701	**800-843-6664**	512-476-3700
Omni Austin Hotel Southpark 4140 Governors Row	Austin	TX	78744	**800-843-6664**	512-448-2222
Park Plaza Austin 6000 Middle Fiskville Rd	Austin	TX	78752	**888-201-1803**	512-451-5757
Radisson Hotel & Suites Austin 111 E Cesar Chavez St	Austin	TX	78701	**800-333-3333**	512-478-9611
Red Lion Hotel Austin 6121 I-35 N at 290 E	Austin	TX	78752	**800-733-5466**	512-323-5466
Renaissance Austin Hotel 9721 Arboretum Blvd	Austin	TX	78759	**800-228-9290**	512-343-2626
Residence Inn Austin/Arboretum 3713 Tudor Blvd	Austin	TX	78759	**800-331-3131**	512-502-8200
Summerfield Suites by Wyndham Northwest Austin 7685 Northcross Dr	Austin	TX	78757	**800-851-9111**	512-452-9391
Wingate Inn Austin North 8500 N IH-35	Austin	TX	78753	**800-228-1000**	512-821-0707
Best Western Rose Garden Inn 845 North Expy	Brownsville	TX	78520	**800-528-1234**	956-546-5501
Four Points by Sheraton Brownsville 3777 North Exwy	Brownsville	TX	78520	**800-325-3535**	956-547-1500
LaSalle Hotel 120 S Main St	Bryan	TX	77803	**866-822-2000**	979-822-2000
Best Western Marina Grand Hotel 300 N Shoreline Blvd	Corpus Christi	TX	78401	**800-937-8376**	361-883-5111
Christy Estates Suites 3942 Holly Rd	Corpus Christi	TX	78415	**800-678-4836**	361-854-1091
Clarion Hotel Corpus Christi 5224 IH-37 at Navigation Blvd	Corpus Christi	TX	78407	**888-882-3355**	361-883-6161
Embassy Suites Corpus Christi 4337 S Padre Island Dr	Corpus Christi	TX	78411	**800-362-2779**	361-853-7899
Holiday Inn Emerald Beach 1102 S Shoreline Blvd	Corpus Christi	TX	78401	**800-465-4329**	361-883-5731
Holiday Inn SunSpree Resort Corpus Christi 15202 Windward Dr	Corpus Christi	TX	78418	**888-949-8041**	361-949-8041
La Quinta Inn Corpus Christi North 5155 IH-37 North	Corpus Christi	TX	78408	**800-531-5900**	361-888-5721
La Quinta Inn Corpus Christi South 6225 S Padre Island Dr	Corpus Christi	TX	78412	**800-531-5900**	361-991-5730
Omni Corpus Christi Hotel Bayfront Tower 900 N Shoreline Blvd	Corpus Christi	TX	78401	**800-843-6664**	361-887-1600
Omni Corpus Christi Hotel Marina Tower 707 N Shoreline Blvd	Corpus Christi	TX	78401	**800-843-6664**	361-882-1700
Ramada Inn Corpus Christi Bayfront 601 N Water St	Corpus Christi	TX	78401	**800-688-0334**	361-882-8100
Residence Inn Corpus Christi 5229 Blanche Moore Dr	Corpus Christi	TX	78411	**800-331-3131**	361-985-1113
Adam's Mark Dallas 400 N Olive St	Dallas	TX	75201	**800-444-2326**	214-922-8000
Adolphus The 1321 Commerce St	Dallas	TX	75202	**800-221-9083**	214-742-8200
AmeriSuites Dallas West End 1907 N Lamar St	Dallas	TX	75202	**800-833-1516**	214-999-0500
Comfort Inn & Suites Market Center 7138 N Stemmons Fwy	Dallas	TX	75247	**800-424-6423**	214-461-2677
Courtyard Dallas Central Expressway 10325 N Central Expy	Dallas	TX	75231	**800-321-2211**	214-739-2500
Courtyard Dallas LBJ at Josey 2930 Forest Ln	Dallas	TX	75234	**800-321-2211**	972-620-8000
Courtyard Dallas Market Center 2150 Market Ctr Blvd	Dallas	TX	75207	**800-321-2211**	214-653-1166
Courtyard Dallas-Northwest 2383 Stemmons Trail	Dallas	TX	75220	**800-321-2211**	214-352-7676
Crowne Plaza Hotel Dallas Market Center 7050 Stemmons Fwy	Dallas	TX	75247	**800-227-6963**	214-630-8500
Crowne Plaza Suites Dallas 7800 Alpha Rd	Dallas	TX	75240	**800-227-6963**	972-233-7600
Doubletree Hotel Dallas-Campbell Centre 8250 N Central Expy	Dallas	TX	75206	**800-222-8733**	214-691-8700
Doubletree Hotel Dallas Near the Galleria 4099 Valley View Ln	Dallas	TX	75244	**800-222-8733**	972-385-9000
Embassy Suites Dallas Near the Galleria 14021 Noel Rd	Dallas	TX	75240	**800-362-2779**	972-364-3640
Fairmont Dallas 1717 N Akard St	Dallas	TX	75201	**800-527-4727**	214-720-2020
Guest Lodge at Cooper Aerobic Center Clinic 12230 Preston Rd	Dallas	TX	75230	**800-444-5187**	972-386-0306
Hilton Dallas Lincoln Centre 5410 LBJ Fwy	Dallas	TX	75240	**800-222-8733**	972-934-8400
Hilton Dallas-Park Cities 5954 Luther Ln	Dallas	TX	75225	**800-445-8667**	214-368-0400
Hilton Dallas Parkway 4801 LBJ Fwy	Dallas	TX	75244	**866-444-7666**	972-661-3600
Hilton Garden Inn Dallas/Market Center 2325 N Stemmons Fwy	Dallas	TX	75207	**877-782-9444**	214-634-8200
Holiday Inn Aristocrat Hotel 1933 Main St	Dallas	TX	75201	**800-231-4235**	214-741-7700
Holiday Inn Select Dallas LBJ NE 11350 LBJ Fwy	Dallas	TX	75238	**800-346-0660**	214-341-5400
Holiday Inn Select Dallas Love Field 3300 W Mockingbird Ln	Dallas	TX	75235	**800-465-4329**	214-357-8500
Holiday Inn Select Dallas North Park 10650 N Central Expy	Dallas	TX	75231	**800-465-4329**	214-373-6000
Holiday Inn Select North Dallas 2645 LBJ Fwy	Dallas	TX	75234	**800-465-4329**	972-243-3363
Hotel Crescent Court 400 Crescent Ct	Dallas	TX	75201	**800-654-6541**	214-871-3200
Hotel Lawrence 302 S Houston St	Dallas	TX	75202	**877-396-0334**	214-761-9090
Hotel Saint Germain 2516 Maple Ave	Dallas	TX	75201	**800-683-2516**	214-871-2516
Hyatt Regency Dallas 300 Reunion Blvd	Dallas	TX	75207	**800-233-1234**	214-651-1234
Hyatt Regency DFW Airport International Pkwy PO Box 619014 Terminal C	Dallas	TX	75261	**800-233-1234**	972-453-1234
Magnolia Hotel Dallas 1401 Commerce St	Dallas	TX	75201	**888-915-1110**	214-915-6500
Mansion on Turtle Creek 2821 Turtle Creek Blvd	Dallas	TX	75219	**800-527-5432**	214-559-2100
Marriott Dallas-Addison Quorum Galleria 14901 N Dallas Pkwy	Dallas	TX	75254	**800-228-9290**	972-661-2800
Marriott Suites Dallas Market Center 2493 N Stemmons Fwy	Dallas	TX	75207	**800-228-9290**	214-905-0050
Melrose Hotel Dallas 3015 Oak Lawn Ave	Dallas	TX	75219	**800-635-7673**	214-521-5151
Omni Dallas Hotel Park West 1590 LBJ Fwy	Dallas	TX	75234	**800-843-6664**	972-869-4300
Radisson Hotel Central Dallas 6060 N Central Expy	Dallas	TX	75206	**800-333-3333**	214-750-6060
Ramada Plaza Hotel Dallas Downtown Convention Center 1011 S Akard St	Dallas	TX	75215	**800-272-6232**	214-421-1083
Renaissance Dallas Hotel 2222 N Stemmons Fwy	Dallas	TX	75207	**800-468-3571**	214-631-2222
Residence Inn Dallas-Park Central 7642 LBJ Fwy	Dallas	TX	75251	**800-331-3131**	972-503-1333
Sheraton Dallas Brookhollow Hotel 1241 W Mockingbird Ln	Dallas	TX	75247	**800-325-3535**	214-630-7000
Sheraton Park Central Hotel Dallas 7750 LBJ Fwy	Dallas	TX	75251	**800-325-3535**	972-233-4421
Sheraton Suites Market Center 2101 N Stemmons Fwy	Dallas	TX	75207	**800-325-3535**	214-747-3000
SpringHill Suites Dallas 2363 Stemmons Trail	Dallas	TX	75220	**800-252-7466**	214-350-2300
Stoneleigh Hotel 2927 Maple Ave	Dallas	TX	75201	**800-255-9299**	214-871-7111
Westin City Center Dallas 650 N Pearl St	Dallas	TX	75201	**888-625-5144**	214-979-9000
Westin Park Central 12720 Merit Dr	Dallas	TX	75251	**800-937-8461**	972-385-3000
Wingate Inn Dallas Market Center 8650 N Stemmons Fwy	Dallas	TX	75247	**800-228-1000**	214-267-8400
Wyndham Anatole 2201 Stemmons Fwy	Dallas	TX	75207	**800-996-3426**	214-748-1200
Wyndham Dallas Market Center 2015 Market Center Blvd	Dallas	TX	75207	**800-996-3426**	214-741-7481
Wyndham Garden Hotel Dallas Park Central 8051 LBJ Fwy	Dallas	TX	75251	**800-996-3426**	972-680-3000
AmeriSuites El Paso Airport 6030 Gateway Blvd E	El Paso	TX	79905	**800-833-1516**	915-771-0022
Camino Real El Paso 101 S El Paso St	El Paso	TX	79901	**800-769-4300**	915-534-3000

Name / Address	City	State	ZIP	Toll-Free	Phone
Courtyard El Paso Airport 6610 International Rd	El Paso	TX	79925	**800-321-2211**	915-772-5000
Embassy Suites El Paso 6100 Gateway Blvd E	El Paso	TX	79905	**800-362-2779**	915-779-6222
Hilton El Paso Airport 2027 Airway Blvd	El Paso	TX	79925	**800-742-7248**	915-778-4241
Marriott El Paso 1600 Airway Blvd	El Paso	TX	79925	**800-228-9290**	915-779-3300
Radisson Suite Inn El Paso Airport 1770 Airway Blvd	El Paso	TX	79925	**800-333-3333**	915-772-3333
Courtyard Fort Worth Downtown 601 Main St	Fort Worth	TX	76102	**800-321-2211**	817-885-8700
Courtyard Fort Worth South University 3150 Riverfront Dr	Fort Worth	TX	76107	**800-321-2211**	817-335-1300
Doral Tesoro Hotel & Golf Club 3300 Championship Pkwy	Fort Worth	TX	76177	**866-983-7676**	817-961-0800
Green Oaks Hotel 6901 West Fwy	Fort Worth	TX	76116	**800-433-2174**	817-738-7311
Hilton Garden Inn Fort Worth North 4400 North Fwy	Fort Worth	TX	76137	**877-782-9444**	817-222-0222
Holiday Inn Fort Worth North Hotel & Conference Center 2540 Meacham Blvd	Fort Worth	TX	76106	**800-465-4329**	817-625-9911
Marriott Dallas-Fort Worth Airport South 4151 Centreport Dr	Fort Worth	TX	76155	**800-228-9290**	817-358-1700
Park Central Hotel 1010 Houston St	Fort Worth	TX	76102	**800-848-7275**	817-336-2011
Radisson Plaza Hotel Fort Worth 815 Main St	Fort Worth	TX	76102	**800-333-3333**	817-870-2100
Ramada Plaza Hotel Fort Worth Downtown 1701 Commerce St	Fort Worth	TX	76102	**800-272-6232**	817-335-7000
Renaissance Worthington Hotel 200 Main St	Fort Worth	TX	76102	**800-468-3571**	817-870-1000
Stockyards Hotel 109 E Exchange Ave	Fort Worth	TX	76106	**800-423-8471**	817-625-6427
Flagship Hotel Over the Water 2501 Seawall Blvd	Galveston	TX	77550	**800-392-6542**	409-762-9000
Harbor House 28 Pier 21	Galveston	TX	77550	**800-874-3721**	409-763-3321
Hotel Galvez - A Wyndham Historic Hotel 2024 Seawall Blvd	Galveston	TX	77550	**800-996-3426**	409-765-7721
Moody Gardens Hotel 7 Hope Blvd	Galveston	TX	77554	**888-388-8484**	409-741-8484
Victorian Condo-Hotel & Conference Center 6300 Seawall Blvd	Galveston	TX	77551	**800-231-6363**	409-740-3555
Rough Creek Lodge PO Box 2400	Glen Rose	TX	76043	**800-864-4705***	254-965-3700
*Resv					
AmeriSuites Houston Intercontinental Airport/Greenspoint 300 Ronan Park Pl	Houston	TX	77060	**800-833-1516**	281-820-6060
Courtyard Houston/Brookhollow 2504 North Loop W	Houston	TX	77092	**800-321-2211**	713-688-7711
Crowne Plaza Hotel Houston Brookhollow 12801 Northwest Fwy	Houston	TX	77040	**800-227-6963**	713-462-9977
Crowne Plaza Hotel Houston-Medical Center 6701 S Main St	Houston	TX	77030	**800-227-6963**	713-797-1110
Doubletree Guest Suites Houston 5353 Westheimer Rd	Houston	TX	77056	**800-222-8733**	713-961-9000
Doubletree Hotel Houston-Allen Center 400 Dallas St	Houston	TX	77002	**800-222-8733**	713-759-0202
Doubletree Hotel Houston-Post Oak 2001 Post Oak Blvd	Houston	TX	77056	**800-222-8733**	713-961-9300
Embassy Suites Houston 9090 Southwest Fwy	Houston	TX	77074	**800-553-3417**	713-995-0123
Four Points by Sheraton Houston Southwest 2828 Southwest Fwy	Houston	TX	77098	**800-325-3535**	713-942-2111
Four Seasons Hotel Houston 1300 Lamar St	Houston	TX	77010	**800-332-3442**	713-650-1300
Hilton Garden Inn Houston Northwest 7979 Willow Chase Blvd	Houston	TX	77070	**877-782-9444**	832-912-1000
Hilton Garden Inn Houston/Bush Intercontinental Airport 15400 John F Kennedy Blvd	Houston	TX	77032	**877-782-9444**	281-449-4148
Hilton Garden Inn Houston/Woodlands 9301 Six Pines Dr	Houston	TX	77380	**877-782-9444**	281-364-9300
Hilton Houston Hobby Airport 8181 Airport Blvd	Houston	TX	77061	**800-445-8667**	713-645-3000
Hilton Houston NASA Clear Lake 3000 NASA Rd 1	Houston	TX	77058	**800-445-8667**	281-333-9300
Hilton Houston Plaza 6633 Travis St	Houston	TX	77030	**800-445-8667**	713-313-4000
Hilton Houston Southwest 6780 Southwest Fwy	Houston	TX	77074	**800-445-8667**	713-977-7911
Hilton Houston Westchase & Towers 9999 Westheimer Rd	Houston	TX	77042	**800-445-8667**	713-974-1000
Holiday Inn Select Houston-Greenway Plaza Area 2712 Southwest Fwy	Houston	TX	77098	**800-465-4329**	713-523-8448
Holiday Inn Select Houston I-10 W 14703 Park Row	Houston	TX	77079	**800-465-4329**	281-558-5580
Hotel Derek 2525 West Loop S	Houston	TX	77027	**866-292-4100**	713-961-3000
Hotel Sofitel Houston 425 N Sam Houston Pkwy E	Houston	TX	77060	**800-763-4835**	281-445-9000
Hyatt Regency Houston 1200 Louisiana St	Houston	TX	77002	**800-233-1234**	713-654-1234
Hyatt Regency Houston Airport 15747 JFK Blvd	Houston	TX	77032	**800-233-1234**	281-987-1234
InterContinental Houston 2222 West Loop S	Houston	TX	77027	**800-316-8645**	713-627-7600
JW Marriott Hotel on Westheimer by the Galleria 5150 Westheimer Rd	Houston	TX	77056	**800-228-9290**	713-961-1500
Lancaster Hotel 701 Texas St	Houston	TX	77002	**800-231-0336**	713-228-9500
Marriott Houston Airport 18700 JFK Blvd	Houston	TX	77032	**800-228-9290**	281-443-2310
Marriott Houston Medical Center 6580 Fannin St	Houston	TX	77030	**800-228-9290**	713-796-0080
Marriott Houston North at Greenspoint 255 N Sam Houston Pkwy E	Houston	TX	77060	**800-228-9290**	281-875-4000
Marriott Houston West Loop by the Galleria 1750 West Loop S	Houston	TX	77027	**800-228-9290**	713-960-0111
Omni Houston Hotel 4 Riverway Dr	Houston	TX	77056	**800-843-6664**	713-871-8181
Omni Houston Hotel Westside 13210 Katy Fwy	Houston	TX	77079	**800-843-6664**	281-558-8338
Park Plaza Hotel Reliant Center 8686 Kirby Dr	Houston	TX	77054	**800-814-7000**	713-748-3221
Renaissance Houston Hotel 6 Greenway Plaza E	Houston	TX	77046	**800-228-9290**	713-629-1200
Saint Regis Houston 1919 Briar Oaks Ln	Houston	TX	77027	**800-325-3589**	713-840-7600
Sheraton Houston Brookhollow Hotel 3000 North Loop W	Houston	TX	77092	**800-325-3535**	713-688-0100
Sheraton North Houston at George Bush Intercontinental Airport 15700 JFK Blvd	Houston	TX	77032	**800-325-3535**	281-442-5100
SpringHill Suites Houston Medical Center/Reliant Park 1400 Old Spanish Trail	Houston	TX	77054	**877-439-7275**	713-796-1000
Westin Galleria Houston 5060 W Alabama St	Houston	TX	77056	**800-937-8461**	713-960-8100
Westin Oaks 5011 Westheimer Rd	Houston	TX	77056	**800-937-8461**	713-960-8100
Wingate Inn Houston Airport 15615 JFK Blvd	Houston	TX	77032	**800-228-1000**	281-987-8777
Wingate Inn Houston Southwest 11050 Southwest Fwy	Houston	TX	77074	**800-228-1000**	281-568-6969
Wingate Inn Houston-Willowbrook 9050 Mills Rd	Houston	TX	77070	**800-228-1000**	281-477-8000
Wyndham Greenspoint 12400 Greenspoint Dr	Houston	TX	77060	**800-996-3426**	281-875-2222
AmeriSuites Dallas Las Colinas/Hidden Ridge 333 W John W Carpenter Fwy	Irving	TX	75039	**800-833-1516**	972-910-0302
Courtyard Dallas DFW Airport North/Irving 4949 Regent Blvd	Irving	TX	75063	**800-321-2211**	972-929-4004
Courtyard Dallas Las Colinas 1151 W Walnut Hill Ln	Irving	TX	75038	**800-321-2211**	972-550-8100
Harvey Suites DFW Airport 4550 W John Carpenter Fwy	Irving	TX	75063	**800-922-9222**	972-929-4499
Hilton Garden Inn Las Colinas 7516 Las Colinas Blvd	Irving	TX	75063	**877-782-9444**	972-444-8434
Holiday Inn Select Dallas/Fort Worth Airport South 4440 W Airport Fwy	Irving	TX	75062	**800-465-4329**	972-399-1010
Marriott Dallas-Fort Worth Airport North 8440 Freeport Pkwy	Irving	TX	75063	**800-228-9290**	972-929-8800
Marriott Dallas Las Colinas 223 W Las Colinas Blvd	Irving	TX	75039	**800-228-9290**	972-831-0000
Omni Mandalay Hotel at Las Colinas 221 E Las Colinas Blvd	Irving	TX	75039	**800-843-6664**	972-556-0800
Sheraton Grand Hotel DFW Airport 4440 W John Carpenter Fwy	Irving	TX	75063	**800-325-3535**	972-929-8400
Summerfield Suites by Wyndham Irving-Las Colinas 5901 N MacArthur Blvd	Irving	TX	75039	**800-833-4353**	972-831-0909
Wingate Inn Irving-DFW Airport 8220 Esters Blvd	Irving	TX	75063	**800-228-1000**	972-929-4600
Wingate Inn Irving-Las Colinas 850 W Walnut Hill Ln	Irving	TX	75038	**800-228-1000**	972-751-1031
Wyndham Garden Hotel Las Colinas 110 W John Carpenter Fwy	Irving	TX	75039	**800-996-3426**	972-650-1600
La Posada Hotel & Suites 1000 Zaragoza St	Laredo	TX	78040	**800-444-2099**	956-722-1701
Ashmore Inn & Suites 4019 S Loop 289	Lubbock	TX	79423	**800-785-0061**	806-785-0060
Comfort Suites Lubbock 5113 S Loop 289	Lubbock	TX	79424	**800-228-5150**	806-798-0002
Courtyard Lubbock 4011 S Loop 289	Lubbock	TX	79423	**800-321-2211**	806-795-1633
Embassy Suites Lubbock 5215 S Loop 289	Lubbock	TX	79424	**800-362-2779**	806-794-5353
Fairfield Inn Lubbock 4007 S Loop 289	Lubbock	TX	79423	**800-228-2800**	806-795-1288
Four Points by Sheraton Lubbock 505 Ave Q	Lubbock	TX	79401	**800-325-3535**	806-747-0171
Holiday Inn Lubbock Hotel & Towers 801 Ave Q	Lubbock	TX	79401	**800-465-4329**	806-763-1200
Holiday Inn Lubbock Park Plaza 3201 S Loop 289	Lubbock	TX	79423	**800-465-4329**	806-797-3241
Koko Inn 5201 Ave Q	Lubbock	TX	79412	**800-782-3254**	806-747-2591
La Quinta Inn Lubbock Civic Center 601 Ave Q	Lubbock	TX	79401	**800-531-5900**	806-763-9441
La Quinta Inn Lubbock West Medical Center 4115 Brownfield Hwy	Lubbock	TX	79407	**800-531-5900**	806-792-0065
Lubbock Inn 3901 19th St	Lubbock	TX	79410	**800-545-8226**	806-792-5181
Residence Inn Lubbock 2551 S Loop 289	Lubbock	TX	79423	**800-331-3131**	806-745-1963
Renaissance Casa de Palmas Hotel 101 N Main St	McAllen	TX	78501	**800-468-3571**	956-631-1101
AmeriSuites Plano 3100 N Dallas Pkwy	Plano	TX	75093	**800-833-1516**	972-378-3997
Courtyard Dallas Plano 4901 W Plano Pkwy	Plano	TX	75093	**800-321-2211**	972-867-8000
Courtyard Dallas Plano in Legacy Park 6840 N Dallas Pkwy	Plano	TX	75024	**800-321-2211**	972-403-0802
Residence Inn Dallas-Plano 5001 Whitestone Ln	Plano	TX	75024	**800-331-3131**	972-473-6761
Southfork Hotel 1600 N Central Expy	Plano	TX	75074	**866-665-2680**	972-578-8555
Courtyard Dallas/Richardson at Spring Valley 1000 S Sherman St	Richardson	TX	75081	**800-321-2211**	972-235-5000
Holiday Inn Select Richardson 1655 N Central Expy	Richardson	TX	75080	**800-465-4329**	972-238-1900
Renaissance Dallas Richardson Hotel 900 E Lookout Dr	Richardson	TX	75082	**800-468-3571***	972-367-2000
*Resv					
Hilton Garden Inn Austin/Round Rock 2310 N IH-35	Round Rock	TX	78681	**877-782-9444**	512-341-8200
Marriott Austin North 2600 La Frontera Blvd	Round Rock	TX	78681	**800-228-9290**	512-733-6767
Alamo Inn 2203 E Commerce St	San Antonio	TX	78203	**888-222-7666**	210-227-2203
AmeriSuites San Antonio Airport 7615 Jones-Maltsberger Rd	San Antonio	TX	78216	**800-833-1516**	210-930-2333
AmeriSuites San Antonio Northwest 4325 Amerisuites Dr	San Antonio	TX	78230	**800-833-1516**	210-561-0099
Courtyard San Antonio Airport 8615 Broadway St	San Antonio	TX	78217	**800-321-2211**	210-828-7200
Courtyard San Antonio/Medical Center 8585 Marriott Dr	San Antonio	TX	78229	**800-321-2211**	210-614-7100
Crowne Plaza Hotel San Antonio Riverwalk 111 E Pecan St	San Antonio	TX	78205	**800-444-2326**	210-354-2800
Doubletree Club San Antonio Airport 1111 NE Loop 410	San Antonio	TX	78209	**800-222-8733**	210-828-9031
Doubletree Hotel San Antonio Airport 37 NE Loop 410	San Antonio	TX	78216	**800-535-1980**	210-366-2424
Drury Inn & Suites San Antonio Riverwalk 201 N Saint Mary's St	San Antonio	TX	78205	**800-378-7946**	210-212-5200
Embassy Suites San Antonio International Airport 10110 US Hwy 281 N	San Antonio	TX	78216	**800-362-2779**	210-525-9999
Fairmount The - A Wyndham Historic Hotel 401 S Alamo St	San Antonio	TX	78205	**800-996-3426**	210-224-8800
Havana Riverwalk Inn 1015 Navarro St	San Antonio	TX	78205	**888-224-2008**	210-222-2008
Hilton Palacio del Rio 200 S Alamo St	San Antonio	TX	78205	**800-445-8667**	210-222-1400
Holiday Inn Crockett Hotel 320 Bonham St	San Antonio	TX	78205	**800-292-1050**	210-225-6500
Holiday Inn San Antonio Riverwalk 217 N Saint Mary's St	San Antonio	TX	78205	**800-465-4329**	210-224-2500
Holiday Inn Select San Antonio International Airport 77 NE Loop 410	San Antonio	TX	78216	**800-445-8475**	210-349-9900
Hyatt Regency San Antonio 123 Losoya St	San Antonio	TX	78205	**800-233-1234**	210-222-1234
La Mansion del Rio 112 College St	San Antonio	TX	78205	**800-292-7300**	210-518-1000
Marriott Plaza San Antonio 555 S Alamo St	San Antonio	TX	78205	**800-727-3239**	210-229-1000
Marriott San Antonio Northwest 3233 NW Loop 410	San Antonio	TX	78213	**800-228-9290**	210-377-3900
Marriott San Antonio Rivercenter 101 Bowie St	San Antonio	TX	78205	**800-648-4462**	210-223-1000
Marriott San Antonio Riverwalk 889 E Market St	San Antonio	TX	78205	**800-228-9290**	210-224-4555
Menger Hotel 204 Alamo Plaza	San Antonio	TX	78205	**800-345-9285**	210-223-4361
Omni San Antonio Hotel 9821 Colonnade Blvd	San Antonio	TX	78230	**800-843-6664**	210-691-8888
Radisson Hotel San Antonio Downtown Market Square 502 W Durango Blvd	San Antonio	TX	78207	**800-333-3333**	210-224-7155
Saint Anthony The - A Wyndham Historic Hotel 300 E Travis St	San Antonio	TX	78205	**800-996-3426**	210-227-4392
Sheraton Gunter Hotel 205 E Houston St	San Antonio	TX	78205	**888-999-2089**	210-227-3241

Texas (Cont'd)

	City	State	Zip	Toll-Free	Phone
Sierra Royale All Suite Hotel 6300 Rue Marielyne	San Antonio	TX	78238	**800-289-2444**	210-647-0041
Westin Riverwalk 420 W Market St	San Antonio	TX	78205	**888-627-8396**	210-224-6500
Comfort Suites South Padre Island 912 Padre Blvd	South Padre Island	TX	78597	**877-774-7848**	956-772-9020
Sheraton South Padre Island Beach Hotel 310 Padre Blvd.	South Padre Island	TX	78597	**888-627-7105**	956-761-6551
Marriott Dallas Solana 5 Village Cir	Westlake	TX	76262	**800-228-9290**	817-430-3848

Utah

	City	State	Zip	Toll-Free	Phone
Alta Peruvian Lodge PO Box 8017 Little Cottonwood Canyon	Alta	UT	84092	**800-453-8488**	801-742-3000
Best Rest Inn 1206 W 21st St	Ogden	UT	84401	**800-343-8644**	801-393-8644
Best Western High Country Inn 1335 W 1200 South	Ogden	UT	84404	**800-594-8979**	801-394-9474
Comfort Suites Ogden 2250 S 1200 West	Ogden	UT	84401	**800-462-9925**	801-621-2545
Marriott Ogden 247 24th St	Ogden	UT	84401	**800-421-7599**	801-627-1190
Sleep Inn Ogden 1155 S 1700 West	Ogden	UT	84404	**800-753-3746**	801-731-6500
Best Western Landmark Inn 6560 N Landmark Dr	Park City	UT	84098	**800-548-8824**	435-649-7300
Goldener Hirsch Inn 7570 Royal St E	Park City	UT	84060	**800-252-3373**	435-649-7770
Lodge at the Mountain Village 1415 Lowell Ave	Park City	UT	84060	**800-754-2002**	435-649-0800
Marriott Park City 1895 Sidewinder Dr	Park City	UT	84060	**800-234-9003**	435-649-2900
Prospector Square Hotel & Conference Center 2200 Sidewinder Dr	Park City	UT	84060	**800-453-3812**	435-649-7100
Silver King Hotel 1485 Empire Ave	Park City	UT	84060	**800-331-8652**	435-649-5500
Yarrow Resort Hotel 1800 Park Ave	Park City	UT	84060	**800-927-7694**	435-649-7000
Best Western Columbian Inn 70 E 300 South	Provo	UT	84606	**800-321-0055**	801-373-8973
Best Western Cotton Tree Inn 2230 N University Pkwy	Provo	UT	84604	**800-662-6886**	801-373-7044
Courtyard Provo 1600 N Freedom Blvd	Provo	UT	84604	**800-321-2211**	801-373-2222
Holiday Inn Provo 1460 S University Ave	Provo	UT	84601	**800-465-4329**	801-374-9750
Marriott Provo Hotel & Conference Center 101 W 100 North	Provo	UT	84601	**800-777-7144**	801-377-4700
Residence Inn Provo 252 W 2230 North	Provo	UT	84604	**800-331-3131**	801-374-1000
Best Western Salt Lake Plaza Hotel 122 W South Temple	Salt Lake City	UT	84101	**800-366-3684**	801-521-0130
Courtyard Salt Lake City/Downtown 130 W 400 South	Salt Lake City	UT	84101	**800-321-2211**	801-531-6000
Crystal Inn Salt Lake City Downtown 230 W 500 South	Salt Lake City	UT	84101	**800-366-4466**	801-328-4466
Embassy Suites Salt Lake City 110 W 600 South	Salt Lake City	UT	84101	**800-362-2779**	801-359-7800
Grand America Hotel 555 S Main St	Salt Lake City	UT	84111	**800-621-4505**	801-258-6000
Hilton Salt Lake City Airport 5151 Wiley Post Way	Salt Lake City	UT	84116	**800-999-3736**	801-539-1515
Hilton Salt Lake City Center 255 S West Temple	Salt Lake City	UT	84101	**800-445-8667**	801-328-2000
Holiday Inn Salt Lake City Downtown 999 S Main St	Salt Lake City	UT	84111	**800-465-4329**	801-359-8600
Hotel Monaco Salt Lake City 15 W 200 South	Salt Lake City	UT	84101	**877-294-9710**	801-595-0000
Inn at Temple Square 71 W South Temple	Salt Lake City	UT	84101	**800-843-4668**	801-531-1000
Little America Hotel & Towers Salt Lake City 500 S Main St	Salt Lake City	UT	84101	**800-453-9450**	801-363-6781
Marriott Salt Lake City Downtown 75 S West Temple	Salt Lake City	UT	84101	**800-228-9290**	801-531-0800
Marriott Salt Lake City University Park 480 Wakara Way	Salt Lake City	UT	84108	**800-637-4390**	801-581-1000
Peery Hotel 110 W 300 South	Salt Lake City	UT	84101	**800-331-0073**	801-521-4300
Prime Hotel Salt Lake City Convention Center 215 W South Temple	Salt Lake City	UT	84101	**866-937-7746**	801-531-7500
Radisson Hotel Salt Lake City Airport 2177 W North Temple St	Salt Lake City	UT	84116	**800-333-3333**	801-364-5800
Red Lion Hotel Salt Lake Downtown 161 W 600 South	Salt Lake City	UT	84101	**800-733-5466**	801-521-7373
Residence Inn Salt Lake City-City Center 285 W Broadway	Salt Lake City	UT	84101	**800-331-3131**	801-355-3300
Sheraton City Centre Hotel Salt Lake 150 W 500 South	Salt Lake City	UT	84101	**800-421-7602**	801-401-2000
Shilo Inn Hotel Salt Lake City 206 S West Temple	Salt Lake City	UT	84101	**800-222-2244**	801-521-9500

Vermont

	City	State	Zip	Toll-Free	Phone
Twin Farms Stage Rd PO box 115	Barnard	VT	05031	**800-894-6327**	802-234-9999
Hollow Inn 278 S Main St	Barre	VT	05641	**800-998-9444**	802-479-9313
Wyndham Burlington 60 Battery St	Burlington	VT	05401	**800-996-3426**	802-658-6500
Inn at Essex 70 Essex Way	Essex Junction	VT	05452	**800-727-4295**	802-878-1100
Cortina Inn & Resort 103 US Rt 4	Killington	VT	05751	**800-451-6108**	802-773-3333
Grey Bonnet Inn 831 Rt 100 N	Killington	VT	05751	**800-342-2086**	802-775-2537
Inn of the Six Mountains 2617 Killington Rd	Killington	VT	05751	**800-228-4676**	802-422-4302
Rabbit Hill Inn Lower Waterford Rd	Lower Waterford	VT	05848	**800-762-8669**	802-748-5168
Barnstead Inn PO Box 988 Bonnet St	Manchester Center	VT	05255	**800-331-1619**	802-362-1619
Middlebury Inn 14 Courthouse Sq	Middlebury	VT	05753	**800-842-4666**	802-388-4961
Capitol Plaza Hotel & Conference Center 100 State St	Montpelier	VT	05602	**800-274-5252**	802-223-5252
Sheraton Burlington Hotel & Conference Center 870 Williston Rd	South Burlington	VT	05403	**800-325-3535**	802-865-6600
Hartness House Inn 30 Orchard St	Springfield	VT	05156	**800-732-4789**	802-885-2115
Golden Eagle Resort 511 Mountain Rd PO Box 1090	Stowe	VT	05672	**800-626-1010**	802-253-4811
Green Mountain Inn 18 Main St PO Box 60	Stowe	VT	05672	**800-253-7302**	802-253-7301
Pitcher Inn 275 Main St	Warren	VT	05674	**888-867-4824**	802-496-6350
Inn at Sawmill Farm Crosstown Rd & Rt 100 PO Box 367	West Dover	VT	05356	**800-493-1133**	802-464-8131

Virginia

	City	State	Zip	Toll-Free	Phone
Martha Washington Inn 150 W Main St	Abingdon	VA	24210	**800-555-8000**	276-628-3161
Embassy Suites Alexandria-Old Town 1900 Diagonal Rd	Alexandria	VA	22314	**800-362-2779**	703-684-5900
Hilton Alexandria Mark Center 5000 Seminary Rd	Alexandria	VA	22311	**800-445-8667**	703-845-1010
Holiday Inn Hotel & Suites Alexandria (Historic District) 625 1st St	Alexandria	VA	22314	**877-732-3318**	703-548-6300
Holiday Inn Select Alexandria Old Town 480 King St	Alexandria	VA	22314	**800-465-4329**	703-549-6080
Home-Style Inn 6461 Edsall Rd	Alexandria	VA	22312	**888-223-9454**	703-354-4400
Morrison House 116 S Alfred St	Alexandria	VA	22314	**800-367-0800**	703-838-8000
Sheraton Pentagon South 4641 Kenmore Ave	Alexandria	VA	22304	**800-325-3535**	703-751-4510
Sheraton Suites Alexandria 801 N Saint Asaph St	Alexandria	VA	22314	**800-325-3535**	703-836-4700
Washington Suites 100 S Reynolds St	Alexandria	VA	22304	**877-736-2500**	703-370-9600
Best Western Key Bridge 1850 N Fort Myers Dr	Arlington	VA	22209	**800-539-2743**	703-522-0400
Courtyard Arlington Crystal City 2899 Jefferson Davis Hwy	Arlington	VA	22202	**800-321-2211**	703-549-3434
Courtyard Rosslyn 1533 Clarendon Blvd.	Arlington	VA	22209	**800-627-7468**	703-528-2222
Crowne Plaza Hotel Washington National Airport 1480 Crystal Dr	Arlington	VA	22202	**800-465-4329**	703-416-1600
Doubletree Hotel Crystal City 300 Army Navy Dr	Arlington	VA	22202	**800-222-8733**	703-416-4100
Embassy Suites Crystal City-National Airport 1300 Jefferson Davis Hwy	Arlington	VA	22202	**800-362-2779**	703-979-9799
Hilton Arlington & Towers 950 N Stafford St	Arlington	VA	22203	**800-445-8667**	703-528-6000
Hilton Crystal City at Ronald Reagan National Airport 2399 Jefferson Davis Hwy	Arlington	VA	22202	**800-445-8667**	703-418-6800
Hilton Garden Inn Arlington Courthouse Plaza 1333 N Courthouse Rd	Arlington	VA	22201	**877-782-9444**	703-528-4444
Hyatt Arlington 1325 Wilson Blvd	Arlington	VA	22209	**800-233-1234**	703-525-1234
Hyatt Regency Crystal City 2799 Jefferson Davis Hwy	Arlington	VA	22202	**800-418-1234**	703-418-1234
Marriott Crystal City 1999 Jefferson Davis Hwy	Arlington	VA	22202	**800-228-9290**	703-413-5500
Marriott Crystal Gateway 1700 Jefferson Davis Hwy	Arlington	VA	22202	**800-228-9290**	703-920-3230
Marriott Key Bridge 1401 Lee Hwy	Arlington	VA	22209	**800-228-9290**	703-524-6400
Residence Inn Arlington-Rosslyn 1651 N Oak St	Arlington	VA	22209	**800-331-3131**	703-812-8400
Ritz-Carlton Pentagon City 1250 S Hayes St	Arlington	VA	22202	**800-241-3333**	703-415-5000
Sheraton Crystal City Hotel 1800 Jefferson Davis Hwy	Arlington	VA	22202	**800-325-3535**	703-486-1111
Sheraton National Hotel 900 S Orme St	Arlington	VA	22204	**800-325-3535**	703-521-1900
Virginian Suites 1500 Arlington Blvd	Arlington	VA	22209	**800-275-2866**	703-522-9600
Wingate Inn Dulles Airport 3940 Centerview Dr	Chantilly	VA	20151	**800-228-1000**	571-203-0999
Omni Charlottesville Hotel 235 W Main St	Charlottesville	VA	22902	**800-843-6664**	434-971-5500
Comfort Suites Chesapeake 1550 Crossways Blvd.	Chesapeake	VA	23320	**800-228-5150**	757-420-1600
Fairfield Inn Chesapeake 1560 Crossways Blvd.	Chesapeake	VA	23320	**800-228-2800**	757-420-1300
Hilton Garden Inn Chesapeake/Greenbrier 1565 Crossways Blvd.	Chesapeake	VA	23320	**877-782-9444**	757-420-1212
Holiday Inn Chesapeake 725 Woodlake Dr	Chesapeake	VA	23320	**800-465-4329**	757-523-1500
Driftwood Lodge 7105 Maddox Blvd	Chincoteague Island	VA	23336	**800-553-6117**	757-336-6557
Hilton Garden Inn Richmond South/Southpark 800 Southpark Blvd	Colonial Heights	VA	23834	**877-782-9444**	804-520-0600
Marriott Washington Dulles Airport 45020 Aviation Dr	Dulles	VA	20166	**800-228-9290**	703-471-9500
Hilton Garden Inn Fairfax 3950 Fair Ridge Dr	Fairfax	VA	22033	**877-782-9444**	703-385-7774
Hyatt Fair Lakes 12777 Fair Lakes Cir	Fairfax	VA	22033	**800-233-1234**	703-818-1234
Doubletree Hotel Falls Church/Tysons Corner 7801 Leesburg Pike	Falls Church	VA	22043	**800-222-8733**	703-893-1340
Marriott Fairview Park 3111 Fairview Park Dr	Falls Church	VA	22042	**800-228-9290**	703-849-9400
Holiday Inn Select Fredericksburg 2801 Plank Rd	Fredericksburg	VA	22401	**800-682-1049**	540-786-8321
Hilton Garden Inn Richmond Innsbrook 4050 Cox Rd	Glen Allen	VA	23060	**877-782-9444**	804-521-2900
Radisson Hotel Hampton 700 Settlers Landing Rd	Hampton	VA	23669	**800-333-3333**	757-727-9700
Hilton Washington Dulles Airport 13869 Park Center Rd	Herndon	VA	20171	**800-445-8667**	703-478-2900
Hyatt Dulles 2300 Dulles Corner Blvd	Herndon	VA	20171	**800-233-1234**	703-713-1234
Marriott Suites Washington Dulles Airport 13101 Worldgate Dr	Herndon	VA	20170	**800-228-9290**	703-709-0400
Staybridge Suites Herndon/Dulles 13700 Coppermine Rd	Herndon	VA	20171	**800-238-8000**	703-713-6800
Keswick Hall at Monticello 701 Club Dr	Keswick	VA	22947	**800-274-5391**	434-979-3440
Holiday Inn Leesburg 1500 E Market St	Leesburg	VA	20176	**888-850-8545**	703-771-9200
Radisson Hotel Lynchburg 2900 Candler's Mountain Rd	Lynchburg	VA	24502	**800-333-3333**	434-237-6333
Ritz-Carlton Tysons Corner 1700 Tyson Blvd	McLean	VA	22102	**800-241-3333**	703-506-4300
Brandermill Inn 13550 Harbour Pointe Pkwy	Midlothian	VA	23112	**800-554-0130**	804-739-8871
Comfort Inn Newport News 12330 Jefferson Ave	Newport News	VA	23602	**800-368-2477**	757-249-0200
Hilton Garden Inn Newport News 180 Regal Way	Newport News	VA	23602	**877-782-9444**	757-947-1080
Omni Newport News Hotel 1000 Omni Blvd	Newport News	VA	23606	**800-843-6664**	757-873-6664
Point Plaza Suites & Conference Hotel 950 J Clyde Morris Blvd	Newport News	VA	23601	**800-841-1112**	757-599-4460
Best Western Center Inn 235 N Military Hwy	Norfolk	VA	23502	**800-528-1234**	757-461-6600
Clarion Hotel James Madison 345 Granby St	Norfolk	VA	23510	**800-424-6423**	757-622-6682
Doubletree Club Norfolk Airport 880 N Military Hwy Suite 35	Norfolk	VA	23502	**800-933-9600**	757-461-9192
Hilton Norfolk Airport 1500 N Military Hwy	Norfolk	VA	23502	**800-422-7474**	757-466-8000
Marriott Norfolk Waterside 235 E Main St	Norfolk	VA	23510	**800-228-9290**	757-627-4200
Radisson Hotel Norfolk 700 Monticello Ave	Norfolk	VA	23510	**800-333-3333**	757-627-5555
Sheraton Norfolk Waterside Hotel 777 Waterside Dr	Norfolk	VA	23510	**800-325-3535**	757-622-6664
Mountain Lake Hotel 115 Hotel Cir	Pembroke	VA	24136	**800-346-3334**	540-626-7121
Holiday Inn Portsmouth Olde Towne Waterfront 8 Crawford Pkwy	Portsmouth	VA	23704	**800-465-4269**	757-393-2573
Hyatt Regency Reston 1800 Presidents St	Reston	VA	20191	**800-233-1234**	703-709-1234
Sheraton Reston Hotel 11810 Sunrise Valley Dr	Reston	VA	20191	**800-325-3535**	703-620-9000
AmeriSuites Richmond Arboretum 201 Arboretum Pl	Richmond	VA	23236	**800-833-1516**	804-560-1566
Berkeley Hotel 1200 E Cary St	Richmond	VA	23219	**888-780-4422**	804-780-1300

Classified Section

Listing	City	State	ZIP	Toll-Free	Phone
Best Western Governor's Inn Motel 9826 Midlothian Tpke	Richmond	VA	23235	**800-528-1234**	804-323-0007
Commonwealth Park Suites Hotel 901 Bank St	Richmond	VA	23219	**888-343-7301**	804-343-7300
Courtyard Richmond West 6400 W Broad St	Richmond	VA	23230	**800-228-2100**	804-282-1881
Crowne Plaza Hotel Richmond-E Canal 555 E Canal St	Richmond	VA	23219	**800-227-6963**	804-788-0900
Embassy Suites Richmond-The Commerce Center 2925 Emerywood Pkwy	Richmond	VA	23294	**800-362-2779**	804-672-8585
Holiday Inn Richmond 6531 W Broad St	Richmond	VA	23230	**800-465-4329**	804-285-9951
Holiday Inn Select Richmond/Koger South Conference Center 1021 Koger Center Blvd	Richmond	VA	23235	**800-465-4329**	804-379-3800
Jefferson Hotel 101 West Franklin St	Richmond	VA	23220	**800-424-8014**	804-788-8000
Linden Row Inn 100 E Franklin St	Richmond	VA	23219	**800-348-7424**	804-783-7000
Marriott Richmond 500 E Broad St	Richmond	VA	23219	**800-228-9290**	804-643-3400
Omni Richmond Hotel 100 S 12th St	Richmond	VA	23219	**800-843-6664**	804-344-7000
Radisson Hotel Historic Richmond 301 W Franklin St	Richmond	VA	23220	**800-333-3333**	804-644-9871
Sheraton Park South Hotel 9901 Midlothian Tpke	Richmond	VA	23235	**800-325-3535**	804-323-1144
Sheraton Richmond West Hotel 6624 W Broad St	Richmond	VA	23230	**800-325-3535**	804-285-2000
Wingate Inn Richmond Airport 491 International Centre Dr	Richmond	VA	23150	**800-228-1000**	804-222-1499
AmeriSuites Roanoke Valley View Mall 5040 Valley View Blvd	Roanoke	VA	24012	**800-833-1516**	540-366-4700
Jefferson Lodge 616 S Jefferson St	Roanoke	VA	24011	**800-950-2580**	540-342-2951
Ramada Inn Roanoke-River's Edge 1927 Franklin Rd	Roanoke	VA	24014	**800-272-6232**	540-343-0121
Wyndham Roanoke Airport 2801 Hershberger Rd NW	Roanoke	VA	24017	**800-996-3426**	540-563-9300
Hilton Springfield 6550 Loisdale Rd	Springfield	VA	22150	**800-445-8667**	703-971-8900
Hotel Strasburg 213 S Holliday St	Strasburg	VA	22657	**800-348-8327**	540-465-9191
Marriott Tysons Corner 8028 Leesburg Pike	Vienna	VA	22182	**800-228-9290**	703-734-3200
Sheraton Premiere at Tysons Corner 8661 Leesburg Pike	Vienna	VA	22182	**800-325-3535**	703-448-1234
Alamar Resort Inn 311 16th St	Virginia Beach	VA	23451	**800-346-5681**	757-428-7582
Barclay Towers 809 Atlantic Ave	Virginia Beach	VA	23451	**800-344-4473**	757-491-2700
Best Western Oceanfront 1101 Atlantic Ave	Virginia Beach	VA	23451	**800-631-5000**	757-422-5000
Breakers Resort Inn 1503 Atlantic Ave	Virginia Beach	VA	23451	**800-237-7532**	757-428-1821
Clarion Hotel Virginia Beach 4453 Bonney Rd	Virginia Beach	VA	23462	**800-424-6423**	757-473-1700
Clarion Resort & Conference Center 501 Atlantic Ave	Virginia Beach	VA	23451	**800-345-3186**	757-422-3186
Courtyard Virginia Beach/Norfolk 5700 Greenwich Rd	Virginia Beach	VA	23462	**800-321-2211**	757-490-2002
Dolphin Inn 1705 Atlantic Ave	Virginia Beach	VA	23451	**800-365-3467**	757-491-1420
Doubletree Hotel Virginia Beach 1900 Pavilion Dr	Virginia Beach	VA	23451	**800-222-8733**	757-422-8900
Four Sails Resort Hotel 3301 Atlantic Ave	Virginia Beach	VA	23451	**800-227-4213**	757-491-8100
Hilton Garden Inn Virginia Beach Town Center 252 Town Center Dr	Virginia Beach	VA	23462	**877-782-9444**	757-326-6200
Holiday Inn Virginia Beach Executive Center Hotel 5655 Greenwich Rd	Virginia Beach	VA	23462	**800-465-4329**	757-499-4400
Holiday Inn Virginia Beach Oceanside 2101 Atlantic Ave	Virginia Beach	VA	23451	**800-882-3224**	757-491-1500
Ocean Key Resort 424 Atlantic Ave	Virginia Beach	VA	23451	**800-955-9700**	757-425-2200
Ramada Plaza Resort Oceanfront Virginia Beach 5700 Atlantic Ave	Virginia Beach	VA	23451	**800-365-3032**	757-428-7025
Sea Gull Motel on the Beach 2613 Atlantic Ave	Virginia Beach	VA	23451	**800-426-4855**	757-425-5711
Sheraton Oceanfront Hotel 3501 Atlantic Ave	Virginia Beach	VA	23451	**800-325-3535**	757-425-9000
Surfside Inn 1211 Atlantic Ave	Virginia Beach	VA	23451	**800-437-2497**	757-428-1183
Wynnwood Suites 1909 Atlantic Ave	Virginia Beach	VA	23451	**800-372-4900**	757-425-0650
Clarion Historic Hotel & Conference Center 500 Merrimac Trail	Williamsburg	VA	23185	**800-666-8888**	757-220-1410
Courtyard Williamsburg 470 McLaws Cir	Williamsburg	VA	23185	**800-321-2211**	757-221-0700
Embassy Suites Williamsburg 3006 Mooretown Rd	Williamsburg	VA	23185	**800-362-2779**	757-229-6800
Heritage Inn 1324 Richmond Rd	Williamsburg	VA	23185	**800-782-3800**	757-229-6220
Hilton Garden Inn Williamsburg 1624 Richmond Rd	Williamsburg	VA	23185	**877-782-9444**	757-253-9400
Holiday Inn Williamsburg Downtown 814 Capitol Landing Rd	Williamsburg	VA	23185	**800-465-4329**	757-229-0200
Marriott Williamsburg 50 Kingsmill Rd	Williamsburg	VA	23185	**800-228-9290**	757-220-2500
Motel Rochambeau 929 Capitol Landing Rd	Williamsburg	VA	23185	**800-368-1055**	757-229-2851
Princess Anne The 1350 Richmond Rd	Williamsburg	VA	23185	**800-552-5571**	757-229-2455
Quarterpath Inn 620 York St	Williamsburg	VA	23185	**800-446-9222**	757-220-0960
Radisson Fort Magruder Hotel & Conference Center 6945 Pocahontas Trail	Williamsburg	VA	23185	**800-333-3333**	757-220-2250
Ramada Inn Central Williamsburg 5351 Richmond Rd	Williamsburg	VA	23185	**800-446-9200**	757-565-2000
White Lion Motel 912 Capitol Landing Rd	Williamsburg	VA	23185	**800-368-1055**	757-229-3931
Williamsburg Hospitality House 415 Richmond Rd	Williamsburg	VA	23185	**800-932-9192**	757-229-4020
Williamsburg Lodge 310 S England St	Williamsburg	VA	23185	**800-447-8679**	757-229-1000

Washington

Listing	City	State	ZIP	Toll-Free	Phone
Bellevue Club Hotel 11200 SE 6th St	Bellevue	WA	98004	**800-579-1110**	425-454-4424
Coast Bellevue Hotel 625 116th Ave NE	Bellevue	WA	98004	**800-325-4000**	425-455-9444
Doubletree Hotel Bellevue 300 112th Ave SE	Bellevue	WA	98004	**800-222-8733**	425-455-1300
Embassy Suites Seattle-Bellevue 3225 158th Ave SE	Bellevue	WA	98008	**800-633-0100**	425-644-2500
Hyatt Regency Bellevue 900 Bellevue Way NE	Bellevue	WA	98004	**800-233-1234**	425-462-1234
Best Western Lakeway Inn 714 Lakeway Dr	Bellingham	WA	98226	**888-671-1011**	360-671-1011
Chrysalis Inn & Spa 804 10th St	Bellingham	WA	98225	**888-808-0005**	360-756-1005
Carson Hot Mineral Springs Resort 372 St Martin Rd	Carson	WA	98610	**800-607-3678**	509-427-8292
Woodmark Hotel on Lake Washington 1200 Carillon Point	Kirkland	WA	98033	**800-822-3700**	425-822-3700
Comfort Inn Lacey 4700 Park Center Ave NE	Lacey	WA	98516	**800-228-5150**	360-456-6300
Embassy Suites Seattle-Lynnwood 20610 44th Ave W	Lynnwood	WA	98036	**800-628-0611**	425-775-2500
Coachman Inn 32959 SR-Hwy 20	Oak Harbor	WA	98277	**800-635-0043**	360-675-0727
Ramada Inn Olympia-Governor House 621 S Capitol Way	Olympia	WA	98501	**800-272-6232**	360-352-7700
Red Lion Hotel Olympia 2300 Evergreen Park Dr SW	Olympia	WA	98502	**800-733-5466**	360-943-4000
Resort at Ludlow Bay 1 Heron Rd	Port Ludlow	WA	98365	**800-732-1239**	360-437-0411
Residence Inn Redmond 7575 164th Ave NE	Redmond	WA	98052	**800-331-3131**	425-497-9226
Hilton Garden Inn Seattle/Renton 1801 E Valley Rd	Renton	WA	98055	**877-782-9444**	425-430-1414
Holiday Inn Select Seattle-Renton 1 S Grady Way	Renton	WA	98055	**800-521-1412**	425-226-7700
Alexis Hotel 1007 1st Ave	Seattle	WA	98104	**800-264-8482**	206-624-4844
Best Western Executive Inn Seattle 200 Taylor Ave N	Seattle	WA	98109	**800-351-9444**	206-448-9444
Best Western Pioneer Square Hotel 77 Yesler Way	Seattle	WA	98104	**800-800-5514**	206-340-1234
Best Western University Tower Hotel 4507 Brooklyn Ave NE	Seattle	WA	98105	**800-899-0251**	206-634-2000
Coast Gateway Hotel 18415 International Blvd	Seattle	WA	98188	**800-663-1144**	206-248-8200
Commodore Motor Hotel 2013 2nd Ave	Seattle	WA	98121	**800-714-8868**	206-448-8868
Courtyard Seattle Downtown/Lake Union 925 Westlake Ave N	Seattle	WA	98109	**800-321-2211**	206-213-0100
Crowne Plaza Hotel Seattle Downtown 1113 6th Ave	Seattle	WA	98101	**800-521-2762**	206-464-1980
Doubletree Guest Suites Seattle-Southcenter 16500 Southcenter Pkwy	Seattle	WA	98188	**800-222-8733**	206-575-8220
Doubletree Hotel Seattle Airport 18740 International Blvd	Seattle	WA	98188	**800-222-8733**	206-246-8600
Four Seasons Hotel Seattle 411 University St	Seattle	WA	98101	**800-223-8772**	206-621-1700
Hilton Seattle 1301 6th Ave	Seattle	WA	98101	**800-426-0535**	206-624-0500
Holiday Inn Seattle-Tacoma Airport 17338 International Blvd	Seattle	WA	98188	**800-465-4329**	206-248-1000
Hotel Andra 2000 4th Ave	Seattle	WA	98121	**877-448-8600**	206-448-8600
Hotel Edgewater 2411 Alaskan Way Pier 67	Seattle	WA	98121	**800-624-0670**	206-728-7000
Hotel Monaco Seattle 1101 4th Ave	Seattle	WA	98101	**800-715-6513**	206-621-1770
Hotel Vintage Park 1100 5th Ave	Seattle	WA	98101	**800-853-3914**	206-624-8000
Inn at the Market 86 Pine St	Seattle	WA	98101	**800-446-4484**	206-443-3600
Inn at Queen Anne 505 1st Ave N	Seattle	WA	98109	**800-952-5043**	206-282-7357
MarQueen Hotel 600 Queen Anne Ave N	Seattle	WA	98109	**888-445-3076**	206-282-7407
Marriott Sea-Tac Airport 3201 S 176th St	Seattle	WA	98188	**800-314-0925**	206-241-2000
Mayflower Park Hotel 405 Olive Way	Seattle	WA	98101	**800-426-5100**	206-623-8700
Pacific Plaza Hotel 400 Spring St	Seattle	WA	98104	**800-426-1165**	206-623-3900
Paramount Hotel 724 Pine St	Seattle	WA	98101	**800-716-6199**	206-292-9500
Quality Inn & Suites Seattle 225 Aurora Ave N	Seattle	WA	98109	**800-255-7932**	206-728-7666
Radisson Hotel Seattle Airport 17001 Pacific Hwy S	Seattle	WA	98188	**800-333-3333**	206-244-6000
Ramada Inn Seattle Downtown 2200 5th Ave	Seattle	WA	98121	**800-272-6232**	206-441-9785
Red Lion Hotel on Fifth Avenue 1415 5th Ave	Seattle	WA	98101	**800-325-4000**	206-971-8000
Red Lion Hotel Seattle Airport 18220 International Blvd	Seattle	WA	98188	**800-733-5466**	206-246-5535
Renaissance Madison Hotel 515 Madison St	Seattle	WA	98104	**800-278-4159**	206-583-0300
Residence Inn Seattle-Lake Union 800 Fairview Ave N	Seattle	WA	98109	**800-331-3131**	206-624-6000
Sheraton Seattle Hotel & Towers 1400 6th Ave	Seattle	WA	98101	**800-325-3535**	206-621-9000
Silver Cloud Inn Seattle-Lake Union 1150 Fairview Ave N	Seattle	WA	98109	**800-330-5812**	206-447-9500
Sixth Avenue Inn 2000 6th Ave	Seattle	WA	98121	**800-648-6440**	206-441-8300
Sorrento Hotel 900 Madison St	Seattle	WA	98104	**800-426-1265**	206-622-6400
Summerfield Suites by Wyndham Seattle Downtown 1011 Pike St	Seattle	WA	98101	**800-833-4353**	206-682-8282
W Hotel Seattle 1112 4th Ave	Seattle	WA	98101	**877-946-8357**	206-264-6000
Warwick Hotel Seattle 401 Lenora St	Seattle	WA	98121	**800-426-9280**	206-443-4300
WestCoast Vance Hotel 620 Stewart St	Seattle	WA	98101	**800-426-0670**	206-441-4200
Westin Seattle 1900 5th Ave	Seattle	WA	98101	**800-937-8461**	206-728-1000
Red Lion Hotel Silverdale 3073 NW Bucklin Hill Rd	Silverdale	WA	98383	**800-733-5466**	360-698-1000
Salish Lodge & Spa 6501 Railroad Ave PO Box 1109	Snoqualmie	WA	98065	**800-272-5474**	425-888-2556
Apple Tree Inn 9508 N Division St	Spokane	WA	99218	**800-323-5796**	509-466-3020
Courtyard Spokane 401 N Riverpoint Blvd	Spokane	WA	99202	**800-321-2211**	509-456-7600
Davenport Hotel 10 S Post St	Spokane	WA	99201	**800-899-1482**	509-455-8888
Doubletree Hotel Spokane-City Center 322 N Spokane Falls Ct	Spokane	WA	99201	**800-222-8733**	509-455-9600
Hilton Garden Inn Spokane Airport 9015 W Hwy 2	Spokane	WA	99224	**877-782-9444**	509-244-5866
Hotel Lusso 1 N Post St	Spokane	WA	99201	**800-525-4800**	509-747-9750
Red Lion Grand Hotel at the Park 303 W North River Dr	Spokane	WA	99201	**800-325-4000**	509-326-8000
Red Lion River Inn N 700 Division St	Spokane	WA	99202	**800-733-5466**	509-326-5577
Shilo Inn Hotel Spokane 923 E 3rd Ave	Spokane	WA	99202	**800-222-2244**	509-535-9000
WestCoast Ridpath Hotel 515 W Sprague Ave	Spokane	WA	99201	**800-325-4000**	509-838-2711
Wolff Corporate Housing 9514 E Montgomery Rd Suite 20	Spokane	WA	99206	**800-528-9519**	509-444-1690
Best Western Fife Hotel & Conference Center 5700 Pacific Hwy E	Tacoma	WA	98424	**888-820-3555**	253-922-3555
Ramada Inn Tacoma Dome/Civic Center 2611 E 'E' St	Tacoma	WA	98421	**800-755-1547**	253-572-7272
Royal Coachman Inn 5805 Pacific Hwy E	Tacoma	WA	98424	**800-422-3051**	253-922-2500
Sheraton Tacoma Hotel 1320 Broadway Plaza	Tacoma	WA	98402	**800-845-9466**	253-572-3200
Best Western Tumwater Inn 5188 Capitol Blvd	Tumwater	WA	98501	**800-848-4992**	360-956-1235
Comfort Inn Vancouver 13207 NE 20th Ave	Vancouver	WA	98686	**800-228-5150**	360-574-6000
Comfort Suites Vancouver 4714 NE 94th Ave	Vancouver	WA	98662	**877-424-6423**	360-253-3100
Heathman Lodge 7801 NE Greenwood Dr	Vancouver	WA	98662	**888-475-3100**	360-254-3100
Phoenix Inn Vancouver 12712 SE 2nd Cir	Vancouver	WA	98684	**888-988-8100**	360-891-9777
Red Lion Hotel Vancouver 100 Columbia St	Vancouver	WA	98660	**800-733-5466**	360-694-8341
Residence Inn Portland-Vancouver 8005 NE Parkway Dr	Vancouver	WA	98662	**800-331-3131**	360-253-4800
Willows Lodge 14580 NE 145th St	Woodinville	WA	98072	**877-424-3930**	425-424-3900

West Virginia

Listing	City	State	ZIP	Toll-Free	Phone
Embassy Suites Charleston 300 Court St	Charleston	WV	25301	**800-362-2779**	304-347-8700
Fairfield Inn Charleston 1000 Washington St E	Charleston	WV	25301	**800-228-2800**	304-343-4661
Holiday Inn Charleston House 600 Kanawha Blvd E	Charleston	WV	25301	**800-465-4329**	304-344-4092
Marriott Charleston Town Center 200 Lee St E	Charleston	WV	25301	**800-228-9290**	304-345-6500
Sleep Inn Charleston-Cross Lanes 15 Goff Crossing Dr	Cross Lanes	WV	25313	**800-799-9946**	304-776-7711

West Virginia (Cont'd)

Name / Address	City	State	Zip	Toll-Free	Phone
Comfort Inn Morgantown 225 Comfort Inn Dr	Morgantown	WV	26508	**800-228-5150**	304-296-9364
Euro-Suites Hotel 501 Chestnut Ridge Rd	Morgantown	WV	26505	**800-678-4837**	304-598-1000
Holiday Inn Morgantown 1400 Saratoga Ave	Morgantown	WV	26505	**800-465-4329**	304-599-1680
Ramada Plaza Charleston 400 2nd Ave	South Charleston	WV	25303	**800-272-6232**	304-744-4641
Wingate Inn Charleston 402 2nd Ave	South Charleston	WV	25303	**800-228-1000**	304-744-4444
Ramada Plaza Wheeling City Center 1200 Market St	Wheeling	WV	26003	**800-862-5873**	304-232-0300

Wisconsin

Name / Address	City	State	Zip	Toll-Free	Phone
Embassy Suites Milwaukee West 1200 S Moorland Rd	Brookfield	WI	53008	**800-362-2779**	262-782-2900
Sheraton Milwaukee Brookfield Hotel 375 S Moorland Rd	Brookfield	WI	53005	**800-325-3535**	262-364-1100
Wyndham Garden Hotel Brookfield 18155 Bluemound Rd	Brookfield	WI	53045	**800-996-3426**	262-792-1212
Best Western Midway Hotel Green Bay 780 Packer Dr	Green Bay	WI	54304	**800-482-3885**	920-499-3161
Hilton Garden Inn Green Bay 1015 Lombardi Ave	Green Bay	WI	54304	**877-782-9444**	920-405-0400
Holiday Inn Green Bay City Centre 200 E Main St	Green Bay	WI	54301	**800-465-4329**	920-437-5900
Radisson Hotel & Conference Center Green Bay 2040 Airport Dr	Green Bay	WI	54313	**800-333-3333**	920-494-7300
Regency Suites Green Bay 333 Main St	Green Bay	WI	54301	**800-236-3330**	920-432-4555
Residence Inn Green Bay 335 W Saint Joseph St	Green Bay	WI	54301	**800-331-3131**	920-435-2222
Settle Inn Airport 2620 S Packerland Dr	Green Bay	WI	54313	**800-688-9052**	920-499-1900
Wingate Inn Green Bay Airport 2065 Airport Dr	Green Bay	WI	54313	**800-228-1000**	920-617-2000
Best Western Inn on the Park 22 S Carroll St	Madison	WI	53703	**800-279-8811**	608-257-8811
Best Western Inntowner & The Highland Club 2424 University Ave	Madison	WI	53726	**800-937-8376**	608-233-8778
Crowne Plaza Hotel Madison-East Towne 4402 E Washington Ave	Madison	WI	53704	**800-404-7630**	608-244-4703
Edgewater The 666 Wisconsin Ave	Madison	WI	53703	**800-922-5512**	608-256-9071
Holiday Inn Hotel & Suites Madison West 1109 Fourier Dr	Madison	WI	53717	**888-522-9472**	608-826-0500
Holiday Inn Madison East 3841 E Washington Ave	Madison	WI	53704	**800-465-4329**	608-244-2481
Howard Johnson Plaza Hotel Madison 525 W Johnson St	Madison	WI	53703	**800-446-4656**	608-251-5511
Madison Concourse Hotel & Governors Club 1 W Dayton St	Madison	WI	53703	**800-356-8293**	608-257-6000
Sheraton Madison Hotel 706 John Nolen Dr	Madison	WI	53713	**800-325-3535**	608-251-2300
Wingate Inn Madison 3510 Mill Pond Rd	Madison	WI	53718	**800-510-3510**	608-224-1500
Hilton Garden Inn Madison West/Middleton 1801 Deming Way	Middleton	WI	53562	**877-782-9444**	608-831-2220
Marriott Madison West 1313 John Q Hammons Dr	Middleton	WI	53562	**800-228-9290**	608-831-2000
AmeriSuites West 11777 W Silver Spring Dr	Milwaukee	WI	53225	**800-723-8280**	414-462-3500
AmerSuites Milwaukee Airport 200 W Grange Ave	Milwaukee	WI	53207	**800-833-1516**	414-744-3600
Astor Hotel The 924 E Juneau Ave	Milwaukee	WI	53202	**800-558-0200**	414-271-4220
Best Western Inn Towne Hotel 710 N Old World 3rd St	Milwaukee	WI	53203	**800-528-1234**	414-224-8400
Clarion Hotel Milwaukee Airport 5311 S Howell Ave	Milwaukee	WI	53207	**800-252-7466**	414-481-2400
Courtyard Milwaukee Downtown 300 W Michigan St	Milwaukee	WI	53203	**800-321-2211**	414-291-4122
Four Points by Sheraton Milwaukee Airport 4747 S Howell Ave	Milwaukee	WI	53207	**800-325-3535**	414-481-8000
Hilton Garden Inn Milwaukee Park Place 11600 W Park Pl	Milwaukee	WI	53224	**877-782-9444**	414-359-9823
Hilton Milwaukee City Center 509 W Wisconsin Ave	Milwaukee	WI	53203	**800-445-8667**	414-271-7250
Hospitality Inn 4400 S 27th St	Milwaukee	WI	53221	**800-825-8466**	414-282-8800
Hotel Metro 411 E Mason St	Milwaukee	WI	53202	**877-638-7620**	414-272-1937
Hyatt Regency Milwaukee 333 W Kilbourn Ave	Milwaukee	WI	53203	**800-233-1234**	414-276-1234
Manchester East Hotel & Suites 7065 N Port Washington Rd	Milwaukee	WI	53217	**800-723-8280**	414-351-6960
Park East Hotel 916 E State St	Milwaukee	WI	53202	**800-328-7275**	414-276-8800
Pfister Hotel 424 E Wisconsin Ave	Milwaukee	WI	53202	**800-558-8222**	414-273-8222
Plaza Hotel & Apartments 1007 N Cass St	Milwaukee	WI	53202	**800-340-9590**	414-276-2101
Radisson Hotel Milwaukee Airport 6331 S 13th St	Milwaukee	WI	53221	**800-333-3333**	414-764-1500
Wyndham Milwaukee Center 139 E Kilbourn Ave	Milwaukee	WI	53202	**800-996-3426**	414-276-8686
Pioneer Resort & Marina 1000 Pioneer Dr	Oshkosh	WI	54902	**800-683-1980**	920-233-1980
Marriott Racine 7111 Washington Ave	Racine	WI	53406	**800-228-9290**	262-886-6100
Voyageur Inn 200 Viking Dr	Reedsburg	WI	53959	**800-444-4493**	608-524-6431
Hotel Mead 451 E Grand Ave	Wisconsin Rapids	WI	54494	**800-843-6323**	715-423-1500

Wyoming

Name / Address	City	State	Zip	Toll-Free	Phone
First Interstate Inn 20 SE Wyoming Blvd	Casper	WY	82609	**800-462-4667**	307-234-9125
Holiday Inn Casper-Convention Center 300 W 'F' St	Casper	WY	82601	**800-465-4329**	307-235-2531
Parkway Plaza Hotel 123 W 'E' St	Casper	WY	82601	**800-270-7829**	307-235-1777
Radisson Hotel Casper 800 N Poplar St	Casper	WY	82601	**800-333-3333**	307-266-6000
Best Western Hitching Post Inn Resort & Conference Center 1700 W Lincolnway	Cheyenne	WY	82001	**800-221-0125**	307-638-3301
Comfort Inn Cheyenne 2245 Etchepare Dr	Cheyenne	WY	82007	**800-777-7218**	307-638-7202
Fairfield Inn Cheyenne 1415 Stillwater Ave	Cheyenne	WY	82001	**800-228-2800**	307-637-4070
Holiday Inn Cheyenne 204 W Fox Farm Rd	Cheyenne	WY	82007	**800-465-4329**	307-638-4466
La Quinta Inn Cheyenne 2410 W Lincolnway	Cheyenne	WY	82009	**800-531-5900**	307-632-7117
Little America Hotel & Resort Cheyenne 2800 W Lincolnway	Cheyenne	WY	82001	**888-709-8384**	307-775-8400
Plains Hotel 1600 Central Ave	Cheyenne	WY	82001	**866-275-2467**	307-638-3311
Quality Inn Cheyenne 5401 Walker Rd	Cheyenne	WY	82009	**800-228-5151**	307-632-8901
Comfort Inn Casper-Evansville 480 Lathrop Rd	Evansville	WY	82636	**800-228-5150**	307-235-3038
Angler's Inn 265 N Millward St PO Box 1247	Jackson	WY	83001	**800-867-4667**	307-733-3682
Antler Inn 43 W Pearl St PO Box 575	Jackson	WY	83001	**800-483-8667**	307-733-2535
Best Western Lodge at Jackson Hole 80 Scott Ln	Jackson	WY	83001	**800-458-3866**	307-739-9703
Cowboy Village Resort 120 S Flat Creek Dr PO Box 8040	Jackson	WY	83001	**800-962-4988**	307-733-3121
Inn on the Creek 295 N Millward St PO Box 445	Jackson	WY	83001	**800-669-9534**	307-739-1565
Jackson Hole Lodge 420 W Broadway PO Box 1805	Jackson	WY	83001	**800-604-9404**	307-733-2992
Painted Buffalo Inn 400 W Broadway	Jackson	WY	83001	**800-288-3866**	307-733-4340
Parkway Inn 125 N Jackson St PO Box 494	Jackson	WY	83001	**800-247-8390**	307-733-3143
Ranch Inn 45 E Pearl St	Jackson	WY	83001	**800-348-5599**	307-733-6363
Rawhide Motel 75 S Millward St PO Box 4800	Jackson	WY	83001	**800-835-2999**	307-733-1216
Red Lion Wyoming Inn Jackson 930 W Broadway	Jackson	WY	83001	**800-844-0035**	307-734-0035
Spring Creek Ranch 1800 Spirit Dance Rd	Jackson	WY	83001	**800-443-6139**	307-733-8833
Wagon Wheel Village 435 N Cache St	Jackson	WY	83001	**800-323-9279**	307-733-2357
Wort Hotel 50 N Glenwood	Jackson	WY	83001	**800-322-2727**	307-733-2190
Virginian Lodge 750 W Broadway PO Box 1052	Jackson Hole	WY	83001	**800-262-4999**	307-733-2792
Alpenhof Lodge 3255 W Village Dr	Teton Village	WY	83025	**800-732-3244**	307-733-3242
Best Western Inn at Jackson Hole 3345 W Village Dr PO Box 328	Teton Village	WY	83025	**800-842-7666**	307-733-2311

374 ICE - MANUFACTURED

Name / Address	City	State	Zip	Toll-Free	Phone
Hanover Foods Corp 1550 York St PO Box 334	Hanover	PA	17331	**800-888-4646**	717-632-6000
Icemakers Inc PO Box 321755	Birmingham	AL	35232	**800-467-2181**	205-591-2791
Reddy Ice & Cassco Refrigerated Services PO Box 548	Harrisonburg	VA	22801	**800-999-4231**	540-433-2751
Reddy Ice Ltd 8450 N Central Expy Suite 1800	Dallas	TX	75231	**800-683-4423**	214-526-6740

375 IMAGING EQUIPMENT & SYSTEMS - MEDICAL

SEE ALSO Medical Instruments & Apparatus - Mfr

Name / Address	City	State	Zip	Toll-Free	Phone
ACMI Corp 136 Turnpike Rd	Southborough	MA	01772	**866-879-0640**	508-804-2600
AFP Imaging Corp 250 Clearbrook Rd	Elmsford	NY	10523	**800-592-6666**	914-592-6100
Applied Imaging Corp 2380 Walsh Ave Bldg B *NASDAQ: AICX*	Santa Clara	CA	95051	**800-634-3622**	408-562-0250
Bio-Imaging Technologies Inc 826 Newtown-Yardley Rd Suite 101 *NASDAQ: BITI*	Newtown	PA	18940	**800-748-9032**	267-757-3000
Bioscan Inc 4590 MacArthur Blvd NW	Washington	DC	20007	**800-255-7226**	202-338-0974
BrainLAB Inc 3 Westbrook Corp Ctr Suite 400	Westchester	IL	60154	**800-784-7700**	708-409-1343
Camtronics Medical Systems 900 Walnut Ridge Dr	Hartland	WI	53029	**800-634-5151**	262-367-0700
CIVCO Medical Instruments 102 1st St S	Kalona	IA	52247	**800-445-6741**	319-656-4447
Clarient Inc 33171 Paseo Cerveza *NASDAQ: CLRT*	San Juan Capistrano	CA	92675	**888-443-3310**	949-443-3355
CTI Molecular Imaging Inc 810 Innovation Dr	Knoxville	TN	37932	**800-841-7226**	865-218-2000
Dent-X Corp 250 Clearbrook Rd	Elmsford	NY	10523	**800-592-6666**	914-592-6100
Dentsply International Inc 221 W Philadelphia St PO Box 872 *NASDAQ: XRAY*	York	PA	17405	**800-877-0020**	717-845-7511
Dentsply International Inc Gendex Products Div 901 W Oakton St	Des Plaines	IL	60018	**800-800-2888**	847-640-4800
Digirad Corp 13950 Stowe Dr *NASDAQ: DRAD*	Poway	CA	92064	**800-947-6134**	858-726-1600
Dornier MedTech America Inc 1155 Roberts Blvd	Kennesaw	GA	30144	**800-367-6437**	770-426-1315
Eastman Kodak Co 343 State St *NYSE: EK*	Rochester	NY	14650	**800-242-2424**	585-724-4000
Eastman Kodak Co Health Imaging Div 343 State St Bldg 20 4th Fl *Cust Svc	Rochester	NY	14650	**800-677-9933***	585-588-9003
Emageon Inc 1200 Corporate Dr Suite 200 *NASDAQ: EMAG*	Birmingham	AL	35242	**866-362-4366**	205-980-9222
Fischer Imaging Corp 12300 N Grant St *NASDAQ: FIMG*	Denver	CO	80241	**800-825-8434**	303-452-6800
Fluoroscan Imaging Systems Inc 35 Crosby Dr	Bedford	MA	01730	**800-343-9729**	781-999-7300
GE Healthcare PO Box 414	Milwaukee	WI	53201	**800-558-5102**	262-544-3011
GE OEC Medical Systems Inc 384 Wright Brothers Dr	Salt Lake City	UT	84116	**800-365-1366**	801-328-9300
Given Imaging Ltd 5555 Oakbrook Pkwy Oakbrook Technology Ctr Suite 355 *NASDAQ: GIVN*	Norcross	GA	30093	**800-448-3644**	770-662-0870
Hitachi Medical Systems America Inc 1959 Summit Commerce Pk	Twinsburg	OH	44087	**800-800-3106**	330-425-1313
Hologic Inc 35 Crosby Dr *NASDAQ: HOLX*	Bedford	MA	01730	**800-343-9729**	781-999-7300
iCAD Inc 4 Townsend W Suite 17 *NASDAQ: ICAD*	Nashua	NH	03063	**800-444-6983**	603-882-5200
IGC-Medical Advances Inc 10437 Innovation Dr	Milwaukee	WI	53226	**800-657-0891**	414-258-3808
Imaging Diagnostic Systems Inc 6531 NW 18th Ct	Plantation	FL	33313	**800-992-9008**	954-581-9800
IRIS International Inc 9172 Eton Ave *NASDAQ: IRIS*	Chatsworth	CA	91311	**800-776-4747**	818-709-1244
IVOW Inc 2101 Faraday Ave *NASDAQ: IVOW*	Carlsbad	CA	92008	**800-510-8090**	760-603-9120
Kodak Co 343 State St *NYSE: EK*	Rochester	NY	14650	**800-242-2424**	585-724-4000

	City	State	Zip	Toll-Free	Phone
Medrad Inc 1 Medrad Dr *Cust Svc	Indianola	PA	15051	800-633-7237*	412-767-2400
Merge Technologies Inc 1126 S 70th St Suite S-107B *NASDAQ: MRGE*	Milwaukee	WI	53214	877-446-3743	414-977-4000
Neoprobe Corp 425 Metro Place N Suite 300	Dublin	OH	43017	800-793-0079	614-793-7500
Nichols Institute Diagnostics 1311 Calle Batido	San Clemente	CA	92673	800-286-4643	949-940-7200
Olympus America Inc 2 Corporate Ctr Dr	Melville	NY	11747	800-446-5967	631-844-5000
Philips Medical Systems 3000 Minuteman Rd	Andover	MA	01810	866-246-7306	978-687-1501
Philips Ultrasound 22100 Bothell Everett Hwy *Cust Svc	Bothell	WA	98021	800-433-3246*	425-487-7000
Positron Corp 1304 Langham Creek Dr Suite 300	Houston	TX	77084	800-766-2984	281-492-7100
Precision Optics Corp Inc 22 E Broadway *NASDAQ: POCI*	Gardner	MA	01440	800-447-2812	978-630-1800
S & S X-Ray Products Inc 10625 Telge Rd	Houston	TX	77095	800-347-9729	800-231-1747
Shimadzu Medical Systems 20101 S Vermont Ave	Torrance	CA	90502	800-228-1429	310-217-8855
Siemens Medical Solutions Inc 51 Valley Stream Pkwy	Malvern	PA	19355	866-872-9745	610-448-6300
Siemens Medical Solutions Ultrasound Div 1230 Shorebird Way	Mountain View	CA	94043	800-422-8766	650-969-9112
SonoSite Inc 21919 30th Dr SE *NASDAQ: SONO*	Bothell	WA	98021	888-482-9449	425-951-1200
Stentor Inc 5000 Marina Blvd Suite 100 *Cust Svc	Brisbane	CA	94005	877-328-2808*	650-866-4100
Topcon Medical Systems Inc 37 W Century Rd	Paramus	NJ	07652	800-223-1130	201-261-9450
Toshiba America Medical Systems Inc 2441 Michelle Dr	Tustin	CA	92780	800-421-1968	714-730-5000
Toshiba America MRI Inc 300 Utah Ave Suite 100	South San Francisco	CA	94080	800-477-4674	650-872-2722
Trex Enterprises 10455 Pacific Center Ct	San Diego	CA	92121	800-626-5885	858-646-5300
TriPath Imaging Inc 780 Plantation Dr *NASDAQ: TPTH*	Burlington	NC	27215	800-426-2176	336-222-9707
Vision-Sciences Inc 9 Strathmore Rd *NASDAQ: VSCI*	Natick	MA	01760	800-874-9975	508-650-9971
Xillix Technologies Corp 13775 Commerce Pkwy Suite 100	Richmond	BC	V6V2V4	800-665-2236	604-278-5000

376 IMAGING SERVICES - DIAGNOSTIC

	City	State	Zip	Toll-Free	Phone
Alliance Imaging Inc 1900 S State College Blvd Suite 600 *NYSE: AIQ*	Anaheim	CA	92806	800-544-3215	714-688-7100
Center for Diagnostic Imaging 5775 Wayzata Blvd Suite 400	Saint Louis Park	MN	55416	877-566-6500	952-543-6500
InfiMed Inc 121 Metropolitan Dr	Liverpool	NY	13088	800-825-8845	315-453-4545
InSight Health Services Corp 26250 Enterprise Ct Suite 100	Lake Forest	CA	92630	800-874-8634	949-282-6000
Medical Resources Inc 125 State St	Hackensack	NJ	07601	800-537-7272	201-488-6230
Raytel Medical Corp 7 Waterside Crossing	Windsor	CT	06095	800-367-1095	860-298-6100
USA Diagnostics Inc 4630 N University Dr PMB 310	Coral Springs	FL	33067	800-273-8798	954-970-3934
Wendt-Bristol Health Services Corp 921 Jasonway Ave	Columbus	OH	43214	800-230-7990	614-221-6000

377 INCENTIVE PROGRAM MANAGEMENT SERVICES

SEE ALSO Conference & Events Coordinators

	City	State	Zip	Toll-Free	Phone
ADI Meetings & Incentives Inc 1223 E Broadway Rd Suite 100	Tempe	AZ	85282	800-944-2359	480-350-9090
Beatty Group International 9800 SW Beaverton Hillsdale Hwy Suite 105	Beaverton	OR	97005	800-285-6215	503-644-3340
Compass Travel Service Inc 840 Ogden Ave	Westmont	IL	60559	800-300-1606	630-986-1606
Destination Success 15 W Central Pkwy	Cincinnati	OH	45202	888-301-3866	513-763-3070
Fennell Promotions Inc 951 Hornet Dr	Hazelwood	MO	63042	800-495-9765	314-592-3300
Fields Group Inc 9124 Technology Dr	Fishers	IN	46038	800-600-2969	317-578-4414
Fraser & Hoyt Group Incentive Div 1505 Barrington St Suite 107	Halifax	NS	B3J3K5	800-565-8747	902-421-1113
Global Incentives Inc 2120 Main St Suite 130	Huntington Beach	CA	92648	800-292-7348	714-960-2300
Incentive Solutions 2337 Perimeter Park Dr Suite 220	Atlanta	GA	30341	800-463-5836	770-457-4597
ITAGroup 4800 Westown Pkwy Suite 300	West Des Moines	IA	50266	800-257-1985	515-224-3400
Maritz Travel Co 1395 N Highway Dr	Fenton	MO	63099	800-253-7562	636-827-4000
Marketing Innovators International Inc 9701 W Higgins Rd Suite 400	Rosemont	IL	60018	800-633-8747	847-696-1111
Mayer Motivations Inc 2434 E Las Olas Blvd	Fort Lauderdale	FL	33301	888-611-4376	954-523-0074
MotivAction 16355 36th Ave N Suite 100	Minneapolis	MN	55446	800-326-2226	763-525-5200
Motivation Through Incentives Inc PO Box 481097	Kansas City	MO	64148	800-826-3464	816-942-0122
Premier Incentives Inc 2 Market Sq	Marblehead	MA	01945	888-255-0000	781-639-4444
Premier Meetings & Incentives 2150 S Washburn St	Oshkosh	WI	54903	800-236-5095	920-236-8030
Robbins Co 400 O'Neil Blvd	Attleboro	MA	02703	800-343-3970	508-222-2900
Travel Marketing Inc PO Box 69629	Portland	OR	97239	800-283-1022	503-222-1020
Travelcorp 917 Duke St	Alexandria	VA	22314	800-770-6910	703-299-9003
USMotivation 7840 Roswell Rd Bldg 100 Suite 300	Atlanta	GA	30350	800-476-0496	770-290-4700

378 INDUSTRIAL EQUIPMENT & SUPPLIES (MISC) - WHOL

	City	State	Zip	Toll-Free	Phone
Abatix Corp 8201 Eastpoint Dr Suite 500 *NASDAQ: ABIX*	Dallas	TX	75227	800-426-3983	214-381-1146
Accurate Air Engineering Inc 2712 N Alameda St	Compton	CA	90224	800-438-5577	310-537-1350
ACG Direct 14660 23-Mile Rd	Shelby Township	MI	48315	800-968-7101	586-247-7100
AIM Supply Co 7337 Bryan Dairy Rd	Largo	FL	33777	800-999-0125	
Aimco 10000 SE Pine St	Portland	OR	97216	800-852-1368	503-255-7364
Alamo Iron Works Inc 943 SBC Center Pkwy *Cust Svc	San Antonio	TX	78219	800-292-7817*	210-223-6161
Ames Supply Co 1936 University Ln	Lisle	IL	60532	800-323-3856	630-964-2440
Berendsen Fluid Power 401 S Boston Ave 1200 Mid Continent Tower	Tulsa	OK	74103	800-360-2327	918-592-3781
Berk O Co 3 Milltown Ct	Union	NJ	07083	800-631-7392	908-851-9500
Brake Supply Co Inc 1300 W Lloyd Expy	Evansville	IN	47708	800-457-5788	812-467-1000
Briggs Equipment 2777 Stemmons Fwy Suite 1525	Dallas	TX	75207	800-606-1833	214-630-0808
C & H Distributors LLC 770 S 70th St *Sales	Milwaukee	WI	53214	800-558-9966*	414-443-1700
Canadian Bearings Ltd 1401 Courtney Park Dr E	Mississauga	ON	L5T2E4	800-229-2327	905-670-6700
Carlson Systems LLC PO Box 3036	Omaha	NE	68103	800-325-8343	402-593-5300
Cascade Machinery & Electric Inc PO Box 3575	Seattle	WA	98124	800-289-0500	206-762-0500
Connell Gatco Co 1 Connell Dr	Berkeley Heights	NJ	07922	800-233-3240	908-673-3700
Davis Wink Equipment Co Inc 4938 S Atlanta Rd Suite 800	Atlanta	GA	30080	800-341-5459	404-266-2290
Detroit Pump & Mfg Co 18943 John R St	Detroit	MI	48203	800-686-1662	313-893-4242
DoALL Co 254 N Laurel Ave	Des Plaines	IL	60016	800-955-8191	847-824-8191
Duncan Equipment Co Inc 3450 S MacArthur Blvd	Oklahoma City	OK	73179	800-375-5216	405-688-2300
Eastern Lift Truck Co Inc PO Box 307	Maple Shade	NJ	08052	888-779-8880	856-779-8880
Ellison Machine Co Inc 9912 S Pioneer Blvd	Santa Fe Springs	CA	90670	800-358-4828	562-949-8311
Engman-Taylor Co Inc W142 N9351 Fountain Blvd	Menomonee Falls	WI	53051	800-236-1975	
Enovation Graphic Systems Inc 200 Summit Lake Dr	Valhalla	NY	10595	800-755-3854	914-749-4800
Fairmont Supply Co 401 Technology Dr	Canonsburg	PA	15317	800-245-9900	724-514-3900
FCx Performance Inc 3000 E 14th Ave	Columbus	OH	43219	800-253-6223	614-253-1996
FD Stella Products Co 7000 Fenkell St	Detroit	MI	48238	800-447-7356	313-341-6400
Forklifts of Minnesota Inc 501 W 78th St	Bloomington	MN	55420	800-752-4300	952-887-5400
FW Webb 237 Albany St	Boston	MA	02118	800-453-1100	617-227-2240
Gas Equipment Supply Co Inc 1440 Lakes Pkwy Suite 300	Lawrenceville	GA	30043	800-241-4155	770-995-1131
General Tool & Supply Co Inc 2705 NW Nicolai St	Portland	OR	97210	800-783-3411	503-226-3411
Goodall Rubber Co 790 Birney Hwy Suite 100	Aston	PA	19014	800-562-8002	610-361-0800
Gosiger Inc 108 McDonough St	Dayton	OH	45402	800-888-4188	937-228-5174
Grady W Jones Co 3965 Old Getwell Rd	Memphis	TN	38118	800-727-5118	901-365-8830
Hackett J Lee Co 23550 Haggerty Rd	Farmington Hills	MI	48335	800-422-5388	248-478-0200
Haggard & Stocking Industrial Supplies 5318 Victory Dr	Indianapolis	IN	46203	800-622-4824	317-788-4661
Hahn Systems Co Inc 2401 Production Dr	Indianapolis	IN	46241	800-589-3796	317-243-3796
Hanover Compressor Co 8150 N Central Expy Suite 1550 *NYSE: HC* ■ *Sales	Dallas	TX	75206	800-522-9270*	214-528-9270
Harrington Industrial Plastics LLC 14480 Yorba Ave	Chino	CA	91710	800-669-8641	909-597-8641
Herc-U-Lift Inc 5655 Hwy 12 W	Maple Plain	MN	55359	800-362-3500	763-479-2501
Holox Ltd 1500C Indian Trail Rd	Norcross	GA	30093	800-554-8306	770-925-4640
Hub Supply Inc 2546 S Leonine St	Wichita	KS	67217	800-482-8665	316-265-9608
Hughes RS Co Inc 10639 Glenoaks Blvd	Pacoima	CA	91331	877-774-8443	818-686-9111
Hull Lift Truck Inc 28747 Old US 33 W	Elkhart	IN	46516	800-860-4855	574-293-8651
IBT Inc 9400 W 55th St	Merriam	KS	66203	800-332-2114	913-677-3151
Illinois Auto Electric Co 700 Enterprise St	Aurora	IL	60504	800-683-9312	630-862-3300
Indusco Group 1200 W Hamburg St	Baltimore	MD	21230	800-727-0665	410-727-0665
Industrial Services of America Inc 7100 Grade Ln *NASDAQ: IDSA*	Louisville	KY	40213	800-824-2144	502-368-1661
Industrial Supply Solutions Inc 520 Elizabeth St	Charleston	WV	25311	800-346-5341	304-346-5341
Industrial Truck Sales & Service Inc 4100 Randleman Rd	Greensboro	NC	27401	800-632-0333	336-275-9121
J Lee Hackett Co 23550 Haggerty Rd	Farmington Hills	MI	48335	800-422-5388	248-478-0200
Jabo Supply Corp 5164 Braley St	Huntington	WV	25705	800-334-5226	304-736-8333
Jefferds Corp US Rt 35 W PO Box 757	Saint Albans	WV	25177	800-735-8111	304-755-8111
JLK Direct Distribution Inc 31800 Industrial Rd	Livonia	MI	48150	800-645-6878	734-458-7000
Jones Grady W Co 3965 Old Getwell Rd	Memphis	TN	38118	800-727-5118	901-365-8830
Kaman Industrial Technologies Inc 1 Waterside Crossing	Windsor	CT	06095	800-526-2626	860-687-5000
Kennametal Inc 1600 Technology Way *NYSE: KMT* ■ *Cust Svc	Latrobe	PA	15650	800-446-7738*	724-539-5000
Kimball Midwest 582 W Goodale St	Columbus	OH	43215	800-233-1294	614-228-6701
Kinecor 451 Lebeau Blvd	Saint-Laurent	QC	H4N1S2	866-546-3267	514-333-7010
L & H Technologies Inc 11616 Wilmar Blvd	Charlotte	NC	28273	800-753-4576	704-588-3670
Lawson Products Inc 1666 E Touhy Ave *NASDAQ: LAWS*	Des Plaines	IL	60018	800-718-1221	847-827-9666
Lewis-Goetz & Co Inc 650 Washington Rd Suite 210	Pittsburgh	PA	15228	800-289-1236	412-787-4154
Lister-Petter Inc 815 E 56 Hwy	Olathe	KS	66061	800-888-3512	913-764-3512
Logan Corp 555 7th Ave	Huntington	WV	25706	888-853-4751	304-526-4700
Mac-Gray Corp 22 Water St *NYSE: TUC*	Cambridge	MA	02141	800-622-4729	617-492-4040
Martin Supply Co 200 Appleton Ave	Sheffield	AL	35660	800-828-8116	
McJunkin Corp 835 Hillcrest Dr E	Charleston	WV	25311	800-624-8603	304-348-5211
Medart Inc 126 Manufacturers Dr	Arnold	MO	63010	800-888-7181	636-282-2300
MEE Material Handling Equipment 11721 W Carmen Ave	Milwaukee	WI	53225	800-992-0292	414-353-3300
Minnesota Supply Co Inc 6470 Flying Cloud Dr	Eden Prairie	MN	55344	800-869-1058	952-828-7300
Modern Group Ltd 2501 Durham Rd	Bristol	PA	19007	800-223-3827	215-943-9100
Morris Robert E Co Inc 17 Talcott Notch Rd	Farmington	CT	06032	800-223-0785	860-678-0200
Motion Industries Inc 1605 Alton Rd	Birmingham	AL	35210	800-526-9328	205-956-1122
MSC Industrial Direct Co 75 Maxess Rd *NYSE: MSM*	Melville	NY	11747	800-645-7270	516-812-2000
Multiquip Inc 18910 Wilmington Ave	Carson	CA	90746	800-421-1244	310-537-3700
National Waterworks Inc 200 W Hwy 6 Suite 620	Waco	TX	76712	800-817-5355	254-772-5355
National Welders Supply Co Inc 810 Gesco St	Charlotte	NC	28208	800-866-4422	704-333-5475
NC Machinery Co 17035 W Valley Hwy	Tukwila	WA	98188	800-562-4735	425-251-9800
Nebraska Machinery Co Inc PO Box 809	North Platte	NE	69103	800-494-9560	308-532-3100
Nelson-Jameson Inc 2400 E 5th St	Marshfield	WI	54449	800-826-8302	715-387-1151

Company / Address	City	State	ZIP	Toll-Free	Phone
Newman's Inc 1300 Gazin St	Houston	TX	77020	**800-231-3505**	713-675-8631
NSC International 7090 Central Ave	Hot Springs	AR	71913	**800-643-1520**	501-525-0133
O Berk Co 3 Milltown Ct	Union	NJ	07083	**800-631-7392**	908-851-9500
Ohio Transmission & Pump Co 1900 Jetway Blvd	Columbus	OH	43219	**800-837-6827**	614-342-6123
Pabco Fluid Power Co Inc 5750 Hillside Ave	Cincinnati	OH	45233	**800-727-2226**	513-941-6200
Pacific Detroit Diesel Allison 600 S 56th Pl	Ridgefield	WA	98642	**800-882-3860**	360-887-7400
Phenix Supply Co 5330 Dividend Dr	Decatur	GA	30035	**800-688-3032**	770-981-2800
Precision Industries Inc 4611 S 96th St	Omaha	NE	68127	**800-373-7777**	402-593-7000
Proctor Stanley Co 2016 Midway Dr	Twinsburg	OH	44087	**800-352-0123**	330-425-7814
Production Tool Supply 8655 E Eight Mile Rd	Warren	MI	48089	**800-366-3600**	586-755-7770
R & M Energy Systems PO Box 2871 *Sales	Borger	TX	79008	**800-858-4158***	806-274-5293
Rem Sales Inc 34 Bradley Park Rd	East Granby	CT	06026	**800-808-1020**	860-653-0071
Rex Supply Co 3715 Harrisburg Blvd	Houston	TX	77003	**800-369-0669**	713-222-2251
Robert E Morris Co Inc 17 Talcott Notch Rd	Farmington	CT	06032	**800-223-0785**	860-678-0200
RS Hughes Co Inc 10639 Glenoaks Blvd	Pacoima	CA	91331	**877-774-8443**	818-686-9111
Ryan Herco Products Corp 3010 N San Fernando Blvd	Burbank	CA	91504	**800-848-1141**	818-841-1141
Sheplar's 9103 E Almeda Rd	Houston	TX	77054	**800-729-1150**	713-799-1150
Sooner Pipe Inc 1331 Lamar St 4 Houston Ctr Suite 970	Houston	TX	77010	**800-888-9161**	713-759-1200
Southern Pump & Tank Co 4800 N Graham St *Cust Svc	Charlotte	NC	28269	**800-477-2826***	704-596-4373
Stanley M Proctor Co 2016 Midway Dr	Twinsburg	OH	44087	**800-352-0123**	330-425-7814
Stella FD Products Co 7000 Fenkell St	Detroit	MI	48238	**800-447-7356**	313-341-6400
Stewart & Stevenson Services Inc 2707 North Loop W *NYSE: SVC*	Houston	TX	77008	**800-527-3246**	713-868-7700
Tate Engineering Systems Inc 1560 Caton Ctr Dr	Baltimore	MD	21227	**800-800-8283**	410-242-8800
Texas Process Equipment Co 5880 Bingle Rd	Houston	TX	77092	**800-828-4114**	713-460-5555
Travers Tool Co Inc 128-15 26th Ave *Cust Svc	Flushing	NY	11354	**800-221-0270***	718-886-7200
Valley Welders Supply 320 N 11th St	Billings	MT	59101	**800-821-9470**	406-256-3330
Vellano Brothers Inc 7 Hemlock St	Latham	NY	12110	**800-342-9855**	518-785-5537
Voto Manufacturers Sales Co 500 N 3rd St	Steubenville	OH	43952	**800-848-4010**	740-282-3621
Webb FW 237 Albany St	Boston	MA	02118	**800-453-1100**	617-227-2240
Werres Corp 807 E South St	Frederick	MD	21701	**800-638-6563**	301-620-4000
Wilson Supply Co PO Box 1492	Houston	TX	77251	**800-228-2893**	713-237-3700
Windsor Factory Supply Ltd 730 N Service Rd	Windsor	ON	N8X3J3	**800-387-2659**	519-966-2202
Wink Davis Equipment Co Inc 4938 S Atlanta Rd Suite 800	Atlanta	GA	30080	**800-341-5459**	404-266-2290
Zuckerman-Honickman Inc 191 S Gulph Rd	King of Prussia	PA	19406	**800-523-1475**	610-962-0100

379 INDUSTRIAL MACHINERY & EQUIPMENT (MISC) - MFR

SEE ALSO Conveyors & Conveying Equipment; Food Products Machinery; Furnaces & Ovens - Industrial Process; Machine Shops; Material Handling Equipment; Packaging Machinery & Equipment; Paper Industries Machinery; Printing & Publishing Equipment & Systems; Rolling Mill Machinery; Textile Machinery; Woodworking Machinery

Company / Address	City	State	ZIP	Toll-Free	Phone
ABB Inc 501 Merritt 7 *Prod Info	Norwalk	CT	06851	**800-626-4999***	203-750-2200
Allen-Sherman-Hoff Co 185 Great Valley Pkwy	Malvern	PA	19355	**888-274-7278**	610-647-9900
Allentown Equipment 421 Schantz Rd	Allentown	PA	18104	**800-553-3414**	610-398-0451
American Baler Co 800 E Centre St	Bellevue	OH	44811	**800-843-7512**	419-483-5790
AO Smith Water Products Co 500 Lindahl Pkwy	Ashland City	TN	37015	**800-365-8170**	615-792-4371
Assembly Technology & Test 12841 Stark Rd	Livonia	MI	48150	**800-373-8634**	734-522-9680
Besser Co 801 Johnson St	Alpena	MI	49707	**800-530-9980**	989-354-4111
Besser Lithibar Co 13521 Quality Dr	Holland	MI	49424	**800-626-0415**	616-399-5215
Central Sprinkler Corp 451 N Cannon Ave	Lansdale	PA	19446	**800-523-6512**	215-362-0700
Charles Ross & Son Co 710 Old Willets Path	Hauppauge	NY	11788	**800-243-7677**	631-234-0500
Chemineer Inc 5870 Poe Ave	Dayton	OH	45414	**800-643-0641**	937-454-3200
Chief Automotive Systems Inc 1924 E 4th St	Grand Island	NE	68801	**800-445-9262**	308-384-9747
CUNO Inc 400 Research Pkwy *NASDAQ: CUNO*	Meriden	CT	06450	**800-243-6894**	203-237-5541
Diamond Power International Inc 2600 E Main St	Lancaster	OH	43130	**800-848-5086**	740-687-6500
Dorr-Oliver Eimco USA Inc 2850 S Becker Lake Dr	Salt Lake City	UT	84119	**800-257-0552**	801-526-2000
Engis Corp 105 W Hintz Rd	Wheeling	IL	60090	**800-993-6447**	847-808-9400
FANUC Robotics North America Inc 3900 W Hamlin Rd	Rochester Hills	MI	48309	**800-477-6268**	248-377-7000
Fluid Management Inc 1023 S Wheeling Rd	Wheeling	IL	60090	**800-462-2466**	847-537-0880
Forward Technology Industries Inc 3050 Ranchview Ln N *Cust Svc	Minneapolis	MN	55447	**800-307-6040***	763-559-1785
Fusion Inc 4658 E 355th St	Willoughby	OH	44094	**800-626-9501**	440-946-3300
Galbreath Inc 461 E Rosser Dr	Winamac	IN	46996	**800-285-0666**	574-946-6631
Gamajet Cleaning Systems Inc PO Box 626 *Sales	Devault	PA	19432	**800-289-5387***	610-408-9940
GEA Niro Inc 9165 Rumsey Rd	Columbia	MD	21045	**800-446-4231**	410-997-8700
General Equipment Co PO Box 334 *Cust Svc	Owatonna	MN	55060	**800-533-0524***	507-451-5510
George Koch Sons LLC 10 S 11th Ave	Evansville	IN	47744	**888-873-5624**	812-465-9600
Gougler Industries Inc 705 Lake St	Kent	OH	44240	**800-527-2282**	330-673-5821
Graham Corp 20 Florence Ave *AMEX: GHM* ■ *Orders	Batavia	NY	14020	**800-828-8150***	585-343-2216
Hamon Research-Cottrell Inc 58 E Main St	Somerville	NJ	08876	**800-722-3048**	908-685-4000
Hosokawa Polymer Systems 63 Fuller Way	Berlin	CT	06037	**800-233-6112**	860-828-0541
Illinois Tool Works Inc (ITW) 3600 W Lake Ave *NYSE: ITW*	Glenview	IL	60025	**800-724-6166**	847-724-7500
ITW (Illinois Tool Works Inc) 3600 W Lake Ave *NYSE: ITW*	Glenview	IL	60025	**800-724-6166**	847-724-7500
Johnson Corp 805 Wood St	Three Rivers	MI	49093	**800-657-5940**	269-278-1715
KJ Brewco Collision Repair Systems Inc 309 Exchange Ave	Conway	AR	72032	**800-582-5215**	501-505-2794
Koch George Sons LLC 10 S 11th Ave	Evansville	IN	47744	**888-873-5624**	812-465-9600
Koch Membrane Systems Inc 850 Main St	Wilmington	MA	01887	**800-343-0499**	978-694-7000
Komline-Sanderson Engineering Corp 12 Holland Ave	Peapack	NJ	07977	**800-225-5457**	908-234-1000
Littleford Day Inc 7451 Empire Dr	Florence	KY	41042	**800-365-8555**	859-525-7600
Lubriquip Inc 18901 Cranwood Pkwy	Cleveland	OH	44128	**800-872-5823**	216-581-2000
Lynch Systems Inc 601 Independent St	Bainbridge	GA	39817	**800-428-6333**	229-248-2345
Marathon Equipment Co 909 County Hwy 9 S PO Box 1798	Vernon	AL	35592	**800-269-7237**	205-695-9105
McNeil & NRM Inc 96 E Crosier St	Akron	OH	44311	**800-669-2525**	330-253-2525
MEGTEC Systems Co 830 Prosper Rd *Cust Svc	De Pere	WI	54115	**800-558-5535***	920-336-5715
Met-Pro Corp PO Box 144 *NYSE: MPR*	Harleysville	PA	19438	**800-722-3267**	215-723-6751
Minuteman International Inc 111 S Rohlwing Rd	Addison	IL	60101	**800-323-9420**	630-627-6900
Mueller Paul Co 1600 W Phelps St *NASDAQ: MUEL*	Springfield	MO	65802	**800-641-2830**	417-831-3000
Mueller Steam Specialty 1491 NC Hwy 20 W	Saint Pauls	NC	28384	**800-334-6259**	910-865-8241
National Super Service Co Inc 3115 Frenchman Rd *Cust Svc	Toledo	OH	43607	**800-677-1663***	419-531-2121
Nilfisk-Advance Group 14600 21st Ave N *Cust Svc	Plymouth	MN	55447	**800-989-2235***	763-745-3500
Nordson Corp 28601 Clemens Rd *NASDAQ: NDSN*	Westlake	OH	44145	**800-321-2881**	440-892-1500
Norwood Kingsley Machine Co 2538 Wisconsin Ave	Downers Grove	IL	60515	**800-421-0995**	630-968-0647
Pall Corp 2200 Northern Blvd *NYSE: PLL*	East Hills	NY	11548	**800-645-6532**	516-484-5400
Park Industries Inc 6600 Saukview Dr	Saint Cloud	MN	56303	**800-328-2309**	320-251-5077
Paul Mueller Co 1600 W Phelps St *NASDAQ: MUEL*	Springfield	MO	65802	**800-641-2830**	417-831-3000
PDQ Mfg Inc 1698 Scheuring Rd	De Pere	WI	54115	**800-227-3373**	920-983-8333
Peterson Machine Tool Inc 5425 Antioch Dr	Merriam	KS	66202	**800-255-6308**	913-432-7500
Pioneer/Eclipse Corp 1 Eclipse Rd *Cust Svc	Sparta	NC	28675	**800-367-3550***	336-372-8080
Porter International 388 Newburyport Tpke	Rowley	MA	01969	**800-343-8138**	978-922-2611
PTI Technologies Inc 501 Del Norte Blvd	Oxnard	CA	93030	**800-331-2701**	805-604-3700
Pullman/Holt Corp 10702 N 46th St	Tampa	FL	33617	**800-237-7582**	813-971-2223
Quipp Inc 4800 NW 157th St *NASDAQ: QUIP*	Miami	FL	33014	**800-345-9680**	305-623-8700
Randell Mfg Inc 520 S Coldwater Rd	Weidman	MI	48893	**800-621-8560**	989-644-3331
Ransco Industries 1801 Solar Dr Suite 190	Oxnard	CA	93030	**800-828-9903**	805-981-1518
Rotary Lift 2700 Lanier Dr	Madison	IN	47250	**800-640-5438**	812-273-1622
RPA Process Technologies 9151 Shaver Rd	Portage	MI	49024	**800-525-4214**	269-323-1313
RTS Wright Industries LLC PO Box 17914	Nashville	TN	37217	**800-782-4202**	615-361-6600
Schutte & Koerting LLC 2233 State Rd	Bensalem	PA	19020	**800-752-8558**	215-639-0900
Smith AO Water Products Co 500 Lindahl Pkwy	Ashland City	TN	37015	**800-365-8170**	615-792-4371
SPX Process Equipment 611 Sugar Creek Rd	Delavan	WI	53115	**800-252-5200**	262-728-1900
Sterling Production Control Units 2280 W Dorothy Ln	Dayton	OH	45439	**800-968-7728**	937-299-5594
Stewart & Stevenson Services Inc Power Products Div 5840 Dahlia St	Commerce City	CO	80022	**800-727-7441**	303-287-7441
Super Products Corp 17000 W Cleveland Ave	New Berlin	WI	53151	**800-837-9711**	262-784-7100
Synventive Molding Solutions Inc 10 Centennial Dr	Peabody	MA	01960	**800-367-5662**	978-750-8065
Talley Defense Systems Inc 4153 N Higley Rd	Mesa	AZ	85277	**800-444-8837**	480-898-2200
Tennant Co 701 N Lilac Dr *NYSE: TNC* ■ *Cust Svc	Minneapolis	MN	55422	**800-553-8033***	763-540-1200
Thomas Engineering Inc 575 W Central Rd	Hoffman Estates	IL	60195	**800-634-9910**	847-358-5800
Timesavers Inc 11123 89th Ave N	Maple Grove	MN	55369	**800-537-3611**	763-488-6600
United Silicone Inc 4471 Walden Ave	Lancaster	NY	14086	**800-365-8222**	716-681-8222
USM Corp 32 Stevens St	Haverhill	MA	01830	**800-343-0772**	978-374-0303
Vacudyne Inc 375 E Joe Orr Rd	Chicago Heights	IL	60411	**800-459-9591**	708-757-5200
Van Air Systems Inc 2950 Mechanic St	Lake City	PA	16423	**800-840-9906**	814-774-2631
Videojet Technologies Inc 1500 Mittel Blvd *Cust Svc	Wood Dale	IL	60191	**800-843-3610***	630-860-7300
Windsor Industries Inc 1351 W Stanford Ave	Englewood	CO	80110	**800-444-7654**	303-762-1800

380 INFORMATION RETRIEVAL SERVICES (GENERAL)

SEE ALSO Investigative Services

Company / Address	City	State	ZIP	Toll-Free	Phone
Amigos Library Services 14400 Midway Rd	Dallas	TX	75244	**800-843-8482**	972-851-8000
Burrelle's/Luce LLC 75 E Northfield Rd	Livingston	NJ	07039	**800-631-1160**	973-992-6600
Cal Info 316 W 2nd St Suite 1102	Los Angeles	CA	90012	**877-687-8710**	213-687-8710
Chemical Abstracts Service (CAS) PO Box 3012	Columbus	OH	43210	**800-848-6538**	614-447-3600
ClariNet Communications Corp 4880 Stevens Creek Blvd Suite 206 *Sales	San Jose	CA	95129	**800-873-6387***	408-296-0366
CompetitivEdge 196 S Main St	Colchester	CT	06415	**888-881-3343**	860-537-6731
Data Transmission Network Corp 9110 W Dodge Rd Suite 200	Omaha	NE	68114	**800-485-4000**	402-390-2328
DataWorld Inc 7700 Old Georgetown Rd Bldg 2 Box 1	Bethesda	MD	20814	**800-368-5754**	301-652-8822
Dialog Corp 11000 Regency Pkwy Suite 10	Cary	NC	27511	**800-334-2564**	919-462-8600
Environmental Data Resources Inc 3530 Post Rd	Southport	CT	06890	**800-352-0050**	203-255-6606
FIND/SVP Inc 625 Ave of the Americas 2nd Fl *Cust Svc	New York	NY	10011	**800-346-3688***	212-645-4500
FRANdata Corp 1725 'I' St NW Suite 600	Washington	DC	20006	**800-485-9570**	202-336-7632
Infotrieve Inc 10850 Wilshire Blvd 8th Fl	Los Angeles	CA	90024	**800-422-4633**	310-234-2000
infoUSA Inc 5711 S 86th Cir *NASDAQ: IUSA*	Omaha	NE	68127	**800-321-0869**	402-593-4500
Insurance Reference Systems Inc DBA SilverPlume 4775 Walnut St Suite 2-B	Boulder	CO	80301	**800-677-4442**	303-444-0695
LexisNexis Group 9443 Springboro Pike	Miamisburg	OH	45342	**800-227-9597**	937-865-6800

Company	City	State	ZIP	Toll-Free	Phone
LexisNexis Martindale-Hubbell 121 Chanlon Rd	New Providence	NJ	07974	**800-526-4902**	908-464-6800
Marshall & Swift/Boeckh 2885 S Calhoun Rd	New Berlin	WI	53151	**800-285-1288**	262-780-2800
National Technical Information Service (NTIS) 5285 Port Royal Rd *Orders	Springfield	VA	22161	**800-553-6847***	703-605-6000
Newsbank Inc 5020 Tamiami Trail N Suite 110 *Cust Svc	Naples	FL	34103	**800-243-7694***	239-263-6004
Ovid Technologies Inc 333 7th Ave 4th Fl	New York	NY	10001	**800-950-2035**	646-674-6300
ProQuest Information & Learning Co 300 N Zeeb Rd	Ann Arbor	MI	48106	**800-521-0600**	734-761-4700
Questia Media America Inc 24 Greenway Plaza Suite 450	Houston	TX	77046	**888-950-2580**	713-358-2500
Regional Information & Communication Exchange Rice University Library 6100 S Main St MS 240	Houston	TX	77005	**800-359-7030**	713-348-3553
Research on Demand Inc PO Box 479	Santa Barbara	CA	93102	**800-227-0750**	805-963-4095
SilverPlume 4775 Walnut St Suite 2-B	Boulder	CO	80301	**800-677-4442**	303-444-0695
Sopheon Corp 2850 Metro Dr Suite 600	Minneapolis	MN	55425	**800-367-8358**	952-851-7581
Thomson Financial 22 Thomson Pl	Boston	MA	02210	**888-837-4636**	617-345-2000
West Group PO Box 64526 *Cust Svc	Saint Paul	MN	55164	**800-328-4880***	651-687-7000

381 INK

Company	City	State	ZIP	Toll-Free	Phone
3M Commercial Graphics Div 3M General Offices Bldg 220-6W-06	Saint Paul	MN	55144	**800-328-3908**	
AJ Daw Printing Ink Co 3559 Greenwood Ave	Los Angeles	CA	90040	**800-432-9465**	323-723-3253
ANI Printing Inks 15500 28th Ave N	Plymouth	MN	55447	**800-328-7838**	763-559-5911
BASF Corp 3000 Continental Dr N *NYSE: BF*	Mount Olive	NJ	07828	**800-526-1072**	973-426-2600
Bomark Inks Inc 601 S 6th Ave	City of Industry	CA	91746	**800-323-5174**	626-968-1666
Braden Sutphin Ink Co 3650 E 93rd St	Cleveland	OH	44105	**800-289-6872**	216-271-2300
Central Ink Corp 1100 N Harvester Rd	West Chicago	IL	60185	**800-345-2541**	630-231-6500
Coates Screen Inc 631 Central Ave	East Rutherford	NJ	07073	**800-999-4657**	201-933-6100
Color Converting Industries Co 3535 SW 56th St	Des Moines	IA	50321	**800-728-8200**	515-471-2100
Color Resolutions International 575 Quality Blvd	Fairfield	OH	45014	**800-346-8570**	513-552-7200
Daw AJ Printing Ink Co 3559 Greenwood Ave	Los Angeles	CA	90040	**800-432-9465**	323-723-3253
DuPont EI de Nemours & Co Inc 1007 Market St *NYSE: DD*	Wilmington	DE	19898	**800-441-7515**	302-774-1000
EI DuPont de Nemours & Co Inc 1007 Market St *NYSE: DD*	Wilmington	DE	19898	**800-441-7515**	302-774-1000
Formulabs Inc 529 W 4th Ave	Escondido	CA	92025	**800-642-2345**	760-741-2345
Gans Ink & Supply Co Inc 1441 Boyd St	Los Angeles	CA	90033	**800-372-7410**	323-264-2200
Graphic Sciences Inc 7515 NE Ambassador Pl Suite L	Portland	OR	97220	**888-546-4465**	503-460-0203
Independent Ink Inc 13700 S Gramercy Pl	Gardena	CA	90249	**800-446-5538**	310-523-4657
International Coatings Co 13929 E 166th St	Cerritos	CA	90702	**800-423-4103**	562-926-1010
INX International Ink Co 651 Bonnie Ln	Elk Grove Village	IL	60007	**800-631-7956**	847-981-9399
Keystone Printing Ink Co 2700 Roberts Ave	Philadelphia	PA	19129	**800-523-0111**	215-228-8100
Kohl & Madden Printing Ink Corp 651 Garden St	Carlstadt	NJ	07072	**800-793-0022**	201-886-1203
Kramer Ink Co Inc 9900 Jordan Cir	Santa Fe Springs	CA	90670	**800-543-8792**	562-946-8847
Miller-Cooper Co 5187 Merriam Dr	Merriam	KS	66203	**800-289-6246**	913-312-5020
Nazdar 8501 Hedge Lane Terr	Shawnee	KS	66227	**800-767-9942**	913-422-1888
Nor-Cote International Inc 506 Lafayette Ave	Crawfordsville	IN	47933	**800-488-9180**	765-362-9180
Sensient Technologies Corp 777 E Wisconsin Ave 11th Fl *NYSE: SXT*	Milwaukee	WI	53202	**800-558-9892**	414-271-6755
Sericol Inc 1101 W Cambridge Dr	Kansas City	KS	66103	**800-737-4265**	913-342-4060
Spectrachem Corp 10 Dell Glen Ave Suite 3A	Lodi	NJ	07644	**800-524-2806**	973-253-3553
Toyo Ink America LLC 710 W Belden	Addison	IL	60101	**800-227-8696**	630-930-5100
US Ink Corp 651 Garden St	Carlstadt	NJ	07072	**800-423-8838**	201-935-8666
Van Son Holland Ink Corp of America 185 Oval Dr	Islandia	NY	11749	**800-645-4182**	

382 INSULATION & ACOUSTICAL PRODUCTS

Company	City	State	ZIP	Toll-Free	Phone
Acoustic Systems Inc 415 E St Elmo Rd	Austin	TX	78745	**800-749-1460**	512-444-1961
Anco Products Inc 2500 S 17th St	Elkhart	IN	46517	**800-837-2626**	574-293-5574
Applegate Insulation Mfg Inc 1000 Highview Dr	Webberville	MI	48892	**800-627-7536**	517-521-3545
CertainTeed Corp 750 E Swedesford Rd *Prod Info	Valley Forge	PA	19482	**800-782-8777***	610-341-7000
Claremont Co Inc 35 Winsome Dr PO Box 430	Durham	CT	06422	**800-222-4448**	860-349-4499
Dryvit Systems Inc 1 Energy Way	West Warwick	RI	02893	**800-556-7752**	401-822-4100
Fibrex Insulations Inc 561 Scott Rd PO Box 2079 *Cust Svc	Sarnia	ON	N7T7L4	**800-265-7514***	519-336-7770
Firstline Corp 511 Highland Ave	Valdosta	GA	31603	**800-243-2451**	229-247-1717
Interface Solutions Inc 216 Wohlsen Way	Lancaster	PA	17603	**800-942-7538**	717-207-6000
Isolatek International Inc 41 Furnace St	Stanhope	NJ	07874	**800-631-9600**	973-347-1200
ITW Insulation Systems 919 N Trenton St	Ruston	LA	71270	**800-551-4866**	318-251-2920
Johns Manville Corp PO Box 5108 *Prod Info	Denver	CO	80217	**800-654-3103***	303-978-2000
Knauf Insulation 1 Knauf Dr	Shelbyville	IN	46176	**800-825-4434**	317-398-4434
Nu-Wool Co Inc 2472 Port Sheldon St	Jenison	MI	49428	**800-748-0128**	616-669-0100
Pittsburgh Corning Corp 800 Presque Isle Dr	Pittsburgh	PA	15239	**800-245-1217**	724-327-6100
Rock Wool Mfg Co PO Box 506 *Sales	Leeds	AL	35094	**800-874-7625***	205-699-6121
Saint-Gobain Corp 750 E Swedesford Rd	Valley Forge	PA	19482	**800-274-8530**	610-341-7000
Scott Industries Inc PO Box 7	Henderson	KY	42419	**800-951-9276**	270-831-2037
Thermafiber Inc 3711 W Mill St	Wabash	IN	46992	**888-834-2371**	260-563-2111
Thermoguard Insulation Co N 125 Dyer Rd	Spokane	WA	99212	**800-541-0579**	509-535-4600
Thermwell Products Co 420 Rt 17 S	Mahwah	NJ	07430	**800-526-5265**	201-684-4400
TIGHITCO Inc 2300 Marietta Blvd NW	Atlanta	GA	30318	**800-223-1205**	404-355-1205
USG Interiors Inc 125 S Franklin St	Chicago	IL	60606	**800-621-9622**	312-606-4000

383 INSURANCE AGENTS, BROKERS, SERVICES

Company	City	State	ZIP	Toll-Free	Phone
ABD Insurance & Financial Services 305 Walnut St	Redwood City	CA	94063	**800-542-7676**	650-839-6000
Acordia Inc 150 N Michigan Ave Suite 4100	Chicago	IL	60601	**866-226-7342**	312-423-2500
Allied North America 390 N Broadway	Jericho	NY	11753	**800-861-9452**	516-733-9200
Anco Insurance Managers Inc 1733 Briarcrest Dr	Bryan	TX	77802	**800-749-1733**	979-776-2626
Andreini & Co 220 W 20th Ave	San Mateo	CA	94403	**800-969-2522**	650-573-1111
Aon Risk Services Inc 200 E Randolph St	Chicago	IL	60601	**800-432-3672**	312-381-4000
Associated Agencies Inc 1701 Golf Rd Tower 3 Suite 700	Rolling Meadows	IL	60008	**800-443-2827**	847-427-8400
Automobile Protection Corp 6010 Atlantic Blvd	Norcross	GA	30071	**800-458-7071**	770-394-6610
BB & T Insurance Services Inc 3605 Glenwood Ave	Raleigh	NC	27612	**800-821-1284**	919-716-9777
Berwanger Overmyer Assoc 2245 Northbank Dr	Columbus	OH	43220	**800-837-0503**	614-457-7000
BGS & G Cos 44 Baltimore St *Cust Svc	Cumberland	MD	21502	**800-684-2474***	301-784-2410
Bollinger Insurance 101 JFK Pkwy	Short Hills	NJ	07078	**800-526-1379**	973-467-0444
Bolton & Co 245 S Los Robles Ave Suite 105	Pasadena	CA	91101	**888-700-1444**	626-799-7000
Brown & Brown Inc 220 S Ridgewood Ave *NYSE: BRO*	Daytona Beach	FL	32114	**800-877-2769**	386-252-9601
Burnham John Insurance Services PO Box 85802	San Diego	CA	92186	**800-421-6744**	619-231-1010
Cal-Surance Associates Inc 681 S Parker St Suite 200	Orange	CA	92868	**800-762-7800**	714-939-0800
Calco Insurance Brokers & Agents Inc 2000 Alameda de las Pulgas	San Mateo	CA	94403	**800-800-8290**	650-295-4600
Cameron M Harris & Co 6400 Fairview Rd	Charlotte	NC	28210	**800-868-8834**	704-366-8834
CBCI Inc 4150 International Plaza Suite 800	Fort Worth	TX	76109	**800-759-0101**	817-737-1700
Charles L Crane Agency Co 100 S 4th St Suite 800	Saint Louis	MO	63102	**800-363-9827**	314-241-8700
Clair Odell Group 2 W Lafayette St Suite 400	Norristown	PA	19401	**800-220-3008**	610-825-5555
Commerce National Insurance Services Inc 1701 Rt 70 E Commerce Atrium	Cherry Hill	NJ	08034	**888-751-9000**	856-489-7000
Crane Charles L Agency Co 100 S 4th St Suite 800	Saint Louis	MO	63102	**800-363-9827**	314-241-8700
Crawford & Co 5620 Glenridge Dr NE *NYSE: CRDa*	Atlanta	GA	30342	**800-241-2541**	404-256-0830
Crystal Frank & Co Inc 40 Broad St 15th Fl	New York	NY	10004	**800-221-5830**	212-344-2444
Dann Insurance 1500 S Lakeside Dr	Bannockburn	IL	60015	**800-323-0371**	847-444-1060
Davis J Rolfe Insurance Agency Inc 850 Concourse Pkwy S Suite 200	Maitland	FL	32751	**800-896-0554**	407-691-9600
DavisBaldwin Inc 4600 W Cypress St 2nd Fl	Tampa	FL	33607	**800-282-0467**	813-287-1936
Eastern Insurance Agency Inc 233 W Central St	Natick	MA	01760	**800-333-7234**	508-651-7700
Esurance Inc 747 Front St 4th Fl	San Francisco	CA	94111	**800-926-6012**	415-875-4500
Frank Crystal & Co Inc 40 Broad St 15th Fl	New York	NY	10004	**800-221-5830**	212-344-2444
Fred A Moreton & Co 709 E South Temple	Salt Lake City	UT	84102	**800-594-8949**	801-531-1234
Fringe Benefits Management Co 3101 Sessions Rd	Tallahassee	FL	32303	**800-847-8286**	850-425-6200
Frontier Adjusters of America Inc PO Box 7610	Phoenix	AZ	85011	**800-528-1187**	602-264-1061
Gallagher Healthcare Insurance Services Inc 2000 W Sam Houston Pkwy S Suite 2000	Houston	TX	77042	**800-733-4474**	713-461-4000
Graham Co 1 Penn Sq W Graham Bldg	Philadelphia	PA	19102	**888-472-4262**	215-567-6300
Guaranty Insurance Services Inc 1300 S Mopac Expy	Austin	TX	78746	**800-331-8959**	512-434-8464
Haas & Wilkerson Inc PO Box 2946	Shawnee Mission	KS	66201	**800-821-7703**	913-432-4400
Hamilton Dorsey Alston Co 4401 Northside Pkwy Suite 400	Atlanta	GA	30327	**888-717-4393**	770-850-0050
Hanafin Robert J Inc PO Box 509	Endicott	NY	13761	**800-448-4826**	607-754-3500
Harris Cameron M & Co 6400 Fairview Rd	Charlotte	NC	28210	**800-868-8834**	704-366-8834
Hibbs Hallmark & Co PO Box 8357	Tyler	TX	75711	**800-765-6767**	903-561-8484
Holmes Murphy & Assoc Inc 3001 Westown Pkwy	West Des Moines	IA	50266	**800-247-7756**	515-223-6800
HUB International Ltd 55 E Jackson Blvd Suite 14A	Chicago	IL	60604	**800-432-2558**	877-402-6601
Hylant Group 811 Madison Ave	Toledo	OH	43624	**800-449-5268**	419-255-1020
Insurance Management Assoc Inc 250 N Water St	Wichita	KS	67202	**800-333-8913**	316-267-9221
Insurance Services Office Inc (ISO) 545 Washington Blvd	Jersey City	NJ	07310	**800-888-4476**	201-469-2000
Insurance.com Insurance Agency LLC 29001 Solon Rd	Solon	OH	44139	**866-533-0227**	
Interstate National Dealer Services Inc 333 Earle Ovington Blvd Suite 700	Uniondale	NY	11553	**800-942-0400**	516-228-8600
InterWest Insurance Services Inc 3636 American River Dr	Sacramento	CA	95864	**800-444-4134**	916-488-3100
ISO (Insurance Services Office Inc) 545 Washington Blvd	Jersey City	NJ	07310	**800-888-4476**	201-469-2000
J Rolfe Davis Insurance Agency Inc 850 Concourse Pkwy S Suite 200	Maitland	FL	32751	**800-896-0554**	407-691-9600
J Smith Lanier & Co 300 W 10th St	West Point	GA	31833	**800-226-4522**	706-645-2211
James B Oswald Co 1360 E 9th St Suite 600	Cleveland	OH	44114	**800-466-0468**	216-241-0468
John Burnham Insurance Services PO Box 85802	San Diego	CA	92186	**800-421-6744**	619-231-1010
John L Wortham & Son LLP 2727 Allen Pkwy	Houston	TX	77019	**888-896-5623**	713-526-3366
Kaye Group Inc 1065 Ave of the Americas	New York	NY	10018	**800-456-5293**	212-338-2000
Kelter-Alliant Insurance Services Inc 210 S Old Woodward Ave Suite 200	Birmingham	MI	48009	**800-888-9088**	248-540-3131
Knox RC & Co Inc 1 Goodwin Sq 24th Fl	Hartford	CT	06103	**800-742-2765**	860-524-7600
Kraus-Anderson Insurance 420 Gateway Blvd	Burnsville	MN	55337	**800-207-9261**	952-707-8200
Lanier J Smith & Co 300 W 10th St	West Point	GA	31833	**800-226-4522**	706-645-2211
Lewer Agency Inc 4534 Wornall Rd	Kansas City	MO	64111	**800-821-7715**	816-753-4390
Loomis Co 850 Park Rd	Wyomissing	PA	19610	**800-782-0392**	610-374-4040

				Toll-Free	Phone
Lovitt & Touche Inc 7202 E Rosewood St	Tucson	AZ	85710	**800-426-2756**	520-722-3000
Marshall & Sterling Inc 110 Main St	Poughkeepsie	NY	12601	**800-333-3766**	845-454-0800
McGriff Seibels & Williams Inc 2211 7th Ave S PO Box 10265	Birmingham	AL	35202	**800-476-2211**	205-252-9871
Mesirow Insurance Services Inc 350 N Clark St	Chicago	IL	60610	**888-973-2323**	312-595-6200
MLW Services Inc 100 William St	New York	NY	10038	**800-962-5524**	212-797-9600
Moreton Fred A & Co 709 E South Temple	Salt Lake City	UT	84102	**800-594-8949**	801-531-1234
National Council on Compensation Insurance 901 Peninsula Corporate Cir *Cust Svc	Boca Raton	FL	33487	**800-622-4123***	561-893-1000
NCCI Holdings Inc 901 Peninsula Corporate Cir *Cust Svc	Boca Raton	FL	33487	**800-622-4123***	561-893-1000
Near North Insurance Brokerage Inc 875 N Michigan Ave Suite 1900	Chicago	IL	60611	**800-859-6719**	312-280-5600
NIA Group Inc 66 Rt 17 N	Paramus	NJ	07652	**800-321-2122**	201-845-6600
Northwest Administrators Inc 2323 Eastlake Ave E	Seattle	WA	98102	**800-552-7334**	206-329-4900
Oswald James B Co 1360 E 9th St Suite 600	Cleveland	OH	44114	**800-466-0468**	216-241-0468
Palmer & Cay Inc 25 Bull St	Savannah	GA	31401	**800-755-9594**	912-234-6621
Parker Smith & Feek Inc 2233 112th Ave NE	Bellevue	WA	98004	**800-457-0220**	425-709-3600
POMCO 2425 James St	Syracuse	NY	13206	**800-766-2687**	315-432-9171
Proctor Financial Insurance Corp 295 Kirts Blvd Suite 100	Troy	MI	48084	**800-521-6800**	248-269-5700
Property Damage Appraisers Inc PO Box 9230	Fort Worth	TX	76147	**800-749-7324**	817-731-5555
Protegrity Services Inc PO Box 914700	Longwood	FL	32791	**800-883-4000**	407-788-1717
Quotesmith.com Inc 8205 S Cass Ave Suite 102 *NASDAQ: QUOT*	Darien	IL	60561	**800-556-9393**	630-515-0170
RC Knox & Co Inc 1 Goodwin Sq 24th Fl	Hartford	CT	06103	**800-742-2765**	860-524-7600
Rebsamen Insurance Inc 1500 Riverfront Dr	Little Rock	AR	72202	**800-542-0226**	501-661-4800
Rigg William Co 777 Main St Suite C-50	Fort Worth	TX	76102	**800-275-4449**	817-335-4444
Robert J Hanafin Inc PO Box 509	Endicott	NY	13761	**800-448-4826**	607-754-3500
Rutherfoord Thomas Inc 1 S Jefferson St	Roanoke	VA	24011	**800-283-1478**	540-982-3511
Seitlin 9800 NW 41st St Suite 300	Miami	FL	33178	**800-677-7348**	305-591-0090
SilverStone Group 11516 Miracle Hills Dr Suite 102	Omaha	NE	68154	**800-288-5501**	402-964-5400
Starkweather & Shepley Inc 60 Catamore Blvd	East Providence	RI	02914	**800-854-4625**	401-435-3600
Sullivan Curtis Monroe 2100 Main St Suite 350	Irvine	CA	92614	**800-427-3253**	949-250-7172
Summit Global Partners Inc 1445 Ross Ave Suite 4200	Dallas	TX	75202	**800-494-9418**	214-443-3500
Talbot Financial Corp 7770 Jefferson St NE Suite 200	Albuquerque	NM	87109	**800-800-5661**	505-828-4000
Trover Solutions Inc 1930 Bishop Ln Suite 1500	Louisville	KY	40218	**800-456-7318**	502-454-1340
Van Gilder Insurance Corp 700 Broadway Suite 1000	Denver	CO	80203	**800-873-8500**	303-837-8500
Van Meter Insurance 1240 Fair Way St	Bowling Green	KY	42103	**800-960-3560**	270-781-2020
Wells Fargo Insurance Inc 600 S Hwy 169 12th Fl	Saint Louis Park	MN	55426	**800-328-2791**	612-667-5600
Wharton Group 101 S Livingston Ave	Livingston	NJ	07039	**800-521-2725**	973-992-5775
William Rigg Co 777 Main St Suite C-50	Fort Worth	TX	76102	**800-275-4449**	817-335-4444
Willis Group Holdings Ltd 7 Hanover Sq *NASDAQ: WSH*	New York	NY	10004	**800-234-8596**	212-344-8888
Wortham John L & Son LLP 2727 Allen Pkwy	Houston	TX	77019	**888-896-5623**	713-526-3366

384 INSURANCE COMPANIES

SEE ALSO Service Contracts & Warranties - Home; Viatical Settlement Companies

384-1 Animal Insurance

				Toll-Free	Phone
Ark Agency Animal Insurance Services PO Box 223	Paynesville	MN	56362	**800-328-8894**	320-243-7250
Canadian Livestock Insurance 75 The Donway W Suite 708	Don Mills	ON	M3C2E9	**800-727-1502**	416-510-8191
Equisport Agency Inc PO Box 269	Bloomfield Hills	MI	48303	**800-432-1215**	248-644-1215
Georgia Walker & Assoc Inc PO Box 584	Raymore	MO	64083	**800-385-2423**	816-331-3211
Henry Equestrian Insurance Brokers 28 Victoria St	Aurora	ON	L4G3L6	**800-565-4321**	905-727-1144
Markel Insurance Co 4600 Cox Rd	Glen Allen	VA	23060	**800-431-1270**	804-527-2700
Petcare Insurance Brokers Ltd 710 Dorval Dr Suite 400	Oakville	ON	L6K3V7	**877-738-4584**	905-842-2615
Pet's Health Plan PO Box 2847	North Canton	OH	44720	**877-592-7387**	330-305-1352
Premier Pet Insurance PO Box 96	Minneapolis	MN	55440	**877-774-2273**	
Veterinary Pet Insurance Inc 3060 Saturn St	Brea	CA	92821	**800-872-7387**	
Walker Georgia & Assoc Inc PO Box 584	Raymore	MO	64083	**800-385-2423**	816-331-3211

384-2 Life & Accident Insurance

				Toll-Free	Phone
Abraham Lincoln Insurance Co 5250 S 6th St	Springfield	IL	62703	**800-323-0050**	217-241-6300
Acacia Life Insurance Co 7315 Wisconsin Ave	Bethesda	MD	20814	**800-444-1889**	301-280-1000
Acacia National Life 7315 Wisconsin Ave	Bethesda	MD	20814	**800-444-1889**	301-280-1000
Aegon Special Markets Group Inc 20 Moores Rd	Frazer	PA	19355	**800-523-7900**	610-648-5000
Aetna Health & Life Insurance Co 151 Farmington Ave	Hartford	CT	06156	**800-872-3862**	860-273-0123
Aetna Inc 151 Farmington Ave *NYSE: AET*	Hartford	CT	06156	**800-872-3862**	860-273-0123
Aetna Life Insurance & Annuity Co 151 Farmington Ave	Hartford	CT	06156	**800-872-3862**	860-273-0123
AFLAC (American Family Life Assurance Co of Columbus) 1932 Wynnton Rd	Columbus	GA	31999	**800-992-3522**	706-323-3431
AGC Life Insurance Co 2000 American General Way	Brentwood	TN	37027	**800-888-2452**	615-749-1000
AIG Life Insurance Co PO Box 2226	Wilmington	DE	19899	**800-441-7468**	302-594-2000
All American Life Insurance Co PO Box 4373	Houston	TX	77210	**800-487-5433**	
Alliance Insurance Co 5250 S 6th St	Springfield	IL	62705	**800-323-0050**	217-241-6300
Allianz Life Insurance Co of North America 5701 Golden Hills Dr	Minneapolis	MN	55416	**800-328-5600**	763-765-6500
Allmerica Life Insurance Co 440 Lincoln St	Worcester	MA	01653	**800-533-7881**	508-855-1000
Allstate Life Insurance Co 3100 Sanders Rd Allstate West Plaza *Cust Svc	Northbrook	IL	60062	**800-366-1411***	847-402-5000
Allstate Life Insurance Co of New York PO Box 80469	Lincoln	NE	68501	**800-347-5433**	
American Amicable Life Insurance Co PO Box 2549	Waco	TX	76702	**800-736-7311**	254-297-2777
American Capitol Insurance Co 10555 Richmond Ave 2nd Fl	Houston	TX	77042	**800-527-2567**	713-974-2242
American Community Mutual Insurance Co 39201 Seven-Mile Rd	Livonia	MI	48152	**800-991-2642**	734-591-9000
American Equity Investment Life Insurance Co 5000 Westown Pkwy Suite 440	West Des Moines	IA	50266	**888-221-1234**	515-221-0002
American Family Life Assurance Co of Columbus (AFLAC) 1932 Wynnton Rd	Columbus	GA	31999	**800-992-3522**	706-323-3431
American Family Life Insurance Co 6000 American Pkwy	Madison	WI	53783	**800-374-0008**	608-249-2111
American Family Mutual Insurance Co 6000 American Pkwy *Cust Svc	Madison	WI	53783	**800-374-0008***	608-249-2111
American Fidelity Assurance Co 2000 N Classen Blvd	Oklahoma City	OK	73106	**800-654-8489**	405-523-2000
American Founders Life Insurance Co PO Box 52121	Phoenix	AZ	85072	**800-531-5067**	480-425-5100
American General Life & Accident Insurance Co 2000 American General Way	Brentwood	TN	37027	**800-888-2452**	615-749-1000
American General Life Insurance Co 2929 Allen Pkwy	Houston	TX	77019	**800-231-3655**	713-522-1111
American Health & Life Insurance Co PO Box 1876	Fort Worth	TX	76101	**800-711-3454**	817-348-7573
American Heritage Life Insurance Co 1776 American Heritage Life Dr	Jacksonville	FL	32224	**800-521-3535**	904-992-1776
American Income Life Insurance Co 1200 Wooded Acres	Waco	TX	76710	**800-433-3405**	254-772-3050
American Investors Life Insurance Co 555 S Kansas Ave	Topeka	KS	66603	**800-435-4884**	785-232-6945
American Life & Casualty Insurance Co 11815 N Pennsylvania St	Carmel	IN	46032	**800-544-0467**	317-817-6300
American Life Insurance Co 600 King St 1 ALICO Plaza	Wilmington	DE	19801	**800-441-7468**	302-594-2000
American National Insurance Co 1 Moody Plaza *NASDAQ: ANAT* ■ *Cust Svc	Galveston	TX	77550	**800-899-6806***	409-763-4661
American Progressive Life & Health Insurance Co of New York 6 International Dr Suite 190	Rye Brook	NY	10573	**800-332-3377**	914-934-8300
American Republic Insurance Co 601 6th Ave	Des Moines	IA	50309	**800-247-2190**	515-245-2000
American Standard Insurance Co of Wisconsin 6000 American Pkwy	Madison	WI	53783	**800-374-0008**	608-249-2111
American United Life Insurance Co PO Box 368	Indianapolis	IN	46206	**800-537-6442**	317-285-1877
Americo Financial Life & Annuity Insurance Co PO Box 410288 *Cust Svc	Kansas City	MO	64141	**800-366-6565***	816-391-2000
Ameritas Direct 5900 'O' St	Lincoln	NE	68510	**800-283-9588**	402-467-1122
Ameritas Life Insurance Corp 5900 'O' St	Lincoln	NE	68510	**800-283-9588**	402-467-1122
Ameritas Variable Life Insurance Co 5900 'O' St	Lincoln	NE	68510	**800-634-8353**	402-467-1122
AmerUs Life Insurance Co 611 5th Ave	Des Moines	IA	50309	**800-800-9882**	515-283-2371
Amica Life Insurance Co PO Box 6008	Providence	RI	02940	**800-242-6422**	
Anthem Insurance Cos Inc 120 Monument Cir Suite 200	Indianapolis	IN	46204	**800-331-1476**	317-488-6000
Appalachian Life Insurance Co PO Box 5147	Springfield	IL	62705	**800-323-0050**	217-241-6300
Assurant Employee Benefits 2323 Grand Blvd	Kansas City	MO	64108	**800-733-7879**	816-474-2345
Assurant Life Insurance Co 308 Maltbie St Suite 200	Syracuse	NY	13204	**800-745-7100**	315-451-0066
Atlanta Life Insurance Co PO Box 2222	Decatur	AL	35609	**800-235-5422**	404-659-2100
Aurora National Life Assurance Co PO Box 4490	Hartford	CT	06147	**800-265-2652**	
AUSA Life Insurance Co Inc 4333 Edgewood Rd NE *Cust Svc	Cedar Rapids	IA	52499	**800-625-4213***	319-398-8511
Auto-Owners Life Insurance Co 6101 Anacapri Blvd	Lansing	MI	48917	**800-288-8740**	517-323-1200
AXA Equitable Life Insurance Co 1290 Ave of the Americas	New York	NY	10104	**888-855-5100**	212-554-1234
Baltimore Life Cos 10075 Red Run Blvd	Owings Mills	MD	21117	**800-628-5433**	410-581-6600
Bank of America Insurance Services Inc PO Box 21848	Greensboro	NC	27420	**800-288-7647**	336-805-8800
Bankers Fidelity Life Insurance Co PO Box 105652	Atlanta	GA	30348	**800-241-1439**	
Bankers Insurance Co 360 Central Ave	Saint Petersburg	FL	33701	**800-627-0000**	727-823-4000
Bankers Life & Casualty Co 222 Merchandise Mart Plaza	Chicago	IL	60654	**800-621-3724**	312-396-6000
Bankers National Life Insurance Co 11815 N Pennsylvania St	Carmel	IN	46032	**800-888-4918**	317-817-6300
Bankers United Life Assurance Co 4333 Edgewood Rd NE *Cust Svc	Cedar Rapids	IA	52499	**800-625-4213***	319-398-8511
Banner Life Insurance Co 1701 Research Blvd	Rockville	MD	20850	**800-638-8428**	301-279-4800
Beneficial Life Insurance Co 36 S State St	Salt Lake City	UT	84136	**800-233-7979**	801-933-1100
Beneficial Standard Life Insurance Co 11815 N Pennsylvania St	Carmel	IN	46032	**800-288-4096**	317-817-6200
Benevolent Life Insurance Co Inc 1624 Milam St	Shreveport	LA	71103	**800-435-1522**	318-425-1522
Berkshire Hathaway Life Insurance Co of Nebraska 3024 Harney St	Omaha	NE	68131	**800-786-6426**	402-536-3000
Berkshire Life Insurance Co of America 700 South St	Pittsfield	MA	01201	**800-819-2468**	413-499-4321
Booker T Washington Insurance Co PO Box 697	Birmingham	AL	35201	**800-228-4180**	205-328-5454

Company / Address	City	State	Zip	Toll-Free	Phone
Boston Mutual Life Insurance Co 120 Royall St	Canton	MA	02021	**800-669-2668**	781-828-7000
Catholic Family Life Insurance PO Box 11563	Milwaukee	WI	53211	**800-227-2354**	414-961-0500
Central Benefits Mutual Insurance Co PO Box 850658	Richardson	TX	75085	**800-777-3377**	614-797-5200
Central Security Life Insurance Co PO Box 833879	Richardson	TX	75083	**866-629-2677**	972-699-2770
Central States Health & Life Co of Omaha PO Box 34350	Omaha	NE	68134	**800-541-2363**	402-397-1111
Chase Insurance Co 2500 Westfield Drive	Elgin	IL	60123	**800-321-9313**	847-930-7000
Chesapeake Life Insurance Co 1331 W Memorial Rd Suite 112	Oklahoma City	OK	73114	**800-725-7887**	405-848-0179
CIGNA Reinsurance 900 Cottage Grove Rd	Hartford	CT	06152	**888-244-6237**	860-226-6000
Cincinnati Life Insurance Co PO Box 145496	Cincinnati	OH	45250	**800-783-4479**	513-870-2000
Citizens Insurance Co of America PO Box 149151	Austin	TX	78714	**800-880-5044**	512-836-9730
Citizens Security Life Insurance Co PO Box 436149	Louisville	KY	40253	**800-843-7752**	502-244-2420
CNA Valley Forge Life Insurance Co 100 CNA Dr	Nashville	TN	37214	**800-437-8854**	615-871-1400
Colonial Life & Accident Insurance Co 1200 Colonial Life Blvd	Columbia	SC	29210	**800-325-4368**	803-798-7000
Colonial Penn Life Insurance Co 399 Market St	Philadelphia	PA	19181	**800-523-9100**	215-928-8000
Columbus Life Insurance Co 400 E 4th St PO Box 5737 *Cust Svc	Cincinnati	OH	45201	**800-677-9595***	513-361-6700
Combined Insurance Co of America 5050 N Broadway	Chicago	IL	60640	**800-428-5466**	
Companion Life Insurance Co 3316 Farnam St	Omaha	NE	68175	**800-775-6000**	
Companion Life Insurance Co 7909 Parklane Rd Suite 200	Columbia	SC	29223	**800-753-0404**	803-735-1251
Concord Group Insurance Co 4 Bouton St	Concord	NH	03301	**800-852-3380**	603-224-4086
Connecticut General Life Insurance Co 900 Cottage Grove Rd	Hartford	CT	06152	**800-444-2363**	860-226-6000
Conseco Annuity Assurance Co 11815 N Pennsylvania St	Carmel	IN	46032	**800-541-2254**	317-817-6100
Conseco Health Insurance Co 11815 N Pennsylvania St	Carmel	IN	46932	**800-541-2254**	317-817-6100
Continental General Insurance Co PO Box 247007	Omaha	NE	68124	**800-545-8905**	402-397-3200
Cotton States Life Insurance Co 244 Perimeter Center Pkwy NE	Atlanta	GA	30346	**800-282-6536**	770-391-8600
Country Cos 1701 N Towanda Ave	Bloomington	IL	61701	**888-211-2555**	309-557-3000
Desjardins Financial Security Life Assurance Co 200 Ave des Commandeurs	Levis	QC	G6V6R2	**866-838-7553**	
EMC National Life Co 4095 NW Urbandale Dr	Urbandale	IA	50322	**800-232-5818**	515-645-4000
Empire General Life Assurance Corp 7400 W 130th St Suite 400	Overland Park	KS	66213	**800-688-3518**	913-897-9733
Employers Insurance Co of Wausau A Mutual Co 2000 Westwood Dr	Wausau	WI	54401	**800-435-4401**	715-845-5211
Employers Reinsurance Corp 5200 Metcalf Ave	Overland Park	KS	66202	**800-255-6931**	913-676-5200
Epic Life Insurance Co 1765 W Broadway *Sales	Madison	WI	53713	**800-236-8809***	608-223-2100
Equitable Distributors Inc 1290 Ave of the Americas	New York	NY	10104	**888-855-5100**	212-554-1234
Equitable Life & Casualty Insurance Co 3 Triad Ctr Suite 200 *Cust Svc	Salt Lake City	UT	84180	**800-352-5150***	801-521-2500
Erie Family Life Insurance Co 100 Erie Insurance Pl	Erie	PA	16530	**800-458-0811**	814-870-2000
Family Life Insurance Co 6500 River Place Blvd	Austin	TX	78730	**800-925-6000**	512-404-5000
Farm Bureau Life Insurance Co 5400 University Ave	West Des Moines	IA	50266	**800-247-4170**	515-225-5400
Farm Family Life Insurance Co PO Box 656	Albany	NY	12201	**800-948-3276**	518-431-5000
Farmers & Traders Life Insurance Co 960 James St PO Box 1056	Syracuse	NY	13201	**800-347-0960**	315-471-5656
Farmers Union Mutual Insurance Co PO Box 2020	Jamestown	ND	58402	**800-366-6338**	701-252-2701
Federated Life Insurance Co PO Box 328	Owatonna	MN	55060	**800-533-0472**	507-455-5200
Federated Mutual Insurance Co PO Box 328	Owatonna	MN	55060	**800-533-0472**	507-455-5200
FIC Insurance Group 6500 River Place Blvd Bldg 1	Austin	TX	78730	**800-925-6000**	512-404-5000
Fidelity & Guaranty Life Insurance Co PO Box 1137 *Sales	Baltimore	MD	21203	**800-445-6758***	410-895-0100
Financial Benefit Life Insurance Co 555 S Kansas Ave	Topeka	KS	66603	**800-332-7732**	785-232-6945
First Alexander Hamilton Life Insurance Co PO Box 21008	Greensboro	NC	27420	**800-950-2454**	336-691-3000
First Colony Life Insurance Co 3100 Albert Lankford Dr	Lynchburg	VA	24501	**888-325-5433**	434-845-0911
First Investors Life Insurance Co 95 Wall St 22nd Fl	New York	NY	10005	**800-832-7783**	212-858-8200
First Penn-Pacific Life Insurance Co 10 N Martingale Rd	Schaumburg	IL	60173	**800-450-3067**	847-466-8000
First UNUM Life Insurance Co 2211 Congress St	Portland	ME	04122	**800-658-8686**	
Forethought Financial Services Inc Forethought Ctr *Cust Svc	Batesville	IN	47006	**800-881-2430***	812-934-7139
Fort Dearborn Life Insurance Co 1020 W 31st St	Downers Grove	IL	60515	**800-633-3696**	
Franklin Life Insurance Co The 1 Franklin Sq	Springfield	IL	62713	**800-528-2011**	217-528-2011
Fremont Life Insurance Co PO Box 410288	Kansas City	MO	64141	**800-231-0801**	816-391-2000
Garden State Life Insurance Co 2450 S Shore Blvd Suite 401	League City	TX	77573	**800-638-8565**	281-538-1037
GE Capital Assurance Co Long Term Care Div 1650 Los Gamos Dr	San Rafael	CA	94903	**800-456-7766**	415-492-7500
GE Financial Assurance Holdings Inc 6604 W Broad St	Richmond	VA	23230	**800-844-6543**	804-281-6000
General Reinsurance Corp 695 E Main St Financial Ctr	Stamford	CT	06901	**800-431-9994**	203-328-5000
Genworth Financial Inc 6610 W Broad St *NYSE: GNW*	Richmond	VA	23230	**888-436-9678**	804-484-3821
Gerber Life Insurance Co 1311 Mamaroneck Ave	White Plains	NY	10605	**800-704-2180**	914-272-4000

Company / Address	City	State	Zip	Toll-Free	Phone
Globe Life & Accident Insurance Co 204 N Robinson Ave Globe Life Ctr	Oklahoma City	OK	73102	**800-654-5433**	405-270-1400
Golden State Mutual Life Insurance Co 1999 W Adams Blvd	Los Angeles	CA	90018	**800-225-5476**	323-731-1131
Grange Life Insurance Co 650 S Front St	Columbus	OH	43206	**800-422-0550**	614-445-2900
Great American Life Assurance Co of Puerto Rico Inc PO Box 363786	San Juan	PR	00936	**800-980-7651**	787-758-4888
Great American Life Insurance Co 525 Vine St 7th Fl	Cincinnati	OH	45202	**800-854-3649**	513-357-3300
Great Southern Life Insurance Co PO Box 410288	Kansas City	MO	64141	**800-231-0801**	816-391-2000
Great-West Life & Annuity Insurance Co PO Box 1700	Denver	CO	80201	**800-537-2033**	303-737-3000
Guarantee Trust Life Insurance Co 1275 Milwaukee Ave	Glenview	IL	60025	**800-338-7452**	847-699-0600
Guardian Insurance & Annuity Co 7 Hanover Sq	New York	NY	10004	**888-482-7342**	212-598-8000
Guardian Life Insurance Co of America 7 Hanover Sq	New York	NY	10004	**888-482-7342**	212-598-8000
GuideOne Mutual Insurance Co 1111 Ashworth Rd	West Des Moines	IA	50265	**877-448-4331**	515-267-5000
GuideOne Specialty Mutual Insurance Co 1111 Ashworth Rd	West Des Moines	IA	50265	**800-247-4181**	515-267-5000
Hannover Life Reassurance Co of America 800 N Magnolia Ave Suite 1400	Orlando	FL	32803	**800-327-1910**	407-649-8411
Harleysville Mutual Insurance Co 355 Maple Ave	Harleysville	PA	19438	**800-523-6344**	215-256-5000
Hartford Life & Accident Insurance Co 200 Hopmeadow St	Simsbury	CT	06089	**800-833-5575**	860-525-8555
Harvey Watt & Co Atlanta Airport PO Box 20787	Atlanta	GA	30320	**800-241-6103**	404-767-7501
HealthExtras Inc 800 King Farm Blvd 4th Fl *NASDAQ: HLEX*	Rockville	MD	20850	**800-323-6640**	301-548-2900
Highmark Life & Casualty 5th Ave Pl 120 5th Ave	Pittsburgh	PA	15222	**800-833-1115**	412-544-2000
Horace Mann Insurance Co 1 Horace Mann Plaza	Springfield	IL	62715	**800-999-1030**	217-789-2500
Horace Mann Life Insurance Co 1 Horace Mann Plaza	Springfield	IL	62715	**800-999-1030**	217-789-2500
Humana Inc 500 W Main St *NYSE: HUM*	Louisville	KY	40202	**800-486-2620**	502-580-1000
Indiana Farm Bureau Insurance Co 225 S East St	Indianapolis	IN	46202	**800-866-1160**	317-692-7200
Indianapolis Life Insurance Co 9200 Keystone Crossing Suite 800	Indianapolis	IN	46204	**800-428-7031**	317-927-6500
Industrial-Alliance Life Insurance Co 1080 Chemin Saint-Louis	Sillery	QC	G1K7M3	**800-463-6236**	418-684-5000
ING Life of Georgia PO Box 105006	Atlanta	GA	30348	**888-968-5433**	770-980-5100
ING Northern Annuity 2000 21st Ave NW	Minot	ND	58703	**877-884-5050**	
ING Southland Life Insurance Co 2000 21st Ave NW	Minot	ND	58703	**877-241-5050**	701-858-2000
Insurance Companies at American General Financial PO Box 39	Evansville	IN	47701	**800-325-2147**	
Integrity Life Insurance Co 515 W Market St 8th Fl	Louisville	KY	40202	**800-325-8583**	502-582-7900
Investors Heritage Life Insurance Co 200 Capital Ave	Frankfort	KY	40602	**800-422-2011**	502-223-2361
Investors Life Insurance Co of Indiana 6500 River Pl Blvd Bldg 1	Austin	TX	78730	**800-925-6000**	512-404-5000
Investors Life Insurance Co of North America 6500 River Pl Blvd Bldg 1	Austin	TX	78730	**800-925-6000**	512-404-5000
Jackson National Life Insurance Co 1 Corporate Way	Lansing	MI	48951	**800-644-4565**	517-381-5500
Jefferson-Pilot Financial Insurance Co 100 N Greene St	Greensboro	NC	27401	**800-487-1485**	336-691-3000
Jefferson-Pilot Life Insurance Co 100 N Greene St	Greensboro	NC	27401	**800-487-1485**	336-691-3000
John Hancock Life Insurance Co PO Box 111	Boston	MA	02117	**800-732-5543**	617-572-6000
John Hancock Variable Life Insurance Co PO Box 111	Boston	MA	02117	**800-732-5543**	617-572-6000
Kanawha Insurance Co PO Box 610	Lancaster	SC	29721	**800-635-4252**	803-283-5300
Keyport Life Insurance Co 1 Sun Life Executive Pk	Wellesley Hills	MA	02481	**800-225-3950**	781-237-6030
Knights of Columbus 1 Columbus Plaza	New Haven	CT	06510	**800-524-3611**	203-752-4000
Lafayette Life Insurance Co PO Box 7007 *Cust Svc	Lafayette	IN	47903	**800-243-6631***	765-477-7411
Liberty National Life Insurance Co PO Box 2612	Birmingham	AL	35202	**800-333-0637**	205-325-2722
Life Insurance Co of the Southwest PO Box 569080	Dallas	TX	75356	**800-543-3794**	214-638-7100
Life Investors Insurance Co of America 4333 Edgewood Rd NE	Cedar Rapids	IA	52499	**800-625-4213**	319-398-8511
Lincoln Insurance Group 1526 K St	Lincoln	NE	68508	**800-747-7191**	402-423-7191
Lincoln National Life Insurance Co 1300 S Clinton St	Fort Wayne	IN	46802	**800-454-6265**	260-455-2000
London Insurance Group Corp PO Box 29045	Phoenix	AZ	85038	**800-433-8181**	
London Life Insurance Co 255 Dufferin Ave	London	ON	N6A4K1	**800-667-3733**	519-432-5281
Loyal American Life Insurance Co PO Box 559004	Austin	TX	78755	**800-633-6752**	
MAMSI Life & Health Insurance Co 4 Taft Ct	Rockville	MD	20850	**800-544-2853**	301-762-8205
Mann Horace Insurance Co 1 Horace Mann Plaza	Springfield	IL	62715	**800-999-1030**	217-789-2500
Mann Horace Life Insurance Co 1 Horace Mann Plaza	Springfield	IL	62715	**800-999-1030**	217-789-2500
Manufacturers Life Insurance Co of New York 100 Summit Lake Dr 2nd Fl	Valhalla	NY	10595	**800-551-2078**	914-773-0708
Manufacturers Life Insurance Co USA 38500 N Woodward Ave Suite 325	Bloomfield Hills	MI	48304	**800-968-8761**	248-644-1444
Manulife New York 100 Summit Lake Dr 2nd Fl	Valhalla	NY	10595	**800-551-2078**	914-773-0708
Massachusetts Mutual Life Insurance Co 1295 State St	Springfield	MA	01111	**800-272-2216**	413-788-8411
Medico Life Insurance Co 1515 S 75th St	Omaha	NE	68124	**800-228-6080**	402-391-6900
MEGA Life & Health Insurance Co 9151 Grapevine Hwy	North Richland Hills	TX	76180	**800-527-2845**	817-255-3100
Merrill Lynch Life Insurance Co 4804 Deer Lake Dr E	Jacksonville	FL	32246	**800-535-5549**	904-218-7000
MetLife Inc 27-01 Queens Plaza North 1 MetLife Plaza *NYSE: MET*	Long Island City	NY	11101	**800-638-5433**	212-578-2211
MetLife Investors Insurance Co 22 Corporate Plaza Dr	Newport Beach	CA	92660	**800-848-3854**	949-629-1300

Life & Accident Insurance (Cont'd)

Company / Address	City	State	Zip	Toll-Free	Phone
Metropolitan Life Insurance Co					
1 Madison Ave	New York	NY	10010	**800-638-5433**	212-578-2211
Mid-Century Insurance Co					
4680 Wilshire Blvd	Los Angeles	CA	90010	**888-516-5656**	323-932-3200
Mid-West National Life Ins Co of					
Tennessee 9151 Grapevine Hwy	North Richland Hills	TX	76182	**800-733-1110**	
Middlesex Insurance Co 3 Carlisle Rd	Westford	MA	01886	**800-225-1390**	978-392-7000
Minnesota Life Insurance Co					
400 Robert St N	Saint Paul	MN	55101	**800-328-6124**	651-665-3500
MML Bay State Life Insurance Co					
1295 State St	Springfield	MA	01111	**800-767-1000***	413-788-8411
*Cust Svc					
Modern Woodmen Co of America					
1701 1st Ave	Rock Island	IL	61201	**800-447-9811**	309-786-6481
Monumental Life Insurance Co 2 E Chase St	Baltimore	MD	21202	**800-638-3080**	410-685-2900
MONY Life Insurance Co of America					
1290 Ave of the Americas	New York	NY	10104	**800-487-6669**	212-544-1234
Mutual of America Life Insurance Co					
320 Park Ave	New York	NY	10022	**800-468-3785**	212-224-1600
Mutual of Omaha Insurance Co					
Mutual of Omaha Plaza	Omaha	NE	68175	**800-775-6000**	402-342-7600
Mutual Protective Insurance Co					
1515 S 75th St	Omaha	NE	68124	**800-228-6080**	402-391-6900
Mutual Savings Life Insurance Co					
2801 Hwy 31 S	Decatur	AL	35603	**800-239-6754***	256-552-7011
*Cust Svc					
Mutual Trust Life Insurance Co					
1200 Jorie Blvd	Oak Brook	IL	60522	**800-323-7320**	630-990-1000
National Benefit Life Insurance Co					
333 W 34th St 10th Fl	New York	NY	10001	**800-222-2062**	212-615-7500
National General Insurance Co					
1 GMAC Plaza	Saint Louis	MO	63045	**800-847-6442**	314-493-8000
National Guardian Life Insurance Co					
PO Box 1191	Madison	WI	53701	**800-548-2962**	608-257-5611
National Health Insurance Co PO Box 619999	Dallas	TX	75261	**800-237-1900**	817-640-1900
National Life Insurance Co					
1 National Life Dr	Montpelier	VT	05604	**800-732-8939**	802-229-3333
National Mutual Benefit Inc					
6522 Grand Teton Plaza	Madison	WI	53719	**800-779-1936**	608-833-1936
National Security Life & Accident Insurance Co					
PO Box 149151	Austin	TX	78714	**800-880-5044**	512-837-7100
National Western Life Insurance Co					
850 E Anderson Ln	Austin	TX	78752	**800-531-5442**	512-836-1010
NASDAQ: NWLIA					
Nationwide Life & Annuity Insurance Co					
5100 Rings Rd	Dublin	OH	43017	**800-882-2822**	614-249-7111
Nationwide Life Insurance Co 5100 Rings Rd	Dublin	OH	43017	**800-882-2822**	614-249-7111
Nationwide Provident 1000 Chesterbrook Blvd	Berwyn	PA	19312	**800-523-4681**	610-889-1717
NCRIC Insurance Agency Inc					
1115 30th St NW	Washington	DC	20007	**800-613-3615**	202-969-1866
New England Financial 501 Boylston St	Boston	MA	02116	**800-388-4000***	617-578-2000
*Cust Svc					
New England Life Insurance Co					
501 Boylston St	Boston	MA	02116	**800-388-4000**	617-578-2000
New York Life Insurance & Annuity Corp					
51 Madison Ave	New York	NY	10010	**800-598-2019**	212-576-7000
Nippon Life Insurance Co of America					
521 5th Ave 5th Fl	New York	NY	10175	**800-252-7174**	212-682-3000
North American Co for Life & Health Insurance					
525 W Van Buren St	Chicago	IL	60607	**800-800-3656**	312-648-7600
North Carolina Mutual Life Insurance Co					
411 W Chapel Hill St	Durham	NC	27701	**800-626-1899**	919-682-9201
Ohio Life Insurance Co PO Box 410288	Kansas City	MO	64141	**800-456-6446**	816-391-2000
Ohio National Life Insurance Co					
1 Financial Way Suite 100	Cincinnati	OH	45242	**800-366-6654**	513-794-6100
Old American Insurance Co					
3520 Broadway	Kansas City	MO	64111	**800-733-6242**	816-753-4900
Oxford Life Insurance Co 2721 N Central Ave	Phoenix	AZ	85004	**800-528-0463**	602-263-6666
Pacific Life Insurance Co					
700 Newport Ctr Dr	Newport Beach	CA	92660	**800-347-7787**	949-219-3011
Pan-American Life Insurance Co					
601 Poydras St	New Orleans	LA	70130	**800-999-0514***	504-566-1300
*Life Ins					
Paragon Life Insurance Co					
190 Carondelet Plaza	Saint Louis	MO	63105	**800-685-0124**	
Paul Revere Life Insurance Co					
18 Chestnut St	Worcester	MA	01608	**800-799-0990**	508-799-4441
Pekin Life Insurance Co 2505 Court St	Pekin	IL	61558	**800-322-0160**	309-346-1161
Penn Insurance & Annuity Co					
600 Dresher Rd	Horsham	PA	19044	**800-523-0650***	215-956-8000
*Cust Svc					
Penn Mutual Life Insurance Co					
600 Dresher Rd	Horsham	PA	19044	**800-523-0650***	215-956-8000
*Cust Svc					
Penn Treaty Network America Insurance Co					
3440 Lehigh St	Allentown	PA	18103	**800-362-0700**	610-965-2222
PFL Life Insurance Co					
4333 Edgewood Rd NE	Cedar Rapids	IA	52499	**800-247-3615**	319-398-8511
Pharmacists Mutual Insurance Co					
808 US Hwy 18 W	Algona	IA	50511	**800-247-5930**	515-295-2461
Philadelphia Life Insurance Co					
11815 N Pennsylvania St	Carmel	IN	46032	**800-525-7662**	317-817-6100
Phoenix Life Insurance Co 1 American Row	Hartford	CT	06102	**800-628-1936***	860-403-5000
*Cust Svc					
Physicians Life Insurance Co 2600 Dodge St	Omaha	NE	68131	**800-228-9100**	402-633-1000
Physicians Mutual Insurance Co					
2600 Dodge St	Omaha	NE	68131	**800-228-9100**	402-633-1000
Pioneer Life Insurance Co					
11815 N Pennsylvania St	Carmel	IN	46032	**800-759-7007**	317-817-6100
Pioneer Mutual Life Insurance Co PO Box 2546	Fargo	ND	58108	**800-437-4692**	701-297-5700
Presidential Life Insurance Co 69 Lydecker St	Nyack	NY	10960	**800-926-7599**	845-358-2300
Principal Life Insurance Co 711 High St	Des Moines	IA	50392	**800-986-3343**	515-247-5111
Property-Owners Insurance Co PO Box 30660	Lansing	MI	48909	**800-288-8740**	517-323-1200
Protective Life & Annuity Insurance Co					
2801 Hwy 280 S	Birmingham	AL	35223	**800-866-3555**	205-879-9230
Protective Life Insurance Co					
2801 Hwy 280 S	Birmingham	AL	35223	**800-866-3555**	205-879-9230
Provident American Insurance Co Inc					
10501 N Central Expy Suite 200	Dallas	TX	75231	**800-933-9456**	214-696-9091
Prudential Financial Inc 751 Broad St	Newark	NJ	07102	**800-843-7625**	973-802-6000
NYSE: PRU					
Pyramid Life Insurance Co PO Box 12922	Pensacola	FL	32591	**800-777-1126**	
RBC Insurance 2300 Main St Suite 450	Kansas City	MO	64108	**800-262-5433**	816-218-6500
Reassure America Life Insurance Co					
PO box 360	Hartford	CT	06141	**800-323-8764**	
Reliance Standard Life Insurance					
2001 Market St Suite 1500	Philadelphia	PA	19103	**800-351-7500**	267-256-3500
Reserve National Insurance Co Inc					
PO Box 18448	Oklahoma City	OK	73154	**800-654-9106**	405-848-7931
Security Benefit Group of Cos					
1 Security Benefit Pl	Topeka	KS	66636	**800-888-2461**	785-438-3000
Security Benefit Life Insurance Co					
1 Security Benefit Pl	Topeka	KS	66636	**800-888-2461**	785-438-3000
Security Financial Life Insurance Co					
4000 Pine Lake Rd	Lincoln	NE	68516	**800-284-8575**	402-434-9500
Security Life Insurance Co of America					
10901 Red Circle Dr	Minnetonka	MN	55343	**800-328-4667**	952-544-2121
Security Mutual Life Insurance Co of New					
York PO Box 1625	Binghamton	NY	13902	**800-346-7171**	607-723-3551
Sentry Life Insurance Co					
1800 N Point Dr	Stevens Point	WI	54481	**800-533-7827***	715-346-6000
*Cust Svc					
Settlers Life Insurance Co PO Box 8600	Bristol	VA	24203	**800-523-2650**	276-645-4300
Shelter Life Insurance Co 1817 W Broadway	Columbia	MO	65218	**800-743-5837***	573-445-8441
*Claims					
Shenandoah Life Insurance Co					
2301 Brambleton Ave	Roanoke	VA	24015	**800-848-5433**	540-985-4400
Sierra Health & Life Insurance Co					
PO Box 15645	Las Vegas	NV	89114	**800-888-2264**	702-242-7000
Southern Security Life Insurance Co					
755 Rinehart Rd Suite 200	Lake Mary	FL	32746	**800-336-9558**	407-321-7113
NASDAQ: SSLI					
Southwestern Life Insurance Co					
8710 Freeport Pkwy Suite 150	Irving	TX	75063	**800-792-4368**	
Standard Life & Accident Insurance Co					
PO Box 1800	Galveston	TX	77553	**888-350-1488**	
Standard Life Insurance Co of Indiana					
10689 N Pennsylvania St	Indianapolis	IN	46280	**800-767-7749***	317-574-6200
*Mktg					
State Life Insurance Co					
1 American Sq PO Box 368	Indianapolis	IN	46206	**800-428-9198**	317-285-2300
Stonebridge Life Insurance Co					
2700 W Plano Pkwy	Plano	TX	75075	**800-527-9027**	972-881-6000
Sun Life Insurance & Annuity Co of New					
York PO Box 9133	Wellesley Hills	MA	02481	**800-447-7569**	
SunAmerica Life Insurance Co					
1 SunAmerica Ctr	Los Angeles	CA	90067	**800-445-7862**	310-772-6000
Sunset Life Insurance Co of America					
PO Box 219139	Kansas City	MO	64121	**800-678-6898**	
Texas Life Insurance Co PO Box 830	Waco	TX	76703	**800-283-9233**	254-752-6521
Thrivent Financial for Lutherans					
4321 N Ballard Rd	Appleton	WI	54919	**800-847-4836**	920-734-5721
TIAA-CREF 730 3rd Ave	New York	NY	10017	**800-842-2776**	212-490-9000
Transamerica Financial Life Insurance Co					
4 Manhattanville Rd Mail Drop 2-50	Purchase	NY	10577	**888-617-6781**	914-697-8000
Transamerica Life Insurance & Annuity Co					
1150 S Olive St	Los Angeles	CA	90015	**800-346-1608**	213-742-3111
Transamerica Occidental Life Insurance Co					
1150 S Olive St	Los Angeles	CA	90015	**800-852-4678***	213-742-2111
*Cust Svc					
Travelers Life & Annuity Co 1 Cityplace	Hartford	CT	06103	**800-334-4298**	860-308-1000
Trustmark Insurance Co 400 Field Dr	Lake Forest	IL	60045	**800-877-9077**	847-615-1500
Union Central Life Insurance Co					
1876 Waycross Rd	Cincinnati	OH	45240	**800-825-1551**	513-595-2200
Union Fidelity Life Insurance Co					
500 Virginia Dr	Fort Washington	PA	19034	**800-523-5758**	
Union Labor Life Insurance Co					
8403 Colesville Rd	Silver Spring	MD	20910	**800-431-5425**	202-682-0900
Union National Life Insurance Co					
8282 Goodwood Blvd	Baton Rouge	LA	70806	**800-765-0550**	225-927-3430
United American Insurance Co Inc					
PO Box 8080	McKinney	TX	75070	**800-331-2512**	972-529-5085
United Healthcare Insurance Co					
9900 Bren Rd E	Minnetonka	MN	55343	**800-328-5979**	952-936-1300
United Heritage Mutual Life Insurance Co					
PO Box 7777	Meridian	ID	83680	**800-657-6351**	208-466-7856
United Investors Life Insurance Co					
2001 3rd Ave S	Birmingham	AL	35233	**800-318-4542**	205-325-4300
United Life Insurance Co PO Box 73909	Cedar Rapids	IA	52407	**800-332-7977**	319-399-5700
United of Omaha Life Insurance Co					
Mutual of Omaha Plaza	Omaha	NE	68175	**800-775-6000**	402-342-7600
United World Life Insurance Co					
Mutual of Omaha Plaza	Omaha	NE	68175	**800-775-6000**	402-342-7600
Unity Mutual Life Insurance Co					
PO Box 5000	Syracuse	NY	13250	**800-836-7100**	315-448-7000
USAA Life Insurance Co					
9800 Fredericksburg Rd	San Antonio	TX	78288	**800-531-8000**	210-498-8000
USG Annuity & Life Co 909 Locust St	Des Moines	IA	50309	**800-369-3690**	515-698-7100
Utica National Insurance Group					
180 Genesee St	New Hartford	NY	13413	**800-274-1914**	315-734-2000
Utica National Life Insurance Co					
180 Genesee St	New Hartford	NY	13413	**800-274-1914**	315-734-2000
VALIC (Variable Annuity Life Insurance Co)					
2929 Allen Pkwy	Houston	TX	77019	**800-633-8960**	713-522-1111
Variable Annuity Life Insurance Co (VALIC)					
2929 Allen Pkwy	Houston	TX	77019	**800-633-8960**	713-522-1111
Vulcan Life Insurance Co PO Box 1980	Carmel	IN	46032	**800-544-0467**	
Wabash Life Insurance Co PO Box 1917	Carmel	IN	46032	**800-525-7662**	317-817-6100
Washington Booker T Insurance Co					
PO Box 697	Birmingham	AL	35201	**800-228-4180**	205-328-5454
Washington National Insurance Co					
11815 N Pennsylvania St	Carmel	IN	46032	**800-933-9301**	
Watt Harvey & Co					
Atlanta Airport PO Box 20787	Atlanta	GA	30320	**800-241-6103**	404-767-7501
West Coast Life Insurance Co					
343 Sansome St	San Francisco	CA	94104	**800-366-9378**	415-591-8200
Western American Life PO Box 833879	Richardson	TX	75083	**866-629-2677**	972-699-2770
Western Fraternal Life Assn					
1900 1st Ave NE	Cedar Rapids	IA	52402	**800-535-5472**	319-363-2653
Western Reserve Life Assurance Co of					
Ohio 570 Carillon Pkwy	Saint Petersburg	FL	33716	**800-851-9777**	727-299-1800
Western-Southern Life Assurance Co					
400 Broadway	Cincinnati	OH	45202	**800-333-5222**	513-629-1800
Western & Southern Life Insurance Co					
400 Broadway	Cincinnati	OH	45202	**800-333-5222**	513-629-1800

Name / Address	City	State	ZIP	Toll-Free	Phone
Western United Life Assurance Co					
PO Box 9000	Post Falls	ID	83877	**800-247-2045**	208-292-3900
William Penn Life Insurance Co of New York					
100 Quentin Roosevelt Blvd.	Garden City	NY	11530	**800-346-4773**	516-794-3700
Wisconsin National Life Insurance Co					
2801 Hwy 280 S	Birmingham	AL	35223	**800-955-4304**	205-879-9230
Woman's Life Insurance Society					
1338 Military St PO Box 5020	Port Huron	MI	48061	**800-521-9292**	810-985-5191
Woodmen Accident & Life Co 1526 K St.	Lincoln	NE	68508	**800-869-0355**	402-476-6500
Woodmen of the World/Omaha Woodmen Life					
Insurance Society 1700 Farnam St	Omaha	NE	68102	**800-225-3108**	402-342-1890

384-3 Medical & Hospitalization Insurance

Name / Address	City	State	ZIP	Toll-Free	Phone
AARP Health Care Options					
PO Box 1017	Montgomeryville	PA	18936	**800-523-5800**	
Aetna Inc 151 Farmington Ave	Hartford	CT	06156	**800-872-3862**	860-273-0123
NYSE: AET					
Aetna US Healthcare Inc 980 Jolly Rd.	Blue Bell	PA	19422	**800-962-6842**	
Alberta Blue Cross 10009 108th St NW	Edmonton	AB	T5J3C5	**800-661-6995**	780-498-8100
Alliance Blue Cross Blue Shield					
1831 Chestnut St.	Saint Louis	MO	63103	**800-366-2583**	314-923-4444
Alliance PPO LLC 4 Taft Ct	Rockville	MD	20850	**800-544-2853**	301-762-8205
Altius Health Plans					
10421 S Jordan Gateway Suite 400	South Jordan	UT	84095	**800-365-1334**	801-355-1234
America Service Group Inc					
105 Westpark Dr Suite 200	Brentwood	TN	37027	**800-729-0069**	615-373-3100
NASDAQ: ASGR					
American Community Mutual Insurance Co					
39201 Seven-Mile Rd.	Livonia	MI	48152	**800-991-2642**	734-591-9000
American National Insurance Co					
1 Moody Plaza	Galveston	TX	77550	**800-899-6806***	409-763-4661
NASDAQ: ANAT ■ *Cust Svc					
American WholeHealth Networks Inc					
45999 Ctr Oak Plaza Suite 100	Sterling	VA	20166	**800-274-7526**	703-547-5100
AMERIGROUP Corp 4425 Corporation Ln	Virginia Beach	VA	23462	**800-600-4441**	757-490-6900
NYSE: AGP					
Ameritas Managed Dental Plan Inc					
5900 'O' St.	Lincoln	NE	68510	**800-404-8019**	402-467-1122
Anthem Blue Cross & Blue Shield					
2015 Staples Mill Rd	Richmond	VA	23230	**888-744-6647***	804-354-7000
*Hum Res					
Anthem Blue Cross Blue Shield in Colorado					
700 Broadway	Denver	CO	80273	**800-654-9338**	303-831-2131
Anthem Blue Cross & Blue Shield of					
Connecticut 370 Bassett Rd	North Haven	CT	06473	**800-545-0948**	203-239-4911
Anthem Blue Cross & Blue Shield of					
Maine 2 Gannett Dr.	South Portland	ME	04106	**800-482-0966***	207-822-7272
*Cust Svc					
Anthem Blue Cross & Blue Shield of the					
Midwest 1351 William Howard Taft Rd	Cincinnati	OH	45204	**888-426-8436**	513-872-8100
Anthem Blue Cross & Blue Shield of Nevada					
6900 Westcliffe Dr Suite 600	Las Vegas	NV	89145	**800-992-6907***	702-228-2583
*Cust Svc					
Anthem Blue Cross & Blue Shield of New					
Hampshire 3000 Goffs Falls Rd	Manchester	NH	03111	**800-225-2666**	603-695-7000
Anthem Blue Cross & Blue Shield of					
Virginia 277 Bendix Rd Suite 100	Virginia Beach	VA	23452	**800-640-0007**	757-326-5130
Arkansas Blue Cross Blue Shield					
PO Box 2181	Little Rock	AR	72203	**800-238-8379**	501-378-2000
Av-Med Health Plan Inc PO Box 749	Gainesville	FL	32602	**800-535-9355**	352-372-8400
AvMed PO Box 749	Gainesville	FL	32602	**800-346-0231**	352-372-8400
Blue Care Network of Michigan					
25925 Telegraph Rd.	Southfield	MI	48086	**800-662-6667**	248-354-7450
Blue Cross & Blue Shield of Alabama					
450 Riverchase Pkwy E	Birmingham	AL	35298	**800-292-8868**	205-988-2200
Blue Cross & Blue Shield of Alaska					
PO Box 91080	Seattle	WA	98111	**800-345-6784**	425-670-4000
Blue Cross Blue Shield of Arizona					
PO Box 2924	Phoenix	AZ	85062	**800-232-2345**	602-864-4400
Blue Cross & Blue Shield of Delaware					
PO Box 1991	Wilmington	DE	19899	**800-633-2563**	302-421-3000
Blue Cross & Blue Shield of Florida Health					
Options Div PO Box 1798	Jacksonville	FL	32231	**800-734-6656**	
Blue Cross & Blue Shield of Florida Inc					
PO Box 1798	Jacksonville	FL	32231	**800-477-3736**	904-791-6111
Blue Cross & Blue Shield of Georgia					
3350 Peachtree Rd NE.	Atlanta	GA	30326	**800-441-2273***	404-842-8000
*Cust Svc					
Blue Cross & Blue Shield of Kansas					
1133 SW Topeka Blvd	Topeka	KS	66629	**800-432-0216**	785-291-7000
Blue Cross & Blue Shield of Kansas City					
2301 Main St	Kansas City	MO	64108	**800-892-6048**	816-395-2222
Blue Cross & Blue Shield of Louisiana					
5525 Reitz Ave.	Baton Rouge	LA	70898	**800-599-2583**	225-295-3307
Blue Cross & Blue Shield of Massachusetts					
401 Park Dr	Boston	MA	02215	**800-262-2583**	
Blue Cross & Blue Shield of Minnesota					
PO Box 64560	Saint Paul	MN	55164	**800-382-2000**	651-662-8000
Blue Cross & Blue Shield of Mississippi					
PO Box 1043	Jackson	MS	39215	**800-222-8046**	601-932-3704
Blue Cross & Blue Shield of Montana					
404 Fuller Ave	Helena	MT	59601	**800-447-7828**	406-444-8200
Blue Cross & Blue Shield of Nebraska					
7261 Mercy Rd	Omaha	NE	68180	**800-642-8980**	402-390-1820
Blue Cross & Blue Shield of New Mexico					
PO Box 27630	Albuquerque	NM	87125	**800-835-8699**	505-291-3500
Blue Cross & Blue Shield of North Carolina					
PO Box 2291	Durham	NC	27702	**800-311-2583***	919-489-7431
*Cust Svc					
Blue Cross Blue Shield of North Dakota					
4510 13th Ave SW.	Fargo	ND	58121	**800-342-4718**	701-282-1100
Blue Cross & Blue Shield of Oklahoma					
1215 S Boulder Ave.	Tulsa	OK	74119	**800-942-5837***	918-560-3500
*Cust Svc					
Blue Cross & Blue Shield of Rhode Island					
444 Westminster St.	Providence	RI	02903	**800-527-7290**	401-459-1000
Blue Cross & Blue Shield of South Carolina					
I-20 E at Alpine Rd	Columbia	SC	29219	**800-288-2227**	803-788-0222
Blue Cross Blue Shield of Tennessee					
801 Pine St	Chattanooga	TN	37402	**800-565-9140**	423-755-5600
Blue Cross & Blue Shield of Texas Inc					
PO Box 655730	Dallas	TX	75265	**800-521-2227***	972-766-6900
*Cust Svc					
Blue Cross & Blue Shield United of Wisconsin					
401 W Michigan St	Milwaukee	WI	53203	**800-558-1584**	414-226-5000
Blue Cross & Blue Shield of Vermont					
445 Industrial Ln	Montpelier	VT	05602	**800-457-6648**	802-223-6131
Blue Cross & Blue Shield of Western New York					
PO Box 80	Buffalo	NY	14240	**800-888-0757**	716-887-6900
Blue Cross & Blue Shield of Wyoming					
PO Box 2266	Cheyenne	WY	82003	**800-851-9145***	307-634-1393
*Cust Svc					
Blue Cross of California					
21555 Oxnard St	Woodland Hills	CA	91365	**800-999-3643**	818-703-2345
Blue Cross of Idaho 3000 E Pine Ave	Meridian	ID	83642	**800-365-2345***	208-345-4550
*Cust Svc					
Blue Cross of Northeastern Pennsylvania					
19 N Main St	Wilkes-Barre	PA	18711	**800-829-8599***	570-200-4300
*Cust Svc					
BlueCross BlueShield of the Rochester Area					
165 Court St	Rochester	NY	14647	**800-847-1200**	585-454-1700
Capital Blue Cross 2500 Elmerton Ave.	Harrisburg	PA	17110	**800-958-5558***	610-820-2700
*Cust Svc					
Capital District Physicians' Health Plan Inc					
1223 Washington Ave	Albany	NY	12206	**800-777-2273**	518-641-3000
Capital Health Plan 2140 Centerville Pl	Tallahassee	FL	32308	**800-390-1434**	850-383-3333
Carelink Health Plans					
141 Summers Square PO Box 1711	Charleston	WV	25326	**800-348-2922**	
Centene Corp					
7711 Carondelet Ave Suite 800	Saint Louis	MO	63105	**800-225-2573**	314-725-4477
NYSE: CNC					
Central Reserve Life 17800 Royalton Rd.	Strongsville	OH	44136	**800-321-3997**	440-572-2400
Chiropractic Health Plan of California					
PO Box 190	Clayton	CA	94517	**800-995-2442**	925-672-0106
ChiroSource Inc 6200 Center St Suite 260	Clayton	CA	94517	**800-680-9997**	925-844-3100
CIGNA Healthcare 900 Cottage Grove Rd	Hartford	CT	06152	**800-832-3211**	860-226-6000
CIGNA Healthcare of Arizona					
11001 N Black Canyon Hwy	Phoenix	AZ	85029	**800-572-9990**	602-942-4462
CIGNA Healthcare of California					
400 N Brand Blvd	Glendale	CA	91203	**800-344-7421**	818-500-6262
CIGNA Healthcare of Florida Inc Tampa					
5404 Cypress Ctr Dr	Tampa	FL	33609	**800-832-3211**	
CIGNA Healthcare of New Hampshire					
2 College Pk Dr	Hooksett	NH	03106	**800-531-3121**	
CIGNA Healthcare of San Diego					
3636 Noble Dr Suite 150	San Diego	CA	92122	**800-368-2471**	858-625-5600
CIGNA Healthcare of South Carolina Inc					
146 Fairchild Dr	Charleston	SC	29492	**800-962-8811**	843-884-4063
Cole Managed Vision 1925 Enterprise Pkwy	Twinsburg	OH	44087	**800-282-3931**	330-486-4000
Community Blue HMO of Blue Cross & Blue					
Shield of Western New York Inc					
PO Box 159	Buffalo	NY	14240	**800-544-2583**	716-884-2800
Community Care 218 W 6th St.	Tulsa	OK	74119	**800-278-7563**	918-594-5200
CompDent Corp 100 Mansell Ct E Suite 400	Roswell	GA	30076	**800-633-1262**	770-552-7101
Comprehensive Health Services Inc DBA Wellness					
Plan The 2888 W Grand Blvd	Detroit	MI	48202	**800-680-9355***	313-875-4200
*Cust Svc					
ConnectiCare Inc 30 Batterson Park Rd	Farmington	CT	06032	**800-251-7722**	860-674-5700
Consumer Health Network					
3525 Quakerbridge Rd	Hamilton	NJ	08619	**800-225-4246**	
Continental General Insurance Co					
PO Box 247007	Omaha	NE	68124	**800-545-8905**	402-397-3200
Coventry Health Care of Delaware Inc					
2751 Centerville Rd Suite 400	Wilmington	DE	19808	**800-727-9951**	302-995-6100
Coventry Health Care of Georgia Inc					
1100 Circle 75 Pkwy Suite 1400	Atlanta	GA	30339	**800-470-2004**	678-202-2100
Coventry Health Care Inc					
6705 Rockledge Dr Suite 900	Bethesda	MD	20817	**800-843-7421**	301-581-0600
NYSE: CVH					
Coventry Health Care of Iowa Inc					
4600 Westown Pkwy Regency 6					
Suite 200	West Des Moines	IA	50266	**800-470-6352**	515-225-1234
Coventry Health Care of Kansas Inc					
2300 Main St Suite 700	Kansas City	MO	64108	**800-468-1442**	816-221-8400
Coventry Health Care of Louisiana Inc					
2424 Edenborn Ave Suite 350	Metairie	LA	70001	**800-245-8327**	504-834-0840
Coventry Health Care of Nebraska Inc					
13305 Birch Dr Suite 100	Omaha	NE	68164	**800-471-0420**	402-498-9030
Coventry HealthCare Management Corp					
9881 Mayland Dr	Richmond	VA	23233	**800-424-0077**	804-747-3700
DAKOTACARE 1323 S Minnesota Ave	Sioux Falls	SD	57105	**800-325-5598**	605-334-4000
Davis Vision Inc 159 Express St.	Plainview	NY	11803	**800-328-4728**	516-932-9500
Dean Health Plan 1277 Deming Way	Madison	WI	53717	**800-279-1301**	608-836-1400
Deere John Health Plan Inc					
1300 River Dr Suite 200	Moline	IL	61265	**800-224-6599**	309-765-1200
Delta Dental Insurance Co PO Box 1809	Alpharetta	GA	30023	**800-521-2651**	770-645-8700
Delta Dental Insurance Co - Alaska					
257 E 200 South Suite 375	Salt Lake City	UT	84111	**800-521-2651**	801-575-5168
Delta Dental of Pennsylvania					
1 Delta Dr.	Mechanicsburg	PA	17055	**800-932-0783**	717-766-8500
Delta Dental Plan of Alabama					
1000 Mansell Exchange W Bldg 100					
Suite 100	Alpharetta	GA	30022	**800-521-2651**	770-645-8700
Delta Dental Plan of Arizona PO Box 43026	Phoenix	AZ	85080	**800-352-6132**	
Delta Dental Plan of Arkansas					
1513 Country Club Rd	Sherwood	AR	72120	**800-462-5410**	501-835-3400
Delta Dental Plan of California					
PO Box 7736	San Francisco	CA	94120	**888-335-8227**	415-972-8300
Delta Dental Plan of Colorado					
4582 S Ulster St Suite 800	Denver	CO	80237	**800-233-0860**	303-741-9300
Delta Dental Plan of Connecticut					
PO Box 222	Parsippany	NJ	07054	**800-346-5377**	973-285-4000
Delta Dental Plan of Delaware					
1 Delta Dr.	Mechanicsburg	PA	17055	**800-932-0783**	717-766-8500
Delta Dental Plan of Florida PO Box 1809	Alpharetta	GA	30022	**800-521-2651**	
Delta Dental Plan of Georgia PO Box 1809	Alpharetta	GA	30023	**800-521-2651**	
Delta Dental Plan of Idaho PO Box 2870	Boise	ID	83701	**800-388-3490**	208-344-4546
Delta Dental Plan of Illinois PO Box 5402	Lisle	IL	60532	**800-323-1743**	630-964-2400
Delta Dental Plan of Indiana PO Box 30416	Lansing	MI	48909	**800-524-0149**	
Delta Dental Plan of Iowa					
2401 SE Tones Dr Suite 13	Ankeny	IA	50021	**800-532-1514**	515-963-4100
Delta Dental Plan of Kansas PO Box 49198	Wichita	KS	67201	**800-234-3375**	316-264-4511
Delta Dental Plan of Kentucky					
PO Box 242810	Louisville	KY	40224	**800-955-2023**	502-736-5000

Medical & Hospitalization Insurance (Cont'd)

Company / Address	City	State	ZIP	Toll-Free	Phone
Delta Dental Plan of Louisiana PO Box 1809	Alpharetta	GA	30023	**800-521-2651**	
Delta Dental Plan of Maine PO Box 2002	Concord	NH	03302	**800-832-5700**	
Delta Dental Plan of Maryland 1 Delta Dr.	Mechanicsburg	PA	17055	**800-932-0783**	717-766-8500
Delta Dental Plan of Massachusetts 465 Medford St *Cust Svc	Boston	MA	02129	**800-872-0500***	617-886-1000
Delta Dental Plan of Michigan PO Box 30416	Lansing	MI	48909	**800-524-0149**	
Delta Dental Plan of Minnesota PO Box 330	Minneapolis	MN	55440	**800-553-9536**	651-406-5918
Delta Dental Plan of Minnesota Corp PO Box 59238	Minneapolis	MN	55459	**800-448-3815**	651-406-5901
Delta Dental Plan of Mississippi PO Box 1809	Alpharetta	GA	30023	**800-521-2651**	
Delta Dental Plan of Missouri PO Box 8690	Saint Louis	MO	63126	**800-392-1167**	314-656-3000
Delta Dental Plan of Montana PO Box 1809	Alpharetta	GA	30023	**800-521-2651**	
Delta Dental Plan of Nebraska PO Box 245	Minneapolis	MN	55440	**800-553-9536**	
Delta Dental Plan of Nevada PO Box 1809	Alpharetta	GA	30023	**800-521-2651**	
Delta Dental Plan of New Hampshire 1 Delta Dr PO Box 2002	Concord	NH	03302	**800-537-1715**	603-223-1000
Delta Dental Plan of New Jersey Inc 1639 Rt 10 E	Parsippany	NJ	07054	**800-346-5377**	973-285-4000
Delta Dental Plan of New Mexico 2500 Louisiana Blvd NE Suite 600	Albuquerque	NM	87110	**800-999-0963**	505-883-4777
Delta Dental Plan of New York 1 Delta Dr.	Mechanicsburg	PA	17055	**800-932-0783**	717-766-8500
Delta Dental Plan of North Carolina 333 Six Forks Rd Suite 180	Raleigh	NC	27609	**800-662-8856**	919-832-6015
Delta Dental Plan of North Dakota 3560 Delta Dental Dr	Eagan	MN	55122	**800-328-1188**	651-406-5900
Delta Dental Plan of Ohio PO Box 30416	Lansing	MI	48909	**800-524-0149**	
Delta Dental Plan of Oklahoma 16 NW 63rd St Suite 301	Oklahoma City	OK	73116	**800-522-0188**	405-607-2100
Delta Dental Plan of South Carolina PO Box 8690	Saint Louis	MO	63126	**800-392-1167**	314-656-3000
Delta Dental Plan of South Dakota 720 N Euclid Ave PO Box 1157	Pierre	SD	57501	**800-627-3961**	605-224-7345
Delta Dental Plan of Tennessee 240 Venture Cir	Nashville	TN	37228	**800-223-3104**	615-255-3175
Delta Dental Plan of Texas 1000 Mansell Exchange W Bldg 100 Suite 100	Alpharetta	GA	30022	**800-521-2651**	770-645-8700
Delta Dental Plan of Utah 1000 Mansell Exchange W Bldg 100 Suite 100	Alpharetta	GA	30022	**800-521-2651**	770-645-8700
Delta Dental Plan of Virginia 4818 Starkey Rd SW	Roanoke	VA	24014	**800-367-3531**	540-989-8000
Delta Dental Plan of Wisconsin 2801 Hoover Rd.	Stevens Point	WI	54481	**800-236-3713**	715-344-6087
Delta Dental Plan of Wyoming 320 W 25th St Suite 100	Cheyenne	WY	82001	**800-735-3379**	307-632-3313
Delta Dental of Rhode Island PO Box 1517	Providence	RI	02901	**800-843-3582**	401-752-6100
Delta Dental of West Virginia 1 Delta Dr.	Mechanicsburg	PA	17055	**800-932-0783**	717-766-8500
Doral Dental USA LLC 12121 N Corporate Pkwy	Mequon	WI	53092	**800-417-7140**	262-241-7140
Empire Blue Cross & Blue Shield 11 W 42 St *NYSE: WC*	New York	NY	10036	**800-261-5962**	212-476-1000
Empire Deluxe PPO 11 W 42nd St	New York	NY	10036	**800-261-5962**	212-476-1000
Excellus BlueCross BlueShield of Central New York 344 S Warren St	Syracuse	NY	13202	**800-633-6066**	315-671-6400
Excellus BlueCross BlueShield of Utica 12 Rhoads Dr.	Utica	NY	13502	**800-544-1450**	
EyeMed Vision Care 4000 Luxottica Pl.	Mason	OH	45040	**888-439-3633**	
First Choice Health Plan 600 University St 13th Fl	Seattle	WA	98101	**800-783-7312**	206-268-2406
First Commonwealth Inc 444 N Wells St Suite 600	Chicago	IL	60610	**800-788-3384**	312-644-1800
First Priority Health 19 N Main St	Wilkes-Barre	PA	18711	**800-822-8753**	
Geisinger Health Plan 100 N Academy Ave	Danville	PA	17822	**800-447-4000**	570-271-8760
Georgia Healthcare Partnership Inc 7135 Hodgson Memorial Dr Suite 12	Savannah	GA	31406	**800-566-6710**	912-350-6710
Golden West Dental & Vision Plan Inc 888 W Ventura Blvd.	Camarillo	CA	93010	**800-995-4124**	805-987-8941
Great-West Healthcare 8525 E Orchard Rd	Greenwood Village	CO	80111	**800-839-6631**	
Group Health Co-op 521 Wall St.	Seattle	WA	98121	**888-901-4636**	206-448-5600
Group Health Plan Inc 111 Corporate Office Dr Suite 400	Earth City	MO	63045	**800-743-3901**	314-506-1700
Hanover Insurance Co 100 North Pkwy	Worcester	MA	01605	**800-922-8427**	508-853-7200
Harvard Pilgrim Health Care Inc 93 Worcester St.	Wellesley	MA	02481	**888-888-4742**	617-509-1000
Hawaii Medical Service Assn 818 Keeaumoku St.	Honolulu	HI	96814	**800-648-3190**	808-948-6111
Health Alliance Medical Plans 102 E Main St	Urbana	IL	61801	**800-851-3379**	217-337-8000
Health Alliance Plan 2850 W Grand Blvd	Detroit	MI	48202	**800-422-4641**	313-872-8100
Health Care Savings Inc 4530 Park Rd Suite 110	Charlotte	NC	28209	**800-833-8464**	704-527-6261
Health Net Inc 21650 Oxnard St. *NYSE: HNT*	Woodland Hills	CA	91367	**800-291-6911**	818-676-6000
Health Options Div Blue Cross & Blue Shield of Florida PO Box 1798	Jacksonville	FL	32231	**800-734-6656**	
Health Plan of Upper Ohio Valley Inc 52160 National Rd E	Saint Clairsville	OH	43950	**800-624-6961**	740-695-3585
HealthAmerica Pennsylvania Inc 3721 Tecport Dr.	Harrisburg	PA	17111	**800-788-6445**	717-540-4260
HealthCare USA Inc 10 S Broadway Suite 1200	Saint Louis	MO	63102	**800-213-7792**	314-241-5300
HealthLink Inc 12443 Olive Blvd.	Saint Louis	MO	63141	**800-624-2356**	314-989-6000
HealthPartners Inc PO Box 1309	Minneapolis	MN	55440	**800-883-2177**	952-883-5000
Healthplex Inc 60 Charles Lindbergh Blvd	Uniondale	NY	11553	**800-468-0608**	516-794-3000
HealthPlus of Michigan 2050 S Linden Rd	Flint	MI	48532	**800-332-9161**	810-230-2000
Healthsource North Carolina Inc 701 Corporate Center Dr	Raleigh	NC	27607	**800-849-9300**	919-854-7000
Heritage Summit HealthCare of Florida Inc PO Box 3623	Lakeland	FL	33802	**800-282-7644**	863-665-6629
HIP Health Plans 7 W 34th St	New York	NY	10001	**800-447-8255**	212-630-5000
HMO Illinois Inc 300 E Randolph St.	Chicago	IL	60601	**800-892-2803**	312-938-6600
Horizon Blue Cross Blue Shield of New Jersey 3 Penn Plaza E.	Newark	NJ	07105	**800-466-2583**	973-466-4000
Humana HMO 500 W Main St	Louisville	KY	40202	**800-448-6262**	502-580-1000
Humana Inc 500 W Main St *NYSE: HUM*	Louisville	KY	40202	**800-486-2620**	502-580-1000
Humana Military Healthcare Services 500 W Main St.	Louisville	KY	40201	**800-964-5482**	502-580-3200
IHC Health Plans Inc PO Box 30192	Salt Lake City	UT	84130	**800-538-5038**	801-442-5000
Independence Blue Cross 1901 Market St.	Philadelphia	PA	19103	**800-227-3114**	215-241-2400
Independent Health Assn 511 Farber Lakes Dr	Buffalo	NY	14221	**800-247-1466**	716-631-3001
John Deere Health Care Inc 1300 River Dr Suite 200	Moline	IL	61265	**800-224-6599**	309-765-1200
Kaiser Foundation Health Plan Inc 1 Kaiser Plaza 27th Fl	Oakland	CA	94612	**800-464-4000**	510-271-5910
Kaiser Permanente 1 Kaiser Plaza 27th Fl	Oakland	CA	94612	**800-464-4000**	510-271-5910
Kaiser Permanente California 1950 Franklin St.	Oakland	CA	94612	**800-464-4000**	510-987-1000
Kaiser Permanente Colorado Denver/Boulder 10350 E Dakota Ave	Denver	CO	80231	**800-632-9700**	303-344-7200
Kaiser Permanente Hawaii 711 Kapiolani Blvd	Honolulu	HI	96813	**800-966-5955**	808-432-5955
Kaiser Permanente Mid-Atlantic States Inc 2101 E Jefferson St.	Rockville	MD	20849	**800-368-5784**	301-468-6000
Kaiser Permanente Northwest 500 NE Multnomah St Suite 100	Portland	OR	97232	**800-813-2000**	503-813-2800
Kaiser Permanente Ohio 1001 Lakeside Ave N Pt Tower Suite 1200	Cleveland	OH	44114	**888-571-4141**	216-621-5600
Kanawha Insurance Co PO Box 610	Lancaster	SC	29721	**800-635-4252**	803-283-5300
Keystone Health Plan Central 3815 Tecport Dr.	Harrisburg	PA	17111	**800-622-2843**	
Keystone Health Plan East Inc 1901 Market St	Philadelphia	PA	19101	**800-227-3114**	215-241-2400
Long Term Preferred Care Inc 801 Crescent Ctr Dr Suite 200	Franklin	TN	37067	**800-251-2148**	
Lovelace Health Plan 4101 Indian School Rd NE *Hum Res	Albuquerque	NM	87110	**800-877-7526***	505-262-7363
M-Care 2301 Commonwealth Blvd	Ann Arbor	MI	48105	**800-527-5549**	734-747-8700
MAMSI Life & Health Insurance Co 4 Taft Ct	Rockville	MD	20850	**800-544-2853**	301-762-8205
MD IPA 4 Taft Ct	Rockville	MD	20850	**800-638-8898**	301-762-8205
MEDICA PO Box 9310 *Cust Svc	Minneapolis	MN	55440	**800-952-3455***	952-992-2900
MetLife Inc 27-01 Queens Plaza North 1 MetLife Plaza *NYSE: MET*	Long Island City	NY	11101	**800-638-5433**	212-578-2211
Molina Healthcare Inc 1 Golden Shore Dr. *NYSE: MOH*	Long Beach	CA	90802	**800-526-8196**	562-435-3666
Mountain State Blue Cross & Blue Shield 700 Market St	Parkersburg	WV	26102	**800-344-5514**	304-424-7700
MSC 3900 E Sprague Ave	Spokane	WA	99202	**800-835-3510**	509-536-4700
MVP Health Plan 625 State St	Schenectady	NY	12305	**800-777-4793**	518-370-4793
Nationwide Health Plans 5525 Parkcenter Cir	Dublin	OH	43017	**800-259-4458**	614-854-3001
Neighborhood Health Partnership Inc 7600 Corporate Ctr Dr	Miami	FL	33126	**800-354-0222**	305-715-2200
Northeast Delta Dental PO Box 2002	Concord	NH	03302	**800-537-1715**	603-223-1000
ODS Health Plans Inc 601 SW 2nd Ave	Portland	OR	97204	**800-852-5195**	503-228-6554
OmniCare Health Plan 1155 Brewery Pk Blvd Suite 250 *Cust Svc	Detroit	MI	48207	**800-477-6664***	313-393-0200
Optimum Choice Inc 4 Taft Ct	Rockville	MD	20850	**800-544-2853**	301-545-5900
Optimum Health Services Inc 707 60th St Ct E Suite A	Bradenton	FL	34208	**800-841-1585**	941-747-1585
Oxford Health Insurance Inc 48 Monroe Tpk	Trumbull	CT	06611	**800-889-7546**	203-459-9100
Oxford Health Plans (CT) Inc 48 Monroe Tpk	Trumbull	CT	06611	**800-889-7546**	203-459-9100
Oxford Health Plans Inc 48 Monroe Tpke	Trumbull	CT	06611	**800-444-6222**	203-459-9100
Oxford Health Plans (NH) Inc 10 Tara Blvd	Nashua	NH	03062	**800-889-7630**	603-891-7000
Oxford Health Plans (NJ) Inc 111 Wood Ave 2nd Fl	Iselin	NJ	08830	**800-201-6920**	732-623-1000
Oxford Health Plans (NY) Inc 1133 Ave of the Americas	New York	NY	10036	**800-889-7622**	212-805-3400
Pacific Union Dental 1390 Willow Pass Rd Suite 800	Concord	CA	94520	**800-999-3367**	925-363-6000
PacifiCare of Arizona PO Box 52078	Phoenix	AZ	85072	**800-347-8600**	602-244-8200
PacifiCare of California 5701 Katella Ave	Cypress	CA	90630	**800-624-8822**	714-952-1121
PacifiCare of Colorado 6455 S Yosemite St.	Greenwood Village	CO	80111	**800-877-9777**	303-220-5800
PacifiCare Dental PO Box 25187	Santa Ana	CA	92704	**800-622-6388**	
PacifiCare Health Systems Inc 5995 Plaza Dr. *NYSE: PHS* ■ *Cust Svc	Cypress	CA	90630	**800-624-8822***	714-952-1121
PacifiCare of Nevada 700 E Warm Spring	Las Vegas	NV	89119	**800-826-4347**	702-269-7500
PacifiCare of Oklahoma 7666 E 61st St Suite 500	Tulsa	OK	74133	**800-459-8890**	918-459-1100
PacifiCare of Oregon 5 Centerpointe Dr Suite 600	Lake Oswego	OR	97035	**800-922-1444**	
Pacificare of Texas 6200 NW Pkwy	San Antonio	TX	78249	**800-624-7272**	210-474-5000
PacifiCare Vision PO Box 66033	Anaheim	CA	92816	**800-622-6388**	
PacifiCare of Washington 7525 SE 24th St Suite 200	Mercer Island	WA	98040	**800-829-2925**	206-236-2500
Paramount Health Care PO Box 928	Toledo	OH	43697	**800-462-3589**	419-887-2525
Partners National Health Plans of North Carolina Inc PO Box 24907	Winston-Salem	NC	27114	**800-942-5695**	336-760-4822
Physicians Health Plan Inc PO Box 30377	Lansing	MI	48909	**800-832-9186**	517-364-8400
Physicians Healthcare Plans Inc 55 Alhambra Plaza 7th Fl.	Coral Gables	FL	33134	**800-577-1072**	305-441-9400
Physicians Plus Insurance Corp 22 E Mifflin St Suite 200	Madison	WI	53703	**800-545-5015**	608-282-8900
PlanVista Corp 4010 Boy Scout Blvd Suite 200	Tampa	FL	33607	**866-318-6564**	813-353-2300
PMI Dental Health Plan 12898 Towne Ctr Dr	Cerritos	CA	90703	**800-422-4234**	562-924-8311
PPOM LLC 28588 Northwestern Hwy	Southfield	MI	48034	**800-831-1166**	248-357-7766
ppoNEXT Inc 1501 Hughes Way Suite 400	Long Beach	CA	90802	**866-776-6398**	
Preferred Care Inc 259 Monroe Ave	Rochester	NY	14607	**800-950-3224**	585-325-3920
Preferred CommunityChoice PPO 218 W 6th St	Tulsa	OK	74119	**800-278-7563**	918-594-5200
Preferred Health Systems Inc 8535 E 21st St N	Wichita	KS	67206	**800-990-0345**	316-609-2345
Premera Blue Cross DBA Blue Cross & Blue Shield of Alaska PO Box 91080	Seattle	WA	98111	**800-345-6784**	425-670-4000
Premera Blue Cross DBA MSC 3900 E Sprague Ave	Spokane	WA	99202	**800-835-3510**	509-536-4700
Premera HealthPlus PO Box 2113 *Cust Svc	Seattle	WA	98111	**800-527-6675***	425-918-4700
Primary Health 800 Park Blvd Suite 760	Boise	ID	83712	**800-688-5008**	208-344-1811
Priority Health 1231 E Beltline Ave NE	Grand Rapids	MI	49525	**800-942-0954**	616-942-0954

				Toll-Free	Phone
Priority Health Managed Benefits Inc 1231 E Beltline NE	Grand Rapids	MI	49525	**800-942-0954**	616-942-0954
Prison Health Services 105 Westpark Dr Suite 200	Brentwood	TN	37027	**800-729-0069**	615-373-3100
Provident American Insurance Co Inc 10501 N Central Expy Suite 200	Dallas	TX	75231	**800-933-9456**	214-696-9091
Provider Networks of America Inc PO Box 101387	Fort Worth	TX	76185	**800-462-7554**	
QualChoice Health Plan Inc 6000 Parkland Blvd	Cleveland	OH	44124	**800-208-1232**	440-460-0093
Regence Blue Cross Blue Shield of Oregon PO Box 1271	Portland	OR	97207	**800-547-0939**	503-225-5364
Regence Blue Shield 1800 9th Ave	Seattle	WA	98101	**800-544-4246**	206-464-3600
Regence Blue Shield of Idaho 1602 21st Ave	Lewiston	ID	83501	**800-632-2022**	208-746-2671
Regence BlueCross BlueShield of Utah 2890 E Cottonwood Pkwy *Cust Svc	Salt Lake City	UT	84121	**800-624-6519***	801-333-2100
RightCHOICE Managed Care Inc DBA Alliance Blue Cross Blue Shield 1831 Chestnut St	Saint Louis	MO	63103	**800-366-2583**	314-923-4444
Rocky Mountain Health Plans PO Box 10600	Grand Junction	CO	81502	**800-843-0719**	970-244-7760
SafeGuard Health Enterprises Inc 95 Enterprise Suite 100	Aliso Viejo	CA	92656	**800-880-1800**	949-425-4300
Sagamore Health Network 11555 N Meridian St Suite 400	Carmel	IN	46032	**800-364-3469**	317-573-2886
Scott & White Health Plan 2401 S 31st St	Temple	TX	76508	**800-321-7947**	254-298-3000
Security Health Plan of Wisconsin Inc 1515 St Joseph Ave	Marshfield	WI	54449	**800-472-2363**	715-387-5621
Sloans Lake Managed Care Inc 6501 S Fiddler's Green Cir Suite 300	Greenwood Village	CO	80111	**800-850-2249**	303-691-2200
Southern Health Services Inc 9881 Mayland Dr	Richmond	VA	23233	**800-424-0077**	804-747-3700
Spectera Inc 2811 Lord Baltimore Dr	Baltimore	MD	21244	**800-638-3120**	410-265-6084
Spectera Vision 100 Corporate Pt Suite 285	Culver City	CA	90230	**800-305-0230**	310-242-6200
STAR Human Resources Group Inc 2222 W Dunlap Ave Suite 350	Phoenix	AZ	85021	**800-308-5948**	602-956-4200
Tufts Associated Health Plans Inc 333 Wyman St	Waltham	MA	02451	**800-462-0224**	781-466-9400
UHP Healthcare 3405 W Imperial Hwy	Inglewood	CA	90303	**800-544-0088**	310-671-3465
Union Pacific Railroad Employees' Health Systems 795 N 400 West	Salt Lake City	UT	84103	**800-547-0421**	801-595-4300
United Concordia Cos Inc 2000 Town Ctr Suite 2200	Southfield	MI	48075	**800-944-6432**	248-353-6410
UnitedHealth Group Inc 9900 Bren Rd East *NYSE: UNH*	Minnetonka	MN	55343	**800-328-5979**	952-936-1300
UnitedHealthcare PO Box 1459	Minneapolis	MN	55440	**800-328-5979**	952-936-1300
Unity Health Plans 840 Carolina St	Sauk City	WI	53583	**800-362-3308**	608-643-2491
Univera Healthcare 205 Park Club Ln	Buffalo	NY	14221	**800-628-8451**	716-847-1480
Universal Care Inc 1600 E Hill St	Signal Hill	CA	90755	**800-635-6668**	562-424-6200
USA Managed Care Organization 7301 N 16th St Suite 201	Phoenix	AZ	85020	**800-872-0020**	602-371-3860
Valley Health Plan Inc 2270 Eastridge Ctr	Eau Claire	WI	54701	**800-472-5411**	715-836-1254
Vision Service Plan (VSP) 3333 Quality Dr *Cust Svc	Rancho Cordova	CA	95670	**800-852-7600***	916-851-5000
Vista Health Plan 300 S Park Rd	Hollywood	FL	33021	**800-447-5116**	954-962-3008
Washington Dental Service 9706 4th Ave NE	Seattle	WA	98115	**800-554-1907**	206-522-1300
Well Path Community Health Plans 6330 Quadrangle Dr Suite 500	Chapel Hill	NC	27517	**800-935-7284**	919-493-1210
WellCare of New York PO Box 1652	Newburgh	NY	12551	**800-288-5441**	
WellChoice Inc 11 W 42 St *NYSE: WC*	New York	NY	10036	**800-261-5962**	212-476-1000
Wellmark Blue Cross & Blue Shield of Iowa 636 Grand Ave	Des Moines	IA	50309	**800-526-8995**	515-245-4500
Wellmark Blue Cross & Blue Shield of South Dakota 1601 W Madison St	Sioux Falls	SD	57104	**800-952-1976**	605-373-7200
Wellmark Inc 636 Grand Ave	Des Moines	IA	50309	**800-362-1697**	515-245-4500
Wellmark of South Dakota Inc DBA Wellmark Blue Cross & Blue Shield of South Da 1601 W Madison St	Sioux Falls	SD	57104	**800-952-1976**	605-373-7200
Wellness Plan The 2888 W Grand Blvd *Cust Svc	Detroit	MI	48202	**800-680-9355***	313-875-4200
WellPath Select Inc 6 Coliseum Ctr 2815 Coliseum Ctr Dr Suite 550	Charlotte	NC	28217	**800-470-4523**	704-357-1421
WellPoint Inc 120 Monument Cir Suite 200 *NYSE: WLP*	Indianapolis	IN	46204	**800-331-1476**	317-488-6000

384-4 Property & Casualty Insurance

				Toll-Free	Phone
21st Century Casualty Co 6301 Owensmouth Ave	Woodland Hills	CA	91367	**800-443-3100**	818-704-3700
21st Century Insurance Co 6301 Owensmouth Ave	Woodland Hills	CA	91367	**800-443-3100**	818-704-3700
Acceptance Insurance Cos Inc 300 W Broadway Suite 3600	Council Bluffs	IA	51503	**800-228-7217**	712-329-3600
Access Group PO Box 250367	Atlanta	GA	30325	**877-353-9837**	770-234-3600
Accident Fund Co 232 S Capitol Ave	Lansing	MI	48901	**800-888-0616**	517-342-4200
Acuity Insurance PO Box 58	Sheboygan	WI	53082	**800-242-7666**	920-458-9131
Addison Insurance Co 118 2nd Ave SE	Cedar Rapids	IA	52401	**800-332-7977**	319-399-5700
Ag States Agency 5500 Cenex Dr	Inver Grove Heights	MN	55077	**800-548-1494**	651-355-3700
All Nation Insurance Co Inc 29621 Northwestern Hwy	Southfield	MI	48034	**800-254-8144**	
Allegiance Insurance Co 1 Horace Mann Plaza	Springfield	IL	62715	**800-999-1030**	217-789-2500
Allianz Insurance Co 2350 Empire Ave	Burbank	CA	91504	**800-421-0504**	818-260-7500
Allied Insurance 3820 109th St	Des Moines	IA	50391	**800-532-1436**	515-508-4211
Allmerica Property & Casualty Cos Inc 440 Lincoln St	Worcester	MA	01653	**800-407-5222**	508-855-1000
Allstate Indemnity Co 2775 Sanders Rd	Northbrook	IL	60062	**800-366-2958**	847-402-5000
Allstate Insurance Co 2775 Sanders Rd Allstate Plaza	Northbrook	IL	60062	**800-366-2958**	847-402-5000
American Alternative Insurance Corp 685 College Rd E	Princeton	NJ	08543	**800-305-4954**	609-951-8295
American Commerce Insurance Co 3590 Twin Creeks Dr	Columbus	OH	43204	**800-848-2945**	614-272-6951
American Family Mutual Insurance Co 6000 American Pkwy *Cust Svc	Madison	WI	53783	**800-374-0008***	608-249-2111
American Federation Insurance Co 25400 US Hwy 19 N Suite 185	Clearwater	FL	33763	**800-527-3907**	727-712-2115
American Fire & Casualty Co 9450 Seward Rd	Fairfield	OH	45014	**800-843-6446**	513-867-3000
American Hardware Mutual Insurance Co PO Box 435	Minneapolis	MN	55440	**800-227-4663**	952-935-1400
American Manufacturers Mutual Insurance Co 1 Kemper Dr	Long Grove	IL	60049	**800-833-0355**	847-320-2000
American Motorists Insurance Co 1 Kemper Dr	Long Grove	IL	60049	**800-833-0355**	847-320-2000
American Physicians Assurance Corp 1301 N Hagadorn Rd	East Lansing	MI	48823	**800-748-0465**	517-351-1150
American Protection Insurance Co 1 Kemper Dr	Long Grove	IL	60049	**800-833-0355**	847-320-2000
American Reinsurance Co 555 College Rd E	Princeton	NJ	08543	**800-255-5676**	609-243-4200
American Road Insurance Co 4 Park Ln Blvd Suite 460	Dearborn	MI	48126	**800-234-2722**	313-845-5850
American Southern Insurance Co 3715 Northside Pkwy NW Bldg 400 8th Fl	Atlanta	GA	30327	**800-241-1172**	404-266-9599
AMERISAFE Inc 2301 Hwy 190 W	DeRidder	LA	70634	**800-256-9052**	337-463-9052
Amerisure Insurance Co PO Box 2060	Farmington Hills	MI	48333	**800-257-1900**	248-615-9000
Amica Mutual Insurance Co 100 Amica Way	Lincoln	RI	02865	**800-652-6422**	
Arbella Indemnity Insurance Co PO Box 699103	Quincy	MA	02269	**800-972-5348**	617-328-2800
Arbella Mutual Insurance Co PO Box 699103	Quincy	MA	02269	**800-972-5348**	617-328-2800
Arbella Protection Insurance Co PO Box 699103	Quincy	MA	02269	**800-972-5348**	617-328-2800
Argonaut Insurance Co 250 Middlefield Rd	Menlo Park	CA	94025	**800-222-7811**	650-326-0900
Armed Forces Insurance Exchange (AFI) PO Box G	Fort Leavenworth	KS	66027	**800-828-7732**	913-651-5000
Association Casualty Insurance Co PO Box 9728	Austin	TX	78766	**800-252-9641**	512-345-7500
Association Risk Management General Agency PO Box 9728 Suite 160	Austin	TX	78766	**800-252-9641**	512-345-7500
Audubon Insurance Group PO Drawer 15989	Baton Rouge	LA	70895	**800-274-9830**	225-293-5900
Auto-Owners Insurance Co PO Box 30660	Lansing	MI	48909	**800-346-0346**	517-323-1200
Avemco Insurance Co 411 Aviation Way	Frederick	MD	21701	**800-874-9125**	301-694-5700
Avomark Insurance Co 9450 Seward Rd	Fairfield	OH	45014	**800-843-6446**	513-603-7400
AXA Canada Inc 2020 University St 6th Fl	Montreal	QC	H3A2A5	**800-361-1594**	514-282-1914
Baldwin & Lyons Inc 1099 N Meridian St Suite 700 *NASDAQ: BWINB*	Indianapolis	IN	46204	**800-231-6024**	317-636-9800
Bank of America Insurance Services Inc PO Box 21848	Greensboro	NC	27420	**800-288-7647**	336-805-8800
Bankers Insurance Co 360 Central Ave	Saint Petersburg	FL	33701	**800-627-0000**	727-823-4000
Brotherhood Mutual Insurance Co 6400 Brotherhood Way	Fort Wayne	IN	46825	**800-333-3735**	260-482-8668
California Automobile Insurance Co 4484 Wilshire Blvd	Los Angeles	CA	90010	**800-431-6654**	323-857-7191
California Casualty Insurance Group PO Box M	San Mateo	CA	94402	**800-288-7765**	650-574-4000
Canada Life Financial Corp 330 University Ave	Toronto	ON	M5G1R8	**888-252-1847**	416-597-1456
Capitol Indemnity Corp 4610 University Ave Suite 1400	Madison	WI	53705	**800-475-4450**	608-231-4450
Capitol Specialty Insurance Corp 4610 University Ave Suite 1400	Madison	WI	53705	**800-475-4450**	608-231-4450
Carolina Casualty Insurance Co 4600 Touchton Rd E Bldg 100	Jacksonville	FL	32246	**800-874-8053**	904-363-0900
Central Insurance Cos 800 S Washington St	Van Wert	OH	45891	**800-736-7000**	419-238-1010
Century-National Insurance Co 12200 Sylvan St	North Hollywood	CA	91606	**800-733-0880**	818-760-0880
Chubb & Son 15 Mountain View Rd	Warren	NJ	07059	**800-252-4670**	908-903-2000
Church Mutual Insurance Co 3000 Schuster Ln	Merrill	WI	54452	**800-542-3465**	715-536-5577
Citizens Insurance Co of America 645 W Grand River Ave	Howell	MI	48843	**800-388-1300**	517-546-2160
Civil Service Employees Insurance Co 50 California St Suite 2550	San Francisco	CA	94111	**800-282-6848**	925-817-6300
CNA 40 Wall St	New York	NY	10005	**800-331-6053**	212-440-3000
CNA Insurance Co 333 S Wabash Ave	Chicago	IL	60685	**800-262-2000**	312-822-5000
Commerce Insurance Co 211 Main St	Webster	MA	01570	**800-221-1605**	508-943-9000
Concord Group Insurance Co 4 Bouton St	Concord	NH	03301	**800-852-3380**	603-224-4086
Continental Casualty Co 333 S Wabash Ave	Chicago	IL	60685	**800-262-2000**	312-822-5000
Continental Western Group 11201 Douglas Ave	Urbandale	IA	50322	**800-235-2942**	515-278-3000
Converium 1 Chase Manhattan Plaza	New York	NY	10005	**866-900-2762**	212-898-5000
Coregis Insurance Co 525 W Van Buren St Suite 500	Chicago	IL	60607	**800-879-4428**	312-821-4000
Cornhusker Casualty Co 9290 W Dodge Rd Suite 300	Omaha	NE	68114	**800-488-2930**	402-393-7255
Cotton States Life Insurance Co 244 Perimeter Center Pkwy NE	Atlanta	GA	30346	**800-282-6536**	770-391-8600
Cotton States Mutual Insurance Co 244 Perimeter Ctr Pkwy NE	Atlanta	GA	30346	**800-282-6536**	770-391-8600
Country Casualty Insurance Co 1701 Towanda Ave	Bloomington	IL	61701	**888-211-2555**	309-557-3000
Country Cos 1701 N Towanda Ave	Bloomington	IL	61701	**888-211-2555**	309-557-3000
Country Mutual Insurance Co 1701 Towanda Ave	Bloomington	IL	61701	**888-211-2555**	309-557-3000
Crum & Forster Insurance Inc 305 Madison Ave	Morristown	NJ	07962	**800-227-3745**	973-490-6600
Cumberland Insurance Group 633 Shiloh Pike	Bridgeton	NJ	08302	**800-232-6992**	856-451-4050
Cumberland Mutual Fire Insurance Co 633 Shiloh Pike	Bridgeton	NJ	08302	**800-232-6992**	856-451-4050
Direct General Corp 1281 Murfreesboro Rd *NASDAQ: DRCT* ■ *Cust Svc	Nashville	TN	37217	**800-627-8006***	615-399-4700
Donegal Mutual Insurance Co 1195 River Rd PO Box 302	Marietta	PA	17547	**800-877-0600**	717-426-1931
Employers Insurance Co of Wausau A Mutual Co 2000 Westwood Dr	Wausau	WI	54401	**800-435-4401**	715-845-5211
Employers Reinsurance Corp 5200 Metcalf Ave	Overland Park	KS	66202	**800-255-6931**	913-676-5200
Erie Insurance Co 100 Erie Insurance Pl	Erie	PA	16530	**800-458-0811**	814-870-2000
Erie Insurance Co of New York 100 Erie Insurance Pl	Erie	PA	16530	**800-458-0811**	814-870-2000
Erie Insurance Exchange 100 Erie Insurance Pl	Erie	PA	16530	**800-458-0811**	814-870-2000
Erie Insurance Property & Casualty Co 100 Erie Insurance Pl	Erie	PA	16530	**800-458-0811**	814-870-2000

Property & Casualty Insurance (Cont'd)

Company	City	State	Zip	Toll-Free	Phone
Everest Reinsurance Co 477 Martinsville Rd	Liberty Corner	NJ	07938	**800-269-6660**	908-604-3000
Factory Mutual Insurance Co 1301 Atwood Ave	Johnston	RI	02919	**800-343-7722**	401-275-3000
Farm & City Insurance Co PO Box 712	Des Moines	IA	50303	**800-362-2296**	515-362-7600
Farm Family Casualty Insurance Co PO Box 656	Albany	NY	12201	**800-843-3276**	518-431-5000
Farmers Alliance Mutual Insurance Co PO Box 1401	McPherson	KS	67460	**800-362-1075**	620-241-2200
Farmers Automobile Insurance Assn 2505 Court St	Pekin	IL	61558	**800-322-0160**	309-346-1161
Farmers Casualty Insurance Co PO Box 65150	West Des Moines	IA	50265	**800-666-3226**	515-223-9438
Farmers Insurance Exchange 4680 Wilshire Blvd	Los Angeles	CA	90010	**888-516-5656**	323-932-3200
Farmers Mutual Hail Insurance Co of Iowa 2323 Grand Ave	Des Moines	IA	50312	**800-247-5248**	515-282-9104
Farmers Mutual Insurance Co of Nebraska 1220 Lincoln Mall	Lincoln	NE	68508	**800-742-7433**	402-434-8300
Farmers Union Mutual Insurance Co PO Box 2020	Jamestown	ND	58402	**800-366-6338**	701-252-2701
Farmland Mutual Insurance Co 1100 Locust St Dept 3010	Des Moines	IA	50391	**800-228-6700**	515-280-4211
FCCI Insurance Group 6300 University Pkwy	Sarasota	FL	34240	**800-226-3224**	941-907-3224
FCCI Mutual Insurance Co 6300 University Pkwy	Sarasota	FL	34240	**800-226-3224**	941-907-3224
Federal Insurance Co 15 Mountain View Rd	Warren	NJ	07059	**800-252-4670**	908-903-2000
Federated Mutual Insurance Co PO Box 328	Owatonna	MN	55060	**800-533-0472**	507-455-5200
Federated Service Insurance Co PO Box 328	Owatonna	MN	55060	**800-533-0472**	507-455-5200
FIC Insurance Group 6500 River Place Blvd Bldg 1	Austin	TX	78730	**800-925-6000**	512-404-5000
Financial Indemnity Co 21650 Oxnard St Suite 1800	Woodland Hills	CA	91367	**800-777-4342**	818-313-8500
Fireman's Fund Insurance Co 777 San Marin Dr	Novato	CA	94998	**800-227-1700**	415-899-2000
Fireman's Fund McGee Marine Underwriters 75 Wall St	New York	NY	10005	**800-235-6029**	212-524-8600
Firemen's Insurance Co of Washington DC 420 Lake Brook Dr	Glen Allen	VA	23060	**800-283-1153**	804-285-2700
First Insurance Co of Hawaii Ltd 1100 Ward Ave	Honolulu	HI	96814	**800-272-5202**	808-527-7777
First National Insurance Co of America 4333 Brooklyn Ave NE Safeco Plaza	Seattle	WA	98185	**800-332-3226**	206-545-5000
FM Global 1301 Atwood Ave	Johnston	RI	02919	**800-343-7722**	401-275-3000
Foremost Insurance Co PO Box 2450 *Cust Svc	Grand Rapids	MI	49501	**800-527-3905***	616-942-3000
Foremost Property & Casualty Insurance Co PO Box 2450	Grand Rapids	MI	49501	**800-527-3905**	616-942-3000
Foremost Signature Insurance Co PO Box 2450	Grand Rapids	MI	49501	**800-527-3905**	616-942-3000
Frankenmuth Mutual Insurance Co 1 Mutual Ave *Cust Svc	Frankenmuth	MI	48787	**800-234-1133***	989-652-6121
Franklin Mutual Insurance Co PO Box 400	Branchville	NJ	07826	**800-842-0551**	973-948-3120
GE Colonial Penn PO Box 8110	Fort Washington	PA	19034	**800-523-4040**	267-468-2000
GE Financial Assurance Holdings Inc 6604 W Broad St	Richmond	VA	23230	**800-844-6543**	804-281-6000
GEICO (Government Employees Insurance Co) 1 GEICO Plaza	Washington	DC	20076	**800-841-3000**	301-986-3000
GEICO Casualty Co 1 GEICO Plaza	Washington	DC	20076	**800-841-3000**	301-986-2300
GEICO General Insurance Co 1 GEICO Plaza	Washington	DC	20076	**800-841-3000**	301-986-2300
General Casualty Co of Wisconsin 1 General Dr	Sun Prairie	WI	53596	**800-362-5448**	608-837-4440
General Reinsurance Corp 695 E Main St Financial Ctr	Stamford	CT	06901	**800-431-9994**	203-328-5000
General Star National Insurance Co 695 E Main St Financial Ctr	Stamford	CT	06901	**800-431-9994**	203-328-5000
Georgia Casualty & Surety Co 4370 Peachtree Rd NE	Atlanta	GA	30319	**866-458-7506**	404-266-5500
Germania Farm Mutual Insurance Assn PO Box 645	Brenham	TX	77834	**800-392-2202**	979-836-5224
Globe Indemnity Co 9300 Arrowpoint Blvd *Cust Svc	Charlotte	NC	28273	**800-523-5451***	704-522-2000
GMAC Insurance 500 W 5th St	Winston Salem	NC	27102	**877-468-3466**	336-770-2000
Golden Eagle Insurance Corp 525 B St	San Diego	CA	92101	**800-688-8661**	619-744-6000
Gotham Insurance Co 913 3rd Ave 10th Fl	New York	NY	10022	**800-367-0224**	212-551-0600
Government Employees Insurance Co (GEICO) 1 GEICO Plaza	Washington	DC	20076	**800-841-3000**	301-986-3000
Grange Guardian 650 S Front St	Columbus	OH	43206	**800-422-0550**	614-445-2900
Grange Mutual Casualty Co 650 S Front St	Columbus	OH	43206	**800-422-0550**	614-445-2900
Graphic Arts Mutual Insurance Co PO Box 530	Utica	NY	13503	**800-274-1914**	315-734-2000
Great Central Insurance Co 3625 N Sheridan Rd	Peoria	IL	61633	**800-447-1972**	309-688-8571
Great Northern Insurance Co 15 Mountain View Rd	Warren	NJ	07059	**800-252-4670**	908-903-2000
Great West Casualty Co 1100 W 29th St	South Sioux City	NE	68776	**800-228-8602**	402-494-2411
Grinnell Mutual Reinsurance Co 4215 Highway 146	Grinnell	IA	50112	**800-362-2041**	641-269-8000
GuideOne Insurance Co 1111 Ashworth Rd	West Des Moines	IA	50265	**877-448-4331**	515-267-5000
GuideOne Mutual Insurance Co 1111 Ashworth Rd	West Des Moines	IA	50265	**877-448-4331**	515-267-5000
GuideOne Specialty Mutual Insurance Co 1111 Ashworth Rd	West Des Moines	IA	50265	**800-247-4181**	515-267-5000
Hanover Insurance Co 100 North Pkwy	Worcester	MA	01605	**800-922-8427**	508-853-7200
Harco National Insurance Co PO Box 68309	Schumburg	IL	60168	**800-448-4642**	847-321-4800
Harleysville Atlantic Insurance Co 107 Southern Blvd	Savannah	GA	31405	**800-543-6355**	912-234-1281
Harleysville Insurance Co of New Jersey 308 Harper Dr Suite 200	Morristown	NJ	08057	**888-595-9876**	856-642-1646
Harleysville Insurance Co of New York 120 Washington St	Watertown	NY	13601	**800-962-1006**	315-782-1160
Hartford Steam Boiler Inspection & Insurance Co 1 State St PO Box 5024	Hartford	CT	06102	**800-472-1866**	860-722-1866
Hartford's Omni Auto Plan PO Box 105440	Atlanta	GA	30348	**800-777-6664**	770-952-4500
HealthLink Inc 12443 Olive Blvd	Saint Louis	MO	63141	**800-624-2356**	314-989-6000
Hingham Mutual Fire Insurance Co 230 Beal St	Hingham	MA	02043	**800-341-8200**	781-749-0841
Horace Mann Insurance Co 1 Horace Mann Plaza	Springfield	IL	62715	**800-999-1030**	217-789-2500
Hortica Insurance PO Box 428	Edwardsville	IL	62025	**800-851-7740**	618-656-4240
HSB Group Inc 1 State St PO Box 5024	Hartford	CT	06102	**800-472-1866**	860-722-1866
Huron Insurance Co 355 Maple Ave	Harleysville	PA	19438	**800-523-6344**	215-256-5000
ICW Group 11455 El Camino Real	San Diego	CA	92130	**800-877-1111**	858-350-2400
IMT Insurance Co PO Box 1336	Des Moines	IA	50305	**800-274-3531**	515-327-2777
Indiana Farmers Mutual Insurance Group 10 W 106th St	Indianapolis	IN	46290	**800-666-6460**	317-846-4211
Infinity Insurance Co PO Box 830189	Birmingham	AL	35283	**800-334-1661**	205-870-4000
Infinity Property & Casualty Corp 11700 Great Oaks Way *NASDAQ: IPCC*	Alpharetta	GA	30022	**800-225-8930**	678-627-6000
ING Canada Inc 181 University Ave 9th Fl	Toronto	ON	M5H3M7	**866-817-2138**	416-941-5151
Insurance Co of the West 11455 El Camino Real	San Diego	CA	92130	**800-877-1111**	858-350-2400
Interstate Fire & Casualty Co 33 W Monroe St 12th Fl	Chicago	IL	60603	**800-628-8574**	312-346-6400
Investors Underwriting Managers Inc 310 Hwy 35S	Red Bank	NJ	07701	**800-243-6869**	732-224-0500
Kemper Insurance Cos 1 Kemper Dr	Long Grove	IL	60049	**800-833-0355**	847-320-2000
Kingsway Financial Services Inc 5310 Explorer Dr Suite 200 *NYSE: KFS*	Mississauga	ON	L4W5H8	**800-265-5458**	905-629-7888
Koch Supply & Trading LP 4111 E 37th St N	Wichita	KS	67220	**800-245-2243**	316-828-5500
Lake States Insurance Co 12935 S West Bay Shore Dr	Traverse City	MI	49684	**800-968-2090**	231-946-6390
Lawrenceville Property & Casualty Co 2 Princess Rd	Lawrenceville	NJ	08648	**800-234-6449**	609-896-2404
Lawrenceville Re 2 Princess Rd	Lawrenceville	NJ	08648	**800-234-6449**	609-896-2404
Leader Insurance Co 5205 N O'Connor Blvd Suite 700	Irving	TX	75039	**877-953-2337**	214-526-3876
Legion Insurance 1 Logan Sq Suite 1400	Philadelphia	PA	19103	**800-255-6738**	215-963-1200
Lexington Insurance Co Inc 100 Summer St	Boston	MA	02110	**800-355-4891**	617-330-1100
Lititz Mutual Insurance Co 2 N Broad St	Lititz	PA	17543	**800-626-4751**	717-626-4751
Lujan Manuel Insurance Inc PO Box 3727	Albuquerque	NM	87190	**888-652-7771**	505-758-2206
Lumbermen's Underwriting Alliance 2501 N Military Trail	Boca Raton	FL	33431	**800-327-0630**	561-994-1900
Lykes Insurance Inc PO Box 2879	Tampa	FL	33601	**800-243-0491**	813-223-3911
Lynn Insurance Group 2501 N Military Trail	Boca Raton	FL	33431	**800-327-0630**	561-994-1900
Magna Carta Co 1 Park Ave	New York	NY	10016	**888-663-7275**	212-591-9500
Main Street America Group 55 West St	Keene	NH	03431	**800-258-5310**	603-352-4000
Mann Horace Insurance Co 1 Horace Mann Plaza	Springfield	IL	62715	**800-999-1030**	217-789-2500
Manuel Lujan Insurance Inc PO Box 3727	Albuquerque	NM	87190	**888-652-7771**	505-758-2206
Markel Insurance Co 4600 Cox Rd	Glen Allen	VA	23060	**800-431-1270**	804-527-2700
Markel Insurance Co 4521 Highwoods Pkwy	Glen Allen	VA	23060	**800-446-6671**	804-747-0136
Mendota Insurance Co 1285 Northland Dr	Mendota Heights	MN	55120	**800-422-0792**	651-688-4100
Mercer Insurance Group Inc 10 N Hwy 31 *NASDAQ: MIGP*	Pennington	NJ	08534	**800-223-0534**	609-737-0426
Merchants Insurance Group PO Box 903	Buffalo	NY	14240	**800-462-1077**	716-849-3333
Mercury General Corp 4484 Wilshire Blvd *NYSE: MCY*	Los Angeles	CA	90010	**800-431-6654**	323-937-1060
MetLife Auto & Home Insurance Co 700 Quaker Ln	Warwick	RI	02886	**800-422-4272**	401-827-2400
Michigan Millers Mutual Insurance Co PO Box 30060	Lansing	MI	48909	**800-888-1914**	517-482-6211
Mid-Century Insurance Co 4680 Wilshire Blvd	Los Angeles	CA	90010	**888-516-5656**	323-932-3200
Mid-Continent Casualty Co PO Box 1409	Tulsa	OK	74101	**800-722-4994**	918-587-7221
Middlesex Insurance Co 3 Carlisle Rd	Westford	MA	01886	**800-225-1390**	978-392-7000
Middlesex Mutual Assurance Co 213 Court St PO Box 891	Middletown	CT	06457	**800-899-0032**	860-347-4621
Midwest Employers Casualty Co 14755 N Outer 40 Dr Suite 300	Chesterfield	MO	63017	**877-632-2474**	636-449-7000
Millers First Insurance Co 111 E 4th St	Alton	IL	62002	**800-558-0500**	618-463-3636
Millers Mutual Insurance Assn 111 E 4th St	Alton	IL	62002	**800-558-0500**	618-463-3636
Milwaukee Mutual Insurance Co 400 S Executive Dr Suite 200	Brookfield	WI	50005	**800-733-7366**	262-207-8500
Minnesota Fire & Casualty Co 7900 W 78th St	Edina	MN	55439	**800-727-5353**	952-829-1400
Montgomery Mutual Insurance Co 17810 Meeting House Rd	Sandy Spring	MD	20860	**800-638-8933**	301-924-4700
Motors Insurance Corp 1 GMAC Insurance Plaza	Saint Louis	MO	63045	**800-642-6464**	314-492-8000
Mutual of Enumclaw Insurance Co 1460 Wells St	Enumclaw	WA	98022	**800-366-5551**	360-825-2591
National Farmers Union Property & Casualty Co 11900 E Cornell Ave	Aurora	CO	80014	**800-669-0622**	303-337-5500
National General Insurance Co 1 GMAC Plaza	Saint Louis	MO	63045	**800-847-6442**	314-493-8000
National Grange Mutual Insurance Co 55 West St	Keene	NH	03431	**800-258-5310**	603-352-4000
National Interstate Corp 3250 Interstate Dr *NASDAQ: NATL*	Richfield	OH	44286	**800-929-1500**	330-659-8900
Nationwide Mutual Fire Insurance Co 1 Nationwide Plaza	Columbus	OH	43215	**800-882-2822**	614-249-7111
Nationwide Property & Casualty Insurance Co 1 Nationwide Plaza	Columbus	OH	43215	**800-882-2822**	614-249-7111
Nautilus Insurance Co 7273 E Butherus Dr	Scottsdale	AZ	85260	**800-842-8972**	480-951-0905
New Jersey Manufacturers Insurance Co 301 Sullivan Way	West Trenton	NJ	08628	**800-232-6600**	609-883-1300
New York Central Mutual Fire Insurance Co 1899 Central Plaza E	Edmeston	NY	13335	**800-234-6926**	607-965-8321
New York Marine & General Insurance Co 913 3rd Ave 10th Fl	New York	NY	10022	**800-367-0224**	212-551-0600
Nobel Insurance 12225 Greenville Ave Suite 750	Dallas	TX	75243	**800-766-6235**	972-644-0434
North American Specialty Insurance Co 650 Elm St 6th Fl	Manchester	NH	03101	**800-542-9200**	603-644-6600
Northern Security Insurance Co PO Box 188	Montpelier	VT	05601	**800-451-5000**	802-223-2341
Northland Insurance Co PO Box 64816	Saint Paul	MN	55164	**800-237-9334**	651-688-4100
Northwestern Pacific Indemnity Co 15 Mountain View Rd *Claims	Warren	NJ	07059	**800-252-4670***	908-903-2000
Odyssey Re Holdings Corp 300 1st Stamford Pl *NYSE: ORH*	Stamford	CT	06902	**866-246-9945**	203-977-8000
Ohio Casualty Insurance Co 9450 Seward Rd	Fairfield	OH	45014	**800-843-6446**	513-603-2400
Ohio Farmers Insurance Co 1 Park Cir	Westfield Center	OH	44251	**800-243-0210**	330-887-0101
Ohio Security Insurance Co 9450 Seward Rd	Fairfield	OH	45014	**800-843-6446**	513-867-3000

Company / Address	City	State	ZIP	Toll-Free	Phone
Oklahoma Surety Co 1437 S Boulder Ave Suite 200	Tulsa	OK	74119	**800-722-4994**	918-587-7221
Old Dominion Insurance Co 4601 Touchton Rd E Suite 330 PO Box 16100	Jacksonville	FL	32245	**800-226-0875**	904-642-3000
Omaha Property & Casualty Insurance Co 3102 Farnam St	Omaha	NE	68131	**800-788-9488**	402-342-3326
OneBeacon Insurance Group 1 Beacon St	Boston	MA	02108	**800-327-6286**	617-725-6000
Oregon Mutual Insurance Co PO Box 808	McMinnville	OR	97128	**800-888-2141**	503-565-2141
Oregon Mutual Insurance Group PO Box 808	McMinnville	OR	97128	**800-888-2141**	503-565-2141
Orion Auto PO Box 118090	Charleston	SC	29423	**800-462-6342**	843-561-0510
Pacific Indemnity Co 801 S Figueroa St 24th Fl	Los Angeles	CA	90017	**800-262-4459**	213-612-0880
Pekin Insurance Co 2505 Court St	Pekin	IL	61558	**800-322-0160**	309-346-1161
Penn National Insurance Co 2 N 2nd St Penn National Plaza	Harrisburg	PA	17101	**800-388-4764**	717-234-4941
Pennland Insurance Co 355 Maple Ave	Harleysville	PA	19438	**800-523-6344**	215-256-5000
Pennsylvania Manufacturers Assn Insurance Co 380 Sentry Pkwy	Blue Bell	PA	19422	**800-222-2749**	610-397-5000
Permanent General Cos Inc 2636 Elm Hill Pike	Nashville	TN	37214	**800-280-1466**	615-242-1961
Pharmacists Mutual Insurance Co 808 US Hwy 18 W	Algona	IA	50511	**800-247-5930**	515-295-2461
Philadelphia Insurance Cos 1 Bala Plaza Suite 100	Bala Cynwyd	PA	19004	**800-525-7662**	610-617-7900
Preferred Employers Group Inc 10800 Biscayne Blvd 10th Fl	Miami	FL	33161	**800-433-5755**	305-893-4040
Preferred Employers Insurance Co PO Box 85478	San Diego	CA	92186	**888-472-9224**	619-688-3900
Preferred Mutual Insurance Co 1 Preferred Way	New Berlin	NY	13411	**800-333-7642**	607-847-6161
Preserver Insurance Co 95 Rt 17 S	Paramus	NJ	07653	**800-242-0332**	201-291-2000
Princeton Excess & Surplus Lines Insurance Co 555 College Rd E	Princeton	NJ	08543	**800-255-5676**	609-243-4200
Princeton Insurance Cos 746 Alexander Rd	Princeton	NJ	08540	**800-433-0157**	800-334-0588
Proformance Insurance Co 4 Paragon Way	Freehold	NJ	07728	**800-298-5742**	732-665-1100
Progressive Casualty Insurance Co 6300 Wilson Mills Rd Campus E	Mayfield Village	OH	44143	**800-321-9843**	440-461-5000
Protective Insurance Co 1099 N Meridian St Suite 700	Indianapolis	IN	46204	**800-231-6024**	317-636-9800
Providence Mutual Fire Insurance Co 340 East Ave	Warwick	RI	02886	**877-763-1800**	401-827-1800
Providence Washington Insurance Co 88 Boyd Ave	East Providence	RI	02914	**800-752-4549**	401-453-7000
Prudential Financial Inc 751 Broad St *NYSE: PRU*	Newark	NJ	07102	**800-843-7625**	973-802-6000
Quincy Mutual Fire Insurance Co 57 Washington St	Quincy	MA	02169	**800-899-1116**	617-472-8770
Ranger Insurance Co 10777 Westheimer Rd Suite 500	Houston	TX	77042	**800-392-1970**	713-954-8100
Republic Indemnity Co of America 15821 Ventura Blvd Suite 370	Encino	CA	91436	**800-821-4520**	818-990-9860
Republic Insurance Co Inc 2727 Turtle Creek Blvd	Dallas	TX	75219	**800-344-2275**	214-559-1222
Republic Western Insurance Co 2721 N Central Ave *Claims	Phoenix	AZ	85004	**800-528-7134***	602-263-6755
Risk Planners Inc PO Box 240	Minneapolis	MN	55440	**800-328-7475**	952-914-5777
RLI Insurance Co 9025 N Lindbergh Dr	Peoria	IL	61615	**800-331-4929**	309-692-1000
Royal & SunAlliance Insurance Co of Canada 10 Wellington St E	Toronto	ON	M5E1L5	**800-268-8406**	416-366-7511
Royal & SunAlliance USA 9300 Arrowpoint Blvd	Charlotte	NC	28273	**800-523-5451**	704-522-2000
RTW Inc 8500 Normandale Lake Blvd Suite 1400 *NASDAQ: RTWI*	Bloomington	MN	55437	**800-789-2242**	952-893-0403
Safe Auto Insurance Co 3883 E Broad St	Columbus	OH	43213	**800-723-3288**	614-231-0200
Safety National Casualty Corp 2043 Woodland Pkwy	Saint Louis	MO	63146	**800-289-7224**	314-995-5300
Safeway Insurance Group 790 Pasquinelli Dr	Westmont	IL	60559	**800-273-0300**	630-887-8300
Sagamore Insurance Co 1099 N Meridian St Suite 700	Indianapolis	IN	46204	**800-231-6024**	317-636-9800
Saint Paul Fire & Marine Insurance Co 385 Washington St	Saint Paul	MN	55102	**800-328-2189**	651-310-7911
Savers Property & Casualty Insurance Co 11880 College Blvd Suite 500	Overland Park	KS	66210	**800-351-1411**	913-339-5000
Scottsdale Insurance Co 8877 N Gainey Ctr Dr	Scottsdale	AZ	85258	**800-423-7675**	480-365-4000
Secura Insurance Cos PO Box 819	Appleton	WI	54912	**800-558-3405**	920-739-3161
Seibels Bruce Group Inc 1501 Lady St	Columbia	SC	29201	**800-525-8835**	803-748-2000
Selective Insurance Co of America 40 Wantage Ave	Branchville	NJ	07890	**800-777-9656**	973-948-3000
Selective Way Insurance Co 40 Wantage Ave	Branchville	NJ	07890	**800-777-9656**	973-948-3000
Shelter Mutual Insurance Co 1817 W Broadway	Columbia	MO	65218	**800-743-5837**	573-445-8441
Sierra Insurance Group 2716 N Tenaya Way 6th Fl	Las Vegas	NV	89128	**800-230-3904**	702-838-8244
Signature Group 200 N Martingale Rd	Schaumburg	IL	60173	**800-621-0393**	847-605-3000
Sompo Japan Insurance Co of America 2 World Financial Ctr 225 Liberty St 43rd Fl	New York	NY	10281	**800-444-6870**	212-416-1200
Southern Farm Bureau Casualty Insurance Co 1800 E County Line Rd Suite 400	Ridgeland	MS	39157	**800-272-7977**	601-957-7777
Southern Guaranty Insurance Co PO Box 235004	Montgomery	AL	36123	**800-633-5606**	334-270-6000
Star Insurance Co 26600 Telegraph Rd	Southfield	MI	48034	**800-482-2726**	248-358-1100
State Auto National Insurance Co 518 E Broad St	Columbus	OH	43215	**800-444-9950**	614-464-5000
State Auto Property & Casualty Insurance Co 518 E Broad St	Columbus	OH	43215	**800-444-9950**	614-464-5000
State Automobile Mutual Insurance Co 518 E Broad St	Columbus	OH	43215	**800-444-9950**	614-464-5000
STOPS Inc 8855 Grissom Pkwy	Titusville	FL	32780	**800-487-0521**	321-383-0499
Swiss Re America Corp 175 King St	Armonk	NY	10504	**877-794-7773**	914-828-8000
Texas Pacific Indemnity Co 15 Mountain View Rd	Warren	NJ	07059	**800-252-4670**	908-903-2000
TIG Specialty Insurance Solutions 5205 N O'Connor Blvd	Irving	TX	75039	**800-472-7583**	972-831-5000
Toa Reinsurance Co of America 177 Madison Ave PO Box 1930	Morristown	NJ	07962	**800-898-7977**	973-898-9480
Tokio Marine Life 230 Park Ave	New York	NY	10169	**800-628-2796**	212-297-6600
Topa Insurance Corp 1800 Ave of the Stars 12th Fl	Los Angeles	CA	90067	**800-949-6505**	310-201-0451
Transcontinental Insurance Co 333 S Wabash Ave CNA Ctr	Chicago	IL	60685	**800-262-2000**	312-822-5000
Transportation Insurance Co 333 S Wabash Ave	Chicago	IL	60604	**800-262-2000**	312-822-5000
Trenwick America Re Corp 1 Canterbury Green	Stamford	CT	06901	**866-330-6719**	203-353-5500
Tri-State Insurance Co of Minnesota 10 Roundwind Rd PO Box 500	Luverne	MN	56156	**800-533-0303**	507-283-9561
Trinity Universal Insurance Co 10000 N Central Expy	Dallas	TX	75231	**800-777-2249**	214-360-8000
Ulico Casualty Co 8403 Colesville Rd	Silver Springs	MD	20910	**800-431-5425**	202-682-0900
Underwriters MGA Inc PO Box 5488	McAllen	TX	78502	**888-560-3240**	956-364-3066
Underwriters Reinsurance Co 26050 Mureau Rd	Calabasas	CA	91302	**800-332-2801**	818-878-9500
Unigard Security Insurance Co 15805 NE 24th St	Bellevue	WA	98008	**800-777-1757**	425-641-4321
Union National Fire Insurance Co 8282 Goodwood Blvd	Baton Rouge	LA	70806	**800-765-0550**	225-927-3430
Union Standard Insurance Co 122 W Carpenter Fwy Suite 350	Irving	TX	75039	**800-444-0049**	972-719-2400
United Casualty Insurance Co 1 E Wacker Dr Suite 1313	Chicago	IL	60601	**800-777-8467**	312-661-4600
United Fire & Casualty Co PO Box 73909 *NASDAQ: UFCS*	Cedar Rapids	IA	52407	**800-332-7977**	319-399-5700
United Heartland Inc PO Box 3026	Milwaukee	WI	53201	**800-258-2667**	262-787-7700
United National Group 3 Bala Plaza E Suite 300	Bala Cynwyd	PA	19004	**800-333-0352**	610-664-1500
United National Insurance Co 3 Bala Plaza E Suite 300	Bala Cynwyd	PA	19004	**800-333-0352**	610-664-1500
Universal Underwriters Group 7045 College Blvd	Overland Park	KS	66211	**800-821-7803**	913-339-1000
USA Workers' Injury Network 916 S Capital of Texas Hwy	Austin	TX	78746	**800-872-0820**	512-306-0201
USAA Property & Casualty Insurance Group 9800 Fredericksburg Rd	San Antonio	TX	78288	**800-531-8111**	
Utica National Insurance Group 180 Genesee St	New Hartford	NY	13413	**800-274-1914**	315-734-2000
Valley Forge Insurance Co 100 CNA Dr	Nashville	TN	37214	**800-437-8854**	615-871-1400
Valley Group Inc PO Box 1119	Albany	OR	97321	**800-456-6343**	541-928-2344
Vermont Mutual Insurance Co PO Box 188	Montpelier	VT	05601	**800-451-5000**	802-223-2341
Vigilant Insurance Co 15 Mountain View Rd	Warren	NJ	07059	**800-252-4670**	908-903-2000
Wausau Business Insurance Co 2000 Westwood Dr	Wausau	WI	54401	**800-435-4401**	715-845-5211
Wausau General Insurance Co 2000 Westwood Dr	Wausau	WI	54401	**800-435-4401**	715-845-5211
Wausau Service Corp 2000 Westwood Dr	Wausau	WI	54401	**800-435-4401**	715-845-5211
Wausau Underwriters Insurance Co 2000 Westwood Dr	Wausau	WI	54401	**800-435-4401**	715-845-5211
West American Insurance Co 9450 Seward Rd	Fairfield	OH	45014	**800-843-6446**	513-867-3000
West Bend Mutual Insurance Co 1900 S 18th Ave	West Bend	WI	53095	**800-236-5010**	262-334-5571
Westchester Fire Insurance Co 305 Madison Ave PO Box 1973	Morristown	NJ	07962	**800-227-3745**	973-490-6600
Western Diversified Casualty Insurance Co 2345 Waukegan Rd Suite 210	Bannockburn	IL	60015	**800-323-5771**	847-948-8988
Western National Mutual Insurance Co 5350 W 78th St	Edina	MN	55439	**877-862-8808**	952-835-5350
Western Reserve Group 1685 Cleveland Rd	Wooster	OH	44691	**800-362-0426**	330-262-9060
Westfield Cos PO Box 5001	Westfield Center	OH	44251	**800-368-3530**	330-887-0101
Westfield Group 1 Park Cir PO Box 5001	Westfield Center	OH	44251	**800-243-0210**	330-887-0101
Westfield National Insurance Co PO Box 5001	Westfield Center	OH	44251	**800-368-3530**	330-887-0101
Windsor Group 11700 Great Oak Way	Atlanta	GA	30022	**800-852-8055**	678-627-6000
Worcester Insurance Co 120 Front St Suite 400	Worcester	MA	01608	**800-225-7387**	508-751-8100
Zenith Insurance Co PO Box 9055	Van Nuys	CA	91409	**800-448-4356**	818-713-1000
Zenithstar Insurance Co 1101 Capital of Texas Hwy S Bldg J	Austin	TX	78746	**800-841-3987**	512-306-1700
ZNAT Insurance Co PO Box 9055	Van Nuys	CA	91409	**800-448-4256**	818-713-1000

384-5 Surety Insurance

Company / Address	City	State	ZIP	Toll-Free	Phone
AMBAC Assurance Corp 1 State St Plaza 15th Fl	New York	NY	10004	**800-221-1854**	212-668-0340
American Fire & Casualty Co 9450 Seward Rd	Fairfield	OH	45014	**800-843-6446**	513-867-3000
American Healthcare Specialty Insurance Co 1888 Century Pk E Suite 800	Los Angeles	CA	90067	**800-962-5549**	310-551-5900
American Physicians Assurance Corp 1301 N Hagadorn Rd	East Lansing	MI	48823	**800-748-0465**	517-351-1150
American Physicians Insurance Exchange (API) 1301 S Capitol of Texas Hwy Suite C-300	Austin	TX	78746	**800-252-3628**	512-328-0888
American Southern Insurance Co 3715 Northside Pkwy NW Bldg 400 8th Fl	Atlanta	GA	30327	**800-241-1172**	404-266-9599
API (American Physicians Insurance Exchange) 1301 S Capitol of Texas Hwy Suite C-300	Austin	TX	78746	**800-252-3628**	512-328-0888
Balboa Life & Casualty Insurance Co 3349 Michelson Dr Suite 200	Irvine	CA	92612	**800-854-6115**	949-222-8000
Central Insurance Cos 800 S Washington St	Van Wert	OH	45891	**800-736-7000**	419-238-1010
Central States Indemnity Co of Omaha PO Box 34350	Omaha	NE	68134	**800-445-6500**	402-397-1111
Century Insurance Group 465 Cleveland Ave	Westerville	OH	43082	**800-878-7389**	614-895-2000
Chubb Specialty Insurance 82 Hopmeadow St	Simsbury	CT	06070	**800-432-8168**	860-408-2000
CNA 40 Wall St	New York	NY	10005	**800-331-6053**	212-440-3000
CNA Surety Corp 333 S Wabash Ave CNA Plaza *NYSE: SUR*	Chicago	IL	60604	**877-672-6115**	312-822-5000
Copic Insurance Co 7351 Lowry Blvd	Denver	CO	80230	**800-421-1834**	
Coregis Insurance Co 525 W Van Buren St Suite 500	Chicago	IL	60607	**800-879-4428**	312-821-4000
Crum & Forster Insurance Inc 305 Madison Ave	Morristown	NJ	07962	**800-227-3745**	973-490-6600
Cumberland Casualty & Surety Co 4311 W Waters Ave Suite 401	Tampa	FL	33614	**800-723-0171**	813-885-2112

Surety Insurance (Cont'd)

Company / Address	City	State	Zip	Toll-Free	Phone
Dentists Insurance Co 1201 K St 17th Fl.	Sacramento	CA	95814	**800-733-0635**	916-443-4501
Doctors' Co The 185 Greenwood Rd	Napa	CA	94558	**800-421-2368**	707-226-0100
Employers Reinsurance Corp 5200 Metcalf Ave	Overland Park	KS	66202	**800-255-6931**	913-676-5200
Euler American Credit Indemnity Co 800 Red Brook Blvd 4th Fl	Owings Mills	MD	21117	**800-866-5551**	410-753-0753
Everest Reinsurance Co 477 Martinsville Rd	Liberty Corner	NJ	07938	**800-269-6660**	908-604-3000
Federated Mutual Insurance Co PO Box 328	Owatonna	MN	55060	**800-533-0472**	507-455-5200
Financial Guaranty Insurance Co 125 Park Ave 6th Fl	New York	NY	10017	**800-352-0001**	212-312-3000
Financial Security Assurance Inc 350 Park Ave 13th Fl	New York	NY	10022	**800-846-4372**	212-826-0100
Fireman's Fund Insurance Co 777 San Marin Dr	Novato	CA	94998	**800-227-1700**	415-899-2000
First Insurance Co of Hawaii Ltd 1100 Ward Ave	Honolulu	HI	96814	**800-272-5202**	808-527-7777
First National Insurance Co of America 4333 Brooklyn Ave NE Safeco Plaza	Seattle	WA	98185	**800-332-3226**	206-545-5000
First Professionals Insurance Co 1000 Riverside Ave Suite 800	Jacksonville	FL	32204	**800-741-3742**	904-354-5910
GE Mortgage Insurance Corp 6601 Six Forks Rd	Raleigh	NC	27615	**800-334-9270**	919-846-4100
Heritage Insurance Managers Inc PO Box 659570	San Antonio	TX	78265	**800-456-7480**	210-829-7467
HUM Div of Medical Liability Mutual Insurance Co 8 British-American Blvd	Latham	NY	12110	**800-635-0666**	518-786-2700
Illinois State Medical Inter-Insurance Exchange (ISMIE) 20 N Michigan Ave Suite 700	Chicago	IL	60602	**800-782-4767**	312-782-2749
Indemnity Co of California 17780 Fitch Suite 200	Irvine	CA	92614	**800-782-1546**	949-263-3300
Insco Dico Group 17780 Fitch Suite 200	Irvine	CA	92614	**800-782-1546**	949-263-3300
Insurance Co of the West 11455 El Camino Real	San Diego	CA	92130	**800-877-1111**	858-350-2400
International Fidelity Insurance Co 1 Newark Center 20th Fl	Newark	NJ	07102	**800-333-4167**	973-624-7200
Investors Heritage Life Insurance Co 200 Capital Ave	Frankfort	KY	40602	**800-422-2011**	502-223-2361
ISMIE (Illinois State Medical Inter-Insurance Exchange) 20 N Michigan Ave Suite 700	Chicago	IL	60602	**800-782-4767**	312-782-2749
KaMMCO (Kansas Medical Mutual Insurance Co) 623 SW 10th Ave Suite 200	Topeka	KS	66612	**800-232-2259**	785-232-2224
Kansas Medical Mutual Insurance Co (KaMMCO) 623 SW 10th Ave Suite 200	Topeka	KS	66612	**800-232-2259**	785-232-2224
Lexington Insurance Co Inc 100 Summer St	Boston	MA	02110	**800-355-4891**	617-330-1100
Life of the South Insurance Co 100 W Bay St	Jacksonville	FL	32202	**800-888-2738**	904-350-9660
Louisiana Medical Mutual Insurance Co 1 Galleria Blvd Suite 700	Metairie	LA	70001	**800-452-2120**	504-831-3756
Markel Insurance Co 4600 Cox Rd	Glen Allen	VA	23060	**800-431-1270**	804-527-2700
MBIA Insurance Corp 113 King St	Armonk	NY	10504	**800-765-6242**	914-273-4545
Medical Assurance 20 Allen Ave Suite 420	Saint Louis	MO	63119	**800-492-7212**	314-961-7700
Medical Assurance Inc 100 Brookwood Pl Suite 300	Birmingham	AL	35209	**800-282-6242**	205-877-4400
Medical Liability Mutual Insurance Co (MLMIC) 2 Park Ave 25th Fl	New York	NY	10016	**800-275-6564**	212-576-9800
Medical Liability Mutual Insurance Co HUM Div 8 British-American Blvd	Latham	NY	12110	**800-635-0666**	518-786-2700
Medical Mutual Insurance Co of Maine PO Box 15275	Portland	ME	04112	**800-942-2791**	
Medical Mutual Liability Insurance Society of Maryland 225 International Cir	Hunt Valley	MD	21030	**800-492-0193**	410-785-0050
Medical Protective Co PO Box 15021	Fort Wayne	IN	46885	**800-463-3776**	260-485-9622
MIIX Insurance Co of New York 2 Princess Rd	Lawrenceville	NJ	08648	**800-234-6449**	609-896-2404
MIIX Insurance Cos 2 Princess Rd	Lawrenceville	NJ	08648	**800-234-6449**	609-896-2404
Monumental General Insurance Co 520 Park Ave	Baltimore	MD	21201	**800-233-4624**	410-685-5500
Mortgage Guaranty Insurance Corp 270 E Kilbourn Ave	Milwaukee	WI	53202	**800-558-9900**	414-347-6480
NCMIC Insurance Co 14001 University Ave	Clive	IA	50325	**800-769-2000**	515-313-4500
NCRIC Inc 1115 30th St NW	Washington	DC	20007	**800-613-3615**	202-969-1866
Nobel Insurance 12225 Greenville Ave Suite 750	Dallas	TX	75243	**800-766-6235**	972-644-0434
Norcal Mutual Insurance Co Inc 560 Davis St	San Francisco	CA	94111	**800-652-1051**	415-397-9700
Northwest Physicians Mutual Insurance Co 2965 Ryan Dr SE	Salem	OR	97301	**800-243-3503**	503-371-8228
OHIC Insurance Co 155 E Broad St 4th Fl	Columbus	OH	43215	**800-666-6442**	614-221-7777
Oklahoma Surety Co 1437 S Boulder Ave Suite 200	Tulsa	OK	74119	**800-722-4994**	918-587-7221
Old Republic Minnehoma Insurance Co 8282 S Memorial Dr	Tulsa	OK	74133	**800-331-4065**	918-307-1000
Old Republic Surety 445 S Moorlands Rd Suite 301	Brookfield	WI	53005	**800-217-1792**	262-797-2640
Pekin Life Insurance Co 2505 Court St	Pekin	IL	61558	**800-322-0160**	309-346-1161
Penn National Insurance Co 2 N 2nd St Penn National Plaza	Harrisburg	PA	17101	**800-388-4764**	717-234-4941
Pennsylvania Medical Society Liability Insurance Co 777 E Park Dr	Harrisburg	PA	17111	**800-445-1212**	717-558-7500
Pharmacists Mutual Insurance Co 808 US Hwy 18 W	Algona	IA	50511	**800-247-5930**	515-295-2461
Physicians' Reciprocal Insurers 111 E Shore Rd	Manhasset	NY	11030	**800-632-6040**	516-365-6690
PMI Mortgage Insurance Co 3003 Oak Rd	Walnut Creek	CA	94597	**800-288-1970**	925-658-7878
Podiatry Insurance Co of America DBA PICA Group 110 Westwood Pl Suite 100	Brentwood	TN	37027	**866-742-2477**	615-371-8776
Pre-Paid Legal Services Inc 1 Pre-Paid Way *AMEX: PPD*	Ada	OK	74820	**800-654-7757**	580-436-1234
Princeton Insurance Cos 746 Alexander Rd	Princeton	NJ	08540	**800-433-0157**	800-334-0588
Pro Insurance Co 2600 Professionals Dr	Okemos	MI	48864	**800-292-1036**	517-349-6500
Progressive Casualty Insurance Co 6300 Wilson Mills Rd Campus E	Mayfield Village	OH	44143	**800-321-9843**	440-461-5000
ProMutual Group 101 Arch St 4th Fl	Boston	MA	02110	**800-225-6168**	617-330-1755
Protective Insurance Co 1099 N Meridian St Suite 700	Indianapolis	IN	46204	**800-231-6024**	317-636-9800
Radian Asset Assurance Inc 335 Madison Ave 25th Fl	New York	NY	10017	**800-523-1988**	212-983-3100
Radian Group Inc 1601 Market St *NYSE: RDN*	Philadelphia	PA	19103	**800-523-1988**	215-564-6600
Radian Guaranty Inc 1601 Market St	Philadelphia	PA	19103	**800-523-1988**	215-564-6600
Ranger Insurance Co 10777 Westheimer Rd Suite 500	Houston	TX	77042	**800-392-1970**	713-954-8100
Reciprocal of America 4200 Innslake Dr	Glen Allen	VA	23060	**800-284-8847**	804-747-8600
Republic Mortgage Insurance Co 190 Oak Plaza Blvd	Winston-Salem	NC	27105	**800-999-7642**	336-661-0015
RLI Insurance Co 9025 N Lindbergh Dr	Peoria	IL	61615	**800-331-4929**	309-692-1000
Scottsdale Insurance Co 8877 N Gainey Ctr Dr	Scottsdale	AZ	85258	**800-423-7675**	480-365-4000
SCPIE Indemnity Co 1888 Century Pk E Suite 800 *Sales	Los Angeles	CA	90067	**800-962-5549***	310-551-5900
State Volunteer Mutual Insurance Co 101 W Park Dr Suite 300	Brentwood	TN	37027	**800-342-2239**	615-377-1999
Surety Assoc 120 Grace Dr	Easley	SC	29640	**800-922-0445**	864-220-9884
Surety Group Inc 1900 Emery St NW Suite 120	Atlanta	GA	30318	**800-486-8211**	404-352-8211
Texas Hospital Insurance Exchange 6300 La Calma Dr Suite 550	Austin	TX	78752	**800-792-0060**	512-451-5775
TIG Specialty Insurance Solutions 5205 N O'Connor Blvd	Irving	TX	75039	**800-472-7583**	972-831-5000
Triad Guaranty Insurance Corp 101 S Stratford Rd *Cust Svc	Winston-Salem	NC	27104	**888-691-8074***	336-723-1282
Ulico Casualty Co 8403 Colesville Rd	Silver Springs	MD	20910	**800-431-5425**	202-682-0900
United Guaranty Corp 230 N Elm St	Greensboro	NC	27401	**800-334-8966**	336-373-0232
United National Group 3 Bala Plaza E Suite 300	Bala Cynwyd	PA	19004	**800-333-0352**	610-664-1500
Universal Surety of America 950 Echo Ln Suite 250	Houston	TX	77024	**888-736-9704**	713-722-4600
US Liability Insurance Group 190 S Warner Rd	Wayne	PA	19087	**800-523-5545**	610-688-2535
Utica National Insurance Group 180 Genesee St	New Hartford	NY	13413	**800-274-1914**	315-734-2000
XL Specialty Insurance Co 20 N Martingale Rd Suite 200	Schaumburg	IL	60173	**800-394-3909**	847-517-2990
Zurich North America 1400 American Ln	Schaumburg	IL	60196	**800-382-2150**	

384-6 Title Insurance

Company / Address	City	State	Zip	Toll-Free	Phone
Alamo Title Insurance 10010 San Pedro Blvd Suite 700	San Antonio	TX	78216	**800-292-5320**	210-340-0456
Attorney's Title Insurance Fund Inc 6545 Corporate Ctr Blvd	Orlando	FL	32822	**800-336-3863**	407-240-3863
Chicago Title Insurance Co 171 N Clark St	Chicago	IL	60601	**800-621-1919**	312-223-2000
Chicago Title & Trust Co 171 N Clark St	Chicago	IL	60601	**800-621-1919**	312-223-2000
Commerce Title Co 1551 N Tustin Ave Suite 430	Santa Ana	CA	92705	**800-244-4322**	714-347-7000
Commonwealth Land Title Insurance Co 101 Gateway Center Pkwy Gateway 1	Richmond	VA	23235	**800-388-8822**	804-267-8000
Community Title & Escrow Ltd 2600 State St Bldg D	Alton	IL	62002	**800-854-4049**	618-466-7755
Dakota Homestead Title Insurance Co 315 S Phillips Ave	Sioux Falls	SD	57104	**800-425-0388**	605-336-0388
Diversified Title & Escrow Services Co 222 S Harbor Blvd 8th Fl	Anaheim	CA	92805	**800-266-9485**	714-999-1800
Fidelity National Title Insurance Co 4050 Calle Real Suite 100	Santa Barbara	CA	93110	**800-815-3969**	805-696-7000
First American Corp 2 First American Way *NYSE: FAF*	Santa Ana	CA	92707	**800-854-3643**	714-558-3211
First American Title Co of Los Angeles 520 N Central Ave	Glendale	CA	91203	**800-328-2652**	818-242-5800
First American Title Insurance Co 2 First American Way	Santa Ana	CA	92707	**800-854-3643**	714-558-3211
First American Title Insurance Co of Oregon 1700 SW 4th Ave Suite 102	Portland	OR	97201	**800-929-3651**	503-222-3651
First American Title Insurance Co of Texas 1500 S Dairy Ashford St Suite 300	Houston	TX	77077	**800-347-7826**	281-588-2200
Gateway Title Co 1405 N San Fernando Blvd	Burbank	CA	91504	**800-660-6992**	818-953-2300
Hanover Insurance Co 100 North Pkwy	Worcester	MA	01605	**800-922-8427**	508-853-7200
Investors Title Insurance Co 121 N Columbia St	Chapel Hill	NC	27514	**800-326-4842**	919-968-2200
LandAmerica OneStop Inc 600 Clubhouse Dr	Moon Township	PA	15108	**866-226-8616**	
Landata Inc of Illinois 2055 W Army Trail Rd	Addison	IL	60101	**888-534-4461**	630-889-4088
Lawyers Title Co 251 S Lake Ave Suite 400	Pasadena	CA	91101	**800-347-7800**	626-304-2700
Lawyers Title Insurance Corp 101 Gateway Center Pkwy	Richmond	VA	23235	**800-446-7086**	804-267-8000
Mississippi Valley Title Insurance Co 315 Tom Bigbee St	Jackson	MS	39201	**800-647-2124**	601-969-0222
Monroe Title Insurance Corp 47 W Main St	Rochester	NY	14614	**800-966-6763**	585-232-4950
North American Title Co 2185 N California Blvd Suite 575	Walnut Creek	CA	94596	**800-869-3434**	925-935-5599
Ohio Bar Title Insurance Co 8425 Pulsar Pl Suite 210	Columbus	OH	43240	**800-628-4853**	614-825-4029
Old Republic National Title Insurance Co 400 2nd Ave S	Minneapolis	MN	55401	**800-328-4441**	612-371-1111
Pacific Northwest Title Co of Washington Inc 215 Columbia St	Seattle	WA	98104	**877-285-6423**	206-622-1040
Southland Title Co 7530 N Glenoaks Blvd	Burbank	CA	91504	**800-747-7777**	818-767-2000
Stewart Information Services Corp 1980 Post Oak Blvd Suite 800 *NYSE: STC*	Houston	TX	77056	**800-729-1900**	713-625-8100
Stewart Title Co 1980 Post Oak Blvd Suite 800	Houston	TX	77056	**800-729-1900**	713-625-8100
Stewart Title Guaranty Co 1980 Post Oak Blvd Suite 800	Houston	TX	77056	**800-729-1900**	713-625-8100
Ticor Title Insurance Co 203 N LaSalle St Suite 2200	Chicago	IL	60601	**800-879-1167**	312-621-5000
Title Guaranty of Hawaii Inc 235 Queen St	Honolulu	HI	96813	**888-352-7389**	808-533-6261
Title Resources Guaranty Co 8111 LBJ Fwy Suite 1200	Dallas	TX	75251	**800-526-8018**	972-644-6500
Transnation Title Insurance Co 101 Gateway Ctr Pkwy Gateway 1	Richmond	VA	23205	**800-388-8822**	804-267-8000

384-7 Travel Insurance

Company / Address	City	State	Zip	Toll-Free	Phone
Access America 2805 N Parham Rd	Richmond	VA	23294	**800-729-6021**	804-285-3300
All Aboard Benefits 6162 E Mockingird Ln Suite 104	Dallas	TX	75214	**800-462-2322**	214-821-6677
CSA Travel Protection 5454 Ruffin Rd	San Diego	CA	92123	**800-873-9855**	

	City	State	Zip	Toll-Free	Phone
Highway To Health Inc 1 Radnor Corporate Ctr Suite 100	Radnor	PA	19087	**888-243-2358**	610-254-8700
Ingle International 5255 Yonge St Suite 218	Toronto	ON	M2N6P4	**800-360-3234**	416-730-8488
Insurance Consultants International 7405 Campstool Dr Suite 101	Colorado Springs	CO	80922	**800-576-2674**	281-587-9884
International SOS Assistance Inc 3600 Horizon Blvd Suite 300	Trevose	PA	19053	**800-523-8930**	215-244-1500
Pacific Indemnity Co 801 S Figueroa St 24th Fl	Los Angeles	CA	90017	**800-262-4459**	213-612-0880
Pan-American Life Insurance Co 601 Poydras St *Life Ins	New Orleans	LA	70130	**800-999-0514***	504-566-1300
Travel Guard International 1145 Clark St	Stevens Point	WI	54481	**800-826-1300**	715-345-0505
Travel Insured International 52-S Oakland Ave PO Box 280568	East Hartford	CT	06128	**800-243-3174**	860-528-7663
Travelex Insurance Services Inc 2121 N 117th Ave Suite 300	Omaha	NE	68164	**888-457-4602**	402-491-3200
Virginia Risk Co 9200 Keystone Crossing Suite 300	Indianapolis	IN	46240	**800-523-6944**	317-818-2089
Wallach & Co Inc 107 W Federal St	Middleburg	VA	20118	**800-237-6615**	540-687-3166

385 INTERCOM EQUIPMENT & SYSTEMS

	City	State	Zip	Toll-Free	Phone
Anacom General Corp 1240 S Claudina St	Anaheim	CA	92805	**800-955-9540**	714-774-8080
Anacom Med-Tek 1240 S Claudina St	Anaheim	CA	92805	**800-955-9540**	714-774-8484
Auth-Florence Mfg 591 Mitchell Rd	Glendale Heights	IL	60139	**800-275-1747**	630-545-5500
Clever Devices Ltd 5 Aerial Way	Syosset	NY	11791	**800-872-6129**	516-433-6100
Crest Healthcare Supply 195 S 3rd St *Cust Svc	Dassel	MN	55325	**800-328-8908***	320-275-3382
David Clark Co Inc 360 Franklin St *Cust Svc	Worcester	MA	01615	**800-298-6235***	508-751-5800
INOVA Corp 110 Avon St	Charlottesville	VA	22902	**800-637-1077**	434-817-8000
Lee Dan Communications Inc 155 Adams Ave	Hauppauge	NY	11788	**800-231-1414**	631-231-1414
M & S Systems Inc 2861 Congressman Ln	Dallas	TX	75220	**800-877-6631**	214-358-3196
Rauland-Borg Corp 3450 W Oakton St	Skokie	IL	60076	**800-621-0087**	847-679-0900
Trine Products Corp 1430 Ferris Pl	Bronx	NY	10461	**800-858-8501**	718-829-4796

386 INTERIOR DESIGN

	City	State	Zip	Toll-Free	Phone
Atlanta Architectural Textile 737 Miami Cir NE	Atlanta	GA	30324	**800-241-0178**	404-237-4246
Curran Assoc 737 Miami Cir NE	Atlanta	GA	30324	**800-241-0178**	404-237-4246
Decorating Den Systems Inc 19100 Montgomery Village Ave Suite 200	Montgomery Village	MD	20886	**800-428-1366**	301-272-1500
MGM Mirage Design Group Inc 3260 Industrial Rd	Las Vegas	NV	89109	**800-477-5110**	702-792-4600
Villa Lighting Supply Inc 1218 S Vandeventer Ave	Saint Louis	MO	63110	**800-325-0963**	314-531-2600

387 INTERNET BACKBONE PROVIDERS

	City	State	Zip	Toll-Free	Phone
AboveNet Communications Inc 1735 Lundy Ave	San Jose	CA	95131	**866-859-6971**	408-521-5619
Cincinnati Bell Inc 201 E 4th St *NYSE: CBB*	Cincinnati	OH	45202	**800-422-1199**	513-397-9900
Cogent Communications Group Inc 1015 31st St NW *AMEX: COI*	Washington	DC	20007	**877-875-4432**	202-295-4200
Electric Lightwave 4400 NE 77th Ave	Vancouver	WA	98662	**800-622-4354**	360-816-3000
Epoch Internet Inc 555 Anton Blvd	Costa Mesa	CA	92626	**888-443-7624**	714-327-2000
ICG Communications Inc 161 Inverness Dr W	Englewood	CO	80112	**888-424-1144**	303-414-5000
Infonet Services Corp 2160 E Grand Ave *NYSE: IN*	El Segundo	CA	90245	**877-325-2876**	310-335-2600
Internap Network Services Corp 250 Williams St Suite E-100 *AMEX: IIP*	Atlanta	GA	30303	**877-843-7627**	404-302-9700
Level 3 Communications Inc 1025 Eldorado Blvd *NASDAQ: LVLT*	Broomfield	CO	80021	**877-453-8353**	720-888-1000
n|Frame Inc 701 Congressional Blvd Suite 100	Carmel	IN	46032	**888-223-8633**	317-805-3759
NEON Communications Inc 2200 W Park Dr Suite 200	Westborough	MA	01581	**800-891-5080**	508-616-7800
SAVVIS Inc 12851 Worldgate Dr *NASDAQ: SVVS*	Herndon	VA	20170	**800-728-8471**	703-234-8000
Servint Internet Services 6861 Elm St Suite 2B	McLean	VA	22101	**800-573-7846**	703-847-1381
SunGard Availability Services 550 E 84th Ave Suite E5	Thornton	CO	80229	**877-246-3569**	303-942-2800
Teleglobe International Holdings Ltd 1000 de la Gauchetiere St W *NASDAQ: TLGB*	Montreal	QC	H3B4X5	**800-465-7551**	514-868-7272
Verio Inc 8005 S Chester St Suite 200	Centennial	CO	80112	**888-558-3746**	303-645-1900
VisiNet 715 Middle Ground Blvd *Cust Svc	Newport News	VA	23606	**800-286-0674***	757-873-4500
WilTel Communications LLC 1 Technology Ctr	Tulsa	OK	74103	**800-945-5426**	918-547-6000
Xspedius Communication LLC 555 Winghaven Blvd Suite 300	O Fallon	MO	63368	**877-962-9100**	636-625-7000

388 INTERNET BROADCASTING

	City	State	Zip	Toll-Free	Phone
Audible Inc 65 Willowbrook Blvd 3rd Fl *NASDAQ: ADBL*	Wayne	NJ	07470	**888-283-5051**	973-890-4070
Eatsleepmusic Network 301 Moodie Dr Suite 306	Ottawa	ON	K2H9C4	**877-867-8668**	

389 INTERNET DOMAIN NAME REGISTRARS

	City	State	Zip	Toll-Free	Phone
AITDomains 421 Maiden Ln	Fayetteville	NC	28301	**877-549-2881**	910-321-1327
All West Registry 329 E 2100 S	Salt Lake City	UT	84115	**877-734-6263**	
Best Registration Services Inc DBA BestRegistrar.com 1418 S 3rd St	Louisville	KY	40208	**800-977-3475**	502-637-4528
BestRegistrar.com 1418 S 3rd St	Louisville	KY	40208	**800-977-3475**	502-637-4528
BulkRegister.com 10 E Baltimore St Suite 1500	Baltimore	MD	21202	**800-361-2682**	410-779-1400
Domain Bank Inc 23 W 4th St	Bethlehem	PA	18015	**888-583-3382**	610-317-9606
Domain Direct Div TUCOWS Inc 96 Mowat Ave	Toronto	ON	M6K3M1	**800-371-6992**	416-531-2697
Domain Registration Services DBA dotEarth.com PO Box 447	Palmyra	NJ	08065	**888-339-9001**	
DomainPeople Inc 555 W Hastings St Harbour Ctr Suite 1440	Vancouver	BC	V6B4N6	**877-734-3667**	604-639-1680
dotEarth.com PO Box 447	Palmyra	NJ	08065	**888-339-9001**	
Global Knowledge Group Inc (GKG) 2700 Earl Rudder Fwy S Suite 1300	College Station	TX	77845	**800-617-0412**	979-693-5447
MarkMonitor Inc 391 N Ancestor Pl *Cust Svc	Boise	ID	83704	**800-337-7520***	208-389-5740
Names4ever.com 10350 Barnes Canyon Rd *Sales	San Diego	CA	92121	**877-275-8763***	858-410-6929
NameSecure LLC PO Box 27096	Concord	CA	94527	**800-299-1288**	925-609-1111
Network Solutions LLC 13200 Woodland Pk Rd	Herndon	VA	20171	**800-638-9759**	703-742-0400
Register.com Inc 575 8th Ave 11th Fl *NASDAQ: RCOM*	New York	NY	10018	**800-899-9703**	212-798-9100
Stargate Holdings Corp 2805 Butterfield Rd Suite 100	Oak Brook	IL	60523	**800-282-6541**	630-572-2242
The Registry at Info Avenue LLC PO Box 698	Fort Mill	SC	29716	**800-950-4726**	803-802-4600
TierraNet Inc 9573 Chesapeake Dr 1st Fl	San Diego	CA	92123	**877-843-7721**	858-560-9416
TUCOWS Inc 96 Mowat Ave	Toronto	ON	M6K3M1	**800-371-6992**	416-535-0123
TUCOWS Inc Domain Direct Div 96 Mowat Ave	Toronto	ON	M6K3M1	**800-371-6992**	416-531-2697
.TV Corp International 21345 Ridge Top Cir	Dulles	VA	20166	**800-255-2218**	703-948-3200
Verio Inc 8005 S Chester St Suite 200	Centennial	CO	80112	**888-558-3746**	303-645-1900
VeriSign Inc 487 E Middlefield Rd *NASDAQ: VRSN* ■ *Sales	Mountain View	CA	94043	**866-893-6565***	650-961-7500

390 INTERNET SERVICE PROVIDERS (ISPS)

	City	State	Zip	Toll-Free	Phone
711.NET Inc 2063 N Lecanto Hwy	Lecanto	FL	34461	**866-558-6778**	
A+Net Internet Services 10350 Barnes Canyon Rd	San Diego	CA	92121	**877-275-8763**	858-410-6929
ABT Internet 525 Northern Blvd Suite 302	Great Neck	NY	11021	**800-367-3414**	516-829-5484
Access US 712 N 2nd St Suite 300	Saint Louis	MO	63102	**800-638-6373**	314-655-7700
Adelphia PowerLink 1 N Main St *Cust Svc	Coudersport	PA	16915	**888-683-1000***	888-233-5638
America Online Inc (AOL) 22000 AOL Way *Orders	Dulles	VA	20166	**888-265-8002***	703-265-1000
America Online Latin America Inc 6600 N Andrews Ave Suite 400	Fort Lauderdale	FL	33309	**800-827-6364**	954-689-3000
AOL (America Online Inc) 22000 AOL Way *Orders	Dulles	VA	20166	**888-265-8002***	703-265-1000
AT & T Business Internet Services PO Box 30021	Tampa	FL	33630	**877-485-1500**	
AT & T WorldNet Service 32 Ave of the Americas *Tech Supp	New York	NY	10013	**800-400-1447***	800-967-5363
ATX Communications Inc 2100 Renaissance Blvd	King of Prussia	PA	19406	**800-220-2891**	610-755-4000
Aurora Cable Internet 350 Industrial Pkwy S	Aurora	ON	L4G3H3	**877-452-6743**	905-727-1981
BlueRibbon.com 625 Walnut Ridge Dr Suite 108	Hartland	WI	53029	**800-788-1298**	262-369-0600
Cayuse Networks Inc 3019 117th Ave Ct E	Edgewood	WA	98372	**888-245-9691**	
ChristianLiving.net 1302 Clear Springs Trace *Tech Supp	Louisville	KY	40223	**877-486-2660***	888-772-7355
Cincinnati Bell Inc 201 E 4th St *NYSE: CBB*	Cincinnati	OH	45202	**800-422-1199**	513-397-9900
ClearSail Communications LLC DBA Family.NET 5160 Timber Creek Rd	Houston	TX	77017	**888-905-0888**	713-230-2800
CompuServe Interactive Services Inc 5000 Arlington Ctr Blvd *Cust Svc	Columbus	OH	43220	**800-848-8990***	614-457-8600
ConnectTo.Net 150 Professional Ctr Dr Suite H	Rohnert Park	CA	94928	**877-586-3538**	707-696-2365
Covad Communications Group Inc 110 Rio robles *Tech Supp	San Jose	CA	95134	**888-642-6823***	408-952-6400
DirecPC 11717 Exploration Ln	Germantown	MD	20876	**800-347-3272**	301-428-5500
Direct Internet Access PO Box 7263	Monroe	LA	71211	**800-296-2249**	
DSL.net Inc 545 Long Wharf Dr 5th Fl *AMEX: BIZ*	New Haven	CT	06511	**800-455-5546**	203-772-1000
DSLextreme.com 20847 Sherman Way	Winnetka	CA	91306	**800-774-3379**	818-902-4821
EarthLink Inc 1375 Peachtree St NE *NASDAQ: ELNK*	Atlanta	GA	30309	**800-332-4892**	404-815-0770
Epoch Internet Inc 555 Anton Blvd	Costa Mesa	CA	92626	**888-443-7624**	714-327-2000
Expedient 40 24th St Suite 300	Pittsburgh	PA	15222	**800-969-0099**	412-316-7800
Family.NET 5160 Timber Creek Rd	Houston	TX	77017	**888-905-0888**	713-230-2800
FASTNET Corp 3864 Courtney St Suite 130	Bethlehem	PA	18017	**888-321-3278**	610-954-5910
Internet America Inc 350 N Saint Paul St 1 Dallas Ctr Suite 3000	Dallas	TX	75201	**800-232-4335**	214-861-2662
Ionix Internet 266 Sutter St	San Francisco	CA	94108	**888-884-6649**	415-288-9940
iSelect Internet Inc 420 W Pine St	Lodi	CA	95240	**888-677-8679**	209-334-0496
MacConnect Inc 81 Larkfield Rd *Sales	East Northport	NY	11731	**866-622-2666***	888-660-3010
MegaPath Networks Inc 6691 Owens Dr	Pleasanton	CA	94588	**877-634-2728**	925-201-2500
MichTel Communications LLC 10 W Huron St	Pontiac	MI	48343	**888-244-6381**	248-771-5000
Microsoft Network (MSN) 1 Microsoft Way *Sales	Redmond	WA	98052	**800-426-9400***	425-882-8080

	City	State	Zip	Toll-Free	Phone
Millenicom 1735 SW Miles St Suite 2000	Portland	OR	97219	**888-925-4221**	503-768-3063
MSN (Microsoft Network) 1 Microsoft Way	Redmond	WA	98052	**800-426-9400***	425-882-8080
*Sales					
NetZero Inc 21301 Burbank Blvd	Woodland Hills	CA	91367	**877-638-3117**	818-287-3000
New Edge Networks 3000 Columbia House Blvd Suite 106	Vancouver	WA	98661	**877-725-3343**	360-693-9009
Nova Internet Services Inc 12225 Greenville Ave SUite 230	Dallas	TX	75243	**877-668-2663**	214-904-9600
PeoplePC Inc 100 Pine St Suite 1100	San Francisco	CA	94111	**800-736-7537**	415-732-4400
ProtoSource Network 2511 W Shaw Ave Suite 102	Fresno	CA	93711	**866-490-8600**	559-486-8638
Provo International Inc 1 Bluehill Plaza PO Box 1548	Pearl River	NY	10965	**888-559-5550**	845-623-8553
SafeBrowse.com Inc 315 Northpoint Pkwy Suite F	Acworth	GA	30102	**877-944-7070**	
SBC Prodigy 6500 River Place Blvd Bldg 3	Austin	TX	78730	**800-776-3449***	512-527-1500
*Cust Svc					
ServUsa Internet PO Box 745	Laurinburg	NC	28353	**877-467-3788***	910-276-1633
*Tech Supp					
Speakeasy Inc 2222 2nd Ave	Seattle	WA	98121	**800-556-5829**	206-728-9770
Spire Communications Inc PO Box 1989	Apopka	FL	32704	**877-797-7473**	
TOAST.net 4841 Monroe St Suite 307	Toledo	OH	43623	**888-862-7863**	419-292-2200
True Vine Online 50 Damsite Rd	Center Barnstead	NH	03225	**877-878-3846**	
Verio Inc 8005 S Chester St Suite 200	Centennial	CO	80112	**888-558-3746**	303-645-1900
Verizon Online 4055 Corporate Dr Suite 400	Grapevine	TX	76051	**877-483-3648**	
VIA NET.WORKS Inc 3575 Piedmont Rd Suite 710	Atlanta	GA	30305	**800-749-1706**	404-926-3611
NASDAQ: VNWI					
WorldKey.net Inc 837 E Ave Suite Q-9	Palmdale	CA	93550	**888-776-2930**	661-274-4443
Xspedius Communication LLC 555 Winghaven Blvd Suite 300	O Fallon	MO	63368	**877-962-9100**	636-625-7000
ZDial Inc PO Box 626	West Chester	PA	19380	**888-737-1001**	610-692-9205

391 INVENTORY SERVICES

	City	State	Zip	Toll-Free	Phone
Douglas-Guardian Services Corp 14800 St Mary's Ln	Houston	TX	77079	**800-255-0552**	281-531-0500
MSI Inventory Service Corp PO Box 230129	Flowood	MS	39232	**800-820-1460**	601-939-0130
RGIS Inventory Specialists 2000 E Taylor Rd	Auburn Hills	MI	48326	**800-521-3102**	248-651-2511
Western Inventory Service Ltd 192 Bridgeland Ave	Toronto	ON	M6A1Z4	**800-268-6848**	416-781-5563

392 INVESTIGATIVE SERVICES

SEE ALSO Information Retrieval Services (General); Public Records Search Services; Security & Protective Services

	City	State	Zip	Toll-Free	Phone
Alliance Investigations LLC 240 S Montezuma St Suite 100	Prescott	AZ	86303	**800-717-1196**	928-717-1196
Allington International Inc 20160 Center Ridge Rd Suite 206	Cleveland	OH	44116	**800-747-5202**	440-333-0505
American Professional Services Inc 5350 S Western Ave Suite 500	Oklahoma City	OK	73109	**800-219-9120**	405-636-4222
Bishops Services Inc 20283 SR 7 Suite 400	Boca Raton	FL	33498	**800-373-5294**	561-237-4242
Bombet Cashio & Assoc 11220 N Harrells Ferry Rd	Baton Rouge	LA	70816	**800-256-5333**	225-275-0796
Bontecou Investigative Services Inc PO Box 2448	Jackson	WY	83001	**877-733-2639**	307-733-2637
Brabston Legal Investigations Inc 3746 Halls Mills Rd	Mobile	AL	36693	**800-239-4939**	251-666-5666
Capitol Detective Agency 2922 N 18th Pl	Phoenix	AZ	85016	**800-346-0347**	602-277-0770
Cleveland Legal Support PO Box 5358	Central Point	OR	97502	**800-888-6629**	541-665-5162
Confidential Services PO Box 91034	Columbus	OH	43209	**800-752-4581**	614-252-4646
DataTrace Investigations Inc PO Box 95322	South Jordan	UT	84095	**800-748-5335**	801-253-2400
Douglas Baldwin & Assoc PO Box 1249	La Canada	CA	91012	**800-392-3950**	818-952-4433
Elliott & Assoc Ltd PO Box 13282	Albuquerque	NM	87192	**800-538-0111**	505-293-8896
Gietzen & Assoc Inc 1302 N Marion St	Tampa	FL	33602	**888-779-2345**	813-223-3233
Graymark Security Group 7301 NW 4th St Suite 110	Plantation	FL	33317	**800-881-3242**	954-581-5575
Gregg Investigations Inc 6320 Monona Dr	Madison	WI	53716	**800-866-1976**	608-256-1074
Heartland Information Services Inc DBA Heartland Business Intelligence 821 Marquette Ave 404 Foshay Tower	Minneapolis	MN	55402	**800-967-1882**	612-371-9255
International Investigators Inc 3216 N Pennsylvania St	Indianapolis	IN	46205	**800-403-8111**	317-925-1496
Johnson Rick & Assoc of Colorado 1649 Downing St	Denver	CO	80218	**800-530-2300**	303-296-2200
Kessler International 45 Rockefeller Plaza Suite 2000	New York	NY	10111	**800-932-2221**	212-286-9100
MacIntire & Assoc Inc 531 W Plata St Suite 200	Tucson	AZ	85705	**800-641-2737**	520-622-2737
Michael Ramey & Assoc Inc PO Box 744	Danville	CA	94526	**800-321-0505**	925-820-8900
North Winds Investigations Inc PO Box 1654	Rogers	AR	72757	**800-530-4514**	479-925-1612
Northwest Location Services Inc DBA Legal Locate Services PO Box 1345	Puyallup	WA	98371	**800-916-3724**	253-848-7767
Owens & Assoc Investigations 2245 San Diego Ave Suite 225	San Diego	CA	92110	**800-297-1343**	619-297-1343
PADIC Inc 1609 E Broadway	Gainesville	TX	76240	**800-679-5727**	940-665-6130
Palmer Investigative Services 624 W Gurley St Suite A	Prescott	AZ	86305	**800-280-2951**	928-778-2951
PI & Information Services LLC PO Box 157	Beaverton	OR	97075	**800-649-7530**	503-643-4274
Pinkerton's Inc 4330 Park Terrace Dr	Westlake Village	CA	91361	**800-232-7465**	818-706-6800
Ramey Michael & Assoc Inc PO Box 744	Danville	CA	94526	**800-321-0505**	925-820-8900
Research Assoc Inc 27999 Clemens Rd	Westlake	OH	44145	**800-255-9693**	440-892-1000
Rick Johnson & Assoc of Colorado 1649 Downing St	Denver	CO	80218	**800-530-2300**	303-296-2200
Shawver & Assoc PO Box 1592	Corpus Christi	TX	78403	**800-364-2333**	361-880-8968
Source Resources PO Box 88	Cookeville	TN	38503	**800-678-8774**	931-537-3641
Southern Research Co Inc 2850 Centenary Blvd	Shreveport	LA	71104	**888-772-6952**	318-227-9700
Specialized Investigations 14530 Delano St	Van Nuys	CA	91411	**800-714-3728**	818-909-9607
State Information Bureau 842 E Park Ave	Tallahassee	FL	32301	**800-881-1742**	850-561-3990
Stewart & Assoc Inc 50 W Douglas St Suite 1200	Freeport	IL	61032	**800-442-3807**	815-235-3807
VISTA Inc 29516 Southfield Rd Suite 104	Southfield	MI	48076	**888-873-8478**	248-559-3500
VTS Investigations LLC PO Box 971	Elgin	IL	60121	**800-538-4464**	847-888-4464
Wood & Tait Inc PO Box 6180	Kamuela	HI	96743	**800-774-8585**	

393 INVESTMENT ADVICE & MANAGEMENT

SEE ALSO Commodity Contracts Brokers & Dealers; Investment Guides - Online; Mutual Funds; Securities Brokers & Dealers

	City	State	Zip	Toll-Free	Phone
Advent Capital Management LLC 1065 Ave of the Americas 31st Fl	New York	NY	10018	**888-523-8368**	212-482-1600
AGF Management Ltd 2920 Matheson Blvd E	Mississauga	ON	L4W5J4	**800-268-8583**	905-214-8203
Alger Fred Management Inc 30 Montgomery St 11th Fl	Jersey City	NJ	07302	**800-223-3810**	201-547-3600
Alliance Capital Management LP 1345 Ave of the Americas	New York	NY	10105	**800-221-5672***	212-969-1000
*Cust Svc					
Allianz Global Investors of America LP 800 Newport Ctr Dr Suite 100	Newport Beach	CA	92660	**800-225-1970**	949-219-2200
American Century Investments Inc 4500 Main St	Kansas City	MO	64111	**800-345-2021**	816-531-5575
American Express Asset Management Group AXP Financial Ctr	Minneapolis	MN	55440	**800-328-8300**	612-671-3131
American Express Financial Advisors Inc AXP Financial Ctr	Minneapolis	MN	55440	**800-328-8300**	612-671-3131
American Express Financial Corp AXP Financial Ctr	Minneapolis	MN	55440	**800-328-8300**	612-671-3131
Amerindo Investment Advisors Inc 1 Embarcadero Ctr Suite 2300	San Francisco	CA	94111	**888-832-4386**	415-362-0292
Amivest Capital Management 275 Broad Hollow Rd	Melville	NY	11747	**800-426-4837**	631-844-0572
AMR Investment Services Inc PO Box 619003 MD 2450	DFW Airport	TX	75261	**800-967-9009**	817-967-3509
Analytic Investors Inc 500 S Grand Ave 23rd Fl	Los Angeles	CA	90017	**800-618-1872**	213-688-3015
Ariel Capital Management LLC 200 E Randolph Dr Suite 2900	Chicago	IL	60601	**800-292-7435**	312-726-0140
Atlantic Trust 300 E Lombard St Suite 1100	Baltimore	MD	21202	**888-880-1621**	410-539-4660
Babson David L & Co Inc 1 Memorial Dr Suite 1100	Cambridge	MA	02142	**877-766-0014**	617-225-3800
Babson-United Inc 400 Talcott Ave	Watertown	MA	02472	**888-223-7412**	781-235-0900
Bailard Biehl & Kaiser Group 950 Tower Ln Suite 1900	Foster City	CA	94404	**800-882-8383**	650-571-5800
Bank of Ireland Asset Management (US) Ltd 75 Holly Hill Ln	Greenwich	CT	06830	**888-473-2275**	203-869-0111
Baring Asset Management Co Inc 125 High St High St Tower Suite 2700	Boston	MA	02110	**800-533-7432**	617-951-0052
Bartlett & Co 36 E 4th St	Cincinnati	OH	45202	**800-800-4612**	513-621-4612
Boston Advisors Inc 1 Federal St 26th Fl	Boston	MA	02110	**800-523-5903**	617-348-3100
Boston Financial Data Services 2 Heritage Dr	North Quincy	MA	02171	**888-772-2337**	617-483-5000
Bramwell Capital Management 745 5th Ave 16th Fl	New York	NY	10151	**800-272-6227**	212-308-0505
Brandes Investment Partners LP 11988 El Camino Real Suite 500	San Diego	CA	92191	**800-237-7119**	858-755-0239
Brandywine Asset Management Inc 201 N Walnut St Suite 1200	Wilmington	DE	19801	**800-348-2499**	302-654-6162
Brown Capital Management Inc 1201 N Calvert St	Baltimore	MD	21202	**800-809-3863**	410-837-3234
Cadence Capital Management 265 Franklin St 11th Fl	Boston	MA	02110	**800-298-2194**	617-367-7400
Callan Assoc Inc 101 California St Suite 3500	San Francisco	CA	94111	**800-227-3288**	415-974-5060
Cambiar Investors Inc 2401 E 2nd Ave Suite 400	Denver	CO	80206	**888-673-9950**	303-302-9000
Capital Group Cos Inc 333 S Hope St	Los Angeles	CA	90071	**800-421-8511**	213-486-9200
Capital Growth Management LP 1 International Pl 45th Fl	Boston	MA	02110	**800-334-6440**	617-737-3225
Capital Resource Advisors 200 W Adams Suite 1800	Chicago	IL	60606	**888-677-4272**	
Cargill Asset Investment & Finance Group 12700 Whitewater Dr	Minnetonka	MN	55343	**800-227-4455**	952-984-3444
CI Fund Management Inc 151 Yonge St 11th Fl	Toronto	ON	M5C2W7	**800-268-9374**	416-364-1145
TSE: CIX					
Citigroup Global Markets Holdings Inc 300 First Stamford Pl 2nd Fl	Stamford	CT	06902	**888-777-0102***	203-961-6000
*Sales					
Cohen & Steers Inc 757 3rd Ave 20th Fl	New York	NY	10017	**800-330-7348**	212-832-3232
NYSE: CNS					
Colony Capital Management 3060 Peachtree Rd NW Suite 1550	Atlanta	GA	30305	**877-365-5050**	404-365-5050
Columbia Funds Distributor Inc 1 Fincial Ctr	Boston	MA	02111	**800-225-2365**	
Columbia Management Assoc Inc 1 Financial Ctr	Boston	MA	02111	**800-225-2365**	617-426-3750
Columbus Circle Investors Inc 1 Station Pl Metro Ctr 8th Fl	Stamford	CT	06902	**888-826-5247**	203-353-6000
Connell Finance Co Inc 1 Connell Dr	Berkeley Heights	NJ	07922	**800-233-3240**	908-673-3700
Connell Technologies Co LLC 350 Lindbergh Ave	Livermore	CA	94550	**888-301-0300**	925-455-6790
Crown Financial Ministries 601 Broad St SE	Gainesville	GA	30501	**800-722-1976**	770-534-1000
David L Babson & Co Inc 1 Memorial Dr Suite 1100	Cambridge	MA	02142	**877-766-0014**	617-225-3800
Davis Hamilton Jackson & Assoc 1401 McKinney St Suite 1600	Houston	TX	77010	**800-594-0438**	713-853-2322
Dean Investment Assoc Kettering Tower Suite 2480	Dayton	OH	45423	**800-327-3656**	937-222-0282
Delaware Investments 2005 Market St	Philadelphia	PA	19103	**800-362-7500**	215-255-1200
Deutsche Asset Management 345 Park Ave	New York	NY	10154	**800-232-9727**	212-326-6200

Classified Section

Company	City	State	Zip	Toll-Free	Phone
Dodge & Cox 555 California St 40th Fl	San Francisco	CA	94104	**800-621-3979**	415-981-1710
Driehaus Capital Management Inc 25 E Erie St	Chicago	IL	60611	**800-688-8819**	312-587-3800
Eagle Asset Management 880 Carillon Pkwy	Saint Petersburg	FL	33716	**800-237-3101**	727-573-2453
Earnest Partners LLC 75 14th St Suite 2300	Atlanta	GA	30309	**800-322-0068**	404-815-8772
Eaton Vance Corp 255 State St *NYSE: EV*	Boston	MA	02109	**800-225-6265**	617-482-8260
Edgar Lomax Co 6564 Loisdale Ct Suite 310	Springfield	VA	22150	**866-205-0524**	703-719-0026
Engemann Asset Management 600 N Rosemead Blvd	Pasadena	CA	91107	**800-882-2855**	626-351-9686
Essex Investment Management Co LLC 125 High St 29th Fl	Boston	MA	02110	**800-342-3202**	617-342-3200
Fayez Sarofim & Co 2 Houston Ctr Suite 2907	Houston	TX	77010	**800-288-7125**	713-654-4484
Federated Investors 1001 Liberty Ave Federated Investors Tower *NYSE: FII*	Pittsburgh	PA	15222	**800-245-0242**	412-288-1900
Fidelity Investments 82 Devonshire St	Boston	MA	02109	**800-522-7297**	617-563-7000
Fiduciary Management Assoc LLC 55 W Monroe St Suite 2550	Chicago	IL	60603	**800-793-0848**	312-930-6850
First Investors Management Co Inc 95 Wall St *Cust Svc	New York	NY	10005	**800-423-4026***	212-858-8000
First Pacific Advisors Inc 11400 W Olympic Blvd Suite 1200	Los Angeles	CA	90064	**800-982-4372**	310-473-0225
Fischer Francis Trees & Watts Inc 200 Park Ave 46th Fl	New York	NY	10166	**888-367-3389**	212-681-3000
Fisher Investments 13100 Skyline Blvd	Woodside	CA	94062	**800-851-8845**	650-851-3334
FMR Corp 82 Devonshire St	Boston	MA	02109	**800-522-7297**	617-563-7000
Founders Asset Management LLC 210 University Blvd Suite 800	Denver	CO	80206	**800-525-2440**	303-394-4404
Frank Russell Co PO Box 1616	Tacoma	WA	98402	**800-426-7969**	253-572-9500
Franklin Resources Inc DBA Franklin Templeton Investments 1 Franklin Pkwy *NYSE: BEN*	San Mateo	CA	94403	**800-342-5236**	650-312-2000
Franklin Templeton Investments 1 Franklin Pkwy *NYSE: BEN*	San Mateo	CA	94403	**800-342-5236**	650-312-2000
Fred Alger Management Inc 30 Montgomery St 11th Fl	Jersey City	NJ	07302	**800-223-3810**	201-547-3600
Freedom Capital LLC 1 Beacon St 5th Fl	Boston	MA	02108	**800-861-8088**	617-722-4700
Gabelli Asset Management Inc 1 Corporate Ctr *NYSE: GBL*	Rye	NY	10580	**800-422-3554**	914-921-5681
Gannett Welsh & Kotler Inc 222 Berkeley St Suite 1500	Boston	MA	02116	**800-225-4236**	617-236-8900
Gartmore Morley Financial Services Inc 5665 SW Meadows Rd Suite 400	Lake Oswego	OR	97035	**800-548-4806**	503-620-7899
Gemini Fund Services LLC 150 Motor Pkwy Suite 205	Hauppauge	NY	11788	**800-368-3322**	631-951-0500
Glenmede Trust Co 1650 Market St Suite 1200	Philadelphia	PA	19103	**800-966-3200**	215-419-6000
Goldman Sachs Asset Management 32 Old Slip 17th Fl	New York	NY	10005	**800-292-4726**	212-902-1000
H & R Block Financial Advisors Inc 719 Griswold St	Detroit	MI	48226	**800-521-1111**	313-628-1300
Harris Assoc LP 2 N La Salle St Suite 500	Chicago	IL	60602	**800-731-0700**	312-621-0600
HD Vest Financial Services 6333 N State Hwy 161 4th Fl	Irving	TX	75038	**800-821-8254**	972-870-6000
Heitman LLC 191 N Wacker Dr Suite 2500	Chicago	IL	60606	**800-225-5435**	312-855-5700
Holland Capital Management LP 1 N Wacker Dr Suite 700	Chicago	IL	60606	**800-522-2711**	312-553-4830
HSBC Asset Management Inc 452 5th Ave	New York	NY	10018	**800-759-0315**	212-525-5000
Hyperion Capital Management Inc 165 Broadway 36th Fl	New York	NY	10006	**800-497-3746**	212-549-8400
ICM Asset Management Inc 601 W Main Ave Suite 600	Spokane	WA	99201	**800-488-4075**	509-455-3588
Independence Investment LLC 53 State St 28th Fl	Boston	MA	02109	**800-858-6635**	617-228-8700
INVESCO Capital Management Inc 1360 Peachtree St NE 1 Midtown Plaza Suite 100	Atlanta	GA	30309	**800-241-5477**	404-892-0896
INVESCO-NAM 400 W Market St Suite 2500	Louisville	KY	40202	**877-581-6262**	502-581-7668
Investment Counselors of Maryland LLC 803 Cathedral St	Baltimore	MD	21201	**800-638-7983**	410-539-3838
J & W Seligman & Co Inc 100 Park Ave	New York	NY	10017	**800-221-7844**	212-850-1864
John Hancock Funds 101 Huntington Ave 10th Fl *Cust Svc	Boston	MA	02199	**800-225-5291***	617-375-1500
Johnson Asset Management 555 Main St Suite 440	Racine	WI	53403	**800-407-5500**	262-681-4770
JPMorgan Fleming Asset Management PO Box 219392	Kansas City	MO	64121	**800-348-4782**	816-435-1000
Kopp Investment Advisors Inc 7701 France Ave S Suite 500	Edina	MN	55435	**800-333-9128**	952-841-0400
Leerink Swann & Co 1 Federal St 37th Fl	Boston	MA	02110	**800-808-7525**	617-248-1601
Lehman Brothers Asset Management LLC 200 S Wacker Dr Suite 2100	Chicago	IL	60606	**800-764-9336**	312-559-2880
Liberty Funds Group 1 Financial Ctr	Boston	MA	02111	**800-225-2365**	617-426-3750
Loomis Sayles & Co Inc LP 1 Financial Ctr	Boston	MA	02111	**800-225-2365**	617-482-2450
Lord Abbett & Co 90 Hudson St	Jersey City	NJ	07302	**800-874-3733**	
M & I Wealth Management 1000 N Water St	Milwaukee	WI	53202	**800-342-2265**	414-287-8700
Mackenzie Financial Corp 150 Bloor St W Suite M111	Toronto	ON	M5S3B5	**888-653-7070**	416-922-5322
Marvin & Palmer Assoc Inc 1201 N Market St Suite 2300	Wilmington	DE	19801	**800-775-4259**	302-573-3570
McGlinn Capital Management 850 N Wyomissing Blvd	Wyomissing	PA	19610	**800-783-1478**	610-374-5125
MDL Capital Management Inc 309 Smithville St 5th Fl	Pittsburgh	PA	15222	**877-635-3863**	215-893-8800
MFS Investment Management 500 Boylston St	Boston	MA	02116	**800-637-2929**	617-954-5000
Navellier Securities Corp 1 E Liberty St 3rd Fl	Reno	NV	89501	**800-887-8671**	775-785-2300
Neuberger Berman LLC 605 3rd Ave	New York	NY	10158	**800-223-6448**	212-476-9000
Nicholas-Applegate Capital Management 600 W Broadway 30th Fl	San Diego	CA	92101	**800-551-8045**	619-687-8100
Northern Trust Co of Connecticut 300 Atlantic St Suite 400	Stamford	CT	06901	**800-722-4609**	203-977-7000
Payden & Rygel 333 S Grand Ave	Los Angeles	CA	90071	**800-572-9336**	213-625-1900
Peninsula Asset Management Inc 1111 3rd Ave W Suite 340	Bradenton	FL	34205	**800-269-6417**	941-748-8680
PLM International Inc 3988 N Central Expy Bldg 5 6th Fl	Dallas	TX	75204	**800-626-7549**	
Primerica Financial Services 3120 Breckinridge Blvd	Duluth	GA	30099	**800-257-4725**	770-381-1000
Princor Financial Services Corp PO Box 10423	Des Moines	IA	50306	**800-247-4123**	515-247-5111
Prudential Financial Inc 751 Broad St *NYSE: PRU*	Newark	NJ	07102	**800-843-7625**	973-802-6000
Putnam Investments 1 Post Office Sq	Boston	MA	02109	**888-478-8626**	617-292-1000
Putnam Lovell NBF 65 E 55th St Park Ave Tower 34th Fl	New York	NY	10022	**800-531-5190**	212-546-7500
PVG Asset Management Corp 24918 Genesee Trail Rd	Golden	CO	80401	**800-777-0818**	303-526-0548
Reed Conner & Birdwell Inc 11111 Santa Monica Blvd Suite 1700	Los Angeles	CA	90025	**877-478-4722**	310-478-4005
Retirement System Group Inc 150 E 42nd St 27th Fl	New York	NY	10017	**800-446-7774**	212-503-0100
Rittenhouse Financial Services Inc 5 Radnor Corporate Ctr Suite 300	Radnor	PA	19087	**800-847-6369**	610-254-9600
RNC Capital Management LLC 11601 Wilshire Blvd 25th Fl	Los Angeles	CA	90025	**800-877-7624**	310-477-6543
Royce & Assoc LLC 1414 Ave of the Americas 9th Fl	New York	NY	10019	**800-348-1414**	212-486-1445
RREEF 101 California St 26th Fl	San Francisco	CA	94111	**800-222-5885**	415-781-3300
Russell Investment Group 909 A St	Tacoma	WA	98402	**800-787-7354**	
Sarofim Fayez & Co 2 Houston Ctr Suite 2907	Houston	TX	77010	**800-288-7125**	713-654-4484
SEI Investments Co 1 Freedom Valley Dr *NASDAQ: SEIC*	Oaks	PA	19456	**800-610-1114**	610-676-1000
Seligman J & W & Co Inc 100 Park Ave	New York	NY	10017	**800-221-7844**	212-850-1864
Seneca Capital Management LLC 909 Montgomery St Suite 500	San Francisco	CA	94133	**800-828-1212**	415-486-6500
Signalert Corp 150 Great Neck Rd Suite 301	Great Neck	NY	11021	**800-829-6229**	516-829-6444
Simms Capital Management Inc 55 Railroad Ave	Greenwich	CT	06830	**888-258-6365**	203-252-5700
Sirach Capital Management Inc 520 Pike St Suite 2800	Seattle	WA	98101	**800-788-9078**	206-624-3800
Smith Graham & Co 600 Travis St Suite 6900	Houston	TX	77002	**800-739-4470**	713-227-1100
Standard & Poor's 55 Water St 45th Fl *Cust Svc	New York	NY	10041	**800-344-3014***	212-438-2000
State Street Research & Management 1 Financial Ctr 31st Fl	Boston	MA	02111	**800-882-0052**	617-357-7800
Strong Financial Corp PO Box 2936	Milwaukee	WI	53201	**800-368-1030**	414-359-1400
Systematic Financial Management LP 300 Frank W Burr Blvd 7th Fl Glenpoint Ctr E	Teaneck	NJ	07666	**800-258-0497**	201-928-1982
T Rowe Price Assoc Inc 100 E Pratt St	Baltimore	MD	21202	**800-638-7890**	410-345-2000
Thompson Siegel & Walmsley Inc 5000 Monument Ave	Richmond	VA	23230	**800-697-1056**	804-353-4500
Todd Investment Advisors Inc 101 S 5th St Suite 3160	Louisville	KY	40202	**888-544-8633**	502-585-3121
Torch Energy Advisors Inc 1221 Lamar St Suite 1600	Houston	TX	77010	**800-324-8672**	713-650-1246
Transamerica Investment Management 1150 S Olive St Suite 2700	Los Angeles	CA	90015	**866-846-1800**	720-941-9124
Trinity Investment Management Corp 10 St James Ave	Boston	MA	02116	**800-422-1854**	617-728-7200
US Global Investors Inc PO Box 781234 *NASDAQ: GROW*	San Antonio	TX	78278	**800-873-8637**	210-308-1234
US Trust Corp 114 W 47th St	New York	NY	10036	**800-878-7878**	212-852-1000
Value Line Asset Management 220 E 42nd St 6th Fl	New York	NY	10017	**800-634-3583**	212-907-1500
Value Line Inc 220 E 42nd St 6th Fl *NASDAQ: VALU* ■ *Cust Svc	New York	NY	10017	**800-634-3583***	212-907-1500
Van Kampen Investments Inc 1 Parkview Plaza	Oakbrook Terrace	IL	60181	**800-225-2222**	630-684-6000
Vanguard Group 455 Devon Park Dr	Wayne	PA	19087	**800-662-7447**	610-669-1000
Vest HD Financial Services 6333 N State Hwy 161 4th Fl	Irving	TX	75038	**800-821-8254**	972-870-6000
Vontobel Asset Management Inc 450 Park Ave 7th Fl	New York	NY	10022	**800-445-8872**	212-415-7000
Voyageur Asset Management Inc 100 S 5th St Suite 2300	Minneapolis	MN	55402	**800-553-2143**	612-376-7000
Waddell & Reed Financial Inc 6300 Lamar Ave *NYSE: WDR*	Shawnee Mission	KS	66202	**888-923-3355**	913-236-2000
Wellington West Capital Inc 200 Waterfront Dr Suite 400	Winnipeg	MB	R3B3P1	**800-461-6314**	204-925-2250
Woodbury Financial Services Inc PO Box 64271	Saint Paul	MN	55164	**800-800-2000**	651-738-4000
Wright Investors' Service 440 Wheelers Farms Rd	Milford	CT	06460	**800-232-0013**	203-783-4400
Yacktman Asset Management Co 1110 W Lake Cook Rd Suite 385	Buffalo Grove	IL	60089	**800-356-6356**	847-325-0707

394 INVESTMENT COMPANIES - SMALL BUSINESS

Company	City	State	Zip	Toll-Free	Phone
Allied Capital Corp 1919 Pennsylvania Ave NW 3rd Fl *NYSE: ALD*	Washington	DC	20006	**888-818-5298**	202-331-1112
Domestic Capital Corp 815 Reservoir Ave	Cranston	RI	02910	**800-556-6600**	401-946-3310
East-West Mortgage 1568 Spring Hill Rd Suite 100	McLean	VA	22102	**800-844-1015**	703-442-0150
Elk Assoc Funding Corp 747 3rd Ave 4th Fl	New York	NY	10017	**800-214-1047**	212-355-2449
Galliard Capital Management Inc 800 La Salle Ave Suite 2060	Minneapolis	MN	55402	**800-717-1617**	612-667-3210
GamePlan Financial Marketing LLC 300 ParkBrooke Pl Suite 200	Woodstock	GA	30189	**866-766-3855**	770-517-2765
Impact Seven Inc 147 Lake Almena Dr	Almena	WI	54805	**800-685-9353**	715-357-3334
Mason Wells 770 N Water St 11th Fl	Milwaukee	WI	53202	**800-342-2265**	414-765-7800
UMB Capital Corp 1010 Grand Blvd	Kansas City	MO	64106	**800-821-2171**	816-860-7914

395 INVESTMENT COMPANIES - SPECIALIZED SMALL BUSINESS

Company	City	State	Zip	Toll-Free	Phone
Far East Capital Corp 350 S Grand Ave	Los Angeles	CA	90071	**800-753-8449**	213-687-1260

	City	State	Zip	Toll-Free	Phone
Sun-Delta Capital Access Center Inc 819 Main St	Greenville	MS	38701	800-829-5338	662-335-5291
Transportation Capital Corp 437 Madison Ave 38th Fl	New York	NY	10022	800-829-4867	212-328-2100
Women's Growth Capital Fund 1054 31st St NW Suite 110	Washington	DC	20007	888-640-8051	202-342-1431

396 INVESTMENT GUIDES - ONLINE

SEE ALSO Buyer's Guides - Online

	City	State	Zip	Toll-Free	Phone
BestCalls.com 12 Clock Tower Pl	Maynard	MA	01754	800-990-6397	
Briefing.com Inc 555 S Airport Blvd Suite 150	Burlingame	CA	94010	800-752-3013	650-347-2220
Canada Stockwatch 609 Granville St Suite 1550	Vancouver	BC	V7Y1J6	800-268-6397	604-687-1500
EDGAR Online Inc 50 Washington St *NASDAQ: EDGR*	Norwalk	CT	06854	800-416-6651	203-852-5666
FactSet Research Systems Inc 1 Greenwich Plaza 2nd Fl *NYSE: FDS*	Greenwich	CT	06830	877-322-8738	203-863-1500
Hoover's Inc 5800 Airport Blvd	Austin	TX	78752	800-486-8666	512-374-4500
IPO Monitor 5200 W Century Blvd Suite 470	Los Angeles	CA	90045	800-266-0126	
myCFO Inc 1700 Seaport Blvd 4th Fl	Redwood City	CA	94063	877-692-3609	650-210-5000
Nasdaq Trader 9513 Key West Ave	Rockville	MD	20850	800-777-5606	
Prophet Financial Systems Inc 115 Everett Ave	Palo Alto	CA	94301	800-772-8040	650-322-4183
TheStreet.com Inc 14 Wall St 15th Fl *NASDAQ: TSCM*	New York	NY	10005	800-562-9571	212-321-5000

397 INVESTMENT (MISC)

SEE ALSO Banks - Commercial & Savings; Commodity Contracts Brokers & Dealers; Franchises; Investment Guides - Online; Mortgage Lenders & Loan Brokers; Mutual Funds; Newsletters - Investment Newsletters; Real Estate Investment Trusts (REITs); Royalty Trusts; Securities Brokers & Dealers; Venture Capital Firms

	City	State	Zip	Toll-Free	Phone
ABRY Partners LLC 111 Huntington Ave 30th Fl	Boston	MA	02199	800-578-2279	617-859-2959
Adams Express Co 7 Saint Paul St Suite 1140 *NYSE: ADX*	Baltimore	MD	21202	800-638-2479	410-752-5900
BKF Capital Group Inc 1 Rockefeller Plaza 19th Fl *NYSE: BKF*	New York	NY	10020	800-253-1891	212-332-8400
Columbia Ventures Corp 16703 SE McGillivray Blvd Suite 210	Vancouver	WA	98683	866-204-0747	360-882-1052
Dundee Wealth Management Inc 40 King St W Suite 5500 *TSE: DW*	Toronto	ON	M5H4A9	800-301-6745	416-350-3489
Enerplus Resources Fund 333 7th Ave SW Suite 3000 *TSE: ERF.UN*	Calgary	AB	T2P2Z1	800-319-6462	403-298-2200
Fidelity Investments Charitable Gift Fund PO Box 55158	Boston	MA	02205	800-682-4438	
General American Investors Co Inc 450 Lexington Ave Suite 3300	New York	NY	10017	800-436-8401	212-916-8400
Hillman Co 330 Grant Bldg Suite 1900	Pittsburgh	PA	15219	800-445-5626	412-281-2620
InvestPrivate.com 500 5th Ave 56th Fl	New York	NY	10110	877-669-4732	212-739-7700
Lee Thomas H Co 100 Federal St Suite 3500	Boston	MA	02110	800-227-1050	617-227-1050
MML Investors Services Inc 1414 Main St	Springfield	MA	01144	800-542-6767	413-737-8400
Peacock Hislop Staley & Given Inc 2999 N 44th St Suite 100	Phoenix	AZ	85018	800-999-1818	602-952-6800
Pembina Pipeline Income Fund 700 9th Ave SW Suite 2000 *TSE: PIF.UN*	Calgary	AB	T2P3V4	888-428-3222	403-231-7500
Petroleum & Resources Corp 7 Saint Paul St Suite 1140 *NYSE: PEO*	Baltimore	MD	21202	800-638-2479	410-752-5900
Smith Barney Asset Management 300 1st Stamford Pl	Stamford	CT	06902	888-772-9996	
Sterling Capital Corp 635 Madison Ave 18th Fl *AMEX: SPR*	New York	NY	10022	800-949-3456	212-980-3360
Superior Plus Income Fund 605 5th Ave SW Suite 2820 *TSE: SPF.UN*	Calgary	AB	T2P3H5	866-490-7587	403-218-2970
Thomas H Lee Co 100 Federal St Suite 3500	Boston	MA	02110	800-227-1050	617-227-1050
Tri-Continental Corp 100 Park Ave 3rd Fl *NYSE: TY*	New York	NY	10017	800-221-7844	212-850-1864

398 JANITORIAL & CLEANING SUPPLIES - WHOL

	City	State	Zip	Toll-Free	Phone
American Sanitary Inc (AmSan) 3 Parkway N Suite 120 N	Deerfield	IL	60015	888-468-1555	847-607-2300
Brady Industries Inc 4175 S Arville St	Las Vegas	NV	89103	800-293-4698	702-876-3990
Fitch Co 2201 Russell St	Baltimore	MD	21230	800-933-4824	410-539-1953
Florida Sanitary Suppliers 3031 N Andrews Ave Ext	Pompano Beach	FL	33064	800-940-0900	954-972-1700
HP Products Corp 4220 Saguaro Trail	Indianapolis	IN	46268	800-382-5326	317-298-9950
Kellermeyer Co 1025 Brown Ave	Toledo	OH	43607	800-462-9552	419-255-3022
Manny's Sanitary Supplies Inc 4866 Tchoupitoulas St	New Orleans	LA	70115	800-256-2398	504-899-2358
Rose Products & Services Inc 545 Stimmel Rd	Columbus	OH	43223	800-264-1568	614-443-7647
Unisource Maintenance Supply Systems Inc 13217 S Figueroa St	Los Angeles	CA	90061	888-242-1827	310-527-3000

399 JEWELERS' FINDINGS & MATERIALS

	City	State	Zip	Toll-Free	Phone
ARC Traders Inc PO Box 3429	Scottsdale	AZ	85271	800-528-2374	480-945-0769
BA Ballou & Co Inc 800 Waterman Ave	East Providence	RI	02914	800-729-3347	401-438-7000
Ballou BA & Co Inc 800 Waterman Ave	East Providence	RI	02914	800-729-3347	401-438-7000
David H Fell & Co Inc 6009 Bandini Blvd	Commerce	CA	90040	800-822-1996	323-722-9992
Eastern Reproduction Corp 1250 Main St	Waltham	MA	02154	800-343-0217	781-893-0555
Fell David H & Co Inc 6009 Bandini Blvd	Commerce	CA	90040	800-822-1996	323-722-9992
Findings Inc PO Box 462	Keene	NH	03431	800-343-0806	603-352-3717
Gesswein Paul H & Co 255 Hancock Ave	Bridgeport	CT	06605	800-544-2043	203-366-5400
James A Murphy & Son Inc PO Box 3006	South Attleboro	MA	02703	800-422-3237	508-761-5060
Karbra Co 131 W 35th St 8th Fl	New York	NY	10001	800-527-2721	212-736-9300
Krohn Industries Inc 303 Veterans Blvd	Carlstadt	NJ	07072	800-526-6299	201-933-9696
Lazare Kaplan International Inc 529 5th Ave 10th Fl *AMEX: LKI* ■ *Cust Svc	New York	NY	10017	800-554-3325*	212-972-9700
Leach & Garner General Findings 57 John L Dietsch Sq PO Box 200	North Attleboro	MA	02761	800-345-1105	508-695-7800
Lee's Mfg Co 1700 Smith St	North Providence	RI	02911	800-821-1700	401-353-1740
MS Co PO Box 480	Attleboro	MA	02703	800-675-4657	508-222-1700
Murphy James A & Son Inc PO Box 3006	South Attleboro	MA	02703	800-422-3237	508-761-5060
Newall Mfg Co 30 E Adams St	Chicago	IL	60603	800-621-6296	312-236-2789
Paul H Gesswein & Co 255 Hancock Ave	Bridgeport	CT	06605	800-544-2043	203-366-5400
Providence Chain 225 Carolina Ave	Providence	RI	02905	800-783-1499	401-781-1330
Romanoff International Supply Corp 9 Deforest St *Cust Svc	Amityville	NY	11701	800-221-7448*	631-842-2400
Stuller Settings Inc 302 Rue Louis XIV	Lafayette	LA	70598	800-877-7777	

400 JEWELRY - COSTUME

	City	State	Zip	Toll-Free	Phone
1928 Jewelry Co 3000 W Empire Ave	Burbank	CA	91504	800-227-1928	818-841-1928
A & Z Hayward Co 655 Waterman Ave	East Providence	RI	02914	800-556-7462	401-438-0550
Accessories Assoc Inc 500 George Washington Hwy	Smithfield	RI	02917	800-388-0258	401-231-3800
C & J Jewelry Co Inc 100 Dupont Dr	Providence	RI	02907	800-556-7494	401-944-2200
Carolee Designs Inc 19 E Elm St	Greenwich	CT	06830	800-227-6533	203-629-1139
Donald Bruce & Co 3600 N Talman Ave	Chicago	IL	60618	800-621-6017	773-477-8100
Howard Eldon Ltd 20333 Gilmore St	Winnetka	CA	91306	800-685-1533	818-340-9371
Imperial-Deltah Inc 795 Waterman Ave	East Providence	RI	02914	800-556-7738	401-434-2250
P & B Mfg Co Inc 655 Waterman Ave	East Providence	RI	02914	800-556-7462	401-438-0550
Roman Research Inc 430 Court St	Plymouth	MA	02362	800-225-8652	508-747-8220
Speidel Corp 25 Fairmount Ave	East Providence	RI	02914	800-441-2200	401-519-2000
Swarovski Consumer Goods Ltd 1 Kenney Dr	Cranston	RI	02920	800-289-4900	401-463-6400
Uncas Mfg Co 150 Niantic Ave *Cust Svc	Providence	RI	02907	800-776-0980*	401-944-4700

401 JEWELRY - PRECIOUS METAL

	City	State	Zip	Toll-Free	Phone
Anthony Michael Jewelers Inc 124 S Terrace Ave	Mount Vernon	NY	10550	800-966-8800	914-699-0000
Armbrust International 735 Allens Ave	Providence	RI	02905	800-255-2631	401-781-3300
Aurafin OroAmerica 6701 N Nob Hill Rd	Tamarac	FL	33321	800-327-1808	954-718-3200
Avery James Craftsman Inc PO Box 291367	Kerrville	TX	78029	800-283-1770	830-895-1122
Balfour LG Co 7211 Circle S Rd	Austin	TX	78745	888-225-3687	512-444-2090
Black Hills Jewelry Mfg Co DBA Landstroms Blackhills Gold Creations 405 Canal St	Rapid City	SD	57701	800-843-0009	605-343-0157
Bondanza Michael Inc 10 W 46th St 12th Fl	New York	NY	10036	800-835-0041	212-869-0043
Brogan Byard F Inc 124 S Keswick Ave	Glenside	PA	19038	800-232-7642	215-885-3550
Burr Patterson & Auld Co PO Box 800	Elwood	IN	46036	800-422-4348	765-552-7366
Cartier Inc 2 E 52nd St *Sales	New York	NY	10022	800-227-8437*	212-753-0111
Colibri Group 100 Niantic Ave *Cust Svc	Providence	RI	02907	800-556-7354*	401-943-2100
Cordova Inc PO Box 521831 *Cust Svc	Flushing	NY	11352	800-221-0744*	718-961-1020
Creed Rosary Mfg Inc 15 Kenneth Miner Rd *Orders	Wrentham	MA	02093	800-255-7439*	508-384-7600
David Yurman Designs Inc 729 Madison Ave	New York	NY	10021	800-226-1400	212-896-1550
Diablo Mfg Co Inc PO Box 1108 *Sales	Grass Valley	CA	95945	800-551-2233*	530-272-2241
Excell Mfg Co 70 Royal Little Dr	Providence	RI	02904	800-343-8410	401-854-1700
F Byard Brogan Inc 124 S Keswick Ave	Glenside	PA	19038	800-232-7642	215-885-3550
Fisher Robert S & Co Inc 19 Liberty St	Newark	NJ	07102	800-526-8052	973-622-2658
Freeman Harold & Co 275 7th Ave	New York	NY	10001	800-221-4092	212-989-9001
Fuller George H & Son Co 151 Exchange St	Pawtucket	RI	02860	800-237-0043	401-722-6530
Garden Jewelry Co Inc 579 5th Ave Suite 420	New York	NY	10017	800-321-0259	212-421-7700
Gem East Corp 2124 2nd Ave	Seattle	WA	98121	800-426-0605	206-441-1700
Gemveto Jewelry Co Inc 16 E 52nd St	New York	NY	10022	800-221-4438	212-755-2522
George H Fuller & Son Co 151 Exchange St	Pawtucket	RI	02860	800-237-0043	401-722-6530
Gold Lance Inc 148 E Broadway	Owatonna	MN	55060	800-252-5777	507-455-6100
Goodman IB Mfg Co 120 E 3rd St	Newport	KY	41071	800-543-1945	859-261-2086
Hallmark Sweet 49 Pearl St	Attleboro	MA	02703	800-225-2706	508-222-9234
Hammerman Brothers Inc 40 W 57th St	New York	NY	10019	800-223-6436	212-956-2800
Harold Freeman & Co 275 7th Ave	New York	NY	10001	800-221-4092	212-989-9001
Harry Winston Inc 718 5th Ave	New York	NY	10019	800-988-4110	212-245-2000

Company	City	State	ZIP	Toll-Free	Phone
IB Goodman Mfg Co 120 E 3rd St	Newport	KY	41071	**800-543-1945**	859-261-2086
Ira Green Inc 177 Georgia Ave	Providence	RI	02905	**800-959-0180**	401-467-4770
J Jenkins Sons Co Inc 1801 Whitehead Rd	Baltimore	MD	21207	**800-296-3468**	410-265-5200
Jabel Inc 365 Coit St	Irvington	NJ	07111	**800-526-4597**	973-374-6000
James Avery Craftsman Inc PO Box 291367	Kerrville	TX	78029	**800-283-1770**	830-895-1122
Jenkins J Sons Co Inc 1801 Whitehead Rd	Baltimore	MD	21207	**800-296-3468**	410-265-5200
Jewelmont Corp 119 W 40th St	New York	NY	10018	**800-328-7173**	212-220-4222
Johns R Ltd PO Box 149107	Austin	TX	78714	**800-521-9493**	
Jostens Inc 5501 American Blvd W	Minneapolis	MN	55437	**800-235-4774**	952-830-3300
Kaspar & Esh Inc 11-25 45th Ave	Long Island City	NY	11101	**800-223-2614**	718-786-0771
Kinsley & Sons Inc PO Box 8539	Saint Louis	MO	63126	**800-468-4428**	314-843-0400
Klitzner Industries Inc 44 Warren St	Providence	RI	02907	**800-556-6860**	401-751-7500
Landstroms Blackhills Gold Creations 405 Canal St	Rapid City	SD	57701	**800-843-0009**	605-343-0157
Leach & Garner General Findings 57 John L Dietsch Sq PO Box 200	North Attleboro	MA	02761	**800-345-1105**	508-695-7800
LG Balfour Co 7211 Circle S Rd	Austin	TX	78745	**888-225-3687**	512-444-2090
Loren Industries Inc 2801 Greene St	Hollywood	FL	33020	**800-772-8085**	954-920-6622
Masters of Design 81 John Dietsch Blvd PO Box 2719	Attleboro Falls	MA	02763	**800-542-3728**	508-695-0201
Maui Divers of Hawaii Ltd 1520 Liona St	Honolulu	HI	96814	**800-462-4454**	808-946-7979
Mendelson & Assoc 2615 S Hill St	Los Angeles	CA	90007	**800-421-8250**	213-746-0745
Michael Anthony Jewelers Inc 124 S Terrace Ave	Mount Vernon	NY	10550	**800-966-8800**	914-699-0000
Michael Bondanza Inc 10 W 46th St 12th Fl	New York	NY	10036	**800-835-0041**	212-869-0043
Novell Design Studio Inc 129 Chestnut St	Roselle	NJ	07203	**888-916-6835**	908-245-4200
OC Tanner Co 1930 S State St	Salt Lake City	UT	84115	**800-453-7490**	801-486-2430
Original Designs/Famor Inc 44-40 11th St	Long Island City	NY	11101	**800-458-4300**	718-706-8989
Oro-Cal Mfg Co Inc 1720 Bird St	Oroville	CA	95965	**800-367-6225**	530-533-5085
Ostbye & Anderson Inc 10055 51st Ave N	Minneapolis	MN	55442	**800-328-4368**	763-553-1515
R Johns Ltd PO Box 149107	Austin	TX	78714	**800-521-9493**	
Ring Specialty Co 2691 30th St	Boulder	CO	80301	**800-328-6330**	303-440-5507
Robert S Fisher & Co Inc 19 Liberty St	Newark	NJ	07102	**800-526-8052**	973-622-2658
Rolyn Inc 189 Macklin St	Cranston	RI	02920	**800-824-2683**	401-944-0844
Sandberg Sikorski Jaffe 37 W 26th St 11th Fl	New York	NY	10010	**800-223-0553**	212-843-7464
Sardelli T & Sons Inc 195 Dupont Dr	Providence	RI	02907	**800-327-4641**	401-944-8510
Stamper Black Hills Gold Jewelry 7201 S Hwy 16 *Cust Svc	Rapid City	SD	57702	**800-523-7515***	605-342-0751
Stanley Creations Inc 1414 Willow Ave	Melrose Park	PA	19027	**800-220-1414**	215-635-6200
T Sardelli & Sons Inc 195 Dupont Dr	Providence	RI	02907	**800-327-4641**	401-944-8510
Tanner OC Co 1930 S State St	Salt Lake City	UT	84115	**800-453-7490**	801-486-2430
Terryberry Co 2033 Oak Industrial Dr NE	Grand Rapids	MI	49505	**800-253-0882**	616-458-1391
Tiara Corp 2425 Oakton St	Evanston	IL	60202	**800-323-6510**	847-570-4700
Tiffany & Co 727 5th Ave *NYSE: TIF* ■ *Orders	New York	NY	10022	**800-526-0649***	212-755-8000
Trebor Enterprises Ltd PO Box 88	Freeport	IL	61032	**800-552-6470**	815-235-1700
Tru-Kay Mfg Co 2 Carol Dr	Lincoln	RI	02865	**800-795-2105**	401-333-2105
Uncas Mfg Co 150 Niantic Ave *Cust Svc	Providence	RI	02907	**800-776-0980***	401-944-4700
Wheeler Mfg 107 Main Ave PO Box 629 *Orders	Lemmon	SD	57638	**800-843-1937***	605-374-3848
Winston Harry Inc 718 5th Ave	New York	NY	10019	**800-988-4110**	212-245-2000
Yurman David Designs Inc 729 Madison Ave	New York	NY	10021	**800-226-1400**	212-896-1550

402 JEWELRY STORES

Company	City	State	ZIP	Toll-Free	Phone
Adler Coleman E & Sons Inc 722 Canal St	New Orleans	LA	70130	**800-925-7912**	504-523-5292
Ashford.com 14001 NW 4th St	Sunrise	FL	33325	**888-922-9039**	954-453-2874
Bailey Banks & Biddle Div Zale Corp 901 W Walnut Hill Ln *Cust Svc	Irving	TX	75038	**800-651-4222***	972-580-4000
Ben Bridge Jeweler Inc PO Box 1908 *Cust Svc	Seattle	WA	98111	**888-448-1912***	206-448-8800
Ben Moss Jewellers 300-201 Portage Ave	Winnipeg	MB	R3B3K6	**888-236-6677**	204-947-6682
Blue Nile Inc 705 5th Ave S Suite 900 *NASDAQ: NILE*	Seattle	WA	98104	**800-242-2728**	206-336-6700
Borsheim's Inc 120 Regency Pkwy	Omaha	NE	68114	**800-642-4438**	402-391-0400
Bridge Ben Jeweler Inc PO Box 1908 *Cust Svc	Seattle	WA	98111	**888-448-1912***	206-448-8800
Bromberg & Co Inc 123 N 20th St	Birmingham	AL	35203	**800-633-4616**	205-252-0221
Carl Greve Jeweler Inc 731 SW Morrison St	Portland	OR	97205	**800-284-2044**	503-223-7121
Cartier Inc 2 E 52nd St *Sales	New York	NY	10022	**800-227-8437***	212-753-0111
Coleman E Adler & Sons Inc 722 Canal St	New Orleans	LA	70130	**800-925-7912**	504-523-5292
Crescent Jewelry Co 315 11th St	Oakland	CA	94607	**800-588-4367**	510-874-7600
DGSE Cos Inc 2817 Forest Ln *NASDAQ: DGSE*	Dallas	TX	75234	**800-527-5307**	972-484-3662
Don Roberto Jewelers Inc 1020 Calle Recodo Suite 100	San Clemente	CA	92673	**888-466-5300**	949-361-6700
Finks Jewelry Inc 3545 Electric Rd	Roanoke	VA	24018	**800-699-7464**	540-342-2991
Foland Jewelry Brokers 630 E 11 Mile Rd	Royal Oak	MI	48067	**877-365-2637**	248-336-6666
Fortunoff 70 Charles Lindbergh Blvd *Cust Svc	Uniondale	NY	11553	**800-777-2807***	516-832-9000
Fred Meyer Jewelers Inc 3800 SE 22nd Ave	Portland	OR	97202	**800-858-9202**	503-797-5550
Freeman Jewelers Inc 76 Merchants Row	Rutland	VT	05701	**800-949-2792**	802-773-2792
Friedman's Inc 171 Crossroads Pkwy	Savannah	GA	31407	**800-545-9033**	912-233-9333
Gordon's Jewelers Div Zale Corp 901 W Walnut Hill Ln *Cust Svc	Irving	TX	75038	**888-467-3661***	972-580-4000
Greve Carl Jeweler Inc 731 SW Morrison St	Portland	OR	97205	**800-284-2044**	503-223-7121
H Stern Jewelers Inc 645 5th Ave	New York	NY	10022	**800-747-8376**	212-688-0300
Haltoms Jewelers 317 Main St	Fort Worth	TX	76102	**800-850-2303**	817-336-4051
Harry Ritchie's Jewelers Inc 956 Willamette St *Cust Svc	Eugene	OR	97401	**800-935-2850***	541-686-1787
Harry Winston Inc 718 5th Ave	New York	NY	10019	**800-988-4110**	212-245-2000
Helzberg Diamonds 1825 Swift Ave	North Kansas City	MO	64116	**800-669-7780**	816-842-7780
JewelryWeb.com Inc 305 Northern Blvd Suite 101	Great Neck	NY	11021	**800-955-9245**	
Karten's Jewelers 901 W Walnut Hill Ln	Irving	TX	75038	**800-333-6739**	972-580-4000
Kay Jewelers 375 Ghent Rd	Akron	OH	44333	**800-681-8796**	330-668-5000
Levy Jewelers Inc 101 E Broughton St	Savannah	GA	31401	**800-237-5389**	912-233-1163
Lux Bond & Green Inc 46 Lasalle Rd	West Hartford	CT	06107	**800-524-7336**	860-521-3015
Mayor's Jewelers Inc 14051 NW 14th St Suite 200 *AMEX: MYR*	Sunrise	FL	33323	**800-223-6964**	954-846-8000
Meyer Fred Jewelers Inc 3800 SE 22nd Ave	Portland	OR	97202	**800-858-9202**	503-797-5550
Mondera.com 45 W 45th St 15th Fl	New York	NY	10036	**800-666-3372**	212-997-9350
Moss Ben Jewellers 300-201 Portage Ave	Winnipeg	MB	R3B3K6	**888-236-6677**	204-947-6682
Odimo Inc 14001 NW 4th St *NASDAQ: ODMO*	Sunrise	FL	33325	**888-342-6663**	954-835-2233
Osterman Jewelers 375 Ghent Rd	Akron	OH	44333	**800-681-8796**	330-668-5000
Reeds Jewelers Inc 2525 S 17th St *Orders	Wilmington	NC	28401	**877-406-3266***	910-350-3100
Rogers Ltd 1050 Central Ave	Middletown	OH	45044	**800-888-8805**	513-422-5407
Ross Simons Jewelers Inc 9 Ross Simons Dr	Cranston	RI	02920	**800-835-0919**	401-463-3100
Samuels Jewelers Inc 2914 Montopolis Dr Suite 200	Austin	TX	78741	**877-726-8357**	512-369-1400
Smyth Jewelers 29 Greenmeadow Dr	Timonium	MD	21093	**800-638-3333**	410-252-6666
Stern H Jewelers Inc 645 5th Ave	New York	NY	10022	**800-747-8376**	212-688-0300
Tiffany & Co 727 5th Ave *NYSE: TIF* ■ *Orders	New York	NY	10022	**800-526-0649***	212-755-8000
Van Cleef & Arpels Inc 744 5th Ave	New York	NY	10019	**800-822-5797**	212-644-9500
Whitehall Jewellers Inc 155 N Wacker Dr Suite 500 *NYSE: JWL*	Chicago	IL	60606	**800-621-0771**	312-782-6800
Winston Harry Inc 718 5th Ave	New York	NY	10019	**800-988-4110**	212-245-2000
Zale Corp 901 W Walnut Hill Ln *NYSE: ZLC* ■ *Cust Svc	Irving	TX	75038	**800-866-9700***	972-580-4000
Zale Corp Bailey Banks & Biddle Div 901 W Walnut Hill Ln *Cust Svc	Irving	TX	75038	**800-651-4222***	972-580-4000
Zale Corp Gordon's Jewelers Div 901 W Walnut Hill Ln *Cust Svc	Irving	TX	75038	**888-467-3661***	972-580-4000
Zale Corp Zales Jewelers Div 901 W Walnut Hill Ln *Cust Svc	Irving	TX	75038	**800-866-9700***	972-580-4000
Zales Jewelers Div Zale Corp 901 W Walnut Hill Ln *Cust Svc	Irving	TX	75038	**800-866-9700***	972-580-4000

403 JEWELRY, WATCHES, GEMS - WHOL

Company	City	State	ZIP	Toll-Free	Phone
Antwerp Diamond Distributors 6 E 45th St Suite 302	New York	NY	10017	**800-223-0444**	212-319-3300
Blank Joseph Inc 62 W 47th St Suite 808	New York	NY	10036	**800-223-7666**	212-575-9050
Citra Trading Corp 590 5th Ave 14th Fl *Orders	New York	NY	10036	**800-223-6515***	212-354-1000
Cliff Weil Inc 8043 Industrial Pk Rd	Mechanicsville	VA	23116	**800-446-9345**	804-746-1321
Continental Coin Corp 5627 Sepulveda Blvd	Van Nuys	CA	91411	**888-367-9456**	818-781-4232
Empire Diamond Corp 350 5th Ave Suite 7619	New York	NY	10118	**800-728-3425**	212-564-4777
Genender International Imports Inc 44 Century Dr	Wheeling	IL	60090	**800-547-3333**	847-541-3333
Gerson Co 1450 S Lone Elm Rd	Olathe	KS	66061	**800-999-7401**	913-262-7400
Joseph Blank Inc 62 W 47th St Suite 808	New York	NY	10036	**800-223-7666**	212-575-9050
Lazare Kaplan International Inc 529 5th Ave 19th Fl *AMEX: LKI* ■ *Cust Svc	New York	NY	10017	**800-554-3325***	212-972-9700
Marcel Watch Corp/Oleg Cassini Watch Co 200 Meadowland Pkwy	Secaucus	NJ	07094	**800-422-6053**	201-330-5600
Paramount Sales Co Inc 10140 Gallows Point Dr *Cust Svc	Knoxville	TN	37931	**800-251-9183***	865-470-9977
Seiko Corp of America 1111 MacArthur Blvd *Cust Svc	Mahwah	NJ	07430	**800-782-2510***	201-529-5730
Smyth Jewelers 29 Greenmeadow Dr	Timonium	MD	21093	**800-638-3333**	410-252-6666
Swiss Army Brands Inc 1 Research Dr PO Box 874 *Cust Svc	Shelton	CT	06484	**800-243-4057***	203-929-6391
Webster Watch Co Assoc 44 E 32nd St 7th Fl *Orders	New York	NY	10016	**800-289-8963***	212-889-3560
Weil Cliff Inc 8043 Industrial Pk Rd	Mechanicsville	VA	23116	**800-446-9345**	804-746-1321
World Minerals Inc 130 Castilian Dr	Santa Barbara	CA	93117	**800-893-4445**	805-562-0200

LABELS - FABRIC

SEE Textile Mills - Narrow Fabric Mills

404 LABELS - OTHER THAN FABRIC

Company	City	State	ZIP	Toll-Free	Phone
Acro Labels Inc 2530 Wyandotte Rd	Willow Grove	PA	19090	**800-355-2235**	215-657-5366
American Law Label Inc 4135 S Pulaski Rd	Chicago	IL	60632	**800-529-5223**	773-523-2222
Arch Crown Tags Inc 177 Main St	West Orange	NJ	07052	**800-526-8353**	973-731-6300
Art Style Printing Inc Dataware Div 7570 Renwick Dr	Houston	TX	77081	**800-426-4844**	713-432-1023
Artisan Press 726 Jefferson Ave	Ashland	OR	97520	**800-424-9364**	541-482-3373
Artistic Direct Inc 1316 College Ave *Cust Svc	Elmira	NY	14901	**800-845-3720***	607-733-5541
Atlas Tag & Label Inc 2361 Industrial Dr	Neenah	WI	54956	**800-634-2705**	920-722-1557
Avery Dennison Business Media Div 685 Howard St	Buffalo	NY	14206	**800-777-2879**	716-852-2155
Avery Dennison Corp 150 N Orange Grove Blvd *NYSE: AVY* ■ *Cust Svc	Pasadena	CA	91103	**800-252-8379***	626-304-2000
Best Label Co 2943 Whipple Rd	Union City	CA	94587	**800-637-5333**	510-489-5400
Blue Ribbon Label Corp 241 Hudson St	Hackensack	NJ	07601	**800-223-2400**	201-489-6003
Blue Ribbon Tag & Label Corp 4035 N 29th Ave	Hollywood	FL	33020	**800-433-4974**	954-922-9292

				Toll-Free	Phone
Brady Corp 6555 W Good Hope Rd	Milwaukee	WI	53223	**800-537-8791***	414-358-6600
NYSE: BRC ■ *Cust Svc					
Brady Identification Solutions 6555 W Good Hope Rd	Milwaukee	WI	53223	**800-537-8791***	414-358-6600
*Cust Svc					
Cellotape Inc 47623 Fremont Blvd	Fremont	CA	94538	**800-231-0608**	510-651-5551
Chicago Decal Co 101 Tower Dr	Burr Ridge	IL	60527	**888-332-2577**	630-850-2122
Clamp Swing Pricing Co Inc 8386 Capwell Dr	Oakland	CA	94621	**800-227-7615**	510-567-1600
Continental Identification Products Inc PO Box 98	Sparta	MI	49345	**800-247-2499**	616-887-7341
Data Label Inc 1000 Spruce St	Terre Haute	IN	47807	**800-457-0676**	812-232-0408
Dataware Div Art Style Printing Inc 7570 Renwick Dr	Houston	TX	77081	**800-426-4844**	713-432-1023
DeskTop Labels 7277 Boone Ave N	Minneapolis	MN	55428	**800-241-9730**	763-531-5800
Discount Labels Inc 4115 Profit Ct	New Albany	IN	47150	**800-995-9500**	812-945-2617
East-West Label Co Inc 1000 E Hector St	Conshohocken	PA	19428	**800-441-7333**	610-825-0410
Ennis Tag & Label 118 W Main St	Wolfe City	TX	75496	**800-527-1008**	903-496-2244
General Data Co Inc 4354 Ferguson Dr	Cincinnati	OH	45245	**800-733-5252**	513-752-7978
Gilbreth Packaging Systems 3001 State Rd	Croydon	PA	19021	**800-758-5888**	215-785-3350
Grand Rapids Label Co 2351 Oak Industrial Dr NE	Grand Rapids	MI	49505	**800-552-5215**	616-459-8134
Graphic Technology Inc 301 Gardner Dr	New Century	KS	66031	**800-767-9930**	913-829-8000
Green Bay Packaging Inc 1700 N Webster Ct	Green Bay	WI	54302	**800-558-4008**	920-433-5111
Hooven-Dayton Corp 8060 Technology Blvd	Dayton	OH	45424	**800-621-9291**	937-233-4473
Impact Label Corp 3434 S Burdick St	Kalamazoo	MI	49001	**800-820-0362**	269-381-4280
International Label & Printing Co Inc 2550 United Ln	Elk Grove Village	IL	60007	**800-244-1442**	630-595-1442
ITW Auto-Sleeve 2003 Case Pkwy S Unit 3	Twinsburg	OH	44087	**800-852-4571**	330-487-2200
Label Art 1 Riverside Way	Wilton	NH	03086	**800-258-1050**	603-654-6131
Labelmaster Co 5724 N Pulaski Rd	Chicago	IL	60646	**800-621-5808**	773-478-0900
Labeltape Inc 4489 E Paris Ave SE	Grand Rapids	MI	49512	**800-928-4537**	616-698-1830
Lancer Label 301 S 74th St	Omaha	NE	68114	**800-228-7074***	402-390-9119
*Cust Svc					
LGInternational 6700 SW Bradbury Ct	Portland	OR	97224	**800-345-0534**	503-620-0520
MACtac 4560 Darrow Rd	Stow	OH	44224	**800-762-2822**	330-688-1111
McCourt Label Co 20 Egbert Ln	Lewis Run	PA	16738	**800-458-2390**	814-362-3851
Mepco Label Systems PO Box 932	Stockton	CA	95201	**800-975-2235**	209-946-0201
Metro Label Corp 1395 Chattahoochee Ave NW	Atlanta	GA	30318	**800-235-8814**	404-351-5044
Morgan Adhesives Co DBA MACtac 4560 Darrow Rd	Stow	OH	44224	**800-762-2822**	330-688-1111
MPI Label Systems Inc 450 Courtney Rd	Sebring	OH	44672	**800-837-2134**	330-938-2134
Nashua Corp Label Products Div 3838 S 108th St	Omaha	NE	68144	**800-533-8806**	402-397-3600
National Label Co Inc 2025 Joshua Rd	Lafayette Hill	PA	19444	**800-872-5223**	610-825-3250
National Printing Converters Inc 18 S Murphy Ave	Brazil	IN	47834	**800-877-6724**	812-448-2555
Paxar Corp 105 Corporate Park Dr	White Plains	NY	10604	**888-447-2927**	914-697-6800
NYSE: PXR					
Paxar Corp Systems Group 1 Wilcox St	Sayre	PA	18840	**800-947-2927**	570-888-6641
Print-O-Tape Inc 755 Tower Rd	Mundelein	IL	60060	**800-346-6311**	847-362-1476
Printed Systems 1271 Gillingham Rd	Neenah	WI	54956	**800-352-2332***	920-886-2000
*Sales					
Quikstik Label Mfg Co 210 Broadway	Everett	MA	02149	**800-225-3496**	617-389-7570
Reidler Decal Corp 1 Reidler Rd	Saint Clair	PA	17970	**800-628-7770**	570-429-1812
Rydin Decal Co 660 Pond Dr	Wood Dale	IL	60191	**800-448-1991**	630-766-8410
Salem Label Co 1472 Salem Pkwy	Salem	OH	44460	**888-274-7465**	330-332-1591
Shamrock Scientific Specialty Systems Inc 34 Davis Dr	Bellwood	IL	60104	**800-323-0249**	708-547-9005
Smyth Cos Inc 1085 Snelling Ave N	Saint Paul	MN	55180	**800-642-4544**	651-646-4544
Spec Print Inc 1710 N Mt Juliet Rd	Mount Juliet	TN	37122	**800-989-3325**	615-758-5913
Spectrum Label Corp 30803 San Clemente St	Hayward	CA	94544	**800-545-2235**	510-477-0707
Spinnaker Coating Inc 518 E Water St	Troy	OH	45373	**800-543-9452**	937-332-6500
Spinnaker Industries Inc 4846 Jennings Ln	Louisville	KY	40218	**800-932-6210**	
Tag-It Pacific Inc 21900 Burbank Blvd Suite 270	Woodland Hills	CA	91367	**800-335-4443**	818-444-4100
AMEX: TAG					
Tape & Label Converters Inc 8231 Allport Ave	Santa Fe Springs	CA	90670	**888-285-2462**	562-945-3486
Tapecon Inc 10 Latta Rd	Rochester	NY	14612	**800-333-2408**	585-621-8400
TAPEMARK Co 150 E Marie Ave	West Saint Paul	MN	55118	**800-535-1998**	651-455-1611
United Ad Label Inc 30 Hazelwood Dr Suite 100	Amherst	NY	14228	**800-992-5755**	
Weber Marking Systems Inc 711 W Algonquin Rd	Arlington Heights	IL	60005	**800-225-0883***	847-364-8500
*Sales					
West Coast Tag & Label Co PO Box 4099	West Hills	CA	91308	**800-742-8247**	818-710-8484
Whitlam Label Co Inc 24800 Sherwood Ave	Center Line	MI	48015	**800-755-2235**	586-757-5100
Wise Tag & Label Co Inc 7035 Central Hwy	Pennsauken	NJ	08109	**800-222-1327**	856-663-2400
Wright of Thomasville Corp 5115 Prospect St	Thomasville	NC	27360	**800-678-9019**	336-472-4200
WS Packaging Group Inc 1102 Jefferson St	Algoma	WI	54201	**800-236-3424**	920-487-3424
YORK Label 405 Willow Springs Ln	York	PA	17402	**888-800-9675***	717-266-9675
*Cust Svc					

405 LABOR UNIONS

				Toll-Free	Phone
AFT Healthcare 555 New Jersey Ave NW	Washington	DC	20001	**800-238-1133**	202-879-4491
Air Line Pilots Assn 535 Herndon Pkwy	Herndon	VA	20170	**800-359-2572**	703-689-2270
Amalgamated Transit Union (ATU) 5025 Wisconsin Ave NW 3rd Fl	Washington	DC	20016	**888-240-1196**	202-537-1645
American Federation of Musicians of the US & Canada (AFM) 1501 Broadway Suite 600	New York	NY	10036	**800-762-3444**	212-869-1330
American Federation of Teachers (AFT) 555 New Jersey Ave NW	Washington	DC	20001	**800-238-1133**	202-879-4400
Association of Professional Flight Attendants 1004 W Euless Blvd	Euless	TX	76040	**800-395-2732**	817-540-0108
Directors Guild of America 7920 W Sunset Blvd	Los Angeles	CA	90046	**800-421-4173**	310-289-2000
Florida Education Assn 213 S Adams St	Tallahassee	FL	32301	**888-807-8007**	850-201-2800
International Alliance of Theatrical Stage Employees Moving Picture Technicians (IATSE) 1430 Broadway 20th Fl	New York	NY	10018	**800-223-6872**	212-730-1770
International Assn of Bridge Structural Ornamental & Reinforcing Iron Workers 1750 New York Ave NW Suite 400	Washington	DC	20006	**800-368-0105**	202-383-4800
International Union of Bricklayers & Allied Craftworkers (BAC) 1776 'I' St NW Suite 500	Washington	DC	20006	**888-880-8222**	202-783-3788
International Union of Industrial Service Transport Health Employees 254 W 31st St	New York	NY	10001	**800-331-1070**	212-696-5545
International Union of Petroleum & Industrial Workers 8131 E Rosecrans Ave	Paramount	CA	90723	**800-624-5842**	562-630-6232
International Union of Police Associations 1421 Prince St Suite 400	Alexandria	VA	22314	**800-247-4872**	703-549-7473
International Union of Security Officers 2201 Broadway Suite 101	San Leandro	CA	94612	**800-772-3326**	510-625-9913
International Union Security Police & Fire Professionals of America 25510 Kelly Rd	Roseville	MI	48066	**800-228-7492**	586-772-7250
National Air Traffic Controllers Assn (NATCA) 1325 Massachusetts Ave NW	Washington	DC	20005	**800-266-0895**	202-628-5451
National Football League Players Assn (NFLPA) 2021 L St NW Suite 600	Washington	DC	20036	**800-372-2000**	202-463-2200
National Hockey League Players Assn (NHLPA) 777 Bay St Suite 2400	Toronto	ON	M5G2C8	**800-363-4625**	416-408-4040
Newspaper Guild CWA 501 3rd St NW Suite 250	Washington	DC	20001	**800-585-5864**	202-434-7177
Office & Professional Employees International Union 265 W 14th St Suite 610	New York	NY	10011	**800-346-7348**	212-675-3210
Seafarers International Union 5201 Auth Way	Camp Springs	MD	20746	**800-252-4674**	301-899-0675
Service Employees International Union 1313 L St NW	Washington	DC	20005	**800-424-8592**	202-898-3200
Sheet Metal Workers International Assn (SMWIA) 1750 New York Ave NW 6th Fl	Washington	DC	20006	**800-457-7694**	202-783-5880
UFCW Textile & Garment Council 4207 Lebanon Pike Suite 200	Hermitage	TN	37076	**888-462-4892**	615-889-9221
UNITE HERE 275 7th Ave	New York	NY	10001	**800-238-6483**	212-265-7000
United Food & Commercial Workers International Union (UFCW) 1775 K St NW	Washington	DC	20006	**800-551-4010**	202-223-3111
United Transportation Union 14600 Detroit Ave	Lakewood	OH	44107	**800-558-8842**	216-228-9400
Writers Guild of America West (WGAw) 7000 W 3rd St	Los Angeles	CA	90048	**800-548-4532**	323-951-4000

406 LABORATORIES - DENTAL

SEE ALSO Laboratories - Medical

				Toll-Free	Phone
Americus Dental Lab Inc 150-15 Hillside Ave	Jamaica	NY	11432	**888-263-7428**	718-658-6655
Boos Dental Laboratories 801 12th Ave N	Minneapolis	MN	55411	**800-333-2667**	612-529-9655
CeraMed Dental LLC 12860 W Cedar Dr Suite 110	Lakewood	CO	80228	**800-426-7836**	303-985-0800
Certified Dental Laboratory Inc 3206 N Kilpatrick Ave	Chicago	IL	60641	**800-458-3384**	773-205-6600
Keller Laboratories Inc 10966 Gravois Industrial Ct	Saint Louis	MO	63128	**800-325-3056**	314-919-4000
Life Like Dental Laboratory 1640 Cobb International Blvd Suite 4	Kennesaw	GA	30152	**800-241-0632**	770-499-1024
Posca Brothers Dental Laboratory Inc 641 W Willow St	Long Beach	CA	90806	**800-537-672.**	562-427-1811
Roe Dental Laboratory Inc 9565 Midwest Ave	Garfield Heights	OH	44125	**800-228-6663**	216-663-2233
Thoele Dental Laboratories Inc 540 Progress Dr	Waite Park	MN	56387	**800-899-1115**	320-252-2070

407 LABORATORIES - DRUG-TESTING

SEE ALSO Laboratories - Medical

				Toll-Free	Phone
Bio-Reference Laboratories Inc 481 Edward H Ross Dr	Elmwood Park	NJ	07407	**800-229-5227**	201-791-2600
NASDAQ: BRLI					
DRUGPROOF 1229 Madison St Suite 500	Seattle	WA	98104	**800-898-0182**	206-386-2661
Employee Information Services Inc 12600 W Colfax Ave Suite A 501	Lakewood	CO	80215	**800-373-2145**	303-238-0189
General Medical Laboratories 36 S Brook St	Madison	WI	53715	**800-236-0465**	608-267-6529
Kroll Laboratory Specialists Inc 1111 Newton St	Gretna	LA	70053	**800-433-3823**	504-361-8989
MecStat Laboratories 1700 S Mt Prospect Rd	Des Plaines	IL	60018	**800-235-2367**	847-375-0770
MEDTOX Scientific Inc 402 W County Rd D	Saint Paul	MN	55112	**800-832-3244**	651-636-7466
AMEX: TOX					
National Medical Services Inc 3701 Welsh Rd	Willow Grove	PA	19090	**800-522-6671**	215-657-4900
PharmChem Inc 4600 N Beach St	Haltom City	TX	76137	**800-446-5177**	817-605-5300
Psychemedics Corp 1280 Massachusetts Ave	Cambridge	MA	02138	**800-628-8073**	617-868-7455
AMEX: PMD					
SED Medical Laboratories 5601 Office Blvd	Albuquerque	NM	87109	**800-999-5227**	505-727-6300
US Drug Testing Laboratories DBA MecStat Laboratories 1700 S Mt Prospect Rd	Des Plaines	IL	60018	**800-235-2367**	847-375-0770

408 LABORATORIES - GENETIC TESTING

SEE ALSO Laboratories - Medical

				Toll-Free	Phone
Blood Systems Laboratories 2424 W Erie Dr	Tempe	AZ	85282	**866-342-4275**	602-343-7000

				Toll-Free	Phone
BRT Laboratories Inc 400 W Franklin St	Baltimore	MD	21201	**800-765-5170**	410-225-9595
Center for Genetic Testing at Saint Francis OU Shusterman Ctr 4502 E 41st St	Tulsa	OK	74135	**800-299-7919**	918-660-3838
Commonwealth Biotechnologies Inc 601 Biotech Dr. *NASDAQ: CBTE*	Richmond	VA	23235	**800-735-9224**	804-648-3820
DNA Diagnostics Center 205 Corporate Ct.	Fairfield	OH	45014	**800-362-2368**	513-881-7800
Genecare Medical Genetics Center 201 Sage Rd Suite 300	Chapel Hill	NC	27514	**800-277-4363**	919-942-0021
Genelex Corp 3000 1st Ave Suite 1	Seattle	WA	98121	**800-523-6487**	206-382-9591
Genetic Profiles Corp 10675 Treena St Suite 103	San Diego	CA	92131	**800-551-7763**	858-623-0840
Genetica DNA Laboratories Inc 8740 Montgomery Rd	Cincinnati	OH	45236	**800-433-6848**	513-985-9777
Genetics & IVF Institute 3020 Javier Rd	Fairfax	VA	22031	**800-552-4363**	703-698-7355
GenQuest DNA Analysis Laboratory Univ of Nevada - Reno 1664 N Virginia St	Reno	NV	89557	**877-362-5227**	775-784-4494
Genzyme Corp 500 Kendall St. *NASDAQ: GENZ*	Cambridge	MA	02142	**800-326-7002**	617-252-7500
Genzyme Genetics 3400 Computer Dr	Westborough	MA	01581	**800-326-7002**	508-898-9001
Identigene Inc 5615 Kirby Dr Suite 800.	Houston	TX	77005	**800-362-8973**	713-798-9510
Identity Genetics Inc 801 32nd Ave.	Brookings	SD	57006	**800-861-1054**	605-697-5300
Laboratories at Bonfils 717 Yosemite St 2nd Fl.	Denver	CO	80230	**800-321-6088**	303-365-9000
Laboratory Corp of America Paternity Testing Services 1440 York Ct.	Burlington	NC	27215	**800-742-3944**	336-222-7566
Long Beach Genetics 2384 E Pacifica Pl	Rancho Dominguez	CA	90220	**800-824-2699**	310-632-8900
Maxxam Analytics Inc 335 Laird Rd Unit 2	Guelph	ON	N1H6J3	**888-266-7889**	519-836-2400
Medical Genetics Consultants 910 Washington Ave	Ocean Springs	MS	39564	**800-362-4363**	228-872-3680
Molecular Pathology Laboratory 250 E Broadway	Maryville	TN	37804	**800-932-2943**	865-380-9746
Orchid GeneScreen 2600 Stemmons Fwy Suite 133	Dallas	TX	75207	**800-362-8378**	214-631-8152
Paternity Testing Corp 300 Portland St	Columbia	MO	65201	**888-837-8323**	573-442-9948
Pediatrix Screening PO Box 219	Bridgeville	PA	15017	**866-463-6436**	412-220-2300
RELIAGENE Technologies Inc 5525 Mounes St Suite 101	New Orleans	LA	70123	**800-256-4106**	504-734-9700
Rhode Island Blood Center 405 Promenade St	Providence	RI	02908	**800-283-8385**	401-453-8360
South Texas Blood & Tissue Center 6211 IH-10 W	San Antonio	TX	78201	**800-292-5534**	210-731-5555
University of North Texas DNA Identity Laboratory Health Science Ctr 3500 Camp Bowie Blvd	Fort Worth	TX	76107	**800-687-5301**	817-735-5015

409 LABORATORIES - MEDICAL

SEE ALSO Blood Centers; Laboratories - Dental; Laboratories - Drug-Testing; Laboratories - Genetic Testing; Organ & Tissue Banks

				Toll-Free	Phone
American Medical Laboratories Inc 14225 Newbrook Dr.	Chantilly	VA	20153	**800-336-3718**	703-802-6900
Associated Pathologists Laboratories 4230 Burnham Ave	Las Vegas	NV	89119	**800-433-2750**	702-733-7866
Bio-Reference Laboratories Inc 481 Edward H Ross Dr *NASDAQ: BRLI*	Elmwood Park	NJ	07407	**800-229-5227**	201-791-2600
Calvert Laboratories Inc 100 Discovery Dr Scott Technology Pk.	Olyphant	PA	18447	**800-300-8114**	570-586-2411
Canadian Medical Laboratories Ltd 6560 Kennedy Rd	Mississauga	ON	L5T2X4	**800-263-0801**	905-565-0043
DIANON Systems Inc 200 Watson Blvd	Stratford	CT	06615	**800-328-2666**	203-381-4000
Franciscan Shared & Medical Science Laboratories Inc 11020 W Plank Ct Suite 100	Wauwatosa	WI	53226	**800-256-1522**	414-476-3400
Great Smokies Diagnostic Laboratory 63 Zillicoa St	Asheville	NC	28801	**800-522-4762**	828-253-0621
Impath Inc 521 W 57th St 6th Fl	New York	NY	10019	**800-447-8881**	212-698-0300
LabCorp (Laboratory Corp of America Holdings) 1447 York Ct. *NYSE: LH ■ *Cust Svc*	Burlington	NC	27215	**800-334-5161***	336-584-5171
Laboratory Corp of America Holdings (LabCorp) 1447 York Ct. *NYSE: LH ■ *Cust Svc*	Burlington	NC	27215	**800-334-5161***	336-584-5171
MDS Pharma Services Inc 2350 Cohen St.	Saint-Laurent	QC	H4R2N6	**800-724-5941**	514-333-0033
MEDTOX Scientific Inc 402 W County Rd D *AMEX: TOX*	Saint Paul	MN	55112	**800-832-3244**	651-636-7466
Pathology Center 8303 Dodge St.	Omaha	NE	68114	**888-432-8980**	402-354-4540
Quest Diagnostics Inc 1 Malcolm Ave *NYSE: DGX*	Teterboro	NJ	07608	**800-631-1390**	
Quest Diagnostics at Nichols Institute 33608 Ortega Hwy	San Juan Capistrano	CA	92690	**800-642-4657**	949-728-4000
SED Medical Laboratories 5601 Office Blvd	Albuquerque	NM	87109	**800-999-5227**	505-727-6300
South Bend Medical Foundation 530 N Lafayette Blvd	South Bend	IN	46601	**800-544-0925**	574-234-4176
Specialty Laboratories Inc 2211 Michigan Ave *NYSE: SP ■ *Sales*	Santa Monica	CA	90404	**800-421-7110***	310-828-6543
Unilab Corp 18408 Oxnard St.	Tarzana	CA	91356	**800-696-7502**	818-996-7300
VCA Antech Inc 12401 W Olympic Blvd *NASDAQ: WOOF*	Los Angeles	CA	90064	**800-966-1822**	310-571-6500

LABORATORIES - RESEARCH

SEE Research Centers & Organizations

410 LABORATORY ANALYTICAL INSTRUMENTS

SEE ALSO Glassware - Laboratory & Scientific; Laboratory Apparatus & Furniture

				Toll-Free	Phone
Abaxis Inc 3240 Whipple Rd. *NASDAQ: ABAX*	Union City	CA	94587	**800-822-2947**	510-675-6500
ACLARA BioSciences Inc 1288 Pear Ave *NASDAQ: ACLA*	Mountain View	CA	94043	**800-257-7121**	650-210-1200
Advanced Measurement Technology 801 S Illinois Ave.	Oak Ridge	TN	37831	**800-251-9750**	865-482-4411
Agilent Technologies Inc 395 Page Mill Rd. *NYSE: A*	Palo Alto	CA	94306	**877-424-4536**	650-752-5000
Alltech Assoc Inc 2051 Waukegan Rd **Cust Svc*	Deerfield	IL	60015	**800-255-8324***	847-948-8600
American Biologics 1180 Walnut Ave	Chula Vista	CA	91911	**800-227-4458**	619-429-8200
Amersham Biosciences 800 Centennial Ave PO Box 1327	Piscataway	NJ	08854	**800-526-3593**	732-457-8000
Applied Biosystems Group 850 Lincoln Ctr Dr. *NYSE: ABI*	Foster City	CA	94404	**800-874-9868**	650-570-6667
Arcturus Engineering Inc 400 Logue Ave.	Mountain View	CA	94043	**888-446-7911**	650-962-3020
Barnstead/Thermolyne Corp 2555 Kerper Blvd.	Dubuque	IA	52001	**800-446-6060**	563-556-2241
BBI Source Scientific Inc 7390 Lincoln Way	Garden Grove	CA	92841	**800-888-9285**	714-898-9001
BD Biosciences 2350 Qume Dr	San Jose	CA	95131	**800-223-8226**	408-432-9475
Beckman Coulter Inc 4300 N Harbor Blvd. *NYSE: BEC ■ *Cust Svc*	Fullerton	CA	92835	**800-742-2345***	714-871-4848
Bioanalytical Systems Inc 2701 Kent Ave *NASDAQ: BASI*	West Lafayette	IN	47906	**800-845-4246**	765-463-4527
Buehler Ltd 41 Waukegan Rd **Sales*	Lake Bluff	IL	60044	**800-283-4537***	847-295-6500
CEM Corp PO Box 200	Matthews	NC	28106	**800-726-3331**	704-821-7015
Cepheid 904 E Caribbean Dr. *NASDAQ: CPHD*	Sunnyvale	CA	94089	**888-838-3222**	408-541-4191
Cetac Technologies Inc 14306 Industrial Rd.	Omaha	NE	68144	**800-369-2822**	402-733-2829
CMI Inc 316 E 9th St	Owensboro	KY	42303	**866-835-0690**	270-685-6545
CompuMed Inc 5777 W Century Blvd Suite 1285	Los Angeles	CA	90045	**800-421-3395**	310-258-5000
Corning Inc Life Sciences Div 45 Nagog Park.	Acton	MA	01720	**800-492-1110**	978-635-2200
Datacolor 5 Princess Rd	Lawrenceville	NJ	08648	**800-433-1885**	609-924-2189
DiaSys Corp 81 W Main St 5th Fl *AMEX: DYX*	Waterbury	CT	06702	**800-360-2003**	203-755-5083
Dionex Corp 1228 Titan Way. *NASDAQ: DNEX ■ *Cust Svc*	Sunnyvale	CA	94085	**800-346-6390***	408-737-0700
FEI Co 5350 NE Dawson Creek Dr *NASDAQ: FEIC*	Hillsboro	OR	97124	**888-466-6455**	503-640-7500
Gambro BCT 10811 W Collins Ave	Lakewood	CO	80215	**877-339-4228**	303-232-6800
Genomic Solutions Inc 4355 Varsity Dr Suite E.	Ann Arbor	MI	48108	**877-436-6642**	734-975-4800
Gretag Macbeth LLC 617 Little Britain Rd.	New Windsor	NY	12553	**800-622-2384**	845-565-7660
Hach Co PO Box 389.	Loveland	CO	80539	**800-227-4224**	970-669-3050
Harvard Bioscience Inc 84 October Hill Rd *NASDAQ: HBIO*	Holliston	MA	01746	**800-272-2775**	508-893-8999
Helena Laboratories Inc 1530 Lindbergh Dr	Beaumont	TX	77704	**800-231-5663**	409-842-3714
Horiba Instruments Inc 17671 Armstrong Ave.	Irvine	CA	92614	**800-446-7422**	949-250-4811
i-STAT Corp 104 Windsor Center Dr	East Windsor	NJ	08520	**800-827-7828**	609-443-9300
Illumina Inc 9885 Towne Centre Dr *NASDAQ: ILMN*	San Diego	CA	92121	**800-809-4566**	858-202-4500
Instrumentation Laboratory Inc 101 Hartwell Ave **Sales*	Lexington	MA	02421	**800-955-9525***	781-861-0710
IRIS International Inc 9172 Eton Ave. *NASDAQ: IRIS*	Chatsworth	CA	91311	**800-776-4747**	818-709-1244
Isco Inc 4700 Superior St PO Box 82531	Lincoln	NE	68501	**800-228-4250**	402-464-0231
LaMotte Co 802 Washington Ave	Chestertown	MD	21620	**800-344-3100**	410-778-3100
Leco Corp 3000 Lakeview Ave	Saint Joseph	MI	49085	**800-292-6141**	269-985-5496
Leica Inc 2345 Waukegan Rd 3rd Fl	Bannockburn	IL	60015	**800-248-0123**	847-405-0123
Luminex Corp 12212 Technology Blvd *NASDAQ: LMNX*	Austin	TX	78727	**888-219-8020**	512-219-8020
Mandel Scientific Co Ltd 2 Admiral Pl	Guelph	ON	N1G4N4	**800-265-8356**	519-763-2145
Molecular Devices Corp 1311 Orleans Dr Suite 408 *NASDAQ: MDCC*	Sunnyvale	CA	94089	**800-635-5577**	408-747-1700
MPD Inc 316 E 9th St.	Owensboro	KY	42303	**866-225-5673**	270-685-6200
Nanogen Inc 10398 Pacific Ctr Ct. *NASDAQ: NGEN*	San Diego	CA	92121	**877-626-6436**	858-410-4600
Nova Biomedical Corp 200 Prospect St Suite 3.	Waltham	MA	02454	**800-458-5813**	781-894-0800
OI Analytical 151 Graham Rd *NASDAQ: OICO*	College Station	TX	77845	**800-653-1711**	979-690-1711
OI Corp DBA OI Analytical 151 Graham Rd *NASDAQ: OICO*	College Station	TX	77845	**800-653-1711**	979-690-1711
Olis Inc 130 Conway Dr Suite A	Bogart	GA	30622	**800-852-3504**	706-353-6547
Olympus America Inc 2 Corporate Ctr Dr.	Melville	NY	11747	**800-446-5967**	631-844-5000
ONIX Systems Inc 9303 W Sam Houston Pkwy S	Houston	TX	77099	**877-290-7422**	713-272-0404
Pall Life Sciences Inc 600 S Wagner Rd.	Ann Arbor	MI	48103	**800-521-1520**	734-665-0651
Panalaytical 12 Michigan Dr	Natick	MA	01760	**800-279-7297**	508-647-1100
Particle Measuring Systems Inc 5475 Airport Blvd. **Cust Svc*	Boulder	CO	80301	**800-238-1801***	303-443-7100
PerkinElmer Instruments Inc 710 Bridgeport Ave	Shelton	CT	06484	**800-762-4000**	203-925-4600
Pfeiffer Vacuum Inc 24 Trafalgar Sq **Orders*	Nashua	NH	03063	**800-248-8254***	603-578-6500
Physical Electronics Inc 18725 Lake Dr E.	Chanhassen	MN	55317	**800-328-7515**	952-828-6100
Response Biomedical Corp 8081 Lougheed Hwy	Burnaby	BC	V5A1W9	**888-591-5577**	604-681-4101
Roche Diagnostics Corp 9115 Hague Rd PO Box 50457 **Cust Svc*	Indianapolis	IN	46256	**800-428-5076***	317-521-2000
Schleicher & Schuell Bioscience Inc 10 Optical Ave **Cust Svc*	Keene	NH	03431	**800-245-4024***	603-352-3810
Shimadzu Scientific Instruments Inc 7102 Riverwood Dr	Columbia	MD	21046	**800-477-1227**	410-381-1227
Smiths Detection 30 Hook Mountain Rd	Pine Brook	NJ	07058	**800-536-2277**	973-830-2100
Spectrum Laboratories Inc 18617 Broadwick St.	Rancho Dominguez	CA	90220	**800-634-3300**	310-885-4600
Spectrum Systems Inc 3410 W Nine-Mile Rd.	Pensacola	FL	32526	**877-837-6644**	850-944-3392
StatSpin Inc 85 Morse St.	Norwood	MA	02062	**800-782-8774**	781-551-0100
Stratagene Inc 11011 N Torrey Pines Rd. *NASDAQ: STGN*	La Jolla	CA	92037	**800-894-1304**	858-535-5400
Supelco Inc 595 N Harrison Rd Supelco Pk.	Bellefonte	PA	16823	**800-247-6628**	814-359-3441

Company	City	State	ZIP	Toll-Free	Phone
Temptronic Corp 4 Commercial St	Sharon	MA	02067	**800-558-5080***	781-688-2300
*Cust Svc					
Thermo Electron Corp 81 Wyman St PO Box 9056	Waltham	MA	02454	**800-678-5599**	781-622-1000
NYSE: TMO					
Thermo Elemental 27 Forge Pkwy	Franklin	MA	02038	**800-229-4087**	508-520-1880
Thermo Finnigan 355 River Oaks Pkwy	San Jose	CA	95134	**800-456-4552**	408-965-6000
Thermo LabSystems 100 Cummings Ctr Suite 407J	Beverly	MA	01915	**888-888-8173**	978-524-1400
Thermo Mattson 5225 Verona Rd Bldg 5	Madison	WI	53711	**800-423-6641**	608-276-6100
Thermo MeasureTech Inc 2555 N I-35	Round Rock	TX	78664	**800-736-0801**	512-388-9100
Thermo Nicolet 5225 Verona Rd	Madison	WI	53711	**800-642-6538**	608-276-6100
Thermo Orion 166 Cummings Ctr	Beverly	MA	01915	**800-225-1480**	978-922-4400
Thermo Shandon 171 Industry Dr	Pittsburgh	PA	15275	**800-547-7429**	412-788-1133
Transgenomic Inc 12325 Emmet St	Omaha	NE	68164	**888-233-9283**	402-452-5400
NASDAQ: TBIO					
Waters Corp 34 Maple St	Milford	MA	01757	**800-252-4752**	508-478-2000
NYSE: WAT					
Westover Scientific Inc 18421 Bothell-Everett Hwy Suite 110	Bothell	WA	98012	**800-304-3202**	425-398-1298
Whatman Inc 9 Bridewell Pl	Clifton	NJ	07014	**800-441-6555**	973-773-5800
X-Rite Inc 3100 44th St SW	Grandville	MI	49418	**800-248-9748**	616-534-7664
NASDAQ: XRIT					

411 LABORATORY APPARATUS & FURNITURE

SEE ALSO Glassware - Laboratory & Scientific; Laboratory Analytical Instruments; Scales & Balances

Company	City	State	ZIP	Toll-Free	Phone
Baker Co Inc 161 Gatehouse Rd PO Drawer E	Sanford	ME	04073	**800-992-2537**	207-324-8773
Barnstead/Thermolyne Corp 2555 Kerper Blvd	Dubuque	IA	52001	**800-446-6060**	563-556-2241
Becton Dickinson & Co 1 Becton Dr	Franklin Lakes	NJ	07417	**888-237-2762***	201-847-6800
NYSE: BDX ■ *Cust Svc					
Bel-Art Products Inc 6 Industrial Rd	Pequannock	NJ	07440	**800-423-5278**	973-694-0500
Boekel Industries Inc 855 Pennsylvania Blvd	Feasterville	PA	19053	**800-336-6929**	215-396-8200
Brinkmann Instruments Inc 1 Cantiague Rd PO Box 1019	Westbury	NY	11590	**800-645-3050**	516-334-7500
Briot 5360 NW 35th Ave	Fort Lauderdale	FL	33309	**800-852-8089**	954-733-2300
Corning Inc Life Sciences Div 45 Nagog Park	Acton	MA	01720	**800-492-1110**	978-635-2200
Edstrom Industries Inc 819 Bakke Ave	Waterford	WI	53185	**800-558-5913**	262-534-5181
Fisher Hamilton Inc 1316 18th St	Two Rivers	WI	54241	**800-762-7587**	920-793-1121
Harlan Sprague Dawley Inc 298 S Carroll Rd	Indianapolis	IN	46229	**800-793-7287**	317-894-7521
Infolab Inc PO Box 1309	Clarksdale	MS	38614	**800-647-8222**	662-627-2283
Kalamazoo Technical Furniture 6450 Valley Industrial Dr	Kalamazoo	MI	49009	**800-832-5227**	269-372-6000
Kendro Laboratory Products 275 Aiken Rd	Asheville	NC	28804	**800-252-7100**	828-658-2711
Labconco Corp 8811 Prospect Ave	Kansas City	MO	64132	**800-821-5525***	816-333-8811
*Cust Svc					
Leica Inc 2345 Waukegan Rd 3rd Fl	Bannockburn	IL	60015	**800-248-0123**	847-405-0123
Millipore Corp 80 Ashby Rd	Bedford	MA	01730	**800-221-1975**	781-533-6000
NYSE: MIL					
Nalge Nunc International 75 Panorama Creek Dr	Rochester	NY	14625	**800-625-4327**	585-586-8800
New Brunswick Scientific Co Inc 44 Talmadge Rd	Edison	NJ	08818	**800-631-5417***	732-287-1200
NASDAQ: NBSC ■ *Cust Svc					
Omnicell Inc 1201 Charleston Rd	Mountain View	CA	94043	**800-850-6664**	650-843-6100
NASDAQ: OMCL					
Pacific Combustion Engineering Co 2107 Border Ave	Torrance	CA	90501	**800-342-4442**	310-212-6300
Parr Instrument Co 211 53rd St	Moline	IL	61265	**800-872-7720**	309-762-7716
Pfeiffer Vacuum Inc 24 Trafalgar Sq	Nashua	NH	03063	**800-248-8254***	603-578-6500
*Orders					
Precision Scientific Inc 170 Marcel Dr	Winchester	VA	22602	**800-621-8820***	540-869-9892
*Cust Svc					
Samco Scientific Corp 1050 Arroyo Ave	San Fernando	CA	91340	**800-522-3359**	818-838-2400
Sargent-Welch 911 Commerce Ct	Buffalo Grove	IL	60089	**800-727-4368**	
Thermo Forma 401 Millcreek Rd	Marietta	OH	45750	**800-848-3080**	740-373-4763
ThermoGenesis Corp 2711 Citrus Rd	Rancho Cordova	CA	95742	**800-783-8357**	916-858-5100
NASDAQ: KOOL					
Thomas Scientific 99 Highville Rd	Swedesboro	NJ	08085	**800-345-2100**	856-467-2000
Westfalia Separator Inc 100 Fairway Ct	Northvale	NJ	07647	**800-722-6622**	201-767-3900

412 LADDERS

Company	City	State	ZIP	Toll-Free	Phone
ALACO Ladder Co 5167 G St	Chino	CA	91710	**888-310-7040**	909-591-7561
Ballymore Co 220 Garfield Ave	West Chester	PA	19380	**800-762-8327**	610-696-3250
Cotterman Co PO Box 168	Croswell	MI	48422	**800-552-3337**	810-679-4400
Green Bull Inc 11225 Bluegrass Pkwy	Louisville	KY	40299	**800-558-2855**	502-267-5577
Johnson Ladders Inc 700 S Ewing St	Dallas	TX	75203	**800-523-1881***	214-943-7494
*Cust Svc					
Lynn Ladder & Scaffolding Co Inc PO Box 346	Lynn	MA	01905	**800-596-6717**	781-598-6010
Miscellaneous Metals Inc 5719 Industry Ln PO Box 3818	Frederick	MD	21705	**800-492-7828**	301-695-8820
Werner Co 93 Werner Rd	Greenville	PA	16125	**888-532-3770**	724-588-2550
Wing Enterprises Inc PO Box 3100	Springville	UT	84663	**800-453-1192**	801-489-3684

413 LANDSCAPING SERVICES

Company	City	State	ZIP	Toll-Free	Phone
Brickman Group Ltd 375 S Flowers Mill Rd	Langhorne	PA	19047	**800-451-7272**	215-757-9400
Environmental Earthscapes Inc 5075 S Swan Rd	Tucson	AZ	85706	**800-571-1575**	520-571-1575
Landscape Concepts Inc 31745 N Alleghany Rd	Grayslake	IL	60030	**866-655-3800**	847-223-3800
Stiles Landscape Co 1080 SW 12 Ave	Pompano Beach	FL	33069	**866-250-4074**	954-781-0247

414 LANGUAGE SCHOOLS

SEE ALSO Translation Services

Company	City	State	ZIP	Toll-Free	Phone
AmeriSpan Unlimited PO Box 58129	Philadelphia	PA	19102	**800-879-6640**	215-751-1100
Berlitz International Inc 400 Alexander Pk	Princeton	NJ	08540	**800-257-9449**	609-514-9650
Cultural Center for Language Studies Corp 3191 Coral Way Suite 114	Miami	FL	33145	**800-704-3131**	305-529-8563
ELS Language Centers 400 Alexander Pk	Princeton	NJ	08540	**800-468-8978**	609-750-3500
Foundation for European Language & Educational Centres USA 101 N Union St Suite 300	Alexandria	VA	22314	**888-387-6236**	703-684-1494
Kaplan International 888 7th Ave 21st Fl	New York	NY	10106	**800-527-8378**	212-492-5800
Language Exchange International 500 NE Spanish River Blvd Suite 19	Boca Raton	FL	33431	**800-223-5836**	561-368-3913
Olin Center 342 Newbury St	Boston	MA	02115	**800-778-7669**	617-247-3033

415 LASER EQUIPMENT & SYSTEMS - MEDICAL

SEE ALSO Medical Instruments & Apparatus - Mfr

Company	City	State	ZIP	Toll-Free	Phone
American Medical Technologies Inc 5555 Bear Ln	Corpus Christi	TX	78405	**800-440-0310**	361-289-1145
NASDAQ: ADLI					
Big Sky Laser Technologies Inc 601 Haggerty Ln	Bozeman	MT	59715	**800-224-4759**	406-586-0131
BioLase Technology Inc 981 Calle Amanecer	San Clemente	CA	92673	**800-699-9462**	949-361-1200
NASDAQ: BLTI					
Candela Corp 530 Boston Post Rd	Wayland	MA	01778	**800-733-8550**	508-358-7637
NASDAQ: CLZR					
CardioGenesis Corp 26632 Towne Centre Dr Suite 320	Foothill Ranch	CA	92610	**800-238-2205**	714-649-5000
Continuum 3150 Central Expy	Santa Clara	CA	95051	**800-956-7757**	408-727-3240
Convergent Laser Technologies 900 Alice St	Oakland	CA	94607	**800-848-8200**	510-832-2130
IntraLase Corp 3 Morgan	Irvine	CA	92618	**877-393-2020**	949-859-5230
NASDAQ: ILSE					
Iridex Corp 1212 Terra Bella Ave	Mountain View	CA	94043	**800-388-4747***	650-940-4700
NASDAQ: IRIX ■ *Cust Svc					
Lambda Physik Inc 3201 W Commercial Blvd Suite 110	Fort Lauderdale	FL	33309	**800-392-4637**	954-486-1500
Laserscope 3070 Orchard Dr	San Jose	CA	95134	**800-356-7600**	408-943-0636
NASDAQ: LSCP					
LaserSight Inc 6848 Stapoint Ct	Winter Park	FL	32792	**888-527-3235**	407-678-9900
LaserSight Technologies Inc 6848 Stapoint Ct	Winter Park	FL	32792	**888-527-3235**	407-678-9900
Lightwave Electronics Corp 2400 Charleston Rd	Mountain View	CA	94043	**888-544-4892**	650-962-0755
Lumenis Ltd 2400 Condensa St	Santa Clara	CA	95051	**800-227-1914**	408-764-3000
Palomar Medical Technologies Inc 82 Cambridge St	Burlington	MA	01803	**800-725-6627**	781-993-2300
NASDAQ: PMTI					
Paradigm Medical Industries Inc 2355 S 1070 West	Salt Lake City	UT	84119	**800-742-0671**	801-977-8970
PhotoMedex Inc 147 Keystone Dr	Montgomeryville	PA	18936	**800-366-4758**	215-619-3600
NASDAQ: PHMD					
PLC Medical Systems Inc 10 Forge Pk	Franklin	MA	02038	**800-232-8422**	508-541-8800
PLC Systems Inc 10 Forge Pk	Franklin	MA	02038	**800-232-8422**	508-541-8800
AMEX: PLC					
Spectranetics Corp 96 Talamine Ct	Colorado Springs	CO	80907	**800-633-0960**	719-633-8333
NASDAQ: SPNC					
Sunrise Technologies International Inc 3400 W Warren AVe	Fremont	CA	94538	**800-789-4949**	510-623-9001
Trex Enterprises 10455 Pacific Center Ct	San Diego	CA	92121	**800-626-5885**	858-646-5300
Trimedyne Inc 15091 Bake Pkwy	Irvine	CA	92618	**800-733-5273**	949-559-5300
VISX Inc 3400 Central Expy	Santa Clara	CA	95051	**800-998-2020**	408-733-2020
NYSE: EYE					

416 LASERS - INDUSTRIAL

Company	City	State	ZIP	Toll-Free	Phone
AGL Corp 2202 Redmond Rd	Jacksonville	AR	72076	**800-643-9696**	501-982-4433
Big Sky Laser Technologies Inc 601 Haggerty Ln	Bozeman	MT	59715	**800-224-4759**	406-586-0131
Coherent Inc 5100 Patrick Henry Dr	Santa Clara	CA	95054	**800-527-3786***	408-764-4000
NASDAQ: COHR ■ *Sales					
Continuum 3150 Central Expy	Santa Clara	CA	95051	**800-956-7757**	408-727-3240
Electro Scientific Industries Inc 13900 NW Science Pk Dr	Portland	OR	97229	**800-547-5746***	503-641-4141
NASDAQ: ESIO ■ *Cust Svc					
JDS Uniphase Corp 1768 Automation Pkwy	San Jose	CA	95131	**800-644-8674**	408-546-5000
NASDAQ: JDSU					
Jodon Inc 62 Enterprise Dr	Ann Arbor	MI	48103	**800-989-5636**	734-761-4044
Lambda Physik Inc 3201 W Commercial Blvd Suite 110	Fort Lauderdale	FL	33309	**800-392-4637**	954-486-1500
Leica Geosystems LLC 6330 28th St SE	Grand Rapids	MI	49546	**800-367-9453***	616-949-7430
*Sales					
Lightwave Electronics Corp 2400 Charleston Rd	Mountain View	CA	94043	**888-544-4892**	650-962-0755
Melles Griot Inc 2051 Talomar Airport Rd Suite 200	Carlsbad	CA	92009	**800-645-2737***	760-268-5131
*Cust Svc					
PRIMA North America Inc 711 E Main St	Chicopee	MA	01020	**800-722-1133***	413-598-5200
*Cust Svc					
PTR-Precision Technologies Inc 120 Post Rd	Enfield	CT	06082	**888-478-7832**	860-741-2281

				Toll-Free	Phone
Spectra-Physics Inc					
1335 Terra Bella Ave	Mountain View	CA	94043	**800-456-2552**	650-961-2550
Synrad Inc 4600 Campus Pl	Mukilteo	WA	98275	**800-796-7231**	425-349-3500
Trimble Engineering & Construction Div					
5475 Kellenburger Rd	Dayton	OH	45424	**800-538-7800**	937-233-8921

417 LAUNDRY & DRYCLEANING SERVICES

SEE ALSO Linen & Uniform Supply

				Toll-Free	Phone
1 Hour Martinizing Dry Cleaning Stores					
422 Wards Corner Rd	Loveland	OH	45140	**800-827-0207**	513-351-6211
Apparelmaster 123 Harrison Ave	Harrison	OH	45030	**877-543-1678**	513-202-1600
Dryclean USA Inc 290 NE 68th St	Miami	FL	33138	**800-746-4583**	305-758-0066
AMEX: DCU					
Horlander Enterprises Inc DBA Nu-Yale					
Cleaners 6300 Hwy 62	Jeffersonville	IN	47130	**888-644-7400**	812-285-7400
Nu-Yale Cleaners 6300 Hwy 62	Jeffersonville	IN	47130	**888-644-7400**	812-285-7400
Pressed4Time Inc 8 Clock Tower Pl Suite 110	Maynard	MA	01754	**800-423-8711**	978-823-8300

LAUNDRY EQUIPMENT - HOUSEHOLD

SEE Appliance & Home Electronics Stores; Appliances - Major - Mfr; Appliances - Whol

418 LAUNDRY EQUIPMENT & SUPPLIES - COMMERCIAL & INDUSTRIAL

				Toll-Free	Phone
Braun GA Inc PO Box 70	Syracuse	NY	13205	**800-432-7286**	315-475-3123
Cissell Mfg Co 831 S 1st St	Louisville	KY	40203	**800-882-6665**	502-587-1292
Colmac Industries Inc PO Box 72	Colville	WA	99114	**800-926-5622**	509-684-4506
Edro Corp 37 Commerce St	East Berlin	CT	06023	**800-628-6434***	860-828-0311
*Sales					
Ellis Corp 1400 W Bryn Mawr Ave	Itasca	IL	60143	**800-611-6806**	630-250-9222
GA Braun Inc PO Box 70	Syracuse	NY	13205	**800-432-7286**	315-475-3123
Hoyt Corp 251 Forge Rd	Westport	MA	02790	**800-343-9411**	508-636-8811
Minnesota Chemical Co 2285 Hampden Ave	Saint Paul	MN	55114	**800-328-5689**	651-646-7521
Washex Inc 5000 Central Fwy N	Wichita Falls	TX	76306	**800-433-0933***	940-855-3990
*Sales					

419 LAW FIRMS

SEE ALSO Arbitration Services - Legal; Associations & Organizations - Professional & Trade - Legal Professionals Associations; Bar Associations - State; Litigation Support Services

				Toll-Free	Phone
Adams & Reese LLP					
1 Shell Sq Suite 4500	New Orleans	LA	70139	**800-725-1990**	504-581-3234
Armstrong Teasdale LLP					
1 Metropolitan Sq Suite 2600	Saint Louis	MO	63102	**800-243-5070**	314-621-5070
Baker & Daniels					
300 N Meridian St Suite 2700	Indianapolis	IN	46204	**800-428-9506**	317-237-0300
Barnes & Thornburg 11 S Meridian St	Indianapolis	IN	46204	**800-753-5139**	317-236-1313
Blackwell Sanders Peper Martin LLP					
4801 Main St Suite 1000	Kansas City	MO	64112	**800-437-7309**	816-983-8000
Buchanan Ingersoll PC					
301 Grant St 1 Oxford Ctr 20th Fl	Pittsburgh	PA	15219	**800-444-6738**	412-562-8800
Burr & Forman LLP					
420 N 20th St Suite 3100	Birmingham	AL	35203	**800-438-2877**	205-251-3000
Carlton Fields PA 4221 W Boy Scout Blvd	Tampa	FL	33607	**888-223-9191**	813-223-7000
Choate Hall & Stewart 53 State St Exchange Pl	Boston	MA	02109	**800-520-2427**	617-248-5000
Clausen Miller PC 10 S La Salle St Suite 1600	Chicago	IL	60603	**800-826-3505**	312-855-1010
Cooley Godward LLP					
1 Maritime Plaza 20th Fl	San Francisco	CA	94111	**866-226-6539**	415-693-2000
Cozen O'Connor 1900 Market St	Philadelphia	PA	19103	**800-523-2900**	215-665-2000
Davis Polk & Wardwell 450 Lexington Ave	New York	NY	10017	**888-765-5529**	212-450-4000
Dorsey & Whitney LLP					
50 S 6th St Suite 1500	Minneapolis	MN	55402	**800-759-4929**	612-340-2600
Faegre & Benson LLP					
90 S 7th St Suite 20 Wells Fargo Bldg	Minneapolis	MN	55402	**800-328-4393**	612-766-7000
Fenwick & West LLP 801 California St	Mountain View	CA	94041	**800-816-6136**	650-988-8500
Fish & Richardson PC 225 Franklin St 31st Fl	Boston	MA	02110	**800-818-5070**	617-542-5070
Foley & Lardner 777 E Wisconsin Ave	Milwaukee	WI	53202	**800-558-1548**	414-271-2400
Godfrey & Kahn SC 780 N Water St	Milwaukee	WI	53202	**877-455-2900**	414-273-3500
Gray Cary Ware & Freidenrich LLP					
401 B St Suite 2000	San Diego	CA	92101	**888-429-4293**	619-699-2700
Harris Beach LLP 805 3rd Ave	New York	NY	10022	**888-999-0529**	212-687-0100
Hodgson Russ LLP 1 M&T Plaza Suite 2000	Buffalo	NY	14203	**800-724-5184**	716-856-4000
Holme Roberts & Owen LLP					
1700 Lincoln St Suite 4100	Denver	CO	80203	**800-334-4124**	303-861-7000
Katten Muchin Zavis Rosenman					
525 W Monroe St Suite 1300	Chicago	IL	60661	**800-346-7400**	312-902-5200
KMZ Rosenman 525 W Monroe St Suite 1300	Chicago	IL	60661	**800-346-7400**	312-902-5200
Kramer Levin Naftalis & Frankel LLP					
919 3rd Ave	New York	NY	10022	**800-766-4707**	212-715-9100
Milberg Weiss Bershad & Schulman LLP					
1 Pennsylvania Plaza 49th Fl	New York	NY	10119	**800-320-5081**	212-594-5300
Miles & Stockbridge PC 10 Light St	Baltimore	MD	21202	**800-344-2532**	410-727-6464
Nelson Mullins Riley & Scarborough LLP					
1320 Main St 17th Fl	Columbia	SC	29201	**800-237-2000**	803-799-2000
Paul Hastings Janofsky & Walker LLP					
515 S Flower St 25th Fl	Los Angeles	CA	90071	**888-745-9557**	213-683-6000
Perkins Coie LLP					
1201 3rd Ave 40th Fl Suite 4800	Seattle	WA	98101	**800-829-1177**	206-583-8888
Pillsbury Winthrop LLP 50 Fremont St	San Francisco	CA	94105	**800-477-0770**	415-983-1000
Pitney Hardin Kipp & Szuch LLP					
200 Campus Dr	Florham Park	NJ	07932	**800-343-7457**	973-966-6300
Porter Wright Morris & Arthur LLP					
41 S High St 29th Fl	Columbus	OH	43215	**800-533-2794**	614-227-2000
Powell Goldstein LLP					
1201 W Peachtree St NW 14th Fl	Atlanta	GA	30309	**800-769-3552**	404-572-6600
Preston Gates & Ellis LLP					
925 4th Ave Suite 2900	Seattle	WA	98104	**800-551-4613**	206-623-7580
Reinhart Boerner Van Deuren SC					
1000 N Water St Suite 2100	Milwaukee	WI	53202	**800-553-6215**	414-298-1000
Robins Kaplan Miller & Ciresi LLP					
800 LaSalle Ave 2800 LaSalle Plaza	Minneapolis	MN	55402	**800-553-9910**	612-349-8500
Robinson & Cole LLP 280 Trumbull St	Hartford	CT	06103	**800-826-3579**	860-275-8200
Roetzel & Andress 222 S Main St	Akron	OH	44308	**800-837-2701**	330-376-2700
Saul Ewing LLP					
1500 Market St Centre Sq W 38th Fl	Philadelphia	PA	19102	**800-355-7777**	215-972-7777
Schiff Hardin & Waite LLP					
233 S Wacker Dr 6600 Sears Tower	Chicago	IL	60606	**800-258-7799**	312-258-5500
Schnader Harrison Segal & Lewis LLP					
1600 Market St Suite 3600	Philadelphia	PA	19103	**800-541-5997**	215-751-2000
Sedgwick Detert Moran & Arnold LLP					
1 Embarcadero Ctr 16th Fl	San Francisco	CA	94111	**800-826-3262**	415-781-7900
Seyfarth Shaw LLP					
55 E Monroe St Suite 4200	Chicago	IL	60603	**800-342-4432**	312-346-8000
Shearman & Sterling LLP 599 Lexington Ave	New York	NY	10022	**800-521-2918**	212-848-4000
Shook Hardy & Bacon LLP					
2555 Grand Blvd	Kansas City	MO	64108	**800-821-7962**	816-474-6550
Snell & Wilmer LLP					
400 E Van Buren St 1 Arizona Ctr	Phoenix	AZ	85004	**800-322-0430**	602-382-6000
Squire Sanders & Dempsey LLP					
127 Public Sq 4900 Key Tower	Cleveland	OH	44114	**800-743-2773**	216-479-8500
Stoel Rives LLP 900 SW 5th Ave Suite 2600	Portland	OR	97204	**800-887-8635**	503-224-3380
Troutman Sanders LLP					
600 Peachtree St NE Suite 5200	Atlanta	GA	30308	**800-255-8752**	404-885-3000
Venable LLP					
1800 Mercantile Bank & Trust Bldg 2					
Hopkins Plaza	Baltimore	MD	21201	**800-966-9877**	410-244-7400
Wachtell Lipton Rosen & Katz					
51 W 52nd St	New York	NY	10019	**800-848-0301**	212-403-1000
Williams Mullin					
1021 E Cary St 2 James Ctr 16th Fl	Richmond	VA	23219	**888-783-8181**	804-643-1991
Winstead Sechrest & Minick PC					
1201 Elm St Suite 5400	Dallas	TX	75270	**800-850-8737**	214-745-5400
Winston & Strawn					
35 W Wacker Dr Suite 4200	Chicago	IL	60601	**800-946-7866**	312-558-5600

420 LAWN & GARDEN EQUIPMENT

SEE ALSO Farm Machinery & Equipment - Mfr

				Toll-Free	Phone
American Biophysics Corp					
140 Frenchtown Rd	North Kingstown	RI	02852	**877-699-8727**	401-884-3500
Ames True Temper Inc 465 Railroad Ave	Camp Hill	PA	17011	**800-393-1846**	717-737-1500
Armatron International Inc 15 Highland Ave	Malden	MA	02148	**800-343-3280**	781-321-2300
Blount Inc Oregon Cutting Systems Div					
4909 SE International Way	Portland	OR	97222	**800-223-5168**	503-653-8881
Blount Outdoor Products Group					
4909 SE International Way	Portland	OR	97222	**800-223-5168**	503-653-8881
Bluemkes Inc PO Box 149	Rosendale	WI	54974	**800-236-2133**	920-872-2131
Brinly-Hardy Co Inc 3230 Industrial Pkwy	Jeffersonville	IN	47130	**800-626-5329**	812-218-6080
California Flexrake Corp 9620 Gidley St	Temple City	CA	91780	**800-266-4200**	626-443-4026
CMD Products 1410 Flightline Dr Suite D	Lincoln	CA	95648	**800-210-9949**	916-434-0228
Commerce Corp 7603 Energy Pkwy	Baltimore	MD	21226	**800-289-0982**	410-255-3500
Continental AFA Corp 135 Pine St	Forest City	NC	28043	**800-325-0005**	828-245-1160
Corona Clipper Co 1540 E 6th St	Corona	CA	92879	**800-847-7863**	951-737-6515
Cub Cadet Corp 1620 Welch St	Brownsville	TN	38012	**888-986-2288**	731-772-5600
Dixon Industries Inc Hwy 169 PO Box 1569	Coffeyville	KS	67337	**877-288-6673**	620-251-2000
EarthWay Products Inc PO Box 547	Bristol	IN	46507	**800-678-0671**	574-848-7491
Echo Inc 400 Oakwood Rd	Lake Zurich	IL	60047	**800-673-1558**	847-540-8400
Fiskars Brands Inc Garden Tools Div					
780 Carolina St	Sauk City	WI	53583	**800-500-4849**	608-643-4389
Frederick Mfg Corp 4840 E 12th St	Kansas City	MO	64127	**800-743-3150**	816-231-5007
Gilmour Mfg Group PO Box 838	Somerset	PA	15501	**800-458-0107***	814-443-4802
*Cust Svc					
Gravely International Inc 655 W Ryan St	Brillion	WI	54110	**888-927-4367***	920-756-2141
*Cust Svc					
Harnack Co 6016 Nordic Dr	Cedar Falls	IA	50613	**800-772-2022***	319-277-0660
*Cust Svc					
Hoffco Inc 358 NW 'F' St	Richmond	IN	47374	**800-999-8161**	765-966-8161
Hound Dog Products Inc					
6811 Shady Oak Rd	Eden Prairie	MN	55344	**800-694-6863**	952-828-9008
Husqvarna Turf Care Co 700 Park St	Beatrice	NE	68310	**877-368-8873**	402-223-2391
Kenney Corp 8420 Zionsville Rd	Indianapolis	IN	46268	**800-878-8676**	317-872-4793
Lawn-Boy Inc 8111 S Lyndale Ave	Bloomington	MN	55420	**800-526-6937**	952-888-8801
Lawn & Golf Supply Co Inc 647 Nutt Rd	Phoenixville	PA	19460	**800-362-5650**	610-933-5801
LESCO Inc 15885 Sprague Rd	Strongsville	OH	44136	**800-321-5325**	440-783-9250
NASDAQ: LSCO					
LR Nelson Corp 1 Sprinkler Ln	Peoria	IL	61615	**800-635-7668***	309-690-2200
*Sales					
Master Mark Plastic Products Inc PO Box 662	Albany	MN	56307	**800-535-4838***	320-845-2111
*Cust Svc					
Maxim Mfg Co PO Box 110	Sebastopol	MS	39359	**800-621-2789**	601-625-7471
MTD Products Inc PO Box 368022	Cleveland	OH	44136	**800-800-7310**	330-225-2600
Nelson LR Corp 1 Sprinkler Ln	Peoria	IL	61615	**800-635-7668***	309-690-2200
*Sales					
Oregon Cutting Systems Div Blount Inc					
4909 SE International Way	Portland	OR	97222	**800-223-5168**	503-653-8881
Precision Products Inc 316 Limit St	Lincoln	IL	62656	**800-225-5891***	217-735-1590
*Cust Svc					
Rio Delmar Enterprises PO Box 1409	Easton	MD	21601	**800-638-4402**	410-822-8866
Roeder Implement Co Inc 1010 Skyline Dr	Hopkinsville	KY	42240	**800-844-3994**	270-886-3994
Rotary Corp PO Box 747	Glennville	GA	30427	**800-841-3989**	912-654-3433
Rugg Mfg Co Inc PO Box 428	Greenfield	MA	01302	**800-633-8772**	413-773-5471

	City	State	Zip	Toll-Free	Phone
Snapper Inc 535 Macon St *Cust Svc	McDonough	GA	30253	**800-935-2967***	770-957-9141
Stens Corp PO Box 490	Jasper	IN	47547	**800-457-7444**	812-482-2526
Stihl Inc 536 Viking Dr *Cust Svc	Virginia Beach	VA	23452	**800-467-8445***	757-486-9100
Telsco Industries Inc Weathermatic 3301 W Kingsley Rd	Garland	TX	75041	**888-484-3776**	972-278-6131
Toro Co 8111 Lyndale Ave *NYSE: TTC*	Bloomington	MN	55420	**800-595-6841**	952-888-8801
Weathermatic 3301 W Kingsley Rd	Garland	TX	75041	**888-484-3776**	972-278-6131
Woods Equipment Co 2606 S Illinois Rt 2	Oregon	IL	61061	**800-319-6637**	815-732-2141

421 LAWN SERVICES

SEE ALSO Landscaping Services; Tree Services

	City	State	Zip	Toll-Free	Phone
Chemlawn Canada 70 Ronson Dr *Cust Svc	Etobicoke	ON	M9W1B9	**800-565-5296***	416-614-6677
Green Lawn Care 476 Evans Ave	Etobicoke	ON	M8W2T9	**800-387-3426**	416-253-6540
Greenspace Services Ltd 70 Ronson Dr	Etobicoke	ON	M9W1B9	**800-565-5296**	416-614-6677
Groundskeeper PO Box 43820	Tucson	AZ	85706	**800-571-1575**	520-571-1575
Lawn Doctor Inc 142 SR 34	Holmdel	NJ	07733	**800-631-5000**	732-946-0029
NaturaLawn of America Inc 1 E Church St	Frederick	MD	21701	**800-989-5444**	301-694-5440
Nutrilawn Inc 5397 Eglinton Ave W Suite 110	Toronto	ON	M9C5K6	**800-396-6096**	416-620-7100
Scotts Lawn Service 14111 Scottslawn Rd	Marysville	OH	43041	**888-872-6887**	937-644-0011
Spring-Green Lawn Care Corp 11909 Spaulding School Dr	Plainfield	IL	60544	**800-435-4051**	815-436-8777
Teufel Nursery Inc Landscape Div 12345 NW Barnes Rd	Portland	OR	97229	**800-483-8335**	503-646-1111
TruGreen ChemLawn 860 Ridge Lake Blvd	Memphis	TN	38120	**800-878-4733**	901-681-1800

422 LEATHER GOODS - PERSONAL

SEE ALSO Clothing & Accessories - Mfr; Footwear; Handbags, Totes, Backpacks; Leather Goods (Misc); Luggage Stores; Luggage, Bags, Cases

	City	State	Zip	Toll-Free	Phone
Berman Leather Co 117 Beaver St	Waltham	MA	02453	**800-992-3762**	781-736-0870
Bosca Hugo Co Inc 1905 W Jefferson St	Springfield	OH	45506	**800-732-6722**	937-323-5523
Bottega Veneta Inc 635 Madison Ave	New York	NY	10022	**877-362-1715**	212-371-5511
Buxton Co PO Box 1650	Springfield	MA	01102	**800-962-2813**	413-734-5900
California Optical Leather Inc 2992 Alvarado St	San Leandro	CA	94577	**800-523-5567**	510-352-4774
Carroll Companies Inc PO Box 1549	Boone	NC	28607	**800-884-2521**	828-264-2521
Coach Inc 516 W 34th St *NYSE: COH*	New York	NY	10001	**800-444-3611**	212-594-1850
Dooney & Bourke Inc 1 Regent St *Cust Svc	East Norwalk	CT	06855	**800-347-5000***	203-853-7515
Enger Kress Co 6510 Aurora Rd Suite C *Cust Svc	West Bend	WI	53090	**800-367-7547***	262-629-1553
Etienne Aigner Group Inc 47 Brunswick Ave	Edison	NJ	08818	**800-537-7463**	732-248-9200
Hadley-Roma Watchband Corp 106 Corporate Pk Dr	White Plains	NY	10604	**800-800-7662**	914-694-2000
Humphreys Inc 2009 W Hastings St *Cust Svc	Chicago	IL	60608	**800-621-8541***	312-997-2358
Penmar Inc PO Box 299	Haverstraw	NY	10927	**800-431-7890**	845-429-2600
Stone Mountain Accessories 10 W 33rd St Suite 728 *Cust Svc	New York	NY	10001	**866-865-0786***	212-563-2500
Terner's of Miami Inc 3050 NW 40th St	Miami	FL	33142	**800-662-4395**	305-638-7778
TGL 300 Wilson Ave	Norwalk	CT	06854	**800-587-1584**	203-853-4747
Trafalgar Ghurka Ltd 300 Wilson Ave	Norwalk	CT	06854	**800-587-1584**	203-853-4747
Westport Corp 10 E 34th St	New York	NY	10016	**800-457-7782**	212-779-5900

423 LEATHER GOODS (MISC)

	City	State	Zip	Toll-Free	Phone
Action Co 1425 N Tennessee St *Sales	McKinney	TX	75069	**800-937-3700***	972-542-8700
Auburn Leather Co PO Box 338	Auburn	KY	42206	**800-635-0617**	270-542-4116
Brauer Brothers Mfg Co 1520 Washington Ave 4th Fl	Saint Louis	MO	63103	**800-527-2837**	314-231-2864
Carroll Companies Inc PO Box 1549	Boone	NC	28607	**800-884-2521**	828-264-2521
Chace Leather Products 507 Alden St	Fall River	MA	02723	**800-272-4223**	508-678-7556
Champion Turf Equipment Inc 330 S Mission Rd	Los Angeles	CA	90033	**800-421-6171**	323-264-0746
Circle Y of Yoakum Inc 201 W Morris St	Yoakum	TX	77995	**800-531-3600**	361-293-5251
Colorado Saddlery Co PO Box 8538 *Cust Svc	Denver	CO	80201	**800-521-2465***	303-572-8350
Gould & Goodrich Leather Inc 709 E McNeil St	Lillington	NC	27546	**800-277-0732**	910-893-2071
Hunter Co Inc 3300 W 71st Ave	Westminster	CO	80030	**800-676-4868**	303-427-4626
Klein Tools Inc Fort Smith Div 5721-A S Zero St	Fort Smith	AR	72903	**800-325-5723**	479-646-7347
LH Lincoln & Son Inc 87 West St	Galeton	PA	16922	**800-845-4626**	814-274-9200
Page Belting Co 24 Chenell Dr	Concord	NH	03301	**800-258-3654**	603-225-5523
Petco Inc 3050 Walkent Ave NW	Grand Rapids	MI	49544	**800-437-3826**	616-784-5868
Safariland Ltd Inc 3120 E Mission Blvd	Ontario	CA	91761	**800-347-1200**	909-923-7300
Shoemaker Tex & Son Inc 714 W Cienega Ave	San Dimas	CA	91773	**800-345-9959**	909-592-2071
Simco Longhorn Leather Co Inc 1800 Daisy St *Cust Svc	Chattanooga	TN	37406	**800-251-6294***	423-624-3331
Strong Group Inc 39 Grove St *Orders	Gloucester	MA	01930	**800-225-0724***	978-281-3300
Tex Shoemaker & Son Inc 714 W Cienega Ave	San Dimas	CA	91773	**800-345-9959**	909-592-2071
Tex Tan Western Leather Co 808 S US Hwy 77A *Cust Svc	Yoakum	TX	77995	**800-531-3608***	361-293-2314

424 LEATHER TANNING & FINISHING

	City	State	Zip	Toll-Free	Phone
Hermann Oak Leather Co 4050 N 1st St	Saint Louis	MO	63147	**800-325-7950**	314-421-1173
Place WB LLC 368 W Sumner St	Hartford	WI	53027	**800-826-4433**	262-673-3130
WB Place LLC 368 W Sumner St	Hartford	WI	53027	**800-826-4433**	262-673-3130
Westan Inc 360 Church St	Westfield	PA	16950	**800-352-8952**	814-367-5951
Western Saddlery & Moser Leather Co 1191 Hooven Ave *Cust Svc	Hamilton	OH	45015	**800-874-1167***	513-889-0500

425 LEGISLATION HOTLINES

	City	State	Zip	Toll-Free	Phone
Arizona Bill Status Capitol Complex 1700 W Washington St	Phoenix	AZ	85007	**800-352-8404**	602-542-4900
Florida Bill Status 111 W Madison St Rm 704	Tallahassee	FL	32399	**800-342-1827**	850-488-4371
Louisiana Bill Status State Capitol 13th Fl	Baton Rouge	LA	70804	**800-256-3793**	225-342-2456
Maine Bill Status State House 100 State House Station	Augusta	ME	04333	**800-301-3178**	207-287-1692
Maryland Bill Status 90 State Cir	Annapolis	MD	21401	**800-492-7122**	410-946-5400
Massachusetts Bill Status 1 Ashburton Pl Rm 1611	Boston	MA	02108	**800-392-6090**	617-727-7030
Nebraska Bill Status 2018 State Capitol Bldg	Lincoln	NE	68509	**800-724-7456**	402-471-2877
Nevada Bill Status 401 S Carson St	Carson City	NV	89701	**800-992-6761**	775-684-6800
New Jersey Bill Status State House Annex PO Box 068	Trenton	NJ	08625	**800-792-8630**	609-292-4840
New York (State) Bill Status 55 Elk St	Albany	NY	12210	**800-342-9860**	518-455-7545
Texas Bill Status State Capitol 1100 Congress Ave Rm 2N-3	Austin	TX	78711	**877-824-7038**	512-463-2182
Washington Bill Status PO Box 40600	Olympia	WA	98504	**800-562-6000**	360-786-7573
West Virginia Bill Status State Capitol Rm MB27	Charleston	WV	25305	**800-642-8650**	304-347-4831
Wisconsin Bill Status 1 E Main St	Madison	WI	53708	**800-362-9472**	608-266-9960
Wyoming Bill Status State Capitol Bldg Rm 213	Cheyenne	WY	82002	**800-342-9570**	307-777-7881

426 LIBRARIES

SEE ALSO Library Systems - Regional - Canadian

	City	State	Zip	Toll-Free	Phone
Alliance Library System 600 High Point Ln Suite 1	East Peoria	IL	61611	**800-700-4857**	309-694-9200
Bangor Public Library 145 Harlow St	Bangor	ME	04401	**800-427-8336**	207-947-8336
Bolivar County Library 104 S Leflore Ave	Cleveland	MS	38732	**888-268-8076**	662-843-2774
Brooke-Gould Memorial Library 450 S Barron St	Eaton	OH	45320	**800-241-7731**	937-456-4331
Carnegie Regional Library 49 W 7th St	Grafton	ND	58237	**800-568-5964**	701-352-2754
Central Massachusetts Regional Library System 8 Flagg Rd	Shrewsbury	MA	01545	**800-922-8326**	508-757-4110
Cuyahoga County Public Library 2111 Snow Rd	Parma	OH	44134	**800-749-5560**	216-398-1800
Daniel Boone Regional Library 100 W Broadway	Columbia	MO	65203	**800-324-4806**	573-443-3161
Dwight D Eisenhower Presidential Library & Museum 200 SE 4th St	Abilene	KS	67410	**877-746-4453**	785-263-6700
Finger Lakes Library System 119 E Green St	Ithaca	NY	14850	**800-909-3557**	607-273-4074
Franklin D Roosevelt Library & Museum 4079 Albany Post Rd	Hyde Park	NY	12538	**800-337-8474**	845-229-8114
Harry S Truman Presidential Library & Museum 500 W Hwy 24	Independence	MO	64050	**800-833-1225**	816-833-1400
Highland Rim Regional Library Center 2118 E Main St	Murfreesboro	TN	37130	**800-257-7323**	615-893-3380
Jackson/Hinds Library System 300 N State St	Jackson	MS	39201	**800-968-5803**	601-968-5811
John F Kennedy Library & Museum Columbia Point	Boston	MA	02125	**866-535-1960**	617-514-1600
Kitsap Regional Library 1301 Sylvan Way	Bremerton	WA	98310	**877-883-9900**	360-405-9110
Linda Hall Library 5109 Cherry St	Kansas City	MO	64110	**800-662-1545**	816-363-4600
Lorain Public Library System 351 6th St	Lorain	OH	44052	**800-322-7323**	440-244-1192
Manhattan Public Library 629 Poyntz Ave	Manhattan	KS	66502	**800-432-2796**	785-776-4741
Massanutten Regional Library 174 S Main St	Harrisonburg	VA	22801	**877-695-4272**	540-434-4475
McNeese State University Frazar Library PO Box 91415	Lake Charles	LA	70609	**800-622-3352**	337-475-5723
Metropolitan Library System 125 Tower Dr	Burr Ridge	IL	60527	**866-734-2004**	630-734-5000
Mississippi Library Commission 1221 Ellis Ave	Jackson	MS	39209	**800-647-7542**	601-961-4111
Monroe County Library System 3700 S Custer Rd	Monroe	MI	48161	**800-462-2050**	734-241-5277
National Library of Education 400 Maryland Ave SW	Washington	DC	20202	**800-424-1616**	202-205-5015
National Library of Medicine 8600 Rockville Pike	Bethesda	MD	20894	**888-346-3656**	301-594-5983
North Suburban Library System 200 W Dundee Rd	Wheeling	IL	60090	**800-374-7134**	847-459-1300
Northern Arizona University Cline Library PO Box 6022	Flagstaff	AZ	86011	**800-247-3380**	928-523-6802
Northern Waters Library Service 3200 E Lakeshore Dr	Ashland	WI	54806	**800-228-5684**	715-682-2365
Oil Creek District Library Center 2 Central Ave	Oil City	PA	16301	**888-645-2489**	814-678-3054
Oklahoma Dept of Libraries 200 NE 18th St	Oklahoma City	OK	73105	**800-522-8116**	405-521-2502
Pickaway County District Public Library 1160 N Court St	Circleville	OH	43113	**888-268-3756**	740-477-1644

Name / Address	City	State	ZIP	Toll-Free	Phone
Portage County District Library 10482 South St	Garrettsville	OH	44231	**800-500-5179**	330-527-4378
Prairie Area Library System 4021 Morsay Dr	Rockford	IL	61107	**877-542-7257**	815-229-0330
Putnam County Library System 601 College Rd	Palatka	FL	32177	**800-231-4045**	386-329-0126
Ronald Reagan Presidential Library & Museum 40 Presidential Dr	Simi Valley	CA	93065	**800-410-8354**	805-577-4000
Rutherford B Hayes Presidential Center Spiegel Grove	Fremont	OH	43420	**800-998-7737**	419-332-2081
Saint Mary Parish Library 206 Iberia St	Franklin	LA	70538	**800-732-8698**	337-828-1624
South Dakota State Library 800 Governors Dr	Pierre	SD	57501	**800-423-6665**	605-773-3131
Southeastern Library Network 1438 W Peachtree St NW Suite 200	Atlanta	GA	30309	**800-999-8558**	404-892-0943
State Library of Ohio 274 E 1st Ave	Columbus	OH	43201	**800-686-1532**	614-644-7061
University of Wisconsin Eau Claire McIntyre Library 105 Garfield Ave	Eau Claire	WI	54702	**877-267-1384**	715-836-3715
University of Wisconsin Stout Library 315 10th Ave E	Menomonie	WI	54751	**800-787-8688**	715-232-1215
Vernon Parish Library 1401 Nolan Trace	Leesville	LA	71446	**800-737-2231**	337-239-2027
Weber County Library 2464 Jefferson Ave	Ogden	UT	84401	**888-618-0564**	801-337-2617
Western New England College D'Amour Library 1215 Wilbraham Rd	Springfield	MA	01119	**800-325-1122**	413-782-1535
Wisconsin Dept of Public Instruction Library Services Div 125 S Webster St PO Box 7841	Madison	WI	53707	**800-441-4563**	608-266-3390

427 LIBRARY ASSOCIATIONS - STATE & PROVINCE

Name / Address	City	State	ZIP	Toll-Free	Phone
Alabama Library Assn (ALLA) 400 S Union St Suite 395	Montgomery	AL	36104	**877-563-5146**	334-263-1272
Library Assn of Alberta (LAA) 80 Baker Crescent NW	Calgary	AB	T2L1R4	**877-522-5550**	403-284-5818
Iowa Library Assn (ILA) 3636 Westown Pkwy Suite 202	West Des Moines	IA	50266	**800-452-5507**	515-273-5322
Minnesota Library Assn (MLA) 1619 Dayton Ave Suite 314	Saint Paul	MN	55104	**877-867-0982**	651-641-0982
New York Library Assn (NYLA) 252 Hudson Ave	Albany	NY	12210	**800-252-6952**	518-432-6952
Ohio Library Council (OLC) 2 Easton Oval Suite 525	Columbus	OH	43215	**800-436-5423**	614-416-2258
Ontario Library Assn (OLA) 100 Lombard St Suite 303	Toronto	ON	M5CIM3	**866-873-9867**	416-363-3388
Texas Library Assn (TLA) 3355 Bee Cave Rd Suite 401	Austin	TX	78746	**800-580-2852**	512-328-1518

428 LIBRARY SYSTEMS - REGIONAL - CANADIAN

Name / Address	City	State	ZIP	Toll-Free	Phone
Ontario Library Service North - Kirkland Lake 11 Station Rd S	Kirkland Lake	ON	P2N3H2	**800-461-6348**	705-567-3341
Parkland Regional Library 5404 56th Ave	Lacombe	AB	T4L1G1	**800-567-9024**	403-782-3850
Southern Ontario Library Service 151 Bloor St W 5th Fl	Toronto	ON	M5S1T6	**800-387-5765**	416-961-1669

429 LIGHT BULBS & TUBES

Name / Address	City	State	ZIP	Toll-Free	Phone
Advanced Lighting Technologies Inc 32000 Aurora Rd	Solon	OH	44139	**800-965-2677**	440-248-3510
AETEK UV Systems 1200 Windham Pkwy *Sales	Romeoville	IL	60446	**800-333-2304***	630-226-4200
American Power Products Inc 5525 Brooks St	Montclair	CA	91763	**800-533-2929**	909-988-0819
Emess Design Group LLC 1 Early St	Ellwood City	PA	16117	**800-688-2579**	724-758-0707
Eye Lighting International NA 9150 Hendricks Rd	Mentor	OH	44060	**888-665-2677**	440-350-7000
GE Consumer Products Appliance Pk	Louisville	KY	40225	**800-626-2000**	502-452-4311
Hanovia Corp 825 Lehigh Ave	Union	NJ	07083	**800-229-3666**	908-688-0050
Interlectric Corp 1401 Lexington Ave	Warren	PA	16365	**800-722-2184**	814-723-6061
Ledtronics Inc 23105 Kashiwa Ct	Torrance	CA	90505	**800-579-4875**	310-534-1505
Light Sources Inc 37 Robinson Blvd	Orange	CT	06477	**800-245-4458**	203-799-7877
Litetronics International Inc 4101 W 123rd St	Alsip	IL	60803	**800-860-3392**	708-389-8000
OSRAM Sylvania Glass Technologies 131 Portsmouth Ave	Exeter	NH	03833	**800-258-8290**	603-772-4331
Philips Lighting Co 200 Franklin Sq Dr	Somerset	NJ	08875	**800-555-0050**	732-563-3000
Sun Ergoline Inc 1 Walter Kratz Dr	Jonesboro	AR	72401	**800-643-0086**	870-935-1130
Technical Consumer Products Inc 300 Lena Dr	Aurora	OH	44202	**800-324-1496**	330-995-6111
Trojan Inc PO Box 850	Mount Sterling	KY	40353	**800-264-0526**	859-498-0526
Ushio America Inc 5440 Cerritos Ave	Cypress	CA	90630	**800-326-1960**	714-236-8600
UVP Inc 2066 W 11th St	Upland	CA	91786	**800-452-6788**	909-946-3197
Westinghouse Lighting Corp 12401 McNulty Rd *Orders	Philadelphia	PA	19154	**800-999-2226***	215-671-2000

430 LIGHTING EQUIPMENT - VEHICULAR

Name / Address	City	State	ZIP	Toll-Free	Phone
Astronics Corp 1801 Elmwood Ave *NASDAQ: ATRO*	Buffalo	NY	14207	**800-666-3722**	716-447-9013
ATC Lighting & Plastics Inc 107 N Eagle St	Geneva	OH	44041	**800-543-1943**	440-466-7670
Avtec Inc 6 Industrial Park	Cahokia	IL	62206	**800-552-8832**	618-337-7800
JW Speaker Corp PO Box 489	Germantown	WI	53022	**800-558-7288**	262-251-6660
OSRAM Sylvania Automotive Lighting Div 275 W Main St	Hillsboro	NH	03244	**800-729-3777**	603-464-5533
Peterson Mfg Co 4200 E 135th St	Grandview	MO	64030	**800-821-3490**	816-765-2000
Pyramid Technologies Inc 48 Elm St	Meriden	CT	06450	**888-479-7264**	203-238-0550
Speaker JW Corp PO Box 489	Germantown	WI	53022	**800-558-7288**	262-251-6660
Truck-Lite Co Inc 310 E Elmwood Ave *Cust Svc	Falconer	NY	14733	**800-562-5012***	716-665-6214
Vehicle Safety Mfg LLC 408 Central Ave	Newark	NJ	07107	**800-832-7233**	973-643-3000

431 LIGHTING FIXTURES & EQUIPMENT

Name / Address	City	State	ZIP	Toll-Free	Phone
Adjusta-Post Lighting Co 3960 Summit Rd	Norton	OH	44203	**800-321-2132**	330-745-1692
ALP Lighting Components Inc 6333 Gross Point Rd	Niles	IL	60714	**877-257-5841**	773-774-9550
American Fluorescent Corp 2345 N Ernie Krueger Cir	Waukegan	IL	60087	**800-873-2326**	847-249-5970
American Louver Co 7700 Austin Ave	Skokie	IL	60077	**800-323-4250**	847-470-3300
Ashley Lighting Inc 405 Industrial Dr	Trumann	AR	72472	**800-343-5267**	870-483-6181
Bieber Lighting Corp 970 W Manchester Blvd	Inglewood	CA	90301	**800-243-2375**	310-645-6789
Brinkmann Corp 4215 McEwen Rd	Dallas	TX	75244	**800-527-0717**	972-387-4939
Burton Medical Products Inc 21100 Lassen St *Cust Svc	Chatsworth	CA	91311	**800-444-9909***	818-701-8700
Canlyte 3015 Louis Amos	Lachine	QC	H8T1C4	**800-565-5486**	514-636-0670
Casual Lamps of California Inc 15000 S Broadway	Gardena	CA	90248	**800-824-8228**	310-323-0105
Catalina Lighting Inc 18191 NW 68th Ave	Miami	FL	33015	**800-966-7074**	305-558-4777
Chloride Systems 272 W Stage Park Service Rd	Burgaw	NC	28425	**800-403-6927**	910-259-1000
Color Kinetics Inc 10 Milk St Suite 1100 *NASDAQ: CLRK*	Boston	MA	02108	**888-385-5742**	617-423-9999
Commercial Lighting Industries 72650 Dinah Shore Dr	Palm Desert	CA	92260	**800-755-0155**	760-328-9431
Con-Tech Lighting 2783 Shermer Rd	Northbrook	IL	60062	**800-728-0312**	847-559-5500
Cooper Frederick Lamp Co Inc 2545 W Diversey Ave	Chicago	IL	60647	**800-693-5234**	773-384-0800
Corbett Lighting Inc 14625 E Clark Ave	City of Industry	CA	91745	**800-533-8769**	626-336-4511
Coronet Lighting 16210 S Avalon Blvd	Gardena	CA	90248	**800-421-2748**	310-327-6700
Day-Brite/Capri/Omega 776 S Green St	Tupelo	MS	38804	**800-955-5352**	662-842-7212
Dazor Mfg Corp 4483 Duncan Ave	Saint Louis	MO	63110	**800-345-9103**	314-652-2400
Dinico Products Inc 220 Goffle Rd	Hawthorne	NJ	07506	**800-225-0497**	973-636-9050
Doane LC Co PO Box 975	Essex	CT	06426	**800-447-5006**	860-767-8295
Edison Price Lighting Inc 41-50 22nd St	Long Island City	NY	11101	**800-275-8548**	718-685-0700
El Products 52 2nd St	Maxwell	TX	78656	**800-669-6766**	512-357-2776
ExceLine 2345 Vauxhall Rd	Union	NJ	07083	**800-334-2212**	908-964-7000
Fiberstars Inc 44259 Noble Dr *NASDAQ: FBST*	Fremont	CA	94538	**800-327-7877**	510-490-0719
Forecast 1600 Fleetwood Dr	Elgin	IL	60123	**800-234-0416**	847-622-0416
Frederick Cooper Lamp Co Inc 2545 W Diversey Ave	Chicago	IL	60647	**800-693-5234**	773-384-0800
Fulton Industries Inc 135 E Linfoot St	Wauseon	OH	43567	**800-537-5012**	419-335-3015
Gardco Lighting 2661 Alvarado St	San Leandro	CA	94577	**800-227-0758**	510-357-6900
Garrity Industries Inc 14 New Rd	Madison	CT	06443	**800-872-5483**	203-245-8383
GE Lighting Systems Inc 3010 Spartanburg Hwy	East Flat Rock	NC	28726	**877-798-6702**	828-693-2000
Genlyte Thomas Group LLC 10350 Ormsby Park Pl Suite 601	Louisville	KY	40223	**800-626-2847**	502-420-9500
Hanover Lantern Inc 350 Kindig Ln	Hanover	PA	17331	**800-233-7196**	717-632-6464
High End Systems Inc 2105 Gracy Farms Ln	Austin	TX	78758	**800-890-8989**	512-836-2242
Hinkley Lighting 12600 Berea Rd	Cleveland	OH	44111	**800-446-5539**	216-671-3300
Hipwell Mfg Co 831 W North Ave	Pittsburgh	PA	15233	**800-447-9355**	412-231-7310
Honeywell Airport Systems 2162 Union Pl	Simi Valley	CA	93065	**800-581-5591**	805-581-5591
Hydrel 12881 Bradley Ave	Sylmar	CA	91342	**800-750-9773**	818-362-9465
Indy Lighting Inc 12001 Exit 5 Pkwy	Fishers	IN	46038	**800-428-5212**	317-849-1233
International Lighting 1825 N 19th St	Saint Louis	MO	63106	**800-235-7050**	314-621-0600
Jimco Lamp & Mfg Co PO Box 490	Bono	AR	72416	**888-565-1388**	870-935-6820
Juno Lighting Inc 1300 S Wolf Rd *NASDAQ: JUNO*	Des Plaines	IL	60017	**800-323-5068**	847-827-9880
Justice Design Group Inc 261 S Figueroa St Suite 450 *Cust Svc	Los Angeles	CA	90012	**800-533-4799***	213-437-0102
Kenall Mfg 1020 Lakeside Dr	Gurnee	IL	60031	**800-453-6255**	847-360-8200
Kichler Lighting 7711 E Pleasant Valley Rd PO Box 318010	Cleveland	OH	44131	**888-659-8809**	216-573-1000
Koehler-Bright Star Inc 380 Stewart Rd *Cust Svc	Hanover Township	PA	18706	**800-631-3814***	570-825-1900
Kurtzon Lighting 1420 S Talman Ave	Chicago	IL	60608	**800-837-8937**	773-277-2121
Lamplight Farms Inc 4900 N Lilly Rd	Menomonee Falls	WI	53051	**800-645-5267**	262-781-9590
LC Doane Co PO Box 975	Essex	CT	06426	**800-447-5006**	860-767-8295
Legion Lighting Co Inc 221 Glenmore Ave	Brooklyn	NY	11207	**800-453-4466**	718-498-1770
Lightolier 631 Airport Rd	Fall River	MA	02720	**800-217-7722**	508-679-8131
Lights of America 611 Reyes Dr *Cust Svc	Walnut	CA	91789	**800-321-8100***	909-594-7883
Lithonia Lighting Co 1400 Lester Rd *Cust Svc	Conyers	GA	30012	**800-858-7763***	770-922-9000
LSI Industries Inc 10000 Alliance Rd *NASDAQ: LYTS*	Cincinnati	OH	45242	**800-274-2840**	513-793-3200
LSI Midwest Lighting Co PO Box 15097	Kansas City	KS	66115	**800-743-5483**	913-281-1100
Luxo Corp 200 Clearbrook Rd	Elmsford	NY	10523	**800-222-5896**	914-345-0067
Mag Instrument Inc 1950 S Sterling Ave	Ontario	CA	91761	**800-289-6241**	909-947-1006
Mario Industries Inc 2490 Paterson Ave SW	Roanoke	VA	24016	**800-458-1244**	540-342-1111
Mercury Lighting Products Co Inc 20 Audrey Pl	Fairfield	NJ	07004	**800-637-2879**	973-244-9444
Minka Group 1151 W Bradford Ct	Corona	CA	92882	**800-221-7977**	951-735-9220
Mule Lighting Inc 46 Baker St	Providence	RI	02905	**800-556-7690**	401-941-4446
Musco Lighting 100 1st Ave W	Oskaloosa	IA	52577	**800-825-6030**	641-673-0411
National Lighting Co Inc 522 Cortlandt St	Belleville	NJ	07109	**800-969-6285**	973-751-1600
Nightscaping 1705 E Colton Ave	Redlands	CA	92374	**800-544-4840**	909-794-2121
North Star Lighting Inc 2150 Parkes Dr	Broadview	IL	60155	**800-229-4330**	708-681-4330
Nulco Lighting PO Box 1328	Pawtucket	RI	02862	**800-668-5269**	401-728-5200
Omniglow Corp 96 Windsor St *Cust Svc	West Springfield	MA	01089	**800-762-7548***	413-739-8252
Paramount Industries Inc 304 N Howard St	Croswell	MI	48422	**800-521-5405**	810-679-2551
Pentair Pool Products Inc 1620 Hawkins Ave	Sanford	NC	27330	**800-831-7133**	919-566-8000
Prestigeline Inc 5 Inez Dr	Bay Shore	NY	11706	**800-776-5483**	631-273-3636
Quality Lighting 11500 Melrose Ave	Franklin Park	IL	60131	**800-545-1326**	847-451-0040
RAB Electric Mfg Inc 170 Ludlow Ave	Northvale	NJ	07647	**800-938-1010**	201-784-8600
Rayovac Corp 601 Rayovac Dr *NYSE: ROV*	Madison	WI	53711	**800-237-7000**	608-275-3340

Company / Address	City	State	ZIP	Toll-Free	Phone
Rejuvenation Inc 1100 SE Grand	Portland	OR	97214	**888-401-1900**	503-231-1900
Renova Lighting Systems Inc 300 High Point Ave	Portsmouth	RI	02871	**800-635-6682**	401-682-1850
Sea Gull Lighting Products Inc 301 W Washington St	Riverside	NJ	08075	**800-347-5483**	856-764-0500
Siemens Airfield Solutions Inc 977 Gahanna Pkwy	Columbus	OH	43230	**800-545-4157**	614-861-1304
SIMKAR Corp 700 Ramona Ave	Philadelphia	PA	19120	**800-523-3602**	215-831-7700
Spaulding Lighting Inc 1736 Dreman Ave *Cust Svc	Cincinnati	OH	45223	**800-221-5666***	513-541-3486
Sterner Lighting Systems Inc 351 Lewis Ave W PO Box 805	Winsted	MN	55395	**800-328-7480**	
Strand Lighting Inc 6603 Darin Way	Cypress	CA	90630	**800-733-0564**	714-230-8200
Tech Lighting LLC 7401 N Hamlin	Skokie	IL	60076	**800-522-5315**	847-410-4400
Tensor Corp 285 Commandants Way Suite 10	Chelsea	MA	02150	**800-872-5267**	617-884-7744
TIR Systems Ltd 7700 Riverfront Gate *TSE: TIR*	Burnaby	BC	V5J5M4	**800-663-2036**	604-294-8477
Translite Sonoma 22678 Broadway Suite 1	Sonoma	CA	95476	**800-473-3242**	707-996-6906
Tri-Lite Inc 1642 Besley Ct	Chicago	IL	60622	**800-322-5250**	773-384-7765
Troy-CSL Lighting Inc 14625 E Clark Ave	City of Industry	CA	91745	**800-533-8769**	626-336-4511
Uspar Enterprises Inc 13404 S Monte Vista Ave	Chino	CA	91710	**800-251-4612**	909-591-7506
Western Reflections 261 Commerce Way *Cust Svc	Gallatin	TN	37066	**800-521-2004***	615-451-9700
Westinghouse Lighting Corp 12401 McNulty Rd *Orders	Philadelphia	PA	19154	**800-999-2226***	215-671-2000
Wide-Lite Corp PO Box 606	San Marcos	TX	78667	**800-235-3214**	512-392-5021
Wilshire Mfg Co 645 Myles Standish Blvd	Taunton	MA	02780	**800-443-4695**	508-824-1970

432 LIME

Company / Address	City	State	ZIP	Toll-Free	Phone
Arkansas Lime Co 600 Limedale Rd *Cust Svc	Batesville	AR	72501	**800-252-5580***	870-793-2301
Ash Grove Cement Co PO Box 25900	Overland Park	KS	66225	**800-545-1886**	913-451-8900
Austin White Lime Co PO Box 9556 *Sales	Austin	TX	78766	**800-553-5463***	512-255-3646
Carmeuse North America 11 Stanwix St 11th Fl	Pittsburgh	PA	15222	**800-445-3930**	412-995-5500
Chemical Lime Co PO Box 985004	Fort Worth	TX	76185	**800-365-6724**	817-732-8164
Cheney Lime & Cement 478 Graystone Rd	Allgood	AL	35013	**800-752-8282**	205-625-3031
CLM Corp PO Box 16807	Duluth	MN	55816	**800-232-1302**	218-722-3981
Cutler-Magner Co PO Box 16807	Duluth	MN	55816	**800-232-1302**	218-722-3981
Dillon E & Co PO Box 160	Swords Creek	VA	24649	**800-234-8970**	276-873-6816
E Dillon & Co PO Box 160	Swords Creek	VA	24649	**800-234-8970**	276-873-6816
Global Stone Chemstone Corp 1696 Oranda Rd	Strasburg	VA	22657	**800-541-3172**	540-465-5161
Global Stone Saint Clair PO Box 160	Marble City	OK	74945	**800-366-5106**	918-775-4466
Global Stone Tenn Luttrell 486 Clinch Valley Rd *Sales	Luttrell	TN	37779	**800-467-5463***	865-992-3841
Graymont Dolime (OH) Inc PO Box 158	Genoa	OH	43430	**800-537-4489**	419-855-8336
Graymont PA Inc PO Box 448 *Orders	Bellefonte	PA	16823	**888-472-9086***	814-355-4744
Graymont Western US Inc 3950 S 700 E Suite 301	Salt Lake City	UT	84107	**800-814-7532**	801-262-3942
Greer Industries Inc PO Box 1900	Morgantown	WV	26507	**800-773-0412**	304-296-1751
Greer Lime Co PO Box 1900	Morgantown	WV	26507	**800-773-0412**	304-296-1751
LWB Refractories Co PO Box 1189	York	PA	17405	**800-233-1991**	717-848-1501
Mississippi Lime Co 7 Alby St	Alton	IL	62002	**800-437-5463**	618-465-7741
Rockwell Lime Co Inc 4110 Rockwood Rd	Manitowoc	WI	54220	**800-558-7711**	920-682-7771
Texas Lime Co PO Box 851 *Orders	Cleburne	TX	76033	**800-772-8000***	817-641-4433
US Lime & Minerals Inc 13800 Montfort Dr Suite 330 *NASDAQ: USLM*	Dallas	TX	75240	**800-991-5463**	972-991-8400
Western Lime Corp PO Box 57	West Bend	WI	53095	**800-433-0036**	262-334-3005

433 LIMOUSINE SERVICES

Company / Address	City	State	ZIP	Toll-Free	Phone
1st Corporate Limousine DBA Carey Executive Limousine 245 University Ave SW	Atlanta	GA	30315	**800-743-5466**	770-933-9000
A1 Worldwide Limousine Inc 69 Yorkville Ave Suite 205	Toronto	ON	M5R1B8	**877-537-5466**	416-922-5466
A Family Limousine 6311 Stirling Rd	Davie	FL	33314	**877-599-5466**	954-522-7455
Advantage Limousine Services Inc DBA ALS Transportation Inc 4605 Post Oak Pl Suite 211	Houston	TX	77027	**866-355-5466**	713-355-5466
Air Brook Limousine Inc 318 Overlook Ave	Rochelle Park	NJ	07662	**800-800-1990**	201-843-6100
AirportsPickup.com PO Box 652	New York	NY	10040	**877-800-6500**	212-927-7152
Alliance Limousine Inc 1800 N Highland Ave Suite 220	Los Angeles	CA	90028	**800-679-5466**	323-465-9406
ALS Transportation Inc 4605 Post Oak Pl Suite 211	Houston	TX	77027	**866-355-5466**	713-355-5466
Ambassador Limousine 3215 S Cinder Ln	Las Vegas	NV	89103	**888-519-5466**	702-362-6200
American Car Services 10853 N Central Expy Suite 2125	Dallas	TX	75231	**800-410-1399**	214-637-6600
American Coach Limousine 1433 W Jeffrey Dr	Addison	IL	60101	**888-709-5466**	630-629-0001
Arizona Limousines Inc 8900 N Central Ave Suite 101	Phoenix	AZ	85020	**800-678-0033**	602-267-7097
Avalon Executive Transportation Inc 6611 Hillcrest Ave Suite 333	Dallas	TX	75205	**866-513-5466**	214-824-1455
Bayview Limousine Service 15701 Nelson Pl S	Seattle	WA	98188	**800-606-7880**	206-824-6200
Bethany Limousine & Bus 2120 West Virginia Ave NE	Washington	DC	20037	**800-424-2971**	202-857-0440
BostonCoach 69 Norman St	Everett	MA	02149	**800-672-7676**	617-394-3900
Broward Limousine & Airport Service Inc 7540 NW 5th St	Plantation	FL	33317	**800-276-9274**	954-791-3000
Burgundy Global 336 W Passaic St 2nd Fl	Rochelle Park	NJ	07662	**800-546-6236**	201-291-4290
Carefree Lifestyle Inc 1031 5th St	Miami Beach	FL	33139	**866-589-8796**	305-534-3531
Carey Executive Limousine 245 University Ave SW	Atlanta	GA	30315	**800-743-5466**	770-933-9000
Carey International Inc 4530 Wisconsin Ave NW 5th Fl	Washington	DC	20016	**800-336-4646**	202-895-1200
Carey Limo International PO Box 3823	Bellevue	WA	98009	**888-227-3903**	212-777-2111
Classic Transportation Group 1600 Locust Ave	Bohemia	NY	11716	**800-666-4949**	631-567-5100
Connecticut Limousine LLC 230 Old Gate Ln	Milford	CT	06460	**800-472-5466**	203-878-6867
Cosmopolitan Limousine 1601 S Preston St	Louisville	KY	40217	**800-603-6594**	502-634-5466
Dav El Chauffeured Transportation Network 200 2nd St	Chelsea	MA	02150	**800-922-0343**	617-887-0900
DispatchOne 2835 Belvidere Rd Suite 309 PO Box 8787	Waukegan	IL	60079	**800-942-9363**	847-662-8802
Elite Limousine Service Inc 1059 12th Ave Suite E	Honolulu	HI	96816	**800-776-2098**	808-735-2431
Empire International Ltd 55 Walnut St	Norwood	NJ	07648	**800-451-5466**	201-784-1200
Executive Transportation Brokers Inc DBA AirportsPickup.com PO Box 652	New York	NY	10040	**877-800-6500**	212-927-7152
Executive Transportation Service Inc 7108 DeSoto Ave Suite 204	Canoga Park	CA	91303	**800-348-4010**	818-716-7727
Four Seasons Limousine Co 2432 W Peoria Ave Bldg 5 Suite 1112	Phoenix	AZ	85029	**877-548-1612**	623-979-8473
Gateway Limousines 1550 Gilbreth Rd	Burlingame	CA	94010	**800-486-7077**	650-345-7077
International Chauffeured Service Worldwide 53 E 34th St	New York	NY	10016	**800-266-5254**	212-213-0302
Leros First Class 6 Skyline Dr	Hawthorne	NY	10532	**800-825-3767**	914-747-2300
Limo One 1342 Shoulder Creek Ln	San Bruno	CA	94066	**877-490-5466**	415-531-6180
Marriton Limousine 13900 N IH-35 Suite J	Austin	TX	78728	**800-940-7007**	512-329-7007
Mears Transportation Group 324 W Gore St	Orlando	FL	32806	**800-759-5219**	407-422-4501
Olympic Limousine Service Inc 5005 Rts 33 & 34	Farmingdale	NJ	07727	**800-822-9797**	732-938-6666
Omni Limousine Inc 4440 E Cheyenne Ave Suite A	Las Vegas	NV	89115	**800-325-8003**	702-367-1000
PHL Limousine 101 Rt 130 Suite 6	Cinnaminson	NJ	08077	**866-264-5466**	856-786-7151
Pioneer Limousine Service 15643 Sherman Way	Van Nuys	CA	91406	**800-640-0700**	818-609-1566
Pontarelli Limousine Service 2225 W Hubbard St	Chicago	IL	60612	**800-322-5466**	312-226-5466
Regency Limousine International 23-57 83rd St	East Elmhurst	NY	11370	**866-754-5466**	718-507-4000
Royal Coachman Worldwide 540 Thomas Blvd	Orange	NJ	07050	**800-472-7433**	973-676-0200
Seattle Limousine Service PO Box 80205	Seattle	WA	98108	**800-274-3339**	206-762-3339
Starlite Limousines LLC 15111 N Hayden Rd Suite 300	Scottsdale	AZ	85260	**800-875-4104**	480-905-1234
US Coachways Inc 36 Richmond Terr Suite 304	Staten Island	NY	10301	**800-359-5991**	718-477-4242
VIPride.com 15111 N Hayden Rd Suite 300	Scottsdale	AZ	85260	**877-474-4847**	480-905-1234

434 LINEN & UNIFORM SUPPLY

Company / Address	City	State	ZIP	Toll-Free	Phone
Ace-Tex Enterprises 7601 Central St	Detroit	MI	48210	**800-444-3800**	313-834-4000
Alltex Inc 324 Taylor St	Manchester	NH	03103	**800-255-8391**	603-625-9722
AmeriPride Service Inc 10801 Wayzata Blvd *Cust Svc	Minnetonka	MN	55305	**800-595-3913***	952-738-4252
Arrow Uniform Rental Inc 6400 Monroe Blvd	Taylor	MI	48180	**800-552-7769**	313-299-5000
Capitol Uniform & Linen Service 195 Commerce Way	Dover	DE	19901	**800-323-1511**	302-674-1511
Cintas Corp 6800 Cintas Blvd *NASDAQ: CTAS*	Mason	OH	45262	**800-786-4367**	513-459-1200
Continental Linen Services 4200 Manchester Rd	Kalamazoo	MI	49001	**800-875-4636**	269-343-2551
Coyne Textile Services Inc 140 Cortland Ave	Syracuse	NY	13202	**800-672-6963**	315-475-1626
Domestic Linen Supply & Laundry Inc 3800 18th St	Detroit	MI	48208	**800-430-0871**	313-831-6700
G & K Services Inc 5995 Opus Pkwy Suite 500 *NASDAQ: GKSRA*	Minnetonka	MN	55343	**800-452-2737**	952-912-5500
Healthcare Services Group Inc 3220 Tillman Dr Suite 300 *NASDAQ: HCSG*	Bensalem	PA	19020	**800-523-2248**	215-639-4274
Industrial Towel & Uniform Inc 2700 S 160th St	New Berlin	WI	53151	**800-767-2487**	262-782-1950
Iron City Uniform Rental 6640 Frankstown Ave	Pittsburgh	PA	15206	**800-532-2010**	412-661-2001
Linens of the Week 713 Lamont St NW	Washington	DC	20010	**800-355-8874**	202-291-9200
Mission Linen Supply 702 E Montecito St *Hum Res	Santa Barbara	CA	93103	**877-641-3626***	805-682-8588
Model Coverall Service Inc 100 28th St SE	Grand Rapids	MI	49548	**800-968-6491**	616-241-6491
Morgan Services Inc 323 N Michigan Ave	Chicago	IL	60601	**888-966-7426**	312-346-3181
National Linen Service 1420 Peachtree St NE Suite 200	Atlanta	GA	30309	**800-225-4636**	404-853-6000
Nixon Uniform Service Inc 2925 Northeast Blvd *Sales	Wilmington	DE	19802	**888-649-6687***	302-764-7550
Overall Laundry Service Inc 7200 Hardeson Rd	Everett	WA	98203	**800-683-7255**	425-353-0800
Progress Linen Inc LLC 711 E Vermont St Suite 200	Indianapolis	IN	46202	**888-297-8049**	317-263-5260
Rental Uniform Co Inc 2117 Berry St	Kingsport	TN	37664	**800-214-5614**	423-247-4101
Roscoe Co 3535 W Harrison St *Cust Svc	Chicago	IL	60624	**800-722-5010***	773-722-5000
S & R Uniforms Inc 1833 14th St W	Bradenton	FL	34205	**800-553-4065**	941-748-1245
Sitex Corp 705 Pennel St	Henderson	KY	42420	**800-278-3537**	270-827-3537
Spirit Services 1021 Ware St	Albany	GA	31705	**888-774-7484**	229-436-1811
Sterling Textile Services 5909 Blair Rd NW	Washington	DC	20011	**800-626-9280**	202-723-9535
Textilease Corp 10733 Tucker St	Beltsville	MD	20705	**800-299-9708**	301-937-4555
UniFirst Corp 68 Jonspin Rd *NYSE: UNF*	Wilmington	MA	01887	**800-347-7888**	978-658-8888
Valiant Products Corp 2727 5th Ave W *Cust Svc	Denver	CO	80204	**800-347-2727***	303-892-1234
Van Dyne Crotty Inc 3233 Newmark Dr	Miamisburg	OH	45342	**800-236-9555**	937-236-1500
Western Uniform & Towel Service Inc 1707 N Mosley St	Wichita	KS	67214	**800-214-2342**	316-264-2342

435 LIQUOR STORES

Name / Address	City	State	Zip	Toll-Free	Phone
ABC Fine Wines & Spirits 8989 S Orange Ave	Orlando	FL	32824	**800-854-7283**	407-851-0000
BK Miller Co Inc 4501 B Auth Place	Suitland	MD	20746	**800-801-7632**	301-423-6200
Crown Liquors of Fort Lauderdale 910 NW 10th Pl	Fort Lauderdale	FL	33311	**888-563-9463**	954-763-6831
Jackson CB & Co Inc DBA Spec's Liquor Warehouse 2410 Smith St	Houston	TX	77006	**888-526-8787**	713-526-8787
Spec's Liquor Warehouse 2410 Smith St	Houston	TX	77006	**888-526-8787**	713-526-8787
Touring & Tasting 207 E Victoria St	Santa Barbara	CA	93101	**800-850-4370**	805-965-2813
Wine Club 2110 E McFadden Ave Suite E	Santa Ana	CA	92705	**800-966-5432**	714-835-6485
Wine.com Inc 114 Sansome St 6th Fl	San Francisco	CA	94104	**877-289-6886**	
Zachys Wine & Liquor Inc 16 East Pkwy	Scarsdale	NY	10583	**800-723-0241**	914-723-0241

436 LITIGATION SUPPORT SERVICES

Name / Address	City	State	Zip	Toll-Free	Phone
Alderson Reporting Co 1111 14th St NW Suite 400	Washington	DC	20004	**800-367-3376**	202-289-2260
Allied Court Reporters Inc 115 Phenix Ave	Cranston	RI	02920	**888-443-3767**	401-946-5500
Atkinson-Baker Inc 330 N Brand Blvd Suite 250	Glendale	CA	91203	**800-288-3376**	818-551-7300
Bowne DecisionQuest 2050 W 190th St Suite 205	Torrance	CA	90504	**800-327-2449**	310-618-9600
Compex Legal Services Inc 325 Maple Ave *Cust Svc	Torrance	CA	90503	**800-426-6739***	310-782-1801
CT Corp 3 Winners Cir 3rd Fl	Albany	NY	12205	**800-624-0099**	518-451-8000
Depobook Reporting Services 713 10th St	Modesto	CA	95354	**800-830-8885**	209-544-6466
DepoNet 25 A Vreeland Rd	Florham Park	NJ	07932	**800-337-6638**	
FTI Consulting Inc 900 Bestgate Rd Suite 100 *NYSE: FCN*	Annapolis	MD	21401	**800-334-5701**	410-224-8770
Hahn & Bowersock Inc 151 Kalmus Dr Suite L-1	Costa Mesa	CA	92626	**800-660-3187**	714-549-3700
Hutchings Court Reporters LLC 5701 S Eastern Ave Suite 530	Los Angeles	CA	90040	**800-697-3210**	323-888-6300
Jane Rose Reporting 74 5th Ave	New York	NY	10011	**800-825-3341**	715-472-4631
Jury Research Institute 2617 Danville Blvd PO Box 100	Alamo	CA	94507	**800-233-5879**	925-932-5663
Lawyer Concierge Ltd 2155 Fairway Cir	Duluth	GA	30096	**888-852-5651**	770-638-1888
LegaLink 160 Commonwealth Ave Suite U-3	Boston	MA	02116	**800-662-1466**	617-262-7717
Professional Shorthand Reporters Inc 601 Poydras St Suite 1615	New Orleans	LA	70130	**800-536-5255**	504-529-5255
Quorum A Lanier Co 950 Blue Gentian Rd Suite 100	Eagan	MN	55121	**800-328-4454**	651-234-5678
Starr Litigation Services Inc 1201 Grand Ave	West Des Moines	IA	50265	**800-627-8277**	515-224-1616
TrialGraphix Inc 155 NE 40th St	Miami	FL	33137	**800-334-5403**	305-576-5400
US Legal Support Inc 519 N Sam Houston Pkwy E Suite 200	Houston	TX	77060	**800-622-1107**	713-653-7100
Z-Axis Corp 5445 DTC Pkwy Suite 450	Greenwood Village	CO	80111	**800-827-2947**	303-713-0200

437 LIVESTOCK - WHOL

SEE ALSO Agricultural Products - Cattle Ranches, Farms, Feedlots (Beef Cattle); Agricultural Products - Hog Farms

Name / Address	City	State	Zip	Toll-Free	Phone
Blue Grass Stockyard 375 Lisle Industrial Ave	Lexington	KY	40511	**800-621-3972**	859-255-7701
Central Livestock Assn 310 Market Ln	South Saint Paul	MN	55075	**800-733-1844**	651-451-1844
D & S Cattle Co 2167 SR 66 PO Box 172	Zolfo Springs	FL	33890	**800-522-0534**	863-735-1112
Empire Livestock Marketing LLC 5001 Brittonfield Pkwy	East Syracuse	NY	13035	**800-462-8802**	315-433-9129
Equity Co-op Livestock Sales Assn E 10890 Penny Ln	Baraboo	WI	53913	**800-362-3989**	608-356-8311
Farmers Livestock Marketing Assn 840 IL Rt 127 PO Box 435	Greenville	IL	62246	**800-743-9110**	618-664-1432
High Plains Livestock Exchange LLC 28601 Hwy 34 PO Box 218	Brush	CO	80723	**866-842-5115**	970-842-5115
Kidron Auction Inc 4885 Kidron Rd	Kidron	OH	44636	**800-589-9749**	330-857-2641
Lewiston Sales Inc 21241 Dutchmans Crossing Rd	Lewiston	MN	55952	**800-732-6334**	507-523-2112
Meridian Order Buyers Inc 5125 Hwy 45 N PO Box 1566	Meridian	MS	39301	**800-833-4566**	601-483-8207
Mo-Kan Livestock Markets Inc RR 2 Box 152	Butler	MO	64730	**800-887-8156**	660-679-6535
O & S Cattle Co 100 Stockyards Rd Suite 106	South Saint Paul	MN	55075	**800-328-0124**	651-455-1102
Prairie Livestock Inc Barton Ferry Rd	West Point	MS	39773	**800-647-6350**	662-494-5651
Producers Livestock Marketing Assn 4809 S 114th St	Omaha	NE	68137	**800-257-4046**	402-597-9189
Stockmen's Livestock Market Inc E Hwy 50 PO Box 280	Yankton	SD	57078	**800-532-0952**	605-665-9641
Thomas Cattle Co Inc 14451 NE 20 St	Williston	FL	32696	**800-654-1871**	352-528-4518
United Producers Inc 5909 Cleveland Ave	Columbus	OH	43231	**800-456-3276**	614-890-6666
Winner Livestock Auction Co 31690 Livestock Barn Rd	Winner	SD	57580	**800-201-0451**	605-842-0451

438 LIVESTOCK & POULTRY FEEDS - PREPARED

Name / Address	City	State	Zip	Toll-Free	Phone
Acco Feeds Inc 1025 China St	Abilene	TX	79602	**800-592-4472**	325-672-3271
ADM Alliance Nutrition Inc 1000 N 30th St	Quincy	IL	62301	**800-292-3333**	217-222-7100
AG Partners Inc PO Box 467	Lake City	MN	55041	**800-772-2990**	651-345-3328
AG Processing Inc PO Box 2047	Omaha	NE	68103	**800-247-1345**	402-496-7809
Agri-King Inc 18246 Waller Rd	Fulton	IL	61252	**800-435-9560**	815-589-2525
AL Gilbert Co 304 N Yosemite Ave	Oakdale	CA	95361	**800-847-1721**	209-847-1721
Alabama Farmers Co-op Inc 121 Somerville Rd NE	Decatur	AL	35601	**800-737-6843**	256-353-6843
Albion Laboratories Inc 101 N Main St	Clearfield	UT	84015	**800-453-2406**	801-773-4631
Alderman Cave Feeds 158 N Main St PO Box 217	Winters	TX	79567	**800-588-3333**	325-754-4546
American Proteins Inc 4705 Leland Dr	Cumming	GA	30041	**800-346-7476**	770-886-2250
Bagdad Roller Mills Inc 5740 Elmburg Rd PO Box 7	Bagdad	KY	40003	**800-928-3333**	502-747-8968
Belstra Milling Co Inc 424 15th St PO Box 460	Demotte	IN	46310	**800-276-2789**	219-987-4343
Bioproducts Inc 320 Springside Dr Suite 300	Fairlawn	OH	44333	**800-722-7242**	330-665-1999
BioZyme Inc 6010 Stockyards Expy	Saint Joseph	MO	64504	**800-821-3070**	816-238-3326
Blair Milling & Elevator Co 1000 Main St PO Box 437	Atchison	KS	66002	**800-633-2931**	913-367-2310
Blue Seal Feeds Inc 15 Buttrick Rd *Cust Svc	Londonderry	NH	03053	**800-367-2730***	603-437-3400
Buckeye Nutrition 330 E Schultz Ave PO Box 505	Dalton	OH	44618	**800-417-6460**	330-828-2251
Cargill Inc Animal Nutrition Div 15407 McGinty Rd W	Wayzata	MN	55391	**800-227-4455**	952-984-1920
Cargill Inc North America 15407 McGinty Rd	Wayzata	MN	55391	**800-227-4455**	952-742-7575
Cumberland Valley Co-op Assn 908 Mt Rock Rd	Shippensburg	PA	17257	**800-488-2197**	717-532-2191
Cutler-Dickerson Co Inc 507 College Ave	Adrian	MI	49221	**800-968-5191**	517-265-5191
Dairymen's Feed & Supply Co-op 323 E Washington St	Petaluma	CA	94952	**800-862-4699**	707-763-1585
Darling International Inc 251 O'Connor Ridge Blvd Suite 300 *AMEX: DAR*	Irving	TX	75038	**800-800-4841**	972-717-0300
DSM Food Specialties Inc 2675 Eisenhower Ave Valley Forge Corporate Ctr	Eagleville	PA	19403	**800-662-4478**	610-650-8480
Eagle Roller Mill Co 1101 Airport Rd	Shelby	NC	28150	**800-223-9108**	704-487-5061
Eastern Farmers Co-op 401 S Railroad Ave	Jasper	MN	56144	**800-865-2773**	507-348-3911
Effingham Equity Inc 201 W Roadway	Effingham	IL	62401	**800-223-1337**	217-342-4101
Elenbaas Co 411 W Front St	Sumas	WA	98295	**800-808-6954**	360-988-5811
Farm Service Elevator Co 3735 County Rd 5 SW	Willmar	MN	56201	**800-328-8842**	320-235-8870
Farmer's Co-op 201 E Orin St	Gordon	NE	69343	**800-252-0898**	308-282-0898
Farmland Industries Inc 12200 N Ambassador Dr	Kansas City	MO	64163	**800-821-8000**	816-713-7000
Feed Products Inc 1000 W 47th Ave	Denver	CO	80211	**800-332-8285**	303-455-3646
First Cooperative Assn 113 S Lewis Ave	Cleghorn	IA	51014	**800-594-9424**	712-436-2224
FL Emmert Co Inc 2007 Dunlap St	Cincinnati	OH	45214	**800-441-3343**	513-721-5808
Flint River Mills Inc PO Box 280 *Cust Svc	Bainbridge	GA	39818	**800-841-8502***	229-246-2232
FM Brown's Sons Inc 127 S Furnace St PO Box 67	Birdsboro	PA	19508	**800-362-6455**	610-582-2741
Form-A-Feed Inc 740 Bowman St	Stewart	MN	55385	**800-422-3649**	320-562-2413
Formax Feeds Co 980 Molly Pond Rd	Augusta	GA	30901	**800-241-2200**	706-722-6681
Franklin Feed & Supply Co 1977 Philadelphia Ave	Chambersburg	PA	17201	**800-722-2074**	717-264-6148
Friona Industries LP 500 S Taylor St Suite 601	Amarillo	TX	79101	**800-658-6014**	806-374-1811
Furst-McNess Co 120 E Clark St	Freeport	IL	61032	**800-435-5131**	815-235-6151
Goldsboro Milling Co 938 Millers Chapel Rd	Goldsboro	NC	27534	**800-768-7823**	919-778-3130
Grange Co-op Supply Assn 89 Alder St	Central Point	OR	97502	**800-888-6317**	541-664-1261
Griffin Industries 4221 Alexandria Pike	Cold Spring	KY	41076	**800-743-7413**	859-781-2010
Harvest Land Co-op 711 Front St	Morgan	MN	56266	**800-245-5819**	507-249-3196
Hogslat Midwest Inc 200 N Meridian Line Rd	Camden	IN	46917	**800-735-4135**	574-686-2573
Hubbard Feeds Inc 424 N Riverfront Dr	Mankato	MN	56001	**800-869-7219**	507-388-9400
JD Heiskell & Co 116 W Cedar St	Tulare	CA	93274	**800-366-1886**	559-757-3135
John A Van Den Bosch Co 4511 Holland Ave *Cust Svc	Holland	MI	49422	**800-968-6477***	616-848-2000
JS West Milling Co Inc 501 9th St *Cust Svc	Modesto	CA	95353	**800-675-9378***	209-577-3221
Kay Dee Feed Co Inc 1919 Grand Ave	Sioux City	IA	51106	**800-831-4815**	712-277-2011
Kemin Industries Inc 2100 Maury St	Des Moines	IA	50317	**800-247-7496**	515-266-2111
Lakeland Animal Nutrition 2725 S Combee Rd	Lakeland	FL	33803	**800-682-6144**	863-682-4995
Land O'Lakes Farmland Feed LLC 4001 Lexington Ave N	Arden Hills	MN	55112	**800-328-9680**	651-481-2222
Land O'Lakes Inc Western Feed Div PO Box 818	Caldwell	ID	83606	**800-452-4052**	208-459-3689
Lucta USA Inc 1829 Stanley St	Northbrook	IL	60062	**800-323-5341**	847-272-6650
M & M Livestock Products Co 310 E Broadway St	Eagle Grove	IA	50533	**800-247-4820**	515-448-5371
Manna Pro Corp 707 Spirit 40 Pk Dr Suite 150	Chesterfield	MO	63005	**800-690-9908**	636-681-1700
Mark Hershey Farms Inc 479 Horseshoe Pike	Lebanon	PA	17042	**888-801-3301**	717-867-4624
Merrick's Inc 2415 Parview Rd PO Box 620307	Middleton	WI	53562	**800-637-7425**	608-831-3440
Midland-Impact LLC 103 Lincoln St	Danville	IN	46122	**800-525-0272**	317-745-4491
Milk Specialties Co PO Box 278	Dundee	IL	60118	**800-323-5424**	847-426-3411
Morgan Grain & Feed Co 260 Front St PO Box 248	Morgan	MN	56266	**800-449-3157**	507-249-3157
Mountaire Farms of North Carolina 203 Morris Farm Rd	Candor	NC	27229	**800-284-4528**	910-974-3232
Moyer & Son Inc 113 E Reliance Rd	Souderton	PA	18964	**800-345-0419**	215-723-6000
Novus International Inc 530 Maryville Center Dr	Saint Louis	MO	63141	**888-906-6887**	314-576-8886
Oberbeck Feed Co 700 Walnut St	Highland	IL	62249	**800-632-2012**	618-654-2387
OMCO Inc 214 E Mill St	Odon	IN	47562	**800-274-0203**	812-636-7362
Pennfield Corp 711 Rohrerstown Rd	Lancaster	PA	17604	**800-732-0467**	717-299-2561
Pied Piper Mills Inc 423 E Lake Dr	Hamlin	TX	79520	**800-338-4610**	325-576-3684
Prairie Lakes Co-op 524 Pulp St PO Box 580	Starbuck	MN	56381	**800-808-1626**	320-239-2226
Preble Feed & Grain Inc Werling Dr PO Box 52	Preble	IN	46782	**800-566-4452**	260-547-4452
Producers Co-op Assoc 300 E Buffalo PO Box 323	Girard	KS	66743	**800-442-2809**	620-724-8241
Ralco-Mix Products Inc 1600 Hahn Rd	Marshall	MN	56258	**800-533-5306**	507-532-5748
Rangen Inc 115 13th Ave S	Buhl	ID	83316	**800-657-6446**	208-543-6421
Rivard's Quality Seeds Inc 103 Main St	Argyle	MN	56713	**888-543-6638**	218-437-6638
RMC Inc 1040 S High St	Harrisonburg	VA	22801	**800-726-7625**	540-434-5333
Seminole Stores Inc PO Box 940	Ocala	FL	34478	**800-683-1881**	352-732-4143
Star Milling Co 24067 Water St	Perris	CA	92570	**800-733-6455**	951-657-3143
Stillwater Milling Co 512 E 6th St	Stillwater	OK	74074	**800-364-6804**	405-372-3445
Strauss Inc 648 E 1100 N PO Box 149	North Manchester	IN	46962	**800-982-7172**	260-982-2181
Texas Farm Products Co 915 S Fredonia St	Nacogdoches	TX	75961	**800-392-3110**	936-564-3711

				Toll-Free	Phone
Triple Crown Nutrition Inc 319 Barry Ave S Suite 303	Wayzata	MN	55391	**800-451-9916**	952-473-6330
Trouw Nutrition 115 Executive Dr.	Highland	IL	62249	**800-870-9233**	618-654-2070
Ursa Farmers Co-op Inc 202 Maple Ave PO Box 8	Ursa	IL	62376	**800-964-2115**	217-964-2111
Van Den Bosch John A Co 4511 Holland Ave *Cust Svc	Holland	MI	49422	**800-968-6477***	616-848-2000
Vita Plus Corp 1508 W Badger Rd	Madison	WI	53713	**800-362-8334**	608-256-1988
Wendland's Farm Products Inc 405 S 2nd St	Temple	TX	76504	**800-792-3038**	254-773-5211
Western Stockmens Inc 223 Rodeo Ave	Caldwell	ID	83605	**800-624-9425**	208-459-0777
Wolfkill Feed & Fertilizer Corp PO Box 578	Monroe	WA	98272	**800-525-4539**	360-794-7065
Zeigler Brothers Inc 400 Gardner Station Rd	Gardners	PA	17324	**800-841-6800**	717-677-6181

439 LOGGING

				Toll-Free	Phone
Canal Wood LLC PO Box 260010	Conway	SC	29528	**866-587-1460**	843-488-9663
Greif Inc 425 Winter Rd *NYSE: GEF*	Delaware	OH	43015	**800-354-7343**	740-549-6000
Herbert C Haynes Inc Box 96	Winn	ME	04495	**800-432-7867**	207-736-3412
Klukwan Inc PO Box 209	Haines	AK	99827	**800-558-5926**	907-766-2211
Midwest Walnut Co 1914 Postevin St	Council Bluffs	IA	51503	**800-592-5688**	712-325-9191
Roseburg Forest Products Co PO Box 1088	Roseburg	OR	97470	**800-245-1115**	541-679-3311
Western Forest Products Inc 435 Trunk Rd 3rd Fl *TSE: WEF*	Duncan	BC	V9L2P9	**800-880-7471**	250-748-3711

440 LOGISTICS SERVICES (TRANSPORTATION & WAREHOUSING)

SEE ALSO Freight Forwarders; Marine Services; Rail Transport Services; Trucking Companies; Warehousing & Storage - Commercial Warehousing

				Toll-Free	Phone
A Duie Pyle Inc PO Box 564	West Chester	PA	19381	**800-523-5020**	610-696-5800
Access Business Group LLC 7575 Fulton St E *Cust Svc	Ada	MI	49355	**800-253-6500***	616-787-5358
AIMS Logistics 311 Moore Ln	Collierville	TN	38017	**877-406-9966**	901-854-5777
AN Deringer Inc PO Box 1309	Saint Albans	VT	05478	**800-448-8108**	802-524-8110
Associated Global Systems Inc 3333 New Hyde Park Rd *Cust Svc	New Hyde Park	NY	11042	**800-645-8300***	516-627-8910
BAX Global Inc 440 Exchange	Irvine	CA	92602	**800-225-5229**	714-442-4500
BDP International Inc 510 Walnut St	Philadelphia	PA	19106	**888-999-2379**	215-629-8900
BDS Worldwide Inc 9362 Dielman Industrial Dr	Saint Louis	MO	63132	**800-325-4074**	314-817-0051
Bender Group 345 Parr Cir	Reno	NV	89512	**800-621-9402**	775-788-8800
CaseStack Inc 2850 Ocean Pk Blvd Suite 100	Santa Monica	CA	90405	**800-684-0522**	310-473-8885
Caterpillar Logistics Services Inc 500 N Morton Ave	Morton	IL	61550	**800-447-6434**	800-240-2126
CH Robinson Worldwide Inc 8100 Mitchell Rd Suite 200 *NASDAQ: CHRW*	Eden Prairie	MN	55344	**800-247-5644**	952-937-8500
Clipper Exxpress Inc 9014 Heritage Pkwy Suite 300	Woodridge	IL	60517	**800-678-2547**	630-739-0700
Crowley Logistics Inc 9487 Regency Sq Blvd	Jacksonville	FL	32225	**800-874-6769**	904-727-2200
CSX Intermodal Inc 301 W Bay St	Jacksonville	FL	32202	**800-542-2754**	904-633-1000
Deringer AN Inc PO Box 1309	Saint Albans	VT	05478	**800-448-8108**	802-524-8110
DHL Logistics 3435 Airborne Rd	Wilmington	OH	45177	**800-637-5502**	
DSC Logistics Inc 1750 S Wolf Rd	Des Plaines	IL	60018	**800-372-1960**	847-390-6800
Eagle Global Logistics 15350 Vickery Dr *NASDAQ: EAGL*	Houston	TX	77032	**800-821-9956**	281-618-3100
EGL Inc DBA Eagle Global Logistics 15350 Vickery Dr *NASDAQ: EAGL*	Houston	TX	77032	**800-821-9956**	281-618-3100
Exel 570 Polaris Pkwy	Westerville	OH	43082	**800-272-1052**	614-865-8500
Expeditors International of Washington Inc 1015 3rd Ave 12th Fl *NASDAQ: EXPD*	Seattle	WA	98104	**800-284-7474**	206-674-3400
FedEx Supply Chain Services Inc 5455 Darrow Rd	Hudson	OH	44236	**800-588-3020**	330-342-3000
GeoLogistics Corp 1251 E Dyer Rd Suite 200	Santa Ana	CA	92705	**888-543-1239**	714-513-3000
Horizon Air Freight 152-15 Rockaway Blvd	Jamaica	NY	11434	**800-221-6028**	718-528-3800
Hub Group Inc 3050 Highland Pkwy Suite 100 *NASDAQ: HUBG*	Downers Grove	IL	60515	**800-964-2515**	630-271-3600
Hunt JB Transport Services Inc 615 JB Hunt Corporate Dr *NASDAQ: JBHT*	Lowell	AR	72745	**800-643-3622**	479-820-0000
JB Hunt Transport Services Inc 615 JB Hunt Corporate Dr *NASDAQ: JBHT*	Lowell	AR	72745	**800-643-3622**	479-820-0000
Kenco Group Inc 2001 Riverside Dr	Chattanooga	TN	37401	**800-365-7189**	423-756-5552
Kintetsu World Express USA Inc 100 Jericho Quadrangle Suite 326	Jericho	NY	11753	**800-275-4045**	516-933-7100
Landstar Logistics Inc 13410 Sutton Park Dr S	Jacksonville	FL	32224	**800-872-9400**	904-399-8909
Leicht Transfer & Storage Co 1401 State St PO Box 2447	Green Bay	WI	54306	**800-338-5665**	920-432-8632
Matson Integrated Logistics Inc 17 W 635 Butterfield Rd Suite 600	Villa Park	IL	60181	**800-325-0325**	630-203-3500
Menlo Worldwide Inc 1 Lagoon Dr Suite 400	Redwood City	CA	94065	**800-227-1981**	650-596-4000
MHF Logistical Solutions Inc 800 Cranberry Woods Dr Suite 450	Cranberry Township	PA	16066	**877-452-9300**	724-772-9800
National Freight Inc 71 W Park Ave	Vineland	NJ	08360	**800-922-5088**	856-691-7000
Navis Logistics Network 5675 DTC Blvd Suite 280	Greenwood Village	CO	80111	**800-525-6309**	303-741-6626
Pacer Global Logistics 6805 Perimeter Dr	Dublin	OH	43016	**800-837-7584**	614-923-1400
Panalpina Inc 1776 On-the-Green 67 E Park Pl	Morristown	NJ	07960	**866-202-0377**	973-683-9000
Pilot Air Freight Corp 314 N Middletown Rd *Cust Svc	Lima	PA	19037	**800-447-4568***	610-891-8100
Progistix-Solutions Inc 20 Norelco Dr	North York	ON	M9L1S2	**800-277-6447**	416-401-7000
Pyle A Duie Inc PO Box 564	West Chester	PA	19381	**800-523-5020**	610-696-5800
ROACO Logistics Services 970 N Oaklawn Ave	Elmhurst	IL	60126	**877-941-0400**	630-941-0400
Robinson CH Worldwide Inc 8100 Mitchell Rd Suite 200 *NASDAQ: CHRW*	Eden Prairie	MN	55344	**800-247-5644**	952-937-8500
Ryder System Inc 3600 NW 82nd Ave *NYSE: R*	Miami	FL	33166	**800-327-3399**	305-593-3726
Schneider Logistics Inc 3101 S Packerland Dr	Green Bay	WI	54313	**800-525-9358**	920-592-2000
Seko Worldwide Inc 1100 Arlington Heights Rd	Itasca	IL	60143	**800-323-1235**	630-919-4800
SOS (Store Opening Solutions) 800 Middle Tennessee Blvd	Murfreesboro	TN	37129	**877-388-9262**	615-867-0858
Store Opening Solutions (SOS) 800 Middle Tennessee Blvd	Murfreesboro	TN	37129	**877-388-9262**	615-867-0858
Thoroughbred Direct Intermodal Services 2260 Butler Pike Suite 400	Plymouth Meeting	PA	19462	**877-250-2902**	610-567-3360
TNT Logistics North America 10751 Deerwood Park Blvd Suite 200	Jacksonville	FL	32256	**888-564-4789**	904-928-1400
UPS Supply Chain Solutions 12380 Morris Rd	Alpharetta	GA	30005	**866-822-5336**	678-746-4365
USF Logistics Inc 2122 York Rd Suite 300	Oak Brook	IL	60523	**800-723-9100**	630-754-3000
Vimich Traffic Logistics Inc 12201 Tecumseh Rd E	Tecumseh	ON	N8N1M3	**800-284-1045**	519-735-6933

441 LONG-TERM CARE FACILITIES

SEE ALSO Long-Term Care Facilities Operators; Retirement Communities; Veterans Nursing Homes - State

				Toll-Free	Phone
Braintree Landing Skilled Nursing & Rehabilitation Center 95 Commercial St	Braintree	MA	02184	**800-498-8322**	781-848-3678
Briarcliff Haven Healthcare & Rehabiliation Center 1000 Briarcliff Rd NE	Atlanta	GA	30306	**800-454-5909**	404-875-6456
Cambridge Manor 8530 Township Line Rd	Indianapolis	IN	46260	**800-454-5909**	317-876-9955
Casa Colina Center for Rehabilitation 255 E Bonita Ave	Pomona	CA	91767	**800-926-5462**	909-596-7733
Heartland Health Care Center Miami Lakes 5725 NW 186th St	Hialeah	FL	33015	**800-427-4397**	305-625-9857
Heatherbank Rehabilitation & Skilled Nursing Center 745 Chiques Hill Rd	Columbia	PA	17512	**800-840-9075**	717-684-7555
Heritage Center 1201 W Buena Vista Rd	Evansville	IN	47710	**800-704-0700**	812-429-0700
Holyoke Rehabilitation Center 260 Easthampton Rd	Holyoke	MA	01040	**800-394-9733**	413-538-9733
Kindred Hospital Greensboro 2401 Southside Blvd	Greensboro	NC	27406	**877-836-2671**	336-271-2800
Lowell Health Care Center 19 Varnum St	Lowell	MA	01850	**800-966-5644**	978-454-5644
ManorCare Health Services - Arlington Heights 715 W Central Rd	Arlington Heights	IL	60005	**888-427-8020**	847-392-2020
ManorCare Health Services - Oak Lawn East 9401 S Kostner Ave	Oak Lawn	IL	60453	**800-427-1902**	708-423-7882
Middleton Village Nursing & Rehabilitation Center 6201 Elmwood Ave	Middleton	WI	53562	**877-836-2676**	608-831-8300
North Adams Common Nursing Home 175 Franklin St	North Adams	MA	01247	**800-278-0021**	413-664-4041
Presbyterian SeniorCare-Westminster Place 1215 Hulton Rd	Oakmont	PA	15139	**877-772-6500**	412-828-5600
South Davis Community Hospital 401 South 400 E	Bountiful	UT	84010	**877-913-2847**	801-295-2361
South Mountain Restoration Center 10058 S Mountain Rd	South Mountain	PA	17261	**877-765-0331**	717-749-3121
Twinbrook Medical Center 3805 Field St	Erie	PA	16511	**800-427-9149**	814-898-5600
Voorhees Pediatric Facility 1304 Laurel Oak Rd	Voorhees	NJ	08043	**888-877-3100**	856-346-3300

442 LONG-TERM CARE FACILITIES OPERATORS

				Toll-Free	Phone
Active Services Corp 1500 Urban Center Dr Suite 200	Vestavia Hills	AL	35242	**800-805-7430**	205-970-3300
Advocat Inc 277 Mallory Station Rd Suite 130	Franklin	TN	37067	**800-771-7576**	615-771-7575
American Religious Town Hall Inc 745 N Buckner Blvd	Dallas	TX	75218	**800-783-9828**	214-328-9828
Atria Retirement & Assisted Living 501 S 4th St Suite 140	Louisville	KY	40202	**877-719-1600**	502-719-1600
Balanced Care Corp 1215 Manor Dr	Mechanicsburg	PA	17055	**888-227-3145**	717-796-6100
Beverly Enterprises Inc 1000 Beverly Way *NYSE: BEV*	Fort Smith	AR	72919	**877-238-3759**	479-201-2000
CabelTel International Corp 14185 Dallas Pkwy Suite 650 *AMEX: GBR*	Dallas	TX	75254	**888-407-8400**	972-407-8400
Centennial HealthCare Corp 303 Perimeter Ctr N Suite 500	Atlanta	GA	30346	**800-334-1488**	770-698-9040
Diversified Senior Services Inc 915 W 4th St	Winston-Salem	NC	27101	**800-721-8182**	336-724-1000
ElderWood Senior Care 7 Limestone Dr	Williamsville	NY	14221	**888-826-9663**	716-633-3900
Emeritus Corp 3131 Elliott Ave Suite 500 *AMEX: ESC*	Seattle	WA	98121	**800-429-4828**	206-298-2909
Genesis ElderCare 101 E State St	Kennett Square	PA	19348	**800-699-1520**	610-444-6350
Genesis HealthCare Corp 101 E State St *NASDAQ: GHCI*	Kennett Square	PA	19348	**800-699-1520**	610-444-6350
HCF Inc 1100 Shawnee Rd	Lima	OH	45805	**800-999-2110**	419-999-2010
Kindred Healthcare Inc 680 S 4th Ave *NASDAQ: KIND*	Louisville	KY	40202	**800-545-0749**	502-596-7300
Mariner Health Care Inc 1 Ravinia Dr Suite 1500	Atlanta	GA	30346	**800-929-4762**	678-443-7000

Classified Section

	City	State	ZIP	Toll-Free	Phone
Regent Assisted Living Inc 121 SW Morrison St Suite 1000	Portland	OR	97204	**888-853-7468**	503-227-4000
Sun Healthcare Group Inc 101 Sun Ave NE *NASDAQ: SUNH*	Albuquerque	NM	87109	**800-856-2512**	505-821-3355
Sunrise Senior Living Inc 7902 Westpark Dr *NYSE: SRZ*	McLean	VA	22102	**800-929-4124**	703-273-7500

443 LOTTERIES, GAMES, SWEEPSTAKES

SEE ALSO Games & Gaming

	City	State	ZIP	Toll-Free	Phone
Colorado Lottery 201 W 8th St Suite 600	Pueblo	CO	81003	**800-999-2959**	719-546-2400
Illinois Lottery 101 W Jefferson St	Springfield	IL	62702	**800-252-1775**	217-524-5155
Pennsylvania State Lottery 2850 Turnpike Industrial Dr	Middletown	PA	17057	**800-692-7481**	717-986-4699
pogo.com Inc 300 California St 8th Fl	San Francisco	CA	94104	**800-804-0836**	415-778-3500
Texas Lottery Commission PO Box 16630	Austin	TX	78761	**800-375-6886**	512-344-5000
WinDough.com Inc 11669 Countryview Ln	Boca Raton	FL	33428	**888-668-6278**	
Youbet.com Inc 1950 Sawtelle Blvd Suite 180 *NASDAQ: UBET*	Los Angeles	CA	90025	**888-968-2388**	310-444-3300

444 LUGGAGE, BAGS, CASES

SEE ALSO Handbags, Totes, Backpacks; Leather Goods - Personal

	City	State	ZIP	Toll-Free	Phone
Airway Industries Inc/Atlantic Products Corp Airway Pk *Cust Svc	Ellwood City	PA	16117	**800-245-1750***	724-752-0012
Anvil Cases 15730 Salt Lake Ave	City of Industry	CA	91745	**800-359-2684**	626-968-4100
Calzone Case Co 225 Black Rock Ave *Cust Svc	Bridgeport	CT	06605	**800-243-5152***	203-367-5766
CH Ellis Co Inc 2432 Southeastern Ave *Sales	Indianapolis	IN	46201	**800-466-3351***	317-636-3351
Coach Inc 516 W 34th St *NYSE: COH*	New York	NY	10001	**800-444-3611**	212-594-1850
Delsey Luggage 6735 Business Pkwy Suite A	Elkridge	MD	21075	**800-558-3344**	410-796-5655
Eagle Creek Inc 3055 Enterprise Ct *Cust Svc	Vista	CA	92081	**800-874-9925***	760-599-6500
Forward Industries Inc 1801 Green Rd Suite E *NASDAQ: FORD*	Pompano Beach	FL	33064	**800-872-3935**	954-419-9544
High Sierra Sport Co 880 Corporate Woods Pkwy	Vernon Hills	IL	60061	**800-323-9590**	847-913-1100
Johnston Mfg 753 Arrow Grand Cir	Covina	CA	91722	**877-891-8899**	626-967-1511
LC Industries 401 N Western Ave	Chicago	IL	60612	**800-539-6255**	312-455-0500
Leather Specialty Co 2690 W Airport Blvd	Sanford	FL	32771	**888-771-0200**	407-323-1830
LeSportsac Inc 358 5th Ave 8th Fl	New York	NY	10001	**800-486-2247**	212-736-6262
Mercury Luggage Mfg Co DBA Mercury Luggage/Seward Trunk 4843 Victor St	Jacksonville	FL	32207	**800-874-1885**	904-733-9595
Mercury Luggage/Seward Trunk 4843 Victor St	Jacksonville	FL	32207	**800-874-1885**	904-733-9595
Monarch Luggage Co Inc 2580 Prospect Ct	Aurora	IL	60504	**800-747-2802**	630-585-6030
Pedro Companies 106 E 10th St	Saint Paul	MN	55101	**800-328-9284**	651-224-9491
Platt Luggage Inc 4051 W 51st St	Chicago	IL	60632	**800-222-1555**	773-838-2000
RJ Singer International Inc 4801 W Jefferson Blvd *Sales	Los Angeles	CA	90016	**800-824-9035***	323-735-1717
Robert Mfg Co Inc 4000 E 10th Ct	Hialeah	FL	33013	**800-780-3684**	305-691-5311
Samsonite Corp 11200 E 45th Ave	Denver	CO	80239	**800-223-7267**	303-373-2000
Singer RJ International Inc 4801 W Jefferson Blvd *Sales	Los Angeles	CA	90016	**800-824-9035***	323-735-1717
SKB Corp 434 W Levers Pl	Orange	CA	92867	**800-410-2024**	714-637-1252
Targus Inc 1211 N Miller St	Anaheim	CA	92806	**800-950-5122**	714-765-5555
TGL 300 Wilson Ave	Norwalk	CT	06854	**800-587-1584**	203-853-4747
Travelpro USA 700 Banyan Trail	Boca Raton	FL	33431	**888-741-7471**	561-998-2824
Vera Bradley Designs 2208 Production Rd	Fort Wayne	IN	46808	**800-975-8372**	260-482-4673
Zero Mfg Inc 500 W 200 North	North Salt Lake	UT	84054	**800-545-1030**	801-298-5900

445 LUGGAGE STORFS

	City	State	ZIP	Toll-Free	Phone
Bottega Veneta Inc 635 Madison Ave	New York	NY	10022	**877-362-1715**	212-371-5511
Coach Inc 516 W 34th St *NYSE: COH*	New York	NY	10001	**800-444-3611**	212-594-1850
Crouch & Fitzgerald 400 Madison Ave	New York	NY	10017	**800-627-6824**	212-755-5888
Fendi NA Inc 720 5th Ave 5th Fl	New York	NY	10019	**800-336-3469**	212-767-0100
Louis Vuitton NA Inc 19 E 57th St *Cust Svc	New York	NY	10022	**866-884-8866***	212-931-2000
Vuitton Louis NA Inc 19 E 57th St *Cust Svc	New York	NY	10022	**866-884-8866***	212-931-2000

446 MACHINE SHOPS

	City	State	ZIP	Toll-Free	Phone
American Grinding & Machine Co 2000 N Mango Ave	Chicago	IL	60639	**877-988-4343**	773-889-4343
Bowe Machine Co 2527 State St	Bettendorf	IA	52722	**800-822-2693**	563-355-4777
Brisco Inc 251 Buckeye Cove Rd	Swannanoa	NC	28778	**877-585-2737**	828-298-1510
Carlson Tool & Mfg Corp PO Box 85	Cedarburg	WI	53012	**800-532-2252**	262-377-2020
Chalmers & Kubeck Inc 150 Commerce Dr	Aston	PA	19014	**800-242-5637**	610-494-4300
Craft Machine Works Inc 2102 48th St	Hampton	VA	23661	**888-350-6006**	757-380-8615
EBW Inc 2814 McCracken St	Muskegon	MI	49441	**800-475-5151**	231-755-1671
Femco Machine Co 754 S Main St Ext	Punxsutawney	PA	15767	**800-458-3445**	814-938-9763
Furmanite America 101 Old Underwood Rd Suite F	La Porte	TX	77571	**800-444-5572**	281-842-5100
Highway Machine Co Inc (HMC) RR 1 Box 208A	Princeton	IN	47670	**800-803-0112**	812-385-3639
Hughes RS Co Inc Saunders Div 905 Allen Ave *Sales	Glendale	CA	91201	**800-845-6500***	818-953-3000
Industrial Tool Inc 9210 52nd Ave N *Sales	Minneapolis	MN	55428	**800-776-4455***	763-533-7244
Keystone Honing Co PO Box 187	Titusville	PA	16354	**800-458-3847**	814-827-9641
Kurt Mfg Co 5280 Main St NE	Minneapolis	MN	55421	**800-458-7811**	763-572-1500
LaVezzi Precision Inc 999 Regency Dr	Glendale Heights	IL	60139	**800-323-1772**	630-582-1230
Lemco Tool Corp 1850 Metzger Ave	Cogan Station	PA	17728	**800-233-8713**	570-494-0620
Lindquist Machine Corp PO Box 2327	Green Bay	WI	54306	**888-499-0831**	920-713-4100
Lith-O-Roll Corp 9521 Telstar Ave	El Monte	CA	91731	**800-423-4176**	626-579-0340
Machine Works at Essex Inc 75 Crystal Ave	New London	CT	06320	**800-724-0528**	860-447-3935
Meyer Tool Inc 3055 Colerain Ave	Cincinnati	OH	45225	**800-286-7362**	513-681-7362
Micro Instrument Corp 1199 Emerson St	Rochester	NY	14606	**800-200-3150**	585-458-3150
Myrmo & Sons Inc PO Box 3215	Eugene	OR	97403	**800-683-7040**	541-747-4561
Onamac Industries Inc 11504 Airport Rd Bldg G	Everett	WA	98204	**877-742-2718**	425-743-6676
PCI Energy Services 1 Energy Dr	Lake Bluff	IL	60044	**800-345-6108**	847-680-8100
Precision Screw Thread Corp S 82 W 19275 Apollo Dr	Muskego	WI	53150	**800-828-3431**	262-679-9000
Process Equipment Co 6555 S SR-202	Tipp City	OH	45371	**800-424-0325**	937-667-4451
Process Industries 3860 N River Rd	Schiller Park	IL	60176	**800-860-1631**	847-671-1631
Saunders Div RS Hughes Co Inc 905 Allen Ave *Sales	Glendale	CA	91201	**800-845-6500***	818-953-3000
Scheirer Machine Co Inc 3200 Industrial Blvd	Bethel Park	PA	15102	**800-448-4590**	412-833-6500
Scheu & Kniss Inc PO Box 2947	Louisville	KY	40201	**800-635-6303**	502-635-6303
Schmiede Corp 1865 Riley Creek Rd PO Box 1630	Tullahoma	TN	37388	**800-535-1851**	931-455-4801
Special Projects Mfg Co 7601 Wyatt Dr	Fort Worth	TX	76108	**800-342-7458**	817-246-2461
Standard Locknut Inc 1045 E 169th St	Westfield	IN	46074	**800-783-6887**	317-867-0100
Steward Machine Co Inc 3911 13th Ave N	Birmingham	AL	35234	**800-394-6461**	205-841-6461
TurboCare Chicopee 2140 Westover Rd	Chicopee	MA	01022	**800-887-2622**	413-593-0500
Twin City EDM 7940 Rancher Rd	Fridley	MN	55432	**800-269-8919**	763-783-7808
Van Dusen & Meyer Inc 50 Parrott Dr	Shelton	CT	06484	**800-760-6242**	203-929-6355
Vescio Threading Co 14002 Anson Ave	Santa Fe Springs	CA	90670	**800-361-4218**	562-802-1868
Walco Tool & Engineering Co 18954 Airport Rd	Lockport	IL	60441	**800-808-9365**	815-834-0225
Weaver Industries Inc 425 S 4th St	Denver	PA	17517	**800-292-7670**	717-336-7507
Xtek Inc 11451 Reading Rd	Cincinnati	OH	45241	**888-332-9835**	513-733-7800

447 MACHINE TOOLS - METAL CUTTING TYPES

SEE ALSO Machine Tools - Metal Forming Types; Metalworking Devices & Accessories

	City	State	ZIP	Toll-Free	Phone
Abbco Inc 26 N Garden Ave	Bensenville	IL	60106	**866-986-6546**	630-595-7115
Acme Mfg Co 4240 N Atlantic Blvd	Auburn Hills	MI	48326	**888-340-2263**	248-393-7300
Agie Ltd 9009-G Perimeter Woods Dr	Charlotte	NC	28216	**800-438-5021**	704-927-8900
Allied Tool Products 9334 N 107th St	Milwaukee	WI	53224	**800-558-5147**	414-355-8280
Amada America 7025 Firestone Blvd	Buena Park	CA	90621	**800-854-3567**	714-739-2111
Amada Cutting Technologies 14849 E Northam St	La Mirada	CA	90638	**800-877-4729**	714-670-1704
American Heller Corp 15825 Leone Dr	Macomb	MI	48042	**800-950-2487**	586-677-2300
Automation Assoc Inc 416 Campus Dr	Arlington Heights	IL	60004	**800-927-7348**	847-255-4500
Babin Machine Works Inc PO Box 2007	Beaumont	TX	77704	**800-269-1274**	409-892-1231
Boyar-Schultz Div WA Whitney Corp 650 Race St	Rockford	IL	61105	**800-435-2823**	815-964-6771
Charmilles Technologies Corp 560 Bond St	Lincolnshire	IL	60069	**800-282-1336**	847-913-5300
Cincinnati Lamb 2200 Litton Ln	Hebron	KY	41048	**800-934-0735**	859-534-4600
Cincinnati Lamb 5523 E Nine-Mile Rd	Warren	MI	48091	**800-521-0166**	586-497-6000
Crafts Technologies 91 Joey Dr	Elk Grove Village	IL	60007	**800-323-6802**	847-758-3100
Cross Huller 13900 Lakeside Cir	Sterling Heights	MI	48313	**800-243-8620**	586-566-2400
Darex Corp PO Box 277	Ashland	OR	97520	**800-547-0222**	541-488-2224
Davenport Industries LLC 167 Ames St	Rochester	NY	14611	**800-344-5748**	585-235-4545
Detroit Broach Co 2750 Paldan Dr	Auburn Hills	MI	48326	**800-383-6978**	248-370-0600
DeVlieg Bullard II Inc 10100 Forest Hills Rd	Rockford	IL	61115	**800-248-8120**	815-282-4100
DoALL Co 254 N Laurel Ave	Des Plaines	IL	60016	**800-955-8191**	847-824-8191
DS Technology Inc 7861 Palace Dr	Cincinnati	OH	45249	**800-531-0135**	513-247-2590
EH Wachs Co 100 Shepard St	Wheeling	IL	60090	**800-323-8185**	847-537-8800
Ex-Cell-O Machine Tools 6015 Center Dr	Sterling Heights	MI	48312	**800-837-6277**	586-939-1330
Extrude Hone Corp 1 Industry Blvd PO Box 1000	Irwin	PA	15642	**800-367-1109**	724-863-5900
Flow International Corp 23500 64th Ave S *NASDAQ: FLOW*	Kent	WA	98032	**800-446-3569**	253-850-3500
Giddings & Lewis LLC 142 Doty St PO Box 590	Fond du Lac	WI	54936	**800-343-2847**	920-921-9400
Giddings & Lewis Machine Tools 142 Doty St PO Box 590	Fond du Lac	WI	54936	**800-343-2847**	920-921-9400
Gould & Eberhardt Gear Machinery Corp 2 Sutton Rd PO Box 190	Webster	MA	01570	**888-241-4757**	508-943-5001
Grob Inc 1731 10th Ave	Grafton	WI	53024	**800-225-6481**	262-377-1400
Hanchett Mfg Inc 906 N State St	Big Rapids	MI	49307	**800-454-7463**	231-796-7678
Hardinge Inc 1 Hardinge Dr *NASDAQ: HDNG*	Elmira	NY	14902	**800-843-8801**	607-734-2281
Hause Machines Inc 809 S Pleasant St	Montpelier	OH	43543	**800-932-8665**	419-485-3158
Hudson Machinery Worldwide PO Box 831	Haverhill	MA	01831	**800-346-5113**	978-374-0303
Huffman Corp 1050 Huffman Way	Clover	SC	29710	**800-523-4833**	803-222-4561
Hurco Cos Inc 1 Technology Way *NASDAQ: HURC* ■ *Sales	Indianapolis	IN	46268	**800-634-2416***	317-293-5309
Hydromat Inc 11600 Adie Rd	Saint Louis	MO	63043	**888-432-0070**	314-432-4644
Hypertherm Inc PO Box 5010	Hanover	NH	03755	**800-643-0030**	603-643-3441
ITW Heartland 3600 W Lake Ave	Glenview	IL	60025	**800-724-6166**	847-724-7500

Company	City	State	ZIP	Toll-Free	Phone
Jasco Cutting Tools 195 Saint Paul St	Rochester	NY	14604	**800-868-1074**	585-546-1254
John J Adams Die Corp 10 Nebraska St	Worcester	MA	01604	**800-356-0110**	508-757-3894
Kennametal Inc 1600 Technology Way *NYSE: KMT* ■ *Cust Svc	Latrobe	PA	15650	**800-446-7738***	724-539-5000
Kennametal Inc Metalworking Systems Development 1600 Technology Way	Latrobe	PA	15650	**800-446-7738**	724-539-5000
Kennametal Inc Mining & Construction Div 1600 Technology Way	Latrobe	PA	15650	**800-446-7738**	724-539-5000
Koike Aronson Inc PO Box 307	Arcade	NY	14009	**800-252-5232**	585-492-2400
Komatsu America Corp Cutting Technologies Div 265 Ballardvale St	Wilmington	MA	01887	**800-707-2767**	978-658-1640
Kyocera Tycom Corp 17862 Fitch Ave	Irvine	CA	92614	**888-848-9266**	
Makino Inc 7680 Innovation Way	Mason	OH	45040	**888-625-4661**	513-573-7200
Manchester Tool Co 5142 Manchester Rd *Cust Svc	Akron	OH	44319	**800-237-8789***	330-644-8853
McLean Inc 3409 E Miraloma Ave *Cust Svc	Anaheim	CA	92806	**800-451-2424***	714-996-5451
Meyers WF Co 1017 14th St PO Box 426	Bedford	IN	47421	**800-457-4055**	812-275-4485
NNT Corp 1320 Norwood Ave	Itasca	IL	60143	**800-556-9999**	630-875-9600
North American Products Corp 1180 Wernsing Rd *Cust Svc	Jasper	IN	47546	**800-634-8665***	812-482-2000
Oliver Instrument Co 831 Division St PO Box 189	Adrian	MI	49221	**877-668-0885**	517-263-2132
Pioneer Broach Co 6434 Telegraph Rd	Los Angeles	CA	90040	**800-621-1945**	323-728-1263
Republic-Lagun Machine Tool Co 1000 E Carson St	Carson	CA	90745	**800-421-2105**	310-518-1100
Rex-Buckeye Co Inc 1230A W 58th St	Cleveland	OH	44102	**800-932-0011**	216-939-9000
Rogers Tool Works Inc PO Box 9	Rogers	AR	72757	**800-525-9855**	479-636-1515
Rottler Mfg 8029 S 200th St	Kent	WA	98032	**800-452-0534**	253-872-7050
S & M Machine Service Inc 206 E Highland Dr	Oconto Falls	WI	54154	**800-323-1579**	920-846-8130
S & S Machinery Co 140 53rd St	Brooklyn	NY	11232	**800-540-9723**	718-492-7400
Sandvik Coromant Co 1702 Nevins Rd *Cust Svc	Fair Lawn	NJ	07410	**800-726-3845***	201-794-5000
Savage WJ Co Inc 100 Indel Ave PO Box 156	Rancocas	NJ	08073	**877-779-8763**	609-267-8000
Servo Products Co 34940 Lakeland Blvd	East Lake	OH	44095	**800-521-7359**	440-975-9684
Setco Sales Co 5880 Hillside Ave	Cincinnati	OH	45233	**800-543-0470**	513-941-5110
Snappy Air Distribution Products 1011 11th Ave SE	Detroit Lakes	MN	56501	**800-328-2044**	218-847-9258
South Bend Lathe 3300 W Sample St Suite 1200	South Bend	IN	46619	**800-245-2843**	574-289-7771
Southwestern Industries Inc 2615 Homestead Pl	Rancho Dominguez	CA	90220	**800-421-6875**	310-608-4422
Sunnen Products Co 7910 Manchester Ave	Saint Louis	MO	63143	**800-325-3670**	314-781-2100
Technidrill Systems Inc 429 Portage Blvd	Kent	OH	44240	**800-914-5863**	330-724-5516
Thermal Dynamics Corp 82 Benning St	West Lebanon	NH	03784	**800-752-7621**	603-298-5711
Tornos Technologies US Corp 70 Pocono Rd	Brookfield	CT	06804	**800-243-5027**	203-775-4319
Toyoda Machinery USA Inc 316 W University Dr	Arlington Heights	IL	60004	**800-257-2985**	847-253-0340
Turmatic Systems Inc 11600 Adie Rd	Saint Louis	MO	63043	**888-432-0070**	314-993-0600
Valenite Inc 1675 Whitcomb Ave *Cust Svc	Madison Heights	MI	48071	**800-488-9112***	248-589-1000
Vernon Tool Co Ltd 503 Jones Rd	Oceanside	CA	92054	**800-452-1542**	760-433-5860
WA Whitney Corp Boyar-Schultz Div 650 Race St	Rockford	IL	61105	**800-435-2823**	815-964-6771
Wachs EH Co 100 Shepard St	Wheeling	IL	60090	**800-323-8185**	847-537-8800
WF Meyers Co 1017 14th St PO Box 426	Bedford	IN	47421	**800-457-4055**	812-275-4485
Whitney Tool Co Inc 906 R St	Bedford	IN	47421	**800-536-1971**	812-275-4491
Wisconsin Machine Tool Corp 3225 Gateway Rd Suite 100	Brookfield	WI	53045	**800-243-3078**	262-317-3048
WJ Savage Co Inc 100 Indel Ave PO Box 156	Rancocas	NJ	08073	**877-779-8763**	609-267-8000

448 MACHINE TOOLS - METAL FORMING TYPES

SEE ALSO Machine Tools - Metal Cutting Types; Metalworking Devices & Accessories; Rolling Mill Machinery; Tool & Die Shops

Company	City	State	ZIP	Toll-Free	Phone
Alva Allen Industries Inc 1001-15 N 3rd St PO Box 427 *Cust Svc	Clinton	MO	64735	**800-343-5657***	660-885-3331
Amada America Inc 7025 Firestone Blvd	Buena Park	CA	90621	**800-626-6612**	714-739-2111
Atlas Technologies Inc 201 S Alloy Dr	Fenton	MI	48430	**800-536-3162**	810-629-6663
Badge A Minit Ltd 345 N Lewis Ave	Oglesby	IL	61348	**800-223-4103**	815-883-8822
Bliss Clearing Niagara 1004 E State St	Hastings	MI	49058	**800-642-5477**	269-948-3300
Bradbury Co Inc PO Box 667	Moundridge	KS	67107	**800-397-6394**	620-345-6394
CA Lawton Co Inc 1860 Enterprise Dr	De Pere	WI	54115	**800-842-6888**	920-337-2470
CJ Winter Machine Technologies Inc 167 Ames St	Rochester	NY	14611	**800-288-7655**	585-429-5000
Cleveland Steel Tool Co 474 E 105th St *Cust Svc	Cleveland	OH	44108	**800-446-4402***	216-681-7400
Cyril Bath Co 1610 Airport Rd	Monroe	NC	28110	**800-801-1418**	704-289-8531
DR Sperry & Co 112 N Grant St	North Aurora	IL	60542	**888-997-9297**	630-892-4361
Edwards Mfg Co 1107 Sykes St PO Box 166	Albert Lea	MN	56007	**800-373-8206**	507-373-8206
Eitel Presses Inc 97 Pinedale Industrial Rd	Orwigsburg	PA	17961	**800-458-2218**	570-366-0585
Erie Press Systems 1253 W 12th St PO Box 4061	Erie	PA	16512	**800-222-3608**	814-455-3941
Grant Assembly Technologies 90 Silliman Ave	Bridgeport	CT	06605	**800-227-2150**	203-366-4557
Greenerd Press & Machine Co Inc 41 Crown St	Nashua	NH	03061	**800-877-9110**	603-889-4101
Grob Inc 1731 10th Ave	Grafton	WI	53024	**800-225-6481**	262-377-1400
H & H Tooling Inc 30505 Clemens Rd	Westlake	OH	44145	**800-808-6840**	440-250-3204
Hudson Machinery Worldwide PO Box 831	Haverhill	MA	01831	**800-346-5113**	978-374-0303
JA Richards Co 903 N Pitcher St	Kalamazoo	MI	49007	**800-253-3288**	269-343-4684
JF Helmold & Brothers Inc 901 Morse Ave	Elk Grove Village	IL	60007	**800-323-8898**	847-437-7085
Kinefac Corp 156 Goddard Memorial Dr	Worcester	MA	01603	**800-458-5941**	508-754-6891
L & F Industries Corp Div of Erie Press Systems 1253 W 12th St PO Box 4061	Erie	PA	16512	**800-222-3608**	814-455-3941
Lawton CA Co Inc 1860 Enterprise Dr	De Pere	WI	54115	**800-842-6888**	920-337-2470
Magnum Integrated Technologies 4 Thomas Dr Unit 5	Westbrook	ME	04092	**800-830-0642**	207-854-9791
Mate Precision Tooling Inc 1295 Lund Blvd	Anoka	MN	55303	**800-328-4492**	763-421-0230
Murata Machinery USA Inc 2120 I-85 S	Charlotte	NC	28208	**800-428-8469**	704-875-9280

Company	City	State	ZIP	Toll-Free	Phone
National Diecasting Machinery & Kard Trim Presses 33 Plan Way Bldg 7	Warwick	RI	02886	**800-242-1253**	401-737-3005
Pacific Press Technologies 714 Walnut St	Mount Carmel	IL	62863	**800-851-3586**	618-262-8666
Pacific Roller Die Co 1321 W Winton Ave	Hayward	CA	94545	**800-253-6463**	510-782-7242
PCC Specialty Products Inc Reed-Rico Div 18 Industrial Dr *Cust Svc	Holden	MA	01520	**800-343-6068***	508-829-4491
Reed-Rico Div PCC Specialty Products Inc 18 Industrial Dr *Cust Svc	Holden	MA	01520	**800-343-6068***	508-829-4491
Richards JA Co 903 N Pitcher St	Kalamazoo	MI	49007	**800-253-3288**	269-343-4684
Sperry DR & Co 112 N Grant St	North Aurora	IL	60542	**888-997-9297**	630-892-4361
Strippit/LVD 12975 Clarence Ctr Rd	Akron	NY	14001	**800-828-1527**	585-542-4511
Tetrahedron Assoc Inc PO Box 710157	San Diego	CA	92171	**800-958-3872**	619-661-0552
Threaded Rod Co Inc 1929 Columbia Ave	Indianapolis	IN	46202	**800-354-3330**	317-921-3000
Tools for Bending Inc 194 W Dakota Ave *Cust Svc	Denver	CO	80223	**800-873-3305***	303-777-7170
US Machine Tools Corp 94 Custer St	West Hartford	CT	06110	**800-664-0013**	860-953-8306
WA Whitney Co 650 Race St	Rockford	IL	61105	**800-435-2823**	815-964-6771
Williams White & Co 600 River Dr	Moline	IL	61265	**877-797-7650**	309-797-7650
Winter CJ Machine Technologies Inc 167 Ames St	Rochester	NY	14611	**800-288-7655**	585-429-5000
Wrentham Steel Products Co 30 Kendrick St	Wrentham	MA	02093	**800-251-2166**	508-384-2166
Wysong & Miles Co Inc 4820 US 29 N	Greensboro	NC	27405	**800-299-7664**	336-621-3960

449 MAGAZINES & JOURNALS

SEE ALSO Publishing Companies - Periodicals Publishers

449-1 Agriculture & Farming Magazines

Company	City	State	ZIP	Toll-Free	Phone
American Quarter Horse Journal PO Box 200	Amarillo	TX	79168	**800-291-7323**	806-376-4811
Beef 7900 International Dr Suite 300 *Cust Svc	Minneapolis	MN	55425	**800-441-0294***	952-851-9329
Breeders Journal 1525 River Rd	DeForest	WI	53532	**800-356-5331**	608-846-6211
Cooperative Partners PO Box 64089	Saint Paul	MN	55164	**800-867-6747**	651-355-5151
Dairy Herd Management Magazine 10901 W 84th Terr	Shawnee Mission	KS	66201	**800-255-5113**	913-438-8700
Farm Industry News 7900 International Dr Suite 300 *Cust Svc	Minneapolis	MN	55425	**800-441-0294***	952-851-9329
Farm Journal 1818 Market St 31st Fl	Philadelphia	PA	19103	**800-523-1538**	215-557-8900
Farm & Ranch Living 5400 S 60th St	Greendale	WI	53129	**800-344-6913**	414-423-0100
Farm Show PO Box 1029	Lakeville	MN	55044	**800-834-9665**	952-469-5572
Iowa Farm Bureau Spokesman 5400 University Ave	West Des Moines	IA	50266	**800-442-3276**	515-225-5413
Kansas Living 2627 KFB Plaza	Manhattan	KS	66503	**800-406-3053**	785-587-6000
Pork Report PO Box 9114	Des Moines	IA	50306	**800-456-7675**	515-223-2600
Progressive Farmer 2100 Lakeshore Dr	Birmingham	AL	35209	**800-366-4712**	205-445-6000
Soybean Digest 7900 International Dr Suite 300 *Cust Svc	Minneapolis	MN	55425	**800-441-0294***	952-851-4677
Successful Farming 1716 Locust St *Cust Svc	Des Moines	IA	50309	**800-374-3276***	515-284-3000

449-2 Art & Architecture Magazines

Company	City	State	ZIP	Toll-Free	Phone
American Artist Magazine 770 Broadway	New York	NY	10003	**800-745-8922**	646-654-5500
Architectural Digest 6300 Wilshire Blvd 11th Fl	Los Angeles	CA	90048	**800-234-2347**	323-965-3400
Architectural Record 2 Penn Plaza 9th Fl *Cust Svc	New York	NY	10121	**888-867-6395***	212-904-2594
Architecture 770 Broadway	New York	NY	10003	**800-745-8922**	646-654-5500
Art in America Magazine 575 Broadway *Cust Svc	New York	NY	10012	**800-925-8059***	212-941-2800
Art & Antiques Magazine 9 E 40th St 7th Fl	New York	NY	10016	**800-533-8484**	212-686-5557
Art & Auction Magazine 11 E 36th St 9th Fl *Cust Svc	New York	NY	10016	**800-777-8718***	212-447-9555
Artforum International Magazine 350 7th Ave 19th Fl	New York	NY	10001	**800-783-4903**	212-475-4000
Artist's Magazine The 4700 E Galbraith Rd	Cincinnati	OH	45236	**800-283-0963**	513-531-2690
ARTnews Magazine 48 W 38th St 9th Fl *Cust Svc	New York	NY	10018	**800-284-4625***	212-398-1690
Bomb Magazine 594 Broadway Suite 905	New York	NY	10012	**888-475-5987**	212-431-3943
HOW Design 4700 E Galbraith Rd *Cust Svc	Cincinnati	OH	45036	**800-333-1115***	513-531-2690
Interior Design Magazine PO Box 16898	North Hollywood	CA	91615	**800-900-0804**	
Metropolis Magazine 61 W 23rd St 4th Fl	New York	NY	10010	**800-344-3046**	212-627-9977
Pastel Journal 4700 E Galbraith Rd	Cincinnati	OH	45236	**800-283-0963**	513-531-2690
Preservation Magazine 1785 Massachusetts Ave NW	Washington	DC	20036	**800-944-6847**	202-588-6000
Southwest Art Magazine 5444 Westheimer St Suite 1440	Houston	TX	77056	**800-621-3963**	713-296-7900
Step Inside Design Magazine 6000 N Forest Park Dr	Peoria	IL	61614	**800-255-8800**	309-688-8800
Watercolor Magic 4700 E Galbraith Rd *Cust Svc	Cincinnati	OH	45236	**800-811-9834***	513-531-2690
Wildlife Art Magazine 1428 E Cliff Rd	Burnsville	MN	55337	**800-221-6547**	952-736-1020

449-3 Automotive Magazines

Company	City	State	ZIP	Toll-Free	Phone
4-Wheel & Off-Road Magazine 6420 Wilshire Blvd	Los Angeles	CA	90048	**800-800-4294**	323-782-2000
American Motorcyclist 13515 Yarmouth Dr	Pickerington	OH	43147	**800-262-5646**	614-856-1900
AutoWeek 1155 Gratiot Ave *Circ	Detroit	MI	48207	**800-678-9595***	313-446-6000

				Toll-Free	Phone
Canadian Biker 735 Market St	Victoria	BC	V8T2E2	**800-667-5667**	250-384-0333
Car Craft 6420 Wilshire Blvd	Los Angeles	CA	90048	**800-800-8326**	323-782-2000
Car & Driver 2002 Hogback Rd	Ann Arbor	MI	48105	**800-666-9485**	734-971-3600
Car Stereo Review 1633 Broadway 45th Fl	New York	NY	10019	**800-498-1993**	212-767-6000
Cycle World 1499 Monrovia Ave	Newport Beach	CA	92663	**800-876-8316**	949-720-5300
Dirt Rider 6420 Wilshire Blvd *Orders	Los Angeles	CA	90048	**800-800-3478***	323-782-2000
Dirt Wheels 25233 Anza Dr	Valencia	CA	91355	**800-767-0345**	661-295-1910
Easyriders 28210 Dorothy Dr	Agoura Hills	CA	91301	**800-247-6246**	818-889-8740
Four Wheeler 6420 Wilshire Blvd	Los Angeles	CA	90048	**800-777-0555**	323-782-2000
Hemmings Motor News 222 Main St	Bennington	VT	05201	**800-227-4373**	802-442-3101
Hot Rod Magazine 6420 Wilshire Blvd *Orders	Los Angeles	CA	90048	**800-800-4681***	323-782-2000
Motor Age Magazine 859 Williamette St	Eugene	OR	97401	**800-822-6678**	541-984-5299
Motor Trend 6420 Wilshire Blvd 7th Fl	Los Angeles	CA	90048	**800-800-6848**	323-782-2000
Motorcyclist 6420 Wilshire Blvd	Los Angeles	CA	90048	**800-800-7433**	323-782-2000
NASCAR Winston Cup Illustrated 120 W Morehead St Suite 320	Charlotte	NC	28202	**800-883-7323**	704-371-3966
National Speed Sport News PO Box 1210	Harrisburg	NC	28075	**866-455-2531**	704-455-2531
Road & Track 1499 Monrovia Ave *Cust Svc	Newport Beach	CA	92663	**800-876-8316***	949-720-5300
Special Interest Autos PO Box 196	Bennington	VT	05201	**800-227-4373**	802-442-3101
Sports Car 16842 Von Karman Ave Suite 125	Irvine	CA	92706	**800-722-7140**	949-417-6700
Stock Car Racing 5555 Concord Pkwy S Suite 326	Concord	NC	28075	**800-333-2633**	863-644-0449

449-4 Boating Magazines

				Toll-Free	Phone
Boating 1633 Broadway 41st Fl *Cust Svc	New York	NY	10019	**800-289-0399***	212-767-4823
Motor Boating & Sailing 18 Marshall St Suite 114	South Norwalk	CT	06834	**800-888-9123**	203-299-5950
Power & Motoryacht 260 Madison Ave 8th Fl	New York	NY	10016	**800-284-8036**	917-256-2200
SAIL Magazine 98 N Washington St 2nd Fl	Boston	MA	02114	**800-745-7245**	617-720-8600
Sailing World 5 John Clarke Rd *Cust Svc	Newport	RI	02840	**866-436-2460***	401-847-1588
Showboats International 1600 SE 17th St Suite 200 *Cust Svc	Fort Lauderdale	FL	33316	**800-876-6976***	954-525-8626
Yachting 18 Marshall St Suite 114	South Norwalk	CT	06854	**800-999-0869**	203-299-5900

449-5 Business & Finance Magazines

				Toll-Free	Phone
Accounting Today PO Box 4871	Chicago	IL	60694	**800-260-2793**	
Advertising Age 360 N Michigan Ave	Chicago	IL	60601	**800-678-2724**	312-649-5200
Adweek 770 Broadway	New York	NY	10003	**800-722-6658**	646-654-5500
AHA News 1 N Franklin St Suite 2800	Chicago	IL	60606	**800-621-6902**	312-893-6800
Alaska Business Monthly 501 W Northern Lights Blvd Suite 100	Anchorage	AK	99503	**800-770-4373**	907-276-4373
American Agent & Broker 6000 Lombardo Center Dr Suite 420	Seven Hills	OH	44131	**888-772-8926**	
American Journalism Review University of Maryland 1117 Journalism Bldg Room 2116	College Park	MD	20742	**800-827-0771**	301-405-8803
American Statistician 1429 Duke St	Alexandria	VA	22314	**888-231-3473**	703-684-1221
Area Development 400 Post Ave Suite 304	Westbury	NY	11590	**800-735-2732**	516-338-0900
Arkansas Business Journal 122 E 2nd St	Little Rock	AR	72203	**888-322-6397**	501-372-1443
ASID Professional Designer 608 Massachusetts Ave NE	Washington	DC	20002	**800-775-2743**	202-546-3480
Barron's The Dow Jones Business & Financial Weekly 200 Liberty St	New York	NY	10281	**800-369-2834**	212-416-2700
Black Enterprise Magazine 130 5th Ave	New York	NY	10011	**800-727-7777**	212-242-8000
Blue Ridge Business Journal 347 W Campbell Ave	Roanoke	VA	24016	**866-542-6198**	540-777-6460
Broadcasting & Cable 360 Park Ave S	New York	NY	10010	**800-554-5729**	646-746-6965
Business Credit 8840 Columbia 100 Pkwy	Columbia	MD	21045	**800-955-8815**	410-740-5560
Business Examiner 1517 S Fawcett Ave Suite 350	Tacoma	WA	98402	**800-540-8322**	253-404-0891
Business Facilities 44 Apple St Suite 3	Tinton Falls	NJ	07724	**800-524-0337**	732-842-7433
Business First 501 S 4th St Suite 130	Louisville	KY	40202	**800-704-3757**	502-583-1731
Business & Health 5 Paragon Dr	Montvale	NJ	07645	**800-232-7379**	201-358-7200
Business Insurance 360 N Michigan Ave	Chicago	IL	60601	**800-678-2724**	312-649-5200
Business Journal The 25 E Boardman St	Youngstown	OH	44501	**800-837-6397**	330-744-5023
Business Magazine 1450 Don Mills Rd	Don Mills	ON	M3B3R5	**800-668-7678**	416-383-2300
Business Opportunities Journal PO Box 60762	San Diego	CA	92166	**800-809-1763**	
Business in Vancouver 1155 W Pender St Suite 500	Vancouver	BC	V6E2P4	**800-208-2011**	604-688-2398
BusinessWeek 1221 Ave of the Americas 43rd Fl *Cust Svc	New York	NY	10020	**800-635-1200***	212-512-2511
Canadian Business 1 Mt Pleasant Rd 11th Fl	Toronto	ON	M4Y2Y5	**800-465-0700**	416-764-1200
CFO 253 Summer St	Boston	MA	02210	**800-877-5416**	617-345-9700
Charlotte Business Journal 120 W Morehead St Suite 200	Charlotte	NC	28202	**800-948-5323**	704-973-1100
CIO 492 Old Connecticut Path	Framingham	MA	01701	**800-788-4605**	508-872-8200
Contract Design 770 Broadway	New York	NY	10003	**800-950-1314**	646-654-5500
CPA Journal 3 Park Ave 18th Fl	New York	NY	10016	**800-633-6320**	212-719-8300
Crain's Chicago Business 360 N Michigan Ave	Chicago	IL	60601	**800-678-2724**	312-649-5200
Crain's Cleveland Business 700 W St Clair Ave Suite 310	Cleveland	OH	44113	**888-909-9111**	216-522-1383
Crain's Detroit Business 1155 Gratiot Ave	Detroit	MI	48207	**888-909-9111**	313-446-6000
Crain's New York Business 711 3rd Ave	New York	NY	10017	**800-283-2724**	212-210-0100
Credit Union Magazine 5710 Mineral Pt Rd *Cust Svc	Madison	WI	53705	**800-356-9655***	608-231-4000
Daily Business Review 1 SE 3rd Ave Suite 900	Miami	FL	33131	**800-777-7300**	305-347-6672
Drug Topics 5 Paragon Dr	Montvale	NJ	07645	**800-232-7379**	201-358-7200
E-Commerce Times 15821 Ventura Blvd Suite 635	Encino	CA	91436	**877-328-5500**	818-461-9700
Eastern Pennsylvania Business Journal 65 E Elizabeth Ave Suite 700	Bethlehem	PA	18018	**800-328-1026**	610-807-9619
Economist The 111 W 57th St 8th Fl	New York	NY	10019	**800-456-6086**	212-541-5730
Editor & Publisher 770 Broadway	New York	NY	10003	**800-783-4903**	646-654-5270
Electronic Business Today 275 Washington St *Cust Svc	Newton	MA	02458	**800-446-6551***	617-964-3030
Electronic Publishing 1421 S Sheridan Rd	Tulsa	OK	74112	**800-331-4463**	918-835-3161
Employee Benefit News 1325 G St NW Suite 970	Washington	DC	20005	**888-280-4820**	202-504-1122
Entrepreneur Magazine 2445 McCabe Way	Irvine	CA	92614	**800-274-6229**	949-261-2325
Expansion Management 1300 E 9th St	Cleveland	OH	44114	**800-539-7263**	216-931-9860
Fairfield County Business Journal 3 Gannett Dr Suite G7	White Plains	NY	10604	**800-784-4564**	914-694-3600
Fleet Owner 11 Riverbend Dr S PO Box 4211	Stamford	CT	06907	**800-776-1246**	203-358-9900
Forbes 60 5th Ave	New York	NY	10011	**800-888-9896**	212-620-2200
Fortune Rockefeller Ctr Time & Life Bldg	New York	NY	10020	**800-621-8000**	212-522-1212
Foundation News & Commentary 1828 L St NW Suite 300	Washington	DC	20036	**800-771-8187**	202-467-0445
Franchising World 1350 New York Ave NW Suite 900	Washington	DC	20005	**800-543-1038**	202-628-8000
FSB Rockefeller Ctr 1271 Ave of the Americas 4th Fl *Cust Svc	New York	NY	10020	**800-771-1444***	212-522-3263
Futures 833 W Jackson Blvd 7th Fl	Chicago	IL	60607	**800-972-9316**	312-846-4600
Harvard Business Review 60 Harvard Way	Boston	MA	02163	**800-274-3214**	617-783-7500
Health Facilities Management 1 N Franklin Suite 2800	Chicago	IL	60606	**800-621-6902**	312-893-6800
Healthcare Informatics 4530 W 77th St Suite 350 *Cust Svc	Minneapolis	MN	55435	**800-525-5003***	952-835-3222
Hispanic Business 425 Pine Ave *Sales	Santa Barbara	CA	93117	**888-447-7287***	805-964-4554
Hospitals & Health Networks 1 N Franklin Suite 2700	Chicago	IL	60606	**800-621-6902**	312-893-6800
HRMagazine 1800 Duke St	Alexandria	VA	22314	**800-283-7476**	703-548-3440
Human Resource Executive 747 Dresher Rd Suite 500	Horsham	PA	19044	**800-341-7874**	215-784-0860
Inc 375 Lexington Ave	New York	NY	10017	**800-234-0999**	212-499-2000
Independent Agent 127 S Peyton St	Alexandria	VA	22314	**800-221-7917**	703-683-4422
Indiana Business Magazine 55 Monument Cir Suite 300	Indianapolis	IN	46204	**800-473-2526**	317-692-1200
Indianapolis Business Journal 41 E Washington St Suite 200	Indianapolis	IN	46204	**800-968-1225**	317-634-6200
Journal of Accountancy 201 Plaza III Harborside Financial Ctr	Jersey City	NJ	07311	**888-777-7077**	201-938-3000
Journal of Financial Planning 4100 E Mississippi Ave Suite 400	Denver	CO	80246	**800-322-4237**	303-759-4900
Journal of Housing & Community Development 630 'I' St NW	Washington	DC	20001	**877-866-2476**	202-289-3500
Journal of Property Management 430 N Michigan Ave 7th Fl	Chicago	IL	60611	**800-837-0706**	312-329-6000
Law Enforcement Technology 1233 Janesville Ave	Fort Atkinson	WI	53538	**800-547-7377**	920-563-6388
Leadership 465 Gundersen Dr	Carol Stream	IL	60188	**800-777-3136**	630-260-6200
Life Assn News 2901 Telestar Ct	Falls Church	VA	22042	**800-247-4074**	703-770-8477
Management Accounting Quarterly 10 Paragon Dr *Cust Svc	Montvale	NJ	07645	**800-638-4427***	201-573-9000
Marketing News 311 S Wacker Dr Suite 5800	Chicago	IL	60606	**800-262-1150**	312-542-9000
Materials Management in Health Care 1 N Franklin St Suite 2700	Chicago	IL	60606	**800-621-6902**	312-893-6800
Meeting News 770 Broadway	New York	NY	10003	**800-950-1314**	646-654-4420
Meetings & Conventions 500 Plaza Dr	Secaucus	NJ	07094	**800-446-6551**	201-902-2000
Mergers & Acquisitions 1 State Street Plaza *Cust Svc	New York	NY	10004	**800-455-5844***	212-803-6051
Minneapolis-Saint Paul CityBusiness 527 Marquette Ave Suite 300	Minneapolis	MN	55402	**800-704-3757**	612-288-2141
Mississippi Business Journal 5120 Galaxie Dr	Jackson	MS	39206	**800-283-4625**	601-364-1000
Modern Healthcare 360 N Michigan Ave	Chicago	IL	60601	**800-678-9595**	312-649-5200
National Notary 9350 DeSoto Ave *Cust Svc	Chatsworth	CA	91311	**800-876-6827***	818-739-4000
National Underwriter 3341 Newark St	Hoboken	NJ	07030	**800-543-0874**	201-963-2300
Northern Colorado Business Report 141 S College Ave	Fort Collins	CO	80524	**800-440-3506**	970-221-5400
Orlando Business Journal 315 E Robinson St Suite 250	Orlando	FL	32801	**888-649-6251**	407-649-8470
Palm Beach Daily Business Review 324 Datura St Suite 140	West Palm Beach	FL	33401	**800-777-7300**	561-820-2060
Pensions & Investments 711 3rd Ave *Cust Svc	New York	NY	10017	**888-446-1422***	212-210-0115
Pharmaceutical Representative 2 Northfield Plaza Suite 300	Northfield	IL	60093	**800-451-7838**	847-441-3700
Philadelphia Business Journal 400 Market St Suite 1200	Philadelphia	PA	19106	**800-220-3202**	215-238-1450
Plants Sites & Parks PO Box 2754	High Point	NC	27261	**800-561-5681**	336-605-1055
Potentials 50 S 9th St *Cust Svc	Minneapolis	MN	55402	**800-328-4329***	612-333-0471
Practical Accountant PO Box 408	Congers	NY	10920	**800-260-2793**	
Print 700 E State St	Iola	WI	54990	**800-258-0929**	715-445-2214
Purchasing Magazine 275 Washington St *Cust Svc	Newton	MA	02458	**800-446-6551***	617-964-3030
Rio Grande Valley Business Journal 1300 Wild Rose Ln	Brownsville	TX	78520	**800-556-9876**	956-546-5113
Rough Notes 11690 Technology Dr	Carmel	IN	46032	**800-428-4384**	317-582-1600
San Diego Business Journal 4909 Murphy Canyon Rd Suite 200	San Diego	CA	92123	**888-425-7325**	858-277-6359
Selling Power 1140 International Pkwy	Fredericksburg	VA	22406	**800-752-7355**	540-752-7000
Signal 4400 Fair Lakes Ct	Fairfax	VA	22033	**800-336-4583**	703-631-6100
Sloan Management Review 77 Massachusetts Ave E60-100	Cambridge	MA	02139	**800-876-5764**	617-253-7170
South Sound Business Examiner 1517 S Fawcett St Suite 350	Tacoma	WA	98402	**800-540-6899**	253-404-0891
Tempdigest 7474 S Kirkwood Suite 108	Houston	TX	77072	**800-444-0674**	281-498-2913
Today's Realtor 430 N Michigan Ave 9th Fl	Chicago	IL	60610	**800-874-6500**	312-329-8458
Training Magazine 50 S 9th St *Cust Svc	Minneapolis	MN	55402	**800-328-4329***	612-333-0471
US Banker 1 State St 27th Fl	New York	NY	10004	**800-221-1809**	212-967-7000
Utah Business Magazine 1245 E Brickyard Rd Suite 90	Salt Lake City	UT	84106	**800-823-0038**	801-568-0114

449-6 Children's & Youth Magazines

				Toll-Free	Phone
AppleSeeds Magazine 30 Grove St Suite C	Peterborough	NH	03458	**800-821-0115**	603-924-7209
Ask Magazine 30 Grove St Suite C	Peterborough	NH	03458	**800-821-0115**	603-924-7209
Babybug Magazine 30 Grove St Suite C	Peterborough	NH	03458	**800-821-0115**	603-924-7209
Calliope Magazine 30 Grove St Suite C	Peterborough	NH	03458	**800-821-0115**	603-924-7209

Children's & Youth Magazines (Cont'd)

Name / Address	City	State	ZIP	Toll-Free	Phone
Child Life Magazine Children's Better Health Institute 1100 Waterway Blvd	Indianapolis	IN	46202	**800-558-2376**	317-636-8881
Children's Digest Children's Better Health Institute 1100 Waterway Blvd	Indianapolis	IN	46202	**800-558-2376**	317-636-8881
Children's Playmate Magazine Children's Better Health Institute 1100 Waterway Blvd	Indianapolis	IN	46202	**800-558-2376**	317-636-8881
Cicada Magazine 30 Grove St Suite C	Peterborough	NH	03458	**800-821-0115**	603-924-7209
Click Magazine 30 Grove St Suite C	Peterborough	NH	03458	**800-821-0115**	603-924-7209
Cobblestone Magazine 30 Grove St Suite C	Peterborough	NH	03458	**800-821-0115**	603-924-7209
Creative Kids Magazine PO Box 8813	Waco	TX	76714	**800-998-2208**	254-756-3337
Cricket Magazine 30 Grove St Suite C	Peterborough	NH	03458	**800-821-0115**	603-924-7209
Dig Magazine 30 Grove St Suite C	Peterborough	NH	03458	**800-821-0115**	603-924-7209
Disney Adventures 114 5th Ave *Cust Svc	New York	NY	10011	**800-829-5146***	212-633-4400
Faces Magazine About People 30 Grove St Suite C	Peterborough	NH	03458	**800-821-0115**	603-924-7209
FamilyFun 114 5th Ave	New York	NY	10011	**800-829-5146**	212-633-3620
Footsteps Magazine 30 Grove St Suite C	Peterborough	NH	03458	**800-821-0115**	603-924-7209
Girl's Life Magazine 4517 Hartford Rd	Baltimore	MD	21214	**888-999-3222**	410-426-9600
Highlights for Children 1800 Watermark Dr *Cust Svc	Columbus	OH	43215	**800-255-9517***	614-486-0631
Humpty Dumpty's Magazine 1100 Waterway Blvd	Indianapolis	IN	46202	**800-558-2376**	317-636-8881
Jack & Jill 1100 Waterway Blvd	Indianapolis	IN	46202	**800-558-2376**	317-636-8881
Ladybug Magazine 30 Grove St Suite C	Peterborough	NH	03458	**800-821-0115**	603-924-7209
Muse Magazine 30 Grove St Suite C	Peterborough	NH	03458	**800-821-0115**	603-924-7209
National Geographic World 1145 17th St NW	Washington	DC	20036	**800-647-5463**	202-857-7000
New Moon Magazine 34 E Superior St Suite 200	Duluth	MN	55802	**800-381-4743**	218-728-5507
Odyssey 30 Grove St Suite C	Peterborough	NH	03458	**800-821-0115**	603-924-7209
Ranger Rick 11100 Wildlife Ctr Dr	Reston	VA	20190	**800-822-9919**	
Seventeen 1440 Broadway 13th Fl	New York	NY	10018	**800-388-1749**	917-934-6500
Spider Magazine 30 Grove St Suite C	Peterborough	NH	03458	**800-821-0115**	603-924-7209
Sports Illustrated for Kids 135 W 50th St *Cust Svc	New York	NY	10020	**800-992-0196***	212-522-1212
Stone Soup Magazine PO Box 83	Santa Cruz	CA	95063	**800-447-4569**	831-426-5557
Teen People 1271 6th Ave Time & Life Bldg	New York	NY	10020	**800-284-0200**	212-522-1212
Turtle Magazine 1100 Waterway Blvd	Indianapolis	IN	46202	**800-558-2376**	317-636-8881
Twist 270 Sylvan Ave *Cust Svc	Englewood Cliffs	NJ	07632	**800-757-7053***	201-569-6699
US Kids Magazine 1100 Waterway Blvd	Indianapolis	IN	46202	**800-558-2376**	317-636-8881
Wild Animal Baby 8925 Leesburg Pike	Vienna	VA	22184	**800-822-9910**	
Writing Magazine 3001 Cindel Dr	Delran	NJ	08075	**800-446-3355**	856-786-5500
Your Big Backyard 8925 Leesburg Pike	Vienna	VA	22184	**800-611-1599**	

449-7 Computer & Internet Magazines

Name / Address	City	State	ZIP	Toll-Free	Phone
BYTE.com 600 Community Dr	Manhasset	NY	11030	**800-645-6278**	516-562-5000
Computer 10662 Los Vaqueros Cir *Orders	Los Alamitos	CA	90720	**800-272-6657***	714-821-8380
Computer Graphics World 98 Spit Brook Rd	Nashua	NH	03062	**800-331-4463**	603-891-0123
Computer Shopper Magazine 28 E 28th St	New York	NY	10016	**800-274-6384**	646-472-4000
Computers in Libraries 143 Old Marlton Pike	Medford	NJ	08055	**800-300-9868**	609-654-6266
Computerworld 1 Speen St	Framingham	MA	01701	**800-343-6474**	508-879-0700
Darwin Magazine 492 Old Connecticut Path PO Box 9208	Framingham	MA	01701	**800-942-4672**	508-872-0080
Dr Dobb's Journal 2800 Campus Dr	San Mateo	CA	94403	**800-289-9839**	650-513-4300
DV: Digital Video Magazine 7300 N Linder Ave	Skokie	IL	60076	**888-776-7002**	847-763-9581
e-doc 1100 Wayne Ave Suite 1100	Silver Spring	MD	20910	**800-477-2446**	301-587-8202
eContent 88 Danbury Rd Suite 1-D	Wilton	CT	06897	**800-248-8466**	203-761-1466
eWEEK Magazine 28 E 28th St 8th Fl	New York	NY	10016	**888-663-8438**	212-503-3500
IEEE Computer Graphics & Applications 10662 Los Vaqueros Cir	Los Alamitos	CA	90720	**800-272-6657**	714-821-8380
IEEE Micro 10662 Los Vaqueros Cir	Los Alamitos	CA	90720	**800-272-6657**	714-821-8380
Information Today Magazine 143 Old Marlton Pike	Medford	NJ	08055	**800-300-9868**	609-654-6266
InformationWeek 600 Community Dr	Manhasset	NY	11030	**800-645-6278**	516-562-7911
InfoWorld 501 2nd St Suite 120	San Francisco	CA	94107	**800-227-8365**	415-243-4344
Intelligent Enterprise 2800 Campus Dr *Cust Svc	San Mateo	CA	94403	**800-289-9839***	650-513-4300
Law Technology News 345 Park Ave S *Cust Svc	New York	NY	10010	**800-274-2893***	212-779-9200
MacHome 200 Folsom St Suite 150	San Francisco	CA	94105	**800-800-6542**	415-957-1911
Macworld Magazine 501 2nd St Suite 120 *Cust Svc	San Francisco	CA	94107	**800-873-4941***	415-243-4141
Manufacturing Systems 2000 Clearwater Dr	Oak Brook	IL	60523	**800-662-7776**	630-320-7000
MultiMedia Schools 143 Old Marlton Pike	Medford	NJ	08055	**800-300-9868**	609-654-6266
Network World 118 Turnpike Rd	Southborough	MA	01772	**800-622-1108**	508-875-6400
Online 143 Old Marlton Pike	Medford	NJ	08055	**800-300-9868**	609-654-6266
PC Magazine 28 E 28th St	New York	NY	10016	**800-289-0429**	212-503-5100
PC World Magazine 501 2nd St Suite 600	San Francisco	CA	94107	**800-234-3498**	415-243-0500
Scientific Computing & Instrumentation Magazine 100 Enterprise Dr Suite 600	Rockaway	NJ	07866	**800-662-7776**	973-920-7000
Searcher: The Magazine for Database Professionals 143 Old Marlton Pike	Medford	NJ	08055	**800-300-9868**	609-654-6266
Wired Magazine 520 3rd St 3rd Fl	San Francisco	CA	94107	**800-769-4733**	415-276-5000

449-8 Education Magazines & Journals

Name / Address	City	State	ZIP	Toll-Free	Phone
Academe 1012 14th St NW Suite 500	Washington	DC	20005	**800-424-2973**	202-737-5900
Advocate 100 E Edwards St	Springfield	IL	62704	**800-252-8076**	217-544-0706
AEA Advocate 4000 N Central Ave Suite 1600	Phoenix	AZ	85012	**800-352-5411**	602-264-1774
Alabama School Journal PO Box 4177	Montgomery	AL	36103	**800-392-5839**	334-834-9790
American Educator 555 New Jersey Ave NW	Washington	DC	20001	**800-238-1133**	202-879-4400
American Libraries 50 E Huron St	Chicago	IL	60611	**800-545-2433**	312-944-6780
American Teacher 555 New Jersey Ave NW	Washington	DC	20001	**800-238-1133**	202-879-4400
Chronicle of Higher Education 1255 23rd St NW Suite 700 *Sales	Washington	DC	20037	**800-728-2803***	202-466-1000
Colorado School Journal 1500 Grant St	Denver	CO	80203	**800-332-5939**	303-837-1500
Dance Teacher Magazine 250 W 57th St Suite 420	New York	NY	10107	**800-362-6765**	
Education Center Inc 3515 W Market St Suite 200	Greensboro	NC	27403	**800-714-7991**	336-854-0309
Education Digest PO Box 8623	Ann Arbor	MI	48107	**800-530-9673**	734-975-2800
Education Week 6935 Arlington Rd	Bethesda	MD	20814	**800-346-1834**	301-280-3100
Educational Leadership 1703 N Beauregard St	Alexandria	VA	22311	**800-933-2723**	703-578-9600
Educators' Advocate 411 E Capitol Ave	Pierre	SD	57501	**800-529-0090**	605-224-9263
FOCUS 1529 18th St NW	Washington	DC	20036	**800-741-9415**	202-387-5200
Harvard Educational Review 8 Story St 1st Fl	Cambridge	MA	02138	**800-513-0763**	617-495-3432
Instructor 557 Broadway	New York	NY	10012	**800-544-2917**	212-343-6100
ISTA Advocate 150 W Market St Suite 900	Indianapolis	IN	46204	**800-382-4037**	317-263-3400
Journal of Physical Education Recreation & Dance 1900 Association Dr	Reston	VA	20191	**800-213-7193**	703-476-3477
KEA News 401 Capital Ave	Frankfort	KY	40601	**800-231-4532**	502-875-2889
Mailbox Bookbag 3515 W Market St Suite 200	Greensboro	NC	27403	**800-714-7991**	336-854-0309
Maine Educator 35 Community Dr	Augusta	ME	04330	**800-452-8709**	207-622-5866
MEA Voice PO Box 2573	East Lansing	MI	48826	**800-292-1934**	517-332-6551
Media & Methods Magazine 1429 Walnut St 10th Fl	Philadelphia	PA	19102	**800-555-5657**	215-563-6005
Minnesota Educator 41 Sherburne Ave	Saint Paul	MN	55103	**800-652-9073**	651-227-9541
Mississippi Educator 775 N State Ct	Jackson	MS	39202	**800-530-7998**	601-354-4463
MTA Today Magazine 20 Ashburton Pl	Boston	MA	02108	**800-392-6175**	617-742-7950
NCAE News Bulletin PO Box 27347	Raleigh	NC	27611	**800-662-7924**	919-832-3000
NEA Today 1201 16th St NW	Washington	DC	20036	**800-229-4200**	202-822-7207
NSEA Voice 605 S 14th St	Lincoln	NE	68508	**800-742-0047**	402-475-7611
On Campus 555 New Jersey Ave NW	Washington	DC	20001	**800-238-1133**	202-879-4400
Scholastic Coach 557 Broadway	New York	NY	10012	**800-724-6527**	212-343-6100
School & Community PO Box 458	Columbia	MO	65205	**800-392-0532**	573-442-3127
Teaching Exceptional Children 1110 N Glebe Rd Suite 300	Arlington	VA	22201	**888-232-7733**	703-620-3660
Teaching K-8 40 Richards Ave *Cust Svc	Norwalk	CT	06854	**800-678-8793***	203-855-2650
TSTA Advocate 316 W 12th St	Austin	TX	78701	**800-324-5355**	512-476-5355
Virginia Journal of Education 116 S 3rd St	Richmond	VA	23219	**800-552-9554**	804-648-5801
Voice 400 N 3rd St PO Box 1724	Harrisburg	PA	17105	**800-944-7732**	717-255-7134
West Virginia School Journal 1558 Quarrier St	Charleston	WV	25311	**800-642-8261**	304-346-5315

449-9 Entertainment & Music Magazines

Name / Address	City	State	ZIP	Toll-Free	Phone
American Cinematographer Magazine 1782 N Orange Dr	Hollywood	CA	90028	**800-448-0145**	323-969-4333
Amusement Business 5055 Wilshire Blvd	Los Angeles	CA	90036	**800-745-8922**	323-525-2350
Back Stage Magazine 770 Broadway *Subscriptions	New York	NY	10003	**800-437-3183***	646-654-5500
Bass Player 2800 Campus Dr *Cust Svc	San Mateo	CA	94403	**800-234-1831***	650-513-4300
Billboard Magazine 770 Broadway *Cust Svc	New York	NY	10003	**800-437-3183***	646-654-5500
Casino Player 8025 Black Horse Pike Suite 470	West Atlantic City	NJ	08232	**800-969-0711**	609-484-8866
Dance Magazine 333 7th Ave 11th Fl	New York	NY	10001	**800-331-1750**	212-979-4814
Down Beat 102 N Haven Rd	Elmhurst	IL	60126	**800-535-7496**	630-941-2030
Entertainment Design Magazine 249 W 17th St *Sales	New York	NY	10011	**800-827-0315***	212-204-1813
Film Comment 70 Lincoln Ctr Plaza *Cust Svc	New York	NY	10023	**800-783-4903***	212-875-5610
Guitar Player 2800 Campus Dr *Cust Svc	San Mateo	CA	94403	**800-289-9839***	650-513-4300
International Musician 1501 Broadway Suite 600	New York	NY	10036	**800-762-3444**	212-869-1330
Jazziz 2650 N Military Trail Suite 140 Fountain Square II Bldg	Boca Raton	FL	33431	**800-742-3252**	561-893-6868
JazzTimes 8737 Colesville Rd 9th Fl	Silver Spring	MD	20910	**800-866-7664**	301-588-4114
Keyboard Magazine 2800 Campus Dr *Cust Svc	San Mateo	CA	94403	**800-289-9919***	650-513-4300
Metal Edge 333 7th Ave 11th Fl	New York	NY	10001	**800-741-1289**	212-780-3500
Multichannel News 360 Park Ave S *Cust Svc	New York	NY	10010	**888-343-5563***	646-746-6400
OnSat PO Box 2347 *Cust Svc	Shelby	NC	28151	**800-234-0021***	704-482-9673
Playbill 525 7th Ave Suite 1801	New York	NY	10018	**800-533-4330**	212-557-5757
Pollstar 4697 W Jacquelyn Ave	Fresno	CA	93722	**800-344-7383**	559-271-7900
Premiere 1633 Broadway *Cust Svc	New York	NY	10019	**800-274-4027***	212-767-6000
Satellite Direct PO Box 310156	Newington	CT	06131	**800-234-4220**	206-262-8183
Satellite Orbit 701 5th Ave 42nd Fl	Seattle	WA	98104	**800-234-4220**	206-262-8183
Sheet Music Magazine 2 Depot Plaza Suite 301 *Claims	Bedford Hills	NY	10507	**800-759-3036***	914-244-8500
Showbiz Magazine 2290 Corporate Circle Suite 250	Henderson	NV	89074	**800-746-9484**	702-383-7185
Singing News 330 University Hall Dr	Boone	NC	28607	**800-255-2810**	828-264-3700
Soap Opera Digest 261 Madison Ave 10th Fl	New York	NY	10016	**800-829-9095**	212-716-2700
Soap Opera Weekly 261 Madison Ave 9th Fl	New York	NY	10016	**800-829-9096**	212-716-8400
Spin 205 Lexington Ave 3rd Fl *Cust Svc	New York	NY	10016	**800-274-7597***	212-231-7400
Stereo Review 1633 Broadway 45th Fl *Cust Svc	New York	NY	10019	**800-876-9011***	212-767-6000
Take One 86 Elm St	Peterborough	NH	03458	**800-677-8847**	603-924-7271
TV Guide 100 Matsonford Rd 4 Radnor Corp Ctr *Cust Svc	Radnor	PA	19088	**800-866-1400***	610-293-8500
Variety 5700 Wilshire Blvd Suite 120	Los Angeles	CA	90036	**800-552-3632**	323-857-6600
Video Event 86 Elm St	Peterborough	NH	03458	**800-677-8847**	603-924-7271
Videomaker Magazine 1350 E 9th St	Chico	CA	95928	**888-884-3226**	530-891-8410

449-10 Fraternal & Special Interest Magazines

Name / Address	City	State	ZIP	Toll-Free	Phone
AARP Modern Maturity 601 'E' St NW	Washington	DC	20049	**800-424-3410**	202-434-6880

Classified Section

				Toll-Free	Phone
AAUW Outlook 1111 16th St NW	Washington	DC	20036	800-326-2289	202-785-7700
Adoptive Families Magazine 39 W 37th St	New York	NY	10018	800-372-3300	646-366-0830
American Scholar 1606 New Hampshire Ave NW	Washington	DC	20009	800-821-4567	202-265-3808
Civitan Magazine 1 Civitan Pl PO Box 130744	Birmingham	AL	35213	800-248-4826	205-591-8910
Commentary 165 E 56th St	New York	NY	10022	800-829-6270	212-891-1400
Disabled American Veterans Magazine 3725 Alexandria Pike	Cold Spring	KY	41076	877-426-2838	859-441-7300
Gettysburg Review 300 N Washington St	Gettysburg	PA	17325	800-431-0803	717-337-6000
Girl Scout Leader 420 5th Ave	New York	NY	10018	800-223-0624	212-852-8000
Girlfriends Magazine 3415 Cesar Chavez Suite 101	San Francisco	CA	94110	800-475-3763	415-648-9464
Hispanic 999 Ponce de Leon Blvd Suite 600	Coral Gables	FL	33134	800-251-2688*	305-442-2462
*Cust Svc					
Irish America 875 Ave of the Americas Suite 2100	New York	NY	10001	800-582-6642	212-725-2993
Journal Francais 944 Market St Suite 210	San Francisco	CA	94102	800-232-1549*	415-981-9088
*Cust Svc					
Kiwanis Magazine 3636 Woodview Trace	Indianapolis	IN	46268	800-549-2647	317-875-8755
Lion Magazine 300 W 22nd St	Oak Brook	IL	60523	800-710-7822*	630-571-5466
*Circ					
Military History Magazine 741 Miller Dr SE Suite D2	Leesburg	VA	20175	800-829-3340	703-771-9400
Optimist Magazine 4494 Lindell Blvd	Saint Louis	MO	63108	800-500-8130	314-371-6000
Phi Delta Kappan PO Box 789	Bloomington	IN	47402	800-766-1156	812-339-1156
Sample Case 632 N Park St	Columbus	OH	43215	800-848-0123	614-228-3276
Twins Magazine 11211 E Arapahoe Rd Suite 101	Centennial	CO	80112	888-558-9467	303-290-8500
WOODMEN 1700 Farnam St	Omaha	NE	68102	800-225-3108	402-342-1890

449-11 General Interest Magazines

				Toll-Free	Phone
Adventure 1145 17th St NW	Washington	DC	20036	800-647-5463	202-857-7000
Alfred Hitchcock Mystery Magazine 475 Park Ave S 11th Fl	New York	NY	10016	800-333-3311	212-686-7188
Allure 4 Times Sq	New York	NY	10036	800-223-0780	212-286-2860
American Baby 125 Park Ave	New York	NY	10017	800-678-1208	212-557-6600
American Heritage 90 5th Ave	New York	NY	10011	800-777-1222	212-206-5500
American Profile 341 Cool Springs Blvd Suite 400	Franklin	TN	37067	800-720-6323	615-468-6000
Asimov's Science Fiction 475 Park Ave S 11th Fl	New York	NY	10016	800-333-4108	212-686-7188
Atlantic Monthly 711 3rd Ave 12th Fl	New York	NY	10017	800-234-2411	646-695-8500
BabyTalk 530 5th Ave 4th Fl	New York	NY	10036	800-234-0847	212-522-8989
Barron's The Dow Jones Business & Financial Weekly 200 Liberty St	New York	NY	10281	800-369-2834	212-416-2700
Better Homes & Gardens 1716 Locust St	Des Moines	IA	50309	800-374-4244	515-284-3000
Better Investing PO Box 220	Royal Oak	MI	48068	877-275-6242	248-583-6242
Black Enterprise Magazine 130 5th Ave	New York	NY	10011	800-727-7777	212-242-8000
Black Romance 333 7th Ave 11th Fl	New York	NY	10001	888-668-8783	212-979-4800
Bon Appetit 6300 Wilshire Blvd 10th Fl	Los Angeles	CA	90048	800-765-9419	323-965-3400
Booklist 50 E Huron St	Chicago	IL	60611	800-545-2433	312-944-6780
Bridal Guide 3 E 54th St 15th Fl	New York	NY	10022	800-472-7744	212-838-2570
Bride's 4 Times Sq	New York	NY	10036	800-223-0780	212-286-2860
BusinessWeek 1221 Ave of the Americas 43rd Fl	New York	NY	10020	800-635-1200*	212-512-2511
*Cust Svc					
Campus Life 465 Gundersen Dr	Carol Stream	IL	60188	800-678-6083*	630-260-6200
*Cust Svc					
Canadian Living 25 Sheppard Ave W Suite 100	Toronto	ON	M2N6S7	800-387-6332	416-733-7600
Capper's 1503 SW 42nd St	Topeka	KS	66609	800-678-5779	785-274-4300
Cargo Magazine 4 Times Sq	New York	NY	10036	800-223-0780	212-286-2860
Chatelaine 1 Mt Pleasant Rd 8th Fl	Toronto	ON	M4Y2Y5	800-268-9119	416-764-1888
Child 375 Lexington Ave 9th Fl	New York	NY	10017	800-777-0222	212-499-2000
College Outlook & Career Opportunities 20 E Gregory Blvd	Kansas City	MO	64114	800-274-8867	816-361-0616
Consumer Reports 101 Truman Ave	Yonkers	NY	10703	800-288-7898*	914-378-2000
*Orders					
Cook's Illustrated 17 Station St	Brookline	MA	02445	800-526-8442*	617-232-1000
*Circ					
Cosmopolitan 224 W 57th St	New York	NY	10019	800-888-2676	212-649-2000
Country 5400 S 60th St	Greendale	WI	53129	800-344-6913	414-423-0100
Country Home 1716 Locust St	Des Moines	IA	50309	800-374-9431*	515-284-3000
*Cust Svc					
Country Living 224 W 57th St	New York	NY	10019	800-888-0128	212-649-2000
Coup de Pouce 2001 ave University Suite 900	Montreal	QC	H3A2A6	800-528-3836	514-499-0561
Delicious! 1401 Pearl St Suite 200	Boulder	CO	80302	800-431-1255	303-939-8440
Economist The 111 W 57th St 8th Fl	New York	NY	10019	800-456-6086	212-541-5730
Elle 1633 Broadway 44th Fl	New York	NY	10019	800-876-8775	212-767-5800
Elle Decor 1633 Broadway 44th Fl	New York	NY	10019	800-274-4687	212-767-5800
Ellery Queen Mystery Magazine 475 Park Ave S 11th Fl	New York	NY	10016	800-333-3053	212-686-7188
Entrepreneur Magazine 2445 McCabe Way	Irvine	CA	92614	800-274-6229	949-261-2325
Esquire 250 W 55th St	New York	NY	10019	800-888-5400	212-649-2000
Essence Magazine 1500 Broadway 6th Fl	New York	NY	10036	800-274-9398	212-642-0600
Family Circle 375 Lexington Ave 9th Fl	New York	NY	10017	800-627-4444	212-499-2000
Food & Wine 1120 Ave of the Americas	New York	NY	10036	800-333-6569	212-382-5600
Forbes 60 5th Ave	New York	NY	10011	800-888-9896	212-620-2200
Fortune Rockefeller Ctr Time & Life Bldg	New York	NY	10020	800-621-8000	212-522-1212
Futurist 7910 Woodmont Ave Suite 450	Bethesda	MD	20814	800-989-8274	301-656-8274
Glamour 4 Times Sq	New York	NY	10036	800-274-7410	212-286-2860
Globe 1000 American Media Way	Boca Raton	FL	33467	800-749-7733	561-997-7733
Good Housekeeping 250 W 55th St	New York	NY	10019	800-888-7788	212-649-2000
Gourmet 4 Times Sq	New York	NY	10036	800-365-2454	212-286-2860
GQ: Gentlemen's Quarterly 4 Times Sq	New York	NY	10036	800-289-9330	212-286-2860
Grit 1503 SW 42nd St	Topeka	KS	66609	800-678-7741	785-274-4300
Harper's Bazaar 1700 Broadway	New York	NY	10019	800-888-3045	212-903-5000
Harper's Magazine 666 Broadway	New York	NY	10012	800-444-4653	212-420-5720
Hispanic Business 425 Pine Ave	Santa Barbara	CA	93117	888-447-7287*	805-964-4554
*Sales					
Home Magazine 1633 Broadway 44th Fl	New York	NY	10019	800-950-7370	212-767-6000
House Beautiful 1700 Broadway 29th Fl	New York	NY	10019	800-444-6873	212-903-5000
Inc 375 Lexington Ave	New York	NY	10017	800-234-0999	212-499-2000
Interview 575 Broadway 5th Fl	New York	NY	10012	800-925-9574	212-941-2900
Jane 7 W 34th St 6th Fl	New York	NY	10001	800-219-5294*	212-630-4000
*Cust Svc					
Kiplinger's Personal Finance Magazine 1729 H St NW	Washington	DC	20006	800-544-0155	202-887-6400
Ladies' Home Journal 125 Park Ave	New York	NY	10017	800-374-4545	212-557-6600
Life Magazine Rockefeller Ctr Time & Life Bldg	New York	NY	10020	800-541-1000	212-522-1212
Lucky 4 Times Sq	New York	NY	10036	800-223-0780	212-286-2860
Mad Magazine 1700 Broadway	New York	NY	10019	800-462-3624	212-506-4850
Marie Claire 1790 Broadway 3rd Fl	New York	NY	10019	800-777-3287	212-649-5000
Martha Stewart Living 11 W 42nd St	New York	NY	10036	800-999-6518	212-827-8000
Maxim 1040 Avenue of the Americas 16th Fl	New York	NY	10018	800-829-5572	212-302-2626
Metropolitan Home 1633 Broadway 44th Fl	New York	NY	10019	800-374-4638	212-767-4500
Modern Bride 4 Times Square	New York	NY	10036	800-777-5786*	212-286-2860
*Cust Svc					
Money Rockefeller Ctr Time & Life Bldg	New York	NY	10020	800-633-9970	212-522-1212
More 125 Park Ave	New York	NY	10017	888-699-4036	212-557-6600
Ms 1600 Wilson Blvd Suite 801	Arlington	VA	22209	866-672-6363	703-522-4201
National Examiner 1000 American Media Way	Boca Raton	FL	33467	800-749-7733	561-997-7733
National Geographic Adventure 1145 17th St NW	Washington	DC	20036	800-647-5463	202-857-7000
National Geographic Magazine 1145 17th St NW	Washington	DC	20036	800-647-5463	202-857-7000
New York Review of Books 1755 Broadway 5th Fl	New York	NY	10019	800-829-5088	212-757-8070
Newsweek 251 W 57th St	New York	NY	10019	800-631-1040*	212-445-4000
*Cust Svc					
North Light 4700 E Galbraith Rd	Cincinnati	OH	45236	800-289-0963*	513-531-2690
*Orders					
O The Oprah Magazine PO Box 7831	Red Oak	IA	51591	888-446-4438	
Parenting 530 5th Ave 4th Fl	New York	NY	10036	800-234-0847*	212-522-8989
*Circ					
Parents 375 Lexington Ave 10th Fl	New York	NY	10017	800-727-3682	212-499-2000
Penthouse 2 Penn Plaza Suite 1125	New York	NY	10121	800-289-7368	212-702-6000
People Rockefeller Ctr Time & Life Bldg	New York	NY	10020	800-541-9000	212-522-1212
People en Espanol Magazine Rockefeller Ctr Time & Life Bldg	New York	NY	10020	800-950-8100	212-522-1212
Personal Excellence Magazine 1366 East 1120 South	Provo	UT	84606	800-304-9782	801-375-4060
Playboy 680 N Lake Shore Dr	Chicago	IL	60611	800-999-4438	312-751-8000
Playgirl 801 2nd Ave 9th Fl	New York	NY	10017	800-877-6139	212-661-7878
Psychology Today 115 E 23 St 9th Fl	New York	NY	10010	800-234-8361*	212-260-7210
*Sales					
Publishers Weekly 360 Park Ave S	New York	NY	10010	800-278-2991*	646-746-6758
*Cust Svc					
Quick Cooking 5400 S 60th St	Greendale	WI	53129	800-344-6913	414-423-0100
Reader's Digest Reader's Digest Rd	Pleasantville	NY	10570	800-234-9000*	914-238-1000
*Cust Svc					
Redbook 224 W 57th St	New York	NY	10019	800-888-0008	212-649-2000
Reminisce 5400 S 60th St	Greendale	WI	53129	800-344-6913	414-423-0100
Saturday Evening Post 1100 Waterway Blvd	Indianapolis	IN	46202	800-558-2376	317-634-1100
Scholastic Parent & Child 557 Broadway	New York	NY	10012	800-724-6527	212-343-6100
Self 4 Times Sq	New York	NY	10036	800-274-6111	212-286-2860
SmartMoney 250 W 55th St	New York	NY	10019	800-444-4204	212-765-7323
Smithsonian 750 9th St NW Suite 7100	Washington	DC	20001	800-766-2149	202-275-2000
Sun 1000 American Media Way	Boca Raton	FL	33467	800-749-7733	561-997-7733
Sunset Magazine 80 Willow Rd	Menlo Park	CA	94025	800-777-0117	650-321-3600
Taste Of Home 5400 S 60th St	Greendale	WI	53129	800-344-6913	414-423-0100
The New Yorker 4 Times Sq	New York	NY	10036	800-825-2510	212-286-5400
Time Rockefeller Ctr Time & Life Bldg	New York	NY	10020	800-541-2000	212-522-1212
Town & Country 1700 Broadway	New York	NY	10019	800-289-8696	212-903-5000
Traditional Home 1716 Locust St	Des Moines	IA	50309	800-374-8791*	515-284-3000
*Circ					
Us Weekly Magazine 1290 Ave of the Americas 2nd Fl	New York	NY	10104	800-283-3956*	212-484-1616
*Cust Svc					
USA Weekend 535 Madison Ave 21st Fl	New York	NY	10022	800-487-2956*	212-715-2100
*Edit					
Utne Reader 1624 Harmon Pl Suite 330	Minneapolis	MN	55403	800-736-8863*	612-338-5040
*Cust Svc					
Vanity Fair 4 Times Sq	New York	NY	10036	800-690-6115	212-286-2860
Vogue 4 Times Sq	New York	NY	10036	800-690-6115	212-286-2860
W 7 W 34th St 3rd Fl	New York	NY	10001	800-289-0390	212-630-4000
Weekly World News 1000 American Media Way	Boca Raton	FL	33467	800-628-5632	561-989-1227
Wilson Quarterly 1300 Pennsylvania Ave NW 1 Woodrow Wilson Plaza	Washington	DC	20004	800-829-5108*	202-691-4000
*Orders					
Woman's Day 1633 Broadway 44th Fl	New York	NY	10019	800-234-2960	212-767-6000
Woman's World 270 Sylvan Ave	Englewood Cliffs	NJ	07632	800-216-6981	201-569-0006
Women's Wear Daily 7 W 34th St 3rd Fl	New York	NY	10001	800-289-0273	212-630-4000
Working Mother 60 E 42nd St 27th Fl	New York	NY	10165	800-627-0690	212-351-6400
Worth Magazine 1177 Ave of the Americas 10th Fl	New York	NY	10036	800-777-1851*	212-223-3100
*Circ					
Your Money 520 Lake Cook Rd Suite 500	Deerfield	IL	60015	800-777-0025	847-607-3000

449-12 Government & Military Magazines

				Toll-Free	Phone
Air Force Magazine 1501 Lee Hwy	Arlington	VA	22209	800-727-3337	703-247-5800
Air Force Times 6883 Commercial Dr	Springfield	VA	22159	800-424-9335	703-750-9000
ARMY Magazine 2425 Wilson Blvd	Arlington	VA	22201	800-336-4570	703-841-4300
Army Times 6883 Commercial Dr	Springfield	VA	22159	800-424-9335	703-750-9000
Governing 1100 Connecticut Ave NW Suite 1300	Washington	DC	20036	800-944-0922	202-862-8802
Government Executive 1501 M St NW Suite 300	Washington	DC	20005	800-207-8001	202-739-8400
Military & Aerospace Electronics 98 Spit Brook Rd	Nashua	NH	03062	800-225-0556	603-891-0123
Military Engineer 607 Prince St	Alexandria	VA	22314	800-336-3097	703-549-3800
Naval Affairs 125 N West St	Alexandria	VA	22314	800-372-1924	703-683-1400
Navy Times 6883 Commercial Dr	Springfield	VA	22159	800-424-9335	703-750-9000
Retired Officer Magazine 201 N Washington St	Alexandria	VA	22314	800-245-8762	703-549-2311
Soldier of Fortune 5735 Arapahoe Ave Suite A-5	Boulder	CO	80303	800-800-7630	303-449-3750

449-13 Health & Fitness Magazines

Name / Address	City	State	Zip	Toll-Free	Phone
American Fitness 15250 Ventura Blvd Suite 200	Sherman Oaks	CA	91403	**800-446-2322**	818-905-0040
Cooking Light 2100 Lakeshore Dr	Birmingham	AL	35209	**800-366-4712**	205-445-6000
Diabetes Self-Management 150 W 22nd St. *Circ	New York	NY	10011	**800-234-0923***	212-989-0200
Fitness 15 E 26th St 5th Fl *Cust Svc	New York	NY	10010	**800-888-1181***	646-758-0600
Flex 21100 Erwin St	Woodland Hills	CA	91367	**800-423-5590**	818-884-6800
Ironman Magazine 1701 Ives Ave.	Oxnard	CA	93033	**800-570-4766**	805-385-3500
Let's Live 11050 Santa Monica Blvd 3rd Fl.	Los Angeles	CA	90025	**800-676-4333**	310-445-7500
Men's Fitness 21100 Erwin St *Orders	Woodland Hills	CA	91367	**800-340-8958***	818-884-6800
Men's Health 33 E Minor St	Emmaus	PA	18098	**800-666-2303**	610-967-5171
Monster Muscle Magazine PO Box 2561	Spokane	WA	99220	**800-268-2248**	509-534-4489
Muscle & Fitness 21100 Erwin St *Orders	Woodland Hills	CA	91367	**800-423-5590***	818-884-6800
Organic Style Magazine 33 Minor St	Emmaus	PA	18098	**800-848-4735**	610-967-8154
Prevention 33 E Minor St	Emmaus	PA	18098	**800-813-8070**	610-967-5171
Rodale's Heart & Soul 315 Park Ave S 11th Fl	New York	NY	10010	**800-666-1716**	646-654-4200
Runner's World 33 E Minor St *Cust Svc	Emmaus	PA	18098	**800-666-2828***	610-967-5171
Vegetarian Times PO Box 1327 *Orders	Elmhurst	IL	60126	**800-829-3340***	630-516-4008
Vim & Vigor 1010 E Missouri Ave	Phoenix	AZ	85014	**[illegible]**	602-395-5850

449-14 Hobby & Personal Interests Magazines

Name / Address	City	State	Zip	Toll-Free	Phone
American History Illustrated 6405 Flank Dr.	Harrisburg	PA	17112	**800-829-3340**	717-657-9555
American Photo 1633 Broadway	New York	NY	10019	**800-274-4514**	212-767-6006
American Square Dance Magazine 34 E Main St	Apopka	FL	32703	**888-588-2362**	407-886-7151
Antiques 575 Broadway 5th Fl *Cust Svc	New York	NY	10012	**800-925-9271***	212-941-2800
AOPA Pilot 421 Aviation Way	Frederick	MD	21701	**800-872-2672**	301-695-2000
Aquarium Fish 3 Burroughs *Cust Svc	Irvine	CA	92618	**800-365-4421***	949-855-8822
Arabian Horse World 1316 Tamson Drive Suite 101	Cambria	CA	94328	**800-955-9423**	805-771-2300
Astronomy 21027 Crossroads Cir	Waukesha	WI	53186	**888-350-2413**	262-796-8776
Backpacker 33 E Minor St *Subcriptions	Emmaus	PA	18098	**800-666-3434***	610-967-5171
Beadwork Magazine 201 E 4th St *Cust Svc	Loveland	CO	80537	**800-849-8753***	970-669-7672
Better Homes & Gardens WOOD Magazine 1716 Locust St	Des Moines	IA	50309	**800-374-9663**	
Bicycling 33 E Minor St *Cust Svc	Emmaus	PA	18098	**800-666-2806***	610-967-5171
Bird Breeder 3 Burroughs *Cust Svc	Irvine	CA	92618	**800-365-4421***	949-855-8822
Bird Talk 3 Burroughs *Cust Svc	Irvine	CA	92618	**800-365-4421***	949-855-8822
Blood-Horse PO Box 911088	Lexington	KY	40591	**800-866-2361**	859-278-2361
British Heritage 6405 Flank Dr	Harrisburg	PA	17112	**800-829-3340**	717-657-9555
Cat Fancy 3 Burroughs *Cust Svc	Irvine	CA	92618	**800-365-4421***	949-855-8822
Chess Life 3068 Rt 9W Suite 100 *Sales	New Windsor	NY	12553	**800-388-5464***	845-562-8350
Cigar Aficionado 387 Park Ave S 8th Fl. *Sales	New York	NY	10016	**800-992-2442***	212-684-4224
Classic Toy Trains 21027 Crossroads Cir	Waukesha	WI	53186	**888-350-2413**	262-796-8776
Coin Prices 700 E State St	Iola	WI	54990	**800-258-0929**	715-445-2214
Collector's Mart 700 E State St	Iola	WI	54990	**800-258-0929**	715-445-2214
Computer Gaming World Magazine 28 E 28th St 9th Fl	New York	NY	10016	**800-827-4450**	212-503-5371
Country Woman Magazine 5400 S 60th St	Greendale	WI	53129	**800-344-6913**	414-423-0100
Crafts 'n Things PO Box 420235	Palm Coast	FL	32142	**800-444-0441**	386-447-6309
Daily Racing Form 100 Broadway 7th Fl *Cust Svc	New York	NY	10005	**800-306-3676***	212-366-7600
Decorative Artist's Workbook 4700 E Galbraith Rd	Cincinnati	OH	45236	**800-289-0963**	513-531-2690
Dog Fancy 3 Burroughs *Cust Svc	Irvine	CA	92618	**800-365-4421***	949-855-8822
Dog World 3 Burroughs	Irvine	CA	92618	**800-365-4421**	949-855-8822
Dollhouse Miniatures PO Box 595	Boston	MA	02117	**800-437-5828**	617-536-0100
Family Handyman Magazine Commerce Dr Suite 700	Eagan	MN	55121	**800-285-4961**	651-454-9200
Fine Cooking Magazine 63 S Main St	Newtown	CT	06470	**800-477-8727**	203-426-8171
Fine Woodworking 63 S Main St PO Box 5507	Newtown	CT	06470	**800-888-8286**	203-426-8171
FineScale Modeler 21027 Crossroads Cir	Waukesha	WI	53186	**888-350-2413**	262-796-8776
Flyer PO Box 39099	Lakewood	WA	98439	**800-426-8538**	253-471-9888
Flying Magazine 1633 Broadway 43rd Fl *Cust Svc	New York	NY	10019	**800-274-6793***	212-767-6000
Freshwater & Marine Aquarium 144 W Sierra Madre Blvd	Sierra Madre	CA	91024	**800-523-1736**	626-355-1476
Growing Edge Magazine PO Box 1027	Corvallis	OR	97339	**800-888-6785**	541-757-8477
Horse Illustrated 3 Burroughs	Irvine	CA	92618	**800-365-4421**	949-855-8822
Horse & Rider 4101 International Pkwy	Carrollton	TX	75007	**877-717-8928**	972-309-5700
Model Airplane News PO Box 428	Mount Morris	IL	61054	**800-877-5160**	815-734-1243
Model Railroader Magazine 21027 Crossroads Cir	Waukesha	WI	53186	**888-350-2413**	262-796-8776
Mountain Bike 33 E Minor St	Emmaus	PA	18098	**800-666-1817**	610-967-5171
Nuts & Volts Magazine 430 Princeland Ct *Orders	Corona	CA	92879	**800-783-4624***	951-371-8497
Organic Gardening 33 E Minor St *Circ	Emmaus	PA	18098	**800-666-2206***	610-967-5171
Outdoor Life 2 Park Ave	New York	NY	10016	**800-227-2224**	212-779-5000
Outdoor Photographer 12121 Wilshire Blvd Suite 1200 *Cust Svc	Los Angeles	CA	90025	**800-283-4410***	310-820-1500
Outside 400 Market St	Santa Fe	NM	87501	**800-688-7433**	505-989-7100
PC Gamer Magazine 150 N Hill Dr	Brisbane	CA	94005	**800-898-7159**	415-468-4684
Petersen's Photographic Magazine 6420 Wilshire Blvd *Cust Svc	Los Angeles	CA	90048	**800-800-3686***	323-782-2000
Plane & Pilot 12121 Wilshire Blvd Suite 1200	Los Angeles	CA	90025	**800-283-4330**	310-820-1500
Popular Mechanics 224 W 57th St	New York	NY	10019	**800-333-4948**	212-649-2000
Practical Horseman 665 Quince Orchard Rd Suite 600 *Cust Svc	Gaithersburg	MD	20878	**877-717-8929***	301-977-3900
Radio Control Boat Modeler PO Box 433	Mount Morris	IL	61054	**800-877-5160**	815-734-1243
R/C Modeler 144 W Sierra Madre Blvd.	Sierra Madre	CA	91024	**800-523-1736**	626-355-1476
Reptiles 3 Burroughs	Irvine	CA	92618	**800-365-4421**	949-855-8822
Rubber Stamper Magazine 207 Commercial Ct	Morganville	NJ	07751	**800-969-7176**	732-536-5160
Rug Hooking Magazine 1300 Market St Suite 202	Lemoyne	PA	17043	**800-233-9055**	717-234-5091
Shutterbug 1419 Chaffee Dr Suite 1	Titusville	FL	32780	**800-829-3340**	386-447-6318
Trains 21027 Crossroads Cir.	Waukesha	WI	53186	**888-350-2413**	262-796-8776
Wine Spectator 387 Park Ave S 8th Fl. *Orders	New York	NY	10016	**800-752-7799***	212-684-4224
Woodsmith 2200 Grand Ave	Des Moines	IA	50312	**800-333-5075**	515-282-7000
Workbench 2200 Grand Ave	Des Moines	IA	50312	**800-311-3991**	515-282-7000

449-15 Law Magazines & Journals

Name / Address	City	State	Zip	Toll-Free	Phone
ABA Journal 750 N Lake Shore Dr	Chicago	IL	60611	**800-285-2221**	312-988-5000
American Lawyer 345 Park Ave S	New York	NY	10010	**800-888-8300**	212-779-9200
Banking Law Journal 1001 Fort Myer Dr Suite 702 *Cust Svc	Arlington	VA	22209	**800-572-2797***	703-528-0145
Compleat Lawyer 750 N Lake Shore Dr	Chicago	IL	60611	**800-285-2221**	312-988-5000
Family Advocate 750 N Lake Shore Dr	Chicago	IL	60611	**800-285-2221**	312-988-5000
Florida Bar Journal 650 Apalachee Pkwy	Tallahassee	FL	32399	**800-342-8060**	850-561-5600
Maryland Bar Journal 520 W Fayette St.	Baltimore	MD	21201	**800-492-1964**	410-685-7878
National Jurist PO Box 939039	San Diego	CA	92913	**800-465-3462**	858-503-7572
National Law Journal 345 Park Ave S	New York	NY	10010	**800-888-8300**	212-779-9200
New York Law Journal 345 Park Ave S	New York	NY	10010	**800-888-8300**	212-779-9200
Ohio Lawyer PO Box 16562	Columbus	OH	43216	**800-282-6556**	614-487-2050
Oregon State Bar Bulletin 5200 SW Meadows Rd	Lake Oswego	OR	97035	**800-452-8260**	503-620-0222
Practical Lawyer 4025 Chestnut St	Philadelphia	PA	19104	**800-253-6397**	215-243-1600
Practical Real Estate Lawyer 4025 Chestnut St	Philadelphia	PA	19104	**800-253-6397**	215-243-1600
Student Lawyer 750 N Lake Shore Dr	Chicago	IL	60611	**800-285-2221**	312-988-5000
Trial 1050 31st St NW	Washington	DC	20007	**800-424-2725**	202-965-3500
Washington State Bar News 2101 4th Ave 4th Fl	Seattle	WA	98121	**800-945-9722**	206-727-8215

449-16 Medical Magazines & Journals

Name / Address	City	State	Zip	Toll-Free	Phone
Alabama MD 19 S Jackson St.	Montgomery	AL	36104	**800-239-6272**	334-263-6441
American Family Physician 11400 Tomahawk Creek Pkwy	Leawood	KS	66211	**800-274-2237**	913-906-6000
American Journal of Nursing 345 Hudson St 16th Fl	New York	NY	10014	**800-777-2295**	212-886-1200
American Journal of Psychiatry 1000 Wilson Blvd Suite 1825	Arlington	VA	22209	**800-368-5777**	703-907-7300
American Nurse 600 Maryland Ave SW Suite 100W	Washington	DC	20024	**800-274-4262**	202-651-7000
American Psychologist 750 1st St NE	Washington	DC	20002	**800-374-2721**	202-336-5500
Annals of Internal Medicine 190 North Independence Mall W	Philadelphia	PA	19106	**800-523-1546**	215-351-2400
CA-A Cancer Journal for Clinicians 345 Hudson St 16th Fl	New York	NY	10014	**800-777-2295**	212-886-1226
California Physician PO Box 7690	San Francisco	CA	94120	**800-882-1262**	415-541-0900
Connecticut Medicine 160 Saint Ronan St	New Haven	CT	06511	**800-635-7740**	203-865-0587
Contemporary OB/GYN 5 Paragon Dr	Montvale	NJ	07645	**888-581-8052**	973-944-7777
Contemporary Pediatrics 5 Paragon Dr	Montvale	NJ	07645	**888-581-8052**	973-944-7777
Contemporary Urology 5 Paragon Dr	Montvale	NJ	07645	**888-581-8052**	973-944-7777
Dental Economics 1421 S Sheridan Rd	Tulsa	OK	74112	**800-331-4463**	918-835-3161
Dental Practice Report 2 Northfield Plaza Suite 300	Northfield	IL	60093	**800-323-3337**	847-441-3700
Dental Products Report 2 Northfield Plaza Suite 300	Northfield	IL	60093	**800-323-3337**	847-441-3700
Diabetes Advisor 1701 N Beauregard St	Alexandria	VA	22311	**800-342-2383**	703-549-1500
Emergency Medicine 26 Main St	Chatham	NJ	07928	**800-976-4040**	973-701-8900
Female Patient 26 Main St	Chatham	NJ	07928	**800-976-4040**	973-701-8900
Internal Medicine News 12230 Wilkins Ave.	Rockville	MD	20852	**800-445-6975**	301-816-8700
Iowa Medicine 1001 Grand Ave	West Des Moines	IA	50265	**800-747-3070**	515-223-1401
JAMA (Journal of the American Medical Assn) 515 N State St	Chicago	IL	60610	**800-262-2350**	312-464-5000
Journal of the American Dental Assn 211 E Chicago Ave.	Chicago	IL	60611	**800-621-8099**	312-440-2740
Journal of the American Dietetic Assn 120 S Riverside Plaza Suite 2000	Chicago	IL	60606	**800-877-1600**	312-899-0040
Journal of the American Medical Assn (JAMA) 515 N State St	Chicago	IL	60610	**800-262-2350**	312-464-5000
Journal of the American Veterinary Medical Assn 1931 N Meacham Rd Suite 100	Schaumburg	IL	60173	**800-248-2862**	847-925-8070
Journal of the Arkansas Medical Society PO Box 55088	Little Rock	AR	72215	**800-524-1058**	501-224-8967
Journal of the Florida Medical Assn 123 S Adams St.	Tallahassee	FL	32301	**800-762-0233**	850-224-6496
Journal of the Louisiana State Medical Society 6767 Perkins Rd	Baton Rouge	LA	70808	**800-375-9508**	225-763-8500
Journal of the Medical Assn of Georgia 1330 W Peachtree St NW Suite 500	Atlanta	GA	30309	**800-282-0224**	404-876-7535
Journal of the Mississippi State Medical Assn PO Box 2548	Ridgeland	MS	39158	**800-898-0251**	601-853-6733
Journal of Oklahoma State Medical Assn 601 NW Grand Blvd.	Oklahoma City	OK	73118	**800-522-9452**	405-843-9571
Journal of the South Carolina Medical Assn 3210 Fernandina Rd.	Columbia	SC	29210	**800-327-1021**	803-798-6207
Laboratory Medicine 2100 W Harrison St	Chicago	IL	60612	**800-621-4142**	312-738-1336
Mayo Clinic Proceedings 200 1st St SW Siebens Bldg 770	Rochester	MN	55905	**800-707-7040**	507-284-2094
Medical Economics 5 Paragon Dr	Montvale	NJ	07645	**888-581-8052**	973-944-7777
Michigan Medicine 1300 Godward St NE Suite 2500	Minneapolis	MN	55413	**800-342-5662**	612-378-1875
NASW News 750 1st St NE Suite 700	Washington	DC	20002	**800-638-8799**	202-408-8600
NCMS Bulletin 222 N Person St	Raleigh	NC	27601	**800-722-1350**	919-833-3836

Classified Section

Name / Address	City	State	Zip	Toll-Free	Phone
New England Journal of Medicine 10 Shattuck St	Boston	MA	02115	**800-843-6356**	617-734-9800
Nurseweek 1156 Aster Ave Suite C	Sunnyvale	CA	94086	**800-859-2091**	408-249-5877
Nursing 2004 323 Norristown Rd Suite 200	Ambler	PA	19002	**800-346-7844**	215-646-8700
Nursing Management 323 Norristown Rd Suite 200	Ambler	PA	19002	**800-346-7844**	215-646-8700
Ohio Medicine 3401 Mill Run Dr	Hilliard	OH	43026	**800-766-6762**	614-527-6762
Patient Care 5 Paragon Dr	Montvale	NJ	07645	**888-581-8052**	973-944-7777
Pharmacy Today 2215 Constitution Ave NW	Washington	DC	20037	**800-327-2742**	202-429-7557
Physician & Sportsmedicine 4530 W 77th St	Minneapolis	MN	55435	**800-525-5003**	952-835-3222
Postgraduate Medicine 4530 W 77th St	Minneapolis	MN	55435	**800-525-5003**	952-835-3222
Psychotherapy Networker 7705 13th St NW	Washington	DC	20012	**888-883-3782**	202-829-2452
RN 5 Paragon Dr	Montvale	NJ	07645	**888-581-8052**	973-944-7777
Social Work 750 1st St NE Suite 700	Washington	DC	20002	**800-638-8799**	202-408-8600
Southern Medical Journal 35 Lakeshore Dr	Birmingham	AL	35209	**800-423-4992**	205-945-1840
Texas Medicine 401 W 15th St	Austin	TX	78701	**800-880-1300**	512-370-1300
US Pharmacist 100 Ave of the Americas 9th Fl	New York	NY	10013	**877-529-1746**	212-274-7000
Veterinary Economics 8033 Flint St	Lenexa	KS	66214	**800-255-6864**	913-492-4300
Veterinary Medicine 8033 Flint St	Lenexa	KS	66214	**800-255-6864**	913-492-4300
Virginia Medical News 4205 Dover Rd	Richmond	VA	23221	**800-746-6768**	804-353-2721
Wisconsin Medical Journal 330 E Lakeside St	Madison	WI	53715	**800-362-9080**	608-257-6781

449-17 Political & Current Events Magazines

Name / Address	City	State	Zip	Toll-Free	Phone
American Spectator 1611 N Kent St Suite 901	Arlington	VA	22209	**800-524-3469**	703-807-2011
Commonweal 475 Riverside Dr Suite 405	New York	NY	10115	**888-495-6755**	212-662-4200
Criminal Politics Magazine PO Box 37432	Cincinnati	OH	45222	**800-543-0486**	513-475-0100
Foreign Affairs 58 E 68th St	New York	NY	10021	**800-829-5539**	212-434-9525
Freeman The 30 S Broadway *Sales	Irvington-on-Hudson	NY	10533	**800-452-3518***	914-591-7230
Human Events 1 Massachusetts Ave NW Suite 600 *Cust Svc	Washington	DC	20001	**800-787-7557***	202-216-0600
Maclean's Magazine 1 Mt Pleasant Rd 11th Fl	Toronto	ON	M4Y2Y5	**800-268-9119**	416-764-1300
Media Bypass Magazine 4900 Tippecanoe Dr	Evansville	IN	47715	**800-429-7277**	812-477-8670
Mother Jones 731 Market St Suite 600	San Francisco	CA	94103	**800-438-6656**	415-665-6637
Nation 33 Irving Pl 8th Fl *Cust Svc	New York	NY	10003	**800-333-8536***	212-209-5400
National Journal 600 New Hampshire Ave NW	Washington	DC	20037	**800-356-4838**	202-266-7230
New Republic 1331 H St Suite 700 *Cust Svc	Washington	DC	20005	**800-827-1289***	202-508-4444
Newsweek 251 W 57th St *Cust Svc	New York	NY	10019	**800-631-1040***	212-445-4000
Reason 3415 S Sepulveda Blvd Suite 400 *Cust Svc	Los Angeles	CA	90034	**888-732-7668***	310-391-2245
Time Rockefeller Ctr Time & Life Bldg	New York	NY	10020	**800-541-2000**	212-522-1212
US News & World Report 1050 Thomas Jefferson St NW	Washington	DC	20007	**800-436-6520**	202-955-2000
Weekly Standard 1150 17th St NW Suite 505 *Cust Svc	Washington	DC	20036	**800-274-7293***	202-293-4900
World Press Review 700 Broadway 3rd Fl	New York	NY	10003	**800-862-2966**	212-982-8880

449-18 Religious & Spiritual Magazines

Name / Address	City	State	Zip	Toll-Free	Phone
Biblical Archaeology Review 4710 41st St NW	Washington	DC	20016	**800-221-4644**	202-364-3300
Body & Soul 42 Pleasant St	Watertown	MA	02472	**800-755-1178**	617-926-0200
Charisma 600 Rinehart Rd	Lake Mary	FL	32746	**800-829-3346**	407-333-0600
Christian Reader 465 Gundersen Dr	Carol Stream	IL	60188	**800-223-3161**	630-260-6200
Christianity Today 465 Gundersen Dr *Sales	Carol Stream	IL	60188	**800-999-1704***	630-260-6200
Crisis 1814 1/2 'N' St NW *Cust Svc	Washington	DC	20036	**800-746-8073***	202-861-7790
Episcopal Life 815 2nd Ave Episcopal Church Ctr	New York	NY	10017	**800-334-7626**	
Guideposts Magazine 39 Seminary Hill Rd	Carmel	NY	10512	**800-431-2344**	845-225-3681
Hope Magazine PO Box 160 *Cust Svc	Brooklin	ME	04616	**800-513-0869***	207-359-4651
Jewish Family & Life Magazine 90 Oak St PO Box 9129	Newton Upper Falls	MA	02464	**888-458-8535**	617-965-7700
Lutheran 8765 W Higgins Rd	Chicago	IL	60631	**800-638-3522**	773-380-2540
Moody Magazine 820 N La Salle Blvd *Cust Svc	Chicago	IL	60610	**800-284-9551***	312-329-2164
Presbyterians Today 100 Witherspoon St	Louisville	KY	40202	**800-227-2872**	502-569-5637
Saint Anthony Messenger 28 W Liberty St	Cincinnati	OH	45202	**800-488-0488**	513-241-5616
Today's Christian Woman 465 Gundersen Dr *Orders	Carol Stream	IL	60188	**800-365-9484***	630-260-6200
US Catholic Magazine 205 W Monroe *Cust Svc	Chicago	IL	60606	**800-328-6515***	312-236-7782
Woman's Touch Magazine 1445 Boonville Ave	Springfield	MO	65802	**877-840-4800**	417-862-1271

449-19 Science & Nature Magazines

Name / Address	City	State	Zip	Toll-Free	Phone
American Forests 734 15th St NW Suite 800	Washington	DC	20005	**800-368-5748**	202-955-4500
American Scientist PO Box 13975	Research Triangle Park	NC	27709	**800-282-0444**	919-549-0097
Archaeology Magazine 36-36 33rd St *Cust Svc	Long Island City	NY	11106	**877-275-9782***	718-472-3050
Audubon Magazine 700 Broadway 5th Fl *Cust Svc	New York	NY	10003	**800-274-4201***	212-979-3000
Aviation Week & Space Technology 1200 G St NW Suite 922	Washington	DC	20005	**800-525-5003**	202-383-2314
BioScience 1444 'I' St NW Suite 200	Washington	DC	20005	**800-992-2427**	202-628-1500
Discover Magazine 114 5th Ave 15th Fl *Circ	New York	NY	10011	**800-829-9132***	212-633-4400
Friends of the Earth Magazine 1717 Massachusetts Ave Suite 600	Washington	DC	20005	**877-843-8687**	202-783-7400
NASA Tech Briefs 317 Madison Ave Suite 1900	New York	NY	10017	**800-944-6272**	212-490-3999
National Parks Magazine 1300 19th St NW Suite 300	Washington	DC	20036	**800-628-7275**	202-223-6722
National Wildlife Magazine 11100 Wildlife Ctr Dr *Cust Svc	Reston	VA	22090	**800-822-9919***	703-438-6000
Natural History Magazine American Museum of Natural History 175-208 Central Pk W	New York	NY	10024	**800-234-5252**	212-769-5500
Nature National Press Bldg 529 14th St NW Suite 968	Washington	DC	20045	**800-524-0384**	202-737-2355
Orion Magazine 187 Main St	Great Barrington	MA	01230	**888-909-6568**	413-528-4422
Physics Today 1 Physics Ellipse	College Park	MD	20740	**800-344-6902**	301-209-3040
Popular Science Magazine Time Life Bldg Rockefeller Ctr *Cust Svc	New York	NY	10020	**800-289-9399***	212-779-5000
R & D Magazine 100 Enterprise Dr Suite 600 Box 912	Rockaway	NJ	07866	**800-222-0289**	973-920-7000
Science 1200 New York Ave NW	Washington	DC	20005	**800-731-4939**	202-326-6500
Science News 1719 'N' St NW *Sales	Washington	DC	20036	**800-552-4412***	202-785-2255
Scientific American Magazine 415 Madison Ave *Orders	New York	NY	10017	**800-333-1199***	212-754-8550
Sky & Telescope Magazine 49 Bay State Rd	Cambridge	MA	02138	**800-253-0245**	617-864-7360
Smithsonian Air & Space Magazine 750 9th St NW Suite 7100 *Cust Svc	Washington	DC	20560	**800-766-2149***	202-275-1230
Wildlife Conservation Magazine 2300 Southern Blvd	Bronx	NY	10460	**800-786-8226**	718-220-6876

449-20 Sports Magazines

Name / Address	City	State	Zip	Toll-Free	Phone
American Hunter 11250 Waples Mill Rd	Fairfax	VA	22030	**800-672-3888**	703-267-1300
American Rifleman 11250 Waples Mill Rd	Fairfax	VA	22030	**800-672-3888**	703-267-1379
Baseball Digest 990 Grove St	Evanston	IL	60201	**800-877-5893**	847-491-6440
Basketball Digest 990 Grove St *Cust Svc	Evanston	IL	60201	**800-877-5893***	847-491-6440
Bowhunting World 14505 21st Ave N Suite 202	Plymouth	MN	55447	**800-766-0039**	763-473-5800
Bowling Digest 990 Grove St	Evanston	IL	60201	**800-877-5893**	847-491-6440
Climbing Magazine 0326 Hwy 133 Suite 190	Carbondale	CO	81623	**800-493-4569**	970-963-9449
Discovery YMCA 101 N Wacker Dr	Chicago	IL	60606	**800-872-9622**	312-977-0031
Ducks Unlimited Magazine 1 Waterfowl Way	Memphis	TN	38120	**800-453-8257**	901-758-3825
ESPN Magazine 19 E 34th St *Cust Svc	New York	NY	10016	**888-267-3684***	212-515-1000
Field & Stream 2 Park Ave *Cust Svc	New York	NY	10016	**800-999-0869***	212-779-5000
Football Digest 990 Grove St	Evanston	IL	60201	**800-877-5893**	847-491-6440
Golf Digest 20 Westport Rd PO Box 850	Wilton	CT	06897	**800-962-5513**	203-761-5100
Golf Magazine 2 Park Ave	New York	NY	10016	**800-227-2224**	212-779-5000
Golf Tips Magazine 12121 Wilshire Blvd Suite 1200	Los Angeles	CA	90025	**800-283-4330**	310-820-1500
Golf for Women 201 Westport Rd PO Box 850	Wilton	CT	06897	**800-962-5513**	203-761-5100
Golf World 210 Westport Rd PO Box 850	Wilton	CT	06897	**800-962-5513**	203-761-5100
Guns & Ammo 6420 Wilshire Blvd 14th Fl	Los Angeles	CA	90048	**800-800-2666**	323-782-2000
Hockey Digest 990 Grove St	Evanston	IL	60201	**800-877-5893**	847-491-6440
Hockey News 100-25 Sheppard Ave W	Toronto	ON	M2N6F7	**888-361-9768**	416-733-7600
In-Fisherman 7819 Highland Scenic Rd	Baxter	MN	56425	**800-441-1740**	218-829-1648
Journal of the Philosophy of Sport 1607 N Market St	Champaign	IL	61820	**800-747-4457**	217-351-5076
North American Fisherman 12301 Whitewater Dr Suite 260	Minnetonka	MN	55343	**800-843-6232**	952-936-9333
North American Hunter 12301 Whitewater Dr Suite 260	Minnetonka	MN	55343	**800-922-4868**	952-936-9333
Petersen's Hunting 6420 Wilshire Blvd	Los Angeles	CA	90048	**800-800-8326**	323-782-2000
Salt Water Sportsman 263 Summer St 3rd Fl	Boston	MA	02210	**888-888-3217**	617-303-3660
Shooting Times PO Box 1790 *Orders	Peoria	IL	61656	**800-727-4353***	309-682-6626
Ski Magazine 2 Park Ave	New York	NY	10016	**800-227-2224**	212-779-5000
Skiing Magazine 2 Park Ave	New York	NY	10016	**800-227-2224**	212-779-5000
Snowboarder PO Box 1028 *Orders	Dana Point	CA	92629	**800-955-9120***	949-496-5922
Snowmobile 6420 Sycamore Ln Suite 100 *Cust Svc	Maple Grove	MN	55369	**800-848-6247***	763-383-4400
Sport Aviation 3000 Poberezny Rd	Oshkosh	WI	54902	**800-843-3612**	920-426-4800
Sporting Classics PO Box 23707	Columbia	SC	29224	**800-849-1004**	803-736-2424
Sporting News 10176 Corporate Sq Dr Suite 200	Saint Louis	MO	63132	**800-443-1886**	314-997-7111
Sports Illustrated 135 W 50th St Time & Life Bldg	New York	NY	10020	**800-541-1000**	212-522-4044
Sports Spectrum PO Box 2037	Indian Trail	NC	28709	**866-821-2971**	
Surfer PO Box 420235	Palm Coast	FL	32142	**800-289-0636**	386-447-6383
Surfing 950 Calle Amanecer Suite C	San Clemente	CA	92673	**800-879-0484**	949-492-7873
T & L Golf 1120 6th Ave	New York	NY	10036	**800-947-7961**	212-382-5600
TransWorld SNOWboarding 353 Airport Rd	Oceanside	CA	92054	**800-788-7072**	760-722-7777
TransWorld Surf 353 Airport Rd	Oceanside	CA	92054	**800-788-7072**	760-722-7777

449-21 Trade & Industry Magazines

Name / Address	City	State	Zip	Toll-Free	Phone
AAPG Explorer 1444 S Boulder Ave	Tulsa	OK	74119	**800-364-2274**	918-584-2555
Aerospace America 1801 Alexander Bell Dr Suite 500	Reston	VA	20191	**800-639-2422**	703-264-7500
Air Conditioning Heating & Refrigeration News 2401 W Big Beaver Rd Suite 700	Troy	MI	48084	**800-837-8337**	248-362-3700
Air Transport World 1350 Connecticut Ave NW Suite 902	Washington	DC	20036	**800-366-1901**	202-659-8500
American Salon 1 Park Ave 2nd Fl	New York	NY	10016	**800-342-8244**	212-951-6600
American Trucker 7355 N Woodland Dr	Indianapolis	IN	46278	**800-827-7468**	317-297-5500
ASCE News 1801 Alexander Bell Dr Suite 100	Reston	VA	20191	**800-548-2723**	703-295-6215

Trade & Industry Magazines (Cont'd)

				Toll-Free	Phone
Automotive Executive 8400 Westpark Dr	McLean	VA	22102	**800-252-6232**	703-821-7150
Automotive News 1155 Gratiot Ave	Detroit	MI	48207	**800-678-9595**	313-446-6000
AV Video & Multi Media Producer					
701 Westchester Ave Suite 101 W	White Plains	NY	10604	**800-800-5474***	914-328-9157
*Cust Svc					
Bartender Magazine PO Box 158	Liberty Corner	NJ	07938	**800-463-7465***	908-766-6006
*Sales					
Boating Industry					
6420 Sycamore Ln Suite 100	Maple Grove	MN	55369	**800-848-6247**	763-383-4400
Business & Commercial Aviation					
6 International Dr Suite 310	Rye Brook	NY	10573	**800-525-5003***	914-939-0300
*Cust Svc					
Chemical Engineering					
110 William St 11th Fl	New York	NY	10038	**800-340-6539**	212-621-4900
Chemical & Engineering News					
1155 16th St NW	Washington	DC	20036	**800-227-5558**	202-872-4600
Chemical Equipment 301 Gibraltar Dr	Morris Plains	NJ	07950	**800-446-6551***	973-292-5100
*Cust Svc					
Chemical Processing					
555 W Pierce Rd Suite 301	Itasca	IL	60143	**800-984-7644**	630-467-1300
Chemical Week 110 William St	New York	NY	10038	**800-927-3430***	212-621-4900
*Cust Svc					
Civil Engineering					
1801 Alexander Bell Dr Suite 100	Reston	VA	20191	**800-548-2723**	703-295-6000
Control 555 W Pierce Rd Suite 301	Itasca	IL	60143	**800-904-7641**	630-467-1300
Control Engineering 2000 Clearwater Dr	Oak Brook	IL	60523	**800-862-2670**	630-320-7000
Controller PO Box 85310	Lincoln	NE	68510	**800-247-4890**	402-479-2143
DaySpa Magazine 7628 Densmore Ave	Van Nuys	CA	91406	**800-442-5667**	818-782-7328
EC & M 9800 Metcalf Ave	Overland Park	KS	66212	**800-814-9511***	913-341-1300
*Acctg					
EDN 275 Washington St	Newton	MA	02458	**800-446-6551***	617-964-3030
*Orders					
EE Product News 45 Eisenhower Dr 5th Fl	Paramus	NJ	07652	**800-829-9028**	201-393-6060
EE Times 600 Community Dr	Manhasset	NY	10030	**800-645-6278**	516-562-5000
Electronic Design 45 Eisenhower Dr 5th Fl	Paramus	NJ	07652	**800-829-9028**	201-393-6060
Electronic News PO Box 15908	Hollywood	CA	91615	**800-353-9118**	818-487-4555
ENR/Engineering News-Record					
2 Penn Plaza 9th Fl	New York	NY	10121	**800-525-5003**	212-904-2000
EPRI Journal 3412 Hillview Ave	Palo Alto	CA	94304	**800-313-3774**	650-855-2000
Equipment Today 1233 Janesville Ave	Fort Atkinson	WI	53538	**800-547-7377**	920-563-6388
Fine Homebuilding 63 S Main St	Newtown	CT	06470	**800-888-8286**	203-426-8171
Giftware News 20 W Kinzie 12th Fl	Chicago	IL	60610	**800-229-1967**	312-849-2220
Healthcare Foodservice PO Box 470067	Celebration	FL	34747	**800-525-2015**	407-343-9333
Heavy Duty Trucking 38 Executive Pk Suite 300	Irvine	CA	92614	**800-233-1911**	949-261-1636
HFN 7 W 34th St	New York	NY	10001	**800-424-8698**	212-630-4000
Homes & Land Magazine/Rental Guide					
1600 Capital Cir SW	Tallahassee	FL	32310	**800-277-4357***	850-574-2111
*Cust Svc					
JEMS Communications Inc					
525 B St Suite 1900	San Diego	CA	92101	**800-266-5367***	619-687-3272
*Cust Svc					
Job Shop Technology Magazine					
16 Waterbury Rd	Prospect	CT	06712	**800-317-0474**	203-758-4474
Journal of Petroleum Technology					
222 Palisades Creek Dr	Richardson	TX	75080	**800-456-6863**	972-952-9393
Journal of Protective Coatings & Linings					
2100 Wharton St Suite 310	Pittsburgh	PA	15203	**800-837-8303**	412-431-8300
Laboratory Equipment 301 Gibraltar Dr	Morris Plains	NJ	07950	**800-547-7377**	973-292-5100
Land Line 1 NW OOIDA Dr	Grain Valley	MO	64029	**800-444-5791**	816-229-5791
Manufacturing Engineering 1 SME Dr	Dearborn	MI	48128	**800-733-4763**	313-271-1500
Mechanical Engineering 3 Park Ave	New York	NY	10016	**800-843-2763***	212-591-7000
*Cust Svc					
Modern Machine Shop 6915 Valley Ave	Cincinnati	OH	45244	**800-950-8020**	513-527-8800
Modern Plastics 110 William St 11th Fl	New York	NY	10038	**800-257-9402**	212-621-4900
Modern Salon 400 Knightsbridge Pkwy	Lincolnshire	IL	60069	**800-621-2845**	847-634-2600
Motorcycle Industry Magazine					
1521 Church St	Gardnerville	NV	89410	**800-576-4624**	775-782-0222
Nailpro Magazine 7628 Densmore Ave	Van Nuys	CA	91406	**800-442-5667**	818-782-7328
National Jeweler 770 Broadway	New York	NY	10003	**800-250-2430**	646-654-4500
Oil & Gas Journal PO Box 1260	Tulsa	OK	74101	**800-331-4463**	918-835-3161
Overdrive 3200 Rice Mine Rd NE	Tuscaloosa	AL	35406	**800-633-5953**	205-349-2990
Photo Insider 11 Vreeland Rd	Florham Park	NJ	07932	**800-631-0300**	973-377-1003
Proceedings of the IEEE 445 Hoes Ln	Piscataway	NJ	08855	**800-678-4333**	732-562-5478
Product Design & Development					
301 Gilbraltar Dr	Morris Plains	NJ	07950	**800-547-7377**	973-292-5100
Publishers Weekly 360 Park Ave S	New York	NY	10010	**800-278-2991***	646-746-6758
*Cust Svc					
Qualified Remodeler 1233 Janesville Ave	Fort Atkinson	WI	53538	**800-547-7377**	920-563-6388
Quality Progress PO Box 3005	Milwaukee	WI	53201	**800-248-1946**	414-272-8575
RCR: Radio Communications Report					
777 E Speer Blvd	Denver	CO	80203	**800-678-9595**	303-733-2500
Remodeling 1 Thomas Cir NW Suite 600	Washington	DC	20005	**888-269-8410**	202-452-0800
Road King 28 Whitebridge Rd Suite 209	Nashville	TN	37205	**800-385-9745**	615-627-2200
Telecommunications 685 Canton St	Norwood	MA	02062	**800-225-9978**	781-769-9750
Telephony Magazine					
330 N Wabash Ave Suite 2300	Chicago	IL	60611	**800-458-0479**	312-595-1080
Travel Weekly Crossroads 500 Plaza Dr	Secaucus	NJ	07094	**800-742-7076**	201-902-2000
U & LC Magazine 200 Ballardvalle Rd	Wilmington	MA	01887	**800-424-8973**	
Video Store Magazine					
201 E Sandpointe Ave Suite 600	Santa Ana	CA	92707	**800-854-3112**	714-513-8400
Water & Wastes Digest					
380 E Northwest Hwy Suite 200	Des Plaines	IL	60016	**800-220-7851**	847-391-1000
Women's Wear Daily 7 W 34th St 3rd Fl	New York	NY	10001	**800-289-0273**	212-630-4000
Writer's Digest 4700 E Galbraith Rd	Cincinnati	OH	45236	**800-888-6880***	513-531-2690
*Cust Svc					

449-22 Travel & Regional Interest Magazines

				Toll-Free	Phone
AAA Travel Topics 2023 Market St	Harrisburg	PA	17103	**877-848-9990**	717-236-4021
Alaska 301 Arctic Slope Ave Suite 300	Anchorage	AK	99518	**800-458-4010**	907-272-6070
Arizona Highways 2039 W Lewis Ave	Phoenix	AZ	85009	**800-543-5432**	602-712-2000
Atlanta Magazine 2600 Peachtree St Suite 300	Atlanta	GA	30303	**800-930-3019**	404-527-5500
Baltimore Magazine					
1000 Lancaster St Suite 400	Baltimore	MD	21202	**800-935-0838***	410-752-4200
*Cust Svc					
Boston Magazine 300 Massachusetts Ave	Boston	MA	02115	**800-333-2003**	617-262-9700
Business Travel News 770 Broadway	New York	NY	10003	**800-950-1314***	646-654-4500
*Cust Svc					
Cape Cod Life					
270 Communications Way Bldg 6	Hyannis	MA	02601	**800-698-1717**	508-775-9800
Caribbean Travel & Life					
460 N Orlando Ave Suite 200	Winter Park	FL	32789	**800-588-1689***	407-628-5662
*Circ					
Chesapeake Bay Magazine					
1819 Bay Ridge Ave Suite 158	Annapolis	MD	21403	**800-584-5066**	410-263-2662
Cincinnati					
705 Central Ave 1 Centennial Plaza					
Suite 175	Cincinnati	OH	45202	**800-846-4333***	513-421-4300
*Cust Svc					
Cleveland Magazine					
1422 Euclid Ave Suite 730	Cleveland	OH	44115	**800-210-7293**	216-771-2833
Coastal Living 2100 Lakeshore Dr	Birmingham	AL	35209	**888-252-3529***	205-445-6000
*Cust Svc					
Conde Nast Traveler 4 Times Sq	New York	NY	10036	**800-223-0780**	212-286-2860
Connecticut 35 Nutmeg Dr	Trumbull	CT	06611	**800-974-2001**	203-380-6600
Cruise Travel 990 Grove St	Evanston	IL	60201	**800-877-5893**	847-491-6440
Departures Magazine					
1120 Ave of the Americas 11th Fl	New York	NY	10036	**800-333-7483**	212-382-5600
Down East: The Magazine of Maine					
680 Commercial St	Rockport	ME	04856	**800-727-7422**	207-594-9544
Family Motor Coaching 8291 Clough Pike	Cincinnati	OH	45244	**800-543-3622**	513-474-3622
Frequent Flyer					
3025 Highland Pkwy Suite 200	Downers Grove	IL	60515	**800-525-1138**	630-515-5300
GO Magazine 6600 AAA Dr	Charlotte	NC	28212	**800-477-4222**	704-377-3600
Guest Informant 21200 Erwin St	Woodland Hills	CA	91367	**800-275-5885**	818-716-7484
Hana Hou (Hawaiian Airlines)					
3465 Waialae Ave Suite 340	Honolulu	HI	96816	**888-733-3336**	808-733-3333
Home & Away Nebraska 10703 J St	Omaha	NE	68127	**800-842-7201**	402-592-5000
Honolulu Magazine 1000 Bishop St Suite 405	Honolulu	HI	96813	**800-788-4230**	808-537-9500
Hudson Valley 22 IBM Rd Suite 108	Poughkeepsie	NY	12601	**800-274-7844**	845-463-0542
Indianapolis Monthly					
40 Monument Cir Suite 100	Indianapolis	IN	46204	**888-403-9005***	317-237-9288
*Circ					
Inland Empire Magazine					
3769 Tibbetts St Suite A	Riverside	CA	92506	**877-357-2005**	951-682-3026
InsideFlyer Magazine					
1930 Frequent Flyer Point	Colorado Springs	CO	80915	**800-767-8896**	719-597-8889
Islands PO Box 4728	Santa Barbara	CA	93140	**800-284-7958**	805-745-7100
Jacksonville 534 Lancaster St	Jacksonville	FL	32204	**800-962-0214***	904-358-8330
*Circ					
Leisure Travel News 770 Broadway	New York	NY	10003	**800-950-1314***	646-654-4500
*Cust Svc					
Los Angeles Magazine					
5900 Wilshire Blvd 10th Fl	Los Angeles	CA	90036	**800-876-5222***	323-801-0100
*Cust Svc					
Louisiana Life					
111 Veterans Memorial Blvd Suite 1800	Metairie	LA	70005	**877-221-3512***	504-834-9292
*Edit					
Michigan Out-of-Doors PO Box 30235	Lansing	MI	48909	**800-777-6720**	517-371-1041
Midwest Living 1716 Locust St	Des Moines	IA	50309	**800-678-8093**	515-284-2662
Midwest Motorist 12901 N 40th Dr	Saint Louis	MO	63141	**800-222-7623**	314-523-7350
Milwaukee Magazine 417 E Chicago St	Milwaukee	WI	53202	**800-662-4818**	414-273-1101
Minneapolis-Saint Paul					
220 S 6th St Suite 500	Minneapolis	MN	55402	**800-788-0204**	612-339-7571
MotorHome 2575 Vista Del Mar Dr	Ventura	CA	93001	**800-678-1201***	805-667-4100
*Cust Svc					
National Geographic Traveler					
1145 17th St NW	Washington	DC	20036	**800-647-5463**	202-857-7000
Nevada Magazine 401 N Carson St	Carson City	NV	89701	**800-495-3281**	775-687-5416
New Jersey Monthly 55 Park Pl Box 920	Morristown	NJ	07963	**888-419-0419***	973-539-8230
*Cust Svc					
New Mexico Magazine 495 Old Santa Fe Trail	Santa Fe	NM	87501	**800-898-6639**	505-476-0202
New Orleans Magazine					
111 Veterans Memorial Blvd Suite 1800	Metairie	LA	70005	**877-221-3512***	504-831-3731
*Edit					
New York 444 Madison Ave	New York	NY	10022	**800-678-0900***	212-508-0700
*Circ					
Ohio Magazine 1422 Euclid Ave Suite 730	Cleveland	OH	44115	**800-210-7293**	216-771-2833
Oregon Coast Magazine					
4969 Hwy 101 Suite 2	Florence	OR	97439	**800-348-8401**	541-997-8401
Orlando Magazine					
11900 Biscayne Blvd Suite 300	Miami	FL	33181	**800-243-0609**	305-892-6644
Palm Beach Illustrated					
1000 N Dixie Hwy Suite C	West Palm Beach	FL	33401	**800-308-7346**	561-659-0210
Philadelphia Magazine					
1818 Market St 36th Fl	Philadelphia	PA	19103	**800-777-1003**	215-564-7700
Phoenix Magazine					
8501 E Princess Dr Suite 190	Scottsdale	AZ	85255	**800-228-6540**	480-664-3960
Pittsburgh Magazine 4802 5th Ave	Pittsburgh	PA	15213	**800-495-7323***	412-622-6440
*Sales					
Porthole Cruise Magazine					
4517 NW 31st Ave	Fort Lauderdale	FL	33309	**888-774-4768**	954-377-7777
San Diego Magazine 1450 Front St	San Diego	CA	92101	**800-600-2489**	619-230-9292
Southern Accents 2100 Lakeshore Dr	Birmingham	AL	35209	**800-366-4712**	205-445-6000
Southern Living 2100 Lakeshore Dr	Birmingham	AL	35209	**800-366-6700**	205-445-6000
Texas Monthly 701 Brazos St	Austin	TX	78701	**800-759-2000**	512-320-6900
Trailer Life 2575 Vista Del Mar Dr	Ventura	CA	93001	**800-765-7070**	805-667-4100
Travel + Leisure					
1120 Ave of the Americas 10th Fl	New York	NY	10036	**800-888-8728**	212-382-5600
Travel Agent Magazine 1 Park Ave 2nd Fl	New York	NY	10016	**800-342-8244**	212-951-6600
Travel Holiday 1633 Broadway	New York	NY	10019	**800-937-9241***	212-767-6000
*Circ					
TravelAge West 9911 W Pico Blvd 11th Fl	Los Angeles	CA	90035	**800-585-7321**	310-772-7430
Travelhost 10701 N Stemmons Fwy	Dallas	TX	75220	**800-527-1782**	972-556-0541
Vermont Life 6 Baldwin St	Montpelier	VT	05602	**800-284-3243**	802-828-3241
Washingtonian 1828 L St NW Suite 200	Washington	DC	20036	**877-532-6083**	202-296-3600
Waterway Guide 326 1st St Suite 400	Annapolis	MD	21403	**800-233-3359**	443-482-9377
Western Outdoors 185 Avenida La Plata	San Clemente	CA	92673	**800-290-2929***	949-366-0030
*Cust Svc					
Where Baltimore 301 S 19th St Suite 1-S	Philadelphia	PA	19103	**866-368-3604**	215-893-5100
Where New York 79 Madison Ave	New York	NY	10016	**800-666-8336**	212-636-2700
Where Philadelphia					
301 S 19th St Suite 1-S	Philadelphia	PA	19103	**866-368-3604**	215-893-5100
Wisconsin Trails					
1131 Mills St PO Box 317	Black Earth	WI	53515	**800-236-8088**	608-767-8000
Yankee 1121 Main St	Dublin	NH	03444	**800-288-4284**	603-563-8111

450 MAGNETS - PERMANENT

Company	City	State	Zip	Toll-Free	Phone
Arnold Engineering Co 300 N West St	Marengo	IL	60152	**800-545-4578**	815-568-2000
Electron Energy Corp 924 Links Ave	Landisville	PA	17538	**800-824-2735**	717-898-2294
Flexmag Industries Inc 107 Industry Rd	Marietta	OH	45750	**800-543-4426**	740-374-8024
Hitachi Magnetics Corp 7800 Neff Rd	Edmore	MI	48829	**800-955-9321**	989-427-5151
Jobmaster Corp 1505 Serpentine Rd *Cust Svc	Baltimore	MD	21209	**800-642-1400***	410-655-1400
Magnetic Component Engineering Inc 2830 Lomita Blvd	Torrance	CA	90505	**800-989-5656**	
Permanent Magnet Co Inc 4437 Bragdon St	Indianapolis	IN	46226	**800-547-1336**	317-547-1336

451 MAIL ORDER HOUSES

SEE ALSO Art Supply Stores; Book, Music, Video Clubs; Checks - Personal & Business; Computer Stores; Seed Companies

Company	City	State	Zip	Toll-Free	Phone
1-800 Contacts Inc 66 E Wadsworth Pk Dr 3rd Fl *NASDAQ: CTAC*	Draper	UT	84020	**800-266-8228**	801-924-9800
Aerobic Life Industries Inc 2800 E Chambers Suite 700 *Orders	Phoenix	AZ	85044	**800-798-0707***	602-283-0755
Allied Marketing Group Inc 1555 Regal Row *Cust Svc	Dallas	TX	75247	**800-762-3302***	214-915-7000
Allpets Inc 1 Maplewood Dr *Orders	Hazleton	PA	18201	**800-346-0749***	570-384-5555
American Blind & Wallpaper Factory 909 N Sheldon Rd *Cust Svc	Plymouth	MI	48170	**800-575-9019***	734-207-5800
America's Hobby Center Inc 8300 Tonnelle Ave	North Bergen	NJ	07047	**800-242-1931**	201-662-8500
Artistic Direct Inc 1316 College Ave *Cust Svc	Elmira	NY	14901	**800-845-3720***	607-733-5541
Backcountry.com 1136 S 3600 W Suite 600 *Orders	Salt Lake City	UT	84104	**800-409-4502***	801-973-4553
Barrie Pace Catalog 101 N Wacker Dr	Chicago	IL	60606	**800-441-6011**	312-372-6300
Bean LL Inc 15 Casco St *Cust Svc	Freeport	ME	04033	**800-341-4341***	207-865-4761
Bedford Fair Lifestyles 421 Landmark Dr	Wilmington	NC	28410	**800-964-9030**	
Blair Corp 220 Hickory St *AMEX: BL* ■ *Cust Svc	Warren	PA	16366	**800-458-6057***	814-723-3600
Boston Proper 6500 Park of Commerce Blvd	Boca Raton	FL	33487	**800-327-3627**	561-241-1700
Brawn of California Inc 741 F St	San Diego	CA	92101	**800-293-9333**	619-544-9900
Campmor Inc 28 Parkway *Orders	Upper Saddle River	NJ	07458	**800-526-4784***	201-825-8300
Chadwick's of Boston 35 United Dr	West Bridgewater	MA	02379	**800-677-0340**	508-583-8110
Childcraft Education Corp 2920 Old Tree Dr	Lancaster	PA	17603	**800-631-5652**	717-397-1717
Coldwater Creek Inc 1 Coldwater Creek Dr *NASDAQ: CWTR* ■ *Cust Svc	Sandpoint	ID	83864	**800-262-0040***	208-263-2266
Company Store 500 Company Store Rd	La Crosse	WI	54601	**800-285-3696**	608-785-1400
Concepts Direct Inc 2950 Colorful Ave *NASDAQ: CDIR*	Longmont	CO	80504	**800-773-0208**	303-772-9171
Crest Fruit Co 100 N Tower Rd	Alamo	TX	78516	**800-695-2253**	956-787-9971
Crutchfield Corp 1 Crutchfield Pk *Sales	Charlottesville	VA	22911	**800-955-3000***	434-817-1000
Current USA Inc 1005 E Woodmen Rd *Cust Svc	Colorado Springs	CO	80920	**800-525-7170***	719-594-4100
dELiA*s Corp 435 Hudson St 3rd Fl	New York	NY	10014	**800-335-4269**	212-807-9060
Digi-Key Corp 701 Brooks Ave S	Thief River Falls	MN	56701	**800-344-4539**	218-681-6674
Eastbay Inc PO Box 8066	Wausau	WI	54402	**800-628-6301**	
ET Wright & Co Inc 1356 Williams St	Chippewa Falls	WI	54729	**800-934-1022**	
Everglades Direct 720 International Pkwy	Sunrise	FL	33345	**800-999-9111**	954-846-8899
Figi's Inc 3200 S Maple Ave	Marshfield	WI	54449	**800-344-4353**	715-387-1771
Fingerhut Cos Inc 4400 Baker Rd *Orders	Minnetonka	MN	55343	**800-233-3588***	952-932-3100
Forestry Suppliers Inc 205 W Rankin St PO Box 8397 *Cust Svc	Jackson	MS	39201	**800-752-8460***	601-354-3565
Franklin Mint Corp 105 Commerce Dr	Aston	PA	19014	**800-523-7622**	610-459-6000
Gaiam Inc 360 Interlocken Blvd Suite 300 *NASDAQ: GAIA*	Broomfield	CO	80021	**800-869-3446**	303-464-3600
Geerlings & Wade Inc 960 Turnpike St	Canton	MA	02021	**800-782-9463**	781-821-4152
Gump's 135 Post St	San Francisco	CA	94108	**800-766-7628**	415-982-1616
Hammacher Schlemmer & Co 303 W Erie St	Chicago	IL	60610	**800-233-4800**	312-664-8170
Hanna Andersson Corp 1010 NW Flanders St *Cust Svc	Portland	OR	97209	**800-222-0544***	503-242-0920
Harry & David Co 2500 S Pacific Hwy *Cust Svc	Medford	OR	97501	**800-345-5655***	541-776-2121
HearthSong 3700 Wyse Rd *Orders	Dayton	OH	45414	**800-533-4397***	540-948-7100
Hello Direct Inc 74 Northeastern Blvd	Nashua	NH	03062	**800-444-3556**	
Helm Inc 14310 Hamilton Ave	Highland Park	MI	48203	**800-782-4356**	313-865-5000
Highsmith Inc W 5527 SR 106 PO Box 800	Fort Atkinson	WI	53538	**800-558-3899**	920-563-9571
Houston Numismatic Exchange Inc 2486 Times Blvd	Houston	TX	77005	**800-231-3650**	713-528-2135
HSN Improvements 23297 Commerce Pk	Beachwood	OH	44122	**800-944-8870**	216-831-6191
J Crew Group Inc 770 Broadway	New York	NY	10003	**800-932-0043**	212-209-2500
J Jill Group Inc The 4 Batterymarch Park *NASDAQ: JILL*	Quincy	MA	02169	**800-642-9989**	617-376-4300
Jackson & Perkins 2500 S Pacific Hwy PO Box 1028 *Cust Svc	Medford	OR	97501	**800-872-7673***	541-776-2000
JC Whitney & Co 225 N Michigan Ave	Chicago	IL	60601	**800-529-4486**	312-431-6000
JDR Microdevices Inc 1850 S 10th St *Sales	San Jose	CA	95112	**800-538-5000***	408-494-1450
Johnny Appleseed's Inc 30 Tozer Rd *Cust Svc	Beverly	MA	01915	**800-767-6666***	978-922-2040
Kimball Miles Co 41 W 8th Ave	Oshkosh	WI	54901	**800-546-2255**	920-231-3800
Lands' End Inc 1 Lands' End Ln *Orders	Dodgeville	WI	53595	**800-356-4444***	608-935-9341
Levenger 420 S Congress Ave *Cust Svc	Delray Beach	FL	33445	**800-544-0880***	561-276-2436
Lillian Vernon Corp 1 Theall Rd	Rye	NY	10580	**800-545-5426**	914-925-1200
LL Bean Inc 15 Casco St *Cust Svc	Freeport	ME	04033	**800-341-4341***	207-865-4761
Mary Maxim Inc 2001 Holland Ave PO Box 5019	Port Huron	MI	48061	**800-962-9504**	810-987-2000
MBI Inc 47 Richards Ave	Norwalk	CT	06857	**800-243-5160**	203-853-2000
MediaBay Inc 2 Ridgedale Ave Suite 300 *NASDAQ: MBAY*	Cedar Knolls	NJ	07927	**800-688-4442**	973-539-9528
Miles Kimball Co 41 W 8th Ave	Oshkosh	WI	54901	**800-546-2255**	920-231-3800
Movies Unlimited Inc 3015 Darnell Rd	Philadelphia	PA	19154	**800-668-4344**	215-637-4444
NASCO International Inc 901 Janesville Ave *Orders	Fort Atkinson	WI	53538	**800-558-9595***	920-563-2446
National Wholesale Co Inc 400 National Blvd	Lexington	NC	27292	**800-480-4673**	336-248-5904
Newport News Inc 711 3rd Ave 4th Fl *Sales	New York	NY	10017	**800-894-9639***	212-986-2585
Norm Thompson Outfitters Inc 3188 NW Aloclek Dr	Hillsboro	OR	97124	**800-547-1160**	503-614-4600
NRC Sports Inc 603 Pleasant St	Paxton	MA	01612	**800-243-5033**	508-852-8206
Oriental Trading Co Inc 5455 S 90th St	Omaha	NE	68127	**800-225-6440**	402-596-1200
Patagonia Inc 259 W Santa Clara Dr PO Box 150 *Cust Svc	Ventura	CA	93001	**800-638-6464***	805-643-8616
PETsMART Direct 1989 Transit Way	Brockport	NY	14420	**800-785-0504**	585-637-7508
Popular Club 22 Lincoln Pl	Garfield	NJ	07026	**800-767-2582**	973-470-3800
Professional Cutlery Direct LLC 242 Branford Rd	North Branford	CT	06471	**800-859-6994**	203-871-1000
Publishers Clearing House 101 Channel Dr	Port Washington	NY	11050	**800-645-9242**	516-883-5432
Real Goods Trading Corp 360 Interlocken Blvd Suite 300	Broomfield	CO	80021	**800-762-7325**	303-222-3600
Roaman's 2300 Southeastern Ave	Indianapolis	IN	46283	**800-459-1025**	
S & S Worldwide Inc 75 Mill St *Orders	Colchester	CT	06415	**800-243-9232***	860-537-3451
Sara Lee Direct 450 W Hanes Mill Rd *Cust Svc	Winston-Salem	NC	27105	**800-522-1151***	336-519-8360
ShopNBC 6740 Shady Oak Rd	Eden Prairie	MN	55344	**800-676-5523**	952-943-6000
SkyMall Inc 1520 E Pima St	Phoenix	AZ	85034	**800-759-6255**	602-254-9777
Specialty Catalog Corp 21 Bristol Dr	South Easton	MA	02375	**800-472-4017**	508-238-0199
Spiegel Inc 3500 Lacey Rd *Orders	Downers Grove	IL	60515	**800-345-4500***	630-986-8800
Sportsman's Guide Inc 411 Farwell Ave *NASDAQ: SGDE* ■ *Cust Svc	South Saint Paul	MN	55075	**800-888-5222***	651-451-3030
Thompson Norm Outfitters Inc 3188 NW Aloclek Dr	Hillsboro	OR	97124	**800-547-1160**	503-614-4600
Tog Shop Inc Lester Sq *Orders	Americus	GA	31710	**800-367-8647***	229-924-8800
TravelSmith Outfitters Inc 60 Leveroni Ct	Novato	CA	94949	**800-950-1600**	415-382-1855
Unicover Corp 1 Unicover Ctr *Cust Svc	Cheyenne	WY	82008	**800-443-4225***	307-771-3000
Van Dyke Supply Co 39771 Hwy 34 E	Woonsocket	SD	57385	**800-843-3320**	605-796-4425
Victoria's Secret Direct LLC 3425 Morse Crossing	Columbus	OH	43219	**800-888-1500**	614-337-5000
Viking Office Products Inc 950 W 190 St *Cust Svc	Torrance	CA	90502	**800-421-1222***	310-225-4500
WearGuard Corp 141 Longwater Dr	Norwell	MA	02061	**800-272-0308**	781-871-4100
Whitney JC & Co 225 N Michigan Ave	Chicago	IL	60601	**800-529-4486**	312-431-6000
Williams-Sonoma Inc 3250 Van Ness Ave *NYSE: WSM* ■ *Cust Svc	San Francisco	CA	94109	**800-541-1262***	415-421-7900
Willow Ridge 421 Landmark Dr	Wilmington	NC	28410	**800-388-2012**	
Wintersilks Inc 14 S Carroll St	Madison	WI	53703	**800-648-7455**	608-280-9000
Woodcraft Supply Co 560 Airport Industrial Park *Cust Svc	Parkersburg	WV	26102	**800-535-4482***	304-428-4866
Wright ET & Co Inc 1356 Williams St	Chippewa Falls	WI	54729	**800-934-1022**	
Zappos.com 271 Omega Pkwy Suite 104	Shepherdsville	KY	40165	**888-492-7767**	502-543-7200

452 MALLS - SHOPPING

Company	City	State	Zip	Toll-Free	Phone
Buy.com Inc 85 Enterprise St	Aliso Viejo	CA	92656	**877-880-1030**	949-389-2000
Columbus City Center 111 S 3rd St	Columbus	OH	43215	**800-882-4900**	614-221-4900
Concord Mills 8111 Concord Mills Blvd	Concord	NC	28027	**877-626-4557**	704-979-3000
Crossgates Mall 1 Crossgates Mall Rd	Albany	NY	12203	**800-439-2011**	518-869-9565
DCOTA (Design Center of the Americas) 1855 Griffin Rd	Dania Beach	FL	33004	**800-573-2682**	954-920-7997
Design Center of the Americas (DCOTA) 1855 Griffin Rd	Dania Beach	FL	33004	**800-573-2682**	954-920-7997
Fairlane Town Center 18900 Michigan Ave	Dearborn	MI	48126	**800-992-9500**	313-593-3330
Fashion Island Shopping Center 401 Newport Ctr Dr	Newport Beach	CA	92660	**800-495-4753**	949-721-2000
Festival Bay Mall at International Drive 5250 International Dr	Orlando	FL	32819	**800-481-1944**	407-351-7718
Franklin Mills 1455 Franklin Mills Cir	Philadelphia	PA	19114	**800-336-6255**	215-632-1500
Great Mall of the Bay Area 447 Great Mall Dr	Milpitas	CA	95035	**800-625-5229**	408-945-4022
Great Mall of the Great Plains 20700 W 151st St	Olathe	KS	66061	**888-386-6255**	913-829-6748
Gurnee Mills 6170 W Grand Ave	Gurnee	IL	60031	**800-937-7467**	847-263-7500
Hanes Mall 3320 Silas Creek Pkwy Suite 264	Winston-Salem	NC	27103	**800-443-6255**	336-765-8323
Internet Shopping Outlet Inc 55 John St 11th Fl	New York	NY	10038	**800-757-3015**	212-619-3353
Lakeside Mall 14000 Lakeside Cir	Sterling Heights	MI	48313	**800-334-5573**	586-247-4131
Northwest Plaza 650-A Northwest Plaza	Saint Ann	MO	63074	**800-264-7841**	314-298-0071
Ontario Mills 1 Mills Cir Suite 1	Ontario	CA	91764	**888-526-4557**	909-484-8300
Prime Outlets Ellenton 5461 Factory Shops Blvd	Ellenton	FL	34222	**888-260-7608**	941-723-1150
Sawgrass Mills 12801 W Sunrise Blvd	Sunrise	FL	33323	**800-356-4557**	954-846-2300
SouthPark Mall 4400 Sharon Rd	Charlotte	NC	28211	**888-364-4411**	704-364-4411
Stanford Shopping Center 180 El Camino Real	Palo Alto	CA	94304	**800-772-9332**	650-617-8585
Supermall of the Great Northwest 1101 SuperMall Way	Auburn	WA	98001	**800-729-8258**	253-833-9500

				Toll-Free	Phone
Tysons Corner Center					
1961 Chain Bridge Rd Suite 105	McLean	VA	22102	**888-289-7667**	703-893-9400
Valley View Mall 4802 Valley View Blvd	Roanoke	VA	24012	**800-321-1711**	540-563-4400

453 MALTING PRODUCTS

SEE ALSO Breweries & Microbreweries

				Toll-Free	Phone
Cargill Malt - Specialty Products Group					
704 S 15th St	Sheboygan	WI	53081	**800-669-6258***	920-459-4148
*Sales					
Froedtert Malting Co PO Box 712	Milwaukee	WI	53201	**800-646-6258**	414-671-1166
Premier Malt Products Inc					
25760 Groesbeck Hwy Suite 103	Warren	MI	48089	**800-521-1057***	586-443-3355
*Cust Svc					

454 MANAGED CARE - BEHAVIORAL HEALTH

				Toll-Free	Phone
Allen Group					
2965 W State Rd 434 Suite 100	Longwood	FL	32779	**800-272-7252**	407-788-8822
American Behavioral Benefits Managers					
550 Montgomery Hwy	Birmingham	AL	35216	**800-677-4544**	205-871-7814
American Psych Systems					
8403 Colesville Rd Suite 1600	Silver Spring	MD	20910	**800-305-3720**	301-571-0633
APC Hegeman 50 Dietz St Suite K	Oneonta	NY	13820	**800-327-0085**	607-432-9039
APS Healthcare Inc 8403 Colesville Rd	Silver Spring	MD	20910	**800-305-3720**	301-563-5633
Associated Behavioral Health Care Inc					
4701 41st Ave SW Suite 120	Seattle	WA	98116	**800-858-6702**	206-935-1282
Bensinger DuPont & Assoc					
20 N Wacker Dr Suite 920	Chicago	IL	60606	**800-227-8620**	312-726-8620
CIGNA Behavioral Health Inc					
11095 Viking Dr Suite 350	Eden Prairie	MN	55344	**800-433-5768**	952-996-2000
Comprehensive EAP 5 Militia Dr	Lexington	MA	02421	**800-344-1011**	781-863-8283
ComPsych Corp					
455 N City Front Plaza Dr NBC Tower					
13th Fl	Chicago	IL	60611	**800-272-7255**	312-595-4000
Contact Behavioral Health Services					
1400 E Southern Ave Suite 800	Tempe	AZ	85282	**800-888-1477**	480-730-3023
COPE Inc 1120 G St NW Suite 550	Washington	DC	20005	**800-247-3054**	202-628-5100
CorpCare Assoc Inc					
7000 Peachtree Dunwoody Rd Bldg 4					
Suite 300	Atlanta	GA	30328	**800-728-9444**	770-396-5253
CorpHealth Inc 1300 Summit Ave Suite 600	Fort Worth	TX	76102	**800-240-8388**	817-332-2519
Corporate Care Works					
8665 Baypine Rd Suite 100	Jacksonville	FL	32256	**800-327-9757**	904-296-9436
EAP Consultants Inc					
3901 Roswell Rd Suite 340	Marietta	GA	30062	**800-869-0276**	770-951-8021
EAP Systems 500 W Cummings Pk Suite 6000	Woburn	MA	01801	**800-327-6721**	781-935-8850
FEI Behavioral Health					
11700 W Lake Park Dr	Milwaukee	WI	53224	**800-221-3726**	414-359-1055
FHC Health Systems 240 Corporate Blvd	Norfolk	VA	23502	**800-451-3581**	757-459-5100
Holman Group 21050 Vanowen St	Canoga Park	CA	91303	**800-321-2843**	818-704-1444
Horizon Behavioral Services					
1500 Waters Ridge Dr	Lewisville	TX	75057	**800-931-4646**	972-420-8200
Horizon Health Corp 1500 Waters Ridge Dr	Lewisville	TX	75057	**800-931-4646**	972-420-8200
NASDAQ: HORC					
Human Management Services Inc					
1463 Dunwoody Dr	Westchester	PA	19380	**800-343-2186**	610-644-6000
Hurst Place 555 Sanatorium Rd	Hamilton	ON	L8N3Z5	**888-521-8300**	905-521-8300
Integrated Insights					
9370 Sky Park Ct Suite 140	San Diego	CA	92123	**800-372-4472**	858-571-1698
Interface EAP Inc					
10370 Richmond Ave Suite 1100	Houston	TX	77042	**800-324-4327**	713-781-3364
Interpersonal Dynamics Inc					
2265 Teton Plaza	Idaho Falls	ID	83404	**800-658-3837**	208-529-1737
Lexington Group 185 Main St Suite 401	New Britain	CT	06051	**800-571-0197**	860-225-3993
Magellan Health Services Inc					
6950 Columbia Gateway Dr	Columbia	MD	21046	**800-458-2740**	410-953-1000
NASDAQ: MGLN					
Managed Health Network Inc					
1600 Los Gamos Dr Suite 300	San Rafael	CA	94903	**800-327-2133**	
Midwest EAP Solutions Inc					
1010 W Saint Germain St Suite 580	Saint Cloud	MN	56301	**800-383-1908**	320-253-1909
National Employee Assistance Services Inc					
N 17 W 24100 Riverwood Dr Suite 300	Waukesha	WI	53188	**800-634-6433**	262-798-3900
National MENTOR Inc DBA MENTOR					
313 Congress St	Boston	MA	02210	**800-388-5150**	617-790-4800
New Directions Behavioral Health LLC					
PO Box 6729	Leawood	KS	66206	**800-528-5763**	913-982-8200
PacifiCare Behavioral Health Inc					
3120 Lake Ctr Dr	Santa Ana	CA	92704	**800-357-5850**	714-445-0300
Perspectives Ltd 20 N Clark Suite 2650	Chicago	IL	60602	**800-456-6327**	312-558-1560
Plan 21 2000 W Loop S Suite 600	Houston	TX	77027	**800-622-7276**	713-621-6500
Preferred Mental Health Management Inc					
401 E Douglas Ave Suite 300	Wichita	KS	67202	**800-776-4357**	316-262-0444
Providence Service Corp 620 N Craycroft Rd	Tucson	AZ	85711	**800-489-0064**	520-748-7108
NASDAQ: PRSC					
Stuecker & Assoc Inc					
1169 Eastern Pkwy Suite 2243	Louisville	KY	40217	**800-799-9327**	502-452-9227
United Behavioral Health Inc					
425 Market St 27th Fl	San Francisco	CA	94105	**800-888-2998**	415-547-5000
ValueOptions Inc					
12369 Sunrise Valley Dr Suite C	Reston	VA	20191	**800-236-4648**	703-390-6800
Wellpoint Behavioral Health/Blue Cross					
9655 Granite Ridge Dr 6th Fl	San Diego	CA	92123	**800-999-7222**	858-571-8300

455 MANAGEMENT SERVICES

SEE ALSO Association Management Companies; Educational Institution Operators & Managers; Facilities Management Services; Hotel & Resort Operation & Management; Incentive Program Management Services; Investment Advice & Management; Pharmacy Benefits Management Services; Restaurant Operation & Management; Retail Store Operation & Management

				Toll-Free	Phone
2 Places At 1 Time Inc					
512 Means St Suite 350	Atlanta	GA	30318	**877-275-2237**	404-815-9980
AimNet Solutions Inc 125 Jeffrey Ave	Holliston	MA	01746	**888-332-5746**	508-429-0700
Ajilon Services Inc					
210 W Pennsylvania Ave 5th Fl	Towson	MD	21204	**800-626-8082**	410-821-0435
American Dental Partners Inc					
201 Edgewater Dr Suite 285	Wakefield	MA	01880	**877-252-7414**	781-224-0880
NASDAQ: ADPI					
American Imaging Management					
40 Skokie Blvd Suite 500	Northbrook	IL	60062	**800-340-0010**	847-564-8500
AmeriPath Inc					
7111 Fairway Dr Suite 400	Palm Beach Gardens	FL	33418	**800-330-6565**	561-845-1850
Aspen Systems Corp 2277 Research Blvd	Rockville	MD	20850	**800-685-6867**	301-519-5000
Care Choices 34605 12-Mile Rd	Farmington Hills	MI	48331	**800-261-3452***	248-489-6203
*Sales					
Castle Dental Centers Inc					
3701 Kriby Dr Suite 550	Houston	TX	77098	**800-867-6453**	713-490-8400
Ceridian Canada Ltd 125 Garry St	Winnipeg	MB	R3C3P2	**866-975-1808**	204-946-0770
Coast Dental Services Inc					
2502 Rocky Point Rd Suite 1000	Tampa	FL	33607	**800-983-3848**	813-288-1999
NASDAQ: CDEN					
Concentra Inc 5080 Spectrum Dr Suite 400 W	Addison	TX	75001	**800-232-3550**	972-364-8000
Correctional Medical Services Inc					
12647 Olive Blvd	Saint Louis	MO	63141	**800-325-4809**	314-878-1810
CRAssociates Inc					
8580 Cinderbed Rd Suite 2400	Newington	VA	22122	**877-272-8960**	703-550-8145
EmCare Holdings Inc 1717 Main St Suite 5200	Dallas	TX	75201	**800-527-2145**	214-712-2000
Emergency Consultants Inc					
2240 S Airport Rd W	Traverse City	MI	49684	**800-253-1795**	231-946-8970
File Keepers LLC 6277 E Slauson Ave	Los Angeles	CA	90040	**800-332-3453**	323-728-3151
First Health Group Corp					
3200 Highland Ave	Downers Grove	IL	60515	**800-445-1425**	630-241-7900
Focus Healthcare Management Inc					
720 Cool Springs Blvd Suite 300	Franklin	TN	37067	**800-873-0055**	615-778-4000
Fortune Practice Management					
9888 Carroll Centre Rd Suite 100	San Diego	CA	92126	**800-628-1052**	858-535-6287
Group Management Services Inc					
3296 Columbia Rd Suite 101	Richfield	OH	44286	**800-456-2885**	330-659-0100
Healthrisk Group Inc					
1551 N Tustin Ave Suite 300	Santa Ana	CA	92705	**800-955-9600**	714-953-9600
Hill Physicians Medical Group Inc					
PO Box 5080	San Ramon	CA	94583	**800-445-5747**	925-820-8300
Infocrossing Inc 2 Christie Heights St	Leonia	NJ	07605	**800-431-1912**	201-840-4700
NASDAQ: IFOX					
Ingenix Inc 12125 Technology Dr	Eden Prairie	MN	55344	**888-445-8745**	952-833-7100
(i)Structure Inc 11707 Miracle Hills Dr	Omaha	NE	68154	**888-757-7501**	402-496-8500
Johnson & Johnson Health Care Systems Inc					
425 Hoes Ln	Piscataway	NJ	08854	**800-255-2500**	732-562-3000
Matria Healthcare Inc					
1850 Parkway Pl 12th Fl	Marietta	GA	33067	**800-456-4060**	770-767-4500
NASDAQ: MATR					
Med-Emerg International Inc					
6711 Mississauga Rd Suite 404	Mississauga	ON	L5N2W3	**800-265-3429**	905-858-1368
Metropolitan Health Networks Inc					
250 Australian Ave S Suite 400	West Palm Beach	FL	33401	**888-663-8227**	561-805-8500
MHM Services Inc					
1593 Spring Hill Rd Suite 610	Vienna	VA	22182	**800-416-3649**	703-749-4600
Modis Inc 1 Independent Dr Suite 215	Jacksonville	FL	32202	**800-372-2788**	904-360-2300
MSS* Group Inc 960 I-25 S Suite F	Castle Rock	CO	80104	**800-873-5790**	303-814-6774
National Flood Services Inc					
451 Hungerford Dr Suite 408	Rockville	MD	20850	**800-251-6274**	301-251-1880
OCA Inc 3850 N Causeway Blvd Suite 1040	Metairie	LA	70031	**800-626-8666**	
NYSE: OCA					
Occupational Health & Rehabilitation Inc					
175 Derby St Suite 36	Hingham	MA	02043	**800-622-4584**	781-741-5175
Paradigm Health Corp					
1001 Galaxy Way Suite 300	Concord	CA	94520	**800-676-6777**	925-676-2300
Patricia Seybold Group 210 Commercial St	Boston	MA	02109	**800-826-2424**	617-742-5200
Pediatrix Medical Group Inc					
PO Box 559001	Fort Lauderdale	FL	33355	**800-243-3839**	954-384-0175
NYSE: PDX					
Per-Se Technologies Inc					
1145 Sanctuary Pkwy Suite 200	Alpharetta	GA	30004	**877-736-3773**	770-237-4300
NASDAQ: PSTI					
PFSweb Inc 500 N Central Expwy Suite 500	Plano	TX	75074	**888-330-5504**	972-881-2900
NASDAQ: PFSW					
Physician Computer Network Inc					
180 Passaic Ave	Fairfield	NJ	07004	**800-844-2131**	973-808-0088
Pitney Bowes Management Services					
220 E 42 St 4th Fl	New York	NY	10017	**800-669-0800**	917-351-2900
Radiation Management Consultants					
3019 Darnell Rd	Philadelphia	PA	19154	**800-793-1304**	215-824-1300
Radiologix Inc 2200 Ross Ave Suite 3600	Dallas	TX	75201	**800-908-9302**	214-303-2776
AMEX: RGX					
Select Medical Corp					
4716 Old Gettysburg Rd	Mechanicsburg	PA	17055	**888-735-6332**	717-972-1100
Sheridan Healthcare Inc					
1613 N Harrison Pkwy Bldg C Suite 200	Sunrise	FL	33323	**800-437-2672**	954-838-2371
Shred First LLC 160 Discovery Dr	Roebuck	SC	29376	**800-387-2009**	864-577-9645
Sourcecorp Inc 3232 McKinney Ave Suite 1000	Dallas	TX	75204	**888-339-4462**	214-740-6500
NASDAQ: SRCP					
Specialized Services Inc					
23077 Greenfield Rd Suite 470	Southfield	MI	48075	**866-774-2004**	248-557-1030
Spectrum Healthcare Resources Inc					
12647 Olive Blvd Suite 600	Saint Louis	MO	63141	**800-325-3982**	314-744-4100
Sterling Healthcare					
1000 Park Forty Plaza Suite 500	Durham	NC	27713	**800-476-4587**	919-383-0355
STI Knowledge Inc					
4 Concourse Pkwy Suite 290	Atlanta	GA	30328	**888-243-5733**	770-280-2630
Sun Solution Consulting 101 Sun Ave NE	Albuquerque	NM	87109	**800-729-6600**	505-821-3355

Company	City	State	Zip	Toll-Free	Phone
Surgical Services Inc 5776 Hoffner Ave Suite 200	Orlando	FL	32822	**800-349-4374**	407-249-1946
Sykes HealthPlan Services Inc 11405 Bluegrass Pkwy	Louisville	KY	40299	**888-421-7477**	502-267-4900
Techmar Communications Inc 45 Dan Rd	Canton	MA	02021	**800-832-4627**	781-821-8324
Transcend Services Inc 945 E Paces Ferry Rd NE Suite 1475 *NASDAQ: TRCR*	Atlanta	GA	30326	**800-225-7552**	404-836-8000
US Oncology Inc 16825 Northchase Dr Suite 1300 *NASDAQ: USON*	Houston	TX	77060	**800-381-2637**	832-601-8766
Verizon Logistics 5615 High Point Dr	Irving	TX	75038	**800-433-4837**	972-751-4100
VHA Inc 220 E Las Colinas Blvd	Irving	TX	75039	**800-842-5146**	972-830-0000
Volt VIEWtech Inc 5109 E La Palma	Anaheim	CA	92807	**800-998-8658**	714-695-3300
VTA Management Services Inc 1901 Emmons Ave Suite 200	Brooklyn	NY	11235	**800-874-3469**	718-615-0049
Xand Corp 11 Skyline Dr	Hawthorne	NY	10532	**800-522-2823**	914-592-8282

456 MANNEQUINS

Company	City	State	Zip	Toll-Free	Phone
Siegel & Stockman Inc 126 W 25th St	New York	NY	10001	**888-515-8949**	212-633-1508
Silvestri Studio Inc 8125 Beach St	Los Angeles	CA	90001	**800-647-8874**	323-277-4420

457 MARINE SERVICES

SEE ALSO Freight Transport - Deep Sea (Domestic Ports); Freight Transport - Deep Sea (Foreign Ports); Freight Transport - Inland Waterways; Logistics Services (Transportation & Warehousing)

Company	City	State	Zip	Toll-Free	Phone
Allied Towing Corp 500 E Indian River Rd	Norfolk	VA	23523	**800-446-8241**	757-545-7301
Bay Houston Towing Co 2243 Milford St	Houston	TX	77098	**800-324-3755**	713-529-3755
Boston Towing & Transportation Co LP 36 New St	East Boston	MA	02128	**800-836-8847**	617-567-9100
Brown Marine Service Inc 40 Audusson Ave	Pensacola	FL	32507	**800-234-3471**	850-453-3471
Campbell Towing Co PO Box 170	Wrangell	AK	99929	**800-399-4869**	907-874-3318
Candies Otto LLC 17271 Hwy 90	Des Allemands	LA	70030	**800-535-4563**	504-469-7700
Cenac Towing Co Inc PO Box 2617	Houma	LA	70361	**800-942-5476**	985-872-2413
Coastal Tug & Barge Inc 1020 Port Blvd Suite 2	Miami	FL	33132	**800-323-2495**	305-579-5013
Cooper/T Smith Stevedoring Co 118 N Royal St Commerce Bldg Suite 1100	Mobile	AL	36602	**800-239-8484**	251-431-6100
Crescent Towing & Salvage Co Inc 1240 Patterson St	New Orleans	LA	70130	**800-843-3930**	504-366-1521
Crowley Marine Services Inc 1102 SW Massachusetts St	Seattle	WA	98134	**800-248-8632**	206-332-8000
Crowley Maritime Corp 155 Grand Ave Suite 700	Oakland	CA	94612	**800-276-9539**	510-251-7500
Dunlap Towing Co PO Box 593	La Conner	WA	98257	**800-476-3114**	360-466-3114
Eckstein Marine Services LLC 5135 Storey St	Harahan	LA	70123	**800-735-5845**	504-733-5845
Edison Chouest Offshore LLC 16201 E Main St	Galliano	LA	70354	**800-417-7144**	985-632-7144
Foss Maritime Co 660 W Ewing St	Seattle	WA	98119	**800-426-2885**	206-281-3800
Great Lakes Towing Co 50 Public Sq 1800 Terminal Tower	Cleveland	OH	44113	**800-321-3663**	216-621-4854
Hawaiian Tug & Barge PO Box 3288	Honolulu	HI	96801	**800-572-2743**	808-543-9311
Kinder Morgan Bulk Terminals Inc 7116 Hwy 22	Sorrento	LA	70778	**800-535-8170**	225-675-5387
Leboeuf Brothers Towing Co Inc PO Box 9036	Houma	LA	70361	**800-256-5088**	985-594-6692
MEMCO Barge Line 16090 Wingley Ridge Rd	Chesterfield	MO	63017	**800-207-8011**	636-530-2100
Mon River Towing Inc 200 Speers St	Belle Vernon	PA	15012	**800-245-8051**	724-483-8051
New York State Canal Corp 200 Southern Blvd	Albany	NY	12201	**800-422-6254**	518-471-5010
Otto Candies Inc 17271 Hwy 90	Des Allemands	LA	70030	**800-535-4563**	504-469-7700
Parker Towing Co Inc 100 1/2 Greensboro Ave PO Box 20908	Tuscaloosa	AL	35402	**800-329-1677**	205-349-1677
Sause Brothers Ocean Towing Co Inc 3710 NW Front Ave	Portland	OR	97210	**800-488-4167**	503-222-1811
Sea Tow Services International Inc 1560 Youngs Ave	Southold	NY	11971	**800-473-2869**	631-765-3660
SSA Marine 1131 SW Klickitat Way	Seattle	WA	98134	**800-422-3505**	206-623-0304
Teco Barge Line PO Box 790	Metropolis	IL	62960	**800-455-5731**	618-524-3100
Tidewater Inc 601 Poydras St Suite 1900 *NYSE: TDW*	New Orleans	LA	70130	**800-678-8433**	504-568-1010
Virginia International Terminals Inc PO Box 1387	Norfolk	VA	23501	**800-541-2431**	757-440-7000
Western Towboat Co Inc 617 NW 40th St	Seattle	WA	98107	**800-932-9651**	206-789-9000

458 MARKET RESEARCH FIRMS

Company	City	State	Zip	Toll-Free	Phone
Burke Inc 805 Central Ave 5th Fl	Cincinnati	OH	45202	**800-688-2674**	513-241-5663
C & R Research Services Inc 500 N Michigan Ave Suite 1200	Chicago	IL	60611	**800-621-5022**	312-828-9200
Catalina Marketing Research Solutions 2845 Chancellor Dr	Crestview Hills	KY	41017	**800-801-2425**	859-344-0077
Cheskin Research 255 Shoreline Dr Suite 350	Redwood City	CA	94065	**888-802-8300**	650-802-2100
Gallup Organization 901 F St NW	Washington	DC	20004	**877-242-5587**	202-715-3030
Gartner Inc 56 Top Gallant Rd *NYSE: IT*	Stamford	CT	06904	**800-328-2776**	203-316-1111
GFK Custom Research Inc 8401 Golden Valley Rd PO Box 27900	Minneapolis	MN	55427	**800-328-6784**	763-542-0800
Greenfield Online Inc 21 River Rd Suite 2000 *NASDAQ: SRVY*	Wilton	CT	06897	**888-291-9997**	203-834-8585
Harris Interactive Inc 135 Corporate Woods *NASDAQ: HPOL*	Rochester	NY	14623	**800-866-7655**	585-272-8400
IDC (International Data Corp) 5 Speen St	Framingham	MA	01701	**800-343-4935**	508-872-8200
International Communications Research 53 W Baltimore Pike	Media	PA	19063	**800-633-1986***	484-840-4300
*Cust Svc					
International Data Corp (IDC) 5 Speen St	Framingham	MA	01701	**800-343-4935**	508-872-8200
M/A/R/C Group 1660 NW Ridge Cir	Irving	TX	75038	**800-527-2680**	972-983-0400
Maritz Research Inc 1355 N Highway Dr	Fenton	MO	63099	**800-446-1690**	636-827-4000
Market Decisions 50 W Rivercenter Blvd Suite 600	Covington	KY	41011	**800-248-2770**	859-905-4800
Marketing Analysts Inc 176 Croghan Spur Rd Suite 100	Charleston	SC	29407	**800-513-4247**	843-797-8900
Marketing & Planning Systems 201 Jones Rd	Waltham	MA	02451	**800-696-6605**	781-642-6277
Marketing Research Services Inc 720 Pete Rose Way Suite 200	Cincinnati	OH	45202	**800-729-6774**	513-579-1555
Marketing Workshop Inc 3725 Da Vinci Ct Suite 200	Norcross	GA	30092	**800-284-7707**	770-449-6767
MORPACE International Inc 31700 Middlebelt Rd Suite 200	Farmington Hills	MI	48334	**800-878-7223**	248-737-5300
NetRatings Inc 890 Hillview Ct Suite 300 *NASDAQ: NTRT*	Milpitas	CA	95035	**888-634-1222**	408-941-2900
RDA Group 450 Enterprise Ct	Bloomfield Hills	MI	48302	**800-669-7324**	248-332-5000
Reis Inc 5 W 37th St 12th Fl	New York	NY	10018	**800-366-7347**	212-921-1122
Simmons Market Research Bureau Inc 700 W Hillsboro Blvd Bldg 4 Suite 201	Deerfield Beach	FL	33441	**800-999-7672**	954-427-4104
TeleSight Inc 820 N Franklin St	Chicago	IL	60610	**800-608-3651**	312-640-2532
Walker Information Inc 3939 Priority Way S Dr	Indianapolis	IN	46240	**800-334-3939**	317-843-3939
Westat Inc 1650 Research Blvd	Rockville	MD	20850	**800-937-8281**	301-251-1500
Yankelovich Inc 20 Glover Ave 2nd Fl N	Norwalk	CT	06850	**800-926-5356**	203-846-0100

459 MARKING DEVICES

Company	City	State	Zip	Toll-Free	Phone
American Marking Systems Inc PO Box 1677	Clifton	NJ	07015	**800-782-6766**	973-478-5600
Automark Marking Systems 13475 Lakefront Dr	Earth City	MO	63045	**888-777-2303**	314-739-0430
Cable Markers Co Inc 22600-F Lambert St Suite 1204	Lake Forest	CA	92630	**800-746-7655**	949-699-1636
CH Hanson Co 3630 N Wolf Rd	Franklin Park	IL	60131	**800-827-3398**	847-451-0500
Cosco Industries Inc 7220 W Wilson Ave	Harwood Heights	IL	60706	**800-323-0253**	708-457-2410
Excelsior Marking Products 4524 Hudson Dr	Stow	OH	44224	**800-433-3615**	330-929-2802
GB Products International Corp 5650 Imhoff Dr Suite B	Concord	CA	94520	**800-650-0341**	925-825-3040
Hampton Technologies LLC 19 Industrial Blvd	Medford	NY	11763	**800-229-1019**	631-924-1335
Hitt Marking Devices Inc 3231 MacArthur Blvd Bldg 709	Santa Ana	CA	92704	**800-969-6699**	714-979-1405
Huntington Park Rubber Stamp 2761 E Slauson Ave	Huntington Park	CA	90255	**800-882-0129**	323-582-6461
Jackson Marking Products Co 9105 N Rainbow Ln	Mount Vernon	IL	62864	**800-782-6722**	618-242-1334
La-Co/Markal Co 1201 Pratt Blvd	Elk Grove Village	IL	60007	**800-621-4025**	847-956-7600
Mark Master Inc 11111 N 46th St	Tampa	FL	33617	**800-441-6275**	813-988-6000
Markem Corp 150 Congress St PO Box 2100	Keene	NH	03431	**800-462-7536**	603-352-1130
MECCO Marking & Traceability PO Box 307	Ingomar	PA	15127	**888-369-9199**	412-369-9199
Menke Marking Devices PO Box 2986	Santa Fe Springs	CA	90670	**800-231-6023**	562-921-1380
Meyercord Revenue 475 Village Dr	Carol Stream	IL	60188	**800-223-6269**	630-682-6200
New Method Steel Stamps Inc 31313 Kendall Ave	Fraser	MI	48026	**888-318-6677**	586-293-0200
Norwood Marking Systems Kingsley Div 2538 Wisconsin Ave	Downers Grove	IL	60515	**800-626-3464**	630-968-0646
Paterson Stamp Works PO Box 1677	Clifton	NJ	07015	**800-782-6766**	973-478-5600
Schwaab Inc 11415 W Burleigh St	Milwaukee	WI	53222	**800-935-9877**	414-771-4150
Schwerdtle Inc 166 Elm St	Bridgeport	CT	06604	**800-535-0004**	203-330-2750
Signet Marking Devices 3121 Red Hill Ave	Costa Mesa	CA	92626	**800-421-5150**	714-549-0341
Stamp-Rite Inc 154 S Larch St	Lansing	MI	48912	**800-328-1988**	517-487-5071
Tacoma Rubber Stamp Co 919 Market St	Tacoma	WA	98402	**800-544-7281**	253-383-5433
Telesis Technologies Inc 740 Welch Rd	Commerce Township	MI	48390	**800-654-5696***	248-624-4249
*Sales					
Volk Corp 23936 Industrial Park Dr	Farmington Hills	MI	48335	**800-521-6799***	248-477-6700
*Cust Svc					
Wendell's Inc 6601 Bunker Lake Blvd NW	Ramsey	MN	55303	**800-328-3692**	763-576-8200

460 MASS TRANSPORTATION (LOCAL & SUBURBAN)

SEE ALSO Bus Services - Intercity & Rural

Company	City	State	Zip	Toll-Free	Phone
Alaska Marine Highway System	Juneau	AK	99801	**800-642-0066**	907-465-3941
Altamont Commuter Express (ACE) 5000 Airport Way Stockton Metropolitan Airport Suite 201	Stockton	CA	95206	**800-411-7245**	209-468-5600
Badger Bus 200 W Beltline Hwy	Madison	WI	53713	**800-442-8259**	608-255-1511
Cape Cod Regional Transit Authority (CCRTA) PO Box 1988	Hyannis	MA	02601	**800-352-7155**	508-775-8504
Catalina Express Berth 95	San Pedro	CA	90731	**800-481-3470***	310-519-1212
*Resv					
Dallas Area Rapid Transit Authority (DART) PO Box 660163	Dallas	TX	75266	**888-557-6669**	214-749-3278
Delaware Transit Corp 400 S Madison St	Wilmington	DE	19801	**800-652-3278**	302-577-3278
Metrolink 700 S Flower St Suite 2600	Los Angeles	CA	90017	**800-371-5465**	213-347-2800
Metropolitan Transportation Authority (MTA) PO Box 194	Los Angeles	CA	90001	**800-266-6883**	213-922-2000
MTA (Metropolitan Transportation Authority) PO Box 194	Los Angeles	CA	90001	**800-266-6883**	213-922-2000
New Jersey Transit Corp 1 Penn Plaza E	Newark	NJ	07105	**800-772-3606***	973-491-7000
*Cust Svc					
Northern Indiana Commuter Transportation District 33 E US Hwy 12	Chesterton	IN	46304	**800-356-2079**	219-926-5744

Classified Section

				Toll-Free	Phone
Pierce Transit 3701 96th St SW PO Box 99070	Lakewood	WA	98499	**800-562-8109**	253-581-8000
rabbittransit 1230 Roosevelt Ave	York	PA	17404	**800-632-9063**	717-846-5562
Regional Transportation District (RTD) 1600 Blake St	Denver	CO	80202	**800-877-7433**	303-628-9000
Riverside Transit Agency (RTA) 1825 3rd St PO Box 59968	Riverside	CA	92517	**800-800-7821**	951-682-1234
San Mateo County Transit District 1250 San Carlos Ave	San Carlos	CA	94070	**800-660-4287**	650-508-6200
Santa Clara Valley Transportation Authority (VTA) 3331 N 1st St	San Jose	CA	95134	**800-894-9908**	408-321-5555
Sonoma County Transit 355 W Robles Ave	Santa Rosa	CA	95407	**800-345-7433**	707-585-7516
Southern California Regional Rail Authority 700 S Flower St Suite 2600	Los Angeles	CA	90017	**800-371-5465**	213-347-2800
Utah Transit Authority 3600 South 700 W PO Box 30810	Salt Lake City	UT	84130	**800-743-3882**	801-262-5626
VIA Metropolitan Transit 800 W Myrtle St	San Antonio	TX	78212	**866-362-4200**	210-362-2000
Virginia Railway Express (VRE) 1500 King St Suite 200	Alexandria	VA	22314	**800-743-3873**	703-684-1001
York County Transportation Authority 1230 Roosevelt Ave	York	PA	17404	**800-632-9063**	717-846-5562

461 MATCHES & MATCHBOOKS

				Toll-Free	Phone
Atlas Match LLC 1801 S Airport Cir	Euless	TX	76040	**800-628-2426**	817-267-1500
DD Bean & Sons Co 207 Peterborough St	Jaffrey	NH	03452	**800-326-8311**	603-532-8311
Maryland Match Corp 605 Alluvion St	Baltimore	MD	21230	**800-423-0013**	410-752-8164

462 MATERIAL HANDLING EQUIPMENT

SEE ALSO Conveyors & Conveying Equipment

				Toll-Free	Phone
Abell-Howe Crane Inc 375 W South Frontage Rd Suite A	Bolingbrook	IL	60440	**800-366-0068**	630-626-5520
Acco Chain & Lifting PO Box 792	York	PA	17405	**800-967-7333**	717-741-4863
Adrian Fabricators Inc Cargotainer Div PO Box 518	Adrian	MI	49221	**800-221-3794**	517-266-5700
Advance Lifts Inc 701 S Kirk Rd	Saint Charles	IL	60174	**800-843-3625**	630-584-9881
Air Technical Industries 7501 Clover Ave	Mentor	OH	44060	**800-321-9680**	440-951-5191
American Crane & Equipment Corp 531 Old Swede Rd	Douglassville	PA	19518	**877-877-6778**	610-385-6061
American Lifts 601 W McKee St	Greensburg	IN	47240	**800-426-9772**	812-663-4085
American Power Pull Corp PO Box 109	Wauseon	OH	43567	**800-808-5922**	419-335-7050
Anchor Crane & Hoist Service Co Inc 2020 E Grauwyler Rd	Irving	TX	75061	**800-275-2624**	972-438-5100
Ancra International LLC 4880 W Rosecrans Ave	Hawthorne	CA	90250	**800-973-5091**	310-973-5000
Autoquip Corp PO Box 1058	Guthrie	OK	73044	**888-811-9876**	405-282-5200
Bayhead Products Corp 173 Crosby Rd	Dover	NH	03820	**800-603-0053**	603-742-3000
Berns Co 1250 W 17th St	Long Beach	CA	90813	**800-421-3773**	562-437-0471
BloApCo (Blower Application Co Inc) N 114 W 19125 Clinton Dr	Germantown	WI	53022	**800-959-0880**	262-255-5580
Blower Application Co Inc (BloApCo) N 114 W 19125 Clinton Dr	Germantown	WI	53022	**800-959-0880**	262-255-5580
Breeze-Eastern Div TransTechnology Corp 700 Liberty Ave *Sales	Union	NJ	07083	**800-929-1919***	908-686-4000
Can Lines Inc PO Box 7039	Downey	CA	90241	**800-233-4597**	323-773-5676
Cannon Equipment Co 15100 Business Pkwy	Rosemount	MN	55068	**800-825-8501**	651-322-6300
Cargotainer Div Adrian Fabricators PO Box 518	Adrian	MI	49221	**800-221-3794**	517-266-5700
Cascade Corp PO Box 20187 *NYSE: CAE*	Portland	OR	97294	**800-227-2233**	503-669-6300
Champion Co 400 Harrison St *Sales	Springfield	OH	45505	**800-328-0115***	937-324-5681
Charnstrom WA Co 5391 12th Ave E *Cust Svc	Shakopee	MN	55379	**800-328-2962***	952-403-0303
Clark Material Handling Co 2317 Alumni Park Plaza Suite 500	Lexington	KY	40517	**866-252-5275**	859-422-6400
Columbus McKinnon Corp 140 John James Audubon Pkwy *NASDAQ: CMCO*	Amherst	NY	14228	**800-888-0985**	716-689-5400
Conveyor & Material Handling Systems 4598 SR 37	Mitchell	IN	47446	**800-551-3195**	812-849-5647
Craneveyor Corp 1524 N Potrero Ave PO Box 3727	South El Monte	CA	91733	**800-423-4180**	626-442-1524
Crosby McKissick PO Box 3128	Tulsa	OK	74101	**800-772-1500**	918-834-4611
Crysteel Mfg Inc PO Box 178 *Orders	Lake Crystal	MN	56055	**800-533-0494***	507-726-2728
Delco Office Systems 55 Old Field Point Rd PO Box 423	Greenwich	CT	06830	**800-243-8528**	203-661-5101
Detroit Hoist Co 6650 Sterling Dr N	Sterling Heights	MI	48312	**800-521-9126**	586-268-2600
Downs Crane & Hoist Co Inc 8827 S Juniper St	Los Angeles	CA	90002	**800-748-5994**	323-589-6061
Duff Norton Co 9415 Pioneer Ave	Charlotte	NC	28273	**800-477-5009**	704-588-0510
Elwell-Parker Ltd 6499 W 65th St *Cust Svc	Bedford Park	IL	60638	**800-848-4373***	708-563-6200
Escalera Inc 708 S Industrial Dr	Yuba City	CA	95993	**800-622-1359**	530-673-6318
Excellon Automation Inc 24751 Crenshaw Blvd	Torrance	CA	90505	**800-392-3556**	310-534-6300
Fairfield Engineering Co Inc PO Box 526	Marion	OH	43302	**800-827-3364**	740-387-3327
Faultless Nutting Co Div FKI Industries 505 W Airport Dr	Watertown	SD	57201	**800-533-0337**	605-882-3000
FKI Industries Faultless Nutting Co Div 505 W Airport Dr	Watertown	SD	57201	**800-533-0337**	605-882-3000
FL Smidth Inc 2040 Ave C	Bethlehem	PA	18017	**800-523-9482**	610-264-6011
Flexible Material Handling 9501 Granger Rd	Cleveland	OH	44125	**800-669-1501**	216-587-1575
Genie Industries Inc PO Box 97030 *Sales	Redmond	WA	98073	**800-536-1800***	425-881-1800
Gunnebo-Johnson Corp 1240 N Harvard Ave *Sales	Tulsa	OK	74115	**800-331-5460***	918-832-8933
Harlan Materials Handling Corp PO Box 15159	Kansas City	KS	66115	**800-255-4262**	913-342-5650
Harlo Corp PO Box 129	Grandville	MI	49468	**800-391-4151**	616-538-0550
Hilman Inc 12 Timber Ln *Cust Svc	Marlboro	NJ	07746	**888-276-5548***	732-462-6277
Hyster New England 159 Rangeway Rd	North Billerica	MA	01862	**800-234-5438**	978-670-3000
Indusco Group 1200 W Hamburg St	Baltimore	MD	21230	**800-727-0665**	410-727-0665
Interlake Material Handling Inc 1230 E Diehl Rd Suite 400 *Sales	Naperville	IL	60563	**800-282-8032***	630-245-8800
Iowa Mold Tooling Co Inc 500 Hwy 18 W	Garner	IA	50438	**800-247-5958**	641-923-3711
Irvington-Moore Div USNR Corp PO Box 40666	Jacksonville	FL	32203	**800-289-8767**	904-354-2301
Jervis B Webb Co 34375 W 12-Mile Rd	Farmington Hills	MI	48331	**800-526-9322**	248-553-1220
Kelly Systems Inc 422 N Western Ave	Chicago	IL	60612	**800-258-8237**	312-733-3224
Kingway Material Handling 240 Northpoint Pkwy	Acworth	GA	30102	**800-554-6632**	770-917-9700
Konecranes America 7300 Chippewa Blvd	Houston	TX	77086	**800-231-0241**	281-445-2225
Kornylak Corp 400 Heaton St	Hamilton	OH	45011	**800-837-5676**	513-863-1277
Landoll Corp 1900 North St *Cust Svc	Marysville	KS	66508	**800-446-5175***	785-562-5381
Leebaw Mfg Co Inc PO Box 553	Canfield	OH	44406	**800-841-8083**	330-533-3368
Lift-All Co Inc 1909 McFarland Dr	Landisville	PA	17538	**800-433-0396**	717-898-6615
Lift-Tech International 414 W Broadway Ave *Cust Svc	Muskegon	MI	49443	**800-955-5541***	231-733-0821
Liftex Inc 443 Ivyland Rd	Warminster	PA	18974	**800-448-3079**	215-957-0810
Linvar LLC 245 Hamilton St	Hartford	CT	06106	**800-282-5288**	860-951-3818
Luker Inc 514 National Ave	Augusta	GA	30901	**800-982-9534**	706-724-0244
Magline Inc 503 S Mercer St	Pinconning	MI	48650	**800-624-5463**	989-879-2411
Manitou North America 6401 Imperial Dr *Cust Svc	Waco	TX	76712	**800-433-3304***	254-799-0232
Maxon Industries Inc 11921 Slauson Ave	Santa Fe Springs	CA	90670	**800-227-4116**	562-464-0099
Mazzella Lifting Technologies 21000 Aerospace Pkwy	Cleveland	OH	44142	**800-362-4601**	440-239-7000
Mertz Inc 1701 N Waverly	Ponca City	OK	74601	**800-654-6433**	580-762-5646
Multiton MIC Corp 5701 Eastport Blvd	Richmond	VA	23231	**800-229-7400**	804-737-7400
Nissan Forklift Corp North America (NFC) 240 N Prospect St	Marengo	IL	60152	**800-871-5438**	815-568-0061
NMC-Wollard Inc 2021 Truax Blvd	Eau Claire	WI	54703	**800-656-6867**	715-835-3151
Noell Crane & Service Inc 2030 Ponderosa St	Portsmouth	VA	23701	**800-996-6355**	757-405-0311
North American Industries Inc 80 Holton St	Woburn	MA	01801	**800-847-8470**	781-721-4446
Ohio Magnetics Inc 5400 Dunham Rd	Maple Heights	OH	44137	**800-486-6446**	216-662-8484
Paltier Div Lyon Metal Products Inc 1701 Kentucky St	Michigan City	IN	46360	**800-348-3201**	219-872-7238
Philadelphia Tramrail Co 2207 E Ontario St	Philadelphia	PA	19134	**800-523-3654**	215-533-5100
Positech Corp 191 N Rush Lake Rd	Laurens	IA	50554	**800-831-6026**	712-841-4548
Production Equipment Co 401 Liberty St	Meriden	CT	06450	**800-758-5697**	203-235-5795
Progressive Crane Inc 13721 Bennington Ave	Cleveland	OH	44135	**800-832-7263**	216-251-6126
Pucel Enterprises Inc 1440 E 36th St	Cleveland	OH	44114	**800-336-4986**	216-881-4604
Raymond Corp 8-20 S Canal St	Greene	NY	13778	**800-235-7200**	607-656-2311
Rohn Industries Inc 6718 W Plank Rd	Peoria	IL	61604	**800-862-4849**	309-697-4400
Shepard Niles Inc 220 N Genesee St	Montour Falls	NY	14865	**800-481-2260**	607-535-7111
Sherman & Reilly Inc PO Box 11267 *Sales	Chattanooga	TN	37401	**800-251-7780***	423-756-5300
Siemens Dematic Material Handling Automation Div 507 Plymouth Ave NE *Cust Svc	Grand Rapids	MI	49505	**800-530-9153***	616-913-6200
Smidth FL Inc 2040 Ave C	Bethlehem	PA	18017	**800-523-9482**	610-264-6011
Spandeck Inc 129 Confederate Dr	Franklin	TN	37064	**800-272-3325**	615-794-4556
SPX Dock Products 1612 Hutton Dr Suite 140	Carrollton	TX	75006	**866-691-1377**	972-466-0707
Streator Dependable Mfg Co 410 W Broadway St	Streator	IL	61364	**800-795-0551**	815-672-0551
Taylor-Dunn Mfg Co Inc 2114 W Ball Rd	Anaheim	CA	92804	**800-688-8680**	714-956-4040
Terex Corp Crane Div 202 Raleigh St	Wilmington	NC	28412	**800-250-2726**	910-395-8500
Thern Inc 5712 Industrial Park Rd	Winona	MN	55987	**800-843-7648**	507-454-2996
Tiffin Parts 235 Miami St	Tiffin	OH	44883	**800-219-6354**	419-447-6545
Toyoshima Special Steel USA 735 S Saint Paul St	Indianapolis	IN	46203	**800-428-4599**	317-638-3511
Trans Technology Corp Breeze-Eastern Div 700 Liberty Ave *Sales	Union	NJ	07083	**800-929-1919***	908-686-4000
Triple/S Dynamics Inc PO Box 151027	Dallas	TX	75315	**800-527-2116**	214-828-8600
UpRight Inc 2686 S Maple Ave *Cust Svc	Fresno	CA	93725	**800-926-5438***	559-443-6600
USNR Corp Irvington-Moore Div PO Box 40666	Jacksonville	FL	32203	**800-289-8767**	904-354-2301
Valley Craft Inc 2001 S Hwy 61 *Cust Svc	Lake City	MN	55041	**800-328-1480***	651-345-3386
WA Charnstrom Co 5391 12th Ave E *Cust Svc	Shakopee	MN	55379	**800-328-2962***	952-403-0303
Waldon/Laymore Inc 401 Capacity Dr	Longview	TX	75604	**800-323-0135**	903-759-0610
Waste Technology Corp 5400 Rio Grande Ave	Jacksonville	FL	32254	**800-231-9286**	904-355-5558
WB McGuire Co 1 Hudson Ave	Hudson	NY	12534	**800-624-8473**	518-828-7652
Webb Jervis B Co 34375 W 12-Mile Rd	Farmington Hills	MI	48331	**800-526-9322**	248-553-1220
Wesco Industrial Products Inc PO Box 47	Lansdale	PA	19446	**800-445-5681**	215-699-7031
Western Hoist Inc 2200 Haffly Ave	National City	CA	91950	**888-994-6478**	619-474-3361
Whiting Corp 26000 Whiting Way	Monee	IL	60449	**800-255-8594**	708-587-2000
Wiggins Lift Co Inc PO Box 5187	Oxnard	CA	93031	**800-350-7821**	805-485-7821

463 MATTRESSES & ADJUSTABLE BEDS

SEE ALSO Furniture - Mfr - Household Furniture

				Toll-Free	Phone
Ackerman Mfg Co/Spring Air 4140 Park Ave	Saint Louis	MO	63110	**800-264-3052**	314-771-3052
Aero Products International Inc 1225 Karl Ct *Cust Svc	Wauconda	IL	60084	**800-237-6233***	847-487-7158

Company / Address	City	State	ZIP	Toll-Free	Phone
American Bedding Industries 500 S Falkenburg Rd	Tampa	FL	33619	**800-780-1084**	813-651-2233
Bechik Products Inc 1140 Homer St	Saint Paul	MN	55116	**800-328-6569**	651-698-0364
Bowles Mattress Co Inc 1220 Watt St	Jeffersonville	IN	47130	**800-223-7509**	812-288-8614
Chittenden & Eastman Co 100 New Rand Rd	Sweet Springs	MO	65351	**800-553-5623***	319-753-2811
*Cust Svc					
Claude Gable Co 322 Fraley Rd	High Point	NC	27263	**800-422-5331**	336-883-1351
Clearwater Mattress Inc 1185 Gooden Crossing	Largo	FL	33778	**800-274-6288**	727-539-1600
Comfortex Inc PO Box 850	Winona	MN	55987	**800-445-4007**	507-454-6579
Continental Silverline Products Inc 710 N Drennan St	Houston	TX	77003	**800-392-9205**	713-222-7394
Corsicana Bedding Inc PO Box 1050	Corsicana	TX	75151	**800-323-4349**	903-872-2591
Cotton Belt Inc 401 E Sater St	Pinetops	NC	27864	**800-849-4192**	252-827-4192
Craftmatic Organization Inc 2500 Interplex Dr	Trevose	PA	19053	**800-677-8200***	215-639-1310
*Cust Svc					
Dreamline Mfg Co PO Box 1250	Cabot	AR	72023	**800-888-3585**	501-843-3585
Flexi-Mat Corp 14420 N Van Dyke Rd	Plainfield	IL	60544	**800-338-7392**	815-609-4600
Fraenkel Co Inc PO Box 15385	Baton Rouge	LA	70895	**800-847-2580**	225-275-8111
Gable Claude Co 322 Fraley Rd	High Point	NC	27263	**800-422-5331**	336-883-1351
Gold Bond Mattress Co 261 Weston St	Hartford	CT	06120	**800-873-8498**	860-549-2000
Herr Mfg Div Serta Inc 18 Prestige Ln	Lancaster	PA	17603	**800-626-6249**	717-392-4168
IBC Group Inc 730 W McNab Rd	Fort Lauderdale	FL	33309	**800-776-1166**	954-968-2333
Jackson Mattress Co Inc PO Box 64609	Fayetteville	NC	28306	**800-763-7378**	910-425-0131
Jamison Bedding Inc PO Box 681948	Franklin	TN	37068	**800-255-1883**	615-794-1883
King Koil Licensing Co Inc 15 Salt Creek Ln Suite 210	Hinsdale	IL	60521	**800-525-8331**	630-230-9744
Kingsdown Inc PO Box 388	Mebane	NC	27302	**800-354-5464***	919-563-3531
*Cust Svc					
Kolcraft Enterprises Inc 10832 NC Hwy 211 E	Aberdeen	NC	28315	**800-453-7673***	910-944-9345
*Cust Svc					
Leggett & Platt Inc PO Box 757	Carthage	MO	64836	**800-888-4569**	417-358-8131
NYSE: LEG					
Lemoyne Sleeper Co Inc PO Box 227	Lemoyne	PA	17043	**800-382-1217**	717-763-1630
Meridian Mattress Factory Inc PO Box 5127	Meridian	MS	39302	**800-844-3875**	601-693-3875
National Bedding Co 61 Leona Dr	Middleboro	MA	02346	**800-343-1006**	508-946-4700
National Bedding Co Div Serta Inc 1500 Lee Lane	Beloit	WI	53511	**800-767-6267**	608-365-6266
Northwest Bedding Co 6102 S Hayford Rd	Spokane	WA	99224	**800-456-7686**	509-244-3000
Paramount Industrial Cos Inc 1112 Kingwood Ave	Norfolk	VA	23502	**800-777-5337**	757-855-3321
Peerless Mattress & Furniture Co PO Box 7650	Flint	MI	48507	**800-253-0937**	810-230-7440
Penfield Mfg Co 1710 N Salina St	Syracuse	NY	13208	**800-724-1868**	315-471-7145
Restonic Mattress Corp 385 Court St Suite 210	Plymouth	MA	02360	**800-898-6075**	508-732-9805
Riverside Mattress Co Inc 225 Dunn Rd	Fayetteville	NC	28312	**888-288-5195**	910-483-0461
Sanitary Mattress Co Inc 5808 Berry Brook Dr	Houston	TX	77017	**800-603-3375**	713-227-0121
Sealy Corp 1 Office Pkwy at Sealy Dr	Trinity	NC	27370	**800-697-3259***	336-861-3500
*Cust Svc					
Select Comfort Corp 6105 Trenton Ln N	Plymouth	MN	55442	**800-472-7185**	763-551-7000
NASDAQ: SCSS					
Serta Inc 325 Spring Lake Dr	Itasca	IL	60143	**888-557-3782**	630-285-9300
Serta Inc Herr Mfg Div 18 Prestige Ln	Lancaster	PA	17603	**800-626-6249**	717-392-4168
Serta Inc National Bedding Co Div 1500 Lee Lane	Beloit	WI	53511	**800-767-6267**	608-365-6266
Serta Mattress/AW Inc 8415 Ardmore Rd	Landover	MD	20785	**800-638-0520**	301-322-1000
Sleepmaster Products Co LP 2001 Lower Rd	Linden	NJ	07036	**800-524-0856**	908-986-5000
Southerland Inc 1973 Southerland Dr	Nashville	TN	37207	**888-226-9009**	615-226-9650
Standard Mattress Co Inc 261 Weston St	Hartford	CT	06120	**800-873-8498**	860-549-2000
Stearns & Foster Bedding Co 1 Office Pkwy at Sealy Dr	Trinity	NC	27370	**800-867-3259**	336-861-3500
Symbol Mattress Co 1814 High Point Ave	Richmond	VA	23230	**800-446-2791**	804-353-8965
Taylor Bedding Inc 1133 MacArthur Ave	New Orleans	LA	70058	**800-826-2839**	504-341-0059
Ther-A-Pedic Midwest Inc 2350 5th St	Rock Island	IL	61201	**800-322-1054**	309-788-0401
United Sleep Products Inc 412 Oak St	Denver	PA	17517	**800-447-2119**	717-336-2846
Western Mattress & Furniture Co 117 E Concho Ave	San Angelo	TX	76903	**800-880-4507**	325-653-4507
White Dove Ltd 3201 Harvard Ave	Cleveland	OH	44105	**888-649-6061**	216-341-0200
World Sleep Products Inc 12 Esquire Rd	North Billerica	MA	01862	**800-370-8700**	978-667-6648

464 MEASURING, TESTING, CONTROLLING INSTRUMENTS

SEE ALSO Electrical Signals Measuring & Testing Instruments

Company / Address	City	State	ZIP	Toll-Free	Phone
AAI ACL Technologies Inc 3200 Enterprise St	Brea	CA	92821	**800-521-4987**	714-223-5100
ABB Inc 501 Merritt 7	Norwalk	CT	06851	**800-626-4999***	203-750-2200
*Prod Info					
Adcole Corp 669 Forest St	Marlborough	MA	01752	**800-858-5802**	508-485-9100
Aero Systems Engineering Inc 358 E Fillmore Ave	Saint Paul	MN	55107	**800-321-0288**	651-227-7515
NASDAQ: AERS					
AMETEK Inc Test & Calibration Instruments Div 8600 Somerset Dr	Largo	FL	33773	**800-527-9999**	727-536-7831
Bently Nevada Corp 1631 Bently Pkwy S	Minden	NV	89423	**800-227-5514**	775-782-3611
Beta LaserMike Inc 8001 Technology Blvd	Dayton	OH	45424	**800-886-9935**	937-233-9935
Bicron 12345 Kinsman Rd	Newbury	OH	44065	**800-472-5656**	440-564-2251
Bruel & Kjaer Instruments Inc 2815-A Colonnades Ct	Norcross	GA	30071	**800-241-9188**	770-209-6907
Canberra Industries Inc 800 Research Pkwy	Meriden	CT	06450	**800-243-4422**	203-238-2351
Clayton Industries 4213 N Temple City Blvd	El Monte	CA	91731	**800-423-4585**	626-443-9381
Control Screening LLC 2 Gardner Rd	Fairfield	NJ	07004	**800-231-6414**	973-276-6161
Crane Nuclear Inc 2825 Cobb International Blvd	Kennesaw	GA	30152	**800-795-8013**	770-424-6343
Emerson Process Management CSI 835 Innovation Dr	Knoxville	TN	37932	**800-675-4726**	865-675-2110
Endevco Corp 30700 Rancho Viejo Rd	San Juan Capistrano	CA	92675	**800-982-6732**	949-493-8181
Enidine Inc 7 Centre Dr	Orchard Park	NY	14127	**800-852-8508**	716-662-1900
Fairfield Industries Inc 14100 Southwest Frwy Suite 600	Sugar Land	TX	77478	**800-231-9809**	281-275-7500
FARO Technologies Inc 125 Technology Pk	Lake Mary	FL	32746	**800-736-0234**	407-333-9911
NASDAQ: FARO					
Fiber Instruments Sales Inc 161 Clear Rd	Oriskany	NY	13424	**800-500-0347***	315-736-2206
*Sales					
Fisher Research Laboratory Inc 200 W Willmott Rd	Los Banos	CA	93635	**800-672-6738**	209-826-3292
Fluke Biomedical Radiation Management Services 6045 Cochran Rd	Solon	OH	44139	**800-850-4608**	440-248-9300
Garrett Metal Detectors 1881 W State St	Garland	TX	75042	**800-234-6151**	972-494-6151
GE Infrastructure Security 205 Lowell St	Wilmington	MA	01887	**800-433-5346**	978-658-3767
GE Ion Track 205 Lowell St	Wilmington	MA	01887	**800-433-5346**	978-658-3767
Goodrich Corp 2730 W Tyvola Rd 4 Coliseum Ctr	Charlotte	NC	28217	**800-784-7009**	704-423-7000
NYSE: GR					
Goodrich Corp Fuel & Utility Systems Div 100 Patton Rd	Vergennes	VT	05491	**800-722-7251**	802-877-2111
GSE Tech-motive Tool 42860 Nine-Mile Rd	Novi	MI	48375	**800-795-7875**	248-596-0600
Herman H Sticht Co Inc 45 Main St Suite 701	Brooklyn	NY	11201	**800-221-3203**	718-852-7602
Honeywell Sensotec 2080 Arlingate Ln	Columbus	OH	43228	**800-298-9228**	614-850-5000
Industrial Dynamics Co Ltd 3100 Fujita St	Torrance	CA	90505	**888-434-5832**	310-325-5633
Instron Corp Wilson Instruments Div 100 Royall St	Canton	MA	02021	**800-695-4273**	781-575-6000
Instron Industrial Products Group 900 Liberty St	Grove City	PA	16127	**800-726-8378**	724-458-9610
Interface Inc 7401 E Butherus Dr	Scottsdale	AZ	85260	**800-947-5598**	480-948-5555
Kistler Instrument Corp 75 John Glenn Dr	Amherst	NY	14228	**888-547-8537**	716-691-5100
L-3 Avionics Systems 5353 52nd St SE	Grand Rapids	MI	49512	**800-253-9525**	616-949-6600
Leica Geosystems LLC 6330 28th St SE	Grand Rapids	MI	49546	**800-367-9453***	616-949-7430
*Sales					
Ludlum Measurements Inc 501 Oak St	Sweetwater	TX	79556	**800-622-0828**	325-235-5494
Meteorlogix LLC 11400 Rupp Dr	Burnsville	MN	55337	**800-328-2278**	952-890-0609
Metrix Instrument Co 1711 Townhurst Dr	Houston	TX	77043	**800-638-7494**	713-461-2131
Metrosonics 1060 Corporate Center Dr	Oconomowoc	WI	53066	**800-245-0779**	262-567-9157
Metrotech Corp 488 Tasman Dr	Sunnyvale	CA	94089	**800-446-3392**	408-734-1400
MSI Entran Devices Inc 10 Washington Ave	Fairfield	NJ	07004	**888-836-8726**	973-227-1002
MTS Systems Corp 14000 Technology Dr	Eden Prairie	MN	55344	**800-328-2255***	952-937-4000
NASDAQ: MTSC ■ *Cust Svc					
Mustang Dynamometer 2300 Pinnacle Pkwy	Twinsburg	OH	44087	**888-468-7826**	330-963-5400
Nanometrics Inc 1550 Buckeye Dr	Milpitas	CA	95035	**800-955-6266**	408-435-9600
NASDAQ: NANO					
Ohmart/VEGA Corp 4241 Allendorf Dr	Cincinnati	OH	45209	**800-543-8668**	513-272-0131
Oxford Instruments Measurement Systems 945 Busse Rd	Elk Grove Village	IL	60007	**800-678-1117**	847-439-4404
Panalaytical 12 Michigan Dr	Natick	MA	01760	**800-279-7297**	508-647-1100
Perceptron Inc 47827 Halyard Dr	Plymouth	MI	48170	**800-333-7753**	734-414-6100
NASDAQ: PRCP					
Princeton Gamma-Tech Inc 1026 Rt 518	Rocky Hill	NJ	08553	**800-229-7484**	609-924-7310
Radiation Monitoring Devices 44 Hunt St Suite 2	Watertown	MA	02472	**800-532-3763**	617-926-1167
Rochester Gauges Inc of Texas 11616 Harry Hines Blvd	Dallas	TX	75229	**800-821-1829**	972-241-2161
Schenck Pegasus Corp 2890 John R Rd	Troy	MI	48083	**800-899-5119**	248-689-9000
Sensor Systems LLC 2800 Anvil St	Saint Petersburg	FL	33710	**800-688-2181**	727-347-2181
Setra Systems Inc 159 Swanson Rd	Boxborough	MA	01719	**800-257-3872**	978-263-1400
Sorrento Electronics Inc 4949 Greencraig Ln	San Diego	CA	92123	**800-252-1180**	858-522-8300
SPECTRO Analytical Instruments Inc 1515 N Hwy 281	Marble Falls	TX	78654	**800-580-6608**	830-798-8786
Sticht Herman H Co Inc 45 Main St Suite 701	Brooklyn	NY	11201	**800-221-3203**	718-852-7602
SuperFlow Corp 3512 N Tejon St	Colorado Springs	CO	80907	**800-471-7701**	719-471-1746
Taylor Hobson Inc 2100 Golf Rd Suite 350	Rolling Meadows	IL	60008	**800-872-7265**	847-290-8090
Testing Machines Inc 2 Fleetwood Ct	Ronkonkoma	NY	11749	**800-678-3221**	631-439-5400
Thermo Electron Corp 81 Wyman St PO Box 9056	Waltham	MA	02454	**800-678-5599**	781-622-1000
NYSE: TMO					
Thermo Radiometrie Corp 10010 Mesa Rim Rd	San Diego	CA	92121	**800-488-4399**	
Trimble Engineering & Construction Div 5475 Kellenburger Rd	Dayton	OH	45424	**800-538-7800**	937-233-8921
Unilux Inc 59 N 5th St	Saddle Brook	NJ	07663	**800-522-0801**	201-712-1266
Vaisala-GAI 2705 E Medina Rd Suite 111	Tucson	AZ	85706	**800-283-4557**	520-741-2838
Vaisala Inc 10-D Gill St	Woburn	MA	01801	**888-824-7252**	781-933-4500
White's Electronics Inc 1011 Pleasant Valley Rd	Sweet Home	OR	97386	**800-547-6911***	541-367-6121
*Sales					

465 MEAT PACKING PLANTS

SEE ALSO Poultry Processing

Company / Address	City	State	ZIP	Toll-Free	Phone
Allen Brothers Inc 3737 S Halsted St	Chicago	IL	60609	**800-548-7777**	773-890-5100
Alpine Packing Co 9900 Lower Sacramento Rd	Stockton	CA	95210	**800-399-6328**	209-477-2691
American Foods Group Inc PO Box 8547	Green Bay	WI	54308	**800-345-0293**	920-437-6330
Berliner & Marx Inc 275 Morgan Ave	Brooklyn	NY	11211	**800-222-8325**	718-599-6400
Best Packers Inc 1122 Bronson St	Palatka	FL	32177	**800-771-9378***	386-328-5127
*Sales					
Brown Packing Co Inc 1 Dutch Valley Dr	South Holland	IL	60473	**800-832-8325**	708-849-7990
Buchy Charles G Packing Co PO Box 899	Greenville	OH	45331	**800-762-1060**	937-548-2128
Carolina Packers Inc PO Box 1109	Smithfield	NC	27577	**800-682-7675**	919-934-2181
Cattleman's Meat Co 1825 Scott St	Detroit	MI	48207	**800-766-5699**	313-833-2700
Central Nebraska Packing Inc PO Box 550	North Platte	NE	69103	**800-445-2881***	308-532-1250
*Cust Svc					
Charles G Buchy Packing Co PO Box 899	Greenville	OH	45331	**800-762-1060**	937-548-2128
Chip Steak & Provision Co 232 Dewey St	Mankato	MN	56001	**888-244-7783**	507-388-6277
Chisesi Brothers Meat Packing Co PO Box 19083	New Orleans	LA	70179	**800-966-3550**	504-822-3550
Cimpl Meats Inc PO Box 80	Yankton	SD	57078	**800-829-3311**	605-665-1665
Clougherty Packing Co DBA Farmer John Meats 3049 E Vernon Ave	Los Angeles	CA	90058	**800-432-7637***	323-583-4621
*Sales					
Comer Packing PO Box 33	Aberdeen	MS	39730	**800-748-8916**	662-369-9325
ConAgra Foods Retail Products Co Deli Foods Group 2001 Butterfield Rd	Downers Grove	IL	60515	**800-325-7424**	630-512-1000
Cudahy Patrick Inc 1 Sweet Apple-Wood Ln	Cudahy	WI	53110	**800-486-6900**	414-744-2000
Demakes Enterprises Inc DBA Old Neighborhood Foods 37 Waterhill St	Lynn	MA	01905	**800-628-3529**	781-595-1557
DL Lee & Sons Inc PO Box 206	Alma	GA	31510	**800-673-9339***	912-632-4406
*Cust Svc					

Name / Address	City	State	ZIP	Toll-Free	Phone
EA Miller Inc 410 N 200 West	Hyrum	UT	84319	**800-873-0939**	435-245-6456
Eddy Packing Co Inc PO Box 392	Yoakum	TX	77995	**800-292-2361**	361-293-2361
Esskay Inc PO Box 587	Riderwood	MD	21139	**800-638-7350**	410-823-2100
EW Knauss & Sons Inc 625 E Broad St	Quakertown	PA	18951	**800-648-4220**	215-536-4220
Excel Process Pork 1915 W Canal St	Milwaukee	WI	53233	**800-558-4242**	414-410-8200
Farm Boy Meats PO Box 996	Evansville	IN	47706	**800-852-3976**	812-425-5231
Farmer John Meats 3049 E Vernon Ave *Sales	Los Angeles	CA	90058	**800-432-7637***	323-583-4621
Freirich Foods Inc PO Box 1529	Salisbury	NC	28145	**800-554-4788**	704-636-2621
Fresh Mark Inc 1888 Southway St SE	Massillon	OH	44646	**800-860-6777**	330-832-7491
GFI America Inc 2815 Blaisdell Ave S	Minneapolis	MN	55408	**800-669-8996**	612-872-6262
Gibbon Packing Inc PO Box 730	Gibbon	NE	68840	**800-652-1910**	308-468-5771
Greater Omaha Packing Co PO Box 7566	Omaha	NE	68107	**800-747-5400**	402-731-3480
Gwaltney of Smithfield Ltd 601 N Church St	Smithfield	VA	23430	**800-888-7521**	757-357-3131
Hansel 'n Gretel Brand Inc 79-36 Cooper Ave	Glendale	NY	11385	**800-635-3354**	718-326-0041
Harris Ranch Beef Co PO Box 220	Selma	CA	93662	**800-742-1955**	559-896-3081
Hausman Sam Meat Packer Inc PO Box 2422	Corpus Christi	TX	78403	**800-364-5521**	361-883-5521
JH Routh Packing Co Inc 4413 W Bogart Rd	Sandusky	OH	44870	**800-446-6759**	419-626-2251
Knauss EW & Sons Inc 625 E Broad St	Quakertown	PA	18951	**800-648-4220**	215-536-4220
L & H Packing Co PO Box 813368	San Antonio	TX	78283	**800-999-3241**	210-532-3241
Land O'Frost Inc 16850 Chicago Ave	Lansing	IL	60438	**800-323-3308**	708-474-7100
Mariah Foods 1333 Indiana Ave	Columbus	IN	47201	**800-227-6328**	812-378-3366
Miller EA Inc 410 N 200 West	Hyrum	UT	84319	**800-873-0939**	435-245-6456
Morrilton Packing Co Inc 51 Blue Diamond Dr	Morrilton	AR	72110	**800-264-2475**	501-354-2474
Moyer Packing Co PO Box 64395	Souderton	PA	18964	**800-876-6722**	215-723-5555
National Beef Packing Co Inc PO Box 20046	Kansas City	MO	64195	**800-449-2333**	
New City Packing & Provision 2600 Church Rd	Aurora	IL	60504	**800-621-0397**	630-851-8800
Ohio Packing Co PO Box 30961	Columbus	OH	43230	**800-282-6403**	614-239-1600
Old Neighborhood Foods 37 Waterhill St	Lynn	MA	01905	**800-628-3529**	781-595-1557
Packerland Inc PO Box 247	Plainwell	MI	49080	**800-841-2961**	269-685-6886
Packerland Packing Co Inc PO Box 23000	Green Bay	WI	54305	**800-753-7724**	920-468-4000
Palo Duro Meat PO Box 31117	Amarillo	TX	79120	**800-625-4785**	806-372-5781
Pearl Meat Packing Co Inc 196 Quincy St	Boston	MA	02121	**800-462-3022**	617-445-6020
Plumrose USA Inc 7 Lexington Ave	East Brunswick	NJ	08816	**800-526-4909**	732-257-6600
Quality Meats & Seafoods 700 Center St	West Fargo	ND	58078	**800-959-4250**	701-282-0202
Raber Packing Co 1413 N Raber Rd	Peoria	IL	61604	**800-331-0545**	309-673-0721
RL Ziegler Co Inc PO Box 1640	Tuscaloosa	AL	35403	**800-392-6328**	205-758-3621
Roode Packing Co Inc PO Box 510	Fairbury	NE	68352	**800-245-5808**	402-729-2253
Rose Packing Co Inc 65 S Barrington Rd	South Barrington	IL	60010	**800-323-7363**	847-381-5700
Routh JH Packing Co Inc 4413 W Bogart Rd	Sandusky	OH	44870	**800-446-6759**	419-626-2251
Sam Hausman Meat Packer Inc PO Box 2422	Corpus Christi	TX	78403	**800-364-5521**	361-883-5521
Sam Kane Beef Processors Inc 9001 Leopard St	Corpus Christi	TX	78409	**800-242-4142**	361-241-5000
Schwab & Co Inc 1111 Linwood Blvd *Cust Svc	Oklahoma City	OK	73106	**800-364-6328***	405-235-2377
Sioux-Preme Packing Co PO Box 255	Sioux Center	IA	51250	**800-735-7675**	712-722-2555
Skylark Meats Inc 4430 S 110th St	Omaha	NE	68137	**800-228-2248**	402-592-0300
Smithfield Foods Inc 200 Commerce St *NYSE: SFD*	Smithfield	VA	23430	**800-276-6158**	757-365-3000
Smithfield Packing Co Inc 501 N Church St	Smithfield	VA	23430	**800-444-9180**	757-357-4321
Square H Brands 2731 S Soto St *Cust Svc	Los Angeles	CA	90023	**800-424-6339***	323-267-4600
Sun Land Beef Co 651 S 91st Ave PO Box 99	Tolleson	AZ	85353	**888-573-2038**	623-936-7177
Superior Packing Co 1477 Drew Ave Suite 101	Davis	CA	95616	**800-228-5262**	530-758-3091
Taylor Excel PO Box 188	Wyalusing	PA	18853	**800-828-9527**	570-746-3000
Thompson Packers Inc 550 Carnation St	Slidell	LA	70460	**800-989-6328**	985-641-6640
Travis Meats Inc PO Box 670	Powell	TN	37849	**800-247-7606**	865-938-9051
Washington Beef Inc PO Box 832	Toppenish	WA	98948	**800-289-2333**	509-865-2121
Wolverine Packing Co Inc 2535 Rivard St	Detroit	MI	48207	**800-521-1390**	313-259-7500
Zeigler RL Co Inc PO Box 1640	Tuscaloosa	AL	35403	**800-392-6328**	205-758-3621

466 MEDICAL ASSOCIATIONS - STATE

SEE ALSO Associations & Organizations - Professional & Trade - Health & Medical Professionals Associations

Name / Address	City	State	ZIP	Toll-Free	Phone
Alabama Medical Assn 19 S Jackson St	Montgomery	AL	36104	**800-239-6272**	334-263-6441
Arizona Medical Assn 810 W Bethany Home Rd	Phoenix	AZ	85013	**800-482-3480**	602-246-8901
Arkansas Medical Society PO Box 55088	Little Rock	AR	72215	**800-542-1058**	501-224-8967
Colorado Medical Society 7351 Lowry Blvd	Denver	CO	80230	**800-654-5653**	720-859-1001
Connecticut State Medical Society 160 Saint Ronan St	New Haven	CT	06511	**800-635-7740**	203-865-0587
Delaware Medical Society 131 Continental Dr Suite 405	Newark	DE	19713	**800-348-6800**	302-658-7596
Florida Medical Assn 123 S Adams St	Tallahassee	FL	32301	**800-762-0233**	850-224-6496
Georgia Medical Assn 1330 W Peachtree St NW Suite 500	Atlanta	GA	30309	**800-282-0224**	404-876-7535
Hawaii Medical Assn 1360 S Beretania St Suite 200	Honolulu	HI	96814	**866-536-8666**	808-536-7702
Indiana State Medical Assn 322 Canal Walk	Indianapolis	IN	46202	**800-257-4762**	317-261-2060
Iowa Medical Society 1001 Grand Ave	West Des Moines	IA	50265	**800-747-3070**	515-223-1401
Kansas Medical Society 623 SW 10th Ave	Topeka	KS	66612	**800-332-0156**	785-235-2383
Kentucky Medical Assn 4965 US Hwy 42 KMA Bldg Suite 2000	Louisville	KY	40222	**800-686-9923**	502-426-6200
Louisiana State Medical Society 6767 Perkins Rd Suite 100	Baton Rouge	LA	70808	**800-375-9508**	225-763-8500
Maine Medical Assn 30 Associate Dr	Manchester	ME	04351	**800-772-0815**	207-622-3374
Maryland State Medical Society 1211 Cathedral St	Baltimore	MD	21201	**800-492-1056**	410-539-0872
Massachusetts Medical Society 860 Winter St	Waltham	MA	02451	**800-322-2303**	781-893-4610
Minnesota Medical Assn 1300 Godward St NE Suite 2500	Minneapolis	MN	55413	**800-342-5662**	612-378-1875
Mississippi State Medical Assn 408 W Parkway Pl	Ridgeland	MS	39157	**800-898-0251**	601-853-6733
Missouri State Medical Assn 113 Madison St	Jefferson City	MO	65101	**800-869-6762**	573-636-5151
Montana Medical Assn 2021 11th Ave Suite 1	Helena	MT	59601	**877-443-4000**	406-443-4000
New Hampshire Medical Society 7 N State St	Concord	NH	03301	**800-564-1909**	603-224-1909
New Jersey Medical Society 2 Princess Rd	Lawrenceville	NJ	08648	**800-322-6765**	609-896-1766
New Mexico Medical Society 7770 Jefferson NE Suite 400	Albuquerque	NM	87109	**800-748-1596**	505-828-0237
New York State Medical Society 420 Lakeville Rd PO Box 5404	Lake Success	NY	11042	**800-523-4405**	516-488-6100
North Carolina Medical Society 222 N Person St	Raleigh	NC	27601	**800-722-1350**	919-833-3836
Ohio State Medical Assn 3401 Mill Run Dr	Hilliard	OH	43026	**800-766-6762**	614-527-6762
Oklahoma State Medical Assn 601 NW Grand Blvd	Oklahoma City	OK	73118	**800-522-9452**	405-843-9571
South Carolina Medical Assn 132 W Park Blvd	Columbia	SC	29210	**800-327-1021**	803-798-6207
Tennessee Medical Assn 2301 21st Ave A	Nashville	TN	37212	**800-659-1862**	615-385-2100
Texas Medical Assn 401 W 15th St	Austin	TX	78701	**800-880-1300**	512-370-1300
Vermont Medical Society 134 Main St	Montpelier	VT	05601	**800-640-8767**	802-223-7898
Virginia Medical Society 4205 Dover Rd	Richmond	VA	23221	**800-746-6768**	804-353-2721
Washington State Medical Assn 2033 6th Ave Suite 1100	Seattle	WA	98121	**800-552-0612**	206-441-9762
West Virginia State Medical Assn 4301 MacCorkle Ave	Charleston	WV	25364	**800-257-4747**	304-925-0342
Wisconsin State Medical Society 330 E Lakeside St	Madison	WI	53701	**866-442-3800**	608-257-6781

467 MEDICAL & DENTAL EQUIPMENT & SUPPLIES - WHOL

Name / Address	City	State	ZIP	Toll-Free	Phone
Armstrong Medical Industries Inc 575 Knightsbridge Pkwy *Cust Svc	Lincolnshire	IL	60069	**800-323-4220***	847-913-0101
Buffalo Hospital Supply Co Inc 4039 Genesee St	Buffalo	NY	14225	**800-724-0530**	716-626-9400
Burkhart Dental Supply Co 2502 S 78th St *Cust Svc	Tacoma	WA	98409	**800-828-2089***	253-474-7761
Burns Veterinary Supply Inc 635 Prior Ave N	Saint Paul	MN	55104	**800-922-8767**	651-646-8788
Caligor Medical & Office Supplies Inc 846 Pelham Pkwy	Pelham Manor	NY	10803	**800-225-9906**	914-738-8400
Derma Sciences Inc 214 Carnegie Ctr Suite 100	Princeton	NJ	08540	**800-825-4325**	609-514-4744
Dunn Safety Products Inc 37 S Sangamon St	Chicago	IL	60607	**800-451-3866**	312-666-5800
Estorge Surgical Supplies 112 S Pierce St	Lafayette	LA	70501	**800-256-8990**	337-232-8920
Evans-Sherratt Co 13050 Northend Ave	Oak Park	MI	48237	**800-248-3826**	248-584-5500
Grogans Health Care Supply Inc 1016 S Broadway St	Lexington	KY	40504	**800-365-1020**	859-254-6661
Gulf South Medical Supply Inc 173 E Marketridge Dr	Ridgeland	MS	39157	**800-347-2456**	601-856-5900
Henry Schein Inc 135 Duryea Rd *NASDAQ: HSIC*	Melville	NY	11747	**800-582-2702**	631-843-5500
Iowa Veterinary Supply Co 124 Country Club Rd	Iowa Falls	IA	50126	**800-392-5636**	641-648-2529
Kentec Medical Inc 17871 Fitch	Irvine	CA	92614	**800-825-5996**	949-863-0810
Laboratory Supply Co 250 Ottawa Ave *Cust Svc	Louisville	KY	40209	**800-888-5227***	502-363-1891
Leeches USA Ltd 300 Shames Dr	Westbury	NY	11590	**800-645-3569**	516-333-2570
Liberty Medical Supply Inc 10045 SE Federal Hwy	Port Saint Lucie	FL	34952	**800-633-2001**	772-398-5800
Mabis Healthcare Inc 1931 Norman Dr	Waukegan	IL	60085	**800-728-6811**	847-680-6811
MacGill William V & Co 1000 N Lombard Rd	Lombard	IL	60148	**800-323-2841**	630-889-0500
McKesson Medical Group Extended Care 8121 10th Ave N	Golden Valley	MN	55427	**800-328-8111**	763-595-6000
McKesson Medical-Surgical 8741 Landmark Rd	Richmond	VA	23228	**800-446-3008**	804-264-7500
Medicore Inc 2337 W 76th St *NASDAQ: MDKI*	Hialeah	FL	33016	**800-327-8894**	305-558-4000
Mesa Laboratories Inc 12100 W 6th Ave *NASDAQ: MLAB* ■ *Sales	Lakewood	CO	80228	**800-992-6372***	303-987-8000
Micro Bio-Medics Inc 846 Pelham Pkwy	Pelham Manor	NY	10803	**800-431-2743**	914-738-8400
Midland Hospital Supply Inc 2011 Great Northern Dr	Fargo	ND	58102	**800-747-4450**	701-235-4451
Midwest Veterinary Supply Inc 11965 Larc Industrial Blvd	Burnsville	MN	55337	**800-328-2975**	952-894-4350
Moore Medical Corp 389 John Downey Dr *Sales	New Britain	CT	06050	**800-234-1464***	860-826-3600
National Logistics Services LLC 11445 G Cronridge Dr	Owings Mills	MD	21117	**800-638-8672**	410-581-1800
NLS Animal Health 11445 G Cronridge Dr	Owings Mills	MD	21117	**800-638-8674**	410-581-1800
Oakworks Inc 923 E Wellspring Rd	New Freedom	PA	17349	**800-558-8850**	717-235-6807
Omron Healthcare Inc 300 Lakeview Pkwy	Vernon Hills	IL	60061	**800-323-1482**	847-680-6200
Patterson Cos Inc 1031 Mendota Heights Rd *NASDAQ: PDCO*	Saint Paul	MN	55120	**800-328-5536**	651-686-1600
PolyMedica Corp 11 State St *NASDAQ: PLMD*	Woburn	MA	01801	**800-886-4050**	781-933-2020
PracticeWares Dental Supply 11291 Sunrise Pk Dr	Rancho Cordova	CA	95742	**800-800-4939**	916-638-8020
PrimeSource Healthcare Inc 3708 E Columbia St	Tucson	AZ	85714	**888-842-6999**	520-512-1100
Radiometer America Inc 810 Sharon Dr	Westlake	OH	44145	**800-736-0600**	440-871-8900
Sammons Preston Inc 4 Sammons Ct	Bolingbrook	IL	60440	**800-323-5547**	630-226-1300
Schein Henry Inc 135 Duryea Rd *NASDAQ: HSIC*	Melville	NY	11747	**800-582-2702**	631-843-5500
Somagen Diagnostics Inc 9220 25th Ave	Edmonton	AB	T6N1E1	**800-661-9993**	780-702-9500
Southern Prosthetic Supply Co 6025 Shiloh Rd Suite A *Cust Svc	Alpharetta	GA	30005	**800-767-7776***	678-455-8888
Sten Corp 13828 Lincoln St NE *NASDAQ: STEN*	Ham Lake	MN	55304	**800-328-7958**	763-755-9516
Sullivan-Schein Dental 10920 W Lincoln Ave	West Allis	WI	53227	**800-648-6684**	414-321-8881
Sun Healthcare Group Inc Pharmaceutical Services 101 Sun Ave NE	Albuquerque	NM	87109	**800-729-6600**	505-468-4168
Tetra Medical Supply Corp 6364 W Gross Pt Rd *Cust Svc	Niles	IL	60714	**800-621-4041***	847-647-0590
VWR Scientific Products Corp 1310 Goshen Pkwy	West Chester	PA	19380	**800-932-5000**	610-431-1700
William V MacGill & Co 1000 N Lombard Rd	Lombard	IL	60148	**800-323-2841**	630-889-0500
Wise El Santo Co Inc 11000 Linpage Pl	Saint Louis	MO	63132	**800-727-8541**	314-428-3100

Company / Address	City	State	Zip	Toll-Free	Phone
Zee Medical Inc 22 Corporate Pk	Irvine	CA	92606	**800-841-8417**	949-252-9500

MEDICAL FACILITIES

SEE Developmental Centers; Health Care Providers - Ancillary; Hospices; Hospitals; Imaging Services - Diagnostic; Substance Abuse Treatment Centers

468 MEDICAL INSTRUMENTS & APPARATUS - MFR

SEE ALSO Imaging Equipment & Systems - Medical; Medical Supplies - Mfr

Company / Address	City	State	Zip	Toll-Free	Phone
3M Medical-Surgical Markets Div 3M Health Care Ctr Bldg 275-4 W-02	Saint Paul	MN	55144	**800-228-3957**	
Abbott Laboratories 100 Abbott Pk Rd *NYSE: ABT*	Abbott Park	IL	60064	**800-323-9100**	847-937-6100
Accurate Surgical & Scientific Instruments Corp 300 Shames Dr	Westbury	NY	11590	**800-645-3569**	516-333-2570
Acme United Corp 1931 Black Rock Tpke *AMEX: ACU*	Fairfield	CT	06825	**800-835-2263**	203-332-7330
AESCULAP Inc 3773 Corporate Pkwy **Cust Svc*	Center Valley	PA	18034	**800-282-9000***	800-258-1946
Akorn Inc 2500 Millbrook Dr	Buffalo Grove	IL	60089	**800-932-5676**	847-279-6100
Aksys Ltd 2 Marriott Dr *NASDAQ: AKSY*	Lincolnshire	IL	60069	**877-229-5700**	847-229-2020
ALARIS Medical Systems Inc 10221 Wateridge Cir	San Diego	CA	92121	**800-854-7128**	858-458-7000
Allied Healthcare Products Inc 1720 Sublette Ave *NASDAQ: AHPI*	Saint Louis	MO	63110	**800-444-3940**	314-771-2400
AngioDynamics Inc 603 Queensbury Ave *NASDAQ: ANGO*	Queensbury	NY	12804	**800-772-6446**	518-798-1215
Antares Pharma Inc 13755 1st Ave N Suite 100 *NASDAQ: ANTR*	Minneapolis	MN	55441	**800-328-3077**	763-475-7700
Arrow International Inc 2400 Bernville Rd *NASDAQ: ARRO*	Reading	PA	19605	**800-233-3187**	610-378-0131
ATEK Medical Mfg 620 Watson St SW	Grand Rapids	MI	49504	**800-253-1540**	616-643-5200
Atrion Corp 1 Allentown Pkwy *NASDAQ: ATRI*	Allen	TX	75002	**800-627-0226**	972-390-9800
B Braun of America Inc 824 12th Ave	Bethlehem	PA	18018	**800-523-9676**	610-691-5400
Ballard Medical Products 12050 Lone Peak Pkwy	Draper	UT	84020	**800-528-5591**	801-572-6800
Bard Access Systems Inc 5425 W Amelia Earhart Dr	Salt Lake City	UT	84116	**800-443-5505**	801-595-0700
Bard CR Inc 730 Central Ave *NYSE: BCR ■ *Cust Svc*	Murray Hill	NJ	07974	**800-526-4455***	908-277-8000
Bard CR Inc Endoscopic Technologies Div 129 Concord Rd Bldg 3 PO Box 7031	Billerica	MA	01821	**800-225-1332**	978-663-8989
Bard CR Inc Medical Div 8195 Industrial Blvd	Covington	GA	30014	**800-526-4455**	770-784-6100
Bard CR Inc Peripheral Vascular Div PO Box 1740	Tempe	AZ	85281	**800-321-4254**	
Bard CR Inc Urological Div 8195 Industrial Blvd	Covington	GA	30014	**800-526-4455**	770-786-9051
Bausch & Lomb Surgical Inc 180 Via Verde Dr **Cust Svc*	San Dimas	CA	91773	**800-338-2020***	909-971-5100
Bayer Healthcare Diagnostics Div 511 Benedict Ave	Tarrytown	NY	10591	**800-431-1970**	914-631-8000
BD Medical 9450 S State St	Sandy	UT	84070	**888-237-2762**	801-565-2300
Becton Dickinson & Co 1 Becton Dr *NYSE: BDX ■ *Cust Svc*	Franklin Lakes	NJ	07417	**888-237-2762***	201-847-6800
Becton Dickinson Consumer Healthcare 1 Becton Dr	Franklin Lakes	NJ	07417	**888-237-2762**	201-847-6800
Becton Dickinson Pharmaceutical Systems 1 Becton Dr	Franklin Lakes	NJ	07417	**888-237-2762**	201-847-6800
Beere Precision Medical Instruments Inc 5307 95th Ave	Kenosha	WI	53144	**800-295-8505**	262-657-2800
Bioject Medical Technologies Inc 20245 SW 95 Ave *NASDAQ: BJCT*	Tualatin	OR	97062	**800-683-7221**	503-692-8001
BioMerieux Inc 595 Anglum Rd	Hazelwood	MO	63042	**800-638-4835**	314-731-8500
Biosense Webster Inc 3333 Diamond Canyon Rd	Diamond Bar	CA	91765	**800-729-9010**	909-839-8500
Boston Scientific Corp 1 Boston Scientific Pl *NYSE: BSX*	Natick	MA	01760	**800-272-3737**	508-650-8000
Braemar Inc 11481 Rupp Dr	Burnsville	MN	55337	**800-328-2719**	952-890-5135
Cambridge Heart Inc 1 Oak Park Dr *NASDAQ: CAMH*	Bedford	MA	01730	**888-226-9283**	781-271-1200
Cardima Inc 47266 Benicia St *NASDAQ: CRDM*	Fremont	CA	94538	**888-354-0300**	510-354-0300
Cardinal Health Automation & Information Services 3750 Torrey View Ct	San Diego	CA	92130	**800-367-9947**	858-480-6000
CAS Medical Systems Inc 44 E Industrial Rd	Branford	CT	06405	**800-227-4414**	203-488-6056
Celsion Corp 10220-L Old Columbia Rd *AMEX: CLN*	Columbia	MD	21046	**800-262-0394**	410-290-5390
Chad Therapeutics Inc 21622 Plummer St *AMEX: CTU*	Chatsworth	CA	91311	**800-423-8870**	818-882-0883
Chronimed Inc 10900 Red Cir Dr Suite 300	Minnetonka	MN	55343	**800-444-5951**	952-979-3600
CNS Inc PO Box 39802 *NASDAQ: CNXS*	Minneapolis	MN	55439	**800-441-0417**	952-229-1500
COBE Cardiovascular Inc 14401 W 65th Way	Arvada	CO	80004	**800-650-2623**	303-425-5508
Codman & Shurtleff Inc 325 Paramount Dr	Raynham	MA	02767	**800-225-0460**	508-880-8100
Conceptus Inc 1021 Howard Ave *NASDAQ: CPTS*	San Carlos	CA	94070	**800-434-7240**	650-802-7240
Conmed Corp 525 French Rd *NASDAQ: CNMD*	Utica	NY	13502	**800-448-6506**	315-797-8375
Cook Critical Care 750 Daniels Way	Bloomington	IN	47404	**800-457-4500**	812-339-2235
Cook Inc PO Box 489	Bloomington	IN	47402	**800-457-4500**	812-339-2235
Cook OB/GYN 1100 W Morgan St	Spencer	IN	47460	**800-541-5591**	812-829-6500
Cook Surgical PO Box 489	Bloomington	IN	47402	**800-457-4500**	812-339-2235
Cook Urological Inc 1100 W Morgan St	Spencer	IN	47460	**800-457-4500**	812-339-2235
Cook Vascular Inc Rt 66 River Rd PO Box 529	Leechburg	PA	15656	**800-245-4715**	724-845-8621
Cooper Cos Inc 21062 Bake Pkwy Suite 200 *NYSE: COO*	Lake Forest	CA	92630	**888-822-2660**	949-597-4700
CooperSurgical Inc 95 Corporate Dr	Trumbull	CT	06611	**800-645-3760**	203-929-6321
Cordis Corp PO Box 025700	Miami	FL	33102	**800-327-2490**	786-313-2000
CR Bard Inc 730 Central Ave *NYSE: BCR ■ *Cust Svc*	Murray Hill	NJ	07974	**800-526-4455***	908-277-8000
CR Bard Inc Endoscopic Technologies Div 129 Concord Rd Bldg 3 PO Box 7031	Billerica	MA	01821	**800-225-1332**	978-663-8989
CR Bard Inc Medical Div 8195 Industrial Blvd	Covington	GA	30014	**800-526-4455**	770-784-6100
CR Bard Inc Peripheral Vascular Div PO Box 1740	Tempe	AZ	85281	**800-321-4254**	
CR Bard Inc Urological Div 8195 Industrial Blvd	Covington	GA	30014	**800-526-4455**	770-786-9051
Criticare Systems Inc 20925 Crossroads Cir Suite 100 *AMEX: CMD*	Waukesha	WI	53186	**800-458-4615**	262-798-8282
Cygnus Inc 400 Penobscot Dr	Redwood City	CA	94063	**866-459-2824**	650-369-4300
Daig Corp 14901 DeVeau Pl	Minnetonka	MN	55345	**800-328-3873**	952-933-4700
Datascope Corp 14 Philips Pkwy *NASDAQ: DSCP*	Montvale	NJ	07645	**800-288-2121**	201-391-8100
Davol Inc PO Box 8500	Cranston	RI	02920	**800-556-6756**	401-463-7000
Deltec Inc 1265 Grey Fox Rd	Saint Paul	MN	55112	**800-426-2448**	651-633-2556
Dexterity Surgical Inc 5444 W Heimer Suite 1970	Houston	TX	77056	**800-840-3339**	713-622-0516
Dolphin Medical Inc 12525 Chadron Ave	Hawthorne	CA	90250	**866-588-9539**	310-978-3073
Empi Inc 599 Cardigan Rd	Saint Paul	MN	55126	**800-328-2536**	651-415-9000
Endocare Inc 201 Technology Dr	Irvine	CA	92618	**800-683-8938**	949-450-5400
Endologix Inc 13900 Alton Pkwy Suite 122 *NASDAQ: ELGX*	Irvine	CA	92618	**800-983-2284**	949-457-9546
Enpath Medical Inc 15301 Hwy 55 W *NASDAQ: NPTH*	Plymouth	MN	55447	**800-559-2613**	763-559-2613
EP Technologies 2710 Orchard Pkwy **Cust Svc*	San Jose	CA	95134	**800-552-6700***	408-895-3500
Ethicon Endo-Surgery Inc 4545 Creek Rd	Cincinnati	OH	45242	**800-556-8451**	513-786-7000
ev3 Inc 4600 Nathan Ln N *NASDAQ: EVVV*	Plymouth	MN	55442	**800-716-6700**	763-398-7000
Gaymar Industries Inc 10 Centre Dr	Orchard Park	NY	14127	**800-828-7341**	716-662-2551
Getinge USA Inc 1777 E Henrietta Rd **Cust Svc*	Rochester	NY	14623	**800-950-9912***	585-475-1400
Graham-Field Health Products Inc 2935 Northeast Pkwy	Atlanta	GA	30360	**800-235-4661**	770-447-1609
Grason-Stadler Inc 5225 Verona Rd Bldg 2	Madison	WI	53711	**800-700-2282**	608-441-2323
Guidant Corp PO Box 44906 *NYSE: GDT*	Indianapolis	IN	46244	**800-405-9611**	317-971-2000
Gyrus Medical Inc 6655 Wedgwood Rd Suite 160	Maple Grove	MN	55311	**800-852-9361**	763-416-3000
Haemonetics Corp 400 Wood Rd *NYSE: HAE*	Braintree	MA	02184	**800-225-5242**	781-848-7100
HNS International Inc 17662 Irvine Blvd Suite 20	Tustin	CA	92780	**877-474-6539**	714-508-6408
Hoggan Health Industries Inc 8020 S 1300 West	West Jordan	UT	84088	**800-678-7888**	801-572-6500
Hudson RCI 27711 Diaz Rd **Cust Svc*	Temecula	CA	92589	**800-848-3766***	951-676-5611
Hypertension Diagnostics Inc 2915 Waters Rd Suite 108 *NASDAQ: HDII*	Eagan	MN	55121	**888-785-7392**	651-687-9999
Integra LifeSciences Holdings Corp 311 Enterprise Dr *NASDAQ: IART*	Plainsboro	NJ	08536	**800-654-2873**	609-275-0500
Intuitive Surgical Inc 950 Kifer Rd *NASDAQ: ISRG*	Sunnyvale	CA	94086	**888-868-4647**	408-523-2100
Invacare ICCG 1644 Lotsie Blvd	Saint Louis	MO	63132	**800-347-5440**	314-253-5440
Inverness Corp 17-10 Willow St	Fair Lawn	NJ	07410	**800-631-0860**	201-794-3400
Jenckes Machine Co PO Box 364	Warren	RI	02885	**866-941-1455**	401-247-1999
Johnson Matthey Medical Products 1401 King Rd	West Chester	PA	19380	**800-442-1405**	610-648-8000
Kendall Co 15 Hampshire St **Cust Svc*	Mansfield	MA	02048	**800-962-9888***	508-261-8000
Kensey Nash Corp 55 E Uwchlan Ave *NASDAQ: KNSY*	Exton	PA	19341	**800-524-1984**	610-524-0188
Linvatec Corp 11311 Concept Blvd	Largo	FL	33773	**800-325-5900**	727-392-6464
Mallinckrodt Inc 675 McDonnell Blvd	Hazelwood	MO	63042	**888-744-1414**	314-654-2000
Manan Medical Products Inc 241 W Palatine Rd	Wheeling	IL	60090	**800-424-6779**	847-637-3333
McKinley Medical LLP 4080 Youngfield St	Wheat Ridge	CO	80033	**800-578-0555**	303-420-9569
Medex Inc 2231 Rutherford Rd	Carlsbad	CA	92008	**800-848-1757**	760-602-4400
Medex Inc 6250 Shier Rings Rd **Cust Svc*	Dublin	OH	43016	**800-848-1757***	614-889-2220
Medical Device Technologies Inc 3600 SW 47th Ave	Gainesville	FL	32608	**800-338-0440**	352-338-0440
Medrad Inc 1 Medrad Dr **Cust Svc*	Indianola	PA	15051	**800-633-7237***	412-767-2400
Medtronic Arterial Vascular Engineering 3576 Unocal Pl	Santa Rosa	CA	95403	**800-308-7868**	707-525-0111
Medtronic Inc 710 Medtronic Pkwy NE *NYSE: MDT ■ *Cust Svc*	Minneapolis	MN	55432	**800-328-2518***	763-574-4000
Medtronic Neurosurgery 125 Cremona Dr **Cust Svc*	Goleta	CA	93117	**800-468-9710***	805-968-1546
Medtronic Perfusion Systems 7611 Northland Dr	Brooklyn Park	MN	55428	**800-328-3320**	763-391-9000
Medtronic Powered Surgical Solutions 4620 N Beach St	Fort Worth	TX	76137	**800-433-7639**	817-788-6400
Medwave Inc 4382 Round Lake Rd W *NASDAQ: MDWV*	Arden Hills	MN	55112	**800-894-7601**	651-639-1227
Meridian Medical Technologies Inc 6350 Stevens Forest Rd Suite 301	Columbia	MD	21046	**800-638-8093**	443-259-7800
Merit Medical Systems Inc 1600 W Merit Pkwy *NASDAQ: MMSI*	South Jordan	UT	84095	**800-356-3748**	801-253-1600
Micro Therapeutics Inc 2 Goodyear Bldg A *NASDAQ: MTIX*	Irvine	CA	92618	**800-684-6733**	949-837-3700
MicroAire Surgical Instruments Inc 1641 Edlich Dr	Charlottesville	VA	22911	**800-538-5561**	434-975-8000
Minntech Corp 14605 28th Ave N	Minneapolis	MN	55447	**800-328-3345**	763-553-3300
Miravant Medical Technologies 336 Bollay Dr	Santa Barbara	CA	93117	**800-685-2959**	805-685-9880
Novosci 2828 N Crescent Ridge Dr	The Woodlands	TX	77381	**800-322-2273**	281-363-4950

				Toll-Free	Phone
Novoste Corp 4350 International Blvd Suite E *NASDAQ: NOVT*	Norcross	GA	30093	**800-668-6783**	770-717-0904
NuVasive Inc 10065 Old Grove Rd *NASDAQ: NUVA*	San Diego	CA	92131	**800-455-1476**	858-271-7070
Ortho-Clinical Diagnostics Inc 1001 US Rt 202 N PO Box 350	Raritan	NJ	08869	**800-828-6316**	908-218-1300
Osteomed Corp 3885 Arapaho Rd *Cust Svc	Addison	TX	75001	**800-456-7779***	972-677-4600
Osteometer MediTech Inc 12515 Chadron Ave	Hawthorne	CA	90250	**866-421-7762**	310-978-3073
Physiometrix Inc 101 Billerica Ave 5 Billerica Pk *NASDAQ: PHYX*	North Billerica	MA	01862	**800-474-9746**	978-670-2422
Pilling Surgical 200 Precision Rd Suite 200 *Cust Svc	Horsham	PA	19044	**800-523-6507***	215-442-8700
Possis Medical Inc 9055 Evergreen Blvd NW *NASDAQ: POSS*	Minneapolis	MN	55433	**800-810-7677**	763-780-4555
Propper Mfg Co Inc 36-04 Skillman Ave *Cust Svc	Long Island City	NY	11101	**800-832-4300***	718-392-6650
ResMed Inc 14040 Danielson St *NYSE: RMD*	Poway	CA	92064	**800-424-0737**	858-746-2400
Rochester Medical Corp 1 Rochester Medical Dr *NASDAQ: ROCM*	Stewartville	MN	55976	**800-243-3315**	507-533-9600
Siemens Medical Solutions Inc 51 Valley Stream Pkwy	Malvern	PA	19355	**866-872-9745**	610-448-6300
Smith & Nephew Inc Endoscopy Div 150 Minuteman Rd	Andover	MA	01810	**800-343-8386**	978-749-1000
Smiths Medical ASD Inc 10 Bowman Dr	Keene	NH	03431	**800-258-5361**	603-352-3812
SS White Medical Products Inc 151 Old New Brunswick Rd *Cust Svc	Piscataway	NJ	08854	**888-779-4483***	732-752-8300
STERIS Corp 5960 Heisley Rd *NYSE: STE*	Mentor	OH	44060	**800-548-4873**	440-354-2600
Stryker Corp 2725 Fairfield Rd *NYSE: SYK*	Kalamazoo	MI	49002	**800-726-2725**	269-385-2600
Stryker Instruments 4100 E Milham Ave *Cust Svc	Kalamazoo	MI	49001	**800-253-3210***	269-323-7700
Sunrise Medical Continuing Care Group 5001 Joerns Dr	Stevens Point	WI	54481	**800-972-7581**	715-341-3600
Surgical Specialties Corp 100 Dennis Dr	Reading	PA	19606	**800-523-3332**	610-404-1000
Teleflex Medical Group 2917 Weck Dr	Research Triangle Park	NC	27709	**800-334-9751**	919-544-8000
Terumo Cardiovascular Systems Corp 6200 Jackson Rd	Ann Arbor	MI	48103	**800-262-3304**	734-663-4145
Terumo Medical Corp 2101 Cottontail Ln	Somerset	NJ	08873	**800-283-7866**	732-302-4900
TFX Medical Inc 50 Plantation Dr	Jaffrey	NH	03452	**800-548-6600**	603-532-7706
Topcon Medical Systems Inc 37 W Century Rd	Paramus	NJ	07652	**800-223-1130**	201-261-9450
Tyco Healthcare/Mallinckrodt 3600 N 2nd St PO Box 5840	Saint Louis	MO	63134	**888-744-1414**	314-654-2000
Urologix Inc 14405 21st Ave N *NASDAQ: ULGX*	Minneapolis	MN	55447	**800-475-1403**	763-475-1400
US Surgical Corp 150 Glover Ave	Norwalk	CT	06856	**800-722-8772**	203-845-1000
Utah Medical Products Inc 7043 S 300 West *NASDAQ: UTMD*	Midvale	UT	84047	**800-533-4984**	801-566-1200
Ventana Medical Systems Inc 1910 Innovation Pk Dr *NASDAQ: VMSI*	Tucson	AZ	85737	**800-227-2155**	520-887-2155
ViaCirq 400 South Point Blvd Bldg 501 Suite 230 *Cust Svc	Canonsburg	PA	15317	**877-952-6100***	724-745-2362
Vital Signs Inc 20 Campus Rd *NASDAQ: VITL*	Totowa	NJ	07512	**800-932-0760**	973-790-1330
Walco International Inc 520 S Main St	Grapevine	TX	76051	**877-289-9252**	817-601-6000
Weck Closure Systems LLC 2917 Weck Dr	Research Triangle Park	NC	27709	**800-334-9751**	919-544-8000
White SS Medical Products Inc 151 Old New Brunswick Rd *Cust Svc	Piscataway	NJ	08854	**888-779-4483***	732-752-8300
Wilson-Cook Medical Inc 4900 Bethania Stn Rd	Winston-Salem	NC	27105	**800-245-4717**	336-744-0157
ZLB Behring LLC 1020 1st Ave	King of Prussia	PA	19406	**800-683-1288**	610-878-4000

469 MEDICAL SUPPLIES - MFR

SEE ALSO Personal Protective Equipment & Clothing

				Toll-Free	Phone
3M Health Care Solutions 3M Ctr Health Care Service Ctr *Prod Info	Saint Paul	MN	55144	**800-364-3577***	651-733-1110
3M Medical-Surgical Markets Div 3M Health Care Ctr Bldg 275-4 W-02	Saint Paul	MN	55144	**800-228-3957**	
Adhesives Research Inc 400 Seaks Run Rd	Glen Rock	PA	17327	**800-445-6240**	717-235-7979
Advanced Sterilization Products 33 Technology Dr	Irvine	CA	92618	**800-595-0200**	949-581-5799
AESCULAP Inc 3773 Corporate Pkwy *Cust Svc	Center Valley	PA	18034	**800-282-9000***	800-258-1946
Allied Healthcare Products Inc 1720 Sublette Ave *NASDAQ: AHPI*	Saint Louis	MO	63110	**800-444-3940**	314-771-2400
American Medical Systems Holdings Inc 10700 Bren Rd W *NASDAQ: AMMD*	Minnetonka	MN	55343	**800-328-3881**	952-933-4666
Animas Corp 200 Lawrence Dr *NASDAQ: PUMP*	West Chester	PA	19380	**877-937-7867**	610-644-8990
Arizant Inc 10393 W 70th St	Eden Prairie	MN	55344	**800-800-4346**	952-947-1200
Arthrex Inc 1370 Creekside Blvd	Naples	FL	34108	**800-934-4404**	239-643-5553
ATS Medical Inc 3905 Annapolis Ln Suite 105 *NASDAQ: ATSI*	Minneapolis	MN	55447	**866-287-6331**	763-553-7736
Avery Dennison Corp 150 N Orange Grove Blvd *NYSE: AVY* ■ *Cust Svc	Pasadena	CA	91103	**800-252-8379***	626-304-2000
Avitar Inc 65 Dan Rd *AMEX: AVR*	Canton	MA	02021	**800-255-0511**	781-821-2440
Ballard Medical Products 12050 Lone Peak Pkwy	Draper	UT	84020	**800-528-5591**	801-572-6800
Bard CR Inc 730 Central Ave *NYSE: BCR* ■ *Cust Svc	Murray Hill	NJ	07974	**800-526-4455***	908-277-8000
Bard CR Inc Urological Div 8195 Industrial Blvd	Covington	GA	30014	**800-526-4455**	770-786-9051
Battle Creek Equipment Co 307 W Jackson St *Cust Svc	Battle Creek	MI	49017	**800-253-0854***	269-962-6181
Bausch & Lomb Inc 1 Bausch & Lomb Pl *NYSE: BOL*	Rochester	NY	14604	**800-344-8815**	585-338-6000
Bausch & Lomb Surgical Inc 180 Via Verde Dr *Cust Svc	San Dimas	CA	91773	**800-338-2020***	909-971-5100
Becton Dickinson & Co 1 Becton Dr *NYSE: BDX* ■ *Cust Svc	Franklin Lakes	NJ	07417	**888-237-2762***	201-847-6800
Becton Dickinson Consumer Healthcare 1 Becton Dr	Franklin Lakes	NJ	07417	**888-237-2762**	201-847-6800
Beiersdorf North America 187 Danbury Rd	Wilton	CT	06897	**800-233-2340**	203-563-5800
Beltone Electronics Corp 4201 W Victoria St	Chicago	IL	60646	**800-235-8663**	773-583-3600
BioCore Medical Technologies Inc 11800 Tech Rd Suite 240	Silver Spring	MD	20904	**888-689-5655**	301-625-6818
BioHorizons Implant Systems Inc One Perimeter Pk S Suite 230 S	Birmingham	AL	35243	**888-246-8338**	205-967-7880
Biomet Inc 56 E Bell Dr *NASDAQ: BMET*	Warsaw	IN	46582	**800-348-9500**	574-267-6639
BSN-Jobst Inc 5825 Carnegie Blvd	Charlotte	NC	28209	**800-221-7573**	704-554-9933
BSN Medical Inc 5825 Carnegie Blvd	Charlotte	NC	28209	**800-598-5370**	704-331-0600
Burke Mobility Products Inc 1800 Merriam Ln *Sales	Kansas City	KS	66106	**800-255-4147***	913-722-5658
CarboMedics Inc 1300 E Anderson Ln	Austin	TX	78752	**800-648-1579**	512-435-3200
Chattanooga Group 4717 Adams Rd	Hixson	TN	37343	**800-592-7329**	423-870-2281
CMS Industries Ltd 1320 Alberta Ave	Saskatoon	SK	S7K1R5	**800-668-8821**	306-955-8821
COBE Cardiovascular Inc 14401 W 65th Way	Arvada	CO	80004	**800-650-2623**	303-425-5508
Codman & Shurtleff Inc 325 Paramount Dr	Raynham	MA	02767	**800-225-0460**	508-880-8100
CR Bard Inc 730 Central Ave *NYSE: BCR* ■ *Cust Svc	Murray Hill	NJ	07974	**800-526-4455***	908-277-8000
CR Bard Inc Urological Div 8195 Industrial Blvd	Covington	GA	30014	**800-526-4455**	770-786-9051
Cramer Products Inc PO Box 1001	Gardner	KS	66030	**800-345-2231**	913-856-7511
Cyberonics Inc Cyberonics Bldg 100 Cyberonics Blvd *NASDAQ: CYBX*	Houston	TX	77058	**800-332-1375**	281-228-7200
Davol Inc PO Box 8500	Cranston	RI	02920	**800-556-6756**	401-463-7000
Depuy Acromed Inc 325 Paramount Dr	Raynham	MA	02767	**800-451-2006**	508-880-8100
DePuy Inc 700 Orthopedic Dr	Warsaw	IN	46581	**800-473-3789**	574-267-8143
DeRoyal Industries Inc 200 DeBusk Ln	Powell	TN	37849	**800-251-9864**	865-938-7828
dj Orthopedics Inc 2985 Scott St *NYSE: DJO*	Vista	CA	92081	**800-321-9549**	760-727-1280
EBI Medical Systems LP 100 Interpace Pkwy	Parsippany	NJ	07054	**800-526-2579**	973-299-9300
Electric Mobility Corp 1 Mobility Plaza *Cust Svc	Sewell	NJ	08080	**800-257-7955***	856-468-0270
Ergodyne Corp 1410 Energy Pk Dr Suite 1	Saint Paul	MN	55108	**800-225-8238**	651-642-9889
Everest & Jennings 2935 Northeast Pkwy	Atlanta	GA	30360	**800-235-4661**	770-447-1609
Exactech Inc 2320 NW 66th Ct *NASDAQ: EXAC*	Gainesville	FL	32653	**800-392-2832**	352-377-1140
Female Health Co 515 N State St Suite 2225	Chicago	IL	60610	**800-635-0844**	312-595-9123
Ferno-Washington Inc 70 Weil Way	Wilmington	OH	45177	**800-733-3766**	937-382-1451
Freeman Mfg Co 900 W Chicago Rd	Sturgis	MI	49091	**800-253-2091**	269-651-2371
Gambro Renal Products 10810 W Collins Ave	Lakewood	CO	80215	**800-525-2623**	303-232-6800
Genzyme Biosurgery 1 Kendall Sq	Cambridge	MA	02139	**800-326-7002**	617-252-7500
Genzyme Corp 500 Kendall St *NASDAQ: GENZ*	Cambridge	MA	02142	**800-326-7002**	617-252-7500
Gish Biomedical Inc 22942 Arroyo Vista	Rancho Santa Margarita	CA	92688	**800-938-0531**	949-635-6200
Graham-Field Health Products Inc 2935 Northeast Pkwy	Atlanta	GA	30360	**800-235-4661**	770-447-1609
Gyrus Medical Inc ENT Div 2925 Appling Rd	Bartlett	TN	38133	**800-262-3540**	901-373-0200
Hanger Orthopedic Group Inc 2 Bethesda Metro Ctr Suite 1200 *NYSE: HGR*	Bethesda	MD	20814	**800-765-3822**	301-986-0701
HearUSA Inc 1250 Northpoint Pkwy *AMEX: EAR* ■ *Cust Svc	West Palm Beach	FL	33407	**800-731-3277***	561-478-8770
Helvoet Pharma Inc 9012 Pennsauken Hwy	Pennsauken	NJ	08110	**800-874-3586**	856-663-2202
Hollister Inc 2000 Hollister Dr	Libertyville	IL	60048	**800-323-4060**	847-680-1000
Hospira Inc 275 N Field Dr *NYSE: HSP*	Lake Forest	IL	60045	**877-946-7747**	224-212-2000
Hoveround Corp 2151 Whitfield Industrial Way	Sarasota	FL	34243	**800-755-4331**	941-739-6200
Hudson RCI 27711 Diaz Rd *Cust Svc	Temecula	CA	92589	**800-848-3766***	951-676-5611
Hy-Tape International Inc PO Box 540	Patterson	NY	12563	**800-248-0101**	845-878-4848
I-Flow Corp 20202 Windrow Dr *NASDAQ: IFLO*	Lake Forest	CA	92630	**800-448-3569**	949-206-2700
ICU Medical Inc 951 Calle Amanecer *NASDAQ: ICUI*	San Clemente	CA	92673	**800-824-7890**	949-366-2183
Ideal Tape Co 1400 Middlesex St	Lowell	MA	01851	**800-284-3325**	978-458-6833
INAMED Aesthetics 700 Ward Dr	Santa Barbara	CA	93111	**800-624-4261**	805-683-6761
INAMED Corp 5540 Ekwill St Suite D *NASDAQ: IMDC*	Santa Barbara	CA	93111	**800-624-6261**	805-692-5400
Independence Technology LLC 45 Technology Dr	Warren	NJ	07059	**888-463-3000**	
International Technidyne Corp 8 Olsen Ave	Edison	NJ	08820	**800-631-5945**	732-548-6677
Interpore Spine Ltd 181 Technology Dr	Irvine	CA	92618	**800-722-4489**	949-453-3200
Invacare Corp 1 Invacare Way *NYSE: IVC*	Elyria	OH	44036	**800-333-6900**	440-329-6000
Johnson & Johnson Consumer Products Co 199 Grandview Rd	Skillman	NJ	08558	**800-526-3967**	908-874-1000
K-Tube Corp 13400 Kirkham Way	Poway	CA	92064	**800-394-0058**	858-513-9229
Kimberly-Clark 6625 Industrial Park Blvd	Fort Worth	TX	76180	**800-742-1996**	817-581-6424
Kimberly-Clark Corp Professional Health Care Business 1400 Holcomb Bridge Rd	Roswell	GA	30076	**800-558-6452**	770-587-8000
Kinetic Concepts Inc (KCI Inc) 8023 Vantage Dr *NYSE: KCI*	San Antonio	TX	78230	**800-531-5346**	210-524-9000
Kyphon Inc 1221 Crossman Ave *NASDAQ: KYPH*	Sunnyvale	CA	94089	**877-459-7466**	408-548-6500
Langer Inc 450 Commack Rd *NASDAQ: GAIT*	Deer Park	NY	11729	**800-233-2687**	631-667-1200

Company / Address	City	State	Zip	Toll-Free	Phone
LecTec Corp 10701 Red Circle Dr	Minnetonka	MN	55343	**800-777-2291**	952-933-2291
Leisure Lift 1800 Merriam Ln	Kansas City	KS	66106	**800-255-0285**	913-722-5658
LPS Industries Inc 10 Caesar Pl *Sales	Moonachie	NJ	07074	**800-275-4577***	201-438-3515
Ludlow Tape 2 Ludlow Pk Dr	Chicopee	MA	01022	**800-445-5025**	413-593-6400
M & C Specialties Co 90 James Way *Cust Svc	Southampton	PA	18966	**800-441-6996***	215-322-1600
Medegen Medical Products 209 Medegen Dr *Cust Svc	Gallaway	TN	38036	**800-233-1987***	901-867-2951
Medical Action Industries Inc 800 Prime Pl NASDAQ: MDCI	Hauppauge	NY	11788	**800-645-7042**	631-231-4600
Medline Industries Inc 1 Medline Pl *Cust Svc	Mundelein	IL	60060	**800-323-6284***	847-949-5500
Medrad Inc 1 Medrad Dr *Cust Svc	Indianola	PA	15051	**800-633-7237***	412-767-2400
Medtronic Inc 710 Medtronic Pkwy NE NYSE: MDT ■ *Cust Svc	Minneapolis	MN	55432	**800-328-2518***	763-574-4000
Medtronic Inc Heart Valve Div 1851 E Deere Ave	Santa Ana	CA	92705	**800-326-3330**	949-474-3943
Medtronic MiniMed Inc 18000 Devonshire St	Northridge	CA	91325	**800-933-3322**	818-362-5958
Medtronic Powered Surgical Solutions 4620 N Beach St	Fort Worth	TX	76137	**800-433-7639**	817-788-6400
Medtronic Sofamor Danek Inc 1800 Pyramid Pl	Memphis	TN	38132	**800-763-2667**	901-396-2695
Medtronic Xomed Inc 6743 Southpoint Dr N	Jacksonville	FL	32216	**800-874-5797**	904-296-9600
Mentor Corp 201 Mentor Dr NYSE: MNT	Santa Barbara	CA	93111	**800-525-0245**	805-681-6000
Microtek Medical Holdings Inc 1850 Beaver Ridge Cir Suite E NASDAQ: MTMD	Norcross	GA	30071	**800-777-7977**	770-806-9898
Microtek Medical Inc 512 Lehmberg Rd	Columbus	MS	39702	**800-824-3027**	662-327-1863
Miracle-Ear Inc 5000 Cheshire Ln N	Plymouth	MN	55446	**800-234-7714**	763-268-4000
Mitek Products 249 Vanderbilt Ave	Norwood	MA	02062	**800-356-4835**	
MPL Technologies 9400 King St *Cust Svc	Franklin Park	IL	60131	**800-323-0970***	847-678-7555
NELCO Inc 98 Baldwin Ave	Woburn	MA	01801	**800-635-2613**	781-933-1940
Nice-Pak Products Inc 2 Nice-Pak Pk	Orangeburg	NY	10962	**800-999-6423**	845-365-1700
NMT Medical Inc 27 Wormwood St NASDAQ: NMTI	Boston	MA	02210	**800-666-6484**	617-737-0930
NorMed 4310 S 131 Pl	Seattle	WA	98168	**800-288-8200**	206-242-8228
Orthofix Inc 1720 Bray Central Dr	McKinney	TX	75069	**800-527-0404**	469-742-2500
OrthoLogic Corp 1275 W Washington St NASDAQ: OLGC	Tempe	AZ	85281	**800-937-5520**	602-286-5520
Orthovita Inc 45 Great Valley Pkwy NASDAQ: VITA	Malvern	PA	19355	**800-676-8482**	610-640-1775
Osteomed Corp 3885 Arapaho Rd *Cust Svc	Addison	TX	75001	**800-456-7779***	972-677-4600
Perclose Inc 400 Saginaw Dr	Redwood City	CA	94063	**800-587-7965**	650-474-3000
Perma-Type Co Inc 83 Northwest Dr	Plainville	CT	06062	**800-243-4234**	860-747-9999
Phonic Ear Inc 3880 Cypress Dr	Petaluma	CA	94954	**800-227-0735**	707-769-1110
Posey Co 5635 Peck Rd	Arcadia	CA	91006	**800-767-3933**	626-443-3143
Precision Dynamics Corp 13880 Del Sur St	San Fernando	CA	91340	**800-847-0670**	818-897-1111
Rehab Plus Therapeutics Products Inc 105 Industrial Dr	Levelland	TX	79336	**800-288-8059**	806-791-2288
Retractable Technologies Inc 511 Lobo Ln AMEX: RVP	Little Elm	TX	75068	**888-806-2626**	972-294-1010
Rite-Hite Corp 4343 Chavenelle Dr	Dubuque	IA	52004	**800-456-0600**	563-556-2020
Rockford Medical & Safety Co 2420 Harrison Ave	Rockford	IL	61108	**800-541-2528**	815-394-4809
Rusch Inc 2450 Meadowbrook Pkwy	Duluth	GA	30096	**800-553-5214**	770-623-0816
Saint Jude Medical Inc 1 Lillehei Plaza NYSE: STJ	Saint Paul	MN	55117	**800-328-9634**	651-483-2000
SCOOTER Store Inc 1650 Independence Dr	New Braunfels	TX	78132	**800-723-4535**	830-626-5600
SeaFab 9561 Satellite Blvd Suite 350	Orlando	FL	32837	**877-265-1491**	407-852-6170
Seattle Systems Inc 26296 Twelve Trees Ln NW	Poulsbo	WA	98370	**800-248-6463**	360-697-5656
Siemens Hearing Instruments Inc 10 Constitution Ave	Piscataway	NJ	08855	**800-766-4500**	732-562-6600
SIMS Respiratory Support Products 9255 Custom House Plaza Suite L	San Diego	CA	92154	**800-258-5361**	619-710-1000
Smith & Nephew Inc 1450 E Brooks Rd *Cust Svc	Memphis	TN	38116	**800-238-7538***	901-396-2121
Smith & Nephew Inc Orthopaedic Div 1450 Brooks Rd	Memphis	TN	38116	**800-821-5700**	901-396-2121
Smith & Nephew Inc Wound Management Div 11775 Starkey Rd *Cust Svc	Largo	FL	33773	**800-876-1261***	727-392-1261
Smiths Medical ASD Inc 160 Weymouth St	Rockland	MA	02370	**800-553-8351**	781-878-8011
Smiths Medical ASD Inc 10 Bowman Dr	Keene	NH	03431	**800-258-5361**	603-352-3812
Sonic Innovations Inc 2795 E Cottonwood Pkwy Suite 660 NASDAQ: SNCI ■ *Cust Svc	Salt Lake City	UT	84121	**888-423-7834***	801-365-2800
Span-America Medical Systems Inc 70 Commerce Ctr NASDAQ: SPAN	Greenville	SC	29615	**800-888-6752**	864-288-8877
Spenco Medical Corp PO Box 2501	Waco	TX	76702	**800-877-3626**	254-772-6000
SSL Americas Inc 3585 Engineering Dr Suite 200	Norcross	GA	30092	**888-387-3927**	770-582-2222
Standard Textile Co Inc 1 Knollcrest	Cincinnati	OH	45237	**800-888-5000**	513-761-9255
Starkey Laboratories Inc 6700 Washington Ave S	Eden Prairie	MN	55344	**800-328-8602**	952-941-6401
STERIS Corp 5960 Heisley Rd NYSE: STE	Mentor	OH	44060	**800-548-4873**	440-354-2600
Stryker Corp 2725 Fairfield Rd NYSE: SYK	Kalamazoo	MI	49002	**800-726-2725**	269-385-2600
Sunrise Medical Inc 2382 Faraday Ave Suite 200	Carlsbad	CA	92008	**800-278-6747**	760-930-1500
Surgical Appliance Industries Inc 3960 Rosslyn Dr	Cincinnati	OH	45209	**800-888-0458**	513-271-4594
Synovis Life Technologies Inc 2575 University Ave W Suite 180 NASDAQ: SYNO	Saint Paul	MN	55114	**800-487-9627**	651-603-3700
Synthes USA 1690 Russell Rd	Paoli	PA	19301	**800-523-0322**	610-647-9700
TAPEMARK Co 150 E Marie Ave	West Saint Paul	MN	55118	**800-535-1998**	651-455-1611
Tefron USA Inc 201 St Germain Ave SW	Valdese	NC	28690	**800-554-5541**	828-879-6500
TIDI Products LLC 570 Enterprise Dr	Neenah	WI	54956	**800-215-5464**	920-751-4300
Tillotson Healthcare Corp 8025 S Willow St Suite 203	Manchester	NH	03103	**800-445-6830**	603-472-6600
Tri-State Hospital Supply Corp 301 Catrell Dr	Howell	MI	48843	**800-248-4058**	517-546-5400
Utah Medical Products Inc 7043 S 300 West NASDAQ: UTMD	Midvale	UT	84047	**800-533-4984**	801-566-1200
Venture Tape Corp 30 Commerce Rd	Rockland	MA	02370	**800-343-1076**	781-331-5900
Vital Signs Inc 20 Campus Rd NASDAQ: VITL	Totowa	NJ	07512	**800-932-0760**	973-790-1330
West Pharmaceutical Services Inc 101 Gordon Dr NYSE: WST	Lionville	PA	19341	**800-345-9800**	610-594-2900
Wright Medical Group Inc 5677 Airline Rd NASDAQ: WMGI	Arlington	TN	38002	**800-238-7188**	901-867-9971
Wright Medical Technology Inc 5677 Airline Rd	Arlington	TN	38002	**800-238-7188**	901-867-9971
Young Innovations Inc 13705 Shoreline Ct E NASDAQ: YDNT	Earth City	MO	63045	**800-325-1881**	314-344-0010
ZEVEX International Inc 4314 ZEVEX Pk Ln NASDAQ: ZVXI	Salt Lake City	UT	84123	**800-970-2337**	801-264-1001
Zimmer Holdings Inc 1800 W Center St NYSE: ZMH	Warsaw	IN	46581	**800-613-6131**	574-267-6131

470 MEDICINAL CHEMICALS & BOTANICAL PRODUCTS

SEE ALSO Biotechnology Companies; Diagnostic Products; Pharmaceutical Companies; Pharmaceutical Companies - Generic Drugs; Vitamins & Nutritional Supplements

Company / Address	City	State	Zip	Toll-Free	Phone
Acic Fine Chemicals Inc 131 Clarence St Suite 200	Brantford	ON	N3T2V6	**800-265-6727**	519-751-3668
Adams Laboratories Inc DBA Adams Respiratory Therapeutics 14801 Sovereign Rd	Fort Worth	TX	76155	**800-770-5270**	817-354-3858
Adams Respiratory Therapeutics 14801 Sovereign Rd	Fort Worth	TX	76155	**800-770-5270**	817-354-3858
Advitech Inc 1165 boul Lebourgneuf Suite 140	Quebec	QC	G2K2C9	**888-686-7498**	418-686-7498
Alpharma Inc Fine Chemicals Div 1 Executive Dr 4th Fl	Fort Lee	NJ	07024	**800-645-4216**	201-947-7774
Alpharma Inc US Pharmaceuticals Div 7205 Windsor Blvd *Cust Svc	Baltimore	MD	21244	**800-638-9096***	410-298-1000
AM Todd Co 1717 Douglas Ave	Kalamazoo	MI	49005	**800-968-2603**	269-343-2603
American Distilling & Mfg Inc 31 E High St	East Hampton	CT	06424	**800-203-4444**	860-267-4444
American Laboratories Inc 4410 S 102nd St *Cust Svc	Omaha	NE	68127	**800-445-5989***	402-339-2494
Array BioPharma Inc 1885 33rd St NASDAQ: ARRY	Boulder	CO	80301	**877-633-2436**	303-381-6600
Bachem Bioscience Inc 3700 Horizon Dr	King of Prussia	PA	19406	**800-634-3183**	610-239-0300
BASF Corp 3000 Continental Dr N NYSE: BF	Mount Olive	NJ	07828	**800-526-1072**	973-426-2600
BCN Chemicals Inc 1320 Rt 9	Champlain	NY	12919	**800-661-1226**	514-630-1044
Bedford Laboratories Inc 300 Northfield Rd	Bedford	OH	44146	**800-562-4797**	440-232-3320
Bio-Botanica Inc 75 Commerce Dr	Hauppauge	NY	11788	**800-645-5720**	631-231-5522
Blessed Herbs Inc 109 Barre Plains Rd	Oakham	MA	01068	**800-489-4372**	508-882-3839
Boehringer Ingelheim Chemicals Inc 2820 N Normandy Dr	Petersburg	VA	23805	**800-820-6015**	804-504-8700
Cambrex Charles City Inc 1205 11th St	Charles City	IA	50616	**800-247-1833**	641-257-1000
Cambrex North Brunswick Inc 661 Hwy 1 Bldg 661 *Sales	North Brunswick	NJ	08902	**866-286-9133***	732-447-1900
Carrington Laboratories Inc 2001 Walnut Hill Ln NASDAQ: CARN ■ *Cust Svc	Irving	TX	75038	**800-527-5216***	972-518-1300
Cyanotech Corp 73-4460 Queen Kaahumanu Hwy Suite 102 NASDAQ: CYAN ■ *Sales	Kailua-Kona	HI	96740	**800-453-1187***	808-326-1353
Ferro Pfanstiehl Laboratories Inc 1219 Glen Rock Ave	Waukegan	IL	60085	**800-383-0126**	847-623-0370
Fytokem Products Inc 110 Research Dr Suite 101	Saskatoon	SK	S7N3R3	**877-457-3986**	306-668-2552
Garden State Nutritionals 8 Henderson Dr	West Caldwell	NJ	07006	**800-526-9095**	973-575-9200
George Uhe Co Inc 12 Rt 17 N	Paramus	NJ	07653	**800-850-4075**	201-843-4000
Greer Laboratories Inc 639 Nuway Cir *Cust Svc	Lenoir	NC	28645	**800-378-3906***	828-754-5327
H Reisman Corp 377 Crane St	Orange	NJ	07051	**800-631-3424**	973-677-9200
Heico Chemicals Inc PO Box 730	Delaware Water Gap	PA	18327	**800-344-3426**	570-420-3900
ICC Industries Inc 460 Park Ave	New York	NY	10022	**800-422-1720**	212-521-1700
Lannett Co Inc 9000 State Rd AMEX: LCI	Philadelphia	PA	19136	**800-325-9994**	215-333-9000
Mallinckrodt Baker Inc 222 Red School Ln	Phillipsburg	NJ	08865	**800-582-2537**	908-859-2151
Mallinckrodt Inc 675 McDonnell Blvd	Hazelwood	MO	63042	**888-744-1414**	314-654-2000
Mallinckrodt Pharmaceutical Group 675 McDonnell Blvd	Hazelwood	MO	63042	**800-554-5343**	314-654-2000
Multisorb Technologies Inc 325 Harlem Rd *Cust Svc	West Seneca	NY	14224	**800-445-9890***	716-824-8900
Nepera Inc 41 Arden House Rd	Harriman	NY	10926	**800-963-7372**	845-782-1200
Nutraceutix Inc 9609 153rd Ave NE	Redmond	WA	98052	**800-548-3222**	425-883-9518
Nutrition 21 Inc 4 Manhattanville Rd NASDAQ: NXXI	Purchase	NY	10577	**800-699-3533**	914-701-4500
Paddock Laboratories Inc 3940 Quebec Ave N *Orders	Minneapolis	MN	55427	**800-328-5113***	763-546-4676
Patheon Inc 2100 Syntex Ct	Mississauga	ON	L5N7K9	**888-728-4366**	905-821-4001
Savient Pharmaceuticals Inc 1 Tower Center Blvd 14th Fl NASDAQ: SVNT	East Brunswick	NJ	08816	**800-284-2480**	732-418-9300
Scientific Protein Laboratories Inc PO Box 158	Waunakee	WI	53597	**800-334-4775**	608-849-5944
SICOR Inc 19 Hughes	Irvine	CA	92618	**800-729-9991**	949-455-4700
Siegfried USA Inc 33 Industrial Pk Rd *Cust Svc	Pennsville	NJ	08070	**877-763-8630***	856-678-3601
Sigma-Aldrich Chemical Co 3050 Spruce St *Sales	Saint Louis	MO	63103	**800-325-3010***	314-771-5765

Company / Address	City	State	Zip	Toll-Free	Phone
Sigma-Aldrich Corp 3050 Spruce St	Saint Louis	MO	63103	**800-325-3010**	314-771-5765
NASDAQ: SIAL					
SPI Pharma 321 Cherry Ln	New Castle	DE	19720	**800-789-9755**	302-576-8554
SST Corp 635 Brighton Rd	Clifton	NJ	07012	**800-222-0921**	973-473-4300
Tapestry Pharmaceuticals Inc 4840 Pearl E Cir Suite 300W	Boulder	CO	80301	**800-976-2776**	303-516-8500
NASDAQ: TPPH					
Technical Sourcing International Inc 7168 Expy	Missoula	MT	59808	**877-549-9123**	406-549-9123
Terry Laboratories Inc 390 N Wickham Rd Suite F	Melbourne	FL	32935	**800-367-2563**	321-259-1630
Tri-K Industries Inc 151 Veterans Dr	Northvale	NJ	07647	**800-526-0372**	201-750-1055
Uhe George Co Inc 12 Rt 17 N	Paramus	NJ	07653	**800-850-4075**	201-843-4000
United-Guardian Inc PO Box 18050	Hauppauge	NY	11788	**800-645-5566**	631-273-0900
AMEX: UG					
Xechem International Inc 100 Jersey Ave Bldg B Suite 310	New Brunswick	NJ	08901	**800-858-5854**	732-247-3300
Zeeland Chemicals Inc 215 N Centennial St	Zeeland	MI	49464	**800-223-0453**	616-772-2193

471 METAL - STRUCTURAL (FABRICATED)

Company / Address	City	State	Zip	Toll-Free	Phone
Aerospace America Inc 900 Harry Truman Pkwy PO Box 189	Bay City	MI	48707	**800-237-6414**	989-684-2121
Afco Mfg Corp 428 Cogshall St PO Box 230	Holly	MI	48442	**800-743-4415**	248-634-4415
Alamo Steel Co 2784 Old Dallas Rd	Waco	TX	76705	**800-810-3166**	254-799-2471
Amerimax Building Products Inc 5208 Tennyson Pkwy Suite 100	Plano	TX	75024	**800-258-6295**	469-366-3200
Amerimax Home Products Inc 450 Richardson Dr	Lancaster	PA	17603	**800-347-2586**	717-299-3711
Barker Steel Co Inc 55 Sumner St	Milford	MA	01757	**800-370-0132**	508-473-8484
Bethesda Iron Works Inc 650 Lofstrand Ln	Rockville	MD	20850	**800-762-1383**	301-762-9100
Bouras Industries Inc 25 DeForest Ave	Summit	NJ	07901	**800-631-1215**	908-277-1617
Braden Mfg LLC 5199 N Mingo Rd	Tulsa	OK	74117	**800-272-3360**	918-272-5371
BW Fabricators LP 4140 Reilly Rd	Wichita Falls	TX	76305	**800-508-2710**	940-855-2710
Canam Steel Corp 4010 Clay St	Point of Rocks	MD	21777	**800-638-4293**	301-874-5141
Capitol City Steel Co Inc 900 N IH-35	Buda	TX	78610	**800-333-8820**	512-282-8820
Carolina Steel Corp 1451 S Elm Eugene St	Greensboro	NC	27406	**800-632-0286**	336-275-9711
CENTRIA 1005 Beaver Grade Rd	Moon Township	PA	15108	**800-759-7474**	412-299-8000
Clark Steel Framing Systems 101 Clark Blvd	Middle Town	OH	45044	**800-882-7883**	513-539-2900
DeKalb Steel Inc 3476 Lawrenceville Hwy	Tucker	GA	30084	**877-646-7623**	770-939-2300
Economy Forms Corp 1800 NE Broadway	Des Moines	IA	50313	**888-289-3326**	515-266-1141
Enco Materials Inc 110 N 1st St	Nashville	TN	37213	**800-876-3626**	615-256-3199
Fabral Inc 3449 Hempland Rd	Lancaster	PA	17601	**800-477-2741**	717-397-2741
Frey John S Enterprises Inc 1900 E 64th St	Los Angeles	CA	90001	**800-377-3322**	323-583-4061
General Steel Fabricators 927 Schifferdecker Rd	Joplin	MO	64801	**800-820-8644**	417-623-2224
Havens Steel Co 7219 E 17th St	Kansas City	MO	64126	**800-279-4283**	816-231-5724
Hirschfeld Steel Co Inc 112 W 29th St	San Angelo	TX	76902	**800-375-3216**	325-486-4201
Hunt Rodney Co Inc 46 Mill St	Orange	MA	01364	**800-448-8860**	978-544-2511
InterLock Industries Inc 7800 State Rd 60	Sellersburg	IN	47172	**800-406-7387**	812-246-1935
JH Industries Inc 1981 E Aurora Rd	Twinsburg	OH	44087	**800-321-4968**	330-963-4105
John S Frey Enterprises Inc 1900 E 64th St	Los Angeles	CA	90001	**800-377-3322**	323-583-4061
LSI Metal Fabrication Inc 3871 Turkeyfoot Rd	Erlanger	KY	41018	**800-546-1513**	859-342-9944
McElroy Metal Mill Inc 1500 Hamilton Rd	Bossier City	LA	71111	**800-950-6531**	318-747-8000
Norlen Inc 900 Grossman Dr	Schofield	WI	54476	**800-648-6594**	715-359-0506
Owen Industries Inc 501 Ave H	Carter Lake	IA	51510	**800-831-9252**	712-347-5500
Owens Corning Fabricating Solutions 426 N Main St	Elkhart	IN	46516	**877-632-2935**	574-522-8473
Paxton & Vierling Steel Co 501 Ave H	Carter Lake	IA	51510	**800-831-9252**	712-347-5500
Ranor Inc 1 Bella Dr	Westminster	MA	01473	**800-225-9552**	978-874-0591
Rodney Hunt Co Inc 46 Mill St	Orange	MA	01364	**800-448-8860**	978-544-2511
SMI Rebar of North Carolina 2528 N Chester St	Gastonia	NC	28052	**800-476-6975**	704-865-8571
Southeastern Steel Co 211 N Koppers Rd	Florence	SC	29506	**800-476-7372**	843-662-5236
Structural Metals Inc 1 Steel Mill Dr	Seguin	TX	78156	**800-227-6489***	830-372-8200
*Sales					
Stupp Brothers Inc 3800 Weber Rd	Saint Louis	MO	63125	**800-899-1856**	314-638-5000
Unistrut Corp 4205 Elizabeth St	Wayne	MI	48184	**800-521-7730***	734-721-4040
*Cust Svc					

472 METAL COATING, PLATING, ENGRAVING

Company / Address	City	State	Zip	Toll-Free	Phone
American Nickeloid Co 2900 W Main St	Peru	IL	61354	**800-645-5643**	815-223-0373
American Performance Industries 109 McNeil Rd PO Box 250	Sanford	NC	27330	**800-438-3348**	919-775-7321
Apollo Metals Ltd 1001 14th Ave	Bethlehem	PA	18018	**800-338-0199**	610-867-5826
Ardco Corp 8250 E 40th Ave	Denver	CO	80207	**800-544-9013**	303-399-2934
Chicago Metallic Corp 4849 S Austin Ave	Chicago	IL	60638	**800-323-7164**	708-563-4600
Decorated Products Co 1 Arch Rd	Westfield	MA	01086	**800-639-4909**	413-568-0944
Donham Craft Inc 15 E Waterbury Rd	Naugatuck	CT	06770	**800-739-1919**	203-729-8244
Foster LB Co 415 Holiday Dr	Pittsburgh	PA	15220	**800-255-4500**	412-928-3400
NASDAQ: FSTR					
GM Nameplate Inc 2040 15th Ave W	Seattle	WA	98119	**800-366-7668**	206-284-2200
LB Foster Co 415 Holiday Dr	Pittsburgh	PA	15220	**800-255-4500**	412-928-3400
NASDAQ: FSTR					
Lorin Industries 125 E Keating Ave	Muskegon	MI	49443	**800-678-1215**	231-722-1631
Magnetic Metals Corp 1900 Hayes Ave	Camden	NJ	08105	**800-257-8174**	856-964-7842
Master Finish Co 2020 Nelson Ave SE	Grand Rapids	MI	49507	**888-372-2913**	616-245-1228
Material Sciences Corp 2200 E Pratt Blvd	Elk Grove Village	IL	60007	**800-877-9078**	847-439-8270
NYSE: MSC					
Metal Cladding Inc 230 S Niagara St	Lockport	NY	14094	**800-432-5513**	716-434-5513
Mills Cos Inc 5215 Gershwin Ave N	Saint Paul	MN	55128	**800-367-9045**	651-770-6660
Premier Die Casting Co 1177 Rahway Ave	Avenel	NJ	07001	**800-394-3006**	732-634-3000
Rimex Metals (USA) Inc 2850 Woodbridge Ave	Edison	NJ	08837	**800-526-7600**	732-549-3800
Roesch Inc 100 N 24th St	Belleville	IL	62222	**800-423-6243**	618-233-2760
Sapa Inc 7933 NE 21st Ave	Portland	OR	97211	**800-547-0790**	503-972-1404
Siegel-Robert Inc 8645 S Broadway	Saint Louis	MO	63111	**800-433-1030**	314-638-8300
State Plating 450 N 9th St	Elwood	IN	46036	**800-428-6340**	765-552-5047
Summit Corp of America 1430 Waterbury Rd	Thomaston	CT	06787	**800-854-0176**	860-283-4391
Triumph Industries 8687 S 77th Ave	Bridgeview	IL	60455	**800-752-9957**	708-598-5100
US Chrome Corp 175 Garfield Ave	Stratford	CT	06615	**800-637-9019**	203-378-9622

473 METAL FABRICATING - CUSTOM

Company / Address	City	State	Zip	Toll-Free	Phone
Afco Industries Inc 3400 Roy Ave	Alexandria	LA	71302	**800-551-6576**	318-448-1651
Aldine Metal Products Corp PO Box 246	Brookfield	CT	06804	**877-775-2551**	203-775-2551
American Aluminum Co Inc 230 Sheffield St	Mountainside	NJ	07092	**800-315-3977**	908-233-3500
Brakewell Steel Fabricator Inc 55 Leone Ln	Chester	NY	10918	**888-914-9131**	845-469-9131
Clark Steel Framing Systems 101 Clark Blvd	Middle Town	OH	45044	**800-882-7883**	513-539-2900
CSM Metal Fabricating & Engineering Inc 1800 S San Pedro St	Los Angeles	CA	90015	**800-272-4806**	213-748-7321
Demsey Mfg Co 78 New Wood Rd	Watertown	CT	06795	**800-533-6739**	860-274-6209
Dynamic Materials Corp 5405 Spine Rd	Boulder	CO	80301	**800-821-2666**	303-665-5700
NASDAQ: BOOM					
Fabricated Components Inc PO Box 431	Stroudsburg	PA	18360	**800-233-8163**	570-421-4110
Harford Systems Inc 2225 Pulaski Hwy PO Box 700	Aberdeen	MD	21001	**800-664-7620**	410-272-3400
Hurtt Fabricating Corp PO Box 128	Marceline	MO	64658	**800-844-3010**	660-376-3501
Johnson Matthey Noble Metals 1401 King Rd	West Chester	PA	19380	**800-441-8159**	610-648-8000
Lucasey Mfg Corp PO Box 14023	Oakland	CA	94614	**800-582-2739**	510-534-1435
Southwire Co Machinery Div 401 Fertilla St	Carrollton	GA	30117	**800-444-1700**	770-832-4900
White River Distributors Inc PO Box 2037	Batesville	AR	72503	**800-548-7219**	870-793-2374

474 METAL FORGINGS

Company / Address	City	State	Zip	Toll-Free	Phone
Alcoa Wheel Products International 1600 Harvard Ave	Cleveland	OH	44105	**800-242-9898**	216-641-3600
Aluminum Precision Products Inc 3333 W Warner St	Santa Ana	CA	92704	**800-411-8983**	714-546-8125
Anchor-Harvey Components Inc 600 W Lamm Rd	Freeport	IL	61032	**888-367-4464**	815-235-4400
Buchanan Metal Forming Inc 103 W Smith St	Buchanan	MI	49107	**800-253-0585**	269-695-3836
Commercial Forged Products Div Wozniak Industries Inc 5757 W 65th St	Bedford Park	IL	60638	**800-637-2695**	708-458-1220
Conley Frog Switch & Forge Co 387 E Bodley St	Memphis	TN	38109	**800-332-4457**	901-948-4591
Cornell Forge Co 6666 W 66th St	Chicago	IL	60638	**800-356-0204**	708-458-1582
Coulter Steel & Forge Co PO Box 8008	Emeryville	CA	94662	**800-648-4884**	510-420-3500
Ellwood City Forge PO Box 31	Ellwood City	PA	16117	**800-843-0166**	724-752-0055
Federal Flange 4014 Pinemont St	Houston	TX	77018	**800-231-0150**	713-681-0606
Federal Forge Inc 2807 S ML King Jr Blvd	Lansing	MI	48910	**800-968-2932**	517-393-5300
Firth Rixson Viking 1 Erik Cir	Verdi	NV	89439	**800-648-4870**	775-345-0345
Forged Products Inc 6505 N Houston Rosslyn Rd	Houston	TX	77091	**800-876-3416**	713-462-3416
Forged Vessel Connections Inc 2525 DeSoto St	Houston	TX	77091	**800-231-2701***	713-688-9705
*Cust Svc					
H & L Tooth Co Inc 10055 E 56 St N	Tulsa	OK	74117	**800-458-6684**	
Kerkau Mfg Co 910 Harry S Truman Pkwy	Bay City	MI	48706	**800-248-5060**	989-686-0350
KomTeK 40 Rockdale St	Worcester	MA	01606	**800-756-6835**	508-853-4500
Liberty Forge Inc PO Drawer 1210	Liberty	TX	77575	**800-231-2377**	936-336-5785
Machine Specialty & Mfg Inc 215 Rousseau Rd	Youngsville	LA	70592	**800-256-1292**	337-837-0020
McKees Rocks Forgings Inc 75 Nichol Ave	McKees Rocks	PA	15136	**800-223-2818**	412-778-2020
National Flange & Fitting Co 4420 Creekmont Dr	Houston	TX	77091	**800-231-1424**	713-688-2515
Nonferrous Products Inc PO Box 349	Franklin	IN	46131	**800-423-5612**	317-738-2558
Norforge & Machining Inc 195 N Dean St	Bushnell	IL	61422	**800-457-7699**	309-772-3124
Nortrak Inc DBA VAE Nortrak North America Inc 3422 1st Ave S	Seattle	WA	98134	**800-638-4657**	206-622-0125
Parish International Inc PO Box 468	Hempstead	TX	77445	**877-496-8378**	979-826-8222
Patriot Forge Co 1802 Cranberry St	Erie	PA	16502	**877-495-9542**	814-456-2088
Phoenix Forging Co Inc 800 Front St	Catasauqua	PA	18032	**800-444-3674**	610-264-2861
Saint Croix Forge Inc 5195 Scandia Trail	Forest Lake	MN	55025	**800-966-3668**	651-464-8967
Scot Forge Co PO Box 8	Spring Grove	IL	60081	**800-435-6621**	815-675-1000
Steel Industries Inc 12600 Beech-Daly Rd	Redford	MI	48239	**877-783-3599**	313-535-8505
Sypris Technologies PO Box 32160	Louisville	KY	40232	**800-626-5655**	502-774-6011
Thoro'Bred Inc 5020 E La Palma Ave	Anaheim	CA	92807	**800-854-6059**	714-779-2581
VAE Nortrak North America Inc 3422 1st Ave S	Seattle	WA	98134	**800-638-4657**	206-622-0125
Western Forge & Flange Co PO Box 327	Santa Clara	CA	95052	**800-352-6433**	408-727-7000
Wozniak Industries Inc Commercial Forged Products Div 5757 W 65th St	Bedford Park	IL	60638	**800-637-2695**	708-458-1220
Wyman-Gordon Co 244 Worcester St	North Grafton	MA	01536	**800-343-6070**	508-839-4441

475 METAL HEAT TREATING

Company / Address	City	State	Zip	Toll-Free	Phone
Alfred Heller Heat Treating Co 5 Wellington St	Clifton	NJ	07015	**800-946-8847**	973-772-4200
Bodycote North America Inc 5001 LBJ Fwy Suite 800	Dallas	TX	75244	**800-234-8422**	214-904-2420
FPM LLC 1501 S Lively Blvd	Elk Grove Village	IL	60007	**800-875-3316**	847-228-2525
Gibraltar Industries Inc 3556 Lakeshore Rd	Buffalo	NY	14219	**800-777-0675**	716-826-6500
NASDAQ: ROCK					
Heller Alfred Heat Treating Co 5 Wellington St	Clifton	NJ	07015	**800-946-8847**	973-772-4200
HI TecMetal Group Inc 1101 E 55th St	Cleveland	OH	44103	**877-484-2867**	216-881-8100
MACSTEEL 1 Jackson Sq Suite 500	Jackson	MI	49204	**800-888-7833***	517-782-0415
*Sales					
Milastar Corp 7317 W Lake St	Minneapolis	MN	55426	**877-888-8874**	952-929-7815
Miller Consolidated Industries Inc 2221 Arbor Blvd	Dayton	OH	45439	**800-589-4133**	937-294-2681

Company	City	State	ZIP	Toll-Free	Phone
Quanex Corp 1900 West Loop S Suite 1500	Houston	TX	77027	**800-231-8176**	713-961-4600
NYSE: NX					
Rex Heat Treat					
8th St & Valley Forge Rd PO Box 270	Lansdale	PA	19446	**800-220-6053**	215-855-1131
Sun Steel Treating Inc 55 N Mill St	South Lyon	MI	48178	**877-471-0844**	248-471-0844
ThyssenKrupp Stahl Co					
11 E Pacific PO Box 6	Kingsville	MO	64061	**888-395-1042**	816-597-3322
Trutec Industries Inc 4700 Gateway Blvd	Springfield	OH	45502	**800-933-8832**	937-323-8833
Wall Colmonoy Corp					
30261 Stephenson Hwy	Madison Heights	MI	48071	**800-521-2412**	248-585-6400
Ward Aluminum Casting Co					
642 Growth Ave	Fort Wayne	IN	46808	**866-427-8700**	260-426-8700

476 METAL INDUSTRIES (MISC)

SEE ALSO Foundries - Investment; Foundries - Iron & Steel; Foundries - Nonferrous (Castings); Metal Heat Treating; Metal Tube & Pipe; Steel - Mfr; Wire & Cable

Company	City	State	ZIP	Toll-Free	Phone
Alcoa Mill Products 4879 State St	Riverdale	IA	52722	**800-237-3254**	563-459-3000
Alcoa Primary Metals					
900 S Gay St Riverview Tower Suite 1100	Knoxville	TN	37902	**800-852-0238**	865-594-4700
Allegheny Technologies Inc					
6 PPG Pl Suite 1000	Pittsburgh	PA	15222	**800-258-3586***	412-394-2800
NYSE: ATI ■ *Sales					
Allvac Inc 2020 Ashcraft Ave	Monroe	NC	28110	**800-537-5551**	704-289-4511
Ampco Metal Inc					
1117 E Algonquin Rd	Arlington Heights	IL	60005	**800-437-6100**	847-437-6000
Anaheim Extrusion Co Inc					
1330 N Kraemer Blvd	Anaheim	CA	92806	**800-660-3318**	714-630-3111
Ansonia Copper & Brass Inc 75 Liberty St	Ansonia	CT	06401	**800-521-1703***	203-732-6600
*Cust Svc					
Arkansas Aluminum Alloys Inc					
4400 Malvern Rd	Hot Springs	AR	71901	**800-643-1302***	501-262-3420
*Cust Svc					
Arvinyl Metal Laminates Corp					
233 N Sherman Ave	Corona	CA	92882	**800-278-4695**	951-371-7800
Big River Zinc Corp 2401 Mississippi Ave	Sauget	IL	62201	**800-274-4002**	618-274-5000
Bonnell William L Co 25 Bonnell St	Newnan	GA	30263	**800-846-8885**	770-253-2020
Broco Inc 8690 Red Oak St	Rancho Cucamonga	CA	91730	**800-845-7259**	909-483-3222
Bunting Magnetics Co 500 S Spencer Ave	Newton	KS	67114	**800-835-2526***	316-284-2020
*Cust Svc					
Cabot Supermetals					
County Line Rd PO Box 1608	Boyertown	PA	19512	**800-531-3676**	610-367-1500
Cannon-Muskegon Corp 2875 Lincoln St	Muskegon	MI	49441	**800-253-0371**	231-755-1681
Cardinal Aluminum Co 6910 Preston Hwy	Louisville	KY	40219	**800-398-7833***	502-969-9302
*Cust Svc					
CCMA LLC 300 Corporate Pkwy Suite 216-N	Amherst	NY	14226	**800-828-6621**	716-446-8800
Century Aluminum Co					
2511 Garden Rd Bldg A Suite 200	Monterey	CA	93940	**888-642-9300**	831-642-9300
NASDAQ: CENX					
Century Aluminum Inc					
Willow Grove Rd PO Box 68	Ravenswood	WV	26164	**800-258-6686**	304-273-6241
Certified Alloy Products Inc					
3245 Cherry Ave	Long Beach	CA	90807	**800-421-3763**	562-595-6621
Chase Brass & Copper Co					
14212 County Rd 50 PO Box 152	Montpelier	OH	43543	**800-537-4291**	419-485-3193
Chicago Extruded Metals Co 1601 S 54th Ave	Cicero	IL	60804	**800-323-8102***	708-656-7900
*Cust Svc					
Cookson Electronics Assembly Materials					
600 Rte 440	Jersey City	NJ	07304	**800-367-5460**	201-434-6778
Croft Metals LLC 107 Oliver Emmerich Dr	McComb	MS	39648	**800-222-3195**	601-684-6121
Custom Aluminum Products Inc					
414 W Division St	South Elgin	IL	60177	**800-745-6333**	847-741-6333
Danaher Motion 1500 Mittel Blvd	Wood Dale	IL	60191	**866-993-2624**	630-860-7300
Doe Run Co 1801 Park 270 Dr Suite 300	Saint Louis	MO	63146	**800-356-3786**	314-453-7110
Dynamet Inc 195 Museum Rd	Washington	PA	15301	**800-237-9655**	724-228-1000
Eastern Alloys Inc					
Henry Henning Dr PO Box Q	Maybrook	NY	12543	**800-456-1496**	845-427-2151
Elkem Metals Co					
2700 Lake Rd E PO Box 40	Ashtabula	OH	44004	**800-848-9795**	440-993-2300
Elmet Technologies Inc 1560 Lisbon St	Lewiston	ME	04240	**800-343-8008**	207-784-3591
Extruded Metals Inc 302 Ashfield St	Belding	MI	48809	**800-428-7296**	616-794-1200
Futura Industries Corp					
Freeport Ctr Bldg H-11 PO Box 160350	Clearfield	UT	84016	**800-824-2049***	801-773-6282
*Cust Svc					
GARMCO USA 55 Triangle St	Danbury	CT	06810	**800-722-3645**	203-743-2731
Glines & Rhodes Inc 189 East St	Attleboro	MA	02703	**800-343-1196**	508-226-2000
Gulf Reduction Corp 6020 Navigation Blvd	Houston	TX	77011	**800-899-1705**	713-926-1705
H Kramer & Co 1345 W 21st St	Chicago	IL	60608	**800-621-2305**	312-226-6600
Hawk Precision Components Group					
31005 Solon Rd	Solon	OH	44139	**866-429-5724**	440-248-5456
Haynes International Inc					
1020 W Park Dr PO Box 9013	Kokomo	IN	46901	**800-354-0806**	765-456-6000
Hoover & Strong Inc 10700 Trade Rd	Richmond	VA	23236	**800-759-9997***	804-794-3700
*Cust Svc					
Hussey Copper Ltd 100 Washington St	Leetsdale	PA	15056	**800-733-8866**	724-251-4200
Hydro Aluminum North America					
801 International Dr	Linthicum	MD	21090	**888-935-5752**	410-487-4500
IMC Group					
165 Township Line Rd 1 Pitcairn Pl					
Suite 1200	Jenkintown	PA	19046	**800-220-6800**	215-517-6000
Indalex Aluminum Solutions Group					
3000 Lakeside Dr Suite 309S	Bannockburn	IL	60015	**877-276-1802**	847-295-0895
Industrial Alloys Inc 3880 W Valley Blvd	Walnut	CA	91789	**800-255-6974**	909-594-7511
Industrial Tectonics Inc					
7222 W Huron River Dr	Dexter	MI	48130	**800-482-2255**	734-426-4681
Intalco Aluminum Corp					
4050 Mountain View Rd	Ferndale	WA	98248	**800-752-0852**	360-384-7061
JW Aluminum Co 435 Old Mount Holly Rd	Mount Holly	SC	29445	**800-568-1100**	843-572-1100
Keymark Corp 1188 Cayadutta Rd	Fonda	NY	12068	**800-833-1609**	518-853-3421
Kramer H & Co 1345 W 21st St	Chicago	IL	60608	**800-621-2305**	312-226-6600
Loxcreen Co Inc 1630 Old Dunbar Rd	West Columbia	SC	29172	**800-394-8667**	803-822-8200
Lucas-Milhaupt Inc 5656 S Pennsylvania Ave	Cudahy	WI	53110	**800-558-3856**	414-769-6000
Magnat Rolls Inc					
52 O'Neil St PO Box 1310	Easthampton	MA	01027	**800-370-4256**	413-527-4256
Magnesium Elektron 1001 College St	Madison	IL	62060	**800-851-3145***	618-452-5190
*Sales					
MD-Both Industries 40 Nickerson Rd	Ashland	MA	01721	**800-288-2684**	508-881-4100
Memry Corp 3 Berkshire Blvd	Bethel	CT	06801	**866-466-3679**	203-739-1100
AMEX: MRY					
Metallurgical Products Co					
810 Lincoln Ave PO Box 598	West Chester	PA	19381	**800-659-4672**	610-696-6770
Metglas Inc 440 Allied Dr	Conway	SC	29526	**800-581-7654**	843-349-7319
Midland Industries Inc 1424 N Halsted St	Chicago	IL	60622	**800-662-8228**	312-664-7300
Mueller Brass Co 2199 Lapeer Ave	Port Huron	MI	48060	**800-553-3336**	810-987-7770
Mueller Industries Inc					
8285 Tournament Dr Suite 150	Memphis	TN	38125	**800-348-8464**	901-753-3200
NYSE: MLI					
Nichols Aluminum 1725 Rockingham Rd	Davenport	IA	52802	**800-553-5508**	563-336-4801
Noranda Aluminum Inc					
801 Crescent Ctr Dr Suite 600	Franklin	TN	37067	**800-344-7522**	615-771-5700
Ormet Primary Aluminum Corp					
43840 State Rd 7 PO Box 176	Hannibal	OH	43931	**800-282-9701**	740-483-1381
Outokumpu American Brass Inc 70 Sayre St	Buffalo	NY	14207	**800-642-7277***	716-879-6700
*Sales					
Pacal LLC 2500 W County Rd B	Roseville	MN	55113	**800-328-9836**	651-631-1111
Patrick Industries Inc Patrick Metals Div					
5020 Lincolnway E	Mishawaka	IN	46544	**800-922-9692**	574-255-9692
Patrick Metals Div Patrick Industries Inc					
5020 Lincolnway E	Mishawaka	IN	46544	**800-922-9692**	574-255-9692
Penn Aluminum International Inc					
1117 N 2nd St PO Box 490	Murphysboro	IL	62966	**800-445-7366**	618-684-2146
PerkinElmer Fluid Sciences Inc					
11642 Old Baltimore Pike	Beltsville	MD	20705	**800-691-4666**	301-937-4010
Quanex Corp 1900 West Loop S Suite 1500	Houston	TX	77027	**800-231-8176**	713-961-4600
NYSE: NX					
Remacor Inc PO Box 366 Rt 168	West Pittsburg	PA	16160	**800-422-2366**	724-535-4357
Revere Copper Products Inc 1 Revere Pk	Rome	NY	13440	**800-448-1776**	315-338-2022
Rollex Aluminum 1100 Richmond St	Jackson	TN	38301	**800-238-3953**	731-424-2000
Ross Metals Corp 54 W 47th St	New York	NY	10036	**800-654-7677**	212-869-4433
Sanders Lead Co 1 Sanders Rd PO Box 707	Troy	AL	36081	**800-633-8744**	334-566-1563
Shieldalloy Metallurgical Corp					
545 Beckett Rd Suite 201	Swedesboro	NJ	08085	**800-762-2020**	856-692-4200
Simcala Inc PO Box 68	Mount Meigs	AL	36057	**800-321-9828**	334-215-7560
Sipi Metals Corp 1720 N Elston Ave	Chicago	IL	60622	**800-621-8013**	773-276-0070
Southern Metals Co					
111 N Raleigh Ave PO Box 471	Sheffield	AL	35660	**800-843-2771**	256-383-3261
Southwire Co 1 Southwire Dr	Carrollton	GA	30119	**800-444-1700**	770-832-4242
Special Metals Corp					
4317 Middle Settlement Rd	New Hartford	NY	13413	**800-334-8351**	315-798-2900
Spectro Alloys Corp 13220 Doyle Path	Rosemount	MN	55068	**800-328-9321**	651-437-2815
Tifton Aluminum Co Inc 250 Southwell Blvd	Tifton	GA	31794	**800-841-2030***	229-382-7330
*Sales					
Universal Molding Co Inc					
10807 Stanford Ave	Lynwood	CA	90262	**888-437-1750**	310-886-1750
US Bronze Powders Inc					
408 Rt 202 N PO Box 31	Flemington	NJ	08822	**800-544-0186**	908-782-5454
Valleycast Inc 553 Carter Ct	Kimberly	WI	54136	**800-747-2912**	920-749-3820
Valmont Industries Inc 1 Valmont Plaza	Omaha	NE	68154	**800-825-6668**	402-963-1000
NYSE: VMI					
Victory White Metal Co 6100 Roland Ave	Cleveland	OH	44127	**800-635-5050**	216-271-1400
Wabash Alloys LLP PO Box 466	Wabash	IN	46992	**800-348-0571**	260-563-7461
Wah Chang 1600 Old Salem Rd NE	Albany	OR	97321	**888-926-4211**	541-926-4211
Werner Co 100 National Dr	Anniston	AL	36207	**800-225-5630**	256-831-8600
Werner Co 93 Werner Rd	Greenville	PA	16125	**888-532-3770**	724-588-2550
William L Bonnell Co 25 Bonnell St	Newnan	GA	30263	**800-846-8885**	770-253-2020
Williams Advanced Materials 2978 Main St	Buffalo	NY	14214	**800-327-1355**	716-837-1000
Zinc Corp of America 300 Frankfort Rd	Monaca	PA	15061	**800-648-8897***	724-774-1020
*Cust Svc					

477 METAL PRODUCTS - HOUSEHOLD

Company	City	State	ZIP	Toll-Free	Phone
All-Clad Metalcrafters Inc					
424 Morganza Rd	Canonsburg	PA	15317	**800-255-2523***	724-745-8300
*Cust Svc					
Calphalon Corp 6100 Benore Rd	Toledo	OH	43612	**800-955-7687**	419-666-8700
Chantal Cookware Corp					
2030 West Sam Houston Pkwy N	Houston	TX	77043	**800-365-4354**	713-467-9949
Chicago Metallic Products Inc 800 Ela Rd	Lake Zurich	IL	60047	**800-323-3966**	847-438-2171
Farberware Div Lifetime Hoan Corp					
1 Merrick Ave	Westbury	NY	11590	**800-252-3390**	516-683-6000
Heuck ME Co Inc 3274 Beekman St	Cincinnati	OH	45223	**800-359-3200***	513-681-1774
*Cust Svc					
Hoffritz Div Lifetime Hoan Corp					
1 Merrick Ave	Westbury	NY	11590	**800-252-3390**	516-683-6000
Le Creuset of America Inc					
114 Bob Gifford Blvd	Early Branch	SC	29916	**800-827-1798**	803-943-4308
Lifetime Hoan Corp 1 Merrick Ave	Westbury	NY	11590	**800-252-3390**	516-683-6000
NASDAQ: LCUT					
Lifetime Hoan Corp Farberware Div					
1 Merrick Ave	Westbury	NY	11590	**800-252-3390**	516-683-6000
Lifetime Hoan Corp Hoffritz Div					
1 Merrick Ave	Westbury	NY	11590	**800-252-3390**	516-683-6000
ME Heuck Co Inc 3274 Beekman St	Cincinnati	OH	45223	**800-359-3200***	513-681-1774
*Cust Svc					
Meyer Corp 525 Curtola Pkwy	Vallejo	CA	94590	**800-388-3872***	707-551-2800
*Cust Svc					
Newell Rubbermaid Inc Home & Family Group					
10B Glenlake Pkwy Suite 600	Atlanta	GA	30328	**800-434-4314**	770-407-3800
Nordic Products Inc DBA NORPRO					
2215 Merrill Creek Pkwy	Everett	WA	98203	**800-722-0202**	425-261-1000
Nordic Ware Inc 5005 Hwy 7	Minneapolis	MN	55416	**800-328-4310**	952-920-2888
Northland Aluminum Products Inc DBA					
Nordic Ware Inc 5005 Hwy 7	Minneapolis	MN	55416	**800-328-4310**	952-920-2888
OXO International 75 9th Ave 5th Fl	New York	NY	10011	**800-545-4411**	212-242-3333
Saladmaster Inc 230 Westway Pl Suite 101	Arlington	TX	76018	**800-765-5795**	817-633-3555
T-Fal Corp 1 Boland Dr Suite 101	West Orange	NJ	07052	**800-395-8325**	973-736-0300
Wilton Armetale Co PO Box 600	Mount Joy	PA	17552	**800-553-2048**	717-653-4444
Wilton Industries Inc 2240 W 75th St	Woodridge	IL	60517	**800-994-5866**	630-963-7100
Wilton Industries Inc Rowoco Div					
2240 W 75th St	Woodridge	IL	60517	**800-772-7100**	630-963-7100
Zyliss USA Corp 19751 Descartes	Foothill Ranch	CA	92610	**888-794-7623**	949-699-1884

478 METAL PRODUCTS (MISC)

Company / Address	City	State	ZIP	*Toll-Free*	*Phone*
Amatom Electronic Hardware LLC 5 Pasco Hill Rd	Cromwell	CT	06416	**800-243-6032**	860-828-0847
Bagshaw WH Co Inc PO Box 766	Nashua	NH	03061	**800-343-7467**	603-883-7758
Bead Industries Inc 11 Cascade Blvd	Milford	CT	06460	**800-297-4851**	203-301-0270
Eagle Group 100 Industrial Blvd	Clayton	DE	19938	**800-441-8440**	302-653-3000
Hamilton Precision Metals Inc 1780 Rohrerstown Rd	Lancaster	PA	17601	**800-476-7065**	717-569-7061
Helmick Corp PO Box 71	Fairmont	WV	26555	**800-624-3808**	304-366-3520
Lawton Industries Inc 4353 Pacific St	Rocklin	CA	95677	**800-692-2600**	916-624-7894
Lechler Inc 445 Kautz Rd *Cust Svc	Saint Charles	IL	60174	**800-777-2926***	630-377-6611
Nanophase Technologies Corp 1319 Marquette Dr *NASDAQ: NANX*	Romeoville	IL	60446	**877-653-8100**	630-771-6708
OPW Fueling Components PO Box 405003	Cincinnati	OH	45240	**800-422-2525**	513-870-3100
Polar Ware Co Inc PO Box 211 *Cust Svc	Sheboygan	WI	53082	**800-237-3655***	920-458-3561
Precision Valve Corp PO Box 309	Yonkers	NY	10702	**800-431-2697**	914-969-6500
Sommer Metalcraft Corp 315 Poston Dr	Crawfordsville	IN	47933	**800-654-3124**	765-362-6200
Spraying Systems Co PO Box 7900	Wheaton	IL	60189	**800-957-7729**	630-665-5000
Uni-Form Components Co 16969 Old Beaumont Hwy 90	Houston	TX	77049	**800-231-3272**	281-456-9310
WH Bagshaw Co Inc PO Box 766	Nashua	NH	03061	**800-343-7467**	603-883-7758

479 METAL STAMPINGS

SEE ALSO Closures - Metal or Plastics; Electronic Enclosures; Metal Stampings - Automotive

Company / Address	City	State	ZIP	*Toll-Free*	*Phone*
Accurate Perforating Co 3636 S Kedzie Ave	Chicago	IL	60632	**800-621-0273**	773-254-3232
Acme Metal Cap Inc Co 33-53 62nd St	Woodside	NY	11377	**800-338-3581**	718-335-3000
Admiral Craft Equipment Corp 940 S Oyster Bay Rd	Hicksville	NY	11801	**800-223-7750**	516-433-3535
AK Stamping Inc 1159 US Rt 22 *Cust Svc	Mountainside	NJ	07092	**800-227-3258***	908-232-7300
Alinabal Inc 28 Woodmont Rd	Milford	CT	06460	**800-254-6763**	203-877-3241
All New Stamping Co 10801 Lower Azusa Rd	El Monte	CA	91731	**800-877-7775**	626-443-8813
American Metalcraft Inc 2074 George St	Melrose Park	IL	60160	**800-333-9133**	708-345-1177
American Performance Industries 109 McNeil Rd PO Box 250	Sanford	NC	27330	**800-438-3348**	919-775-7321
Arrow Tru-Line Inc 2211 S Defiance St	Archbold	OH	43502	**877-285-7253**	419-446-2785
Bazz Houston Co 12700 Western Ave	Garden Grove	CA	92841	**800-385-9608**	714-898-2666
Chilton Products Div Western Industries Inc 300 E Breed St	Chilton	WI	53014	**877-671-7063**	920-849-2381
Connecticut Stamping & Bending Co 206 Newington Ave	New Britain	CT	06051	**800-966-6964**	860-225-4637
Dayton Rogers Mfg Co 8401 W 35 'W' Service Dr	Blaine	MN	55449	**800-677-8881**	763-784-7714
Dee Zee Inc 1572 NE 58th Ave	Des Moines	IA	50313	**800-779-2102**	515-265-7331
Delta Consolidated Industries Inc 2728 Capital Blvd	Raleigh	NC	27604	**800-643-0084**	919-832-6351
Diamond Mfg Co 243 W 8th St	Wyoming	PA	18644	**800-233-9601**	570-693-0300
Diamond Perforated Metals Inc 7300 W Sunnyview Ave	Visalia	CA	93291	**800-642-4334**	559-651-1889
East Moline Metal Products Co 1201 7th St *Sales	East Moline	IL	61244	**800-325-4151***	309-752-1350
Fraen Corp 80 Newcrossing Rd	Reading	MA	01867	**800-370-0078**	781-942-2223
Fulton Industries Inc 135 E Linfoot St	Wauseon	OH	43567	**800-537-5012**	419-335-3015
Gilco Inc 16000 Common Rd	Roseville	MI	48066	**800-424-4526**	586-779-5850
Hannibal Industries Inc 3851 S Santa Fe Ave	Los Angeles	CA	90058	**800-433-3166**	323-588-4261
Hendrick Mfg Co 1 7th Ave *Cust Svc	Carbondale	PA	18407	**800-225-7373***	570-282-1010
Heyco Products 1800 Industrial Way North	Toms River	NJ	08755	**800-526-4182**	732-286-1800
HMC Holdings LLC 720 Dartmouth Ln	Buffalo Grove	IL	60089	**800-874-6625**	847-541-5070
Hobson & Motzer Inc 30 Air Line Dr PO Box 427	Durham	CT	06422	**800-476-5111**	860-349-1756
Innovative Stamping Corp 2068 Gladwick St	Compton	CA	90220	**800-400-0047**	310-537-6996
Kendale Industries Inc 7600 Hub Pkwy	Cleveland	OH	44125	**800-321-9308**	216-524-5400
Kennedy Mfg Co 520 E Sycamore St	Van Wert	OH	45891	**800-413-8665**	419-238-2442
Kilmartin Industries DBA Roger Williams Mint 79 Walton St	Attleboro	MA	02703	**800-225-2734**	508-226-3310
Knaack Mfg Co 420 E Terra Cotta Ave	Crystal Lake	IL	60014	**800-456-7865**	815-459-6020
Matco Tools 4403 Allen Rd	Stow	OH	44224	**800-368-6651**	330-929-4949
Metal Box International 11600 W King St	Franklin Park	IL	60131	**800-622-2697**	847-455-8500
Midwest Wire Products LLC PO Box 770	Sturgeon Bay	WI	54235	**800-445-0225**	920-743-6591
Oberg Industries Inc 2301 Silverville Rd	Freeport	PA	16229	**800-286-1275**	724-295-2121
OSRAM Sylvania Electronic Components & Materials 100 Endicott St	Danvers	MA	01923	**800-544-4828**	978-777-1900
P & G Steel Products Co Inc 54 Gruner Rd	Buffalo	NY	14227	**800-952-3696**	716-896-7900
Peerless Industries Inc 1980 Hawthorne Ave	Melrose Park	IL	60160	**800-729-0307**	708-865-8870
Quality Perforating Inc 166 Dundaff St	Carbondale	PA	18407	**800-872-7373**	570-282-4344
RES Mfg Co Inc 7801 N 73rd St	Milwaukee	WI	53223	**800-334-8044**	414-354-4530
Roger Williams Mint 79 Walton St	Attleboro	MA	02703	**800-225-2734**	508-226-3310
Saunders Mfg Co Inc 61 Nickerson Hill Rd *Cust Svc	Readfield	ME	04355	**800-341-4674***	207-685-3385
Stack-On Products Co PO Box 489	Wauconda	IL	60084	**800-323-9601**	847-526-1611
Stanco Metal Products Inc 2101 168th Ave	Grand Haven	MI	49417	**800-530-9655**	616-842-5000
Steel City Corp 190 N Meridian Rd	Youngstown	OH	44501	**800-321-0350**	330-792-7663
Stewart EFI LLC 45 Old Waterbury Rd	Thomaston	CT	06787	**800-393-5387**	860-283-8213
T & D Metal Products Co 602 E Walnut St	Watseka	IL	60970	**800-634-7267**	815-432-4938
Wallace Metal Products 1800 Roberts Dr	Anniston	AL	36207	**888-831-9675**	256-831-4826
Waterloo Industries Inc 100 E 4th St	Waterloo	IA	50703	**800-833-8851**	319-235-7131
Western Industries Inc Chilton Products Div 300 E Breed St	Chilton	WI	53014	**877-671-7063**	920-849-2381
York Stamping DBA Wallace Metal Products 1800 Roberts Dr	Anniston	AL	36207	**888-831-9675**	256-831-4826

480 METAL STAMPINGS - AUTOMOTIVE

SEE ALSO Automotive Parts & Supplies - Mfr

Company / Address	City	State	ZIP	*Toll-Free*	*Phone*
Brown Corp of America Inc 401 S Steele St	Ionia	MI	48846	**800-530-9570**	616-527-4050
C Cowles & Co Inc 83 Water St	New Haven	CT	06511	**800-624-4483**	203-865-3117
Cowles C & Co Inc 83 Water St	New Haven	CT	06511	**800-624-4483**	203-865-3117
Means Industries Inc 1860 S Jefferson Ave	Saginaw	MI	48601	**800-869-1433**	989-754-3300
Stanco Metal Products Inc 2101 168th Ave	Grand Haven	MI	49417	**800-530-9655**	616-842-5000
Stewart EFI LLC 45 Old Waterbury Rd	Thomaston	CT	06787	**800-393-5387**	860-283-8213
Syracuse Stamping Co Inc 1054 S Clinton St	Syracuse	NY	13202	**800-581-5555**	315-476-5306
Taber Bushnell Inc 7709 Winpark Dr	Minneapolis	MN	55427	**800-811-9362**	763-546-0994
United Receptacle Inc PO Box 870	Pottsville	PA	17901	**800-233-0314**	570-622-7715
Welarco Fabrications Inc 7400 W Plank Rd	Peoria	IL	61604	**800-447-6464**	309-697-9400

481 METAL TUBE & PIPE

Company / Address	City	State	ZIP	*Toll-Free*	*Phone*
AK Tube LLC 30400 E Broadway	Walbridge	OH	43465	**800-955-8031**	419-661-4150
Alliance Mid-West Co 640 Keystone St *Cust Svc	Alliance	OH	44601	**800-521-9694***	330-821-5700
Allied Tube & Conduit Inc 16100 S Lathrop Ave	Harvey	IL	60426	**800-882-5543**	708-339-1610
American Cast Iron Pipe Co (ACIPCO) 2916 16th St N	Birmingham	AL	35207	**800-442-2347**	205-325-7701
Berg Steel Pipe Corp 5315 W 19th St	Panama City	FL	32401	**800-874-0384**	850-769-2273
Bull Moose Tube Co 1819 Clarkson Rd Suite 100	Chesterfield	MO	63017	**800-325-4467**	636-537-2600
California Steel & Tube 16049 Stephens St	City of Industry	CA	91745	**800-338-8823**	626-968-5511
Cerro Flow Products Inc 3000 Mississippi Ave	Sauget	IL	62206	**888-237-7611**	618-337-6000
Charlotte Pipe & Foundry Co 2109 Randolph Rd	Charlotte	NC	28207	**800-432-6172**	704-372-5030
Crucible Materials Corp Trent Tube Div 2015 Energy Dr PO Box 77	East Troy	WI	53120	**800-558-2260**	262-642-7321
Dekoron Unitherm Inc 1531 Commerce Creek Blvd	Cape Coral	FL	33909	**800-633-5015**	239-995-8111
Earle M Jorgensen Co 10650 S Alameda St *NYSE: JOR*	Lynwood	CA	90262	**800-336-5365**	323-567-1122
Eugene Welding Co 2420 Wills St	Marysville	MI	48040	**800-959-0857**	810-364-7421
Felker Brothers Corp 22 N Chestnut Ave	Marshfield	WI	54449	**800-826-2304**	715-384-3121
Handy & Harman Tube Co Inc 701 W Township Line Rd	Norristown	PA	19403	**800-766-8823**	610-539-3900
Hannibal Industries Inc 3851 S Santa Fe Ave	Los Angeles	CA	90058	**800-433-3166**	323-588-4261
Hydro Aluminum North America 801 International Dr	Linthicum	MD	21090	**888-935-5752**	410-487-4500
International Metal Hose Co 520 Goodrich Rd	Bellevue	OH	44811	**800-458-6855**	419-483-7690
John Maneely Co 900 Haddon Ave	Collingswood	NJ	08108	**800-257-8182**	856-854-5400
Keystone Tube Co 13527 S Halsted St *Cust Svc	Riverdale	IL	60827	**800-323-9493***	708-841-2450
LeFiell Mfg Co 13700 Firestone Blvd	Santa Fe Springs	CA	90670	**800-451-5971**	562-921-3411
Lock Joint Tube Inc 515 W Ireland Rd	South Bend	IN	46614	**800-257-6859**	574-299-5326
Maneely John Co 900 Haddon Ave	Collingswood	NJ	08108	**800-257-8182**	856-854-5400
Maverick Tube Corp 16401 Swingley Ridge Rd Suite 700 *NYSE: MVK*	Chesterfield	MO	63017	**888-628-8823**	636-733-1600
Morris Coupling Co 2240 W 15th St	Erie	PA	16505	**800-426-1579**	814-459-1741
Newport Steel Corp 530 W 9th St	Newport	KY	41071	**800-348-7751**	859-292-6000
Northwest Pipe Co 200 SW Market St Suite 1800 *NASDAQ: NWPX*	Portland	OR	97201	**800-989-9631**	503-946-1200
Plymouth Tube Co 29 W 150 Warrenville Rd	Warrenville	IL	60555	**800-323-9506**	630-393-3550
PTC Alliance Copperleaf Corporate Ctr 6051 Wallace Rd Ext Sutie 200	Wexford	PA	15090	**888-299-8823**	412-299-7900
Quanex Corp 1900 West Loop S Suite 1500 *NYSE: NX*	Houston	TX	77027	**800-231-8176**	713-961-4600
Reading Tube Corp PO Box 14026	Reading	PA	19612	**800-523-8263**	610-926-4141
Sharon Tube Co 134 Mill St	Sharon	PA	16146	**800-245-8115**	724-981-5200
Southern Metals Co 111 N Raleigh Ave PO Box 471	Sheffield	AL	35660	**800-843-2771**	256-383-3261
Stupp Corp 12555 Ronaldson Rd	Baton Rouge	LA	70807	**800-535-9999**	225-775-8800
Synalloy Corp 2155 W Croft Cir *NASDAQ: SYNL* ■ *Orders	Spartanburg	SC	29302	**800-763-1001***	864-585-3605
Tube Processing Corp 604 E Le Grande Ave	Indianapolis	IN	46203	**800-776-4119**	317-787-1321
UNR-Leavitt 1717 W 115th St	Chicago	IL	60643	**800-532-8488**	773-239-7700
Valmont Industries Inc 1 Valmont Plaza *NYSE: VMI*	Omaha	NE	68154	**800-825-6668**	402-963-1000
Wheatland Tube Co 900 Haddon Ave	Collingswood	NJ	08108	**800-257-8182**	856-854-5400
Wolverine Tube Inc 200 Clinton Ave W Suite 1000 *NYSE: WLV*	Huntsville	AL	35801	**800-633-3972**	256-890-0460

482 METAL WORK - ARCHITECTURAL & ORNAMENTAL

Company / Address	City	State	ZIP	*Toll-Free*	*Phone*
2nd Ave Design 737 W 2nd Ave	Mesa	AZ	85210	**800-843-1602**	480-464-8366
AEP-Span Corp 5100 E Grand Ave	Dallas	TX	75223	**800-527-2503**	214-827-1740

Company / Address	City	State	Zip	Toll-Free	Phone
Airolite Co 114 Westview Ave.	Marietta	OH	45750	**800-247-6548**	740-373-7676
Alabama Metal Industries Corp					
3245 Fayette Ave	Birmingham	AL	35208	**800-366-2642**	205-787-2611
Alvarado Mfg Co Inc 12660 Colony St.	Chino	CA	91710	**800-423-4143**	909-591-8431
American Stair Corp Inc					
642 Forestwood Dr	Romeoville	IL	60446	**800-872-7824**	815-886-9600
ATAS International Inc 6612 Snowdrift Rd	Allentown	PA	18106	**800-468-1441**	610-395-8445
BETCO (Builders Equipment & Tool Co)					
1617 Enid St	Houston	TX	77009	**800-908-8778**	713-869-3491
Bil-Jax Inc 125 Taylor Pkwy	Archbold	OH	43502	**800-537-0540**	419-445-8915
Builders Equipment & Tool Co (BETCO)					
1617 Enid St	Houston	TX	77009	**800-908-8778**	713-869-3491
Chicago Metallic Corp 4849 S Austin Ave.	Chicago	IL	60638	**800-323-7164**	708-563-4600
Construction Specialties Inc 3 Werner Way	Lebanon	NJ	08833	**800-972-7214**	908-236-0800
Duvinage Corp 60 W Oak Ridge Dr	Hagerstown	MD	21740	**800-541-2645**	301-733-8255
Forms & Surfaces 30 Pine St	Pittsburgh	PA	15223	**800-553-7722**	412-781-9003
Gadsden Scaffold Co Inc 137 Ewing Ave	Gadsden	AL	35901	**800-538-1780**	256-547-6918
GS Metals Corp 3764 Longspur Rd	Pinckneyville	IL	62274	**800-582-3643**	618-357-5353
Hapco Inc 26252 Hillman Hwy	Abingdon	VA	24210	**800-368-7171**	276-628-7171
Hart & Cooley Inc 500 E 8th St	Holland	MI	49423	**800-748-0392**	616-392-7855
Hunter Douglas Architectural Products Inc					
5015 Oakbrook Pkwy Suite 100	Norcross	GA	30093	**800-366-4327**	770-806-9557
IKG Industries 1 Mack Ctr Dr	Paramus	NJ	07652	**800-969-5600***	201-261-5600
*Cust Svc					
Irvine Access Floors Inc					
9425 Washington Blvd Suite Y-WW	Laurel	MD	20723	**800-969-8870**	410-781-7190
Laurel Steel Products Co					
1 Mount Pleasant Rd	Scottdale	PA	15683	**800-426-1983**	724-887-8090
Lawrence Metal Products Inc					
260 Spur Dr S PO Box 400-M.	Bay Shore	NY	11706	**800-441-0019***	631-666-0300
*Sales					
LL Building Products Inc					
4501 Circle 75 Pkwy Suite E5300	Atlanta	GA	30339	**800-755-9397**	770-953-6366
Marwas Steel Co DBA Laurel Steel Products Co					
1 Mount Pleasant Rd	Scottdale	PA	15683	**800-426-1983**	724-887-8090
McGregor Industries Inc					
46 Line St Keystone Industrial Pk	Dunmore	PA	18512	**800-326-6786**	570-343-2436
Miscellaneous Metals Inc					
5719 Industry Ln PO Box 3818	Frederick	MD	21705	**800-492-7828**	301-695-8820
Moultrie Mfg Co PO Box 2948	Moultrie	GA	31776	**800-841-8674**	229-985-1312
Overly Mfg Co 574 W Otterman St	Greensburg	PA	15601	**800-979-7300**	724-834-7300
Patent Construction Systems					
1 Mack Centre Dr	Paramus	NJ	07652	**800-969-5600**	201-261-5600
Perry Mfg Co Inc 1233 W 18th St	Indianapolis	IN	46202	**800-428-7200**	317-231-9037
Spider Staging Corp 365 Upland Dr	Tukwila	WA	98188	**800-428-7887**	206-575-6445
Steel Ceilings Inc 500 N 3rd St	Coshocton	OH	43812	**800-848-0496**	740-622-4655
Tate Access Floors Inc 7510 Montevideo Rd	Jessup	MD	20794	**800-231-7788**	410-799-4200
Tru-Weld Grating Inc 2000 Corporate Dr	Wexford	PA	15090	**800-445-7093**	724-934-5320
Universal Builders Supply Inc					
216 S Terrace Ave	Mount Vernon	NY	10550	**800-582-0070**	914-699-2400
Universal Mfg Corp PO Box 220	Zelienople	PA	16063	**800-836-8780**	724-452-8300
Velux-Greenwood Inc 450 Old Brickyard Rd	Greenwood	SC	29648	**800-688-3589**	864-941-4700
Waco Scaffolding & Equipment Co					
PO Box 318028	Cleveland	OH	44131	**800-901-2282**	216-749-8900
Wooster Products Inc 1000 Spruce St	Wooster	OH	44691	**800-321-4936**	330-264-2844

483 METALS SERVICE CENTERS

Company / Address	City	State	Zip	Toll-Free	Phone
ABC Metals Inc 500 W Clinton St	Logansport	IN	46947	**800-238-8470**	574-753-0471
Alamo Iron Works Inc					
943 SBC Center Pkwy	San Antonio	TX	78219	**800-292-7817***	210-223-6161
*Cust Svc					
Alaskan Copper & Brass Co 3223 6th Ave S	Seattle	WA	98134	**800-552-7661**	206-623-5800
Alro Steel Corp 3100 E High St	Jackson	MI	49203	**800-877-2576**	517-787-5500
AM Castle & Co 3400 N Wolf Rd	Franklin Park	IL	60131	**800-289-2785**	847-455-7111
AMEX: CAS					
American Steel LLC 4033 NW Yeon Ave	Portland	OR	97210	**800-547-9032**	503-226-1511
American Strip Steel Inc 55 Passaic Ave	Kearny	NJ	07032	**800-526-1216**	201-991-1500
AMI Metals Inc					
1738 General George Patton Dr	Brentwood	TN	37027	**800-727-1903**	615-377-0400
Art Iron Inc 860 Curtis St	Toledo	OH	43609	**800-472-1113**	419-241-1261
Bing Metals Group Steel Processing Div					
1500 E Euclid	Detroit	MI	48211	**800-521-1564**	313-875-2022
Bobco Metals Co 2000 S Alameda St	Los Angeles	CA	90058	**800-262-2605**	
Bohler-Uddeholm North America					
4902 Tollview Dr	Rolling Meadows	IL	60008	**800-638-2520**	847-577-2220
Bouras Industries Inc 25 DeForest Ave	Summit	NJ	07901	**800-631-1215**	908-277-1617
Bralco Metals Div Reliance Steel & Aluminum Co 15090 Northam St	La Mirada	CA	90638	**800-628-1864**	714-736-4800
Brown-Strauss Steel 2495 Uravan St	Aurora	CO	80011	**800-677-2778***	303-371-2200
*Sales					
Cambridge-Lee Industries Inc					
1340 Soldiers Field Rd	Brighton	MA	02135	**800-225-4378**	617-783-3100
Castle AM & Co 3400 N Wolf Rd	Franklin Park	IL	60131	**800-289-2785**	847-455-7111
AMEX: CAS					
Castle Metals Inc 3400 N Wolf Rd	Franklin Park	IL	60131	**800-289-2785**	847-455-7111
Central Steel & Wire Co 3000 W 51st St	Chicago	IL	60632	**800-621-8510**	773-471-3800
Chatham Steel Corp 501 W Boundary St	Savannah	GA	31402	**800-546-2650**	912-233-4182
Chicago Tube & Iron Co 2531 W 48th St	Chicago	IL	60632	**800-972-0217***	773-523-1441
*Cust Svc					
Clayton Metals Inc 546 Clayton Ct	Wood Dale	IL	60191	**800-323-7628**	
Coilplus Pennsylvania Inc 5135 Bleigh St	Philadelphia	PA	19136	**800-355-5200**	215-331-5200
Columbia Pipe & Supply Co					
1120 W Pershing Rd	Chicago	IL	60609	**888-361-7700**	773-927-6600
Commonwealth Metal Corp					
560 Sylvan Ave	Englewood Cliffs	NJ	07632	**800-772-2119**	201-569-2000
Consolidated Pipe & Supply Inc					
1205 Hilltop Pkwy	Birmingham	AL	35201	**800-467-7261***	205-323-7261
*Sales					
Contractors Steel Co PO Box 33881	Detroit	MI	48232	**800-521-3946**	734-464-4000
Coral Sales Co 9838 SE 17th Ave	Milwaukie	OR	97222	**800-538-7245**	503-655-6351
Corus America Inc					
475 N Martingale Rd Suite 400	Schaumburg	IL	60173	**800-542-6244**	847-619-0400
Crucible Service Centers 5639 W Genesee St	Camillus	NY	13031	**800-365-1185**	315-487-0800
Decker Steel & Supply Inc 4500 Train Ave	Cleveland	OH	44102	**800-321-6100**	216-281-7900
Duhig & Co Inc PO Box 226966	Los Angeles	CA	90022	**800-690-1776**	323-263-7161
East Coast Metal Distributors Inc					
1313 S Briggs Ave	Durham	NC	27703	**800-334-9708**	919-598-5030
Eaton Steel Corp 10221 Capital Ave	Oak Park	MI	48237	**800-527-3851**	248-398-3434
Edgcomb Metals Co 555 State Rd	Bensalem	PA	19020	**800-562-6777**	215-639-4000
Energy & Process Corp 2146B Flintstone Dr	Tucker	GA	30084	**800-241-9460**	770-934-3101
Farwest Steel Corp 2000 Henderson Ave	Eugene	OR	97403	**800-542-5091**	541-686-2000
Friedman Industries Inc PO Box 21147	Houston	TX	77226	**800-899-7695**	713-672-9433
AMEX: FRD					
Future Metals Inc 10401 State St	Tamarac	FL	33321	**800-733-0960**	954-724-1400
Gerber Metal Supply Co 2 Boundary Rd	Somerville	NJ	08876	**800-836-4672**	908-823-9150
Gibbs Wire & Steel Co Inc PO Box 520	Southington	CT	06489	**800-800-4422**	860-621-0121
Gibraltar Metals Corp 1050 Military Rd	Buffalo	NY	14217	**800-873-6322**	716-875-7920
Integris Metals Inc 455 85th Ave NW	Minneapolis	MN	55433	**800-328-7800**	763-717-9000
JM Tull Metals Co Inc PO Box 4725	Norcross	GA	30091	**800-243-8855**	770-368-4311
Kane Steel Co PO Box 829	Millville	NJ	08332	**800-223-5263**	856-825-2200
Kasle Steel Corp 4343 Wyoming Ave	Dearborn	MI	48126	**800-225-2753**	313-943-2500
Ken-Mac Metals Inc 17901 Englewood Dr	Cleveland	OH	44130	**800-831-9503**	440-234-7500
Kenwal Steel Corp 8223 W Warren Ave	Dearborn	MI	48126	**800-521-7522**	313-935-7942
Klein Steel Service 105 Vanguarden Pkwy	Rochester	NY	14606	**800-477-6789**	585-328-4000
Kreher Steel Co LLC 1550 N 25th Ave	Melrose Park	IL	60160	**800-323-0745**	708-345-8180
LaBarge Pipe & Steel Co					
500 N Broadway Suite 1600	Saint Louis	MO	63102	**800-325-3363**	314-231-3400
Lapham-Hickey Steel Corp 5500 W 73rd St	Chicago	IL	60638	**800-323-8443***	708-496-6111
*Cust Svc					
Lindquist Steels Inc 1050 Woodend Rd	Stratford	CT	06615	**800-243-9637**	203-377-2828
Lofland Co 2920 N Stemmons Fwy	Dallas	TX	75247	**800-288-5250**	214-631-5250
Lyon Conklin & Co					
7030 Troy Hill Dr Suite 700A	Elkridge	MD	21075	**800-759-5966**	410-540-2800
Maas-Hansen Steel Corp 2435 E 37th St	Vernon	CA	90058	**800-647-8335**	323-583-6321
Macsteel Service Centers USA					
888 San Clemente Dr Suite 250	Newport Beach	CA	92660	**866-622-7833**	949-219-9000
Marmon/Keystone Corp PO Box 992	Butler	PA	16003	**800-544-1748**	724-283-3000
McNichols Co 5505 W Gray St	Tampa	FL	33609	**800-237-3828**	813-282-3828
Merit USA 620 Clark Ave	Pittsburg	CA	94565	**800-445-6374**	925-432-6900
MetalCenter Inc					
12034 S Greenstone Ave	Santa Fe Springs	CA	90670	**800-448-0001**	562-944-3322
Metals USA Inc 3 Riverway Suite 600	Houston	TX	77056	**888-871-8701**	713-965-0990
NASDAQ: MUSA					
Metrolina Steel Inc PO Box 790465	Charlotte	NC	28206	**800-849-7835**	704-598-7007
Mineral & Pigment Solutions Inc					
1000 Coolidge St	South Plainfield	NJ	07080	**800-732-0562**	908-561-6100
New Process Steel Corp 5800 Westview Dr	Houston	TX	77055	**800-392-4989**	713-686-9631
Nippon Steel USA Inc 80 3rd Ave 34th Fl	New York	NY	10017	**800-345-6477**	212-486-7150
Olympic Steel Inc 5080 Richmond Rd	Bedford Heights	OH	44146	**800-321-6290**	216-292-3800
NASDAQ: ZEUS					
O'Neal Steel Inc 744 41st St N	Birmingham	AL	35222	**800-292-4090**	205-599-8000
Owen Industries Inc 501 Ave H	Carter Lake	IA	51510	**800-831-9252**	712-347-5500
Pacesetter Steel Service Inc					
3300 Town Point Dr	Kennesaw	GA	30144	**800-749-6505**	770-919-8000
Pacific Steel & Recycling 1401 3rd St NW	Great Falls	MT	59404	**800-889-6264**	406-727-6222
Peterson Steel Corp 61 W Mountain St	Worcester	MA	01606	**800-325-3245**	508-853-3630
Pipe Distributors Inc 5400 Mesa Dr	Houston	TX	77028	**800-989-7473**	713-635-4200
Precision Steel Warehouse Inc					
3500 N Wolf Rd	Franklin Park	IL	60131	**800-323-0740**	847-455-7000
Rancocas Metals Corp 35 Indel Ave	Rancocas	NJ	08073	**800-762-6382**	609-267-4120
Reliance Steel & Aluminum Co Bralco Metals Div 15090 Northam St	La Mirada	CA	90638	**800-628-1864**	714-736-4800
Rolled Alloys Inc 125 W Sterns Rd	Temperance	MI	48182	**800-521-0332**	734-847-0561
Russel Metals Bahcall Group PO Box 1054	Appleton	WI	54912	**800-236-0500***	920-734-9271
*Sales					
Russel Metals Inc					
1900 Minnesota Ct Suite 210	Mississauga	ON	L5N3C9	**800-268-0750**	905-819-7777
TSE: RUS					
Sabel Steel Industries Inc PO Box 4747	Montgomery	AL	36103	**800-392-5754***	334-265-6771
*Sales					
Service Steel & Pipe Inc 1130 Fullerton St	Shreveport	LA	71107	**800-256-8598**	318-222-9462
Shamrock Steel Sales Inc 238 W County Rd S	Odessa	TX	79763	**800-299-2317**	432-337-2317
Siskin Steel & Supply Co Inc					
PO Box 1191	Chattanooga	TN	37401	**800-756-3671***	423-756-3671
*Sales					
Smith Pipe & Steel Inc 735 N 19th Ave	Phoenix	AZ	85009	**800-352-4596***	602-257-9494
*Cust Svc					
State Pipe & Supply Co					
9615 S Norwalk Blvd	Santa Fe Springs	CA	90670	**800-733-6410**	562-695-5555
Staub Metals Corp PO Box 1425	Paramount	CA	90723	**800-447-8282**	562-602-2200
Steel Engineers Inc 716 W Mesquite Ave	Las Vegas	NV	89106	**800-838-4043**	702-386-0023
Steel & Pipe Supply Co 555 Poyntz Ave	Manhattan	KS	66502	**800-521-2345**	785-537-2222
Steel Warehouse Co Inc					
2722 W Tucker Dr	South Bend	IN	46619	**800-348-2529**	574-236-5100
Texas Pipe & Supply Co Inc 2330 Holmes Rd	Houston	TX	77051	**800-233-8736**	713-799-9235
Tioga Pipe Supply Co Inc					
2450 Wheatsheaf Ln	Philadelphia	PA	19137	**800-523-3678**	215-831-0700
Titan Steel Corp 2500-B Broening Hwy	Baltimore	MD	21224	**800-359-4678**	410-631-5200
Titanium Industries Inc 181 E Halsey Rd	Parsippany	NJ	07054	**888-482-6486**	973-428-1900
Toyota Tsusho America Inc					
437 Madison Ave 29th Fl	New York	NY	10022	**800-883-0100**	212-418-0100
Transtar Metals 14400 S Figueroa St	Gardena	CA	90248	**800-344-4972**	323-321-1700
Tubular Steel Inc 1031 Executive Pkwy Dr	Saint Louis	MO	63141	**800-882-8527**	314-851-9200
Universal Steel Co 6600 Grant Ave	Cleveland	OH	44105	**800-927-2659**	216-883-4972
West Central Steel Inc					
2011 W Gorton Ave NW	Willmar	MN	56201	**800-992-8853**	320-235-4070
Wrisco Industries Inc					
355 Hiatt Dr Suite B	Palm Beach Gardens	FL	33418	**800-627-2646**	561-626-5700

484 METALWORKING DEVICES & ACCESSORIES

SEE ALSO Machine Tools - Metal Cutting Types; Machine Tools - Metal Forming Types; Tool & Die Shops

Company / Address	City	State	Zip	Toll-Free	Phone
Acme Industrial Co 441 Maple Ave	Carpentersville	IL	60110	**800-323-5582**	847-428-3911
Advanced Machine & Engineering Co					
2500 Latham St	Rockford	IL	61103	**800-255-2331**	815-962-6076
Allied Machine & Engineering Corp					
120 Deeds Dr	Dover	OH	44622	**800-321-5537**	330-343-4283

Company / Address	City	State	Zip	Toll-Free	Phone
American Cutting Edge Inc 4455 Infirmary Rd	West Carrollton	OH	45449	**800-543-6860**	937-866-5986
American Drill Bushing Co 2000 Camfield Ave	Los Angeles	CA	90040	**800-423-4425**	323-725-1515
ASKO Inc 501 W 7th Ave	Homestead	PA	15120	**800-321-1310**	412-461-4110
Besly Products Corp 100 Dearborn Ave	South Beloit	IL	61080	**800-435-2965**	815-389-2231
Brubaker Tool Corp 200 Front St	Millersburg	PA	17061	**800-522-8665**	717-692-2113
Buck Forkardt Inc 4169 Commercial Ave	Portage	MI	49002	**800-228-2825**	269-327-8200
Carl Zeiss Inc Industrial Measuring Technology Div 6250 Sycamore Ln N	Maple Grove	MN	55369	**800-752-6181**	763-744-2400
CJT Koolcarb Inc 494 Mission St	Carol Stream	IL	60188	**800-323-2299**	630-690-5933
ClappDiCO Corp 6325 Industrial Pkwy	Whitehouse	OH	43571	**800-537-6445**	419-877-5358
Climax Portable Machine Tools Inc 2712 E 2nd St	Newberg	OR	97132	**800-333-8311**	503-538-2185
Cushion Cut Inc 2565 W 237th St	Torrance	CA	90505	**800-421-2222**	
Deltronic Corp 3900 W Segerstrom Ave	Santa Ana	CA	92704	**800-451-6922**	714-545-0401
DeVlieg Bullard II Inc 10100 Forest Hills Rd	Rockford	IL	61115	**800-248-8120**	815-282-4100
Dundick Corp 4616 W 20th St	Cicero	IL	60804	**800-322-4243**	708-656-6363
Duramet Corp 11350 Stephens Dr	Warren	MI	48089	**800-783-2280**	586-759-2280
Fastcut Tool Corp 200 Front St	Millersburg	PA	17061	**800-682-8832**	717-692-2222
Fullerton Tool Co Inc 121 Perry St	Saginaw	MI	48602	**800-248-8315**	989-799-4550
Garr Tool Co 7800 N Alger Rd	Alma	MI	48801	**800-248-9003**	989-463-6171
Giddings & Lewis Machine Tools 142 Doty St PO Box 590	Fond du Lac	WI	54936	**800-343-2847**	920-921-9400
Gilman Russell T Inc 1230 Cheyenne Ave	Grafton	WI	53024	**800-445-6267**	262-377-2434
Glastonbury Southern Gage Co Inc 46 Industrial Park Rd	Erin	TN	37061	**800-251-4243**	931-289-4243
Greenfield Industries Inc 470 Old Evans Rd	Evans	GA	30809	**888-434-4311**	706-863-7708
Guhring Inc 1445 Commerce Ave	Brookfield	WI	53045	**800-776-6170**	262-784-6730
Hardinge Inc 1 Hardinge Dr *NASDAQ: HDNG*	Elmira	NY	14902	**800-843-8801**	607-734-2281
Hayden Twist Drill & Tool Co Inc 22822 Globe St	Warren	MI	48089	**800-521-1780**	586-754-7700
Hoppe Tool Inc 107 1st Ave *Sales	Chicopee	MA	01020	**800-742-6571***	413-592-9213
Hougen Mfg Inc 3001 Hougen Dr *Orders	Swartz Creek	MI	48473	**800-462-7818***	810-635-7111
Huron Machine Products Inc 228 SW 21st Terr	Fort Lauderdale	FL	33312	**800-327-8186**	954-587-4541
Industrial Tools Inc 1111 S Rose Ave	Oxnard	CA	93033	**800-266-5561**	805-483-1111
Invo Spline Inc 2357 E Nine-Mile Rd *Cust Svc	Warren	MI	48090	**800-959-0884***	586-757-8840
ITW Workholding Group 2155 Traverse Field Dr	Traverse City	MI	49686	**800-828-5755**	231-947-5755
Jasco Cutting Tools 195 Saint Paul St	Rochester	NY	14604	**800-868-1074**	585-546-1254
Jasco Tools Inc 1390 Mt Read Blvd PO Box 60497	Rochester	NY	14606	**800-724-5497**	585-254-7000
Jergens Inc 15700 S Waterloo Rd	Cleveland	OH	44110	**800-537-4367**	216-486-2100
Kaiser Precision Tooling Inc 641 Fargo Ave	Elk Grove Village	IL	60007	**800-553-5113**	847-228-7660
Kennametal Inc 1600 Technology Way *NYSE: KMT* ■ *Cust Svc	Latrobe	PA	15650	**800-446-7738***	724-539-5000
KEO Cutters Inc 25040 Easy St	Warren	MI	48089	**888-771-2062**	586-771-2050
KPT/Kaiser Precision Tooling Inc 641 Fargo Ave	Elk Grove Village	IL	60007	**800-553-5113**	847-228-7660
Lancaster Knives Inc 165 Court St PO Box 268	Lancaster	NY	14086	**800-869-9666**	716-683-5050
Lovejoy Tool Co Inc 133 Main St	Springfield	VT	05156	**800-843-8376**	802-885-2194
Melin Tool Co 5565 Venture Dr Unit C	Cleveland	OH	44130	**800-521-1078**	216-362-4200
NED Corp 18 Grafton St 2nd Fl	Worcester	MA	01604	**800-343-6086**	508-798-8546
Newcomer Products Inc PO Box 272	Latrobe	PA	15650	**800-245-6880**	724-537-5531
Niagara Cutter Inc 200 John James Audubon Pkwy	Amherst	NY	14228	**888-689-8400**	716-689-8400
North American Tool Corp 215 Elmwood Ave	South Beloit	IL	61080	**800-872-8277**	815-389-2300
Norton Co Diamond Tool Div 65 Beale Rd *Cust Svc	Arden	NC	28704	**800-438-4773***	828-684-2500
Onsrud Cutter Inc 800 Liberty Dr	Libertyville	IL	60048	**800-234-1560**	847-362-1560
OSG Tap & Die Inc 676 E Fullerton Ave	Glendale Heights	IL	60139	**800-837-2223**	630-790-1400
Precitech Precision Inc 44 Blackbrook Rd	Keene	NH	03431	**800-295-2510**	603-357-2511
Quinco Tool Products Co 21000 Hubbell Rd	Oak Park	MI	48237	**800-521-1910**	248-968-5000
Reiff & Nestor Co PO Box 147	Lykens	PA	17048	**800-521-3422**	717-453-7113
RMT Technology 435 Eastern Ave	Bellwood	IL	60104	**800-228-9949**	708-544-1017
Russell T Gilman Inc 1230 Cheyenne Ave	Grafton	WI	53024	**800-445-6267**	262-377-2434
S-T Industries Inc 301 Armstrong Blvd N	Saint James	MN	56081	**800-326-2039**	507-375-3211
Scotchman Industries Inc 180 E Hwy 14	Philip	SD	57567	**800-843-8844**	605-859-2542
Scully-Jones Corp 1901 S Rockwell St	Chicago	IL	60608	**800-752-8665**	773-247-5900
Seibert Inc 1901 S Rockwell St *Sales	Chicago	IL	60608	**800-435-4530***	815-945-2411
Smith TM Tool International Corp PO Box 1065	Mount Clemens	MI	48046	**800-521-4894**	586-468-1465
Spiralock Corp 25235 Dequindre Rd Madison Tech Ctr	Madison Heights	MI	48071	**800-521-2688**	248-543-7800
Stocker Yale Inc Stilson Die-Draulic Div 15935 Sturgeon St	Roseville	MI	48066	**877-784-5766**	586-778-1100
Strong Tool Co 1251 E 286th St	Cleveland	OH	44132	**800-362-0293**	216-289-2450
Tapmatic Corp 802 Clearwater Loop	Post Falls	ID	83854	**800-854-6019**	208-773-8048
Target Products Inc 17400 W 119th St	Olathe	KS	66061	**800-288-5040**	913-928-1000
Thread Check Inc 390 Oser Ave	Hauppauge	NY	11788	**800-767-7633**	631-231-1515
TM Smith Tool International Corp PO Box 1065	Mount Clemens	MI	48046	**800-521-4894**	586-468-1465
Tools for Bending Inc 194 W Dakota Ave *Cust Svc	Denver	CO	80223	**800-873-3305***	303-777-7170
Union Butterfield Corp PO Box 9000	Crystal Lake	IL	60039	**800-222-8665**	
United Drill Bushing Corp 12200 Woodruff Ave	Downey	CA	90241	**800-486-3466**	562-803-1521
Valenite Inc 1675 Whitcomb Ave *Cust Svc	Madison Heights	MI	48071	**800-488-9112***	248-589-1000
Viking Drill & Tool Inc 355 State St	Saint Paul	MN	55107	**800-328-4655**	651-227-8911
WA Whitney Co 650 Race St	Rockford	IL	61105	**800-435-2823**	815-964-6771
Walker Magnetics Group Inc 20 Rockdale St	Worcester	MA	01606	**800-962-4638**	508-853-3232
Walter Waukesha Inc 1111 Sentry Dr	Waukesha	WI	53186	**800-945-5554**	262-542-4426
Weldon Tool Co 200 Front St	Millersburg	PA	17061	**800-622-7742**	717-692-2113
Wisconsin Machine Tool Corp 3225 Gateway Rd Suite 100	Brookfield	WI	53045	**800-243-3078**	262-317-3048
Zeiss Carl Inc Industrial Measuring Technology Div 6250 Sycamore Ln N	Maple Grove	MN	55369	**800-752-6181**	763-744-2400

485 METALWORKING MACHINERY

SEE ALSO Rolling Mill Machinery

Company / Address	City	State	Zip	Toll-Free	Phone
Belvac Production Machinery Inc 237 Graves Mill Rd	Lynchburg	VA	24502	**800-423-5822**	434-239-0358
Pannier Corp 207 Sandusky St	Pittsburgh	PA	15212	**800-233-2009**	412-323-4900
Pines Mfg Inc 30505 Clemens Rd	Westlake	OH	44145	**800-207-2840**	440-835-5553
Red Bud Industries 200 B & E Industrial Dr	Red Bud	IL	62278	**800-851-4612**	618-282-3801
Rowe Machinery & Automation Inc 76 Hinckley Rd	Clinton	ME	04927	**800-247-2645**	207-426-2351
Superior Machine Co of South Carolina Inc 692 N Cashua Rd	Florence	SC	29502	**800-736-9898**	843-664-3001
Sweed Machinery Inc 653 2nd Ave PO Box 228 *Sales	Gold Hill	OR	97525	**800-888-1352***	541-855-1512
Tridan International Inc 130 N Jackson St	Danville	IL	61832	**800-369-3544**	217-443-3592
Wright-K Technology Inc 2025 E Genesee Ave	Saginaw	MI	48601	**800-752-3103**	989-752-3103

486 METERS & OTHER COUNTING DEVICES

Company / Address	City	State	Zip	Toll-Free	Phone
American Meter Co 132 Welsh Rd Suite 140	Horsham	PA	19044	**888-295-7928**	215-830-1800
AMETEK Inc Dixson Div 287 27 Rd	Grand Junction	CO	81503	**888-302-0639**	970-244-1241
AMETEK Sensor Technology Drexelbrook Div 205 Keith Valley Rd *Cust Svc	Horsham	PA	19044	**800-527-6297***	215-674-1234
Badger Meter Inc 4545 W Brown Deer Rd *AMEX: BMI*	Milwaukee	WI	53223	**800-876-3837**	414-355-0400
Controlotron Corp 155 Plant Ave	Hauppauge	NY	11788	**800-275-8479**	631-231-3600
Danaher Controls 1675 Delany Rd	Gurnee	IL	60031	**800-873-8731**	847-662-2666
Dixson Div AMETEK Inc 287 27 Rd	Grand Junction	CO	81503	**888-302-0639**	970-244-1241
Drexelbrook Div AMETEK Sensor Technology 205 Keith Valley Rd *Cust Svc	Horsham	PA	19044	**800-527-6297***	215-674-1234
Duncan Parking Technologies Inc 340 Industrial Park Rd *Cust Svc	Harrison	AR	72601	**800-338-6226***	870-741-5481
Electro-Sensors Inc 6111 Blue Circle Dr *NASDAQ: ELSE*	Minnetonka	MN	55343	**800-328-6170**	952-930-0100
EMCO (Engineering Measurements Co) 1401 Ken Pratt Blvd	Longmont	CO	80501	**800-356-9362**	303-651-0550
Engineering Measurements Co (EMCO) 1401 Ken Pratt Blvd	Longmont	CO	80501	**800-356-9362**	303-651-0550
FMC Measurement Solutions 1602 Wagner Ave	Erie	PA	16510	**800-867-6484**	814-898-5000
Greenwald Industries 212 Middlesex Ave	Chester	CT	06412	**800-221-0982**	860-526-0800
Invensys 33 Commercial St	Foxboro	MA	02035	**866-746-6477**	508-543-8750
Isspro Inc 2515 NE Riverside Way PO Box 11177	Portland	OR	97211	**888-447-7776**	503-288-4488
Laser Technology Inc 7070 S Tucson Way	Englewood	CO	80112	**800-280-6113**	303-649-1000
McKesson Automated Prescription Systems 4333 Shreveport Hwy	Pineville	LA	71360	**800-551-6578**	318-640-8114
Metretek Inc 300 North Dr	Melbourne	FL	32934	**800-327-8559**	321-259-9700
Minarik Corp 905 E Thompson Ave	Glendale	CA	91201	**800-427-2757**	818-637-7500
Pierburg Instruments Inc 47519 Halyard Dr	Plymouth	MI	48170	**800-394-3569**	734-446-8360
PMP Corp 25 Security Dr *Cust Svc	Avon	CT	06001	**800-243-6628***	860-677-9656
POM Inc 200 S Elmira Ave PO Box 430	Russellville	AR	72802	**800-331-7275**	479-968-2880
Racine Federated Inc Hedland Div 2200 South St	Racine	WI	53404	**800-433-5263**	262-639-6770
Sparling Instruments Co Inc 4097 N Temple City Blvd *Sales	El Monte	CA	91731	**800-800-3569***	626-444-0571
Thomas G Faria Corp 385 Norwich-New London Tpke	Uncasville	CT	06382	**800-473-2742**	860-848-9271
Woodward FST 700 N Centennial St	Zeeland	MI	49464	**800-253-3295**	616-772-9171

487 MICROGRAPHICS PRODUCTS & SERVICES

Company / Address	City	State	Zip	Toll-Free	Phone
Bay Microfilm Inc DBA BMI Imaging Systems 1115 E Arques Ave *Cust Svc	Sunnyvale	CA	94085	**800-359-3456***	408-736-7444
BMI Imaging Systems 1115 E Arques Ave *Cust Svc	Sunnyvale	CA	94085	**800-359-3456***	408-736-7444
Comstor Productivity Center Inc 2219 N Dickey Rd	Spokane	WA	99212	**800-776-2451**	509-534-5080
DPF Data Services Group Inc 1990 Swarthmore Ave	Lakewood	NJ	08701	**800-431-4416**	732-370-8840
Eye Communication Systems Inc 455 E Industrial Dr	Hartland	WI	53029	**800-558-2153**	262-367-1360
Indus International Inc 340 S Oak St PO Box 890	West Salem	WI	54669	**800-843-9377**	608-786-0300
Information Imaging Corp 20 S Linden Ave Bldg 2-B	South San Francisco	CA	94080	**800-373-1834**	650-244-9911
MicroFilm Products Co 157 Avalon Gardens Dr	Nanuet	NY	10954	**800-642-7668**	845-371-3780
Mohr Microfilm Corp 20 S Linden Ave Bldg 2-B	South San Francisco	CA	94080	**800-373-1834**	650-244-9911

488 MILITARY SERVICE ACADEMIES

Company / Address	City	State	Zip	Toll-Free	Phone
US Air Force Academy Dept of the Air Force Headquarters USAFA	USAF Academy	CO	80840	**800-379-1455**	719-333-1110
US Military Academy Admissions Bldg 606	West Point	NY	10996	**800-822-8762**	845-938-5746
US Naval Academy 117 Decatur Rd	Annapolis	MD	21402	**888-249-7707**	410-293-1000

489 MILLWORK

SEE ALSO Construction Materials - Lumber & Building Supplies; Doors & Windows - Wood; Home Improvement Centers; Shutters - Window (All Types)

Company	City	State	ZIP	Toll-Free	Phone
Allen Millwork Inc PO Box 6480	Shreveport	LA	71136	**800-551-8737**	318-868-6541
Black Millwork Co Inc 230 W Crescent Ave	Allendale	NJ	07401	**800-864-2356**	201-934-0100
Brockway-Smith Co (BWAY) 146 Dascomb Rd.	Andover	MA	01810	**800-225-7912**	978-475-7100
BWAY (Brockway-Smith Co) 146 Dascomb Rd.	Andover	MA	01810	**800-225-7912**	978-475-7100
Causeway Lumber Co 2601 S Andrews Ave	Fort Lauderdale	FL	33316	**800-375-5050**	954-763-1224
Central Woodwork Inc 870 Keough Rd	Collierville	TN	38017	**800-788-3775**	901-363-4141
Clopay Corp 8585 Duke Blvd	Mason	OH	45040	**800-262-2260**	513-770-4800
Colonial Craft 2270 Woodale Dr.	Mounds View	MN	55112	**800-727-5187**	763-231-4000
Contact Lumber Co 9200 SE Sunnybrook Blvd Suite 200	Clackamas	OR	97015	**800-547-1038**	503-228-7361
Cox Interior Inc 1751 Old Columbia Rd	Campbellsville	KY	42718	**800-733-1751**	270-789-3129
CW Ohio Inc 1209 Maple Ave	Conneaut	OH	44030	**800-677-5801**	440-593-5800
Do+Able Products Inc 5150 Edison Ave.	Chino	CA	91710	**800-829-3648**	909-590-4444
Graves Lumber Co 1315 S Cleveland-Massillon Rd	Copley	OH	44321	**877-500-5515**	330-666-1115
Horner Millwork Corp 1255 Grand Army Hwy	Somerset	MA	02726	**800-543-5403**	508-679-6479
Huttig Building Products Inc 555 Maryville University Dr *NYSE: HBP*	Saint Louis	MO	63141	**800-325-4466**	314-216-2600
Jeld-Wen Inc 401 Harbor Isles Blvd.	Klamath Falls	OR	97601	**800-535-3462**	541-882-3451
Lafayette Wood-Works Inc 3004 Cameron St	Lafayette	LA	70506	**800-960-3311**	337-233-5250
Liberty Wood & Construction Inc 3300 Benzing Rd	Orchard Park	NY	14127	**800-448-2200**	716-824-6067
Louisiana-Pacific Corp 414 Union St Suite 2000 *NYSE: LPX*	Nashville	TN	37219	**877-744-5600**	615-986-5600
Merrimack Valley Wood Products Co B St Derry Industrial Park	Derry	NH	03038	**800-955-0702**	603-432-2581
Milliken Millwork Inc 6361 Sterling Dr N.	Sterling Heights	MI	48312	**800-686-9218**	586-264-0950
Monarch Industries Inc 99 Main St	Warren	RI	02885	**800-669-9663**	401-247-5200
MW Manufacturers Inc 433 N Main St	Rocky Mount	VA	24151	**888-999-8400**	540-483-0211
New England Door Corp 15 Campanelli Cir.	Canton	MA	02021	**800-969-5151**	781-821-2737
Norwood Sash & Door Mfg Co 4953 Section Ave.	Norwood	OH	45212	**800-599-5043**	513-531-5700
Ohline Corp 1930 W 139th St.	Gardena	CA	90249	**800-585-3197**	310-327-4630
Randall Brothers Inc 665 Marietta St NW *Cust Svc	Atlanta	GA	30313	**800-476-4539***	404-892-6666
Raynor Garage Doors 1101 E River Rd	Dixon	IL	61021	**800-472-9667**	815-288-1431
ROW Window Co 612 Moen Ave.	Joliet	IL	60434	**800-966-3769**	815-725-5491
Schuck Component Systems Inc 8205 N 67th Ave	Glendale	AZ	85302	**800-666-3661**	623-931-3661
Shuster's Building Components 2920 Clay Pike	Irwin	PA	15642	**800-366-6733**	724-446-7000
Somerset Door & Column Co 174 Sagamore St.	Somerset	PA	15501	**800-242-7916**	814-444-9427
Taylor Brothers Inc PO Box 11198.	Lynchburg	VA	24506	**800-288-6767**	434-237-8100
Trus Joist MacMillan LP 200 E Mallard Dr *Cust Svc	Boise	ID	83706	**800-338-0515***	208-364-1200
Walpole Woodworkers Inc 767 East St PO Box 151	Walpole	MA	02081	**800-343-6948**	508-668-2800
Wayne-Dalton Corp 1 Door Dr PO Box 67	Mount Hope	OH	44660	**800-827-3667**	330-674-7015
Werzalit of America Inc PO Box 373	Bradford	PA	16701	**800-999-3730**	814-362-3881
Woodgrain Millworks Inc PO Box 566	Fruitland	ID	83619	**800-452-3801**	208-452-3801
Young Mfg Co Inc PO Box 167.	Beaver Dam	KY	42320	**800-545-6595**	270-274-3306

490 MINERAL PRODUCTS - NONMETALLIC

SEE ALSO Insulation & Acoustical Products

Company	City	State	ZIP	Toll-Free	Phone
3M Industrial Mineral Products Div 3M Ctr Bldg 225-2N-07	Saint Paul	MN	55144	**800-447-2914**	
Big River Industries Inc PO Box 66377	Baton Rouge	LA	70896	**800-969-5634**	225-627-4242
Burgess Pigment Co Inc PO Box 4146.	Macon	GA	31208	**800-841-8999**	478-746-5658
Eagle-Picher Minerals Inc PO Box 12130 *Cust Svc	Reno	NV	89510	**800-228-3865***	775-824-7600
GE Quartz 4901 Campbell Rd	Willoughby	OH	44094	**800-438-2100**	800-258-3803
Graphel Corp 6115 Centre Pk Dr	West Chester	OH	45071	**800-255-1104**	513-779-6166
Graphite Sales Inc 16710 W Park Circle Dr.	Chagrin Falls	OH	44023	**800-321-4147**	440-543-8221
Harborlite Corp PO Box 100.	Vicksburg	MI	49097	**800-403-4869**	269-649-1352
Hill & Griffith Co 1085 Summer St	Cincinnati	OH	45204	**800-543-0425**	513-921-1075
Kocour Co 4800 S St Louis Ave	Chicago	IL	60632	**888-562-6871**	773-847-1111
La Habra Products Inc 4125 E La Palma Ave Suite 250	Anaheim	CA	92807	**800-649-8933**	714-778-2266
Metallics Systems 31935 Aurora Rd	Solon	OH	44139	**800-638-2859**	440-349-8800
Miller & Co LLC 9700 W Higgins Rd Suite 1000.	Rosemont	IL	60018	**800-727-9847**	847-696-2400
Multicoat Corp 23331 Antonio Pkwy	Rancho Santa Margarita	CA	92688	**877-685-8426**	949-888-7100
San Jose Delta Assoc Inc 482 Sapena Ct	Santa Clara	CA	95054	**800-809-4308**	408-727-1448
Silbrico Corp 6300 River Rd.	Hodgkins	IL	60525	**800-323-4287**	708-354-3350
Solite LLC 3900 Shannon St.	Chesapeake	VA	23324	**888-854-9634**	757-494-5200
Tec Minerals Inc Hwy 787	Cleveland	TX	77327	**800-833-5442**	281-592-6428
US Diamond Wheel Co 101 Kendall Point Dr	Oswego	IL	60543	**800-223-0457**	630-898-9000
USG Corp 125 S Franklin St. *NYSE: USG*	Chicago	IL	60606	**800-621-9622**	312-606-4000
Von Roll Isola USA 1 W Campbell Rd	Schenectady	NY	12306	**800-654-7652**	518-344-7100
Winter Brothers Material Co 13098 Gravois Rd	Saint Louis	MO	63127	**800-722-5424**	314-843-1400

491 MINING - COAL

Company	City	State	ZIP	Toll-Free	Phone
Arch Coal Inc 1 City Place Suite 300 *NYSE: ACI*	Saint Louis	MO	63141	**800-238-7398**	314-994-2700
Blattner DH & Sons Inc 400 CR 50	Avon	MN	56310	**800-877-2866**	320-356-7351
Cleveland-Cliffs Inc 1100 Superior Ave 18th Fl. *NYSE: CLF*	Cleveland	OH	44114	**800-521-5701**	216-694-5700
DH Blattner & Sons Inc 400 CR 50	Avon	MN	56310	**800-877-2866**	320-356-7351
Electric Fuels Corp 1 Progress Plaza	Saint Petersburg	FL	33733	**800-999-3835**	727-824-6600
Kennecott Energy Co PO Box 3009	Gillette	WY	82717	**800-305-1142**	307-687-6000

492 MINING - METALS

Company	City	State	ZIP	Toll-Free	Phone
Barrick Gold Corp 161 Bay St BCE Place Suite 3700 *NYSE: ABX*	Toronto	ON	M5J2S1	**800-720-7415**	416-861-9911
Brush Engineered Materials Inc 17876 St Clair Ave. *NYSE: BW* ■ *Cust Svc	Cleveland	OH	44110	**800-321-2076***	216-486-4200
Cleveland-Cliffs Inc 1100 Superior Ave 18th Fl. *NYSE: CLF*	Cleveland	OH	44114	**800-521-5701**	216-694-5700
Coeur d'Alene Mines Corp PO Box 'I' *NYSE: CDE*	Coeur d'Alene	ID	83816	**800-624-2824**	208-667-3511
Constellation Copper Corp 1776 Lincoln St. *TSE: CCU*	Denver	CO	80203	**877-370-5400**	303-861-5400
Eldorado Gold Corp 550 Burrard St Suite 1188. *AMEX: EGO*	Vanouver	BC	V6C2B5	**888-353-8166**	604-687-4018
First Quantum Minerals Ltd 543 Granville St Suite 800. *TSE: FM*	Vancouver	BC	V6C1X8	**888-688-6577**	604-688-6577
Glamis Gold Ltd 5190 Neil Rd Suite 310 *NYSE: GLG*	Reno	NV	89502	**800-452-6472**	775-827-4600
Gold Reserve Inc 926 W Sprague Ave Suite 200 *AMEX: GRZ*	Spokane	WA	99201	**800-625-9550**	509-623-1500
Goldcorp Inc 145 King St W Suite 2700 *NYSE: GG*	Toronto	ON	M5H1J8	**800-813-1412**	416-865-0326
Great Basin Gold Ltd 800 W Pender St Suite 1020. *AMEX: GBN*	Vancouver	BC	V6C2V6	**800-667-2114**	604-684-6365
IAMGOLD Corp 220 Bay St 5th Fl *AMEX: IAG*	Toronto	ON	M5J2W4	**888-464-9999**	416-360-4710
Kinross Gold USA Inc 670 Sierra Rose Dr	Reno	NV	89511	**800-644-3547**	775-829-1000
Meridian Gold Co 9670 Gateway Dr Suite 200. *NYSE: MDG*	Reno	NV	89521	**800-557-4699**	775-850-3777
Miramar Mining Corp 889 Harbourside Dr Suite 300. *AMEX: MNG*	North Vancouver	BC	V7P3S1	**800-663-8780**	604-985-2572
MK Resources Co 60 E South Temple St Suite 1225	Salt Lake City	UT	84111	**800-664-6528**	801-297-6900
NA Degerstrom Inc 3303 N Sullivan Rd	Spokane	WA	99216	**800-637-3773**	509-928-3333
Nord Resources Corp 3048 N Seven Dash Rd PO Box 384.	Dragoon	AZ	85609	**800-543-2599**	520-586-2241
NovaGold Resources Inc 1055 Dunsmuir St Suite 3454. *AMEX: NG*	Vancouver	BC	V7X1K8	**866-699-6227**	604-663-6227
Oglebay Norton Co 1001 Lakeside Ave 15th Fl.	Cleveland	OH	44114	**800-321-4230**	216-861-3300
Pacific Rim Mining Co 625 Howe St Suite 410 *AMEX: PMU*	Vancouver	BC	V6C2T6	**888-775-7097**	604-689-1976
Phelps Dodge Corp 1 N Central Ave. *NYSE: PD*	Phoenix	AZ	85004	**800-528-1182**	602-366-8100
Phelps Dodge Mining Co 1 N Central Ave	Phoenix	AZ	85004	**800-528-1182**	602-366-8100
PT Freeport Indonesia Co 1615 Poydras St	New Orleans	LA	70112	**800-535-7094**	504-582-4000
Stratcor Inc 4955 Steubenville Pike Suite 305	Pittsburgh	PA	15205	**800-573-6052**	412-787-4500
Tenke Mining Corp 885 W Georgia St Suite 2101 *TSE: TNK*	Vancouver	BC	V6C3E8	**888-689-7842**	604-689-7842
United Taconite LLC PO Box 180.	Eveleth	MN	55734	**800-560-4532**	218-744-7800
Wheaton River Minerals Ltd 200 Burrard St Suite 1560. *TSE: WRM*	Vancouver	BC	V6C3L6	**800-567-6223**	604-696-3000
Yamana Gold Inc 150 York St Suite 1902 *AMEX: AUY*	Toronto	ON	M5H3S5	**888-809-0925**	416-815-0220

493 MINING - MINERALS

493-1 Chemical & Fertilizer Minerals Mining

Company	City	State	ZIP	Toll-Free	Phone
American Borate Corp 5700 Cleveland St Suite 420	Virginia Beach	VA	23462	**800-486-1072**	757-490-2242
Mississippi Chemical Corp 3622 Hwy 49 E PO Box 388	Yazoo City	MS	39194	**800-433-1351**	662-746-4131
New Riverside Ochre Co Inc PO Box 460 *Orders	Cartersville	GA	30120	**800-248-0176***	770-382-4568
OCI Chemical Corp 2 Corporate Dr Suite 440	Shelton	CT	06484	**800-865-1774**	203-225-3100
Potash Corp 1101 Skokie Blvd	Northbrook	IL	60062	**800-645-2183**	847-849-4200
Potash Corp of Saskatchewan Inc 122 1st Ave S Suite 500 *NYSE: POT*	Saskatoon	SK	S7K7G3	**800-667-3930**	306-933-8500
Solvay Minerals Inc 3333 Richmond Ave.	Houston	TX	77098	**800-443-2785**	713-525-6800
United Salt Corp 4800 San Felipe St	Houston	TX	77056	**800-554-8658**	713-877-2600
US Borax Inc 26877 Tourney Rd.	Valencia	CA	91355	**800-533-4872**	661-287-5400

493-2 Clay, Ceramic, Refractory Minerals Mining

Company	City	State	ZIP	Toll-Free	Phone
AMCOL International Corp 1500 W Shure Dr. *NYSE: ACO*	Arlington Heights	IL	60004	**800-323-0629**	847-392-4600

Clay, Ceramic, Refractory Minerals Mining (Cont'd)

	City	State	ZIP	Toll-Free	Phone
American Colloid Co					
1500 W Shure Dr	Arlington Heights	IL	60004	**800-323-0629**	847-392-4600
Black Hills Bentonite Co 55 Saltcreek Hwy	Casper	WY	82601	**800-788-9443***	307-265-3740
*Orders					
CT Harris Inc 9411 Deepstep Rd	Sandersville	GA	31082	**800-547-6404**	478-552-5070
Harris CT Inc 9411 Deepstep Rd	Sandersville	GA	31082	**800-547-6404**	478-552-5070
IMERYS 100 Mansell Ct E Suite 300	Roswell	GA	30076	**800-374-3224**	770-594-0660
Kentucky-Tennessee Clay Co					
1441 Donelson Pike	Nashville	TN	37217	**800-814-4538**	615-365-0852
Milwhite Inc 5487 South Padre Island Hwy	Brownsville	TX	78521	**800-442-0082**	956-547-1970
Riverside Clay Co Inc 201 Truss Ferry Rd	Pell City	AL	35128	**800-226-4542**	205-338-3366
RT Vanderbilt Co Inc 30 Winfield St	Norwalk	CT	06855	**800-243-6064***	203-853-1400
*Cust Svc					
Southern Clay Products Inc 1212 Church St	Gonzales	TX	78629	**800-324-2891**	830-672-2891
US Silica Co PO Box 187	Berkeley Springs	WV	25411	**800-243-7500**	304-258-2500
Wyo-Ben Inc 1345 Discovery Dr	Billings	MT	59102	**800-548-7055***	406-652-6351
*Cust Svc					

493-3 Minerals Mining (Misc)

	City	State	ZIP	Toll-Free	Phone
Gouverneur Talc Co Inc					
1837 State Hwy 812	Gouverneur	NY	13642	**800-243-6064**	315-287-0100
Luzenac America Inc					
345 Inverness Dr S Suite 310	Centennial	CO	80112	**800-525-8252**	303-643-0400
Milwhite Inc 5487 South Padre Island Hwy	Brownsville	TX	78521	**800-442-0082**	956-547-1970
RT Vanderbilt Co Inc 30 Winfield St	Norwalk	CT	06855	**800-243-6064***	203-853-1400
*Cust Svc					
Stornoway Diamond Corp					
625 Howe St Suite 860	Vancouver	BC	V6C2T6	**888-338-2200**	604-331-2259
TSE: SWY					
Tahera Diamond Corp					
121 Richmond St W Suite 803	Toronto	ON	M5H2K1	**877-777-2004**	416-777-1998
TSE: TAH					
WGI Heavy Minerals Inc					
1875 N Lakewood Dr Suite 201	Coeur d'Alene	ID	83814	**888-542-7638**	208-666-6000
TSE: WG					

493-4 Sand & Gravel Pits

	City	State	ZIP	Toll-Free	Phone
Best Sand Corp PO Box 87	Chardon	OH	44024	**800-237-4986**	440-285-3132
Boxley Co Inc PO Box 13527	Roanoke	VA	24035	**800-442-8878**	540-777-7600
Branscome Inc 4551 John Tyler Hwy	Williamsburg	VA	23185	**888-229-2504**	757-229-2504
Cadman Inc PO Box 97038	Redmond	WA	98073	**888-322-6847**	425-868-1234
Fairfax Sand & Crushed Stone Co					
8490 Garrett Hwy	Oakland	MD	21550	**800-325-8663**	301-334-8101
Fisher Sand & Gravel Co PO Box 1034	Dickinson	ND	58602	**800-932-8740**	701-456-9184
Florida Rock Industries Inc 155 E 21st St	Jacksonville	FL	32206	**800-874-8382**	904-355-1781
NYSE: FRK					
Frank W Whitcomb Construction Corp					
PO Box 1000	Walpole	NH	03608	**800-238-7283**	603-445-5555
Hilltop Basic Resources Inc					
1 W 4th St Suite 1100	Cincinnati	OH	45202	**800-701-7973**	513-651-5000
Janesville Sand & Lycon Co					
1110 Harding St	Janesville	WI	53547	**800-955-7702**	608-754-7701
Mark Sand & Gravel Co PO Box 458	Fergus Falls	MN	56538	**800-427-8316**	218-736-7523
Material Service Corp					
222 N LaSalle St Suite 1200	Chicago	IL	60601	**800-642-8936**	312-372-3600
Pike Industries Inc 3 Eastgate Park Rd	Belmont	NH	03220	**800-283-7453**	603-527-5100
Pounding Mill Quarry Corp					
171 St Clair's Crossing	Bluefield	VA	24605	**888-661-7625**	276-326-1145
Standard Sand & Silica Co PO Box 1059	Davenport	FL	33836	**877-444-7263**	863-422-7100
Thelen Sand & Gravel Inc 28955 W SR-173	Antioch	IL	60002	**800-537-2324**	847-395-3313
Unimin Corp 258 Elm St	New Canaan	CT	06840	**800-223-2236**	203-966-8880
US Silica Co PO Box 187	Berkeley Springs	WV	25411	**800-243-7500**	304-258-2500
Whibco Inc 87 E Commerce St	Bridgeton	NJ	08302	**800-631-8010**	856-455-9200
Whitcomb Frank W Construction Corp					
PO Box 1000	Walpole	NH	03608	**800-238-7283**	603-445-5555

493-5 Stone Quarries - Crushed & Broken Stone

	City	State	ZIP	Toll-Free	Phone
Arkansas Lime Co 600 Limedale Rd	Batesville	AR	72501	**800-252-5580***	870-793-2301
*Cust Svc					
Berks Products Corp 726 Spring St	Reading	PA	19604	**800-282-2375**	610-374-5131
Boxley Co Inc PO Box 13527	Roanoke	VA	24035	**800-442-8878**	540-777-7600
Cessford Construction Co 3808 Old Hwy 61	Burlington	IA	52601	**800-747-2297**	319-753-2297
Fairfax Sand & Crushed Stone Co					
8490 Garrett Hwy	Oakland	MD	21550	**800-325-8663**	301-334-8101
Florida Crushed Stone Co PO Box 490300	Leesburg	FL	34749	**800-767-0608**	352-787-0608
Florida Rock Industries Inc 155 E 21st St	Jacksonville	FL	32206	**800-874-8382**	904-355-1781
NYSE: FRK					
Frank W Whitcomb Construction Corp					
PO Box 1000	Walpole	NH	03608	**800-238-7283**	603-445-5555
Franklin Industrial Minerals 612 10th Ave N	Nashville	TN	37203	**800-626-8147**	615-259-4222
Graymont Western US Inc					
3950 S 700 E Suite 301	Salt Lake City	UT	84107	**800-814-7532**	801-262-3942
Greer Industries Inc PO Box 1900	Morgantown	WV	26507	**800-773-0412**	304-296-1751
Hamm NR Quarry Inc PO Box 17	Perry	KS	66073	**888-597-5464**	785-597-5111
Hanson Building Products North America					
3500 Maple Ave	Dallas	TX	75219	**800-527-2362**	214-525-5500
Iowa Limestone Co 500 New York Ave	Des Moines	IA	50313	**800-247-2133**	515-243-8106
Material Service Corp					
222 N LaSalle St Suite 1200	Chicago	IL	60601	**800-642-8936**	312-372-3600
NR Hamm Quarry Inc PO Box 17	Perry	KS	66073	**888-597-5464**	785-597-5111
Pike Industries Inc 3 Eastgate Park Rd	Belmont	NH	03220	**800-283-7453**	603-527-5100
Pounding Mill Quarry Corp					
171 St Clair's Crossing	Bluefield	VA	24605	**888-661-7625**	276-326-1145
Texas Crushed Stone Co 5300 S IH-35	Georgetown	TX	78628	**800-772-8272**	512-863-5511
US Lime & Minerals Inc					
13800 Montfort Dr Suite 330	Dallas	TX	75240	**800-991-5463**	972-991-8400
NASDAQ: USLM					
Whitcomb Frank W Construction Corp					
PO Box 1000	Walpole	NH	03608	**800-238-7283**	603-445-5555

493-6 Stone Quarries - Dimension Stone

	City	State	ZIP	Toll-Free	Phone
APAC Inc 900 Ashwood Pkwy Suite 700	Atlanta	GA	30338	**800-241-7074**	770-392-5300
Cadman Inc PO Box 97038	Redmond	WA	98073	**888-322-6847**	425-868-1234
Cold Spring Granite Inc 202 S 3rd Ave	Cold Spring	MN	56320	**800-328-5040**	320-685-3621
Fletcher Granite Co Inc 534 Groton Rd	Westford	MA	01886	**800-253-8168**	978-251-4031
Pounding Mill Quarry Corp					
171 St Clair's Crossing	Bluefield	VA	24605	**888-661-7625**	276-326-1145

494 MISSILES, SPACE VEHICLES, PARTS

	City	State	ZIP	Toll-Free	Phone
ATK Integrated Defense Co					
4700 Nathan Ln N	Plymouth	MN	55442	**800-456-8933**	763-744-5000
Esterline Mason 13955 Balboa Blvd	Sylmar	CA	91342	**800-232-7700**	818-361-3366
Honeywell Space Systems					
13350 US Hwy 19 N	Clearwater	FL	33764	**888-561-5665**	727-539-4000
Kaiser Electroprecision Corp					
17000 S Red Hill Ave	Irvine	CA	92614	**800-866-5775**	949-250-1015
Lourdes Industries Inc 65 Hoffman Ave	Hauppauge	NY	11788	**800-368-3728**	631-234-6600
Mason Controls 13955 Balboa Blvd	Sylmar	CA	91342	**800-232-7700**	818-361-3366
Orbital Sciences Corp 21839 Atlantic Blvd	Dulles	VA	20166	**877-672-4825**	703-406-5000
NYSE: ORB					
Pratt & Whitney Government Engines & Space Propulsion Div					
PO Box 109600	West Palm Beach	FL	33410	**800-327-3246**	561-796-2000

495 MOBILE HOMES & BUILDINGS

	City	State	ZIP	Toll-Free	Phone
Astro Homes PO Box 190	Shippenville	PA	16254	**800-222-7876**	814-226-6822
Buccaneer Homes of Alabama Inc					
PO Box 1418	Hamilton	AL	35570	**800-326-2822**	205-921-3135
Burlington Homes of Maine Inc 620 Main St	Oxford	ME	04270	**800-255-5218**	207-539-4406
Cavco Industries Inc					
1001 N Central Ave 8th Fl	Phoenix	AZ	85004	**800-790-9111**	602-256-6263
NASDAQ: CVCO					
Commodore Corp 1423 Lincolnway E	Goshen	IN	46526	**800-554-4285**	574-533-7100
Fleetwood Homes of Idaho Inc PO Box 1550	Nampa	ID	83653	**800-334-8958**	208-466-2438
Fleetwood Homes of Washington Inc					
211 5th St	Woodland	WA	98674	**800-275-6869***	360-225-9461
*Sales					
Franklin Homes Inc 10655 Hwy 43	Russellville	AL	35653	**800-332-4511**	256-332-4510
Fuqua Homes Inc 7100 S Cooper St	Arlington	TX	76001	**800-336-0874**	817-465-3211
Homes of Merit Inc PO Box 1606	Bartow	FL	33831	**800-589-8942**	863-533-0593
Horton Homes Inc 101 Industrial Blvd	Eatonton	GA	31024	**800-282-2680**	706-485-8506
Jacobsen Homes PO Box 368	Safety Harbor	FL	34695	**800-843-1559***	727-726-1138
*Sales					
Liberty Homes Inc 1101 Eisenhower Dr N	Goshen	IN	46526	**800-733-0431**	574-533-0431
NASDAQ: LIBHA					
Manufactured Housing Enterprises Inc					
09302 US SR 6	Bryan	OH	43506	**800-821-0220**	419-636-4511
McGrath RentCorp DBA Mobile Modular Management Corp 5700 Las Positas Rd	Livermore	CA	94551	**800-352-2900**	925-606-9200
NASDAQ: MGRC					
Mobile Modular Management Corp					
5700 Las Positas Rd	Livermore	CA	94551	**800-352-2900**	925-606-9200
NASDAQ: MGRC					
Mobile/Modular Express Inc					
1301 Trimble Rd	Edgewood	MD	21040	**800-321-7971**	410-676-3700
Nobility Homes Inc 3741 SW 7th St	Ocala	FL	34474	**800-476-6624**	352-732-5157
NASDAQ: NOBH					
Oxford Homes Inc PO Box 679	Oxford	ME	04270	**800-341-0436**	
R-Anell Custom Homes Inc 35439 Hwy 16 N	Denver	NC	28037	**800-951-5511**	704-483-5511
Resun Leasing Inc 22810 Quicksilver Dr	Dulles	VA	20166	**800-554-6506**	703-709-8880
Ritz-Craft Corp of Pennsylvania Inc					
15 Industrial Pk Rd	Mifflinburg	PA	17844	**800-326-9836**	570-966-1053
Satellite Industries Inc 2530 Xenium Ln N	Minneapolis	MN	55441	**800-328-3332**	763-553-1900
Schult Homes Corp 221 US 20 W	Middlebury	IN	46540	**800-516-7392**	574-825-5881
Skyline Corp 2520 By-Pass Rd	Elkhart	IN	46514	**800-348-7469**	574-294-6521
NYSE: SKY					
Victorian Homes 109 14th St	Middlebury	IN	46540	**800-999-5841**	574-825-5841
Wick Building Systems Inc 405 Walter Rd	Mazomanie	WI	53560	**800-356-9682**	608-795-4281
Williams Scotsman Inc 8211 Town Ctr Dr	Baltimore	MD	21236	**800-782-1500**	410-931-6000

496 MODEMS

SEE ALSO Computer Networking Products & Systems; Telecommunications Equipment & Systems

	City	State	ZIP	Toll-Free	Phone
3Com Corp 5403 Betsy Ross Dr	Santa Clara	CA	95054	**800-638-3266***	408-326-5000
NASDAQ: COMS ■ *Cust Svc					
ActionTec Electronics Inc 760 N Mary Ave	Sunnyvale	CA	94085	**800-752-7820**	408-752-7700
Arescom Inc 47338 Fremont Blvd	Fremont	CA	94538	**800-575-4736**	510-445-3638
Avocent Corp 4991 Corporate Dr	Huntsville	AL	35805	**800-932-9239**	256-430-4000
NASDAQ: AVCT					
Aztech Labs Inc 43264 Christy St	Fremont	CA	94538	**800-886-8859**	510-683-9800
Biscom Inc 321 Billerica Rd	Chelmsford	MA	01824	**800-477-2472**	978-250-1800
Castelle 855 Jarvis Dr Suite 100	Morgan Hill	CA	95037	**800-289-7555**	408-852-8000
NASDAQ: CSTL					
Cermetek Microelectronics Inc					
406 Tasman Dr	Sunnyvale	CA	94089	**800-882-6271**	408-752-5000
Com21 Inc 750 Tasman Dr	Milpitas	CA	95035	**888-266-2111**	408-953-9100
Comspec Digital Products Inc					
PO Box 178	Jacksonville	TX	75766	**800-490-6893**	832-443-4487
Connecticut microComputer Inc					
150 Pocono Rd	Brookfield	CT	06804	**800-426-2872**	203-740-9890

Classified Section

Company	City	State	Zip	Toll-Free	Phone
Copia International Ltd 1220 Iroquois Dr Suite 180	Naperville	IL	60563	**800-689-8898***	630-778-8898
*Sales					
CXR Telcom Corp 894 Faulstich Ct	San Jose	CA	95112	**800-537-5762**	510-657-8810
Dataforth Corp 3331 E Hemisphere Loop	Tucson	AZ	85706	**800-444-7644**	520-741-1404
DEI Inc 230 N Market Pl	Escondido	CA	92029	**800-732-8344**	760-743-8344
GRE America Inc 425 Harbor Blvd	Belmont	CA	94002	**800-233-5973**	650-591-1400
Internet Commerce Corp 805 3rd Ave 9th Fl	New York	NY	10022	**888-422-4401**	212-271-7640
NASDAQ: ICCA					
Konexx 5550 Oberlin Dr	San Diego	CA	92121	**800-275-6354**	858-622-1400
Motorola Canada Ltd 8133 Warden Ave	Markham	ON	L6G1B3	**800-268-3395**	905-948-5200
Motorola Inc 1301 E Algonquin Rd	Schaumburg	IL	60196	**800-331-6456**	847-576-5000
NYSE: MOT					
Multi-Tech Systems 2205 Woodale Dr	Mounds View	MN	55112	**800-328-9717***	763-785-3500
*Cust Svc					
Music Telecom Inc 580 Howard Ave	Somerset	NJ	08873	**800-648-3647**	732-469-0880
NEC USA Inc 8 Corporate Ctr Dr	Melville	NY	11747	**800-338-9549**	631-753-7000
Novatel Wireless Inc 9255 Towne Centre Dr Suite 225	San Diego	CA	92121	**888-888-9231**	858-320-8800
NASDAQ: NVTL					
SMART Modular Technologies Inc 4211 Starboard Dr	Fremont	CA	94538	**800-956-7627**	510-623-1231
Terayon Communication Systems Inc 4988 Great America Pkwy	Santa Clara	CA	95054	**888-783-7296**	408-235-5500
NASDAQ: TERN					
Toshiba America Information Systems Inc 9740 Irvine Blvd	Irvine	CA	92618	**800-457-7777***	949-583-3000
*Cust Svc					
Unlimited Systems Corp Inc DBA Konexx 5550 Oberlin Dr	San Diego	CA	92121	**800-275-6354**	858-622-1400
US Robotics Corp 935 National Pkwy	Schaumburg	IL	60173	**877-710-0884**	847-874-2000
Verilink Corp 127 Jetplex Cir	Madison	AL	35758	**800-926-0085**	256-327-2001
NASDAQ: VRLK					
Western Datacom Co Inc 959 Bassett Rd	Cleveland	OH	44145	**800-262-3311**	440-835-1510
Western Telematic Inc 5 Sterling	Irvine	CA	92618	**800-854-7226**	949-586-9950
Wi-LAN Inc 2891 Sunridge Way NE	Calgary	AB	T1Y7K7	**800-258-6876**	403-273-9133
Zoom Technologies Inc 207 South St	Boston	MA	02111	**800-666-6191**	617-423-1072
NASDAQ: ZOOM					
ZyXEL Communications Inc 1130 N Miller St	Anaheim	CA	92806	**800-255-4101**	714-632-0882

497 MOPS, SPONGES, WIPING CLOTHS

SEE ALSO Brushes & Brooms; Cleaning Products

Company	City	State	Zip	Toll-Free	Phone
A & B Wiper Supply Inc 5601 Paschall Ave	Philadelphia	PA	19143	**800-333-7247**	215-482-6100
ABCO Products Corp 6800 NW 36th Ave	Miami	FL	33147	**888-694-2226**	305-694-2226
Bro-Tex Inc 800 Hampden Ave	Saint Paul	MN	55114	**800-328-2282**	651-645-5721
Butler Home Products Inc 311 Hopping Brook Rd PO Box 8000	Holliston	MA	01746	**800-343-3368**	508-429-8100
Continental Mfg Co 305 Rock Industrial Pk Dr	Bridgeton	MO	63044	**800-325-1051**	314-656-4301
Disco Inc 1895 Brannan Rd	McDonough	GA	30253	**800-548-5150**	770-474-7575
Ettore Products Co 8469 Pardee Dr	Oakland	CA	94621	**800-438-8673**	510-638-4870
Golden Star Inc 400 E 10th Ave	North Kansas City	MO	64116	**800-821-2792**	816-842-0233
Greenwood Mop & Broom Inc PO Drawer 1426	Greenwood	SC	29648	**800-635-6849**	864-227-8411
Houston Wiper & Mill Supply Co 9800 Market St	Houston	TX	77029	**800-633-5968**	713-672-0571
Intex Supply Co 670 Alpha Dr	Highland Heights	OH	44143	**800-753-5822***	440-449-6550
*Cust Svc					
Kleen-Tex Industries Inc 1516 Orchard Hill Rd	LaGrange	GA	30240	**800-241-2323**	706-882-8134
Libman Co 220 N Sheldon St	Arcola	IL	61910	**800-646-6262**	217-268-4200
Magla Products LLC 159 South St	Morristown	NJ	07960	**800-247-5281**	973-984-7998
Mednik Riverbend 4245 Forest Pk Blvd	Saint Louis	MO	63108	**800-325-7193**	314-535-9090
Milliken & Co KEX Div 201 Lukken Industrial Dr W MS 801	LaGrange	GA	30240	**800-342-5539**	
O-Cedar Brands Inc 505 N Railroad Ave	North Lake	IL	60164	**800-332-8690**	
Plezall Wipers Inc 9869 NW 79th Ave	Hialeah Gardens	FL	33016	**800-237-8724**	305-556-3744
Signature Works Inc 1 Signature Dr	Hazlehurst	MS	39083	**800-647-2468**	601-894-1771
Southern Wipers 100 Fairview Rd	Asheville	NC	28803	**800-544-9387**	828-274-2100
Spontex Inc 100 Spontex Dr	Columbia	TN	38401	**800-251-4222**	931-388-5632
Tranzonic Cos 670 Alpha Dr	Highland Heights	OH	44143	**800-553-7979**	440-449-6550
TxF Products PO Box 1118	Brownwood	TX	76804	**800-441-7894**	325-646-1504
United Textile Co Inc 2225 Grant Ave	San Lorenzo	CA	94580	**800-233-0077**	510-276-2288
Wipe-Tex International Corp 110 E 153rd St	Bronx	NY	10451	**800-643-9607**	718-665-0013

498 MORTGAGE LENDERS & LOAN BROKERS

SEE ALSO Banks - Commercial & Savings

Company	City	State	Zip	Toll-Free	Phone
AAA Financial Corp 9601 W Sample Rd	Coral Springs	FL	33065	**800-881-2530**	954-344-2530
Aames Financial Corp 350 S Grand Ave 43rd Fl	Los Angeles	CA	90071	**800-829-2929**	323-210-5000
ABN AMRO Mortgage Group Inc 1643 N Harrison Pkwy Bldg H	Sunrise	FL	33323	**877-406-2967**	954-320-1000
Accredited Home Lenders Inc 15030 Ave of Science Suite 100	San Diego	CA	92128	**800-690-6000**	858-676-2100
NASDAQ: LEND					
AccuBanc Mortgage Corp 12377 Merit Dr Suite 600	Dallas	TX	75251	**800-457-1600**	972-982-7000
Ace Mortgage Funding Inc 777 Beachway Dr	Indianapolis	IN	46224	**888-223-9975**	317-246-5740
American Business Financial Services Inc PO Box11716 Suite 215	Philadelphia	PA	19101	**800-776-4001**	
American Home Mortgage Investment Corp 520 Broadhollow Rd	Melville	NY	11747	**800-755-3100**	516-949-3900
NYSE: AHM					
American Mortgage Express 3570 Camino Del Rio N Suite 300	San Diego	CA	92108	**800-700-0263**	619-521-3000
BRT Realty Trust 60 Cutter Mill Rd Suite 303	Great Neck	NY	11021	**800-450-5816**	516-466-3100
NYSE: BRT					
California Mortgage Service 400 N Tustin Ave Suite 220	Santa Ana	CA	92705	**800-995-8267**	714-835-1500
CapitalSource Inc 4445 Willard Ave 12th Fl	Chevy Chase	MD	20815	**866-876-8723**	301-841-2700
NYSE: CSE					
Carteret Mortgage Corp 6211 Centreville Rd Suite 800	Centreville	VA	20121	**877-227-8373**	703-802-8000
Cendant Mortgage 6000 Atrium Way	Mount Laurel	NJ	08054	**866-684-7334**	
Centex Home Equity Corp PO Box 199400	Dallas	TX	75219	**888-480-2432**	214-981-5000
Charter One Mortgage 10561 Telegraph Rd	Glen Allen	VA	23059	**800-876-2434**	804-627-4000
CharterMac 625 Madison Ave	New York	NY	10022	**800-600-6422**	212-421-5333
AMEX: CHC					
Chase Manhattan Mortgage Corp 343 Thornall St	Edison	NJ	08837	**800-848-9136**	732-205-0600
CIBC Mortgage Inc 100 University Ave	Toronto	ON	M5J2X4	**800-465-2422**	416-785-3255
Citi Financial Mortgage Co 5901 E Fowler Ave	Tampa	FL	33617	**800-217-1000**	813-984-8801
CitiMortgage Inc 15851 Clayton Rd	Ballwin	MO	63011	**800-283-7918**	
Colony Mortgage Corp 22983 Lorraine Rd	Fairview Park	OH	44026	**800-423-3085**	440-777-9999
Columbia National Inc 7142 Columbia Gateway Dr	Columbia	MD	21046	**800-444-7963**	410-872-2000
Continental Wingate Co Inc 63 Kendrick St	Needham	MA	02494	**800-332-0372**	781-707-9000
Countrywide Financial Corp 4500 Park Granada	Calabasas	CA	91302	**800-669-6607**	818-225-3000
NYSE: CFC					
CRIIMI MAE Inc 11200 Rockville Pike	Rockville	MD	20852	**800-266-0535**	301-816-2300
NYSE: CMM					
CTX Mortgage Co 3100 McKinnon St	Dallas	TX	75201	**800-666-5363**	214-981-5000
ditech.com 3200 Park Center Dr Suite 150	Costa Mesa	CA	92626	**800-803-7656**	714-800-5800
E-LOAN Inc 6230 Stone Ridge Mall Rd	Pleasanton	CA	94588	**888-356-2622**	925-847-6900
NASDAQ: EELN					
Emigrant Mortgage Co Inc 5 E 42nd St	New York	NY	10017	**888-364-4726**	212-850-4361
EverHome Mortgage Co 8100 Nations Way	Jacksonville	FL	32256	**800-669-9721***	904-281-6000
*Cust Svc					
Extraco Mortgage 7503 Bosque Blvd	Waco	TX	76712	**800-227-4894**	254-772-0202
Fannie Mae 3900 Wisconsin Ave NW	Washington	DC	20016	**800-732-6643**	202-752-7000
NYSE: FNM					
Farmer Mac (Federal Agricultural Mortgage Corp) 1133 21st St NW Suite 600	Washington	DC	20036	**800-879-3276**	202-872-7700
NYSE: AGM					
Federal Agricultural Mortgage Corp (Farmer Mac) 1133 21st St NW Suite 600	Washington	DC	20036	**800-879-3276**	202-872-7700
NYSE: AGM					
Federal Home Loan Mortgage Corp 8200 Jones Branch Dr	McLean	VA	22102	**800-373-3343**	703-903-3000
NYSE: FRE					
Finance America 16802 Aston St	Irvine	CA	92606	**800-690-8200**	949-440-1000
Financial Freedom Senior Funding Corp 7595 Irvine Ctr Dr Suite 250	Irvine	CA	92618	**800-500-5150**	949-341-9200
First Connecticut Capital Corp 1000 Bridgeport Ave	Shelton	CT	06484	**800-401-3222**	203-944-5400
First Eastern Mortgage Corp 100 Brickstone Sq	Andover	MA	01810	**800-777-2240**	978-749-3100
First NLC Financial Services Inc 700 W Hillsboro Blvd Bldg 1 Suite 204	Deerfield Beach	FL	33441	**800-950-3314**	954-420-0060
First Residential Mortgage Network Inc 9500 Ormsby Station Rd	Louisville	KY	40223	**800-585-9005**	502-315-4700
Freddie Mac 8200 Jones Branch Dr	McLean	VA	22102	**800-373-3343**	703-903-3000
NYSE: FRE					
North Central Region 333 W Wacker Dr Suite 2500	Chicago	IL	60606	**800-373-3343**	312-407-7400
Northeast Region 8200 Jones Branch Dr	McLean	VA	22102	**800-373-3343**	703-902-7700
Southeast/Southwest Region 2300 Windy Ridge Pkwy Suite 200N	Atlanta	GA	30339	**800-373-3343**	770-857-8800
Gershman Investment Corp 7 N Bemiston Ave	Clayton	MO	63105	**800-457-2357**	314-889-0600
GMAC Mortgage Corp 100 Witmer Rd	Horsham	PA	19044	**800-627-0128**	215-682-1000
Green Tree Servicing LLC 345 Saint Peter St Suite 600	Saint Paul	MN	55102	**800-423-9527**	651-293-3400
Guaranty Residential Lending Inc 1300 S Mopac Expy	Austin	TX	78746	**800-964-9420**	512-434-8000
H & R Block Mortgage Corp 3 Burlington Woods 2nd Fl	Burlington	MA	01803	**800-974-1899**	781-852-5600
HomeAdvisor 1 Microsoft Way	Redmond	WA	98052	**800-642-7676**	425-882-8080
HomeBanc Mortgage Corp 2002 Summit Blvd Suite 100	Atlanta	GA	30319	**866-926-8466**	404-459-7400
HomePath c/o FannieMae 3900 Wisconsin Ave NW	Washington	DC	20016	**800-732-6643**	202-752-7016
HomeSteps 500 Plano Pkwy	Carrollton	TX	75010	**800-972-7555**	
HSBC Mortgage Corp (USA) 2929 Walden Ave	Depew	NY	14043	**800-338-4626**	
Huntington Mortgage Co 7575 Huntington Park Dr	Columbus	OH	43235	**800-323-4695**	614-480-6505
IMX Inc 2305 Camino Ramon Suite 200	San Ramon	CA	94583	**800-401-4639**	
IndyMac Bank 1 Banting	Irvine	CA	92618	**800-731-0383**	949-585-3301
Inland Mortgage Corp 2901 Butterfield Rd	Oak Brook	IL	60523	**800-828-8999**	630-218-8000
Intuit Lender Services Inc PO Box 7850	Mountain View	CA	94039	**888-565-2488**	650-944-6000
Irwin Mortgage Corp 10300 Kincaid Dr	Fishers	IN	46038	**800-984-5363**	317-594-8900
JI Kislak Inc 7900 Miami Lakes Dr W	Miami Lakes	FL	33016	**800-233-7164**	305-364-4100
Kaufman & Broad Mortgage Co 10990 Wilshire Blvd 9th Fl	Los Angeles	CA	90024	**800-446-2624**	310-893-7300
Kislak JI Inc 7900 Miami Lakes Dr W	Miami Lakes	FL	33016	**800-233-7164**	305-364-4100
LendingTree Inc 11115 Rushmore Dr	Charlotte	NC	28277	**877-510-2659**	704-541-5351
Lennar Financial Services Inc 700 NW 107th Ave 3rd Fl	Miami	FL	33172	**800-741-8262**	305-223-9966
Lion Inc 2000 S Colorado Blvd Suite 350	Denver	CO	80222	**800-786-8083**	303-455-1800
LoanSurfer.com 12140 Woodcrest Executive Dr	Saint Louis	MO	63141	**877-434-4555**	314-628-2000
M & I Home Lending Solutions 4121 NW Urbandale Dr	Urbandale	IA	50322	**800-827-2654**	515-281-2807
M & I Mortgage Corp W 57 N 14280 Doerr Way	Cedarburg	WI	53012	**800-236-1221**	262-376-8484
M & T Mortgage Corp 1 Fountain Plaza	Buffalo	NY	14203	**800-724-7575**	716-848-7600
Market Street Mortgage Corp PO Box 22128	Tampa	FL	33622	**800-669-3210**	727-724-7000
Mercantile Mortgage Corp 2 Hopkins Plaza Suite 900	Baltimore	MD	21201	**800-874-7880**	410-347-8940
MidCoast Credit Corp 1926 10th Ave N Suite 400	Lake Worth	FL	33461	**800-218-5919**	561-540-6224
Midland Loan Services Inc 10851 Mastin	Overland Park	KS	66210	**800-327-8083**	913-253-9000
Midland Mortgage Co PO Box 26648	Oklahoma City	OK	73126	**800-654-4566**	

Company	City	State	Zip	Toll-Free	Phone
MortgageIT Holdings Inc 33 Maiden Ln *NYSE: MHL*	New York	NY	10038	**877-684-4826**	212-651-7700
MSN House & Home 1 Microsoft Way	Redmond	WA	98052	**800-642-7676**	425-882-8080
Municipal Mortgage & Equity LLC (MuniMae) 621 E Pratt St Suite 300 *NYSE: MMA*	Baltimore	MD	21202	**888-788-3863**	
MuniMae (Municipal Mortgage & Equity LLC) 621 E Pratt St Suite 300 *NYSE: MMA*	Baltimore	MD	21202	**888-788-3863**	
National City Mortgage Co 3232 Newmark Dr *Cust Svc	Miamisburg	OH	45342	**800-253-7313***	937-297-3600
National Rural Utilities Cooperative Finance Corp 2201 Cooperative Way Woodland Pk	Herndon	VA	20171	**800-424-2954**	703-709-6700
New Century Financial Corp 18400 Von Karman Ave Suite 1000 *NYSE: NEW*	Irvine	CA	92612	**800-967-7623**	949-440-7030
New South Federal Savings Bank 1900 Crestwood Blvd	Irondale	AL	35210	**800-366-3030**	205-951-4000
Nexstar Financial Corp 19 Research Pk Ct	Saint Charles	MO	63304	**877-706-7382**	636-685-9100
Option One Mortgage Corp 3 Ada	Irvine	CA	92618	**800-704-0800**	949-790-3600
Origen Financial Inc 27777 Franklin Rd Suite 1700 *NASDAQ: ORGN*	Southfield	MI	48034	**866-467-4436**	248-746-7000
Pulte Mortgage LLC 7475 S Joliet St	Englewood	CO	80112	**800-488-0053**	303-740-8800
Quicken Loans 20555 Victor Pkwy	Livonia	MI	48152	**888-565-2488**	734-805-7285
QuickenMortgage PO Box 7850	Mountain View	CA	94039	**888-565-2488**	650-944-6000
RBC Prism 222 Merchandise Mart Plaza Suite 550	Chicago	IL	60654	**877-217-9988**	312-494-0020
Regions Mortgage Inc 605 S Perry St	Montgomery	AL	36104	**800-392-5669**	334-223-3701
Reilly Mortgage Group Inc 2010 Corporate Ridge Suite 1000	McLean	VA	22102	**877-724-7792**	703-760-4700
Resource Bancshares Mortgage Group Inc 9710 Two Notch Rd	Columbia	SC	29223	**800-627-1991**	803-462-8000
Saxon Mortgage Inc 4880 Cox Rd	Glen Allen	VA	23060	**800-538-8202**	804-967-7400
SDF Realty Corp 1650 Hotel Circle N Suite 215	San Diego	CA	92108	**800-809-1952**	619-209-4777
Security Savings Mortgage Corp 217 2nd St NW Suite 1000	Canton	OH	44702	**800-421-8059**	330-455-5600
Shorewood CenTrust Mortgage Corp 1926 10th Ave N Suite 400	Lake Worth	FL	33461	**800-218-5919**	561-540-6224
SouthTrust Mortgage Corp 210 Wildwood Pkwy Suite 200	Birmingham	AL	35209	**800-239-2322**	205-667-8100
Sovereign Bank Wholesale Lending Div 1022 E Lancaster Ave	Rosemont	PA	19010	**888-696-8879**	610-525-1860
SunTrust Mortgage Inc 1001 Semmes Ave	Richmond	VA	23224	**800-634-7928**	804-291-0740
Transnational Financial Network Inc 401 Taraval St 2nd Fl *AMEX: TFN*	San Francisco	CA	94116	**888-229-2344**	415-242-7800
Universal American Mortgage Co 311 Park Place Blvd Suite 500	Clearwater	FL	33759	**800-696-4619**	727-791-2111
USA Lending Group 10542 S Jordan Gateway Suite 300	Salt lake City	UT	84095	**877-434-8042**	801-676-1200
Vanderbilt Mortgage & Finance Inc 500 Alcoa Trail	Maryville	TN	37804	**800-970-7250**	865-380-3000
Vestin Group Inc 2901 El Camino Ave Suite 206 *NASDAQ: VSTN*	Las Vegas	NV	89102	**800-232-7613**	702-227-0965
Wachovia Mortgage Corp 1100 Corporate Ctr Dr	Raleigh	NC	27607	**800-654-9322**	
Washington Mutual Mortgage Loan Corp 4305 Harrison Blvd Suite 10	Ogden	UT	84403	**800-756-8000**	801-626-2203
Waterfield Mortgage Co Inc 7500 W Jefferson Blvd	Fort Wayne	IN	46804	**800-444-9847**	260-434-8411
Wells Fargo Home Mortgage 405 SW 5th St	Des Moines	IA	50328	**800-288-3212**	515-237-6000

499 MORTUARY, CREMATORY, CEMETERY COMPANIES

Company	City	State	Zip	Toll-Free	Phone
AJ Desmond & Sons Funeral Directors 2600 Crooks Rd	Troy	MI	48084	**800-210-7135**	248-362-2500
Alderwoods Group Inc 259 Yorkland Rd *NASDAQ: AWGI*	Toronto	ON	M2J5R2	**800-206-6404**	416-498-2430
Baue Funeral Homes 620 Jefferson St	Saint Charles	MO	63301	**888-724-0073**	636-724-0073
Carriage Services Inc 1900 St James Pl 4th Fl *NYSE: CSV*	Houston	TX	77056	**800-692-3092**	713-332-8450
Cornerstone Family Services 155 Rittenhouse Cir *NASDAQ: STON*	Bristol	PA	19007	**877-857-8890**	215-826-2800
Dignity Memorial 1929 Allen Pkwy	Houston	TX	77019	**800-894-2024**	713-522-5141
Earthman Funeral Directors 2420 Fannin St	Houston	TX	77002	**800-654-2609**	713-659-3000
Forest Lawn Memorial-Parks & Mortuaries 1712 S Glendale Ave	Glendale	CA	91205	**800-204-3131**	323-254-7251
Neptune Society 4312 Woodman Ave 3rd Fl	Sherman Oaks	CA	91423	**888-637-8863**	818-953-9995
Palm Mortuary Inc 1325 N Main St	Las Vegas	NV	89101	**800-542-2902**	702-464-8300
Restland Funeral Home & Cemetary 13005 Greenville Ave	Dallas	TX	75243	**800-749-7379**	972-238-7111
Rose Hills Co 3888 S Workman Mill Rd	Whittier	CA	90601	**800-328-7526**	562-699-0921
Spring Grove Cemetery 4521 Spring Grove Ave	Cincinnati	OH	45232	**888-853-2230**	513-681-6680
Stewart Enterprises Inc 1333 S Clearview Pkwy *NASDAQ: STEI*	Jefferson	LA	70121	**800-257-1610**	504-729-1400
StoneMor Partners LP DBA Cornerstone Family Services 155 Rittenhouse Cir *NASDAQ: STON*	Bristol	PA	19007	**877-857-8890**	215-826-2800

500 MOTION PICTURE DISTRIBUTION & RELATED SERVICES

Company	City	State	Zip	Toll-Free	Phone
ABC News VideoSource 125 West End Ave 5th Fl	New York	NY	10023	**800-789-1250**	212-456-5421
Aims Multimedia 20765 Superior St	Chatsworth	CA	91311	**800-367-2467**	818-773-4300
Alliance Atlantis Communications Inc 121 Bloor St E Suite 1500 *NASDAQ: AACB*	Toronto	ON	M4W3M5	**877-345-9195**	416-967-1174
Alliance Entertainment Corp 4250 Coral Ridge Dr	Coral Springs	FL	33065	**800-329-7664**	954-255-4000
Anchor Bay Entertainment Inc 1699 Stutz Dr	Troy	MI	48084	**800-786-8777**	248-816-0909
Baker & Taylor Inc 2550 W Tyvola Rd Suite 300	Charlotte	NC	28217	**800-775-1800**	704-998-3100
Bridgestone Multimedia Group Inc 300 N McKemy Ave *Cust Svc	Chandler	AZ	85226	**800-622-3070***	480-940-5777
Central Park Media Corp 250 W 57th St Suite 317	New York	NY	10107	**800-833-7456**	212-977-7456
Clearvue & SVE 6465 N Avondale Ave	Chicago	IL	60631	**800-829-1900**	773-775-9433
Crown Media Holdings Inc 6430 S Fiddlers Green Cir Suite 225 *NASDAQ: CRWN*	Greenwood Village	CO	80111	**800-820-7990**	303-220-7990
Deluxe Media Services Inc 568 Atrium Dr	Vernon Hills	IL	60061	**800-745-7265**	847-990-4100
Desert Island Films 11 Coggeshall Cir	Middletown	RI	02842	**800-766-8550**	401-846-3453
Facets Multimedia Inc 1517 W Fullerton Ave	Chicago	IL	60614	**800-331-6197**	773-281-9075
Films for the Humanities & Sciences PO Box 2053	Princeton	NJ	08543	**800-257-5126**	609-275-1400
Home Vision Entertainment 4423 N Ravenswood Ave	Chicago	IL	60640	**800-826-3456**	773-878-2600
Image Entertainment Inc 20525 Nordhoff St Suite 200 *NASDAQ: DISK*	Chatsworth	CA	91311	**800-473-3475**	818-407-9100
Ingram Entertainment Inc 2 Ingram Blvd	La Vergne	TN	37089	**800-759-5000**	615-287-4000
Insight Media 2162 Broadway	New York	NY	10024	**800-233-9910**	212-721-6316
Inspired Corp 103 Eisenhower Pkwy	Roseland	NJ	07068	**800-738-3747**	973-226-1234
Kultur International Films Ltd 195 Hwy 36	West Long Branch	NJ	07764	**800-458-5887**	732-229-2343
Lions Gate Films Inc 4553 Glencoe Ave Suite 200	Marina del Rey	CA	90292	**800-424-7070**	310-449-9200
MPI Media Group 16101 S 108th Ave	Orland Park	IL	60467	**800-777-2223**	708-460-0555
Pyramid Media PO Box 1048	Santa Monica	CA	90406	**800-421-2303**	310-828-7577
Questar Inc 680 N Lake Shore Dr Suite 900	Chicago	IL	60611	**800-544-8422**	312-266-9400
Resolution Inc 19 Gregory Dr	South Burlington	VT	05403	**800-862-8900**	802-862-8881
Scholastic Corp 557 Broadway *NASDAQ: SCHL* ■ *Cust Svc	New York	NY	10012	**800-724-6527***	212-343-6100
Swank Motion Pictures Inc 201 S Jefferson Ave	Saint Louis	MO	63103	**800-876-5577**	314-534-6300
Terra Entertainment 12335 Santa Monica Blvd Suite 336	Los Angeles	CA	90025	**877-788-3772**	310-268-1210
Video Products Distributors 150 Parkshore Dr	Folsom	CA	95630	**800-366-2111**	916-605-1500
WRS Motion Picture & Video Laboratory 1000 Napor Blvd *Cust Svc	Pittsburgh	PA	15205	**800-345-6977***	412-937-7700

501 MOTION PICTURE PRE- & POST-PRODUCTION SERVICES

Company	City	State	Zip	Toll-Free	Phone
Avatar Studios Inc 2675 Scott Ave Suite G	Saint Louis	MO	63103	**800-737-6065**	314-533-2242
Century III at Universal Studios 2000 Universal Studios Plaza Suite 100	Orlando	FL	32819	**800-281-7501**	407-354-1000
Crawford Communications Inc 3845 Pleasantdale Rd	Atlanta	GA	30340	**800-831-8027**	404-876-7149
Crossman Post Production LLC DBA Crossman Digital Post 35 Lone Hollow	Sandy	UT	84092	**888-553-1958**	801-553-1958
DeLuxe Laboratories Inc 1377 N Serrano Ave	Hollywood	CA	90027	**800-233-5893**	323-462-6171
FPC Inc 6677 Santa Monica Blvd	Hollywood	CA	90038	**800-814-1333**	323-468-5774
GTN Inc 13320 Northend Ave	Oak Park	MI	48237	**888-225-5486**	248-548-2500
Match Frame 8531 Fairhaven	San Antonio	TX	78229	**800-929-2790**	210-614-5678
Post Group Inc 6335 Homewood Ave	Hollywood	CA	90028	**800-827-7896**	323-462-2300
Rainmaker LP 50 W 2nd Ave	Vancouver	BC	V5Y1B3	**800-616-4433**	604-874-8700
Resolution Inc 19 Gregory Dr	South Burlington	VT	05403	**800-862-8900**	802-862-8881
Saul Zaentz Co 2600 10th St	Berkeley	CA	94710	**800-227-0466**	510-549-1528
Saul Zaentz Film Center 2600 10th St	Berkeley	CA	94710	**800-227-0466**	510-549-1528
Victory Studios 2247 15th Ave W	Seattle	WA	98119	**888-282-1776**	206-282-1776
WRS Motion Picture & Video Laboratory 1000 Napor Blvd *Cust Svc	Pittsburgh	PA	15205	**800-345-6977***	412-937-7700
Zaentz Saul Co 2600 10th St	Berkeley	CA	94710	**800-227-0466**	510-549-1528

502 MOTION PICTURE PRODUCTION - SPECIAL INTEREST

SEE ALSO Animation Companies; Motion Picture & Television Production

Company	City	State	Zip	Toll-Free	Phone
Active Parenting Publishers 810 Franklin Ct SE Suite B	Marietta	GA	30067	**800-825-0060**	770-429-0565
Aims Multimedia 20765 Superior St	Chatsworth	CA	91311	**800-367-2467**	818-773-4300
American Educational Products Inc 401 W Hickory St PO Box 2121	Fort Collins	CO	80522	**800-446-8767**	970-484-7445
Automotive Services Training Network 4101 International Pkwy	Carrollton	TX	75007	**800-223-2786**	972-309-4000
AVW - TELAV Audio Visual Solutions 4545 W Davis St	Dallas	TX	75211	**800-225-5289**	214-634-9060
Baby Einstein Co LLC 1201 Grand Central Ave	Glendale	CA	91201	**800-793-1454**	818-265-6050
Bankers Training & Consulting Co 12250 Weber Hill Rd Suite 200	Saint Louis	MO	63127	**800-264-7600**	314-843-5656
Clearvue & SVE 6465 N Avondale Ave	Chicago	IL	60631	**800-829-1900**	773-775-9433
CRM Learning 2215 Faraday Ave Suite F	Carlsbad	CA	92008	**800-421-0833**	760-431-9800
Disney Educational Productions 105 Terry Dr Suite 120	Newtown	PA	18940	**800-295-5010**	
DSAT 30151 Tomas St	Rancho Santa Margarita	CA	92688	**800-729-7234**	
Fire & Emergency Training Network 4101 International Pkwy	Carrollton	TX	75007	**800-845-2443**	972-309-4000
Gail & Rice Productions Inc 21301 Civic Ctr Dr	Southfield	MI	48076	**800-860-1931**	248-799-5000

	City	St	Zip	Toll-Free	Phone
Grace & Wild Inc 23689 Industrial Park Dr	Farmington Hills	MI	48335	**800-451-6010**	248-471-6010
Hammond Communications Group Inc 173 Trade St	Lexington	KY	40511	**888-424-1878**	859-254-1878
Industrial Training Systems Corp 4101 International Pkwy	Carrollton	TX	75007	**800-727-2487**	972-309-4000
Intaglio Visual Arts & Technology 3855 Eastern Ave SE	Grand Rapids	MI	49508	**800-632-9153**	616-243-3300
Keystone Learning Systems Corp 5300 Westview Dr Suite 405	Frederick	MD	21703	**800-658-3358**	301-624-5590
Kultur International Films Ltd 195 Hwy 36	West Long Branch	NJ	07764	**800-458-5887**	732-229-2343
Law Enforcement Television Network 4101 International Pkwy	Carrollton	TX	75007	**800-535-5386**	972-309-4000
LearnCom Inc 714 Industrial Dr	Bensenville	IL	60106	**800-824-8889**	630-227-1080
Medcom Trainex 6060 Phyllis Dr	Cypress	CA	90630	**800-877-1443***	714-891-1443
*Cust Svc					
Medialink Worldwide Inc 708 3rd Ave 8th Fl	New York	NY	10017	**800-843-0677**	212-682-8300
NASDAQ: MDLK					
National Film Board of Canada PO Box 6100 Station Centre-Ville	Montreal	QC	H3C3H5	**800-267-7710**	514-283-9000
Nightingale-Conant Corp 6245 W Howard St	Niles	IL	60714	**800-323-3938***	847-647-0300
*Cust Svc					
Novations Training Solutions 4621 121st St	Urbandale	IA	50323	**888-776-8268**	515-224-0919
NTN Communications Inc 5966 La Place Ct Suite 100	Carlsbad	CA	92008	**888-752-9686**	760-438-7400
AMEX: NTN					
Questar Inc 680 N Lake Shore Dr Suite 900	Chicago	IL	60611	**800-544-8422**	312-266-9400
Trinity Workplace Learning 4101 International Pkwy	Carrollton	TX	75007	**800-624-2272**	972-309-4000
Veritech Corp 37 Prospect St	East Longmeadow	MA	01028	**800-525-5912**	413-525-3368

503 MOTION PICTURE & TELEVISION PRODUCTION

SEE ALSO Animation Companies; Motion Picture Production - Special Interest

	City	St	Zip	Toll-Free	Phone
Alliance Atlantis Communications Inc 121 Bloor St E Suite 1500	Toronto	ON	M4W3M5	**877-345-9195**	416-967-1174
NASDAQ: AACB					
Avatar Studios Inc 2675 Scott Ave Suite G	Saint Louis	MO	63103	**800-737-6065**	314-533-2242
Chicago Story 401 W Superior St	Chicago	IL	60610	**800-642-3173**	312-642-3173
Crawford Communications Inc 3845 Pleasantdale Rd	Atlanta	GA	30340	**800-831-8027**	404-876-7149
Guthy-Renker Corp 41550 Eclectic St Suite 200	Palm Desert	CA	92260	**800-321-4730**	760-773-9022
Hallmark Hall of Fame Productions Inc 12001 Ventura Pl Suite 300	Studio City	CA	91604	**800-425-5627**	818-505-9191
Lions Gate Entertainment Corp 595 Burrard St	Vancouver	BC	V7J3S5	**888-609-6120**	604-609-6100
NYSE: LGF					
Lions Gate Entertainment Corp Lions Gate Television Div 4553 Glencoe Ave Suite 200	Marina del Rey	CA	90292	**800-424-7070**	310-449-9200
Lions Gate Films Inc 4553 Glencoe Ave Suite 200	Marina del Rey	CA	90292	**800-424-7070**	310-449-9200
Peace Arch Entertainment Group Inc 150 W 1st Ave Suite 200	Vancouver	BC	V5Y1A4	**888-588-3608**	604-681-9308
AMEX: PAE					
Pixar Animation Studios 1200 Park Ave	Emeryville	CA	94608	**800-888-9856**	510-752-3000
NASDAQ: PIXR					
PRIMEDIA Productions 4101 International Pkwy	Carrollton	TX	75007	**800-761-4386**	972-309-4700
Voodoo Films Inc 728 E Hennepin Ave	Minneapolis	MN	55414	**888-866-3666**	612-617-0000

MOTION PICTURE THEATERS

SEE Theaters - Motion Picture

504 MOTOR SPEEDWAYS

	City	St	Zip	Toll-Free	Phone
Bandimere Speedway 3051 S Rooney Rd	Morrison	CO	80465	**800-664-8946**	303-697-6001
Big Daddy's South Boston Speedway 1188 James D Hagood Hwy PO Box 1066	South Boston	VA	24592	**877-440-1540**	434-572-4947
California Speedway 9300 Cherry Ave	Fontana	CA	92335	**800-944-7223**	909-429-5000
Elko Speedway 26350 France Ave	Elko	MN	55020	**800-479-3630**	952-461-7223
Heartland Park Topeka 1805 SW 71st St	Topeka	KS	66619	**800-437-2237**	785-862-4781
Infineon Raceway Hwys 37 & 121	Sonoma	CA	95476	**800-870-7223**	707-938-8448
Las Vegas Motor Speedway 7000 Las Vegas Blvd N	Las Vegas	NV	89115	**800-644-4444**	702-644-4444
Lime Rock Park 497 Lime Rock Rd	Lakeville	CT	06039	**800-722-3577**	860-435-5000
Marion County International Raceway 2303 Richwood-LaRue Rd	La Rue	OH	43332	**800-422-6247**	740-499-3666
Memphis Motorsports Park 5500 Taylor-Forge DR	Millington	TN	38053	**866-407-7333**	901-358-7223
Michigan International Speedway 12626 US 12	Brooklyn	MI	49230	**800-354-1010**	517-592-6666
Mid-Ohio Sports Car Course 7721 Steam Corners Rd PO Box 3108	Lexington	OH	44904	**800-643-6446**	419-884-4000
Nazareth Speedway Hwy 191	Nazareth	PA	18064	**888-629-7223**	610-759-8000
Pocono Raceway Long Pond Rd PO Box 500	Long Pond	PA	18334	**800-722-3929**	570-646-2300
Road America PO Box P	Elkhart Lake	WI	53020	**800-365-7223**	920-892-4576
Road Atlanta Raceway 5300 Winder Hwy	Braselton	GA	30517	**800-849-7223**	770-967-6143
Speedway of Southern New Mexico 3590 W Picacho Ave	Las Cruces	NM	88005	**800-658-9650**	505-524-7913
Texas Motorplex PO Box 1439	Ennis	TX	75120	**800-668-6775**	972-878-2641

505 MOTOR VEHICLES - COMMERCIAL & SPECIAL PURPOSE

SEE ALSO All-Terrain Vehicles; Automobiles - Mfr; Campers, Travel Trailers, Motor Homes; Motorcycles & Motorcycle Parts & Accessories; Snowmobiles; Weapons & Ordnance (Military)

	City	St	Zip	Toll-Free	Phone
Allied Body Works Inc 625 S 96th St	Seattle	WA	98108	**800-733-7450**	206-763-7811
American LaFrance Corp 8500 Palmetto Commerce Pkwy	Lodson	SC	29456	**888-253-8725**	843-486-7400
ASV Inc 840 Lilly Ln	Grand Rapids	MN	55744	**800-346-5954**	218-327-3434
NASDAQ: ASVI					
Auto Truck Inc 1200 N Ellis St	Bensenville	IL	60106	**877-284-4440**	630-860-5600
Benson International Inc Rt 14 S PO Box 970	Mineral Wells	WV	26150	**877-489-9020**	304-489-9020
Blue Bird Corp 402 Blue Bird Blvd	Fort Valley	GA	31030	**800-486-7122**	478-825-2021
Bowie Mfg Inc 313 S Hancock	Lake City	IA	51449	**800-831-0960**	712-464-3191
Capacity of Texas Inc 401 Capacity Dr	Longview	TX	75604	**800-323-0135**	903-759-0610
Carnegie Body Co 9500 Brookpark Rd	Cleveland	OH	44129	**800-362-1989**	216-749-5000
Champion Bus Inc 331 Graham Rd	Imlay City	MI	48444	**800-776-4943**	810-724-6474
Chance Rides Mfg Inc 4219 Irving St	Wichita	KS	67209	**800-242-6231**	316-942-7411
Club Car Inc PO Box 204658	Augusta	GA	30917	**800-227-0739**	706-863-3000
Columbia ParCar Corp 350 N Dewey Ave	Reedsburg	WI	53959	**800-222-4653**	608-524-8888
Curtis Tractor Cab Inc 111 Higgins St	Worcester	MA	01606	**800-343-7676**	508-853-2200
Dealers Truck Equipment Co 2460 Midway St	Shreveport	LA	71108	**800-259-7569**	318-635-7567
Diamond Coach Corp 2300 W 4th St	Oswego	KS	67356	**800-442-4645**	620-795-2191
Douglass Truck Bodies Inc 231 21st St	Bakersfield	CA	93301	**800-635-7641**	661-327-0258
DST Industries Inc 34364 Goddard Rd	Romulus	MI	48174	**800-327-6174**	734-941-0300
Electric Golf Car Co 1022 Douglas Blvd	Roseville	CA	95678	**800-700-8857**	916-773-2244
Elliott Machine Works Inc 146 Rensch Ave	Galion	OH	44833	**800-299-0412**	419-468-4709
Erie Vehicle Co 60 E 51st St	Chicago	IL	60615	**888-550-3743**	773-536-6300
Featherlite Luxury Coaches Inc 4441 Orange Blvd	Sanford	FL	32771	**888-826-8273**	407-323-1120
Fleet Engineers Inc 1800 E Keating Ave	Muskegon	MI	49442	**800-333-7890***	231-777-2537
*Cust Svc					
Florig Equipment Inc 906 W Ridge Pike	Conshohocken	PA	19428	**800-345-6172**	610-825-0900
Fontaine Modification Co 9827 Mt Holly Rd	Charlotte	NC	28214	**800-989-2113**	704-391-1355
Fontaine Truck Equipment Co 2490 Pinson Valley Pkwy	Birmingham	AL	35217	**800-824-3033**	205-841-8582
Freightliner Corp 4747 N Channel Ave	Portland	OR	97217	**800-385-4357***	503-735-8000
*Cust Svc					
GEMTOP Mfg Inc 8811 SE Herbert Ct	Clackamas	OR	97015	**800-547-9706**	503-659-3733
Gillig Corp 25800 Clawiter Rd	Hayward	CA	94545	**800-735-1500**	510-785-1500
Hackney & Sons Inc 400 Hackney Ave	Washington	NC	27889	**800-763-0700**	252-946-6521
Heil Environmental Industries Ltd 5751 Cornelison Rd Bldg B	Chattanooga	TN	37411	**800-824-4345**	423-899-9100
Hercules Mfg Co 800 Bob Posey St	Henderson	KY	42420	**800-633-3031**	270-826-9501
Hesse Inc 6700 St John Ave	Kansas City	MO	64123	**800-821-5562**	816-483-7808
HME Inc 1950 Byron Ctr Ave	Wyoming	MI	49519	**800-669-9192**	616-534-1463
IC Corp 751 S Harkrider St	Conway	AR	72032	**800-993-7686***	501-327-7761
*Cust Svc					
Jerr-Dan Corp 1080 Hykes Rd	Greencastle	PA	17225	**800-926-9666***	717-597-7111
*Sales					
Johnson Truck Bodies LLC 215 E Allen St	Rice Lake	WI	54868	**800-922-8360***	715-234-7071
*Sales					
Kidron Inc PO Box 17	Kidron	OH	44636	**800-321-5421**	330-857-3011
KME Fire Apparatus 68 Sicker Rd	Latham	NY	12110	**800-394-5593**	518-861-8535
Les Entreprises Michel Corbeil Inc 830 12th Ave	Saint-Lin-Laurentides	QC	J5M2V9	**888-439-3577**	450-439-3577
Lodal Inc 620 N Hooper St	Kingsford	MI	49802	**800-435-3500**	906-779-1700
LZ Truck Equipment Co Inc 1881 Rice St	Roseville	MN	55113	**800-247-1082**	651-488-2571
Masterack-Crown Inc 4171 B Lincolnway E	Wooster	OH	44691	**800-321-4934***	330-262-6010
*Cust Svc					
Meyer Truck Equipment Inc 196 W State Rd 56	Jasper	IN	47546	**800-456-3451**	812-695-3451
Mickey Truck Bodies Inc 1305 Trinity Ave PO Box 2044	High Point	NC	27261	**800-334-9061**	336-882-6806
Miller Industries Inc 8503 Hilltop Dr	Ooltewah	TN	37363	**800-292-0330**	423-238-4171
NYSE: MLR					
Monroe Truck Equipment Inc 1051 W 7th St	Monroe	WI	53566	**800-356-8134**	608-328-8127
Morgan Corp 35 Thousand Oaks Blvd	Morgantown	PA	19543	**800-666-7426**	610-286-5025
Morgan Olson Corp 1801 S Nottawa Rd	Sturgis	MI	49091	**800-624-9005**	269-659-0200
Motor Coach Industries International Co 1700 E Golf Rd	Schaumburg	IL	60173	**800-743-3624**	847-285-2000
Ottawa Truck Inc 415 E Dundee St	Ottawa	KS	66067	**888-229-6300**	785-242-2200
Parco-Hesse Corp 1060 Andre-Line Rd	Granby	QC	J2J1J9	**800-363-5975**	450-378-4696
Parkhurst Mfg Co 18997 Hwy Y	Sedalia	MO	65302	**800-821-7380**	660-826-8685
Pierce Mfg Inc 2600 American Dr	Appleton	WI	54914	**888-974-3723***	920-832-3000
*Cust Svc					
Prevost Car Inc 35 boul Gagnon	Sainte-Claire	QC	G0R2V0	**800-463-8876**	418-883-3391
R & S/Godwin Truck Body Co LLC 5168 S US Hwy 23	Ivel	KY	41642	**800-826-7413**	606-874-2151
Reading Truck Body Inc 10 Hancock Blvd	Reading	PA	19611	**800-458-2226**	610-775-3301
Road Rescue Inc 2914 Spartan Pl	Marion	SC	29571	**800-328-3804**	843-676-2900
Rocket Supply Corp 404 N Hwy 115	Roberts	IL	60962	**800-252-6871**	217-395-2278
Saf-T-Cab Inc 3241 S Parkway Dr	Fresno	CA	93725	**800-344-7491**	559-268-5541
Scania USA Inc 121 Interpark Blvd Suite 601	San Antonio	TX	78216	**800-272-2642**	210-403-0007
Schetky Northwest Sales Inc 8430 NE Killingsworth St	Portland	OR	97220	**800-255-8341**	503-287-4141
Segway LLC 14 Technology Dr	Bedford	NH	03110	**866-473-4929**	603-222-6000
Shealy's Truck Center Inc 1340 Bluff Rd	Columbia	SC	29201	**800-951-8580**	803-771-0176
Somerset Welding & Steel Inc 10558 Somerset Pike	Somerset	PA	15501	**800-598-8552***	814-445-9312
*Sales					
Specialized Vehicles Corp 400 Hackney Ave	Washington	NC	97889	**800-763-0700**	252-946-6521
STAHL A Scott Fetzer Co 3201 W Old Lincoln Way	Wooster	OH	44691	**800-392-7251**	330-264-7441
Sterling Truck Corp 4420 Sherwin Rd	Willoughby	OH	44094	**888-785-4357***	440-269-5500
*Cust Svc					
Supreme Corp 2581 E Kerchen Rd PO Box 463	Goshen	IN	46527	**800-642-4889**	574-642-4888
Supreme Industries Inc 2581 E Kerchen Rd PO Box 463	Goshen	IN	46527	**800-642-4889**	574-642-3070
AMEX: STS					
Sutphen Corp 7000 Columbus-Marysville Rd	Amlin	OH	43002	**800-726-7030**	614-889-1005
Tafco Equipment Co Inc 1304 W 1st St	Blue Earth	MN	56013	**800-328-3189***	507-526-3247
*Sales					
Tesco Williamsen Inc 1925 W Indiana Ave	Salt Lake City	UT	84104	**800-828-9847**	801-973-9400

	City	State	Zip	Toll-Free	Phone
Trail King Industries Inc 147 Industrial Pk Rd	Brookville	PA	15825	**800-545-1549**	814-849-2342
Truck Utilities Inc 2370 English St	Saint Paul	MN	55109	**800-869-1075**	651-484-3305
Tymco Inc 225 E Industrial Blvd	Waco	TX	76705	**800-258-9626**	254-799-5546
Unicell Body Co 571 Howard St	Buffalo	NY	14206	**800-628-8914***	716-853-8628
*Cust Svc					
Union City Body Co 301 S Jackson Pike	Union City	IN	47390	**888-990-8222**	765-964-3121
Wheeled Coach Industries Inc 2737 N Forsyth Rd	Winter Park	FL	32792	**800-342-0720**	407-677-7777
Wittke Inc 1496 Brier Park Crescent NW	Medicine Hat	AB	T1C1T8	**877-948-8531**	403-527-8806
Worldwide Equipment Inc Kentucky Rt 1428 E PO Box 1370	Prestonsburg	KY	41653	**800-307-4746**	606-874-2172

506 MOTORCYCLES & MOTORCYCLE PARTS & ACCESSORIES

	City	State	Zip	Toll-Free	Phone
Answer Products Inc 28209 Ave Stanford	Valencia	CA	91355	**800-423-0273***	661-257-4411
*Cust Svc					
Corbin 2360 Technology Pkwy	Hollister	CA	95023	**800-538-5035**	831-634-1100
CycoActive Inc 701 34th Ave	Seattle	WA	98122	**800-491-2926**	206-323-2349
Edelbrock Corp 2700 California St	Torrance	CA	90503	**800-739-3737**	310-781-2222
NASDAQ: EDEL					
Fulmer Co 122 Gayoso Ave	Memphis	TN	38103	**800-467-2400**	901-525-5711
Harley-Davidson Inc 3700 W Juneau Ave	Milwaukee	WI	53208	**800-443-2153**	414-342-4680
NYSE: HDI					
National Cycle Inc 2200 Maywood Dr	Maywood	IL	60153	**877-972-7336**	708-343-0400
Rivco Products Inc 440 S Pine St	Burlington	WI	53105	**888-801-8222**	262-763-8222
Summit Industries Inc 1220 W Railroad St	Corona	CA	92882	**800-347-8664**	951-371-1744
Yamaha Motor Corp USA 6555 Katella Ave	Cypress	CA	90630	**800-962-7926***	714-761-7300
*Cust Svc					

MOTORS - FLUID POWER

SEE Pumps & Motors - Fluid Power

507 MOTORS (ELECTRIC) & GENERATORS

SEE ALSO Automotive Parts & Supplies - Mfr

	City	State	Zip	Toll-Free	Phone
Alaska Diesel Electric Inc 4420 14th Ave NW	Seattle	WA	98107	**800-762-0165**	206-789-3880
AMK Drives & Controls Inc 5631 S Laburnum Ave	Richmond	VA	23231	**800-385-3929**	804-222-0323
AO Smith Corp 11270 W Park Pl Suite 170	Milwaukee	WI	53224	**800-359-4065**	414-359-4000
NYSE: AOS					
Apex Microtechnology Corp 5980 N Shannon Rd	Tucson	AZ	85741	**800-421-1865**	520-690-8600
Arco Electric Products Corp 2325 E Michigan Rd	Shelbyville	IN	46176	**800-428-4370**	317-398-9713
Aura Systems Inc 2335 Alaska Ave	El Segundo	CA	90245	**800-909-2872***	310-643-5300
*Cust Svc					
Autotrol Corp PO Box 557	Crystal Lake	IL	60039	**800-228-6207**	815-459-3080
Axsys Technologies Motion Control Products 7603 St Andrew Ave Suite H	San Diego	CA	92154	**800-777-3393***	619-671-5400
*Cust Svc					
Bodine Electric Co 2500 W Bradley Pl	Chicago	IL	60618	**800-726-3463**	773-478-3515
Bosch Rexroth Corp 5150 Prairie Stone Pkwy	Hoffman Estates	IL	60192	**800-860-1055**	847-645-3600
Briggs & Stratton Power Products Group LLC PO Box 239	Jefferson	WI	53549	**800-270-1408**	920-674-3750
CALEX Mfg Co 2401 Stanwell Dr	Concord	CA	94520	**800-542-3355**	925-687-4411
Cleveland Motion Controls Inc Torque Systems Div 6 Enterprise Rd	Billerica	MA	01821	**800-669-5112**	978-667-5100
Danaher Motion 1500 Mittel Blvd	Wood Dale	IL	60191	**866-993-2624**	630-860-7300
Ducommun Technologies Inc 23301 Wilmington Ave	Carson	CA	90745	**800-421-5032**	310-513-7200
Dumore Corp 1030 Veterans St	Mauston	WI	53948	**888-467-8288**	608-847-6420
Electrical Products Co 531 N 4th St	Tipp City	OH	45371	**800-543-9450**	937-667-2431
Electro Sales Inc 100 Fellsway W	Somerville	MA	02145	**888-789-0500**	617-666-0500
Electro-Tec Corp 1501 N Main St	Blacksburg	VA	24060	**800-382-5366**	540-552-2111
Elwood Corp Gettys Group 2701 N Green Bay Rd	Racine	WI	53404	**800-566-5274**	262-637-6591
Emoteq Corp 10002 E 43rd St	Tulsa	OK	74146	**800-221-7572***	918-627-1845
*Sales					
Franklin Electric Co Inc 400 E Spring St	Bluffton	IN	46714	**800-269-0063**	260-824-2900
NASDAQ: FELE					
GE Consumer Products Appliance Pk	Louisville	KY	40225	**800-626-2000**	502-452-4311
Glentek Inc 208 Standard St	El Segundo	CA	90245	**800-232-4485**	310-322-3026
Howell Electric Motors 900 North Ave	Plainfield	NJ	07061	**800-346-9350**	908-756-8800
Joliet Equipment Corp PO Box 114	Joliet	IL	60434	**800-435-9350**	815-727-6606
Katolight Corp 100 Power Dr	Mankato	MN	56001	**800-325-5450**	507-625-7973
Kirkwood Industries Inc 4855 W 130th St	Cleveland	OH	44135	**800-262-2266***	216-267-6200
*Cust Svc					
Kraft WA Corp 199 Wildwood Ave	Woburn	MA	01801	**800-969-6121**	781-938-9100
Kurz Electric Solutions Inc 736 Ford St	Kimberly	WI	54136	**800-776-3629**	920-734-5644
Lincoln Motors 28300 Euclid Ave	Cleveland	OH	44092	**800-668-6748**	216-731-4790
Louis Allis Large Motor Corp PO Box 610	Hayden	AL	35079	**866-568-4700**	205-590-2986
Minarik Corp 905 E Thompson Ave	Glendale	CA	91201	**800-427-2757**	818-637-7500
Molon Motor & Coil Corp 3737 Industrial Ave	Rolling Meadows	IL	60008	**800-526-6867**	847-253-6000
Motor Appliance Corp 555 Spirit of St Louis Blvd	Chesterfield	MO	63005	**800-622-3406**	636-532-3406
Motor Products Owosso Corp 201 S Delaney Rd	Owosso	MI	48867	**800-248-3841**	989-725-5151
PennEngineering & Mfg Corp 5190 Old Easton Rd	Danboro	PA	18916	**800-237-4736**	215-766-8853
Phytron Inc 1347 Main St	Waltham	MA	02451	**800-967-4987**	781-647-3581
Piller Inc 334 CR 49	Middletown	NY	10940	**800-597-6937**	845-355-5000
RAE Corp 4615 W Prime Pkwy	McHenry	IL	60050	**800-323-7049**	815-385-3500
Smith AO Corp 11270 W Park Pl Suite 170	Milwaukee	WI	53224	**800-359-4065**	414-359-4000
NYSE: AOS					
Specialty Motors Inc 25060 Ave Tibbitts	Valencia	CA	91355	**800-232-2612**	661-257-7388
Sterling Electric Inc 16752 Armstrong Ave	Irvine	CA	92606	**800-654-6220***	949-474-0520
*Cust Svc					
Stimple & Ward Co 3400 Babcock Blvd	Pittsburgh	PA	15237	**800-792-6457**	412-364-5200
Swiger Coils Systems Inc 4677 Manufacturing Rd	Cleveland	OH	44135	**800-321-3310**	216-362-7500
Toshiba International Corp 13131 W Little York Rd	Houston	TX	77041	**800-231-1412**	713-466-0277
Transicoil 2560 General Armistead Ave	Norristown	PA	19403	**800-323-7115**	610-539-4400
Unico Inc 3725 Nicholson Rd	Franksville	WI	53126	**800-245-1859**	262-886-5678
Unitron Inc PO Box 38902	Dallas	TX	75238	**800-527-1279**	214-340-8600
US Electrical Motors 8100 W Florissant Ave Bldg K	Saint Louis	MO	63136	**888-637-7333**	314-553-2000
Vicor Corp 25 Frontage Rd	Andover	MA	01810	**800-869-5300**	978-470-2900
NASDAQ: VICR					
WA Kraft Corp 199 Wildwood Ave	Woburn	MA	01801	**800-969-6121**	781-938-9100
Warfield Electric Co Inc 175 Industry Ave	Frankfort	IL	60423	**800-435-9346**	815-469-4094
Welco Technologies 200 Technicenter Dr Suite 205	Milford	OH	45150	**800-715-6006**	513-831-5335
Yamaha Motor Corp USA 6555 Katella Ave	Cypress	CA	90630	**800-962-7926***	714-761-7300
*Cust Svc					
Yaskawa Electric America Inc 2121 Norman Dr	Waukegan	IL	60085	**800-927-5292**	847-887-7000

508 MOVING COMPANIES

SEE ALSO Trucking Companies

	City	State	Zip	Toll-Free	Phone
Ace World Wide Moving 1900 E College Ave	Cudahy	WI	53110	**800-223-6683**	414-764-1000
Air Van Moving Group 10510 NE Northup Way Suite 110	Kirkland	WA	98033	**800-877-1442**	425-629-4101
Allied International NA Inc 700 Oakmont Ln	Westmont	IL	60559	**800-323-1909**	630-570-3500
Allied Van Lines Inc 700 Oakmont Ln	Westmont	IL	60559	**800-762-4689***	630-570-3000
*Cust Svc					
American Red Ball International Inc 9750 3rd Ave NE Suite 200	Seattle	WA	98115	**800-669-6424**	206-526-1730
American Red Ball Transit Co Inc 1335 Sadlier Circle E Dr	Indianapolis	IN	46239	**800-733-8077**	317-353-8331
Amodio Moving & Storage Inc 1 Hartford Sq	New Britain	CT	06052	**800-326-6346**	860-223-2725
Andrews Van Lines Inc 310 S 7th St	Norfolk	NE	68701	**800-228-8146***	402-371-5440
*Cust Svc					
Arnoff Moving & Storage Inc 1282 Dutchess Tpke	Poughkeepsie	NY	12603	**800-633-6683**	845-471-1504
Arpin Paul Van Lines 99 James P Murphy Hwy	West Warwick	RI	02893	**800-343-3500**	401-828-8111
Atlantic Relocation Systems Inc 1314 Chattahoochee Ave NW	Atlanta	GA	30318	**800-241-1140***	404-351-5311
*Cust Svc					
Atlas Van Lines Inc 1212 St George Rd	Evansville	IN	47711	**800-638-9797**	812-424-2222
B Von Paris & Sons Inc 8691 Larkin Rd	Savage	MD	20763	**800-866-6355**	410-888-8500
Barrett Moving & Storage Co 7100 Washington Ave S	Eden Prairie	MN	55344	**800-879-1283**	952-944-6550
Bay State Moving Systems Inc 60 Haynes Cir	Chicopee	MA	01020	**800-388-7411**	413-592-6381
Bekins Van Lines LLC 330 S Mannheim Rd	Hillside	IL	60162	**800-723-5467**	708-547-2000
Berger Transfer & Storage Inc 2950 Long Lake Rd	Saint Paul	MN	55113	**800-328-2459**	651-639-2260
Beverly Hills Transfer & Storage Co 15500 S Main St	Gardena	CA	90248	**800-999-7114**	310-276-1121
Bisson Moving & Storage 76 New Meadows Rd	West Bath	ME	04530	**800-370-4011**	207-442-7991
Bohrens United Van Lines 3 Applegate Dr	Robbinsville	NJ	08691	**800-326-4736**	609-208-1470
Bolliger Inc 120 Viaduct Rd	Stamford	CT	06907	**800-243-9517**	203-324-5999
Buehler Moving & Storage Co 3899 Jackson St	Denver	CO	80205	**800-234-6683**	303-388-4000
Cartwright Transportation Services 11901 Cartwright Ave	Grandview	MO	64030	**877-455-5991**	816-763-2700
Castine Movers 1235 Chestnut St	Athol	MA	01331	**800-225-8068**	978-249-9105
Coast to Coast Moving & Storage Co 470 Pulaski St	Brooklyn	NY	11221	**800-872-6683**	718-443-5800
Cook Moving Systems Inc 1845 Dale Rd	Buffalo	NY	14225	**800-828-7144**	716-897-0700
Corrigan Moving Systems 23923 Research Dr	Farmington Hills	MI	48335	**800-446-1996**	248-471-4000
Davidson Transfer & Storage Co 6600 Frankford Ave	Baltimore	MD	21206	**800-285-4387**	410-488-9200
DeVries Moving Packing & Storage 3808 N Sullivan Rd Spokane Industrial Pk Bldg 22	Spokane Valley	WA	99216	**800-333-6352**	509-924-6000
East Side Moving & Storage PO Box 86216	Portland	OR	97286	**800-547-4600**	503-777-4181
Fogarty Van Lines 1103 E Cumberland Ave	Tampa	FL	33602	**800-237-7529**	813-228-7481
Giant Van Lines 8215 Patuxent Range Rd	Jessup	MD	20794	**866-442-6863**	301-490-5790
Graebel Van Lines Inc 16346 E Airport Circle	Aurora	CO	80011	**800-723-6683**	303-214-6680
Hilford Moving & Storage 1595 S Arundell Ave	Ventura	CA	93003	**800-739-6683**	805-642-0221
Hollister Moving & Storage 1650 Lana Way	Hollister	CA	95023	**800-696-6250**	831-637-6250
I-Go Van & Storage 9820 S 142nd St	Omaha	NE	68138	**800-228-9276**	402-891-1222
Interdean.Interconex 55 Hunter Ln	Elmsford	NY	10523	**800-952-7230**	914-347-6600
Johnson Storage & Moving Co 221 Broadway	Denver	CO	80203	**800-289-6683**	303-785-4310
King Relocation Services 13535 Larwin Cir	Santa Fe Springs	CA	90670	**800-854-3679**	562-921-0555
Leppla Moving & Storage Co 303 W Southern Ave	Mesa	AZ	85210	**800-922-6344**	480-964-1444
Mayflower Transit Inc 1 Mayflower Dr	Fenton	MO	63026	**800-428-1234**	636-305-4000
McCollister's Transportation Group Inc 1800 Rt 130 N	Burlington	NJ	08016	**800-257-9595**	609-386-0600
Moving Express 9180 Kelvin Ave	Chatsworth	CA	91311	**800-844-3977**	818-591-8579
Nassau World Wide Movers Inc 63 Lamar St	West Babylon	NY	11704	**800-327-9343**	631-420-8340
National Van Lines Inc 2800 W Roosevelt Rd	Broadview	IL	60155	**800-323-1962**	708-450-2900
Nationwide Van Lines Inc 5450 S State Rd 7 Suite 39	Hollywood	FL	33314	**800-310-0056**	954-585-3945
Nelson Westerberg Inc 1500 Arthur Ave Suite 200	Elk Grove Village	IL	60007	**800-245-2080**	847-437-2080
NorthStar Moving Corp 9324 Corbin Ave	Northridge	CA	91324	**800-275-7767**	818-727-0128
Palmer Moving & Storage Co 24660 Dequindre Rd	Warren	MI	48091	**800-521-3954**	586-834-3400

Name / Address	City	State	Zip	Toll-Free	Phone
Paul Arpin Van Lines 99 James P Murphy Hwy	West Warwick	RI	02893	**800-343-3500**	401-828-8111
Paxton Van Lines Inc 5300 Port Royal Rd.	Springfield	VA	22151	**800-336-4536**	703-321-7600
Pickens-Kane Moving Co 410 N Milwaukee Ave	Chicago	IL	60610	**800-853-6462**	312-942-0330
S & M Moving Systems Inc 12128 Burke St	Santa Fe Springs	CA	90670	**800-336-5556**	562-567-2100
Security Storage Co 1701 Florida Ave NW	Washington	DC	20009	**800-736-6825**	202-234-5600
Smith Dray Line 320 Frontage Rd.	Greenville	SC	29611	**800-327-5673**	864-269-3696
Starving Students Moving & Storage Co 1850 Sawtelle Blvd 3rd Fl	Los Angeles	CA	90025	**800-441-6683**	310-854-4464
Stevens Worldwide Van Lines 527 Morley Dr	Saginaw	MI	48601	**800-678-3836**	989-755-3000
Suddath Cos 815 S Main St	Jacksonville	FL	32207	**800-395-7100**	904-390-7100
Truckin Movers Corp 1031 Harvest St	Durham	NC	27704	**800-334-1651**	919-682-2300
Two Men & A Truck International Inc 3400 Belle Chase Way	Lansing	MI	48911	**800-345-1070**	517-394-7210
UniGroup Inc 1 Premier Dr	Fenton	MO	63026	**800-325-3924**	636-305-5000
UniGroup Worldwide UTS 1 Worldwide Dr	Saint Louis	MO	63026	**800-325-3924**	636-349-3600
United Van Lines Inc 1 United Dr.	Fenton	MO	63026	**800-325-3924**	636-326-3100
Wald Relocation Services Ltd 8708 W Little York Rd Suite 190	Houston	TX	77040	**800-527-1408**	713-512-4800
Wheaton Van Lines Inc PO Box 50800	Indianapolis	IN	46250	**800-932-7799**	317-849-7900

509 MUSEUMS

SEE ALSO Museums & Halls of Fame - Sports; Museums - Children's

Name / Address	City	State	Zip	Toll-Free	Phone
ABA Museum of Law 321 N Clark St	Chicago	IL	60610	**800-285-2221**	312-988-5000
African American Historical Museum & Cultural Center of Iowa 55 12th Ave SE	Cedar Rapids	IA	52406	**877-526-1863**	319-862-2101
Airline History Museum 201 Lou Holland Dr Hangar 9	Kansas City	MO	64116	**800-513-9484**	816-421-3401
Alabama Constitution Village 109 Gates Ave	Huntsville	AL	35801	**800-678-1819**	256-564-8100
Alaska Native Heritage Center 8800 Heritage Center Dr	Anchorage	AK	99506	**800-315-6608**	907-330-8000
American Civil War Museum 297 Steinwehr Ave.	Gettysburg	PA	17325	**800-877-7775**	717-334-6245
American Numismatic Assn Money Museum 818 N Cascade Ave	Colorado Springs	CO	80903	**800-367-9723**	719-632-2646
American Presidential Museum 3107 W Hwy 76	Branson	MO	65616	**866-334-8683**	417-334-8683
American Quarter Horse Heritage Center & Museum 2601 I-40 E	Amarillo	TX	79104	**888-209-8322**	806-376-5181
American Royal Museum & Visitors Center 1701 American Royal Ct	Kansas City	MO	64102	**800-821-5857**	816-221-9800
American Saddlebred Museum 4083 Iron Works Pkwy	Lexington	KY	40511	**800-829-4438**	859-259-2746
American Swedish Institute 2600 Park Ave *Sales	Minneapolis	MN	55407	**800-579-3336***	612-871-4907
Amon Carter Museum 3501 Camp Bowie Blvd	Fort Worth	TX	76107	**800-573-1933**	817-738-1933
Antique Car Museum/Grovewood Gallery 111 Grovewood Rd	Asheville	NC	28804	**877-622-7238**	828-253-7651
Arabia Steamboat Museum 400 Grand Blvd	Kansas City	MO	64106	**800-471-1856**	816-471-1856
Arizona Memorial Museum Assn 1 Arizona Memorial Pl	Honolulu	HI	96818	**888-485-1941**	808-422-5664
Arizona State Capitol Museum 1700 W Washington St	Phoenix	AZ	85007	**800-255-5841**	602-542-4675
Ark-La-Tex Antique & Classic Vehicle Museum 601 Spring St	Shreveport	LA	71101	**888-664-4854**	318-222-0227
Arkansas Arts Center 501 E 9th St	Little Rock	AR	72202	**800-264-2787**	501-372-4000
Arkansas Museum of Science & History Museum of Discovery 500 President Clinton Ave Suite 150	Little Rock	AR	72201	**800-880-6475**	501-396-7050
Arkansas River Historical Society Museum 5350 Cimarron Rd	Catoosa	OK	74015	**888-512-7678**	918-266-2291
Bailey Matthews Shell Museum 3075 Sanibel-Captiva Rd PO Box 1580	Sanibel	FL	33957	**888-679-6450**	239-395-2233
Banneker-Douglas Museum 84 Franklin St.	Annapolis	MD	21401	**866-521-6173**	410-216-6180
Battles for Chattanooga Museum 1110 E Brow Rd	Lookout Mountain	TN	37350	**800-854-0675**	423-821-2812
Belle Meade Plantation 5025 Harding Rd *Info	Nashville	TN	37205	**800-270-3991***	615-356-0501
Biltmore House One N Pack Sq	Asheville	NC	28801	**800-543-1895**	828-225-6300
Birmingham Civil Rights Institute 520 16th St N	Birmingham	AL	35203	**866-328-9696**	205-328-9696
Black Cultural Centre for Nova Scotia 1149 Main St	Dartmouth	NS	B2Z1A8	**800-465-0767**	902-434-6223
Bob Bullock Texas State History Museum 1800 N Congress Ave	Austin	TX	78701	**866-369-7108**	512-936-8746
Bonanzaville USA 1351 W Main Ave	West Fargo	ND	58078	**800-700-5317**	701-282-2822
Bragg-Mitchell Mansion 1906 Springhill Ave.	Mobile	AL	36607	**866-471-6364**	251-471-6364
Canadian Museum of Civilization PO Box 3100 Station B	Hull	QC	J8X4H2	**800-555-5621**	819-776-7000
Canadian Museum of Contemporary Photography 1 Rideau Canal	Ottawa	ON	K1N9N6	**877-541-8888**	613-990-8257
Canadian Museum of Nature 240 McLeod St	Ottawa	ON	K1P6P4	**800-263-4433**	613-566-4700
Canterbury Shaker Village 288 Shaker Rd.	Canterbury	NH	03224	**866-783-9511**	603-783-9511
Carnegie Science Center 1 Allegheny Ave.	Pittsburgh	PA	15212	**877-975-6787**	412-237-3400
Carter Amon Museum 3501 Camp Bowie Blvd	Fort Worth	TX	76107	**800-573-1933**	817-738-1933
Cattle Raisers Museum 1301 W 7th St	Fort Worth	TX	76102	**800-242-7420**	817-332-8551
Center for Western Studies 2101 S Summit Ave Augustana College	Sioux Falls	SD	57197	**800-727-2844**	605-274-4007
Challenger Learning Center 316 Washington Ave Wheeling Jesuit University	Wheeling	WV	26003	**800-624-6992**	304-243-4325
Charlotte Nature Museum 1658 Sterling Rd	Charlotte	NC	28209	**800-935-0553**	704-372-6261
Cherokee Heritage Center & National Museum 21992 S Keeler Rd.	Park Hill	OK	74451	**888-999-6007**	918-456-6007
Children's Museum of Indianapolis 3000 N Meridian St	Indianapolis	IN	46208	**800-826-5431**	317-924-5431
Chrysler Walter P Museum 1 Chrysler Dr	Auburn Hills	MI	48326	**888-456-1924**	248-944-0001
Cincinnati Art Museum 953 Eden Park Dr	Cincinnati	OH	45202	**877-472-4226**	513-721-5204
Cincinnati History Museum 1301 Western Ave Cincinnati Museum Ctr	Cincinnati	OH	45203	**800-733-2077**	513-287-7000
Circus World Museum 550 Water St	Baraboo	WI	53913	**866-693-1500**	608-356-8341
Cleveland Museum of Art 11150 East Blvd *Sales	Cleveland	OH	44106	**888-262-7175***	216-421-7340
Cleveland Museum of Natural History 1 Wade Oval Dr University Cir	Cleveland	OH	44106	**800-317-9155**	216-231-4600
Coleman Factory Outlet Store & Museum 235 N Saint Francis St	Wichita	KS	67202	**800-835-3278**	316-264-0836
Colorado Railroad Museum 17155 W 44th Ave	Golden	CO	80402	**800-365-6263**	303-279-4591
Conner Prairie Living History Museum 13400 Allisonville Rd	Fishers	IN	46038	**800-966-1836**	317-776-6000
Corcoran Gallery of Art 500 17th St NW	Washington	DC	20006	**800-267-2672**	202-639-1700
Corning Museum of Glass 1 Museum Way *Cust Svc	Corning	NY	14830	**800-732-6845***	607-937-5371
COSI Columbus 333 W Broad St	Columbus	OH	43215	**888-819-2674**	614-228-2674
Country Music Hall of Fame & Museum 222 5th Ave S	Nashville	TN	37203	**800-852-6437**	615-416-2001
Cranbrook Art Museum 39221 Woodward Ave	Bloomfield Hills	MI	48303	**800-462-7262**	248-645-3319
Dali Salvador Museum 1000 3rd St S	Saint Petersburg	FL	33701	**800-442-3254**	727-823-3767
Dayton Art Institute 456 Belmonte Pk N	Dayton	OH	45405	**800-296-4426**	937-223-5277
DeGrazia Gallery in the Sun 6300 N Swan Rd.	Tucson	AZ	85718	**800-545-2185**	520-299-9191
Denver Museum of Nature & Science 2001 Colorado Blvd	Denver	CO	80205	**800-925-2250**	303-370-6357
Depot The Saint Louis County Heritage & Arts Center 506 W Michigan St	Duluth	MN	55802	**888-733-5833**	218-727-8025
DeWitt Wallace Decorative Arts Museum 325 Francis St	Williamsburg	VA	23185	**800-447-8679**	757-220-7724
Doak House Museum 690 Erwin Hwy.	Greeneville	TN	37743	**800-729-0256**	423-636-8554
Doyle New York 175 E 87th St	New York	NY	10128	**800-808-0902**	212-427-2730
Dutton Family Theatre 3454 W Hwy 76	Branson	MO	65616	**800-942-4626**	417-332-2772
Dwight D Eisenhower Presidential Library & Museum 200 SE 4th St	Abilene	KS	67410	**877-746-4453**	785-263-6700
Edgar Allan Poe Museum 1914-16 E Main St.	Richmond	VA	23223	**888-213-2763**	804-648-5523
Eisenhower Dwight D Presidential Library & Museum 200 SE 4th St	Abilene	KS	67410	**877-746-4453**	785-263-6700
EnergyExplorium 13339 Hagers Ferry Rd MG03E	Huntersville	NC	28078	**800-777-0003**	704-875-5600
Fieldcrest Cannon Textile Museum Cannon Village Visitor Center 200 West Ave	Kannapolis	NC	28081	**800-438-6111**	704-938-3200
Fireworks Fine Crafts Gallery 3307 Utah Ave S	Seattle	WA	98134	**800-505-8882**	206-682-8707
Fitger's Brewery Complex Museum 600 E Superior St	Duluth	MN	55802	**888-348-4377**	218-722-0410
Florida Holocaust Museum 55 5th St S	Saint Petersburg	FL	33701	**800-960-7448**	727-820-0100
Florida International Museum 100 2nd St N	Saint Petersburg	FL	33701	**800-777-9882**	727-821-1448
Ford Henry Museum 20900 Oakwood Blvd.	Dearborn	MI	48124	**800-835-5237**	313-271-1620
Forest Lawn Museum 1712 S Glendale Ave	Glendale	CA	91205	**800-204-3131**	
Fort Henry Historic Site PO Box 213 *Cust Svc	Kingston	ON	K7L4V8	**800-437-2233***	613-542-7388
Fort Worth Museum of Science & History 1501 Montgomery St	Fort Worth	TX	76107	**888-255-9300**	817-255-9300
Franklin D Roosevelt Library & Museum 4079 Albany Post Rd	Hyde Park	NY	12538	**800-337-8474**	845-229-8114
Frazier Historical Arms Museum 829 W Main St	Louisville	KY	40202	**866-886-7103**	502-412-2280
Garland Landmark Museum 200 Museum Plaza Dr	Garland	TX	75040	**888-879-0264**	972-205-2749
Georgia Music Hall of Fame 200 ML King Jr Blvd	Macon	GA	31202	**888-427-6257**	478-750-8555
Gilcrease Museum 1400 N Gilcrease Museum Rd	Tulsa	OK	74127	**888-655-2278**	918-596-2700
Gold Coast Railroad Museum 12450 SW 152nd St	Miami	FL	33177	**888-608-7246**	305-253-0063
Graceland (Elvis Presley Mansion) 3734 Elvis Presley Blvd	Memphis	TN	38186	**800-238-2000**	901-332-3322
Grandmother's Buttons Museum 9814 Royal St	Saint Francisville	LA	70775	**800-580-6941**	225-635-4107
Greenfield Village 20900 Oakwood Blvd	Dearborn	MI	48124	**800-835-5237**	313-271-1620
Hale Farm & Village 2686 Oakhill Rd	Bath	OH	44210	**800-589-9703**	330-666-3711
Harry S Truman Presidential Library & Museum 500 W Hwy 24	Independence	MO	64050	**800-833-1225**	816-833-1400
Headley-Whitney Museum 4435 Old Frankfort Pike	Lexington	KY	40510	**800-310-5085**	859-255-6653
Henry Ford Museum 20900 Oakwood Blvd.	Dearborn	MI	48124	**800-835-5237**	313-271-1620
Heritage Hill Living History Museum 2640 S Webster Ave	Green Bay	WI	54301	**800-721-5150**	920-448-5150
Hillwood Museum & Gardens 4155 Linnean Ave NW	Washington	DC	20008	**877-445-5966**	202-686-8500
Historic Annapolis Foundation Museum 77 Main St	Annapolis	MD	21401	**800-603-4020**	410-268-5576
Historic Huntsville Depot 404 Madison St	Huntsville	AL	35801	**800-678-1819**	256-564-8100
Historical Lawmen Museum 750 N Motel Blvd	Las Cruces	NM	88007	**800-332-2121**	505-525-1911
Hollywood Wax Museum 3030 W Hwy 76	Branson	MO	65616	**800-720-4110**	417-337-8277
Hook's Discovery & Learning Center 1305 W 29th St	Indianapolis	IN	46208	**877-924-5886**	317-951-2222
House of Broel's Historic Mansion & Dollhouse Museum 2220 St Charles Ave	New Orleans	LA	70130	**800-827-4325**	504-525-1000
Huntsville Museum of Art 300 Church St S	Huntsville	AL	35801	**800-786-9095**	256-535-4350
Hywet Stan Hall & Gardens 714 N Portage Path	Akron	OH	44403	**888-836-5533**	330-836-5533
Idaho Historical Museum 610 N Julia Davis Dr	Boise	ID	83702	**877-653-4367**	208-334-2120
Illinois American Historical Water Museum 100 Lorentz St	Peoria	IL	61614	**800-422-2782**	309-671-3701
Indian Pueblo Cultural Center 2401 12th St NW	Albuquerque	NM	87104	**800-766-4405**	505-843-7270
Institute of American Indian Arts Museum 108 Cathedral Pl	Santa Fe	NM	87501	**800-804-6423**	505-983-8900
Institute of Texan Cultures 801 S Bowie St HemisFair Pk	San Antonio	TX	78205	**800-776-7651**	210-458-2300
Intel Museum 2200 Mission College Blvd.	Santa Clara	CA	95052	**800-628-8686**	408-765-0503
International Civil Rights Center & Museum 134 S Elm St	Greensboro	NC	27401	**800-748-7116**	336-274-9199
International Museum of the Horse 4089 Iron Works Pkwy	Lexington	KY	40511	**800-678-8813**	859-259-4231
International Spy Museum 800 F St NW	Washington	DC	20004	**866-779-6873**	202-393-7798
Inventure Place 221 S Broadway	Akron	OH	44308	**800-968-4332**	330-762-4463
Ironworld Discovery Center 801 SW Hwy 169 Suite 1	Chisholm	MN	55719	**800-372-6437**	218-254-7959
Japanese American National Museum 369 E 1st St	Los Angeles	CA	90012	**800-461-5266**	213-625-0414

Name / Address	City	State	Zip	Toll-Free	Phone
Jewish Museum of Maryland 15 Lloyd St	Baltimore	MD	21202	**877-376-7190**	410-732-6400
Kennedy John F Library & Museum Columbia Point	Boston	MA	02125	**866-535-1960**	617-514-1600
Kentucky Military History Museum 125 E Main St	Frankfort	KY	40601	**877-444-7867**	502-564-3265
Kings Landing Historical Settlement 20 Kings Landing Service Entrance Rd Unit 2	Kings Lndg Hist Settlemnt	NB	E6K3W3	**888-666-5547**	506-363-4999
Kirkpatrick Science & Air Space Museum at Omniplex 2100 NE 52nd St	Oklahoma City	OK	73111	**800-532-7652**	405-602-6664
Knights of Columbus Museum 1 State St	New Haven	CT	06510	**800-524-3611**	203-772-2130
Kruger Street Toy & Train Museum 144 Kruger St	Wheeling	WV	26003	**877-242-8133**	304-242-8133
Laura Ingalls Wilder Museum & Home 3068 Hwy A	Mansfield	MO	65704	**877-924-7126**	417-924-3626
Leanin' Tree Museum of Western Art 6055 Longbow Dr	Boulder	CO	80301	**800-777-8716**	303-530-1442
Legends of Harley Drag Racing Museum 1126 S Saunders St	Raleigh	NC	27603	**800-394-2758**	919-832-2261
Lincoln County Historical Society Museum of Pioneer History 717 Manvel Ave	Chandler	OK	74834	**888-258-2809**	405-258-2425
Louisiana State Museum 751 Chartres St	New Orleans	LA	70116	**800-568-6968**	504-568-6968
Louisville Science Center 727 W Main St	Louisville	KY	40202	**800-591-2203**	502-561-6100
Manitou Cliff Dwellings Museum Hwy 24 W	Manitou Springs	CO	80829	**800-354-9971**	719-685-5242
Mariners' Museum 100 Museum Dr	Newport News	VA	23606	**800-581-7245**	757-596-2222
May Natural History Museum & Museum of Space Exploration 710 Rock Creek Canyon Rd	Colorado Springs	CO	80926	**800-666-3841**	719-576-0450
McWane Center Science Museum 200 19th St N	Birmingham	AL	35203	**877-462-9263**	205-714-8300
Messianic Museum 1928 Hamill Rd	Hixson	TN	37343	**888-876-8150**	423-876-8150
Meteor Crater & Museum of Astrogeology Exit 233 off I-40 Meteor Crater Rd	Winslow	AZ	86047	**800-289-5898**	928-289-2362
Mid-America Science Museum 500 Mid-America Blvd	Hot Springs	AR	71913	**800-632-0583**	501-767-3461
Minneapolis Institute of Arts 2400 3rd Ave S	Minneapolis	MN	55404	**888-642-2787**	612-870-3000
Minnesota Historical Society History Center Museum 345 Kellogg Blvd W	Saint Paul	MN	55102	**800-657-3773**	651-296-6126
Miramont Castle Museum 9 Capitol Hill Ave	Manitou Springs	CO	80829	**888-685-1011**	719-685-1011
Mississippi Agriculture & Forestry Museum/National Agricultural Aviation Museum 1150 Lakeland Dr	Jackson	MS	39216	**800-844-8687**	601-354-6113
Mississippi River Museum 101 Mud Island Dr	Memphis	TN	38103	**800-507-6507**	901-576-7230
Missouri State Museum Capitol Bldg Room B2	Jefferson City	MO	65101	**800-336-6946**	573-751-2854
Montana Historical Society Museum 225 N Roberts St	Helena	MT	59620	**800-243-9900**	406-444-2694
Montreal Museum of Decorative Arts 1379 rue Sherbrook O	Montreal	QC	H3G1J5	**800-899-6873**	514-285-1600
Montreal Science Centre Saint-Laurent Blvd & de la Commune St King-Edward Pier	Montreal	QC	H2Y2E2	**877-496-4724**	514-496-4724
Musee Conti-Wax Museum of Louisiana Legends 917 Rue Conti French Quarter	New Orleans	LA	70112	**800-233-5405**	504-525-2605
Musee de l'Amerique Francaise 2 cote de la Fabrique	Quebec	QC	G1R4R7	**866-710-8031**	418-692-2843
Musee du Quebec Parc des Champs-de-Bataille	Quebec	QC	G1R5H3	**866-220-2150**	418-643-2150
Museum of American Financial History 28 Broadway	New York	NY	10004	**877-983-4626**	212-908-4110
Museum of American Illustration 128 E 63rd St	New York	NY	10021	**800-746-8738**	212-838-2560
Museum of Beverage Containers & Advertising 1055 Ridgecrest Dr	Millersville	TN	37072	**800-826-4929**	615-859-5236
Museum of Early Southern Decorative Arts 924 S Main St	Winston-Salem	NC	27101	**800-441-5305**	336-721-7360
Museum of Fine Arts 220 State St	Springfield	MA	01103	**800-625-7738**	413-263-6800
Museum of Fine Arts 1001 Bissonnet St	Houston	TX	77005	**888-733-6324**	713-639-7300
Museum of Geology 501 E Saint Joseph St South Dakota School of Mines & Technology	Rapid City	SD	57701	**800-544-8162**	605-394-2467
Museum of Glass 1801 E Dock St	Tacoma	WA	98402	**866-468-7386**	253-284-4750
Museum of Making Music 5790 Armada Dr	Carlsbad	CA	92008	**877-551-9976**	760-438-5996
Museum of Natural History & Science 1301 Western Ave Cincinnati Museum Ctr	Cincinnati	OH	45203	**800-733-2077**	513-287-7000
Museum of Nebraska History 131 Centennial Mall N	Lincoln	NE	68508	**800-833-6747**	402-471-4754
Museum of Northern Arizona 3101 N Fort Valley Rd	Flagstaff	AZ	86001	**800-423-1069**	928-774-5211
Museum of Science Science Pk	Boston	MA	02114	**866-770-4363**	617-589-0100
Museum of Science & Industry 4801 E Fowler Ave	Tampa	FL	33617	**800-995-6674**	813-987-6300
Museum of Science & Industry 5700 S Lake Shore Dr	Chicago	IL	60637	**800-468-6674**	773-684-1414
Museum of the Cherokee Indian PO Box 1599	Cherokee	NC	28719	**888-665-7249**	828-497-3481
Museum of the Mountain Man 700 E Hennick St	Pinedale	WY	82941	**877-686-6266**	307-367-4101
Mystic Seaport Museum Inc 75 Greenmanville Ave PO Box 6000	Mystic	CT	06355	**888-973-2767**	860-572-0711
National Afro-American Museum & Cultural Center 1350 Brush Row Rd PO Box 578	Wilberforce	OH	45384	**800-752-2603**	937-376-4944
National Border Patrol Museum 4315 Transmountain Rd	El Paso	TX	79924	**877-276-8738**	915-759-6060
National Cleveland-Style Polka Hall of Fame 605 E 22nd St	Euclid	OH	44123	**866-667-6552**	216-261-3263
National Constitution Center 525 Arch St Independence Mall	Philadelphia	PA	19106	**866-917-1787**	215-409-6600
National Corvette Museum 350 Corvette Dr	Bowling Green	KY	42101	**800-538-3883**	270-781-7973
National Cowgirl Museum & Hall of Fame 1720 Gendy St	Fort Worth	TX	76107	**800-476-3263**	817-336-4475
National Geographic Society Explorers Hall 1145 17th St NW	Washington	DC	20036	**800-647-5463**	202-857-7589
National Inventors Hall of Fame 221 S Broadway St Inventure Place	Akron	OH	44308	**800-968-4332**	330-762-4463
National Mississippi River Museum & Aquarium 550 E 3rd St Ice Harbor	Dubuque	IA	52001	**800-226-3369**	563-557-9545

Name / Address	City	State	Zip	Toll-Free	Phone
National Museum of Naval Aviation 1750 Radford Blvd Suite C	Pensacola	FL	32508	**800-327-5002**	850-452-3604
National Museum of Patriotism 1405 Spring St NW	Atlanta	GA	30309	**877-276-1692**	404-875-0691
National Museum of the American Indian (Smithsonian Institution) 1 Bowling Green	New York	NY	10004	**800-242-6624**	212-514-3700
National Museum of Wildlife Art 2820 Rungius Rd PO Box 6825	Jackson	WY	83002	**800-313-9553**	307-733-5771
National Museum of Women in the Arts 1250 New York Ave NW	Washington	DC	20005	**800-222-7270**	202-783-5000
National Science Center Fort Discovery 1 7th St	Augusta	GA	30901	**800-325-5445**	706-821-0200
National Underground Railroad Freedom Center 50 E Freedom Way	Cincinnati	OH	45202	**877-648-4838**	513-333-7500
New Hampshire Institute of Art 148 Concord St	Manchester	NH	03104	**866-241-4918**	603-623-0313
New Mexico Museum of Space History PO Box 5430	Alamogordo	NM	88311	**877-333-6589**	505-437-2840
New York Historical Society 170 Central Park W	New York	NY	10024	**888-860-6947**	212-873-3400
Newark Museum 49 Washington St	Newark	NJ	07102	**800-768-7386**	973-596-6550
North American Black Historical Museum Inc 277 King St	Amherstburg	ON	N9V2C7	**800-713-6336**	519-736-5433
Nottoway Plantation 30970 Hwy 405	White Castle	LA	70788	**866-428-4748**	225-346-8263
Octave Chanute Aerospace Museum 1011 Pacesetter Dr	Rantoul	IL	61866	**877-726-8685**	217-893-1613
Oglebay Institute's Mansion & Glass Museums The Burton Center Oglebay Pk	Wheeling	WV	26003	**800-624-6988**	304-242-7272
Ohio Historical Center 1982 Velma Ave	Columbus	OH	43211	**800-686-6124**	614-297-2300
Oklahoma City Museum of Art 415 Couch Dr	Oklahoma City	OK	73102	**800-579-9278**	405-236-3100
Oklahoma Jazz Hall of Fame 322 N Greenwood Ave	Tulsa	OK	74120	**800-348-9336**	918-596-1001
Old Barracks Museum Barrack St	Trenton	NJ	08608	**888-227-7225**	609-396-1776
Old Florida Museum 254-D San Marco Ave	Saint Augustine	FL	32084	**800-813-3208**	904-824-8874
Old Jail Museum 167 San Marco Ave	Saint Augustine	FL	32084	**800-397-4071**	904-829-3800
Old State Capitol Museum 100 W Broadway	Frankfort	KY	40601	**877-444-7867**	502-564-3016
Omniplex 2100 NE 52nd St	Oklahoma City	OK	73111	**800-532-7652**	405-602-6664
Oneida Nation Museum W892 County Rd EE PO Box 365	De Pere	WI	54155	**800-236-2214**	920-869-2768
Orange County Regional History Center 65 E Central Blvd	Orlando	FL	32801	**800-965-2030**	407-836-8500
Oregon Museum of Science & Industry 1945 SE Water Ave	Portland	OR	97214	**800-955-6674**	503-797-4000
Orlando Science Center 777 E Princeton St	Orlando	FL	32803	**888-672-4386**	407-514-2000
Palm Springs Air Museum 745 N Gene Autry Trail	Palm Springs	CA	92262	**800-562-2604**	760-778-6262
Patriots Point Naval & Maritime Museum Charleston Harbor 40 Patriots Point Rd	Mount Pleasant	SC	29464	**800-248-3508**	843-884-2727
Philbrook Museum of Art & Gardens 2727 S Rockford Rd	Tulsa	OK	74114	**800-324-7941**	918-749-7941
Pierpont Morgan Library 29 E 36th St *Orders	New York	NY	10016	**800-861-0001***	212-685-0008
Plaquemine Lock Museum 57730 Main St	Plaquemine	LA	70764	**877-987-7158**	225-687-7158
Poe Edgar Allan Museum 1914-16 E Main St	Richmond	VA	23223	**888-213-2763**	804-648-5523
Polynesian Cultural Center 55-370 Kamehameha Hwy	Laie	HI	96762	**800-367-7060**	808-293-3000
Pony Express National Memorial 914 Penn St	Saint Joseph	MO	64503	**800-530-5930**	816-279-5059
Port Townsend Marine Science Center 532 Battery Way	Port Townsend	WA	98368	**800-566-3932**	360-385-5582
Potter's Wax Museum 17 King St	Saint Augustine	FL	32084	**800-584-4781**	904-829-9056
Public Museum of Grand Rapids 272 Pearl St NW Van Andel Museum Ctr	Grand Rapids	MI	49504	**800-459-4253**	616-456-3977
Pueblo Grande Museum & Archaeological Park 4619 E Washington St	Phoenix	AZ	85034	**877-706-4408**	602-495-0901
Queen Mary Seaport 1126 Queens Hwy	Long Beach	CA	90802	**800-437-2934**	562-435-3511
Reagan Ronald Presidential Library & Museum 40 Presidential Dr	Simi Valley	CA	93065	**800-410-8354**	805-577-4000
Reynolda House Museum of American Art 2250 Reynolda Rd	Winston-Salem	NC	27106	**888-663-1149**	336-725-5325
Reynolds-Alberta Museum PO Box 6360	Wetaskiwin	AB	T9A2G1	**800-661-4726**	780-361-1351
Ripley's Believe It or Not! Museum 3326 W Hwy 76	Branson	MO	65616	**800-998-4418**	417-337-5300
Ripley's Believe It or Not! Museum New York Ave & Boardwalk	Atlantic City	NJ	08401	**877-713-4233**	609-347-2001
Roberson Museum & Science Center 30 Front St	Binghamton	NY	13905	**888-269-5325**	607-772-0660
Robert C Williams American Museum of Papermaking 500 10th St NW	Atlanta	GA	30318	**800-558-6611**	404-894-7840
Rock & Roll Hall of Fame & Museum 1 Key Plaza	Cleveland	OH	44114	**800-349-7625**	216-781-7625
Rocky Mount Museum 200 Hyder Hill Rd	Piney Flats	TN	37686	**888-538-1791**	423-538-7396
Ronald Reagan Presidential Library & Museum 40 Presidential Dr	Simi Valley	CA	93065	**800-410-8354**	805-577-4000
Roosevelt Franklin D Library & Museum 4079 Albany Post Rd	Hyde Park	NY	12538	**800-337-8474**	845-229-8114
Roscoe Village 381 Hill St	Coshocton	OH	43812	**800-877-1830**	740-622-9310
Royal British Columbia Museum 675 Belleville St	Victoria	BC	V8W9W2	**888-447-7977**	250-356-7226
Royal Canadian Military Institute 426 University Ave	Toronto	ON	M5G1S9	**800-585-1072**	416-597-0286
Royal Canadian Mounted Police Centennial Museum 6101 Dewdney Ave	Regina	SK	S4P3J7	**877-526-0585**	306-780-5838
Royal Tyrrell Museum of Palaeontology Hwy 838 Midland Provincial Pk	Drumheller	AB	T0J0Y0	**888-440-4240**	403-823-7707
Saint Louis Science Center 5050 Oakland Ave	Saint Louis	MO	63110	**800-456-7572**	314-289-4400
Salem Witch Museum 19 1/2 Washington Sq N	Salem	MA	01970	**800-544-1692**	978-744-1692
Salvador Dali Museum 1000 3rd St S	Saint Petersburg	FL	33701	**800-442-3254**	727-823-3767
San Bernardino County Museum 2024 Orange Tree Ln	Redlands	CA	92374	**888-247-3344**	909-307-2669
Sci-Port Discovery Center 820 Clyde Fant Pkwy	Shreveport	LA	71101	**877-724-7678**	318-424-3466
Science Central 1950 N Clinton St	Fort Wayne	IN	46805	**800-442-6376**	260-424-2400
Science Museum of Virginia 2500 W Broad St	Richmond	VA	23220	**800-659-1727**	804-864-1400
Shaker Village of Pleasant Hill 3501 Lexington Rd	Harrodsburg	KY	40330	**800-734-5611**	859-734-5411
Sixth Floor Museum 411 Elm St Dealey Plaza	Dallas	TX	75202	**888-485-4854**	214-747-6660

Name / Address	City	State	ZIP	Toll-Free	Phone
Smithsonian Institution 1000 Jefferson Dr SW	Washington	DC	20560	**800-766-2149**	202-357-2700
Southern University Museum of Art 610 Texas St Suite 110	Shreveport	LA	71101	**800-458-1472**	318-678-4631
Spanish Military Hospital Museum 3 Aviles St	Saint Augustine	FL	32084	**800-597-7177**	904-827-0807
Stan Hywet Hall & Gardens 714 N Portage Path	Akron	OH	44403	**888-836-5533**	330-836-5533
Strategic Air & Space Museum 28210 W Park Hwy	Ashland	NE	68003	**800-358-5029**	402-944-3100
Studebaker National Museum 525 S Main St	South Bend	IN	46601	**888-391-5600**	574-235-9714
Teddy Bear Museum 2511 Pine Ridge Rd	Naples	FL	34109	**866-365-2327**	239-598-2711
Tennessee State Museum 505 Deaderick St	Nashville	TN	37243	**800-407-4324**	615-741-2692
Texas Maritime Museum 1202 Navigation Cir	Rockport	TX	78382	**866-729-2469**	361-729-1271
Toledo Museum of Art 2445 Monroe St	Toledo	OH	43620	**800-644-6862**	419-255-8000
Truman Harry S Presidential Library & Museum 500 W Hwy 24	Independence	MO	64050	**800-833-1225**	816-833-1400
Upper Room Chapel & Museum 1908 Grand Ave	Nashville	TN	37212	**800-972-0433**	615-340-7207
US Space & Rocket Center 1 Tranquility Base	Huntsville	AL	35805	**800-637-7223**	256-837-3400
USS Lexington Museum on the Bay 2914 N Shoreline Blvd	Corpus Christi	TX	78403	**800-523-9539**	361-888-4873
Walter P Chrysler Museum 1 Chrysler Dr	Auburn Hills	MI	48326	**888-456-1924**	248-944-0001
Washington National Cathedral 3101 Wisconsin Ave NW	Washington	DC	20016	**800-622-6304**	202-537-6200
Washington Pavilion of Arts & Science 301 S Main Ave	Sioux Falls	SD	57104	**877-927-4728**	605-367-7397
Washington State History Museum 1911 Pacific Ave	Tacoma	WA	98402	**888-238-4373**	253-272-3500
Wax Museum at Fisherman's Wharf 145 Jefferson St Suite 500	San Francisco	CA	94133	**800-439-4305**	415-885-4834
Wells Fargo History Museum 420 Montgomery St	San Francisco	CA	94163	**800-411-4932**	415-396-2619
West Feliciana Historical Society Museum 11757 Ferdinand St	Saint Francisville	LA	70775	**800-789-4221**	225-635-6330
Western Museum of Mining & Industry 1025 N Gate Rd	Colorado Springs	CO	80921	**800-752-6588**	719-488-0880
Westville 1850's Village 1 ML King Blvd	Lumpkin	GA	31815	**888-733-1850**	229-838-6310
Wheelwright Museum of the American Indian 704 Camino Lejo	Santa Fe	NM	87505	**800-607-4636**	505-982-4636
Wilder Laura Ingalls Museum & Home 3068 Hwy A	Mansfield	MO	65704	**877-924-7126**	417-924-3626
Will Rogers Memorial Museum 1720 W Will Rogers Blvd	Claremore	OK	74017	**800-324-9455**	918-341-0719
Williams Robert C American Museum of Papermaking 500 10th St NW	Atlanta	GA	30318	**800-558-6611**	404-894-7840
Wilton House Museum 215 S Wilton Rd	Richmond	VA	23226	**877-994-5866**	804-282-5936
Winterthur Museum Garden & Library 5105 Kennett Pike	Winterthur	DE	19735	**800-448-3883**	302-888-4600
Wisconsin Maritime Museum 75 Maritime Dr	Manitowoc	WI	54220	**866-724-2356**	920-684-0218
Woolaroc Ranch Museum & Wildlife Preserve Hwy 123 S	Bartlesville	OK	74003	**888-966-5276**	918-336-0307
Youngstown Historical Center of Industry & Labor 151 W Wood St	Youngstown	OH	44503	**800-262-6137**	330-743-5934

510 MUSEUMS - CHILDREN'S

Name / Address	City	State	ZIP	Toll-Free	Phone
Children's Hands-On Museum 2213 University Blvd	Tuscaloosa	AL	35401	**877-349-4235**	205-349-4235
Children's Museum of Richmond 2626 W Broad St	Richmond	VA	23220	**877-295-2667**	804-474-7000
Cinergy Children's Museum 1301 Western Ave Cincinnati Museum Ctr	Cincinnati	OH	45203	**800-733-2077**	513-287-7000
Discovery Place 301 N Tryon St	Charlotte	NC	28202	**800-935-0553**	704-372-6261
Don Harrington Discovery Center 1200 Streit Dr	Amarillo	TX	79106	**800-784-9548**	806-355-9547
Exploration Place 300 N McLean Blvd	Wichita	KS	67203	**877-904-1444**	316-263-3373
Gulf Coast Exploreum Science Center 65 Government St	Mobile	AL	36602	**877-625-4386**	251-208-6883
Harrington Don Discovery Center 1200 Streit Dr	Amarillo	TX	79106	**800-784-9548**	806-355-9547
Kansas Cosmosphere & Space Center 1100 N Plum	Hutchinson	KS	67501	**800-397-0330**	620-662-2305

511 MUSEUMS & HALLS OF FAME - SPORTS

Name / Address	City	State	ZIP	Toll-Free	Phone
American Water Ski Hall of Fame & Museum 1251 Holy Cow Rd	Polk City	FL	33868	**800-533-2972**	863-324-2472
Baseball Hall of Fame 910 S 3rd St	Minneapolis	MN	55415	**888-375-9707**	612-375-9707
Bob Feller Museum 310 Mill St PO Box 95	Van Meter	IA	50261	**866-996-2806**	515-996-2806
Canadian Baseball Hall of Fame & Museum 386 Church St PO Box 1838	Saint Marys	ON	N4X1C2	**877-250-2255**	519-284-1838
Canadian Golf Hall of Fame & Museum Glen Abbey Golf Club 1333 Dorval Dr	Oakville	ON	L6J4Z3	**800-310-7242**	905-849-9700
College Football Hall of Fame 111 Saint Joseph St	South Bend	IN	44601	**800-440-3263**	574-235-9999
Don Garlits Museums 13700 SW 16th Ave	Ocala	FL	34473	**877-271-3278**	352-245-8661
Georgia Golf Hall of Fame 1 11th St	Augusta	GA	30901	**888-874-4443**	706-724-4443
Greyhound Hall of Fame 407 S Buckeye Ave	Abilene	KS	67410	**800-932-7881**	785-263-3000
Hendrick Motorsports Museum 4411 Papa Joe Hendrick Blvd	Charlotte	NC	28262	**877-467-4890**	704-455-3400
International Bowling Museum & Hall of Fame 111 Stadium Plaza Dr	Saint Louis	MO	63102	**800-966-2695**	314-231-6340
International Tennis Hall of Fame & Museum 194 Bellevue Ave	Newport	RI	02840	**800-457-1144**	401-849-3990
International Women's Sports Hall of Fame Eisenhower Pk Parking Field 6	East Meadow	NY	11554	**800-227-3988**	516-542-4700
Mississippi Sports Hall of Fame & Museum 1152 Lakeland Dr	Jackson	MS	39216	**800-280-3263**	601-982-8264
Missouri Sports Hall of Fame 3861 E Stan Musial Dr	Springfield	MO	65809	**800-498-5678**	417-889-3100
Motorcycle Hall of Fame Museum 13515 Yarmouth Dr	Pickerington	OH	43147	**800-262-5646**	614-856-1900
Motorsports Hall of Fame of America 43700 Expo Center Dr	Novi	MI	48375	**800-250-7223**	248-349-7223
Naismith Memorial Basketball Hall of Fame 1000 W Columbus Ave	Springfield	MA	01105	**877-446-6752**	413-231-5490
National Baseball Hall of Fame & Museum 25 Main St	Cooperstown	NY	13326	**888-425-5633**	607-547-7200
National Fresh Water Fishing Hall of Fame 10360 Hall of Fame Dr	Hayward	WI	54843	**866-268-4333**	715-634-4440
National Jousting Hall of Fame 94 Natural Chimneys Ln	Mount Solon	VA	22843	**888-430-2267**	540-350-2510
National Museum of Racing & Hall of Fame 191 Union Ave	Saratoga Springs	NY	12866	**800-562-5394**	518-584-0400
National Softball Hall of Fame & Museum 2801 NE 50th St	Oklahoma City	OK	73111	**800-654-8337**	405-424-5266
National Sprint Car Hall of Fame & Museum 1 Sprint Capital Pl	Knoxville	IA	50138	**800-874-4488**	641-842-6176
NCAA Hall of Champions 1 NCAA Plaza 700 W Washington St	Indianapolis	IN	46204	**800-735-6222**	317-916-4255
Negro Leagues Baseball Museum 1616 E 18th St	Kansas City	MO	64108	**888-221-6526**	816-221-1920
Nolan Ryan Exhibit Center 2925 S Hwy 35	Alvin	TX	77511	**800-350-7926**	281-388-1134
Paul W Bryant Museum 300 Paul W Bryant Dr	Tuscaloosa	AL	35487	**866-772-2327**	205-348-4668
Skate Canada Hall of Fame 865 Shefford Rd	Ottowa	ON	K1J1H9	**877-211-2372**	613-747-1007
Texas Sports Hall of Fame 1108 S University Parks Dr	Waco	TX	76706	**800-567-9561**	254-756-1633
University of Iowa Athletics Hall of Fame KHF Bldg 446	Iowa City	IA	52242	**866-469-2326**	319-384-1031
US Golf Assn Museum 77 Liberty Corner Rd	Far Hills	NJ	07931	**800-222-8742**	908-234-2300
US Hockey Hall of Fame PO Box 657	Eveleth	MN	55734	**800-443-7825**	218-744-5167
US Olympic Hall of Fame 1750 E Boulder St	Colorado Springs	CO	80909	**888-659-8687**	719-866-4500

512 MUSIC DISTRIBUTORS

Name / Address	City	State	ZIP	Toll-Free	Phone
Allegro Corp 14134 NE Airport Way	Portland	OR	97230	**800-288-2007**	503-257-8480
Alliance Entertainment Corp 4250 Coral Ridge Dr	Coral Springs	FL	33065	**800-329-7664**	954-255-4000
Alternative Distribution Alliance 72 Spring St 12th Fl	New York	NY	10012	**800-239-3232**	212-343-2485
Baker & Taylor Inc 2550 W Tyvola Rd Suite 300	Charlotte	NC	28217	**800-775-1800**	704-998-3100
Caroline Distribution 104 W 29th St 4th Fl	New York	NY	10001	**800-275-2250**	212-886-7500
EMI Christian Music Group 101 Winners Cir	Brentwood	TN	37024	**800-669-8586**	615-371-6800
Gotham Distributing Corp 60 Portland Rd	Conshohocken	PA	19428	**800-446-8426**	610-649-7650
Inspired Corp 103 Eisenhower Pkwy	Roseland	NJ	07068	**800-738-3747**	973-226-1234
K-Tel International Inc 2655 Cheshire Ln N Suite 100	Plymouth	MN	55447	**800-328-6640**	763-559-5566
Koch Entertainment Distribution 22 Harbor Pk Dr	Port Washington	NY	11050	**800-332-7553**	516-484-1000
Malaco Music Group Inc 3023 W Northside Dr *Cust Svc	Jackson	MS	39213	**800-272-7936***	601-982-4522
Music City Record Distributors Inc 25 Lincoln St	Nashville	TN	37210	**800-467-1050**	615-255-7315
Navarre Corp 7400 49th Ave N *NASDAQ: NAVR*	New Hope	MN	55428	**800-728-4000**	763-535-8333
Provident-Integrity Distribution 741 Cool Springs Blvd *Sales	Franklin	TN	37067	**800-333-9000***	615-261-6500
RED Distribution 79 5th Ave 15th Fl	New York	NY	10003	**800-733-1966**	212-404-0600
Select-O-Hits Inc 1981 Fletcher Creek Dr	Memphis	TN	38133	**800-346-0723**	901-388-1190

513 MUSIC PROGRAMMING SERVICES

Name / Address	City	State	ZIP	Toll-Free	Phone
DMX Music Inc 11400 W Olympic Blvd Suite 1100	Los Angeles	CA	90064	**800-700-4412**	310-444-1744
Jones Radio Network Inc 8200 S Akron St Suite 103	Englewood	CO	80112	**800-609-5663**	303-784-8700
Muzak LLC 3318 Lakemont Blvd	Fort Mill	SC	29708	**800-331-3340**	803-396-3000
PlayNetwork Inc 8727 148th Ave NE *Sales	Redmond	WA	98052	**888-567-7529***	425-497-8100

514 MUSIC STORES

SEE ALSO Book, Music, Video Clubs

Name / Address	City	State	ZIP	Toll-Free	Phone
Amazon.com Inc PO Box 81226 *NASDAQ: AMZN* ■ *Cust Svc	Seattle	WA	98108	**800-201-7575***	206-622-2335
Archambault Group Inc 500 rue Sainte-Catherine E	Montreal	QC	H2L2C6	**877-849-8589**	514-849-6206
Beatnik Inc 2600 S El Camino Real	San Mateo	CA	94403	**877-295-6593**	650-295-2300
Best Buy Co Inc 7601 Penn Ave S *NYSE: BBY*	Richfield	MN	55423	**800-369-5050**	612-291-1000
Borders Inc 100 Phoenix Dr *Cust Svc	Ann Arbor	MI	48108	**800-566-6616***	734-477-1100
CD Universe 101 N Plains Industrial Rd	Wallingford	CT	06492	**800-231-7937**	203-294-1648
CD Warehouse Inc 900 N Broadway	Oklahoma City	OK	73102	**800-641-9394**	405-236-8742
Circuit City Group 9950 Mayland Dr	Richmond	VA	23233	**800-251-2665**	804-527-4000
Coconuts Music & Movies 38 Corporate Cir	Albany	NY	12203	**800-540-1242**	518-452-1242
FirstCom Music 1325 Capital Pkwy Suite 109	Carrollton	TX	75006	**800-858-8880**	972-446-8742

Classified Section

Name / Address	City	State	Zip	Toll-Free	Phone
For Your Entertainment 38 Corporate Cir	Albany	NY	12203	**800-540-1242**	518-452-1242
Global Electronic Music Marketplace PO Box 4062	Palm Springs	CA	92262	**800-207-4366**	760-318-6250
Half.com Inc 500 S Gravers Rd *Cust Svc	Plymouth Meeting	PA	19462	**800-545-9857***	610-567-1090
Hastings Entertainment Inc 3601 Plains Blvd *NASDAQ: HAST* ■ *Cust Svc	Amarillo	TX	79102	**877-427-8464***	806-351-2300
IndiSonic Inc 126 N 3rd St Suite 512	Minneapolis	MN	55401	**877-492-7916**	612-349-9013
Inspired Distribution LLC 103 Eisenhower Pkwy	Roseland	NJ	07068	**800-272-4214**	973-226-1234
J & R Music World 23 Park Row	New York	NY	10038	**800-221-8180**	212-732-8600
Media Play 10400 Yellow Circle Dr *Cust Svc	Minnetonka	MN	55343	**800-371-4425***	952-932-7700
Mississippi Music Inc 222 S Main St	Hattiesburg	MS	39401	**800-844-5821**	601-544-5821
Musica Obscura PO Box 1571	Longmont	CO	80502	**800-655-8563**	303-702-0482
Musicland Group Inc 10400 Yellow Circle Dr *Cust Svc	Minnetonka	MN	55343	**800-371-4425***	952-932-7700
Musicnotes Inc 8020 Excelsior Dr Suite 201	Madison	WI	53717	**800-944-4667**	608-662-1680
Sam Goody 10400 Yellow Circle Dr *Cust Svc	Minnetonka	MN	55343	**800-371-4225***	952-932-7700
Spec's Music Inc 501 Collins Ave	Miami Beach	FL	33139	**800-540-1242**	305-534-3667
Strawberries Music & Video 38 Corporate Cir	Albany	NY	12203	**800-540-1242**	518-452-1242
Tower Records 2500 Del Monte St Bldg C	West Sacramento	CA	95691	**800-225-0880**	916-373-2500
Trans World Entertainment Corp 38 Corporate Cir *NASDAQ: TWMC*	Albany	NY	12203	**800-540-1242**	518-452-1242
Transcontinent Record Sales Inc DBA Record Theatre 1762 Main St	Buffalo	NY	14208	**800-836-0751**	716-883-9520
Virgin Megastores USA c/o SJ Communications 17012 Enadia Way	Lake Balboa	CA	91406	**877-484-7446**	818-881-3889
YesAsia.com Inc 1192 Cherry Ave	San Bruno	CA	94066	**888-716-5753**	650-517-5100

515 MUSICAL INSTRUMENT STORES

Name / Address	City	State	Zip	Toll-Free	Phone
Alamo Music Center 425 N Main Ave	San Antonio	TX	78205	**800-822-5010**	210-224-1010
American Musical Supply PO Box 152	Spicer	MN	56288	**800-458-4076**	320-796-2088
Amro Music Stores 2918 Poplar Ave	Memphis	TN	38111	**800-661-2676**	901-323-8888
Apollo's Axes LLC 19228 Wind Dancer St	Lutz	FL	33558	**800-827-9196**	813-920-7363
Ash Sam Music Corp PO Box 9047	Hicksville	NY	11802	**888-615-5904**	516-932-6400
Bizamo Music 12524 W Atlantic Blvd	Coral Springs	FL	33071	**888-924-9266**	
Bodine's Inc 6436 Penn Ave S	Richfield	MN	55423	**800-535-6424**	612-866-2025
Brook Mays Music Co 8605 John Carpenter Fwy *Cust Svc	Dallas	TX	75247	**800-637-8966***	214-631-0928
Buddy Rogers Music Inc 6891 Simpson Ave	Cincinnati	OH	45239	**888-276-8742**	513-729-1950
Elderly Instruments 1100 N Washington Ave	Lansing	MI	48906	**888-473-5810**	517-372-7890
Fletcher Music Centers Inc 3966 Airway Cir	Clearwater	FL	33762	**800-258-1088**	727-571-1088
Foxes Music Co 416 S Washington St	Falls Church	VA	22046	**800-446-4414**	703-533-7393
Giardinelli PO Box 4370	Medford	OR	97501	**800-249-8361**	541-772-5173
Graves Piano & Organ Co Inc 5798 Karl Rd	Columbus	OH	43229	**800-686-4322**	614-847-4322
Guitar Center Inc 5795 Lindero Canyon Rd *NASDAQ: GTRC*	Westlake Village	CA	91362	**800-905-0585**	818-735-8800
Guitar Imports 887 N McCormick Way 3	Layton	UT	84041	**877-544-4060**	801-544-4060
H & H Music Co 10303 Katy Fwy	Houston	TX	77024	**800-446-8742**	281-531-9222
Hume Music Inc 3660 SW Topeka Blvd	Topeka	KS	66611	**800-657-5748**	785-266-6366
International Violin Co Ltd 1421 Clarkview Rd	Baltimore	MD	21209	**800-542-3538**	410-832-2525
JW Pepper & Son Inc 2480 Industrial Blvd	Paoli	PA	19301	**800-345-6296**	610-648-0500
Ken Stanton Music Inc 119 Cobb Pkwy N	Marietta	GA	30062	**800-282-9011**	770-427-2491
Keyboard World Inc 23-25 E Main St	Frostburg	MD	21532	**800-947-4266**	301-729-1817
Ludwig Music House Inc 3600 Rider Trail S	Earth City	MO	63045	**800-783-7007**	314-298-9696
Music123 1 Cherry Hill Suite 800	Cherry Hill	NJ	08002	**888-590-9700**	856-779-6300
Music & Arts Centers Inc 4626 Wedgewood Blvd	Frederick	MD	21703	**800-237-7760**	301-620-4040
Musician's Friend Inc PO Box 4370	Medford	OR	97501	**800-391-8762**	541-772-5173
Musiciansbuy.com Inc 11-7830 Byron Dr	West Palm Beach	FL	33404	**877-778-7845**	561-842-7451
Sam Ash Music Corp PO Box 9047	Hicksville	NY	11802	**888-615-5904**	516-932-6400
SameDayMusic 65 Greenwood Ave	Midland Park	NJ	07432	**866-744-7736**	
Schmitt Music Co 100 N 6th St Suite 850B	Minneapolis	MN	55403	**800-767-3434**	612-339-4811
Stanton's Sheet Music 330 S 4th St	Columbus	OH	43215	**800-426-8742**	614-224-4257
Strait Music Co 2428 W Ben White Blvd	Austin	TX	78704	**800-725-8877**	512-476-6927
US Music Corp 444 E Courtland St	Mundelein	IL	60060	**800-877-6863**	847-949-0444
West Music Inc 1212 5th St PO Box 5521	Coralville	IA	52241	**800-373-2000**	319-351-2000
Woodwind & Brasswind 4004 Technology Dr	South Bend	IN	46628	**800-348-5003**	574-251-3500
zZounds Music 65 Greenwood Ave	Midland Park	NJ	07432	**800-996-8637**	

516 MUSICAL INSTRUMENTS

Name / Address	City	State	Zip	Toll-Free	Phone
Avedis Zildjian Co 22 Longwater Dr	Norwell	MA	02061	**800-229-8672**	781-871-2200
Baldwin Piano Co 309 Plus Park Blvd	Nashville	TN	37219	**800-444-2766**	615-871-4500
Carvin Guitars 12340 World Trade Dr	San Diego	CA	92128	**800-854-2235**	858-487-1600
Casio Inc 570 Mt Pleasant Ave *Cust Svc	Dover	NJ	07801	**800-634-1895***	973-361-5400
CF Martin & Co Inc DBA Martin Guitar Co 510 Sycamore St	Nazareth	PA	18064	**800-345-3103**	610-759-2837
Chesbro Music Co Inc PO Box 2009 *Cust Svc	Idaho Falls	ID	83403	**800-243-7276***	208-522-8691
Chime Master Systems PO Box 936	Lancaster	OH	43130	**800-344-7464**	740-746-8500
Commercial Music Co Inc 1550 Edison St	Dallas	TX	75207	**800-442-7281**	214-741-6381
Conn-Selmer Inc 600 Industrial Pkwy	Elkhart	IN	46515	**800-759-9124**	574-295-0079
Davitt & Hanser Music Co 4940 Delhi Pike	Cincinnati	OH	45238	**800-999-5558**	513-451-5000
Deering Banjo Co 3733 Kenora Dr	Spring Valley	CA	91977	**800-845-7791**	619-464-8252
E & O Mari Inc 256 Broadway	Newburgh	NY	12550	**800-750-3034**	845-562-4400
Edwards Instrument Co 530 S Hwy H	Elkhorn	WI	53121	**800-366-5584**	262-723-4221
Emerson Flutes USA 600 Industrial Pkwy	Elkhart	IN	46515	**800-759-9124**	574-522-1675
Ernie Ball 151 Suburban Rd	San Luis Obispo	CA	93401	**800-543-2255**	
Fender Musical Instruments Corp 8860 E Chaparral Rd Suite 100	Scottsdale	AZ	85250	**800-488-1818**	480-596-9690
Fernandez Guitars International Inc 8163 Lankershim Blvd	North Hollywood	CA	91605	**800-318-8599**	818-252-6799
General Music Corp 1164 Tower Ln	Bensenville	IL	60106	**800-323-0280**	630-766-8230
Getzen Co Inc 530 S Hwy H PO Box 440	Elkhorn	WI	53121	**800-366-5584**	262-723-4221
GHS Corp 2813 Wilber Ave	Battle Creek	MI	49015	**800-388-4447**	269-968-3351
Gibson Guitar Corp DBA Gibson Musical Instruments 309 Plus Park Blvd	Nashville	TN	37217	**800-444-2766**	615-871-4500
Gibson Musical Instruments 309 Plus Park Blvd	Nashville	TN	37217	**800-444-2766**	615-871-4500
Gibson Piano Ventures Inc DBA Baldwin Piano Co 309 Plus Park Blvd	Nashville	TN	37219	**800-444-2766**	615-871-4500
Hammond Suzuki USA 733 Annoreno Dr	Addison	IL	60101	**800-466-2286**	630-543-0277
Hohner Inc 1000 Technology Pk Dr	Glen Allen	VA	23059	**800-446-6010**	804-515-1900
J D'Addario & Co Inc 595 Smith St	Farmingdale	NY	11735	**800-323-2746**	631-439-3300
JD Calato Mfg Co Inc 4501 Hyde Park Blvd *Cust Svc	Niagara Falls	NY	14305	**800-358-4590***	716-285-3546
Kaman Music Corp 20 Old Windsor Rd	Bloomfield	CT	06002	**800-647-2244**	860-509-8888
Kawai America Corp 2055 E University Dr	Compton	CA	90220	**800-421-2177**	310-631-1771
La Bella Strings 256 Broadway	Newburgh	NY	12550	**800-750-3034**	845-562-4400
Leblanc Inc 7001 Leblanc Blvd	Kenosha	WI	53141	**800-558-9421**	262-658-1644
Lowrey Organ Co 825 E 26th St	La Grange Park	IL	60526	**800-451-5939**	708-352-3388
Lyon & Healy Harps Inc 168 N Ogden Ave	Chicago	IL	60607	**800-621-3881**	312-786-1881
Maas-Rowe Carillons Inc 2255 Meyers Ave	Escondido	CA	92029	**800-854-2023**	760-743-1311
Manhasset Specialty Co 3505 Fruitvale Blvd	Yakima	WA	98902	**800-795-0965**	509-248-3810
Martin Guitar Co 510 Sycamore St	Nazareth	PA	18064	**800-345-3103**	610-759-2837
Meisel Music Inc PO Box 90	Springfield	NJ	07081	**800-634-7350**	973-379-5000
Music Industries Corp 625 Locust St *Orders	Garden City	NY	11530	**800-431-6699***	516-794-1888
Musicorp PO Box 30819	Charleston	SC	29417	**800-845-1922**	843-763-9083
Organ Supply Industries Inc 2320 W 50th St	Erie	PA	16506	**800-458-0289**	814-835-2244
Ovation Guitars 37 Greenwoods Rd *Cust Svc	New Hartford	CT	06057	**800-552-4681***	860-379-7575
PianoDisc 4111 N Freeway Blvd	Sacramento	CA	95834	**800-566-3472**	916-567-9999
Prestini Musical Instruments Inc 2020 N Aurora Dr	Nogales	AZ	85628	**800-528-6569**	520-287-4931
Remo Inc 28101 Industry Dr	Valencia	CA	91355	**800-525-5134**	661-294-5600
Saint Louis Music Inc 1400 Ferguson Ave	Saint Louis	MO	63133	**800-727-4512**	314-727-4512
Schulmerich Carillons Inc 35 Carillon Hill Rd	Sellersville	PA	18960	**800-772-3557**	215-257-2771
Selmer Co Inc 600 Industrial Pkwy	Elkhart	IN	46515	**800-348-7426**	574-522-1675
Sound Enhancements Inc 185 Detroit St	Cary	IL	60013	**800-284-5172**	847-639-4646
Steinway & Sons 1 Steinway Pl	Long Island City	NY	11105	**800-366-1853**	718-721-2600
Suzuki Musical Instrument Corp PO Box 261030 *Cust Svc	San Diego	CA	92196	**800-854-1594***	858-566-9710
Ultimate Support Systems Inc 2506 Zurich Dr	Fort Collins	CO	80524	**800-525-5628**	970-493-4488
US Music Corp 444 E Courtland St	Mundelein	IL	60060	**800-877-6863**	847-949-0444
Wenger Corp 555 Park Dr	Owatonna	MN	55060	**800-733-0393**	507-455-4100
Wicks Pipe Organ Co 1100 5th St *Cust Svc	Highland	IL	62249	**800-444-9425***	618-654-2191

517 MUTUAL FUNDS

Name / Address	City	State	Zip	Toll-Free	Phone
AARP Investment Funds PO Box 219735	Kansas City	MO	64121	**800-253-2277**	
ABN AMRO Funds PO Box 9765	Providence	RI	02940	**800-992-8151**	
AIM Family of Funds 11 Greenway Plaza Suite 100	Houston	TX	77046	**800-347-1919**	713-626-1919
Alger Fund 30 Montgomery St	Jersey City	NJ	07302	**800-992-3863**	201-547-3600
American AAdvantage Funds 4151 Amon Carter Blvd MD 2450	Fort Worth	TX	76155	**800-388-3344**	817-967-3509
American Century Funds PO Box 419200	Kansas City	MO	64141	**800-345-2021**	816-531-5575
American Express Mutual Funds 70100 AXP Financial Ctr	Minneapolis	MN	55474	**800-328-8300**	612-671-3131
American Funds Group 135 S State College Blvd	Brea	CA	92821	**800-421-0180**	714-671-7000
American Skandia PO Box 8012	Boston	MA	02266	**800-752-6342**	
AMF Funds 230 W Monroe St Suite 2810	Chicago	IL	60606	**800-527-3713**	
AmSouth Funds 3435 Stelzer Rd	Columbus	OH	43219	**800-451-8382**	614-470-8000
Aquila Group of Funds 380 Madison Ave Suite 2300	New York	NY	10017	**800-762-5955**	212-697-6666
Armada Funds PO Box 8421	Boston	MA	02266	**800-622-3863**	
Artisan Funds PO Box 8412	Boston	MA	02266	**800-344-1770**	
Asset Management Fund 230 W Monroe St Suite 2810	Chicago	IL	60606	**800-527-3713**	
Barclays Global Investors Funds 45 Fremont St 5th Fl	San Francisco	CA	94105	**888-204-3956**	415-597-2000
Baron Funds 767 5th Ave 49th Fl	New York	NY	10153	**800-992-2766**	212-583-2000
Bear Stearns Inc 383 Madison Ave	New York	NY	10179	**800-766-4111**	212-272-2000
BlackRock Funds 40 E 52nd St	New York	NY	10022	**888-825-2257**	212-754-5300
BNY Hamilton Funds PO Box 182785	Columbus	OH	43218	**800-426-9363**	
Brandywine Funds PO Box 701	Milwaukee	WI	53201	**800-656-3017**	
Brazos Mutual Funds 5949 Sherry Ln Suite 1600	Dallas	TX	75225	**800-426-9157**	214-365-5214
Calvert Group Mutual Funds 4550 Montgomery Ave Suite 1000N	Bethesda	MD	20814	**800-727-5578**	301-951-4800
CDC Nvest Funds PO Box 219579	Kansas City	MO	64121	**800-225-5478**	
CGM Funds 222 Berkeley St Suite 1013	Boston	MA	02116	**800-345-4048**	617-859-7714
Citifunds PO Box 9083	Boston	MA	02266	**800-331-1792**	
Citizens Funds 1 Harbor Pl Suite 400	Portsmouth	NH	03801	**800-223-7010**	603-436-5152
Clipper Fund 9601 Wilshire Blvd Suite 800	Beverly Hills	CA	90210	**800-776-5033**	310-247-3940
Columbia Funds Services Inc PO Box 8081	Boston	MA	02266	**800-345-6611**	
Davis Funds PO Box 8406	Boston	MA	02266	**800-279-0279**	
Delaware Investments Funds 2005 Market St	Philadelphia	PA	19103	**800-523-1918**	215-255-1200
Delaware Pooled Trust Funds Delaware Investments 2005 Market St 1 Commerce Sq	Philadelphia	PA	19103	**800-231-8002**	
Diversified Funds 4 Manhattanville Rd	Purchase	NY	10577	**800-926-0044**	914-697-8000
Dodge & Cox Funds 555 California St 40th Fl	San Francisco	CA	94104	**800-621-3979**	415-981-1710
Domini Social Investments PO Box 9785	Providence	RI	02940	**800-582-6757**	
Dreyfus Family of Funds 200 Park Ave	New York	NY	10166	**800-645-6561**	212-922-6000
Eaton Vance Mutual Funds 255 State St	Boston	MA	02109	**800-225-6265**	617-482-8260
Eclipse Funds 169 Lackawanna Ave	Parsippany	NJ	07054	**866-232-5477**	973-394-3000

Name / Address	City	State	Zip	Toll-Free	Phone
Enterprise Group of Funds 3343 Peachtree Rd NE East Tower Suite 450	Atlanta	GA	30326	**800-432-4320**	404-261-1116
Evergreen Investments PO Box 8400	Boston	MA	02266	**800-343-2898**	
Excelsior Funds PO Box 8529	Boston	MA	02266	**800-446-1012**	
Federated Funds PO Box 8606	Boston	MA	02266	**800-245-4770**	
Fidelity Advisor Funds PO Box 770002	Cincinnati	OH	45277	**800-522-7297**	
Fidelity Freedom Funds PO Box 770001	Cincinnati	OH	45277	**800-343-3548**	
Fidelity Investment Funds PO Box 770001	Cincinnati	OH	45277	**800-343-3548**	
Fidelity Select Funds PO Box 770002	Cincinnati	OH	45277	**800-544-8888**	
Fidelity Spartan Funds PO Box 770002	Cincinnati	OH	45277	**800-544-8888**	
Fifth Third Funds PO Box 182706	Columbus	OH	43218	**800-282-5706**	
First American Funds PO Box 3011	Milwaukee	WI	53201	**800-677-3863**	
First Eagle Funds PO Box 219324	Kansas City	MO	64121	**800-334-2143**	
First Eagle SoGen Funds PO Box 219324	Kansas City	MO	64121	**800-334-2143**	
First Funds PO Box 8050	Boston	MA	02266	**800-442-1941**	
First Investors Funds 95 Wall St	New York	NY	10005	**800-423-4026**	212-858-8000
Firsthand Funds PO Box 8356	Boston	MA	02266	**888-883-3863**	
Franklin Templeton Mutual Funds PO Box 33030	Saint Petersburg	FL	33733	**800-632-2301**	
Gabelli Funds 1 Corporate Ctr	Rye	NY	10580	**800-422-3554**	914-921-5100
Gartmore Funds PO Box 182205	Columbus	OH	43218	**800-848-0920**	
Gateway Funds 3805 Edwards Rd Suite 600	Cincinnati	OH	45209	**800-354-6339**	513-719-1100
GE Elfun Funds 101 Savings St	Pawtucket	RI	02860	**800-242-0134**	
GE Mutual Funds 101 Savings St	Pawtucket	RI	02860	**800-242-0134**	
Glenmede Funds 1650 Market St One Liberty Pl Suite 1200	Philadelphia	PA	19103	**800-966-3200**	215-419-6000
Goldman Sachs Funds PO Box 219711	Kansas City	MO	64121	**800-526-7384**	312-655-4435
Guardian Group of Funds PO Box 219611	Kansas City	MO	64121	**800-343-0817**	
Hartford Mutual Funds PO Box 64387	Saint Paul	MN	55164	**888-843-7824**	
Heartland Funds 789 N Water St Suite 500	Milwaukee	WI	53202	**800-432-7856**	414-347-7777
HighMark Funds PO Box 8416	Boston	MA	02266	**800-433-6884**	
Horace Mann Growth Fund 1 Horace Mann Plaza	Springfield	IL	62715	**800-999-1030**	217-789-2500
ICAP Family of Funds PO Box 2160	Milwaukee	WI	53201	**888-221-4227**	
ING Funds 7337 E Doubletree Ranch Rd	Scottsdale	AZ	85258	**800-334-3444**	480-477-3000
INVESCO Funds Group Inc 4350 S Monaco St	Denver	CO	80237	**800-525-8085**	303-930-6300
Ivy Funds 6300 Lamar Ave	Overland Park	KS	66202	**888-923-3355**	913-236-2000
Janus Funds 100 Fillmore St	Denver	CO	80206	**800-525-3713**	303-333-3863
Japan Fund PO Box 446	Portland	ME	04112	**800-535-2726**	
John Hancock Funds 101 Huntington Ave 10th Fl	Boston	MA	02199	**800-338-8080**	617-375-1500
Kaufmann Fund 140 E 45th St 43rd Fl	New York	NY	10017	**800-261-0551**	212-922-0123
Kopp Funds 7701 France Ave S Suite 500	Edina	MN	55435	**888-533-5677**	952-841-0400
Lazard Funds 30 Rockefeller Plaza 57th Fl	New York	NY	10112	**800-823-6300**	
Legg Mason Family of Funds 100 Light St	Baltimore	MD	21202	**800-368-2558**	410-539-0000
Loomis Sayles Funds 1 Financial Ctr	Boston	MA	02111	**800-633-3330**	617-482-2450
Lord Abbett Family of Funds 90 Hudson St	Jersey City	NJ	07302	**800-201-6984**	201-395-2000
MainStay Funds 169 Lackawanna Ave	Parsippany	NJ	07054	**800-695-9950**	
Mairs & Power Funds 332 Minnesota St Suite W-1520	Saint Paul	MN	55101	**800-304-7404**	651-222-8478
Marshall Funds PO Box 1348	Milwaukee	WI	53201	**800-236-3863**	
Marsico Funds PO Box 3210	Milwaukee	WI	53201	**888-860-8686**	
MAS Funds 100 Front St Suite 1100	West Conshohocken	PA	19428	**800-354-8185**	610-940-5000
MassMutual Funds 1295 State St	Springfield	MA	01111	**800-542-6767**	413-788-8411
Merger Fund PO Box 701	Milwaukee	WI	53201	**800-343-8959**	414-765-4124
Merrill Lynch Family of Funds PO Box 45289	Jacksonville	FL	32232	**800-637-3863**	
Morgan Stanley Family of Funds 1585 Broadway	New York	NY	10036	**800-869-6397**	212-761-4000
Morgan Stanley Institutional Funds 73 Tremont St	Boston	MA	02108	**800-548-7786**	617-557-8000
Munder Funds 480 Pierce St	Birmingham	MI	48009	**800-468-6337**	248-647-9200
Nations Funds PO Box 34602	Charlotte	NC	28254	**800-321-7854**	
Neuberger Berman Funds PO Box 8403	Boston	MA	02266	**800-877-9700**	212-476-8800
Nicholas Family of Funds 700 N Water St Suite 1010	Milwaukee	WI	53202	**800-227-5987**	414-272-6133
Northeast Investors Funds 150 Federal St	Boston	MA	02110	**800-225-6704**	617-523-3588
Northern Funds PO Box 75986	Chicago	IL	60675	**800-595-9111**	312-557-2790
Northern Institutional Funds 801 S Canal St C5S	Chicago	IL	60607	**800-637-1380**	
Nuveen Mutual Funds PO Box 463	East Syracuse	NY	13057	**800-257-8787**	
Oak Assoc Funds PO Box 219441	Kansas City	MO	64121	**888-462-5386**	
Oakmark Family of Funds 2 N La Salle St Suite 500	Chicago	IL	60602	**800-625-6275**	312-621-0600
OppenheimerFunds Inc PO Box 5270	Denver	CO	80217	**800-525-7048**	303-671-3200
Pax World Fund Family 222 State St	Portsmouth	NH	03801	**800-767-1729**	603-431-8022
PBHG Funds Inc 1400 Liberty Ridge Dr	Wayne	PA	19087	**800-433-0051**	610-647-4100
Phoenix Mutual Funds PO Box 8301	Boston	MA	02266	**800-243-1574**	
PIMCO Funds 2187 Atlantic St	Stamford	CT	06902	**800-628-1237**	
PIMCO Institutional Funds PO Box 219024	Kansas City	MO	64121	**800-927-4648**	
Pioneer Funds 60 State St	Boston	MA	02109	**800-225-6292**	617-742-7825
Preferred Group of Mutual Funds PO Box 8320	Boston	MA	02266	**800-662-4769**	
Price T Rowe Mutual Funds 100 E Pratt St	Baltimore	MD	21202	**800-638-5660**	410-345-2000
Putnam Family of Funds PO Box 41203	Providence	RI	02940	**800-225-1581**	
Rainier Investment Management Mutual Funds 601 Union St Suite 2801	Seattle	WA	98101	**800-248-6314**	206-464-0400
Royce Funds 1414 Ave of the Americas	New York	NY	10019	**800-337-6923**	
RS Investments PO Box 219717	Kansas City	MO	64121	**800-766-3863**	
Rydex Funds 9601 Blackwell Rd Suite 500	Rockville	MD	20850	**800-820-0888**	301-296-5100
SAFECO Mutual Funds PO Box 34890	Seattle	WA	98124	**800-624-5711**	
Salomon Brothers Investment Series 100 First Stamford Pl	Stamford	CT	06902	**866-811-7256**	
Schwab Mutual Funds 101 Montgomery St	San Francisco	CA	94104	**800-435-4000**	415-627-7000
Scudder Funds PO Box 219669	Kansas City	MO	64121	**800-728-3337**	
Security Funds 1 Security Benefit Pl	Topeka	KS	66636	**800-888-2461**	785-438-3000
SEI Mutual Funds Services PO Box 1098	Oaks	PA	19456	**800-342-5734**	
Selected Funds PO Box 8243	Boston	MA	02266	**800-243-1575**	
Seligman Group of Funds 100 Park Avenue	New York	NY	10017	**800-221-7844**	212-850-1864
Sentinel Funds PO Box 1499	Montpelier	VT	05601	**800-282-3863**	802-229-7355
Sequoia Fund Inc 767 5th Ave Suite 4701	New York	NY	10153	**800-686-6884**	212-832-5280
Smith Barney Family of Funds PO Box 9699	Providence	RI	02940	**800-451-2010**	
Sound Shore Fund PO Box 1810	Greenwich	CT	06836	**800-551-1980**	203-629-1980
Spectra Fund Alger Shareholder Services 30 Montgomery St	Jersey City	NJ	07302	**800-711-6141**	
SSgA funds 1 Lincoln St	Boston	MA	02111	**800-997-7327**	617-664-6089
State Farm Mutual Funds PO Box 219548	Kansas City	MO	64121	**800-447-4930**	
State Street Research Funds PO Box 8408	Boston	MA	02266	**800-882-3302**	617-357-7800
STI Classic Funds PO Box 4418 MC 712	Atlanta	GA	30302	**800-428-6970**	
SunAmerica Mutual Funds 733 3rd Ave 4th Fl	New York	NY	10017	**800-858-8850**	212-551-5100
T Rowe Price Mutual Funds 100 E Pratt St	Baltimore	MD	21202	**800-638-5660**	410-345-2000
Tamarack Funds PO Box 219757	Kansas City	MO	64121	**800-422-2766**	
TARGET Funds PO Box 8098	Philadelphia	PA	19101	**800-225-1852**	
TCW Galileo Funds PO Box 9821	Providence	RI	02940	**800-386-3829**	
Third Avenue Funds PO Box 9802	Providence	RI	02940	**800-443-1021**	212-888-6685
Thornburg Investment Management Funds 119 E Marcy St Suite 202	Santa Fe	NM	87501	**800-533-9337**	505-984-0200
TIAA-CREF Mutual Funds PO Box 8009	Boston	MA	02266	**800-223-1200**	
Torray Fund 7501 Wisconsin Ave Suite 1100	Bethesda	MD	20814	**800-443-3036**	301-493-4600
Transamerica IDEX Mutual Funds PO Box 9015 *Cust Svc	Clearwater	FL	33758	**800-233-4339***	727-299-1800
Trizec Canada Inc 181 Bay St Suite 3820 *TSE: TZC.SV*	Toronto	ON	M5J2T3	**877-239-7200**	416-361-7200
TRUST for Credit Unions (TCU) 4900 Sears Tower 51st Fl	Chicago	IL	60606	**800-621-2550**	312-655-4400
Turner Funds 1205 Westlakes Dr Suite 100	Berwyn	PA	19312	**800-424-4865**	610-251-0268
Tweedy Browne Funds 350 Park Ave 9th Fl	New York	NY	10022	**800-432-4789**	212-916-0600
UBS Global Asset Management Mutual Funds PO Box 9786	Providence	RI	02940	**800-647-1568**	
USAA Funds 9800 Fredericksburg Rd USAA Bldg	San Antonio	TX	78288	**800-531-8448**	210-498-7290
Value Line Funds PO Box 219729	Kansas City	MO	64121	**800-223-0818**	
Van Kampen Funds 2800 Post Oak Blvd	Houston	TX	77056	**800-341-2911**	713-438-4000
Van Wagoner Funds PO Box 9682	Providence	RI	02940	**800-228-2121**	
Vanguard Funds PO Box 1110	Valley Forge	PA	19482	**800-871-3879**	
VantagePoint Funds 777 N Capitol St NW	Washington	DC	20002	**800-669-7400**	202-962-4600
Victory Funds PO Box 182593	Columbus	OH	43218	**800-539-3863**	
W & R Funds 6300 Lamar Ave	Shawnee Mission	KS	66202	**800-366-5465**	913-236-2000
Waddell & Reed Advisors Funds 6300 Lamar Ave	Shawnee Mission	KS	66202	**800-366-5465**	913-236-2000
Warburg Pincus Funds 466 Lexington Ave	New York	NY	10017	**800-888-3697**	212-878-0600
Weitz Funds 1125 S 103rd St Suite 600	Omaha	NE	68124	**800-304-9745**	402-391-1980
Wells Fargo Funds PO Box 8266	Boston	MA	02266	**800-222-8222**	
Wilshire Target Funds Inc PO Box 9807	Providence	RI	02940	**888-200-6796**	
WM Group of Funds PO Box 9757	Providence	RI	02940	**800-222-5852**	
WWW Internet Fund PO Box 25910	Lexington	KY	40524	**888-999-8331**	

518 NATURE STORES

SEE ALSO Gift Shops

Name / Address	City	State	Zip	Toll-Free	Phone
A2Z Science & Nature Store 57 King St	Northampton	MA	01060	**877-261-6171**	413-586-1611
Nature Store Roger Tory Peterson Institute 311 Curtis St	Jamestown	NY	14701	**800-758-6841**	716-665-2473
Wild Bird Centers of America Inc 7370 MacArthur Blvd	Glen Echo	MD	20812	**800-945-3247**	301-229-9585
Wild Bird Shop 123 S Hemlock	Cannon Beach	OR	97110	**800-281-9806**	503-436-9806
Wild Birds Unlimited 11711 N College Ave Suite 146	Carmel	IN	46032	**800-326-4928**	317-571-7100

519 NAVIGATION & GUIDANCE INSTRUMENTS & SYSTEMS

Name / Address	City	State	Zip	Toll-Free	Phone
AAI Corp PO Box 126	Hunt Valley	MD	21030	**800-626-6283**	410-666-1400
Acterna Corp 1 Milestone Center Dr	Germantown	MD	20876	**800-543-1550**	301-353-1550
Alpine Electronics of America 19145 Gramercy Pl	Torrance	CA	90501	**800-257-4631**	310-326-8000
AMS (ASI) Inc 11300 W 89th St	Overland Park	KS	66214	**800-765-0861**	913-495-2600
ATK Integrated Defense Co 4700 Nathan Ln N	Plymouth	MN	55442	**800-456-8933**	763-744-5000
BAE SYSTEMS Infrared Imaging Systems 2 Forbes Rd	Lexington	MA	02421	**800-250-9494**	781-863-3199
BEI Technologies Inc Systron Donner Inertial Div 2700 Systron Dr	Concord	CA	94518	**800-227-1625**	925-671-6400
Benthos Inc 49 Edgerton Dr *NASDAQ: BTHS* ■ *Sales	North Falmouth	MA	02556	**800-446-1222***	508-563-1000
Boeing Sunnyvale 84 Hermosa Ct	Sunnyvale	CA	94086	**800-332-2201**	408-737-1000
Brunswick New Technologies Marine Electronics 30 Sudbury Rd	Acton	MA	01720	**800-628-4487**	978-897-6600
CMI Inc 316 E 9th St	Owensboro	KY	42303	**866-835-0690**	270-685-6545
Del Mar Avionics 1601-C Alton Pkwy	Irvine	CA	92606	**800-854-0481**	949-250-3200
DRS Infrared Technologies LP 13544 N Central Expy	Dallas	TX	75243	**877-377-4783**	972-560-6000
DRS Training & Control Systems 645 Anchors St NW	Fort Walton Beach	FL	32548	**800-326-6724**	850-302-3000
EDO Corp 60 E 42nd St 42nd Fl *NYSE: EDO*	New York	NY	10165	**800-621-3677**	212-716-2000
FLIR Systems Inc 16505 SW 72nd Ave *NASDAQ: FLIR*	Portland	OR	97224	**800-322-3731**	503-684-3731
Frontier Electronic Systems Corp 4500 W 6th Ave	Stillwater	OK	74074	**800-677-1769**	405-624-1769
Garmin Ltd 1200 E 151st St *NASDAQ: GRMN*	Olathe	KS	66062	**888-442-7646**	913-397-8200
General Dynamics Decision Systems 8201 E McDowell Rd	Scottsdale	AZ	85257	**877-466-9467**	480-441-8630
Gilfillan Div ITT Industries Inc 7821 Orion Ave	Van Nuys	CA	91406	**800-264-9234**	818-988-2600
Goodrich Corp 2730 W Tyvola Rd 4 Coliseum Ctr *NYSE: GR*	Charlotte	NC	28217	**800-784-7009**	704-423-7000
Honeywell Aerospace 1944 E Sky Harbor Cir	Phoenix	AZ	85034	**800-601-3099**	
Honeywell Aerospace Electronic Systems 1944 E Sky Harbor Cir	Phoenix	AZ	85034	**800-601-3099**	
Honeywell Defense Avionics Systems 9201 San Mateo Blvd NE	Albuquerque	NM	87113	**800-376-5311**	505-828-5000
Honeywell Space Systems 13350 US Hwy 19 N	Clearwater	FL	33764	**888-561-5665**	727-539-4000
Interstate Electronics Corp 602 E Vermont Ave	Anaheim	CA	92805	**800-854-6979**	714-758-0500

				Toll-Free	Phone
ITT Industries Inc Gilfillan Div					
7821 Orion Ave	Van Nuys	CA	91406	**800-264-9234**	818-988-2600
Jewell Instruments LLC 850 Perimeter Rd	Manchester	NH	03103	**800-227-5955**	603-669-6400
Kearfott Guidance & Navigation Corp					
150 Totowa Rd	Wayne	NJ	07470	**800-785-6000**	973-785-6000
Kollsman Inc 220 Daniel Webster Hwy	Merrimack	NH	03054	**800-258-1350**	603-889-2500
KVH Industries Inc 50 Enterprise Ctr	Middletown	RI	02842	**888-584-4773**	401-847-3327
NASDAQ: KVHI					
L-3 Avionics Systems 5353 52nd St SE	Grand Rapids	MI	49512	**800-253-9525**	616-949-6600
L-3 Communications Corp Telemetry & Instrumentation Div 9020 Balboa Ave	San Diego	CA	92123	**800-351-8483**	858-694-7500
Laitram Corp 220 Laitram Ln	Harahan	LA	70123	**800-533-8253**	504-733-6000
Lockheed Martin Management & Data Systems Western Region 3200 Zanker Rd	San Jose	CA	95134	**800-537-2188**	408-473-3000
Lockheed Martin Naval Electronics & Surveillance Systems Manassas					
9500 Godwin Dr	Manassas	VA	20110	**800-325-4019**	703-367-2121
Lowrance Electronics Inc 12000 E Skelly Dr	Tulsa	OK	74128	**800-234-4738**	918-437-6881
NASDAQ: LEIX					
Meggitt/S-TEC 1 S-Tec Way	Mineral Wells	TX	76067	**800-872-7832**	940-325-9406
Motorola Inc 1301 E Algonquin Rd	Schaumburg	IL	60196	**800-331-6456**	847-576-5000
NYSE: MOT					
MPD Inc 316 E 9th St	Owensboro	KY	42303	**866-225-5673**	270-685-6200
Narco Avionics 270 Commerce Dr	Fort Washington	PA	19034	**800-223-3636***	215-643-2900
*Sales					
NavCom Defense Electronics Inc					
4323 Arden Dr	El Monte	CA	91731	**800-729-8191**	626-442-0123
Northrop Grumman Information Technology					
4800 Hampden Ln Suite 200	Bethesda	MD	20814	**800-366-4822**	301-961-0500
Orbit International Corp 80 Cabot Ct	Hauppauge	NY	11788	**800-663-5366**	631-435-8300
NASDAQ: ORBT					
Orbital Sciences Corp 21839 Atlantic Blvd	Dulles	VA	20166	**877-672-4825**	703-406-5000
NYSE: ORB					
Raymarine Inc 21 Manchester St	Merrimack	NH	03054	**800-539-5539**	603-881-5200
Raytheon Intelligence & Information Systems					
1200 S Jupiter Rd	Garland	TX	75042	**800-752-6163**	972-205-5409
Rockwell Collins Inc 400 Collins Rd NE	Cedar Rapids	IA	52498	**888-265-5467**	319-295-1000
NYSE: COL					
Rostra Precision Controls Inc					
2519 Dana Dr	Laurinburg	NC	28352	**800-782-3379***	910-276-4853
*Cust Svc					
SEA/Datamarine Inc					
7030 220th St SW	Mountlake Terrace	WA	98043	**800-426-1330**	425-771-2182
Sparton Corp 2400 E Ganson St	Jackson	MI	49202	**800-248-9579**	517-787-8600
NYSE: SPA					
Sperry Marine 1070 Seminole Trail	Charlottesville	VA	22901	**800-368-2010***	434-974-2000
*Cust Svc					
Stewart & Stevenson Services Inc					
2707 North Loop W	Houston	TX	77008	**800-527-3246**	713-868-7700
NYSE: SVC					
Systron Donner Inertial Div BEI Technologies Inc 2700 Systron Dr	Concord	CA	94518	**800-227-1625**	925-671-6400
Telair International Inc 4175 Guardian St	Simi Valley	CA	93063	**800-989-4827**	805-306-8066
Telephonics Corp 815 Broad Hollow Rd	Farmingdale	NY	11735	**877-755-7700**	631-755-7000
Thales ATM 23501 W 84th St	Shawnee	KS	66227	**800-526-3433**	913-422-2600
Trimble Navigation Ltd 749 N Mary Ave	Sunnyvale	CA	94085	**800-827-8000**	408-481-8000
NASDAQ: TRMB					
Whistler Group Inc 13016 N Walton Blvd	Bentonville	AR	72712	**800-531-0004***	479-273-6012
*Cust Svc					
XATA Corp 151 E Cliff Rd Suite 10	Burnsville	MN	55337	**800-262-9282***	952-894-3680
NASDAQ: XATA ■ *Tech Supp					

520 NEWS SYNDICATES, SERVICES, BUREAUS

				Toll-Free	Phone
AccuWeather Inc 385 Science Park Rd	State College	PA	16803	**800-566-6606***	814-235-8650
*Sales					
American Baptist News Service					
PO Box 851	Valley Forge	PA	19482	**800-222-3872**	610-768-2077
Bloomberg News 499 Park Ave 15th Fl	New York	NY	10022	**800-448-5678**	212-318-2000
Business Wire					
44 Montgomery St 39th Fl	San Francisco	CA	94104	**800-227-0845**	415-986-4422
California Newspaper Service Bureau					
915 E 1st St	Los Angeles	CA	90012	**800-788-7840**	213-229-5500
Comics.com 200 Madison Ave 4th Fl	New York	NY	10016	**800-221-4816**	212-293-8500
Copley News Service					
123 Camino de la Reina Suite E-250	San Diego	CA	92108	**800-238-6196**	619-293-1818
Disaster News Network					
9195-C Red Branch Rd	Columbia	MD	21045	**888-203-9119**	410-884-7350
Federal News Services					
1000 Vermont Ave NW 5th Fl	Washington	DC	20005	**800-221-4020**	202-347-1400
HyperFeed Technologies Inc					
300 S Wacker Dr Suite 300	Chicago	IL	60606	**800-225-5657**	312-913-2800
NASDAQ: HYPR					
King Features Syndicate Inc					
888 7th Ave 2nd Fl	New York	NY	10019	**800-526-5464**	212-455-4000
Knight Ridder/Tribune Information Services					
700 12th St NW Suite 1000	Washington	DC	20005	**800-346-8798**	202-383-6080
KRT Direct 700 12th St NW Suite 1000	Washington	DC	20005	**800-346-8798**	202-383-6080
Market Wire Inc					
5757 W Century Blvd 2nd Fl	Los Angeles	CA	90045	**800-774-9473**	310-846-3600
Mortgage Market Information Services Inc					
53 E Saint Charles Rd	Villa Park	IL	60181	**800-509-4636**	630-834-7555
New Yorker Magazine Cartoon Bank Div					
145 Palisade St Suite 373	Dobbs Ferry	NY	10522	**800-897-8666**	914-478-5527
Newspaper Enterprise Assn					
200 Madison Ave 4th Fl	New York	NY	10016	**800-221-4816**	212-293-8500
PR Newswire 810 7th Ave 35th Fl	New York	NY	10019	**800-832-5522**	212-596-1500
Religion News Service					
1101 Connecticut Ave NW Suite 350	Washington	DC	20036	**800-767-6781**	202-463-8777
Sports Network 2200 Byberry Rd	Hatboro	PA	19040	**800-583-5499**	215-441-8444
SportsTicker Enterprises					
ESPN Plaza Bldg B 4th Fl	Bristol	CT	06010	**800-367-8935**	860-766-1899
Stats Inc 8130 Lehigh Ave	Morton Grove	IL	60053	**800-637-8287***	847-677-3322
*Orders					
Stephens Media Group Washington News Bureau 666 11th St NW Rm 535	Washington	DC	20001	**800-366-7390**	202-783-1760
Tribune Media Services Inc					
435 N Michigan Ave Suite 1500	Chicago	IL	60611	**800-245-6536**	312-222-4444
United Feature Syndicate Inc					
200 Madison Ave 4th Fl	New York	NY	10016	**800-221-4816**	212-293-8500
United Media 200 Madison Ave 4th Fl	New York	NY	10016	**800-221-4816**	212-293-8500
United Press International (UPI)					
1510 H St NW	Washington	DC	20005	**800-783-4874**	202-898-8000
Universal Press Syndicate					
4520 Main St Suite 700	Kansas City	MO	64111	**800-255-6734**	816-932-6600
Washington Post Writers Group					
1150 15th St NW	Washington	DC	20071	**800-879-9794**	202-334-6375
Wireless Flash News Service					
827 Washington St	San Diego	CA	92103	**800-790-2444**	619-220-7191

521 NEWSLETTERS

521-1 Banking & Finance Newsletters

				Toll-Free	Phone
Asset Sales Report 1 State St Plaza	New York	NY	10004	**888-280-4820**	212-803-8200
Bank Asset/Liability Management					
807 Las Cimas Pkwy Suite 300	Austin	TX	78746	**800-572-2797**	
Bank Network News					
1 State Street Plaza 27th Fl	New York	NY	10004	**800-535-8403**	212-803-8200
Consumer Credit & Truth-In-Lending Compliance Report 807 Las Cimas Pkwy Suite 300	Austin	TX	78756	**800-572-2797**	800-753-7577
Controller's Report 3 Park Ave 30th Fl	New York	NY	10016	**800-401-5937**	212-244-0360
Credit Card News					
1 State Street Plaza 27th Fl	New York	NY	10004	**800-535-8403**	212-803-8200
Credit Union Directors Newsletter					
5710 Mineral Point Rd	Madison	WI	53705	**800-356-8010**	608-231-4000
Credit Union Information Service					
11300 Rockville Pike Suite 1100	Rockville	MD	20852	**800-929-4824***	301-816-8950
*Cust Svc					
Debit Card News 1 State Street Plaza 27th Fl	New York	NY	10004	**800-535-8403**	212-803-8200
Defined Contribution News					
225 Park Ave S 7th Fl	New York	NY	10003	**800-543-4444**	212-224-3800
Equipment Leasing Newsletter					
1617 JFK Blvd Suite 1750	Philadelphia	PA	19103	**800-999-1916**	215-557-2310
Executive 5710 Mineral Point Rd	Madison	WI	53705	**800-356-8010***	608-231-4000
*Circ					
Global Money Management					
225 Park Ave S 7th Fl	New York	NY	10003	**800-715-9195**	212-224-3800
Insurance Accountant 1 State St Plaza	New York	NY	10004	**800-221-1809**	212-803-8200
Internal Auditing Alert 395 Hudson St 4th Fl	New York	NY	10014	**800-950-1205**	212-367-6300
Lender Liability Law Report					
1901 Fort Myer Dr Suite 501	Arlington	VA	22209	**800-572-2797***	703-528-0145
*Cust Svc					
Loan Market Week 225 Park Ave S 7th Fl	New York	NY	10003	**800-543-4444**	212-224-3300
Managing 401K Plans 30 Park Ave 30th Fl	New York	NY	10016	**800-401-5937**	212-244-0360
Managing Accounts Payable					
3 Park Ave 30th Fl	New York	NY	10016	**800-401-5937**	212-244-0360
Managing Benefits Plans 3 Park Ave 30th Fl	New York	NY	10016	**800-401-5937**	212-244-0360
Managing Credit Receivables & Collections					
3 Park Ave 30th Fl	New York	NY	10016	**800-401-5937**	212-244-0360
Price Perceptions					
3030 NW Expy Suite 725	Oklahoma City	OK	73112	**800-231-0477**	405-604-8726
Regulatory Risk Monitor					
11300 Rockville Pike Suite 1100	Rockville	MD	20852	**800-929-4824**	301-816-8950
SEC Accounting Report					
395 Hudson St 4th Fl	New York	NY	10014	**800-431-9025**	212-367-6300
Smart Card Alert 300 S Wacker Dr Suite 1800	Chicago	IL	60606	**800-535-8403**	312-913-1334
VentureWire					
800 Plaza 2 Harborside Finanacial Ctr	Jersey City	NJ	07311	**800-326-3613**	866-291-1800

521-2 Business & Professional Newsletters

				Toll-Free	Phone
Accounting Dept Management & Administration Report 3 Park Ave 30th Fl	New York	NY	10016	**800-401-5937**	212-244-0360
Accounting for Law Firms 345 Park Ave S	New York	NY	10010	**800-888-8300**	212-779-9200
Accounting Office Management & Administration Report 3 Park Ave 30th Fl	New York	NY	10016	**800-401-5937**	212-244-0360
American Nurse					
8515 Georgia Ave Suite 400	Silver Spring	MD	20910	**800-274-4262**	301-628-5000
ATLA Advocate 1050 31st St NW	Washington	DC	20007	**800-424-2727**	202-965-3500
Business Crimes Bulletin					
1617 JFK Blvd Suite 1750	Philadelphia	PA	19103	**800-888-8300**	800-999-1916
C2M 858 Longview Rd	Burlingame	CA	94010	**800-221-2557**	650-342-1954
Communication at Work					
360 Hiatt Dr	Palm Beach Gardens	FL	33418	**800-621-5463**	561-622-9914
Consultants News					
1 Phoenix Mill Ln 3rd FL	Peterborough	NH	03458	**800-531-0007**	603-924-0900
Corporate Counsellor					
1617 JFK Blvd Suite 1750	Philadelphia	PA	19103	**800-999-1916**	215-557-2310
Cross Border Monitor 111 W 57th St 9th Fl	New York	NY	10019	**800-938-4685**	212-554-0600
Customer Communicator					
28 W 25th St 8th Fl	New York	NY	10010	**800-232-4317**	212-228-0246
Customers First 360 Hiatt Dr	Palm Beach Gardens	FL	33418	**800-621-5463**	561-622-9914
Daily Report for Executives					
1231 25th St NW	Washington	DC	20037	**800-372-1033**	202-452-4262
Distribution Center Management					
28 W 25th St 8th Fl	New York	NY	10010	**800-232-4317**	212-228-0246
Downtown Idea Exchange					
28 W 25th St 8th Fl	New York	NY	10003	**800-232-4317**	212-228-0246
Economic Opportunity Report					
8737 Colesville Rd Suite 1100	Silver Spring	MD	20910	**800-274-6737**	301-587-6300
Effective Telephone Techniques					
360 Hiatt Dr	Palm Beach Gardens	FL	33418	**800-621-5463**	561-622-9914
Executive Excellence 1366 East 1120 S	Provo	UT	84604	**800-304-9782**	801-375-4060
Executive Recruiter News					
1 Phoenix Mill Ln 5th Fl	Peterborough	NH	03458	**800-531-0007**	603-924-0900
Executive Strategies PO Box 9070	McLean	VA	22102	**800-543-2053**	703-905-8000
First Line Supervisor 360 Hiatt Dr	Palm Beach Gardens	FL	33418	**800-621-5463**	561-622-9914
From 9 To 5 360 Hiatt Dr	Palm Beach Gardens	FL	33418	**800-621-5463**	561-622-9914
Getting Along 360 Hiatt Dr	Palm Beach Gardens	FL	33418	**800-621-5463**	561-622-9914
Human Resources Dept Management Report					
3 Park Ave 30th Fl	New York	NY	10016	**800-401-5937**	212-244-0360

Name / Address	City	State	ZIP	Toll-Free	Phone
Law Firm Partnership & Benefits Report 1617 JFK Blvd Suite 1750	Philadelphia	PA	19103	**800-999-1916**	215-557-2310
Law Office Management & Administration Report 3 Park Ave 30th Fl	New York	NY	10016	**800-401-5937**	212-244-0360
Law Officer's Bulletin 610 Opperman Dr	Eagan	MN	55123	**800-344-5008**	651-687-7000
Leadership For The Front Lines 7201 McKinney Cir	Frederick	MD	21704	**800-243-0876**	301-698-7100
Legislative Network for Nurses 8737 Colesville Rd Suite 1100	Silver Spring	MD	20910	**800-274-6737**	301-587-6300
Mail Center Management Report 3 Park Ave 30th Fl	New York	NY	10016	**800-401-5937**	212-244-0360
Maintenance Management 7201 McKinney Cir	Frederick	MD	21704	**800-243-0876**	301-698-7100
Manager's Intelligence Report 316 N Michigan Ave Suite 300	Chicago	IL	60601	**800-878-5331**	312-960-4100
Managing Customer Service 3 Park Ave 30th Fl	New York	NY	10016	**800-401-5937**	212-244-0360
Managing International Credit & Collections Newsletter 3 Park Ave 30th Fl	New York	NY	10016	**800-401-5937**	212-244-0360
Managing Logistics 3 Park Ave 30th Fl	New York	NY	10016	**800-401-5937**	212-244-0360
Minorities in Business Insider 8204 Fenton St	Silver Spring	MD	20910	**800-666-6380**	301-588-6380
Motivational Manager 316 N Michigan Ave Suite 300	Chicago	IL	60601	**800-878-5331**	312-960-4100
Pay for Performance 3 Park Ave 30th Fl	New York	NY	10016	**800-401-5937**	212-244-0360
Payroll Manager's Report 3 Park Ave 30th Fl	New York	NY	10016	**800-401-5937**	212-244-0360
Positive Leadership 316 N Michigan Ave Suite 300	Chicago	IL	60601	**800-878-5331**	312-960-4140
Preventing Business Fraud 3 Park Ave 30th Fl	New York	NY	10016	**800-401-5937**	212-244-0360
Professional Apartment Management 149 5th Ave 16th Fl	New York	NY	10010	**800-643-8095**	800-519-3692
Quality First 360 Hiatt Dr	Palm Beach Gardens	FL	33418	**800-621-5463**	561-622-6520
Ragan Report 316 N Michigan Ave Suite 300 *Cust Svc	Chicago	IL	60601	**800-878-5331***	312-960-4100
Recruiting Trends 1 Phoenix Mill Ln 3rd FL	Peterborough	NH	03458	**800-531-0007**	603-924-0900
Report on Salary Surveys 3 Park Ave 30th Fl	New York	NY	10016	**800-401-5937**	212-244-0360
Successful Supervisor 360 Hiatt Dr	Palm Beach Gardens	FL	33418	**800-621-5463**	561-622-9914
Supplier Selection & Management Report 3 Park Ave 30th Fl	New York	NY	10016	**800-401-5937**	212-244-0360
Team Leader 360 Hiatt Dr	Palm Beach Gardens	FL	33418	**800-621-5463**	561-622-9914
Teamwork 360 Hiatt Dr	Palm Beach Gardens	FL	33418	**800-621-5463**	561-622-6520
Tradeshow Week 5700 Wilshire Blvd Suite 120	Los Angeles	CA	90036	**800-375-4212**	323-965-5300
Working Together 360 Hiatt Dr	Palm Beach Gardens	FL	33418	**800-621-5463**	561-622-6520
Your New Pryor Report: Managers Edge 2807 N Parham Rd Suite 200 *Cust Svc	Richmond	VA	23294	**800-722-9221***	804-762-9600

521-3 Computer & Internet Newsletters

Name / Address	City	State	ZIP	Toll-Free	Phone
Biotechnology Software 140 Huguenot St 3rd Fl	New Rochelle	NY	10801	**800-654-3237**	914-740-2100
Computer Economics Report 2082 Business Center Dr Suite 240	Irvine	CA	92612	**800-326-8100**	949-831-8700
Data Management Strategies 37 Broadway Suite 1	Arlington	MA	02474	**800-964-8702**	781-648-8700
DemoLetter 177 Bovet Rd Suite 400	San Mateo	CA	94402	**800-633-4312**	650-577-2700
EDP Weekly 1150 Connecticut Ave NW	Washington	DC	20036	**888-739-8500**	202-862-4375
eMarketer 75 Broad St 32nd Fl	New York	NY	10004	**800-405-0844**	212-763-6010
eWatch Report 810 7th Ave 35th Fl	New York	NY	10019	**888-857-6842**	212-832-9400
Insider Weekly for AS/400 Managers 990 Washington St Suite 308	Dedham	MA	02026	**888-400-4768**	781-320-9460
Internet Newsletter 1617 JFK Blvd Suite 1750	Philadelphia	PA	19103	**800-999-1916**	215-557-2300
Intranet Report 316 N Michigan Ave Suite 300	Chicago	IL	60601	**800-878-5331**	312-960-4100
IT Metrics 37 Broadway Suite 1	Arlington	MA	02474	**800-964-8702**	781-648-8702
Legal Tech Newsletter 1617 JFK Blvd Suite 1750	Philadelphia	PA	19103	**800-999-1916**	215-557-2310
Microprocessor Report 298 S Sunnyvale Ave Suite 101	Sunnyvale	CA	94086	**800-527-0288**	408-328-3900
Object-Oriented Strategies 37 Broadway Suite 1	Arlington	MA	02474	**800-964-8702**	781-648-8700
Software Industry Report 1150 Connecticut Ave NW Suite 900	Washington	DC	20036	**888-739-8500**	202-862-4375
Software Success 990 Washington St Suite 308	Dedham	MA	02026	**888-479-6663**	781-320-9460
Web Content Report 316 N Michigan Ave Suite 400	Chicago	IL	60601	**800-878-5331**	312-960-4100

521-4 Education Newsletters

Name / Address	City	State	ZIP	Toll-Free	Phone
Aid for Education Report 8204 Fenton St	Silver Spring	MD	20910	**800-666-6380**	301-588-6380
California School Law Digest 747 Dresher Rd Suite 500	Horsham	PA	19044	**800-341-7874**	215-784-0860
Campus Crime 8737 Colesville Rd Suite 1100	Silver Spring	MD	20910	**800-274-6737**	301-587-6300
Education Technology News 8737 Colesville Rd Suite 1100	Silver Spring	MD	20910	**800-274-6737**	301-587-6300
Education USA 747 Dresher Rd Suite 500 *Cust Svc	Horsham	PA	19044	**800-341-7874***	215-784-0860
Federal Research Report 8737 Colesville Rd Suite 1100	Silver Spring	MD	20910	**800-274-6737**	301-587-6300
New Jersey Education Law Report PO Box 241	Burtonsville	MD	20866	**800-359-6049**	301-384-1573
New York Education Law Report 360 Hiatt Dr	Palm Beach	FL	33418	**800-341-7874**	561-622-6520
Report on Literacy Programs 8737 Colesville Rd Suite 1100	Silver Spring	MD	20910	**800-274-6737**	301-587-6300
Report on Preschool Programs 8737 Colesville Rd Suite 1100	Silver Spring	MD	20910	**800-274-6737**	301-587-6300
Research Libraries Group News 1200 Villa St	Mountain View	CA	94041	**800-537-7546**	650-962-9951
School Law News 360 Hiatt Dr	Palm Beach Gardens	FL	33418	**800-638-8437**	800-341-7874
School-to-Work Report 8737 Colesville Rd Suite 1100	Silver Spring	MD	20910	**800-274-6737**	301-587-6300
Special Education Report 360 Hiatt Dr *Sales	Palm Beach Gardens	FL	33418	**800-621-5463***	561-622-6520
Student Aid News 360 Hiatt Dr	Palm Beach Gardens	FL	33418	**800-638-8437**	800-341-7874
Vocational Training News 360 Hiatt Dr	Palm Beach Gardens	FL	33418	**800-638-8437**	800-341-7874
What Works in Teaching & Learning 360 Hiatt Dr *Sales	Palm Beach Gardens	FL	33418	**800-621-5463***	561-622-6520

521-5 Energy & Environmental Newsletters

Name / Address	City	State	ZIP	Toll-Free	Phone
Asbestos & Lead Abatement Report 8737 Colesville Rd Suite 1100	Silver Spring	MD	20910	**800-274-6737**	301-589-5103
Electric Utility Week 2 Penn Plaza 25th Fl	New York	NY	10121	**800-752-8878**	212-904-6410
Energy Daily 1325 G St NW Suite 1003	Washington	DC	20005	**800-926-5464**	202-638-4260
Environmental Compliance Bulletin 1231 25th St NW	Washington	DC	20037	**800-372-1033**	202-452-4200
Environmental Compliance & Litigation Strategy 1617 JFK Blvd Suite 1750	Philadelphia	PA	19103	**800-999-1916**	215-557-2310
Environmental Regulation PO Box 7376	Alexandria	VA	22307	**800-876-2545**	703-768-9600
Global Power Report 2 Penn Plaza 25th Fl	New York	NY	10121	**800-223-6180**	800-752-8878
Ground Water Monitor 8737 Colesville Rd Suite 1100	Silver Spring	MD	20910	**800-274-6737**	301-587-6300
Hazardous Waste News 8737 Colesville Rd Suite 1100	Silver Spring	MD	20910	**800-274-6737**	301-587-6300
HazMat Transportation News 8737 Colesville Rd Suite 1100	Silver Spring	MD	20910	**800-274-6737**	301-587-6300
Inside Energy 2 Penn Plaza 25th Fl	New York	NY	10121	**800-223-6180**	800-752-8872
Inside FERC 2 Penn Plaza 25th Fl	New York	NY	10121	**800-223-6180**	800-752-8872
Inside FERC's Gas Market Report 2 Penn Plaza 25th Fl	New York	NY	10121	**800-223-6180**	212-904-6410
Inside NRC 2 Penn Plaza 25th Fl	New York	NY	10121	**800-223-6180**	800-752-8872
Land Use Law Report 8737 Colesville Rd Suite 1100	Silver Spring	MD	20910	**800-274-6767**	301-587-6300
Noise Regulation Report 8737 Colesville Rd Suite 1100	Silver Spring	MD	20910	**800-274-6737**	301-587-6300
Northeast Power Report 2 Penn Plaza 25th FL	New York	NY	10121	**800-223-6180**	800-752-8872
Nuclear News PO Box 97781	Chicago	IL	60678	**800-323-3044**	708-352-6611
Nuclear Waste News 8737 Colesville Rd Suite 1100	Silver Spring	MD	20910	**800-274-6737**	301-589-5103
Nuclearfuel 1200 G St NW Suite 1000	Washington	DC	20005	**800-223-6180**	202-383-2100
Nucleonics Week 1200 G St NW Suite 1100	Washington	DC	20005	**800-223-6180**	202-383-2100
Oil Express 11300 Rockville Pike Suite 1100	Rockville	MD	20852	**800-929-4824**	301-816-8950
Oil Price Information Service 3349 Hwy 138 Bldg D Suite D *Cust Svc	Wall	NJ	07719	**888-301-2645***	732-901-8800
Pesticide & Toxic Chemical News 1725 K St NW Suite 506	Washington	DC	20006	**888-732-7070**	202-887-6320
Sludge 8737 Colesville Rd Suite 1100	Silver Spring	MD	20910	**800-274-6737**	301-587-6300
Solid Waste Report 8737 Colesville Rd Suite 1100	Silver Spring	MD	20910	**800-274-6737**	301-587-6300
SWANA-Solid Waste Assn of North America Newsletter 1100 Wayne Ave Suite 700	Silver Spring	MD	20910	**800-467-9262**	301-585-2898
Utility Environment Report 2 Penn Plaza 25th Fl	New York	NY	10121	**800-223-6180**	800-752-8872

521-6 General Interest Newsletters

Name / Address	City	State	ZIP	Toll-Free	Phone
ARTnewsletter 48 W 38th St 9th Fl *Cust Svc	New York	NY	10018	**800-284-4625***	212-398-1690
Bottom Line/Personal 281 Tresser Blvd *Cust Svc	Stamford	CT	06901	**800-274-5611***	203-973-5900
Frm Weekly 224 7th St	Garden City	NY	11530	**800-229-6700**	516-746-6700
Kiplinger California Letter 1729 H St NW	Washington	DC	20006	**800-544-0155**	202-887-6400
Kiplinger Retirement Report 1729 H St NW	Washington	DC	20006	**800-544-0155**	202-887-6400
Older Americans Report 8737 Colesville Rd Suite 1100	Silver Spring	MD	20910	**800-274-6737**	301-587-6300
Passport 5315 N Clark St PMB 501	Chicago	IL	60640	**800-542-6670**	773-769-6760
Retirement Letter 7811 Montrose Rd *Cust Svc	Potomac	MD	20854	**800-804-0940***	301-340-2100

521-7 Government & Law Newsletters

Name / Address	City	State	ZIP	Toll-Free	Phone
Alcoholic Beverage Control PO Box 7376	Alexandria	VA	22307	**800-876-2545**	703-768-9600
ATLA Law Reporter 1050 31st St NW	Washington	DC	20007	**800-424-2727**	202-965-3500
Bankruptcy Law Letter 610 Opperman Dr	Eagan	MN	55123	**800-937-8529**	651-687-7000
Bankruptcy Strategist 345 Park Ave S	New York	NY	10010	**800-888-8300**	212-779-9200
Campaign Insider 1414 22nd St NW *Cust Svc	Washington	DC	20037	**800-432-2250***	202-887-6279
Civil Rights PO Box 7376	Alexandria	VA	22307	**800-876-2545**	703-768-9600
Commercial Lease Law Insider 149 5th Ave 16th Fl	New York	NY	10010	**800-643-8095**	212-473-8200
Commercial Leasing Law & Strategy 345 Park Ave S	New York	NY	10010	**800-888-8300**	212-779-9200
Community Development Digest 8204 Fenton St	Silver Spring	MD	20910	**800-666-6380**	301-588-6380
Community Health Funding Report 8204 Fenton St	Silver Spring	MD	20910	**800-666-6380**	301-588-6380
Computer Law Strategist 345 Park Ave S	New York	NY	10010	**800-888-8300**	212-779-9200
Congress Daily 1501 'M' St NW Suite 300	Washington	DC	20005	**800-207-8001**	202-739-8541
Defense Today 1325 G St NW Suite 1003	Washington	DC	20005	**800-926-5464**	202-638-4260
Development Director's Letter 8204 Fenton St	Silver Spring	MD	20910	**800-666-6380**	301-588-6380
Disability Law Compliance Report 610 Opperman Dr *Cust Svc	Saint Paul	MN	55123	**800-328-4880***	651-687-7000
DWI Journal PO Box 340	Fanwood	NJ	07023	**800-359-6049**	908-889-6336
Economic Development PO Box 7376	Alexandria	VA	22307	**800-876-2545**	703-768-9600

Government & Law Newsletters (Cont'd)

Name / Address	City	State	ZIP	Toll-Free	Phone
Emergency Preparedness News 8737 Colesville Rd Suite 1100	Silver Spring	MD	20910	**800-274-6737**	301-587-6300
Employee Policy PO Box 7376	Alexandria	VA	22307	**800-876-2545**	703-768-9600
Employment Law Strategist 345 Park Ave S	New York	NY	10010	**800-888-8300**	212-779-9200
FBO Weekly Release Newsletter 11300 Rockville Pike Suite 1100 *Cust Svc	Rockville	MD	20852	**800-824-1195***	301-287-2700
Federal Action Affecting the States PO Box 7376	Alexandria	VA	22307	**800-876-2545**	703-768-9600
Federal Assistance Monitor 8204 Fenton St	Silver Spring	MD	20910	**800-666-6380**	301-588-6380
Federal Computer Market Report 1150 Connecticut Ave NW Suite 900	Washington	DC	20036	**888-739-8500**	202-862-4375
Government Accounting & Auditing Update 395 Hudson St	New York	NY	10014	**800-431-9025**	212-367-6300
Government Contracts Update 11300 Rockville Pike Suite 1100 *Cust Svc	Rockville	MD	20852	**888-287-2223***	301-287-2700
Hospital Litigation Reporter 590 Dutch Valley Rd NE	Atlanta	GA	30324	**800-926-7926**	404-881-1141
Housing & Development Reporter Newsletter 610 Opperman Dr	Eagan	MN	55123	**800-937-8529**	651-687-7000
Insurance Regulation PO Box 7376	Alexandria	VA	22307	**800-876-2545**	703-768-9600
Intellectual Property Strategist Newsletter 345 Park Ave S	New York	NY	10010	**800-883-8300**	212-779-9200
IRS Practice & Policy Bulletin 1231 25th St NW *Cust Svc	Washington	DC	20037	**800-372-1033***	202-452-4200
Kiplinger Tax Letter 1729 H St NW	Washington	DC	20006	**800-544-0155**	202-887-6400
Kiplinger Washington Letter 1729 H St NW	Washington	DC	20006	**800-544-0155**	202-887-6400
Landlord Law Report 8204 Fenton St	Silver Spring	MD	20910	**800-666-6380**	301-588-6380
Medical Malpractice Law & Strategy 345 Park Ave S	New York	NY	10010	**800-888-8300**	212-779-9200
Medicare Compliance Alert 11300 Rockville Pike Suite 1100	Rockville	MD	20852	**800-929-4824**	301-287-2700
Motor Vehicle Regulation PO Box 7376	Alexandria	VA	22307	**800-876-2545**	703-768-9600
Municipal Litigation Reporter 590 Dutch Valley Rd NE	Atlanta	GA	30324	**800-926-7926**	404-881-1141
Native American Report 8737 Colesville Rd Suite 1100	Silver Spring	MD	20910	**800-274-6737**	301-587-6300
Outlook from the State Capitals PO Box 7376	Alexandria	VA	22307	**800-876-2545**	703-768-9600
Postal World 11300 Rockville Pike Suite 1100	Rockville	MD	20852	**800-929-4824**	301-287-2700
Private Security Case Law Reporter 590 Dutch Valley Rd NE	Atlanta	GA	30324	**800-926-7926**	404-881-1141
Product Liability Law & Strategy 345 Park Ave S	New York	NY	10010	**800-888-8300**	212-779-9200
Public Safety & Justice Policies PO Box 7376	Alexandria	VA	22307	**800-876-2545**	703-768-9600
Real Estate Law Report 610 Opperman Dr *Cust Svc	Eagan	MN	55123	**800-328-4880***	651-687-7000
Superfund Week 8737 Colesville Rd Suite 1100 *Cust Svc	Silver Spring	MD	20910	**800-274-6737***	301-587-6300
Taxation & Revenue Policies PO Box 7376	Alexandria	VA	22307	**800-876-2545**	703-768-9600
Taxes-Property PO Box 7376	Alexandria	VA	22307	**800-876-2545**	703-768-9600
Physician Practice Coder 11300 Rockville Pike Suite 1100	Rockville	MD	20852	**800-929-4824**	301-287-2700
Public Assistance & Welfare Trends PO Box 7376	Alexandria	VA	22307	**800-876-2545**	703-768-9600
Report on Disability Programs 8737 Colesville Rd Suite 1100	Silver Spring	MD	20910	**800-274-6737**	301-587-6300
Substance Abuse Funding Week 8204 Fenton St	Silver Spring	MD	20910	**800-666-6380**	301-588-6384

521-8 Health & Social Issues Newsletters

Name / Address	City	State	ZIP	Toll-Free	Phone
Aging News Alert 8204 Fenton St	Silver Spring	MD	20910	**800-666-6380**	301-588-6380
AICR Newsletter 1759 R St NW	Washington	DC	20009	**800-843-8114**	202-328-7744
American Parkinson's Disease Assn 1250 Hylan Blvd Suite 4B	Staten Island	NY	10305	**800-223-2732**	718-981-8001
Amnesty Action 322 8th Ave	New York	NY	10001	**800-266-3789**	212-807-8400
APCO Bulletin 351 N Williamson Blvd	Daytona Beach	FL	32114	**888-272-6911**	386-322-2500
Bottom Line/Health 281 Tresser Blvd *Cust Svc	Stamford	CT	06901	**800-289-0409***	203-973-5900
Cancer Economics PO Box 9905	Washington	DC	20016	**800-513-7042**	202-362-1809
Cancer Letter PO Box 9905	Washington	DC	20016	**800-513-7042**	202-362-1809
Child Protection Law Report 8737 Colesville Rd Suite 1100	Silver Spring	MD	20910	**800-274-6737**	301-587-6300
Children & Youth Funding Report 8204 Fenton St	Silver Spring	MD	20910	**800-666-6380**	301-588-6380
Clinical Cancer Letter PO Box 9905	Washington	DC	20016	**800-513-7042**	202-362-1809
CTD News 747 Dresher Rd Suite 500	Horsham	PA	19044	**800-341-7874**	215-784-0860
Dairy Council Digest 10255 W Higgins Rd Suite 900 *Cust Svc	Rosemont	IL	60018	**800-426-8271***	847-803-2000
Disabilities in The Workplace PO Box 64833	Saint Paul	MN	55164	**800-328-4880**	847-948-7000
Disability Funding Week 8204 Fenton St	Silver Spring	MD	20910	**800-666-6380**	301-588-6380
Drug Detection Report 8737 Colesville Rd Suite 1100	Silver Spring	MD	20910	**800-274-6737**	301-587-6300
Environment of Care Leader 11300 Rockville Pike Suite 1100	Rockville	MD	20852	**800-929-4824**	301-287-2700
Family Relations PO Box 7376	Alexandria	VA	22307	**800-876-2545**	703-768-9600
Health & Healing 7811 Montrose Rd	Potomac	MD	20854	**800-861-5967**	301-340-2100
Health Law Week 590 Dutch Valley Rd NE	Atlanta	GA	30324	**800-926-7926**	404-881-1141
Heartsense 7811 Montrose Rd	Potomac	MD	20854	**800-861-5970**	301-340-2100
Home Care Accreditation Alert 11300 Rockville Pike Suite 1100	Rockville	MD	20852	**800-929-4824**	301-287-2700
Home Health Line 11300 Rockville Pike Suite 1100	Rockville	MD	20852	**800-929-4824**	301-287-2700
International Medical Device Regulatory Monitor 9700 Philadelphia Ct	Lanham	MD	20706	**800-774-6809**	301-731-5200
Medicare Compliance Alert 11300 Rockville Pike Suite 1100	Rockville	MD	20852	**800-929-4824**	301-287-2700
Mental Health Law Reporter 8737 Colesville Rd Suite 1100	Silver Spring	MD	20910	**800-274-6737**	301-587-6300
Mental Health Report 8737 Colesville Rd Suite 1100	Silver Spring	MD	20910	**800-274-6737**	301-587-6300
Nutrition Research 605 3rd Ave	New York	NY	10158	**800-825-7550**	201-748-6000
OSHA Up-to-Date 1121 Spring Lake Dr *Cust Svc	Itasca	IL	60143	**800-621-7619***	630-285-1121
Physician Office Lab News 11300 Rockville Pike Suite 1100	Rockville	MD	20852	**800-929-4824**	301-287-2700

521-9 Investment Newsletters

Name / Address	City	State	ZIP	Toll-Free	Phone
AIC Investment Bulletin 30 Stockbridge Rd	Great Barrington	MA	01230	**800-532-4999**	413-528-9779
Blue Chip Economic Indicators 1333 H St NW Suite 100E *Cust Svc	Washington	DC	20005	**800-234-1660***	202-312-6112
Blue Chip Financial Forecasts 1333 H St NW Suite 100E *Cust Svc	Washington	DC	20005	**800-234-1660***	202-312-6112
Bondweek 225 Park Ave S 7th Fl	New York	NY	10003	**800-543-4444**	212-224-3800
Cabot Market Letter 176 North St PO Box 2049 *Orders	Salem	MA	01970	**800-777-2658***	978-745-5532
Chartist 6621 E Pacific Coast Hwy Suite 200	Long Beach	CA	90803	**800-942-4278**	562-596-2385
Elliott Wave Theorist PO Box 1618	Gainesville	GA	30503	**800-336-1618**	770-536-0309
Fabian's Investment Resources 2100 Main St Suite 300	Huntington Beach	CA	92648	**800-950-8765**	714-536-1931
Future Market Service 330 S Wells St Suite 1112	Chicago	IL	60606	**800-621-5271**	312-554-8456
Global Market Perspective PO Box 1618	Gainesville	GA	30503	**800-336-1618**	770-536-0309
Gold Newsletter 2400 Jefferson Hwy Suite 600	Jefferson	LA	70121	**800-877-8847**	504-837-3033
Granville Market Letter PO Box 413006	Kansas City	MO	64141	**800-876-5388**	816-474-5353
Growth Fund Guide PO Box 6600	Rapid City	SD	57709	**800-621-8322**	605-341-1971
Growth Stock Outlook 4405 East-West Hwy Suite 305	Bethesda	MD	20814	**800-742-5476**	301-654-5205
Investor Relations 1 Phoenix Mill Ln	Peterborough	NH	03458	**800-531-0007**	603-924-0900
John Dessauer's Investor's World 7811 Montrose Rd	Potomac	MD	20854	**800-804-0942**	301-340-2100
Louis Rukeyser's Mutual Funds 1750 Old Meadow Rd Suite 300	McLean	VA	22102	**800-892-9702**	703-905-8000
Option Advisor 1259 Kemper Meadow Dr	Cincinnati	OH	45240	**800-448-2080**	513-589-3800
Personal Finance 1750 Old Meadow Rd Suite 300	McLean	VA	22102	**800-832-2330**	703-905-8000
Prudent Speculator 32392 Coast Hwy Suite 260	Laguna Beach	CA	92651	**800-258-7786**	949-497-7657
Richard Band's Profitable Investing 7811 Montrose Rd	Potomac	MD	20854	**800-211-8565**	301-340-2100
Richard Young's Intelligence Report 7811 Montrose Rd	Potomac	MD	20854	**800-301-8969**	301-340-2100
Standard & Poor's Outlook 55 Water St	New York	NY	10041	**800-221-5277**	212-438-2000
Standard & Poor's Stock Reports 55 Water St	New York	NY	10041	**800-221-5277**	212-438-2000
Timer Digest PO Box 1688	Greenwich	CT	06836	**800-356-2527**	203-629-3503
Utility Forecaster 1750 Old Meadow Rd Suite 300	McLean	VA	22102	**800-832-2330**	703-905-8000
Wall Street Digest 8830 S Tamiami Trail Suite 110	Sarasota	FL	34238	**800-785-5050**	941-954-5500
Young's Richard Intelligence Report 7811 Montrose Rd	Potomac	MD	20854	**800-301-8969**	301-340-2100

521-10 Marketing & Sales Newsletters

Name / Address	City	State	ZIP	Toll-Free	Phone
Book Marketing Update 135 E Plumstead Ave	Lansdowne	PA	19050	**800-989-1400**	610-259-1070
CPA Marketing Report 2700 Lake Cook Rd	Riverwoods	IL	60015	**800-224-7977**	847-267-7000
Downtown Promotion Reporter 28 W 25th St 8th Fl	New York	NY	10010	**800-232-4317**	212-228-0246
eMarketer 75 Broad St 32nd Fl	New York	NY	10004	**800-405-0844**	212-763-6010
Friday Report 224 7th St	Garden City	NY	11530	**800-229-6700**	516-746-6700
Marketing for Lawyers 345 Park Ave S	New York	NY	10010	**800-888-8300**	212-779-9200
Marketing Library Services 143 Old Marlton Pike	Medford	NJ	08055	**800-300-9868**	609-654-6266
Overcoming Objections 360 Hiatt Dr	Palm Beach Gardens	FL	33418	**800-621-5463**	561-622-9914
Sales Management Report 316 N Michigan Ave Suite 300	Chicago	IL	60601	**800-878-5331**	312-960-4100
Salesmanship 360 Hiatt Dr	Palm Beach Gardens	FL	33418	**800-621-5463**	561-622-9914
Selling to Seniors 8204 Fenton St	Silver Spring	MD	20910	**800-666-6380**	301-588-6380
Successful Closing Techniques 360 Hiatt Dr	Palm Beach Gardens	FL	33418	**800-621-5463**	561-622-9914

521-11 Media & Communications Newsletters

Name / Address	City	State	ZIP	Toll-Free	Phone
Accuracy in Media Report 4455 Connecticut Ave NW Suite 330	Washington	DC	20008	**800-787-4567**	202-364-4401
Book Publishing Report 11 River Bend Dr S	Stamford	CT	06907	**800-307-2529**	203-358-4100
Cable Regulation Monitor 2115 Ward Ct NW	Washington	DC	20037	**800-771-9200**	202-872-9200
Children's Book Insider 901 Columbia Rd	Fort Collins	CO	80525	**800-807-1916**	970-495-0056
Communication Briefings 1101 King St Suite 110	Alexandria	VA	22314	**800-888-2084**	703-548-3800
Communications Daily 2115 Ward Ct NW	Washington	DC	20037	**800-771-9202**	202-872-9200
Editorial Eye 66 Canal Center Plaza Suite 200	Alexandria	VA	22314	**800-683-8380**	703-683-0683
Entertainment Law & Finance 345 Park Ave S	New York	NY	10010	**800-888-8300**	212-779-9200
First Draft 316 N Michigan Ave Suite 300	Chicago	IL	60601	**800-878-5331**	312-960-4100
Ideas Unlimited for Editors 9700 Philadelphia Ct	Lanham	MD	20706	**800-774-6809**	301-731-5200
Intellectual Property Strategist Newsletter 345 Park Ave S	New York	NY	10010	**800-883-8300**	212-779-9200
Interactive Public Relations 316 N Michigan Ave Suite 300	Chicago	IL	60601	**800-878-5331**	312-960-4100

Name / Address	City	State	Zip	Toll-Free	Phone
Media Relations 316 N Michigan Ave Suite 300	Chicago	IL	60601	**800-878-5331**	312-960-4100
PR Intelligence 316 N Michigan Ave Suite 300	Chicago	IL	60601	**800-878-5331**	312-960-4100
PR Reporter 316 N Michigan Ave Suite 300	Chicago	IL	60601	**800-493-4867**	312-960-4140
Speechwriter's Newsletter 316 N Michigan Ave Suite 300	Chicago	IL	60601	**800-878-5331**	312-960-4100
Strategic Employee Publications 316 N Michigan Ave Suite 300	Chicago	IL	60601	**800-878-5331**	312-960-4100
Telecommunications Report 7201 McKinney Cir *Cust Svc	Frederick	MD	21704	**800-822-6338***	301-698-7100
TR's Last-Mile Telecom Report 7201 McKinney Cir	Frederick	MD	21704	**800-822-6338**	301-698-7100

521-12 Science & Technology Newsletters

Name / Address	City	State	Zip	Toll-Free	Phone
Advanced Coatings & Surface Technology 7550 W I-10 Suite 400	San Antonio	TX	77229	**877-463-7678**	210-348-1000
Advanced Mfg Technology 7550 W I-10 Suite 400	San Antonio	TX	77229	**877-463-7678**	210-348-1000
Futuretech: Emerging Technologies 7550 W I-10 Suite 400	San Antonio	TX	77229	**877-463-7678**	210-348-1000
Genetic Engineering News 2 Madison Ave.	Larchmont	NY	10538	**800-654-3237**	914-834-3100
Genetic Technology News 7550 W I-10 Suite 400	San Antonio	TX	77229	**877-463-7678**	210-348-1000
Geophysical Research Letter 2000 Florida Ave NW	Washington	DC	20009	**800-966-2481**	202-462-6900
High-Tech Materials 7550 W I-10 Suite 400	San Antonio	TX	77229	**877-463-7678**	210-348-1000
Industrial Bioprocessing 7550 W I-10 Suite 400	San Antonio	TX	77229	**877-463-7678**	210-348-1000
International Pharmaceutical Regulatory Monitor 9700 Philadelphia Ct	Lanham	MD	20706	**800-345-2611**	301-731-5200
Microelectronics Technology Alert 7550 W 1-10 Suite 400	San Antonio	TX	77220	**877-463-7678**	210-348-1000
Nanotech Alert 7550 W I-10 Suite 400	San Antonio	TX	77229	**877-463-7678**	210-348-1000
New Technology Week 1325 G St Suite 1003	Washington	DC	20005	**800-926-5464**	202-638-4260
Sensor Technology 7550 W I-10 Suite 400	San Antonio	TX	77229	**877-463-7678**	210-348-1000
World Food Chemical News 1725 K St NW Suite 506	Washington	DC	20006	**800-272-7737**	202-887-6320

521-13 Trade & Industry Newsletters

Name / Address	City	State	Zip	Toll-Free	Phone
Airports 1200 G St NW Suite 900	Washington	DC	20005	**800-752-4959**	202-383-2350
Aviation Daily 1200 G St NW Suite 900	Washington	DC	20005	**800-752-4959**	202-383-2350
Car Dealer Insider Newsletter 11300 Rockville Pike Suite 1100 *Cust Svc	Rockville	MD	20852	**800-929-4824***	301-816-8950
Construction Claims Monthly 8737 Colesville Rd Suite 1100	Silver Spring	MD	20910	**800-274-6737**	301-589-5103
Cotton's Week 1918 North Pkwy	Memphis	TN	38112	**800-377-9030**	901-274-9030
Doane's Agricultural Report 11701 Borman Dr Suite 300	Saint Louis	MO	63146	**800-535-2342**	314-569-2700
Fashion Newsletter 9700 Philadelphia Ct	Lanham	MD	20706	**800-345-2611**	301-731-5200
Food Chemical News 1725 K St NW Suite 506	Washington	DC	20006	**888-272-7737**	202-887-6320
Funeral Service Insider 11300 Rockville Pike Suite 1100	Rockville	MD	20852	**800-929-4824**	301-287-2700
Industry Report 301 N Fairfax St	Alexandria	VA	22314	**800-542-6672**	703-549-9040
Kane's Beverage Week 313 South Ave Suite 202	Fanwood	NJ	07023	**800-359-6049**	908-889-6336
Kiplinger Agriculture Letter 1729 H St NW *Circ	Washington	DC	20006	**800-544-0155***	202-887-6400
Leisure Beverage Insider 313 South Ave Suite 202	Fanwood	NJ	07023	**800-359-6049**	908-889-6336
Metals Week 55 Water St	New York	NY	10041	**800-223-6180**	212-438-2000
National Farmers Union News 11900 E Cornell Ave	Aurora	CO	80014	**800-347-1961**	303-337-5500
PhotoLetter 1910 35th Ave Pine Lake Farm	Osceola	WI	54020	**800-624-0266**	715-248-3800
Pro Farmer 6612 Chancellor Dr Suite 300 *Cust Svc	Cedar Falls	IA	50613	**800-772-0023***	319-277-1278
Uniform Commercial Code Law Letter 610 Opperman Dr *Cust Svc	Eagan	MN	55123	**800-328-4880***	651-687-7000
Urban Transport News 8737 Colesville Rd Suite 1100	Silver Spring	MD	20910	**800-274-6737**	301-589-5103
US Rail News 8737 Colesville Rd Suite 1100	Silver Spring	MD	20910	**800-274-6737**	301-589-5103
Weekly of Business Aviation 1200 G St NW Suite 900	Washington	DC	20005	**800-752-4959**	202-383-2350

522 NEWSPAPERS

SEE ALSO Publishing Companies - Newspaper Publishers

522-1 Daily Newspapers - Canada

Name / Address	City	Prov	Postal Code	Toll-Free	Phone
Edmonton Journal PO Box 2421	Edmonton	AB	T5J2S6	**800-663-7810**	780-429-5100
Gazette The 1010 St Catherine St W Suite 200	Montreal	QC	H3B5L1	**800-361-8478**	514-987-2222
Le Journal de Montreal 4545 rue Frontenac	Montreal	QC	H2H2R7	**800-521-4545**	514-521-4545
Ottawa Citizen 1101 Baxter Rd PO Box 5020	Ottawa	ON	K2C3M4	**800-267-6100**	613-829-9100
Prince Rupert Daily News 801 2nd Ave W	Prince Rupert	BC	V8J1H6	**800-343-0022**	250-624-6781
Recorder & Times 1600 California Ave.	Brockville	ON	K6V5T8	**800-267-4434**	613-342-4441
Spectator The 44 Frid St.	Hamilton	ON	L8N3G3	**800-263-6902**	905-526-3333

522-2 Daily Newspapers - US

Name / Address	City	State	Zip	Toll-Free	Phone
Andalusia Star News 207 Dunson St PO Box 430	Andalusia	AL	36420	**866-735-5289**	334-222-2402
Anniston Star 4305 McClellan Blvd PO Box 189	Anniston	AL	36202	**888-649-1551**	256-236-1551
News Courier PO Box 670	Athens	AL	35612	**800-844-5480**	256-232-2720
Birmingham News 2200 4th Ave N	Birmingham	AL	35203	**800-283-4015**	205-325-2222
Birmingham Post-Herald 2200 4th Ave N.	Birmingham	AL	35203	**800-283-4255**	205-325-2343
Cullman Times 300 4th Ave SE	Cullman	AL	35055	**800-844-5369**	256-734-2131
Decatur Daily 201 1st Ave SE	Decatur	AL	35601	**888-353-4612**	256-353-4612
Dothan Eagle PO Box 1968	Dothan	AL	36302	**800-811-1771**	334-792-3141
Times Journal PO Box 680349	Fort Payne	AL	35968	**800-348-4637**	256-845-2550
Gadsden Times 401 Locust St	Gadsden	AL	35901	**800-762-2464**	256-549-2000
Huntsville Times 2317 S Memorial Pkwy	Huntsville	AL	35801	**800-239-5271**	256-532-4000
Daily Mountain Eagle 1301 Viking Dr	Jasper	AL	35502	**800-518-6397**	205-221-2840
Mobile Register 401 N Water St	Mobile	AL	36602	**800-239-1340**	251-219-5400
Selma Times-Journal PO Box 611	Selma	AL	36702	**800-522-1681**	334-875-2110
Tuscaloosa News 315 28th Ave	Tuscaloosa	AL	35401	**800-888-8639**	205-345-0505
Anchorage Daily News 1001 Northway Dr	Anchorage	AK	99508	**800-555-1212**	907-257-4200
Mohave Valley Daily News PO Box 21209	Bullhead City	AZ	86439	**800-571-3835**	928-763-2505
Today's News-Herald 2225 W Acoma Blvd	Lake Havasu City	AZ	86403	**800-894-2109**	928-453-4237
East Valley Tribune The 120 W 1st Ave *Cust Svc	Mesa	AZ	85210	**888-887-4286***	480-898-6500
Arizona Republic 200 E Van Buren	Phoenix	AZ	85004	**800-331-9303**	602-444-8000
Daily Courier 1958 Commerce Ctr Cir	Prescott	AZ	86304	**888-349-3436**	928-445-3333
Arizona Daily Star 4850 S Park Ave	Tucson	AZ	85714	**800-695-4111**	520-573-4220
Tucson Citizen 4850 S Park Ave	Tucson	AZ	85714	**800-695-4492**	520-573-4560
Yuma Daily Sun 2055 Arizona Ave	Yuma	AZ	85364	**800-995-9862**	928-783-3333
Batesville Guard 258 W Main St PO Box 2036	Batesville	AR	72503	**800-559-2383**	870-793-2383
Northwest Arkansas Times PO Box 1607	Fayetteville	AR	72702	**800-498-1991**	479-571-6400
Times Record 3600 Wheeler Ave	Fort Smith	AR	72901	**888-274-4051**	479-785-7700
Jonesboro Sun 518 Carson St.	Jonesboro	AR	72401	**800-237-5341**	870-935-5525
Arkansas Democrat-Gazette 121 E Capital St *Cust Svc	Little Rock	AR	72201	**800-482-1121***	501-378-3400
Malvern Daily Record 219 Locust St	Malvern	AR	72104	**800-582-5794**	501-337-7523
Pine Bluff Commercial PO Box 6469	Pine Bluff	AR	71611	**800-669-3110**	870-534-3400
Courier The 201 E 2nd St PO Box 887	Russellville	AR	72811	**800-369-5252**	479-968-5252
Daily Citizen 3000 E Race Ave	Searcy	AR	72143	**800-400-3142**	501-268-8621
Morning News of Northwest Arkansas PO Box 7	Springdale	AR	72765	**888-692-1222**	479-751-6200
Bakersfield Californian 1707 Eye St	Bakersfield	CA	93302	**800-953- 533**	661-395-7500
Desert Dispatch 130 Coolwater Ln	Barstow	CA	92311	**800-676-7585**	760-256-2257
Chico Enterprise Record 400 E Park Ave PO Box 9	Chico	CA	95927	**800-827-1421**	530-891-1234
Los Angeles Times Orange County 1375 Sunflower Ave	Costa Mesa	CA	92626	**800-528-4637**	714-966-5600
North County Times 207 E Pennsylvania Ave. *News Rm	Escondido	CA	92025	**800-200-0704***	760-745-6611
Argus The 39737 Paseo Padre Pkwy	Fremont	CA	94538	**800-595-9595**	510-661-2600
Fresno Bee 1626 'E' St	Fresno	CA	93786	**800-877-7300**	559-441-6111
Union The 464 Sutton Way	Grass Valley	CA	95945	**800-899-9561**	530-273-9561
Sentinel The 300 W 6th St	Hanford	CA	93230	**800-582-0471**	559-582-0471
Daily Review 22533 Foothill Blvd	Hayward	CA	94541	**800-595-9595**	510-783-6111
Daily Commerce 915 E 1st St	Los Angeles	CA	90012	**800-788-7840**	213-229-5300
Investor's Business Daily 12655 Beatrice St	Los Angeles	CA	90066	**800-831-2525**	310-448-6000
Los Angeles Times 202 W 1st St	Los Angeles	CA	90012	**800-528-4637**	213-237-5000
Appeal-Democrat 1530 Ellis Lake Dr	Marysville	CA	95901	**800-831-2345**	530-741-2345
Modesto Bee 1325 H St PO Box 5256	Modesto	CA	95354	**800-776-4233**	209-578-2000
Monterey County Herald 8 Upper Ragsdale	Monterey	CA	93940	**888-646-4422**	831-372-3311
Napa Valley Register PO Box 150	Napa	CA	94559	**800-504-6397**	707-226-3711
Marin Independent Journal PO Box 6150	Novato	CA	94948	**800-782-5277**	415-883-8600
Oroville Mercury Register PO Box 651	Oroville	CA	95965	**800-827-1421**	530-533-3131
Desert Sun 750 N Gene Autry Trail	Palm Springs	CA	92263	**800-233-3741**	760-322-8889
Antelope Valley Press 37404 Sierra Hwy PO Box 4050	Palmdale	CA	93590	**888-874-2527**	661-273-2700
Pasadena Star-News 911 E Colorado Blvd	Pasadena	CA	91109	**800-788-1200**	626-578-6300
Red Bluff Daily News 545 Diamond Ave	Red Bluff	CA	96080	**800-497-6397**	530-527-2151
Redlands Daily Facts 700 Brookside Ave	Redlands	CA	92373	**800-922-0922**	909-793-3221
Press-Enterprise 3512 14th St	Riverside	CA	92501	**800-933-1400**	951-684-1200
Sacramento Bee 2100 Q St *Cust Svc	Sacramento	CA	95816	**800-284-3233***	916-321-1000
Sun The 399 N 'D' St	San Bernardino	CA	92401	**800-922-0922**	909-889-9666
San Diego Daily Transcript 2131 3rd Ave	San Diego	CA	92101	**800-697-6397**	619-232-4381
San Diego Union-Tribune 350 Camino De La Reina	San Diego	CA	92112	**800-244-6397**	619-299-3131
San Francisco Chronicle 901 Mission St	San Francisco	CA	94103	**866-732-4766**	415-777-7100
San Francisco Examiner 450 Mission St	San Francisco	CA	94105	**866-733-7232**	415-826-1100
Tribune The PO Box 112	San Luis Obispo	CA	93406	**800-477-8799**	805-781-7800
San Mateo County Times 1080 S Amphlett Blvd	San Mateo	CA	94402	**800-595-9595**	650-348-4321
Orange County Register 625 N Grand Ave	Santa Ana	CA	92701	**877-469-7344**	714-796-7000
Santa Barbara News-Press 715 Anacapa St	Santa Barbara	CA	93101	**800-654-3292**	805-564-5200
Press Democrat PO Box 569	Santa Rosa	CA	95402	**800-675-5056**	707-546-2020
Record The 530 E Market St	Stockton	CA	95201	**800-606-9741**	209-943-6397
Ukiah Daily Journal PO Box 749	Ukiah	CA	95482	**800-729-0123**	707-468-3500
Vallejo Times Herald 440 Curtola Pkwy	Vallejo	CA	94590	**800-600-1141**	707-644-1141
Ventura County Star 5250 Ralston St	Ventura	CA	93003	**800-221-7827**	805-650-2900
Daily Press 13891 Park Ave PO Box 1389	Victorville	CA	92393	**800-553-2006**	760-241-7744
San Gabriel Valley Tribune 1210 N Azusa Canyon Rd	West Covina	CA	91790	**800-788-1200**	626-962-8811
Whittier Daily News 7612 Green Leaf Ave	Whittier	CA	90602	**800-788-1200**	562-698-0955
Daily News of Los Angeles 21221 Oxnard St	Woodland Hills	CA	91367	**800-346-6397**	818-713-3000
Siskiyou Daily News PO Box 129	Yreka	CA	96097	**800-540-5905**	530-842-5777
Aspen Daily News 517 E Hopkins Ave	Aspen	CO	81611	**800-889-9020**	970-925-2220
Boulder Daily Camera 1048 Pearl St	Boulder	CO	80302	**800-783-1202**	303-442-1202
Gazette The 30 S Prospect St. *News Rm	Colorado Springs	CO	80903	**800-800-4899***	719-632-5511
Denver Post 1560 Broadway	Denver	CO	80202	**800-336-7678**	303-820-1010
Rocky Mountain News 400 W Colfax Ave	Denver	CO	80204	**800-933-1990**	303-892-5000
Durango Herald 1275 Main Ave	Durango	CO	81301	**800-530-8318**	970-247-3504
Glenwood Springs Post Independent 2014 Grand Ave	Glenwood Springs	CO	81601	**866-850-9937**	970-945-8515
Greeley Tribune 501 8th Ave	Greeley	CO	80631	**800-275-0321**	970-352-0211
Daily Times-Call 350 Terry St.	Longmont	CO	80501	**800-796-8201**	303-776-2244
Loveland Daily Reporter-Herald 201 E 5th St	Loveland	CO	80537	**800-216-0680**	970-669-5050

Classified Section

Daily Newspapers - US (Cont'd)

Newspaper / Address	City	State	Zip	Toll-Free	Phone
Pueblo Chieftain 825 W 6th St PO Box 440	Pueblo	CO	81003	**800-279-6397**	719-544-3520
Connecticut Post 410 State St	Bridgeport	CT	06604	**800-542-5620***	203-333-0161
*Edit					
Bristol Press 99 Main St	Bristol	CT	06010	**800-220-6229**	860-584-0501
Hartford Courant 285 Broad St	Hartford	CT	06115	**800-524-4242**	860-241-6200
Journal Inquirer					
306 Progress Dr PO Box 510	Manchester	CT	06045	**800-237-3606**	860-646-0500
New Haven Register 40 Sargent Dr	New Haven	CT	06511	**800-925-2509**	203-789-5200
Day The					
47 Eugene O'Neil Dr PO Box 1231	New London	CT	06320	**800-542-3354**	860-442-2200
Republican-American 389 Meadow St	Waterbury	CT	06702	**800-992-3232**	203-574-3636
Chronicle The 1 Chronicle Rd	Willimantic	CT	06226	**800-992-8466**	860-423-8466
Delaware State News PO Box 737	Dover	DE	19903	**800-282-8586**	302-674-3600
News Journal 950 W Basin Rd	New Castle	DE	19720	**800-235-9100**	302-324-2500
Washington Post 1150 15th St NW	Washington	DC	20071	**800-627-1150**	202-334-6000
Sun Herald 23170 Harborview Rd	Charlotte Harbor	FL	33980	**800-830-7861**	941-206-1000
Citrus County Chronicle					
1624 N Meadowcrest Blvd	Crystal River	FL	34429	**888-852-2340**	352-563-6363
Miami Herald Broward Edition					
1520 E Sunrise Blvd	Fort Lauderdale	FL	33304	**800-441-0444**	954-462-3000
South Florida Sun-Sentinel					
200 E Las Olas Blvd	Fort Lauderdale	FL	33301	**800-548-6397***	954-356-4000
*Cust Svc					
News-Press 2442 Dr ML King Jr Blvd	Fort Myers	FL	33901	**800-468-0350***	239-335-0200
*News Rm					
Tribune 600 Edwards Rd	Fort Pierce	FL	34982	**800-444-8742**	772-461-2050
Northwest Florida Daily News					
PO Box 2949	Fort Walton Beach	FL	32549	**800-755-1185**	850-863-1111
Gainesville Sun 2700 SW 13th St	Gainesville	FL	32614	**800-443-9493***	352-378-1411
*Circ					
Florida Times-Union 1 Riverside Ave	Jacksonville	FL	32202	**800-472-6397**	904-359-4111
Ledger The 300 W Lime St	Lakeland	FL	33815	**888-431-7323**	863-802-7000
Daily Commercial 212 E Main St	Leesburg	FL	34748	**877-702-0600**	352-365-8200
Florida Today 1 Gannett Plaza	Melbourne	FL	32940	**800-633-8449**	321-242-3500
El Nuevo Herald 1 Herald Plaza	Miami	FL	33132	**800-437-2535**	305-376-3535
Miami Herald 1 Herald Plaza	Miami	FL	33132	**800-437-2535**	305-350-2111
Ocala Star-Banner PO Box 490	Ocala	FL	34478	**800-541-2171**	352-867-4010
Orlando Sentinel 633 N Orange Ave	Orlando	FL	32801	**800-347-6868**	407-420-5000
Palatka Daily News 1825 St Johns Ave	Palatka	FL	32178	**800-881-7355**	386-328-2721
News-Herald 501 W 11th St	Panama City	FL	32401	**800-345-8688**	850-747-5000
Pensacola News Journal 101 E Romana St	Pensacola	FL	32508	**800-288-2021**	850-435-8500
Saint Petersburg Times					
490 1st Ave S	Saint Petersburg	FL	33701	**800-333-7505**	727-893-8111
Sarasota Herald-Tribune 801 S Tamiami Trail	Sarasota	FL	34236	**866-284-7102**	941-953-7755
Stuart News PO Box 9009	Stuart	FL	34995	**800-381-6397**	772-287-1550
Tallahassee Democrat 277 N Magnolia Dr	Tallahassee	FL	32301	**800-777-2154**	850-599-2100
Tampa Tribune 202 S Parker St	Tampa	FL	33606	**800-282-5588**	813-259-7600
Vero Beach Press-Journal PO Box 1268	Vero Beach	FL	32961	**888-988-8376**	772-562-2315
Palm Beach Post 2751 S Dixie Hwy	West Palm Beach	FL	33405	**800-432-7595**	561-820-4100
Albany Herald 126 N Washington St	Albany	GA	31701	**800-685-4639**	229-888-9300
Americus Times-Recorder 101 Hwy 27 E	Americus	GA	31709	**800-924-2751**	229-924-2751
Athens Banner-Herald 1 Press Pl	Athens	GA	30601	**800-533-4252**	706-549-0123
Atlanta Journal-Constitution 72 Marietta St	Atlanta	GA	30303	**800-846-6672**	404-526-5151
Augusta Chronicle 725 Broad St	Augusta	GA	30901	**800-822-4077**	706-724-0851
Columbus Ledger-Enquirer 17 W 12th St	Columbus	GA	31902	**800-282-7859**	706-324-5526
Cordele Dispatch					
306 W 13th Ave PO Box 1058	Cordele	GA	31010	**888-273-2278**	229-273-2277
Daily Citizen 308 S Thornton Ave	Dalton	GA	30722	**877-217-6397**	706-217-6397
Courier Herald 115 S Jefferson St	Dublin	GA	31021	**800-833-2504**	478-272-5522
Gainesville Times 345 Green St NW	Gainesville	GA	30501	**800-395-5005**	770-532-1234
Macon Telegraph 120 Broadway	Macon	GA	31201	**800-679-6397**	478-744-4200
Thomasville Times-Enterprise PO Box 650	Thomasville	GA	31799	**888-224-2402**	229-226-2400
Tifton Gazette PO Box 708	Tifton	GA	31793	**888-382-4321**	229-382-4321
Valdosta Daily Times PO Box 968	Valdosta	GA	31603	**800-600-4838**	229-244-1880
Honolulu Advertiser PO Box 3110	Honolulu	HI	96801	**877-233-1133**	808-525-8000
Honolulu Star-Bulletin					
500 Ala Moana Blvd 7 Waterfront Plaza					
Suite 210	Honolulu	HI	96813	**800-417-3484**	808-529-4700
West Hawaii Today PO Box 789	Kailua-Kona	HI	96745	**800-355-3911**	808-329-9311
Garden Island Newspaper 3-3137 Kuhio Hwy	Lihue	HI	96766	**800-296-2880**	808-245-3681
Maui News PO Box 550	Wailuku	HI	96793	**800-827-0347**	808-244-3981
Idaho Statesman 1200 N Curtis Rd	Boise	ID	83706	**800-635-8934**	208-377-6400
South Idaho Press 230 E Main St	Burley	ID	83318	**800-817-5480**	208-678-2201
Post-Register PO Box 1800	Idaho Falls	ID	83403	**800-574-6397**	208-522-1800
Idaho State Journal 305 S Arthur	Pocatello	ID	83204	**800-275-0774**	208-232-4161
Times-News PO Box 548	Twin Falls	ID	83303	**800-658-3883**	208-733-0931
Telegraph The PO Box 278	Alton	IL	62002	**800-477-1447**	618-463-2500
Beacon News 101 S River St	Aurora	IL	60506	**800-244-5844**	630-844-5800
Belleville News-Democrat 120 S Illinois St	Belleville	IL	62220	**877-338-7416**	618-234-1000
Pantagraph PO Box 2907	Bloomington	IL	61702	**800-747-7323**	309-829-9411
Southern Illinoisan PO Box 2108	Carbondale	IL	62902	**800-228-0429**	618-529-5454
Centralia Sentinel 232 E Broadway	Centralia	IL	62801	**800-371-9892**	618-532-5604
Chicago Tribune 435 N Michigan Ave	Chicago	IL	60611	**800-874-2863**	312-222-3232
Northwest Herald PO Box 250	Crystal Lake	IL	60039	**800-589-8910**	815-459-4122
Commercial-News 17 W North St	Danville	IL	61832	**800-729-2992**	217-446-1000
Daily Chronicle 1586 Barber Greene Rd	DeKalb	IL	60115	**877-688-4841**	815-756-4841
DuQuoin Evening Call					
9 N Division St PO Box 184	DuQuoin	IL	62832	**800-455-2133**	618-542-2133
Effingham Daily News 201 N Bankers St	Effingham	IL	62401	**800-526-7205**	217-347-7151
Courier-News 300 Lake St PO Box 531	Elgin	IL	60121	**800-445-3538**	847-888-7800
Daily Clay County Advocate-Press					
105 W North Ave	Flora	IL	62839	**800-804-9383**	618-662-2108
Journal-Standard 27 S State St	Freeport	IL	61032	**800-325-6397**	815-232-1171
Register-Mail 140 S Prairie St PO Box 310	Galesburg	IL	61401	**800-747-7181**	309-343-7181
Daily Register 35 S Vine St PO Box 248	Harrisburg	IL	62946	**800-283-8117**	618-253-7146
Jacksonville Journal-Courier					
235 W State St	Jacksonville	IL	62650	**800-682-9132**	217-245-6121
Herald-News 300 Caterpillar Dr	Joliet	IL	60436	**800-397-9397**	815-729-6161
Daily Journal 8 Dearborn Sq	Kankakee	IL	60901	**800-892-1861**	815-937-3300
Star-Courier PO Box A	Kewanee	IL	61443	**800-397-7827**	309-852-2181
News-Tribune 426 2nd St	La Salle	IL	61301	**800-892-6452**	815-223-3200
Courier The 601 Pulaski St PO Box 740	Lincoln	IL	62656	**800-747-5462**	217-732-2101
Macomb Journal 203 N Randolph St	Macomb	IL	61455	**800-237-6858**	309-833-2114
Marion Daily Republican PO Box 490	Marion	IL	62959	**800-238-3853**	618-993-2626
Morris Daily Herald PO Box 749	Morris	IL	60450	**800-215-9778**	815-942-3221
Olney Daily Mail PO Box 340	Olney	IL	62450	**800-804-9383**	618-393-2931
Paris Daily Beacon News PO Box 100	Paris	IL	61944	**800-587-5955**	217-465-6424
Peoria Journal Star 1 News Plaza	Peoria	IL	61643	**800-225-5757**	309-686-3000
Quincy Herald-Whig PO Box 909	Quincy	IL	62306	**800-373-9444**	217-223-5100
Rockford Register Star 99 E State St	Rockford	IL	61104	**800-383-7827**	815-987-1200
State Journal-Register 1 Copley Plaza	Springfield	IL	62701	**800-397-6397**	217-788-1300
Herald Bulletin 1133 Jackson St	Anderson	IN	46015	**800-750-5049**	765-622-1212
News-Banner PO Box 436	Bluffton	IN	46714	**800-579-7476**	260-824-0224
Brazil Times 100 N Meridian St	Brazil	IN	47834	**800-489-5090**	812-446-2216
Republic The 333 2nd St	Columbus	IN	47201	**800-876-7811**	812-372-7811
Connersville News-Examiner					
406 N Central Ave	Connersville	IN	47331	**888-906-1700**	765-825-0581
Journal Review 119 N Green St	Crawfordsville	IN	47933	**800-488-4414**	765-362-1200
Truth The PO Box 487	Elkhart	IN	46515	**800-585-5416**	574-294-1661
Evansville Courier & Press 300 E Walnut St	Evansville	IN	47713	**800-288-3200**	812-424-7711
Journal Gazette 600 W Main St	Fort Wayne	IN	46802	**800-444-3303**	260-461-8222
News-Sentinel 600 W Main St	Fort Wayne	IN	46802	**800-444-3303**	260-461-8222
Daily Journal 2575 N Morton St	Franklin	IN	46131	**888-736-7101**	317-736-7101
Goshen News 114 S Main St PO Box 569	Goshen	IN	46527	**800-487-2151**	574-533-2151
Banner-Graphic					
100 N Jackson St PO Box 509	Greencastle	IN	46135	**888-778-8877**	765-653-5151
Indianapolis Star 307 N Pennsylvania St	Indianapolis	IN	46204	**800-669-7827**	317-444-4000
Herald The 216 E 4th St	Jasper	IN	47546	**877-482-2424**	812-482-2426
News-Sun The PO Box 39	Kendallville	IN	46755	**800-717-4679**	260-347-0400
Kokomo Tribune 300 N Union St	Kokomo	IN	46901	**800-382-0696**	765-459-3121
La Porte Herald-Argus 701 State St	La Porte	IN	46350	**866-362-2167**	219-362-2161
Journal & Courier 217 N 6th St	Lafayette	IN	47901	**800-407-5813***	765-423-5511
*News Rm					
Linton Daily Citizen PO Box 129	Linton	IN	47441	**800-947-4487**	812-847-4487
Pharos-Tribune PO Box 210	Logansport	IN	46947	**800-676-4125**	574-722-5000
Madison Courier 310 Courier Sq	Madison	IN	47250	**800-333-2885**	812-265-3641
Chronicle-Tribune 610 S Adams St	Marion	IN	46953	**800-955-7888**	765-664-5111
Post-Tribune 1433 E 83rd Ave	Merrillville	IN	46410	**800-876-8974**	219-648-3055
News-Dispatch 121 W. Michigan Blvd	Michigan City	IN	46360	**800-489-9292**	219-874-7211
Herald Journal 114 S Main St	Monticello	IN	47960	**800-541-7906**	574-583-5121
Muncie Star-Press PO Box 2408	Muncie	IN	47307	**800-783-7827**	765-213-5700
Times The 601 45th Ave	Munster	IN	46321	**800-837-3232**	219-933-3200
Courier Times The 201 S 14th St	New Castle	IN	47362	**800-489-2472**	765-529-1111
Peru Tribune 26 W 3rd St	Peru	IN	46970	**800-737-4488**	765-473-6641
Pilot-News PO Box 220	Plymouth	IN	46563	**800-933-0356**	574-936-3101
Princeton Daily Clarion					
100 N Gibson St PO Box 30	Princeton	IN	47670	**800-467-5130**	812-385-2525
Rochester Sentinel PO Box 260	Rochester	IN	46975	**800-686-2112**	574-223-2111
Tribune The PO Box 447	Seymour	IN	47274	**800-800-8212**	812-522-4871
Shelbyville News PO Box 750	Shelbyville	IN	46176	**800-362-0114**	317-398-6631
South Bend Tribune 225 W Colfax Ave	South Bend	IN	46626	**800-220-7378**	574-235-6161
Tribune-Star PO Box 149	Terre Haute	IN	47808	**800-783-8742**	812-231-4200
Vincennes Sun-Commercial PO Box 396	Vincennes	IN	47591	**800-876-9955**	812-886-9955
Wabash Plain Dealer 123 W Canal St	Wabash	IN	46992	**800-659-6321**	260-563-2131
Washington Times-Herald PO Box 471	Washington	IN	47501	**800-235-4113**	812-254-0480
Winchester News-Gazette PO Box 429	Winchester	IN	47394	**800-782-2508**	765-584-4501
Tribune The 317 5th St PO Box 380	Ames	IA	50010	**800-234-8742**	515-232-2160
Boone News-Republican					
2136 E Mamie Eisenhower Ave	Boone	IA	50036	**888-270-0090**	515-432-1234
Hawk Eye 800 S Main St	Burlington	IA	52601	**800-397-1708**	319-754-8461
Daily Times Herald 508 N Court St	Carroll	IA	51401	**800-262-5495**	712-792-3573
Gazette The 500 3rd Ave SE	Cedar Rapids	IA	52401	**800-397-8212**	319-398-8313
Clinton Herald 221 6th Ave S	Clinton	IA	52733	**800-729-7101**	563-242-7101
Daily Nonpareil					
535 W Broadway Suite 300	Council Bluffs	IA	51503	**800-283-1882**	712-328-1811
Quad-City Times 500 E 3rd St	Davenport	IA	52801	**800-437-4641**	563-383-2200
Des Moines Register 715 Locust St	Des Moines	IA	50304	**800-247-5346**	515-284-8000
Telegraph Herald 801 Bluff St	Dubuque	IA	52001	**800-553-4801**	563-588-5611
Fairfield Ledger 112 E Broadway	Fairfield	IA	52556	**800-369-0340**	641-472-4129
Messenger The 713 Central Ave	Fort Dodge	IA	50501	**800-622-6613**	515-573-2141
Daily Democrat 1226 Ave H PO Box 160	Fort Madison	IA	52627	**800-798-8819**	319-372-6421
Daily Gate City 1016 Main St	Keokuk	IA	52632	**800-779-8819**	319-524-8300
Le Mars Daily Sentinel 41 1st Ave NE	Le Mars	IA	51031	**800-728-0066**	712-546-7031
Times-Republican PO Box 1300	Marshalltown	IA	50158	**800-542-7893**	641-753-6611
Globe-Gazette					
300 N Washington St PO Box 271	Mason City	IA	50402	**800-421-0546**	641-421-0500
Mount Pleasant News PO Box 240	Mount Pleasant	IA	52641	**800-373-2411**	319-385-3131
Muscatine Journal 301 E 3rd St	Muscatine	IA	52761	**800-383-3198**	563-263-2331
Oelwein Daily Register PO Box 511	Oelwein	IA	50662	**800-211-1076**	319-283-2144
Oskaloosa Herald PO Box 530	Oskaloosa	IA	52577	**888-672-2581**	641-672-2581
Ottumwa Courier 213 E 2nd St	Ottumwa	IA	52501	**800-532-1504**	641-684-4611
Valley News Today PO Box 369	Shenandoah	IA	51601	**800-369-3097**	712-246-3097
Sioux City Journal 515 Pavonia St	Sioux City	IA	51102	**800-397-3530**	712-293-4300
Daily Reporter					
310 E Milwaukee St PO Box 197	Spencer	IA	51301	**800-383-0964**	712-262-6610
Pilot Tribune PO Box 1187	Storm Lake	IA	50588	**800-798-6397**	712-732-3130
Washington Evening Journal PO Box 471	Washington	IA	52353	**800-369-0341**	319-653-2191
Waterloo Cedar Falls Courier PO Box 540	Waterloo	IA	50704	**800-798-1730**	319-291-1400
Atchison Daily Globe					
1015 Main St PO Box 247	Atchison	KS	66002	**800-748-7615**	913-367-0583
Dodge City Daily Globe					
705 2nd Ave PO Box 820	Dodge City	KS	67801	**800-279-8795**	620-225-4151
Fort Scott Tribune 6 E Wall St PO Box 150	Fort Scott	KS	66701	**800-658-1753**	620-223-1460
Garden City Telegram 310 N 7th St	Garden City	KS	67846	**800-475-8600**	620-275-8500
Great Bend Tribune					
2012 Forest St PO Box 228	Great Bend	KS	67530	**800-950-8742**	620-792-1211
Hays Daily News 507 Main St PO Box 857	Hays	KS	67601	**800-657-6017**	785-628-1081
Hiawatha World 607 Utah St	Hiawatha	KS	66434	**800-803-3321**	785-742-2111
Hutchinson News 300 W 2nd St	Hutchinson	KS	67504	**800-766-3311**	620-694-5700
Iola Register 302 S Washington St PO Box 767	Iola	KS	66749	**800-365-1901**	620-365-2111
Daily Union 222 W 6th St PO Box 129	Junction City	KS	66441	**800-657-6096**	785-762-5000
Lawrence Journal-World					
609 New Hampshire St	Lawrence	KS	66044	**800-578-8748**	785-843-1000
Leavenworth Times 422 Seneca St	Leavenworth	KS	66048	**800-466-0305**	913-682-0305
Southwest Daily Times PO Box 889	Liberal	KS	67905	**800-279-5826**	620-624-2541
Newton Kansan PO Box 268	Newton	KS	67114	**888-526-7261**	316-283-1500
Ottawa Herald 104 S Cedar St	Ottawa	KS	66067	**800-467-8383**	785-242-4700
Parsons Sun PO Box 836	Parsons	KS	67357	**800-530-5723**	620-421-2000
Morning Sun PO Drawer H	Pittsburg	KS	66762	**800-794-6536**	620-231-2600
Topeka Capital-Journal 616 SE Jefferson St	Topeka	KS	66607	**800-777-7171**	785-295-1111
Daily Independent 224 17th St	Ashland	KY	41105	**800-955-5860**	606-326-2600
Daily News					
813 Center St PO Box 90012	Bowling Green	KY	42102	**800-599-6397**	270-781-1700
Advocate Messenger 330 S 4th St	Danville	KY	40423	**800-428-0409**	859-236-2551
News-Enterprise 408 W Dixie Ave	Elizabethtown	KY	42701	**800-653-6344**	270-769-1200
Lexington Herald-Leader 100 Midland Ave	Lexington	KY	40508	**800-274-7355**	859-231-3100
Courier-Journal 525 W Broadway	Louisville	KY	40202	**800-765-4011**	502-582-4011
Messenger The PO Box 529	Madisonville	KY	42431	**800-726-6397**	270-821-6833
Ledger-Independent PO Box 518	Maysville	KY	41056	**800-264-9091**	606-564-9091
Paducah Sun PO Box 2300	Paducah	KY	42002	**800-959-1771**	270-575-8600
Alexandria Daily Town Talk PO Box 7558	Alexandria	LA	71306	**800-523-8391**	318-487-6397
American Press 4900 Hwy 90 E	Lake Charles	LA	70615	**800-531-4080***	337-494-4000
*News Rm					
News-Star 411 N 4th St	Monroe	LA	71201	**800-259-7788**	318-322-5161
Daily Iberian 926 E Main St	New Iberia	LA	70560	**800-365-6773**	337-365-6773

Classified Section

				Toll-Free	Phone
Times-Picayune 3800 Howard Ave	New Orleans	LA	70125	**800-925-0000**	504-826-3279
Times 222 Lake St	Shreveport	LA	71130	**800-551-8892**	318-459-3200
Daily Comet 705 W 5th St	Thibodaux	LA	70301	**800-256-1305**	985-447-4055
Kennebec Journal 274 Western Ave	Augusta	ME	04330	**800-537-5508**	207-623-3811
Journal Tribune 457 Alfred St	Biddeford	ME	04005	**888-429-1535**	207-282-1535
Times Record PO Box 10	Brunswick	ME	04011	**800-879-3311**	207-729-3311
Sun-Journal PO Box 4400	Lewiston	ME	04243	**800-482-0759**	207-784-5411
Morning Sentinel 31 Front St	Waterville	ME	04901	**800-452-4666**	207-873-3341
Baltimore Sun 501 N Calvert St	Baltimore	MD	21278	**800-829-8000**	410-332-6000
Daily Banner 1000 Goodwill Rd	Cambridge	MD	21613	**800-282-8586**	410-228-3131
Cumberland Times-News 19 Baltimore St	Cumberland	MD	21502	**800-742-8149**	301-722-4600
Cecil Whig Newspaper PO Box 429	Elkton	MD	21922	**800-220-3311**	410-398-3311
Frederick News Post 200 E Patrick St	Frederick	MD	21701	**800-486-1177**	301-662-1177
Herald-Mail 100 Summit Ave	Hagerstown	MD	21740	**888-851-2553**	301-733-5131
Daily Times 115 E Carroll St	Salisbury	MD	21801	**877-335-6278**	410-749-7171
Boston Herald 1 Herald Sq	Boston	MA	02118	**800-225-2040**	617-426-3000
Haverhill Gazette PO Box 991	Haverhill	MA	01831	**800-370-0321**	978-374-0321
Lowell Sun 15 Kearny Sq	Lowell	MA	01852	**800-694-7100**	978-458-7100
Daily News-Tribune 254 Beckon Ave	Needham	MA	02494	**800-982-4023**	781-647-7898
Berkshire Eagle 75 S Church St PO Box 1171	Pittsfield	MA	01202	**800-234-7404**	413-447-7311
Telegram & Gazette 20 Franklin St PO Box 15012	Worcester	MA	01615	**800-678-6680**	508-793-9100
Daily Telegram 133 N Winter St	Adrian	MI	49221	**800-968-5111**	517-265-5111
Ann Arbor News 340 E Huron St	Ann Arbor	MI	48104	**800-466-6989**	734-994-6989
Battle Creek Enquirer 155 W Van Buren St	Battle Creek	MI	49017	**800-333-4139**	269-964-7161
Pioneer The 502 N State St	Big Rapids	MI	49307	**800-968-1114**	231-796-4831
Cadillac News 130 N Mitchell St	Cadillac	MI	49601	**888-584-6564**	231-775-6565
Detroit Free Press 600 W Fort St	Detroit	MI	48226	**800-678-6400**	313-222-6400
Detroit News 615 W Lafayette Blvd	Detroit	MI	48226	**800-678-6400**	313-222-6400
Daily Press 600 Ludington St	Escanaba	MI	49829	**800-743-0609**	906-786-2021
Flint Journal 200 E 1st St	Flint	MI	48502	**800-875-6200***	810-766-6100
*Circulation					
Grand Haven Tribune 101 N 3rd St	Grand Haven	MI	49417	**800-874-7180**	616-842-6400
Grand Rapids Press 155 Michigan St NW	Grand Rapids	MI	49503	**800-878-1400**	616-459-1400
Daily News PO Box 340	Greenville	MI	48838	**800-968-9301**	616-754-9301
Holland Sentinel 54 W 8th St	Holland	MI	49423	**800-968-3495**	616-392-2311
Daily Mining Gazette 206 Sheldon Ave	Houghton	MI	49931	**800-682-7607**	906-482-1500
Daily News 215 E Ludington St PO Box 460	Iron Mountain	MI	49801	**800-743-2088**	906-774-2772
Jackson Citizen Patriot 214 S Jackson St	Jackson	MI	49201	**800-878-6397**	517-787-2300
Kalamazoo Gazette 401 S Burdick St	Kalamazoo	MI	49007	**800-466-6397**	269-345-3511
Lansing State Journal 120 E Lenawee St	Lansing	MI	48919	**800-234-1719**	517-377-1000
Ludington Daily News 202 N Rath St	Ludington	MI	49431	**800-748-0407**	231-845-5181
Manistee News-Advocate PO Box 317	Manistee	MI	49660	**888-723-3592**	231-723-3592
Midland Daily News 124 S McDonald St	Midland	MI	48640	**800-835-6679**	989-835-7171
Muskegon Chronicle PO Box 59	Muskegon	MI	49443	**800-783-3161**	231-722-3161
Dowagiac Daily News 217 N 4th St	Niles	MI	49020	**888-725-0108**	269-782-2101
Niles Daily Star 217 N 4th St	Niles	MI	49120	**888-725-0108**	269-683-2100
Argus-Press 201 E Exchange St	Owosso	MI	48867	**800-444-4850**	989-725-5136
Petoskey News-Review PO Box 528	Petoskey	MI	49770	**800-968-2544**	231-347-2544
Daily Tribune 210 E 3rd St	Royal Oak	MI	48067	**877-373-2387**	248-541-3000
Saginaw News 203 S Washington Ave	Saginaw	MI	48607	**800-875-6397**	989-752-7171
Herald-Palladium 7450 Hollywood Rd PO Box 128	Saint Joseph	MI	49085	**800-356-4262**	269-429-2400
Sturgis Journal PO Box 660	Sturgis	MI	49091	**800-686-5653**	269-651-5407
Albert Lea Tribune 808 W Front St PO Box 60	Albert Lea	MN	56007	**800-657-4996**	507-373-1411
Brainerd Dispatch 506 James St	Brainerd	MN	56401	**800-432-3703**	218-829-4705
Duluth News-Tribune 424 W 1st St	Duluth	MN	55802	**800-456-8080***	218-723-5281
*Circ					
Sentinel PO Box 681	Fairmont	MN	56031	**800-598-5597**	507-235-3303
Free Press 418 S 2nd St	Mankato	MN	56002	**800-657-4662**	507-625-4451
Marshall Independent PO Box 411	Marshall	MN	56258	**800-640-6148**	507-537-1551
Star Tribune 425 Portland Ave	Minneapolis	MN	55488	**800-827-8742**	612-673-4000
Republican Eagle PO Box 15	Red Wing	MN	55066	**800-535-1660**	651-388-8235
Post-Bulletin 18 1st Ave SE	Rochester	MN	55903	**800-562-1758**	507-285-7600
Saint Cloud Times PO Box 768	Saint Cloud	MN	56302	**800-272-8770**	320-255-8700
Saint Paul Pioneer Press 345 Cedar St	Saint Paul	MN	55101	**800-950-9080**	651-222-1111
West Central Tribune PO Box 839	Willmar	MN	56201	**800-450-1150**	320-235-1150
Winona Daily News 601 Franklin St	Winona	MN	55987	**800-328-2182**	507-454-6500
Daily Globe 300 11th St	Worthington	MN	56187	**800-642-3243**	507-376-9711
Daily Leader 128 N Railroad Ave PO Box 551	Brookhaven	MS	39602	**800-833-6961**	601-833-6961
Commercial Dispatch 516 Main St	Columbus	MS	39703	**888-477-1555**	662-328-2424
Sun Herald 205 DeBuys Rd	Gulfport	MS	39507	**800-346-5022**	228-896-2100
Hattiesburg American 825 N Main St	Hattiesburg	MS	39401	**800-844-2637**	601-582-4321
Clarion-Ledger 201 S Congress St	Jackson	MS	39201	**800-367-3384**	601-961-7000
Meridian Star PO Box 1591	Meridian	MS	39302	**800-232-2525**	601-693-1551
Natchez Democrat PO Box 1447	Natchez	MS	39121	**888-878-9101**	601-442-9101
Northeast Mississippi Daily Journal 1242 S Green St	Tupelo	MS	38804	**800-264-6397**	662-842-2611
Lake Sun Leader 918 N State Hwy 5	Camdenton	MO	65020	**866-346-2132**	573-346-2132
Southeast Missourian PO Box 699	Cape Girardeau	MO	63702	**800-879-1210**	573-335-6611
Constitution-Tribune The 818 Washington St PO Box 707	Chillicothe	MO	64601	**800-373-0256**	660-646-2411
Columbia Daily Tribune 101 N 4th St	Columbia	MO	65201	**800-333-6799**	573-449-3811
Hannibal Courier-Post 200 N 3rd St PO Box A	Hannibal	MO	63401	**800-748-7025**	573-221-2800
Branson Daily News 200 Industrial Pk Dr	Hollister	MO	65672	**800-490-8020**	417-334-3161
Daily Capital News 210 Monroe St	Jefferson City	MO	65101	**866-865-1690**	573-636-3131
Jefferson City Post-Tribune 210 Monroe St	Jefferson City	MO	65101	**866-896-8088**	573-636-3131
Joplin Globe 117 E 4th St	Joplin	MO	64801	**800-444-8514**	417-623-3480
Kansas City Star 1729 Grand Ave	Kansas City	MO	64108	**800-726-2340**	816-234-4141
Lebanon Daily Record 100 E Commercial St	Lebanon	MO	65536	**800-665-8875**	417-532-9131
Maryville Daily Forum PO Box 188	Maryville	MO	64468	**800-582-7863**	660-562-2424
Mexico Ledger PO Box 8	Mexico	MO	65265	**800-246-0050**	573-581-1111
Daily Journal 1513 St Joe Dr	Park Hills	MO	63601	**800-660-8166**	573-431-2010
Saint Joseph News-Press PO Box 29	Saint Joseph	MO	64502	**800-779-6397**	816-271-8500
Saint Louis Post-Dispatch 900 N Tucker Blvd	Saint Louis	MO	63101	**800-365-0820**	314-340-8000
Springfield News Leader 651 Boonville Ave	Springfield	MO	65806	**800-695-2005***	417-836-1100
*Circ					
Billings Gazette 401 N Broadway	Billings	MT	59107	**800-543-2505**	406-657-1200
Montana Standard PO Box 627	Butte	MT	59703	**800-877-1074**	406-496-5500
Great Falls Tribune 205 River Dr S	Great Falls	MT	59405	**800-438-6600**	406-791-1444
Havre Daily News 119 2nd St PO Box 431	Havre	MT	59501	**800-993-2459**	406-265-6795
Helena Independent Record 317 Cruse Ave	Helena	MT	59604	**800-523-2272**	406-447-4000
Livingston Enterprise 401 S Main St	Livingston	MT	59047	**800-345-8412**	406-222-2000
Miles City Star PO Box 1216	Miles City	MT	59301	**800-323-6505**	406-234-0450
Missoulian PO Box 8029	Missoula	MT	59807	**800-366-7102**	406-523-5200
Beatrice Daily Sun 200 N 7th St PO Box 847	Beatrice	NE	68310	**800-666-5233**	402-223-5233

				Toll-Free	Phone
Columbus Telegram 1254 27th St PO Box 648	Columbus	NE	68602	**800-279-1123**	402-564-2741
Fremont Tribune 135 N Main St	Fremont	NE	68025	**800-927-7598**	402-721-5000
Grand Island Independent 422 W 1st St PO Box 1208	Grand Island	NE	68802	**800-658-3160**	308-382-1000
Hastings Tribune 908 W 2nd St	Hastings	NE	68901	**800-742-6397**	402-462-2131
Lincoln Journal-Star 926 P St	Lincoln	NE	68508	**800-742-7315**	402-475-4200
McCook Daily Gazette PO Box 1268	McCook	NE	69001	**800-269-1426**	308-345-4500
Nebraska City News-Press PO Box 757	Nebraska City	NE	68410	**877-269-3358**	402-873-3334
Norfolk Daily News PO Box 977	Norfolk	NE	68702	**877-371-1020**	402-371-1020
North Platte Telegraph PO Box 370	North Platte	NE	69103	**800-753-7092**	308-532-6000
Omaha World-Herald 1334 Dodge St	Omaha	NE	68102	**800-284-6397**	402-444-1000
Star-Herald PO Box 1709	Scottsbluff	NE	69363	**800-846-6102**	308-632-9000
Sidney Sun-Telegraph PO Box 193	Sidney	NE	69162	**888-254-2818**	308-254-2818
York News-Times PO Box 279	York	NE	68467	**800-334-4530**	402-362-4478
Nevada Appeal 580 Mallory Way	Carson City	NV	89701	**800-221-8013**	775-882-2111
Reno Gazette-Journal 955 Kuenzli St	Reno	NV	89502	**800-648-5048**	775-788-6200
Daily Sparks Tribune 1002 C St	Sparks	NV	89431	**800-669-1338**	775-358-8061
Eagle Times 401 River Rd	Claremont	NH	03743	**800-545-0347**	603-543-3100
Foster's Daily Democrat 333 Central Ave	Dover	NH	03820	**800-660-8310**	603-742-4455
Keene Sentinel 60 West St PO Box 546	Keene	NH	03431	**800-765-9994**	603-352-1234
Citizen The 171 Fair St	Laconia	NH	03246	**800-564-3806**	603-524-3800
Union Leader 100 William Loeb Dr	Manchester	NH	03109	**800-562-8218**	603-668-4321
Portsmouth Herald 111 Maplewood Ave	Portsmouth	NH	03801	**800-439-0303**	603-436-1800
Courier-News 1201 Rt 22 W	Bridgewater	NJ	08807	**800-675-0298**	908-722-8800
Courier-Post PO Box 5300	Cherry Hill	NJ	08034	**800-677-6289**	856-663-6000
Home News Tribune 35 Kennedy Blvd	East Brunswick	NJ	08816	**800-627-4663**	732-246-5500
Star-Ledger The 1 Star Ledger Plaza	Newark	NJ	07102	**800-501-2100**	973-877-4141
Daily Journal 891 E Oak Rd	Vineland	NJ	08360	**800-222-0104**	856-691-5000
Albuquerque Journal 7777 Jefferson St NE	Albuquerque	NM	87109	**800-990-5765**	505-823-7777
Albuquerque Tribune 7777 Jefferson St NE	Albuquerque	NM	87109	**800-665-8742**	505-823-3653
Clovis News Journal 521 Pile St	Clovis	NM	88101	**800-819-9925**	505-763-3431
Daily Times 201 N Allen Ave	Farmington	NM	87401	**800-395-6397**	505-325-4545
Gallup Independent 500 N 9th St	Gallup	NM	87305	**800-545-3817**	505-863-6811
Hobbs News-Sun PO Box 850	Hobbs	NM	88241	**800-993-2123**	505-393-2123
Las Cruces Sun-News 256 W Las Cruces Ave	Las Cruces	NM	88005	**800-745-5851**	505-541-5400
Las Vegas Optic 614 Lincoln St	Las Vegas	NM	87701	**800-767-6796**	505-425-6796
Portales News-Tribune PO Box 848	Portales	NM	88130	**800-658-6944**	505-356-4481
Amsterdam Recorder 1 Venner Rd	Amsterdam	NY	12010	**800-453-6397**	518-843-1100
Daily News 2 Apollo Dr PO Box 870	Batavia	NY	14021	**888-217-6397**	585-343-8000
Press & Sun Bulletin PO box 1270	Binghamton	NY	13902	**800-365-0077**	607-798-1234
Buffalo News 1 News Plaza PO Box 100	Buffalo	NY	14240	**800-777-8680**	716-849-3434
Daily Messenger 73 Buffalo St	Canandaigua	NY	14424	**800-724-2099**	585-394-0770
Evening Observer 8-10 E 2nd St PO Box 391	Dunkirk	NY	14048	**800-836-0931**	716-366-3000
Star-Gazette 201 Baldwin St	Elmira	NY	14902	**800-836-8970**	607-734-5151
Finger Lakes Times 218 Genesee St	Geneva	NY	14456	**800-388-6652**	315-789-3333
Post-Star PO Box 2157	Glens Falls	NY	12801	**800-724-2543**	518-792-3131
Register-Star 364 Warren St	Hudson	NY	12534	**800-836-4069**	518-828-1616
Post-Journal PO Box 190	Jamestown	NY	14702	**866-756-9600**	716-487-1111
Newsday Inc 235 Pinelawn Rd	Melville	NY	11747	**800-639-7329**	631-843-4000
Times Herald-Record 40 Mulberry St PO Box 2046	Middletown	NY	10940	**800-295-2181**	845-341-1100
Financial Times 1330 Ave of the Americas	New York	NY	10019	**800-628-8088**	212-641-6500
New York Post 1211 Ave of the Americas	New York	NY	10036	**800-552-7678**	212-930-8000
New York Sun 105 Chambers St 2nd Fl	New York	NY	10007	**866-692-7861**	212-406-2000
Evening Sun PO Box 151	Norwich	NY	13815	**800-836-6780**	607-334-3276
Olean Times-Herald 639 Norton Dr	Olean	NY	14760	**800-722-8812**	716-372-3121
Daily Star 102 Chestnut St PO Box 250	Oneonta	NY	13820	**800-721-1000**	607-432-1000
Press-Republican 170 Margaret St	Plattsburgh	NY	12901	**800-288-7323**	518-561-2300
Poughkeepsie Journal 85 Civic Ctr Plaza	Poughkeepsie	NY	12601	**800-765-1120**	845-437-4800
Democrat & Chronicle 55 Exchange Blvd	Rochester	NY	14614	**800-473-5274**	585-232-7100
Salamanca Press PO Box 111	Salamanca	NY	14779	**800-474-9874**	716-945-1644
Daily Gazette 2345 Maxon Rd Ext	Schenectady	NY	12308	**800-262-2211**	518-374-4141
Post-Standard PO Box 4915	Syracuse	NY	13221	**800-765-4569**	315-470-0011
Observer-Dispatch 221 Oriskany Plaza	Utica	NY	13501	**800-765-5303**	315-792-5000
Watertown Daily Times 260 Washington St	Watertown	NY	13601	**800-642-6222**	315-782-1000
Rockland Journal-News PO Box 300	West Nyack	NY	10994	**800-942-1010**	845-358-2200
Journal News 1 Gannett Dr	White Plains	NY	10604	**800-942-1010**	914-694-9300
Courier-Tribune 500 Sunset Ave	Asheboro	NC	27203	**800-967-1838**	336-625-2101
Asheville Citizen Times 14 O'Henry Ave	Asheville	NC	28801	**800-800-4204**	828-252-5622
Times-News PO Box 481	Burlington	NC	27216	**800-488-0085**	336-227-0131
Charlotte Observer 600 S Tryon St	Charlotte	NC	28202	**800-332-0686**	704-358-5000
Herald-Sun 2828 Pickett Rd	Durham	NC	27705	**800-672-0061**	919-419-6500
Fayetteville Observer 458 Whitfield St	Fayetteville	NC	28306	**800-345-9895**	910-323-4848
Daily Courier 601 Oak St	Forest City	NC	28043	**888-761-1898**	828-245-6431
Gaston Gazette 1893 Remount Rd	Gastonia	NC	28054	**800-273-3315**	704-869-1700
News & Record 200 E Market St	Greensboro	NC	27401	**800-553-6880**	336-373-7000
Daily Reflector PO Box 1967	Greenville	NC	27835	**800-849-6166**	252-752-6166
Times-News PO Box 490	Hendersonville	NC	28793	**800-849-8050**	828-692-0505
Hickory Daily Record 1100 Park Pl	Hickory	NC	28603	**800-849-8586**	828-322-4510
High Point Enterprise 210 Church Ave	High Point	NC	27262	**800-933-5760**	336-888-3500
Daily News 724 Bell Fork Rd PO Box 196	Jacksonville	NC	28541	**800-659-2873**	910-353-1171
Exchange The PO Box 459	Laurinburg	NC	28353	**800-334-2311**	910-276-2311
Mount Airy News PO Box 808	Mount Airy	NC	27030	**800-826-6397**	336-786-4141
News & Observer 215 S McDowell St	Raleigh	NC	27601	**800-365-3115**	919-829-4500
Salisbury Post 131 W Innes St	Salisbury	NC	28144	**800-633-8957**	704-633-8950
Star-News PO Box 840	Wilmington	NC	28402	**800-272-1277**	910-343-2000
Wilson Daily Times PO Box 2447	Wilson	NC	27894	**800-849-8811**	252-243-5151
Winston-Salem Journal 418 N Marshall St	Winston-Salem	NC	27102	**800-642-0925**	336-727-7211
Bismarck Tribune 707 E Front Ave	Bismarck	ND	58506	**866-476-5348**	701-223-2500
Dickinson Press 1815 1st St PO Box 1367	Dickinson	ND	58602	**800-279-9150**	701-225-8111
Forum The 101 N 5th St	Fargo	ND	58102	**800-747-7311**	701-235-7311
Jamestown Sun 121 3rd St NW	Jamestown	ND	58401	**800-657-8067**	701-252-3120
Minot Daily News 301 4th St SE	Minot	ND	58701	**800-735-3119**	701-857-1900
Valley City Times-Record PO Box 697	Valley City	ND	58072	**800-254-0674**	701-845-0463
Daily News PO Box 760	Wahpeton	ND	58074	**800-666-4492**	701-642-8585
Williston Daily Herald PO Box 1447	Williston	ND	58802	**800-950-2165**	701-572-2165
Akron Beacon Journal 44 E Exchange St	Akron	OH	44309	**800-777-2442**	330-996-3000
Ashland Times-Gazette 40 E 2nd St	Ashland	OH	44805	**888-463-9711**	419-281-0581
Star Beacon PO Box 2100	Ashtabula	OH	44005	**800-554-6768**	440-998-2323
Bryan Times 127 S Walnut St	Bryan	OH	43506	**800-589-5520**	419-636-1111
Telegraph-Forum 119 W Rensselaer St	Bucyrus	OH	44820	**877-838-6329**	419-562-3333
Repository 500 Market Ave S	Canton	OH	44702	**877-580-8300**	330-580-8300
Daily Standard 123 E Market St	Celina	OH	45822	**877-525-3680**	419-586-2371
Cincinnati Enquirer 312 Elm St	Cincinnati	OH	45202	**800-876-4500**	513-721-2700
Kentucky Post 125 E Court St	Cincinnati	OH	45202	**800-937-4954**	859-292-2600
Plain Dealer 1801 Superior Ave	Cleveland	OH	44114	**800-688-4802**	216-999-4800
Columbus Dispatch 34 S 3rd St	Columbus	OH	43215	**800-848-1110**	614-461-5000
Coshocton Tribune 550 Main St PO Box 10	Coshocton	OH	43812	**800-589-8689**	740-622-1122
Crescent-News 624 W 2nd St PO Box 249	Defiance	OH	43512	**800-589-5441**	419-784-5441

Daily Newspapers - US (Cont'd)

Newspaper	City	State	ZIP	Toll-Free	Phone
Delphos Daily Herald 405 N Main St	Delphos	OH	45833	**800-589-6950**	419-695-0015
Chronicle-Telegram 225 East Ave	Elyria	OH	44035	**800-633-4623**	440-329-7000
Review Times PO Box 947	Fostoria	OH	44830	**800-457-2796**	419-435-6641
News-Messenger 1700 Cedar St	Fremont	OH	43420	**800-766-6397**	419-332-5511
Ironton Tribune 2903 S 5th St	Ironton	OH	45638	**866-532-1441**	740-532-1441
Kenton Times 201 E Columbus St PO Box 230	Kenton	OH	43326	**800-886-2412**	419-674-4066
Lancaster Eagle-Gazette 138 W Chestnut St	Lancaster	OH	43130	**888-420-3883**	740-681-4500
Lima News 3515 Elida Rd	Lima	OH	45807	**800-686-9924**	419-223-1010
Morning Journal 308 W Maple St	Lisbon	OH	44432	**800-862-6224**	330-424-9541
Madison Press PO Box 390	London	OH	43140	**800-282-3838**	740-852-1616
Morning Journal 1657 Broadway Ave	Lorain	OH	44052	**800-765-6901**	440-245-6901
News Journal 70 W 4th St	Mansfield	OH	44902	**800-472-5547**	419-522-3311
Marietta Times 700 Channel Ln	Marietta	OH	45750	**800-531-1215**	740-373-2121
Star The Marion 150 Court St	Marion	OH	43302	**800-626-1331**	740-387-0400
Times Leader 200 S 4th St	Martins Ferry	OH	43935	**800-244-5671**	740-633-1131
Medina Gazette 805 W Liberty St	Medina	OH	44256	**800-633-4623**	330-725-4166
Middletown Journal PO Box 490	Middletown	OH	45042	**888-397-6397**	513-422-3611
Northwest Signal PO Box 567	Napoleon	OH	43545	**800-559-6779**	419-592-5055
Times Reporter 629 Wabash Ave NW	New Philadelphia	OH	44663	**800-837-8666**	330-364-5577
Advocate The 22 N 1st St	Newark	OH	43055	**800-555-8350**	740-345-4053
Norwalk Reflector 61 E Monroe St PO Box 71	Norwalk	OH	44857	**800-589-3771**	419-668-3771
Portsmouth Daily Times PO Box 581	Portsmouth	OH	45662	**800-298-5232**	740-353-3101
Record-Courier 126 N Chestnut St PO Box 1201	Ravenna	OH	44266	**800-560-9657**	330-296-9657
Salem News PO Box 268	Salem	OH	44460	**877-332-4601**	330-332-4601
Sandusky Register 314 W Market St	Sandusky	OH	44870	**800-466-1243**	419-625-5500
Sidney Daily News PO Box 4099	Sidney	OH	45365	**800-688-4820**	937-498-8088
Springfield News-Sun 202 N Limestone St	Springfield	OH	45503	**888-890-7323**	937-328-0300
Blade 541 N Superior St	Toledo	OH	43660	**888-252-3301**	419-724-6000
Times-Bulletin PO Box 271	Van Wert	OH	45891	**800-727-2036**	419-238-2285
Tribune Chronicle 240 Franklin St SE	Warren	OH	44482	**888-550-8742**	330-841-1600
Record Herald 138 S Fayette St	Washington Court House	OH	43160	**800-200-4968**	740-335-3611
News-Herald 7085 Mentor Ave	Willoughby	OH	44094	**800-947-2737**	440-951-0000
Daily Record 212 E Liberty St PO Box 918	Wooster	OH	44691	**800-686-2958**	330-264-1125
Vindicator The 107 Vindicator Sq PO Box 780	Youngstown	OH	44501	**800-686-5199**	330-747-1471
Times Recorder 34 S 4th St	Zanesville	OH	43701	**800-886-7326**	740-452-4561
Altus Times 218 W Commerce St PO Box 578	Altus	OK	73522	**800-303-1221**	580-482-1221
Anadarko Daily News 117-119 E Broadway	Anadarko	OK	73005	**800-256-2763**	405-247-3331
Daily Ardmoreite 117 W Broadway St	Ardmore	OK	73401	**800-873-0211**	580-223-2200
Cushing Daily Citizen 115 S Cleveland St PO Box 1031	Cushing	OK	74023	**800-780-6397**	918-225-3333
Duncan Banner 1001 W Elm St PO Box 1268	Duncan	OK	73534	**800-893-8718**	580-255-5354
Durant Daily Democrat 200 W Beech St PO Box 250	Durant	OK	74702	**800-729-4388**	580-924-4388
Enid News & Eagle 227 W Broadway	Enid	OK	73702	**800-299-6397**	580-233-6600
Guthrie News Leader 107 W Harrison St PO Box 879	Guthrie	OK	73044	**888-851-8717**	405-282-2222
Guymon Daily Herald 515 N Ellison St	Guymon	OK	73942	**866-430-6397**	580-338-3355
Hugo Daily News 128 E Jackson St	Hugo	OK	74743	**800-900-3311**	580-326-3311
Lawton Constitution 102 SW 3rd St Po Box 2069	Lawton	OK	73502	**800-364-3636**	580-353-0620
McAlester News-Capital & Democrat PO Box 987	McAlester	OK	74502	**877-307-4237**	918-423-1700
Miami News-Record PO Box 940	Miami	OK	74355	**800-611-1032**	918-542-5533
Muskogee Daily Phoenix PO Box 1968	Muskogee	OK	74402	**800-730-3649**	918-684-2828
Oklahoman The 9000 N Broadway	Oklahoma City	OK	73114	**800-375-6397**	405-475-3311
Perry Daily Journal PO Box 311	Perry	OK	73077	**888-709-2197**	580-336-2222
Ponca City News PO Box 191	Ponca City	OK	74602	**866-765-3311**	580-765-3311
Shawnee News-Star PO Box 1688	Shawnee	OK	74802	**800-332-2305**	405-273-4200
Tahlequah Daily Press PO Box 888	Tahlequah	OK	74465	**800-725-8866**	918-456-8833
Tulsa World 315 S Boulder Ave	Tulsa	OK	74103	**800-897-3557**	918-583-2161
Woodward News PO Box 928	Woodward	OK	73802	**888-389-6960**	580-256-2200
Albany Democrat-Herald 600 Lyons St SW	Albany	OR	97321	**800-677-3993**	541-926-2211
Daily Astorian 949 Exchange St	Astoria	OR	97103	**800-781-3211**	503-325-3211
Baker City Herald 1915 1st St PO Box 807	Baker City	OR	97814	**888-318-7508**	541-523-3673
Bulletin The 1777 SW Chandler Ave	Bend	OR	97702	**800-503-3933**	541-382-1811
Corvallis Gazette-Times 600 SW Jefferson St PO Box 368	Corvallis	OR	97339	**800-653-3755**	541-753-2641
Daily Courier 409 SE 7th St	Grants Pass	OR	97526	**800-228-0457**	541-474-3700
Herald & News PO Box 788	Klamath Falls	OR	97601	**800-275-0982**	541-885-4410
Observer The 1406 5th St	La Grande	OR	97850	**800-422-3110**	541-963-3161
Medford Mail Tribune PO Box 1108	Medford	OR	97501	**800-366-2527**	541-776-4411
Argus Observer 1160 SW 4th St	Ontario	OR	97914	**800-945-4223**	541-889-5387
East Oregonian 211 SE Byers St PO Box 1089	Pendleton	OR	97801	**800-522-0255**	541-276-2211
News-Review 345 NE Winchester St	Roseburg	OR	97470	**800-683-3321**	541-672-3321
Dalles Chronicle 315 Federal St	The Dalles	OR	97058	**800-375-7832**	541-296-2141
Morning Call 101 N 6th St	Allentown	PA	18101	**800-666-5492**	610-820-6500
Altoona Mirror 301 Cayuga Ave	Altoona	PA	16602	**800-222-1962**	814-946-7411
Bedford Gazette 424 W Penn St	Bedford	PA	15522	**800-242-4250**	814-623-1151
Dispatch The 116 E Market St	Blairsville	PA	15717	**888-636-1116**	724-459-6100
Sentinel The 457 E North St	Carlisle	PA	17013	**800-829-5570**	717-243-2611
Daily Courier 127 W Apple St	Connellsville	PA	15425	**800-801-9000**	724-628-2000
Danville News 14 E Mahoning St	Danville	PA	17821	**800-792-2303**	570-275-3235
Courier-Express The 500 Jeffers St	Du Bois	PA	15801	**800-442-4217**	814-371-4200
Express-Times 30 N 4th St	Easton	PA	18042	**800-360-3601**	610-258-7171
Erie Times-News 205 W 12th St	Erie	PA	16534	**800-352-0043**	814-870-1600
Record-Argus 10 Penn Ave	Greenville	PA	16125	**800-542-3100**	724-588-5000
Evening Sun 135 Baltimore St	Hanover	PA	17331	**800-877-3786**	717-637-3736
Patriot-News 812 Market St	Harrisburg	PA	17101	**800-692-7207**	717-255-8100
Hazleton Standard Speaker 21 N Wyoming St	Hazleton	PA	18201	**800-843-6680**	570-455-3636
Daily News 325 Penn St	Huntingdon	PA	16652	**800-634-5692**	814-643-4040
Tribune-Democrat 425 Locust St	Johnstown	PA	15907	**800-473-0998**	814-532-5050
Intelligencer Journal 8 W King St	Lancaster	PA	17603	**800-809-4666**	717-291-8811
Lancaster New Era 8 W King St	Lancaster	PA	17608	**800-809-4666**	717-291-8733
Times News 594 Blakeslee Blvd Dr W	Lehighton	PA	18235	**800-443-0377**	610-377-2051
Meadville Tribune 947 Federal Ct	Meadville	PA	16335	**800-879-0006**	814-724-6370
Derrick The 1510 W 1st St PO Box 928	Oil City	PA	16301	**800-352-1002**	814-676-7444
News-Herald PO Box 928	Oil City	PA	16301	**800-352-1002**	814-676-7444
Pittsburgh Tribune-Review 503 Martindale St 3rd Fl	Pittsburgh	PA	15212	**800-433-3045**	412-321-6460
Pottsville Republican 111 Mahantongo St	Pottsville	PA	17901	**800-622-1737**	570-622-3456
Reading Eagle 345 Penn St	Reading	PA	19601	**800-633-7222**	610-371-5000
Morning Times 201 N Lehigh Ave	Sayre	PA	18840	**800-459-6397**	570-888-9643
Scranton Times-Tribune 149 Penn Ave	Scranton	PA	18503	**800-228-4637**	570-348-9100
Herald The 52 S Dock St	Sharon	PA	16146	**800-981-1692**	724-981-6100
Daily American 111 S Emma St PO Box 617	Somerset	PA	15501	**800-452-0823**	814-444-5900
Centre Daily Times 3400 E College Ave	State College	PA	16804	**800-327-5500**	814-238-5000
Pocono Record 511 Lenox St	Stroudsburg	PA	18360	**800-756-4237**	570-421-3000
Daily Item 200 Market St PO Box 607	Sunbury	PA	17801	**800-792-2303**	570-286-5671
Valley News Dispatch 210 4th Ave	Tarentum	PA	15084	**877-698-2553**	724-226-1006
Daily Review 116 Main St	Towanda	PA	18848	**800-253-3662**	570-265-2151
Daily Herald 1067 Pennsylvania Ave PO Box 246	Tyrone	PA	16686	**800-524-7108**	814-684-4000
Herald-Standard 8-18 E Church St PO Box 848	Uniontown	PA	15401	**800-342-8254**	724-439-7500
Observer-Reporter 122 S Main St	Washington	PA	15301	**800-222-6397**	724-222-2200
Daily Local News 250 N Bradford Ave	West Chester	PA	19382	**800-456-6397**	610-696-1775
Williamsport Sun-Gazette 252 W 4th St	Williamsport	PA	17701	**800-339-0289**	570-326-1551
York Daily Record PO Box 15122	York	PA	17405	**800-682-1334**	717-771-2000
York Dispatch 205 N George St	York	PA	17401	**800-483-5517**	717-854-1575
Providence Journal 75 Fountain St	Providence	RI	02902	**888-697-7656**	401-277-7000
Westerly Sun The 56 Main St	Westerly	RI	02891	**800-937-8759**	401-596-7791
Anderson Independent-Mail PO Box 2507	Anderson	SC	29622	**800-859-6397**	864-224-4321
Island Packet 10 Buck Island Rd	Bluffton	SC	29910	**877-706-8100**	843-706-8100
State The 1401 Shop Rd	Columbia	SC	29201	**800-888-5353**	803-771-6161
Greenville News 305 S Main St	Greenville	SC	29601	**800-800-5116**	864-298-4100
Sun News 914 Frontage Rd E	Myrtle Beach	SC	29578	**800-568-1800**	843-626-8555
Times & Democrat PO Box 1766	Orangeburg	SC	29116	**877-534-1060**	803-533-5500
Spartanburg Herald-Journal 189 W Main St	Spartanburg	SC	29304	**800-922-4158**	864-582-4511
Aberdeen American News 124 S 2nd St	Aberdeen	SD	57402	**800-925-4100**	605-225-4100
Madison Daily Leader PO Box 348	Madison	SD	57042	**877-635-7323**	605-256-4555
Capital Journal 333 N Dakota Ave	Pierre	SD	57501	**800-658-3063**	605-224-7301
Rapid City Journal 507 Main St	Rapid City	SD	57701	**800-843-2300**	605-394-8300
Argus Leader 200 S Minnesota Ave	Sioux Falls	SD	57104	**800-530-6397**	605-331-2200
Black Hills Pioneer 315 Seaton Cir	Spearfish	SD	57783	**800-676-2761**	605-642-2761
Watertown Public Opinion PO Box 10	Watertown	SD	57201	**800-658-5401**	605-886-6901
Yankton Daily Press & Dakotan PO Box 56	Yankton	SD	57078	**800-743-2968**	605-665-7811
Jackson Sun 245 W LaFayette St	Jackson	TN	38301	**800-372-3922**	731-427-3333
Kingsport Times-News 701 Lynn Garden Dr	Kingsport	TN	37660	**800-251-0328**	423-246-8121
Knoxville News-Sentinel 2332 News Sentinel Dr	Knoxville	TN	37921	**800-237-5821**	865-523-3131
Commercial Appeal 495 Union Ave	Memphis	TN	38103	**800-444-6397**	901-529-2345
Citizen Tribune 1609 W 1st North St PO Box 625	Morristown	TN	37815	**800-624-0281**	423-581-5630
Tennessean 1100 Broadway	Nashville	TN	37203	**800-342-8237**	615-259-8800
Union City Daily Messenger PO Box 430	Union City	TN	38281	**866-885-0744**	731-885-0744
Abilene Reporter-News 101 Cypress St	Abilene	TX	79601	**800-588-6397**	325-673-4271
Brownsville Herald 11 E Van Buren St	Brownsville	TX	78520	**800-488-4301**	956-542-4301
Brownsville Herald The 1135 E Van Buren St	Brownsville	TX	78520	**800-488-4301**	956-542-4301
Brownwood Bulletin 700 Carnegie PO Box 1189	Brownwood	TX	76804	**800-283-0998**	325-646-2541
Brazosport Facts 720 S Main St	Clute	TX	77531	**800-864-8340**	979-265-7411
Courier The PO Box 609	Conroe	TX	77305	**800-659-8313**	936-756-6671
Caller-Times 820 N Lower Broadway	Corpus Christi	TX	78401	**800-827-2011**	361-884-2011
Dallas Morning News 508 Young St	Dallas	TX	75202	**800-431-0010**	214-977-8222
Denton Record-Chronicle 314 E Hickory St	Denton	TX	76201	**800-275-1722**	940-387-3811
El Paso Times 300 N Campbell St Times Plaza	El Paso	TX	79901	**800-351-6007**	915-546-6100
Fort Worth Star-Telegram 685 John B Sias Pkwy	Fort Worth	TX	76134	**800-776-7827**	817-390-7400
Galveston County Daily News PO Box 628	Galveston	TX	77553	**800-561-3611**	409-683-5200
Valley Morning Star PO Box 511	Harlingen	TX	78551	**866-578-7827**	956-430-6212
Houston Chronicle 801 Texas Ave	Houston	TX	77002	**800-735-3800**	713-362-7171
Laredo Morning Times 111 Esperanza Dr	Laredo	TX	78041	**800-728-3118**	956-728-2500
Longview News-Journal 320 E Methvin St	Longview	TX	75601	**800-825-9799**	903-757-3311
Lubbock Avalanche-Journal 710 Ave J	Lubbock	TX	79401	**800-692-4021**	806-762-8844
Monitor The 1400 E Nolana Loop	McAllen	TX	78504	**800-366-4343**	956-683-4000
Midland Reporter-Telegram PO Box 1650	Midland	TX	79702	**800-542-3952**	432-682-5311
New Braunfels Herald-Zeitung 707 Landa St	New Braunfels	TX	78130	**877-409-9860**	830-625-9144
Odessa American PO Box 2952	Odessa	TX	79760	**888-375-6262**	432-337-4661
Paris News PO Box 1078	Paris	TX	75461	**800-683-1929**	903-785-8744
San Antonio Express-News Ave 'E' & 3rd St	San Antonio	TX	78205	**800-555-1551**	210-250-3000
Herald Democrat 603 S Sam Rayburn Fwy	Sherman	TX	75090	**800-827-7183**	903-893-8181
Sulphur Springs New Telegram 401 Church St	Sulphur Springs	TX	75482	**800-245-2149**	903-885-8663
Sweetwater Reporter PO Box 750	Sweetwater	TX	79556	**800-401-3763**	325-236-6677
Temple Daily Telegram PO Box 6114	Temple	TX	76503	**800-460-6397**	254-778-4444
Texarkana Gazette PO Box 621	Texarkana	TX	75504	**800-955-8518**	903-794-3311
Tyler Morning Telegraph PO Box 2030	Tyler	TX	75710	**800-333-8411**	903-597-8111
Vernon Daily Record 3214 Wilbarger St	Vernon	TX	76384	**800-234-9014**	940-552-5454
Victoria Advocate PO Box 1518	Victoria	TX	77902	**800-234-8108**	361-575-1451
Waco Tribune-Herald PO Box 2588	Waco	TX	76702	**800-678-8742**	254-757-5757
Times Record News PO Box 120	Wichita Falls	TX	76307	**800-627-1646**	940-767-8341
Herald Journal 75 W 300 North PO Box 487	Logan	UT	84323	**800-275-0423**	435-752-2121
Standard-Examiner 332 Standard Way	Ogden	UT	84412	**800-234-5505**	801-625-4200
Daily Herald 1555 N Freedom Blvd	Provo	UT	84604	**800-880-8075**	801-373-5050
Bennington Banner 245 Main St PO Box 5027	Bennington	VT	05201	**800-491-7567**	802-447-7567
Brattleboro Reformer 62 Black Mountain Rd Box 802	Brattleboro	VT	05302	**800-649-2311**	802-254-2311
Burlington Free Press 191 College St	Burlington	VT	05401	**800-427-3124**	802-863-3441
Newport Daily Express PO Box 347	Newport	VT	05855	**800-464-6568**	802-334-6568
Rutland Herald PO Box 668	Rutland	VT	05702	**800-776-5512**	802-775-5511
Caledonian-Record The 195 Federal St	Saint Johnsbury	VT	05819	**800-523-6397**	802-748-8121
Valley News PO Box 877	White River Junction	VT	05001	**800-874-2226**	603-298-8711
Washington Examiner 6408 Edsall Rd	Alexandria	VA	22312	**800-531-1223**	703-560-4000
Bristol Herald-Courier 320 Bob Morrison Blvd	Bristol	VA	24201	**888-228-2098**	276-669-2181
Free Lance Star 616 Amelia St	Fredericksburg	VA	22401	**800-877-0500**	540-374-5000
News & Advance PO Box 10129	Lynchburg	VA	24506	**800-275-8831**	434-385-5512
Martinsville Bulletin PO Box 3711	Martinsville	VA	24115	**800-234-6575**	276-638-8801
Virginian-Pilot 150 N Bramelton Ave	Norfolk	VA	23510	**800-446-2004**	757-446-2000
Richmond Times-Dispatch 333 E Franklin St	Richmond	VA	23219	**800-468-3382**	804-649-6990
Roanoke Times 201 W Campbell Ave SW	Roanoke	VA	24011	**800-346-1234**	540-981-3100
News Leader 11 N Central Ave	Staunton	VA	24402	**800-793-2459**	540-885-7281
Northern Virginia Daily 152 N Holliday St	Strasburg	VA	22657	**800-296-5137**	540-465-5137
Suffolk News-Herald PO Box 1220	Suffolk	VA	23439	**866-828-9237**	757-539-3437
News-Virginian The PO Box 1027	Waynesboro	VA	22980	**800-368-0509**	540-949-8213
Winchester Star 2 N Kent St	Winchester	VA	22601	**800-296-8639**	540-667-3200
Daily World 315 S Michigan St	Aberdeen	WA	98520	**800-829-7880**	360-532-4000
Sun The PO Box 259	Bremerton	WA	98337	**888-377-3711**	360-377-3711
Chronicle The 321 N Pearl St	Centralia	WA	98531	**800-562-6084**	360-736-3311
King County Journal 600 Washington Ave S	Kent	WA	98032	**888-399-3999**	253-872-6600
Daily News 770 11th Ave	Longview	WA	98632	**800-341-4745**	360-577-2500
Skagit Valley Herald PO Box 578	Mount Vernon	WA	98273	**800-683-3300**	360-424-3251
Peninsula Daily News PO Box 1330	Port Angeles	WA	98362	**800-826-7714**	360-452-2345
Spokesman Review 999 W Riverside Ave	Spokane	WA	99201	**800-338-8801**	509-459-5000
Tri-City Herald PO Box 2608	Tri-Cities	WA	99302	**800-411-5085**	509-582-1500
Columbian 701 W 8th St	Vancouver	WA	98660	**800-743-3391**	360-694-3391

Name / Address	City	State	Zip	Toll-Free	Phone
Walla Walla Union-Bulletin PO Box 1358	Walla Walla	WA	99362	**800-423-5617**	509-525-3300
Wenatchee World 14 N Mission St	Wenatchee	WA	98801	**800-572-4433**	509-663-5161
Yakima Herald-Republic PO Box 9668	Yakima	WA	98909	**800-343-2799**	509-248-1251
Register-Herald 801 N Kanawha St	Beckley	WV	25801	**800-950-0250**	304-255-4400
Bluefield Daily Telegraph 928 Bluefield Ave	Bluefield	WV	24701	**800-763-2459**	304-327-2800
Charleston Daily Mail 1001 Virginia St E	Charleston	WV	25301	**800-982-6397**	304-348-5140
Charleston Gazette 1001 Virginia St E	Charleston	WV	25301	**800-982-6397**	304-348-5140
Clarksburg Exponent Telegram 324 Hewes Ave	Clarksburg	WV	26301	**800-982-6034**	304-626-1400
Times-West Virginian PO Box 2530	Fairmont	WV	26555	**800-846-3798**	304-367-2500
Herald-Dispatch 946 5th Ave	Huntington	WV	25720	**800-444-2446**	304-526-4000
Journal The 207 W King St	Martinsburg	WV	25401	**800-448-1895**	304-263-8931
Dominion Post 1251 Earl L Core Rd	Morgantown	WV	26505	**800-654-4676**	304-292-6301
Parkersburg News PO Box 1787	Parkersburg	WV	26102	**800-642-1997**	304-485-1891
Post-Crescent 306 W Washington St	Appleton	WI	54912	**800-236-6397**	920-733-4411
Baraboo News Republic 219 1st St PO Box 9	Baraboo	WI	53913	**800-773-4808**	608-356-4808
Daily Citizen 805 Park Ave PO Box 558	Beaver Dam	WI	53916	**888-887-0111**	920-887-0321
Beloit Daily News 149 State St	Beloit	WI	53511	**800-356-3411**	608-365-8811
Chippewa Herald 321 Frenette Dr PO Box 9	Chippewa Falls	WI	54729	**800-236-5515**	715-723-5515
Leader-Telegram 701 S Farwell St	Eau Claire	WI	54701	**800-236-8808**	715-833-9200
Reporter The PO Box 630	Fond du Lac	WI	54936	**800-261-7323**	920-922-4600
Daily Jefferson County Union 28 W Milwaukee Ave PO Box 801	Fort Atkinson	WI	53538	**800-236-1013**	920-563-5553
Green Bay Press-Gazette PO Box 23430	Green Bay	WI	54305	**800-289-8221**	920-431-8400
Janesville Gazette 1 S Parker Dr PO Box 5001	Janesville	WI	53547	**800-362-6712**	608-754-3311
Kenosha News 5800 7th Ave	Kenosha	WI	53140	**800-292-2700**	262-657-1000
La Crosse Tribune 401 N 3rd St	La Crosse	WI	54601	**800-262-0420**	608-782-9710
Capital Times 1901 Fish Hatchery Rd	Madison	WI	53713	**800-362-8333**	608-252-6400
Wisconsin State Journal 1901 Fish Hatchery Rd	Madison	WI	53713	**800-362-8333**	608-252-6100
Herald Times Reporter 902 Franklin St	Manitowoc	WI	54221	**800-783-7323**	920-684-4433
EagleHerald The 1809 Dunlap Ave PO Box 77	Marinette	WI	54143	**800-777-0345**	715-735-6611
Marshfield News-Herald PO Box 70	Marshfield	WI	54449	**800-967-2087**	715-384-3131
Milwaukee Journal Sentinel 333 W State St	Milwaukee	WI	53203	**800-456-5943**	414-224-2318
Monroe Times PO Box 230	Monroe	WI	53566	**800-236-2240**	608-328-4202
Oshkosh Northwestern PO Box 2926	Oshkosh	WI	54903	**800-924-6168**	920-235-7700
Daily Register PO Box 470	Portage	WI	53901	**800-236-2110**	608-742-2111
Daily News 34 Courtney St PO Box 778	Rhinelander	WI	54501	**888-886-8135**	715-365-6397
Shawano Leader 1464 E Green Bay St	Shawano	WI	54166	**800-236-2105**	715-526-2121
Sheboygan Press PO Box 358	Sheboygan	WI	53082	**800-686-3900**	920-457-7711
Wausau Daily Herald PO Box 1286	Wausau	WI	54402	**800-477-4838**	715-842-2101
Daily News 100 S 6th Ave PO Box 478	West Bend	WI	53095	**800-924-3142**	262-306-5000
Daily Tribune 220 1st Ave S	Wisconsin Rapids	WI	54495	**800-362-8315**	715-423-7200
Wyoming Tribune-Eagle 702 W Lincolnway	Cheyenne	WY	82001	**800-561-6268**	307-634-3361
Rawlins Daily Times 522 W Buffalo St PO Box 370	Rawlins	WY	82301	**800-541-3411**	307-324-3411
Riverton Ranger PO Box 993	Riverton	WY	82501	**800-428-7229**	307-856-2244
Daily Rocket-Miner 215 D St PO Box 98	Rock Springs	WY	82902	**888-443-3736**	307-362-3736
Northern Wyoming Daily News PO Box 508	Worland	WY	82401	**800-788-4679**	307-347-3241

522-3 National Newspapers

Name / Address	City	State	Zip	Toll-Free	Phone
Christian Science Monitor 1 Norway St	Boston	MA	02115	**800-288-7090**	617-450-2000
USA Today 7950 Jones Branch Dr *Cust Svc	McLean	VA	22108	**800-872-0001***	703-854-3400
Wall Street Journal PO Box 300 *Cust Svc	Princeton	NJ	08543	**800-568-7625***	609-520-4000

522-4 Weekly Newspapers

Name / Address	City	State	Zip	Toll-Free	Phone
Aegis The PO Box 189	Bel Air	MD	21014	**888-879-1710**	410-838-4400
Bay News 1733 Sheepshead Bay Rd	Brooklyn	NY	11235	**800-564-5433**	718-615-2500
Biddeford-Saco-OOB Courier PO Box 1894	Biddeford	ME	04005	**800-617-3984**	207-282-4337
Boca Times 1701 Green Rd Suite B	Deerfield Beach	FL	33064	**800-275-8820**	954-698-6397
Boynton Beach Times 1701 Green Rd Suite B	Deerfield Beach	FL	33064	**800-275-8820**	954-698-6397
Bridgeport News 1000 Bridgeport Ave	Shelton	CT	06484	**800-843-6791**	203-926-2080
Bulletin The 24417 75th St	Paddock Lake	WI	53168	**800-846-1101**	262-843-1535
Camden Publications 331 E Bell St	Camden	MI	49232	**800-222-6336**	517-368-0365
Chapel Hill News 505 W Franklin St	Chapel Hill	NC	27516	**800-365-6115**	919-932-2000
Clay Today 1560 Kingsley Ave Suite 1	Orange Park	FL	32073	**888-424-6220**	904-264-3200
Coastal Journal PO Box 705	Bath	ME	04530	**800-649-6241**	207-443-6241
Collinsville Journal 2 Executive Dr	Collinsville	IL	62234	**800-766-3278**	618-344-0264
Columbia News Times 4272 Washington Rd Suite 3B	Evans	GA	30809	**888-464-9988**	706-863-6165
Country Today PO Box 570	Eau Claire	WI	54702	**800-236-4004**	715-833-9270
Creative Loafing Atlanta 750 Willoughby Way	Atlanta	GA	30312	**800-950-5623**	404-688-5623
Cuyahoga Falls News-Press PO Box 1549	Stow	OH	44224	**800-966-6565**	330-688-0088
Daily Sun 1153 Main St	The Villages	FL	32159	**800-726-6592**	352-753-1119
Deerfield Times 1701 Green Rd Suite B *Sales	Deerfield Beach	FL	33064	**800-275-8820***	954-698-6397
Delray Beach Times 1701 Green Rd Suite B	Deerfield Beach	FL	33064	**800-275-8820**	954-698-6397
Dover Post PO Box 664	Dover	DE	19903	**800-942-1616**	302-678-3616
Early Bird The 5312 Sebring Warner Rd	Greenville	OH	45331	**800-548-5312**	937-548-3330
Eastsider 1701 Green Rd Suite B	Deerfield Beach	FL	33064	**800-275-8820**	954-698-6397
Elkhart County the Paper PO Box 188	Milford	IN	46542	**800-733-4111**	574-658-4111
Forum Gazette 4801 S University Dr Suite 101	Davie	FL	33328	**800-275-8820**	954-680-4460
Gardena Valley News 16417 S Western Ave	Gardena	CA	90247	**800-329-6351**	310-329-6351
Gateway Press 1619 Commerce Dr	Stow	OH	44224	**800-966-6565**	330-688-0088
Gazette The PO Box 319	Galena	IL	61036	**800-373-6397**	815-777-0019
Granite City Journal 2 Executive Dr	Collinsville	IL	62234	**800-766-3278**	618-877-7700
Greenville Advocate PO Box 507	Greenville	AL	36037	**888-246-8237**	334-382-3111
Hartford Advocate 100 Constitution Plaza	Hartford	CT	06103	**800-442-4266**	860-548-9300
Hendricks County Flyer 8109 Kingston St Suite 500	Avon	IN	46123	**800-359-3747**	317-272-5800
Home & Store News PO Box 329	Ramsey	NJ	07446	**877-237-7855**	201-327-1212
Independent Weekly PO Box 2690	Durham	NC	27715	**800-948-8699**	919-286-1972
Kings Courier 1733 Sheepshead Bay Rd	Brooklyn	NY	11235	**800-564-5433**	718-615-2500
LA Weekly 6715 Sunset Blvd	Los Angeles	CA	90028	**800-304-4414**	323-465-4414
Lake Worth Herald/Coastal Observer PO Box 191	Lake Worth	FL	33460	**888-544-0047**	561-585-9387
Lebanon Reporter 117 E Washington St	Lebanon	IN	46052	**888-482-4650**	765-482-4650
Meade County Times-Tribune PO Box 129	Sturgis	SD	57785	**800-253-3656**	605-347-2503
Mechanicsville Local PO Box 1118	Mechanicsville	VA	23111	**800-476-0197**	804-746-1235
Messenger The PO Box 1190	Hillsboro	NH	03244	**800-281-2859**	603-464-3388
Milford Mirror 1000 Bridgeport Ave	Shelton	CT	06484	**800-843-6791**	203-926-2080
Monday Magazine 818 Broughton St	Victoria	BC	V8W1E4	**800-661-6335**	250-382-6188
Morrison County Record 216 SE 1st St	Little Falls	MN	56345	**888-637-2345**	320-632-2345
New York Harbor Watch 1733 Sheepshead Bay Rd	Brooklyn	NY	11235	**800-564-5433**	718-615-2500
News Sun 32 Park St	Berea	OH	44017	**800-362-8008**	216-986-7550
North Country Free Press PO Box 330	Granville	NY	12832	**800-354-4232**	518-642-1234
North County Journal 7751 N Lindbergh Blvd	Hazelwood	MO	63042	**866-440-4500**	314-972-1111
North Side Journal 7751 N Lindbergh Blvd	Hazelwood	MO	63042	**866-440-4500**	314-972-1111
Northeast Times Booster 409 Washington Ave	Towson	MD	21204	**877-696-0660**	410-337-2400
Northeast Times Reporter 409 Washington Ave	Towson	MD	21204	**877-696-0660**	410-337-2400
Osceola News-Gazette PO Box 422068	Kissimmee	FL	34742	**800-327-2166**	407-846-7600
Paradise Post PO Drawer 70	Paradise	CA	95967	**800-924-0908**	530-877-4413
Plains Reporter PO Box 1447	Williston	ND	58802	**800-950-2165**	701-572-2165
Plattsburgh Free Trader PO Box 338	Elizabethtown	NY	12932	**800-277-6567**	518-873-6368
Press Journal 14522 S Outer 40 Dr	Chesterfield	MO	63017	**866-440-4500**	314-821-1110
Reminder The PO Box 210	Vernon	CT	06066	**888-456-2211**	860-875-3366
San Luis Obispo New Times 505 Higuera St	San Luis Obispo	CA	93401	**800-215-0300**	805-546-8208
Shoppers Guide PO Box 328	Everett	PA	15537	**800-596-5428**	814-652-5191
Standard Examiner 2072 Layton Hills Mall	Layton	UT	84041	**800-651-2105**	801-629-5220
Stratford Star 1000 Bridgeport Ave	Shelton	CT	06484	**800-843-6791**	203-926-2080
Suburban Press & Metro Press PO Box 169	Millbury	OH	43447	**800-300-6158**	419-836-2221
Suburban Review PO Box 912	Athens	GA	30603	**800-533-4252**	706-549-0123
Sun Herald 28895 Lorain Rd	North Olmsted	OH	44070	**800-466-7861**	216-986-6070
Suncoast News 6214 US Hwy 19	New Port Richey	FL	34652	**800-376-4786**	727-815-1000
Sussex Post PO Box 737	Dover	DE	19903	**800-282-8586**	302-934-9261
Texas Observer 307 W 7th St	Austin	TX	78701	**800-939-6620**	512-477-0746
Times Record 219 S College Ave	Aledo	IL	61231	**800-582-4373**	309-582-5112
Tribune PO Box 419000	Melbourne	FL	32941	**800-633-8449**	321-242-3801
Valley Town Crier 1811 N 23rd St	McAllen	TX	78501	**800-556-9876**	956-682-2423
Venice Gondolier 200 E Venice Ave	Venice	FL	34285	**800-799-7861**	941-207-1000
Village Voice 36 Cooper Sq *Cust Svc	New York	NY	10003	**800-875-2997***	212-475-3300
Virginia Gazette 216 Ironbound Rd	Williamsburg	VA	23188	**800-944-6908**	757-220-1736
Washington Missourian PO Box 336	Washington	MO	63090	**888-239-7701**	636-239-7701
Wednesday Magazine 20 E Gregory St	Kansas City	MO	64114	**800-274-8867**	816-361-0616
Weekender The PO Box 189	Bel Air	MD	21014	**888-879-1710**	410-838-4400
West Boca Times 1701 Green Rd Suite B	Deerfield Beach	FL	33064	**800-275-8820**	954-698-6397
Wisconsin State Farmer PO Box 152	Waupaca	WI	54981	**800-236-3313**	715-258-5546
Yorba Linda Star 1771 S Lewis St	Anaheim	CA	92805	**877-469-7344**	714-634-1567
York Sunday News 205 N George St	York	PA	17401	**800-483-5517**	717-854-1575

523 OFFICE SUPPLIES

SEE ALSO Office Supply Stores; Paper - Mfr - Writing Paper; Pens, Pencils, Parts; Printing & Photocopying Supplies; School Supplies

Name / Address	City	State	Zip	Toll-Free	Phone
3M Consumer & Office Div 3M Ctr *NYSE: MMM*	Saint Paul	MN	55144	**800-364-3577**	651-733-1110
A & W Products Co Inc 14 Gardner St	Port Jervis	NY	12771	**800-223-5156**	845-856-5156
American Solutions for Business 31 E Minnesota Ave	Glenwood	MN	56334	**800-862-3690**	320-634-5471
Ames Supply Co 1936 University Ln	Lisle	IL	60532	**800-323-3856**	630-964-2440
Angler's Roslyn Group Ltd 45-25 162nd St	Flushing	NY	11358	**800-221-0675**	718-961-7744
Apex Office Products Inc 5209 N Howard Ave	Tampa	FL	33603	**800-227-1563**	813-871-2010
Arlington Industries Inc 1001 Technology Way	Libertyville	IL	60048	**800-323-4147**	847-362-1001
Arthur Brown & Brother Inc 2 W 46th St	New York	NY	10036	**800-772-7367**	212-575-5555
Avery Dennison Corp 150 N Orange Grove Blvd *NYSE: AVY* ■ *Cust Svc	Pasadena	CA	91103	**800-252-8379***	626-304-2000
Avery Dennison Worldwide Office Products Div 50 Pointe Dr	Brea	CA	92821	**800-462-8379**	714-674-8500
Bartizan Corp 217 Riverdale Ave	Yonkers	NY	10705	**800-431-2682**	914-965-7977
Baumgarten's 144 Ottley Dr	Atlanta	GA	30324	**800-247-5547**	404-874-7675
Best Computer Supplies 895 E Patriot Blvd Suite 110	Reno	NV	89511	**800-544-3472**	775-850-2600
Brodart Co Library Supplies & Furnishings Div 500 Arch St	Williamsport	PA	17701	**800-233-8467**	570-326-2461
C-Line Products Inc 1100 Business Ctr Dr	Mount Prospect	IL	60056	**800-323-6084**	847-827-6661
Cardinal Brands 643 Massachusetts Suite 200	Lawrence	KS	66044	**800-444-3508**	785-344-1400
Cardinal Office Systems Inc 576 E Main St	Frankfort	KY	40601	**800-930-2280**	502-875-3300
Case Logic Inc 6303 Dry Creek Pkwy	Longmont	CO	80503	**800-447-4848**	303-652-1000
CDP Computer Supplier Inc 378 Page St	Stoughton	MA	02072	**800-366-6283**	781-341-3985
Champion Industries Inc 2450-90 1st Ave *NASDAQ: CHMP*	Huntington	WV	25703	**800-624-3431**	304-528-2791
CPP International LLC PO Box 7525	Charlotte	NC	28241	**800-888-3190**	704-588-3190
Dahle North America Inc 375 Jaffrey Rd	Peterborough	NH	03458	**800-243-8145**	603-924-0003
Dart Mfg Co Inc 4012 Bronze Way	Dallas	TX	75237	**800-345-3278**	214-333-4221
Datavision & Devices PO Box 7445	Charlottesville	VA	22906	**800-237-5658**	434-977-0651
Deflect-O Corp PO Box 50057	Indianapolis	IN	46250	**800-428-4328**	317-849-9555
Eaton Office Supply Co Inc 180 John Glenn Dr	Amherst	NY	14228	**800-365-3237**	716-691-6100
Eldon 1401 W Badger Rd	Madison	WI	53713	**800-356-8368**	608-216-3000
Fellowes Inc 1789 Norwood Ave	Itasca	IL	60143	**800-945-4545**	630-893-1600
Great North American Cos 2828 Forest Ln Suite 2000	Dallas	TX	75234	**800-527-2782**	972-481-6100
Highsmith Inc W 5527 SR 106 PO Box 800	Fort Atkinson	WI	53538	**800-558-3899**	920-563-9571
IIMAK 310 Commerce Dr	Amherst	NY	14228	**888-464-4625**	716-691-6333
International Imaging Materials Inc 310 Commerce Dr	Amherst	NY	14228	**888-464-4625**	716-691-6333
Kensington Technology Group 333 Twin Dolphin Dr 6th Fl	Redwood Shores	CA	94065	**800-243-2972**	650-572-2700
Lee Products Co 800 E 80th St	Minneapolis	MN	55420	**800-989-3544**	952-854-3544
Magna Visual Inc 9400 Watson Rd	Saint Louis	MO	63126	**800-843-3399**	314-843-9000
McGill Inc 131 E Prairie St	Marengo	IL	60152	**800-982-9884**	815-568-7244
Mod-Systems Inc 2172-B River Rd PO Box 585	Greer	SC	29652	**800-637-2937**	864-879-3850
New England Newspaper Supply Co 9 Railroad Ave	Millbury	MA	01527	**800-347-7377**	508-865-0800

				Toll-Free	Phone
Nina Enterprises 1350 S Leavitt St	Chicago	IL	60608	**800-886-8688**	312-733-6400
OfficeMax Inc 150 E Pierce Rd	Itasca	IL	60143	**800-472-6473**	630-773-5000
NYSE: OMX					
PerfectData Corp 110 W Easy St	Simi Valley	CA	93065	**800-973-7332**	805-581-4000
Promedia Computer Supplies Ltd Co					
12806 Schabarum Ave Unit C-D	Irwindale	CA	91706	**800-583-5833**	626-960-5778
Protector Corp 337 S Arthur Ave	Louisville	CO	80027	**800-438-1012**	303-926-5400
Quill Corp PO Box 94081	Palatine	IL	60094	**800-789-1331***	847-634-4800
*Orders					
Reliable Corp 150 E Pierce Rd	Itasca	IL	60143	**800-359-5000***	630-438-8888
*Cust Svc					
Richards SP Co 6300 Highlands Pkwy	Smyrna	GA	30082	**888-436-6881**	770-436-6881
Sierra Office Supply & Printing					
4007 Transport St	Palo Alto	CA	94303	**800-433-0282**	650-845-2091
SP Richards Co 6300 Highlands Pkwy	Smyrna	GA	30082	**888-436-6881**	770-436-6881
Staples Business Advantage					
45 E Wesley St	South Hackensack	NJ	07606	**888-333-6494***	201-488-2900
*Orders					
Staples National Advantage					
45 E Wesley St	South Hackensack	NJ	07606	**800-999-9077**	201-488-2900
TAB Products Co 605 4th St	Mayville	WI	53050	**888-822-9777**	920-387-3131
United Stationers Inc 2200 E Golf Rd	Des Plaines	IL	60016	**800-424-4003**	847-699-5000
NASDAQ: USTR					
Van Ausdall & Farrar Inc					
1214 N Meridian St	Indianapolis	IN	46204	**800-467-7474**	317-634-2913
Weeks-Lerman Group 58-38 Page Pl	Maspeth	NY	11378	**800-544-5959**	718-803-5000

524 OFFICE SUPPLY STORES

				Toll-Free	Phone
Allied Office Products Inc 100 Delawanna Ave	Clifton	NJ	07014	**800-275-2554**	973-594-3000
Arctic Office Products 100 W Fireweed Ln	Anchorage	AK	99503	**800-478-2322**	907-276-2322
Ashland Office Supply Co Inc 2100 29th St	Ashland	KY	41101	**800-926-1267**	606-329-1400
Choice Office Products 5090 State St	Saginaw	MI	48603	**866-726-2678**	989-793-9860
Church & Stagg Office Supply Co Inc					
3421 6th Ave	Birmingham	AL	35222	**800-239-5336**	205-251-2951
Corporate Express Inc					
1 Environmental Way	Broomfield	CO	80021	**888-664-3945**	303-664-2000
Eakes Office Plus 617 W 3rd St	Grand Island	NE	68802	**800-652-9396**	308-382-8026
Egyptian Stationers Inc 107 W Main St	Belleville	IL	62220	**800-642-3949**	618-234-2323
Friend HA & Co Inc 1535 Lewis Ave	Zion	IL	60099	**800-323-4394**	847-746-1248
Great American Office LLC 337 Rt 101	Bedford	NH	03110	**888-596-9996**	603-472-9996
HA Friend & Co Inc 1535 Lewis Ave	Zion	IL	60099	**800-323-4394**	847-746-1248
Halsey & Griffith Inc 313 Datura St	West Palm Beach	FL	33401	**800-466-1921**	561-820-8000
Hurst Office Suppliers Inc 257 E Short St	Lexington	KY	40507	**800-926-4423**	859-255-4422
Iowa Office Supply Inc 731 Lake Ave	Storm Lake	IA	50588	**800-373-9182**	712-732-4801
Kennedy Office Supply Co 4211-A Atlantic Ave	Raleigh	NC	27604	**800-733-9401**	919-878-5400
Koch Brothers 325 Grand Ave	Des Moines	IA	50309	**800-944-5624**	515-283-2451
Laser Tek Industries 4909 US Hwy 12	Richmond	IL	60071	**800-322-8137**	815-675-1199
Latta Inc 1502 4th Ave	Huntington	WV	25701	**800-624-3501**	304-523-8400
Lincoln Office Supply Co Inc 77 Commerce Dr	Morton	IL	61550	**800-468-6868**	309-263-7777
Louisiana Office Supply Co					
5550 Florida Blvd	Baton Rouge	LA	70806	**800-738-2218**	225-927-1110
Midwest Office Furniture & Supply Co					
987 S West Temple	Salt Lake City	UT	84101	**800-351-4553**	801-359-7681
Office Depot Inc					
2200 Old Germantown Rd	Delray Beach	FL	33445	**800-937-3600**	561-278-4800
NYSE: ODP					
Office Suppliers Inc 13716 Crayton Blvd	Hagerstown	MD	21742	**800-225-2723**	301-797-3120
Patrick & Co 611 Mission St	San Francisco	CA	94520	**800-792-0755**	415-392-2640
Phillips Group 501 Fulling Mill Rd	Middletown	PA	17057	**800-538-7500**	717-944-0400
Prime Office Products 7500 Lindbergh Dr	Gaithersburg	MD	20879	**800-478-7782**	301-721-4300
Printers & Stationers Inc 113 N Court St	Florence	AL	35630	**800-233-5514**	256-764-8061
Sav-On Discount Office Supplies					
6601 Will Rogers Blvd Suite B	Fort Worth	TX	76140	**866-571-8177**	817-568-5200
Smith & Butterfield Co Inc 2800 Lynch Rd	Evansville	IN	47711	**800-321-6543**	812-422-3261
Staples Inc 500 Staples Dr	Framingham	MA	01702	**877-235-9088**	508-253-5000
NASDAQ: SPLS					
Stationers Inc 1945 5th Ave	Huntington	WV	25703	**800-862-7200**	304-528-2780
Supply Room Cos Inc					
14140 N Washington Hwy	Ashland	VA	23005	**800-849-7239**	804-412-1200
Triplett Office Essentials Corp					
3553 109th St	Des Moines	IA	50322	**800-437-5034**	515-270-9150
Wist Office Products Co 107 W Julie Dr	Tempe	AZ	85283	**800-999-9478**	480-921-2900
Xpedx Paper Store 3351 W Addison St	Chicago	IL	60618	**800-866-6332**	773-463-6423

525 OIL & GAS EXTRACTION

				Toll-Free	Phone
Apache Corp 2000 Post Oak Blvd Suite 100	Houston	TX	77056	**800-272-2434**	713-296-6000
NYSE: APA					
Aramco Services Co 9009 West Loop S	Houston	TX	77096	**800-343-4272**	713-432-4000
Belden & Blake Corp 5200 Stoneham Rd	North Canton	OH	44720	**800-837-4344**	330-497-5471
Calpine Energy Inc 717 Texas Ave Suite 1000	Houston	TX	77002	**800-251-6165**	713-830-2000
Canadian Superior Energy Inc					
400 3rd Ave SW Suite 3300	Calgary	AB	T2P4H2	**877-294-1411**	403-294-1411
TSE: SNG					
CGAS Exploration Inc 4770 Indianola Ave	Columbus	OH	43214	**800-686-2427**	614-888-9588
Chevron Corp 6001 Bollinger Canyon Rd	San Ramon	CA	94583	**800-243-8766***	925-842-1000
NYSE: CVX ■ *Cust Svc					
Comstock Resources Inc					
5300 Town & Country Blvd Suite 500	Frisco	TX	75034	**800-877-1322**	972-668-8800
NYSE: CRK					
Credo Petroleum Corp					
1801 Broadway Suite 900	Denver	CO	80202	**800-297-2366**	303-297-2200
NASDAQ: CRED					
Denbury Resources Inc					
5100 Tennyson Pkwy Suite 3000	Plano	TX	75024	**800-364-5482**	972-673-2000
NYSE: DNR					
Dugan Production Corp 709 E Murray Dr	Farmington	NM	87499	**800-618-1821**	505-325-1821
Duncan Oil Inc 1777 S Harrison St Suite P1	Denver	CO	80210	**800-359-3303**	303-759-3303
DuPont El de Nemours & Co Inc					
1007 Market St	Wilmington	DE	19898	**800-441-7515**	302-774-1000
NYSE: DD					
El DuPont de Nemours & Co Inc					
1007 Market St	Wilmington	DE	19898	**800-441-7515**	302-774-1000
NYSE: DD					
EnCana Oil & Gas USA Inc					
555 17th St Suite 1850	Denver	CO	80202	**800-829-3408**	303-260-5000
ExxonMobil Corp 5959 Las Colinas Blvd	Irving	TX	75039	**800-252-1800***	972-444-1000
NYSE: XOM ■ *Hum Res					
Flying J Inc 1104 Country Hill Dr	Ogden	UT	84403	**800-842-6428**	801-624-1000
GeoResources Inc					
1407 W Dakota Pkwy Suite 1-B	Williston	ND	58802	**800-735-5984**	701-572-2020
NASDAQ: GEOI					
Giant Industries Inc 23733 N Scottsdale Rd	Scottsdale	AZ	85255	**800-937-4937**	480-585-8888
NYSE: GI					
Grey Wolf Inc 10370 Richmond Ave Suite 600	Houston	TX	77042	**800-553-7563**	713-435-6100
AMEX: GW					
Headington Oil Co 7557 Rambler Rd Suite 1100	Dallas	TX	75231	**800-245-5773**	214-696-0606
Houston Exploration Co					
1100 Louisiana St Suite 2000	Houston	TX	77002	**800-261-3283**	713-830-6800
NYSE: THX					
Hunt Oil Co					
1445 Ross Ave Fountain Pl Suite 1500	Dallas	TX	75202	**800-435-7794**	214-978-8000
Ivanhoe Energy Inc					
999 Canada Pl Suite 654	Vancouver	BC	V6C3E1	**888-273-9999**	604-688-8323
TSE: IE					
KCS Energy Inc					
5555 San Felipe St Suite 1200	Houston	TX	77056	**800-848-9844**	713-877-8006
NYSE: KCS					
Kerr-McGee Rocky Mountain Corp					
1999 Broadway Suite 3600	Denver	CO	80202	**800-275-8966**	303-296-3600
King Ranch Inc PO Box 1090	Kingsville	TX	78364	**800-375-6411**	361-592-6411
Lario Oil & Gas Co 301 S Market St	Wichita	KS	67202	**800-865-5611**	316-265-5611
Mack Energy Co 1202 N 10th St	Duncan	OK	73533	**800-299-5580**	580-252-5580
Maguire Oil Co 1201 Elm St Suite 4000	Dallas	TX	75270	**800-969-6248**	214-741-5137
McGoldrick Oil Co 8808 McGoldrick Dr	Shreveport	LA	71129	**800-844-6490**	318-687-6490
McMoRan Oil & Gas Co 1615 Poydras St	New Orleans	LA	70112	**800-535-7094**	504-582-4000
Mission Resources Corp					
1331 Lamar St Suite 1455	Houston	TX	77010	**888-454-4105**	713-495-3000
NASDAQ: MSSN					
Murphy Exploration & Production Co					
131 S Robertson St	New Orleans	LA	70161	**800-765-9501**	504-561-2811
Murphy Oil Corp 200 Peach St	El Dorado	AR	71730	**800-643-2364**	870-862-6411
NYSE: MUR					
Newfield Exploration Co					
363 N Sam Houston Pkwy Suite 2020	Houston	TX	77060	**800-419-4789**	281-847-6000
NYSE: NFX					
NGAS Resources Inc					
120 Prosperous Pl Suite 201	Lexington	KY	40509	**800-977-2363**	859-263-3948
NASDAQ: NGAS					
North Coast Energy Inc 1993 Case Pkwy	Twinsburg	OH	44087	**800-645-6427**	330-425-2330
Northwest Natural Gas Development Corp					
220 NW 2nd Ave	Portland	OR	97209	**800-422-4012**	503-226-4211
Parallel Petroleum Corp					
1004 N Big Spring St Suite 400	Midland	TX	79701	**800-299-3727**	432-684-3727
NASDAQ: PLLL					
Patina Oil & Gas Corp					
1625 Broadway Suite 2000	Denver	CO	80202	**866-404-8161**	303-389-3600
NYSE: POG					
Petroleum Development Corp					
103 E Main St	Bridgeport	WV	26330	**800-624-3821**	304-842-6256
NASDAQ: PETD					
Pioneer Natural Resources Co					
303 W Wall St Suite 101	Midland	TX	79701	**800-532-5291**	432-683-4768
NYSE: PXD					
Plains Exploration & Production Co					
700 Milam St Suite 3100	Houston	TX	77002	**800-934-6083**	832-239-6000
NYSE: PXP					
Pure Resources 500 W Illinois Ave	Midland	TX	79701	**800-725-6612**	432-498-8600
Remington Oil & Gas Corp					
8201 Preston Rd Suite 600	Dallas	TX	75225	**800-521-5481**	214-210-2650
NYSE: REM					
Royal Oil & Gas Corp 1 Indian Spring Rd	Indiana	PA	15701	**800-346-0246**	724-463-0246
Samson Energy Co LP 2 W 2nd St Samson Plaza	Tulsa	OK	74103	**800-283-1791**	918-583-1791
Samson Investment Co					
2 W 2nd St Samson Plaza	Tulsa	OK	74103	**800-283-1791**	918-583-1791
Seneca Resources Corp					
1201 Louisiana St Suite 400	Houston	TX	77002	**800-622-6695**	713-654-2650
Shell Oil Co PO Box 2463	Houston	TX	77252	**888-467-4355**	713-241-6161
Statex Petroleum Inc 1801 Royal Ln Suite 606	Dallas	TX	75229	**800-989-3427**	972-869-2800
Stone Energy Corp 625 E Kaliste Saloom Rd	Lafayette	LA	70508	**800-551-3340**	337-237-0410
NYSE: SGY					
Sunoco Inc 1801 Market St	Philadelphia	PA	19103	**800-786-6261**	215-977-3000
NYSE: SUN					
Swift Energy Co					
16825 Northchase Dr Suite 400	Houston	TX	77060	**800-777-2412**	281-874-2700
NYSE: SFY					
Toreador Resources Corp					
4809 Cole Ave Suite 108	Dallas	TX	75205	**800-966-2141**	214-559-3933
NASDAQ: TRGL					
Unit Corp 7130 S Lewis Ave Suite 1000	Tulsa	OK	74136	**800-722-3612**	918-493-7700
NYSE: UNT					
Wagner & Brown Ltd					
300 N Marienfeld St Suite 1100	Midland	TX	79702	**800-777-7936**	432-682-7936
Wagner Oil Co 500 Commerce St Suite 600	Fort Worth	TX	76102	**800-457-5332**	817-335-2222

526 OIL & GAS FIELD EQUIPMENT

				Toll-Free	Phone
ABB Vetco Gray Inc					
3010 Briarpark Dr Suite 300	Houston	TX	77042	**800-231-6828**	713-821-5000
Airtek Inc PO Box 466	Irwin	PA	15642	**800-424-7835**	724-863-1350
Baker Hughes Inc 3900 Essex Ln Suite 1200	Houston	TX	77027	**800-229-7447**	713-439-8600
NYSE: BHI					
Baker Oil Tools Inc PO Box 40129	Houston	TX	77240	**800-229-7447**	713-466-1322
Cooper Mfg Corp 1221 E Houston St	Broken Arrow	OK	74012	**866-496-0369**	918-258-7300
David Industries Inc Petrotherm Div					
4122 E Chapman Ave Suite 10	Orange	CA	92869	**888-468-8645**	714-744-9234
Drillers Service Inc PO Box 1407	Hickory	NC	28603	**800-334-2308**	828-322-1100
Failing George E Co 2215 S Van Buren St	Enid	OK	73701	**800-759-7441**	580-234-4141
FMC Technologies Inc 1803 Gears Rd	Houston	TX	77067	**800-869-6999**	281-591-4000
NYSE: FTI					

Company	City	State	Zip	Toll-Free	Phone
Gearench Inc PO Box 192	Clifton	TX	76634	**800-221-1848**	254-675-8651
George E Failing Co 2215 S Van Buren St	Enid	OK	73701	**800-759-7441**	580-234-4141
Gulf Island Fabrication Inc 583 Thompson Rd	Houma	LA	70363	**888-465-2100**	985-872-2100
NASDAQ: GIFI					
Harbison-Fischer Mfg PO Box 2477	Fort Worth	TX	76113	**800-364-7867**	817-297-2211
Hydril Co 3300 N Sam Houston Pkwy E	Houston	TX	77032	**800-231-0023**	281-449-2000
NASDAQ: HYDL					
M & M Supply Co PO Box 548	Duncan	OK	73534	**800-404-7879**	580-252-7879
Martin/Decker Totco Instrumentation Inc 1200 Cypress Creek Rd	Cedar Park	TX	78613	**800-423-3319**	512-340-5000
Morris Industries Inc 777 Rt 23 PO Box 278	Pompton Plains	NJ	07444	**800-835-0777**	973-835-6600
Morrison Brothers Co PO Box 238	Dubuque	IA	52004	**800-553-4840***	563-583-5701
*Cust Svc					
National Oilwell Varco Inc 10000 Richmond Ave Suite 400	Houston	TX	77042	**888-262-8645**	713-346-7500
NYSE: NOV					
Natural Gas Services Group Inc 2911 S CR 1260	Midland	TX	79706	**888-891-6275**	432-563-3947
AMEX: NGS					
Omsco ShawCor 6418 Esperson St	Houston	TX	77011	**800-426-6726**	713-844-3700
Perry Equipment Corp 118 Washington Walters Industrial Pk	Mineral Wells	TX	76067	**800-877-7326**	940-325-2575
Smith International Inc PO Box 60068	Houston	TX	77205	**800-877-6484**	281-443-3370
NYSE: SII					
Southern Co Inc 3101 Carrier St	Memphis	TN	38116	**800-264-7626**	901-345-2531
Southwest Oilfield Products 10340 Wallisville Rd	Houston	TX	77013	**800-392-4600**	713-675-7541
Standco Industries Inc Oilfield Products Div 2701 Clinton Dr	Houston	TX	77020	**800-231-6018**	713-224-6311
TD Williamson Inc 5725 S Lewis St Suite 300	Tulsa	OK	74105	**888-839-6766**	918-447-5001
Titan Specialties Inc PO Box 2316	Pampa	TX	79066	**800-692-4486***	806-665-3781
*Sales					
Total Energy Services Ltd 520 5th Ave SW Suite 2410	Calgary	AB	T2P3R7	**877-818-6825**	403-216-3939
TSE: TOT					
Weatherford International Inc 515 Post Oak Blvd Suite 200	Houston	TX	77027	**800-257-3826**	713-693-4000
NYSE: WFT					
Williamson TD Inc 5725 S Lewis St Suite 300	Tulsa	OK	74105	**888-839-6766**	918-447-5001
Winston F2S Corp 1604 Cherokee Trace	White Oak	TX	75693	**800-527-8465**	903-757-7341

527 OIL & GAS FIELD EXPLORATION SERVICES

Company	City	State	Zip	Toll-Free	Phone
Anchor Gasoline 114 E 5th St	Tulsa	OK	74103	**800-321-4086**	918-584-5291
Arctic Slope Regional Corp PO Box 129	Barrow	AK	99723	**800-770-2772**	907-852-8633
Columbia Natural Resources Inc 900 Pennsylvania Ave	Charleston	WV	25302	**800-962-6645**	304-353-5000
Dawson Geophysical Co 508 W Wall St Suite 800	Midland	TX	79701	**800-332-9766**	432-684-3000
NASDAQ: DWSN					
EnCana Oil & Gas USA Inc 555 17th St Suite 1850	Denver	CO	80202	**800-829-3408**	303-260-5000
EOG Resources Inc 333 Clay St Suite 4200	Houston	TX	77002	**877-363-3647**	713-651-7000
NYSE: EOG					
Exploration Co The 500 North Loop 1604 E Suite 250	San Antonio	TX	78232	**877-912-8926**	210-496-5300
NASDAQ: TXCO					
Fidelity Exploration & Production Co 1700 Lincoln St Suite 4600	Denver	CO	80203	**800-986-3133**	303-893-3133
GlobalSantaFe Corp 15375 Memorial Dr	Houston	TX	77079	**800-231-5754**	281-925-6000
NYSE: GSF					
MarkWest Hydrocarbon Inc 155 Inverness Dr W Suite 200	Englewood	CO	80112	**800-730-8388**	303-290-8700
AMEX: MWP					
McMoRan Exploration Co 1615 Poydras St	New Orleans	LA	70112	**800-535-7094**	504-582-4000
NYSE: MMR					
New Jersey Natural Gas Co 1415 Wyckoff Rd	Wall	NJ	07719	**800-221-0051**	732-938-1480
Patterson-UTI Energy Inc 4510 Lamesa Hwy	Snyder	TX	79549	**800-245-0167**	325-573-1104
NASDAQ: PTEN					
PetroQuest Energy Inc 400 E Kaliste Saloom Rd Suite 6000	Lafayette	LA	70508	**800-755-8381**	337-232-7028
NASDAQ: PQUE					
Sanchez Oil & Gas Corp 1920 Sandman St	Laredo	TX	78041	**800-292-7699**	956-722-8092
Superior Energy Services Inc 1105 Peters Rd	Harvey	LA	70058	**800-259-7774**	504-362-4321
NYSE: SPN					
Veritas DGC Inc 10300 Townpark Dr	Houston	TX	77072	**800-344-4266**	832-351-8300
NYSE: VTS					
Walter Oil & Gas Corp 1100 Louisiana St Suite 200	Houston	TX	77002	**888-756-7880**	713-659-1221
Williams Energy Services 1 Williams Ctr PO Box 2400	Tulsa	OK	74102	**800-945-5426**	918-573-2000

528 OIL & GAS FIELD SERVICES

SEE ALSO Oil & Gas Field Exploration Services

Company	City	State	Zip	Toll-Free	Phone
Badger Daylighting Inc 6740 65th Ave	Red Deer	AB	T4P1A5	**800-465-4273**	403-343-0303
Baker Hughes Inc 3900 Essex Ln Suite 1200	Houston	TX	77027	**800-229-7447**	713-439-8600
NYSE: BHI					
BJ Services Co 5500 NW Central Dr	Houston	TX	77092	**800-234-6487**	713-462-4239
NYSE: BJS					
Cal Dive International Inc 400 N Sam Houston Pkwy E Suite 400	Houston	TX	77060	**888-345-2347**	281-618-0400
NASDAQ: CDIS					
Central Industries Inc PO Box 1380	Scott	LA	70583	**800-326-3171**	337-233-3171
Colloid Environmental Technologies Co (CETCO) 1500 W Shure Dr	Arlington Heights	IL	60004	**800-527-9948**	847-392-5800
Columbia Natural Resources Inc 900 Pennsylvania Ave	Charleston	WV	25302	**800-962-6645**	304-353-5000
Crain Brothers Inc PO Box 118	Grand Chenier	LA	70643	**800-737-2767**	337-538-2411
Danos & Curole Marine Contractors Inc PO Box 1460	Larose	LA	70373	**800-487-5971**	985-693-3313
Diamond Services Inc 503 S DeGravelle Rd	Amelia	LA	70340	**800-879-1162**	985-631-2187
Fidelity Exploration & Production Co 1700 Lincoln St Suite 4600	Denver	CO	80203	**800-986-3133**	303-893-3133
Global Industries Ltd PO Box 442	Sulphur	LA	70664	**800-525-3483**	337-583-5000
NASDAQ: GLBL					
Goodrich Petroleum Corp 808 Travis St Suite 1320	Houston	TX	77002	**800-256-2380**	713-780-9494
NYSE: GDP					
Hanover Inc 11000 Corporate Ctr Dr Suite 200	Houston	TX	77041	**800-366-0980**	281-854-3000
Houma Industries PO Box 685	Harvey	LA	70059	**800-348-5340**	504-347-4585
ICO Inc 5333 Westheimer Rd Suite 600	Houston	TX	77056	**877-777-0877**	713-351-4100
NASDAQ: ICOC					
Indel-Davis Inc 4401 S Jackson Ave	Tulsa	OK	74107	**800-331-6300**	918-587-2151
Koch Specialty Plant Services 12221 E Sam Houston Pkwy N	Houston	TX	77044	**800-497-1789**	713-427-7700
Matrix Service Co 10701 E Ute St	Tulsa	OK	74116	**800-866-8822**	918-838-8822
NASDAQ: MTRX					
Milbar Hydro-Test Inc 651 Aero Dr	Shreveport	LA	71107	**800-259-8210**	318-227-8210
Nabors Industries Ltd 515 W Greens Rd Suite 1200	Houston	TX	77067	**888-622-6777**	281-874-0035
AMEX: NBR					
Oceaneering International Inc 11911 FM 529	Houston	TX	77041	**800-527-1865**	713-329-4500
NYSE: OII					
Pool Co Texas Ltd PO Box 2545	Hobbs	NM	88241	**800-299-1388**	505-392-6591
Pride International Inc 5847 San Felipe Suite 3300	Houston	TX	77057	**800-645-2067**	713-789-1400
NYSE: PDE					
Production Management Industries LLC 9761 Hwy 90 E	Morgan City	LA	70380	**800-229-3837**	985-631-3837
Stanley TK Inc PO Box 31	Waynesboro	MS	39367	**800-477-2855**	601-735-2855
Stolt Offshore Inc 10787 Clay Rd Suite 110	Houston	TX	77041	**800-299-3483**	713-430-1100
NASDAQ: SOSA					
TK Stanley Inc PO Box 31	Waynesboro	MS	39367	**800-477-2855**	601-735-2855
Veco Corp 3601 C St Suite 1000	Anchorage	AK	99503	**800-284-2812**	907-264-8100
Weatherford Completion Systems 11420 W Hwy 80 E	Midland	TX	79711	**800-777-7957**	432-563-7957
Williams Energy Services 1 Williams Ctr PO Box 2400	Tulsa	OK	74102	**800-945-5426**	918-573-2000

529 OIL & GAS WELL DRILLING

Company	City	State	Zip	Toll-Free	Phone
Applied Drilling Technology Inc 15375 Memorial Dr Suite A-200	Houston	TX	77079	**800-990-2384**	281-925-7100
Atwood Oceanics Inc 15835 Park Ten Place Dr Suite 200	Houston	TX	77084	**800-231-5924**	281-749-7800
NYSE: ATW					
Cyclone Drilling Inc PO Box 908	Gillette	WY	82717	**800-318-3724**	307-682-4161
Diamond Offshore Drilling Inc 15415 Katy Fwy	Houston	TX	77094	**800-848-1980**	281-492-5300
NYSE: DO					
Ensco International Inc 500 N Akard St Suite 4300	Dallas	TX	75201	**800-423-8006**	214-397-3000
NYSE: ESV					
Exploration Co The 500 North Loop 1604 E Suite 250	San Antonio	TX	78232	**877-912-8926**	210-496-5300
NASDAQ: TXCO					
Fairman Drilling Co PO Box 288	Du Bois	PA	15801	**800-225-6540**	814-371-8410
Friede Halter Inc PO Box 1328	Pascagoula	MS	39568	**800-877-0029**	228-696-6888
GlobalSantaFe Corp 15375 Memorial Dr	Houston	TX	77079	**800-231-5754**	281-925-6000
NYSE: GSF					
Grey Wolf Inc 10370 Richmond Ave Suite 600	Houston	TX	77042	**800-553-7563**	713-435-6100
AMEX: GW					
Helmerich & Payne Inc 1437 S Boulder Ave	Tulsa	OK	74119	**800-331-7250**	918-742-5531
NYSE: HP					
Justiss Oil Co Inc PO Box 2990	Jena	LA	71342	**800-256-2501**	318-992-4111
Leonard Hudson Drilling Co 601 N Price Rd	Pampa	TX	79065	**800-826-9587**	806-665-1816
Nabors Drilling International Ltd 515 W Greens Rd Suite 1000	Houston	TX	77067	**877-622-6777**	281-874-0035
Nabors Drilling USA Inc 515 W Greens Rd Suite 1000	Houston	TX	77067	**888-622-6777**	281-874-0035
Nabors Industries Ltd 515 W Greens Rd Suite 1200	Houston	TX	77067	**888-622-6777**	281-874-0035
AMEX: NBR					
Noble Corp 13135 S Dairy Ashford Rd Suite 800	Sugar Land	TX	77478	**800-231-6326**	281-276-6100
NYSE: NE					
Parker Drilling Co 1401 Enclave Pkwy Suite 600	Houston	TX	77077	**800-545-3645**	281-406-2000
NYSE: PKD					
Patterson Drilling Co PO Box 1416	Snyder	TX	79550	**800-245-0167**	325-574-6300
Patterson-UTI Energy Inc 4510 Lamesa Hwy	Snyder	TX	79549	**800-245-0167**	325-573-1104
NASDAQ: PTEN					
Pride Offshore Inc 410 S Van Ave	Houma	LA	70363	**800-624-1106**	985-872-4700
Reliance Well Service PO Box 787	Magnolia	AR	71754	**800-458-6451**	870-234-2700
Shell Oil Co PO Box 2463	Houston	TX	77252	**888-467-4355**	713-241-6161
Total Energy Services Ltd 520 5th Ave SW Suite 2410	Calgary	AB	T2P3R7	**877-818-6825**	403-216-3939
TSE: TOT					
Transocean Inc 4 Greenway Plaza	Houston	TX	77046	**888-748-6334**	713-232-7500
NYSE: RIG					
Union Drilling Inc PO Drawer 40	Buckhannon	WV	26201	**800-352-3839**	304-472-4610
Unit Corp 7130 S Lewis Ave Suite 1000	Tulsa	OK	74136	**800-722-3612**	918-493-7700
NYSE: UNT					
Vermilion Energy Trust 2800 400 4th Ave SW	Calgary	AB	T2P0J4	**866-895-8101**	403-269-4884
TSE: VET.un					

530 OILS & GREASES - LUBRICATING

SEE ALSO Chemicals - Specialty; Petroleum Refineries

Company	City	State	Zip	Toll-Free	Phone
Acheson Colloids Co 1600 Washington Ave	Port Huron	MI	48060	**800-255-1908**	810-984-5581

Company	City	State	Zip	Toll-Free	Phone
American Grease Stick Co 2651 Hoyt St	Muskegon Heights	MI	49444	**800-253-0403**	231-733-2101
American Polywater Corp 5630 Memorial Ave Suite 2	Stillwater	MN	55082	**800-328-9384**	651-430-2270
Amsoil Inc 925 Tower Ave	Superior	WI	54880	**800-777-7094***	715-392-7101
*Sales					
Anderol Inc 215 Merry Ln PO Box 518	East Hanover	NJ	07936	**888-263-3765**	973-887-7410
Benz Oil Inc 2724 W Hampton Ave	Milwaukee	WI	53209	**800-991-2369**	414-442-2900
BG Products Inc 740 S Wichita St PO Box 1282	Wichita	KS	67201	**800-961-6228**	316-265-2686
Blachford Corp 401 Center Rd	Frankfort	IL	60423	**800-435-5942**	815-464-2100
BP Chemicals 150 W Warrenville Rd	Naperville	IL	60563	**877-701-2726**	630-420-5111
Castrol Heavy Duty Lubricants 9300 Pulaski Hwy	Baltimore	MD	21220	**800-777-1466**	410-574-5000
Castrol Industrial North America Inc 1100 W 31st St	Downers Grove	IL	60515	**800-621-2661**	630-241-4000
Castrol North America Inc 1500 Valley Rd	Wayne	NJ	07470	**800-633-6163**	973-633-2200
Cenex 5500 Cenex Dr	Inver Grove Heights	MN	55077	**800-232-3639**	651-355-6000
Chem-Trend Inc PO Box 860	Howell	MI	48844	**800-727-7730**	517-546-4520
Colorado Petroleum Products Co 4080 Globeville Rd	Denver	CO	80216	**800-580-4080**	303-294-0302
Condat Corp 250 S Industrial Dr	Saline	MI	48176	**800-883-7876**	734-944-4994
CRC Industries Inc 885 Louis Dr	Warminster	PA	18974	**800-272-4620***	215-674-4300
*Cust Svc					
D-A Lubricant Co 1340 W 29th St	Indianapolis	IN	46208	**800-873-2582**	317-923-5321
DA Stuart Co 4580 Weaver Pkwy	Warrenville	IL	60555	**800-323-1438**	630-393-0833
Dylon Industries 7700 Clinton Rd	Cleveland	OH	44144	**800-237-8246**	216-651-1300
Elco Corp 1000 Belt Line Ave	Cleveland	OH	44109	**800-321-0467**	216-749-2605
Ergon Inc Petroleum Specialties Marketing Div PO Box 1639	Jackson	MS	39215	**800-824-2626**	601-933-3000
Fiske Brothers Refining Co 129 Lockwood St	Newark	NJ	07105	**800-733-4755**	973-589-9150
Fuchs Lubricants Co 17050 Lathrop Ave	Harvey	IL	60426	**800-323-7755**	708-333-8900
Fuchs Lubricants Co Grand Kal Div 760 36th St SE	Grand Rapids	MI	49548	**800-247-0364**	616-247-0363
Fuchs Lubricants Co LUBRITECH Div 2140 S 88th St	Kansas City	KS	66111	**800-800-6457**	913-422-4022
Fuchs Lubricants Co Midlantic Div 1700 S Caton Ave	Baltimore	MD	21227	**800-776-0368**	410-368-5000
Fuchs Lubricants Co Montgomery Div 17191 Chrysler Fwy	Detroit	MI	48203	**800-368-5991**	313-891-3700
Fuchs Lubricants Co Southeast Div 2601 New Cut Rd	Spartanburg	SC	29303	**800-442-5666**	864-574-9300
GC Quality Lubricants Inc 1403 6th St	Macon	GA	31206	**800-768-5823**	478-738-3900
Hangsterfer's Laboratories Inc 175 Ogden Rd	Mantua	NJ	08051	**800-433-5823**	856-468-0216
Hercules Chemical Co Inc 111 South St	Passaic	NJ	07055	**800-221-9330**	973-778-5000
Houghton International Inc 950 Madison St PO Box 930	Valley Forge	PA	19482	**888-459-9844**	610-666-4000
Hydrotex Inc 1825 Monetary Ln Suite 100	Carrollton	TX	75006	**800-527-9439**	972-389-8500
JD Streett & Co Inc 144 Weldon Pkwy	Maryland Heights	MO	63043	**800-678-6600**	314-432-6600
Jesco Resources Inc PO Box 12337	North Kansas City	MO	64116	**800-421-4590**	816-471-4590
Jet-Lube Inc PO Box 21258	Houston	TX	77226	**800-538-5823**	713-674-7617
Kluber Lubrication North America LP 32 Industrial Dr	Londonderry	NH	03053	**888-455-8237**	603-434-7704
LPS Laboratories 4647 Hugh Howell Rd	Tucker	GA	30084	**800-241-8334**	770-934-7800
Lubrication Engineers Inc 3851 Airport Fwy	Fort Worth	TX	76111	**800-537-7683**	817-834-6321
Lubrication Technologies Inc 900 Mendelssohn Ave N	Golden Valley	MN	55427	**800-328-5573**	763-545-0707
Lubrizol Corp 29400 Lakeland Blvd	Wickliffe	OH	44092	**800-522-4125**	440-943-4200
NYSE: LZ					
Magie Brothers Oil Co 9101 Fullerton Ave	Franklin Park	IL	60131	**800-624-4347**	847-455-4500
Master Chemical Corp PO Box 10001	Perrysburg	OH	43552	**800-874-6329***	419-874-7902
*Sales					
Mayco Oil Co 775 Louis Dr	Warminster	PA	18974	**800-523-3903**	215-672-6600
McCollister & Co 2200 South Ave	Council Bluffs	IA	51503	**800-798-6457**	712-322-4038
Metalworking Lubricants Co 25 W Silverdome Industrial Pk	Pontiac	MI	48342	**800-394-5494**	248-332-3500
Northland Products Co PO Box 418	Waterloo	IA	50704	**800-772-1724**	319-234-5585
Oil Center Research Inc 106 Montrose Ave	Lafayette	LA	70503	**800-256-8977**	337-232-2496
Orelube Corp 201 E Bethpage Rd	Plainview	NY	11803	**800-645-9124**	516-249-6500
Primrose Oil Co Inc PO Box 29665	Dallas	TX	75229	**800-275-2772**	972-241-1100
Schaeffer Mfg Co Inc 102 Barton St	Saint Louis	MO	63104	**800-325-9962***	314-865-4100
*Cust Svc					
Sentinel Lubricants Corp PO Box 694240	Miami	FL	33269	**800-842-6400**	305-625-6400
Shell Lubricants 5700 S Lee Rd	Cleveland	OH	44137	**800-321-8577**	216-332-4200
Southwestern Petroleum Corp 534 N Main St	Fort Worth	TX	76106	**800-877-9372**	817-332-2336
Streett JD & Co Inc 144 Weldon Pkwy	Maryland Heights	MO	63043	**800-678-6600**	314-432-6600
Stuart DA Co 4580 Weaver Pkwy	Warrenville	IL	60555	**800-323-1438**	630-393-0833
Sun Drilling Products Corp PO Box 129	Belle Chasse	LA	70037	**800-962-6490**	504-393-2778
Texas Refinery Corp 840 N Main St	Fort Worth	TX	76106	**800-827-0711**	817-332-1161
Total Lubricants USA 5 N Stiles St	Linden	NJ	07036	**800-344-2241**	908-862-9300
Valvoline Co 3499 Blazer Pkwy	Lexington	KY	40509	**800-354-9061**	859-357-7777
Wallover Oil Co Inc 1032 Pennsylvania Ave	East Liverpool	OH	43920	**800-662-9626***	330-385-9336
*Sales					
WD-40 Co 1061 Cudahy Pl	San Diego	CA	92110	**800-448-9340**	619-275-1400
NASDAQ: WDFC					
Wolf's Head Oil Co PO Box 2967	Houston	TX	77252	**800-468-6457**	713-546-4000
Wynn Oil Co 1050 W 5th St	Azusa	CA	91702	**800-989-8363**	626-334-0231

531 OPHTHALMIC GOODS - MFR

SEE ALSO Personal Protective Equipment & Clothing

Company	City	State	Zip	Toll-Free	Phone
AAI Foster Grant 500 George Washington Hwy	Smithfield	RI	02917	**800-388-0258**	401-231-3800
Aearo Co 5457 W 79th St	Indianapolis	IN	46268	**800-327-3431***	317-692-6666
*Cust Svc					
Alcon Laboratories Inc Surgical Div 6201 South Fwy	Fort Worth	TX	76134	**800-862-5266***	817-293-0450
*Orders					
American Contact Lens Inc 15970 Bernardo Ctr	San Diego	CA	92127	**800-959-4448**	858-487-8684
Art-Craft Optical Co Inc 57 Goodway Dr S	Rochester	NY	14623	**800-828-8288**	585-546-6640
Bausch & Lomb Inc 1 Bausch & Lomb Pl	Rochester	NY	14604	**800-344-8815**	585-338-6000
NYSE: BOL					
Bausch & Lomb Inc Vision Care Div 1400 N Goodman St	Rochester	NY	14609	**800-344-8815**	585-338-6000
Bolle Inc 9200 Cody St	Overland Park	KS	66214	**800-222-6553**	913-752-3400
Bouton HL Co Inc 11 Kendrick Rd	Wareham	MA	02571	**800-426-1881***	508-295-3300
*Cust Svc					
Carl Zeiss Optical Inc 13017 N Kingston Ave	Chester	VA	23836	**800-338-2984***	804-530-8300
*Cust Svc					
Charmant Group Inc 400 American Rd	Morris Plains	NJ	07950	**800-645-2121**	973-538-1511
CIBA Vision Corp 11460 Johns Creek Pkwy	Duluth	GA	30097	**800-227-1524**	770-476-3937
Conforma Laboratories Inc 4705 Colley Ave	Norfolk	VA	23508	**800-426-1700**	757-423-5807
Cooper Cos Inc 21062 Bake Pkwy Suite 200	Lake Forest	CA	92630	**888-822-2660**	949-597-4700
NYSE: COO					
CooperVision Inc 21062 Bake Pkwy Suite 200	Lake Forest	CA	92630	**800-341-2030**	949-597-8130
Costa Del Mar 123 N Orchard St Bldg 6	Ormond Beach	FL	32174	**800-447-3700**	386-677-3700
Cumberland Optical Laboratory 806 Olympic St	Nashville	TN	37203	**800-888-8316**	615-254-5868
DAC Vision 3930 Miller Park Dr	Garland	TX	75042	**800-800-1550**	972-494-4555
Dakota Smith Signature Eyewear 498 N Oak St	Inglewood	CA	90302	**800-765-3937**	310-330-2700
Dispensers Optical Service Corp 1815 Plantside Dr	Louisville	KY	40299	**800-626-4545***	502-491-3440
*Cust Svc					
Duffens Langley Optical Co 8140 Marshall Dr	Lenexa	KS	66214	**800-888-5379**	913-492-5379
Dynoptic Inc 4399 35th St N	Saint Petersburg	FL	33714	**800-648-7463**	727-812-3000
Essilor of America Inc 2400 118th Ave N	Saint Petersburg	FL	33716	**800-843-3937**	727-572-0844
Eye-Kraft Optical Inc PO Box 400	Saint Cloud	MN	56302	**888-455-2022**	320-251-0141
Eyetech 7016 6th St N	Oakdale	MN	55128	**800-328-9060**	651-501-8114
Gateway Safety Inc 4722 Spring Rd	Cleveland	OH	44131	**800-822-5347**	216-749-1100
Gentex Optics Inc 324 Main St	Simpson	PA	18407	**800-343-6062**	570-282-3550
Hilsinger Co 33 W Bacon St	Plainville	MA	02762	**800-955-6544**	508-699-4406
HL Bouton Co Inc 11 Kendrick Rd	Wareham	MA	02571	**800-426-1881***	508-295-3300
*Cust Svc					
Icare Industries Inc 4399 35th St N	Saint Petersburg	FL	33714	**800-648-7463**	727-812-3000
Johnson & Johnson Vision Care Inc 7500 Centurion Pkwy	Jacksonville	FL	32256	**800-874-5278**	904-443-1000
LBI Eyewear 20801 Nordhoff St	Chatsworth	CA	91311	**800-423-5175**	818-407-1890
Luxottica Group 44 Harbor Park Dr	Port Washington	NY	11050	**800-422-2020**	516-484-3800
Magnivision 3700 Commerce Pkwy	Miramar	FL	33025	**800-237-4231**	954-986-9000
Marchon Eyewear Inc 35 Hub Dr	Melville	NY	11747	**800-645-1300**	631-755-2020
Maui Jim Inc 721 Wainee St	Lahaina	HI	96761	**800-848-3644**	808-661-8841
Oakley Inc 1 Icon	Foothill Ranch	CA	92610	**800-403-7449***	949-951-0991
NYSE: OO ■ *Cust Svc					
Ocular Sciences Inc 475 Eccles Ave	South San Francisco	CA	94080	**800-628-5367**	650-583-1400
Omega Optical Co Inc 13515 N Stemmons Fwy	Dallas	TX	75234	**800-366-6342**	972-241-4141
Orange 21 Inc 2070 Las Palmas Dr	Carlsbad	CA	92009	**800-779-3937**	760-804-8420
NASDAQ: ORNG					
Parmelee Industries Inc US Safety Div 8101 Lenexa Dr	Lenexa	KS	66214	**800-821-5218**	913-599-5555
Rite-Style Optical Co PO Box 3068	Omaha	NE	68103	**800-373-3200**	402-492-8822
Scott USA Inc PO Box 2030	Sun Valley	ID	83353	**800-292-5874**	208-622-1000
Sellstrom Mfg Co 1 Sellstrom Dr	Palatine	IL	60067	**800-323-7402**	847-358-2000
Serengeti Eyewear Inc 9200 Cody St	Overland Park	KS	66214	**888-838-1449***	913-752-3400
*Cust Svc					
Signet Armorlite Inc 130 N Bingham Dr	San Marcos	CA	92069	**800-950-5367**	760-744-4000
Soderberg Inc 230 Eva St	Saint Paul	MN	55107	**800-755-5655**	651-291-1400
SOLA Optical USA Inc 2277 Pine View Way	Petaluma	CA	94954	**800-533-5368**	707-763-9911
Southern Optical Co Inc 1909 N Church St	Greensboro	NC	27405	**800-888-8842**	336-272-8146
STAAR Surgical Co 1911 Walker Ave	Monrovia	CA	91016	**800-292-7902**	626-303-7902
NASDAQ: STAA					
Sun Rams Products Inc 8736 Lion St	Rancho Cucamonga	CA	91730	**800-866-7267**	909-980-1160
Titmus Optical Inc 3811 Corporate Dr	Petersburg	VA	23805	**800-446-1802***	804-732-6121
*Cust Svc					
Transitions Optical Inc 9251 Belcher Rd	Pinellas Park	FL	33782	**800-848-1506**	727-545-0400
Universal/Univis Inc 23 W Bacon St	Plainville	MA	02762	**800-899-5432**	508-695-3584
US Safety Div Parmelee Industries Inc 8101 Lenexa Dr	Lenexa	KS	66214	**800-821-5218**	913-599-5555
Uvex Safety Inc 10 Thurber Blvd	Smithfield	RI	02917	**800-343-3411**	401-232-1200
Vision-Ease Lens Inc 700 54th Ave N	Saint Cloud	MN	56302	**800-328-3449***	320-251-8782
*Cust Svc					
Viva International Group 3140 Rt 22 W	Branchburg	NJ	08876	**800-345-8482**	908-595-6200
Walman Optical Co Inc 801 12th Ave N	Minneapolis	MN	55411	**800-873-9256**	612-520-6000
WOS Inc 2985 S Ridge Rd Suite B	Green Bay	WI	54304	**800-888-4454**	920-336-0690
X-Cel Optical Co Inc 806 S Benton Dr	Sauk Rapids	MN	56379	**800-747-9235**	320-251-8404
Younger Optics 2925 California St	Torrance	CA	90503	**800-366-5367**	310-783-1533
Zeiss Carl Optical Inc 13017 N Kingston Ave	Chester	VA	23836	**800-338-2984***	804-530-8300
*Cust Svc					

532 OPHTHALMIC GOODS - WHOL

Company	City	State	Zip	Toll-Free	Phone
Bell Optical Laboratory Inc 2510 Lance Dr	Kettering	OH	45409	**800-543-4864**	937-294-8022
De'Vons Optics Inc 10823 Bell Ct	Rancho Cucamonga	CA	91730	**888-333-8667**	909-466-4700
Eye Care Inc 5858 Line Ave	Shreveport	LA	71106	**800-533-9638**	318-869-4443
Frames Data Inc 100 Ave of the Americas 14th Fl	New York	NY	10013	**800-821-6069**	949-788-0150
Homer Optical Co Inc 2401 Linden Ln	Silver Spring	MD	20910	**800-627-2710**	301-585-9060
Neostyle Eyewear Corp 2605 State St	San Diego	CA	92103	**800-854-2782**	619-299-0755
SAX North Atlantic Services Inc 432 Fairfield Ave	Stamford	CT	06902	**800-223-5127**	203-348-3645
Swift Instruments Inc 952 Dorchester Ave	Boston	MA	02125	**800-446-1116**	617-436-2960
Western Ophthalmics Corp 19019 36th Ave W Suite G	Lynnwood	WA	98036	**800-426-9938**	425-672-9332

533 OPTICAL GOODS STORES

Company	City	State	Zip	Toll-Free	Phone
America's Best Contacts & Eyeglasses 7255 N Crescent Blvd	Pennsauken	NJ	08110	**800-896-7247**	856-486-4300

				Toll-Free	Phone
Bard Optical 7722 N Crestline Dr	Peoria	IL	61615	**800-752-3295**	309-693-9540
Consolidated Vision Group Inc DBA America's Best Contacts & Eyeglasses 7255 N Crescent Blvd	Pennsauken	NJ	08110	**800-896-7247**	856-486-4300
Cooperative Optical 2424 E Eight-Mile Rd	Detroit	MI	48234	**800-368-5160**	313-366-5100
DOC Optics Corp 19800 W Eight-Mile Rd	Southfield	MI	48075	**800-289-3937**	248-354-7100
Empire Vision Centers 2921 Erie Blvd E	Syracuse	NY	13224	**877-446-3145**	315-446-5120
Europtics Inc 2960 E 2nd Ave Suite C	Denver	CO	80206	**800-564-2179**	303-322-7507
Eye Glass World Inc 3801 S Congress Ave	Lake Worth	FL	33461	**800-529-4345**	561-965-9110
Eye-Mart Express Inc 2110 Hutton Dr Suite 100	Carrollton	TX	75006	**800-755-3936**	972-488-2002
Eye-Mate Inc 77 N Centre Ave	Rockville Centre	NY	11570	**800-393-6283**	516-678-9613
For Eyes/Insight Optical 285 W 74th Pl	Hialeah	FL	33014	**800-367-3937**	305-557-9004
General Vision Services LLC 520 8th Ave 9th Fl	New York	NY	10018	**800-847-4661**	212-594-2580
Henry Ford OptimEyes 655 W 13-Mile Rd	Madison Heights	MI	48071	**800-792-3262**	248-588-9300
JC Penney Optical Co 1 Harmon Dr Glen Oaks Industrial Park	Glendora	NJ	08012	**800-524-0789**	856-228-1000
LensCrafters Inc 4000 Luxottica Pl	Mason	OH	45040	**800-283-5367**	513-765-6000
Magnifying Center 10086 W McNab Rd	Tamarac	FL	33321	**800-364-1612**	954-722-1580
Malbar Vision Center 409 N 78th St	Omaha	NE	68114	**800-701-3937**	402-393-4500
Optical Shop of Aspen International 25 Brookline	Aliso Viejo	CA	92656	**800-647-2345**	949-360-1010
Palmetto Optical 1727 Laurel St	Columbia	SC	29201	**800-845-2231**	803-799-8168
Pearle Vision Inc 1925 Enterprise Pkwy	Twinsburg	OH	44087	**800-282-3931**	330-486-3000
Penney JC Optical Co 1 Harmon Dr Glen Oaks Industrial Park	Glendora	NJ	08012	**800-524-0789**	856-228-1000
ProCare Vision Centers Inc 1949 Newark-Granville Rd	Granville	OH	43023	**800-837-5569**	740-587-3937
Rite-Style Optical Co PO Box 3068	Omaha	NE	68103	**800-373-3200**	402-492-8822
Rx Optical 1700 S Park St	Kalamazoo	MI	49001	**800-792-2737**	269-342-0003
Southern Optical 501 Merritt Ave	Nashville	TN	37203	**800-333-8498**	615-256-6631
Sterling Optical 100 Quentin Roosevelt Blvd	Garden City	NY	11530	**800-332-6302**	516-390-2100
Sunglass Hut International Inc 4000 Luxottica Pl	Mason	OH	45040	**800-767-0990**	513-765-6000
SVS Vision 140 Macomb Pl	Mount Clemens	MI	48043	**800-225-3095**	586-468-7370
Today's Vision 6970 FM 1960 W Suite A	Houston	TX	77069	**800-733-8632**	281-469-2020
Union Eyecare Centers 9700 Rockside Rd Suite 190	Valley View	OH	44125	**800-443-9699**	216-986-9700
Wisconsin Vision Inc 6310 W Blue Mound Rd	Milwaukee	WI	53213	**800-705-7011**	414-778-5360

534 OPTICAL INSTRUMENTS & LENSES

SEE ALSO Laboratory Analytical Instruments

				Toll-Free	Phone
3M Precision Optics Inc 4000 McMann Rd	Cincinnati	OH	45245	**800-877-0787**	513-752-7000
Allergan Inc PO Box 19534 *NYSE: AGN*	Irvine	CA	92623	**800-347-4500**	714-246-4500
Applied Fiber Inc 1300 W Oakridge Dr	Albany	GA	31707	**800-226-5394**	229-888-3212
Burris Co Inc 331 E 8th St	Greeley	CO	80631	**888-228-7747**	970-356-1670
Bushnell Corp DBA Bushnell Performance Optics 9200 Cody St	Overland Park	KS	66214	**800-423-3537**	913-752-3400
Bushnell Performance Optics 9200 Cody St	Overland Park	KS	66214	**800-423-3537**	913-752-3400
Coherent Auburn Group 2303 Lindbergh St *Sales	Auburn	CA	95602	**800-343-4912***	530-823-9550
CST/Berger Corp 255 W Fleming St	Watseka	IL	60970	**800-435-1859**	815-432-5237
Daedal Div Parker Hannifin Corp 1140 Sandy Hill Rd	Irwin	PA	15642	**800-245-6903**	724-861-8200
Deltronic Corp 3900 W Segerstrom Ave	Santa Ana	CA	92704	**800-451-6922**	714-545-0401
Diversified Optical Products Inc 282 Main St	Salem	NH	03079	**800-230-1600**	603-898-1880
Edmund Optics Inc 101 E Gloucester Pike	Barrington	NJ	08007	**800-363-1992**	856-547-3488
EXFO Burleigh Products Group Inc 7647 Main St Fishers	Victor	NY	14564	**800-663-3936**	585-924-9355
Fujinon Inc 10 High Point Dr	Wayne	NJ	07470	**800-872-0196**	973-633-5600
G-S Supplies 408 Saint Paul St	Rochester	NY	14605	**800-295-3050**	585-295-0250
Intevac Inc 3560 Bassett St *NASDAQ: IVAC*	Santa Clara	CA	95054	**800-468-3822**	408-986-9888
ITT Night Vision 7635 Plantation Rd	Roanoke	VA	24019	**800-533-5502**	540-563-0371
JML Optical Industries Inc 690 Portland Ave *Sales	Rochester	NY	14621	**800-456-5462***	585-342-8900
Leica Inc 2345 Waukegan Rd 3rd Fl	Bannockburn	IL	60015	**800-248-0123**	847-405-0123
Meade Instruments Corp 6001 Oak Canyon *NASDAQ: MEAD*	Irvine	CA	92618	**800-626-3233**	949-451-1450
Melles Griot Inc 2051 Talomar Airport Rd Suite 200 *Cust Svc	Carlsbad	CA	92009	**800-645-2737***	760-268-5131
Microvision Inc 19910 N Creek Pkwy *NASDAQ: MVIS*	Bothell	WA	98011	**888-822-6847**	425-415-6847
New Focus Inc 2584 Junction Ave *Sales	San Jose	CA	95134	**866-683-6287***	408-919-1500
Newport Corp 1791 Deere Ave *NASDAQ: NEWP* ■ *Sales	Irvine	CA	92606	**800-222-6440***	949-863-3144
Olympus America Inc 2 Corporate Ctr Dr	Melville	NY	11747	**800-446-5967**	631-844-5000
Oriel Instruments Corp 150 Long Beach Blvd	Stratford	CT	06615	**800-714-5393**	203-377-8282
Paradigm Medical Industries Inc 2355 S 1070 West	Salt Lake City	UT	84119	**800-742-0671**	801-977-8970
Parker Hannifin Corp Daedal Div 1140 Sandy Hill Rd	Irwin	PA	15642	**800-245-6903**	724-861-8200
Ross Optical Industries Inc 1410 Gail Borden Pl Suite A-3	El Paso	TX	79935	**800-880-5417**	915-595-5417
Schott Fiber Optics Inc 122 Charlton St	Southbridge	MA	01550	**800-343-6120**	508-765-9744
Seiler Instrument & Mfg Co Inc 170 E Kirkham Ave	Saint Louis	MO	63119	**800-489-2282**	314-968-2282
Stevens Water Monitoring Systems 5465 SW Western Ave Suite F	Beaverton	OR	97005	**800-452-5272**	503-469-8000
StockerYale Inc 32 Hampshire Rd *NASDAQ: STKR*	Salem	NH	03079	**800-843-8011**	603-893-8778
Telesensory Inc 520 Almanor Ave *Cust Svc	Sunnyvale	CA	94085	**800-804-8004***	408-616-8700
Zygo Corp Laurel Brook Rd *NASDAQ: ZIGO*	Middlefield	CT	06455	**800-994-6669**	860-347-8506

535 ORGAN & TISSUE BANKS

SEE ALSO Eye Banks

				Toll-Free	Phone
Alabama Tissue Center 1900 University Blvd 855 Tinsley Harrison Towers	Birmingham	AL	35294	**800-227-2907**	205-934-4314
Alamo Tissue Service Ltd 4414 Centerview Suite 167	San Antonio	TX	78228	**800-226-9091**	210-738-2663
AlloSource 6278 S Troy Cir	Centennial	CO	80111	**888-873-8330**	720-873-0213
Andrology Laboratory & Sperm Bank 9500 Euclid Ave Cleveland Clinic Foundation Desk A19.1	Cleveland	OH	44195	**800-223-2273**	216-444-3019
AppTec Laboratory Services 2540 Executive Dr	Saint Paul	MN	55120	**888-794-0077**	651-675-2000
Bio-Tissue 7000 SW 97th Ave Suite 211	Miami	FL	33173	**888-296-8858**	305-412-4430
Bone Bank Allografts 4808 Research Dr	San Antonio	TX	78240	**800-397-0088**	210-696-7616
Caitlin Raymond International Registry University of Massachusetts Medical Ctr 55 Lake Ave N	Worcester	MA	01655	**800-726-2824**	508-334-8969
California Cryobank Inc 1019 Gayley Ave	Los Angeles	CA	90024	**800-231-3373**	310-443-5244
California Cryobank Inc 950 Massachusetts Ave	Cambridge	MA	02139	**800-231-3373**	617-497-8646
Central Florida Tissue & Eye Bank Inc 8663 Commodity Cir	Orlando	FL	32819	**800-753-9109**	407-226-3888
Community Tissue Services 3425 N 1st St Suite 103	Fresno	CA	93726	**800-201-8477**	559-224-1168
Community Tissue Services 7770 E 88th St	Indianapolis	IN	46256	**800-984-7783**	317-842-0009
Community Tissue Services 349 S Main St	Dayton	OH	45402	**800-684-7783**	937-222-0228
Community Tissue Services 2736 N Holland-Sylvania Rd	Toledo	OH	43615	**866-684-7783**	419-536-4924
Community Tissue Services 16361 NE Cameron Blvd	Portland	OR	97230	**800-545-8668**	503-408-9394
Community Tissue Services 7821 Bartram Ave Suite E	Philadelphia	PA	19153	**800-456-5445**	215-937-9662
Community Tissue Services 328 S Adams St	Fort Worth	TX	76104	**800-905-2556**	817-332-1898
Cryobiology Inc 4830D Knightsbridge Blvd	Columbus	OH	43214	**800-359-4375**	614-451-4375
Cryogenic Laboratories Inc 1944 Lexington Ave N	Roseville	MN	55113	**800-466-2796**	651-489-8000
Doheny Eye & Tissue Transplant Bank 1127 Wilshire Blvd Suite 602	Los Angeles	CA	90017	**877-348-2020**	213-482-3937
Donor Alliance Inc 720 Colorado Blvd Suite 800-N	Denver	CO	80246	**888-868-4747**	303-329-4747
Gift of Hope Organ & Tissue Donor Network 660 N Industrial Dr	Elmhurst	IL	60126	**800-545-4438**	630-758-2600
Indiana Organ Procurement Organization 429 N Pennsylvania St Suite 201	Indianapolis	IN	46204	**888-275-4676**	317-685-0389
Interpore Cross International 181 Technology Dr	Irvine	CA	92618	**800-722-4489**	949-453-3200
IsoTis OrthoBiologics US 2 Goodyear	Irvine	CA	92618	**800-550-7155**	949-595-8710
Kentucky Organ Donor Affiliates 106 E Broadway	Louisville	KY	40202	**800-525-3456**	502-581-9511
Legacy of Life Tissue Foundation 4804 Research Dr	San Antonio	TX	78240	**800-397-3077**	210-696-7677
LifeBanc 20600 Chagrin Blvd Suite 350	Cleveland	OH	44122	**888-558-5433**	216-752-5433
LifeCell Corp 1 Millennium Way *NASDAQ: LIFC*	Branchburg	NJ	08876	**800-367-5737**	908-947-1100
Lifeline of Ohio 770 Kinnear Rd Suite 200	Columbus	OH	43212	**800-525-5667**	614-291-5667
LifeLink Tissue Bank 8510 Sunstate St	Tampa	FL	33634	**800-683-2400**	813-886-8111
LifeNet 5809 Ward Ct	Virginia Beach	VA	23455	**800-847-7831**	757-464-4761
LifeShare of the Carolinas 5000 D Airport Ctr Pkwy	Charlotte	NC	28208	**800-932-4483**	704-697-3303
LifeShare Transplant Donor Services of Oklahoma 5801 N Broadway Suite 300	Oklahoma City	OK	73118	**888-580-5680**	405-840-5551
Lost Mountain Tissue Bank 3175 Cherokee St NW	Kennesaw	GA	30144	**800-243-1070**	770-428-1070
Louisiana Organ Procurement Agency 3501 N Causeway Blvd Suite 940	Metairie	LA	70002	**800-521-4483**	504-837-3355
Mid-America Transplant Services 1139 Olivette Executive Pkwy	Saint Louis	MO	63132	**888-376-4854**	314-991-1661
Mid-South Tissue Bank 5600 Pleasant View Rd Suite 107	Memphis	TN	38134	**888-366-6775**	901-683-6566
Musculoskeletal Transplant Foundation 125 May St Suite 300	Edison	NJ	08837	**800-433-6576**	732-661-0202
New England Organ Bank 1 Gateway Ctr Suite 202	Newton	MA	02458	**800-446-6362**	617-244-8000
Northwest Tissue Center 921 Terry Ave	Seattle	WA	98104	**800-858-2282**	206-292-1879
Nu Med Technologies Inc 7225 S 85th E Ave Suite 200	Tulsa	OK	74133	**800-640-3131**	918-249-2697
Regional Tissue Bank QEII Health Sciences 5788 University Ave Rm 431 McKenzie Bldg Ctr	Halifax	NS	B3H1V7	**800-314-6515**	902-473-7360
ReproTech Ltd 1944 Lexington Ave N	Roseville	MN	55113	**888-489-8944**	651-489-0827
Rocky Mountain Tissue Bank 2993 S Peoria St Suite 390	Aurora	CO	80014	**800-424-5169**	303-337-3330
ScienceCare Anatomical Inc 2020 W Melinda Ln	Phoenix	AZ	85027	**800-417-3747**	602-331-3641
Sierra Eye & Tissue Donor Services 1700 Alhambra Blvd Suite 112	Sacramento	CA	95816	**800-762-8819**	916-456-1450
South Texas Blood & Tissue Center 6211 IH-10 W	San Antonio	TX	78201	**800-292-5534**	210-731-5555
Tennessee/DCI Donor Services 1714 Hayes St	Nashville	TN	37203	**800-969-4438**	615-234-5200
Tissue Banks International (TBI) 815 Park Ave	Baltimore	MD	21201	**800-756-4824**	410-752-3800
Transplant Services Center University of Texas 5323 Harry Hines Blvd MC 9074	Dallas	TX	75390	**800-433-6667**	214-648-2609
University of Miami Dept of Orthopedic Rehabilitation Tissue Bank 1600 NW 10th Ave Rm 8080	Miami	FL	33136	**888-684-7783**	305-243-6465
US Tissue & Cell Inc (East Div) 2925 Vernon Pl Suite 301	Cincinnati	OH	45219	**800-558-5004**	513-558-6400
Wright Medical Technology Inc 5677 Airline Rd	Arlington	TN	38002	**800-238-7188**	901-867-9971

536 PACKAGE DELIVERY SERVICES

Company / Address	City	State	Zip	Toll-Free	Phone
Air Courier Dispatch 1700 Enterprise Way Suite 110	Atlanta	GA	30348	**800-257-7162**	770-933-9496
AirNet Systems Inc 3939 International Gateway *NYSE: ANS*	Columbus	OH	43219	**888-888-8463**	614-237-2057
Caribbean Transportation Services 7304 W Market St	Greensboro	NC	27409	**800-767-2494**	336-668-7500
Central Delivery Service 5501 Virginia Manor Rd	Beltsville	MD	20705	**800-938-4151**	301-210-0100
Corporate Express Inc 1 Environmental Way	Broomfield	CO	80021	**888-664-3945**	303-664-2000
Deutsche Post Global Mail Ltd 196 Van Buren St 2nd Fl	Herndon	VA	20170	**800-426-7478**	703-450-5777
DHL Airways DBA DHL Worldwide Express 1200 S Pine Island Rd	Plantation	FL	33324	**800-225-5345**	
DHL Worldwide Express 1200 S Pine Island Rd	Plantation	FL	33324	**800-225-5345**	
Dynamics Inc 1455 Estes	Elk Grove Village	IL	60007	**800-323-6850**	847-264-2580
Federal Express Corp DBA FedEx Express PO Box 727	Memphis	TN	38194	**800-463-3339**	901-369-3600
FedEx Custom Critical Inc 1475 Boettler Rd *Cust Svc	Uniontown	OH	44685	**800-762-3787***	234-310-4090
FedEx Express PO Box 727	Memphis	TN	38194	**800-463-3339**	901-369-3600
International Bonded Couriers Inc 3333 New Hyde Park Rd Suite 300	New Hyde Park	NY	11042	**800-422-4124**	516-627-8200
Network Courier Service Corp 9010 Bellanca Ave	Los Angeles	CA	90045	**800-938-1801**	310-410-7700
Priority Express Courier Service 5 Chelsea Pkwy	Boothwyn	PA	19061	**800-526-4646**	610-364-3300
Purolator Courier Ltd 5995 Avebury Rd	Mississauga	ON	L5R3T8	**888-744-7123**	905-712-1084
Quick International Courier 212 5th Ave 18th Fl	New York	NY	10010	**800-488-4400**	212-689-4151
Sterling Courier Systems Inc 1110 Herndon Pkwy 2nd Fl	Herndon	VA	20170	**800-633-6666**	703-471-4488
TNT Express Worldwide Corp 3 Huntington Quadrangle Suite 201S *Cust Svc	Melville	NY	11747	**800-558-5555***	631-760-0700
Tricor America Inc 717 Airport Blvd	South San Francisco	CA	94080	**800-669-7631**	650-877-3650
Unishippers Assn 746 E Winchester Suite 200	Salt Lake City	UT	84107	**800-999-8721**	801-487-0600
United Parcel Service Inc (UPS) 55 Glenlake Pkwy NE *NYSE: UPS* ■ *Cust Svc	Atlanta	GA	30328	**800-742-5877***	404-828-6000
Velocity Express Corp 512 Sharptown Rd *NASDAQ: VEXP*	Bridgeport	NJ	08014	**877-990-0199**	856-294-0111
Washington Express Service LLC 12240 Indian Creek Ct Suite 100	Beltsville	MD	20705	**800-939-5463**	301-210-0899
World Courier Inc 1313 4th Ave	New Hyde Park	NY	11040	**800-223-4461**	516-354-2600
Worldwide Express 2501 Cedar Springs Rd Suite 450	Dallas	TX	75201	**800-758-7447**	214-720-2400
WPX Delivery Solutions 3320 W Valley Hwy N Suite 110	Auburn	WA	98001	**800-562-1091**	253-796-2301
Yamato Transport USA Inc 80 Seaview Dr	Secaucus	NJ	07094	**800-492-6286**	201-583-9696

537 PACKAGING MACHINERY & EQUIPMENT

Company / Address	City	State	Zip	Toll-Free	Phone
A-B-C Packaging Machine Corp 811 Live Oak St	Tarpon Springs	FL	34689	**800-237-5975**	727-937-5144
Accraply Div Barry-Wehmiller Cos Inc 3580 Holly Ln N	Plymouth	MN	55447	**800-328-3997**	763-557-1313
ACMA USA Inc 501 Southlake Blvd	Richmond	VA	23236	**800-525-2735**	804-794-9777
Automated Packaging Systems Inc 10175 Phillip Pkwy *Sales	Streetsboro	OH	44241	**800-527-0733***	330-528-2000
B & H Mfg Co 3461 Roeding Rd	Ceres	CA	95307	**888-643-0444**	209-537-5785
Barry-Wehmiller Cos Inc 8020 Forsyth Blvd	Clayton	MO	63105	**800-862-8200**	314-862-8000
Barry-Wehmiller Cos Inc Accraply Div 3580 Holly Ln N	Plymouth	MN	55447	**800-328-3997**	763-557-1313
Belco Packaging Systems Inc 910 S Mountain Ave	Monrovia	CA	91016	**800-833-1833**	626-357-9566
Bosch Robert Corp Packaging Technology Div 9890 Red Arrow Hwy	Bridgman	MI	49106	**800-292-6724**	269-466-4000
Campbell Wrapper Corp 1415 Fortune Ave	De Pere	WI	54115	**800-727-4210**	920-983-7100
ComTal Machine & Engineering Inc 5000 Township Pkwy	Saint Paul	MN	55110	**800-635-2507**	651-426-0177
Damrow Co PO Box 750	Fond du Lac	WI	54936	**800-236-1501**	920-922-1500
Data Technology Inc 260-J Fordham Rd	Wilmington	MA	01887	**800-331-5797**	978-694-0055
Dynaric Inc 5740 Bayside Rd	Virginia Beach	VA	23455	**800-526-0827**	757-363-5850
Elmar Worldwide Inc PO Box 245 *Cust Svc	Depew	NY	14043	**800-433-3562***	716-681-5650
GMA Industries 444 Innovation Way	Allentown	PA	18109	**800-667-5531**	610-694-9494
Hartness International Inc PO Box 26509	Greenville	SC	29616	**800-845-8791**	864-297-1200
Hoppmann Corp 13129 Airpark Dr Suite 120 *Cust Svc	Elkwood	VA	22718	**800-368-3582***	540-829-2654
ITW Angleboard 595 Telser Rd Suite 100	Lake Zurich	IL	60047	**800-252-4777**	800-457-5777
Krones Inc 9600 S 58th St PO Box 321801	Franklin	WI	53132	**800-752-3787**	414-409-4000
Lantech Inc 11000 Bluegrass Pkwy	Louisville	KY	40299	**800-866-0322**	502-267-4200
Liberty Industries Inc 840 McClurg Rd	Youngstown	OH	44512	**800-860-4744**	330-729-2100
Loveshaw Corp PO Box 83 *Cust Svc	South Canaan	PA	18459	**800-747-1586***	570-937-4921
Matthews International Corp Graphics Systems Div 252 Park West Dr	Pittsburgh	PA	15275	**800-245-1129**	412-788-2111
Medical Technology Systems Inc 2003 Gandy Blvd N Suite 800 *AMEX: MPP*	Saint Petersburg	FL	33702	**800-334-6663**	727-571-1616
Moen Industries 12333 E Los Nietos Rd	Santa Fe Springs	CA	90670	**800-423-4747**	562-946-6381
National Instrument Co Inc 4119 Fordleigh Rd	Baltimore	MD	21215	**800-526-1301**	410-764-0900
New Jersey Machine Inc 56 Etna Rd *Sales	Lebanon	NH	03766	**800-432-2990***	603-448-0300
Packaging Systems International Inc 4990 Acoma St *Parts	Denver	CO	80216	**800-525-6110***	303-296-4445
Packaging Technologies 807 W Kimberly Rd *Sales	Davenport	IA	52806	**800-257-5622***	563-391-1100
Pearson RA Co 8120 W Sunset Hwy	Spokane	WA	99224	**800-732-7766**	509-838-6226
RA Pearson Co 8120 W Sunset Hwy	Spokane	WA	99224	**800-732-7766**	509-838-6226
Ro-An Industries Corp 64-20 Admiral Ave	Middle Village	NY	11379	**800-255-7626**	718-821-1115
Robert Bosch Corp Packaging Technology Div 9890 Red Arrow Hwy	Bridgman	MI	49106	**800-292-6724**	269-466-4000
SCA Consumer Packaging 1401 Pleasant St	DeKalb	IL	60115	**800-756-7638**	815-756-8451
Slidell Inc 2355 Lemond Rd PO Box 710	Owatonna	MN	55060	**800-298-3990**	507-451-0365
Standard Knapp Inc 63 Pickering St *Cust Svc	Portland	CT	06480	**800-628-9565***	860-342-1100
Tri-Pak Machinery Inc 1102 N Commerce St	Harlingen	TX	78550	**800-531-7343**	956-423-5140
Triangle Package Machinery Co 6655 W Diversey Ave	Chicago	IL	60707	**800-621-4170**	773-889-0200
Waste Technology Corp 5400 Rio Grande Ave	Jacksonville	FL	32254	**800-231-9286**	904-355-5558

538 PACKAGING MATERIALS - PAPER OR PLASTICS

SEE ALSO Bags - Paper; Bags - Plastics; Blister Packaging; Paper - Mfr - Coated & Laminated Paper; Plastics Foam Products

Company / Address	City	State	Zip	Toll-Free	Phone
Aldelano Packaging Corp 3525 Walnut Ave Suite A	Chino	CA	91710	**800-509-9212**	909-861-3970
Alliance Rubber Co 210 Carpenter Dam Rd	Hot Springs	AR	71901	**800-626-5940**	501-262-2700
American Transparent Plastics Corp 180 National Rd *Orders	Edison	NJ	08817	**800-942-8725***	732-287-3000
Automated Packaging Systems Inc 10175 Phillip Pkwy *Sales	Streetsboro	OH	44241	**800-527-0733***	330-528-2000
Badger Paper Mills Inc 200 W Front St *NASDAQ: BPMI*	Peshtigo	WI	54157	**800-826-0494**	715-582-4551
Bagcraft Packaging LLC 3900 W 43rd St	Chicago	IL	60632	**800-621-8468**	773-254-8000
Beaverite Corp 128 Main St *Cust Svc	Beaver Falls	NY	13305	**800-424-6337***	315-346-6011
Bedford Industries Inc 1659 Rowe Ave *Cust Svc	Worthington	MN	56187	**800-533-5314***	507-376-4136
Bryce Corp 4505 Old Lamar Ave PO Box 18338	Memphis	TN	38118	**800-238-7277**	901-369-4400
Cello-Pack Corp 55 Innsbruck Dr	Cheektowaga	NY	14227	**800-778-3111**	716-668-3111
Clear Lam Packaging Inc 1950 Pratt Blvd	Elk Grove Village	IL	60007	**800-305-4409**	847-439-8570
Command Plastic Corp 124 West Ave	Tallmadge	OH	44278	**800-321-8001**	330-434-3497
Crowell Corp PO Box 3227	Newport	DE	19804	**800-441-7525**	302-998-0557
Cryovac Div Sealed Air Corp 100 Rogers Bridge Rd Bldg A	Duncan	SC	29334	**800-845-7551**	864-433-2000
Danco Industries Inc PO Box 948	Westfield	MA	01086	**800-225-7960**	413-568-0980
DuPont Packaging & Industrial Polymers Barley Mill Plaza 26-2122 PO Box 80026	Wilmington	DE	19880	**800-438-7225**	302-774-1161
Exopack LLC 3070 Southport Rd PO Box 5687	Spartanburg	SC	29304	**877-447-3539**	864-596-7140
Fibercel Corp 46 Brooklyn St PO Box 610	Portville	NY	14770	**800-545-8546**	716-933-8703
Flextron Industries Inc 720 Mount Rd	Aston	PA	19014	**800-633-2181**	610-459-4600
Fortifiber Corp 1001 Tahoe Blvd	Incline Village	NV	89451	**800-443-4079**	775-833-6161
FP International 1090 Mills Way	Redwood City	CA	94063	**800-866-9946**	650-261-5300
Free-Flow Packaging Corp DBA FP International 1090 Mills Way	Redwood City	CA	94063	**800-866-9946**	650-261-5300
General Plastic Extrusions Inc 1238 Kasson Dr	Prescott	WI	54021	**800-532-3888**	715-262-3806
Green Bay Packaging Inc 1700 N Webster Ct	Green Bay	WI	54302	**800-558-4008**	920-433-5111
Highland Supply Corp 1111 6th St	Highland	IL	62249	**800-472-3645**	618-654-2161
Honeywell Specialty Films 98 Westwood Rd *Cust Svc	Pottsville	PA	17901	**800-934-5679***	570-621-6000
International Paper Co 400 Atlantic St *NYSE: IP* ■ *Prod Info	Stamford	CT	06921	**800-223-1268***	203-541-8000
Kimberly-Clark Corp Technical Paper Div 1400 Holcomb Bridge Rd	Roswell	GA	30076	**800-544-1847**	770-587-8000
LallyPak Inc 1209 Central Ave	Hillside	NJ	07205	**800-523-8484**	908-351-4141
Laminations 3010 E Venture Dr	Appleton	WI	54911	**800-925-2626**	920-831-0596
Letica Corp PO Box 5005	Rochester	MI	48308	**866-538-4221**	248-652-0557
LPS Industries Inc 10 Caesar Pl *Sales	Moonachie	NJ	07074	**800-275-4577***	201-438-3515
Menominee Paper 144 1st St	Menominee	MI	49858	**800-258-3781**	906-863-5595
Multifilm Packaging Corp 1040 N McLean Blvd	Elgin	IL	60123	**800-837-9727**	847-695-7600
New High Glass Inc 12713 SW 125th Ave	Miami	FL	33186	**800-452-7787**	305-232-0840
Novacel 55 Tower Rd	Newton	MA	02464	**800-561-7906**	617-527-4980
NTP Republic PO Box 2448	Holyoke	MA	01041	**800-739-1129**	413-493-6800
Pactiv Corp 1900 W Field Ct *NYSE: PTV*	Lake Forest	IL	60045	**888-828-2850**	847-482-2000
Paper-Pak Products Inc 545 Terrace Dr	San Dimas	CA	91773	**800-635-4560**	909-971-5000
Papercon Inc 2700 Apple Valley Rd NE	Atlanta	GA	30319	**800-241-0619**	404-261-7205
Paramount Paper Ltd 953 Alma Rd *Cust Svc	Maxton	NC	28364	**800-727-9444***	910-844-5293
Perfecseal Inc 9800 Bustleton Ave	Philadelphia	PA	19115	**888-673-4100**	215-673-4500
Polyair Inter Pack Inc 258 Attwell Dr *AMEX: PPK*	Toronto	ON	M9W5B2	**800-456-4348**	416-740-2687
Printpack Inc 4335 Wendell Dr	Atlanta	GA	30336	**800-241-9984**	404-691-5830
Printpack Inc Film Products Div PO Box 110	New Castle	DE	19720	**800-572-4345**	302-323-0900
Rexam Inc 4201 Congress St Suite 340	Charlotte	NC	28209	**800-289-2800**	704-551-1500
Rexam Medical Packaging 1919 S Butterfield Rd	Mundelein	IL	60060	**800-543-8604**	847-362-9000
Robinson Industries Inc 3051 Curtis Rd	Coleman	MI	48618	**800-525-0391**	989-465-6111
Rollprint Packaging Products Inc 320 Stewart Ave	Addison	IL	60101	**800-276-7629**	630-628-1700
SCA Packaging North America 800 5th Ave	New Brighton	PA	15066	**800-887-2276**	724-843-8200
Sealed Air Corp Cryovac Div 100 Rogers Bridge Rd Bldg A	Duncan	SC	29334	**800-845-7551**	864-433-2000

				Toll-Free	Phone
Sealed Air Corp Packaging Products Div					
301 Mayhill St	Saddle Brook	NJ	07663	800-346-5855	201-712-7000
Shields Bag & Printing Co 1009 Rock Ave	Yakima	WA	98902	800-541-8630	509-248-7500
SI Jacobson Mfg Co 1414 Jacobson Dr	Waukegan	IL	60085	800-621-5492	847-623-1414
Sonoco Products Co 1 N 2nd St	Hartsville	SC	29550	800-377-2692	843-383-7000
NYSE: SON					
Unger Co 12401 Berea Rd	Cleveland	OH	44111	800-321-1418	216-252-1400
Union Industries Inc 10 Admiral St	Providence	RI	02908	800-556-6454	401-274-7000
Viskase Corp					
625 Willowbrook Centre Pkwy	Willowbrook	IL	60527	800-323-8562	630-789-4900
Warp Bros Flex-O-Glass Inc					
4647 W Augusta Blvd	Chicago	IL	60651	800-621-3345	773-261-5200
WS Packaging Group Inc 1102 Jefferson St	Algoma	WI	54201	800-236-3424	920-487-3424

539 PACKING & CRATING

				Toll-Free	Phone
Fapco Inc 216 Post Rd	Buchanan	MI	49107	800-782-0167	269-695-6889
Navis Logistics Network					
5675 DTC Blvd Suite 280	Greenwood Village	CO	80111	800-525-6309	303-741-6626
Navis Pack & Ship Centers					
5675 DTC Blvd Suite 280	Greenwood Village	CO	80111	800-525-6309	303-741-6626
Neff Packaging Solutions 2001 Kuntz Rd	Dayton	OH	45404	800-445-4383	937-233-3333
Pierce Distribution Services Inc					
PO Box 15600	Loves Park	IL	61132	800-466-7397	815-636-5650
Tri-Wall 2626 County Rd 71	Butler	IN	46721	888-874-9255	260-868-2151

540 PAINTS, VARNISHES, RELATED PRODUCTS

				Toll-Free	Phone
3M Transportation Div 3M Ctr	Saint Paul	MN	55144	888-364-3577	651-733-1110
Akron Paint & Varnish Inc 1390 Firestone Pkwy	Akron	OH	44301	800-772-3452	330-773-8911
Akzo Nobel Inc 525 W Van Buren St	Chicago	IL	60607	800-227-7070*	312-544-7000
*Cust Svc					
American Safety Technologies Inc					
565 Eagle Rock Ave	Roseland	NJ	07068	800-631-7841	973-403-2600
Ardco Corp 8250 E 40th Ave	Denver	CO	80207	800-544-9013	303-399-2934
Barr WM & Co Inc 205 Channel Ave	Memphis	TN	38113	800-782-9928	901-775-0100
Behr Process Corp 3400 W Segerstrom Ave	Santa Ana	CA	92704	800-854-0133	714-545-7101
Benjamin Moore & Co 51 Chestnut Ridge Rd	Montvale	NJ	07645	800-344-0400	201-573-9600
Bondo Corp 3700 Atlanta Industrial Pkwy NW	Atlanta	GA	30331	800-622-8754	404-696-2730
California Products Corp 150 Dascomb Rd	Andover	MA	01810	800-225-1141	978-623-9980
Carboline Co 350 Hanley Industrial Ct	Saint Louis	MO	63144	800-848-4645	314-644-1000
Chemical Coatings Inc 22 S Center St	Hickory	NC	28603	800-522-8266	828-728-8266
Coronado Paint Co Inc					
308 S Old County Rd	Edgewater	FL	32132	800-883-4193	386-428-6461
DAP Inc 2400 Boston St Suite 200	Baltimore	MD	21224	800-584-3840*	410-675-2100
*Cust Svc					
Davis Paint Co Inc 1311 Iron St	Kansas City	MO	64116	800-821-2029	816-471-4447
Day-Glo Color Corp 4515 St Clair Ave	Cleveland	OH	44103	800-289-3294	216-391-7070
Diamond Vogel Paint & Wax Co					
1020 Albany Pl SE	Orange City	IA	51041	800-728-6435	712-737-4116
Duckback Products Inc 2644 Hegan Ln	Chico	CA	95928	800-825-5382	530-343-3261
Dunn-Edwards Corp 4885 E 52nd Pl	Los Angeles	CA	90040	800-537-4098	323-771-3330
DuPont Automotive 950 Stephenson Hwy	Troy	MI	48083	800-441-0575	248-583-8000
DuPont EI de Nemours & Co Inc					
1007 Market St	Wilmington	DE	19898	800-441-7515	302-774-1000
NYSE: DD					
DuPont Performance Coatings					
1007 Market St	Wilmington	DE	19898	800-441-7515	302-774-1000
Duron Inc 10406 Tucker St	Beltsville	MD	20705	800-723-8766	301-937-4700
EI DuPont de Nemours & Co Inc					
1007 Market St	Wilmington	DE	19898	800-441-7515	302-774-1000
NYSE: DD					
Ferro Corp Liquid Coatings & Dispersions Div					
1301 N Flora St	Plymouth	IN	46563	800-882-1456	574-935-5131
Ferro Corp Plastic Colorants Div					
103 Railroad Ave	Stryker	OH	43557	800-521-9094	419-682-3311
FinishMaster Inc					
54 Monument Cir Suite 600	Indianapolis	IN	46204	888-311-3678	317-237-3678
NASDAQ: FMST					
Finnaren & Haley Inc					
901 Washington St	Conshohocken	PA	19428	800-843-9800	610-825-1900
Flex Bon Paints 2131 Andrea Ln	Fort Myers	FL	33912	800-226-3539	239-489-2332
Frazee Industries Inc 6625 Miramar Rd	San Diego	CA	92121	800-477-9991	619-276-9500
General Coatings Technology Inc					
24 Woodward Ave	Flushing	NY	11385	800-522-3664	718-821-1232
George PD Co Inc 5200 N 2nd St	Saint Louis	MO	63147	800-325-7492	314-621-5700
GMG Distributors Inc 1995 Davis St	San Leandro	CA	94577	800-468-4420	510-430-2940
Harrison Paint Co 1329 Harrison Ave SW	Canton	OH	44706	800-321-0680	330-455-5125
HB Fuller Co					
1200 Willow Lake Blvd PO Box 64683	Saint Paul	MN	55164	800-828-2981	651-236-5900
NYSE: FUL					
ICI American Holdings Inc					
10 Finderne Ave	Bridgewater	NJ	08807	800-998-9986	908-203-2800
ICI Paints North America 925 Euclid Ave	Cleveland	OH	44115	800-221-4100*	216-344-8000
*Cust Svc					
Insl-X Products Corp 50 Holt Dr	Stony Point	NY	10980	800-225-5554	845-786-5000
Iowa Paint Mfg Co Inc 1625 Grand Ave	Des Moines	IA	50309	800-659-4455	515-283-1501
Jones-Blair Co 2728 Empire Central	Dallas	TX	75235	800-492-9400	214-353-1600
Kelly-Moore Paint Co Inc					
987 Commercial St	San Carlos	CA	94070	800-874-4436	650-592-8337
Kwal-Howells Paint 3900 Joliet St	Denver	CO	80239	800-383-8406*	303-371-5600
*Cust Svc					
Lancaster Distributing Co 1310 Union St	Spartanburg	SC	29302	800-845-8287	864-583-3011
Landers Segal Color Co 305 W Grand Ave	Montvale	NJ	07645	888-452-6726	201-307-5995
Lansco Colors 305 W Grand Ave	Montvale	NJ	07645	888-452-6726	201-307-5995
MAB Paints 600 Reed Rd	Broomall	PA	19008	800-622-1899	610-353-5100
Mantros-Haeuser & Co Inc 1175 Post Rd E	Westport	CT	06880	800-344-4229	203-454-1800
Martin-Senour Paints 101 Prospect Ave NW	Cleveland	OH	44115	800-542-8468	216-566-2000
Masterchem Industries 3135 Hwy M	Imperial	MO	63052	800-325-3552	636-942-2510
Michelman Inc 9080 Shell Rd	Cincinnati	OH	45236	800-477-0498	513-793-7766
Minwax Co 10 Mountainview Rd	Upper Saddle River	NJ	07458	800-526-0495	201-818-7500
Mobile Paint Mfg Co 4775 Hamilton Blvd	Theodore	AL	36582	800-621-6952	251-443-6110
Mohawk Finishing Products Inc					
22 S Center St	Hickory	NC	28603	800-545-0047	828-261-0325
Moore Benjamin & Co 51 Chestnut Ridge Rd	Montvale	NJ	07645	800-344-0400	201-573-9600
Muralo Co Inc 148 E 5th St	Bayonne	NJ	07002	800-631-3440	201-437-0770
Norton & Son Inc 148 E 5th St	Bayonne	NJ	07002	800-631-3440	201-437-0770
O'Leary Paint 300 E Oakland	Lansing	MI	48906	800-477-2066	517-487-2066
Parker Paint Mfg Co Inc 3003 S Tacoma Way	Tacoma	WA	98409	800-826-4308	253-473-1122
Parks Corp 1 West St	Fall River	MA	02720	800-225-8543	508-679-5938
PD George Co Inc 5200 N 2nd St	Saint Louis	MO	63147	800-325-7492	314-621-5700
Penn Color Inc 400 Old Dublin Pike	Doylestown	PA	18901	800-523-6032	215-345-6550
Pioneer Mfg 4529 Industrial Pkwy	Cleveland	OH	44135	800-877-1500	216-671-5500
Plasti-Kote Co Inc 1000 Lake Rd	Medina	OH	44256	800-431-5928	330-725-4511
Porter Paints Inc 400 S 13th St	Louisville	KY	40203	800-332-6270	502-588-9200
Progress Paint Co Inc 201 E Market St	Louisville	KY	40202	800-626-6407	502-584-0151
Republic Powdered Metals Inc 2628 Pearl Rd	Medina	OH	44256	800-551-7081	330-225-3192
RPM International Inc 2628 Pearl Rd	Medina	OH	44256	800-776-4488	330-273-5090
NYSE: RPM					
Rust-Oleum Corp 11 Hawthorn Pkwy	Vernon Hills	IL	60061	800-323-3584*	847-367-7700
*Cust Svc					
Samuel Cabot Inc 100 Hale St	Newburyport	MA	01950	800-877-8246	978-465-1900
Sherwin-Williams Co 101 Prospect Ave NW	Cleveland	OH	44115	800-996-7566	216-566-2000
NYSE: SHW					
Sigma Coatings USA 1401 Destrehan Ave	Harvey	LA	70058	800-221-7978	504-347-4321
Sterling-Clark-Lurton Corp 184 Commercial St	Malden	MA	02148	800-225-4444	781-322-0163
Surface Protection Industries Inc Zolatone					
Div 3360 E Pico Blvd	Los Angeles	CA	90023	800-372-6292	323-269-9231
TCI Powder Coatings Inc 4036 Dixon Dr	Ellaville	GA	31806	800-533-9067	229-937-5411
Technical Coatings Laboratory LLC					
205 Old Farms Rd	Avon	CT	06001	800-782-8704	860-673-3245
Trowelon Inc 973 Haven Pl Suite D	Green Bay	WI	54313	800-975-8778	920-499-8778
United Gilsonite Laboratories PO Box 70	Scranton	PA	18501	800-272-3235	570-344-1202
Valspar Corp 1101 S 3rd St	Minneapolis	MN	55415	800-328-8044	612-332-7371
NYSE: VAL					
Valspar Refinish Inc 210 Crosby St	Picayune	MS	39466	800-556-1347*	601-798-4731
*Cust Svc					
Vista Paint Corp 2020 E Orangethorpe Ave	Fullerton	CA	92831	800-698-4782	714-680-3800
Willamette Valley Co 1075 Arrowsmith St	Eugene	OR	97402	800-333-9826	541-484-9621
WM Barr & Co Inc 205 Channel Ave	Memphis	TN	38113	800-782-9928	901-775-0100
Wolf Gordon Inc 33-00 47th Ave	Long Island City	NY	11101	800-347-0550	718-361-6611
Yenkin-Majestic Paint Corp					
1920 Leonard Ave	Columbus	OH	43219	800-848-1898	614-253-8511
Zolatone Div Surface Protection Industries					
Inc 3360 E Pico Blvd	Los Angeles	CA	90023	800-372-6292	323-269-9231

541 PALLETS & SKIDS

				Toll-Free	Phone
American Pallet Inc 1001 Knox Rd	Oakdale	CA	95361	800-840-6122	209-847-6122
Brunswick Box Co Inc PO Box 7	Lawrenceville	VA	23868	800-343-9913	434-848-2222
Clinch-Tite Corp PO Box 456	Sandy Lake	PA	16145	800-241-0900	724-376-7315
Daniel Lumber Co Inc					
309 Pierce St PO Box 340	LaGrange	GA	30241	800-251-0398	706-884-5686
Eastern Wood Products Inc PO Box 1056	Williamsport	PA	17703	800-445-5428	570-326-1946
Hunter Woodworks Inc PO Box 4937	Carson	CA	90749	800-966-4751	323-775-2544
Ifco Systems 6829 Flintlock Rd	Houston	TX	77040	800-771-1148	713-332-6145
Industrial Timber & Land Co					
23925 Commerce Pk	Beachwood	OH	44122	800-829-9663	216-831-3140
Nepa Pallet & Container Co Inc					
PO Box 399	Snohomish	WA	98291	800-562-3932	360-568-3185
Packing Material Co					
27280 Haggerty Rd Suite C-16	Farmington Hills	MI	48331	888-927-4797	248-489-7000
Pallet Masters Inc 655 E Florence Ave	Los Angeles	CA	90001	800-675-2571	323-758-6559
PalletOne Inc 1470 US Hwy 17 S	Bartow	FL	33831	800-771-1148	863-533-1147
Potomac Supply Corp 1398 Kinsale Rd	Kinsale	VA	22488	800-365-3900*	804-472-2527
*Sales					
Precision Pallet Co 721 Parkwood Ave	Romeoville	IL	60446	800-255-8532	815-886-1061
Precision Wood Products Inc PO Box 529	Vancouver	WA	98660	877-743-9663	360-694-8322
Remmey the Pallet Co PO Box 558	Willow Grove	PA	19090	800-725-5385	267-913-0002
Savanna Pallets Co PO Box 308	McGregor	MN	55760	800-348-5708	218-768-2077
Seaman Timber Co Inc PO Box 372	Montevallo	AL	35115	800-782-8155	205-665-2536
United Wholesale Lumber Co 8009 Doe Ave	Visalia	CA	93291	800-651-2037	559-651-2037
Walczak Lumber Inc PO Box 340	Clifford	PA	18413	800-445-1215	570-222-9651
Williamsburg Millwork Corp					
PO Box 427	Bowling Green	VA	22427	888-699-8900	804-994-2151

542 PAPER - MFR

SEE ALSO Packaging Materials - Paper or Plastics

542-1 Coated & Laminated Paper

				Toll-Free	Phone
Appleton Papers Inc PO Box 359	Appleton	WI	54912	800-558-8390	920-734-9841
Arkwright Inc 538 Main St	Fiskeville	RI	02823	800-942-5900*	401-821-1000
*Cust Svc					
Avery Dennison Worldwide Graphics Div					
250 Chester St Bldg 6	Painesville	OH	44077	800-443-9380	440-358-3700
Azon Corp 720 Azon Rd	Johnson City	NY	13790	800-847-9374	
Badger Paper Mills Inc 200 W Front St	Peshtigo	WI	54157	800-826-0494	715-582-4551
NASDAQ: BPMI					
Cardinal Industries Inc 37 W 750 Rt 64	Saint Charles	IL	60175	800-323-5018	630-513-5400
FaxBond International 112 Basaltic Rd Unit 3	Concord	ON	L4K1G6	800-263-3175	905-669-0966
Fortifiber Corp 1001 Tahoe Blvd	Incline Village	NV	89451	800-443-4079	775-833-6161
Fraser Papers Inc 70 Seaview Ave	Stamford	CT	06902	877-237-2737	203-705-2800
French Paper Co 100 French St	Niles	MI	49120	800-253-5952	269-683-1100
IntelliCoat Technologies 28 Gaylord St	South Hadley	MA	01075	800-628-9285	413-536-7800
Kimberly-Clark Corp Technical Paper Div					
1400 Holcomb Bridge Rd	Roswell	GA	30076	800-544-1847	770-587-8000
Mepco Label Systems PO Box 932	Stockton	CA	95201	800-975-2235	209-946-0201
Nashua Corp 11 Trafalgar Sq 2nd Fl	Nashua	NH	03063	800-258-1370	603-880-2323
NYSE: NSH					
Permalin Products Corp					
205 W 39th St 16th Fl	New York	NY	10018	800-417-3762	212-768-7400

Coated & Laminated Paper (Cont'd)

Company / Address	City	State	ZIP	Toll-Free	Phone
Stora Enso North America Corp 2 Landmark Sq 3rd Fl	Stamford	CT	06901	888-807-8672	203-356-2300
NYSE: SEO					
TST/Impreso Inc 652 Southwestern Blvd	Coppell	TX	75019	800-527-2878	972-462-0100

542-2 Wrapping Paper (Decorative)

Company / Address	City	State	ZIP	Toll-Free	Phone
American Greetings Corp 1 American Rd.	Cleveland	OH	44144	800-321-3040*	216-252-7300
NYSE: AM ■ *Sales					
American Greetings Corp Carlton Cards Div 1 American Rd	Cleveland	OH	44144	800-321-3040*	216-252-7300
*Sales					
Berwick Offray Inc Bombay Ln & 9th St	Berwick	PA	18603	800-327-0350	570-752-5934
Carlton Cards Div American Greetings Corp 1 American Rd	Cleveland	OH	44144	800-321-3040*	216-252-7300
*Sales					
Cleo Inc 4025 Viscount Ave	Memphis	TN	38118	800-289-2536	901-369-6300
Current USA Inc 1005 E Woodmen Rd.	Colorado Springs	CO	80920	800-525-7170*	719-594-4100
*Cust Svc					
Field Container Co LP Saint Clair Pakwell Div 120 25th Ave	Bellwood	IL	60104	800-323-1922*	708-547-7500
*Cust Svc					
Flower City Tissue Mills Inc PO Box 13497	Rochester	NY	14613	800-595-2030	585-458-9200
Gift Box Corp of America 225 5th Ave Rm 1223	New York	NY	10010	800-443-8269	212-684-5113
Gift Wrap Co 338 Industrial Blvd	Midway	GA	31320	800-443-4429	912-884-9727
Hallmark Cards Inc 2501 McGee St	Kansas City	MO	64108	800-425-5627	816-274-5111
Indiana Ribbon Inc 106 N 2nd St	Wolcott	IN	47995	800-531-3100	219-279-2112
Mafcote Industries Inc 108 Main St	Norwalk	CT	06851	800-526-4280*	203-847-8500
*Cust Svc					
Saint Clair Pakwell Div Field Container Co LP 120 25th Ave	Bellwood	IL	60104	800-323-1922*	708-547-7500
*Cust Svc					
Schurman Fine Papers 500 Chadbourne Rd Box 6030	Fairfield	CA	94533	800-333-6724*	707-428-0200
*Sales					

542-3 Writing Paper

Company / Address	City	State	ZIP	Toll-Free	Phone
3M Consumer & Office Div 3M Ctr	Saint Paul	MN	55144	800-364-3577	651-733-1110
NYSE: MMM					
American Greetings Corp 1 American Rd.	Cleveland	OH	44144	800-321-3040*	216-252-7300
NYSE: AM ■ *Sales					
American Pad & Paper Co LLC 3101 E George Bush Hwy Suite 200	Plano	TX	75082	800-426-1368	
Artistic Products Inc 125 Commerce Dr	Hauppauge	NY	11788	800-223-8336	718-665-5510
Case Stationery Co Inc 179 Saw Mill River Rd.	Yonkers	NY	10701	800-431-2422	914-965-5100
CPP International LLC PO Box 7525	Charlotte	NC	28241	800-888-3190	704-588-3190
CR Gibson Inc 404 BNA Dr Bldg 200 Suite 600	Nashville	TN	37217	800-243-6004	615-724-2900
Crane & Co Inc 30 South St.	Dalton	MA	01226	800-572-0024*	413-684-2600
*Cust Svc					
Domtar Inc 395 boul de Maisonneuve O.	Montreal	QC	H3A1L6	800-267-2040	514-848-5400
NYSE: DTC					
Fay Paper Products Inc PO Box 38	Norwood	MA	02062	800-765-4620	781-769-4620
Geographics LLC 93 North Ave.	Garwood	NJ	07027	800-526-4280	
Mafcote Industries Inc 108 Main St	Norwalk	CT	06851	800-526-4280*	203-847-8500
*Cust Svc					
MeadWestvaco Consumer & Office Products 10 W 2nd St	Dayton	OH	45402	800-648-6323	937-495-6323
Neenah Paper Inc 1400 Holcomb Bridge Rd	Roswell	GA	30076	800-558-5061*	770-587-8000
*Cust Svc					
Paper Conversions Inc 6761 Thompson Rd N	Syracuse	NY	13211	800-729-2823	315-437-1641
Performance Office Papers 21673 Cedar Ave	Lakeville	MN	55044	800-458-7189	952-469-1400
Pratt & Austin Co Inc 1 Cabot St.	Holyoke	MA	01040	800-848-8020	413-532-0106
Roaring Spring Blank Book Co 740 Spang St.	Roaring Spring	PA	16673	800-441-1653*	814-224-5141
*Cust Svc					
Rytex Co 100 N Park Ave	Peru	IN	46970	800-277-5458	
Schurman Fine Papers 500 Chadbourne Rd Box 6030	Fairfield	CA	94533	800-333-6724*	707-428-0200
*Sales					
Southworth Co 265 Main St	Agawam	MA	01001	800-225-1839	413-789-1200
Top Flight Paper Products Inc 1300 Central Ave	Chattanooga	TN	37408	800-777-3740	423-266-8171
TOPS 2275 Cabot Dr	Lisle	IL	60532	800-444-4660	630-588-6000
William Arthur Inc 7 Alewive Park Rd PO Box 460	West Kennebunk	ME	04094	800-985-6581	207-985-6581

543 PAPER - WHOL

Company / Address	City	State	ZIP	Toll-Free	Phone
Abitibi-Consolidated Sales Corp 4 Gannett Dr	White Plains	NY	10604	800-848-7213	914-640-8600
Anchor Paper Co Inc 480 Broadway St	Saint Paul	MN	55101	800-652-9755	651-298-1311
AT Clayton & Co Inc 2 Pickwick Plaza	Greenwich	CT	06830	800-282-5298	203-861-1190
Atlantic Corp 806 N 23rd St.	Wilmington	NC	28405	800-722-5841	910-343-0624
Bradner Smith & Co 2300 Arthur Ave	Elk Grove Village	IL	60007	800-678-1852	847-290-8485
CJ Duffey Paper Co Inc 528 Washington Ave N	Minneapolis	MN	55401	800-752-8190	612-338-8701
Clampitt Paper Co of Dallas 9207 Ambassador Row	Dallas	TX	75247	800-856-0138	214-638-3300
Clayton AT & Co Inc 2 Pickwick Plaza	Greenwich	CT	06830	800-282-5298	203-861-1190
Cole Papers Inc 1300 N 38th St.	Fargo	ND	58102	800-800-8090	701-282-5311
Eastern Data Paper Inc PO Box 202	Little Falls	NJ	07424	800-524-2528	973-472-5252
Frank Parsons Paper Co Inc 2270 Beaver Rd	Landover	MD	20785	800-944-9940	301-386-4700
Gould Paper Corp 11 Madison Ave 14th Fl.	New York	NY	10010	800-275-4685	212-301-0000
GPA 1151 W 40th St	Chicago	IL	60609	800-395-9000	312-243-6860
GreenLine Paper Co 631 S Pine St.	York	PA	17403	800-641-1117	717-845-8697
Hearn Paper Co 556 N Meridian Rd	Youngstown	OH	44509	800-225-2989	330-792-6533
Hudson Valley Paper Co 981 Broadway	Albany	NY	12207	800-473-5525	518-471-5111
Kelly Paper Co 288 Brea Canyon Rd	City of Industry	CA	91789	800-675-3559	909-859-8200
Lindenmeyr Munroe Paper Corp 115 Moonachie Ave	Moonachie	NJ	07074	800-631-0193	201-440-6491
Mac Papers Inc 3300 Phillips Hwy.	Jacksonville	FL	32207	800-622-2968	904-348-3300
Midland Paper 101 E Palatine Rd.	Wheeling	IL	60090	800-523-7477	847-777-2700
Millcraft Paper Co 6800 Grant Ave	Cleveland	OH	44105	800-826-4444	216-441-5500
Newell Paper Co 1212 Grand Ave PO Box 631	Meridian	MS	39301	800-844-8894	601-693-1783
PaperDirect Inc 1005 E Woodmen Rd.	Colorado Springs	CO	80920	800-272-7377	719-594-4100
Parsons Frank Paper Co Inc 2270 Beaver Rd	Landover	MD	20785	800-944-9940	301-386-4700
Perez Trading Co Inc 3490 NW 125th St.	Miami	FL	33167	800-999-7599	305-769-0761
Quimby-Walstrom Paper Co PO Box 1806	Grand Rapids	MI	49501	800-632-5930	616-784-4700
Roosevelt Paper Co 1 Roosevelt Dr	Mount Laurel	NJ	08054	800-523-3470	856-303-4100
Spicers Paper Inc 12310 E Slauson Ave.	Santa Fe Springs	CA	90670	800-774-2377	562-698-1199
Tayloe Paper Co Inc 6717 E 13th St	Tulsa	OK	74112	800-825-6911	918-835-6911
Unisource Worldwide Inc 6600 Governors Lake Pkwy	Norcross	GA	30071	800-282-7958	770-447-9000
Websource 161 Ave of the Americas 3rd Fl	New York	NY	10013	800-221-3213	212-255-1600
Wisconsin Paper & Products Co PO Box 13455	Milwaukee	WI	53213	800-242-0790	414-771-3771

544 PAPER CONVERTERS

SEE ALSO Paper Products - Mfr - Pressed & Molded Paper Products

Company / Address	City	State	ZIP	Toll-Free	Phone
Ameri-Fax Corp 7709 W 20th Ave	Hialeah	FL	33014	800-969-1601	305-828-1701
Artistic Industries Inc 6395 SR 103 N Bldg 5	Lewistown	PA	17044	800-424-4433	717-242-2926
Burrows Paper Corp Packaging Div 1722 53rd St	Fort Madison	IA	52627	800-779-7779	319-372-4241
Case Paper Co Inc 500 Mamaroneck Ave 2nd Fl.	Harrison	NY	10528	800-222-2922	718-361-9000
Chargeurs Inc 421 S Union St	Troy	OH	45373	800-561-7981	937-335-5611
Cindus Corp 515 Station Ave	Cincinnati	OH	45215	800-543-4691	513-948-9951
Delta Craft Paper Co 99 Bud-Mill Dr	Buffalo	NY	14206	800-735-5735	716-856-5135
Extra Packaging Corp 631 Golden Harbour Dr	Boca Raton	FL	33432	800-872-7548	561-416-2060
Fabricon Products 4101 N American St.	Philadelphia	PA	19140	800-676-9727	215-455-3300
Fay Paper Products Inc PO Box 38	Norwood	MA	02062	800-765-4620	781-769-4620
Fonda Group Inc 2920 N Main St.	Oshkosh	WI	54901	888-898-3988*	920-235-9330
*Cust Svc					
Genpak Processor Div PO Box 727	Glens Falls	NY	12801	800-626-6695	518-798-9511
Graphic Converting Inc 6701 W Oakton St	Niles	IL	60714	800-447-1935	847-967-3300
Hampden Papers Inc PO Box 149	Holyoke	MA	01041	800-456-0200	413-536-1000
Holyoke Card & Paper Co 95 Fisk Ave.	Springfield	MA	01107	877-217-2737	413-732-2107
International Converter Inc 721 Farson St	Belpre	OH	45714	800-962-8572	740-423-7525
Label Art Southeast Div 100 Clover Green	Peachtree City	GA	30269	800-232-7833	770-631-7324
Mac Paper Converters PO Box 5369	Jacksonville	FL	32247	800-334-7026	904-733-9660
Mafcote Industries Inc 108 Main St	Norwalk	CT	06851	800-526-4280*	203-847-8500
*Cust Svc					
Mail Advertising Supply Co Inc 1450 S West Ave	Waukesha	WI	53189	800-558-2126	262-549-1730
Newark Paperboard Products Inc 20 Jackson Dr	Cranford	NJ	07016	800-777-7890	908-276-4000
PAC Paper Inc 6416 NW Whitney Rd.	Vancouver	WA	98665	800-223-4981	360-695-7771
Pacon Corp 2525 N Casaloma Dr	Appleton	WI	54912	800-333-2545	920-830-5050
Paper Systems Inc 185 S Pioneer Blvd	Springboro	OH	45066	888-564-6774	937-746-6841
PM Co 1500 Kemper Meadow Dr	Cincinnati	OH	45240	800-327-4359	513-825-7626
RiteMade Paper Converters 1015 Tyler St.	Fredericksburg	VA	22401	800-368-3485*	540-371-8626
*Cust Svc					
Riverside Paper Co 110 N Kensington Dr	Appleton	WI	54915	800-443-6326*	920-991-2212
*Cust Svc					
Rollsource Papers 2392 S Wolf Rd	Des Plaines	IL	60018	800-525-7785	847-699-3100
Smith-Lee Co Inc 537 Fitch St	Oneida	NY	13421	800-448-3363	315-363-2500
Spinnaker Coating Inc 518 E Water St	Troy	OH	45373	800-543-9452	937-332-6500
TimeMed Labeling Systems Inc 144 Tower Dr.	Burr Ridge	IL	60527	800-323-4840*	630-986-1800
*Cust Svc					
Tufco Technologies Inc PO Box 23500	Green Bay	WI	54305	800-558-8145	920-336-0054
NASDAQ: TFCO					

545 PAPER FINISHERS (EMBOSSING, COATING, GILDING, STAMPING)

Company / Address	City	State	ZIP	Toll-Free	Phone
Colad Group 801 Exchange St.	Buffalo	NY	14210	800-950-1755	716-961-1776
Complemar Partners 175 Humboldt St.	Rochester	NY	14610	800-388-5126	585-647-5800
Madison Cutting Die Inc 2547 Progress Rd	Madison	WI	53716	800-395-9405	608-221-3422
Malahide Design & Mfg Inc 209 Griffith Rd	Stratford	ON	N5A6S4	800-867-5077	519-273-0603
McGraphics Inc 601 Hagan St	Nashville	TN	37203	888-280-8200	615-242-8779
Walton Press 402 Mayfield Dr	Monroe	GA	30655	800-354-0235	770-267-2596

546 PAPER INDUSTRIES MACHINERY

Company / Address	City	State	ZIP	Toll-Free	Phone
Baumfolder Corp 1660 Campbell Rd	Sidney	OH	45365	800-543-6107	937-492-1281
Butler Automatic Inc 41 Leona Dr	Middleboro	MA	02346	800-544-0070	508-923-0544
Cranston Machinery Co Inc 2251 SE Oak Grove Blvd PO Box 68207	Oak Grove	OR	97267	800-547-1012	503-654-7751
Geschmay Corp 525 Old Piedmont Hwy	Greenville	SC	29605	800-845-6774	864-220-7500

Company	City	State	Zip	Toll-Free	Phone
LE Sauer Machine Co 3535 Tree Ct Industrial Blvd	Saint Louis	MO	63122	**800-745-4107**	636-225-5358
Mokry-Tesmer Inc 707 Maryetta St	Middletown	OH	45042	**800-383-5135**	513-424-5135
Montague Machine Co 15 Rastallis St	Turners Falls	MA	01376	**800-555-6891**	413-863-4301
Rice Barton Corp 25 Southgate St	Worcester	MA	01610	**800-225-9415**	508-752-2821
Sauer LE Machine Co 3535 Tree Ct Industrial Blvd	Saint Louis	MO	63122	**800-745-4107**	636-225-5358
Sherwood Tool Inc 10 Main St	Kensington	CT	06037	**888-313-0954**	860-828-4161
Shreiner Co 1 Taylor Dr PO Box 347	Killbuck	OH	44637	**800-722-9915**	330-276-6135
Standard Paper Box Machine Co Inc 347 Coster St	Bronx	NY	10474	**800-367-8755**	718-328-3300
Ward Machinery Co 10615 Beaver Dam Rd	Hunt Valley	MD	21030	**800-847-9273**	410-584-7700
Zerand Corp 15800 W Overland Dr	New Berlin	WI	53151	**800-889-9984**	262-827-3800

547 PAPER MILLS

SEE ALSO Paperboard Mills; Pulp Mills

Company	City	State	Zip	Toll-Free	Phone
Badger Paper Mills Inc 200 W Front St *NASDAQ: BPMI*	Peshtigo	WI	54157	**800-826-0494**	715-582-4551
Blue Heron Paper 427 Main St	Oregon City	OR	97045	**800-331-9991**	503-650-4211
Bowater Inc Newsprint & Directory Div PO Box 1028	Greenville	SC	29602	**800-845-6002**	864-271-7733
Burrows Paper Corp 501 W Main St	Little Falls	NY	13365	**800-272-7122**	315-823-2300
Cauthorne Paper Co 205 Hull St	Richmond	VA	23224	**800-552-3011**	804-232-6736
Climax Mfg Co 7840 SR 26	Lowville	NY	13367	**800-225-4629**	315-376-8000
FiberMark Inc Technical Specialities Div 1 CR 519 *Cust Svc	Bloomsbury	NJ	08804	**800-784-8558***	908-995-2424
Finch Pruyn & Co Inc 1 Glen St	Glens Falls	NY	12801	**800-833-9981**	518-793-2541
Fox River Paper Co 100 W Lawrence St	Appleton	WI	54911	**800-993-7300**	920-733-7341
Fox Valley Corp PO Box 727	Appleton	WI	54912	**800-993-7300**	920-739-8982
Gilbert Paper Co 100 W Lawrence St	Appleton	WI	54911	**866-452-8777**	920-733-7807
International Paper Co 400 Atlantic St *NYSE: IP ■ *Prod Info*	Stamford	CT	06921	**800-223-1268***	203-541-8000
Kimberly-Clark Corp 351 Phelps Dr *NYSE: KMB*	Irving	TX	75038	**800-544-1847**	972-281-1200
Madison Paper Industries PO Box 129	Madison	ME	04950	**800-323-3443**	207-696-3307
Manistique Papers Inc 453 S Mackinac Ave	Manistique	MI	49854	**800-743-2389**	906-341-2175
Marcal Paper Mills Inc 1 Market St	Elmwood Park	NJ	07407	**800-631-8451**	201-796-4000
Mohawk Paper Mills Inc 465 Saratoga St	Cohoes	NY	12047	**800-843-6455**	518-237-1740
Monadnock Paper Mills Inc 117 Antrim Rd *Orders	Bennington	NH	03442	**800-221-2159***	603-588-3311
Norbord Industries Inc 1 Toronto St 6th Fl *TSE: NBD*	Toronto	ON	M5C2W4	**877-263-9367**	416-643-8820
Parsons Paper Co PO Box 309	Holyoke	MA	01041	**800-842-9029**	413-532-3222
Riverside Paper Corp 800 S Lawe St *Cust Svc	Appleton	WI	54915	**800-443-6326***	920-991-2200
Robbins Sabin Paper Co 497 Circle Freeway Dr Suite 490	Cincinnati	OH	45246	**800-424-5574**	513-874-5270
Sabin Robbins Paper Co 497 Circle Freeway Dr Suite 490	Cincinnati	OH	45246	**800-424-5574**	513-874-5270
Schweitzer-Mauduit International Inc 100 North Point Ctr E Suite 600 *NYSE: SWM*	Alpharetta	GA	30022	**800-514-0186**	770-569-4272
Stora Enso North America Corp 2 Landmark Sq 3rd Fl *NYSE: SEO*	Stamford	CT	06901	**888-807-8672**	203-356-2300
Wausau Papers Otis Mill Inc 1 Mill St	Jay	ME	04239	**800-876-5772**	207-897-7200

548 PAPER PRODUCTS - MFR

SEE ALSO Envelopes; Paper Converters

548-1 Pressed & Molded Paper Products

Company	City	State	Zip	Toll-Free	Phone
Amscan Inc 80 Grasslands Rd	Elmsford	NY	10523	**800-284-4333**	914-345-2020
Designware Inc 1 American Rd	Cleveland	OH	44144	**800-321-3040**	216-252-7300
Fonda Group Inc 2920 N Main St *Cust Svc	Oshkosh	WI	54901	**888-898-3988***	920-235-9330
Huhtamaki Americas 9201 Packaging Dr	DeSoto	KS	66018	**800-255-4243**	913-583-3025
Insulair Inc 35275 Welty Rd	Vernalis	CA	95385	**800-343-3402**	209-839-0911
International Paper Food Service Business 3 Paragon Dr	Montvale	NJ	07645	**800-852-2425**	201-391-1776
Letica Corp PO Box 5005	Rochester	MI	48308	**866-538-4221**	248-652-0557
Premier Industries Inc 1320 Russell St	Covington	KY	41011	**800-354-9817**	859-581-1390
Solo Cup Co 1505 E Main St *Cust Svc	Urbana	IL	61802	**800-367-2877***	217-384-1800
Winthrop-Atkins Co Inc 35 E Main St	Middleboro	MA	02346	**888-463-7888**	508-947-4600

548-2 Sanitary Paper Products

Company	City	State	Zip	Toll-Free	Phone
American Tissue Corp 80 Orville Dr	Bohemia	NY	11716	**800-282-7922**	631-435-9000
Associated Hygienic Products LLC 3400 River Green Ct Suite 600	Duluth	GA	30096	**888-639-5863**	770-497-9800
Bright of America Inc 300 Greenbrier Rd	Summersville	WV	26651	**800-877-1925**	304-872-3000
EMJA Co Inc PO Box 767189	Roswell	GA	30076	**800-992-3652**	770-992-9464
Erving Paper Mills 97 E Main St	Erving	MA	01344	**800-225-8014**	413-422-2700
Hoffmaster PO Box 2038	Oshkosh	WI	54903	**800-558-9300**	920-235-9330
Hospital Specialty Co 7501 Carnegie Ave	Cleveland	OH	44103	**800-321-9832**	216-361-1230
Kimberly-Clark Corp 351 Phelps Dr *NYSE: KMB*	Irving	TX	75038	**800-544-1847**	972-281-1200
Kleen Test Products Inc 8225 W Parkland Ct	Milwaukee	WI	53223	**800-558-6842**	414-357-7444
Marcal Paper Mills Inc 1 Market St	Elmwood Park	NJ	07407	**800-631-8451**	201-796-4000
Nice-Pak Products Inc 2 Nice-Pak Pk	Orangeburg	NY	10962	**800-999-6423**	845-365-1700
Orchids Paper Products Co 4826 Hunt St	Pryor	OK	74361	**800-832-4908**	918-825-0616
Paper-Pak Products Inc 545 Terrace Dr	San Dimas	CA	91773	**800-635-4560**	909-971-5000
Playtex Products Inc 300 Nyala Farms Rd *NYSE: PYX*	Westport	CT	06880	**800-999-9700**	203-341-4000
Principle Business Enterprises Inc PO Box 129 *Cust Svc	Dunbridge	OH	43414	**800-467-3224***	419-352-1551
SCA North America Inc 500 Baldwin Tower *Cust Svc	Eddystone	PA	19022	**800-992-9939***	610-499-3700
SCA Tissue North America 1451 McMahon Dr PO Box 2400	Neenah	WI	54957	**866-722-6659**	920-725-7031
Tranzonic Cos 670 Alpha Dr	Highland Heights	OH	44143	**800-553-7979**	440-449-6550
Tyco Healthcare Retail Group Inc 601 Allendale Rd PO Box 61930	King of Prussia	PA	19406	**800-262-0042**	610-265-5000

549 PAPER PRODUCTS - WHOL

Company	City	State	Zip	Toll-Free	Phone
A & M Tape & Packaging 5201 Nob Hill Rd	Sunrise	FL	33351	**800-231-8806**	954-572-2500
AD Schinner Co Inc 4901 W State St	Milwaukee	WI	53208	**800-776-4709**	414-771-4300
American Hotel Register Co 100 S Milwaukee Ave	Vernon Hills	IL	60061	**800-323-5686**	847-743-3000
American Paper & Twine Co 7400 Cockrill Bend Blvd	Nashville	TN	37209	**800-251-2437**	615-350-9000
Brame Specialty Co Inc 2021 S Briggs Ave	Durham	NC	27703	**800-672-0011**	919-598-1500
Bunzl/Grossman Paper Co Inc 1305 Jersey Ave	North Brunswick	NJ	08902	**800-234-0169**	732-846-6500
Conley Paper & Packaging 1312 4th St SE	Canton	OH	44707	**800-362-6001**	330-456-8243
Dacotah Paper Co 3940 15th Ave NW	Fargo	ND	58102	**800-726-1767**	701-277-3300
Ernest Paper Products 5777 Smithway St	Commerce	CA	90040	**800-233-7788**	323-583-6561
First Choice Distribution 1770 NE 58th Ave	Des Moines	IA	50313	**800-369-8733**	515-262-9776
Fleetwood-Signode 2222 Windsor Ct	Addison	IL	60101	**800-862-7997**	630-268-9999
Garland C Norris Co 1101 Terry Rd	Apex	NC	27502	**800-331-8920**	919-387-1059
GreenLine Paper Co 631 S Pine St	York	PA	17403	**800-641-1117**	717-845-8697
Harder Paper & Packaging 5301 Verona Rd	Madison	WI	53711	**800-261-3400**	608-271-5127
Heartland Paper Co 808 W Cherokee St *Cust Svc	Sioux Falls	SD	57104	**800-843-7922***	605-336-1190
Houston Paper & Janitorial Supply Inc 600 Monument St	Dothan	AL	36303	**800-239-7561**	334-794-7561
Johnston Paper Co 1 Eagle Dr	Auburn	NY	13021	**800-800-7123**	315-253-8435
Joseph Weil & Sons Inc 825 E 26th St	La Grange Park	IL	60526	**800-621-5955**	708-579-9595
Lagasse Inc 1122 Longford Rd	Oaks	PA	19456	**800-345-6020**	610-933-9015
Leonard Paper Co 725 N Haven St *Cust Svc	Baltimore	MD	21205	**800-327-5547***	410-563-0800
M Conley Co 1312 4th St SE	Canton	OH	44707	**800-362-6001**	330-456-8243
Mayfield Paper Co 1115 S Hill St	San Angelo	TX	76903	**800-725-1441**	325-653-1444
National Paper & Sanitary Supply 2511 S 156th Cir	Omaha	NE	68130	**800-647-2737**	402-330-5507
Norris Garland C Co 1101 Terry Rd	Apex	NC	27502	**800-331-8920**	919-387-1059
Northwest Arkansas Paper Co 2400 Cantrell Rd Suite 116	Little Rock	AR	72202	**800-643-3068**	501-374-5884
Pacific Packaging Products Inc 24 Industrial Way	Wilmington	MA	01887	**800-777-0300**	978-657-9100
Packaging Distribution Services Inc (PDS) 2308 Sunset Rd	Des Moines	IA	50321	**800-747-2699**	515-243-3156
Paper Products Co Inc 36 Terminal Way	Pittsburgh	PA	15219	**800-837-2702**	412-481-6200
Paterson Pacific Parchment Co 625 Greg St	Sparks	NV	89431	**800-678-8104**	775-353-3000
PDS (Packaging Distribution Services Inc) 2308 Sunset Rd	Des Moines	IA	50321	**800-747-2699**	515-243-3156
Perez Trading Co Inc 3490 NW 125th St	Miami	FL	33167	**800-999-7599**	305-769-0761
Phillips Distribution Inc 3000 E Houston St PO Box 200067	San Antonio	TX	78220	**800-580-2397**	210-227-2397
Pollock Paper & Packaging 1 Pollock Pl	Grand Prairie	TX	75050	**800-843-7320**	972-263-2126
Saint Louis Paper & Box Co 3843 Garfield Ave	Saint Louis	MO	63113	**800-779-7901**	314-531-7900
Schinner AD Co Inc 4901 W State St	Milwaukee	WI	53208	**800-776-4709**	414-771-4300
Schwarz 8338 Austin Ave	Morton Grove	IL	60053	**800-323-4903**	847-966-2550
Shorr Packaging Inc 800 N Commerce St	Aurora	IL	60504	**888-978-1122**	630-978-1000
Snyder Paper Corp 250 26th St Dr SE	Hickory	NC	28602	**800-222-8562**	828-328-2501
Tayloe Paper Co Inc 6717 E 13th St	Tulsa	OK	74112	**800-825-6911**	918-835-6911
TEC Products Co Inc 100 Middlesex Ave PO Box 309	Carteret	NJ	07008	**800-922-1998**	732-969-8700
Tricorbraun Inc 10330 Old Olive St Rd	Saint Louis	MO	63141	**800-325-7782**	314-569-3633
TSN Inc 4001 Salazar Way PO Box 679	Frederick	CO	80530	**800-800-4131**	303-530-0600
Unisource Worldwide Inc 6600 Governors Lake Pkwy	Norcross	GA	30071	**800-282-7958**	770-447-9000
Weil Joseph & Sons Inc 825 E 26th St	La Grange Park	IL	60526	**800-621-5955**	708-579-9595
White River Paper Co 118 Rt 14	Hartford	VT	05047	**800-639-7226**	802-295-3188
Wurzburg Inc 710 S 4th St PO Box 710	Memphis	TN	38101	**800-274-4885**	901-525-1441

550 PAPERBOARD & CARDBOARD - DIE-CUT

Company	City	State	Zip	Toll-Free	Phone
Alvah Bushnell Co 519 E Chelten Ave	Philadelphia	PA	19144	**800-255-7434**	215-842-9520
Blanks/USA Inc 8625 Xylon Ct	Minneapolis	MN	55445	**800-328-7311**	763-391-8001
Cardinal Brands 643 Massachusetts Suite 200	Lawrence	KS	66044	**800-444-3508**	785-344-1400
Chilcote Co 2140-60 Superior Ave *Sales	Cleveland	OH	44114	**800-827-5679***	216-781-6000
Chilcote Co Taprell Loomis Div 2160 Superior Ave	Cleveland	OH	44114	**800-827-5679**	216-781-6000
Crescent Cardboard Co LLC 100 W Willow Rd	Wheeling	IL	60090	**800-323-1055**	847-537-3400
Demco Inc 4810 Forest Run Rd *Orders	Madison	WI	53704	**800-356-1200***	608-241-1201
Esselte Corp 48 S Service Rd Suite 400 *Cust Svc	Melville	NY	11747	**800-645-6051***	631-675-5700
GBS Filing Systems 224 Morges Rd	Malvern	OH	44644	**800-873-4427**	330-863-1828
Gussco Mfg Inc 5112 2nd Ave	Brooklyn	NY	11232	**800-248-7726**	718-492-7900
Kruysman Inc 32-00 Skillman Ave	Long Island City	NY	11101	**800-221-3218**	718-433-3800
Smead Mfg Co 600 Smead Blvd *Cust Svc	Hastings	MN	55033	**888-737-6323***	651-437-4111
Southern Folder & Index Co 475 Bailey Rd	El Dorado	AR	71730	**888-368-6432**	870-863-5184

				Toll-Free	Phone
Tabbies Div Xertrex International Inc 1530 W Glenlake Ave	Itasca	IL	60143	800-822-2437	630-773-4020
University Products Inc PO Box 101 *Cust Svc	Holyoke	MA	01041	800-628-1912*	413-532-3372
Xertrex International Inc 1530 W Glenlake Ave	Itasca	IL	60143	800-822-2437	630-773-4020
Xertrex International Inc Tabbies Div 1530 W Glenlake Ave	Itasca	IL	60143	800-822-2437	630-773-4020

551 PAPERBOARD MILLS

SEE ALSO Paper Mills; Pulp Mills

				Toll-Free	Phone
Brownville Specialty Paper Products Inc 1 Bridge St	Brownville	NY	13615	800-724-0299	315-782-4500
Domtar Inc 395 boul de Maisonneuve O. *NYSE: DTC*	Montreal	QC	H3A1L6	800-267-2040	514-848-5400
Evanite Fiber Corp PO Box E *Cust Svc	Corvallis	OR	97339	800-441-5567*	541-753-1211
FiberMark Inc Technical Specialities Div 1 CR 519 *Cust Svc	Bloomsbury	NJ	08804	800-784-8558*	908-995-2424
Green Bay Packaging Inc Mill Div 1700 N Webster Ct	Green Bay	WI	54302	800-558-4008	920-433-5111
International Paper Co 400 Atlantic St *NYSE: IP* ■ *Prod Info	Stamford	CT	06921	800-223-1268*	203-541-8000
Lydall Inc 1 Colonial Rd *NYSE: LDL*	Manchester	CT	06045	800-365-9325	860-646-1233
Menominee Paper 144 1st St	Menominee	MI	49858	800-258-3781	906-863-5595
Newark Group 20 Jackson Dr	Cranford	NJ	07016	800-777-7890	908-276-4000
Newman & Co Inc 6101 Tacony St	Philadelphia	PA	19135	800-523-3256	215-333-8700
Packaging Corp of America 1900 W Field Ct *NYSE: PKG*	Lake Forest	IL	60045	888-828-2850	847-482-2000
Pactiv Corp 1900 W Field Ct *NYSE: PTV*	Lake Forest	IL	60045	888-828-2850	847-482-2000
Rock-Tenn Co 504 Thrasher St *NYSE: RKT*	Norcross	GA	30071	800-762-5836	770-448-2193
Smurfit-Stone Container Corp 150 N Michigan Ave 17th Fl *NASDAQ: SSCC*	Chicago	IL	60601	877-772-2999	312-346-6600
Sonoco Products Co 1 N 2nd St *NYSE: SON*	Hartsville	SC	29550	800-377-2692	843-383-7000
Temple-Inland Forest Products Corp 303 S Temple Dr	Diboll	TX	75941	800-262-5512	936-829-5511

552 PARKING SERVICE

				Toll-Free	Phone
Ace Parking Management Inc 645 Ash St	San Diego	CA	92101	800-925-7275	619-233-6624
Central Parking Corp 2401 21st Ave S Suite 200 *NYSE: CPC*	Nashville	TN	37212	800-423-6613	615-297-4255
Diamond Parking Inc 3161 Elliott Ave Suite 200	Seattle	WA	98121	800-340-7275	206-284-3100
Edison Properties LLC 100 Washington St	Newark	NJ	07102	800-248-7275	973-643-7700
Park Air Express 18931 Snow Rd	Cleveland	OH	44142	800-522-0750	216-362-7275
Park To Fly Inc 7855 N Frontage Rd	Orlando	FL	32812	888-851-8875	407-851-8044
Park 'N Fly 2060 Mt Paran Rd Suite 207	Atlanta	GA	30327	800-325-4863	404-264-1000
Parking Co of America 11101 Lakewood Blvd	Downey	CA	90241	866-727-5728	562-862-2118
Standard Parking Corp 900 N Michigan Ave Suite 1600 *NASDAQ: STAN*	Chicago	IL	60611	888-700-7275	312-274-2000
SunPark Inc 6 Fountain Plaza	Buffalo	NY	14202	866-400-7275	716-332-4200

PARKS - AMUSEMENT

SEE Amusement Parks

553 PARKS - NATIONAL - CANADA

				Toll-Free	Phone
Parks Canada 25 Eddy St MC 25-7 N 7th Fl	Gatineau	QC	K1A0M5	888-773-8888	819-997-0055
Banff National Park Box 900	Banff	AB	T1L1K2	800-762-1599	403-762-1550
Fundy National Park PO Box 1001 *Campground Resv	Alma	NB	E4H1B4	800-414-6765*	506-887-6000
Gros Morne National Park PO Box 130 *Campground Resv	Rocky Harbour	NL	A0K4N0	800-563-6353*	709-458-2417
Gwaii Haanas National Park Reserve/Haida Heritage Site PO Box 37 *Resv	Queen Charlotte	BC	V0T1S0	800-435-5622*	250-559-8818
Kootenay National Park PO Box 220	Radium Hot Springs	BC	V0A1M0	800-748-7275	250-347-9615
Prince Albert National Park PO Box 100	Waskesiu Lake	SK	S0J2Y0	877-255-7267	306-663-4522
Riding Mountain National Park General Delivery *Campground Resv	Wasagaming	MB	R0J2H0	800-707-8480*	204-848-7272
Wapusk National Park PO Box 127	Churchill	MB	R0B0E0	888-748-2928	204-675-8863

554 PARKS - NATIONAL & STATE - US

				Toll-Free	Phone
Acadia National Park Rt 233 Eagle Lake Rd *Campground Resv	Bar Harbor	ME	04609	800-365-2267*	207-288-3338
Barren River Lake State Resort Park 1149 State Park Rd	Lucas	KY	42156	800-325-0057	270-646-2151
Brice's Crossroads National Battlefield Site 2680 Natchez Trace Pkwy	Tupelo	MS	38804	800-305-7417	662-680-4025
Crissey Field State Recreation Site c/o Harris Beach State Park 1655 Hwy 101	Brookings	OR	97415	800-551-6949	541-469-0224
First Missouri State Capitol State Historic Site 200-216 S Main St	Saint Charles	MO	63301	800-334-6946	636-946-9282
Fort Vancouver National Historic Site 10001 E 5th St	Vancouver	WA	98661	800-832-3599	360-696-7655
Gates of the Arctic National Park & Preserve 201 1st Ave	Fairbanks	AK	99701	866-869-6887	907-457-5752
Kentucky Dam Village State Resort Park PO Box 69	Gilbertsville	KY	42044	800-325-0146	270-362-4271
Kobuk Valley National Park PO Box 1029	Kotzebue	AK	99752	800-478-7252	907-442-3890
Mastodon State Historic Site 1050 Museum Dr	Imperial	MO	63052	800-334-6946	636-464-2976
Myakka River State Park 13207 State Rd 72	Sarasota	FL	34241	800-326-3521	941-361-6511
Natchez Trace Parkway 2680 Natchez Trace Pkwy	Tupelo	MS	38804	800-305-7417	662-680-4025
Nickerson State Park 3488 Main St	Brewster	MA	02631	877-422-6762	508-896-3491
Oklahoma City National Memorial PO Box 323	Oklahoma City	OK	73101	888-542-4673	405-235-3313
Oleta River State Park 3400 NE 163rd St	North Miami Beach	FL	33160	800-326-3521	305-919-1846
Paris Mountain State Park 2401 State Park Rd	Greenville	SC	29609	866-345-7275	864-244-5565
Pipestem Resort State Park PO Box 150	Pipestem	WV	25979	800-225-5982	304-466-1800
Poverty Point National Monument c/o Poverty Point State Historic Site 6859 Hwy 577	Pioneer	LA	71226	888-926-5492	318-926-5492
Steamtown National Historic Site 150 S Washington Ave	Scranton	PA	18503	888-693-9391	570-340-5200
Tupelo National Battlefield c/o Natchez Trace Pkwy 2680 Natchez Trace Pkwy	Tupelo	MS	38804	800-305-7417	662-680-4027
White River State Park 801 W Washington St	Indianapolis	IN	46204	800-665-9056	317-233-2434

555 PARTY SUPPLY STORES

				Toll-Free	Phone
Balloons Everywhere Inc 16474 Greeno Rd	Fairhope	AL	36532	800-239-2000	251-210-2100
Birthday Express 11220 120th Ave NE *NASDAQ: BDAY*	Kirkland	WA	98033	800-424-7843	425-250-1064
Celebrate Express Inc DBA Birthday Express 11220 120th Ave NE *NASDAQ: BDAY*	Kirkland	WA	98033	800-424-7843	425-250-1064
Cooper Decoration Co 200 Maple St	Syracuse	NY	13217	800-632-4997	315-475-1661
iParty Corp 270 Bridge St Suite 301 *AMEX: IPT*	Dedham	MA	02026	888-727-8970	781-329-3952
Party City Corp 400 Commons Way *NASDAQ: PCTY*	Rockaway	NJ	07866	800-883-2100	973-983-0888
Party Concepts Inc 5730 Technology Cir	Appleton	WI	54914	800-296-2160	920-738-3600
Party Land Inc 5215 Militia Hill Rd	Plymouth Meeting	PA	19462	800-778-9563	610-941-6200
Stumps Inc 1 Party Pl PO Box 305	South Whitley	IN	46787	800-348-5084	260-723-5171

556 PATTERNS - INDUSTRIAL

				Toll-Free	Phone
D & F Corp 42455 Merrill Rd	Sterling Heights	MI	48314	800-959-3456	586-254-5300
Freeman Mfg & Supply Co 1101 Moore Rd	Avon	OH	44011	800-321-8511	440-934-1902
Hub Pattern Corp 2113 Salem Ave	Roanoke	VA	24016	800-482-3505	540-342-3505

557 PATTERNS - SEWING

				Toll-Free	Phone
Bonfit America Inc 8460 Higuera St	Culver City	CA	90232	800-526-6348	310-204-7880
Kwik-Sew Pattern Co Inc 3000 Washington Ave N	Minneapolis	MN	55411	888-594-5739	612-521-7651
McCall Pattern Co 615 McCall Rd	Manhattan	KS	66502	800-255-2762	785-776-4041
Simplicity Pattern Co Inc 2 Park Ave 12th Fl	New York	NY	10016	888-588-2700	212-372-0500
Stretch & Sew Inc PO Box 25306	Tempe	AZ	85282	800-547-7717	480-966-1462

558 PAWN SHOPS

				Toll-Free	Phone
Camco Inc DBA SuperPawn 3021 Business Ln	Las Vegas	NV	89103	800-511-2568	702-735-4444
Cash America International Inc 1600 W 7th St *NYSE: PWN*	Fort Worth	TX	76102	800-223-8738	817-335-1100
EZCORP Inc 1901 Capital Pkwy *NASDAQ: EZPW*	Austin	TX	78746	800-873-7296	512-314-3400
EZPAWN 1901 Capital Pkwy	Austin	TX	78746	800-873-7296	512-314-3400
PawnMart Inc 6400 Atlantic Blvd Suite 190	Norcross	GA	30071	800-729-6261	678-720-0660
SuperPawn 3021 Business Ln	Las Vegas	NV	89103	800-511-2568	702-735-4444

559 PAYROLL SERVICES

SEE ALSO Data Processing & Related Services; Professional Employer Organizations (PEOs)

Name / Address	City	State	Zip	Toll-Free	Phone
Advantage Payroll Services Inc 126 Merrow Rd PO Box 1330 *Cust Svc	Auburn	ME	04211	800-876-0178*	207-784-0178
Automatic Data Processing Inc (ADP) 1 ADP Blvd *NYSE: ADP*	Roseland	NJ	07068	800-225-5237	973-994-5000
Ceridian Canada Ltd 125 Garry St	Winnipeg	MB	R3C3P2	866-975-1808	204-946-0770
Ceridian Corp 3311 E Old Shakopee Rd *NYSE: CEN*	Minneapolis	MN	55425	800-767-4969	952-853-8100
CheckPoint HR 2035 Lincoln Hwy Suite 1080	Edison	NJ	08817	800-385-0331	732-287-8270
DSI Payroll Services 300 Atrium Dr	Somerset	NJ	08873	800-254-0780	732-748-1700
Media Services 500 S Sepulveda Blvd 4th Fl	Los Angeles	CA	90049	800-333-7518	310-440-9600
Paychex Inc 911 Panorama Trail S *NASDAQ: PAYX*	Rochester	NY	14625	800-828-4411	585-385-6666
PayMaxx Inc 302 S Royal Oaks Blvd	Franklin	TN	37064	877-729-6299	615-791-4000
Payroll 1 Inc 333 W 7th St	Royal Oak	MI	48067	888-999-7291	248-548-7020
Paywise Inc 122 E 42nd St Suite 520	New York	NY	10168	800-975-8607	212-953-1287
SurePayroll 4709 Golf Rd Suite 900	Skokie	IL	60076	877-954-7873	847-676-8420
TeamStaff Inc 300 Atrium Dr *NASDAQ: TSTF*	Somerset	NJ	08873	800-374-1001	732-748-1700
TTS Payrolls Inc 21 Penn Plaza Suite 1008	New York	NY	10001	866-887-4749	

560 PENS, PENCILS, PARTS

SEE ALSO Art Materials & Supplies - Mfr; Office Supplies; School Supplies

Name / Address	City	State	Zip	Toll-Free	Phone
Accutec Inc 168 Main Ave	Wallington	NJ	07057	800-222-8832	973-471-3131
Alvin & Co Inc 1335 Blue Hills Ave	Bloomfield	CT	06002	800-444-2584	860-243-8991
AT Cross Co 1 Albion Rd *AMEX: ATX*	Lincoln	RI	02865	800-722-1719	401-333-1200
Avery Dennison Corp 150 N Orange Grove Blvd *NYSE: AVY ■ *Cust Svc*	Pasadena	CA	91103	800-252-8379*	626-304-2000
BIC Corp 500 BIC Dr	Milford	CT	06460	800-546-1111	203-783-2000
Cross AT Co 1 Albion Rd *AMEX: ATX*	Lincoln	RI	02865	800-722-1719	401-333-1200
Dixon Ticonderoga Co 195 International Pkwy *AMEX: DXT*	Heathrow	FL	32746	800-824-9430	407-829-9000
Dri Mark Products Inc 15 Harbor Pk Dr	Port Washington	NY	11050	800-645-9118	516-484-6200
Fisher Space Pen Co 711 Yucca St	Boulder City	NV	89005	800-634-3494	702-293-3011
Harcourt Pencil Co 7765 S 175 W	Milroy	IN	46156	800-215-4024	765-629-2244
HPC Global 14 Inudstrial Dr	Hanover	PA	17331	800-233-4463	717-637-6681
Hub Pen Co Inc 230 Quincy Ave	Quincy	MA	02169	800-388-2323	617-471-9900
Listo Pencil Corp 1925 Union St	Alameda	CA	94501	800-547-8648	510-522-2910
Montblanc North America 430 Mountain Ave	Murray Hill	NJ	07974	800-995-4810	908-508-2300
Moon Products Inc 1150 5th Ave N PO Box 1309	Lewisburg	TN	37091	800-541-3758	931-359-1501
Musgrave Pencil Co Inc PO Box 290	Shelbyville	TN	37162	800-736-2450	931-684-3611
National Pen Corp 16885 Via Del Compo Ct Suite 100	San Diego	CA	92127	800-854-1000	858-675-3000
Pencoa Mfg Corp 117 State St *Cust Svc	Westbury	NY	11590	800-989-7527*	516-997-2330
Pentel of America Ltd 2805 Columbia St	Torrance	CA	90503	800-262-1127	310-320-3831
Sanford Corp 2707 Butterfield Rd *Cust Svc	Oak Brook	IL	60523	800-438-3703*	800-323-0749
Sargent Art Inc 100 E Diamond Ave	Hazleton	PA	18201	800-424-3596	570-454-3596
Sheaffer Pen Corp 301 Ave H	Fort Madison	IA	52627	800-346-3736	319-372-3300
Staedtler Inc 21900 Plummer St	Chatsworth	CA	91311	800-800-3691	818-882-6000
Union Pen Co PO Box 220	Hagaman	NY	12086	800-846-6600	

561 PEOPLE

Name / Address	City	State	Zip	Toll-Free	Phone
Aun Michael A 2901 E Irlo Bronson Memorial Hwy Suite D	Kissimmee	FL	34744	800-356-0567	407-870-0030
Bergman Marilyn Pres & Chm ASCAP 1 Lincoln Plaza	New York	NY	10023	800-952-7227	212-621-6000
Blanchard Ken Ken Blanchard Cos 125 State Pl	Escondido	CA	92029	800-728-6000	760-839-8070
Boyd Ty Ty Boyd Executive Learning Systems 1727 Garden Terr	Charlotte	NC	28203	800-336-2693	704-333-9999
Boyle Father Gregory J Homeboy Industries 1916 E 1st St	Los Angeles	CA	90033	800-526-1254	
Brown Les Les Brown Enterprises 20700 Civic Center Dr Suite 170	Southfield	MI	48076	800-733-4226	313-653-4110
Canfield Jack Canfield Group & Chicken Soup for the Soul Enterprises PO Box 30880	Santa Barbara	CA	93130	800-237-8336	
Cayne James E 383 Madison Ave Chm/CEO Bear Stearns Cos Inc	New York	NY	10179	800-999-2000	212-272-2000
Chopra Deepak Chopra Center at La Costa Resort & Spa 2013 Costa del Mar Rd	Carlsbad	CA	92009	888-424-6772	760-931-7566
Evanson Paul J 800 Cabin Hill Dr Chm/Pres/CEO Allegheny Energy Inc	Greensburg	PA	15601	800-255-3443	724-837-3000
Fairbank Richard D 1680 Capital One Dr Fndr/Chm/CEO Capital One Financial	McLean	VA	22102	800-801-1164	703-720-1000
Frankfort Lew 516 W 34th St Chm/CEO Coach Inc	New York	NY	10001	800-444-3611	212-594-1850
Fripp Patricia 527 Hugo St	San Francisco	CA	94122	800-634-3035	415-753-6556
Gingrich Candace Youth Outreach Mgr Human Rights Campaign 1640 Rhode Island Ave NW	Washington	DC	20036	800-777-4723	202-628-4160
Greshes Warren 202 Telluride Tr	Chapel Hill	NC	27514	800-858-1516	919-933-5900
Hopkins Tom Tom Hopkins International 7531 E 2nd St	Scottsdale	AZ	85251	800-528-0446	480-949-0786
Hutson Don Don Hutson Organization 516 Tennessee St Suite 219	Memphis	TN	38103	800-647-9166	901-767-0000
Jeffries Michael S CEO Abercrombie & Fitch Co 6301 Fitch Pass	New Albany	OH	43054	800-666-2595	614-283-6500
Johnson Spencer Who Moved My Cheese LLC 1775 West 2300 S Suite B	Salt Lake City	UT	84119	800-851-9311	801-924-0260
Karatz Bruce 10990 Wilshire Blvd Chm/CEO KB Home	Los Angeles	CA	90024	800-344-6637	310-231-4000
Kovacevich Richard M Chm/Pres/CEO Wells Fargo & Co 420 Montgomery St	San Francisco	CA	94104	800-869-3557	
LaDuke Winona White Earth Land Recovery Project 32033 E Round Lake Rd	Ponsford	MN	56575	888-779-3577	218-573-3448
Lauren Ralph Chm/CEO/Dir Polo Ralph Lauren Corp 650 Madison Ave	New York	NY	10022	800-377-7656	
Lewis Kenneth D Pres/CEO Bank of America Corp 100 N Tyron St	Charlotte	NC	28255	800-299-2265	
Lomax Michael Pres/CEO United Negro College Fund Inc 8260 Willow Oaks Corporate Dr	Fairfax	VA	22031	800-331-2244	703-205-3400
Mitchell W 12014 W 54th Dr Suite 100	Arvada	CO	80002	800-421-4840	303-425-1800
Moreno Arturo Owner Anaheim Angels 2000 Gene Autry Way	Anaheim	CA	92806	888-796-4256	714-634-2000
Morgenstern Julie Julie Morgenstern's Professional Organizers 300 W 53rd St Suite 1L	New York	NY	10019	866-742-6473	212-544-8722
Munk Peter Fndr/Chm Barrick Gold Corp Canada Trust Tower 161 Bay St Suite 3700	Toronto	ON	M5J2S1	800-720-7415	
Neas Ralph G Pres People for the American Way 2000 M St NW Suite 400	Washington	DC	20036	800-326-7329	202-467-4999
Pelletier Ray Pelletier Management Group PO Box 810	Zionsville	IN	46077	800-662-4625	
Poses Frederic M 1 Centennial Ave Chm/CEO American Standard Cos Inc	Piscataway	NJ	08854	800-223-0068	732-980-6000
Qubein Nido Creative Services Inc PO Box 6008	High Point	NC	27262	800-989-3010	336-889-3010
Robbins Anthony 9888 Carroll Centre Rd	San Diego	CA	92126	800-445-8183	858-535-9900
Rohn Jim Jim Rohn International 2835 Exchange Blvd Suite 200	Southlake	TX	76092	800-929-0434	817-442-5407
Samueli Susan Owner Mighty Ducks of Anaheim 2695 Katella Ave Arrowhead Pond of Anaheim	Anaheim	CA	92806	877-945-3946	714-704-2700
Sanborn Mark Sanborn & Associates Inc 818 Summer Dr	Highlands Ranch	CO	80126	800-650-3343	303-683-0714
Slutsky Jeff Street Fighter Marketing Inc 467 Waterbury Ct	Gahanna	OH	43230	800-758-8759	614-337-7474
Solomon Howard 909 3rd Ave 23rd Fl Chm/CEO Forest Laboratories Inc	New York	NY	10022	800-947-5227	212-421-7850
Toll Robert I 250 Gibraltar Rd Chm/CEO Toll Brothers Inc	Horsham	PA	19044	800-289-8655	215-938-8000
Upshaw Gene Exec Dir National Football League Players Assn 2021 L St NW Suite 600	Washington	DC	20036	800-372-2000	202-463-2200
Ziglar Zig Ziglar Training Systems 15303 Dallas Pkwy Suite 550	Addison	TX	75001	800-527-0306	972-233-9191

562 PERFORMING ARTS FACILITIES

SEE ALSO Convention Centers; Stadiums & Arenas; Theaters - Broadway; Theaters - Resident

Alabama

Name / Address	City	State	Zip	Toll-Free	Phone
Birmingham-Jefferson Convention Complex 2100 Richard Arrington Jr Blvd	Birmingham	AL	35203	877-843-2522	205-458-8400

Alaska

Name / Address	City	State	Zip	Toll-Free	Phone
Palace Theatre & Saloon Airport Way & Peger Rd	Fairbanks	AK	99709	800-354-7274	907-452-7274

Arkansas

				Toll-Free	Phone
Arkansas Repertory Theatre 601 Main St	Little Rock	AR	72203	**866-684-3737**	501-378-0445
Robinson Center 426 W Markham St 7 Statehouse Plaza	Little Rock	AR	72201	**800-844-4781**	501-376-4781
Wildwood Park for the Performing Arts 20919 Denny Rd	Little Rock	AR	72223	**888-278-7727**	501-821-7275

California

				Toll-Free	Phone
California Center for the Arts 340 N Escondido Blvd	Escondido	CA	92025	**800-988-4253**	760-839-4138
California Theatre of Performing Arts 562 W 4th St	San Bernardino	CA	92402	**800-511-6449**	909-386-7361
Montgomery Theater 271 S Market St	San Jose	CA	95113	**800-533-2345**	408-277-3900
Redding Civic Auditorium 777 Auditorium Dr	Redding	CA	96001	**888-225-4130**	530-225-4130
Robert and Margrit Mondavi Center for the Performing Arts 1 Shields Ave	Davis	CA	95616	**866-754-2787**	530-754-2787
San Jose Center for the Performing Arts 408 Almaden Ave	San Jose	CA	95110	**800-533-2345**	408-277-5277
San Jose Convention & Cultural Facilities 408 Almaden Blvd	San Jose	CA	95110	**800-533-2345**	408-277-5277

Colorado

				Toll-Free	Phone
Denver Center for the Performing Arts 1245 Champa St	Denver	CO	80204	**800-641-1222**	303-893-4100

Connecticut

				Toll-Free	Phone
Lincoln Theater 200 Bloomfield Ave University of Hartford Campus	West Hartford	CT	06117	**800-274-8587**	860-768-4228
Long Wharf Theatre 222 Sargent Dr	New Haven	CT	06511	**800-782-8497**	203-787-4284
Quick Center for the Arts Fairfield University 1073 Benson Rd	Fairfield	CT	06430	**877-278-7396**	203-254-4242

Delaware

				Toll-Free	Phone
DuPont Theatre 10th & Market Sts DuPont Bldg	Wilmington	DE	19801	**800-338-0881**	302-656-4401
Grand Opera House 818 N Market St	Wilmington	DE	19801	**800-374-7263**	302-652-5577

District of Columbia

				Toll-Free	Phone
John F Kennedy Center for the Performing Arts 2700 F St NW	Washington	DC	20566	**800-444-1324**	202-416-8000
National Theatre 1321 Pennsylvania Ave NW	Washington	DC	20004	**800-447-7400**	202-628-6161
Shakespeare Theatre 516 8th St SE	Washington	DC	20003	**877-487-8849**	202-547-3230

Florida

				Toll-Free	Phone
Barbara B Mann Performing Arts Hall 8099 College Pkwy SW	Fort Myers	FL	33919	**800-440-7469**	239-489-3033
Broward Center for the Performing Arts 201 SW 5th Ave	Fort Lauderdale	FL	33312	**800-564-9539**	954-462-0222
Charlotte County Memorial Auditorium 75 Taylor St	Punta Gorda	FL	33950	**800-329-9988**	941-639-5833
Eckerd Ruth Hall 1111 McMullen Booth Rd	Clearwater	FL	33759	**800-875-8682**	727-791-7060
Kravis Raymond F Center for the Performing Arts 701 Okeechobee Blvd	West Palm Beach	FL	33401	**800-572-8471**	561-832-7469
Lakeland Center 701 W Lime St	Lakeland	FL	33815	**800-200-4870**	863-834-8100
Mahaffey Theater for the Performing Arts 400 1st St S	Saint Petersburg	FL	33701	**800-874-9015**	727-892-5798
Mann Barbara B Performing Arts Hall 8099 College Pkwy SW	Fort Myers	FL	33919	**800-440-7469**	239-489-3033
Ocean Center 101 N Atlantic Ave	Daytona Beach	FL	32118	**800-858-6444**	386-254-4500
Peabody Auditorium 600 Auditorium Blvd	Daytona Beach	FL	32118	**866-605-4276**	386-671-3460
Raymond F Kravis Center for the Performing Arts 701 Okeechobee Blvd	West Palm Beach	FL	33401	**800-572-8471**	561-832-7469
Ruth Eckerd Hall 1111 McMullen Booth Rd	Clearwater	FL	33759	**800-875-8682**	727-791-7060
Seaside Music Theater 176 Northbeach St	Daytona Beach	FL	32114	**800-854-5592**	386-252-6200
Tallahassee-Leon County Civic Center 505 W Pensacola St	Tallahassee	FL	32301	**800-322-3602**	850-487-1691
Tampa Bay Performing Arts Center 1010 N WC MacInnes Pl	Tampa	FL	33602	**800-955-1045**	813-222-1000
Van Wezel Performing Arts Center 777 N Tamiami Trail	Sarasota	FL	34236	**800-826-9303**	941-953-3368

Georgia

				Toll-Free	Phone
Gwinnett Center 6400 Sugarloaf Pkwy Bldg 100	Duluth	GA	30097	**800-224-6422**	770-813-7500
Macon City Auditorium 415 1st St	Macon	GA	31201	**877-532-6144**	478-751-9152

Illinois

				Toll-Free	Phone
Krannert Center for the Performing Arts 500 S Goodwin Ave	Urbana	IL	61801	**800-527-2849**	217-333-6700
Symphony Center 220 S Michigan Ave	Chicago	IL	60604	**800-223-7114**	312-294-3333

Indiana

				Toll-Free	Phone
American Cabaret Theatre 401 E Michigan St	Indianapolis	IN	46204	**800-375-8887**	317-631-0334
Christel DeHaan Fine Arts Center 1400 E Hanna Ave University of Indianapolis	Indianapolis	IN	46227	**800-232-8634**	317-788-3566
Indianapolis Artsgarden Above the intersection of Washington & Illinois St	Indianapolis	IN	46204	**800-965-2787**	317-631-3301
Morris Performing Arts Center 211 N Michigan St	South Bend	IN	46601	**800-537-6415**	574-235-9190

Louisiana

				Toll-Free	Phone
Preservation Hall 726 Saint Peter St	New Orleans	LA	70116	**888-946-5299**	504-522-2841
Strand Theatre 619 Louisiana Ave	Shreveport	LA	71101	**800-313-6373**	318-226-1481

Maryland

				Toll-Free	Phone
Joseph Meyerhoff Symphony Hall 1212 Cathedral St	Baltimore	MD	21201	**800-442-1198**	410-783-8100

Michigan

				Toll-Free	Phone
Grand Rapids Civic Theatre 30 N Division Ave	Grand Rapids	MI	49503	**866-455-4728**	616-222-6650
Wharton Center for the Performing Arts Michigan State University	East Lansing	MI	48824	**800-942-7866**	517-432-2000
Whiting Auditorium 1241 E Kearsley St	Flint	MI	48503	**888-823-6837**	810-237-7333

Minnesota

				Toll-Free	Phone
Guthrie Theater 725 Vineland Pl	Minneapolis	MN	55403	**877-447-8243**	612-347-1100
Mayo Civic Center 30 Civic Center Dr SE	Rochester	MN	55904	**800-422-2199**	507-281-6184
Renegade Center for the Arts 404 W Superior St	Duluth	MN	55802	**888-722-6627**	218-722-6775

Missouri

				Toll-Free	Phone
Andy Williams Moon River Theatre 2500 W Hwy 76	Branson	MO	65616	**800-666-6094**	417-334-4500
Champagne Theatre 1984 Hwy 165 Welk Resort Ctr	Branson	MO	65616	**800-505-9355**	
Country Tonite Theatre 3600 W Hwy 76	Branson	MO	65616	**800-468-6648**	417-334-2422
Jim Stafford Theatre 3440 W Hwy 76	Branson	MO	65616	**800-677-8533**	417-335-8080
Juanita K Hammons Hall for the Performing Arts 901 S National Ave	Springfield	MO	65804	**888-476-7849**	417-836-6776
Kansas City Music Hall 201 W 13th St	Kansas City	MO	64105	**800-821-7060**	816-513-5000
Legends Theater 3216 W Hwy 76	Branson	MO	65616	**800-374-7469**	417-339-3003
Powell Symphony Hall 718 N Grand Blvd	Saint Louis	MO	63103	**800-232-1880**	314-533-2500
Remington Theatre 3701 W Hwy 76	Branson	MO	65616	**800-884-4536**	417-336-1220
Shepherd of the Hills Homestead & Outdoor Theatre 5586 W Hwy 76	Branson	MO	65616	**800-653-6288**	417-334-4191
Stafford Jim Theatre 3440 W Hwy 76	Branson	MO	65616	**800-677-8533**	417-335-8080

Montana

				Toll-Free	Phone
Alberta Bair Theater for the Performing Arts 2722 3rd Ave N Suite 400	Billings	MT	59101	**877-321-2074**	406-256-8915

New Jersey

				Toll-Free	Phone
New Jersey Performing Arts Center 1 Center St	Newark	NJ	07102	**888-466-5722**	973-642-8989
State Theatre 15 Livingston Ave	New Brunswick	NJ	08901	**877-782-8311**	732-247-7200

New York

				Toll-Free	Phone
Artpark 450 S 4th St	Lewiston	NY	14092	**800-659-7275**	716-754-9000
Shea's Performing Arts Center 646 Main St	Buffalo	NY	14202	**800-217-4327**	716-847-1410

North Dakota

				Toll-Free	Phone
Chester Fritz Auditorium Yale Dr & University Ave PO Box 9028 University of North Dakota	Grand Forks	ND	58202	**800-375-4068**	701-777-3076

Ohio

				Toll-Free	Phone
Benjamin & Marian Schuster Performing Arts Center 109 Main St	Dayton	OH	45402	**888-228-3630**	937-228-3630
Henry H Stambaugh Auditorium 1000 5th Ave	Youngstown	OH	44504	**866-582-8963**	330-747-5175
Playhouse Square Center 1501 Euclid Ave Suite 200	Cleveland	OH	44115	**800-888-9941**	216-771-4444
Veterans Memorial Civic & Convention Center 7 Town Sq	Lima	OH	45801	**877-377-0674**	419-224-5222
Victoria Theatre 138 N Main St	Dayton	OH	45402	**888-228-3630**	937-228-3630

Oklahoma

				Toll-Free	Phone
Tulsa Performing Arts Center 110 E 2nd St	Tulsa	OK	74103	**800-364-7122**	918-596-7122

Oregon

				Toll-Free	Phone
Florence Events Center 715 Quince St	Florence	OR	97439	**888-968-4086**	541-997-1994

Pennsylvania

				Toll-Free	Phone
Academy of Music Broad & Locust Sts	Philadelphia	PA	19102	**800-457-8354**	215-893-1935
Fulton Opera House 12 N Prince St	Lancaster	PA	17608	**888-480-1265**	717-397-7425

South Carolina

				Toll-Free	Phone
Alabama Theatre 4750 Hwy 17 S	North Myrtle Beach	SC	29582	**800-342-2262**	843-272-1111
Carolina Opry 8901 Hwy 17 N Suite A	Myrtle Beach	SC	29577	**800-843-6779**	843-238-8888
Dock Street Theatre 135 Church St	Charleston	SC	29401	**800-454-7093**	843-577-5967
Palace Theater 1420 Celebrity Cir Broadway at the Beach	Myrtle Beach	SC	29577	**800-905-4228**	843-448-9224

South Dakota

				Toll-Free	Phone
Washington Pavilion of Arts & Science 301 S Main Ave	Sioux Falls	SD	57104	**877-927-4728**	605-367-7397

Tennessee

				Toll-Free	Phone
Memphis Cook Convention Center 255 N Main St	Memphis	TN	38103	**800-726-0915**	901-576-1200

Texas

				Toll-Free	Phone
Alley Theatre 615 Texas Ave	Houston	TX	77002	**800-259-2553**	713-228-9341
El Paso Convention & Performing Arts Center 1 Civic Center Plaza	El Paso	TX	79901	**800-351-6024**	915-534-0600
Grand 1894 Opera House 2020 Postoffice St	Galveston	TX	77550	**800-821-1894**	409-765-1894
Julie Rogers Theatre 765 Pearl St	Beaumont	TX	77701	**800-782-3081**	409-838-3435
Rogers Julie Theatre 765 Pearl St	Beaumont	TX	77701	**800-782-3081**	409-838-3435
University of Texas at Austin Performing Arts Center E 23rd St & E Robert Dedman Dr	Austin	TX	78705	**800-687-6010**	512-471-1444

Utah

				Toll-Free	Phone
Capitol Theatre 50 W 200 South	Salt Lake City	UT	84101	**888-451-2787**	801-323-6800
Maurice Abravanel Hall 123 W South Temple	Salt Lake City	UT	84101	**888-451-2787**	801-533-5626
Salt Lake County Center for the Arts 50 W 200 South	Salt Lake City	UT	84101	**888-451-2787**	801-323-6800

Virginia

				Toll-Free	Phone
Landmark Theater 6 N Laurel St	Richmond	VA	23220	**877-297-5729**	804-646-4213
Mill Mountain Theatre 1 Market Sq 2nd Fl	Roanoke	VA	24011	**800-317-6455**	540-342-5740
Willett Hall 3701 Willett Dr	Portsmouth	VA	23707	**800-488-6761**	757-393-5460

Washington

				Toll-Free	Phone
Pantages Theater 901 Broadway	Tacoma	WA	98402	**800-291-7593**	253-591-5890
Rialto Theater 310 S 9th St	Tacoma	WA	98402	**800-291-7593**	253-591-5890
Spokane Civic Theatre 1020 N Howard St	Spokane	WA	99205	**800-446-9576**	509-325-1413

West Virginia

				Toll-Free	Phone
Capitol Music Hall 1015 Main St	Wheeling	WV	26003	**800-624-5456**	304-234-0050
Victoria Vaudeville Theater 1228 Market St	Wheeling	WV	26003	**800-505-7464**	304-233-7464

Wisconsin

				Toll-Free	Phone
Pabst Theater 144 E Wells St	Milwaukee	WI	53202	**800-511-1552**	414-286-3665
Weidner Center for the Performing Arts 2420 Nicolet Dr University of Wisconsin at Green Bay	Green Bay	WI	54311	**800-328-8587**	920-465-2726

Wyoming

				Toll-Free	Phone
Casper Events Center 1 Events Dr	Casper	WY	82601	**800-442-2256**	307-235-8441

563 PERFORMING ARTS ORGANIZATIONS

SEE ALSO Associations & Organizations - General - Arts & Artists Organizations

563-1 Dance Companies

				Toll-Free	Phone
Ballet Arizona 3645 E Indian School Rd	Phoenix	AZ	85018	**888-322-5538**	602-381-0184
Ballet Florida 500 Fern St	West Palm Beach	FL	33401	**800-540-0172**	561-659-1212
Columbia City Ballet PO Box 11898	Columbia	SC	29211	**800-899-7408**	803-799-7605
Nai-Ni Chen Dance Co PO Box 1121	Fort Lee	NJ	07024	**800-650-0246**	
New York City Ballet Inc 20 Lincoln Center New York State Theatre	New York	NY	10023	**800-580-8730**	212-870-5656
Sarasota Ballet of Florida 5555 N Tamiami Trail	Sarasota	FL	34243	**866-269-6334**	941-359-0099

563-2 Opera Companies

				Toll-Free	Phone
Arizona Opera Co 4600 N 12th St	Phoenix	AZ	85014	**877-473-1497**	602-266-7464
Atlanta Opera 728 West Peachtree St NW	Atlanta	GA	30308	**800-356-7372**	404-881-8801
Central City Opera 400 S Colorado Blvd Suite 530	Denver	CO	80246	**800-851-8175**	303-292-6500
Dayton Opera 138 N Main St	Dayton	OH	45402	**888-228-3630**	937-228-0662
Florentine Opera Co 700 N Water St Suite 950	Milwaukee	WI	53202	**800-326-7372**	414-291-5700
Florida Grand Opera 1200 Coral Way	Miami	FL	33145	**800-741-1010**	305-854-1643
Houston Grand Opera 510 Preston St Suite 500	Houston	TX	77002	**800-626-7372**	713-546-0200
Kentucky Opera Assn 101 S 8th St	Louisville	KY	40202	**800-690-9236**	502-584-4500
Minnesota Opera 620 N 1st St	Minneapolis	MN	55401	**800-676-6737**	612-333-2700
Mississippi Opera PO Box 1551	Jackson	MS	39215	**877-676-7372**	601-960-1528
New Orleans Opera Assn 305 Baronne St Suite 500	New Orleans	LA	70112	**800-881-4459**	504-529-2278
Opera Omaha 1625 Farnam St Suite 100	Omaha	NE	68102	**877-346-7372**	402-346-0357
Opera Pacific 600 W Warner Ave	Santa Ana	CA	92707	**800-346-7372**	714-546-6000
Opera Santa Barbara 123 W Padre St Suite A	Santa Barbara	CA	93105	**800-563-7181**	805-898-3890
Opera Theatre at Wildwood 20919 Denny Rd	Little Rock	AR	72223	**888-278-7727**	501-821-7275
Orlando Opera 1111 N Orange Ave	Orlando	FL	32804	**800-336-7372**	407-426-1717
Santa Fe Opera PO Box 2408	Santa Fe	NM	87504	**800-280-4654**	505-986-5900
Sarasota Opera 61 N Pineapple Ave	Sarasota	FL	34236	**888-673-7212**	941-366-8450
Seattle Opera PO Box 9248	Seattle	WA	98109	**800-426-1619***	206-389-7600
*Sales					
Toledo Opera 425 Jefferson Ave Suite 415	Toledo	OH	43604	**866-860-9048**	419-255-7464
Washington National Opera 2600 Virginia Ave NW Suite 104	Washington	DC	20037	**800-876-7372**	202-295-2420

563-3 Orchestras

				Toll-Free	Phone
Abilene Philharmonic Orchestra 402 Cypress St Suite 130	Abilene	TX	79601	**800-460-0610**	325-677-6710
Anderson Symphony Orchestra PO Box 741	Anderson	IN	46015	**888-644-9490**	765-644-2111
Austin Symphony Orchestra 1101 Red River St	Austin	TX	78701	**888-462-3787**	512-476-6064
Baltimore Symphony Orchestra 1212 Cathedral St	Baltimore	MD	21201	**800-422-1198**	410-783-8100
Bangor Symphony Orchestra 51-A Main St PO Box 1441	Bangor	ME	04402	**800-639-3221**	207-942-5555
Boston Pops 301 Massachusetts Ave Symphony Hall	Boston	MA	02115	**888-266-1200**	617-266-1492
Boston Symphony Orchestra 301 Massachusetts Ave Symphony Hall	Boston	MA	02115	**888-266-1200**	617-266-1492
Cedar Rapids Symphony Orchestra 119 3rd Ave Se	Cedar Rapids	IA	52401	**800-369-8863**	319-366-8206
Chicago Symphony Orchestra 220 S Michigan Ave	Chicago	IL	60604	**800-223-7114**	312-294-3000
Cleveland Orchestra 11001 Euclid Ave Severance Hall	Cleveland	OH	44106	**800-686-1141**	216-231-7300
Corpus Christi Symphony Orchestra 555 N Carancahua St Suite 410	Corpus Christi	TX	78478	**877-286-6683**	361-882-2717
Da Camera of Houston 1427 Branard St	Houston	TX	77006	**800-233-2226**	713-524-7601
Edmonton Symphony Orchestra 4 Sir Winston Churchill Sq Winspear Centre	Edmonton	AB	T5J4X8	**800-563-5081**	780-428-1414
Flagstaff Symphony Orchestra PO Box 122	Flagstaff	AZ	86002	**888-520-7214**	928-774-5107
Florida Orchestra 101 S Hoover Blvd Suite 100	Tampa	FL	33609	**800-662-7286**	813-286-1170
Florida West Coast Symphony 709 N Tamiami Trail	Sarasota	FL	34236	**800-287-9634**	941-953-4252
Henry Mancini Institute 10811 Washington Blvd Suite 250	Culver City	CA	90232	**888-464-1903**	310-845-1900
Illinois Symphony Orchestera 524 1/2 Capitol Ave	Springfield	IL	62705	**800-401-7222**	217-522-2838
Indianapolis Symphony Orchestra 32 E Washington St Suite 600	Indianapolis	IN	46204	**800-366-8457**	317-262-1100
Lexington Philharmonic 161 N Mill St	Lexington	KY	40507	**888-494-4226**	859-233-4226

Orchestras (Cont'd)

Organization	City	State	ZIP	Toll-Free	Phone
Louisville Orchestra 300 W Main St Suite 100	Louisville	KY	40202	**800-775-7777**	502-587-8681
Mancini Henry Institute 10811 Washington Blvd Suite 250	Culver City	CA	90232	**888-464-1903**	310-845-1900
Milwaukee Symphony Orchestra 700 N Water St Suite 700	Milwaukee	WI	53202	**800-291-7605**	414-291-6010
Mississippi Symphony Orchestra 201 E Pascagoula St	Jackson	MS	39201	**800-898-5050**	601-960-1565
Naples Philharmonic Orchestra 5833 Pelican Bay Blvd Philharmonic Center for the Arts	Naples	FL	34108	**800-597-1900**	239-597-1900
New Jersey Symphony Orchestra 2 Central Ave.	Newark	NJ	07102	**888-255-3476**	973-624-3713
New Mexico Symphony Orchestra 4407 Menaul Blvd NE	Albuquerque	NM	87110	**800-251-6676**	505-881-9590
New West Symphony 2100 E Thousand Oaks Blvd Suite D	Thousand Oaks	CA	91362	**866-776-8400**	805-497-5800
New World Symphony 541 Lincoln Rd	Miami Beach	FL	33139	**800-597-3331**	305-673-3330
Northeastern Pennsylvania Philharmonic 957 Broadcast Ctr	Avoca	PA	18641	**800-836-3413**	570-457-8301
Orchestra New England College & Elm Sts Battell Chapel Yale University	New Haven	CT	06510	**800-476-9040**	
Oregon Symphony Orchestra 921 SW Washington St Suite 200	Portland	OR	97205	**800-228-7343**	503-228-1294
Philadelphia Orchestra 260 S Broad St Suite 1600	Philadelphia	PA	19102	**800-457-8354**	215-893-1900
Phoenix Symphony 455 N 3rd St Suite 390	Phoenix	AZ	85004	**800-776-9080**	602-495-1999
River City Brass Band 885 Progress St	Pittsburgh	PA	15212	**800-292-7222**	412-322-7222
Roanoke Symphony 541 Luck Ave Suite 200	Roanoke	VA	24016	**866-277-9127**	540-343-6221
Rochester Orchestra & Chorale 301 N Broadway	Rochester	MN	55906	**877-286-8742**	507-286-8742
Saint Louis Symphony Orchestra 718 N Grand Blvd	Saint Louis	MO	63103	**800-232-1880**	314-533-2500
Santa Fe Symphony 211 W San Francisco St	Santa Fe	NM	87501	**800-480-1319**	505-983-1414
South Dakota Symphony Orchestra 300 N Dakota Ave Suite 116	Sioux Falls	SD	57104	**866-681-7376**	605-335-7933
Syracuse Symphony Orchestra 411 Montgomery St Suite 40	Syracuse	NY	13202	**800-724-3810**	315-424-8222
Toledo Symphony 1838 Parkwood Ave Suite 310	Toledo	OH	43624	**800-348-1253**	419-246-8000
Vermont Symphony Orchestra 2 Church St Suite 19	Burlington	VT	05401	**800-876-9293**	802-864-5741
Wheeling Symphony Orchestra 1025 Main St Suite 811	Wheeling	WV	26003	**800-395-9241**	304-232-6100

563-4 Theater Companies

Organization	City	State	ZIP	Toll-Free	Phone
Charleston Stage Co 135 Church St	Charleston	SC	29401	**800-454-7093**	843-577-5967
Corn Stock Theatre 1700 Park Rd	Peoria	IL	61604	**800-220-1185**	309-676-2196
Fargo-Moorhead Community Theatre 333 4th St S	Fargo	ND	58103	**877-687-7469**	701-235-6778
Garden Grove Playhouse 12001 Saint Mark St	Garden Grove	CA	92845	**866-468-3399**	714-897-5122
Missouri Repertory Theatre 4949 Cherry St	Kansas City	MO	64110	**888-502-2700**	816-235-2727
Omaha Community Playhouse 6915 Cass St	Omaha	NE	68132	**888-782-4338**	402-553-0800
Paper Bag Players 225 W 99th St	New York	NY	10025	**800-777-2247**	212-663-0390
Santa Fe Stages 422 W San Francisco St	Santa Fe	NM	87501	**877-222-3022**	505-982-6683
Seaside Music Theater 176 Northbeach St	Daytona Beach	FL	32114	**800-854-5592**	386-252-6200
Seattle Repertory Theatre 155 Mercer St PO Box 900923	Seattle	WA	98109	**877-900-9285**	206-443-2210
Second City Chicago 1616 N Wells St	Chicago	IL	60614	**877-778-4707**	312-664-4032
Studio Arena Theatre 710 Main St	Buffalo	NY	14202	**800-777-8243**	716-856-8025
Theatre Under the Stars 800 Bagby Suite 200	Houston	TX	77002	**800-678-5440**	713-558-2600
West Virginia Public Theatre PO Box 4270	Morgantown	WV	26504	**877-999-9878**	304-598-0144

564 PERFUMES

Company	City	State	ZIP	Toll-Free	Phone
Avon Products Inc 1251 Ave of the Americas *NYSE: AVP* ■ *Cust Svc	New York	NY	10020	**800-367-2866***	212-282-5000
Bijan Boutique 420 N Rodeo Dr	Beverly Hills	CA	90210	**800-992-4526**	310-273-6544
Body Shop The 5036 One World Way *Cust Svc	Wake Forest	NC	27587	**800-747-4827***	919-554-4900
Calvin Klein Cosmetics 725 5th Ave Trump Tower	New York	NY	10022	**800-715-4023**	212-326-6800
Chanel Inc 9 W 57th St 44th Fl	New York	NY	10019	**800-550-0005**	212-688-5055
Charles of the Ritz 237 Park Ave *Consumer Info	New York	NY	10017	**800-473-8566***	212-527-4000
Crabtree & Evelyn Ltd 102 Peake Brook Rd	Woodstock	CT	06281	**800-624-5211**	860-928-2761
Eagle Marketing Inc Perfume Originals Products Div 2412 Sequoia Pk	Yukon	OK	73099	**800-233-7424**	405-354-1027
Elizabeth Arden Inc 14100 NW 60th Ave *NASDAQ: RDEN*	Miami Lakes	FL	33014	**800-227-2445**	305-818-8000
FragranceNet.com Inc 909 Motor Pkwy	Hauppauge	NY	11788	**800-987-3738**	631-582-5204
H2O Plus Inc 845 W Madison St *Cust Svc	Chicago	IL	60607	**800-690-2284***	312-850-9283
Inter Parfums Inc 551 5th Ave Suite 1500 *NASDAQ: IPAR*	New York	NY	10176	**800-533-6010**	212-983-2640
Key West Fragrance & Cosmetics Factory Inc 540 Greene St *Orders	Key West	FL	33040	**800-445-2563***	305-293-1885
Klein Calvin Cosmetics 725 5th Ave Trump Tower	New York	NY	10022	**800-715-4023**	212-326-6800
Noville Essential Oil Co 124 Case Dr	South Plainfield	NJ	07080	**888-668-4553**	908-754-2222
Parfums de Coeur Ltd 85 Old Kings Hwy N	Darien	CT	06820	**800-887-2738**	203-655-8807
Parfums Givenchy Inc 19 E 57th St	New York	NY	10022	**800-479-6427**	212-931-2600
Perfumania Inc 251 International Pkwy	Sunrise	FL	33325	**866-600-3600**	954-335-9100
Perfume Originals Products Div Eagle Marketing Inc 2412 Sequoia Pk	Yukon	OK	73099	**800-233-7424**	405-354-1027

Company	City	State	ZIP	Toll-Free	Phone
Quest International Fragrances USA Inc 400 International Dr	Mount Olive	NJ	07828	**800-598-5986**	973-691-7100
Ulta3 Inc 1135 Arbor Dr	Romeoville	IL	60446	**866-858-2266**	630-226-0020

565 PERSONAL EMERGENCY RESPONSE SYSTEMS

Company	City	State	ZIP	Toll-Free	Phone
AlertOne Services Inc 24 W 4th St	Williamsport	PA	17701	**800-693-5433**	570-321-5433
American Medical Alert Corp 3265 Lawson Blvd *NASDAQ: AMAC*	Oceanside	NY	11572	**800-645-3244**	516-536-5850
Health Watch Inc 6400 Park of Commerce Blvd Suite 1-A	Boca Raton	FL	33487	**888-994-1835**	561-994-6699
Life Alert 16027 Ventura Blvd Suite 400	Encino	CA	91436	**800-700-7000**	818-700-7000
LifeFone 16 Yellowstone Ave	White Plains	NY	10607	**800-882-2280**	914-948-0282
LifeGard of America Inc 141 W Main St	Westminster	MD	21157	**800-448-5697**	410-875-2126
Lifeline Systems Inc 111 Lawrence St *NASDAQ: LIFE*	Framingham	MA	01702	**800-451-0525**	508-988-1000
Medic Aid Response Systems Ltd 167 Village Rd	Harring Cove	NS	B3V1H2	**800-565-9135**	902-454-8877
Pioneer Medical Systems 37 Washington St	Melrose	MA	02176	**800-338-2303**	781-662-2222
Response USA Inc 535 Rt 38 Suite 500	Cherry Hill	NJ	08002	**800-777-9807**	856-661-0700

566 PERSONAL PROTECTIVE EQUIPMENT & CLOTHING

SEE ALSO Medical Supplies - Mfr; Safety Equipment - Mfr; Safety Equipment - Whol; Sporting Goods

Company	City	State	ZIP	Toll-Free	Phone
3M Occupational Health & Environmental Safety Products Div 3M Ctr Bldg 235-2W-75	Saint Paul	MN	55144	**800-328-1667**	651-733-8029
3M Safety Security & Protection Services Div 3M Ctr	Saint Paul	MN	55144	**800-364-3577**	651-733-1110
Aearo Co 5457 W 79th St *Cust Svc	Indianapolis	IN	46268	**800-327-3431***	317-692-6666
AHPC Holdings Inc 500 Park Blvd Suite 1260 *NASDAQ: GLOV*	Itasca	IL	60143	**800-828-2964**	630-285-9191
American Body Armor & Equipment Inc 13386 International Pkwy	Jacksonville	FL	32218	**800-654-9943**	904-741-5400
American Health Products Corp 500 Park Blvd Suite 1260	Itasca	IL	60143	**800-828-2964**	630-285-9191
Ansell Healthcare Inc 200 Schulz Dr	Red Bank	NJ	07701	**800-232-1309**	732-345-5400
Ansell Occupational Healthcare 1300 Walnut St *Cust Svc	Coshocton	OH	43812	**800-800-0444***	740-622-4311
Athletic Supporter Ltd 24601 Hallwood Ct	Farmington Hills	MI	48335	**800-521-6500**	248-474-6000
Bacou-Dalloz 910 Douglas Pike	Smithfield	RI	02917	**800-343-3411**	401-233-0333
Bell Sports Corp 6225 N State Hwy 161 Suite 300	Irving	TX	75038	**866-525-2355**	469-417-6600
Best Mfg Co 579 Edison St *Cust Svc	Menlo	GA	30731	**800-241-0323***	706-862-2302
Bike Athletic Co 3303 Cumberland Blvd	Atlanta	GA	30339	**800-251-9230**	678-742-8255
Biomarine Inc 456 Creamery Way	Exton	PA	19341	**800-378-2287**	610-524-8800
Bouton HL Co Inc 11 Kendrick Rd *Cust Svc	Wareham	MA	02571	**800-426-1881***	508-295-3300
Bullard Co 1898 Safety Way	Cynthiana	KY	41031	**800-827-0423**	859-234-6611
Carleton Technologies Inc 10 Cobham Dr	Orchard Park	NY	14127	**800-395-4074**	716-662-0006
David Clark Co Inc 360 Franklin St *Cust Svc	Worcester	MA	01615	**800-298-6235***	508-751-5800
DHB Industries Inc 4031 NE 12th Terr *AMEX: DHB*	Oakland Park	FL	33334	**800-979-4343**	954-566-0040
Dispensers Optical Service Corp 1815 Plantside Dr *Cust Svc	Louisville	KY	40299	**800-626-4545***	502-491-3440
Diversified Optical Products Inc Cairns Advanced Technologies Div 282 Main St	Salem	NH	03079	**800-230-1600**	603-898-1880
DuPont Personal Protection 884 S 7th St	McBee	SC	29101	**800-931-3456**	843-335-8211
Encon Safety Products Co 6825 W Sam Houston Pkwy N	Houston	TX	77041	**800-283-6266**	713-466-1449
Fibre-Metal Products Co Rt 1 at S Brinton Wake Rd PO Box 248	Concordville	PA	19331	**800-523-7048**	610-459-5300
Fire-End & Croker Corp 7 Westchester Plaza	Elmsford	NY	10523	**800-759-3473**	914-592-3640
Fisher Scientific International Inc Safety Div 2000 Park Ln *Cust Svc	Pittsburgh	PA	15275	**800-766-7000***	412-490-8300
Flight Suits Ltd 1675 Pioneer Way	El Cajon	CA	92020	**800-748-6693**	619-440-6976
Galls Inc 2680 Palumbo Dr	Lexington	KY	40509	**800-477-7766**	859-266-7227
Gateway Safety Inc 4722 Spring Rd	Cleveland	OH	44131	**800-822-5347**	216-749-1100
General Econopak Inc 1725 N 6th St	Philadelphia	PA	19122	**888-871-8568**	215-763-8200
Gerson Louis M Co Inc 15 Sproat St	Middleboro	MA	02346	**800-225-8623**	508-947-4000
Gexco 7209 Arlington Ave Suite D	Riverside	CA	92503	**800-829-8222**	951-637-0546
Globe Mfg Co Inc PO Box 128 37 Loudon Rd	Pittsfield	NH	03263	**800-232-8323**	603-435-8323
GRABBER Performance Group 4600 Danvers Dr SE	Grand Rapids	MI	49512	**800-423-1233**	616-940-1914
Graham Professional Div Little Rapids Corp 2273 Larsen Rd PO Box 19100 *Cust Svc	Green Bay	WI	54304	**800-558-6765***	920-494-8701
H Koch & Sons Co 5410 E La Palma Ave	Anaheim	CA	92807	**800-433-5787**	714-779-7000
Handgards Inc 901 Hawkins Blvd	El Paso	TX	79915	**800-351-8161**	915-779-6606
HeatMax Inc 505 Hill Rd	Dalton	GA	30721	**800-432-8629**	706-226-1800
Helmet House Inc 26855 Malibu Hill Rd	Calabasas Hills	CA	91301	**800-421-7247**	818-880-0000
HL Bouton Co Inc 11 Kendrick Rd *Cust Svc	Wareham	MA	02571	**800-426-1881***	508-295-3300
ILC Dover Inc 1 Moonwalker Rd	Frederica	DE	19946	**800-631-9567**	302-335-3911
Jackson Products Inc 801 Corporate Ctr Dr Suite 300	Saint Charles	MO	63304	**800-253-7281**	636-300-2700
Kappler Protective Apparel & Fabrics 115 Grimes Dr	Guntersville	AL	35976	**800-600-4019**	256-505-4000
Kimberly-Clark 6625 Industrial Park Blvd	Fort Worth	TX	76180	**800-742-1996**	817-581-6424

Company / Address	City	State	ZIP	Toll-Free	Phone
Kimberly-Clark Corp Professional Health Care					
Business 1400 Holcomb Bridge Rd	Roswell	GA	30076	**800-558-6452**	770-587-8000
Koch H & Sons Co 5410 E La Palma Ave	Anaheim	CA	92807	**800-433-5787**	714-779-7000
Lakeland Industries Inc					
711-2 Koehler Ave	Ronkonkoma	NY	11779	**800-645-9291**	631-981-9700
NASDAQ: LAKE					
Landauer Inc 2 Science Rd	Glenwood	IL	60425	**800-323-8830**	708-755-7000
NYSE: LDR					
Lion Apparel Inc 6450 Poe Ave	Dayton	OH	45414	**800-548-6614**	937-898-1949
Little Rapids Corp 2273 Larsen Rd	Green Bay	WI	54303	**800-496-3040**	920-496-3040
Little Rapids Corp Graham Professional Div					
2273 Larsen Rd PO Box 19100	Green Bay	WI	54304	**800-558-6765***	920-494-8701
*Cust Svc					
Louis M Gerson Co Inc 15 Sproat St	Middleboro	MA	02346	**800-225-8623**	508-947-4000
Magid Products LLC 159 South St	Morristown	NJ	07960	**800-247-5281**	973-984-7998
MAPA Spontex Inc 100 Spontex Dr	Columbia	TN	38401	**800-537-2897***	931-388-5632
*Cust Svc					
MCR Safety 5321 E Shelby Dr	Memphis	TN	38118	**800-955-6887**	901-795-5810
Med-Eng Systems Inc 2400 St Laurent Blvd	Ottawa	ON	K1G6C4	**800-644-9078**	613-739-9646
Medline Industries Inc 1 Medline Pl	Mundelein	IL	60060	**800-323-6284***	847-949-5500
*Cust Svc					
Miller Products Co Inc 2220 91st St	North Bergen	NJ	07047	**800-782-7437**	201-662-2010
Mine Safety Appliances Co (MSA)					
121 Gamma Dr	Pittsburgh	PA	15238	**800-672-2222**	412-967-3000
NYSE: MSA					
Moldex Metric Inc 10111 W Jefferson Blvd	Culver City	CA	90232	**800-421-0668**	310-837-6500
MTS Safety Products Inc 150 2nd St	Belmont	MS	38827	**800-647-8168**	662-454-9245
National Safety Apparel Inc					
3865 W 150th St	Cleveland	OH	44111	**800-553-0672**	216-941-1111
Newtex Industries Inc 8050 Victor Mendon Rd	Victor	NY	14564	**800-836-1001**	585-924-9135
Niedner Ltd 675 Merrill St	Coaticook	QC	J1A2S2	**800-567-2703**	514-637-5572
Norcross Safety Products LLC					
1136 2nd St	Rock Island	IL	61201	**800-777-9021***	309-786-7741
*Cust Svc					
North Safety Products 2000 Plainfield Pike	Cranston	RI	02921	**800-430-4110***	401-943-4400
*Cust Svc					
Parmelee Industries Inc 8101 Lenexa Dr	Lenexa	KS	66214	**800-821-5218**	913-599-5555
Parmelee Industries Inc US Safety Div					
8101 Lenexa Dr	Lenexa	KS	66214	**800-821-5218**	913-599-5555
Plastic Safety Systems Inc 2444 Baldwin Rd	Cleveland	OH	44104	**800-662-6338**	216-231-8590
PolyConversions Inc 505 Condit Dr	Rantoul	IL	61866	**888-893-3330**	217-893-3330
Precept Medical Products Inc 370 Airport Rd	Arden	NC	28704	**800-851-4431**	828-681-0209
Protech Armored Products					
13386 International Pkwy	Jacksonville	FL	32218	**800-428-0588**	904-741-5400
Right-Gard Corp 531 N 4th St PO Box 286	Denver	PA	17517	**800-535-1122**	
Saf-T-Gard International Inc 205 Huehl Rd	Northbrook	IL	60062	**800-548-4273**	847-291-1600
Safariland Ltd Inc 3120 E Mission Blvd	Ontario	CA	91761	**800-347-1200**	909-923-7300
Safe-T-Gard Corp 12105 W Cedar Dr	Lakewood	CO	80228	**800-356-9026***	303-763-8900
*Cust Svc					
Salisbury WH & Co 7520 N Long Ave	Skokie	IL	60077	**877-406-4501**	847-679-6700
Schutt Sports 1200 E Union Ave PO Box 426	Litchfield	IL	62056	**800-637-2047**	217-324-2712
Scott Health & Safety PO Box 569	Monroe	NC	28111	**800-247-7257**	704-291-8300
Seattle Mfg Corp 6930 Salashan Pkwy	Ferndale	WA	98248	**800-426-6251**	360-366-5534
Sellstrom Mfg Co 1 Sellstrom Dr	Palatine	IL	60067	**800-323-7402**	847-358-2000
SSL Americas Inc					
3585 Engineering Dr Suite 200	Norcross	GA	30092	**888-387-3927**	770-582-2222
Standard Textile Co Inc 1 Knollcrest	Cincinnati	OH	45237	**800-888-5000**	513-761-9255
Stearns Inc 1100 Stearns Dr	Sauk Rapids	MN	56379	**800-333-1179**	320-252-1642
Steel Grip Inc 700 Garfield St	Danville	IL	61832	**800-223-1595**	217-442-6240
Steiner Industries 5801 N Tripp Ave	Chicago	IL	60646	**800-621-4515**	773-588-3444
Strong Enterprises Inc 11236 Satellite Blvd	Orlando	FL	32837	**800-344-6319**	407-859-9317
Switlik Parachute Co Inc PO Box 1328	Trenton	NJ	08607	**800-525-2747**	609-587-3300
TASER International Inc 17800 N 85th St	Scottsdale	AZ	85255	**800-978-2737**	480-905-2000
NASDAQ: TASR					
Tillotson Healthcare Corp					
8025 S Willow St Suite 203	Manchester	NH	03103	**800-445-6830**	603-472-6600
Tingley Rubber Corp 1 Cragwood Rd	South Plainfield	NJ	07080	**800-631-5498***	908-757-7474
*Cust Svc					
Titmus Optical Inc 3811 Corporate Dr	Petersburg	VA	23805	**800-446-1802***	804-732-6121
*Cust Svc					
United Pioneer Co 10 W 33rd St	New York	NY	10001	**800-466-9823**	212-279-3931
US Safety Div Parmelee Industries Inc					
8101 Lenexa Dr	Lenexa	KS	66214	**800-821-5218**	913-599-5555
Uvex Safety Inc 10 Thurber Blvd	Smithfield	RI	02917	**800-343-3411**	401-232-1200
WH Salisbury & Co 7520 N Long Ave	Skokie	IL	60077	**877-406-4501**	847-679-6700
White Knight Engineered Products					
94 Glenn Bridge Rd	Arden	NC	28704	**800-743-4700**	828-687-0940
Wilshire Technologies 5861 Edison Pl	Carlsbad	CA	92008	**800-433-3340**	760-929-7200
Wolf X-Ray Corp					
420 Hempstead Tpke	West Hempstead	NY	11552	**800-356-9729***	516-485-7000
*Cust Svc					

567 PEST CONTROL SERVICES

Company / Address	City	State	ZIP	Toll-Free	Phone
Antimite Assoc Inc					
7365 Hellman Ave	Rancho Cucamonga	CA	91730	**800-675-6483**	909-483-5300
Arrow Exterminators Inc 8613 Roswell Rd	Atlanta	GA	30350	**800-281-8978**	770-993-8705
Cats USA Pest Control PO Box 151	North Hollywood	CA	91603	**800-924-3626**	818-506-1000
Copesan Services Inc 3490 N 127th St	Brookfield	WI	53005	**800-267-3726**	262-783-6261
Dodson Brothers Exterminating Co Inc					
PO Box 10249	Lynchburg	VA	24506	**800-446-0977**	434-847-9051
Ecolab Inc 370 N Wabasha St	Saint Paul	MN	55102	**800-392-3392**	651-293-2233
NYSE: ECL					
Ecolab Pest Elimination Services					
370 N Wabasha St	Saint Paul	MN	55102	**800-352-5326**	651-293-2233
Ehrlich JC Co Inc PO Box 13848	Reading	PA	19612	**800-488-9495**	610-372-9700
Fischer Environmental Service Inc					
PO Box 1319	Mandeville	LA	70471	**800-391-2565**	985-626-7378
Home Paramount Pest Control Companies Inc					
2011 Rock Spring Rd PO Box 850	Forest Hill	MD	21050	**800-492-5544**	410-510-0700
Horizon Termite & Pest Control Corp					
45 Cross Ave	Midland Park	NJ	07432	**888-612-2847**	201-447-2530
JC Ehrlich Co Inc PO Box 13848	Reading	PA	19612	**800-488-9495**	610-372-9700
Knockout Pest Control Inc 1009 Front St	Uniondale	NY	11553	**800-244-7378**	516-489-7817
Massey Services Inc 610 N Wymore Rd	Maitland	FL	32751	**800-432-1820**	407-645-2500
McCall Service Inc 2861 College St	Jacksonville	FL	32205	**800-342-6948**	904-389-5561
McCloud WB & Co					
2500 W Higgins Rd Suite 850	Hoffman Estates	IL	60195	**800-332-7805***	847-585-0650
*Cust Svc					
Orkin Exterminating Co Inc					
2170 Piedmont Rd NE	Atlanta	GA	30324	**800-346-7546**	404-888-2000
PermaTreat Pest Control Inc					
10745 Courthouse Rd	Fredericksburg	VA	22408	**800-944-8592**	540-891-7811
Presto-X Co PO Box 2578	Omaha	NE	68103	**800-759-1942**	402-554-1942
Schendel Pest Services 1824 S Kansas Ave	Topeka	KS	66612	**800-233-3956**	785-232-9357
Smithereen Exterminators Inc					
3451 Church St	Evanston	IL	60203	**800-336-3500**	847-675-0010
Terminix International Co					
860 Ridge Lake Blvd	Memphis	TN	38120	**800-654-7848**	901-766-1333
Truly Nolen of America Inc					
3636 E Speedway Blvd	Tucson	AZ	85716	**800-528-3442**	520-327-3447
Waltham Services Inc 817 Moody St	Waltham	MA	02453	**800-562-9287**	781-893-1810
WB McCloud & Co					
2500 W Higgins Rd Suite 850	Hoffman Estates	IL	60195	**800-332-7805***	847-585-0650
*Cust Svc					
Western Exterminator Co					
305 N Crescent Way	Anaheim	CA	92801	**800-640-0694**	714-517-9000

PESTICIDES

SEE Fertilizers & Pesticides

568 PET PRODUCTS

SEE ALSO Leather Goods - Personal; Livestock & Poultry Feeds - Prepared

Company / Address	City	State	ZIP	Toll-Free	Phone
American Nutrition Inc 2890 Reeves Ave	Ogden	UT	84402	**800-257-4530**	801-394-3477
Applica Consumer Products Inc					
3633 Flamingo Rd	Miramar	FL	33027	**800-231-9786***	954-883-1000
*Cust Svc					
Applica Inc 3633 Flamingo Rd	Miramar	FL	33027	**800-557-9463**	954-883-1000
NYSE: APN					
Aquatrol Inc 237-H N Euclid Way	Anaheim	CA	92801	**800-237-7735**	714-533-3381
Barr Enterprises Inc 7276 W Chickadee Rd	Greenwood	WI	54437	**800-826-2341**	715-267-6335
Bioproducts Inc 320 Springside Dr Suite 300	Fairlawn	OH	44333	**800-722-7242**	330-665-1999
BioZyme Inc 6010 Stockyards Expy	Saint Joseph	MO	64504	**800-821-3070**	816-238-3326
Central Pet 301 Island Rd	Mahwah	NJ	07430	**800-631-7724**	201-529-5050
Dad's Pet Care Inc 18746 Mill St	Meadville	PA	16335	**800-458-1801**	814-724-7710
Doane Pet Care Co					
210 Westwood Pl S Suite 400	Brentwood	TN	37027	**800-789-4639**	615-373-7774
Doctors Foster & Smith Inc					
2253 Air Pk Rd	Rhinelander	WI	54501	**800-381-7179**	715-369-3305
Doskocil Mfg Co Inc 4209 Barnett Blvd	Arlington	TX	76017	**800-433-5185**	817-467-5116
Eagle Pack Pet Foods Inc 1025 W 11th St	Mishawaka	IN	46544	**800-255-5959**	574-259-7834
Edstrom Industries Inc 819 Bakke Ave	Waterford	WI	53185	**800-558-5913**	262-534-5181
Ethical Products Inc 27 Federal Plaza	Bloomfield	NJ	07003	**800-223-7768**	973-748-8282
FL Emmert Co Inc 2007 Dunlap St	Cincinnati	OH	45214	**800-441-3343**	513-721-5808
Golden Sun Feeds Inc 1842 Hwy 4 S	Estherville	IA	51334	**800-831-5040**	712-362-3551
Great Western Pet Supply					
2001 N Black Canyon Hwy	Phoenix	AZ	85009	**800-646-3611**	602-255-0166
Hartz Mountain Corp 400 Plaza Dr	Secaucus	NJ	07094	**800-929-6700**	201-271-4800
Heath Mfg Co 140 Mill St	Coopersville	MI	49404	**800-678-8183**	616-997-8181
Hill's Pet Nutrition Inc PO Box 148	Topeka	KS	66601	**800-255-0449**	785-354-8523
Iams Co 7250 Poe Ave	Dayton	OH	45414	**800-525-4267***	937-898-7387
*Cust Svc					
John A Van Den Bosch Co 4511 Holland Ave	Holland	MI	49422	**800-968-6477***	616-848-2000
*Cust Svc					
Karem Inc 549 Karem Dr	Marshall	WI	53559	**800-655-1705**	608-655-3439
Kaytee Products Inc 521 Clay St	Chilton	WI	53014	**800-669-9580**	920-849-2321
Kennel-Aire Inc 801 E North St	Ottawa	KS	66067	**800-346-0134**	785-242-8484
Manna Pro Corp					
707 Spirit 40 Pk Dr Suite 150	Chesterfield	MO	63005	**800-690-9908**	636-681-1700
Mark Hershey Farms Inc 479 Horseshoe Pike	Lebanon	PA	17042	**888-801-3301**	717-867-4624
Masterfoods USA 800 High St	Hackettstown	NJ	07840	**800-222-0293**	908-852-1000
Merrick Pet Foods PO Box 2257	Hereford	TX	79045	**800-664-7387**	806-364-2565
MFM Industries Inc 3951 NW County Rd 329	Reddick	FL	32686	**800-922-6369***	352-854-0070
*Cust Svc					
Morning Song Wild Bird Food 4824 Tazer Dr	Lafayette	IN	47905	**800-552-2516**	765-446-1466
Moyer & Son Inc 113 E Reliance Rd	Souderton	PA	18964	**800-345-0419**	215-723-6000
Multipet International Inc					
265 W Commercial Ave	Moonachie	NJ	07074	**800-900-6738**	201-438-6600
Natural Life Pet Products Inc					
412 W Saint John St PO Box 159	Girard	KS	66743	**800-367-2391**	620-724-8012
Nestle Purina PetCare Co Checkerboard Sq	Saint Louis	MO	63164	**800-835-6369**	314-982-1000
North States Industries Inc 1507 92nd Ln NE	Blaine	MN	55449	**800-848-8421**	763-486-1754
Novalek Inc 2242 Davis Ct	Hayward	CA	94545	**800-877-7387**	510-782-4058
Nutro Products Inc 445 Wilson Way	City of Industry	CA	91744	**800-833-5330**	626-968-0532
Orrco Inc 228 W Chestnut St	Orrville	OH	44667	**800-321-3085**	330-683-5015
Pet Food Express 2131 Williams St	San Leandro	CA	94577	**877-472-7777**	510-346-7777
Pet Supermarket Inc 13700 NW 2nd St	Sunrise	FL	33325	**800-361-0049**	954-351-0834
Pet Supplies "Plus" Inc					
22670 Haggerty Rd Suite 200	Farmington Hills	MI	48335	**866-477-7747**	248-374-1900
PETCO Animal Supplies Inc 9125 Rehco Rd	San Diego	CA	92121	**877-738-6742**	858-453-7845
NASDAQ: PETC					
PetFoodDirect.com 203 Progress Dr	Montgomeryville	PA	18936	**800-865-1333***	215-699-4535
*Cust Svc					
Petland Inc 250 Riverside St	Chillicothe	OH	45601	**800-221-5935**	740-775-2464
PetMed Express Inc					
1441 SW 26th Ave	Pompano Beach	FL	33069	**800-738-6337**	954-979-5995
NASDAQ: PETS					
PETsMART Inc 19601 N 27th Ave	Phoenix	AZ	85027	**800-738-1385***	623-580-6100
NASDAQ: PETM ■ *Cust Svc					
Pied Piper Mills Inc 423 E Lake Dr	Hamlin	TX	79520	**800-338-4610**	325-576-3684
Prevue Pet Products Inc					
224 N Maplewood Ave	Chicago	IL	60612	**800-243-3624**	312-243-3624
Prince Corp 8351 County Rd H	Marshfield	WI	54449	**800-777-2486**	715-384-3105
Pro-Pet LLC 1400 McKinley Rd	Saint Marys	OH	45885	**800-245-4125**	419-394-3374
Radio Systems Corp 10427 Electric Ave	Knoxville	TN	37932	**800-732-2677***	865-777-5404
*Cust Svc					
Ralco-Mix Products Inc 1600 Hahn Rd	Marshall	MN	56258	**800-533-5306**	507-532-5748
RMC Inc 1040 S High St	Harrisonburg	VA	22801	**800-726-7625**	540-434-5333
Royal Canin USA Inc					
500 Fountain Lakes Blvd Suite 100	Saint Charles	MO	63301	**800-592-6687**	636-926-0003

				Toll-Free	Phone
Sergeant's Pet Care Products					
2637 S 158th Plaza Suite 100	Omaha	NE	68130	**800-224-7387**	402-938-7000
Simmons Allied Pet Foods Inc 1450 Hills Pl	Atlanta	GA	30318	**800-241-8504**	404-351-2400
Star Milling Co 24067 Water St	Perris	CA	92570	**800-733-6455**	951-657-3143
Sunshine Mills Inc 500 6th St SW	Red Bay	AL	35582	**800-633-3349**	256-356-9541
Tetra Holdings US Inc 3001 Commerce St	Blacksburg	VA	24060	**800-526-0650**	540-951-5400
Texas Farm Products Co					
915 S Fredonia St	Nacogdoches	TX	75961	**800-392-3110**	936-564-3711
Triumph Pet Industries Inc 7 Lake Station Rd	Warwick	NY	10990	**800-331-5144**	845-469-5125
Van Den Bosch John A Co 4511 Holland Ave	Holland	MI	49422	**800-968-6477***	616-848-2000
*Cust Svc					
Virbac Corp 3200 Meacham Blvd	Fort Worth	TX	76137	**800-338-3659**	817-831-5030
Wells Pet Food Corp 617 S 'D' St	Monmouth	IL	61462	**800-447-8435**	309-734-3121

569 PETROLEUM & PETROLEUM PRODUCTS - WHOL

				Toll-Free	Phone
Ada Resources Inc 6603 Kirbyville St	Houston	TX	77033	**800-945-6113**	713-644-2111
Agri Co-op 310 Logan St	Holdrege	NE	68949	**800-658-4089**	308-995-8626
Allied Oil & Supply Inc 2209 S 24th St	Omaha	NE	68103	**800-333-3717**	402-344-4343
Arkansas Valley Petroleum Inc					
8336 E 73rd St Suite 100	Tulsa	OK	74133	**800-888-1389**	918-252-0508
Blue Rhino Corp					
104 Cambridge Plaza Dr	Winston-Salem	NC	27104	**800-258-7466**	336-659-6900
Boncosky Oil Co Inc 739 N State St	Elgin	IL	60123	**800-628-7231**	847-741-2577
Campbell Oil Co Inc 611 Erie St S	Massillon	OH	44646	**800-589-8555**	330-833-8555
Cargill Energy PO Box 9300	Minneapolis	MN	55440	**800-227-4455**	952-742-7575
Carson Oil Co Inc 3125 NW 35th Ave	Portland	OR	97210	**800-998-7767**	503-224-8500
Castrol North America Inc 1500 Valley Rd	Wayne	NJ	07470	**800-633-6163**	973-633-2200
Colonial Oil Industries Inc PO Box 576	Savannah	GA	31402	**800-944-3835**	912-236-1331
Condon Oil Co Inc PO Box 184	Ripon	WI	54971	**800-452-1212**	920-748-3186
Drake Petroleum Co Inc PO Box 72616	Providence	RI	02907	**800-456-9427**	401-781-9900
Englefield Oil Co 447 James Pkwy	Heath	OH	43056	**800-282-1675**	740-928-8215
Evans Systems Inc PO Box 2480	Bay City	TX	77404	**800-392-6402**	979-245-2981
Ever-Ready Oil Co PO Box 25845	Albuquerque	NM	87125	**800-259-6120**	505-842-6120
Farm & Home Oil Co PO Box 389	Telford	PA	18969	**800-473-1562**	215-257-0131
Flying J Inc 1104 Country Hill Dr	Ogden	UT	84403	**800-842-6428**	801-624-1000
Global Cos LLC 800 South St Suite 200	Waltham	MA	02454	**800-685-7222**	781-894-8800
Gulf Oil LP 90 Everett Ave	Chelsea	MA	02150	**800-256-4853**	617-889-9000
Gull Industries 3404 4th Ave S	Seattle	WA	98134	**800-866-4855**	206-624-5900
Hicks Oil & Hicks Gas Inc 204 N Rt 54	Roberts	IL	60962	**800-252-6871**	217-395-2281
Inergy LP 2 Brush Creek Blvd Suite 200	Kansas City	MO	64112	**877-446-3749**	816-842-8181
NASDAQ: NRGY					
Inter City Oil Co Inc PO Box 3048	Duluth	MN	55803	**800-642-5542**	218-728-3641
Jardine Petroleum Co					
1117 N 400 East	North Salt Lake	UT	84054	**800-777-9251**	801-298-3252
JH Williams Oil Co Inc 1237 E Twiggs St	Tampa	FL	33602	**800-683-0536**	813-228-7776
Keystops LLC PO Box 2809	Franklin	KY	42135	**800-346-6456**	270-586-8283
Lakeside Oil Co Inc 555 W Brown Deer Rd	Milwaukee	WI	53217	**800-289-3835**	414-540-4000
Leffler Energy Inc PO Box 278	Richland	PA	17087	**800-222-2531**	717-866-2105
Lucky Lady Oil Co 107 NW 28th St	Fort Worth	TX	76106	**800-303-1412**	817-740-7400
Lyden Oil Co Inc 3711 Lee Harps Rd	Youngstown	OH	44515	**800-362-9410**	330-792-1100
Miller Oil Co PO Box 1858	Norfolk	VA	23501	**800-333-4645**	757-623-6600
Montour Oil Service Co					
112 Broad St PO Box 128	Montoursville	PA	17754	**800-332-8915**	570-368-8611
National Oil & Gas Inc PO Box 476	Bluffton	IN	46714	**800-322-8454**	260-824-2220
NOCO Energy Corp 2440 Sheridan Dr	Tonawanda	NY	14150	**800-500-6626**	716-874-6200
Phoenix Fuel Co Inc					
2502 N Black Canyon Hwy	Phoenix	AZ	85009	**800-444-5823**	602-278-6271
Ramos Oil Co Inc 1515 S River Rd	West Sacramento	CA	95691	**800-477-7266**	916-371-2570
Risser Oil Corp 2865 Executive Dr	Clearwater	FL	33762	**800-572-0075**	727-573-4000
Rite Way Oil & Gas Co Inc PO Box 27049	Omaha	NE	68127	**800-279-6401**	402-331-6400
River City Petroleum Inc					
PO Box 235	West Sacramento	CA	95691	**800-441-2108**	916-371-4960
Sapp Brothers Petroleum Inc					
660 S Main St	West Point	NE	68788	**800-922-0382**	402-372-5485
Sasol Wax Americas Inc					
2 Corporate Dr Suite 434	Shelton	CT	06484	**800-423-7071**	203-925-4300
Shank Services 9000 Emmott Rd Suite A	Houston	TX	77040	**800-406-3835**	713-896-4300
Shell Oil Co PO Box 2463	Houston	TX	77252	**888-467-4355**	713-241-6161
Sierra Energy					
1020 Winding Creek Rd Suite 100	Roseville	CA	95678	**800-552-0748**	916-218-1600
Silco Oil Co Inc 181 E 56th Ave Suite 600	Denver	CO	80216	**800-707-4526**	303-292-0500
Sinclair Marketing 550 E South Temple	Salt Lake City	UT	84102	**800-325-3265**	801-524-2700
Sinclair Oil Corp 550 E South Temple	Salt Lake City	UT	84102	**800-552-8695**	801-524-2700
Southern Maryland Oil Co Inc (SMO)					
6355 Crain Hwy	La Plata	MD	20646	**800-492-3420**	301-932-3600
Spencer Cos Inc 120 Woodson St NW	Huntsville	AL	35801	**800-633-2910**	256-533-1150
Sprague Energy					
2 International Dr Suite 200	Portsmouth	NH	03801	**800-225-1560**	603-431-1000
Sun Coast Resources Inc 6922 Cavalcade St	Houston	TX	77028	**800-677-3835**	713-844-9600
Tesoro Refining & Marketing Co					
3450 S 344th Way Suite 201	Auburn	WA	98001	**800-473-1123**	253-896-8700
Time Oil Co 2737 W Commodore Way	Seattle	WA	98199	**800-552-0748**	206-285-2400
Truman Arnold Cos 701 S Robison Rd	Texarkana	TX	75504	**800-243-5343**	903-794-3835
United Energy Inc					
8040 NE Sandy Blvd Suite 300	Portland	OR	97213	**800-291-1793**	503-287-4000
US Oil Co Inc 425 S Washington St	Combined Locks	WI	54113	**800-444-0202**	920-739-6101
Vesco Oil Corp 16055 W 12-Mile Rd	Southfield	MI	48076	**800-527-5358**	248-557-1600
Webber Energy Fuels 700 Main St	Bangor	ME	04401	**800-932-2371**	207-942-5501
Western Petroleum Co					
9531 W 78th St Suite 102	Eden Prairie	MN	55344	**800-972-3835**	952-941-9090
Williams JH Oil Co Inc 1237 E Twiggs St	Tampa	FL	33602	**800-683-0536**	813-228-7776
World Fuel Services Corp					
9800 NW 41st St Suite 400	Miami	FL	33178	**800-345-3818**	305-428-8000
NYSE: INT					

570 PETROLEUM REFINERIES

				Toll-Free	Phone
Calumet Lubricants Co					
2780 Waterfront Pkwy Dr E Suite 200	Indianapolis	IN	46214	**800-437-3188**	317-328-5660
Chevron Canada Ltd					
1050 W Pender St Suite 1500	Vancouver	BC	V6E3T4	**800-663-1650**	604-668-5300
Chevron Corp 6001 Bollinger Canyon Rd	San Ramon	CA	94583	**800-243-8766***	925-842-1000
NYSE: CVX ■ *Cust Svc					
CITGO Asphalt Refining Co					
620 W Germantown Pike	Plymouth Meeting	PA	19462	**800-443-4232**	484-530-4020
Cross Oil Refining & Marketing Inc					
484 E 6th St	Smackover	AR	71762	**800-725-3066**	870-881-8700
ExxonMobil Corp 5959 Las Colinas Blvd	Irving	TX	75039	**800-252-1800***	972-444-1000
NYSE: XOM ■ *Hum Res					
Farmland Industries Inc					
12200 N Ambassador Dr	Kansas City	MO	64163	**800-821-8000**	816-713-7000
Flying J Inc 1104 Country Hill Dr	Ogden	UT	84403	**800-842-6428**	801-624-1000
Giant Industries Inc 23733 N Scottsdale Rd	Scottsdale	AZ	85255	**800-937-4937**	480-585-8888
NYSE: GI					
Hunt Oil Co					
1445 Ross Ave Fountain Pl Suite 1500	Dallas	TX	75202	**800-435-7794**	214-978-8000
Imperial Oil Ltd 111 St Clair Ave W	Toronto	ON	M5W1K3	**800-567-3776**	
AMEX: IMO					
International Group Inc					
85 Old Eagle School Rd	Wayne	PA	19087	**800-852-6537**	610-687-9030
Lion Oil Co PO Box 1639	Jackson	MS	39215	**800-824-2626**	601-933-3000
Murphy Oil Corp 200 Peach St	El Dorado	AR	71730	**800-643-2364**	870-862-6411
NYSE: MUR					
Murphy Oil USA Inc 200 Peach St	El Dorado	AR	71730	**800-643-2364**	870-862-6411
Petro-Canada 150 6th Ave SW	Calgary	AB	T2P3E3	**800-668-0220**	403-296-8000
NYSE: PCZ					
Shell Oil Co PO Box 2463	Houston	TX	77252	**888-467-4355**	713-241-6161
Silver Eagle Refining 2355 S 1100 W	Woods Cross	UT	84087	**800-927-0736**	801-298-3211
Sinclair Oil Corp 550 E South Temple	Salt Lake City	UT	84102	**800-552-8695**	801-524-2700
Southland Oil Co 5170 Galaxie Dr	Jackson	MS	39206	**800-222-7630**	601-981-4151
Sunoco Inc 1801 Market St	Philadelphia	PA	19103	**800-786-6261**	215-977-3000
NYSE: SUN					
Tesoro Alaska Petroleum Co					
2700 Gambell St Suite 500	Anchorage	AK	99503	**800-478-4447**	907-561-5521
Texas Oil & Chemical Co 7752 FM 418	Silsbee	TX	77656	**800-324-1123**	409-385-1400
Ultramar Diamond Shamrock Corp					
2200 ave McGill College	Montreal	QC	H3A3L3	**800-361-4253**	514-499-6111
United Refining Co Inc 15 Bradley St	Warren	PA	16365	**800-458-6097**	814-723-1500
US Oil & Refining Co 3001 Marshall Ave	Tacoma	WA	98421	**800-424-2012**	253-383-1651
Valero Energy Corp 1 Valero Way	San Antonio	TX	78249	**800-531-7911**	210-370-2000
NYSE: VLO					
World Oil Co 9302 Garfield Ave	South Gate	CA	90280	**800-266-6551**	562-928-0100

571 PETROLEUM STORAGE TERMINALS

				Toll-Free	Phone
Gottry Corp 175 Ensminger Rd	Tonawanda	NY	14150	**800-836-6720**	716-876-3800
LBC Houston LP 11666 Port Rd	Seabrook	TX	77586	**888-922-4433**	281-474-4433
RKA Petroleum 28340 Wick Rd	Romulus	MI	48174	**800-875-3835**	734-946-2199

572 PHARMACEUTICAL COMPANIES

SEE ALSO Biotechnology Companies; Diagnostic Products; Medicinal Chemicals & Botanical Products; Pharmaceutical & Diagnostic Products - Veterinary; Pharmaceutical Companies - Generic Drugs; Vitamins & Nutritional Supplements

				Toll-Free	Phone
aaiPharma Inc 2320 Scientific Pk Dr	Wilmington	NC	28405	**800-575-4224**	910-254-7000
NASDAQ: AAIIE					
Abbott Laboratories 100 Abbott Pk Rd	Abbott Park	IL	60064	**800-323-9100**	847-937-6100
NYSE: ABT					
Abbott Laboratories Pharmaceutical Products Div 100 Abbott Park Rd	Abbott Park	IL	60064	**800-255-5162**	847-937-6100
Accucaps Industries Ltd 2125 Ambassador Dr	Windsor	ON	N9C3R5	**800-665-7210**	519-969-5404
Akorn Inc 2500 Millbrook Dr	Buffalo Grove	IL	60089	**800-932-5676**	847-279-6100
AkPharma Inc PO Box 111	Pleasantville	NJ	08232	**800-994-4711**	609-645-5100
Alcon Laboratories Inc 6201 South Fwy	Fort Worth	TX	76134	**800-757-9195**	817-293-0450
NYSE: ACL					
Allergan Canada Inc 110 Cochrane Dr	Markham	ON	L3R9S1	**800-668-6424**	905-940-1660
Allergan Inc PO Box 19534	Irvine	CA	92623	**800-347-4500**	714-246-4500
NYSE: AGN					
Allergan Inc North America Region					
PO Box 19534	Irvine	CA	92623	**800-347-4500**	714-246-4500
Allergan Inc Worldwide Operations					
PO Box 19534	Irvine	CA	92623	**800-347-4500**	714-246-4500
Alpharma Inc 1 Executive Dr	Fort Lee	NJ	07024	**800-645-4216**	201-947-7774
NYSE: ALO					
Altana Inc Savage Laboratories Div					
60 Baylis Rd	Melville	NY	11747	**800-231-0206**	631-454-7677
Alva-Amco Pharmacal Cos Inc					
7711 N Merrimac Ave	Niles	IL	60714	**800-792-2582**	847-663-0700
Amphastar Pharmaceuticals Inc					
11570 6th St	Rancho Cucamonga	CA	91730	**800-423-4136**	909-980-9484
Apotex Inc 150 Signet Dr	Weston	ON	M9L1T9	**800-268-4623**	416-749-9300
Apothecus Pharmaceutical Corp					
220 Townsend Sq	Oyster Bay	NY	11771	**800-227-2393**	516-624-8200
AstraZeneca Canada Inc					
1004 Middlegate Rd	Mississauga	ON	L4Y1M4	**800-565-5877**	905-277-7111
AstraZeneca LP PO Box 15437	Wilmington	DE	19850	**800-456-3669**	302-886-3000
NYSE: AZN					
Aventis Pharma Inc 2150 St Elzear Blvd W	Laval	QC	H7L4A8	**800-363-6364**	514-331-9220
Axcan Pharma Inc 597 Laurier Blvd	Mont-Saint-Hilaire	QC	J3H6C4	**800-565-3255**	450-467-5138
NASDAQ: AXCA					
Banner Pharmacaps Inc 4125 Premier Dr	High Point	NC	27265	**800-447-1140**	336-812-4729
Banner Pharmacaps Ltd 5807 47th Ave	Olds	AB	T4H1S7	**866-507-3483**	403-556-2531
Bausch & Lomb Inc 1 Bausch & Lomb Pl	Rochester	NY	14604	**800-344-8815**	585-338-6000
NYSE: BOL					
Bausch & Lomb Pharmaceuticals Inc					
8500 Hidden River Pkwy	Tampa	FL	33637	**800-323-0000**	813-975-7700
Bayer Corp 100 Bayer Rd	Pittsburgh	PA	15205	**800-662-2927**	412-777-2000
NYSE: BAY					
Bayer Inc 77 Belfield Rd	Toronto	ON	M9W1G6	**800-622-2937**	416-248-0771
Berlex Laboratories Inc 6 W Belt	Wayne	NJ	07470	**888-237-2394**	973-694-4100

Company	City	State	Zip	Toll-Free	Phone
Bertek Pharmaceuticals Inc 781 Chestnut Ridge Rd	Morgantown	WV	26505	**888-823-7835**	304-598-5420
Blistex Inc 1800 Swift Dr *Cust Svc	Oak Brook	IL	60523	**800-837-1800***	630-571-2870
Boehringer Ingelheim Ltd 5180 S Service Rd	Burlington	ON	L7L5H4	**800-263-9107**	905-639-0333
Boehringer Ingelheim Pharmaceuticals Inc 900 Ridgebury Rd	Ridgefield	CT	06877	**800-243-0127**	203-798-9988
Bradley Pharmaceuticals Inc 383 Rt 46 W *NYSE: BDY*	Fairfield	NJ	07004	**800-929-9300**	973-882-1505
Brioschi Inc 19-01 Pollitt Dr	Fair Lawn	NJ	07410	**800-274-6724**	201-796-4226
Bristol-Myers Squibb Canada Inc 2365 Cote de Liesse Rd	Montreal	QC	H4N2M7	**800-267-1088**	514-333-3200
Care-Tech Laboratories Inc 3224 S Kingshighway Blvd	Saint Louis	MO	63139	**800-325-9681**	314-772-4610
Carrington Laboratories Inc 2001 Walnut Hill Ln *NASDAQ: CARN* ■ *Cust Svc	Irving	TX	75038	**800-527-5216***	972-518-1300
Carter-Horner Inc 6600 Kitimat Rd	Mississauga	ON	L5N1L9	**800-387-2130**	905-826-6200
CB Fleet Inc 4615 Murray Pl PO Box 11349	Lynchburg	VA	24502	**800-999-9711**	434-528-4000
Centocor Inc 200 Great Valley Pkwy	Malvern	PA	19355	**888-874-3083**	610-651-6000
Chattem Inc 1715 W 38th St *NASDAQ: CHTT*	Chattanooga	TN	37409	**800-366-6077**	423-821-4571
Chronimed Inc 10900 Red Cir Dr Suite 300	Minnetonka	MN	55343	**800-444-5951**	952-979-3600
Cirrus Healthcare Products LLC 60 Main St PO Box 220	Cold Spring Harbor	NY	11724	**800-327-6151**	631-692-7600
Combe Inc 1101 Westchester Ave	White Plains	NY	10604	**800-873-7400**	914-694-5454
Daiichi Pharmaceutical Corp 11 Philips Pkwy	Montvale	NJ	07645	**800-374-5589**	201-573-7000
Darby Group Cos Inc 300 Jericho Quad	Jericho	NY	11753	**800-468-1001**	516-683-1800
Del Laboratories Inc 178 EAB Plaza West Tower	Uniondale	NY	11556	**800-952-5080**	516-844-2020
Dermik Laboratories Inc 1050 Westlakes Dr	Berwyn	PA	19312	**800-666-6030**	484-595-2700
Dey LP 2751 Napa Valley Corporate Dr	Napa	CA	94558	**800-869-9005**	707-224-3200
Dickinson Brands Inc 31 E High St	East Hampton	CT	06424	**888-860-2279**	860-267-2279
Doak Dermatologics 383 Rt 46 W	Fairfield	NJ	07004	**800-929-9300**	973-882-1505
Edwards Lifesciences Corp 1 Edwards Way *NYSE: EW*	Irvine	CA	92614	**800-424-3278**	949-250-2500
Eisai Inc 500 Frank W Burr Blvd Glenpointe Ctr W 5th Fl	Teaneck	NJ	07666	**888-793-4724**	201-692-1100
Eli Lilly Canada Inc 3650 Danforth Ave	Toronto	ON	M1N2E8	**800-268-4446**	416-694-3221
Eli Lilly & Co Lilly Corporate Ctr *NYSE: LLY* ■ *Prod Info	Indianapolis	IN	46285	**800-545-5979***	317-276-2000
Endo Pharmaceuticals Holdings Inc 100 Endo Blvd *NASDAQ: ENDP*	Chadds Ford	PA	19317	**800-462-3636**	610-558-9800
F & F Foods Inc 3501 W 48th Pl	Chicago	IL	60632	**800-621-0225**	773-927-3737
Ferndale Laboratories Inc 780 W Eight-Mile Rd	Ferndale	MI	48220	**800-621-6003**	248-548-0900
First Horizon Pharmaceutical Corp 6195 Shiloh Rd *NASDAQ: FHRX*	Alpharetta	GA	30005	**800-849-9707**	770-442-9707
Fleet CB Inc 4615 Murray Pl PO Box 11349	Lynchburg	VA	24502	**800-999-9711**	434-528-4000
Forest Laboratories Inc 909 3rd Ave 23rd Fl *AMEX: FRX*	New York	NY	10022	**800-947-5227**	212-421-7850
Forest Pharmaceutical Inc 13600 Shoreline Dr	Saint Louis	MO	63045	**800-678-1605**	314-493-7000
Fujisawa Canada Inc 625 Cochrane Dr Suite 1000 *Cust Svc	Markham	ON	L3R9R9	**800-888-7704***	905-470-7990
Fujisawa Healthcare 3 Parkway N	Deerfield	IL	60015	**800-888-7704**	847-317-8800
G & W Laboratories Inc 111 Coolidge St	South Plainfield	NJ	07080	**800-922-1038**	908-753-2000
Galderma Laboratories Inc 14501 N Fwy	Fort Worth	TX	76177	**800-582-8225**	817-961-5000
Germiphene Corp PO Box 1748	Brantford	ON	N3T5V7	**800-265-9931**	519-759-7100
GlaxoSmithKline PO Box 13398 *NYSE: GSK*	Research Triangle Park	NC	27709	**888-825-5249**	919-248-2100
GlycoGenesys Inc 31 St James Ave Suite 810 *NASDAQ: GLGS*	Boston	MA	02116	**800-260-6843**	617-422-0674
Hi-Tech Pharmacal Co Inc 369 Bayview Ave *NASDAQ: HITK*	Amityville	NY	11701	**800-262-9010**	631-789-8228
Hoffmann-LaRoche Inc 340 Kingsland St	Nutley	NJ	07110	**800-526-6367**	973-235-5000
Hoffmann-La Roche Ltd 2455 Meadowpine Blvd	Mississauga	ON	L5N6L7	**800-561-1759**	905-542-5555
Hope Pharmaceuticals Inc 8260 E Gelding Dr Suite 104	Scottsdale	AZ	85260	**800-755-9595**	480-607-1970
Hospira Inc 275 N Field Dr *NYSE: HSP*	Lake Forest	IL	60045	**877-946-7747**	224-212-2000
Humco Holding Group Inc 7400 Alumax Dr	Texarkana	TX	75501	**800-662-3435**	903-831-7808
Immtech International Inc 150 Fairway Dr Suite 150 *AMEX: IMM*	Vernon Hills	IL	60061	**877-898-8038**	847-573-0033
Innovative Health Products Inc 6950 Bryan Dairy Rd	Largo	FL	33777	**800-654-2347**	727-544-8866
Janssen-Ortho Inc 19 Green Belt Dr	North York	ON	M3C1L9	**800-387-8781**	416-382-5000
Janssen Pharmaceutica Inc 1125 Trenton-Harbourton Rd	Titusville	NJ	08560	**800-526-7736**	609-730-2000
Kenwood Therapeutics 383 Rt 46 W	Fairfield	NJ	07004	**800-929-9300**	973-882-1505
King Bio Pharmaceuticals Inc 3 Westside Dr	Asheville	NC	28806	**888-827-6414**	828-255-9818
King Pharmaceuticals Inc 501 5th St *NYSE: KG*	Bristol	TN	37620	**800-776-3637**	423-989-8000
Konsyl Pharmaceuticals Inc 8050 Industrial Park Rd	Easton	MD	21601	**800-356-6795**	410-822-5192
Kramer Laboratories Inc 8778 SW 8th St	Miami	FL	33174	**800-824-4894**	305-223-1287
Leiner Health Products Inc 901 E 233rd St	Carson	CA	90745	**800-421-1168**	310-835-8400
Ligand Pharmaceuticals Inc 10275 Science Ctr Dr *NASDAQ: LGND*	San Diego	CA	92121	**800-964-5793**	858-550-7500
Lilly Eli Canada Inc 3650 Danforth Ave	Toronto	ON	M1N2E8	**800-268-4446**	416-694-3221
Lilly Eli & Co Lilly Corporate Ctr *NYSE: LLY* ■ *Prod Info	Indianapolis	IN	46285	**800-545-5979***	317-276-2000
Major Pharmaceutical Co 31778 Enterprise Dr	Livonia	MI	48150	**800-521-5098**	734-525-8700
McNeil Consumer & Specialty Pharmaceuticals 7050 Camp Hill Rd	Fort Washington	PA	19034	**800-962-5357**	215-273-7000
Medicis Pharmaceutical Corp 8125 N Hayden Rd *NYSE: MRX* ■ *Cust Svc	Scottsdale	AZ	85258	**800-550-5115***	602-808-8800
Melaleuca Inc 3910 S Yellowstone Hwy *Sales	Idaho Falls	ID	83402	**800-282-3000***	208-522-0700
Mentholatum Co Inc 707 Sterling Dr	Orchard Park	NY	14127	**800-688-7660**	716-677-2500
Merck & Co Inc 1 Merck Dr PO Box 100 *NYSE: MRK* ■ *Cust Svc	Whitehouse Station	NJ	08889	**800-672-6372***	908-423-1000
Merz Pharmaceuticals Inc 4215 Tudor Ln	Greensboro	NC	27410	**800-334-0514**	336-856-2003
MGI Pharma Inc 5775 W Old Shakopee Rd Suite 100 *NASDAQ: MOGN* ■ *Orders	Bloomington	MN	55437	**800-562-4531***	952-346-4700
Mission Pharmacal PO Box 786099	San Antonio	TX	78278	**800-531-3333**	210-696-8400
Monarch Pharmaceuticals Inc 501 5th St	Bristol	TN	37620	**800-776-3637**	423-989-8000
Novartis Pharmaceuticals Canada Inc 385 boul Bouchard	Dorval	QC	H9S1A9	**800-465-2244**	514-631-6775
Novartis Pharmaceuticals Corp 1 Health Plaza *Cust Svc	East Hanover	NJ	07936	**888-669-6682***	862-778-8300
Noven Pharmaceuticals Inc 11960 SW 144th St *NASDAQ: NOVN*	Miami	FL	33186	**800-253-5099**	305-253-5099
Novo Nordisk of North America Inc 100 College Rd W	Princeton	NJ	08540	**800-727-6500**	
Novo Nordisk Pharmaceuticals Inc 100 College Rd W *Cust Svc	Princeton	NJ	08540	**800-727-6500***	609-987-5800
Numark Laboratories Inc 164 Northfield Ave	Edison	NJ	08837	**800-338-8079**	732-417-1870
Organon Inc 375 Mt Pleasant Ave	West Orange	NJ	07052	**800-631-1253**	973-325-4500
Ortho BioTech Products LP PO Box 6914 *Cust Svc	Bridgewater	NJ	08807	**800-325-7504***	908-541-4000
Parkedale Pharmaceuticals Inc 870 Parkdale Rd *Sales	Rochester	MI	48307	**800-615-5464***	248-651-9081
PDK Labs Inc 145 Ricefield Ln	Hauppauge	NY	11788	**800-221-0855**	631-273-2630
Pfizer Canada Inc 17300 TransCanada Hwy	Kirkland	QC	H9J2M5	**800-463-6001**	514-695-0500
Pfizer Canada Inc Consumer Healthcare 2200 Eglinton Ave E	Toronto	ON	M1L2N3	**800-387-6577**	416-288-2200
Pfizer Inc 235 E 42nd St *NYSE: PFE* ■ *Prod Info	New York	NY	10017	**800-733-4717***	212-573-2323
Pharmion Corp 2525 28th St Suite 200 *NASDAQ: PHRM*	Boulder	CO	80301	**866-742-7646**	720-564-9100
Pharmos Corp 99 Wood Ave S Suite 311 *NASDAQ: PARS*	Iselin	NJ	08830	**888-308-5520**	732-452-9556
Procter & Gamble Pharmaceuticals Canada Inc PO Box 355 Station A	Toronto	ON	M5W1C5	**800-668-0150**	416-730-4711
ProCyte Corp PO Box 808 *Cust Svc	Redmond	WA	98073	**888-966-1010***	425-869-1239
Prometheus Laboratories Inc 5739 Pacific Center Blvd	San Diego	CA	92121	**888-423-5227**	858-824-0895
Purdue Pharma LP 1 Stamford Forum *Cust Svc	Stamford	CT	06901	**800-877-5666***	203-588-8000
Quigley Corp 621 Shady Retreat Rd *NASDAQ: QGLY*	Doylestown	PA	18091	**877-265-3339**	215-345-0919
Quintiles Canada Inc 100 Alexis-Nihon Suite 800	Saint Laurent	QC	H4M2P4	**800-799-6166**	514-855-0888
Quintiles Transnational Corp PO Box 13979	Research Triangle Park	NC	27709	**800-875-2888**	919-998-2000
Roxane Laboratories Inc 1809 Wilson Rd *Cust Svc	Columbus	OH	43228	**800-520-1631***	614-276-4000
Savage Laboratories Div Altana Inc 60 Baylis Rd	Melville	NY	11747	**800-231-0206**	631-454-7677
Scherer Labs Inc 84 Church St Suite C	Marietta	GA	33063	**800-310-5357**	770-514-1333
Schering-Plough Corp 2000 Galloping Hill Rd *NYSE: SGP* ■ *Mktg	Kenilworth	NJ	07033	**888-793-7253***	908-298-4000
Schering-Plough HealthCare Products Corp PO Box 377 *Cust Svc	Memphis	TN	38151	**800-842-4090***	901-320-2011
Schering-Plough Pharmaceuticals 2000 Galloping Hill Rd *Mktg	Kenilworth	NJ	07033	**888-793-7253***	908-298-4000
Schwarz Pharma Inc PO Box 2038	Milwaukee	WI	53201	**800-558-5114**	262-238-5400
SciClone Pharmaceuticals Inc 901 Mariners Island Blvd Suite 205 *NASDAQ: SCLN*	San Mateo	CA	94404	**800-724-2566**	650-358-3456
Shionogi Qualicaps Inc 6505 Franz Warner Pkwy	Whitsett	NC	27377	**800-227-7853**	336-449-3900
Solvay America Inc 3333 Richmond Ave	Houston	TX	77098	**800-231-6313**	713-525-6000
Solvay Pharma Inc 60 Columbia Way Suite 102	Markham	ON	L3R0C9	**800-268-4276**	905-944-2480
Solvay Pharmaceuticals Inc 901 Sawyer Rd	Marietta	GA	30062	**800-241-1643**	770-578-9000
Somerset Pharmaceuticals Inc 2202 NW Shore Blvd Suite 450	Tampa	FL	33607	**800-892-8889**	813-288-0040
Stiefel Laboratories Inc 255 Alhambra Cir Suite 1000	Coral Gables	FL	33134	**888-784-3335**	305-443-3807
Taisho Pharmaceutical California Inc 3878 Carson St Suite 216	Torrance	CA	90503	**877-531-4559**	310-543-2035
Taro Pharmaceuticals Inc 130 East Dr	Brampton	ON	L6T1C1	**800-268-1975**	905-791-8276
UCB Pharma Inc 1950 Lake Park Dr	Smyrna	GA	30080	**800-477-7877**	770-970-7500
Upsher-Smith Laboratories Inc 6701 Evenstad Dr	Maple Grove	MN	55369	**800-328-3344**	763-473-4412
Valeant Pharmaceuticals International 3300 Hyland Ave *NYSE: VRX*	Costa Mesa	CA	92626	**800-548-5100**	714-545-0100
Vivus Inc 1172 Castro St *NASDAQ: VVUS*	Mountain View	CA	94040	**888-367-6873**	650-934-5200
Watson Pharmaceuticals Inc 311 Bonnie Cir *NYSE: WPI*	Corona	CA	92880	**800-272-5525**	951-493-5300
WF Young Inc PO Box 1990	East Longmeadow	MA	01028	**800-628-9653**	413-526-9999
Wyeth BioPharm 1 Burtt Rd	Andover	MA	01810	**800-934-5556**	978-475-9214
Wyeth Consumer Health Care International Inc 5 Giralda Farms *Cust Svc	Madison	NJ	07940	**800-322-3129***	973-660-5000
Xechem International Inc 100 Jersey Ave Bldg B Suite 310	New Brunswick	NJ	08901	**800-858-5854**	732-247-3300
ZLB Behring LLC 1020 1st Ave	King of Prussia	PA	19406	**800-683-1288**	610-878-4000

573 PHARMACEUTICAL COMPANIES - GENERIC DRUGS

SEE ALSO Biotechnology Companies; Diagnostic Products; Medicinal Chemicals & Botanical Products; Pharmaceutical & Diagnostic Products - Veterinary; Pharmaceutical Companies; Vitamins & Nutritional Supplements

Company	City	State	Zip	Toll-Free	Phone
Allerderm Laboratories Inc PO Box 9295	Phoenix	AZ	85010	**800-365-6868**	707-664-8777

Company / Address	City	State	ZIP	Toll-Free	Phone
Altana Inc 60 Baylis Rd	Melville	NY	11747	**800-645-9833**	631-454-7677
American Pharmaceutical Partners Inc 2020 Ruby St *NASDAQ: APPX*	Melrose Park	IL	60160	**800-888-7704**	708-345-6170
Andrx Corp 4955 Orange Dr *NASDAQ: ADRX*	Davie	FL	33314	**800-331-2632**	954-585-1400
Barr Pharmaceuticals Inc 2 Quaker Rd PO Box 2900 *NYSE: BRL*	Pomona	NY	10970	**800-222-4043**	845-362-1100
E Fougera & Co 60 Baylis Rd	Melville	NY	11747	**800-645-9833**	631-454-6996
Eon Labs Inc 227-15 N Conduit Ave *NASDAQ: ELAB*	Laurelton	NY	11413	**800-526-0225**	718-276-8600
Ethex Corp 10888 Metro Ct	Saint Louis	MO	63043	**800-321-1705**	314-567-3307
Fougera E & Co 60 Baylis Rd	Melville	NY	11747	**800-645-9833**	631-454-6996
Genpharm Inc 85 Advance Rd	Etobicoke	ON	M8Z2S6	**800-668-3174**	416-236-2631
Glades Pharmaceuticals Inc 6340 Sugarloaf Pkwy Suite 400	Duluth	GA	30097	**888-445-2337**	770-945-0708
Glenwood LLC 111 Cedar Ln	Englewood	NJ	07631	**800-542-0772**	201-569-0050
Healthpoint Ltd 3909 Hulen St	Fort Worth	TX	76107	**800-441-8227**	817-900-4000
Impax Laboratories Inc 3735 Castor Ave *NASDAQ: IPXL*	Philadelphia	PA	19124	**800-296-5227**	215-289-2220
IVAX Pharmaceuticals Inc 4400 Biscayne Blvd	Miami	FL	33137	**800-327-4114**	305-575-4100
Martec Pharmaceutical Inc 1800 N Topping	Kansas City	MO	64120	**800-822-6782**	816-241-4144
Mericon Industries Inc 8819 N Pioneer Rd	Peoria	IL	61615	**800-242-6464**	309-693-2150
Morton Grove Pharmaceuticals Inc 6451 Main St	Morton Grove	IL	60053	**800-346-6854**	847-967-5600
Nephron Pharmaceuticals Corp 4121 SW 34th St	Orlando	FL	32811	**800-443-4313**	407-246-1389
Par Pharmaceutical Inc 1 Ram Ridge Rd	Spring Valley	NY	10977	**800-828-9393**	845-425-7100
Pedinol Pharmacal Inc 30 Banfi Plaza N	Farmingdale	NY	11735	**800-733-4665**	631-293-9500
Perrigo Co 515 Eastern Ave *NASDAQ: PRGO*	Allegan	MI	49010	**800-253-3606**	269-673-8451
Perrigo International Inc 515 Eastern Ave	Allegan	MI	49010	**800-827-2296**	269-673-8451
Pharmics Inc PO Box 27554	Salt Lake City	UT	84127	**800-456-4138**	801-966-4138
Pliva Inc 72 Eagle Rock Ave	East Hanover	NJ	10736	**800-922-0547**	973-386-5566
Sandoz Inc 506 Carnegie Ctr Suite 400	Princeton	NJ	08540	**800-525-8747**	609-627-8500
Seneca Pharmaceutical Inc 8621 Barefoot Industrial Rd	Raleigh	NC	27617	**800-545-3701**	919-783-6936
Stada Pharmaceuticals Inc 5 Cedar Brook Dr	Cranbury	NJ	08512	**800-542-6682**	609-409-5999
Steris Laboratories Inc 620 N 51st Ave *Cust Svc	Phoenix	AZ	85043	**800-272-5525***	602-278-1400
Stratus Pharmaceuticals Inc 14377 SW 142nd St	Miami	FL	33186	**800-442-7882**	305-254-6793
Taro Pharmaceuticals USA Inc 5 Skyline Dr *NASDAQ: TARO*	Hawthorne	NY	10532	**800-544-1449**	914-345-9001
Teva Pharmaceutical USA 1090 Horsham Rd *NASDAQ: TEVA*	North Wales	PA	19454	**800-545-8800**	215-591-3000
UDL Laboratories Inc 1718 Northrock Ct	Rockford	IL	61103	**800-435-5272**	815-282-1201
USL Pharma 301 S Cherokee St	Denver	CO	80223	**800-445-8091**	303-607-4500
Warner Chilcott Laboratories 100 Enterprise Dr Rockaway 80 Corporate Ctr Suite 280	Rockaway	NJ	07866	**800-521-8813**	973-442-3200
Watson Laboratories Inc 311 Bonnie Cir	Corona	CA	92880	**800-272-5525**	951-270-1400
West-Ward Pharmaceutical Corp 465 Industrial Way W *Cust Svc	Eatontown	NJ	07724	**800-631-2174***	732-542-1191
X-Gen Pharmaceuticals Inc PO Box 445	Big Flats	NY	14814	**866-390-4411**	607-732-4411
Xanodyne Pharmaceuticals Inc 7300 Turfway Rd Suite 300	Florence	KY	41042	**877-926-6396**	859-371-6383

574 PHARMACEUTICAL & DIAGNOSTIC PRODUCTS - VETERINARY

Company / Address	City	State	ZIP	Toll-Free	Phone
Abbott Laboratories Animal Health Div 1401 Sheridan Rd	North Chicago	IL	60064	**888-299-7416**	847-937-6100
Addison Biological Laboratory Inc 507 N Cleveland Ave	Fayette	MO	65248	**800-331-2530**	660-248-2215
ADM Animal Health & Nutrition Div 1877 NE 58th Ave	Des Moines	IA	50313	**800-247-5450**	515-262-9763
Alltech Inc 3031 Catnip Hill Pike	Nicholasville	KY	40356	**800-289-8324**	859-885-9613
Alpharma Inc Animal Health Div 1 Executive Dr 3rd Fl	Fort Lee	NJ	07024	**800-834-6470**	201-947-7774
BASF Corp 3000 Continental Dr N *NYSE: BF*	Mount Olive	NJ	07828	**800-526-1072**	973-426-2600
Bell Pharmaceuticals PO Box 128	Belle Plaine	MN	56011	**800-328-5890**	952-873-2288
Bio-Serv 1 8th St Suite 1	Frenchtown	NJ	08825	**800-996-9908**	908-996-2155
Biomune Inc 8906 Rosehill Rd	Lenexa	KS	66215	**800-846-0230**	913-894-0230
Bioniche Animal Health Canada Inc 231 Dundas St E	Belleville	ON	K8N1E2	**800-265-5464**	613-966-8058
Biovet Inc 2900 ave Beaudry	Saint-Hyacinthe	QC	J2S8W2	**888-824-6838**	450-771-7291
Biovet USA Inc 3055 Old Hwy 8 Suite 100	Saint Anthony	MN	55418	**877-824-6838**	612-781-2952
Boehringer Ingelheim Vetmedica Inc 2621 N Belt Hwy	Saint Joseph	MO	64506	**800-821-7467**	816-233-2571
Cut-Heal Animal Care Products Inc 923 S Cedar Hill Rd	Cedar Hill	TX	75104	**800-288-4325**	972-293-9700
Dairy Assn Co Inc 91 Williams St	Lyndonville	VT	05851	**800-232-3610**	802-626-3610
Darby Group Cos Inc 300 Jericho Quad	Jericho	NY	11753	**800-468-1001**	516-683-1800
Dawe's Laboratories Inc 3355 N Arlington Heights Rd	Arlington Heights	IL	60004	**800-323-4317**	847-577-2020
Delmont Laboratories Inc 715 Harvard Ave PO Box 269	Swarthmore	PA	19081	**800-562-5541**	610-543-3365
DiagXotics Inc PO Box 160295	Nashville	TN	37216	**800-676-2927**	615-226-1832
Diamond Animal Health Inc 2538 SE 43rd St *Cust Svc	Des Moines	IA	50327	**800-924-8601***	515-263-8600
DMS Laboratories Inc 2 Darts Mill Rd	Flemington	NJ	08822	**800-567-4367**	908-782-3353
Dominion Veterinary Laboratories Inc 1199 Sanford St	Winnipeg	MB	R3E3A1	**800-465-7122**	204-589-7361
DVM Pharmaceuticals Inc 50 NW 176th St	Miami	FL	33169	**800-367-4902**	305-575-6950
EVSCO Pharmaceuticals Div IGI Inc 101 Lincoln Ave	Buena	NJ	08310	**800-387-2607**	
Farnam Cos Inc PO Box 34820	Phoenix	AZ	85067	**800-234-2269**	602-285-1660
Fort Dodge Animal Health 9225 Indian Creek Pkwy Bldg 32 Suite 400	Overland Park	KS	66210	**800-477-1365**	913-664-7000
Heska Corp 2601 Midpoint Dr Suite D *NASDAQ: HSKA*	Fort Collins	CO	80525	**800-464-3752**	970-493-7272
IDEXX Pharmaceuticals Inc 1 Idexx Dr	Westbrook	ME	04092	**800-548-6733**	207-856-0300
IMMVAC Inc 6080 Bass Ln	Columbia	MO	65201	**800-944-7563**	573-443-5363
Ivy Animal Health Inc 8857 Bond St	Overland Park	KS	66214	**800-828-2192**	913-888-2192
King Bio Pharmaceuticals Inc 3 Westside Dr	Asheville	NC	28806	**888-827-6414**	828-255-9818
Lake Immunogenics Inc 348 Berg Rd	Ontario	NY	14519	**800-648-9990**	585-265-1973
Lloyd Inc 604 W Thomas Ave	Shenandoah	IA	51601	**800-831-0004**	712-246-4000
Luitpold Pharmaceuticals Inc 1 Luitpold Dr PO Box 9001	Shirley	NY	11967	**800-645-1706**	631-924-4000
MVP Laboratories Inc 5510 Miller Ave	Ralston	NE	68127	**800-856-4648**	402-331-5106
Nelson Laboratories Ltd 4001 N Lewis Ave	Sioux Falls	SD	57104	**800-843-3322**	605-336-2451
Novartis Animal Vaccine 1447 140th St	Larchwood	IA	51241	**800-843-3386**	712-477-2811
Nutra-Blend Inc 3200 E 2nd St	Neosho	MO	64850	**800-657-5657**	417-451-6111
PM Resources Inc 13001 St Charles Rock Rd *Cust Svc	Bridgeton	MO	63044	**800-447-5463***	314-291-6720
Qualis Inc 4600 Park Ave	Des Moines	IA	50321	**800-334-4514**	515-243-3000
Schering-Plough Corp Animal Health Div 1095 Morris Ave *Cust Svc	Union	NJ	07083	**800-521-5767***	908-298-4000
Synbiotics Corp 11011 Via Frontera	San Diego	CA	92127	**800-228-4305**	858-451-3771
Texas Vet Lab Inc 1702 N Bell St	San Angelo	TX	76903	**800-284-8403**	325-653-4505
Thomas Veterinary Drug 9165 W VanBuren St	Tolleson	AZ	85353	**800-359-8387**	623-936-3363
TW Medical Veterinary Supply 3610 Lohman Ford Rd	Lago Vista	TX	78645	**888-787-4483**	512-267-8800
Veterinary Pharmacies of America 2854 Antoine Dr	Houston	TX	77092	**877-838-7979**	713-688-3321
VetLife 1001 Office Pk Rd Suite 201	West Des Moines	IA	50265	**888-462-3493**	515-224-0788
Vetoquinol Canada Inc 2000 ch Georges	Lavaltrie	QC	J0K1H0	**800-363-1700**	450-586-2252
Vetoquinol EVSCO Pharmaceuticals 101 Lincoln Ave	Buena	NJ	08310	**800-387-2607**	
VetriCare 590 Main St Suite B	Templeton	CA	93465	**800-238-5999**	805-434-5999
WA Butler Co 5600 Blazer Pkwy	Dublin	OH	43017	**800-848-5983**	614-761-9095
Wildlife Pharmaceuticals Inc 1635 Blue Spruce Dr Suite 202	Fort Collins	CO	80524	**877-883-9283**	970-484-6267
Wyeth Corp Fort Dodge Animal Health Div 9225 Indian Creek Pkwy Bldg 32 Suite 400	Overland Park	KS	66210	**800-477-1365**	913-664-7000

575 PHARMACY BENEFITS MANAGEMENT SERVICES

Company / Address	City	State	ZIP	Toll-Free	Phone
Aetna US Healthcare Pharmacy Management 11100 Wayzata Blvd Suite 400 MC F615	Minnetonka	MN	55035	**800-872-3862**	952-594-6250
AmeriScript Inc 4301 Darrow Rd	Stow	OH	44224	**800-681-6912**	330-686-7000
BeneScript Services Inc 3720 DaVinci Ct Suite 200	Norcross	GA	30092	**800-345-3189**	770-448-4344
BioScrip Inc 100 Clearbrook Rd *NASDAQ: BIOS*	Elmsford	NY	10523	**888-818-3939**	914-460-1600
Caremark Rx Inc 211 Commerce St Suite 800 *NYSE: CMX*	Nashville	TN	37201	**800-633-9509**	615-743-6600
CuraScript Pharmacy Inc 6272 Lee Vista Blvd	Orlando	FL	32822	**800-950-2840**	407-852-4903
Express Scripts Inc 13900 Riverport Dr *NASDAQ: ESRX*	Maryland Heights	MO	63043	**800-332-5455**	314-770-1666
First Health Services Corp 4300 Cox Rd	Glen Allen	VA	23060	**800-884-2822**	804-965-7400
Health Resources Inc 10 E Baltimore St Suite 1404	Baltimore	MD	21202	**800-932-4648**	410-347-1540
Maxor National Pharmacy Services Corp 320 S Polk St Suite 100	Amarillo	TX	79101	**800-658-6146**	806-324-5400
Medco Health Solutions Inc 100 Parsons Pond Dr *NYSE: MHS* ■ *Cust Svc	Franklin Lakes	NJ	07417	**800-248-2268***	201-269-3400
MedImpact Healthcare Systems Inc 10680 Treena St Suite 500	San Diego	CA	92131	**800-788-2949**	858-566-2727
National Medical Health Card Systems Inc DBA NMHCrx Pharmacy Benefits Manager 26 Harbor Park Dr *NASDAQ: NMHC*	Port Washington	NY	11050	**800-645-3332**	516-626-0007
National Prescription Administrators Inc 711 Ridgedale Ave	East Hanover	NJ	07936	**800-526-7813**	973-503-1000
NMHCrx Pharmacy Benefits Manager 26 Harbor Park Dr *NASDAQ: NMHC*	Port Washington	NY	11050	**800-645-3332**	516-626-0007
PharmaCare Management Services Inc 695 George Washington Hwy	Lincoln	RI	02865	**800-237-6184**	401-334-0069
Pharmaceutical Care Network 9343 Tech Center Dr Suite 200	Sacramento	CA	95826	**800-777-9216**	916-361-4400
Prescription Solutions 3515 Harbor Blvd	Costa Mesa	CA	92626	**800-562-6223**	714-825-3600
Prime Therapeutics Inc 1020 Discovery Rd Suite 100	Eagan	MN	55121	**800-858-0723**	651-286-4000
RESTAT 724 Elm St *Cust Svc	West Bend	WI	53095	**800-248-1062***	262-338-5760
RxAmerica LLC 221 N Charles Lindbergh Dr	Salt Lake City	UT	84116	**800-770-8014**	801-961-6000
Script Care Inc 6380 Folsom Dr	Beaumont	TX	77706	**800-880-9902**	409-833-9061
ScriptSave 333 E Wetmore Rd 4th Fl	Tucson	AZ	85705	**800-347-5985**	520-888-8070
Serve You Custom Prescription Management 9051 W Heather Ave	Milwaukee	WI	53224	**888-243-6890**	414-410-8100
WellPoint Pharmacy Management 8407 Fallbrook Ave	West Hills	CA	91304	**800-700-2533**	

576 PHARMACY MANAGEMENT SERVICES

Company / Address	City	State	ZIP	Toll-Free	Phone
Accredo Health Inc 1640 Century Center Pkwy Suite 101 *NASDAQ: ACDO*	Memphis	TN	38134	**877-222-7336**	901-385-3688
Compscript Inc 1225 Broken Sound Pkwy NW Suite A	Boca Raton	FL	33487	**800-832-8585**	561-994-8585
McKesson Health Systems 1 Post St	San Francisco	CA	94104	**800-571-2889**	415-983-8300
McKesson Medication Management 7115 Northland Terr Suite 500	Brooklyn Park	MN	55428	**877-806-7888**	763-354-1200

Classified Section

	City	State	ZIP	Toll-Free	Phone
MedExpress Pharmacy Ltd 1431 W Innes St	Salisbury	NC	28144	**800-808-8060**	704-633-3113
NeighborCare Inc 7 E Lee St	Baltimore	MD	21202	**888-872-3030**	410-752-2600
NASDAQ: NCRX					
Omnicare Inc					
100 E RiverCenter Blvd Suite 1600	Covington	KY	41011	**800-342-5627**	859-392-3300
NYSE: OCR					
PharMerica Inc 175 Kelsey Ln	Tampa	FL	33619	**800-237-7676**	877-975-2273
Priority Healthcare Corp					
250 Technology Pk Suite 124	Lake Mary	FL	32746	**800-942-5999**	407-804-6700
NASDAQ: PHCC					

577 PHOTO PROCESSING & STORAGE

	City	State	ZIP	Toll-Free	Phone
ABC Photo & Imaging Services Inc					
9016 Prince William St	Manassas	VA	20110	**800-368-4044**	703-369-2566
Advanced Photographic Solutions LLC					
1525 Hardeman Ln NE	Cleveland	TN	37312	**800-241-9234**	423-479-5481
Burrell Professional Labs					
1311 Merrillville Rd	Crown Point	IN	46307	**800-348-8732**	219-663-3210
Candid Color Systems Inc					
1300 Metropolitan Ave	Oklahoma City	OK	73108	**800-336-4550**	405-947-8747
Dale Laboratories 2960 Simms St	Hollywood	FL	33020	**800-327-1776**	954-925-0103
Express Digital Graphics Inc DBA					
PhotoReflect 9780 Mt Pyramid Ct					
Suite 120	Englewood	CO	80112	**888-584-0089**	303-790-1004
FLM Graphics 123 Lehigh Dr	Fairfield	NJ	07004	**800-257-9757**	973-575-9450
FotoTime Inc 6711 Atlanta Dr	Colleyville	TX	76034	**888-705-0389**	469-361-3441
Fujicolor Processing Inc 174 S Main St	Mansfield	OH	44902	**800-558-1678**	419-525-1678
H & H Color Lab Inc 8906 E 67th St	Raytown	MO	64133	**800-821-1305**	816-358-6677
McKenna Professional Imaging Inc					
2815 Falls Ave	Waterloo	IA	50701	**800-238-3456**	319-235-6265
Meisel Visual Imaging 433 Regal Row	Dallas	TX	75247	**800-527-5186**	214-688-4900
Moto Photo Inc 4444 Lake Center Dr	Dayton	OH	45426	**800-733-6686**	937-854-6686
Mystic Color Lab Inc					
Masons Island Rd PO Box 144	Mystic	CT	06355	**800-367-6061**	
Ofoto Inc 1480 64th St Suite 300	Emeryville	CA	94608	**800-360-9098**	510-229-1200
Photo USA 3736 Franklin Rd	Roanoke	VA	24014	**888-234-6320**	540-344-0961
PhotoFun.com Inc 10201 E Cholla St	Scottsdale	AZ	85260	**888-746-8638**	
PhotoWorks Inc 1260 16th Ave W	Seattle	WA	98119	**800-345-6967**	206-281-1390
Prolab Visual Imaging Services Inc					
123 NW 36th St	Seattle	WA	98107	**800-426-6770**	206-547-5447
Reliance Color Labs Inc PO Box 3640	Hampton Park	MD	20791	**800-332-6567**	
Yahoo! Photos 701 1st Ave	Sunnyvale	CA	94089	**888-267-7574**	408-349-3300

578 PHOTOCOPYING EQUIPMENT

SEE ALSO Business Machines - Whol

	City	State	ZIP	Toll-Free	Phone
Brother International Corp					
100 Somerset Corporate Blvd	Bridgewater	NJ	08807	**800-276-7746***	908-704-1700
*Cust Svc					
Canon USA Inc 1 Canon Plaza	Lake Success	NY	11042	**800-828-4040**	516-488-6700
NYSE: CAJ					
Daisy Wheel Ribbon Co Inc					
10742 Edison Ct	Rancho Cucamonga	CA	91730	**800-266-5585**	909-989-5585
Dietzgen 250 S Northwest Hwy Suite 203	Park Ridge	IL	60068	**800-473-1270***	800-473-1200
*Cust Svc					
Eastman Kodak Co 343 State St	Rochester	NY	14650	**800-242-2424**	585-724-4000
NYSE: EK					
Kodak Co 343 State St	Rochester	NY	14650	**800-242-2424**	585-724-4000
NYSE: EK					
Konica Minolta Business Solutions					
500 Day Hill Rd	Windsor	CT	06095	**800-456-6422**	860-683-2222
Konica Minolta Photo Imaging USA Inc					
725 Darlington Ave	Mahwah	NJ	07430	**800-285-6422**	201-574-4000
Oce-USA Inc 5450 N Cumberland Ave 6th Fl	Chicago	IL	60656	**800-877-6232**	773-714-8500
Pitney Bowes Inc 1 Elmcroft Rd	Stamford	CT	06926	**800-672-6937**	203-356-5000
NYSE: PBI					
Ricoh Corp 5 Dedrick Pl	West Caldwell	NJ	07006	**800-637-4264**	973-882-2000
Samsung Electronics America Inc					
105 Challenger Rd	Ridgefield Park	NJ	07660	**800-726-7864**	201-229-4000
Sharp Electronics Corp 1 Sharp Plaza	Mahwah	NJ	07430	**800-237-4277**	201-529-8200
Toshiba America Inc					
1251 Ave of the Americas 41st Fl	New York	NY	10020	**800-457-7777**	212-596-0600
Xerox Canada Inc 5650 Yonge St	North York	ON	M2M4G7	**800-275-9376**	416-229-3769
Xerox Corp 800 Long Ridge Rd	Stamford	CT	06904	**800-842-0024**	203-968-3000
NYSE: XRX					

579 PHOTOGRAPH STUDIOS - PORTRAIT

	City	State	ZIP	Toll-Free	Phone
Bryn-Alan Studios Inc 606 W Kennedy Blvd	Tampa	FL	33606	**800-749-2796**	813-253-2891
CPI Corp 1706 Washington Ave	Saint Louis	MO	63103	**800-669-9699**	314-231-1575
NYSE: CPY					
Glamour Shots 1300 Metropolitan Ave	Oklahoma City	OK	73108	**800-336-4550**	
Jostens Inc 5501 American Blvd W	Minneapolis	MN	55437	**800-235-4774**	952-830-3300
Olan Mills Inc Box 23456	Chattanooga	TN	37422	**800-251-6320**	423-622-5141
PCA International Inc					
815 Mathews Mint Hill Rd	Matthews	NC	28105	**877-763-4456***	704-847-8011
*Cust Svc					
Picture People 1157 Triton Dr Suite B	Foster City	CA	94404	**800-827-4686**	650-578-9291
Root Studios Inc 1131 W Sheridan Rd	Chicago	IL	60660	**800-962-8089**	773-761-5500
Shugart Studios Inc 812 College Ave	Levelland	TX	79336	**800-888-4322**	806-894-4322

580 PHOTOGRAPHIC EQUIPMENT & SUPPLIES

SEE ALSO Cameras & Related Supplies - Retail

	City	State	ZIP	Toll-Free	Phone
3M Meeting & Presentation Solutions Div					
6801 River Place Blvd 3M Austin Ctr	Austin	TX	78726	**800-328-1371**	
AFP Imaging Corp 250 Clearbrook Rd	Elmsford	NY	10523	**800-592-6666**	914-592-6100
Agfa Corp 100 Challenger Rd	Ridgefield Park	NJ	07660	**800-581-2432**	201-440-2500
Alan Gordon Enterprises Inc					
5625 Melrose Ave	Hollywood	CA	90038	**800-825-6684**	323-466-3561
Apollo Presentation Products					
300 Tower Pkwy	Lincolnshire	IL	60069	**800-777-3750**	
Avant Inc 238 Bemis Rd	Fitchburg	MA	01420	**800-433-6843**	978-345-8200
Ballantyne of Omaha Inc 4350 McKinley St	Omaha	NE	68112	**800-262-5016**	402-453-4444
BenQ America Corp 53 Discovery	Irvine	CA	92618	**866-600-2367**	949-255-9500
Beta Screen Corp 707 Commercial Ave	Carlstadt	NJ	07072	**800-272-7336**	201-939-2400
Blue Grass Chemical Specialties LP					
895 Industrial Blvd	New Albany	IN	47150	**800-638-7197**	812-948-1115
Boxlight Corp					
19472 Powder Hill Pl NE Suite 100	Poulsbo	WA	98370	**800-762-5757**	360-779-7901
Burgess Industries Inc 2700 Campus Dr	Plymouth	MN	55441	**800-233-2589***	763-553-7800
*Cust Svc					
Canon Consumer Imaging & Information Systems					
Group 15955 Alton Pkwy	Irvine	CA	92618	**800-848-4123***	949-753-4000
*Sales					
Canon USA Inc 1 Canon Plaza	Lake Success	NY	11042	**800-828-4040**	516-488-6700
NYSE: CAJ					
Carr Corp 1547 11th St	Santa Monica	CA	90401	**800-952-2398**	310-587-1113
Ceiva Logic Inc 214 E Magnolia Blvd	Burbank	CA	91502	**877-693-7263***	818-562-1495
*Tech Supp					
Century Precision Optics 7701 Haskell Ave	Van Nuys	CA	91406	**800-228-1254**	818-766-3715
Champion Photochemistry					
1760 Meyerside Dr	Mississauga	ON	L5T1A3	**800-387-3430**	905-670-7900
Charles Beseler Co 1501 Oakland Ave	Millville	NJ	08332	**800-237-3537**	
Concord Camera Corp					
4000 Hollywood Blvd Suite 650N	Hollywood	FL	33021	**800-339-4215**	954-331-4200
NASDAQ: LENS					
Da-Lite Screen Co Inc 3100 N Detroit St	Warsaw	IN	46581	**800-622-3737**	574-267-8101
Draper Shade & Screen Co 411 S Pearl St	Spiceland	IN	47385	**800-238-7999**	765-987-7999
DRS Hadland Inc					
4000 Moorpark Ave Suite 110	San Jose	CA	95117	**800-248-4686**	408-244-0901
Ducommun Technologies Inc					
23301 Wilmington Ave	Carson	CA	90745	**800-421-5032**	310-513-7200
Dycam Inc					
22425 Ventura Blvd Suite 12	Woodland Hills	CA	91364	**800-883-9226**	818-998-8008
Eastman Kodak Co 343 State St	Rochester	NY	14650	**800-242-2424**	585-724-4000
NYSE: EK					
Eastman Kodak Co Commercial & Government					
Systems Div 1447 Saint Paul St	Rochester	NY	14653	**800-698-3324**	
Eastman Kodak Co Digital & Applied Imaging					
Div 343 State St	Rochester	NY	14650	**800-242-2424**	800-698-3324
Eastman Kodak Co Kodak Professional Div					
343 State St	Rochester	NY	14650	**800-242-2424**	800-698-3324
Eastman Kodak Co Professional Motion					
Imaging Div 343 State St	Rochester	NY	14650	**800-621-3456**	800-698-3324
Epson America Inc					
3840 Kilroy Airport Way	Long Beach	CA	90806	**800-533-3731***	562-981-3840
*Cust Svc					
Fuji Photo Film USA Inc 200 Summit Lake Dr	Valhalla	NY	10595	**800-755-3854**	914-789-8100
Gordon Alan Enterprises Inc					
5625 Melrose Ave	Hollywood	CA	90038	**800-825-6684**	323-466-3561
Identatronics Inc 165 Lively Blvd	Elk Grove Village	IL	60007	**800-323-5403***	847-437-2654
*Cust Svc					
InFocus Corp 27700-B SW Parkway Ave	Wilsonville	OR	97070	**800-294-6400**	503-685-8888
NASDAQ: INFS					
Joseph Merritt & Co 650 Franklin Ave	Hartford	CT	06114	**800-344-4477**	860-296-2500
Kodak Co 343 State St	Rochester	NY	14650	**800-242-2424**	585-724-4000
NYSE: EK					
Konica Minolta Graphic Imaging USA Inc					
71 Charles St	Glen Cove	NY	11542	**800-645-6252**	516-674-2500
Konica Minolta Photo Imaging USA Inc					
725 Darlington Ave	Mahwah	NJ	07430	**800-285-6422**	201-574-4000
Kyocera Optics Inc 2301-200 Cottontail Ln	Somerset	NJ	08873	**800-526-0266***	732-560-0060
*Cust Svc					
Merritt Joseph & Co 650 Franklin Ave	Hartford	CT	06114	**800-344-4477**	860-296-2500
Navitar Inc 200 Commerce Dr	Rochester	NY	14623	**800-828-6778***	585-359-4000
*Cust Svc					
NEC Solutions (America) Inc					
1250 N Arlington Heights Rd Suite 400	Itasca	IL	60143	**800-632-4636**	630-467-5000
Neumade Products Corp 30-40 Pecks Ln	Newtown	CT	06470	**800-645-6687**	203-270-1100
Neumade Products Corp Xetron Div					
30-40 Pecks Ln	Newtown	CT	06470	**800-526-0722**	203-270-1100
Nikon Inc 1300 Walt Whitman Rd	Melville	NY	11747	**800-645-6687***	631-547-4200
*Cust Svc					
Olympus America Inc 2 Corporate Ctr Dr	Melville	NY	11747	**800-446-5967**	631-844-5000
Owen Mfg Inc PO Box 398	Owen	WI	54460	**800-524-0105**	715-229-2123
Panavision Inc 6219 DeSoto Ave	Woodland Hills	CA	91367	**800-367-7262**	818-316-1000
Pentax Imaging Co 600 12th St Suite 300	Golden	CO	80401	**800-543-6144**	303-799-8000
Phase One Inc 200 Broadhollow Rd Suite 312	Melville	NY	11747	**888-742-7366**	631-757-0400
Photo Control Corp 4800 Quebec Ave N	Minneapolis	MN	55428	**800-787-8078**	763-537-3601
NASDAQ: PHOC					
Pic-Mount Imaging Corp					
2300 Arrowhead Dr	Carson City	NV	89706	**800-458-6875**	775-887-5100
Pictorvision 7701 Haskel Ave Suite B	Van Nuys	CA	91406	**800-876-5583**	818-785-9881
Polaroid Corp 1265 Main St Suite W-7	Waltham	MA	02451	**800-343-5000***	781-386-2000
*Cust Svc					
QuickSet International Inc					
3650 Woodhead Dr	Northbrook	IL	60062	**800-247-6563***	847-498-0700
*Orders					
Redlake MASD Inc 5295 Ferris Sq Suite A	San Diego	CA	92121	**800-453-1223**	858-481-8182
Reprogrphics Once Inc 36060 Industrial Rd	Livonia	MI	48150	**800-968-7788**	734-542-8800
Research Technology International Inc					
4700 W Chase Ave	Lincolnwood	IL	60712	**800-323-7520***	847-677-3000
*Sales					
Ricoh Corp 5 Dedrick Pl	West Caldwell	NJ	07006	**800-637-4264**	973-882-2000
Sharp Electronics Corp 1 Sharp Plaza	Mahwah	NJ	07430	**800-237-4277**	201-529-8200
Sony Corp of America 550 Madison Ave	New York	NY	10022	**800-282-2848**	212-833-6800
Stewart Filmscreen Corp					
1161 W Sepulveda Blvd	Torrance	CA	90502	**800-762-4999**	310-326-1422
Tatung Co of America Inc					
2850 El Presidio St	Long Beach	CA	90810	**800-827-2850**	310-637-2105

Company / Address	City	State	ZIP	Toll-Free	Phone
Tiffen Mfg Corp 90 Oser Ave	Hauppauge	NY	11788	**800-645-2522**	631-273-2500
Toshiba America Inc 1251 Ave of the Americas 41st Fl	New York	NY	10020	**800-457-7777**	212-596-0600
Toshiba America Information Systems Inc 9740 Irvine Blvd. *Cust Svc	Irvine	CA	92618	**800-457-7777***	949-583-3000
Visual Departures Ltd PO Box 1326	Passaic	NJ	07055	**800-628-2003**	973-405-6455
Vutec Corp 2741 NE 4th Ave	Pompano Beach	FL	33064	**800-770-4700**	954-545-9000
Wolf X-Ray Corp 420 Hempstead Tpke *Cust Svc	West Hempstead	NY	11552	**800-356-9729***	516-485-7000
X-Rite Inc 3100 44th St SW *NASDAQ: XRIT*	Grandville	MI	49418	**800-248-9748**	616-534-7664
Xetron Div Neumade Products Corp 30-40 Pecks Ln	Newtown	CT	06470	**800-526-0722**	203-270-1100

581 PHOTOGRAPHY - COMMERCIAL

Company / Address	City	State	ZIP	Toll-Free	Phone
Kreber Enterprises 221 Swathmore Ave	High Point	NC	27263	**800-775-3801**	336-861-2700
Modernage Photo Service Inc 1381 E 6th St	Los Angeles	CA	90021	**800-974-3686**	213-628-8194
Sports Section Inc 2150 Boggs Rd Suite 200	Duluth	GA	30096	**800-321-9127**	770-622-4900
Universal Convention Photography Inc 7121 Grand National Dr Suite 104	Orlando	FL	32819	**800-553-5499**	407-352-5302

582 PHOTOGRAPHY - STOCK

Company / Address	City	State	ZIP	Toll-Free	Phone
Alaska Stock Images 2505 Fairbanks St	Anchorage	AK	99503	**800-487-4285**	907-276-1343
Bruce Coleman Inc 117 E 24th St 5th Fl	New York	NY	10010	**800-942-7917**	212-979-6252
Coleman Bruce Inc 117 E 24th St 5th Fl	New York	NY	10010	**800-942-7917**	212-979-6252
Comstock Images Inc 244 Sheffield St	Mountainside	NJ	07092	**800-225-2727**	908-518-6200
Corbis Corp 710 2nd Ave Suite 200	Seattle	WA	98104	**800-260-0444**	206-373-6000
Custom Medical Stock Photo Inc 3660 W Irving Park Rd	Chicago	IL	60618	**800-373-2677**	773-267-3100
Film & Video Stock Shots 10442 Burbank Blvd.	North Hollywood	CA	91601	**888-436-6824**	818-760-2098
Great American Stock 5200 Pasadena Ave Suite C	Albuquerque	NM	87113	**800-624-5834**	505-892-7747
Image Works 1679 Rt 212	Woodstock	NY	12498	**800-475-8801**	845-679-8500
ImageState New York 29 E 19th St 4th Fl	New York	NY	10003	**800-821-9600**	212-505-2500
Index Stock Imagery Inc 23 W 18th St 3rd Fl.	New York	NY	10011	**800-729-7466**	212-929-4644
Ink Jet Art Solutions Inc 346 S 500 East Suite 200	Salt Lake City	UT	84102	**800-777-2076**	801-363-9700
Midwestock 9218 Metcalf Suite 145	Overland Park	KS	66212	**800-474-9974**	816-474-0229
Photo Researchers Inc 60 E 56th St	New York	NY	10022	**800-833-9033**	212-758-3420
Photo Resource Hawaii 111 Hekili St Suite 241	Kailua	HI	96734	**888-599-7773**	808-599-7773
Photri 3701 S George Mason Dr Suite C-2N	Falls Church	VA	22041	**800-544-0385**	703-931-8600
Picture Arts 99 Pasadena Ave	South Pasadena	CA	91030	**800-720-9755**	323-257-4400
PictureQuest 8280 Greensboro Dr Suite 520	McLean	VA	22102	**800-764-7427**	
Picturesque Stock Photo Agency 1520-3 Brookside Dr	Raleigh	NC	27604	**800-450-3377**	919-828-0023
PunchStock 8517 Excelsior Dr Suite 200	Madison	WI	53717	**800-390-0461**	608-828-2700
Rainbow 61 Entrada	Santa Fe	NM	87507	**800-810-3686**	505-820-3434
Stockyard Photos 1410 Hutchins St.	Houston	TX	77003	**800-238-4105**	713-520-0898

583 PIECE GOODS & NOTIONS

SEE ALSO Fabric Stores

Company / Address	City	State	ZIP	Toll-Free	Phone
A Meyers & Sons Corp 325 W 38th St.	New York	NY	10018	**800-666-5577**	212-279-6632
Allen Robert Fabrics Inc 55 Cabot Blvd.	Mansfield	MA	02048	**800-333-3777**	508-339-9151
Aplix Inc PO Box 7505	Charlotte	NC	28241	**800-438-0424**	704-588-1920
B Berger Co 1380 Highland Rd. *Cust Svc	Macedonia	OH	44056	**800-288-8400***	330-425-3838
Barrow Industries 3 Edgewater Dr	Norwood	MA	02062	**800-332-2776**	781-828-6750
Blank Textiles Inc 2 Bridge St Suite 220	Irvington	NY	10533	**800-237-3717**	914-478-3100
Blumenthal Lansing Co 1 Palmer Terr	Carlstadt	NJ	07072	**800-448-9749**	201-935-6220
Brookwood Cos Inc 232 Madison Ave 10th Fl.	New York	NY	10016	**800-426-5468**	212-551-0100
Brunschwig & Fils 75 Virginia Rd	North White Plains	NY	10603	**800-538-8280**	914-684-5800
Burch Fabrics Group 4200 Brockton Dr SE	Grand Rapids	MI	49512	**800-841-8111**	616-698-2800
Carolyn Fabrics Inc 1948 W Green Dr	High Point	NC	27261	**800-333-8400**	336-887-3101
Custom Metal Crafters Inc 815 N Mountain Rd	Newington	CT	06111	**800-262-3140**	860-953-4210
Dunlap Industries Inc PO Box 459	Dunlap	TN	37327	**800-251-7214**	423-949-4021
Duralee Fabrics Ltd Inc 1775 5th Ave *Cust Svc	Bay Shore	NY	11706	**800-275-3872***	631-273-8800
EE Schenck Co PO Box 5200	Portland	OR	97208	**800-433-0722**	503-284-4124
Glick Textiles Inc 2327 SW Fwy	Houston	TX	77098	**800-231-7246**	713-942-9191
Haber Fabrics Corp 1745 Hayden Dr	Carrollton	TX	75006	**800-527-1980**	972-416-8479
Hanes Industries 500 N McLin Creek Rd	Conover	NC	28613	**800-438-9124**	828-464-4673
Hoffman California Fabrics Inc 25792 Obrero Dr	Mission Viejo	CA	92691	**800-547-0100**	949-770-2922
Ideal Fastener Corp PO Box 548	Oxford	NC	27565	**800-334-6653**	919-693-3115
Janlynn Corp 2070 Westover Rd	Chicopee	MA	01022	**800-445-5565**	413-206-0002
JHB International Inc 1955 S Quince St	Denver	CO	80247	**800-525-9007**	303-751-8100
John K Burch Co 4200 Brockton Dr SE	Grand Rapids	MI	49512	**800-841-8111**	616-698-2800
Komar Apparel Supply Co LLC 6900 Washington Blvd.	Montebello	CA	90640	**800-872-7397**	323-890-3000
Kravet Fabrics Inc 225 Central Ave S *Cust Svc	Bethpage	NY	11714	**800-648-5728***	516-293-2000
Logantex Inc 70 W 36th St Suite 1001	New York	NY	10018	**800-223-2004**	212-221-3900
Maharam 45 Rasons Ct.	Hauppauge	NY	11788	**800-645-3943**	631-582-3434
Mainzer Minton Co Inc 144 Main St	Hackettstown	NJ	07840	**800-944-7632**	908-979-0800
Marcus Brothers Textiles Inc 980 Ave of the Americas	New York	NY	10018	**800-548-8295**	212-354-8700
McKee Button Co Inc PO Box 230 *Cust Svc	Muscatine	IA	52761	**800-553-9662***	563-263-2421
Meyers A & Sons Corp 325 W 38th St.	New York	NY	10018	**800-666-5577**	212-279-6632
Peachtree Fabrics Inc 1400 English St	Atlanta	GA	30318	**800-732-2437**	404-351-5400
Prym-Dritz Corp 950 Brisack Rd *Cust Svc	Spartanburg	SC	29303	**800-255-7796***	864-576-5050
Robert Allen Fabrics Inc 55 Cabot Blvd.	Mansfield	MA	02048	**800-333-3777**	508-339-9151
Saint Louis Trimming Div Trimtex 400 Park Ave	Williamsport	PA	17701	**800-326-9135**	570-326-9135
Sanderson & Sons Ltd 285 Grand Ave 3 Patriot Ctr	Englewood	NJ	07631	**800-894-6185**	201-894-8400
Schenck EE Co PO Box 5200	Portland	OR	97208	**800-433-0722**	503-284-4124
Schott International Inc 2850 Gilchrist Rd	Akron	OH	44305	**800-321-2178**	330-773-7851
Scovill Fasteners Inc 1802 Scovill Dr *Cust Svc	Clarkesville	GA	30523	**800-756-4734***	706-754-1000
Spradling International Inc 200 Cahaba Valley Pkwy PO Box 1668	Pelham	AL	35124	**800-333-0955**	205-985-4206
Stroheim & Romann Inc 31-11 Thomson Ave.	Long Island City	NY	11101	**800-974-8444**	718-706-7000
Tag-It Pacific Inc 21900 Burbank Blvd Suite 270 *AMEX: TAG*	Woodland Hills	CA	91367	**800-335-4443**	818-444-4100
Tiger Button Co Inc 307 W 38th St 4th Fl	New York	NY	10018	**800-223-2754**	212-594-0570
Tingue Brown & Co 535 N Midland Ave *Sales	Saddle Brook	NJ	07663	**800-829-4636***	201-796-4100
Trimtex Saint Louis Trimming Div 400 Park Ave	Williamsport	PA	17701	**800-326-9135**	570-326-9135
United Notions Inc 13800 Hutton St	Dallas	TX	75234	**800-527-9447**	972-484-8901
Universal Fasteners Inc PO Box 240	Lawrenceburg	KY	40342	**800-786-2561**	502-839-6971
US Button Corp 328 Kennedy Dr.	Putnam	CT	06260	**800-243-1842**	860-928-2707
Velcro USA Inc 406 Brown Ave	Manchester	NH	03108	**800-225-0180**	603-669-4880
Westgate Payne Fabrics Inc 1517 W North Carrier Pkwy Suite 116	Grand Prairie	TX	75050	**800-527-2517**	972-647-2323

584 PIPE & PIPE FITTINGS - METAL (FABRICATED)

SEE ALSO Metal Tube & Pipe

Company / Address	City	State	ZIP	Toll-Free	Phone
Acme Mfg Co 7601 State Rd	Philadelphia	PA	19136	**800-899-2850**	215-338-2850
Alloy Stainless Products Co 611 Union Blvd.	Totowa	NJ	07512	**800-631-8372**	973-256-1616
AY McDonald Mfg Co 4800 Chavenelle Rd. *Cust Svc	Dubuque	IA	52002	**800-292-2737***	563-583-7311
Beck Mfg 330 E 9th St	Waynesboro	PA	17268	**800-742-6621**	717-762-9141
Bent Tube Inc 9649 W Van Buren Rd	Fowlerville	MI	48836	**888-797-1931**	517-521-4330
Burner Systems International Inc 3600 Cummings Rd.	Chattanooga	TN	37419	**800-251-6318**	423-822-3600
Campbell Mfg Inc 129 E Spring St.	Bechtelsville	PA	19505	**800-523-0224**	610-367-2107
Carpenter & Paterson Inc 225 Merrimac St	Woburn	MA	01801	**800-342-6437**	781-935-2950
Carpenter Special Products Corp 1717 Cuyamaca St.	El Cajon	CA	92020	**866-466-6584**	619-448-1000
Champion Manufacturing Industries Inc. 6021 N Galena Rd	Peoria	IL	61614	**800-452-7473**	309-685-1031
Cobra Pipe Supply Inc 100 Brook St	Elmwood	CT	06110	**877-474-7332**	860-233-1231
Colonial Engineering Inc 6400 Corporate Ave	Portage	MI	49002	**800-374-0234**	269-323-2495
Connecticut Stamping & Bending Co 206 Newington Ave	New Britain	CT	06051	**800-966-6964**	860-225-4637
Continental Industries Inc 4102 S 74th East Ave.	Tulsa	OK	74145	**800-558-1373**	918-627-5210
Douglas Brothers 423 Riverside Industrial Pkwy	Portland	ME	04103	**800-341-0927**	207-797-6771
Elkhart Products Corp 1255 Oak St	Elkhart	IN	46514	**800-284-4851**	574-264-3181
Empire Industries Inc 180 Olcott St	Manchester	CT	06040	**800-243-4844**	860-647-1431
Excelsior Mfg & Supply Corp 1465 E Industrial Dr	Itasca	IL	60143	**800-548-8135**	630-773-5500
General Plug & Mfg Co Inc 455 N Main St PO Box 26	Grafton	OH	44044	**800-289-7584**	440-926-2411
Grant Prideco Inc 400 N San Houston Pkwy E Suite 900 *NYSE: GRP*	Houston	TX	77060	**866-472-6861**	281-878-8000
H-P Products Inc 512 W Gorgas St	Louisville	OH	44641	**800-860-8823**	330-875-5556
Kelly Pipe Co LLC 11680 Bloomfield Ave	Santa Fe Springs	CA	90670	**800-305-3559**	562-868-0456
McDonald AY Mfg Co 4800 Chavenelle Rd. *Cust Svc	Dubuque	IA	52002	**800-292-2737***	563-583-7311
Micro Group Inc 7 Industrial Pk Rd	Medway	MA	02053	**800-255-8823**	508-533-4925
Mills Iron Works Inc 14834 Maple St	Gardena	CA	90247	**800-421-2281**	323-321-6520
Milwaukee Valve Co Inc 2375 S Burrell St	Milwaukee	WI	53207	**800-348-6544**	414-744-5240
National Tube Form Inc 3405 Engle Rd	Fort Wayne	IN	46809	**800-752-1458**	260-478-2363
NIBCO Inc 1516 Middlebury St	Elkhart	IN	46515	**800-234-0227**	574-295-3000
Nor-Cal Products Inc 1967 S Oregon St	Yreka	CA	96097	**800-824-4166**	530-842-4458
NPC Inc 250 Elm St.	Milford	NH	03055	**800-626-2180**	603-673-8680
Parker Hannifin Corp Brass Products Div 300 Parker Dr	Otsego	MI	49078	**800-272-7537**	269-694-9411
Penn Machine Co 106 Station St	Johnstown	PA	15905	**800-763-0406**	814-288-1547
Pure-Flo Solutions Group 110-B W Cochran St	Simi Valley	CA	93065	**800-926-8884**	805-520-7200
Richards Industries Inc 3170 Wasson Rd *Cust Svc	Cincinnati	OH	45209	**800-543-7311***	513-533-5600
Robert Mfg Co Inc 10667 Jersey Blvd	Rancho Cucamonga	CA	91730	**800-877-6237**	909-987-4654
Romac Industries Inc 21919 20th Ave SE Suite 100	Bothell	WA	98021	**800-426-9341**	425-951-6200
Roscoe Moss Co 4360 Worth St.	Los Angeles	CA	90063	**800-767-2634**	323-261-4185
Rovanco Piping Systems Inc 20535 SE Frontage Rd.	Joliet	IL	60431	**800-289-7473**	815-741-6700
Shaw Group Inc 4171 Essen Ln *NYSE: SGR*	Baton Rouge	LA	70809	**800-747-3322**	225-932-2500
Snap-Tite Inc 8325 Hessinger Dr	Erie	PA	16509	**800-458-0409**	814-838-5700
Synalloy Corp 2155 W Croft Cir *NASDAQ: SYNL* ■ *Orders	Spartanburg	SC	29302	**800-763-1001***	864-585-3605
Tolco Inc 1375 Sampson Ave.	Corona	CA	92879	**800-786-5266**	951-737-5599
Trinity Fitting Group Inc 2525 Stemmons Fwy	Dallas	TX	75207	**800-527-4500**	214-589-8177
Tru-Flex Metal Hose Corp PO Box 247	West Lebanon	IN	47991	**800-255-6291**	765-893-4403
Tube Forming Inc 2101 W Belt Line Rd.	Carrollton	TX	75006	**800-513-0022**	972-512-2400
Tube Processing Corp 604 E Le Grande Ave.	Indianapolis	IN	46203	**800-776-4119**	317-787-1321

				Toll-Free	Phone
Victaulic Co of America 4901 Kesslersville Rd *Sales	Easton	PA	18040	**800-742-5842***	610-559-3300
Wolverine Tube Inc 200 Clinton Ave W Suite 1000 *NYSE: WLV*	Huntsville	AL	35801	**800-633-3972**	256-890-0460
Woolf Aircraft Products Inc 6401 Cogswell Rd	Romulus	MI	48174	**800-367-5475**	734-721-5330

585 PIPE & PIPE FITTINGS - PLASTICS

				Toll-Free	Phone
Advanced Drainage Systems Inc 4640 Trueman Blvd	Hilliard	OH	43026	**800-821-6710**	614-658-0050
Ameron International Fiberglass Composite Pipe Group PO Box 801148	Houston	TX	77280	**800-542-4070**	713-690-7777
CANTEX Inc PO Box 365	Auburndale	FL	33823	**800-765-8704**	863-967-4161
CertainTeed Corp 750 E Swedesford Rd *Prod Info	Valley Forge	PA	19482	**800-782-8777***	610-341-7000
Charlotte Pipe & Foundry Co Plastics Div PO Box 1339 *Sales	Monroe	NC	28111	**800-438-6091***	704-289-2531
Chemtrol Div NIBCO Inc 1516 Middlebury St	Elkhart	IN	46516	**800-343-5455**	574-295-3316
Chevron Phillips Chemical Co Performance Pipe Div 5085 W Park Blvd Suite 500	Plano	TX	75093	**800-527-0662**	972-599-6600
Dura-Line Corp 835 Innovation Dr	Knoxville	TN	37932	**800-847-7661**	865-218-3460
Dura Plastics Products Inc PO Box 2097	Beaumont	CA	92223	**800-854-2323**	951-845-3161
Excalibur Extrusions Inc 110 E Crowther Ave	Placentia	CA	92670	**800-648-6804**	714-528-8834
Fernco PlumbQwik Inc 300 S Dayton St	Davison	MI	48423	**800-521-1283**	810-653-9626
FiberCast Inc 25 S Main St	Sand Springs	OK	74063	**800-331-4406**	918-245-6651
Freedom Plastics Inc 3206 Enterprise Rd	Fort Pierce	FL	34982	**800-432-6143**	772-465-1222
Genova Products Inc 7034 E Court St	Davison	MI	48423	**800-521-7488**	810-744-4500
George Fischer Sloane Mfg Co Inc 7777 Sloane Dr	Little Rock	AR	72206	**800-423-2686**	501-490-7777
Isco Industries 926 Baxter Ave	Louisville	KY	40204	**800-345-4726**	502-583-6591
J-M Mfg Co Inc 9 Peach Tree Hill Rd	Livingston	NJ	07039	**800-621-4404**	973-535-1633
Lasco Fittings Inc PO Box 116	Brownsville	TN	38012	**800-776-2756**	731-772-3180
Maloney Technical Products 1300 E Berry St	Fort Worth	TX	76119	**800-231-7236**	817-923-3344
National Pipe & Plastics Inc 3421 Old Vestal Rd	Vestal	NY	13850	**800-836-4350**	607-729-9381
Nebraska Plastics Inc PO Box 45	Cozad	NE	69130	**800-445-2887**	308-784-2500
Normandy Industries Inc PO Box 40	Verona	PA	15147	**800-322-9463**	412-826-1825
Oil Creek Plastics Inc PO Box 385	Titusville	PA	16354	**800-537-3661**	814-827-3661
Rehau Inc PO Box 1706	Leesburg	VA	20177	**800-247-9445**	703-777-5255
Special Plastics Systems Inc 385 W Valley St	San Bernardino	CA	92401	**800-423-4422**	909-888-2531
Teel Plastics Inc 426 Hitchcock St	Baraboo	WI	53913	**800-322-8335**	608-355-3080
Texas United Pipe Inc 11627 N Houston Rosslyn Rd *Sales	Houston	TX	77086	**800-966-8741***	281-448-3276
Uponor Aldyl Co 7901 N Kickapoo St	Shawnee	OK	74804	**800-454-0480**	405-273-0900
Weiler Welding Co Inc 324 E 2nd St	Dayton	OH	45402	**800-526-9353**	937-222-8312

586 PIPELINES (EXCEPT NATURAL GAS)

				Toll-Free	Phone
Colonial Pipeline Co PO Box 1624	Alpharetta	GA	30009	**800-275-3004**	678-762-2200
Country Mark Co-op 1200 Refinery Rd	Mount Vernon	IN	47620	**800-832-5490**	812-838-4341
Enbridge Energy Partners LP 1100 Louisiana Suite 3300 *NYSE: EEP* ■ *PR	Houston	TX	77002	**800-525-3999***	888-650-8900
Genesis Energy LP 500 Dallas St Suite 2500 *AMEX: GEL*	Houston	TX	77002	**800-284-3365**	713-860-2500
Giant Industries Arizona Inc 23733 N Scottsdale Rd	Scottsdale	AZ	85255	**800-937-4937**	480-585-8888
Kaneb Pipe Line Partners LP 2435 N Central Expy Suite 700 *NYSE: KPP*	Richardson	TX	75080	**866-769-2987**	972-699-4000
Kinder Morgan Energy Partners LP 500 Dallas St Suite 1000 *NYSE: KMP*	Houston	TX	77002	**888-844-5657**	713-369-9000
Kinder Morgan Management LLC 500 Dallas St 1 Allen Ctr Suite 1000 *NYSE: KMR*	Houston	TX	77002	**800-324-2900**	713-369-9000
Magellan Midstream Partners LP 1 Williams Ctr *NYSE: MMP*	Tulsa	OK	74172	**800-574-6671**	
MarkWest Energy Partners LP 155 Inverness Dr W Suite 200 *AMEX: MWE*	Englewood	CO	80112	**800-730-8388**	303-290-8700
Newpark Drilling Fluids LLC 5560B NW 72nd St	Oklahoma City	OK	73132	**800-444-0682**	405-721-0207
Olympic Pipeline Co 2319 Lind Ave SW	Renton	WA	98055	**877-659-7473**	425-235-7736
Plains All American Pipeline LP 333 Clay St Suite 1600 *NYSE: PAA* ■ *Mktg	Houston	TX	77002	**800-564-3036***	713-646-4100
Sunoco Inc 1801 Market St *NYSE: SUN*	Philadelphia	PA	19103	**800-786-6261**	215-977-3000
Texas Eastern Products Pipeline Co (TEPPCO) 2929 Allen Pkwy	Houston	TX	77019	**800-877-3636**	713-759-3636
Ultramar Diamond Shamrock Corp 2200 ave McGill College	Montreal	QC	H3A3L3	**800-361-4253**	514-499-6111

587 PLANETARIUMS

				Toll-Free	Phone
Dreyfuss Planetarium 49 Washington St	Newark	NJ	07102	**800-768-7386**	973-596-6529
Ethyl IMAX Dome & Planetarium 2500 W Broad St	Richmond	VA	23220	**800-659-1727**	804-864-1400
Meyer Robert R Planetarium 900 Arkadelphia Rd Birmingham Southern College PO Box 549036	Birmingham	AL	35254	**800-523-5793**	205-226-4770
Noble Planetarium 1501 Montgomery St Museum of Science & History	Fort Worth	TX	76107	**888-255-9300**	817-732-1631
Robert R Meyer Planetarium 900 Arkadelphia Rd Birmingham Southern College PO Box 549036	Birmingham	AL	35254	**800-523-5793**	205-226-4770

588 PLASTICS - LAMINATED - PLATE, SHEET, PROFILE SHAPES

				Toll-Free	Phone
American Thermoplastic Extrusion Co 4851 NW 128th Street Rd	Opa Locka	FL	33054	**800-426-9605**	305-769-9566
Applied Plastics Co Inc 7320 S 6th St	Oak Creek	WI	53154	**800-959-0445**	414-764-2900
Atlantis Plastics Inc Linear Films Div 6940 W 76th St S *Cust Svc	Tulsa	OK	74157	**800-332-4437***	918-446-1651
Bravo Sports 6600 Katella Ave *Cust Svc	Cypress	CA	90630	**800-773-1111***	714-850-8800
Columbus Cello-Poly Corp 4041 Roberts Rd	Columbus	OH	43228	**800-837-1204**	614-876-1204
Conimar Corp 1724 NE 22nd Ave	Ocala	FL	34470	**800-874-9735**	352-732-7235
Connecticut Laminating Co Inc 162 James St	New Haven	CT	06513	**800-753-9119**	203-787-2184
Current Inc 30 Tyler St PO Box 120183	East Haven	CT	06512	**877-436-6542**	203-469-1337
DuPont Surfaces 4417 Lancaster Pike Chestnut Run Plaza Maple Run 721	Wilmington	DE	19805	**800-426-7426**	302-774-1000
Edlon Inc 150 Pomeroy Ave *Sales	Avondale	PA	19311	**800-753-3566***	610-268-3101
Formica Corp 10155 Reading Rd	Cincinnati	OH	45241	**800-367-6422**	513-786-3400
Franklin Fibre-Lamitex Corp 903 E 13th St	Wilmington	DE	19802	**800-233-9739**	302-652-3621
GE Structured Products 1 Plastics Ave	Pittsfield	MA	01201	**800-451-3147**	413-448-5400
Insulfab Plastics Inc 834 Hayne St	Spartanburg	SC	29301	**800-845-7599**	864-582-7506
Insultab Inc 45 Industrial Pkwy *Cust Svc	Woburn	MA	01801	**800-468-4822***	781-935-0800
Iten Industries 4602 Benefit Ave *Orders	Ashtabula	OH	44004	**800-227-4836***	440-997-6134
Lakeland Plastics Inc 1550 McCormick Blvd	Mundelein	IL	60060	**800-225-2508**	847-680-1550
Lamart Corp 16 Richmond St	Clifton	NJ	07015	**800-526-2789**	973-772-6262
Linear Films Div Atlantis Plastics Inc 6940 W 76th St S *Cust Svc	Tulsa	OK	74157	**800-332-4437***	918-446-1651
Madico Inc 45 Industrial Pkwy *Cust Svc	Woburn	MA	01801	**800-456-4331***	781-935-7850
Olon Industries Inc 42 Armstrong Ave	Georgetown	ON	L7G4R9	**800-387-2319**	905-877-7300
Petro Plastics Co Inc 450 South Ave	Garwood	NJ	07027	**800-486-4738**	908-789-1200
Rochling Engineered Plastics 120 Rochling St PO Box 2729 *Cust Svc	Gastonia	NC	28053	**800-541-4419***	704-922-7814
Rowmark Inc 2040 Industrial Dr	Findlay	OH	45840	**800-243-3339**	419-425-2407
Sabin Corp 3800 Constitution Ave	Bloomington	IN	47402	**800-264-4510**	812-323-4500
Spaulding Composites Co 55 Nadeau Dr	Rochester	NH	03867	**800-964-0555**	603-332-0555
V-T Industries Inc 1000 Industrial Pk	Holstein	IA	51025	**800-827-1615**	712-368-4381
Vytech Industries Inc 5201 Old Pearman Dairy Rd	Anderson	SC	29625	**800-225-8531**	864-224-8771
Wilmington Fibre Specialty Co 700 Washington St	New Castle	DE	19720	**800-220-5132**	302-328-7525
Wilsonart International Inc 2400 Wilson Pl *Cust Svc	Temple	TX	76504	**800-433-3222***	254-207-7000

589 PLASTICS - UNSUPPORTED - FILM, SHEET, PROFILE SHAPES

SEE ALSO Blister Packaging

				Toll-Free	Phone
3M Commercial Graphics Div 3M General Offices Bldg 220-6W-06	Saint Paul	MN	55144	**800-328-3908**	
3M Display & Graphics Div 3M Ctr	Saint Paul	MN	55144	**800-364-3577**	651-733-1110
3M Safety Security & Protection Services Div 3M Ctr	Saint Paul	MN	55144	**800-364-3577**	651-733-1110
3M Traffic Control Materials Div 3M Ctr Bldg 225-5S-08	Saint Paul	MN	55144	**800-553-1380**	
AEP Industries Inc 125 Phillips Ave *NASDAQ: AEPI*	South Hackensack	NJ	07606	**800-999-2374**	201-641-6600
Allen Extruders Inc 1305 Lincoln Ave	Holland	MI	49423	**800-833-1305**	616-392-9004
Anaheim Custom Extruders 4640 E La Palma Ave *Cust Svc	Anaheim	CA	92807	**800-229-2760***	714-693-8508
Applied Extrusion Technologies Inc 15 Reads Way *NASDAQ: AETC*	New Castle	DE	19720	**800-688-2044**	302-326-5500
Arlon Adhesives & Films 2811 S Harbor Blvd	Santa Ana	CA	92704	**800-854-0361**	714-540-2811
Atlantic Extrusions Corp 96 Swampscott Rd	Salem	MA	01970	**800-331-8441**	978-744-8000
Atlantis Plastics Inc 1870 The Exchange Suite 200 *NASDAQ: ATPL*	Atlanta	GA	30339	**800-497-7659**	770-953-4567
Atlas Roofing Falcon Foam Div 8240 Byron Center Rd SW	Byron Center	MI	49315	**800-917-9138**	616-878-1568
Avery Dennison Worldwide Graphics Div 250 Chester St Bldg 6	Painesville	OH	44077	**800-443-9380**	440-358-3700
Bemis Co Inc Bemis Polyethylene Packaging Div 1350 N Fruitridge Ave	Terre Haute	IN	47804	**800-457-0861**	812-466-2213
BER Plastic Corp PO Box 2	Riverdale	NJ	07457	**877-237-3456**	973-839-2100
Bixby International Corp 1 Preble Rd	Newburyport	MA	01950	**800-466-4102**	978-462-4100
Brandywine Investment Group Homalite Div 11 Brookside Dr	Wilmington	DE	19804	**800-346-7802**	302-652-3686
Bunzl Extrusion Inc 1625 Ashton Park Dr	Colonial Heights	VA	23834	**800-755-7528**	804-518-1124
Catalina Graphic Films Inc 27001 Agoura Rd Suite 100	Calabasas Hills	CA	91301	**800-333-3136**	818-880-8060
Clopay Corp 8585 Duke Blvd	Mason	OH	45040	**800-262-2260**	513-770-4800

Company / Address	City	State	Zip	Toll-Free	Phone
Clopay Plastic Products Co 8585 Duke Blvd	Mason	OH	45040	**800-282-2260**	513-770-4800
Conwed Corp 2810 Weeks Ave SE	Minneapolis	MN	55414	**800-426-0149**	612-623-1700
CUE Inc 11 Leonberg Rd	Cranberry Township	PA	16066	**800-283-4621**	724-772-5225
D & B Plastics Inc PO Box 26	Fairmont	MN	56031	**800-405-2247**	507-235-5950
Danafilms Inc 5 Otis St PO Box 624	Westborough	MA	01581	**800-634-8289**	508-366-8884
Dielectrics Industries Inc 300 Burnett Rd	Chicopee	MA	01020	**800-472-7286**	413-594-8111
Dunmore Corp 145 Wharton Rd *Cust Svc	Bristol	PA	19007	**888-386-6673***	215-781-8895
Enbee Plastics Inc 31-35 31st St	Long Island City	NY	11106	**800-255-9170**	718-721-3700
Enflo Corp 315 Lake Ave	Bristol	CT	06010	**888-887-4093**	860-589-0014
Falcon Foam Div Atlas Roofing 8240 Byron Center Rd SW	Byron Center	MI	49315	**800-917-9138**	616-878-1568
Farber Plastics Inc 162 Hanse Ave	Freeport	NY	11520	**800-338-6315**	516-378-4860
Favorite Plastic Corp 1465 Utica Ave *Cust Svc	Brooklyn	NY	11234	**800-221-8077***	718-253-7000
Film Technologies International Inc 2544 Terminal Dr S	Saint Petersburg	FL	33712	**800-777-1770**	727-327-2544
Fluoro Plastics Inc 3601 G St *Cust Svc	Philadelphia	PA	19134	**800-262-1910***	215-425-5500
Gary Plastic Packaging Corp 1340 Viele Ave	Bronx	NY	10474	**800-221-8150**	718-893-2200
General Formulations Inc 309 S Union St	Sparta	MI	49345	**800-253-3664**	616-887-7387
Glasforms Inc 271 Barnard Ave	San Jose	CA	95125	**888-297-3800**	408-297-9300
GSE Lining Technology Inc 19103 Gundle Rd	Houston	TX	77073	**800-435-2008**	281-443-8564
Holm Industries Inc Saint Charles Div 315 N 9th St	Saint Charles	IL	60174	**800-221-2209**	630-584-1880
Homalite Div Brandywine Investment Group 11 Brookside Dr	Wilmington	DE	19804	**800-346-7802**	302-652-3686
Impact Plastics Inc 154 West St Bldg 3 Unit C	Cromwell	CT	06416	**800-625-7224**	860-632-3550
Intermex Inc 9330 LBJ Fwy Suite 260	Dallas	TX	75243	**800-527-2303**	214-575-0572
JPS Elastomerics Corp 9 Sullivan Rd	Holyoke	MA	01040	**800-621-7663**	413-533-8100
Kama Corp 600 Dietrich Ave	Hazleton	PA	18201	**800-628-7598**	570-455-2022
Karolina Polymers Inc 1508 S Center St	Hickory	NC	28602	**800-280-2247**	828-328-2247
Kayline Processing Inc 31 Coates St *Sales	Trenton	NJ	08611	**800-367-5546***	609-695-1449
Kendall Packaging Corp 10200 N Port Washington Rd	Mequon	WI	53092	**800-237-0951**	262-404-1200
Lavanture Products Co PO Box 2058	Elkhart	IN	46515	**800-348-7625**	574-264-0658
Mitsubishi Polyester Film LLC 2001 Hood Rd	Greer	SC	29650	**800-845-2009**	864-879-5000
MPI Technologies 37 East St	Winchester	MA	01890	**888-674-8088**	781-729-8300
Natvar 8720 US 70 W	Clayton	NC	27520	**800-395-6288**	919-553-4151
New Hampshire Plastics Inc 1 Bouchard St	Manchester	NH	03103	**800-258-3036**	603-669-8523
Northland Plastics Inc PO Box 290	Sheboygan	WI	53082	**800-776-7163**	920-458-0732
Orcon Corp 1570 Atlantic St	Union City	CA	94587	**800-227-0505**	510-489-8100
Penn Fibre Plastics 2434 Bristol Rd *Cust Svc	Bensalem	PA	19020	**800-662-7366***	215-702-9551
Plaskolite Inc 1770 Joyce Ave	Columbus	OH	43219	**800-848-9124**	614-294-3281
Primex Plastics Corp 1235 N 'F' St	Richmond	IN	47374	**800-222-5116**	765-966-7774
Prinsco Inc 108 W Hwy 7 PO Box 265	Prinsburg	MN	56281	**800-992-1725**	320-978-4116
Quality Films Inc 321 Duncan St PO Box 459	Schoolcraft	MI	49087	**800-306-5263**	269-679-5263
Raven Industries Inc 205 E 6th St *NASDAQ: RAVN*	Sioux Falls	SD	57104	**800-227-2836**	605-336-2750
Ross & Roberts Inc 1299 W Broad St	Stratford	CT	06615	**800-822-4220**	203-378-9363
Sheffield Plastics Inc 119 Salisbury Rd *Cust Svc	Sheffield	MA	01257	**800-254-1707***	413-229-8711
Shepherd CE Co Inc 2221 Canada Dry St	Houston	TX	77023	**800-324-6733**	713-928-3763
Sinclair & Rush Inc 123 Manufacturers Dr	Arnold	MO	63010	**800-827-2277**	636-282-6800
SLM Mfg Corp 215 Davidson Ave	Somerset	NJ	08873	**800-526-3708**	732-469-7500
Soliant LLC 1872 Hwy 9 Bypass	Lancaster	SC	29720	**800-288-9401**	
Southern Film Extruders Inc 1829 Eastchester Dr Suite 100	High Point	NC	27265	**800-334-6101**	336-885-8091
Sto-Cote Products Inc 218 South Rd	Genoa City	WI	53128	**800-435-2621**	262-279-6000
Summit Plastics Inc 107 Laurel St	Summit	MS	39666	**800-790-7117**	601-276-7500
Thatcher Tubes LLC 1005 Courtaulds Dr	Woodstock	IL	60098	**888-842-8243**	815-334-1200
Thermoplastic Processes Inc 1268 Valley Rd	Stirling	NJ	07980	**888-554-6400**	908-561-3000
Transilwrap Co Inc 9201 W Belmont Ave	Franklin Park	IL	60131	**800-745-5802**	847-678-1800
Tredegar Corp Film Products Div 1100 Boulders Pkwy	Richmond	VA	23225	**800-411-7441**	804-330-1222
Tulox Plastics Corp 401 S Miller Ave *Cust Svc	Marion	IN	46953	**800-234-1118***	765-664-5155
Tyco Plastics Inc 1401 W 94th St	Bloomington	MN	55431	**800-873-3941**	952-884-7281
Valley Decorating Co 2829 E Hamilton Ave	Fresno	CA	93721	**800-245-2817**	559-495-1100
VCF Films Inc 1100 Sutton Ave	Howell	MI	48843	**888-823-4141**	517-546-2300
Victory Plastics International 25 Shelley Rd *Cust Svc	Haverhill	MA	01835	**800-541-5108***	978-373-1551
Vinylex Corp 2636 Byington Rd	Knoxville	TN	37931	**800-624-4435**	865-690-2211
VPI LLC 3123 S 9th St *Orders	Sheboygan	WI	53081	**800-874-4240***	920-458-4664
Watersaver Co Inc 5870 E 56th Ave	Commerce City	CO	80022	**800-525-2424**	303-289-1818
Winzen Film Inc 1212 Elm St	Sulphur Springs	TX	75482	**800-779-7595**	903-885-7595
Zippertubing Co 13000 S Broadway	Los Angeles	CA	90061	**800-321-8178**	310-527-0488

590 PLASTICS FOAM PRODUCTS

Company / Address	City	State	Zip	Toll-Free	Phone
AASR Inc 2219 McKinney St *Cust Svc	Houston	TX	77003	**800-621-0685***	713-223-4474
Adams RL Plastics Inc 5955 Crossroads Commerce Pkwy	Wyoming	MI	49517	**800-968-2241**	616-261-4400
Advanced Materials Group Inc 20211 S Susana Rd *Cust Svc	Rancho Dominguez	CA	90221	**800-395-3626***	310-537-5444
American Converters Inc 5360 Main St NE	Fridley	MN	55421	**888-360-8050**	763-574-1044
American Excelsior Co PO Box 5067	Arlington	TX	76005	**800-777-7645**	817-640-1555
Astrofoam Molding Co Inc 4117 Calle Tesoro	Camarillo	CA	93012	**800-339-0967**	805-482-7276
Blue Ridge Products Inc PO Box 2028	Hickory	NC	28603	**800-345-1367**	828-322-7990
Bontex Inc 1 Bontex Dr	Buena Vista	VA	24416	**800-733-4234**	540-261-2181
Burnett WT & Co Inc 1500 Bush St	Baltimore	MD	21230	**800-638-0606**	410-837-3000
Carlon Products Co PO Box 377 *Cust Svc	Derby	CT	06418	**800-243-6682***	203-735-7474
Carpenter Co 5016 Monument Ave	Richmond	VA	23230	**800-288-3830**	804-359-0800
Cellofoam North America Inc PO Box 406	Conyers	GA	30012	**800-241-3634**	770-929-3688
Cellox Corp 1200 Industrial St	Reedsburg	WI	53959	**888-217-6631**	608-524-2316
Chestnut Ridge Foam Inc PO Box 781	Latrobe	PA	15650	**800-234-2734**	724-537-9000
Clayton Corp 866 Horan Dr *Cust Svc	Fenton	MO	63026	**800-325-6180***	636-349-5333
Creative Foam Corp 300 N Alloy Dr	Fenton	MI	48430	**800-837-0630**	810-629-4149
Custom Pack Inc 443 Creamery Way	Exton	PA	19341	**800-722-7005**	610-524-4222
Dart Container Corp 500 Hogsback Rd	Mason	MI	48854	**800-248-5960**	517-676-3800
Diversifoam Products 9091 County Rd 50	Rockford	MN	55373	**800-669-0100**	763-477-5854
Dow Thermoset Systems 1881 W Oak Pkwy	Marietta	GA	30062	**800-735-3129**	770-428-2684
Duraco Inc 7400 W Industrial Dr	Forest Park	IL	60130	**800-852-1025**	708-488-1025
E-A-R Specialty Composites 5457 W 79th St	Indianapolis	IN	46268	**800-544-5180**	317-692-6666
Elliott Co of Indianapolis Inc 9200 Zionsville Rd *Orders	Indianapolis	IN	46268	**800-545-1213***	317-291-1213
Elm Packaging Co 1261 Brukner Dr *Cust Svc	Troy	OH	45373	**800-962-0635***	937-339-2655
Fairmont Corp 2245 W Pershing Rd	Chicago	IL	60609	**800-621-6907**	773-376-1300
Federal Foam Technologies Inc 600 Wisconsin Dr	New Richmond	WI	54017	**800-898-9559**	715-246-9500
Flextron Industries Inc 720 Mount Rd	Aston	PA	19014	**800-633-2181**	610-459-4600
FloraCraft Corp PO Box 400	Ludington	MI	49431	**800-253-0409**	231-845-5127
Foam Rubber Products Inc 2000 Troy Ave	New Castle	IN	47362	**800-878-3774**	765-521-2000
Foamade Industries Inc 2550 Auburn Ct	Auburn Hills	MI	48326	**800-221-7388**	248-852-6010
Foamex International Inc 1000 Columbia Ave *NASDAQ: FMXI*	Linwood	PA	19061	**800-355-3626**	610-859-3000
Fomo Products Inc 2775 Barber Rd	Norton	OH	44203	**800-321-5585**	330-753-4585
FP International 1090 Mills Way	Redwood City	CA	94063	**800-866-9946**	650-261-5300
Free-Flow Packaging Corp DBA FP International 1090 Mills Way	Redwood City	CA	94063	**800-866-9946**	650-261-5300
Future Foam Inc 400 N 10th St	Council Bluffs	IA	51503	**800-733-8067**	712-323-6718
Fypon Ltd 3846 Green Valley Rd	Seven Valleys	PA	17360	**800-955-5748**	717-993-2593
G & T Industries Inc 3413 Eastern Ave SE	Grand Rapids	MI	49508	**800-686-2659**	616-452-8611
Gaco Western Inc PO Box 88698 *Cust Svc	Seattle	WA	98138	**800-456-4226***	206-575-0450
General Plastics Mfg Co 4910 Burlington Way	Tacoma	WA	98409	**800-806-6051**	253-473-5000
Genpak Corp 68 Warren St	Glens Falls	NY	12801	**800-626-6695**	518-798-9511
Gilman Brothers Co PO Box 38	Gilman	CT	06336	**800-852-4220**	860-889-8444
Guardian Packaging Inc 3615 Security St	Garland	TX	75042	**800-259-1502**	214-349-1500
Hibco Plastics Inc PO Box 157	Yadkinville	NC	27055	**800-849-8683**	336-463-2391
Kerr Group Inc 1706 Hempstead Rd	Lancaster	PA	17601	**800-367-1876**	717-299-6511
King & Co Inc PO Box 10 *Cust Svc	Clarksville	AR	72830	**800-643-9530***	479-754-6090
Life-Like Products Inc 1600 Union Ave *Cust Svc	Baltimore	MD	21211	**800-638-1470***	410-889-1023
Minnesota Diversified Products Inc DBA Diversifoam Products 9091 County Rd 50	Rockford	MN	55373	**800-669-0100**	763-477-5854
North Carolina Foam Industries Inc 1515 Carter St	Mount Airy	NC	27030	**800-346-8229**	336-789-9161
OPCO Inc PO Box 101	Latrobe	PA	15650	**800-229-6726**	724-537-9300
Pacific Packaging Products Inc 24 Industrial Way	Wilmington	MA	01887	**800-777-0300**	978-657-9100
Perry Chemical & Mfg Co Inc PO Box 6419	Lafayette	IN	47903	**800-592-6614**	765-474-3404
Plastics Mfg Inc 7301 Caldwell Rd	Harrisburg	NC	28075	**800-446-5191**	704-455-5191
PMC Global Inc 12243 Branford St	Sun Valley	CA	91352	**800-423-5632**	818-896-1101
Poly Molding Corp 96 4th Ave	Haskell	NJ	07420	**800-229-7161**	973-835-7161
RL Adams Plastics Inc 5955 Crossroads Commerce Pkwy	Wyoming	MI	49517	**800-968-2241**	616-261-4400
Robbie Mfg Inc 10810 Mid America Ave	Lenexa	KS	66219	**800-255-6328**	913-492-3400
Sekisui America Corp Voltek Div 100 Shepard St *Cust Svc	Lawrence	MA	01843	**800-225-0668***	978-685-2557
Spongex Corp 6 Bridge St	Shelton	CT	06484	**800-782-7749**	203-924-9335
Stephenson & Lawyer Inc 3831 Patterson Ave SE	Grand Rapids	MI	49512	**800-968-5535**	616-949-8100
Storopack Inc 12007 S Woodruff Ave	Downey	CA	90241	**800-829-1491**	562-803-1584
StyroChem International 3607 N Sylvania Ave	Fort Worth	TX	76111	**800-448-6232**	817-759-4400
Styrotek Inc PO Box 1180	Delano	CA	93216	**800-936-2611**	661-725-4957
Texas Fiber-Poly Foam Inc 1200 Rink St	Brenham	TX	77833	**800-798-6729**	979-836-6625
Thermo-Serv Inc 3901 Pipestone Rd	Dallas	TX	75212	**800-527-2648**	214-631-0307
ThermoSafe Brands 3930 Ventura Dr Suite 450	Arlington Heights	IL	60004	**800-323-7442**	847-398-0110
Vita Foam Inc 1900 Stuart St *Cust Svc	Chattanooga	TN	37406	**800-627-3972***	423-698-3408
Vita Olympic Inc 2222 Surrett Dr	High Point	NC	27263	**800-431-1171**	336-431-1171
Voltek Div Sekisui America Corp 100 Shepard St *Cust Svc	Lawrence	MA	01843	**800-225-0668***	978-685-2557
WinCup 7980 W Buckeye Rd	Phoenix	AZ	85043	**800-292-2877**	623-936-1791
WT Burnett & Co Inc 1500 Bush St	Baltimore	MD	21230	**800-638-0606**	410-837-3000

591 PLASTICS MACHINING & FORMING

SEE ALSO Plastics Molding - Custom

Company / Address	City	State	Zip	Toll-Free	Phone
Bardes Plastics Inc 5225 W Clinton Ave *Cust Svc	Milwaukee	WI	53223	**800-558-5161***	414-354-5300
Bo-Mer Mfg Co 13 Pulaski St	Auburn	NY	13021	**800-221-6563**	315-252-7216
Comco Plastics Inc 98-34 Jamaica Ave	Woodhaven	NY	11421	**800-849-0731**	718-849-9000
Conroy & Knowlton Inc 2000 S Hoefner Ave	Commerce	CA	90040	**888-295-9500**	323-665-5288
EGC Corp 11718 McGallion Rd	Houston	TX	77076	**800-342-7677**	281-774-6100
Elixir Industries Inc Custom Aluminum Div 5600 NE 121st Ave	Vancouver	WA	98682	**800-426-1782**	360-254-5077
Empire West Inc 9270 Graton Rd PO Box 511	Graton	CA	95444	**800-521-4261**	707-823-1190
Engineered Plastics Inc 211 Chase St PO Box 227	Gibsonville	NC	27249	**800-711-1740**	336-449-4121
Ensinger Hyde Co 1 Main St	Grenloch	NJ	08032	**800-234-4933**	856-227-0500
Fabri-Form Co 200 S Friendship Dr	New Concord	OH	43762	**800-837-2574**	740-826-5000
Fabri-Kal Corp Plastics Pl	Kalamazoo	MI	49001	**800-888-5054**	269-385-5050
FNW Industrial Plastics Inc 740 S 28th St	Washougal	WA	98671	**800-634-5082**	360-835-2129
Formall Inc 3908 Fountain Valley Ln	Knoxville	TN	37918	**800-643-3676**	865-922-7514
Gage Industries Inc PO Box 1318	Lake Oswego	OR	97035	**800-443-4243**	503-639-2177
GML Inc 500 Oak Grove Pkwy	Saint Paul	MN	55127	**800-344-8899**	651-490-0000
Inline Plastics Corp 42 Canal St	Shelton	CT	06484	**800-826-5567**	203-924-5933
Laich Industries Corp 1000 Laich Pkwy	Cleveland	OH	44135	**800-551-0053**	216-898-9900
Mantex Corp 611 Industrial Pkwy	Imlay City	MI	48444	**800-666-2689**	810-721-2100
McNeal Enterprises Inc 2031 Ringwood Ave	San Jose	CA	95131	**800-562-6325**	408-922-7290
Meyer Plastics Inc 5167 E 65th St	Indianapolis	IN	46220	**800-968-4131**	317-259-4131
Morgan Hill Plastics Inc 640 E Dunne Ave	Morgan Hill	CA	95037	**800-449-0322**	408-779-2118
Parsons Mfg Corp 1055 O'Brien Dr	Menlo Park	CA	94025	**800-221-0823**	650-324-4726

Company	City	State	ZIP	Toll-Free	Phone
Perkasie Industries Corp PO Box 179 *Sales	Perkasie	PA	18944	**800-523-6747***	215-257-6581
Placon Corp 6096 McKee Rd	Madison	WI	53719	**800-541-1535**	608-271-5634
Polygon Co 103 Industrial Pk Dr PO Box 176	Walkerton	IN	46574	**800-918-9261**	574-586-3145
Quadrant Engineering Plastic Products PO Box 14235	Reading	PA	19612	**800-366-0300**	610-320-6600
Ray Products Co Inc 1700 Chablis Ave	Ontario	CA	91761	**800-423-7859**	909-390-9906
Spaulding Composites Co Fab Div 55 Nadeau Dr	Rochester	NH	03867	**800-964-0555**	603-332-0555
Speck Plastics Inc PO Box 421	Nazareth	PA	18064	**800-755-2922**	610-759-1807
Total Plastics Inc 3316 Pagosa Ct	Indianapolis	IN	46226	**800-382-4635**	317-543-3540
Vinyl Source Inc 427 Thatcher Ln	Youngstown	OH	44515	**800-824-4067**	330-792-6511

592 PLASTICS MATERIALS - WHOL

Company	City	State	ZIP	Toll-Free	Phone
A Daigger Co Inc 620 Lakeview Pkwy	Vernon Hills	IL	60061	**800-621-7193**	847-816-5060
Aetna Plastics Corp 1702 Saint Clair Ave	Cleveland	OH	44114	**800-634-3074**	216-781-4421
AIN Plastics Inc 23235 Telegraph Rd *Cust Svc	Southfield	MI	48034	**800-521-1757***	248-356-4000
Bamberger Polymers Inc 2 Jericho Plaza	Jericho	NY	11753	**800-888-8959**	516-622-3600
Buckley Industries Inc 1850 E 53rd St N	Wichita	KS	67219	**800-835-2779**	316-744-7587
Calsak Corp 200 W Artesia Blvd *Sales	Compton	CA	90220	**800-743-2595***	310-637-2000
Cope Plastics Inc 4441 Industrial Dr	Godfrey	IL	62035	**800-851-5510**	618-466-0221
El Mar Plastics Inc 840 E Walnut St	Carson	CA	90746	**800-255-5210**	310-327-3180
GE Polymerland 9930 Kincey Ave	Huntersville	NC	28078	**800-752-7842**	
GLS Corp 833 Ridgeview Dr	McHenry	IL	60050	**800-457-8777**	815-385-8500
Gulf-Wandes Corp 8325 S Choctaw Dr	Baton Rouge	LA	70815	**800-211-7613**	225-927-1920
H Muehlstein & Co Inc 800 Connecticut Ave	Norwalk	CT	06854	**800-257-3746**	203-855-6000
Laird Plastics Inc 1400 Centrepark Blvd Suite 500	West Palm Beach	FL	33401	**800-610-1016**	561-684-7000
Leed Plastics Corp 1425 Palomares Ave	La Verne	CA	91750	**800-421-9880**	909-596-1927
Louisiana Utilities Supply PO Box 3531	Baton Rouge	LA	70821	**800-743-8916**	225-383-8916
M Holland Co 400 Skokie Blvd Suite 600	Northbrook	IL	60062	**800-872-7370**	847-272-7370
Momentum Technologies Inc 1507 Boettler Rd	Uniontown	OH	44685	**800-720-0261**	330-896-5900
Plastic Sales Southern Inc 6490 Fleet St	Los Angeles	CA	90040	**800-257-7747**	323-728-8309
Polymer Plastics Corp 645 National Ave	Mountain View	CA	94043	**800-369-2213**	650-968-2212
Port Plastics Inc 16750 Chestnut St	City of Industry	CA	91748	**800-800-0039**	626-333-7678
Regal Plastic Supply Co 111 E 10th Ave	North Kansas City	MO	64116	**800-627-2102**	816-421-6290
Regal Plastic Supply Co Southern Div 2356 Merrell Rd	Dallas	TX	75229	**800-441-1553**	972-484-0741
Ryan Herco Products Corp 3010 N San Fernando Blvd	Burbank	CA	91504	**800-848-1141**	818-841-1141
Seelye Plastics Inc 9700 Newton Ave S	Bloomington	MN	55431	**800-328-2728**	952-881-2658
Sekisui America Corp 666 5th Ave 12th Fl	New York	NY	10103	**800-866-4005**	212-489-3500
Superior Oil Co Inc 400 W Regent St	Indianapolis	IN	46225	**800-553-5480**	317-781-4400
Tekra Corp 16700 W Lincoln Ave	New Berlin	WI	53151	**800-448-3572**	262-784-5533

593 PLASTICS MOLDING - CUSTOM

Company	City	State	ZIP	Toll-Free	Phone
AJ Plastic Products 19919 Shawnee Mission Pkwy	Shawnee	KS	66218	**800-999-5518**	913-422-2027
Allegheny Plastics Inc 17 Ave A	Leetsdale	PA	15056	**800-966-5152**	412-749-0700
American Plastic Molding Corp 965 S Elm St	Scottsburg	IN	47170	**877-527-8427**	812-752-7000
ASK Plastics Inc 9750 Ashton Rd	Philadelphia	PA	19114	**888-948-1862**	215-969-0800
BMJ Mold & Engineering Co Inc 1104 N Touby Pike	Kokomo	IN	46901	**800-238-7785**	765-457-1166
Chilton Products Div Western Industries Inc 300 E Breed St	Chilton	WI	53014	**877-671-7063**	920-849-2381
Chris Kaye Plastics Corp 715 W Park Rd	Union	MO	63084	**800-325-9927**	636-583-2583
Confer Plastics Inc 97 Witmer Rd	North Tonawanda	NY	14120	**800-635-3213**	716-693-2056
Cuyahoga Molded Plastics Corp 1265 Babbitt Rd	Cleveland	OH	44132	**800-805-9549**	216-261-2744
D-M-E Co 29111 Stephenson Hwy	Madison Heights	MI	48071	**800-626-6653**	248-398-6000
Double H Plastics Inc 50 W Street Rd	Warminster	PA	18974	**800-523-3932**	215-674-4100
EFP Corp 223 Middleton Run Rd	Elkhart	IN	46516	**800-205-8537**	574-295-4690
Elgin Molded Plastics 909 Grace St	Elgin	IL	60120	**800-548-5483**	847-931-2455
Evco Plastics Inc 100 W North St	DeForest	WI	53532	**800-507-6000**	608-846-6000
Filtertek Inc 11411 Price Rd	Hebron	IL	60034	**800-248-2461**	815-648-2416
Flambeau Inc 15981 Valplast Rd	Middlefield	OH	44062	**800-457-5252**	440-632-1631
FPI Thermoplastic Technologies PO Box 1907	Morristown	NJ	07962	**800-932-0715**	973-539-4200
Gruber Systems Inc 25636 Ave Stanford	Valencia	CA	91355	**800-257-4070**	661-257-4060
Jarden Plastic Solutions PO Box 2750	Greenville	SC	29602	**888-291-5755**	864-879-7600
Kaye Chris Plastics Corp 715 W Park Rd	Union	MO	63084	**800-325-9927**	636-583-2583
Lehigh Valley Plastics Inc 1075 N Gilmore St	Allentown	PA	18109	**800-354-5344**	610-439-8573
M & Q Plastic Products 1120 Welsh Rd Suite 170	North Wales	PA	19454	**800-600-3068**	267-498-4000
Molding Corp of America 2701 N Ontario St	Burbank	CA	91504	**800-634-3991**	818-840-9288
MXL Industries Inc 1764 Rohrerstown Rd	Lancaster	PA	17601	**800-233-0159**	717-569-8711
National Molding Corp 5 Dubon Ct	Farmingdale	NY	11735	**800-544-7162**	631-293-8696
National Molding Corp Security Plastics Div 14427 NW 60th Ave	Miami Lakes	FL	33014	**800-327-3787**	305-823-5440
New England Plastics Corp 126 Duchaine Blvd *Cust Svc	New Bedford	MA	02745	**800-292-3500***	508-998-3111
ORC Plastics 920 E Raleigh St	Siler City	NC	27344	**800-214-0942**	
Plastech Corp 56 E Broadway Ave Suite 210	Forest Lake	MN	55025	**800-223-0462**	651-407-5700
Precise Technology Inc 501 Mosside Blvd	North Versailles	PA	15137	**800-949-2101**	412-823-2100
Putnam Precision Molding Inc 11 Danco Rd	Putnam	CT	06260	**800-752-7865**	860-928-7911
Royal Plastics Inc 9410 Pineneedle Dr	Mentor	OH	44060	**800-533-2163**	440-352-1357
Sabin Corp 3800 Constitution Ave	Bloomington	IN	47402	**800-264-4510**	812-323-4500
Schiffmayer Plastics Corp 1201 Armstrong St	Algonquin	IL	60102	**800-621-1092**	847-658-8140
Shape Global Technology Inc 90 Community Dr *Cust Svc	Sanford	ME	04073	**800-627-5836***	207-324-5200
Steere Enterprises Inc 285 Commerce St	Tallmadge	OH	44278	**800-875-4926**	330-633-4926
Toledo Molding & Die Inc 4 E Laskey Rd	Toledo	OH	43612	**800-437-5116**	419-476-0581
Tuthill Corp Plastics Group 2050 Sunnydale Blvd	Clearwater	FL	33765	**800-447-5278**	727-446-8593
Vaupell Industrial Plastics Inc 1144 NW 53rd St	Seattle	WA	98107	**800-426-7738**	206-784-9050
Wescon Products Co 2533 S West St	Wichita	KS	67217	**800-835-0160**	316-942-7266
Western Industries Inc Chilton Products Div 300 E Breed St	Chilton	WI	53014	**877-671-7063**	920-849-2381
Westlake Plastics Co PO Box 127	Lenni	PA	19052	**800-999-1700**	610-459-1000
Williams Industries Inc 2201 E Michigan Rd	Shelbyville	IN	46176	**800-383-4701**	317-392-4701
Winzeler Gear Inc 7355 W Wilson Ave	Harwood Heights	IL	60706	**800-621-2397**	708-867-7971

594 PLASTICS & OTHER SYNTHETIC MATERIALS

594-1 Synthetic Fibers & Filaments

Company	City	State	ZIP	Toll-Free	Phone
Barnet William & Son Inc 1300 Hayne St	Arcadia	SC	29320	**800-922-7638**	864-576-7154
Carlee Corp 28 Piermont Rd	Rockleigh	NJ	07647	**800-822-7533**	201-768-6800
Contex Inc 8100 South Blvd	Charlotte	NC	28273	**800-243-8621**	704-554-8621
Fairfield Processing Corp PO Box 1157	Danbury	CT	06813	**800-980-8000**	203-744-2090
Hexcel Corp 281 Tresser Blvd 2 Stamford Plaza 16th Fl *NYSE: HXL*	Stamford	CT	06901	**800-444-3923**	203-969-0666
Honeywell Nylon Inc 4824 Pkwy Plaza Blvd Suite 300	Charlotte	NC	28217	**800-247-0557**	704-423-2000
Honeywell Specialty Materials 101 Columbia Rd	Morristown	NJ	07962	**800-222-0094**	973-455-2145
International Fiber Corp 50 Bridge St	North Tonawanda	NY	14120	**888-698-1936**	716-693-4040
INVISTA 4123 E 37th St North	Wichita	KS	67220	**877-446-8478**	316-828-1000
Martin Color-Fi Inc 320 Neeley St	Sumter	SC	29150	**800-843-6382**	803-436-4200
Noble Fiber Technologies 300 Palm St	Scranton	PA	18505	**877-978-2842**	570-558-5309
Nylon Corp of America 333 Sundial Ave	Manchester	NH	03103	**800-851-2001**	603-627-5150
Performance Fibers 15801 Woods Edge Rd	Colonial Heights	VA	23834	**800-486-0148**	
Specialty Filaments Inc 1 Howard St	Burlington	VT	05401	**800-451-3448**	802-863-6333
Stein Fibers Ltd 4 Computer Dr W Suite 200	Albany	NY	12205	**888-489-2790**	518-489-5700
TC Thiolon USA Corp 1131 Broadway St	Dayton	TN	37321	**800-251-1033**	423-775-0792
William Barnet & Son Inc 1300 Hayne St	Arcadia	SC	29320	**800-922-7638**	864-576-7154

594-2 Synthetic Resins & Plastics Materials

Company	City	State	ZIP	Toll-Free	Phone
A Schulman Inc 3550 W Market St *NASDAQ: SHLM*	Akron	OH	44333	**800-662-3751**	330-666-3751
Akcros Chemicals America 500 Jersey Ave *Cust Svc	New Brunswick	NJ	08903	**800-500-7890***	732-247-2202
Albis Plastics Corp 445 Hwy 36 N PO Box 711	Rosenberg	TX	77471	**888-252-4748**	281-342-3311
AlphaGary Corp 170 Pioneer Dr	Leominster	MA	01453	**800-232-9741**	978-537-8071
Asahi Thermofil Inc 1 Thermofil Way	Fowlerville	MI	48836	**800-444-4408**	517-223-2000
ATOFINA Chemicals Inc 2000 Market St	Philadelphia	PA	19103	**800-533-5552**	215-419-7000
Basell North America Inc 912 Appleton Rd	Elkton	MD	21921	**800-458-1416**	410-996-1600
BASF Corp Chemical Div 333 Mount Hope Ave *Cust Svc	Rockaway	NJ	07866	**800-669-2273***	973-895-8000
Bayer Corp 100 Bayer Rd *NYSE: BAY*	Pittsburgh	PA	15205	**800-662-2927**	412-777-2000
Bayer Inc 77 Belfield Rd	Toronto	ON	M9W1G6	**800-622-2937**	416-248-0771
Bayer MaterialScience LLC 100 Bayer Rd	Pittsburgh	PA	15205	**800-662-2927**	412-777-2000
BP Solvay Polyethylene North America 3333 Richmond Ave	Houston	TX	77098	**800-231-6313**	713-525-4000
Chevron Phillips Chemical Co LP 10001 Six Pines Dr	The Woodlands	TX	77380	**800-231-1212**	832-813-4100
Colorite Specialty Resins PO Box 116	Burlington	NJ	08016	**800-215-1497**	609-386-9200
Cook Composites & Polymers Co 820 E 14th Ave	North Kansas City	MO	64116	**800-821-3590**	816-391-6000
Daikin America Inc 20 Olympic Dr *Cust Svc	Orangeburg	NY	10962	**800-365-9570***	845-365-9500
Day Michael Enterprise Inc PO Box 179	Wadsworth	OH	44282	**800-758-0960**	330-336-7611
Dow Chemical Canada Inc 250 6th Ave SW Suite 2200	Calgary	AB	T2P3H7	**800-433-4398**	403-267-3500
Dow Chemical Co 2030 Dow Ctr *NYSE: DOW* ■ *Cust Svc	Midland	MI	48674	**800-331-6451***	989-636-1000
DSM Engineering Plastics Inc 2267 W Mill Rd	Evansville	IN	47720	**800-333-4237**	812-435-7500
DuPont Air Products NanoMaterials LLC 1969 Palomar Oaks Way	Carlsbad	CA	92009	**866-265-0058**	760-931-9555
DuPont El de Nemours & Co Inc 1007 Market St *NYSE: DD*	Wilmington	DE	19898	**800-441-7515**	302-774-1000
DuPont Engineering Polymers Lancaster Pike Rt 141 Barley Mill Plaza Bldg 22	Wilmington	DE	19805	**800-441-0575**	302-999-4592
DuPont Packaging & Industrial Polymers Barley Mill Plaza 26-2122 PO Box 80026	Wilmington	DE	19880	**800-438-7225**	302-774-1161
Dyneon LLC 50 Milton Dr	Aston	PA	19014	**800-554-6782**	610-497-8899
Eastman Chemical Co PO Box 431 *NYSE: EMN* ■ *Cust Svc	Kingsport	TN	37662	**800-327-8626***	423-229-2000
El DuPont de Nemours & Co Inc 1007 Market St *NYSE: DD*	Wilmington	DE	19898	**800-441-7515**	302-774-1000
Engineered Polymer Solutions Inc 1400 N State St	Marengo	IL	60152	**800-654-4242**	815-568-3020
Gallagher Corp 3908 Morrison Dr	Gurnee	IL	60031	**800-249-3473**	847-249-3440
GE Plastics 1 Plastics Ave	Pittsfield	MA	01201	**800-451-3147**	413-448-7484
Goldsmith & Eggleton Inc 300 1st St	Wadsworth	OH	44281	**800-321-0954**	330-336-6616

Classified Section

Synthetic Resins & Plastics Materials (Cont'd)

				Toll-Free	Phone
Hercules Inc 1313 N Market St Hercules Plaza *NYSE: HPC*	Wilmington	DE	19894	**800-441-7600**	302-594-5000
Heritage Plastics Inc 1002 Hunt St	Picayune	MS	39466	**800-245-4623**	601-798-8663
Huntsman Corp 500 Huntsman Way *NYSE: HUN*	Salt Lake City	UT	84108	**800-421-2411**	801-584-5700
Interplastic Corp 1225 Willow Lake Blvd	Saint Paul	MN	55110	**800-736-5497**	651-481-6860
Lewcott Corp 86 Providence Rd *Sales	Millbury	MA	01527	**800-225-7725***	508-865-1791
Lord Corp 111 Lord Dr	Cary	NC	27511	**800-524-2885**	919-468-5979
Markel Corp 435 School Ln	Plymouth Meeting	PA	19462	**800-462-4479**	610-272-8960
Mer-Kote Products Inc 501 S Van Ness Ave	Torrance	CA	90501	**800-851-6303**	323-775-2461
Michael Day Enterprises Inc PO Box 179	Wadsworth	OH	44282	**800-758-0960**	330-336-7611
Minova USA Inc 150 Carley Ct	Georgetown	KY	40324	**800-626-2948**	502-863-6800
Mitsui Chemicals America Inc 2500 Westchester Ave Suite 110	Purchase	NY	10577	**800-682-2377**	914-253-0777
Modern Dispersions Inc 78 Marguerite Ave	Leominster	MA	01453	**800-633-6434**	978-534-3370
NeoResins 730 Main St	Wilmington	MA	01887	**800-225-0947**	978-658-6600
Neville Chemical Co 2800 Neville Rd *Cust Svc	Pittsburgh	PA	15225	**877-704-4200***	412-331-4200
Occidental Chemical Corp 5005 LBJ Fwy	Dallas	TX	75244	**800-570-8880**	972-404-3300
Perstorp Polyols Inc 600 Matzinger Rd *Cust Svc	Toledo	OH	43612	**800-537-0280***	419-729-5448
Plastics Color & Compounding Inc 349 Lake Rd	Dayville	CT	06241	**888-549-7820**	860-774-3770
Plastomer Technologies 23 Friends Ln	Newtown	PA	18940	**800-798-1288**	215-968-5011
Poly Hi Solidur Inc 2710 American Way	Fort Wayne	IN	46809	**877-476-5944**	260-479-4100
PolyOne Corp 33587 Walker Rd *NYSE: POL*	Avon Lake	OH	44012	**866-765-9663**	440-930-1000
Reichhold Inc 2400 Ellis Rd	Durham	NC	27703	**800-448-3482**	919-990-7500
Resinall Corp 3065 High Ridge Rd *Cust Svc	Stamford	CT	06905	**800-421-0561***	203-329-7100
Rhe Tech Inc 1500 E North Territorial Rd	Whitmore Lake	MI	48189	**800-837-4921**	734-769-0585
Rogers Corp 1 Technology Dr *NYSE: ROG*	Rogers	CT	06263	**800-227-6437**	860-774-9605
RTP Co 580 E Front St	Winona	MN	55987	**800-433-4787**	507-454-6900
Rutland Plastic Technologies 10021 Rodney St	Pineville	NC	28134	**800-438-5134**	704-553-0046
Sartomer Co 502 Thomas Jones Way	Exton	PA	19341	**800-345-8247**	610-363-4100
Schulman A Inc 3550 W Market St *NASDAQ: SHLM*	Akron	OH	44333	**800-662-3751**	330-666-3751
Spartech Corp 120 S Central Ave Suite 1700 *NYSE: SEH*	Clayton	MO	63105	**888-721-4242**	314-721-4242
Sterling Fibers Inc 5005 Sterling Way *Cust Svc	Pace	FL	32571	**800-874-8593***	850-994-5311
Thermagon Inc 4707 Detroit Ave	Cleveland	OH	44102	**888-246-9050**	216-939-2300
Ticona LLC 8040 Dixie Hwy	Florence	KY	41042	**800-833-4882**	859-525-4740
Vi-Chem Corp 55 Cottage Grove St SW	Grand Rapids	MI	49507	**800-477-8501**	616-247-8501

594-3 Synthetic Rubber

				Toll-Free	Phone
Akrochem Corp 255 Fountain St	Akron	OH	44304	**800-321-2260**	330-535-2108
American Synthetic Rubber Corp PO Box 32960 *Cust Svc	Louisville	KY	40232	**800-262-9253***	502-449-8300
Associated Rubber Co PO Box 245	Tallapoosa	GA	30176	**800-277-8231**	770-574-2321
Diamond US Elastomer 161 Marble Mill Rd	Marietta	GA	30060	**800-394-8735**	770-424-4850
Firestone Polymers 381 W Wilbeth Rd *Cust Svc	Akron	OH	44319	**800-282-0222***	330-379-7000
Goodyear Tire & Rubber Co 1144 E Market St *NYSE: GT* ■ *Cust Svc	Akron	OH	44316	**800-321-2136***	330-796-2121
ISP Elastomers 1615 Main St	Port Neches	TX	77651	**800-847-1625**	409-722-8321
Midwest Elastomers Inc PO Box 412	Wapakoneta	OH	45895	**800-786-3539**	419-738-8844
Teknor Apex Co 505 Central Ave	Pawtucket	RI	02861	**800-556-3864**	401-725-8000
Textile Rubber & Chemical Co Inc 1300 Tiarco Dr SW	Dalton	GA	30721	**800-727-8453**	706-277-1300
US Elastomer 161 Marble Mill Rd	Marietta	GA	30060	**800-394-8735**	770-424-4850

595 PLASTICS PRODUCTS - FIBERGLASS REINFORCED

				Toll-Free	Phone
AO Smith Corp 11270 W Park Pl Suite 170 *NYSE: AOS*	Milwaukee	WI	53224	**800-359-4065**	414-359-4000
Bowie Mfg Inc 313 S Hancock	Lake City	IA	51449	**800-831-0960**	712-464-3191
Ershigs Inc PO Box 1707	Bellingham	WA	98227	**888-377-4447**	360-733-2620
Ewald Red Inc PO Box 519	Karnes City	TX	78118	**800-242-3524**	830-780-3304
Fiber-Tech Industries Inc 2000 Kenskill Ave	Washington Court House	OH	43160	**800-879-4377**	740-335-9400
Fibergrate Composite Structures Inc 5151 Beltline Rd Suite 700	Dallas	TX	75254	**800-527-4043**	972-250-1633
Glastic Corp 4321 Glenridge Rd	Cleveland	OH	44121	**800-360-1319**	216-486-0100
GMI Composites Inc 1355 W Sherman Blvd	Muskegon	MI	49441	**800-330-4045**	231-755-1611
Kemlite Co 23525 W Eames St	Channahon	IL	60410	**800-435-0080**	815-467-8600
Lasco Bathware 8101 E Kaiser Blvd Suite 130	Anaheim	CA	92808	**800-877-2005**	714-993-1220
McClarin Plastics Inc 600 Linden Ave PO Box 486	Hanover	PA	17331	**800-233-3189**	717-637-2241
Smith AO Corp 11270 W Park Pl Suite 170 *NYSE: AOS*	Milwaukee	WI	53224	**800-359-4065**	414-359-4000

596 PLASTICS PRODUCTS - HOUSEHOLD

				Toll-Free	Phone
Aero Plastics Inc 163 Pioneer Dr	Leominster	MA	01453	**800-458-0116**	978-537-4363
Alladin Plastics Inc 140 Industrial Dr	Surgoinsville	TN	37873	**800-960-2351**	423-345-2351
American Household Products Inc 8220 Dunnavant Rd SE PO Box 310	Leeds	AL	35094	**800-325-3895**	205-699-5144
Blitz USA Inc 404 26th Ave NW *Cust Svc	Miami	OK	74354	**800-331-3795***	918-540-1515
Carthage Cup 505 E Cotton St	Carthage	TX	75633	**800-527-8440**	903-693-7151
Contico International LLC 305 Rock Industrial Pk Dr	Saint Louis	MO	63044	**800-831-7077**	314-656-4349
Dart Container Corp 500 Hogsback Rd	Mason	MI	48854	**800-248-5960**	517-676-3800
Dial Industries Inc 3616 Noakes St	Los Angeles	CA	90023	**800-624-8682**	323-263-6878
Duraco Products Inc 1109 E Lake St	Streamwood	IL	60107	**800-888-7687**	630-837-6615
Eagle Affiliates Inc 1000 S 2nd St	Plainfield	NJ	07063	**800-221-0434**	908-757-4464
Fiskars Brands Inc 2537 Daniels St	Madison	WI	53718	**800-500-4849**	608-259-1649
GT Water Products Inc 5239 N Commerce Ave	Moorpark	CA	93021	**800-862-5647**	805-529-2900
Home Products International Inc 4501 W 47th St *NASDAQ: HOMZ*	Chicago	IL	60632	**800-327-3534**	773-890-1010
Igloo Products Corp 777 Igloo Rd *Cust Svc	Katy	TX	77494	**800-324-2653***	713-465-2571
Jet Plastica Inc 1100 Schwab Rd	Hatfield	PA	19440	**800-220-5381**	215-362-1501
King Plastics Inc 840 N Elm St	Orange	CA	92867	**800-997-7540**	714-997-7540
Kraftware Corp 270 Cox St	Roselle	NJ	07203	**800-221-1728**	908-259-8883
Majestic 60 Cherry St	Bridgeport	CT	06605	**800-673-2543**	203-367-7900
Maryland Plastics Inc 251 E Central Ave *Cust Svc	Federalsburg	MD	21632	**800-544-5582***	410-754-5566
Meese Inc 1745 Cragmont St	Madison	IN	47250	**800-829-4535**	812-273-3232
Newell Rubbermaid Inc Home & Family Group 10B Glenlake Pkwy Suite 600	Atlanta	GA	30328	**800-434-4314**	770-407-3800
Prolon Inc PO Box 568	Port Gibson	MS	39150	**800-628-7749**	601-437-4211
Sterilite Corp PO Box 524	Townsend	MA	01469	**800-225-1046**	978-597-8702
TAP Plastics Inc 6475 Sierra Ln	Dublin	CA	94568	**800-894-0827**	925-829-4889
Thermos Co 2550 W Golf Rd Suite 800 *Cust Svc	Rolling Meadows	IL	60008	**800-243-0745***	847-439-7821
Tupperware Corp PO Box 2353 *NYSE: TUP* ■ *Cust Svc	Orlando	FL	32802	**800-772-4001***	407-847-3111
US Can Co 98 Amlajack Blvd	Newnan	GA	30265	**800-929-4274**	770-253-7176
Venturi Inc PO Box 6348 *Cust Svc	Traverse City	MI	49696	**800-968-0104***	231-929-7732
WNA Comet East Inc 6 Stuart Rd	Chelmsford	MA	01824	**800-225-0939**	978-256-6551

597 PLASTICS PRODUCTS (MISC)

				Toll-Free	Phone
Aigner Index Inc 218 MacArthur Ave	New Windsor	NY	12553	**800-242-3919**	845-562-4510
AJ Siris Corp Inc PO Box AV	Paterson	NJ	07509	**800-526-5300**	973-684-7700
Alexander Plastics Inc 11937 Denton Dr	Dallas	TX	75234	**800-421-4171**	972-241-4171
All States Inc 1801 W Foster Ave *Cust Svc	Chicago	IL	60640	**800-621-5837***	773-728-0525
Allied Plastics Inc 9445 E River Rd	Coon Rapids	MN	55433	**800-328-3113**	763-862-4500
Avery Dennison Fastener Div 224 Industrial Rd	Fitchburg	MA	01420	**800-225-5913**	978-353-2100
Beemak Plastics Inc 18554 S Susana Rd	Rancho Dominguez	CA	90221	**800-421-4393**	310-886-5880
Bemis Mfg Co PO Box 901	Sheboygan Falls	WI	53085	**800-558-7651**	920-467-4621
Concept Plastics Inc PO Box 847	High Point	NC	27260	**800-225-9553**	336-889-2001
DelStar Technologies Inc 220 E St Elmo Rd	Austin	TX	78745	**800-531-5112**	512-447-7000
Evergreen Scientific Co 2300 E 49th St	Los Angeles	CA	90058	**800-421-6261**	323-583-1331
Fiberglass Specialties Inc PO Box 1340	Henderson	TX	75653	**800-527-1459**	903-657-6522
Gabriel Mfg Co Inc 125 S Liberty Dr	Stony Point	NY	10980	**800-454-3387**	845-942-0100
General Polymeric Corp PO Box 380	Reading	PA	19607	**800-654-4391**	610-374-5171
Goodrich Corp Engineered Polymer Products Div 6061 Goodrich Blvd	Jacksonville	FL	32226	**800-366-8945**	904-757-3660
Hygolet Inc 349 SE 2nd Ave	Deerfield Beach	FL	33441	**800-494-6538**	954-481-8601
Kalwall Corp 1111 Candia Rd	Manchester	NH	03109	**800-258-9777**	603-627-3861
M & D Industries International Inc 7700 Anagram Dr	Eden Prairie	MN	55344	**888-469-5277**	
MOCAP Inc 13100 Manchester Rd	Saint Louis	MO	63131	**800-633-6775**	314-543-4000
NEXPAK Corp 3475 Forest Lake Dr Suite 200	Uniontown	OH	44685	**800-442-5742**	330-896-3050
PI Inc PO Box 669 *Cust Svc	Athens	TN	37371	**800-951-3542***	423-745-6213
Plastomer Technologies 23 Friends Ln	Newtown	PA	18940	**800-798-1288**	215-968-5011
Plastpro Inc 9 Peach Tree Hill Rd	Livingston	NJ	07039	**800-779-0561**	973-994-7708
Porex Technologies Corp 500 Bohannon Rd *Cust Svc	Fairburn	GA	30213	**800-241-0195***	770-964-1421
PSI Inc 10630 Marina Dr	Olive Branch	MS	38654	**866-638-7926**	662-895-8777
Richco Inc 8145 River Dr	Morton Grove	IL	60053	**800-466-8301**	773-539-4060
Rogan Corp 3455 Woodhead Dr	Northbrook	IL	60062	**800-423-1543**	847-498-2300
Rubbermaid Commercial Products 3124 Valley Ave	Winchester	VA	22601	**800-347-9800**	540-667-8700
Shakespeare Composites & Electronics 19845 US Hwy 76	Newberry	SC	29108	**800-800-9008**	803-276-5504
Shakespeare Monofilaments & Specialty Polymers PO Box 4060	Columbia	SC	29240	**800-845-2110**	803-754-7011
Smith McDonald Corp 304 Sonwil Dr	Buffalo	NY	14225	**800-753-8548**	716-684-7200
Spir-It Inc 159 Rangeway Rd	North Billerica	MA	01862	**800-321-7667**	978-964-1551
Thombert Inc 316 E 7th St N	Newton	IA	50208	**800-433-3572**	641-792-4449
Triad Products Co 1801 W 'B' St	Hastings	NE	68901	**800-241-3704**	402-462-2181
Value Plastics Inc 3325 Timberline Rd	Fort Collins	CO	80525	**888-404-5837**	970-223-8306
Wiedemann Church Products PO Box 677	Muscatine	IA	52761	**800-553-9664**	563-263-6642

598 PLUMBING FIXTURES & FITTINGS - METAL

				Toll-Free	Phone
Acorn Engineering Co Inc PO Box 3527	City of Industry	CA	91744	**800-488-8999**	626-336-4561
Alsons Corp PO Box 282	Hillsdale	MI	49242	**800-421-0001**	517-439-1411
American Brass Mfg Co 5000 Superior Ave	Cleveland	OH	44103	**800-431-6440**	216-431-6565
American Standard Inc 1 Centennial Ave PO Box 6820	Piscataway	NJ	08855	**800-223-0068**	732-980-6000
Anderson Copper & Brass Co 4325 Frontage Rd	Oak Forest	IL	60452	**800-323-5284**	708-535-9030
Bath Unlimited 1578 Sussex Tpk	Randolph	NJ	07869	**800-635-2731**	973-598-4300
Bradley Corp PO Box 309	Menomonee Falls	WI	53051	**800-272-3539**	262-251-6000
Brasstech Inc 2001 E Carnegie Ave	Santa Ana	CA	92705	**888-436-0805**	949-417-5207
Central Brass Mfg Co Inc 2950 E 55th St	Cleveland	OH	44127	**800-321-8630**	216-883-0220
Champion Irrigation Products Inc 3141 N Maxson Rd	El Monte	CA	91732	**800-332-4267**	323-221-2108

Classified Section

				Toll-Free	Phone
Chicago Faucet Co 2100 S Clearwater Dr	Des Plaines	IL	60018	**800-323-5060**	847-803-5000
CSI Bath Accessories Div Moen Inc 25300 Al Moen Dr	North Olmsted	OH	44070	**800-321-8809**	440-962-2000
Eljer Plumbingware Inc 14801 Quorum Dr	Dallas	TX	75254	**800-423-5537**	972-560-2000
Fisher Mfg Co PO Box 60	Tulare	CA	93275	**800-421-6162**	559-685-5200
Fluidmaster Inc 30800 Rancho Viejo Rd	San Juan Capistrano	CA	92675	**800-631-2011**	949-728-2000
Hansgrohe Inc 1490 Bluegrass Lakes Pkwy Suite 200	Alpharetta	GA	30004	**800-334-0455**	770-360-9880
In-Sink-Erator 4700 21st St	Racine	WI	53406	**800-558-5712**	262-554-5432
Josam Co PO Box T	Michigan City	IN	46361	**800-365-6726**	219-872-5531
Keeney Mfg Co 1170 Main St	Newington	CT	06111	**800-243-0526***	860-666-3342
*Cust Svc					
Keystone Maax PO Box 544	Southampton	PA	18966	**800-355-5397**	215-825-5250
Kohler Canada Co 180 Creditview Rd	Vaughan	ON	L4L9N4	**800-964-5590**	905-762-6599
Kohler Plumbing North America 444 Highland Dr	Kohler	WI	53044	**800-456-4537**	920-457-4441
Macristy Industries Inc 206 Newington Ave	New Britain	CT	06051	**800-966-6964**	860-225-4637
Microphor Inc 452 E Hill Rd	Willits	CA	95490	**800-358-8280***	707-459-5563
*Orders					
Moen Inc 25300 Al Moen Dr	North Olmsted	OH	44070	**800-289-6636***	440-962-2000
*Cust Svc					
Moen Inc CSI Bath Accessories Div 25300 Al Moen Dr	North Olmsted	OH	44070	**800-321-8809**	440-962-2000
Norman Supply Co 825 SW 5th St	Oklahoma City	OK	73109	**800-375-3457**	405-235-9511
Oatey Co 4700 W 160th St	Cleveland	OH	44135	**800-321-9532***	216-267-7100
*Cust Svc					
Price Pfister Inc 19701 Da Vinci St	Lake Forest	CA	92610	**800-732-8238**	949-672-4000
Sloan Valve Co 10500 Seymour Ave	Franklin Park	IL	60131	**800-982-5839**	847-671-4300
Speakman Co 400 Anchor Mill Rd	New Castle	DE	19720	**800-537-2107**	302-764-9100
Steinen William Mfg Co 29 E Halsey Rd	Parsippany	NJ	07054	**800-724-3343**	973-887-6400
Sterling Plumbing Group Inc 444 Highland Dr	Kohler	WI	53044	**888-783-7546***	920-457-4441
*Cust Svc					
Symmons Industries Inc 31 Brooks Dr	Braintree	MA	02184	**800-796-6667**	781-848-2250
T & S Brass & Bronze Works Inc PO Box 1088	Travelers Rest	SC	29690	**800-476-4103***	864-834-4102
*Cust Svc					
Water Saver Faucet Co 701 W Erie St 2nd Fl	Chicago	IL	60610	**800-973-7278***	312-666-5500
*Parts					
William Steinen Mfg Co 29 E Halsey Rd	Parsippany	NJ	07054	**800-724-3343**	973-887-6400
Woodford Mfg Co 2121 Waynoka Rd	Colorado Springs	CO	80915	**800-621-6032***	719-574-0600
*Sales					

599 PLUMBING FIXTURES & FITTINGS - PLASTICS

				Toll-Free	Phone
AmBath Corp 1055 S Country Club Dr	Mesa	AZ	85210	**888-826-2284**	480-844-2596
Florestone Products Co Inc 2851 Falcon Dr	Madera	CA	93637	**800-446-8827**	559-661-4171
Lasco Bathware 8101 E Kaiser Blvd Suite 130	Anaheim	CA	92808	**800-877-2005**	714-993-1220
Maax Inc 1010 Sherbrooke St W Suite 1610	Montreal	QC	H3A2R7	**800-463-6229**	
TSE: MXA					
Olsonite Corp 25 Dart Rd	Newnan	GA	30265	**800-521-8266**	770-253-3930
Sanderson Plumbing Products Inc PO Box 1367	Columbus	MS	39705	**800-647-1042**	662-328-4000
Softub Inc 27615 Ave Hopkins	Valencia	CA	91355	**800-554-1120***	661-702-1401
*Sales					
Thetford Corp PO Box 1285	Ann Arbor	MI	48106	**800-521-3032**	734-769-6000
Tomkins Industries Inc LASCO Products Group 151 Industrial St	Lancaster	TX	75134	**800-876-3044**	972-227-6692

600 PLUMBING FIXTURES & FITTINGS - VITREOUS CHINA & EARTHENWARE

				Toll-Free	Phone
American Standard Inc 1 Centennial Ave PO Box 6820	Piscataway	NJ	08855	**800-223-0068**	732-980-6000
Briggs Plumbing Products 300 Eagle Rd	Goose Creek	SC	29445	**800-888-4458**	843-569-7887
Eljer Plumbingware Inc 14801 Quorum Dr	Dallas	TX	75254	**800-423-5537**	972-560-2000
ITT Industries Jabsco 20 Icon	Foothill Ranch	CA	92610	**800-235-6538**	949-609-5106
Kohler Canada Co 180 Creditview Rd	Vaughan	ON	L4L9N4	**800-964-5590**	905-762-6599
Kohler Plumbing North America 444 Highland Dr	Kohler	WI	53044	**800-456-4537**	920-457-4441
Microphor Inc 452 E Hill Rd	Willits	CA	95490	**800-358-8280***	707-459-5563
*Orders					
Norman Supply Co 825 SW 5th St	Oklahoma City	OK	73109	**800-375-3457**	405-235-9511
Peerless Pottery Inc PO Box 145	Rockport	IN	47635	**800-457-5785**	812-649-6430
Sunrise Specialty Co 930 98th Ave	Oakland	CA	94603	**800-646-9117**	510-729-7277
TOTO USA Inc 1155 Southern Rd	Morrow	GA	30260	**888-295-8134**	770-282-8686

601 PLUMBING, HEATING, AIR CONDITIONING EQUIPMENT & SUPPLIES - WHOL

SEE ALSO Refrigeration Equipment - Whol

				Toll-Free	Phone
AB Young Cos Inc 15305 Stony Creek Way	Noblesville	IN	46060	**800-886-7001**	317-565-5000
Air Monitor Corp 1050 Hopper Ave	Santa Rosa	CA	95403	**800-247-3569**	707-544-2706
American Granby Inc 7645 Henry Clay Blvd	Liverpool	NY	13088	**800-776-2266**	315-451-1100
Arizona Wholesale Supply Co 2020 E University Dr	Phoenix	AZ	85062	**800-877-4954**	602-258-7901
Automatic Firing Co Inc 2100 Fillmore Ave	Buffalo	NY	14214	**866-836-0300**	716-836-0300
Baker Distributing Co 7892 Baymeadows Way	Jacksonville	FL	32256	**877-733-9633**	904-733-9633
Barnett Inc 3333 Lenox Ave	Jacksonville	FL	32254	**800-288-2000**	904-384-6530
Bayonne Plumbing 250 Ave E	Bayonne	NJ	07002	**800-713-7473**	201-339-8000
Brauer Supply Co 4260 Forest Park Ave	Saint Louis	MO	63108	**800-392-8776**	314-534-7150
Butcher Distributors Inc 101 Boyce Rd	Broussard	LA	70518	**800-960-0008**	337-837-2088
Coastline Distribution Inc 317 S Northlake Blvd Suite 1024	Altamonte Springs	FL	32701	**800-741-5531**	407-323-8500
Coburn Supply Co Inc 550 Fannin St Suite 950	Beaumont	TX	77701	**800-832-8492**	409-838-6363
Comfort Supply Inc 407 Garden Oaks Blvd	Houston	TX	77018	**800-281-7511**	713-845-4705
Consolidated Supply Co 7337 SW Kable Ln	Tigard	OR	97224	**800-929-5810**	503-620-7050
Cooper Harry Supply Co Inc 605 N Sherman Pkwy	Springfield	MO	65802	**800-426-6737**	417-865-8392
Dana Kepner Co Inc 700 Alcott St	Denver	CO	80204	**800-332-3079**	303-623-6161
Duncan Supply Co Inc 910 N Illinois St	Indianapolis	IN	46204	**800-382-5528**	317-634-1335
Eastern Pennsylvania Supply Co 700 Scott St PO Box 1126	Wilkes-Barre	PA	18773	**800-432-8075**	570-823-1181
Emerson-Swan Inc 300 Pond St	Randolph	MA	02368	**800-346-9219**	781-986-2000
Engineering & Equipment Co Inc 910 N Washington St	Albany	GA	31701	**800-688-8816**	229-435-5601
Everett J Prescott Inc 32 Prescott St	Gardiner	ME	04345	**800-876-1357**	207-582-1851
First Supply LLC 6800 Gisholt Dr	Madison	WI	53713	**800-236-9795**	608-222-7799
Four Seasons Inc 1801 Waters Ridge Dr	Lewisville	TX	75057	**800-433-7508**	972-316-8100
Fresno Distributing Co Inc 2055 E McKinley Ave	Fresno	CA	93703	**800-655-2542**	559-442-8800
Gateway Supply Co Inc 1312 Hamrick St	Columbia	SC	29202	**800-922-5312**	803-771-7160
Gensco Inc 4402 20th St E	Tacoma	WA	98424	**800-729-3003**	253-922-3003
Goodin Co 2700 N 2nd St	Minneapolis	MN	55411	**800-328-8433**	612-588-7811
Granite Group Wholesalers LLC 6 Storrs St	Concord	NH	03301	**800-258-3690**	603-224-1901
Hajoca Corp 127 Coulter Ave	Ardmore	PA	19003	**800-284-3164**	610-649-1430
Hajoca Corp Keenan Supply Div 1341 Philadelphia St	Pomona	CA	91766	**800-437-6593**	909-613-1363
Handy NB Co 65 10th St	Lynchburg	VA	24504	**800-284-6242**	434-847-4495
Harrison Piping Supply Co Inc 38777 Schoolcraft Rd	Livonia	MI	48150	**800-482-3929**	734-464-4400
Harry Cooper Supply Co Inc 605 N Sherman Pkwy	Springfield	MO	65802	**800-426-6737**	417-865-8392
Hercules Industries Inc 1310 W Evans Ave	Denver	CO	80223	**800-356-5350**	303-937-1000
Indiana Supply Corp 3835 E 21st St	Indianapolis	IN	46218	**800-686-0195**	317-359-5451
Interline Brands Inc 801 W Bay St	Jacksonville	FL	32204	**800-288-2000**	904-421-1400
NYSE: IBI					
J & B Supply Inc 4915 S Zero St	Fort Smith	AR	72903	**800-345-5752**	479-649-4915
JH Larson Co 10200 51st Ave N	Plymouth	MN	55442	**800-292-7970**	763-545-1717
John M Frey Co Inc 2735 62nd St Ct	Bettendorf	IA	52722	**800-397-3739**	563-332-9200
Johnson Supply & Equipment Inc 10151 Stella Link Rd	Houston	TX	77025	**800-833-5455**	713-661-6666
Keenan Supply Div Hajoca Corp 1341 Philadelphia St	Pomona	CA	91766	**800-437-6593**	909-613-1363
Keller Supply Co Inc 3209 17th Ave W	Seattle	WA	98119	**800-285-3302**	206-285-3300
Kelly's Pipe & Supply Co Inc 2124 Industrial Rd	Las Vegas	NV	89102	**888-382-4957**	702-382-4957
Koch Air LLC PO Box 1167	Evansville	IN	47706	**877-456-2422**	812-962-5200
Larson JH Co 10200 51st Ave N	Plymouth	MN	55442	**800-292-7970**	763-545-1717
Lee Supply Corp 6610 Guion Rd	Indianapolis	IN	46268	**800-873-1103**	317-290-2500
Michel RE Co Inc 1 RE Michel Dr	Glen Burnie	MD	21060	**800-283-7362**	410-760-4000
Mid-Lakes Distributing Inc 1029 W Adams St	Chicago	IL	60607	**888-733-2700**	312-733-1033
Mid-States Supply Co 1716 Guinotte Ave	Kansas City	MO	64120	**800-825-1410**	816-842-4290
Milwaukee Stove & Furnace Supply Co 5070 W State St	Milwaukee	WI	53208	**800-677-0213**	414-258-0300
Mingledorffs Inc 6675 Jones Mill Ct	Norcross	GA	30092	**800-282-4911**	770-446-6311
Morley-Murphy Co 200 S Washington St Suite 305	Green Bay	WI	54301	**877-499-3171**	920-499-3171
Mountainland Supply Co 1505 W 130 South	Orem	UT	84058	**800-666-5434**	801-224-6050
NB Handy Co 65 10th St	Lynchburg	VA	24504	**800-284-6242**	434-847-4495
Noland Co 80 29th St	Newport News	VA	23607	**800-446-8960**	757-928-9000
NASDAQ: NOLD					
Parnell-Martin Co Inc 1315 N Graham St	Charlotte	NC	28206	**800-849-2443**	704-375-8651
Plumb Supply Co 1622 NE 51st Ave	Des Moines	IA	50313	**800-483-9511**	515-262-9511
Plumbers Supply Co 1000 E Main St	Louisville	KY	40206	**800-626-5133**	502-582-2261
Plumbing Distributors Inc 20 Collins Industrial Way	Lawrenceville	GA	30046	**800-262-9231**	770-963-9231
Prescott Everett J Inc 32 Prescott St	Gardiner	ME	04345	**800-876-1357**	207-582-1851
RE Michel Co Inc 1 RE Michel Dr	Glen Burnie	MD	21060	**800-283-7362**	410-760-4000
Redlon & Johnson 172-174 Saint John St	Portland	ME	04102	**800-905-5250**	207-773-4755
Ridgewood Corp 270 Rt 17 S	Mahwah	NJ	07430	**800-562-0214***	201-529-5500
*Cust Svc					
Roosevelt WA Co 2727 Commerce St	La Crosse	WI	54603	**800-279-2726**	608-781-2000
Sauna Warehouse Inc 20902 Bake Pkwy Suite 110	Lake Forest	CA	92630	**800-906-2242**	949-699-0820
Security Supply Corp 196 Maple Ave	Selkirk	NY	12158	**800-333-2226**	518-767-2226
SG Supply Co 12900 S Throop St	Calumet Park	IL	60827	**800-626-9130**	708-371-8800
Standard Air & Lite Corp 2406 Woodmere Dr	Pittsburgh	PA	15205	**800-472-2458**	412-920-6505
Temperature Systems Inc 5001 Voges Rd	Madison	WI	53718	**800-366-0930**	608-271-7500
Three States Supply Co LLC 666 EH Crump Blvd	Memphis	TN	38101	**800-666-1565**	901-948-8651
Torrington Supply Co Inc 100 N Elm St	Waterbury	CT	06723	**800-445-9936**	203-756-3641
United Pipe & Supply Co Inc 90099 Prairie Rd	Eugene	OR	97402	**800-288-6511**	541-688-6511
UP Electric/Wittock Supply Co 2201 E Industrial Dr	Iron Mountain	MI	49801	**800-562-7102**	906-774-4455
US Airconditioning Distributors 16900 Chestnut St	City of Industry	CA	91748	**800-937-7222**	626-854-4500
Vamac Inc 4201 Jacque St	Richmond	VA	23230	**800-768-2622**	804-353-7811
WA Roosevelt Co 2727 Commerce St	La Crosse	WI	54603	**800-279-2726**	608-781-2000
Waxman Industries Inc 24460 Aurora Rd	Bedford Heights	OH	44146	**800-531-3342**	440-439-1830
Western Nevada Supply Co 950 S Rock Blvd	Sparks	NV	89431	**800-648-1230**	775-359-5800
Wilmar Industries Inc 200 E Park Dr Suite 200	Mount Laurel	NJ	08054	**800-345-3000**	856-439-1222
Woodhill Supply Inc 4665 Beidler Rd	Willoughby	OH	44094	**800-362-6111**	440-269-1100
Young AB Cos Inc 15305 Stony Creek Way	Noblesville	IN	46060	**800-886-7001**	317-565-5000
Young Supply Co 888 W Baltimore St	Detroit	MI	48202	**800-872-3280**	313-875-3280

602 PLYWOOD & VENEERS

SEE ALSO Construction Materials - Lumber & Building Supplies; Home Improvement Centers

				Toll-Free	Phone
Atlantic Veneer Corp 2457 Lennoxville Rd PO Box 660	Beaufort	NC	28516	**800-334-7723**	252-728-3169
California Panel & Veneer Co PO Box 3250	Cerritos	CA	90703	**800-451-1745**	562-926-5834
Capitol Plywood Inc 160 Commerce Cir	Sacramento	CA	95815	**800-326-1505**	916-922-8861

Name / Address	City	State	ZIP	Toll-Free	Phone
Chesapeake Hardwood Products Inc 201 Dexter St W	Chesapeake	VA	23324	**800-446-8162**	757-543-1601
Cleveland Plywood Co Inc 5900 Harvard Ave	Cleveland	OH	44105	**800-727-2759**	216-641-6600
Coastal Wood Products Inc 13285 Temple Ave	City of Industry	CA	91746	**800-852-9663**	626-333-1104
Columbia Forest Products Inc 222 SW Columbia St Suite 1575	Portland	OR	97201	**800-547-4261**	503-224-5300
Columbia Forest Products Inc Columbia Plywood Div PO Box 1780	Klamath Falls	OR	97601	**800-547-1791**	541-882-7281
Constantine's Wood Center 1040 E Oakland Pk Blvd	Fort Lauderdale	FL	33334	**800-443-9667**	954-561-1716
Darlington Veneer Co Inc PO Box 1087	Darlington	SC	29540	**800-845-2388**	843-393-3861
Dean Co Inc PO Box 1239	Princeton	WV	24740	**800-624-6153**	304-425-8701
Fiber-Tech Industries Inc 2000 Kenskill Ave	Washington Court House	OH	43160	**800-879-4377**	740-335-9400
Flexible Materials Inc 1202 Port Rd	Jeffersonville	IN	47130	**800-359-9663**	812-280-7000
G-L Veneer Co Inc 2224 E Slauson Ave	Huntington Park	CA	90255	**800-588-5003**	323-582-5203
Harbor Sales Co Inc 1000 Harbor Ct	Sudlersville	MD	21668	**800-345-1712**	
Hardel Mutual Plywood Corp PO Box 566	Chehalis	WA	98532	**800-562-6344**	360-740-0232
Inland Plywood Co 375 N Cass Ave	Pontiac	MI	48342	**800-521-4355**	248-334-4706
International Wood Industries Inc 250 D St	Turlock	CA	95380	**800-458-5545**	209-632-3300
Louisiana-Pacific Corp 414 Union St Suite 2000 *NYSE: LPX*	Nashville	TN	37219	**877-744-5600**	615-986-5600
MacBeath Hardwood Co 2150 Oakdale Ave	San Francisco	CA	94124	**800-233-0782**	415-401-7046
McKnight Plywood Inc 201 N 1st St	West Helena	AR	72390	**800-566-2145**	870-572-2501
Norbord Industries Inc 1 Toronto St 6th Fl *TSE: NBD*	Toronto	ON	M5C2W4	**877-263-9367**	416-643-8820
Norbord Industries Inc 1 Toronto St Suite 600	Toronto	ON	M5C2W4	**800-387-1740**	416-365-0710
North American Plywood Corp 12343 Hawkins St *Sales	Santa Fe Springs	CA	90670	**800-421-1372***	562-941-7575
Pavco Industries Inc PO Box 612	Pascagoula	MS	39568	**800-346-7206**	228-762-3172
Phillips Plywood Co Inc 13599 Desmond St	Pacoima	CA	91331	**800-649-6410**	818-897-7736
Plywood Supply Inc 7036 NE 175th St	Kenmore	WA	98028	**800-683-9663**	425-485-8585
Roseburg Forest Products Co PO Box 1088	Roseburg	OR	97470	**800-245-1115**	541-679-3311
RS Bacon Veneer Co 6951 High Grove Blvd	Burr Ridge	IL	60527	**800-443-7995**	630-323-1414
Rutland Plywood 1 Ripley Rd	Rutland	VT	05701	**800-457-0023**	802-747-4000
Scotch Lumber Co PO Box 38	Fulton	AL	36446	**800-936-4424**	334-636-4424
States Industries Inc PO Box 7037	Eugene	OR	97401	**800-626-1981**	541-688-7871
Stimson Lumber Co 520 SW Yamhill St Suite 700	Portland	OR	97204	**800-445-9758**	503-222-1676
United Plywood & Lumber Inc 1640 Mims Ave SW	Birmingham	AL	35211	**800-272-6486**	205-925-7601

603 POINT-OF-SALE (POS) & POINT-OF-INFORMATION (POI) SYSTEMS

Name / Address	City	State	ZIP	Toll-Free	Phone
3M Electro & Communications Div 3M Ctr	Saint Paul	MN	55144	**800-364-3577**	651-733-1110
Debitek Inc 2115 Chapman Rd Suite 159	Chattanooga	TN	37421	**800-332-4835**	423-894-6177
Frank Mayer & Assoc Inc 1975 Wisconsin Ave	Grafton	WI	53024	**800-225-3987**	262-377-4700
Hypercom Corp 2851 W Kathleen Rd *NYSE: HYC*	Phoenix	AZ	85053	**800-577-5501**	602-504-5000
Ingenico Corp 1003 Mansell Rd	Roswell	GA	30076	**800-435-3014**	770-594-6000
Mayer Frank & Assoc Inc 1975 Wisconsin Ave	Grafton	WI	53024	**800-225-3987**	262-377-4700
Mercury Online Solutions Inc 600 Ericksen Ave NE Suite 200	Bainbridge Island	WA	98110	**888-460-8866**	206-285-0347
Micros Systems Inc 7031 Columbia Gateway Dr *NASDAQ: MCRS*	Columbia	MD	21046	**800-937-2211**	443-285-6000
MTi Inc 1050 NW 229th Ave	Hillsboro	OR	97124	**800-426-6844**	503-648-6500
NCR Corp 1700 S Patterson Blvd *NYSE: NCR* ■ *Cust Svc	Dayton	OH	45479	**800-531-2222***	937-445-5000
Omron Systems Inc 55 E Commerce Dr *Tech Supp	Schaumburg	IL	60173	**800-706-6766***	847-884-0322
PAR Technology Corp 8383 Seneca Tpke *NYSE: PTC*	New Hartford	NY	13413	**800-448-6505**	315-738-0600
PSC Inc 959 Terry St	Eugene	OR	97402	**800-695-5700**	541-683-5700
Radiant Systems Inc 3925 Brookside Pkwy *NASDAQ: RADS*	Alpharetta	GA	30022	**800-229-0991**	770-576-6000
TouchSystems Corp 220 Tradesmen Dr	Hutto	TX	78634	**800-320-5944**	512-846-2424
Ultimate Technology Corp 100 Rawson Rd	Victor	NY	14564	**800-349-0546**	585-924-9500
VeriFone Inc 2455 Augustine Dr *NYSE: PAY*	Santa Clara	CA	95054	**800-837-4366**	408-232-7800

604 POLITICAL ACTION COMMITTEES

SEE ALSO Associations & Organizations - General - Civic & Political Organizations

Name / Address	City	State	ZIP	Toll-Free	Phone
American Assn of Orthodontists PAC 401 N Lindbergh Blvd	Saint Louis	MO	63141	**800-424-2841**	314-993-1700
American Chiropractic Assn PAC (ACA-PAC) 1701 Clarendon Blvd	Arlington	VA	22209	**800-986-4636**	703-276-8800
American Federation of Teachers Committee on Political Education 555 New Jersey Ave NW	Washington	DC	20001	**800-238-1133**	202-879-4400
American Pharmacists Assn PAC 2215 Constitution Ave NW	Washington	DC	20037	**800-237-2742**	202-628-4410
American Society of Travel Agents PAC 1101 King St Suite 200	Alexandria	VA	22314	**800-275-2782**	703-739-2782
American Speech-Language-Hearing Assn PAC 10801 Rockville Pike	Rockville	MD	20852	**800-638-8255**	301-897-5700
Associated General Contractors PAC (AGC PAC) 333 John Carlyle St Suite 200	Alexandria	VA	22314	**800-242-1766**	703-548-3118
Black America's Political Action Committee 2029 P St NW Suite 202	Washington	DC	20036	**877-722-6722**	202-785-9619
BUSPAC 700 13th St NW Suite 575	Washington	DC	20005	**800-283-2877**	202-842-1645
College of American Pathologists PAC 1350 'I' St NW Suite 590	Washington	DC	20005	**800-392-9994**	202-354-7100
Committee for a Strong Economy 9300 Livingston Rd	Fort Washington	MD	20744	**800-248-6862**	301-248-6200
Dealers Election Action Committee 8400 Westpark Dr 3rd Fl MS 3	McLean	VA	22102	**877-501-3322**	703-821-7110
FRAN-PAC 1350 New York Ave NW Suite 900	Washington	DC	20005	**800-543-1038**	202-628-8000
Human Rights Campaign PAC 1640 Rhode Island Ave NW	Washington	DC	20036	**800-777-4723**	202-628-4160
IATSE PAC 1430 Broadway 20th Fl	New York	NY	10018	**800-223-6972**	212-730-1770
Independent Community Bankers of America PAC 1 Thomas Cir NW Suite 400	Washington	DC	20005	**800-422-8439**	202-659-8111
Ironworkers Political Action League 1750 New York Ave NW Suite 400	Washington	DC	20006	**800-368-0105**	202-383-4800
Manufactured Housing Institute PAC (MHI PAC) 2101 Wilson Blvd Suite 610	Arlington	VA	22201	**800-505-5500**	703-558-0400
Marriott International PAC 1 Marriott Dr	Washington	DC	20058	**800-228-9290**	301-380-3000
MassMutual PAC 1295 State St	Springfield	MA	01111	**800-272-2216**	413-788-8411
Mechanical Contractors Assn of America PAC 1385 Piccard Dr	Rockville	MD	20850	**800-556-3653**	301-869-5800
NAADAC PAC 901 N Washington St Suite 600	Alexandria	VA	22314	**800-548-0497**	703-741-7686
National Assn of Chain Drug Stores PAC (NACDS PAC) 413 N Lee St	Alexandria	VA	22314	**800-678-6223**	703-549-3001
National Assn of Retired Federal Employees 606 N Washington St	Alexandria	VA	22314	**800-627-3394**	703-838-7760
National Confectioners Assn PAC 8320 Old Courthouse Rd Suite 300	Vienna	VA	22182	**800-433-1200**	703-790-5750
National Court Reporters Assn PAC 8224 Old Courthouse Rd	Vienna	VA	22182	**800-272-6272**	703-556-6272
National Federation of Independent Business SAFE Trust 1201 F St NW Suite 200	Washington	DC	20004	**800-552-6342**	202-554-9000
National Ground Water Assn PAC 601 Dempsey Rd	Westerville	OH	43081	**800-551-7379**	614-898-7791
National Pork Producers Council PAC 122 C St NW Suite 875	Washington	DC	20001	**866-701-6388**	202-347-3600
National Restaurant Assn PAC 1200 17th St NW	Washington	DC	20036	**800-424-5156**	202-331-5900
National Sunflower Assn PAC 4023 State St	Bismarck	ND	58503	**888-718-7033**	701-328-5100
NRA Institute for Legislative Action 11250 Waples Mill Rd	Fairfax	VA	22030	**800-672-3888**	703-267-1000
Petroleum Marketers Assn of America's Small Business Community 1901 N Fort Myer Dr Suite 500	Arlington	VA	22209	**800-300-7622**	703-351-8000
Print PAC 100 Daingerfield Rd 4th Fl	Alexandria	VA	22314	**800-742-2666**	703-519-8113
Society of American Florists PAC 1601 Duke St	Alexandria	VA	22314	**800-336-4743**	703-836-8700
Southwest Airlines PAC 2702 Love Field Fr	Dallas	TX	75235	**800-435-9792**	214-792-4000
Title Industry PAC 1828 L St NW Suite 705	Washington	DC	20036	**800-787-2582**	202-296-3671

605 POLITICAL PARTIES (MAJOR)

SEE ALSO Associations & Organizations - General - Civic & Political Organizations

Name / Address	City	State	ZIP	Toll-Free	Phone
Democratic National Committee 430 S Capitol St SE	Washington	DC	20003	**800-934-8683**	202-863-8000
Greens/Green Party USA (G/GPUSA) PO Box 1406	Chicago	IL	60690	**866-473-3672**	708-524-1741
Libertarian Party 2600 Virginia Ave NW Suite 100	Washington	DC	20037	**800-682-1776**	202-333-0008
Republican National Committee 310 1st St SE	Washington	DC	20003	**800-445-5768**	202-863-8500

605-1 Democratic State Committees

Name / Address	City	State	ZIP	Toll-Free	Phone
Alabama PO Box 950	Montgomery	AL	36104	**800-995-3386**	334-262-2221
Florida PO Box 1758	Tallahassee	FL	32302	**800-925-3411**	850-222-3411
Georgia 1100 Spring St Suite 710	Atlanta	GA	30309	**800-894-1996**	404-870-8201
Idaho PO Box 445	Boise	ID	83701	**800-542-4737**	208-336-1815
Indiana 1 N Capital St Suite 200	Indianapolis	IN	46204	**800-223-3387**	317-231-7100
Minnesota 255 E Plato Blvd	Saint Paul	MN	55107	**800-999-7457**	651-293-1200
Mississippi PO Box 1583	Jackson	MS	39215	**888-674-3367**	601-969-2913
Nebraska 633 S 9th St Suite 201	Lincoln	NE	68508	**800-677-7068**	402-434-2180
North Carolina 220 Hillsborough St	Raleigh	NC	27603	**800-229-3367**	919-821-2777
South Carolina PO Box 5965	Columbia	SC	29250	**800-841-1817**	803-799-7798
Wyoming 254 N Center St Suite 205	Casper	WY	82601	**800-729-3367**	307-473-1457

605-2 Republican State Committees

Name / Address	City	State	ZIP	Toll-Free	Phone
Alabama 2019 Holland Ave S	Birmingham	AL	35255	**877-919-2002**	205-212-5900
Arizona 3501 N 24th St	Phoenix	AZ	85016	**800-844-4065**	602-957-7770
Colorado 1777 S Harrison St Suite 100	Denver	CO	80210	**800-236-3769**	303-758-3333
Connecticut 97 Elm St Rear	Hartford	CT	06106	**888-982-8467**	860-547-0589
Florida PO Box 311	Tallahassee	FL	32302	**800-777-7920**	850-222-7920
Georgia 3110 Maple Dr Suite 200-E	Atlanta	GA	30305	**877-464-2467**	404-257-5559
Idaho PO Box 2267	Boise	ID	83701	**800-658-3898**	208-343-6405
Indiana 47 S Meridian St Suite 200	Indianapolis	IN	46204	**800-466-1087**	317-635-7561
Kansas 2025 SW Gage Blvd	Topeka	KS	66604	**888-482-9051**	785-234-3456
Louisiana 11440 N Lake Sherwood Ave Suite A	Baton Rouge	LA	70816	**800-376-7245**	225-928-2998
Michigan 2121 E Grand River Ave	Lansing	MI	48912	**877-644-6704**	517-487-5413
Nebraska 1610 N St	Lincoln	NE	68508	**800-829-3459**	402-475-2122
Utah 117 E South Temple St	Salt Lake City	UT	84111	**800-230-8824**	801-533-9777

606 PORTALS - VOICE

Company	City	State	Zip	Toll-Free	Phone
BeVocal Inc 685 Clyde Ave	Mountain View	CA	94043	**800-428-6225**	650-210-8600
GoSolo Technologies Inc 1901 Ulmerton Rd Suite 400	Clearwater	FL	33762	**888-551-7656**	727-821-6565
NetByTel Inc 1141 S Rogers Cir Suite 9	Boca Raton	FL	33487	**800-638-2983**	561-988-5050
Tellme Networks Inc 1310 Villa St	Mountain View	CA	94041	**800-555-8355**	650-930-9000

607 PORTS & PORT AUTHORITIES

SEE ALSO Airports; Cruise Lines

Company	City	State	Zip	Toll-Free	Phone
Detroit-Wayne County Port Authority 8109 E Jefferson Ave	Detroit	MI	48214	**800-249-7678**	313-331-3842
Georgia Ports Authority PO Box 2406	Savannah	GA	31402	**800-342-8012**	912-964-3811
Illinois International Port District 3600 E 95th St	Chicago	IL	60617	**800-843-7678**	773-646-4400
Indiana Port Commission 150 W Market St Suite 100	Indianapolis	IN	46204	**800-232-7678**	317-232-9200
Mississippi State Port Authority at Gulfport 1 Hancock Plaza Suite 1401	Gulfport	MS	39503	**877-881-4367**	228-865-4300
North Carolina State Ports Authority 2202 Burnett Blvd PO Box 9002	Wilmington	NC	28402	**800-334-0682**	910-763-1621
Port of Astoria 1 Portway St	Astoria	OR	97103	**800-860-4093**	503-325-4521
Port of Baltimore Maryland Port Administration 401 E Pratt St World Trade Ctr	Baltimore	MD	21202	**800-638-7519**	410-385-4484
Port of Brownsville 1000 Foust Rd	Brownsville	TX	78521	**800-378-5395**	956-831-4592
Port Canaveral 200 George King Blvd	Cape Canaveral	FL	32920	**888-767-8226**	321-783-7831
Port of Corpus Christi 222 Power St	Corpus Christi	TX	78401	**800-580-7110**	361-882-5633
Port of Duluth Duluth Seaway Port Authority 1200 Port Terminal Dr	Duluth	MN	55802	**800-232-0703**	218-727-8525
Port of Everett 2911 Bond St Suite 202	Everett	WA	98201	**800-729-7678**	425-259-3164
Port Freeport PO Box 615	Freeport	TX	77542	**800-362-5473**	979-233-2667
Port of Houston 111 E Loop N *Cust Svc	Houston	TX	77029	**800-688-3625***	713-670-2400
Port of Lake Charles 150 Marine St	Lake Charles	LA	70601	**800-845-7678**	337-439-3661
Port of New Orleans 1350 Port of New Orleans Pl *Mktg	New Orleans	LA	70130	**800-776-6652***	504-522-2551
Port of Norfolk Virginia Port Authority 600 World Trade Ctr	Norfolk	VA	23510	**800-446-8098**	757-683-8000
Port of Pittsburgh 425 6th Ave Suite 2990	Pittsburgh	PA	15219	**877-609-9870**	412-201-7330
Port of Portland 121 NW Everett St	Portland	OR	97209	**800-547-8411**	503-944-7000
Port of Sacramento 3251 Beacon Blvd Suite 210	West Sacramento	CA	95691	**888-258-7969**	916-371-8000
Port of Saint Petersburg 300 2nd Ave SE	Saint Petersburg	FL	33701	**800-782-8350**	727-893-7329
Port of San Diego PO Box 120488	San Diego	CA	92112	**800-854-2757**	619-686-6200
Port of Seattle PO Box 1209	Seattle	WA	98111	**800-426-7817**	206-728-3000
Port of South Louisiana 171 Belle Terre Blvd Suite 100	LaPlace	LA	70069	**888-752-7678**	985-652-9278
Port of Stockton 2201 W Washington St	Stockton	CA	95203	**800-344-3213**	209-946-0246
South Carolina State Ports Authority 176 Concord St	Charleston	SC	29401	**800-845-7106**	843-723-8651
Tampa Port Authority 1101 Channelside Dr	Tampa	FL	33602	**800-741-2297**	813-905-7678
Vancouver Port Authority 100 The Point 999 Canada Pl	Vancouver	BC	V6C3T4	**888-767-8826**	604-665-9000

608 POULTRY PROCESSING

SEE ALSO Meat Packing Plants

Company	City	State	Zip	Toll-Free	Phone
Amick Farms Inc PO Box 2309	Leesville	SC	29070	**800-926-4257**	803-532-1400
Cagle's Inc 2000 Hills Ave NW *AMEX: CGLa*	Atlanta	GA	30318	**800-476-2820**	404-355-2820
Cargill Inc North America 15407 McGinty Rd	Wayzata	MN	55391	**800-227-4455**	952-742-7575
Cargill Turkey Products 1 Kratzer Rd *Cust Svc	Harrisonburg	VA	22802	**800-233-8457***	540-568-1400
Carolina Turkeys 1628 Garner Chapel Rd PO Box 589	Mount Olive	NC	28365	**800-523-4559**	919-658-6743
ConAgra Foods International 2 Jericho Plaza Suite 304	Jericho	NY	11753	**800-275-5454**	516-949-7500
Cutler at Abbeville LLC 496 Industrial Park Rd	Abbeville	AL	36310	**800-633-7565**	334-585-2268
Downs Food Group 400 Armstrong Blvd N	Saint James	MN	56081	**800-533-0452**	507-375-3111
Durbin Marshall Food Corp 2830 Commerce Blvd	Irondale	AL	35210	**800-768-2456**	205-956-3505
Echo Lake Farm Produce Co PO Box 279	Burlington	WI	53105	**800-888-3447**	262-763-9551
Empire Kosher Poultry Inc RD 5 Box 228	Mifflintown	PA	17059	**800-233-7177**	717-436-5921
Gold'n Plump Poultry 4150 2nd St S	Saint Cloud	MN	56301	**800-328-8236**	320-251-6568
House of Raeford Farms Inc PO Box 100	Raeford	NC	28376	**800-888-7539**	910-875-5161
ISE America Inc 33335 Galena Sassafras	Galena	MD	21635	**800-343-7926**	410-755-6300
Jennie-O Turkey Store 2505 Willmar Ave SW	Willmar	MN	56201	**800-328-1756**	320-235-2622
JFC Inc PO Box 1106	Saint Cloud	MN	56302	**800-328-8236**	320-251-3570
Koch Foods LLC 1300 Higgins Rd Suite 100	Park Ridge	IL	60068	**800-837-2778**	847-384-5940
Mar-Jac Poultry Inc PO Box 1017	Gainesville	GA	30503	**800-226-0561**	770-536-0561
Marshall Durbin Food Corp 2830 Commerce Blvd	Irondale	AL	35210	**800-768-2456**	205-956-3505
Michael Foods Inc 301 Carlson Pkwy Suite 400	Minnetonka	MN	55305	**800-325-4270**	952-258-4000
Mountaire Farms 17269 NC Hwy 71 N	Lumber Bridge	NC	28357	**800-962-0720**	910-843-5942
OK Foods Inc PO Box 1119	Fort Smith	AR	72902	**800-635-9441**	479-783-0244
Park Farms Inc 1925 30th St NE	Canton	OH	44705	**800-683-6511**	330-455-0241
Pennfield Corp 711 Rohrerstown Rd	Lancaster	PA	17604	**800-732-0467**	717-299-2561
Perdue Farms Inc PO Box 1537	Salisbury	MD	21802	**800-457-3738**	410-543-3000
Petaluma Poultry Processors PO Box 7368	Petaluma	CA	94955	**800-556-6789**	707-763-1904
Randall Foods Inc 2905 E 50th St	Vernon	CA	90058	**800-372-6581**	323-587-2383
Simmons Industries Inc 601 N Hico St	Siloam Springs	AR	72761	**888-831-7007**	479-524-8151
Sonstegard Foods Inc 707 E 41st St Suite 222	Sioux Falls	SD	57105	**800-533-3184**	605-338-4642
Sunny Fresh Foods Inc 206 W 4th St	Monticello	MN	55362	**800-872-3447**	763-271-5600
Sylvest Farms Inc 3500 Western Blvd	Montgomery	AL	36108	**800-277-2473**	334-281-0400
Tyson Foods Inc 2210 W Oaklawn Dr *NYSE: TSN*	Springdale	AR	72762	**800-643-3410**	479-290-4000
Valley Fresh Inc 680 D St	Turlock	CA	95380	**800-526-3189**	209-668-3695
Watson Quality Food Inc PO Box 215	Blackwood	NJ	08012	**800-257-7870**	856-227-0594
Wayne Farms Enterprises LLC 1020 County Rd 114	Jack	AL	36346	**800-223-2569**	334-897-3435
Willow Brook Foods Inc PO Box 50190	Springfield	MO	65805	**800-423-2366**	417-862-3612

609 POWER TRANSMISSION EQUIPMENT - MECHANICAL

SEE ALSO Bearings - Ball & Roller

Company	City	State	Zip	Toll-Free	Phone
A-1 Carbide Corp 1649 Miraloma Ave	Placentia	CA	92870	**800-222-9422**	714-630-9422
Allied-Locke Industries 1088 Corregidor Rd	Dixon	IL	61021	**800-435-7752**	815-288-1471
American Metal Bearing Co 7191 Acacia Ave	Garden Grove	CA	92841	**800-888-3048**	714-892-5527
Avon Bearings 1500 Nagle Rd	Avon	OH	44011	**800-286-6274**	440-871-2500
Barden Corp 200 Park Ave	Danbury	CT	06813	**800-243-1060**	203-744-2211
Beemer Precision Inc 230 New York Dr PO Box 3080	Fort Washington	PA	19034	**800-836-2340**	215-646-8440
Bird Precision PO Box 540569 *Cust Svc	Waltham	MA	02454	**800-454-7369***	781-894-0160
Bishop-Wisecarver Corp 2104 Martin Way	Pittsburg	CA	94565	**888-580-8272**	925-439-8272
Brenco Inc PO Box 389	Petersburg	VA	23804	**800-238-4712**	804-732-0202
Cangro Industries Long Island Transmission Co 495 Smith St	Farmingdale	NY	11735	**800-899-2264**	631-454-9000
Carlyle Johnson Machine Co 291 Boston Tpke	Bolton	CT	06043	**888-629-4867**	860-643-1531
Certified Power Inc 970 Campus Dr	Mundelein	IL	60060	**800-877-8350**	847-573-3800
Diamond Chain Co 402 Kentucky Ave *Cust Svc	Indianapolis	IN	46225	**800-872-4246***	317-638-6431
Don Dye Co Inc PO Box 107	Kingman	KS	67068	**800-901-3131**	620-532-3131
Drives Inc 1009 1st St	Fulton	IL	61252	**800-435-0782**	815-589-2211
Force Control Industries Inc 3660 Dixie Hwy	Fairfield	OH	45014	**800-829-3244**	513-868-0900
Funk Mfg Co PO Box 577	Coffeyville	KS	67337	**800-844-1337**	620-251-3400
General Bearing Corp 44 High St *NASDAQ: GNRL* ■ *Sales	West Nyack	NY	10994	**800-431-1766***	845-358-6000
Horton Inc 2565 Walnut St	Roseville	MN	55113	**800-843-7445**	651-361-6400
Kamatics Corp 1330 Blue Hills Ave	Bloomfield	CT	06002	**800-468-4735**	860-243-9704
Kingsbury Inc 10385 Drummond Rd	Philadelphia	PA	19154	**800-898-8912**	215-824-4000
Linn Gear Co 100 N 8th St PO Box 397	Lebanon	OR	97355	**800-547-2471**	541-259-1211
Lovejoy Inc 2655 Wisconsin Ave	Downers Grove	IL	60515	**800-334-9659**	630-852-0500
Magtrol Inc 70 Gardenville Pkwy W	Buffalo	NY	14224	**800-828-7844**	716-668-5555
Nook Industries 4950 E 49th St	Cuyahoga Heights	OH	44125	**800-321-7800**	216-271-7900
NSK Corp 4200 Goss Rd	Ann Arbor	MI	48105	**800-521-0605**	734-761-9500
NTN Bearing Corp of America 1600 E Bishop Ct Suite 100	Mount Prospect	IL	60056	**800-468-6528**	847-298-7500
OPW Engineered Systems Inc 2726 Henkle Dr *Cust Svc	Lebanon	OH	45036	**800-547-9393***	513-932-9114
Peer Bearing Co 2200 Norman Dr S	Waukegan	IL	60085	**800-433-7337**	847-578-1000
PerkinElmer Fluid Sciences Inc Pressure Science 11642 Old Baltimore Pike	Beltsville	MD	20705	**800-691-4666**	301-937-4010
Pic Design Corp 86 Benson Rd PO Box 1004	Middlebury	CT	06762	**800-243-6125**	203-758-8272
RBC Transport Dynamics Corp 3131 W Segerstrom Ave PO Box 1953	Santa Ana	CA	92704	**800-854-3922**	714-546-3131
Renold Ajax Inc 100 Bourne St *Cust Svc	Westfield	NY	14787	**800-879-2529***	716-326-3121
Siemens Power Transmission & Distribution Inc 7000 Siemens Rd	Wendell	NC	27591	**800-347-6659**	919-365-2200
SKF USA Inc 1111 Adams Ave	Norristown	PA	19403	**800-440-4753**	610-630-2800
SS White Technologies Inc 151 Old New Brunswick Rd	Piscataway	NJ	08854	**800-872-2673**	732-752-8300
Stock Drive Products/Sterling Instrument 2101 Jericho Tpke	New Hyde Park	NY	11040	**800-354-1144**	516-328-3300
TB Wood's Inc 440 N 5th Ave *NASDAQ: TBWC*	Chambersburg	PA	17201	**888-829-6637**	717-264-7161
Tuthill Corp 8500 S Madison St	Burr Ridge	IL	60527	**800-888-4455**	630-382-4900
Tuthill Linkage Group 2110 Summit St	New Haven	IN	46774	**800-233-6213**	260-749-5105
US Tsubaki Inc 301 E Marquardt Dr	Wheeling	IL	60090	**800-323-7790**	847-459-9500
Wampfler Inc 8091 Production Ave	Florence	KY	41042	**800-326-2899**	859-814-2100
Warner Electric 449 Gardner St	South Beloit	IL	61080	**800-234-3369**	815-389-3771
Wheeler Industries 7261 Investment Dr *Sales	North Charleston	SC	29418	**800-343-0803***	843-552-1251
White SS Technologies Inc 151 Old New Brunswick Rd	Piscataway	NJ	08854	**800-872-2673**	732-752-8300
Whittet-Higgins Co 33 Higginson Ave PO Box 8 *Sales	Central Falls	RI	02863	**800-972-8070***	401-728-0700
Zero-Max Inc 13200 6th Ave N	Plymouth	MN	55441	**800-533-1731**	763-546-4300

610 PRECISION MACHINED PRODUCTS

SEE ALSO Aircraft Parts & Auxiliary Equipment

Company	City	State	Zip	Toll-Free	Phone
Accellent 200 W 7th Ave	Collegeville	PA	19426	**800-321-6285**	610-489-0300
Alger Mfg Co Inc 724 S Bon View Ave	Ontario	CA	91761	**800-854-9833**	909-986-4591
Amsco-Wire Products Co 610 Grand Ave	Ridgefield	NJ	07657	**800-255-7467**	201-945-5700
Anderson Automatics Inc 6401 Welcome Ave N	Minneapolis	MN	55429	**800-959-0316**	763-533-2206
ATEC Inc 12600 Executive Dr	Stafford	TX	77477	**866-753-2384**	281-240-1919
Automatic Products Corp 2735 Forest Ln	Garland	TX	75042	**800-788-2726**	972-272-6422
Bay Swiss Mfg Co Inc 5 Airpark Vista Blvd	Dayton	NV	89403	**800-247-3207**	775-246-7100
Betar Inc 1524 Millstone River Rd	Hillsborough	NJ	08844	**800-841-8841**	908-359-4200
Betty Machine Co 324 Freehill Rd	Hendersonville	TN	37075	**800-264-3480**	615-826-6004
Biddle Precision Components Inc 701 S Main St	Sheridan	IN	46069	**800-428-4387**	317-758-4451

				Toll-Free	Phone
CNW Inc 4710 Madison Rd	Cincinnati	OH	45227	**800-327-5900**	513-321-2775
Cox Mfg Co 5500 N Loop 1604 E	San Antonio	TX	78247	**800-900-7981**	210-657-7731
Enoch Mfg Co PO Box 98	Clackamas	OR	97015	**888-659-6565**	503-659-2660
Fairchild Auto-mated Parts Inc 10 White St	Winsted	CT	06098	**800-927-2545**	860-379-2725
Fluidyne Ansonia 1 Riverside Dr *Cust Svc	Ansonia	CT	06401	**800-765-2676***	203-735-9311
Golden States Engineering Inc 15338 S Garfield Ave	Paramount	CA	90723	**800-292-2838**	562-634-3125
H & H Swiss Screw Machine Products Co Inc 1478 Chestnut Ave	Hillside	NJ	07205	**800-826-9985**	908-688-6390
Hall Industries Inc 514 Mecklem Ln	Ellwood City	PA	16117	**800-828-5519**	724-752-2000
Horspool & Romine Mfg Inc 5850 Marshall St	Oakland	CA	94608	**800-446-2263**	510-652-1844
IW Industries Inc 35 Melville Park Rd	Melville	NY	11747	**800-252-8202**	631-293-9494
Kerr Lakeside Inc 26841 Tungsten Rd	Euclid	OH	44132	**800-487-5377**	216-261-2100
Lakeshore Automatic Products Inc 1865 Industrial Park Dr	Grand Haven	MI	49417	**800-851-6411**	616-846-5090
Lehr Precision Inc 11230 Deerfield Rd	Cincinnati	OH	45242	**800-966-5060**	513-489-9800
Liberty Brass Turning Co Inc 38-01 Queens Blvd	Long Island City	NY	11101	**800-345-5939**	718-784-2911
MagStar Technologies 410 11th Ave S	Hopkins	MN	55343	**800-473-8837**	952-935-6921
Marvel Screw Machine Products 58 Lafayette St	Waterbury	CT	06708	**800-394-6767**	203-756-7058
Modern Machine & Engineering Corp 1707 Jefferson St NE	Minneapolis	MN	55413	**800-218-8838**	612-781-3347
Mount Vernon Screw Products Inc PO Box 250	Mount Vernon	IN	47620	**800-880-5502**	812-838-5501
MSK Precision Parts Inc 4100 NW 10th Ave	Fort Lauderdale	FL	33309	**800-992-5018**	954-776-0770
Multimatic Products Inc 390 Oser Ave	Hauppauge	NY	11788	**800-767-7633**	631-231-1515
New Castle Industries Inc PO Box 7359	New Castle	PA	16107	**800-897-2830**	724-656-5600
Ohio Cast Products Inc 2408 13th St NE	Canton	OH	44705	**800-909-2278**	330-456-4784
Precisionform Inc 148 W Airport Rd	Lititz	PA	17543	**800-233-3821**	717-560-7610
Production Products Co 6176 E Molloy Rd	East Syracuse	NY	13057	**800-800-6652**	315-431-7200
Roberts Automatic Products Inc 880 Lake Dr	Chanhassen	MN	55317	**800-879-9837**	952-949-1000
Sperry Automatics Co Inc PO Box 717	Naugatuck	CT	06770	**800-923-3709**	203-729-4589
Talladega Machinery & Supply Co Inc PO Box 736 *Cust Svc	Talladega	AL	35161	**800-289-8672***	256-362-4124
TCR Corp 1600 67th Ave N *Cust Svc	Minneapolis	MN	55430	**800-328-8961***	763-560-2200
Thuro Metal Products Inc 21-25 Grand Blvd N	Brentwood	NY	11717	**800-238-3929**	631-435-0444
Wells Mfg Co 2100 W Lake Shore Dr	Woodstock	IL	60098	**800-227-6455**	815-338-3900

611 PREPARATORY SCHOOLS

SEE ALSO Preparatory Schools - Non-boarding

				Toll-Free	Phone
All Saints' Episcopal School 2717 Confederate Ave	Vicksburg	MS	39180	**800-748-9957**	601-636-5266
Andrews School 38588 Mentor Ave	Willoughby	OH	44094	**800-753-4683**	440-942-3606
Annie Wright School 827 N Tacoma Ave	Tacoma	WA	98403	**800-847-1582**	253-272-2216
Army & Navy Academy 2605 Carlsbad Blvd PO Box 3000	Carlsbad	CA	92018	**888-762-2338**	760-729-2385
Avon Old Farms School 500 Old Farms Rd	Avon	CT	06001	**800-464-2866**	860-404-4100
Baylor School PO Box 1337	Chattanooga	TN	37401	**800-222-9567**	423-267-5902
Ben Lippen School 7401 Monticello Rd	Columbia	SC	29203	**888-236-5476**	803-786-7200
Brewster Academy 80 Academy Dr	Wolfeboro	NH	03894	**800-842-9961**	603-569-7200
Canyonville Christian Academy 250 E 1st St PO Box 1100	Canyonville	OR	97417	**888-222-6379**	541-839-4401
Chaminade College Preparatory School 425 S Lindbergh Blvd	Saint Louis	MO	63131	**877-378-6847**	314-993-4400
Christ School 500 Christ School Rd	Arden	NC	28704	**800-422-3212**	828-684-6232
Christchurch School 49 Seahorse Ln	Christchurch	VA	23031	**800-296-2306**	804-758-2306
Crested Butte Academy 505 Whiterock Ave PO Box 1180	Crested Butte	CO	81224	**888-633-0222**	970-349-1805
Culver Academies 1300 Academy Rd	Culver	IN	46511	**800-528-5837**	574-842-7000
Darlington School 1014 Cave Spring Rd	Rome	GA	30161	**800-368-4437**	706-235-6051
Dunn School 2555 Hwy 154 PO Box 98	Los Olivos	CA	93441	**800-287-9197**	805-688-6471
Episcopal High School 1200 N Quaker Ln	Alexandria	VA	22302	**877-933-4347**	703-933-4062
Fay School 48 Main St	Southborough	MA	01772	**800-933-2925**	508-485-0100
Foxcroft School PO Box 5555	Middleburg	VA	20118	**800-858-2364**	540-687-5555
Fryeburg Academy 152 Main St	Fryeburg	ME	04037	**877-935-2013**	207-935-2013
Girard College 2101 S College Ave Suite 311	Philadelphia	PA	19121	**877-344-7273**	215-787-2600
Happy Valley School PO Box 850	Ojai	CA	93024	**800-900-0437**	805-646-4343
Hargrave Military Academy 200 Military Dr	Chatham	VA	24531	**800-432-2480**	434-432-2481
Hebron Academy Rt 119 PO Box 309	Hebron	ME	04238	**888-432-7664**	207-966-2100
Hill School 717 E High St	Pottstown	PA	19464	**888-445-5150**	610-326-1000
Howe Military Academy PO Box 240	Howe	IN	46746	**888-462-4693**	260-562-2131
Indian Springs School 190 Woodward Dr	Indian Springs	AL	35124	**888-843-3477**	205-988-3350
Kent School PO Box 2006	Kent	CT	06757	**800-538-5368**	860-927-6111
Kiski School 1888 Brett Ln	Saltsburg	PA	15681	**877-547-5448**	724-639-3586
Lawrenceville School 2500 Main St PO Box 6008	Lawrenceville	NJ	08648	**800-735-2030**	609-896-0400
Lee Academy 26 Winn Rd	Mee	ME	04455	**888-433-2852**	207-738-2255
Leelanau School 1 Old Homestead Rd	Glen Arbor	MI	49636	**800-533-5262**	231-334-5800
Linden Hall School for Girls 212 E Main St	Lititz	PA	17543	**800-258-5778**	717-626-8512
Linden Hill School 154 S Mountain Rd	Northfield	MA	01360	**888-254-6336**	413-498-2906
Marvelwood School 476 Skiff Mountain Rd PO Box 3001	Kent	CT	06757	**800-440-9107**	860-927-0047
McCallie School 500 Dodds Rd	Chattanooga	TN	37404	**800-234-2163**	423-624-8300
Milton Hershey School PO Box 830	Hershey	PA	17033	**800-322-3248**	717-520-2100
New York Military Academy 78 Academy Ave	Cornwall-on-Hudson	NY	12520	**888-275-6962**	845-534-3710
Oakwood Friends School 22 Spackenkill Rd	Poughkeepsie	NY	12603	**800-843-3341**	845-462-4200
Ojai Valley School 723 El Paseo Rd	Ojai	CA	93023	**800-433-4687**	805-646-1423
Olney Friends School 61830 Sandy Ridge Rd	Barnesville	OH	43713	**800-303-4291**	740-425-3655
Rabun Gap-Nacoochee School 339 Nacoochee Dr	Rabun Gap	GA	30568	**800-543-7467**	706-746-7467
Randolph-Macon Academy 200 Academy Dr	Front Royal	VA	22630	**800-272-1172**	540-636-5200
Riverside Military Academy 2001 Riverside Dr	Gainsville	GA	30501	**800-462-2338**	770-532-6251
Saint Andrew's College 15800 Yonge St	Aurora	ON	L4G3H7	**877-378-1899**	905-727-3178
Saint Bernard Preparatory School 1600 Saint Bernard Dr SE	Cullman	AL	35055	**800-722-0999**	256-739-6682
Saint Catherine's School 6001 Grove Ave	Richmond	VA	23226	**800-648-4982**	804-288-2804
Saint John's Military School 110 E Otis Ave PO Box 827	Salina	KS	67402	**866-704-5294**	785-823-7231
Saint John's Northwestern Military Academy 1101 N Genesee St	Delafield	WI	53018	**800-752-2338**	262-646-7115
Saint John's Preparatory School 1857 Watertower Rd PO Box 4000	Collegeville	MN	56321	**800-525-7737**	320-363-3321
Saint John's=Ravenscourt School 400 South Dr	Winnipeg	MB	R3T3K5	**800-437-0040**	204-477-2400
Saint Mary's School 900 Hillsborough St	Raleigh	NC	27603	**800-948-2557**	919-424-4100
Saint Michael's University School 3400 Richmond Rd	Victoria	BC	V8P4P5	**800-661-5199**	250-592-2411
Saint Stanislaus College 304 S Beach Blvd	Bay Saint Louis	MS	39520	**800-517-6257**	228-467-9057
Saint Stephen's Episcopal School 2900 Bunny Run	Austin	TX	78746	**888-377-7937**	512-327-1213
Saint Timothy's School 8400 Greenspring Ave	Stevenson	MD	21153	**800-467-8846**	410-486-7400
Salem Academy 500 Salem Ave	Winston-Salem	NC	27101	**877-407-2536**	336-721-2643
San Marcos Baptist Academy 2801 Ranch Rd 12	San Marcos	TX	78666	**800-428-5120**	512-753-8000
Scattergood Friends School 1951 Delta Ave	West Branch	IA	52358	**888-737-4636**	319-643-7628
Shattuck-Saint Mary's School 1000 Shumway Ave PO Box 218	Faribault	MN	55021	**800-421-2724**	507-333-1616
Storm King School 314 Mountain Rd	Cornwall-on-Hudson	NY	12520	**800-225-9144**	845-534-9860
Stuart Hall 235 E Frederick St PO Box 210	Staunton	VA	24402	**888-306-8926**	540-885-0356
Subiaco Academy 405 N Subiaco Ave	Subiaco	AR	72865	**800-364-7824**	479-934-1025
Valley Forge Military Academy & College 1001 Eagle Rd	Wayne	PA	19087	**800-234-8362**	610-989-1300
Vermont Academy PO Box 500	Saxtons River	VT	05154	**800-560-1876**	802-869-6229
Wasatch Academy 120 S 100 W	Mount Pleasant	UT	84647	**800-634-4690**	435-462-1400
Wayland Academy 101 N University Ave	Beaver Dam	WI	53916	**800-860-7725**	920-885-3373
Webb School PO Box 488	Bell Buckle	TN	37020	**888-733-9322**	931-389-9322
West Nottingham Academy 1079 Firetower Rd	Colora	MD	21917	**800-962-1744**	410-658-5556
Western Reserve Academy 115 College St	Hudson	OH	44236	**800-784-3776**	330-650-9717
White Mountain School 371 W Farm Rd	Bethlehem	NH	03574	**800-545-7813**	603-444-2928
Woodberry Forest School 241 Woodberry Station	Woodberry Forest	VA	22989	**888-798-9371**	540-672-3900
Wyoming Seminary 201 N Sprague Ave	Kingston	PA	18704	**877-996-7364**	570-270-2160

612 PRESS CLIPPING SERVICES

				Toll-Free	Phone
Bacon's Information Inc 332 S Michigan Ave Suite 900	Chicago	IL	60604	**800-621-0561**	312-922-2400
Clipping Bureau of Florida PO Box 2190	Palm Harbor	FL	34682	**800-442-0332**	727-442-0332
CompetitivEdge 196 S Main St	Colchester	CT	06415	**888-881-3343**	860-537-6731
Luce Press Clippings Inc 42 S Center St	Mesa	AZ	85210	**800-528-8226**	480-834-4884
New England Newsclip Agency Inc 5 Auburn St	Framingham	MA	01701	**800-235-3879**	508-879-4460
New Jersey Clipping Service 75 E Northfield Rd	Livingston	NJ	07039	**800-631-1160**	973-994-3333
New York State Clipping Service 200 Central Park Ave N	Hartsdale	NY	10530	**800-772-5477**	914-948-2525
Newsclip 363 W Erie St 7th Fl	Chicago	IL	60610	**800-544-8433**	312-751-7300
South Carolina Press Services Inc PO Box 11429	Columbia	SC	29211	**888-727-7377**	803-750-9561
South Dakota Newspaper Services 527 Main Ave Suite 202	Brookings	SD	57006	**800-658-3697**	605-692-4300
Virginia Press Services Inc 11529 Nuckols Rd	Glen Allen	VA	23059	**800-849-8717**	804-521-7570
West Virginia Press Services Inc 3422 Pennsylvania Ave	Charleston	WV	25302	**800-235-6881**	304-342-6908

613 PRINTED CIRCUIT BOARDS

SEE ALSO Electronic Components & Accessories - Mfr; Semiconductors & Related Devices

				Toll-Free	Phone
3Com Corp 5403 Betsy Ross Dr *NASDAQ: COMS* ■ *Cust Svc	Santa Clara	CA	95054	**800-638-3266***	408-326-5000
3Dlabs Inc 1901 McCarthy Blvd	Milpitas	CA	94035	**800-464-3348**	408-432-6700
Adaptec Inc 691 S Milpitas Blvd *NASDAQ: ADPT* ■ *Tech Supp	Milpitas	CA	95035	**800-959-7274***	408-945-8600
Antex Electronics Corp 1125 W 190th St	Gardena	CA	90248	**800-338-4231**	310-532-3092
Appian Graphics Inc 18047 NE 68th St Suite B-100 *Tech Supp	Redmond	WA	98052	**800-422-7369***	425-882-2020
Chrislin Industries Inc 31312 Via Colinas Suite 108	Westlake Village	CA	91362	**800-468-0736**	818-991-2254
Creative Labs Inc 1901 McCarthy Blvd *Cust Svc	Milpitas	CA	95035	**800-998-1000***	408-428-6600
Crucial Technology 3475 E Commercial Ct	Meridian	ID	83642	**800-336-8915**	208-363-5790
Cytec Corp 10385 Brockwood Rd	Dallas	TX	75238	**888-349-8881**	214-349-8881
Data Translation Inc 100 Locke Dr	Marlborough	MA	01752	**800-525-8528**	508-481-3700
Dataram Corp 186 Rt 571 *NASDAQ: DRAM*	West Windsor	NJ	08550	**800-328-2726**	609-799-0071
Diamond Flower Electric Instrument Co USA Inc (DFI) 732-C Striker Ave	Sacramento	CA	95834	**800-909-4334**	916-568-1234
Diversified Technology Inc 476 Highland Colony Pkwy	Ridgeland	MS	39157	**800-443-2667**	601-856-4121
Dynatem Inc 23263 Madero Suite C	Mission Viejo	CA	92691	**800-543-3830**	949-855-3235
GoldenRAM Computer Products 8 Whatney	Irvine	CA	92618	**800-222-8861**	949-460-9000
Guillemot North America 5500 rue Saint-Laurent Suite 5000	Montreal	QC	H2T1S6	**877-484-5536**	514-279-9960

				Toll-Free	Phone
Hauppauge Computer Works Inc					
91 Cabot Ct	Hauppauge	NY	11788	**800-443-6284**	631-434-1600
Hauppauge Digital Inc 91 Cabot Ct	Hauppauge	NY	11788	**800-443-6284**	631-434-1600
NASDAQ: HAUP					
Hitachi Computer Products (America) Inc					
(HICAM) 1800 E Imhoff Rd	Norman	OK	73071	**800-448-2244**	405-360-5500
I-Bus Corp 2391 Zanker Rd Suite 370	San Jose	CA	95131	**800-382-4229**	408-428-6100
Intel Corp 2200 Mission College Blvd	Santa Clara	CA	95052	**800-628-8686***	408-765-8080
NASDAQ: INTC ■ *Cust Svc					
Kimball Electronics Group 1038 E 15th St	Jasper	IN	47549	**800-634-4005**	812-634-4200
Kontron Communications Inc					
616 Cure-Boivin	Boisbriand	QC	J7G2A7	**800-354-4223**	450-437-5682
McDonald Technologies International Inc					
1920 Diplomat Dr	Farmers Branch	TX	75234	**800-678-7046**	972-243-6767
Micro Industries Corp					
8399 Green Meadow Dr N	Westerville	OH	43081	**800-722-1845**	740-548-7878
Motorola Computer Group 2900 S Diablo Way	Tempe	AZ	85282	**800-759-1107**	602-438-3000
Motorola Inc 1301 E Algonquin Rd	Schaumburg	IL	60196	**800-331-6456**	847-576-5000
NYSE: MOT					
Nitto Denko America Inc 48500 Fremont Blvd	Fremont	CA	94538	**800-356-4880**	510-445-5400
NVIDIA Corp 2701 San Tomas Expy	Santa Clara	CA	95050	**877-768-4342**	408-486-2000
NASDAQ: NVDA					
Parallax Inc 599 Menlo Dr Suite 100	Rocklin	CA	95765	**888-512-1024**	916-624-8333
PEMSTAR Inc 3535 Technology Dr NW	Rochester	MN	55901	**888-736-7827**	507-288-6720
NASDAQ: PMTR					
Promise Technology Inc 1745 McCandless Dr	Milpitas	CA	95035	**800-888-0245***	408-228-6300
*Sales					
Quatech Inc 5675 Hudson Industrial Pkwy	Hudson	OH	44236	**800-553-1170**	330-655-9000
RadiSys Corp 5445 NE Dawson Creek Dr	Hillsboro	OR	97124	**800-950-0044**	503-615-1100
NASDAQ: RSYS					
Reptron Electronics Inc 13700 Reptron Blvd	Tampa	FL	33626	**800-800-5441**	813-854-2000
Samsung Semiconductors Inc 3655 N 1st St	San Jose	CA	95134	**800-726-7864**	408-544-4000
SBS Technologies Inc					
2400 Louisiana Blvd NE AFC Bldg 5					
Suite 600	Albuquerque	NM	87110	**800-727-1553**	505-875-0600
NASDAQ: SBSE					
Sigma Designs Inc 1221 California Cir	Milpitas	CA	95035	**800-845-8086***	408-262-9003
NASDAQ: SIGM ■ *Sales					
SMART Modular Technologies Inc					
4211 Starboard Dr	Fremont	CA	94538	**800-956-7627**	510-623-1231
Socket Communications Inc 37400 Central Ct	Newark	CA	94560	**800-552-3300**	510-744-2700
NASDAQ: SCKT					
Spectrum Signal Processing Inc					
2700 Production Way Suite 200	Burnaby	BC	V5A4X1	**800-663-8986**	604-421-5422
NASDAQ: SSPI					
Suntron Corp 2401 W Grandview Rd Suite 1	Phoenix	AZ	85023	**866-554-1223**	602-789-6600
NASDAQ: SUNN					
TechWorks 4030 W Braker Ln Suite 120	Austin	TX	78759	**800-688-7466***	512-794-8533
*Cust Svc					
Unigen Corp 45388 Warm Springs Blvd	Fremont	CA	94539	**800-826-0808**	510-657-2680
Viking Components Inc					
30200 Avenida de					
Las Banderas	Rancho Santa Margarita	CA	92688	**800-338-2361**	949-643-7255
VisionTek Inc 1610 Colonial Pkwy	Inverness	IL	60067	**800-680-4424**	224-836-3000
Voyetra Turtle Beach Inc 5 Odell Plaza	Yonkers	NY	10701	**800-233-9377**	914-966-0600
Western Electronics LLC 1550 S Tech Ln	Meridian	ID	83642	**888-857-5775**	208-377-1557
Xycom Automation Inc 750 N Maple Rd	Saline	MI	48176	**800-289-9266**	734-429-4971
Z-World Inc 2900 Spafford St	Davis	CA	95616	**888-362-3387**	530-757-4616

614 PRINTING COMPANIES - BOOK PRINTERS

				Toll-Free	Phone
Adair Printing Technologies 7850 2nd St	Dexter	MI	48130	**800-637-5025**	734-426-2822
Amidon Graphics 1966 Benson Ave	Saint Paul	MN	55116	**800-328-6502**	651-690-2401
Bang Printing Inc 3323 Oak St	Brainerd	MN	56401	**800-328-0450**	218-829-2877
Banta Book Group PO Box 60	Menasha	WI	54952	**800-291-1171**	920-751-7771
Berryville Graphics PO Box 272	Berryville	VA	22611	**800-606-6467**	540-955-2750
Boyd Printing Co Inc 49 Sheridan Ave	Albany	NY	12210	**800-877-2693**	518-436-9686
Bradford & Bigelow Inc					
1 Electronic Ave Danvers Industrial Pk	Danvers	MA	01923	**800-882-9503**	978-777-1200
Cadmus Communications Port City Press Div					
1323 Greenwood Rd	Baltimore	MD	21208	**800-858-7678**	410-486-3000
CJ Krehbiel Co Inc 3962 Virginia Ave	Cincinnati	OH	45227	**800-598-7808**	513-271-6035
Claitor's Law Books & Publishing Inc					
3165 S Acadian Thwy	Baton Rouge	LA	70808	**800-274-1403**	225-344-0476
Command Web Offset Inc 100 Castle Rd	Secaucus	NJ	07094	**800-466-2932**	201-863-8100
Cookbook Publishers Inc 10800 Lakeview Ave	Lenexa	KS	66219	**800-227-7282**	913-492-5900
Courier Kendallville Inc 2500 Marion Dr	Kendallville	IN	46755	**800-228-9577**	260-347-3044
Courier Westford Inc 22 Town Farm Rd	Westford	MA	01886	**800-666-8772**	978-692-6321
Cushing-Malloy Inc 1350 N Main St	Ann Arbor	MI	48104	**888-295-7244**	734-663-8554
Darby Printing Co 6215 Purdue Dr	Atlanta	GA	30336	**800-241-5292**	404-344-2665
Deaton-Kennedy Co Inc 927 Gardner St	Joliet	IL	60434	**800-637-9665**	815-726-6234
Fidlar Doubleday Inc 6255 Technology Ave	Kalamazoo	MI	49009	**800-632-2259**	269-544-3600
Gospel Publishing House					
1445 N Boonville Ave	Springfield	MO	65802	**800-641-4310***	417-862-2781
*Orders					
Griffin Publishing Group 18022 Cowan	Irvine	CA	92614	**800-472-9741**	949-263-3733
Hamilton Printing Co Inc PO Box 232	Rensselaer	NY	12144	**800-242-4222**	518-732-4491
Henry John Co 5800 W Grand River Ave	Lansing	MI	48906	**800-748-0517**	517-323-9000
Joe Christensen Inc 1540 Adams St	Lincoln	NE	68521	**800-228-5030**	402-476-7535
John Henry Co 5800 W Grand River Ave	Lansing	MI	48906	**800-748-0517**	517-323-9000
Jostens Inc 5501 American Blvd W	Minneapolis	MN	55437	**800-235-4774**	952-830-3300
Kirby Lithographic Co Inc 2900 S Eads St	Arlington	VA	22202	**800-932-3594**	703-684-7600
KNI Inc 1261 S State College Pkwy	Anaheim	CA	92806	**800-886-7301**	714-956-7300
Krehbiel CJ Co Inc 3962 Virginia Ave	Cincinnati	OH	45227	**800-598-7808**	513-271-6035
Library Reproduction Service					
14214 S Figueroa St	Los Angeles	CA	90061	**800-255-5002**	310-354-2610
Malloy Lithographing Inc PO Box 1124	Ann Arbor	MI	48106	**800-722-3231**	734-665-6113
Moran Printing Inc 5425 Florida Blvd	Baton Rouge	LA	70806	**800-211-8335**	225-923-2550
National Publishing Co					
11311 Roosevelt Blvd	Philadelphia	PA	19154	**800-333-1863**	215-676-1863
Phillips Brothers Inc 1555 W Jefferson St	Springfield	IL	62702	**800-637-9327**	217-787-3014
Phoenix Color Corp					
540 Western Maryland Pkwy	Hagerstown	MD	21740	**800-632-4111**	301-733-0018
Port City Press Div Cadmus Communications					
1323 Greenwood Rd	Baltimore	MD	21208	**800-858-7678**	410-486-3000
Publishers Press Inc					
100 Frank E Simon Ave	Shepherdsville	KY	40165	**800-627-5801**	502-955-6526
RCL Enterprises 200 E Bethany Dr	Allen	TX	75002	**877-275-4725**	972-390-6400
Rose Printing Co Inc					
2503 Jackson Bluff Rd	Tallahassee	FL	32304	**800-227-3725**	850-576-4151
Sheridan Books Inc 613 E Industrial Dr	Chelsea	MI	48118	**800-999-2665**	734-475-9145
Smith-Edwards-Dunlap Co					
2867 E Allegheny Ave	Philadelphia	PA	19134	**800-829-0020**	215-425-8800
Stinehour Press 853 Lancaster Rd	Lunenburg	VT	05906	**800-331-7753**	802-328-2507
Transcontinental Printing Inc					
395 Lebeau Blvd	Saint-Laurent	QC	H4N1S2	**800-337-8560**	514-337-8560
Versa Press Inc 1465 Springbay Rd	East Peoria	IL	61611	**800-447-7829**	309-822-8272
Victor Graphics Inc 1211 Bernard Dr	Baltimore	MD	21223	**800-899-8303**	410-233-8300
Von Hoffmann Corp 1000 Camera Ave	Saint Louis	MO	63126	**800-325-2463**	314-966-0909
Webcrafters Inc 2211 Fordem Ave	Madison	WI	53704	**800-356-8200**	608-244-3561
Whitehall Printing Co 4244 Corporate Sq	Naples	FL	34104	**800-321-9290**	239-643-6464
Williamson Law Book Co 790 Canning Pkwy	Victor	NY	14564	**800-733-9522**	585-924-3400
Wright Color Graphics 626 Sonora Ave	Glendale	CA	91201	**800-695-3355**	818-246-8877

615 PRINTING COMPANIES - COMMERCIAL PRINTERS

				Toll-Free	Phone
Acme Printing Co Inc 30 Industrial Way	Wilmington	MA	01887	**800-829-0800**	978-658-0800
Allegra Network LLC 21680 Haggerty Rd	Northville	MI	48167	**800-726-9050**	248-596-8600
AlphaGraphics Inc					
268 S State St Suite 300	Salt Lake City	UT	84111	**800-955-6246**	801-595-7270
American Color Graphics Inc					
100 Winners Cir Suite 300	Brentwood	TN	37027	**800-621-7746**	615-377-0377
American Press LLC 1 American Pl	Gordonsville	VA	22942	**800-289-4602**	540-832-2253
American Stationery Co Inc 100 N Park Ave	Peru	IN	46970	**800-822-2577***	765-473-4438
*Sales					
Anderson Lithograph Co					
3217 S Garfield Ave	Los Angeles	CA	90040	**800-727-5846**	323-727-7767
Arandell Corp PO Box 405	Menomonee Falls	WI	53052	**800-558-8724**	262-255-4400
Banta Catalog Group 7401 Kilmer Ln	Maple Grove	MN	55369	**888-882-2682**	763-424-7446
Banta Direct Marketing Group					
12 Salt Creek Ln Suite 350	Hinsdale	IL	60521	**800-323-6112***	630-323-9490
*Cust Svc					
Brown Printing Co 2300 Brown Ave	Waseca	MN	56093	**800-533-0475**	507-835-2410
Cadmus Communications Corp Whitehall Group					
Div 2750 Whitehall Park Dr	Charlotte	NC	28273	**800-733-4318**	704-583-6600
Cadmus Professional Communications					
1801 Bayberry Ct Suite 200	Richmond	VA	23226	**877-422-3687**	804-287-5680
CadmusMack 2901 Byrdhill Rd	Richmond	VA	23228	**800-888-2973**	804-264-2711
Champion Industries Inc 2450-90 1st Ave	Huntington	WV	25703	**800-624-3431**	304-528-2791
NASDAQ: CHMP					
Color-Art Inc 10300 Watson Rd	Saint Louis	MO	63127	**800-800-8845**	314-966-2000
ColorDynamics 200 E Bethany Dr	Allen	TX	75002	**800-445-0017**	972-390-6500
Concord Litho Group 92 Old Turnpike Rd	Concord	NH	03301	**800-258-3662**	603-225-3328
Consolidated Graphics Group Inc					
1614 E 40th St	Cleveland	OH	44103	**888-884-9191**	216-881-9191
Dingley Press 119 Lisbon St	Lisbon	ME	04250	**888-346-4539**	207-353-4151
E & D Web Inc 4633 W 16th St	Cicero	IL	60804	**800-323-5733**	708-656-6600
EBSCO Media 801 5th Ave S	Birmingham	AL	35233	**800-765-0852**	205-323-1508
EU Services 649 N Horners Ln	Rockville	MD	20850	**800-230-3362**	301-424-3300
FedEx Kinko's Office & Print Services Inc					
13155 Noel Rd Suite 1600	Dallas	TX	75240	**800-254-6567***	214-550-7000
*Cust Svc					
Fort Dearborn Co 6035 W Gross Point Rd	Niles	IL	60714	**888-332-7746**	773-774-4321
Gannett Co Inc Gannett Offset Div					
6883 Commercial Dr	Springfield	VA	22159	**800-255-1457**	703-642-1800
Henry Wurst Inc 1331 Saline St	North Kansas City	MO	64116	**800-775-5851**	816-842-3113
Hickory Printing Group Inc PO Box 69	Hickory	NC	28603	**800-442-5679**	828-465-3431
Holden Graphic Services					
607 Washington Ave N	Minneapolis	MN	55401	**800-423-1099**	612-339-0241
IGI Earth Color Group 527 W 34th St	New York	NY	10001	**800-407-6449**	212-967-9720
IntegraColor PO Box 180218	Dallas	TX	75218	**800-433-8247**	972-289-0705
Intelligencer Printing Co 330 Eden Rd	Lancaster	PA	17601	**800-233-0107**	717-291-3100
Intermountain Color Inc 1840 Range St	Boulder	CO	80301	**800-678-9785**	303-443-3800
Japs-Olson Co 7500 Excelsior Blvd	Saint Louis Park	MN	55426	**800-548-2897**	952-932-9393
John Roberts Co 9687 E River Rd	Coon Rapids	MN	55433	**800-551-1534**	763-755-5500
Keller Crescent Co Inc 1100 E Louisiana St	Evansville	IN	47711	**800-457-3837**	812-464-2461
K/P Corp 12647 Alcosta Blvd Suite 425	San Ramon	CA	94583	**877-957-2677**	925-543-5200
Lake County Press Inc 98 Noll St	Waukegan	IL	60085	**800-369-4333**	847-336-4333
Lane Press Inc PO Box 130	Burlington	VT	05402	**800-733-3740**	802-863-5555
Litho-Krome Co 5700 Old Brim Dr	Midland	GA	31820	**800-572-8028**	706-225-6600
Lithographix Inc 13500 S Figueroa St	Los Angeles	CA	90061	**800-848-2449**	323-770-1000
LP Thebault Co					
249 Pomeroy Rd PO Box 169	Parsippany	NJ	07054	**800-843-2285**	973-884-1300
Merrill Corp 1 Merrill Cir	Saint Paul	MN	55108	**800-688-4400**	651-646-4501
Merrill/Daniels Printing Co 40 Commercial St	Everett	MA	02149	**800-553-7733**	617-389-7900
Meyers Co Inc 7277 Boone Ave N	Brooklyn Park	MN	55428	**800-927-9709**	763-533-9730
Network Communications Inc					
2305 New Point Pkwy	Lawrenceville	GA	30043	**800-841-3401**	770-962-7220
Nielsen Co 7405 Industrial Rd	Florence	KY	41042	**800-877-7405**	859-525-7405
Panel Prints Inc 1001 Moosic Rd	Old Forge	PA	18518	**800-557-2635**	570-457-8334
PBM Graphics Inc PO Box 13603	Durham	NC	27709	**800-849-8100**	919-544-6222
Perry Judd's Inc 575 W Madison St	Waterloo	WI	53594	**800-737-7948**	920-478-3551
ProForma 8800 E Pleasant Valley Rd	Independence	OH	44131	**800-825-1525**	216-520-8400
Progress Printing Co 2677 Waterlick Rd	Lynchburg	VA	24502	**800-572-7804**	434-239-9213
Publishers Printing Co					
100 Frank E Simon Ave	Shepherdsville	KY	40165	**800-627-5801**	502-543-2251
Quebecor World Inc 612 rue Saint-Jacques	Montreal	QC	H3C4M8	**800-567-7070**	514-954-0101
NYSE: IQW					
Saint Ives Cleveland Inc 4437 E 49th St	Cleveland	OH	44125	**800-634-1262**	216-271-5300
Saint Joseph Corp 50 MacIntosh Blvd	Concord	ON	L4K4P3	**877-660-3111**	905-660-3111
Schawk Inc 1695 S River Rd	Des Plaines	IL	60018	**800-621-1909**	847-827-9494
NYSE: SGK					
Shakopee Valley Printing					
5101 Valley Industrial Blvd S	Shakopee	MN	55379	**800-752-9906**	952-445-8260
Sir Speedy Inc 26722 Plaza Dr	Mission Viejo	CA	92691	**800-854-8297**	949-348-5000
Smith Litho 1029 E Gude Dr	Rockville	MD	20850	**800-622-2577**	301-424-1400
Solar Communications Inc					
1120 Frontenac Rd	Naperville	IL	60563	**800-323-2751**	630-983-1400
Spencer Press Inc 90 Spencer Dr	Wells	ME	04090	**800-765-0039**	207-646-9926
Strine Printing Co Inc 30 Grumbacher Rd	York	PA	17402	**800-477-8746**	717-767-6602
Tanagraphics Inc 263 9th Ave	New York	NY	10001	**800-606-6876**	212-255-6876
Transcontinental Printing Inc					
395 Lebeau Blvd	Saint-Laurent	QC	H4N1S2	**800-337-8560**	514-337-8560
Valassis Communications Inc					
19975 Victor Pkwy	Livonia	MI	48152	**800-437-0479**	734-591-3000
NYSE: VCI					

				Toll-Free	Phone
Vertis Inc 250 W Pratt St 18th Fl	Baltimore	MD	21201	**800-577-3569**	410-528-9800
Weldon Williams & Lick Inc PO Box 168	Fort Smith	AR	72902	**800-242-4995**	479-783-4113
Whitehall Group Div Cadmus Communications Corp 2750 Whitehall Park Dr	Charlotte	NC	28273	**800-733-4318**	704-583-6600
Williamson Printing Corp 6700 Denton Dr	Dallas	TX	75235	**800-843-5423**	214-352-1122

616 PRINTING & PHOTOCOPYING SUPPLIES

				Toll-Free	Phone
Abco Distribution Inc 6282 Proprietors Rd	Worthington	OH	43085	**800-821-9435**	614-848-4899
American Ribbon & Toner Co 2895 W Prospect Rd	Fort Lauderdale	FL	33309	**800-327-1013**	954-733-4552
Atlantic Exchange Inc 10405 NW 37th Terr	Miami	FL	33178	**800-327-2822**	305-593-1176
Automated Office Products Inc 9730-EE ML King Jr Hwy	Lanham	MD	20706	**800-929-2528**	301-731-4000
Barouh Eaton Allen Corp 67 Kent Ave	Brooklyn	NY	11211	**800-366-6767**	718-782-2601
Buckeye Business Products Inc 3830 Kelley Ave	Cleveland	OH	44114	**800-837-4323**	216-391-6300
Canon USA Inc 1 Canon Plaza	Lake Success	NY	11042	**800-828-4040**	516-488-6700
NYSE: CAJ					
Capital Imaging Co Inc 2745 W 5th North St	Summerville	SC	29483	**800-868-6780**	843-871-6084
Charts Inc 12977 Arroyo St	San Fernando	CA	91340	**800-882-9357**	818-898-3707
Chromaline Corp 4832 Grand Ave	Duluth	MN	55807	**800-328-4261**	218-628-2217
Colonial Carbon Co PO Box 498	Barrington	IL	60011	**800-345-9313**	847-299-0111
ColorImaging Inc 4350 Peachtree Industrial Blvd Suite 100	Norcross	GA	30071	**800-783-1090**	770-840-1090
Corporate Express Imaging & Computer Graphic Supplies Inc 1096 E Newport Center Dr Suite 300	Deerfield Beach	FL	33442	**800-828-9949**	954-379-5500
Curtis-Young Corp 2704 Cindel Dr	Cinnaminson	NJ	08077	**800-282-6650**	856-665-6650
Domino Amjet Inc 1290 Lakeside Dr	Gurnee	IL	60031	**800-444-4512**	847-244-2501
DuraLine Imaging Inc 110 Commercial Blvd	Flat Rock	NC	28731	**800-982-3872**	828-692-1301
Encore Ribbon Inc 3721 Santa Rosa Ave Suite B-1	Santa Rosa	CA	95407	**800-431-4969**	707-206-9600
Epson America Inc 3840 Kilroy Airport Way	Long Beach	CA	90806	**800-533-3731***	562-981-3840
*Cust Svc					
Frye Tech Inc 110 Industrial Rd	New Windsor	NY	12553	**800-705-3793**	
General Ribbon Corp 20650 Prairie St	Chatsworth	CA	91311	**800-423-5400**	818-709-1234
Guy Brown Products 9003 Overlook Blvd	Brentwood	TN	37027	**877-794-5906**	615-777-1500
Hurst Chemical Co 2500 N San Fernando Rd	Los Angeles	CA	90065	**800-723-2004**	323-223-4121
Image One Corp 13201 Capital Ave	Oak Park	MI	48237	**800-799-5377**	248-414-9955
ImageTek Corp 420 E Easy St Suite 2	Simi Valley	CA	93065	**800-584-2503**	805-584-2100
International Communication Materials Inc Rt 119 S	Connellsville	PA	15425	**800-438-2530**	724-628-1014
IRIS Graphics Inc 3 Federal St	Billerica	MA	01821	**800-666-8990**	978-313-4747
Ko-Rec-Type Div Barouh Eaton Allen Corp 67 Kent Ave	Brooklyn	NY	11211	**800-366-6767**	718-782-2601
Kodak Polychrome Graphics 770 Canning Pkwy	Victor	NY	14564	**800-677-9943**	585-742-5700
Kroy LLC 3830 Kelley Ave	Cleveland	OH	44114	**888-888-5769**	216-426-5600
LexJet Corp 1680 Fruitville Rd Suite 202	Sarasota	FL	34236	**800-453-9538**	941-330-1210
Micro Solutions Enterprises 9111 Mason Ave	Chatsworth	CA	91311	**800-673-4968**	818-407-7500
MKG Cartridge Systems Inc 1090 Lorimar Dr	Mississauga	ON	L5S1R8	**800-881-7545**	905-564-9218
NER Data Products Inc 307 S Delsea Dr	Glassboro	NJ	08028	**800-257-5235**	856-881-5524
Nukote International Inc 200 Beasley Dr	Franklin	TN	37064	**800-251-1910**	615-794-9000
Oasis Imaging Products Inc 460 Amherst St	Nashua	NH	03063	**888-627-6555**	603-880-3991
Perfecopy Co 103 W 61st St	Westmont	IL	60559	**800-323-4030***	630-769-9901
*Cust Svc					
Rayven Inc 431 Griggs St N	Saint Paul	MN	55104	**800-878-3776***	651-642-1112
*Cust Svc					
Repeat-O-Type Mfg Corp 665 State Hwy 23	Wayne	NJ	07470	**800-288-3330***	973-696-3330
*Cust Svc					
Ricoh Printing Systems America Inc 2635-A Park Center Dr	Simi Valley	CA	93065	**800-887-8848***	805-578-4000
*Cust Svc					
Sercomp Corp 21050 Lassen St	Chatsworth	CA	91311	**800-477-7372**	818-341-1680
Weber-Valentine Co 1099 E Morse Ave	Elk Grove Village	IL	60007	**800-323-9642***	847-439-7111
*Cust Svc					
Western Numerical Control 983 Golden Gate Terr	Grass Valley	CA	95945	**800-538-5108**	530-477-7575

617 PRINTING & PUBLISHING EQUIPMENT & SYSTEMS

SEE ALSO Computer Equipment - Printers

				Toll-Free	Phone
AB Dick Co 7400 Caldwell Ave	Niles	IL	60714	**800-422-3616**	847-779-1900
Accel Graphic Systems Inc 11103 Indian Trail	Dallas	TX	75229	**800-666-8803**	972-484-6808
Agfa Corp 100 Challenger Rd	Ridgefield Park	NJ	07660	**800-581-2432**	201-440-2500
Autographic Business Forms Inc 31 Industrial Ave	Mahwah	NJ	07430	**800-526-5309**	201-327-6200
Bingham Co 12827 E Imperial Hwy	Santa Fe Springs	CA	90670	**800-635-9490***	562-903-3006
*Sales					
Brackett Inc PO Box 19306	Topeka	KS	66619	**800-255-3506**	785-862-2205
Brandtjen & Kluge Inc 539 Blanding Woods Rd	Saint Croix Falls	WI	54024	**800-826-7320**	715-483-3265
Dauphin Graphic Machines Inc PO Box 573	Elizabethville	PA	17023	**800-346-6119**	717-362-3243
Diamond Roller 150 Marr Ave	Marietta	GA	30060	**800-247-5290**	770-590-0152
Dick AB Co 7400 Caldwell Ave	Niles	IL	60714	**800-422-3616**	847-779-1900
Didde Press Systems 6499 S Potomac St	Centennial	CO	80112	**800-225-5799**	303-708-9044
GMI (Graphics Microsystems Inc) 484 Oakmead Pkwy	Sunnyvale	CA	94085	**800-336-1464**	408-745-7745
Graphics Microsystems Inc (GMI) 484 Oakmead Pkwy	Sunnyvale	CA	94085	**800-336-1464**	408-745-7745
Gravograph-New Hermes Inc 2200 Northmont Pkwy	Duluth	GA	30096	**800-843-7637**	770-623-0331
Heidelberg USA Inc 1000 Gutenberg Dr	Kennesaw	GA	30144	**800-437-7388**	770-419-6500
MAN Roland Inc 800 E Oak Hill Dr	Westmont	IL	60559	**800-700-2344**	630-920-2000
Mark Andy Inc 18081 Chesterfield Airport Rd	Chesterfield	MO	63005	**800-700-6275**	636-532-4433
NexPress Solutions LLC 1447 Saint Paul St	Rochester	NY	14653	**877-446-3977**	585-253-5224
Pamarco Global Graphics 209 E 11th Ave	Roselle	NJ	07203	**800-526-2180**	908-665-8500
Rosback Co 125 Hawthorne Ave	Saint Joseph	MI	49085	**800-542-2420**	269-983-2582
Townsend Industries Inc 6650 NE 41st Ave	Altoona	IA	50009	**877-868-3544**	515-967-4261
Web Press Corp 22023 68th Ave S	Kent	WA	98032	**800-424-1411**	253-395-3343
Xerox Corp 800 Long Ridge Rd	Stamford	CT	06904	**800-842-0024**	203-968-3000
NYSE: XRX					

618 PRISON INDUSTRIES

				Toll-Free	Phone
Alabama Correctional Industries 1400 Lloyd St	Montgomery	AL	36107	**800-224-7007**	334-261-3600
Arizona Correctional Industries 3701 W Cambridge Ave	Phoenix	AZ	85009	**800-992-1738**	602-272-7600
Big House Products & Services PO Box 47	Camp Hill	PA	17001	**877-673-3724**	717-731-7132
Colorado Correctional Industries DBA Juniper Valley Products 2862 S Circle Dr	Colorado Springs	CO	80906	**800-685-7891***	719-226-4206
*Cust Svc					
Cornhusker State Industries 800 Pioneers Blvd	Lincoln	NE	68502	**800-348-7537**	402-471-4597
Correctional Enterprises of Connecticut 24 Wolcott Hill Rd	Wethersfield	CT	06109	**800-842-1146**	860-692-7480
DEPTCOR PO Box 863	Trenton	NJ	08625	**800-321-6524**	609-292-4036
Georgia Correctional Industries 2984 Clifton Springs Rd	Decatur	GA	30034	**800-282-7130**	404-244-5100
Iowa Prison Industries 420 Watson Powell Jr Way	Des Moines	IA	50309	**800-670-4537***	515-242-5702
*Sales					
Juniper Valley Products 2862 S Circle Dr	Colorado Springs	CO	80906	**800-685-7891***	719-226-4206
*Cust Svc					
MINNCOR Industries 1450 Energy Park Dr Suite 110	Saint Paul	MN	55108	**800-646-6267**	651-603-0118
Missouri Vocational Enterprises PO Box 1898	Jefferson City	MO	65102	**800-392-8486***	573-751-6663
*Sales					
Montana Correctional Enterprises 300 Conley Lake Rd	Deer Lodge	MT	59722	**800-815-6252**	406-846-1320
New Jersey Bureau of State Use Industries PO Box 863	Trenton	NJ	08625	**800-321-6524**	609-292-4036
New Mexico Correctional Industries 4337 SR 14	Santa Fe	NM	87505	**800-568-8789**	505-827-8838
Ohio Penal Industries 1221 McKinley Ave	Columbus	OH	43222	**800-237-3454**	614-752-0287
Oklahoma Correctional Industries 3402 ML King Blvd	Oklahoma City	OK	73111	**800-522-3565**	405-425-7500
Pennsylvania Bureau of Correctional Industries DBA Big House Products & Services PO Box 47	Camp Hill	PA	17001	**877-673-3724**	717-731-7132
PRIDE (Prison Rehabilitative Industries & Diversified Enterprises Inc) 12425 28th St N Suite 103	Saint Petersburg	FL	33716	**800-643-8495**	727-572-1987
Prison Rehabilitative Industries & Diversified Enterprises Inc (PRIDE) 12425 28th St N Suite 103	Saint Petersburg	FL	33716	**800-643-8495**	727-572-1987
Rough Rider Industries 3303 E Main Ave	Bismarck	ND	58506	**800-732-0557**	701-328-6161
Silver State Industries PO Box 7011	Carson City	NV	89702	**800-648-7578**	775-887-3303
Tennessee Rehabilitative Initiative in Correction (TRICOR) 240 Great Circle Rd Suite 310	Nashville	TN	37228	**800-958-7426**	615-741-5705
TRICOR (Tennessee Rehabilitative Initiative in Correction) 240 Great Circle Rd Suite 310	Nashville	TN	37228	**800-958-7426**	615-741-5705
West Virginia Correctional Industries 617 Leon Sullivan Way	Charleston	WV	25301	**800-525-5381**	304-558-6054

619 PROFESSIONAL EMPLOYER ORGANIZATIONS (PEOS)

				Toll-Free	Phone
Accord Human Resources Inc 210 Park Ave Suite 1200	Oklahoma City	OK	73102	**800-725-4004**	405-232-9888
Adams Keegan Inc 6055 Primacy Pkwy Suite 300	Memphis	TN	38119	**800-621-1308**	901-683-5353
Administaff Inc 19001 Crescent Springs Dr	Kingwood	TX	77339	**800-465-3800**	281-358-8986
NYSE: ASF					
ADP TotalSource Co 10200 Sunset Dr	Miami	FL	33173	**800-447-3237**	305-630-1000
AdvanTech Solutions 1410 N Westshore Blvd Suite 600	Tampa	FL	33607	**888-340-9442**	813-289-9442
Alcott Group 71 Executive Blvd PO Box 160	Farmingdale	NY	11735	**888-425-2688**	
All Staffing Inc 100 W Ridge St PO Box 219	Lansford	PA	18232	**800-442-4538**	570-645-5000
Allied Employer Group 4400 Buffalo Gap Rd Suite 4500	Abilene	TX	79606	**800-729-7823**	325-695-5822
AlphaStaff Inc 1801 Clint Moore Rd Suite 115	Boca Raton	FL	33487	**888-335-9545**	561-241-9545
ALTRES Inc 967 Kapiolani Blvd	Honolulu	HI	96814	**800-373-1955**	808-591-4900
AmStaff Human Resources Inc 6723 Plantation Rd	Pensacola	FL	32504	**800-888-0472**	850-477-7022
Axiom HR Solutions 8345 Lenexa Dr Suite 100	Lenexa	KS	66214	**800-801-7557**	913-383-2999
Barrett Business Services Inc 4724 SW Macadam Ave	Portland	OR	97239	**800-676-4710**	503-220-0988
NASDAQ: BBSI					
Bowles Group of Cos DBA Workforce 2000 1903 Central Dr Suite 200	Bedford	TX	76021	**800-522-9778**	817-868-7277
Century II Staffing Inc 278 Franklin Rd Suite 350	Brentwood	TN	37027	**800-972-9630**	615-665-9060
Ceridian Corp 3311 E Old Shakopee Rd	Minneapolis	MN	55425	**800-767-4969**	952-853-8100
NYSE: CEN					
Certified HR Services 5101 NW 21st Ave Suite 350	Fort Lauderdale	FL	33309	**800-793-2872**	954-677-0202
Checks & Balances Inc 10328 Battleview Pkwy	Manassas	VA	20109	**800-624-3698**	703-361-2220

Company	City	State	Zip	Toll-Free	Phone
Co-Advantage Resources 111 W Jefferson St Suite 100	Orlando	FL	32801	**888-278-6055**	407-422-8448
Diversified Human Resources Inc 2735 E Camelback Rd	Phoenix	AZ	85016	**888-870-5588**	480-941-5588
Doherty Employment Group 7625 Parklawn Ave	Edina	MN	55435	**800-910-8822**	952-832-8383
EBDS (Employee Benefits Data Services Inc) 420 Fort Duquesne Blvd 1 Gateway Ctr Suite 1250	Pittsburgh	PA	15222	**800-472-2738**	412-394-6300
EHRI (Employer's Human Resources Inc) PO Box 1072	Wagoner	OK	74477	**800-878-0515**	918-485-9404
Employee Benefits Data Services Inc (EBDS) 420 Fort Duquesne Blvd 1 Gateway Ctr Suite 1250	Pittsburgh	PA	15222	**800-472-2738**	412-394-6300
Employee Professionals 6320 Trail Blvd	Naples	FL	34108	**888-592-9700**	239-592-9700
Employer's Human Resources Inc (EHRI) PO Box 1072	Wagoner	OK	74477	**800-878-0515**	918-485-9404
Executive Staffing Group The 4101 Lake Boone Trail Suite 112	Raleigh	NC	27607	**888-374-4364**	919-783-6695
Genesis Consolidated Services Inc 76 Blanchard Rd	Burlington	MA	01803	**800-367-8367**	781-272-4900
Gevity HR Inc 600 301 Blvd W	Bradenton	FL	34205	**800-243-8489**	941-748-4540
NASDAQ: GVHR					
HR America 1833 Magnavox Way	Fort Wayne	IN	46804	**800-837-4787**	260-436-3878
Human Capital 28777 Northwestern Hwy Suite 125	Southfield	MI	48034	**888-736-9071**	248-353-3444
Kelly Staff Leasing 110 W 'A' St Suite 1700	San Diego	CA	92101	**800-877-8233**	619-615-7500
KimStaff HR 17872 Cowan Ave	Irvine	CA	92614	**800-601-4800**	949-752-2995
Merit Resources Inc 4165 120th St	Des Moines	IA	50323	**800-336-1931**	515-278-1931
Moresource Inc 401 Vandiver Dr	Columbia	MO	65202	**800-495-5678**	573-814-1234
Oasis Outsourcing Inc 4400 N Congress Ave Suite 250	West Palm Beach	FL	33407	**800-627-4735**	561-627-4735
Odyssey OneSource Inc 204 N Ector Dr	Euless	TX	76039	**800-580-3090**	817-267-6090
Pay Plus Benefits Inc 1110 N Center Pkwy Suite B	Kennewick	WA	99336	**888-531-5781**	509-735-1143
Paychex Business Solutions 10105 Dr Martin Luthur King Jr St N	Saint Petersburg	FL	33716	**800-741-6277**	727-579-0505
PaySource Inc 251 New Karner Rd	Albany	NY	12205	**888-452-9743**	518-452-9743
PayTech 640 E Purdue Dr Suite 102	Phoenix	AZ	85020	**800-972-6064**	602-788-1317
Persidion Solutions 1 Harbison Way Suite 114	Columbia	SC	29212	**800-948-8524**	803-781-7810
Personnel Management Inc PO Box 6657	Shreveport	LA	71136	**800-259-4126**	318-869-4555
Professional Staff Management Inc 224 S 5th St Suite C	Richmond	IN	47374	**800-967-5515**	765-935-1515
Progressive Employer Services 2469 Enterprise Rd Suite B	Clearwater	FL	33763	**800-741-7848**	727-712-9121
Reserves Network The 22021 Brookpark Rd	Fairview Park	OH	44126	**866-876-2020**	440-779-1400
Sequent Inc 222 E Campus View Blvd	Columbus	OH	43235	**888-456-3627**	614-436-5880
Shaw & Shaw 2421 N Glassell St	Orange	CA	92865	**800-933-6756**	714-921-5442
Staff Management Inc 5919 Spring Creek Rd	Rockford	IL	61114	**800-535-3518**	815-282-3900
Staff One Inc 1100 W Main St	Durant	OK	74701	**800-771-7823**	580-920-1212
Staff Resources Inc 870 Manzanita Ct Suite A	Chico	CA	95926	**888-835-5774***	530-345-2487
*Sales					
Staffing Plus 555 E Butterfield Rd Suite 330	Lombard	IL	60148	**800-782-3346**	630-515-0500
Strategic Outsourcing Inc 5260 Parkway Plaza Blvd Suite 140	Charlotte	NC	28217	**800-572-2412**	704-523-2191
Tilson HR Inc 1499 Windhorst Way Suite 100	Greenwood	IN	46143	**800-276-3976**	317-885-3838
TriNet Group Inc 1100 San Leandro Blvd Suite 300	San Leandro	CA	94577	**800-638-0461**	510-352-5000
USPersonnel 2300 Valley View Ln Suite 300	Irving	TX	75062	**888-506-7785**	972-871-0400
Workforce 2000 1903 Central Dr Suite 200	Bedford	TX	76021	**800-522-9778**	817-868-7277

620 PUBLIC BROADCASTING ORGANIZATIONS

SEE ALSO Radio Networks; Television Networks

Organization	City	State	Zip	Toll-Free	Phone
Alabama Educational Television Commission 2112 11th Ave S Suite 400	Birmingham	AL	35205	**800-239-5233**	205-328-8756
Alabama Public Television (APT) 2112 11th Ave S Suite 400	Birmingham	AL	35205	**800-239-5233**	205-328-8756
Alaska One PO Box 755620	Fairbanks	AK	99775	**800-727-6543**	907-474-7491
Annenberg/CPB Projects c/o Learner Online 1301 Pennsylvania Ave NW Suite 302	Washington	DC	20004	**800-532-7637**	202-783-0500
Arkansas Educational Television Network (AETN) PO Box 1250	Conway	AR	72033	**800-662-2386**	501-682-2386
Association of Independents in Radio (AIR) 328 Flatbush Ave Suite 322	Brooklyn	NY	11238	**888-937-2477**	
Blue Ridge Public Television 1215 McNeil Dr	Roanoke	VA	24015	**888-332-7788**	540-344-0991
Boise State Radio 1910 University Drive	Boise	ID	83725	**888-859-5278**	208-947-5660
Commonwealth Club of California 595 Market St 2nd Fl	San Francisco	CA	94105	**800-933-7548**	415-597-6700
Connecticut Public Broadcasting Inc (CPBI) 1049 Asylum Ave	Hartford	CT	06105	**800-683-2112**	860-278-5310
Corporation for Public Broadcasting (CPB) 401 9th St NW	Washington	DC	20004	**800-272-2190**	202-879-9600
Development Exchange Inc (DEI) 1645 Hennepin Ave Suite 312	Minneapolis	MN	55403	**888-454-2314**	612-677-1505
East Tennessee Public Communications Corp 1611 E Magnolia Ave	Knoxville	TN	37917	**800-595-0220**	865-595-0220
Georgia Public Broadcasting (GPB) 260 14th St NW	Atlanta	GA	30318	**800-222-6006**	404-685-2400
GPB Education 260 14th St NW	Atlanta	GA	30318	**888-501-8960**	404-685-2550
Idaho Public Television (IPTV) 1455 N Orchard St	Boise	ID	83706	**800-543-6868**	208-373-7220
Indiana Higher Education Telecommunication System (IHETS) 714 N Senate Ave	Indianapolis	IN	46202	**800-776-4438**	317-263-8900
Iowa Public Television (IPTV) 6450 Corporate Dr PO Box 6450	Johnston	IA	50131	**800-532-1290**	515-242-3100
Kentucky Educational Television (KET) 600 Cooper Dr	Lexington	KY	40502	**800-432-0951**	859-258-7000
Louisiana Educational Television Authority 7733 Perkins Rd	Baton Rouge	LA	70810	**800-272-8161**	225-767-5660
Louisiana Public Broadcasting (LPB) 7733 Perkins Rd	Baton Rouge	LA	70810	**800-272-8161**	225-767-5660
Maine Public Broadcasting Corp (MPBC) 65 Texas Ave	Bangor	ME	04401	**800-884-1717**	207-941-1010
Maryland Public Television (MPT) 11767 Owings Mills Blvd	Owings Mills	MD	21117	**800-223-3678**	410-356-5600
Metropolitan Indianapolis Public Broadcasting Corp 1401 N Meridian St	Indianapolis	IN	46202	**800-633-7419**	317-636-2020
Minnesota Public Radio (MPR) 45 E 7th St	Saint Paul	MN	55101	**800-228-7123**	651-290-1212
Mississippi Public Broadcasting 3825 Ridgewood Rd	Jackson	MS	39211	**800-922-9698**	601-432-6565
Montana Public Radio 32 Campus Dr University of Montana	Missoula	MT	59812	**800-325-1565**	406-243-4931
Montana Public Television PO Box 10715	Bozeman	MT	59715	**800-426-8243**	406-994-3437
Nebraska Educational Telecommunications (NET) 1800 N 33rd St	Lincoln	NE	68503	**800-228-4630**	402-472-3611
New Hampshire Public Television (NHPTV) 268 Mast Rd	Durham	NH	03824	**800-639-8408**	603-868-1100
New Jersey Public Broadcasting PO Box 777	Trenton	NJ	08625	**800-792-8645**	609-777-5000
NJN Public Television & Radio PO Box 777	Trenton	NJ	08625	**800-792-8645**	609-777-5000
Oklahoma Educational TV Authority (OETA) 7403 N Kelley St	Oklahoma City	OK	73111	**800-879-6382**	405-848-8501
Prairie Public Broadcasting Inc 207 N 5th St	Fargo	ND	58102	**800-359-6900**	701-241-6900
Public Broadcasting Council of Central New York PO Box 2400	Syracuse	NY	13220	**800-451-9269**	315-453-2424
Public Broadcasting Northwest Pennsylvania 8425 Peach St	Erie	PA	16509	**800-727-8854**	814-864-3001
Rhode Island PBS 50 Park Lane	Providence	RI	02907	**800-613-8836**	401-222-3636
Rocky Mountain Public Broadcasting Network (RMPB) 1089 Bannock St	Denver	CO	80204	**800-274-6666**	303-892-6666
South Carolina Educational Television Commission PO Box 11000	Columbia	SC	29211	**800-922-5437**	803-737-3200
South Dakota Public Broadcasting (SDPB) 555 N Dakota St PO Box 5000	Vermillion	SD	57069	**800-456-0766**	605-677-5861
South Texas Public Broadcasting System Inc 4455 S Padre Island Dr Suite 38	Corpus Christi	TX	78411	**800-307-5338**	361-855-2213
Texas Public Radio (TPR) 8401 Datapoint Dr Suite 800	San Antonio	TX	78229	**800-622-8977**	210-614-8977
TRAC Media Services 4380 N Campbell Ave Suite 205	Tucson	AZ	85718	**888-299-1866**	520-299-1866
University of North Carolina Center for Public Television (UNC-TV) 10 TW Alexander Dr PO Box 14900	Research Triangle Park	NC	27709	**800-906-5050**	919-549-7060
Vermont Public Television (VPT) 204 Ethan Allen Ave	Colchester	VT	05446	**800-639-7811**	802-655-4800
Virginia Satellite Educational Network (VSEN) PO Box 2120	Richmond	VA	23218	**800-246-8736**	804-692-0335
WAMC/Northeast Public Radio 318 Central Ave	Albany	NY	12206	**800-323-9262**	518-465-5233
Wisconsin Public Radio (WPR) 821 University Ave	Madison	WI	53706	**800-442-7110**	608-263-3970
Wisconsin Public Television (WPT) 821 University Ave	Madison	WI	53706	**800-422-9707**	608-263-2121
Wyoming Public Television 2660 Peck Ave	Riverton	WY	82501	**800-495-9788**	307-856-6944

621 PUBLIC RECORDS SEARCH SERVICES

SEE ALSO Investigative Services

Company	City	State	Zip	Toll-Free	Phone
Accufax PO Box 35563	Tulsa	OK	74153	**800-256-8898**	918-627-2226
All-Search & Inspection Inc 1108 E South Union Ave	Midvale	UT	84047	**800-227-3152**	801-984-8160
American Background Information Services Inc 629 Cedar Creek Grade Suite C	Winchester	VA	22601	**800-669-2247**	540-665-8056
American Driving Records Inc 2860 Gold Tailings Ct	Rancho Cordova	CA	95670	**800-766-6877**	916-456-3200
AmeriSearch 1232 Q St	Sacramento	CA	95814	**800-877-2877**	916-443-0795
AmRent PO Box 771176	Houston	TX	77215	**800-324-3681**	713-266-1870
Applicant Insight Ltd PO Box 458	New Port Richey	FL	34656	**800-771-7703**	
Apscreen Inc 2043 Westcliff Dr Suite 300	Newport Beach	CA	92660	**800-277-2733**	949-646-4003
Background Bureau Inc 2019 Alexandria Pike	Highland Heights	KY	41076	**800-854-3990**	859-781-3400
Background Information Services Inc 1800 30th St Suite 204	Boulder	CO	80301	**800-433-6010**	303-442-3960
Barry Shuster Information Services 1157 Tucker Rd	North Dartmouth	MA	02747	**877-852-2507**	508-999-5436
Canadian Securities Registration Systems 4126 Norland Ave Suite 200	Burnaby	BC	V5G3S8	**800-561-1404**	604-637-4000
Capitol Lien Records & Research Inc 1010 N Dale St	Saint Paul	MN	55167	**800-845-4077**	651-488-0100
Capitol Services Inc 800 Brazos St Suite 1100	Austin	TX	78701	**800-345-4647**	512-474-8377
CARCO Group Inc 17 Flowerfield Industrial Pk	Saint James	NY	11780	**800-645-4556**	631-862-9300
CCH Corsearch 345 Hudson St 16th Fl	New York	NY	10014	**800-732-7241**	917-408-5000
CCH Legal Information Services 111 8th Ave	New York	NY	10011	**800-223-7567**	212-894-8940
CCH Washington Service Bureau Inc 1015 15th St NW 10th Fl	Washington	DC	20005	**800-955-5219**	202-312-6600
CDI Credit Inc 6160 Peachtree Dunwoody Rd NE Suite B-210	Atlanta	GA	30328	**800-633-3961**	770-350-5070
Charles Jones Inc PO Box 8488	Trenton	NJ	08650	**800-792-8888**	609-538-1000
ChoicePoint Inc 1000 Alderman Dr	Alpharetta	GA	30005	**877-317-5000**	770-752-6000
NYSE: CPS					
Colby Attorneys Service Co Inc 41 State St	Albany	NY	12207	**800-832-1220**	518-463-4426
Corporation Service Co 2711 Centerville Rd Suite 400	Wilmington	DE	19808	**800-927-9800**	302-636-5400
Corporation Service Co 801 Adlai Stevenson Dr	Springfield	IL	62703	**800-634-9738**	217-529-5599
CourtEXPRESS 701 Pennsylvania Ave NW Suite C-100	Washington	DC	20004	**800-542-3320**	202-737-7111
CT Corp 111 8th Ave	New York	NY	10011	**800-223-7567**	212-894-8940
DCS Information Services Inc 500 N Central Expy Suite 280	Plano	TX	75074	**800-299-3647**	972-422-3600
Doc-U-Search Inc 63 Pleasant St	Concord	NH	03301	**877-524-3034**	603-224-2871
Driving Records Facilities PO Box 1086	Glen Burnie	MD	21061	**800-772-5510**	410-761-5510
Edge Information Management Inc 100 Rialto Pl Suite 800	Melbourne	FL	32901	**800-725-3343**	321-722-3343

				Toll-Free	Phone
Employment Screening Services Inc 627 E Sprague St Suite 100	Spokane	WA	99202	800-473-7778	509-624-3851
Explore Information Services Inc 2945 Lone Oak Dr Suite 150	Eagan	MN	55121	800-531-9125	651-681-4460
Federal Research Corp 1030 15th St NW Suite 920	Washington	DC	20005	800-846-3190	202-783-2700
Fidelifacts 42 Broadway 15th Fl	New York	NY	10004	800-678-0007	212-425-1520
Find People Fast 4600 Chippewa Suite 244	Saint Louis	MO	63116	800-829-1807	314-351-4000
First American Real Estate Solutions 5601 E La Palma Ave	Anaheim	CA	92807	800-345-7334	714-701-2100
Government Liaison Services Inc 200 N Glebe Rd Suite 321	Arlington	VA	22203	800-642-6564	703-524-8200
HireCheck Inc 805 Executive Center Dr W Suite 300	Saint Petersburg	FL	33702	800-881-3924	727-535-4473
HRPlus 2902 Evergreen Pkwy Suite 100	Evergreen	CO	80439	800-827-2479	303-670-8177
Human Resource Profile Inc 8506 Beechmont Ave	Cincinnati	OH	45255	800-969-4300	513-388-4300
IMI Data Search Inc 275 E Hillcrest Dr Suite 102	Thousand Oaks	CA	91360	800-860-7779	805-495-1149
Info-Center Inc 940 North St Ext	Feeding Hills	MA	01030	800-462-3033	413-786-7987
Information Management Systems Inc 114 W Main St Suite 202	New Britain	CT	06050	888-403-8347	860-229-1119
Information Source LLC 627 E Sprague Ave Suite 111	Spokane	WA	99202	800-548-8847	509-624-2229
InfoTrack Information Services Inc 111 Deerlake Rd	Deerfield	IL	60015	800-275-5594	847-444-1177
Insured Aircraft Title Service Inc 4848 SW 36th St	Oklahoma City	OK	73179	800-654-4882	405-681-6663
Intelnet Inc 320 Westcott St Suite 108	Houston	TX	77007	888-636-3693	713-880-3693
Jones Charles Inc PO Box 8488	Trenton	NJ	08650	800-792-8888	609-538-1000
KnowX LLC 730 Peachtree St Suite 700	Atlanta	GA	30308	877-317-5000	404-541-0221
Kroll Background America Inc 1900 Church St Suite 400	Nashville	TN	37203	800-697-7189	615-320-9800
Laborchex Co 2506 Lakeland Dr Suite 200	Jackson	MS	39232	800-880-0366	601-664-6760
Legal Data Resources Inc 2816 W Summerdale Ave	Chicago	IL	60625	800-735-9207	773-561-2468
LegalEase Inc 139 Fulton St Suite 1013	New York	NY	10038	800-393-1277	212-393-9070
Liberty Corporate Services Inc 11285 Elkins Rd Suite G1B	Roswell	GA	30076	800-334-2735	770-794-6600
Merlin Information Services 215 S Complex Dr	Kalispell	MT	59901	800-367-6646	406-755-8550
MicroPatent LLC 250 Dodge Ave	East Haven	CT	06512	800-648-6787	203-466-5055
MLQ Attorney Services 2110 Powers Ferry Rd Suite 305	Atlanta	GA	30339	800-446-8794	770-984-7007
National Data Access Corp 2 Office Park Ct Suite 103	Columbia	SC	29223	800-528-8790	803-699-6130
National Public Records Inc 4426 Hugh Howell Rd Suite B314	Tucker	GA	30084	800-343-6641	770-938-1050
Nationwide Information Services Inc 52 James St 5th Fl	Albany	NY	12207	800-873-3482	518-449-8429
OPENonline 1650 Lake Shore Dr Suite 350	Columbus	OH	43204	888-381-5656	614-481-6999
Pacific Corporate & Title Services 914 S St	Sacramento	CA	95814	800-230-4988	916-558-4988
Parasec Inc 640 Bercut Dr Suite A	Sacramento	CA	95814	800-533-7272	916-441-1001
Penncorp Servicegroup Inc 600 N 2nd St Suite 500	Harrisburg	PA	17101	800-544-9050	717-234-2300
Professional Research Services Inc 4901 W 77th St Suite 135	Minneapolis	MN	55435	800-886-4777	952-941-9040
Property Owners Exchange Inc 6630 Baltimore National Pike Suite 208	Baltimore	MD	21228	800-869-3200	410-719-0100
Questel Orbit 7925 Jones Branch Dr	McLean	VA	22102	800-456-7248	703-873-4700
Quick Search 4155 Buena Vista	Dallas	TX	75204	800-473-2840	214-358-2840
Record Search America Inc 5527 Kendall St	Boise	ID	83706	866-865-8003	208-375-1906
Rental Research Services Inc 11300 Minnetonka Mills Rd	Minnetonka	MN	55305	800-328-0333	952-935-5700
Search Co International 1535 Grant St Suite 140	Denver	CO	80203	800-727-2120	303-863-1800
Search Network Ltd 1501 42nd St 2 Corporate Pl Suite 210	West Des Moines	IA	50266	800-383-5050	515-223-1153
SearchTec Inc 211 N 13th St 6th Fl	Philadelphia	PA	19107	800-762-5018	215-963-0888
Securitech Inc 8230 E Broadway Suite E-10	Tucson	AZ	85710	800-805-4473	520-721-0305
Security Search & Abstract Co 201 N Presidential Blvd Suite 102	Bala Cynwyd	PA	19004	800-345-9494	610-664-5912
Sterling Testing Systems Inc 249 W 17th St 6th Fl	New York	NY	10011	800-899-2272	212-736-5100
Superior Information Services Inc 300 Phillips Blvd Suite 500	Trenton	NJ	08618	800-848-0489	609-883-7000
TABB Inc PO Box 10	Chester	NJ	07930	800-887-8222	908-879-2323
Thomson & Thomson 500 Victory Rd	North Quincy	MA	02171	800-692-8833	617-479-1600
Title First Agency Inc 555 S Front St Suite 400	Columbus	OH	43215	800-837-4032	614-224-9207
TML Information Services Inc 116-55 Queens Blvd Suite 210	Forest Hills	NY	11375	800-733-9777	718-793-3737
UCC Direct Services 2727 Allen Pkwy Suite 1000	Houston	TX	77019	800-833-5778	713-533-4600
UCC Filing & Search Services Inc 526 E Park Ave	Tallahassee	FL	32302	800-822-5436	850-681-6528
Unisearch Inc 1780 Barnes Blvd SW	Tumwater	WA	98512	800-722-0708	360-956-9500
US Corporate Services 380 Jackson St Suite 418	Saint Paul	MN	55101	800-327-1186	651-227-7575
US Datalink Inc 6711 Bayway Dr	Baytown	TX	77520	800-527-7930	281-424-7223
US Investigations Services Inc 1137 Branchton Rd	Annandale	PA	16018	888-794-8747	724-794-5612
US Search.com Inc 5401 Beethoven St	Los Angeles	CA	90066	877-327-2450	310-302-6300
USIS Commercial Services 6365 Taft St Suite 2000	Hollywood	FL	33024	800-881-5993	954-989-9965
Vantage Data Solutions 5889 S Greenwood Plaza Blvd Suite 201	Englewood	CO	80111	800-568-5665	
Vericon Resources Inc 2358 Perimeter Park Dr Suite 370	Atlanta	GA	30341	800-795-3784	770-457-9922
Verified Credentials Inc 20890 Kenbridge Ct	Lakeville	MN	55044	800-473-4934	952-985-7200
Washington Document Service Inc 1023 15th St NW 12th Fl	Washington	DC	20005	800-728-5201	202-628-5200

622 PUBLIC RELATIONS FIRMS

SEE ALSO Advertising Agencies

				Toll-Free	Phone
Access Communications 101 Howard St	San Francisco	CA	94105	800-393-7737	415-904-7070
Ackermann Public Relations & Marketing 1111 Northshore Dr Suite N-400	Knoxville	TN	37919	888-414-7787	865-584-0550
B & B Media Group 109 S Main St	Corsicana	TX	75110	800-927-0517	903-872-0517
Bite Communications 345 Spear St Suite 750	San Francisco	CA	94105	888-329-7059	415-365-0222
Burson-Marsteller 230 Park Ave S	New York	NY	10003	800-342-5692	212-614-4000
Carmichael Lynch Spong 800 Hennepin Ave	Minneapolis	MN	55403	800-835-9624	612-334-6000
Charles Ryan Assoc Inc 300 Summer St Suite 1100	Charleston	WV	25301	877-342-0161	304-342-0161
Edward Howard & Co 1360 E 9th St 7th Fl	Cleveland	OH	44114	800-868-2045	216-781-2400
Environics Communications Inc 33 Bloor St E Suite 900	Toronto	ON	M4W3H1	888-863-3377	416-920-9000
Euro RSCG Worldwide 350 Hudson St 6th Fl	New York	NY	10014	800-263-7590	212-886-2000
FitzGerald Communications Inc 855 Boylston St 5th Fl	Boston	MA	02116	888-494-9501	617-488-9500
GCI Group Inc 825 3rd Ave 24th Fl	New York	NY	10022	800-883-9525	212-537-8000
Howard Edward & Co 1360 E 9th St 7th Fl	Cleveland	OH	44114	800-868-2045	216-781-2400
Lois Paul & Partners 150 Presidential Way	Woburn	MA	01801	800-989-1550	781-782-5000
MWW Group 1 Meadowlands Plaza 6th Fl	East Rutherford	NJ	07073	800-724-7602	201-507-9500
Paul Lois & Partners 150 Presidential Way	Woburn	MA	01801	800-989-1550	781-782-5000
Rogers & Assoc 1875 Century Park E Suite 300	Los Angeles	CA	90067	800-554-6901	310-552-6922
Ryan Charles Assoc Inc 300 Summer St Suite 1100	Charleston	WV	25301	877-342-0161	304-342-0161
Sterling Communications Inc 221 Sun Valley Blvd Suite G	Lincoln	NE	68528	888-438-0316	402-438-0316

PUBLICATIONS

SEE Magazines & Journals; Newsletters; Newspapers

623 PUBLISHING COMPANIES

SEE ALSO Book Producers; Magazines & Journals; Newsletters; Newspapers

623-1 Atlas & Map Publishers

				Toll-Free	Phone
American Hagstrom Langenscheidt DBA Hagstrom Map 46-35 54th Rd	Maspeth	NY	11378	800-432-6277	718-784-0055
Arrow Publishing Co 50 Scotland Blvd	Bridgewater	MA	02324	800-343-7500	508-279-1177
DeLorme 2 DeLorme Dr *Sales	Yarmouth	ME	04096	800-452-5931*	207-846-7000
George F Cram Co Inc 301 S LaSalle St	Indianapolis	IN	46201	800-227-4199	317-635-5564
Hagstrom Map 46-35 54th Rd	Maspeth	NY	11378	800-432-6277	718-784-0055
Hammond World Atlas Corp 95 Progress St	Union	NJ	07083	800-526-4953	908-206-1300
MARCOA Publishing Inc 9955 Black Mountain Rd	San Diego	CA	92126	800-854-2935	858-695-9600
Nystrom 3333 Elston Ave	Chicago	IL	60618	800-621-8086	773-463-1144
Rand McNally & Co 8255 N Central Park Ave	Skokie	IL	60076	800-333-0136	847-329-8100
Sanborn Map Co 629 5th Ave	Pelham	NY	10803	800-930-3298	914-738-1649
Universal Map 795 Progress Ct	Williamston	MI	48895	800-829-6277	517-655-5641

623-2 Book Publishers

				Toll-Free	Phone
101 Publishing 1033 Oregon Ave Suite 101 *Orders	Palo Alto	CA	94303	800-852-4890*	650-493-2221
Abacus Software Inc 5130 Patterson St SE *Sales	Grand Rapids	MI	49512	800-451-4319*	616-698-0330
ABC-CLIO Inc 130 Cremona Dr	Santa Barbara	CA	93117	800-368-6868	805-968-1911
Abrams & Co Publishers Inc PO Box 10025 *Cust Svc	Waterbury	CT	06725	800-227-9120*	203-756-3580
Abrams Harry N Inc 100 5th Ave 7th Fl	New York	NY	10011	800-345-1359	212-206-7715
Adams Media Corp 57 Littlefield St	Avon	MA	02322	800-872-5627	
Addison-Wesley Higher Education Group 75 Arlington St	Boston	MA	02116	800-447-2226	617-848-6000
Albert Whitman & Co 6340 Oakton St	Morton Grove	IL	60053	800-255-7675	847-581-0033
Allyn & Bacon/Longman Publishers Pearson Education Inc 75 Arlington St Suite 300 *Orders	Boston	MA	02116	800-852-8024*	617-848-7090
American Printing House for the Blind 1839 Frankfort Ave PO Box 6085	Louisville	KY	40206	800-223-1839	502-895-2405
Antique Collectors' Club 116 Pleasant St Eastworks Bldg	Easthampton	MA	01027	800-252-5231	413-529-0861
Aspen Publishers Inc 111 8th Ave 7th Fl *Orders	New York	NY	10011	800-638-8437*	212-771-0600
Auerbach Publications 2000 NW Corporate Blvd *Cust Svc	Boca Raton	FL	33431	800-272-7737*	561-994-0555
Author House 1663 Liberty Dr	Bloomington	IN	47403	800-839-8640	812-339-6000
Avon Books Div HarperCollins Publishers 10 E 53rd St	New York	NY	10022	800-242-7737	212-207-7000
Barron's Educational Series Inc 250 Wireless Blvd	Hauppauge	NY	11788	800-645-3476	631-434-3311
Berkley Publishing Group 375 Hudson St *Cust Svc	New York	NY	10014	800-631-8571*	212-366-2000
Bernard C Harris Publishing Co Inc 2500 Westchester Ave Suite 400	Purchase	NY	10577	800-326-6600	
Black Classic Press PO Box 13414	Baltimore	MD	21203	800-476-8870	410-358-0980
Blackwell Publishers Inc 350 Main St	Malden	MA	02148	800-835-6770	781-388-8250
Blackwell Publishing Professional 2121 S State Ave	Ames	IA	50014	800-862-6657	515-292-0140
BNA Books Div Bureau of National Affairs Inc 1231 25th St *Sales	Washington	DC	20037	800-960-1220*	202-452-4200
Books On Tape Inc PO Box 25122	Santa Ana	CA	92799	800-882-6657	714-825-0021
BRB Publications Inc PO Box 27869	Tempe	AZ	85285	800-929-3811	480-829-7475

				Toll-Free	Phone
Brooks/Cole Publishing Co 60 Garden Ct Suite 205	Monterey	CA	93940	**800-354-0092**	831-373-0728
Bureau of National Affairs Inc 1231 25th St NW	Washington	DC	20037	**800-372-1033**	202-452-4200
Bureau of National Affairs Inc BNA Books Div 1231 25th St *Sales	Washington	DC	20037	**800-960-1220***	202-452-4200
Carroll Publishing Co 4701 Sangamore Rd Suite S-155	Bethesda	MD	20816	**800-336-4240**	301-263-9800
CCH Inc 2700 Lake Cook Rd *Cust Svc	Riverwoods	IL	60015	**800-835-5224***	847-267-7000
Charles C Thomas Publisher 2600 S 1st St *Sales	Springfield	IL	62704	**800-258-8980***	217-789-8980
Children's Press 90 Old Sherman Tpke	Danbury	CT	06816	**800-621-1115**	203-797-3500
Chronicle Books 85 2nd St 6th Fl	San Francisco	CA	94105	**800-722-6657**	415-537-4200
Clarion Books 215 Park Ave S *Cust Svc	New York	NY	10003	**800-225-3362***	212-420-5800
Congressional Quarterly Inc 1255 22nd St NW	Washington	DC	20037	**800-432-2250**	202-419-8500
Cornell Maritime Press PO Box 456	Centreville	MD	21617	**800-638-7641**	410-758-1075
Corwin Press Inc 2455 Teller Rd *Orders	Thousand Oaks	CA	91320	**800-818-7243***	805-499-9734
CRC Press LLC 6000 Broken Sound Pkwy NW Suite 300 *Cust Svc	Boca Raton	FL	33487	**800-272-7737***	561-994-0555
Curriculum Assoc Inc PO Box 2001	North Billerica	MA	01862	**800-225-0248**	978-667-8000
Davis FA Co 1915 Arch St	Philadelphia	PA	19103	**800-523-4049**	215-568-2270
Dearborn Financial Publishing Inc DBA Dearborn A Kaplan Professional Co 30 S Wacker Dr	Chicago	IL	60606	**800-621-9621**	312-836-4400
Dekker Marcel Inc 270 Madison Ave *Sales	New York	NY	10016	**800-228-1160***	212-696-9000
Delacorte Press 1745 Broadway	New York	NY	10019	**800-200-3552**	212-782-9000
Delmar Learning 5 Maxwell Dr	Clifton Park	NY	12065	**800-998-7498**	518-464-3500
Disney Consumer Products 500 S Buena Vista St *PR	Burbank	CA	91521	**800-723-4763***	818-560-1000
Donning Co Publishers 184 Business Pk Dr Suite 206	Virginia Beach	VA	23462	**800-296-8572**	757-497-1789
Dorling Kindersley Publishing 375 Hudson St *Cust Svc	New York	NY	10014	**877-342-5357***	212-213-4800
Doubleday Broadway Publishing Group 1745 Broadway	New York	NY	10019	**800-726-0600**	212-782-9000
Douglas Publications Inc 2807 N Parham Rd Suite 200	Richmond	VA	23294	**800-223-1797**	804-762-9600
Dover Publications Inc 31 E 2nd St	Mineola	NY	11501	**800-223-3130**	516-294-7000
Educators Publishing Service Inc PO Box 9031	Cambridge	MA	02139	**800-225-5750**	617-547-6706
Eerdmans William B Publishing Co 255 Jefferson Ave SE	Grand Rapids	MI	49503	**800-253-7521**	616-459-4591
EMC-Paradigm Publishing Co 875 Montreal Way	Saint Paul	MN	55102	**800-328-1452**	651-290-2800
Encyclopaedia Britannica Inc 310 S Michigan Ave	Chicago	IL	60604	**800-323-1229**	312-347-7000
F & W Publications Inc 4700 E Galbraith Rd *Sales	Cincinnati	OH	45236	**800-289-0963***	513-531-2690
FA Davis Co 1915 Arch St	Philadelphia	PA	19103	**800-523-4049**	215-568-2270
Facts on File Inc 132 W 31st St 17th Fl *Cust Svc	New York	NY	10001	**800-322-8755***	212-967-8800
Financial Publishing Co PO Box 570 *Cust Svc	South Bend	IN	46624	**800-247-3214***	574-243-6040
Fodor's Travel Publications Inc 1745 Broadway	New York	NY	10019	**800-726-0600**	212-751-2600
Forbes Inc 60 5th Ave	New York	NY	10011	**800-888-9896**	212-620-2200
Franklin Watts PO Box 1795 *Cust Svc	Danbury	CT	06816	**800-621-1115***	203-797-3500
Freeman WH & Co 41 Madison Ave 35th Fl	New York	NY	10010	**800-903-3019**	212-576-9400
Gale Group 27500 Drake Rd *Cust Svc	Farmington Hills	MI	48331	**800-877-4253***	248-699-4253
Garland Publishing Inc 270 Madison Ave	New York	NY	10016	**800-797-3803**	917-351-7100
Glencoe/McGraw-Hill 8787 Orion Pl	Columbus	OH	43240	**800-848-1567**	614-430-4000
Golden Books 1745 Broadway *Cust Svc	New York	NY	10019	**800-558-9427***	212-782-9000
Goodheart-Willcox Publisher 18604 W Creek Dr	Tinley Park	IL	60477	**800-323-0440**	708-687-5000
Government Information Services 1725 K St NW Suite 700	Washington	DC	20006	**800-677-3789**	202-872-4000
Government Research Service PO Box 2067	Topeka	KS	66601	**800-346-6898**	785-232-7720
Greenwillow Books 1350 Ave of the Americas	New York	NY	10019	**800-242-7737**	212-261-6500
Greenwood-Heinemann 361 Hanover St	Portsmouth	NH	03801	**800-541-2086**	603-431-7894
Greenwood Publishing Group Inc 88 Post Rd W *Orders	Westport	CT	06881	**800-225-5800***	203-226-3571
Grolier Inc 90 Old Sherman Tpke *Cust Svc	Danbury	CT	06816	**800-955-9877***	203-797-3500
Harcourt Achieve 6277 Sea Harbor Dr	Orlando	FL	32887	**800-531-5015**	
Harcourt Inc 6277 Sea Harbor Dr	Orlando	FL	32887	**800-782-4479**	407-345-2000
Harlequin Enterprises Ltd 225 Duncan Mill Rd	Don Mills	ON	M3B3K9	**800-387-0112**	416-445-5860
HarperCollins Canada Ltd 1995 Markham Rd	Scarborough	ON	M1B5M8	**800-387-0117**	416-321-2241
HarperCollins Children's Books Group 1350 Ave of the Americas *Cust Svc	New York	NY	10019	**800-242-7737***	212-261-6500
HarperCollins Publishers Avon Books Div 10 E 53rd St	New York	NY	10022	**800-242-7737**	212-207-7000
HarperCollins Publishers Inc 10 E 53rd St *Cust Svc	New York	NY	10022	**800-242-7737***	212-207-7000
Harris Bernard C Publishing Co Inc 2500 Westchester Ave Suite 400	Purchase	NY	10577	**800-326-6600**	
Harry N Abrams Inc 100 5th Ave 7th Fl	New York	NY	10011	**800-345-1359**	212-206-7715
Health Communications Inc (HCI) 3201 SW 15th St *Cust Svc	Deerfield Beach	FL	33442	**800-851-9100***	954-360-0909
Hein William S & Co Inc 1285 Main St	Buffalo	NY	14209	**800-828-7571**	716-882-2600
Holt Rinehart & Winston Inc 10801 N MoPac Expy Bldg 3	Austin	TX	78759	**800-992-1627**	512-721-7000
Howard W Sams 9850 E 30th St *Cust Svc	Indianapolis	IN	46229	**800-428-7267***	317-396-9850
Human Kinetics 1607 N Market St	Champaign	IL	61820	**800-747-4457**	217-351-5076
HW Wilson Co 950 University Ave	Bronx	NY	10452	**800-367-6770**	718-588-8400
Inner Traditions International 1 Park St	Rochester	VT	05767	**800-246-8648**	802-767-3174

				Toll-Free	Phone
Island Press 1718 Connecticut Ave NW Suite 300	Washington	DC	20009	**800-828-1302**	202-232-7933
iUniverse 2021 Pine Lake Rd Suite 100	Lincoln	NE	68512	**800-288-4677**	402-323-7800
J Weston Walch Publisher PO Box 658	Portland	ME	04104	**800-558-2846**	207-772-2846
Jane's Information Group 110 N Royal St Suite 200	Alexandria	VA	22314	**800-824-0768**	703-683-3700
Jeppesen Sanderson Inc 55 Inverness Dr E	Englewood	CO	80112	**800-621-5377**	303-799-9090
John Wiley & Sons Inc 111 River St *NYSE: JWa* ■ *Sales	Hoboken	NJ	07030	**800-225-5945***	201-748-6000
Kalmbach Publishing Co 21027 Crossroads Cir *Cust Svc	Waukesha	WI	53187	**800-446-5489***	262-796-8776
Kendall/Hunt Publishing Co 4050 Westmark Dr *Cust Svc	Dubuque	IA	52002	**800-228-0810***	563-589-1000
Kensington Publishing Corp 850 3rd Ave	New York	NY	10022	**877-422-3665**	212-407-1500
Key Curriculum Press 1150 65th St	Emeryville	CA	94608	**800-338-7638**	510-595-7000
Klutz 455 Portage Ave	Palo Alto	CA	94306	**800-737-4123**	650-857-0888
Lark Books 67 Broadway St *Orders	Asheville	NC	28801	**800-284-3388***	828-253-0467
Lawyers Diary & Manual 240 Mulberry St	Newark	NJ	07102	**800-444-4041**	973-642-1440
LexisNexis Matthew Bender 744 Broad St	Newark	NJ	07102	**800-252-9257**	973-820-2000
Linden Publishing 2006 S Mary St *Sales	Fresno	CA	93721	**800-345-4447***	559-233-6633
Lippincott Williams & Wilkins 530 Walnut St	Philadelphia	PA	19106	**800-638-3030**	215-521-8300
Little Brown & Co 1271 Ave of the Americas *Cust Svc	New York	NY	10020	**800-759-0190***	212-522-1212
Llewellyn Worldwide Inc PO Box 64383	Saint Paul	MN	55164	**800-843-6666**	651-291-1970
Lonely Planet Publications 150 Linden St	Oakland	CA	94607	**800-275-8555**	510-893-8555
LRP Publications 360 Hiatt Dr	Palm Beach Gardens	FL	33418	**800-621-5463**	561-622-6520
Marcel Dekker Inc 270 Madison Ave *Sales	New York	NY	10016	**800-228-1160***	212-696-9000
Marquis Who's Who 562 Central Ave	New Providence	NJ	07974	**800-473-7020**	
Matthew Bender & Co (now LexisNexis Matthew Bender) 744 Broad St	Newark	NJ	07102	**800-252-9257**	973-820-2000
McDougal Littell PO Box 1667	Evanston	IL	60204	**800-323-5435**	847-869-2300
McGraw-Hill Higher Education Group 1333 Burr Ridge Pkwy	Burr Ridge	IL	60527	**800-634-3963**	630-789-4000
McGraw-Hill Professional Publishing Group 2 Penn Plaza 11th Fl	New York	NY	10121	**800-262-4729**	212-512-2000
ME Sharpe Inc 80 Business Park Dr Suite 202 *Orders	Armonk	NY	10504	**800-541-6563***	914-273-1800
Means RS Co Inc 63 Smiths Ln	Kingston	MA	02364	**800-334-3509**	781-585-7880
Mel Bay Publications Inc 4 Industrial Dr	Pacific	MO	63069	**800-863-5229**	636-257-3970
Merriam-Webster Inc PO Box 281	Springfield	MA	01102	**800-828-1880**	413-734-3134
Microsoft Press 1 Microsoft Way *Cust Svc	Redmond	WA	98052	**800-426-9400***	425-882-8080
Millbrook Press Inc 2 Old New Milford Rd	Brookfield	CT	06804	**800-462-4703**	203-740-2220
Modern Library 1745 Broadway *Cust Svc	New York	NY	10019	**800-726-0600***	212-751-2600
National Academy Press 2101 Constitution Ave NW PO Box 285	Washington	DC	20055	**800-624-6242**	202-334-3313
National Braille Press Inc 88 Saint Stephens St	Boston	MA	02115	**888-965-8965**	617-266-6160
National Geographic Society 1145 17th St NW *Orders	Washington	DC	20036	**800-647-5463***	202-857-7000
National Register Publishing Co 562 Central Ave	New Providence	NJ	07974	**800-473-7020**	
National Underwriter Co 5081 Olympic Blvd	Erlanger	KY	41018	**800-543-0874**	859-692-2100
Nerdy Books 135 Main St	Flemington	NJ	08822	**866-843-8477**	908-788-4676
New Readers Press 1320 Jamesville Ave	Syracuse	NY	13210	**800-448-8878**	315-422-9121
Nightingale-Conant Corp 6245 W Howard St *Cust Svc	Niles	IL	60714	**800-323-3938***	847-647-0300
Nolo.com 950 Parker St *Cust Svc	Berkeley	CA	94710	**800-728-3555***	510-549-1976
Norton WW & Co Inc 500 5th Ave	New York	NY	10110	**800-223-2584**	212-354-5500
Oceana Publications Inc 75 Main St *Orders	Dobbs Ferry	NY	10522	**800-831-0758***	914-693-8100
Omnigraphics Inc 615 Griswold St Ford Bldg Suite 1400 *Orders	Detroit	MI	48226	**800-234-1340***	313-961-1340
Oxmoor House Inc 2100 Lakeshore Dr	Birmingham	AL	35209	**800-633-4910**	205-445-6000
Pathway Press 1080 Montgomery Ave NE *Sales	Cleveland	TN	37311	**800-553-8506***	423-476-4512
Peachpit Press 1249 8th St	Berkeley	CA	94710	**800-283-9444**	510-524-2178
Pearson Education Inc 1 Lake St *Cust Svc	Upper Saddle River	NJ	07458	**800-922-0579***	201-236-7000
Pearson Education Inc Allyn & Bacon/Longman Publishers 75 Arlington St Suite 300 *Orders	Boston	MA	02116	**800-852-8024***	617-848-7090
Penguin Books Canada Ltd 10 Alcorn Ave Suite 300	Toronto	ON	M4V3B2	**800-810-3104**	416-925-2249
Penguin Group (USA) Inc 375 Hudson St *Cust Svc	New York	NY	10014	**800-631-8571***	212-366-2000
Perseus Inc 387 Park Ave S	New York	NY	10016	**800-386-5656**	212-340-8100
Peterson's Guides Inc Princeton Pike Corporate Ctr 2000 Lenox Dr	Lawrenceville	NJ	08648	**800-338-3282**	609-896-1800
Pike & Fischer Inc 1010 Wayne Ave Suite 1400	Silver Spring	MD	20910	**800-255-8131**	301-562-1530
Pocket Books 1230 Ave of the Americas 13th Fl *Cust Svc	New York	NY	10020	**800-223-2336***	212-698-7000
Praeger Publishers 88 Post Rd W *Sales	Westport	CT	06881	**800-225-5800***	203-226-3571
Prentice-Hall Inc 1 Lake St	Upper Saddle River	NJ	07458	**800-947-7700**	201-236-7000
Prentice Hall-Professional Technical Reference 1 Lake St	Upper Saddle River	NJ	07458	**800-947-7700**	201-236-7000
Price Books & Forms Inc 751 N Coney Ave	Azusa	CA	91702	**800-423-8961**	626-334-0348
Publications International Ltd 7373 N Cicero Ave	Lincolnwood	IL	60712	**800-745-9299**	847-676-3470
Rand McNally & Co 8255 N Central Park Ave	Skokie	IL	60076	**800-333-0136**	847-329-8100
Random House Inc 1745 Broadway *Cust Svc	New York	NY	10019	**800-733-3000***	212-782-9000
Random House Reference & Information Publishing 1745 Broadway *Orders	New York	NY	10019	**800-733-3000***	212-751-2600
Reader's Digest Assn Inc Reader's Digest Rd *NYSE: RDA*	Pleasantville	NY	10570	**800-635-5006**	914-238-1000
Reed Elsevier Inc 121 Chanlon Rd	New Providence	NJ	07974	**800-526-4902**	908-464-6800

Book Publishers (Cont'd)

Company	City	State	ZIP	Toll-Free	Phone
Regnery Publishing Inc 1 Massachusetts Ave NW	Washington	DC	20001	**800-462-6420**	202-216-0600
RIA Group 395 Hudson St *Cust Svc	New York	NY	10014	**800-950-1205***	212-367-6300
Rodale Inc 33 E Minor St *Cust Svc	Emmaus	PA	18098	**800-848-4735***	610-967-8154
RR Bowker LLC 630 Central Ave	New Providence	NJ	07974	**800-521-8110**	908-286-1090
RS Means Co Inc 63 Smiths Ln	Kingston	MA	02364	**800-334-3509**	781-585-7880
Running Press Book Publishers 125 S 22nd St	Philadelphia	PA	19103	**800-345-5359**	215-567-5080
Rutledge Hill Press PO Box 141000	Nashville	TN	37214	**800-251-4000**	615-889-9000
Sadlier William H Inc 9 Pine St 2nd Fl	New York	NY	10005	**800-582-5437**	212-227-2120
Sage Publications Inc 2455 Teller Rd	Thousand Oaks	CA	91320	**800-818-7243**	805-499-9774
Saint Martin's Press Inc 175 5th Ave *Cust Svc	New York	NY	10010	**888-330-8477***	212-674-5151
Sams Technical Publishing 9850 E 30th St *Cust Svc	Indianapolis	IN	46229	**800-428-7267***	317-396-9850
Scholastic Corp 557 Broadway *NASDAQ: SCHL* ■ *Cust Svc	New York	NY	10012	**800-724-6527***	212-343-6100
School Annual Publishing Co 500 Science Pk Rd Suite B	State College	PA	16803	**800-436-6030**	
Scientific American Inc 415 Madison Ave *Cust Svc	New York	NY	10017	**800-333-1199***	212-451-8550
Scott Foresman 1900 E Lake Ave *Cust Svc	Glenview	IL	60025	**800-554-4411***	847-729-3000
Sharpe ME Inc 80 Business Park Dr Suite 202 *Orders	Armonk	NY	10504	**800-541-6563***	914-273-1800
Simon & Schuster Inc 1230 Ave of the Americas *Cust Svc	New York	NY	10020	**800-223-2336***	212-698-7000
Slack Inc 6900 Grove Rd	Thorofare	NJ	08086	**800-257-8290**	856-848-1000
South-Western Thomson Learning 5191 Natorp Blvd	Mason	OH	45040	**800-543-0487**	513-543-0487
Springer-Verlag New York Inc 233 Spring St	New York	NY	10013	**800-777-4643**	212-460-1500
SRDS 1700 Higgins Rd	Des Plaines	IL	60018	**800-851-7737**	847-375-5000
Stackpole Books 5067 Ritter Rd *Sales	Mechanicsburg	PA	17055	**800-732-3669***	717-796-0411
Standard Educational Corp 900 Northshore Dr Suite 252 *Cust Svc	Lake Bluff	IL	60044	**800-332-8755***	847-283-0301
Standard & Poor's Corp 55 Water St	New York	NY	10041	**800-289-8000**	212-438-2000
Steck-Vaughn Co 10801 N MoPac Expy Bldg 3	Austin	TX	78759	**800-531-5015**	512-343-8227
Sterling Publishing Co Inc 387 Park Ave S 5th Fl *Cust Svc	New York	NY	10016	**800-367-9692***	212-532-7160
Storey Communications Inc 210 Mass Moca Way	North Adams	MA	01247	**800-335-3432**	413-346-2100
Sunset Publishing Corp 80 Willow Rd	Menlo Park	CA	94025	**800-227-7346**	650-321-3600
Sybex Inc 1151 Marina Village Pkwy	Alameda	CA	94501	**800-227-2346**	510-523-8233
T & F Informa 6000 NW Broken Sound Pkwy Suite 300	Boca Raton	FL	33487	**800-272-7737**	561-994-0555
Taylor & Francis Group LLC DBA T & F Informa 6000 NW Broken Sound Pkwy Suite 300	Boca Raton	FL	33487	**800-272-7737**	561-994-0555
Taylor & Francis Routledge Publishers Inc 270 Madison Ave	New York	NY	10016	**800-634-7064**	917-351-7100
Taylor Publishing Co 1550 W Mockingbird Ln	Dallas	TX	75235	**800-677-2800**	214-637-2800
Technology Marketing Corp 1 Technology Plaza *Cust Svc	Norwalk	CT	06854	**800-243-6002***	203-852-6800
Ten Speed Press PO Box 7123	Berkeley	CA	94707	**800-841-2665**	510-559-1600
TFH Publications Inc 3rd & Union Aves 1 TFH Plaza	Neptune	NJ	07753	**800-631-2188**	732-988-8400
Thomas Charles C Publisher 2600 S 1st St *Sales	Springfield	IL	62704	**800-258-8980***	217-789-8980
Thomas Publishing Co 5 Penn Plaza	New York	NY	10001	**800-699-9822**	212-695-0500
Thomson Corp 1 Station Pl Metro Ctr	Stamford	CT	06902	**800-354-9706**	203-539-8000
Thomson Financial Publishing Inc 4709 W Golf Rd 6th Fl	Skokie	IL	60076	**800-321-3373**	847-676-9600
Thomson Learning 10650 Tobben Dr	Independence	KY	41051	**800-354-9706**	
Thomson Learning Wadsworth PO Box 6904	Florence	KY	41022	**800-354-9706**	
Thorndike Press 295 Kennedy Memorial Dr	Waterville	ME	04901	**800-223-1244**	207-859-1000
Time Warner Book Group Inc 1271 Ave of the Americas	New York	NY	10020	**800-759-0190**	212-522-7200
Tor Books 175 5th Ave 14th Fl *Cust Svc	New York	NY	10010	**800-221-7945***	212-388-0100
Triumph Learning 136 Madison Ave	New York	NY	10016	**800-221-9372**	212-652-0200
Tuttle Publishing 364 Innovation Dr Airport Industrial Pk *Sales	North Clarendon	VT	05759	**800-526-2778***	802-773-8930
United Nations Publications 2 UN Plaza Suite DC2-853	New York	NY	10017	**800-253-9646**	212-963-8302
University Press of America 4501 Forbes Blvd Suite 200	Lanham	MD	20706	**800-462-6420**	301-459-3366
US Government Printing Office (GPO) 732 N Capitol St NW	Washington	DC	20401	**866-512-1800**	202-512-0000
Vantage Press Inc 419 Park Ave S 18th Fl	New York	NY	10016	**800-882-3273**	212-736-1767
Verso Books 180 Varick St 10th Fl *Sales	New York	NY	10014	**800-233-4830***	212-807-9680
Vintage Books 1745 Broadway *Orders	New York	NY	10019	**800-733-3000***	212-751-2600
VNU Business Publications USA 770 Broadway	New York	NY	10003	**800-451-1741**	646-654-5500
Walch J Weston Publisher PO Box 658	Portland	ME	04104	**800-558-2846**	207-772-2846
Walsworth Publishing Co Inc 306 N Kansas Ave	Marceline	MO	64658	**800-369-2646**	660-376-3543
West Group PO Box 64526 *Cust Svc	Saint Paul	MN	55164	**800-328-4880***	651-687-7000
Western Psychological Services 12031 Wilshire Blvd	Los Angeles	CA	90025	**800-648-8857**	310-478-2061
WH Freeman & Co 41 Madison Ave 35th Fl	New York	NY	10010	**800-903-3019**	212-576-9400
Wheatmark Inc 610 E Delano St Suite 104	Tucson	AZ	85705	**888-934-0888**	520-798-0888
White Wolf Publishing Co 1554 Litton Dr *Orders	Stone Mountain	GA	30083	**800-454-9653***	404-292-1819
Whitman Albert & Co 6340 Oakton St	Morton Grove	IL	60053	**800-255-7675**	847-581-0033
Wiley John & Sons Inc 111 River St *NYSE: JWa* ■ *Sales	Hoboken	NJ	07030	**800-225-5945***	201-748-6000
William B Eerdmans Publishing Co 255 Jefferson Ave SE	Grand Rapids	MI	49503	**800-253-7521**	616-459-4591
William H Sadlier Inc 9 Pine St 2nd Fl	New York	NY	10005	**800-582-5437**	212-227-2120
William Morrow & Co 10 E 53rd St *Cust Svc	New York	NY	10022	**800-242-7737***	212-207-7000
William S Hein & Co Inc 1285 Main St	Buffalo	NY	14209	**800-828-7571**	716-882-2600
Wilson HW Co 950 University Ave	Bronx	NY	10452	**800-367-6770**	718-588-8400
Wimmer Cos 4650 Shelby Air Dr	Memphis	TN	38118	**800-548-2537**	901-362-8900
Workman Publishing 708 Broadway	New York	NY	10003	**800-722-7202**	212-254-5900
World Book Publishing 233 N Michigan Ave Suite 2000 *Sales	Chicago	IL	60601	**800-967-5325***	312-729-5800
Wright Group/McGraw-Hill 19201 120th Ave NE Suite 100 *Sales	Bothell	WA	98011	**800-523-2371***	425-486-8011
WW Norton & Co Inc 500 5th Ave	New York	NY	10110	**800-223-2584**	212-354-5500
Xlibris Corp International Plaza 2 Suite 340	Philadelphia	PA	19113	**888-795-4274**	610-915-5214
Zaner-Bloser Inc PO Box 16764	Columbus	OH	43216	**800-421-3018**	614-486-0221
Zebra Books Kensington Publishing Corp 850 3rd Ave	New York	NY	10022	**800-221-2647**	212-407-1500
Ziff Davis Media Inc 28 E 28th St	New York	NY	10016	**800-336-2423**	212-503-3500

623-3 Book Publishers - Comic Books

Company	City	State	ZIP	Toll-Free	Phone
Dark Horse Comics Inc 10956 SE Main St	Milwaukie	OR	97222	**800-862-0052**	503-652-8815
Fantagraphics Books 7563 Lake City Way NE	Seattle	WA	98115	**800-657-1100**	206-524-1967
Marvel Enterprises Inc 417 5th Ave *NYSE: MVL*	New York	NY	10016	**800-217-9158**	212-576-4000

623-4 Book Publishers - Religious & Spiritual Books

Company	City	State	ZIP	Toll-Free	Phone
Abbey Press Inc 1 Hill Dr *Sales	Saint Meinrad	IN	47577	**800-962-4760***	812-357-6611
American Bible Society 1865 Broadway	New York	NY	10023	**800-322-4253**	212-408-1200
Augsburg Fortress Publishers PO Box 1209	Minneapolis	MN	55440	**800-426-0115**	612-330-3300
Baker Book House Co Inc 6030 E Fulton St *Orders	Ada	MI	49301	**800-877-2665***	616-676-9185
Baker Book House Co Inc Revell Div 6030 E Fulton St *Orders	Ada	MI	49301	**800-877-2665***	616-676-9185
Bethany House Publishers 11400 Hampshire Ave S *Cust Svc	Bloomington	MN	55438	**800-328-6109***	952-829-2500
Brethren Press 1451 Dundee Ave	Elgin	IL	60120	**800-441-3712**	847-742-5100
Broadman & Holman Publishers 1 Lifeway Plaza	Nashville	TN	37234	**800-251-3225**	615-251-2000
Christian Publications Inc 3825 Hartzdale Dr *Orders	Camp Hill	PA	17011	**800-233-4443***	717-761-7044
Concordia Publishing House Inc 3558 S Jefferson Ave *Cust Svc	Saint Louis	MO	63118	**800-325-3040***	314-268-1000
Cook Communications Ministries 4050 Lee Vance View	Colorado Springs	CO	80918	**800-708-5550**	719-536-0100
CRC Publications Co 2850 Kalamazoo Ave SE	Grand Rapids	MI	49560	**800-333-8300**	616-224-0727
Deseret Book Co PO Box 30178 *Sales	Salt Lake City	UT	84130	**800-453-4532***	801-534-1515
DeVore & Sons Inc DBA Heirloom Bible Publishers PO Box 780189	Wichita	KS	67278	**800-676-2448**	316-267-3211
Gospel Light Publications 1957 Eastman Ave	Ventura	CA	93003	**800-235-3415**	805-644-9721
Guideposts Inc 39 Seminary Hill Rd *Cust Svc	Carmel	NY	10512	**800-431-2344***	845-225-3681
Hay House Inc PO Box 5100	Carlsbad	CA	92018	**800-654-5126**	760-431-7695
Heirloom Bible Publishers PO Box 780189	Wichita	KS	67278	**800-676-2448**	316-267-3211
Jewish Publication Society 2100 Arch St 2nd Fl	Philadelphia	PA	19103	**800-234-3151**	215-832-0600
Light & Life Communications PO Box 535002	Indianapolis	IN	46253	**800-348-2513**	317-244-3660
Mennonite Publishing House 616 Walnut Ave *Sales	Scottdale	PA	15683	**800-245-7894***	724-887-8500
Multnomah Publishers PO Box 1720	Sisters	OR	97759	**800-929-0910**	541-549-1144
NavPress PO Box 35001 *Cust Svc	Colorado Springs	CO	80935	**800-366-7788***	719-548-9222
Nazarene Publishing House Inc PO Box 419527	Kansas City	MO	64141	**800-877-0700**	816-931-1900
Nelson Bibles PO Box 141000	Nashville	TN	37214	**800-251-4000**	615-889-9000
Nelson Thomas Inc PO Box 141000 *NYSE: TNM*	Nashville	TN	37214	**800-251-4000**	615-889-9000
Nelson Tommy 402 BNA Dr Bldg 100 Suite 600	Nashville	TN	37217	**800-251-4000**	615-889-9000
New Leaf Press PO Box 726	Green Forest	AR	72638	**800-999-3777**	870-438-5288
New World Library 14 Pamaron Way	Novato	CA	94949	**800-972-6657**	415-884-2100
Northwestern Publishing House 1250 N 113th St *Orders	Milwaukee	WI	53226	**800-662-6022***	414-475-6600
Oregon Catholic Press 5536 NE Hassalo St	Portland	OR	97213	**800-548-8749**	503-281-1191
Our Sunday Visitor Inc 200 Noll Plaza	Huntington	IN	46750	**800-348-2440**	260-356-8400
Pacific Press Publishing Assn 1350 N Kings Rd *Cust Svc	Nampa	ID	83687	**800-545-2449***	208-465-2500
Pauline Books & Media 50 Saint Paul's Ave *Sales	Boston	MA	02130	**800-876-4463***	617-522-8911
Review & Herald Publishing Assn 55 W Oak Ridge Dr	Hagerstown	MD	21740	**800-456-3991**	301-393-3000
Standard Publishing Co 8121 Hamilton Ave *Orders	Cincinnati	OH	45231	**800-543-1353***	513-931-4050
Strang Communications 600 Rinehart Rd *Sales	Lake Mary	FL	32746	**800-451-4598***	407-333-0600
Thomas Nelson Inc PO Box 141000 *NYSE: TNM*	Nashville	TN	37214	**800-251-4000**	615-889-9000
Tommy Nelson 402 BNA Dr Bldg 100 Suite 600	Nashville	TN	37217	**800-251-4000**	615-889-9000
Tyndale House Publishers Inc 351 Executive Dr	Carol Stream	IL	60188	**800-323-9400**	630-668-8300

				Toll-Free	Phone
United Methodist Publishing House PO Box 801 *Cust Svc	Nashville	TN	37202	**800-672-1789***	615-749-6000
W Publishing Group PO Box 141000 *Cust Svc	Nashville	TN	37214	**800-251-4000***	615-889-9000
Whitaker House/Anchor Distributors 30 Hunt Valley Cir *Orders	New Kensington	PA	15068	**800-444-4484***	724-334-7000
Zondervan 5300 Patterson Ave SE *Cust Svc	Grand Rapids	MI	49530	**800-727-1309***	616-698-6900

623-5 Book Publishers - University Presses

				Toll-Free	Phone
Cambridge University Press 40 W 20th St	New York	NY	10011	**800-221-4512**	212-924-3900
Columbia University Press 61 W 62nd St 3rd Fl	New York	NY	10023	**800-944-8648**	212-459-0600
Cornell University Press 750 Cascadilla St *Sales	Ithaca	NY	14850	**800-666-2211***	607-277-2338
Duke University Press 905 W Main St *Cust Svc	Durham	NC	27701	**888-651-0122***	919-687-3600
Harvard Business School Publishing 60 Harvard Way	Boston	MA	02163	**800-545-7685**	617-783-7400
Harvard University Press 79 Garden St *Cust Svc	Cambridge	MA	02138	**800-448-2242***	617-495-2600
Indiana University Press 601 N Morton St	Bloomington	IN	47404	**800-842-6796**	812-855-8817
Johns Hopkins University Press 2715 N Charles St *Orders	Baltimore	MD	21218	**800-537-5487***	410-516-6900
Mercer University Press 1400 Coleman Ave	Macon	GA	31207	**800-637-2378**	478-301-2880
Michigan State University Press 1405 S Harrison Rd Suite 25	East Lansing	MI	48823	**800-678-2120**	517-355-9543
MIT Press 55 Hayward St *Sales	Cambridge	MA	02142	**800-356-0343***	617-253-5646
Naval Institute Press 2062 Generals Hwy	Annapolis	MD	21401	**800-233-8764**	410-224-3378
Ohio University Press Scott Quadrangle *Sales	Athens	OH	45701	**800-621-2736***	740-593-1155
Oregon State University Press 500 Kerr Administration Bldg *Orders	Corvallis	OR	97331	**800-426-3797***	541-737-3166
Oxford University Press 198 Madison Ave	New York	NY	10016	**800-334-4249**	212-726-6000
Pennsylvania State University Press 820 N University Dr USBI Suite C	University Park	PA	16802	**800-326-9180**	814-865-1327
Princeton University Press 41 William St *Sales	Princeton	NJ	08540	**800-777-4726***	609-258-4900
Purdue University Press 1407 Campus Courts Bldg E *Orders	West Lafayette	IN	47907	**800-247-6553***	765-494-2038
Rutgers University Press 100 Joyce Kilmer Ave *Orders	Piscataway	NJ	08854	**800-446-9323***	732-445-7762
Southern Illinois University Press 1915 University Press Dr	Carbondale	IL	62901	**800-346-2680**	618-453-2281
Southern Methodist University Press 6404 Hilltop Ln 314 Fondren Library W	Dallas	TX	75275	**800-826-8911**	214-768-1432
Stanford University Press 1450 Page Mill Rd	Palo Alto	CA	94304	**800-621-2736**	650-723-9434
State University of New York Press 194 Washington Ave Suite 305 *Orders	Albany	NY	12210	**800-666-2211***	518-472-5000
Temple University Press 1601 N Broad St USB 305	Philadelphia	PA	19122	**800-447-1656**	215-204-8787
Texas A & M University Press John H Lindsey Bldg 4354 TAMUS *Orders	College Station	TX	77843	**800-826-8911***	979-845-1436
Texas Tech University Press 2903 4th St	Lubbock	TX	79409	**800-832-4042**	806-742-2982
University of Alabama Press 20 Research Dr Rm 201 McMillan Bldg *Orders	Tuscaloosa	AL	35487	**800-621-2736***	205-348-5180
University of Alaska Press Box 756240	Fairbanks	AK	99775	**888-252-6657**	907-474-5831
University of Arizona Press 355 S Euclid Ave Suite 103 *Orders	Tucson	AZ	85719	**800-426-3797***	520-621-1441
University of Arkansas Press McIlroy House 201 Ozark Ave	Fayetteville	AR	72701	**800-626-0090**	479-575-3246
University of California Press 2120 Berkeley Way	Berkeley	CA	94704	**800-822-6657**	510-642-4247
University of Chicago Press 1427 E 60th St *Sales	Chicago	IL	60637	**800-621-2736***	773-702-7700
University of Georgia Press 330 Research Dr Suite B-100 *Orders	Athens	GA	30602	**800-266-5842***	706-369-6163
University of Hawaii Press 2840 Kolowalu St	Honolulu	HI	96822	**888-847-7377**	808-956-8255
University of Illinois Press 1325 S Oak St *Orders	Champaign	IL	61820	**800-545-4703***	217-333-0950
University of Minnesota Press 111 3rd Ave S Suite 290	Minneapolis	MN	55401	**800-621-2736**	612-627-1942
University of Missouri Press 2910 LeMone Blvd	Columbia	MO	65201	**800-828-1894**	573-882-7641
University of Nebraska Press 1111 Lincoln Mall *Orders	Lincoln	NE	68588	**800-755-1105***	402-472-3581
University of Nevada Press MS 166 *Orders	Reno	NV	89557	**877-682-6657***	775-784-6573
University of New Mexico Press 3721 Spirit Dr SE *Orders	Albuquerque	NM	87106	**800-249-7737***	505-277-4810
University of North Carolina Press 116 S Boundary St	Chapel Hill	NC	27514	**800-848-6224**	919-966-3561
University of North Texas Press 1820 Highland Ave Bain Hall Rm 101 *Sales	Denton	TX	76201	**800-826-8911***	940-565-2142
University of Oklahoma Press 2800 Venture Dr *Orders	Norman	OK	73069	**800-627-7377***	405-325-2000
University of Pennsylvania Press 4200 Pine St *Cust Svc	Philadelphia	PA	19104	**800-537-5487***	215-898-6261
University of Pittsburgh Press 3400 Forbes Ave 5th Fl *Sales	Pittsburgh	PA	15261	**800-666-2211***	412-383-2456
University Press of Colorado 5589 Arapahoe Ave Suite 206C *Mktg	Boulder	CO	80303	**800-627-7377***	720-406-8849
University Press of Florida 15 NW 15th St *Sales	Gainesville	FL	32611	**800-226-3822***	352-392-1351
University Press of Kentucky 663 S Limestone St *Sales	Lexington	KY	40508	**800-839-6855***	859-257-8400
University Press of Mississippi 3825 Ridgewood Rd	Jackson	MS	39211	**800-737-7788**	601-432-6205
University Press of New England 37 Lafayette St *Orders	Lebanon	NH	03766	**800-421-1561***	603-643-5585
University Press of Virginia 210 Sprigg Ln *Sales	Charlottesville	VA	22903	**800-831-3406***	434-924-3469
University of South Carolina Press 1600 Hampton St 5th Fl *Orders	Columbia	SC	29208	**800-768-2500***	803-777-5243
University of the South Press 735 University Ave Fulford Hall	Sewanee	TN	37383	**800-289-4919**	931-598-1286
University of Texas Press 2100 Comal St *Sales	Austin	TX	78722	**800-252-3206***	512-471-7233
University of Washington Press 1326 5th Ave Suite 555	Seattle	WA	98101	**800-441-4115**	206-543-4050
Wesleyan University Press 215 Long Ln *Orders	Middletown	CT	06459	**800-421-1561***	860-685-7711
Yale University Press 302 Temple St *Sales	New Haven	CT	06511	**800-987-7323***	203-432-0960

623-6 Directory Publishers

				Toll-Free	Phone
1-800-ATTORNEY Inc 186 Industrial Center Dr	Lake Helen	FL	32744	**800-644-3458**	386-228-1000
ALLTEL Publishing Corp 100 Executive Pkwy	Hudson	OH	44236	**800-235-3386**	330-650-7100
AroundCampus Inc 1000 Conshohocken Rd 4th Fl	Conshohocken	PA	19428	**800-466-2221**	610-940-1515
ASD Data Services LLC 180 Freedom Ave	Murfreesboro	TN	37129	**800-929-2612**	866-273-7297
Bacon's Information Inc 332 S Michigan Ave Suite 900	Chicago	IL	60604	**800-621-0561**	312-922-2400
BellSouth Advertising & Publishing Corp 2247 Northlake Pkwy	Tucker	GA	30084	**877-573-2597**	
Bresser's Cross Index Directory Co 684 W Baltimore St	Detroit	MI	48202	**800-878-3333**	313-874-0570
Burrelle's/Luce LLC 75 E Northfield Rd	Livingston	NJ	07039	**800-631-1160**	973-992-6600
Capitol Advantage LLC 2751 Prosperity Ave 6th Fl	Fairfax	VA	22031	**800-659-8708**	703-289-4670
Cole Information Services 901 W Bond St	Lincoln	NE	68521	**877-414-3332**	402-323-3500
College Directory Publishing Inc 1000 Conshohocken Rd	Conshohocken	PA	19428	**800-466-2221**	610-940-1515
Commonwealth Business Media Inc 50 Millstone Rd Bldg 400 Suite 200	East Windsor	NJ	08520	**888-215-6084**	609-371-7700
Community Directory Publishing Service 2025 E Beltline Ave SE Suite 101	Grand Rapids	MI	49546	**888-831-2800**	616-831-2800
Contractors Register Inc 800 E Main St	Jefferson Valley	NY	10535	**800-431-2584**	914-245-0200
CSG Information Services 3922 Coconut Palm Dr	Tampa	FL	33619	**800-927-9292**	813-627-6800
DAG Media Inc 125-10 Queens Blvd Suite 14 *NASDAQ: DAGM*	Kew Gardens	NY	11415	**800-261-2799**	718-263-8454
DataNational 3800 Concorde Pkwy Suite 500	Chantilly	VA	20151	**800-888-7823**	703-818-0120
Dex Media Inc 198 Inverness Dr W *NYSE: DEX*	Englewood	CO	80112	**800-243-2960**	303-784-2900
Dickman Directories Inc 6145 Columbus Pike	Lewis Center	OH	43035	**877-836-4154**	740-548-6130
DirectoryNet LLC 4555 Mansell Rd Suite 230	Alpharetta	GA	30022	**800-733-1212**	770-521-0100
Feist Publications Inc 306 Main St	Spearville	KS	67876	**800-536-2612**	620-385-2612
Grey House Publishing 185 Millerton Rd PO Box 860	Millerton	NY	12546	**800-562-2139**	518-789-8700
Haines & Co Inc 8050 Freedom Ave NW	North Canton	OH	44720	**800-843-8452**	330-494-9111
Harris InfoSource 2057 E Aurora Rd	Twinsburg	OH	44087	**800-888-5900**	330-425-9000
Hill-Donnelly Information Services 10126 Windhorst Rd	Tampa	FL	33619	**800-925-4654**	813-832-1600
InterStudy Publications 210 12th Ave S Suite 100	Nashville	TN	37203	**800-844-3351**	888-293-9675
LexisNexis Martindale-Hubbell 121 Chanlon Rd	New Providence	NJ	07974	**800-526-4902**	908-464-6800
Manufacturers Group Inc 1084 Wellington Way PO Box 4310	Lexington	KY	40544	**800-264-3303**	859-223-6703
Marc Publishing Co 600 Germantown Pike Suite B	Lafayette Hill	PA	19444	**800-432-5478**	610-834-8585
Nelson Information 195 Broadway	New York	NY	10007	**800-333-6357**	646-822-6499
Real Yellow Pages Online 754 Peachtree St	Atlanta	GA	30308	**888-935-8818**	877-573-2597
Rich's Business Directories Inc 2551 Casey Ave Suite A	Mountain View	CA	94043	**800-969-7424**	650-564-9464
SBC Smart Yellow Pages 100 E Big Beaver Rd	Troy	MI	48083	**800-434-7778**	248-524-7300
Stewart Directories Inc 10540 J York Rd	Cockeysville	MD	21030	**800-311-0786**	410-628-5988
SunShine Pages 3445 N Causeway Blvd Suite 1000	Metairie	LA	70002	**800-259-9835**	504-832-9835
T & F Informa 6000 NW Broken Sound Pkwy Suite 300	Boca Raton	FL	33487	**800-272-7737**	561-994-0555
Taylor & Francis Group LLC DBA T & F Informa 6000 NW Broken Sound Pkwy Suite 300	Boca Raton	FL	33487	**800-272-7737**	561-994-0555
TransWestern Publishing Co LLC 8344 Clairemont Mesa Blvd	San Diego	CA	92111	**800-333-1111**	858-467-2800
United Communications Group 11300 Rockville Pike Suite 1100	Rockville	MD	20852	**800-929-4824**	301-816-8950
United Yellow Pages Inc 12442 Knott St 2nd Fl	Garden Grove	CA	92841	**800-343-2046**	714-889-5200
Valley Yellow Pages 1850 N Gateway Blvd Suite 132	Fresno	CA	93727	**800-350-8887**	559-251-8888
Verizon Directories 2200 W Airfield Dr *Orders	DFW Airport	TX	75261	**800-888-8448***	972-453-7000
Verizon Information Services 2200 W Airfield Dr	DFW Airport	TX	75261	**877-814-6854**	972-453-7000
Volt Directory Systems & Services 1 Sentry Pkwy Suite 1000	Blue Bell	PA	19422	**800-897-2508**	610-825-7720
West Legal Directory 610 Opperman Dr	Eagan	MN	55123	**800-328-9378**	651-687-7000

Directory Publishers (Cont'd)

Name / Address	City	State	ZIP	Toll-Free	Phone
White Directory Publishers Inc 1945 Sheridan Dr	Buffalo	NY	14223	**800-388-8255**	716-875-9100
World Aviation Directory 1200 G St NW Suite 900	Washington	DC	20005	**800-551-2015**	609-426-5000
Yellow Book USA 193 EAB Plaza	Uniondale	NY	11556	**877-512-7710**	516-730-1900
YP Corp 4840 E Jasmine St Suite 105	Mesa	AZ	85205	**800-300-3209**	480-654-9646

623-7 Music Publishers (Sheet Music)

Name / Address	City	State	ZIP	Toll-Free	Phone
Alfred Publishing Co 16320 Roscoe Blvd Suite 100	Van Nuys	CA	91406	**800-292-6122**	818-891-5999
Carl Fischer Inc 65 Bleecker St	New York	NY	10012	**800-762-2328**	212-777-0900
Hal Leonard Corp PO Box 227	Winona	MN	55987	**800-321-3408**	507-454-2920
Lorenz Corp PO Box 802	Dayton	OH	45401	**800-444-1144**	937-228-6118
Malaco Music Group Inc 3023 W Northside Dr *Cust Svc	Jackson	MS	39213	**800-272-7936***	601-982-4522
Mel Bay Publications Inc 4 Industrial Dr	Pacific	MO	63069	**800-863-5229**	636-257-3970
Nazarene Publishing House Inc PO Box 419527	Kansas City	MO	64141	**800-877-0700**	816-931-1900
Warner Bros Publications 15800 NW 48th Ave	Miami	FL	33014	**800-327-7643**	305-620-1500
Warner/Chappell Music Inc 10585 Santa Monica Blvd	Los Angeles	CA	90025	**800-327-7643**	310-441-8600

623-8 Newspaper Publishers

Name / Address	City	State	ZIP	Toll-Free	Phone
Alameda Newspaper Group PO Box 28884	Oakland	CA	94604	**800-595-9595**	510-208-6300
Albany Herald Publishing Co Inc 126 N Washington St	Albany	GA	31702	**800-685-4639**	229-888-9300
Albert Lea Newspapers Inc PO Box 60	Albert Lea	MN	56007	**800-657-4996**	507-373-1411
Amos Press Inc PO Box 4129	Sidney	OH	45365	**800-327-1259**	937-498-2111
ASP Westward LP 907B E Main St	Humble	TX	77338	**866-446-5979**	281-446-5979
Auburn Publishers Inc 25 Dill St	Auburn	NY	13021	**800-878-5311**	315-253-5311
AUS Inc PO Box 1050	Moorestown	NJ	08057	**800-925-4287**	856-234-9200
Beckley Newspapers Inc 801 N Kanawha St	Beckley	WV	25801	**800-950-0250**	304-255-4400
Belo Corp 400 Record St *NYSE: BLC*	Dallas	TX	75202	**800-431-0010**	214-977-8222
Belo Corp Newspaper Group 400 S Record St	Dallas	TX	75205	**800-431-0010**	214-977-6606
Brethren Missionary Herald 1104 Kings Hwy	Winona Lake	IN	46590	**800-348-2756**	574-267-7158
Burlington Hawk Eye Co PO Box 10	Burlington	IA	52601	**800-397-1708**	319-754-8461
Butler TB Publishing Co 410 W Erwin St	Tyler	TX	75702	**800-333-9141**	903-597-8111
Casa Grande Valley Newspaper Inc PO Box 15002	Casa Grande	AZ	85230	**800-821-1746**	520-836-7461
Chattanooga Publishing Co 400 E 11th St	Chattanooga	TN	37403	**800-733-2637**	423-756-6900
Cheyenne Newspaper Inc 702 W Lincolnway	Cheyenne	WY	82001	**800-561-6268**	307-634-3361
Christian Science Publishing Society 1 Norway St	Boston	MA	02115	**800-288-7090**	617-450-2000
Citizen Publishing Co Inc 805 Park Ave PO box 558	Beaver Dam	WI	53916	**800-777-9470**	920-887-0321
Community Newspaper Holdings Inc 3500 Colonnade Pkwy Suite 600	Birmingham	AL	35243	**800-951-2644**	205-298-7100
Cox Newspapers Inc 6205 Peachtree Dunwoody Dr	Atlanta	GA	30328	**800-950-3739**	678-645-0000
Daily Journal Corp 915 E 1st St *NASDAQ: DJCO*	Los Angeles	CA	90012	**800-788-7840**	213-229-5300
Daily Record Co 11 E Saratoga St	Baltimore	MD	21202	**800-296-8181**	410-752-3849
Daily Reflector Inc PO Box 1967	Greenville	NC	27835	**800-849-6166**	252-752-6166
Day Publishing Co 47 Eugene O'Neill Dr	New London	CT	06320	**800-542-3354**	860-442-2200
Delphos Herald Inc 405 N Main St	Delphos	OH	45833	**800-589-6950**	419-695-0015
Denver Newspaper Agency 1560 Broadway	Denver	CO	80202	**800-933-1990**	303-892-2745
Derrick Publishing Co 1510 W 1st St	Oil City	PA	16301	**800-352-1002**	814-676-7444
Desert Sun Publishing Co PO Box 2734 *Advertising	Palm Springs	CA	92263	**800-233-3741***	760-322-8889
Detroit Legal News Co 2001 W Lafayette Blvd	Detroit	MI	48216	**800-875-5275**	313-961-3949
Dispatch Printing Co 34 S 3rd St	Columbus	OH	43215	**800-282-0263**	614-461-5000
DMG World Media 27 N Jefferson St	Knightstown	IN	46148	**800-876-5133**	765-345-5133
Eagle Publications Inc RR 2 River Rd Box 301	Claremont	NH	03743	**800-545-0347**	603-542-5121
Edward A Sherman Publishing Co 101 Malbone Rd	Newport	RI	02840	**800-320-2378**	401-849-3300
Enterprise Newspapers 4303 198th St SW	Lynnwood	WA	98036	**800-944-3630**	425-673-6500
EW Scripps Co 312 Walnut St Suite 2800 *NYSE: SSP*	Cincinnati	OH	45202	**800-888-3000**	513-977-3000
Express-News Corp Ave 'E' & 3rd St	San Antonio	TX	78205	**800-555-1551**	210-250-3000
Finger Lakes Printing Co PO Box 393	Geneva	NY	14456	**800-388-6652**	315-789-3333
Flashes Publishers Inc 595 Jenner Dr	Allegan	MI	49010	**800-968-4415**	269-673-2141
Fort Wayne Newspapers Inc 600 W Main St	Fort Wayne	IN	46802	**800-444-3303**	260-461-8444
Forum Communications Co 101 5th St N	Fargo	ND	58102	**800-747-7311**	701-235-7311
Forum Publishing Group 1701 Green Rd Suite B	Deerfield Beach	FL	33064	**800-275-8820**	954-698-6397
Forward Publishing 45 E 33rd St	New York	NY	10016	**800-266-0773**	212-889-8200
Foster George J Co Inc 333 Central Ave	Dover	NH	03820	**800-660-8310**	603-742-4455
Gazette Newspapers Inc 1200 Quince Orchard Blvd	Gaithersburg	MD	20878	**888-670-7100**	301-948-3120
George J Foster Co Inc 333 Central Ave	Dover	NH	03820	**800-660-8310**	603-742-4455
Herald Mail Co Inc 100 Summit Ave	Hagerstown	MD	21740	**888-851-2553**	301-733-5131
Herald-Star 401 Herald Sq	Steubenville	OH	43952	**800-526-7987**	740-283-4711
Herald-Sun Newspapers PO Box 2092	Durham	NC	27702	**800-672-0061**	919-419-6900
Hersam Acorn Newspapers PO Box 1019	Ridgefield	CT	06877	**800-372-2790**	203-438-6545
Hickory Publishing Co Inc PO Box 968	Hickory	NC	28603	**800-849-8586**	828-322-4510
High Plains Publishers Inc PO Box 760	Dodge City	KS	67801	**800-452-7171**	620-227-7171
Home News Enterprises 333 2nd St	Columbus	IN	47201	**800-876-7811**	812-372-7811
Home Town Newspapers PO Box 230	Howell	MI	48844	**888-999-1288**	517-548-2000
Huse Publishing Co PO Box 977	Norfolk	NE	68702	**800-672-8351**	402-371-1020
Indianapolis Newspapers Inc 307 N Pennsylvania St	Indianapolis	IN	46204	**800-669-7827**	317-633-1240
Journal Communications Inc 333 W State St *NYSE: JRN*	Milwaukee	WI	53203	**800-456-5943**	414-224-2000
Journal Publishing Co PO Box 909	Tupelo	MS	38802	**800-264-6397**	662-842-2611
Keene Publishing Corp PO Box 546	Keene	NH	03431	**800-765-9994**	603-352-1234
Kingsport Publishing Co 701 Lynn Garden Dr	Kingsport	TN	37660	**800-251-0328**	423-246-8121
Kline William J & Son Inc 1 Venner Rd	Amsterdam	NY	12010	**800-453-6397**	518-843-1100
Knight Publishing Co 600 S Tryon St	Charlotte	NC	28202	**800-332-0686**	704-358-5000
Lancaster Newspapers Inc 8 W King St	Lancaster	PA	17603	**800-809-4666**	717-291-8811
Landmark Community Newspapers Inc 601 Taylorsville Rd	Shelbyville	KY	40065	**800-939-9322**	502-633-4334
Lawrence Daily Journal-World Co 609 New Hampshire St	Lawrence	KS	66044	**800-578-8748**	785-843-1000
Lee Publications Inc 6113 State Hwy 5	Palatine Bridge	NY	13428	**800-218-5586**	518-673-3237
Lehman Communications Corp 350 Terry St	Longmont	CO	80501	**800-796-8201**	303-776-2244
Lewiston Daily Sun Corp 104 Park St	Lewiston	ME	04240	**800-482-0753**	207-784-5411
Longview Newspapers Inc 320 E Methvin St	Longview	TX	75601	**800-627-4716**	903-757-3311
Lowell Sun Publishing Co 15 Kearney Sq	Lowell	MA	01852	**800-694-7100**	978-458-7100
Madison Newspapers Inc 1901 Fish Hatchery Rd *Classified	Madison	WI	53713	**800-252-7723***	608-252-6200
Magic Valley Newspapers 132 Fairfield St W	Twin Falls	ID	83301	**800-658-3883**	208-733-0931
Maverick Media Inc 123 W 17th St	Syracuse	NE	68446	**800-742-7662**	402-269-2135
McCormick & Co Inc 1201 3rd St	Alexandria	LA	71301	**800-523-8391**	318-487-6397
Memphis Publishing Co 495 Union Ave *Cust Svc	Memphis	TN	38103	**800-444-6397***	901-529-2211
Meridian Star Inc 814 22nd Ave	Meridian	MS	39301	**800-232-2525**	601-693-1551
Messenger Publishing Co 9300 Johnson Rd	Athens	OH	45701	**800-233-6611**	740-592-6612
Metro Group Inc PO Box 211	Buffalo	NY	14225	**800-836-7262**	716-668-5223
Mineral Daily News Tribune Inc 24 Armstrong St	Keyser	WV	26726	**800-788-4026**	304-788-3333
Missourian Publishing Co 14 W Main St	Washington	MO	63090	**888-239-7701**	636-239-7701
Mobile Press Register Inc PO Box 2488	Mobile	AL	36652	**800-239-1340**	251-433-1551
Morning Call Inc 101 N 6th St	Allentown	PA	18101	**800-666-5492**	610-820-6500
Morning Star Publishing Co 711 W Pickard St	Mount Pleasant	MI	48858	**800-616-6397**	989-772-2971
Morris Communications Co LLC 725 Broad St	Augusta	GA	30901	**800-622-6358**	706-724-0851
Natchez Newspapers Inc 503 N Canal St	Natchez	MS	39120	**888-878-9101**	601-442-9101
New Mexico Newspapers Inc PO Box 450	Farmington	NM	87499	**800-395-6397**	505-325-4545
News Journal Co PO Box 15505	Wilmington	DE	19850	**800-235-9100**	302-324-2500
Nittany Printing & Publishing Co 3400 E College Ave	State College	PA	16801	**800-327-5500**	814-238-5000
Northwest Herald Inc PO Box 250	Crystal Lake	IL	60039	**800-589-8910**	815-459-4040
Northwest Publications 99 E State St	Rockford	IL	61104	**800-383-7827**	815-987-1200
Oakland Press Co 48 W Huron St	Pontiac	MI	48342	**800-686-2236**	248-332-8181
Observer Publishing Co 122 S Main St	Washington	PA	15301	**800-222-6397**	724-222-2200
Oklahoma Publishing Co 9000 N Broadway Ext	Oklahoma City	OK	73114	**800-375-3450**	405-475-3311
Oshkosh Northwestern Co 224 State St	Oshkosh	WI	54901	**800-924-6168**	920-235-7700
Our Sunday Visitor Inc 200 Noll Plaza	Huntington	IN	46750	**800-348-2440**	260-356-8400
Paducah Newspapers Inc PO Box 2300	Paducah	KY	42002	**800-959-1771**	270-575-8600
Palm Beach Newspapers Inc PO Box 24700	West Palm Beach	FL	33416	**800-432-7597**	561-820-4100
Pamplin Communications Corp 10209 SE Division St	Portland	OR	97266	**866-233-7102**	503-251-1597
Patuxent Publishing Co 10750 Little Patuxent Pkwy	Columbia	MD	21044	**800-884-8797**	410-730-3620
Pennysaver 27101 Puerto Real Suite 250	Mission Viejo	CA	92691	**800-873-5548**	949-614-2600
Peoria Journal-Star Inc 1 News Plaza	Peoria	IL	61643	**800-225-5757**	309-686-3000
PG Publishing Co 34 Blvd of the Allies *Cust Svc	Pittsburgh	PA	15222	**800-228-6397***	412-263-1100
Phoenix Newspapers Inc 200 E Van Buren St	Phoenix	AZ	85004	**800-331-9303**	602-444-8000
Pipestone Publishing Co PO Box 277	Pipestone	MN	56164	**800-325-6440**	507-825-3333
Post Publishing Co PO Box 4639	Salisbury	NC	28145	**800-633-8957**	704-633-8950
Press-Enterprise Co PO Box 792	Riverside	CA	92502	**800-933-1400**	951-684-1200
Press-Enterprise Inc 3185 Lackawanna Ave	Bloomsburg	PA	17815	**800-228-3483**	570-784-2121
Pulitzer Inc 900 N Tucker Blvd *NYSE: PTZ*	Saint Louis	MO	63101	**800-365-0820**	314-340-8000
Quincy Newspapers Inc 130 S 5th St	Quincy	IL	62301	**800-373-9444**	217-223-5100
Reminder Press Inc 130 Old Town Rd	Vernon	CT	06066	**888-456-2211**	860-875-3366
Republican-American Inc 389 Meadow St	Waterbury	CT	06702	**800-992-3232**	203-574-3636
Richmond Newspapers Inc PO Box 85333	Richmond	VA	23293	**800-468-3383**	804-649-6000
Rivertown Newspaper Group 2760 N Service Dr PO Box 15	Red Wing	MN	55066	**800-535-1660**	651-388-8235
Roanoke Chowan Publishing PO Box 1325	Ahoskie	NC	27910	**888-639-7437**	252-332-2123
Saint Joseph News Press & Gazette Co PO Box 29	Saint Joseph	MO	64502	**800-779-6397**	816-271-8500
San Angelo Standard Times Inc PO Box 5111	San Angelo	TX	76902	**800-588-1884**	325-653-1221
San Mateo Times Group Newspapers 1080 S Amphlett Blvd	San Mateo	CA	94402	**800-843-6397**	650-348-4321
Santa Barbara News-Press Publishing Co 715 Anacapa St	Santa Barbara	CA	93101	**800-654-3292**	805-564-5200
Scotsman Publishing Co PO Box 352	Cambridge	MN	55008	**800-473-1981**	763-689-1981
Scranton Times Co 149 Penn Ave	Scranton	PA	18503	**800-228-4637**	570-348-9100
Scripps Howard Inc PO Box 5380	Cincinnati	OH	45201	**800-888-3000**	513-977-3000
Sherman Edward A Publishing Co 101 Malbone Rd	Newport	RI	02840	**800-320-2378**	401-849-3300
Shore Line Newspapers 1100 Boston Post Rd	Guilford	CT	06437	**800-922-7066**	203-453-2711
South Jersey Shopper's Guide Inc 8 Ranoldo Terr	Cherry Hill	NJ	08034	**800-229-8775**	856-616-4900
Star-News Newspapers PO Box 840	Wilmington	NC	28402	**800-222-2385**	910-343-2296
Stonebridge Press Inc 25 Elm St	Southbridge	MA	01550	**800-536-5836**	508-764-4325
Sun Co 399 N 'D' St	San Bernardino	CA	92401	**800-548-5448**	909-889-9666
Sun Newspapers 5510 Cloverleaf Pkwy	Cleveland	OH	44125	**800-362-8008**	216-986-2600
Sun Post Newspaper Group 1688 Meridian Ave Suite 404	Miami Beach	FL	33139	**888-769-7678**	305-538-9700
Sun Publishing Corp 201 N Thorp St	Hobbs	NM	88240	**800-993-2123**	505-393-2123
Sun-Sentinel Co 200 E Las Olas Blvd	Fort Lauderdale	FL	33301	**800-548-6397**	954-356-4000
TB Butler Publishing Co 410 W Erwin St	Tyler	TX	75702	**800-333-9141**	903-597-8111
Tennessee Valley Printing Co Inc PO Box 2213	Decatur	AL	35609	**888-353-4612**	256-353-4612
Terry Newspapers Inc 108 W 1st St	Geneseo	IL	61254	**888-422-3837**	309-944-2119
Times Herald Inc 410 Markley St PO Box 591	Norristown	PA	19404	**800-887-2501**	610-272-2500
Times News Publishing Co 707 S Main St	Burlington	NC	27215	**800-488-0085**	336-227-0131
Times Publishing Co 222 Lake St	Shreveport	LA	71101	**800-525-4335**	318-459-3200
Trader Publications Inc 185 Kisco Ave	Mount Kisco	NY	10549	**800-689-5933**	914-666-6222
Tri-State Livestock News 1022 Main St PO Box 129	Sturgis	SD	57785	**800-253-3656**	605-347-2585
Tribune Review Publishing Co 622 Cabin Hill Dr	Greensburg	PA	15601	**800-433-3045**	724-834-1151
Troy Publishing Co 501 Broadway	Troy	NY	12180	**800-934-4304**	518-270-1200
Truth Publishing Co Inc 421 S 2nd St	Elkhart	IN	46516	**800-585-5416**	574-294-1661
Union-Tribune Publishing Co PO Box 120191	San Diego	CA	92112	**800-244-6397**	619-299-3131
Uniontown Newspapers Inc 8-18 E Church St	Uniontown	PA	15401	**800-342-8254**	724-439-7500

Company	City	State	ZIP	Toll-Free	Phone
West Virginia Newspaper Publishing Co 1251 Earl L Core Rd	Morgantown	WV	26505	**800-654-4676**	304-292-6301
Western States Weeklies Inc PO Box 600600	San Diego	CA	92160	**800-280-2985**	619-280-2985
Wick Communications Inc 333 W Wilcox Dr Suite 302	Sierra Vista	AZ	85635	**800-777-9425**	520-458-0200
William J Kline & Son Inc 1 Venner Rd	Amsterdam	NY	12010	**800-453-6397**	518-843-1100
Worcester Telegram & Gazette Inc PO Box 15012	Worcester	MA	01615	**800-678-6680**	508-793-9100
Yankton Printing Co PO Box 56	Yankton	SD	57078	**800-743-2968**	605-665-7811

623-9 Periodicals Publishers

Company	City	State	ZIP	Toll-Free	Phone
Access Intelligence LLC 1201 Seven Locks Rd Suite 300	Potomac	MD	20854	**800-777-5006**	301-354-2000
Advanstar Communications Inc 7500 Old Oak Blvd	Cleveland	OH	44130	**800-225-4569**	440-243-8100
Advanstar Medical Economics Healthcare Communications 5 Paragon Dr	Montvale	NJ	07645	**800-526-4870**	201-358-7200
Advanstar Veterinary Healthcare Communications 8033 Flint St	Lenexa	KS	66214	**800-255-6864**	913-492-4300
Advisor Media Inc 4849 Viewridge Ave Suite 200	San Diego	CA	92123	**800-336-6060**	858-278-5600
Adweek Directories 770 Broadway	New York	NY	10003	**800-468-2395**	646-654-5000
Agora Publishing Inc 14 W Monument St	Baltimore	MD	21201	**800-433-1528**	410-783-8499
Alexander Communications Group Inc 28 W 25th St 8th Fl	New York	NY	10010	**800-232-4317**	212-228-0246
Alexander Hamilton Institute Inc 70 Hilltop Rd *Orders	Ramsey	NJ	07446	**800-879-2441***	201-825-3377
American Banker Newsletters 1 State St Plaza 27th Fl	New York	NY	10004	**800-221-1809**	212-803-8350
American Banker/Bond Buyer 1 State Street Plaza 26th Fl	New York	NY	10004	**800-362-3807**	212-803-8200
American City Business Journals Inc 120 W Moorehead St Suite 400	Charlotte	NC	28202	**800-704-3757**	704-973-1000
American Lawyer Media Inc 345 Park Ave S 8th Fl	New York	NY	10010	**800-888-8300**	212-545-6000
American Media Inc 1000 American Media Way	Boca Raton	FL	33464	**800-749-7733**	561-997-7733
Amos Press Inc PO Box 4129	Sidney	OH	45365	**800-327-1259**	937-498-2111
Andrews Publications Inc 175 Strafford Ave Bldg 4 Suite 140	Wayne	PA	19087	**800-345-1101**	610-225-0510
Annual Reviews 4139 El Camino Way	Palo Alto	CA	94303	**800-523-8635**	650-493-4400
Army Times Publishing Co 6883 Commercial Dr	Springfield	VA	22159	**800-424-9335**	703-750-9000
AS Pratt & Sons 1901 Fort Myer Dr Suite 501 *Cust Svc	Arlington	VA	22209	**800-572-2797***	703-528-0145
Aspen Publishers Inc 111 8th Ave 7th Fl *Orders	New York	NY	10011	**800-638-8437***	212-771-0600
Atlantic Information Services Inc 1100 17th St NW Suite 300	Washington	DC	20036	**800-521-4323**	202-775-9008
Augsburg Fortress Publishers PO Box 1209	Minneapolis	MN	55440	**800-426-0115**	612-330-3300
Boucher Communications Inc 1300 Virginia Dr Suite 400	Fort Washington	PA	19034	**800-306-6332**	215-643-8000
Brownstone Publishers Inc 149 5th Ave 16th Fl	New York	NY	10010	**800-643-8095**	212-473-8200
Bureau of National Affairs Inc 1231 25th St NW	Washington	DC	20037	**800-372-1033**	202-452-4200
Business & Legal Reports Inc 141 Mill Rock Rd E	Old Saybrook	CT	06475	**800-727-5257**	860-510-0100
Business News Publishing Co 2401 W Big Beaver Rd Suite 700	Troy	MI	48084	**800-837-7370**	248-362-3700
Business Publishers Inc 8737 Colesville Rd Suite 1100	Silver Spring	MD	20910	**800-274-6737**	301-587-6300
CCH Inc 2700 Lake Cook Rd *Cust Svc	Riverwoods	IL	60015	**800-835-5224***	847-267-7000
CD Publications 8204 Fenton St	Silver Spring	MD	20910	**800-666-6380**	301-588-6380
Challenge Publications Inc 9509 Vassar Ave Suite A	Chatsworth	CA	91311	**800-562-9182**	818-700-6868
Chemical Week Assoc 110 William St	New York	NY	10038	**800-774-5733**	212-621-4900
Children's Better Health Institute 1100 Waterway Blvd	Indianapolis	IN	46202	**800-558-2376**	317-636-8881
Christian Board of Publication PO Box 179 Suite 1200	Saint Louis	MO	63166	**800-366-3383**	314-231-8500
Christianity Today Inc 465 Gundersen Dr *Cust Svc	Carol Stream	IL	60188	**800-999-1704***	630-260-6200
CMP Media LLC 600 Community Dr	Manhasset	NY	11030	**800-645-6278**	516-562-5000
Cobblestone Publishing Co 30 Grove St Suite C	Peterborough	NH	03458	**800-821-0115**	603-924-7209
Commodity Information Systems Inc 3030 Northwest Expy Suite 725	Oklahoma City	OK	73112	**800-231-0477**	405-604-8726
ComputerUser.com Inc 220 S 6th St Suite 500	Minneapolis	MN	55402	**800-788-0204**	612-339-7571
Conde Nast Publications Inc 4 Times Sq	New York	NY	10036	**800-223-0780**	212-286-2860
Congressional Quarterly Inc 1255 22nd St NW	Washington	DC	20037	**800-432-2250**	202-419-8500
Connell Communications Inc 86 Elm St	Peterborough	NH	03458	**800-677-8847**	603-924-7271
Consumers Union of US Inc 101 Truman Ave	Yonkers	NY	10703	**800-234-1645**	914-378-2000
Cook Communications Ministries 4050 Lee Vance View	Colorado Springs	CO	80918	**800-708-5550**	719-536-0100
CRC Press LLC 6000 Broken Sound Pkwy NW Suite 300 *Cust Svc	Boca Raton	FL	33487	**800-272-7737***	561-994-0555
Cutter Information Corp 37 Broadway Suite 1	Arlington	MA	02474	**800-964-5118**	781-648-8700
Davis Dick Publishing Co 3333 W Commercial Blvd Suite 113	Fort Lauderdale	FL	33309	**800-654-1514**	954-733-3996
Deal LLC 105 Madison Ave 4th Fl *Cust Svc	New York	NY	10016	**888-667-3325***	212-313-9200
Dekker Marcel Inc 270 Madison Ave *Sales	New York	NY	10016	**800-228-1160***	212-696-9000
Desert Publications Inc 303 N Indian Canyon Dr PO Box 2724	Palm Springs	CA	92262	**800-775-7256**	760-325-2333
Dick Davis Publishing Co 3333 W Commercial Blvd Suite 113	Fort Lauderdale	FL	33309	**800-654-1514**	954-733-3996
Disney Consumer Products 500 S Buena Vista St *PR	Burbank	CA	91521	**800-723-4763***	818-560-1000
Disney Magazine Publishing 114 5th Ave *Cust Svc	New York	NY	10011	**800-333-8734***	212-633-4400
Doane Agricultural Services 11701 Borman Dr Suite 300	Saint Louis	MO	63146	**800-535-2342**	314-569-2700
Earl G Graves Ltd 130 5th Ave 10th Fl	New York	NY	10011	**800-727-7777**	212-242-8000
Economist Intelligence Unit 111 W 57th St 7th Fl	New York	NY	10019	**800-938-4685**	212-554-0600
EGW Publishing Co Inc 1041 Shary Cir *Cust Svc	Concord	CA	94518	**800-546-4754***	925-671-9852
Ehlert Publishing Group Inc 6420 Sycamore Ln Suite 100	Maple Grove	MN	55369	**800-848-6247**	763-383-4400
Eli Journals 2272 Airport Rd	Naples	FL	34112	**800-508-2582**	239-280-2383
Elliott Wave International PO Box 1618 *Sales	Gainesville	GA	30503	**800-336-1618***	770-536-0309
Elsevier Science Ltd 360 Park Ave S	New York	NY	10010	**888-437-4636**	212-989-5800
Energy Intelligence Group 5 E 37th St 5th Fl	New York	NY	10016	**888-427-7496**	212-532-1112
Entrepreneur Media Inc 2445 McCabe Way	Irvine	CA	92614	**800-357-7299**	949-261-2325
EPM Communications Inc 160 Mercer St 3rd Fl	New York	NY	10012	**888-852-9467**	212-941-0099
Ernst Publishing Co LLC 1937 Delaware Tpke Suite B	Clarksville	NY	12041	**800-345-3822**	
Essence Communications Inc 1500 Broadway 6th Fl *Circ	New York	NY	10036	**800-274-9398***	212-642-0600
F & W Publications Inc 4700 E Galbraith Rd *Sales	Cincinnati	OH	45236	**800-289-0963***	513-531-2690
Fairchild Publications Inc 7 W 34th St 3rd Fl	New York	NY	10001	**800-289-0273**	212-630-4000
Famfare Media Works Inc 25300 Rye Canyon Rd	Valencia	CA	91355	**800-935-0090**	661-257-4000
Farm Progress Co Inc 191 S Gary Ave	Carol Stream	IL	60188	**800-441-1410**	630-690-5600
FCN Publishing 1725 K St NW Suite 506	Washington	DC	20006	**888-732-7070**	202-887-6320
FDC Reports Inc 5550 Friendship Blvd Suite 1	Chevy Chase	MD	20815	**800-332-1370**	301-657-9830
Feistritzer Publications 4401A Connecticut Ave NW Suite 212	Washington	DC	20008	**866-778-2784**	202-362-3444
First Marketing 3300 Gateway Dr	Pompano Beach	FL	33069	**800-641-9251**	954-979-0700
Forbes Inc 60 5th Ave	New York	NY	10011	**800-888-9896**	212-620-2200
Forecast International/DMS Inc 22 Commerce Rd	Newtown	CT	06470	**800-451-4975**	203-426-0800
Frequent Flyer Services 1930 Frequent Flyer Pt	Colorado Springs	CO	80915	**800-209-2870**	719-597-8889
Gardner Publications Inc 6915 Valley Ave	Cincinnati	OH	45244	**800-950-8020**	513-527-8800
Government Information Services 1725 K St NW Suite 700	Washington	DC	20006	**800-677-3789**	202-872-4000
Grand View Media Group Inc 200 Croft St Suite 1	Birmingham	AL	35242	**888-431-2877**	205-262-4600
Grass Roots Publishing Co Inc Hochman Assoc 908 Oaktree Rd Suite H	South Plainfield	NJ	07080	**877-207-9007**	908-222-1811
Graves Earl G Ltd 130 5th Ave 10th Fl	New York	NY	10011	**800-727-7777**	212-242-8000
Guest Informant Inc 21200 Erwin St	Woodland Hills	CA	91367	**800-275-5885**	818-716-7484
Guideposts Inc 39 Seminary Hill Rd *Cust Svc	Carmel	NY	10512	**800-431-2344***	845-225-3681
Gulf Publishing Co Inc 2 Greenway Plaza Suite 1020	Houston	TX	77046	**800-231-6275**	713-529-4301
Hart Publications Inc 4545 Post Oak Pl Suite 210	Houston	TX	77027	**800-874-2544**	713-993-9320
Hatton Brown Publishing Co 225 Hanrick St	Montgomery	AL	36104	**800-669-5613**	334-834-1170
Healthy Directions LLC 7811 Montrose Rd	Rockville	MD	20854	**800-340-7788**	301-340-2100
Hearst Magazines Div 959 8th Ave	Manhattan	NY	10019	**800-678-7767**	212-649-2000
Highlights for Children Inc 1800 Watermark Dr *Cust Svc	Columbus	OH	43215	**800-255-9517***	614-486-0631
Hobsons CollegeView 10200 Alliance Rd Suite 301	Cincinnati	OH	45242	**800-927-8439**	513-891-5444
Hoke Communications Inc 224 7th St	Garden City	NY	11530	**800-229-6700**	516-746-6700
Homes & Land Publishing Ltd 1830 E Park Ave	Tallahassee	FL	32301	**800-466-3546**	850-574-2111
Honolulu Publishing Co Ltd 707 Richards St Suite 525	Honolulu	HI	96813	**800-272-5245**	808-524-7400
Horizon House Publications Inc 685 Canton St	Norwood	MA	02062	**800-225-9977**	781-769-9750
House of White Birches Inc 306 E Parr Rd *Orders	Berne	IN	46711	**800-347-9887***	260-589-8741
HW Wilson Co 950 University Ave	Bronx	NY	10452	**800-367-6770**	718-588-8400
IEEE Computer Society Publications Office 10662 Los Vaqueros Cir	Los Alamitos	CA	90720	**800-272-6657**	714-821-8380
Information Today Inc 143 Old Marlton Pike	Medford	NJ	08055	**800-300-9868**	609-654-6266
InfoWorld Media Group Inc 501 2nd St Suite 120	San Francisco	CA	94107	**800-227-8365**	415-243-4344
Inside Washington Publishers Inc 1225 South Clark St Suite 1400	Arlington	VA	22202	**800-424-9068**	703-416-8500
Institute of Management & Administration Inc (IOMA Inc) 3 Park Ave 30th Fl	New York	NY	10016	**800-401-5937**	212-244-0360
Institutional Investor Newsletters 225 Park Ave S 8th Fl	New York	NY	10003	**800-715-9197**	212-224-3800
IOMA Inc (Institute of Management & Administration Inc) 3 Park Ave 30th Fl	New York	NY	10016	**800-401-5937**	212-244-0360
Journal of Commerce Group 33 Washington St 13th Fl *Cust Svc	Newark	NJ	07103	**800-223-0243***	973-848-7000
Kagan World Media 1 Lower Ragsdale Dr Bldg 1 Suite 130	Monterey	CA	93940	**800-307-2529**	831-624-1536
Kalmbach Publishing Co 21027 Crossroads Cir *Cust Svc	Waukesha	WI	53187	**800-446-5489***	262-796-8776
KCI Communications 1750 Old Meadow Rd Suite 300 *Cust Svc	McLean	VA	22102	**800-832-2330***	703-905-8000
Kennedy Information 1 Phoenix Mill Ln 5th Fl	Peterborough	NH	03458	**800-531-1026**	603-924-1006
King Publishing Group 1325 G St NW Suite 1003	Washington	DC	20005	**800-926-5464**	202-638-4260
Kiplinger Washington Editors Inc 1729 H St NW	Washington	DC	20006	**800-544-0155**	202-887-6400
Krause Publications Inc 700 E State St *Cust Svc	Iola	WI	54990	**800-942-0673***	715-445-2214
Lawrence Ragan Communications Inc 316 N Michigan Ave Suite 300	Chicago	IL	60601	**800-878-5331**	312-960-4140
Liebert Mary Ann Publishers Inc 140 Huguenot St 3rd Fl	New Rochelle	NY	10801	**800-654-3237**	914-740-2100

Periodicals Publishers (Cont'd)

	City	State	ZIP	Toll-Free	Phone
Lippincott Williams & Wilkins 530 Walnut St	Philadelphia	PA	19106	**800-638-3030**	215-521-8300
Liturgical Publications Inc 2875 S James Dr	New Berlin	WI	53151	**800-876-4574**	262-785-1188
LRP Publications 360 Hiatt Dr	Palm Beach Gardens	FL	33418	**800-621-5463**	561-622-6520
M Shanken Communications Inc 387 Park Ave S 8th Fl	New York	NY	10016	**800-866-0775**	212-684-4224
MacAddict Network c/o Imagine Media Inc 150 N Hill Dr Suite 40 *Cust Svc	Brisbane	CA	94005	**888-771-6222***	415-468-4684
Marcel Dekker Inc 270 Madison Ave *Sales	New York	NY	10016	**800-228-1160***	212-696-9000
Mary Ann Liebert Publishers Inc 140 Huguenot St 3rd Fl	New Rochelle	NY	10801	**800-654-3237**	914-740-2100
McGraw-Hill Construction 2 Penn Plaza	New York	NY	10121	**800-221-0088**	
Meister Publishing Co 37733 Euclid Ave *Orders	Willoughby	OH	44094	**800-572-7740***	440-942-2000
Mergent Inc 60 Madison Ave 6th Fl	New York	NY	10010	**888-411-0893**	212-413-7700
Metal Bulletin Inc 1250 Broadway 26th Fl	New York	NY	10001	**800-638-2525**	212-213-6202
Microsoft Press 1 Microsoft Way *Cust Svc	Redmond	WA	98052	**800-426-9400***	425-882-8080
Miles Media Group Inc 6751 Professional Pkwy W Suite 200	Sarasota	FL	34240	**800-683-0010**	941-342-2300
Millin Publishing Group Inc 1150 Connecticut Ave NW Suite 900	Washington	DC	20036	**888-739-8500**	202-862-4375
Morningstar Inc 225 W Wacker Dr. *NASDAQ: MORN* ■ *Orders	Chicago	IL	60606	**800-735-0700***	312-696-6000
National Braille Press Inc 88 Saint Stephens St	Boston	MA	02115	**888-965-8965**	617-266-6160
National Catholic Reporter Publishing Co 115 E Armour Blvd	Kansas City	MO	64111	**800-333-7373**	816-531-0538
National Geographic Society 1145 17th St NW *Orders	Washington	DC	20036	**800-647-5463***	202-857-7000
National Journal Group Inc 600 New Hampshire Ave NW 4th Fl	Washington	DC	20037	**800-207-8001**	202-739-8400
Nazarene Publishing House Inc PO Box 419527	Kansas City	MO	64141	**800-877-0700**	816-931-1900
Newsweek Inc 251 W 57th St *Cust Svc	New York	NY	10019	**800-634-6842***	212-445-4000
North American Publishing Co 1500 Springarden St Suite 1200	Philadelphia	PA	19130	**800-627-2689**	215-238-5482
NORTHSTAR Travel Media LLC 500 Plaza Dr	Secaucus	NJ	07094	**800-742-7076**	201-902-2000
Omniprint 9700 Philadelphia Ct	Lanham	MD	20706	**800-774-6809**	301-731-5200
Online Inc 88 Danbury Rd Suite D	Wilton	CT	06897	**800-248-8466**	203-761-1466
Our Sunday Visitor Inc 200 Noll Plaza	Huntington	IN	46750	**800-348-2440**	260-356-8400
Oxmoor House Inc 2100 Lakeshore Dr	Birmingham	AL	35209	**800-633-4910**	205-445-6000
Pacific Press Publishing Assn 1350 N Kings Rd *Cust Svc	Nampa	ID	83687	**800-545-2449***	208-465-2500
Paisano Publications 28210 Dorothy Dr	Agoura Hills	CA	91301	**800-247-6246**	818-889-8740
PC World Communications Inc 501 2nd St	San Francisco	CA	94107	**800-997-2967**	415-243-0500
PennWell Publishing Co 1421 S Sheridan Rd	Tulsa	OK	74112	**800-331-4463**	918-835-3161
Photosource International 1910 35th Rd Pine Lake Farm	Osceola	WI	54020	**800-624-0266**	715-248-3800
Pike & Fischer Inc 1010 Wayne Ave Suite 1400	Silver Spring	MD	20910	**800-255-8131**	301-562-1530
Platts 2 Penn Plaza 25th Fl	New York	NY	10121	**800-752-8878**	212-904-3070
Pohly & Partners Inc 27 Melcher St 2nd Fl	Boston	MA	02210	**877-687-6459**	617-451-1700
Post-Newsweek Tech Media Group 10 G St NE Suite 500	Washington	DC	20002	**866-447-6864**	202-772-2500
Pratt AS & Sons 1901 Fort Myer Dr Suite 501 *Cust Svc	Arlington	VA	22209	**800-572-2797***	703-528-0145
Publications & Communications Inc 11675 Jollyville Rd Suite 150	Austin	TX	78759	**800-678-9724**	512-250-9023
Publications International Ltd 7373 N Cicero Ave	Lincolnwood	IL	60712	**800-745-9299**	847-676-3470
Publishing Group of America Inc 341 Cool Springs Blvd Suite 400	Franklin	TN	37067	**800-720-6323**	615-468-6000
Putman Media Inc 555 W Pierce Rd Suite 301	Itasca	IL	60143	**800-984-7644**	630-467-1300
Ragan Lawrence Communications Inc 316 N Michigan Ave Suite 300	Chicago	IL	60601	**800-878-5331**	312-960-4140
Randall Publishing Co 3200 Rice Mine Rd NE *Cust Svc	Tuscaloosa	AL	35406	**800-633-5953***	205-349-2990
Reader's Digest Assn Inc Reader's Digest Rd *NYSE: RDA*	Pleasantville	NY	10570	**800-635-5006**	914-238-1000
Reed Business Information 100 Enterprise Dr Suite 600	Rockaway	NJ	07866	**800-446-6551**	973-920-7000
Reed Elsevier Inc 121 Chanlon Rd	New Providence	NJ	07974	**800-526-4902**	908-464-6800
Reiman Publications 5400 S 60th St	Greendale	WI	53129	**800-344-6913**	414-423-0100
Review & Herald Publishing Assn 55 W Oak Ridge Dr	Hagerstown	MD	21740	**800-456-3991**	301-393-3000
RIA Group 395 Hudson St *Cust Svc	New York	NY	10014	**800-950-1205***	212-367-6300
Rodale Inc 33 E Minor St *Cust Svc	Emmaus	PA	18098	**800-848-4735***	610-967-8154
Rough Notes Co Inc 11690 Technology Dr	Carmel	IN	46032	**800-428-4384**	317-582-1600
Sage Publications Inc 2455 Teller Rd	Thousand Oaks	CA	91320	**800-818-7243**	805-499-9774
Saint Croix Press Inc 1185 S Knowles Ave	New Richmond	WI	54017	**800-826-6622**	715-246-5811
Sandhills Publishing 120 W Harvest Dr	Lincoln	NE	68521	**800-544-1382**	402-479-2181
Saturday Evening Post Society 1100 Waterway Blvd	Indianapolis	IN	46202	**800-558-2376**	317-636-8881
Schaeffer's Investment Research Inc 5151 Pfeiffer Dr Suite 250	Cincinnati	OH	45242	**800-448-2080**	513-589-3800
Scholastic Corp 557 Broadway *NASDAQ: SCHL* ■ *Cust Svc	New York	NY	10012	**800-724-6527***	212-343-6100
Scientific American Inc 415 Madison Ave *Cust Svc	New York	NY	10017	**800-333-1199***	212-451-8550
Shanken M Communications Inc 387 Park Ave S 8th Fl	New York	NY	10016	**800-866-0775**	212-684-4224
Simmons-Boardman Publishing Corp 345 Hudson St 12th Fl	New York	NY	10014	**800-895-4389**	212-620-7200
Sky Publishing Corp 49 Bay State Rd	Cambridge	MA	02138	**800-253-0245**	617-864-7360
Slack Inc 6900 Grove Rd	Thorofare	NJ	08086	**800-257-8290**	856-848-1000
Southern Progress Corp 2100 Lakeshore Dr	Birmingham	AL	35209	**800-366-4712**	205-445-6000
Springer-Verlag New York Inc 233 Spring St	New York	NY	10013	**800-777-4643**	212-460-1500
ST Media Group International Inc 407 Gilbert Ave	Cincinnati	OH	45202	**800-925-1110**	513-421-2050
Stamats Communications Inc 615 5th St SE	Cedar Rapids	IA	52401	**800-553-8878**	319-364-6167
Standard & Poor's Corp 55 Water St	New York	NY	10041	**800-289-8000**	212-438-2000
Standard Publishing Co 8121 Hamilton Ave *Orders	Cincinnati	OH	45231	**800-543-1353***	513-931-4050
Sterling/MacFadden Partnership 333 7th Ave 11th Fl	New York	NY	10001	**800-741-1289**	212-979-4800
Strafford Publications Inc PO Box 13729	Atlanta	GA	30324	**800-926-7926**	404-881-1141
Strang Communications 600 Rinehart Rd *Sales	Lake Mary	FL	32746	**800-451-4598***	407-333-0600
Sunset Publishing Corp 80 Willow Rd	Menlo Park	CA	94025	**800-227-7346**	650-321-3600
Taunton Press Inc 63 S Main St	Newtown	CT	06470	**800-243-7252**	203-426-8171
Tax Management Inc 1231 25th St NW	Washington	DC	20037	**800-372-1033**	202-452-4200
Testa Communications 25 Willowdale Ave	Port Washington	NY	11050	**800-937-7678**	516-767-2500
Thompson American Health Consultants Inc 3525 Piedmont Rd NE Bldg 6 Suite 400 *Cust Svc	Atlanta	GA	30305	**800-688-2421***	404-262-7436
Thompson Publishing Group Inc 1725 K St NW Suite 700 *Cust Svc	Washington	DC	20006	**800-677-3789***	202-872-4000
Thomson Media 1 State Street Plaza 27th Fl	New York	NY	10004	**800-535-8403**	212 803 8200
Thomson Scientific 3501 Market St	Philadelphia	PA	19104	**800-523-1850**	215-386-0100
Times Mirror Magazines Inc 2Park Ave	New York	NY	10016	**800-227-2224**	212-779-5000
TL Enterprises Inc 2575 Vista Del Mar Dr	Ventura	CA	93001	**800-765-1912**	805-667-4100
Transcontinental Media 1100 Rene-Levesque Blvd W 24th fl	Montreal	QC	H3B4X9	**800-461-3773**	514-392-9000
TransWorld Media 353 Airport Rd	Oceanside	CA	92054	**800-788-7072**	760-722-7777
Travelhost Inc 10701 N Stemmons Fwy	Dallas	TX	75220	**800-527-1782**	972-556-0541
United Communications Group 11300 Rockville Pike Suite 1100	Rockville	MD	20852	**800-929-4824**	301-816-8950
United Methodist Publishing House PO Box 801 *Cust Svc	Nashville	TN	37202	**800-672-1789***	615-749-6000
United Nations Publications 2 UN Plaza Suite DC2-853	New York	NY	10017	**800-253-9646**	212-963-8302
University of Chicago Press Journals Div PO Box 37005	Chicago	IL	60637	**877-705-1878**	773-753-3347
US Government Printing Office (GPO) 732 N Capitol St NW	Washington	DC	20401	**866-512-1800**	202-512-0000
Value Line Inc 220 E 42nd St 6th Fl *NASDAQ: VALU* ■ *Cust Svc	New York	NY	10017	**800-634-3583***	212-907-1500
Vance Publishing Corp 400 Knightsbridge Pkwy	Lincolnshire	IL	60069	**800-621-2845**	847-634-2600
Wakeman/Walworth Inc PO Box 7376	Alexandria	VA	22307	**800-876-2545**	703-768-9600
Warren Communications News Inc 2115 Ward Ct NW	Washington	DC	20037	**800-771-9202**	202-872-9200
Weider Publications Inc 21100 Erwin St	Woodland Hills	CA	91367	**800-423-5590**	818-884-6800
Whitaker Newsletters Inc PO Box 241	Burtonsville	MD	20866	**800-359-6049**	301-384-1573
Wilson HW Co 950 University Ave	Bronx	NY	10452	**800-367-6770**	718-588-8400
Working Mother Media Inc 60 E 42nd St 27th	New York	NY	10165	**800-627-0690**	212-351-6400
Yankee Publishing Inc PO Box 520	Dublin	NH	03444	**800-729-9265**	603-563-8111
Ziff Davis Media Inc 28 E 28th St	New York	NY	10016	**800-336-2423**	212-503-3500

623-10 Publishers (Misc)

	City	State	ZIP	Toll-Free	Phone
American Printing House for the Blind 1839 Frankfort Ave PO Box 6085	Louisville	KY	40206	**800-223-1839**	502-895-2405
Art Publishing Group 165 Chubb Ave	Lyndhurst	NJ	07071	**800-760-3058**	201-842-8500
Associated Press Information Services 450 W 33rd St	New York	NY	10001	**800-272-2551**	212-621-1585
Bernan Assoc 4611 F Assembly Dr	Lanham	MD	20706	**800-865-3457**	301-459-2255
Britannica.com Inc 310 S Michigan Ave *Cust Svc	Chicago	IL	60604	**800-747-8503***	312-347-7000
Brodart Co Automation Div 500 Arch St	Williamsport	PA	17701	**800-233-8467**	570-326-2461
Cathedral Press Inc 600 NE 6th St *Cust Svc	Long Prairie	MN	56347	**800-874-8332***	320-732-6143
Chalk & Vermilion Fine Arts Inc 55 Old Post Rd #2	Greenwich	CT	06830	**800-877-2250**	203-869-9500
Channing L Bete Co Inc 1 Community Pl	South Deerfield	MA	01373	**800-628-7733**	413-665-7611
Clement Communications Inc 10 LaCrue Ave	Concordville	PA	19331	**888-358-5858**	610-459-4200
CoreData Group 2108 W Laburnum Ave	Richmond	VA	23227	**800-775-8118**	804-278-6700
CPP Inc 1055 Joaquin Rd Suite 200	Mountain View	CA	94043	**800-624-1765**	650-969-8901
Dorland Healthcare Information 1500 Walnut St Suite 1000	Philadelphia	PA	19102	**800-784-2332**	215-875-1212
Dow Jones Reuters Business Interactive LLC DBA Factiva PO Box 300 *Cust Svc	Princeton	NJ	08543	**800-369-7466***	609-627-2000
Drivers License Guide Co 1492 Oddstad Dr	Redwood City	CA	94063	**800-227-8827**	650-369-4849
EBSCO Publishing Inc 10 Estes St	Ipswich	MA	01938	**800-653-2726**	978-356-6500
Entertainment Publications Inc 1414 E Maple Rd	Troy	MI	48083	**800-926-0565**	248-404-1000
Factiva PO Box 300 *Cust Svc	Princeton	NJ	08543	**800-369-7466***	609-627-2000
Facts & Comparisons Inc 77 W Port Plaza Suite 450	Saint Louis	MO	63146	**800-223-0554**	314-216-2100
Forecast International/DMS Inc 22 Commerce Rd	Newtown	CT	06470	**800-451-4975**	203-426-0800
Hadley Cos 11300 Hampshire Ave S *Sales	Bloomington	MN	55438	**800-927-0880***	952-943-8474
IGN Entertainment Inc 8000 Marina Blvd 4th Fl	Brisbane	CA	94005	**800-994-2275**	415-508-2000
Krames Communication/Staywell 780 Township Line Rd *Sales	Yardley	PA	19067	**800-333-3032***	267-685-2500
Lifetouch Church Directories 1371 State Rt 598	Galion	OH	44833	**800-521-4611**	419-468-4739
Liturgical Publications of Saint Louis Inc 160 Old State Rd	Ballwin	MO	63021	**800-876-7000**	636-394-7000
MeansBusiness Inc 374 Congress St Suite 603	Boston	MA	02210	**800-231-8338**	617-956-9921
Mergent FIS Inc 60 Madison Ave 6th Fl	New York	NY	10010	**800-342-5647**	212-413-7700
New York Graphic Society Ltd 129 Glover Ave	Norwalk	CT	06850	**800-677-6947**	203-847-2000

	City	State	Zip	Toll-Free	Phone
OAG Worldwide 3025 Highland Pkwy Suite 200	Downers Grove	IL	60515	**800-323-3537**	630-515-5300
OneSource Information Services Inc 300 Baker Ave	Concord	MA	01742	**800-333-8036**	978-318-4300
Parish Publications Inc 6503 19 1/2 Mile Rd	Sterling Heights	MI	48314	**800-521-4486**	586-997-4241
ProQuest Information & Learning Co 300 N Zeeb Rd	Ann Arbor	MI	48106	**800-521-0600**	734-761-4700
Psychological Corp 19500 Bulverdy Rd	San Antonio	TX	78259	**800-228-0752**	210-339-5000
San Dieguito Printers 1880 Diamond St	San Marcos	CA	92069	**800-321-5794**	760-744-0910
Somerset House Publishing 10688 Haddington	Houston	TX	77043	**800-444-2540***	713-932-6847
*Sales					
TechTarget 117 Kendrick St Suite 800	Needham	MA	02111	**888-274-4111**	781-657-1000
Thomson CenterWatch Inc 22 Thomson Pl 47th Fl	Boston	MA	02210	**800-765-9647***	617-856-5900
*Cust Svc					
Winn Devon Art Group 6015 6th Ave S	Seattle	WA	98108	**800-875-4150**	206-763-9544
Wonderlic Inc 1795 N Butterfield Rd	Libertyville	IL	60048	**800-323-3742**	847-680-4900
Workman Publishing 708 Broadway	New York	NY	10003	**800-722-7202**	212-254-5900
Zagat Survey LLC 4 Columbus Cir 3rd Fl	New York	NY	10019	**800-333-3421**	212-977-6000

623-11 Technical Publishers

	City	State	Zip	Toll-Free	Phone
Aircraft Technical Publishers 101 S Hill Dr	Brisbane	CA	94005	**800-227-4610**	415-330-9500
American Chemical Society Publications 1155 16th St NW Publications Support Services	Washington	DC	20036	**800-227-5558**	202-872-4600
American Technical Publishers Inc 1155 W 175th St	Homewood	IL	60430	**800-323-3471**	708-957-1100
Applied Computer Research Inc PO Box 82266	Phoenix	AZ	85071	**800-234-2227**	602-216-9100
Cambridge Information Group 7200 Wisconsin Ave Suite 601	Bethesda	MD	20814	**800-843-7751**	301-961-6700
Center for Communications Management Information 11300 Rockville Pike Suite 1100	Rockville	MD	20852	**888-275-2264**	301-287-2835
Course Technology 25 Thomson Pl	Boston	MA	02210	**800-648-7450**	617-757-7900
DevX Inc 150 Executive Pk Blvd Suite 4100	San Francisco	CA	94134	**800-887-2702**	415-467-0305
Electronic Trend Publications 1975 Hamilton Ave Suite 6	San Jose	CA	95125	**800-726-6858**	408-369-7000
Faulkner Information Services 7905 Browning Rd Suite 116	Pennsauken	NJ	08109	**800-843-0460**	856-662-2070
Fawcette Technical Publications 2600 S El Camino Real Suite 300	San Mateo	CA	94403	**800-848-5523**	650-378-7100
Information Gatekeepers Inc 320 Washington St Suite 302	Brighton	MA	02135	**800-323-1088**	617-782-5033
JJ Keller & Assoc Inc PO Box 368	Neenah	WI	54957	**800-558-5011**	920-722-2848
Keller JJ & Assoc Inc PO Box 368	Neenah	WI	54957	**800-558-5011**	920-722-2848
knovel.com 13 Eaton Ave	Norwich	NY	13815	**888-238-1626**	607-337-5600
McGraw-Hill Osborne 2100 Powell St 10th Fl	Emeryville	CA	94608	**800-227-0900**	510-420-7700
McGraw-Hill Professional Publishing Group 2 Penn Plaza 11th Fl	New York	NY	10121	**800-262-4729**	212-512-2000
Mitchell 1 14145 Danielson St	Poway	CA	92064	**888-724-6742**	858-391-5000
Mitchell International Inc 9889 Willow Creek Rd	San Diego	CA	92131	**800-854-7030**	858-578-6550
O'Reilly & Assoc Inc 1005 Gravenstein Hwy N	Sebastopol	CA	95472	**800-998-9938**	707-829-0515
Thompson Publishing Group Inc 1725 K St NW Suite 700	Washington	DC	20006	**800-677-3789***	202-872-4000
*Cust Svc					

624 PULP MILLS

SEE ALSO Paper Mills; Paperboard Mills

	City	State	Zip	Toll-Free	Phone
Alberta-Pacific Forest Industries Inc Hwy 63 N	Boyle	AB	T0A0M0	**800-661-5210**	780-525-8000
Daishowa America Co Ltd PO Box 271	Port Angeles	WA	98362	**800-331-6314***	360-457-4474
*Sales					
Domtar Inc 395 boul de Maisonneuve O	Montreal	QC	H3A1L6	**800-267-2040**	514-848-5400
NYSE: DTC					
International Paper Co 400 Atlantic St	Stamford	CT	06921	**800-223-1268***	203-541-8000
NYSE: IP ■ *Prod Info					
Kimberly-Clark Corp 351 Phelps Dr	Irving	TX	75038	**800-544-1847**	972-281-1200
NYSE: KMB					
MeadWestvaco Fiber Sales Courthouse Plaza NE	Dayton	OH	45463	**800-345-6323**	937-495-3379
Norbord Industries Inc 1 Toronto St 6th Fl	Toronto	ON	M5C2W4	**877-263-9367**	416-643-8820
TSE: NBD					
Western Forest Products Inc 435 Trunk Rd 3rd Fl	Duncan	BC	V9L2P9	**800-880-7471**	250-748-3711
TSE: WEF					

625 PUMPS - MEASURING & DISPENSING

	City	State	Zip	Toll-Free	Phone
Bennett Pump Co 1218 E Pontaluna Rd	Spring Lake	MI	49456	**800-423-6638**	231-798-1310
Dresser Inc Wayne Div 3814 Jarrett Way	Austin	TX	78728	**800-289-2963**	512-388-8311
Gasboy International Inc 7300 W Friendly Ave	Greensboro	NC	27420	**800-444-5579***	336-547-5000
*Sales					
Graco Inc 88 11th Ave	Minneapolis	MN	55413	**800-328-0211***	612-623-6000
NYSE: GGG ■ *Cust Svc					
Great Plains Industries Inc 5252 E 36th St N	Wichita	KS	67220	**800-835-0113***	316-686-7361
*Sales					
O'Day Equipment Inc 1301 40th St NW	Fargo	ND	58102	**800-654-6329**	701-282-9260
Red Jacket Div Veeder-Root 125 Powder Forest Dr	Simsbury	CT	06070	**800-873-3313**	860-651-2700
Veeder-Root Red Jacket Div 125 Powder Forest Dr	Simsbury	CT	06070	**800-873-3313**	860-651-2700
Wayne Div Dresser Inc 3814 Jarrett Way	Austin	TX	78728	**800-289-2963**	512-388-8311

626 PUMPS & MOTORS - FLUID POWER

	City	State	Zip	Toll-Free	Phone
Applied Energy Co Inc 11431 Chairman Dr	Dallas	TX	75243	**800-284-3166**	214-349-1171
ARO Fluid Products Div Ingersoll-Rand Co 1 Aro Ctr PO Box 151	Bryan	OH	43506	**800-495-0276***	419-636-4242
*Cust Svc					
Bosch Rexroth Corp 5150 Prairie Stone Pkwy	Hoffman Estates	IL	60192	**800-860-1055**	847-645-3600
Cross Mfg Inc 11011 King St Suite 210	Overland Park	KS	66210	**800-542-7677**	913-451-1233
Fluid Metering Inc 5 Aerial Way Suite 500	Syosset	NY	11791	**800-223-3388**	516-922-6050
Haldex Hydraulic Systems 2222 15th St	Rockford	IL	61104	**800-572-7867**	815-398-4400
Ingersoll-Rand Co ARO Fluid Products Div 1 Aro Ctr PO Box 151	Bryan	OH	43506	**800-495-0276***	419-636-4242
*Cust Svc					
ITT Industries Jabsco 20 Icon	Foothill Ranch	CA	92610	**800-235-6538**	949-609-5106
Jetstream of Houston LLP 4930 Cranswick	Houston	TX	77041	**800-231-8192**	713-462-7000
Liquid Drive Corp 418 Hadley St	Holly	MI	48442	**800-523-4443**	248-634-5382
Oilgear Co PO Box 343924	Milwaukee	WI	53234	**800-276-5356***	414-327-1700
NASDAQ: OLGR ■ *Sales					
Permco Inc 1500 Frost Rd	Streetsboro	OH	44241	**800-628-2801**	330-626-2801
RG Group 258 W Market St	York	PA	17405	**866-744-7687**	717-849-0320
TII Network Technologies Inc 1385 Akron St	Copiague	NY	11726	**888-844-4720**	631-789-5000
NASDAQ: TIII					

627 PUMPS & PUMPING EQUIPMENT (GENERAL USE)

SEE ALSO Industrial Machinery & Equipment (Misc) - Mfr

	City	State	Zip	Toll-Free	Phone
Acme Dynamics Inc 3608 Sydney Rd	Plant City	FL	33566	**800-622-9355**	813-752-3137
Aermotor Pumps Inc 293 Wright St	Delavan	WI	53115	**800-265-7241**	800-230-1816
Afton Pumps Inc 7335 Ave N	Houston	TX	77011	**800-829-9731**	713-923-9731
American Machine & Tool Co Inc 400 Spring St	Royersford	PA	19468	**888-268-7867**	610-948-3800
AR Wilfley & Sons Inc 7350 E Progress Pl Suite 200	Englewood	CO	80111	**800-525-9930**	303-779-1777
ASM Industries Inc Pacer Pumps Div 41 Industrial Cir	Lancaster	PA	17601	**800-233-3861***	717-656-2161
*Cust Svc					
Beckett Corp 5931 Campus Circle Dr W	Irving	TX	75063	**888-232-5388**	972-871-8000
Berkeley Pumps 293 Wright St	Delavan	WI	53115	**888-237-5353***	262-728-5551
*Cust Svc					
Calvert Engineering Inc 28606 W Livingston Ave	Valencia	CA	91355	**800-225-1339**	661-257-7330
Centrilift Inc 200 W Stuart Roosa Dr	Claremore	OK	74017	**800-633-5088**	918-341-9600
CH & E Mfg Co 3849 N Palmer St	Milwaukee	WI	53212	**800-236-0666***	414-964-3400
*Cust Svc					
Corcoran RS Co 500 N Vine St	New Lenox	IL	60451	**800-637-1067**	815-485-2156
Corken Inc 3805 NW 36th St	Oklahoma City	OK	73112	**800-631-4929**	405-946-5576
David Brown Union Pumps Co 4600 W Dickman Rd	Battle Creek	MI	49015	**800-877-7867**	269-966-4600
Dempster Industries Inc 711 S 6th St	Beatrice	NE	68310	**800-777-0212**	402-223-4026
Dosmatic USA Inc 1230 Crowley Cir	Carrollton	TX	75006	**800-344-6767**	972-245-9765
Evans-Hydro 18128 S Santa Fe Ave	Rancho Dominguez	CA	90221	**800-429-7867**	310-608-5801
Flint & Walling Inc 95 N Oak St	Kendallville	IN	46755	**800-927-0360***	260-347-1600
*Sales					
Fybroc Div Met-Pro Corp 700 Emlen Way	Telford	PA	18969	**800-392-7621**	215-723-8155
Gardner Denver Pump Div 4747 S 83rd E Ave	Tulsa	OK	74145	**800-637-8099**	918-664-1151
GIW Industries Inc 5000 Wrightsboro Rd	Grovetown	GA	30813	**800-241-2702**	706-863-1011
Graco Inc 88 11th Ave	Minneapolis	MN	55413	**800-328-0211***	612-623-6000
NYSE: GGG ■ *Cust Svc					
Great Plains Industries Inc 5252 E 36th St N	Wichita	KS	67220	**800-835-0113***	316-686-7361
*Sales					
Grundfos Pumps Corp 5900 E Shields Ave	Fresno	CA	93727	**800-333-1366***	559-292-8000
*Cust Svc					
Hale Products Inc 700 Spring Mill Ave	Conshohocken	PA	19428	**800-220-4253**	610-825-6300
Harben Inc 2010 Ronald Regan Blvd	Cumming	GA	30041	**800-327-5387**	770-889-9535
Haskel International Inc 100 E Graham Pl	Burbank	CA	91502	**800-743-2720**	818-843-4000
Hypro 375 5th Ave NW	New Brighton	MN	55112	**800-424-9776***	651-766-6300
*Cust Svc					
ITT Industries Jabsco 20 Icon	Foothill Ranch	CA	92610	**800-235-6538**	949-609-5106
Kerr Pump & Supply 12880 Cloverdale St	Oak Park	MI	48237	**800-482-8259**	248-543-3880
Krogh Pump Co 251 W Channel Rd	Benicia	CA	94510	**800-225-7644**	707-747-7585
KSB Inc 4415 Sarellen Rd	Richmond	VA	23231	**800-945-7867**	804-222-1818
Little Giant Pump Co 3810 N Tulsa Ave	Oklahoma City	OK	73112	**800-621-7264**	405-947-2511
Maass Midwest Inc 11283 Dundee Rd	Huntley	IL	60142	**800-323-6259**	847-669-5135
Madden Mfg Co 1317 Princeton Blvd	Elkhart	IN	46516	**800-369-6233**	574-295-4292
McNally Industries LLC 340 W Benson Ave PO Box 129	Grantsburg	WI	54840	**800-473-0053**	715-463-8300
Met-Pro Corp Fybroc Div 700 Emlen Way	Telford	PA	18969	**800-392-7621**	215-723-8155
Met-Pro Corp Sethco Div 70 Arkay Dr	Hauppauge	NY	11788	**800-645-0500**	631-435-0530
Micropump Inc 1402 NE 136th Ave	Vancouver	WA	98684	**800-671-6269***	360-253-2008
*Sales					
Moyno Inc 1895 W Jefferson St	Springfield	OH	45506	**800-325-1331**	937-327-3111
MP Pumps Inc 34800 Bennett Dr	Fraser	MI	48026	**800-563-8006**	586-293-8240
Pacer Pumps Div ASM Industries Inc 41 Industrial Cir	Lancaster	PA	17601	**800-233-3861***	717-656-2161
*Cust Svc					
PACO Pumps Inc 800 Koomey Rd	Brookshire	TX	77423	**800-926-6688**	281-934-6014
Pentair Pool Products Inc 1620 Hawkins Ave	Sanford	NC	27330	**800-831-7133**	919-566-8000
Red Jacket Div Veeder-Root 125 Powder Forest Dr	Simsbury	CT	06070	**800-873-3313**	860-651-2700
REDA PO Box 1181	Bartlesville	OK	74005	**800-331-0970**	918-661-2000
Roper Pump Co PO Box 269	Commerce	GA	30529	**800-944-6769***	706-335-5551
*Sales					
Roth Pump Co PO Box 4330	Rock Island	IL	61204	**888-444-7684**	309-787-1791
RS Corcoran Co 500 N Vine St	New Lenox	IL	60451	**800-637-1067**	815-485-2156
Scot Pump 6437 Pioneer Rd	Cedarburg	WI	53012	**888-835-0600**	262-377-7000
seepex Inc 511 Speedway Dr	Enon	OH	45323	**800-695-3659**	937-864-7150

Name / Address	City	State	ZIP	Toll-Free	Phone
Serfilco Ltd 2900 MacArthur Blvd	Northbrook	IL	60062	**800-323-5431**	847-559-1777
Sethco Div Met-Pro Corp 70 Arkay Dr	Hauppauge	NY	11788	**800-645-0500**	631-435-0530
SHURflo Pump Mfg Co Inc 5900 Katella Ave Suite A	Cypress	CA	90630	**800-854-3218**	562-795-5200
SPX Process Equipment 611 Sugar Creek Rd	Delavan	WI	53115	**800-252-5200**	262-728-1900
Standard Alloys & Mfg PO Box 969	Port Arthur	TX	77640	**800-231-8240**	409-983-3201
Sturm Rapid Response Center 1305 Main St	Barboursville	WV	25504	**800-624-3485**	304-736-3476
Syncroflo Inc 6700 Best Friend Rd	Norcross	GA	30071	**800-886-4443**	770-447-4443
Taco Inc 1160 Cranston St	Cranston	RI	02920	**800-822-6007**	401-942-8000
Thompson Pump & Mfg Co Inc 4620 City Ctr Dr	Port Orange	FL	32129	**800-767-7310**	386-767-7310
Tramco Pump Co 1500 W Adams St	Chicago	IL	60607	**877-872-6260**	312-243-5800
Tuthill Corp 8500 S Madison St	Burr Ridge	IL	60527	**800-888-4455**	630-382-4900
Vaughan Co Inc 364 Monte-Elma Rd	Montesano	WA	98563	**888-249-2467**	360-249-4042
Veeder-Root Red Jacket Div 125 Powder Forest Dr	Simsbury	CT	06070	**800-873-3313**	860-651-2700
Waterous Co 125 Hardman Ave	South Saint Paul	MN	55075	**800-488-1228**	651-450-5000
Waukesha Cherry-Burrell Corp 611 Sugar Creek Rd	Delavan	WI	53115	**800-252-5200**	262-728-1900
Whitten Pumps Inc 502 County Line Rd	Delano	CA	93215	**800-287-4578**	661-725-0250
Wilfley AR & Sons Inc 7350 E Progress Pl Suite 200	Englewood	CO	80111	**800-525-9930**	303-779-1777
Zoeller Co 3649 Kane Run Rd	Louisville	KY	40211	**800-928-7867**	502-778-2731

628 RACING & RACETRACKS

SEE ALSO Motor Speedways

Name / Address	City	State	ZIP	Toll-Free	Phone
Batavia Downs 8315 Park Rd	Batavia	NY	14020	**800-724-2000**	585-343-3750
Beulah Park Race Track 3664 Grant Ave	Grove City	OH	43123	**800-433-6905**	614-871-9600
Calder Race Course Inc 21001 NW 27th Ave	Miami	FL	33056	**800-333-3227**	305-625-1311
Canterbury Park Holding Corp 1100 Canterbury Rd *AMEX: ECP*	Shakopee	MN	55379	**800-340-6361**	952-445-7223
Charles Town Races & Slots US Rt 340	Charles Town	WV	25414	**800-795-7001**	
Colonial Holdings Inc 10515 Colonial Downs Pkwy	New Kent	VA	23124	**888-482-8722**	804-966-7223
Columbus Races 822 15th St	Columbus	NE	68601	**800-314-2983**	402-564-0133
Dairyland Greyhound Park 5522 104th Ave	Kenosha	WI	53144	**800-233-3357**	262-657-8200
Delaware North Cos Gaming & Entertainment 40 Fountain Plaza	Buffalo	NY	14202	**800-828-7240**	716-858-5000
Delaware Park Racetrack & Slots Casino 777 Delaware Pk Blvd	Wilmington	DE	19804	**800-417-5687**	302-994-2521
Delaware Racing Assn 777 Delaware Park Blvd. *Mktg	Wilmington	DE	19804	**800-441-6587***	302-994-2521
Delta Downs Racing Assn Inc 2717 Delta Downs Dr	Vinton	LA	70668	**800-589-7441**	337-589-7441
Dover Downs Gaming & Entertainment Inc 1131 N DuPont Hwy *NYSE: DDE*	Dover	DE	19901	**800-711-5882**	302-674-4600
Dover Motorsports Inc 1131 N Dupont Hwy *NYSE: DVD*	Dover	DE	19901	**800-441-7223**	302-674-4600
Dubuque Greyhound Park & Casino 1855 Greyhound Park Dr	Dubuque	IA	52001	**800-373-3647**	563-582-3647
Fair Grounds Corp 1751 Gentilly Blvd	New Orleans	LA	70119	**800-786-0010**	504-944-5515
Greenetrack Greyhound Park I-59 at Exit 45 - Union Rd PO Drawer 471	Eutaw	AL	35462	**800-633-5942**	205-372-9318
Hawthorne Race Course 3501 S Laramie Ave	Cicero	IL	60804	**800-780-0701**	708-780-3700
Hoosier Park 4500 Dan Patch Cir	Anderson	IN	46013	**800-526-7223**	765-642-7223
Jackson Harness Raceway 200 W Ganson St	Jackson	MI	49201	**877-316-0283**	517-788-4500
Laurel Racing Assn Inc Rt 198 & Racetrack Rd	Laurel	MD	20724	**800-638-1859**	301-725-0400
Lone Star Park at Grand Prairie 1000 Lone Star Pkwy	Grand Prairie	TX	75050	**800-795-7223**	972-263-7223
Maywood Park 8600 W North Ave	Melrose Park	IL	60160	**800-748-5782**	708-343-4800
MetraPark 308 6th Ave N PO Box 2514	Billings	MT	59103	**800-366-8538**	406-256-2422
Midstate Raceway Inc 14 Ruth St PO Box 860	Vernon	NY	13476	**877-777-8559**	315-829-2201
Mountaineer Racetrack Rt 2 PO Box 358	Chester	WV	26034	**800-804-0468**	304-387-2400
MTR Gaming Group Inc PO Box 358 *NASDAQ: MNTG*	Chester	WV	26034	**800-804-0468**	304-387-8300
Multnomah Greyhound Park PO Box 9	Fairview	OR	97024	**800-888-7576**	503-667-7700
Oaklawn Park 2705 Central Ave	Hot Springs	AR	71901	**800-625-5296**	501-623-4411
Pacific Racing Assn Inc 1100 Eastshore Hwy	Albany	CA	94706	**800-675-7001**	510-559-7300
Portland Meadows Horse Track 1001 N Schmeer Rd	Portland	OR	97217	**800-944-3127**	503-285-9144
Rosecroft Raceway 6336 Rosecroft Dr	Fort Washington	MD	20744	**877-818-9467**	301-567-4000
Saginaw Harness Raceway 2701 E Genesee St	Saginaw	MI	48601	**800-636-7223**	989-755-3451
Sam Houston Race Park 7575 N Sam Houston Pkwy W	Houston	TX	77064	**800-807-7223**	281-807-7223
Southland Racing Corp 1550 N Ingram Blvd	West Memphis	AR	72301	**800-467-6182**	870-735-3670
Sunflower Racing Inc 9700 Leavenworth Rd	Kansas City	KS	66109	**800-695-7223**	913-299-9797
Tampa Bay Downs Inc 11225 Racetrack Rd	Tampa	FL	33626	**800-200-4434**	813-855-4401
Vernon Downs 14 Ruth St	Vernon	NY	13476	**877-777-8559**	315-829-2201
Woodlands The 9700 Leavenworth Rd	Kansas City	KS	66109	**800-695-7223**	913-299-3434

629 RADIO COMPANIES

Name / Address	City	State	ZIP	Toll-Free	Phone
American Family Radio PO Drawer 2440	Tupelo	MS	38803	**800-326-4543**	662-844-8888
Bible Broadcasting Network Inc 11530 Carmel Commons Blvd	Charlotte	NC	28226	**800-888-7077**	704-523-5555
Bott Radio Network 10550 Barkley St	Overland Park	KS	66212	**800-875-1903**	913-642-7770
Bristol Broadcasting Co Inc PO Box 1389	Bristol	VA	24203	**800-253-8112**	276-669-8112
Canadian Broadcasting Corp (CBC) 181 Queen St	Ottawa	ON	K1P1K9	**866-306-4636**	613-288-6000
CBC (Canadian Broadcasting Corp) 181 Queen St	Ottawa	ON	K1P1K9	**866-306-4636**	613-288-6000
Clear Channel Radio 200 E Basse Rd	San Antonio	TX	78209	**888-937-6131**	210-822-2828
Communications Corp of America 700 Saint John St Suite 300	Lafayette	LA	70501	**800-237-1142**	337-237-1142
CSN International PO Box 391	Twin Falls	ID	83303	**800-357-4226**	208-734-2049
Educational Media Foundation 5700 W Oaks Blvd	Rocklin	CA	95765	**800-434-8400**	916-251-1600
Family Life Broadcasting System DBA Family Life Radio 7355 N Oracle Rd	Tucson	AZ	85704	**800-776-1070**	520-742-6976
Family Radio 290 Hegenberger Rd	Oakland	CA	94621	**800-543-1495**	510-568-6200
Family Stations Radio Network 290 Hegenberger Rd	Oakland	CA	94621	**800-543-1495**	510-568-6200
Far East Broadcasting Co Inc PO Box 1	La Mirada	CA	90637	**800-523-3480**	562-947-4651
Fisher Communications Inc 100 4th Ave N Suite 510 *NASDAQ: FSCI*	Seattle	WA	98109	**800-443-0073**	206-404-7000
Georgia Public Broadcasting (GPB) 260 14th St NW	Atlanta	GA	30318	**800-222-6006**	404-685-2400
GPB (Georgia Public Broadcasting) 260 14th St NW	Atlanta	GA	30318	**800-222-6006**	404-685-2400
Metropolitan Radio Group Inc 2010 S Stewart Ave	Springfield	MO	65804	**800-961-5595**	417-862-0852
Midwest Communications Inc 904 Grand Ave	Wausau	WI	54403	**877-903-2171**	715-842-1437
Minnesota Public Radio (MPR) 45 E 7th St	Saint Paul	MN	55101	**800-228-7123**	651-290-1212
Morris Communications Co LLC 725 Broad St	Augusta	GA	30901	**800-622-6358**	706-724-0851
MPR (Minnesota Public Radio) 45 E 7th St	Saint Paul	MN	55101	**800-228-7123**	651-290-1212
Northern Star Broadcasting LLC 1356 Mackinaw Ave	Cheboygan	MI	49721	**888-847-2346**	231-627-2341
Pamplin Communications Corp 10209 SE Division St	Portland	OR	97266	**866-233-7102**	503-251-1597
Saga Communications Inc 73 Kercheval Ave *NYSE: SGA*	Grosse Pointe Farms	MI	48236	**888-886-7070**	313-886-7070
Shamrock Communications Inc 149 Penn Ave	Scranton	PA	18503	**800-228-4637**	570-348-9108
Susquehanna Radio Corp 140 E Market St	York	PA	17401	**800-367-8261**	717-848-5500
Waitt Media Inc 1125 S 103rd St Suite 200	Omaha	NE	68124	**888-656-0634**	402-697-8000
Withers Broadcasting Co PO Box 1508	Mount Vernon	IL	62864	**800-333-1577**	618-242-3500

630 RADIO NETWORKS

Name / Address	City	State	ZIP	Toll-Free	Phone
American Family Radio PO Drawer 2440	Tupelo	MS	38803	**800-326-4543**	662-844-8888
American Public Media 45 7th St E	Saint Paul	MN	55101	**877-276-8400**	651-290-1225
AP Broadcast Services 1825 K St NW Suite 800	Washington	DC	20006	**800-821-4747**	202-736-1100
Bible Broadcasting Network Inc 11530 Carmel Commons Blvd	Charlotte	NC	28226	**800-888-7077**	704-523-5555
Bloomberg Radio Network 499 Park Ave 15th Fl	New York	NY	10022	**800-448-5678**	212-318-2350
Bott Radio Network 10550 Barkley St	Overland Park	KS	66212	**800-875-1903**	913-642-7770
CSN International PO Box 391	Twin Falls	ID	83303	**800-357-4226**	208-734-2049
Family Life Broadcasting System DBA Family Life Radio 7355 N Oracle Rd	Tucson	AZ	85704	**800-776-1070**	520-742-6976
Family Life Communications Inc PO Box 35300	Tucson	AZ	85740	**800-776-1070**	520-742-6976
Family Radio 290 Hegenberger Rd	Oakland	CA	94621	**800-543-1495**	510-568-6200
Family Stations Radio Network 290 Hegenberger Rd	Oakland	CA	94621	**800-543-1495**	510-568-6200
Far East Broadcasting Co Inc PO Box 1	La Mirada	CA	90637	**800-523-3480**	562-947-4651
Jones International Ltd 9697 E Mineral Ave	Englewood	CO	80112	**800-525-7002**	303-792-3111
Jones Media Networks Ltd 9697 E Mineral Ave	Englewood	CO	80112	**800-525-7000**	303-792-3111
New Dimensions Radio Broadcasting Network PO Box 569	Ukiah	CA	95482	**800-935-8273**	707-468-5215
Radio America 1030 15th St NW Suite 1040	Washington	DC	20005	**800-807-4703**	202-408-0944
Sirius Satellite Radio Inc 1221 Ave of the Americas *NASDAQ: SIRI*	New York	NY	10020	**888-539-7474**	212-584-5100
Tiger Financial News Network 2401 W Bay Dr Suite 126	Largo	FL	33770	**877-518-9190**	727-518-9190
Tribune Radio Network 435 N Michigan Ave	Chicago	IL	60611	**800-654-8597**	312-222-3342
XM Satellite Radio Holdings Inc 1500 Eckington Pl NE *NASDAQ: XMSR*	Washington	DC	20002	**877-967-2346**	202-380-4000

631 RADIO STATIONS

SEE ALSO Internet Broadcasting

Name / Address	City	State	ZIP	Toll-Free	Phone
CHIN-AM 1540 (Ethnic) 622 College St	Toronto	ON	M6G1B6	**888-944-2446**	416-531-9991
CHIN-FM 100.7 (Ethnic) 622 College St	Toronto	ON	M6G1B6	**888-944-2446**	416-531-9991
CHQR-AM 770 (N/T) 630 3rd Ave SW Suite 105	Calgary	AB	T2P4L4	**800-563-7770**	403-716-6500
CHRI-FM 99.1 (Rel) 1010 Thomas Spratt Pl Suite 3	Ottawa	ON	K1G5L5	**866-247-1440**	613-247-1440
CJRT-FM 91.1 (Jazz) 150 Mutual St	Toronto	ON	M5B2M1	**888-595-0404**	416-595-0404
CKIK-FM 107.3 (CHR) 630 3rd Ave SW Suite 105	Calgary	AB	T2P4L4	**800-563-7770**	403-716-6500
CKRY-FM 105.1 (Ctry) 630 3rd Ave SW Suite 105	Calgary	AB	T2P4L4	**800-563-7770**	403-716-6500
KACV-FM 89.9 (Alt) 2408 S Jackson St	Amarillo	TX	79109	**800-766-0176**	806-371-5222
KAFF-AM 930 (Ctry) 1117 W Rt 66	Flagstaff	AZ	86001	**888-893-5646**	928-774-5231
KAFF-FM 92.9 (Ctry) 1117 W Rt 66	Flagstaff	AZ	86001	**888-412-5233**	928-774-5231
KAJA-FM 97.3 (Ctry) 6222 NW IH-10	San Antonio	TX	78201	**800-707-5597**	210-736-9700
KAMA-AM 750 (Span) 2211 E Missouri Ave Suite S-300	El Paso	TX	79903	**800-880-9797**	915-544-9797
KANU-FM 91.5 (NPR) 1120 W 11th St University of Kansas	Lawrence	KS	66044	**888-577-5268**	785-864-4530
KATZ-FM 100.3 (Urban) 1001 Highlands Plaza Dr W Suite 100	Saint Louis	MO	63110	**800-541-0036**	314-333-8300
KAZU-FM 90.3 (NPR) 167 Central Ave PO Box 210	Pacific Grove	CA	93950	**800-903-6624**	831-375-7275
KBHE-FM 89.3 (NPR) 555 N Dakota St	Vermillion	SD	57069	**800-456-0766**	605-677-5861
KBIA-FM 91.3 (NPR) 409 Jesse Hall	Columbia	MO	65211	**800-292-9136**	573-882-3431

	City	State	Zip	Toll-Free	Phone
KBIG-FM 104.3 (AC)					
3400 W Olive Ave Suite 550	Burbank	CA	91505	**800-524-4104**	818-559-2252
KBLG-AM 910 (N/T) 2075 Central Ave	Billings	MT	59102	**866-627-5483**	406-652-8400
KBLX-FM 102.9 (Urban AC)					
55 Hawthorne St Suite 900	San Francisco	CA	94105	**800-683-5259**	415-284-1029
KBMX-FM 107.7 (AC) 14 E Central Entrance	Duluth	MN	55811	**866-266-2649**	218-727-4500
KBNA-FM 97.5 (Span AC)					
2211 E Missouri Ave Suite S-300	El Paso	TX	79903	**800-880-9797**	915-544-9797
KBSG-FM 97.3 (Oldies) 1820 Eastlake Ave E	Seattle	WA	98102	**877-668-9797**	206-726-7000
KBSX-FM 91.5 (NPR) 1910 University Dr	Boise	ID	83725	**888-859-5278**	208-947-5660
KCBS-AM 740 (N/T)					
865 Battery St 3rd Fl	San Francisco	CA	94111	**800-400-3697**	415-765-4000
KCFR-AM 1340 (NPR) 7409 S Alton Ct	Centennial	CO	80112	**800-722-4449**	303-871-9191
KCLR-FM 99.3 (Ctry)					
3215 Lemone Industrial Blvd Suite 200	Columbia	MO	65201	**800-455-5257**	573-875-1099
KCMP-FM 89.3 (NPR) 45 E 7th St	Saint Paul	MN	55101	**888-798-9225**	651-290-1212
KCMQ-FM 96.7 (CR)					
3215 Lemone Industrial Blvd Suite 200	Columbia	MO	65201	**800-455-1967**	573-875-1099
KCMS-FM 105.3 (Rel) 19303 Fremont Ave N	Shoreline	WA	98133	**877-275-1053**	206-546-7350
KCND-FM 90.5 (NPR) 1814 N 15th St	Bismarck	ND	58501	**800-359-5566**	701-224-1700
KCOL-AM 600 (N/T) 1612 LaPorte Ave	Fort Collins	CO	80521	**866-888-5449**	970-482-5991
KCPW-FM 88.3 (NPR) PO Box 510730	Salt Lake Cityu	UT	84151	**888-359-5279**	801-359-5279
KCRW-FM 89.9 (NPR) 1900 Pico Blvd	Santa Monica	CA	90405	**888-600-5279**	310-450-5183
KCSD-FM 90.9 (NPR) PO Box 5000	Vermillion	SD	57069	**800-456-0766**	605-677-5861
KDAL-AM 610 (N/T) 715 E Central Entrance	Duluth	MN	55811	**888-532-5610**	218-722-4321
KDAL-FM 95.7 (AC) 715 E Central Entrance	Duluth	MN	55811	**800-532-5610**	218-722-4321
KDAQ-FM 89.9 (NPR) 1 University Pl	Shreveport	LA	71115	**800-552-8502**	318-797-5150
KDNW-FM 97.3 (Rel) 1101 E Central Entrance	Duluth	MN	55811	**888-322-5369**	218-722-6700
KDON-FM 102.5 (CHR) 903 N Main St	Salinas	CA	93906	**888-558-5366**	831-755-8181
KDSU-FM 91.9 (NPR)					
1301 12th Ave N NDSU Memorial Union Bldg	Fargo	ND	58102	**800-359-6900**	701-241-6900
KDVV-FM 100.3 (Rock)					
825 S Kansas Ave Suite 100	Topeka	KS	66612	**866-297-1003**	785-272-2122
KEAN-FM 105.1 (Ctry) 3911 S 1st St	Abilene	TX	79605	**800-588-5326**	325-676-7711
KEDT-FM 90.3 (NPR)					
4455 S Padre Island Dr Suite 38	Corpus Christi	TX	78411	**800-307-5338**	361-855-2213
KELO-AM 1320 (N/T) 500 S Phillips Ave	Sioux Falls	SD	57104	**800-888-5356**	605-331-5350
KEMC-FM 91.7 (NPR) 1500 University Dr	Billings	MT	59101	**800-441-2941**	406-657-2941
KERA-FM 90.1 (NPR) 3000 Harry Hines Blvd	Dallas	TX	75201	**800-456-5372**	214-871-1390
KERN-AM 1410 (N/T)					
1400 Easton Dr Suite 144	Bakersfield	CA	93309	**800-840-5376**	661-328-1410
KEX-AM 1190 (Var) 4949 SW Macadam Ave	Portland	OR	97239	**800-990-0750**	503-225-1190
KFAL-AM 900 (Ctry) 1805 Westminster Ave	Fulton	MO	65251	**800-769-5274**	573-642-3341
KFFG-FM 97.7 (AAA)					
55 Hawthorne St Suite 1100	San Francisco	CA	94105	**800-300-5364**	415-543-1045
KFIS-FM 104.1 (Rel)					
6400 SE Lake Rd Suite 350	Portland	OR	97222	**866-320-1041**	503-786-0600
KFLX-FM 105.1 (AAA) 112 E Rt 66 Suite 105	Flagstaff	AZ	86001	**877-600-5359**	928-779-1177
KFMB-AM 760 (N/T) 7677 Engineer Rd	San Diego	CA	92111	**800-760-5362**	858-292-7600
KFNK-FM 104.9 (Alt)					
351 Elliott Ave W Suite 300	Seattle	WA	98119	**800-482-1049**	206-494-2000
KFNW-FM 97.9 (Rel) 5702 52nd Ave S	Fargo	ND	58104	**800-979-1200**	701-282-5910
KFOG-FM 104.5 (AAA)					
55 Hawthorne St Suite 1100	San Francisco	CA	94105	**800-300-5304**	415-543-1045
KFPW-AM 1230 (AC) 321 N Greenwood Ave	Fort Smith	AR	72901	**800-352-1047**	479-783-5379
KFRC-AM 610 (Oldies) 865 Battery St	San Francisco	CA	94111	**888-456-5372**	415-391-9970
KFRC-FM 99.7 (Oldies)					
875 Battery St 4th Fl	San Francisco	CA	94111	**888-456-5372**	415-391-9970
KFSH-FM 95.9 (Rel)					
701 N Brand Blvd Suite 550	Glendale	CA	91203	**866-347-4959**	818-956-5552
KFUO-FM 99.1 (Clas) 85 Founders Ln	Clayton	MO	63105	**800-844-0524**	314-505-7899
KGGN-AM 890 (Rel)					
1734 E 63rd St Suite 600	Kansas City	MO	64110	**800-924-3177**	816-333-0092
KGMS-AM 940 (Rel) 3222 S Richey Ave	Tucson	AZ	85713	**866-725-5467**	520-790-2440
KGNC-AM 710 (N/T) PO Box 710	Amarillo	TX	79189	**800-285-0710**	806-355-9801
KGNC-FM 97.9 (Ctry) PO Box 710	Amarillo	TX	79189	**877-765-9790**	806-355-9801
KGNZ-FM 88.1 (Rel) 542 Butternut St	Abilene	TX	79602	**800-588-8801**	325-673-3045
KGON-FM 92.3 (CR) 0700 SW Bancroft St	Portland	OR	97239	**800-222-9236**	503-223-1441
KGY-AM 1240 (AC) 1700 Marine Dr NW	Olympia	WA	98501	**800-310-7625**	360-943-1240
KGY-FM 96.9 (Ctry) 1700 Marine Dr NW	Olympia	WA	98501	**800-310-7625**	360-943-1240
KHAK-FM 98.1 (Ctry)					
425 2nd St SE 4th Fl	Cedar Rapids	IA	52401	**800-747-5425**	319-365-9431
KHAR-AM 590 (Nost)					
301 Arctic Slope Ave Suite 300	Anchorage	AK	99518	**800-896-1669**	907-344-9622
KHCC-FM 90.1 (NPR)					
815 N Walnut St Suite 300	Hutchinson	KS	67501	**800-723-4657**	620-662-6646
KHHO-AM 850 (Sports)					
351 Elliott Ave W Suite 300	Seattle	WA	98119	**877-829-0850**	206-285-2295
KHOZ-FM 102.9 (Ctry) 1111 Radio Ave	Harrison	AR	72601	**800-553-6103**	870-741-3103
KHVN-AM 970 (Rel)					
5787 S Hampton Rd Suite 285	Dallas	TX	75232	**866-856-5447**	972-572-5447
KINK-FM 101.9 (AAA) 1501 SW Jefferson St	Portland	OR	97201	**877-567-5465**	503-517-6000
KIOI-FM 101.3 (AC)					
340 Townsend St 4th Fl	San Francisco	CA	94107	**800-800-1013**	415-975-5555
KIQK-FM 104.1 (Ctry)					
306 1/2 E Saint Joseph St	Rapid City	SD	57701	**800-456-2613**	605-343-0888
KISQ-FM 98.1 (Urban AC)					
340 Townsend St 4th Fl	San Francisco	CA	94107	**888-354-7736**	415-975-5555
KIXI-AM 880 (Nost)					
3650 131st Ave SE Suite 550	Bellevue	WA	98006	**866-880-5494**	425-373-5536
KIYX-FM 106.1 (AC) PO Box 1	Platteville	WI	53818	**800-362-2224**	608-348-2775
KJMN-FM 92.1 (Span AC) 777 Grant St 5th Fl	Denver	CO	80203	**888-874-2656**	303-832-0050
KJR-AM 950 (Sports)					
351 Elliott Ave W Suite 300	Seattle	WA	98119	**800-829-0950**	206-285-2295
KJTY-FM 88.1 (Rel) 1005 SW 10th St	Topeka	KS	66604	**888-569-5589**	785-357-8888
KJZZ-FM 91.5 (NPR) 2323 W 14th St	Tempe	AZ	85281	**800-266-1111**	480-834-5627
KKAD-AM 1550 (Nost)					
888 SW 5th Ave Suite 790	Portland	OR	97204	**866-517-1550**	503-228-5523
KKCB-FM 105.1 (Ctry) 14 E Central Entrance	Duluth	MN	55811	**800-928-2105**	218-727-4500
KKDV-FM 95.7 (Ctry)					
201 3rd St Suite 1200	San Francisco	CA	94103	**800-905-9570**	415-957-0957
KKHT-AM 1070 (Rel)					
6161 Savoy St Suite 1200	Houston	TX	77036	**800-625-1070**	713-260-3600
KKJZ-FM 88.1 (Jazz)					
1288 N Bellflower Blvd	Long Beach	CA	90815	**800-767-3688**	562-985-5566
KKRZ-FM 100.3 (CHR) 4949 SW Macadam Ave	Portland	OR	97239	**888-843-0100**	503-225-1190
KKSF-FM 103.7 (NAC)					
340 Townsend St 4th Fl	San Francisco	CA	94107	**866-900-1037**	415-975-5555
KLDJ-FM 101.7 (Oldies) 14 E Central Entrance	Duluth	MN	55811	**888-564-1017**	218-727-4500
KLJC-FM 88.5 (Rel) 15800 Calvary Rd	Kansas City	MO	64147	**800-466-5552**	816-331-8700
KLLC-FM 97.3 (AC) 865 Battery St 3rd Fl	San Francisco	CA	94111	**800-400-3697**	415-765-4000
KLNV-FM 106.5 (Span)					
600 W Broadway Suite 2150	San Diego	CA	92101	**877-570-1065**	619-235-0600

	City	State	Zip	Toll-Free	Phone
KLNZ-FM 103.5 (Span)					
501 N 44th St Suite 425	Phoenix	AZ	85008	**888-874-2656**	602-266-2005
KLO-AM 1430 (N/T)					
4155 Harrison Blvd Suite 206	Ogden	UT	84403	**866-627-1430**	801-627-1430
KLOB-FM 94.7 (Span)					
41601 Corporate Way	Palm Desert	CA	92260	**888-331-2667**	760-341-5837
KLOK-FM 99.5 (Span) 67 Garden Ct	Monterey	CA	93940	**888-874-2656**	831-333-9735
KLOS-FM 95.5 (CR)					
3321 S La Cienega Blvd	Los Angeles	CA	90016	**800-955-5567**	310-840-4900
KLQV-FM 102.9 (Span AC)					
600 W Broadway Suite 2150	San Diego	CA	92101	**877-570-1065**	619-235-0600
KLSE-FM 91.7 (Clas)					
206 S Broadway Suite 735	Rochester	MN	55904	**800-652-9700**	507-282-0910
KLSY-FM 92.5 (AC)					
3650 131st Ave SE Suite 550	Bellevue	WA	98006	**866-649-9250**	425-653-9462
KLTY-FM 94.9 (Rel)					
6400 N Beltline Rd Suite 120	Irving	TX	75063	**866-562-1949**	972-870-9949
KMAJ-AM 1440 (N/T)					
825 S Kansas Ave Suite 100	Topeka	KS	66612	**877-297-1077**	785-272-2122
KMAJ-FM 107.7 (AC)					
825 S Kansas Ave Suite 100	Topeka	KS	66612	**877-297-1077**	785-272-2122
KMBX-AM 700 (Span Oldies) 67 Garden Ct	Monterey	CA	93940	**866-434-4084**	831-333-9735
KMEL-FM 106.1 (Urban)					
340 Townsend St 4th Fl	San Francisco	CA	94107	**800-955-5635**	415-975-5555
KMFC-FM 92.1 (Rel) 1249 E Hwy 22	Centralia	MO	65240	**800-769-5632**	573-682-5525
KMGN-FM 93.9 (CR) 1117 W Rt 66	Flagstaff	AZ	86001	**888-893-5646**	928-774-5231
KMPS-FM 94.1 (Ctry)					
1000 Dexter Ave N Suite 100	Seattle	WA	98109	**800-464-9436**	206-805-1100
KMTT-FM 103.7 (AAA)					
1100 Olive Way Suite 1650	Seattle	WA	98101	**800-676-5688**	206-233-1037
KMVP-AM 860 (Sports) 5300 N Central Ave	Phoenix	AZ	85012	**800-729-3776**	602-274-6200
KMXA-AM 1090 (Span) 777 Grant St 5th Fl	Denver	CO	80203	**888-874-2656**	303-832-0050
KNDD-FM 107.7 (Alt)					
1100 Olive Way Suite 1650	Seattle	WA	98101	**800-423-1077**	206-622-3251
KNDR-FM 104.7 (Rel) 1400 NE 3rd St	Mandan	ND	58554	**800-767-5095**	701-663-2345
KNIS-FM 91.3 (Rel) 6363 Hwy 50 E	Carson City	NV	89701	**800-541-5647**	775-883-5647
KNLE-FM 88.1 (Rel)					
12703 Research Blvd Suite 222	Austin	TX	78759	**800-322-5653**	512-257-8881
KNML-AM 610 (Sports)					
500 4th St NW Suite 500	Albuquerque	NM	87102	**888-922-0610**	505-767-6700
KNOW-FM 91.1 (NPR) 45 E 7th St	Saint Paul	MN	55101	**800-228-7123**	651-290-1500
KNRK-FM 94.7 (Alt) 0700 SW Bancroft St	Portland	OR	97239	**800-777-0947**	503-223-1441
KOCN-FM 105.1 (Urban) 903 N Main St	Salinas	CA	93906	**888-896-5626**	831-755-8181
KOIT-AM 1260 (AC)					
201 3rd St Suite 1200	San Francisco	CA	94103	**800-564-8965**	415-777-0965
KOIT-FM 96.5 (AC)					
201 3rd St Suite 1200	San Francisco	CA	94103	**800-564-8965**	415-777-0965
KOMO-AM 1000 (N/T) 140 4th Ave N Suite 340	Seattle	WA	98109	**877-869-6469**	206-404-4000
KPBX-FM 91.1 (NPR) 2319 N Monroe St	Spokane	WA	99205	**800-328-5729**	509-328-5729
KPDQ-FM 93.7 (Rel)					
6400 SE Lake Rd Suite 350	Portland	OR	97222	**800-845-2162**	503-786-0600
KPLU-FM 88.5 (NPR)					
Pacific Lutheran University	Tacoma	WA	98447	**800-677-5758**	253-535-7758
KPLZ-FM 101.5 (AC) 140 4th Ave N Suite 340	Seattle	WA	98109	**888-821-1015**	206-404-4000
KPOJ-AM 620 (N/T) 4949 SW Macadam Ave	Portland	OR	97239	**866-452-0620**	503-225-1190
KPRF-FM 98.7 (CHR) 6214 W 34th St	Amarillo	TX	79109	**888-368-1212**	806-355-9777
KPSI-FM 100.5 (AC)					
2100 Tahquitz Canyon Way	Palm Springs	CA	92262	**877-282-2648**	760-325-2582
KQBZ-FM 100.7 (N/T)					
1100 Olive Way suite 1650	Seattle	WA	98101	**888-647-1007**	206-285-7625
KQCV-AM 800 (Rel) 1919 N Broadway	Oklahoma City	OK	73103	**888-909-5728**	405-521-0800
KQV-AM 1410 (N/T)					
650 Smithfield St Centre City Towers	Pittsburgh	PA	15222	**800-424-1410**	412-562-5900
KRCC-FM 91.5 (NPR)					
912 N Weber St	Colorado Springs	CO	80903	**800-748-2727**	719-473-4801
KRKX-FM 94.1 (Rock) 2075 Central Ave	Billings	MT	59102	**866-627-5483**	406-652-8400
KRLD-AM 1080 (N/T) 1080 Ballpark Way	Arlington	TX	76011	**800-289-1080**	817-543-5400
KROL-FM 99.5 (Rel) 6900 Commerce St	El Paso	TX	79915	**800-840-5765**	915-779-0016
KRSK-FM 105.1 (AC) 0700 SW Bancroft St	Portland	OR	97239	**888-733-5105**	503-223-1441
KRTH-FM 101.1 (Oldies)					
5670 Wilshire Blvd Suite 200	Los Angeles	CA	90036	**800-232-5834**	323-936-5784
KRVS-FM 88.7 (NPR) PO Box 42171	Lafayette	LA	70504	**800-892-6827**	337-482-5787
KRWG-FM 90.7 (NPR) PO Box 3000	Las Cruces	NM	88003	**800-245-5794**	505-646-4525
KRZN-FM 96.3 (Rock) 2075 Central Ave	Billings	MT	59102	**866-627-5483**	406-652-8400
KSAN-FM 107.7 (CR)					
55 Hawthorne St Suite 1100	San Francisco	CA	94105	**888-303-2663**	415-981-5726
KSED-FM 107.5 (Ctry) 112 E Rt 66 Suite 105	Flagstaff	AZ	86001	**800-799-5658**	928-779-1177
KSES-FM 107.1 (Span) 67 Garden Ct	Monterey	CA	93942	**866-434-4084**	831-333-9735
KSGN-FM 89.7 (Rel) 11498 Pierce St	Riverside	CA	92505	**800-321-5746**	951-687-5746
KSHE-FM 94.7 (Rock)					
800 St Louis Union Stn	Saint Louis	MO	63103	**800-842-5743**	314-621-0095
KSKY-AM 660 (N/T)					
6400 N Beltline Rd Suite 110	Irving	TX	75063	**800-949-5973**	214-561-9660
KSLZ-FM 107.7 (CHR)					
1001 Highlands Plaza Dr W Suite 1100	Saint Louis	MO	63110	**888-570-1077**	314-333-8000
KSMB-FM 94.5 (CHR) 202 Galbert Rd	Lafayette	LA	70506	**800-299-2100**	337-232-1311
KSMS-FM 90.5 (NPR)					
Southwest Missouri State University 901 S National Ave	Springfield	MO	65804	**800-767-5768**	417-836-5878
KSMU-FM 91.1 (NPR)					
Southwest Missouri State University 901 S National Ave	Springfield	MO	65804	**800-767-5768**	417-836-5878
KSOL-FM 98.9 (Span)					
750 Battery St Suite 200	San Francisco	CA	94111	**888-880-5765**	415-733-5765
KSON-FM 97.3 (Ctry)					
1615 Murray Canyon Rd Suite 710	San Diego	CA	92108	**800-243-1973**	619-291-9797
KSTX-FM 89.1 (NPR)					
8401 Datapoint Dr Suite 800	San Antonio	TX	78229	**800-622-8977**	210-614-8977
KSWV-AM 810 (Span) 102 Taos St	Santa Fe	NM	87505	**800-794-5798**	505-989-7441
KTCY-FM 101.7 (Span CHR)					
5307 E Mockingbird Ln Suite 500	Dallas	TX	75206	**800-420-2757**	214-887-9107
KTLI-FM 99.1 (Rel)					
125 N Market St Suite 1900	Wichita	KS	67202	**800-525-5683**	316-303-9999
KTNO-AM 1440 (Span Rel)					
5787 S Hampton Rd Suite 340	Dallas	TX	75232	**877-292-2431**	214-330-5866
KTOM-FM 92.7 (Ctry) 903 N Main St	Salinas	CA	93906	**888-660-5866**	831-755-8181
KTOO-FM 104.3 (NPR) 360 Egan Dr	Juneau	AK	99801	**800-870-5866**	907-586-1670
KTOQ-AM 1340 (N/T)					
306 1/2 E Saint Joseph St	Rapid City	SD	57701	**800-456-2613**	605-343-0888
KTPK-FM 106.9 (Ctry) 2121 SW Chelsea Dr	Topeka	KS	66614	**888-291-1069**	785-273-1069
KTRR-FM 102.5 (AC) 600 Main St	Windsor	CO	80550	**800-964-1025**	970-686-2791
KTRS-AM 550 (N/T) 638 W Port Plaza	Saint Louis	MO	63146	**888-550-5877**	314-453-5500
KTSA-AM 550 (N/T) 4050 Eisenhauer Rd	San Antonio	TX	78218	**800-299-5872**	210-599-5500
KTSD-FM 91.1 (NPR) PO Box 5000	Vermillion	SD	57069	**800-456-0766**	605-677-5861

Station / Address	City	State	Zip	Toll-Free	Phone
KTTS-FM 94.7 (Ctry) 2330 W Grand St	Springfield	MO	65802	**800-765-5887**	417-865-6614
KTXR-FM 101.3 (AC) 3000 E Chestnut Expy	Springfield	MO	65802	**800-749-8001**	417-862-3751
KTXY-FM 106.9 (AC)					
3215 Lemone Industrial Blvd Suite 200	Columbia	MO	65201	**800-500-9107**	573-875-1099
KUAD-FM 99.1 (Ctry) 600 Main St	Windsor	CO	80550	**800-500-2599**	970-686-2791
KUAF-FM 91.3 (NPR)					
747 W Dickson St Suite 2	Fayetteville	AR	72701	**800-522-5823**	479-575-2556
KUAR-FM 89.1 (NPR) 2801 S University Ave	Little Rock	AR	72204	**800-952-2528**	501-569-8485
KUAT-FM 90.5 (Clas) PO Box 210067	Tucson	AZ	85721	**800-521-5828**	520-621-5828
KUAZ-FM 89.1 (NPR) PO Box 210067	Tucson	AZ	85721	**800-521-5828**	520-621-5828
KUBE-FM 93.3 (CHR) 351 Elliott Ave W	Seattle	WA	98119	**877-933-9393**	206-285-2295
KUCV-FM 91.1 (Var) 1800 N 33rd St	Lincoln	NE	68583	**800-290-6850**	402-472-2200
KUER-FM 90.1 (NPR)					
101 S Wasatch Dr Rm 270	Salt Lake City	UT	84112	**800-313-5937**	801-581-6625
KUFO-FM 101.1 (Rock) 2040 SW 1st Ave	Portland	OR	97201	**800-344-5836**	503-222-1011
KUHM-FM 91.7 (NPR)					
32 Campus Dr University of Montana	Missoula	MT	59812	**800-325-1565**	406-243-4931
KULL-FM 92.5 (Oldies) 3911 S 1st St	Abilene	TX	79605	**800-659-1965**	325-676-7711
KUMD-FM 103.3 (Var) 1201 Ordean Ct Rm 130	Duluth	MN	55812	**800-566-5863**	218-726-7181
KUND-FM 89.3 (NPR) PO Box 8117	Grand Forks	ND	58202	**800-359-6900**	701-777-4595
KUOP-FM 91.3 (NPR) 7055 Folsom Blvd	Sacramento	CA	95826	**800-800-5867**	916-278-8900
KUOW-FM 94.9 (NPR)					
4518 University Way NE Suite 310	Seattle	WA	98105	**800-289-5869**	206-543-2710
KUSP-FM 88.9 (NPR) 203 8th Ave	Santa Cruz	CA	95026	**800-655-5877**	831-476-2800
KUT-FM 90.5 (NPR)					
University of Texas 1 University Station					
Box A-0704	Austin	TX	78712	**800-435-8836**	512-471-1631
KUVO-FM 89.3 (Jazz) PO Box 2040	Denver	CO	80201	**800-574-5886**	303-480-9272
KUWJ-FM 90.3 (NPR) PO Box 3984	Laramie	WY	82071	**800-729-5897**	307-766-4240
KUWR-FM 91.9 (NPR)					
1000 E University Ave Dept 3984	Laramie	WY	82071	**800-729-5897**	307-766-4240
KUWS-FM 91.3 (NPR)					
1800 Grand Ave PO Box 2000	Superior	WI	54880	**800-300-8530**	715-394-8530
KVI-AM 570 (N/T) 140 4th Ave N Suite 340	Seattle	WA	98109	**888-421-5757**	206-404-4000
KVLC-FM 101.1 (Oldies)					
105 E Idaho Ave Suite B	Las Cruces	NM	88005	**800-527-1170**	505-527-1111
KVMX-FM 107.5 (Oldies) 2040 SW 1st Ave	Portland	OR	97201	**800-567-1075**	503-222-1011
KVPR-FM 89.3 (NPR)					
3437 W Shaw Ave Suite 101	Fresno	CA	93711	**800-275-0764**	559-275-0764
KVRP-FM 97.1 (Ctry) PO Box 1118	Haskell	TX	79521	**800-460-5877**	940-864-8505
KVTT-FM 91.7 (Rel) 11061 Shady Trail	Dallas	TX	75229	**866-787-1917**	214-351-6655
KVVA-FM 107.1 (Span AC)					
501 N 44th St Suite 425	Phoenix	AZ	85008	**800-420-2757**	602-266-2005
KWGS-FM 89.5 (NPR) 600 S College Ave	Tulsa	OK	74104	**888-594-5947**	918-631-2577
KWJJ-FM 99.5 (Ctry) 0700 SW Bancroft St	Portland	OR	97239	**866-239-9653**	503-223-1441
KWRT-AM 1370 (Ctry) 1600 Radio Hill Rd	Boonville	MO	65233	**800-887-6686**	660-882-6686
KWTO-AM 560 (N/T) 3000 E Chestnut Expy	Springfield	MO	65802	**800-749-8001**	417-862-3751
KWWK-FM 96.5 (Ctry) 122 SW 4th St	Rochester	MN	55902	**888-599-5965**	507-286-1010
KWWR-FM 95.7 (Ctry) 1705 E Liberty St	Mexico	MO	65265	**800-264-5997**	573-581-5500
KWYR-FM 93.7 (AC) PO Box 491	Winner	SD	57580	**800-388-5997**	605-842-3333
KXEG-AM 1280 (Rel)					
2800 N 44th St Suite 100	Phoenix	AZ	85008	**888-294-4321**	602-254-5001
KXJM-FM 95.5 (Urban) 0234 SW Bancroft St	Portland	OR	97239	**800-990-0750**	503-243-7595
KXJZ-FM 88.9 (NPR) 7055 Folsom Blvd	Sacramento	CA	95826	**877-480-5900**	916-278-8900
KXL-AM 750 (N/T) 0234 SW Bancroft St	Portland	OR	97239	**800-990-0750**	503-243-7595
KXPK-FM 96.5 (Span) 777 Grant St 5th Fl	Denver	CO	80203	**888-874-2656**	303-832-0050
KXPR-FM 90.9 (Clas) 7055 Folsom Blvd	Sacramento	CA	95826	**877-480-5900**	916-278-8900
KXTA-AM 1150 (Sports)					
3400 W Olive Ave Suite 550	Burbank	CA	91505	**866-987-8570**	818-559-2252
KYCC-FM 90.1 (Rel) 9019 West Ln	Stockton	CA	95210	**800-654-5254**	209-477-3690
KYLD-FM 94.9 (Urban)					
340 Townsend St 4th Fl	San Francisco	CA	94107	**888-333-9490**	415-975-5555
KYXY-FM 96.5 (AC) 8033 Linda Vista Rd	San Diego	CA	92111	**888-560-9650**	858-571-7600
KYYA-FM 93.3 (AC) 2075 Central Ave	Billings	MT	59102	**866-627-5483**	406-652-8400
KZBD-FM 105.7 (CR) 1601 E 57th Ave	Spokane	WA	99223	**800-718-7874**	509-448-1000
KZKZ-FM 106.3 (Rel) 6420 S Zero St	Fort Smith	AR	72903	**800-583-7960**	479-646-6700
KZOK-FM 102.5 (CR)					
1000 Dexter Ave N Suite 100	Seattle	WA	98109	**800-252-1025**	206-805-1100
KZSE-FM 90.7 (NPR)					
206 S Broadway Suite 735	Rochester	MN	55904	**800-652-9700**	507-282-0910
WABB-FM 97.5 (CHR) 1551 Springhill Ave	Mobile	AL	36604	**800-678-9736**	251-432-5572
WABX-FM 107.5 (CR) 20 NW 3rd St	Evansville	IN	47708	**800-879-1372**	812-424-8284
WADO-AM 1280 (Span)					
485 Madison Ave 3rd Fl	New York	NY	10022	**800-999-1280**	212-310-6000
WAER-FM 88.3 (Jazz) 795 Ostram Ave	Syracuse	NY	13244	**888-918-3688**	315-443-4021
WAEZ-FM 94.9 (CHR) 901 E Valley Dr	Bristol	VA	24201	**888-937-4487**	276-669-8112
WAMC-FM 90.3 (NPR) 318 Central Ave	Albany	NY	12206	**800-323-9262**	518-465-5233
WAVA-FM 105.1 (Rel)					
1901 N Moore St Suite 200	Arlington	VA	22209	**888-293-9282**	703-807-2266
WAXQ-FM 104.3 (CR) 1180 6th Ave 6th Fl	New York	NY	10036	**888-872-1043**	212-575-1043
WAYJ-FM 88.7 (Rel)					
1860 Boyscout Dr Suite 202	Fort Myers	FL	33907	**888-936-1929**	239-936-1929
WAYZ-FM 104.7 (Ctry)					
10960 John Wayne Dr	Greencastle	PA	17225	**888-950-1047**	717-597-9200
WBCT-FM 93.7 (Ctry)					
77 Monroe Center St NW Suite 1000	Grand Rapids	MI	49503	**800-633-9393**	616-459-1919
WBDX-FM 102.7 (Rel)					
5512 Ringgold Rd Suite 214	Chattanooga	TN	37412	**877-262-5103**	423-892-1200
WBGL-FM 91.7 (Rel)					
2108 W Springfield Ave	Champaign	IL	61821	**866-917-9245**	217-359-8232
WBHM-FM 90.3 (NPR) 650 11th St S	Birmingham	AL	35294	**800-444-9246**	205-934-2606
WBHT-FM 97.1 (CHR) 600 Baltimore Dr	Wilkes-Barre	PA	18702	**800-447-5000**	570-824-9000
WBHY-FM 88.5 (Rel) PO Box 1328	Mobile	AL	36633	**888-473-8488**	251-473-8488
WBNI-FM 89.1 (NPR) 3204 Clairmont Ct	Fort Wayne	IN	46808	**800-471-9264**	260-452-1189
WBSN-FM 89.1 (Rel) 3939 Gentilly Blvd	New Orleans	LA	70126	**800-480-3600**	504-816-8000
WBUD-AM 1260 (Oldies) 109 Walters Ave	Trenton	NJ	08638	**800-678-9599**	609-771-8181
WBUR-FM 90.9 (NPR) 890 Commonwealth Ave	Boston	MA	02215	**800-909-9287**	617-353-2790
WCAA-FM 105.9 (Span)					
485 Madison Ave 3rd Fl	New York	NY	10022	**866-927-1059**	212-310-6000
WCBM-AM 680 (N/T)					
1726 Reisterstown Rd Suite 117	Baltimore	MD	21208	**800-922-6680**	410-580-6800
WCBU-FM 89.9 (NPR) 1501 W Bradley Ave	Peoria	IL	61625	**888-488-9228**	309-677-3690
WCIC-FM 91.5 (Rel) 3902 W Baring Trace	Peoria	IL	61615	**800-353-9191**	309-282-9191
WCNY-FM 91.3 (NPR) 506 Old Liverpool Rd	Liverpool	NY	13088	**800-451-9269**	315-453-2424
WCQR-FM 88.3 (Rel) 2312 Pine St	Gray	TN	37659	**888-477-5676**	423-477-5676
WCQS-FM 88.1 (NPR) 73 Broadway	Asheville	NC	28801	**800-768-6698**	828-253-6875
WCRF-FM 103.3 (Rel) 9756 Barr Rd	Cleveland	OH	44141	**800-283-9273**	440-526-1111
WDAS-AM 1480 (Rel) 23 W City Line Ave	Bala Cynwyd	PA	19004	**877-894-1480**	610-617-8500
WDAS-FM 105.3 (Urban AC)					
23 W City Line Ave	Bala Cynwyd	PA	19004	**877-894-1053**	610-617-8500
WDCO-FM 89.7 (NPR) 260 14th St NW	Atlanta	GA	30318	**800-222-4788**	404-685-2400
WDEL-AM 1150 (N/T) 2727 Shipley Rd	Wilmington	DE	19810	**800-544-1150**	302-478-2700
WDJA-AM 1420 (N/T)					
2710 W Atlantic Ave	Delray Beach	FL	33445	**888-278-0098**	561-278-1420
WDNA-FM 88.9 (Jazz) 4848 SW 74th Ct	Miami	FL	33155	**866-688-9362**	305-662-8889
WDSD-FM 92.9 (Ctry) 1575 McKee Rd Suite 206	Dover	DE	19904	**888-929-9373**	302-674-1410
WEBC-AM 560 (N/T) 14 E Central Entrance	Duluth	MN	55811	**888-932-2560**	218-727-4500
WEBN-FM 102.7 (Rock)					
8044 Montgomery Rd Suite 650	Cincinnati	OH	45236	**800-616-9236**	513-686-8300
WEDR-FM 99.1 (Urban) 2741 N 29th Ave	Hollywood	FL	33020	**866-991-5269**	954-584-7117
WEGW-FM 107.5 (Rock) 1015 Main St	Wheeling	WV	26003	**800-668-7426**	304-232-1170
WEKU-FM 88.9 (Clas)					
521 Lancaster Ave 102 Perkins Bldg-EKU	Richmond	KY	40475	**800-621-8890**	859-622-1660
WEMU-FM 89.1 (NPR) PO Box 980350	Ypsilanti	MI	48198	**888-299-8910**	734-487-2229
WEMX-FM 94.1 (Urban)					
650 Wooddale Blvd	Baton Rouge	LA	70806	**800-499-9410**	225-926-1106
WEPN-AM 1050 (Sports)					
2 Penn Plaza 17th Fl	New York	NY	10121	**800-919-3776**	212-613-3800
WERN-FM 88.7 (NPR) 821 University Ave	Madison	WI	53706	**800-747-7444**	608-263-2121
WETS-FM 89.5 (NPR)					
89 Drive East Tennessee					
State University	Johnson City	TN	37614	**888-895-9387**	423-439-6440
WEVO-FM 89.1 (N/T) 207 N Main St	Concord	NH	03301	**800-262-1816**	603-228-8910
WFAE-FM 90.7 (NPR)					
8801 JM Keynes Dr Suite 91	Charlotte	NC	28262	**800-876-9323**	704-549-9323
WFDD-FM 88.5 (NPR)					
56 Wake Forest Rd	Winston-Salem	NC	27109	**800-262-8850**	336-758-8850
WFIU-FM 103.7 (Clas)					
Indiana University 1229 E 7th St	Bloomington	IN	47405	**877-285-9348**	812-855-1357
WFLC-FM 97.3 (AC) 2741 N 29th Ave	Hollywood	FL	33020	**866-227-9730**	954-584-7117
WFMF-FM 102.5 (CHR)					
5555 Hilton Ave Suite 500	Baton Rouge	LA	70808	**888-235-6673**	225-231-1860
WFRE-FM 99.9 (Ctry) 5966 Grove Hill Rd	Frederick	MD	21703	**877-999-9373**	301-663-4181
WFRN-AM 1270 (Rel) 25802 CR 26	Elkhart	IN	46517	**800-522-9376**	574-875-5166
WFSQ-FM 91.5 (Clas)					
1600 Red Barber Plaza	Tallahassee	FL	32310	**800-829-8809**	850-487-3086
WFSU-FM 88.9 (NPR)					
1600 Red Barber Plaza	Tallahassee	FL	32310	**800-829-8809**	850-487-3086
WFUM-FM 91.1 (NPR)					
535 W William St Suite 110	Ann Arbor	MI	48103	**800-728-9386**	734-764-9210
WFYR-FM 97.3 (Ctry) 120 Eaton St	Peoria	IL	61603	**866-673-0973**	309-676-5000
WGBG-FM 98.5 (CR) 20200 Dupont Blvd	Georgetown	DE	19947	**888-780-0970**	302-856-2567
WGCU-FM 90.1 (NPR) 10501 FGCU Blvd	Fort Myers	FL	33965	**888-824-0030**	239-590-2500
WGCX-FM 95.7 (N/T) 2070 N Palafox St	Pensacola	FL	32501	**800-441-2636**	850-434-1230
WGET-AM 1320 (AC) 1560 Fairfield Rd	Gettysburg	PA	17325	**800-366-9489**	717-334-3101
WGLO-FM 95.5 (CR) 120 Eaton St	Peoria	IL	61603	**888-676-9595**	309-676-5000
WGNA-FM 107.7 (Ctry)					
800 New Loudon Rd Suite 4200	Latham	NY	12110	**800-476-1077**	518-782-1474
WGRD-FM 97.9 (Rock)					
50 Monroe Ave NW Suite 500	Grand Rapids	MI	49503	**800-957-3979**	616-451-4800
WGST-AM 640 (N/T)					
1819 Peachtree Rd NE Suite 700	Atlanta	GA	30309	**800-776-4638**	404-367-0640
WGTE-FM 91.3 (NPR) 1270 S Detroit Ave	Toledo	OH	43614	**800-243-9483**	419-380-4600
WGTS-FM 91.9 (Rel) 7600 Flower Ave	Takoma Park	MD	20912	**877-948-7919**	301-891-4200
WGTY-FM 107.7 (Ctry) 1560 Fairfield Rd	Gettysburg	PA	17325	**800-366-9489**	717-334-3101
WGVU-FM 88.5 (NPR) 301 W Fulton St	Grand Rapids	MI	49504	**800-442-2771**	616-331-6666
WGZO-FM 103.1 (AC)					
401 Mall Blvd Suite 101D	Savannah	GA	31406	**888-844-1031**	912-351-9830
WHAD-FM 90.7 (NPR)					
111 E Kilbourn Ave Suite 2375	Milwaukee	WI	53202	**800-486-8655**	414-227-2040
WHIL-FM 91.3 (NPR) PO Box 8509	Mobile	AL	36689	**800-239-9445**	251-380-4685
WHNN-FM 96.1 (Oldies)					
1740 Champagne Dr N	Saginaw	MI	48604	**877-479-9466**	989-776-2100
WHOT-FM 101.1 (CHR) 4040 Simon Rd	Youngstown	OH	44512	**800-989-9468**	330-783-1000
WHQT-FM 105.1 (Urban) 2741 N 29th Ave	Hollywood	FL	33020	**888-550-9105**	954-584-7117
WHTZ-FM 100.3 (CHR) PO Box 7100	New York	NY	10150	**800-242-0100**	212-239-2300
WHUR-FM 96.3 (Urban AC)					
529 Bryant St NW	Washington	DC	20059	**800-221-9487**	202-806-3500
WHXT-FM 103.9 (Urban) 1900 Pineview Rd	Columbia	SC	29209	**877-874-1039**	803-376-1039
WHYN-AM 560 (N/T) 1331 Main St	Springfield	MA	01103	**800-331-9496**	413-781-1011
WHYN-FM 93.1 (AC) 1331 Main St	Springfield	MA	01103	**888-293-9310**	413-781-1011
WIHT-FM 99.5 (CHR)					
1801 Rockville Pike 6th Fl	Rockville	MD	20852	**877-995-4681**	301-231-8231
WIKY-FM 104.1 (AC) 1162 Mt Auburn Rd	Evansville	IN	47736	**800-454-9459**	812-424-8284
WIOQ-FM 102.1 (CHR)					
1 Bala Plaza Suite 243	Bala Cynwyd	PA	19004	**800-521-1021**	610-667-8100
WITF-FM 89.5 (NPR) 1982 Locust Ln	Harrisburg	PA	17109	**800-366-9483**	717-236-6000
WITL-FM 100.7 (Ctry) 3200 Pine Tree Rd	Lansing	MI	48911	**800-968-7749**	517-393-1010
WJAB-FM 90.9 (Jazz)					
Alabama A&M University					
Telecommunications Ctr PO Box 1687	Normal	AL	35762	**800-845-9746**	256-372-5795
WJBX-FM 99.3 (Alt) 20125 S Tamiami Trail	Estero	FL	33928	**800-937-7465**	239-495-2100
WJFK-FM 106.7 (N/T) 10800 Main St	Fairfax	VA	22030	**800-636-1067**	703-691-1900
WJQK-FM 99.3 (Rel)					
425 Centerstone Ct Suite 1	Zeeland	MI	49464	**888-993-1260**	616-931-9930
WJRF-FM 89.5 (Rel)					
425 W Superior St Suite 300	Duluth	MN	55802	**800-727-4487**	218-722-3017
WJWL-AM 900 (Nost) 20200 Dupont Blvd	Georgetown	DE	19947	**888-780-0970**	302-856-2567
WJZW-FM 105.9 (NAC)					
4400 Jenifer St NW 4th Fl	Washington	DC	20015	**800-779-1059**	202-686-3100
WKAP-AM 1470 (Oldies)					
1541 Alta Dr Suite 400	Whitehall	PA	18052	**800-659-1965**	610-434-1742
WKCQ-FM 98.1 (Ctry) 2000 Whittier St	Saginaw	MI	48601	**800-262-0098**	989-752-8161
WKGM-AM 940 (Rel) 13379 Great Spring Rd	Smithfield	VA	23430	**800-706-4769**	757-357-9546
WKIT-FM 100.3 (Rock) 861 Broadway	Bangor	ME	04401	**800-287-1003**	207-990-2800
WKKT-FM 96.9 (Ctry) 801 Wood Ridge Ctr Dr	Charlotte	NC	28217	**800-332-1029**	704-714-9444
WKLB-FM 99.5 (Ctry) 55 Morrissey Blvd	Boston	MA	02125	**888-784-0995**	617-822-9600
WKLQ-FM 94.5 (Rock)					
60 Monroe Center St NW 3rd Fl	Grand Rapids	MI	49503	**800-785-1073**	616-774-8461
WKNN-FM 99.1 (Ctry) 286 DeBuys Rd	Biloxi	MS	39531	**800-898-9900**	228-388-2323
WKNO-FM 91.1 (NPR)					
900 Getwell Rd PO Box 241880	Memphis	TN	38124	**800-766-9566**	901-325-6544
WKRR-FM 92.3 (CR) 192 E Lewis St	Greensboro	NC	27406	**800-762-5923**	336-274-8042
WKSU-FM 89.7 (NPR) 1613 E Summit St	Kent	OH	44240	**800-672-2132**	330-672-3114
WKTU-FM 103.5 (CHR)					
525 Washington Blvd 16th Fl	Jersey City	NJ	07310	**800-245-1035**	201-420-3700
WKXU-FM 101.1 (Ctry) 1109 Tower Dr	Burlington	NC	27215	**800-272-6404**	336-584-0126
WKXW-FM 101.5 (N/T) 109 Walters Ave	Trenton	NJ	08638	**800-678-9599**	609-771-8181
WKZL-FM 107.5 (CHR) 192 E Lewis St	Greensboro	NC	27406	**800-682-1075**	336-274-8042
WLAT-AM 910 (Span) 330 Main St	Hartford	CT	06106	**866-910-6342**	860-524-0001
WLBW-FM 92.1 (Oldies) 351 Tilghman Rd	Salisbury	MD	21804	**800-762-0105**	410-742-1923
WLCL-FM 105.7 (Oldies)					
1819 Peachtree Rd NE Suite 700	Atlanta	GA	30309	**800-776-4638**	404-367-0640
WLDE-FM 101.7 (Oldies)					
347 W Berry St Suite 417	Fort Wayne	IN	46802	**888-450-1017**	260-423-3676
WLIB-AM 1190 (N/T) 3 Park Ave 41st Fl	New York	NY	10016	**866-303-2270**	212-447-1000
WLLL-AM 930 (Rel) PO Box 11375	Lynchburg	VA	24506	**888-224-9809**	434-385-9555

				Toll-Free	Phone
WLRH-FM 89.3 (NPR) University of Alabama-Huntsville John Wright Dr	Huntsville	AL	35899	800-239-9574	256-895-9574
WLVE-FM 93.9 (NAC) 7601 Riviera Blvd	Miramar	FL	33023	877-456-8394	954-862-2000
WLYT-FM 102.9 (AC) 801 Wood Ridge Ctr Dr	Charlotte	NC	28217	800-332-1029	704-714-9444
WMAE-FM 89.5 (NPR) 3825 Ridgewood Rd	Jackson	MS	39211	800-922-9698	601-432-6565
WMAH-FM 90.3 (NPR) 3825 Ridgewood Rd	Jackson	MS	39211	800-922-9698	601-432-6800
WMAL-AM 630 (N/T) 4400 Jenifer St NW 4th Fl	Washington	DC	20015	888-630-9625	202-686-3100
WMBD-AM 1470 (N/T) 331 Fulton St Suite 1200	Peoria	IL	61602	800-698-1470	309-637-3700
WMBM-AM 1490 (Rel) 13242 NW 7th Ave	North Miami	FL	33168	888-599-9626	305-769-1100
WMBS-AM 590 (Oldies) 44 S Mt Vernon Ave	Uniontown	PA	15401	866-590-9627	724-438-3900
WMBW-FM 88.9 (Rel) PO Box 73026	Chattanooga	TN	37407	800-621-9629	423-629-8900
WMCU-FM 89.7 (Rel) 600 SW 3rd St Suite 2290	Pompano Beach	FL	33060	866-897-9628	954-545-7600
WMEA-FM 90.1 (NPR) 309 Marginal Way	Portland	ME	04101	800-884-1717	207-874-6570
WMEH-FM 90.9 (NPR) 65 Texas Ave	Bangor	ME	04401	800-884-1717	207-941-1010
WMEZ-FM 94.1 (AC) 6085 Quinette Rd	Pace	FL	32571	888-741-0941	850-994-5357
WMGS-FM 92.9 (AC) 600 Baltimore Dr	Wilkes-Barre	PA	18702	800-447-5000	570-824-9000
WMHR-FM 102.9 (Rel) 4044 Makyes Rd	Syracuse	NY	13215	800-677-1881	315-469-5051
WMIT-FM 106.9 (Rel) PO Box 159	Black Mountain	NC	28711	800-330-9648	828-669-8477
WMPI-FM 105.3 (Ctry) 22 E McClain Ave	Scottsburg	IN	47170	800-441-1053	812-752-3688
WMPN-FM 91.3 (NPR) 3825 Ridgewood Rd	Jackson	MS	39211	866-262-9643	601-432-6800
WMT-AM 600 (N/T) 600 Old Marion Rd	Cedar Rapids	IA	52402	800-332-5401	319-395-0530
WMT-FM 96.5 (AC) 600 Old Marion Rd NE	Cedar Rapids	IA	52402	800-332-5401	319-395-0530
WMVX-FM 106.5 (AC) 6200 Oak Tree Blvd 4th Fl	Independence	OH	44131	800-829-1065	216-520-2600
WMXJ-FM 102.7 (Oldies) 20450 NW 2nd Ave	Miami	FL	33169	800-226-1027	305-521-5100
WMZQ-FM 98.7 (Ctry) 1801 Rockville Pike 6th Fl	Rockville	MD	20852	800-505-0098	301-231-8231
WNEW-FM 102.7 (AC) 888 7th Ave 9th Fl	New York	NY	10106	877-649-1027	212-489-1027
WNJN-FM 89.7 (NPR) PO Box 777	Trenton	NJ	08625	800-792-8645	609-777-5000
WNNH-FM 99.1 (Oldies) 11 Kimball Dr Unit 114	Hooksett	NH	03106	800-228-9664	603-225-1160
WNOE-FM 101.1 (Ctry) 929 Howard Ave	New Orleans	LA	70113	800-543-9663	504-679-7300
WNSR-AM 560 (Sports) 435 37th Ave N	Nashville	TN	37209	888-228-6123	615-844-1039
WNVY-AM 1090 (Rel) 2070 N Palafox St	Pensacola	FL	32501	800-441-2636	850-434-1230
WOCQ-FM 103.9 (CHR) 20200 Dupont Blvd	Georgetown	DE	19947	888-780-0970	302-856-2567
WOGG-FM 94.9 (Ctry) 123 Blaine Rd	Brownsville	PA	15417	866-937-6449	724-938-2000
WOI-AM 640 (NPR) Iowa State University 2022 Communications Bldg	Ames	IA	50011	800-861-8000	515-294-2025
WOKO-FM 98.9 (Ctry) PO Box 4489	Burlington	VT	05406	800-354-9890	802-658-1230
WOLC-FM 102.5 (Rel) 11890 Crisfield Ln PO Box 130	Princess Anne	MD	21853	877-569-9652	410-543-9652
WORD-FM 101.5 (Rel) 7 Parkway Ctr Suite 625	Pittsburgh	PA	15220	800-320-8255	412-937-1500
WOSC-FM 95.9 (Rock) 351 Tilghman Rd	Salisbury	MD	21804	800-762-0105	410-742-1923
WOWO-AM 1190 (N/T) 2915 Maples Rd	Fort Wayne	IN	46816	800-333-1190	260-447-5511
WPBG-FM 93.3 (Oldies) 331 Fulton St Suite 1200	Peoria	IL	61602	800-310-0930	309-637-3700
WPCS-FM 89.5 (Rel) 250 Brent Ln	Pensacola	FL	32503	800-726-1191	850-479-6570
WPEO-AM 1020 (Rel) 1708 Highview Rd	East Peoria	IL	61611	800-728-1020	309-698-9736
WPKX-FM 97.9 (Ctry) 1331 Main St	Springfield	MA	01103	800-345-9759	413-781-1011
WPLM-FM 99.1 (AC) 17 Columbus	Plymouth	MA	02360	877-327-9991	508-746-1390
WPLN-FM 90.3 (NPR) 630 Mainstream Dr	Nashville	TN	37228	877-760-2903	615-760-2903
WPNN-AM 790 (N/T) 3801 N Pace Blvd	Pensacola	FL	32505	888-433-1141	850-433-1141
WPRO-AM 630 (N/T) 1502 Wampanoag Trail	East Providence	RI	02915	800-321-9776	401-433-4200
WPTF-AM 680 (N/T) 3012 Highwoods Blvd Suite 200	Raleigh	NC	27604	800-662-7979	919-876-0674
WQCD-FM 101.9 (NAC) 395 Hudson St 7th Fl	New York	NY	10014	800-423-1019	212-352-1019
WQDR-FM 94.7 (Ctry) 3012 Highwoods Blvd Suite 200	Raleigh	NC	27604	800-233-9470	919-876-0674
WQED-FM 89.3 (Clas) 4802 5th Ave	Pittsburgh	PA	15213	800-876-1316	412-622-1436
WQHQ-FM 104.7 (AC) 351 Tilghman Rd	Salisbury	MD	21804	800-762-0105	410-742-1923
WQHT-FM 97.1 (Urban) 395 Hudson St 7th Fl	New York	NY	10014	800-223-9797	212-229-9797
WQKC-FM 93.7 (Ctry) PO Box 806	Seymour	IN	47274	800-633-9370	812-522-1390
WQLN-FM 91.3 (NPR) 8425 Peach St	Erie	PA	16509	800-727-8854	814-864-3001
WQSA-FM 99.9 (N/T) 1006 1st St	Perry	GA	31069	800-705-8770	478-218-7756
WRAL-FM 101.5 (AC) 711 Hillsborough St	Raleigh	NC	27603	800-849-6101	919-890-6101
WRBS-FM 95.1 (Rel) 3600 Georgetown Rd	Baltimore	MD	21227	800-899-0951	410-247-4100
WRFX-FM 99.7 (CR) 801 Wood Ridge Ctr Dr	Charlotte	NC	28217	800-332-1029	704-714-9444
WRKF-FM 89.3 (NPR) 3050 Valley Creek Dr	Baton Rouge	LA	70808	888-926-3050	225-926-3050
WRKS-FM 98.7 (Urban) 395 Hudson St 7th Fl	New York	NY	10014	800-288-5477	212-242-9870
WRNE-AM 980 (Urban) 312 E Nine-Mile Rd Suite 29D	Pensacola	FL	32514	866-478-8866	850-478-6000
WRNX-FM 100.9 (AAA) 98 Lower Westfield Rd 3rd Fl	Holyoke	MA	01040	800-977-1009	413-536-1105
WROL-AM 950 (Rel) PO Box 9121	Boston	MA	02171	888-659-0590	617-423-0213
WRTI-FM 90.1 (NPR) 1509 Cecil B Moore Ave 3rd Fl	Philadelphia	PA	19122	800-245-8776	215-204-8405
WSBY-FM 98.9 (Urban AC) 351 Tilghman Rd	Salisbury	MD	21804	800-762-0105	410-742-1923
WSCL-FM 89.5 (NPR) PO Box 2596 Salisbury University	Salisbury	MD	21801	800-543-6895	410-543-6895
WSHA-FM 88.9 (Jazz) 118 E South St	Raleigh	NC	27601	800-241-0421	919-546-8430
WSHU-FM 91.1 (NPR) 5151 Park Ave	Fairfield	CT	06825	800-937-6045	203-365-6604
WSKO-AM 790 (Sports) 1502 Wampanoag Trail	East Providence	RI	02915	888-345-0790	401-433-4200
WSM-AM 650 (Ctry) 2804 Opryland Dr	Nashville	TN	37214	877-878-4650	615-889-6595
WSOS-FM 94.1 (AC) 2715 Stratton Blvd	Saint Augustine	FL	32084	877-829-9767	904-824-0833
WSTH-FM 106.1 (Ctry) 1501 13th Ave	Columbus	GA	31901	800-445-4106	706-576-3000
WSTO-FM 96.1 (CHR) 20 NW 3rd St 13th Fl	Evansville	IN	47708	800-879-1372	812-424-8284
WSTW-FM 93.7 (CHR) 2727 Shipley Rd	Wilmington	DE	19810	800-544-9370	302-478-2700
WSUA-AM 1260 (Span) 2100 Coral Way 2nd Fl	Miami	FL	33145	800-441-1260	305-285-1260
WSVH-FM 91.1 (NPR) 12 Ocean Science Cir	Savannah	GA	31411	800-673-7332	912-598-3300
WSWT-FM 106.9 (AC) 331 Fulton St Suite 1200	Peoria	IL	61602	800-579-1069	309-637-3700
WTBC-AM 1230 (N/T) 2110 McFarland Blvd E Suite C	Tuscaloosa	AL	35404	800-518-1977	205-758-5523
WTKE-FM 98.1 (Sports) 21 Miracle Strip Pkwy	Fort Walton Beach	FL	32548	877-981-0981	850-244-1400
WTKX-FM 101.5 (Rock) 6485 Pensacola Blvd	Pensacola	FL	32505	888-357-7625	850-473-0400
WTSU-FM 89.9 (NPR) Troy State University Wallace Hall	Troy	AL	36082	800-800-6616	334-670-3268
WTWR-FM 98.3 (CHR) 14930 LaPlaisance Rd Suite 113	Monroe	MI	48161	888-578-0098	734-242-6600
WTZR-FM 99.3 (Alt) 901 E Valley Dr	Bristol	VA	24201	866-770-7625	276-669-8112
WUAL-FM 91.5 (NPR) University of Alabama Phifer Hall Suite 166	Tuscaloosa	AL	35487	800-654-4262	205-348-6644
WUIS-FM 91.9 (NPR) University of Illinois at Springfield 1 University Plaza	Springfield	IL	62703	866-206-9847	217-206-6516
WUMB-FM 91.9 (Folk) 100 Morrissey Blvd	Boston	MA	02125	800-573-2100	617-287-6900
WUNC-FM 91.5 (NPR) University of North Carolina Box 0915	Chapel Hill	NC	27599	800-962-9862	919-966-5454
WUSF-FM 89.7 (NPR) 4202 E Fowler Ave WRB 219	Tampa	FL	33620	800-741-9090	813-974-8700
WUWF-FM 88.1 (NPR) University of West Florida 11000 University Pkwy	Pensacola	FL	32514	800-239-9893	850-474-2787
WVAA-AM 1390 (Ctry) 272 Dorset St	South Burlington	VT	05403	800-286-9537	802-863-1010
WVKF-FM 95.7 (CHR) 1015 Main St	Wheeling	WV	26003	800-668-7426	304-232-1170
WVKS-FM 92.5 (CHR) 125 S Superior St	Toledo	OH	43602	877-547-7366	419-244-8321
WVPE-FM 88.1 (NPR) 2424 California Rd	Elkhart	IN	46514	888-399-9873	574-262-5660
WVPN-FM 88.5 (NPR) 600 Capitol St	Charleston	WV	25301	888-596-9729	304-556-4900
WVPS-FM 107.9 (NPR) 365 Troy Ave	Colchester	VT	05446	800-639-2192	802-655-9451
WVTF-FM 89.1 (NPR) 3520 Kingsbury Ln	Roanoke	VA	24014	800-856-8900	540-231-8900
WVXU-FM 91.7 (NPR) 3800 Victory Pkwy	Cincinnati	OH	45207	800-230-3576	513-731-9898
WWAX-FM 92.1 (CHR) 501 Lake Ave S Suite 200-A	Duluth	MN	55802	877-921-5477	218-728-9500
WWDC-FM 101.1 (Rock) 1801 Rockville Pike Suite 405	Rockville	MD	20852	800-333-2101	301-587-7100
WWDL-FM 104.9 (Oldies) 1049 N Sekol Rd	Scranton	PA	18504	888-577-4487	570-344-1221
WWFE-AM 670 (Span) 330 SW 27th Ave Suite 207	Miami	FL	33135	888-541-9933	305-541-3300
WWFG-FM 99.9 (Ctry) 351 Tilghman Rd	Salisbury	MD	21804	800-762-0105	410-742-1923
WWFM-FM 89.1 (Clas) 1200 Old Trenton Rd	Trenton	NJ	08650	800-622-9936	609-587-8989
WWGR-FM 101.9 (Ctry) 10915 K-Nine Dr	Bonita Springs	FL	34135	877-787-1019	239-495-8383
WWJC-AM 850 (Rel) 1120 E McCuen St	Duluth	MN	55808	877-626-2738	218-626-2738
WWNO-FM 89.9 (NPR) University of New Orleans Lake Front Campus	New Orleans	LA	70148	800-286-7002	504-280-7000
WWPR-FM 105.1 (Urban) 1120 6th Ave	New York	NY	10036	800-585-1051	212-704-1051
WWZZ-FM 103.9 (AC) 1300 Idaho Ave NW Suite 200	Washington	DC	20016	800-987-2104	202-895-5000
WXBM-FM 102.7 (Ctry) 6085 Quintette Rd	Pace	FL	32571	800-626-9926	850-994-5357
WXBQ-FM 96.9 (Ctry) 901 E Valley Dr	Bristol	VA	24201	800-332-3697	276-669-8112
WXCY-FM 103.7 (Ctry) 707 Revolution St	Havre de Grace	MD	21078	800-788-9929	410-939-1100
WXEL-FM 90.7 (NPR) PO Box 6607	West Palm Beach	FL	33405	800-915-9935	561-737-8000
WXOK-AM 1460 (Rel) 650 Wooddale Blvd	Baton Rouge	LA	70806	800-499-1460	225-926-1106
WXTW-FM 102.3 (Alt) 2000 Lower Huntington Rd	Fort Wayne	IN	46819	877-747-7711	260-747-1511
WYCL-FM 107.3 (Oldies) 6485 Pensacola Blvd	Pensacola	FL	32505	888-345-1073	850-473-0400
WYEP-FM 91.3 (Var) 2313 E Carson St	Pittsburgh	PA	15203	877-381-9900	412-381-9131
WZBH-FM 93.5 (Rock) 20200 Dupont Blvd	Georgetown	DE	19947	888-780-0970	302-856-2567
WZEB-FM 101.7 (AC) 20200 Dupont Blvd	Georgetown	DE	19947	888-780-0970	302-856-2567
WZZR-FM 94.3 (N/T) PO Box 0093	Port Saint Lucie	FL	34985	877-927-6969	772-335-9300
XETRA-FM 91.1 (Alt) 9660 Granite Ridge Dr	San Diego	CA	92123	866-690-1150	619-291-9191

632 RADIO SYNDICATORS

				Toll-Free	Phone
AARP Broadcast Dept 601 'E' St NW	Washington	DC	20049	888-687-2277	202-434-2600
AP Broadcast Services 1825 K St NW Suite 800	Washington	DC	20006	800-821-4747	202-736-1100
B & B Media Group 109 S Main St	Corsicana	TX	75110	800-927-0517	903-872-0517
Bloomberg Radio Network 499 Park Ave 15th Fl	New York	NY	10022	800-448-5678	212-318-2350
Car Clinic Productions 5675 N Davis Hwy	Pensacola	FL	32503	800-264-5454	850-478-3139
Environmental Media Broadcasting Radio Network 7302 Pierce Ave	Whittier	CA	90607	800-963-9927	562-945-6469
FamilyNet 6350 West Fwy	Fort Worth	TX	76116	800-292-2287	817-737-4011
Focus on the Family 8605 Explorer Dr *Sales	Colorado Springs	CO	80920	800-232-6459*	719-531-3400
Jones Media Networks Ltd 9697 E Mineral Ave	Englewood	CO	80112	800-525-7000	303-792-3111
New Dimensions Radio Broadcasting Network PO Box 569	Ukiah	CA	95482	800-935-8273	707-468-5215
Premiere Radio Networks Inc 15260 Ventura Blvd Suite 500	Sherman Oaks	CA	91403	800-533-8686	818-377-5300
Radio America 1030 15th St NW Suite 1040	Washington	DC	20005	800-807-4703	202-408-0944
Talk Radio Network PO Box 3755	Central Point	OR	97502	888-383-3733	541-664-8827
Transmedia Productions Inc 719 Battery St	San Francisco	CA	94111	800-229-7234	415-956-3118
Tribune Radio Network 435 N Michigan Ave	Chicago	IL	60611	800-654-8597	312-222-3342
WCLV/Seaway Productions 26501 Renaissance Pkwy	Cleveland	OH	44128	800-491-8863	216-464-0900

633 RADIO & TELEVISION BROADCASTING & COMMUNICATIONS EQUIPMENT

SEE ALSO Audio & Video Equipment; Telecommunications Equipment & Systems

				Toll-Free	Phone
Acrodyne Industries Inc 200 Schell Ln	Phoenixville	PA	19460	800-523-2596	610-917-1300
AheadTek Inc 6410 Via Del Oro	San Jose	CA	95119	800-971-9191	408-226-9991
Amerilink LLC 2 Easton Oval Suite 500	Columbus	OH	43219	800-669-8765	614-479-2500
Andrew Corp 10500 W 153rd St *NASDAQ: ANDW* ■ *Cust Svc	Orland Park	IL	60462	800-255-1479*	708-349-3300
Andrew Corp Decibel Products Div 2601 Telecom Pkwy	Richardson	TX	75082	800-676-5342	972-952-9700
Arris Group Inc 3871 Lakefield Dr *NASDAQ: ARRS*	Suwanee	GA	30024	800-469-6569	770-622-8400

Company	City	State	ZIP	Toll-Free	Phone
Axcera Corp 103 Freedom Dr	Lawrence	PA	15055	**800-215-2614**	724-873-8100
Blonder Tongue Laboratories Inc 1 Jake Brown Rd *AMEX: BDR*	Old Bridge	NJ	08857	**800-523-6049**	732-679-4000
C-COR Inc 60 Decibel Rd *NASDAQ: CCBL*	State College	PA	16801	**800-233-2267**	814-238-2461
CalAmp Corp 1401 N Rice Ave *NASDAQ: CAMP*	Oxnard	CA	93030	**888-767-7988**	805-987-9000
Centurion Wireless Technologies Inc 3425 N 44th St	Lincoln	NE	68504	**800-228-4563**	402-467-4491
Channell Commercial Corp 250 Ynez Rd *NASDAQ: CHNL*	Temecula	CA	92591	**800-423-1863**	951-719-2600
Circuit Research Labs Inc 1302 W Drivers Way	Tempe	AZ	85284	**800-535-7648**	480-403-8300
Cohu Inc Electronics Div 3912 Calle Fortunada	San Diego	CA	92123	**800-735-2648**	858-277-6700
Concurrent Computer Corp 4375 River Green Pkwy Suite 100 *NASDAQ: CCUR*	Duluth	GA	30096	**877-978-7363**	678-258-4000
Conolog Corp 5 Columbia Rd *NASDAQ: CNLG*	Somerville	NJ	08876	**800-526-3984**	908-722-8081
Continental Electronics Corp 4212 S Buckner Blvd	Dallas	TX	75227	**800-733-5011**	214-381-7161
Datron World Communications Inc 3030 Enterprise Ct *Sales	Vista	CA	92081	**800-405-0744***	760-734-5454
Decibel Products Div Andrew Corp 2601 Telecom Pkwy	Richardson	TX	75082	**800-676-5342**	972-952-9700
Dielectric Communications 22 Tower Rd *Sales	Raymond	ME	04071	**800-341-9678***	207-655-4555
Digital Angel Corp 490 Villaume Ave S *AMEX: DOC*	South Saint Paul	MN	55075	**800-328-0118**	651-455-1621
Eagle Comtronics Inc 7665 Henry Clay Blvd	Liverpool	NY	13088	**800-448-7474**	315-622-3402
Earmark LLC 1125 Dixwell Ave *Cust Svc	Hamden	CT	06514	**888-327-6275***	203-777-2130
GAI-Tronics Corp PO Box 1060	Reading	PA	19607	**800-492-1212**	610-777-1374
Globecomm Systems Inc 45 Oser Ave *NASDAQ: GCOM*	Hauppauge	NY	11788	**888-231-9800**	631-231-9800
Harmonic Inc 549 Baltic Way *NASDAQ: HLIT*	Sunnyvale	CA	94089	**800-788-1330**	408-542-2500
Harris Corp 1025 W NASA Blvd *NYSE: HRS*	Melbourne	FL	32919	**800-442-7747**	321-727-9100
Harris Corp Broadcast Communications Div 3200 Wismann Ln	Quincy	IL	62301	**800-622-0022**	217-222-8200
Harris Corp RF Communications Div 1680 University Ave	Rochester	NY	14610	**800-288-4277**	585-244-5830
ICOM America Inc 2380 116th Ave NE	Bellevue	WA	98004	**800-306-1356**	425-454-8155
ICTV Inc 14600 Winchester Blvd	Los Gatos	CA	95032	**800-926-8398**	408-364-9200
Ikegami Electronics USA Inc 37 Brook Ave	Maywood	NJ	07607	**800-368-9171**	201-368-9171
Intelect Technologies Inc 1225 Commerce Dr	Richardson	TX	75081	**888-477-7272**	972-367-2100
Kenwood USA Corp PO Box 22745	Long Beach	CA	90801	**800-536-9663**	310-639-9000
KVH Industries Inc 50 Enterprise Ctr *NASDAQ: KVHI*	Middletown	RI	02842	**888-584-4773**	401-847-3327
L-3 Communications Narda Microwave (East) 435 Moreland Rd	Hauppauge	NY	11788	**800-666-7060**	631-272-5600
Leitch Technology Corp 150 Ferrand Dr Suite 700 *TSE: LTV*	Toronto	ON	M3C3E5	**800-387-0233**	416-445-9640
MCL Inc 501 S Woodcreek Rd *Support	Bolingbrook	IL	60440	**800-743-4625***	630-759-9500
MDI Security Systems Inc 9725 Datapoint Dr Suite 200 *NASDAQ: MDII*	San Antonio	TX	78229	**866-435-7634**	210-477-5400
MFJ Enterprises Inc 300 Industrial Park Rd	Starkville	MS	39759	**800-647-1800**	662-323-5869
Microwave Radio Communications 101 Billerica Ave Bldg 6	North Billerica	MA	01862	**800-490-5700**	978-671-5700
Miller RA Industries Inc 14500 168th Ave	Grand Haven	MI	49417	**888-845-9450**	616-842-9450
Minerva Networks Inc 2111 Tasman Dr	Santa Clara	CA	95054	**800-806-9594**	408-567-9400
Motorola Inc Broadband Communications Sector 101 Tournament Dr	Horsham	PA	19044	**800-523-6678**	215-323-1000
Narco Avionics 270 Commerce Dr *Sales	Fort Washington	PA	19034	**800-223-3636***	215-643-2900
nCube Corp 1825 NW 167th Pl	Beaverton	OR	97006	**800-654-2823**	503-629-5088
Newfound Technology Corp 330 Codman Hill Rd	Boxborough	MA	01719	**800-225-0228**	508-303-8200
ParkerVision Inc 8493 Baymeadows Way *NASDAQ: PRKR*	Jacksonville	FL	32256	**800-532-8034**	904-737-1367
Pelco 3500 Pelco Way	Clovis	CA	93612	**800-289-9100**	559-292-1981
Pico Macom Inc 355 Parkside Dr	San Fernando	CA	91340	**800-421-6511**	818-493-4300
Powerwave Technologies Inc 1801 E Saint Andrew Pl *NASDAQ: PWAV*	Santa Ana	CA	92705	**888-797-9283**	714-466-1000
PTS Corp 5233 Hwy 37 S	Bloomington	IN	47401	**800-844-3291**	812-824-9331
RA Miller Industries Inc 14500 168th Ave	Grand Haven	MI	49417	**888-845-9450**	616-842-9450
RELM Wireless Corp 7100 Technology Dr *Cust Svc	West Melbourne	FL	32904	**800-422-6281***	321-984-1414
RF Scientific Inc 5644 Commerce Dr	Orlando	FL	32839	**800-741-5465**	407-856-1050
Rockwell Collins Inc 400 Collins Rd NE *NYSE: COL*	Cedar Rapids	IA	52498	**888-265-5467**	319-295-1000
Scientific-Atlanta Inc 5030 Sugarloaf Pkwy *NYSE: SFA* ■ *Sales	Lawrenceville	GA	30044	**800-433-6222***	770-236-5000
SeaChange International Inc 124 Acton St *NASDAQ: SEAC*	Maynard	MA	01754	**888-732-2641**	978-897-0100
SEA/Datamarine Inc 7030 220th St SW	Mountlake Terrace	WA	98043	**800-426-1330**	425-771-2182
Shively Labs PO Box 389	Bridgton	ME	04009	**888-744-8359**	207-647-3327
SkyStream Networks Inc 455 DeGuigne Dr *Cust Svc	Sunnyvale	CA	94085	**877-475-9787***	408-616-3300
Space Systems/Loral 3825 Fabian Way	Palo Alto	CA	94303	**800-332-6490**	650-852-4000
Tecom Industries Inc 375 Conejo Ridge Ave	Thousand Oaks	CA	91361	**800-959-0495**	805-267-0100
Telephonics Corp 815 Broad Hollow Rd	Farmingdale	NY	11735	**877-755-7700**	631-755-7000
Ten-Tec Inc 1185 Dolly Parton Pkwy *Cust Svc	Sevierville	TN	37862	**800-833-7373***	865-453-7172
Thales Broadcast & Multimedia Inc 104 Feeding Hills Rd	Southwick	MA	01077	**800-266-9283**	413-569-0116
Thales Communications Inc 22605 Gateway Center Dr	Clarksburg	MD	20871	**800-258-4420**	240-864-7000
TPL Communications 3370 San Fernando Rd Unit 206	Los Angeles	CA	90065	**800-447-6937**	323-256-3000
Transcript International 3900 NW 12th St Suite 200	Lincoln	NE	68521	**800-228-0226**	402-474-4800
Ultra Electronics-DNE Technologies Inc 50 Barnes Park N	Wallingford	CT	06492	**800-370-4485**	203-265-7151
Vicon Industries Inc 89 Arkay Dr *AMEX: VII* ■ *Cust Svc	Hauppauge	NY	11788	**800-645-9116***	631-952-2288
Videotek Inc 243 Shoemaker Rd *Sales	Pottstown	PA	19464	**800-800-5719***	610-327-2292
Viewsonics Inc 3103 N Andrews Ave Ext	Pompano Beach	FL	33064	**800-645-7600**	954-971-8439
Ward Products LLC 633 Nassau St	New Brunswick	NJ	08902	**877-732-4095**	732-846-7500
Wegener Communications Inc 11350 Technology Cir	Duluth	GA	30097	**800-848-9467**	770-623-0096
Wilcom Inc 73 Daniel Webster Hwy	Belmont	NH	03220	**800-222-1898**	603-524-2622
Winegard Co 3000 Kirkwood St *Cust Svc	Burlington	IA	52601	**800-288-8094***	319-754-0600
WJ Communications Inc 401 River Oaks Pkwy *NASDAQ: WJCI*	San Jose	CA	95134	**800-951-4401**	408-577-6200

634 RAIL TRANSPORT SERVICES

SEE ALSO Logistics Services (Transportation & Warehousing)

Company	City	State	ZIP	Toll-Free	Phone
Aberdeen & Rockfish Railroad Co 101 E Main St	Aberdeen	NC	28315	**800-849-5713**	910-944-2341
Amtrak 60 Massachusetts Ave NE	Washington	DC	20002	**800-872-7245**	202-906-3000
BNSF (Burlington Northern & Santa Fe Railway) 2650 Lou Menk Dr	Fort Worth	TX	76131	**800-795-2673**	
Buffalo & Pittsburgh Railroad 1200-C Scottsville Rd Suite 200	Rochester	NY	14624	**800-603-3385**	585-463-3308
Burlington Northern & Santa Fe Railway (BNSF) 2650 Lou Menk Dr	Fort Worth	TX	76131	**800-795-2673**	
Canadian Pacific Railway Co Gulf Canada Sq 401 9th Ave SW *NYSE: CP*	Calgary	AB	T2P4Z4	**888-333-6370**	403-319-7000
CHEP USA 8517 S Park Cir	Orlando	FL	32819	**800-432-2437**	407-370-2437
Columbus & Greenville Railway Co 201 19th St N PO Box 6000	Columbus	MS	39703	**888-601-1222**	662-327-8664
Dardanelle & Russellville Railroad Co 4416 S Arkansas Ave	Russellville	AR	72802	**800-530-7526**	479-968-6455
Florida East Coast Industries Inc 1 Malaga St *NYSE: FLA*	Saint Augustine	FL	32084	**800-342-1131**	904-829-3421
Florida East Coast Railway 1 Malaga St	Saint Augustine	FL	32084	**800-342-1131**	904-829-3421
Georgetown Railroad Co 5300 S IH-35 PO Box 529	Georgetown	TX	78627	**800-772-8272**	512-863-2538
Kansas City Southern Railway Co 427 W 12th St	Kansas City	MO	69405	**800-468-6527**	816-983-1303
Mississippi Export Railroad Co 4519 McInnis Ave	Moss Point	MS	39563	**866-353-3322**	228-475-3322
Montana Rail Link Inc 101 International Way	Missoula	MT	59808	**800-338-4750**	406-523-1500
National Railroad Passenger Corp DBA Amtrak 60 Massachusetts Ave NE	Washington	DC	20002	**800-872-7245**	202-906-3000
New England Central Railway Inc 2 Federal St Suite 201 *Cust Svc	Saint Albans	VT	05478	**800-800-3450***	802-527-3450
New York Susquehanna & Western Railway Corp 1 Railroad Ave	Cooperstown	NY	13326	**800-366-6979**	607-547-2555
Norfolk Southern Railway Co 3 Commercial Pl	Norfolk	VA	23510	**800-635-5768**	757-629-2600
Pioneer Railcorp 1318 S Johanson Rd *NASDAQ: PRRR*	Peoria	IL	61607	**800-914-3810**	309-697-1400
Providence & Worcester Railroad Co 75 Hammond St *AMEX: PWX*	Worcester	MA	01610	**800-447-2003**	508-755-4000
RailAmerica Inc 5300 Broken Sound Blvd NW 2nd Fl *NYSE: RRA*	Boca Raton	FL	33487	**800-211-7245**	561-994-6015
Texas Mexican Railway Co 5810 San Bernardo Ave Suite 350	Laredo	TX	78041	**800-283-9639**	956-728-6700
Triple Crown Services 2720 Dupont Commerce Ct	Fort Wayne	IN	46825	**800-325-6510**	260-416-3600
Union Pacific Railroad Co 1416 Dodge St	Omaha	NE	68179	**888-870-8777**	402-271-5000
Winston-Salem Southbound Railway Co 4550 Overdale Rd	Winston-Salem	NC	27107	**888-631-8223**	336-788-9407

635 RAIL TRAVEL

SEE ALSO Mass Transportation (Local & Suburban)

Company	City	State	ZIP	Toll-Free	Phone
Amtrak 60 Massachusetts Ave NE	Washington	DC	20002	**800-872-7245**	202-906-3000
VIA Rail Canada Inc 3 Place Ville-Marie Suite 500	Montreal	QC	H3B2C9	**800-681-2561**	514-871-6000

636 RAILROAD EQUIPMENT - MFR

SEE ALSO Transportation Equipment & Supplies - Whol

Company	City	State	ZIP	Toll-Free	Phone
A Stucki Co 2600 Neville Rd	Pittsburgh	PA	15225	**800-771-7302**	412-771-7300
American Railcar Industries Inc 100 Clark St	Saint Charles	MO	63301	**800-933-7937**	636-940-6000
Foster LB Co 415 Holiday Dr *NASDAQ: FSTR*	Pittsburgh	PA	15220	**800-255-4500**	412-928-3400

				Toll-Free	Phone
FreightCar America Inc 17 Johns St *NASDAQ: RAIL*	Johnstown	PA	15901	**800-458-2235**	
GE Transportation Rail 2901 E Lake Rd *Prod Info	Erie	PA	16531	**800-626-2000***	814-875-2234
General Motors Corp Electro-Motive Div 9301 W 55th St *Cust Svc	La Grange	IL	60525	**800-255-5354***	708-387-6000
Greenbrier Co 1 Centerpointe Dr Suite 200 *NYSE: GBX*	Lake Oswego	OR	97035	**800-343-7188**	503-684-7000
Gunderson Inc 4350 NW Front Ave	Portland	OR	97210	**800-253-4350**	503-972-5700
Harsco Track Technologies (HTT) 2401 Edmund Rd Box 20	West Columbia	SC	29171	**800-345-9160**	803-822-9160
Holland Co 1000 Holland Dr	Crete	IL	60417	**800-899-7754**	708-672-2300
HTT (Harsco Track Technologies) 2401 Edmund Rd Box 20	West Columbia	SC	29171	**800-345-9160**	803-822-9160
LB Foster Co 415 Holiday Dr *NASDAQ: FSTR*	Pittsburgh	PA	15220	**800-255-4500**	412-928-3400
Morse Automotive East 101 Friction Dr	Cartersville	GA	30120	**800-746-6773**	770-607-2222
MotivePower 4600 Apple St	Boise	ID	83716	**800-272-7702**	208-947-4800
National Railway Equipment Co (NREC) 14400 S Robey St	Dixmoor	IL	60426	**800-253-2905**	708-388-6002
New York Air Brake Co 748 Starbuck Ave	Watertown	NY	13601	**888-836-6922**	315-786-5200
NREC (National Railway Equipment Co) 14400 S Robey St	Dixmoor	IL	60426	**800-253-2905**	708-388-6002
Portec Rail Products Inc PO Box 38250 *NASDAQ: PRPX*	Pittsburgh	PA	15238	**800-722-9960**	412-782-6000
Prime Mfg Corp 1619 Kuntz Rd	Dayton	OH	45404	**800-657-0707**	937-496-3807
Salco Products Inc 20W201 101st St Suite A	Lemont	IL	60439	**800-535-8990**	630-783-2570
Siemens Transportation Systems Inc 7464 French Rd	Sacramento	CA	95828	**800-722-8044**	916-681-3000
Stucki A Co 2600 Neville Rd	Pittsburgh	PA	15225	**800-771-7302**	412-771-7300
Trinity Mining Service 109 48th St	Pittsburgh	PA	15201	**800-245-6206**	412-682-4700
Trinity Rail Group Inc 2525 Stemmons Fwy	Dallas	TX	75207	**800-631-4420**	214-631-4420
Union Tank Car Co 175 W Jackson Blvd Suite 2100	Chicago	IL	60604	**800-635-3770**	312-431-3111
Vapor Bus International 1010 Johnson Dr	Buffalo Grove	IL	60089	**800-631-9200**	847-777-6400

637 RAILROAD SWITCHING & TERMINAL SERVICES

				Toll-Free	Phone
Public Belt Railroad Commission 4822 Tchoupitulas St *Cust Svc	New Orleans	LA	70115	**800-524-3421***	504-896-7410
Rail Link Inc 4337 Pablo Oaks Ct Suite 104	Jacksonville	FL	32224	**888-902-7245**	904-223-1110
Railserve Inc 1691 Phoenix Blvd Suite 110	Atlanta	GA	30349	**800-345-7245**	770-996-6838
Rescar Inc 1101 31st St Suite 250	Downers Grove	IL	60515	**800-851-5196**	630-963-1114

638 REAL ESTATE AGENTS & BROKERS

				Toll-Free	Phone
Assist-2-Sell Inc 1610 Meadow Wood Ln	Reno	NV	89502	**800-528-7816**	775-688-6060
Buy Owner 1192 E Newport Ctr Dr Suite 200	Deerfield Beach	FL	33442	**800-940-7777**	954-771-7777
Century 21 Commercial Investment Network 1 Campus Dr	Parsippany	NJ	07054	**800-221-5737**	973-428-9700
Century 21 Real Estate Corp 1 Campus Dr	Parsippany	NJ	07054	**800-221-5737**	973-428-9700
Chelsea Moore Co 8940 Glendale Milford Rd	Loveland	OH	45140	**888-621-1161**	513-561-5454
Coldwell Banker Gundaker 2458 Old Dorsett Rd Suite 300	Maryland Heights	MO	63043	**800-325-1978**	314-298-5000
Coldwell Banker Relocation 27271 Las Ramblas Suite 233	Mission Viejo	CA	92691	**800-733-1380**	800-292-2656
Coldwell Banker Residential Brokerage 8490 E Crescent Pkwy Suite 250	Greenwood Village	CO	80111	**877-233-8657**	303-409-1500
Coldwell Banker Residential Real Estate 5971 Cattleridge Blvd Suite 202	Sarasota	FL	34232	**800-624-5292**	941-378-8211
Daum Commercial Real Estate Services 4675 McArthur Ct Suite 220	Newport Beach	CA	92660	**888-659-3286**	949-724-1900
Divaris Real Estate Inc 1 Columbus Ctr Suite 700	Virginia Beach	VA	23462	**888-373-0023**	757-497-2113
Dodge NP Real Estate 8701 W Dodge Rd Suite 300	Omaha	NE	68114	**800-642-5008**	402-397-4900
ERA Franchise Systems Inc 1 Campus Dr	Parsippany	NJ	07054	**800-869-1260**	973-428-9700
First Hartford Realty Corp 149 Colonial Rd PO Box 1270	Manchester	CT	06045	**888-646-6555**	860-646-6555
First Service Realty Inc 13155 SW 42nd St Suite 200	Miami	FL	33175	**800-899-8477**	305-551-9400
Heitman LLC 191 N Wacker Dr Suite 2500	Chicago	IL	60606	**800-225-5435**	312-855-5700
Help-U-Sell Real Estate 6800 Jericho Tpke Suite 208 E	Syosset	NY	11791	**800-366-1177**	516-364-9650
HomeGain.com Inc 1250 45th St Suite 200	Emeryville	CA	94608	**888-542-0800**	510-655-0800
HomeLife Realty Services Inc 5752 176th St Unit 203	Surrey	BC	V3S4C8	**800-667-6329**	604-575-3130
Inland Group Inc 2901 Butterfield Rd	Oak Brook	IL	60523	**800-828-8999**	630-218-8000
Inland Real Estate Sales Inc 2901 Butterfield Rd	Oak Brook	IL	60523	**800-828-8999**	630-218-8000
Iowa Realty Co Inc 3501 Westown Pkwy	West Des Moines	IA	50266	**800-247-2430**	515-453-6222
Joyner & Co Realtors 2727 Enterprise Pkwy PO Box 31355	Richmond	VA	23294	**800-446-3858**	804-270-9440
Long & Foster Realtors 11351 Random Hills Rd	Fairfax	VA	22030	**800-237-8800**	703-359-1500
Miller WC & AN Realtors 4910 Massachusetts Ave NW Suite 119	Washington	DC	20016	**877-362-1300**	202-362-1300
NP Dodge Real Estate 8701 W Dodge Rd Suite 300	Omaha	NE	68114	**800-642-5008**	402-397-4900
Patterson-Schwartz & Assoc Inc 913 Delaware Ave	Wilmington	DE	19806	**800-438-2961**	302-656-3141
Prudential Northwest Real Estate 2497 Bethel Rd SE	Port Orchard	WA	98366	**800-463-7768**	360-876-5522
Prudential Real Estate Affiliates Inc 3333 Michelson Dr Suite 1000	Irvine	CA	92612	**800-999-1120**	949-794-7900
Real Estate One Inc 29630 Orchard Lake Rd	Farmington Hills	MI	48334	**800-521-0508**	248-851-2600
Realty Executives International 2398 E Camelback Rd Suite 900	Phoenix	AZ	85016	**800-252-3366**	602-957-0747
Realty One 6000 Rockside Woods Blvd	Cleveland	OH	44131	**877-328-2500**	216-328-2500
Re/MAX Equity Group Inc 84505 SW Nimbus Ave	Beaverton	OR	97008	**800-283-3358**	503-670-3000
RE/MAX International Inc 8390 E Crescent Pkwy Suite 500 *Cust Svc	Greenwood Village	CO	80111	**800-525-7452***	303-770-5531
RE/MAX Ontario-Atlantic 7101 Syntex Dr	Mississauga	ON	L5N6H5	**888-542-2499**	905-542-2400
RE/MAX of Western Canada Inc 1664 Richter St Suite 213	Kelowna	BC	V1Y8N3	**800-563-3622**	250-860-3628
Semonin Realtors 4967 US Hwy 42 Suite 200	Louisville	KY	40222	**800-548-1650**	502-425-4760
Sotheby's International Realty 38 E 61st St	New York	NY	10021	**800-848-2541**	212-606-4100
Staubach Co 15601 Dallas Pkwy Suite 400	Addison	TX	75001	**800-944-0012**	972-361-5000
Towne Realty Inc 710 N Plankinton Ave 12th Fl	Milwaukee	WI	53203	**800-945-4450**	414-273-2200
Watne Inc Realtors 408 N Broadway	Minot	ND	58703	**800-568-5311**	701-852-1156
WC & AN Miller Realtors 4910 Massachusetts Ave NW Suite 119	Washington	DC	20016	**877-362-1300**	202-362-1300
Weichert Realtors 1625 Rt 10 E	Morris Plains	NJ	07950	**800-872-7653**	973-267-7777
Westdale Realty Co 300 E Beltline Ave NE	Grand Rapids	MI	49506	**800-968-8770**	616-949-9400
ZipRealty Inc 2000 Powell St Suite 1555 *NASDAQ: ZIPR*	Emeryville	CA	94608	**800-225-5947**	510-735-2600

639 REAL ESTATE DEVELOPERS

SEE ALSO Construction - Building Contractors - Non-Residential; Construction - Building Contractors - Residential

				Toll-Free	Phone
Al Neyer Inc 10151 Carver Rd Suite 100	Cincinnati	OH	45242	**877-271-6400**	513-271-6400
Alter Group 5500 W Howard St	Skokie	IL	60077	**800-637-4842**	847-676-4300
Amelia Island Co 1501 Lewis St	Amelia Island	FL	32034	**888-261-6161**	904-261-6161
Avatar Holdings Inc 201 Alhambra Cir 12th Fl *NASDAQ: AVTR*	Coral Gables	FL	33134	**800-736-6660**	305-442-7000
Barratt American Inc 5950 Priestly Dr Suite 101	Carlsbad	CA	92008	**800-675-0440**	760-431-0800
Brooks Resources Corp 296 SW Columbia St Suite A	Bend	OR	97702	**888-773-7553**	541-382-1662
Buchan John F Homes 2821 Northup Way Suite 100	Bellevue	WA	98004	**866-528-2426**	425-827-2266
California Pacific Homes 38 Executive Pk Suite 200	Irvine	CA	92614	**800-999-0629**	949-833-6000
Connell Realty & Development Co 1 Connell Dr	Berkeley Heights	NJ	07922	**800-233-3240**	908-673-3700
Cooper Communities Inc 903 N 47th St	Rogers	AR	72756	**800-648-6401**	479-246-6500
CountryTyme Inc 4218 Hoover Rd	Grove City	OH	43123	**800-388-1349**	614-875-1423
Davis Homes Inc 3755 E 82nd St Suite 120	Indianapolis	IN	46240	**888-595-2800**	317-595-2800
Del Webb Corp 15111 N Pima Rd Suite 100	Scottsdale	AZ	85260	**800-808-8088**	
Deltona Corp 8014 SW 135th St Rd	Ocala	FL	34473	**800-935-6378**	352-347-2322
Developers of Nevada 7448 W Sahara Ave	Las Vegas	NV	89117	**888-250-7033**	702-222-1410
Dixon Builders & Developers Inc 7924 Jessie's Way	Hamilton	OH	45011	**877-442-5888**	513-887-6400
Donohoe Cos Inc 2101 Wisconsin Ave NW	Washington	DC	20007	**877-366-6463**	202-333-0880
DR Horton Inc 1901 Ascension Blvd Suite 100 *NYSE: DHI*	Arlington	TX	76006	**800-846-7866**	817-856-8200
EBSCO Development Co 5 Mt Laurel Ave	Birmingham	AL	35242	**888-408-8696**	205-408-8696
Estridge Cos 1041 W Main St	Carmel	IN	46032	**800-473-7326**	317-846-7311
Fieldstone Communities Inc 14 Corporate Plaza	Newport Beach	CA	92660	**800-665-0661**	949-640-9090
First Hartford Realty Corp 149 Colonial Rd PO Box 1270	Manchester	CT	06045	**888-646-6555**	860-646-6555
Forecast Group DBA Forecast Homes 3536 Concours St Suite 100	Ontario	CA	91764	**800-229-4117**	909-483-7320
Fralin & Waldron Inc 2917 Penn Forest Blvd	Roanoke	VA	24018	**888-238-7459**	540-774-4415
Horton DR Inc 1901 Ascension Blvd Suite 100 *NYSE: DHI*	Arlington	TX	76006	**800-846-7866**	817-856-8200
Hunt Midwest Residential Development 8300 NE Underground Dr	Kansas City	MO	64161	**800-551-6877**	816-455-2500
Inland Real Estate Development Corp 2901 Butterfield Rd	Oak Brook	IL	60523	**800-828-8999**	630-218-8000
JMC Communities 2201 4th St N Suite 200	Saint Petersburg	FL	33704	**800-741-4106**	727-823-0022
John F Buchan Homes 2821 Northup Way Suite 100	Bellevue	WA	98004	**866-528-2426**	425-827-2266
John Kavanagh Homes 1810 Pembroke Rd	Greensboro	NC	27408	**800-940-9904**	336-272-9904
John Wieland Homes & Neighborhoods Inc 1950 Sullivan Rd	Atlanta	GA	30337	**800-376-4663**	770-996-2400
Jupiter Realty Corp 919 N Michigan Ave Suite 1500	Chicago	IL	60611	**800-910-2276**	312-642-6000
Kaiser Ventures LLC 3633 E Inland Empire Blvd Suite 480	Ontario	CA	91764	**800-889-3652**	909-483-8500
Kapalua Land Co Ltd 700 Village Rd *Sales	Kapalua	HI	96761	**800-545-8439***	808-669-5622
Kavanagh John Homes 1810 Pembroke Rd	Greensboro	NC	27408	**800-940-9904**	336-272-9904
KB Home 10990 Wilshire Blvd 7th Fl *NYSE: KBH*	Los Angeles	CA	90024	**800-344-6637**	310-231-4000
KB Home Orlando 8403 S Park Cir Suite 670	Orlando	FL	32819	**800-615-2312**	321-354-2500
Lancia Construction 9430 Lima Rd Suite A	Fort Wayne	IN	46818	**800-752-6242**	260-489-4433
Landstar Development Corp 120 Fairway Woods Blvd	Orlando	FL	32824	**800-327-9105**	407-240-0044
Lennar Homes Inc 700 NW 107th Ave Suite 400	Miami	FL	33172	**800-741-4663**	305-559-4000
Martin Stanley Cos Inc 1881 Campus Commons Dr Suite 101	Reston	VA	20191	**800-446-4807**	703-715-7800
Minto Builders 4400 W Sample Rd Suite 200	Coconut Creek	FL	33073	**800-767-4490**	954-973-4490
Mission West Properties 10050 Bandley Dr *AMEX: MSW*	Cupertino	CA	95014	**800-222-5401**	408-725-0700
Newhall Land & Farming Co 23823 Valencia Blvd	Valencia	CA	91355	**800-342-3612**	661-255-4000

Classified Section

	City	State	ZIP	Toll-Free	Phone
Neyer Al Inc 10151 Carver Rd Suite 100	Cincinnati	OH	45242	**877-271-6400**	513-271-6400
Oriole Homes Corp 6400S Congress Ave Suite 2000	Boca Raton	FL	33487	**800-964-6631**	561-999-1860
Polygon Northwest Co 11624 SE 5th St Suite 200	Bellevue	WA	98005	**800-765-9466**	425-586-7700
Post Properties Inc 4401 Northside Pkwy Suite 800 *NYSE: PPS*	Atlanta	GA	30327	**877-644-7678**	404-846-5000
Pringle Development Inc 26600 Ace Ave	Leesburg	FL	34748	**800-325-4471**	352-365-2303
Pulte Home Corp 100 Bloomfield Hills Pkwy Suite 300	Bloomfield Hills	MI	48304	**800-777-8583**	248-644-7300
Richman Group of Cos 599 W Putnam Ave	Greenwich	CT	06830	**800-333-3509**	203-869-0900
Richmond American Homes Inc 6550 S Greenwood Plaza Blvd	Centennial	CO	80111	**888-402-4663**	303-773-2727
Robson Communities 9532 E Riggs Rd	Sun Lakes	AZ	85248	**800-732-9949**	480-895-9200
Ryland Group Inc 24025 Park Sorrento Suite 400 *NYSE: RYL*	Calabasas	CA	91302	**800-267-0998**	818-223-7500
Saint Joe Towns & Resorts 7900 Glades Rd Suite 200	Boca Raton	FL	33434	**800-527-8432**	561-479-1100
Schatten Properties Management Co Inc 1514 South St	Nashville	TN	37212	**800-892-1315**	615-329-3011
Sea Pines Plantation Co Inc 32 Greenwood Dr	Hilton Head Island	SC	29928	**800-925-4653**	843-785-3333
Shapell Industries Inc 8383 Wilshire Blvd Suite 700	Beverly Hills	CA	90211	**800-655-9502**	323-655-7330
Simpson Housing LP 8110 E Union Ave Suite 200	Denver	CO	80237	**888-330-5951**	
Space Center Inc 2501 Rosegate	Saint Paul	MN	55113	**800-548-9737**	651-604-4200
Stanley Martin Cos Inc 1881 Campus Commons Dr Suite 101	Reston	VA	20191	**800-446-4807**	703-715-7800
Stratus Properties Inc 98 San Jacinto Blvd Suite 220 *NASDAQ: STRS*	Austin	TX	78701	**800-690-0315**	512-478-5788
Taylor-Morley Homes 17107 Chesterfield Airport Rd Suite 200	Chesterfield	MO	63005	**888-297-3155**	314-434-9000
Toll Brothers Inc 250 Gibraltar Rd *NYSE: TOL*	Horsham	PA	19044	**800-289-8655**	215-938-8000
TransCon Builders Inc 25250 Rockside Rd	Bedford Heights	OH	44146	**800-362-0371**	440-439-3400
Transeastern Properties Inc 3300 N University Dr Suite 001	Coral Springs	FL	33065	**877-352-4635**	954-346-9700
Village Homes of Colorado Inc 6 W Dry Creek Cir	Littleton	CO	80120	**866-752-2322**	303-795-1976
Villages of Lake Sumter Inc 1100 Main St	The Villages	FL	32159	**800-346-4556**	352-753-2270
Warmington Group 3090 Pullman St Suite A	Costa Mesa	CA	92626	**800-925-9709**	714-557-5511
Washington Homes Inc 1802 Brightseat Rd	Landover	MD	20785	**800-342-5944**	301-772-8900
WCI Communities Inc 24301 Walden Ctr Dr *NYSE: WCI*	Bonita Springs	FL	34134	**800-924-2290**	239-947-2600
Webb Del Corp 15111 N Pima Rd Suite 100	Scottsdale	AZ	85260	**800-808-8088**	
Weiss Homes Inc 828 E Jefferson Blvd	South Bend	IN	46617	**888-336-7373**	574-234-7373
Westrum Development Co Inc 370 Commerce Dr Suite 100	Fort Washington	PA	19034	**800-937-8786**	215-283-2190
Wieland John Homes & Neighborhoods Inc 1950 Sullivan Rd	Atlanta	GA	30337	**800-376-4663**	770-996-2400
Worthington Communities 9240 Marketplace Rd Suite 2	Fort Myers	FL	33912	**877-560-4666**	239-561-4666
Zicka Walker Homes Inc 7861 E Kemper Rd	Cincinnati	OH	45249	**800-652-1745**	513-247-3500

640 REAL ESTATE INVESTMENT TRUSTS (REITS)

	City	State	ZIP	Toll-Free	Phone
Acadia Realty Trust 1311 Mamaroneck Ave Suite 260 *NYSE: AKR*	White Plains	NY	10605	**800-227-5570**	914-288-8100
Affordable Residential Communities Inc 600 Grant St Suite 900 *NYSE: ARC*	Denver	CO	80203	**800-245-5415**	303-291-0222
America First Apartment Investors Inc 1004 Farnam St Suite 100 *NASDAQ: APRO*	Omaha	NE	68102	**800-283-2357**	402-444-1630
American Land Lease Inc 29399 US 19 N Suite 320 *NYSE: ANL*	Clearwater	FL	33761	**800-826-6069**	727-726-8868
AmREIT 8 Greenway Plaza Suite 1000 *AMEX: AMY*	Houston	TX	77046	**800-888-4400**	713-850-1400
Annaly Mortgage Management Inc 1211 Ave of the Americas Suite 2902 *NYSE: NLY*	New York	NY	10036	**800-487-9947**	212-696-0100
Apartment Investment & Management Co 4582 S Ulster Street Pkwy Suite 1100 *NYSE: AIV*	Denver	CO	80237	**888-789-8600**	303-757-8101
Archstone-Smith Trust 9200 E Panorama Cir Suite 400 *NYSE: ASN*	Englewood	CO	80112	**877-272-4786**	303-708-5959
Arizona Land Income Corp 2999 N 44th St Suite 100 *AMEX: AZL*	Phoenix	AZ	85018	**800-999-1818**	602-952-6800
Associated Estates Realty Corp 5025 Swetland Ct *NYSE: AEC*	Richmond Heights	OH	44143	**800-440-2372**	216-261-5000
Berkshire Income Realty Inc 1 Beacon St *AMEX: BIR_pa*	Boston	MA	02108	**888-867-0100**	617-523-7722
BRT Realty Trust 60 Cutter Mill Rd Suite 303 *NYSE: BRT*	Great Neck	NY	11021	**800-450-5816**	516-466-3100
Camden Property Trust 3 Greenway Plaza Suite 1300 *NYSE: CPT*	Houston	TX	77046	**800-922-6336**	713-354-2500
Capital Automotive REIT 8270 Greensboro Dr Suite 950 *NASDAQ: CARS*	McLean	VA	22102	**877-422-7288**	703-288-3075
Capstead Mortgage Corp 8401 N Central Expy Suite 800 *NYSE: CMO*	Dallas	TX	75225	**800-358-2323**	214-874-2323
CarrAmerica Realty Corp 1850 K St NW Suite 500 *NYSE: CRE*	Washington	DC	20006	**800-417-2277**	202-729-1700
Cedar Shopping Centers Inc 44 S Bayles Ave Suite 304 *NYSE: CDR*	Port Washington	NY	11050	**800-564-3128**	516-767-6492
Church Loans & Investment Trust PO Box 8203	Amarillo	TX	79114	**800-692-1111**	806-358-3666
Clarion Commercial Holdings Inc 230 Park Ave 12th Fl	New York	NY	10169	**800-776-4696**	212-883-2500
Commercial Net Lease Realty Inc 450 S Orange Ave *NYSE: NNN*	Orlando	FL	32801	**800-522-3863**	407-650-1000
Commercial Properties Realty Trust 5630 Bankers Ave	Baton Rouge	LA	70808	**800-648-9064**	225-924-7206
Correctional Properties Trust 3300 PGA Blvd Suite 750 *NYSE: CPV*	Palm Beach Gardens	FL	33410	**877-774-7661**	561-630-6336
Cousins Properties Inc 2500 Windy Ridge Pkwy Suite 1600 *NYSE: CUZ*	Atlanta	GA	30339	**800-926-8746**	770-955-2200
CRIIMI MAE Inc 11200 Rockville Pike *NYSE: CMM*	Rockville	MD	20852	**800-266-0535**	301-816-2300
Developers Diversified Realty Corp 3300 Enterprise Pkwy *NYSE: DDR*	Beachwood	OH	44122	**800-258-7289**	216-755-5500
Dividend Capital Trust 518 17th St Suite 1700	Denver	CO	80202	**866-324-7348**	303-228-2200
Duke Realty Corp 600 E 96th St Suite 100 *NYSE: DRE*	Indianapolis	IN	46240	**800 875 3366**	317 808 6000
EastGroup Properties Inc 188 E Capitol St Suite 300 *NYSE: EGP*	Jackson	MS	39201	**800-337-5602**	601-354-3555
ECC Capital Corp 1833 Alton Pkwy *NYSE: ECR*	Irvine	CA	92606	**800-472-2971**	949-856-8300
Entertainment Properties Trust 30 W Pershing Rd Suite 201 *NYSE: EPR*	Kansas City	MO	64108	**888-377-7348**	816-472-1700
Equity One Inc 1696 NE Miami Gardens Dr *NYSE: EQY*	North Miami Beach	FL	33179	**800-867-2777**	305-947-1664
Falcon Financial Investment Trust 15 Commerce Rd	Stamford	CT	06902	**800-771-5400**	203-967-0000
Federal Realty Investment Trust 1626 E Jefferson St *NYSE: FRT*	Rockville	MD	20852	**800-658-8980**	301-998-8100
First Industrial Realty Trust Inc 311 S Wacker Dr Suite 4000 *NYSE: FR*	Chicago	IL	60606	**800-894-8778**	312-344-4300
Friedman Billings Ramsey Group Inc 1001 19th St N 18th Fl *NYSE: FBR*	Arlington	VA	22209	**800-846-5050**	703-312-9500
Health Care Property Investors Inc 3760 Kilroy Airport Way Suite 300 *NYSE: HCP*	Long Beach	CA	90806	**888-604-1990**	562-733-5100
Highwoods Properties Inc 3100 Smoketree Ct Suite 600 *NYSE: HIW*	Raleigh	NC	27604	**866-449-6637**	919-872-4924
Impac Mortgage Holdings Inc 1401 Dove St Suite 100 *NYSE: IMH*	Newport Beach	CA	92660	**800-597-4101**	949-475-3600
Inland Real Estate Corp 2901 Butterfield Rd *NYSE: IRC*	Oak Brook	IL	60523	**888-331-4732**	630-218-8000
InnSuites Hospitality Trust 1615 E Northern Ave Suite 102 *AMEX: IHT*	Phoenix	AZ	85020	**800-842-4242**	602-944-1500
Kimco Realty Corp 3333 New Hyde Pk Rd Suite 100 *NYSE: KIM*	New Hyde Park	NY	11042	**800-285-4626**	516-869-9000
Macerich Co 401 Wilshire Blvd Suite 700 *NYSE: MAC*	Santa Monica	CA	90401	**800-421-7237**	310-394-6911
New Plan Excel Realty Trust Inc 420 Lexington Ave 7th Fl *NYSE: NXL*	New York	NY	10170	**800-468-7526**	646-344-8600
Novastar Financial Inc 8140 Ward Pkwy Suite 300 *NYSE: NFI*	Kansas City	MO	64114	**800-469-4270**	816-237-7000
One Liberty Properties Inc 60 Cutter Mill Rd Suite 303 *NYSE: OLP*	Great Neck	NY	11021	**800-450-5816**	516-466-3100
Pan Pacific Retail Properties Inc 1631-B S Melrose Dr *NYSE: PNP*	Vista	CA	92081	**800-776-1002**	760-727-1002
Parkway Properties Inc 188 E Capitol St Suite 1000 *NYSE: PKY*	Jackson	MS	39201	**800-748-1667**	601-948-4091
PMC Commercial Trust 17950 Preston Rd Suite 600 *AMEX: PCC*	Dallas	TX	75252	**800-486-3223**	972-349-3200
Post Properties Inc 4401 Northside Pkwy Suite 800 *NYSE: PPS*	Atlanta	GA	30327	**877-644-7678**	404-846-5000
Presidential Realty Corp 180 S Broadway *AMEX: PDL/A*	White Plains	NY	10605	**800-948-2977**	914-948-1300
Prime Retail LP 217 E Redwood St 20th Fl	Baltimore	MD	21202	**800-980-7467**	410-234-0782
ProLogis 14100 E 35th Pl *NYSE: PLD*	Aurora	CO	80011	**800-566-2706**	303-375-9292
Public Storage Inc 701 Western Ave *NYSE: PSA* ■ *Cust Svc	Glendale	CA	91201	**800-567-0759***	818-244-8080
Ramco-Gershenson Properties Trust 31500 Northwestern Hwy Suite 300 *NYSE: RPT*	Farmington Hills	MI	48334	**800-225-6765**	248-350-9900
Reckson Assoc Realty Corp 225 Broadhollow Rd Suite 212 *NYSE: RA*	Melville	NY	11747	**888-732-5766**	631-694-6900
Regency Centers 121 W Forsyth St Suite 200 *NYSE: REG*	Jacksonville	FL	32202	**800-950-6333**	904-356-7000
Royal Host Real Estate Investment Trust 5940 Macleod Trail S Suite 500 *TSE: RYL* ■ *Cust Svc	Calgary	AB	T2H2G4	**877-626-4004***	403-259-9800
Shurgard Storage Centers Inc 1155 Valley St Suite 400 *NYSE: SHU*	Seattle	WA	98109	**800-748-7427**	206-624-8100

				Toll-Free	Phone
Starwood Hotels & Resorts Worldwide Inc 1111 Westchester Ave *NYSE: HOT ■ *Cust Svc*	White Plains	NY	10604	**877-443-4585***	914-640-8100
Tanger Factory Outlet Centers Inc 3200 Northline Ave Suite 360 *NYSE: SKT*	Greensboro	NC	27408	**800-438-8474**	336-292-3010
Town & Country Trust 300 E Lombard St Suite 1700 *NYSE: TCT*	Baltimore	MD	21202	**800-735-2468**	410-539-7600
Transcontinental Realty Investors Inc 1800 Valley View Ln 1 Hickory Ctr *NYSE: TCI*	Dallas	TX	75234	**800-400-6407**	469-522-4200
Trustreet Properties Inc 450 S Orange Ave *NYSE: TSY*	Orlando	FL	32801	**877-667-4769**	407-540-2000
United Dominion Realty Trust Inc 400 E Cary St *NYSE: UDR*	Richmond	VA	23219	**800-800-2691**	804-780-2691
Urstadt Biddle Properties Inc 321 Railroad Ave *NYSE: UBP*	Greenwich	CT	06830	**800-323-8216**	203-863-8200
Ventas Inc 10350 Ormsby Pk Pl Suite 300 *NYSE: VTR*	Louisville	KY	40223	**800-877-4836**	502-357-9000
Vornado Realty Trust 210 Rt 4 E *NYSE: VNO*	Paramus	NJ	07652	**800-242-4119**	201-587-1000
Washington Real Estate Investment Trust 6110 Executive Blvd Suite 800 *NYSE: WRE*	Rockville	MD	20852	**800-565-9748**	301-984-9400
Weingarten Realty Investors 2600 Citadel Plaza Dr Suite 300 *NYSE: WRI*	Houston	TX	77008	**800-688-8865**	713-866-6000
Wells Real Estate Investment Trust 6200 The Corners Pkwy	Norcross	GA	30092	**800-282-1581**	770-449-7800
WP Carey & Co LLC 50 Rockefeller Plaza 2nd Fl *NYSE: WPC*	New York	NY	10020	**800-972-2739**	212-492-1100

641 REAL ESTATE MANAGERS & OPERATORS

SEE ALSO Hotel & Resort Operation & Management; Retirement Communities

				Toll-Free	Phone
Acadia Realty Trust 1311 Mamaroneck Ave Suite 260 *NYSE: AKR*	White Plains	NY	10605	**800-227-5570**	914-288-8100
Allred Douglas Co 11512 El Camino Real Suite 100	San Diego	CA	92130	**800-555-6214**	858-793-0202
America First Apartment Investors Inc 1004 Farnam St Suite 100 *NASDAQ: APRO*	Omaha	NE	68102	**800-283-2357**	402-444-1630
American Golf Corp 2951 28th St	Santa Monica	CA	90405	**800-345-4259**	310-664-4000
American Land Lease Inc 29399 US 19 N Suite 320 *NYSE: ANL*	Clearwater	FL	33761	**800-826-6069**	727-726-8868
AmREIT 8 Greenway Plaza Suite 1000 *AMEX: AMY*	Houston	TX	77046	**800-888-4400**	713-850-1400
Apartment Investment & Management Co 4582 S Ulster Street Pkwy Suite 1100 *NYSE: AIV*	Denver	CO	80237	**888-789-8600**	303-757-8101
Archstone-Smith Trust 9200 E Panorama Cir Suite 400 *NYSE: ASN*	Englewood	CO	80112	**877-272-4786**	303-708-5959
Associated Estates Realty Corp 5025 Swetland Ct *NYSE: AEC*	Richmond Heights	OH	44143	**800-440-2372**	216-261-5000
Berkshire Income Realty Inc 1 Beacon St *AMEX: BIR_pa*	Boston	MA	02108	**888-867-0100**	617-523-7722
Berkshire Property Advisors LLC 1 Beacon St Suite 1550	Boston	MA	02108	**888-867-0100**	617-646-2300
Boyle Investment Co 5900 Poplar Ave Suite 100	Memphis	TN	38119	**888-862-6953**	901-767-0100
Bozzuto Group 7850 Walker Dr Suite 400	Greenbelt	MD	20770	**800-718-0200**	301-220-0100
Calista Corp 301 Calista Ct Suite A	Anchorage	AK	99518	**800-277-5516**	907-279-5516
Camden Property Trust 3 Greenway Plaza Suite 1300 *NYSE: CPT*	Houston	TX	77046	**800-922-6336**	713-354-2500
CarrAmerica Realty Corp 1850 K St NW Suite 500 *NYSE: CRE*	Washington	DC	20006	**800-417-2277**	202-729-1700
Cedar Shopping Centers Inc 44 S Bayles Ave Suite 304 *NYSE: CDR*	Port Washington	NY	11050	**800-564-3128**	516-767-6492
Century 21 Commercial Investment Network 1 Campus Dr	Parsippany	NJ	07054	**800-221-5737**	973-428-9700
ClubCorp Inc 3030 LBJ Fwy	Dallas	TX	75234	**800-346-7621**	972-243-6191
ClubLink Corp 15675 Dufferin St *TSE: LNK*	King City	ON	L7B1K5	**800-661-1818**	905-841-3730
Coldwell Banker Commercial 1 Campus Dr	Parsippany	NJ	07054	**800-222-2162**	973-496-7651
Commercial Net Lease Realty Inc 450 S Orange Ave *NYSE: NNN*	Orlando	FL	32801	**800-522-3863**	407-650-1000
Correctional Properties Trust 3300 PGA Blvd Suite 750 *NYSE: CPV*	Palm Beach Gardens	FL	33410	**877-774-7661**	561-630-6336
Cousins Properties Inc 2500 Windy Ridge Pkwy Suite 1600 *NYSE: CUZ*	Atlanta	GA	30339	**800-926-8746**	770-955-2200
Crombie Properties Ltd 115 King St	Stellarton	NS	B0K1S0	**800-463-2406**	902-755-4440
Developers Diversified Realty Corp 3300 Enterprise Pkwy *NYSE: DDR*	Beachwood	OH	44122	**800-258-7289**	216-755-5500
Divaris Real Estate Inc 1 Columbus Ctr Suite 700	Virginia Beach	VA	23462	**888-373-0023**	757-497-2113
Douglas Allred Co 11512 El Camino Real Suite 100	San Diego	CA	92130	**800-555-6214**	858-793-0202
Draper & Kramer Inc 33 W Monroe St Suite 1900	Chicago	IL	60603	**800-621-0776**	312-346-8600
Duke Realty Corp 600 E 96th St Suite 100 *NYSE: DRE*	Indianapolis	IN	46240	**800-875-3366**	317-808-6000

				Toll-Free	Phone
EastGroup Properties Inc 188 E Capitol St Suite 300 *NYSE: EGP*	Jackson	MS	39201	**800-337-5602**	601-354-3555
Entertainment Properties Trust 30 W Pershing Rd Suite 201 *NYSE: EPR*	Kansas City	MO	64108	**888-377-7348**	816-472-1700
Equity One Inc 1696 NE Miami Gardens Dr *NYSE: EQY*	North Miami Beach	FL	33179	**800-867-2777**	305-947-1664
Federal Realty Investment Trust 1626 E Jefferson St *NYSE: FRT*	Rockville	MD	20852	**800-658-8980**	301-998-8100
First Hartford Realty Corp 149 Colonial Rd PO Box 1270	Manchester	CT	06045	**888-646-6555**	860-646-6555
First Industrial Realty Trust Inc 311 S Wacker Dr Suite 4000 *NYSE: FR*	Chicago	IL	60606	**800-894-8778**	312-344-4300
First Republic Corp of America 302 5th Ave	New York	NY	10001	**800-578-2254**	212-279-6100
Forest City Residential Group Inc 50 Public Sq Terminal Tower Suite 1100	Cleveland	OH	44113	**800-726-1800**	216-621-6060
Grady Management Inc 8630 Fenton St Suite 625	Silver Spring	MD	20910	**800-544-7239**	301-587-3330
Gundaker Property Management 2458 Old Dorsett Rd Suite 300	Maryland Heights	MO	63043	**800-325-1978**	314-298-5000
Hallwood Commercial Real Estate LLC 3710 Rawlins St Suite 1500	Dallas	TX	75219	**800-225-0135**	214-528-5588
Health Care Property Investors Inc 3760 Kilroy Airport Way Suite 300 *NYSE: HCP*	Long Beach	CA	90806	**888-604-1990**	562-733-5100
Heitman LLC 191 N Wacker Dr Suite 2500	Chicago	IL	60606	**800-225-5435**	312-855-5700
Highwoods Properties Inc 3100 Smoketree Ct Suite 600 *NYSE: HIW*	Raleigh	NC	27604	**866-449-6637**	919-872-4924
Holiday Retirement Corp 2250 McGilchrist St SE	Salem	OR	97302	**800-860-2249**	503-370-7070
Inland Group Inc 2901 Butterfield Rd	Oak Brook	IL	60523	**800-828-8999**	630-218-8000
Inland Real Estate Corp 2901 Butterfield Rd *NYSE: IRC*	Oak Brook	IL	60523	**888-331-4732**	630-218-8000
Jacobs Richard E Group Inc 25425 Center Ridge Rd	Cleveland	OH	44145	**800-852-9558**	440-871-4800
Kimco Realty Corp 3333 New Hyde Pk Rd Suite 100 *NYSE: KIM*	New Hyde Park	NY	11042	**800-285-4626**	516-869-9000
Kraus-Anderson Realty Co 4210 W Old Shakopee Rd	Bloomington	MN	55437	**800-399-4220**	952-881-8166
Levin Management Corp 893 Rt 22 W	North Plainfield	NJ	07060	**800-488-0768**	908-755-2401
LNR Property Corp 1601 Washington Ave Suite 800	Miami Beach	FL	33139	**800-784-6380**	305-695-5600
Macerich Co 401 Wilshire Blvd Suite 700 *NYSE: MAC*	Santa Monica	CA	90401	**800-421-7237**	310-394-6911
New Plan Excel Realty Trust Inc 420 Lexington Ave 7th Fl *NYSE: NXL*	New York	NY	10170	**800-468-7526**	646-344-8600
One Liberty Properties Inc 60 Cutter Mill Rd Suite 303 *NYSE: OLP*	Great Neck	NY	11021	**800-450-5816**	516-466-3100
Pan Pacific Retail Properties Inc 1631-B S Melrose Dr *NYSE: PNP*	Vista	CA	92081	**800-776-1002**	760-727-1002
Parkway Properties Inc 188 E Capitol St Suite 1000 *NYSE: PKY*	Jackson	MS	39201	**800-748-1667**	601-948-4091
Pier 39 LP Inc Beach & Embarcadero Sts Stairway 2 Level 3	San Francisco	CA	94133	**800-325-7437**	415-705-5500
Price Edwards & Co 210 Park Ave Suite 1000	Oklahoma City	OK	73102	**800-316-7811**	405-843-7474
Prime Retail LP 217 E Redwood St 20th Fl	Baltimore	MD	21202	**800-980-7467**	410-234-0782
Professional Community Management Inc 23726 Birtcher Dr	Lake Forest	CA	92630	**800-369-7260**	949-768-7261
ProLogis 14100 E 35th Pl *NYSE: PLD*	Aurora	CO	80011	**800-566-2706**	303-375-9292
Ramco-Gershenson Properties Trust 31500 Northwestern Hwy Suite 300 *NYSE: RPT*	Farmington Hills	MI	48334	**800-225-6765**	248-350-9900
Reckson Assoc Realty Corp 225 Broadhollow Rd Suite 212 *NYSE: RA*	Melville	NY	11747	**888-732-5766**	631-694-6900
Regency Centers 121 W Forsyth St Suite 200 *NYSE: REG*	Jacksonville	FL	32202	**800-950-6333**	904-356-7000
Richard E Jacobs Group Inc 25425 Center Ridge Rd	Cleveland	OH	44145	**800-852-9558**	440-871-4800
Saint Joe Towns & Resorts 7900 Glades Rd Suite 200	Boca Raton	FL	33434	**800-527-8432**	561-479-1100
Schatten Properties Management Co Inc 1514 South St	Nashville	TN	37212	**800-892-1315**	615-329-3011
Sea Island Co 100 1st St	Sea Island	GA	31561	**800-732-4752**	912-638-3611
Selig Enterprises Inc 1100 Spring St NW Suite 550	Atlanta	GA	30309	**800-830-9965**	404-876-5511
Seligman & Assoc 1 Town Sq Suite 1913	Southfield	MI	48076	**866-864-9824**	248-862-8000
Sen Plex Corp 938 Kohou St	Honolulu	HI	96817	**800-552-4553**	808-848-0111
Stanmar Inc 130 Boston Post Rd	Sudbury	MA	01776	**800-617-3607**	978-443-9922
Staubach Co 15601 Dallas Pkwy Suite 400	Addison	TX	75001	**800-944-0012**	972-361-5000
Stirling Properties 109 Northpark Blvd Suite 300	Covington	LA	70433	**888-261-2022**	985-898-2022
Tanger Factory Outlet Centers Inc 3200 Northline Ave Suite 360 *NYSE: SKT*	Greensboro	NC	27408	**800-438-8474**	336-292-3010
Town & Country Trust 300 E Lombard St Suite 1700 *NYSE: TCT*	Baltimore	MD	21202	**800-735-2468**	410-539-7600
Towne Realty Inc 710 N Plankinton Ave 12th Fl	Milwaukee	WI	53203	**800-945-4450**	414-273-2200
Transcontinental Realty Investors Inc 1800 Valley View Ln 1 Hickory Ctr *NYSE: TCI*	Dallas	TX	75234	**800-400-6407**	469-522-4200
Tucson Realty & Trust Co 335 N Wilmont Rd Suite 505	Tucson	AZ	85711	**877-254-5740**	520-577-7000
United Dominion Realty Trust Inc 400 E Cary St *NYSE: UDR*	Richmond	VA	23219	**800-800-2691**	804-780-2691

	City	State	ZIP	*Toll-Free*	*Phone*
Urstadt Biddle Properties Inc 321 Railroad Ave *NYSE: UBP*	Greenwich	CT	06830	**800-323-8216**	203-863-8200
USAA Real Estate Co 9830 Colonnade Blvd Suite 600	San Antonio	TX	78230	**800-531-8182**	210-498-3222
Ventas Inc 10350 Ormsby Pk Pl Suite 300 *NYSE: VTR*	Louisville	KY	40223	**800-877-4836**	502-357-9000
Vinings Investment Properties Trust 2839 Paces Ferry Rd NW Suite 880	Atlanta	GA	30339	**800-849-5868**	770-984-9500
Vornado Realty Trust 210 Rt 4 E *NYSE: VNO*	Paramus	NJ	07652	**800-242-4119**	201-587-1000
Wal-Mart Realty 2001 SE 10th St	Bentonville	AR	72716	**800-925-6278**	479-273-4000
Warren Properties Inc PO Box 469114	Escondido	CA	92046	**877-927-7361**	760-480-6211
Washington Real Estate Investment Trust 6110 Executive Blvd Suite 800 *NYSE: WRE*	Rockville	MD	20852	**800-565-9748**	301-984-9400
Weingarten Realty Investors 2600 Citadel Plaza Dr Suite 300 *NYSE: WRI*	Houston	TX	77008	**800-688-8865**	713-866-6000
Wentworth Group Inc 901 S Trooper Rd	Norristown	PA	19403	**800-222-7569**	610-650-0600
White Co 1750 S Brentwood Blvd Suite 301	Saint Louis	MO	63144	**888-221-9679**	314-961-4480
WP Carey & Co LLC 50 Rockefeller Plaza 2nd Fl *NYSE: WPC*	New York	NY	10020	**800-972-2739**	212-492-1100

642 REALTOR ASSOCIATIONS - STATE

SEE ALSO Associations & Organizations - Professional & Trade - Real Estate Professionals Associations

	City	State	ZIP	*Toll-Free*	*Phone*
Arizona 255 E Osborne Rd Suite 200	Phoenix	AZ	85012	**800-426-7274**	602-248-7787
Arkansas 204 Executive Ct Suite 300	Little Rock	AR	72205	**888-333-2206**	501-225-2020
Colorado 309 Inverness Way S	Englewood	CO	80112	**800-944-6550**	303-790-7099
Connecticut 111 Founders Plaza 11th Fl	East Hartford	CT	06108	**800-335-4862**	860-290-6601
Delaware 9 E Loockerman St Suite 315	Dover	DE	19901	**800-305-4445**	302-734-4444
Idaho 1450 W Bannock St	Boise	ID	83702	**800-621-7553**	208-342-3585
Iowa 1370 NW 114th St Suite 100	Clive	IA	50325	**800-532-1515**	515-453-1064
Kansas 3644 SW Burlingame Rd	Topeka	KS	66611	**800-366-0069**	785-267-3610
Kentucky 161 Prosperous Pl	Lexington	KY	40509	**800-264-2185**	859-263-7377
Louisiana 4639 Bennington Ave	Baton Rouge	LA	70808	**800-266-8538**	225-923-2210
Maryland 2594 Riva Rd	Annapolis	MD	21401	**800-638-6425**	410-841-6080
Massachusetts 256 2nd Ave	Waltham	MA	02451	**800-725-6272**	781-890-3700
Michigan 720 N Washington Ave	Lansing	MI	48906	**800-454-7842**	517-372-8890
Minnesota 5750 Lincoln Dr	Edina	MN	55436	**800-862-6097**	952-935-8313
Mississippi PO Box 321000	Jackson	MS	39232	**800-747-1103**	601-932-9325
Missouri 2601 Bernadette Pl	Columbia	MO	65203	**800-403-0101**	573-445-8400
Montana 208 N Montana Ave Suite 203	Helena	MT	59601	**800-477-1864**	406-443-4032
Nebraska 145 S 56th St Suite 100	Lincoln	NE	68510	**800-777-5231**	402-323-6500
Nevada 760 Margrave Dr Suite 200	Reno	NV	89502	**800-748-5526**	775-829-5911
New Mexico 2201 Brothers Rd	Santa Fe	NM	87505	**800-224-2282**	505-982-2442
New York 130 Washington Ave	Albany	NY	12210	**800-422-2501**	518-463-0300
North Carolina 4511 Weybridge Ln	Greensboro	NC	27407	**800-443-9956**	336-294-1415
North Dakota 318 W Apollo Ave	Bismarck	ND	58503	**800-279-2361**	701-355-1010
Oklahoma 9807 N Broadway	Oklahoma City	OK	73114	**800-375-9944**	405-848-9944
Oregon 693 Chemeketa St NE	Salem	OR	97308	**800-252-9115**	503-362-3645
South Carolina 3780 Fernandina Rd	Columbia	SC	29210	**800-233-6381**	803-772-5206
Texas 1115 San Jacinto Blvd Suite 200	Austin	TX	78701	**800-873-9155**	512-480-8200
Utah 5710 S Green St	Murray	UT	84123	**800-594-8933**	801-268-4747
Vermont 148 State St	Montpelier	VT	05602	**866-248-6182**	802-229-0513
Virginia 10231 Telegraph Rd	Glen Allen	VA	23059	**800-755-8271**	804-264-5033
Washington 504 E 14th Ave Suite 200	Olympia	WA	98501	**800-562-6024**	360-943-3100
Wyoming PO Box 2312	Casper	WY	82602	**800-676-4085**	307-237-4085

643 RECORDING COMPANIES

	City	State	ZIP	*Toll-Free*	*Phone*
American Gramaphone LLC 9130 Mormon Bridge Rd	Omaha	NE	68152	**800-348-3434**	402-457-4341
Back Porch Records 4650 N Port Washington Rd	Milwaukee	WI	53212	**800-966-3699**	414-961-8350
BMG Heritage 1540 Broadway	New York	NY	10036	**877-264-7744**	
Concord Records Inc 270 N Canon Dr Suite 1212	Beverly Hills	CA	90210	**800-551-5299**	310-385-4455
Fantasy Inc 2600 10th St	Berkeley	CA	94710	**800-227-0466**	510-549-2500
HighBridge Audio 33 S 6th St CC-2205	Minneapolis	MN	55402	**800-755-8532**	612-304-7163
Higher Octave Music 4650 N Port Washington Rd	Milwaukee	WI	53212	**800-966-3699**	414-961-8350
Integrity Media Inc 1000 Cody Rd S *Orders	Mobile	AL	36695	**800-533-6912***	251-633-9000
Interscope Records 2220 Colorado Ave	Santa Monica	CA	90404	**800-982-1812**	310-865-1000
K-Tel International Inc 2655 Cheshire Ln N Suite 100	Plymouth	MN	55447	**800-328-6640**	763-559-5566
Koch Entertainment Distribution 22 Harbor Pk Dr	Port Washington	NY	11050	**800-332-7553**	516-484-1000
Lyric Street Records 1100 Demonbreun St Suite 100	Nashville	TN	37203	**888-814-4934**	615-963-4848
Malaco Music Group Inc 3023 W Northside Dr *Cust Svc	Jackson	MS	39213	**800-272-7936***	601-982-4522
Narada Productions Inc 4650 N Port Washington Rd	Milwaukee	WI	53212	**800-966-3699**	414-961-8350
Nightingale-Conant Corp 6245 W Howard St *Cust Svc	Niles	IL	60714	**800-323-3938***	847-647-0300
Putumayo World Music 411 Lafayette St 4th Fl	New York	NY	10003	**888-788-8629**	212-995-9400
Rhino Records 3400 W Olive Ave	Burbank	CA	91505	**800-827-4466**	818-238-6100
Righteous Babe Records PO Box 95 Ellicott Station	Buffalo	NY	14205	**800-664-3769**	716-852-8020
Rounder Records 1 Camp St	Cambridge	MA	02140	**800-768-6337**	617-354-0700
Smithsonian Folkways Recordings 750 9th St NW Suite 4100	Washington	DC	20560	**800-410-9815**	202-275-1143
Sound of America Records (SOAR) 5200 Constitution NE	Albuquerque	NM	87110	**800-890-7627**	505-268-6110
Sparrow Label Group PO Box 5010	Brentwood	TN	37024	**800-347-4777**	615-371-6800
Sugar Hill Records 501-A Washington St	Durham	NC	27701	**800-996-4455**	919-489-4349
Telarc International Corp 23307 Commerce Pk Rd	Cleveland	OH	44122	**800-801-5810**	216-464-2313

644 RECORDING MEDIA - MAGNETIC & OPTICAL

SEE ALSO Photographic Equipment & Supplies

	City	State	ZIP	*Toll-Free*	*Phone*
Allied Vaughn Inc 7951 Computer Ave	Bloomington	MN	55435	**800-323-0281**	952-832-3200
Americ Disc Inc 2525 rue Canadien	Drummondville	QC	J2C7W2	**800-263-0419**	819-474-2655
Ampex Corp 1228 Douglas Ave	Redwood City	CA	94063	**800-227-8333**	650-367-2011
Athana Inc 24045 Frampton Ave	Harbor City	CA	90710	**800-421-1591**	310-539-7280
Cine Magnetics Inc 100 Business Pk Dr Suite 1	Armonk	NY	10504	**800-431-1102**	914-273-7500
Cinram International Inc 2255 Markham Rd	Scarborough	ON	M1B2W3	**800-387-5146**	416-298-8190
Color Film Corp 770 Connecticut Ave	Norwalk	CT	06854	**800-882-1120**	203-866-2711
Digital Excellence 300 York Ave	Saint Paul	MN	55101	**800-608-8008**	651-772-5100
Digital Media Impressions 3489 W 2100 South Suite 150	Salt Lake City	UT	84119	**800-637-5546**	801-303-6100
Duplication Factory Inc 4275 Norex Dr	Chaska	MN	55318	**800-279-2009**	952-448-9912
Forge Recording Studios Inc 200 Lincoln Ave	Phoenixville	PA	19460	**800-331-0405**	610-935-1422
Fuji Photo Film USA Inc 200 Summit Lake Dr	Valhalla	NY	10595	**800-755-3854**	914-789-8100
Imation Corp 1 Imation Pl *NYSE: IMN*	Oakdale	MN	55128	**888-466-3456**	651-704-4000
JVC Disc America Co 2 JVC Rd	Tuscaloosa	AL	35405	**800-223-5081**	205-556-7111
Komag Inc 1710 Automation Pkwy *NASDAQ: KOMG*	San Jose	CA	95131	**800-576-2000**	408-576-2000
Maxell Corp of America 22-08 Rt 208	Fair Lawn	NJ	07410	**800-533-2836**	201-794-5900
Peripheral Mfg Inc 4775 Paris St	Denver	CO	80239	**800-468-6888**	303-371-8651
Sanyo Laser Products 1767 Sheridan St	Richmond	IN	47374	**800-704-7648**	765-935-7574
TDK Electronics Corp 901 Franklin Ave	Garden City	NY	11530	**800-835-8273**	516-535-2600
TDK USA Corp 901 Franklin Ave	Garden City	NY	11530	**800-835-8273**	516-535-2600
Transco Products Corp PO Box 1025	Linden	NJ	07036	**800-876-0039**	908-862-0030
US Optical Disc Inc 1 Eagle Dr	Sanford	ME	04073	**800-743-1124**	207-324-1124
USA Dubs 29 W 38th St	New York	NY	10018	**800-872-3821**	212-398-6400
Verbatim Corp 1200 West WT Harris Blvd	Charlotte	NC	28262	**800-538-8589**	704-547-6500
VU Media Duplication 1420 Blake St	Denver	CO	80202	**800-637-4336**	303-534-5503
Wabash Computer Products Inc 4720 W 90th St *Cust Svc	Tulsa	OK	74132	**800-323-9868***	918-447-8977

645 RECREATION FACILITY OPERATORS

SEE ALSO Bowling Centers

	City	State	ZIP	*Toll-Free*	*Phone*
Dave & Buster's Inc 2481 Manana Dr *NYSE: DAB*	Dallas	TX	75220	**800-842-5369**	214-357-9588
Jeepers! Inc 800 South St Suite 355	Waltham	MA	02453	**800-533-7377**	781-890-1800
New Horizon Kids Quest Inc 16355 36th Ave N Suite 700	Plymouth	MN	55446	**800-941-1007**	763-557-1111
Putt-Putt Golf Courses of America Inc 6350 Quadrangle Dr Suite 210	Chapel Hill	NC	27517	**888-788-8788**	910-401-9759

646 RECYCLABLE MATERIALS RECOVERY

	City	State	ZIP	*Toll-Free*	*Phone*
American Paper Recycling Corp 301 W Lake St *Cust Svc	Northlake	IL	60164	**800-762-6790***	708-344-6789
Appliance Recycling Centers of America Inc 7400 Excelsior Blvd	Minneapolis	MN	55426	**800-452-8680**	952-930-9000
Batliner Paper Stock Co Inc 2501 Front St	Kansas City	MO	64120	**800-821-8512**	816-483-3343
Better Management Corp PO Box 9755	Youngstown	OH	44513	**877-293-4300**	330-758-5757
Envirosource Inc 1155 Business Center Dr Suite 200	Horsham	PA	19044	**800-523-0781**	215-956-5500
Federal International Inc 7935 Clayton Rd	Saint Louis	MO	63117	**800-972-7277**	314-721-3377
Macon Iron & Paper Stock Co Inc 950 Lower Poplar Rd	Macon	GA	31202	**800-342-1933**	478-743-6773
Mervis Industries Inc 3295 E Main St	Danville	IL	61834	**800-637-3016**	217-442-5300
Pall Corp 2200 Northern Blvd *NYSE: PLL*	East Hills	NY	11548	**800-645-6532**	516-484-5400
Paper Tigers Inc 2121 Waukegan Rd Suite 130	Bannockburn	IL	60015	**800-621-1774**	847-919-6500
Rock-Tenn Co Recycled Fiber Div 504 Thrasher St	Norcross	GA	30071	**800-762-5836**	770-448-2193
US Rubber Reclaiming Inc 2000 Rubber Way Dr	Vicksburg	MS	39810	**800-842-6043**	601-636-7071

647 RECYCLED PLASTICS PRODUCTS

SEE ALSO Flooring - Resilient

	City	State	ZIP	*Toll-Free*	*Phone*
Aeolian Enterprises Inc PO Box 888	Latrobe	PA	15650	**800-269-4672**	724-539-9460
Allen Ventures Inc 517 State Farm Rd	Deerfield	WI	53531	**877-423-9800**	608-423-9800
American Recycled Plastic Inc 1500 Main St	Palm Bay	FL	32905	**866-674-1525**	321-674-1525

Company	City	State	Zip	Toll-Free	Phone
Cascades Re-Plast Inc 1350 ch Quatre-Saisons PO Box 514	Notre-Dame-du-Bon-Conseil	QC	J0C1A0	**888-313-2440**	819-336-2440
NEW Plastics Corp Renew Plastics Div PO Box 480	Luxemburg	WI	54217	**800-666-5207**	920-845-2326
Northern Plastic Lumber 164 Needham St Unit 1	Lindsay	ON	K9V5R7	**888-255-1222**	705-878-5700
Parkland Plastics Inc PO Box 339	Middlebury	IN	46540	**800-835-4110**	574-825-4336
PlasTEAK PO Box 4290	Akron	OH	44321	**800-320-1841**	330-668-2587
Plastic Lumber Co Inc 115 W Bartges St	Akron	OH	44311	**800-886-8990**	330-762-8989
Plastival 1685 Holmes Rd	Elgin	IL	60123	**800-231-9721**	847-931-4771
Polywood Inc 125 National Rd	Edison	NJ	08817	**800-915-0043**	732-248-8810
Recycled Plastic Products Inc 1600 W Evans Ave Unit J	Englewood	CO	80110	**800-235-7940**	303-975-0033
Renew Plastics Div NEW Plastics Corp PO Box 480	Luxemburg	WI	54217	**800-666-5207**	920-845-2326
Resco Plastics Inc 93783 Newport Ln	Coos Bay	OR	97420	**800-266-5097**	541-269-5485
Trex Co Inc 160 Exeter Dr *NYSE: TWP*	Winchester	VA	22603	**800-289-8739**	540-678-4070
US Plastic Lumber Corp 2300 Glades Rd Suite 440W *NASDAQ: USPL*	Boca Raton	FL	33431	**866-272-8775**	561-394-3511

648 REFRACTORIES - CLAY

Company	City	State	Zip	Toll-Free	Phone
BNZ Materials Inc 6901 S Pierce St Suite 260	Littleton	CO	80128	**800-999-0890**	303-978-1199
Mount Savage Specialty Refractories Co 736 W Ingomar Rd	Ingomar	PA	15127	**800-437-6777**	412-367-9100
Reftech Div RENO Refractories Inc 601 Reno Dr	Morris	AL	35116	**800-741-7366**	
RENO Refractories Inc 601 Reno Dr	Morris	AL	35116	**800-741-7366**	205-647-0240
RENO Refractories Inc Reftech Div 601 Reno Dr	Morris	AL	35116	**800-741-7366**	
Resco Products Inc 2 Penn Ctr W Suite 430	Pittsburgh	PA	15276	**888-283-5505**	412-494-4491
Saxonburg Ceramics Inc PO Box 688	Saxonburg	PA	16056	**800-245-1270**	724-352-1561
Utah Refractories Corp 2200 North 1100 W	Lehi	UT	84043	**800-345-6808**	801-768-3591
Whitacre Greer Fireproofing Inc 1400 S Mahoning Ave	Alliance	OH	44601	**800-947-2837**	330-823-1610

649 REFRACTORIES - NONCLAY

Company	City	State	Zip	Toll-Free	Phone
Corhart Refractories Corp 1600 W Lee St	Louisville	KY	40210	**800-233-1421**	502-778-3311
Fedmet Resources Corp PO Box 278 Westmount Stn	Montreal	QC	H3Z2T2	**800-609-5711**	514-931-5711
Inland Refractories Co 38600 Chester Rd	Avon	OH	44011	**800-321-0767**	440-934-6600
LWB Refractories Co PO Box 1189	York	PA	17405	**800-233-1991**	717-848-1501
Morganite Crucible Inc 22 N Plains Industrial Rd Suite 1	Wallingford	CT	06492	**800-936-7550**	203-697-0808
Mount Savage Specialty Refractories Co 736 W Ingomar Rd	Ingomar	PA	15127	**800-437-6777**	412-367-9100
Norton Co Refractories Div 1 New Bond St Box 15008	Worcester	MA	01615	**800-543-4335**	508-795-5000
Plibrico Co 1010 N Hooker St	Chicago	IL	60622	**800-511-6203**	312-337-9000
Ransom & Randolph Co 3535 Briarfield Blvd	Maumee	OH	43537	**800-800-7496**	419-865-9497
Reftech Div RENO Refractories Inc 601 Reno Dr	Morris	AL	35116	**800-741-7366**	
RENO Refractories Inc 601 Reno Dr	Morris	AL	35116	**800-741-7366**	205-647-0240
RENO Refractories Inc Reftech Div 601 Reno Dr	Morris	AL	35116	**800-741-7366**	
Wahl Refractories Inc 767 SR 19 S	Fremont	OH	43420	**800-837-9245**	419-334-2658
Wulfrath Refractories Inc 6th & Center Sts PO Box 28	Tarentum	PA	15084	**800-245-1801**	724-224-8800

650 REFRIGERATION EQUIPMENT - MFR

SEE ALSO Air Conditioning & Heating Equipment - Commercial/Industrial

Company	City	State	Zip	Toll-Free	Phone
A-1 Components Corp 625 W 18th St	Hialeah	FL	33010	**800-759-2872**	305-885-1911
Advance Energy Technologies Inc 1 Solar Dr	Clifton Park	NY	12065	**800-724-0198**	518-371-2140
Aluma Shield Industries Inc Butcher Boy Doors Div 725 Summerhill Dr	Deland	FL	32724	**888-882-5862**	386-626-6789
American Panel Corp 5800 SE 78th St	Ocala	FL	34472	**800-327-3015**	352-245-7055
Arctic Star Refrigeration Mfg Co Inc 3540 W Pioneer Pkwy	Arlington	TX	76013	**800-229-6562**	817-274-1396
Brown WA & Son Inc 209 Long Meadow Dr	Salisbury	NC	28147	**800-438-2316**	704-636-5131
Burch Industries Inc 16780 Airbase Rd	Maxton	NC	28364	**800-322-3688**	910-844-3688
Butcher Boy Doors Div Aluma Shield Industries Inc 725 Summerhill Dr	Deland	FL	32724	**888-882-5862**	386-626-6789
Carrier Refrigeration Operations 700 Bluffington Rd	Spartanburg	SC	29303	**800-845-9800**	864-582-8111
CrownTonka Inc 10700 Hwy 55 Suite 300	Plymouth	MN	55441	**800-523-7337**	763-541-1410
Custom Coolers LLC 5609 Azle Ave	Fort Worth	TX	76114	**800-627-0488**	817-626-3737
Delfield Co 980 S Isabella Rd	Mount Pleasant	MI	48858	**800-733-8821**	989-773-7981
Dole Refrigerating Co 1420 Higgs Rd	Lewisburg	TN	37091	**800-251-8990**	931-359-6211
Edey Mfg Co Inc 2159 E 92nd St	Los Angeles	CA	90002	**800-333-9634**	323-566-6151
Eliason Corp 9229 Shaver Rd *Cust Svc	Portage	MI	49024	**800-828-3655***	269-327-7003
Elliott-Williams Co Inc 3500 E 20th St	Indianapolis	IN	46218	**800-428-9303**	317-453-2295
Federal Industries Div Standex Corp 215 Federal Ave PO Box 290	Belleville	WI	53508	**800-356-4206**	608-424-3331
Follett Corp 801 Church Ln *Cust Svc	Easton	PA	18040	**800-523-9361***	610-252-7301
Gem Refrigerator Co 650 E Erie Ave	Philadelphia	PA	19134	**800-922-1422**	215-426-8700
Harris Environmental Systems Inc 11 Connector Rd	Andover	MA	01810	**888-771-4200**	978-475-0104
Haws Corp 1455 Kleppe Ln	Sparks	NV	89431	**888-640-4297**	775-359-4712
Heatcraft Refrigeration Products 2175 W Park Place Blvd	Stone Mountain	GA	30087	**800-321-1881**	770-465-5600
Hill PHOENIX Inc 709 Sigman Rd	Conyers	GA	30013	**800-518-6630**	770-388-0706
Hussmann Corp 12999 St Charles Rock Rd	Bridgeton	MO	63044	**800-879-1152**	314-291-2000
Ice-O-Matic 11100 E 45th Ave	Denver	CO	80239	**800-423-3367**	303-371-3737
IMI Cornelius Inc 101 Broadway St W	Osseo	MN	55369	**800-238-3600**	763-488-8200
International Cold Storage Co Inc 215 E 13th St	Andover	KS	67002	**800-835-0001**	316-733-1385
KDIndustries 1525 E Lake Rd	Erie	PA	16511	**800-840-9577**	814-453-6761
Kloppenberg & Co 2627 W Oxford Ave	Englewood	CO	80110	**800-346-3246**	303-761-1615
Kolpak Inc 2915 Tennessee Ave N	Parsons	TN	38363	**800-826-7036**	731-847-6361
Kysor Panel Systems 3201 NE Loop 820 Suite 150	Fort Worth	TX	76137	**800-633-3426**	817-281-5121
Lancer Corp 6655 Lancer Blvd *AMEX: LAN*	San Antonio	TX	78219	**800-729-1500**	210-310-7000
Leer LP 206 Leer St *Cust Svc	New Lisbon	WI	53950	**800-766-5337***	608-562-3161
Manitowoc Ice Inc 2110 S 26th St	Manitowoc	WI	54220	**800-545-5720**	920-682-0161
McCann's Engineering & Mfg Co 4570 W Colorado Blvd	Los Angeles	CA	90039	**800-423-2429**	818-637-7200
Micro Matic USA Inc 10726 N 2nd St	Machesney Park	IL	61115	**800-435-6950**	815-968-7557
MicroMetl Corp 3035 N Shadeland Ave	Indianapolis	IN	46226	**800-662-4822**	317-524-5400
Mr Winter Inc 8085 W 26th Ct	Hialeah	FL	33016	**800-327-3371**	305-556-6741
Nor-Lake Inc PO Box 248	Hudson	WI	54016	**800-388-5253**	715-386-2323
Perlick Corp 8300 W Good Hope Rd	Milwaukee	WI	53223	**800-558-5592**	414-353-7060
Scotsman Ice Systems 775 Corporate Woods Pkwy	Vernon Hills	IL	60061	**800-726-8762**	847-215-4500
Seattle Refrigeration & Mfg Co 1057 S Director St	Seattle	WA	98108	**800-228-8881**	206-762-7740
Silver King Refrigeration Inc 1600 Xenium Ln N	Minneapolis	MN	55441	**800-328-3329**	763-923-2441
Springer Penguin Inc 460 Grand Blvd	Westbury	NY	11590	**800-529-4375**	516-333-4400
Standex Corp Federal Industries Div 215 Federal Ave PO Box 290	Belleville	WI	53508	**800-356-4206**	608-424-3331
Starrett Corp 6203 Johns Rd Suite 8	Tampa	FL	33634	**800-237-8350**	813-882-3616
Sunroc Corp 60 Starlifter Ave Kent County Aero Pk	Dover	DE	19901	**800-478-6762**	302-678-7800
True Mfg Co 301 Cannonball Ln	O'Fallon	MO	63366	**800-325-6152**	636-240-2400
Turbo Refrigerating LLC 1815 Shady Oaks Dr	Denton	TX	76205	**800-775-8648**	940-387-4301
Tyler Refrigeration 1329 Lake St	Niles	MI	49120	**800-992-3744**	269-683-2000
Victory Refrigeration Inc 110 Woodcrest Rd	Cherry Hill	NJ	08003	**800-523-5008**	856-428-4200
Vilter Mfg Corp 5555 S Packard Ave PO Box 8904 *Orders	Cudahy	WI	53110	**800-862-2677***	414-744-0111
Vogt Tube Ice 1000 W Ormsby Ave Suite 19	Louisville	KY	40210	**800-853-8648**	502-635-3000
WA Brown & Son Inc 209 Long Meadow Dr	Salisbury	NC	28147	**800-438-2316**	704-636-5131
York Refrigeration Systems Frick 100 CV Ave	Waynesboro	PA	17268	**800-487-2653**	717-762-2121

651 REFRIGERATION EQUIPMENT - WHOL

SEE ALSO Plumbing, Heating, Air Conditioning Equipment & Supplies - Whol

Company	City	State	Zip	Toll-Free	Phone
Abco Refrigeration Supply Corp 49-70 31st St	Long Island City	NY	11101	**800-786-2075**	718-937-9000
Allied Supply Co Inc 1100 E Monument Ave	Dayton	OH	45402	**800-589-5690**	937-224-9833
Automatic Ice & Beverage Inc PO Box 110159	Birmingham	AL	35211	**800-476-4242**	205-787-9640
Baker Distributing Co 7892 Baymeadows Way	Jacksonville	FL	32256	**877-733-9633**	904-733-9633
Brock-McVey Co Inc Refrigeration Supply Div PO Box 55487	Lexington	KY	40555	**800-955-1412**	859-255-1412
Dennis Supply Co PO Box 3376	Sioux City	IA	51102	**800-352-4618**	712-255-7637
Don Stevens Inc 980 Discovery Rd	Eagan	MN	55121	**800-444-2299**	651-452-0872
Ernest F Mariani Co Inc 614 W 600 South	Salt Lake City	UT	84104	**800-453-2927**	801-359-3744
Gulf Refrigeration Supply Inc of Tampa 8920 Sabal Industrial Blvd	Tampa	FL	33619	**888-683-2111**	813-626-5111
Gustave A Larson Co PO Box 910	Pewaukee	WI	53072	**800-829-9609**	262-542-0200
Hart & Price Corp PO Box 36368	Dallas	TX	75235	**800-777-9129**	214-521-9129
Insco Distributing Inc 12501 Network Blvd	San Antonio	TX	78249	**800-203-8400**	210-690-8400
ISI Commercial Refrigeration LP 9136 Viscount Row	Dallas	TX	75247	**800-777-5070**	214-631-7980
Larson Gustave A Co PO Box 910	Pewaukee	WI	53072	**800-829-9609**	262-542-0200
Lewis RE Refrigeration Inc 803 S Lincoln St PO Box 92	Creston	IA	50801	**800-264-0767**	641-782-8183
Mariani Ernest F Co Inc 614 W 600 South	Salt Lake City	UT	84104	**800-453-2927**	801-359-3744
Michel RE Co Inc 1 RE Michel Dr	Glen Burnie	MD	21060	**800-283-7362**	410-760-4000
Midlands Carrier Transicold Inc 10707 S 149th St	Omaha	NE	68138	**800-655-9382**	402-895-5500
Modern Ice Equipment & Supply Co DBA Modern Tour Inc 109 May Dr	Harrison	OH	45030	**800-543-1581**	513-367-2101
Modern Tour Inc 109 May Dr	Harrison	OH	45030	**800-543-1581**	513-367-2101
Preston Refrigeration Co Inc 3200 Fiberglass Rd	Kansas City	KS	66115	**800-621-1813**	913-621-1813
RE Lewis Refrigeration Inc 803 S Lincoln St PO Box 92	Creston	IA	50801	**800-264-0767**	641-782-8183
RE Michel Co Inc 1 RE Michel Dr	Glen Burnie	MD	21060	**800-283-7362**	410-760-4000
Redico Inc 943 Buford Hwy	Buford	GA	30518	**800-242-3920**	770-614-1401
Refron Inc 38-18 33rd St	Long Island City	NY	11101	**800-473-3766**	718-392-8002
Rogers Supply Co Inc PO Box 740	Champaign	IL	61824	**800-252-0406**	217-356-0166
Southern Refrigeration Corp 2026 Salem Ave SW	Roanoke	VA	24016	**800-763-4433**	540-342-3493
Stafford-Smith Inc 3414 S Burdick St	Kalamazoo	MI	49001	**800-968-2442**	269-343-1240
Supermarket Systems Inc PO Box 472513	Charlotte	NC	28247	**800-553-1905**	704-542-6000
SWH Supply Co 242 E Main St	Louisville	KY	40202	**800-866-6672**	502-589-9287
Taylor Freezer Sales Co Inc 2032 Atlantic Ave	Chesapeake	VA	23324	**800-768-6945**	757-545-7900
Taylor Industries Inc 1533 E Euclid Ave	Des Moines	IA	50313	**800-362-2500**	515-262-8221
United Refrigeration Inc 11401 Roosevelt Blvd	Philadelphia	PA	19154	**800-852-5132**	215-698-9100
Wittichen Supply Co Inc 1600 3rd Ave S	Birmingham	AL	35233	**800-239-5294**	205-251-8203

652 RELOCATION CONSULTING SERVICES

Toll-Free | Phone

Arizona Insights Relocation Center Inc
10446 N 74th St Suite 100 .... Scottsdale AZ 85258 **800-899-7356** 480-481-8401
Century 21 Real Estate Corp 1 Campus Dr . . . Parsippany NJ 07054 **800-221-5737** 973-428-9700
Coldwell Banker Gundaker
2458 Old Dorsett Rd Suite 300 ...... Maryland Heights MO 63043 **800-325-1978** 314-298-5000
GMAC Global Relocation Services
150 Mount Bethel Rd. .... Warren NJ 07059 **800-589-7858** 908-542-5400
Hewitt Relocation Services Inc
7901 Stoneridge Dr Suite 390 .... Pleasanton CA 94588 **800-831-3444** 925-734-3434
Joyner & Co Realtors
2727 Enterprise Pkwy PO Box 31355 ...... Richmond VA 23294 **800-446-3858** 804-270-9440
Prudential Real Estate Affiliates Inc
3333 Michelson Dr Suite 1000 .... Irvine CA 92612 **800-999-1120** 949-794-7900
Relo & Mobility Management
161 N Clark St Suite 1250 .... Chicago IL 60601 **800-621-6510** 312-424-0400
Relocation America
25800 Northwestern Hwy Suite 210 .... Southfield MI 48075 **800-521-0508*** 248-208-2900
*Cust Svc
Re/MAX Equity Group Inc
84505 SW Nimbus Ave .... Beaverton OR 97008 **800-283-3358** 503-670-3000
Re/MAX International Relocation Services Inc 8390 E Crescent
Pkwy Suite 500 .... Greenwood Village CO 80111 **800-442-3501** 303-770-5531
Resource Careers 343 W Bagley Rd Suite 302 .... Berea OH 44017 **800-[illegible]-1770*** [illegible]-2810
*Cust Svc
Runzheimer International Runzheimer Pk ..... Rochester WI 53167 **800-558-1702** 262-971-2200
SIRVA Inc 700 Oakmont Ln. .... Westmont IL 60559 **800-234-2788** 630-570-3000
NYSE: SIR
Weichert Relocation Resources Inc
120 Longwater Dr .... Norwell MA 02061 **800-926-8774** 781-871-4500
Welcome Wagon
245 Newtown Rd Suite 500 PO box 9101 ... Plainview NY 11803 **800-779-3526**
Windermere Relocation Inc
4040 Lake Washington Blvd NE Suite 201 .... Kirkland WA 98033 **800-735-7029** 425-216-7100

653 REMEDIATION SERVICES

SEE ALSO Associations & Organizations - General - Environmental Organizations; Consulting Services - Environmental; Waste Management

Toll-Free | Phone

3CI Complete Compliance Corp
1517 W North Carrier Pkwy Suite 104 ... Grand Prairie TX 75050 **800-863-0345** 972-375-0006
Allstate Power Vac Inc 928 E Hazelwood Ave... Rahway NJ 07065 **800-876-9699** 732-815-0220
Aquagenix Inc
1460 SW 3rd St Suite B2 .... Pompano Beach FL 33069 **800-832-5253** 954-943-5118
Brook Environmental & Engineering Corp
11419 Cronridge Dr Suite 10........... Owings Mills MD 21117 **800-381-4434** 410-356-4875
Carylon Corp 2500 W Arthington St........... Chicago IL 60612 **800-621-4342** 312-666-7700
Chem-Nuclear Systems Inc
140 Stoneridge Dr .... Columbia SC 29210 **800-925-1592** 803-256-0450
Clean Harbors Inc
1501 Washington St PO Box 859048 .... Braintree MA 02185 **800-282-0058** 781-849-1800
NASDAQ: CLHB
Clean Venture/Cycle Chem Inc 201 S 1st St.... Elizabeth NJ 07206 **800-347-7672** 908-355-5800
Crosby & Overton Inc 1610 W 17th St...... Long Beach CA 90813 **800-827-6729** 562-432-5445
Delta Environmental Consultants Inc
5910 Rice Creek Pkwy................. Shoreview MN 55126 **800-477-7411** 651-639-9449
Duratek Inc 10100 Old Columbia Rd .... Columbia MD 21046 **800-638-3838** 410-312-5100
NASDAQ: DRTK
Ecology Control Industries Inc
255 Parr Blvd......................... Richmond CA 94801 **800-788-1393** 510-235-1393
Environmental Enterprises Inc
10163 Cincinnati Dayton Rd .... Cincinnati OH 45241 **800-722-2818** 513-772-2818
Handex Group Inc 30941 Suneagle Dr ...... Mount Dora FL 32757 **800-989-3753** 352-735-1800
Kemron Environmental Services Inc
8150 Leesburg Pike Suite 1410.............. Vienna VA 22182 **800-777-1042** 703-893-4106
MARCOR Remediation Inc
246 Cockeysville Rd Suite 1 .... Hunt Valley MD 21030 **800-547-0128** 410-785-0001
Marisol Inc 213 W Union Ave............ Bound Brook NJ 08805 **877-627-4765** 732-469-5100
PDG Environmental Inc
1386 Beulah Rd Bldg 801 .... Pittsburgh PA 15235 **800-972-7341** 412-243-3200
Perma-Fix Environmental Services Inc
1940 NW 67th Pl...................... Gainesville FL 32653 **800-365-6066** 352-373-4200
NASDAQ: PESI
Petroclean Inc PO Box 92 .... Carnegie PA 15106 **800-247-3592** 412-279-9556
PW Stephens Inc
15201 Pipeline Ln Unit B.......... Huntington Beach CA 92649 **800-937-1521** 714-892-2028
Romic Environmental Technologies Corp
2081 Bay Rd .... East Palo Alto CA 94303 **800-766-4248** 650-324-1638
Safety-Kleen Corp
5400 Legacy Dr Cluster 2 Bldg 3 .... Plano TX 75024 **800-669-5740** 972-265-2000
Sevenson Environmental Services Inc
2749 Lockport Rd .... Niagara Falls NY 14305 **800-777-3836** 716-284-0431
Sigma Environmental Services Inc
1300 W Canal St .... Milwaukee WI 53233 **800-732-4671** 414-643-4200
United Oil Recovery Inc 14-16 W Main St...... Meriden CT 06451 **800-631-2099** 203-238-6745
UXB International Inc
1715 Pratt Dr Suite 1300............... Blacksburg VA 24060 **800-422-4892** 540-443-3700
WRR Environmental Services Co Inc
5200 SR-93 .... Eau Claire WI 54701 **800-727-8760** 715-834-9624

654 RESEARCH CENTERS & ORGANIZATIONS

SEE ALSO Laboratories - Genetic Testing; Market Research Firms; Testing Facilities

Toll-Free | Phone

AARP Public Policy Institute
601 'E' St NW .... Washington DC 20049 **888-687-2277** 202-434-2277
AEL Inc PO Box 1348 .... Charleston WV 25325 **800-624-9120** 304-347-0400
Agency for Healthcare Research & Quality
540 Gaither Rd.......................... Rockville MD 20850 **800-358-9295** 301-427-1200
Agency for Toxic Substances & Disease Registry
Centers for Disease Control & Prevention
1600 Clifton Rd NE Bldg 37 MS E-29......... Atlanta GA 30333 **888-422-8737** 404-498-0110
AMC Cancer Research Center 1600 Pierce St.... Denver CO 80214 **800-321-1557** 303-233-6501
American Enterprise Institute for Public Policy Research (AEI) 1150 17th St NW
Suite 1100 .... Washington DC 20036 **800-862-5801** 202-862-5800
American Institute for Cancer Research
1759 R St NW .... Washington DC 20009 **800-843-8114** 202-328-7744
American Institute of Baking
1213 Bakers Way PO Box 3999 .... Manhattan KS 66505 **800-633-5137** 785-537-4750
American Type Culture Collection (ATCC)
10801 University Blvd PO Box 1549........ Manassas VA 20108 **800-638-6597** 703-365-2700
Arthritis Foundation
1330 W Peachtree St Suite 100 .... Atlanta GA 30309 **800-283-7800** 404-872-7100
Ashbrook Center Ashland University........... Ashland OH 44805 **877-289-5411** 419-289-5411
Barbara Ann Karmanos Cancer Institute
4110 John R St .... Detroit MI 48201 **800-527-6266** 313-833-0710
Bell Labs 600 Mountain Ave............... Murray Hill NJ 07974 **877-894-4647** 908-582-8500
Bettis Laboratory
814 Pittsburgh-McKeeseport Blvd .... West Mifflin PA 15122 **800-296-5002** 412-476-5000
Brookings Institution
1775 Massachusetts Ave NW .... Washington DC 20036 **800-275-1447** 202-797-6000
Brown DH Assoc Inc 222 Grace Church St. . . Port Chester NY 10573 **800-253-1799** 914-937-4302
Capital Research Center 1513 16th St NW . . . Washington DC 20036 **800-459-3950** 202-483-6900
CBR (Center for Blood Research Inc)
800 Huntington Ave .... Boston MA 02115 **800-850-2466** 617-278-3000
Center for Blood Research Inc (CBR)
800 Huntington Ave .... Boston MA 02115 **800-850-2466** 617-278-3000
Center for Community Inclusion
University of Maine 5717 Corbett Hall
Rm 114 .... Orono ME 04469 **800-203-6957** 207-581-1084
Center for Technology Commercialization (CTC) 1400 Computer Dr.............. Westborough MA 01581 **800-472-6785** 508-870-0042
Center for Youth & Communities
Brandeis University 60 Turner St 2nd Fl ...... Waltham MA 02453 **800-343-4205** 781-736-3770
Center on Education & Training for Employment Ohio State University 1900
Kenny Rd .... Columbus OH 43210 **800-848-4815** 614-292-4353
Centers for Disease Control & Prevention (CDC) National Center for Environmental Health 4770 Buford Hwy Bldg 101......... Chamblee GA 30341 **888-232-6789** 770-488-7000
Centrifuge Research Center
ATTN: CEERD-PA-Z 3909 Halls Ferry Rd..... Vicksburg MS 39180 **800-522-6937** 601-634-2502
Charles River Laboratories Inc
251 Ballardvale St .... Wilmington MA 01887 **800-522-7287** 978-658-6000
NYSE: CRL
Charles Stark Draper Laboratory Inc
555 Technology Sq .... Cambridge MA 02139 **800-676-1977** 617-258-1000
Cincinnati Children's Hospital Research Foundation Children's Hospital Medical
Center 3333 Burnet Ave.................. Cincinnati OH 45229 **800-344-2462** 513-636-4588
Coastal & Hydraulics Laboratory
ATTN: CEERD-PA-Z 3909 Halls Ferry Rd..... Vicksburg MS 39180 **800-522-6937** 601-634-2502
Construction Engineering Research Laboratory PO Box 9005............ Champaign IL 61826 **800-872-2375** 217-352-6511
Coriell Institute for Medical Research
403 Haddon Ave .... Camden NJ 08103 **800-752-3805** 856-757-9758
Cotton Inc 6399 Weston Pkwy .... Cary NC 27513 **800-334-5868** 919-678-2220
Dana-Farber Cancer Institute 44 Binney St...... Boston MA 02115 **800-757-3324** 617-632-3000
DH Brown Associates Inc
222 Grace Church St.................. Port Chester NY 10573 **800-253-1799** 914-937-4302
Family & Consumer Sciences Research Institute
Iowa State University MacKay Hall Rm 126 ..... Ames IA 50011 **877-891-5349** 515-294-5982
Far West Regional Technology Transfer Center South Hope St Research Annex
3716 Rm 200........................ Los Angeles CA 90007 **800-642-2872** 213-743-2353
Food & Drug Administration (FDA)
Center for Devices & Radiological Health
9200 Corporate Blvd Suite 100E......... Rockville MD 20850 **800-638-2041**
Center for Food Safety & Applied Nutrition
5100 Paint Branch Pkwy .... College Park MD 20740 **888-723-3366** 301-436-1600
Foundation for Economic Education (FEE) 30 S Broadway........... Irvington-on-Hudson NY 10533 **800-960-4333** 914-591-7230
Fox Chase Cancer Center
333 Cottman Ave .... Philadelphia PA 19111 **888-369-2427** 215-728-6900
Friends Research Institute Inc
505 Baltimore Ave .... Baltimore MD 21204 **800-822-3677** 410-823-5116
Gatorade Sports Science Institute
617 W Main St........................ Barrington IL 60010 **800-616-4774** 847-381-1980
Geo-Centers Inc 7 Wells Ave .... Newton MA 02459 **800-347-7592** 617-964-7070
Geotechnical & Structures Laboratory
ATTN: CEERD-PA-Z 3909 Halls Ferry Rd..... Vicksburg MS 39180 **800-522-6937** 601-634-2502
Gould Food Industries Center
Ohio State University Howlett Hall Suite
140 2001 Fyffe Ct .... Columbus OH 43210 **800-752-2751** 614-292-7004
Grain Marketing & Production Research Center USDA/ARS 1515 College Ave ...... Manhattan KS 66502 **800-627-0388** 785-776-2701
Great Lakes Industrial Technology Center
20445 Emerald Pkwy SW Suite 200 .... Cleveland OH 44135 **800-472-6785** 216-898-6400
Great Plains-Rocky Mountain Hazardous Substance Research Center Kansas State
University Ward Hall Rm 104 .... Manhattan KS 66506 **800-798-7796** 785-532-6519
H Lee Moffitt Cancer Center & Research Institute
12902 Magnolia Dr .... Tampa FL 33612 **800-456-3434** 813-972-4673
Heritage Foundation
214 Massachusetts Ave NE............. Washington DC 20002 **800-546-2843** 202-546-4400
Hill Top Research Inc PO Box 138.......... Miamiville OH 45147 **800-785-2693** 513-831-3114
Hoover Institution on War Revolution & Peace
Stanford University 434 Galvez Mall .... Stanford CA 94305 **877-466-8374** 650-723-1754
Hudson Institute
1015 18th St NW Suite 300 .... Washington DC 20036 **800-483-7660** 202-225-7770
Hybridon Inc 345 Vassar St .... Cambridge MA 02139 **800-223-3771** 617-679-5500
AMEX: HBY
Idaho National Engineering & Environmental Laboratory (INEEL) Communications &
Public Affairs 2525 Fremont Avenue PO
Box 1625 .... Idaho Falls ID 83415 **800-708-2680** 208-526-0111
Illinois Waste Management & Research Center 1 E Hazelwood Dr .... Champaign IL 61820 **800-407-0261** 217-333-8940
Independent Institute 100 Swan Way .... Oakland CA 94621 **800-927-8733** 510-632-1366

Classified Section

				Toll-Free	Phone
Institute for Humane Studies 3301 N Fairfax Dr Suite 440	Arlington	VA	22201	**800-697-8799**	703-993-4880
Institute of World Politics 1521 16th St NW	Washington	DC	20036	**888-566-9497**	202-462-2101
International Diabetes Center 3800 Park Nicollet Blvd	Minneapolis	MN	55416	**888-825-6315**	952-993-3393
John Wayne Cancer Institute Saint John's Health Center 2200 Santa Monica Blvd	Santa Monica	CA	90404	**800-262-6259**	
Karmanos Barbara Ann Cancer Institute 4110 John R St	Detroit	MI	48201	**800-527-6266**	313-833-0710
Kendle International Inc 441 Vine St 1200 Carew Tower	Cincinnati	OH	45202	**800-733-1572**	513-381-5550
NASDAQ: KNDL					
Kennedy Space Center Public Inquiries	Kennedy Space Center	FL	32899	**800-561-8618**	321-867-5000
Ktech Corp 1300 Eubank Blvd SE	Albuquerque	NM	87123	**877-998-5830**	505-998-5830
Kurzweil Technologies Inc 15 Walnut St	Wellesley Hills	MA	02481	**877-365-9633**	781-263-0000
Laboratory for Student Success (LSS) Temple University/Center for Research in Human Development & Education 933 Ritter Annex 1301 Cecil B. Moore Ave	Philadelphia	PA	19122	**800-892-5550**	215-204-3030
Lark Technologies Inc 9441 W Sam Houston Pkwy S Suite 103	Houston	TX	77099	**800-288-3720**	713-779-3663
Lerner Research Institute Cleveland Clinic Foundation 9500 Euclid Ave NB 21	Cleveland	OH	44195	**800-223-2273**	216-444-3900
LIMRA International Inc 300 Day Hill Rd	Windsor	CT	06095	**800-285-7792***	860-688-3358
*Cust Svc					
Lucent Technologies Inc Bell Labs 600 Mountain Ave	Murray Hill	NJ	07974	**877-894-4647**	908-582-8500
Manpower Demonstration Research Corp 16 E 34th St 19th Fl	New York	NY	10016	**800-221-3165**	212-532-3200
Mechanical Technology Inc 431 New Karner Rd	Albany	NY	12205	**800-828-8210**	518-533-2200
NASDAQ: MKTY					
Miami Project to Cure Paralysis PO Box 016960 Mail Locator R-48	Miami	FL	33101	**800-782-6387**	305-243-6001
Michigan Manufacturing Technology Center 47911 Halyard Dr	Plymouth	MI	48170	**888-414-6682**	
Mid-Continent Regional Technology Transfer Center 301 Tarrow MS 8000	College Station	TX	77840	**800-472-6785**	979-845-2907
Minnesota Technology Inc 111 3rd Ave S	Minneapolis	MN	55401	**800-325-3073**	612-373-2900
Mote Marine Laboratory 1600 Ken Thompson Pkwy	Sarasota	FL	34236	**800-690-6083**	941-388-4441
National Assn of Home Builders Research Center 400 Prince Georges Blvd	Upper Marlboro	MD	20774	**800-638-8556**	301-249-4000
National Cancer Institute (NCI) 6116 Executive Blvd MSC 8322	Bethesda	MD	20892	**800-422-6237**	301-435-3848
National Center for Complementary & Alternative Medicine (NCCAM) National Institutes of Health 31 Center Dr Bldg 31	Bethesda	MD	20892	**888-644-6226**	301-435-5042
National Center for Genome Resources 2935 Rodeo Pk Dr E	Santa Fe	NM	87505	**800-450-4854**	505-982-7840
National Center for Manufacturing Sciences (NCMS) 3025 Boardwalk	Ann Arbor	MI	48108	**800-222-6267**	734-995-0300
National Center for Toxicological Research 3900 NCTR Rd	Jefferson	AR	72079	**800-638-3321**	870-543-7000
National Energy Research Scientific Computing Center (NERSC) Lawrence Berkeley National Laboratory 1 Cyclotron Rd MS 50C3396	Berkeley	CA	94720	**800-847-6070**	510-486-5849
National Energy Technology Laboratory (NETL) US Dept of Energy 3610 Collins Ferry Rd PO Box 880	Morgantown	WV	26507	**800-432-8330**	304-285-4764
National Foundation for Cancer Research (NFCR) 4600 East West Hwy Suite 525	Bethesda	MD	20814	**800-321-2873**	301-654-1250
National Hansen's Disease Programs (NHDP) 1770 Physicians Park Dr	Baton Rouge	LA	70816	**800-642-2477**	225-756-3773
National Institute for Occupational Safety & Health 200 Independence Ave SW	Washington	DC	20201	**800-356-4674**	202-401-6997
National Institute of Neurological Disorders & Stroke (NINDS) 31 Center Dr Bldg 31 Rm 8A52	Bethesda	MD	20892	**800-352-9424**	301-496-9746
National Jewish Medical & Research Center 1400 Jackson St	Denver	CO	80206	**800-222-5864**	303-388-4461
National Research Center for Coal & Energy PO Box 6064	Morgantown	WV	26506	**800-624-8301**	304-293-2867
National Technical Information Service (NTIS) 5285 Port Royal Rd	Springfield	VA	22161	**800-553-6847***	703-605-6000
*Orders					
National Technology Transfer Center 316 Washington Ave	Wheeling	WV	26003	**800-678-6882**	304-243-2455
Naval Facilities Engineering Service Center (NFESC) 1100 23rd Ave	Port Hueneme	CA	93043	**888-484-3372**	805-982-1393
NEC Research Institute Inc 4 Independence Way	Princeton	NJ	08540	**888-777-6324**	609-520-1555
North Central Regional Educational Laboratory (NCREL) 1120 E Diehl Rd Suite 200	Naperville	IL	60563	**800-356-2735**	630-649-6500
Oklahoma Medical Research Foundation (OMRF) 825 NE 13th St	Oklahoma City	OK	73104	**800-522-0211**	405-271-6673
Omnicare Clinical Research 630 Alledale Rd	King of Prussia	PA	19406	**800-290-5766**	484-679-2400
Pacific Northwest National Laboratory (PNNL) 902 Battelle Blvd PO Box 999	Richland	WA	99352	**888-375-7665**	509-375-2121
PAREXEL International Corp 195 West St	Waltham	MA	02451	**800-727-3935**	781-487-9900
NASDAQ: PRXL					
Pittsburgh Supercomputing Center 4400 5th Ave	Pittsburgh	PA	15213	**800-221-1641**	412-268-4960
Progressive Policy Institute (PPI) 600 Pennsylvania Ave SE Suite 400	Washington	DC	20003	**800-546-0027**	202-547-0001
Quintiles Transnational Corp PO Box 13979	Research Triangle Park	NC	27709	**800-875-2888**	919-998-2000
Research Triangle Institute 3040 Cornwallis Rd PO Box 12194	Research Triangle Park	NC	27709	**800-334-8571**	919-541-6000
Ricerca Biosciences 7528 Auburn Rd	Painesville	OH	44077	**888-742-3722**	440-357-3300
Rockford Institute 928 N Main St	Rockford	IL	61103	**800-383-0680**	815-964-5053
Roswell Park Cancer Institute Elm & Carlton Sts	Buffalo	NY	14263	**800-685-6825**	716-845-2300
Rothe Development Inc 4614 Sinclair Rd	San Antonio	TX	78222	**800-229-5209**	210-648-3131
Schering-Plough Research Institute 2015 Galloping Hill Rd	Kenilworth	NJ	07033	**800-222-7579**	908-298-4000
Shuster Laboratories Inc 85 John Rd	Canton	MA	02021	**800-444-8705**	781-821-2200
Social & Economic Sciences Research Center Washington State University Wilson Hall Rm 133 PO Box 644014	Pullman	WA	99164	**800-833-0867**	509-335-1511
Southern Research Institute 2000 9th Ave S	Birmingham	AL	35205	**800-967-6774**	205-581-2000
Syracuse Research Corp (SRC) 6225 Running Ridge Rd	North Syracuse	NY	13212	**800-724-0451**	315-452-8000
Titan Corp 3033 Science Park Rd	San Diego	CA	92121	**800-359-4404**	858-552-9500
NYSE: TTN					
Transportation Research Center Inc Ohio State University 10820 Rt 347 PO Box B 67	East Liberty	OH	43319	**800-837-7872**	937-666-2011
University of Tennessee Space Institute 411 BH Goethert Pkwy	Tullahoma	TN	37388	**888-822-8874**	931-393-7100
US Army Engineer Research & Development Center (ERDC) 3909 Halls Ferry Rd ATTN: CEERD-PA-Z	Vicksburg	MS	39180	**800-522-6937**	601-634-2502
Centrifuge Research Center ATTN: CEERD-PA-Z 3909 Halls Ferry Rd	Vicksburg	MS	39180	**800-522-6937**	601-634-2502
Coastal & Hydraulics Laboratory ATTN: CEERD-PA-Z 3909 Halls Ferry Rd	Vicksburg	MS	39180	**800-522-6937**	601-634-2502
Construction Engineering Research Laboratory PO Box 9005	Champaign	IL	61826	**800-872-2375**	217-352-6511
Geotechnical & Structures Laboratory ATTN: CEERD-PA-Z 3909 Halls Ferry Rd	Vicksburg	MS	39180	**800-522-6937**	601-634-2502
Information Technology Laboratory 3909 Halls Ferry Rd ATTN: CEERD-IV-Z	Vicksburg	MS	39180	**800-522-6937**	601-634-2502
US Army Research Laboratory (ARL) ATTN: AMSRL-CS-PA 2800 Powder Mill Rd	Adelphi	MD	20783	**800-276-9522**	301-394-1178
West Pharmaceutical Services Inc 101 Gordon Dr	Lionville	PA	19341	**800-345-9800**	610-594-2900
NYSE: WST					
Western Research Institute 365 N 9th St	Laramie	WY	82072	**888-436-6974**	307-721-2011
Wistar Institute 3601 Spruce St	Philadelphia	PA	19104	**800-724-6633**	215-898-3700

655 RESORTS

SEE ALSO Casinos; Dude Ranches; Hotel & Resort Operation & Management; Hotels & Motels (Individual) - Canada; Hotels & Motels (Individual) - US; Hotels - Conference Center; Spas - Health & Fitness; Spas - Hotel & Resort

Alabama

				Toll-Free	Phone
Joe Wheeler Resort Lodge & Convention Center Joe Wheeler State Park 201 McLean Dr	Rogersville	AL	35652	**800-544-5639**	256-247-5461
Legends at Capitol Hill 2500 Legends Cir	Prattville	AL	36066	**888-250-3767**	334-290-1235
Marriott's Grand Hotel Resort & Golf Club 1 Grand Blvd	Point Clear	AL	36564	**800-544-9933**	251-928-9201
Perdido Beach Resort 27200 Perdido Beach Blvd	Orange Beach	AL	36561	**800-634-8001**	251-981-9811
StillWaters Resort 797 Moonbrook Dr	Dadeville	AL	36853	**800-687-3732**	256-825-7021

Alaska

				Toll-Free	Phone
Alyeska Prince Hotel & Resort PO Box 249	Girdwood	AK	99587	**800-880-3880**	907-754-1111
Whalers' Cove Sportfishing Lodge Mile 1 Killisnoo Rd PO Box 101	Angoon	AK	99820	**800-423-3123**	907-788-3123

Alberta

				Toll-Free	Phone
Delta Lodge at Kananaskis 1 Centennial Dr	Kananaskis Village	AB	T0L2H0	**888-244-8666**	403-591-7711
Fairmont Banff Springs PO Box 960	Banff	AB	T1L1J4	**800-441-1414**	403-762-2211
Fairmont Chateau Lake Louise 111 Lake Louise Dr	Lake Louise	AB	T0L1E0	**800-441-1414**	403-522-3511
Fairmont Jasper Park Lodge 1 Lodge Rd	Jasper	AB	T0E1E0	**800-441-1414**	780-852-3301
Rimrock Resort Hotel 300 Mountain Ave PO Box 1110	Banff	AB	T1L1J2	**800-661-1587**	403-762-3356
Waterton Lakes Lodge Box 4 101 Clematis Ave	Waterton Park	AB	T0K2M0	**888-985-6343**	403-859-2150

Arizona

				Toll-Free	Phone
Arizona Biltmore Resort & Spa 2400 E Missouri Ave	Phoenix	AZ	85016	**800-950-0086**	602-955-6600
Arizona Golf Resort & Conference Center 425 S Power Rd	Mesa	AZ	85206	**800-528-8282**	480-832-3202
Boulders Resort & Golden Door Spa - A Wyndham Luxury Resort 34631 N Tom Darlington Dr PO Box 2090	Carefree	AZ	85377	**800-553-1717**	480-488-9009
Camelback Inn JW Marriott Resort Golf Club & Spa 5402 E Lincoln Dr	Scottsdale	AZ	85253	**800-242-2635**	480-948-1700
Chaparral Suites Resort & Conference Center 5001 N Scottsdale Rd	Scottsdale	AZ	85250	**800-528-1456**	480-949-1414
CopperWynd Resort & Club 13225 N Eagle Ridge Dr	Fountain Hills	AZ	85268	**877-707-7760**	480-333-1900
Doubletree Paradise Valley Resort 5401 N Scottsdale Rd	Scottsdale	AZ	85250	**800-222-8733**	480-947-5400
Doubletree La Posada Resort 4949 E Lincoln Dr	Scottsdale	AZ	85253	**800-222-8733**	602-952-0420

Arizona (Cont'd)

Name / Address	City	State	ZIP	Toll-Free	Phone
Enchantment Resort 525 Boynton Canyon Rd	Sedona	AZ	86336	**800-826-4180**	928-282-2900
Fairmont Scottsdale Princess 7575 E Princess Dr	Scottsdale	AZ	85255	**800-344-4758**	480-585-4848
Four Seasons Resort Scottsdale at Troon North 10600 E Crescent Moon Dr	Scottsdale	AZ	85262	**800-332-3442**	480-515-5700
Gold Canyon Golf Resort 6100 S Kings Ranch Rd	Gold Canyon	AZ	85218	**800-624-6445**	480-982-9090
Harrah's Ak-Chin Casino Resort 15406 Maricopa Rd	Maricopa	AZ	85239	**888-302-3293**	480-802-3091
Hilton Sedona Resort & Spa 90 Ridge Trail Dr	Sedona	AZ	86351	**800-222-8733**	928-284-4040
Hilton Tucson El Conquistador Golf & Tennis Resort 10000 N Oracle Rd	Tucson	AZ	85737	**800-325-7832**	520-544-5000
Hyatt Regency Scottsdale Resort at Gainey Ranch 7500 E Doubletree Ranch Rd	Scottsdale	AZ	85258	**800-233-1234**	480-991-3388
Lake Powell Resorts & Marinas 100 Lakeshore Dr	Page	AZ	86040	**800-528-6154**	928-645-2433
Legacy Golf Resort 6808 S 32nd St	Phoenix	AZ	85042	**888-828-3673**	602-305-5500
Lodge at Ventana Canyon - A Wyndham Luxury Resort 6200 N Clubhouse Ln	Tucson	AZ	85750	**800-828-5701**	520-577-1400
Loews Ventana Canyon Resort 7000 N Resort Dr	Tucson	AZ	85750	**800-234-5117**	520-299-2020
Los Abrigados Resort 160 Portal Ln	Sedona	AZ	86336	**800-521-3131**	928-282-1777
Millennium Resort Scottsdale McCormick Ranch 7401 N Scottsdale Rd	Scottsdale	AZ	85253	**800-243-1332**	480-948-5050
Orange Tree Golf & Conference Resort 10601 N 56th St	Scottsdale	AZ	85254	**800-228-0386**	480-948-6100
Phoenician The 6000 E Camelback Rd	Scottsdale	AZ	85251	**800-888-8234**	480-941-8200
Pointe Hilton Resort at Tapatio Cliffs 11111 N 7th St	Phoenix	AZ	85020	**800-876-4683**	602-866-7500
Pointe Hilton at Squaw Peak Resort 7677 N 16th St	Phoenix	AZ	85020	**800-685-0550**	602-997-2626
Pointe South Mountain Resort 7777 S Pointe Pkwy	Phoenix	AZ	85044	**877-800-4888**	602-438-9000
Radisson Resort & Spa Scottsdale 7171 N Scottsdale Rd	Scottsdale	AZ	85253	**800-333-3333**	480-991-3800
Rancho de los Caballeros 1551 S Vulture Mine Rd	Wickenburg	AZ	85390	**800-684-5030**	928-684-5484
Rio Rico Resort & Country Club 1069 Camino Caralampi	Rio Rico	AZ	85648	**800-288-4746**	520-281-1901
Royal Palms Resort & Spa 5200 E Camelback Rd	Phoenix	AZ	85018	**800-672-6011**	602-840-3610
Sanctuary on Camelback Mountain 5700 E McDonald Dr	Paradise Valley	AZ	85253	**800-245-2051**	480-948-2100
Scottsdale Camelback Resort 6302 E Camelback Rd	Scottsdale	AZ	85251	**800-891-8585**	480-947-3300
Scottsdale Plaza Resort 7200 N Scottsdale Rd	Scottsdale	AZ	85253	**800-832-2025**	480-948-5000
Sheraton San Marcos Golf Resort & Conference Center 1 San Marcos Pl	Chandler	AZ	85225	**800-528-8071**	480-812-0900
Sheraton Wild Horse Pass Resort & Spa 5594 W Wild Horse Pass Blvd	Chandler	AZ	85226	**888-218-8989**	602-225-0100
SunBurst Resort 4925 N Scottsdale Rd	Scottsdale	AZ	85251	**800-528-7867**	480-945-7666
Tanque Verde Guest Ranch 14301 E Speedway Blvd	Tucson	AZ	85748	**800-234-3833**	520-296-6275
Westin Kierland Resort & Spa 6902 E Greenway Pkwy	Scottsdale	AZ	85254	**888-625-5144**	480-624-1000
Westin La Paloma Resort & Spa 3800 E Sunrise Dr	Tucson	AZ	85718	**888-627-7201**	520-742-6000
Westward Look Resort 245 E Ina Rd	Tucson	AZ	85704	**800-722-2500**	520-297-1151
Wigwam Resort 300 Wigwam Blvd	Litchfield Park	AZ	85340	**800-327-0396**	623-935-3811

Arkansas

Name / Address	City	State	ZIP	Toll-Free	Phone
Arlington Resort Hotel & Spa 239 Central Ave	Hot Springs	AR	71901	**800-643-1502**	501-623-7771
Best Western Inn of the Ozarks 297 W Van Buren	Eureka Springs	AR	72632	**800-552-3785**	479-253-9768

British Columbia

Name / Address	City	Province	Postal Code	Toll-Free	Phone
Aerie Resort PO Box 108	Malahat	BC	V0R2L0	**800-518-1933**	250-743-7115
Delta Victoria Ocean Pointe Resort Hotel & Spa 45 Songhees Rd	Victoria	BC	V9A6T3	**800-667-4677**	250-360-2999
Delta Whistler Resort 4050 Whistler Way	Whistler	BC	V0N1B4	**888-244-8666**	604-932-1982
Delta Whistler Village Suites 4308 Main St	Whistler	BC	V0N1B4	**888-244-8666**	604-905-3987
Echo Valley Ranch & Spa Clinton PO Box 16	Jesmond	BC	V0K1K0	**800-253-8831**	250-459-2386
Fairmont Chateau Whistler 4599 Chateau Blvd	Whistler	BC	V0N1B4	**800-441-1414**	604-938-8000
Fairwinds Schooner Cove Resort & Marina 3521 Dolphin Dr	Nanoose Bay	BC	V9P9J7	**800-663-7060**	250-468-7691
Harrison Hot Springs Resort & Spa 100 Esplanade Ave	Harrison Hot Springs	BC	V0M1K0	**800-663-2266**	604-796-2244
Holiday Inn SunSpree Resort Whistler Village 4295 Blackcomb Way	Whistler	BC	V0N1B4	**800-229-3188**	604-938-0878
Oak Bay Beach Hotel & Marine Resort 1175 Beach Dr	Victoria	BC	V8S2N2	**800-668-7758**	250-598-4556
Pan Pacific Lodge Whistler 4320 Sundial Crescent	Whistler	BC	V0N1B4	**888-905-9995**	604-905-2999
Tantalus Lodge 4200 Whistler Way	Whistler	BC	V0N1B4	**888-633-4046**	604-932-4146
Westin Resort & Spa Whistler 4090 Whistler Way	Whistler	BC	V0N1B4	**888-634-5577**	604-905-5000
Whistler Blackcomb Mountain Ski Resort 4545 Blackcomb Way	Whistler	BC	V0N1B4	**800-766-0449**	604-932-3434

California

Name / Address	City	State	ZIP	Toll-Free	Phone
Alisal Guest Ranch & Resort 1054 Alisal Rd	Solvang	CA	93463	**800-425-4725**	805-688-6411
Alpine Meadows Ski Resort 2600 Alpine Meadows Rd PO Box 5279	Tahoe City	CA	96145	**800-441-4423**	530-583-4232
Bacara Resort & Spa 8301 Hollister Ave	Santa Barbara	CA	93117	**877-422-4245**	805-968-0100
Bahia Resort Hotel 998 W Mission Bay Dr	San Diego	CA	92109	**800-576-4229**	858-488-0551
Balboa Bay Club & Resort 1221 W Coast Hwy	Newport Beach	CA	92663	**888-445-7153**	949-645-5000
Barona Valley Ranch Resort & Casino 1932 Wildcat Canyon Rd	Lakeside	CA	92040	**888-722-7662**	619-443-2300
Calistoga Ranch 580 Lommel Rd	Calistoga	CA	94515	**800-942-4220**	707-254-2800
Carmel Valley Ranch Resort - A Wyndham Luxury Resort 1 Old Ranch Rd	Carmel	CA	93923	**800-422-7635**	831-625-9500
Casa Palmero 1518 Cypress Dr	Pebble Beach	CA	93953	**800-654-9300**	831-647-7500
Claremont Resort & Spa 41 Tunnel Rd	Berkeley	CA	94705	**800-551-7266**	510-843-3000
Costanoa Coastal Lodge & Camp 2001 Rossi Rd	Pescadero	CA	94060	**877-262-7848**	650-879-1100
Crowne Plaza Resort Anaheim-Garden Grove 12021 Harbor Blvd	Garden Grove	CA	92840	**800-227-6963**	714-867-5555
Desert Hot Springs Spa Hotel 10805 Palm Dr	Desert Hot Springs	CA	92240	**800-808-7727**	760-329-6000
Desert Springs Marriott Resort & Spa 74855 Country Club Dr	Palm Desert	CA	92260	**800-331-3112**	760-341-2211
Doral Desert Princess Palm Springs Resort 67-967 Vista Chino	Cathedral City	CA	92234	**888-386-4677**	760-322-7000
Doubletree Golf Resort San Diego 14455 Penasquitos Dr	San Diego	CA	92129	**800-222-8733**	858-672-9100
Fairmont Sonoma Mission Inn & Spa 100 Boyes Blvd PO Box 1447	Boyes Hot Springs	CA	95416	**800-862-4945**	707-938-9000
Flamingo Resort Hotel & Conference Center 2777 4th St	Santa Rosa	CA	95405	**800-848-8300**	707-545-8530
Four Seasons Resort Aviara 7100 Four Seasons Pt	Carlsbad	CA	92009	**800-332-3442**	760-603-6800
Four Seasons Resort Santa Barbara 1260 Channel Dr	Santa Barbara	CA	93100	**000-424 6066**	806 060-2261
Gardiner's Resort 114 Carmel Valley Rd	Carmel Valley	CA	93924	**800-453-6225**	831-659-2207
Grand Pacific Palisades Resort & Hotel 5805 Armada Dr	Carlsbad	CA	92008	**800-725-4723**	760-827-3200
Greenhorn Creek Resort 711 McCauley Ranch Rd	Angels Camp	CA	95222	**888-736-5900**	209-736-6201
Handlery Hotel & Resort 950 Hotel Cir N	San Diego	CA	92108	**800-676-6567**	619-298-0511
Harrah's Rincon Casino & Resort 777 Harrah's Rincon Way	Valley Center	CA	92082	**877-777-2457**	760-751-3100
Hilton Palm Springs Resort 400 E Tahquitz Canyon Way	Palm Springs	CA	92262	**800-522-6900**	760-320-6868
Hilton San Diego Resort 1775 E Mission Bay Dr	San Diego	CA	92109	**877-414-8019**	619-276-4010
Hilton Waterfront Beach Resort 21100 Pacific Coast Hwy	Huntington Beach	CA	92648	**800-822-7873**	714-845-8000
Hotel Del Coronado 1500 Orange Ave	Coronado	CA	92118	**800-582-2595**	619-522-8000
Hyatt Grand Champions Resort 44-600 Indian Wells Ln	Indian Wells	CA	92210	**800-233-1234**	760-341-1000
Indian Wells Resort Hotel 76-661 Hwy 111	Indian Wells	CA	92210	**800-248-3220**	760-345-6466
Inn at Rancho Santa Fe 5951 Linea Del Cielo PO Box 869	Rancho Santa Fe	CA	92067	**800-843-4661**	858-756-1131
Inn at Spanish Bay 2700 17-Mile Dr	Pebble Beach	CA	93953	**800-654-9300**	831-647-7500
Knott's Berry Farm Resort 7675 Crescent Ave	Buena Park	CA	90620	**866-752-2444**	714-995-1111
La Casa del Zorro 3845 Yaqui Pass Rd	Borrego Springs	CA	92004	**800-824-1884**	760-767-5323
La Costa Resort & Spa 2100 Costa del Mar Rd	Carlsbad	CA	92009	**800-854-5000**	760-438-9111
La Jolla Beach & Tennis Club 2000 Spindrift Dr	La Jolla	CA	92037	**800-237-5211**	858-454-7126
La Mancha Resort Village 444 Avenida Caballeros	Palm Springs	CA	92262	**800-255-1773**	760-323-1773
La Quinta Resort & Club 49-499 Eisenhower Dr	La Quinta	CA	92253	**800-598-3828**	760-564-4111
Laguna Cliffs Marriott Resort 25135 Park Lantern	Dana Point	CA	92629	**800-228-9290**	949-661-5000
Lakeland Village Beach & Mountain Resort 3535 Lake Tahoe Blvd	South Lake Tahoe	CA	96150	**800-822-5969**	530-544-1685
L'Auberge Del Mar Resort & Spa 1540 Camino del Mar	Del Mar	CA	92014	**800-553-1336**	858-259-1515
Lawrence Welks Desert Oasis 34567 Cathedral Canyon Dr	Cathedral City	CA	92234	**800-824-8224**	760-321-9000
Lodge at Pebble Beach 1500 Cypress Dr	Pebble Beach	CA	93953	**800-654-9300**	831-624-3811
Loews Coronado Bay Resort 4000 Coronado Bay Rd	Coronado	CA	92118	**800-815-6397**	619-424-4000
Mammoth Mountain Resort 1 Minaret Rd PO Box 24	Mammoth Lakes	CA	93546	**800-626-6684**	760-934-2571
Marriott Coronado Island Resort 2000 2nd St	Coronado	CA	92118	**800-228-9290**	619-435-3000
Meadowood Napa Valley 900 Meadowood Ln	Saint Helena	CA	94574	**800-458-8080**	707-963-3646
Miramonte Resort & Spa 45000 Indian Wells Ln	Indian Wells	CA	92210	**800-237-2926**	760-341-2200
Montage Resort & Spa 30801 S Coast Hwy	Laguna Beach	CA	92651	**866-271-6953**	949-715-6001
Morgan Run Resort & Club 5690 Cancha de Golf	Rancho Santa Fe	CA	92091	**800-378-4653**	858-756-2471
Mount Shasta Resort 1000 Siskiyou Lake Blvd	Mount Shasta	CA	96067	**800-958-3363**	530-926-3030
Northstar-at-Tahoe PO Box 129	Truckee	CA	96160	**800-466-6784**	530-562-1010
Oasis Villa Resort Hotel 4190 E Palm Canyon Dr	Palm Springs	CA	92264	**800-247-4664**	760-328-1499
Ojai Valley Inn & Spa 905 Country Club Rd	Ojai	CA	93023	**800-422-6524**	805-646-5511
Pacific Palms Conference Resort 1 Industry Hills Pkwy	City of Industry	CA	91744	**800-524-4557**	626-810-4455
Pala Casino Resort & Spa 11154 Hwy 76 PO Box 40	Pala	CA	92059	**877-946-7252**	760-510-5100
Pala Mesa Resort 2001 Old Hwy 395	Fallbrook	CA	92028	**800-722-4700**	760-728-5881
Palm Springs Riviera Resort & Racket Club 1600 N Indian Canyon Dr	Palm Springs	CA	92262	**800-444-8311**	760-327-8311
Paradise Point Resort & Spa 1404 W Vacation Rd	San Diego	CA	92109	**800-344-2626**	858-274-4630
Pechanga Resort & Casino 45000 Pechanga Pkwy	Temecula	CA	92592	**877-711-2946**	951-693-1819
Post Ranch Inn Hwy 1	Big Sur	CA	93920	**800-527-2200**	831-667-2200
Quail Lodge Resort & Golf Club 8205 Valley Greens Dr	Carmel	CA	93923	**800-538-9516**	831-624-2888
Rancho Bernardo Inn 17550 Bernardo Oaks Dr	San Diego	CA	92128	**877-517-9342**	858-675-8500
Rancho Las Palmas Marriott Resort & Spa 41000 Bob Hope Dr	Rancho Mirage	CA	92270	**800-458-8786**	760-568-2727
Rancho Valencia Resort 5921 Valencia Cir PO Box 9126	Rancho Santa Fe	CA	92067	**800-548-3664**	858-756-1123
Renaissance Esmeralda Resort 44-400 Indian Wells Ln	Indian Wells	CA	92210	**800-552-4386**	760-773-4444

				Toll-Free	Phone
Resort at Squaw Creek 400 Squaw Creek Rd	Olympic Valley	CA	96146	**800-327-3353**	530-583-6300
Rio Bravo Resort 11200 Lake Ming Rd	Bakersfield	CA	93306	**888-517-5500**	661-872-5000
Ritz-Carlton Half Moon Bay 1 Miramontes Pt Rd	Half Moon Bay	CA	94019	**800-244-3333**	650-712-7000
Ritz-Carlton Laguna Niguel 1 Ritz Carlton Dr	Dana Point	CA	92629	**800-241-3333**	949-240-2000
Saint Regis Monarch Beach Resort & Spa 1 Monarch Beach Resort	Dana Point	CA	92629	**800-722-1543**	949-234-3200
San Vicente Inn & Golf Course 24157 San Vicente Rd	Ramona	CA	92065	**800-776-1289**	760-789-8290
San Ysidro Ranch 900 San Ysidro Ln	Montecito	CA	93108	**800-368-6788**	805-969-5046
Sea Venture Resort 100 Ocean View Ave	Pismo Beach	CA	93449	**800-662-5545**	805-773-4994
Shadow Mountain Resort & Club 45-750 San Luis Rey	Palm Desert	CA	92260	**800-472-3713**	760-346-6123
Silverado Resort 1600 Atlas Peak Rd	Napa	CA	94558	**800-532-0500**	707-257-0200
Singing Hills Resort at Sycuan 3007 Dehesa Rd	El Cajon	CA	92019	**800-457-5568**	619-442-3425
Spa Resort The 100 N Indian Canyon Dr	Palm Springs	CA	92262	**800-854-1279**	760-325-1461
Spa Resort Casino 401 E Amado Rd	Palm Springs	CA	92262	**800-854-1279**	760-883-1000
Squaw Valley USA PO Box 2007	Olympic Valley	CA	96146	**800-545-4350**	530-583-6985
Temecula Creek Inn 44501 Rainbow Canyon Rd	Temecula	CA	92592	**800-962-7335**	951-694-1000
Town & Country Resort & Convention Center 500 Hotel Cir N	San Diego	CA	92108	**800-772-8527**	619-291-7131
Two Bunch Palms Resort & Spa 67425 Two Bunch Palms Trail	Desert Hot Springs	CA	92240	**800-472-4334**	760-329-8791
Ventana Inn 48123 Hwy 1	Big Sur	CA	93920	**800-628-6500**	831-667-2331
Westin Mission Hills Resort 71333 Dinah Shore Dr	Rancho Mirage	CA	92270	**800-937-8461**	760-328-5955

Colorado

				Toll-Free	Phone
Aspen Meadows Resort 845 Meadows Rd	Aspen	CO	81611	**800-452-4240**	970-925-4240
Beaver Run Resort & Conference Center 620 Village Rd	Breckenridge	CO	80424	**800-525-2253**	970-453-6000
Breckenridge Ski Resort 351 County Rd 708	Breckenridge	CO	80424	**800-789-7669**	970-453-5000
Broadmoor The 1 Lake Ave	Colorado Springs	CO	80906	**800-634-7711**	719-634-7711
Copper Mountain Resort 509 Copper Rd PO Box 3001	Copper Mountain	CO	80443	**888-219-2441**	970-968-2882
Crested Butte Mountain Resort 12 Snowmass Rd PO Box 5700	Mount Crested Butte	CO	81225	**800-810-7669**	970-349-2201
Durango Mountain Resort 1 Skier Pl	Durango	CO	81301	**800-693-0175**	970-247-9000
Gold Lake Mountain Resort & Spa 3371 Gold Lake Rd	Ward	CO	80481	**800-450-3544**	303-459-3544
Grand Lodge Crested Butte 6 Emmons Rd	Mount Crested Butte	CO	81225	**888-823-4446**	970-349-8000
Hot Springs Lodge & Pool 415 E 6th St PO Box 308	Glenwood Springs	CO	81602	**800-537-7946**	970-945-6571
Inn at Beaver Creek 10 Elk Track Ln	Beaver Creek	CO	81620	**800-859-8242**	970-845-7800
Inverness Hotel & Golf Club 200 Inverness Dr W	Englewood	CO	80112	**800-346-4891**	303-799-5800
Keystone Resort 21996 Hwy 6	Keystone	CO	80435	**800-239-1639**	970-496-2316
Lion Square Lodge & Conference Center 660 W Lionshead Pl	Vail	CO	81657	**800-525-5788**	970-476-2281
Lodge at Tamarron 40292 Hwy 550 N	Durango	CO	81301	**800-678-1000**	970-259-2000
Lodge at Vail 174 E Gore Creek Dr	Vail	CO	81657	**800-331-5634**	970-476-5011
Manor Vail Lodge 595 E Vail Valley Dr	Vail	CO	81657	**800-950-8245**	970-476-5651
Marriott Mountain Resort at Vail 715 W Lionshead Cir	Vail	CO	81657	**800-648-0720**	970-476-4444
Monarch Mountain Lodge 22720 W US Hwy 50	Monarch	CO	81227	**888-996-7669**	719-539-2581
Mountain Lodge at Telluride 457 Mountain Village Blvd	Telluride	CO	81435	**866-368-6867**	970-369-5000
Omni Interlocken Resort 500 Interlocken Blvd	Broomfield	CO	80021	**800-843-6664**	303-438-6600
Park Hyatt Beaver Creek Resort & Spa 136 E Thomas Pl	Beaver Creek	CO	81620	**800-233-1234**	970-949-1234
Sheraton Steamboat Resort & Conference Center 2200 Village Inn Ct	Steamboat Springs	CO	80487	**800-325-3535**	970-879-2220
Snowmass Club PO Box G-2	Snowmass Village	CO	81615	**800-525-0710**	970-923-5600
Sonnenalp Resort of Vail 20 Vail Rd	Vail	CO	81657	**800-654-8312**	970-476-5656
Steamboat Grand Resort Hotel & Conference Center 2300 Mt Werner Cir	Steamboat Springs	CO	80487	**877-269-2628**	970-871-5500
Steamboat Ski & Resort Corp 2305 Mt Werner Cir	Steamboat Springs	CO	80487	**877-237-2628**	970-879-6111
Torian Plum Condo Resort 1855 Ski Time Square Dr	Steamboat Springs	CO	80487	**800-228-2458**	970-879-8811
Vail Cascade Resort & Spa 1300 Westhaven Dr	Vail	CO	81657	**800-420-2424**	970-476-7111
Village at Breckenridge Resort 535 S Park Ave	Breckenridge	CO	80424	**800-332-0424**	970-453-2000
Winter Park Resort 150 Alpenglobe Way PO Box 36	Winter Park	CO	80482	**800-979-0332**	303-892-0961
Wyndham Peaks Resort & Golden Door Spa 136 Country Club Dr	Telluride	CO	81435	**800-789-2220**	970-728-6800

Connecticut

				Toll-Free	Phone
Dolce Heritage 522 Heritage Rd	Southbury	CT	06488	**800-932-3466**	203-264-8200
Foxwoods Resort Casino 39 Norwich Westerly Rd	Ledyard	CT	06339	**800-752-9244**	860-312-3000
Interlaken Inn 74 Interlaken Rd	Lakeville	CT	06039	**800-222-2909**	860-435-9878
Saybrook Point Inn & Spa 2 Bridge St	Old Saybrook	CT	06475	**800-243-0212**	860-395-2000
Water's Edge Resort 1525 Boston Post Rd	Westbrook	CT	06498	**800-222-5901**	860-399-5901

Florida

				Toll-Free	Phone
Admiral Lehigh Golf Resort & Spa 225 E Joel Blvd	Lehigh Acres	FL	33972	**888-465-3222**	239-369-2121
Amelia Island Plantation 1501 Lewis St	Amelia Island	FL	32034	**800-874-6878**	904-261-6161
Bahia Beach Resort 611 Destiny Dr	Ruskin	FL	33570	**800-327-2773**	813-645-3291
Banana Bay Resort 2319 N Roosevelt Blvd	Key West	FL	33040	**800-226-2621**	305-296-6925
Bay Hill Golf Club & Lodge 9000 Bay Hill Blvd	Orlando	FL	32819	**888-422-9445**	407-876-2429
Bay Point Resort Village Marriott Golf & Yacht Club 4200 Marriott Dr	Panama City Beach	FL	32408	**800-874-7105**	850-236-6000
Belleview Biltmore Resort & Spa 25 Belleview Blvd	Clearwater	FL	33756	**800-237-8947**	727-442-6171
Biltmore Hotel & Conference Center of the Americas 1200 Anastasia Ave	Coral Gables	FL	33134	**800-727-1926**	305-445-1926
Bluewater Bay Resort 1940 Bluewater Blvd	Niceville	FL	32578	**800-874-2128**	850-897-3613
Boca Raton Resort & Club 501 E Camino Real	Boca Raton	FL	33431	**800-327-0101**	561-447-3000
Bonaventure Resort & Spa 250 Racquet Club Rd	Weston	FL	33326	**800-996-3426**	954-389-3300
Breakers The 1 S County Rd	Palm Beach	FL	33480	**800-833-3141**	561-655-6611
Casa Ybel Resort 2255 W Gulf Dr	Sanibel	FL	33957	**800-276-4753**	239-472-3145
Charter Club Resort on Naples Bay 1000 10th Ave S	Naples	FL	34102	**800-494-5559**	239-261-5559
Cheeca Lodge & Spa MM 82 81801 Overseas Hwy	Islamorada	FL	33036	**800-327-2888**	305-664-4651
Club Med Sandpiper 3500 SE Morningside Blvd	Port Saint Lucie	FL	34952	**800-258-2633**	772-335-4400
Colony Beach & Tennis Resort 1620 Gulf of Mexico Dr	Longboat Key	FL	34228	**800-426-5669**	941-383-6464
Colony Reef Club 4670 A1A S	Saint Augustine	FL	32080	**800-624-5965**	904-471-2233
Coral Springs Marriott Hotel 11775 Heron Bay Blvd	Coral Springs	FL	33076	**800-333-3333***	954-753-5598
*Resv					
Crowne Plaza Resort Orlando 12000 International Dr	Orlando	FL	32821	**800-227-6963**	407-239-1222
Deauville Beach Resort 6701 Collins Ave	Miami Beach	FL	33141	**800-327-6656**	305-865-8511
Diplomat Country Club & Spa 501 Diplomat Pkwy	Hallandale Beach	FL	33009	**800-327-1212**	954-883-4000
Don CeSar Beach Resort & Spa 3400 Gulf Blvd	Saint Pete Beach	FL	33706	**800-282-1116**	727-360-1881
Don Shula's Hotel & Golf Club 6842 Main St	Miami Lakes	FL	33014	**800-247-4852**	305-821-1150
Doral Golf Resort & Spa 4400 NW 87th Ave	Miami	FL	33178	**800-713-6725**	305-592-2000
Doubletree Grand Key Resort 3990 S Roosevelt Blvd	Key West	FL	33040	**888-844-0454**	305-293-1818
Eden Roc - A Renaissance Resort & Spa 4525 Collins Ave	Miami Beach	FL	33140	**800-327-8337**	305-531-0000
Fairmount Turnberry Isle Resort & Club 19999 W Country Club Dr	Aventura	FL	33180	**800-327-7028**	305-932-6200
Fisher Island Hotel & Resort 1 Fisher Island Dr	Fisher Island	FL	33109	**800-537-3708**	305-535-6080
Fishermen's Village 1200 W Retta Esplanade	Punta Gorda	FL	33950	**800-639-0020**	941-639-8721
Fontainebleau Hilton Resort 4441 Collins Ave	Miami Beach	FL	33140	**800-548-8886**	305-538-2000
Four Seasons Resort Palm Beach 2800 S Ocean Blvd	Palm Beach	FL	33480	**800-432-2335**	561-582-2800
Galleon Resort & Marina 617 Front St	Key West	FL	33040	**800-544-3030**	305-296-7711
Grand Palms Hotel & Golf Resort 110 Grand Palms Dr	Pembroke Pines	FL	33027	**800-327-9246**	954-431-8800
Grenelefe Golf & Tennis Resort 3200 SR-546	Haines City	FL	33844	**888-808-7410**	863-422-7511
Hawk's Cay Resort & Marina 61 Hawk's Cay Blvd	Duck Key	FL	33050	**800-432-2242**	305-743-7000
Hilton Longboat Key Beach Resort 4711 Gulf of Mexico Dr	Longboat Key	FL	34228	**800-445-8667**	941-383-2451
Hilton Marco Island Beach Resort 560 S Collier Blvd	Marco Island	FL	34145	**800-443-4550**	239-394-5000
Hilton Sandestin Beach Golf Resort & Spa 4000 Sandestin Blvd S	Destin	FL	32550	**800-367-1271**	850-267-9500
Holiday Inn SunSpree Resort Jacksonville Beach 1617 N 1st St	Jacksonville Beach	FL	32250	**800-590-4767**	904-249-9071
Holiday Inn SunSpree Resort Lake Buena Vista 13351 SR 535	Orlando	FL	32821	**800-366-6299**	407-239-4500
Holiday Inn SunSpree Resort Marina Cove 6800 Sunshine Skyway Ln	Saint Petersburg	FL	33711	**800-227-8045**	727-867-1151
Holiday Isle Beach Resort & Marina 84001 Overseas Hwy	Islamorada	FL	33036	**800-327-7070**	305-664-2321
Hyatt Key West Resort & Marina 601 Front St	Key West	FL	33040	**800-554-9288**	305-296-9900
Hyatt Regency Coconut Point Resort & Spa 5001 Coconut Rd	Bonita Springs	FL	34134	**800-233-1234**	239-444-1234
Hyatt Regency Grand Cypress Resort 1 Grand Cypress Blvd	Orlando	FL	32836	**800-233-1234**	407-239-1234
Hyatt Regency Pier 66 2301 SE 17th St Cswy Pier 66	Fort Lauderdale	FL	33316	**800-233-1234**	954-525-6666
Inverrary Plaza Resort 3501 Inverrary Blvd	Fort Lauderdale	FL	33319	**800-241-0363**	954-485-0500
Jupiter Beach Resort 5 N Hwy A1A	Jupiter	FL	33477	**800-228-8810**	561-746-2511
JW Marriott Orlando Grande Lakes Resort 4040 Central Florida Pkwy	Orlando	FL	32837	**800-576-5750**	407-206-2300
Key Largo Bay Marriott Beach Resort 103800 Overseas Hwy	Key Largo	FL	33037	**866-849-3753**	305-453-0000
La Playa Beach & Golf Resort 9891 Gulf Shore Dr	Naples	FL	34108	**800-237-6883**	239-597-3123
Lago Mar Resort & Club 1700 S Ocean Ln	Fort Lauderdale	FL	33316	**800-524-6627**	954-523-6511
Little Palm Island 28500 Overseas Hwy MM 28.5	Little Torch Key	FL	33042	**800-343-8567**	305-872-2524
Lodge & Club at Ponte Vedra Beach 607 Ponte Vedra Blvd	Ponte Vedra Beach	FL	32082	**800-243-4304**	904-273-9500
Longboat Key Club 301 Gulf of Mexico Dr	Longboat Key	FL	34228	**800-237-8821**	941-383-8821
Marco Beach Ocean Resort 480 S Collier Blvd	Marco Island	FL	34145	**800-715-8517**	239-393-1400
Marriott Golf & Yacht Club Bay Point Resort Village 4200 Marriott Dr	Panama City Beach	FL	32408	**800-874-7105**	850-236-6000
Marriott Harbor Beach Resort & Spa 3030 Holiday Dr	Fort Lauderdale	FL	33316	**800-228-9290**	954-525-4000
Marriott Hutchinson Island Beach Resort & Marina 555 NE Ocean Blvd	Stuart	FL	34996	**800-775-5936**	772-225-3700
Marriott Marco Island Resort Golf Club & Spa 400 S Collier Blvd	Marco Island	FL	34145	**800-438-4373**	239-394-2511
Miccosukee Resort & Convention Center 500 SW 177th Ave	Miami	FL	33194	**877-242-6464**	305-925-2555
Mission Inn Golf & Tennis Resort 10400 CR 48	Howey in the Hills	FL	34737	**800-874-9053**	352-324-3101

Florida (Cont'd)

Name / Address	City	State	ZIP	Toll-Free	Phone
Naples Beach Hotel & Golf Club 851 Gulf Shore Blvd N.	Naples	FL	34102	**800-237-7600**	239-261-2222
Nickelodeon Family Suites by Holiday Inn 14500 Continental Gateway	Orlando	FL	32821	**877-387-5437**	407-387-5437
Ocean Hammock Resort 300 Clubhouse Dr	Palm Coast	FL	32137	**800-654-6538**	386-445-3000
Ocean Key - A Noble House Resort Zero Duval St.	Key West	FL	33040	**800-328-9815**	305-296-7701
Omni Orlando Resort at Championsgate 1500 Masters Blvd.	Orlando	FL	33896	**800-843-6664**	407-390-6664
Orlando World Center Marriott Resort & Convention Center 8701 World Ctr Dr	Orlando	FL	32821	**800-621-0638**	407-239-4200
Park Shore Resort 600 Neapolitan Way	Naples	FL	34103	**888-627-1595**	239-263-2222
PGA National Resort & Spa 400 Ave of the Champions	Palm Beach Gardens	FL	33418	**800-633-9150**	561-627-2000
Pier House Resort & Caribbean Spa 1 Duval St	Key West	FL	33040	**800-327-8340**	305-296-4600
Plantation Inn & Golf Resort 9301 W Fort Island Trail	Crystal River	FL	34429	**800-632-6262**	352-795-4211
Plaza Resort & Spa 600 N Atlantic Ave	Daytona Beach	FL	32118	**800-874-7420**	386-255-4471
Ponte Vedra Inn & Club 200 Ponte Vedra Blvd	Ponte Vedra Beach	FL	32082	**800-234-7842**	904-285-1111
Quality Inn & Suites Naples Golf Resort 4100 Golden Gate Pkwy.	Naples	FL	34116	**800-277-0017**	239-455-1010
Radisson Resort Parkway 2900 Parkway Blvd	Kissimmee	FL	34747	**800-333-3333**	407-[illegible]-7000
Registry Resort 475 Seagate Dr	Naples	FL	34103	**800-247-9810**	239-597-3232
Renaissance Orlando Resort 6677 Sea Harbor Dr.	Orlando	FL	32821	**800-380-7917**	407-351-5555
Renaissance Vinoy Resort & Golf Club 501 5th Ave NE	Saint Petersburg	FL	33701	**800-468-3571**	727-894-1000
Renaissance World Golf Village Resort 500 S Legacy Trail	Saint Augustine	FL	32092	**888-740-7020**	904-940-8000
Ritz-Carlton Amelia Island 4750 Amelia Island Pkwy.	Amelia Island	FL	32034	**800-241-3333**	904-277-1100
Ritz-Carlton Key Biscayne 455 Grand Bay Dr	Key Biscayne	FL	33149	**800-241-3333**	305-365-9575
Ritz-Carlton Naples 280 Vanderbilt Beach Rd	Naples	FL	34108	**800-241-3333**	239-598-3300
Ritz-Carlton Naples Golf Resort 2600 Tiburon Dr	Naples	FL	34109	**888-856-2164**	239-593-2000
Ritz-Carlton Palm Beach 100 S Ocean Blvd.	Manalapan	FL	33462	**800-241-3333**	561-533-6000
Saddlebrook Resort 5700 Saddlebrook Way	Wesley Chapel	FL	33543	**800-729-8383**	813-973-1111
Safety Harbor Resort & Spa 105 N Bayshore Dr	Safety Harbor	FL	34695	**888-237-8772**	727-726-1161
Sandestin Golf & Beach Resort 9300 Emerald Coast Pkwy W	Sandestin	FL	32550	**800-277-0800**	850-267-8000
Sanibel Harbour Resort & Spa 17260 Harbour Pointe Dr.	Fort Myers	FL	33908	**800-767-7777**	239-466-4000
Sanibel Inn 937 E Gulf Dr.	Sanibel	FL	33957	**800-237-1491**	239-472-3181
Sawgrass Marriott Resort & Beach Club 1000 PGA Tour Blvd	Ponte Vedra Beach	FL	32082	**800-457-4653**	904-285-7777
Seabonay Beach Resort 1159 Hillsboro Mile	Hillsboro Beach	FL	33062	**800-777-1961**	954-427-2525
Seascape Resort 100 Seascape Dr.	Destin	FL	32550	**800-874-9106**	850-837-9181
Seminole Hard Rock Hotel & Casino Hollywood 1 Seminole Way	Hollywood	FL	33314	**800-937-0010**	954-327-7625
Seminole Hard Rock Hotel & Casino Tampa 5223 N Orient Rd.	Tampa	FL	33610	**800-282-7016**	813-621-1302
Sheraton Bal Harbour Beach Resort 9701 Collins Ave	Miami Beach	FL	33154	**800-325-3535**	305-865-7511
Sheraton Sand Key Resort 1160 Gulf Blvd.	Clearwater Beach	FL	33767	**800-325-3535**	727-595-1611
Sirata Beach Resort & Conference Center 5300 Gulf Blvd.	Saint Pete Beach	FL	33706	**866-587-8538**	727-363-5100
Sonesta Beach Resort & Spa Key Biscayne 350 Ocean Dr.	Key Biscayne	FL	33149	**800-766-3782**	305-361-2021
South Seas Resort 5400 Plantation Rd.	Captiva	FL	33924	**800-965-7772**	239-472-5111
Standard The 40 Island Ave	Miami Beach	FL	33139	**800-327-8363**	305-673-1717
Summer Beach Resort 5456 First Coast Hwy.	Amelia Island	FL	32034	**800-862-9297**	904-277-0905
Sundial Beach & Tennis Resort 1451 Middle Gulf Dr	Sanibel	FL	33957	**800-237-4184**	239-472-4151
Sunset Key Guest Cottages at Hilton Key West Resort 245 Front St.	Key West	FL	33040	**888-477-7786**	305-292-5300
TradeWinds Island Grand Beach Resort 5500 Gulf Blvd.	Saint Pete Beach	FL	33705	**800-360-4016**	727-367-6461
TradeWinds Sandpiper Beach Resort 6000 Gulf Blvd.	Saint Pete Beach	FL	33705	**800-237-0707**	727-360-5551
Vanderbilt Beach Resort 9225 Gulf Shore Dr N	Naples	FL	34108	**800-243-9076**	239-597-3144
Villas of Grand Cypress 1 N Jacaranda	Orlando	FL	32836	**800-835-7377**	407-239-4700
Walt Disney World Dolphin 1500 Epcot Resorts Blvd	Lake Buena Vista	FL	32830	**800-227-1500**	407-934-4000
Walt Disney World Swan 1200 Epcot Resorts Blvd	Lake Buena Vista	FL	32830	**800-248-7926**	407-934-3000
West Wind Inn 3345 W Gulf Dr	Sanibel	FL	33957	**800-824-0476**	239-472-1541
Westin Beach Resort Key Largo 97000 S Overseas Hwy MM 97	Key Largo	FL	33037	**800-937-8461**	305-852-5553
Westin Diplomat Resort & Spa 3555 S Ocean Dr	Hollywood	FL	33019	**888-627-9057**	954-602-6000
Westin Innisbrook Golf Resort 36750 US Hwy 19 N	Palm Harbor	FL	34684	**800-456-2000**	727-942-2000
Wyndham Casa Marina Resort 1500 Reynolds St	Key West	FL	33040	**800-626-0777**	305-296-3535
Wyndham Orlando Resort 8001 International Dr.	Orlando	FL	32819	**800-421-8001**	407-351-2420
Wyndham Palace Resort & Spa in the Walt Disney World Resort 1900 Buena Vista Dr	Lake Buena Vista	FL	32830	**800-996-3426**	407-827-2727
Wyndham Reach Resort 1435 Simonton St	Key West	FL	33040	**800-996-3426**	305-296-5000

Georgia

Name / Address	City	State	ZIP	Toll-Free	Phone
Barnsley Gardens 597 Barnsley Gardens Rd	Adairsville	GA	30103	**877-773-2447**	770-773-7480
Brasstown Valley Resort 6321 US Hwy 76	Young Harris	GA	30582	**800-201-3205**	706-379-9900
Callaway Gardens Resort PO Box 2000	Pine Mountain	GA	31822	**800-225-5292**	706-663-2281
Chateau Elan Resort & Conference Center 100 rue Charlemagne	Braselton	GA	30517	**800-233-9463**	678-425-0900
Cloister The 100 Hudson Pl	Sea Island	GA	31561	**800-732-4752**	912-638-3611
Emerald Pointe Resort 7000 Holiday Rd	Lake Lanier Islands	GA	30518	**800-768-5253**	770-945-8787
Evergreen Marriott Conference Resort 4021 Lakeview Dr	Stone Mountain	GA	30083	**800-228-9290**	770-879-9900
Forrest Hills Mountain Resort & Conference Center 135 Forrest Hills Dr.	Dahlonega	GA	30533	**800-654-6313**	706-864-6456
Jekyll Island Club Hotel 371 Riverview Dr.	Jekyll Island	GA	31527	**800-535-9547**	912-635-2600
King & Prince Beach & Golf Resort 201 Arnold Rd	Saint Simons Island	GA	31522	**800-342-0212**	912-638-3631
Marietta Conference Center & Resort 500 Powder Springs St	Marietta	GA	30064	**888-685-2500**	770-427-2500
Renaissance PineIsle Resort 9000 Holiday Rd	Lake Lanier Islands	GA	30518	**800-468-3571**	770-945-8921
Reynolds Plantation 100 Linger Longer Rd	Greensboro	GA	30642	**800-852-5885**	706-467-3151
Ritz-Carlton Reynolds Plantation 1 Lake Oconee Trail	Greensboro	GA	30642	**800-826-1945**	706-467-0600
Sea Palms Golf & Tennis Resort 5445 Frederica Rd	Saint Simons Island	GA	31522	**800-841-6268**	912-638-3351
Sky Valley Golf Course Resort 696 Sky Valley Way	Sky Valley	GA	30537	**800-437-2416**	706-746-5302
Villas by the Sea Resort 1175 N Beachview Dr	Jekyll Island	GA	31527	**800-841-6262**	912-635-2521
Westin Savannah Harbor Resort & Spa 1 Resort Dr	Savannah	GA	31421	**800-937-8461**	912-201-2000

Hawaii

Name / Address	City	State	ZIP	Toll-Free	Phone
Fairmont Kea Lani Maui 4100 Wailea Alanui Dr	Maui	HI	96753	**800-659-4100**	808-875-4100
Fairmont Orchid Hawaii 1 N Kaniku Dr	Kohala	HI	96743	**800-845-9905**	808-885-2000
Four Seasons Resort Hualalai 100 Ka'upulehu Dr.	Ka'upulehu-Kona	HI	96740	**888-340-5662**	808-325-8000
Four Seasons Resort Maui at Wailea 3900 Wailea Alanui Dr	Wailea	HI	96753	**800-334-6284**	808-874-8000
Grand Wailea Resort & Spa 3850 Wailea Alanui Dr	Wailea	HI	96753	**800-888-6100**	808-875-1234
Hanalei Bay Resort & Suites 5380 Honoiki Rd	Princeville	HI	96722	**800-827-4427**	808-826-6522
Hapuna Beach Prince Hotel 62-100 Kauna'oa Dr.	Kamuela	HI	96743	**800-882-6060**	808-880-1111
Hawaii Prince Hotel Waikiki 100 Holomoana St.	Honolulu	HI	96815	**800-321-6248**	808-956-1111
Hilton Hawaiian Village 2005 Kalia Rd	Honolulu	HI	96815	**800-445-8667**	808-949-4321
Hilton Waikoloa Village 425 Waikoloa Beach Dr.	Waikoloa	HI	96738	**866-223-6574**	808-886-1234
Hotel Hana-Maui PO Box 9	Hana	HI	96713	**800-321-4262**	808-248-8211
Hyatt Regency Kauai Resort & Spa 1571 Poipu Rd.	Koloa	HI	96756	**800-233-1234**	808-742-1234
Hyatt Regency Maui Resort & Spa 200 Nohea Kai Dr	Lahaina	HI	96761	**800-233-1234**	808-661-1234
Hyatt Regency Waikiki Resort & Spa 2424 Kalakaua Ave.	Honolulu	HI	96815	**800-233-1234**	808-923-1234
JW Marriott Resort Ihilani 92-1001 Olani St.	Kapolei	HI	96707	**800-626-4446**	808-679-0079
Kapalua Resort 300 Kapalua Dr	Kapalua	HI	96761	**877-527-2582**	808-669-8044
Kapalua Villas The 500 Office Rd	Maui	HI	96761	**800-545-0018**	808-669-8088
Kaua'i Marriott Resort & Beach Club 3610 Rice St	Lihue	HI	96766	**800-220-2925**	808-245-5050
Kona Village Resort Queen Kaahumanu Hwy.	Kaupulehu-Kona	HI	96740	**800-367-5290**	808-325-5555
Lodge at Koele PO Box 630310	Lanai City	HI	96763	**800-321-4666**	808-565-7300
Makena Resort Maui Prince Hotel 5400 Makena Alanui.	Makena	HI	96753	**800-321-6248**	808-874-1111
Manele Bay Hotel 1 Manele Rd	Lanai City	HI	96763	**800-321-4666**	808-565-7700
Marriott Kaua'i Resort & Beach Club 3610 Rice St	Lihue	HI	96766	**800-220-2925**	808-245-5050
Marriott Maui Resort 100 Nohea Kai Dr	Lahaina	HI	96761	**800-763-1333**	808-667-1200
Maui Prince Hotel 5400 Makena Alanui	Makena	HI	96753	**800-321-6248**	808-874-1111
Mauna Kea Beach Hotel 62-100 Maunakea Beach Dr.	Kohala Coast	HI	96743	**800-882-6060**	808-882-7222
Mauna Lani Bay Hotel & Bungalows 68-1400 Mauna Lani Dr.	Kohala Coast	HI	96743	**800-367-2323**	808-885-6622
Napili Kai Beach Club 5900 Honoapiilani Rd.	Lahaina	HI	96761	**800-367-5030**	808-669-6271
Princeville Resort 5520 Ka Haku Rd	Princeville	HI	96722	**800-826-1260**	808-826-9644
Renaissance Wailea Beach Resort 3550 Wailea Alanui Dr	Kihei	HI	96753	**800-992-4532**	808-879-4900
Royal Lahaina Resort 2780 Kekaa Dr.	Lahaina	HI	96761	**800-447-6925**	808-661-3611
Sheraton Kauai Resort 2440 Hoonani Rd.	Koloa	HI	96756	**888-847-0208**	808-742-1661
Sheraton Moana Surfrider 2365 Kalakaua Ave.	Honolulu	HI	96815	**800-325-3535**	808-922-3111
Sheraton Waikiki 2255 Kalakaua Ave.	Honolulu	HI	96815	**800-325-3535**	808-922-4422
Turtle Bay Resort 57-091 Kamehameha Hwy.	Kahuku	HI	96731	**800-203-3650**	808-293-8811

Idaho

Name / Address	City	State	ZIP	Toll-Free	Phone
Coeur d'Alene Resort 115 S 2nd St PO Box 7200	Coeur d'Alene	ID	83814	**800-688-5253**	208-765-4000
Premier Resorts Sun Valley PO Box 659	Sun Valley	ID	83353	**800-635-4444**	208-727-4000
Red Lion Templin's Hotel on the River 414 E 1st Ave	Post Falls	ID	83854	**800-733-5466**	208-773-1611
Sun Valley Resort 1 Sun Valley Rd	Sun Valley	ID	83353	**800-786-8259**	208-622-2001

Illinois

Name / Address	City	State	ZIP	Toll-Free	Phone
Doral Eaglewood Conference Resort & Spa Chicago 1401 Nordic Rd.	Itasca	IL	60143	**877-285-6150**	630-773-2750
Eagle Ridge Inn & Resort 444 Eagle Ridge Dr.	Galena	IL	61036	**800-892-2269**	815-777-2444
Indian Lakes Resort 250 W Schick Rd.	Bloomingdale	IL	60108	**800-334-3417**	630-529-0200
Marriott's Lincolnshire Resort 10 Marriott Dr	Lincolnshire	IL	60069	**800-228-9290**	847-634-0100
Pheasant Run Resort & Spa 4051 E Main St	Saint Charles	IL	60174	**800-999-3319**	630-584-6300

Indiana

				Toll-Free	Phone
Belterra Casino Resort 777 Belterra Dr	Belterra	IN	47020	**888-235-8377***	812-427-7777
*Resv					
Eagle Pointe Golf Resort 2250 E Pointe Rd	Bloomington	IN	47401	**877-324-7683**	812-824-4040
Fourwinds Resort & Marina 9301 Fairfax Rd	Bloomington	IN	47401	**800-538-1187**	812-824-9904
French Lick Springs Resort & Spa 8670 W SR-56	French Lick	IN	47432	**800-457-4042**	812-936-9300
Grand Victoria Casino & Resort by Hyatt 600 Grand Victoria Dr	Rising Sun	IN	47040	**800-472-6311**	812-438-1234
Potawatomi Inn Pokagan State Park 6 Lane 100A Lake James	Angola	IN	46703	**877-768-2928**	260-833-1077

Iowa

				Toll-Free	Phone
Grand Harbor Resort & Waterpark 350 Bell St	Dubuque	IA	52001	**866-690-4006**	563-609-4000

Kentucky

				Toll-Free	Phone
Barren River Lake State Resort Park 1149 State Park Rd	Lucas	KY	42156	**800-325-0057**	270-646-2151
Carter Caves State Resort Park 344 Caveland Dr	Olive Hill	KY	41164	**800-325-0059**	606-286-4411
General Butler State Resort Park PO Box 325	Carrollton	KY	41008	**866-462-8853**	502-732-4384
Kentucky Dam Village State Resort Park PO Box 69	Gilbertsville	KY	42044	**800-325-0146**	270-362-4271
Lake Barkley State Resort Park 3500 State Park Rd Box 790	Cadiz	KY	42211	**800-325-1708**	270-924-1131
Lake Cumberland State Resort Park 5465 State Park Rd	Jamestown	KY	42629	**800-325-1709**	270-343-3111
Marriott's Griffin Gate Resort 1800 Newtown Pike	Lexington	KY	40511	**800-228-9290**	859-231-5100

Louisiana

				Toll-Free	Phone
Emerald Hills Golf Resort 42618 Hwy 171 S	Florien	LA	71429	**800-533-5031**	318-586-4661

Maine

				Toll-Free	Phone
Atlantic Oakes 119 Eden St	Bar Harbor	ME	04609	**800-336-2463**	207-288-5801
Bethel Inn & Country Club PO Box 49	Bethel	ME	04217	**800-654-0125**	207-824-2175
Black Point Inn Resort 510 Black Point Rd	Scarborough	ME	04074	**800-258-0003**	207-883-2500
Colony Hotel 140 Ocean Ave	Kennebunkport	ME	04046	**800-552-2363**	207-967-3331
Holiday Inn SunSpree Bar Harbor Regency Resort 123 Eden St	Bar Harbor	ME	04609	**800-234-6835**	207-288-9723
Inn by the Sea 40 Bowery Beach Rd	Cape Elizabeth	ME	04107	**800-888-4287**	207-799-3134
Samoset Resort 220 Warrenton St	Rockport	ME	04856	**800-341-1650**	207-594-2511
Sebasco Harbor Resort 27 Keynon Rd	Phippsburg	ME	04562	**800-225-3819**	207-389-1161
Spruce Point Inn 88 Grandview Ave PO Box 237	Boothbay Harbor	ME	04538	**800-553-0289**	207-633-4152
Stage Neck Inn 8 Stage Neck Rd Rt 1A Box 70	York Harbor	ME	03911	**800-222-3238**	207-363-3850
Sugarloaf/USA 5092 Access Rd	Carrabassett Valley	ME	04947	**800-843-5623**	207-237-2000
Sunday River Ski Resort 15 S Ridge Rd	Newry	ME	04261	**800-543-2754**	207-824-3000

Maryland

				Toll-Free	Phone
Harbourtowne Golf Resort & Conference Center 9784 Martingham Dr	Saint Michaels	MD	21663	**800-446-9066**	410-745-9066
Turf Valley Resort & Conference Center 2700 Turf Valley Rd	Ellicott City	MD	21042	**800-666-8873**	410-465-1500
Wisp Mountain Resort Hotel & Conference Center Deep Creek Lake 290 Marsh Hill Rd	McHenry	MD	21541	**800-462-9477**	301-387-5581

Massachusetts

				Toll-Free	Phone
Best Western Blue Rock Golf Resort 39 Todd Rd	South Yarmouth	MA	02664	**800-227-3263**	508-398-6962
Cape Codder Resort & Spa 1225 Iyanough Rd	Hyannis	MA	02601	**888-297-2200**	508-771-3000
Chatham Bars Inn 297 Shore Rd	Chatham	MA	02633	**800-527-4884**	508-945-0096
Cranwell Resort Spa & Golf Club 55 Lee Rd	Lenox	MA	01240	**800-272-6935**	413-637-1364
Harbor House Village South Beach St	Nantucket	MA	02554	**800-475-2637**	508-228-1500
New Seabury Resort 20 Red Brook Rd	Mashpee	MA	02649	**800-999-9033**	508-477-9111
Ocean Edge Resort & Golf Club 2907 Main St	Brewster	MA	02631	**800-343-6074**	508-896-9000
Sea Crest Resort & Conference Center 350 Quaker Rd	North Falmouth	MA	02556	**800-225-3110**	508-540-9400
Sheraton Ferncroft Resort 50 Ferncroft Rd	Danvers	MA	01923	**800-325-3535**	978-777-2500
Sheraton Hyannis Resort West End Cir	Hyannis	MA	02601	**800-325-3535**	508-775-7775
Wequassett Inn Resort & Golf Club 2173 Rt 28	East Harwich	MA	02645	**800-225-7125**	508-432-5400

Michigan

				Toll-Free	Phone
Bay Valley Hotel & Resort 2470 Old Bridge Rd	Bay City	MI	48706	**800-292-5028**	989-686-3500
Boyne Highlands Resort 600 Highlands Dr	Harbor Springs	MI	49740	**800-462-6963**	231-526-3000
Boyne Mountain Resort PO Box 19	Boyne Falls	MI	49713	**800-462-6963**	231-549-6000
Crystal Mountain Resort 12500 Crystal Mountain Dr	Thompsonville	MI	49683	**800-968-7686**	231-378-2000
Garland Resort 4700 N Red Oak Rd	Lewiston	MI	49756	**800-968-0042**	989-786-2211
Grand Hotel 286 Grand Dr	Mackinac Island	MI	49757	**800-334-7263**	906-847-3331
Grand Traverse Resort & Spa 100 Grand Traverse Village Blvd PO Box 404	Acme	MI	49610	**800-748-0303**	231-938-2100
Indianhead Mountain Resort 500 Indianhead Rd	Wakefield	MI	49968	**800-346-3426**	906-229-2229
Inn at Bay Harbor 3600 Village Harbor Dr	Bay Harbor	MI	49770	**800-462-6963**	231-439-4000
Lakewood Shores Resort 7751 Cedar Lake Rd	Oscoda	MI	48750	**800-882-2493**	989-739-2073
Marsh Ridge Resort 4815 Old US Hwy 27 S	Gaylord	MI	49735	**800-743-7529**	989-732-5552
McGuire's Resort 7880 Mackinaw Trail	Cadillac	MI	49601	**800-632-7302**	231-775-9947
Mission Point Resort 1 Lake Shore Dr PO Box 430	Mackinac Island	MI	49757	**800-833-7711**	906-847-3312
Otsego Club 696 M-32 E Main St PO Box 556	Gaylord	MI	49734	**800-752-5510**	989-732-5181
Shanty Creek Resort 1 Shanty Creek Rd	Bellaire	MI	49615	**800-678-4111**	231-533-8621
Soaring Eagle Casino & Resort 6800 E Soaring Eagle Blvd	Mount Pleasant	MI	48858	**877-232-4532**	989-775-5777
Treetops Resort 3962 Wilkinson Rd	Treetops Village	MI	49735	**800-444-6711**	989-732-6711

Minnesota

				Toll-Free	Phone
Arrowwood Resort 2100 Arrowwood Ln NW	Alexandria	MN	56308	**866-386-5263**	320-762-1124
Breezy Point Resort 9252 Breezy Point Dr	Breezy Point	MN	56472	**800-432-3777**	218-562-7811
Caribou Highlands Lodge 371 Ski Hill Rd	Lutsen	MN	55612	**800-642-6036**	218-663-7241
Cragun's Conference & Golf Resort 11000 Cragun's Dr	Brainerd	MN	56401	**800-272-4867**	218-829-3591
Driftwood Resort 6020 Driftwood Ln	Pine River	MN	56474	**800-950-3540**	218-568-4221
Eagle's Nest Resort 6103 LaVaque Rd	Duluth	MN	55803	**800-348-4575**	218-721-4147
Fair Hills Resort 24270 County Hwy 20	Detroit Lakes	MN	56501	**800-323-2849**	218-847-7638
Grand Casino Hinckley 777 Lady Luck Dr	Hinckley	MN	55037	**800-472-6321**	320-384-7777
Grand Casino Mille Lacs 777 Grand Ave PO Box 343	Onamia	MN	56359	**800-626-5825**	320-532-7777
Grand Portage Lodge & Casino PO Box 233	Grand Portage	MN	55605	**800-543-1384**	218-475-2401
Grand View Lodge 23521 Nokomis Ave	Nisswa	MN	56468	**800-432-3788**	218-963-2234
Izatys Golf & Yacht Club 40005 85th Ave	Onamia	MN	56359	**800-533-1728**	320-532-3101
Lake Breeze Motel Resort 9000 Congdon Blvd	Duluth	MN	55804	**800-738-5884**	218-525-6808
Lutsen Resort 5700 W Hwy 61 PO Box 9	Lutsen	MN	55612	**800-258-8736**	218-663-7212
Madden's on Gull Lake 11266 Pine Beach Peninsula	Brainerd	MN	56401	**800-247-1040**	218-829-2811
Ruttger's Bay Lake Lodge 25039 Tame Fish Lake Rd Box 400	Deerwood	MN	56444	**800-450-4545**	218-678-2885

Mississippi

				Toll-Free	Phone
Beau Rivage Resort & Casino 875 Beach Blvd	Biloxi	MS	39530	**888-750-7111**	228-386-7111
Grand Casino Biloxi 265 Beach Blvd	Biloxi	MS	39530	**800-946-2946**	228-436-2946
Grand Casino Gulfport 3215 W Beach Blvd	Gulfport	MS	39501	**800-946-7777**	228-870-7777
Grand Casino Tunica 13615 Old Hwy 61 N	Robinsonville	MS	38664	**800-946-4946**	662-363-2788
Gulf Hills Hotel 13701 Paso Rd	Ocean Springs	MS	39564	**877-875-4211**	228-875-4211
Imperial Palace Mississippi 850 Bayview Ave	Biloxi	MS	39530	**800-436-3000**	228-436-3000
President Casino Broadwater Resort 2110 Beach Blvd	Biloxi	MS	39531	**800-843-7737**	228-388-2211
Treasure Bay Casino Resort 1980 Beach Blvd	Biloxi	MS	39531	**800-747-2839**	228-388-6610

Missouri

				Toll-Free	Phone
Best Western Dogwood Hills Resort Inn & Golf Club 1252 State Hwy KK	Osage Beach	MO	65065	**800-528-1234**	573-348-1735
Holiday Inn SunSpree Resort Lake Ozark 120 Holiday Ln PO Box 1930	Lake Ozark	MO	65049	**800-532-3575**	573-365-2334
Indian Point Lodge 71 Dogwood Pk Trail	Branson	MO	65616	**800-888-1891**	417-338-2250
Lilleys' Landing Resort 367 River Ln	Branson	MO	65616	**800-284-2916**	417-334-6380
Lodge of Four Seasons Horseshoe Bend Pkwy PO Box 215	Lake Ozark	MO	65049	**800-843-5253**	573-365-3000
Plantation at Fall Creek Resort 1-A Fall Creek Dr	Branson	MO	65616	**800-510-7472**	417-334-6404
Tan-Tar-A Resort Golf Club & Spa PO Box 188 TT	Osage Beach	MO	65065	**800-826-8272***	573-348-3131
*Resv					
Welk Resort Branson 1984 State Hwy 165	Branson	MO	65616	**800-505-9355**	417-336-3575

Montana

				Toll-Free	Phone
Big Sky Resort 1 Lone Mountain Trail	Big Sky	MT	59716	**800-548-4486**	406-995-5000
Fairmont Hot Springs Resort 1500 Fairmont Rd	Fairmont	MT	59711	**800-332-3272**	406-797-3241
Meadow Lake Resort 100 St Andrews Dr	Columbia Falls	MT	59912	**800-321-4653**	406-892-8700
Rock Creek Resort HC 49 Box 3500	Red Lodge	MT	59068	**800-667-1119**	406-446-1111

Nevada

				Toll-Free	Phone
Aladdin Resort & Casino 3667 Las Vegas Blvd S	Las Vegas	NV	89109	**877-333-9474**	702-785-5555
Bally's Las Vegas 3645 Las Vegas Blvd S	Las Vegas	NV	89109	**800-225-5977***	702-739-4111
*Resv					
Bellagio Hotel & Casino 3600 Las Vegas Blvd S	Las Vegas	NV	89109	**888-987-7111**	702-693-7111
Buffalo Bill's Resort & Casino 31700 S Las Vegas Blvd	Primm	NV	89019	**800-386-7867**	702-382-1111
Cal-Neva Resort 2 Stateline Rd PO Box 368	Crystal Bay	NV	89402	**800-225-6382**	775-832-4000
Casablanca Resort 950 W Mesquite Blvd	Mesquite	NV	89027	**800-459-7529**	702-346-7529

Classified Section

Nevada (Cont'd)

	City	State	Zip	Toll-Free	Phone
Club Cal Neva Hotel Casino 38 E 2nd St	Reno	NV	89501	**877-777-7303**	775-954-4540
Don Laughlin's Riverside Resort & Casino 1650 Casino Dr	Laughlin	NV	89029	**800-227-3849**	702-298-2535
Flamingo Las Vegas 3555 Las Vegas Blvd S *Resv	Las Vegas	NV	89109	**800-732-2111***	702-733-3111
Flamingo Laughlin 1900 S Casino Dr *Resv	Laughlin	NV	89029	**800-352-6464***	702-298-5111
Golden Nugget Hotel 129 E Fremont St	Las Vegas	NV	89101	**800-634-3454**	702-385-7111
Golden Nugget Laughlin 2300 S Casino Dr	Laughlin	NV	89029	**800-237-1739**	702-298-7111
Hard Rock Hotel & Casino 4455 Paradise Rd	Las Vegas	NV	89109	**800-473-7625**	702-693-5000
Harrah's Las Vegas 3475 Las Vegas Blvd S	Las Vegas	NV	89109	**800-427-7247**	702-369-5000
Harrah's Laughlin 2900 S Casino Dr PO Box 33000	Laughlin	NV	89029	**800-427-7247**	702-298-4600
Hilton Reno Resort & Casino 2500 E 2nd St	Reno	NV	89595	**800-501-2651**	775-789-2000
Hyatt Regency Lake Las Vegas Resort 101 MonteLago Blvd	Henderson	NV	89011	**800-233-1234**	702-567-1234
Hyatt Regency Lake Tahoe Resort & Casino 111 Country Club Dr	Incline Village	NV	89451	**800-233-1234**	775-832-1234
John Ascuaga's Nugget Hotel Casino 1100 Nugget Ave	Sparks	NV	89431	**800-648-1177**	775-356-3300
JW Marriott Resort Las Vegas 221 N Rampart Blvd	Las Vegas	NV	89145	**877-869-8777**	702-869-7777
Mandalay Bay Resort & Casino 3950 Las Vegas Blvd S	Las Vegas	NV	89119	**877-632-7800**	702-632-7777
MGM Grand Hotel & Casino 3799 Las Vegas Blvd S	Las Vegas	NV	89109	**800-929-1111**	702-891-1111
Mirage The 3400 Las Vegas Blvd S	Las Vegas	NV	89109	**800-627-6667**	702-791-7111
Monte Carlo Resort & Casino 3770 Las Vegas Blvd S	Las Vegas	NV	89109	**800-311-8999**	702-730-7777
Oasis Resort Casino Golf & Spa 897 W Mesquite Blvd	Mesquite	NV	89027	**800-621-0187**	702-346-5232
Primm Valley Resort & Casino 31900 S Las Vegas Blvd	Primm	NV	89019	**800-386-7867**	702-382-1212
Ridge Tahoe 400 Ridge Club Dr PO Box 5790	Stateline	NV	89449	**800-334-1600**	775-588-3553
Rio All-Suite Hotel & Casino 3700 W Flamingo Rd	Las Vegas	NV	89103	**888-746-7482**	702-777-7777
Riviera Hotel & Casino 2901 Las Vegas Blvd S *Resv	Las Vegas	NV	89109	**800-634-6753***	702-734-5110
Silver Legacy Resort & Casino 407 N Virginia St	Reno	NV	89501	**800-687-8733**	775-329-4777
Treasure Island Hotel & Casino 3300 Las Vegas Blvd S	Las Vegas	NV	89109	**800-944-7444**	702-894-7111
Tropicana Resort & Casino 3801 Las Vegas Blvd S *Resv	Las Vegas	NV	89109	**888-826-8767***	702-739-2222
Venetian Resort Hotel & Casino 3355 Las Vegas Blvd S	Las Vegas	NV	89109	**877-283-6423**	702-414-1000

New Brunswick

	City	State	Zip	Toll-Free	Phone
Fairmont Algonquin 184 Adolphus St	Saint Andrews	NB	E5B1T7	**800-441-1414**	506-529-8823

New Hampshire

	City	State	Zip	Toll-Free	Phone
BALSAMS The Rt 26	Dixville Notch	NH	03576	**800-255-0600**	603-255-3400
Cranmore Mountain Resort 1 Skimobile Rd PO Box 1640	North Conway	NH	03860	**800-786-6754**	603-356-5544
Margate on Winnipesaukee 76 Lake St	Laconia	NH	03246	**800-627-4283**	603-524-5210
Mount Washington Hotel & Resort Rt 302	Bretton Woods	NH	03575	**800-314-1752**	603-278-1000
Valley Inn Tecumseh Rd PO Box 1	Waterville Valley	NH	03215	**800-343-0969**	603-236-8336
Waterville Valley Resort 1 Ski Area Rd PO Box 540	Waterville Valley	NH	03215	**800-468-2553**	603-236-8311
White Mountain Hotel & Resort West Side Rd	North Conway	NH	03860	**800-533-6301**	603-356-7100

New Jersey

	City	State	Zip	Toll-Free	Phone
Bally's Atlantic City 1900 Boardwalk & Park Pl	Atlantic City	NJ	08401	**800-772-7777**	609-340-2000
Caesars Atlantic City 2100 Pacific Ave	Atlantic City	NJ	08401	**800-443-0104**	609-348-4411
Legends Resort & Country Club 430 Rt 517 PO Box 637	McAfee	NJ	07428	**800-835-2555**	973-827-6000
Montreal Inn Beach Dr & Madison Ave	Cape May	NJ	08204	**800-525-7011**	609-884-7011
Ocean Place Resort & Spa 1 Ocean Blvd	Long Branch	NJ	07740	**800-411-6493**	732-571-4000
Resorts Atlantic City 1133 Boardwalk	Atlantic City	NJ	08401	**800-336-6378**	609-344-6000
Seaview Marriott Resort & Spa 401 S New York Rd	Galloway	NJ	08205	**800-228-9290**	609-652-1800
Trump Taj Mahal Casino Resort 1000 Boardwalk & Virginia Ave *Resv	Atlantic City	NJ	08401	**800-825-8786***	609-449-1000

New Mexico

	City	State	Zip	Toll-Free	Phone
Angel Fire Resort PO Drawer B	Angel Fire	NM	87710	**800-633-7463**	505-377-6401
Bishop's Lodge Resort & Spa 1297 Bishop's Lodge Rd PO Box 2367	Santa Fe	NM	87501	**800-732-2240**	505-983-6377
Hyatt Regency Tamaya Resort & Spa 1300 Tuyuna Trail	Santa Ana Pueblo	NM	87004	**800-233-1234**	505-867-1234
Inn of the Mountain Gods 287 Carrizo Canyon Rd	Mescalero	NM	88340	**800-545-9011**	505-464-5141
La Posada de Santa Fe Resort & Spa 330 E Palace Ave	Santa Fe	NM	87501	**800-727-5276**	505-986-0000
Lifts West Condominium Resort Hotel PO Box 330	Red River	NM	87558	**800-221-1859**	505-754-2778
Lodge at Cloudcroft 1 Corona Pl	Cloudcroft	NM	88317	**800-395-6343**	505-682-2566
Quail Ridge Inn Taos Ski Valley Rd PO Box 707	Taos	NM	87571	**800-624-4448**	505-776-2211

New York

	City	State	Zip	Toll-Free	Phone
Bonnie Castle Resort 31 Holland St	Alexandria Bay	NY	13607	**800-955-4511**	315-482-4511
Concord Resort & Golf Club Concord Rd	Kiamesha Lake	NY	12751	**888-448-9686**	845-794-4000
Danfords Inn Marina & Conference Center 25 E Broadway	Port Jefferson	NY	11777	**800-332-6367**	631-928-5200
Doral Arrowwood Conference Resort 975 Anderson Hill Rd	Rye Brook	NY	10573	**800-223-6725**	914-939-5500
Friar Tuck Resort & Convention Center 4858 SR-32	Catskill	NY	12414	**800-832-7600**	518-678-2271
Gurney's Inn Resort & Spa 290 Old Montauk Hwy	Montauk	NY	11954	**800-848-7639**	631-668-2345
Hilton Lake Placid Resort 1 Mirror Lake Dr	Lake Placid	NY	12946	**800-755-5598**	518-523-4411
Holiday Valley Resort PO Box 370 Rt 219	Ellicottville	NY	14731	**800-323-0020**	716-699-2345
Kutsher's Country Club Resort Kutchers Rd PO Box 432	Monticello	NY	12701	**800-431-1273**	845-794-6000
Lodge at Woodcliff 199 Woodcliff Dr	Fairport	NY	14450	**800-365-3065**	585-381-4000
Mohonk Mountain House 1000 Mountain Rest Rd	New Paltz	NY	12561	**800-772-6646**	845-255-1000
Montauk Yacht Club Resort & Marina 32 Star Island Rd	Montauk	NY	11954	**888-692-8668**	631-668-3100
Nevele Grande Resort & Country Club 1 Nevele Rd	Ellenville	NY	12428	**800-647-6000**	845-647-6000
Otesaga The PO Box 311	Cooperstown	NY	13326	**800-348-6222**	607-547-9931
Pine Tree Point Resort 70 Anthony St PO Box 99	Alexandria Bay	NY	13607	**888-746-3229**	315-482-9911
Point The PO Box 1327	Saranac Lake	NY	12983	**800-255-3530**	518-891-5674
Rocking Horse Ranch Resort 600 Rt 44-55	Highland	NY	12528	**800-647-2624**	845-691-2927
Sagamore The 110 Sagamore Rd	Bolton Landing	NY	12814	**800-358-3585**	518-644-9400
Villa Roma Resort & Conference Center 356 Villa Roma Rd	Callicoon	NY	12723	**800-727-8455**	845-887-4880
Whiteface Club & Resort PO Box 231 Whiteface Inn Rd	Lake Placid	NY	12946	**800-422-6757**	518-523-2551

North Carolina

	City	State	Zip	Toll-Free	Phone
Ballantyne Resort Hotel 10000 Ballantyne Commons Pkwy	Charlotte	NC	28277	**866-248-4824**	704-248-4000
Chetola Resort PO Box 17 N Main St	Blowing Rock	NC	28605	**800-243-8652**	828-295-5500
Eseeola Lodge 175 Linville Ave PO Box 99	Linville	NC	28646	**800-742-6717**	828-733-4311
Fontana Village Resort Hwy 28 PO Box 68	Fontana Dam	NC	28733	**800-849-2258**	828-498-2211
Greystone Inn Greystone Ln	Lake Toxaway	NC	28747	**800-824-5766**	828-966-4700
Grove Park Inn Resort & Spa 290 Macon Ave	Asheville	NC	28804	**800-438-5800**	828-252-2711
High Hampton Inn & Country Club 1525 Hwy 107 S	Cashiers	NC	28717	**800-334-2551**	828-743-2450
Holiday Inn SunSpree Resort Great Smokies 1 Holiday Inn Dr	Asheville	NC	28806	**800-733-3211**	828-254-3211
Holiday Inn SunSpree Resort Wrightsville Beach 1706 N Lumina Ave	Wrightsville Beach	NC	28480	**877-330-5050**	910-256-2231
Maggie Valley Resort & Country Club 1819 Country Club Dr	Maggie Valley	NC	28751	**800-438-3861**	828-926-1616
Mid Pines Inn & Golf Club 1010 Midland Rd	Southern Pines	NC	28387	**800-323-2114**	910-692-2114
Pine Needles Lodge & Golf Club PO Box 88	Southern Pines	NC	28388	**800-747-7272**	910-692-7111
Pinehurst Resort & Country Club 80 Carolina Vista Dr	Pinehurst	NC	28374	**800-487-4653**	910-295-6811
Pinnacle Inn Resort 301 Pinnacle Inn Rd	Banner Elk	NC	28604	**800-405-7888**	828-387-2231
Sanderling Resort & Spa 1461 Duck Rd	Duck	NC	27949	**800-701-4111**	252-261-4111
Waynesville Country Club Inn 176 Country Club Dr	Waynesville	NC	28786	**800-627-6250**	828-456-3551
Wolf Laurel Ski Resort 578 Valley View Cir	Mars Hill	NC	28754	**800-817-4111**	828-689-4111

Nova Scotia

	City	State	Zip	Toll-Free	Phone
Inverary Resort PO Box 190	Baddeck	NS	B0E1B0	**800-565-5660**	902-295-3500
Oak Island Resort & Spa PO Box 6	Western Shore	NS	B0J3M0	**800-565-5075**	902-627-2600
Pines Resort The 103 Shore Rd	Digby	NS	B0V1A0	**800-667-4637**	902-245-2511

Ohio

	City	State	Zip	Toll-Free	Phone
Atwood Lake Resort PO Box 96	Dellroy	OH	44620	**800-362-6406**	330-735-2211
Avalon Inn & Resort 9519 E Market St	Warren	OH	44484	**800-828-2566**	330-856-1900
Glenmoor Country Club 4191 Glenmoor Rd NW	Canton	OH	44718	**888-456-6667**	330-966-3600
Hueston Woods Resort & Conference Center 5201 Lodge Rd	College Corner	OH	45003	**800-282-7275**	513-664-3500
Renaissance Quail Hollow Resort 11080 Concord-Hambden Rd	Painesville	OH	44077	**800-792-0258**	440-497-1100
Sawmill Creek Resort 400 Sawmill Creek	Huron	OH	44839	**800-729-6455**	419-433-3800

Oklahoma

	City	State	Zip	Toll-Free	Phone
Lake Murray Resort Park 3323 Lodge Rd	Ardmore	OK	73401	**800-257-0322**	580-223-6600
Lake Texoma Resort Park PO Box 248	Kingston	OK	73439	**800-528-0593**	580-564-2311
Quartz Mountain Resort & Conference Center 22469 Lodge Rd	Lone Wolf	OK	73655	**877-999-5567**	580-563-2424
Shangri-La Resort 57401 E Hwy 125	Afton	OK	74331	**800-331-4060**	918-257-4204

Ontario

	City	State	Zip	Toll-Free	Phone
Deerhurst Resort 1235 Deerhurst Dr	Huntsville	ON	P1H2E8	**800-461-4390**	705-789-6411
Delta Meadowvale Resort & Conference Centre 6750 Mississauga Rd	Mississauga	ON	L5N2L3	**800-268-1133**	905-821-1981
Pinestone Resort PO Box 809	Haliburton	ON	K0M1S0	**800-461-0357**	705-457-1800

Classified Section

				Toll-Free	Phone
White Oaks Conference Resort & Spa 253 Taylor Rd	Niagara-on-the-Lake	ON	L0S1J0	**800-263-5766**	905-688-2550

Oregon

				Toll-Free	Phone
Black Butte Ranch 12930 Hawks Beard Rd	Black Butte Ranch	OR	97759	**800-452-7455**	541-595-6211
Gearhart By The Sea PO Box 2700	Gearhart	OR	97138	**800-547-0115**	503-738-8331
Inn of the Seventh Mountain 18575 SW Century Dr	Bend	OR	97702	**800-452-6810**	541-382-8711
Mount Bachelor Village Resort & Conference Center 19717 Mt Bachelor Dr	Bend	OR	97702	**800-452-9846**	541-389-5900
Resort at the Mountain 68010 E Fairway Ave	Welches	OR	97067	**800-669-7666**	503-622-3101
Salishan Lodge & Golf Resort PO Box 118	Gleneden Beach	OR	97388	**800-452-2300**	541-764-2371
Sunriver Resort 1 Center Dr PO Box 3609	Sunriver	OR	97707	**800-547-3922**	541-593-1000
Timberline Lodge 88 Hwy 150	Timberline Lodge	OR	97028	**800-547-1406**	503-272-3311

Pennsylvania

				Toll-Free	Phone
Allenberry Resort 1559 Boiling Springs Rd	Boiling Springs	PA	17007	**800-430-5468**	717-258-3211
Brookdale on the Lake 1 Brookdale Rd	Scotrun	PA	18355	**800-233-4141**	570-839-8843
Caesars Cove Haven Resort 194 Lakeview Dr	Lakeville	PA	18438	**800-233-4141**	570-226-4506
Caesars Paradise Stream Rt 940 PO Box 99	Mount Pocono	PA	18344	**800-233-4141**	570-839-8881
Caesars Pocono Palace Resort Rt 209	Marshalls Creek	PA	18335	**800-233-4141**	570-588-6692
Carroll Valley Golf Resort 121 Sanders Rd	Fairfield	PA	17320	**800-548-8504**	717-642-8211
Felicita Resort 2201 Fishing Creek Valley Rd	Harrisburg	PA	17112	**888-321-3713**	717-599-5301
Fernwood Resort & Country Club Rt 209 N	Bushkill	PA	18324	**888-337-6966**	570-588-9500
Heritage Hills Golf Resort & Conference Center 2700 Mount Rose Ave	York	PA	17402	**877-782-9752**	717-755-0123
Hidden Valley Resort & Conference Center 1 Craighead Dr	Hidden Valley	PA	15502	**800-458-0175**	814-443-8000
Hotel Hershey 100 Hotel Rd	Hershey	PA	17033	**800-533-3131**	717-533-2171
Lancaster Host Resort 2300 Lincoln Hwy E	Lancaster	PA	17602	**800-233-0121***	717-299-5500
*Resv					
Mountain Laurel Resort & Spa Rt 940 PO Box 9	White Haven	PA	18661	**800-255-7625**	570-443-8411
Mountain Manor Inn & Golf Club Creek Rd PO Box 1067	Marshalls Creek	PA	18335	**800-626-6747**	570-223-8098
Nemacolin Woodlands Resort & Spa 1001 Lafayette Dr	Farmington	PA	15437	**800-422-2736**	724-329-8555
Penn Hills Resort Rt 447 & 191 PO Box 309	Analomink	PA	18320	**800-233-8240**	570-421-6464
Pocono Manor Golf Resort & Spa Rt 314	Pocono Manor	PA	18349	**800-233-8150**	570-839-7111
Seven Springs Mountain Resort 777 Waterwheel Dr	Champion	PA	15622	**800-452-2223**	814-352-7777
Shadowbrook Inn & Resort 615 SR 6 E	Tunkhannock	PA	18657	**800-955-0295**	570-836-2151
Shawnee Inn & Golf Resort PO Box 67 1 River Rd	Shawnee on Delaware	PA	18356	**800-742-9633**	570-424-4000
Skytop Lodge 1 Skytop	Skytop	PA	18357	**800-345-7759**	570-595-7401
Split Rock Resort 1 Lake Dr	Lake Harmony	PA	18624	**800-255-7625**	570-722-9111
Tamiment Resort & Conference Center Bush Kills Fall Rd	Tamiment	PA	18371	**800-532-8280**	570-588-6652
Toftrees Resort & Conference Center 1 Country Club Ln	State College	PA	16803	**800-252-3551**	814-234-8000
Willow Valley Resort & Conference Center 2416 Willow Street Pike	Lancaster	PA	17602	**800-444-1714**	717-464-2711

Puerto Rico

				Toll-Free	Phone
Candalero Resort at Palmas Del Mar 270 Harborside Dr Suite 1	Humacao	PR	00791	**800-725-6273**	787-852-6000
Caribe Hilton Los Rosales St San Geronimo Grounds	San Juan	PR	00901	**800-445-8667**	787-721-0303
Hyatt Dorado Beach Resort & Country Club Hwy 693	Dorado	PR	00646	**800-233-1234**	787-796-1234
Las Casitas Village & Golden Door Spa 1000 El Conquistador Ave	Fajardo	PR	00738	**800-996-3426**	787-863-1000
Wyndham Condado Plaza Hotel & Casino 999 Ashford Ave	San Juan	PR	00907	**800-468-5228**	787-721-1000
Wyndham El Conquistador Resort & Country Club 1000 El Conquistador Ave	Fajardo	PR	00738	**800-996-3426**	787-863-1000
Wyndham El San Juan Hotel & Casino 6063 Isla Verde Ave	Carolina	PR	00979	**800-996-3426**	787-791-1000

Quebec

				Toll-Free	Phone
Fairmont Le Chateau Montebello 392 rue Notre Dame	Montebello	QC	J0V1L0	**800-441-1414**	819-423-6341
Gray Rocks Resort & Convention Center 2322 rue Labelle	Mont-Tremblant	QC	J8E1T8	**800-567-6767**	819-425-2771
Hotel Cheribourg 2603 ch du Parc	Orford	QC	J1X8C8	**800-567-6132**	819-843-3308
Hotel Club Tremblant 121 rue Cuttle	Mont-Tremblant	QC	J8E1B9	**800-567-8341**	819-425-2731
Manoir du Lac Delage 40 ave du Lac	Lac Delage	QC	G0A4P0	**888-202-3242**	418-848-2551
Westin Resort Tremblant 100 ch Kandahar	Mont-Tremblant	QC	J8E1E2	**800-937-8461**	819-681-8000

Rhode Island

				Toll-Free	Phone
Inn on the Harbor 359 Thames St	Newport	RI	02840	**800-225-3522**	401-849-6789
Inn on Long Wharf 142 Long Wharf	Newport	RI	02840	**800-225-3522**	401-847-7800

South Carolina

				Toll-Free	Phone
Beach Colony Resort 5308 N Ocean Blvd	Myrtle Beach	SC	29577	**800-222-2141**	843-449-4010
Blue Water Resort 2001 S Ocean Blvd	Myrtle Beach	SC	29577	**800-845-6994**	843-626-8345
Caravelle Resort Hotel & Villas 6900 N Ocean Blvd	Myrtle Beach	SC	29572	**800-845-0893**	843-918-8000
Caribbean Resort & Villas 3000 N Ocean Blvd	Myrtle Beach	SC	29577	**800-552-8509**	843-448-7181
Compass Cove Ocean Resort 2311 S Ocean Blvd	Myrtle Beach	SC	29577	**800-228-9894**	843-448-8373
Coral Beach Resort & Suites 1105 S Ocean Blvd	Myrtle Beach	SC	29577	**800-843-2684**	843-448-8421
Crowne Plaza Resort Hilton Head Island 130 Shipyard Dr	Hilton Head Island	SC	29928	**800-334-1881**	843-842-2400
Disney's Hilton Head Island Resort 22 Harborside Ln	Hilton Head Island	SC	29928	**800-453-4911**	843-341-4100
Fairfield Ocean Ridge Resort 1 King Cotton Rd	Edisto Beach	SC	29438	**877-296-6335**	843-869-2561
Harbour Town Resort & Yacht Club 149 Lighthouse Rd	Hilton Head Island	SC	29928	**800-541-7375**	843-671-1400
Hilton Charleston Harbor Resort & Marina 20 Patriots Point Rd	Mount Pleasant	SC	29464	**800-445-8667**	843-856-0028
Hilton Head Island Beach & Tennis Resort 40 Folly Field Rd	Hilton Head Island	SC	29928	**800-475-2631**	843-842-4402
Hilton Myrtle Beach Resort 10000 Beach Club Dr	Myrtle Beach	SC	29572	**877-887-9549**	843-449-5000
Hilton Oceanfront Resort Hilton Head Island 23 Ocean Ln	Hilton Head Island	SC	29928	**800-845-8001**	843-842-8000
Holiday Inn SunSpree Resort Myrtle Beach 1601 N Ocean Blvd	Surfside Beach	SC	29575	**877-245-1360**	843-238-5601
Kiawah Island Resort 12 Kiawah Beach Dr	Kiawah Island	SC	29455	**800-654-2924**	843-768-2121
Landmark Resort 1501 S Ocean Blvd	Myrtle Beach	SC	29577	**800-845-0658**	843-448-9441
Legends Resort 1500 Legends Dr PO Box 2038	Myrtle Beach	SC	29578	**888-246-9809**	843-236-9318
Litchfield Beach & Golf Resort 14276 Ocean Highway	Pawleys Island	SC	29585	**800-845-1897**	843-237-3000
Mystic Sea Resort 2105 S Ocean Blvd	Myrtle Beach	SC	29577	**800-443-7050**	843-448-8446
Palmetto Dunes Resort 4 Queen Folly Rd	Hilton Head Island	SC	29938	**800-845-6130**	843-785-1161
Palms Resort 2500 N Ocean Blvd	Myrtle Beach	SC	29578	**800-528-0451**	843-626-8334
Patricia Grand Resort 2710 N Ocean Blvd	Myrtle Beach	SC	29577	**800-255-4763**	843-448-8453
Pawleys Plantation 70 Tanglewood Dr	Pawleys Island	SC	29585	**800-367-9959**	843-237-6009
Reef Resort 2101 S Ocean Blvd	Myrtle Beach	SC	29577	**800-845-1212**	843-448-1765
Resort at Seabrook Island 3772 Seabrook Island Rd	Seabrook Island	SC	29455	**800-845-2475**	843-768-2500
Sea Mist Resort 1200 S Ocean Blvd	Myrtle Beach	SC	29577	**800-732-6478**	843-448-1551
Sea Pines Resort 32 Greenwood Dr	Hilton Head Island	SC	29928	**800-732-7463**	843-785-3333
Tropical Winds 705 S Ocean Blvd	Myrtle Beach	SC	29578	**800-843-3466**	843-448-4304
Westin Resort Hilton Head Island 2 Grasslawn Ave	Hilton Head Island	SC	29928	**800-937-8461**	843-681-4000
Wild Dunes Resort 5757 Palm Blvd	Isle of Palms	SC	29451	**800-845-8880**	843-886-6000
Woodlands Resort & Inn 125 Parsons Rd	Summerville	SC	29483	**800-774-9999**	843-875-2600

South Dakota

				Toll-Free	Phone
Blue Bell Lodge & Resort Hwy 87 Custer State Pk	Custer	SD	57730	**800-658-3530**	605-255-4535
Spearfish Canyon Resort 10619 Roughlock Falls Rd	Lead	SD	57754	**877-975-6343**	605-584-3435

Tennessee

				Toll-Free	Phone
Blackberry Farm 1471 W Millers Cove Rd	Walland	TN	37886	**800-273-6004**	865-380-2260
Marriott MeadowView Conference Resort & Convention Center 1901 Meadowview Pkwy	Kingsport	TN	37660	**800-820-5055**	423-578-6600

Texas

				Toll-Free	Phone
Bahia Mar Resort & Conference Center 6300 Padre Blvd	South Padre Island	TX	78597	**800-997-2373**	956-761-1343
Barton Creek Conference Resort 8212 Barton Club Dr	Austin	TX	78735	**800-336-6158**	512-329-4000
Columbia Lakes Resort & Conference Center 188 Freeman Blvd	West Columbia	TX	77486	**800-231-1030**	979-345-5151
Del Lago Waterfront Conference Center & Resort 600 Del Lago Blvd	Montgomery	TX	77356	**800-863-9208**	936-582-7510
Four Seasons Resort & Club Dallas at Las Colinas 4150 N MacArthur Blvd	Irving	TX	75038	**800-332-3442**	972-717-0700
Hilton Galveston Island Resort 5400 Seawall Blvd	Galveston	TX	77551	**800-475-3386**	409-744-5000
Holiday Inn SunSpree Resort South Padre Island 100 Padre Blvd	South Padre Island	TX	78597	**800-531-7405**	956-761-5401
Horseshoe Bay Resort & Conference Center PO Box 7766	Horseshoe Bay	TX	78657	**800-531-5105**	830-598-2511
Houstonian Hotel Club & Spa 111 N Post Oak Ln	Houston	TX	77024	**800-231-2759**	713-680-2626
Hyatt Regency Hill Country Resort 9800 Hyatt Resort Dr	San Antonio	TX	78251	**800-233-1234**	210-647-1234
Inn of the Hills River Resort 1001 Junction Hwy	Kerrville	TX	78028	**800-292-5690**	830-895-5000
Lakeway Inn & Resort 101 Lakeway Dr	Austin	TX	78734	**800-525-3929**	512-261-6600
Radisson Resort South Padre Island 500 Padre Blvd	South Padre Island	TX	78597	**800-333-3333**	956-761-6511
Rancho Viejo Resort & Country Club 1 Rancho Viejo Dr	Rancho Viejo	TX	78575	**800-531-7400**	956-350-4000
San Luis Resort Spa & Conference Center 5222 Seawall Blvd	Galveston Island	TX	77551	**800-445-0090**	409-744-1500
Tanglewood Resort Hotel & Conference Center 290 Tanglewood Cir	Pottsboro	TX	75076	**800-833-6569**	903-786-2968
Tapatio Springs Golf Resort & Conference Center PO Box 550	Boerne	TX	78006	**800-999-3299**	830-537-4611

Texas (Cont'd)

Name / Address	City	State	ZIP	Toll-Free	Phone
Waterwood National Resort 1 Waterwood Pkwy	Huntsville	TX	77320	**877-441-5211**	936-891-5211
Westin La Cantera Resort 16641 La Cantera Pkwy	San Antonio	TX	78256	**800-937-8461**	210-558-6500
Westin Stonebriar Resort 1549 Legacy Dr	Frisco	TX	75034	**800-937-8461**	972-668-8000
Woodlands Resort & Conference Center 2301 N Millbend Dr	The Woodlands	TX	77380	**800-433-2624**	281-367-1100

Utah

Name / Address	City	State	ZIP	Toll-Free	Phone
Alta Lodge 1 Main St PO Box 8040	Alta	UT	84092	**800-707-2582**	801-742-3500
Brighton Ski Resort 12601 E Big Cottonwood Canyon	Brighton	UT	84121	**800-873-5512**	801-532-4731
Canyons Resort 4000 The Canyons Resort Dr	Park City	UT	84098	**888-226-9667**	435-615-8040
Deer Valley 1375 Deer Valley Dr S	Park City	UT	84060	**800-453-3833**	435-649-4040
Green Valley Resort 1871 W Canyon View Dr	Saint George	UT	84770	**800-237-1068**	435-628-8060
Homestead The 700 N Homestead Dr	Midway	UT	84049	**800-327-7220**	435-654-1102
Inn on the Creek 375 Rainbow Lane PO Box 1000	Midway	UT	84049	**800-654-0892**	435-654-0892
Park City Mountain Resort 1310 Lowell Ave PO Box 39	Park City	UT	84060	**800-222-7275**	435-649-8111
Rustler Lodge Hwy 210 PO Box 8030	Alta	UT	84092	**888-532-2582**	801-742-2200
Snowbird Ski & Summer Resort Hwy 210 PO Box 929000	Snowbird	UT	84092	**800-453-3000**	801-742-2222
Solitude Mountain Ski Resort 12000 Big Cottonwood Canyon	Solitude	UT	84121	**800-748-4754**	801-534-1400
Stein Eriksen Lodge 7700 Stein Way	Park City	UT	84060	**800-453-1302**	435-649-3700
Sundance Ski Resort North Fork Provo Canyon	Provo	UT	84604	**800-892-1600**	801-225-4107

Vermont

Name / Address	City	State	ZIP	Toll-Free	Phone
Ascutney Mountain Resort 485 Hotel Rd	Brownsville	VT	05037	**800-243-0011**	802-484-7711
Basin Harbor Club 4800 Basin Harbor Rd	Vergennes	VT	05491	**800-622-4000**	802-475-2311
Equinox The 3567 Main St	Manchester Village	VT	05254	**800-362-4747**	802-362-4700
Hawk Inn & Mountain Resort HCR 70 Box 64	Plymouth	VT	05056	**800-685-4295**	802-672-3811
Inn at Stratton Mountain 61 Middle Ridge Rd	Stratton Mountain	VT	05155	**800-777-1700**	802-297-2500
Jay Peak Ski & Summer Resort 4850 Rt 242	Jay	VT	05859	**800-451-4449**	802-988-2611
Killington Resort & Pico Mountain 4763 Killington Rd	Killington	VT	05751	**800-621-6867**	802-422-6200
Lake Morey Resort Club House Rd PO Box 48	Fairlee	VT	05045	**800-423-1211**	802-333-4311
Mount Snow Resort Rt 100	West Dover	VT	05356	**800-451-4211**	802-464-3333
Smugglers' Notch Resort 4323 Vermont Rt 108 S	Jeffersonville	VT	05464	**800-451-8752**	802-644-8851
Stowe Mountain Resort 5781 Mountain Rd	Stowe	VT	05672	**800-253-4754**	802-253-3000
Stoweflake Mountain Resort & Spa 1746 Mountain Rd PO Box 369	Stowe	VT	05672	**800-253-2232**	802-253-7355
Sugarbush Resort & Inn 1840 Sugarbush Access Rd	Warren	VT	05674	**800-537-8427**	802-583-6300
Topnotch at Stowe Resort & Spa 4000 Mountain Rd	Stowe	VT	05672	**800-451-8686**	802-253-8585
Trapp Family Lodge 700 Trapp Hill Rd PO Box 1428	Stowe	VT	05672	**800-826-7000**	802-253-8511
Woodstock Inn & Resort 14 The Green	Woodstock	VT	05091	**800-448-7900**	802-457-1100

Virginia

Name / Address	City	State	ZIP	Toll-Free	Phone
Boar's Head Inn 200 Ednam Dr	Charlottesville	VA	22903	**800-476-1988**	434-296-2181
Cavalier Hotel 4201 Atlantic Ave	Virginia Beach	VA	23451	**800-446-8199**	757-425-8555
Holiday Inn SunSpree Resort Virginia Beach 3900 Atlantic Ave	Virginia Beach	VA	23451	**800-942-3224**	757-428-1711
Homestead The Rt 220 Main St PO Box 2000	Hot Springs	VA	24445	**800-838-1766**	540-839-1766
Kingsmill Resort & Spa 1010 Kingsmill Rd	Williamsburg	VA	23185	**800-832-5665**	757-253-1703
Lansdowne Resort 44050 Woodridge Pkwy	Leesburg	VA	20176	**800-541-4801**	703-729-8400
Shenvalee Golf Resort 9660 Fairway Dr PO Box 930	New Market	VA	22844	**888-339-3181**	540-740-3181
Tides Resort 480 King Carter Dr	Irvington	VA	22480	**800-843-3746**	804-438-5000
Virginia Beach Resort Hotel & Conference Center 2800 Shore Dr	Virginia Beach	VA	23451	**800-468-2722**	757-481-9000
Virginia Crossings Resort 1000 Virginia Ctr Pkwy	Glen Allen	VA	23059	**888-444-6553**	804-262-1010
Williamsburg Inn 136 E Francis St	Williamsburg	VA	23185	**800-447-8679**	757-229-1000

Washington

Name / Address	City	State	ZIP	Toll-Free	Phone
Alderbrook Resort 7101 E SR-106	Union	WA	98592	**800-622-9370**	360-898-2200
Campbell's Resort PO Box 278	Chelan	WA	98816	**800-553-8225**	509-682-2561
Desert Canyon Golf Resort 1201 Desert Canyon Blvd	Orondo	WA	98843	**800-258-4173**	509-784-1111
Freestone Inn at Wilson Ranch 31 Early Winters Dr	Mazama	WA	98833	**800-639-3809**	509-996-3906
Lake Quinault Lodge 345 S Shore Rd PO Box 7	Quinault	WA	98575	**800-562-6672**	360-288-2900
Polynesian Resort The 615 Ocean Shores Blvd NW	Ocean Shores	WA	98569	**800-562-4836**	360-289-3361
Resort at Deer Harbor 31 Jack & Jill Ln PO Box 200	Deer Harbor	WA	98243	**888-376-4480**	360-376-4420
Resort at Ludlow Bay 1 Heron Rd	Port Ludlow	WA	98365	**877-805-0868**	360-437-2222
Resort Semiahmoo 9565 Semiahmoo Pkwy	Blaine	WA	98230	**800-770-7992**	360-318-2000
Rosario Resort & Spa 1400 Rosario Rd	Eastsound	WA	98245	**800-562-8820**	360-376-2222
Sun Mountain Lodge 604 Patterson Lake Rd PO Box 1000	Winthrop	WA	98862	**800-572-0493**	509-996-2211

West Virginia

Name / Address	City	State	ZIP	Toll-Free	Phone
Canaan Valley Resort & Conference Center HC 70 Box 330	Davis	WV	26260	**800-622-4121**	304-866-4121
Coolfont Resort 3621 Cold Run Valley Rd	Berkeley Springs	WV	25411	**800-888-8768**	304-258-4500
Glade Springs Resort 200 Lake Dr	Daniels	WV	25832	**800-634-5233**	304-763-2000
Greenbrier The 300 W Main St	White Sulphur Springs	WV	24986	**800-453-4858**	304-536-1110
Lakeview Scanticon Resort & Conference Center 1 Lakeview Dr	Morgantown	WV	26508	**800-624-8300**	304-594-1111
Oglebay Resort & Conference Center Rt 88 N Oglebay Pk	Wheeling	WV	26003	**800-624-6988**	304-243-4000
Pipestem Resort State Park PO Box 150	Pipestem	WV	25979	**800-225-5982**	304-466-1800
Snowshoe Mountain Resort 10 Snowshoe Dr	Snowshoe	WV	26209	**877-441-4386**	304-572-1000
Stonewall Resort 940 Resort Dr	Roanoke	WV	26447	**888-278-8150**	304-269-7400
Woods Resort & Conference Center Mountain Lake Rd PO Box 5	Hedgesville	WV	25427	**800-248-2222**	304-754-7977

Wisconsin

Name / Address	City	State	ZIP	Toll-Free	Phone
Abbey Resort & Fontana Spa 269 Fontana Blvd	Fontana	WI	53125	**800-558-2405**	262-275-6811
American Club The 444 Highland Dr	Kohler	WI	53044	**800-344-2838**	920-457-8000
Chanticleer Inn 1458 E Dollar Lake Rd	Eagle River	WI	54521	**800-752-9193**	715-479-4486
Chula Vista Resort 4031 N River Rd	Wisconsin Dells	WI	53965	**800-388-4782**	608-254-8366
Devil's Head Resort & Convention Center S6330 Bluff Rd	Merrimac	WI	53561	**800-472-6670**	608-493-2251
Fox Hills Resort & Convention Center 250 W Church St	Mishicot	WI	54228	**800-950-7615**	920-755-2376
Grand Geneva Resort & Spa 7036 Grand Geneva Way	Lake Geneva	WI	53147	**800-558-3417**	262-248-8811
Heidel House Resort 643 Illinois Ave	Green Lake	WI	54941	**800-444-2812**	920-294-3344
Holiday Acres Resort & Conference Center 4060 S Shore Dr	Rhinelander	WI	54501	**800-261-1500**	715-369-1500
Inn on Woodlake 705 Woodlake Rd	Kohler	WI	53044	**800-919-3600**	920-452-7800
Interlaken Resort & Country Spa W 4240 SR-50	Lake Geneva	WI	53147	**800-225-5558**	262-248-9121
Lake Lawn Resort 2400 E Geneva St	Delavan	WI	53115	**800-338-5253**	262-728-7950
Landmark Resort 7643 Hillside Rd	Egg Harbor	WI	54209	**800-273-7877**	920-868-3205
Olympia Resort & Spa 1350 Royale Mile Rd	Oconomowoc	WI	53066	**800-558-9573**	262-567-0311
Osthoff Resort 101 Osthoff Ave	Elkhart Lake	WI	53020	**800-876-3399**	920-876-3366

Wyoming

Name / Address	City	State	ZIP	Toll-Free	Phone
Amangani Resort 1535 NE Butte Rd	Jackson	WY	83001	**877-734-7333**	307-734-7333
Cowboy Village Resort at Togwotee PO Box 91	Moran	WY	83013	**800-543-2847**	307-543-2847
Grand Targhee Resort PO Box SKI	Alta	WY	83422	**800-827-4433**	307-353-2300
Jackson Hole Mountain Resort PO Box 290	Teton Village	WY	83025	**888-333-7766**	307-733-2292
Jackson Hole Racquet Club Resort 3535 Moose-Wilson Rd	Wilson	WY	83014	**800-443-8613**	307-733-3990
Jackson Lake Lodge PO Box 250	Moran	WY	83013	**800-628-9988**	307-543-2811
Jenny Lake Lodge PO Box 250	Moran	WY	83013	**800-628-9988**	307-733-4647
Rusty Parrot Lodge & Spa PO Box 1657	Jackson	WY	83001	**800-458-2004**	307-733-2000
Snake River Lodge & Spa 7710 Granite Loop Rd	Teton Village	WY	83025	**800-445-4655**	307-733-3657
Snow King Resort 400 E Snow King Ave PO Box SKI	Jackson	WY	83001	**800-522-5464**	307-733-5200
Teton Pines Resort & Country Club 3450 N Clubhouse Dr	Wilson	WY	83014	**800-238-2223**	307-733-1005

656 RESTAURANT OPERATION & MANAGEMENT

Name / Address	City	State	ZIP	Toll-Free	Phone
AFC Enterprises Inc 6 Concourse Pkwy Suite 1700 *NASDAQ: AFCE*	Atlanta	GA	30328	**866-232-4401**	770-391-9500
AJS Assoc 1003 Jordan Ln	Huntsville	AL	35816	**800-227-0340**	256-830-2423
Al Copeland Investments 1405 Airline Hwy	Metairie	LA	70001	**800-401-0401**	504-830-1000
Avado Brands Inc 150 Hancock St	Madison	GA	30650	**800-609-1255**	706-342-4552
BAB Inc 500 Lake Cook Rd Suite 475	Deerfield	IL	60015	**800-251-6101**	847-948-7522
Back Bay Restaurant Group Inc 284 Newberry St	Boston	MA	02115	**800-367-2424**	617-536-2800
Benihana Inc 8685 NW 53rd Terr Suite 201 *NASDAQ: BNHN*	Miami	FL	33166	**800-327-3369**	305-593-0770
Big Boy Restaurants International LLC 4199 Marcy St	Warren	MI	48091	**800-837-3003**	586-759-6000
Bob Evans Farms Inc 3776 S High St *NASDAQ: BOBE*	Columbus	OH	43207	**800-272-7675**	614-491-2225
Bobby Cox Cos Inc 4055 International Plaza Suite 450	Fort Worth	TX	76109	**800-897-8723**	817-377-6200
Bravo! Development Inc 4644 Kenny Rd	Columbus	OH	43220	**888-452-7286**	614-326-7944
Bridgeman Foods Inc 1903 Stanley Gault Pkwy	Louisville	KY	40223	**800-254-7130**	502-254-7130
Brinker International Inc 6820 LBJ Fwy *NYSE: EAT*	Dallas	TX	75240	**800-983-4637**	972-980-9917
Buca Inc 1300 Nicollet Mall Suite 5003 *NASDAQ: BUCA*	Minneapolis	MN	55403	**800-273-1388**	612-288-2382
Buffet Partners LP 2701 E Plano Pkwy	Plano	TX	75074	**800-804-7151**	214-291-2900
Cafe Express LLC 5858 Westheimer Rd Suite 110	Houston	TX	77057	**800-552-1999**	713-977-1922
Carisch Inc 641 E Lake St Suite 226	Wayzata	MN	55391	**800-952-7297**	952-473-4291
Carlson Restaurants Worldwide Inc 4201 Marsh Ln	Carrollton	TX	75007	**800-374-3297**	972-662-5400
Champps Entertainment Inc 10375 Park Meadows Dr Suite 560 *NASDAQ: CMPP*	Littleton	CO	80124	**800-461-5965**	303-804-1333
Checkers Drive-In Restaurants Inc 4300 W Cypress St Suite 600 *NASDAQ: CHKR*	Tampa	FL	33607	**800-800-8072**	813-283-7000

				Toll-Free	*Phone*
CKE Restaurants Inc					
401 W Carl Karcher Way	Anaheim	CA	92801	**800-758-2275**	714-774-5796
NYSE: CKR					
Claremont Restaurant Group 129 Fast Ln	Mooresville	NC	28117	**877-704-5939**	704-660-5939
CMT Cos Inc					
125 Plantation Centre Dr S Suite 100	Macon	GA	31210	**800-767-7253**	478-474-5633
Consolidated Restaurant Operations Inc					
12200 N Stemmons Fwy Suite 100	Dallas	TX	75234	**800-275-1337**	972-241-5500
Copeland Al Investments 1405 Airline Hwy	Metairie	LA	70001	**800-401-0401**	504-830-1000
DavCo Restaurants Inc 1657 Crofton Blvd	Crofton	MD	21114	**800-523-1411**	410-721-3770
Denny's Corp 203 E Main St	Spartanburg	SC	29319	**800-733-6697***	864-597-8000
*Cust Svc					
Doctor's Assoc Inc 325 Bic Dr	Milford	CT	06460	**800-888-4848**	203-877-4281
Dynaco Inc 2246 E Date Ave	Fresno	CA	93706	**800-230-4985**	559-485-8520
Dynamic Management LLC 1210 Briarville Rd	Madison	TN	37115	**800-306-1748**	615-277-1234
Eat'n Park Hospitality Group Inc					
285 E Waterfront Dr PO Box 3000	Pittsburgh	PA	15230	**800-947-4033**	412-461-2000
Elmer's Restaurants Inc 11802 SE Stark St	Portland	OR	97216	**800-325-5188**	503-252-1485
NASDAQ: ELMS					
Family Sports Concepts Inc					
5510 W La Salle St Suite 200	Tampa	FL	33607	**800-728-8878**	813-226-2333
Fox & Hound Restaurant Group					
1551 N Waterfront Pkwy Suite 310	Wichita	KS	67206	**800-229-2118**	316-634-0505
NASDAQ: FOXX					
Fresh Enterprises Inc					
100 Moody Ct Suite 200	Thousand Oaks	CA	91360	**877-225-2373**	805-495-4704
Garden Fresh Restaurant Corp					
15822 Bernardo Ctr Dr Suite A	San Diego	CA	92127	**800-874-1600**	858-675-1600
GCF Food Services Inc					
658 Danforth Ave Suite 201	Toronto	ON	M4J5B9	**800-465-3324**	416-778-8028
Grill Concepts Inc					
11661 San Vincente Blvd Suite 404	Los Angeles	CA	90049	**888-999-9156**	310-820-5559
NASDAQ: GRIL					
IHOP Corp 450 N Brand Blvd 7th Fl	Glendale	CA	91203	**800-241-4467**	818-240-6055
NYSE: IHP					
Interfoods of America Inc					
9400 S Dadeland Blvd Suite 720	Miami	FL	33156	**866-476-7393**	305-670-0746
International Dairy Queen Inc					
7505 Metro Blvd	Minneapolis	MN	55439	**866-793-7582**	952-830-0200
International Restaurant Management Group					
Inc 4104 Aurora St	Coral Gables	FL	33146	**800-662-1668**	305-476-1611
Investors Management Corp					
5151 Glenwood Ave	Raleigh	NC	27612	**800-284-5673**	919-781-9310
Jack in the Box Inc 9330 Balboa Ave	San Diego	CA	92123	**800-500-5225**	858-571-2121
NYSE: JBX					
Jan Cos 35 Sockanosset Cross Rd	Cranston	RI	02920	**800-937-1800**	401-946-4000
Johnny Rockets Group Inc					
26970 Aliso Viejo Pkwy Suite 100	Aliso Viejo	CA	92656	**888-236-9100**	949-643-6100
JRN Inc 201 W 7th St	Columbia	TN	38401	**800-251-8035**	931-381-3000
K-Mac Enterprises Inc 1820 S Zero St	Fort Smith	AR	72906	**800-345-5622**	479-646-2053
Kelsey's Operations Ltd 6303 Airport Rd	Mississauga	ON	L4V1R8	**800-860-4082**	905-405-6500
Kimpton Hotel & Restaurant Group LLC					
222 Kearny St Suite 200	San Francisco	CA	94108	**800-546-2686**	415-397-5572
Kirtac Inc 111 Carey Dr	Noblesville	IN	46060	**800-776-1646**	317-773-7855
Landry's Restaurants Inc 1510 W Loop South	Houston	TX	77027	**800-552-6379**	713-850-1010
NYSE: LNY					
Lone Star Steakhouse & Saloon Inc					
224 E Douglas Ave	Wichita	KS	67202	**800-234-0888**	316-264-8899
NASDAQ: STAR					
Main Street Restaurant Group Inc					
5050 N 40th St Suite 200	Phoenix	AZ	85018	**888-677-5080**	602-852-9000
NASDAQ: MAIN					
Malnati Organization Inc					
3685 Woodhead Dr	Northbrook	IL	60062	**800-568-8646**	847-562-1814
Manchu Wok Canada Inc					
85 Citizen Ct Unit 9	Markham	ON	L6G1A8	**800-361-8864**	905-946-7200
Mexican Restaurants Inc 1135 Edgebrook St	Houston	TX	77034	**800-741-7574**	713-943-7574
NASDAQ: CASA					
Morgan's Foods Inc					
24200 Chagrin Blvd Suite 126	Beachwood	OH	44122	**800-869-8691**	216-360-7500
AMEX: MR					
Mrs Fields Original Cookies Inc					
2855 E Cottonwood Pkwy Suite 400	Salt Lake City	UT	84121	**800-348-6311**	801-736-5600
New World Restaurant Group Inc					
100 Horizon Center Blvd	Hamilton	NJ	08691	**800-859-3090**	609-631-7000
Nu-Ventures Inc 1324 W Milham St	Portage	MI	49024	**888-432-8379**	269-226-4400
Palm Management Corp					
1730 Rhode Island Ave NW Suite 900	Washington	DC	20036	**800-388-7256**	202-775-7256
Panda Restaurant Group					
1683 Walnut Grove Ave	Rosemead	CA	91770	**800-877-8988**	626-799-9898
Pappas Restaurants Inc 642 Yale St	Houston	TX	77007	**877-277-2748**	713-869-0151
Prime Restaurant Group Inc					
10 Kingsbridge Garden Cir Suite 600	Mississauga	ON	L5R3K6	**800-613-1111**	905-568-0000
Quality Dining Inc 4220 Edison Lakes Pkwy	Mishawaka	IN	46545	**800-589-3820**	574-271-4600
Rare Hospitality International Inc					
8215 Roswell Rd Bldg 600	Atlanta	GA	30350	**800-434-6245**	770-399-9595
NASDAQ: RARE					
Restaurant Developers Corp					
5755 Granger Rd Suite 200	Independence	OH	44131	**800-837-9599**	216-398-1101
Restaurants Unlimited Inc					
1818 N Northlake Way	Seattle	WA	98103	**877-855-6106**	206-634-0550
Rock Bottom Restaurants Inc					
248 Centennial Pkwy	Louisville	CO	80027	**800-273-9827**	303-664-4000
Romacorp Inc 9304 Forest Ln Suite 200	Dallas	TX	75243	**800-286-7662**	214-343-7800
RPM Pizza LLC 15384 5th St	Gulfport	MS	39503	**800-622-6000**	228-832-4000
Shoney's Inc 1717 Elm Hill Pike Suite B1	Nashville	TN	37202	**877-474-6639**	615-391-5395
Smith & Sons Foods Inc 2124 Riverside Dr	Macon	GA	31204	**800-841-5385**	478-745-4759
Sonic Corp 300 Johnny Bench Dr	Oklahoma City	OK	73104	**800-569-6656**	405-280-7654
NASDAQ: SONC					
SunQuesT Systems 7170 Zionsville Rd	Indianapolis	IN	46268	**800-808-4774**	317-299-3391
SWH Corp					
17852 E 17th St South Bldg Suite 108	Tustin	CA	92780	**866-566-6464**	714-544-4826
Taco Maker Inc 4605 Harrison Blvd	Ogden	UT	84403	**800-207-5804**	801-476-9780
Thompson Hospitality					
505 Huntmar Pk Dr Suite 350	Herndon	VA	20170	**800-842-2737**	703-709-0145
Triarc Restaurant Group					
1000 Corporate Dr	Fort Lauderdale	FL	33334	**800-487-2729**	954-351-5100
Una Mas Restaurants Inc 25064 Viking St	Hayward	CA	94545	**888-862-2627**	408-747-7000
Val Ltd Inc 2601 S 70th St	Lincoln	NE	68506	**800-556-8150**	402-434-9350
Western Sizzlin Inc 1338 Plantation Rd	Roanoke	VA	24012	**800-247-8325**	540-345-3195
Yum! Brands Inc 1441 Gardiner Ln	Louisville	KY	40213	**800-225-5532**	502-874-8300
NYSE: YUM					

657 RESTAURANTS

SEE ALSO Bakeries; Dairy Product Stores; Food Service; Franchises; Restaurant Operation & Management

				Toll-Free	*Phone*
Acapulco Restaurants Inc					
4001 Via Oro Ave Suite 200	Long Beach	CA	90810	**800-735-3501**	310-513-7500
Ale House Management Inc					
612 N Orange Ave Suite C-6	Jupiter	FL	33458	**866-743-2299**	561-743-2299
American Cafe 150 W Church Ave	Maryville	TN	37801	**800-325-0755**	865-379-5700
Arby's Inc 1000 Corporate Dr	Fort Lauderdale	FL	33334	**800-487-2729**	954-351-5100
Back Yard Burgers Inc					
1657 Shelby Oaks Dr N Suite 105	Memphis	TN	38134	**800-292-6939**	901-367-0888
NASDAQ: BYBI					
Bahama Breeze 5900 Lake Ellenor Dr	Orlando	FL	32809	**866-475-5666**	407-245-4000
Bailey's Sports Grill					
1551 N Waterfront Pkwy Suite 310	Wichita	KS	67206	**800-229-2118**	316-634-0505
Baja Fresh Mexican Grill					
100 Moody Ct Suite 200	Thousand Oaks	CA	91360	**800-932-5309**	805-495-4704
Bakers Square Restaurants Inc					
400 W 48th Ave	Denver	CO	80216	**800-800-3644**	303-296-2121
Barnhill's Buffet Inc 226 Palafox Pl 5th Fl	Pensacola	FL	32502	**888-738-3808**	850-435-9914
Beef O'Bradys 5510 W LaSalle St Suite 200	Tampa	FL	33607	**800-728-8878**	813-226-2333
Bellacino's Corp 10096 Shaver Rd	Portage	MI	49024	**877-379-0700**	269-329-0782
Benihana Inc 8685 NW 53rd Terr Suite 201	Miami	FL	33166	**800-327-3369**	305-593-0770
NASDAQ: BNHN					
Bennigan's 6500 International Pkwy Suite 1000	Plano	TX	75093	**800-727-8355**	972-588-5000
Bertolini's 350 W Hubbard St Suite 610	Chicago	IL	60610	**800-486-4791**	312-923-0030
Bickford's Family Restaurants Inc					
1330 Soldiers Field Rd	Boston	MA	02135	**800-969-5653**	617-782-4010
Big Bowl 6820 LBJ Fwy	Dallas	TX	75240	**800-983-4637**	972-980-9917
Big Boy Restaurants International LLC					
4199 Marcy St	Warren	MI	48091	**800-837-3003**	586-759-6000
Bill Miller Bar-B-Q 430 S Santa Rosa St	San Antonio	TX	78207	**800-339-3111**	210-225-4461
Bishop's Buffet					
1520 Midland Ct NE Suite 300	Cedar Rapids	IA	52402	**866-393-4766**	319-393-4766
BJ's Restaurants Inc					
16162 Beach Blvd Suite 100	Huntington Beach	CA	92647	**800-223-1255**	714-848-3747
NASDAQ: BJRI					
Blimpie International Inc					
145 Huguenot St Suite 410	New Rochelle	NY	10801	**800-447-6258**	914-576-1006
Bob Evans Farms Inc 3776 S High St	Columbus	OH	43207	**800-272-7675**	614-491-2225
NASDAQ: BOBE					
Bojangles' Restaurants Inc					
9432 Southern Pine Blvd	Charlotte	NC	28273	**800-366-9921**	704-527-2675
Bonanza Restaurants					
6500 International Pkwy Suite 1000	Plano	TX	75093	**800-727-8355**	972-588-5000
Bonefish Grill 2202 N West Shore Blvd	Tampa	FL	33607	**866-880-2226**	813-282-1225
Boston Market Corp 14103 Denver West Pkwy	Golden	CO	80401	**800-877-2870**	303-278-9500
Bravo Cucina Italiana 4644 Kenny Rd	Columbus	OH	43220	**888-452-7286**	614-326-7944
Breadeaux Pisa Inc 3308 S Leonard Rd	Saint Joseph	MO	64503	**800-835-6534**	816-364-1088
Brio Tuscan Grille 4644 Kenny Rd	Columbus	OH	43220	**888-452-7286**	614-326-7944
Brown's Chicken & Pasta Inc					
489 W Fullerton Ave	Elmhurst	IL	60126	**888-582-7700**	630-617-8800
Bruchi's Cheesesteaks & Subs					
11801 NE 65th St	Vancouver	WA	98682	**877-488-9045**	360-882-8823
Bubba Gump Shrimp Co LLC					
940 Calle Negocio Suite 250	San Clemente	CA	92673	**877-729-4867**	949-366-6260
Buck's Pizza Franchising Corp Inc					
53 Industrial Dr	Du Bois	PA	15801	**800-310-8848**	814-371-3076
Buddy's Bar-B-Q 5806 Kingston Pike	Knoxville	TN	37919	**800-368-9208**	865-584-1924
Buffalo Wild Wings Inc					
1600 Utica Ave S Suite 700	Minneapolis	MN	55416	**800-499-9586**	952-593-9943
NASDAQ: BWLD					
Buffalo's Franchise Concepts Inc					
707 Whitlock Ave SW Bldg H Suite 13	Marietta	GA	30064	**800-459-4647**	770-420-1800
Buffet Partners LP 2701 E Plano Pkwy	Plano	TX	75074	**800-804-7151**	214-291-2900
Bugaboo Creek Steak House Inc					
8215 Roswell Rd Bldg 600	Atlanta	GA	30350	**800-434-6245**	770-399-9595
Burger King Restaurants of Canada Inc					
401 The West Mall 7th Fl	Etobicoke	ON	M9C5J4	**888-252-8280**	416-626-6464
Cafe Express LLC					
5858 Westheimer Rd Suite 110	Houston	TX	77057	**800-552-1999**	713-977-1922
Cajun & Grill of America 4104 Aurora St	Coral Gables	FL	33146	**800-662-1668**	305-476-1611
California Pizza Kitchen Inc					
6053 W Century Blvd Suite 1100	Los Angeles	CA	90045	**800-275-8255**	310-342-5000
NASDAQ: CPKI					
Capital Grille 8215 Roswell Rd Bldg 600	Atlanta	GA	30350	**800-434-6245**	770-399-9595
Captain D's LLC 1717 Elm Hill Pike Suite A-1	Nashville	TN	37210	**800-314-4819**	615-391-5461
Captain Tony's Inc					
2607 S Woodland Blvd Suite 300	DeLand	FL	32720	**800-332-8669**	386-736-9855
Carl's Jr Restaurants					
401 W Carl Karcher Way	Anaheim	CA	92803	**800-422-4141**	714-774-5796
Carson's Inc 5970 N Ridge Ave	Chicago	IL	60660	**888-999-7427**	773-271-4000
Casa Ole 1135 Edgebrook St	Houston	TX	77034	**800-741-7574**	713-943-7574
Casey's Bar & Grill					
10 Kingsbridge Garden Cir Suite 600	Mississauga	ON	L5R3K6	**800-361-3111**	905-568-0000
CB & Potts					
10013 59th Ave SW PO Box 99010	Lakewood	WA	98499	**888-898-4050**	253-588-1788
Champps Restaurants & Bar					
10375 Park Meadows Dr Suite 560	Littleton	CO	80124	**800-461-5965**	303-804-1333
Charley's Eating & Drinking Saloon					
284 Newbury St	Boston	MA	02115	**800-424-2753**	617-536-2800
Charley's Grilled Subs					
2500 Farmers Dr Suite 140	Columbus	OH	43235	**800-437-8325**	614-923-4700
Charley's Steakery 2500 Farmers Dr	Columbus	OH	43235	**800-437-8325**	614-923-4700
Charlie Brown's Steakhouse Inc					
1450 Rt 22 W	Mountainside	NJ	07092	**800-518-1855**	908-518-1800
Chart House Restaurants 1510 W Loop South	Houston	TX	77027	**800-552-6379**	713-850-1010
Checkers Drive-In Restaurants Inc					
4300 W Cypress St Suite 600	Tampa	FL	33607	**800-800-8072**	813-283-7000
NASDAQ: CHKR					
Cheeburger Cheeburger Restaurants Inc					
15951 McGregor Blvd Suite 2A	Fort Myers	FL	33908	**800-487-6211**	239-437-1611
Chevys Inc 2000 Powell St Suite 300	Emeryville	CA	94608	**800-424-3897**	510-768-1400
Chick-fil-A Inc 5200 Buffington Rd	Atlanta	GA	30349	**800-232-2677**	404-765-8000
Chicken Out Rotisserie					
15952 Shady Grove Rd	Gaithersburg	MD	20877	**800-328-4663**	301-921-0600
Chili's Grill & Bar 6820 LBJ Fwy	Dallas	TX	75240	**800-983-4637**	972-980-9917

Name / Address	City	State	ZIP	Toll-Free	Phone
Chinese Cafes of America 4104 Aurora St	Coral Gables	FL	33146	**800-662-1668**	305-476-1611
ChopHouse & Brewery 248 Centennial Pkwy	Louisville	CO	80027	**800-273-9827**	303-664-4000
Church's Chicken Inc 980 Hammond Dr NE Suite 1100	Atlanta	GA	30328	**866-232-9402**	770-350-3800
Chuy's Comida Deluxe 1623 Toomey Rd	Austin	TX	78704	**800-439-2489**	512-473-2783
Claim Jumper Restaurants 16721 Millikan Ave	Irvine	CA	92606	**800-949-4538**	949-756-9001
Copeland's of New Orleans 1405 Airline Dr	Metairie	LA	70001	**800-401-0401**	504-830-1000
Country Kitchen International 801 Deming Way	Madison	WI	53717	**888-359-3235**	608-833-9633
Country Pride Restaurants 24601 Center Ridge Rd Suite 200	Westlake	OH	44145	**800-872-7024**	440-808-9100
Cousins Subs Inc N 83 W 13400 Leon Rd	Menomonee Falls	WI	53051	**800-238-9736**	262-253-7700
Crab House 1510 W Loop South	Houston	TX	77027	**800-552-6379**	713-850-1010
Cracker Barrel Old Country Store Inc 305 Hartmann Dr	Lebanon	TN	37087	**800-333-9566**	615-444-5533
Daily Grill 11661 San Vincente Blvd Suite 404	Los Angeles	CA	90049	**888-999-9156**	310-820-5559
Damon's International Inc 4645 Executive Dr	Columbus	OH	43220	**800-226-7427**	614-442-7900
D'Angelo Sandwich Shops 600 Providence Hwy	Dedham	MA	02026	**800-727-2446**	781-461-1200
Dave & Buster's Inc 2481 Manana Dr *NYSE: DAB*	Dallas	TX	75220	**800-842-5369**	214-357-9588
Del Frisco's 224 E Douglas Ave	Wichita	KS	67202	**800-234-0888**	316-264-8899
Del Taco Inc 25521 Commercentre Dr Suite 200 *Cust Svc	Lake Forest	CA	92630	**800-852-7204***	949-462-9300
Desert Moon Cafe 612 Corporate Way Suite 1M	Valley Cottage	NY	10989	**877-564-6362**	845-267-3300
Dickey's Barbecue Restaurants Inc 4514 Cole Ave Suite 1000	Dallas	TX	75205	**866-340-6188**	972-248-9899
Dixie Restaurants Inc 1215 Rebsamen Pk Rd	Little Rock	AR	72202	**800-508-1242**	501-666-3494
Dolly's Pizza Franchising Inc 1097-B Union Lake Rd	White Lake	MI	48386	**866-336-5597**	248-360-6440
Domino's Pizza Inc 30 Frank Lloyd Wright Dr *NYSE: DPZ*	Ann Arbor	MI	48106	**888-366-4667**	734-930-3030
Don Pablo's Mexican Kitchen 150 Hancock St	Madison	GA	30650	**800-765-7894**	706-342-4552
Donatos Pizza 935 Taylor Stn Rd	Columbus	OH	43230	**800-366-2867**	614-864-2444
Durango Steakhouse 2325 Ulmerton Rd Suite 20	Clearwater	FL	33762	**800-525-8643**	727-576-6424
Eat'n Park Hospitality Group Inc 285 E Waterfront Dr PO Box 3000	Pittsburgh	PA	15230	**800-947-4033**	412-461-2000
Edwardo's Natural Pizza Restaurants 600 W Jackson Blvd Suite 200	Chicago	IL	60661	**800-344-5455**	312-463-1210
El Chico Restaurants Inc 12200 N Stemmons Fwy Suite 100	Dallas	TX	75234	**800-275-1334**	972-241-5500
El Fenix Corp 11075 Harry Hines Blvd	Dallas	TX	75229	**877-591-1918**	972-241-2171
El Torito Restaurants Inc 4001 Via Oro Ave Suite 200	Long Beach	CA	90810	**800-735-3501**	310-513-7500
Elmer's Restaurants Inc 11802 SE Stark St *NASDAQ: ELMS*	Portland	OR	97216	**800-325-5188**	503-252-1485
Famous Dave's of America Inc 8091 Wallace Rd *NASDAQ: DAVE*	Eden Prairie	MN	55344	**800-210-4040**	952-294-1300
Farmer Boys Food Inc 3452 University Ave	Riverside	CA	92501	**800-930-3276**	951-275-9900
Figaro's Italian Pizza Inc 1500 Liberty St SE Suite 160	Salem	OR	97302	**888-344-2767**	503-371-9318
First Watch Inc 6910 Professional Pkwy E	Sarasota	FL	34240	**800-774-0724**	941-907-9800
Fox's Distribution Inc 3243 Old Frankstown Rd	Pittsburgh	PA	15239	**800-899-3697**	724-733-7888
Fox's Pizza Den Inc 3243 Old Frankstown Rd	Pittsburgh	PA	15239	**800-899-3697**	724-733-7888
Fresh Choice Inc 485 Cochrane Cir	Morgan Hill	CA	95037	**800-859-8693**	408-776-0799
Freshens Frozen Treats 1750 The Exchange	Atlanta	GA	30339	**800-633-4519**	678-627-5400
Friendly's Restaurants 1855 Boston Rd	Wilbraham	MA	01095	**800-966-9970**	413-543-2400
Frisch's Restaurants Inc 2800 Gilbert Ave *AMEX: FRS*	Cincinnati	OH	45206	**800-873-3633**	513-961-2660
Frullati Cafe & Bakery 7730 E Greenway Rd Suite 104	Scottsdale	AZ	85260	**800-438-2590**	480-443-0200
Gates Bar-B-Q 4621 Paseo Blvd	Kansas City	MO	64110	**800-662-7427**	816-923-0900
Godfather's Pizza Inc 9140 W Dodge Rd	Omaha	NE	68114	**800-456-8347**	402-391-1452
Gold Star Chili 650 Lunken Pk Dr	Cincinnati	OH	45226	**800-643-0465**	513-231-4541
Golden Corral Corp 5151 Glenwood Ave	Raleigh	NC	27612	**800-284-5673**	919-781-9310
Good Eats Inc 12200 Stemmons Fwy Suite 100	Dallas	TX	75234	**800-275-1337**	972-241-5500
Gorin's Homemade Cafe & Grill 4 Executive Pk E Suite 315	Atlanta	GA	30329	**888-489-7277**	404-248-9900
Grady's American Grill 4220 Edison Lakes Pkwy	Mishawaka	IN	46545	**800-589-3820**	574-271-4600
Great Wraps! 4 Executive Pk E Suite 315	Atlanta	GA	30329	**888-489-7277**	404-248-9900
Green Burrito 401 Carl Karcher Way	Anaheim	CA	92801	**800-422-4141**	714-774-5796
Grisanti's Inc 9300 Shelbyville Rd Suite 508	Louisville	KY	40222	**800-436-6323**	502-429-0341
Hacienda Mexican Restaurants 1501 N Ironwood Dr	South Bend	IN	46635	**800-541-3227**	574-272-5922
Hard Rock Cafe International Inc 6100 Old Park Ln	Orlando	FL	32835	**800-235-7625**	407-445-7625
Hardee's Food Systems Inc 505 N 7th St	Saint Louis	MO	63101	**800-711-4274**	314-259-6200
Hibachi-San Japanese Grill 1683 Walnut Grove Ave	Rosemead	CA	91770	**800-487-2632**	626-799-9898
Ho-Lee-Chow 658 Danforth Ave Suite 201	Toronto	ON	M4J5B9	**800-465-3324**	416-778-8028
Hogi Yogi Corp 4833 N Edgewood Dr	Provo	UT	84604	**800-653-4581**	801-222-9004
Home Run Inn Inc 1300 Internationale Pkwy	Woodridge	IL	60517	**800-636-9696**	630-783-9696
Hoss's Steak & Sea House 170 Patch Way Rd	Duncansville	PA	16635	**800-992-4677**	814-695-7600
Hot Dog on a Stick 5601 Palmer Way	Carlsbad	CA	92008	**800-321-8400**	760-930-0456
Hot Stuff Pizza 2930 W Maple St	Sioux Falls	SD	57107	**800-648-6227**	605-336-6961
House of Blues Entertainment Inc 6255 Sunset Blvd 16th Fl	Hollywood	CA	90028	**800-843-2583**	323-769-4600
Houston's Restaurants 2425 E Camelback Rd Suite 200	Phoenix	AZ	85016	**866-418-8583**	602-553-2111
Huddle House Inc 2969 E Ponce de Leon Ave	Decatur	GA	30030	**800-418-9555**	404-377-5700
Humperdinks 10013 59th Ave SW	Lakewood	WA	98499	**888-898-4050**	253-588-1788
Humpty's Restaurants International Inc 2505 Macleod Tr S	Calgary	AB	T2G5J4	**800-661-7589**	403-269-4675
Hungry Howie's Pizza & Subs Inc 30300 Stephenson Hwy Suite 200	Madison Heights	MI	48071	**800-624-8122**	248-414-3300
I Can't Believe It's Yogurt 8300 Woodbine Ave 5th Fl	Markham	ON	L3R9Y7	**800-528-0727**	905-479-8762
Il Fornaio America Corp 770 Tamalpais Dr Suite 400	Corte Madera	CA	94925	**800-291-1505**	415-945-0500
In-N-Out Burger Inc 4199 Campus Dr Suite 900 *Cust Svc	Irvine	CA	92612	**800-786-1000***	949-509-6200
International House of Pancakes (IHOP) 450 N Brand Blvd 7th Fl	Glendale	CA	91203	**800-241-4467**	818-240-6055
Iron Skillet 6080 Surety Dr	El Paso	TX	79905	**800-331-8809**	915-779-4711
J Alexander's Corp 3401 West End Ave Suite 260 *AMEX: JAX*	Nashville	TN	37203	**888-285-2539**	615-269-1900
Jack in the Box Restaurants 9330 Balboa Ave	San Diego	CA	92123	**800-500-5225**	858-571-2121
Jack's Family Restaurants Inc 124 W Oxmoor Rd	Birmingham	AL	35209	**800-422-3893**	205-945-8167
Jake's Over the Top 4605 Harrison Blvd	Ogden	UT	84403	**800-207-5804**	801-476-9780
Jake's Pizza Enterprises Inc 1931 Rohlwing Rd Suite B	Rolling Meadows	IL	60008	**800-425-2537**	847-368-1990
Jerry's Subs & Pizza 15942 Shady Grove Rd	Gaithersburg	MD	20877	**800-990-9176**	301-921-8777
Jersey Mike's Franchise Systems Inc 2251 Landmark Pl	Manasquan	NJ	08736	**800-321-7676**	732-282-2323
Jet's America Inc 37177 Mound Rd	Sterling Heights	MI	48130	**888-446-5870**	586-268-5870
Jillian's Restaurants 4500 Bowling Blvd Suite 200	Louisville	KY	40207	**888-594-8231**	502-638-9008
Jimmy John's Franchise Inc 600 Tollgate Rd	Elgin	IL	60123	**800-546-6904**	847-888-7206
Joe's Crab Shack 1510 W Loop South	Houston	TX	77027	**800-552-6379**	713-850-1010
Joey's Only Seafood Franchising Corp 514 42nd Ave SE	Calgary	AB	T2G1Y6	**800-661-2123**	403-243-4584
Johnny Rockets the Original Hamburger 26970 Aliso Viejo Pkwy Suite 100	Aliso Viejo	CA	92656	**888-236-9100**	949-643-6100
Johnny's Pizza House Inc 2920 N 7th St	West Monroe	LA	71291	**800-256-5453**	318-323-0518
Kahunaville Management Inc 500 S Madison St	Wilmington	DE	19801	**888-453-3990**	302-571-6200
KC Masterpiece Restaurants 9537 Alden St	Lenexa	KS	66215	**800-467-9206**	913-888-5210
Kelsey's Operations Ltd 6303 Airport Rd	Mississauga	ON	L4V1R8	**800-860-4082**	905-405-6500
Kenny Rogers Roasters 1400 Old Country Rd Suite 400	Westbury	NY	11590	**800-628-4267**	516-338-8500
Kettle Country Kitchen Inc 350 Oaks Trail Suite 142	Garland	TX	75043	**800-929-2391**	972-203-6222
KFC 1441 Gardiner Ln	Louisville	KY	40213	**800-544-5774**	502-874-8300
Krystal Co 1 Union Sq	Chattanooga	TN	37402	**800-458-5841**	423-757-1550
La Madeleine Inc 6688 N Central Expy Suite 700	Dallas	TX	75206	**800-400-5840**	214-696-6962
La Salsa Inc 6307 Carpinteria Ave Suite A	Carpinteria	CA	93013	**800-527-2572**	805-745-7500
La Senorita 1135 Edgebrook St	Houston	TX	77034	**800-741-7574**	713-943-7574
Landry's Restaurants Inc 1510 W Loop South *NYSE: LNY*	Houston	TX	77027	**800-552-6379**	713-850-1010
Leeann Chin Inc 3600 American Blvd W Suite 418	Bloomington	MN	55431	**800-784-0029**	952-896-3606
Legal Sea Foods Inc 1 Seafood Way	Boston	MA	02210	**800-477-5342**	617-783-8088
Leverock Seafood House PO Box 20466	Tampa	FL	33622	**888-538-3762**	813-637-8663
Libby Hill Seafood Restaurants Inc 4517-B W Market St	Greensboro	NC	27407	**800-452-2071**	336-294-0505
Li'l Dino Corp 5601 Roanne Way Suite 100	Greensboro	NC	27409	**800-525-6782**	336-297-4440
Little Caesars Inc 2211 Woodward Ave	Detroit	MI	48201	**800-722-3727**	313-983-6000
Little King Inc 11811 'I' St	Omaha	NE	68137	**800-788-9478**	402-330-8019
Logan's Roadhouse Inc 3011 Armory Dr Suite 300	Nashville	TN	37204	**800-815-9056**	615-885-9056
Lone Star Steakhouse & Saloon Inc 224 E Douglas Ave *NASDAQ: STAR*	Wichita	KS	67202	**800-234-0888**	316-264-8899
LongHorn Steakhouse 8215 Roswell Rd Bldg 600	Atlanta	GA	30350	**800-434-6245**	770-399-9595
Luby's Inc PO Box 33069 *NYSE: LUB*	San Antonio	TX	78265	**800-886-4600**	210-654-9000
MacGregor's Market 2930 W Maple St	Sioux Falls	SD	57107	**800-648-6227**	605-336-6961
Manchu Wok 85 Citizen Ct Unit 9	Markham	ON	L6G1A8	**800-361-8864**	905-946-7200
Marco's Pizza 5252 Monroe St	Toledo	OH	43623	**800-262-7267**	419-885-4844
Margaritaville Inc 424-A Fleming St	Key West	FL	33040	**800-262-6835**	305-296-9089
Marie Callender Inc 27081 Aliso Creek Rd Suite 200	Aliso Viejo	CA	92656	**800-776-7437**	949-448-5300
Maui Tacos International Inc 180 Interstate N Pkwy SE Suite 500	Atlanta	GA	30339	**888-628-4822**	770-226-8226
McAlister's Corp 731 S Pear Orchard Rd Suite 51	Ridgeland	MS	39157	**888-855-3354**	601-952-1100
McDonald's Corp 1 McDonald's Plaza *NYSE: MCD*	Oak Brook	IL	60523	**800-234-6227**	630-623-3000
MCL Cafeterias Inc 2730 E 62nd St	Indianapolis	IN	46220	**800-530-9625**	317-257-5425
Me-N-Ed's Pizzerias 5701 N West Ave	Fresno	CA	93711	**888-636-3373**	559-432-0399
Mean Gene's Burgers 2930 W Maple St	Sioux Falls	SD	57107	**800-648-6227**	605-336-6961
Melting Pot Restaurants Inc 8810 Twin Lakes Blvd	Tampa	FL	33614	**800-783-0867**	813-881-0055
Mikes Restaurants Inc 8250 Decarie Blvd Suite 310	Montreal	QC	H4P2P5	**866-346-4537**	514-341-5544
Monical Pizza Corp 530 N Kinzie Ave	Bradley	IL	60915	**800-929-3227**	815-937-1890
Montana's Cookhouse Saloon 6303 Airport Rd	Mississauga	ON	L4V1R8	**800-860-4082**	905-405-6500
Monterey's Little Mexico 1135 Edgebrook St	Houston	TX	77034	**800-741-7574**	713-943-7574
Monterey's Tex-Mex Cafe 1135 Edgebrook St	Houston	TX	77034	**800-741-7574**	713-943-7574
Mountain Jack 10200 Willow Creek Rd	San Diego	CA	92131	**800-570-9159**	858-689-2333
Mozzarella's Cafe 150 W Church Ave	Maryville	TN	37801	**800-325-0755**	865-379-5700
Mr Goodcents Franchise Systems Inc 8997 Commerce Dr	DeSoto	KS	66018	**800-648-2368**	913-583-8400
Mr Hero 5755 Granger Rd Suite 200	Independence	OH	44131	**800-837-9599**	216-398-1101
Mr Jim's Pizza Inc 4276 Kellway Cir	Addison	TX	75001	**800-583-5960**	972-267-5467
Mr Sub 4576 Yonge St	Toronto	ON	M2N6P1	**800-668-7827**	416-225-5545
Mr Subb Franchise Corp 601 Columbia St	Cohoes	NY	12047	**800-267-7822**	518-783-0276
Mrs Winner's Chicken & Biscuits 6055 Barfield Rd	Atlanta	GA	30328	**877-733-5577**	404-459-5805
My Friend's Place 106 Hammond Dr	Atlanta	GA	30328	**800-882-9436**	404-843-2803
Nancy's Pizzeria 8200 W 185th St Suite J	Tinley Park	IL	60477	**800-626-2977**	708-444-4411
Napa Valley Grill 2200 Powell St Suite 750	Emeryville	CA	94608	**800-294-9323**	510-594-4262
Nathan's Famous Inc 1400 Old Country Rd Suite 400 *NASDAQ: NATH*	Westbury	NY	11590	**800-628-4267**	516-338-8500
Nature's Table Franchise Co 800 N Magnolia Ave	Orlando	FL	32803	**800-222-6090**	407-481-2544
Noble Roman's Pizza Inc 1 Virginia Ave Suite 800	Indianapolis	IN	46204	**800-585-0669**	317-634-3377
Office Beer Bar & Grill 1450 Rt 22 W	Mountainside	NJ	07092	**800-518-1855**	908-518-1800
Old Chicago Restaurants 248 Centennial Pkwy	Louisville	CO	80027	**800-273-9827**	303-664-4000
Olga's Kitchen Inc 1940 Northwood Dr	Troy	MI	48084	**800-336-5427**	248-362-0001
On the Border Mexican Cafe 6820 LBJ Fwy	Dallas	TX	75240	**800-983-4637**	972-980-9917
Orange Julius of America 7505 Metro Blvd	Minneapolis	MN	55439	**800-679-6556**	952-830-0200

Name / Address	City	State	ZIP	Toll-Free	Phone
Palm Restaurant					
1730 Rhode Island Ave NW Suite 900	Washington	DC	20036	**800-795-7256**	202-775-7256
Panchero's Mexican Grill					
2475 Coral Ct Suite B	Coraville	IA	52241	**888-639-2378**	319-545-6565
Pancho's Mexican Buffet Inc					
3500 Noble Ave	Fort Worth	TX	76111	**800-433-7670**	817-831-0081
Panda Express 1683 Walnut Grove Ave	Rosemead	CA	91770	**800-487-2632**	626-799-9898
Panda Inn 1683 Walnut Grove Ave	Rosemead	CA	91770	**800-487-2632**	626-799-9898
Papa Gino's Inc 600 Providence Hwy	Dedham	MA	02026	**800-727-2446**	781-461-1200
Papa John's International Inc					
2002 Papa John's Blvd	Louisville	KY	40299	**877-547-7272**	502-261-7272
NASDAQ: PZZA					
Papa Razzi 284 Newbury St	Boston	MA	02115	**800-424-2753**	617-536-2800
Pappadeaux Seafood Kitchen 642 Yale St	Houston	TX	77007	**877-277-2748**	713-869-0151
Pappas Restaurants Inc 642 Yale St	Houston	TX	77007	**877-277-2748**	713-869-0151
Pappas Seafood House 642 Yale St	Houston	TX	77077	**877-277-2748**	713-869-0151
Pappasito's Cantina 642 Yale St	Houston	TX	77007	**877-277-2748**	713-869-0151
Pasta Connections 1000 Corporate Dr	Fort Lauderdale	FL	33334	**800-487-2729**	954-351-5100
Pasta House Co 1143 Macklind Ave	Saint Louis	MO	63110	**800-467-2782**	314-535-6644
Pat & Mario's					
10 Kingsbridge Garden Cir Suite 600	Mississauga	ON	L5R3K6	**800-361-3111**	905-568-0000
Pat O'Brien's International Inc					
718 Saint Peter St	New Orleans	LA	70116	**800-597-4823**	504-525-4823
Penguin Point Franchise Systems Inc					
2691 E US 30	Warsaw	IN	46580	**800-577-5755**	574-267-3107
Pepperoni Grill 1220 S Santa Fe Ave	Edmond	OK	73003	**800-679-3607**	405-705-5000
Perkins Restaurant & Bakery					
6075 Poplar Ave Suite 800	Memphis	TN	38119	**800-877-7375**	901-766-6400
Perko's Cafe 2246 E Date Ave	Fresno	CA	93706	**800-230-4985**	559-485-8520
Peter Piper Inc					
14635 N Kierland Blvd Suite 160	Scottsdale	AZ	85254	**800-899-3425**	480-609-6400
Petro's Chili & Chips					
5614 Kingston Pike 2nd Fl	Knoxville	TN	37919	**800-738-7639**	865-588-1076
Phillips Seafood Restaurants					
1215 E Fort Ave	Baltimore	MD	21230	**800-648-7067**	443-263-1200
Philly Franchising Co					
120 Interstate N Pkwy E Suite 112	Atlanta	GA	30339	**800-886-8826**	770-952-6152
Piccadilly Cafeterias Inc					
3232 Sherwood Forest Blvd	Baton Rouge	LA	70816	**800-535-9974**	225-293-9440
Piccadilly Circus Pizza 1007 Okoboji Ave	Milford	IA	51351	**800-338-4340**	712-338-2771
Pick Up Stix Inc 1330 Calle Avanzado	San Clemente	CA	92673	**800-400-7849**	949-361-3189
Pizza Boli's 5725 Falls Rd	Baltimore	MD	21209	**800-234-2654**	
Pizza Factory Inc 49430 Rd 426	Oakhurst	CA	93644	**800-654-4840**	559-683-3377
Pizza Hut Inc 14841 N Dallas Pkwy	Dallas	TX	75254	**800-948-8488**	972-338-7700
Pizza Inn Inc 3551 Plano Pkwy	The Colony	TX	75056	**800-880-9955**	469-384-5000
NASDAQ: PZZI					
Pizza Pizza Ltd 580 Jarvis St	Toronto	ON	M4Y2H9	**800-265-9762**	416-967-1010
Pizza Plus Pizza Inc 1816 Volunteer Pkwy	Bristol	TN	37620	**800-675-1220**	423-652-2336
Pizza Pro Inc 2107 N 2nd St PO Box 1285	Cabot	AR	72023	**800-777-7554**	501-605-1175
Pizza Ranch Inc 1121 Main St	Hull	IA	51239	**800-321-3401**	712-439-1150
PoFolks Restaurants 508 Harmon Ave	Panama City	FL	32401	**888-876-3655**	850-763-0501
Pollo Tropical Inc 7300 N Kendall Dr 8th Fl	Miami	FL	33156	**888-778-7696**	305-670-7696
Ponderosa Steakhouses					
6500 International Pkwy Suite 1000	Plano	TX	75093	**800-727-8355**	972-588-5000
Popeyes Chicken & Biscuits					
5555 Glenridge Connector NE Suite 300	Atlanta	GA	30342	**866-232-4403**	404-459-4450
Pretzelmaker					
2855 E Cottonwood Pkwy Suite 400	Salt Lake City	UT	84121	**800-266-5437**	801-736-5600
Prime Pubs Inc					
10 Kingsbridge Garden Cir Suite 600	Mississauga	ON	L5R3K6	**800-361-3111**	905-568-0000
Prime Sirloin Steak House 129 Fast Ln	Mooresville	NC	28117	**877-704-5939**	704-660-5939
Qdoba Restaurant Corp					
4865 Ward Rd Suite 500	Wheat Ridge	CO	80033	**877-261-4783**	720-898-2300
Rainforest Cafe 1510 W Loop South	Houston	TX	77027	**800-552-6379**	713-850-1010
Rally's Hamburgers Inc					
4300 W Cypress St Suite 600	Tampa	FL	33607	**800-800-8072**	813-283-7000
Ram The 10013 59th Ave SW	Lakewood	WA	98499	**888-898-4050**	253-588-1788
Red Hot & Blue Restaurants Inc					
1701 Clarendon Blvd Suite 105	Arlington	VA	22209	**800-723-0745**	703-276-8833
Redfish America LLC					
5050 N 40th St Suite 200	Phoenix	AZ	85018	**888-677-5080**	602-852-9000
Rib Crib Corp 4535 S Harvard St	Tulsa	OK	74135	**800-275-9677**	918-712-7427
RJ Boar's Franchising Corp					
3127 Brady St Suite 3	Davenport	IA	52803	**877-395-8910**	563-322-2627
RJ Gator's Hometown Grill & Bar					
609 Hepburn Ave Suite 103	Jupiter	FL	33458	**800-438-4286**	561-575-0326
Roadhouse Grill Inc					
2703-A Gateway Dr	Pompano Beach	FL	33069	**800-680-2279**	954-957-2600
Rock Bottom Restaurants Inc					
248 Centennial Pkwy	Louisville	CO	80027	**800-273-9827**	303-664-4000
Rocky Rococo 105 E Wisconsin Ave	Oconomowoc	WI	53066	**800-888-7625**	262-569-5580
Romano's Macaroni Grill 6820 LBJ Fwy	Dallas	TX	75240	**800-983-4637**	972-980-9917
Ruby Tuesday Inc 150 W Church Ave	Maryville	TN	37801	**800-325-0755**	865-379-5700
NYSE: RI					
Ruby's Diner Inc					
660 Newport Ctr Dr Suite 850	Newport Beach	CA	92660	**800-439-7829**	949-644-7829
Runza Drive-Ins of America Inc					
5931 S 58th St Suite D	Lincoln	NE	68516	**800-929-2394**	402-423-2394
Russ' Restaurants Inc 390 E 8th St	Holland	MI	49423	**800-521-1778**	616-396-6571
Rusty Pelican					
940 Calle Negocio Suite 250	San Clemente	CA	92673	**877-729-4867**	949-366-6260
Ruth's Chris Steak House 3321 Hessmer Ave	Metairie	LA	70002	**800-487-4785**	504-454-6560
S & S Cafeterias 2124 Riverside Dr	Macon	GA	31204	**800-841-5385**	478-745-4759
Sagebrush Steakhouse 129 Fast Ln	Mooresville	NC	28117	**877-704-5939**	704-660-5939
Saltgrass Steak House Corp					
1510 W Loop South	Houston	TX	77027	**800-552-6379**	713-850-1010
Samuel Mancino's Italian Eatery					
1324 W Milham St	Portage	MI	49024	**888-432-8379**	269-226-4400
Sandella's LLC 9 Brookside Pl	West Redding	CT	06896	**888-544-9984**	203-544-9984
Sbarro Inc 401 Broadhollow Rd	Melville	NY	11747	**800-766-4949***	631-715-4100
*Cust Svc					
Schlotzsky's Ltd 203 Colorado St	Austin	TX	78701	**800-846-2867***	512-236-3600
*Sales					
Shakey's USA 2200 W Valley Blvd	Alhambra	CA	91803	**888-444-6686**	626-537-0737
Shari's Restaurants 9400 SW Gemini Dr	Beaverton	OR	97008	**800-433-5334**	503-605-4299
Shoney's Inc 1717 Elm Hill Pike Suite B1	Nashville	TN	37202	**877-474-6639**	615-391-5395
Shula's Steak House					
7601 Miami Lakes Dr	Miami Lakes	FL	33014	**800-247-4852**	305-820-8102
Simple Simon's Pizza 6650 S Lewis St	Tulsa	OK	74136	**800-261-6375**	918-496-1272
Skyline Chili Inc 4180 Thunderbird Ln	Fairfield	OH	45014	**800-443-4371**	513-874-1188
Smash Hit Subs 2930 W Maple St	Sioux Falls	SD	57107	**800-648-6227**	605-336-6961
Smokey Bones BBQ 5900 Lake Ellenor Dr	Orlando	FL	32809	**800-421-3035**	407-245-4000
Snappy Tomato Pizza Co 7230 Turfway Rd	Florence	KY	41042	**888-463-7627**	859-525-4680
Sonic Drive-In Restaurants					
101 Park Ave Suite 1400	Oklahoma City	OK	73102	**800-569-6656**	405-280-7654
Souper Salad Inc					
140 Heimer Rd Suite 400	San Antonio	TX	78232	**800-346-7687**	210-495-9644
Souplantation					
15822 Bernardo Ctr Dr Suite A	San Diego	CA	92127	**800-874-1600**	858-675-1600
Spaghetti Warehouse Inc					
12200 Stemmons Fwy Suite 100	Dallas	TX	75234	**800-929-4000***	972-241-5500
*Cust Svc					
Steak & Ale 6500 International Pkwy Suite 1000	Plano	TX	75093	**800-727-8355**	972-588-5000
Steak n Shake Co					
36 S Pennsylvania St Suite 500	Indianapolis	IN	46204	**800-437-2406**	317-633-4100
NYSE: SNS					
Steak-Out Franchising Inc					
6801 Governors Lake Pkwy Suite 100	Norcross	GA	30071	**877-878-3257**	678-533-6000
Stuart Anderson's Black Angus					
4410 El Camino Real Suite 201	Los Altos	CA	94022	**800-750-0211**	650-949-6400
Stuckey's Corp 8555 16th St Suite 850	Silver Spring	MD	20910	**800-423-6171**	301-585-8222
Sub Station II Inc 425 N Main St	Sumter	SC	29150	**800-779-2970**	803-773-4711
Subway Restaurants 325 Bic Dr	Milford	CT	06460	**800-888-4848**	203-877-4281
Sullivan's 224 E Douglas Ave	Wichita	KS	67227	**800-234-0888**	316-264-8899
SunShine Cafe Restaurants					
7112 Zionsville Rd	Indianapolis	IN	46268	**800-808-4774**	317-299-3391
Sushi Doraku 8685 NW 53rd Terr Suite 201	Miami	FL	33166	**800-327-3369**	305-593-0770
Sweet Tomatoes					
15822 Bernardo Ctr Dr Suite A	San Diego	CA	92127	**800-874-1600**	858-675-1600
Swiss Chalet Rotisserie & Grill					
6303 Airport Rd	Mississauga	ON	L4V1R8	**800-860-4082**	905-405-6500
Taco Bueno Restaurants Inc					
3033 Kellway Dr Suite 122	Carrollton	TX	75006	**800-440-0778**	972-417-4800
Taco Cabana Inc					
8918 Tesoro Dr Suite 200	San Antonio	TX	78217	**800-357-9924**	210-804-0990
Taco John's International Inc					
808 W 20th St	Cheyenne	WY	82001	**800-854-0819**	307-635-0101
Taco Maker Inc 4605 Harrison Blvd	Ogden	UT	84403	**800-207-5804**	801-476-9780
Taco Mayo Inc 10405 Greenbriar Pl	Oklahoma City	OK	73159	**800-291-8226**	405-691-8226
Taco Tico Inc 2118 N Tyler St Suite B-100	Wichita	KS	67212	**877-681-0220**	316-681-0220
Taco Time International Inc					
7730 E Greenway Rd Suite 104	Scottsdale	AZ	85260	**800-547-8907**	480-443-0200
Tacone 950 S Flower St Suite 105	Los Angeles	CA	90015	**877-482-2663**	213-236-0950
Texas Roadhouse Inc					
6040 Dutchmans Ln Suite 400	Louisville	KY	40205	**800-839-7623**	502-426-9984
NASDAQ: TXRH					
TGI Friday's Worldwide Inc 4201 Marsh Ln	Carrollton	TX	75007	**800-374-3297**	972-662-5400
Thundercloud Subs 1102 W 6th St	Austin	TX	78703	**800-256-7895**	512-479-8805
Tia's Tex Mex					
1101 N Union Bower Rd Suite 160	Irving	TX	75061	**800-486-5322**	972-554-6886
Todai Franchising LLC					
3700 Wilshire Blvd Suite 560	Los Angeles	CA	90010	**888-558-6324**	213-628-1858
Togo's Eateries Inc 130 Royal St	Canton	MA	02021	**800-859-5339**	781-737-3000
Tony Roma's Famous for Ribs					
9304 Forest Ln Suite 200	Dallas	TX	75243	**800-286-7662**	214-343-7800
Tortuga Coastal Cantina 1135 Edgebrook St	Houston	TX	77034	**800-741-7574**	713-943-7574
Trader Vic's Inc 2 Fifer Ave Suite 130	Corte Madera	CA	94925	**877-762-4824**	415-927-9788
Tubby's Inc 35807 Moravian	Clinton Township	MI	48035	**800-752-0644**	586-792-2369
Una Mas Restaurants Inc 25064 Viking St	Hayward	CA	94545	**888-862-2627**	408-747-7000
Uno Chicago Grill 100 Charles Park Rd	Boston	MA	02132	**866-600-8667**	617-323-9200
Valentino's 2601 S 70th St	Lincoln	NE	68506	**888-240-8257**	402-434-9350
Village Inn 400 W 48th Ave	Denver	CO	80216	**800-800-3644**	303-296-2121
Waffle House Inc 5986 Financial Dr	Norcross	GA	30071	**800-882-9235**	770-729-5700
Weathervane Seafood Restaurant					
31 Badgers Island W	Kittery	ME	03904	**800-654-4639**	207-439-0335
Western Sizzlin Inc 1338 Plantation Rd	Roanoke	VA	24012	**800-247-8325**	540-345-3195
Western Steer Family Steakhouse					
129 Fast Ln PO Box 3130	Mooresville	NC	28117	**877-704-5939**	704-660-5939
WG Grinders 9002 Cotter St	Lewis Center	OH	43035	**877-447-3354**	614-766-2313
White Castle System Inc 555 W Goodale St	Columbus	OH	43215	**866-272-8372**	614-228-5781
Willie G's 1510 W Loop South	Houston	TX	77027	**800-552-6379**	713-850-1010
Wings To Go Inc					
846 Ritchie Hwy Suite 1 B	Severna Park	MD	21146	**800-552-9464**	
World Wrapps 401 2nd Ave S Suite 150	Seattle	WA	98104	**888-233-9727**	206-233-9727
Yaya's Flame Broiled Chicken 521 S Dort Hwy	Flint	MI	48503	**800-754-1242**	810-235-6550
Yoshinoya Beef Bowl 1603 W Sepulveda Blvd	Torrance	CA	90501	**800-576-8017**	310-539-8319
Zaxby's Franchising Inc 1040 Sounder's Blvd	Athens	GA	30606	**866-892-9297**	706-353-8107
Zero's Subs					
2859 Virginia Beach Blvd Suite 105	Virginia Beach	VA	23452	**800-588-0782**	757-486-8338
Zyng Inc 4710 rue St Ambroise Suite 320	Montreal	QC	H4C2C7	**888-966-6353**	514-288-8800

658 RETAIL STORE OPERATION & MANAGEMENT

Name / Address	City	State	ZIP	Toll-Free	Phone
B Moss Clothing Co Ltd					
550 Meadowland Pkwy	Secaucus	NJ	07094	**800-524-0639**	201-866-6677
Clark Cos NA 156 Oak St	Newton Upper Falls	MA	02464	**800-425-2757***	617-964-1222
*Cust Svc					
Cole Vision Corp 1925 Enterprise Pkwy	Twinsburg	OH	44087	**800-282-3931**	330-486-3000
E Com Ventures Inc 251 International Pkwy	Sunrise	FL	33325	**866-600-3600**	954-335-9100
NASDAQ: ECMV					
Emerging Vision Inc					
100 Quentin Roosevelt Blvd Suite 508	Garden City	NY	11530	**800-332-6302**	516-390-2100
Exprezit! Convenience Stores LLC					
6320 Quadrangle Dr Suite 200	Chapel Hill	NC	27517	**800-424-2067**	919-477-4200
Eye Care Centers of America Inc					
11103 West Ave	San Antonio	TX	78213	**800-669-1183**	210-340-3531
FFP Marketing Co Inc DBA Kwik Pantry					
2801 Glenda Ave	Fort Worth	TX	76117	**800-695-3282**	817-838-4700
Footstar Inc 933 MacArthur Blvd	Mahwah	NJ	07430	**866-208-7027**	201-934-2000
Gap Inc 2 Folsom St	San Francisco	CA	94105	**800-333-7899**	650-952-4400
NYSE: GPS					
Katz Group 10104 103rd Ave Suite 1702	Edmonton	AB	T5J0H8	**800-267-8877**	780-990-0505
Limited Brands Inc 3 Limited Pkwy	Columbus	OH	43230	**800-945-9000**	614-415-7000
NYSE: LTD					
MTS Inc 2500 Del Monte St	West Sacramento	CA	95691	**800-225-0880**	916-373-2500
National Vision Inc 296 Grayson Hwy	Lawrenceville	GA	30045	**800-571-5202**	770-822-3600
AMEX: NVI					
OptiCare Health Systems Inc					
87 Grandview Ave	Waterbury	CT	06708	**800-225-5393**	203-574-2020
AMEX: OPT					

Company / Address	City	State	Zip	Toll-Free	Phone
Provide Commerce Inc 5005 Wateridge Vista Dr Suite 200 *NASDAQ: PRVD* ■ *Cust Svc	San Diego	CA	92121	**888-373-7437***	858-638-4900
RadioShack Corp 300 RadioShack Cir *NYSE: RSH*	Fort Worth	TX	76102	**800-843-7422**	817-415-3700
Schottenstein Stores Corp 1800 Moler Rd	Columbus	OH	43207	**800-743-4577**	614-221-9200
Stage Stores Inc 10201 S Main St *NASDAQ: STGS*	Houston	TX	77025	**800-315-7257**	713-667-5601
Target Corp 33 S 6th St *NYSE: TGT* ■ *Cust Svc	Minneapolis	MN	55402	**800-440-0680***	612-304-6073
Too Inc 8323 Walton Pkwy *NYSE: TOO*	New Albany	OH	43054	**800-934-4496**	614-775-3500
United Retail Group Inc 365 W Passaic St *NASDAQ: URGI*	Rochelle Park	NJ	07662	**877-708-8740**	201-845-0880
US Vision Inc 1 Harmon Dr Glen Oaks Industrial Pk	Glendora	NJ	08012	**800-524-0789**	856-228-1000
Wilsons The Leather Experts Inc 7401 Boone Ave N *NASDAQ: WLSN*	Brooklyn Park	MN	55428	**800-967-6270**	763-391-4000
Winmark Corp 4200 Dahlberg Dr Suite 100 *NASDAQ: WINA*	Minneapolis	MN	55422	**800-433-2540**	763-520-8500

659 RETIREMENT COMMUNITIES

SEE ALSO Long-Term Care Facilities

Company / Address	City	State	Zip	Toll-Free	Phone
Friendship Village of Tempe 2645 E Southern Ave	Tempe	AZ	85282	**800-824-1112**	480-831-5000
Terraces of Phoenix 7550 N 16th St	Phoenix	AZ	85020	**877-279-6207**	602-944-4455
Butterfield Trail Village 1923 E Joyce Blvd	Fayetteville	AR	72703	**800-441-9996**	479-442-7220
Carlsbad by the Sea 2855 Carlsbad Blvd	Carlsbad	CA	92008	**800-255-1556**	760-729-2377
Carmel Valley Manor 8545 Carmel Valley Rd	Carmel	CA	93923	**800-544-5546**	831-624-1281
Covenant Village of Turlock 2125 N Olive Ave	Turlock	CA	95382	**800-485-7844**	209-632-9976
Eskaton Village 3939 Walnut Ave	Carmichael	CA	95608	**800-300-3929**	916-974-2000
Freedom Village 23442 El Toro Rd	Lake Forest	CA	92630	**800-584-8084**	949-472-4700
Hillcrest Homes 2705 Mountain View Dr *Mktg	La Verne	CA	91750	**800-566-4636***	909-593-4917
Morningside of Fullerton 800 Morningside Dr	Fullerton	CA	92835	**800-499-6010**	714-529-2952
O'Connor Woods 3400 Wagner Heights Rd	Stockton	CA	95209	**800-249-6637**	209-956-3400
Park Lane Classic Residence by Hyatt 200 Glenwood Cir	Monterey	CA	93940	**800-782-5730**	831-373-6126
Pilgrim Haven 373 Pine Ln	Los Altos	CA	94022	**877-284-7635**	650-948-8291
Redwood Terrace 710 W 13th Ave *Mktg	Escondido	CA	92025	**800-842-6775***	760-747-4306
Smith Ranch Homes 500 Deer Valley Rd *Mktg	San Rafael	CA	94903	**800-772-6264***	415-492-4900
Spring Lake Village 5555 Montgomery Dr	Santa Rosa	CA	95409	**800-795-1267**	707-538-8400
White Sands of La Jolla 7450 Olivetas Ave	La Jolla	CA	92037	**800-892-7817**	858-454-4201
Heritage Club 2020 S Monroe St	Denver	CO	80210	**877-756-0025**	303-757-1404
Villas at Sunny Acres 2501 E 104th Ave	Denver	CO	80233	**800-447-2092**	303-452-4181
Arbors The 403 W Center St	Manchester	CT	06040	**888-227-2677**	860-647-9343
Duncaster 40 Loeffler Rd	Bloomfield	CT	06002	**800-545-5065**	860-726-2000
East Hill Woods 611 E Hill Rd	Southbury	CT	06488	**800-435-4249**	203-262-6161
Westfield Court 77 3rd St	Stamford	CT	06905	**800-443-3245**	203-327-4551
Methodist Manor House 1001 Middleford Rd	Seaford	DE	19973	**800-775-4593**	302-629-4593
Abbey Delray 2000 Lowson Blvd	Delray Beach	FL	33445	**800-936-7397**	561-454-2000
Azalea Trace 10100 Hillview DR	Pensacola	FL	32514	**800-828-8274**	850-478-5200
East Ridge Retirement Village 19301 SW 87th Ave	Miami	FL	33157	**800-605-7778**	305-256-3564
Fleet Landing Retirement Community 1 Fleet Landing Blvd	Atlantic Beach	FL	32233	**800-872-8761**	904-246-9900
Freedom Village 6501 17th Ave W	Bradenton	FL	34209	**800-841-4676**	941-798-8122
Harbour's Edge 401 E Linton Blvd	Delray Beach	FL	33483	**800-232-1358**	561-272-7979
Indian River Estates 2250 Indian Creek Blvd W *Mktg	Vero Beach	FL	32966	**800-544-0277***	772-562-7400
Mayflower Retirement Community 1620 Mayflower Ct	Winter Park	FL	32792	**800-228-6518**	407-672-1620
Saint Andrews Estates 6152 Verde Trail N *Mktg	Boca Raton	FL	33433	**800-850-2287***	561-487-5500
Shell Point Village 15000 Shell Point Blvd *Mktg	Fort Myers	FL	33908	**800-780-1131***	239-466-1111
Stratford Court 45 Katherine Blvd	Palm Harbor	FL	34684	**800-772-2622**	727-787-1500
Village on the Green 500 Village Pl *Mktg	Longwood	FL	32779	**800-432-8833***	407-788-2300
Clark-Lindsey Village 101 W Windsor Rd	Urbana	IL	61802	**800-998-2581**	217-344-2144
Westminster Place 3200 Grant St	Evanston	IL	60201	**800-896-9095**	847-492-4800
Larksfield Place 7373 E 29th St N	Wichita	KS	67226	**877-636-1234**	316-636-1000
Asbury Methodist Village 201 Russell Ave	Gaithersburg	MD	20877	**800-327-2879**	301-330-3000
Fairhaven 7200 3rd Ave	Sykesville	MD	21784	**800-241-9997**	410-795-8800
Heron Point of Chestertown 501 E Campus Ave	Chestertown	MD	21620	**800-327-9138**	410-778-7300
Loomis Communities 246 N Main St	South Hadley	MA	01075	**800-865-7655**	413-532-5325
Willows The 1 Lyman St	Westborough	MA	01581	**800-464-4730**	508-366-4730
Friendship Village 1400 N Drake Rd	Kalamazoo	MI	49006	**800-613-3984**	269-381-0560
Naval Home 1800 Beach Dr	Gulfport	MS	39507	**800-332-3527**	228-897-4026
John Knox Village 400 NW Murray Rd	Lee's Summit	MO	64081	**800-892-5669**	816-524-8400
Laclede Groves Retirement Community 723 S Laclede Station Rd	Saint Louis	MO	63119	**877-363-1211**	314-968-5570
Hillcrest Terrace 200 Alliance Way	Manchester	NH	03102	**800-862-9490**	603-645-6500
RiverMead Retirement Community 150 RiverMead Rd	Peterborough	NH	03458	**800-200-5433**	603-924-0062
Applewood Estates 1 Applewood Dr *Mktg	Freehold	NJ	07728	**800-438-0888***	732-780-7370
Cadbury Retirement Community 2150 Rt 38	Cherry Hill	NJ	08002	**800-422-3287**	856-667-4550
Classic Residence by Hyatt 655 Pomander Walk	Teaneck	NJ	07666	**800-292-7474**	201-836-7474
Crestwood Manor 50 Lacey Rd	Whiting	NJ	08759	**800-526-1665**	732-849-4900
Evergreens The 309 Bridgeboro Rd	Moorestown	NJ	08057	**800-371-4918**	856-439-2000
Meadowlakes 300 Meadow Lakes	Hightstown	NJ	08520	**800-222-0609**	609-448-4100
Medford Leas 1 Medford Leas Way	Medford	NJ	08055	**800-331-4302**	609-654-3000
Monroe Village 1 David Brainerd Dr	Monroe Township	NJ	08831	**800-833-4447**	732-521-6400
La Vida Llena 10501 Lagrima de Oro NE	Albuquerque	NM	87111	**800-922-1344**	505-293-4001
Fountains at Millbrook 79 Flint Rd	Millbrook	NY	12545	**800-433-6092**	845-677-8550
Kendal at Ithaca 2230 N Triphammer Rd	Ithaca	NY	14850	**800-253-6325**	607-266-5300
Bermuda Village 142 Bermuda Village Dr *Mktg	Advance	NC	27006	**800-843-5433***	336-998-6535
Carol Woods Retirement Community 750 Weaver Dairy Rd	Chapel Hill	NC	27514	**800-518-9333**	919-968-4511
Carolina Meadows 100 Carolina Meadows	Chapel Hill	NC	27517	**800-458-6756**	919-942-4014
First Community Village 1800 Riverside Dr	Columbus	OH	43212	**888-328-9511**	614-486-9511
Kendal at Oberlin 600 Kendal Dr *Mktg	Oberlin	OH	44074	**800-548-9469***	440-775-0094
Laurel Lake Retirement Community 200 Laurel Lake Dr	Hudson	OH	44236	**866-650-0681**	866-650-2100
Maple Knoll Village 11100 Springfield Pike	Cincinnati	OH	45246	**800-789-6008**	513-782-2717
Epworth Villa 14901 N Pennsylvania Ave	Oklahoma City	OK	73134	**800-579-8776**	405-752-1200
Golden Oaks Village 5801 N Oakwood Rd	Enid	OK	73703	**800-259-0914**	580-234-2817
Capital Manor 1955 Dallas Hwy NW	Salem	OR	97304	**800-637-0327**	503-362-4101
Rogue Valley Manor 1200 Mira Mar Ave	Medford	OR	97504	**800-848-7868**	541-857-7777
Terwilliger Plaza 2545 SW Terwilliger Blvd	Portland	OR	97201	**800-875-4211**	503-226-4911
Willamette View 12705 SE River Rd	Milwaukie	OR	97222	**800-446-0670**	503-654-6581
Foxdale Village 500 E Marylyn Ave	State College	PA	16801	**800-253-4951**	814-238-3322
Martins Run 11 Martins Run	Media	PA	19063	**800-327-3875**	610-353-7660
American Retirement Corp 111 Westwood Pl Suite 200 *NYSE: ACR*	Brentwood	TN	37027	**888-221-7317**	615-221-2250
John Knox Village of the Rio Grande Valley 1300 S Border Ave *Mktg	Weslaco	TX	78596	**800-245-6526***	956-968-4575
Manor Park Inc 2208 North Loop 250 W	Midland	TX	79707	**800-523-9898**	432-689-9898
Culpeper Baptist Retirement Community 12425 Village Loop	Culpeper	VA	22701	**800-894-2411**	540-825-2411
Shenandoah Valley Westminster-Canterbury 300 Westminster-Canterbury Dr	Winchester	VA	22603	**800-492-9463**	540-665-5914
Westminster-Canterbury Richmond 1600 Westbrook Ave	Richmond	VA	23227	**800-445-9904**	804-264-6000
Judson Park 23600 Marine View Dr S	Des Moines	WA	98198	**877-263-8484**	206-824-4000

660 RETREATS - SPIRITUAL

Company / Address	City	State	Zip	Toll-Free	Phone
Cenacle Retreat House & Spirituality Center 29 W 012 Batavia Rd	Warrenville	IL	60555	**800-240-6702**	630-393-1231
Chopra Center at La Costa Resort & Spa 2013 Costa del Mar Rd	Carlsbad	CA	92009	**888-424-6772**	760-931-7566
Elat Chayyim 99 Mill Hook Rd	Accord	NY	12404	**800-398-2630**	845-626-0157
Expanding Light 14618 Tyler Foote Rd	Nevada City	CA	95959	**800-346-5350**	530-478-7518
Hollyhock Box 127	Mansons Landing	BC	V0P1K0	**800-933-6339**	250-935-6576
Kalani Oceanside Retreat RR 2 Box 4500	Pahoa	HI	96778	**800-800-6886**	808-965-7828
Kordes Enrichment Center 841 E 14th St	Ferdinand	IN	47532	**800-880-2777**	812-367-2777
Laurelville Mennonite Church Center Rt 5 Box 145	Mount Pleasant	PA	15666	**800-839-1021**	724-423-2056
Living Water Worship & Teaching Center 595 N Aspaas Rd *Mktg	Cornville	AZ	86325	**888-627-5631***	928-634-4421
Merritt Center PO Box 2087	Payson	AZ	85547	**800-414-9880**	928-474-4268
Omega Institute for Holistic Studies 150 Lake Dr	Rhinebeck	NY	12572	**800-944-1001**	845-266-4444
Pendle Hill 338 Plush Mill Rd	Wallingford	PA	19086	**800-742-3150**	610-566-4507
Pumpkin Hollow Farm 1184 Rt 11	Craryville	NY	12521	**877-325-3583**	518-325-3583
Shambhala Mountain Center 4921 County Rd 68C	Red Feather Lakes	CO	80545	**888-788-7221**	970-881-2184
Sivananda Ashram Yoga Ranch Budd Rd Box 195	Woodbourne	NY	12788	**800-783-9642**	845-436-6492
Still Life Retreat 394591 Concession 2 RR1	Durham	ON	N0G1R0	**877-584-8880**	519-369-3663

661 ROLLING MILL MACHINERY

SEE ALSO Metalworking Machinery

Company / Address	City	State	Zip	Toll-Free	Phone
Bradbury Co Inc PO Box 667	Moundridge	KS	67107	**800-397-6394**	620-345-6394
Engel Industries Inc 8122 Reilly Ave	Saint Louis	MO	63111	**800-428-6046**	314-638-0100
Formtek Metal Forming Inc 26565 Miles Rd Suite 200	Cleveland	OH	44128	**800-631-0520**	216-292-4460
Littell International Inc 145 N Swift Rd	Addison	IL	60101	**800-548-8355**	630-916-6662
Rosemont Industries Inc 1700 West St	Cincinnati	OH	45215	**800-782-9958**	513-733-4277
Waterbury Farrel Technologies Inc 200 1st Gulf Blvd	Brampton	ON	L6W4T5	**800-387-3834**	905-455-0402
Weatherford-Enterra-Pearland Mfg Co 3810 Magnolia St	Pearland	TX	77581	**800-331-3387**	281-652-1300
WHEMCO Inc 5 Hot Metal St	Pittsburgh	PA	15203	**800-800-7686**	412-390-2700

662 ROYALTY TRUSTS

Company / Address	City	State	Zip	Toll-Free	Phone
Acclaim Energy Trust 255 5th Ave SW Suite 1900 *TSE: AE.DB*	Calgary	AB	T2P2Z1	**877-539-6300**	403-539-6300
APF Energy Trust 144 4th Ave SW Suite 2100	Calgary	AB	T2P3N4	**800-838-9206**	403-294-1000
ARC Energy Trust 440 2nd Ave SW Suite 2100 *TSE: AET.UN*	Calgary	AB	T2P5E9	**888-272-4900**	403-503-8600
Cross Timbers Royalty Trust 901 Main St Bank of America Plaza 17th Fl *NYSE: CRT*	Dallas	TX	75202	**877-228-5084**	214-209-2400
Dominion Resources Black Warrior Trust 901 Main St Bank of America Plaza 17th Fl *NYSE: DOM*	Dallas	TX	75202	**800-365-6548**	214-209-2400
Freehold Royalty Trust 144 4th Ave SW Suite 400	Calgary	AB	T2P3N4	**888-257-1873**	403-221-0848
Hugoton Royalty Trust 901 Main St Bank of America Plaza 17th Fl *NYSE: HGT*	Dallas	TX	75202	**877-228-5083**	214-209-2400

				Toll-Free	Phone
Marine Petroleum Trust					
901 Main St Bank of America Plaza 17th Fl	Dallas	TX	75202	**800-985-0794**	214-209-2310
NASDAQ: MARPS					
Pengrowth Energy Trust					
111 5th Ave SW 29th Fl	Calgary	AB	T2P3Y6	**800-223-4122**	403-233-0224
NYSE: PGH					
Petrofund Energy Trust					
444 7th Ave SW Suite 600	Calgary	AB	T2P0X8	**888-318-1457**	403-218-8625
TSE: PTF.UN					
PrimeWest Energy Trust					
150 6th Ave SW Suite 5100	Calgary	AB	T2P3Y7	**877-968-7878**	403-234-6600
Sabine Royalty Trust					
901 Main St 17th Fl Bank of America Plaza	Dallas	TX	75202	**800-365-6541**	214-209-2400
NYSE: SBR					
San Juan Basin Royalty Trust					
2525 Ridgmar Blvd Suite 100	Fort Worth	TX	76116	**866-809-4553**	
NYSE: SJT					
Tidelands Royalty Trust PO Box 830650	Dallas	TX	75202	**800-985-0794**	214-209-2400
Torch Energy Royalty Trust					
1221 Lamar Suite 1600	Houston	TX	77010	**800-536-7453**	
NYSE: TRU					
Viking Energy Royalty Trust					
330 5th Ave SW Calgary Pl Suite 400	Calgary	AB	T2P0L4	**877-292-2527**	403-268-3175
Williams Coal Seam Gas Royalty Trust					
901 Main St Bank of America Plaza 17th Fl	Dallas	TX	75202	**800-365-6544**	214-209-2364
NYSE: WTU					

663 RUBBER GOODS

				Toll-Free	Phone
3M Commercial Care Div					
3M Center Bldg 223-4N-14	Saint Paul	MN	55144	**800-847-3021**	800-626-8578
Aero Tec Labs Inc 45 Spear Rd Industrial Pk	Ramsey	NJ	07446	**800-526-5330**	201-825-1400
Alliance Rubber Co					
210 Carpenter Dam Rd	Hot Springs	AR	71901	**800-626-5940**	501-262-2700
Barry Controls 40 Guest St	Brighton	MA	02135	**800-227-7962**	617-787-1555
Biltrite Corp 51 Sawyer Rd	Waltham	MA	02454	**800-245-8748**	781-647-1700
BRP Mfg Co 637 N Jackson St	Lima	OH	45801	**800-858-0482**	419-228-4441
Carlisle Tire & Wheel Mfg 23 Windham Blvd	Aiken	SC	29805	**800-827-1001***	803-643-2900
*Sales					
Creative Urethanes Inc PO Box 919	Purcellville	VA	20134	**800-343-6591***	540-338-7139
*Sales					
Dodge-Regupol Inc 715 Fountain Ave	Lancaster	PA	17601	**800-322-1923**	717-295-3400
Fiskars Brands Inc Royal Floor Mats Div					
3000 W Orange Ave	Apopka	FL	32703	**800-621-4253**	407-889-5533
Griswold Rubber Co Inc PO Box 638	Moosup	CT	06354	**800-472-8788***	860-564-3321
*Cust Svc					
Kent Elastomer Products Inc 1500 St Claire Ave	Kent	OH	44240	**800-331-4762***	330-673-1011
*Cust Svc					
Koneta Inc 1400 Lunar Dr	Wapakoneta	OH	45895	**800-331-0775**	419-739-4200
Kraco Enterprises Inc 505 E Euclid Ave	Compton	CA	90224	**800-678-1910**	310-639-0666
Ludlow Composites Corp 2100 Commerce Dr	Fremont	OH	43420	**800-628-5463**	419-332-5531
Monarch Rubber Co 3500 Pulaski Hwy	Baltimore	MD	21224	**800-638-6312**	410-342-8510
MSM Industries Inc 802 Swan Dr	Smyrna	TN	37167	**800-648-6648**	615-355-4355
Musson RC Rubber Co Inc					
1320 E Archwood Ave	Akron	OH	44306	**800-321-2381***	330-773-7651
*Cust Svc					
NRI Industries Inc 394 Symington Ave	Toronto	ON	M6N2W3	**800-387-8501**	416-657-1111
Pawling Corp 157 Charles Colman Blvd	Pawling	NY	12564	**800-431-0101**	845-855-1000
Plasticoid Co 249 W High St	Elkton	MD	21921	**800-398-2806**	410-398-2800
R & K Industrial Products Co 1945 N 7th St	Richmond	CA	94801	**800-842-7655***	510-234-7212
*Cust Svc					
RC Musson Rubber Co Inc					
1320 E Archwood Ave	Akron	OH	44306	**800-321-2381***	330-773-7651
*Cust Svc					
Rex-Hide Inc 705 S Lyons Ave	Tyler	TX	75702	**800-527-8403**	903-593-7387
Royal Floor Mats Div Fiskars Brands Inc					
3000 W Orange Ave	Apopka	FL	32703	**800-621-4253**	407-889-5533
Seismic Energy Products LP 518 Progress Way	Athens	TX	75751	**800-603-8766**	903-675-8571
SMR Technologies Inc 93 Nettie Fenwick Rd	Fenwick	WV	26202	**800-767-6899**	304-846-2554
Teknor Apex Co 505 Central Ave	Pawtucket	RI	02861	**800-556-3864**	401-725-8000
Tennessee Mat Co Inc 1414 4th Ave S	Nashville	TN	37210	**800-264-3030**	615-254-8381
Vulcan Corp 30 Garfield Pl Suite 1040	Cincinnati	OH	45202	**800-447-1146***	513-621-2850
*Sales					

664 RUBBER GOODS - MECHANICAL

				Toll-Free	Phone
AirBoss Polymer Products Corp					
200 Veterans Blvd	South Haven	MI	49090	**888-258-7252**	269-637-2181
Alert Mfg & Supply Co					
520 S 18th St	West Des Moines	IA	50265	**800-247-4178**	515-223-5843
American National Rubber Co Main & High St	Ceredo	WV	25507	**800-624-3410***	304-453-1311
*Cust Svc					
Ames Rubber Corp 19 Ames Blvd	Hamburg	NJ	07419	**800-697-9101**	973-827-9101
Armada Rubber Mfg Co					
24586 Armada Ridge Rd PO Box 579	Armada	MI	48005	**800-842-8311**	586-784-9135
Atlantic India Rubber Co					
1437 Kentucky Rt 1428	Hager Hills	KY	41222	**800-476-6638**	606-789-9115
Boyd Corp 600 S McClure Rd	Modesto	CA	95357	**800-554-0200**	209-236-1111
Chardon Rubber Co 373 Washington St	Chardon	OH	44024	**800-322-0193**	440-285-2161
Chemprene Inc 483 Fishkill Ave	Beacon	NY	12508	**800-431-9981**	845-831-2800
Chicago Manifold Products Co					
171 E Marquardt Dr	Wheeling	IL	60090	**800-323-7735***	847-459-6000
*Sales					
Colonial Diversified Polymer Products LLC					
2055 Forrest St Ext	Dyersburg	TN	38024	**800-303-3606**	731-287-3636
Fabreeka International Inc					
1023 Turnpike St	Stoughton	MA	02072	**800-322-7352***	781-341-3655
*Cust Svc					
Finzer Roller Co 129 Rawls Rd	Des Plaines	IL	60018	**888-486-1900**	847-390-6200
Griffith Rubber Mills 2625 NW Industrial St	Portland	OR	97210	**800-321-9677**	503-226-6971
Groendyk Mfg Co Inc 19318 Main St	Buchanan	VA	24066	**800-879-4395**	540-254-1010
Hiawatha Rubber Co 1700 67th Ave N	Minneapolis	MN	55430	**800-728-3845**	763-566-0900
Holz Rubber Co Inc 1129 S Sacramento St	Lodi	CA	95240	**800-285-1600**	209-368-7171
Jasper Rubber Products Inc 1010 1st Ave W	Jasper	IN	47546	**800-457-7457**	812-482-3242
Johnson Rubber Co					
16025 Johnson St PO Box 67	Middlefield	OH	44062	**800-362-1951**	440-632-1611
Lauren Mfg 2228 Reiser Ave SE	New Philadelphia	OH	44663	**800-683-0676**	330-339-3373
Lavelle Industries Inc 665 McHenry St	Burlington	WI	53105	**800-528-3553**	262-763-2434
Longwood Elastomers Inc					
706 Green Valley Rd Suite 212	Greensboro	NC	27408	**800-374-2837**	336-272-3710
Lord Corp 111 Lord Dr	Cary	NC	27511	**800-524-2885**	919-468-5979
Mantaline Corp 4754 E High St	Mantua	OH	44255	**800-321-0948**	330-274-2264
Minor Rubber Co Inc 49 Ackerman St	Bloomfield	NJ	07003	**800-433-6886**	973-338-6800
MOCAP Inc 13100 Manchester Rd	Saint Louis	MO	63131	**800-633-6775**	314-543-4000
Molded Rubber & Plastic Corp					
13161 W Glendale Ave	Butler	WI	53007	**888-781-7122**	262-781-7122
Precision Assoc Inc					
740 Washington Ave N	Minneapolis	MN	55401	**800-394-6590***	612-333-7464
*Cust Svc					
Prince Rubber & Plastics Co Inc 137 Arthur St	Buffalo	NY	14207	**800-225-8505**	716-877-7400
Rubber Engineering PO Box 26188	Salt Lake City	UT	84126	**800-453-6403***	801-530-7887
*Cust Svc					
Sperry & Rice Mfg Co LLC 9146 US Hwy 52	Brookville	IN	47012	**800-541-9277**	765-647-4141
Thermodyn Corp 3550 Silica Rd	Sylvania	OH	43560	**800-654-6518**	419-841-7782
Universal Polymer & Rubber Ltd					
15730 S Madison Rd	Middlefield	OH	44062	**800-782-2375**	440-632-1691
Vernay Laboratories Inc					
120 E South College St	Yellow Springs	OH	45387	**800-837-6291**	937-767-7261
YUSA Corp					
151 Jamison Rd SW	Washington Court House	OH	43160	**800-395-0335**	740-335-0335

665 SAFES, VAULTS, DEPOSIT BOXES, ETC - MFR

				Toll-Free	Phone
Allied Fire & Security Inc 425 W 2nd Ave	Spokane	WA	99201	**800-448-8338**	509-624-3152
American Locker Group Inc 608 Allen St	Jamestown	NY	14701	**800-828-9118**	716-664-9600
NASDAQ: ALGI					
American Locker Security Systems Inc					
608 Allen St	Jamestown	NY	14701	**800-828-9118***	716-664-9600
*Sales					
American Security Products Inc					
11925 Pacific Ave	Fontana	CA	92337	**800-421-6142**	951-685-9680
Armor Safe Technologies LLC					
PO Box 560275	The Colony	TX	75056	**800-487-2766**	972-624-5734
Center Mfg Co 540 Goodrich Rd	Bellevue	OH	44811	**800-377-7736**	419-483-4852
Diebold Inc 5995 Mayfair Rd	North Canton	OH	44720	**800-999-3600**	330-490-4000
NYSE: DBD					
Engage Technologies Inc 8419 Sunstate St	Tampa	FL	33634	**800-388-2219**	813-885-6615
FireKing International Inc					
101 Security Pkwy	New Albany	IN	47150	**800-528-9900**	812-948-8400
FKI Security Group 101 Security Pkwy	New Albany	IN	47150	**800-457-2424**	812-948-8400
MMF Industries Inc 370 Alice St	Wheeling	IL	60090	**800-445-8293***	847-537-7890
*Cust Svc					
National Safe Corp					
4400 34th St N Unit G	Saint Petersburg	FL	33714	**800-634-8174**	727-525-7800
ProSteel 1400 S State St	Provo	UT	84606	**877-501-7233**	801-373-2385
Schwab Corp PO Box 5088	Lafayette	IN	47903	**800-428-7678**	765-447-9470
Sentry Group 900 Linden Ave	Rochester	NY	14625	**800-828-1438**	585-381-4900
Tread Corp PO Box 13207	Roanoke	VA	24032	**800-900-6881**	540-982-6881

666 SAFETY EQUIPMENT - MFR

SEE ALSO Medical Supplies - Mfr; Personal Protective Equipment & Clothing

				Toll-Free	Phone
3M Safety Security & Protection Services Div					
3M Ctr	Saint Paul	MN	55144	**800-364-3577**	651-733-1110
ACR Electronics Inc					
5757 Ravenswood Rd	Fort Lauderdale	FL	33312	**800-432-0227**	954-981-3333
Am-Safe Inc 1043 N 47th Ave	Phoenix	AZ	85043	**800-228-1567**	602-850-2850
Ansul Inc 1 Stanton St	Marinette	WI	54143	**800-862-6785**	715-735-7411
Badger Fire Protection Inc					
4251 Seminole Tr	Charlottesville	VA	22911	**800-446-3857**	
Bradley Corp PO Box 309	Menomonee Falls	WI	53051	**800-272-3539**	262-251-6000
Buckeye Fire Equipment Co					
110 Kings Rd	Kings Mountain	NC	28086	**800-438-1028**	704-739-7415
Carsonite International Corp					
605 Bob Gifford Blvd	Early Branch	SC	29916	**800-648-7974**	803-943-9115
DBI/SALA & Protecta 3965 Pepin Ave	Red Wing	MN	55066	**800-328-6146**	651-388-8282
Encon Safety Products Co					
6825 W Sam Houston Pkwy N	Houston	TX	77041	**800-283-6266**	713-466-1449
Flag Fire Equipment Ltd 1 Stanton St	Marinette	WI	54143	**800-265-0804**	
Gemtor Inc 1 Johnson Ave	Matawan	NJ	07747	**800-405-9048**	732-583-6200
H Koch & Sons Co 5410 E La Palma Ave	Anaheim	CA	92807	**800-433-5787**	714-779-7000
Hawkins Traffic Safety Supply					
1255 E Shore Hwy	Berkeley	CA	94710	**800-772-3995**	510-525-4040
ITW Shippers Products					
1203 N Main St	Mount Pleasant	TN	38474	**800-933-7731**	931-379-7731
Kinedyne Inc 151 Industrial Pkwy	North Branch	NJ	08876	**800-848-6057**	908-231-1800
Koch H & Sons Co 5410 E La Palma Ave	Anaheim	CA	92807	**800-433-5787**	714-779-7000
Larsen's Mfg Co 7421 Commerce Ln NE	Minneapolis	MN	55432	**800-527-7367**	763-571-1181
Niedner Ltd 675 Merrill St	Coaticook	QC	J1A2S2	**800-567-2703**	514-637-5572
Ocenco Inc 10225 82nd Ave	Pleasant Prairie	WI	53158	**800-932-2293**	262-947-9000
Peck & Hale LLC 180 Division Ave	West Sayville	NY	11796	**800-448-7325**	631-589-2510
Plastic Safety Systems Inc 2444 Baldwin Rd	Cleveland	OH	44104	**800-662-6338**	216-231-8590
Potter-Roemer PO Box 3527	City of Industry	CA	91744	**800-366-3473**	626-855-4890
Quixote Corp 35 E Wacker Dr Suite 1100	Chicago	IL	60601	**888-323-6374**	312-467-6755
NASDAQ: QUIX					
Reflexite North America 315 South St	New Britain	CT	06051	**800-654-7570**	860-223-9297
Security Chain Co PO Box 949	Clackamas	OR	97015	**800-547-6806**	503-656-5400
United Rental Highway Technology					
880 N Addison Rd	Villa Park	IL	60181	**800-323-2462***	630-932-4600
*Cust Svc					

667 SAFETY EQUIPMENT - WHOL

				Toll-Free	Phone
Allstar Fire Equipment Inc 12328 Lower Azusa Rd	Arcadia	CA	91006	**800-425-5787**	626-652-0900
Alltype Fire Protection Co 9495 Page Ave PO Box 32432	Saint Louis	MO	63132	**800-369-7101**	314-426-7100
Ally Industries Inc 30-A Progress Ave	Seymour	CT	06483	**800-772-3389**	203-888-7873
American Cleanroom Supply LLC 1042-B El Camino Real Suite 414	Encinitas	CA	92024	**888-901-3220**	
Brooks Equipment Co Inc 9700 Research Dr	Charlotte	NC	28262	**800-826-3473**	704-596-9438
Broward Fire Equipment & Service Inc 101 SW 6th St	Fort Lauderdale	FL	33301	**800-866-3473**	954-467-6625
Calolympic Glove & Safety Co Inc 1720 Delilah St	Corona	CA	92879	**800-421-6630**	951-340-2229
Continental Safety Equipment Inc 899 Apollo Rd	Eagan	MN	55121	**800-844-7003**	651-454-7233
Empire Safety & Supply Inc 4321 Anthony Ct Unit 5	Rocklin	CA	95677	**800-376-6337**	
Fire Fighters Equipment Co 3038 Lenox Ave	Jacksonville	FL	32254	**800-488-8542**	904-388-8542
Graves Fire Protection PO Box 451	Lunenburg	MA	01462	**800-214-1456**	978-345-0165
Industrial Safety & Supply Co Inc 176 Newington Rd	West Hartford	CT	06110	**800-243-2316**	860-233-9881
Lab Safety Supply Inc PO Box 1368	Janesville	WI	53547	**800-356-0783**	608-754-2345
LaFrance Equipment Corp 516 Erie St	Elmira	NY	14904	**800-873-8808**	607-733-5511
Minnesota Conway 314 W 86th St Suite 101	Bloomington	MN	55420	**800-223-2587**	952-345-3473
Nardini Fire Equipment Co Inc 405 County Rd 'E' W	Saint Paul	MN	55126	**888-627-3464**	651-483-6631
Orr Safety Corp 11601 Interchange Dr	Louisville	KY	40229	**800-726-6789**	502-774-5791
PK Safety Supply 2005 Clement Ave Bldg 9	Alameda	CA	94501	**800-829-9580**	510-337-8880
Saf-T-Gard International Inc 205 Huehl Rd	Northbrook	IL	60062	**800-548-4273**	847-291-1600
Safety Products Inc 3517 Craftsman Blvd	Lakeland	FL	33803	**800-248-6860**	863-665-3601
Safety Solutions Inc 6161 Shamrock Ct PO Box 8100	Dublin	OH	43016	**800-232-7463**	614-799-9900
Safety Supply South Inc 100 Centrum Dr	Irmo	SC	29063	**800-522-8344**	803-732-1500
Safety Today 2425 Speigel Dr Suite A	Groveport	OH	43125	**800-837-5900**	614-409-7200
Safeware Inc 3200 Hubbard Rd	Landover	MD	20785	**800-331-6707**	301-683-1234
Sanderson Safety Supply Co 1101 SE 3rd Ave	Portland	OR	97214	**800-547-0927**	503-238-5700
Skaggs Cos 3828 S Main St	Murray	UT	84115	**800-879-1787**	801-261-4400
Sun Devil Fire Equipment Inc 2211 S 3rd Dr	Phoenix	AZ	85003	**800-536-3845**	623-245-0636
United Fire Equipment Co 335 N 4th Ave	Tucson	AZ	85705	**800-362-0150**	520-622-3639
Vallen Corp 521 N Sam Houston Pkwy E Suite 300	Houston	TX	77060	**800-372-3389**	281-500-4500
Wayest Safety Inc 3745 NW 37th Pl	Oklahoma City	OK	73112	**800-256-1003**	405-942-7101
Wenaas AGS Inc 202 E Larkspur St	Victoria	TX	77904	**888-576-2668**	361-576-2668
Wise El Santo Co Inc 11000 Linpage Pl	Saint Louis	MO	63132	**800-727-8541**	314-428-3100
Zink Safety Equipment 15101 W 110th St	Lenexa	KS	66219	**800-255-1101**	913-492-9444

668 SALT

SEE ALSO Food Products - Mfr - Spices, Seasonings, Herbs

				Toll-Free	Phone
Cargill Inc North America 15407 McGinty Rd	Wayzata	MN	55391	**800-227-4455**	952-742-7575
Cargill Salt Inc 400 S Hwy 169 Suite 600	Saint Louis Park	MN	55426	**888-385-7258**	952-984-8280
Compass Minerals International Inc 8300 College Blvd *NYSE: CMP* ■ *Cust Svc	Overland Park	KS	66210	**800-253-7934***	913-344-9200
Cutler-Magner Co PO Box 16807	Duluth	MN	55816	**800-232-1302**	218-722-3981
Morton Salt Group PO Box 1496	New Iberia	LA	70562	**800-551-9086**	337-867-4231
United Salt Corp 4800 San Felipe St	Houston	TX	77056	**800-554-8658**	713-877-2600

669 SATELLITE COMMUNICATIONS SERVICES

SEE ALSO Cable & Other Pay Television Services; Internet Service Providers (ISPs); Telecommunications Services

				Toll-Free	Phone
Aliant Inc PO Box 880 *TSE: AIT*	Halifax	NS	B3J2W3	**800-688-9811**	877-225-4268
ARINC Inc 2551 Riva Rd	Annapolis	MD	21401	**800-492-2182**	410-266-4000
Globalstar LP 461 S Milpitas Blvd Bldg 5	Milpitas	CA	95035	**877-245-6225**	408-933-4000
International Satellite Services Inc 1004 Collier Ctr Way Suite 205	Naples	FL	34110	**888-511-3403**	239-598-2241
Loral Skynet Ltd 500 Hills Dr	Bedminster	NJ	07921	**800-242-2422**	908-470-2300
Motient Corp 300 Knightsbridge Pkwy	Lincolnshire	IL	60069	**800-872-6222**	847-478-4200
MTN/ATC Teleports 3044 N Commerce Pkwy	Miramar	FL	33025	**877-464-4686**	954-538-4000
ORBCOMM LLC 21700 Atlantic Blvd	Dulles	VA	20166	**800-672-2666**	703-433-6300
SES Americom Inc 4 Research Way *Sales	Princeton	NJ	08540	**800-273-0329***	609-987-4000
SpaceCom Systems Inc 1950 E 71st St	Tulsa	OK	74136	**800-950-6690**	
StarBand Communciations Inc 1760 Old Meadow Rd *Cust Svc	McLean	VA	22102	**800-478-2722***	703-287-3000
Vyvx Integrated Transmission Services 1 Technology Ctr	Tulsa	OK	74103	**800-364-0807**	918-547-5760
XM Satellite Radio Holdings Inc 1500 Eckington Pl NE *NASDAQ: XMSR*	Washington	DC	20002	**877-967-2346**	202-380-4000

670 SAW BLADES & HANDSAWS

SEE ALSO Tools - Hand & Edge

				Toll-Free	Phone
Armstrong-Blum Mfg Co Inc 3501 Marvel Dr	Oshkosh	WI	54902	**800-472-9464**	920-236-7200
Atlanta Sharptech 1594 Evans Dr SW	Atlanta	GA	30310	**800-241-5296**	404-752-6000
Blount Outdoor Products Group 4909 SE International Way	Portland	OR	97222	**800-223-5168**	503-653-8881
Contour Saws Inc 1217 Thacker St *Sales	Des Plaines	IL	60016	**800-458-9034***	847-824-1146
Diamond Saw Works Inc 12290 Olean Rd	Chaffee	NY	14030	**800-828-1180**	716-496-7417
Disston Precision Inc 6795 State Rd *Cust Svc	Philadelphia	PA	19135	**800-238-1007***	215-338-1200
Great Neck Saw Mfg Inc 165 E 2nd St *Cust Svc	Mineola	NY	11501	**800-457-0600***	516-746-5352
ICS Blount Inc 4909 SE International Way	Portland	OR	97222	**800-321-1240**	503-653-8881
International Knife & Saw Inc 3940 Olympic Blvd Suite 350	Erlanger	KY	41018	**800-354-9872**	859-371-0333
MK Diamond Products Inc 1315 Storm Pkwy	Torrance	CA	90501	**800-421-5830**	310-539-5221
MK Morse Co 1101 11th St SE	Canton	OH	44707	**800-733-3377**	330-453-8187
Simonds International 135 Intervale Rd	Fitchburg	MA	01420	**800-343-1616**	978-343-3731
Vermont American Corp 101 S 5th St Suite 2300	Louisville	KY	40202	**800-626-2834**	502-625-2000

671 SAWMILLS & PLANING MILLS

				Toll-Free	Phone
Ainsworth Lumber Co Ltd 1055 Dunsmuir St Suite 3194 *TSE: ANS*	Vancouver	BC	V7X1L3	**877-661-3200**	604-661-3200
Anthony Forest Products Co 309 N Washington Ave	El Dorado	AR	71730	**800-221-2326**	870-862-3414
Averitt Hardwoods International PO Box 2217	Clarksville	TN	37042	**800-647-8394**	931-647-8394
Beadles Lumber Co Inc PO Box 3457	Moultrie	GA	31776	**800-763-2400**	229-985-6996
Buse Timber & Sales Inc 3812 28th Pl NE	Everett	WA	98205	**800-305-2577**	425-258-2577
Buskirk Lumber Co 319 Oak St	Freeport	MI	49325	**800-860-9663**	616-765-5103
Cersosimo Lumber Co Inc 1103 Vernon St	Brattleboro	VT	05301	**800-326-5647**	802-254-4508
Collins Cos 1618 SW 1st Ave Suite 500	Portland	OR	97201	**800-329-1219**	503-227-1219
Davidson Industries Inc PO Box 7	Mapleton	OR	97453	**800-845-5516**	541-268-4422
Domtar Inc 395 boul de Maisonneuve O *NYSE: DTC*	Montreal	QC	H3A1L6	**800-267-2040**	514-848-5400
Feldman Lumber Co Inc 228 Buckeye Rd	Lancaster	KY	40444	**800-325-0459**	859-792-2141
Forest Grove Lumber Co 2700 Orchard Ave	McMinnville	OR	97128	**800-647-9663**	503-472-3195
Fulghum Industries Inc 317 S Main St PO Box 909	Wadley	GA	30477	**800-841-5980**	478-252-5223
Gulf Lumber Co Inc PO Box 1663	Mobile	AL	36633	**800-496-3307**	251-457-6872
Hampton Affiliates 9600 SW Barnes Rd Sunset Business Pk Suite 200	Portland	OR	97225	**888-310-1464**	503-297-7691
Hunt Forest Products PO Box 1263	Ruston	LA	71273	**800-390-8589**	318-255-2245
Indian Country Inc 791 Airport Rd	Deposit	NY	13754	**800-414-3801**	607-467-3801
JV Wells Inc PO Box 520	Sharptown	MD	21861	**800-638-7697**	410-883-3196
Kessel Lumber Supply Inc HC 84 Box 4	Keyser	WV	26726	**800-543-9479**	304-788-3371
Langdale Forest Products Co PO Box 1088	Valdosta	GA	31603	**800-864-6909**	229-242-7450
Lewisohn Sales Co Inc PO Box 192 *Orders	North Bergen	NJ	07047	**800-631-3196***	201-864-0300
Louisiana-Pacific Corp 414 Union St Suite 2000 *NYSE: LPX*	Nashville	TN	37219	**877-744-5600**	615-986-5600
MacBeath Hardwood Co 2150 Oakdale Ave	San Francisco	CA	94124	**800-233-0782**	415-401-7046
Manke Lumber Co Inc 1717 Marine View Dr NE	Tacoma	WA	98422	**800-426-8488**	253-572-6252
McQuesten Co 600 Iron Horse Pk	North Billerica	MA	01862	**800-752-0129**	978-663-3435
Memphis Hardwood Flooring Co 1551 N Thomas St	Memphis	TN	38107	**800-346-3010**	901-526-7306
Middleton Building Supply Inc 5 Kings Hwy	Middleton	NH	03887	**800-647-8989**	603-473-2314
Miller TR Mill Co Inc PO Box 708	Brewton	AL	36427	**800-633-6740**	251-867-4331
New South Cos Inc 3700 Clay Pond Rd	Myrtle Beach	SC	29579	**800-346-8675**	843-236-9399
Parton Lumber Co Inc 251 Parton Rd	Rutherfordton	NC	28139	**800-624-1510**	828-287-4257
Pike Lumber Co Inc PO Box 247	Akron	IN	46910	**800-356-4554**	574-893-4511
Robbins Inc 4777 Eastern Ave	Cincinnati	OH	45226	**800-543-1913**	513-871-8988
Robbins Lumber Inc PO Box 9	Searsmont	ME	04973	**800-287-5067**	207-342-5221
Roseburg Forest Products Co PO Box 1088	Roseburg	OR	97470	**800-245-1115**	541-679-3311
Scotch Lumber Co PO Box 38	Fulton	AL	36446	**800-936-4424**	334-636-4424
Scott Industries Inc PO Box 7	Henderson	KY	42419	**800-951-9276**	270-831-2037
Stimson Lumber Co 520 SW Yamhill St Suite 700	Portland	OR	97204	**800-445-9758**	503-222-1676
Swaner Hardwood Co Inc PO Box 4200	Burbank	CA	91503	**800-368-1108**	818-953-5350
Temple-Inland Forest Products Corp 303 S Temple Dr	Diboll	TX	75941	**800-262-5512**	936-829-5511
Tolleson Lumber Co Inc 903 Jernigan St	Perry	GA	31069	**800-768-2105**	478-988-3800
TR Miller Mill Co Inc PO Box 708	Brewton	AL	36427	**800-633-6740**	251-867-4331
Universal Forest Products Inc 2801 E Beltline Ave NE *NASDAQ: UFPI*	Grand Rapids	MI	49525	**800-598-9663**	616-364-6161
Wadena Timberroots PO Box 109 *Sales	Wadena	MN	56482	**800-982-4863***	218-631-2607
Webster Industries Inc PO Box 297 *Sales	Bangor	WI	54614	**800-284-2173***	608-486-2341
Wells JV Inc PO Box 520	Sharptown	MD	21861	**800-638-7697**	410-883-3196
Western Forest Products Inc 435 Trunk Rd 3rd Fl *TSE: WEF*	Duncan	BC	V9L2P9	**800-880-7471**	250-748-3711

672 SCALES & BALANCES

SEE ALSO Laboratory Apparatus & Furniture

				Toll-Free	Phone
BRK Brands Inc 3901 Liberty Street Rd	Aurora	IL	60504	**800-323-9005**	630-851-7330
Cardinal Detecto Scale Mfg Co PO Box 151 *Cust Svc	Webb City	MO	64870	**800-641-2008***	417-673-4631
Detecto Scale Co 203 E Daugherty St PO Box 151	Webb City	MO	64870	**800-641-2008**	417-673-4631
Fairbanks Scales Inc 821 Locust St	Kansas City	MO	64106	**800-451-4107**	816-471-0231

Company	City	State	ZIP	Toll-Free	Phone
Industrial Data Systems Inc 590 W Freedom Ave	Orange	CA	92865	**800-854-3311**	714-921-9212
Intercomp Co 14465 23rd Ave N	Minneapolis	MN	55447	**800-328-3336**	763-476-2531
Johnson Scale Co 235 Fairfield Ave	West Caldwell	NJ	07006	**800-572-2531**	973-226-2100
Measurement Specialties Inc 710 Rt 46 E Suite 206 *AMEX: MSS*	Fairfield	NJ	07004	**800-236-6746**	973-808-3020
Merrick Industries Inc 10 Arthur Dr	Lynn Haven	FL	32444	**800-345-8440**	850-265-3611
Nicol Scales Inc 7239 Envoy Ct	Dallas	TX	75247	**800-225-8181**	214-428-8181
Ohaus Corp 19-A Chapin Rd PO Box 2033	Pine Brook	NJ	07058	**800-672-7722**	973-377-9000
Pelouze Scale Co 7400 W 100 Pl	Bridgeview	IL	60455	**800-654-8330**	708-598-9100
Pelstar LLC 7400 W 100th Pl	Bridgeview	IL	60455	**800-638-3722**	708-598-9100
Pennsylvania Scale Co 1042 New Holland Ave	Lancaster	PA	17601	**800-233-0473**	717-295-6935
Rice Lake Weighing Systems 230 W Coleman St	Rice Lake	WI	54868	**800-472-6703**	715-234-9171
Scale-Tronix Inc 200 E Post Rd	White Plains	NY	10601	**800-873-2001**	914-948-8117
Schenck Trebel Corp 535 Acorn St	Deer Park	NY	11729	**800-873-2357**	631-242-4010
Scientech Inc 5649 Arapahoe Ave	Boulder	CO	80303	**800-525-0522**	303-444-1361
Setra Systems Inc 159 Swanson Rd	Boxborough	MA	01719	**800-257-3872**	978-263-1400
SI Technologies Inc 14192 Franklin Ave *Cust Svc	Tustin	CA	92780	**800-872-4784***	714-731-1234
Sterling Scale Co Inc 20950 Boening Dr	Southfield	MI	48075	**800-331-9931**	248-358-0590
Tanita Corp of America Inc 2625 S Clearbrook Dr	Arlington Heights	IL	60005	**800-826-4828**	847-640-9241
TCI Scales 4208 Russell Rd Unit E	Mukilteo	WA	98275	**800-522-2206**	425-353-4384
Thayer Scale Corp 91 Schoosett St	Pembroke	MA	02359	**800-225-0450**	781-826-8101
Triner Scale & Mfg Co 2842 Sanderwood Dr	Memphis	TN	38118	**800-238-0152**	901-795-0746
Weigh-Tronix Inc 1000 Armstrong Dr	Fairmont	MN	56031	**800-533-0456**	507-238-4461
Yamato Corp PO Box 15070	Colorado Springs	CO	80935	**800-538-1702**	719-591-1500

673 SCHOOL SUPPLIES

Company	City	State	ZIP	Toll-Free	Phone
ABC School Supply Inc 3312 N Berkeley Lake Rd	Duluth	GA	30096	**800-669-4222**	770-497-0001
Binney & Smith Inc 1100 Church Ln	Easton	PA	18044	**800-272-9652**	610-253-6271
Carolina Biological Supply Co 2700 York Rd	Burlington	NC	27215	**800-334-5551**	336-584-0381
Cascade School Supplies Inc 1 Brown St PO Box 780	North Adams	MA	01247	**800-628-5078**	413-663-3716
ClassroomDirect.com PO Box 830677	Birmingham	AL	35283	**800-599-3040**	205-251-9171
CPP International LLC PO Box 7525	Charlotte	NC	28241	**800-888-3190**	704-588-3190
Douglas Stewart Co 2402 Advance Rd	Madison	WI	53718	**800-279-2795**	608-221-1155
Educational Supplies Inc 1506 S Salisbury Blvd	Salisbury	MD	21801	**800-797-8775**	410-543-2519
Educators Resource Inc 2575 Schillingers Rd	Semmes	AL	36575	**800-868-8181**	251-645-8800
Fisher Scientific International Inc Science Education Div 4500 Turnberry Dr	Hanover Park	IL	60133	**800-955-1177**	630-259-1200
Hammett's Learning World 1 Hammett Pl	Braintree	MA	02184	**800-955-2200**	781-848-1000
Highsmith Inc W 5527 SR 106 PO Box 800	Fort Atkinson	WI	53538	**800-558-3899**	920-563-9571
Holcomb's Education Resource 3205 Harvard Ave	Cleveland	OH	44105	**800-362-9907**	216-341-3000
JL Hammett Co 1 Hammett Pl *Cust Svc	Braintree	MA	02184	**800-955-2200***	781-848-1000
JR Holcomb & Co Inc PO Box 94636	Cleveland	OH	44101	**800-362-9907**	216-341-3000
Kaplan School Supply Corp 1310 Lewisville-Clemmons Rd	Lewisville	NC	27023	**800-334-2014**	336-766-7374
Learning How 8895 McGaw Rd	Columbia	MD	21045	**800-675-7627**	410-381-0828
National School Products 101 E Broadway	Maryville	TN	37804	**800-627-9393**	865-984-3960
School & Preschool Inc DBA Learning How 8895 McGaw Rd	Columbia	MD	21045	**800-675-7627**	410-381-0828
School Specialty Inc PO Box 1579 *NASDAQ: SCHS*	Appleton	WI	54912	**888-388-3224**	920-734-5712
Stewart Douglas Co 2402 Advance Rd	Madison	WI	53718	**800-279-2795**	608-221-1155

674 SCRAP METAL

SEE ALSO Recyclable Materials Recovery

Company	City	State	ZIP	Toll-Free	Phone
Alma Iron & Metal Co Inc PO Box 729	Alma	MI	48801	**800-572-6357**	989-463-2131
Alter Trading Corp 689 Craig Rd	Saint Louis	MO	63141	**888-887-6005**	314-872-2400
AMG Resources Corp 4100 Grand Ave	Pittsburgh	PA	15225	**800-633-3606**	412-331-0770
Annaco Inc PO Box 1148	Akron	OH	44309	**800-394-1300**	330-376-1400
Auto Shred Recycling LLC PO Box 17188	Pensacola	FL	32522	**800-277-6964**	850-432-0977
Baker Iron & Metal Co Inc 740 Rock Castle Ave	Lexington	KY	40505	**800-398-2537**	859-255-5676
Behr Joseph & Sons Inc PO Box 740	Rockford	IL	61105	**800-332-2347**	815-987-2600
Calbag Metals Co PO Box 10067	Portland	OR	97296	**800-398-3441**	503-226-3441
Cohen Brothers Inc PO Box 957	Middletown	OH	45044	**800-878-3697**	513-422-3696
Connell LP 1 International Pl 31st Fl	Boston	MA	02110	**800-276-4746**	617-737-2700
CSR Inc PO Box 389	York	PA	17405	**800-839-0931**	717-843-0931
Cycle Systems Inc PO Box 611	Roanoke	VA	24004	**800-542-7000**	540-981-1211
Duggan Industries Inc 3901 S Lamar St	Dallas	TX	75215	**877-428-8336**	214-428-8336
Franklin Iron & Metal Corp 1939 E 1st St	Dayton	OH	45403	**800-255-8184**	937-253-8184
Gachman Metals & Recycling Co Inc 2600 Shamrock Ave	Fort Worth	TX	76107	**800-749-0423**	817-334-0211
Grossman Iron & Steel Co Inc 5 N Market St	Saint Louis	MO	63102	**800-969-9423**	314-231-9423
Horsehead Resource Development Co Inc 900 Delaware Ave *Sales	Palmerton	PA	18071	**800-962-7500***	610-826-2111
International Mill Service Inc 1155 Business Ctr Dr Suite 200	Horsham	PA	19044	**800-523-0781**	215-956-5500
Iron & Metals Inc 5555 Franklin St	Denver	CO	80216	**800-776-7910**	303-292-5555
Joe Krentzman & Son Inc PO Box 508	Lewistown	PA	17044	**800-543-2000**	717-543-5635
Joseph Behr & Sons Inc PO Box 740	Rockford	IL	61105	**800-332-2347**	815-987-2600
Joseph Simon & Sons 2202 E River St	Tacoma	WA	98421	**800-562-8464**	253-272-9364
K & F Industries Inc PO Box 1206	Indianapolis	IN	46206	**800-359-2385**	317-783-4154
Kendallville Iron & Metal Inc PO Box 69	Kendallville	IN	46755	**800-530-5564**	260-347-1958
Krentzman Joe & Son Inc PO Box 508	Lewistown	PA	17044	**800-543-2000**	717-543-5635
Liberty Iron & Metal Co PO Box 1391	Erie	PA	16512	**800-836-0259**	814-453-6758
Louis Padnos Iron & Metal Co PO Box 1979	Holland	MI	49422	**800-442-3509**	616-396-6521
Mayer Pollock Steel Corp PO Box 759	Pottstown	PA	19464	**800-323-5502**	610-323-5500
Mervis Industries Inc 3295 E Main St	Danville	IL	61834	**800-637-3016**	217-442-5300
Metal Management Inc 500 N Dearborn St Suite 400 *NASDAQ: MTLM*	Chicago	IL	60610	**888-645-0700**	312-645-0700
Midland Iron & Steel Co 3301 4th Ave	Moline	IL	61265	**800-223-5942**	309-764-6723
Morris Scrap Metal Inc PO Box 460	Sherman	MS	38869	**800-467-5865**	662-844-6441
OmniSource Corp 1610 N Calhoun St	Fort Wayne	IN	46808	**800-666-4789**	260-422-5541
Padnos Louis Iron & Metal Co PO Box 1979	Holland	MI	49422	**800-442-3509**	616-396-6521
Progress Rail Services 1600 Progress Dr	Albertville	AL	35950	**800-476-8769**	256-593-1260
Regional Recycling LLC 897 Adamson St SW *Cust Svc	Atlanta	GA	30315	**800-800-6733***	404-332-1750
Richman SD Sons Inc 2435 Wheatsheaf Ln	Philadelphia	PA	19137	**800-648-3576**	215-535-5100
Riverside Scrap Iron PO Box 5288	Riverside	CA	92517	**800-399-4766**	951-686-2120
Sadoff & Rudoy Industries LLP 240 W Arndt St	Fond du Lac	WI	54935	**800-236-5700**	920-921-2070
SD Richman Sons Inc 2435 Wheatsheaf Ln	Philadelphia	PA	19137	**800-648-3576**	215-535-5100
Segel & Son Inc 107 S South St	Warren	PA	16365	**800-252-1215**	814-723-4900
Simon Joseph & Sons 2202 E River St	Tacoma	WA	98421	**800-562-8464**	253-272-9364
Simon Resources Inc 2525 Trenton Ave	Williamsport	PA	17701	**800-822-2001**	570-326-9041
Sims Bros Inc PO Box 1170	Marion	OH	43301	**800-536-7461**	740-387-9041
Solomon Metal Co 580 Lynnway	Lynn	MA	01905	**800-326-8959**	781-581-7000
South Bend Scrap & Processing Div Sturgis Iron & Metal Co 1305 Prairie Ave	South Bend	IN	46613	**800-232-2441**	574-287-3311
Southern Holdings Inc 4801 Florida Ave	New Orleans	LA	70117	**800-467-2727**	504-944-3371
Southern Scrap Material Co Inc 6847 Scenic Hwy	Baton Rouge	LA	70807	**800-355-4453**	225-355-4453
Sturgis Iron & Metal Co PO Box 579	Sturgis	MI	49091	**800-446-0794**	269-651-7851
Sturgis Iron & Metal Co South Bend Scrap & Processing Div 1305 Prairie Ave	South Bend	IN	46613	**800-232-2441**	574-287-3311
Sugar Creek Scrap Inc PO Box 208	West Terre Haute	IN	47885	**800-466-7462**	812-533-2147
Tri-State Iron & Metal Co PO Box 775	Texarkana	AR	75504	**800-773-8409**	870-773-8409
Wabash Alloys LLP PO Box 466	Wabash	IN	46992	**800-348-0571**	260-563-7461
Wise Metals Group 857 Elkridge Landing Rd Suite 600	Linthicum	MD	21090	**800-818-9473**	410-636-6500
Yaffe Iron & Metal Co Inc PO Box 916	Muskogee	OK	74402	**800-759-2333**	918-687-7543

675 SCREEN PRINTING

Company	City	State	ZIP	Toll-Free	Phone
Airmate Co Inc 16280 County Rd D	Bryan	OH	43506	**800-544-3614**	419-636-3184
Allen Co 712 E Main St	Blanchester	OH	45107	**800-783-2491**	937-783-2491
B & B Adcrafters Inc 1712 Marshall St NE	Minneapolis	MN	55413	**888-788-9461**	612-788-9461
Barton Nelson Inc 13700 Wyandotte St	Kansas City	MO	64145	**800-821-6697**	816-942-3100
Celia Corp 140 E Averill St	Sparta	MI	49345	**800-253-3664**	616-887-7341
Champion Awards Inc 3649 Winplace Rd	Memphis	TN	38118	**800-242-6781**	901-365-4830
College House Inc 1400 Chamberlayne Ave	Richmond	VA	23222	**800-888-7606**	804-643-4240
Color Arts Inc PO Box 081158	Racine	WI	53408	**800-236-7751**	262-633-7751
Designer Decal Inc 1120 E 1st Ave	Spokane	WA	99202	**800-622-6333**	509-535-0267
FB Johnston Graphics 300 E Boundary St	Chapin	SC	29036	**800-800-8160**	803-345-5481
Holoubek Inc W 238 N 1800 Rockwood Dr	Waukesha	WI	53188	**800-558-0566**	262-547-0500
M & M Designs Inc 1981 Quality Blvd	Huntsville	TX	77320	**800-627-0656**	936-295-2682
Motson Graphics Inc 1717 Bethlehem Pike	Flourtown	PA	19031	**800-972-1986**	215-233-0500
Ram Graphics Inc 2408 S Park Ave	Alexandria	IN	46001	**800-531-4656**	
Serigraph Inc 3801 E Decorah Road	West Bend	WI	53095	**800-279-6060**	262-335-7200
Stratecom Graphics 235 Conway Dr	Bogart	GA	30622	**800-205-9159**	706-546-8840
Trau & Loevner Inc 5817 Centre Ave	Pittsburgh	PA	15206	**800-245-6207**	412-361-7700

676 SCREENING - WOVEN WIRE

Company	City	State	ZIP	Toll-Free	Phone
ACS Industries Inc 191 Social St	Woonsocket	RI	02895	**800-237-1939**	401-769-4700
Belleville Wire Cloth Inc 18 Rutgers Ave	Cedar Grove	NJ	07009	**800-631-0490**	973-239-0074
Buffalo Wire Works Co 1165 Clinton St	Buffalo	NY	14206	**800-828-7028**	716-826-4666
CCX Inc 500 E Middle St	Hanover	PA	17331	**800-323-5585**	717-637-3795
Century Fireplace Furnishings Inc 856 N Main St Ext	Wallingford	CT	06492	**800-448-0409**	203-265-1686
Cleveland Wire Cloth & Mfg Co 3573 E 78th St	Cleveland	OH	44105	**800-321-3234**	216-341-1832
Darby Edward J & Son Inc PO Box 50049	Philadelphia	PA	19133	**800-875-6374**	215-236-2203
Edward J Darby & Son Inc PO Box 50049	Philadelphia	PA	19133	**800-875-6374**	215-236-2203
Gerard Daniel Worldwide 34 Barnhart Dr	Hanover	PA	17331	**800-233-3017**	717-637-5901
Halliburton Screen Co 1815 Shearn St	Houston	TX	77007	**800-527-4772**	713-869-5771
Hanover Wire Cloth 500 E Middle St PO Box 473	Hanover	PA	17331	**800-323-5585**	717-637-3795
Jelliff Corp 354 Pequot Ave	Southport	CT	06890	**800-364-9502**	203-259-1615
National-Standard Co 1631 Lake St	Niles	MI	49120	**800-777-1618**	269-683-8100
National Wire Fabric 701 Arkansas St	Star City	AR	71667	**800-643-1558**	870-628-4201
New York Wire Co 152 Main St	Mount Wolf	PA	17347	**800-699-4732**	717-266-5626
Newark Wire Cloth Co 160 Verona Ave	Newark	NJ	07013	**800-221-0392**	973-483-7700
Phoenix Wire Cloth Inc 585 Stephenson Hwy	Troy	MI	48083	**800-458-3286**	248-585-6350
Sherman Wire Co 428 Gibbons Rd	Sherman	TX	75092	**800-527-4637**	903-893-0191
TWP Inc 2831 10th St	Berkeley	CA	94710	**800-227-1570**	510-548-4434
Universal Wire Cloth Co 16 N Steel Rd	Morrisville	PA	19067	**800-523-0575**	215-736-8981
Wayne Wire Cloth Products Inc 200 E Dresden St	Kalkaska	MI	49646	**800-654-7688**	231-258-9187
Western Wire Group 4025 NW Express Ave	Portland	OR	97210	**800-547-9192**	503-222-1644

677 SEARCH ENGINES, PORTALS, DIRECTORIES

Company	City	State	ZIP	Toll-Free	Phone
Ancestry.com Inc 360 W 4800 North *Cust Svc	Provo	UT	84606	**800-262-3787***	801-705-7000
AnyWho Online Directory c/o AT & T Corp 1 AT & T Way	Bedminster	NJ	07921	**800-222-0300**	908-221-2000
AOL (America Online Inc) 22000 AOL Way *Orders	Dulles	VA	20166	**888-265-8002***	703-265-1000
Bankrate Inc 11760 US Hwy 1 Suite 101 *NASDAQ: RATE*	North Palm Beach	FL	33408	**800-243-7720**	561-630-2400

Classified Section

Name / Address	City	State	Zip	Toll-Free	Phone
Bio Online Inc 1900 Powell St Suite 230	Emeryville	CA	94608	**800-246-3010**	510-601-7194
BioSpace Inc 564 Market St	San Francisco	CA	94104	**888-246-7722**	239-659-0100
Congress.Org					
Capitol Advantage PO Box 2018	Merrifield	VA	22116	**800-659-8708**	703-289-4670
Domainsearch.com					
9525 Kenwood Rd Suite 328	Cincinnati	OH	45242	**866-927-3624**	513-351-4222
Encarta 1 Microsoft Way	Redmond	WA	98052	**800-426-9400**	425-882-8080
Essential Links					
Essentix Inc 13807 SE McLoughlin Suite 626	Portland	OR	97222	**800-401-6970**	503-659-0707
FindWhat.com Inc 143 Varick St	New York	NY	10013	**800-823-3477**	212-255-1500
NASDAQ: FWHT					
Genealogy.com 360 W 4800 North	Provo	UT	84606	**800-262-3787**	801-705-7000
GoHip.com Inc					
8306 Wilshire Blvd Suite 54	Beverly Hills	CA	90211	**866-739-5517**	213-596-6248
Great Web Sites for Kids					
American Library Assn 50 E Huron St	Chicago	IL	60611	**800-545-2433**	312-944-6780
Hollywood Media Corp					
2255 Glades Rd Suite 221A	Boca Raton	FL	33431	**888-861-8898**	561-998-8000
NASDAQ: HOLL					
Hotelrooms.com Inc 108-18 Queens Blvd	Forest Hills	NY	11375	**800-486-7000**	718-730-6000
ImproveNet Inc 10799 N 90th St Suite 200	Scottsdale	AZ	85260	**877-517-2928**	480-346-0000
Law.com Inc					
10 United Nations Plaza 3rd Fl	San Francisco	CA	94102	**800-903-9872**	
LookSmart Ltd 625 2nd St	San Francisco	CA	94107	**877-512-5665**	415-348-7000
NASDAQ: LOOK					
Mamma.com Inc					
384 Saint Jacques St W Suite 100	Montreal	QC	H2Y1S1	**888-841-2372**	514-844-2700
NASDAQ: MAMA					
MetaCrawler 601 108th Ave NE Suite 1200	Bellevue	WA	98004	**866-438-4677**	425-201-6100
MSN Encarta 1 Microsoft Way	Redmond	WA	98052	**800-426-9400**	425-882-8080
MSN Search 1 Microsoft Way	Redmond	WA	98052	**800-386-5550**	425-882-8080
MyFamily.com Inc 360 W 4800 North	Provo	UT	84606	**800-262-3787**	801-705-7000
NewsHub 96 Mowat Ave	Toronto	ON	M6K3M1	**800-371-6992**	416-535-0123
Nursing Center 323 Norristown Rd Suite 200	Ambler	PA	19002	**800-346-7844**	215-646-8700
Rhapsody.com 2012 16th St	San Francisco	CA	94103	**866-311-0228**	415-934-2000
RootsWeb.com 360 W 4800 North	Provo	UT	84606	**800-262-3787**	801-705-7000
ServiceMagic Inc					
14023 Denver W Pkwy Bldg 64 Suite 200	Golden	CO	80401	**800-474-1596**	303-963-7200
SMARTpages.com PO Box 567	Saint Louis	MO	63188	**877-647-6278**	
Switchboard Inc 120 Flanders Rd	Westborough	MA	01581	**800-343-1511**	508-898-8000
Yahoo! Search Marketing Solutions					
74 N Pasadena Ave 3rd Fl	Pasadena	CA	91103	**888-811-4686**	626-685-5600
YP.Com 4840 E Jasmine St Suite 105	Mesa	AZ	85205	**800-300-3209**	480-654-9646

678 SEATING - VEHICULAR

Name / Address	City	State	Zip	Toll-Free	Phone
Bostrom HO Co Inc 818 Progress Ave	Waukesha	WI	53186	**800-332-5415**	262-542-0222
Bostrom Seating Inc					
50 Nances Creek Industrial Blvd	Piedmont	AL	36272	**800-459-7328**	256-447-9051
Freedman Seating Co 4545 W Augusta Blvd	Chicago	IL	60651	**800-443-4540**	773-524-2440
HO Bostrom Co Inc 818 Progress Ave	Waukesha	WI	53186	**800-332-5415**	262-542-0222
Milsco Mfg Co 9009 N 51st St	Brown Deer	WI	53223	**800-645-7261**	414-354-0500
National Seating Co 200 National Dr	Vonore	TN	37885	**800-222-7328**	423-884-6651
Precision Pattern Inc 1643 S Maize Rd	Wichita	KS	67209	**800-448-5127**	316-721-3100
Sears Mfg Co					
1718 S Concord St PO Box 3667	Davenport	IA	52808	**800-553-3013***	563-383-2800
*Cust Svc					
Seats Inc 1515 Industrial St PO Box 60	Reedsburg	WI	53959	**800-443-0615**	608-524-4316
Villa Furniture Mfg 502 E Julianna St	Anaheim	CA	92801	**888-707-7272**	714-535-7273
Wise Co Inc 5535 Pleasant View Rd	Memphis	TN	38134	**800-251-2622**	901-388-0155

679 SECURITIES BROKERS & DEALERS

SEE ALSO Commodity Contracts Brokers & Dealers; Electronic Communications Networks (ECNs); Investment Advice & Management; Mutual Funds

Name / Address	City	State	Zip	Toll-Free	Phone
AB Watley Inc 90 Park Ave 26th Fl	New York	NY	10016	**888-229-2853**	212-500-6500
ABN AMRO Inc 135 S La Salle St	Chicago	IL	60603	**800-643-9600**	312-904-2000
Accutrade Inc PO Box 2227	Omaha	NE	68103	**800-228-3011***	402-970-7400
*Cust Svc					
Adams Harkness Inc 99 High St 12th Fl	Boston	MA	02110	**800-225-6201**	617-371-3900
Advest Group Inc 90 State House Sq	Hartford	CT	06103	**800-243-8115**	860-509-1000
America First Assoc 94 Covert Ave	Stewart Manor	NY	11530	**888-588-0400**	516-437-0866
American Express Brokerage					
70400 AXP Financial Ctr	Minneapolis	MN	55474	**800-297-7378**	612-671-3131
Ameritas Investment Corp PO Box 81889	Lincoln	NE	68501	**800-228-8712**	402-466-4565
Ameritrade Inc 4211 S 102nd St	Omaha	NE	68127	**800-237-8692***	402-331-2744
*Cust Svc					
Baird Patrick & Co Inc					
20 Exchange Pl 11th Fl	New York	NY	10005	**800-221-7747**	212-493-6600
Baird Robert W & Co Inc PO Box 672	Milwaukee	WI	53201	**800-792-2473**	414-765-3500
Bank of America Securities LLC					
600 Montgomery St	San Francisco	CA	94111	**800-227-4786**	415-627-2000
Barclays Capital Inc 200 Park Ave	New York	NY	10166	**888-227-2275**	212-412-4000
Baum George K & Co					
120 W 12th St 8th Fl	Kansas City	MO	64105	**800-821-7195**	816-474-1100
BB & T Capital Markets 2 S 9th St	Richmond	VA	23219	**800-476-3819**	804-649-3900
Bear Stearns & Co Inc 383 Madison Ave	New York	NY	10179	**800-999-2000**	212-272-2000
Bear Stearns Cos Inc 383 Madison Ave	New York	NY	10179	**800-999-2000**	212-272-2000
NYSE: BSC					
Bernard L Madoff Investment Securities Co					
885 3rd Ave 18th Fl	New York	NY	10022	**800-334-1343**	212-230-2424
BISYS Fund Services					
3435 Stelzer Rd Suite 1000	Columbus	OH	43219	**800-852-0045**	614-470-8000
Blair William & Co LLC 222 W Adams St	Chicago	IL	60606	**800-621-0687**	312-236-1600
Boston Institutional Services Inc					
100 Summer St 16th Fl	Boston	MA	02110	**800-325-5323**	617-223-5600
Broadview International 520 Madison Ave	New York	NY	10022	**800-346-9616**	212-284-8100
Brown & Co Securities Corp					
1 Beacon St 18th Fl	Boston	MA	02108	**800-822-2021**	617-357-4410
Butler Wick & Co Inc					
100 Federal Plaza E City Ctr 1	Youngstown	OH	44503	**800-229-1643**	330-744-4351
BUYandHOLD.com Securities Corp					
PO Box 6498	Edison	NJ	08837	**800-646-8212**	
Charles Schwab & Co Inc					
101 Montgomery St	San Francisco	CA	94104	**800-435-4000***	415-627-7000
*Cust Svc					
CIBC World Markets 300 Madison Ave	New York	NY	10017	**800-999-6726**	212-856-4000
Citicorp Venture Capital Ltd					
399 Park Ave 14th Fl Zone 4	New York	NY	10022	**800-285-3000**	212-559-1127
CitiStreet PO Box 6723	Summerset	NJ	08875	**800-537-6517**	732-514-2000
City Securities Corp PO Box 44992	Indianapolis	IN	46244	**800-800-2489**	317-634-4400
Comerica Securities 201 W Fort St 3rd Fl	Detroit	MI	48226	**800-232-6983**	313-222-5580
Credit Suisse First Boston Corp					
11 Madison Ave	New York	NY	10010	**877-775-2732**	212-325-2000
Crowell Weedon & Co					
624 S Grand Ave 1 Wilshire Bldg Suite 2600	Los Angeles	CA	90017	**800-227-0319**	213-620-1850
Crown Financial Group Inc					
525 Washington Blvd	Jersey City	NJ	07303	**800-333-3113**	201-459-9600
CyberTrader Inc					
12401 Research Blvd Bldg 2 Suite 350	Austin	TX	78759	**888-762-9237**	
DA Davidson & Co Inc 8 3rd St N	Great Falls	MT	59401	**800-332-5915**	406-727-4200
Davenport & Co LLC 901 E Cary St	Richmond	VA	23219	**800-846-6666**	804-780-2000
Davidson DA & Co Inc 8 3rd St N	Great Falls	MT	59401	**800-332-5915**	406-727-4200
Deutsche Bank Securities Inc 60 Wall St	New York	NY	10005	**800-334-1898**	
Domestic Securities Inc 160 Summit Ave	Montvale	NJ	07645	**877-429-2111**	201-782-0888
Dougherty & Co LLC					
90 S 7th St Suite 4300	Minneapolis	MN	55402	**800-328-4005**	612-376-4000
Dresdner Kleinwort Wasserstein					
1301 Ave of the Americas	New York	NY	10019	**800-457-0245**	212-429-2000
Duncan-Williams Inc					
6750 Poplar Ave Suite 300	Memphis	TN	38138	**800-827-0827**	901-260-6800
E*Trade Financial Corp 4500 Bohannon Dr	Menlo Park	CA	94025	**800-786-2575***	650-331-6000
NYSE: ET ■ *Orders					
Eaton Vance Distributors Inc 255 State St	Boston	MA	02109	**800-225-6265**	617-482-8260
eChapman Inc 5850 Waterloo Rd Suite 140	Columbia	MD	21045	**800-752-1013**	410-480-7095
Empire Financial Group Inc					
2170 W SR 434 Suite 100	Longwood	FL	32779	**800-569-3337**	407-774-1300
AMEX: EFH					
Ferris Baker Watts Inc					
1700 Pennsylvania Ave NW Suite 700	Washington	DC	20006	**800-227-0308**	202-661-9500
Fidelity Brokerage Services Inc					
82 Devonshire St	Boston	MA	02109	**800-828-6680**	617-563-7000
Fidelity Personal Investments & Brokerage Group					
82 Devonshire St	Boston	MA	02109	**800-828-6680**	617-563-7000
Fidelity Spartan Brokerage Services Inc					
82 Devonshire St	Boston	MA	02109	**800-828-6680**	617-563-7000
Financial Service Corp					
2300 Windy Ridge Pkwy Suite 1100	Atlanta	GA	30339	**800-352-4372**	770-916-6500
First Albany Corp 677 Broadway	Albany	NY	12207	**800-462-6242**	518-447-8500
First Options of Chicago Inc					
440 S La Salle St Suite 1600	Chicago	IL	60605	**800-621-3436**	312-362-3000
First Southwest Co					
325 N Saint Paul St Suite 800	Dallas	TX	75201	**800-678-3792**	214-953-4000
Frank Russell Co PO Box 1616	Tacoma	WA	98402	**800-426-7969**	253-572-9500
Franklin Templeton Investments					
3344 Quality Dr	Rancho Cordova	CA	95670	**800-632-2350**	650-312-2000
Freedom Investments Inc 375 Raritan Ctr Pkwy	Edison	NJ	08837	**800-944-4033**	732-934-3113
Friedman Billings Ramsey Group Inc					
1001 19th St N 18th Fl	Arlington	VA	22209	**800-846-5050**	703-312-9500
NYSE: FBR					
Garban Corp 1100 Plaza 5 12th Fl	Jersey City	NJ	07311	**800-427-6859**	201-369-5663
George K Baum & Co					
120 W 12th St 8th Fl	Kansas City	MO	64105	**800-821-7195**	816-474-1100
Gilford Securities Inc 777 3rd Ave 17th Fl	New York	NY	10017	**800-445-3673**	212-888-6400
Glickenhaus & Co 6 E 43rd St 10th Fl	New York	NY	10017	**800-559-8540**	212-953-7800
Goldman Sachs & Co 85 Broad St	New York	NY	10004	**800-323-5678**	212-902-1000
Goldman Sachs Group Inc 85 Broad St	New York	NY	10004	**800-323-5678**	212-902-1000
NYSE: GS					
Hambrecht WR & Co					
539 Bryant St Suite 100	San Francisco	CA	94107	**877-673-6476***	415-551-8600
*Cust Svc					
Hanauer JB & Co 4 Gatehall Dr	Parsippany	NJ	07054	**800-631-1094**	973-829-1000
Harrisdirect					
501 Plaza II Harborside Financial Ctr	Jersey City	NJ	07311	**800-825-5873**	
HC Wainwright & Co Inc					
245 Park Ave 44th Fl	New York	NY	10167	**800-727-7176**	212-856-5700
Hilliard JJB WL Lyons Inc					
501 S 4th St Hilliard Lyons Ctr	Louisville	KY	40202	**800-444-1854**	502-588-8400
Hoenig Group Inc 4 International Dr 2nd Fl	Rye Brook	NY	10573	**800-999-9558**	914-312-2300
Howard Weil 1100 Poydras St Suite 3500	New Orleans	LA	70163	**800-322-3005**	504-582-2500
Howe Barnes Investments Inc					
222 S Riverside Plaza 7th Fl	Chicago	IL	60606	**800-275-4693**	312-655-3000
Hummer Wayne Investments LLC					
300 S Wacker Dr Suite 1500	Chicago	IL	60606	**800-621-4477**	312-431-1700
ING Altus Group 230 Park Ave 14th Fl	New York	NY	10169	**800-621-6626**	212-309-8200
ING Barings 1325 Ave of the Americas	New York	NY	10019	**800-221-5855**	646-424-6000
Ingalls & Snyder 61 Broadway 31st Fl	New York	NY	10006	**800-221-2598**	212-269-7800
Integrated Fund Services Inc					
221 E 4th St Suite 300	Cincinnati	OH	45202	**800-543-8721**	
Investment Technology Group					
380 Madison Ave 4th Fl	New York	NY	10017	**800-215-4484**	212-588-4000
NYSE: ITG					
Investors Capital Corp					
230 Broadway Suite 205	Lynnfield	MA	01940	**800-949-1422**	781-593-8565
Investrade Discount Securities					
950 N Milwaukee Ave Suite 102	Glenview	IL	60025	**800-498-7120**	847-375-6080
ITG Inc 380 Madison Ave 4th Fl	New York	NY	10017	**800-215-4484**	212-588-4000
Jackson Securities					
100 Peachtree St NW Suite 2250	Atlanta	GA	30303	**866-888-4574**	404-522-5766
Janney Montgomery Scott LLC					
1801 Market St	Philadelphia	PA	19103	**800-526-6397**	215-665-6000
JB Hanauer & Co 4 Gatehall Dr	Parsippany	NJ	07054	**800-631-1094**	973-829-1000
Jefferies & Co Inc					
11100 Santa Monica Blvd	Los Angeles	CA	90025	**800-421-0160**	310-445-1199
Jefferies Group Inc					
11100 Santa Monica Blvd	Los Angeles	CA	90025	**800-421-0160**	310-445-1199
NYSE: JEF					
Jefferson-Pilot Securities Corp PO Box 515	Concord	NH	03302	**800-258-3648**	603-226-5000
JJB Hilliard WL Lyons Inc					
501 S 4th St Hilliard Lyons Ctr	Louisville	KY	40202	**800-444-1854**	502-588-8400
Johnston Lemon & Co Inc					
1101 Vermont Ave NW Suite 800	Washington	DC	20005	**800-424-5158**	202-842-5500

	City	State	Zip	Toll-Free	Phone
Keefe Bruyette & Woods Inc					
1 Constitution Plaza 17th Fl	Hartford	CT	06103	**800-726-0006**	860-722-5900
Kirkpatrick Pettis Inc					
10250 Regency Cir Suite 500	Omaha	NE	68114	**800-776-5777**	402-397-5777
Knight Capital Group Inc					
525 Washington Blvd Newport Tower					
23rd Fl	Jersey City	NJ	07310	**800-544-7508**	201-222-9400
NASDAQ: NITE					
Ladenburg Thalmann Financial Services Inc					
590 Madison Ave	New York	NY	10022	**800-523-8425**	212-409-2000
AMEX: LTS					
Lebenthal & Co Inc 120 Broadway 12th Fl	New York	NY	10271	**800-425-6116**	212-425-6116
Legg Mason Inc 100 Light St	Baltimore	MD	21202	**800-368-2558**	410-539-0000
NYSE: LM					
Lehman Brothers Inc 70 Hudson St	Jersey City	NJ	07302	**800-666-2388**	201-524-2000
Lepercq de Neuflize & Co					
40 W 57th St 19th Fl	New York	NY	10019	**800-697-3863**	212-698-0700
Loop Capital Markets LLC					
200 W Jackson Blvd 16th Fl	Chicago	IL	60606	**888-294-8898**	312-913-4900
LPL Financial Services 1 Beacon St 22nd Fl	Boston	MA	02108	**800-775-4575**	617-423-3644
Lynch Jones & Ryan Inc 3 Times Sq 8th Fl	New York	NY	10036	**800-992-7526***	212-310-9500
*Sales					
Madoff Bernard L Investment Securities					
885 3rd Ave 18th Fl	New York	NY	10022	**800-334-1343**	212-230-2424
Marshall Miller & Schroeder Inc					
150 S 5th St Suite 3000	Minneapolis	MN	55402	**800-328-6122**	612-376-1500
Mesirow Financial Inc 350 N Clark St	Chicago	IL	60610	**800-453-0600**	312-595-6000
Miller Johnson Steichen Kinnard Inc					
60 S 6th St Suite 3000	Minneapolis	MN	55402	**800-444-7884**	612-455-5555
Morgan Keegan & Co Inc					
50 N Front St 17th Fl	Memphis	TN	38103	**800-366-7426**	901-524-4100
Morgan Stanley 1585 Broadway	New York	NY	10036	**800-223-2440**	212-761-4000
NYSE: MWD					
Morgan Stanley Investment Management					
1221 Ave of the Americas 22nd Fl	New York	NY	10020	**800-419-2861**	212-762-7400
Muriel Siebert & Co Inc					
885 3rd Ave Suite 1720	New York	NY	10022	**800-872-0444***	212-644-2400
*Cust Svc					
Natexis Bleichroeder Inc					
1345 Ave of the Americas	New York	NY	10105	**800-435-0336**	212-698-3000
NBC Capital Markets Group Inc					
850 Ridge Lake Blvd Suite 400	Memphis	TN	38120	**800-795-2421**	901-842-3700
Needham & Co Inc 445 Park Ave 3rd Fl	New York	NY	10022	**800-903-3268**	212-371-8300
New England Securities Corp					
485 E Rt 1 S 4th Fl	Iselin	NJ	08830	**800-472-7227**	
Northern Trust Securities					
50 S La Salle St 12th Fl	Chicago	IL	60675	**800-621-2253**	312-557-2000
Nuveen Investments Inc 333 W Wacker Dr	Chicago	IL	60606	**800-257-8787**	312-917-7700
NYSE: JNC					
NYLIFE Securities Inc					
335 Madison Ave Suite 200	New York	NY	10017	**800-695-4785**	212-351-6000
Oberweis Securities Inc					
951 Ice Cream Dr Suite 200	North Aurora	IL	60542	**800-323-6166**	630-801-6000
Paulson Capital Corp					
811 SW Naito Pkwy Suite 200	Portland	OR	97204	**800-458-5667***	503-243-6000
NASDAQ: PLCC ■ *Cust Svc					
Paulson Investment Co Inc					
811 SW Naito Pkwy Suite 200	Portland	OR	97204	**800-458-5667***	503-243-6000
*Cust Svc					
PDI Financial Group 601 N Lynndale Dr	Appleton	WI	54914	**800-234-7341**	920-739-2303
Penson Financial Services Inc					
1700 Pacific Ave Suite 1400	Dallas	TX	75201	**800-696-3585**	214-765-1100
People's Securities Inc 1000 Lafayette Blvd	Bridgeport	CT	06601	**800-772-4400**	203-338-0800
Pioneer Investment Management Inc					
60 State St 4th Fl	Boston	MA	02109	**800-225-6292**	617-742-7825
Piper Jaffray Cos					
800 Nicollet Mall Suite 800	Minneapolis	MN	55402	**800-333-6000**	612-303-6000
NYSE: PJC					
Quick & Reilly Inc 26 Broadway 14th Fl	New York	NY	10004	**800-672-7220**	212-747-1200
Ragen Mackenzie Group Inc					
999 3rd Ave Suite 4000	Seattle	WA	98104	**800-456-4457**	206-343-5000
Raymond James Financial Inc					
880 Carillon Pkwy	Saint Petersburg	FL	33716	**800-248-8863**	727-573-3800
NYSE: RJF					
RBC Capital Markets 1 Liberty Plaza	New York	NY	10006	**888-886-8296**	212-428-6200
Robert W Baird & Co Inc PO Box 672	Milwaukee	WI	53201	**800-792-2473**	414-765-3500
Royal Alliance Assoc Inc 733 3rd Ave 4th Fl	New York	NY	10017	**800-821-5100**	212-551-5100
Ryan Beck & Co 18 Columbia Tpke	Florham Park	NJ	07932	**800-342-2325**	973-549-4000
Schwab Charles & Co Inc					
101 Montgomery St	San Francisco	CA	94104	**800-435-4000***	415-627-7000
*Cust Svc					
Scotia Capital Markets 1 Liberty Plaza	New York	NY	10006	**800-472-6842**	212-225-5000
Scott & Stringfellow Inc 909 E Main St	Richmond	VA	23219	**800-552-7757**	804-643-1811
Seasongood & Mayer LLC					
414 Walnut St Suite 300	Cincinnati	OH	45202	**800-767-7207**	513-621-2000
Seidler Cos Inc					
515 S Figueroa St Suite 1100	Los Angeles	CA	90071	**800-840-1090**	213-683-4500
SG Cowen Securities Corp					
1221 Ave of the Americas	New York	NY	10020	**800-942-7575**	212-278-6000
ShareBuilder Corp 1445 120th Ave NE	Bellevue	WA	98005	**866-747-2537**	425-451-4440
Shelby Cullom Davis & Co					
609 5th Ave 11th Fl	New York	NY	10017	**800-232-0303**	212-207-3500
Siebert Muriel & Co Inc					
885 3rd Ave Suite 1720	New York	NY	10022	**800-872-0444***	212-644-2400
*Cust Svc					
Smith Barney 388 Greenwich St 16th Fl	New York	NY	10013	**800-221-3636**	
Standard & Poor's 55 Water St 45th Fl	New York	NY	10041	**800-344-3014***	212-438-2000
*Cust Svc					
Stephens Inc 111 Center St	Little Rock	AR	72201	**800-643-9691**	501-377-2000
Sterne Agee & Leach Inc					
800 Shades Creek Pkwy Suite 700	Birmingham	AL	35209	**800-240-1438**	205-949-3500
Stifel Financial Corp 501 N Broadway	Saint Louis	MO	63102	**800-488-0970**	314-342-2000
NYSE: SF					
Stifel Nicolaus & Co Inc 501 N Broadway	Saint Louis	MO	63102	**800-488-0970**	314-342-2000
SunTrust Robinson Humphrey Capital Markets					
3333 Peachtree Rd NE Atlanta Financial Ctr	Atlanta	GA	30326	**877-266-6501**	404-926-5000
TD Waterhouse Group Inc 100 Wall St	New York	NY	10005	**800-835-0245**	212-806-3500
TradeStation Group Inc					
8050 SW 10th St Suite 2000	Plantation	FL	33324	**800-871-3577**	954-652-7000
NASDAQ: TRAD					
TradeStation Securities Inc					
8050 SW 10th St Suite 2000	Plantation	FL	33324	**800-515-3238**	954-652-7000
Trading Direct 160 Broadway E Bldg 7th Fl	New York	NY	10038	**800-925-8566**	212-766-0230
UBS Capital Markets					
111 Pavonia Ave E Newport Financial Ctr	Jersey City	NJ	07310	**800-543-7995**	201-963-9100
UBS Financial Services Inc					
1285 Ave of the Americas	New York	NY	10019	**800-221-3260**	212-713-2000
UBS Warburg LLC 677 Washington Blvd	Stamford	CT	06901	**800-221-3260**	203-719-3000
Utendahl Capital Management LP					
30 Broad St 21st Fl	New York	NY	10004	**877-941-4900**	212-797-2688
Vanguard Brokerage Services					
PO Box 2600	Valley Forge	PA	19482	**800-992-8327**	610-669-1000
Wainwright HC & Co Inc					
245 Park Ave 44th Fl	New York	NY	10167	**800-727-7176**	212-856-5700
Walnut Street Securities Inc					
260 Madison Ave 11th Fl	New York	NY	10016	**800-873-7702**	212-354-8800
Watley AB Inc 90 Park Ave 26th Fl	New York	NY	10016	**888-229-2853**	212-500-6500
Wayne Hummer Investments LLC					
300 S Wacker Dr Suite 1500	Chicago	IL	60606	**800-621-4477**	312-431-1700
Wells Fargo Investments					
420 Montgomery St 5th Fl	San Francisco	CA	94104	**800-621-7609**	
William Blair & Co LLC 222 W Adams St	Chicago	IL	60606	**800-621-0687**	312-236-1600
WM Financial Services Inc PO Box 145432	Cincinnati	OH	45290	**800-331-3426**	
WR Hambrecht & Co					
539 Bryant St Suite 100	San Francisco	CA	94107	**877-673-6476***	415-551-8600
*Cust Svc					

680 SECURITIES & COMMODITIES EXCHANGES

	City	State	Zip	Toll-Free	Phone
American Stock Exchange (AMEX)					
86 Trinity Pl	New York	NY	10006	**800-843-2639**	212-306-1000
Arbinet-thexchange Inc					
120 Albany St Tower II 4th Fl	New Brunswick	NJ	08901	**800-272-4638**	732-509-9100
NASDAQ: ARBX					
Chicago Board Options Exchange					
400 S La Salle St	Chicago	IL	60605	**800-678-4667**	312-786-5600
Chicago Board of Trade (CBOT)					
141 W Jackson Blvd	Chicago	IL	60604	**800-572-3276**	312-435-3500
Chicago Mercantile Exchange Holdings Inc					
(CME) 20 S Wacker Dr	Chicago	IL	60606	**800-331-3332**	312-930-1000
NYSE: CME					
International Monetary Market					
20 S Wacker Dr	Chicago	IL	60606	**800-331-3332**	312-930-3170
Kansas City Board of Trade					
4800 Main St Suite 303	Kansas City	MO	64112	**800-821-5228**	816-753-7500
Minneapolis Grain Exchange					
400 S 4th St Rm 130	Minneapolis	MN	55415	**800-827-4746**	612-321-7101
Montreal Exchange					
800 Victoria Sq PO Box 61	Montreal	QC	H4Z1A9	**800-361-5353**	514-871-2424
Nasdaq Stock Market Inc 9600 Blackwell Rd	Rockville	MD	20850	**877-536-2737**	301-978-8008
National Stock Exchange (NSX)					
440 S LaSalle St Suite 2600	Chicago	IL	60605	**800-843-3924**	312-786-8803
New York Board of Trade					
1 N End Ave 13th Fl	New York	NY	10282	**800-433-4348**	212-748-4000
NSX (National Stock Exchange)					
440 S LaSalle St Suite 2600	Chicago	IL	60605	**800-843-3924**	312-786-8803
Pacific Exchange					
115 Samsone St 3rd Fl	San Francisco	CA	94104	**877-729-7291**	415-393-4000
Philadelphia Stock Exchange					
1900 Market St	Philadelphia	PA	19103	**800-843-7459**	215-496-5404
Toronto Stock Exchange 130 King St W	Toronto	ON	M5X1J2	**888-873-8392**	416-947-4700

681 SECURITY, FIRE, DETECTION SYSTEMS - MFR

SEE ALSO Security Systems Services; Signals & Sirens - Electric

	City	State	Zip	Toll-Free	Phone
Aamp of America Inc					
13160 56th Ct Suite 508	Clearwater	FL	33760	**800-477-2267**	727-572-9255
ADT Security Systems Inc					
14200 E Exposition Ave	Aurora	CO	80012	**800-662-5378**	303-338-8200
Advanced Security Link 1690 Scenic Ave	Costa Mesa	CA	92626	**800-576-4275**	714-825-1818
Advantor Systems Corp					
1707 Orlando Central Pkwy Suite 350	Orlando	FL	32809	**800-238-2686***	407-859-3350
*Sales					
AMAG Technology Inc 20701 Manhattan Pl	Torrance	CA	90501	**800-889-9138**	310-518-2380
American Dynamics Corp 6795 Flanders Dr	San Diego	CA	92121	**800-854-2057**	858-642-2400
American Science & Engineering Inc					
829 Middlesex Tpke	Billerica	MA	01821	**800-225-1608**	978-262-8700
NASDAQ: ASEI					
Ansul Inc 1 Stanton St	Marinette	WI	54143	**800-862-6785**	715-735-7411
APi Systems Group Inc 2366 Rose Pl	Saint Paul	MN	55113	**800-223-4922**	651-636-4320
BI Inc 6400 Lookout Rd	Boulder	CO	80301	**800-241-2911**	303-218-1000
Bosch Security Systems 130 Perinton Pkwy	Fairport	NY	14450	**800-289-0096**	585-223-4060
BRK Brands Inc 3901 Liberty Street Rd	Aurora	IL	60504	**800-323-9005**	630-851-7330
Chamberlain Group 845 Larch Ave	Elmhurst	IL	60126	**800-282-6225**	630-279-3600
Checkpoint Systems Inc 101 Wolf Dr	Thorofare	NJ	08086	**800-257-5540**	856-848-1800
NYSE: CKP					
Chemetron Fire Systems					
4801 Southwick Dr 3rd Fl	Matteson	IL	60443	**800-878-5631***	708-748-1503
*Cust Svc					
Chubb Americas Sector 5201 Explorer Dr	Mississauga	ON	L4W4H1	**800-661-4149**	905-629-2600
Computerized Security Systems Inc					
1950 Austin Dr	Troy	MI	48083	**877-272-3565***	248-680-8484
*Sales					
Corby Industries Inc 1501 E Pennsylvania St	Allentown	PA	18109	**800-652-6729**	610-433-1412
Counter Technology Inc					
4733 Bethesda Ave Suite 800	Bethesda	MD	20814	**800-783-4284**	301-907-0127
Crest Electronics Inc 3706 Alliance Dr	Greensboro	NC	27407	**800-873-2121**	336-855-6422
Detector Electronics Corp					
6901 W 110th St	Minneapolis	MN	55438	**800-765-3473**	952-941-5665
Detex Corp 302 Detex Dr	New Braunfels	TX	78130	**800-729-3839**	830-629-2900
Digital Products of Delaware Inc					
625 SW 9th Terr	Pompano Beach	FL	33069	**800-671-0299**	954-941-0903
Driven Technologies 2345 S Michigan Ave	Chicago	IL	60616	**877-437-4836**	312-842-1880

Company / Address	City	State	ZIP	Toll-Free	Phone
Edwards Systems Technology 90 Fieldstone Ct	Cheshire	CT	06410	**800-655-4497**	203-699-3000
Faraday LLC 805 S Maumee St	Tecumseh	MI	49286	**800-465-7115**	517-423-2111
Federal APD Inc 42775 Nine-Mile Rd	Novi	MI	48375	**800-521-9330**	248-374-9600
Fire-Lite Alarms 1 Fire-Lite Pl	Northford	CT	06472	**800-289-3473**	203-484-7161
Firecom Inc 39-27 59th St	Woodside	NY	11377	**800-347-3266**	718-899-6100
First Alert Inc 3901 Liberty Street Rd	Aurora	IL	60504	**800-323-9005**	630-851-7330
FMJ/Pad.Lock Computer Security Systems Inc 741 E 223rd St	Carson	CA	90745	**800-322-3365**	310-549-3221
Force Inc 825 Park St	Christiansburg	VA	24073	**800-732-5252**	540-382-0462
Frisco Bay Industries Ltd 160 Graveline St	Saint-Laurent	QC	H4T1R7	**800-463-7472**	514-738-7300
Gamewell Co 12 Clintonville Rd	Northford	CT	06472	**800-866-1456**	203-484-7161
GE Security 300 W 6th St Suite 1850	Austin	TX	78701	**877-526-0885**	512-381-2760
General Monitors Inc 26776 Simpatica Cir	Lake Forest	CA	92630	**866-686-0741**	949-581-4464
Genie Co 22790 Lake Park Blvd *Cust Svc	Alliance	OH	44601	**800-995-1111***	330-821-5360
Gentex Corp 600 N Centennial St *NASDAQ: GNTX*	Zeeland	MI	49464	**800-444-4689**	616-772-1800
George Risk Industries Inc 802 S Elm St *Sales	Kimball	NE	69145	**800-523-1227***	308-235-4645
Harrington Signal Co 2519 4th Ave	Moline	IL	61265	**800-577-5758**	309-762-0731
Honeywell ACS 11 W Spring St	Freeport	IL	61032	**800-328-5111**	
Honeywell Aerospace 1944 E Sky Harbor Cir	Phoenix	AZ	85034	**800-601-3099**	
Honeywell Automation & Control Solutions 11 W Spring St	Freeport	IL	61032	**800-328-5111**	
Honeywell Fire Solutions DBA Fire-Lite Alarms 1 Fire-Lite Pl	Northford	CT	06472	**800-289-3473**	203-484-7161
Honeywell Security Inc 165 Eileen Way *Cust Svc	Syosset	NY	11791	**800-573-0154***	516-921-6704
IDenticard Systems Inc 40 Citation Ln	Lancaster	PA	17601	**800-233-0298**	717-569-5797
International Electronics Inc 427 Turnpike St *NASDAQ: IEIB*	Canton	MA	02021	**800-343-9502**	781-821-5566
JAI Pulnix Inc 1330 Orleans Dr	Sunnyvale	CA	94089	**800-445-5444**	408-747-0300
Johnson Controls Fire & Security Solutions 1757 Tapo Canyon Rd	Simi Valley	CA	93063	**800-229-4076**	805-522-5555
KM Systems Inc 4910 Starcrest Dr *Sales	Monroe	NC	28111	**800-438-1937***	704-289-9212
Larco 1902 13th St SE *Cust Svc	Brainerd	MN	56401	**800-523-6996***	218-829-9797
Linear LLC 2055 Corte del Nogal *Cust Svc	Carlsbad	CA	92009	**800-421-1587***	760-438-7000
Logiplex Corp 4855 N Lagoon	Portland	OR	97217	**800-735-0555**	503-978-6726
LoJack Corp 200 Lowder Brook Dr Suite 1000 *NASDAQ: LOJN*	Westwood	MA	02090	**800-456-5225**	781-326-4700
Mace Security International Inc 160 Benmont Ave Suite 1 *NASDAQ: MACE*	Bennington	VT	05201	**800-255-2634**	802-447-1503
MAXxess Systems Inc 1515 S Manchester Ave	Anaheim	CA	92802	**800-842-0221**	714-772-1000
MDI Security Systems Inc 9725 Datapoint Dr Suite 200 *NASDAQ: MDII*	San Antonio	TX	78229	**866-435-7634**	210-477-5400
Merrill Lynch Family of Funds PO Box 45289	Jacksonville	FL	32232	**800-637-3863**	
MILCOM Systems Corp 532 Viking Dr	Virginia Beach	VA	23452	**800-967-0966**	757-463-2800
Namco Controls Corp 6095 Parkland Blvd Suite 310 *Cust Svc	Mayfield Heights	OH	44124	**800-626-8324***	440-460-1360
NAPCO Security Systems Inc 333 Bayview Ave *NASDAQ: NSSC*	Amityville	NY	11701	**800-645-9445**	631-842-9400
Optex America Inc 1845 W 205th St	Torrance	CA	90501	**800-966-7839**	310-533-1500
Potter Electric Signal Co Inc 2081 Craig Rd	Saint Louis	MO	63146	**800-325-3936**	314-878-4321
Rapiscan Security Products Inc 3232 El Segundo Blvd	Hawthorne	CA	90250	**800-318-7226**	310-978-1457
Rostra Precision Controls Inc 2519 Dana Dr *Cust Svc	Laurinburg	NC	28352	**800-782-3379***	910-276-4853
Seco-Larm USA Inc 16842 Millikan Ave	Irvine	CA	92606	**800-662-0800**	949-261-2999
Security Defense Systems Corp 160 Park Ave	Nutley	NJ	07110	**800-325-6339**	973-235-0606
Security Services & Technologies 2450 Blvd of the Generals Valley Forge Business Ctr	Norristown	PA	19403	**888-446-7781**	610-630-6790
Sensormatic Electronics Corp 6600 Congress Ave	Boca Raton	FL	33487	**800-327-1765**	561-912-6000
Sentry Technology Corp 1881 Lakeland Ave	Ronkonkoma	NY	11779	**800-645-4224**	631-739-2100
Siemens Building Technologies Inc Fire Safety Div 8 Fernwood Rd	Florham Park	NJ	07932	**800-222-0108**	973-593-2600
Silent Knight 7550 Meridian Cir Suite 100	Maple Grove	MN	55369	**800-328-0103**	763-493-6400
SimplexGrinnell Ltd 50 Technology Dr	Westminster	MA	01441	**800-746-7539**	978-731-2500
SIRCHIE Finger Print Laboratories Inc 100 Hunter Pl	Youngsville	NC	27596	**800-356-7311**	919-554-2244
Software House 70 Westview St	Lexington	MA	02421	**800-550-6660**	781-466-6660
Sola Communications Inc 113 N Patch St	Scott	LA	70583	**800-458-8301**	337-235-1515
Sparton Corp 2400 E Ganson St *NYSE: SPA*	Jackson	MI	49202	**800-248-9579**	517-787-8600
Unisec Inc 2555 Nicholson St	San Leandro	CA	94577	**800-982-4587**	510-352-5610
Universal Security Instruments Inc 7-A Gwynns Mill Ct	Owings Mills	MD	21117	**800-390-4321**	410-363-3000
UTC Fire & Security 5201 Explorer Dr	Mississauga	ON	L4W4H1	**800-661-4149**	905-629-2600
Verint Video Solutions 9105 Guilford Rd	Columbia	MD	21046	**800-638-5969**	301-483-8930
Viking Corp 210 N Industrial Pk Dr	Hastings	MI	49058	**800-968-9501**	269-945-9501
Wheelock Inc 273 Branchport Ave *Cust Svc	Long Branch	NJ	07740	**800-631-2148***	732-222-6880
Whistler Group Inc 13016 N Walton Blvd *Cust Svc	Bentonville	AR	72712	**800-531-0004***	479-273-6012
Winner International LLC 32 W State St	Sharon	PA	16146	**800-258-2321**	724-981-1152

682 SECURITY & PROTECTIVE SERVICES

SEE ALSO Investigative Services

Company / Address	City	State	ZIP	Toll-Free	Phone
AlliedBarton Security Services 3606 Horizon Dr	King of Prussia	PA	19406	**888-239-1104**	610-239-1100
Analytic Services Inc 2900 S Quincy St Suite 800	Arlington	VA	22206	**866-226-5697**	703-416-2000
Chubb Americas Sector 5201 Explorer Dr	Mississauga	ON	L4W4H1	**800-661-4149**	905-629-2600
Deter Security Inc 233 S Main St	Rutland	VT	05701	**800-696-3383**	802-773-7305
Diversco Inc 105 Diversco Dr	Spartanburg	SC	29307	**800-277-3420**	864-579-3420
Doyle Protective Services Inc 792 Calkins Rd	Rochester	NY	14623	**800-836-9538**	585-244-3400
Garda World Security Corp 705 Bourget St Suite 200 *TSE: GW*	Montreal	QC	H4C2M6	**800-334-2732**	514-937-7487
Guard Systems Inc 12124 Ramona Blvd	El Monte	CA	91732	**800-307-0031**	626-433-4999
Guardsmark Inc 22 S 2nd St	Memphis	TN	38103	**800-238-5878**	901-522-6000
Initial Security 3355 Cherry Ridge St Suite 200	San Antonio	TX	78230	**800-683-7771**	210-349-6321
International Claim Specialists 530 W Lockport St	Plainfield	IL	60544	**800-822-8220**	815-254-0600
IPC International Corp 2111 Waukegan Rd	Bannockburn	IL	60015	**800-323-1228**	847-444-2000
Levy Security Corp 8750 W Bryn Mawr Ave Suite 1200	Chicago	IL	60631	**800-649-5389**	773-867-9204
Loomis Fargo & Co 1655 Vilbig Rd	Dallas	TX	75208	**800-725-7475**	214-742-2554
Murray Guard Inc 58 Murray Guard Dr	Jackson	TN	38305	**800-238-3830**	731-668-3400
MVM Inc 1593 Spring Hill Rd Suite 700	Vienna	VA	22182	**800-727-1949**	703-790-3138
Northwest Protective Service Inc 2700 Elliott Ave	Seattle	WA	98121	**888-981-4040**	206-448-4040
Pinkerton's Inc 4330 Park Terrace Dr	Westlake Village	CA	91361	**800-232-7465**	818-706-6800
Shield Security 150 W Wardlow Rd	Long Beach	CA	90807	**800-793-3354**	562-283-1100
Smith Protective Services Inc 8918 John W Carpenter Fwy	Dallas	TX	75247	**800-634-1381**	214-631-4444
US Security Assoc Inc 200 Mansell Ct 5th Fl	Roswell	GA	30076	**800-241-0267**	770-625-1400
UTC Fire & Security 5201 Explorer Dr	Mississauga	ON	L4W4H1	**800-661-4149**	905-629-2600
Vance 10467 White Granite Dr Suite 210	Oakton	VA	22124	**800-533-6754**	703-592-1400
Wackenhut Airline Services Inc 4200 Wackenhut Dr Suite 100	Palm Beach Gardens	FL	33410	**800-683-6853**	561-622-5656
Wackenhut Corp 4200 Wackenhut Dr Suite 100	Palm Beach Gardens	FL	33410	**800-922-6488**	561-622-5656
Wackenhut Corp Nuclear Services Div 4200 Wackenhut Dr Suite 100	Palm Beach Gardens	FL	33410	**800-683-6853**	561-622-5656
Wackenhut International Inc 4200 Wackenhut Dr Suite 100	Palm Beach Gardens	FL	33410	**800-683-6853**	561-622-5656
Wackenhut Services Inc 4200 Wackenhut Dr Suite 100	Palm Beach Gardens	FL	33410	**800-922-6488**	561-622-5656
Wackenhut Sports Security Inc 4200 Wackenhut Dr Suite 100	Palm Beach Gardens	FL	33410	**800-683-6853**	561-622-5656

683 SECURITY SYSTEMS SERVICES

Company / Address	City	State	ZIP	Toll-Free	Phone
ADT Security Systems Inc 14200 E Exposition Ave	Aurora	CO	80012	**800-662-5378**	303-338-8200
Akal Security Inc PO Box 1197	Santa Cruz	NM	87567	**888-325-2527**	505-753-7832
AlliedBarton Security Services 3606 Horizon Dr	King of Prussia	PA	19406	**888-239-1104**	610-239-1100
Brink's Home Security Inc 8880 Esters Blvd	Irving	TX	75063	**800-874-1190**	972-871-3500
Central Signaling Inc 2033 Hamilton Rd	Columbus	GA	31904	**800-554-1104**	706-322-3756
Chubb Americas Sector 5201 Explorer Dr	Mississauga	ON	L4W4H1	**800-661-4149**	905-629-2600
EMERgency 24 Inc 4179 W Irving Park Rd	Chicago	IL	60641	**800-877-3624**	773-777-0707
Fire Electrical Services 2500 Brookpark Rd	Cleveland	OH	44134	**877-741-6001**	216-741-6001
First Action Security 18702 Crestwood Dr	Hagerstown	MD	21742	**800-342-4243**	301-797-2124
Guardian Alarm Co 20800 Southfield Rd	Southfield	MI	48075	**800-782-9688**	248-423-1000
Honeywell ACS 11 W Spring St	Freeport	IL	61032	**800-328-5111**	
Honeywell Automation & Control Solutions 11 W Spring St	Freeport	IL	61032	**800-328-5111**	
Integrated Alarm Services Group Inc 99 Pine St 5th Fl *NASDAQ: IASG*	Albany	NY	12207	**888-305-4090**	518-426-1515
Matrix Security Systems LLC 109 S Old Dupont Rd	Wilmington	DE	19805	**800-498-5581**	302-683-9101
Monitronics International Inc 12801 Stemmons Fwy Suite 821 *Cust Svc	Dallas	TX	75234	**800-447-9239***	972-243-7443
New England Security Inc 10 Industrial Dr PO Box 562	Westerly	RI	02891	**800-556-7395**	401-596-0660
Norment Security Group Inc 3224 Mobile Hwy	Montgomery	AL	36108	**800-633-1968**	334-281-8440
Per Mar Security 1910 E Kimberly Rd	Davenport	IA	52807	**800-473-7627**	563-326-6291
Protection One Inc 1035 N 3rd St Suite 101	Lawrence	KS	66044	**800-438-4357**	785-856-5500
Response USA Inc 535 Rt 38 Suite 500	Cherry Hill	NJ	08002	**800-777-9807**	856-661-0700
Security Assoc International Inc 2101 S Arlington Heights Rd Suite 150	Arlington Heights	IL	60005	**800-323-7601**	847-956-8650
Security Corp 22325 Roethel Dr	Novi	MI	48375	**888-374-5789**	248-374-5700
Security Services & Technologies 2450 Blvd of the Generals Valley Forge Business Ctr	Norristown	PA	19403	**888-446-7781**	610-630-6790
Security Solutions Inc 3224 Lake Woodard Dr	Raleigh	NC	27604	**888-531-1018**	919-828-1018
UTC Fire & Security 5201 Explorer Dr	Mississauga	ON	L4W4H1	**800-661-4149**	905-629-2600

684 SEED COMPANIES

SEE ALSO Farm Supplies

Company / Address	City	State	ZIP	Toll-Free	Phone
AgriGold Hybrids RR 1 Box 203	Saint Francisville	IL	62460	**800-262-7333**	618-943-5776
Albert Lea Seed House 1414 W Main St	Albert Lea	MN	56007	**800-352-5247**	507-373-3161
Ampac Seed Co 32727 Hwy 99 E	Tangent	OR	97389	**800-547-3230**	541-928-1651
Applewood Seed Co 5380 Vivian St	Arvada	CO	80002	**888-778-7333**	303-431-7333
Ball Seed Co 622 Town Rd	West Chicago	IL	60185	**800-879-2255**	630-231-3500
Barenbrug USA Inc 33477 Hwy 99 E	Tangent	OR	97389	**800-547-4101**	541-926-5801
Burpee W Atlee Co 300 Park Ave *Cust Svc	Warminster	PA	18974	**800-333-5808***	215-674-4900
Cascade International Seed Co 8483 W Stayton Rd	Aumsville	OR	97325	**800-826-6799**	503-749-1822

Classified Section

Company	City	State	Zip	Toll-Free	Phone
Croplan Genetics PO Box 64281 MS 5850	Saint Paul	MN	55164	**800-328-9680**	651-765-5712
Garst Seed Co 2369 230th St PO Box 500	Slater	IA	50244	**888-464-2778**	515-685-5000
Gries Seed Farms Inc 2348 N 5th St	Fremont	OH	43420	**800-472-4797**	419-332-5571
Harris Moran Seed Co 555 Codoni Ave	Modesto	CA	95352	**800-808-7333**	209-579-7333
Johnston Seed Co 415 W Chestnut St	Enid	OK	73701	**800-375-4613**	580-233-5800
JW Jung Seed Co 335 S High St	Randolph	WI	53956	**800-297-3123**	920-326-3121
Latham Seed Co 131 180th St	Alexander	IA	50420	**800-798-3258**	641-692-3258
Lebanon Seaboard Corp 1600 E Cumberland St	Lebanon	PA	17042	**800-233-0628**	717-273-1685
Loft Seed Inc 9327 US Rt 1 Suite J	Laurel	MD	20723	**800-732-3332**	
Nunhems USA Inc 1200 Anderson Corner Rd *Cust Svc	Parma	ID	83660	**800-733-9505***	208-674-4000
Olds Seed Solutions 2901 Tackers Ave	Madison	WI	53707	**800-356-7333**	608-249-9291
Park Seed Co 1 Parkton Ave *Orders	Greenwood	SC	29647	**800-845-3369***	864-223-8555
Pennington Seed Inc 1280 Atlantic Hwy	Madison	GA	30650	**800-277-1412**	706-342-1234
Red River Commodities Inc 501 42nd St NW	Fargo	ND	58102	**800-437-5539**	701-282-2600
Renee's Garden Seeds Inc 7389 W Zayante Rd	Felton	CA	95018	**888-880-7228**	831-335-7228
Sand Seed Service Inc 4765 Hwy 143	Marcus	IA	51035	**800-352-2228**	712-376-4135
Schlessman Seed Co 11513 US Rt 250	Milan	OH	44846	**888-534-7333**	419-499-2572
Seedway Inc 1734 Railroad Pl	Hall	NY	14463	**800-836-3710**	585-526-6391
Seminis Inc 2700 Camino del Sol	Oxnard	CA	93030	**800-647-7386**	805-647-1572
Sharp Brothers Seed Co 2005 S Sycamore	Healy	KS	67850	**800-462-8483**	620-398-2231
Stock Seed Farms 28008 Mill Rd	Murdock	NE	68407	**800-759-1520**	402-867-3771
Stratton Seed Co 1530 Hwy 79 S PO box 1088	Stuttgart	AR	72160	**800-264-4433**	870-673-4433
Syngenta Corp 2200 Concord Pike	Wilmington	DE	19803	**800-759-4500**	302-425-2000
Syngenta Seeds Inc 7500 Olson Memorial Hwy	Golden Valley	MN	55427	**800-445-0956**	763-593-7333
Syngenta Seeds Inc Flowers Div 5300 Katrine Ave	Downers Grove	IL	60515	**800-323-7253**	630-969-6300
Thorp Seed Co RR 3 Box 257	Clinton	IL	61727	**800-648-2676**	217-935-2171
Triumph Seed Co Hwy 62 Bypass PO Box 1050	Ralls	TX	79357	**800-530-4789**	806-253-2584
W Atlee Burpee Co 300 Park Ave *Cust Svc	Warminster	PA	18974	**800-333-5808***	215-674-4900
Weeks Seed Co Inc 2103 Chestnut St	Greenville	NC	27834	**800-322-1234**	252-757-1234
Wetsel Inc 961 Liberty St	Harrisonburg	VA	22802	**800-572-4018**	540-434-6753

685 SEMICONDUCTOR MANUFACTURING SYSTEMS & EQUIPMENT

Company	City	State	Zip	Toll-Free	Phone
ADE Corp 80 Wilson Way *NASDAQ: ADEX*	Westwood	MA	02090	**800-343-2332**	781-467-3500
Advanced Energy Industries Inc 1625 Sharp Pt Dr *NASDAQ: AEIS*	Fort Collins	CO	80525	**800-446-9167**	970-221-4670
Aehr Test Systems 400 Kato Terr *NASDAQ: AEHR*	Fremont	CA	94539	**800-522-7200**	510-623-9400
ASML 8555 S River Pkwy *NASDAQ: ASML*	Tempe	AZ	85284	**800-227-6462**	480-383-4422
Asyst Technologies Inc 48761 Kato Rd *NASDAQ: ASYT*	Fremont	CA	94538	**800-345-7643**	510-661-5000
ATMI Inc 7 Commerce Dr *NASDAQ: ATMI*	Danbury	CT	06810	**800-766-2681**	203-794-1100
BOC Edwards 301 Ballardvale St	Wilmington	MA	01887	**800-848-9800**	978-658-5410
BTU International Inc 23 Esquire Rd *NASDAQ: BTUI*	North Billerica	MA	01862	**800-998-0666**	978-667-4111
Data I/O Corp 10525 Willows Rd NE *NASDAQ: DAIO*	Redmond	WA	98052	**800-426-1045**	425-881-6444
Ebara Technologies Inc 51 Main Ave	Sacramento	CA	95838	**800-535-5376**	916-920-5451
Electroglas Inc 6024 Silver Creek Valley Rd *NASDAQ: EGLS*	San Jose	CA	95138	**800-538-5124**	408-528-3000
FSI International Inc 3455 Lyman Blvd *NASDAQ: FSII*	Chaska	MN	55318	**800-274-5440**	952-448-5440
Genus Inc 1139 Karlstad Dr	Sunnyvale	CA	94089	**800-366-0989**	408-747-7120
KDF Inc 10 Volvo Dr	Rockleigh	NJ	07647	**877-533-3343**	201-784-5005
Kokusai Semiconductor Equipment Group 2450 N 1st St Suite 290	San Jose	CA	95131	**800-800-5321**	408-456-2750
Kulicke & Soffa Industries Inc 2101 Blair Mill Rd *NASDAQ: KLIC*	Willow Grove	PA	19090	**800-445-5671**	215-784-6000
Lam Research Corp 4650 Cushing Pkwy *NASDAQ: LRCX*	Fremont	CA	94538	**800-526-7678**	510-659-0200
LogicVision Inc 101 Metro Dr 3rd Fl *NASDAQ: LGVN*	San Jose	CA	95110	**888-584-2478**	408-453-0146
Mattson Technology Inc 47131 Bayside Pkwy *NASDAQ: MTSN*	Fremont	CA	94538	**800-628-8766**	510-657-5900
Micro Component Technology Inc 2340 W County Rd C	Saint Paul	MN	55113	**800-628-1628**	651-697-4000
Mykrolis Corp 129 Concord Rd Bldg 2 *NYSE: MYK*	Billerica	MA	01821	**877-695-7654**	978-436-6500
Novellus Systems Inc 4000 N 1st St *NASDAQ: NVLS*	San Jose	CA	95134	**800-800-3079**	408-943-9700
RVSI Inspection LLC 425 Rabro Dr E	Hauppauge	NY	11788	**800-669-5234**	631-273-9700
Semitool Inc 655 W Reserve Dr *NASDAQ: SMTL*	Kalispell	MT	59901	**800-548-8495**	406-752-2107
Siemens Dematic Electronics Assembly Systems Inc 3140 Northwoods Pkwy Suite 300	Norcross	GA	30071	**888-768-4357**	770-797-3000
Small Precision Tools Inc 1330 Clegg St	Petaluma	CA	94954	**800-346-4927**	707-765-4545
Solitec Wafer Processing Inc 685 River Oaks Pkwy	San Jose	CA	95134	**800-648-4040**	408-955-9939
Spire Corp 1 Patriots Pk *NASDAQ: SPIR*	Bedford	MA	01730	**800-510-4815**	781-275-6000
Sputtered Films Inc 320 Nopal St	Santa Barbara	CA	93103	**888-734-3456**	805-963-9651
Tokyo Electron America Inc 2400 Grove Blvd	Austin	TX	78741	**800-828-6596**	512-424-1000
Trikon Technologies Inc 17835 New Hope St Suite A *NASDAQ: TRKN*	Fountain Valley	CA	92708	**800-727-5585**	714-968-4299
Ultratech Inc 3050 Zanker Rd *NASDAQ: UTEK*	San Jose	CA	95134	**800-222-1213**	408-321-8835
Universal Instruments Corp 90 Bevier St	Binghamton	NY	13904	**800-842-9732**	607-779-7522
Varian Semiconductor Equipment Assoc Inc 35 Dory Rd *NASDAQ: VSEA*	Gloucester	MA	01930	**800-447-1762**	978-282-2000

686 SEMICONDUCTORS & RELATED DEVICES

SEE ALSO Electronic Components & Accessories - Mfr; Printed Circuit Boards

Company	City	State	Zip	Toll-Free	Phone
Actel Corp 2061 Stierlin Ct *NASDAQ: ACTL*	Mountain View	CA	94043	**800-262-1060**	650-318-4200
Advanced Micro Devices Inc PO Box 3453 *NYSE: AMD*	Sunnyvale	CA	94088	**800-538-8450**	408-732-2400
Advanced Power Technology Inc 405 SW Columbia St *NASDAQ: APTI*	Bend	OR	97702	**800-522-0809**	541-382-8028
Agere Systems Inc 1110 American Pkwy NE *NYSE: AGR*	Allentown	PA	18109	**800-372-2447**	610-712-6011
Agilent Technologies Inc 395 Page Mill Rd *NYSE: A*	Palo Alto	CA	94306	**877-424-4536**	650-752-5000
Alliance Semiconductor Corp 2575 Augustine Dr *NASDAQ: ALSC*	Santa Clara	CA	95054	**888-383-4900**	408-855-4900
Altera Corp 101 Innovation Dr *NASDAQ: ALTR* ■ *Cust Svc	San Jose	CA	95134	**800-767-3753***	408-544-7000
Analog Devices Inc 1 Technology Way PO Box 9106 *NYSE: ADI*	Norwood	MA	02062	**800-262-5643**	781-329-4700
Applied Micro Circuits Corp 6290 Sequence Dr *NASDAQ: AMCC*	San Diego	CA	92121	**800-935-2622**	858-450-9333
California Micro Devices Corp 430 N McCarthy Blvd Suite 100 *NASDAQ: CAMD*	Milpitas	CA	95035	**800-325-4966**	408-263-3214
Catalyst Semiconductor Inc 1250 Borregas Ave *NASDAQ: CATS*	Sunnyvale	CA	94089	**800-258-5991**	408-542-1000
Centillium Communications Inc 215 Fourier Ave *NASDAQ: CTLM*	Fremont	CA	94539	**877-879-7500**	510-771-3700
Centrovision 2088 Anchor Ct	Newbury Park	CA	91320	**800-700-2088**	805-499-5902
Cirrus Logic Inc 2901 Via Fortuna *NASDAQ: CRUS*	Austin	TX	78746	**800-888-5016**	512-851-4000
Conexant Systems Inc 4000 MacArthur Blvd *NASDAQ: CNXT*	Newport Beach	CA	92660	**800-854-8099**	949-483-4600
Cree Inc 4600 Silicon Dr *NASDAQ: CREE*	Durham	NC	27703	**800-533-2583**	919-313-5300
Cypress Semiconductor Corp 3901 N 1st St *NYSE: CY*	San Jose	CA	95134	**800-541-4736**	408-943-2600
DPAC Technologies Corp 7321 Lincoln Way *NASDAQ: DPAC*	Garden Grove	CA	92841	**800-642-4477**	714-898-0007
Enhanced Memory Systems Inc 1850 Ramtron Dr	Colorado Springs	CO	80921	**800-545-3726**	719-481-7000
Epson Electronics America Inc 150 River Oaks Pkwy	San Jose	CA	95134	**800-228-3964**	408-922-0200
Evergreen Solar Inc 259 Cedar Hill St *NASDAQ: ESLR*	Marlborough	MA	01752	**800-357-2221**	508-357-2221
Fairchild Semiconductor Corp 333 Western Ave *NYSE: FCS*	South Portland	ME	04106	**800-341-0392**	207-775-8100
FerroTec (USA) Corp 40 Simon St	Nashua	NH	03060	**800-258-1788**	603-883-9800
Freescale Semiconductor Inc 6501 William Cannon Dr W *NYSE: FSL* ■ *Tech Supp	Austin	TX	78735	**800-521-6274***	512-895-2000
Fujitsu Microelectronics America Inc 1250 E Arques Ave	Sunnyvale	CA	94088	**800-637-0683**	408-737-5600
HEI Inc 1495 Steiger Lake Ln *NASDAQ: HEII*	Victoria	MN	55386	**800-778-7773**	952-443-2500
Hitachi Canada Ltd 2495 Meadowpine Blvd	Mississauga	ON	L5N6C3	**800-906-4482**	905-821-4545
Hynix Semiconductor America Inc 3101 N 1st St	San Jose	CA	95134	**800-627-7978**	408-232-8000
Integrated Device Technology Inc 2975 Stender Way *NASDAQ: IDTI*	Santa Clara	CA	95054	**800-345-7015**	408-727-6116
Integrated Silicon Solution Inc (ISSI) 2231 Lawson Ln *NASDAQ: ISSI*	Santa Clara	CA	95054	**800-379-4774**	408-969-6600
Intel Corp 2200 Mission College Blvd *NASDAQ: INTC* ■ *Cust Svc	Santa Clara	CA	95052	**800-628-8686***	408-765-8080
InterDigital Communications Corp 781 3rd Ave *NASDAQ: IDCC*	King of Prussia	PA	19406	**800-669-4737**	610-878-7800
Irvine Sensors Corp 3001 Redhill Ave Bldg 3 Suite 108 *NASDAQ: IRSN*	Costa Mesa	CA	92626	**800-468-4612**	714-549-8211
ISSI (Integrated Silicon Solution Inc) 2231 Lawson Ln *NASDAQ: ISSI*	Santa Clara	CA	95054	**800-379-4774**	408-969-6600
Kyocera Solar Inc 7812 E Acoma Dr Suite 2	Scottsdale	AZ	86260	**800-223-9580**	480-948-8003
Lattice Semiconductor Corp 5555 NE Moore Ct *NASDAQ: LSCC*	Hillsboro	OR	97124	**800-327-8636**	503-681-0118
Legerity Inc 4509 Frederick Ln Suite 200	Austin	TX	78744	**800-432-4009**	512-228-5400
Logic Devices Inc 395 W Java Dr *NASDAQ: LOGC*	Sunnyvale	CA	94089	**800-851-0767**	408-542-5400
LSI Logic Corp 1621 Barber Ln *NYSE: LSI*	Milpitas	CA	95035	**866-574-5741**	408-433-8000
Maxim Integrated Products Inc 120 San Gabriel Dr *NASDAQ: MXIM*	Sunnyvale	CA	94086	**800-659-5909**	408-737-7600
Medtronic Microelectronics Center 2343 W Medtronic Way	Tempe	AZ	85281	**800-633-8766**	480-929-5507
Micrel Inc 1849 Fortune Dr *NASDAQ: MCRL*	San Jose	CA	95131	**800-800-2045**	408-944-0800
Micro Linear Corp 2050 Concourse Dr *NASDAQ: MLIN*	San Jose	CA	95131	**800-998-5200**	408-433-5200
Microchip Technology Inc 2355 W Chandler Blvd *NASDAQ: MCHP*	Chandler	AZ	85224	**800-437-2767**	480-792-7200
Microsemi Corp 2381 Morse Ave *NASDAQ: MSCC*	Irvine	CA	92614	**800-713-4113**	949-221-7100
Motorola Inc 1301 E Algonquin Rd *NYSE: MOT*	Schaumburg	IL	60196	**800-331-6456**	847-576-5000

				Toll-Free	Phone
NEC Electronics Inc 2880 Scott Blvd	Santa Clara	CA	95052	**800-366-9782**	408-588-6000
NeoPhotonics Corp 2911 Zanker Rd	San Jose	CA	95134	**800-499-7519**	408-232-9200
NetSilicon Inc					
411 Waverly Oaks Rd Suite 304	Waltham	MA	02452	**800-243-2333**	781-647-1234
Nitto Denko America Inc 48500 Fremont Blvd	Fremont	CA	94538	**800-356-4880**	510-445-5400
Omron Electronics Inc 1 Commerce Dr	Schaumburg	IL	60173	**800-556-6766**	847-843-7900
ON Semiconductor Corp 5005 E McDowell Rd	Phoenix	AZ	85008	**800-282-9855**	602-244-6600
NASDAQ: ONNN					
Optek Technology Inc 1645 Wallace Dr	Carrollton	TX	75006	**800-341-4747**	972-323-2200
Pericom Semiconductor Corp 3545 N 1st St	San Jose	CA	95134	**800-435-2336**	408-435-0800
NASDAQ: PSEM					
PerkinElmer Optoelectronics Inc					
2175 Mission College Blvd	Santa Clara	CA	95054	**800-775-6786**	408-565-0850
Philips Semiconductors 1109 McKay Dr	San Jose	CA	95131	**800-447-1500**	408-434-3000
PLX Technology Inc 870 W Maude Ave	Sunnyvale	CA	94085	**800-759-3735**	408-774-9060
NASDAQ: PLXT					
Powerex Inc 200 Hillis St	Youngwood	PA	15697	**800-451-1415**	724-925-7272
Praxair MRC 542 Rt 303	Orangeburg	NY	10962	**800-827-4387**	845-359-4200
QLogic Corp 26650 Aliso Viejo Pkwy	Aliso Viejo	CA	92656	**800-662-4471**	949-389-6000
NASDAQ: QLGC					
Rambus Inc 4440 El Camino Real	Los Altos	CA	94022	**800-726-2879**	650-947-5000
NASDAQ: RMBS					
Ramtron International Corp					
1850 Ramtron Dr	Colorado Springs	CO	80921	**800-545-3726**	719-481-7000
NASDAQ: RMTR					
Raytek Inc 1201 Shaffer Rd Bldg 2	Santa Cruz	CA	95060	**800-227-8074**	831-458-1110
Samsung Electronics America Inc					
105 Challenger Rd	Ridgefield Park	NJ	07660	**800-726-7864**	201-229-4000
Samsung Semiconductors Inc 3655 N 1st St	San Jose	CA	95134	**800-726-7864**	408-544-4000
Scientific Technologies Inc					
6550 Dumbarton Cir	Fremont	CA	94555	**800-221-7060**	510-608-3400
NASDAQ: STIZ					
Seiko Instruments USA Inc					
2990 W Lomita Blvd	Torrance	CA	90505	**800-358-0880**	310-517-7050
Sheldahl Inc 1150 Sheldahl Rd	Northfield	MN	55057	**800-533-0505**	507-663-8000
Sigma Designs Inc 1221 California Cir	Milpitas	CA	95035	**800-845-8086***	408-262-9003
NASDAQ: SIGM ■ *Sales					
Silicon Laboratories Inc 4635 Boston Ln	Austin	TX	78735	**877-444-3032**	512-416-8500
NASDAQ: SLAB					
Sirenza Microdevices Inc					
303 S Technology Ct	Broomfield	CO	80021	**800-764-6642**	303-327-3030
NASDAQ: SMDI					
Skyworks Solutions Inc 20 Sylvan Rd	Woburn	MA	01801	**800-411-3619***	781-935-5150
NASDAQ: SWKS ■ *Sales					
Southland Micro Systems 7 Morgan	Irvine	CA	92618	**800-255-4200**	949-380-1958
Supertex Inc 1235 Bordeaux Dr	Sunnyvale	CA	94089	**800-487-8737**	408-744-0100
NASDAQ: SUPX					
Telephonics Corp 815 Broad Hollow Rd	Farmingdale	NY	11735	**877-755-7700**	631-755-7000
Texas Instruments Inc 12500 TI Blvd	Dallas	TX	75243	**800-336-5236***	972-995-2011
NYSE: TXN ■ *Cust Svc					
Toshiba America Electronic Components Inc					
19900 MacArthur Blvd Suite 400	Irvine	CA	92612	**800-879-4963***	949-455-2000
*Cust Svc					
Tosoh SMD Inc 3600 Gantz Rd	Grove City	OH	43123	**800-678-8942**	614-875-7912
Tripath Technology Inc 2560 Orchard Pkwy	San Jose	CA	95131	**877-874-7284**	408-750-3000
NASDAQ: TRPH					
TriQuint Semiconductor Inc					
2300 NE Brookwood Pkwy	Hillsboro	OR	97124	**888-258-5873**	503-615-9000
NASDAQ: TQNT					
Tundra Semiconductor Corp 603 March Rd	Ottawa	ON	K2K2M5	**800-267-7231**	613-592-0714
TSE: TUN					
Virage Logic Corp 47100 Bayside Pkwy	Fremont	CA	94538	**877-360-6690**	510-360-8000
NASDAQ: VIRL					
Vitesse Semiconductor Corp 741 Calle Plano	Camarillo	CA	93012	**800-848-3773**	805-388-3700
NASDAQ: VTSS					
Wacker Siltronic Corp 7200 NW Front Ave	Portland	OR	97210	**800-922-5371**	503-243-2020
White Electronic Designs Corp					
3601 E University Dr	Phoenix	AZ	85034	**800-326-9556**	602-437-1520
NASDAQ: WEDC					
Winbond Electronics Corp America					
2727 N 1st St	San Jose	CA	95134	**800-825-4473**	408-943-6666
Xilinx Inc 2100 Logic Dr	San Jose	CA	95124	**800-494-5469**	408-559-7778
NASDAQ: XLNX					
Zarlink Semiconductor Inc 400 March Rd	Ottawa	ON	K2K3H4	**800-325-4927**	613-592-0200
NYSE: ZL					
ZiLOG Inc 532 Race St	San Jose	CA	95126	**800-662-6211**	408-558-8500

687 SERVICE CONTRACTS & WARRANTIES - HOME

				Toll-Free	Phone
American Home Shield 889 Ridge Lake Blvd	Memphis	TN	38120	**800-247-1644**	901-537-8000
Aon Warranty Group Inc					
1000 Milwaukee Ave 6th Fl	Glenview	IL	60025	**800-747-5152**	847-953-2025
Blue Ribbon Home Warranty Inc					
95 S Wadsworth Blvd	Lakewood	CO	80226	**800-571-0475**	303-986-3900
Cross Country Home Services					
1625 NW 136th Ave Suite 200	Fort Lauderdale	FL	33323	**800-327-9787**	954-845-9100
Fidelity National Home Warranty Inc					
2950 Euskirk Ave	Walnut Creek	CA	94596	**800-862-6837**	925-934-4450
First American Home Buyers Protection Corp					
7833 Haskell Ave PO Box 10180	Van Nuys	CA	91410	**800-444-9030**	818-781-5050
HMS National Inc					
1625 NW 136th Ave Suite 200	Fort Lauderdale	FL	33323	**800-432-1033**	954-845-9100
Home Security of America Inc					
310 N Midvale Blvd	Madison	WI	53705	**800-367-1448**	608-231-0010
ServiceCare 3680 Leeds Ave	Charleston	SC	29405	**800-796-8889**	
Warrantech Consumer Products Services Inc					
2200 Hwy 121	Bedford	TX	76021	**800-544-9510**	817-283-7267
Warrantech Corp Inc 2200 Hwy 121	Bedford	TX	76021	**800-544-9510**	817-283-7267
Warrantech Home Service Co 2200 Hwy 121	Bedford	TX	76021	**800-544-9510**	817-283-7267
Warrantech International Inc 2200 Hwy 121	Beford	TX	76021	**800-544-9510**	817-283-7267

688 SHEET METAL WORK

SEE ALSO Construction - Special Trade Contractors - Plumbing, Heating, Air Conditioning Contractors; Construction - Special Trade Contractors - Roofing, Siding, Sheet Metal Contractors

				Toll-Free	Phone
Abalon Precision Mfg Corp 1040 Home St	Bronx	NY	10459	**800-888-2225**	718-589-5682
Acme Mfg Co 7601 State Rd	Philadelphia	PA	19136	**800-899-2850**	215-338-2850
Air Comfort Corp 2550 Braga Dr	Broadview	IL	60155	**800-466-3779**	708-345-1900
Air Systems Inc 7400 S 28th St	Fort Smith	AR	72908	**800-643-2980**	479-646-8386
Aircom Mfg Inc 6205 E 30th St	Indianapolis	IN	46219	**800-925-2426**	317-545-5383
Airolite Co 114 Westview Ave	Marietta	OH	45750	**800-247-6548**	740-373-7676
Aluminum Line Products Co 24460 Sperry Cir	Westlake	OH	44145	**800-321-3154**	440-835-8880
ArcRon Div IEA					
W 141 N 9501 Fountain Blvd	Menomonee Falls	WI	53051	**800-886-4151**	262-255-4150
Arizona Precision Sheet Metal					
2140 W Pinnacle Peak Rd	Phoenix	AZ	85027	**800-443-7039**	623-516-3700
ASC Profiles Inc					
2110 Enterprise Blvd	West Sacramento	CA	95691	**800-726-2727***	916-372-6851
*Cust Svc					
Associated Materials Inc					
3773 State Rd	Cuyahoga Falls	OH	44223	**800-257-4335**	330-929-1811
Berger Bros Co 805 Pennsylvania Blvd	Feasterville	PA	19053	**800-523-8852***	215-355-1200
*Cust Svc					
Berger Holdings Ltd 805 Pennsylvania Blvd	Feasterville	PA	19053	**800-523-8852**	215-355-1200
Buffalo Sheet Metals Inc PO Box 191	Buffalo	NY	14240	**800-724-0750**	716-895-2324
Childers Products Co 1370 E 40th St	Houston	TX	77022	**800-231-1024**	713-691-7002
Christen Fred & Sons Co 714 George St	Toledo	OH	43608	**800-243-4161**	419-243-4161
Cinnabar Solution Inc					
155 Sunnynoll Ct Suite 300	Winston-Salem	NC	27106	**800-782-2171**	
Clark Specialty Co Inc 8440 Rt 54	Hammondsport	NY	14840	**888-569-2128**	607-569-2191
Connell LP 1 International Pl 31st Fl	Boston	MA	02110	**800-276-4746**	617-737-2700
Consolidated Systems Inc 650 Rosewood Dr	Columbia	SC	29201	**800-654-1912**	803-771-7920
Contech Construction Products Inc					
1001 Grove St	Middletown	OH	45044	**800-338-1122**	513-425-5896
Crown Products Co Inc 6390 Phillips Hwy	Jacksonville	FL	32216	**800-683-7144**	904-737-7144
CWR Mfg Corp 7000 Fly Rd	Syracuse	NY	13220	**800-724-0311***	315-437-1032
*Sales					
Dura-Bilt Products Inc PO Box 188	Wellsburg	NY	14894	**800-233-4251**	570-596-2000
Edco & Arrowhead Products Inc					
8700 Excelsior Blvd	Hopkins	MN	55343	**800-333-2580**	952-938-6313
Elixir Industries Inc 17925 S Broadway	Gardena	CA	90247	**800-421-1942**	310-767-3400
Fisher Skylights Inc					
5005 Veterans Memorial Hwy	Holbrook	NY	11741	**800-431-1586**	631-563-4001
Foster LB Co 415 Holiday Dr	Pittsburgh	PA	15220	**800-255-4500**	412-928-3400
NASDAQ: FSTR					
Frank M Booth Inc 222 3rd St	Marysville	CA	95901	**800-540-9369**	530-742-7134
Fred Christen & Sons Co 714 George St	Toledo	OH	43608	**800-243-4161**	419-243-4161
Gentek Building Products Inc					
3773 State Rd	Cuyahoga Falls	OH	44223	**800-548-4542**	
Gilbert Mechanical Contractors Inc					
4451 W 76th St	Edina	MN	55435	**800-701-0986**	952-835-3810
H & H Industrial Corp 7612 N Rt 130	Pennsauken	NJ	08110	**800-982-0341**	856-663-4444
Hi Pro International Inc 5049 S National Dr	Knoxville	TN	37914	**800-947-0997**	865-637-1711
HiMEC Inc 1400 7th St NW	Rochester	MN	55901	**888-454-4632**	507-281-4000
IEA ArcRon Div					
W 141 N 9501 Fountain Blvd	Menomonee Falls	WI	53051	**800-886-4151**	262-255-4150
Industrial Louvers Inc 511 7th St S	Delano	MN	55328	**800-328-3421**	763-972-2981
John W McDougall Co Inc					
3731 Amy Lynn Dr	Nashville	TN	37218	**800-264-1122**	615-321-3900
Jones Metal Products Inc 3201 3rd Ave	Mankato	MN	56001	**800-967-1750**	507-625-4436
Juniper Industries Inc					
72-15 Metropolitan Ave	Middle Village	NY	11379	**800-221-4664**	718-326-2546
Knox RF Co Inc PO Box 1337	Smyrna	GA	30081	**800-989-7401**	770-434-7401
LB Foster Co 415 Holiday Dr	Pittsburgh	PA	15220	**800-255-4500**	412-928-3400
NASDAQ: FSTR					
LL Building Products Inc					
4501 Circle 75 Pkwy Suite E5300	Atlanta	GA	30339	**800-755-9397**	770-953-6366
Maddox Metal Works Inc 4116 Bronze Way	Dallas	TX	75237	**800-952-1984**	214-333-2311
Mapes Industries Inc 2929 Cornhusker Hwy	Lincoln	NE	68504	**800-228-2391**	402-466-1985
Mayco Industries LLC 18 W Oxmoor Rd	Birmingham	AL	35209	**800-749-6061**	205-942-4242
Maysteel LLC					
N89 W14700 Patrita Dr PO Box 1240	Menomonee Falls	WI	53052	**800-255-1247**	262-255-2400
McCorvey Sheet Metal Works Inc					
PO Box 405	Galena Park	TX	77547	**800-580-7545**	713-672-7545
McDougall John W Co Inc					
3731 Amy Lynn Dr	Nashville	TN	37218	**800-264-1122**	615-321-3900
Metal-Fab Inc 3025 May St	Wichita	KS	67213	**800-835-2830**	316-943-2351
Metaltech Inc 206 Prospect Ave	Kirkwood	MO	63122	**800-325-9886**	314-965-4550
Micro Industries Inc 2990 S Main St	Salt Lake City	UT	84115	**800-446-3902**	801-466-2232
Milcor Inc 1150 N Cable Rd	Lima	OH	45805	**800-528-1411**	
Mitchell Metal Products Inc PO Box 789	Kosciusko	MS	39090	**800-258-6137**	662-289-7110
Murray Sheet Metal Co Inc 3112 7th St	Parkersburg	WV	26101	**800-464-8801**	304-422-5431
Napco Inc 125 McFann Rd	Valencia	PA	16059	**800-786-2726**	724-898-1511
National Metal Fabricators					
2395 Greenleaf Ave	Elk Grove Village	IL	60007	**800-323-8849**	847-439-5321
New Columbia Joist Co					
2093 Old Hwy 15	New Columbia	PA	17856	**800-233-3199**	570-568-6761
Owens Corning Fabricating Solutions					
426 N Main St	Elkhart	IN	46516	**877-632-2935**	574-522-8473
Pemberton Fabricators Inc 30 Indel Ave	Rancocas	NJ	08073	**800-573-6322**	609-267-0922
Petersen Aluminum Corp					
1005 Tonne Rd	Elk Grove Village	IL	60007	**800-323-1960**	847-228-7150
Platt & Labonia Co 70 Stoddard Ave	North Haven	CT	06473	**800-505-9099**	203-239-5681
Quality Metal Products Inc					
11500 W 13th Ave	Lakewood	CO	80215	**800-700-4730**	303-232-4242
Ready Metal Mfg Co Inc 4500 W 47th St	Chicago	IL	60632	**800-638-7334**	773-376-9700
RF Knox Co Inc PO Box 1337	Smyrna	GA	30081	**800-989-7401**	770-434-7401
Rollex Corp 2001 Lunt Ave	Elk Grove Village	IL	60007	**800-251-3300***	847-437-3000
*Cust Svc					
Saint Regis Culvert Inc 202 Morrell St	Charlotte	MI	48813	**800-527-4604**	517-543-3430
Simpson Dura-Vent Inc 877 Cotting Ct	Vacaville	CA	95688	**800-227-7374**	707-446-1786
Southwark Metal Mfg Co Inc					
2800 Red Lion Rd	Philadelphia	PA	19114	**800-523-1052**	215-735-3401
Standex International Corp Air Distribution Products Group 7601 State Rd	Philadelphia	PA	19136	**800-899-2850**	215-338-2850
Structures Unlimited Inc 88 Pine St	Manchester	NH	03103	**800-225-3895**	603-645-6539
Swanson Engineering & Mfg Co					
1133 E Redondo Blvd	Inglewood	CA	90302	**800-633-1158**	310-671-6915

				Toll-Free	Phone
Texas Aluminum Industries Inc 2900 Patio Dr	Houston	TX	77017	800-231-4009	713-946-9000
Thybar Corp 913 S Kay Ave	Addison	IL	60101	800-666-2872	630-543-5300
Trinity Industries Inc Highway Safety Products Div 2525 N Stemmons Fwy	Dallas	TX	75207	800-527-6050	214-589-8814
Valley Joist 3019 Gault Ave N	Fort Payne	AL	35967	800-633-2258	256-845-2330
Vent Products Co Inc 1901 S Kilbourn Ave	Chicago	IL	60623	800-368-8368	773-521-1900
Western Metal Lath & Steel Framing Systems Inc 6510 General Dr	Riverside	CA	92509	800-365-5284	951-360-3500
Wisco Products Inc 109 Commercial St	Dayton	OH	45402	800-367-6570	937-228-2101

689 SHIP BUILDING & REPAIRING

				Toll-Free	Phone
Atlantic Marine Inc 8500 Heckscher Dr	Jacksonville	FL	32226	800-395-6446	904-251-1545
Bay Ship & Yacht Co 310 W Cutting Blvd	Point Richmond	CA	94804	800-900-6646	510-237-0140
Boland Marine & Mfg Co Inc 1000 Tchoupitoulas St	New Orleans	LA	70130	888-265-2631	504-581-5800
Cascade General Inc 5555 N Channel Ave	Portland	OR	97217	800-505-1930	503-285-1111
Colonna's Shipyard Inc 400 E Indian River Rd	Norfolk	VA	23523	800-265-6627	757-545-2414
Detyens Shipyards Inc 1670 Drydock Ave Bldg 236 Suite 200	North Charleston	SC	29405	800-745-2811	843-308-8000
First Wave Marine Inc 2616 South Loop W Suite 665	Houston	TX	77054	800-399-9283	713-847-4600
Friede Halter Inc PO Box 1328	Pascagoula	MS	39568	800-877-0029	228-696-6888
Goltens New York Corp 160 Van Brunt St	Brooklyn	NY	11231	877-204-1088	718-855-7200
Greenbrier Co 1 Centerpointe Dr Suite 200 *NYSE: GBX*	Lake Oswego	OR	97035	800-343-7188	503-684-7000
Gunderson Inc 4350 NW Front Ave	Portland	OR	97210	800-253-4350	503-972-5700
Tecnico Corp 831 Industrial Ave	Chesapeake	VA	23324	800-786-2207	757-545-4013

690 SHUTTERS - WINDOW (ALL TYPES)

				Toll-Free	Phone
All Broward Hurricane Panel Co 450 W McNab Rd	Fort Lauderdale	FL	33309	800-432-1803	954-974-3300
Atlantic Shutter Systems 3239 Hwy 301 N	Latta	SC	29565	877-437-0608	
Hurst Awning Co Inc 6865 NW 36th Ave	Miami	FL	33147	800-327-0905	
Mid-America Building Products Co 29797 Beck Rd	Wixom	MI	48393	800-521-8486	
Perfect Shutters Inc 12213 Hwy 173	Hebron	IL	60034	800-548-3336	815-648-2401
Roll-A-Way Inc 10601 Oak St NE	Saint Petersburg	FL	33716	800-683-9505	727-576-1143
Roll Shutter Systems Inc 21633 N 14th Ave	Phoenix	AZ	85027	800-551-7655	623-869-7057
Rolladen Inc 550 Ansin Blvd	Hallandale	FL	33009	800-748-8837	954-921-1522
Rolling Shield Inc 2500 NW 74th Ave	Miami	FL	33122	800-474-9404	305-470-9404
Rolsafe 5845 Corporation Cir	Fort Myers	FL	33905	800-833-5486	239-694-5400
Seaview Industries Inc 4595 NW 37th Ct	Miami	FL	33142	800-282-8688	305-633-9650
Shutter Mill Inc 8517 S Perkins Rd	Stillwater	OK	74074	800-416-6455	405-377-6455
Storm Safe Shutters 3593 Veronica Shoemaker Blvd	Fort Myers	FL	33916	800-257-8676	239-432-9181
Vantage Products Corp 960 Almon Rd	Covington	GA	30014	800-481-3303	770-788-0136

691 SIGNALS & SIRENS - ELECTRIC

				Toll-Free	Phone
ADDCO Inc 240 Arlington Ave E	Saint Paul	MN	55117	888-616-4408	651-488-8600
ALSTOM Signaling Inc 1025 John St *Cust Svc	West Henrietta	NY	14586	800-717-4477*	585-783-2000
ECCO 833 W Diamond St	Boise	ID	83705	800-635-5900	208-395-8000
GE Transportation Rail Global Signaling PO Box 8900	Melbourne	FL	32904	800-342-5434	321-435-7000
Jenkins WL Co 1445 Whipple Ave SW	Canton	OH	44710	800-426-7021	330-477-3407
Safetran Systems Corp 2400 Nelson Miller Pkwy	Louisville	KY	40223	800-626-2710	502-244-7400
Siemens ITS 8004 Cameron Rd	Austin	TX	78754	800-388-6882	512-837-8310
Signal Communications Inc 6555 NW 9th Ave Suite 108	Fort Lauderdale	FL	33309	800-400-3220	954-493-6363
Traffic Control Corp 780 W Belden Ave Suite D	Addison	IL	60101	800-996-6511	630-543-1300
Union Switch & Signal Inc 1000 Technology Dr	Pittsburgh	PA	15219	800-351-1520	412-688-2400
Unitrol 1108 Raymond Way	Anaheim	CA	92801	800-854-3375	714-871-3336
US Traffic Corp 9603 S John St	Santa Fe Springs	CA	90670	800-733-7872	562-923-9600
Webb Murray & Assoc Inc 2615 Beltway 8 E	Pasadena	TX	77503	800-288-7428	281-991-4227
WL Jenkins Co 1445 Whipple Ave SW	Canton	OH	44710	800-426-7021	330-477-3407

692 SIGNS

SEE ALSO Displays - Exhibit & Trade Show; Displays - Point-of-Purchase; Signals & Sirens - Electric

				Toll-Free	Phone
Ace Sign Systems Inc 3621 W Royerton Rd	Muncie	IN	47304	800-607-6010	765-288-1000
Advance Corp Braille-Tac Div 8200 97th St S	Cottage Grove	MN	55016	800-328-9451	651-771-9297
Allen Industries Corp 6434 Burnt Poplar Rd	Greensboro	NC	27409	800-967-2553	336-668-2791
Artcraft Signs Co 1717 S Acoma St	Denver	CO	80223	800-278-7771	303-777-7771
Brady Corp 6555 W Good Hope Rd *NYSE: BRC* ■ *Cust Svc	Milwaukee	WI	53223	800-537-8791*	414-358-6600
Braille-Tac Div Advance Corp 8200 97th St S	Cottage Grove	MN	55016	800-328-9451	651-771-9297
California Neon Products Inc 4530 Mission Gorge Pl	San Diego	CA	92120	800-822-6366	619-283-2191
Century Graphics & Metals Inc 3497 All American Blvd	Orlando	FL	32810	800-327-5664	407-295-7818
Certified Electronic Display Inc 3121 N Adart Rd	Stockton	CA	95215	800-350-7773	209-931-7850
Clearr Corp 6325 Sandburg Rd	Minneapolis	MN	55427	800-948-3269	763-398-5400
Colorado Time Systems LLC 1551 E 11th St	Loveland	CO	80537	800-920-9332	970-667-1000
Couch & Philippi Inc PO Box A *Orders	Stanton	CA	90680	800-854-3360*	714-527-2261
DeeSign Co 1010 Raymond Way	Anaheim	CA	92801	800-824-2565	714-871-5115
DiAZiT Co Inc PO Box 276 *Cust Svc	Youngsville	NC	27596	800-334-6641*	919-556-5188
Doyle Signs Inc 232 Interstate Rd	Addison	IL	60101	800-344-9490	630-543-9490
Eastern Metal/USA-SIGN 1430 Sullivan St *Sales	Elmira	NY	14901	800-872-7446*	607-734-2295
Everbrite Inc PO Box 20020	Greenfield	WI	53220	800-558-3888	414-529-3500
FASTSIGNS International Inc 2550 Midway Rd Suite 150	Carrollton	TX	75006	800-827-7446	972-447-0777
FLOORgraphics Inc 5 Vaughn Dr Suite 200	Princeton	NJ	08540	888-356-6723	609-514-0404
GableSigns Inc 7440 Fort Smallwood Rd	Baltimore	MD	21226	800-854-0568	410-255-6400
Gemini Inc 103 Mensing Ave	Cannon Falls	MN	55009	800-533-3631	507-263-3957
General Sign Co PO Box 999 *Cust Svc	Cape Girardeau	MO	63702	800-325-0205*	573-334-5041
Globe Transportation Graphics 7127 Rutherford Rd	Baltimore	MD	21244	800-755-6750	410-685-6750
Gopher Sign Co 1310 Randolph Ave	Saint Paul	MN	55105	800-383-3156	651-698-5095
Gordon Sign Co Inc 2930 W 9th Ave	Denver	CO	80204	800-323-6121	303-629-6121
Grandwell Industries Inc 121 Quantum St	Holly Springs	NC	27540	800-338-6554	919-557-1221
Graphic Specialties Inc 3110 Washington Ave N	Minneapolis	MN	55411	800-486-4605	612-522-5287
Hall Signs Inc PO Box 2267 Dept 15 *Cust Svc	Bloomington	IN	47402	800-284-7446*	812-332-9355
Hawkins Traffic Safety Supply 1255 E Shore Hwy	Berkeley	CA	94710	800-772-3995	510-525-4040
Hi*Tech Electronic Displays 13900 US Hwy 19N	Clearwater	FL	33764	800-723-9402	727-531-4800
Hy-Ko Products Co 60 Meadow Ln	Northfield	OH	44067	800-292-0550	330-467-7446
Icon Identity Solutions 1418 Elmhurst Rd	Elk Grove Village	IL	60007	800-633-8181	847-364-2250
Image National Inc 444 E Amity Rd	Boise	ID	83716	800-592-8058	208-345-4020
ImagePoint Inc 445 S Gay St	Knoxville	TN	37902	800-444-7446	865-938-1511
Insignia Systems Inc 6470 Sycamore Ct N *NASDAQ: ISIG*	Maple Grove	MN	55369	800-874-4648	763-392-6200
International Display Systems Inc 5008 Veterans Memorial Hwy	Holbrook	NY	11741	800-542-9779	631-218-1802
International Patterns Inc 50 Inez Dr	Bay Shore	NY	11706	800-471-6368	631-952-2000
Jarob Design Inc 2601 Elmridge Dr NW	Grand Rapids	MI	49544	800-843-2508	616-453-5419
JM Stewart Corp 2201 Cantu Ct Suite 217-218	Sarasota	FL	34232	800-237-3928	941-378-4242
KCS Industries Inc 340 Maple Ave	Hartland	WI	53029	800-777-5111	262-369-9995
Kieffer & Co Inc 3322 Washington Ave	Sheboygan	WI	53081	800-458-4354	920-458-4394
Kux Graphic Systems Inc 12675 Burt Rd	Detroit	MI	48223	800-521-9534	313-255-6460
Lake Shores Industries Inc PO Box 59	Erie	PA	16512	800-458-0463	814-456-4277
Lawrence Sign Inc 945 Pierce Butler Rt	Saint Paul	MN	55104	800-998-8901	651-488-6711
Leotek Electronics USA Corp 1330 Memorex Dr	Santa Clara	CA	95050	888-806-1188	408-988-4668
LSI Industries Inc 10000 Alliance Rd *NASDAQ: LYTS*	Cincinnati	OH	45242	800-274-2840	513-793-3200
Lyle Signs Inc 6294 Bury Dr	Eden Prairie	MN	55346	800-367-8560	952-934-7653
Lynn Sign Co 3 Liberty St	Merrimac	MA	01860	800-225-5764	978-346-8182
M-R Sign Co Inc 1706 1st Ave N	Fergus Falls	MN	56537	800-231-5564	218-736-5681
Marketing Displays International 38271 W 12-Mile Rd *Sales	Farmington Hills	MI	48331	800-228-8925*	248-553-1900
McLoone Metal Graphics Co 75 Sumner St	La Crosse	WI	54602	800-624-6641	608-784-1260
Mulholland Harper Co Inc 24778 Meeting House Rd PO Box C	Denton	MD	21629	800-882-3052	410-479-1300
National Print Group Inc PO Box 5968	Chattanooga	TN	37406	800-624-0408	423-622-2254
National Stock Sign Co 1040 El Dorado Ave	Santa Cruz	CA	95062	800-462-7726	831-476-2020
Pannier Graphics 345 Oak Rd	Gibsonia	PA	15044	800-544-8428	724-265-4900
Philadelphia Sign Co Inc 707 W Spring Garden St	Palmyra	NJ	08065	800-355-1460	856-829-1460
Poblocki Sign Co LLC 922 S 70th St	West Allis	WI	53214	800-776-7064	414-453-4010
Precision Solar Controls Inc 2985 Market St	Garland	TX	75041	800-686-7414	972-278-0553
Prismaflex Inc 1645 Queens Way E	Mississauga	ON	L4X3A3	800-526-1488	905-279-9793
Protection Services Inc 635 Lucknow Rd	Harrisburg	PA	17110	866-489-1234	717-236-9307
Quality Mfg Inc 969 Labore Industrial Ct	Saint Paul	MN	55110	800-243-5473	651-483-5473
SA-SO Co PO Box 67484	Saint Paul	MN	55164	800-527-2450	
Safeway Sign Co 9875 Yucca Rd	Adelanto	CA	92301	800-637-7233	760-246-7070
Scioto Sign Co Inc 6047 US Rt 68 N	Kenton	OH	43326	800-572-4686	419-673-1261
Scott Sign Systems Inc 7524 Commerce Pl	Sarasota	FL	34243	800-237-9447	941-355-5171
Sign Builders Inc 4800 Jefferson Ave PO Box 28380	Birmingham	AL	35221	800-222-7330	
Sign Designs Inc 204 Campus Way	Modesto	CA	95350	800-421-7446	209-524-4484
Sign Resource Inc 6135 District Blvd	Maywood	CA	90270	800-423-4283	323-771-2098
Sign*A*Rama 1801 S Australian Ave	West Palm Beach	FL	33409	800-286-8671	561-640-5570
Signs First PO Box 11569	Memphis	TN	38111	800-852-2163	901-682-2264
Signs & More in 24 1739 St Marys Ave	Parkersburg	WV	26101	800-358-2358	304-424-7446
Signs Now Corp 4900 Manatee Ave W Suite 201	Bradenton	FL	34209	800-356-3373	941-747-7747
Signs by Tomorrow-USA Inc 6460 Dobbin Rd	Columbia	MD	21045	800-765-7446	410-992-7192
Signtronix Inc 1445 W Sepulveda Blvd	Torrance	CA	90501	800-729-4853	
Spectrum Corp 10048 Easthaven Blvd	Houston	TX	77075	800-392-5050	713-944-6200
Stout Marketing Inc 6425 W Florissant Ave	Saint Louis	MO	63136	800-325-8530	314-385-4600
Total Image Specialists 1877 E 17th Ave	Columbus	OH	43219	800-366-7446	614-564-1300
Tube Art Displays Inc 2730 Occidental Ave S	Seattle	WA	98134	800-562-2854	206-223-1122
Visual Graphic Systems Inc 500 10th Ave 7th Fl	New York	NY	10018	800-203-0301	212-563-5600
Vomela Specialty Co 380 Saint Peter St Suite 705	Saint Paul	MN	55102	800-645-1012	651-228-2200
Walter Haas & Sons Inc 123 W 23rd St	Hialeah	FL	33010	800-552-3845	305-883-2257
Wayne Industries 1400 8th St N	Clanton	AL	35045	800-225-3148	205-755-5580
White Way Sign 1317 N Clybourn Ave	Chicago	IL	60610	800-621-4122	312-642-6580
Worldwide Sign Systems 446 N Cecil St PO Box 338	Bonduel	WI	54107	800-874-3334	715-758-2146
Zimmerman Sign Co 1500 N Bolton St	Jacksonville	TX	75766	800-888-1327	903-589-2100
Zumar Industries Inc PO Box 2883	Santa Fe Springs	CA	90670	800-654-7446	562-941-4633

693 SILVERWARE

SEE ALSO Cutlery; Metal Stampings

Company	City	State	Zip	Toll-Free	Phone
Dansk International Designs Ltd 100 Lenox Dr *Cust Svc	Lawrenceville	NJ	08648	**800-293-2675***	609-896-2800
Empire Silver Co Inc 6520 New Utrecht Ave	Brooklyn	NY	11219	**800-255-9475**	718-232-3389
Eureka Mfg Co 47 Elm St	Norton	MA	02766	**800-376-8209**	508-285-9881
Great American Products Inc 1661 S Seguin Ave	New Braunfels	TX	78130	**800-341-4436**	830-620-4400
Lenox Inc 100 Lenox Dr *Cust Svc	Lawrenceville	NJ	08648	**800-635-3669***	609-896-2800
Lunt Silversmiths 298 Federal St	Greenfield	MA	01301	**800-242-2774**	413-774-2774
Mikasa Inc 1 Mikasa Dr *Cust Svc	Secaucus	NJ	07096	**800-833-4681***	201-867-9210
Old Newbury Crafters Inc 36 Main St	Amesbury	MA	01913	**800-343-1388**	978-388-0983
Olde Country Reproductions Inc 722 W Market St *Cust Svc	York	PA	17405	**800-358-3997***	717-848-1859
Oneida Ltd 163-181 Kenwood Ave	Oneida	NY	13421	**800-877-6667**	315-361-3000
Pfaltzgraff Co 140 E Market St	York	PA	17401	**800-999-2811**	717-848-5500
Reed & Barton Silversmiths Corp 144 W Britannia St	Taunton	MA	02780	**800-822-1824**	508-824-6611
Rogers Lunt & Bowlen Co DBA Lunt Silversmiths 298 Federal St	Greenfield	MA	01301	**800-242-2774**	413-774-2774
Salisbury Pewter Co 29085 Airpark Dr	Easton	MD	21601	**800-824-4708**	410-770-4901
Utica Cutlery Co 820 Noyes St	Utica	NY	13502	**800-888-4223**	315-733-4663
Woodbury Pewterers Inc 860 Main St S	Woodbury	CT	06798	**800-648-2014**	203-263-2668

694 SIMULATION & TRAINING SYSTEMS

Company	City	State	Zip	Toll-Free	Phone
Amherst Systems Inc 1740 Wehrle Dr *Cust Svc	Buffalo	NY	14221	**800-477-0181***	716-631-0610
CAE Inc Royal Bank Plaza Suite 3060 *TSE: CAE*	Toronto	ON	M5J2J1	**800-760-0667**	416-865-0070
Cubic Simulation Systems 2001 W Oakridge Rd	Orlando	FL	32809	**800-327-1020**	407-859-7410
DRS Training & Control Systems 645 Anchors St NW	Fort Walton Beach	FL	32548	**800-326-6724**	850-302-3000
Energy Concepts Inc 404 Washington Blvd	Mundelein	IL	60060	**800-621-1247**	847-837-8191
Evans & Sutherland Computer Corp 600 Komas Dr *NASDAQ: ESCC* ■ *Sales	Salt Lake City	UT	84108	**800-367-7460***	801-588-1000
Firearms Training Systems Inc 7340 McGinnis Ferry Rd	Suwanee	GA	30024	**800-813-9046**	770-813-0180
IDEAS Simulation Inc 125 Clairemont Ave Suite 570	Decatur	GA	30030	**800-567-4332**	404-370-1350
Immersion Medical 55 W Watkins Mills Rd	Gaithersburg	MD	20878	**800-929-4709**	301-984-3706
Lab-Volt Systems 1710 Hwy 34 PO Box 686	Farmingdale	NJ	07727	**800-522-9658**	732-938-2000
Nida Corp 300 S John Rodes Blvd	Melbourne	FL	32904	**800-327-6432**	321-727-2265

695 SMART CARDS

Company	City	State	Zip	Toll-Free	Phone
ActivCard Inc 6623 Dumbarton Cir *NASDAQ: ACTI*	Fremont	CA	94555	**800-529-9499**	510-574-0100
Credit Card Systems Inc 180 Shepard Ave	Wheeling	IL	60090	**800-747-1269**	847-459-8320
DataCard Corp 11111 Bren Rd W	Minnetonka	MN	55343	**800-328-8623**	952-933-1223
Gemplus Corp 1350 Old Bayshore Hwy Suite 445	Burlingame	CA	94010	**888-436-7627**	650-373-0200
Greenwald Industries 212 Middlesex Ave	Chester	CT	06412	**800-221-0982**	860-526-0800
Indala 6850-B Santa Teresa Blvd *Sales	San Jose	CA	95119	**800-779-8663***	408-361-4700
QualTeq Inc 800 Montros Ave MS CN1037	South Plainfield	NJ	07080	**800-257-5347**	908-668-0999
SPYRUS Inc 2355 Oakland Rd Suite 1	San Jose	CA	95131	**800-277-9787**	408-953-0700

696 SNOWMOBILES

SEE ALSO Sporting Goods

Company	City	State	Zip	Toll-Free	Phone
Yamaha Motor Corp USA 6555 Katella Ave *Cust Svc	Cypress	CA	90630	**800-962-7926***	714-761-7300

SOFTWARE

SEE Computer Software

697 SPAS - HEALTH & FITNESS

SEE ALSO Health & Fitness Centers; Spas - Hotel & Resort; Weight Loss Centers & Services

Company	City	State	Zip	Toll-Free	Phone
Black Hills Health & Education Center Box 19	Hermosa	SD	57744	**800-658-5433**	605-255-4101
Cal-a-Vie Spa 29402 Spa Havens Way	Vista	CA	92084	**866-772-4283**	760-945-2055
Calistoga Spa Hot Springs 1006 Washington St	Calistoga	CA	94515	**866-822-5772**	707-942-6269
Canyon Ranch in the Berkshires 165 Kemble St *Resv	Lenox	MA	01240	**800-742-9000***	413-637-4100
Canyon Ranch Health Resort 8600 E Rockcliff Rd	Tucson	AZ	85750	**800-742-9000**	520-749-9000
Cooper Wellness Program 12230 Preston Rd	Dallas	TX	75230	**800-444-5192**	972-386-4777
Deerfield Spa 650 Resica Falls Rd	East Stroudsburg	PA	18301	**800-852-4494**	570-223-0160
Duke Diet & Fitness Center 804 W Trinity Ave	Durham	NC	27701	**800-235-3853**	919-688-3079
Grand Wailea Resort & Spa 3850 Wailea Alanui Dr	Wailea	HI	96753	**800-888-6100**	808-875-1234
Green Mountain at Fox Run PO Box 164	Ludlow	VT	05149	**800-448-8106**	802-228-8885
Green Valley Spa 1871 W Canyon View Dr	Saint George	UT	84770	**800-237-1068**	435-628-8060
Healing Center of Arizona 25 Wilson Canyon Rd	Sedona	AZ	86336	**877-723-2811**	928-282-7710
Heartland Spa 1237 E 1600 North Rd	Gilman	IL	60938	**800-545-4853**	
Hills Health Ranch PO Box 26	108 Mile Ranch	BC	V0K2Z0	**800-668-2233**	250-791-5225
Hilton Head Health Institute 14 Valencia Rd	Hilton Head Island	SC	29928	**800-292-2440**	843-785-7292
Hippocrates Health Institute Life-Change Center 1443 Palmdale Ct	West Palm Beach	FL	33411	**800-842-2125**	561-471-8876
Interlaken Resort & Country Spa W 4240 SR-50	Lake Geneva	WI	53147	**800-225-5558**	262-248-9121
Kripalu Center for Yoga & Health 57 Interlaken Rd	Stockbridge	MA	01262	**800-741-7353**	413-448-3400
Lake Austin Spa Resort 1705 S Quinlan Pk Rd	Austin	TX	78732	**800-847-5637**	512-266-2444
Lifestyle Center of America Rt 1 Box 4001	Sulphur	OK	73086	**800-213-8955**	580-993-2327
Lodge & Spa at Cordillera 2205 Cordillera Way	Edwards	CO	81632	**800-877-3529**	970-926-2200
Mineral Springs Resort 11000 Palm Dr	Desert Hot Springs	CA	92240	**800-635-8660**	760-329-6484
Miraval Life in Balance 5000 E Via Estancia Miraval	Catalina	AZ	85739	**800-825-4000**	520-825-4000
Mountain Trek Fitness Retreat & Health Spa Ltd 4952 North St	Ainsworth Hot Springs	BC	V0G1A0	**800-661-5161**	250-229-5636
New Age Health Spa 7491 SR 55	Neversink	NY	12765	**800-682-4348**	845-985-7601
New Life Hiking Spa 2617 Killington Rd	Killington	VT	05751	**800-228-4676**	802-422-4302
Oaks at Ojai 122 E Ojai Ave	Ojai	CA	93023	**800-753-6257**	805-646-5573
Ocean Waters Spa 600 N Atlantic Ave	Daytona Beach	FL	32118	**800-767-4471**	386-267-1660
Ojo Caliente Mineral Springs Resort 50 Los Banos Dr PO Box 68	Ojo Caliente	NM	87549	**800-222-9162**	505-583-2233
Optimum Health Institute 6970 Central Ave	Lemon Grove	CA	91945	**800-993-4325**	619-464-3346
Palms at Palm Springs 572 N Indian Canyon Dr	Palm Springs	CA	92262	**800-753-7256**	760-325-1111
Pritikin Longevity Center & Spa 19735 Turnberry Way	Aventura	FL	33180	**800-327-4914**	305-935-7131
Raj The 1734 Jasmine Ave	Fairfield	IA	52556	**800-248-9050**	641-472-9580
Red Mountain Spa 1275 E Red Mountain Cir	Ivins	UT	84738	**800-407-3002**	435-673-4905
Regency House Natural Health Spa 2000 S Ocean Dr	Hallandale Beach	FL	33009	**800-454-0003**	954-454-2220
Rex Ranch Resort & Spa 131 Alamo Rd	Amado	AZ	85645	**800-547-2696**	520-398-2914
Sivananda Ashram Yoga Ranch Budd Rd Box 195	Woodbourne	NY	12788	**800-783-9642**	845-436-6492
Spa-Atlantis 1350 N Ocean Blvd	Pompano Beach	FL	33062	**800-583-3500**	954-941-6688
Spa at Coeur d'Alene 115 S 2nd St	Coeur d'Alene	ID	83814	**800-688-5253**	208-765-4000
Spa Concept Bromont 90 Stanstead St	Bromont	QC	J2L1K6	**800-567-7727**	450-534-2717
Spa at Grand Lake 1667 Exeter Rd	Lebanon	CT	06249	**800-843-7721**	860-642-4306
Structure House 3017 Pickett Rd	Durham	NC	27705	**800-553-0052**	919-493-4205
Tennessee Fitness Spa 299 Natural Bridge Pk Rd	Waynesboro	TN	38485	**800-235-8365**	931-722-5589
Two Bunch Palms Resort & Spa 67425 Two Bunch Palms Trail	Desert Hot Springs	CA	92240	**800-472-4334**	760-329-8791
Vail Cascade Resort & Spa 1300 Westhaven Dr	Vail	CO	81657	**800-420-2424**	970-476-7111
Vatra Mountain Valley Health Resort Rt 214 Box F	Hunter	NY	12442	**800-232-2772**	518-263-4919
Westglow Spa 2845 Hwy 221 S	Blowing Rock	NC	28605	**800-562-0807**	828-295-4463
White Sulphur Springs Resort & Spa 3100 White Sulphur Springs Rd	Saint Helena	CA	94574	**800-593-8873**	707-963-8588

698 SPAS - HOTEL & RESORT

SEE ALSO Spas - Health & Fitness

Company	City	State	Zip	Toll-Free	Phone
100 Fountain Spa at the Pillar & Post Inn 48 John St PO Box 1011	Niagara-on-the-Lake	ON	L0S1J0	**888-669-5566**	905-468-0515
Abbey Resort & Fontana Spa 269 Fontana Blvd	Fontana	WI	53125	**800-558-2405**	262-275-6811
Agave the Arizona Spa at the Westin Kierland Resort & Spa 6902 E Greenway Pkwy	Scottsdale	AZ	85254	**888-625-5144**	480-624-1500
Allegria Spa at the Park Hyatt Beaver Creek 100 E Thomas Pl	Beaver Creek	CO	81620	**800-233-1234**	970-748-7500
Allegria Spa at the Ventana Inn & Spa Hwy 1	Big Sur	CA	93920	**800-628-6500**	831-667-4222
Alvadora Spa at the Royal Palms Resort & Spa 5200 E Camelback Rd	Phoenix	AZ	85018	**800-672-6011**	602-977-6400
Ancient Cedars Spa at the Wickaninnish Inn Osprey Ln at Chesterman Beach Box 250	Tofino	BC	V0R2Z0	**800-333-4604**	250-725-3113
Aquae Sulis Spa at the JW Marriott Resort Las Vegas 221 N Rampart Blvd	Las Vegas	NV	89145	**877-869-8777**	702-869-7807
Aria Spa & Club at the Vail Cascade Resort 1300 Westhaven Dr	Vail	CO	81657	**888-824-5772**	970-479-5942
Arizona Biltmore Resort & Spa 2400 E Missouri Ave	Phoenix	AZ	85016	**800-950-0086**	602-955-6600
Au Naturel Wellness & Medical Spa at the Brookstreet Hotel 525 Legget Dr	Ottawa	ON	K2K2W2	**888-826-2220**	613-271-3393
Avanyu Spa at the Casa Madrona Hotel 801 Bridgeway	Sausalito	CA	94965	**866-709-7625**	415-354-8308
Avanyu Spa at the Cheeca Lodge Mile Marker 82 PO Box 527	Islamorada	FL	33036	**800-327-2888**	305-517-4485
Avanyu Spa at the Equinox Resort 3567 Main St	Manchester Village	VT	05254	**800-362-4747**	802-362-7881

Name / Address	City	State	Zip	Toll-Free	Phone
Avanyu Spa at the Lodge at Rancho Mirage Resort 68-900 Frank Sinatra Dr	Rancho Mirage	CA	92270	**866-518-6870**	760-321-8989
Avanyu Spa at La Posada de Santa Fe Resort 330 E Palace Ave	Santa Fe	NM	87501	**866-331-7625**	505-954-9630
Avanyu Spa at the Rosario Resort 1400 Rosario Rd	Eastsound	WA	98245	**800-562-8820**	360-376-2222
Avanyu Spa at the Snake River Lodge 7710 Granite Loop Rd PO Box 348	Teton Village	WY	83025	**800-445-4655**	307-732-6070
Bathhouse at Calistoga Ranch 580 Lommel Rd	Calistoga	CA	94515	**800-942-4220**	707-254-2820
Boutique Spa at the Ritz-Carlton Georgetown 3100 South St NW	Washington	DC	20007	**800-241-3333**	202-912-4175
Canyon Ranch SpaClub at the Gaylord Palms Resort 6000 W Osceola Pkwy	Kissimmee	FL	34746	**800-742-9000**	407-586-2051
Canyon Ranch SpaClub at the Venetian 3355 Las Vegas Blvd S Suite 1159	Las Vegas	NV	89109	**877-220-2688**	702-414-3600
Cape Codder Resort & Spa 1225 Iyanough Rd	Hyannis	MA	02601	**888-297-2200**	508-771-3000
Centre for Well-Being at the Phoenician 6000 E Camelback Rd	Scottsdale	AZ	85251	**800-843-2392**	480-423-2452
Chaminade 1 Chaminade Ln	Santa Cruz	CA	95065	**800-283-6569**	831-475-5600
Chateau Elan Spa at the Chateau Elan Atlanta 100 Rue Charlemagne	Braselton	GA	30542	**800-233-9463**	678-425-6064
Cliff Spa at Snowbird Hwy 210 PO Box 929000	Snowbird	UT	84092	**800-453-3000**	801-933-2225
Cranwell Resort Spa & Golf Club 55 Lee Rd	Lenox	MA	01240	**800-272-6935**	413-637-1364
Echo Valley Ranch & Spa Clinton PO Box 16	Jesmond	BC	V0K1K0	**800-253-8831**	250-459-2386
Elizabeth Arden Red Door Spa at Mystic Marriott Hotel & Spa 625 North Rd	Groton	CT	06340	**866-449-7390**	860-446-2500
Elizabeth Arden Red Door Spa at the Seaview Marriot Resort & Spa 400 E Fairway Ln	Galloway	NJ	08205	**800-205-6518**	609-404-4100
Farmhouse Spa at Blackberry Farm 1471 W Millers Cove Rd	Walland	TN	37886	**800-273-6004**	865-379-9819
Felicita Resort 2201 Fishing Creek Valley Rd	Harrisburg	PA	17112	**888-321-3713**	717-599-5301
Four Seasons Spa at the Four Seasons Hotel Las Vegas 3960 Las Vegas Blvd S	Las Vegas	NV	89119	**800-819-5053**	702-632-5302
Four Seasons Spa at the Four Seasons Hotel Los Angeles at Beverly Hills 300 S Doheny Dr	Los Angeles	CA	90048	**800-819-5053**	310-786-2229
Four Seasons Spa at the Four Seasons Resort Aviara 7100 Four Seasons Pt	Carlsbad	CA	92009	**800-819-5053**	760-603-6902
Four Seasons Spa at the Four Seasons Resort Jackson Hole 7680 Granite Loop Rd PO Box 544	Teton Village	WY	83025	**800-819-5053**	307-732-5120
Four Seasons Spa at the Four Seasons Resort Maui 3900 Wailea Alanui Dr	Kihei	HI	96753	**800-819-5053**	808-874-2925
Four Seasons Spa at the Four Seasons Resort Santa Barbara 1260 Channel Dr	Santa Barbara	CA	93108	**800-819-5053**	805-565-8250
Four Seasons Spa at the Four Seasons Scottsdale at Troon North 10600 E Crescent Moon Dr	Scottsdale	AZ	85262	**800-819-5053**	480-513-5145
Garden Spa at MacArthur Place 29 E MacArthur St	Sonoma	CA	95476	**800-722-1866**	707-933-3193
Golden Door Spa at the Wyndham Peaks Resort 136 Country Club Dr Box 2702	Telluride	CO	81435	**800-772-5482**	970-728-2590
Greenbrier The 300 W Main St	White Sulphur Springs	WV	24986	**800-453-4858**	304-536-1110
Grove Park Inn Resort & Spa 290 Macon Ave	Asheville	NC	28804	**800-438-5800**	828-252-2711
Health Spa at Meadowood Napa Valley 900 Meadowood Ln	Saint Helena	CA	94574	**800-458-8080**	707-967-1275
Health Spa at the Regent Beverly Wilshire 9500 Wilshire Blvd	Beverly Hills	CA	90212	**800-545-4000**	310-385-7023
Homestead The 700 N Homestead Dr	Midway	UT	84049	**800-327-7220**	435-654-1102
Hualalai Sports Club & Spa at the Four Seasons Resort Hualalai 100 Kaupulehu Dr	Kaupulehu-Kona	HI	96740	**888-340-5662**	808-325-8440
Indies Spa at the Hawks Cay Resort & Marina 61 Hawk's Cay Blvd	Duck Key	FL	33050	**800-432-2242**	305-289-4810
Indulgence Spa at Taboo 1209 Muskoka Beach Rd RR 1	Gravenhurst	ON	P1P1R1	**800-461-0236**	705-687-2233
Kea Lani Spa at the Fairmont Kea Lani Maui 4100 Wailea Alanui Dr	Maui	HI	96753	**800-659-4100**	808-875-2229
Kohler Waters Spa 501 Highlands Dr	Kohler	WI	53044	**866-928-3777**	920-457-7777
La Prairie at the Ritz-Carlton Spa New York (Central Park) 50 Central Pk S 2nd Fl	New York	NY	10019	**800-241-3333**	212-521-6135
Lafayette Park Hotel 3287 Mt Diablo Blvd	Lafayette	CA	94549	**800-368-2468**	925-283-3700
Los Willows Inn & Spa 530 Stewart Canyon Rd	Fallbrook	CA	92028	**888-731-9400**	760-728-8121
Massage Center at Mohonk Mountain House 1000 Mountain Rest Rd	New Paltz	NY	12561	**800-772-6646**	845-256-2751
Mauna Lani Spa at Mauna Lani Resort 68-1365 Pauoa Rd	Kohala Coast	HI	96743	**866-877-6982**	808-881-7922
Mii Amo at Enchantment Resort 525 Boynton Canyon Rd	Sedona	AZ	86336	**888-749-2137**	928-282-2900
Mirbeau Inn & Spa 851 W Genesee St	Skaneateles	NY	13152	**877-647-2328**	315-685-5006
Moonlight Spa at Moonlight Lodge 1 Mountain Loop Rd	Big Sky	MT	59716	**800-845-4428**	406-995-7700
Mountain Laurel Spa at Stonewall Resort 940 Resort Dr	Roanoke	WV	26447	**888-278-8150**	304-269-8881
Na Hoola Spa at Hyatt Regency Waikiki Resort 2424 Kalakaua Ave	Honolulu	HI	96815	**800-233-1234**	808-921-6097
Nob Hill Spa at the Huntington Hotel 1075 California St	San Francisco	CA	94108	**800-227-4683**	415-345-2888
Ojai Valley Inn & Spa 905 Country Club Rd	Ojai	CA	93023	**800-422-6524**	805-646-5511
Omni Interlocken Resort 500 Interlocken Blvd	Broomfield	CO	80021	**800-843-6664**	303-438-6600
Pala Casino Resort & Spa 11154 Hwy 76 PO Box 40	Pala	CA	92059	**877-946-7252**	760-510-5100
Raindance Spa at the Lodge at Sonoma Renaissance Resort 1325 Broadway	Sonoma	CA	95476	**888-710-8008**	707-931-2034
Resort at Squaw Creek 400 Squaw Creek Rd	Olympic Valley	CA	96146	**800-327-3353**	530-583-6300
Revive Spa at the JW Marriott Desert Ridge Resort Phoenix 5350 E Marriott Dr	Phoenix	AZ	85054	**866-738-4834**	480-293-3700
Safety Harbor Resort & Spa 105 N Bayshore Dr	Safety Harbor	FL	34695	**888-237-8772**	727-726-1161
Scottsdale Resort & Conference Center 7700 E McCormick Pkwy	Scottsdale	AZ	85258	**800-528-0293**	480-991-9000
Sea Island Spa at the Cloister 100 Hudson Pl	Sea Island	GA	31561	**800-732-4752**	912-638-5148
Secret Garden Spa at the Prince of Wales Hotel 6 Picton St PO Box 46	Niagara-on-the-Lake	ON	L0S1J0	**888-669-5566**	905-468-0515
Senator Inn and Spa of Augusta 284 Western Ave	Augusta	ME	04330	**877-772-2224**	207-622-8800
ShaNah Spa at the Bishop's Lodge 1297 Bishop's Lodge Rd	Santa Fe	NM	87504	**800-974-2624**	505-819-4000
Sonwai Spa at the Hyatt Regency Scottsdale Resort at Gainey Ranch 7500 E Doubletree Ranch Rd	Scottsdale	AZ	85258	**800-233-1234**	480-483-5558
Spa at the Amelia Island Plantation 60 Amelia Village	Amelia Island	FL	32034	**877-843-7722**	904-432-2220
Spa at the Arizona Biltmore Resort 2400 E Missouri Ave	Phoenix	AZ	85016	**800-950-0086**	602-955-6600
Spa & Athletic Club at the Lodge at Breckinridge 112 Overlook Dr	Breckenridge	CO	80424	**800-736-1607**	970-453-4274
Spa at the Bacara Resort 8103 Hollister Ave	Santa Barbara	CA	93117	**877-422-4245**	805-571-4210
Spa at the Beau Rivage Resort & Casino 875 Beach Blvd	Biloxi	MS	39530	**888-750-7111**	228-386-7474
Spa at Bernardus Lodge 415 Carmel Valley Rd PO Box 80	Carmel Valley	CA	93924	**888-648-9463**	831-658-3514
Spa at the Bodega Bay Lodge 103 Coast Hwy 1	Bodega Bay	CA	94923	**800-368-2468**	707-875-3525
Spa at Bonaventure Resort & Spa 250 Racquet Club Rd	Weston	FL	33326	**800-787-7248**	954-349-5515
Spa at the Breakers 1 S County Rd	Palm Beach	FL	33480	**888-273-2537**	561-653-6656
Spa at the Broadmoor 1 Lake Ave	Colorado Springs	CO	80906	**800-634-7711**	719-577-5770
Spa at the Camelback Inn JW Marriott Resort Golf Club & Spa 5402 E Lincoln Dr	Scottsdale	AZ	85253	**800-922-2635**	480-596-7040
Spa at Carefree Resort & Villas 37220 Mule Train Rd	Carefree	AZ	85377	**888-488-9034**	480-595-3853
Spa at the Chattanoogan 1201 S Broad St	Chattanooga	TN	37402	**800-619-0018**	423-424-3779
Spa at the Chrysalis Inn 804 10th St	Bellingham	WA	98225	**888-808-0005**	360-392-5515
Spa Claremont at the Claremont Resort 41 Tunnel Rd	Berkeley	CA	94705	**800-551-7266**	510-549-8566
Spa at the CopperWynd Resort & Club 13225 N Eagle Ridge Dr	Fountain Hills	AZ	85268	**877-707-7760**	480-333-1835
Spa at Cordillera 2206 Cordillera Way	Edwards	CO	81623	**800-877-6419**	800-877-3529
Spa at La Costa 2100 Costa del Mar Rd	Carlsbad	CA	92009	**800-729-4772**	760-931-7570
Spa at the Delta Victoria Ocean Pointe Resort 45 Songhees Rd	Victoria	BC	V9A6T3	**800-575-8882**	250-360-5858
Spa at the Diplomat Country Club 501 Diplomat Pkwy	Hallandale	FL	33009	**800-327-1212**	954-883-4905
Spa at the Don CeSar Beach Resort 3400 Gulf Blvd	Saint Pete Beach	FL	33706	**800-282-1116**	727-360-1883
Spa at Eagle Crest Resort 1522 Cline Falls Hwy PO Box 1215	Redmond	OR	97756	**800-682-4786**	541-923-9647
Spa at Eden Roc A Renaissance Resort & Spa 4525 Collins Ave	Miami Beach	FL	33140	**800-327-8337**	305-674-5585
Spa Esmeralda at the Renaissance Esmeralda Resort 44-400 Indian Wells Ln	Indian Wells	CA	92210	**800-468-3571**	760-836-1265
Spa at the Fairmont Inn Sonoma Mission Inn 100 Boyes Blvd	Sonoma	CA	95476	**877-289-7354**	
Spa & Fitness Club at the Four Seasons Hotel Washington 2800 Pennsylvania Ave NW	Washington	DC	20007	**800-819-5053**	202-944-2022
Spa at Fox Harb'r 1337 Fox Harbour Rd	Wallace	NS	B0K1Y0	**866-257-1801**	902-257-4307
Spa Fusion at the Hilton San Francisco 333 O'Farrell St	San Francisco	CA	94102	**800-445-8667**	415-923-5014
Spa Gaucin at the Saint Regis Monarch Beach 1 Monarch Beach Resort	Dana Point	CA	92629	**800-722-1543**	949-234-3367
Spa Grande at the Grand Wailea Resort Maui 3850 Wailea Alanui Dr	Wailea	HI	96753	**800-772-1933**	808-875-1234
Spa at Gurney's Inn Resort 290 Old Montauk Hwy	Montauk	NY	11954	**800-848-7639**	631-668-1892
Spa at the Hilton Sedona Resort 10 Ridge View Dr	Sedona	AZ	86351	**877-273-3762**	928-284-6975
Spa at the Hilton Short Hills Hotel 41 JFK Pkwy	Short Hills	NJ	07078	**800-445-8667**	973-912-7956
Spa at the Homestead Rt 220 Main St PO Box 2000	Hot Springs	VA	24445	**800-838-1766**	540-839-7547
Spa at the Hotel Hershey 100 Hotel Rd	Hershey	PA	17033	**877-772-9988**	717-520-5888
Spa Internazionale at Fisher Island Hotel & Resort 1 Fisher Island Dr	Miami	FL	33109	**800-537-3708**	305-535-6030
Spa at the JW Marriott Denver at Cherry Creek 150 Clayton Ln	Denver	CO	80206	**800-228-9290**	303-316-2700
Spa at the JW Marriott Desert Springs Resort Palm Desert 74855 Country Club Dr	Palm Desert	CA	92260	**800-331-3112**	760-341-1856
Spa at the JW Marriott Ihilani Resort 92-1001 Olani St	Kapolei	HI	96707	**800-626-4446**	808-679-3321
Spa at the Kauai Marriott Resort & Beach Club 3610 Rice St	Lihue	HI	96766	**800-220-2925**	808-246-4918
Spa at Kingsmill Resort 1010 Kingsmill Rd	Williamsburg	VA	23185	**800-965-4772**	757-253-8230
Spa at the Laguna Cliffs Marriott Resort 25135 Park Lantern	Dana Point	CA	92629	**800-228-9290**	949-487-7576
Spa at the Lansdowne Resort 44050 Woodridge Pkwy	Leesburg	VA	20176	**800-541-4801**	703-729-4036
Spa Las Palmas at the Marriott Rancho Las Palmas Resort 41000 Bob Hope Dr	Rancho Mirage	CA	92270	**877-843-7720**	760-836-3106
Spa Las Palmas at Marriott's Rancho Las Palmas Resort 41000 Bob Hope Dr	Rancho Mirage	CA	92270	**800-932-2198**	760-836-3106
Spa at the Loews Santa Monica Beach Hotel 1700 Ocean Ave	Santa Monica	CA	90401	**800-325-6397**	310-899-4040
Spa at the Loews Ventana Canyon Resort 7000 N Resort Dr	Tucson	AZ	85750	**800-235-6397**	520-529-7830
Spa Luana at Turtle Bay Resort 57-091 Kamehameha Hwy	Kahuku	HI	96731	**800-203-3650**	808-447-6868
Spa at the Mandarin Oriental Miami 500 Brickell Key Dr	Miami	FL	33131	**800-526-6566**	305-913-8332
Spa at the Marriott Harbor Beach Resort 3030 Holiday Dr	Fort Lauderdale	FL	33316	**800-222-6543**	954-765-3032
Spa at the Marriott Marco Island Resort Golf Club & Spa 400 S Collier Blvd	Marco Island	FL	34145	**800-438-4373**	239-642-2686
Spa at the Marriott Tampa Waterside 700 S Florida Ave	Tampa	FL	33602	**888-268-1616**	813-204-6300
Spa at the Marriott's Grand Hotel & Resort 1 Grand Blvd PO Box 639	Point Clear	AL	36564	**800-544-9933**	251-928-9201
Spa at Le Merigot JW Marriott Beach Hotel Santa Monica 1740 Ocean Ave	Santa Monica	CA	90401	**877-637-4468**	310-395-9700
Spa Moana at the Hyatt Regency Maui Resort 200 Nohea Kai Dr	Lahaina	HI	96761	**800-233-1234**	808-667-4725

Name / Address	City	State	ZIP	Toll-Free	Phone
Spa at Montage Resort 30801 S Coast Hwy	Laguna Beach	CA	92651	**866-271-6953**	949-715-6010
Spa at Monterey Plaza Hotel 400 Cannery Row	Monterey	CA	93940	**800-334-3999**	831-645-4098
Spa at the Moody Gardens Hotel 7 Hope Blvd	Galveston	TX	77554	**888-388-8484**	409-683-4440
Spa Moulay at the Hyatt Regency Lake Las Vegas Resort 101 Montelago Blvd	Henderson	NV	89011	**800-233-1234**	702-567-6049
Spa Mystique at the Westin Century Plaza Hotel 10220 Constellation Ave	Los Angeles	CA	90067	**800-937-8461**	310-551-3251
Spa at Nemacolin Woodlands Resort 1001 Lafayette Dr	Farmington	PA	15437	**800-422-2736**	724-329-6772
Spa at the Norwich Inn 607 W Thames St	Norwich	CT	06360	**800-275-4772**	860-886-2401
Spa Olakino at the Waikiki Beach Marriott Resort 2552 Kalakaua Ave	Honolulu	HI	96815	**800-367-5370**	808-924-2121
Spa at the Omni Orlando Resort at Championsgate 1500 Masters Blvd	Champions Gate	FL	33896	**800-843-6664**	407-390-6664
Spa at the Omni Tucson National Golf Resort & Spa 2727 W Club Dr	Tucson	AZ	85742	**800-297-2000**	520-877-2367
Spa at the Orlando World Center Marriott Resort & Convention Center 8701 World Ctr Dr	Orlando	FL	32821	**800-621-0638**	407-238-8705
Spa Pallazo at the Boca Raton Resort & Club 501 E Camino Real	Boca Raton	FL	33432	**888-491-2622**	561-347-4772
Spa at Pebble Beach 17 Mile Dr PO Box 1128	Pebble Beach	CA	93953	**888-565-7615**	831-649-7615
Spa at Pechanga Resort & Casino 45000 Pechanga Pkwy	Temecula	CA	92592	**888-732-4264**	951-719-8501
Spa at the PGA National Resort 450 Avenue of the Champions	Palm Beach Gardens	FL	33418	**800-633-9150**	561-627-3111
Spa at Pinehurst Resort 180 Barrett Rd E	Pinehurst	NC	28374	**800-487-4653**	910-235-8320
Spa at the Ponte Vedra Inn & Club 200 Ponte Vedra Blvd	Ponte Vedra Beach	FL	32082	**800-234-7842**	904-273-7700
Spa La Quinta at La Quinta Resort 49-499 Eisenhower Dr PO Box 69	La Quinta	CA	92253	**800-598-3828**	760-777-4800
Spa at the Ritz-Carlton Amelia Island 4750 Amelia Island Pkwy	Amelia Island	FL	32034	**800-241-3333**	904-277-1087
Spa at the Ritz-Carlton Bachelor Gulch 0130 Daybreak Ridge	Avon	CO	81620	**800-241-3333**	970-343-1138
Spa at the Ritz-Carlton Coconut Grove 3300 SW 27th Ave	Coconut Grove	FL	33133	**800-241-3333**	305-644-4680
Spa at the Ritz-Carlton Half Moon Bay 1 Miramontes Pt Rd	Half Moon Bay	CA	94019	**800-241-3333**	650-712-7091
Spa at the Ritz-Carlton Huntington Hotel 1401 S Oak Knoll Ave	Pasadena	CA	91106	**800-241-3333**	626-585-6414
Spa at the Ritz-Carlton Key Biscayne 455 Grand Bay Dr	Key Biscayne	FL	33149	**800-241-3333**	305-365-4158
Spa at the Ritz-Carlton Naples 280 Vanderbilt Beach Rd	Naples	FL	34108	**800-241-3333**	239-514-6100
Spa at the Ritz-Carlton New Orleans 921 Canal St	New Orleans	LA	70112	**800-241-3333**	504-670-2929
Spa at the Ritz-Carlton Orlando Grande Lakes 4012 Central Florida Pkwy	Orlando	FL	32837	**800-241-3333**	407-393-4200
Spa at the Ritz-Carlton Reynolds Plantation 1 Lake Oconee Tr	Greensboro	GA	30642	**800-241-3333**	706-467-7181
Spa at the Ritz-Carlton Sarasota 1111 Ritz-Carlton Dr	Sarasota	FL	34236	**800-241-3333**	941-309-2000
Spa at the Ritz-Carlton South Beach 1 Lincoln Rd	Miami Beach	FL	33139	**800-241-3333**	786-276-4090
Spa at the Ritz-Carlton Tysons Corner 1700 Tysons Blvd	McLean	VA	22102	**800-241-3333**	703-744-3924
Spa at the Saddlebrook Resort 5700 Saddlebrook Way	Wesley Chapel	FL	33543	**800-729-8383**	813-907-4419
Spa at the Sagamore 110 Sagamore Rd	Bolton Landing	NY	12814	**800-358-3585**	518-743-6081
Spa at the Saint Regis Aspen 315 E Dean St	Aspen	CO	81611	**888-625-5144**	970-920-3300
Spa at the Salish Lodge 6501 Railroad Ave PO Box 1109	Snoqualmie	WA	98065	**800-272-5474**	425-831-6535
Spa Samadhi at Inn at Sunrise Springs 242 Los Pinos Rd	Santa Fe	NM	87507	**800-955-0028**	505-428-3614
Spa at the Sanctuary on Camelback Mountain 5700 E McDonald Dr	Paradise Valley	AZ	85253	**800-245-2051**	480-948-2100
Spa at the Sanderling Resort 1461 Duck Rd	Duck	NC	27949	**800-701-4111**	252-261-7744
Spa at Sanibel Harbour Resort 17260 Harbour Pointe Dr	Fort Myers	FL	33908	**800-676-7777**	239-466-2156
Spa at Saybrook Point Inn 2 Bridge St	Old Saybrook	CT	06475	**800-243-0212**	860-395-3245
Spa Shiki at the Lodge of Four Seasons Horseshoe Bend Pkwy PO Box 215	Lake Ozark	MO	65049	**800-843-5253**	573-365-8108
Spa du Soleil at the Auberge du Soleil 180 Rutherford Hill Rd	Rutherford	CA	94573	**800-348-5406**	707-967-3159
Spa at the Sonesta Beach Resort Key Biscayne 350 Ocean Dr	Key Biscayne	FL	33149	**800-766-3782**	305-365-2949
Spa at the Stoweflake Mountain Resort 1746 Mountain Rd PO Box 369	Stowe	VT	05672	**800-253-2232**	802-760-1083
Spa Suites at Kahala Mandarin Oriental Hawaii Resort 5000 Kahala Ave	Honolulu	HI	96816	**800-367-2525**	808-739-8938
Spa Terre at the Hotel Viking 1 Bellevue Ave	Newport	RI	02840	**800-556-7126**	401-848-4848
Spa Terre at the Inn & Spa at Loretto 211 Old Santa Fe Trail	Santa Fe	NM	87501	**800-727-5531**	505-984-7997
Spa Terre at the Little Palm Island Resort 28500 Overseas Hwy	Little Torch Key	FL	33042	**800-343-8567**	305-515-3028
Spa Terre at Paradise Point Resort 1404 Vacation Rd	San Diego	CA	92109	**800-344-2626**	858-581-5998
Spa Terre at SunBurst Resort 4925 N Scottsdale Rd	Scottsdale	AZ	85251	**800-528-7867**	480-424-6072
Spa Toccare at Borgata Hotel Casino 1 Borgata Way	Atlantic City	NJ	08401	**866-692-6742**	609-317-7555
Spa at Topnotch at Stowe Resort 4000 Mountain Rd	Stowe	VT	05672	**800-451-8686**	802-253-6463
Spa Torrey Pines at the Lodge at Torrey Pines 11480 N Torrey Pines Rd	La Jolla	CA	92037	**800-656-0087**	858-777-6690
Spa at the Vail Marriott Mountain Resort 715 W Lionshead Cir	Vail	CO	81657	**800-648-0720**	970-479-5004
Spa at the Vail Mountain Lodge 352 E Meadow Dr	Vail	CO	81657	**866-476-0700**	970-476-7721
Spa at the Villagio Inn 6481 Washington St	Yountville	CA	94599	**800-351-1133**	707-948-5050
Spa Vita di Lago at The Ritz Carlton Lake Las Vegas 1610 Lake Las Vegas Pkwy	Henderson	NV	89011	**800-241-3333**	702-567-4600
Spa at the Watermark Hotel 212 W Crockett St	San Antonio	TX	78205	**866-605-1212**	210-396-5840
Spa at the Westin Maui Resort 2365 Kaanapali Pkwy	Lahaina	HI	96761	**866-500-8313**	808-661-2588
Spa at White Oaks Conference Resort 253 Taylor Rd	Niagara-on-the-Lake	ON	L0S1J0	**800-263-5766**	905-641-2599
Spa Without Walls at the Fairmont Orchid Hawaii 1 N Kaniku Dr	Kohala Coast	HI	96743	**800-845-9905**	808-885-2000
SpaHalekulani at the Halekulani Hotel 2199 Kalia Rd	Honolulu	HI	96815	**800-367-2343**	808-931-5322
Stillwater Spa at the Hyatt Regency Newport 1 Goat Island	Newport	RI	02840	**800-233-1234**	401-851-3225
Turtle Cove Spa at Mountain Harbor Resort 994 Mountain Harbor Rd PO Box 1268	Mount Ida	AR	71957	**800-832-2276**	870-867-1220
Village Bay Spa at Lake Arrowhead Resort 27984 Hwy 189	Lake Arrowhead	CA	92352	**800-800-6792**	909-744-3000
Well Spa at Miramonte Resort 45-000 Indian Wells Ln	Indian Wells	CA	92210	**800-237-2926**	760-837-1652
Willow Stream Spa at the Fairmont Banff Springs 405 Spray Ave	Banff	AB	T1L1J4	**800-404-1772**	403-762-1772
Willow Stream Spa at the Fairmont Empress 633 Humboldt St	Victoria	BC	V8W1A6	**866-854-7444**	250-995-4650
Willow Stream Spa at Fairmont Scottsdale Princess 7575 E Princess Dr	Scottsdale	AZ	85255	**800-257-7544**	480-585-2732
Willow Stream Spa at the Turnberry Isle Resort & Club 19999 W Country Club Dr	Aventura	FL	33180	**800-327-7028**	305-933-6930
Wintergarden Spa & Fitness Center at Wintergreen Resort Rt 664 PO Box 706	Wintergreen	VA	22958	**800-266-2444**	434-325-8185
Wyndham Peaks Resort & Golden Door Spa 136 Country Club Dr	Telluride	CO	81435	**800-789-2220**	970-728-6800
Za Spa at Hotel Zaza 2332 Leonard St	Dallas	TX	75201	**800-597-8399**	214-550-9492

699 SPEAKERS BUREAUS

Name / Address	City	State	ZIP	Toll-Free	Phone
AEI Speakers Bureau 214 Lincoln St Suite 113	Boston	MA	02134	**800-447-7325**	617-782-3111
Agricultural Speakers Network 10436 Oak Ridge Dr	Zionsville	IN	46077	**800-222-1556***	317-873-9797
*Sales					
All-Star Agency Speakers Bureau 4829 Powell Rd	Fairfax	VA	22032	**800-736-0031**	703-503-9438
American Program Bureau Inc 36 Crafts St	Newton	MA	02458	**800-225-4575**	617-965-6600
Atlantic Speakers Bureau 980 Rt 730	Scotch Ridge	NB	E3L5L2	**866-465-0990**	506-465-0990
Barclay Steven Agency 12 Western Ave	Petaluma	CA	94952	**888-965-7323**	707-773-0654
Capitol City Speakers Bureau 1620 S 5th St	Springfield	IL	62703	**800-397-3183**	217-544-8552
Eagles Talent Connection Inc 57 W South Orange Ave	South Orange	NJ	07079	**800-345-5607**	973-376-3737
Executive Speakers Bureau 8470 Deerfield Ln	Germantown	TN	38138	**800-754-9404**	901-754-9404
Financial Forum 90 N 100 East Suite 4	Logan	UT	84321	**800-500-5119**	435-750-0062
Garrett Speakers International Inc PO Box 153448	Irving	TX	75015	**800-787-2840**	972-513-0054
Greater Talent Network Inc 437 5th Ave 7th Fl	New York	NY	10016	**800-326-4211**	212-645-4200
International Speakers Bureau Inc 2528 Elm St Suite 200	Dallas	TX	75226	**800-842-4483**	214-744-3885
Leading Authorities Inc 1220 L St NW Suite 850	Washington	DC	20005	**800-773-2537**	202-783-0300
National Speakers Bureau 1663 W 7th Ave	Vancouver	BC	V6J1S4	**800-661-4110**	604-734-3663
National Speakers Bureau Inc 14047 W Petronalla Dr Suite 102	Libertyville	IL	60048	**800-323-9442**	847-295-1122
Professional Speakers Network 10436 Oak Ridge Dr	Zionsville	IN	46077	**800-222-1556**	317-873-9840
Speakers Guild Inc PO Box 1540	Sandwich	MA	02563	**800-343-4530**	508-888-6702
Steven Barclay Agency 12 Western Ave	Petaluma	CA	94952	**888-965-7323**	707-773-0654

700 SPEED CHANGERS, INDUSTRIAL HIGH SPEED DRIVES, GEARS

SEE ALSO Aircraft Parts & Auxiliary Equipment; Automotive Parts & Supplies - Mfr; Controls & Relays - Electrical; Machine Shops; Motors (Electric) & Generators; Power Transmission Equipment - Mechanical

Name / Address	City	State	ZIP	Toll-Free	Phone
Alten Engineering Div Westerman Cos 245 N Broad St	Bremen	OH	43107	**800-338-8265**	740-569-4143
Bison Gear & Engineering Corp 3850 Ohio Ave	Saint Charles	IL	60174	**800-282-4766**	630-377-4327
Bond Charles Co 11 Green St PO Box 105	Christiana	PA	17509	**800-922-0125***	610-593-5171
*Cust Svc					
Boston Gear 14 Hayward St	Quincy	MA	02171	**888-999-9860***	617-328-3300
*Cust Svc					
Charles Bond Co 11 Green St PO Box 105	Christiana	PA	17509	**800-922-0125***	610-593-5171
*Cust Svc					
Cleveland Gear Co 3249 E 80th St	Cleveland	OH	44104	**800-423-3169**	216-641-9000
Columbia Gear Corp 530 County Rd 50	Avon	MN	56310	**800-323-9838**	320-356-7301
Dalton Gear Co 212 Colfax Ave N	Minneapolis	MN	55405	**800-328-7485**	612-374-2150
Danaher Motion 1500 Mittel Blvd	Wood Dale	IL	60191	**866-993-2624**	630-860-7300
Designatronics Inc 2101 Jericho Tpke	New Hyde Park	NY	11040	**800-345-1144***	516-328-3300
*Orders					
Electra-Gear Div Regal-Beloit Corp 1110 N Anaheim Blvd	Anaheim	CA	92801	**800-877-4327**	714-535-6061
Electro Sales Inc 100 Fellsway W	Somerville	MA	02145	**888-789-0500**	617-666-0500
Euclid Universal Corp 30500 Bruce Industrial Pkwy Suite B	Solon	OH	44139	**800-280-2616**	440-349-4083
Fairchild Industrial Products Co 3920 West Point Blvd	Winston-Salem	NC	27103	**800-423-1093**	336-659-3400
Falk Corp 3001 W Canal St	Milwaukee	WI	53208	**800-852-3255**	414-342-3131
Flender Corp 950 Tollgate Rd	Elgin	IL	60123	**800-867-3766**	847-931-1990
Hub City Inc PO Box 1089	Aberdeen	SD	57402	**800-482-2489**	605-225-0360
Invensys 33 Commercial St	Foxboro	MA	02035	**866-746-6477**	508-543-8750
Kurz Electric Solutions Inc 736 Ford St	Kimberly	WI	54136	**800-776-3629**	920-734-5644
Molon Motor & Coil Corp 3737 Industrial Ave	Rolling Meadows	IL	60008	**800-526-6867**	847-253-6000
Nuttall Gear LLC PO Box 1032	Niagara Falls	NY	14302	**800-432-0121**	716-731-5180
Peerless-Winsmith Inc 1401 W Market St	Warren	OH	44485	**800-676-3651**	330-399-3651

				Toll-Free	Phone
Perfection Gear Inc 9 N Bear Creek Rd	Asheville	NC	28806	**800-532-5314**	828-253-0000
Piller Inc 334 CR 49	Middletown	NY	10940	**800-597-6937**	845-355-5000
Regal-Beloit Corp Electra-Gear Div 1110 N Anaheim Blvd	Anaheim	CA	92801	**800-877-4327**	714-535-6061
Richmond Gear PO Box 238 *Sales	Liberty	SC	29657	**800-476-6446***	864-843-9231
Rush Gears Inc 550 Virginia Dr	Fort Washington	PA	19034	**800-523-2576**	215-542-9000
Sterling Electric Inc 16752 Armstrong Ave *Cust Svc	Irvine	CA	92606	**800-654-6220***	949-474-0520
Sumitomo Machinery Corp of America 4200 Holland Blvd	Chesapeake	VA	23323	**800-762-9256**	757-485-3355
Textron Power Transmission 240 E 12th St *Sales	Traverse City	MI	49685	**888-994-2663***	231-946-8410
Toshiba International Corp 13131 W Little York Rd	Houston	TX	77041	**800-231-1412**	713-466-0277
Westerman Cos Alten Engineering Div 245 N Broad St	Bremen	OH	43107	**800-338-8265**	740-569-4143

701 SPORTING GOODS

SEE ALSO All-Terrain Vehicles; Bicycles & Bicycle Parts & Accessories; Boats - Recreational; Cord & Twine; Exercise & Fitness Equipment; Firearms & Ammunition (Non-Military); Gym & Playground Equipment; Handbags, Totes, Backpacks; Motor Vehicles - Commercial & Special Purpose; Personal Protective Equipment & Clothing; Snowmobiles; Swimming Pools - Above-Ground; Tarps, Tents, Covers

				Toll-Free	Phone
Abel Quality Products 165 Aviador St	Camarillo	CA	93010	**800-848-7335**	805-484-8789
Acushnet Co 333 Bridge St	Fairhaven	MA	02719	**800-225-8500**	508-979-2000
AcuSport Corp 1 Hunter Pl	Bellefontaine	OH	43311	**800-543-3150**	937-593-7010
Adams USA Inc 610 S Jefferson Ave	Cookeville	TN	38501	**800-251-6857**	931-526-2109
AK Bommer Custom Snowboards PO Box 1444	Valdez	AK	99686	**888-252-6637**	907-835-3846
Aldila Inc 13450 Stowe Dr *NASDAQ: ALDA*	Poway	CA	92064	**800-854-2786**	858-513-1801
Altamonte Billiard Factory Inc 700 N Hwy 17-92	Longwood	FL	32750	**800-780-7799**	407-339-8700
American Classic Sales 1142 S 2475 West	Salt Lake City	UT	84104	**888-733-5763**	801-977-3935
American Sports 74 Albe Dr Suite 1	Newark	DE	19702	**800-977-6786**	302-369-9480
AMF Bowling Worldwide Inc 8100 AMF Dr	Mechanicsville	VA	23111	**800-342-5263**	804-730-4000
Aqua-Leisure Industries Inc 525 Bodwell St Ext PO Box 239	Avon	MA	02322	**888-807-2998**	508-587-5400
Aqualung America Inc 2340 Cousteau Ct	Vista	CA	92083	**800-635-3483**	760-597-5000
Armour Tommy Golf Co 36 Dufflaw Rd *Cust Svc	Toronto	ON	M6A2W1	**800-723-4653***	416-630-4996
Atomic Ski USA Inc 9 Columbia Dr	Amherst	NH	03031	**800-258-5020**	603-880-6143
Bankshot Organization 785 F Rockville Pike Suite 504	Rockville	MD	20852	**800-933-0140**	301-309-0260
Bare Sportswear Corp 1755 Grant Ave	Blaine	WA	98230	**800-663-0111**	360-332-2700
Barrecrafters 700 Bernard	Granby	QC	J269H7	**800-451-3240**	
Bauer Nike Hockey Inc 150 Ocean Rd	Greenland	NH	03840	**800-362-3146**	603-430-2111
Bauer Premium Fly Reels 401 Corral de Tierra Rd	Salinas	CA	93908	**888-484-4165**	831-484-0536
Bear Creek Canoes Inc 72 Swamp Rd & Rt 107	Sebago	ME	04029	**800-241-2268**	207-647-5850
Bell Sports Corp 6225 N State Hwy 161 Suite 300	Irving	TX	75038	**866-525-2355**	469-417-6600
Ben Hogan Co 425 Meadow St	Chicopee	MA	01021	**800-772-5346**	413-536-1200
Biscayne Rod Manufacturing Inc 425 E 9th St	Hialeah	FL	33010	**888-866-7637**	305-884-0808
Bison Inc 603 L St	Lincoln	NE	68508	**800-247-7668**	402-474-3353
Black Knight USA 5355 Sierra Rd	San Jose	CA	95132	**800-535-3300**	408-923-7777
Brass Eagle Inc 1201 SE 30th St	Bentonville	AR	72712	**877-877-4263**	479-464-8700
Brine Inc 47 Sumner St	Milford	MA	01757	**800-227-2722**	508-478-3250
Burton Golf Inc 654 Anchors St	Fort Walton Beach	FL	32548	**800-633-4630**	850-244-8651
Burton Snowboards Inc 80 Industrial Pkwy	Burlington	VT	05401	**800-881-3138**	802-862-4500
Callaway Golf Co 2180 Rutherford Rd *NYSE: ELY*	Carlsbad	CA	92008	**800-228-2767**	760-931-1771
Cape Fear Rod Co 302-A Raleigh St	Wilmington	NC	28412	**888-886-2064**	910-350-0494
Cascade Designs Inc 4000 1st Ave S *Cust Svc	Seattle	WA	98134	**800-877-9677***	206-624-8573
Caviness Woodworking Co 200 N Aycock Ave PO Box 710	Calhoun City	MS	38916	**800-626-5195**	662-628-5195
Century Inc 1000 Century Blvd *Sales	Midwest City	OK	73110	**800-626-2787***	405-732-2226
Century Sports Inc 1995 Rutgers University Blvd *Sales	Lakewood	NJ	08701	**800-526-7548***	732-905-4422
Century Tool & Mfg Co Inc PO Box 188	Cherry Valley	IL	61016	**800-435-4525**	815-332-4951
Champion Shuffleboard Ltd 7216 Burns St	Richland Hills	TX	76118	**800-598-2881**	817-284-3499
Cleveland Golf Co 5630 Cerritos Ave *Cust Svc	Cypress	CA	90630	**800-999-6263***	714-821-4200
Cobra Golf Inc 1812 Aston Ave *Cust Svc	Carlsbad	CA	92008	**800-223-3537***	760-929-0377
Cobra Mfg 7909 E 148th St S PO Box 667	Bixby	OK	74008	**800-352-6272**	918-366-7624
Coleman Co Inc 211 E 37th St N *Cust Svc	Wichita	KS	67219	**800-835-3278***	316-832-2653
Colorado Classic Co DBA Pappy's Golf Shop 4030 N Sinton Rd	Colorado Springs	CO	80907	**800-530-2345**	719-633-2064
Columbia 300 Inc 5005 West Ave *Cust Svc	San Antonio	TX	78213	**800-531-5920***	210-344-9211
Columbia Industries Inc DBA Columbia 300 Inc 5005 West Ave *Cust Svc	San Antonio	TX	78213	**800-531-5920***	210-344-9211
Confluence Watersports Co 3761 Old Glenola Rd	Trinity	NC	27370	**800-311-7245**	336-434-7470
Connelly Billiard Mfg 1440 S Euclid Ave	Tucson	AZ	85713	**800-861-8619**	520-624-6000
Connelly Skis Inc 20621 52nd Ave W	Lynnwood	WA	98036	**800-234-7547**	425-775-5416
Cortland Line Co Inc 3736 Kellogg Rd	Cortland	NY	13045	**800-847-6787**	607-756-2851
Current Designs PO Box 247	Winona	MN	55987	**877-655-1822**	507-454-5430
Da Kine International 408 Columbia St Suite 300	Hood River	OR	97031	**800-827-7466**	541-386-3166
Daisy Mfg Co Inc 400 W Stribling Dr	Rogers	AR	72756	**800-643-3458**	479-636-1200
Daiwa Corp 12851 Midway Pl	Cerritos	CA	90703	**800-736-4653**	562-802-9589
Dana Design 19215 Vashon Hwy SW	Vashon	WA	98070	**888-357-3262**	206-463-3631
DeBeer J & Son Inc 5 Burdick Dr	Albany	NY	12205	**800-833-3535**	518-438-7871
Dolomite USA Corp 5 Commerce Ave	West Lebanon	NH	03784	**800-257-2008**	603-298-5592
Donek Snowboards Inc 35907 E 88 Ave PO Box 580	Watkins	CO	80137	**877-533-6635**	303-261-0100
Douglas Industries Co 3441 S 11th Ave	Eldridge	IA	52748	**800-553-8907**	563-285-4162
Dynacraft Golf Products Inc 107 Pine St *Cust Svc	Newark	OH	43058	**800-423-2968***	740-344-1191
E-Force 7920 Arjons Dr Suite A	San Diego	CA	92126	**800-433-6723**	858-547-3720
Eagle Claw Fishing Tackle 4245 E 46th Ave	Denver	CO	80216	**800-628-0108**	303-321-1481
Eagle Sports 6020 N Sam Houston Pkwy E	Humble	TX	77396	**800-862-4424**	281-441-4220
Easton Sports Inc 7855 Haskell Ave	Van Nuys	CA	91406	**800-632-7866**	818-782-6445
Easton Tru-Flite LLC 2709 S Freeman Rd	Monticello	IN	47960	**800-348-2224**	574-583-5131
Ebonite International Inc PO Box 746	Hopkinsville	KY	42241	**800-626-8350**	270-881-1200
EBSCO Industries Inc PRADCO Outdoor Brands Div 3601 Jenny Lind Rd	Fort Smith	AR	72901	**800-531-1201**	479-782-8971
Elan USA 5 Commerce Ave	West Lebanon	NH	03784	**800-950-8900**	603-298-9017
Ellett Brothers Inc 267 Columbia Ave *Sales	Chapin	SC	29036	**800-845-3711***	803-345-3751
Eppinger Mfg Corp 6340 Schaefer Rd	Dearborn	MI	48126	**888-771-8277**	313-582-3205
Escalade Inc DBA Escalade Sports PO Box 889 *NASDAQ: ESCA* ■ *Cust Svc	Evansville	IN	47706	**800-426-1421***	812-467-1200
Fly Logic Inc PO Box 270	Melba	ID	83641	**888-359-5644**	208-495-2090
FMP International 1800 Industrial Pk Dr PO Box 732	Grand Haven	MI	49417	**800-560-7795**	616-847-9121
Folbot Inc 4209 Pace St	Charleston	SC	29405	**800-533-5099**	843-744-3483
Forten Corp 7815 Silverton Ave Suite 2-A	San Diego	CA	92126	**800-722-5588**	858-693-9888
Franklin Sports Industry Inc 17 Campanelli Pkwy	Stoughton	MA	02072	**800-225-8647**	781-344-1111
G & H Decoys Inc PO Box 1208 *Orders	Henryetta	OK	74437	**800-443-3269***	918-652-3314
G Loomis Inc 1359 Down River Dr	Woodland	WA	98674	**800-456-6647**	360-225-6516
Gamma Racquet Sports 200 Waterfront Dr	Pittsburgh	PA	15222	**800-333-0337**	412-323-0335
Gared Sports Inc 1107 Mullanphy St	Saint Louis	MO	63106	**800-325-2682**	314-421-0044
GeoDesic Corp 400 Commerce Rd	Alice	TX	78332	**800-824-4153**	361-668-3766
Gexco 7209 Arlington Ave Suite D	Riverside	CA	92503	**800-829-8222**	951-637-0546
Gill Athletics Inc 2808 Gemini Ct *Cust Svc	Champaign	IL	61822	**800-637-3090***	217-367-8438
Goal Oriented Inc 7935 E 14th Ave	Denver	CO	80220	**888-393-0888**	303-393-6040
Goal Sporting Goods Inc 37 Industrial Pk Rd Box 236	Essex	CT	06426	**800-334-4625**	860-767-9112
Goalsetter Systems Inc PO Box 552	Pella	IA	50219	**800-362-4625**	641-628-2628
GolfCoach Inc 5060 N Royal Atlanta Dr Suite 28	Tucker	GA	30084	**800-772-3813**	770-414-9508
Golfsmith International Inc 11000 N IH-35 *Sales	Austin	TX	78753	**800-396-0099***	512-837-4810
H O Sports Inc 17622 NE 67th Ct	Redmond	WA	98052	**800-938-4040**	425-885-3505
Harmony Sports 22 Village Dr	Riverside	RI	02915	**800-882-3448**	401-490-9334
Harrison Hoge Industries 19 N Columbia St	Port Jefferson	NY	11777	**800-852-0925**	631-473-7308
HEAD USA 1 Selleck St	Norwalk	CT	06855	**800-874-3235**	203-855-0631
HEAD/Penn Racquet Sports 306 S 45th Ave	Phoenix	AZ	85043	**800-289-7366**	602-269-1492
Hillerich & Bradsby Co Inc 800 W Main St	Louisville	KY	40232	**800-282-2287**	502-585-5226
Hobie Cat Co 4925 Oceanside Blvd	Oceanside	CA	92056	**800-462-4349**	760-758-9100
Hockey Co 3500 Maison Neuve W Suite 800 *Cust Svc	Westmount	QC	H3Z3C1	**800-451-4600***	514-932-1118
Hogan Ben Co 425 Meadow St	Chicopee	MA	01021	**800-772-5346**	413-536-1200
Hoops Sporting Equipment Inc 22047 Lutheran Church Rd	Tomball	TX	77375	**800-294-4667**	281-351-9822
Huffy Sports Co N 53 W 24700 South Corporate Cir *Cust Svc	Sussex	WI	53089	**800-558-5234***	262-820-3440
Hunter Co Inc 3300 W 71st Ave	Westminster	CO	80030	**800-676-4868**	303-427-4626
International Billiards Inc 2311 Washington Ave	Houston	TX	77007	**800-255-6386**	713-869-3237
Intex Corp 4130 Santa Fe Ave	Long Beach	CA	90801	**800-234-6839**	310-549-5400
J DeBeer & Son Inc 5 Burdick Dr	Albany	NY	12205	**800-833-3535**	518-438-7871
Jayhawk Bowling Supply Inc 355 N Iowa St	Lawrence	KS	66044	**800-255-6436**	785-842-3237
Jerry's Sport Center Inc PO Box 121 *Sales	Forest City	PA	18421	**800-234-2612***	570-785-9400
JKP Sports Inc 19333 SW 18th Ave	Tualatin	OR	97062	**800-547-6843**	503-692-1635
Johnson Outdoors Inc 555 Main St *NASDAQ: JOUT*	Racine	WI	53403	**800-299-2592**	262-631-6600
K2 Inc 2051 Palomar Airport Rd Suite 100 *NYSE: KTO*	Carlsbad	CA	92009	**800-972-4063**	760-494-1000
K-2 Skis 19215 Vashon Hwy SW	Vashon	WA	98070	**800-972-4937**	206-463-3631
Kalispel Case Line PO Box 267	Cusick	WA	99119	**800-398-0338**	509-445-1121
Kangaroo Products Co 111 Kangaroo Dr PO Box 607	Columbus	NC	28722	**800-438-3011**	828-894-8241
Karsten Mfg Corp 2201 W Desert Cove Ave	Phoenix	AZ	85029	**800-474-6434**	602-870-5000
Kent Sporting Goods Co Inc 433 Park Ave S	New London	OH	44851	**800-537-2970**	419-929-7021
KL Industries 1790 Sun Dolphin Dr	Muskegon	MI	49444	**800-733-2727**	231-733-2725
Knight & Hale Game Calls PO Box 1587	Fort Smith	AR	72901	**800-500-9357**	479-782-8971
Kolpin Outdoors Inc 205 N Depot St	Fox Lake	WI	53933	**877-956-5746**	920-928-3118
KR Strikeforce Inc 1200 S 54th Ave	Cicero	IL	60804	**800-297-8555**	708-863-1200
Kwik Goal Ltd 140 Pacific Dr	Quakertown	PA	18951	**800-531-4252**	215-536-2200
Kwikee Kwiver Co 7292 Peaceful Valley Rd PO Box 130	Acme	MI	49610	**800-346-7001**	231-938-1690
Lamartek Inc DBA Dive Right 175 NW Washington St *Orders	Lake City	FL	32055	**800-495-1046***	386-752-1087
Life-Link International Inc PO Box 2913	Jackson	WY	83001	**800-443-8620**	307-733-2266
Lifetime Products Inc PO Box 160010 Freeport Ctr Bldg D-11	Clearfield	UT	84016	**800-225-3865**	801-776-1532
Local Motion Inc 424 Sumner St	Honolulu	HI	96817	**800-841-7613**	808-523-7873
Loomis G Inc 1359 Down River Dr	Woodland	WA	98674	**800-456-6647**	360-225-6516
Louisville Golf Co 2500 Grassland Dr	Louisville	KY	40299	**800-456-1631**	502-491-5490
Luhr Jensen & Sons Inc 400 Portway Ave PO Box 297	Hood River	OR	97031	**800-366-3811**	541-386-3811
MacGregor Golf Co Inc 1000 Pecan Grove Dr	Albany	GA	31707	**800-841-4358**	229-420-7000
Maravia Corp of Idaho 602 E 45th St	Boise	ID	83714	**800-223-7238**	208-322-4949
Mares America Corp 1 Selleck St	Norwalk	CT	06855	**800-874-3236**	203-855-0631
Martin Archery Inc 3134 W Hwy 12	Walla Walla	WA	99362	**800-541-8902**	509-529-2554
Master Industries Inc 14420 Myford Rd *Cust Svc	Irvine	CA	92606	**800-854-3794***	949-660-0644
Master Pitching Machine 4200 NE Birmingham Rd	Kansas City	MO	64117	**800-878-8228**	816-452-0228
Masterfit Golf Ltd 4128 S 3rd St	Jacksonville Beach	FL	32250	**888-501-7834**	904-246-3100
McHenry Metals Golf Corp 4502 Marquette Ave	Jacksonville	FL	32210	**866-410-2544**	

				Toll-Free	Phone
Michaels of Oregon 1710 Redsoils Ct	Oregon City	OR	97045	**800-962-5757**	503-557-0536
MicroMarine Ltd 7 Industrial Pk Rd	Medway	MA	02053	**800-451-8746**	508-634-0205
Miller Golf Inc 835 Bill Jones Industrial Dr	Springfield	TN	37172	**800-343-1000**	615-384-1286
Mister Twister LLC 1401 Commerce St	Minden	LA	71055	**800-344-6331**	318-377-8818
Mizuno USA 4925 Avalon Ridge Pkwy	Norcross	GA	30071	**800-333-7888**	770-441-5553
Mohawk Canoes 963 County Rd 427N	Longwood	FL	32750	**800-686-6429**	407-834-3233
Moultrie Feeders 150 Industrial Rd	Alabaster	AL	35007	**800-653-3334**	205-664-6700
Murrey International USA 14150 S Figueroa St	Los Angeles	CA	90061	**800-421-1022**	310-532-6091
Nash Mfg Inc 315 W Ripy St	Fort Worth	TX	76110	**800-433-2901**	817-926-5223
Natural Golf Corp 1200 E Business Center Dr Suite 400	Mount Prospect	IL	60056	**888-628-4653**	847-321-4000
Nitro USA 5 Commerce Ave	Lebanon	NH	03784	**877-648-7666**	603-298-9867
Nocona Athletic Goods Co 208 W Walnut St	Nocona	TX	76255	**800-433-0957**	940-825-3326
North Face Inc 2013 Farallon Dr	San Leandro	CA	94577	**800-535-3331**	510-618-3500
O'Brien International 14615 NE 91st St	Redmond	WA	98052	**800-662-7436**	425-202-2100
Ocean Kayak 2460 Salashan Loop	Ferndale	WA	98248	**800-852-9257**	360-366-4003
Oceanic USA 2002 Davis St	San Leandro	CA	94577	**800-435-3483**	510-562-0500
Old Town Canoe Co PO Box 548	Old Town	ME	04468	**800-343-1555**	207-827-5514
Olin Skis 19215 Vashon Hwy SW	Vashon	WA	98070	**800-522-7547**	206-463-3631
O'Neill Inc 1071 41st Ave PO Box 6300	Santa Cruz	CA	95063	**800-538-0764**	831-475-7500
Orlimar Golf Equipment Co 1385 Park Center Dr	Vista	CA	92081	**877-675-4627*** *Cust Svc	760-305-0013
Orvis Co Inc PO Box 798	Manchester	VT	05254	**800-541-3541**	802-362-3622
Osborne Innovative Products Inc 2221 2nd St	Enumclaw	WA	98022	**800-325-7238**	360-825-4299
Pappy's Golf Shop 4030 N Sinton Rd	Colorado Springs	CO	80907	**800-530-2345**	719-633-2064
Perception Inc 111 Kayaker Way	Easley	SC	29642	**800-595-2925**	864-859-7518
Poolmaster Inc 770 W Del Paso Rd Suite W	Sacramento	CA	95834	**800-854-1776**	916-567-9800
Porter Athletic Equipment Co 2500 S 25th Ave	Broadview	IL	60155	**800-947-6783**	708-338-2000
Powell Skate One Corp 30 S La Patera Ln	Santa Barbara	CA	93117	**800-884-3813**	805-964-1330
PRADCO Outdoor Brands Div EBSCO Industries Inc 3601 Jenny Lind Rd	Fort Smith	AR	72901	**800-531-1201**	479-782-8971
Prince Sports Inc 1 Advantage Ct	Bordentown	NJ	08505	**800-283-6647**	609-291-5800
Priva Sport 8505 Devonshire Rd	Montreal	QC	H4P2L3	**877-568-8662**	514-341-9548
Pro-Kennex Inc 5122 Avenida Encinas Suite 120	Carlsbad	CA	92008	**800-854-1908**	760-804-8322
Pure Fishing America 1900 18th St	Spirit Lake	IA	51360	**877-777-3850**	712-336-1520
Ralph Maltby's GolfWorks 4820 Jacksontown Rd	Newark	OH	43055	**800-848-8358**	740-328-4193
Rawlings Sporting Goods Co PO Box 22000	Saint Louis	MO	63126	**800-729-5464**	636-349-3500
Remington Arms Co Inc Stren Fishing Lines Div PO Box 700	Madison	NC	27025	**800-243-9700**	336-548-8700
Resilite Sports Products PO Box 764	Sunbury	PA	17801	**800-326-9307**	570-473-3529
Ride Snowboards 19215 Vashon Hwy SW	Vashon	WA	98070	**800-757-5806**	206-463-3631
Riedell Shoes Inc 122 Cannon River Ave	Red Wing	MN	55066	**800-698-6893**	651-388-8251
Rio Products Inc 5050 S Yellowstone Hwy	Idaho Falls	ID	83402	**800-553-0838**	208-524-7760
RL Winston Rod Co 500 S Main St	Twin Bridges	MT	59754	**800-237-8763**	406-684-5674
Rollerblade Inc 1 Advantage Ct	Bordentown	NJ	08505	**800-232-7655**	609-291-5800
Rome Specialty Co Inc Rosco Div 501 W Embargo St	Rome	NY	13440	**800-794-8357**	315-337-8200
Ross Reels 1 Ponderosa Ct	Montrose	CO	81401	**800-336-1050**	970-249-1212
Royal Precision Inc 535 Migeon Ave	Torrington	CT	06790	**800-920-4848**	860-489-9254
Sage Mfg Corp 8500 NE Day Rd	Bainbridge Island	WA	98110	**800-533-3004**	206-842-6608
Saint Croix of Park Falls Ltd PO Box 279	Park Falls	WI	54552	**800-826-7042**	715-762-3226
Saunders Archery Co 1874 14th Ave PO Box 1707	Columbus	NE	68601	**800-228-1408*** *Cust Svc	402-564-7176
Schutt Sports 1200 E Union Ave PO Box 426	Litchfield	IL	62056	**800-637-2047**	217-324-2712
Scott Fly Rod Co 2355 Air Park Way	Montrose	CO	81401	**800-728-7208**	970-249-3180
Scott USA Inc PO Box 2030	Sun Valley	ID	83353	**800-292-5874**	208-622-1000
Seeker Rod Co Inc 1340 W Cowles St	Long Beach	CA	90813	**800-373-3537**	562-491-0076
Sevylor USA Inc 4398 Corporate Center Dr	Los Alamitos	CA	90720	**800-821-4645**	714-503-6300
Shakespeare Fishing Tackle Co 3801 Westmore Dr	Columbia	SC	29223	**800-347-3759*** *Cust Svc	803-754-7000
Sierra Designs Inc 2011 Cherry St Suite 202	Louisville	CO	80027	**800-635-0461**	
Spalding 150 Brookdale Dr	Springfield	MA	01104	**800-772-5346*** *Cust Svc	413-735-1400
Sport Supply Group Inc 1901 Diplomat Dr	Dallas	TX	75234	**800-527-7510**	972-484-9484
Standard Golf Co 6620 Nordic Dr	Cedar Falls	IA	50613	**800-553-1707**	319-266-2638
Stearns Inc 1100 Stearns Dr	Sauk Rapids	MN	56379	**800-333-1179**	320-252-1642
Stockli Ski USA Inc PO Box 370206	Denver	CO	80237	**800-638-6284**	303-220-9737
Stone Legacy Corp S1075 Westland Ct E	Spring Valley	WI	54767	**877-563-6465*** *Sales	715-778-5079
Storm Products Inc 165 S 800 West	Brigham City	UT	84302	**800-369-4402**	435-723-0403
Straight Line Sports LLC 19011 Woodinville-Snohomish Rd Suite 130	Woodinville	WA	98072	**800-248-5564**	425-527-1148
Tampa G Mfg Co 5105 S Lois Ave	Tampa	FL	33611	**800-365-1559**	813-229-1559
Taylor Made Golf Co 5545 Fermi Ct	Carlsbad	CA	92008	**800-456-8633*** *Cust Svc	760-918-6000
Team Cobra Products 7240 W Erie St Suite 3	Chandler	AZ	85226	**800-336-7784**	480-889-1035
Tecnica USA 19 Technology Dr	West Lebanon	NH	03784	**800-258-3897**	603-298-8032
Tommy Armour Golf Co 36 Dufflaw Rd	Toronto	ON	M6A2W1	**800-723-4653*** *Cust Svc	416-630-4996
Toobs Inc 349 B Quintana Rd	Morro Bay	CA	93442	**800-795-8662**	805-772-5742
Top-Flite Golf Co 425 Meadow St	Chicopee	MA	01021	**866-834-6532**	413-536-1200
True Temper Sports 8275 Tournament Dr Suite 200	Memphis	TN	38125	**800-355-8783**	901-746-2000
Tuf-Wear USA 1001 Industrial Ave	North Platte	NE	69101	**800-445-5210**	308-532-0187
Underwater Kinetics 13400 Danielson St	Poway	CA	92064	**800-852-7483**	858-513-9100
US Line Co 16 Union Ave	Westfield	MA	01085	**800-456-4665**	413-562-3629
Variflex Inc 5152 N Commerce Ave *NASDAQ: VFLX*	Moorpark	CA	93021	**800-327-0821**	805-523-0322
Virtual Turf 1800 Industrial Pk Dr PO Box 732	Grand Haven	MI	49417	**800-560-7795**	616-847-9121
Volkl Sport America 19 Technology Dr	West Lebanon	NH	03784	**800-264-4579**	603-298-0314
Weed USA Inc 275 Old County Line Rd Suite D	Westerville	OH	43081	**800-933-3758**	614-568-0060
Wileys Custom Water Skis 1417 S Trenton	Seattle	WA	98108	**800-962-0785**	206-762-1300
Winston Rods 500 S Main St	Twin Bridges	MT	59754	**800-237-8763**	406-684-5674
Wittek Golf Supply Co Inc 3650 N Avondale Ave	Chicago	IL	60618	**800-869-1800**	773-463-2636
Women's Golf Unlimited Inc 18 Gloria Ln	Fairfield	NJ	07004	**800-526-2250**	973-227-7783
Worth Co PO Box 88	Stevens Point	WI	54481	**800-944-1899**	715-344-6081
Worth Sports PO Box 88104	Tullahoma	TN	37388	**800-282-9637*** *Cust Svc	931-455-0691
Wright & McGill Co DBA Eagle Claw Fishing Tackle 4245 E 46th Ave	Denver	CO	80216	**800-628-0108**	303-321-1481
Yamaha Motor Corp USA 6555 Katella Ave	Cypress	CA	90630	**800-962-7926*** *Cust Svc	714-761-7300
Yonex Corp 20140 S Western Ave	Torrance	CA	90501	**800-449-6639**	310-793-3800
Zebco Corp 6101 E Apache St	Tulsa	OK	74115	**800-588-9030**	918-836-5581

702 SPORTING GOODS STORES

				Toll-Free	Phone
Academy Sports & Outdoors 1800 N Mason Rd	Katy	TX	77449	**877-999-9856**	281-646-5200
Adventure 16 Inc 4620 Alvarado Canyon Rd	San Diego	CA	92120	**800-854-2672**	619-283-2362
Alpina Sports USA PO Box 23	Hanover	NH	03755	**800-425-7462**	603-448-3101
Altrec.com Inc 135 Lake St S Suite 1000	Kirkland	WA	90833	**800-369-3949**	425-827-5159
Any Mountain Ltd 71 Tamal Vista Blvd	Corte Madera	CA	94925	**800-992-4844**	415-927-2400
Aspen Sports Ltd 408 E Cooper Ave	Aspen	CO	81611	**800-544-6648**	970-925-6331
Baseball Express Inc 1051 E Nakoma St	San Antonio	TX	78216	**800-937-4824*** *Cust Svc	210-348-7000
Big 5 Sporting Goods Corp 2525 E El Segundo Blvd *NASDAQ: BGFV*	El Segundo	CA	90245	**800-367-2445**	310-536-0611
Bob Ward & Sons Inc 3015 Paxson St	Missoula	MT	59801	**800-800-5083**	406-728-3220
Boyne Country Sports 1200 Bay View Rd	Petoskey	MI	49770	**800-462-6963**	231-439-4906
Brady's Sportsman's Surplus Inc 2315 Brooks St	Missoula	MT	59801	**800-473-4867**	406-721-5501
Cabela's Inc 1 Cabela Dr *NYSE: CAB*	Sidney	NE	69160	**800-237-8888**	308-254-5505
Camping World Inc 650 Three Springs Rd	Bowling Green	KY	42104	**800-626-3636*** *Cust Svc	270-781-2718
Campmor Inc 28 Parkway	Upper Saddle River	NJ	07458	**800-526-4784*** *Orders	201-825-8300
Century Inc 1000 Century Blvd	Midwest City	OK	73110	**800-626-2787*** *Sales	405-732-2226
Champs Sports 311 Manatee Ave W	Bradenton	FL	34205	**800-991-6813**	941-748-0577
Copeland's Enterprises Inc PO Box 1348	San Luis Obispo	CA	93406	**800-619-2853**	805-543-0660
D & R Sports Center Inc 8178 W Main St	Kalamazoo	MI	49009	**800-992-1520**	269-372-2277
Dick's Sporting Goods Inc 300 Industry Dr *NYSE: DKS*	Pittsburgh	PA	15275	**800-690-7655**	412-809-0100
Dixie Bocock Sporting Goods DBA Dixie Sporting Goods 501 Deacon Blvd	Winston-Salem	NC	27105	**888-262-6251**	336-724-2421
Dixie Gun Works Inc PO Box 130	Union City	TN	38281	**800-238-6785*** *Orders	731-885-0700
Eastern Mountain Sports Inc 1 Vose Farm Rd	Peterborough	NH	03458	**888-463-6367**	603-924-9571
Edwin Watts Golf Shops Inc 20 Hill Ave NW	Fort Walton Beach	FL	32548	**800-874-0146**	850-244-2066
Erie Sport Store Inc 701 State St	Erie	PA	16501	**800-333-6812**	814-452-2289
Fanzz 1832 W 2770 South Suite 10	Salt Lake City	UT	84119	**888-326-9946**	801-325-2700
Fitness Zone 2630 6th Ave S	Birmingham	AL	35233	**800-875-9145*** *Cust Svc	205-324-1955
Galyan's Trading Co Inc 1 Galyan's Pkwy *NASDAQ: GLYN*	Plainfield	IN	46168	**888-425-9267**	317-532-0200
Gander Mountain Co 4567 American Blvd W *NASDAQ: GMTN*	Bloomington	MN	55437	**800-745-7411**	952-830-8700
Gerry Cosby & Co Inc 3 Pennsylvania Plaza	New York	NY	10001	**877-563-6464**	212-563-6464
Golf Shack Inc 1631 N Bell School Rd	Rockford	IL	61107	**888-446-5390**	815-397-3709
Golf USA 3705 W Memorial Rd Suite 801	Oklahoma City	OK	73134	**800-488-1107**	405-751-0015
Golfsmith International Inc 11000 N IH-35	Austin	TX	78753	**800-396-0099*** *Sales	512-837-4810
Gym Source 40 E 52nd St	New York	NY	10022	**800-496-7687**	212-688-4222
In The Swim Inc 320 Industrial Dr	West Chicago	IL	60185	**800-288-7946**	
Island Water Sports Inc 1985 NE 2nd St	Deerfield Beach	FL	33441	**800-873-0375**	954-427-4929
Jan's Mountain Outfitters 1600 Park Ave PO Box 280	Park City	UT	84060	**800-745-1020**	435-649-4949
Kittery Trading Post 301 US Rt 1	Kittery	ME	03904	**888-587-6246**	207-439-2700
Langhorne Ski Shop 543 Lincoln Hwy	Fairless Hills	PA	19030	**800-523-8850**	215-295-4240
Leslie's Swimming Pool Supplies 3925 E Broadway Rd Suite 100	Phoenix	AZ	85040	**800-233-8063**	602-366-3999
MC Sports 3070 Shaffer Ave SE	Grand Rapids	MI	49512	**800-626-1762**	616-942-2600
Modell's Sporting Goods 498 7th Ave 20th Fl	New York	NY	10018	**800-250-7405**	212-822-1000
NRC Sports Inc 603 Pleasant St	Paxton	MA	01612	**800-243-5033**	508-852-8206
OMNI Fitness Equipment Inc 2344 Summer St	Stamford	CT	06902	**877-875-6664**	203-978-5200
Performance Inc 1 Performance Way	Chapel Hill	NC	27514	**800-727-2433*** *Cust Svc	919-933-9113
Peter Glenn Ski & Sports 2901 W Oakland Pk Blvd	Fort Lauderdale	FL	33311	**800-818-0946**	954-484-7800
Play It Again Sports 4200 Dahlberg Dr Suite 100	Minneapolis	MN	55422	**800-433-2540**	763-520-8500
Pro Golf of America Inc 32751 Middlebelt Rd	Farmington Hills	MI	48334	**800-521-6388**	248-737-0553
Ramsey Outdoor Store 240 SR 17 N	Paramus	NJ	07652	**800-699-5874**	201-261-5000
Recreational Equipment Inc (REI) 6750 S 228th St	Kent	WA	98032	**800-426-4840*** *Orders	253-395-3780
SailNet 3864 Leeds Ave	Charleston	SC	29405	**866-724-5638*** *Cust Svc	843-972-2010
Sport Chalet Inc 1 Sport Chalet Dr *NASDAQ: SPCH*	La Canada	CA	91011	**888-801-9162**	818-790-2717
Sports Endeavors Inc 431 US Hwy 70-A E	Hillsborough	NC	27278	**800-934-3876**	919-644-6800
Tri-State Distributors 1104 W Pullman Rd	Moscow	ID	83843	**877-878-2835**	208-882-4555
Val Surf Inc 4810 Whitsett Ave	Valley Village	CA	91607	**888-825-7873**	818-769-6977
Wheel & Sprocket Inc 5722 S 108th St	Hales Corners	WI	53130	**800-362-4537**	414-529-6600
World of Golf 4500 Tamiami Trail N	Naples	FL	34103	**800-505-9998**	239-263-4999

SPORTS FACILITIES

SEE Motor Speedways; Racing & Racetracks; Stadiums & Arenas

703 SPORTS TEAMS

SEE ALSO Associations & Organizations - General - Sports Organizations

Name / Address	City	State	ZIP	Toll-Free	Phone
Major League Baseball (Office of the Commissioner) 245 Park Ave 31st Fl *Cust Svc	New York	NY	10167	**800-704-2937***	212-931-7800
Arizona Cardinals 8701 S Hardy Dr	Tempe	AZ	85284	**800-999-1402**	602-379-0101
Atlanta Falcons 4400 Falcon Pkwy	Flowery Branch	GA	30542	**800-241-3489**	770-965-3115
Baltimore Orioles 333 W Camden St Oriole Pk at Camden Yards	Baltimore	MD	21201	**888-848-2473**	410-685-9800
Buffalo Sabres HSBC Arena 1 Seymour H Knox III Plaza	Buffalo	NY	14203	**888-467-2273**	716-855-4100
Calgary Flames Pengrowth Saddledome 555 Saddledome Rise SE	Calgary	AB	T2G2W1	**888-535-2637**	403-777-2177
Chicago Fire 980 N Michigan Ave Suite 1998	Chicago	IL	60611	**888-657-3473**	312-705-7200
Chicago Rush 8735 W Higgins Rd Suite 160	Chicago	IL	60631	**888-682-3434**	773-243-3434
Cincinnati Bengals 1 Paul Brown Stadium	Cincinnati	OH	45202	**866-621-8383**	513-621-3550
Cleveland Browns 76 Lou Groza Blvd *Sales	Berea	OH	44017	**888-891-1999***	440-891-5000
Cleveland Cavaliers 1 Center Ct Gund Arena	Cleveland	OH	44115	**800-332-2260**	216-420-2000
Cleveland Indians Jacobs Field 2401 Ontario St	Cleveland	OH	44115	**866-488-7743**	216-420-4200
Club Deportivo Chivas USA Home Depot Center 18400 Avalon Blvd Suite 500	Carson	CA	90746	**877-244-8271**	310-630-4550
Colorado Rockies Coors Field 2001 Blake St	Denver	CO	80205	**800-388-7625**	303-292-0200
Columbus Blue Jackets Nationwide Arena 200 W Nationwide Blvd 3rd Fl	Columbus	OH	43215	**800-645-2657**	614-246-4625
Columbus Crew Crew Stadium 1 Black & Gold Blvd	Columbus	OH	43211	**800-273-9326**	614-447-2739
Connecticut Sun 1 Mohegan Sun Blvd	Uncasville	CT	06382	**877-786-8499**	860-862-4000
Detroit Lions 222 Republic Dr	Allen Park	MI	48101	**800-616-7627**	313-216-4000
Edmonton Eskimos 9023 111th Ave	Edmonton	AB	T5B0C3	**800-667-3757**	780-448-1525
Florida Marlins Dolphins Stadium 2267 Dan Marino Blvd	Miami	FL	33056	**877-627-5467**	305-626-7400
Golden State Warriors 1011 Broadway	Oakland	CA	94607	**888-479-4667**	510-986-2200
Grand Rapids Rampage 130 Fulton St W	Grand Rapids	MI	49503	**888-595-4878**	616-559-1871
Hamilton Tiger-Cats 75 Balsam Ave N Ivor Wynne Stadium	Hamilton	ON	L8L8C1	**800-714-7627**	905-547-2418
Houston Astros Minute Maid Park 501 Crawford St	Houston	TX	77002	**877-927-8768**	713-259-8000
Indianapolis Colts 7001 W 56th St	Indianapolis	IN	46254	**800-805-2658**	317-297-2658
Jacksonville Jaguars 1 Alltel Stadium Pl	Jacksonville	FL	32202	**877-452-4784**	904-633-6000
Kansas City Royals Kauffman Stadium 1 Royal Way *Sales	Kansas City	MO	64129	**800-676-9257***	816-921-8000
Los Angeles Avengers 12100 W Olympic Blvd Suite 400	Los Angeles	CA	90064	**888-283-6437**	310-788-7744
Los Angeles Galaxy 18400 Avalon Blvd Suite 200	Carson	CA	90746	**877-342-5299**	310-630-2200
Los Angeles Kings Staples Ctr 1111 S Figueroa St	Los Angeles	CA	90015	**888-546-4752**	213-742-7100
Mighty Ducks of Anaheim 2695 Katella Ave Arrowhead Pond of Anaheim	Anaheim	CA	92806	**877-945-3946**	714-704-2700
Minnesota Twins Hubert H Humphrey Metrodome 34 Kirby Puckett Pl	Minneapolis	MN	55415	**800-338-9467**	612-375-1366
New England Revolution 1 Patriot Pl Gillette Stadium	Foxboro	MA	02035	**877-438-7387**	508-543-5001
New Jersey Devils Continental Airlines Arena 50 Rt 120N	East Rutherford	NJ	07073	**800-653-3845**	201-935-6050
New Jersey Nets 390 Murray Hill Pkwy Nets Champion Ctr	East Rutherford	NJ	07073	**800-765-6387**	201-935-8888
New York Dragons 1535 Old Country Rd	Plainview	NY	11803	**800-882-4753**	516-501-6700
New York Mets Shea Stadium 123-01 Roosevelt Ave	Flushing	NY	11368	**800-221-1155**	718-507-6387
New York/New Jersey MetroStars 1 Harmon Plaza 3rd Fl	Secaucus	NJ	07094	**800-638-7684**	201-583-7000
Ottawa Senators Corel Ctr 1000 Palladium Dr *Orders	Kanata	ON	K2V1A5	**888-688-7367***	613-599-0250
Pittsburgh Penguins 1 Chatham Ctr Suite 400	Pittsburgh	PA	15219	**800-642-7366**	412-642-1300
Saint Louis Rams 1 Rams Way *Cust Svc	Earth City	MO	63045	**800-246-7267***	314-982-7267
San Diego Chargers 4020 Murphy Canyon Rd	San Diego	CA	92123	**877-242-7437**	858-874-4500
Saskatchewan Roughriders 2940 10th Ave Taylor Field * Box 1277	Regina	SK	S4P3B8	**888-474-3377**	306-569-2323
Seattle Seahawks 11220 NE 53rd St	Kirkland	WA	98033	**888-635-4295**	425-827-9777
Seattle Storm 351 Elliott Ave W Suite 500	Seattle	WA	98119	**800-743-7021**	206-281-5800
Seattle SuperSonics 351 Elliott Ave W Suite 500	Seattle	WA	98119	**800-743-7021**	206-281-5800
Tampa Bay Devil Rays Tropicana Field 1 Tropicana Dr	Saint Petersburg	FL	33705	**888-697-2373**	727-825-3137
Texas Rangers Ameriquest Field in Arlington 1000 Ballpark Way	Arlington	TX	76011	**888-968-3927**	817-273-5222
Toronto Blue Jays 1 Blue Jays Way	Toronto	ON	M5V1J1	**888-654-6529**	416-341-1000
Utah Jazz 301 W South Temple St Delta Ctr	Salt Lake City	UT	84101	**800-358-7328**	801-325-2500
Vancouver Canucks General Motors Pl 800 Griffiths Way	Vancouver	BC	V6B6G1	**888-672-2229**	604-899-4600
Washington Wizards 601 F St NW	Washington	DC	20004	**800-551-7328**	202-661-5000

704 SPRINGS - HEAVY-GAUGE

Name / Address	City	State	ZIP	Toll-Free	Phone
Barnes Group Inc 123 Main St *NYSE: B*	Bristol	CT	06011	**800-877-8803**	860-583-7070
General Wire Spring Co 1101 Thompson Ave	McKees Rocks	PA	15136	**800-245-6200**	412-771-6300
Southern Spring & Stamping Inc 401 Sub Station Rd	Venice	FL	34292	**800-450-5882**	941-488-2276

705 SPRINGS - LIGHT-GAUGE

Name / Address	City	State	ZIP	Toll-Free	Phone
Century Spring Corp PO Box 15287	Los Angeles	CA	90015	**800-237-5225**	213-749-1466
Connecticut Spring & Stamping Corp 48 Spring Ln	Farmington	CT	06034	**800-255-8590**	860-677-1341
Flex-O-Lators Inc 1460 Jackson Dr	Carthage	MO	64836	**800-641-4363**	417-358-4095
Hickory Springs Mfg Co 235 2nd Ave NW	Hickory	NC	28601	**800-438-5341**	828-328-2201
Lee Spring Co Inc 1462 62nd St	Brooklyn	NY	11219	**800-426-0272**	718-236-2222
Leggett & Platt Inc PO Box 757 *NYSE: LEG*	Carthage	MO	64836	**800-888-4569**	417-358-8131
Mid-West Spring & Stamping Co 1404 Joliet Rd Unit C	Romeoville	IL	60446	**800-838-7812**	630-739-3800
Spring Engineers Inc 9740 Tanner Rd	Houston	TX	77041	**800-899-9488**	713-690-9488
Sterling Spring Corp 5432 W 54th St	Chicago	IL	60638	**800-969-7884**	773-582-6464
Yost Superior Co PO Box 1487	Springfield	OH	45501	**800-544-4570**	937-323-7591

706 STADIUMS & ARENAS

SEE ALSO Convention Centers; Performing Arts Facilities

Name / Address	City	State	ZIP	Toll-Free	Phone
Alamodome 100 Montana St	San Antonio	TX	78203	**800-884-3663**	210-207-3663
Alltel Stadium 1 Alltel Stadium Pl	Jacksonville	FL	32202	**877-452-4784**	904-633-6000
Ameriquest Field in Arlington 1000 Ballpark Way Suite 400	Arlington	TX	76011	**888-968-3927**	817-273-5222
Canal Park Stadium 300 S Main St	Akron	OH	44308	**800-972-3767**	330-253-5151
Cleveland Browns Stadium 100 Alfred Lerner Way *Sales	Cleveland	OH	44114	**888-891-1999***	440-891-5000
Columbus Civic Center 400 4th St	Columbus	GA	31901	**800-711-3986**	706-653-4482
Coors Field 2001 Blake St	Denver	CO	80205	**800-388-7625**	303-762-5437
Corel Centre 1000 Palladium Dr	Kanata	ON	K2V1A5	**800-444-7367**	613-599-0250
Cowtown Coliseum 121 E Exchange Ave	Fort Worth	TX	76106	**888-269-8696**	817-625-1025
Golden Spike Event Center 1000 N 1200 West	Ogden	UT	84404	**800-442-7362**	801-399-8544
Gund Arena 1 Center Ct	Cleveland	OH	44115	**800-332-2287**	216-420-2000
HP Pavilion at San Jose 525 W Santa Clara St	San Jose	CA	95113	**800-366-4423**	408-287-7070
Kemper Arena 1800 Genessee St	Kansas City	MO	64102	**800-634-3942**	816-513-4000
Louisiana Superdome 1500 Poydras PO Box 52439	New Orleans	LA	70152	**800-756-7074**	504-587-3663
MetraPark Arena 308 6th Ave N	Billings	MT	59101	**800-366-8538**	406-256-2400
Municipal Auditorium Arena 301 W 13th St Suite 100	Kansas City	MO	64105	**800-821-7060**	816-513-5000
Olympic Center Arena 2634 Main St	Lake Placid	NY	12946	**800-462-6236**	518-523-1655
Olympic Stadium 4549 Pierre-de-Coubertin Ave	Montreal	QC	H1V3N7	**800-463-9767**	514-252-4679
Oriole Park at Camden Yards 333 W Camden St	Baltimore	MD	21201	**888-848-2473**	410-576-0300
PNC Park 115 Federal St	Pittsburgh	PA	15212	**800-289-2827**	412-321-2827
Rose Garden 1 Center Ct	Portland	OR	97227	**800-231-8750**	503-797-9619
Sioux Falls Arena 1201 West Ave N	Sioux Falls	SD	57104	**800-338-3177**	605-367-7288
Superdome 1500 Poydras PO Box 52439	New Orleans	LA	70152	**800-756-7074**	504-587-3663
Tropicana Field 1 Tropicana Dr	Saint Petersburg	FL	33705	**888-326-7297**	727-825-3120

707 STAFFING SERVICES

SEE ALSO Employment Services - Online; Executive Recruiting Firms; Professional Employer Organizations (PEOs)

Name / Address	City	State	ZIP	Toll-Free	Phone
AccountingSolutions Div Career Blazers Inc 222 W Las Colinas Blvd Suite 1250E	Irving	TX	75039	**800-787-6750**	214-296-6700
Adecco Inc 175 Broad Hollow Rd *NYSE: ADO*	Melville	NY	11747	**877-632-9169**	631-844-7800
Aerotek Inc 7301 Parkway Dr	Hanover	MD	21076	**800-435-2029**	410-540-7000
All Medical Personnel 4651 Sheridan St	Hollywood	FL	33021	**800-706-2378**	954-922-9696
Allied Health Group 145 Technology Pkwy NW	Norcross	GA	30092	**800-741-4674**	770-246-9191
AllStates Technical Services 1777 Sentry Pkwy W Suite 304	Blue Bell	PA	19422	**800-432-8006**	215-591-3870
ALTRES Inc 967 Kapiolani Blvd	Honolulu	HI	96814	**800-373-1955**	808-591-4900
AMN Healthcare Services Inc 12400 High Bluff Dr Suite 100 *NYSE: AHS*	San Diego	CA	92130	**866-510-1904**	
APEX Systems Inc 2235 Staples Mill Rd Suite 200	Richmond	VA	23230	**800-452-7391**	804-254-2600
AppleOne Employment Services Inc 327 W Broadway	Glendale	CA	91204	**800-872-2677**	818-240-8688
AppleOne Employment Services Inc 50 Paxman Rd Unit 8	Etobicoke	ON	M9C1B7	**800-564-5644**	416-622-0100
Aquent LLC 711 Boylston St	Boston	MA	02116	**800-878-0900**	617-535-6000
ARC Industries Inc 2879 Johnstown Rd	Columbus	OH	43219	**800-734-7007**	614-475-7007
Aspire Group 4510 Executive Dr Suite 206	San Diego	CA	92121	**800-487-2967**	858-526-1530
ATC Travelers 1983 Marcus Ave Suite E122	Lake Success	NY	11042	**800-797-8707**	
Atlantic Group 5426 Robin Hood Rd	Norfolk	VA	23513	**800-446-8131**	757-857-6400

	City	State	Zip	Toll-Free	Phone
ATS Services Inc 9700 Phillips Hwy Suite 101	Jacksonville	FL	32256	**800-346-5574**	904-645-9505
Bartech Group 17199 N Laurel Pk Dr Suite 224	Livonia	MI	48152	**800-828-4410**	734-953-5050
Bartech Technical Services 3980 Chicago Dr	Grandville	MI	49418	**800-968-5776**	616-532-5555
Bay Area Anesthesia Inc PO Box 1547	Ukiah	CA	95482	**800-327-8427**	707-462-1557
C & A Industries Inc 11825 Q St	Omaha	NE	68137	**800-574-9829**	402-891-0009
Calian Technology Ltd 2 Beaverbrook Rd	Kanata	ON	K2K1L1	**877-225-4264**	613-599-8600
TSE: CTY					
Career Blazers Inc 222 W Las Colinas Blvd Suite 1250E	Irving	TX	75039	**800-787-6750**	214-296-6700
Career Blazers Inc AccountingSolutions Div 222 W Las Colinas Blvd Suite 1250E	Irving	TX	75039	**800-787-6750**	214-296-6700
Career Blazers Inc Personnel One Div 222 W Las Colinas Blvd Suite 1250E	Irving	TX	75039	**800-787-6750**	214-296-6700
Career Blazers Inc ProDrivers Div 222 W Las Colinas Blvd Suite 1250E	Irving	TX	75039	**800-787-6750**	214-296-6700
Career Blazers Inc ResourceMFG Div 222 W Las Colinas Blvd Suite 1250E	Irving	TX	75039	**800-787-6750**	214-296-6700
Career Blazers Inc StaffingSolutions Div 222 W Las Colinas Blvd Suite 1250E	Irving	TX	75039	**800-787-6750**	214-296-6700
Career Blazers Inc Telesource Div 222 W Las Colinas Blvd Suite 1250E	Irving	TX	75039	**800-787-6750**	214-296-6700
CareerBuilder Inc 8420 W Bryn Mawr Ave Suite 900	Chicago	IL	60631	**888-622-9022**	773-527-3600
CareerStaff Unlimited Inc 2600 S Gessner Suite 300	Houston	TX	77063	**800-443-1221**	713-297-9000
Cejka & Co 222 S Central Ave Suite 400	Saint Louis	MO	63105	**800-678-7858**	314-726-1603
COMFORCE Corp 415 Crossways Park Dr	Woodbury	NY	11797	**877-266-3672**	
AMEX: CFS					
CompHealth Inc 4021 S 700 E Suite 300	Salt Lake City	UT	84107	**800-453-3030**	801-264-6400
Compunnel Software Group Inc 1000 Rt 9 N Suite 102	Woodbridge	NJ	07095	**800-692-4440**	732-636-1999
Compuware Corp Professional Services Div 505 Hwy 169 N Suite 750	Plymouth	MN	55441	**800-292-7432***	763-541-9575
*Cust Svc					
Comsys IT Partners Inc 4400 Post Oak Pkwy Suite 1800	Houston	TX	77027	**877-626-6797**	713-386-1400
NASDAQ: CITP					
Consultis 4401 N Federal Hwy Suite 100	Boca Raton	FL	33431	**800-275-2667**	561-362-9104
Contract Counsel 1025 N Campbell Rd	Royal Oak	MI	48067	**877-526-8673**	248-597-0400
CPC Logistics Inc 14528 S Outer 40 Rd Suite 210	Chesterfield	MO	63017	**800-274-3746**	314-542-2266
Cross Country Healthcare Inc 6551 Park of Commerce Blvd Suite 200	Boca Raton	FL	33487	**800-530-6125**	561-998-2232
NASDAQ: CCRN					
CyberStaff America Ltd 253 W 35th St 16th Fl	New York	NY	10001	**888-244-2300**	212-244-2300
Davis Cos 33 Boston Post Rd W	Marlborough	MA	01752	**800-482-9494**	508-481-9500
Design Group Staffing Services Inc 10155 102nd St Suite 2380	Edmonton	AB	T5J4G8	**800-770-1228**	780-428-1505
Devon Consulting 950 W Valley Rd Suite 2602	Wayne	PA	19087	**800-229-5709**	610-964-2700
Diversified Medical Staffing LLC 3410 Belle Chase Way Suite 600	Lansing	MI	48911	**800-881-3205**	517-702-4030
Dunhill Staffing Systems Inc 9190 Priority Way W Suite 204	Indianapolis	IN	46240	**800-386-7823**	317-818-4910
Durham Cos Inc 6300 Transit Rd	Depew	NY	14043	**800-633-7724**	716-684-3333
Eagle Professional Resources Inc 67 Yonge St Suite 200	Toronto	ON	M5E1J8	**800-281-2339**	416-861-0636
Emergency Consultants Inc 2240 S Airport Rd W	Traverse City	MI	49684	**800-253-1795**	231-946-8970
enherent Corp 80 Lamberton Rd 1st Fl	Windsor	CT	06095	**877-778-4768**	860-687-2200
Ensearch Management Consultants 905 E Cotati Ave	Cotati	CA	94931	**800-473-6776**	707-795-3800
EuroSoft Inc 1705 Capital of Texas Hwy Suite 200	Austin	TX	78746	**888-329-8100**	512-329-8100
Express Services Inc 8516 Northwest Expy	Oklahoma City	OK	73162	**800-652-6400**	405-840-5000
First Assist Inc 4720 Montgomery Ln Suite 300	Bethesda	MD	20814	**800-426-1724**	301-718-2200
Gibson Arnold & Assoc 1776 Yorktown St Suite 350	Houston	TX	77056	**800-879-2007**	713-572-3000
Gonzer LJ Assoc Inc 1225 Raymond Blvd	Newark	NJ	07102	**800-631-4218**	973-624-5600
HireKnowledge 1 Harry St	Providence	RI	02907	**800-937-3622**	401-942-0570
Interim HealthCare Inc 1601 Sawgrass Corporate Pkwy	Sunrise	FL	33323	**800-338-7786**	954-858-6000
Joule Inc 1235 US Rt 1 S	Edison	NJ	08837	**800-341-0341**	732-548-5444
AMEX: JOL					
Judge Group Inc 300 Conshohocken State Rd Suite 300	West Conshohocken	PA	19428	**888-228-7162**	610-667-7700
Kforce Inc 75 Rowland Way Suite 200	Novato	CA	94945	**800-880-4611**	415-895-2200
Kforce Inc 1001 E Palm Ave	Tampa	FL	33605	**888-663-3626**	813-552-5000
NASDAQ: KFRC					
Labor Finders International Inc 3910 RCA Blvd Suite 1001	Palm Beach Gardens	FL	33410	**800-864-7749**	561-627-6507
Labor Ready Inc PO Box 2910	Tacoma	WA	98401	**800-991-4991**	253-383-9101
NYSE: LRW					
Legal Network Ltd 425 6th Ave Suite 1830	Pittsburgh	PA	15219	**800-737-3436**	412-201-7470
LJ Gonzer Assoc Inc 1225 Raymond Blvd	Newark	NJ	07102	**800-631-4218**	973-624-5600
Med-Emerg International Inc 6711 Mississauga Rd Suite 404	Mississauga	ON	L5N2W3	**800-265-3429**	905-858-1368
Medical Staffing Assoc Inc 6731 Whittier Ave Suite A300	McLean	VA	22101	**800-235-5105**	703-893-1773
Medstaff National Medical Staffing Inc 1000 Pk 40 Plaza	Durham	NC	27713	**800-476-3275**	
National Engineering Service Corp 72 Mirona Rd	Portsmouth	NH	03801	**800-562-3463**	603-431-9740
North Star Communications Group Inc 1900 International Pk Dr	Birmingham	AL	35243	**888-836-6784**	877-862-8682
Nursefinders Inc 1701 E Lamar Blvd Suite 200	Arlington	TX	76006	**800-445-0459**	817-460-1181
On Assignment Inc 26651 W Agoura Rd	Calabasas	CA	91302	**800-995-7378**	818-878-7900
NASDAQ: ASGN					
Orion International Consulting Group Inc 1250 Capital of Texas Hwy S Bldg 1 Suite 270	Austin	TX	78746	**800-336-7466**	512-327-7111
Oxford Global Resources Inc 100 Cummings Ctr Suite 206L	Beverly	MA	01915	**800-426-9196**	978-236-1182
PDS Technical Services 1320 Greenway Dr Suite 550	Dallas	TX	75038	**800-270-4737**	972-550-1212
Peak Technical Services Inc 300 Penn Ctr Blvd Suite 800	Pittsburgh	PA	15235	**800-825-8088**	412-824-2000
Personnel Management Inc 1499 Windhorst Way Suite 220	Greenwood	IN	46143	**888-967-5764**	317-888-4400
Personnel One Div Career Blazers Inc 222 W Las Colinas Blvd Suite 1250E	Irving	TX	75039	**800-787-6750**	214-296-6700
Plus Group Inc 555 E Butterfield Rd Suite 330	Lombard	IL	60148	**800-782-3346**	630-515-0500
Pomeroy IT Solutions Inc 1020 Petersburg Rd	Hebron	KY	41048	**800-846-8727**	859-586-1515
NASDAQ: PMRY					
Principal Technical Services Inc 24102 Brookfield Cir	Lake Forest	CA	92630	**888-787-3711**	949-457-9035
Pro Staff Personnel Services 50 S 10th St Suite 500	Minneapolis	MN	55403	**800-829-5369**	612-373-2600
ProDrivers Div Career Blazers Inc 222 W Las Colinas Blvd Suite 1250E	Irving	TX	75039	**800-787-6750**	214-296-6700
Productive Data Systems Inc 6160 S Syracuse Way Suite 300	Greenwood Village	CO	80111	**800-404-7165**	303-220-7165
Professional Placement Resources 333 1st St N Suite 200	Jacksonville Beach	FL	32250	**888-909-5038**	
Quantum Resources 300 Arboretum Pl Suite 500	Richmond	VA	23236	**800-446-9852**	804-320-4800
RehabWorks Inc 103 Corporate Dr E	Langhorne	PA	19047	**800-563-1103**	215-504-5100
Remedy Temp Inc 101 Enterprise Suite 100	Aliso Viejo	CA	92656	**800-828-3726**	949-425-7600
NASDAQ: REMX					
Research Pharmaceutical Services Inc 610 W Germantown Pike Suite 200	Plymouth Meeting	PA	19462	**866-777-1151**	215-540-0700
ResourceMFG Div Career Blazers Inc 222 W Las Colinas Blvd Suite 1250E	Irving	TX	75039	**800-787-6750**	214-296-0700
Resources Global Professionals 695 Town Center Dr Suite 600	Costa Mesa	CA	92626	**800-900-1131**	714-430-6400
NASDAQ: RECN					
Roth Staffing Cos Inc 333 City Blvd W Suite 100	Orange	CA	92868	**888-304-4684**	714-939-8600
Sigma Systems Inc 201 Boston Post Rd Suite 201	Marlborough	MA	01752	**888-867-4462**	508-357-6300
Silicon Valley Staffing 2200 Powell St Suite 510	Emeryville	CA	94608	**877-660-6000**	510-923-9898
Snelling Personnel Services 12801 N Central Expy Suite 700	Dallas	TX	75243	**800-766-5556**	972-239-7575
Softworld Inc 395 Totten Pond Rd Suite 201	Waltham	MA	02451	**877-899-1166**	781-466-8882
Solomon-Page Group LLC 1140 Ave of the Americas 9th Fl	New York	NY	10036	**800-296-7646**	212-403-6100
SOS Staffing Services Inc 2650 Decker Lake Blvd Suite 500	Salt Lake City	UT	84119	**800-474-1722**	801-484-4400
Southwest Medical Assoc Inc PO Box 2168	Rockport	TX	78382	**800-929-4854**	361-729-0646
Special Counsel 1 Independent Dr Suite 112	Jacksonville	FL	32202	**800-737-3436**	904-737-3436
Spherion Corp 2050 Spectrum Blvd	Fort Lauderdale	FL	33309	**866-435-7456**	954-308-7600
NYSE: SFN					
StaffingSolutions Div Career Blazers Inc 222 W Las Colinas Blvd Suite 1250E	Irving	TX	75039	**800-787-6750**	214-296-6700
Stone Legal Resources Group 100 Summer St 10th Fl	Boston	MA	02110	**877-529-5627**	617-482-4100
Stratus Services Group Inc 500 Craig Rd Suite 201	Manalapan	NJ	07726	**800-777-1557**	732-866-0300
Superior Design International Inc 6365 NW 6th Way Suite 360	Fort Lauderdale	FL	33309	**800-850-4222**	954-938-5400
Superior Technical Resources Inc 250 International Dr	Williamsville	NY	14231	**800-568-8310**	716-631-8310
Surgical Staff Inc PO Box 192	San Mateo	CA	94401	**800-339-9599**	650-558-3999
Symphony Health Services 11350 McCormick Rd Executive Plaza IV Suite 600	Hunt Valley	MD	21031	**800-359-5971**	443-886-2200
TAC Worldwide Cos 888 Washington St	Dedham	MA	02026	**800-588-0707**	781-251-8000
Talent Tree 9703 Richmond Ave	Houston	TX	77042	**800-999-1515**	713-789-1818
Tandem Staffing Solutions Inc 1690 S Congress Ave Suite 210	Delray Beach	FL	33445	**800-275-5000**	561-454-3500
Team Health Inc 1900 Winston Rd Suite 300	Knoxville	TN	37919	**800-342-2898**	865-693-1000
TeamStaff Inc 300 Atrium Dr	Somerset	NJ	08873	**800-374-1001**	732-748-1700
NASDAQ: TSTF					
TeamStaff Rx 1901 Ulmerton Rd Suite 800	Clearwater	FL	33762	**800-345-9642**	
Technisource Inc 2300 Cottondale Ln Suite 250	Little Rock	AR	72202	**877-664-1101**	501-664-1100
Telesource Div Career Blazers Inc 222 W Las Colinas Blvd Suite 1250E	Irving	TX	75039	**800-787-6750**	214-296-6700
Temporary Solutions Inc 10515 Crestwood Dr	Manassas	VA	20109	**888-874-5627**	703-368-3800
Thinkpath Inc 201 W Creek Blvd	Brampton	ON	L6T5S6	**800-334-3911**	905-460-3040
Thompson Technologies Inc 114 Townpark Dr Suite 100	Kennesaw	GA	30144	**888-794-7947**	770-794-8380
TRC Staffing Services Inc 100 Ashford Ctr N Suite 500	Atlanta	GA	30338	**800-488-8008**	770-392-1411
UltraStaff 3730 Kirby Dr Suite 900	Houston	TX	77098	**800-522-7707**	713-522-7100
US Legal Support Inc 519 N Sam Houston Pkwy E Suite 200	Houston	TX	77060	**800-622-1107**	713-653-7100
Vedior North America 60 Harvard Mill Sq	Wakefield	MA	01880	**800-648-2469**	781-213-1500
Vista RMS 950 Herndon Pkwy Suite 360	Herndon	VA	20170	**888-535-7401**	703-481-6030
Volt Services Group 1212 Ave of the Americas 9th Fl	New York	NY	10036	**800-367-8658**	212-719-7800
Westaff Inc 298 N Wiget Ln	Walnut Creek	CA	94598	**800-872-8367**	925-930-5300
NASDAQ: WSTF					
Workstream Inc 495 March Rd Suite 300	Ottawa	ON	K2K3G1	**877-327-8483**	613-270-0619
NASDAQ: WSTM					

708 STAGE EQUIPMENT & SERVICES

	City	State	Zip	Toll-Free	Phone
Angstrom Lighting 837 N Cahuenga Blvd	Hollywood	CA	90038	**866-275-9211**	323-462-4246
Apollo Design Technology Inc 4130 Fourier Dr	Fort Wayne	IN	46818	**800-288-4626**	260-497-9191
Chapman/Leonard Studio Equipment Inc 12950 Raymer St	North Hollywood	CA	91605	**888-883-6559**	818-764-6726
Dreamworld Backdrops 6450 Lusk Blvd Suite E-106	San Diego	CA	92121	**800-737-9869**	858-452-4922
Gerriets International 29 Hutchinson Rd	Allentown	NJ	08501	**800-369-3695**	609-758-9121
Grosh Scenic Rentals 4114 Sunset Blvd	Hollywood	CA	90029	**877-363-7998**	323-662-1134
High End Systems Inc 2105 Gracy Farms Ln	Austin	TX	78758	**800-890-8989**	512-836-2242
Hollywood Rentals Production Services 19731 Nordhoff St	Northridge	CA	91324	**800-233-7830**	818-407-7800

	Toll-Free	Phone
Janson Industries 1200 Garfield Ave SW........Canton OH 44706	**800-548-8982**	330-455-7029
Musson Theatrical Inc 890 Walsh Ave...... Santa Clara CA 95050	**800-843-2837**	408-986-0210
Panavision Inc 6219 DeSoto Ave....... Woodland Hills CA 91367	**800-367-7262**	818-316-1000
Rosco Laboratories Inc 52 Harbor View Ave... Stamford CT 06902	**800-767-2669**	203-708-8900
Secoa Inc 8650 109th Ave N............... Champlin MN 55316	**800-328-5519**	763-506-8800
Syracuse Scenery & Stage Lighting Co Inc 101 Monarch Dr........................ Liverpool NY 13088	**800-453-7775**	315-453-8096

709 STEEL - MFR

	Toll-Free	Phone
A Finkl & Sons Co 2011 N Southport Ave...... Chicago IL 60614	**800-343-2562**	773-975-2510
AK Steel Holding Corp 703 Curtis St....... Middletown OH 45043 NYSE: AKS	**800-331-5050**	513-425-5000
Aleris International Inc 500 W Jefferson St 19th Fl.............. Louisville KY 40202 NYSE: ARS	**866-266-2586**	502-589-8100
Algoma Steel Inc 105 West St....... Sault Sainte Marie ON P6A7B4 TSE: AGA	**800-387-9495**	705-945-2351
Allegheny Ludlum Corp 100 River Rd ..... Brackenridge PA 15014 *Sales	**800-258-3586***	412-394-2800
Allegheny Technologies Inc 6 PPG Pl Suite 1000................... Pittsburgh PA 15222 NYSE: ATI ■ *Sales	**800-258-3586***	412-394-2800
Baron Drawn Steel Corp 1420 Baron Steel Ave... Toledo OH 43607	**800-537-8850**	419-531-5525
Bayou Steel Corp PO Box 5000.............. LaPlace LA 70069	**800-535-7692**	985-652-0370
BCS Cuyahoga LLC 31000 Solon Rd............ Solon OH 44139	**800-362-9132**	440-248-0290
Carlson GO Inc 350 Marshallton Thorndale Rd ....Downingtown PA 19335	**800-338-5622**	610-384-2800
Carpenter Specialty Alloys Operations 101 W Bern St.......................... Reading PA 19601	**800-654-6543**	610-208-2000
Carpenter Technology Corp 2 Meridian Blvd 3rd Fl.................Wyomissing PA 19610 NYSE: CRS ■ *Sales	**800-654-6543***	610-208-2000
Cascade Steel Rolling Mills Inc 3200 N Hwy 99 W.................... McMinnville OR 97128	**800-283-2776**	503-472-4181
Chicago Heights Steel Acquisition Corp 211 E Main St....................Chicago Heights IL 60411	**800-424-4487**	708-754-0410
Corey Steel Co 2800 S 61st Ct................Cicero IL 60804	**800-323-2750**	708-735-8000
Crucible Compaction Metals 1001 Robb Hill Rd....................... Oakdale PA 15071	**888-923-2670**	412-923-2670
Crucible Materials Corp PO Box 977......... Syracuse NY 13201	**800-365-1180**	315-487-4111
Crucible Materials Corp Specialty Metals Div PO Box 977........................... Syracuse NY 13201	**800-365-1180**	315-487-4111
Dofasco Inc 1330 Burlington St E po Box 2460......... Hamilton ON L8N3J5 TSE: DFS	**800-363-2726**	905-544-3761
Dunkirk Specialty Steel Corp 830 Brigham Rd PO Box 319.............. Dunkirk NY 14048	**800-916-9133**	716-366-1000
Electralloy Corp 175 Main St.................Oil City PA 16301	**800-458-7273**	814-678-4100
F & D Head Co 3040 E Peden Rd...........Fort Worth TX 76179	**800-451-2684**	817-236-8773
Finkl A & Sons Co 2011 N Southport Ave...... Chicago IL 60614	**800-343-2562**	773-975-2510
Geneva Steel Holdings Corp PO Box 2500........Provo UT 84603	**800-877-9990**	801-227-9000
Georgetown Steel Corp 420 S Harard St.... Georgetown SC 29440 *Sales	**800-472-7637***	843-546-2525
Gerdau AmeriSteel Corp 5100 W Lemon St Suite 312................ Tampa FL 33609 NYSE: GNA ■ *Sales	**800-637-8144***	813-286-8383
Gibraltar Industries Inc 3556 Lakeshore Rd ..... Buffalo NY 14219 NASDAQ: ROCK	**800-777-0675**	716-826-6500
Gibraltar Metals Corp 1050 Military Rd......... Buffalo NY 14217	**800-873-6322**	716-875-7920
GO Carlson Inc 350 Marshallton Thorndale Rd ....Downingtown PA 19335	**800-338-5622**	610-384-2800
Greer Steel Co 624 Boulevard.................Dover OH 44622 *Sales	**800-388-2868***	330-343-8811
Group Canam Inc 11505 1st Ave Bureau 500........... Saint-Georges QC G5Y7X3 TSE: CAM	**877-499-6049**	418-228-8031
Gulf Coast Machine & Supply Co Inc 6817 Industrial Rd.......................Beaumont TX 77705	**800-231-3032**	409-842-1311
Heckett Multiserv North America 612 N Main St............................ Butler PA 16001	**800-999-7524**	724-283-5741
Huron Valley Steel Corp 41000 E Huron River Dr..................Belleville MI 48111	**800-783-3404**	734-697-3400
Hutchens Industries Inc Steel Process Div 215 N Patterson Ave.....................Springfield MO 65802	**800-654-8824**	417-935-2276
International Steel Group Inc 4020 Kinross Lakes Pkwy................Richfield OH 44286 NYSE: ISG	**866-474-8808**	330-659-9100
Interstate Steel Co 401 E Touhy Ave....... Des Plaines IL 60017	**800-323-9800**	847-827-5151
IPSCO Inc PO Box 1670.................... Regina SK S4P3C7 NYSE: IPS	**800-667-1616**	306-924-7700
Ispat Inland Inc 3210 Watling St......... East Chicago IN 46312	**800-422-9422**	219-399-1200
Kentucky Electric Steel LLC PO Box 2119..... Ashland KY 41105	**800-333-3012**	606-929-1200
Kobe Steel USA Inc 535 Madison Ave........New York NY 10022	**888-562-3872**	212-751-9400
Lone Star Steel Co 15660 N Dallas Pkwy Suite 500.............Dallas TX 75248	**800-527-4615**	972-386-3981
MACSTEEL 1 Jackson Sq Suite 500........... Jackson MI 49204 *Sales	**800-888-7833***	517-782-0415
Marion Steel Co 912 Cheney Ave............. Marion OH 43302	**800-333-4011**	740-383-4011
Metalex Corp 1530 Artaius Pkwy............ Libertyville IL 60048	**800-323-0792**	847-362-8300
Mill Steel Co 5116 36th St SE...........Grand Rapids MI 49512	**800-247-6455**	616-949-6700
Neilsen Mfg Inc 3501 Portland Rd NE...........Salem OR 97303	**800-292-2495**	503-585-0040
Niagara LaSalle Corp 1412 150th St........ Hammond IN 46327	**877-289-2277**	219-853-6000
NS Group Inc 530 W 9th St.................Newport KY 41071 NYSE: NSS	**800-348-7751**	859-292-6809
Nucor Corp Cold Finish Div 2800 N Governor Williams Hwy .... Darlington SC 29540	**800-333-0590**	843-395-8689
Nucor Corp Steel Div 1455 Hagan Ave...........Huger SC 29450	**888-466-8267**	843-336-6000
Nucor-Yamato Steel Co PO Box 1228........Blytheville AR 72316	**800-289-6977**	870-762-5500
Oregon Steel Mills Inc 1000 SW Broadway Suite 2200.............Portland OR 97205 NYSE: OS	**800-547-9451**	503-223-9228
Outokumpu Stainless 425 N Martingale Rd Suite 1600........ Schaumburg IL 60173	**800-833-8703**	847-517-4050
Precision Rolled Products Inc 306 Columbia Tpke..................Florham Park NJ 07932	**800-321-0135**	973-822-9100
Prudential Steel Ltd 140 4th Ave SW Suite 1800................Calgary AB T2P3N3	**800-661-1050**	403-267-0300
Quanex Corp 1900 West Loop S Suite 1500....Houston TX 77027 NYSE: NX	**800-231-8176**	713-961-4600
Republic Engineered Products Inc 3770 Embassy Pkwy.......................Akron OH 44333	**800-232-7157**	330-670-3000
Roanoke Electric Steel Corp 102 Westside Blvd NW...................Roanoke VA 24017 NASDAQ: RESC	**800-765-6567**	540-342-1831
Samuel Son & Co Ltd 20001 Sherwood St....... Detroit MI 48234	**800-521-0870**	313-893-5000
Sandmeyer Steel Co 1 Sandmeyer Ln...... Philadelphia PA 19116	**800-523-3663**	215-464-7100
Schnitzer Steel Industries Inc 3200 NW Yeon Ave......................Portland OR 97210 NASDAQ: SCHN	**800-666-2992**	503-224-9900
Scion Steel Inc 23800 Blackstone St...........Warren MI 48089	**800-288-2127**	586-755-4000
Shalmet Corp 116 Pinedale Industrial Rd.... Orwigsburg PA 17961	**888-278-1414**	570-366-1414
Sheffield Steel Corp 2300 Hwy S 97......Sand Springs OK 74063	**800-331-3304**	918-245-1335
SMI Steel Alabama 101 S 50th St.........Birmingham AL 35212	**800-621-0262**	205-592-8981
Steel Technologies Inc 15415 Shelbyville Rd.. Louisville KY 40245 NASDAQ: STTX	**800-828-2170**	502-245-2110
Steel of West Virginia Inc 17th St & 2nd Ave.....................Huntington WV 25703	**800-624-3492**	304-696-8200
Stelco Inc PO Box 2030.................... Hamilton ON L8N3T1 TSE: STE.a	**800-263-9305**	905-528-2511
Tempel Steel Co 5500 N Wolcott Ave......... Chicago IL 60640	**800-621-7700**	773-250-8000
Thomas Steel Strip Corp Delaware Ave NW......Warren OH 44485	**800-321-7778**	330-841-6111
Timken Co 1835 Dueber Ave SW.............. Canton OH 44706 NYSE: TKR	**800-223-1954**	330-438-3000
Timken Latrobe Steel Co 2626 Ligonier St PO Box 31................Latrobe PA 15650	**800-245-7856**	724-537-7711
Ulbrich Stainless Steels & Special Metals Inc 57 Dodge Ave....................North Haven CT 06473	**800-243-1676**	203-239-4481
USS-POSCO Industries PO Box 471.......... Pittsburg CA 94565	**800-877-7672**	925-439-6000
Wheeling Corrugating Co 1134 Market St..... Wheeling WV 26003 *Sales	**800-922-3325***	304-234-2300
Wheeling-Pittsburgh Corp 1134 Market St..... Wheeling WV 26003 NASDAQ: WPSC	**800-441-8190**	304-234-2400
Worthington Industries Inc 200 Old Wilson Bridge Rd................Columbus OH 43085 NYSE: WOR	**800-944-2255**	614-438-3210
Worthington Steel Co 1127 Dearborn Dr......Columbus OH 43085	**800-944-3733**	614-438-3205

710 STONE (CUT) & STONE PRODUCTS

	Toll-Free	Phone
Biesanz Stone Co Inc 4600 Goodview Rd.......Winona MN 55987	**800-247-8322**	507-454-4336
Bristol Memorial Works Inc 508 Farmington Ave........................ Bristol CT 06010	**877-225-7626**	860-583-1654
Bybee Stone Co Inc 6293 N Matthews Dr.....Ellettsville IN 47429	**800-457-4530**	812-876-2215
Cold Spring Granite Inc Texas Granite Div 2400 Hwy 1431 W....................Marble Falls TX 78654	**800-247-2637**	830-693-4316
Columbus Marble Works Corp PO Box 791....Columbus MS 39703	**800-647-1055**	662-328-1477
Continental Cast Stone Inc 22001 W 83rd St... Shawnee KS 66227	**800-989-7866**	913-422-7575
Dakota Granite Co 14964 484th Ave PO Box 1351............. Milbank SD 57252	**800-843-3333**	605-432-5580
Dakota Marble Inc 902 W 19th St............ Yankton SD 57078	**800-697-7241**	605-665-7241
Granit Bronz Inc 202 S 3rd Ave........... Cold Spring MN 56320	**800-328-2312**	320-685-4628
Harmony Blue Granite Co Inc PO Box 958...... Elberton GA 30635	**800-241-7000**	706-283-3111
Insaco Inc 1365 Canary Rd............... Quakertown PA 18951	**800-497-4531**	215-536-3500
Kollmann Monumental Works Inc 1915 W Division St................... Saint Cloud MN 56301	**800-659-8010**	320-251-8010
Kotecki-Rock of Ages Inc 3636 Pearl Rd..... Cleveland OH 44109	**800-753-2880**	216-749-2880
LeSueur-Richmond Slate Corp PO Box 8 Rt 675.........................Arvonia VA 23004	**800-235-8921**	434-581-3214
Mankato-Kasota Stone Inc 818 N Willow St.... Mankato MN 56001	**800-437-7059**	507-625-2746
Milwaukee Marble & Granite Co Inc 4535 W Mitchell St.................... Milwaukee WI 53214	**877-645-6272**	414-645-0305
North Carolina Granite Corp PO Box 151.....Mount Airy NC 27030 *Sales	**800-227-6242***	336-786-5141
Owatonna Granite Rock of Ages 1300 Hoffman Dr.......................Owatonna MN 55060	**800-422-2397**	507-451-4882
Piqua Materials Inc 1750 W Statler Rd.......... Piqua OH 45356	**800-338-2962**	937-773-4824
Rock of Ages Corp RR 1 Box 1140.........Graniteville VT 05654 NASDAQ: ROAC	**800-421-0166**	802-476-3115
Royal Melrose Granite Co 202 S 3rd Ave... Cold Spring MN 56320	**800-328-7021**	320-685-5101
Texas Granite Div Cold Spring Granite Inc 2400 Hwy 1431 W....................Marble Falls TX 78654	**800-247-2637**	830-693-4316
Tru-Stone Technologies PO Box 430........ Waite Park MN 56387	**800-959-0517**	320-251-7171
Vermont Structural Slate Co Inc 3 Prospect St PO Box 98................ Fair Haven VT 05743	**800-343-1900**	802-265-4933
Vulcan Materials Co Western Div 3200 San Fernando Rd................Los Angeles CA 90065	**800-225-6280**	323-258-2777
Winona Monument Co Inc 174 W 3rd St........Winona MN 55987	**800-657-4411**	507-452-4672
WS Hampshire Inc 365 Keyes Ave.......... Hampshire IL 60140	**800-541-0251**	847-683-4400

711 STUDENT ASSISTANCE PROGRAMS

	Toll-Free	Phone
Alabama Prepaid Affordable College Tuition (PACT) Program 100 N Union St Suite 660.................... Montgomery AL 36130	**800-252-7228**	334-242-7514
Alaska Student Aid Office 3030 Vintage Blvd.... Juneau AK 99801	**800-441-2962**	907-465-2962
Arkansas Financial Aid Office 114 E Capitol St.......................... Little Rock AR 72201	**800-547-8839**	501-371-2013
California Student Aid Commission PO Box 419027...................... Rancho Cordova CA 95741	**888-224-7268**	916-526-8999
Coca-Cola Scholars Foundation PO Box 442..... Atlanta GA 30301	**800-306-2653**	404-733-5420
College Savings Plans Network PO Box 11910........................Lexington KY 40578	**877-277-6496**	859-244-8175
Colorado CollegeInvest 1801 Broadway Suite 1300................. Denver CO 80202	**800-478-5651**	303-295-1981
Department of Education Office of Federal Student Aid 830 1st St NE Union Center Plaza.................................. Washington DC 20202	**800-433-3243**	
District of Columbia Tuition Assistance Grant Program 441 4th St NW Rm 350N........................... Washington DC 20001	**877-485-6751**	202-727-2824

	City	State	ZIP	Toll-Free	Phone
Dollars for Scholars Scholarship America 1 Scholarship Way	Saint Peter	MN	56082	**800-537-4180**	507-931-1682
FastWeb Inc 444 N Michigan Ave Suite 3100	Chicago	IL	60611	**800-327-8932**	312-832-2126
Federal Student Aid Information Center PO Box 84	Washington	DC	20044	**800-433-3243**	
Florida					
Prepaid College Board PO Box 6567	Tallahassee	FL	32314	**800-552-4723**	850-488-8514
Student Financial Assistance Office 1940 N Monroe St Suite 70	Tallahassee	FL	32303	**888-827-2004**	850-410-5200
Free Application for Federal Student Aid (FAFSA) US Dept of Education 400 Maryland Ave SW	Washington	DC	20202	**800-433-3243**	319-337-5665
Georgia Student Finance Commission 2082 E Exchange Pl Suite 200	Tucker	GA	30084	**800-505-4732**	770-724-9000
Hispanic Scholarship Fund 55 2nd St Suite 1500	San Francisco	CA	94105	**877-473-4636**	415-808-2300
Illinois Student Assistance Commission 1755 Lake Cook Rd	Deerfield	IL	60015	**800-899-4722**	847-948-8500
Indiana Students Assistance Commission 150 W Market St Suite 500	Indianapolis	IN	46204	**888-528-4719**	317-232-2350
Iowa College Student Aid Commission 200 10th St 4th Fl	Des Moines	IA	50309	**800-383-4222**	515-281-3501
Kentucky Higher Education Assistance Authority PO Box 798	Frankfort	KY	40602	**800-928-8926**	502-696-7200
Louisiana Student Financial Assistance Office PO Box 91202	Baton Rouge	LA	70821	**800-259-5626**	225-922-1011
Maine Finance Authority of Maine (FAME) PO Box 949	Augusta	ME	04332	**800-228-3734**	207-623-3263
Maryland Student Financial Assistance Office 839 Bestgate Rd Suite 400	Annapolis	MD	21401	**800-974-1024**	410-260-4565
Massachusetts Educational Financing Authority 125 Summer St	Boston	MA	02110	**800-449-6332**	617-261-9760
Michigan					
Education Trust PO Box 30198	Lansing	MI	48909	**800-638-4543**	517-335-4767
Student Financial Services Bureau PO Box 30047	Lansing	MI	48909	**800-642-5626**	517-373-4897
Minnesota Higher Education Services Office 1450 Energy Park Dr Suite 350	Saint Paul	MN	55108	**800-657-3866**	651-642-0567
Mississippi Prepaid Affordable College Tuition Program (MPACT) PO Box 120	Jackson	MS	39205	**800-987-4450**	601-359-5255
Missouri Student Assistance Resource Services (MOSTARS) 3515 Amazonas Dr	Jefferson City	MO	65109	**800-473-6757**	573-751-2361
New Jersey Higher Education Student Assistance Authority 4 Quakerbridge Plaza PO Box 540	Trenton	NJ	08625	**800-792-8670**	609-588-7944
New York (State) Higher Education Services Corp 99 Washington Ave	Albany	NY	12255	**888-697-4372**	518-473-1574
North Carolina State Education Assistance Authority PO Box 14103	Research Triangle Park	NC	27709	**800-700-1775**	919-549-8614
Ohio					
State Grants & Scholarships Office PO Box 182452	Columbus	OH	43218	**888-833-1133**	614-466-7420
Tuition Trust Authority 580 S High St Suite 208 *Cust Svc	Columbus	OH	43215	**800-233-6734***	614-752-9400
Oregon Student Assistance Commission 1500 Valley River Dr Suite 100	Eugene	OR	97401	**800-452-8807**	541-687-7400
Pennsylvania					
Higher Education Assistance Agency 1200 N 7th St	Harrisburg	PA	17102	**800-692-7392**	717-720-2860
Tuition Account Plan (TAP 529) PO Box 42529	Philadelphia	PA	19101	**800-440-4000**	
Rhode Island Higher Education Assistance Authority 560 Jefferson Blvd	Warwick	RI	02886	**800-922-9855**	401-736-1100
Scholarship America 1 Scholarship Way	Saint Peter	MN	56082	**800-537-4180**	507-931-1682
Tennessee					
Baccalaureate Education System Trust (BEST) PO Box 198786	Nashville	TN	37219	**888-486-2378**	615-532-8056
Student Assistance Corp 404 James Robertson Pkwy Suite 1950	Nashville	TN	37243	**800-257-6526**	615-741-1346
United Negro College Fund Inc (UNCF) 8260 Willow Oaks Corporate Dr Suite 400	Fairfax	VA	22031	**800-331-2244**	703-205-3400
Utah Higher Education Assistance Authority 60 S 400 West	Salt Lake City	UT	84101	**877-336-7378**	801-321-7294
Vermont Student Assistance Corp PO Box 2000	Winooski	VT	05404	**800-642-3177**	802-655-9602
Veterans Benefits Administration Education Service 1800 G St NW	Washington	DC	20006	**800-442-4551**	202-273-7132
Virginia College Savings Plan PO Box 607	Richmond	VA	23218	**888-567-0540**	804-786-0719
Wisconsin Education Investment Program (EdVest) PO Box 7871	Madison	WI	53707	**888-338-3789**	608-264-7899

712 SUBSTANCE ABUSE TREATMENT CENTERS

SEE ALSO Associations & Organizations - General - Self-Help Organizations; Hospitals - General Hospitals - US; Hospitals - Psychiatric Hospitals

	City	State	ZIP	Toll-Free	Phone
AdCare Hospital of Worcester 107 Lincoln St	Worcester	MA	01605	**800-345-3552**	508-799-9000
Anchor Hospital 5454 Yorktowne Dr	Atlanta	GA	30349	**800-444-2273**	770-991-6044
Areba Casriel Institute 500 W 57th St	New York	NY	10019	**800-724-4444**	212-293-3000
Arms Acres 75 Seminary Hill Rd	Carmel	NY	10512	**800-989-7581**	845-225-3400
Betty Ford Center 39000 Bob Hope Dr	Rancho Mirage	CA	92270	**800-854-9211**	760-773-4100
Bradford Health Services 2101 Magnolia Ave S Suite 518	Birmingham	AL	35205	**800-217-2849**	205-251-7753
Brighton Hospital 12851 E Grand River Ave	Brighton	MI	48116	**800-523-8198**	810-227-1221
Clear Brook Lodge 890 Bethel Hill Rd	Shickshinny	PA	18655	**800-582-6241**	570-864-3116
Clear Brook Manor 1100 E Northampton St	Wilkes-Barre	PA	18702	**800-582-6241**	570-823-1171
Conifer Park 79 Glenridge Rd	Glenville	NY	12302	**800-989-6446**	518-399-6446
Cornerstone Medical Arts Center Hospital 57 W 57th St	New York	NY	10019	**800-233-9999**	212-755-0200
Cove Forge Behavioral Health Rt 1 Box 79	Williamsburg	PA	16693	**800-873-2131**	814-832-2121
Eagleville Hospital 100 Eagleville Rd	Eagleville	PA	19408	**800-255-2019**	610-539-6000
Fairbanks Hospital 8102 Clearvista Pkwy	Indianapolis	IN	46256	**800-225-4673**	317-849-8222
Family Recovery Inc 555 SW 148th Ave	Sunrise	FL	33325	**800-417-6237**	954-370-0200
Fellowship Hall Inc 5140 Dunstan Rd	Greensboro	NC	27405	**800-659-3381**	336-621-3381
Friary of Lakeview Center 4400 Hickory Shores Blvd	Gulf Breeze	FL	32563	**800-332-2271**	850-932-9375
Gateway Foundation Inc 55 E Jackson St Suite 1500	Chicago	IL	60604	**800-444-1331**	312-663-1130
Gaudenzia Inc Common Ground 2835 N Front St	Harrisburg	PA	17110	**888-237-8984**	717-238-5553
Glenbeigh Health Source 2863 SR 45	Rock Creek	OH	44084	**800-234-1001**	440-563-3400
Hanley-Hazelden 5200 East Ave	West Palm Beach	FL	33407	**800-444-7008**	561-841-1000
Hazelden Foundation 15245 Pleasant Valley Rd	Center City	MN	55012	**800-257-7800**	651-257-4010
Hazelden Springbrook 1901 Esther St *Admissions	Newberg	OR	97132	**800-333-3712***	503-537-7000
HealthSource Saginaw 3340 Hospital Rd	Saginaw	MI	48603	**800-662-6848**	989-790-7700
High Point 5960 SW 106th Ave	Cooper City	FL	33328	**800-523-7773**	954-680-2700
Impact Drug & Alcohol Treatment Center 1680 N Fair Oaks Ave	Pasadena	CA	91103	**888-400-4222**	626-798-0884
Keystone Center 2001 Providence Ave	Chester	PA	19013	**800-558-9600**	610-876-9000
La Hacienda Treatment Center PO Box 1	Hunt	TX	78024	**800-749-6160**	830-238-4222
Livengrin Foundation 4833 Hulmeville Rd	Bensalem	PA	19020	**800-245-4746**	215-638-5200
Malvern Institute 940 King Rd	Malvern	PA	19355	**800-486-0017**	610-647-0330
Mount Regis Center 405 Kimball Ave	Salem	VA	24153	**800-477-3447**	540-389-4761
Mountain Manor Treatment Center Rt 15 PO Box 136	Emmitsburg	MD	21727	**800-537-3422**	301-447-2361
New Directions Inc 30800 Chagrin Blvd	Cleveland	OH	44124	**800-750-6709**	216-591-0324
Phoenix House Foundation Inc 164 W 74th St	New York	NY	10023	**800-262-2463**	212-595-5810
Providence Behavioral Health Hospital 1233 Main St	Holyoke	MA	01040	**800-274-7724**	413-539-2400
Rimrock Foundation 1231 N 29th St	Billings	MT	59101	**800-227-3953**	406-248-3175
Rivervalley Behavioral Health Hospital 1000 Industrial Dr	Owensboro	KY	42301	**800-755-8477**	270-686-8477
Schick Shadel Hospital 12101 Ambaum Blvd SW	Seattle	WA	98146	**800-272-8464**	206-244-8100
Serenity Lane 616 E 16th St	Eugene	OR	97401	**800-543-9905**	541-687-1110
Sierra Tucson Inc 39580 S Lago Del Oro Pkwy	Tucson	AZ	85739	**800-842-4487**	520-624-4000
Spencer Recovery Centers Inc 1316 S Coast Hwy	Laguna Beach	CA	92651	**800-252-6465**	949-376-3705
Starlite Recovery Center PO Box 317	Center Point	TX	78010	**800-292-0148**	830-634-2212
Substance Abuse Foundation 3125 E 7th St	Long Beach	CA	90804	**888-476-2743**	562-439-7755
Talbott Recovery Campus 5448 Yorktowne Dr	Atlanta	GA	30349	**800-445-4232**	770-994-0185
Turning Point Hospital 3015 Veterans Pkwy	Moultrie	GA	31788	**800-342-1075**	229-985-4815
Turning Point of Tampa 6227 Sheldon Rd	Tampa	FL	33615	**800-397-3006**	813-882-3003
Twin Town Treatment Center 1706 University Ave	Saint Paul	MN	55104	**800-645-3662**	651-645-3661
Village South Inc 3180 Biscayne Blvd	Miami	FL	33137	**800-443-3784**	305-573-3784
Warwick Manor Behavioral Health 3680 Warwick Rd	East New Market	MD	21631	**800-344-6423**	410-943-8108
Willingway Hospital 311 Jones Mill Rd	Statesboro	GA	30458	**800-242-9455**	912-764-6236
Wilmington Treatment Center 2520 Troy Dr	Wilmington	NC	28401	**800-992-3671**	910-762-2727

713 SURVEYING, MAPPING, RELATED SERVICES

SEE ALSO Engineering & Design

	City	State	ZIP	Toll-Free	Phone
Abrams Aerial Survey Corp 9659 W Grand Ledge Hwy Suite 1	Sunfield	MI	48890	**800-826-7518**	517-372-8100
C-MAP USA Inc 133 Falmouth Rd	Mashpee	MA	02649	**800-424-2627**	508-477-8010
Day & Zimmermann Group Inc 1818 Market St	Philadelphia	PA	19103	**800-523-0786**	215-299-8000
Greenhorne & O'Mara Inc 9001 Edmonston Rd	Greenbelt	MD	20770	**866-322-8905**	301-982-2800
KCI Technologies Inc 10 N Park Dr	Hunt Valley	MD	21030	**800-572-7496**	410-316-7800
Markhurd Corp 13400 68th Ave N	Minneapolis	MN	55311	**800-627-4873**	763-420-9606
Space Imaging Inc 12076 Grant St	Thornton	CO	80241	**800-697-4454**	303-254-2000
Spot Image Corp 14595 Avion Pkwy Suite 500	Chantilly	VA	20151	**800-275-7768**	703-715-3100
Wade-Trim Group Inc 25251 Northline Rd	Taylor	MI	48180	**800-482-2864**	734-947-9700

714 SWIMMING POOLS - ABOVE-GROUND

	City	State	ZIP	Toll-Free	Phone
Aqua-Leisure Industries Inc 525 Bodwell St Ext PO Box 239	Avon	MA	02322	**888-807-2998**	508-587-5400
Delair Group LLC 8600 River Rd	Delair	NJ	08110	**800-235-0185**	856-663-2900
Fox Pool Corp 3490 Board Rd	York	PA	17402	**800-723-1011**	717-764-8581
Imperial Pools Inc 615 Loudonville Rd	Latham	NY	12110	**800-444-9977**	518-786-1200
Morgan Building Systems Inc 2800 McCree Rd	Garland	TX	75041	**800-935-0321**	972-864-7300
Vogue Pool Products 9031 Salley	LaSalle	QC	H8R2C8	**800-363-3232**	514-363-3232
Zodiac American Pools Inc 265 Industrial Blvd *Cust Svc	Midway	GA	31320	**800-338-1013***	912-880-7665

715 SWITCHGEAR & SWITCHBOARD APPARATUS

SEE ALSO Transformers - Power, Distribution, Specialty; Wiring Devices - Current-Carrying

	City	State	ZIP	Toll-Free	Phone
American Solenoid Co Inc 760 New Brunswick Rd	Somerset	NJ	08873	**800-526-3966**	732-560-1240
Automatic Switch Co 50-60 Hanover Rd	Florham Park	NJ	07932	**800-524-1023**	973-966-2000
Bel Fuse Inc 206 Van Vorst St *NASDAQ: BELFA*	Jersey City	NJ	07302	**800-235-3873**	201-432-0463

Company	City	State	Zip	Toll-Free	Phone
DuraSwitch Industries Inc 234 S Extension Rd Suite 103 *NASDAQ: DSWT*	Mesa	AZ	85210	**800-729-3132**	480-586-3300
Eaton Cutler-Hammer Inc 1 Tuscarawas Rd	Beaver	PA	15009	**800-354-2070**	724-775-2000
Grayhill Inc 561 Hillgrove Ave	La Grange	IL	60525	**800-244-0559**	708-354-1040
Guardian Electric Mfg Co Inc 1425 Lake Ave	Woodstock	IL	60098	**800-762-0369**	815-337-0050
ITW Switches 7301 W Ainslie Ave	Harwood Heights	IL	60706	**800-544-3354**	708-667-3370
Korry Electronics Co 901 Dexter Ave N	Seattle	WA	98109	**800-257-8921**	206-281-1300
Meter Devices Co Inc 3359 Bruening Ave SW PO Box 6382 Stn B	Canton	OH	44706	**888-367-6383**	330-455-0301
Russelectric Inc 99 Industrial Park Rd	Hingham	MA	02043	**800-225-5250**	781-749-6000
Satin American Corp 40 Oliver Terr	Shelton	CT	06484	**800-272-7711**	203-929-6363
Siemens Power Transmission & Distribution Inc 7000 Siemens Rd	Wendell	NC	27591	**800-347-6659**	919-365-2200
SPD Technologies 13500 Roosevelt Blvd	Philadelphia	PA	19116	**800-832-4773**	215-677-4900
Tapeswitch Corp 100 Schmitt Blvd	Farmingdale	NY	11735	**800-234-8273**	631-630-0442
TopWorx Inc 3300 Fern Valley Rd	Louisville	KY	40213	**800-969-9020**	502-969-8000

716 TABLE & KITCHEN SUPPLIES - CHINA & EARTHENWARE

SEE ALSO Glassware & Pottery - Household

Company	City	State	Zip	Toll-Free	Phone
Buffalo China Inc 500 Bailey Ave *Cust Svc	Buffalo	NY	14210	**800-828-7033***	716-824-8515
Dansk International Designs Ltd 100 Lenox Dr *Cust Svc	Lawrenceville	NJ	08648	**800-293-2675***	609-896-2800
Fitz & Floyd Corp Inc 501 Corporate Dr	Lewisville	TX	75057	**800-243-2058**	972-874-3480
Frankoma Pottery 9549 Frankoma Rd	Sapulpa	OK	74066	**800-331-3650**	918-224-5511
Hall China Co 1 Anna St PO Box 989 *Cust Svc	East Liverpool	OH	43920	**800-445-4255***	330-385-2900
Hartstone Inc PO Box 2310	Zanesville	OH	43701	**800-339-4278**	740-452-9000
Heartland China Inc PO Box 8156	Topeka	KS	66608	**888-383-3163**	785-354-8080
Homer Laughlin China Co 672 Fiesta Dr	Newell	WV	26050	**800-452-4462**	304-387-1300
Laughlin Homer China Co 672 Fiesta Dr	Newell	WV	26050	**800-452-4462**	304-387-1300
Lenox Inc 100 Lenox Dr *Cust Svc	Lawrenceville	NJ	08648	**800-635-3669***	609-896-2800
Lipper International Inc 235 Washington St	Wallingford	CT	06492	**800-243-3129**	203-269-8588
Luna Garcia 201 San Juan Ave	Venice	CA	90291	**800-905-9975**	310-396-8026
Martin's Herend Imports Inc 21440 Pacific Blvd	Sterling	VA	20167	**800-643-7363**	703-450-1601
Mikasa Inc 1 Mikasa Dr *Cust Svc	Secaucus	NJ	07096	**800-833-4681***	201-867-9210
Noritake Co Inc 15-22 Fair Lawn Ave	Fair Lawn	NJ	07410	**888-296-3423**	
Oneida Ltd 163-181 Kenwood Ave	Oneida	NY	13421	**800-877-6667**	315-361-3000
Pfaltzgraff Co 140 E Market St	York	PA	17401	**800-999-2811**	717-848-5500
Royal China & Porcelain Cos Inc 1265 Glen Ave *Orders	Moorestown	NJ	08057	**800-631-7120***	856-866-2900
Royal Doulton USA Inc 200 Cottontail Ln	Somerset	NJ	08873	**800-682-4462**	732-356-7880
Sterling China USA LLC 511 12th St	Wellsville	OH	43968	**800-682-7628**	330-532-1544
Syracuse China Co 2900 Court St	Syracuse	NY	13208	**800-448-5711**	315-455-5671
Waterford Wedgwood USA Inc 1330 Campus Pkwy *Cust Svc	Wall	NJ	07719	**888-938-7911***	732-938-5800

TAPE - ADHESIVE

SEE Medical Supplies - Mfr

717 TAPE - CELLOPHANE, GUMMED, MASKING, PRESSURE SENSITIVE

SEE ALSO Medical Supplies - Mfr

Company	City	State	Zip	Toll-Free	Phone
3M Adhesives & Tapes Div 3M Ctr Bldg 220-8E-04	Saint Paul	MN	55144	**800-362-3550**	
3M Automotive Aftermarket Div 3M Center Bldg 223-6N-01	Saint Paul	MN	55144	**800-364-3577**	
3M Canada Co PO Box 5757	London	ON	N6A4T1	**800-265-1840**	519-451-2500
3M Consumer & Office Div 3M Ctr *NYSE: MMM*	Saint Paul	MN	55144	**800-364-3577**	651-733-1110
3M Display & Graphics Div 3M Ctr	Saint Paul	MN	55144	**800-364-3577**	651-733-1110
3M Personal Care & Related Products Div 3M Ctr Bldg 220-3W-10	Saint Paul	MN	55144	**866-212-5083**	
Avery Dennison Corp 150 N Orange Grove Blvd *NYSE: AVY* ■ *Cust Svc	Pasadena	CA	91103	**800-252-8379***	626-304-2000
Beiersdorf North America 187 Danbury Rd	Wilton	CT	06897	**800-233-2340**	203-563-5800
Bemis Co Inc Industrial Products Div 2200 Badger Ave PO Box 2968	Oshkosh	WI	54903	**800-328-4550**	920-303-7830
Brady Coated Products 6555 W Good Hope Rd	Milwaukee	WI	53223	**800-635-7557**	414-358-6600
Cantec Industries Inc 455 Cote Vertu Rd *Orders	Montreal	QC	H4N1E8	**800-334-1567***	514-334-1510
Compac Corp 103 Bilby Rd	Hackettstown	NJ	07840	**800-631-9350**	908-498-0660
Compac Industries Inc 103 Bilby Rd	Hackettstown	NJ	07840	**800-631-9350**	908-498-0660
Crowell Corp PO Box 3227	Newport	DE	19804	**800-441-7525**	302-998-0557
Custom Tapes Inc 7125 W Gunnison St	Harwood Heights	IL	60706	**800-621-7994**	708-867-6060
Decker Tape Products Inc 6 Stewart Pl	Fairfield	NJ	07004	**800-227-5252**	973-227-5350
DeWAL Industries Inc 15 Ray Trainor Dr	Narragansett	RI	02882	**800-366-8356**	401-789-9736
Dielectric Polymers Inc 218 Race St	Holyoke	MA	01040	**800-628-9007**	413-532-3288
Eternabond 16 Saint John Dr	Hawthorn Woods	IL	60047	**888-336-2663**	847-540-0600
Gaska-Tape Inc 1810 W Lusher Ave	Elkhart	IN	46517	**800-423-1571**	574-294-5431
Henkel Consumer Adhesives Inc 32150 Just Imagine Dr	Avon	OH	44011	**800-321-1733**	440-937-7000
Holland Mfg Co Inc 15 Main St PO Box 404	Succasunna	NJ	07876	**800-454-2606**	973-584-8141
Industrial Adhesives Inc 4244 W 6th Ave	Eugene	OR	97402	**800-451-2580**	541-683-6677
JHL Industries 10012 Nevada Ave	Chatsworth	CA	91311	**800-255-6636**	818-882-2233
Kruse Adhesive Tape Inc 16582 Burke Ln	Huntington Beach	CA	92647	**800-992-7702**	714-596-0707
M & C Specialties Co 90 James Way *Cust Svc	Southampton	PA	18966	**800-441-6996***	215-322-1600
MACtac 4560 Darrow Rd	Stow	OH	44224	**800-762-2822**	330-688-1111
Morgan Adhesives Co DBA MACtac 4560 Darrow Rd	Stow	OH	44224	**800-762-2822**	330-688-1111
Neptco Inc 30 Hamlet St	Pawtucket	RI	02861	**800-354-5445**	401-722-5500
Patco Corp 51 Ballou Blvd *Cust Svc	Bristol	RI	02809	**800-343-7875***	401-254-0600
Permacel US Hwy 1 S Box 671	North Brunswick	NJ	08902	**800-755-8273**	732-418-2400
PolyMask Corp 500 Thornburg Dr	Conover	NC	28613	**800-624-4772**	828-465-3053
Presto Tape Inc 1626 Bridgewater Rd	Bensalem	PA	19020	**800-331-1373**	215-245-8555
Pro Tapes & Specialties 100 Northfield Ave	Edison	NJ	08837	**800-345-0234**	732-346-0900
Scapa Tapes North America 746 Gotham Pkwy	Carlstadt	NJ	07072	**800-801-0323**	201-939-0565
Shurtape Technologies Inc 1506 Highland Ave NE	Hickory	NC	28601	**800-438-5779**	828-322-2700
Stik-II Products Inc 41 O'Neill St	Easthampton	MA	01027	**800-356-3572**	413-527-7120
Tesa Tape Inc 5825 Carnegie Blvd	Charlotte	NC	28209	**800-873-8825**	704-554-0707
Tommy Tape Mfg Inc 135 Redstone St	Southington	CT	06489	**800-866-8273**	860-378-0111
Tyco Adhesives 25 Forge Pkwy	Franklin	MA	02038	**800-248-7659**	508-918-1600
Venture Tape Corp 30 Commerce Rd	Rockland	MA	02370	**800-343-1076**	781-331-5900
Witchcraft Tape Products Inc 100 Klitchman Dr	Coloma	MI	49038	**800-521-0931**	269-468-3399
Zepak Corp 26755 SW 95th Ave PO Box 789	Wilsonville	OR	97070	**800-248-7732**	503-682-1248

718 TARPS, TENTS, COVERS

SEE ALSO Bags - Textile; Sporting Goods

Company	City	State	Zip	Toll-Free	Phone
Aero Industries Inc 3010 W Morris St *Sales	Indianapolis	IN	46241	**800-535-9545***	317-244-2433
American Recreation Products Inc 1224 Fern Ridge Pkwy	Saint Louis	MO	63141	**800-325-4121**	314-576-8000
Anchor Industries Inc 1100 Burch Dr	Evansville	IN	47725	**800-544-4445**	812-867-2421
Canvas Products Co 2340 Lafayette Blvd W *Cust Svc	Detroit	MI	48216	**800-624-6671***	313-496-1000
Carefree of Colorado 2145 W 6th Ave	Broomfield	CO	80020	**800-621-2617**	303-469-3324
Clamshell Structures Inc DBA Clamshell Buildings 1990 Knoll Dr	Ventura	CA	93003	**800-360-8853**	805-650-1700
Commonwealth Canvas Corp 310 Andover St	Danvers	MA	01923	**877-922-6827**	978-646-9400
CR Daniels Inc 3451 Ellicott Ctr Dr	Ellicott City	MD	21043	**800-933-2638**	410-461-2100
DC Humphrys Inc 5744 Woodland Ave *Sales	Philadelphia	PA	19143	**800-523-4503***	215-724-8181
Diamond Brand Canvas Products 145 Cane Creek Industrial Pk Rd Suite 1 *Sales	Fletcher	NC	28732	**800-258-9811***	828-684-9848
Eide Industries Inc 16215 Piuma Ave	Cerritos	CA	90703	**800-422-6827**	562-402-8335
Estex Mfg Co Inc 402 E Broad St PO Box 368	Fairburn	GA	30213	**800-749-1224**	770-964-3322
Fisher Canvas Products Inc 415 Saint Mary St	Burlington	NJ	08016	**800-892-6688**	609-239-2733
Harry Miller Co Inc 850 Albany St	Boston	MA	02119	**800-225-5598**	617-427-2300
John Johnson Co 1481 14th St	Detroit	MI	48216	**800-991-1394**	313-496-0600
Johnson Outdoors Inc 555 Main St *NASDAQ: JOUT*	Racine	WI	53403	**800-299-2592**	262-631-6600
Loop-Loc Ltd 390 Motor Pkwy	Hauppauge	NY	11788	**800-562-5667**	631-582-2626
M Putterman & Co Inc 4834 S Oakley St	Chicago	IL	60609	**800-621-0146**	773-927-4120
Mauritzon Inc 3939 W Belden Ave	Chicago	IL	60647	**800-621-4352**	773-235-6000
Midwest Canvas Corp 4635 W Lake St	Chicago	IL	60644	**800-433-4701**	773-287-4400
Miller Harry Canvas Co Inc 850 Albany St	Boston	MA	02119	**800-225-5598**	617-427-2300
Rainier Industries Ltd 18435 Olympic Ave S	Tukwila	WA	98188	**800-869-7162**	425-251-1800
Robertson Mfg Inc 112 Woodland Ave	West Grove	PA	19390	**800-260-5423**	610-869-9600
Shur-Co Inc 2309 Shur-Lok St PO Box 713	Yankton	SD	57078	**800-437-4172**	605-665-6000
Steele Canvas Basket Corp 201 William St PO Box 6267 IMCN	Chelsea	MA	02150	**800-541-8929**	617-889-0202
Sullivan & Brampton Inc 1688 Abram Ct	San Leandro	CA	94577	**800-257-5900**	510-483-7771
Trimaco LLC 2800 Meridian Pkwy Suite 185	Durham	NC	27713	**866-874-6226**	919-433-4010
Troy Sunshade Co 607 Riffle Ave	Greenville	OH	45331	**800-833-8769**	937-548-2466
Universal Fabric Structures Inc 2200 Kumry Rd	Quakertown	PA	18951	**800-634-8368**	215-529-9921
Webb Mfg Co 1241 Carpenter St	Philadelphia	PA	19147	**800-932-2634**	215-336-5570

719 TAX RETURN PREPARATION

Company	City	State	Zip	Toll-Free	Phone
EconoTax Inc 5846 Ridgewood Rd Suite B-101	Jackson	MS	39211	**800-748-9106**	601-956-0500
Fiducial Franchising 10480 Little Patuxent Pkwy 3rd Fl	Columbia	MD	21044	**800-323-9000**	410-910-5885
Fiducial Inc 450 Park Ave 15th Fl	New York	NY	10022	**800-283-1040**	212-207-4700
H & R Block Tax Services Inc 4400 Main St	Kansas City	MO	64111	**800-869-9220**	816-753-6900
Jackson Hewitt Inc 7 Sylvan Way *NYSE: JTX*	Parsippany	NJ	07054	**800-234-1040**	973-496-1040
LedgerPlus Inc 401 Saint Francis St	Tallahassee	FL	32301	**888-643-1348**	850-681-1941
Liberty Tax Service Inc 4575 Bonney Rd Suite 1040	Virginia Beach	VA	23462	**800-790-3863**	757-493-8855
TaxPro Inc DBA EconoTax Inc 5846 Ridgewood Rd Suite B-101	Jackson	MS	39211	**800-748-9106**	601-956-0500

720 TELECOMMUNICATIONS EQUIPMENT & SYSTEMS

SEE ALSO Modems; Radio & Television Broadcasting & Communications Equipment

				Toll-Free	Phone
ACE*COMM Corp					
704 Quince Orchard Rd Suite 100	Gaithersburg	MD	20878	**800-989-5566**	301-721-3000
NASDAQ: ACEC					
Acterna Corp 1 Milestone Center Dr	Germantown	MD	20876	**800-543-1550**	301-353-1550
ADC Telecommunications Inc					
13625 Technology Dr	Eden Prairie	MN	55344	**800-366-3891**	952-938-8080
NASDAQ: ADCT					
ADTRAN Inc 901 Explorer Blvd	Huntsville	AL	35806	**800-923-8726**	256-963-8000
NASDAQ: ADTN					
Advanced Fibre Communications Inc					
1465 N McDowell Blvd	Petaluma	CA	94954	**800-690-2324**	707-794-7700
NASDAQ: AFCI					
AirNet Communications Corp 3950 Dow Rd	Melbourne	FL	32934	**800-984-1990**	321-984-1990
NASDAQ: ANCC					
Alcatel Canada Inc					
600 March Rd PO Box 13600	Kanata	ON	K2K2E6	**888-662-3425**	613-591-3600
Alcatel USA Inc 3400 W Plano Pkwy	Plano	TX	75075	**800-252-2835**	972-519-3000
AltiGen Communications Inc					
4555 Cushing Pkwy	Fremont	CA	94538	**888-258-4436**	510-252-9712
NASDAQ: ATGN					
Amtelco 4800 Curtin Dr	McFarland	WI	53558	**800-356-9148**	608-838-4194
Appairent Technologies Inc					
150 Lucius Gordon Dr Suite 211	West Henrietta	NY	14586	**866-357-6210**	585-214-2460
Applied Innovation Inc 5800 Innovation Dr	Dublin	OH	43016	**800-247-9482**	614-798-2000
NASDAQ: AINN					
Aspect Communications Corp					
1310 Ridder Park Dr	San Jose	CA	95131	**800-391-2341**	408-325-2200
NASDAQ: ASPT					
Astrocom Corp 3500 Holly Ln N Suite 60	Minneapolis	MN	55447	**800-669-6242**	763-694-9949
Audiovox Corp 150 Marcus Blvd	Hauppauge	NY	11788	**800-645-4994**	631-231-7750
NASDAQ: VOXX					
Broadwing Corp 7015 Albert Einstein Dr	Columbia	MD	21046	**877-926-7847**	443-259-4000
NASDAQ: BWNG					
Carrier Access Corp 5395 Pearl Pkwy	Boulder	CO	80301	**800-495-5455**	303-442-5455
NASDAQ: CACS					
Casabyte Inc 222 Williams Ave S	Renton	WA	98055	**888-352-9527***	425-254-9925
*Cust Svc					
Ceragon Networks Inc 10 Forest Ave	Paramus	NJ	07652	**877-342-3247***	201-845-6955
*Tech Supp					
Charles Industries Ltd					
5600 Apollo Dr	Rolling Meadows	IL	60008	**800-458-4747**	847-806-6300
CiDRA Corp 50 Barnes Park N	Wallingford	CT	06492	**877-243-7277**	203-265-0035
CIENA Corp 1201 Winterson Rd	Linthicum	MD	21090	**800-921-1144**	410-694-5700
NASDAQ: CIEN					
ClearOne Communications Inc					
1825 W Research Way	Salt Lake City	UT	84119	**800-945-7730**	801-975-7200
Comarco Wireless Technologies Inc 2 Cromwell	Irvine	CA	92618	**800-697-1500***	949-599-7400
*Cust Svc					
Comdial Corp 106 Cattlemen Rd	Sarasota	FL	34232	**800-266-3425**	941-554-5000
Command Communications Inc					
7025 S Fulton St Suite 120	Centennial	CO	80112	**800-288-3491**	303-792-0890
Communication Technologies Inc DBA COMTek					
14151 Newbrook Dr Suite 400	Chantilly	VA	20151	**888-266-8358**	703-961-9080
Communications Systems Inc 213 S Main St	Hector	MN	55342	**800-852-8662**	320-848-6231
AMEX: JCS					
Communications Test Design Inc					
1373 Enterprise Dr	West Chester	PA	19380	**800-223-3910**	610-436-5203
Compunetix Inc 2420 Mosside Blvd	Monroeville	PA	15146	**800-879-4266**	412-373-8110
COMTek 14151 Newbrook Dr Suite 400	Chantilly	VA	20151	**888-266-8358**	703-961-9080
Concerto Software 6 Technology Pk Dr	Westford	MA	01886	**800-999-4458**	978-952-0200
Conklin Corp 199 West Rd	Pleasant Valley	NY	12569	**800-266-5546**	845-635-2136
Copper Mountain Networks Inc					
1850 Embarcadero Rd	Palo Alto	CA	94303	**888-267-7374**	650-687-3300
CopperCom Inc 3600 FAU Blvd	Boca Raton	FL	33431	**866-267-7371**	561-322-4000
Digital Lightwave Inc 15550 Lightwave Dr	Clearwater	FL	33760	**800-548-9283**	727-442-6677
NASDAQ: DIGL					
Digital Voice Corp 13700 Hutton Dr	Farmers Branch	TX	75234	**800-777-8329***	972-888-6300
*Cust Svc					
Ditech Communications Corp					
825 E Middlefield Rd	Mountain View	CA	94043	**800-770-0117**	650-623-1300
NASDAQ: DITC					
DynaMetric Inc 717 S Myrtle Ave	Monrovia	CA	91016	**800-525-6925**	626-358-2559
Dynamic Concepts Inc 1730 17th St NE	Washington	DC	20002	**800-634-4385**	202-944-8787
ECI Telecom Ltd					
605 Crescent Executive Ct Suite 416	Lake Mary	FL	32746	**800-321-2662**	407-829-8600
Electronic Tele-Communications Inc					
1915 MacArthur Rd	Waukesha	WI	53188	**888-746-4382**	262-542-5600
eOn Communications Corp					
4105 Royal Dr Suite 100	Kennesaw	GA	30144	**800-955-5321**	770-423-2200
NASDAQ: EONC					
FiberNet Telecom Group Inc					
570 Lexington Ave	New York	NY	10022	**800-342-3768**	212-405-6200
NASDAQ: FTGX					
GAI-Tronics Corp PO Box 1060	Reading	PA	19607	**800-492-1212**	610-777-1374
Genesys Telecommunications Laboratories Inc					
2001 Junipero Serra Blvd	Daly City	CA	94014	**888-436-3797**	650-466-1100
Glenayre Electronics Inc 11360 Lakefield Dr	Duluth	GA	30097	**800-688-4001**	770-283-1000
Glenayre Technologies Inc 11360 Lakefield Dr	Duluth	GA	30097	**800-866-4002**	770-283-1000
NASDAQ: GEMS					
GN Netcom Inc 77 Northeastern Blvd	Nashua	NH	03062	**800-345-8639**	603-598-1100
Harmonic Inc 549 Baltic Way	Sunnyvale	CA	94089	**800-788-1330**	408-542-2500
NASDAQ: HLIT					
Harris Corp 1025 W NASA Blvd	Melbourne	FL	32919	**800-442-7747**	321-727-9100
NYSE: HRS					
iDirect Technologies Inc 10803 Parkridge Blvd	Reston	VA	20191	**888-362-5475**	703-648-8080
Inter-Tel Inc 1615 S 52nd St	Tempe	AZ	85281	**800-669-5858**	480-449-8900
NASDAQ: INTL					
Intervoice Inc 17811 Waterview Pkwy	Dallas	TX	75252	**800-955-3675**	972-454-8000
NASDAQ: INTV					
InterWorks Systems Inc					
1233 Old Walt Whitman Rd	Melville	NY	11747	**800-814-9757**	631-424-9757
ISCO International Inc					
1001 Cambridge Dr	Elk Grove Village	IL	60007	**888-472-3458**	847-391-9400
AMEX: ISO					

				Toll-Free	Phone
JTech Communications Inc					
6413 Congress Ave Suite 150	Boca Raton	FL	33487	**800-321-6221**	561-997-0772
Lantronix Corp 15353 Barranca Pkwy	Irvine	CA	92618	**800-422-7055***	949-453-3990
NASDAQ: LTRX ■ *Orders					
Larscom Inc 39745 Eureka Dr	Newark	CA	94560	**888-527-7266**	510-492-0800
NASDAQ: LARS					
Magnasync Corp 1135 N Mansfield Ave	Hollywood	CA	90038	**800-366-3564**	323-962-0382
Metro-Tel Corp 11422 Miracle Hills Dr	Omaha	NE	68154	**888-998-8300**	402-498-2964
Midcom Inc 121 Airport Dr	Watertown	SD	57201	**800-643-2661**	605-886-4385
Mitel Networks Corp 350 Legget Dr	Kanata	ON	K2K2W7	**800-267-6244**	613-592-2122
Molex Premise Networks 8 Executive Dr	Hudson	NH	03051	**800-866-3827**	603-324-0200
Motorola Canada Ltd 8133 Warden Ave	Markham	ON	L6G1B3	**800-268-3395**	905-948-5200
Motorola Inc 1301 E Algonquin Rd	Schaumburg	IL	60196	**800-331-6456**	847-576-5000
NYSE: MOT					
Motorola Inc Cellular Subscriber Sector					
600 N US Hwy 45	Libertyville	IL	60048	**800-331-6456**	847-523-5000
Motorola Inc Land Mobile Products Sector					
1301 E Algonquin Rd	Schaumburg	IL	60196	**800-247-2346**	847-576-5000
NDS Americas					
3501 Jamboree Rd Suite 200	Newport Beach	CA	92660	**866-398-8749**	949-725-2500
NASDAQ: NNDS					
NEC USA Inc 8 Corporate Ctr Dr	Melville	NY	11747	**800-338-9549**	631-753-7000
Network Equipment Technologies Inc					
6900 Paseo Padre Pkwy	Fremont	CA	94555	**888-828-8080**	510-713-7300
NYSE: NWK					
Networld Communications 3221 20th St	San Francisco	CA	94110	**800-284-9519***	415-276-8000
*Cust Svc					
NextiraOne LLC 2800 Post Oak Blvd	Houston	TX	77056	**800-510-0561**	713-307-4000
NICE Systems Inc 301 Rt 17 N 10th Fl	Rutherford	NJ	07070	**888-577-6423**	201-964-2600
NightHawk Systems Inc					
8200 E Pacific Pl Suite 204	Denver	CO	80231	**800-735-3650***	303-337-4811
*Sales					
NMS Communications 100 Crossing Blvd	Framingham	MA	01702	**800-533-6120***	508-271-1000
NASDAQ: NMSS ■ *Sales					
Nokia Inc 6000 Connection Dr	Irving	TX	75039	**800-547-9810**	972-894-5000
NYSE: NOK					
Norsat International Inc					
4401 Still Creek Dr Suite 300	Burnaby	BC	V5C6G9	**888-830-4223**	604-292-9000
Norstan Inc 5101 Shady Oak Rd	Minnetonka	MN	55343	**800-667-7826**	952-352-4000
Nortel Networks Corp					
8200 Dixie Rd Suite 100	Brampton	ON	L6T5P6	**800-666-7835**	905-863-0000
NYSE: NT					
Numerex Corp 1600 Parkwood Cir Suite 200	Atlanta	GA	30339	**800-665-5686**	770-693-5950
NASDAQ: NMRX					
Oki America Inc 785 N Mary Ave	Sunnyvale	CA	94085	**800-654-3282**	408-720-1900
Oki Network Technologies 785 N Mary Ave	Sunnyvale	CA	94085	**800-641-8909**	408-737-6477
Optelecom Inc 12920 Cloverleaf Ctr Dr	Germantown	MD	20874	**800-293-4237**	301-444-2200
NASDAQ: OPTC					
P-Com Inc 3175 S Winchester Blvd	Campbell	CA	95008	**800-646-7266**	408-866-3666
Panasonic Consumer Electronics Co					
1 Panasonic Way	Secaucus	NJ	07094	**888-275-2595**	201-348-7000
Paradyne Networks Inc 8545 126th Ave N	Largo	FL	33773	**800-805-9493***	727-530-2000
NASDAQ: PDYN ■ *Cust Svc					
Plantronics Inc PO Box 635	Santa Cruz	CA	95061	**800-544-4660**	831-426-5858
NYSE: PLT					
Polycom Inc 4750 Willow Rd	Pleasanton	CA	94588	**866-476-5926**	925-924-6000
NASDAQ: PLCM					
Porta Systems Corp					
6851 Jericho Tpke Suite 170	Syosset	NY	11791	**800-937-6782**	516-364-9300
Protel Inc 4150 Kidron Rd	Lakeland	FL	33811	**800-925-8882**	863-644-5558
Proxim Corp 510 DeGuigne Dr	Sunnyvale	CA	94085	**800-229-1630**	408-731-2700
NASDAQ: PROX					
Pulse Communications Inc					
2900 Towerview Rd	Herndon	VA	20171	**800-381-1997***	703-471-2900
*Cust Svc					
RAD Data Communications Ltd					
900 Corporate Dr	Mahwah	NJ	07430	**800-444-7234**	201-529-1100
Radian Communications Services Corp					
2700 Matheson Blvd E West Tower					
Suite 800	Mississauga	ON	L4W4V9	**866-472-3126**	905-212-8200
Redback Networks Inc 300 Holger Way	San Jose	CA	95134	**866-727-5400**	408-750-5000
NASDAQ: RBAK					
Redback Networks Systems Canada Inc					
4190 Still Creek Dr Suite 200	Burnaby	BC	V5C6C6	**877-922-2847**	604-629-7000
Riverstone Networks Inc					
5200 Great America Pkwy	Santa Clara	CA	95054	**888-924-6797**	408-878-6500
Samsung Electronics America Inc					
105 Challenger Rd	Ridgefield Park	NJ	07660	**800-726-7864**	201-229-4000
SBC Communications Inc					
175 E Houston St	San Antonio	TX	78205	**888-875-6388**	210-821-4105
NYSE: SBC					
Shared Technologies Inc 1405 S Beltline Rd	Coppell	TX	75019	**888-835-4444**	972-462-5800
SmarTrunk Systems Inc					
401 W 35th St Bldg B	National City	CA	91950	**866-870-9052**	619-426-6440
Solunet Inc					
1571 Robert J Conlan Blvd Suite 110	Palm Bay	FL	32905	**888-765-8638**	321-676-7947
SpectraLink Corp 5755 Central Ave	Boulder	CO	80301	**800-676-5465**	303-440-5330
NASDAQ: SLNK					
SPL Integrated Solutions					
9180 Rumsey Rd Suite D-4	Columbia	MD	21045	**800-292-4125**	410-992-0998
Startel Corp 17661 Cowan Ave	Irvine	CA	92614	**800-782-7835**	949-863-8700
Stratex Networks Inc 120 Rose Orchard Way	San Jose	CA	95134	**800-362-9283**	408-943-0777
NASDAQ: STXN					
Superior Essex Communications LLC					
150 Interstate North Pkwy	Atlanta	GA	30339	**800-685-4887**	770-657-6000
Suttle PO Box 548	Hector	MN	55342	**800-852-8662**	320-848-6711
Symmetricom Inc 2300 Orchard Pkwy	San Jose	CA	95131	**888-367-7966**	408-433-0910
NASDAQ: SYMM					
Syntellect Inc					
16610 N Black Canyon Hwy Suite 100	Phoenix	AZ	85053	**800-788-9733**	602-789-2800
Tekelec 26580 W Agoura Rd	Calabasas	CA	91302	**800-835-3532**	818-880-5656
NASDAQ: TKLC					
Tel Electronics Inc 705 E Main St	American Fork	UT	84003	**800-564-9424**	801-756-9606
Telco Systems Inc 2 Hampshire St Suite 3A	Foxboro	MA	02035	**800-221-2849**	781-551-0300
Telect Inc 2111 N Molter Rd	Liberty Lake	WA	99019	**800-551-4567**	509-926-6000
Telegenix Inc 1930 Olney Ave Bldg 32	Cherry Hill	NJ	08034	**800-424-5220**	856-424-5220
Telephonics Corp 815 Broad Hollow Rd	Farmingdale	NY	11735	**877-755-7700**	631-755-7000
Telrad Connegy Inc 10 Executive Blvd	Farmingdale	NY	11735	**800-628-3038***	631-420-8800
*Cust Svc					
Teltone Corp PO Box 945	Bothell	WA	98041	**800-426-3926**	425-487-1515
Teltronics Inc 2150 Whitfield Industrial Way	Sarasota	FL	34243	**800-486-7685**	941-753-5000
Terabeam Wireless 8000 Lee Hwy	Falls Church	VA	22042	**888-297-9090**	703-205-0600
Tollgrade Communications Inc 493 Nixon Rd	Cheswick	PA	15024	**800-878-3399***	412-820-1400
NASDAQ: TLGD ■ *Cust Svc					

	City	State	Zip	Toll-Free	Phone
Tone Commander Systems Inc					
11609 49th Pl W	Mukilteo	WA	98275	**800-524-0024**	425-349-1000
Toshiba America Inc					
1251 Ave of the Americas 41st Fl	New York	NY	10020	**800-457-7777**	212-596-0600
Toshiba America Information Systems Inc					
9740 Irvine Blvd	Irvine	CA	92618	**800-457-7777***	949-583-3000
*Cust Svc					
Tut Systems Inc					
6000 SW Meadows Rd Suite 200	Lake Oswego	OR	97035	**877-225-7255**	971-217-0400
NASDAQ: TUTS					
Uniden America Corp					
4700 Amon Carter Blvd	Fort Worth	TX	76155	**800-297-1023***	817-858-3300
*Cust Svc					
Vcon Inc 10535 Boyer Blvd Suite 300	Austin	TX	78758	**800-418-5328***	512-583-7700
*Tech Supp					
Verint Systems Inc 330 S Service Rd	Melville	NY	11747	**800-967-1028**	631-962-9600
NASDAQ: VRNT					
Vodavi Technology Inc					
4717 E Hilton Ave Suite 400	Phoenix	AZ	85034	**800-843-4863**	480-443-6000
NASDAQ: VTEK					
VTech Innovations LP					
9590 SW Gemini Dr Suite 120	Beaverton	OR	97008	**800-835-8023**	503-596-1200
Westell Technologies Inc 750 N Commons Dr	Aurora	IL	60504	**800-323-6883**	630-898-2500
NASDAQ: WSTL					
XETA Technologies Inc					
1814 W Tacoma St	Broken Arrow	OK	74012	**800-845-9145***	918-664-8200
NASDAQ: XETA ■ *Cust Svc					
YDI Wireless Inc DBA Terabeam Wireless					
8000 Lee Hwy	Falls Church	VA	22042	**888-297-9090**	703-205-0600
Zhone Technologies Inc 7001 Oakport St	Oakland	CA	94621	**877-946-6320**	510-777-7000
NASDAQ: ZHNE					

721 TELECOMMUNICATIONS SERVICES

	City	State	Zip	Toll-Free	Phone
AboveNet Inc 360 Hamilton Ave 7th Fl	White Plains	NY	10601	**866-859-6971**	914-421-6700
Acceris Communications Solutions					
1001 Brinton Rd	Pittsburgh	PA	15221	**800-447-2111**	412-244-6600
Access America 673 Emery Valley Rd	Oak Ridge	TN	37830	**800-860-2140**	865-482-2140
ACT Teleconferencing Inc					
1526 Cole Blvd Bldg 3 Suite 300	Golden	CO	80401	**800-228-2554**	303-235-9000
NASDAQ: ACTT					
Advanced TelCom Group Inc					
463 Aviation Blvd Suite 120	Santa Rosa	CA	95403	**800-285-6100***	707-284-5000
*Cust Svc					
Advantage Cellular Systems Inc					
3040 Nashville Hwy	Alexandria	TN	37012	**800-772-8645**	615-464-2355
Alaska Communications Systems Group Inc					
600 Telephone Ave	Anchorage	AK	99503	**800-478-7121**	907-297-3000
NASDAQ: ALSK					
Aliant Inc PO Box 880	Halifax	NS	B3J2W3	**800-688-9811**	877-225-4268
TSE: AIT					
Allstream Corp 200 Wellington St W	Toronto	ON	M5V3G2	**888-288-2273**	416-345-2000
ALLTEL Communications Services					
1 Allied Dr	Little Rock	AR	72202	**800-255-8351***	501-905-8500
*Cust Svc					
ALLTEL Corp 1 Allied Dr	Little Rock	AR	72202	**800-255-8351**	501-905-8000
NYSE: AT					
Amanda Co 4079 Govenor Dr Suite 320	San Diego	CA	92122	**800-410-2745**	
AmeriCom Inc 870 E 9400 S	Sandy	UT	84094	**800-820-6296**	801-571-2446
AT & T Corp 1 AT & T Way	Bedminster	NJ	07921	**800-222-0300**	908-221-2000
ATG Group Inc 463 Aviation Blvd Suite 120	Santa Rosa	CA	95403	**800-285-6100***	707-284-5000
*Cust Svc					
ATI					
30575 Trabuco Canyon Rd					
Suite 200	Trabuco Canyon	CA	92679	**877-757-0000**	949-265-2000
ATX Communications Inc					
2100 Renaissance Blvd	King of Prussia	PA	19406	**800-220-2891**	610-755-4000
Bell Canada					
1000 rue de la Gauchetiere O Bureau 3700	Montreal	QC	H3B4Y7	**888-932-6666**	514-870-8777
BellSouth Long Distance Inc					
28 Perimeter Ctr E	Atlanta	GA	30346	**877-271-7795**	770-352-3000
Birch Telecom Inc 2300 Main St Suite 600	Kansas City	MO	64108	**888-422-4724**	816-300-3000
Bluegrass Cellular Inc 2902 Ring Rd	Elizabethtown	KY	42701	**800-928-2355**	270-769-0339
Broadcast International Inc					
7050 Union Pk Ctr Suite 650	Midvale	UT	84047	**800-722-0400**	801-562-2252
Broadview Networks Holdings Inc					
59 Maiden Ln 27th Fl	New York	NY	10038	**800-260-8766**	212-400-1000
Cal-North Wireless PO Box 627	Fort Jones	CA	96032	**800-499-1863**	530-468-5222
Call-Net Enterprises Inc					
2235 Sheppard Ave E Suite 1800	Toronto	ON	M2J5G1	**800-500-7741**	416-496-1644
TSE: FON					
Cavalier Telephone 2134 W Laburnum Ave	Richmond	VA	23227	**800-683-3944**	804-422-4100
CBC Marketing Group 3000 Cameron St	Monroe	LA	71201	**800-256-6000**	318-387-4621
Cellular One 3650 131st Ave SE Suite 600	Bellevue	WA	98006	**800-873-2349**	425-313-5200
NASDAQ: WWCA					
Cellular One Group (Licensing Management					
Office) 3650 131St Ave SE Suite 600	Bellevue	WA	98006	**800-545-5982**	425-586-8700
Century Interactive LLC					
7502 Greenville Ave Suite 300	Dallas	TX	75231	**800-256-3159**	214-360-6280
Choice One Communications Inc					
100 Chestnut St Suite 600	Rochester	NY	14604	**888-832-5800**	
Cincinnati Bell Inc 201 E 4th St	Cincinnati	OH	45202	**800-422-1199**	513-397-9900
NYSE: CBB					
Cingular Wireless					
5565 Glenridge Connector Suite 1401	Atlanta	GA	30342	**866-246-4852**	404-236-6000
Citizens Communications Co					
3 High Ridge Pk	Stamford	CT	06905	**800-877-4390**	203-614-5600
NYSE: CZN					
Coastal Communications 100 Ryon Ave	Hinesville	GA	31313	**877-702-3030**	912-368-3300
Comcast Business Communications Inc					
650 Centerton Rd	Moorestown	NJ	08057	**888-262-7300**	856-638-4000
Commonwealth Telephone Co 100 CTE Dr	Dallas	PA	18612	**800-544-1530**	570-675-1121
Commonwealth Telephone Enterprises Inc					
100 CTE Dr	Dallas	PA	18612	**800-225-5282**	570-631-2700
NASDAQ: CTCO					
Consolidated Communications Inc					
121 S 17th St	Mattoon	IL	61938	**800-553-9981**	217-235-3311
Convergent Media Systems Corp					
190 Bluegrass Valley Pkwy 1					
Convergent Ctr	Alpharetta	GA	30005	**800-254-7463**	404-262-1555
Conversent Communications Inc					
313 Boston Post Rd W Suite 140	Marlborough	MA	01752	**800-275-2088***	508-486-6300
*Cust Svc					
Cooperative Communciations Inc					
412-420 Washington Ave	Belleville	NJ	07109	**800-833-2700**	973-759-8100
Corporate Telephone 56 Roland St	Boston	MA	02129	**800-274-1211**	617-625-1200
Covista Communications Inc					
4803 Hwy 58 N	Chattanooga	TN	37416	**800-805-1000**	423-648-9700
NASDAQ: CVST					
CT Communications Inc 1000 Progress Pl	Concord	NC	28025	**800-617-8595***	704-722-2500
NASDAQ: CTCI ■ *Cust Svc					
CTC Communications Corp 220 Bear Hill Rd	Waltham	MA	02451	**800-883-6000**	781-466-8080
Cypress Communications Inc					
15 Piedmont Ctr Suite 100	Atlanta	GA	30305	**888-205-6912**	404-869-2500
D & E Communications Inc 124 E Main St	Ephrata	PA	17522	**800-321-6112***	717-733-4101
NASDAQ: DECC ■ *Cust Svc					
Dakota Central Telecommunications Co-op					
630 5th St N	Carrington	ND	58421	**800-771-0974**	701-652-3184
DataWave Systems Inc					
13575 Commerce Pkwy Suite 110	Richmond	BC	V6V2L1	**888-388-7031**	604-295-1800
Davel Communications Inc					
200 Public Sq Suite 700	Cleveland	OH	44114	**800-333-9920**	216-241-2555
deltathree Inc 75 Broad St 31st Fl	New York	NY	10004	**888-335-8230**	212-500-4850
NASDAQ: DDDC					
Deutsche Telekom Inc					
600 Lexington Ave 17th Fl	New York	NY	10022	**888-382-4872**	212-424-2900
NYSE: DT					
Dial-Thru International Corp					
17383 Sunset Blvd Suite 350	Pacific Palisades	CA	90272	**800-378-9045**	310-566-1700
Dobson Communications Corp					
14201 Wireless Way	Oklahoma City	OK	73134	**888-575-9427***	405-529-8500
NASDAQ: DCEL ■ *Cust Svc					
Dynegy Global Communications					
1000 Louisiana St Suite 5800	Houston	TX	77002	**800-922-2104**	713-507-6400
EATELCORP Inc 913 S Burnside Ave	Gonzales	LA	70737	**800-621-4211**	225-621-4300
eircom (US) Ltd 1 Landmark Sq Suite 1105	Stamford	CT	06901	**888-387-6731**	203-363-7171
Elantic Networks Inc					
2134 W Laburnum Ave	Richmond	VA	23227	**888-854-2138**	804-422-4100
Electric Lightwave 4400 NE 77th Ave	Vancouver	WA	98662	**800-622-4354**	360-816-3000
Enventis Telecom Inc 30 W Superior St	Duluth	MN	55802	**888-436-8683**	218-720-2686
Eureka-GGN 39 Broadway 19th Fl	New York	NY	10006	**800-562-4206**	212-404-5000
Evercom Inc 8201 Tristar Dr	Irving	TX	75063	**800-947-0899**	972-988-3737
Excel Telecommunications 2440 Marsh Ln	Carrollton	TX	75006	**800-589-5884***	972-478-3000
*Tech Supp					
FairPoint Communications Inc					
521 E Morehead St Suite 250	Charlotte	NC	28202	**888-235-3242**	704-344-8150
NYSE: FRP					
Farmers Telephone Co-op Inc					
1101 E Main St	Kingstree	SC	29556	**888-218-5050**	843-382-2333
Fax Source 2 W Dry Creek Cir Suite 270	Littleton	CO	80210	**800-256-2753**	303-730-9396
Faxaway 417 2nd Ave W	Seattle	WA	98119	**800-906-4329**	206-301-7000
FaxBack Inc 7405 SW Tech Ctr Dr Suite 100	Tigard	OR	97223	**800-329-2225**	503-645-1114
FDN Communications					
2301 Lucien Way Suite 200	Maitland	FL	32751	**877-225-5336**	407-835-0300
Focal Communications Corp					
200 N LaSalle St 10th Fl	Chicago	IL	60601	**800-895-8400**	312-895-8400
Frontier Corp 180 S Clinton Ave	Rochester	NY	14646	**800-836-0342**	585-777-1000
Fusion Telecommunications International Inc					
420 Lexington Ave Suite 518	New York	NY	10170	**800-503-3325**	212-972-2000
AMEX: FSN					
General Communication Inc					
2550 Denali St Suite 1000	Anchorage	AK	99503	**800-770-7886**	907-265-5600
NASDAQ: GNCMA					
Genesys Conferencing Inc					
9139 S Ridgeline Blvd	Highlands Ranch	CO	80129	**800-685-1995**	303-267-1272
Global Crossing Conferencing					
1499 W 121 Ave	Westminster	CO	80234	**800-525-8244**	303-633-3000
Golden State Cellular					
17400 High School Rd	Jamestown	CA	95327	**800-453-8255**	209-533-8844
Golden West Telecommunications Co-op Inc					
415 Crown St	Wall	SD	57790	**877-610-7040**	605-279-2161
Graphnet Inc 40 Foltron St 28th Fl	New York	NY	10038	**800-327-1800**	212-994-1100
GT Com 502 5th St Caller Box 9001	Port Saint Joe	FL	32456	**800-772-7288**	850-229-7231
Guadalupe Valley Telephone Co-op					
36101 FM 3159	New Braunfels	TX	78132	**800-367-4882**	830-885-4411
Hargray Communications					
PO Box 5986	Hilton Head Island	SC	29938	**800-726-1266**	843-686-5000
Harrisonville Telephone Co					
213 S Main St PO Box 149	Waterloo	IL	62298	**888-482-8353**	618-939-6112
Hector Communications Corp 211 S Main St	Hector	MN	55342	**800-992-8857**	320-848-6611
AMEX: HCT					
Horry Telephone Co-op Inc 3480 Hwy 701 N	Conway	SC	29526	**800-824-6779**	843-365-2151
ILD Telecommunications Inc					
16200 Addison Rd Suite 180	Addison	TX	75001	**800-749-1229**	972-267-0100
InPhonic Inc					
1010 Wisconsin Ave NW Suite 600	Washington	DC	20007	**800-300-7066***	202-333-0001
NASDAQ: INPC ■ *Sales					
Integra Telecom					
1201 NE Lloyd Blvd Suite 500	Portland	OR	97232	**800-727-8484**	503-453-8000
Intercall Inc 8420 W Bryn Mawr Suite 400	Chicago	IL	60631	**800-374-2441***	773-399-1600
*Resv					
ITC^DeltaCom Inc 1791 OG Skinner Dr	West Point	GA	31833	**800-239-3000**	706-385-8000
j2 Global Communications Inc					
6922 Hollywood Blvd 8th Fl	Hollywood	CA	90028	**888-718-2000***	323-817-3217
NASDAQ: JCOM ■ *Sales					
KDDI America 375 Park Ave 7th Fl	New York	NY	10152	**888-696-9533**	212-702-3720
KMC Telecom Holdings Inc					
1545 Rt 206 Suite 300	Bedminster	NJ	07921	**877-470-2100**	908-470-2100
Leap Wireless International Inc					
10307 Pacific Center Ct	San Diego	CA	92121	**877-977-5327**	858-882-6000
Lexcom Inc DBA Lexcom Communications					
200 N State St PO Box 808	Lexington	NC	27293	**888-234-1663**	336-249-9901
Locus Telecommunications Inc					
111 Sylvan Ave	Englewood Cliffs	NJ	07632	**888-823-7587**	201-585-3600
Manitoba Telecom Services Inc 333 Main St	Winnipeg	MB	R3C3V6	**800-565-1936**	204-941-8244
TSE: MBT					
MCI Inc 22001 Loudoun County Pkwy	Ashburn	VA	20147	**877-624-1000**	703-886-5600
NASDAQ: MCIP					
MetroPCS Communications Inc					
8144 Walnut Hill Ln Suite 800	Dallas	TX	75231	**888-863-8768***	214-265-2550
*Cust Svc					

Company / Address	City	State	ZIP	Toll-Free	Phone
Midcontinent Communications					
PO Box 5010	Sioux Falls	SD	57117	**800-888-1300**	605-229-1775
Mpower Communications Corp					
175 Sully's Trail Suite 300	Pittsford	NY	14534	**888-777-5802**	585-218-6550
Multi-Link Communications Inc					
4704 Harlan St Suite 420	Denver	CO	80212	**888-968-5465**	303-831-1977
Multiband Corp 9449 Science Ctr Dr	New Hope	MN	55428	**800-475-7135**	763-504-3000
NASDAQ: MBND					
Net2Phone Inc 520 Broad St	Newark	NJ	07102	**800-225-5438**	973-438-3111
NASDAQ: NTOP					
Network Communications International Corp					
1809 Judson Rd	Longview	TX	75605	**888-686-3699**	903-757-4455
Network Services LLC 525 S Douglas St	El Segundo	CA	90245	**800-536-0700**	
Network Telephone Corp 3300 N Pace Blvd	Pensacola	FL	32505	**888-432-4855**	850-432-4855
Nextel Communications Inc					
2001 Edmund Halley Dr	Reston	VA	20191	**800-639-8352**	703-433-4000
NASDAQ: NXTL					
Nextel Partners Inc 4500 Carillon Point Rd	Kirkland	WA	98033	**888-566-6111**	425-576-3600
NASDAQ: NXTP					
Nobel 5759 Fleet St	Carlsbad	CA	92008	**800-986-6235**	760-405-0105
NSTAR Communications Inc 800 Boylston St.	Boston	MA	02199	**800-592-2000**	617-424-2000
NTELOS Inc					
401 Spring Ln Suite 300 PO Box 1990	Waynesboro	VA	22980	**800-482-1133**	540-946-3500
NuVox Communications Inc					
16090 Swingley Ridge Rd Suite 500	Chesterfield	MO	63017	**800-800-9681**	636-537-5700
Operator Service Co 5302 Ave Q	Lubbock	TX	79412	**800-658-6041**	806-747-2474
Otoloo Ino 5050 3rd Ave E	Oneonta	AL	35121	**800-286-4600**	205-625-3591
AMEX: OTT					
Pac-West Telecomm Inc 4210 Coronado Ave	Stockton	CA	95204	**800-399-3389**	209-926-3300
NASDAQ: PACW					
PaeTec Communications Inc					
1 PaeTec Plaza 600 Willowbrook Office Pk	Fairport	NY	14450	**877-472-3832**	585-340-2500
Panhandle Telecommunication Systems Inc					
2224 NW Hwy 64	Guymon	OK	73942	**800-327-7525**	580-338-7525
Pioneer Telephone Co-op					
1304 Main St PO Box 631	Philomath	OR	97370	**888-929-1014**	541-929-3135
Pioneer Telephone Co-op Inc					
108 E Roberts Ave PO Box 539	Kingfisher	OK	73750	**800-992-0234**	405-375-4111
Powercom Corp 1807 N Center St	Beaver Dam	WI	53916	**800-444-4014***	920-887-3148
*Cust Svc					
Primus Telecommunications					
7901 Jones Ranch Dr Suite 900	McLean	VA	22102	**800-226-4884**	703-902-2800
NASDAQ: PRTL					
Proximity Inc 99 Swift St Suite 200	South Burlington	VT	05403	**800-433-2900**	802-264-2900
PT-1 Long Distance Inc					
30-50 Whitestone Expwy	Flushing	NY	11354	**888-660-5377***	718-939-9000
*Cust Svc					
Puerto Rico Telephone Co PO Box 360998	San Juan	PR	00936	**800-981-2050**	787-782-8282
PVT Networks Inc 1311 Main St.	Artesia	NM	88210	**866-746-9844**	505-746-9844
Q Comm International Inc					
510 E Technology Ave Bldg C	Orem	UT	84097	**800-626-9941**	801-226-4222
AMEX: QMM					
Questar InfoComm Inc					
180 E 100 South PO Box 45433	Salt Lake City	UT	84145	**800-729-6790**	801-324-5856
RCN Corp 105 Carnegie Ctr	Princeton	NJ	08540	**800-746-4726**	609-734-3700
NASDAQ: RCNI					
Rogers Communications Inc 333 Bloor St E	Toronto	ON	M4W1G9	**888-620-7777**	416-935-7777
NYSE: RG					
Rogers Wireless Communications Inc					
1 Mount Pleasant Rd	Toronto	ON	M4Y2Y5	**800-268-7347**	416-935-1100
Rural Cellular Corp					
3905 Dakota St SW PO Box 2000	Alexandria	MN	56308	**800-450-2000***	320-762-2000
NASDAQ: RCCC ■ *Cust Svc					
Satellink Communications Inc					
1100 Northmeadow Pkwy Suite 100	Roswell	GA	30076	**800-426-2283**	770-625-2599
SBC Communications Inc					
175 E Houston St	San Antonio	TX	78205	**888-875-6388**	210-821-4105
NYSE: SBC					
Seren Innovations Inc					
15 S 5th St Suite 500	Minneapolis	MN	55402	**800-427-8686**	612-395-3500
SkyTel Communications Inc 550 Clinton Ctr Dr.	Clinton	MS	39056	**800-759-8737***	601-944-1300
*Cust Svc					
Smart City Networks					
3720 Howard Hughes Pkwy Suite 190	Las Vegas	NV	89109	**888-446-6911**	702-943-6000
Southern Communications Services Inc DBA					
Southern LINC 5555 Glenridge Connector					
Suite 500	Atlanta	GA	30342	**800-406-0151**	678-443-1500
Southern LINC					
5555 Glenridge Connector Suite 500	Atlanta	GA	30342	**800-406-0151**	678-443-1500
Sprint Canada Inc					
2235 Sheppard Ave E Suite 600	North York	ON	M2J5G1	**800-980-5464***	416-496-1644
*Cust Svc					
Sprint PCS Group 6991 Sprint Pkwy	Overland Park	KS	66251	**800-829-0965**	
SunCom Wireless Holdings Inc					
1100 Cassatt Rd	Berwyn	PA	19312	**800-786-7378***	610-651-5900
NYSE: TPC ■ *Cust Svc					
Supra Telecom Inc 7795 W Flagler St Suite 39	Miami	FL	33144	**888-317-8772**	305-447-5401
Supra Telecommunications & Information Systems					
DBA Supra Telecom Inc 7795 W Flagler St					
Suite 39	Miami	FL	33144	**888-317-8772**	305-447-5401
SureWest Communications 211 Lincoln St	Roseville	CA	95678	**877-686-6141**	916-786-6141
NASDAQ: SURW					
Swisscom North America					
2001 L St NW Suite 750	Washington	DC	20036	**800-966-1145**	202-785-1145
T-Mobile USA Inc 12920 SE 38th St	Bellevue	WA	98006	**800-318-9270**	
TDS Telecommunications Corp					
525 Junction Rd	Madison	WI	53717	**800-358-3648**	608-664-4000
TelCove 712 N Main St	Coudersport	PA	16915	**866-835-2683**	814-260-2000
Telefonica Data USA					
1221 Brickell Ave Suite 600	Miami	FL	33131	**866-839-0926**	305-925-5473
NYSE: TEF					
Teletouch Communications Inc					
1913 Deerbrook Dr	Tyler	TX	75703	**888-800-0232**	903-595-8889
Teligent Inc PO Box 341210	Bethesda	MD	20827	**888-411-1175**	
Telstra Inc 575 5th Ave 39th Fl	New York	NY	10017	**877-835-7872**	212-231-7744
TELUS Corp 3777 Kingsway Ave	Burnaby	BC	V5H3Z7	**888-811-2323**	604-432-2151
NYSE: TU					
Time Warner Telecom Inc					
10475 Park Meadow Dr	Littleton	CO	80124	**800-565-8982**	303-566-1000
NASDAQ: TWTC					
TippingPoint Technologies Inc					
7501-B N Capital of Texas Hwy	Austin	TX	78731	**888-648-9663**	512-681-8000
Titan Wireless Inc 3033 Science Park Rd	San Diego	CA	92121	**800-359-4404**	858-552-9500
TNS Inc DBA Transaction Network Services					
1939 Roland Clarke Pl	Reston	VA	20191	**800-240-2824**	703-453-8300
NYSE: TNS					
Trans National Communications International Inc					
2 Charlesgate W Suite 500	Boston	MA	02215	**800-900-5210**	617-369-1000
Transaction Network Services					
1939 Roland Clarke Pl	Reston	VA	20191	**800-240-2824**	703-453-8300
NYSE: TNS					
Trinsic Inc					
601 S Harbour Island Blvd Suite 220	Tampa	FL	33602	**800-511-4572**	813-273-6261
NASDAQ: TRIN					
Twin Lakes Telephone Co-op					
201 W Gore Ave	Gainesboro	TN	38562	**800-644-8582***	931-268-2151
*Cust Svc					
United Systems Access Inc					
5 Bragdon Ln Suite 200	Kennebunk	ME	04043	**877-872-2800**	207-467-8000
Universal Access Inc					
200 S Wacker Dr Suite 1200	Chicago	IL	60606	**888-482-4669**	312-660-5000
Universal Service Administrative Co					
2000 L St NW Suite 200	Washington	DC	20036	**888-641-8722**	202-776-0200
Universal Service Administrative Co Rural					
Health Care Div 80 S Jefferson Rd.	Whippany	NJ	07981	**800-229-5476**	973-581-6706
Universal Service Administrative Co Schools					
& Libraries Div 2000 L St NW	Washington	DC	20036	**888-203-8100**	
Universal Solutions Inc					
100 Business Park Dr Suite C	Ridgeland	MS	39157	**800-611-7093**	601-899-5000
US LEC Corp					
6801 Morrison Blvd 3 Morrocroft Ctr	Charlotte	NC	28211	**800-588-7380**	704-319-1000
NASDAQ: CLEC					
US Unwired Inc 901 Lakeshore Dr	Lake Charles	LA	70601	**800-673-2200**	337-436-9000
USA Mobility Inc 6910 Richmond Hwy.	Alexandria	VA	22306	**800-344-1004**	703-660-6677
NASDAQ: USMO					
VarTec Telecom Inc 1600 Viceroy Dr	Dallas	TX	75235	**800-583-8832**	214-424-1000
VeriSign Inc 487 E Middlefield Rd	Mountain View	CA	94043	**866-893-6565***	650-961-7500
NASDAQ: VRSN ■ *Sales					
Verizon Airfone 2809 Butterfield Rd	Oak Brook	IL	60522	**800-247-3663***	630-572-1800
*Cust Svc					
Verizon Communications					
1095 Ave of the Americas	New York	NY	10036	**800-621-9900**	212-395-2121
NYSE: VZ					
Verizon Wireless					
180 Washington Valley Rd	Bedminster	NJ	07921	**800-214-3555**	908-306-7000
Voice Power Telecommunications Inc					
PO Box 187	Austin	TX	78767	**800-613-6470**	512-419-4600
Voicecom 5900 Windward Pkwy Suite 500	Alpharetta	GA	30005	**800-384-4357**	404-262-8400
Vycera Communications Inc					
12750 High Bluff Dr Suite 200	San Diego	CA	92130	**800-705-3500***	858-792-2400
*Cust Svc					
Warwick Valley Telephone Co DBA WVT					
Communications 47 Main St PO Bo 592	Warwick	NY	10990	**800-952-7642***	845-986-1101
NASDAQ: WWVY ■ *Cust Svc					
Western Wireless Corp DBA Cellular One					
3650 131st Ave SE Suite 600	Bellevue	WA	98006	**800-873-2349**	425-313-5200
NASDAQ: WWCA					
Wood County Telephone Co					
440 E Grand Ave	Wisconsin Rapids	WI	54494	**800-421-9282**	715-421-8111
Working Assets Long Distance Service					
101 Market St Suite 700	San Francisco	CA	94105	**800-788-0898***	415-369-2000
*Cust Svc					
WQN Inc 14911 Quorum Dr Suite 140	Dallas	TX	75254	**866-661-6176**	972-361-1980
NASDAQ: WQNI					
WVT Communications 47 Main St PO Bo 592	Warwick	NY	10990	**800-952-7642***	845-986-1101
NASDAQ: WWVY ■ *Cust Svc					
XO Communications Inc 11111 Sunset Hills Rd.	Reston	VA	20190	**800-900-6398**	703-547-2000
Xspedius Communication LLC					
555 Winghaven Blvd Suite 300	O Fallon	MO	63368	**877-962-9100**	636-625-7000
Z-Tel Communications Inc					
601 S Harbour Island Blvd Suite 220	Tampa	FL	33602	**800-511-4572**	813-273-6261

722 TELEMARKETING SERVICES

Company / Address	City	State	ZIP	Toll-Free	Phone
Abacus Communications LC					
4456 Corporation Ln Suite 200	Virginia Beach	VA	23462	**800-866-2004**	757-497-2004
Access Worldwide Communications Inc					
4950 Communications Ave Suite 300	Boca Raton	FL	33431	**800-867-2340**	561-226-5000
ACI Telecentrics Inc					
3100 W Lake St Suite 300	Minneapolis	MN	55416	**800-735-1224**	612-928-4700
Advanced Data-Comm Inc 301 Data Ct	Dubuque	IA	52003	**800-582-9501**	563-582-9501
Aegis Communications Group Inc					
7880 Bent Branch Dr Suite 150	Irving	TX	75063	**800-332-0266**	972-830-1800
AFFINA 2001 Ruppman Plaza	Peoria	IL	61614	**800-787-7626**	309-685-5901
Alta Resources 1 Neenah Ctr Suite 500	Neenah	WI	54956	**800-756-7298**	920-727-9925
AmeriCall Corp 550 E Diehl Rd.	Naperville	IL	60563	**800-688-0078**	630-955-9100
APAC Customer Services Inc 6 Parkway N	Deerfield	IL	60015	**800-776-2722**	847-374-4980
NASDAQ: APAC					
Call_Solutions.com Inc					
20825 Swenson Dr Suite 200	Waukesha	WI	53186	**800-669-7711**	262-827-6400
Calling Solutions By Phone Power Inc					
2200 McCullough Ave	San Antonio	TX	78212	**800-321-8582**	210-822-7400
Carlson Marketing Group PO Box 59159	Minneapolis	MN	55459	**888-521-2200**	763-212-4520
Connection The 11351 Rupp Dr	Burnsville	MN	55337	**800-883-5777***	952-948-5488
*Sales					
Consolidated Market Response					
700 W Lincoln Ave Suite 200	Charleston	IL	61920	**800-500-6006**	217-348-7050
Convergys Corp 201 E 4th St	Cincinnati	OH	45202	**888-284-9900**	513-723-7000
NYSE: CVG					
Creative Marketing Strategies Inc					
15 E Center St	Woodbury	NJ	08096	**800-793-2345**	856-853-7718
Dakotah Direct Inc 9317 E Sinto Ave	Spokane	WA	99206	**800-433-3633**	509-789-4500
DialAmerica Marketing Inc					
960 MacArthur Blvd	Mahwah	NJ	07495	**800-526-4679***	201-327-0200
*Cust Svc					
DMS Direct Marketing Services Inc					
2324 E Bell Rd	Phoenix	AZ	85022	**888-225-5367**	602-308-1000
EBSCO TeleServices					
4150 Belden Village Ave NW Suite 401	Canton	OH	44718	**800-456-5105**	330-492-5105
Faneuil Group 1 Bridge St Suite 101	Newton	MA	02458	**800-932-6384**	617-742-4888
Global Response Corp 777 S SR-7	Margate	FL	33068	**800-537-8000**	954-973-7300

Name / Address	City	State	Zip	Toll-Free	Phone
Greene Henry M & Assoc Inc 28457 N Ballard Dr Suite A-1	Lake Forest	IL	60045	**800-356-1300**	847-816-9330
Harte-Hanks Direct Marketing 55 5th Ave 14th Fl	New York	NY	10003	**800-543-2212**	212-889-5000
Harte-Hanks Response Management 2800 Wells Branch Pkwy	Austin	TX	78728	**800-333-3383**	512-434-1100
Henry M Greene & Assoc Inc 28457 N Ballard Dr Suite A-1	Lake Forest	IL	60045	**800-356-1300**	847-816-9330
Holden MSS 5000 Lima St	Denver	CO	80239	**800-343-4717**	720-374-3700
ICT Group Inc 100 Brandywine Blvd *NASDAQ: ICTG*	Newtown	PA	18940	**800-799-6880**	215-757-0200
Integretel Inc 5883 Rue Ferrari	San Jose	CA	95138	**888-302-2750**	408-362-4000
InterMedi@ Marketing Solutions 204 Carter Dr	West Chester	PA	19382	**800-835-3466**	610-696-4646
iSky Inc 6100 Frost Pl	Laurel	MD	20707	**800-351-5055**	240-456-4300
Lester Telemarketing Inc 19 Business Park Dr	Branford	CT	06405	**800-999-5265**	203-488-5265
LiveBridge Inc 7303 SE Lake Rd	Portland	OR	97267	**800-783-6000**	503-652-6000
Midco Call Center Services 4901 E 26th St	Sioux Falls	SD	57110	**800-843-8800**	605-330-4125
Millennium Teleservices LLC 425 Raritan Ctr Pkwy	Edison	NJ	08837	**877-877-7698**	
OKS-Ameridial Inc 4535 Strausser St NW	North Canton	OH	44720	**800-445-7128**	330-497-4888
OnPoint LP 4301 Cambridge Rd	Fort Worth	TX	76155	**800-325-2580**	817-355-8200
Precision Response Corp 8151 Peters Rd Suite 3000	Plantation	FL	33324	**800-866-4443**	954-693-3700
ProCom Inc PO Box 27	Lamoni	IA	50140	**800-433-9893**	641-784-8841
Protocol Marketing Group 1751 Lake Cook Rd Suite 400	Deerfield	IL	60015	**800-867-7892**	847-236-3400
Reese Teleservices Inc 925 Penn Ave	Pittsburgh	PA	15222	**800-365-3500**	412-355-0800
Results Telemarketing Inc 499 Sheridan St 4th Fl	Dania Beach	FL	33004	**800-284-5318**	954-921-2400
RMH Teleservices Inc 15 Campus Blvd	Newtown Square	PA	19073	**800-325-3100**	610-352-3100
Ron Weber & Assoc Inc 185 Plains Rd Suite 302 E	Milford	CT	06460	**800-835-6584**	203-799-0000
SITEL Corp 7277 World Communication Dr *NYSE: SWW*	Omaha	NE	68122	**800-225-4858**	402-963-6810
Smith Co 4455 Connecticut Ave NW Suite 600B	Washington	DC	20008	**800-895-0999**	202-895-0900
TCIM Services Inc 1013 Centre Rd Suite 400	Wilmington	DE	19805	**800-333-2255**	302-633-3000
Telemarketing Co DBA TTC Marketing Solutions 3945 N Neenah Ave	Chicago	IL	60634	**800-777-6340**	773-545-0407
Telemarketing Concepts 80 Triangle Ctr	Yorktown Heights	NY	10598	**800-666-0858**	914-245-0701
TeleNational Marketing 2918 N 72nd St *Cust Svc	Omaha	NE	68134	**800-333-6106***	402-548-1100
Teleperformance USA 200 N 2200 W	Salt Lake City	UT	84116	**800-938-7872**	801-359-6843
Telerx 723 Dresher Rd	Horsham	PA	19044	**800-283-5379**	215-347-5700
TeleServices Direct 6050 Corporate Way	Indianapolis	IN	46278	**800-736-6072**	317-216-2240
TeleSpectrum Worldwide Inc 443 S Gulph Rd	King of Prussia	PA	19406	**888-878-7400**	610-878-7400
TeleSystems Marketing Inc 3600 S Gessner St Suite 259	Houston	TX	77063	**800-622-0190**	713-784-3439
TeleTech Holdings Inc 9197 S Peoria St *NASDAQ: TTEC*	Englewood	CO	80112	**800-835-3832**	303-397-8100
USA 800 Inc PO Box 16795	Raytown	MO	64133	**800-821-7539**	816-358-1303
Weber Ron & Assoc Inc 185 Plains Rd Suite 302 E	Milford	CT	06460	**800-835-6584**	203-799-0000
West Corp 9910 Maple St *NASDAQ: WSTC*	Omaha	NE	68134	**800-542-1000**	402-571-7700
Young America Corp 717 Faxon Rd	Young America	MN	55397	**800-533-4529**	952-467-3366

723 TELEPHONE ANSWERING SERVICES

Name / Address	City	State	Zip	Toll-Free	Phone
American Home Base 428 Childers St	Pensacola	FL	32534	**800-422-4663**	850-857-0860
AnswerNet Network 345 Witherspoon St	Princeton	NJ	08542	**800-411-5777**	609-921-7450
Tele-Serve 409 Main St *Cust Svc	Eau Claire	WI	54701	**800-428-8159***	715-834-3442

724 TELEVISION COMPANIES

Name / Address	City	State	Zip	Toll-Free	Phone
Belo Corp Television Group 400 S Record St	Dallas	TX	75202	**800-431-0010**	214-977-6606
Clear Channel Television 200 E Basse Rd	San Antonio	TX	78209	**888-937-6131**	210-822-2828
Communications Corp of America 700 Saint John St Suite 300	Lafayette	LA	70501	**800-237-1142**	337-237-1142
EW Scripps Co 312 Walnut St Suite 2800 *NYSE: SSP*	Cincinnati	OH	45202	**800-888-3000**	513-977-3000
Fisher Communications Inc 100 4th Ave N Suite 510 *NASDAQ: FSCI*	Seattle	WA	98109	**800-443-0073**	206-404-7000
Forum Communications Co 101 5th St N	Fargo	ND	58102	**800-747-7311**	701-235-7311
Groupe TVA Inc 1600 Maisonneuve Blvd E	Montreal	QC	H2L4P2	**877-304-8828**	514-790-0461
LeSea Broadcasting 61300 S Ironwood Rd	South Bend	IN	46614	**800-365-3732**	574-291-8200
Paxson Communications Corp 601 Clearwater Park Rd *AMEX: PAX*	West Palm Beach	FL	33401	**800-646-7296**	561-659-4122
Pegasus Communications Corp 225 E City Line Ave	Bala Cynwyd	PA	19004	**888-438-7488**	610-934-7000
Quincy Newspapers Inc 130 S 5th St	Quincy	IL	62301	**800-373-9444**	217-223-5100
Saga Communications Inc 73 Kercheval Ave *NYSE: SGA*	Grosse Pointe Farms	MI	48236	**888-886-7070**	313-886-7070
Sunbeam Television Corp 1401 79th Street Cswy	Miami	FL	33141	**800-845-7777**	305-751-6692
Telemundo Communications Group Inc 2290 W 8th Ave	Hialeah	FL	33010	**800-688-8851**	305-884-8200
Withers Broadcasting Co PO Box 1508	Mount Vernon	IL	62864	**800-333-1577**	618-242-3500

725 TELEVISION NETWORKS

Name / Address	City	State	Zip	Toll-Free	Phone
ABS-CBN Global Ltd DBA Filipino Channel 859 Cowan Rd	Burlingame	CA	94010	**800-345-2465**	650-697-3700
Cable Radio Networks Inc (CRN) 10487 Sunland Blvd	Sunland	CA	91040	**800-336-2225**	818-352-7152
Christian Broadcasting Network (CBN) 977 Centerville Tpke CBN Ctr	Virginia Beach	VA	23463	**800-759-0700**	757-226-7000
CNBC Inc 900 Sylvan Ave	Englewood Cliffs	NJ	07632	**800-788-2622**	201-585-2622
CRN (Cable Radio Networks Inc) 10487 Sunland Blvd	Sunland	CA	91040	**800-336-2225**	818-352-7152
Crown Media Holdings Inc 6430 S Fiddlers Green Cir Suite 225 *NASDAQ: CRWN*	Greenwood Village	CO	80111	**800-820-7990**	303-220-7990
Discovery Communications Inc 7700 Wisconsin Ave	Bethesda	MD	20814	**800-762-2189**	
FamilyNet 6350 West Fwy	Fort Worth	TX	76116	**800-292-2287**	817-737-4011
GoodLife TV Network 650 Massachusetts Ave NW	Washington	DC	20001	**800-446-6388**	202-289-6633
Great American Country 9697 E Mineral Ave	Englewood	CO	80112	**800-727-5663**	303-792-3111
Hallmark Channel 12700 Ventura Blvd Suite 200	Studio City	CA	91604	**888-390-7474**	818-755-2400
HGTV (Home & Garden Television) 9721 Sherrill Blvd	Knoxville	TN	37932	**800-448-8275**	865-694-2700
Home & Garden Television (HGTV) 9721 Sherrill Blvd	Knoxville	TN	37932	**800-448-8275**	865-694-2700
HSN LP 1 HSN Dr	Saint Petersburg	FL	33729	**800-284-3900**	727-872-1000
Idea Channel 1502 Powell Ave	Erie	PA	16505	**800-388-0662**	814-464-9068
Inspirational Network The (INSP) 7910 Crescent Executive Dr Suite 500	Charlotte	NC	28217	**800-725-4677**	704-525-9800
Learning Channel The (TLC) 8516 Georgia Ave	Silver Spring	MD	20910	**888-404-5969**	240-662-2000
Lottery Channel Inc 425 Walnut St Suite 2300	Cincinnati	OH	45202	**800-733-2074**	513-381-0777
Ovation The Arts Network 5801 Duke St Suite D-112	Alexandria	VA	22304	**800-682-8466**	703-813-6310
PAX TV 601 Clearwater Park Rd	West Palm Beach	FL	33401	**800-646-7296**	561-659-4122
Product Information Network 9697 E Mineral Ave	Englewood	CO	80112	**800-525-7002**	303-792-3111
QVC Inc 1200 Wilson Dr	West Chester	PA	19380	**800-367-9444**	
Resort Sports Network PO Box 7528	Portland	ME	04112	**800-653-0697**	207-772-5000
Shop at Home LLC 5388 Hickory Hollow Pkwy	Antioch	TN	37013	**800-224-9739**	615-263-8000
ShopNBC 6740 Shady Oak Rd	Eden Prairie	MN	55344	**800-676-5523**	952-943-6000
Telelatino Network Inc (TLN) 5125 Steeles Ave W	Toronto	ON	M9L1R5	**800-551-8401**	416-744-8200
Telemundo Communications Group Inc 2290 W 8th Ave	Hialeah	FL	33010	**800-688-8851**	305-884-8200
TLN (Telelatino Network Inc) 5125 Steeles Ave W	Toronto	ON	M9L1R5	**800-551-8401**	416-744-8200
Travel Channel 8516 Georgia Ave	Silver Spring	MD	20910	**888-404-5969**	240-662-2000
TV Guide Channel 7140 S Lewis Ave	Tulsa	OK	74136	**800-447-7388**	918-488-4450
ValueVision Media Inc 6740 Shady Oak Rd *NASDAQ: VVTV*	Eden Prairie	MN	55344	**800-788-2454**	952-943-6000

726 TELEVISION STATIONS

SEE ALSO Internet Broadcasting

Name / Address	City	State	Zip	Toll-Free	Phone
CBLT-TV Ch 5 (CBC) 250 Front St W	Toronto	ON	M5W1E6	**866-306-4636**	416-205-3311
CBWF-TV Ch 3 (SRC) 541 Portage Ave	Winnipeg	MB	R3C2H1	**866-306-4636**	204-788-3222
CBWT-TV Ch 6 (CBC) 541 Portage Ave	Winnipeg	MB	R3C2H1	**866-306-4636**	204-788-3222
CFTO-TV Ch 9 (CTV) 9 Channel 9 Ct	Toronto	ON	M4A2M9	**800-668-0060**	416-332-5000
CHRO-TV Ch 5 (Ind) 87 George St	Ottawa	ON	K1N9H7	**800-461-2476**	613-789-0606
CICA-TV Ch 19 (Ind) 2180 Yonge St Box 200 Stn Q	Toronto	ON	M4T2T1	**800-613-0513**	416-484-2600
CKVU-TV Ch 10 (Ind) 180 W 2nd Ave	Vancouver	BC	V5Y3T9	**888-336-9978**	604-876-1344
KAAL-TV Ch 6 (ABC) 1701 10th Pl NE	Austin	MN	55912	**800-234-0776**	507-437-6666
KACV-TV Ch 2 (PBS) PO Box 447	Amarillo	TX	79178	**800-999-9243**	806-371-5222
KADN-TV Ch 15 (Fox) 1500 Eraste Landry Rd	Lafayette	LA	70506	**800-738-6736**	337-237-1500
KAFT-TV Ch 13 (PBS) 350 S Donaghey Ave	Conway	AR	72034	**800-662-2386**	501-682-2386
KAID-TV Ch 4 (PBS) 1455 N Orchard St	Boise	ID	83706	**800-543-6868**	208-373-7220
KATU-TV Ch 2 (ABC) 2153 NE Sandy Blvd	Portland	OR	97232	**800-447-6397**	503-231-4222
KBAK-TV Ch 29 (CBS) 1901 Westwind Dr	Bakersfield	CA	93301	**800-229-6397**	661-327-7955
KBDI-TV Ch 12 (PBS) 2900 Welton St 1st Fl	Denver	CO	80205	**800-727-8812**	303-296-1212
KBHE-TV Ch 9 (PBS) PO Box 5000	Vermillion	SD	57069	**800-456-0766**	605-677-5861
KBME-TV Ch 3 (PBS) 207 N 5th St	Fargo	ND	58102	**800-359-6900**	701-241-6900
KBMY-TV Ch 17 (ABC) 3128 E Broadway Ave	Bismarck	ND	58501	**877-563-9369**	701-223-1700
KBTC-TV Ch 28 (PBS) 2320 S 19th St	Tacoma	WA	98405	**888-596-5282**	253-680-7700
KBYU-TV Ch 11 (PBS) 2000 Ironton Blvd Brigham Young University	Provo	UT	84606	**800-298-5298**	801-422-8450
KCBA-TV Ch 35 (Fox) 1550 Moffett St	Salinas	CA	93905	**800-321-5222**	831-422-3500
KCHF-TV Ch 11 (Ind) 27556 I-25 E Frontage Rd	Santa Fe	NM	87508	**800-831-9673**	505-473-1111
KCRG-TV Ch 9 (ABC) 501 2nd Ave SE	Cedar Rapids	IA	52401	**800-332-5443**	319-398-8422
KCTS-TV Ch 9 (PBS) 401 Mercer St	Seattle	WA	98109	**800-443-9991**	206-728-6463
KDAF-TV Ch 33 (WB) 8001 John Carpenter Fwy	Dallas	TX	75247	**877-252-8233**	214-252-9233
KDIN-TV Ch 11 (PBS) 6450 Corporate Dr	Johnston	IA	50131	**800-532-1290**	515-242-3100
KDLT-TV Ch 46 (NBC) 3600 S Westport Ave	Sioux Falls	SD	57106	**800-727-5358**	605-361-5555
KDVR-TV Ch 31 (Fox) 100 E Speer Blvd	Denver	CO	80203	**888-369-4762**	303-595-3131
KEDT-TV Ch 16 (PBS) 4455 S Padre Island Dr Suite 38	Corpus Christi	TX	78411	**800-307-5338**	361-855-2213
KESQ-TV Ch 3 (ABC) 42650 Melanie Pl	Palm Desert	CA	92211	**877-564-9729**	760-568-6830
KETG-TV Ch 9 (PBS) 350 S Donaghey Ave	Conway	AR	72034	**800-662-2386**	501-682-2386
KETS-TV Ch 2 (PBS) 350 S Donaghey Ave	Conway	AR	72032	**800-662-2386**	501-682-2386
KETV-TV Ch 7 (ABC) 2665 Douglas St	Omaha	NE	68131	**800-279-5388**	402-345-7777
KEYE-TV Ch 42 (CBS) 10700 Metric Blvd	Austin	TX	78758	**800-563-9742**	512-835-0042
KFBB-TV Ch 5 (ABC) PO Box 1139	Great Falls	MT	59403	**800-854-7720**	406-453-4377
KFME-TV Ch 13 (PBS) PO Box 3240	Fargo	ND	58108	**800-359-6900**	701-241-6900
KFTV-TV Ch 21 (Uni) 3239 W Ashlan Ave	Fresno	CA	93722	**800-733-5388**	559-222-2121
KFXA-TV Ch 28 (Fox) 600 Old Marion Rd NE	Cedar Rapids	IA	52402	**800-642-6140**	319-393-2800

				Toll-Free	Phone
KGAN-TV Ch 2 (CBS)					
600 Old Marion Rd NE	Cedar Rapids	IA	52402	**800-642-6140**	319-395-9060
KGFE-TV Ch 2 (PBS) PO Box 3240	Fargo	ND	58108	**800-359-6900**	701-241-6900
KGW-TV Ch 8 (NBC) 1501 SW Jefferson St	Portland	OR	97201	**800-288-5498**	503-226-5000
KGWN-TV Ch 5 (CBS) 2923 E Lincolnway	Cheyenne	WY	82001	**877-672-8019**	307-634-7755
KHBS-TV Ch 40 (ABC) 2415 N Albert Pike	Fort Smith	AR	72904	**800-821-9170**	479-783-4040
KICU-TV Ch 36 (Ind) 2102 Commerce Dr	San Jose	CA	95131	**800-464-5428**	408-953-3636
KIII-TV Ch 3 (ABC)					
5002 S Padre Island Dr	Corpus Christi	TX	78411	**800-874-5705**	361-986-8300
KIIN-TV Ch 12 (PBS) 6450 Corporate Dr	Johnston	IA	50131	**800-532-1290**	515-242-3100
KIMO-TV Ch 13 (ABC) 2700 E Tudor Rd	Anchorage	AK	99507	**877-304-1313**	907-561-1313
KION-TV Ch 46 (CBS) 1550 Moffett St	Salinas	CA	93905	**800-321-5222**	831-422-3500
KISU-TV Ch 10 (PBS)					
Idaho State University CB 8111 921 S					
8th Ave	Pocatello	ID	83209	**800-543-6868**	208-282-2857
KJLA-TV Ch 57 (Ind) 2323 Corinth Ave	Los Angeles	CA	90064	**800-588-5788**	310-943-5288
KKPX-TV Ch 65 (PAX) 848 Battery St	San Francisco	CA	94111	**888-467-2988**	415-276-1400
KLPB-TV Ch 24 (PBS) 7733 Perkins Rd	Baton Rouge	LA	70810	**800-272-8161**	225-767-5660
KLRN-TV Ch 9 (PBS) 501 Broadway St	San Antonio	TX	78215	**800-627-8193**	210-270-9000
KMIZ-TV Ch 17 (ABC)					
501 Business Loop 70 E	Columbia	MO	65201	**800-441-4485**	573-449-0917
KMOS-TV Ch 6 (PBS)					
Central Missouri State University	Warrensburg	MO	64093	**800-753-3436**	660-543-4134
KMOV-TV Ch 4 (CBS) 1 Memorial Dr	Saint Louis	MO	63102	**800-477-5668**	314-621-4444
KNDX-TV Ch 26 (Fox) 3130 E Broadway Ave	Bismarck	ND	58501	**877-563-9369**	701-355-0026
KNLJ-TV Ch 25 (Ind) 9810 SR-AE	New Bloomfield	MO	65063	**800-228-5284**	573-896-5105
KNME-TV Ch 5 (PBS)					
1130 University Blvd NE University of					
New Mexico	Albuquerque	NM	87131	**800-328-5663**	505-277-2121
KNXV-TV Ch 15 (ABC) 515 N 44th St	Phoenix	AZ	85008	**800-803-3277**	602-273-1500
KOAT-TV Ch 7 (ABC)					
3801 Carlisle Blvd NE	Albuquerque	NM	87107	**800-421-6159**	505-884-7777
KOLN-TV Ch 10 (CBS) PO Box 30350	Lincoln	NE	68503	**800-475-1011**	402-467-4321
KOMU-TV Ch 8 (NBC) 5550 Hwy 63 S	Columbia	MO	65201	**800-409-0292**	573-884-6397
KOZK-TV Ch 21 (PBS) 901 S National Ave	Springfield	MO	65804	**866-684-5695**	417-836-3500
KPBS-TV Ch 15 (PBS) 5200 Campanile Dr	San Diego	CA	92182	**888-399-5727**	619-594-1515
KPDX-TV Ch 49 (UPN)					
14975 NW Greenbrier Pkwy	Beaverton	OR	97006	**866-906-1249**	503-906-1249
KPLO-TV Ch 6 (CBS) 501 S Phillips Ave	Sioux Falls	SD	57104	**800-888-5356**	605-336-1100
KPTS-TV Ch 8 (PBS) 320 W 21 St	Wichita	KS	67203	**800-794-8498**	316-838-3090
KPTV-TV Ch 12 (Fox)					
14975 NW Greenbrier Pkwy	Beaverton	OR	97006	**866-906-1249**	503-906-1249
KPVI-TV Ch 6 (NBC) 902 E Sherman St	Pocatello	ID	83201	**800-366-5784**	208-232-6666
KPXE-TV Ch 50 (PAX) 4720 Oak St	Kansas City	MO	64112	**800-646-7296**	816-924-5050
KPXN-TV Ch 30 (PAX) 1100 Air Way	Glendale	CA	91201	**800-646-7296**	818-840-2687
KRMA-TV Ch 6 (PBS) 1089 Bannock St	Denver	CO	80204	**800-274-6666**	303-892-6666
KRNV-TV Ch 4 (NBC) 1790 Vassar St	Reno	NV	89502	**877-377-0122**	775-322-4444
KRQE-TV Ch 13 (CBS)					
13 Broadcast Plaza SW	Albuquerque	NM	87104	**800-283-4227**	505-243-2285
KRWG-TV Ch 22 (PBS)					
Jordan St PO Box 30001 MSC TV 22	Las Cruces	NM	88003	**866-457-9488**	505-646-2222
KSAZ-TV Ch 10 (Fox) 511 W Adams St	Phoenix	AZ	85003	**888-369-4762**	602-257-1234
KSCI-TV Ch 18 (Ind)					
1990 S Bundy Dr Suite 850	Los Angeles	CA	90025	**800-841-1818**	310-478-1818
KSEE-TV Ch 24 (NBC) 5035 E McKinley Ave	Fresno	CA	93727	**800-234-5733**	559-454-2424
KSNW-TV Ch 3 (NBC) 833 N Main St	Wichita	KS	67203	**800-949-5769**	316-265-3333
KSPR-TV Ch 33 (ABC) 1359 Saint Louis St	Springfield	MO	65802	**800-220-8222**	417-831-1333
KSPS-TV Ch 7 (PBS) 3911 S Regal St	Spokane	WA	99223	**800-735-2377**	509-354-7800
KTBN-TV Ch 40 (TBN) 2442 Michelle Dr	Tustin	CA	92780	**888-731-1000**	714-832-2950
KTGF-TV Ch 16 (NBC) 118 6th St S	Great Falls	MT	59405	**800-926-5401**	406-761-8816
KTNV-TV Ch 13 (ABC)					
3355 S Valley View Blvd	Las Vegas	NV	89102	**800-463-9713**	702-876-1313
KTOO-TV Ch 3 (PBS) 360 Egan Dr	Juneau	AK	99801	**800-870-5866**	907-586-1670
KTSD-TV Ch 10 (PBS) PO Box 5000	Vermillion	SD	57069	**800-456-0766**	605-677-5861
KTSF-TV Ch 26 (Ind) 100 Valley Dr	Brisbane	CA	94005	**800-488-6226**	415-468-2626
KTTC-TV Ch 10 (NBC) 6301 Bandel Rd NW	Rochester	MN	55901	**800-288-1656**	507-288-4444
KTVB-TV Ch 7 (NBC) PO Box 7	Boise	ID	83707	**800-559-7277**	208-375-7277
KTVI-TV Ch 2 (Fox) 5915 Berthold Ave	Saint Louis	MO	63110	**800-920-0222**	314-647-2222
KTXS-TV Ch 12 (ABC) 4420 N Clack St	Abilene	TX	79601	**800-588-5897**	325-677-2281
KUED-TV Ch 7 (PBS)					
101 Wasatch Dr Rm 215	Salt Lake City	UT	84112	**800-477-5833**	801-581-7777
KUHT-TV Ch 8 (PBS) 4343 Elgin St	Houston	TX	77204	**800-364-5848**	713-748-8888
KUON-TV Ch 12 (PBS) 1800 N 33rd St	Lincoln	NE	68583	**800-698-3426**	402-472-3611
KUSD-TV Ch 2 (PBS) PO Box 5000	Vermillion	SD	57069	**800-456-0766**	605-677-5861
KUSM-TV Ch 9 (PBS)					
Visual Communications Bldg Rm 183	Bozeman	MT	59717	**800-426-8243**	406-994-3437
KVIE-TV Ch 6 (PBS) 2595 Capitol Oaks Dr	Sacramento	CA	95833	**800-347-5843**	916-929-5843
KVII-TV Ch 7 (ABC) 1 Broadcast Ctr	Amarillo	TX	79101	**800-777-5844**	806-373-1787
KVLY-TV Ch 11 (NBC) 1350 21st Ave S	Fargo	ND	58103	**800-450-5844**	701-237-5211
KVOS-TV Ch 12 (Ind) 1151 Ellis St	Bellingham	WA	98225	**800-488-5867**	360-671-1212
KWCH-TV Ch 12 (CBS) 2815 E 37th St North	Wichita	KS	67219	**888-512-6397**	316-838-1212
KXAS-TV Ch 5 (NBC) 3900 Barnett St	Fort Worth	TX	76103	**800-232-5927**	817-429-5555
KXLT-TV Ch 47 (Fox) 6301 Bandel Rd NW	Rochester	MN	55901	**877-369-4788**	507-252-4747
KXMB-TV Ch 12 (CBS) 1811 N 15th St	Bismarck	ND	58501	**800-223-9197**	701-223-9197
KYTV-TV Ch 3 (NBC) PO Box 3500	Springfield	MO	65807	**800-492-4335**	417-268-3000
WAAY-TV Ch 31 (ABC)					
1000 Monte Sano Blvd SE	Huntsville	AL	35801	**877-799-9229**	256-533-3131
WACY-TV Ch 32 (UPN) 1391 North Rd	Green Bay	WI	54313	**800-800-6619**	920-490-0320
WAFB-TV Ch 9 (CBS) 844 Government St	Baton Rouge	LA	70802	**800-223-9232**	225-383-9999
WAGT-TV Ch 26 (NBC) PO Box 1526	Augusta	GA	30903	**800-924-8639**	706-826-0026
WAIQ-TV Ch 26 (PBS) 1255 Madison Ave	Montgomery	AL	36107	**800-239-5239**	334-264-9900
WAKA-TV Ch 8 (CBS) 3020 Eastern Blvd	Montgomery	AL	36116	**800-467-0401**	334-271-8888
WAXN-TV Ch 64 (ABC) 1901 N Tryon St	Charlotte	NC	28206	**800-367-9762**	704-338-9999
WAZE-TV Ch 19 (WB) 1277 N St Joseph Ave	Evansville	IN	47720	**888-488-1900**	812-425-1900
WBAL-TV Ch 11 (NBC) 3800 Hooper Ave	Baltimore	MD	21211	**800-677-9225**	410-467-3000
WBIQ-TV Ch 10 (PBS)					
2112 11th Ave S Suite 400	Birmingham	AL	35205	**800-239-5233**	205-328-8756
WBKI-TV Ch 34 (WB) 1601 Alliant Ave	Louisville	KY	40299	**877-541-3434**	502-809-3400
WBNX-TV Ch 55 (WB) 2690 State Rd	Cuyahoga Falls	OH	44223	**800-367-8855**	330-922-5500
WBSC-TV Ch 40 (WB) 110 Technology Dr	Asheville	NC	28803	**800-288-8813**	864-226-9292
WCBB-TV Ch 10 (PBS) 1450 Lisbon St	Lewiston	ME	04240	**800-884-1717**	207-783-9101
WCCO-TV Ch 4 (CBS) 90 S 11th St	Minneapolis	MN	55403	**800-444-9226**	612-339-4444
WCEU-TV Ch 15 (PBS)					
1200 W International Speedway Blvd	Daytona Beach	FL	32114	**800-638-9238**	386-254-4415
WCHS-TV Ch 8 (ABC) 1301 Piedmont Rd	Charleston	WV	25301	**888-696-9247**	304-346-5358
WCNY-TV Ch 24 (PBS) PO Box 2400	Syracuse	NY	13220	**800-451-9269**	315-453-2424
WCSH-TV Ch 6 (NBC) 1 Congress Sq	Portland	ME	04101	**800-464-1213**	207-828-6666
WCTV-TV Ch 6 (CBS) 4000 County Rd 12	Tallahassee	FL	32312	**800-375-4204**	850-893-6666
WCVE-TV Ch 23 (PBS) 23 Sesame St	Richmond	VA	23235	**800-476-8440**	804-320-1301
WDAM-TV Ch 7 (NBC) PO Box 16269	Hattiesburg	MS	39404	**800-844-9326**	601-544-4730
WDAZ-TV Ch 8 (ABC)					
2220 S Washington St	Grand Forks	ND	58201	**800-732-4361**	701-775-2511
WDBJ-TV Ch 7 (CBS)					
2807 Hershberger Rd NW	Roanoke	VA	24017	**800-777-9325**	540-344-7000

				Toll-Free	Phone
WDCO-TV Ch 29 (PBS) 260 14th St NW	Atlanta	GA	30318	**800-222-6006**	404-685-2400
WDIO-TV Ch 10 (ABC) 10 Observation Rd	Duluth	MN	55811	**800-477-1013**	218-727-6864
WDIV-TV Ch 4 (NBC) 550 W Lafayette Blvd	Detroit	MI	48226	**800-654-8221**	313-222-0500
WDSE-TV Ch 8 (PBS) 632 Niagara Ct	Duluth	MN	55811	**888-563-9373**	218-724-8568
WEAO-TV Ch 49 (PBS) 1750 Campus Center Dr	Kent	OH	44240	**800-544-4549**	330-677-4549
WEAR-TV Ch 3 (ABC) 4990 Mobile Hwy	Pensacola	FL	32506	**866-856-9327**	850-456-3333
WEHT-TV Ch 25 (ABC) 800 Marywood Dr	Henderson	KY	42420	**800-879-8549**	270-826-9566
WEIQ-TV Ch 42 (PBS)					
2112 11th Ave S Suite 400	Birmingham	AL	35205	**800-239-5233**	205-328-8756
WEMT-TV Ch 39 (Fox) 3206 Hanover Rd	Johnson City	TN	37604	**800-376-3939**	423-283-3900
WETK-TV Ch 33 (PBS) 204 Ethan Allen Ave	Colchester	VT	05446	**800-639-7811**	802-655-4800
WETP-TV Ch 2 (PBS) 1611 E Magnolia Ave	Knoxville	TN	37917	**800-595-0220**	865-595-0220
WFFF-TV Ch 44 (Fox)					
298 Mountain View Dr	Colchester	VT	05446	**888-400-4855**	802-660-9333
WFIE-TV Ch 14 (NBC) 1115 Mt Auburn Rd	Evansville	IN	47720	**800-832-0014**	812-426-1414
WFLA-TV Ch 8 (NBC) 200 S Parker St	Tampa	FL	33606	**800-348-9352**	813-228-8888
WFMJ-TV Ch 21 (NBC)					
101 W Boardman St	Youngstown	OH	44503	**800-488-9365**	330-744-8611
WFSU-TV Ch 11 (PBS)					
1600 Red Barber Plaza	Tallahassee	FL	32310	**800-322-9378**	850-487-3170
WFTS-TV Ch 28 (ABC) 4045 N Himes Ave	Tampa	FL	33607	**800-234-9387**	813-354-2800
WFWA-TV Ch 39 (PBS)					
2501 E Coliseum Blvd	Fort Wayne	IN	46805	**888-484-8839**	260-484-8839
WFXP-TV Ch 66 (Fox) 8455 Peach St	Erie	PA	16509	**888-989-9538**	814-864-2400
WGCU-TV Ch 30 (PBS) 10501 FGCU Blvd	Fort Myers	FL	33965	**888-824-0030**	239-590-2300
WGGS-TV Ch 16 (Ind) 3409 Rutherford Rd Ext	Taylors	SC	29687	**800-849-3683**	864-244-1616
WGME-TV Ch 13 (CBS) 1335 Washington Ave	Portland	ME	04103	**800-766-9330**	207-797-1313
WGRZ-TV Ch 2 (NBC) 259 Delaware Ave	Buffalo	NY	14202	**877-849-2200**	716-849-2200
WGTE-TV Ch 30 (PBS) PO Box 30	Toledo	OH	43614	**800-243-9483**	419-380-4600
WGTV-TV Ch 8 (PBS) 260 14th St NW	Atlanta	GA	30318	**800-222-6006**	404-685-2400
WGVU-TV Ch 35 (PBS) 301 W Fulton St	Grand Rapids	MI	49504	**800-442-2771**	616-331-6666
WGXA-TV Ch 24 (Fox) 599 ML King Jr Blvd	Macon	GA	31201	**800-592-4240**	478-745-2424
WHEC-TV Ch 10 (NBC) 191 East Ave	Rochester	NY	14604	**800-284-9432**	585-546-5670
WHIQ-TV Ch 25 (PBS)					
2112 11th Ave S Suite 400	Birmingham	AL	35205	**800-239-5233**	205-328-8756
WHNT-TV Ch 19 (CBS) PO Box 19	Huntsville	AL	35804	**800-533-8819**	256-533-1919
WHO-TV Ch 13 (NBC) 1801 Grand Ave	Des Moines	IA	50309	**800-835-1313**	515-242-3500
WICS-TV Ch 20 (NBC) 2680 E Cook St	Springfield	IL	62703	**800-263-9720**	217-753-5620
WILX-TV Ch 10 (NBC) 500 American Rd	Lansing	MI	48911	**800-968-1024**	517-393-0110
WITF-TV Ch 33 (PBS) 1982 Locust Ln	Harrisburg	PA	17109	**800-366-9483**	717-236-6000
WIWB-TV Ch 14 (WB)					
975 Parkview Rd Suite 4	Green Bay	WI	54304	**877-352-1000**	920-983-9014
WJHL-TV Ch 11 (CBS) 338 E Main St	Johnson City	TN	37601	**800-606-9545**	423-926-2151
WJSP-TV Ch 28 (PBS) 260 14th St NW	Atlanta	GA	30318	**800-222-4788**	404-685-2400
WJXX-TV Ch 25 (ABC) 1070 E Adams St	Jacksonville	FL	32202	**800-352-8812**	904-354-1212
WKBW-TV Ch 7 (ABC) 7 Broadcast Plaza	Buffalo	NY	14202	**800-234-9529**	716-845-6100
WKCF-TV Ch 18 (WB) 31 Skyline Dr	Lake Mary	FL	32746	**877-411-2899**	407-670-3018
WKLE-TV Ch 46 (PBS) 600 Cooper Dr	Lexington	KY	40502	**800-432-0951**	859-258-7000
WKMG-TV Ch 6 (CBS)					
4466 N John Young Pkwy	Orlando	FL	32804	**888-853-6060**	407-291-6000
WKMJ-TV Ch 68 (PBS) 600 Cooper Dr	Lexington	KY	40502	**800-432-0951**	859-258-7000
WKPC-TV Ch 15 (PBS) 600 Cooper Dr	Lexington	KY	40502	**800-432-0951**	859-258-7000
WKRN-TV Ch 2 (ABC) 441 Murfreesboro Rd	Nashville	TN	37210	**800-242-9576**	615-369-7222
WLBZ-TV Ch 2 (NBC) 329 Mt Hope Ave	Bangor	ME	04402	**800-244-6306**	207-942-4821
WLEX-TV Ch 18 (NBC) PO Box 1457	Lexington	KY	40588	**800-255-4566**	859-259-1818
WLOS-TV Ch 13 (ABC) 110 Technology Dr	Asheville	NC	28803	**800-288-8813**	828-684-1340
WLPB-TV Ch 27 (PBS) 7733 Perkins Rd	Baton Rouge	LA	70810	**800-272-8161**	225-767-5660
WLUK-TV Ch 11 (Fox) 787 Lombardi Ave	Green Bay	WI	54304	**800-242-8067**	920-494-8711
WMGT-TV Ch 41 (NBC) 301 Poplar St	Macon	GA	31201	**866-901-6397**	478-745-4141
WMHT-TV Ch 17 (PBS) 17 Fern Ave	Schenectady	NY	12306	**800-477-9648**	518-357-1700
WMPB-TV Ch 67 (PBS)					
11767 Owings Mills Blvd	Owings Mills	MD	21117	**800-223-3678**	410-356-5600
WMPT-TV Ch 22 (PBS)					
11767 Owings Mills Blvd	Owings Mills	MD	21117	**800-223-3678**	410-356-5600
WMTV-Ch 15 (NBC) 615 Forward Dr	Madison	WI	53711	**800-894-4222**	608-274-1515
WNDU-TV Ch 16 (NBC) 54516 US 31 N	South Bend	IN	46637	**800-631-6397**	574-631-1616
WNEM-TV Ch 5 (CBS) 107 N Franklin St	Saginaw	MI	48607	**800-522-9636**	989-755-8191
WNEO-TV Ch 45 (PBS) 1750 Campus Center Dr	Kent	OH	44240	**800-554-4549**	330-677-4549
WNEP-TV Ch 16 (ABC)					
16 Montage Mountain Rd	Moosic	PA	18507	**800-982-4374**	570-346-7474
WNPB-TV Ch 24 (PBS) 191 Scott Ave	Morgantown	WV	26508	**888-596-9729**	304-284-1440
WNYT-TV Ch 13 (NBC) 15 N Pearl St	Albany	NY	12204	**800-999-9698**	518-436-4791
WOIO-TV Ch 19 (CBS) 1717 E 12th St	Cleveland	OH	44114	**877-929-1943**	216-771-1943
WOWK-TV Ch 13 (CBS) 555 5th Ave	Huntington	WV	25701	**800-234-9695**	304-525-1313
WOWT-TV Ch 6 (NBC) 3501 Farnam St	Omaha	NE	68131	**800-688-2431**	402-346-6666
WPBT-TV Ch 2 (PBS) 14901 NE 20th Ave	Miami	FL	33181	**800-222-9728**	305-949-8321
WPDE-TV Ch 15 (ABC) 1194 Atlantic Ave	Conway	SC	29526	**800-698-9733**	843-234-9733
WPGA-TV Ch 58 (ABC) 1691 Forsyth St	Macon	GA	31201	**800-225-5222**	478-745-5858
WPTD-TV Ch 16 (PBS) 110 S Jefferson St	Dayton	OH	45402	**800-247-1614**	937-220-1600
WPXI-TV Ch 11 (NBC) 11 Television Hill	Pittsburgh	PA	15214	**800-237-9794**	412-237-1100
WPXN-TV Ch 31 (PAX)					
1330 Ave of the Americas 32nd Fl	New York	NY	10019	**800-646-7296**	212-757-3100
WPXP-TV Ch 67 (PAX)					
601 Clearwater Rd	West Palm Beach	FL	33401	**800-646-7296**	561-659-4122
WQED-TV Ch 13 (PBS) 4802 5th Ave	Pittsburgh	PA	15213	**800-876-1316**	412-622-1300
WQLN-TV Ch 54 (PBS) 8425 Peach St	Erie	PA	16509	**800-727-8854**	814-864-3001
WRAL-TV Ch 5 (CBS) 2619 Western Blvd	Raleigh	NC	27606	**800-245-9725**	919-821-8555
WRAZ-TV Ch 50 (Fox) 512 S Mangum St	Durham	NC	27701	**877-369-5050**	919-595-5050
WRLK-TV Ch 35 (PBS)					
1101 George Rogers Blvd	Columbia	SC	29201	**800-922-5437**	803-737-3200
WRNN-TV Ch 62 (Ind) 437 5th Ave	New York	NY	10016	**800-824-3302**	212-725-2666
WSAZ-TV Ch 3 (NBC) PO Box 2115	Huntington	WV	25721	**800-834-8515**	304-697-4780
WSBT-TV Ch 22 (CBS)					
300 W Jefferson Blvd	South Bend	IN	46601	**800-872-3141**	574-233-3141
WSEC-TV Ch 14 (PBS) PO Box 6248	Springfield	IL	62708	**800-232-3605**	217-206-6647
WSFJ-TV Ch 51 (PAX)					
3948 Townsfair Way Suite 220	Columbus	OH	43219	**800-517-5151**	614-416-6080
WSKY-TV Ch 4 (Ind)					
1417 N Battlefield Blvd Suite 160	Chesapeake	VA	23320	**800-414-0911**	757-382-0004
WSLS-TV Ch 10 (NBC) PO Box 10	Roanoke	VA	24022	**800-800-9757**	540-981-9110
WSOC-TV Ch 9 (ABC) 1901 N Tryon St	Charlotte	NC	28206	**800-367-9762**	704-338-9999
WSPA-TV Ch 7 (CBS) PO Box 1717	Spartanburg	SC	29304	**800-207-6397**	864-576-7777
WTIU-TV Ch 30 (PBS) 1229 E 7th St	Bloomington	IN	47405	**800-662-3311**	812-855-5900
WTKR-TV Ch 3 (CBS) 720 Boush St	Norfolk	VA	23510	**800-375-0901**	757-446-1000
WTLV-TV Ch 12 (NBC) 1070 E Adams St	Jacksonville	FL	32202	**800-352-8812**	904-354-1212
WTOV-TV Ch 9 (NBC)					
9 Red Donley Plaza	Mingo Junction	OH	43938	**800-288-0799**	740-282-0911
WTRF-TV Ch 7 (CBS) 96 16th St	Wheeling	WV	26003	**800-777-9873**	304-232-7777
WTSP-TV Ch 10 (CBS)					
11450 Gandy Blvd N	Saint Petersburg	FL	33702	**800-393-6610**	727-577-1010
WTTG-TV Ch 5 (Fox)					
5151 Wisconsin Ave NW	Washington	DC	20016	**800-988-4885**	202-244-5151
WTVD-TV Ch 11 (ABC) 411 Liberty St	Durham	NC	27701	**800-467-4440**	919-683-1111
WTVP-TV Ch 47 (PBS) PO Box 1347	Peoria	IL	61654	**800-837-4747**	309-677-4747

	City	State	Zip	Toll-Free	Phone
WTVW-TV Ch 7 (Fox) 477 Carpenter St	Evansville	IN	47708	**800-511-6009**	812-424-7777
WTXF-TV Ch 29 (Fox) 330 Market St	Philadelphia	PA	19106	**800-220-6397**	215-925-2929
WUAB-TV Ch 43 (UPN) 1717 E 12th St	Cleveland	OH	44114	**800-929-0132**	216-771-1943
WUNC-TV Ch 4 (PBS) PO Box 14900	Research Triangle Park	NC	27709	**800-906-5050**	919-549-7000
WUPW-TV Ch 36 (Fox) 4 Seagate Bldg	Toledo	OH	43604	**866-369-6397**	419-244-3600
WUSF-TV Ch 16 (PBS) 4202 E Fowler Ave	Tampa	FL	33620	**800-654-3703**	813-974-4000
WVAN-TV Ch 9 (PBS) 260 14th St NW	Atlanta	GA	30318	**800-222-6006**	404-685-2400
WVCY-TV Ch 30 (Ind) 3434 W Kilbourn Ave	Milwaukee	WI	53208	**800-729-9829**	414-935-3000
WVII-TV Ch 7 (ABC) 371 Target Industrial Cir	Bangor	ME	04401	**800-499-9844**	207-945-6457
WVIT-TV Ch 30 (NBC) 1422 New Britain Ave	West Hartford	CT	06110	**800-523-9848**	860-521-3030
WWMB-TV Ch 21 (UPN) 1194 Atlantic Ave	Conway	SC	29526	**800-698-9733**	843-234-9733
WWMT-TV Ch 3 (CBS) 590 W Maple St	Kalamazoo	MI	49008	**800-875-3333**	269-388-3333
WXEL-TV Ch 42 (PBS) PO Box 6607	West Palm Beach	FL	33405	**800-915-9935**	561-737-8000
WXXA-TV Ch 23 (Fox) 28 Corporate Cir	Albany	NY	12203	**800-999-2882**	518-862-2323
WYOU-TV Ch 22 (CBS) 409 Lackawanna Ave	Scranton	PA	18503	**800-422-9968**	570-961-2222
WYTV-TV Ch 33 (ABC) 3800 Shady Run Rd	Youngstown	OH	44502	**800-686-2930**	330-783-2930
WZPX-TV Ch 43 (PAX) 2610 Horizon Dr Suite E	Grand Rapids	MI	49546	**877-729-8843**	616-222-4343
WZVN-TV Ch 26 (ABC) 3719 Central Ave	Fort Myers	FL	33901	**800-741-8820**	239-939-2020

727 TELEVISION SYNDICATORS

	City	State	Zip	Toll-Free	Phone
AP Broadcast Services 1825 K St NW Suite 800	Washington	DC	20006	**800-821-4747**	202-736-1100
Babe Winkelman Productions PO Box 407	Brainerd	MN	56401	**800-333-0471**	218-822-4424
Georgia Public Broadcasting (GPB) 260 14th St NW	Atlanta	GA	30318	**800-222-6006**	404-685-2400
Information Television Network 621 NW 53rd St Suite 350	Boca Raton	FL	33487	**800-463-6488**	561-997-5433
TV Japan 100 Broadway 15th Fl *Cust Svc	New York	NY	10005	**800-518-8576***	212-262-3377

728 TESTING FACILITIES

	City	State	Zip	Toll-Free	Phone
Accutest Laboratories 2235 Rt 130 Bldg B	Dayton	NJ	08810	**800-329-0204**	732-329-0200
Aguirre Engineers Inc 13276 E Fremont Pl	Centennial	CO	80112	**800-403-7066**	303-799-8378
Altran Corp 451 D St	Boston	MA	02210	**800-281-2506**	617-204-1000
American Standards Testing Bureau Inc PO Box 583	New York	NY	10274	**800-221-5170**	212-943-3160
Analysts Inc 20505 Earl St	Torrance	CA	90503	**800-336-3637**	310-370-2345
Astro Pak Corp 12201 Pangborn Ave	Downey	CA	90241	**800-743-5444**	562-803-3400
Bioanalytical Systems Inc Clinical Research Unit 302 W Fayette St	Baltimore	MD	21201	**800-787-7800**	410-385-4500
Brook Environmental & Engineering Corp 11419 Cronridge Dr Suite 10	Owings Mills	MD	21117	**800-381-4434**	410-356-4875
Brown Dayton T Inc 1175 Church St	Bohemia	NY	11716	**800-232-6300**	631-589-6300
Camin Cargo Control Inc 230 Marion Ave	Linden	NJ	07036	**800-756-8798**	908-862-1899
Construction Technology Laboratories Inc 5400 Old Orchard Rd	Skokie	IL	60077	**800-522-2285**	847-965-7500
Construction Testing & Engineering Inc 242 W Larch Rd Suite F	Tracy	CA	95304	**800-576-2271**	209-839-2890
Dayton T Brown Inc 1175 Church St	Bohemia	NY	11716	**800-232-6300**	631-589-6300
Detroit Testing Lab Inc 7111 E 11-Mile Rd	Warren	MI	48092	**800-820-7009**	586-754-9000
Environmental Enterprises Inc 10163 Cincinnati Dayton Rd	Cincinnati	OH	45241	**800-722-2818**	513-772-2818
Evans Analytical Group 810 Kifer Rd	Sunnyvale	CA	94086	**800-321-4775**	408-530-3500
Idaho National Engineering & Environmental Laboratory (INEEL) Communications & Public Affairs 2525 Fremont Avenue PO Box 1625	Idaho Falls	ID	83415	**800-708-2680**	208-526-0111
Intertek Testing Services North America Inc 3933 US Rt 11	Cortland	NY	13045	**800-345-3851**	607-753-6711
Longview Inspection 5250 Mayfair Rd	North Canton	OH	44720	**800-321-0878**	330-494-9436
Magna Chek Inc 32701 Edward Ave	Madison Heights	MI	48071	**800-582-8947**	248-597-0089
Metcut Research Inc 3980 Rosslyn Dr	Cincinnati	OH	45209	**800-966-2888**	513-271-5100
National Technical Systems Inc 24007 Ventura Blvd Suite 200 *NASDAQ: NTSC*	Calabasas	CA	91302	**800-759-2687**	818-591-0776
New York Testing Group Inc 47 Hudson St	Ossining	NY	10562	**800-282-8701**	631-952-7300
Owensby & Kritikos Inc 671 Whitney Ave Bldg B	Gretna	LA	70056	**800-749-3122**	504-368-3122
Performance Validation LLC 2601 Fortune Cir Suite 200C	Indianapolis	IN	46241	**800-875-8897**	317-248-8848
Pittsburgh Testing Lab Div Professional Service Industries Inc 850 Poplar St	Pittsburgh	PA	15220	**866-842-9637**	412-922-4000
Professional Service Industries Inc Pittsburgh Testing Lab Div 850 Poplar St	Pittsburgh	PA	15220	**866-842-9637**	412-922-4000
Qore Property Science 11420 Johns Creek Pkwy	Duluth	GA	30097	**877-767-3462**	770-476-3555
SGS Canada Inc 6275 Northam Dr Unit 2	Mississauga	ON	L4V1Y8	**800-636-0847**	905-676-9595
SGS US Testing Co Inc 291 Fairfield Ave *Cust Svc	Fairfield	NJ	07004	**800-777-8378***	973-575-5252
Southern Petroleum Lab Inc 8880 Interchange Dr	Houston	TX	77054	**800-969-6775**	713-660-0901
Standard Labs Inc 147 11th Ave Suite 100	South Charleston	WV	25303	**888-216-0239**	304-744-6800
Sypris Test & Measurement 6120 Hanging Moss Rd	Orlando	FL	32807	**800-775-2550**	407-678-6900
Teledyne Brown Engineering Environmental Services PO Box 070007	Huntsville	AL	35807	**800-933-2091**	256-726-1000
Terra Tek Inc 400 Wakara Way	Salt Lake City	UT	84108	**800-372-2522**	801-584-2400
TestAmerica Inc 122 Lyman St	Asheville	NC	28801	**800-344-5759**	828-258-3746
Transportation Research Center Inc Ohio State University 10820 Rt 347 PO Box B 67	East Liberty	OH	43319	**800-837-7872**	937-666-2011
Twin City Testing 662 Cromwell Ave	Saint Paul	MN	55114	**888-645-8378**	651-645-3601
US Biosystems Inc 3231 NW 7th Ave	Boca Raton	FL	33431	**888-862-5227**	561-447-7373
Valley Lea Laboratories 4609 Grape Rd Suite D-4	Mishawaka	IN	46545	**800-822-1283**	574-272-8484

	City	State	Zip	Toll-Free	Phone
WIL Research Laboratories Inc 1407 George Rd *Cust Svc	Ashland	OH	44805	**800-221-9610***	419-289-8700

729 TEXTILE MACHINERY

	City	State	Zip	Toll-Free	Phone
American Performance Industries 109 McNeil Rd PO Box 250	Sanford	NC	27330	**800-438-3348**	919-775-7321
Barudan America Inc 29500 Fountain Pkwy	Solon	OH	44139	**800-627-4776**	440-248-8770
Bowman Hollis Mfg Inc 2925 Old Steele Creek Rd	Charlotte	NC	28208	**888-269-2358**	704-374-1500
Eastman Machine Co 779 Washington St	Buffalo	NY	14203	**800-872-5571**	716-856-2200
Elliott Metal Works Inc PO Box 8675	Greenville	SC	29604	**800-726-1542**	864-269-8930
Embroidery Store 5081 Arden Ct *Cust Svc	Ramseur	NC	27316	**800-727-4244***	336-824-4975
Gerber Technology Inc 24 Industrial Pk Rd W	Tolland	CT	06084	**800-826-3243**	860-871-8082
Gribetz International Inc 13800 NW 4th St	Sunrise	FL	33325	**800-326-4742**	954-846-0300
Hix Corp 1201 E 27th Terr	Pittsburg	KS	66762	**800-835-0606**	620-231-8568
Ioline Corp 14140 NE 200th St	Woodinville	WA	98072	**800-598-0029**	425-398-8282
Knitting Machine & Supply Co Inc 1257 Westfield Ave	Clark	NJ	07066	**877-898-2900**	732-382-9898
Lummus Corp 1 Lummus Dr PO Box 4259	Savannah	GA	31407	**800-458-6687**	912-447-9000
Macpherson Meistergram Inc DBA Embroidery Store 5081 Arden Ct *Cust Svc	Ramseur	NC	27316	**800-727-4244***	336-824-4975
McCoy-Ellison Inc PO Box 967	Monroe	NC	28111	**800-811-5348**	704-289-5413
Monarch Machine Corp Vanguard Supreme Machine Div PO Box 5009	Monroe	NC	28111	**800-222-1971**	704-283-8171
Petty Machine Co Inc 2403 Forbes Rd	Gastonia	NC	28056	**800-343-0960**	704-864-3254
Thermopatch Corp 2204 Erie Blvd E *Cust Svc	Syracuse	NY	13224	**800-252-6555***	315-446-8110
Tidland Corp 2305 SE 8th Ave	Camas	WA	98607	**800-426-1000**	360-834-2345
TrimMaster 4860 N 5th St Hwy	Temple	PA	19560	**800-356-4237**	610-921-0203
Tuftco Corp 2318 S Holtzclaw Ave	Chattanooga	TN	37408	**800-288-3826**	423-698-8601
Vanguard Supreme Machine Div Monarch Machine Corp PO Box 5009	Monroe	NC	28111	**800-222-1971**	704-283-8171

730 TEXTILE MILLS

730-1 Broadwoven Fabric Mills

	City	State	Zip	Toll-Free	Phone
Burlington House Group 3330 W Friendly Ave	Greensboro	NC	27410	**800-523-7888**	336-379-2000
Burlington Industries LLC 804 Green Valley Rd Suite 300	Greensboro	NC	27408	**800-523-7888**	336-379-6220
Carthage Fabrics Corp PO Box 398	Carthage	NC	28327	**800-541-4877**	910-947-2211
Circa 1801 Doblin Fabrics 1 Jacquard Dr *Cust Svc	Connelly Springs	NC	28612	**800-462-9295***	828-397-7003
Cone Mills Corp 804 Green Valley Rd Suite 300	Greensboro	NC	27408	**800-763-0123**	336-379-6220
Cone Mills Corp Denim Group 804 Green Valley Rd Suite 300	Greensboro	NC	27408	**800-763-0123**	336-379-6220
DeRoyal Textiles Inc 125 E York St *Sales	Camden	SC	29020	**800-845-1062***	803-432-2403
Faribault Mills PO Box 369	Faribault	MN	55021	**800-533-0444**	507-334-6444
Galey & Lord Inc 7736 McCloud Rd Suite 300 *Cust Svc	Greensboro	NC	27409	**800-527-9548***	336-665-3000
Greenwood Mills Inc 300 Morgan Ave	Greenwood	SC	29646	**800-847-5929**	864-229-2571
Hoffman Mills Inc 470 Park Ave S 7th Fl	New York	NY	10016	**800-582-1922**	212-684-3700
JB Martin Co 10 E 53rd St	New York	NY	10022	**800-223-0525**	212-421-2020
Kuraray America Inc 101 E 52nd St 26th Fl	New York	NY	10022	**800-879-1676**	212-986-2230
La France Industries Div Mount Vernon Mills Inc 290 Old Anderson Hwy	La France	SC	29656	**800-845-9728**	864-646-3213
Lantal Textiles Inc 1300 Langenthal Dr PO Box 965	Rural Hall	NC	27045	**800-334-3309**	336-969-9551
Leggett & Platt Inc Textile & Fiber Products Div 400 Davidson St	Nashville	TN	37213	**800-888-4136**	615-734-1600
Malden Mills Industries Inc 46 Stafford St	Lawrence	MA	01841	**800-252-6688**	978-685-6341
Martin JB Co 10 E 53rd St	New York	NY	10022	**800-223-0525**	212-421-2020
Mount Vernon Mills Inc PO Box 3478	Greenville	SC	29602	**800-845-8857**	864-233-4151
Mount Vernon Mills Inc La France Industries Div 290 Old Anderson Hwy	La France	SC	29656	**800-845-9728**	864-646-3213
Polymer Group Inc 4055 Saber Pl Suite 201	North Charleston	SC	29405	**800-631-5594**	
Precision Fabrics Group Inc 301 N Elm St Suite 600	Greensboro	NC	27401	**800-284-8001**	336-510-8000
Somerset Industries Inc 68 Harrison St	Gloversville	NY	12078	**800-262-0606**	518-773-7383
Springs Industries Inc 205 N White St	Fort Mill	SC	29715	**800-438-6709**	803-547-1500
Warm Co 954 E Union St	Seattle	WA	98122	**800-234-9276**	206-320-9276

730-2 Coated Fabric

	City	State	Zip	Toll-Free	Phone
Alpha Assoc Inc 2 Amboy Ave	Woodbridge	NJ	07095	**800-563-3136**	732-634-5700
Cooley Group 50 Esten Ave *Cust Svc	Pawtucket	RI	02860	**800-333-3048***	401-724-9000
Deccofelt Corp 555 S Vermont Ave *Cust Svc	Glendora	CA	91740	**800-543-3226***	626-963-8511
Der-Tex Corp 1 Lehner Rd	Saco	ME	04072	**800-669-0364**	207-284-5931
Duracote Corp 350 N Diamond St	Ravenna	OH	44266	**800-321-2252**	330-296-9600
Herculite Products Inc 105 E Sinking Springs Ln	Emigsville	PA	17318	**800-772-0036**	717-764-1192
ICG/Holliston PO Box 478	Kingsport	TN	37662	**800-251-0251**	423-357-6141
John Boyle & Co Inc 1803 Salisbury Rd *Cust Svc	Statesville	NC	28677	**800-438-1061***	704-872-8151
SanduskyAthol International 100 22nd St PO Box 105	Butner	NC	27509	**800-282-6523**	919-575-6523

Coated Fabric (Cont'd)

Company	City	State	Zip	Toll-Free	Phone
Sauquoit Industries LLC 300 Palm St	Scranton	PA	18505	**800-858-5552**	570-348-2751
Seaman Corp 1000 Venture Blvd	Wooster	OH	44691	**800-927-8578**	330-262-1111
Taconic Inc 136 Coonbrook Rd PO Box 69	Petersburgh	NY	12138	**800-833-1805**	518-658-3202
Twitchell Corp 4031 Ross Clark Cir NW	Dothan	AL	36303	**800-633-7550**	334-792-0002
Uniroyal Engineered Products LLC 501 S Water St	Stoughton	WI	53589	**800-873-8800**	608-873-6631
Vintex Inc 1 Mount Forest Dr	Mount Forest	ON	N0G2L2	**800-846-8399**	519-323-0100

730-3 Industrial Fabrics

Company	City	State	Zip	Toll-Free	Phone
Acme Group 1750 Telegraph Rd	Bloomfield Hills	MI	48302	**800-521-8565**	248-203-2000
Albany International Corp 1373 Broadway *NYSE: AIN*	Albany	NY	12204	**800-833-3836**	518-445-2200
Albany International Corp Appleton Wire Div 435 6th St	Menasha	WI	54952	**800-558-3526**	920-725-2600
Albany International Corp Engineered Fabrics Div 214 Kirby Dr	Portland	TN	37148	**800-833-3836**	615-325-6767
Albany International Corp Mount Vernon Dryer Fabrics Div 1373 Broadway	Albany	NY	12204	**800-833-3836**	518-445-2200
Amatex Corp 1032 Stambridge St	Norristown	PA	19404	**800-441-9680**	610-277-6100
AMETEK Inc Chemical Products Div 455 Corporate Blvd *Orders	Newark	DE	19702	**800-441-7777***	302-456-4400
Belton Industries 1205 Hanby Rd PO Box 127	Belton	SC	29627	**800-845-8753**	864-338-5711
BGF Industries Inc 3802 Robert Porcher Way	Greensboro	NC	27410	**800-476-4845**	336-545-0011
Bonn FH Co 4300 Gateway Blvd	Springfield	OH	45502	**800-323-0143**	937-323-7024
Carthage Mills 4243 Hunt Rd *Sales	Cincinnati	OH	45242	**800-543-4430***	513-794-1600
FH Bonn Co 4300 Gateway Blvd	Springfield	OH	45502	**800-323-0143**	937-323-7024
Firestone Fibers & Textiles Co 100 Firestone Ln	Kings Mountain	NC	28086	**800-441-1336**	704-734-2100
Firstline Corp 511 Highland Ave	Valdosta	GA	31603	**800-243-2451**	229-247-1717
Industrial Fabrics Corp 7160 Northland Cir N	Minneapolis	MN	55428	**800-328-3036**	763-535-3220
LINQ Industrial Fabrics Inc 2550 W 5th North St	Summerville	SC	29483	**800-822-8968**	843-873-5800
Mutual Industries Inc 707 W Grange St	Philadelphia	PA	19120	**800-523-0888**	215-927-6000
Newtex Industries Inc 8050 Victor Mendon Rd	Victor	NY	14564	**800-836-1001**	585-924-9135
Sefar America Inc 120 Mt Holly Bypass	Lumberton	NJ	08048	**800-289-8385**	609-613-5000
Southern Mills Inc 6501 Mall Blvd	Union City	GA	30291	**800-241-8630**	770-969-1000
Synthetic Industries Inc 309 LaFayette Rd	Chickamauga	GA	30707	**800-258-3121**	706-375-3121
Ten Cate Nicolon USA 365 S Holland Dr	Pendergrass	GA	30567	**888-795-0808**	706-693-2226
Tex-Tech Industries Inc 105 N Main St PO Box 8	North Monmouth	ME	04265	**800-441-7089**	207-933-4404
Ultrafabrics LLC 400 Executive Blvd	Elmsford	NY	10523	**888-361-9216**	914-460-1730
Weavexx Corp 51 Flex Way	Youngsville	NC	27596	**800-932-8399**	919-556-7235
Wellstone Mills 856 S Pleasantburg Dr	Greenville	SC	29607	**877-867-6455**	864-242-1293

730-4 Knitting Mills

Company	City	State	Zip	Toll-Free	Phone
Apex Mills Corp 168 Doughty Blvd	Inwood	NY	11096	**800-989-2739**	516-239-4400
Burlington Industries LLC 804 Green Valley Rd Suite 300	Greensboro	NC	27408	**800-523-7888**	336-379-6220
Charbert Inc 299 Church St	Alton	RI	02894	**800-570-2184**	401-364-7751
Concord Fabrics Inc 462 7th Ave	New York	NY	10018	**800-223-5678**	212-760-0300
Glenoit LLC 3002 Anaconda Rd	Tarboro	NC	27886	**800-829-0984**	252-823-2124
Guilford Mills Inc 6001 W Market St *Cust Svc	Greensboro	NC	27409	**800-277-0987***	336-316-4000
Monterey Mills Inc 1725 E Delavan Dr	Janesville	WI	53546	**800-255-9665**	608-754-2866
Paris Lace Inc 1500 Main Ave	Clifton	NJ	07011	**800-533-5223**	973-478-9035
Westchester Lace Inc 3901 Liberty Ave	North Bergen	NJ	07047	**800-699-5223**	201-864-2150

730-5 Narrow Fabric Mills

Company	City	State	Zip	Toll-Free	Phone
Advance Fiber Technologies Corp 344 Lodi St	Hackensack	NJ	07601	**800-631-1930**	201-488-2700
AH Rice Corp 55 Spring St *Sales	Pittsfield	MA	01201	**800-765-7423***	413-443-6477
Berwick Offray Inc Bombay Ln & 9th St	Berwick	PA	18603	**800-327-0350**	570-752-5934
Bo-Buck Mills Inc 921 East Blvd	Chesterfield	SC	29709	**800-690-7474**	843-623-2158
Carson & Gebel Ribbon Co 17 Green Pond Rd	Rockaway	NJ	07866	**800-223-8283**	973-627-4200
Conso International Corp 513 N Duncan Bypass	Union	SC	29379	**800-842-6676**	864-427-9004
CT-Nassau Corp 4101 S NC 62	Alamance	NC	27201	**800-397-0090**	336-570-0091
Elastic Corp of America Inc 455 Hwy 70 W	Columbiana	AL	35051	**800-633-4538**	205-669-3101
Fulflex Inc 652 George Washington Hwy	Lincoln	RI	02865	**800-222-1263**	401-333-1212
Hickory Brands Inc 429 27th St NW	Hickory	NC	28601	**800-438-5777**	828-322-2600
Ideal Bias Binding Corp 1637 N Main St	Fall River	MA	02720	**800-532-6600**	508-673-3212
JRM Industries Inc 1 Mattimore St	Passaic	NJ	07055	**800-533-2697**	973-779-9340
Julius Koch USA Inc 387 Church St *Sales	New Bedford	MA	02745	**800-522-3652***	508-995-9565
Koch Julius USA Inc 387 Church St *Sales	New Bedford	MA	02745	**800-522-3652***	508-995-9565
Mitchellace Inc 830 Murray St	Portsmouth	OH	45662	**800-848-8696**	740-354-2813
Murdock Webbing Co 27 Foundry St	Central Falls	RI	02863	**800-375-2052**	401-724-3000
Name Maker Inc PO Box 43821	Atlanta	GA	30336	**800-241-2890**	
Narrow Fabric Industries Inc 7th & W Reading Ave PO Box 6948	West Reading	PA	19611	**800-523-8118**	610-376-2891
Rhode Island Textile Co 211 Columbus Ave	Pawtucket	RI	02861	**800-556-6488**	401-722-3700
Ross Matthews Mills Inc 657 Quarry St	Fall River	MA	02723	**800-753-7677**	508-677-0601
Shelby Elastics Inc 639 N Post Rd	Shelby	NC	28150	**800-562-4507**	704-487-4301
South Carolina Elastic Co 201 South Carolina Elastic Rd	Landrum	SC	29356	**800-845-6700**	864-457-3388
Southern Weaving Co 1005 W Bramlett Rd	Greenville	SC	29611	**800-849-8962**	864-233-1635
Star Binding & Trimming Corp 1109 Grand Ave	North Bergen	NJ	07047	**800-782-7150**	201-864-2220
State Narrow Fabrics Inc 2902 Borden Ave	Long Island City	NY	11101	**800-221-7288**	718-392-8787

Company	City	State	Zip	Toll-Free	Phone
Tape Craft Corp 200 Tape Craft Dr *Cust Svc	Oxford	AL	36203	**800-521-1783***	256-236-2535
Trimtex Co Inc 400 Park Ave	Williamsport	PA	17701	**800-326-9135**	570-326-9135
Venus Industries 41-50 24th St	Long Island City	NY	11101	**800-221-6097**	718-729-4300
Wayne Mills Co Inc 130 W Berkley St	Philadelphia	PA	19144	**800-220-8053**	215-842-2134
William Wright Co 85 South St	West Warren	MA	01092	**800-628-9362**	413-436-7732
Wright William E Ltd 85 South St	West Warren	MA	01092	**800-628-9362**	413-436-7732

730-6 Nonwoven Fabrics

Company	City	State	Zip	Toll-Free	Phone
Aetna Felt Corp 2401 W Emaus Ave	Allentown	PA	18103	**800-526-4451**	610-791-0900
Airtex Consumer Products a Division of Federal Foam Technologies 150 Industrial Pk Blvd	Cokato	MN	55321	**800-851-8887**	320-286-2696
Clark-Cutler-McDermott Co 5 Fisher St PO Box 269	Franklin	MA	02038	**800-922-3019**	508-528-1200
DuPont Nonwovens Bldg 728 PO Box 80728 Chestnut Run Plaza	Wilmington	DE	19805	**800-448-9835**	
Foss Mfg Co Inc 380 Lafayette Rd	Hampton	NH	03842	**800-343-3277**	603-929-6000
Hobbs Bonded Fibers Inc 200 S Commerce St	Waco	TX	76710	**800-433-3357**	254-741-0040
Leggett & Platt Inc Textile & Fiber Products Div 400 Davidson St	Nashville	TN	37213	**800-888-4136**	615-734-1600
National Nonwovens 180 Pleasant St	Easthampton	MA	01027	**800-333-3469**	413-527-3445
PGI Nonwovens/Chicopee Inc 1203 S Chicopee Rd	Benson	NC	27504	**800-631-5594**	919-894-4111
Reliance Upholstery Supply Co 15902 S Main St	Gardena	CA	90248	**800-522-5252**	323-321-2300
Tietex International 3010 N Blackstock Rd	Spartanburg	SC	29301	**800-843-8390**	864-574-0500

730-7 Textile Dyeing & Finishing

Company	City	State	Zip	Toll-Free	Phone
Albert Screen Print Inc 3704 Summit Rd	Norton	OH	44203	**800-759-2774**	330-753-1252
Artex International Inc 1405 Walnut St	Highland	IL	62249	**800-851-8671**	618-654-2113
Aurora Textile Finishing Co PO Box 70	Aurora	IL	60507	**800-864-0303**	630-892-7651
Blumenthal Print Works Inc 905 S Broad St	New Orleans	LA	70125	**800-535-8590**	504-822-4620
Cranston Print Works Co 1381 Cranston St	Cranston	RI	02920	**800-876-2756**	401-943-4800
Harodite Finishing Co 66 South St	Taunton	MA	02780	**800-328-5656**	508-824-6961
Johnston Industries Inc Finished Fabrics Div PO Box 1108	Phenix City	AL	36868	**800-566-0889**	334-298-9351
Rockland Industries Inc PO Box 17293 *Cust Svc	Baltimore	MD	21297	**800-876-2566***	410-522-2505
Western Piece Dyers & Finishers Inc 2845 W 48th Pl	Chicago	IL	60632	**866-493-7839**	773-523-7000

730-8 Textile Fiber Processing Mills

Company	City	State	Zip	Toll-Free	Phone
A Sheftel & Sons Inc 2121 31st St SW *Cust Svc	Allentown	PA	18103	**800-542-2426***	610-797-9420
Acordis Celluosic Fibers Ltd US Hwy 43 N PO Box 171	Axis	AL	36505	**800-633-6720**	251-679-2200
Charles House & Sons Inc 235 Singleton St	Woonsocket	RI	02895	**800-243-7063**	401-769-0189
Fabri-Tech Inc 8236 N 600 W *Cust Svc	McCordsville	IN	46055	**800-332-4797***	317-335-9412
Herndon JE Co Inc 1020 J E Herndon Access Rd	Kings Mountain	NC	28086	**800-277-0500**	704-739-4711
House Charles & Sons Inc 235 Singleton St	Woonsocket	RI	02895	**800-243-7063**	401-769-0189
JE Herndon Co Inc 1020 J E Herndon Access Rd	Kings Mountain	NC	28086	**800-277-0500**	704-739-4711
Leggett & Platt Inc Textile & Fiber Products Div 400 Davidson St	Nashville	TN	37213	**800-888-4136**	615-734-1600
Leigh Fibers Inc 1101 Syphrit Rd	Wellford	SC	29385	**800-274-7707**	864-439-4111
Lewis Industrial Supply Co 3307 N 6th St	Harrisburg	PA	17110	**800-929-2400**	717-234-2409
Norman W Paschall Co Inc 1 Paschall Rd	Peachtree City	GA	30269	**800-849-1820**	770-487-7945
Oklahoma Waste & Wiping Rag Co Inc 2013 SE 18th St *Cust Svc	Oklahoma City	OK	73129	**800-232-4433***	405-670-3100
Sheftel A & Sons Inc 2121 31st St SW *Cust Svc	Allentown	PA	18103	**800-542-2426***	610-797-9420
Slosman Corp 100 Fairview Rd	Asheville	NC	28803	**800-544-9387**	828-274-2100
Triangle Textiles Ltd 1320 E Division St	Slaton	TX	79364	**800-622-8299**	806-828-6573

730-9 Yarn & Thread Mills

Company	City	State	Zip	Toll-Free	Phone
American & Efird Inc PO Box 507	Mount Holly	NC	28120	**800-438-6781**	704-827-4311
Amital Spinning Corp 197 Bosch Blvd	New Bern	NC	28562	**800-548-1922**	252-636-3435
Charles Craft Inc 21381 Charles Craft Ln PO Box 1049	Laurinburg	NC	28352	**800-277-1009**	910-844-3521
Coats North America 3430 Toringdon Way Suite 301	Charlotte	NC	28227	**800-631-0965**	704-329-5800
Eddington Thread Mfg Co 3222 Knights Rd	Bensalem	PA	19020	**800-220-8901**	215-639-8900
Elmore-Pisgah Inc 204 Oak St	Spindale	NC	28160	**800-633-7829**	828-286-3665
Jefferson Mills Inc 27 Valley St *Sales	Pulaski	VA	24301	**800-574-0069***	540-980-1530
Lion Brand Yarn Co 34 W 15th St	New York	NY	10011	**800-795-5466**	212-243-8995
Ludlow Textiles Co Inc PO Box 559	Ludlow	MA	01056	**800-628-9048**	413-583-5051
National Spinning Co Inc 111 W 40th St 28th Fl	New York	NY	10018	**800-868-7764**	212-382-6400
Parkdale Mills Inc 531 Cotton Blossom Cir	Gastonia	NC	28054	**800-331-1843**	704-864-8761
Perfect Thread Co Inc 10 E Merrick Rd	Valley Stream	NY	11580	**800-645-3500**	516-825-6565
Shuford Mills Inc 1985 Tate Blvd SE	Hickory	NC	28601	**800-633-7649**	828-328-2131
Spectrum Dyed Yarns Inc 136 Patterson Rd	Kings Mountain	NC	28086	**800-221-9456**	704-739-7401
Supreme Corp 325 Spence Rd	Conover	NC	28613	**888-604-6975**	828-322-6975
Tuscarora Yarns Inc 8760 E Franklin St	Mount Pleasant	NC	28124	**800-849-6527**	704-436-6527
Universal Fibers Inc PO Box 8930 *Cust Svc	Bristol	VA	24203	**800-457-4759***	276-669-1161

				Toll-Free	Phone
Waverly Mills Inc 23 3rd St *Cust Svc	Laurinburg	NC	28352	**800-496-9276***	910-276-1441
Wehadkee Yarn Mills Inc 802 3rd Ave	West Point	GA	31833	**800-996-9276**	706-645-1331

731 TEXTILE PRODUCTS - HOUSEHOLD

				Toll-Free	Phone
Ado Corp 851 Simuel Rd *Cust Svc	Spartanburg	SC	29301	**800-845-0918***	864-574-2731
Amana Woolen Mill 800 48th Ave	Amana	IA	52203	**800-222-6430**	319-622-3432
American Textile Co 10 N Linden St *Cust Svc	Duquesne	PA	15110	**800-289-2826***	412-948-1020
Arley Corp 1115 W Chestnut St *Cust Svc	Brockton	MA	02301	**800-628-7872***	508-580-4245
Bates of Maine 2 Cedar St	Lewiston	ME	04240	**800-552-2837**	
Blair Mills LP 115 Little St *Cust Svc	Belton	SC	29627	**800-458-8038***	864-338-6611
Carole Fabrics Inc 633 NW Frontage Rd	Augusta	GA	30907	**800-241-0920**	706-863-4742
Carpenter Co Morning Glory Div 302 Highland Dr	Taylor	TX	76574	**800-234-9105**	
Cecil Saydah Co 2935 E 12th St	Los Angeles	CA	90023	**800-221-4617**	323-263-9321
Charles Craft Inc 21381 Charles Craft Ln PO Box 1049	Laurinburg	NC	28352	**800-277-1009**	910-844-3521
CHF Industries Inc 1 Park Ave 9th Fl	New York	NY	10016	**800-243-7090**	212-951-7800
Corona Curtain Mfg Co Inc 401 Neponset St	Canton	MA	02021	**800-828-8906**	617-350-6970
Custom Drapery Blinds & Shutters 3900 Polk St	Houston	TX	77023	**800-929-9211**	713-225-9211
Dakotah Inc 530 Park Ln *Cust Svc	Webster	SD	57274	**800-261-1315***	605-345-4646
Dorothy's Ruffled Originals Inc 6721 Market St	Wilmington	NC	28405	**800-367-6849**	
Earle Industries Inc Hwys 149 & 64 PO Box 28	Earle	AR	72331	**888-944-8667**	870-792-8694
Ex-Cell Home Fashion Inc 295 5th Ave Rm 612	New York	NY	10016	**800-223-1999**	212-213-8000
F Schumacher & Co 79 Madison Ave	New York	NY	10016	**800-556-0040**	212-213-7900
Fantagraph Div Standard Textile Co Inc One Knollcrest Dr	Cincinnati	OH	45237	**800-888-5000**	513-761-9255
Franco Mfg Co Inc 555 Prospect St	Metuchen	NJ	08840	**800-631-4663**	732-494-0500
Hollander Home Fashions Corp 6560 W Rogers Cir Suite 19	Boca Raton	FL	33487	**800-233-7666**	561-997-6900
Kaslen Textiles 5899 Downey Rd	Vernon	CA	90058	**800-423-4448**	323-589-5337
Kay Dee Designs Inc 177 Skunk Hill Rd	Hope Valley	RI	02832	**800-537-3433**	401-539-2405
Kennebunk Home Inc 25 Canal St	Suncook	NH	03275	**800-242-1537**	603-485-7511
Klear-Vu Corp 135 Alden St	Fall River	MA	02723	**800-732-8723**	508-674-5723
Lichtenberg S & Co Inc 295 5th Ave Rm 918 *Cust Svc	New York	NY	10016	**800-682-1959***	212-689-4510
Louisville Bedding Co 10400 Bunsen Way	Louisville	KY	40299	**800-626-2594**	502-491-3370
Manual Woodworkers & Weavers Inc 3737 Howard Gap Rd	Hendersonville	NC	28792	**800-542-3139**	828-692-7333
Marietta Drapery & Window Coverings Co 22 Trammel St	Marietta	GA	30064	**800-241-7974**	770-428-3335
Miller Curtain Co Inc PO Box 240790	San Antonio	TX	78224	**800-741-9020**	210-483-1000
Newport Layton Home Fashions Inc 14546 N Lombard St	Portland	OR	97203	**800-752-2225**	503-283-4864
Paramount Industrial Cos Inc 1112 Kingwood Ave	Norfolk	VA	23502	**800-777-5337**	757-855-3321
Pendleton Woolen Mills Inc 2516 SE Mailwell Dr	Portland	OR	97222	**800-760-4844**	503-226-4801
Perfect Fit Industries Inc 261 5th Ave *Cust Svc	New York	NY	10016	**800-438-1516***	212-679-6656
Phoenix Down Corp 85 Rt 46 W	Totowa	NJ	07512	**800-255-3696**	973-812-8100
Piedmont Home Textile Inc PO Box 267	Walhalla	SC	29691	**800-334-9033**	864-638-3636
Quip Industries Inc 191 Methodist St	Carlyle	IL	62231	**800-851-4013**	618-594-2437
Riegel Consumer Products PO Box E	Johnston	SC	29832	**800-845-3251**	803-275-2541
Rug Barn Inc 234 Industrial Park Rd PO Box 1187	Abbeville	SC	29620	**800-784-2276**	800-626-7033
S Lichtenberg & Co Inc 295 5th Ave Rm 918 *Cust Svc	New York	NY	10016	**800-682-1959***	212-689-4510
Samson Mfg Co PO Box 807	Waynesboro	GA	30830	**800-682-1959**	706-554-2129
Saydah Cecil Co 2935 E 12th St	Los Angeles	CA	90023	**800-221-4617**	323-263-9321
Springs Industries Inc 205 N White St	Fort Mill	SC	29715	**800-438-6709**	803-547-1500
Standard Textile Co Inc Fantagraph Div One Knollcrest Dr	Cincinnati	OH	45237	**800-888-5000**	513-761-9255
Steven Fabrics Co 1400 Van Buren St NE	Minneapolis	MN	55413	**800-328-2558**	612-781-6671
Surefit 939 Marcon Blvd	Allentown	PA	18109	**888-754-7166**	610-264-7300
TexStyle Inc 5555 Murray Ave Suite A	Cincinnati	OH	45227	**800-875-8001**	513-272-1800
United Feather & Down Inc 414 E Golf Rd	Des Plaines	IL	60016	**800-932-3696**	847-296-6500
Wesco Fabrics Inc 4001 Forest St	Denver	CO	80216	**800-950-9372**	303-388-4101

732 THEATERS - BROADWAY

SEE ALSO Performing Arts Facilities; Performing Arts Organizations - Theater Companies; Theaters - Resident

				Toll-Free	Phone
Ambassador Theatre 215 W 49th St	New York	NY	10019	**800-432-7250**	212-239-6200
Barrymore Theatre 243 W 47th St	New York	NY	10036	**800-432-7250**	212-239-6200
Belasco Theatre 111 W 44th St	New York	NY	10036	**800-432-7250**	212-239-6200
Booth Theatre 222 W 45th St	New York	NY	10036	**800-432-7250**	212-239-6200
Broadhurst Theatre 235 W 44th St	New York	NY	10036	**800-432-7250**	212-239-6200
Broadway Theatre 1681 Broadway	New York	NY	10019	**800-432-7250**	212-239-6200
Brooks Atkinson Theatre 256 W 47th St	New York	NY	10036	**800-755-4000**	212-307-4100
Cadillac Winter Garden Theatre 1634 Broadway	New York	NY	10019	**800-432-7250**	212-239-6200
Circle in the Square Theatre 1633 Broadway	New York	NY	10019	**800-432-7250**	212-239-6200
Cort Theatre 138 W 48th St	New York	NY	10036	**800-432-7250**	212-239-6200
Eugene O'Neill Theatre 230 W 49th St	New York	NY	10019	**800-432-7250**	212-239-6200
Ford Center for the Performing Arts 213 W 42nd St	New York	NY	10036	**800-755-4000**	212-307-4100
Gershwin Theatre 222 W 51st St	New York	NY	10019	**800-755-4000**	212-307-4100
Golden Theatre 252 W 45th St	New York	NY	10036	**800-432-7250**	212-239-6200
Helen Hayes Theatre 240 W 44th St	New York	NY	10036	**800-432-7250**	212-239-6200
Imperial Theatre 249 W 45th St	New York	NY	10036	**800-432-7250**	212-239-6200
Longacre Theatre 220 W 48th St	New York	NY	10036	**800-432-7250**	212-239-6200
Lunt-Fontanne Theatre 205 W 46th St	New York	NY	10036	**800-755-4000**	212-307-4100
Lyceum Theatre 149 W 45th St	New York	NY	10036	**800-432-7250**	212-239-6200
Majestic Theatre 245 W 44th St	New York	NY	10036	**800-432-7250**	212-239-6200
Marquis Theatre 211 W 45th St	New York	NY	10036	**800-755-4000**	212-307-4100
Minskoff Theatre 200 W 45th St	New York	NY	10036	**800-755-4000**	212-307-4100
Music Box Theatre 239 W 45th St	New York	NY	10036	**800-432-7250**	212-239-6200
Nederlander Theatre 208 W 41st St	New York	NY	10036	**800-755-4000**	212-307-4100
Neil Simon Theatre 250 W 52nd St	New York	NY	10019	**800-755-4000**	212-307-4100
New Amsterdam Theatre 214 W 42nd St	New York	NY	10036	**800-755-4000**	212-307-4100
Palace Theatre 1564 Broadway	New York	NY	10036	**800-755-4000**	212-307-4100
Plymouth Theatre 236 W 45th St	New York	NY	10036	**800-432-7250**	212-239-6200
Richard Rodgers Theatre 226 W 46th St	New York	NY	10036	**800-755-4000**	212-307-4100
Royale Theatre 242 W 45th St	New York	NY	10036	**800-432-7250**	212-239-6200
Saint James Theatre 246 W 44th St	New York	NY	10036	**800-432-7250**	212-239-6200
Shubert Theatre 225 W 44th St	New York	NY	10036	**800-432-7250**	212-239-6200
Virginia Theatre 245 W 52nd St	New York	NY	10019	**800-432-7250**	212-239-6200
Vivian Beaumont Theatre 150 W 65th St	New York	NY	10023	**800-432-7250**	212-239-6200
Walter Kerr Theatre 219 W 48th St	New York	NY	10036	**800-432-7250**	212-239-6200

733 THEATERS - MOTION PICTURE

				Toll-Free	Phone
AMC Entertainment Inc 920 Main St *AMEX: AEN*	Kansas City	MO	64105	**800-326-2432**	816-221-4000
American Multi-Cinema Inc 920 Main St	Kansas City	MO	64105	**800-326-2432**	816-221-4000
Carmike Cinemas Inc 1301 1st Ave *NASDAQ: CKEC*	Columbus	GA	31901	**800-241-0431**	706-576-3400
Cinemark Inc 3900 Dallas Pkwy Suite 500	Plano	TX	75093	**800-950-2872**	972-665-1000
Eastern Federal Corp 901 East Blvd	Charlotte	NC	28203	**800-394-7368**	704-377-3495
Goodrich Quality Theaters Inc 4417 Broadmoor Ave SE	Kentwood	MI	49512	**800-473-3523**	616-698-7733
Iwerks Entertainment Inc 4520 W Valerio St	Burbank	CA	91505	**800-388-8628**	818-841-7766
Marcus Theatres Corp 100 E Wisconsin Ave Suite 19 *Cust Svc	Milwaukee	WI	53202	**800-274-0099***	414-905-1000
Muvico Theaters 3101 N Federal Hwy 6th Fl	Ft Lauderdale	FL	33306	**800-294-6585**	954-564-6550
Regal Entertainment Group 7132 Regal Ln *NYSE: RGC*	Knoxville	TN	37918	**877-835-5734**	865-922-1123

734 THEATERS - RESIDENT

SEE ALSO Performing Arts Facilities; Performing Arts Organizations - Theater Companies; Theaters - Broadway

				Toll-Free	Phone
Actors Theatre of Louisville 316 W Main St	Louisville	KY	40202	**800-428-5849**	502-584-1265
Alabama Shakespeare Festival 1 Festival Dr	Montgomery	AL	36117	**800-841-4273**	334-271-5300
Alley Theatre 615 Texas Ave	Houston	TX	77002	**800-259-2553**	713-228-9341
Arkansas Repertory Theatre 601 Main St	Little Rock	AR	72203	**866-684-3737**	501-378-0445
Asolo Theatre Co 5555 N Tamiami Tr	Sarasota	FL	34243	**800-361-8388**	941-351-9010
Berkshire Theatre Festival PO Box 797	Stockbridge	MA	01262	**866-811-4111**	413-298-5536
Denver Center Theatre Co 1245 Champa St	Denver	CO	80204	**800-641-1222**	303-893-4000
Florida Stage 262 S Ocean Blvd	Manalapan	FL	33462	**800-514-3837**	561-585-3404
Guthrie Theater 725 Vineland Pl	Minneapolis	MN	55403	**877-447-8243**	612-347-1100
Long Wharf Theatre 222 Sargent Dr	New Haven	CT	06511	**800-782-8497**	203-787-4284
Maltz Jupiter Theatre 1001 E Indiantown Rd	Jupiter	FL	33477	**800-445-1666**	561-743-2666
Missouri Repertory Theatre 4949 Cherry St	Kansas City	MO	64110	**888-502-2700**	816-235-2727
Prince Music Theater 100 S Broad St Suite 650	Philadelphia	PA	19110	**800-964-6895**	215-972-1000
Seattle Repertory Theatre 155 Mercer St PO Box 900923	Seattle	WA	98109	**877-900-9285**	206-443-2210
Shakespeare Theatre 516 8th St SE	Washington	DC	20003	**877-487-8849**	202-547-3230
Studio Arena Theatre 710 Main St	Buffalo	NY	14202	**800-777-8243**	716-856-8025

735 TICKET BROKERS

				Toll-Free	Phone
Acteva.com 1 Bush St 15th Fl *Cust Svc	San Francisco	CA	94104	**877-855-8646***	415-374-8222
All American Ticket Service 2616 Philadelphia Pike Suite E	Claymont	DE	19703	**800-669-0571**	302-798-8556
Americana Tickets NY 115 W 45th St 8th Fl	New York	NY	10036	**800-833-3121**	212-581-6660
Broadway.com 1650 Broadway Suite 910	New York	NY	10019	**800-276-2392**	212-541-8457
Front Row USA Entertainment Inc 18170 W Dixie Hwy 2nd Fl	North Miami Beach	FL	33160	**800-446-8499**	305-940-8499
Good Time Tickets Inc 38 Hadden Field Rd	Palmyra	NJ	08065	**800-774-8499**	856-829-3900
GoTickets.com 201 Shannon Oaks Cir	Cary	NC	27512	**800-775-1617**	919-481-4868
Great Seats Inc 7338 Baltimore Ave Suite 108A	College Park	MD	20740	**800-664-5056**	301-985-6250
HMR Enterprises Inc DBA VIP Tickets 14515 Ventura Blvd Suite 210	Sherman Oaks	CA	91403	**800-328-4253**	818-907-1548
Moviefone Inc 333 Westchester Ave 2nd Fl *Cust Svc	White Plains	NY	10604	**800-745-0009***	914-872-0333
Pacific Northwest Ticket Service 2864 77th Ave SE	Mercer Island	WA	98040	**800-281-0753**	206-232-0150
Premiere Tickets & Tours Inc 201 Shannon Oaks Cir	Cary	NC	27512	**800-775-1617**	919-481-4868
Select-A-Ticket Inc 25 Rt 23 S	Riverdale	NJ	07457	**800-735-3288**	973-839-6100
Shubert Ticketing Services 234 W 44th St	New York	NY	10036	**800-545-2559**	212-944-3700
Ticket Box Inc 2125 Center Ave Suite 509	Fort Lee	NJ	07024	**800-842-5440**	201-461-8771
Ticket Heaven 600 S County Farm Rd Suite 144	Wheaton	IL	60187	**800-260-6616**	630-260-0626

Name / Address	City	State	Zip	Toll-Free	Phone
Ticket Pros USA 245 Peachtree Ctr Ave Suite M-39	Atlanta	GA	30303	**800-962-2985**	404-524-8491
Ticket Source Inc 5516 E Mockingbird Ln Suite 100	Dallas	TX	75206	**800-557-6872**	214-821-9011
Ticketfinder.com 236 W Portal Ave Suite 360	San Francisco	CA	94127	**800-523-1515**	650-757-3514
Ticketmall.com 245 Peachtree Ctr Ave Suite M-39	Atlanta	GA	30303	**800-962-2985**	404-524-8491
Ticketmaster 3701 Wilshire Blvd 7th Fl	Los Angeles	CA	90010	**800-366-8652**	213-381-2000
Ticketmonster Inc 303 Frederick Rd	Catonsville	MD	21228	**800-637-3719**	410-719-0030
Tickets Galore Inc 33 Haddon Ave	Westmont	NJ	08108	**888-849-9663**	856-869-8499
Tickets.com Inc 555 Anton Blvd 11th Fl	Costa Mesa	CA	92626	**800-352-0212**	714-327-5400
TicketWeb Inc PO Box 77250 *Cust Svc	San Francisco	CA	94103	**866-468-7630***	800-965-4827
TNT Tickets Inc 23881 Via Fabricante Suite 505	Mission Viejo	CA	92691	**800-425-5849**	949-458-5744
Total Travel & Tickets Inc 6250 N Andrews Ave Suite 205	Fort Lauderdale	FL	33309	**800-493-8499**	954-493-9151
VIP Tickets 14515 Ventura Blvd Suite 210	Sherman Oaks	CA	91403	**800-328-4253**	818-907-1548
Western States Ticket Service 143 W McDowell Rd	Phoenix	AZ	85003	**800-326-0331**	602-254-3300
Who Needs Two? 707 Lake Cook Rd Suite 115	Deerfield	IL	60015	**888-246-8499**	847-564-8499

736 TILE - CERAMIC (WALL & FLOOR)

Name / Address	City	State	Zip	Toll-Free	Phone
Ann Sacks Tile & Stone Inc 8120 NE 33rd Dr	Portland	OR	97211	**800-278-8453**	503-281-7751
Architectural Shapes & Colors Custom Tile 1201 Millerton St SE	Canton	OH	44707	**877-497-4273**	330-484-0429
Armstrong World Industries Inc 2500 Columbia Ave *Cust Svc	Lancaster	PA	17603	**800-233-3823***	717-397-0611
Dal-Tile International Inc 7834 Hawn Fwy	Dallas	TX	75217	**800-933-8453**	214-398-1411
Endicott Clay Products Co 57120 707 Rd	Endicott	NE	68350	**800-927-9179**	402-729-3315
Endicott Tile LLC 57120 707 Rd	Endicott	NE	68350	**800-927-9179**	402-729-3315
Epro Inc 10890 E CR 6	Bloomville	OH	44818	**866-818-3776**	
Florida Tile Industries Inc 1 Sikes Blvd	Lakeland	FL	33815	**800-352-8453**	863-687-7171
Interstyle Ceramics & Glass Ltd 3625 Brighton Ave	Burnaby	BC	V5A3H5	**800-667-1566**	604-421-7229
Ironrock Capital Inc 1201 Millerton St SE	Canton	OH	44707	**877-497-4273**	330-484-4887
Laufen USA 4244 Mt Pleasant St NW Suite 100	North Canton	OH	44720	**800-321-0684**	330-649-5000
Meredith Collection 1201 Millerton St SE	Canton	OH	44707	**877-497-4273**	330-484-1656
Metropolitan Ceramics 1201 Millerton St SE	Canton	OH	44707	**800-325-3945**	330-484-4887
Monarch Ceramic Tile 4321 Bryson Blvd *Cust Svc	Florence	AL	35630	**800-289-8453***	256-764-6181
Sacks Ann Tile & Stone Inc 8120 NE 33rd Dr	Portland	OR	97211	**800-278-8453**	503-281-7751
US Ceramic Tile Co 4244 Mt Pleasant St NW Suite 720	North Canton	OH	44720	**800-321-0684**	330-649-5000

737 TIMBER TRACTS

Name / Address	City	State	Zip	Toll-Free	Phone
Holiday Tree Farms Inc 800 NW Cornell Ave	Corvallis	OR	97330	**800-289-3684**	541-753-3236
Pike Lumber Co Inc PO Box 247	Akron	IN	46910	**800-356-4554**	574-893-4511

738 TIMESHARE COMPANIES

SEE ALSO Hotel & Resort Operation & Management; Hotels & Motels (Individual) - Canada; Hotels & Motels (Individual) - US

Name / Address	City	State	Zip	Toll-Free	Phone
Bluegreen Corp 4960 Conference Way N Suite 100 *NYSE: BXG*	Boca Raton	FL	33431	**800-456-2582**	561-912-8000
Central Florida Investments Inc 5601 Windhover Dr	Orlando	FL	32819	**800-925-9999**	407-351-3383
Club Intrawest 375 Water St Suite 326	Vancouver	BC	V6B5C6	**800-767-2166**	604-689-8816
Diamond Resorts International 3745 Las Vegas Blvd S	Las Vegas	NV	89109	**866-309-7318**	702-261-1000
Disney Vacation Club 200 Celebration Pl	Celebration	FL	34747	**800-500-3990**	407-566-3100
Fairfield Resorts Inc 8427 S Park Cir *Cust Svc	Orlando	FL	32819	**800-251-8736***	407-370-5200
Fairmont Vacation Villas PO Box 127 *Resv	Fairmont Hot Springs	BC	V0B1L0	**800-663-6333***	250-345-6321
Festiva Resorts 1 Vance Gap Rd *Resv	Asheville	NC	28805	**877-933-7848***	828-254-3378
Four Seasons Vacation Ownership 1165 Leslie St	Toronto	ON	M3C2K8	**800-332-3442**	416-449-1750
Grand Pacific Resorts 5900 Pasteur Ct Suite 200	Carlsbad	CA	92008	**800-444-3515**	760-431-8500
Hilton Grand Vacations Co LLC 6355 Metro West Blvd Suite 180	Orlando	FL	32835	**800-521-3144**	407-521-3100
Hyatt Vacation Ownership Inc 450 Carillon Pkwy Suite 210 *Resv	Saint Petersburg	FL	33716	**800-926-4447***	727-803-9400
ILX Resorts Inc 2111 E Highland Ave Suite 210 *AMEX: ILX*	Phoenix	AZ	85016	**800-822-2589**	602-957-2777
Interval International Inc 6262 Sunset Dr PH 1	Miami	FL	33143	**800-828-8200**	305-666-1861
Island One Resorts 2345 Sand Lake Rd Suite 100	Orlando	FL	32809	**800-892-7523**	407-859-8900
Marriott Vacation Club International 10400 Fernwood Rd	Bethesda	MD	20817	**800-845-5279**	301-380-3000
Monarch Grand Vacations 23091 Mill Creek Dr	Laguna Hills	CA	92653	**800-828-4200**	949-609-2400
One Napili Way 5355 Lower Honoapiilani Hwy	Lahaina	HI	96761	**800-841-6284**	808-669-2007
Resort Condominiums International (RCI) 9998 N Michigan Rd	Carmel	IN	46032	**800-481-5738**	317-805-9000
Royal Aloha Vacation Club 1505 Dillingham Blvd Suite 212	Honolulu	HI	96817	**800-367-5212**	808-847-8050
Silverleaf Resorts Inc 1221 Riverbend Dr	Dallas	TX	75247	**800-613-0310**	214-631-1166
Starwood Vacation Ownership Inc 8800 Vistana Center Dr	Orlando	FL	32821	**800-847-8262**	407-239-3000
Sunterra Corp 3865 W Cheyenne Ave *NASDAQ: SNRR*	North Las Vegas	NV	89032	**800-411-9922**	702-804-8600
Tempus Resorts International 7380 Sand Lake Rd Suite 600	Orlando	FL	32819	**800-463-7256**	407-226-1000
Trendwest Resorts Inc 9805 Willows Rd NE	Redmond	WA	98052	**800-722-3487**	425-498-2500
Vacation Internationale 1417 116th Ave NE	Bellevue	WA	98004	**800-444-6633**	425-454-3065
Westgate Resorts 5601 Windhover Dr	Orlando	FL	32819	**800-925-9999**	407-351-3383
WorldMark The Club 9805 Willows Rd NE	Redmond	WA	98052	**800-722-3487**	425-498-1950

739 TIRES - MFR

Name / Address	City	State	Zip	Toll-Free	Phone
Bridgestone Americas Holding Inc 535 Marriott Dr *Cust Svc	Nashville	TN	37214	**800-543-7522***	615-937-5000
Carlisle Tire & Wheel Mfg 23 Windham Blvd *Sales	Aiken	SC	29805	**800-827-1001***	803-643-2900
Cooper Tire & Rubber Co 701 Lima Ave *NYSE: CTB* ■ *Cust Svc	Findlay	OH	45840	**800-854-6288***	419-423-1321
Denman Tire Corp 400 Diehl South Rd *Cust Svc	Leavittsburg	OH	44430	**800-334-5543***	330-675-4242
Dunlop Tire Corp PO Box 1109	Buffalo	NY	14240	**800-828-7428**	716-639-5200
Galaxy Tire & Wheel Inc 730 Eastern Ave *Sales	Malden	MA	02148	**800-343-3276***	781-321-3910
Goodyear Tire & Rubber Co 1144 E Market St *NYSE: GT* ■ *Cust Svc	Akron	OH	44316	**800-321-2136***	330-796-2121
Hankook Tire America Corp 1450 Valley Rd	Wayne	NJ	07470	**800-426-5665**	973-633-9000
Hercules Tire & Rubber Co 1300 Morrical Blvd	Findlay	OH	45840	**800-677-9535**	419-425-6400
Maine Industrial Tires Ltd 9 Laurence Rd *Sales	Gorham	ME	04038	**800-782-2371***	207-856-6381
Martin Wheel Co Inc 342 West Ave	Tallmadge	OH	44278	**800-462-7846**	330-633-3278
Michelin North America PO Box 19001 *Cust Svc	Greenville	SC	29602	**800-847-3435***	864-458-5000
Mitchell Industrial Tire Co PO Box 71839	Chattanooga	TN	37407	**800-251-7226**	423-698-4442
Pirelli Tire North America 100 Pirelli Dr PO Box 700	Rome	GA	30161	**800-747-3554**	
Purcell Tire & Rubber Co 301 N Hall St	Potosi	MO	63664	**800-326-8410**	573-438-2133
Robbins LLC PO Box 60	Tuscumbia	AL	35674	**800-633-3312**	256-383-5441
Specialty Tires of America Inc 1600 Washington St	Indiana	PA	15701	**800-622-7327**	724-349-9010
Stratham Tire Inc 355 Rt 125	Brentwood	NH	03833	**800-427-7217**	603-679-5840
Superior Tire & Rubber Corp PO Box 308 *Cust Svc	Warren	PA	16365	**800-289-1456***	814-723-2370
Tech International 200 E Coshocton St	Johnstown	OH	43031	**800-336-8324**	740-967-9015
Tech Supply PO Box 56747	Hayward	CA	94545	**800-245-8324**	510-783-7085
Titan Tire Co 2345 E Market St	Des Moines	IA	50317	**800-872-2327**	515-265-9200
Toyo Tire USA Corp 6261 Katella Ave Suite 2B	Cypress	CA	90630	**800-678-3250**	714-236-2080
Trelleborg Wheel Systems America Inc 61 State Rt 43 N	Hartville	OH	44632	**800-666-8473**	330-877-1211
Vogue Tire & Rubber Co Inc 1101 Feehanville Dr	Mount Prospect	IL	60056	**800-323-1466**	847-297-1900
Yokohama Tire Corp 601 S Acacia Ave	Fullerton	CA	92831	**800-423-4544**	714-870-3800

740 TIRES & TUBES - WHOL

Name / Address	City	State	Zip	Toll-Free	Phone
Allied Oil & Supply Inc 2209 S 24th St	Omaha	NE	68103	**800-333-3717**	402-344-4343
Am-Pack Tasco Distributing Ltd PO Box 20305	Waco	TX	76702	**800-548-1075**	254-772-9144
American Tire Distributors Inc 12200 Herbert Wayne Ct Suite 150	Huntersville	NC	28078	**800-277-8473**	704-992-2000
Ball Tire & Gas Inc 620 S Ripley Blvd	Alpena	MI	49707	**800-322-3016**	989-354-4186
Barron's Wholesale Tire Inc 1302 Eastport Rd	Jacksonville	FL	32218	**800-245-1899**	904-751-2449
Bauer Built Inc PO Box 248	Durand	WI	54736	**800-999-0123**	715-672-4295
Ben Tire Distributors Ltd Inc 203 E Madison St PO Box 158	Toledo	IL	62468	**800-252-8961**	217-849-3331
Bob Sumerel Tires & Service Inc 3646 E Broad St	Columbus	OH	43213	**800-858-0421**	614-237-6325
Burggraf Corp 322 Main St	Quapaw	OK	74363	**800-331-2617**	918-674-2281
Capital Tire Inc 1001-17 Cherry St	Toledo	OH	43608	**800-537-0190**	419-241-5111
Clark Tire & Auto Supply Co Inc 220 S Center St	Hickory	NC	28602	**800-968-3092**	828-322-2303
Dapper Tire Co Inc 4025 Lockridge St	San Diego	CA	92102	**800-266-7172**	619-266-1397
Dunlap & Kyle Co Inc PO Box 720	Batesville	MS	38606	**800-647-6133**	662-563-7601
East Bay Tire Co 2200 Huntington Dr Unit C	Fairfield	CA	94533	**800-831-8473**	707-437-4700
Falken Tire Corp 10404 6th St	Rancho Cucamonga	CA	91730	**800-723-2553**	909-466-1116
Friend Tire Co 11 N Industrial Dr	Monett	MO	65708	**800-950-8473**	417-235-7836
Ganin Tire Co Inc 1421 38th St	Brooklyn	NY	11218	**800-344-2788**	718-633-6300
Gateway Tire Co Inc 4 W Crescentville Rd	Cincinnati	OH	45246	**800-837-1405**	513-874-2500
Hanco Corp 3650 Dodd Rd *Cust Svc	Eagan	MN	55123	**800-328-7400***	651-456-5600
Hesselbein Tire Co Inc 4299 Industrial Dr	Jackson	MS	39209	**800-685-6462**	601-974-5959
Jones Ken Tire Inc PO Box 782	Worcester	MA	01613	**800-225-9513**	508-755-5255
Ken Jones Tire Inc PO Box 782	Worcester	MA	01613	**800-225-9513**	508-755-5255
Kenda USA 7095 Americana Pkwy	Reynoldsburg	OH	43068	**866-536-3287**	614-866-9803
Kost Tire Distributors Inc 335 Court St	Binghamton	NY	13904	**800-622-6672**	607-723-1230
Kumho Tire USA Inc 14605 Miller Ave	Fontana	CA	92336	**800-445-8646**	909-428-3999
Lakin Tire West Inc 15305 Spring Ave	Santa Fe Springs	CA	90670	**800-488-2752**	562-802-2752
Laramie Tire Distributors Inc 2000 Campus Ln	East Norristown	PA	19403	**800-523-0430**	610-615-8000
Michelin North America PO Box 19001 *Cust Svc	Greenville	SC	29602	**800-847-3435***	864-458-5000
Parrish Tire Co Inc 5130 Indiana Ave	Winston-Salem	NC	27106	**800-849-8473**	336-767-0202
Pomps Tire Service Inc 1123 Cedar St	Green Bay	WI	54302	**800-236-8911**	920-435-8301
Raben Tire Co Inc 400 NW 4th St	Evansville	IN	47708	**800-322-6247**	812-465-5566

				Toll-Free	Phone
Reliable Tire Co					
805 N Blackhorse Pike PO Box 39	Blackwood	NJ	08012	**800-342-3426**	856-232-0700
Rott-Keller Supply Co Inc PO Box 390	Fargo	ND	58107	**800-342-4709**	701-235-0563
Sehman Tire Service Inc					
814 Atlantic Ave PO Box 889	Franklin	PA	16323	**800-895-8663**	814-437-7878
Snyder Wholesale Tire Co 401 Cadiz Rd	Wintersville	OH	43953	**800-967-8473**	740-264-5543
Southeastern Wholesale Tire Co					
4721 Trademark Dr	Raleigh	NC	27610	**800-849-9215**	919-832-3900
Sumerel Bob Tires & Service Inc					
3646 E Broad St	Columbus	OH	43213	**800-858-0421**	614-237-6325
TBC Corp 4770 Hickory Hill Rd	Memphis	TN	38141	**800-238-6469**	901-363-8030
NASDAQ: TBCC					
Terry's Tire Town Inc 2360 W Main St	Alliance	OH	44601	**800-235-2921**	330-821-5022
Tire Centers LLC 310 Inglesby Pkwy	Duncan	SC	29334	**800-603-2430**	864-329-2700
Tire Rack 7101 Vorden Pkwy	South Bend	IN	46628	**800-428-8359**	574-287-2345
Tire-Rama Inc PO Box 23509	Billings	MT	59104	**800-828-1642**	406-245-4006
Traction Wholesale Center Inc					
1515 Parkway Ave	Trenton	NJ	08628	**800-846-8847**	609-771-9383
Tyres International Inc 619 E Tallmadge Ave	Akron	OH	44310	**800-321-0941**	330-374-1000
University Wholesalers Inc 1945 Main St	Colchester	VT	05446	**800-852-5222**	802-655-8030
WD Tire Warehouse Inc					
3805 E Livingston Ave	Columbus	OH	43227	**800-634-7883**	614-461-8944
Wheels Etc 15186 Foothill Blvd	Fontana	CA	92335	**800-758-4737**	909-350-8200
White Tire Distributors Inc					
1513 Seibel Dr NE	Roanoke	VA	24012	**800-476-9448**	540-342-3183
Wholesale Tire Co PO Box 1637	Victoria	TX	77902	**800-950-8119**	361-578-2945
Wholesale Tire Inc PO Box 1660	Clarksburg	WV	26302	**800-772-5752**	304-624-8465
Woody Tire Co Inc 1606 50th St	Lubbock	TX	79412	**800-530-4818**	806-747-4556

741 TOBACCO PRODUCTS - MFR

741-1 Cigarettes

				Toll-Free	Phone
Carolina Group 714 Green Valley Rd	Greensboro	NC	27408	**888-278-1133**	336-335-7000
NYSE: CG					
Liggett Group Inc 100 Maple Ln	Mebane	NC	27302	**800-334-1686**	919-304-7700
Lorillard Tobacco Co 714 Green Valley Rd	Greensboro	NC	27408	**877-703-0386**	336-335-7000
Philip Morris USA 615 Maury St	Richmond	VA	23224	**800-343-0975***	804-274-2000
*Cust Svc					
Star Scientific Inc 801 Liberty Way	Chester	VA	23836	**800-867-6653**	804-530-0535
NASDAQ: STSI					

741-2 Cigars

				Toll-Free	Phone
Abel Cigar Co 165 Aviador St	Camarillo	CA	93010	**800-848-7335**	805-484-8789
Altadis USA					
5900 N Andrews Ave Suite 1100	Fort Lauderdale	FL	33309	**800-446-5797***	954-772-9000
*Orders					
Conwood Co LP PO Box 217	Memphis	TN	38101	**800-238-2409**	901-248-1700
Finck Cigar Co 414 Vera Cruz St	San Antonio	TX	78207	**800-221-0638***	210-226-4191
*Orders					
General Cigar Co Inc 387 Park Ave S	New York	NY	10016	**800-273-8044**	212-448-3800
House of Windsor Inc PO Box 68	Dallastown	PA	17313	**800-237-4715***	717-244-4501
*Cust Svc					
JC Newman Cigar Co 2701 16th St	Tampa	FL	33605	**800-477-1884***	813-248-2124
*Orders					
John Middleton Inc 418 W Church Rd	King of Prussia	PA	19406	**800-523-1126**	610-265-1400
National Cigar Corp PO Box 97	Frankfort	IN	46041	**800-321-0247**	765-659-3326
Swisher International Group Inc					
PO Box 2230	Jacksonville	FL	32203	**800-843-3731**	904-353-4311
World's Best Rated Cigar Co 6826 NW 77th Ct	Miami	FL	33166	**877-562-4427**	

741-3 Tobacco (Loose) & Snuff

				Toll-Free	Phone
Altadis USA					
5900 N Andrews Ave Suite 1100	Fort Lauderdale	FL	33309	**800-446-5797***	954-772-9000
*Orders					
Conwood Co LP PO Box 217	Memphis	TN	38101	**800-238-2409**	901-248-1700
John Middleton Inc 418 W Church Rd	King of Prussia	PA	19406	**800-523-1126**	610-265-1400
Lane Ltd 2280 Mountain Industrial Blvd	Tucker	GA	30084	**800-221-4134**	770-934-8540
National Tobacco Co LP					
3029 W Muhammad Ali Blvd	Louisville	KY	40212	**800-331-5964***	502-778-4421
*Cust Svc					
RC Owens Co 310 N Blythe St	Gallatin	TN	37066	**800-821-2933**	615-452-5658
Swisher International Group Inc					
PO Box 2230	Jacksonville	FL	32203	**800-843-3731**	904-353-4311

742 TOBACCO STEMMING & REDRYING

				Toll-Free	Phone
Conwood Co LP PO Box 217	Memphis	TN	38101	**800-238-2409**	901-248-1700
Lancaster Leaf Tobacco Co PO Box 897	Lancaster	PA	17608	**800-767-6889**	717-394-2676
Liggett Group Inc 100 Maple Ln	Mebane	NC	27302	**800-334-1686**	919-304-7700

743 TOBACCO STORES

				Toll-Free	Phone
Alfred Dunhill North America Ltd					
645 5th Ave	New York	NY	10022	**800-776-4053**	212-888-4000
Cigar.com Inc 747 N LaSalle Ave 2nd Fl	Chicago	IL	60610	**800-357-9800**	312-334-1010
Cigarettes Cheaper! PO Box 2400	Benicia	CA	94510	**800-243-2737**	707-745-6691
Dunhill Alfred North America Ltd					
645 5th Ave	New York	NY	10022	**800-776-4053**	212-888-4000
Gateway Newstands Inc					
9555 Yonge St Suite 400	Richmond Hill	ON	L4C9M5	**800-942-5351**	905-737-7755
Holts Cigar Co 1522 Walnut St	Philadelphia	PA	19102	**800-523-1641**	215-732-8500
Tinder Box International Ltd					
3 Bala Plaza E Suite 102	Bala Cynwyd	PA	19004	**800-846-3372**	610-668-4220

744 TOBACCO & TOBACCO PRODUCTS - WHOL

				Toll-Free	Phone
800-JR Cigar Inc 301 Rt 10 E	Whippany	NJ	07981	**800-572-4427**	973-884-9555
Albert Guarnieri Co 1133 E Market St	Warren	OH	44483	**800-686-2639**	330-394-5636
Albert H Notini & Sons Inc 225 Aiken St	Lowell	MA	01854	**800-366-8464**	978-459-7151
AMCON Distributing Co 7405 Irvington Rd	Omaha	NE	68122	**800-369-0047**	402-331-3727
AMEX: DIT					
Amster-Kirtz Co 2830 Cleveland Ave NW	Canton	OH	44709	**800-257-9338**	330-493-1800
Anchor Tobacco Co Inc 605 Capitol St	Charleston	WV	25301	**800-213-6134**	304-342-6134
Anter Brothers Co 12501 Elmwood Ave	Cleveland	OH	44111	**800-331-5000**	216-252-4555
AW Marshall Co PO Box 16127	Salt Lake City	UT	84116	**800-273-4713**	801-328-4713
Axton Candy & Tobacco Co PO Box 32219	Louisville	KY	40232	**800-633-7816**	502-634-8000
Boyd-Bluford Inc PO Box 12240	Norfolk	VA	23541	**800-985-2828**	757-855-6036
Burklund Distributors Inc					
2500 N Main St Suite 3	East Peoria	IL	61611	**800-322-2876**	309-694-1900
Charles M Sledd Co 100 E Cove Ext	Wheeling	WV	26003	**800-333-0374**	304-243-1820
Core-Mark International Inc					
395 Oyster Point Blvd					
Suite 415	South San Francisco	CA	94080	**800-622-1713**	650-589-9445
Eby-Brown Co					
280 W Shuman Blvd Suite 280	Naperville	IL	60563	**800-553-8249**	630-778-2800
Farner-Bocken Co 1751 US Hwy 30 E	Carroll	IA	51401	**800-274-8692**	712-792-3503
Franklin Supply Inc 75 Lee St	Franklin	LA	70538	**800-259-3208**	337-828-3208
Fritz Co Inc 1912 Hastings Ave	Newport	MN	55055	**800-328-1652**	651-459-9751
George Melhado & Co 10 Merchant St	Sharon	MA	02067	**800-635-4236**	781-784-5550
Guarnieri Albert Co 1133 E Market St	Warren	OH	44483	**800-686-2639**	330-394-5636
Harold Levinson Assoc Inc 21 Banfi Plaza	Farmingdale	NY	11735	**800-325-2512**	631-962-2400
J Polep Distribution Services Inc					
705 Meadow St	Chicopee	MA	01013	**800-447-6537**	413-592-4141
Keilson-Dayton Co 107 Commerce Park Dr	Dayton	OH	45404	**800-759-3174**	937-236-1070
L & L/Jiroch Distributing Co 1180 58th St	Wyoming	MI	49509	**800-874-5550**	616-530-6600
Levinson Harold Assoc Inc 21 Banfi Plaza	Farmingdale	NY	11735	**800-325-2512**	631-962-2400
Long Wholesale Distribution Center					
PO Box 70	Meridian	MS	39301	**800-748-3847**	601-482-3144
Macon Cigar & Tobacco Co Inc DBA MCT					
Wholesale 575 12th St	Macon	GA	31201	**800-637-0190**	478-743-2236
Marshall AW Co PO Box 16127	Salt Lake City	UT	84116	**800-273-4713**	801-328-4713
MCT Wholesale 575 12th St	Macon	GA	31201	**800-637-0190**	478-743-2236
Notini Albert H & Sons Inc 225 Aiken St	Lowell	MA	01854	**800-366-8464**	978-459-7151
Polep J Distribution Services Inc					
705 Meadow St	Chicopee	MA	01013	**800-447-6537**	413-592-4141
Republic Tobacco 2301 Ravine Way	Glenview	IL	60025	**800-288-8888**	847-832-9700
Saint Joe Distributing 5808 Corporate Dr	Saint Joseph	MO	64507	**800-892-9072**	816-233-8213
Saint Joseph Tobacco Co Inc DBA Saint Joe					
Distributing 5808 Corporate Dr	Saint Joseph	MO	64507	**800-892-9072**	816-233-8213
Tobacco Exporters International USA Ltd					
2280 Mountain Industrial Blvd	Tucker	GA	30084	**800-221-4134**	770-934-8540

745 TOOL & DIE SHOPS

				Toll-Free	Phone
A Finkl & Sons Co 2011 N Southport Ave	Chicago	IL	60614	**800-343-2562**	773-975-2510
A & M Tool & Die Co Inc 64 Mill St	Southbridge	MA	01550	**800-848-4628**	508-764-3241
Ahaus Tool & Engineering Inc PO Box 280	Richmond	IN	47375	**800-962-3571**	765-962-3571
AIP Inc 1290 Maplelawn St	Troy	MI	48084	**800-247-5551**	248-649-7300
Alliance Carolina Tool & Mold Corp					
125 Glenn Bridge Rd	Arden	NC	28704	**800-684-7831**	828-684-7831
Armin Industries 1500 N La Fox St	South Elgin	IL	60177	**800-427-3607**	847-742-1864
Bonell Mfg Co 13521 S Halsted St	Riverdale	IL	60827	**800-323-3110**	708-849-1770
Capitol Technologies Inc					
3615 W Voorde Dr	South Bend	IN	46628	**800-270-5222**	574-232-3311
Carlson Tool & Mfg Corp PO Box 85	Cedarburg	WI	53012	**800-532-2252**	262-377-2020
Chicago Cutting Die Co					
3555 Woodhead Dr	Northbrook	IL	60062	**800-747-3437**	847-509-5800
Cleveland Punch & Die Co					
666 Pratt St PO Box 769	Ravenna	OH	44266	**888-451-4342**	330-296-4342
Cook Technologies Inc N 2nd St	Green Lane	PA	18054	**800-755-2856**	215-234-4535
Custom Mold Engineering Inc					
9780 S Franklin Dr	Franklin	WI	53132	**800-448-2005**	
D-M-E Co 29111 Stephenson Hwy	Madison Heights	MI	48071	**800-626-6653**	248-398-6000
Danly IEM 6779 Engle Rd Suite F	Middleburg Heights	OH	44130	**800-243-2659**	440-239-7600
Danly IEM Punchrite Div					
16065 Industrial Ln SW	Cleveland	OH	44135	**800-232-2659**	216-267-1444
Diamond Tool & Die Inc 508 29th Ave	Oakland	CA	94601	**800-227-1084**	510-534-7050
Die-Namic Inc 12700 Delta Dr	Taylor	MI	48180	**800-817-1270**	734-946-6150
Electro-Magnetic Products Inc					
355 Crider Ave	Moorestown	NJ	08057	**800-234-0071**	856-235-3011
Fansteel Hydro Carbide PO Box 363	Latrobe	PA	15650	**800-245-2476**	724-539-9701
Finkl A & Sons Co 2011 N Southport Ave	Chicago	IL	60614	**800-343-2562**	773-975-2510
Future Products Tool Corp					
885 N Rochester Rd	Clawson	MI	48017	**800-237-5754**	248-588-1060
Genca 9600 18th St N	Saint Petersburg	FL	33716	**800-237-5448**	727-524-3622
General Carbide Corp PO Box C	Greensburg	PA	15601	**800-245-2465**	724-836-3000
General Tool Co 101 Landy Ln	Cincinnati	OH	45215	**800-472-4406**	513-733-5500
Gerber Coburn Optical Inc					
1701 S Cherokee St	Muskogee	OK	74402	**800-262-8761**	918-683-4521
GlobalDie 1130 Minot Ave PO Box 1120	Auburn	ME	04211	**800-910-3747**	
Goodrich Corp Sterling Die Div					
5565 Venture Dr Suite D	Parma	OH	44130	**800-533-1300**	216-267-1300
Hoppe Tool Inc 107 1st Ave	Chicopee	MA	01020	**800-742-6571***	413-592-9213
*Sales					
Hygrade Precision Technologies Inc					
329 Cooke St	Plainville	CT	06062	**800-457-1666**	860-747-5773
Jade Corp 3063 Philmont Ave	Huntingdon Valley	PA	19006	**800-628-4370**	215-947-3333

Classified Section

Company / Address	City	State	ZIP	Toll-Free	Phone
Jasco Tools Inc 1390 Mt Read Blvd PO Box 60497	Rochester	NY	14606	**800-724-5497**	585-254-7000
Jones Metal Products Co 200 N Center St	West Lafayette	OH	43845	**800-552-3468**	740-545-6381
Kell-Strom Tool Co Inc 214 Church St	Wethersfield	CT	06109	**800-851-6851**	860-529-6851
L & F Industries Corp Div of Erie Press Systems 1253 W 12th St PO Box 4061	Erie	PA	16512	**800-222-3608**	814-455-3941
Lempco Industries Inc 5490 Dunham Rd	Cleveland	OH	44137	**800-321-8632**	216-475-2400
Mate Precision Tooling Inc 1295 Lund Blvd	Anoka	MN	55303	**800-328-4492**	763-421-0230
Metco Mfg Co Inc 1993 County Line Rd	Warrington	PA	18976	**888-343-1993**	215-343-1993
Mid-State Machine Products Inc 83 Verti Dr	Winslow	ME	04901	**800-341-4672**	207-873-6136
Millcraft SMS Services LLC PO Box 1107	Oil City	PA	16301	**800-394-4862**	814-677-9400
Moeller Mfg Co Inc Punch & Die Div 43938 Plymouth Oaks Blvd	Plymouth	MI	48170	**800-521-7613**	734-416-0000
Mold-A-Matic Corp DBA MAMCO 147 River St	Oneonta	NY	13820	**800-486-8611**	607-433-2121
Mold Base Industries Inc 7501 Derry St	Harrisburg	PA	17111	**800-241-6656**	717-564-7960
National Tool & Mfg Co Inc 100-124 N 12th St	Kenilworth	NJ	07033	**800-223-0926**	908-276-1600
Oberg Industries Inc 2301 Silverville Rd	Freeport	PA	16229	**800-286-1275**	724-295-2121
OTC Div SPX Corp 655 Eisenhower Dr	Owatonna	MN	55060	**800-533-6127**	507-455-7000
Outokumpu Livernois Engineering Co 25315 Kean St	Dearborn	MI	48124	**800-900-0200**	313-278-0200
Paslin Co 25411 Ryan Rd	Warren	MI	48091	**877-972-7546**	586-758-0200
PCS Co 34488 Doreka Dr	Fraser	MI	48026	**800-521-0546**	586-294-7780
Pennsylvania Tool & Gages Inc PO Box 534	Meadville	PA	16335	**877-827-8285**	814-336-3136
Porter Precision Products Inc 2734 Banning Rd	Cincinnati	OH	45239	**800-543-7041**	513-923-3777
Producto Machine Co 800 Union Ave	Bridgeport	CT	06607	**800-243-9898***	203-367-8675
*Cust Svc					
Prospect Mold Inc 1100 Main St	Cuyahoga Falls	OH	44221	**800-683-3312**	330-929-3311
Remmele Engineering Inc 10 Old Hwy 8 SW	New Brighton	MN	55112	**800-222-7737**	651-635-4100
Rome Tool & Die Co Inc 113 Hemlock St	Rome	GA	30161	**800-241-3369**	706-234-6743
RotoMetrics Group 800 Howerton Ln	Eureka	MO	63025	**800-325-3851**	636-587-3600
RTS Wright Industries LLC PO Box 17914	Nashville	TN	37217	**800-782-4202**	615-361-6600
SB Whistler & Sons Inc PO Box 207	Akron	NY	14001	**800-828-1010**	716-542-4141
Select Tool & Die Corp 60 Heid Ave	Dayton	OH	45404	**800-797-4150**	937-233-9191
SPX Corp OTC Div 655 Eisenhower Dr	Owatonna	MN	55060	**800-533-6127**	507-455-7000
Sterling Die Div Goodrich Corp 5565 Venture Dr Suite D	Parma	OH	44130	**800-533-1300**	216-267-1300
Superior Die Set Corp 900 W Drexel Ave	Oak Creek	WI	53154	**800-558-6040**	414-764-4900
Superior Die Tool & Machine Co 2301 Fairwood Ave	Columbus	OH	43207	**800-292-2181**	614-444-2181
Thor Tool Corp 865 Estabrook St	San Leandro	CA	94577	**800-222-8467**	510-357-6777
Uniloy Milacron Inc 5550 Occidental Hwy	Tecumseh	MI	49286	**800-419-7771**	734-428-8371
Unipunch Products Inc 370 Babcock St	Buffalo	NY	14206	**800-828-7061***	716-825-7960
*Sales					
Walker Tool & Die Inc 2411 Walker Ave NW	Grand Rapids	MI	49544	**888-925-5377**	616-453-5471
Westland Corp PO Box 9268	Wichita	KS	67277	**800-247-1144**	316-721-1144
Whistler SB & Sons Inc PO Box 207	Akron	NY	14001	**800-828-1010**	716-542-4141
Yarema Die & Engineering Co Inc 300 Minnesota Rd	Troy	MI	48083	**800-989-2830**	248-585-2830

746 TOOLS - HAND & EDGE

SEE ALSO Lawn & Garden Equipment; Metalworking Devices & Accessories; Saw Blades & Handsaws

Company / Address	City	State	ZIP	Toll-Free	Phone
Acorn Products Inc 390 W Nationwide Blvd	Columbus	OH	43215	**800-888-4196**	614-222-4400
Allway Tools Inc 1255 Seabury Ave	Bronx	NY	10462	**800-422-5592**	718-792-3636
Ames Taping Tools Inc 3305 Breckenridge Blvd Suite 122	Duluth	GA	30096	**800-408-2801***	770-243-2637
*Cust Svc					
Ames True Temper Inc 465 Railroad Ave	Camp Hill	PA	17011	**800-393-1846**	717-737-1500
Applied Concepts Inc 100 Rudolph Ln	Wexford	PA	15090	**800-466-5028**	724-776-5595
ATI Tools Div Snap-on Inc 2425 Vineyard Ave	Escondido	CA	92029	**800-284-4460**	760-746-8301
Baltimore Tool Works PO Box 27149	Baltimore	MD	21230	**800-752-5533**	410-752-5297
BARCO Industries Inc 1020 MacArthur Rd	Reading	PA	19605	**800-234-8665***	610-374-3117
*Cust Svc					
Bondhus Corp 1400 E Broadway St	Monticello	MN	55362	**800-328-8310***	763-295-2162
*Cust Svc					
Brunner & Lay Inc 9300 King Ave	Franklin Park	IL	60131	**800-872-6899**	847-678-3232
Cal-Van Tools 4300 Waterleaf Ct	Greensboro	NC	27410	**800-537-2636**	336-294-3259
Channellock Inc 1306 S Main St	Meadville	PA	16335	**800-724-3018***	814-724-8700
*Cust Svc					
Charles GG Schmidt & Co Inc 301 W Grand Ave	Montvale	NJ	07645	**800-724-6438**	201-391-5300
Clauss Cutlery Co 223 N Prospect St	Fremont	OH	43420	**800-225-2877***	419-332-7344
*Cust Svc					
Consolidated Devices Inc 19220 San Jose Ave	City of Industry	CA	91748	**800-525-6319**	626-965-0668
Cornwell Quality Tools Co 667 Seville Rd	Wadsworth	OH	44281	**800-321-8356***	330-336-3506
*Cust Svc					
Dasco Pro Inc 340 Blackhawk Park Ave	Rockford	IL	61104	**800-327-2690**	815-962-3727
Duo-Fast Corp 2400 Galvin Dr	Elgin	IL	60123	**888-386-3278***	847-783-5500
*Cust Svc					
Empire Level Mfg Corp 929 Empire Dr	Mukwonago	WI	53149	**800-558-0722**	262-368-2000
Enderes Tool Co Inc 14925 Energy Way	Apple Valley	MN	55124	**800-874-7776**	952-891-1200
Fiskars Brands Inc 2537 Daniels St	Madison	WI	53718	**800-500-4849**	608-259-1649
Fletcher-Terry Co Inc 65 Spring Ln	Farmington	CT	06032	**800-843-3826***	860-677-7331
*Cust Svc					
General Machine Products Co Inc 3111 Old Lincoln Hwy	Trevose	PA	19053	**800-345-6009***	215-357-5500
*Tech Supp					
Grobet File Co of America Inc 750 Washington Ave	Carlstadt	NJ	07072	**800-847-4188**	201-939-6700
Harrington Tools Inc PO Box 39879	Los Angeles	CA	90039	**800-331-6291**	323-245-2142
Hexacon Electric Co 161 W Clay Ave	Roselle Park	NJ	07204	**888-439-2266**	908-245-6200
Huther Brothers Inc 1290 University Ave	Rochester	NY	14607	**888-448-8437**	585-473-9462
Hyde Mfg Co 54 Eastford Rd	Southbridge	MA	01550	**800-872-4933**	508-764-4344
Jensen Tools Inc 7815 S 46th St	Phoenix	AZ	85044	**800-426-1194***	480-968-6241
*Orders					
Kastar Inc PO Box 1616	Racine	WI	53401	**800-645-1142***	262-554-2300
*Cust Svc					
Klein Tools Inc PO Box 599033	Skokie	IL	60659	**800-553-4676***	847-677-9500
*Cust Svc					
Leatherman Tool Group Inc 12106 NE Ainsworth Cir	Portland	OR	97220	**800-847-8665**	503-253-7826
Mac Tools Inc 4635 Hilton Corporate Dr	Columbus	OH	43232	**800-622-8665**	614-755-7000
Malco Products Inc 14080 State Hwy 55 NW	Annandale	MN	55302	**800-328-3530**	320-274-8246
Mann Edge Tool Co PO Box 351	Lewistown	PA	17044	**800-248-8303***	717-248-9628
*Sales					
Marshalltown Co 104 S 8th Ave	Marshalltown	IA	50158	**800-888-0127**	641-753-5999
Matco Tools 4403 Allen Rd	Stow	OH	44224	**800-368-6651**	330-929-4949
Mayhew Steel Products Inc 199 Industrial Blvd	Turners Falls	MA	01376	**800-872-0037**	413-863-4860
Olympia Group Inc 505 S 7th Ave	City of Industry	CA	91746	**800-888-8782**	626-336-4999
QEP Co Inc 1081 Holland Dr	Boca Raton	FL	33487	**800-777-8665**	561-994-5550
NASDAQ: QEPC					
Red Devil Inc 2400 Vauxhall Rd	Union	NJ	07083	**800-423-3845**	908-688-6900
Reed Mfg Co 1425 W 8th St	Erie	PA	16502	**800-666-3691**	814-452-3691
Relton Corp PO Box 60019	Arcadia	CA	91066	**800-423-1505***	626-446-8201
*Cust Svc					
Ripley Co 46 Nooks Hill Rd	Cromwell	CT	06416	**800-528-8665**	860-635-2200
Schmidt Charles GG & Co Inc 301 W Grand Ave	Montvale	NJ	07645	**800-724-6438**	201-391-5300
Seymour Mfg Co Inc 500 N Broadway St	Seymour	IN	47274	**800-457-1909**	812-522-2900
SK Hand Tool Corp 3535 W 47th St	Chicago	IL	60632	**800-822-5575**	773-523-1300
Skyo Industries Inc 171 Brook Ave	Deer Park	NY	11729	**800-645-5535**	631-586-4702
Snap-on Inc ATI Tools Div 2425 Vineyard Ave	Escondido	CA	92029	**800-284-4460**	760-746-8301
Snow & Nealley Co PO Box 876	Bangor	ME	04402	**800-933-6642**	207-947-6642
Stabila Inc 332 Industrial Dr	South Elgin	IL	60177	**800-869-7460**	847-488-0050
Stanley Mechanics Tools 12827 Valley Branch Ln	Dallas	TX	75234	**800-505-4648***	972-247-1367
*Orders					
Stanley Tools Inc 480 Myrtle St	New Britain	CT	06053	**800-262-2161***	860-225-5111
*Cust Svc					
Stanley Tools Worldwide 480 Myrtle St	New Britain	CT	06053	**800-262-2161***	860-225-5111
*Cust Svc					
Stanley Works 1000 Stanley Dr	New Britain	CT	06053	**800-262-2161***	860-225-5111
NYSE: SWK ■ *Cust Svc					
Stride Tool Inc Milbar Div 530 E Washington St	Chagrin Falls	OH	44022	**877-225-8858**	440-247-4600
Superior Tool Co 100 Hayes Dr Unit C	Brooklyn Heights	OH	44131	**800-533-3244**	216-398-8600
Tamco Inc PO Box 371	Monongahela	PA	15063	**800-826-2672**	724-258-6622
UnionTools Inc 390 W Nationwide Blvd	Columbus	OH	43215	**800-848-6657**	614-222-4400
Vaughan & Bushnell Mfg Co 11414 Maple Ave	Hebron	IL	60034	**800-435-6000**	815-648-2446
Vermont American Corp 101 S 5th St Suite 2300	Louisville	KY	40202	**800-626-2834**	502-625-2000
Warner Mfg Co 13435 Industrial Park Blvd	Minneapolis	MN	55441	**800-234-7708**	763-559-4740
Wheeler-Rex PO Box 688	Ashtabula	OH	44005	**800-321-7950**	440-998-2788
Wilton Tool Group 2420 Vantage Dr	Elgin	IL	60123	**800-519-7381**	847-851-1000
WMH Tool Group Inc 2420 Vantage Dr	Elgin	IL	60123	**800-274-6848**	847-649-3010
Wright Tool Co 1 Wright Dr	Barberton	OH	44203	**800-321-2902**	330-848-3702

TOOLS - MACHINE

SEE Machine Tools - Metal Cutting Types; Machine Tools - Metal Forming Types

747 TOOLS - POWER

SEE ALSO Lawn & Garden Equipment; Metalworking Devices & Accessories

Company / Address	City	State	ZIP	Toll-Free	Phone
Air Tool Service Co (ATSCO) 7722 Metric Dr	Mentor	OH	44060	**800-321-3554**	440-942-4475
American Pneumatic Tool Inc 14710 S Maple Ave	Gardena	CA	90248	**800-532-7402**	310-538-2600
Atlas Copco Tools & Assembly Systems 2998 Dutton Rd	Auburn Hills	MI	48326	**800-859-3746**	248-373-3000
Blackstone Industries Inc 16 Stoney Hill Rd	Bethel	CT	06801	**800-441-0625**	203-792-8622
Blount Inc Oregon Cutting Systems Div 4909 SE International Way	Portland	OR	97222	**800-223-5168**	503-653-8881
Chicago Pneumatic Tool Co 1800 Overview Dr	Rock Hill	SC	29730	**800-367-2442**	803-817-7000
DESA International 2701 Industrial Dr	Bowling Green	KY	42101	**800-432-5212***	270-781-9600
*Cust Svc					
Dremel Inc 4915 21st St	Racine	WI	53406	**800-437-3635**	262-554-1390
Dynabrade Inc 8989 Sheridan Dr	Clarence	NY	14031	**800-828-7333***	716-631-0100
*Cust Svc					
Enerpac 6101 N Baker Rd	Milwaukee	WI	53209	**800-433-2766***	262-781-6600
*Cust Svc					
Florida Pneumatic Mfg Corp 851 Jupiter Park Ln	Jupiter	FL	33458	**800-327-9403**	561-744-9500
Greenlee Textron Inc 4455 Boeing Dr	Rockford	IL	61109	**800-435-0786**	815-397-7070
Hilti Inc 5400 S 122nd East Ave	Tulsa	OK	74146	**800-879-8000***	918-252-6000
*Cust Svc					
Hougen Mfg Inc 3001 Hougen Dr	Swartz Creek	MI	48473	**800-462-7818***	810-635-7111
*Orders					
Hydratight Sweeney Products Inc 12508 E Briarwood Ave Unit 1-A	Englewood	CO	80112	**800-448-2524***	303-749-6000
*Cust Svc					
International Staple & Machine Co 629 E Butler Rd	Butler	PA	16002	**800-378-3430**	724-287-7711
Makita USA Inc 14930 Northam St Suite C	La Mirada	CA	90638	**800-462-5482**	714-522-8088
Master Appliance Corp 2420 18th St	Racine	WI	53403	**800-558-9413**	262-633-7791
Milwaukee Electric Tool Corp 13135 W Lisbon Rd	Brookfield	WI	53005	**800-729-3878**	262-781-3600
Oregon Cutting Systems Div Blount Inc 4909 SE International Way	Portland	OR	97222	**800-223-5168**	503-653-8881
Paslode 888 Forest Edge Dr	Vernon Hills	IL	60061	**800-682-3428**	847-634-1900
Pioneer Tool & Forge Inc 101 6th St	New Kensington	PA	15068	**800-359-6408**	724-337-4700
Pneutek Inc 17 Friars Dr	Hudson	NH	03051	**800-431-8665**	603-883-1660
Porter-Cable Corp 4825 Hwy 45 N	Jackson	TN	38305	**800-321-9443**	731-668-8600
Powernail Co 1300 Rose Rd	Lake Zurich	IL	60047	**800-323-1653**	847-634-3000
Precision Twist Drill Co 301 Industrial Ave	Crystal Lake	IL	60012	**800-877-3745**	815-459-2040

				Toll-Free	Phone
Robert Bosch Tool Corp 4300 W Peterson Ave1800 W Central Rd	Mount Prospect	IL	60056	**800-301-8255**	224-223-2000
Ryobi Technologies Inc 1428 Pearman Dairy Rd	Anderson	SC	29625	**800-525-2579**	864-226-6511
SENCO Products Inc 8485 Broadwell Rd	Cincinnati	OH	45244	**800-543-4596***	513-388-2000
*Tech Supp					
Sioux Tools Inc 250 Snap-on Dr	Murphy	NC	28906	**800-722-7290***	828-835-9765
*Orders					
Stihl Inc 536 Viking Dr	Virginia Beach	VA	23452	**800-467-8445***	757-486-9100
*Cust Svc					
Suhner Mfg Inc PO Box 1234	Rome	GA	30162	**800-323-6886**	706-235-8047
Thomas C Wilson Inc 21-11 44th Ave	Long Island City	NY	11101	**800-230-2636**	718-729-3360
WMH Tool Group Inc 2420 Vantage Dr	Elgin	IL	60123	**800-274-6848**	847-649-3010

748 TOUR OPERATORS

SEE ALSO Bus Services - Charter; Travel Agencies

				Toll-Free	Phone
Abercrombie & Kent International Inc 1520 Kensington Rd Suite 212	Oak Brook	IL	60523	**800-323-7308**	630-954-2944
Academy Bus Tours Inc 111 Paterson Ave	Hoboken	NJ	07030	**800-442-7272**	201-339-6000
Adventure Alaska Tours Inc PO Box 64	Hope	AK	99605	**800-365-7057**	907-782-3730
Adventure Center 40 N Main St	Ashland	OR	97520	**800-444-2819**	541-488-2819
Adventure Center Inc 1311 63rd St Suite 200	Emeryville	CA	94608	**800-227-8747**	510-654-1879
Adventure Connection PO Box 475	Coloma	CA	95613	**800-556-6060**	530-626-7385
Adventure Life South America 1655 S 3rd St W Suite 1	Missoula	MT	59801	**800-344-6118**	406-541-2677
Adventures Out West 15001 N 74th St	Scottsdale	AZ	85260	**800-755-0935***	602-996-6100
*Resv					
Africa Adventure Co 5353 N Federal Hwy Suite 300	Fort Lauderdale	FL	33308	**800-882-9453**	954-491-8877
African Travel Inc 1100 E Broadway 2nd Fl	Glendale	CA	91205	**800-421-8907**	818-507-7893
Agape Tours Inc 1210 US Hwy 281	Wichita Falls	TX	76310	**800-460-2641**	940-767-4935
AHI International 6400 Shafer Ct	Rosemont	IL	60018	**800-323-7373**	847-384-4500
Alpha Omega Tours & Charters PO Box 97	Medical Lake	WA	99022	**800-351-1060**	509-624-4116
Alpine Adventure Trails Tours Inc 7495 Lower Thomaston Rd	Macon	GA	31220	**888-478-4004**	478-477-4004
Alyson Adventures Inc 923 White St	Key West	FL	33040	**800-825-9766**	305-296-9935
Ambassadors International Inc 1071 Camelback St	Newport Beach	CA	92660	**800-325-7103**	949-759-5900
NASDAQ: AMIE					
American Coach Lines Inc 2328 10th Ave N Suite 501	Lake Worth	FL	33460	**800-593-1818**	561-721-1170
American Trails West 92 Middle Neck Rd	Great Neck	NY	11021	**800-645-6260**	516-487-2800
AmericanTours International Inc (ATI) 6053 W Century Blvd	Los Angeles	CA	90045	**800-800-8942**	310-641-9953
Ameritours 5018 William Flynn Hwy	Gibsonia	PA	15044	**800-466-3868**	724-443-5600
Anderson Coach & Tour Co 1 Anderson Plaza	Greenville	PA	16125	**800-345-3435**	724-588-8310
ATS Tours 2381 Rosecrans Ave Suite 325	El Segundo	CA	90245	**800-423-2880**	310-643-0044
Australian Pacific Tours (USA) Ltd 4605 Lankershim Blvd Suite 712	North Hollywood	CA	91602	**888-299-1428**	818-755-6392
Backroads 801 Cedar St	Berkeley	CA	94710	**800-462-2848**	510-527-1555
BadgerTour & Travel 200 W Beltline Hwy	Madison	WI	53713	**800-442-8259**	608-255-4040
Banff Adventures Unlimited 207 Caribou St	Banff	AB	T1L1A8	**800-644-8888**	403-762-4554
Bestway Tours & Safaris 8678 Greenall Ave Suite 206	Burnaby	BC	V5J3M6	**800-663-0844**	604-264-7378
Big Five Tours & Expeditions 1551 SE Palm Ct	Stuart	FL	34994	**800-244-3483**	772-287-7995
Bigfoot Adventure Tours Inc 360 Edworthy Way Suite 104	New Westminster	BC	V3L5T8	**888-244-6673**	604-278-8224
Blue Grass Tours Inc 817 Enterprise Dr	Lexington	KY	40510	**800-755-6956**	859-233-2152
Bombard Society Inc 333 Pershing Way	West Palm Beach	FL	33401	**800-862-8537**	561-837-6610
Bonaventure Tours 8 Boudreau Ln	Haute-Aboujagane	NB	E4P5N1	**800-561-1213**	506-532-3674
Borderland Tours 2550 W Calle Padilla	Tucson	AZ	85745	**800-525-7753**	520-882-7650
Breakaway Tours 10 Kingsbridge Garden Cir Suite 400	Mississauga	ON	L5R3K6	**800-465-4257**	905-501-9774
Brendan Worldwide Vacations 21625 Prairie St	Chatsworth	CA	91311	**800-421-8446**	818-428-6000
Brennan Vacations 1402 3rd Ave Suite 717	Seattle	WA	98101	**800-237-7249**	206-622-9155
Brenner Tours 2535 132nd Ave	Hopkins	MI	49328	**800-338-5963**	269-793-7430
Brewster Rocky Mountain Adventures 208 Caribou St	Banff	AB	T1L1A9	**800-691-5085**	403-762-5454
Brewster Transport Co Ltd 100 Gopher St PO Box 1140	Banff	AB	T1L1J3	**800-661-1152**	403-762-6700
Brown Tours 123 Saratoga Rd	Scotia	NY	12303	**800-424-4700**	518-853-4412
Burke International Tours Inc DBA Christian Tours Inc PO Box 890	Newton	NC	28658	**800-476-3900**	828-465-3900
Butterfield & Robinson 70 Bond St Suite 300	Toronto	ON	M5B1X3	**800-678-1147**	416-864-1354
C & E Motorcoach Inc 1470 Bolton Rd	Atlanta	GA	30331	**800-229-0976**	404-799-9979
California Parlor Car Tours 1255 Post St	San Francisco	CA	94109	**800-227-4250**	415-474-7500
CampAlaska Tours PO Box 872247	Wasilla	AK	99687	**800-376-9438**	907-376-9438
Canadian Wild Bird Watching Adventures PO Box 82	Nestor Falls	ON	P0X1K0	**800-561-3166**	
Centennial Travelers 1532 E Mulberry St Suite G	Fort Collins	CO	80524	**800-223-0675**	970-484-4988
Christian Tours Inc PO Box 890	Newton	NC	28658	**800-476-3900**	828-465-3900
Club Europa 802 W Oregon St	Urbana	IL	61801	**800-331-1882**	217-344-5863
Coach Tours Ltd 475 Federal Rd	Brookfield	CT	06804	**800-822-6224**	203-798-8687
Collette Travel Service Inc 162 Middle St	Pawtucket	RI	02860	**800-832-4656**	401-728-3805
Columbia Rafting Adventures Ltd PO Box 942	Fairmont Hot Springs	BC	V0B1L0	**877-706-7238**	250-345-4550
Connection Tours Inc 3596 Lorna Ridge Dr	Birmingham	AL	35216	**888-287-7328**	205-822-7323
Contemporary Tours 125 Mineola Ave Suite 305	Roslyn Heights	NY	11577	**800-627-8873**	516-484-5032
Contiki Holidays 801 E Katella Ave 3rd Fl	Anaheim	CA	92805	**888-266-8454**	
Cox & Kings 25 Davis Blvd	Tampa	FL	33606	**800-999-1758**	813-258-3323
Cultural Experiences Abroad Inc 1400 E Southern Ave Suite B-108	Tempe	AZ	85282	**800-266-4441**	480-557-7900
Cypress Swamp Tours Inc 501 Laroussini St	Westwego	LA	70094	**800-633-0503**	504-581-4501
Cyr Northstar Tours 153 Gilman Falls Ave	Old Town	ME	04468	**800-244-2335**	207-827-2335
Dash Tours 1024 Winnipeg St	Regina	SK	S4R8P8	**800-265-0000**	306-352-2222

				Toll-Free	Phone
DER Travel Services 9501 W Devon Ave Suite 301	Rosemont	IL	60018	**800-782-2424**	847-430-0000
Dipert Travel & Transportation Ltd PO Box 580	Arlington	TX	76004	**800-433-5335**	817-543-3710
Discovery Canada Outdoor Adventure Inc 331 Front St	Kaslo	BC	V0G1M0	**888-300-4453**	250-353-7349
Discovery Charter & Tours 8668 Sunrise Dr	Chilliwack	BC	V2R3J1	**888-468-6877**	604-795-6016
Earthwatch Institute 3 Clock Tower Pl Suite 100	Maynard	MA	01754	**800-776-0188**	978-461-0081
Educational Tours 1123 Sterling Rd	Inverness	FL	34450	**800-343-9003**	352-344-3589
Educational Tours Inc PO Box 828	Northbrook	IL	60065	**800-962-0060**	847-509-0088
Educational Travel Consultants PO Box 1580	Hendersonville	NC	28793	**800-247-7969**	828-693-0412
Educational Travel Tours Inc PO Box 9028	Trenton	NJ	08650	**800-959-9833**	609-587-1550
Especially 4-U Tours & Travel 7303 E Main St Suite 107	Mesa	AZ	85207	**800-331-4968**	480-985-4200
Esplanade Tours 160 Commonwealth Ave Suite L3	Boston	MA	02116	**800-426-5492**	617-266-7465
Fantastic Tours & Travel 6143 Jericho Tpke	Commack	NY	11725	**800-552-6262**	631-462-6262
Flack Tours PO Box 725	Waddington	NY	13694	**800-842-9747**	315-393-7160
Frontier Tours Inc 1923 N Carson St Suite 105	Carson City	NV	89701	**800-648-0912**	775-882-2100
Frontiers International PO Box 959	Wexford	PA	15090	**800-245-1950**	724-935-1577
Gadabout Tours Inc 700 E Tahquitz Canyon Way	Palm Springs	CA	92262	**800-952-5068**	760-325-5556
GAP Adventures 355 Eglinton Ave E	Toronto	ON	M4P1M5	**800-465-5600**	416-260-0999
General Tours 53 Summer St	Keene	NH	03431	**800-221-2216**	603-357-5033
Geographic Expeditions 1008 Gen Kennedy Ave	San Francisco	CA	94129	**800-777-8183**	415-922-0448
Gerber Tours Inc 1400 Old Country Rd Suite 100	Westbury	NY	11590	**800-645-9145**	516-826-5000
GET Travel Group LLC DBA Invasion Tours 3355 Vincent Dr	Pleasant Hill	CA	94523	**800-339-4723**	925-944-5844
GlobalQuest Journeys Ltd 185 Willis Ave 2nd Fl	Mineola	NY	11501	**800-221-3254**	516-739-3690
Globus Cosmos & Monograms 5301 S Federal Cir	Littleton	CO	80123	**800-221-0090**	303-797-2800
Go Ahead Vacations 1 Education St	Cambridge	MA	02141	**800-242-4686**	617-619-1000
Go...With Jo! Tours & Travel Inc 910 Dixieland Rd	Harlingen	TX	78552	**800-999-1446**	956-423-1446
Golden Age Festival Travel 5501 New Jersey Ave	Wildwood Crest	NJ	08260	**800-257-8920**	609-522-6316
Good Time Tours 455 Corday St	Pensacola	FL	32503	**800-446-0886**	850-476-0046
Good Times Travel Club Inc 17132 Magnolia St	Fountain Valley	CA	92708	**888-488-2287**	714-848-1255
Grand European Tours 4000 Kruse Way Pl Bldg 2 Suite 355	Lake Oswego	OR	97035	**800-552-5545**	503-635-9627
Green Tortoise Adventure Travel 494 Broadway	San Francisco	CA	94133	**800-867-8647**	415-956-7500
Greene Coach Charters & Tours Inc 126 Bohannon Ave	Greeneville	TN	37745	**800-338-5469**	423-638-8271
Group Leaders of America Inc 460 E State St	Salem	OH	44460	**800-628-0993**	330-337-1027
Group Tour Co Inc 1110 Vermont Ave NW Suite 407	Washington	DC	20005	**800-424-8895**	202-955-5667
Hesselgrave International PO Box 30768	Bellingham	WA	98228	**800-457-5522**	360-734-3570
Historic Tours of America Inc 201 Front St Suite 224	Key West	FL	33040	**800-868-7482**	305-296-3609
Holiday Expeditions 544 East 3900 S	Salt Lake City	UT	84107	**800-624-6323**	801-266-2087
Holiday Tours Inc 10367 Randleman Rd	Randleman	NC	27317	**800-733-9011**	336-498-9000
Holiday Travel Inc DBA Holiday Vacations 2727 Henry Ave	Eau Claire	WI	54701	**800-826-2266**	715-834-5555
Holiday Vacations 2727 Henry Ave	Eau Claire	WI	54701	**800-826-2266**	715-834-5555
Hospitality Tours 2 Academy Pl	Orleans	MA	02653	**800-966-1331**	508-240-3333
Insight Vacations Inc 801 Katella Ave	Anaheim	CA	92805	**800-582-8380**	
International Expeditions Inc 1 Environs Pk	Helena	AL	35080	**800-633-4734**	205-428-1700
International Student Tours 999 W Broadway Ave Suite 720	Vancouver	BC	V5Z1K5	**888-472-3933**	604-714-1244
Intrav Inc 11969 Westline Industrial Dr	Saint Louis	MO	63146	**800-825-2900**	314-655-6700
Invasion Tours 3355 Vincent Dr	Pleasant Hill	CA	94523	**800-339-4723**	925-944-5844
Isram World of Travel 630 3rd Ave 4th Fl	New York	NY	10017	**800-223-7460**	212-661-1193
ISTours 999 W Broadway Ave Suite 720	Vancouver	BC	V5Z1K5	**888-472-3933**	604-714-1244
Jackson Tour & Travel Inc 4500 55 Highland Village Suite 258	Jackson	MS	39216	**800-873-8572**	601-981-8415
Janssen's Charters & Tours 1623 Woods Rd E	Port Orchard	WA	98366	**800-922-5044**	360-871-2446
Julian Tours 1500 N Beauregard St Suite 110	Alexandria	VA	22311	**800-541-7936**	703-379-2300
Katmai Coastal Bear Tours PO Box 1501	Homer	AK	99603	**800-532-8338**	
KE Adventure Travel 1131 Grand Ave	Glenwood Springs	CO	81601	**800-497-9675**	970-384-0001
Ker & Downey Inc 6703 Highway Blvd	Katy	TX	77494	**800-423-4236**	281-371-2500
Kincaid Coach Lines Inc 9207 Woodend Rd	Edwardsville	KS	66111	**800-998-1901**	913-441-6200
Kootenay River Runners PO Box 81	Edgewater	BC	V0A1E0	**800-599-4399**	250-347-9210
Lamers Tour & Travel 1126 W Boden Ct	Milwaukee	WI	53221	**800-236-8687**	414-281-2002
Lampert Tours Inc 1359 N Wells St	Chicago	IL	60610	**800-331-9640**	312-951-2866
Lindblad Expeditions 96 Morton St 9th Fl	New York	NY	10014	**800-397-3348**	212-765-7740
Magic Bus Co 16 Roncesvalles Ave	Toronto	ON	M6R2K3	**877-371-8747**	416-516-7433
Marketing Services Inc DBA Adventures Out West 15001 N 74th St	Scottsdale	AZ	85260	**800-755-0935***	602-996-6100
*Resv					
Marshall Field's Travel Service 700 Nicollet Mall	Minneapolis	MN	55402	**800-316-6166**	612-375-2884
Maupintour Inc 10650 W Charleston Blvd	Las Vegas	NV	89135	**800-255-4266**	702-260-3600
Mayflower Tours Inc 1225 Warren Ave PO Box 490	Downers Grove	IL	60515	**800-323-7604**	630-435-8500
Micato Safaris 15 W 26th St 11th Fl	New York	NY	10010	**800-642-2861**	212-545-7111
Mid-American Coaches Inc PO Box 1609	Washington	MO	63090	**800-365-8687**	636-239-4700
Midnight Sun Adventure Travel 1845-B Fort St	Victoria	BC	V8R1J6	**800-255-5057**	250-480-9409
Milne Travel 40 Patchen Rd	South Burlington	VT	05403	**800-698-1415**	802-864-0204
Montana River Outfitters 923 10th Ave N	Great Falls	MT	59401	**800-800-8218**	406-761-1677
Morgan Coach Lines Inc 236 Greenfield Rd PO Box 259	South Deerfield	MA	01373	**800-344-3979**	413-665-8036
Mountain Travel Sobek 1266 66th St Suite 4	Emeryville	CA	94608	**888-687-6235**	510-594-6000
Musiker Discovery Programs Inc 1326 Old Northern Blvd	Roslyn	NY	11576	**888-878-6637**	516-621-3939
Nawas International Travel Service Inc 777 Post Rd 3rd Fl	Darien	CT	06820	**800-221-4984**	203-656-3033
New Horizons Tour & Travel Inc 2727 Spring Arbor Rd	Jackson	MI	49203	**800-327-4695**	517-788-6822
New Orleans Hospitality Enterprises Inc 610 S Peter St	New Orleans	LA	70130	**800-543-6332**	504-587-1600
New World Tours Inc 7920 Gainsford Ct	Bristow	VA	20136	**800-322-7733**	703-643-9800

				Toll-Free	Phone
New York Tours 1414 Grand St	Hoboken	NJ	07030	**800-735-8530**	
Nichols Five Star Charters & Tours					
PO Box 709	Fond du Lac	WI	54936	**877-373-6456**	920-929-8030
Northern Light Balloon Expeditions					
PO Box 1695	Sedona	AZ	86339	**800-230-6222**	928-282-2274
Northern Tours 2740 Bauer St	Eau Claire	WI	54701	**800-735-8687**	715-834-1463
Off the Beaten Path 7 E Beall St	Bozeman	MT	59715	**800-445-2995**	406-586-1311
Old West Tours 3432 Limestone Dr	Rosamond	CA	93560	**800-868-7777**	661-256-4091
Olivia Cruises & Resorts					
434 Brannan St	San Francisco	CA	94107	**800-631-6277**	415-962-5700
Onondaga Coach Corp PO Box 277	Auburn	NY	13021	**800-451-1570**	315-255-2216
Orange Belt Stages 2134 E Mineral King Ave	Visalia	CA	93292	**800-266-7433**	559-733-4408
Orion Pacific Inc 8682 N Olive Ave	Orange	CA	92865	**800-827-7890**	714-283-8687
Overseas Adventure Travel 347 Congress St	Boston	MA	02210	**800-493-6824**	
Pacific Delight Tours Inc 3 Park Ave 38th Fl	New York	NY	10016	**800-221-7179**	212-818-1781
Panorama Balloon Tours PO Box 218	Del Mar	CA	92014	**800-455-3592**	760-271-3467
Paragon Tours 25 Market St	Swansea	MA	02777	**800-999-5050**	508-379-1976
ParkEast Tours 100 Environs Pk	Helena	AL	35080	**800-223-6078**	205-428-1700
Perillo Tours 577 Chestnut Ridge Rd	Woodcliff Lake	NJ	07677	**800-431-1515**	201-307-1234
Pilgrim Tours & Travel Inc					
3821 Main St PO Box 268	Morgantown	PA	19543	**800-322-0788**	610-286-0788
Polynesian Adventure Tours Inc					
1049 Kikowaena Pl	Honolulu	HI	96819	**800-622-3011**	808-833-3000
Premier Tours 1430 Walnut St 2nd Fl	Philadelphia	PA	19102	**800-545-1910**	215-893-9966
Presley Tours Inc					
16 Presley Park Dr PO Box 58	Makanda	IL	62958	**800-621-6100**	618-549-0704
Princess Tours 2815 2nd Ave Suite 400	Seattle	WA	98121	**800-426-0442**	206-336-6000
Rail Europe Group 44 S Broadway 11th Fl	White Plains	NY	10601	**800-438-7245**	914-682-2999
Raz Transportation 11655 SW Pacific Hwy	Portland	OR	97223	**888-684-3322**	503-684-3322
Red Sail Sports Inc					
1 Ferry Bldg Suite 255	San Francisco	CA	94111	**877-733-7245**	415-981-4411
REI Adventures PO Box 1938	Sumner	WA	98390	**800-622-2236**	253-437-1100
Rivers Oceans & Mountains Adventures Inc					
(ROAM) 7025 Beggs Rd	Nelson	BC	V1L5P6	**877-271-7626**	250-354-2056
Roberts Hawaii Inc					
680 Iwilei Rd Dole Office Bldg Suite 700	Honolulu	HI	96817	**800-831-5541**	808-523-7750
Rohrer Bus Service 190 Pic Rite Ln	Lewisburg	PA	17837	**800-487-8687**	570-524-5800
Royal Coach Tours 630 Stockton Ave	San Jose	CA	95126	**800-927-6925**	408-279-4801
Royal Tours Inc PO Box 998	Randleman	NC	27317	**800-997-6925**	336-629-9080
RSVP Vacations 2535 25th Ave S	Minneapolis	MN	55406	**800-328-7787**	
Runaway Tours Inc 1040 Vannes Ave	San Francisco	CA	94109	**800-622-0723**	415-268-8200
Sanborn Tours Inc 2015 S 10th St	McAllen	TX	78503	**800-395-8482**	956-682-9872
Scenic Airlines Inc 2705 Airport Dr	North Las Vegas	NV	89032	**800-634-6801**	702-638-3300
Scholastic Tours Inc 3841 Nostrand Ave	Brooklyn	NY	11235	**800-221-6209**	718-934-9400
SeaEurope Holidays Inc					
6801 Lake Worth Rd Suite 103	Lake Worth	FL	33467	**800-533-3755**	561-432-4100
Senior Tours Canada Inc 225 Eglinton Ave W	Toronto	ON	M4R1A9	**800-268-3492**	416-322-1529
Seniors Unlimited LLC 53 W Huron St	Pontiac	MI	48342	**800-837-1333**	248-338-1333
Short Hills Tours PO Box 310	Short Hills	NJ	07078	**800-348-6871**	973-467-2113
Silver Fox Tours & Motorcoaches					
3 Silver Fox Dr	Millbury	MA	01527	**800-342-5998**	508-865-6000
Silverado Tours Inc 241 Prado Rd	San Luis Obispo	CA	93401	**800-478-4287**	805-544-7658
Sky High Red Rock Balloon Adventures					
105 Canyon Diablo	Sedona	AZ	86351	**800-258-3754**	928-284-0040
Southern Coach Co 1300 E Pettigrew St	Durham	NC	27701	**800-222-4793**	919-688-1230
Specialty Tours Inc					
3095 S Parker Rd Suite 150	Aurora	CO	80014	**800-342-4299**	303-337-7488
Sports Leisure Vacations					
9521-H Folsom Blvd	Sacramento	CA	95827	**800-951-5556**	916-361-2051
Sports Travel Inc 60 Main St PO Box 50	Hatfield	MA	01038	**800-662-4424**	413-247-7678
Straight A Tours & Travel					
715 N Ferncreek Ave	Orlando	FL	32803	**800-237-5440**	407-896-1242
Student Tours Inc 2 Webaqua Rd	Vineyard Haven	MA	02568	**800-331-7093**	508-693-5078
Student Travel Services Inc					
1413 Madison Pk Dr	Glen Burnie	MD	21061	**800-648-4849**	410-859-4200
Sundial Special Vacations Inc					
2609 Hwy 101 N Suite 103	Seaside	OR	97138	**800-547-9198**	503-738-3324
Sunny Land Tours Inc 166 Main St	Hackensack	NJ	07601	**800-783-7839**	201-487-2150
Super Holiday Tours 116 Gatlin Ave	Orlando	FL	32806	**800-327-2116**	407-851-0060
Tag-A-Long Expeditions 452 N Main St	Moab	UT	84532	**800-453-3292**	435-259-8946
Talbot Tours Inc 1952 Camden Ave	San Jose	CA	95124	**800-662-9933**	408-879-0101
Tauck World Discovery 10 Norden Pl	Norwalk	CT	06855	**800-468-2825**	203-899-6500
TCS Expeditions 710 2nd Ave Suite 840	Seattle	WA	98104	**800-727-7477**	206-727-7300
Timberwolf Tours Ltd					
51404 RR 264 Suite 34	Spruce Grove	AB	T7Y1E4	**888-467-9697**	780-470-4966
Toto Tours Ltd 1326 W Albion Ave	Chicago	IL	60626	**800-565-1241**	773-274-8686
Tourco Inc 16 E Pond Rd	Nobleboro	ME	04555	**800-537-5378**	207-563-2288
Trafalgar Tours 801 E Katella Ave	Anaheim	CA	92805	**866-544-4434**	
Trans-Bridge Tours 1155 MacArthur Rd	Whitehall	PA	18052	**800-962-9135**	610-776-8687
Transat AT Inc					
1160 Cargo A-1 Rd Montreal					
International Airport	Mirabel	QC	J7N1G9	**877-470-1011**	450-476-1011
TSE: TRZ					
Travcoa 2424 SE Bristol Suite 310	Newport Beach	CA	92660	**800-992-2003**	949-476-2800
Travel Adventures Inc 1175 S Lapeer Rd	Lapeer	MI	48446	**800-356-2737**	810-664-1777
Travel Bound Inc 599 Broadway 12th Fl	New York	NY	10012	**800-808-9541**	212-334-1350
Travel Mates of Virginia Inc PO Box 2	Harrisonburg	VA	22803	**888-262-4863**	540-434-4155
Travel Tours Inc 2111 W Hwy 51 PO Box 40	Wagoner	OK	74477	**800-331-3192**	918-485-4595
Traveland 1055 Wilshire Blvd Suite 1705	Los Angeles	CA	90017	**800-321-6336**	213-482-2323
TravelQuest International 305 Double D Dr	Prescott	AZ	86303	**800-830-1998**	928-445-7754
TrekAmerica PO Box 189	Rockaway	NJ	07866	**800-221-0596**	973-983-1144
Tri-State Travel Inc PO Box 307	Galena	IL	61036	**800-779-4869**	815-777-0820
Tumlare Corp 2128 Bellmore Ave	Bellmore	NY	11710	**800-223-4664**	516-781-0322
Upstate Tours & Travel					
207 Geyser Rd	Saratoga Springs	NY	12866	**800-237-5252**	518-584-5252
USA Student Travel					
5080 Robert J Mathews Pkwy	El Dorado Hills	CA	95762	**888-949-0650**	916-939-6805
VBT Bicycle Vacations 614 Monkton Rd	Bristol	VT	05443	**800-245-3868**	802-453-4811
Venture Travel & Tours Inc 965 Bethel Rd	Columbus	OH	43214	**800-859-8687**	614-442-8687
VentureOut 575 Pierce St Suite 604	San Francisco	CA	94117	**888-431-6789**	415-626-5678
VIP Tour & Charter Bus Co 129-137 Fox St	Portland	ME	04101	**800-337-4457**	207-772-4457
Wade Tours Inc 797 Burdeck St	Schenectady	NY	12306	**800-955-9233**	518-355-4500
Walking Adventures International					
PO Box 871000	Vancouver	WA	98687	**800-779-0353**	360-260-9393
West Coast Connection					
318 Indian Trace Suite 336	Weston	FL	33326	**888-868-7882**	954-888-9780
Western Discovery International					
507 Casazza Dr Suite C	Reno	NV	89502	**800-843-5061**	775-329-9933
White Mountain Adventures					
107 Boulder Crescent Suite 7	Canmore	AB	T1W1K9	**800-408-0005**	403-678-4099
White Star Tours 26 E Lancaster Ave	Reading	PA	19607	**800-437-2323**	610-775-5000
Wilderness Travel 1102 9th St	Berkeley	CA	94710	**800-368-2794**	510-558-2488
Wings Tours Inc					
11350 McCormick Rd Suite 703	Hunt Valley	MD	21031	**800-869-4647**	410-771-0925
Winn Transportation 1831 Westwood Ave	Richmond	VA	23227	**800-296-9466**	804-358-9466
Wisconsin Coach Lines Inc					
1520 Arcadian Ave	Waukesha	WI	53186	**800-236-2015**	262-542-8861
WorldStrides					
590 Peter Jefferson Pkwy Suite 300	Charlottesville	VA	22911	**800-468-5899**	434-982-8600

749 TOY STORES

				Toll-Free	Phone
Build-A-Bear Workshop Inc					
1954 Innerbelt Business Center Dr	Saint Louis	MO	63114	**888-560-2327**	314-423-8000
Creative Kid Stuff 4313 Upton Ave S	Minneapolis	MN	55410	**800-353-0710***	612-929-2431
*Orders					
FAO Schwarz 767 5th Ave Suite 401	New York	NY	10153	**800-426-8697**	
Hobbytown USA 6301 S 58th St	Lincoln	NE	68516	**800-869-0424**	402-434-5385
HobbyTron.com 1053 S 1675 W	Orem	UT	84058	**800-494-1778**	801-434-7664
SmarterKids.com Inc					
2 Lower Ragsdale Rd Suite 200	Monterey	CA	93940	**800-293-9314**	831-333-2000
Toys 'R' Us Inc 1 Geoffrey Way	Wayne	NJ	07470	**800-869-7787**	973-617-3500
NYSE: TOY					

750 TOYS, GAMES, HOBBIES

SEE ALSO Baby Products; Bicycles & Bicycle Parts & Accessories; Computer Software - Games & Entertainment Software

				Toll-Free	Phone
Action Products International Inc					
1101 N Keller Rd Suite E	Orlando	FL	32810	**800-772-2846**	407-481-8007
NASDAQ: APII					
Alexander Doll Co Inc DBA Madame Alexander					
615 W 131st St	New York	NY	10027	**800-229-5192**	212-283-5900
American Plastic Toys Inc 799 Ladd Rd	Walled Lake	MI	48390	**800-521-7080**	248-624-4881
Annalee Mobilitee Dolls Inc 50 Reservoir Rd	Meredith	NH	03253	**800-433-6557***	603-279-6544
*Cust Svc					
Atari Inc 417 5th Ave 8th Fl	New York	NY	10016	**800-898-1438**	212-726-6500
NASDAQ: ATAR					
Atlas Model Railroad Co Inc 378 Florence Ave	Hillside	NJ	07205	**800-872-2521***	908-687-0880
*Orders					
Bachmann Industries Inc 1400 E Erie Ave	Philadelphia	PA	19124	**800-356-3910***	215-533-1600
*Cust Svc					
Binney & Smith Inc 1100 Church Ln	Easton	PA	18044	**800-272-9652**	610-253-6271
BRIO Corp N 120 W 18485 Freistadt Rd	Germantown	WI	53022	**888-274-6869***	262-250-3240
*Cust Svc					
Caron International 111 W 40th St 28th Fl	New York	NY	10018	**800-868-9194**	212-382-6400
Charles Craft Inc					
21381 Charles Craft Ln PO Box 1049	Laurinburg	NC	28352	**800-277-1009**	910-844-3521
Community Products LLC DBA Community					
Playthings 359 Gibson Hill Rd	Chester	NY	10918	**800-777-4244**	845-572-3410
Craft House International 5570 Enterprise Blvd	Toledo	OH	43612	**800-537-0295**	419-536-8351
Creativity for Kids 9450 Allen Dr	Cleveland	OH	44125	**800-311-8684**	216-643-4660
Daisy Mfg Co Inc 400 W Stribling Dr	Rogers	AR	72756	**800-643-3458**	479-636-1200
Dakin LLC 32942 Lyons Ave Suite 215	Newhall	CA	91321	**800-777-6990***	661-222-9900
*Cust Svc					
Dimensions Inc 1801 N 12th St	Reading	PA	19604	**800-523-8452**	610-939-9900
Douglas Cuddle Toys Co Inc					
69 Krif Rd PO Box D	Keene	NH	03431	**800-992-9002**	603-352-3414
Effanbee Doll Co 459 Hurley Ave	Hurley	NY	12443	**888-362-3655**	845-339-8246
Electronic Arts Inc					
209 Redwood Shores Pkwy	Redwood City	CA	94065	**877-324-2637***	650-628-1500
NASDAQ: ERTS ■ *Sales					
Estes-Cox Corp 1295 H St	Penrose	CO	81240	**800-525-7561**	719-372-6565
Fisher-Price Inc 636 Girard Ave	East Aurora	NY	14052	**800-432-5437**	716-687-3000
Fleer/Skybox International LP					
1120 Rt 73 S Suite 300	Mount Laurel	NJ	08054	**800-343-6816**	856-231-6200
Flexible Flyer Inc 100 Tubb Ave	West Point	MS	39773	**800-521-6233***	662-494-4732
*Cust Svc					
Franklin Sports Industry Inc					
17 Campanelli Pkwy	Stoughton	MA	02072	**800-225-8647**	781-344-1111
Gayla Industries Inc 6401 Antoine Dr	Houston	TX	77291	**800-231-7508**	713-681-2411
Goffa International Corp					
5301 11th St	Long Island City	NY	11101	**800-969-7864**	718-361-8883
Goldberger Doll Mfg Co Inc 538 Johnson Ave	Brooklyn	NY	11237	**800-452-3655**	718-366-5800
Great Planes Model Distributors Co					
1608 Interstate Dr	Champaign	IL	61826	**800-637-7660**	217-398-6300
Guidecraft USA 66 Grand Ave Suite 207	Englewood	NJ	07631	**800-544-6526**	201-894-5401
Gund Inc 1 Runyons Ln	Edison	NJ	08817	**800-448-4863***	732-248-1500
*Cust Svc					
Hanover Accessories Inc					
3555 Holly Ln N Suite 60	Plymouth	MN	55447	**888-509-6100**	763-509-6100
Hasbro Inc 1027 Newport Ave	Pawtucket	RI	02861	**800-242-7276**	401-431-8697
NYSE: HAS					
Hasbro Inc Parker Brothers Div					
200 Narragansett Park Dr	Pawtucket	RI	02862	**888-836-7025**	
Hasbro Inc Playskool Div 1027 Newport Ave	Pawtucket	RI	02861	**800-242-7276**	401-431-8697
Hasbro Inc Tiger Electronics Div					
1027 Newport Ave	Pawtucket	RI	02861	**800-844-3733**	401-431-8697
International Playthings Inc					
75D Lackawanna Ave	Parsippany	NJ	07054	**800-631-1272**	973-316-2500
JAKKS Pacific Inc					
22619 Pacific Coast Hwy Suite 250	Malibu	CA	90265	**877-875-2557**	310-456-7799
NASDAQ: JAKK					
Klutz 455 Portage Ave	Palo Alto	CA	94306	**800-737-4123**	650-857-0888
K'NEX Industries 2990 Bergey Rd PO box 700	Hatfield	PA	19440	**800-543-5639**	215-997-7722
LeapFrog Enterprises Inc					
6401 Hollis St Suite 150	Emeryville	CA	94608	**800-701-5327**	510-420-5000
NYSE: LF					
Learning Resources 380 N Fairway Dr	Vernon Hills	IL	60061	**800-222-3909**	847-573-8400
Lee Middleton Original Dolls Inc					
480 Olde Worthington Rd Suite 110	Westerville	OH	43082	**800-242-3285**	614-901-0604
LEGO Systems Inc 555 Taylor Rd	Enfield	CT	06082	**800-243-4870**	860-749-2291
Lionel LLC 26750 23 Mile Rd	Chesterfield	MI	48051	**800-454-6635**	586-949-4100
Little Tikes Co 2180 Barlow Rd	Hudson	OH	44236	**800-321-0183***	330-650-3000
*Cust Svc					

Toll-Free *Phone*

Mag-Nif Inc 8820 East Ave .... Mentor OH 44060 **800-869-5463** 440-946-4308
Maple City Rubber Co 55 Newton St .... Norwalk OH 44857 **800-841-9434** 419-668-8261
Marvel Enterprises Inc 417 5th Ave.......... New York NY 10016 **800-217-9158** 212-576-4000
NYSE: MVL
Mattel Inc 333 Continental Blvd .... El Segundo CA 90245 **800-524-8697*** 310-252-2000
NYSE: MAT ■ *Cust Svc
Midwest Products Co Inc 400 S Indiana St...... Hobart IN 46342 **800-348-3497*** 219-942-1134
*Orders
Newell Rubbermaid Inc Home & Family Group
10B Glenlake Pkwy Suite 600 .... Atlanta GA 30328 **800-434-4314** 770-407-3800
Nintendo of America Inc 4822 150th Ave NE .. Redmond WA 98052 **800-255-3700*** 425-882-2040
*Cust Svc
Ohio Art Co 1 Toy St......................... Bryan OH 43506 **800-641-6226** 419-636-3141
Paris Co Inc 822 Main St .... Oxford ME 04271 **800-678-5112** 207-539-8221
Parker Brothers Div Hasbro Inc
200 Narragansett Park Dr .... Pawtucket RI 02862 **888-836-7025**
Patch Products Inc 1400 E Inman Pkwy .... Beloit WI 53511 **800-524-4263** 608-362-6896
Pioneer National Latex Co 246 E 4th St .... Ashland OH 44805 **800-537-6723** 419-289-3300
Plaid Enterprises Inc 3225 Westech Dr....... Norcross GA 30092 **800-842-4197** 678-291-8100
Playmobil USA Inc 26 Commerce Dr .... Cranbury NJ 08512 **800-752-9662** 609-395-5566
Playskool Div Hasbro Inc 1027 Newport Ave... Pawtucket RI 02861 **800-242-7276** 401-431-8697
Poof-Slinky Inc
45400 Helm St PO Box 701394 .... Plymouth MI 48170 **800-829-9502** 734-454-9552
Pop Rocket Inc 6330 San Vicente Blvd ..... Los Angeles CA 90048 **800-238-0798** 323-932-4300
Princess Soft Toys 7664 W 78th St........ Minneapolis MN 55439 **800-252-7638** 952-829-5772
Processed Plastic Co 1001 Aucutt Rd..... Montgomery IL 60538 **800-323-6165** 630-892-7981
Radica USA Ltd 13628-A Beta Rd............... Dallas TX 75244 **800-803-9611** 972-490-4247
NASDAQ: RADA
Radio Flyer Inc 6515 W Grand Ave .... Chicago IL 60707 **800-621-7613** 773-637-7100
Revell-Monogram LLC 725 Landwehr Rd ..... Northbrook IL 60062 **800-833-3570** 847-770-6100
Rose Art Industries Inc 6 Regent St .... Livingston NJ 07039 **800-272-9667** 973-535-1313
Russ Berrie & Co Inc 111 Bauer Dr........... Oakland NJ 07436 **800-272-7877** 201-337-9000
NYSE: RUS
Scholastic Corp 557 Broadway............. New York NY 10012 **800-724-6527*** 212-343-6100
NASDAQ: SCHL ■ *Cust Svc
SIG Mfg Co Inc 401 S Front St............ Montezuma IA 50171 **800-247-5008*** 641-623-5154
*Sales
Spin Master Ltd 450 Front St W.............. Toronto ON M5V1B6 **800-622-8339** 416-364-6002
Steiff North America 425 Paramont Dr .... Raynham MA 02767 **800-830-0429** 508-828-2377
Swibco Inc 4810 Venture Rd .... Lisle IL 60532 **877-794-2261** 630-968-8900
Tara Toy Corp 40 Adams Ave............... Hauppauge NY 11788 **800-899-8272** 631-273-8697
Team Losi Inc 4710 E Guasti Rd .... Ontario CA 91761 **800-338-4639** 909-390-9595
Testor Corp 440 Blackhawk Park Ave......... Rockford IL 61104 **800-962-3741** 815-962-6654
Tiger Electronics Div Hasbro Inc
1027 Newport Ave...................... Pawtucket RI 02861 **800-844-3733** 401-431-8697
Twin Hills Collectables LLC 70 Hickory Rd...... Hickory KY 42051 **800-210-8230** 270-856-2277
Ty Inc 280 Chestnut Ave.................. Westmont IL 60559 **800-876-8000*** 630-920-1515
*Cust Svc
Uncle Milton Industries Inc
5717 Corsa Ave.................. Westlake Village CA 91362 **800-869-7555** 818-707-0800
Universal Mfg Co Inc 5450 Deramus Ave ... Kansas City MO 64120 **800-821-2724** 816-231-2771
University Games Corp 2030 Harrison St.. San Francisco CA 94110 **800-347-4818** 415-503-1600
US Playing Card Co 4590 Beech St .... Cincinnati OH 45212 **800-863-1333** 513-396-5700
Vermont Teddy Bear Co Inc
6655 Shelburne Rd .... Shelburne VT 05482 **800-988-8277** 802-985-3001
NASDAQ: BEAR
VTech Electronics North America LLC
1155 W Dundee St Suite 130 .... Arlingtn Heights IL 60004 **800-521-2010** 847-400-3600
Walthers William K Inc 5601 W Florist Ave... Milwaukee WI 53218 **800-877-7171** 414-527-0770
Wham-O Inc 5903 Christie Ave............. Emeryville CA 94608 **877-469-4266** 510-596-4202
William K Walthers Inc 5601 W Florist Ave... Milwaukee WI 53218 **800-877-7171** 414-527-0770
Wizards of the Coast Inc 1801 Land Ave SW.... Renton WA 98055 **800-324-6496*** 425-226-6500
*Cust Svc
World Wide Press Inc 801 River Dr S .... Great Falls MT 59405 **800-548-9888** 406-727-7812

TRAILERS - TRUCK

SEE Truck Trailers

751 TRAILERS (TOWING) & TRAILER HITCHES

Toll-Free *Phone*

Cequent Towing Products
47774 Anchor Ct W.................... Plymouth MI 48170 **800-521-0510** 734-656-3000
Cequent Trailer Products 1050 Indianhead Dr... Mosinee WI 54455 **800-604-9466** 715-693-1700
CM Trailers Inc 200 County Rd PO Box 680...... Madill OK 73446 **888-268-7577** 580-795-5536
Creek Hill Welding 50 Mill St............... Christiana PA 17509 **866-593-8188** 610-593-8188
Dethmers Mfg Co Inc 4010 320th St........... Boyden IA 51234 **800-543-3626** 712-725-2302
Exiss Aluminum Trailers Inc
900 Exiss Blvd Box D .... El Reno OK 73036 **877-993-9477** 405-262-6471
EZ Loader Boat Trailers Inc
717 N Hamilton St...................... Spokane WA 99202 **800-398-5623** 509-489-0181
Featherlite Inc PO Box 320 .... Cresco IA 52136 **800-800-1230** 563-547-6000
NASDAQ: FTHR
Gooseneck Trailer Mfg Co 4400 E Hwy 21 .... Bryan TX 77808 **800-688-5490** 979-778-0034
Hawkeye Leisure Trailers Ltd
1419 11th St N .... Humboldt IA 50548 **888-874-9943** 515-332-1802
Load Rite Trailers Inc 265 Lincoln Hwy.... Fairless Hills PA 19030 **800-562-3783** 215-949-0500
Midwest Industries Inc PO Box 235 .... Ida Grove IA 51445 **800-859-3028** 712-364-3365
Quality S Mfg Inc 3801 N 43rd Ave............. Phoenix AZ 85019 **800-521-8181** 602-233-3499
Reese Products Inc 2602 College Ave.......... Goshen IN 46528 **800-326-1090** 574-537-6800
Rigid Hitch Inc 3301 W Burnsville Pkwy ...... Burnsville MN 55337 **800-624-7630*** 952-895-5001
*Cust Svc
Sundowner Trailers Inc 9805 S State Hwy 48... Coleman OK 73432 **800-654-3879** 580-937-4255
Take 3 Trailers Inc 2007 Longwood Dr....... Brenham TX 77833 **866-428-2533** 979-337-9568
Unique Functional Products Corp
135 Sunshine Ln .... San Marcos CA 92069 **800-854-1905** 760-744-1610
Valley Automotive Inc
32501 Dequindre Rd .... Madison Heights MI 48071 **800-344-3112*** 248-588-6900
*Cust Svc

752 TRAINING & CERTIFICATION PROGRAMS - COMPUTER & INTERNET

Toll-Free *Phone*

Canterbury Consulting Group Inc
352 Stokes Rd Suite 200.................. Medford NJ 08055 **800-873-2040** 609-953-0044
NASDAQ: CITI
Career Blazers Inc Learning Centers Div
290 Madison Ave....................... New York NY 10017 **800-284-3232** 212-725-7900
Corporate Solutions 303 Riding Trail Ct....... Leesburg VA 20176 **800-622-4686**
Element K LLC 500 Canal View Blvd.......... Rochester NY 14623 **800-434-3466** 585-240-7500
ET3 LLC DBA ExecuTrain Corp
2500 Northwinds Pkwy Suite 600.......... Alpharetta GA 30004 **800-908-7246** 770-521-1964
Global Knowledge Network Corp
9000 Regency Pkwy Suite 500 .... Cary NC 27512 **800-268-7737** 919-461-8600
Intellinex LLC 925 Euclid Ave Suite 1800...... Cleveland OH 44115 **866-835-3276** 216-685-6000
Learning Tree International Inc
6053 W Century Blvd Suite 200 .... Los Angeles CA 90045 **800-843-8733*** 310-417-9700
NASDAQ: LTRE ■ *Cust Svc
MeasureUp Inc
2325 Lakeview Pkwy Suite 175............ Alpharetta GA 30004 **800-649-1687** 678-356-5000
MindLeaders.com Inc
851 W 3rd Ave Bldg 3................... Columbus OH 43212 **800-223-3732** 614-781-7300
MSI/Canterbury Inc 200 Lanidex Plaza....... Parsippany NJ 07054 **800-638-2252**
NETg Inc 1751 W Diehl Rd 2nd Fl .... Naperville IL 60563 **800-265-1900*** 630-369-3000
*Cust Svc
New Horizons Computer Learning Centers Inc
1900 S State College Blvd Suite 100......... Anaheim CA 92806 **888-222-3380** 714-712-1000
New Horizons Worldwide Inc
1900 S State College Blvd Suite 200......... Anaheim CA 92806 **800-725-3276** 714-940-8000
NASDAQ: NEWH
Productivity Point International Inc
2950 Gateway Center Blvd.............. Morrisville NC 27560 **800-774-2727** 919-379-5611
ProsoftTraining 410 N 44th St Suite 600....... Phoenix AZ 85008 **888-776-7638** 602-794-4199
NASDAQ: POSO
Sento Corp 808 E Utah Valley Dr .... American Fork UT 84003 **800-868-8448** 801-492-2000
NASDAQ: SNTO
SkillSoft PLC 107 Northeastern Blvd............ Nashua NH 03062 **877-545-5763** 603-324-3000
NASDAQ: SKIL

753 TRAINING PROGRAMS - CORPORATE

Toll-Free *Phone*

AchieveGlobal Inc
8875 Hidden River Pkwy Suite 400........... Tampa FL 33637 **800-659-6090** 813-631-5500
American Management Assn (AMA)
1601 Broadway .... New York NY 10019 **800-262-9699** 212-586-8100
American Management Assn International
Keye Productivity Center Div
600 AMA Way .... Saranac Lake NY 12983 **800-262-9699*** 518-891-1500
*Cust Svc
Bob Pike Group 7620 W 78th St .... Edina MN 55439 **800-383-9210** 952-829-1954
Breakthrough Learning Inc
17800 Woodland Ave.................. Morgan Hill CA 95037 **800-221-3637** 408-779-0701
Canterbury Consulting Group Inc
352 Stokes Rd Suite 200.................. Medford NJ 08055 **800-873-2040** 609-953-0044
NASDAQ: CITI
Carlson Marketing Group PO Box 59159.... Minneapolis MN 55459 **888-521-2200** 763-212-4520
Corpedia Corp DBA Corpedia Education
2020 N Central Ave Suite 1050............ Phoenix AZ 85004 **877-629-8724** 602-712-9919
Creative Training Techniques International Inc
7620 W 78th St.......................... Edina MN 55439 **800-383-9210** 952-829-1954
Don Hutson Organization
516 Tennessee St Suite 219 .... Memphis TN 38103 **800-647-9166** 901-767-0000
Elite Business Services PO Box 9630 .. Rancho Santa Fe CA 92067 **800-204-3548**
Executive Enterprises Institute
2 Shaw's Cove........................ New London CT 06320 **800-831-8333** 860-701-5900
Forum Corp 265 Franklin St 4th Fl .... Boston MA 02110 **800-367-8611** 617-523-7300
Franklin Covey Co
2200 W Parkway Blvd .... Salt Lake City UT 84119 **800-827-1776** 801-975-1776
NYSE: FC
Fred Pryor Seminars 9757 Metcalf Ave ... Overland Park KS 66212 **800-780-8476** 913-967-8599
General Physics Corp
6095 Marshalee Dr Suite 300 .... Elkridge MD 21075 **800-727-6677** 410-379-3600
HealthStream Inc 209 10th Ave S Suite 450 ... Nashville TN 37203 **800-933-9293** 615-301-3100
NASDAQ: HSTM
Hinda Incentives Inc 2440 W 34th St .... Chicago IL 60608 **800-621-4412** 773-890-5900
Insight Information Co
214 King St W Suite 300................. Toronto ON M5H3S6 **888-777-1707** 416-777-2020
ITC Learning Corp
1616 Anderson Rd Suite 109 .... McLean VA 22102 **800-638-3757** 703-286-0756
Jones Knowledge Inc 9697 E Mineral Ave.... Englewood CO 80112 **800-453-5663** 303-792-3111
Keye Productivity Center Div American
Management Assn International
600 AMA Way .... Saranac Lake NY 12983 **800-262-9699*** 518-891-1500
*Cust Svc
LearnCom Inc 714 Industrial Dr .... Bensenville IL 60106 **800-824-8889** 630-227-1080
Levinson Institute Inc 28 Main St Suite 100 ..... Jaffrey NH 03452 **800-290-5735** 603-532-4700
MSI/Canterbury Inc 200 Lanidex Plaza....... Parsippany NJ 07054 **800-638-2252**
National Businesswomen's Leadership Assn
PO Box 419107 .... Kansas City MO 64141 **800-258-7246** 913-432-7755
National Seminars Group
6901 W 63rd St................. Shawnee Mission KS 66202 **800-258-7246** 913-432-7755
Nelson Motivation Inc
12245 World Trade Dr Suite C .... San Diego CA 92128 **800-575-5521** 858-487-1046
Novations Group Inc 745 Boylston St Suite 300.... Boston MA 02116 **888-652-9975** 617-247-0214
NTL Institute for Applied Behavioral Science
300 N Lee St Suite 300................ Alexandria VA 22314 **800-777-5227** 703-548-8840
Pacific Institute 1709 Harbor Ave SW.......... Seattle WA 98126 **800-426-3660** 206-628-4800
Priority Management Systems Inc
13251 Delf Pl Suite 420................. Richmond BC V6V2A2 **800-221-9031** 604-214-7772
Productivity Inc 100 Commerce Dr Suite 120.... Shelton CT 06484 **800-966-5423** 203-225-0451
Productivity Point International Inc
2950 Gateway Center Blvd.............. Morrisville NC 27560 **800-774-2727** 919-379-5611
Rockhurst University Continuing Education
Center Inc PO Box 419107............. Kansas City MO 64141 **800-258-7246** 913-432-7755

Name / Address	City	State	ZIP	Toll-Free	Phone
Sandler Sales Institute 10411 Stevenson Rd	Stevenson	MD	21153	**800-638-5686**	410-653-1993
SkillPath Seminars 6900 Squibb Rd	Shawnee Mission	KS	66202	**800-873-7545**	913-362-3900
SkillSoft PLC 107 Northeastern Blvd. *NASDAQ: SKIL*	Nashua	NH	03062	**877-545-5763**	603-324-3000
TeamSource Technical Services 800 Paloma Dr Suite 230	Round Rock	TX	78664	**800-489-0585**	512-275-0941
US Learning Inc 516 Tennessee St Suite 219	Memphis	TN	38103	**800-647-9166**	901-767-5700
Wilson Learning Corp 8000 W 78th St Suite 200	Edina	MN	55439	**800-328-7937**	952-944-2880

754 TRAINING PROGRAMS (MISC)

SEE ALSO Children's Learning Centers; Training & Certification Programs - Computer & Internet; Training Programs - Corporate

Name / Address	City	State	ZIP	Toll-Free	Phone
Academy for Guided Imagery Inc 30765 Pacific Coast Hwy Suite 369	Malibu	CA	90265	**800-726-2070**	
Audio-Digest Foundation DBA Cme Unlimited; Infomedix 1577 E Chevy Chase Dr	Glendale	CA	91206	**800-423-2308**	818-240-7500
Canter & Assoc Inc 12975 Coral Tree Pl **Cust Svc*	Los Angeles	CA	90066	**800-733-1711***	310-578-4700
Ed Necco & Assoc 804 Solida Rd	South Point	OH	45680	**877-506-3226**	740-894-1520
Fourth R Inc 11410 NE 124th St Suite 142	Kirkland	WA	98034	**800-821-8653**	425-814-1001
Fred Astaire Dance Studios Inc 10 Bliss Rd	Longmeadow	MA	01106	**800-278-2473**	413-567-3200
Global University 1211 S Glenstone Ave	Springfield	MO	65804	**800-443-1083**	417-862-9533
Institute for Integral Development PO Box 2172	Colorado Springs	CO	80901	**800-544-9562**	719-634-7943
Learn.com Inc 14000 NW 4th St	Sunrise	FL	33325	**800-544-1023**	954-233-4000
Megatech Corp 555 Woburn St	Tewksbury	MA	01876	**800-767-6342**	978-937-9600
Natural Golf Corp 1200 E Business Center Dr Suite 400	Mount Prospect	IL	60056	**888-628-4653**	847-321-4000
Outward Bound USA 100 Mystery Point Rd	Garrison	NY	10524	**866-467-7651**	845-424-4000
Res-Care Inc 10140 Linn Station Rd *NASDAQ: RSCR*	Louisville	KY	40223	**800-866-0860**	502-394-2100
Smith & Wesson Academy 299 Page Blvd	Springfield	MA	01104	**800-331-0852**	413-846-6461

755 TRANSCRIPTION SERVICES - MEDICAL

Name / Address	City	State	ZIP	Toll-Free	Phone
Heartland Information Services 3103 Executive Pkwy Suite 500	Toledo	OH	43606	**800-626-3830**	419-578-6300
MED-TECH Resource Inc 2053 Franklin Way	Marietta	GA	30067	**800-538-7498**	770-955-7292
MediGrafix Inc 11205 Wright Cir Suite 120	Omaha	NE	68144	**877-284-5147**	402-333-3323
MedQuist Inc 5 Greentree Ctr Suite 311	Marlton	NJ	08053	**800-233-3030**	856-596-8877
Scribes Online 21670 Ridgetop Cir Suite 100	Sterling	VA	20166	**800-873-4710**	
Spheris 720 Cool Springs Blvd Suite 200	Franklin	TN	37067	**800-368-1717**	615-261-1500
Thomas Transcription Services Inc 550 Balmoral Cir Suite 305	Jacksonville	FL	32218	**888-878-2889**	904-751-5058
Transcend Services Inc 945 E Paces Ferry Rd NE Suite 1475 *NASDAQ: TRCR*	Atlanta	GA	30326	**800-225-7552**	404-836-8000
Webmedx Inc 564 Alpha Dr	Pittsburgh	PA	15238	**888-932-6339**	412-968-9244

756 TRANSFORMERS - POWER, DISTRIBUTION, SPECIALTY

Name / Address	City	State	ZIP	Toll-Free	Phone
Advance Transformer Co 10275 W Higgins Rd	Rosemont	IL	60018	**800-322-2086**	847-390-5000
AFP Transformers Inc 206 Talmedge Rd	Edison	NJ	08817	**800-843-1215**	732-248-0305
Bodine Co 236 S Mount Pleasant Rd	Collierville	TN	38027	**800-223-5778**	901-853-7211
Delta Star Inc 270 Industrial Rd	San Carlos	CA	94070	**800-892-8673**	650-508-2850
Johnson Electric Coil Co 821 Watson St	Antigo	WI	54409	**800-826-9741**	715-627-4367
MGM Transformer Co 5701 Smithway St	Commerce	CA	90040	**800-423-4366**	323-726-0888
MTE Corp PO Box 9013	Menomonee Falls	WI	53051	**800-253-8210**	262-253-8200
Niagara Transformer Corp 1747 Dale Rd	Buffalo	NY	14225	**800-817-5652**	716-896-6500
Olsun Electrics Corp 10901 Commercial St	Richmond	IL	60071	**800-336-5786**	815-678-2421
Pauwels Transformers 1 Pauwels Dr	Washington	MO	63090	**800-833-6582**	636-239-6783
Shape LLC 2105 Corporate Dr	Addison	IL	60101	**800-367-5811**	630-620-8394
Siemens Power Transmission & Distribution Inc 7000 Siemens Rd	Wendell	NC	27591	**800-347-6659**	919-365-2200
T & R Electric Supply Co Inc PO Box 180	Colman	SD	57017	**800-843-7994**	605-534-3555
Tech-Tran Corp 50 Indel Ave PO Box 232	Rancocas	NJ	08073	**800-257-9420**	609-267-6750
VanTran Industries Inc PO Box 20128 **Sales*	Waco	TX	76702	**800-433-3346***	254-772-9740
Virginia Transformer Corp 220 Glade View Dr	Roanoke	VA	24012	**800-882-3944**	540-345-9892
Ward Transformer Sales & Service Inc PO Box 90609	Raleigh	NC	27675	**800-334-9600**	919-787-3553
Waukesha Electric Systems Inc 400 S Prairie Ave	Waukesha	WI	53186	**800-835-2732**	262-547-0121

757 TRANSLATION SERVICES

SEE ALSO Language Schools

Name / Address	City	State	ZIP	Toll-Free	Phone
Berlitz International Inc 400 Alexander Pk	Princeton	NJ	08540	**800-257-9449**	609-514-9650
Language Line Services 1 Lower Ragsdale Dr Bldg 2	Monterey	CA	93940	**877-886-3885**	831-648-7541
Linguistics Systems Inc 201 Broadway	Cambridge	MA	02139	**800-654-5006**	617-864-3900
TripleInk 60 S 6th St Suite 2600	Minneapolis	MN	55402	**800-632-1388**	612-342-9800

758 TRANSPLANT CENTERS - BLOOD STEM CELL

Name / Address	City	State	ZIP	Toll-Free	Phone
Barnes-Jewish Hospital Bone Marrow & Stem Cell Transplant Program 1 Barnes-Jewish Hospital Plaza Steinberg Bldg 5th Fl	Saint Louis	MO	63110	**800-635-2371**	314-454-8304
City of Hope National Medical Center Hematology & Hematopoietic Cell Transplantation Div 1500 E Duarte Rd	Duarte	CA	91010	**800-535-7119**	626-256-4673
Froedtert Hospital Bone Marrow Transplant Program 9200 W Wisconsin Ave	Milwaukee	WI	53226	**800-272-3666**	414-805-3666
Indiana Blood & Marrow Transplantation Saint Francis Hospital 1600 Albany St 6th Tower	Beech Grove	IN	46107	**800-361-0016**	317-782-7355
Indiana University Cancer Center Bone Marrow & Stem Cell Transplant Team 550 N University Blvd Suite 6611	Indianapolis	IN	46202	**877-814-7594**	317-274-1114
INOVA Fairfax Hospital Transplant Center 8503 Arlington Blvd Suite 200	Fairfax	VA	22031	**800-358-8831**	703-970-3178
Medical City Hospital Transplant Center 7777 Forest Ln Bldg A 12 S	Dallas	TX	75230	**800-348-4318**	972-566-6547
Presbyterian-Saint Luke's Medical Center Blood & Marrow Transplant Program 1719 E 19th Ave	Denver	CO	80218	**877-268-9300**	303-839-6953
Roswell Park Cancer Institute Blood & Marrow Transplantation Program Elm & Carlton Sts	Buffalo	NY	14263	**800-685-6825**	716-845-3516
Seattle Cancer Care Alliance 825 Eastlake Ave E PO Box 19023	Seattle	WA	98109	**800-804-8824**	206-288-1024
Shands Hospital at the University of Florida Blood & Bone Marrow Transplant Program 1600 SW Archer Rd Box 100403	Gainesville	FL	32610	**800-749-7424**	352-265-0062
Texas Transplant Institute 7700 Floyd Curl Dr	San Antonio	TX	78229	**800-298-7824**	210-575-3817
Tufts-New England Medical Center Bone Marrow Transplant Program 750 Washington St Box 542	Boston	MA	02111	**866-636-5001**	617-636-0154
University of Alabama at Birmingham Bone Marrow Transplant Program 619 S 19th St P302 West Pavilion	Birmingham	AL	35249	**800-822-6478**	205-934-1911
University of Iowa Hospitals & Clinics Blood & Marrow Transplantation Program 200 Hawkins Dr C332 General Hospital	Iowa City	IA	52242	**800-944-8220**	319-356-3337
University Medical Center Blood & Marrow Transplantation Program 1501 N Campbell Ave PO Box 24-5176	Tucson	AZ	85724	**800-831-9205**	520-694-6172
University of Miami Sylvester Comprehensive Cancer Center Blood & Marrow Transplant Program PO Box 016960	Miami	FL	33101	**800-545-2292**	305-243-1000
University of Utah Hospital & Clinics Blood & Marrow Transplant Program 50 N Medical Dr	Salt Lake City	UT	84132	**800-664-8268**	801-585-2044
Veterans Affairs Puget Sound Medical Center Marrow Transplant Unit 1660 S Columbian Way	Seattle	WA	98108	**800-329-8387**	206-764-2189
Western Pennsylvania Hospital Hematology/Oncology Patient Care Unit 4800 Friendship Ave Suite 2303 NT	Pittsburgh	PA	15224	**866-680-0004**	412-578-4707
Winship Cancer Institute Bone Marrow Transplant/Hematology/Leukemia Clinic Emory Univ School of Medicine 1365 Clifton Rd NE Suite B1106	Atlanta	GA	30322	**888-946-7447**	404-778-4342

759 TRANSPORTATION EQUIPMENT & SUPPLIES - WHOL

Name / Address	City	State	ZIP	Toll-Free	Phone
A & K Railroad Materials Inc PO Box 30076	Salt Lake City	UT	84130	**800-453-8812**	801-974-5484
AAR Aircraft Turbine Center 1100 N Wood Dale Rd 1 AAR Pl	Wood Dale	IL	60191	**800-422-2213**	630-227-2000
AAR Corp 1100 N Wood Dale Rd 1 AAR Pl *NYSE: AIR*	Wood Dale	IL	60191	**800-422-2213**	630-227-2000
AAR Distribution 1100 N Wood Dale Rd 1 AAR Pl	Wood Dale	IL	60191	**800-422-2213**	630-227-2000
Aerotech World Trade Corp 11 New King St	White Plains	NY	10604	**800-499-2982**	914-681-3000
Aircraft Instrument & Radio Co Inc 1853 S Eisenhower Ct	Wichita	KS	67209	**800-835-2243**	316-945-0445
AirLiance Materials LLC PO Box 661008	Chicago	IL	60666	**877-233-5800**	847-233-5800
Airparts Co Inc PO Box 9268	Fort Lauderdale	FL	33310	**800-392-4999**	954-739-3575
Alexander/Ryan Marine & Safety Co of Louisiana 7759 Townsend Pl	New Orleans	LA	70126	**800-743-0501**	504-243-0501
Argo International Corp 140 Franklin St	New York	NY	10013	**877-274-6468**	212-431-1700
Atlantic Track & Turnout Co PO Box 1589 **Cust Svc*	Bloomfield	NJ	07003	**800-631-1274***	973-748-5885
Aviall Inc 2750 Regent Blvd *NYSE: AVL*	Dallas	TX	75261	**800-284-2551**	972-586-1000
Birmingham Rail & Locomotive Co Inc PO Box 530157	Birmingham	AL	35253	**800-241-2260**	205-424-7245
Boat Owners Warehouse 311 SW 24th St	Fort Lauderdale	FL	33315	**888-262-8799**	954-522-7998
DAC International Inc 6702 McNeil Dr	Austin	TX	78729	**800-527-2531**	512-331-5323
Defender Industries Inc 42 Great Neck Rd	Waterford	CT	06385	**800-628-8225**	860-701-3400
Dodson Aviation Inc 2110 Montana Rd	Ottawa	KS	66067	**800-255-0034**	785-242-4000
Donovan Marine Inc 6316 Humphreys St	Harahan	LA	70123	**800-347-4464**	504-488-5731
Dreyfus-Cortney & Lowery Brothers Rigging 4500 N Galvez St	New Orleans	LA	70117	**800-228-7660**	504-944-3366
Edmo Distributors Inc 12830 E Mirabeau Pkwy	Spokane	WA	99216	**800-235-3300**	509-535-8280
ERS Industries Inc 1005 Indian Church Rd	West Seneca	NY	14224	**800-993-6446**	716-675-2040
Fisheries Supply Co 1900 N Northlake Way	Seattle	WA	98103	**800-426-6930**	206-632-4462
Freundlich Supply Co Inc 2200 Arthur Kill Rd	Staten Island	NY	10309	**800-221-0260**	718-356-1500
GC Supply Inc 3587 Clover Ln	New Castle	PA	16105	**800-248-4653**	724-658-1741
Heli-Mart Inc 3184 Airway Ave Suite E	Costa Mesa	CA	92626	**800-826-6899**	714-755-2999

	City	State	ZIP	Toll-Free	Phone
Helicopter Support Inc (HSI)					
124 Quarry Rd PO Box 111068	Trumbull	CT	06611	**800-795-6051**	203-416-4000
HSI (Helicopter Support Inc)					
124 Quarry Rd PO Box 111068	Trumbull	CT	06611	**800-795-6051**	203-416-4000
Industry-Railway Suppliers Inc 811 Golf Ln	Bensenville	IL	60106	**800-728-0029**	630-766-5708
Jerry's Marine Service					
100 SW 16th St	Fort Lauderdale	FL	33315	**800-432-2231**	954-525-0311
JMA Railroad Supply Co 381 S Main Pl	Carol Stream	IL	60188	**800-874-0643**	630-653-9224
Kellogg Marine Supply Inc 5 Enterprise Dr	Old Lyme	CT	06371	**800-243-9303**	860-434-6002
Land 'N' Sea Distributing Inc					
3131 N Andrews Ave Ext	Pompano Beach	FL	33064	**800-432-7652**	954-792-5436
Lewis Marine Supply Co Inc					
220 SW 32nd St	Fort Lauderdale	FL	33315	**800-327-3792***	954-523-4371
*Sales					
M & M Aerospace Hardware Inc					
10000 NW 15th Terr	Miami	FL	33172	**800-533-5155**	305-592-5155
Meridian Aerospace Group Ltd					
3796 Vest Mill Rd	Winston-Salem	NC	27103	**800-538-7767**	336-765-5454
National Salvage & Service Corp					
417 S Walnut St	Bloomington	IN	47401	**800-769-8437**	812-339-9000
Ottosen Propeller & Accessories Inc					
105 S 28th St	Phoenix	AZ	85034	**800-528-7551**	602-275-8514
Parker Hannifin Corp Aircraft Wheel & Brake Div					
1160 Center Rd	Avon	OH	44011	**800-272-5464**	440-937-6211
PartsBase Inc 905 Clint Moore Rd	Boca Raton	FL	33487	**888-322-6896**	561-953-0700
Paxton Co 1111 Ingleside Rd	Norfolk	VA	23502	**800-234-7290**	757-853-6781
PTMW Inc 3501 NW US Hwy 24	Topeka	KS	66618	**800-842-1546**	785-232-7792
Rails Co 101 Newark Way	Maplewood	NJ	07040	**800-217-2457**	973-763-4320
Sabine Universal Products Inc PO Box 295	Port Arthur	TX	77641	**800-482-9446**	409-982-9446
Shorty's Truck & Railroad Car Parts Inc					
7744 Alabama Hwy 144 PO Box 270	Alexandria	AL	36250	**800-227-7995**	256-892-3131
SkyTech Inc					
Martin State Airport 701 Wilson Point Rd Hanger 3	Baltimore	MD	21220	**888-386-3596**	410-574-4144
Spencer Industries Inc 19308 68th Ave S	Kent	WA	98032	**800-367-5646**	253-796-1100
Unical Aviation Inc 4775 Irwindale Ave	Irwindale	CA	91706	**800-813-1901**	626-813-1901
Unirex Inc 9310 E 37th St N	Wichita	KS	67226	**800-397-1257**	316-636-1228
United Marine Inc 490 NW South River Dr	Miami	FL	33128	**800-432-8575**	305-545-8445
Valley Power Systems Inc					
425 S Hacienda Blvd	City of Industry	CA	91745	**800-924-4265**	626-333-1243
Valtec International Inc PO Box 747	Ivoryton	CT	06442	**800-825-8321**	860-767-8211
Van Bortel Aircraft Inc 4900 S Collins St	Arlington	TX	76018	**800-759-4295**	817-468-7788
Washington Chain & Supply Inc PO Box 3645	Seattle	WA	98124	**800-851-3429**	206-623-8500
Yingling Aircraft Inc 2010 Airport Rd	Wichita	KS	67277	**800-835-0083**	316-943-3246
ZAP 501 4th St	Santa Rosa	CA	95401	**800-251-4555***	707-525-8658
*Orders					

760 TRAVEL AGENCIES

SEE ALSO Tour Operators; Travel Agency Networks

	City	State	ZIP	Toll-Free	Phone
A1SuperCruises.com					
3380 Fairline Farms Rd Suite 7	West Palm Beach	FL	33414	**866-878-8785**	561-204-2669
ABC Corporate Services					
6400 Shafer Ct Suite 310	Rosemont	IL	60018	**800-722-5179**	847-384-6868
Abercrombie & Kent International Inc					
1520 Kensington Rd Suite 212	Oak Brook	IL	60523	**800-323-7308**	630-954-2944
Abracadabra! Cruises					
1735 Roswell Rd Suite 100	Marietta	GA	30062	**800-474-5678**	770-509-8080
Adelman Travel Group					
6980 N Port Washington Rd	Milwaukee	WI	53217	**800-231-3999**	414-352-7600
ADTRAV Travel Management					
4555 S Lake Pkwy	Birmingham	AL	35244	**800-476-2952**	205-444-4800
AESU Travel Inc 3922 Hickory Ave	Baltimore	MD	21211	**800-638-7640**	410-366-5494
Alamo Travel Group Inc					
9000 Wurzbach Rd	San Antonio	TX	78240	**800-692-5266**	210-593-0084
Alaska Tour & Travel					
9170 Jewel Lake Rd Suite 202	Anchorage	AK	99502	**800-208-0200**	907-245-0200
Alaska Travel Adventures Inc					
18384 Redmond Way	Redmond	WA	98052	**800-323-5757**	425-497-1212
Alaska Vacation Packages PO Box 622	Palmer	AK	99645	**888-745-8872**	907-745-8872
All Aboard Cruise Center					
PO Box 540685	Grand Prairie	TX	75054	**800-567-5379**	972-262-4638
All Aboard Cruises Inc 11114 SW 127th Ct	Miami	FL	33186	**800-883-8657**	305-385-8657
All Cruise Travel 1213 Lincoln Ave Suite 205	San Jose	CA	95125	**800-227-8473**	408-295-1200
All-Inclusive Vacations Inc 1595 Iris St	Lakewood	CO	80215	**866-980-6483**	303-980-6483
All-Waves Cruise & Travel					
20381 Lake Forest Dr Suite B-3	Lake Forest	CA	92630	**800-449-0767**	949-829-8031
Altour-Classic Cruise & Travel					
19720 Ventura Blvd Suite A	Woodland Hills	CA	91364	**800-688-8500**	818-346-8747
Anchors Away Cruise Center					
3702 Independence Pl	Rocklin	CA	95677	**888-516-6306**	916-625-0722
Anchors Away Cruise Outlet					
3750 Caribou St PO Box 871723	Wasilla	AK	99687	**800-580-3494**	907-373-3494
Andavo Travel Inc					
5325 S Valentia Way	Greenwood Village	CO	80111	**800-685-0038**	303-694-3322
Apple Vacations Inc					
101 NW Point Blvd	Elk Grove Village	IL	60007	**800-365-2775**	847-640-1150
Austin Travel 265 Spagnoli Rd	Melville	NY	11747	**800-645-7466**	516-465-1000
Avanti Destinations Inc 851 SW 6th St	Portland	OR	97204	**800-422-5053**	503-295-1100
Azumano Travel Service Inc 400 SW 4th Ave	Portland	OR	97204	**800-777-2018**	503-294-2000
Balboa Travel Management Inc					
5414 Oberlin Dr Suite 300	San Diego	CA	92121	**800-359-8773**	858-678-3700
Best Price Cruises					
8930 S Federal Hwy	Port Saint Lucie	FL	34952	**800-672-7485**	772-344-3330
Best Travel Inc 8600 W Bryn Mawr Ave	Chicago	IL	60631	**800-323-3015**	773-380-0150
Bob's Cruises 635 Fourth Line	Oakville	ON	L6L5W4	**800-361-6688**	905-338-2077
Boeing Travel Management Co					
325 JS McDonnell Blvd Bldg 303 M-S3069236	Hazelwood	MO	63042	**800-243-8292**	314-551-4025
Bon Voyage Travel 1640 E River Rd Suite 115	Tucson	AZ	85718	**800-439-7963**	520-797-1110
Branson Deals 152 Christie Ln	Walnut Shade	MO	65771	**800-221-5692**	
Brennco Travel Services Inc					
6600 College Blvd Suite 130	Overland Park	KS	66211	**800-955-1909**	913-660-0121
Bridge Travel Alliance					
2200 Powell St Suite 130	Emeryville	CA	94608	**800-762-5885**	510-496-8266
Brownell World Travel					
813 Shades Creek Pkwy	Birmingham	AL	35209	**800-999-3960**	205-802-6222
BTS Travel & Tours 323 Silvergrove Dr NW	Calgary	AB	T3B4M4	**877-929-9019**	403-286-1205
Campbell Travel					
14800 Landmark Blvd Suite 155	Dallas	TX	75254	**800-357-7972**	972-716-2500
Caravelle Travel Management Inc					
1900 E Golf Rd Suite 1100	Schaumburg	IL	60173	**800-323-0902**	847-619-8300
Carefree Vacations Inc					
9710 Scranton Rd Suite 300	San Diego	CA	92121	**800-800-8505**	858-450-4060
Cass Tours 109 N Maple St Suite B	Corona	CA	92880	**800-593-6510**	951-371-3511
Casto Travel Inc					
900 Lafayette St Suite 105	Santa Clara	CA	95050	**800-832-3445**	408-984-7000
Certified Vacations Group Inc					
110 E Broward Blvd	Fort Lauderdale	FL	33301	**800-233-7260**	954-522-1440
CI Travel 101 W Main St Suite 800	Norfolk	VA	23510	**800-222-3577**	757-627-8000
City Escape Holidays					
13470 Washington Blvd Suite 101	Marina del Rey	CA	90292	**800-222-0022**	310-827-5031
Classic Custom Vacations 5893 Rue Ferrari	San Jose	CA	95138	**800-221-3949**	408-287-4550
Club Med Inc 75 Valencia Ave	Coral Gables	FL	33134	**800-258-2633**	305-925-9000
Collette Vacations 162 Middle St	Pawtucket	RI	02860	**800-340-5158**	401-727-9000
Compass Travel Service Inc 840 Ogden Ave	Westmont	IL	60559	**800-300-1606**	630-986-1606
Conlin Travel Inc 3270 Washtenaw Ave	Ann Arbor	MI	48104	**800-426-6546**	734-677-0900
Consolidated Cruises 300 Market St	Kingston	PA	18704	**800-732-2628**	570-283-8480
Corporate Travel Management Group					
450 E 22nd St Suite 100	Lombard	IL	60148	**800-323-3800**	630-691-9100
Costamar Travel Inc					
1421 E Oakland Park Blvd	Fort Lauderdale	FL	33334	**800-444-7171**	954-630-0060
Covington International Travel					
4401 Dominion Blvd	Glen Allen	VA	23060	**800-922-9238**	804-747-7077
Creative Leisure International					
951 Transport Way	Petaluma	CA	94954	**800-426-6367**	707-778-1800
Crown Travel & Cruises					
240 Newton Rd Suite 106	Raleigh	NC	27615	**800-869-7447**	919-870-1986
Cruise Brokers 4802 Gunn Hwy Suite 141	Tampa	FL	33624	**800-409-1919**	813-288-9597
Cruise Center The 11713 101st Ave E	Puyallup	WA	98373	**800-454-7174**	253-845-5330
Cruise Concepts 34034 US Hwy 19 N	Palm Harbor	FL	34684	**800-752-7963**	727-784-7245
Cruise Connection LLC					
7932 N Oak Suite 210	Kansas City	MO	64118	**800-572-0004**	816-420-8688
Cruise Connections Inc					
1422 S Stratford Rd	Winston-Salem	NC	27103	**800-248-7447**	336-659-9772
Cruise Holidays International Inc					
701 Carlson Pkwy	Minnetonka	MN	55305	**800-866-7245**	
Cruise Marketing International					
3401 Investment Blvd Suite 3	Hayward	CA	94545	**800-578-7742**	510-784-8500
Cruise People Inc					
10191 W Sample Rd Suite 215	Coral Springs	FL	33065	**800-642-2469**	954-753-0069
Cruise People Ltd					
1252 Lawrence Ave E Suite 210	Don Mills	ON	M3A1C3	**800-268-6523**	416-444-2410
Cruise Shop The 700 Pasquinelli Dr Suite C	Westmont	IL	60559	**800-622-6456**	630-325-7447
Cruise by Sue 1792 Whitecap Cir	Fort Myers	FL	33903	**888-486-1135**	239-997-7874
Cruise & Travel Inc 26212 Carmel St	Laguna Hills	CA	92656	**888-484-3732**	949-360-8081
Cruise & Travel Shoppe					
5809 NW 48th Ave	Coconut Creek	FL	33073	**800-957-4477**	954-427-3216
Cruise Vacation Center PO Box 12304	Huntsville	AL	35815	**800-239-9997**	256-880-6700
Cruise Vacation Center 2042 Central Pk Ave	Yonkers	NY	10710	**800-803-7245**	914-337-8500
Cruise Value Center 6 Edgeboro Rd	East Brunswick	NJ	08816	**800-231-7447**	732-257-4545
Cruise Ventures DBA CI Travel					
101 W Main St Suite 800	Norfolk	VA	23510	**800-222-3577**	757-627-8000
Cruise Web Inc 8100 Corporate Dr Suite 300	Landover	MA	20785	**800-377-9383**	240-487-0155
CruiseOne Inc					
1415 NW 62nd St Suite 205	Fort Lauderdale	FL	33309	**800-832-3592**	954-958-3700
Cruises Cruises 6604 Antoine Dr	Houston	TX	77091	**800-245-9806**	713-681-9866
Cruises Inc 1415 SW 62nd St	Fort Lauderdale	FL	33309	**800-854-0500***	954-958-3700
*Cust Svc					
Cruises by Kay 6903 California Ave SW	Seattle	WA	98136	**800-938-2602**	206-938-2602
CruisesOnly 100 Sylvan Rd Suite 600	Woburn	MA	01801	**800-278-4737**	617-424-7990
CTS Corporate Travel Solutions					
340 Cedar St Suite 1200	Saint Paul	MN	55101	**800-635-5488**	651-287-4900
Cutting Edge Cruises & Tours					
32 Toms Way	Lagrangeville	NY	12540	**888-345-6100**	845-227-2660
Delta Vacations 110 E Broward Blvd	Fort Lauderdale	FL	33301	**800-654-6559**	954-522-1440
E Tour & Travel					
3626 Quadrangle Blvd Suite 400	Orlando	FL	32817	**800-339-5120**	407-658-8285
Elegant Voyages 6348 Skywalker Dr	San Jose	CA	95135	**800-555-3534**	408-239-0300
Euro Lloyd Travel Inc					
1640 Hempstead Tpke	East Meadow	NY	11554	**800-334-2724**	516-228-4970
European Travel Inc					
301 Howard St 4th Fl	San Francisco	CA	94105	**800-635-6463**	415-981-5518
Fantasy Holidays 400 Jericho Tpke Suite 301	Jericho	NY	11753	**800-645-2555**	516-935-8500
First Class International 27156 Burbank	Foothill Ranch	CA	92610	**800-222-9968**	949-829-5300
Fox World Travel Inc 7936 Sheridan Rd	Kenosha	WI	53143	**800-236-8475***	262-654-9116
*Resv					
Freighter World Cruises Inc					
180 South Lake Ave Suite 335	Pasadena	CA	91101	**800-531-7774**	626-449-3106
Friendly Cruises Inc					
3081 S Sycamore Village Dr	Superstition Mountain	AZ	85218	**800-842-1786**	888-842-1786
Fugazy International Travel					
6006 SW 18th St Suite B3	Boca Raton	FL	33433	**800-852-7613**	954-481-2888
Funjet Vacations					
8907 N Port Washington Rd	Milwaukee	WI	53217	**800-558-6654**	414-351-3553
Future Vacations Inc					
110 E Broward Blvd 11th Fl	Fort Lauderdale	FL	33301	**800-456-2323**	954-522-1440
Gant Travel Management					
304 W Kirkwood Ave Suite 1	Bloomington	IN	47404	**800-742-4198**	
Garber Travel Service Inc 27 Boylston St	Chestnut Hill	MA	02467	**800-359-4272**	617-739-2200
Gateway Travel Management					
1501 Ardmore Blvd Suite 400	Pittsburgh	PA	15221	**800-553-0093**	412-244-3740
GE Perfect Getaways PO Box 5007	Carol Stream	IL	60197	**800-621-5505**	800-452-7118
Giselle's Travel Inc					
1300 Ethan Way Suite 100	Sacramento	CA	95825	**800-782-5545**	916-922-5500
Global Philosophy Travel LLC					
61 Parish Farm Rd	Branford	CT	06405	**888-378-9276**	203-315-8200
Global Travel 900 W Jefferson St	Boise	ID	83702	**800-584-8888**	208-387-1000
Global Vacation Travel Packages					
61 Parish Farm Rd	Branford	CT	06405	**888-378-9276**	203-315-8200
GOGO WorldWide Vacations 69 Spring St	Ramsey	NJ	07446	**888-271-1584**	201-934-3500
Golden Bear Travel Inc 16 Digital Dr	Novato	CA	94949	**800-551-1000**	415-382-8900
Golden Sports Tours 301 W Parker Rd Suite 206	Plano	TX	75023	**800-966-8258**	972-578-1166
Golf Packages of the Carolinas					
218 Main St	North Myrtle Beach	SC	29582	**877-833-2255**	877-732-6999
Gwin's Travel Planners Inc					
212 N Kirkwood Rd	Kirkwood	MO	63122	**800-325-1904**	314-822-1957
GWV International 300 1st Ave	Needham	MA	02494	**800-225-5498**	781-449-6500
Hanin Travel					
2681 W Olympic Blvd Suite 101	Los Angeles	CA	90006	**800-839-5929**	213-388-4949
ICE Gallery 10030 N 25th Ave	Phoenix	AZ	85021	**888-320-4234**	602-395-1995

Name / Address	City	State	ZIP	Toll-Free	Phone
InnovAsian Travel Inc 10 North Ln	Armonk	NY	10504	**800-553-4665**	914-273-6716
International Cruise & Excursion Gallery DBA ICE Gallery 10030 N 25th Ave	Phoenix	AZ	85021	**888-320-4234**	602-395-1995
Islands in the Sun Cruises & Tours 348 Thompson Creek Mall Suite 107	Stevensville	MD	21666	**800-278-7786**	301-261-4457
Japan Travel Bureau USA Inc 810 7th Ave 34th Fl	New York	NY	10019	**800-235-3523**	212-698-4900
JourneyCorp 488 Madison Ave 3rd Fl	New York	NY	10022	**800-305-4911**	212-753-5511
Kincaid Coach Lines Inc 9207 Woodend Rd	Edwardsville	KS	66111	**800-998-1901**	913-441-6200
Lawyers' Travel Service 71 5th Ave 10th Fl	New York	NY	10003	**800-431-1112**	212-679-1166
Liberty Travel Inc 69 Spring St	Ramsey	NJ	07446	**800-899-9800**	201-934-3500
Lorraine Travel 377 Alhambra Cir	Coral Gables	FL	33134	**800-666-8911**	305-446-4433
Maine Windjammer Assn 251 Jefferson St MS-06	Waldoboro	ME	04572	**800-807-9463**	
Mark Travel Corp 8907 N Port Washington Rd	Milwaukee	WI	53217	**800-558-3060**	414-228-7472
Marshall Field's Travel Service 700 Nicollet Mall	Minneapolis	MN	55402	**800-316-6166**	612-375-2884
MC & A Inc 615 Piikoi St Suite 1000	Honolulu	HI	96814	**877-589-5501**	808-589-5500
Menno Travel Service Inc DBA MTS Travel Inc 124 E Main St 4th Fl	Ephrata	PA	17522	**800-642-8315**	717-733-4131
Merit Travel Group Inc 145 King St W Suite 2020	Toronto	ON	M5H1J8	**800-268-5940**	416-364-3775
MLT Vacations 4660 W 77th St	Edina	MN	55435	**800-362-3520**	952-474-2540
Montrose Travel 2355 Honolulu Ave	Montrose	CA	91020	**800-766-4687**	818-553-3210
More Hawaii for Less Inc 1200 Quail St Suite 290	Newport Beach	CA	92660	**800-967-6687**	949-724-5050
Morris Murdock Travel 240 E Morris Ave Suite 400	Salt Lake City	UT	84115	**800-888-6699**	801-487-9731
MTS Travel Inc 124 E Main St 4th Fl	Ephrata	PA	17522	**800-642-8315**	717-733-4131
MyTravel Canada Inc 130 Merton St	Toronto	ON	M4S1A4	**800-668-1743**	416-485-1700
National Discount Cruise Co 1401 N Cedar Crest Blvd Suite 56	Allentown	PA	18104	**800-788-8108**	610-439-4883
Navigant International Canada 2810 Matheson Blvd E 3rd FL	Mississauga	ON	L4W4X7	**800-668-1116**	905-629-9975
Nippon Express Travel USA 22 Center Point Dr Suite 110	La Palma	CA	90623	**800-654-8228**	714-521-2050
Northstar Cruises 80 Bloomfield Ave Suite 102	Caldwell	NJ	07006	**800-249-9360**	973-228-5005
NWA WorldVacations 2915 N Broadway	Minot	ND	58703	**800-727-1111**	701-839-5555
Ocean One Cruise Outlet 3264 Marilynn St	Lancaster	CA	93536	**877-362-7770**	661-949-2873
Omega World Travel Inc 3102 Omega Office Pk Dr Suite 100	Fairfax	VA	22031	**800-756-6342**	703-359-8888
Ovation Travel Group 71 5th Ave 11th Fl	New York	NY	10003	**800-431-1112**	212-679-1600
Paradise Island Vacations 1000 S Pine Island Rd Suite 800	Plantation	FL	33324	**800-722-7466**	954-809-2000
Patterson TravelStore 855 Howe Ave Suite 5	Sacramento	CA	95825	**800-283-2772**	916-929-5555
Pleasant Holidays LLC 2404 Townsgate Rd	Westlake Village	CA	91361	**800-242-9244**	818-991-3390
Premier Golf 4355 River Green Pkwy	Duluth	GA	30096	**800-283-4653**	770-291-4100
Prestige Travel & Cruises Inc 6175 Spring Mountain Rd	Las Vegas	NV	89146	**800-553-0204**	702-251-5552
Pro Golf Travel 515 Madison Ave 10th Fl	New York	NY	10022	**888-685-4426**	212-409-9585
Professional Travel Inc 25000 Country Club Blvd Suite 170	North Olmsted	OH	44070	**800-247-0060**	440-734-8800
Protravel International Inc 515 Madison Ave 10th Fl	New York	NY	10022	**800-227-1059**	212-755-4550
Provident Travel Corp 11309 Montgomery Rd	Cincinnati	OH	45249	**800-543-2120**	513-247-1100
Qantas Vacations 300 Continental Blvd Suite 350	El Segundo	CA	90245	**800-348-8145**	310-322-6359
Regal Travel 720 Iwilei Rd Suite 101	Honolulu	HI	96817	**800-817-9920**	808-566-7000
Rich Worldwide Travel Inc 500 Mamaroneck Ave	Harrison	NY	10528	**800-431-1130**	914-835-7600
Robustelli World Travel Inc 460 Summer St	Stamford	CT	06901	**800-243-2654**	203-352-0500
SatoTravel 511 Shaw Rd	Sterling	VA	20166	**800-776-7286**	703-708-9400
Scheduled Airlines Traffic Offices Inc DBA SatoTravel 511 Shaw Rd	Sterling	VA	20166	**800-776-7286**	703-708-9400
Sea Gate Travel LLC 16 E 34th St 3rd Fl	New York	NY	10016	**800-622-6622**	212-689-9525
SGH Golf Inc 9403 Kenwood Rd Suite C110	Cincinnati	OH	45242	**800-284-8884**	513-984-0414
Ship N Shore 100 Sylvan Rd Suite 600 *Cust Svc	Woburn	MA	01801	**866-711-7447***	800-892-5537
Simply Cruises Inc 3814 Hampton Ave	Saint Louis	MO	63109	**888-367-9398**	314-832-8880
Ski-Pak Inc PO Box 30085	Seattle	WA	98113	**800-446-4688**	206-729-8200
Spectacular Sport Specials Inc 5813 Citrus Blvd	New Orleans	LA	70123	**800-451-5772**	504-734-9511
Sports Empire PO Box 6169	Lakewood	CA	90714	**800-255-5258**	562-920-2350
Sterling Cruises & Travel 8700 W Flagler St Suite 105	Miami	FL	33174	**800-435-7967**	305-592-2522
Stevens Travel Management Inc 55 Broad St 17th Fl	New York	NY	10004	**800-275-7400**	212-696-4300
Stratton Travel Management 860 Wyckoff Ave	Mahwah	NJ	07430	**800-223-0599**	201-405-1999
Sun Holidays Inc 7208 Sand Lake Rd Suite 207	Orlando	FL	32819	**800-422-8000**	
Sun Islands Hawaii Inc 2299 Kuhio Ave 1st Fl	Honolulu	HI	96815	**800-560-3338**	808-926-3888
Sunburst Vacations 310 1st Ave	Needham Heights	MA	02494	**800-786-2877**	781-707-2668
SunQuest Vacations 77-6435 Kuakini Hwy	Kailua-Kona	HI	96740	**800-367-5168**	808-329-6438
Sunsational Cruises 710 W Elliot Rd	Tempe	AZ	85284	**800-239-6252**	480-491-6248
SunSpots International 1918 NE 181st Ave	Portland	OR	97230	**800-334-5623**	503-666-3893
SunTrips Inc 2350 Paragon Dr *Resv	San Jose	CA	95131	**800-786-8747***	408-432-1101
Tenenbaum's Vacation Stores Inc 300 Market St	Kingston	PA	18704	**800-545-7099**	570-288-8747
Tower Travel Management 1 Tower Ln Suite 2520	Oakbrook Terrace	IL	60181	**800-542-9700**	630-954-3000
TQ3Navigant 84 Inverness Cir E	Englewood	CO	80112	**877-628-4426**	303-706-0800
TQ3NavigantVacations.com 84 Inverness Cir E	Englewood	CO	80112	**800-783-9200**	303-706-0800
Transat Holidays USA Inc 140 S Federal Hwy	Dania	FL	33004	**866-828-4872**	954-920-0090
Transat AT Inc 1160 Cargo A-1 Rd Montreal International Airport *TSE: TRZ*	Mirabel	QC	J7N1G9	**877-470-1011**	450-476-1011
TransGlobal Vacations 8907 N Port Washington Rd	Milwaukee	WI	53217	**800-699-2080**	414-228-7472
Travel Advisors 7930 Lee Blvd	Leawood	KS	66206	**800-745-6260**	913-649-6266
Travel Authority Inc 702 N Shore Dr Suite 300	Jeffersonville	IN	47130	**800-626-2717**	812-206-5100
Travel Destinations Management Group Inc 110 Painters Mill Rd Suite 36	Owings Mills	MD	21117	**800-635-7307**	410-363-3111
Travel Impressions Ltd 465 Smith St	Farmingdale	NY	11735	**800-284-0044**	631-845-8000
Travel Inc 4355 River Green Pkwy	Duluth	GA	30096	**800-452-6575**	770-291-4100
Travel-Rite International 3000 Dundee Rd Suite 309	North Brooke	IL	60062	**877-880-3033**	847-412-1420
Travel Team Inc 2495 Main St	Buffalo	NY	14214	**800-633-6782**	716-862-7600
Travel & Transport Inc 2120 S 72nd St	Omaha	NE	68124	**800-228-2545**	402-399-4500
TraveLeaders Group Inc 1701 Ponce de Leon Blvd	Coral Gables	FL	33134	**800-327-0180**	305-445-2999
Travelennium Inc 5050 Poplar Ave Suite 115	Memphis	TN	38157	**800-844-4924**	901-767-0761
Traveline Travel Agencies Inc 4074 Erie St	Willoughby	OH	44094	**888-700-8747**	440-946-4040
Travelmore/Carlson-Wagonlit Travel 212 W Colfax Ave	South Bend	IN	46601	**877-543-5752**	574-232-3061
Travelong Inc 225 W 35th St Suite 1501	New York	NY	10001	**800-537-6043**	212-736-2166
TravelStore Inc 11601 Wilshire Blvd	Los Angeles	CA	90025	**800-343-9779**	310-575-5540
TravelVisions 1000 Heritage Ctr Cir	Round Rock	TX	78664	**800-452-2256**	512-238-3166
TRAVIZON Inc 10 State St 2nd Fl	Woburn	MA	01801	**888-781-5200**	781-994-1200
TripQuest Inc 786 N Beal Pkwy Suite 7A	Fort Walton Beach	FL	32548	**888-459-8747**	850-862-8999
Tumlare Corp 2128 Bellmore Ave	Bellmore	NY	11710	**800-223-4664**	516-781-0322
Ultramar Travel Management International 14 E 47th St 5th Fl	New York	NY	10017	**888-856-2929**	212-856-5600
United Vacations 8907 N Port Washington Rd	Milwaukee	WI	53217	**800-377-1816**	414-351-8470
User-Friendly Group Inc DBA Friendly Cruises Inc 3081 S Sycamore Village Dr	Superstition Mountain	AZ	85218	**800-842-1786**	888-842-1786
Vacation Express Inc 301 Perimeter Center N NE Suite 500	Atlanta	GA	30346	**800-309-4717**	404-315-4848
Vacations by Adventure Tours 10670 N Central Expy	Dallas	TX	75231	**800-642-8872**	214-210-6100
Valerie Wilson Travel Inc 475 Park Ave S	New York	NY	10016	**800-776-1116**	212-532-3400
VE Holdings Inc DBA Vacation Express Inc 301 Perimeter Center N NE Suite 500	Atlanta	GA	30346	**800-309-4717**	404-315-4848
Virtuoso 500 Main St Suite 400	Fort Worth	TX	76102	**800-401-4274**	817-870-0300
Wilson Valerie Travel Inc 475 Park Ave S	New York	NY	10016	**800-776-1116**	212-532-3400
World Travel Bureau Inc 620 N Main St	Santa Ana	CA	92701	**800-899-3370**	714-835-8111
World Travel Inc 1724 W Schuylkill Rd	Douglassville	PA	19518	**800-341-2014**	610-327-9000
WorldTravel BTI 1055 Lenox Park Blvd Suite 420	Atlanta	GA	30319	**800-342-3234**	404-841-6600
Worldwide Holidays Inc 7800 Red Rd Suite 112	South Miami	FL	33143	**800-327-9854**	305-665-0841
Worldwide Travel & Cruise Assoc Inc 150 S University Dr Suite E	Plantation	FL	33324	**800-881-8484**	954-452-8800
Wright Travel Inc 2505 21st Ave S Suite 500	Nashville	TN	37212	**800-643-5992**	615-783-1111
YMT Vacations 8831 Aviation Blvd	Inglewood	CA	90301	**800-922-9000**	310-649-3820

761 TRAVEL AGENCY NETWORKS

SEE ALSO Travel Agencies

Name / Address	City	State	ZIP	Toll-Free	Phone
Algonquin Travel Corp 130 Merton St *Cust Svc	Toronto	ON	M4S1A4	**888-599-0789***	416-485-1700
American Express Co Inc World Financial Ctr 200 Vesey St *NYSE: AXP*	New York	NY	10285	**800-666-1775**	212-640-2000
BTI Canada 370 King St W Suite 700	Toronto	ON	M5V1J9	**800-567-4337**	416-593-8866
Carlson Leisure Group 12755 State Hwy 55	Plymouth	MN	55441	**800-335-8747**	763-212-5000
Carlson Wagonlit Travel Assoc 701 Carlson Pkwy	Minnetonka	MN	55305	**800-335-8747**	763-212-4000
Carlson Wagonlit Travel Inc 701 Carlson Pkwy	Minnetonka	MN	55305	**800-335-8747**	763-212-5000
Cruise Planners Inc 3300 University Dr Suite 602	Coral Springs	FL	33065	**800-683-0206**	954-344-8060
CruiseOne Inc 1415 NW 62nd St Suite 205	Fort Lauderdale	FL	33309	**800-832-3592**	954-958-3700
CTS Cruise & Travel 5435 Scotts Valley Dr	Scotts Valley	CA	95066	**800-777-1677**	831-438-6662
Design Travel Management Group Inc 2168 Lake Shore Cir	Arlington Heights	IL	60004	**800-773-7930**	847-577-7930
Ensemble Travel 29 W 36th St 8th Fl	New York	NY	10018	**800-442-6871**	212-545-7460
Global Travel International 2600 Lake Lucien Dr Suite 201	Maitland	FL	32751	**800-951-5979**	407-660-7800
Hickory Travel Systems Inc Park 80 Plaza East	Saddle Brook	NJ	07663	**800-448-0350**	
IT Group Inc 100 Executive Way Suite 202	Ponte Vedra Beach	FL	32082	**888-482-4636**	904-285-9796
MAST Vacation Partners Inc (MAST) 17 W 635 Butterfield Rd Suite 150	Oakbrook Terrace	IL	60181	**888-305-3951**	630-889-9817
Navigant International Inc 84 Inverness Cir E *NASDAQ: FLYR*	Englewood	CO	80112	**877-628-4426**	303-706-0800
Nexion 1625 The Alameda 9th Fl	San Jose	CA	95126	**800-747-6813**	408-280-6410
Riverside Travel Group Inc 13343 SE Stark St Suite 200	Portland	OR	97233	**800-772-2228**	503-255-2950
SYNERGI Global Travel Management 16 E 34th St 3rd Fl	New York	NY	10016	**800-622-6622**	212-404-8814
Thor Inc 382 S Arthur Ave	Louisville	CO	80027	**800-862-2111**	303-876-4100
Tix Travel & Ticket Agency Inc 201 Main St	Nyack	NY	10960	**800-269-6849**	
TQ3 Travel Solutions 84 Inverness Cir E	Englewood	CO	80112	**877-628-4426**	303-706-0800
Travelex International Inc 2500 W Higgins Rd Suite 1065	Hoffman Estates	IL	60195	**800-882-0499**	847-882-0400
Travelsavers Inc 71 Audrey Ave	Oyster Bay	NY	11771	**800-726-7283**	516-624-0500
UNIGLOBE Travel USA LLC 18662 MacArthur Blvd Suite 100	Irvine	CA	92612	**800-863-1606**	949-623-9000
Vacation.com 1650 King St Suite 450	Alexandria	VA	22314	**800-843-0733**	703-535-5505
Virtuoso 500 Main St Suite 400	Fort Worth	TX	76102	**800-401-4274**	817-870-0300
Western Assn of Travel Agencies (WESTA) 5933 NE Win Sivers Dr Suite 202	Portland	OR	97220	**800-288-8191**	503-251-8170
WorldClass Travel Network 7900 Xerxes Ave S 115 Wells Fargo Plaza	Bloomington	MN	55431	**800-234-3576**	952-835-8636
Worldtek Travel Inc 111 Water St	New Haven	CT	06511	**800-243-1723**	203-772-0470
WorldTravel BTI 1055 Lenox Park Blvd Suite 420	Atlanta	GA	30319	**800-342-3234**	404-841-6600

TRAVEL INFORMATION - CITY

SEE Convention & Visitors Bureaus

762 TRAVEL SERVICES - ONLINE

SEE ALSO Hotel Reservations Services

Name / Address	City	State	Zip	Toll-Free	Phone
11th Hour Vacations 15 Century Dr	Greenville	SC	29607	**888-740-1998**	864-331-1140
1800CHEAPSEATS 11145 Tampa Ave Suite 17-B	Northridge	CA	91326	**800-243-2773**	
A & E Travel 3307 Northland Dr Suite 220	Austin	TX	78731	**877-238-6877**	512-244-9883
BedandBreakfast.com 700 Brazos St Suite B-700 *Sales	Austin	TX	78701	**800-462-2632***	512-322-2710
Best Fares USA Inc 1301 S Bowen Rd Suite 400	Arlington	TX	76013	**800-880-1234**	817-860-5573
Bombardier Skyjet 3040 Williams Dr Suite 404 *Cust Svc	Alexandria	VA	22031	**888-275-9538***	703-584-3330
Car Rental Express 3337 W 4th Ave	Vancouver	BC	V6R1N6	**888-557-8188**	604-714-5911
Cheap Tickets Inc 7 Sylvan Way	Parsippany	NJ	07054	**888-922-8849**	
Cruise.com 1701 Eller Dr	Port Everglades	FL	33316	**888-333-3116**	954-763-6828
Cruises.com 100 Sylvan Rd	Woburn	MA	01801	**800-288-6006**	617-424-7990
Excursia.com PO Box 936	Augusta	GA	30903	**800-622-6358**	
Expedia Inc 3150 139th Ave SE	Bellevue	WA	98005	**800-397-3342**	425-564-7200
Fodors.com 1745 Broadway	New York	NY	10019	**888-264-1745**	212-751-2600
GetThere LC 3150 Sabre Dr	Southlake	TX	76092	**800-850-3906**	682-605-1000
Hotwire.com 333 Market St Suite 100	San Francisco	CA	94105	**877-468-9473**	415-343-8400
iExplore Inc 954 W Washington Blvd Suite 3W	Chicago	IL	60607	**800-439-7567**	312-492-9443
LastMinuteTravel.com Inc 220 E Central Pkwy Suite 4010	Altamonte Springs	FL	32701	**800-442-0568**	407-667-8700
Lonely Planet Online 150 Linden St	Oakland	CA	94607	**800-275-8555**	510-893-8555
National Park Service Reservation Center 12501 Willowbrook Rd	Cumberland	MD	21502	**800-365-2267**	
National Recreation Reservation Service PO Box 140	Ballston Spa	NY	12020	**877-444-6777**	
OneTravel Inc 258 Main St 3rd Fl	East Greenville	PA	18041	**800-929-2523**	215-541-1030
OnlineCityGuide.com LLC 1940 Elm Hill Pike	Nashville	TN	37210	**800-467-1218**	615-259-4500
Orbitz LLC 200 S Wacker Dr Suite 1900	Chicago	IL	60606	**888-656-4546**	312-894-5000
Priceline.com Inc 800 Connecticut Ave *NASDAQ: PCLN*	Norwalk	CT	06854	**800-774-2354**	203-299-8000
ReserveAmerica 2480 Meadowvale Blvd Suite 120	Mississauga	ON	L5N8M6	**800-695-4636**	905-286-6600
TravelNow.com Inc 4124 S McCann Ct	Springfield	MO	65804	**800-568-1972**	417-864-3600
Travelocity 3150 Sabre Dr	Southlake	TX	76092	**888-709-5983**	682-605-3000
Vacation.com 1650 King St Suite 450	Alexandria	VA	22314	**800-843-0733**	703-535-5505
WebFlyer.com 1930 Frequent Flyer Pt *Cust Svc	Colorado Springs	CO	80915	**800-209-2870***	719-572-2787

763 TRAVEL & TOURISM INFORMATION - CANADIAN

Name / Address	City	Prov	Postal	Toll-Free	Phone
Newfoundland & Labrador Tourism PO Box 8730	Saint John's	NL	A1B4K2	**800-563-6353**	709-729-2830
Nova Scotia Dept of Tourism & Culture PO Box 456	Halifax	NS	B3J2R5	**800-565-0000**	902-424-5000
Nunavut Tourism PO Box 1450	Iqaluit	NU	X0A0H0	**800-491-7910**	867-979-6551
NWT Tourism Box 610	Yellowknife	NT	X1A2N5	**800-661-0788**	867-873-7200
Ontario Tourism Marketing Partnership Corp 900 Bay St Hearst Block 10th Fl	Toronto	ON	M7A2E1	**800-668-2746**	905-282-1721
Prince Edward Island Tourism PO Box 2000	Charlottetown	PE	C1A7N8	**888-734-7529**	902-368-4000
Tourism New Brunswick 26 Roseberry St	Campbellton	NB	E3N2G4	**800-561-0123**	506-789-4982
Tourism Saskatchewan 1922 Park St	Regina	SK	S4N7M4	**877-237-2273**	306-787-9600
Tourism Yukon PO Box 2703	Whitehorse	YT	Y1A2C6	**800-661-0494**	867-667-5036
Tourisme Quebec 1010 Saint Catherines W 4th Fl	Montreal	QC	H3B1G2	**800-363-7777**	
Travel Alberta 10123 99th St Suite 1600 Sun Life Pl	Edmonton	AB	T5J3H1	**800-252-3782**	780-427-4321
Travel Manitoba 155 Carlton St 7th Fl	Winnipeg	MB	R3C3H8	**800-665-0040**	204-945-3777
travel.bc.ca 4252 Commerce Cir	Victoria	BC	V8Z4M2	**800-663-6000**	866-810-6645
York Region Tourism 17250 Young St Box 147 4th Fl	Newmarket	ON	L3Y6Z1	**888-448-0000**	905-883-3442

764 TRAVEL & TOURISM INFORMATION - FOREIGN TRAVEL

Name / Address	City	State	Zip	Toll-Free	Phone
Antigua & Barbuda Dept of Tourism & Trade 610 5th Ave Suite 311	New York	NY	10020	**888-268-4227**	212-541-4117
Aruba Tourism Authority 1200 Harbor Blvd	Weehawken	NJ	07086	**800-862-7822**	201-330-0800
Bahamas Tourism Office 11400 W Olympic Blvd Suite 204	Los Angeles	CA	90064	**800-439-6993**	310-312-9544
Bahamas Tourism Office 1200 S Pine Island Rd Suite 750	Plantation	FL	33324	**800-224-3681**	954-236-9292
Bahamas Tourism Office 150 E 52nd St 28th Fl N	New York	NY	10022	**800-823-3136**	212-758-2777
Barbados Tourism Authority 3440 Wilshire Blvd Suite 1215	Los Angeles	CA	90010	**800-221-9831**	213-380-2198
Barbados Tourism Authority 150 Alhambra Cir Suite 1000	Coral Gables	FL	33134	**800-221-9831**	305-442-7471
Barbados Tourism Authority 800 2nd Ave 2nd Fl	New York	NY	10017	**800-221-9831**	212-986-6516
Bermuda Dept of Tourism 245 Peachtree Ctr Ave NE Suite 803	Atlanta	GA	30303	**800-223-6106**	404-524-1541
Bermuda Dept of Tourism 675 3rd Ave 20th Fl	New York	NY	10017	**800-223-6106**	212-818-9800
Bonaire Government Tourist Office 10 Rockefeller Plaza Suite 900	New York	NY	10020	**800-266-2473**	212-956-5911
British Virgin Islands Tourist Board 3450 Wilshire Blvd Suite 1202	Los Angeles	CA	90010	**800-835-8530**	213-736-8931
British Virgin Islands Tourist Board 1270 Broadway Suite 705	New York	NY	10017	**800-835-8530**	212-696-0400
Cayman Islands Dept of Tourism 8300 NW 53rd St Suite 103	Miami	FL	33166	**800-346-3313**	305-599-9033
Croatian National Tourist Office 350 5th Ave Suite 4003	New York	NY	10118	**800-829-4416**	212-279-8672
Curacao Tourist Board 7951 SW 6th St Suite 216	Plantation	FL	33324	**800-328-7222**	954-370-5887
Dominica Tourist Office 110-64 Queens Blvd Box 427	Forest Hills	NY	11375	**888-645-5637**	212-949-1711
Dominican Republic Tourist Board 248 NW 42nd Ave	Miami	FL	33126	**888-358-9594**	305-444-4592
Dominican Republic Tourist Board 136 E 57th St Suite 803	New York	NY	10022	**888-374-6361**	212-588-1012
Egyptian Tourist Authority 630 5th Ave Suite 2305	New York	NY	10111	**877-773-4978**	212-332-2570
Fiji Visitors Bureau 5777 W Century Blvd Suite 220	Los Angeles	CA	90045	**800-932-3454**	310-568-1616
Grenada Board of Tourism PO Box 1668	Lake Worth	FL	33460	**800-927-9554**	561-588-8176
Grenada Board of Tourism 305 Madison Ave Suite 2145	New York	NY	10165	**800-927-9554**	212-687-9554
Guam Visitors Bureau c/o Aviso Inc 1336-C Park St	Alameda	CA	94501	**800-873-4826**	510-865-0366
Honduras Tourism Institute 299 Alhambra Cir Suite 226	Coral Gables	FL	33134	**800-410-9608**	305-461-0601
Hong Kong Tourism Board 10940 Wilshire Blvd Suite 2050	Los Angeles	CA	90024	**800-282-4582**	310-208-4582
India Tourist Office 3550 Wilshire Blvd Suite 204	Los Angeles	CA	90010	**800-422-4634**	213-380-8855
India Tourist Office 1270 Ave of the Americas Suite 1808	New York	NY	10020	**800-953-9399**	212-586-4901
Irish Tourist Board 345 Park Ave 17th Fl	New York	NY	10154	**800-669-9967**	212-418-0800
Israel Government Tourist Office 6380 Wilshire Blvd Suite 1700	Los Angeles	CA	90048	**888-774-7723**	323-658-7463
Israel Government Tourist Office 800 2nd Ave 16th Fl	New York	NY	10017	**888-774-7723**	212-499-5650
Jamaica Tourist Board 1320 S Dixie Hwy Suite 1101	Coral Gables	FL	33146	**800-233-4582**	305-665-0557
Jordan Tourism Board 6867 Elm St Suite 102	McLean	VA	22101	**877-733-5673**	703-243-7404
Kenya Tourism Board c/o Carlson Destinationa Marketing Services PO Box 59159	Minneapolis	MN	55459	**866-445-3692**	
Korea National Tourism Organization 4801 Wilshire Blvd Suite 103	Los Angeles	CA	90010	**800-868-7567**	323-634-0280
Korea National Tourism Organization 737 N Michigan Ave Suite 910	Chicago	IL	60611	**800-868-7567**	312-981-1717
Korea National Tourism Organization 2 Executive Dr Suite 750	Fort Lee	NJ	07024	**800-868-7567**	201-585-0909
Macau Government Tourist Office 3601 Aviation Blvd Suite 2100	Manhattan Beach	CA	90266	**866-656-2228**	310-643-2630
Martinique Promotion Bureau 444 Madison Ave 16th Fl	New York	NY	10022	**800-391-4909**	
Mexico Tourism Board 5975 Sunset Dr Suite 305	Miami	FL	33143	**800-446-3942**	786-621-2909
Mexico Tourism Board 225 N Michigan Ave Suite 1850	Chicago	IL	60601	**800-446-3942**	312-228-0517
Mexico Tourism Board 400 Madison Ave Suite 11-C	New York	NY	10017	**800-446-3942**	212-308-2110
Mexico Tourism Board 4507 San Jacinto Suite 308	Houston	TX	77004	**800-446-3942**	713-772-2581
Monaco Government Tourist Office 565 5th Ave	New York	NY	10017	**800-753-9696**	212-286-3330
Netherlands Board of Tourism & Conventions 355 Lexington Ave 19th Fl	New York	NY	10017	**888-464-6552**	212-370-7360
New Zealand Tourism Board 501 Santa Monica Blvd Suite 300	Santa Monica	CA	90401	**866-639-9325**	310-395-7480
Peru Tourist Office 495 Biltmore Way Suite 404	Coral Gables	FL	33134	**866-661-7378**	305-476-1220
Portuguese Trade & Tourism Office 590 5th Ave 4th Fl	New York	NY	10036	**800-767-8842**	646-723-0200
Puerto Rico Tourism Co 3575 W Cahuenga Blvd Suite 405	Los Angeles	CA	90068	**800-874-1230**	323-874-5991
Puerto Rico Tourism Co 901 Ponce de Leon Blvd Suite 101	Coral Gables	FL	33134	**800-815-7391**	305-445-9112
Puerto Rico Tourism Co 666 5th Ave 15th Fl	New York	NY	10103	**800-223-6530**	212-586-6262
Russian National Group 130 W 42nd St Suite 1804	New York	NY	10036	**877-221-7120**	212-575-3431
Russian National Tourist Office 130 W 42nd St Suite 1804	New York	NY	10036	**877-221-7120**	212-575-3431
Saint Kitts Tourism Authority 414 E 75th St Suite 5	New York	NY	10021	**800-582-6208**	212-535-1234
Saint Lucia Tourist Board 800 2nd Ave 9th Fl	New York	NY	10017	**800-456-3984**	212-867-2950
Saint Maarten Tourist Office 675 3rd Ave Suite 1807	New York	NY	10017	**800-786-2278**	212-953-2084
Saint Martin Tourist Office 675 3rd Ave Suite 1807	New York	NY	10017	**877-956-1234**	212-475-8970
Saint Vincent & the Grenadines Tourist Information Office 801 2nd Ave 21st Fl	New York	NY	10017	**800-729-1726**	212-687-4981
Singapore Tourism Board 4929 Wilshire Blvd Suite 510	Beverly Hills	CA	90010	**800-283-9595**	323-677-0808
South African Tourism Board 500 5th Ave 20th Fl Suite 2040	New York	NY	10110	**800-822-5368**	212-730-2929
Switzerland Tourism 608 5th Ave Suite 202	New York	NY	10020	**800-794-7795**	212-757-5944
Tahiti Tourisme 300 Continental Blvd Suite 160	El Segundo	CA	90245	**800-365-4949**	310-414-8484
Tourism Australia 6100 Center Dr Suite 1150	Los Angeles	CA	90045	**800-369-6863**	310-695-3200
Tourism Authority of Thailand 611 N Larchmont Blvd 1st Fl	Los Angeles	CA	90004	**800-842-4526**	323-461-9814
Tourism Malaysia 818 W 7th St Suite 970	Los Angeles	CA	90017	**800-336-6842**	213-689-9702
Tourism Malaysia 120 E 56th St Suite 810	New York	NY	10022	**800-336-6842**	212-754-1113
Tourism New Zealand 501 Santa Monica Blvd Suite 300	Santa Monica	CA	90401	**866-639-9325**	310-395-7480
Turkish Tourist Office 821 UN Plaza 1st Fl	New York	NY	10017	**877-367-8875**	212-687-2194
Turks & Caicos Islands Tourism Office 2715 E Oakland Park Blvd Suite 101	Fort Lauderdale	FL	33306	**800-241-0824**	954-568-6588
US Virgin Islands Dept of Tourism 444 N Capitol St NW Suite 305	Washington	DC	20001	**800-372-8784**	202-624-3590

Company	City	State	Zip	Toll-Free	Phone
US Virgin Islands Dept of Tourism 2655 S LeJeune Rd Suite 907	Coral Gables	FL	33134	**800-372-8784**	305-442-7200
US Virgin Islands Dept of Tourism 500 N Michigan Ave Suite 2030	Chicago	IL	60611	**888-656-8784**	
VisitBritain 551 5th Ave Suite 701	New York	NY	10176	**800-462-2748**	212-986-2266

765 TREE SERVICES

SEE ALSO Landscaping Services; Lawn Services

Company	City	State	Zip	Toll-Free	Phone
Arbor Tree Surgery Inc 802 Paso Robles St	Paso Robles	CA	93446	**800-238-9494**	805-239-1239
Asplundh Tree Expert Co 708 Blair Mill Rd	Willow Grove	PA	19090	**800-248-8733**	215-784-4200
Bartlett FA Tree Expert Co 476 Canal St	Stamford	CT	06902	**877-227-8538**	203-323-1131
Blume Tree Services 708 Blair Mill Rd	Willow Grove	PA	19090	**800-248-8733**	215-784-4200
Davey Tree Expert Co 1500 N Mantua St	Kent	OH	44240	**800-445-8733**	330-673-9511
Davey Tree Surgery Co Inc PO Box 5015	Livermore	CA	94551	**800-972-5261**	925-443-1723
FA Bartlett Tree Expert Co 476 Canal St	Stamford	CT	06902	**877-227-8538**	203-323-1131
Farrens Tree Service 708 Blair Mill Rd	Willow Grove	PA	19090	**800-248-8733**	215-784-4200
Groundskeeper Tree Div PO Box 43820	Tucson	AZ	85733	**800-571-1575**	520-571-1575
Lewis Tree Service Inc 225 Ballantyne Rd	Rochester	NY	14623	**800-333-1593**	585-436-3208
Nelson Tree Service Inc 3300 Office Park Dr	Dayton	OH	45439	**800-522-4311**	937-294-1313
Tamarack Forestry Service Inc PO Box 769	Canton	NY	13617	**800-858-0437**	315-386-2010
Tree Preservation Co 708 Blair Mill Rd	Willow Grove	PA	19090	**800-248-8733**	215-784-4200
Trees Inc 650 N Sam Houston Pkwy E Suite 209	Houston	TX	77060	**800-676-7712**	281-447-1327
Wright Tree Service Inc PO Box 1718	Des Moines	IA	50306	**800-882-1216**	515-277-6291

766 TROPHIES, PLAQUES, AWARDS

Company	City	State	Zip	Toll-Free	Phone
Architectural Bronze & Aluminum Corp 3638 W Oakton St	Skokie	IL	60076	**800-339-6581**	847-674-3638
Au Sable Woodworking Co PO Box 108	Frederic	MI	49733	**800-248-9261**	989-348-7086
Award Products Inc 4830 N Front St	Philadelphia	PA	19120	**800-972-2562**	215-324-0414
Barlow Promotional Products Inc 8700 Bellanca Ave	Los Angeles	CA	90045	**800-227-5691**	310-670-6363
Bruce Fox Inc 1909 McDonald Ln	New Albany	IN	47150	**800-289-3699**	812-945-3511
F & H Ribbon Co Inc PO Box 1338	Hurst	TX	76053	**800-877-5775**	817-283-5891
Fox Bruce Inc 1909 McDonald Ln	New Albany	IN	47150	**800-289-3699**	812-945-3511
Jostens Inc 5501 American Blvd W	Minneapolis	MN	55437	**800-235-4774**	952-830-3300
Metallic Arts Inc 914 N Lake Rd	Spokane	WA	99212	**800-541-3200**	509-489-7173
Neff Athletic Lettering Co 645 Pine St PO Box 218 *Cust Svc	Greenville	OH	45331	**800-232-6333***	937-548-3194
Owens RS & Co 5535 N Lynch Ave	Chicago	IL	60630	**800-282-6200**	773-282-6000
Plastic Dress-Up Co 11077 E Rush St	South El Monte	CA	91733	**800-800-7711**	626-442-7711
Regalia Mfg Co PO Box 4448	Rock Island	IL	61204	**800-798-7471**	309-788-7471
RS Owens & Co 5535 N Lynch Ave	Chicago	IL	60630	**800-282-6200**	773-282-6000
Trophyland USA Inc 7001 W 20th Ave	Hialeah	FL	33014	**800-327-5820**	
Tuff-Weld Wood Specialties 7569 Woodman Pl *Cust Svc	Van Nuys	CA	91405	**800-223-2955***	818-988-0991
US Bronze Sign Co 811 2nd Ave	New Hyde Park	NY	11040	**800-872-5155**	516-352-5155
Western Badge & Trophy Co 1716 W Washington Blvd	Los Angeles	CA	90007	**800-367-4332**	323-735-1201
Wilson Trophy Co 1724 Frienza Ave	Sacramento	CA	95815	**800-325-4911**	916-927-9733

TRUCK BODIES

SEE Motor Vehicles - Commercial & Special Purpose

767 TRUCK RENTAL & LEASING

Company	City	State	Zip	Toll-Free	Phone
Carco National Lease Inc 2905 N 32nd St	Fort Smith	AR	72904	**800-643-2596**	479-441-3200
Daco Corp 1761 E Brooks Rd	Memphis	TN	38116	**800-824-7992**	901-332-4000
DeCarolis Truck Rental Inc 333 Colfax St	Rochester	NY	14606	**800-666-1169**	585-254-1169
Hale Trailer Brake & Wheel Service Inc 5361 Oakview Dr	Allentown	PA	18104	**800-383-8894**	610-395-0371
National Truck Leasing System DBA NationaLease 1 S 450 Summit Ave Suite 300	Oakbrook Terrace	IL	60181	**800-729-6857**	630-953-8878
NationaLease 1 S 450 Summit Ave Suite 300	Oakbrook Terrace	IL	60181	**800-729-6857**	630-953-8878
PACCAR Leasing Corp 777 106th Ave NE PO Box 1518	Bellevue	WA	98009	**800-426-1420**	425-468-7400
Penske Corp Rt 10 Green Hills PO Box 563	Reading	PA	19603	**800-222-0277**	610-775-6000
Penske Truck Leasing Co LP Rt 10 Green Hills PO Box 563	Reading	PA	19603	**800-222-0277**	610-775-6000
Rapid Ways Truck Leasing Inc 3940 Great Midwest Dr	Kansas City	MO	64161	**800-962-7322**	816-455-7262
RUAN Transportation Management Systems 666 Grand Ave Suite 3100	Des Moines	IA	50309	**800-997-7826**	515-245-2500
Rush Enterprises Inc 555 IH 35 S Suite 500 *NASDAQ: RUSHA*	New Braunfels	TX	78130	**800-973-7874**	830-626-5200
Ryder System Inc 3600 NW 82nd Ave *NYSE: R*	Miami	FL	33166	**800-327-3399**	305-593-3726
Salem Leasing Corp PO Box 24788	Winston-Salem	NC	27114	**800-877-2536**	336-768-6800
Star Truck Rentals Inc 3940 Eastern Ave SE	Grand Rapids	MI	49508	**800-748-0468**	616-243-7033
Transport International Pool 426 W Lancaster Ave	Devon	PA	19333	**800-333-2030**	610-647-4900
U-Haul International Inc PO Box 21502	Phoenix	AZ	85036	**800-468-4285**	602-263-6011
XTRA Intermodal 100 Tower Dr	Burr Ridge	IL	60527	**800-344-9872**	630-789-3200

768 TRUCK TRAILERS

SEE ALSO Motor Vehicles - Commercial & Special Purpose

Company	City	State	Zip	Toll-Free	Phone
4-Star Trailers Inc 10000 NW 10th St	Oklahoma City	OK	73127	**800-848-3095**	405-324-7827
American Carrier Equipment Corp 2285 E Date Ave	Fresno	CA	93706	**800-344-2174**	559-442-1500
Arkansas Trailer Mfg Co 3200 S Elm St	Little Rock	AR	72204	**800-666-5417**	501-666-5417
Barrett Trailers Inc 1831 Hardcastle Blvd	Purcell	OK	73080	**888-405-4050**	405-527-5050
Brenner Tank LLC 450 Arlington Ave	Fond du Lac	WI	54935	**800-558-9750**	920-922-5020
Bri-Mar Mfg LLC 1080 S Main St	Chambersburg	PA	17201	**800-732-5845**	717-263-6116
Clement Industries Inc PO Box 914 *Cust Svc	Minden	LA	71058	**800-562-5948***	318-377-2776
CM Trailers Inc 200 County Rd PO Box 680	Madill	OK	73446	**888-268-7577**	580-795-5536
Cottrell Inc 2125 Candler Rd *Sales	Gainesville	GA	30507	**800-827-0132***	770-532-7251
Dakota Mfg Co Inc 1909 S Rowley St	Mitchell	SD	57301	**800-232-5682**	605-996-5571
Dan Hill & Assoc Inc DBA Flow Boy Mfg PO Box 720660	Norman	OK	73070	**800-580-3260**	405-329-3765
Delavan Industries 199 Lein Rd	West Seneca	NY	14224	**888-508-0700**	716-677-4080
Eager Beaver 14893 Hwy 27	Lake Wales	FL	33853	**800-257-8163**	863-638-1421
East Mfg Corp 1871 State Rt 44 PO Box 277	Randolph	OH	44265	**888-405-3278**	330-325-9921
Everlite Inc 607 Fisher Rd	Longview	TX	75604	**800-600-3867**	903-297-3444
Featherlite Inc PO Box 320 *NASDAQ: FTHR*	Cresco	IA	52136	**800-800-1230**	563-547-6000
Florig Equipment Inc 906 W Ridge Pike	Conshohocken	PA	19428	**800-345-6172**	610-825-0900
Flow Boy Mfg PO Box 720660	Norman	OK	73070	**800-580-3260**	405-329-3765
Fontaine Specialized Inc 5398 US Hwy 11	Springville	AL	35146	**800-633-6551**	205-467-6171
Fontaine Trailer Co 430 Letson Rd PO Box 619	Haleyville	AL	35565	**800-821-6535**	205-486-5251
General Trailer Parts LLC 1420 S B St	Springfield	OR	97477	**800-452-9532**	541-746-8218
Heil Trailer International 5741 Cornelison Rd Bldg A	Chattanooga	TN	37411	**800-400-6913**	423-499-1300
Hesse Inc 6700 St John Ave	Kansas City	MO	64123	**800-821-5562**	816-483-7808
Hill Dan & Assoc Inc DBA Flow Boy Mfg PO Box 720660	Norman	OK	73070	**800-580-3260**	405-329-3765
K-Dee Supply Inc 621 E Lake St	Lake Mills	WI	53551	**800-221-6417**	920-648-8202
Kalyn/Siebert LP 1505 W Main St	Gatesville	TX	76528	**800-525-9689**	254-865-7235
Kentucky Trailer 2601 S 3rd St	Louisville	KY	40217	**888-598-7245**	502-637-2551
Kentucky Trailer Technologies 1240 Pontiac Trail	Walled Lake	MI	48390	**800-521-9700**	248-960-9700
Kiefer Built Inc 305 E 1st St	Kanawha	IA	50447	**888-254-3337**	641-762-3201
Liddell Trailers 100 Industrial Dr	Springville	AL	35146	**800-662-9216**	205-467-3990
Load King Div Terex Corp 701 E Rose St PO Box 427	Elk Point	SD	57025	**800-264-5522**	605-356-3301
Mac Trailer Mfg Inc 14599 Commerce St NE	Alliance	OH	44601	**800-795-8454**	330-823-9900
Merritt Equipment Co 9339 Hwy 85	Henderson	CO	80640	**800-634-3036**	303-289-2286
Mickey Truck Bodies Inc 1305 Trinity Ave PO Box 2044	High Point	NC	27261	**800-334-9061**	336-882-6806
Nu Van Technology Inc 2155 Hwy 1187 PO Box 759	Mansfield	TX	76063	**800-487-1734**	817-477-1734
Pace American Inc 11550 Harter Dr	Middlebury	IN	46540	**800-247-5767**	574-825-7223
Parco-Hesse Corp 1060 Andre-Line Rd	Granby	QC	J2J1J9	**800-363-5975**	450-378-4696
Polar Service Centers 7600 E Sam Houston Pkwy N	Houston	TX	77049	**800-955-8558**	281-459-6400
Polar Tank Trailer Inc 12810 CR 17	Holdingford	MN	56340	**800-826-6589**	320-746-2255
Red River Mfg Inc 202 8th St W	West Fargo	ND	58078	**800-762-5557**	701-282-3013
Reliance Trailer Mfg Co 7911 Redwood Dr	Cotati	CA	94931	**800-339-7911**	707-795-0081
Rogers Brothers Corp 100 Orchard St	Albion	PA	16401	**800-441-9880**	814-756-4121
Steco Mfg 2215 S Van Buren St	Enid	OK	73703	**800-627-8326**	580-237-7433
Summit Trailer Sales Inc 1 Summit Plaza	Summit Station	PA	17979	**800-437-3729**	570-754-3511
Talbert Mfg Inc 1628 W SR-114 *Cust Svc	Rensselaer	IN	47978	**800-348-5232***	219-866-7141
Terex Corp Load King Div 701 E Rose St PO Box 427	Elk Point	SD	57025	**800-264-5522**	605-356-3301
Timpte Inc 1827 Industrial Dr	David City	NE	68632	**888-256-4884**	402-367-3056
Towmaster Inc 61381 US Hwy 12	Litchfield	MN	55355	**800-462-4517**	320-693-7900
Trail King Industries Inc 147 Industrial Pk Rd	Brookville	PA	15825	**800-545-1549**	814-849-2342
Trailmobile Corp 1101 Skokie Blvd Suite 350	Northbrook	IL	60062	**800-877-4990**	847-504-2000
Trailmobile Trailer LLC 1101 Skokie Blvd Suite 350	Northbrook	IL	60062	**800-877-4990**	847-504-2000
Trailstar Mfg Corp 20700 Harrisburg-Westville Rd	Alliance	OH	44601	**800-235-5635**	330-821-9900
Transcraft Corp 110 Florsheim Dr	Anna	IL	62906	**800-950-2995**	618-833-5151
Travis Body & Trailer Inc 13955 Furman Rd FM 529	Houston	TX	77041	**800-535-4372**	713-466-5888
Truck Equipment Service Co 800 Oak St	Lincoln	NE	68521	**800-869-0363**	402-476-3225
Vantage Trailers Inc 29335 Hwy 90	Katy	TX	77494	**800-826-8245**	281-391-2664
Wabash National Corp PO Box 6129 *NYSE: WNC* ■ *Sales	Lafayette	IN	47903	**800-937-4784***	765-771-5300
Wells Cargo Inc 1503 W McNaughton St	Elkhart	IN	46514	**800-348-7553**	574-264-9661
Western Trailer Co 6700 Business Way	Boise	ID	83716	**888-344-2539**	208-344-2539
Western World Inc 200 N Kit Ave	Caldwell	ID	83605	**800-247-2535**	208-459-0842
Wilson Trailer Co 4400 S Lewis Blvd	Sioux City	IA	51106	**800-798-2002**	712-252-6500
Witzco Trailers Inc 6101 McIntosh Rd	Sarasota	FL	34238	**888-922-9900**	941-922-5301

769 TRUCKING COMPANIES

SEE ALSO Logistics Services (Transportation & Warehousing); Moving Companies

Company	City	State	Zip	Toll-Free	Phone
AAA Cooper Transportation 1751 Kinsey Rd	Dothan	AL	36303	**800-633-7571**	334-793-2284
Ace Doran Hauling & Rigging Co Inc 1601 Blue Rock St	Cincinnati	OH	45223	**800-829-0929**	513-681-7900
Acme Truck Line Inc 121 Pailet Dr	Harvey	LA	70058	**800-825-6246**	504-368-2510

Company	City	State	ZIP	Toll-Free	Phone
Active Transportation Co 3050 W Broadway	Louisville	KY	46211	**800-685-5638**	502-775-6401
Admiral-Merchants Motor Freight Inc 215 S 11th St	Minneapolis	MN	55403	**800-972-8864**	612-332-4819
Aetna Freight Lines Inc PO Box 350	Warren	OH	44482	**800-837-4995**	330-369-5201
Alan Ritchey Inc 740 S I-35 E Frontage Rd	Valley View	TX	76272	**800-877-0273**	940-726-3276
Alvan Motor Freight Inc 3600 Alvan Rd	Kalamazoo	MI	49001	**800-632-4172**	269-382-1500
Anderson Trucking Service Inc 203 Cooper Ave N PO Box 1377	Saint Cloud	MN	56302	**800-328-2307**	320-255-7400
ARG Trucking Corp 369 Bostwick Rd	Phelps	NY	14532	**800-334-1314**	315-789-8871
Armellini Express Lines Inc 3446 SW Armellini Ave	Palm City	FL	34990	**800-626-1815**	772-287-0575
Arnold Transportation Services Inc 9523 Florida Mining Blvd	Jacksonville	FL	32257	**800-388-8320**	904-262-4285
Associated Petroleum Carriers Inc PO Box 2808	Spartanburg	SC	29304	**800-573-9301**	864-573-9301
Atkinson Freight Lines Co 2950 State Rd PO Box 984	Bensalem	PA	19020	**800-345-8052**	215-638-1130
Autolog Corp 1701 E Linden Ave	Linden	NJ	07036	**800-526-6078**	908-587-9400
Automotive Carrier Services Co LLC 402 S Main St 7th Fl	Joplin	MO	64801	**800-685-7904**	417-206-5900
Autumn Industries Inc 518 Perkins-Jones Rd	Warren	OH	44483	**800-447-2116**	330-372-5002
Averitt Express Inc PO Box 3166	Cookeville	TN	38502	**800-283-7488**	931-526-3306
Baer Howard F Inc 1301 Foster Ave	Nashville	TN	37210	**800-447-7430**	615-255-7351
Baggett Transportation Co 2 S 32nd St	Birmingham	AL	35233	**800-633-8982**	205-322-6501
Barry Trucking Inc 120 E National Ave	Milwaukee	WI	53204	**800-279-8395**	414-274-6150
Beaver Express Service LLC PO Box 1147	Woodward	OK	73802	**800-593-2328**	580-256-6460
Beelman Truck Co 4 Caine Dr *Sales	Madison	IL	62060	**800-541-5918***	618-452-8187
Benton Express Inc PO Box 16709	Atlanta	GA	30321	**888-423-6866**	404-267-2200
Besl Transfer Co 5700 Este Ave	Cincinnati	OH	45232	**800-456-2375**	513-242-3456
Bilkays Express Co 400 S 2nd St	Elizabeth	NJ	07206	**800-526-4006**	908-289-2400
Billings Freight Systems Inc PO Box 2000	Lexington	NC	27293	**800-438-2151**	336-956-1111
BJJ Co Inc PO Box 30010	Stockton	CA	95213	**800-776-2551**	209-941-8361
Black Hills Trucking Inc PO Drawer 2360	Casper	WY	82602	**800-253-8080**	307-237-9301
Blue & Gray Transportation Co Inc 1111 Commerce Rd	Richmond	VA	23234	**800-368-2583**	804-232-2324
Boyd Bros Transportation Inc 3275 Hwy 30 *NASDAQ: BOYD*	Clayton	AL	36016	**800-338-2693**	334-775-1400
Britt Trucking Co Inc PO Drawer 707	Lamesa	TX	79331	**800-448-9098**	806-872-3353
Bulkmatic Transport Co 2001 N Cline Ave	Griffith	IN	46319	**800-535-8505**	219-972-7630
Bunning John Transfer Co Inc PO Box 128	Rock Springs	WY	82902	**800-443-2753**	307-362-3791
Burns Motor Freight Inc PO Box 149	Marlinton	WV	24954	**800-598-5674**	304-799-6106
Butler & Co Inc PO Box 570	Vernon	AL	35592	**800-633-8988**	205-695-7132
Butler Trucking Co PO Box 88	Woodland	PA	16881	**800-458-3777**	814-857-7644
Caldwell Freight Lines Inc PO Box 1950	Lenoir	NC	28645	**800-438-8244**	828-728-9231
California Cartage Co Inc 3545 Long Beach Blvd 5th Fl	Long Beach	CA	90807	**888-537-1432**	562-427-1143
CAR Transportation Brokerage Co PO Box 712	Springdale	AR	72765	**800-648-6588**	479-751-8747
Carlile Transportation Services Inc 1800 E 1st Ave	Anchorage	AK	99501	**800-478-1853**	907-276-7797
Carroll Fulmer Logistics Corp 8340 American Way	Groveland	FL	34736	**800-468-9400**	352-429-5000
Celadon Trucking Services Inc 9503 E 33rd St	Indianapolis	IN	46235	**800-235-2366**	317-972-7000
CenTra 12225 Stephens Rd	Warren	MI	48089	**800-334-4883**	586-939-7000
Central Freight Lines Inc PO Box 2638 *NASDAQ: CENF*	Waco	TX	76702	**800-233-9226**	254-772-2120
Central Petroleum Transport Inc 4036 Southgate Dr *Sales	Sioux City	IA	51111	**800-798-6357***	712-258-6357
Central Transport International Inc 12225 Stephens Rd	Warren	MI	48089	**800-334-4883**	586-939-7000
Chadderton Trucking Inc PO Box 687	Sharon	PA	16146	**800-942-8074**	724-981-5050
Cimarron Express Inc 21611 SR-51 PO Box 185	Genoa	OH	43430	**800-759-8979**	419-855-7713
Clipper Exxpress Inc 9014 Heritage Pkwy Suite 300	Woodridge	IL	60517	**800-678-2547**	630-739-0700
Coastal Transport Co Inc 5714 Star Ln	Houston	TX	77057	**800-256-8897**	713-784-1010
Colonial Freight Systems Inc 10924 McBride Ln	Knoxville	TN	37932	**800-826-1402**	865-966-9711
Colorado-Denver Delivery Inc 7170 Dahlia St	Commerce City	CO	80022	**800-488-3077**	303-289-5577
Combined Transport Inc 5656 Crater Lake Ave	Central Point	OR	97502	**800-547-2870**	541-734-7418
Comcar Industries Inc 502 E Bridgers Ave *Cust Svc	Auburndale	FL	33823	**800-524-1101***	863-967-1101
Con-Way Central Express Inc 4880 Venture Dr	Ann Arbor	MI	48108	**800-421-4007**	734-994-6600
Con-Way Southern Express 14500 Trinity Blvd Suite 118	Fort Worth	TX	76155	**800-525-3117**	817-358-3600
Con-Way Western Express 6301 Beach Blvd Suite 300	Buena Park	CA	90621	**800-545-9683**	714-562-0110
Container Freight Corp 6150 Paramount Blvd	Long Beach	CA	90805	**800-252-7208**	562-220-2433
Contract Freighters Inc PO Box 2547	Joplin	MO	64803	**800-641-4747**	417-623-5229
Cooper Jack Transport Co Inc 2345 Grand Blvd Suite 400	Kansas City	MO	64108	**866-449-6301**	816-983-4000
Covenant Transport Inc 400 Birmingham Hwy *NASDAQ: CVTI*	Chattanooga	TN	37419	**800-334-9686**	423-821-1212
CR England & Sons Inc 4701 W 2100 South	Salt Lake City	UT	84120	**800-453-8826**	801-972-2712
Crescent Truck Lines 2480 Whipple Rd	Hayward	CA	94544	**800-722-3171**	510-471-8900
Cresco Lines Inc 15220 S Halsted St	Harvey	IL	60426	**800-323-4476**	708-596-8310
Crete Carrier Corp 400 NW 56th St	Lincoln	NE	68528	**800-998-4095**	402-475-9521
CRST International Inc 3930 16th Ave SW PO Box 68	Cedar Rapids	IA	52406	**800-366-8460**	319-396-4400
CS Henry Transfer Inc PO Box 2306	Rocky Mount	NC	27802	**800-849-6400**	252-446-5116
CTI PO Box 397	Rillito	AZ	85654	**800-362-4952**	520-624-2348
CTL Distribution Inc PO Drawer 437	Mulberry	FL	33860	**800-237-9088**	863-428-2373
Curtiss Arlin Trucking Inc PO Box 26	Montevideo	MN	56265	**800-328-8940**	320-269-5581
Daggett Truck Line Inc PO Box 158	Frazee	MN	56544	**800-262-9393**	218-334-3711
Dahlsten Truck Line Inc 101 W Edgar PO Box 95	Clay Center	NE	68933	**800-228-4313**	402-762-3511
Daily Express Inc 1072 Harrisburg Pike	Carlisle	PA	17013	**800-735-3136**	717-243-5757
Dallas & Mavis Specialized Carrier Co 625 55th St	Kenosha	WI	53140	**888-878-2504**	
Dana Transport Inc 210 Essex Ave E	Avenel	NJ	07001	**800-733-3262**	732-750-9100
Dart Transit Co Inc PO Box 64110	Saint Paul	MN	55164	**800-366-9000**	651-688-2000
Daylight Transport 1501 Hughes Way	Long Beach	CA	90810	**800-468-9999**	310-507-8200
Del Monte Trucking Operations 2 Nestle Way	Lathrop	CA	95330	**800-634-6300**	209-547-7275
Dennis Trucking Co Inc 6951 Norwich Dr	Philadelphia	PA	19153	**800-333-4961**	215-492-8200
Devine Intermodal 3870 Channel Dr	West Sacramento	CA	95691	**800-371-4430**	916-371-4430

Company	City	State	ZIP	Toll-Free	Phone
Diamond Transportation System Inc 5021 21st St	Racine	WI	53406	**800-927-5702**	262-554-5400
Dick Jones Trucking PO Box 136	Swanton	VT	05488	**800-451-3535**	802-868-3381
Distribution Technologies Inc DBA DistTech 14841 Sperry Rd	Newbury	OH	44065	**800-321-3143**	440-338-1010
DistTech 14841 Sperry Rd	Newbury	OH	44065	**800-321-3143**	440-338-1010
Duffy Brothers Inc PO Box 250	Columbus	WI	53925	**800-242-1887**	920-623-4160
Duncan Machinery Movers Inc 2004 Duncan Machinery Dr	Lexington	KY	40504	**800-331-0116**	859-233-7333
E & L Transport Co LLC 35005 W Michigan Ave	Wayne	MI	48184	**800-833-8322**	734-729-9500
EL Farmer & Co PO Box 3512	Odessa	TX	79760	**800-592-4753**	432-332-1496
Ennis Transportation Co Inc PO Drawer 798	Ennis	TX	75120	**800-527-6772**	972-878-5801
Enterprise Truck Line Inc 1000 Colfax St	Gary	IN	46406	**800-825-0833**	219-977-5200
Epes Carriers Inc 3400 Edgefield Ct	Greensboro	NC	27409	**800-869-3737**	336-668-3358
Erickson Transport Corp PO Box 10068	Springfield	MO	65808	**800-641-4595**	417-862-6741
EW Wylie Corp 222 40th St SW *Cust Svc	Fargo	ND	58103	**800-437-4132***	701-282-5550
Ewell HR Inc 4635 Division Hwy	East Earl	PA	17519	**800-233-0161**	717-354-4556
Farmer EL & Co PO Box 3512	Odessa	TX	79760	**800-592-4753**	432-332-1496
FedEx Freight East PO Box 840	Harrison	AR	72602	**800-874-4723**	870-741-9000
FedEx Freight West 6411 Guadalupe Mines Rd	San Jose	CA	95120	**800-845-4647**	408-268-9600
FFE Transportation Services Inc 1145 Empire Central Pl	Dallas	TX	75247	**800-569-9200**	214-630-8090
Five Star Trucking Inc 4380 Glenbrook Rd	Willoughby	OH	44094	**800-321-3658**	440-953-9300
Floyd & Beasley Transfer Co Inc PO Box 8	Sycamore	AL	35149	**800-952-7599**	256-245-4385
Fort Edward Express Co Inc PO Box 394	Fort Edward	NY	12828	**800-342-1233**	518-792-6571
Forward Air Corp PO Box 1058 *NASDAQ: FWRD*	Greeneville	TN	37744	**800-726-6654**	423-636-7100
Fredericksen Tank Lines Inc PO Box 235	West Sacramento	CA	95691	**800-441-2109**	916-371-4655
Fulmer Carroll Logistics Corp 8340 American Way	Groveland	FL	34736	**800-468-9400**	352-429-5000
Gainey Transportation Services Inc 6000 Clay Ave SW	Grand Rapids	MI	49548	**800-859-4072**	616-530-8551
GI Trucking Co 14727 Alondra Blvd	La Mirada	CA	90638	**800-541-1670**	714-523-1122
Gibco Motor Express Inc PO Box 18	Elberfeld	IN	47613	**800-333-4285**	812-867-0069
Gordon Trucking Inc 151 Stewart Rd SW	Pacific	WA	98047	**800-426-8486**	253-863-7777
Gra-Bell Truck Line Inc PO Box 1019	Holland	MI	49422	**800-632-5300**	616-396-1453
Gray Truck Line Co PO Box 1406	Lake Alfred	FL	33850	**800-282-6884**	863-956-3431
Great Lakes Cartage Co PO Box 4704 *Cust Svc	Youngstown	OH	44515	**800-228-4274***	330-793-9331
Groendyke Transport Inc 2510 Rock Island Blvd	Enid	OK	73701	**800-843-2103**	580-234-4663
H & W Trucking Co Inc 1772 N Andy Griffith Pkwy PO Box 1545	Mount Airy	NC	27030	**800-334-9181**	336-789-2188
Hallamore Motor Transportation Inc 795 Plymouth St	Holbrook	MA	02343	**800-242-1300**	781-767-2000
Heartland Express Inc 2777 Heartland Dr *NASDAQ: HTLD*	Coralville	IA	52241	**800-553-1201**	319-545-2728
Heartland Express Inc 1515 Wherebottom Springs Rd	Chester	VA	23836	**800-444-4929**	804-768-0016
Henry CS Transfer Inc PO Box 2306	Rocky Mount	NC	27802	**800-849-6400**	252-446-5116
Hirschbach Motor Lines Inc 920 W 21st St PO Box 9	South Sioux City	NE	68776	**800-554-2969**	402-494-5000
Hodges Trucking Co Inc 4050 W I-40	Oklahoma City	OK	73108	**800-733-7765**	405-947-7764
Houff Transfer Inc PO Box 220	Weyers Cave	VA	24486	**800-476-4683**	540-234-9233
Howard F Baer Inc 1301 Foster Ave	Nashville	TN	37210	**800-447-7430**	615-255-7351
Howard's Express Inc 369 Bostwick Rd	Phelps	NY	14532	**800-274-1100**	315-789-1900
HR Ewell Inc 4635 Division Hwy	East Earl	PA	17519	**800-233-0161**	717-354-4556
HTL Inc PO Box 988DTS	Omaha	NE	68101	**800-877-4136**	712-328-2393
Interstate Distributor Co 11707 21st Ave S	Tacoma	WA	98444	**800-426-8560**	253-537-9455
Irvin Dick Inc 475 Wilson Ave	Shelby	MT	59474	**800-332-5131**	406-434-5583
Jack B Kelley Inc 8101 W 34th Ave	Amarillo	TX	79121	**800-225-5525**	806-353-3553
Jack Cooper Transport Co Inc 2345 Grand Blvd Suite 400	Kansas City	MO	64108	**866-449-6301**	816-983-4000
Jerry Lipps Trucking Inc 3888 Nash Rd PO Drawer F *Cust Svc	Cape Girardeau	MO	63702	**800-325-3331***	573-335-8204
Jevic Transportation Inc 700 Creek Rd	Delanco	NJ	08075	**800-257-0427**	856-461-7111
JH Walker Trucking Co Inc 152 N Hollywood Rd	Houma	LA	70364	**800-535-5992**	985-868-8330
Jones Dick Trucking PO Box 136	Swanton	VT	05488	**800-451-3535**	802-868-3381
Jones Motor Co Inc 900 W Bridge St	Spring City	PA	19475	**800-825-6637**	610-948-7900
Keller Transfer Line Inc 5635 Clay Ave SW	Grand Rapids	MI	49548	**800-666-0701**	616-531-1850
Kelley Jack B Inc 8101 W 34th Ave	Amarillo	TX	79121	**800-225-5525**	806-353-3553
Kenan Advantage Group Inc 4895 Dressler Rd NW	Canton	OH	44718	**800-969-5149**	330-491-0474
Kenan Transport Co 100 Europa Ctr Suite 320	Chapel Hill	NC	27517	**800-768-8765**	919-967-8221
Key Energy 2210 W Broadway	Sweetwater	TX	79556	**800-749-6613**	325-236-6611
Kings County Truck Lines PO Box 1016	Tulare	CA	93275	**800-842-5285**	559-686-2857
Kinnie Annex Cartage Co 32097 Hollingsworth Ave	Warren	MI	48092	**888-546-6432**	586-939-2880
KLLM Transport Services Inc 135 Riverview Dr	Richland	MS	39218	**800-925-1000**	601-939-2545
Knight Transportation Inc 5601 W Buckeye Rd *NASDAQ: KNGT*	Phoenix	AZ	85043	**800-489-2000**	602-269-2000
Kruepke Trucking Inc 2881 Hwy P	Jackson	WI	53037	**800-798-5000**	262-677-3155
La Rosa Del Monte Express Inc 1133-35 Tiffany St	Bronx	NY	10459	**800-452-7672**	718-991-3300
Land Span Inc 1120 W Griffin Rd	Lakeland	FL	33805	**800-248-4847**	863-688-1102
Land Transportation 1901 Phoenix Blvd Suite 210	Atlanta	GA	30349	**888-831-4448**	678-251-2500
Landair Corp 430 Airport Rd	Greeneville	TN	37745	**888-526-3247**	423-783-1300
Landstar Express America Inc 13410 Sutton Park Dr S	Jacksonville	FL	32224	**800-872-3278**	
Landstar Gemini Inc 13410 Sutton Park Dr S	Jacksonville	FL	32224	**800-862-9232**	
Landstar Inway Inc 1000 Simpson Rd	Rockford	IL	61102	**800-435-4373**	815-972-5000
Landstar Ligon Inc 13410 Sutton Park Dr S	Jacksonville	FL	32224	**800-235-4466**	904-306-2440
Landstar Ranger Inc 13410 Sutton Pk Dr S	Jacksonville	FL	32224	**800-872-9400**	904-398-9400
Landstar System Inc 13410 Sutton Park Dr S *NASDAQ: LSTR*	Jacksonville	FL	32224	**800-872-9400**	904-398-9400
Lanter Co PO Box 68	Madison	IL	62060	**800-966-6137**	618-452-9500
Lawrence Transportation Systems PO Box 7667	Roanoke	VA	24019	**800-336-9626**	540-966-4000
LCT Transportation Services 26444 County Rd 33	Okahumpka	FL	34762	**800-874-3344**	352-326-8900

Company / Address	City	State	ZIP	Toll-Free	Phone
Lee & Eastes Tank Lines Inc 2418 Airport Way S	Seattle	WA	98134	**800-552-7496**	206-623-5403
Linden Bulk Transportation Co Inc 4200 Tremley Point Rd	Linden	NJ	07036	**800-333-2855**	908-862-3883
Lipps Jerry Trucking Inc 3888 Nash Rd PO Drawer F	Cape Girardeau	MO	63702	**800-325-3331***	573-335-8204
*Cust Svc					
Liquid Transport Corp 8470 Allison Pointe Blvd Suite 400	Indianapolis	IN	46250	**800-942-3175**	317-841-4200
Lisa Motor Lines Inc PO Box 4529	Fort Worth	TX	76164	**800-569-9234**	817-336-2900
Lockwood Bros Inc 220 Salters Creek Rd	Hampton	VA	23661	**800-367-5295**	757-722-1946
Lynden Transport Inc 3027 Rampart Dr	Anchorage	AK	99501	**800-327-9390**	907-276-4800
Mail Contractors of America 100 Morgan Keegan Dr Suite 200	Little Rock	AR	72202	**800-294-7743**	501-280-0500
Mainliner Motor Express Inc PO Box 7439	Omaha	NE	68107	**800-228-9887**	402-734-3500
Malone Freight Lines 1901 Floyd Bradford Rd	Trussville	AL	35173	**800-366-6350**	205-951-1900
Market Transport Ltd 110 N Marine Dr	Portland	OR	97217	**800-547-0781**	503-283-2405
Marten Transport Ltd 129 Marten St	Mondovi	WI	54755	**800-395-3000**	715-926-4216
NASDAQ: MRTN					
Martin Howard Inc 4315 Meyer Rd	Fort Wayne	IN	46806	**800-348-4759**	260-447-5591
Martin Trucking Inc PO Box M	Hugoton	KS	67951	**800-737-0047**	620-544-4920
Matheson Trucking Inc 10519 E Stockton Blvd Suite 125	Elk Grove	CA	95624	**800-455-7678**	916-685-2330
Maust Transportation 21848 76th Ave S	Kent	WA	98032	**800-446-2878**	253-479-0261
Maverick Transportation Inc PO Box 15428	Little Rock	AR	72231	**800-289-6600**	501-945-6130
May Trucking Co 4185 Brooklake Rd PO Box 9039	Salem	OR	97305	**800-547-9169**	503-393-7030
Mayfield Transfer Co Inc 3200 W Lake St	Melrose Park	IL	60160	**800-222-2959**	708-681-4440
McClendon Transportation Group PO Box 641	Lafayette	AL	36862	**800-633-7710**	334-864-9311
McLeod Trucking & Rigging PO Box 790376	Charlotte	NC	28206	**800-438-0330**	704-372-3611
McQuaide WC Inc 153 Macridge Ave	Johnstown	PA	15904	**800-456-0292**	814-269-6000
Melton Truck Lines Inc 808 N 161 East Ave	Tulsa	OK	74116	**800-545-6651**	918-234-8000
Mercer Transportation Co Inc PO Box 35610	Louisville	KY	40232	**800-626-5375**	502-584-2301
MGM Transport Corp 1 Railroad Ave	Ridgefield	NJ	07657	**800-646-8726**	201-840-1340
Midwest Coast Transport 1600 E Benson Rd	Sioux Falls	SD	57104	**800-843-6699***	605-339-8400
*Cust Svc					
Midwest Motor Express Inc 5015 E Main Ave	Bismarck	ND	58502	**800-741-4097**	701-223-1880
Milan Express Co Inc 1091 Kefauver Dr PO Box 699	Milan	TN	38358	**800-231-7303**	731-686-7428
Miller Transporters Inc 5500 Hwy 80 W	Jackson	MS	39209	**800-645-5378***	601-922-8331
*Cust Svc					
Motor Cargo Industries Inc 845 W Center St	North Salt Lake	UT	84054	**800-922-4099**	801-936-1111
Murrows Transfer Inc PO Box 4095	High Point	NC	27263	**800-669-2928***	336-475-6101
*Cust Svc					
National Carriers Inc PO Box 1358	Liberal	KS	67905	**800-835-9180**	620-624-1621
Navajo Express Inc PO Box 1780	Denver	CO	80217	**800-525-1969**	303-287-3800
New Penn Motor Express Inc 625 S 5th Ave	Lebanon	PA	17042	**800-285-5000***	717-274-2521
*Cust Svc					
Nick Strimbu Inc 3500 Parkway Rd	Brookfield	OH	44403	**800-446-8785**	330-448-4071
Nussbaum Trucking Inc 2200 N Main St	Normal	IL	61761	**800-322-7305**	309-452-4426
Old Dominion Freight Line Inc 500 Old Dominion Way	Thomasville	NC	27360	**800-432-6335**	336-889-5000
NASDAQ: ODFL					
Oliver Trucking Co Inc PO Box 53	Winchester	KY	40392	**800-354-7421**	859-744-6373
Overnite Corp PO Box 1216	Richmond	VA	23218	**800-334-3343**	804-231-8000
NASDAQ: OVNT					
Ozark Motor Lines Inc 3934 Homewood Rd	Memphis	TN	38118	**800-264-4100**	901-251-9711
PAM Transportation Services Inc PO Box 188	Tontitown	AR	72770	**800-879-7261**	479-361-9111
NASDAQ: PTSI					
Patriot Transportation Holding Inc 1801 Art Museum Dr 3rd Fl	Jacksonville	FL	32207	**877-704-1776**	904-396-5733
NASDAQ: PATR					
Peet Frate Line Inc 650 S Eastwood Dr PO Box 1129	Woodstock	IL	60098	**800-435-6909**	815-338-5500
Perkins Specialized Transportation Inc 5502 W 73rd St	Indianapolis	IN	46268	**800-428-3762**	317-297-3550
Petron Inc PO Box 8718	Alexandria	LA	71306	**800-551-6678**	318-445-5685
Pitt Ohio Express 15 27th St	Pittsburgh	PA	15222	**800-366-7488***	412-281-9883
*Cust Svc					
Powers Transportation Systems Inc PO Box 103	Savannah	GA	31402	**888-673-1287**	912-966-2198
Pozas Brothers Trucking Co Inc 8130 Enterprise Dr	Newark	CA	94560	**800-874-8383**	510-742-9939
Prestera Trucking PO Box 399	South Point	OH	45680	**800-759-9555**	740-894-4770
Prime Inc PO Box 4208	Springfield	MO	65808	**800-848-4560***	417-866-0001
*Cust Svc					
Puget Sound Truck Lines Inc 3720 Airport Way S	Seattle	WA	98134	**800-638-2254**	206-623-1600
Quality Distribution Inc 3802 Corporex Pk Dr Suite 200	Tampa	FL	33619	**800-282-2031**	813-630-5826
NASDAQ: QLTY					
Refrigerated Food Express Inc PO Box 347	Avon	MA	02322	**800-225-2350**	508-587-4600
Reliable Trucking Inc 5141 Commercial Cir	Concord	CA	94520	**800-952-3344**	925-681-6500
RFK Transportation 5650 6th St SW	Cedar Rapids	IA	52404	**800-322-8412**	319-364-8102
Ritchey Alan Inc 740 S I-35 E Frontage Rd	Valley View	TX	76272	**800-877-0273**	940-726-3276
Roadway Express Inc 1077 Gorge Blvd	Akron	OH	44310	**800-762-3929**	330-384-1717
Roehl Transport Inc 1916 E 29th St PO Box 750	Marshfield	WI	54449	**800-826-8367**	715-387-3795
Rountree Transport & Rigging Inc 2640 N Lane Ave	Jacksonville	FL	32254	**800-342-5036**	904-781-1033
Roy Bros Inc 764 Boston Rd	Billerica	MA	01821	**800-225-0830***	978-667-1921
*Cust Svc					
RTI Transport Inc 5635 Clay Ave SW	Grand Rapids	MI	49548	**800-666-0701**	616-531-1467
Saia Motor Freight Line Inc 11465 Johns Creek Pkwy Suite 400	Duluth	GA	30097	**800-950-7242**	770-232-4050
Sammons Trucking 3665 W Broadway	Missoula	MT	59808	**800-548-9276**	406-728-2600
Schilli Transportation Services Inc 6358 W US 24	Remington	IN	47977	**800-759-2101**	219-261-2101
Schneider National Inc 3101 S Packerland Dr PO Box 2545	Green Bay	WI	54306	**800-558-6767***	920-592-2000
*Cust Svc					
SCS Transportation Inc 4435 Main St Suite 930	Kansas City	MO	64111	**800-533-9643**	816-960-3664
NASDAQ: SCST					
Seaboard Tank Lines Inc 124 Monahan Ave	Dunmore	PA	18512	**800-338-4221**	570-343-2491
Shaffer Trucking Inc 49 E Main St PO Box 418	New Kingstown	PA	17072	**800-742-3337***	717-766-4708
*Cust Svc					
Shaw Trucking Inc 7804 Belvedere Rd	West Palm Beach	FL	33411	**800-930-7263**	
Shaw Willis Express Inc 201 N Elm St	Elm Springs	AR	72728	**800-643-3540**	479-248-7261
Sheedy Drayage Co Inc 1215 Michigan St	San Francisco	CA	94107	**800-792-2984**	415-648-7171
Shippers Express Co 1651 Kerr Dr	Jackson	MS	39204	**800-647-2480**	601-948-4251
Short Freight Lines Inc 459 S River Rd	Bay City	MI	48708	**800-248-0625**	989-893-3505
Smithway Motor Xpress Inc 2031 Quail Ave	Fort Dodge	IA	50501	**800-247-4972**	515-576-7418
NASDAQ: SMXC					
South Shore Transportation Inc 4010 Columbus Ave	Sandusky	OH	44870	**800-418-9726**	419-626-6267
Southeastern Freight Lines Inc 420 Davega Rd	Lexington	SC	29073	**800-637-7335**	803-794-7300
Southwestern Motor Transport Inc 4600 Goldfield	San Antonio	TX	78218	**800-531-1071**	210-661-6791
Spectraserv Inc 75 Jacobus Ave	South Kearny	NJ	07032	**800-445-4436**	973-589-0277
Stahly Cartage Co 119 S Main St	Edwardsville	IL	62025	**800-851-5553**	618-656-5070
Star Transportation Inc 1116 Polk Ave	Nashville	TN	37210	**800-333-3060**	615-256-4336
Stevens Transport PO Box 279010	Dallas	TX	75227	**800-233-9369**	972-216-9000
Strimbu Nick Inc 3500 Parkway Rd	Brookfield	OH	44403	**800-446-8785**	330-448-4071
Sullivan RM Transportation 649 Cottage St	Springfield	MA	01104	**800-628-1064**	413-739-2558
Sunbelt Furniture Express Inc PO Box 487	Hickory	NC	28603	**800-766-1117**	828-464-7240
Sunco Carriers Inc 1025 N Chestnut Rd	Lakeland	FL	33805	**800-237-8288**	863-688-1948
Sunflower Carriers Inc PO Box 9	York	NE	68467	**800-775-5000***	402-362-7491
*Cust Svc					
Superior Carriers Inc 2122 York Rd Suite 150	Oak Brook	IL	60523	**800-654-7707**	630-573-2555
Swift Transportation Co Inc 2200 S 75th Ave	Phoenix	AZ	85043	**800-800-2200**	602-269-9700
NASDAQ: SWFT					
T & T Trucking Inc 11396 N Hwy 99	Lodi	CA	95240	**800-692-3457**	209-368-3629
Tank Lines Inc 1357 Diamond Springs Rd	Virginia Beach	VA	23455	**800-969-1357**	757-464-9349
Tankstar USA Inc PO Box 736	Milwaukee	WI	53201	**800-338-5699**	414-671-1600
Tauro Brothers Trucking Co 1775 N State St	Girard	OH	44420	**800-860-9763**	330-545-9763
Telfer Oil Co 211 Foster St	Martinez	CA	94553	**800-624-9917**	925-228-1515
Teresi Trucking Inc PO Box 1270	Lodi	CA	95241	**800-692-3431**	209-368-2472
Thomas WS Transfer Inc 1854 Morgantown Ave	Fairmont	WV	26554	**800-624-8062**	304-363-8050
Tiona Truck Line Inc PO Box 90	Butler	MO	64730	**800-821-3046**	660-679-4197
Trailer Bridge Inc 10405 New Berlin Rd E	Jacksonville	FL	32226	**800-554-1589**	904-751-7100
NASDAQ: TRBR					
TransAm Trucking Inc 15910 S 169th Hwy	Olathe	KS	66051	**800-573-0588**	913-782-5300
Transport Corp of America Inc 1715 Yankee Doodle Rd	Eagan	MN	55121	**800-328-3927**	651-686-2500
NASDAQ: TCAM					
Transport Inc PO Box 400	Moorhead	MN	56561	**800-949-7678**	218-236-6300
Transport Service Co 908 N Elm St Suite 101	Hinsdale	IL	60521	**800-323-5561***	630-920-5800
*Sales					
Trimac Transportation System PO Box 3000	Rapid City	SD	57709	**800-843-4012**	605-348-1063
Triple Crown Services 2720 Dupont Commerce Ct	Fort Wayne	IN	46825	**800-325-6510**	260-416-3600
Truck Transport Inc 2280 Cassens Dr	Fenton	MO	63026	**800-274-5995**	636-343-1877
Underwood Machinery Transport Inc 940 W Troy Ave	Indianapolis	IN	46225	**800-428-2372**	317-783-9235
United Road Services Inc 17 Computer Dr W	Albany	NY	12205	**888-730-7797**	518-446-0140
Universal Truckload Services Inc 11355 Stephens Rd	Warren	MI	48089	**800-233-9445**	586-920-0100
NASDAQ: UACL					
US Cargo & Courier Service 900 Williams Ave	Columbus	OH	43212	**800-234-8608**	614-552-2746
US Xpress Enterprises Inc 4080 Jenkins Rd	Chattanooga	TN	37421	**800-251-6291**	423-510-3000
NASDAQ: XPRSA					
USA Truck Inc 3200 Industrial Pk Rd	Van Buren	AR	72956	**800-872-8782**	479-471-2500
NASDAQ: USAK					
USF Bestway Inc 17200 N Perimeter Dr	Scottsdale	AZ	85255	**800-274-1250**	480-760-1675
USF Dugan Inc 2015 S Meridian Ave	Wichita	KS	67213	**800-888-4151**	316-941-3000
USF Holland Inc 750 E 40th St	Holland	MI	49423	**800-456-6322**	616-395-5000
USF Reddaway Inc PO Box 1035	Clackamas	OR	97015	**800-395-1360**	503-650-1286
Vitran Express Inc 6500 E 30th St	Indianapolis	IN	46219	**800-366-0150**	317-803-6400
Waggoners Trucking PO Box 31357	Billings	MT	59107	**800-999-9097**	406-248-1919
Ward Trucking Corp PO Box 1553	Altoona	PA	16603	**800-458-3625**	814-944-0803
Warren Transport Inc PO Box 420	Waterloo	IA	50704	**800-553-2792**	319-233-6113
Watkins Motor Lines Inc PO Box 95002	Lakeland	FL	33804	**800-284-4544**	863-687-4545
WC McQuaide Inc 153 Macridge Ave	Johnstown	PA	15904	**800-456-0292**	814-269-6000
Weaver Brothers Inc 2230 Spar Ave	Anchorage	AK	99501	**800-478-4600**	907-278-4526
Werner Enterprises Inc PO Box 45308	Omaha	NE	68145	**800-228-2240**	402-895-6640
NASDAQ: WERN					
Western Co-op Transport Assn PO Box 327	Montevideo	MN	56265	**800-992-8817**	320-269-5531
White Brothers Trucking Co PO Box 82	Wasco	IL	60183	**800-323-4762**	630-584-3810
Wildwood Express Trucking 12416 E Swanson Ave	Kingsburg	CA	93631	**800-627-3115**	559-897-1035
Wilhelm Trucking Co PO Box 10363	Portland	OR	97296	**800-275-3974***	503-227-0561
*Cust Svc					
Willis Shaw Express Inc 201 N Elm St	Elm Springs	AR	72728	**800-643-3540**	479-248-7261
Wilson Trucking Corp PO Box 200	Fishersville	VA	22939	**800-494-5766**	540-949-3200
Wispak Transport Inc 11225 W County Line Rd	Milwaukee	WI	53224	**800-558-0560**	414-410-8282
Womeldorf Inc PO Box 829	Du Bois	PA	15801	**800-245-6339**	814-849-8347
Wynne Transport Service Inc 2222 N 11th St	Omaha	NE	68108	**800-383-9330**	402-342-4001
Yanke Group of Cos 2815 Lorne Ave	Saskatoon	SK	S7J0S5	**800-667-7988**	306-955-4221
Yeatts Transfer Co PO Box 687	Altavista	VA	24517	**800-446-0939**	434-369-5695
Yellow Freight System Inc 10990 Roe Ave	Overland Park	KS	66211	**800-458-3323**	913-344-3000
Young's Commercial Transfer 44 S Lotas St	Porterville	CA	93257	**800-289-1639**	559-784-6651
Yourga Trucking Inc 145 JH Yourga Pl	Wheatland	PA	16161	**800-245-1722**	724-981-3600

770 TYPESETTING & RELATED SERVICES

SEE ALSO Graphic Design; Printing Companies - Commercial Printers

Company / Address	City	State	ZIP	Toll-Free	Phone
Ano-Coil Corp 60 E Main St	Rockville	CT	06066	**800-492-7286**	860-871-1200
Artisan Press 726 Jefferson Ave	Ashland	OR	97520	**800-424-9364**	541-482-3373

Classified Section

				Toll-Free	Phone
Auto-Graphics Inc 3201 Temple Ave	Pomona	CA	91768	**800-776-6939**	909-595-7204
Blanks Color Imaging 2343 N Beckley Ave	Dallas	TX	75208	**800-325-7651**	214-741-3905
Carey Digital 1718 Central Pkwy	Cincinnati	OH	45214	**800-767-6071**	513-241-5210
Citiplate Inc 1600 Stewart Ave Suite 201	Westbury	NY	11590	**800-280-9778**	516-484-2000
Cohber Communication PO Box 93100	Rochester	NY	14692	**800-724-3032**	585-272-1100
Color Communication Inc 4000 W Fillmore St	Chicago	IL	60624	**800-458-5743**	773-638-1400
Colorhouse Inc 13010 County Rd 6	Plymouth	MN	55441	**800-328-8046**	763-553-0100
Composing Room of Michigan Inc 678 Front Ave NW Suite 135	Grand Rapids	MI	49504	**800-253-4632**	616-776-7940
Cosco Graphics PO Box 836	Toledo	OH	43697	**800-837-4221**	419-243-4221
GGS Information Services Inc 3265 Farmtrail Rd	York	PA	17402	**800-927-4474**	717-764-2222
IPC Communications Services 501 Colonial Dr	Saint Joseph	MI	49085	**888-563-3220**	269-983-7105
JJ Michael Inc 74 Industrial Ave	Little Ferry	NJ	07643	**800-879-0470**	201-641-3600
KC Photo Engraving Co 2666 E Nina St	Pasadena	CA	91107	**800-660-4127**	323-681-0203
Kreber Graphics Inc 2580 Westbelt Dr	Columbus	OH	43228	**800-777-3501**	614-529-5701
Lastra America Inc 83 Wooster Heights Rd	Danbury	CT	06810	**800-325-3310**	203-744-6720
Ligature 4909 Alcoa Ave	Los Angeles	CA	90058	**800-944-5440**	323-585-6000
Mark Trece Inc 112 Connolly Rd	Fallston	MD	21047	**800-638-1464**	410-893-3903
Memphis Engraving Co 5120 Elmore Rd	Memphis	TN	38134	**800-426-6803**	901-388-8200
Meridian Inc 4805 G St	Omaha	NE	68117	**800-733-7765**	402-733-6400
Michael JJ Inc 74 Industrial Ave	Little Ferry	NJ	07643	**800-879-0470**	201-641-3600
Napp Systems Inc 260 S Pacific St	San Marcos	CA	92078	**800-854-2860**	760-510-6277
National Engraving Co 248 Oxmoor Ct	Birmingham	AL	35209	**800-633-8613**	205-942-2809
NEC Inc 1504 Elm Hill Pike	Nashville	TN	37210	**800-666-8243**	615-367-9110
Peerless Group 823 Main St	Little Rock	AR	72201	**800-880-7671**	501-375-8266
Presstek Inc 55 Executive Dr	Hudson	NH	03051	**877-862-2227**	603-595-7000
NASDAQ: PRST					
Printing Developments Inc 2010 Indiana St	Racine	WI	53405	**800-558-9425**	262-554-1030
Pro Image Corp 1805 Loucks Rd	York	PA	17404	**800-245-7259**	717-764-5880
Progressive Information Technologies 315 Busser Rd	Emigsville	PA	17318	**800-673-2500**	717-764-5908
Ridgways Inc 5711 Hillcroft St	Houston	TX	77036	**800-777-1623**	713-782-8580
Ropkey Graphics Inc 4923 W 78th St	Indianapolis	IN	46268	**800-783-8265**	317-632-5446
Schawkgraphics Inc 1600 E Sherwin Ave	Des Plaines	IL	60018	**800-621-1909**	847-296-6000
Southern Graphic Systems Inc 2823 S Floyd St	Louisville	KY	40209	**800-228-3720**	502-637-5443
Stratford Publishing Services 70 Landmark Hill Dr	Brattleboro	VT	05301	**800-451-4328**	802-254-6073
T & R Graphic Imaging Inc 2535 17th St	Denver	CO	80211	**800-525-2497**	303-458-0626
Thomas Technology & Solutions Inc 1 Progress Dr	Horsham	PA	19044	**800-872-2828**	215-682-5000
Trece Mark Inc 112 Connolly Rd	Fallston	MD	21047	**800-638-1464**	410-893-3903
Typesetting Inc 1144 S Robertson Blvd	Los Angeles	CA	90035	**800-794-8973**	310-273-3330
West Essex Graphics Inc 305 Fairfield Ave	Fairfield	NJ	07004	**800-221-5859**	973-227-2400
Zenith Engraving Co PO Box 870	Chester	SC	29706	**800-551-7535**	803-377-1911

771 ULTRASONIC CLEANING EQUIPMENT

SEE ALSO Dental Equipment & Supplies - Mfr

				Toll-Free	Phone
Crest Ultrasonics Corp PO Box 7266	Trenton	NJ	08628	**800-992-7378**	609-883-4000
Lewis Ultrasonics 102 Willenbroch Rd	Oxford	CT	06478	**800-243-5092**	203-264-3100
Sonicor Instrument Corp 100 Wartburg Ave	Copiague	NY	11726	**800-864-5022**	631-842-3344
Sonics & Materials Inc 53 Church Hill Rd	Newtown	CT	06470	**800-745-1105**	203-270-4600
Sterigenics 2015 Spring Rd Suite 650	Oak Brook	IL	60523	**800-472-4508**	630-928-1700

772 UMBRELLAS & PARTS

SEE ALSO Furniture - Mfr - Outdoor Furniture

				Toll-Free	Phone
Totes Isotoner Corp 9655 International Blvd	Cincinnati	OH	45246	**800-762-8712**	513-682-8200

773 UNIVERSITIES - CANADIAN

				Toll-Free	Phone
Athabasca University 1 University Dr	Athabasca	AB	T9S3A3	**800-788-9041**	780-675-6111
Augustana University College 4901 46th Ave	Camrose	AB	T4V2R3	**800-661-8714**	780-679-1100
Bishop's University rue College	Lennoxville	QC	J1M1Z7	**800-567-2792**	819-822-9600
Laurentian University 935 Ramsey Lake Rd	Sudbury	ON	P3E2C6	**800-461-4030**	705-675-4843
Redeemer University College 777 Garner Rd E	Ancaster	ON	L9K1J4	**877-779-0913**	905-648-2131
Royal Roads University 2005 Sooke Rd	Victoria	BC	V9B5Y2	**800-788-8028**	250-391-2550
Trent University 1600 W Bank Dr	Peterborough	ON	K9J7B8	**888-739-8885**	705-748-1011
Trinity Western University 7600 Glover Rd	Langley	BC	V2Y1Y1	**888-468-6898**	604-888-7511
Universite Laval Pavillion Bonensant	Quebec	QC	G1K7P4	**877-785-2825**	418-656-2131
Universite de Moncton 165 Massey Ave	Moncton	NB	E1A3E9	**800-363-8336**	506-858-4000
University of British Columbia 2329 West Mall	Vancouver	BC	V6T1Z4	**877-272-1422**	604-822-9836
University of Manitoba 66 Chancellors Cir	Winnipeg	MB	R3T2N2	**800-224-7713***	204-474-8880
*Admissions					
University of Ottawa 550 Cumberland St	Ottawa	ON	K1N6N5	**877-868-8292**	613-562-5800
University of Prince Edward Island 550 University Ave	Charlottetown	PE	C1A4P3	**800-606-8734**	902-566-0400

774 UTILITY COMPANIES

SEE ALSO Electric Companies - Cooperatives (Rural); Gas Transmission - Natural Gas

				Toll-Free	Phone
AEP Public Service Co of Oklahoma PO Box 201	Tulsa	OK	74102	**888-216-3523**	
AEP Texas 1 Riverside Dr	Columbus	OH	43215	**866-322-5563**	
AGL Resources Inc 10 Peachtree Pl	Atlanta	GA	30309	**800-427-5463***	404-584-4000
*NYSE: ATG ■ *Cust Svc*					
Alabama Gas Corp (Alagasco) 605 Richard Arrington Jr Blvd N	Birmingham	AL	35203	**800-292-4005**	205-326-8100
Alabama Power Co PO Box 2641	Birmingham	AL	35291	**800-245-2244**	205-257-1000
Alaska Power & Telephone Co 193 Otto St	Port Townsend	WA	98368	**800-982-0136***	360-385-1733
*Cust Svc					
Allegheny Power 800 Cabin Hill Dr	Greensburg	PA	15601	**800-255-3443***	724-837-3000
*Cust Svc					
Alliant Energy Corp 4902 N Biltmore Ln	Madison	WI	53707	**800-521-1725***	608-458-3311
*NYSE: LNT ■ *Cust Svc*					
AmerenUE PO Box 66149	Saint Louis	MO	63166	**800-552-7583**	314-621-3222
American States Water Co 630 E Foothill Blvd	San Dimas	CA	91773	**800-999-4033**	909-394-3600
NYSE: AWR					
APS (Arizona Public Service Co) 400 N 5th St	Phoenix	AZ	85004	**800-253-9405***	602-250-1000
*Cust Svc					
Aquarion Co 835 Main St	Bridgeport	CT	06604	**800-732-9678**	203-336-7624
Aquila Inc 20 W 9th St	Kansas City	MO	64105	**800-303-0752**	816-421-6600
NYSE: ILA					
Arizona Public Service Co (APS) 400 N 5th St	Phoenix	AZ	85004	**800-253-9405***	602-250-1000
*Cust Svc					
Arkansas Western Gas Co 1001 Sain St	Fayetteville	AR	72703	**800-773-2113**	479-521-5400
Atmos Energy Corp PO Box 650205	Dallas	TX	75265	**888-954-4321**	972-934-9227
NYSE: ATO					
Avista Corp 1411 E Mission St	Spokane	WA	99202	**800-727-9170**	509-495-4817
NYSE: AVA					
Avista Utilities 1411 E Mission St	Spokane	WA	99202	**800-227-9187**	509-495-4817
Baltimore Gas & Electric Co 39 W Lexington St	Baltimore	MD	21201	**800-685-0123**	410-234-5000
Bangor Hydro Electric Co 33 State St	Bangor	ME	04402	**800-499-6600**	207-945-5621
Bay State Gas Co 300 Friberg Pkwy	Westborough	MA	01581	**800-882-5454**	508-836-7000
Berkshire Gas Co Inc 115 Cheshire Rd	Pittsfield	MA	01201	**800-292-5012**	413-442-1511
BIW Ltd 230 Beaver St	Ansonia	CT	06401	**800-481-0141**	203-735-1888
AMEX: BIW					
Bonneville Power Administration 905 NE 11th Ave	Portland	OR	97232	**800-282-3713**	503-230-3000
California Water Service Group 1720 N 1st St	San Jose	CA	95112	**800-750-8200**	408-367-8200
NYSE: CWT					
Calpine Corp 50 W San Fernando St 5th Fl	San Jose	CA	95113	**800-359-5115**	408-995-5115
NYSE: CPN					
Cap Rock Energy Corp 500 W Wall St Suite 400	Midland	TX	79701	**800-442-8688**	432-683-5422
AMEX: RKE					
CenterPoint Energy Arkla PO Box 751	Little Rock	AR	72203	**800-992-7552**	501-377-4556
Central Hudson Gas & Electric Corp 284 South Ave	Poughkeepsie	NY	12601	**800-527-2714**	845-452-2000
Central Maine Power Co 83 Edison Dr	Augusta	ME	04336	**800-565-0121**	207-623-3521
Central Vermont Public Service Corp 77 Grove St	Rutland	VT	05701	**800-649-2877***	802-773-2711
*NYSE: CV ■ *Cust Svc*					
Cinergy/CG & E 139 E 4th St	Cincinnati	OH	45201	**800-544-6900***	513-421-9500
*Cust Svc					
Cinergy/PSI 139 E 4th St	Cincinnati	OH	45201	**800-544-6900***	513-421-9500
*Cust Svc					
Cinergy/ULH & P 139 E 4th St	Cincinnati	OH	45202	**800-544-6900***	513-421-9500
*Cust Svc					
Citizens Gas & Coke Utility 2020 N Meridian St	Indianapolis	IN	46202	**800-427-4217**	317-924-3341
City Public Service Board 145 Navarro St	San Antonio	TX	78296	**800-773-3077**	210-353-2222
Cleco Power LLC 2030 Donahue Ferry Rd	Pineville	LA	71361	**800-622-6537***	318-484-7400
*Cust Svc					
CMS Electric & Gas Co 1 Energy Plaza	Jackson	MI	49201	**888-477-5050**	517-788-0550
Colorado Springs Utilities 111 S Cascade Ave	Colorado Springs	CO	80903	**800-238-5434**	719-448-4800
Columbia Gas of Kentucky Inc 2001 Mercer Rd	Lexington	KY	40511	**800-432-9345**	859-288-0210
Columbia Gas of Maryland Inc 501 Technology Dr	Canonsburg	PA	15317	**888-460-4332***	724-416-6300
*Cust Svc					
Columbia Gas of Ohio Inc 200 Civic Center Dr	Columbus	OH	43215	**800-282-3044**	614-460-6000
Columbia Gas of Pennsylvania Inc 501 Technology Dr	Canonsburg	PA	15317	**888-460-4332***	724-416-6300
*Cust Svc					
Columbia Gas of Virginia Inc 1809 Coyote Dr	Chester	VA	23836	**800-543-8911***	804-323-5300
*Cust Svc					
ComEd An Exelon Co PO Box 87522	Chicago	IL	60680	**800-334-7661**	312-394-4321
Conectiv Power Delivery 630 Martin Luther King Blvd	Wilmington	DE	19899	**800-375-7117***	302-454-0300
*Cust Svc					
Connecticut Light & Power Co 107 Selden St	Berlin	CT	06037	**800-286-2000***	860-665-5000
*Cust Svc					
Consolidated Edison Co of New York 4 Irving Pl	New York	NY	10003	**800-752-6633**	212-460-4600
Consumers Energy Co 1 Energy Plaza	Jackson	MI	49201	**800-477-5050***	517-788-0550
*Cust Svc					
Covanta Energy Corp 40 Lane Rd	Fairfield	NJ	07004	**866-268-2682**	973-882-9000
CrossCountry Energy Co 1331 Lamar St Suite 650	Houston	TX	77010	**800-973-6766**	713-853-0300
Dayton Power & Light Co PO Box 1247	Dayton	OH	45401	**800-433-8500**	937-331-3900
Delta Natural Gas Co Inc 3617 Lexington Rd	Winchester	KY	40391	**800-262-2012**	859-744-6171
NASDAQ: DGAS					
Detroit Edison Co 2000 2nd Ave	Detroit	MI	48226	**800-477-4747***	313-235-8000
*Cust Svc					
Dominion East Ohio 701 E Cary St	Richmond	VA	23219	**888-667-3000**	804-771-3000
Dominion Hope 701 E Cary St	Richmond	VA	23219	**888-667-3000**	304-623-8600
Dominion North Carolina Power 701 E Cary St	Richmond	VA	23219	**888-667-3000**	804-771-3000
Dominion Peoples 625 Liberty Ave	Pittsburgh	PA	15222	**800-764-0111**	412-244-2626
Dominion Virginia Power 701 E Cary St	Richmond	VA	23219	**888-667-3000**	804-771-3000
Duke Energy North America 5400 Westheimer Ct	Houston	TX	77056	**800-873-3853**	713-627-5400
Duke Energy Services Group 5400 Westheimer Ct	Houston	TX	77056	**800-873-3853**	713-627-5400
Duke Energy Trading & Marketing 5400 Westheimer Ct	Houston	TX	77056	**800-873-3853**	713-260-1800
Duquesne Light Co 411 7th Ave	Pittsburgh	PA	15230	**888-393-7100***	412-393-6000
*Cust Svc					

Company / Address	City	State	ZIP	Toll-Free	Phone
Edison Sault Electric Co 725 E Portage Ave	Sault Sainte Marie	MI	49783	**800-562-4960**	906-632-2221
El Paso Electric Co 123 W Mills St	El Paso	TX	79901	**800-351-1621**	915-543-5711
NYSE: EE					
Elizabethtown Gas Co 1 Elizabethtown Plaza	Union	NJ	07083	**800-242-5830**	908-289-5000
Empire District Electric Co 602 Joplin St	Joplin	MO	64801	**800-639-0077**	417-625-5100
NYSE: EDE					
Energy America Inc 2225 Sheppard Ave E Main Fl	Toronto	ON	M2J5C2	**888-305-3828**	
Energy West Inc 1 First Ave S	Great Falls	MT	59401	**800-570-5688**	406-791-7500
NASDAQ: EWST					
EnergyUSA-TPC Corp 1500 165th St	Hammond	IN	46324	**800-531-1193**	219-853-5929
Enron Corp 1221 Lamar St	Houston	TX	77010	**800-973-6766**	713-853-6161
Entergy Arkansas Inc 425 W Capitol Ave	Little Rock	AR	72201	**800-368-3749**	501-377-4000
Entergy Louisiana Inc 639 Loyola Ave	New Orleans	LA	70113	**800-368-3749***	504-529-5262
*Cust Svc					
Entergy New Orleans Inc 639 Loyola Ave	New Orleans	LA	70113	**800-368-3749***	504-529-5262
*Cust Svc					
Entergy Texas Inc 350 Pine St	Beaumont	TX	77701	**800-368-3749**	409-838-6631
Environmental Power Corp 1 Cate St 4th Fl	Portsmouth	NH	03801	**888-430-3082**	603-431-1780
Equitable Gas Co 200 Allegheny Ctr Mall	Pittsburgh	PA	15212	**800-654-6335**	412-395-3000
Equitable Utilities 200 Allegheny Center Mall	Pittsburgh	PA	15212	**800-654-6335**	412-395-3000
Florida City Gas 955 E 25th St	Hialeah	FL	33013	**800-993-7546**	305-691-8710
Florida Public Utilities Co 401 S Dixie Hwy	West Palm Beach	FL	33401	**800-427-7712**	561-832-0872
AMEX: FPU					
FPL Energy Inc 700 Universe Blvd	Juno Beach	FL	33408	**888-867-3050**	561-691-7171
Gaz Metro LP 1717 rue du Havre	Montreal	QC	H2K2X3	**800-567-1313**	514-598-3444
TSE: GZM.un					
Georgia Power Co 241 Ralph McGill Blvd NE	Atlanta	GA	30308	**888-660-5890***	404-506-6526
*Cust Svc					
Granite State Electric Co 55 Bearfoot Rd	Northborough	MA	01532	**800-322-3223**	508-357-4501
Green Mountain Energy Co 3815 Capital of Texas Hwy Suite 100	Austin	TX	78704	**800-286-5856***	512-691-6100
*Cust Svc					
Green Mountain Power Corp 163 Acorn Ln	Colchester	VT	05446	**888-835-4672**	802-864-5731
NYSE: GMP					
Gulf Power Co 1 Energy Pl	Pensacola	FL	32520	**800-487-6937**	850-444-6111
Hydro One Inc 483 Bay St	Toronto	ON	M5G2P5	**888-664-9376**	416-345-5000
Idaho Power Co 1221 W Idaho St	Boise	ID	83702	**800-488-6151**	208-388-2200
Illuminating Co 76 S Main St	Akron	OH	44308	**800-646-0400**	216-622-9800
Indianapolis Power & Light Co PO Box 1595	Indianapolis	IN	46206	**888-261-8222***	317-261-8261
*Cust Svc					
Intermountain Gas Co Inc 555 S Cole Rd	Boise	ID	83709	**800-548-3679***	208-377-6000
*Cust Svc					
Kansas Gas Service 7421 W 129th St	Overland Park	KS	66213	**800-794-4780**	913-319-8600
KCS Energy Inc 5555 San Felipe St Suite 1200	Houston	TX	77056	**800-848-9844**	713-877-8006
NYSE: KCS					
Kentucky Utilities Co 1 Quality St	Lexington	KY	40507	**800-981-0600**	859-255-2100
Kinder Morgan Inc 500 Dallas St Suite 1000	Houston	TX	77002	**800-525-3752**	713-369-9000
NYSE: KMI					
Kinder Morgan Inc KN Energy Retail Div 370 Van Gordon St	Lakewood	CO	80228	**800-232-1627**	303-989-1740
KN Energy Retail Div Kinder Morgan Inc 370 Van Gordon St	Lakewood	CO	80228	**800-232-1627**	303-989-1740
Laclede Gas Co 720 Olive St	Saint Louis	MO	63101	**800-887-4173**	314-342-0500
Long Island Power Authority 333 Earle Ovington Blvd Suite 403	Uniondale	NY	11553	**877-275-5472***	516-222-7700
*Cust Svc					
Louisville Gas & Electric Co 220 W Main St	Louisville	KY	40202	**800-331-7370**	502-627-2000
Madison Gas & Electric Co 133 S Blair St	Madison	WI	53703	**800-245-1125**	608-252-7000
Maine & Maritimes Corp 209 State St	Presque Isle	ME	04769	**877-655-4448**	207-768-5811
AMEX: MAM					
Massachusetts Electric Co 25 Research Dr	Westborough	MA	01582	**800-322-3223**	508-389-2000
Merrill Lynch Commodities 20 E Greenway Plaza Suite 700	Houston	TX	77046	**866-820-6000**	713-544-6222
Metretek Technologies Inc 303 E 17th Ave Suite 660	Denver	CO	80203	**800-394-8169**	303-785-8080
Metromedia Energy Inc 6 Industrial Way W Suite F	Eatontown	NJ	07724	**800-828-9427**	732-542-7575
Metropolitan Utilities District 1723 Harney St	Omaha	NE	68102	**800-732-5864**	402-449-8155
Michigan Consolidated Gas Co 2000 2nd Ave	Detroit	MI	48226	**800-477-4747***	313-235-4000
*Cust Svc					
MidAmerican Energy Co 666 Grand Ave	Des Moines	IA	50309	**800-338-8007**	515-242-4300
Middle Tennessee Natural Gas Utility District 1036 W Broad	Smithville	TN	37166	**800-880-6373**	615-597-4300
Middlesex Water Co 1500 Ronson Rd	Iselin	NJ	08830	**800-729-4030**	732-634-1500
NASDAQ: MSEX					
Minnesota Power Inc 30 W Superior St	Duluth	MN	55802	**800-228-4966**	218-722-2641
Mirant Corp 1155 Perimeter Ctr W	Atlanta	GA	30338	**800-334-2726**	678-579-7000
Mississippi Power Co Inc 2992 W Beach Blvd	Gulfport	MS	39501	**800-353-9777**	228-864-1211
Missouri Gas Energy 3420 Broadway	Kansas City	MO	64111	**800-582-1234**	816-360-5500
Montana-Dakota Utilities Co 918 E Divide Ave	Bismarck	ND	58506	**800-638-3278**	701-222-7600
Nantucket Electric Co 2 Fairgrounds Rd	Nantucket	MA	02554	**800-322-3223***	508-325-8000
*Cust Svc					
Narragansett Electric Co 280 Melrose St	Providence	RI	02907	**800-322-3223***	401-784-7000
*Cust Svc					
National Energy & Gas Transmission 7600 Wisconsin Ave	Bethesda	MD	20814	**888-874-3677**	301-280-6800
National Fuel Gas Distribution Corp 6363 Main St	Williamsville	NY	14221	**800-365-3234**	716-857-7000
National Fuel Gas Supply Corp 6363 Main St	Williamsville	NY	14221	**800-365-3234***	716-857-7000
*Cust Svc					
National Fuel Resources Inc 165 Lawrence Bell Dr Suite 120	Williamsville	NY	14221	**800-839-9993**	716-630-6786
Nevada Power Co 6226 W Sahara Ave	Las Vegas	NV	89146	**800-331-3103***	702-367-5000
*Cust Svc					
New England Gas Co 100 Weybosset St	Providence	RI	02903	**800-227-8000**	401-272-5040
New York State Electric & Gas Corp Corporate Dr PO Box 5240	Binghamton	NY	13902	**800-572-1111**	
Nicor Gas 1844 Ferry Rd	Naperville	IL	60563	**888-642-6748**	630-983-8888
NIPSCO (Northern Indiana Public Service Co) 801 E 86th Ave	Merrillville	IN	46410	**800-464-7726***	219-853-5200
*Cust Svc					
North Shore Gas Co 3001 Grand Ave	Waukegan	IL	60085	**866-556-6004**	
Northern Indiana Public Service Co (NIPSCO) 801 E 86th Ave	Merrillville	IN	46410	**800-464-7726***	219-853-5200
*Cust Svc					
Northern Utilities Inc 300 Friberg Pkwy	Westborough	MA	01581	**800-882-5454**	508-836-7000
Northwest Natural Gas Co DBA NW Natural 220 NW 2nd Ave	Portland	OR	97209	**800-422-4012**	503-226-4211
NYSE: NWN					
NorthWestern Energy 600 Market St W	Huron	SD	57350	**800-245-6977**	605-352-8411
Nova Scotia Power Inc PO Box 910	Halifax	NS	B3J2W5	**800-428-6230**	902-428-6230
NRG Energy Inc 901 Marquette Ave Suite 2300	Minneapolis	MN	55402	**800-241-4674**	612-373-5300
NYSE: NRG					
NSTAR Electric 1 Nstar Way	Westwood	MA	02090	**800-592-2000***	781-441-8000
*Cust Svc					
NSTAR Gas 1 NSTAR Way	Westwood	MA	02090	**800-592-2000**	
NW Natural 220 NW 2nd Ave	Portland	OR	97209	**800-422-4012**	503-226-4211
NYSE: NWN					
OG & E Electric Services 3220 S High	Oklahoma City	OK	73124	**800-272-9741**	405-553-3000
Ohio Edison Co 76 S Main St PO Box 3637	Akron	OH	44309	**800-633-4766***	800-646-0400
*Cust Svc					
Oklahoma Natural Gas Co 401 N Harvey	Oklahoma City	OK	73101	**800-664-5463**	405-551-6500
Orange & Rockland Utilities Inc 1 Blue Hill Plaza	Pearl River	NY	10965	**877-434-4100**	845-352-6000
Otter Tail Power Co 215 S Cascade St	Fergus Falls	MN	56537	**800-551-3593**	218-739-8200
Pacific Power & Light 825 NE Multnomah St	Portland	OR	97232	**888-221-7070***	503-813-5000
*Cust Svc					
PacifiCorp 825 NE Multnomah St	Portland	OR	97232	**877-722-5001**	503-813-5000
Park Water Co 9750 Washburn Rd	Downey	CA	90241	**800-727-5987**	562-923-0711
Pennichuck Corp 25 Manchester St	Merrimack	NH	03054	**800-553-5191**	603-882-5191
NASDAQ: PNNW					
Pennsylvania Power Co 76 S Main St	Akron	OH	44308	**800-720-3600***	800-646-0400
*Cust Svc					
Peoples Gas Light & Coke Co 130 E Randolph Dr	Chicago	IL	60601	**866-556-6001**	312-240-4000
Pepco Energy Services Inc 1300 N 17th St Suite 1600	Arlington	VA	22209	**800-363-7499**	703-253-1800
Piedmont Natural Gas 1915 Rexford Rd	Charlotte	NC	28211	**800-752-7504**	704-364-3120
NYSE: PNY					
PNM Resources Inc Alvarado Sq	Albuquerque	NM	87158	**800-687-7854***	505-848-2700
NYSE: PNM ■ *Cust Svc					
Portland General Electric 121 SW Salmon St	Portland	OR	97204	**800-548-8818***	503-464-8000
*Cust Svc					
PPL Electric Utilities Corp 2 N 9th St	Allentown	PA	18101	**800-342-5775***	610-774-5151
*Cust Svc					
PPL EnergyPlus LLC 2 N 9th St	Allentown	PA	18101	**800-342-5775***	610-774-5151
*Cust Svc					
PPL Gas Utilities Corp 57 S 3rd St	Oxford	PA	19363	**800-959-7366**	610-932-2000
PPL Generation LLC 2 N 9th St	Allentown	PA	18101	**800-342-5775***	610-774-5151
*Cust Svc					
Progress Energy Florida Inc 100 Central Ave	Saint Petersburg	FL	33733	**800-700-8744***	727-820-5151
*Cust Svc					
PS Energy Group Inc 2987 Clairmont Rd Suite 450	Atlanta	GA	30329	**800-334-7548**	404-321-5711
PSEG Power LLC 80 Park Plaza	Newark	NJ	07101	**800-436-7734**	973-430-7000
PSNC Energy 800 Gaston Rd	Gastonia	NC	28056	**800-222-1034**	704-864-6731
Public Service Electric & Gas Co 80 Park Plaza	Newark	NJ	07102	**800-436-7734***	973-430-7000
*Cust Svc					
Public Service of New Hampshire 780 N Commercial St	Manchester	NH	03105	**800-662-7764**	603-669-4000
Puget Sound Energy Inc 10608 NE 4th St	Bellevue	WA	98009	**888-225-5773**	425-454-6363
Questar Gas Co PO Box 45360	Salt Lake City	UT	84145	**800-323-5517**	801-324-5111
Reliant Energy Inc PO Box 4932	Houston	TX	77210	**866-872-6646**	713-497-3000
NYSE: RRI					
Roanoke Gas Co 519 Kimball Rd	Roanoke	VA	24030	**800-552-6514**	540-777-3800
Rochester Gas & Electric Corp 89 East Ave	Rochester	NY	14649	**888-253-8888**	585-546-2700
Rockland Electric Co 1 Blue Hill Plaza	Pearl River	NY	10965	**877-434-4100**	845-352-6000
Salt River Project (SRP) 1521 N Project Dr	Tempe	AZ	85281	**800-258-4777**	602-236-5900
San Diego Gas & Electric Co 101 Ash St	San Diego	CA	92101	**800-411-7343**	619-696-2000
Savannah Electric & Power Co 600 E Bay St	Savannah	GA	31401	**800-437-3890**	
SCANA Energy Marketing Inc 1426 Main St MC 092	Columbia	SC	29201	**800-472-1051**	803-217-1300
SEMCO Energy Gas Co 1411 3rd St Suite A	Port Huron	MI	48060	**800-624-2019**	810-987-2200
Sierra Pacific Power Co 6100 Neil Rd	Reno	NV	89511	**800-962-0399**	775-834-4011
South Beloit Water Gas & Electric Co 4902 N Biltmore Ln	Madison	WI	53718	**800-862-6222**	608-458-3311
South Jersey Gas Co 1 S Jersey Plaza Rt 54	Folsom	NJ	08037	**888-766-9900**	609-561-9000
Southern California Edison Co 2244 Walnut Grove Ave	Rosemead	CA	91770	**800-655-4555**	626-302-1212
Southern California Gas Co 555 W 5th St	Los Angeles	CA	90013	**800-427-2200**	213-244-1200
SouthStar Energy Services LLC 817 W Peachtree St NW Suite 1000	Atlanta	GA	30308	**888-442-7288**	404-685-4000
Southwest Gas Corp 4300 W Tropicana Ave	Las Vegas	NV	89103	**800-748-5539**	702-365-1555
NYSE: SWX					
Southwest Gas Corp Northern Nevada Div 400 Eagle Station Ln	Carson City	NV	89701	**800-832-2555**	775-887-2706
Southwest Gas Corp Southern Arizona Div 3401 E Gas Rd	Tucson	AZ	85714	**800-428-7324**	520-794-6596
Southwest Gas Corp Southern California Div 13471 Mariposa Rd	Victorville	CA	92395	**800-443-8093**	760-951-4021
SWEPCo 1 Riverside Plaza	Columbus	OH	43215	**888-216-3523**	
Terasen Inc 1111 W Georgia St	Vancouver	BC	V6E4M4	**800-224-9376**	604-576-7000
TSE: TER					
Texas Gas Service Co 1301 South MoPac Expwy Suite 400	Austin	TX	78746	**800-700-2443**	512-477-5852
Texas-New Mexico Power Co 4100 International Plaza Tower 2 9th Fl	Fort Worth	TX	76109	**800-435-2822**	817-731-0099
Toledo Edison Co 76 S Main St	Akron	OH	44308	**800-447-3333***	800-646-0400
*Cust Svc					
Tucson Electric Power Co PO Box 711	Tucson	AZ	85702	**800-328-8853***	520-571-4000
*Cust Svc					
TXU Electric & Gas 1601 Bryan St	Dallas	TX	75201	**800-242-9113**	214-812-4600
UGI Utilities Inc 100 Kachel Blvd Green Hills Corporate Ctr Suite 400	Reading	PA	19607	**800-276-2722**	610-796-3400
United Illuminating Co 157 Church St	New Haven	CT	06510	**800-722-5584***	203-499-2000
*Cust Svc					
Upper Peninsula Power Co 600 E Lakeshore Dr	Houghton	MI	49931	**800-562-7680**	
Utah Power & Light 825 NE Multnomah St	Portland	OR	97232	**888-221-7070***	503-813-5000
*Cust Svc					
Vectren Corp 20 NW 4th St	Evansville	IN	47708	**800-227-1376**	812-491-4000
NYSE: VVC					

Company	City	State	ZIP	Toll-Free	Phone
Virginia Natural Gas Inc 5100 E Virginia Beach Blvd *Cust Svc	Norfolk	VA	23502	**866-229-3578***	757-466-5400
Washington Gas & Light Co 101 Constitution Ave NW	Washington	DC	20080	**800-752-7520**	703-750-4440
We Energies PO Box 2046	Milwaukee	WI	53201	**800-242-9437**	414-221-2345
Westar Energy 818 S Kansas Ave *NYSE: WR*	Topeka	KS	66612	**800-794-4780**	785-575-8500
Western Gas Resources Inc 1099 18th St Suite 1200 *NYSE: WGR*	Denver	CO	80202	**800-677-5603**	303-452-5603
Western Kentucky Gas Co Inc PO Box 650205	Dallas	TX	75265	**888-954-4321**	972-934-9227
Western Massachusetts Electric Co 1 Federal St Bldg 111-4	Springfield	MA	01105	**800-286-2000**	413-785-5871
Western Water Co 102 Washington Ave	Point Richmond	CA	94801	**877-928-9282**	510-234-7400
Wisconsin Public Service Corp PO Box 19001	Green Bay	WI	54307	**800-450-7260**	
Xcel Energy Inc PO Box 840	Denver	CO	80201	**800-772-7858**	303-571-7511
Xcel Energy Inc 800 Nicollet Mall *NYSE: XEL*	Minneapolis	MN	55401	**800-328-8226**	612-330-5500
Yankee Energy System Inc 107 Selden St	Berlin	CT	06037	**800-286-5000**	203-639-4000
York Water Co 130 E Market St PO Box 15089 *NASDAQ: YORW*	York	PA	17405	**800-750-5561**	717-845-3601

775 VACUUM CLEANERS - HOUSEHOLD

SEE ALSO Appliances - Small - Mfr

Company	City	State	ZIP	Toll-Free	Phone
Beam Industries PO Box 788	Webster City	IA	50595	**800-369-2326**	515-832-4620
CentralVac International Inc 1525 E 5th St	Kimball	NE	69145	**800-666-3133**	308-235-4139
Douglas/Quikut Co 118 E Douglas Rd	Walnut Ridge	AR	72476	**800-982-5233**	870-886-6774
Electrolux LLC 5956 Sherry Ln Suite 1500 *Cust Svc	Dallas	TX	75225	**800-243-9078***	214-361-4300
Eureka Co 807 N Main St *Cust Svc	Bloomington	IL	61701	**800-843-4324***	309-828-2367
HMI Industries Inc 6000 Lombardo Ctr Genesis Bldg Suite 500 *Cust Svc	Seven Hills	OH	44131	**800-344-1840***	216-986-8008
Kirby Co 1920 W 114th St	Cleveland	OH	44102	**800-437-7170**	216-228-2400
Lindsay Mfg Inc PO Box 1708	Ponca City	OK	74602	**800-546-3729**	580-762-2457
Metropolitan Vacuum Cleaner Co Inc 1 Ramapo Ave	Suffern	NY	10901	**800-822-1602**	845-357-1600
Oreck Corp 100 Plantation Rd *Orders	New Orleans	LA	70123	**800-535-8810***	504-733-8761
Panasonic Consumer Electronics Co 1 Panasonic Way	Secaucus	NJ	07094	**888-275-2595**	201-348-7000
Royal Appliance Mfg Co 7005 Cochran Rd	Glenwillow	OH	44139	**888-321-1134**	440-996-2000
Sequoia Vacuum Systems Inc 164 Jefferson Dr	Menlo Park	CA	94025	**800-994-0494**	650-322-7281
Sharp Electronics Corp 1 Sharp Plaza	Mahwah	NJ	07430	**800-237-4277**	201-529-8200

776 VALVES - INDUSTRIAL

Company	City	State	ZIP	Toll-Free	Phone
American Cast Iron Pipe Co (ACIPCO) 2916 16th St N	Birmingham	AL	35207	**800-442-2347**	205-325-7701
Anderson Brass Co 1629 W Bobo Newsome Hwy	Hartsville	SC	29550	**800-476-9876**	843-332-4111
Automatic Switch Co 50-60 Hanover Rd	Florham Park	NJ	07932	**800-524-1023**	973-966-2000
AY McDonald Mfg Co 4800 Chavenelle Rd *Cust Svc	Dubuque	IA	52002	**800-292-2737***	563-583-7311
Barksdale Inc 3211 Fruitland Ave	Los Angeles	CA	90058	**800-835-1060**	323-589-6181
Bonney Forge Corp US Rt 522 S *Cust Svc	Mount Union	PA	17066	**800-345-7546***	814-542-2545
Clow Valve Co 902 S 2nd St	Oskaloosa	IA	52577	**800-829-2569**	641-673-8611
Control Components Inc 22591 Avenida Empresa	Rancho Santa Margarita	CA	92688	**800-788-8762**	949-858-1877
Cooper Cameron Valves 3250 Briarpark Dr Suite 300	Houston	TX	77042	**800-432-8511**	281-499-8511
Crane Co Stockham Div 2129 3rd Ave SE	Cullman	AL	35055	**800-786-2542**	256-775-3800
Cross Mfg Inc 11011 King St Suite 210	Overland Park	KS	66210	**800-542-7677**	913-451-1233
DeZurik Water Controls 250 Riverside Ave N	Sartell	MN	56377	**800-788-0288**	320-259-2000
Dresser Flow Solutions 16240 Port St NW	Houston	TX	77041	**800-847-1099**	832-590-2300
Engineered Valves Div ITT Industries Inc 33 Centerville Rd	Lancaster	PA	17603	**800-366-1111**	717-291-1901
Fleck Controls Inc 20580 Enterprise Ave *Cust Svc	Brookfield	WI	53045	**888-784-9065***	262-784-4490
FMC Technologies Inc 1803 Gears Rd *NYSE: FTI*	Houston	TX	77067	**800-869-6999**	281-591-4000
Gemini Valve Inc 2 Otter Ct	Raymond	NH	03077	**800-370-0936**	603-895-4761
General Valve Co 800 Koomey Rd	Brookshire	TX	77423	**800-926-2288**	281-934-6013
Goulds Pumps Inc Goulds Water Technologies Group E Bayard St Ext	Seneca Falls	NY	13148	**800-327-7700**	315-568-2811
Groth Corp 13650 N Promenade Blvd	Stafford	TX	77477	**800-531-3140**	281-295-6800
Halkey-Roberts Corp 11600 Dr ML King Jr St N *Sales	Saint Petersburg	FL	33716	**800-303-4384***	727-577-1300
Harsco Corp Gas Technologies Group PO Box 8316 *Cust Svc	Camp Hill	PA	17001	**800-821-2975***	717-763-5060
High Vacuum Apparatus LLC 12880 Moya Blvd	Reno	NV	89506	**800-551-4422**	775-359-4442
Hoerbiger Corp of America Inc 3350 Gateway Dr	Pompano Beach	FL	33069	**800-327-8961**	954-974-5700
Hudson Valve Co Inc 5301 Office Pk Dr Suite 330	Bakersfield	CA	93390	**800-748-6218**	661-869-1126
Humphrey Products Co 5070 East N Ave	Kalamazoo	MI	49048	**800-477-8707**	269-381-5500
Hunt Valve Co Inc DBA Hunt Engineering 1913 E State St	Salem	OH	44460	**800-321-2757**	330-337-9535
Hydroseal Valve Co Inc 1610 US Hwy 259 N	Kilgore	TX	75662	**800-256-8574**	903-984-8574
Hyson Products 10367 Brecksville Rd	Brecksville	OH	44141	**800-876-4976**	440-526-5900
ITT Industries Inc Engineered Valves Div 33 Centerville Rd	Lancaster	PA	17603	**800-366-1111**	717-291-1901
Kennedy Valve 1021 E Water St	Elmira	NY	14902	**800-782-5831**	607-734-2211
Kerotest Mfg Corp 5500 2nd Ave	Pittsburgh	PA	15207	**800-825-8371**	412-521-4200
KF Industries Inc 1500 SE 89th St	Oklahoma City	OK	73149	**800-654-4842**	405-631-1533
Lee Co PO Box 424	Westbrook	CT	06498	**800-533-7584**	860-399-6281
Leonard Valve Co 1360 Elmwood Ave	Cranston	RI	02910	**888-797-4456**	401-461-1200
Leslie Controls Inc 12501 Telecom Dr	Tampa	FL	33637	**800-253-7543**	813-978-1000
Mac Valves Inc 30569 Beck Rd	Wixom	MI	48393	**800-622-8587**	248-624-7700
Marotta Controls Inc 78 Boonton Ave	Montville	NJ	07045	**888-627-6882**	973-334-7800
Marshall Gas Controls Inc 1000 Civic Center Loop	San Marcos	TX	78666	**800-447-9513**	512-396-2257
McDonald AY Mfg Co 4800 Chavenelle Rd *Cust Svc	Dubuque	IA	52002	**800-292-2737***	563-583-7311
Milwaukee Valve Co Inc 2375 S Burrell St	Milwaukee	WI	53207	**800-348-6544**	414-744-5240
Mueller Co 500 W Eldorado St	Decatur	IL	62522	**800-432-4471**	217-423-4471
Mueller Refrigeration Co Inc 121 Rogers St PO Box 239 *Cust Svc	Hartsville	TN	37074	**800-251-8983***	615-374-2124
Newport News Industrial Corp 182 Enterprise Dr	Newport News	VA	23603	**800-627-0353**	757-380-7053
NIBCO Inc 1516 Middlebury St	Elkhart	IN	46515	**800-234-0227**	574-295-3000
Ogontz Corp 2835 Terwood Rd	Willow Grove	PA	19090	**800-523-2478**	215-657-4770
Parker Instrumentation Group 6035 Parkland Blvd	Cleveland	OH	44124	**800-272-7537**	216-896-3000
PGI International Ltd 16101 Vallen Dr	Houston	TX	77041	**800-231-0233**	713-466-0056
Plattco Corp 7 White St	Plattsburgh	NY	12901	**800-352-1731**	518-563-4640
Powell William Co 2503 Spring Grove Ave	Cincinnati	OH	45214	**800-888-2583**	513-852-2000
Richards Industries Inc 3170 Wasson Rd *Cust Svc	Cincinnati	OH	45209	**800-543-7311***	513-533-5600
Robert H Wager Co 570 Montroyal Rd	Rural Hall	NC	27045	**800-562-7024**	336-969-6909
Sherwood 2111 Liberty Dr	Niagara Falls	NY	14304	**800-438-2916**	716-283-1010
Snap-Tite Inc 8325 Hessinger Dr	Erie	PA	16509	**800-458-0409**	814-838-5700
Starflo Corp 940 Crosscreek Rd SE	Orangeburg	SC	29115	**800-888-2583**	803-536-9660
Stockham Div Crane Co 2129 3rd Ave SE	Cullman	AL	35055	**800-786-2542**	256-775-3800
Storm Mfg Group Inc 23201 Normandie Ave	Torrance	CA	90501	**800-210-2525**	310-326-8287
Tapco International 11307 W Little York Rd	Houston	TX	77041	**866-827-2660**	713-466-0300
United Brass Works Inc 714 S Main St	Randleman	NC	27317	**800-334-3035**	336-498-2661
Wager Robert H Co 570 Montroyal Rd	Rural Hall	NC	27045	**800-562-7024**	336-969-6909
William Powell Co 2503 Spring Grove Ave	Cincinnati	OH	45214	**800-888-2583**	513-852-2000

777 VALVES & HOSE FITTINGS - FLUID POWER

SEE ALSO Carburetors, Pistons, Piston Rings, Valves

Company	City	State	ZIP	Toll-Free	Phone
Air-Way Mfg Co 586 N Main St *Cust Svc	Olivet	MI	49076	**800-253-1036***	269-749-2161
Bosch Rexroth Corp 5150 Prairie Stone Pkwy	Hoffman Estates	IL	60192	**800-860-1055**	847-645-3600
Bosch Rexroth Corp Mobile Hydraulics Div PO Box 394	Wooster	OH	44691	**866-230-2790**	330-263-3300
Civacon 4304 N Mattox Rd *Sales	Riverside	MO	64150	**888-526-5657***	816-741-6600
Clippard Instrument Lab 7390 Colerain Ave	Cincinnati	OH	45239	**877-245-6247**	513-521-4261
Dixon Valve & Coupling Co 800 High St	Chestertown	MD	21620	**800-876-3822**	410-778-2000
Dynaquip Controls 10 Harris Industrial Pk	Saint Clair	MO	63077	**800-545-3636**	636-629-3700
EKK Eagle America 33 Plan Way Bldg 5	Warwick	RI	02886	**800-314-9246**	401-732-0333
Gould JD Co Inc 4707 Massachusetts Ave	Indianapolis	IN	46218	**800-634-6853**	317-547-5289
Hays Fluid Controls PO Box 580	Dallas	NC	28034	**800-354-4297**	704-922-9565
Henry Pratt Co 401 S Highland Ave	Aurora	IL	60506	**877-436-7728**	630-844-4000
Hunt Valve Co Inc DBA Hunt Engineering 1913 E State St	Salem	OH	44460	**800-321-2757**	330-337-9535
Hyson Products 10367 Brecksville Rd	Brecksville	OH	44141	**800-876-4976**	440-526-5900
JD Gould Co Inc 4707 Massachusetts Ave	Indianapolis	IN	46218	**800-634-6853**	317-547-5289
Jetstream of Houston LLP 4930 Cranswick	Houston	TX	77041	**800-231-8192**	713-462-7000
Morrison Brothers Co PO Box 238 *Cust Svc	Dubuque	IA	52004	**800-553-4840***	563-583-5701
Oilgear Co PO Box 343924 *NASDAQ: OLGR* ■ *Sales	Milwaukee	WI	53234	**800-276-5356***	414-327-1700
OPW Fueling Components PO Box 405003	Cincinnati	OH	45240	**800-422-2525**	513-870-3100
Parker Fluid Connectors Group 6035 Parkland Blvd	Cleveland	OH	44124	**800-272-7537**	216-896-3000
Parker Hannifin Corp Brass Products Div 300 Parker Dr	Otsego	MI	49078	**800-272-7537**	269-694-9411
Parker Hannifin Corp Fluid Power Systems Div 595 Shelter Rd	Lincolnshire	IL	60069	**800-401-5015**	847-821-9478
Parker Hannifin Corp General Valve Div 19 Gloria Ln	Fairfield	NJ	07004	**800-482-8258**	973-575-4844
Parker Hannifin Corp Skinner Valve Div 95 Edgewood Ave	New Britain	CT	06051	**800-825-8305**	860-827-2300
PBM Inc 1070 Sandy Hill Rd	Irwin	PA	15642	**800-967-4726**	724-863-0550
PerkinElmer Fluid Sciences Inc 11642 Old Baltimore Pike	Beltsville	MD	20705	**800-691-4666**	301-937-4010
Plattco Corp 7 White St	Plattsburgh	NY	12901	**800-352-1731**	518-563-4640
Pratt Henry Co 401 S Highland Ave	Aurora	IL	60506	**877-436-7728**	630-844-4000
Precision Dynamics Inc 60 Production Ct	New Britain	CT	06051	**888-840-1230**	860-229-3753
Richards Industries Inc 3170 Wasson Rd *Cust Svc	Cincinnati	OH	45209	**800-543-7311***	513-533-5600
Ritter Technology LLC 100 Williams Dr	Zelienople	PA	16063	**800-374-8837**	724-452-6000
SafeWay Hydraulics Inc 4040 Norex Dr *Cust Svc	Chaska	MN	55318	**800-222-1169***	952-448-2600
Sargent Controls & Aerospace 5675 W Burlingame Rd	Tucson	AZ	85743	**800-932-5273**	520-744-1000
Skinner Valve Div Parker Hannifin Corp 95 Edgewood Ave	New Britain	CT	06051	**800-825-8305**	860-827-2300
SMC Pneumatics Inc 3011 N Franklin Rd	Indianapolis	IN	46226	**800-762-7621**	317-899-4440
Teleflex Fluid Systems Inc One Firestone Dr	Suffield	CT	06078	**800-225-9077**	860-668-1285
Watts Fluidair Inc 9 Cutts Rd	Kittery	ME	03904	**877-467-4323**	207-439-9511

778 VARIETY STORES

Company	City	State	ZIP	Toll-Free	Phone
Alaska Commercial Co 550 W 64th Ave Suite 200	Anchorage	AK	99518	**800-478-4484**	907-273-4600

	City	State	ZIP	Toll-Free	Phone
Andersons Inc Retail Group 480 W Dussel Dr	Maumee	OH	43537	**800-537-3370**	419-893-5050
Army & Air Force Exchange Service (AAFES) 3911 S Walton Walker Blvd	Dallas	TX	75236	**800-527-6790**	214-312-2011
Big Lots Inc 300 Phillipi Rd	Columbus	OH	43228	**800-877-1253**	614-278-6800
NYSE: BLI					
Building No 19 Inc 319 Lincoln St	Hingham	MA	02043	**800-225-5061**	781-749-6900
Dollar Discount Stores of America Inc 1362 Naamans Creek Rd	Boothwyn	PA	19061	**800-227-5314**	610-497-1991
Duckwall-ALCO Stores Inc 401 Cottage Ave	Abilene	KS	67410	**800-334-2526**	785-263-3350
NASDAQ: DUCK					
Fred Meyer Inc 3800 SE 22nd Ave	Portland	OR	97202	**800-858-9202**	503-232-8844
Marden's Inc 184 College Ave	Waterville	ME	04901	**800-564-3337**	207-873-6111
Meyer Fred Inc 3800 SE 22nd Ave	Portland	OR	97202	**800-858-9202**	503-232-8844
Navy Exchange Service Command (NEXCOM) 3280 Virginia Beach Blvd	Virginia Beach	VA	23452	**800-628-3924**	757-463-6200
Orvis Co Inc PO Box 798	Manchester	VT	05254	**800-541-3541**	802-362-3622
Overstock.com Inc 6322 S 3000 East Suite 100	Salt Lake City	UT	84121	**800-843-2446***	801-947-3100
NASDAQ: OSTK ■ *Cust Svc					
Super Dollar Stores 3401 Gresham Lake Rd	Raleigh	NC	27615	**800-366-9144**	919-876-6000
Variety Wholesalers Inc 3401 Gresham Lake Rd	Raleigh	NC	27615	**800-366-9144**	919-876-6000

779 VENTURE CAPITAL FIRMS

	City	State	ZIP	Toll-Free	Phone
Allied Capital Corp 1919 Pennsylvania Ave NW 3rd Fl	Washington	DC	20006	**888-818-5298**	202-331-1112
NYSE: ALD					
American Capital Group Inc 500 N State College Blvd Suite 950	Orange	CA	92868	**800-305-0224**	714-937-4126
Blair William Capital Partners 222 W Adams St	Chicago	IL	60606	**800-621-0687**	312-236-1600
Chell Group Corp 14 Meteor Dr	Toronto	ON	M9W1A4	**866-455-2435**	416-675-0874
Churchill Capital Inc 333 S 7th St Suite 2400	Minneapolis	MN	55402	**888-782-3328**	612-673-6633
Circle Group Holdings Inc 1011 Campus Dr	Mundelein	IL	60060	**800-730-4880**	847-549-6002
AMEX: CXN					
Comdisco Ventures Group 6111 N River Rd	Rosemont	IL	60018	**800-321-1111**	847-698-3000
Cravey Green & Wahlen Inc 12 Piedmont Ctr Suite 210	Atlanta	GA	30305	**800-249-6669**	404-816-3255
Desai Capital Management Inc 410 Park Ave	New York	NY	10022	**800-337-2484**	212-838-9191
Domain Assoc 1 Palmer Sq Suite 515	Princeton	NJ	08542	**800-241-1901**	609-683-5656
Dominion Ventures Inc 1656 N California Blvd Suite 300	Walnut Creek	CA	94596	**800-875-4890**	925-280-6300
Equus Capital Corp 2727 Allen Pkwy 13th Fl	Houston	TX	77019	**800-856-0901**	713-529-0900
Frazier & Co 601 Union St Suite 3200	Seattle	WA	98101	**800-411-4499**	206-621-7200
Frontenac Co 135 S La Salle St Suite 3800	Chicago	IL	60603	**800-368-3681**	312-368-0044
Galen Assoc 610 5th Ave 5th Fl	New York	NY	10020	**800-868-4195**	212-218-4990
Harvard Management Co Inc 600 Atlantic Ave 16th Fl	Boston	MA	02210	**800-723-0044**	617-523-4400
HC Wainwright & Co Inc 245 Park Ave 44th Fl	New York	NY	10167	**800-727-7176**	212-856-5700
Hoak Capital Corp 13355 Noel Rd Suite 1050	Dallas	TX	75240	**800-755-0769**	972-960-4848
Idealab 130 W Union St	Pasadena	CA	91103	**888-433-3522**	626-585-6900
JH Whitney & Co LLC 177 Broad St 15th Fl	Stamford	CT	06901	**800-881-6085**	203-973-1400
JPMorgan H & Q 560 Mission St	San Francisco	CA	94105	**800-227-3958**	415-315-5000
Mesirow Financial Private Equity 350 N Clark St	Chicago	IL	60610	**800-453-0600**	312-595-6099
MRV Communications Inc 20415 Nordhoff St	Chatsworth	CA	91311	**800-858-7815***	818-773-0900
NASDAQ: MRVC ■ *Sales					
Noro-Moseley Partners 4200 Northside Pkwy NW Bldg 9	Atlanta	GA	30327	**800-648-0520**	404-233-1966
Piper Jaffray Ventures 800 Nicollet Mall Suite 800	Minneapolis	MN	55402	**800-333-6000**	612-303-6000
Safeguard Scientifics Inc 435 Devon Park Dr Suite 800	Wayne	PA	19087	**888-733-1200**	610-293-0600
NYSE: SFE					
Sierra Ventures 2884 Sand Hill Rd Suite 100	Menlo Park	CA	94025	**800-819-9665**	650-854-1000
TA Assoc 125 High St High St Tower Suite 2500	Boston	MA	02110	**800-836-8873**	617-574-6700
Technology Funding Inc 460 St Michael's Dr Suite 1000	Santa Fe	NM	87505	**800-821-5323**	505-982-2200
TEOCO Corp 12701 Fair Lakes Cir Suite 350	Fairfax	VA	22033	**888-868-3626**	703-322-9200
US Venture Partners 2735 Sand Hill Rd Suite 300	Menlo Park	CA	94025	**877-773-8787**	650-854-9080
VS & A Communications Partners 350 Park Ave 7th Fl	New York	NY	10022	**800-935-4990**	212-935-4990
Wainwright HC & Co Inc 245 Park Ave 44th Fl	New York	NY	10167	**800-727-7176**	212-856-5700
William Blair Capital Partners 222 W Adams St	Chicago	IL	60606	**800-621-0687**	312-236-1600
Woodside Fund 350 Marine Pkwy Suite 300	Redwood Shores	CA	94065	**888-368-5545**	650-610-8050

780 VETERANS NURSING HOMES - STATE

SEE ALSO Hospitals - Veterans Hospitals

	City	State	ZIP	Toll-Free	Phone
Colorado State Veterans Nursing Home-Homelake 3749 Sherman Ave	Monte Vista	CO	81144	**888-838-2687**	719-852-5118
Colorado State Veterans Nursing Home-Walsenburg 23500 US Hwy 160	Walsenburg	CO	81089	**800-645-8387**	719-738-5133
Hastings Veterans Home 1200 E 18th St	Hastings	MN	55033	**877-838-3803**	651-438-8504
Maine Veterans Home-Bangor 44 Hogan Rd	Bangor	ME	04401	**888-684-4665**	207-942-2333
Maine Veterans Home-Scarborough 290 US Rt 1	Scarborough	ME	04074	**888-684-4666**	207-883-7184
Maine Veterans Home-South Paris 477 High St	South Paris	ME	04281	**888-684-4668**	207-743-6300
Minnesota Veterans Home-Minneapolis 5101 Minnehaha Ave S	Minneapolis	MN	55407	**877-838-6757**	612-721-0600
Minnesota Veterans Home-Silver Bay 45 Banks Blvd	Silver Bay	MN	55614	**877-729-8387**	218-226-6300
New Mexico State Veterans Center 992 S Broadway St	Truth or Consequences	NM	87901	**800-964-3976**	505-894-9081
Ohio Veterans Home 3416 Columbus Ave	Sandusky	OH	44870	**800-572-7934***	419-625-2454
*Admissions					
Oregon Veterans' Home 700 Veterans Dr	The Dalles	OR	97058	**800-846-8460**	541-296-7190
Thomson-Hood Veterans Center 100 Veterans Dr	Wilmore	KY	40390	**800-928-4838**	859-858-2814
Veterans Home of California-Barstow 100 E Veterans Pkwy	Barstow	CA	92311	**800-746-0606**	760-252-6200
Veterans Home of California-Chula Vista 700 E Naples Ct	Chula Vista	CA	91911	**888-857-2146**	619-482-6010
Veterans Home of California-Yountville PO Box 1200	Yountville	CA	94599	**800-404-8387**	707-944-4541

781 VETERINARY HOSPITALS

	City	State	ZIP	Toll-Free	Phone
Banfield The Pet Hospital 11815 NE Glenn Widing Dr	Portland	OR	97220	**800-394-6117**	503-256-7299
National PetCare Centers (NPC) 3540 JFK Pkwy	Fort Collins	CO	80525	**877-738-4677**	970-226-6632
Radiocat 32-A Mellor Ave	Baltimore	MD	21228	**800-323-9729**	410-788-5200
VCA Antech Inc 12401 W Olympic Blvd	Los Angeles	CA	90064	**800-966-1822**	310-571-6500
NASDAQ: WOOF					

782 VETERINARY MEDICAL ASSOCIATIONS - STATE

	City	State	ZIP	Toll-Free	Phone
Colorado 789 Sherman St Suite 550	Denver	CO	80203	**800-228-5429**	303-318-0447
Florida 7131 Lake Ellenor Dr	Orlando	FL	32809	**800-992-3862**	407-851-3862
Georgia 2814 Spring Rd Suite 217	Atlanta	GA	30339	**800-853-1625**	678-309-9800
Louisiana 8550 United Plaza Blvd Suite 1001	Baton Rouge	LA	70809	**800-524-2996**	225-928-5862
Maryland 8015 Corporate Dr Suite A	Baltimore	MD	21236	**888-884-6862**	410-931-3332
New York 9 Highland Ave	Albany	NY	12205	**800-876-9867**	518-437-0787
North Carolina 1611 Jones Franklin Rd Suite 108	Raleigh	NC	27606	**800-446-2862**	919-851-5850
North Dakota 921 S 9th St Suite 120	Bismarck	ND	58504	**877-637-6386**	701-221-7740
Ohio 3168 Riverside Dr	Columbus	OH	43221	**800-662-6862**	614-486-7253
Oregon 1880 Lancaster Dr NE Suite 118	Salem	OR	97305	**800-235-3502**	503-399-0311
Pennsylvania 905 W Governor Rd Suite 320	Hershey	PA	17033	**888-550-7862**	717-533-7934
Rhode Island 11 S Angell St Suite 347	Providence	RI	02906	**877-521-0103**	
South Carolina 1226 Pickens St Suite 203	Columbia	SC	29201	**800-441-7228**	
Tennessee 618 Church St Suite 220	Nashville	TN	37219	**800-697-3587**	615-254-3687
Virginia 2314-C Commerce Ctr Dr	Rockville	VA	23146	**800-937-8862**	804-749-8058
Washington PO Box 962	Bellevue	WA	98009	**800-399-7862**	425-454-8381
Wisconsin 301 N Broom St	Madison	WI	53703	**888-254-5202**	608-257-3665

783 VIATICAL SETTLEMENT COMPANIES

	City	State	ZIP	Toll-Free	Phone
21st Services Inc 200 S 6th St Suite 350	Minneapolis	MN	55402	**877-371-3008**	612-371-3008
Advanced Settlements Inc 2101 Park Center Dr Suite 220	Orlando	FL	32835	**800-561-4148**	407-296-7373
ALIR Co 814 Hwy A1A Suite 303	Ponte Vedra Beach	FL	32082	**888-599-1112**	904-280-1112
American Viatical Services 280 Heritage Walk	Woodstock	GA	30188	**800-699-5326**	770-926-8880
AMG/Neuma Inc 7366 N Lincoln Ave Suite 202	Lincolnwood	IL	60712	**800-457-7828**	847-674-1150
Ardan Group Ltd 111 St Joseph's Terr	Woodbridge	NJ	07095	**800-699-3522**	732-855-0670
Assignable Life Assets 601 N New York Ave Suite 202	Winter Park	FL	32789	**800-334-3211**	
Benefits America 415 East Paces Ferry Rd NE	Atlanta	GA	30305	**800-777-8878**	404-233-5411
Coventry First LLC 7111 Valley Green Rd Suite 320	Fort Washington	PA	19034	**877-836-8300**	215-233-5100
Legacy Benefits Corp 350 5th Ave Suite 4320	New York	NY	10118	**800-875-1000**	212-643-1190
Life Asset Group LLC 1111 Lincoln Rd Suite 801	Miami Beach	FL	33139	**800-481-3481**	305-534-9044
Life Partners Holdings Inc 204 Woodhew Dr	Waco	TX	76712	**800-368-5569**	254-751-7797
NASDAQ: LPHI					
Lifeline Program 1979 Lakeside Pkwy Suite 925	Tucker	GA	30084	**800-572-4346**	800-252-5282
Page & Assoc Inc DBA Lifeline Program 1979 Lakeside Pkwy Suite 925	Tucker	GA	30084	**800-572-4346**	800-252-5282
Peachtree Life Settlements 6501 Park of Commerce Blvd Suite 140-B	Boca Raton	FL	33487	**866-730-4411**	561-962-3900
Stone Street Capital 7316 Wisconsin Ave 5th Fl	Bethesda	MD	20814	**800-586-7786**	
ViaSource Funding Group LLC 81 E Water St	Toms River	NJ	08753	**888-828-4404**	732-280-8500
Viatical Benefactors LLC 100 Galleria Pkwy Suite 440	Atlanta	GA	30339	**888-404-4484**	770-951-4760
Viatical Settlements Inc 10801 NE Reinking Rd	Kansas City	MO	64156	**800-650-3333**	816-792-3663
Welcome Funds Inc 301 Yamato Rd	Boca Raton	FL	33431	**877-227-4484**	561-862-0244

784 VIDEO STORES

SEE ALSO Book, Music, Video Clubs

	City	State	ZIP	Toll-Free	Phone
Amazon.com Inc PO Box 81226	Seattle	WA	98108	**800-201-7575***	206-622-2335
NASDAQ: AMZN ■ *Cust Svc					

	City	State	ZIP	Toll-Free	Phone
Archambault Group Inc					
500 rue Sainte-Catherine E	Montreal	QC	H2L2C6	**877-849-8589**	514-849-6206
Best Buy Co Inc 7601 Penn Ave S	Richfield	MN	55423	**800-369-5050**	612-291-1000
NYSE: BBY					
CD Universe 101 N Plains Industrial Rd	Wallingford	CT	06492	**800-231-7937**	203-294-1648
CinemaNow					
4553 Glencoe Ave Suite 200	Marina del Rey	CA	90292	**800-432-5216**	310-255-3700
Circuit City Group 9950 Mayland Dr	Richmond	VA	23233	**800-251-2665**	804-527-4000
Coconuts Music & Movies 38 Corporate Cir	Albany	NY	12203	**800-540-1242**	518-452-1242
DVD Avenue PO Box 820	Clinton	MD	20735	**800-990-4159**	301-856-4159
DVD Empire 2140 Woodland Rd	Warrendale	PA	15086	**888-383-1880**	724-933-0399
Facets Multimedia Inc 1517 W Fullerton Ave	Chicago	IL	60614	**800-331-6197**	773-281-9075
Gameznflix Inc 6960 Eastgate Blvd	Lebanon	TN	37088	**800-613-1543**	
Half.com Inc 500 S Gravers Rd	Plymouth Meeting	PA	19462	**800-545-9857***	610-567-1090
*Cust Svc					
Hollywood Entertainment Corp DBA Hollywood Video 9275 SW Peyton Ln	Wilsonville	OR	97070	**877-325-8687**	503-570-1600
Hollywood Video 9275 SW Peyton Ln	Wilsonville	OR	97070	**877-325-8687**	503-570-1600
Media Play 10400 Yellow Circle Dr	Minnetonka	MN	55343	**800-371-4425***	952-932-7700
*Cust Svc					
Movie Gallery Inc 900 W Main St	Dothan	AL	36301	**866-209-5533***	334-677-2108
NASDAQ: MOVI ■ *Cust Svc					
Musicland Group Inc					
10400 Yellow Circle Dr	Minnetonka	MN	55343	**800-371-4425***	952-932-7700
*Cust Svc					
NetFlix Inc 970 University Ave	Los Gatos	CA	95032	**888-638-3549***	408-399-3700
NASDAQ: NFLX ■ *Cust Svc					
Strawberries Music & Video 38 Corporate Cir	Albany	NY	12203	**800-540-1242**	518-452-1242
Tower Records					
2500 Del Monte St Bldg C	West Sacramento	CA	95691	**800-225-0880**	916-373-2500
Videoflicks.com Inc 1654 Avenue Rd	Toronto	ON	M5M3Y1	**800-690-2879**	416-782-5084
YesAsia.com Inc 1192 Cherry Ave	San Bruno	CA	94066	**888-716-5753**	650-517-5100

785 VISION CORRECTION CENTERS

	City	State	ZIP	Toll-Free	Phone
Arrowsmith Eye Institute					
210 25th Ave N Suite 900	Nashville	TN	37203	**800-844-2019**	615-327-2020
Barnet-Dulaney Eye Center 4800 N 22nd St	Phoenix	AZ	85016	**800-966-7000**	602-955-1000
Eye Centers of Florida 4101 Evans Ave	Fort Myers	FL	33901	**800-226-3377**	239-939-3456
John-Kenyon Eye Center					
1305 Wall St Suite 200	Jeffersonville	IN	47130	**800-342-5393**	812-288-9011
Jones Eye Clinic					
4405 Hamilton Blvd PO Box 3246	Sioux City	IA	51104	**800-334-2015**	712-239-3937
Laser Vision Centers Inc					
540 Maryville Centre Dr Suite 200	Saint Louis	MO	63141	**800-852-1033**	314-434-6900
LaserSight of Wisconsin 240 1st St	Neenah	WI	54956	**888-774-3937**	920-729-6600
LaserVue Eye Center					
3554 Round Barn Blvd Suite 200	Santa Rosa	CA	95430	**888-527-3745**	707-522-6200
LCA-Vision Inc 7840 Montgomery Rd	Cincinnati	OH	45236	**888-529-2020**	513-792-9292
NASDAQ: LCAV					
Millennium Laser Eye Centers					
1750 Tysons Blvd Suite 120	McLean	VA	22102	**888-565-2737**	703-761-4999
Minnesota Eye Consultants PA					
710 E 24th St Suite 106	Minneapolis	MN	55404	**800-526-7632**	612-813-3600
NovaMed Inc 980 N Michigan Ave Suite 1620	Chicago	IL	60611	**800-388-4133**	312-664-4100
NASDAQ: NOVA					
Ophthalmology Consultants The Center for LASIK					
5800 Colonial Dr Suite 100	Margate	FL	33063	**800-448-8770**	954-977-8770
Pacific Cataract & Laser Institute					
2517 NE Kresky Ave	Chehalis	WA	98532	**800-224-7254**	360-748-8632
Prado Vision Center 7522 N Himes Ave	Tampa	FL	33614	**877-455-2745**	813-931-0500
Southwestern Eye Center 2610 E University Dr	Mesa	AZ	85213	**800-425-8404**	480-892-8400
TLC Vision Corp 5280 Solar Dr Suite 300	Mississauga	ON	L4W5M8	**888-225-5852**	905-602-2020
NASDAQ: TLCV					
Vista Alliance Eye Care Assoc					
160 E 56th St 9th Fl	New York	NY	10022	**888-695-2745**	212-758-3838
Will Vision & Laser Centers					
8100 NE Pkwy Dr Suite 125	Vancouver	WA	98662	**877-542-3937**	360-885-1327

786 VITAMINS & NUTRITIONAL SUPPLEMENTS

SEE ALSO Food Products - Mfr - Diet & Health Foods; Medicinal Chemicals & Botanical Products; Pharmaceutical Companies; Pharmaceutical Companies - Generic Drugs

	City	State	ZIP	Toll-Free	Phone
Abkit Inc 61 Broadway Suite 1310	New York	NY	10006	**800-226-6227**	212-292-1550
Access Business Group LLC 7575 Fulton St E	Ada	MI	49355	**800-253-6500***	616-787-5358
*Cust Svc					
ADM Nutraceutical Div 4666 Faries Pkwy	Decatur	IL	62526	**800-637-5843**	217-424-5200
Advanced American Pharmaceuticals Inc DBA Peak Nutrition 1097 11th St	Syracuse	NE	68446	**800-600-2069**	402-269-2825
Advanced Sports Nutrition (ASN)					
1813 Cascade St	Hood River	OR	97031	**800-800-9119**	541-387-4500
Amazon Herb Co 1002 Jupiter Park Ln Suite 1	Jupiter	FL	33458	**800-535-0850**	561-575-7663
American Sports Nutrition Inc 1501 E Main St	Meriden	CT	06450	**888-462-5671**	203-639-8189
ASN (Advanced Sports Nutrition)					
1813 Cascade St	Hood River	OR	97031	**800-800-9119**	541-387-4500
Aspen Group Inc 10325 N Rt 47	Hebron	IL	60034	**888-227-7361**	815-648-2001
AST Sports Science Inc 120 Capitol Dr	Golden	CO	80401	**800-627-2788**	303-278-1420
Beehive Botanicals Inc 16297 W Nursery Rd	Hayward	WI	54843	**800-233-4483**	715-634-4274
Boehringer Ingelheim Pharmaceuticals Inc Pharmaton Natural Health Products Div					
900 Ridgebury Rd	Ridgefield	CT	06877	**800-451-6688**	203-798-9988
Champion Nutrition 2615 Stanwell Dr	Concord	CA	94520	**800-225-4831**	925-689-1790
Chattem Inc 1715 W 38th St	Chattanooga	TN	37409	**800-366-6077**	423-821-4571
NASDAQ: CHTT					
CV Technologies Inc 9411 20th Ave	Edmonton	AB	T6N1E5	**888-843-7239**	780-432-0022
CytoSport Inc 4795 Industrial Way	Benicia	CA	94510	**888-298-6629**	925-685-6600
Douglas Laboratories Inc 600 Boyce Rd	Pittsburgh	PA	15205	**800-245-4440**	412-494-0122
DuPont Agriculture & Nutrition					
1007 Market St DuPont Bldg	Wilmington	DE	19898	**800-441-7515**	302-774-1000
EAS Inc (Experimental & Applied Science Inc)					
555 Corporate Cir	Golden	CO	80401	**800-297-9776**	303-271-1002
Edom Laboratories Inc 100-M E Jeffryn Blvd	Deer Park	NY	11729	**800-723-3366**	631-586-2266
Enzymatic Therapy 825 Challenger Dr	Green Bay	WI	54311	**800-783-2286**	920-469-1313
Experimental & Applied Science Inc (EAS Inc)					
555 Corporate Cir	Golden	CO	80401	**800-297-9776**	303-271-1002
Foodscience Corp 20 New England Dr	Essex Junction	VT	05453	**800-451-5190**	802-878-5508
Futurebiotics Inc 70 Commerce Dr	Hauppauge	NY	11788	**800-367-5433**	631-272-6300
Garden of Life Inc					
770 Northpoint Pkwy Suite 100	West Palm Beach	FL	33407	**888-622-8986***	561-748-2477
*Orders					
Garden State Nutritionals					
8 Henderson Dr	West Caldwell	NJ	07006	**800-526-9095**	973-575-9200
GeoPharma Inc 6950 Bryan Dairy Rd	Largo	FL	33777	**800-654-2347**	727-544-8866
NASDAQ: GORX					
Ginseng Co 2279 Agate Ct	Simi Valley	CA	93065	**800-284-2598**	805-520-2592
GNC Corp 300 6th Ave	Pittsburgh	PA	15222	**888-462-2548***	412-288-4600
*Cust Svc					
Hammer Nutrition Ltd					
4952 Whitefish Stage Rd	Whitefish	MT	59937	**800-336-1977***	406-862-1877
*Cust Svc					
Herbalist The 2106 NE 65th St	Seattle	WA	98115	**800-694-3727**	206-523-2600
Irwin Naturals 5310 Beethoven St	Los Angeles	CA	90066	**866-544-7946**	310-306-3636
Jamieson Laboratories Ltd					
2 St Clair Ave W Suite 1600	Toronto	ON	M4V1L5	**888-235-8213**	416-960-0052
Jo Mar Laboratories 583-B Division St	Campbell	CA	95008	**800-538-4545**	408-374-5920
Klamath Blue Green Inc					
301 S Old Stage Rd	Mount Shasta	CA	96067	**800-327-1956**	530-926-6684
Labrada Bodybuilding Nutrition					
403 Century Plaza Dr Suite 440	Houston	TX	77073	**800-832-9948**	281-209-2137
Mannatech Inc 600 S Royal Ln Suite 200	Coppell	TX	75019	**800-281-4469**	972-471-7400
NASDAQ: MTEX					
Matol Botanical International Ltd					
290 La Brosse Ave	Pointe-Claire	QC	H9R6R6	**800-363-1890**	514-426-2865
Maximum Human Performance Inc (MHP Inc)					
1376 Pompton Ave	Cedar Grove	NJ	07009	**888-783-8844**	973-785-9055
Mega-Pro International Inc					
251 W Hilton Dr	Saint George	UT	84770	**800-541-9469**	435-673-1001
MET-Rx Nutrition Inc					
851 Broken Sound Pkwy NW	Boca Raton	FL	33487	**800-926-3879**	561-999-1337
Metabolife International Inc					
5643 Copley Dr	San Diego	CA	92111	**800-962-3438***	858-490-5222
*Cust Svc					
MHP Inc (Maximum Human Performance Inc)					
1376 Pompton Ave	Cedar Grove	NJ	07009	**888-783-8844**	973-785-9055
Morinda Inc PO Box 4000	Orem	UT	84059	**800-445-2969**	801-431-6000
National Vitamin Co 2075 W Scranton Ave	Porterville	CA	93257	**800-538-5828**	559-781-8871
Natrol Inc 21411 Prairie St	Chatsworth	CA	91311	**800-262-8765**	818-739-6000
NASDAQ: NTOL					
Naturade Products Inc					
14370 Myford Rd Suite 100	Irvine	CA	92606	**800-367-2880**	714-573-4800
Natural Alternatives International Inc					
1185 Linda Vista Dr Suite D	San Marcos	CA	92069	**800-848-2646**	760-744-7340
NASDAQ: NAII					
Natural Factors Nutritional Products Inc					
1111 80th St Suite 100	Everett	WA	98203	**800-322-8704**	425-513-8800
Natural Factors Nutritional Products Ltd					
1550 United Blvd	Coquitlam	BC	V3K6Y7	**800-663-8900**	604-420-4229
Natural Organics Inc 548 Broadhollow Rd	Melville	NY	11747	**800-645-9500**	631-293-0030
Naturally Vitamin Supplements Inc					
4404 E Elwood St	Phoenix	AZ	85040	**800-899-4499**	480-991-0200
Nature's Life					
900 Larkspur Landing Cir Suite 105	Larkspur	CA	94939	**800-247-6997**	435-655-6790
Nature's Sunshine Products Inc					
75 E 1700 South	Provo	UT	84606	**800-223-8225***	801-342-4300
NASDAQ: NATR ■ *Cust Svc					
Nature's Way 10 Mountain Springs Pkwy	Springville	UT	84663	**800-962-8873**	801-489-1500
NBTY Inc 90 Orville Dr	Bohemia	NY	11716	**800-645-5412**	631-567-9500
NYSE: NTY					
Next Proteins International PO Box 2469	Carlsbad	CA	92018	**800-468-6398**	760-431-8152
Nickers International Ltd PO Box 50066	Staten Island	NY	10305	**800-642-5377**	718-448-6283
Novartis Nutrition					
1600 Utica Ave S Suite 600	Saint Louis Park	MN	55416	**800-999-9978**	952-925-2100
Nutraceutical International Corp					
1400 Kearns Blvd 2nd Fl	Park City	UT	84060	**800-669-8877**	435-655-6000
NASDAQ: NUTR					
Paragon Laboratories 20433 Earl St	Torrance	CA	90503	**800-228-6965**	310-370-1563
Peak Nutrition 1097 11th St	Syracuse	NE	68446	**800-600-2069**	402-269-2825
Perrigo Co 515 Eastern Ave	Allegan	MI	49010	**800-253-3606**	269-673-8451
NASDAQ: PRGO					
Pharmanex Inc 75 W Ctr	Provo	UT	84601	**888-742-7626**	801-345-9800
Pharmaton Natural Health Products Div Boehringer Ingelheim Pharmaceuticals Inc 900 Ridgebury Rd	Ridgefield	CT	06877	**800-451-6688**	203-798-9988
Pharmavite Corp					
8510 Balboa Ave Suite 300 PO Box 9609	Northridge	CA	91325	**800-423-2405**	818-221-6200
Phibro Animal Health Corp					
400 Kelby St 1 Parker Plaza	Fort Lee	NJ	07024	**800-223-0434**	201-944-6020
Prolab Nutrition 11 Britton Dr	Bloomfield	CT	06002	**800-776-5221**	860-769-5550
Randal Nutritional Products Inc					
1595 Hampston Way PO Box 7328	Santa Rosa	CA	95407	**800-221-1697**	707-528-1800
Rexall Sundown Inc					
6111 Broken Sound Pkwy NW	Boca Raton	FL	33487	**800-327-0908**	561-241-9400
Solae Co PO Box 88940	Saint Louis	MO	63188	**800-325-7136**	
Solgar Vitamin Co Inc 500 Willow Tree Rd	Leonia	NJ	07605	**800-645-2246**	201-944-2311
SportPharma USA Inc 111 Speen St	Framingham	MA	01701	**800-654-4246**	508-620-1500
Tishcon Corp 30 New York Ave	Westbury	NY	11590	**800-848-8442**	516-333-3050
TSN Labs Inc PO Box 38	Midvale	UT	84047	**800-769-7290**	801-261-2252
Twinlab Corp 150 Motor Pkwy Suite 210	Hauppauge	NY	11788	**800-645-5626**	631-467-3140
Ultra-Lab Nutrition Inc					
7491 N Federal Hwy Suite 148	Boca Raton	FL	33487	**800-800-0267**	561-367-1474
USANA Health Sciences Inc					
3838 W Parkway Blvd	Salt Lake City	UT	84120	**888-950-9595**	801-954-7100
NASDAQ: USNA					
Wachters' Organic Sea Products Corp					
550 Sylvan St	Daly City	CA	94014	**800-682-7100**	650-757-9851
Wakunaga of America Co Ltd					
23501 Madero	Mission Viejo	CA	92691	**800-421-2998**	949-855-2776
Weider Nutrition International Inc					
2002 S 5070 West	Salt Lake City	UT	84104	**800-453-9542**	801-975-5000
NYSE: WNI					
Windmill Health Products 21 Dwight Pl	Fairfield	NJ	07004	**800-822-4320**	973-575-6591

Classified Section

787 VOCATIONAL & TECHNICAL SCHOOLS

SEE ALSO Children's Learning Centers; Colleges & Universities - Four-Year; Colleges - Business; Colleges - Fine Arts; Colleges - Junior; Language Schools; Military Service Academies; Universities - Canadian

Name / Address	City	State	Zip	Toll-Free	Phone
Herzing College 280 W Valley Ave	Birmingham	AL	35209	**800-425-9432**	205-916-2800
Reid State Technical College I-65 & Hwy 83 PO Box 588	Evergreen	AL	36401	**866-578-1313**	251-578-1313
DeVRY University 2700 3rd Ave SE	Calgary	AB	T2A7W4	**800-363-5558**	403-235-3450
DeVRY University 2149 W Dunlap Ave *Cust Svc	Phoenix	AZ	85021	**800-528-0250***	602-870-9222
ITT Technical Institute 5005 S Wendler Dr	Tempe	AZ	85282	**800-879-4881**	602-437-7500
ITT Technical Institute 1455 W River Rd	Tucson	AZ	85704	**800-870-9730**	520-408-7488
Rainstar University 8370 E Via De Ventura St Suite K-100	Scottsdale	AZ	85258	**888-724-6782**	480-423-0375
Southwest Institute of Healing Arts 1100 E Apache Blvd	Tempe	AZ	85281	**888-504-9106**	480-994-9244
California Culinary Academy Inc 625 Polk St	San Francisco	CA	94102	**800-229-2433**	415-771-3500
DeVRY University 6600 Dumbarton Cir	Fremont	CA	94555	**888-201-9941**	510-574-1200
DeVRY University 3880 Kilroy Airport Way	Long Beach	CA	90806	**800-597-1333**	562-997-5422
DeVRY University 901 Corporate Ctr Dr University Ctr	Pomona	CA	91768	**800-243-3660**	909-622-9800
ITT Technical Institute 10863 Gold Center Dr	Rancho Cordova	CA	95670	**800-488-8466**	916-851-3900
ITT Technical Institute 630 E Brier Dr Suite 150	San Bernardino	CA	92408	**800-888-3801**	909-889-3800
ITT Technical Institute 9680 Granite Ridge Dr	San Diego	CA	92123	**800-883-0380**	858-571-8500
ITT Technical Institute 12669 Encinitas Ave	Sylmar	CA	91342	**800-363-2086**	818-364-5151
ITT Technical Institute of West Covina 1530 W Cameron Ave	West Covina	CA	91790	**800-414-6522**	626-960-8681
National Polytechnic College of Engineering & Oceaneering 272 S Fries Ave	Wilmington	CA	90744	**800-432-3483**	310-834-2501
Bel-Rea Institute of Animal Technology 1681 S Dayton St	Denver	CO	80247	**800-950-8001**	303-751-8700
Denver Automotive & Diesel College 460 S Lipan St	Denver	CO	80223	**800-347-3232**	303-722-5724
DeVRY University 925 S Niagara St	Denver	CO	80224	**888-212-1857**	303-329-3340
Westwood College of Technology 7350 N Broadway	Denver	CO	80221	**800-875-6050**	303-650-5050
International College of Hospitality Management Cesar Ritz 1760 Mapleton Ave	Suffield	CT	06078	**800-955-0809**	860-668-3515
Rensselaer Polytechnic Institute 275 Windsor St	Hartford	CT	06120	**800-433-4723**	860-548-2400
ATI Health Education Center 1395 NW 167th St Suite 200	Miami	FL	33169	**800-275-2725**	305-628-1000
Crane Institute of America Inc 3880 St Johns Pkwy	Sanford	FL	32771	**800-832-2726**	407-322-6800
First Coast Technical Institute 2980 Collins Ave	Saint Augustine	FL	32084	**866-462-3284**	904-824-4401
Florida Culinary Institute 2410 Metro Centre Blvd	West Palm Beach	FL	33407	**800-867-2433**	561-688-2001
Florida Technical College 1450 S Woodland Blvd	DeLand	FL	32720	**888-724-6441**	386-734-3303
Full Sail Center for the Recording Arts 3300 University Blvd Suite 160	Winter Park	FL	32792	**800-226-7625**	407-679-6333
ITT Technical Institute 3401 S University Dr	Fort Lauderdale	FL	33328	**800-488-7797**	954-476-9300
ITT Technical Institute 6600 Youngerman Cir Suite 10	Jacksonville	FL	32244	**800-318-1264**	904-573-9100
ITT Technical Institute 4809 Memorial Hwy	Tampa	FL	33634	**800-825-2831**	813-885-2244
Keiser College 1500 NW 49th St	Fort Lauderdale	FL	33309	**800-749-4456**	954-776-4456
New England Institute of Technology 2410 Metro Centre Blvd	West Palm Beach	FL	33407	**800-826-9986**	561-842-8324
Wackenhut Training Institute 4200 Wackenhut Dr Suite 100	Palm Beach Gardens	FL	33410	**800-922-6488**	561-622-5656
Bauder College 384 N Yard Blvd Suite 190	Atlanta	GA	30313	**800-241-3797**	404-237-7573
DeVRY University 250 N Arcadia Ave	Decatur	GA	30030	**800-221-4771**	404-292-7900
Gupton-Jones College of Funeral Service 5141 Snapfinger Woods Dr	Decatur	GA	30035	**800-848-5352**	770-593-2257
Eastern Idaho Technical College 1600 S 25th E	Idaho Falls	ID	83404	**800-662-0261**	208-524-3000
ITT Technical Institute 12302 W Explorer Dr	Boise	ID	83713	**800-666-4888**	208-322-8844
DeVRY University 1221 N Swift Rd	Addison	IL	60101	**800-346-5420**	630-953-1300
DeVRY University 3300 N Campbell Ave	Chicago	IL	60618	**800-338-7940**	773-929-8500
Midstate College 411 W Northmoor Rd	Peoria	IL	61614	**800-251-4299**	309-692-4092
ITT Technical Institute 4919 Coldwater Rd	Fort Wayne	IN	46825	**800-866-4488**	260-484-4107
ITT Technical Institute 9511 Angola Ct	Indianapolis	IN	46268	**800-937-4488**	317-875-8640
ITT Technical Institute 10999 Stahl Rd	Newburgh	IN	47630	**800-832-4488**	812-858-1600
Ivy Tech State College Columbus 4475 Central Ave	Columbus	IN	47203	**800-922-4838**	812-372-9925
Ivy Tech State College Gary 1440 E 35th Ave	Gary	IN	46409	**800-843-4882**	219-981-1111
Ivy Tech State College Kokomo 1815 E Morgan St	Kokomo	IN	46901	**800-459-0561**	765-459-0561
Ivy Tech State College Muncie 4301 S Cowan Rd	Muncie	IN	47302	**800-589-8324**	765-289-2291
Ivy Tech State College Richmond 2325 Chester Blvd	Richmond	IN	47374	**800-659-4562**	765-966-2656
Ivy Tech State College South Bend 220 Dean Johnson Blvd	South Bend	IN	46601	**888-489-3478**	574-289-7001
Ivy Tech State College Terre Haute 7999 S US 41	Terre Haute	IN	47802	**800-377-4882**	812-299-1121
Lincoln Technical Institute 7225 Winton Dr Bldg 128	Indianapolis	IN	46268	**800-554-4465**	317-632-5553
Western Iowa Tech Community College 4647 Stone Ave	Sioux City	IA	51106	**800-352-4649**	712-274-6400
Concorde Career Colleges Inc 5800 Foxridge Dr Suite 500 *NASDAQ: CCDC*	Mission	KS	66202	**800-515-1007**	913-831-9977
Hazard Community & Technical College *Hazard Campus* 101 Vo Tech Dr	Hazard	KY	41701	**800-246-7521**	606-435-6101
Lees Campus 601 Jefferson Ave	Jackson	KY	41339	**800-246-7521**	606-666-7521
Louisville Technical Institute 3901 Atkinson Square Dr	Louisville	KY	40218	**800-844-6528**	502-456-6509
Paducah Technology College 509 S 30th St	Paducah	KY	42001	**800-995-4438**	270-444-9676
RETS Institute of Technology 300 Highrise Dr	Louisville	KY	40213	**800-999-7387**	502-968-7191
Central Maine Community College 1250 Turner St *Admissions	Auburn	ME	04210	**800-891-2002***	207-755-5100
Northern Maine Community College 33 Edgemont Dr *Admissions	Presque Isle	ME	04769	**800-535-6682***	207-768-2700
Southern Maine Community College 2 Fort Rd	South Portland	ME	04106	**877-282-2182**	207-741-5500
Baltimore International College 17 Commerce St	Baltimore	MD	21202	**800-624-9926**	410-752-4710
Argosy University/Twin Cities 1515 Central Pkwy	Eagan	MN	55121	**888-844-2004**	651-846-2882
Dunwoody College of Technology 818 Dunwoody Blvd	Minneapolis	MN	55403	**800-292-4625**	612-374-5800
Northwest Technical Institute 11995 Singletree Ln	Eden Prairie	MN	55344	**800-443-4223**	952-944-0080
Ridgewater College Willmar Campus 2101 15th Ave NW	Willmar	MN	56201	**800-722-1151**	320-235-5114
Saint Cloud Technical College 1540 Northway Dr	Saint Cloud	MN	56303	**800-222-1009**	320-308-5089
Saint Paul College 235 Marshall Ave	Saint Paul	MN	55102	**800-227-6029**	651-846-1600
DeVRY University 11224 Holmes Rd	Kansas City	MO	64131	**800-821-3766**	816-941-0430
ITT Technical Institute 13505 Lake Front Dr	Earth City	MO	63045	**800-235-5488**	314-298-7800
Vatterott College Kansas City 8955 E 38th Terr	Kansas City	MO	64129	**800-466-3997**	816-861-1000
ITT Technical Institute 9814 M St	Omaha	NE	68127	**800-677-9260**	402-331-2900
Nebraska College of Technical Agriculture RR 3 Box 23A	Curtis	NE	69025	**800-328-7847**	308-367-4124
Southeast Community College-Milford 600 State St	Milford	NE	68405	**800-933-7223**	402-761-2131
New Hampshire Community Technical College *Berlin Campus* 2020 Riverside Dr	Berlin	NH	03570	**800-445-4525**	603-752-1113
Laconia Campus 379 Belmont Rd	Laconia	NH	03246	**800-357-2992**	603-524-3207
New Hampshire Technical Institute 31 College Dr	Concord	NH	03301	**800-247-0179**	603-271-6484
DeVRY University 630 US Hwy 1	North Brunswick	NJ	08902	**800-333-3879**	732-435-4880
Southwestern Indian Polytechnic Institute 9169 Coors Rd	Albuquerque	NM	87184	**800-586-7474**	505-346-2346
Culinary Institute of America 1946 Campus Dr *Admissions	Hyde Park	NY	12538	**800-285-4627***	845-452-9600
Cleveland Institute of Electronics 1776 E 17th St	Cleveland	OH	44114	**800-243-6446**	216-781-9400
DeVRY University 1350 Alum Creek Dr	Columbus	OH	43209	**800-426-2206**	614-253-7291
Hocking College 3301 Hocking Pkwy	Nelsonville	OH	45764	**800-282-4163**	740-753-3591
ITT Technical Institute 3325 Stop Eight Rd	Dayton	OH	45414	**800-568-3241**	937-454-2267
ITT Technical Institute 1030 N Meridian Rd	Youngstown	OH	44509	**800-832-5001**	330-270-1600
North Central State College 2441 Kenwood Circle	Mansfield	OH	44906	**888-755-4899**	419-755-4800
Ohio Institute of Photography & Technology 2029 Edgefield Rd	Dayton	OH	45439	**800-932-9698**	937-294-6155
RETS Tech Center 555 E Alex Bell Rd	Centerville	OH	45459	**800-837-7387**	937-433-3410
Stark State College of Technology 6200 Frank Ave NW	Canton	OH	44720	**800-797-8275**	330-494-6170
Zane State College 1555 Newark Rd	Zanesville	OH	43701	**800-686-8324**	740-454-2501
Oklahoma State University Okmulgee 1801 E 4th St	Okmulgee	OK	74447	**800-722-4471**	918-293-4678
Spartan School of Aeronautics 8820 E Pine St *Admissions	Tulsa	OK	74115	**800-331-1204***	918-836-6886
ITT Technical Institute 6035 NE 78th Ct	Portland	OR	97218	**800-234-5488**	503-255-6500
American College 270 S Bryn Mawr Ave	Bryn Mawr	PA	19010	**888-263-7265**	610-526-1000
Johnson College 3427 N Main Ave	Scranton	PA	18508	**800-293-9675**	570-342-6404
Lincoln Technical Institute 5151 Tilghman St	Allentown	PA	18104	**877-533-2592**	610-398-5301
Lincoln Technical Institute 9191 Torresdale Ave	Philadelphia	PA	19136	**800-806-1917**	215-335-0800
Pennco Tech 3815 Otter St	Bristol	PA	19007	**800-575-9399**	215-824-3200
Pennsylvania College of Technology 1 College Ave *Admissions	Williamsport	PA	17701	**800-367-9222***	570-326-3761
Pennsylvania Institute of Technology 800 Manchester Ave	Media	PA	19063	**800-422-0025**	610-565-7900
Pittsburgh Institute of Aeronautics PO Box 10897	Pittsburgh	PA	15236	**800-444-1440**	412-462-9011
Pittsburgh Institute of Mortuary Science Inc 5808 Baum Blvd	Pittsburgh	PA	15206	**800-933-5808**	412-362-8500
Pittsburgh Technical Institute 1111 McKee Rd	Oakdale	PA	15071	**800-905-9985**	412-809-5100
Thaddeus Stevens College of Technology 750 E King St	Lancaster	PA	17602	**800-842-3832**	717-299-7701
Triangle Tech Inc 1940 Perrysville Ave	Pittsburgh	PA	15214	**800-874-8324**	412-359-1000
Du Bois School PO Box 551	Du Bois	PA	15801	**800-874-8324**	814-371-2090
Erie School 2000 Liberty St	Erie	PA	16502	**800-874-8324**	814-453-6016
Greensburg 222 E Pittsburgh St	Greensburg	PA	15601	**800-533-4224**	724-832-1050
Welder Training & Testing Institute 1144 N Graham St	Allentown	PA	18109	**800-223-9884**	610-820-9551
New England Institute of Technology 2500 Post Rd	Warwick	RI	02886	**800-736-7744**	401-467-7744
Florence-Darlington Technical College 2715 W Lucas St	Florence	SC	29501	**800-228-5745**	843-661-8324
Piedmont Technical College 620 N Emerald Rd	Greenwood	SC	29646	**800-868-5528**	864-941-8324
Spartanburg Technical College PO Box 4386	Spartanburg	SC	29305	**800-922-3679**	864-591-3600
Technical College of the Lowcountry 921 Ribaut Rd	Beaufort	SC	29901	**800-768-8252**	843-525-8324
Trident Technical College 7000 Rivers Ave PO Box 118067	Charleston	SC	29423	**877-349-6184**	843-574-6111
Fountainhead College of Technology 3203 Tazewell Pike	Knoxville	TN	37918	**888-218-7335**	865-688-9422
ITT Technical Institute 10208 Technology Dr	Knoxville	TN	37932	**800-671-2801**	865-671-2800
ITT Technical Institute 2845 Elm Hill Pike	Nashville	TN	37214	**800-331-8386**	615-889-8700
Nashville State Community College 120 White Bridge Rd	Nashville	TN	37209	**800-272-7363**	615-353-3333
Northeast State Technical Community College PO Box 696	Elizabethton	TN	37644	**800-836-7822**	423-547-8450
DeVRY University 4800 Regent Blvd	Irving	TX	75063	**800-633-3879**	972-929-6777
ITT Technical Institute 551 Ryan Plaza Dr	Arlington	TX	76011	**888-288-4950**	817-794-5100
ITT Technical Institute 6330 Hwy 290 E Suite 150	Austin	TX	78723	**800-431-0677**	512-467-6800
ITT Technical Institute 15621 Blue Ash Dr Suite 160	Houston	TX	77090	**800-879-6486**	281-873-0512

				Toll-Free	Phone
ITT Technical Institute 2101 Water View Pkwy	Richardson	TX	75080	**888-488-5761**	972-690-9100
ITT Technical Institute 5700 Northwest Pkwy	San Antonio	TX	78249	**800-880-0570**	210-694-4612
National Center of Continuing Education 1100 Lakeway Dr Suite 200 PO Box 342588	Lakeway	TX	78734	**800-824-1254**	512-261-1937
South Texas Vocational Technical Institute 2419 E Haggar Ave	Weslaco	TX	78596	**888-279-3556**	956-969-1564
Texas State Technical College					
Sweetwater Campus 300 College Dr	Sweetwater	TX	79556	**800-592-8784**	325-235-7300
Waco Campus 3801 Campus Dr	Waco	TX	76705	**800-792-8784**	254-799-3611
ITT Technical Institute 920 W Levoy Dr	Murray	UT	84123	**800-365-2136**	801-263-3313
New England Culinary Institute 250 Main St	Montpelier	VT	05602	**877-223-6324**	802-223-6324
Sterling College PO Box 72	Craftsbury Common	VT	05827	**800-648-3591**	802-586-7711
Vermont Technical College PO Box 500	Randolph Center	VT	05061	**800-442-8821**	802-728-1000
ITT Technical Institute 863 Glenrock Rd Suite 100	Norfolk	VA	23502	**888-253-8324**	757-466-1260
Jefferson College of Health Sciences 920 S Jefferson St PO Box 13186	Roanoke	VA	24031	**888-985-8483**	540-985-8483
ITT Technical Institute 12720 Gateway Dr Suite 100	Seattle	WA	98168	**800-422-2029**	206-244-3300
ITT Technical Institute N 1050 Argonne Rd	Spokane	WA	99212	**800-777-8324**	509-926-2900
Chippewa Valley Technical College 620 W Clairemont Ave	Eau Claire	WI	54701	**800-547-2882**	715-833-6200
Fox Valley Technical College 1825 N Bluemound Dr	Appleton	WI	54912	**800-735-3882**	920-735-5600
Gateway Technical College 3520 30th Ave	Kenosha	WI	53144	**800-247-7122**	262-564-2200
Herzing College 5218 E Terrace Dr	Madison	WI	53718	**800-582-1227**	608-249-6611
ITT Technical Institute 6300 W Layton Ave	Greenfield	WI	53220	**800-388-3368**	414-282-9494
Lakeshore Technical College 1290 North Ave	Cleveland	WI	53015	**800-443-2129**	920-693-8213
Madison Area Technical College 3550 Anderson St	Madison	WI	53704	**800-322-6282**	608-246-6100
Mid-State Technical College 500 32nd St N	Wisconsin Rapids	WI	54494	**888-575-6782**	715-422-5444
Milwaukee Area Technical College 700 W State St	Milwaukee	WI	53233	**800-720-6282**	414-297-6600
Moraine Park Technical College 235 N National Ave	Fond du Lac	WI	54936	**800-472-4554**	920-922-8611
Northcentral Technical College 1000 W Campus Dr	Wausau	WI	54401	**888-682-7144**	715-675-3331
Northeast Wisconsin Technical College 2740 W Mason St	Green Bay	WI	54307	**800-422-6982**	920-498-5400
Southwest Wisconsin Technical College 1800 Bronson Blvd	Fennimore	WI	53809	**800-362-3322**	608-822-3262
Western Wisconsin Technical College 304 N 6th St	La Crosse	WI	54602	**800-248-9982**	608-785-9200
Wisconsin Indianhead Technical College					
Ashland Campus 2100 Beaser Ave	Ashland	WI	54806	**800-243-9482**	715-682-4591
New Richmond Campus 1019 S Knowles Ave	New Richmond	WI	54017	**800-243-9482**	715-246-6561
Rice Lake Campus 1900 College Dr	Rice Lake	WI	54868	**800-243-9482**	715-234-7082
Superior Campus 600 N 21 St	Superior	WI	54880	**800-243-9482**	715-394-6677
WyoTech 4373 N 3rd St	Laramie	WY	82072	**800-521-7158**	307-742-3776

788 VOTING SYSTEMS & SOFTWARE

				Toll-Free	Phone
Diebold Inc 5995 Mayfair Rd	North Canton	OH	44720	**800-999-3600**	330-490-4000
NYSE: DBD					
Election Data Direct Inc PO Box 302021	Escondido	CA	92030	**800-233-9953**	760-751-9900
Election Systems & Software Inc 11208 John Galt Blvd	Omaha	NE	68137	**800-247-8683**	402-593-0101
Election Works Inc 42W349 Hunters Hill Dr	Saint Charles	IL	60175	**888-619-0500**	630-377-1973
Elections USA Inc 1927 E Saw Mill Rd	Quakertown	PA	18951	**800-789-8683**	215-538-0779
Fidlar Software 4450 48th Ave Ct PO Box 6248	Rock Island	IL	61204	**800-747-4600**	309-794-3200
Guardian Voting Systems 1675 Delany Rd	Gurnee	IL	60031	**800-888-9527**	847-662-2666
Hart InterCivic 15500 Wells Port Dr PO Box 80649	Austin	TX	78708	**800-223-4278**	512-252-6400
MicroVote General Corp 6366 Guilford Ave	Indianapolis	IN	46220	**800-257-4901**	317-257-4900

789 WALLCOVERINGS

				Toll-Free	Phone
Blue Mountain Wallcoverings Inc 15 Akron Rd	Toronto	ON	M8W1T3	**800-219-2424**	416-251-1678
Butler Printing & Laminating Inc 250 Hamburg Tpke PO Box 836	Butler	NJ	07405	**800-524-0786**	973-838-8550
Eisenhart Wallcoverings Co 400 Pine St PO Box 464	Hanover	PA	17331	**800-555-2554**	717-632-8024
F Schumacher & Co 79 Madison Ave	New York	NY	10016	**800-556-0040**	212-213-7900
Fashion Wallcoverings 2040 W 110th St	Cleveland	OH	44102	**800-362-9930***	216-631-6700
*Orders					
Goldcrest Wallcoverings 1526 New Scotland Rd	Slingerlands	NY	12159	**800-535-9513**	518-478-7214
Hunter & Co of North Carolina Inc 1945 W Green Dr	High Point	NC	27261	**800-523-8387**	336-883-4161
Seabrook Wallcoverings Inc 1325 Farmville Rd	Memphis	TN	38122	**800-238-9152**	901-320-3500
Sellers & Josephson Inc 86 Rt 4 E	Englewood	NJ	07631	**800-274-3385**	201-567-1353
Thibaut Inc 480 Frelinghuysen Ave	Newark	NJ	07114	**800-223-0704**	973-643-1118
Warner Co 9201 W Belmont Ave	Franklin Park	IL	60131	**800-621-1143**	847-737-8000
York Wallcoverings Inc 750 Linden Ave PO Box 5166	York	PA	17405	**800-453-9281**	717-846-4456

790 WAREHOUSING & STORAGE

SEE ALSO Logistics Services (Transportation & Warehousing)

790-1 Commercial Warehousing

				Toll-Free	Phone
A Duie Pyle Distribution & Warehousing Inc 650 Westtown Rd	West Chester	PA	19381	**800-523-5020**	610-696-5800
Columbian Distribution Services Inc 900 Hall St SW	Grand Rapids	MI	49503	**888-609-8542**	616-514-6000
Dart Warehouse Corp 1430 S Eastman Ave	Los Angeles	CA	90023	**800-963-3278**	323-264-1011
DD Jones Transfer & Warehouse Co Inc 2115 Portlock Rd	Chesapeake	VA	23324	**800-335-4787**	757-494-0200
Distribution Technology Inc 1701 Continental Blvd	Charlotte	NC	28273	**800-264-4771**	704-588-2867
Evans Distribution Systems 18765 Seaway Dr	Melvindale	MI	48122	**888-361-9850**	313-388-3200
Federal Warehouse Co 101 National Rd	East Peoria	IL	61611	**800-747-4100**	309-694-4500
File Keepers LLC 6277 E Slauson Ave	Los Angeles	CA	90040	**800-332-3453**	323-728-3151
Hollister Moving & Storage 1650 Lana Way	Hollister	CA	95023	**800-696-6250**	831-637-6250
Iron Mountain Inc 745 Atlantic Ave	Boston	MA	02111	**800-899-4766**	
NYSE: IRM					
Jones DD Transfer & Warehouse Co Inc 2115 Portlock Rd	Chesapeake	VA	23324	**800-335-4787**	757-494-0200
Keller Transfer/Commerce Distribution Center 31750 Enterprise Dr	Livonia	MI	48151	**800-666-0701**	734-458-5116
Kenco Group Inc 2001 Riverside Dr	Chattanooga	TN	37401	**800-365-7189**	423-756-5552
Pyle A Duie Distribution & Warehousing Inc 650 Westtown Rd	West Chester	PA	19381	**800-523-5020**	610-696-5800
Recall Corp 1 Recall Ctr 180 Technology Pkwy	Norcross	GA	30092	**888-732-2556**	770-776-1200
Robinson Terminal Warehouse Corp 2 Duke St	Alexandria	VA	22314	**800-331-6593**	703-836-8300
Security Storage Co 1701 Florida Ave NW	Washington	DC	20009	**800-736-6825**	202-234-5600
Tejas Warehouse System 324 Pleasant St	Waco	TX	76704	**800-535-9786**	254-752-9241

790-2 Refrigerated Storage

				Toll-Free	Phone
Berkshire Foods Inc 4600 S Packers Ave	Chicago	IL	60609	**800-621-5042**	773-254-2424
Burris Logistics 501 SE 5th St	Milford	DE	19963	**800-805-8135**	302-839-4531
New Orleans Cold Storage & Warehouse Co Inc 3411 Jourdan Rd Terminal	New Orleans	LA	70126	**800-782-2653**	504-944-4400
Perley-Halladay Assoc Inc 1442 Phoenixville Pike	West Chester	PA	19380	**800-248-5800**	610-296-5800
Reddy Ice & Cassco Refrigerated Services PO Box 548	Harrisonburg	VA	22801	**800-999-4231**	540-433-2751
Total Logistic Control Inc 8300 Logistic Dr	Zeeland	MI	49464	**800-333-5599**	616-772-9009

790-3 Self-Storage Facilities

				Toll-Free	Phone
Devon Group DBA Devon Self Storage 2000 Powell St Suite 1240	Emeryville	CA	94068	**800-995-4480**	510-450-1300
Devon Self Storage 2000 Powell St Suite 1240	Emeryville	CA	94068	**800-995-4480**	510-450-1300
Public Storage Inc 701 Western Ave	Glendale	CA	91201	**800-567-0759***	818-244-8080
NYSE: PSA ■ *Cust Svc					
Shurgard Storage Centers Inc 1155 Valley St Suite 400	Seattle	WA	98109	**800-748-7427**	206-624-8100
NYSE: SHU					
Stor-All Systems Inc 1375 W Hillsboro Blvd	Deerfield Beach	FL	33442	**800-937-8673**	954-421-7888
U-Haul International Inc PO Box 21502	Phoenix	AZ	85036	**800-468-4285**	602-263-6011
U-Store-It Trust 6745 Engle Rd Suite 300	Middleburg Heights	OH	44130	**800-234-4494**	440-234-0700
NYSE: YSI					

791 WASTE MANAGEMENT

SEE ALSO Recyclable Materials Recovery; Remediation Services

				Toll-Free	Phone
Athens Disposal Co Inc 14048 Valley Blvd	City of Industry	CA	91746	**888-336-6100***	626-336-3636
*Cust Svc					
Casella Waste Systems Inc PO Box 866	Rutland	VT	05702	**800-227-3552**	802-775-0325
NASDAQ: CWST					
Classic Sanitation Co Inc 375 Rt 1 & 9 S	Jersey City	NJ	07306	**800-386-7783**	201-547-4100
Consolidated Disposal Services Inc 12949 Telegraph Rd	Santa Fe Springs	CA	90670	**800-299-4898**	562-946-6441
Coulter Cos Inc DBA Peoria Disposal Co PO Box 9071	Peoria	IL	61612	**888-988-0760**	309-688-0760
EL Harvey & Sons 68 Hopkinton Rd	Westborough	MA	01581	**800-321-3002**	508-836-3000
EQ-The Environmental Quality Co 36255 Michigan Ave	Wayne	MI	48184	**800-592-5489**	734-329-8000
Harold LeMay Enterprises Inc 13502 Pacific Ave	Tacoma	WA	98444	**800-345-3629**	253-537-8687
Harris Waste Management Group Inc 200 Clover Reach Dr	Peachtree City	GA	30269	**800-468-5657**	770-631-7290
Harrison Industries Inc PO Box 4009	Ventura	CA	93007	**800-418-7274**	805-647-1414
Heritage Environmental Services Inc 7901 W Morris St	Indianapolis	IN	46231	**877-436-8778**	317-243-0811
Industrial Services of America Inc 7100 Grade Ln	Louisville	KY	40213	**800-824-2144**	502-368-1661
NASDAQ: IDSA					
JP Mascaro Inc 600 W Neversink Rd	Reading	PA	19606	**800-334-3403**	610-779-8807
Kaiser Ventures LLC 3633 E Inland Empire Blvd Suite 480	Ontario	CA	91764	**800-889-3652**	909-483-8500

				Toll-Free	Phone
LeMay Harold Enterprises Inc					
13502 Pacific Ave	Tacoma	WA	98444	**800-345-3629**	253-537-8687
Modern Corp 4746 Model City Rd	Model City	NY	14107	**800-662-0012**	716-754-8226
N-Viro International Corp					
3450 W Central Ave Suite 328	Toledo	OH	43606	**800-666-8476**	419-535-6374
National Serv-All Inc 6231 McBeth Rd.	Fort Wayne	IN	46809	**800-876-9001**	260-747-4117
Norcal Waste Systems Inc					
160 Pacific Ave Suite 200	San Francisco	CA	94111	**800-652-1275**	415-875-1000
Oakleaf Waste Management LLC					
800 Connecticut Blvd 1 Oakleaf Ctr.	East Hartford	CT	06108	**888-625-5323**	860-290-1250
Onyx Industrial Services Inc 1980 N Hwy 146	La Porte	TX	77571	**877-719-5086**	713-307-2100
Palm Springs Disposal Co					
4690 E Mesquite Ave	Palm Springs	CA	92264	**800-973-3873**	760-327-1351
Peoria Disposal Co PO Box 9071	Peoria	IL	61612	**888-988-0760**	309-688-0760
Prairie Waste Service Inc 6449 Valley Dr	Bettendorf	IA	52722	**800-233-9634**	563-332-0050
Republic Services Inc					
110 SE 6th St Suite 2800	Fort Lauderdale	FL	33301	**877-241-8396**	954-769-2400
NYSE: RSG					
Rumpke Consolidated Cos Inc					
10795 Hughes Rd	Cincinnati	OH	45251	**800-582-3107**	513-851-0122
Shaw Environmental & Infrastructure Inc					
4171 Essen Ln	Baton Rouge	LA	70809	**800-444-9586**	225-932-2500
Solid Waste Services Inc DBA JP Mascaro Inc					
600 W Neversink Rd	Reading	PA	19606	**800-334-3403**	610-779-8807
Stericycle Inc 28161 N Keith Dr.	Lake Forest	IL	60045	**800-355-8773**	800-643-0240
NASDAQ: SRCL					
Synagro Technologies Inc					
1800 Bering Dr Suite 1000	Houston	TX	77057	**800-370-0035**	713-369-1700
NASDAQ: SYGR					
Texas Disposal Systems Inc 12200 Carl Rd.	Creedmoor	TX	78610	**800-375-8375**	512-392-1515
Urban Services Systems Inc					
2041 ML King Ave SE	Washington	DC	20020	**800-766-0635**	202-678-7393
VFL Technology Corp 16 Hagerty Blvd	West Chester	PA	19382	**800-882-8358**	610-918-1100
Waste Industries Inc					
3301 Benson Dr Suite 601	Raleigh	NC	27609	**800-647-9946**	919-325-3000
Waste Management Inc					
1001 Fannin St Suite 4000	Houston	TX	77002	**800-633-7871**	713-512-6200
NYSE: WMI					
Wheelabrator Technologies Inc					
4 Liberty Ln W.	Hampton	NH	03842	**800-682-0026**	603-929-3000

792 WATER - BOTTLED

				Toll-Free	Phone
Absopure Water Co 8835 General Dr	Plymouth	MI	48170	**800-422-7678**	
Belmont Crystal Springs Water Cos					
PO Box 3229	Lancaster	PA	17604	**800-444-7873**	717-560-6674
Beverage Corp International 3505 NW 107th St	Miami	FL	33167	**800-226-5061**	305-714-7000
Calistoga Mineral Water Co 2767 E Imperial Hwy	Brea	CA	92821	**800-365-4446**	
Carolina Mountain Water Co					
150 Central Ave	Hot Springs	AR	71901	**800-643-1501**	501-623-6671
Crystal Geyser Water Co 501 Washington St.	Calistoga	CA	94515	**800-443-9737***	707-942-0500
*Cust Svc					
Culligan International Co 1 Culligan Pkwy.	Northbrook	IL	60062	**800-285-5442**	847-205-6000
Danone Waters of North America Inc					
3280 E Foothill Blvd.	Pasadena	CA	91107	**800-492-8377**	626-585-1000
Distillata Co 1608 E 24th St.	Cleveland	OH	44114	**800-999-2906***	216-771-2900
*Cust Svc					
Fountainhead Water Co PO Box 570	Salem	SC	29676	**800-874-8595**	864-944-1993
Glacier Clear Enterprises Inc 3291 Thomas St	Innisfil	ON	L9S3W3	**800-668-5118***	705-436-6363
*Cust Svc					
Hinckley Springs 6055 S Harlem Ave.	Chicago	IL	60638	**800-347-9283**	773-586-8600
Kentwood Spring Water Co					
PO Box 52043	New Orleans	LA	70152	**800-235-7873**	504-821-3333
Klarbrunn Inc 860 West St	Watertown	WI	53094	**800-910-2837**	920-262-6300
Mountain Valley Spring Co					
150 Central Ave	Hot Springs	AR	71901	**800-643-1501**	501-623-6671
Nestle Waters North America Inc					
2767 E Imperial Hwy	Brea	CA	92821	**800-877-7775**	714-792-2100
Nicolet Forest Bottling Co Inc					
39 S Barrington Rd	Barrington	IL	60010	**888-928-3756**	847-382-2950
Polar Beverages Inc 1001 Southbridge St.	Worcester	MA	01610	**800-225-7410***	508-753-4300
*Cust Svc					
Pure-Flo Water Co 7737 Mission Gorge Rd.	Santee	CA	92071	**800-787-3356***	619-448-5120
*Cust Svc					
Sparkletts Drinking Water Corp					
3280 E Foothill Blvd Suite 400	Pasadena	CA	91107	**800-492-8377**	626-585-1000
Suntory Water Group Inc					
5660 New Northside Dr Suite 500	Atlanta	GA	30328	**800-444-7873**	770-933-1400
Talking Rain Beverage Co 30520 SE 84th St	Preston	WA	98050	**800-734-0748***	425-222-4900
*Cust Svc					
Universal Beverages PO Box 448	Ponte Vedra Beach	FL	32004	**888-426-7936**	904-280-7795
Vermont Pure Holdings Ltd					
2281 Vermont Rt 66	Randolph	VT	05060	**800-939-9119***	802-728-3600
AMEX: VPS ■ *Cust Svc					
Zephyrhills Natural Spring Water					
777 W Putnam Ave	Greenwich	CT	06830	**800-950-9398**	203-531-4100

793 WATER TREATMENT & FILTRATION EQUIPMENT

				Toll-Free	Phone
Alamo Water Refiners Inc					
13700 Hwy 90 W.	San Antonio	TX	78245	**800-659-8400**	210-677-8400
Andritz-Ruthner Inc 1010 Commercial Blvd S	Arlington	TX	76001	**800-433-5161**	817-465-5611
Aqua-Aerobic Systems Inc 6306 N Alpine Rd	Rockford	IL	61111	**800-940-5008**	815-654-2501
AquaCell Technologies Inc					
10410 Trademark St	Rancho Cucamonga	CA	91730	**800-326-5222**	909-987-0456
AMEX: AQA					
Baker Hydro Filtrations Inc 1864 Tobacco Rd.	Augusta	GA	30906	**800-247-7291**	706-793-7291
Crane Environmental 2600 Eisenhower Ave.	Trooper	PA	19403	**800-633-7435**	610-631-7700
Culligan International Co 1 Culligan Pkwy.	Northbrook	IL	60062	**800-285-5442**	847-205-6000
Dow Liquid Separations PO Box 1206	Midland	MI	48642	**800-447-4369**	989-832-2442
EcoWater Systems Inc PO Box 64420	Saint Paul	MN	55164	**800-942-5415***	651-739-5330
*Cust Svc					
Everpure Inc 1040 Muirfield Dr.	Hanover Park	IL	60133	**800-323-7873**	630-307-3000
Filterspun 624 N Fairfield St.	Amarillo	TX	79107	**800-432-0108**	806-383-3840
Glacier Clear Enterprises Inc 3291 Thomas St	Innisfil	ON	L9S3W3	**800-668-5118***	705-436-6363
*Cust Svc					
Graver Technologies Inc 200 Lake Dr	Glasgow	DE	19702	**800-249-1990**	302-731-1700
Graver Water Systems Inc 750 Walnut Ave	Cranford	NJ	07016	**877-472-8379**	908-653-4200
Ionics Inc 65 Grove St	Watertown	MA	02472	**800-446-6427**	617-926-2500
Keystone Filter Div Met-Pro Corp					
2485 N Penn Rd	Hatfield	PA	19440	**800-811-4424**	215-822-1963
KX Industries 269 S Lambert Rd	Orange	CT	06477	**800-462-8745**	203-799-9000
McNish Corp 840 N Russell Ave	Aurora	IL	60506	**800-992-5537**	630-892-7921
Mechanical Equipment Co Inc					
1615 Poydras St Suite 1400	New Orleans	LA	70112	**800-599-2152**	504-599-4000
Met-Pro Corp Keystone Filter Div					
2485 N Penn Rd	Hatfield	PA	19440	**800-811-4424**	215-822-1963
MSC Liquid Filtration Corp 198 Freshwater Blvd	Enfield	CT	06082	**800-237-7359***	860-745-7475
*Cust Svc					
National Filter Media Corp					
691 N 400 West	Salt Lake City	UT	84103	**800-777-4248**	801-363-6736
Ondeo Degremont Inc					
2924 Emerywood Pkwy	Richmond	VA	23294	**800-446-1150**	804-756-7600
Osmonics Inc 5951 Clearwater Dr.	Minnetonka	MN	55343	**800-328-0992**	952-933-2277
Pall Corp 2200 Northern Blvd	East Hills	NY	11548	**800-645-6532**	516-484-5400
NYSE: PLL					
Plymouth Products Inc 502 Indiana Ave	Sheboygan	WI	53082	**800-222-7558**	920-457-9435
Polaris Pool Systems Inc 2620 Commerce Way	Vista	CA	92081	**800-822-7933***	760-599-9600
*Cust Svc					
Process Efficiency Products Inc					
322 Rolling Hills Rd.	Mooresville	NC	28117	**800-243-4586**	704-662-3133
PUR Water Purification Products					
9300 N 75th Ave	Minneapolis	MN	55428	**800-787-5463**	763-315-5500
Pure Water Inc 3725 Touzalin Ave	Lincoln	NE	68507	**800-875-5915***	402-467-9300
*Cust Svc					
Rainsoft Water Conditioning Co Inc					
2080 E Lunt Ave	Elk Grove Village	IL	60007	**800-860-7638**	847-437-9400
Schreiber Corp 100 Schreiber Dr	Trussville	AL	35173	**800-535-0944**	205-655-7466
Slickbar Products Corp 18 Beach St	Seymour	CT	06483	**800-322-2666**	203-888-7700
Taylor Technologies Inc 31 Loveton Cir	Sparks	MD	21152	**800-837-8548***	410-472-4340
*Cust Svc					
USFilter Corp 40-004 Cook St.	Palm Desert	CA	92211	**800-994-4811**	760-340-0098
USFilter/Zimpro 301 W Military Rd.	Rothschild	WI	54474	**800-826-1476**	715-359-7211
Walker Process Equipment 840 N Russell Ave	Aurora	IL	60506	**800-992-5537**	630-892-7921
Zodiac Pool Care Inc					
2028 NW 25th Ave	Pompano Beach	FL	33069	**800-937-7873**	954-935-8200

794 WEAPONS & ORDNANCE (MILITARY)

SEE ALSO Firearms & Ammunition (Non-Military); Missiles, Space Vehicles, Parts; Simulation & Training Systems

				Toll-Free	Phone
Allied Defense Group Inc					
8000 Towers Crescent Dr Suite 260	Vienna	VA	22182	**800-847-5322**	703-847-5268
AMEX: ADG					
Chamberlain Mfg Corp 845 N Larch Ave	Elmhurst	IL	60126	**800-528-9131**	630-279-3600
United Defense Steel Products Div					
2101 W 10th St	Anniston	AL	36201	**800-468-9731**	256-237-2841

795 WEB HOSTING SERVICES

SEE ALSO Internet Service Providers (ISPs)

				Toll-Free	Phone
@INR.net 379 Amherst St Suite 218	Nashua	NH	03063	**877-880-8120**	603-880-8120
1 2 3 HostMe! 3864 Courtney St Suite 130	Bethlehem	PA	18017	**888-321-3278**	610-266-6700
About Web Services					
1253 N Research Way Suite Q-2500	Orem	UT	84097	**800-396-1999**	801-437-6000
Basiclink Inc 761 D Ave Suite B	Coronado	CA	92118	**877-238-1770**	619-522-6771
Broadspire Services					
1200 W 7th St Suite 410	Los Angeles	CA	90017	**800-323-9585**	213-986-1050
Burlee Networks					
303 Peachtree Ctr Ave Suite 500	Atlanta	GA	30303	**877-467-8464**	404-260-2477
Catalog.com Inc					
6404 International Pkwy Suite 2200	Plano	TX	75093	**888-932-4376**	972-380-2202
Chapel Services Inc 1212 W Main St	Richmond	KY	40475	**888-747-4949**	859-623-1500
CI Host 1851 Central Dr Suite 110	Bedford	TX	76021	**888-820-0688***	817-868-6999
*Tech Supp					
CommuniTech.Net Inc					
303 Peachtree Ctr Ave Suite 500	Atlanta	GA	30303	**877-467-8464**	404-260-2477
DataPipe 80 River St	Hoboken	NJ	07030	**877-773-3306**	201-792-4847
DataRealm Internet Services LLC					
PO Box 726	Glassboro	NJ	08028	**877-227-3783**	602-850-4044
E-Access Inc 840 6th Ave.	Huntington	WV	25701	**800-471-5087***	304-697-4410
*Sales					
EarthLink Inc 1375 Peachtree St NE	Atlanta	GA	30309	**800-332-4892**	404-815-0770
NASDAQ: ELNK					
eStoreManager.com					
c/o American Digital Network Inc 9725 Scranton Rd	San Diego	CA	92121	**877-928-9376**	858-427-2400
Express Technologies Inc DBA HalfPrice Hosting PO Box 22789	Louisville	KY	40252	**800-284-9391**	502-214-4100
Freeservers.com					
1253 N Research Way Suite Q-2500	Orem	UT	84097	**800-396-1999**	801-437-6000
FullWeb Inc					
201 Robert S Kerr Ave Suite 210	Oklahoma City	OK	73102	**888-826-4687**	405-236-8200
Global Knowledge Group Inc (GKG)					
2700 Earl Rudder Fwy S Suite 1300	College Station	TX	77845	**800-617-0412**	979-693-5447
HalfPrice Hosting PO Box 22789	Louisville	KY	40252	**800-284-9391**	502-214-4100
HomeStore Inc					
30700 Russell Ranch Rd	Westlake Village	CA	91362	**800-878-4166***	805-557-2300
NASDAQ: HOMS ■ *Cust Svc					
Host Depot Inc 9732 W Sample Rd	Coral Springs	FL	33065	**888-340-3527**	954-340-3527
Hostcentric Inc					
6757 Edgewater Commerce Pkwy	Orlando	FL	32810	**800-467-8669**	407-445-3033

Company / Address	City	State	ZIP	Toll-Free	Phone
Hostedware Corp 16 Technology Dr Suite 116	Irvine	CA	92618	**800-211-6967**	949-585-1500
Hostway Corp 1 N State St 12th Fl	Chicago	IL	60602	**800-397-2449**	312-236-2132
ICOM (Internet Communications) 303 Peachtree Ctr Ave Suite 500	Atlanta	GA	30303	**877-504-0091**	404-260-2477
INetU Inc 744 Roble Rd Suite 70	Allentown	PA	18019	**888-664-6388**	610-266-7441
Interland Inc 303 Peachtree Ctr Ave Suite 500 *NASDAQ: INLD*	Atlanta	GA	30303	**800-214-1460**	404-260-2477
Internet Communications (ICOM) 303 Peachtree Ctr Ave Suite 500	Atlanta	GA	30303	**877-504-0091**	404-260-2477
Knight Ridder Digital 35 S Market St	San Jose	CA	95113	**877-732-5248**	408-938-6000
Media3 Technologies LLC 33 Riverside Dr N River Commerce Pk	Pembroke	MA	02359	**800-903-9327**	781-826-1213
NetNation Communications Inc 555 W Hastings St Suite 1410	Vancouver	BC	V6B4N6	**888-277-0000**	604-684-6892
OLM LLC 4 Trefoil Dr	Trumbull	CT	06611	**877-265-6638**	203-445-7700
Pacific Internet 105 W Clay St *NASDAQ: PCNTF*	Ukiah	CA	95482	**888-722-8638**	707-468-1005
Pegasus Web Technologies Inc Rt 10 E 17-19B Suite 220	Parsippany	NJ	07054	**888-734-9320**	973-267-4707
Power Surge Technologies Inc 2349 Jamestown Ave	Independence	IA	50644	**800-867-5055**	319-334-4229
Rackspace Ltd 9725 Datapoint Dr Suite 100	San Antonio	TX	78229	**800-961-2888**	210-447-4000
Radiant Communications Corp 1050 W Pender St Suite 1600	Vancouver	BC	V6E4T3	**888-219-2111**	604-257-0500
Real Cities Network 35 S Market St	San Jose	CA	95113	**877-732-5248**	408-938-6000
Solo Web Hosting 10350 Barnes Canyon Rd *Sales	San Diego	CA	92121	**877-275-8763***	858-410-6929
Stargate Holdings Corp 2805 Butterfield Rd Suite 100	Oak Brook	IL	60523	**800-282-6541**	630-572-2242
Superb Internet Corp 700 W Pender St Suite 1400	Vancouver	BC	V6C1G8	**888-354-6128**	604-638-2525
TierraNet Inc 9573 Chesapeake Dr 1st Fl	San Diego	CA	92123	**877-843-7721**	858-560-9416
ValueWeb 3250 W Commercial Blvd Suite 200	Fort Lauderdale	FL	33309	**800-934-6788**	954-429-3449
Verio Inc 8005 S Chester St Suite 200	Centennial	CO	80112	**888-558-3746**	303-645-1900
VPOP Technologies Inc 365 E Avenida de los Arboles PMB 1014 *Sales	Thousand Oaks	CA	91360	**888-811-8767***	805-529-9374
Vstore.com c/o Vcommerce Corp 9977 N 90th St Suite 200	Scottsdale	AZ	85258	**800-821-6034**	480-922-9922
Web Communications LLC 8005 S Chester St Suite 200	Englewood	CO	80112	**888-893-2266**	

796 WEB SITE DESIGN SERVICES

SEE ALSO Advertising Agencies; Advertising Services - Online; Computer Systems Design Services

Company / Address	City	State	ZIP	Toll-Free	Phone
Active Web Corp 3-304 Stone Rd W Suite 155	Guelph	ON	N1G4W4	**866-837-2711**	519-837-2711
Bigstep 2601 Mission St Suite 500	San Francisco	CA	94110	**866-499-2799**	
Braun Consulting Inc 20 W Kinzie St Suite 1600 *NASDAQ: BRNC*	Chicago	IL	60610	**800-682-7286**	312-984-7000
bx.com Inc 3 Davol Sq	Providence	RI	02903	**800-344-8487**	401-274-8991
Fry Inc 650 Avis Dr	Ann Arbor	MI	48108	**800-379-6858**	734-741-0640
Headquarters.Com Inc 625 Walnut Ridge Dr Suite 108	Hartland	WI	53029	**800-788-1298**	262-369-0600
Idea Integration Corp 1 Independent Dr 2nd Fl	Jacksonville	FL	32202	**800-433-2206**	904-360-2700
ISITE Design Inc 615 SW Broadway Suite 200	Portland	OR	97205	**888-269-9103**	503-221-9860
Logical Design Solutions Inc 131 Madison Ave	Morristown	NJ	07960	**800-275-5374**	973-971-0100
uSight 727 N 1550 E	Orem	UT	84097	**800-544-9459**	801-356-3131

797 WEIGHT LOSS CENTERS & SERVICES

SEE ALSO Health & Fitness Centers; Spas - Health & Fitness

Company / Address	City	State	ZIP	Toll-Free	Phone
Barix Clinics 135 S Prospect St	Ypsilanti	MI	48198	**800-282-0066**	734-547-4700
Craig Jenny International Inc 5770 Fleet St	Carlsbad	CA	92008	**800-443-2331**	760-696-4000
Diet Center Worldwide Inc 395 Springside Dr	Akron	OH	44333	**800-656-3294**	330-665-5861
Fit America MD 401 Fairway Dr	Deerfield Beach	FL	33441	**800-940-7546**	954-570-3211
Form-You 3 International Inc 395 Springside Dr	Akron	OH	44333	**800-525-6315**	330-668-1461
Inches-A-Weigh North America Inc 4320 Alpine Ct	Rockford	IL	61107	**800-241-8663**	815-227-4623
Jazzercise Inc 2460 Impala Dr *Cust Svc	Carlsbad	CA	92008	**800-348-4748***	760-476-1750
Jenny Craig International Inc 5770 Fleet St	Carlsbad	CA	92008	**800-443-2331**	760-696-4000
LA Weight Loss Centers 747 Dresher Rd Suite 100	Horsham	PA	19044	**877-524-3571**	215-346-4300
NutriSystem Inc 200 Welsh Rd *AMEX: NSI*	Horsham	PA	19044	**800-321-8446**	215-706-5300
Physicians Weight Loss Centers of America Inc 395 Springside Dr	Akron	OH	44333	**800-205-7887**	330-666-7952
Slender Lady Inc 45 NE Loop 410 Suite 500	San Antonio	TX	78216	**888-227-8187**	210-877-1500
Weight Watchers International Inc 175 Crossways Pk W *NYSE: WTW*	Woodbury	NY	11797	**800-651-6000**	516-390-1400

798 WELDING & SOLDERING EQUIPMENT

Company / Address	City	State	ZIP	Toll-Free	Phone
AGM Industries Inc 16 Jonathan Dr	Brockton	MA	02301	**800-225-9990**	508-587-3900
Arcos Industries 1 Arcos Dr	Mount Carmel	PA	17851	**800-233-8460**	570-339-5200
Argus International Ltd 108 Whispering Pines Dr Suite 110	Scotts Valley	CA	95066	**800-862-7487**	831-461-4700
CK Worldwide Inc PO Box 1636	Auburn	WA	98071	**800-426-0877**	253-854-5820
Cooperheat-MQS Inc 4740 E Park Dr	Houston	TX	77028	**800-526-4233**	713-673-3660
Esab Welding & Cutting Products Inc PO Box 100545	Florence	SC	29501	**800-372-2123**	843-669-4411
Eureka Welding Alloys Inc 2000 E Avis Dr	Madison Heights	MI	48071	**800-962-8560**	248-588-0001
Eutectic Corp N 94 W 14355 Garwin Mace Dr	Menomonee Falls	WI	53051	**800-558-8524**	
Forney Industries Inc PO Box 563	Fort Collins	CO	80522	**800-521-6038**	970-482-7271
Goss Inc 1511 Rt 8	Glenshaw	PA	15116	**800-367-4677**	412-486-6100
Harris Calorific Inc 2345 Murphy Blvd	Gainesville	GA	30504	**800-241-0804**	770-536-8801
IHS Inc 5009 Rondo Dr	Fort Worth	TX	76106	**800-485-5577**	817-625-5577
Industrial Welders & Machinists Inc PO Box 16720	Duluth	MN	55806	**800-689-9520**	218-628-1011
JW Harris Co Inc 4501 Quality Pl	Mason	OH	45040	**800-733-4043**	513-754-2000
Kanox Inc 1200 N Grand St PO Box 3007	Hutchinson	KS	67501	**800-333-6156**	620-665-5551
Merrill Mfg Corp PO Box 566	Merrill	WI	54452	**800-826-5300**	715-536-5533
Milco Mfg Co 2147 E 10-Mile Rd	Warren	MI	48091	**800-697-6452**	586-755-7320
NLC Inc PO Box 348	Jackson	MO	63755	**800-747-4743**	573-243-3141
Palomar Technologies Inc 2230 Oak Ridge Way	Vista	CA	92083	**800-854-3467**	760-931-3600
Pandjiris Inc 5151 Northrup Ave	Saint Louis	MO	63110	**800-237-2006**	314-776-6893
Smith Equipment Mfg Co 2601 Lockheed Ave *Cust Svc	Watertown	SD	57201	**800-328-3363***	605-882-3200
Sonobond Ultrasonics Inc 1191 McDermott Dr	West Chester	PA	19380	**800-323-1269**	610-696-4710
Stulz-Sickles Steel Co PO Box 273	Elizabeth	NJ	07207	**800-351-1776**	908-351-1776
Tuffaloy Products Inc 601 High Tech Ct	Greer	SC	29650	**800-521-3722**	864-879-0763
Uniweld Products Inc 2850 Ravenswood Rd	Fort Lauderdale	FL	33312	**800-323-2111**	954-584-2000
Victor Equipment Co 2800 Airport Rd	Denton	TX	76207	**800-426-1888**	940-566-2000
Weld Mold Co PO Box 298	Brighton	MI	48116	**800-521-9755**	810-229-9521
Weld Tooling Corp 3001 W Carson St	Pittsburgh	PA	15204	**800-245-3186**	412-331-1776
Western Enterprises Inc 875 Bassett Rd	Westlake	OH	44145	**800-783-7890**	

799 WHOLESALE CLUBS

Company / Address	City	State	ZIP	Toll-Free	Phone
BJ's Wholesale Club 1 Mercer Rd *NYSE: BJ*	Natick	MA	01760	**800-257-2582**	508-651-7400
Costco Wholesale Corp 999 Lake Dr *NASDAQ: COST* ■ *Cust Svc	Issaquah	WA	98027	**800-774-2678***	425-313-8100

800 WIRE & CABLE

Company / Address	City	State	ZIP	Toll-Free	Phone
Adirondack Wire & Cable Co Inc 191 Social St	Woonsocket	RI	02895	**800-237-4542**	401-769-1600
AFC Cable Systems Inc 272 Duchaine Blvd	New Bedford	MA	02745	**800-757-6996**	508-998-1131
Allwire Inc PO Box 12602	Fresno	CA	93778	**800-255-2828**	559-485-8120
AmerCable Corp 350 Bailey Rd	El Dorado	AR	71730	**800-643-1516**	870-862-4919
Astro Industries Inc 4403 Dayton-Xenia Rd	Dayton	OH	45432	**800-543-5810**	937-429-5900
BIW Cable Systems Inc 22 Joseph E Warner Blvd	North Dighton	MA	02764	**800-333-4248**	508-822-5444
Cerro Wire & Cable Co Inc 1099 Thompson Rd SE	Hartselle	AL	35640	**800-523-3869**	256-773-2522
Charter Wire 114 N Jackson St	Milwaukee	WI	53202	**800-436-9074**	414-390-3000
Coleman Cable Systems Inc 1530 Shields Dr	Waukegan	IL	60085	**800-323-9355**	847-672-2300
Elektrisola Inc 126 High St	Boscawen	NH	03303	**800-325-2022**	603-796-2114
Encore Wire Corp PO Box 1149 *NASDAQ: WIRE*	McKinney	TX	75069	**800-962-9473**	972-562-9473
Gehr Industries 7400 E Slauson Ave	Los Angeles	CA	90040	**800-688-6606**	323-728-5558
Industrial Wire Products Corp 3880 W Valley Blvd	Walnut	CA	91787	**800-843-9561**	909-594-7511
Kerite Co 49 Day St	Seymour	CT	06483	**800-777-7483**	203-888-2591
Keystone Consolidated Industries Inc 7000 SW Adams St *Sales	Peoria	IL	61641	**800-447-6444***	309-697-7020
Leggett Wire Co 1 Leggett Rd	Carthage	MO	64836	**800-888-4569**	417-358-8131
Mid-South Wire Co Inc 1070 Visco Dr	Nashville	TN	37210	**800-714-7800**	615-244-5258
Nichols Wire Co 1547 Helton Dr	Florence	AL	35630	**800-633-3156**	256-764-4271
Phelps Dodge Magnet Wire Co 2131 S Coliseum Blvd	Fort Wayne	IN	46803	**800-255-2542**	260-421-5400
Raychem Corp 300 Constitution Dr	Menlo Park	CA	94025	**800-729-2436**	650-361-3333
Rea Magnet Wire Co Inc 3600 E Pontiac St	Fort Wayne	IN	46803	**800-732-9473**	260-421-7321
Ribbon Technology Corp PO Box 30758	Gahanna	OH	43230	**800-848-0477**	614-864-5444
S & S Industries Inc 32-00 Skillman Ave	Long Island City	NY	11101	**800-543-9154**	718-585-1333
Seneca Wire & Mfg Co 319 S Vine St *Sales	Fostoria	OH	44830	**800-537-9537***	419-435-9261
Sivaco Wire Group 800 rue Ouellette	Marieville	QC	J3M1P5	**800-876-9473**	450-658-8741
Southwire Co 1 Southwire Dr	Carrollton	GA	30119	**800-444-1700**	770-832-4242
Superior Essex Inc Magnet Wire/Winding Wire Div PO Box 1601 *Cust Svc	Fort Wayne	IN	46802	**800-551-8948***	260-461-4633
Techalloy Co Inc 370 Franklin Tpke	Mahwah	NJ	07430	**800-882-1006**	201-529-0900
Techalloy Co Inc Baltimore Wire Div 2310 Chesapeake Ave	Baltimore	MD	21222	**800-638-1458**	410-633-9300
Times Fiber Communications Inc 358 Hall Ave	Wallingford	CT	06492	**800-677-2288**	203-265-8500
Walker Wire & Steel Co 660 E Ten-Mile Rd	Ferndale	MI	48220	**800-521-2070**	248-399-4800
Wrap-On Co Inc 5550 W 70th Pl	Bedford Park	IL	60638	**800-621-6947**	708-496-2150

801 WIRE & CABLE - ELECTRONIC

Company / Address	City	State	ZIP	Toll-Free	Phone
Alpha Wire Co 711 Lidgerwood Ave	Elizabeth	NJ	07207	**800-522-5742**	908-925-8000

Classified Section

Company	City	State	Zip	Toll-Free	Phone
American Insulated Wire Corp 95 Grand Ave	Pawtucket	RI	02861	**800-366-2492**	401-726-0700
Belden Wire & Cable Co PO Box 1980	Richmond	IN	47375	**800-235-3362**	765-983-5200
Cables to Go Inc 1501 Webster St	Dayton	OH	45404	**800-826-7904**	937-224-8646
Champlain Cable Corp 175 Hercules Dr	Colchester	VT	05446	**800-451-5162**	802-654-4200
CommScope Inc PO Box 1729 *NYSE: CTV*	Hickory	NC	28603	**800-982-1708**	828-324-2200
Comprehensive Video Group 55 Ruta Ct	South Hackensack	NJ	07606	**800-526-0242**	201-229-4270
Consolidated Electronic Wire & Cable Co 11044 King St	Franklin Park	IL	60131	**800-621-4278**	847-455-8830
Corning Cable Systems PO Box 489	Hickory	NC	28603	**800-743-2671**	828-901-5000
CXtec 5404 S Bay Rd *Orders	Syracuse	NY	13212	**800-767-3282***	315-476-3000
Electro Products Inc 26601 79th Ave S	Kent	WA	98032	**800-423-0646**	253-859-0575
Fujikura America Inc 280 Interstate North Cir SE Suite 530	Atlanta	GA	30339	**888-385-4587**	770-956-7200
Judd Wire Inc 124 Turnpike Rd *Cust Svc	Turners Falls	MA	01376	**800-545-5833***	413-863-4357
Madison Cable Corp 125 Goddard Memorial Dr	Worcester	MA	01603	**877-623-4766**	508-752-2884
MNM Group Inc 3235 Sunset Ln	Hatboro	PA	19040	**800-645-3477**	
Mohawk/CDT 9 Mohawk Dr	Leominster	MA	01453	**800-422-9961**	978-537-9961
Montrose/CDT 28 Sword St	Auburn	MA	01501	**800-346-6626**	508-791-3161
Nehring Electric Works Inc 813 E Locust St	DeKalb	IL	60115	**800-435-4481**	815-756-2741
Optical Cable Corp 5290 Concourse Dr *NASDAQ: OCCF*	Roanoke	VA	24019	**800-622-7711**	540-265-0690
Paige Electric Corp 1160 Springfield Rd	Union	NJ	07083	**800-327-2443**	908-687-7810
Phelps Dodge Corp 1 N Central Ave *NYSE: PD*	Phoenix	AZ	85004	**800-528-1182**	602-366-8100
Pirelli Cables & Systems 700 Industrial Dr *Cust Svc	Lexington	SC	29072	**800-845-8507***	803-951-4800
Prestolite Wire Corp 200 Galleria Officentre Suite 212	Southfield	MI	48034	**800-498-3132**	248-355-4422
Siemon Co 101 Siemon Co Dr	Watertown	CT	06795	**866-548-5814**	860-945-4200
Superior Essex Inc 150 Interstate North Pkwy *NASDAQ: SPSX*	Atlanta	GA	30339	**800-685-6543**	770-657-6000
Tensolite Co 100 Tensolite Dr	Saint Augustine	FL	32092	**800-458-9960**	904-829-5600
Trilogy Communications Inc 2910 Hwy 80 E	Pearl	MS	39208	**800-874-5649**	601-932-4461
McGill Electrical Product Group 9377 W Higgins Rd	Rosemont	IL	60018	**888-832-0660**	800-722-8515
Mid-State Mfg Corp 1115 Aldrich Ave N *Cust Svc	Minneapolis	MN	55411	**800-328-7144***	612-522-3631
Mill-Max Mfg Corp 190 Pine Hollow Rd	Oyster Bay	NY	11771	**800-294-8027**	516-922-6000
Ohio Associated Enterprises LLC 1359 W Jackson St	Painesville	OH	44077	**800-863-9014**	440-354-3148
Omnetics Connector Corp 7260 Commerce Cir E *Cust Svc	Minneapolis	MN	55432	**800-343-0025***	763-572-0656
Panduit Corp 17301 S Ridgeland Ave	Tinley Park	IL	60477	**888-506-5400**	708-532-1800
Pass & Seymour/Legrand PO Box 4822	Syracuse	NY	13221	**800-223-4185**	315-468-6211
PolyPhaser Corp 2225 Park Pl *Cust Svc	Minden	NV	89423	**800-325-7170***	775-782-2511
Raychem Corp 300 Constitution Dr	Menlo Park	CA	94025	**800-729-2436**	650-361-3333
Shape LLC 2105 Corporate Dr	Addison	IL	60101	**800-367-5811**	630-620-8394
Technology Research Corp 5250 140th Ave N *NASDAQ: TRCI* ■ *Mktg	Clearwater	FL	33760	**800-780-4324***	727-535-0572
Transtector Systems Inc 10701 Airport Dr	Hayden Lake	ID	83835	**800-882-9110**	208-772-8515
Veetronix Inc 1311 W Pacific	Lexington	NE	68850	**800-445-0007**	308-324-6661
Weidmuller Inc 821 Southlake Blvd *Cust Svc	Richmond	VA	23236	**800-849-9343***	804-794-2877
Wells-CTI Inc 2102 W Quail Ave Suite 2	Phoenix	AZ	85027	**800-348-2505**	623-581-5330
Wiremold Co 60 Woodlawn St *Sales	West Hartford	CT	06110	**800-621-0049***	860-233-6251
Wiremold Co Brooks Electronics Div 13200 Townsend Rd	Philadelphia	PA	19154	**800-523-0130**	215-969-3803
Woodhead LP 3411 Woodhead Dr *Mktg	Northbrook	IL	60062	**800-225-7724***	847-272-7990
Woods Industries Canada Inc 375 Kennedy Rd	Toronto	ON	M1K2A3	**800-561-4321**	416-267-4610
Woods Industries Inc 510 3rd Ave SW	Carmel	IN	46032	**800-428-6168**	317-844-7261

802 WIRE ROPE

Company	City	State	Zip	Toll-Free	Phone
ALP Industries Inc 1229 W Lincoln Hwy	Coatesville	PA	19320	**800-220-2515**	610-384-1300
Peerless Chain Co 1416 E Sanborn St	Winona	MN	55987	**800-533-8056**	507-457-9100
West Coast Wire Rope & Rigging Inc 2900 NW 29th Ave	Portland	OR	97210	**800-275-0482**	503-228-9353
Wire Rope Corp of America Inc PO Box 288	Saint Joseph	MO	64502	**800-343-2808**	816-233-0287
Wirerope Works Inc 100 Maynard St *Cust Svc	Williamsport	PA	17701	**800-541-7673***	570-326-5146

803 WIRING DEVICES - CURRENT-CARRYING

Company	City	State	Zip	Toll-Free	Phone
ALP Lighting Components Inc 6333 Gross Point Rd	Niles	IL	60714	**877-257-5841**	773-774-9550
Amphenol Corp 358 Hall Ave *NYSE: APH*	Wallingford	CT	06492	**877-267-4366**	203-265-8900
Ark-Les Corp 95 Mill St	Stoughton	MA	02072	**800-342-6472**	781-297-6000
Arlington Industries Inc 1 Stauffer Industrial Pk	Scranton	PA	18517	**800-233-4717**	570-562-0270
AVA Electronics Corp 4000 Bridge St *Sales	Drexel Hill	PA	19026	**800-331-8838***	610-284-2500
AVCON Corp 4640 Ironwood Dr	Franklin	WI	53132	**877-423-8725**	414-817-6160
Cinch Connectors Inc 1700 Findley Rd	Lombard	IL	60148	**800-323-9612**	630-705-6000
Cole Hersee Co 20 Old Colony Ave	Boston	MA	02127	**800-365-2653**	617-268-2100
Control Concepts Corp 328 Water St	Binghamton	NY	13902	**800-288-6169**	607-724-2484
Cooper Wiring Devices Inc 203 Cooper Cir *Cust Svc	Peachtree City	GA	30269	**800-441-3177***	
Cord Sets Inc 1015 5th St N	Minneapolis	MN	55411	**800-752-0580**	612-337-9700
Curtis Industries Inc 2400 S 43rd St	Milwaukee	WI	53219	**800-657-0853**	414-649-4200
Dossert Corp 500 Captain Neville Dr	Waterbury	CT	06705	**800-890-8878**	203-573-1616
Edwin Gaynor Corp 200 Charles St	Stratford	CT	06615	**800-342-9667**	203-378-5545
EFI Electronics Corp 1751 S 4800 West	Salt Lake City	UT	84104	**800-877-1174**	801-977-9009
Electroswitch Electronic Products 2010 Yonkers Rd	Raleigh	NC	27604	**888-768-2797**	919-833-0707
ERICO International Corp 30575 Bainbridge Rd Suite 300	Solon	OH	44139	**800-800-9301**	440-349-2630
ERICO Products Inc 34600 Solon Rd	Solon	OH	44139	**800-813-3378**	440-248-0100
Fiskars Brands Inc Newpoint Div 17300 Medina Rd Suite 800	Plymouth	MN	55447	**800-639-7646**	763-557-8889
Fiskars Brands Inc Power Sentry Div 17300 Medina Rd Suite 800	Plymouth	MN	55447	**800-852-4312**	763-557-8889
FTZ Industries Inc 515 Palmetto Dr	Simpsonville	SC	29681	**800-336-8989**	864-963-5000
Gaynor Edwin Corp 200 Charles St	Stratford	CT	06615	**800-342-9667**	203-378-5545
Group Dekko Services LLC 6928 N 400 E	Kendallville	IN	46755	**800-829-0700**	260-347-0700
Hoffman Products 20700 Hubbell Ave	Oak Park	MI	48237	**800-445-6949**	248-395-8462
Hoyt Corp 520 S Dean St	Englewood	NJ	07631	**800-255-4698**	201-894-0707
Hubbell Premise Wiring Inc 14 Lord's Hill Rd	Stonington	CT	06378	**800-626-0005**	
ILSCO 4730 Madison Rd *Sales	Cincinnati	OH	45227	**800-776-9775***	513-533-6200
Independent Protection Co Inc 1607 S Main St	Goshen	IN	46526	**800-860-8388**	574-533-4116
Joslyn Electronics 5900 Eastport Blvd	Richmond	VA	23231	**800-752-8068**	804-236-3300
Joslyn High Voltage Corp 4000 E 116th St	Cleveland	OH	44105	**800-621-5875**	216-271-6600
KDI Precision Products Inc 3975 McMann Rd	Cincinnati	OH	45245	**800-377-3334**	513-943-2000
Keystone Cable Corp 8200 Lynch Rd	Detroit	MI	48234	**800-223-2996**	313-924-9720
Leviton Mfg Co Inc 59-25 Little Neck Pkwy *Tech Supp	Little Neck	NY	11362	**800-824-3005***	718-229-4040
Liebert Corp 1050 Dearborn Dr *Tech Supp	Columbus	OH	43085	**800-543-2778***	614-888-0246

804 WIRING DEVICES - NONCURRENT-CARRYING

Company	City	State	Zip	Toll-Free	Phone
Active Industries Inc 20 Solar Dr	Clifton Park	NY	12065	**800-403-2284**	518-371-2020
Alflex Inc 2630 El Presidio St	Long Beach	CA	90810	**800-755-4232**	310-886-8300
Bedford Materials Co Inc 7676 Allegheny Rd	Manns Choice	PA	15550	**800-773-4276**	814-623-9014
Conduit Pipe Products Co 1504 W Main St	West Jefferson	OH	43162	**800-848-6125**	614-879-9114
Cope TJ Inc 11500 Norcom Rd	Philadelphia	PA	19154	**800-426-4293**	215-961-2570
Cottrell Paper Co Inc PO Box 35	Rock City Falls	NY	12863	**800-948-3559**	518-885-1702
Creftcon Industries DBA Regal Mfg Co 900 S Ajax Ave	City of Industry	CA	91748	**800-582-3092**	626-964-6534
Curlee Mfg Co 13639 Aldine Westfield Rd	Houston	TX	77039	**800-631-6815**	
Electri-Flex Co 222 W Central Ave *Cust Svc	Roselle	IL	60172	**800-323-6174***	630-529-2920
Electro-Term/Hollingsworth 90 Memorial Dr	Springfield	MA	01104	**800-274-6748**	413-734-6469
Flex Cable & Furnace Products Inc 20 W Huron St	Pontiac	MI	48342	**800-245-3539**	248-332-6900
Gaylord Mfg Co PO Box 547	Ceres	CA	95307	**800-375-0091**	209-538-3313
Homaco Inc 1875 W Fullerton Ave	Chicago	IL	60614	**888-446-6226**	773-384-5575
Hubbell Killark 3940 ML King Dr	Saint Louis	MO	63113	**800-545-5275**	314-531-0460
Hubbell Premise Wiring Inc 14 Lord's Hill Rd	Stonington	CT	06378	**800-626-0005**	
Hubbell RACO 3902 W Sample St	South Bend	IN	46619	**800-722-6437**	574-234-7151
Ideal Industries Inc Becker Pl *Cust Svc	Sycamore	IL	60178	**800-435-0705***	815-895-5181
Joslyn Mfg Co 3700 S Morgan St	Chicago	IL	60609	**800-456-7596**	773-927-1420
Lamson & Sessions Co 25701 Science Park Dr *NYSE: LMS*	Cleveland	OH	44122	**800-321-1970**	216-464-3400
MP Husky Corp PO Box 16749	Greenville	SC	29606	**800-277-4810**	864-234-4800
O-Z/Gedney 7770 N Frontage Rd	Skokie	IL	60077	**877-999-7652**	847-679-7800
Opti-Com Mfg Network Co Inc 259 Plauche St	Harahan	LA	70123	**800-345-8774**	504-736-0331
P-W Industries Inc 9415 Kruse Rd	Pico Rivera	CA	90660	**800-452-3023**	562-463-9055
Regal Mfg Co 900 S Ajax Ave	City of Industry	CA	91748	**800-582-3092**	626-964-6534
Rittal Corp 1 Rittal Pl	Springfield	OH	45504	**800-477-4000**	937-399-0500
Saginaw Control & Engineering Inc 95 Midland Rd	Saginaw	MI	48603	**800-234-6871**	989-799-6871
Thomas & Betts Corp 8155 T & B Blvd *NYSE: TNB*	Memphis	TN	38125	**800-888-0211**	901-252-8000
TJ Cope Inc 11500 Norcom Rd	Philadelphia	PA	19154	**800-426-4293**	215-961-2570
US Samica Inc PO Box 848	Rutland	VT	05702	**800-248-5528**	802-775-5528
Virginia Plastics Co Inc 3453 Aerial Way Dr	Roanoke	VA	24018	**888-905-2225**	540-981-9700

805 WOOD MEMBERS - STRUCTURAL

Company	City	State	Zip	Toll-Free	Phone
Armstrong Lumber Co Inc 2709 Auburn Way N	Auburn	WA	98002	**800-868-9066**	253-833-6666
Citation Homes Inc 1100 Lake St	Spirit Lake	IA	51360	**800-831-5090**	712-336-2156
Columbia Forest Products Inc 222 SW Columbia St Suite 1575	Portland	OR	97201	**800-547-4261**	503-224-5300
Davidson Lumber Co 2801 N Morton St	Franklin	IN	46131	**800-787-3211**	317-738-3211
Enwood Structures Inc 5724 McCrimmon Pkwy	Morrisville	NC	27560	**800-777-8648**	919-467-6155
Fullerton Building Systems Inc 34620 250th St	Worthington	MN	56187	**800-450-9782**	507-376-3128
Laminators Inc 3255 Souderton Pike	Hatfield	PA	19440	**800-523-2347**	215-723-8107
Montgomery Truss & Panel Inc 803 W Main St	Grove City	PA	16127	**800-245-0334**	724-458-7500
Olympic Structures Inc 1850 93rd Ave SW	Olympia	WA	98512	**800-562-6066**	360-943-5433
Powell Structural Systems Inc 130 Johnson Dr	Delaware	OH	43015	**800-351-7176**	740-549-0465
Ram Building Components Co 9500 Henry Ct	Zeeland	MI	49464	**800-827-5434**	616-875-8157
Robbins Mfg Co PO Box 17939	Tampa	FL	33682	**800-282-9336**	813-971-3030
Shoffner Industries Inc 5631 S NC 62	Burlington	NC	27215	**800-476-9356**	336-226-9356
Southern Components Inc 7360 Julie Frances Rd	Shreveport	LA	71129	**800-256-2144**	318-687-3330
Standard Structures Inc 340 Standard Ave	Windsor	CA	95492	**800-862-4936**	707-836-8100
Stark Truss Co 109 Miles Ave SW	Canton	OH	44710	**800-933-2258**	330-478-2100
Structural Wood Corp 4000 Labore Rd	Saint Paul	MN	55110	**800-652-9058**	651-426-8111

Company	City	State	Zip	Toll-Free	Phone
Timber Truss Housing Systems Inc PO Box 996	Salem	VA	24153	**800-766-9072**	540-387-0273
Trus Joist MacMillan LP 200 E Mallard Dr *Cust Svc	Boise	ID	83706	**800-338-0515***	208-364-1200
Truss Mfg Co Inc 17317 Westfield Pk Rd	Westfield	IN	46074	**800-467-4525**	317-896-2571
Universal Forest Products Inc 2801 E Beltline Ave NE *NASDAQ: UFPI*	Grand Rapids	MI	49525	**800-598-9663**	616-364-6161
Valley Best-Way Building Supply 118 S Union Rd	Spokane	WA	99206	**800-722-4491**	509-924-1250
Villaume Industries Inc 2926 Lone Oak Cir *Cust Svc	Saint Paul	MN	55121	**800-488-3610***	651-454-3610
Wickes Inc 706 N Deerpath Dr	Vernon Hills	IL	60061	**800-558-1232**	847-367-3400
Windquest Co Inc 3311 Windquest Dr	Holland	MI	49424	**800-562-4257**	616-399-3311
Wood Structures Inc 20 Pomerleau St	Biddeford	ME	04005	**800-341-9612**	207-282-7556

806 WOOD PRESERVING

Company	City	State	Zip	Toll-Free	Phone
Brown Wood Preserving Co Inc 6201 Camp Ground Rd	Louisville	KY	40216	**800-537-1765**	502-448-2337
Building Products Plus 12317 Almeda Rd	Houston	TX	77045	**800-460-8627**	713-434-8008
Cox Industries Inc 860 Cannon Bridge Rd	Orangeburg	SC	29115	**800-476-4401**	803-534-7467
Great Southern Wood Preserving Inc PO Box 610	Abbeville	AL	36310	**800-633-7539**	334-585-2291
JH Baxter & Co 1700 S El Camino Real Suite 200	San Mateo	CA	94402	**800-780-7073**	650-349-0201
McFarland Cascade 1640 E Marc St *Cust Svc	Tacoma	WA	98421	**800-426-8430***	253-572-3033
Osmose Inc 980 Ellicott St	Buffalo	NY	14209	**800-877-7653**	716-882-5905
Robbins Mfg Co PO Box 17939	Tampa	FL	33682	**800-282-9336**	813-971-3030
Seaman Timber Co Inc PO Box 372	Montevallo	AL	35115	**800-782-8155**	205-665-2536
Tolleson Lumber Co Inc 903 Jernigan St	Perry	GA	31069	**800-768-2105**	478-988-3800
Western Wood Preserving Co PO Box 1250	Sumner	WA	98390	**800-472-7714**	253-863-8191
Wood Preservers Inc PO Box 158	Warsaw	VA	22572	**800-368-2536**	804-333-4022

807 WOOD PRODUCTS - RECONSTITUTED

Company	City	State	Zip	Toll-Free	Phone
Collins Cos 1618 SW 1st Ave Suite 500	Portland	OR	97201	**800-329-1219**	503-227-1219
Homasote Co PO Box 7240	West Trenton	NJ	08628	**800-257-9491**	609-883-3300
Panel Processing Inc 120 N Industrial Hwy	Alpena	MI	49707	**800-433-7142**	989-356-9007
Panolam Industries International Inc 20 Progress Dr	Shelton	CT	06484	**800-672-6652**	203-925-1556
Tectum Inc 105 S 6th St	Newark	OH	43055	**888-977-9691**	740-345-9691
Temple-Inland Forest Products Corp 303 S Temple Dr	Diboll	TX	75941	**800-262-5512**	936-829-5511

808 WOOD PRODUCTS - SHAPED & TURNED

Company	City	State	Zip	Toll-Free	Phone
Brown Wood Products Co 7040 N Lawndale Ave	Lincolnwood	IL	60712	**800-328-5858**	847-673-4780
Bruner Ivory Handle Co PO Box 647	Hope	AR	71801	**800-233-1017**	870-777-2304
Chicago Dowel Co Inc 4700 W Grand Ave	Chicago	IL	60639	**800-333-6935**	773-622-2000
Cowee WJ Inc 28 Taylor Ave	Berlin	NY	12022	**800-862-6933**	518-658-2233
Fibron Products Inc 170 Florida St	Buffalo	NY	14208	**800-516-0285**	716-886-2378
Forster Inc PO Box 657 *Cust Svc	Wilton	ME	04294	**800-777-7942***	207-645-2574
Hudson River Inlay 34 State Street	Ossining	NY	10562	**800-745-0744**	914-762-1134
Saunders Brothers Inc 170 Forest St	Westbrook	ME	04092	**800-343-0675**	207-854-2551
Sequatchie Handle Works 219 Handle St	Sequatchie	TN	37374	**800-221-3419**	423-942-5901

809 WOODWORKING MACHINERY

Company	City	State	Zip	Toll-Free	Phone
Biesemeyer Mfg Corp 216 S Alma School Rd Suite 1	Mesa	AZ	85210	**800-782-1831**	480-835-9300
ITW Amp 100 Fairway Dr Suite 114	Vernon Hills	IL	60061	**800-322-4204**	847-918-1970
Kimwood Corp 77684 Hwy 99 S	Cottage Grove	OR	97424	**800-942-4401**	541-942-4401
KVAL Inc 825 Petaluma Blvd S	Petaluma	CA	94952	**800-553-5825**	707-762-7367
Memphis Machinery & Supply Co Inc 2881 Directors Cove	Memphis	TN	38131	**800-388-4485**	901-527-4443
Mereen-Johnson Machine Co 4401 Lyndale Ave N	Minneapolis	MN	55412	**888-465-7297**	612-529-7791
Oliver Machinery Co 1210 Andover Park E	Tukwila	WA	98188	**800-559-5065**	206-575-2722
Pacific Hoe Co 2700 SE Tacoma St	Portland	OR	97202	**800-547-5537**	503-234-9501
Pendu Mfg Inc 718 N Shirk Rd	New Holland	PA	17557	**800-233-0471**	717-354-4348
Safety Speed Cut Mfg Co Inc 13943 Lincoln St NE	Ham Lake	MN	55304	**800-772-2327**	763-755-1600
Shopsmith Inc 6530 Poe Ave *Cust Svc	Dayton	OH	45414	**800-543-7586***	937-898-6070
Thermwood Corp 904 Buffaloville Rd *Mktg	Dale	IN	47523	**800-533-6901***	812-937-4476
US Natural Resources Inc 8000 NE Parkway Dr Suite 100	Vancouver	WA	98662	**800-289-8767**	360-892-2650
USNR Inc 2727 E Grand Ave	Hot Springs	AR	71901	**800-289-8767**	501-262-1010
Viking Engineering & Development Inc 5750 Main St NE *Sales	Fridley	MN	55432	**800-328-2403***	763-571-2400
Voorwood Co 2350 Barney St	Anderson	CA	96007	**800-225-3879**	530-365-3311
Yates-American Machine Co Inc 2880 Kennedy Dr	Beloit	WI	53511	**800-752-6377**	608-364-0333

810 WORLD TRADE CENTERS

Company	City	State	Zip	Toll-Free	Phone
Dallas World Trade Center 2100 Stemmons Fwy	Dallas	TX	75207	**800-325-6587**	214-655-6100
Ronald Reagan Building & International Trade Center 1300 Pennsylvania Ave NW	Washington	DC	20004	**888-393-3306**	202-312-1300
World Trade Center Boston 164 Northern Ave	Boston	MA	02210	**800-367-9822**	617-385-5000
World Trade Center Cleveland Tower City Ctr 50 Public Sq Suite 824	Cleveland	OH	44113	**888-304-4769**	216-621-3300
World Trade Center Rio Grande Valley at McAllen 200 S 10th St Suite 401	McAllen	TX	78501	**888-874-8638**	956-686-1982

811 ZOOS & WILDLIFE PARKS

SEE ALSO Aquariums - Public; Botanical Gardens & Arboreta

Company	City	State	Zip	Toll-Free	Phone
African Lion Safari & Game Farm RR 1	Cambridge	ON	N1R5S2	**800-461-9453**	519-623-2620
African Safari Wildlife Park 267 Lightner Rd	Port Clinton	OH	43452	**800-521-2660**	419-732-3606
Alaska Wildlife Conservation Center Milepost 79 Seward Hwy	Portage Glacier	AK	99587	**866-773-2025**	907-783-2025
Arkansas Alligator Farm & Petting Zoo 847 Whittington Ave	Hot Springs	AR	71901	**800-750-7891**	501-623-6172
Audubon Zoo 6500 Magazine St	New Orleans	LA	70118	**800-774-7394**	504-581-4629
Austin Zoo 10807 Rawhide Trail	Austin	TX	78736	**800-291-1490**	512-288-1490
Birmingham Zoo 2630 Cahaba Rd	Birmingham	AL	35223	**888-966-2426**	205-879-0409
Bolsa Chica Ecological Reserve 3842 Warner Ave	Huntington Beach	CA	92649	**888-265-7248**	714-846-1114
Bronx Zoo 2300 Southern Blvd	Bronx	NY	10460	**800-234-5128**	718-220-5100
Busch Gardens Tampa Bay 3605 Bougainvillea Ave	Tampa	FL	33164	**888-800-5447**	813-987-5082
Busch Gardens Williamsburg 1 Busch Gardens Blvd	Williamsburg	VA	23187	**800-772-8886**	757-253-3350
Caribbean Gardens 1590 Goodlette-Frank Rd	Naples	FL	34102	**888-520-3756**	239-262-5409
Cincinnati Zoo & Botanical Garden 3400 Vine St	Cincinnati	OH	45220	**800-944-4776**	513-281-4701
Clyde Peeling's Reptiland 18628 US Rt 15	Allenwood	PA	17810	**800-737-8452**	570-538-1869
Columbus Zoo & Aquarium 9990 Riverside Dr PO Box 400	Powell	OH	43065	**800-666-5397**	614-645-3400
Discovery Cove 6000 Discovery Cove Way Suite B	Orlando	FL	32821	**877-434-7268**	407-370-1280
Exotic Animal Paradise 124 Jungle Dr	Strafford	MO	65757	**888-570-9898**	417-859-2016
Gator Park 24050 SW 8th St	Miami	FL	33184	**800-559-2205**	305-559-2255
Gatorland 14501 S Orange Blossom Trail	Orlando	FL	32837	**800-393-5297**	407-855-5496
Good Zoo & Benedum Planetarium Rt 88 N Oglebay Pk	Wheeling	WV	26003	**800-624-6988**	304-243-4030
Granby Zoo & Amazoo Water Park 525 St-Hubert St	Granby	QC	J2G5P3	**877-472-6299**	450-372-9113
Grizzly & Wolf Discovery Center 201 S Canyon	West Yellowstone	MT	59758	**800-257-2570**	406-646-7001
Harmony Safari Park 431 Clouds Cove Rd	Huntsville	AL	35803	**877-726-4625**	
Jungle Adventures 26205 E Hwy 50	Christmas	FL	32709	**877-424-2867**	407-568-1354
Kentucky Horse Park 4089 Iron Works Pkwy	Lexington	KY	40511	**800-678-8813**	859-233-4303
Minnesota Zoo 13000 Zoo Blvd	Apple Valley	MN	55124	**800-366-7811**	952-431-9200
North Carolina Zoological Park 4401 Zoo Pkwy	Asheboro	NC	27205	**800-488-0444**	336-879-7000
Pittsburgh Zoo & PPG Aquarium 1 Wild Pl	Pittsburgh	PA	15206	**800-474-4966**	412-665-3639
Safari West Wildlife Preserve & Tent Camp 3115 Porter Creek Rd	Santa Rosa	CA	95404	**800-616-2695**	707-579-2551
Sarasota Jungle Gardens 3701 Bay Shore Dr	Sarasota	FL	34234	**877-861-6547**	941-355-5305
Silver Springs 5656 E Silver Springs Blvd	Silver Springs	FL	34488	**888-422-8727**	352-236-2121
Wild Animal Safari 1300 Oak Grove Rd	Pine Mountain	GA	31822	**800-367-2751**	706-663-8744
Wildlife West Nature Park 87 N Frontage Rd	Edgewood	NM	87015	**877-815-9453**	505-281-7655
Zoo Sauvage de Saint-Felicien 2230 boul du Jardin	Saint-Felicien	QC	G8K2P8	**800-667-5687**	418-679-0543
ZooAmerica North American Wildlife Park 100 W Hersheypark Dr	Hershey	PA	17033	**800-437-7439**	717-534-3860

Index to Classified Headings

Citations provided in this index refer to the subject headings under which listings are organized in the Classified Section. The page number given for each citation refers to the page on which a particular subject category begins rather than to a specific company or organization name. "See" and "See also" references are included to help locate appropriate subject categories.

A

Index citations refer to **page numbers**.

B

Index

Index citations refer to **page numbers.**

Index

C

Index

Index

Index

Index citations refer to **page numbers**.

D

F

Index

Index

Index

G

H

Index

I

Index citations refer to **page numbers.**

Index

N

O

P

Index

Index

S

Index citations refer to **page numbers.**

Index

Index citations refer to **page numbers.**

Index

U

Index

V

W

X

Y

Z

Notes

Notes